Small Business Sourcebook

ISSN 0883-3397

Small Business Sourcebook

The Entrepreneur's Resource

TWENTY-SECOND EDITION

Volume 2

General Small Business Topics

General Small Business Resources

(Includes State and Federal Sections)

(Entries 26104–67863)

Sonya D. Hill,
Project Editor

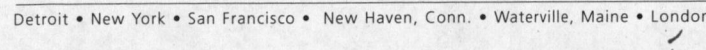

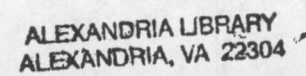

Small Business Sourcebook, 22nd Edition

Project Editor
Sonya D. Hill

Editorial Support Services
Scott Flaugher

Composition and Electronic Prepress
Evi Seoud

Manufacturing
Rita Wimberley

This publication is a creative work fully pro-tected by all applicable copyright laws, as well as by misappropriation, trade secret, unfair competition, and other applicable laws. The authors and editors of this work have added value to the underlying factual material herein through one or more of the following: unique and original selection, coordination, expression, arrangement, and classification of the information.

For permission to use material from this product, submit your request via Web at http://www.gale-edit.com/permissions, or you may download our Permissions Request form and submit your request by fax or mail to:

Permissions Department
Thomson Gale
27500 Drake Rd.
Farmington Hills, MI 48331-3535
Permissions Hotline:
248-699-8006 or 800-877-4253, ext. 8006
Fax: 248-699-8074 or 800-762-4058

While every effort has been made to ensure the reliability of the information presented in this publication, Thomson Gale does not guarantee the accuracy of the data contained herein. Thomson Gale accepts no payment for listing; and inclusion in the publication of any organization, agency, institution, publica-tion, service, or individual does not imply endorsement of the publisher. Errors brought to the attention of the publisher and verified to the satisfaction of the publisher will be corrected in future editions.

ISBN-13:	ISBN-10:
978-0-7876-8856-1 (set)	0-7876-8856-8 (set)
978-0-7876-8857-8 (vol. 1)	0-7876-8857-6 (vol. 1)
978-0-7876-8858-5 (vol. 2)	0-7876-8858-4 (vol. 2)

ISSN 0883-3397

Printed in the United States of America
10 9 8 7 6 5 4 3 2 1

Contents

The appeal of small business ownership remains perpetually entrenched in American culture as one of the most viable avenues for achieving the American Dream. To many entrepreneurs going into business for themselves represents financial independence, an increased sense of identity and self-worth, and the fulfillment of personal goals. Small business owners strive to make their mark in today's competitive marketplace by establishing healthy businesses that can, over time, become legacies handed down from one generation to the next. Entrepreneurs from each generation tackle the obstacles and adversities of the current business and economic climate to test their business savvy and generate opportunities. Today's entrepreneurs face many of the problems of their predecessors, as well as some distinctly new challenges.

With the rightsizing, downsizing, and reorganization of corporate America, many individuals have decided to confront the risks of developing and operating their own businesses. Small business ownership is rapidly becoming a viable alternative to what is perceived as an equally unstable corporate environment. These entrepreneurs, many of whom have first-hand experience with the problems and inefficiencies inherent in today's large corporations, seek to improve upon an archaic business model and to capitalize on their own ingenuity and strengths. Led by their zeal, many would-be entrepreneurs let their desire, drive, and determination overshadow the need for business knowledge and skill. Ironically, aids in obtaining these components of entrepreneurial success are widely available, easily accessible, and often free of charge.

Small Business Sourcebook (*SBS*) is a two-volume annotated guide to more than 26,000 listings of live and print sources of information designed to facilitate the start-up, development, and growth of specific small businesses, as well as over 30,000 similar listings on general small business topics. An additional 10,006 state-specific listings and 1,084 U.S. federal government agencies and offices specializing in small business issues, programs, and assistance are also included. *SBS* covers 340 specific small business profiles and 99 general small business topics.

Contents and Arrangement

The geographical scope of *SBS* encompasses the United States and Canada, with expanded coverage for resources pertaining to international trade and for resources that have a U.S. or Canadian distributor or contact. Internet sites that are maintained outside of the U.S. and Canada are also included if they contain relevant information for North American small businesses. Resources that do not relate specifically to small businesses are generally not included.

The information presented in *SBS* is grouped within four sections: Specific Small Business Profiles, General Small Business Topics, State Listings, and Federal Government Assistance. Detailed outlines of these sections may be found in the Users' Guide following this Introduction. Also included is a Master Index to both Volumes 1 and 2.

Specific Small Business Profiles This section includes the following types of resources: start-up information, associations and other organizations, educational programs, directories of educational programs, reference works, sources of supply, statistical sources, trade periodicals, videocassettes/audiocassettes, trade shows and conventions, consultants, franchises and business opportunities, computerized databases, computer systems/software, Internet databases, libraries, and research centers—all arranged by business type. Entries range from Accounting Service to Word Processing Service, and include such businesses as Airbag Replacement Service Centers, Computer Consulting, Damage Restoration Service, and Web Site Design.

General Small Business Topics This section offers such resources as associations, books, periodicals, articles, pamphlets, educational programs, directories of educational programs, videocassettes/audiocassettes, trade shows and conventions, consultants, computerized databases, Internet databases, software, libraries, and research centers, arranged alphabetically by business topic.

State Listings Entries include government, academic, and commercial agencies and organizations, as well as select coverage of relevant state-specific publications; listings are arranged alphabetically by state, territory, and Canadian province. Some examples include small business development consultants, educational programs, financing and loan programs, better business bureaus, and chambers of commerce.

Federal Government Assistance Listings specializing in small business issues, programs, assistance, and policy are arranged alphabetically by U.S. government agency or office; regional or branch offices are listed alphabetically by state.

Master Index All entries in both Volumes 1 and 2 are arranged in one alphabetic index for convenience.

Entries in *SBS* include (as appropriate and available):

- Organization, institution, or product name

- Contact information, including contact name, address and phone, toll-free, and fax numbers

- Author/editor, date(s), and frequency

- Availability, including price

- Brief description of purpose, services, or content

- Company and/or personal E-mail addresses

- Web site addresses

SBS also features the following:

Guide to Publishers—An alphabetic listing of 3,357 companies, associations, institutions, and individuals that publish the periodicals, directories, guidebooks, and other publications noted in the Small Business Profiles and General Topics sections. Users are provided with full contact information, including address, phone, fax, and e-mail and URL when available. The Guide to Publishers facilitates contact with publishers and provides a one-stop resource for valuable information.

Method of Compilation

SBS was compiled by consulting small business experts and entrepreneurs, as well as a variety of resources, including direct contact with the associations, organizations, and agencies through telephone surveys, Internet research, or through materials provided by those listees; government resources; and data obtained from other relevant Gale directories. *SBS*

was reviewed by a team of small business advisors, all of whom have numerous years of expertise in small business counseling and identification of small business information resources. The last and perhaps most important resource we utilize is direct contact with our readers, who provide valuable comments and suggestions to improve our publication. *SBS* relies on these comprehensive market contacts to provide today's entrepreneurs with relevant, current, and accurate information on all aspects of small business.

Available in Electronic Formats

Licensing. *Small Business Sourcebook* is available for licensing. The complete database is provided in a fielded format and is deliverable on such media as disk or CD-ROM. For more information, contact Gale's Business Development Group at 1-800-877-GALE, or visit our website at www.gale.com/bizdev.

Comments and Suggestions Welcome

Associations, agencies, business firms, publishers, and other organizations that provide assistance and information to the small business community are encouraged to submit material about their programs, activities, services, or products. Comments and suggestions from users of this directory are also welcomed and appreciated. Please contact:

Project Editor
Small Business Sourcebook
Thomson Gale
27500 Drake Rd.
Farmington Hills, MI 48331-3535
Phone: (248) 699-4253
Fax: (248) 699-8070
E-mail: BusinessProducts@gale.com
URL: www.gale.com

Small Business Sourcebook (SBS) provides information in a variety of forms and presentations for comprehensive coverage and ease of use. The directory contains four parts within two volumes:

- Specific Small Business Profiles
- General Small Business Topics
- State Listings
- Federal Government Assistance

Information on specific businesses is arranged by type of business; the many general topics that are of interest to the owners, operators, or managers of all small businesses are grouped in a separate section for added convenience. Users should consult the various sections to benefit fully from the information SBS offers.

For example, an entrepreneur with a talent or interest in the culinary arts could peruse a number of specific small business profiles, such as Restaurant, Catering, Cooking School, Specialty Food/Wine Shop, Bakery/Doughnut Shop, Healthy Restaurant, or Candy/Chocolate Store. Secondly, the General Small Business Topics section could be consulted for any applicable subjects, such as Service Industry, Retailing, Franchising, and other relevant topics. Then, the appropriate state within the State Listings section would offer area programs and offices providing information and support to small businesses, including venture capital firms and small business development consultants. Finally, the Federal Government Assistance section could supply relevant government offices, such as procurement contacts.

Features Included in Volume 1

List of Small Business Profiles. This list provides an alphabetic outline of the small businesses profiled, with cross-references for related profiles and for alternate names by which businesses may be identified. The page number for each profile is indicated.

Standard Industrial Classification (SIC) Codes for Profiled Small Businesses. This section lists four-digit SIC codes and corresponding classification descriptions for the small businesses profiled in this edition. The SIC system, which organizes businesses by type, is a product of the Statistical Policy Division of the U.S. Office of Management and Budget. Statistical data produced by government, public, and private organizations is usually categorized according to SIC codes, thereby facilitating the collection, comparison, and analysis of data as well as providing a uniform method for presenting statistical information. Hence, knowing the SIC code for a particular small business increases access and the use of a variety of statistical data from many sources.

Guide to Publishers. This resource lists alphabetically the companies, associations, institutions, and individuals that publish the periodicals, directories, guidebooks, and other publications noted in the "Small Business Profiles" and "General Topics" sections. Users are provided with full contact information, including address, phone, fax, and e-mail and URL when available. The "Guide" facilitates contact with publishers and provides a one-stop resource for valuable information.

Small Business Profiles A-Z. A total of 340 small businesses is represented in volume one. Profiles are listed alphabetically by business name. Entries within each profile are arranged alphabetically by resource type, within up to 17 subheadings. These subheadings are detailed below:

- *Start-up Information*—Includes periodical articles, books, manuals, book excerpts, kits, and other sources of information. Entries offer title; publisher; address; phone, fax, toll-free numbers; company e-mail and URL addresses; and a description. Bibliographic data is provided for cited periodical articles whenever possible.

- *Associations and Other Organizations*— Includes trade and professional associations whose members gather and disseminate information of interest to small business owners. Entries offer the association's name; address; phone, toll-free and fax numbers; company e-mail address; contact name; purpose and objective; a description of membership; telecommunication services; and a listing of its publications, including publishing frequency.

- **Educational Programs**— Includes university and college programs, schools, training opportunities, association seminars, correspondence courses, and other educational programs. Entries offer name of program or institution, sponsor name, address, phone, toll-free and fax numbers, e-mail and URL addresses; and description of program.

- **Directories of Educational Programs**— Includes directories and other publications that list educational programs. Entries offer name of publication; publisher name, address, and phone, toll-free and fax numbers; editor; frequency or date of publication; price; and description of contents, including directory arrangement and indexes.

- **Reference Works**— Includes handbooks, manuals, textbooks, guides, directories, dictionaries, encyclopedias, and other published reference materials. Entries offer name of publication; publisher name, address, and phone, toll-free and fax numbers; e-mail and URL addresses; and, when available, name of author or editor, publication year or frequency, and price. A brief description is often featured.

- **Sources of Supply**— Includes buyer's guides, directories, special issues of periodicals, and other publications that list sources of equipment, supplies, and services related to the operation of the profiled small business. Entries offer publication name; publisher name, address, and phone, toll-free and fax numbers; e-mail and URL addresses; and, when available, editor's name, frequency or publication year, and price. A brief description of the publication, including directory arrangement and indexes, is often provided.

- **Statistical Sources**— Includes books, reports, pamphlets, and other sources of statistical data of interest to an owner, operator or manager of the profiled small business, such as wage, salary, and compensation data; financial and operating ratios; prices and costs; demographics; and other statistical information. Entries offer publication/data source name; publisher (if applicable); address; phone, toll-free and fax numbers of data source; publication date or frequency; and price. A brief description of the publication/data source is often provided.

- **Trade Periodicals**— Includes trade journals, newsletters, magazines, and other serials that offer information about the management and operation of the profiled small business. Such periodicals often contain industry news; trends and developments; reviews; articles about new equipment and supplies; and other information related to business operations. Entries offer publication name; publisher name, address, phone, toll-free and fax numbers, and e-mail and URL addresses; editor name; publication frequency; and price. A brief description of the publication's content is also included, when known.

- **Videocassettes/Audiocassettes**— Includes videocassettes, audiocassettes, and other audiovisual media offering information on the profiled small business. Entries offer program title; distributor name, address, phone, toll-free and fax numbers, and e-mail and URL addresses; description of program; release date; price; and format(s).

- **Trade Shows and Conventions**— Includes trade shows, exhibitions, expositions, conventions, and other industry meetings that provide prospective and existing business owners with the opportunity to meet and exchange information with their peers, review commercial exhibits, establish business or sales contacts, and attend educational programs. Entries offer event name; sponsor or management company name, address, phone, toll-free and fax numbers, and e-mail and URL addresses; a description of the event, including audience, frequency, principal exhibits, and dates and locations of event for as many years ahead as provided by the event's sponsor.

- **Consultants**— Includes consultants and consulting organizations that provide services specifically related to the profiled small business. Entries offer individual consultant or consulting organization name, address, and phone, toll-free and fax numbers; company and individual e-mail addresses; and a brief description of consulting services. (For e-mail and URL addresses, see the Small Business Development Consultants subheadings in the State Listings section in Volume 2.)

- **Franchises and Business Opportunities**— Includes companies granting franchise licenses for enterprises falling within the scope of the profiled small business, as well as other non-franchised business opportunities that operate within a given network or system. Entries offer franchise name, address, phone, toll-free and fax numbers, and e-mail and URL addresses, as well as a description of the franchise or business opportunity, which has been expanded whenever possible to include the number of existing franchises, the founding date of the franchise, franchise fees, equity capital requirements, royalty fees, any managerial assistance offered, and available training.

- **Computerized Databases**— Includes diskettes, magnetic tapes, CD-ROMs, online systems, and other computer-readable databases. Entries offer database name; producer name, address, phone, toll-free and fax numbers, e-mail and URL addresses; description; and available format(s), including vendor name. (Many university and public libraries offer online information retrieval services that provide searches of databases, including those listed in this category.)

- **Computer Systems/Software**— Includes software and computerized business systems designed to assist in the operation of the profiled small business. Entries offer name of the software or system; publisher name, address, phone, toll-free and fax numbers; price; and description.

- *Libraries*— Includes libraries and special collections that contain material especially applicable to the profiled small business. Entries offer library or collection name; parent organization (where applicable); address; phone, toll-free and fax numbers; e-mail and URL addresses; contact name and title; scope of collection; and description of holdings, subscriptions, and services.

- *Research Centers*— Includes university-related and independently operated research institutes and information centers that generate, through their research programs, data related to the operation of the profiled small business. Also listed are associations and other business-related organizations that conduct research programs. Entries offer name of organization; address; phone, toll-free and fax numbers; company web site address; contact name and personal e-mail; a description of principal fields of research or services; publications, including title and frequency; and related conferences.

Features Included in Volume 2

Glossary of Small Business Terms. This glossary defines nearly 400 small business terms, including financial, governmental, insurance, procurement, technical, and general business definitions. Cross-references and acronyms are also provided.

General Small Business Topics. This section offers chapters on different topics in the operation of any small business, for example, venture capital and other funding, or compensation. Chapters are listed alphabetically by small business topic; entries within each chapter are arranged alphabetically, within up to 14 subheadings, by resource type:

- *Associations and Other Organizations*— Includes trade and professional associations that gather and disseminate information of interest to small business owners. Entries offer the association's name; address; phone, toll-free and fax numbers; organization e-mail and URL addresses; contact name; purpose and objectives; a description of membership; telecommunication services; and a listing of its publications, including publishing frequency.

- *Educational Programs*— Includes university and college programs, schools, training opportunities, association seminars, correspondence courses, and other educational programs. Entries offer name of program or institution, sponsor name, address, phone, toll-free and fax numbers, e-mail and URL addresses, and description of program.

- *Directories of Educational Programs*— Includes directories and other publications that list educational programs. Entries offer name of publication; publisher name, address, phone, toll-free and fax numbers, and e-mail and URL addresses; editor; frequency or date

of publication; price; and description of contents, including arrangement and indexes.

- *Reference Works*— Includes articles, handbooks, manuals, textbooks, guides, directories, dictionaries, encyclopedias, and other published reference materials. Entries offer title of article, including bibliographic information; name of publication; publisher name, address, phone, toll-free and fax numbers, and e-mail and URL addresses; and, when available, name of author or editor, publication year or frequency, and price. A brief description is often featured.

- *Sources of Supply*— Includes buyer's guides, directories, special issues of periodicals, and other publications that list sources of equipment, supplies, and services. Entries offer publication name; publisher name, address, phone, toll-free and fax numbers, and e-mail and URL addresses; editor's name, frequency or publication year, price, and a brief description of the publication, when available.

- *Statistical Sources*— Includes books, reports, pamphlets, and other sources of statistical data of interest to an owner, operator, or manager of a small business, such as wage, salary, and compensation data; financial and operating ratios; prices and costs; demographics; and other statistical information. Entries offer publication/data source name; publisher (if applicable); address; phone, toll-free and fax numbers of data source; publication date or frequency; and price. A brief description is often provided.

- *Trade Periodicals*— Includes journals, newsletters, magazines, and other serials. Entries offer name of publication; publisher name, address, phone, toll-free and fax numbers, and e-mail and URL addresses; and name of editor, frequency, and price. A brief description of the periodical's content is included when known.

- *Videocassettes/Audiocassettes*— Includes videocassettes, audiocassettes, and other audiovisual media. Entries offer program title; distributor name, address, phone, toll-free and fax numbers, and e-mail and URL addresses; price; description of program; release date; and format(s).

- *Trade Shows and Conventions*— Includes trade shows, exhibitions, expositions, seminars, and conventions. Entries offer event name; sponsor or management company name, address, phone, toll-free and fax numbers, and e-mail and URL addresses; frequency of event; and dates and locations of the event for as many years ahead as known.

- *Consultants*— Includes consultants and consulting organizations. Entries offer individual consultant or consulting organization name, address, and phone, toll-free and fax numbers; company and individual e-mail addresses; and a brief description of consulting services. (See also Consultants in the State Listings section.)

- **Computerized Databases**— Includes diskettes, CD-ROMs, magnetic tape, online systems and other computer-readable databases. Entries offer database name; producer, address, phone, toll-free and fax numbers, and e-mail and URL addresses; description; and available format(s), including vendor name. (Many university and public libraries offer online information retrieval services that provide searches of databases, including those listed in this category.)

- **Computer Systems/Software**— Includes software and computerized business systems. Entries offer name of the software or system; publisher name, address, phone, toll-free and fax numbers, and e-mail and URL addresses; price; and description.

- **Libraries**— Includes libraries and special collections that contain material applicable to the small business topic. Entries offer library or collection name, parent organization (where applicable), address, phone and fax numbers, e-mail and URL addresses, scope of collection, and description of holdings and services.

- **Research Centers**— Includes university-related and independently operated research institutes and information centers that generate, through their research programs, data related to specific small business topics. Entries offer name of organization, address, phone, toll-free and fax numbers, e-mail and URL addresses, a description of principal fields of research or services, and related conferences.

State Listings. This section lists various sources of information and assistance available within given states, territories, and Canadian provinces; entries include governmental, academic, and commercial agencies, and are arranged alphabetically within up to 15 subheadings by resource type:

- **Small Business Development Center Lead Office**— Includes the lead small business development center (SBDC) for each state.

- **Small Business Development Centers**— Includes any additional small business development centers (SBDC) in the state, territory, or province. SBDCs provide support services to small businesses, including individual counseling, seminars, conferences, and learning center activities.

- **Small Business Assistance Programs**— Includes state small business development offices and other programs offering assistance to small businesses.

- **SCORE Offices**— Includes SCORE office(s) for each state. The Service Corps of Retired Executives Association (SCORE), a volunteer program sponsored by the Small Business Administration, offers counseling, workshops, and seminars across the U.S. for small business entrepreneurs.

- **Better Business Bureaus**— Includes various better business bureaus within each state. By becoming a member of the local Better Business Bureau, a small business owner can increase the prestige and credibility of his or her business within the community, as well as make valuable business contacts.

- **Chambers of Commerce**— Includes various chambers of commerce within each state. Chambers of Commerce are valuable sources of small business advice and information; often, local chambers sponsor SCORE counseling several times per month for a small fee, seminars, conferences, and other workshops to its members. Also, by becoming a member of the local Chamber of Commerce, a small business owner can increase the prestige and credibility of his or her business within the community, as well as make valuable business contacts.

- **Minority Business Assistance Programs**— Includes minority business development centers and other sources of assistance for minority-owned business.

- **Financing and Loan Programs**— Includes venture capital firms, small business investment companies (SBIC), minority enterprise small business investment companies (MESBIC), and other programs that provide funding to qualified small businesses.

- **Procurement Assistance Programs**— Includes state services such as counseling, set-asides, and sheltered-market bidding, which are designed to aid small businesses in bidding on government contracts.

- **Incubators/Research and Technology Parks**— Includes small business incubators, which provide newly established small business owners with work sites, business services, training, and consultation; also includes research and technology parks, which sponsor research and facilitate commercialization of new technologies.

- **Educational Programs**— Includes university and college programs, as well as those sponsored by other organizations that offer degree, nondegree, certificate, and correspondence programs in entrepreneurship and in small business development.

- **Legislative Assistance**— Includes committees, subcommittees, and joint committees of each state's senate and house of representatives that are concerned with small business issues and regulations.

- **Consultants**— Includes consultants and consulting firms offering expertise in small business development.

- **Publications**— Includes publications related to small business operations within the profiled state.

- **Publishers**— Includes publishers operating in or for the small business arena within the profiled state.

Federal Government Assistance. This section lists federal government agencies and offices, many with additional listings for specific offices, as well as regional or district branches. Main agencies or offices are listed alphabetically; regional, branch, or district offices are listed after each main office or agency.

Master Index. This index provides an alphabetic listing of all entries contained in both Volumes 1 and 2. Citations are referenced by their entry numbers. Publication titles are rendered in italics.

Acknowledgements

The editors would like to extend sincere thanks to the following members of the *Small Business Sourcebook* advisory board for their expert guidance, recommendations, and suggestions for the ongoing development of this title:

Susan C. Awe
Assistant Director,
William J. Parish Memorial Business Library

JoAnn Kosanke
Business Department Manager,
Toledo-Lucas County Public Library

Jules Matsoff
District Manager,
Service Corps of Retired Executives (SCORE)
Milwaukee Chapter

Ken MacKenzie
President,
Southeast Business Appraisal

The editors would also like to thank the individuals from associations and other organizations who provided information for the compilation of this directory.

List of General Small Business Topics

This section covers sources of assistance applicable to a variety of small businesses. Resources are arranged by topic and include associations, educational programs, directories of educational programs, reference works, sources of supply, statistical sources, periodicals, videocassettes/audiocassettes, trade shows and conventions, consultants, computerized databases, computer systems/software, Internet databases, libraries, and research centers.

Absolute liability ▮ Liability that is incurred due to product defects or negligent actions. Manufacturers or retail establishments are held responsible, even though the defect or action may not have been intentional or negligent.

ACE ▮ *See* Active Corps of Executives.

Accident and health benefits ▮ Benefits offered to employees and their families in order to offset the costs associated with accidental death, accidental injury, or sickness.

Account statement ▮ A record of transactions, including payments, new debt, and deposits, incurred during a defined period of time.

Accounting system ▮ System capturing the costs of all employees and/or machinery included in business expenses.

Accounts payable ▮ *See* Trade credit.

Accounts receivable ▮ Unpaid accounts which arise from unsettled claims and transactions from the sale of a company's products or services to its customers.

Active Corps of Executives (ACE) ▮ (*See also* Service Corps of Retired Executives) A group of volunteers for a management assistance program of the U.S. Small Business Administration; volunteers provide one-on-one counseling and teach workshops and seminars for small firms.

ADA ▮ *See* Americans with Disabilities Act.

Adaptation ▮ The process whereby an invention is modified to meet the needs of users.

Adaptive engineering ▮ The process whereby an invention is modified to meet the manufacturing and commercial requirements of a targeted market.

Adverse selection ▮ The tendency for higher-risk individuals to purchase health care and more comprehensive plans, resulting in increased costs.

Advertising ▮ A marketing tool used to capture public attention and influence purchasing decisions for a product or service. Utilizes various forms of media to generate consumer response, such as flyers, magazines, newspapers, radio, and television.

Age discrimination ▮ The denial of the rights and privileges of employment based solely on the age of an individual.

Agency costs ▮ Costs incurred to insure that the lender or investor maintains control over assets while allowing the borrow-

er or entrepreneur to use them. Monitoring and information costs are the two major types of agency costs.

Agribusiness ▮ The production and sale of commodities and products from the commercial farming industry.

America Online ▮ (*See also* Prodigy) An online service which is accessible by computer modem. The service features Internet access, bulletin boards, online periodicals, electronic mail, and other services for subscribers.

Americans with Disabilities Act (ADA) ▮ Law designed to ensure equal access and opportunity to handicapped persons.

Annual report ▮ (*See also* Securities and Exchange Commission) Yearly financial report prepared by a business that adheres to the requirements set forth by the Securities and Exchange Commission (SEC).

Antitrust immunity ▮ (*See also* Collective ratemaking) Exemption from prosecution under antitrust laws. In the transportation industry, firms with antitrust immunity are permitted—under certain conditions—to set schedules and sometimes prices for the public benefit.

Applied research ▮ Scientific study targeted for use in a product or process.

Asians ▮ A minority category used by the U.S. Bureau of the Census to represent a diverse group that includes Aleuts, Eskimos, American Indians, Asian Indians, Chinese, Japanese, Koreans, Vietnamese, Filipinos, Hawaiians, and other Pacific Islanders.

Assets ▮ Anything of value owned by a company.

Audit ▮ The verification of accounting records and business procedures conducted by an outside accounting service.

Average cost ▮ Total production costs divided by the quantity produced.

Balance Sheet ▮ A financial statement listing the total assets and liabilities of a company at a given time.

Bankruptcy ▮ (*See also* Chapter 7 of the 1978 Bankruptcy Act; Chapter 11 of the 1978 Bankruptcy Act) The condition in which a business cannot meet its debt obligations and petitions a federal district court either for reorganization of its debts (Chapter 11) or for liquidation of its assets (Chapter 7).

Basic research ▮ Theoretical scientific exploration not targeted to application.

Basket clause ❚ A provision specifying the amount of public pension funds that may be placed in investments not included on a state's legal list (see separate citation).

BBS ❚ *See* Bulletin Board Service.

BDC ❚ *See* Business development corporation.

Benefit ❚ Various services, such health care, flextime, day care, insurance, and vacation, offered to employees as part of a hiring package. Typically subsidized in whole or in part by the business.

BIDCO ❚ *See* Business and industrial development company

Billing cycle ❚ A system designed to evenly distribute customer billing throughout the month, preventing clerical backlogs.

Birth ❚ *See* Business birth.

Blue chip security ❚ A low-risk, low-yield security representing an interest in a very stable company.

Blue sky laws ❚ A general term that denotes various states' laws regulating securities.

Bond ❚ (*See also* General obligation bond; Taxable bonds; Treasury bonds) A written instrument executed by a bidder or contractor (the principal) and a second party (the surety or sureties) to .assure fulfillment of the principal's obligations to a third party (the obligee or government) identified in the bond. If the principal's obligations are not met, the bond assures payment to the extent stipulated of any loss sustained by the obligee.

Bonding requirements ❚ Terms contained in a bond (see separate citation).

Bonus ❚ An amount of money paid to an employee as a reward for achieving certain business goals or objectives.

Brainstorming ❚ A group session where employees contribute their ideas for solving a problem or meeting a company objective without fear of retribution or ridicule.

Brand name ❚ The part of a brand, trademark, or service mark that can be spoken. It can be a word, letter, or group of words or letters.

Bridge financing ❚ A short-term loan made in expectation of intermediate-term or long-term financing. Can be used when a company plans to go public in the near future.

Broker ❚ One who matches resources available for innovation with those who need them.

Budget ❚ An estimate of the spending necessary to complete a project or offer a service in comparison to cash-on-hand and expected earnings for the coming year, with an emphasis on cost control.

Bulletin Board Service (BBS) ❚ An online service enabling users to communicate with each other about specific topics.

Business birth ❚ The formation of a new establishment or enterprise. The appearance of a new establishment or enterprise in the Small Business Data Base (see separate citation).

Business conditions ❚ Outside factors that can affect the financial performance of a business.

Business contractions ❚ The number of establishments that have decreased in employment during a specified time.

Business cycle ❚ A period of economic recession and recovery. These cycles vary in duration.

Business death ❚ The voluntary or involuntary closure of a firm or establishment. The disappearance of an establishment or enterprise from the Small Business Data Base (see separate citation).

Business development corporation (BDC) ❚ A business financing agency, usually composed of the financial institutions in an area or state, organized to assist in financing businesses unable to obtain assistance through normal channels; the risk is spread among various members of the business development corporation, and interest rates may vary somewhat from those charged by member institutions. A venture capital firm in which shares of ownership are publicly held and to which the Investment Act of 1940 applies.

Business dissolution ❚ For enumeration purposes, the absence of a business that was present in the prior time period from any current record.

Business entry ❚ *See* Business birth.

Business ethics ❚ Moral values and principles espoused by members of the business community as a guide to fair and honest business practices.

Business exit ❚ *See* Business death.

Business expansions ❚ The number of establishments that added employees during a specified time.

Business failure ❚ Closure of a business causing a loss to at least one creditor.

Business format franchising ❚ (*See also* Franchising) The purchase of the name, trademark, and an ongoing business plan of the parent corporation or franchisor by the franchisee.

Business and industrial development company (BIDCO) ❚ A private, for-profit financing corporation chartered by the state to provide both equity and long-term debt capital to small business owners (see separate citations for equity and debt capital).

Business license ❚ A legal authorization issued by municipal and state governments and required for business operations.

Business name ❚ (*See also* Business license; Trademark) Enterprises must register their business names with local governments usually on a "doing business as" (DBA) form. (This name is sometimes referred to as a "fictional name.") The procedure is part of the business licensing process and prevents any other business from using that same name for a similar business in the same locality.

Business norms ❚ *See* Financial ratios.

Business permit ❚ *See* Business license.

Business plan ❚ A document that spells out a company's expected course of action for a specified period, usually including a detailed listing and analysis of risks and uncertainties. For the small busi-ness, it should examine the proposed products, the market, the industry, the management policies, the marketing policies, produc-tion needs, and financial needs. Frequently, it is used as a pros-pectus for potential investors and lenders.

Business proposal ❚ *See* Business plan.

Business service firm ❚ A business primarily engaged in rendering services to other businesses on a fee or contract basis.

Business start ❚ For enumeration purposes, a business with a name or similar designation that did not exist in a prior time period.

Cafeteria plan ❙ *See* Flexible benefit plan.

Capacity ❙ Level of a firm's, industry's, or nation's output corresponding to full practical utilization of available resources.

Capital ❙ Assets less liabilities, representing the ownership interest in a business. A stock of accumulated goods, especially at a specified time and in contrast to income received during a specified time period. Accumulated goods devoted to production. Accumulated possessions calculated to bring income.

Capital expenditure ❙ Expenses incurred by a business for improvements that will depreciate over time.

Capital gain ❙ The monetary difference between the purchase price and the selling price of capital. Capital gains are taxed at a rate of 28% by the federal government.

Capital intensity ❙ (*See also* Debt capital; Equity midrisk venture capital; Informal capital; Internal capital; Owner's capital; Secondhand capital; Seed capital; Venture capital) The relative importance of capital in the production process, usually expressed as the ratio of capital to labor but also sometimes as the ratio of capital to output.

Capital resource ❙ The equipment, facilities and labor used to create products and services.

Caribbean Basin Initiative ❙ An interdisciplinary program to support commerce among the businesses in the nations of the Caribbean Basin and the United States. Agencies involved include: the Agency for International Development, the U.S. Small Business Administration, the International Trade Administration of the U.S. Department of Commerce, and various private sector groups.

Catastrophic care ❙ Medical and other services for acute and long-term illnesses that cost more than insurance coverage limits or that cost the amount most families may be expected to pay with their own resources.

CDC ❙ *See* Certified development corporation.

CD-ROM ❙ Compact disc with read-only memory used to store large amounts of digitized data.

Certified development corporation (CDC) ❙ A local area or statewide corporation or authority (for profit or nonprofit) that packages U.S. Small Business Administration (SBA), bank, state, and/or private money into financial assistance for existing business capital improvements. The SBA holds the second lien on its maximum share of 40 percent involvement. Each state has at least one certified development corporation. This program is called the SBA 504 Program.

Certified lenders ❙ Banks that participate in the SBA guaranteed loan program (see separate citation). Such banks must have a good track record with the U.S. Small Business Administration (SBA) and must agree to certain conditions set forth by the agency. In return, the SBA agrees to process any guaranteed loan application within three business days.

Champion ❙ An advocate for the development of an innovation.

Channel of distribution ❙ The means used to transport merchandise from the manufacturer to the consumer.

Chapter 7 of the 1978 Bankruptcy Act ❙ Provides for a court-appointed trustee who is responsible for liquidating a company's assets in order to settle outstanding debts.

Chapter 11 of the 1978 Bankruptcy Act ❙ Allows the business owners to retain control of the company while working with their creditors to reorganize their finances and establish better business practices to prevent liquidation of assets.

Closely held corporation ❙ A corporation in which the shares are held by a few persons, usually officers, employees, or others close to the management; these shares are rarely offered to the public.

Code of Federal Regulations ❙ Codification of general and permanent rules of the federal government published in the Federal Register.

Code sharing ❙ *See* Computer code sharing.

Coinsurance ❙ (*See also* Cost sharing) Upon meeting the deductible payment, health insurance participants may be required to make additional health care cost-sharing payments. Coinsurance is a payment of a fixed percentage of the cost of each service; copayment is usually a fixed amount to be paid with each service.

Collateral ❙ Securities, evidence of deposit, or other property pledged by a borrower to secure repayment of a loan.

Collective ratemaking ❙ (*See also* Antitrust immunity) The establishment of uniform charges for services by a group of businesses in the same industry.

Commercial insurance plan ❙ *See* Underwriting.

Commercial loans ❙ Short-term renewable loans used to finance specific capital needs of a business.

Commercialization ❙ The final stage of the innovation process, including production and distribution.

Common stock ❙ The most frequently used instrument for purchasing ownership in private or public companies. Common stock generally carries the right to vote on certain corporate actions and may pay dividends, although it rarely does in venture investments. In liquidation, common stockholders are the last to share in the proceeds from the sale of a corporation's assets; bondholders and preferred shareholders have priority. Common stock is often used in first-round start-up financing.

Community development corporation ❙ A corporation established to develop economic programs for a community and, in most cases, to provide financial support for such development.

Competitor ❙ A business whose product or service is marketed for the same purpose/use and to the same consumer group as the product or service of another.

Computer code sharing ❙ An arrangement whereby flights of a regional airline are identified by the two-letter code of a major carrier in the computer reservation system to help direct passengers to new regional carriers.

Consignment ❙ A merchandising agreement, usually referring to secondhand shops, where the dealer pays the owner of an item a percentage of the profit when the item is sold.

Consortium ❙ A coalition of organizations such as banks and corporations for ventures requiring large capital resources.

Consultant ❙ An individual that is paid by a business to provide advice and expertise in a particular area.

Consumer price index ❙ A measure of the fluctuation in prices between two points in time.

Consumer research ❚ Research conducted by a business to obtain information about existing or potential consumer markets.

Continuation coverage ❚ Health coverage offered for a specified period of time to employees who leave their jobs and to their widows, divorced spouses, or dependents.

Contractions ❚ *See* Business contractions.

Convertible preferred stock ❚ A class of stock that pays a reasonable dividend and is convertible into common stock (see separate citation). Generally the convertible feature may only be exercised after being held for a stated period of time. This arrangement is usually considered second-round financing when a company needs equity to maintain its cash flow.

Convertible securities ❚ A feature of certain bonds, debentures, or preferred stocks that allows them to be exchanged by the owner for another class of securities at a future date and in accordance with any other terms of the issue.

Copayment ❚ *See* Coinsurance.

Copyright ❚ A legal form of protection available to creators and authors to safeguard their works from unlawful use or claim of ownership by others. Copyrights may be acquired for works of art, sculpture, music, and published or unpublished manuscripts. All copyrights should be registered at the Copyright Office of the Library of Congress.

Corporate financial ratios ❚ (*See also* Industry financial ratios) The relationship between key figures found in a company's financial statement expressed as a numeric value. Used to evalu-ate risk and company performance. Also known as Financial averages, Operating ratios, and Business ratios.

Corporation ❚ A legal entity, chartered by a state or the federal government, recognized as a separate entity having its own rights, privileges, and liabilities distinct from those of its members.

Cost containment ❚ Actions taken by employers and insurers to curtail rising health care costs; for example, increasing employee cost sharing (see separate citation), requiring second opinions, or preadmission screening.

Cost sharing ❚ The requirement that health care consumers contribute to their own medical care costs through deductibles and coinsurance (see separate citations). Cost sharing does not include the amounts paid in premiums. It is used to control utilization of services; for example, requiring a fixed amount to be paid with each health care service.

Cottage industry ❚ (*See also* Home-based business) Businesses based in the home in which the family members are the labor force and family-owned equipment is used to process the goods.

Credit Rating ❚ A letter or number calculated by an organization (such as Dun & Bradstreet) to represent the ability and disposition of a business to meet its financial obligations.

Customer service ❚ Various techniques used to ensure the satisfaction of a customer.

Cyclical peak ❚ The upper turning point in a business cycle.

Cyclical trough ❚ The lower turning point in a business cycle.

DBA ❚ *See* Business name.

Death ❚ *See* Business death.

Debenture ❚ A certificate given as acknowledgment of a debt (see separate citation) secured by the general credit of the issuing corporation. A bond, usually without security, issued by a corporation and sometimes convertible to common stock.

Debt ❚ (*See also* Long-term debt; Mid-term debt; Securitized debt; Short-term debt) Something owed by one person to another. Financing in which a company receives capital that must be repaid; no ownership is transferred.

Debt capital ❚ Business financing that normally requires periodic interest payments and repayment of the principal within a specified time.

Debt financing ❚ *See* Debt capital.

Debt securities ❚ Loans such as bonds and notes that provide a specified rate of return for a specified period of time.

Deductible ❚ A set amount that an individual must pay before any benefits are received.

Demand shock absorbers ❚ A term used to describe the role that some small firms play by expanding their output levels to accommodate a transient surge in demand.

Demographics ❚ Statistics on various markets, including age, income, and education, used to target specific products or services to appropriate consumer groups.

Demonstration ❚ Showing that a product or process has been modified sufficiently to meet the needs of users.

Deregulation ❚ The lifting of government restrictions; for example, the lifting of government restrictions on the entry of new businesses, the expansion of services, and the setting of prices in particular industries.

Desktop Publishing ❚ Using personal computers and specialized software to produce camera-ready copy for publications.

Digital cash ❚ A system that allows a person to make financial transactions over the Internet. This system allows a person to purchase goods or services by transmitting a number from one computer to another.

Disaster loans ❚ Various types of physical and economic assistance available to individuals and businesses through the U.S. Small Business Administration (SBA). This is the only SBA loan program available for residential purposes.

Discrimination ❚ The denial of the rights and privileges of employ-ment based on factors such as age, race, religion, or gender.

Diseconomies of scale ❚ The condition in which the costs of production increase faster than the volume of production.

Dissolution ❚ *See* Business dissolution.

Distribution ❚ Delivering a product or process to the user.

Distributor ❚ One who delivers merchandise to the user.

Diversified company ❚ A company whose products and services are used by several different markets.

Doing business as (DBA) ❚ *See* Business name.

Dow Jones ❚ An information services company that publishes the Wall Street Journal and other sources of financial information.

Dow Jones Industrial Average ❚ An indicator of stock market performance.

Earned income ❚ A tax term that refers to wages and salaries earned by the recipient, as opposed to monies earned through interest and dividends.

E-commerce ❚ *See* Electronic commerce.

Economic efficiency ❚ The use of productive resources to the fullest practical extent in the provision of the set of goods and services that is most preferred by purchasers in the economy.

Economic indicators ❚ Statistics used to express the state of the economy. These include the length of the average work week, the rate of unemployment, and stock prices.

Economically disadvantaged ❚ *See* Socially and economically disadvantaged.

Economies of scale ❚ *See* Scale economies.

EEOC ❚ *See* Equal Employment Opportunity Commission.

8(a) Program ❚ A program authorized by the Small Business Act that directs federal contracts to small businesses owned and operated by socially and economically disadvantaged individuals.

Electronic mail (e-mail) ❚ The electronic transmission of mail via phone lines.

Electonic commerce (e-commerce) ❚ Buying and selling goods and services through the Internet.

E-mail ❚ *See* Electronic mail.

Employee leasing ❚ A contract by which employers arrange to have their workers hired by a leasing company and then leased back to them for a management fee. The leasing company typically assumes the administrative burden of payroll and provides a benefit package to the workers.

Employee tenure ❚ The length of time an employee works for a particular employer.

Employer identification number ❚ The business equivalent of a social security number. Assigned by the U.S. Internal Revenue Service.

Enterprise ❚ An aggregation of all establishments owned by a parent company. An enterprise may consist of a single, independent establishment or include subsidiaries and other branches under the same ownership and control.

Enterprise zone ❚ A designated area, usually found in inner cities and other areas with significant unemployment, where businesses receive tax credits and other incentives to entice them to establish operations there.

Entrepreneur ❚ A person who takes the risk of organizing and operating a new business venture.

Entry ❚ *See* Business entry

Equal Employment Opportunity Commission (EEOC) ❚ A federal agency that ensures nondiscrimination in the hiring and firing practices of a business.

Equal opportunity employer ❚ An employer who adheres to the standards set by the Equal Employment Opportunity Commission (see separate citation).

Equity ❚ (*See also* Common Stock; Equity midrisk venture capital) The ownership interest. Financing in which partial or total ownership of a company is surrendered in exchange for capital. An

investor's financial return comes from dividend payments and from growth in the net worth of the business.

Equity capital ❚ *See* Equity; Equity midrisk venture capital.

Equity financing ❚ *See* Equity; Equity midrisk venture capital.

Equity midrisk venture capital ❚ An unsecured investment in a company. Usually a purchase of ownership interest in a company that occurs in the later stages of a company's development.

Equity partnership ❚ A limited partnership arrangement for providing start-up and seed capital to businesses.

Equity securities ❚ *See* Equity.

Equity-type ❚ Debt financing subordinated to conventional debt.

Establishment ❚ A single-location business unit that may be independent (a single-establishment enterprise) or owned by a parent enterprise.

Establishment and Enterprise Microdata File ❚ *See* U.S. Establishment and Enterprise Microdata File.

Establishment birth ❚ *See* Business birth.

Establishment Longitudinal Microdata File ❚ *See* U.S. Establishment Longitudinal Microdata File.

Ethics ❚ *See* Business ethics.

Evaluation ❚ Determining the potential success of translating an invention into a product or process.

Experience rating ❚ *See* Underwriting.

Exit ❚ *See* Business exit.

Export ❚ A product sold outside of the country.

Export license ❚ A general or specific license granted by the U.S. Department of Commerce required of anyone wishing to export goods. Some restricted articles need approval from the U.S. Departments of State, Defense, or Energy.

Extranet ❚ (*See also* Intranet) An intranet that provides various levels of accessibility to outsiders. Access to an extranet can only be obtained if you have a valid username and password.

Failure ❚ *See* Business failure.

Fair share agreement ❚ (*See also* Franchising) An agreement reached between a franchisor and a minority business organization to extend business ownership to minorities by either reducing the amount of capital required or by setting aside certain marketing areas for minority business owners.

Feasibility study ❚ A study to determine the likelihood that a proposed product or development will fulfill the objectives of a particular investor.

Federal Trade Commission (FTC) ❚ Federal agency that promotes free enterprise and competition within the U.S.

Federal Trade Mark Act of 1946 ❚ *See* Lanham Act.

Fictional name ❚ *See* Business name.

Fiduciary ❚ An individual or group that hold assets in trust for a beneficiary.

Financial analysis ❚ The techniques used to determine money needs in a business. Techniques include ratio analysis, calculation of return on investment, guides for measuring profitability, and break-even analysis to determine ultimate success.

Financial intermediary ▌ A financial institution that acts as the intermediary between borrowers and lenders. Banks, savings and loan associations, finance companies, and venture capital companies are major financial intermediaries in the United States.

Financial ratios ▌ *See* Corporate financial ratios; Industry financial ratios.

Financial statement ▌ A written record of business finances, including balance sheets and profit and loss statements.

Financing ▌ *See* First-stage financing; Second-stage financing; Third-stage financing.

First-stage financing ▌ (*See also* Second-stage financing; Third-stage financing) Financing provided to companies that have expended their initial capital, and require funds to start full-scale manufacturing and sales. Also known as First-round financing.

Fiscal year ▌ Any twelve-month period used by businesses for accounting purposes.

504 Program ▌ *See* Certified development corporation.

Flexible benefit plan ▌ A plan that offers a choice among cash and/or qualified benefits such as group term life insurance, accident and health insurance, group legal services, dependent care assistance, and vacations.

FOB ▌ *See* Free on board

Format franchising ▌ *See* Business format franchising; Franchising.

401(k) plan ▌ A financial plan where employees contribute a percentage of their earnings to a fund that is invested in stocks, bonds, or money markets for the purpose of saving money for retirement.

Four Ps ▌ Marketing terms: Product, Price, Place, and Promotion.

Franchising ▌ A form of licensing by which the owner—the franchisor—distributes or markets a product, method, or service through affiliated dealers called franchisees. The product, method, or service being marketed is identified by a brand name, and the franchisor maintains control over the marketing methods employed. The franchisee is often given exclusive access to a defined geographic area.

Free on board (FOB) ▌ A pricing term indicating that the quoted price includes the cost of loading goods into transport vessels at a specified place.

Frictional unemployment ▌ *See* Un-employment.

FTC ▌ *See* Federal Trade Commission.

Fulfillment ▌ The systems necessary for accurate delivery of an ordered item, including subscriptions and direct marketing.

Full-time workers ▌ Generally, those who work a regular schedule of more than 35 hours per week.

Garment registration number ▌ A number that must appear on every garment sold in the U.S. to indicate the manufacturer of the garment, which may or may not be the same as the label under which the garment is sold. The U.S. Federal Trade Commission assigns and regulates garment registration numbers.

Gatekeeper ▌ A key contact point for entry into a network.

GDP ▌ *See* Gross domestic product.

General obligation bond ▌ A municipal bond secured by the taxing power of the municipality. The Tax Reform Act of 1986 limits the purposes for which such bonds may be issued and establishes volume limits on the extent of their issuance.

GNP ▌ *See* Gross national product.

Good Housekeeping Seal ▌ Seal appearing on products that signifies the fulfillment of the standards set by the Good Housekeeping Institute to protect consumer interests.

Goods sector ▌ All businesses producing tangible goods, including agriculture, mining, construction, and manufacturing businesses.

GPO ▌ *See* Gross product originating.

Gross domestic product (GDP) ▌ The part of the nation's gross national product (see separate citation) generated by private business using resources from within the country.

Gross national product (GNP) ▌ The most comprehensive single measure of aggregate economic output. Represents the market value of the total output of goods and services produced by a nation's economy.

Gross product originating (GPO) ▌ A measure of business output estimated from the income or production side using employee compensation, profit income, net interest, capital consumption, and indirect business taxes.

HAL ▌ *See* Handicapped assistance loan program.

Handicapped assistance loan program (HAL) ▌ Low-interest direct loan program through the U.S. Small Business Administration (SBA) for handicapped persons. The SBA requires that these persons demonstrate that their disability is such that it is impossible for them to secure employment, thus making it necessary to go into their own business to make a living.

Health maintenance organization (HMO) ▌ Organization of physi-cians and other health care professionals that provides health services to subscribers and their dependents on a prepaid basis.

Health provider ▌ An individual or institution that gives medical care. Under Medicare, an institutional provider is a hospital, skilled nursing facility, home health agency, or provider of certain physical therapy services.

Hispanic ▌ A person of Cuban, Mexican, Puerto Rican, Latin American (Central or South American), European Spanish, or other Spanish-speaking origin or ancestry.

HMO ▌ *See* Health maintenance organization.

Home-based business ▌ (*See also* Cottage industry) A business with an operating address that is also a residential address (usually the residential address of the proprietor).

Hub-and-spoke system ▌ A system in which flights of an airline from many different cities (the spokes) converge at a single airport (the hub). After allowing passengers sufficient time to make connections, planes then depart for different cities.

Human Resources Management ▌ A business program designed to oversee recruiting, pay, benefits, and other issues related to the company's work force, including planning to determine the optimal use of labor to increase production, thereby increasing profit.

Idea ▌ An original concept for a new product or process.

Import ▮ Products produced outside the country in which they are consumed.

Income ▮ Money or its equivalent, earned or accrued, resulting from the sale of goods and services.

Income statement ▮ A financial statement that lists the profits and losses of a company at a given time.

Incorporation ▮ The filing of a certificate of incorporation with the secretary of state, thereby limiting the business owner's liability.

Incubator ▮ A facility designed to encourage entrepreneurship and minimize obstacles to new business formation and growth, particularly for high-technology firms, by housing a number of fledgling enterprises that share an array of services, such as meeting areas, secretarial services, accounting, research library, on-site financial and management counseling, and word processing facilities.

Independent contractor ▮ An individual considered self-employed (see separate citation) and responsible for paying Social Security taxes and income taxes on earnings.

Indirect health coverage ▮ Health insurance obtained through another individual's health care plan; for example, a spouse's employer-sponsored plan.

Industrial development authority ▮ The financial arm of a state or other political subdivision established for the purpose of financing economic development in an area, usually through loans to nonprofit organizations, which in turn provide facilities for manufacturing and other industrial operations.

Industry financial ratios ▮ (*See also* Corporate financial ratios) Corporate financial ratios averaged for a specified industry. These are used for comparison purposes and reveal industry trends and identify differences between the performance of a specific company and the performance of its industry. Also known as Industrial averages, Industry ratios, Financial averages, and Business or Industrial norms.

Inflation ▮ Increases in volume of currency and credit, generally resulting in a sharp and continuing rise in price levels.

Informal capital ▮ Financing from informal, unorganized sources; includes informal debt capital such as trade credit or loans from friends and relatives and equity capital from informal investors.

Initial public offering (IPO) ▮ A corporation's first offering of stock to the public.

Innovation ▮ The introduction of a new idea into the marketplace in the form of a new product or service or an improvement in organization or process.

Intellectual property ▮ Any idea/work that can be considered proprietary in nature and thus protected from infringement by others.

Internal capital ▮ Debt or equity financing obtained from the owner or through retained business earnings.

Internet ▮ A government-designed computer network that contains large amounts of information and is accessible through various vendors for a fee.

Intranet ▮ (*See also* Extranet) A web site belonging to an organization or a corporation, that is accessible only to employees, members, or others that have authorization.

Intrapreneurship ▮ The state of employing entrepreneurial principles to nonentrepreneurial situations.

Invention ▮ The tangible form of a technological idea, which could include a laboratory prototype, drawings, formulas, etc.

IPO ▮ *See* Initial public offering.

Job description ▮ The duties and responsibilities required in a particular position.

Job tenure ▮ A period of time during which an individual is continuously employed in the same job.

Joint marketing agreements ▮ Agree-ments between regional and major airlines, often involving the coordination of flight schedules, fares, and baggage transfer. These agreements help regional carriers operate at lower cost.

Joint venture ▮ Venture in which two or more people combine efforts in a particular business enterprise, usually a single transaction or a limited activity, and agree to share the profits and losses jointly or in proportion to their contributions.

Keogh plan ▮ Designed for self-employed persons and unincorporated businesses as a tax-deferred pension account.

Labor force ▮ Civilians considered eligible for employment who are also willing and able to work.

Labor force participation rate ▮ The civilian labor force as a percentage of the civilian population.

Labor intensity ▮ (*See also* Capital intensity) The relative importance of labor in the production process, usually measured as the capital-labor ratio; i.e., the ratio of units of capital (typically, dollars of tangible assets) to the number of employees. The higher the capital-labor ratio exhibited by a firm or industry, the lower the capital intensity of that firm or industry is said to be.

Labor surplus area ▮ An area in which there exists a high unemployment rate. In procurement (see separate citation), extra points are given to firms in counties that are designated a labor surplus area; this information is requested on procurement bid sheets.

Labor union ▮ An organization of similarly-skilled workers who collectively bargain with management over the conditions of employment.

Laboratory prototype ▮ *See* Prototype.

LAN ▮ *See* Local Area Network.

Lanham Act ▮ Refers to the Federal Trade Mark Act of 1946. Protects registered trademarks, trade names, and other service marks used in commerce.

Large business-dominated industry ▮ Industry in which a minimum of 60 percent of employment or sales is in firms with more than 500 workers.

LBO ▮ *See* Leveraged buy-out.

Leader pricing ▮ A reduction in the price of a good or service in order to generate more sales of that good or service.

Legal list ▮ A list of securities selected by a state in which certain institutions and fiduciaries (such as pension funds, insurance companies, and banks) may invest. Securities not on the list are not eligible for investment. Legal lists typically restrict investments to high quality securities meeting certain specifications. Generally, investment is limited to U.S. securities and investment-grade blue chip securities (see separate citation).

Leveraged buy-out (LBO) ❚ The purchase of a business or a division of a corporation through a highly leveraged financing package.

Liability ❚ An obligation or duty to perform a service or an act. Also defined as money owed.

License ❚ (*See also* Business license) A legal agreement granting to another the right to use a technological innovation.

Limited partnerships ❚ *See* Venture capital limited partnerships

Liquidity ❚ The ability to convert a security into cash promptly.

Loans ❚ *See* Commercial loans; Disaster loans; SBA direct loans; SBA guaranteed loans; SBA special lending institution categories.

Local Area Network (LAN) ❚ Computer networks contained within a single building or small area; used to facilitate the sharing of information.

Local development corporation ❚ An organization, usually made up of local citizens of a community, designed to improve the economy of the area by inducing business and industry to locate and expand there. A local development corporation establishes a capability to finance local growth.

Long-haul rates ❚ Rates charged by a transporter in which the distance traveled is more than 800 miles.

Long-term debt ❚ An obligation that matures in a period that exceeds five years.

Low-grade bond ❚ A corporate bond that is rated below investment grade by the major rating agencies (Standard and Poor's, Moody's).

Macro-efficiency ❚ (*See also* Economic efficiency) Efficiency as it pertains to the operation of markets and market systems.

Managed care ❚ A cost-effective health care program initiated by employers whereby low-cost health care is made available to the employees in return for exclusive patronage to program doctors.

Management and technical assistance ❚ A term used by many programs to mean business (as opposed to technological) assistance.

Management Assistance Programs ❚ *See* SBA Management Assistance Programs

Mandated benefits ❚ Specific treatments, providers, or individuals required by law to be included in commercial health plans.

Market evaluation ❚ The use of market information to determine the sales potential of a specific product or process.

Market failure ❚ The situation in which the workings of a competitive market do not produce the best results from the point of view of the entire society.

Market information ❚ Data of any type that can be used for market evaluation, which could include demographic data, technology forecasting, regulatory changes, etc.

Market research ❚ A systematic collection, analysis, and reporting of data about the market and its preferences, opinions, trends, and plans; used for corporate decision-making.

Market share ❚ In a particular market, the percentage of sales of a specific product.

Marketing ❚ Promotion of goods or services through various media.

Master Establishment List (MEL) ❚ A list of firms in the United States developed by the U.S. Small Business Administration; firms can be selected by industry, region, state, standard metropolitan statistical area (see separate citation), county, and zip code.

Maturity ❚ (*See also* Term) The date upon which the principal or stated value of a bond or other indebtedness becomes due and payable.

Medicaid (Title XIX) ❚ A federally aided, state-operated and administered program that provides medical benefits for certain low-income persons in need of health and medical care who are eligible for one of the government's welfare cash payment programs, including the aged, the blind, the disabled, and members of families with dependent children where one parent is absent, incapacitated, or unemployed.

Medicare (Title XVIII) ❚ A nationwide health insurance program for disabled and aged persons. Health insurance is available to insured persons without regard to income. Monies from payroll taxes cover hospital insurance and monies from general revenues and beneficiary premiums pay for supplementary medical insurance.

MEL ❚ *See* Master Establishment List.

Metropolitan statistical area (MSA) ❚ A means used by the government to define large population centers that may transverse different governmental jurisdictions. For example, the Washington, D.C., MSA includes the District of Columbia and contiguous parts of Maryland and Virginia because all of these geopolitical areas comprise one population and economic operating unit.

Mezzanine financing ❚ *See* Third-stage financing.

MESBIC ❚ *See* Minority enterprise small business investment corporation.

MET ❚ *See* Multiple employer trust.

Micro-efficiency ❚ (*See also* Economic efficiency) Efficiency as it pertains to the operation of individual firms.

Microdata ❚ Information on the characteristics of an individual business firm.

Mid-term debt ❚ An obligation that matures within one to five years.

Midrisk venture capital ❚ *See* Equity midrisk venture capital.

Minimum premium plan ❚ A combination approach to funding an insurance plan aimed primarily at premium tax savings. The employer self-funds a fixed percentage of estimated monthly claims and the insurance company insures the excess.

Minimum wage ❚ The lowest hourly wage allowed by the federal government.

Minority Business Development Agency ❚ Contracts with private firms throughout the nation to sponsor Minority Business Development Centers which provide minority firms with advice and technical assistance on a fee basis.

Minority Enterprise Small Business Investment Corporation (MESBIC) ❚ A federally funded private venture capital firm licensed by the U.S. Small Business Administration to provide capital to minority-owned businesses (see separate citation).

Minority-owned business ∎ Businesses owned by those who are socially or economically disadvantaged (see separate citation).

Mom and Pop business ∎ A small store or enterprise having limited capital, principally employing family members.

Moonlighter ∎ A wage-and-salary worker with a side business.

MSA ∎ *See* Metropolitan statistical area.

Multi-employer plan ∎ A health plan to which more than one employer is required to contribute and that may be maintained through a collective bargaining agreement and required to meet standards prescribed by the U.S. Department of Labor.

Multi-level marketing ∎ A system of selling in which you sign up other people to assist you, and they, in turn, recruit others to help them. Some entrepreneurs have built successful companies on this concept because the main focus of their activities is their product and product sales.

Multimedia ∎ The use of several types of media to promote a product or service. Also refers to the use of several different types of media (sight, sound, pictures, text) in a CD-ROM (see separate citation) product.

Multiple employer trust (MET) ∎ A self-funded benefit plan generally geared toward small employers sharing a common interest.

NAFTA ∎ *See* North American Free Trade Agreement.

NASDAQ ∎ *See* National Association of Securities Dealers Automated Quotations.

National Association of Securities Dealers Automated Quotations ∎ Provides price quotes on over-the-counter securities as well as securities listed on the New York Stock Exchange.

National income ∎ Aggregate earnings of labor and property arising from the production of goods and services in a nation's economy.

Net assets ∎ *See* Net worth.

Net income ∎ The amount remaining from earnings and profits after all expenses and costs have been met or deducted. Also known as Net earnings.

Net profit ∎ Money earned after production and overhead expenses (see separate citations) have been deducted.

Net worth ∎ (*See also* Capital) The difference between a company's total assets and its total liabilities.

Network ∎ A chain of interconnected individuals or organizations sharing information and/or services.

New York Stock Exchange (NYSE) ∎ The oldest stock exchange in the U.S. Allows for trading in stocks, bonds, warrants, options, and rights that meet listing requirements.

Niche ∎ A career or business for which a person is well-suited. Also, a product which fulfills one need of a particular market segment, often with little or no competition.

Nodes ∎ One workstation in a network, either local area or wide area (see separate citations).

Nonbank bank ∎ A bank that either accepts deposits or makes loans, but not both. Used to create many new branch banks.

Noncompetitive awards ∎ A method of contracting whereby the federal government negotiates with only one contractor to supply a product or service.

Nonmember bank ∎ A state-regulated bank that does not belong to the federal bank system.

Nonprofit ∎ An organization that has no shareholders, does not distribute profits, and is without federal and state tax liabilities.

Norms ∎ *See* Financial ratios.

North American Free Trade Agreement (NAFTA) ∎ Passed in 1993, NAFTA eliminates trade barriers among businesses in the U.S., Canada, and Mexico.

NYSE ∎ *See* New York Stock Exchange

Occupational Safety & Health Administration (OSHA) ∎ Federal agency that regulates health and safety standards within the workplace.

Optimal firm size ∎ The business size at which the production cost per unit of output (average cost) is, in the long run, at its minimum.

Organizational chart ∎ A hierarchical chart tracking the chain of command within an organization.

OSHA ∎ *See* Occupational Safety & Health Administration.

Overhead ∎ Expenses, such as employee benefits and building utilities, incurred by a business that are unrelated to the actual product or service sold.

Owner's capital ∎ Debt or equity funds provided by the owner(s) of a business; sources of owner's capital are personal savings, sales of assets, or loans from financial institutions.

P & L ∎ *See* Profit and loss statement.

Part-time workers ∎ Normally, those who work less than 35 hours per week. The Tax Reform Act indicated that part-time workers who work less than 17.5 hours per week may be excluded from health plans for purposes of complying with federal nondiscrimination rules.

Part-year workers ∎ Those who work less than 50 weeks per year.

Partnership ∎ Two or more parties who enter into a legal relationship to conduct business for profit. Defined by the U.S. Internal Revenue Code as joint ventures, syndicates, groups, pools, and other associations of two or more persons organized for profit that are not specifically classified in the IRS code as corporations or proprietorships.

Patent ∎ A grant by the government assuring an inventor the sole right to make, use, and sell an invention for a period of 17 years.

PC ∎ *See* Professional corporation.

Peak ∎ *See* Cyclical peak.

Pension ∎ A series of payments made monthly, semiannually, annually, or at other specified intervals during the lifetime of the pensioner for distribution upon retirement. The term is sometimes used to denote the portion of the retirement allowance financed by the employer's contributions.

Pension fund ∎ A fund established to provide for the payment of pension benefits; the collective contributions made by all of the parties to the pension plan.

Performance appraisal ∎ An established set of objective criteria, based on job description and requirements, that is used to evaluate the performance of an employee in a specific job.

Permit ❚ *See* Business license.

Plan ❚ *See* Business plan.

Pooling ❚ An arrangement for employers to achieve efficiencies and lower health costs by joining together to purchase group health insurance or self-insurance.

PPO ❚ *See* Preferred provider organization

Preferred lenders program ❚ *See* SBA special lending institution categories

Preferred provider organization (PPO) ❚ A contractual arrangement with a health care services organization that agrees to discount its health care rates in return for faster payment and/or a patient base.

Premiums ❚ The amount of money paid to an insurer for health insurance under a policy. The premium is generally paid periodically (e.g., monthly), and often is split between the employer and the employee. Unlike deductibles and coinsurance or copayments, premiums are paid for coverage whether or not benefits are actually used.

Prime-age workers ❚ Employees 25 to 54 years of age.

Prime contract ❚ A contract awarded directly by the U.S. Federal Government.

Private company ❚ *See* Closely held corporation.

Private placement ❚ A method of raising capital by offering for sale an investment or business to a small group of investors (generally avoiding registration with the Securities and Exchange Commis-sion or state securities registration agencies). Also known as Private financing or Private offering.

Pro forma ❚ The use of hypothetical figures in financial statements to represent future expenditures, debts, and other potential financial expenses.

Proactive ❚ Taking the initiative to solve problems and anticipate future events before they happen, instead of reacting to an already existing problem or waiting for a difficult situation to occur.

Procurement ❚ (*See also* 8(a) Program; Small business set asides) A contract from an agency of the federal government for goods or services from a small business.

Prodigy ❚ (*See also* America Online) An online service which is accessible by computer modem. The service features Internet access, bulletin boards, online periodicals, electronic mail, and other services for subscribers.

Product development ❚ The stage of the innovation process where research is translated into a product or process through evaluation, adaptation, and demonstration.

Product franchising ❚ An arrangement for a franchisee to use the name and to produce the product line of the franchisor or parent corporation.

Production ❚ The manufacture of a product.

Production prototype ❚ *See* Prototype.

Productivity ❚ A measurement of the number of goods produced during a specific amount of time.

Professional corporation (PC) ❚ Organized by members of a pro-fession such as medicine, dentistry, or law for the purpose of con-ducting their professional activities as a corporation. Liability of a member or shareholder is limited in the same manner as in a business corporation.

Profit and loss statement (P & L) ❚ The summary of the incomes and costs of a company's operation during a specific period of time. Also known as Income and expense statement.

Proposal ❚ *See* Business plan.

Proprietorship ❚ The most common legal form of business owner-ship; about 85 percent of all small businesses are proprietorships. The liability of the owner is unlimited in this form of ownership.

Prospective payment system ❚ A cost-containment measure included in the Social Security Amendments of 1983 whereby Medicare payments to hospitals are based on established prices, rather than on cost reimbursement.

Prototype ❚ A model that demonstrates the validity of the concept of an invention (laboratory prototype); a model that meets the needs of the manufacturing process and the user (production prototype).

Prudent investor rule or standard ❚ A legal doctrine that requires fiduciaries to make investments using the prudence, diligence, and intelligence that would be used by a prudent person in making similar investments. Because fiduciaries make investments on behalf of third-party beneficiaries, the standard results in very conservative investments. Until recently, most state regulations required the fiduciary to apply this standard to each investment. Newer, more progressive regulations permit fiduciaries to apply this standard to the portfolio taken as a whole, thereby allowing a fiduciary to balance a portfolio with higher-yield, higher-risk invest-ments. In states with more progressive regulations, practically every type of security is eligible for inclusion in the portfolio of investments made by a fiduciary, provided that the portfolio investments, in their totality, are those of a prudent person.

Public equity markets ❚ Organized markets for trading in equity shares such as common stocks, preferred stocks, and warrants. Includes markets for both regularly traded and nonregularly traded securities.

Public offering ❚ General solicitation for participation in an investment opportunity. Interstate public offerings are supervised by the U.S. Securities and Exchange Commission (see separate citation).

Quality control ❚ The process by which a product is checked and tested to ensure consistent standards of high quality.

Rate of return z (See also Yield) The yield obtained on a security or other investment based on its purchase price or its current market price. The total rate of return is current income plus or minus capital appreciation or depreciation.

Real property ❚ Includes the land and all that is contained on it.

Realignment ❚ *See* Resource realignment.

Recession ❚ Contraction of economic activity occurring between the peak and trough (see separate citations) of a business cycle.

Regulated market ❚ A market in which the government controls the forces of supply and demand, such as who may enter and what price may be charged.

Regulation D ❚ A vehicle by which small businesses make small offerings and private placements of securities with limited disclosure requirements. It was designed to ease the burdens imposed on small businesses utilizing this method of capital formation.

Regulatory Flexibility Act ▌ An act requiring federal agencies to evaluate the impact of their regulations on small businesses before the regulations are issued and to consider less burdensome alternatives.

Research ▌ The initial stage of the innovation process, which includes idea generation and invention.

Research and development financing ▌ A tax-advantaged partnership set up to finance product development for start-ups as well as more mature companies.

Resource mobility ▌ The ease with which labor and capital move from firm to firm or from industry to industry.

Resource realignment ▌ The adjustment of productive resources to interindustry changes in demand.

Resources ▌ The sources of support or help in the innovation process, including sources of financing, technical evaluation, market evaluation, management and business assistance, etc.

Retained business earnings ▌ Business profits that are retained by the business rather than being distributed to the shareholders as dividends.

Revolving credit ▌ An agreement with a lending institution for an amount of money, which cannot exceed a set maximum, over a specified period of time. Each time the borrower repays a portion of the loan, the amount of the repayment may be borrowed yet again.

Risk capital ▌ *See* Venture capital.

Risk management ▌ The act of identifying potential sources of financial loss and taking action to minimize their negative impact.

Routing ▌ The sequence of steps necessary to complete a product during production.

S corporations ▌ *See* Sub chapter S corporations.

SBA ▌ *See* Small Business Administration.

SBA direct loans ▌ Loans made directly by the U.S. Small Business Administration (SBA); monies come from funds appropriated specifically for this purpose. In general, SBA direct loans carry interest rates slightly lower than those in the private financial markets and are available only to applicants unable to secure private financing or an SBA guaranteed loan.

SBA 504 Program ▌ *See* Certified development corporation.

SBA guaranteed loans ▌ Loans made by lending institutions in which the U.S. Small Business Administration (SBA) will pay a prior agreed-upon percentage of the outstanding principal in the event the borrower of the loan defaults. The terms of the loan and the interest rate are negotiated between the borrower and the lending institution, within set parameters.

SBA loans ▌ *See* Disaster loans; SBA direct loans; SBA guaranteed loans; SBA special lending institution categories.

SBA Management Assistance Programs ▌ (*See also* Active Corps of Executives; Service Corps of Retired Executives; Small business institutes program) Classes, workshops, counseling, and publications offered by the U.S. Small Business Administration.

SBA special lending institution categories ▌ U.S. Small Business Administration (SBA) loan program in which the SBA promises certified banks a 72-hour turnaround period in giving its approval for a loan, and in which preferred lenders in a pilot program are allowed to write SBA loans without seeking prior SBA approval.

SBDB ▌ *See* Small Business Data Base.

SBDC ▌ *See* Small business development centers.

SBI ▌ *See* Small business institutes program.

SBIC ▌ *See* Small business investment corporation.

SBIR Program ▌ *See* Small Business Innovation Development Act of 1982.

Scale economies ▌ The decline of the production cost per unit of output (average cost) as the volume of output increases.

Scale efficiency ▌ The reduction in unit cost available to a firm when producing at a higher output volume.

SCORE ▌ *See* Service Corps of Retired Executives.

SEC ▌ *See* Securities and Exchange Commission.

SECA ▌ *See* Self-Employment Contribu-tions Act.

Second-stage financing ▌ (*See also* First-stage financing; Third-stage financing) Working capital for the initial expansion of a com-pany that is producing, shipping, and has growing accounts receiv-able and inventories. Also known as Second-round financing.

Secondary market ▌ A market established for the purchase and sale of outstanding securities following their initial distribution.

Secondary worker ▌ Any worker in a family other than the person who is the primary source of income for the family.

Secondhand capital ▌ Previously used and subsequently resold capital equipment (e.g., buildings and machinery).

Securities and Exchange Commission (SEC) ▌ Federal agency charged with regulating the trade of securities to prevent unethical practices in the investor market.

Securitized debt ▌ A marketing technique that converts long-term loans to marketable securities.

Seed capital ▌ Venture financing provided in the early stages of the innovation process, usually during product development.

Self-employed person ▌ One who works for a profit or fees in his or her own business, profession, or trade, or who operates a farm.

Self-Employment Contributions Act (SECA) ▌ Federal law that governs the self-employment tax (see separate citation).

Self-employment income ▌ Income covered by Social Security if a business earns a net income of at least $400.00 during the year. Taxes are paid on earnings that exceed $400.00.

Self-employment retirement plan ▌ *See* Keogh plan.

Self-employment tax ▌ Required tax imposed on self-employed individuals for the provision of Social Security and Medicare. The tax must be paid quarterly with estimated income tax statements.

Self-funding ▌ A health benefit plan in which a firm uses its own funds to pay claims, rather than transferring the financial risks of paying claims to an outside insurer in exchange for premium payments.

Service Corps of Retired Executives (SCORE) ▌ (*See also* Active Corps of Executives) Volunteers for the SBA Management

Assistance Program who provide one-on-one counseling and teach workshops and seminars for small firms.

Service firm ▌ *See* Business service firm.

Service sector ▌ Broadly defined, all U.S. industries that produce intangibles, including the five major industry divisions of transportation, communications, and utilities; wholesale trade; retail trade; finance, insurance, and real estate; and services.

Set asides ▌ *See* Small business set asides.

Short-haul service ▌ A type of transportation service in which the transporter supplies service between cities where the maximum distance is no more than 200 miles.

Short-term debt ▌ An obligation that matures in one year.

SIC codes ▌ *See* Standard Industrial Classification codes.

Single-establishment enterprise ▌ *See* Establishment.

Small business ▌ An enterprise that is independently owned and operated, is not dominant in its field, and employs fewer than 500 people. For SBA purposes, the U.S. Small Business Administration (SBA) considers various other factors (such as gross annual sales) in determining size of a business.

Small Business Administration (SBA) ▌ An independent federal agency that provides assistance with loans, management, and advocating interests before other federal agencies.

Small Business Data Base ▌ (*See also* U.S. Establishment and Enterprise Microdata File; U.S. Establishment Longitudinal Microdata File) A collection of microdata (see separate citation) files on individual firms developed and maintained by the U.S. Small Business Administration.

Small business development centers (SBDC) ▌ Centers that provide support services to small businesses, such as individual counseling, SBA advice, seminars and conferences, and other learning center activities. Most services are free of charge, or available at minimal cost.

Small business development corporation ▌ *See* Certified development corporation.

Small business-dominated industry ▌ Industry in which a minimum of 60 percent of employment or sales is in firms with fewer than 500 employees.

Small Business Innovation Development Act of 1982 ▌ Federal statute requiring federal agencies with large extramural research and development budgets to allocate a certain percentage of these funds to small research and development firms. The program, called the Small Business Innovation Research (SBIR) Program, is designed to stimulate technological innovation and make greater use of small businesses in meeting national innovation needs.

Small business institutes (SBI) program ▌ Cooperative arrangements made by U.S. Small Business Administration district offices and local colleges and universities to provide small business firms with graduate students to counsel them without charge.

Small business investment corporation (SBIC) ▌ A privately owned company licensed and funded through the U.S. Small Business Administration and private sector sources to provide equity or debt capital to small businesses.

Small business set asides ▌ Procure-ment (see separate citation) opportunities required by law to be on all contracts under $10,000 or a certain percentage of an agency's total procurement expenditure.

Smaller firms ▌ For U.S. Department of Commerce purposes, those firms not included in the Fortune 1000.

SMSA ▌ *See* Metropolitan statistical area.

Socially and economically disadvantaged ▌ Individuals who have been subjected to racial or ethnic prejudice or cultural bias without regard to their qualities as individuals, and whose abilities to compete are impaired because of diminished opportunities to obtain capital and credit.

Sole proprietorship ▌ An unincorporated, one-owner business, farm, or professional practice.

Special lending institution categories ▌ *See* SBA special lending institution categories.

Standard Industrial Classification (SIC) codes ▌ Four-digit codes established by the U.S. Federal Government to categorize businesses by type of economic activity; the first two digits correspond to major groups such as construction and manufacturing, while the last two digits correspond to subgroups such as home construction or highway construction.

Standard metropolitan statistical area (SMSA) ▌ *See* Metropolitan statistical area.

Start-up ▌ A new business, at the earliest stages of development and financing.

Start-up costs ▌ Costs incurred before a business can commence operations.

Start-up financing ▌ Financing provided to companies that have either completed product development and initial marketing or have been in business for less than one year but have not yet sold their product commercially.

Stock ▌ (*See also* Common stock; Convertible preferred stock) A certificate of equity ownership in a business.

Stop-loss coverage ▌ Insurance for a self-insured plan that reimburses the company for any losses it might incur in its health claims beyond a specified amount.

Strategic planning ▌ Projected growth and development of a business to establish a guiding direction for the future. Also used to determine which market segments to explore for optimal sales of products or services.

Structural unemployment ▌ *See* Un-employment.

Sub chapter S corporations ▌ Corpora-tions that are considered noncorporate for tax purposes but legally remain corporations.

Subcontract ▌ A contract between a prime contractor and a subcontractor, or between subcontractors, to furnish supplies or services for performance of a prime contract (see separate citation) or a subcontract.

Surety bonds ▌ Bonds providing reimbursement to an individual, company, or the government if a firm fails to complete a contract. The U.S. Small Business Administration guarantees surety bonds in a program much like the SBA guaranteed loan program (see separate citation).

Swing loan ▌ *See* Bridge financing.

Target market ▌ The clients or customers sought for a business' product or service.

Targeted Jobs Tax Credit ▮ Federal legislation enacted in 1978 that provides a tax credit to an employer who hires structurally unemployed individuals.

Tax number ▮ (*See also* Employer identification number) A number assigned to a business by a state revenue department that enables the business to buy goods without paying sales tax.

Taxable bonds ▮ An interest-bearing certificate of public or private indebtedness. Bonds are issued by public agencies to finance economic development.

Technical assistance ▮ *See* Management and technical assistance

Technical evaluation ▮ Assessment of technological feasibility.

Technology ▮ The method in which a firm combines and utilizes labor and capital resources to produce goods or services; the application of science for commercial or industrial purposes.

Technology transfer ▮ The movement of information about a tech-nology or intellectual property from one party to another for use.

Tenure ▮ *See* **Employee tenure.**

Term ▮ (*See also* Maturity) The length of time for which a loan is made.

Terms of a note ▮ The conditions or limits of a note; includes the interest rate per annum, the due date, and transferability and convertibility features, if any.

Third-party administrator ▮ An outside company responsible for handling claims and performing administrative tasks associated with health insurance plan maintenance.

Third-stage financing ▮ (*See also* First-stage financing; Second-stage financing) Financing provided for the major expansion of a company whose sales volume is increasing and that is breaking even or profitable. These funds are used for further plant expansion, marketing, working capital, or development of an improved product. Also known as Third-round or Mezzanine financing.

Time deposit ▮ A bank deposit that cannot be withdrawn before a specified future time.

Time management ▮ Skills and scheduling techniques used to maximize productivity.

Trade credit ▮ Credit extended by suppliers of raw materials or finished products. In an accounting statement, trade credit is referred to as "accounts payable."

Trade name ▮ The name under which a company conducts business, or by which its business, goods, or services are identified. It may or may not be registered as a trademark.

Trade periodical ▮ A publication with a specific focus on one or more aspects of business and industry.

Trade secret ▮ Competitive advantage gained by a business through the use of a unique manufacturing process or formula.

Trade show ▮ An exhibition of goods or services used in a particular industry. Typically held in exhibition centers where exhibitors rent space to display their merchandise.

Trademark ▮ A graphic symbol, device, or slogan that identifies a business. A business has property rights to its trademark from the inception of its use, but it is still prudent to register all trade-marks with the Trademark Office of the U.S. Department of Commerce.

Translation ▮ *See* Product development.

Treasury bills ▮ Investment tender issued by the Federal Reserve Bank in amounts of $10,000 that mature in 91 to 182 days.

Treasury bonds ▮ Long-term notes with maturity dates of not less than seven and not more than twenty-five years.

Treasury notes ▮ Short-term notes maturing in less than seven years.

Trend ▮ A statistical measurement used to track changes that occur over time.

Trough ▮ *See* Cyclical trough.

UCC ▮ *See* Uniform Commercial Code.

UL ▮ *See* Underwriters Laboratories.

Underwriters Laboratories (UL) ▮ One of several private firms that tests products and processes to determine their safety. Although various firms can provide this kind of testing service, many local and insurance codes specify UL certification.

Underwriting ▮ A process by which an insurer determines whether or not and on what basis it will accept an application for insurance. In an experience-rated plan, premiums are based on a firm's or group's past claims; factors other than prior claims are used for community-rated or manually rated plans.

Unfair competition ▮ Refers to business practices, usually unethical, such as using unlicensed products, pirating merch-andise, or misleading the public through false advertising, which give the offending business an unequitable advantage over others.

Unfunded accrued liability ▮ The excess of total liabilities, both present and prospective, over present and prospective assets.

Unemployment ▮ The joblessness of individuals who are willing to work, who are legally and physically able to work, and who are seeking work. Unemploy-ment may represent the temporary joblessness of a worker between jobs (frictional unemployment) or the joblessness of a worker whose skills are not suitable for jobs available in the labor market (structural unemployment).

Uniform Commercial Code (UCC) ▮ A code of laws governing commercial transactions across the U.S., except Louisiana. Their purpose is to bring uniformity to financial transactions.

Uniform product code (UPC symbol) ▮ A computer-readable label comprised of ten digits and stripes that encodes what a product is and how much it costs. The first five digits are assigned by the Uniform Produce Code Council, and the last five digits by the individual manufacturer.

Unit cost ▮ *See* Average cost.

UPC symbol ▮ *See* Uniform product code.

US Establishment and Enterprise Microdata (USEEM) File ▮ A cross-sectional database containing information on employment, sales, and location for individual enterprises and establishments with employees that have a Dun & Bradstreet credit rating.

US Establishment Longitudinal Microdata (USELM) File ▮ A database containing longitudinally linked sample microdata on establishments drawn from the U.S. Establishment and Enterprise Microdata file (see separate citation).

US Small Business Administration 504 Program ∎ *See* Certified development corporation.

USEEM ∎ *See* U.S. Establishment and Enterprise Microdata File.

USELM ∎ *See* U.S. Establishment Longitudinal Microdata File.

VCN ∎ *See* Venture capital network.

Venture capital ∎ (*See also* Equity; Equity midrisk venture capital) Money used to support new or unusual business ventures that exhibit above-average growth rates, significant potential for market expansion, and are in need of additional financing to sustain growth or further research and development; equity or equity-type financing traditionally provided at the commercialization stage, increasingly available prior to commercialization.

Venture capital company ∎ A company organized to provide seed capital to a business in its formation stage, or in its first or second stage of expansion. Funding is obtained through public or private pension funds, commercial banks and bank holding companies, small business investment corporations licensed by the U.S. Small Business Administration, private venture capital firms, insurance companies, investment management companies, bank trust departments, industrial companies seeking to diversify their investment, and investment bankers acting as intermediaries for other investors or directly investing on their own behalf.

Venture capital limited partnerships ∎ Designed for business development, these partnerships are an institutional mechanism for providing capital for young, technology-oriented businesses. The investors' money is pooled and invested in money market assets until venture investments have been selected. The general partners are experienced investment managers who select and invest the equity and debt securities of firms with high growth potential and the ability to go public in the near future.

Venture capital network (VCN) ∎ A computer database that matches investors with entrepreneurs.

WAN ∎ *See* Wide Area Network.

Wide Area Network (WAN) ∎ Computer networks linking systems throughout a state or around the world in order to facilitate the sharing of information.

Withholding ∎ Federal, state, social security, and unemployment taxes withheld by the employer from employees' wages; employers are liable for these taxes and the corporate umbrella and bankruptcy will not exonerate an employer from paying back payroll withholding. Employers should escrow these funds in a separate account and disperse them quarterly to withholding authorities.

Workers' compensation ∎ A state-mandated form of insurance covering workers injured in job-related accidents. In some states, the state is the insurer; in other states, insurance must be acquired from commercial insurance firms. Insurance rates are based on a number of factors, including salaries, firm history, and risk of occupation.

Working capital ∎ Refers to a firm's short-term investment of current assets, including cash, short-term securities, accounts receivable, and inventories.

Yield ∎ (*See also* Rate of return) The rate of income returned on an investment, expressed as a percentage. Income yield is obtained by dividing the current dollar income by the current market price of the security. Net yield or yield to maturity is the current income yield minus any premium above par or plus any discount from par in purchase price, with the adjustment spread over the period from the date of purchase to the date of maturity.

General Topics

START-UP INFORMATION

26104 ■ "Balancing the Books - by the Book" in *Business Week Online* **(February 4, 2002)**
Pub: McGraw-Hill, Inc.
Description: Small business accounting practice and procedures for entrepreneurs are discussed, including the use of software such as QuickBooks and Peachtree.

26105 ■ *The Small Business Start-Up Kit*
Pub: NOLO
Ed: Peri Pakroo. **Released:** April 2004. **Price:** $24.99. **Description:** Entrepreneurial advice for launching a new business. Topics include compliance with state regulations, sole proprietorships, partnerships, corporations, limited liability companies, as well as accounting and tax information.

26106 ■ *Start and Run a Bookkeeping Business*
Pub: Self-Counsel, Incorporated
Ed: Angie Mohr. **Released:** October 2005. **Price:** $17.95 (US), $22.95 (Canadian). **Description:** Advice for starting and running a bookkeeping service business. Includes MS Word and PDF formats for use in Windows-based PC.

ASSOCIATIONS AND OTHER ORGANIZATIONS

26107 ■ Accountants Global Network
2851 S Parker Rd., Ste. 850
Aurora, CO 80014
Ph:(303)743-7880
Fax: (303)743-7660
Co. E-mail: rhood@agn.org
URL: http://www.agn.org
Contact: Rita Hood, Exec. Dir.
Description: Represents and promotes the fields of separate and independent accounting and consulting firms serving business organizations.

26108 ■ Canadian Payroll Association–Association canadienne de la paie
1600 - 250 Bloor St. E
Toronto, ON, Canada M4W 1E6
Ph:(416)487-3380
Free: 800-387-4693
Fax: (416)487-3384
Co. E-mail: membership@payroll.ca
URL: http://www.payroll.ca
Contact: Wendy McLean-Cobban, Marketing/Communication Mgr.
Description: Represents the payroll community in Canada; offers education programs, advocacy efforts, products and services to help members enhance and adapt payroll operations, meet new legislative requirements, address changing workplace needs and take advantage of emerging technologies. **Publications:** *CPA E-Source* (bimonthly); *Dialogue Magazine* (bimonthly).

26109 ■ Clearinghouse for Volunteer Accounting Services
920 Hampshire Rd., Ste. A-29
Westlake Village, CA 91361
Ph:(805)495-6755
Fax: (805)374-2257
Co. E-mail: info@cvas-ca.org
URL: http://www.cvas-usa.org
Contact: Paul H. Glass, Pres./Exec. Dir.
Description: Works to match nonprofit organizations with pro bono accounting services required. **Publications:** Newsletter (quarterly).

26110 ■ Community Banking Advisory Network
10831 Old Mill Rd., Ste. 400
Omaha, NE 68154
Ph:(402)778-7922
Free: 888-475-4476
Fax: (402)778-7931
Co. E-mail: info@bankingcpas.com
URL: http://www.bankingcpas.com
Contact: Nancy Drennen, Exec.Dir.
Membership: Certified Public Accounting (CPA) firms providing financial and consulting services to community banks. **Purpose:** Seeks to advance CPA services to the community banking industry. Sponsors continuing education and training courses; conducts industry and member surveys; facilitates formation of joint ventures; makes available marketing assistance; facilitates resource sharing among members. **Publications:** *Community Banking Advisor* (quarterly).

26111 ■ Construction Industry CPAs/Consultants Association
15011 E Twilight View Dr.
Fountain Hills, AZ 85268
Ph:(480)836-0300
Free: 800-864-0491
Fax: (480)836-0400
Co. E-mail: jcorcoran@cicpac.com
URL: http://www.cicpac.com
Contact: John J. Corcoran CPA, Exec. Dir.
Membership: Certified Public Accounting (CPA) firms providing financial and consulting services to construction companies. **Purpose:** Seeks to advance CPA services to the construction industries. Sponsors continuing education and training courses; conducts industry and member surveys; facilitates formation of joint ventures; makes available marketing assistance; facilitates resource sharing among members. **Publications:** *CICPAC Membership Directory* (periodic).

26112 ■ CPA Auto Dealer Consultants Association
10831 Old Mill Rd., Ste. 400
Omaha, NE 68154
Ph:(402)778-7922
Free: 888-475-4476
Fax: (402)778-7931
Co. E-mail: info@autodealercpas.net
URL: http://www.autodealercpas.net
Contact: Nancy Drennen, Exec. Dir.
Membership: Certified Public Accounting (CPA) firms providing financial and consulting services to automo-

bile dealers. **Purpose:** Seeks to advance CPA services to automobile dealers. Sponsors continuing education and training courses; conducts industry and member surveys; facilitates formation of joint ventures; makes available marketing assistance; facilitates resource sharing among members. **Publications:** *Auto Focus* (quarterly). **Telecommunication Services:** electronic mail, nancyd@autodealercpas.net.

26113 ■ CPA Manufacturing Services Association
10831 Old Mill Rd., Ste. 400
Omaha, NE 68154
Ph:(402)778-7922
Free: 888-475-4476
Fax: (402)778-7931
Co. E-mail: info@manufacturingcpas.com
URL: http://www.manufacturingcpas.com
Contact: Nancy Drennen, Exec.Dir.
Membership: Certified Public Accounting (CPA) firms providing financial and consulting services to the manufacturing industries. **Purpose:** Seeks to advance CPA services to manufacturers. Sponsors continuing education and training courses; conducts industry and member surveys; facilitates formation of joint ventures; makes available marketing assistance; facilitates resource sharing among members. **Publications:** *Client* (periodic); Membership Directory (periodic).

26114 ■ International Budget Project of the Center on Budget and Policy Priorities
820 1st St. NE, Ste. 510
Washington, DC 20002
Ph:(202)408-1080
Fax: (202)408-8173
Co. E-mail: info@internationalbudget.org
URL: http://www.internationalbudget.org
Contact: Warren Krafchik, Proj. Dir.
Description: Works to assist civil society organizations globally to improve budget policies and decision-making processes. **Publications:** *A Guide to Budget Work for NGOs*; *A Taste of Success: Examples of the Budget Work of NGOs* ; *Can Civil Society Add Value to Budget Decision-Making?*; *IBP Newsletter* (bimonthly); *Reports on Budget Transparency*.

26115 ■ International Group of Accounting Firms
3235 Satellite Blvd., Bldg. 400, Ste. 300
Duluth, GA 30096
Ph:(678)417-7730
Fax: (678)999-3959
Co. E-mail: kmead@igafworldwide.org
URL: http://www.igaf.org
Contact: Kevin Mead, Pres./Exec. Dir.
Description: Works to ensure that the standard for accounting, auditing, and management services are maintained. **Publications:** Annual Report (annual).

26116 ■ Law Firm Services Association
10831 Old Mill Rd., Ste. 400
Omaha, NE 68154
Ph:(402)778-7922
Free: 888-475-4476

Fax: (402)778-7931
Co. E-mail: info@lawfirmcpas.com
Contact: Nancy Drennen, Exec.Dir.
Membership: Certified public accountant (CPA) firms providing financial and consulting services to law firms. **Purpose:** Seeks to enhance members' ability to serve the legal community. Facilitates resource sharing and the establishment of joint ventures among members; provides marketing services to members; conducts industry surveys; sponsors continuing professional development and training courses.

26117 ■ Society of Depreciation Professionals
8100-M4 Wyoming Blvd. NE, No. 228
Albuquerque, NM 87113
Ph:(505)867-9513
Fax: (505)867-0917
Co. E-mail: sdp@his.com
URL: http://www.depr.org
Contact: Rod Daniel, Exec. Sec.
Membership: Accountants and other individuals with an interest in the depreciation of assets. **Purpose:** Promotes "professionalism and ethics within the art of depreciation." Serves as a forum for the discussion of issues affecting depreciation; sponsors continuing professional development courses for members. **Publications:** *Journal of the Society of Depreciation Professionals* (annual); Newsletter (triennial). **Telecommunication Services:** electronic bulletin board.

EDUCATIONAL PROGRAMS

26118 ■ Advanced Cost Accounting
American Management Association
1601 Broadway
New York, NY 10019
Ph:(212)586-8100
Free: 800-262-9699
Fax: (212)903-8168
Co. E-mail: customerservice@amanet.org
URL: http://www.amanet.org
Price: $1,895 for non-members; $1,695 for AMA members. **Description:** For cost professionals with two or more years of experience; covers how to effectively determine operating costs as it pertains to pricing, including cost variances, and calculation of total product costs. **Locations:** San Francisco, CA; Atlanta, GA; Washington, DC; and New York, NY.

26119 ■ AMA's Course on Financial Analysis
American Management Association
1601 Broadway
New York, NY 10019
Ph:(212)586-8100
Free: 800-262-9699
Fax: (212)903-8168
Co. E-mail: customerservice@amanet.org
URL: http://www.amanet.org
Price: $1,995.00 for non-members; $1,895.00 for AMA members. **Description:** Four-day seminar for managers with budget responsibilities; covers corporate planning, capital investments, cash flow, balance sheets, mergers and acquisitions, and other financial aspects of business. **Locations:** Cities throughout the United States.

26120 ■ AMA's Course on Financial Forecasting for Dynamic Business Results
American Management Association
1601 Broadway
New York, NY 10019
Ph:(212)586-8100
Free: 800-262-9699
Fax: (212)903-8168
Co. E-mail: customerservice@amanet.org
URL: http://www.amanet.org
Price: $2,095.00 for non-members; $1,895.00 for AMA members. **Description:** Covers forecasting models, business risks, and various approaches to interest rate risk modeling. **Locations:** San Francisco, CA; Washington, DC; and New York, NY.

26121 ■ Budgeting for Publications
EEI Communications
66 Canal Ctr. Plz., Ste. 200
Alexandria, VA 22314-5507
Ph:(703)683-7453
Free: 888-253-2762
Fax: (703)683-7310
Co. E-mail: train@eeicommunications.com
URL: http://www.eeicommunications.com/training
Price: $395. **Description:** Seminar that covers the basics of developing and monitoring budgets for the publications department, including types of publications departments, profit and cost centers, defining profit, margins, revenues, and analysis, budgeting traps, and what you can and cannot control. **Locations:** Alexandria, VA; Silver Spring, MD; and Washington, DC.

26122 ■ CMC's Course on Financial Analysis (Canada)
Canadian Management Centre
150 York St., 5th Fl.
Toronto, ON, Canada M5H 3S5
Ph:(416)214-5678
Free: 800-262-9699
Fax: (416)313-4985
Co. E-mail: cmcinfo@cmctraining.org
URL: http://cmcamai.org
Price: $2,150.00 Canadian. **Description:** Four-day seminar for managers with budget responsibilities; covers corporate planning, capital investments, cash flow, balance sheets, mergers and acquisitions, and other financial aspects of business. **Locations:** Toronto, ON.

26123 ■ The Essentials of Budgeting: From Creation through Application
American Management Association
1601 Broadway
New York, NY 10019
Ph:(212)586-8100
Free: 800-262-9699
Fax: (212)903-8168
Co. E-mail: customerservice@amanet.org
URL: http://www.amanet.org
Price: $1,695.00 for non-members; $1,595.00 for AMA members. **Description:** Three-day seminar for managers with budget responsibilities; covers budget basics, developing a budget, incorporating organizational goals, and the various types of costs and revenues. **Locations:** Washington, DC; and New York, NY.

26124 ■ The Essentials of Budgeting: From Creation Through Application
American Management Association
1601 Broadway
New York, NY 10019
Ph:(212)586-8100
Free: 800-262-9699
Fax: (212)903-8168
Co. E-mail: customerservice@amanet.org
URL: http://www.amanet.org
Price: $1,895 for non-members; $1,695 for AMA members. **Description:** Covers the budgeting skills needed for today's managers, including operating budgets, preparing a revenue budget, and techniques to stay on target. **Locations:** Chicago, IL.

26125 ■ Financial Analysis (Canada)
Canadian Management Centre
150 York St., 5th Fl.
Toronto, ON, Canada M5H 3S5
Ph:(866)400-4941 ext. 2252
Free: 877-CMC-2500
Fax: (416)313-4985
Co. E-mail: cmcinfo@cmctraining.org
URL: http://www.cmcamai.org
Price: $1,895 Canadian. **Description:** Covers financial strategies, and techniques to make knowledgeable decisions for your organization's performance and growth. **Locations:** Toronto, ON.

26126 ■ Fixed Asset Accounting
American Management Association
1601 Broadway
New York, NY 10019

Ph:(212)586-8100
Free: 800-262-9699
Fax: (212)903-8168
Co. E-mail: customerservice@amanet.org
URL: http://www.amanet.org
Price: $1,595.00 for non-members; $1,495.00 for AMA members. **Description:** Two-day seminar for accountants and managers with less than two years of experience in fixed asset accounting; covers tax benefits, transitioning to a computerized system, and getting started with paperwork. **Locations:** Atlanta, GA.

26127 ■ Fundamentals of Cost Accounting
American Management Association
1601 Broadway
New York, NY 10019
Ph:(212)586-8100
Free: 800-262-9699
Fax: (212)903-8168
Co. E-mail: customerservice@amanet.org
URL: http://www.amanet.org
Price: $1,795.00 for non-members; $1,595.00 for AMA members. **Description:** Covers the use of cost accounting, analyzing reports, choosing a cost system, and measuring results. **Locations:** San Francisco, CA; Atlanta, GA; Washington, DC; San Diego, CA; and Chicago, IL.

26128 ■ Fundamentals of Cost Accounting (Canada)
Canadian Management Centre
150 York St., 5th Fl.
Toronto, ON, Canada M5H 3S5
Ph:(416)214-5678
Free: 800-262-9699
Fax: (416)313-4985
Co. E-mail: cmcinfo@cmctraining.org
URL: http://cmcamai.org
Price: $1,750.00 Canadian. **Description:** Covers the use of cost accounting, analyzing reports, choosing a cost system, and measuring results. **Locations:** Toronto, ON.

26129 ■ Fundamentals of Finance and Accounting for Administrative Professionals
American Management Association
1601 Broadway
New York, NY 10019
Ph:(212)586-8100
Free: 800-262-9699
Fax: (212)903-8168
Co. E-mail: customerservice@amanet.org
URL: http://www.amanet.org
Price: $1,695.00; $1,495.00 for AMA members. **Description:** Covers basic accounting principles, cash flow accounting, and learning to understand various financial documents. **Locations:** San Francisco, CA; Washington, DC; Chicago, IL; and New York, NY.

26130 ■ Fundamentals of Finance and Accounting for Non-Financial Managers (Canada)
Canadian Management Centre
150 York St., 5th Fl.
Toronto, ON, Canada M5H 3S5
Ph:(416)214-5678
Free: 800-262-9699
Fax: (416)313-4985
Co. E-mail: cmcinfo@cmctraining.org
URL: http://cmcamai.org
Price: $1,995.00 Canadian. **Description:** Covers basic aspects of the budgeting process. **Locations:** Mississauga, ON; Ottawa, ON; Calgary, AB; and Toronto, ON.

26131 ■ Fundamentals of IT Cost Management
American Management Association
1601 Broadway
New York, NY 10019
Ph:(212)586-8100
Free: 800-262-9699
Fax: (212)903-8168
Co. E-mail: customerservice@amanet.org
URL: http://www.amanet.org
Price: $1,695.00 for non-members; $1,525.00 for AMA members. **Description:** Covers all aspects of

the IT budget, including opportunities for cost reduction, communication with financial staff, and buying and selling IT equipment and services. **Locations:** San Francisco, CA; Washington, DC; and Atlanta, GA.

26132 ■ How to Develop and Administer a Budget
Fred Pryor Seminars
9757 Metcalf Ave.
Overland Park, KS 66212
Free: 800-944-8503
Fax: (913)967-8849
Co. E-mail: customerservice@pryor.com
URL: http://www.careertrack.com
Description: Covers the benefits of budgeting, budgeting concepts, templates, and methods for evaluating budgets. **Locations:** Cities throughout the United States.

26133 ■ How to Sharpen Your Business Math Skills: The Inside Track to Job Empowerment
American Management Association
1601 Broadway
New York, NY 10019
Ph:(212)586-8100
Free: 800-262-9699
Fax: (212)903-8168
Co. E-mail: customerservice@amanet.org
URL: http://www.amanet.org
Price: $1,695.00 for non-members; $1,595.00 for AMA members. **Description:** Covers basic math skills and how to use them in business. **Locations:** Washington, DC; and New York, NY.

26134 ■ Performance Measures for Your Business: How to Determine and Measure What Really Counts
American Management Association
1601 Broadway
New York, NY 10019
Ph:(212)586-8100
Free: 800-262-9699
Fax: (212)903-8168
Co. E-mail: customerservice@amanet.org
URL: http://www.amanet.org
Price: $1,795.00 for non-members; $1,695.00 for AMA members. **Description:** Two-day seminar for upper-level managers; covers performance measurement planning, gaining greater accountability, motivating staff, and applying results. **Locations:** San Francisco, CA; and Atlanta, GA.

26135 ■ Valuation of Information Technology: How to Measure and Create Value from Your IT Investment
American Management Association
1601 Broadway
New York, NY 10019
Ph:(212)586-8100
Free: 800-262-9699
Fax: (212)903-8168
Co. E-mail: customerservice@amanet.org
URL: http://www.amanet.org
Price: $2,195.00 for non-members; $1,995.00 for AMA members. **Description:** Covers IT investments, including challenges, measurements, future planning, and increasing shareholder value. **Locations:** San Francisco, CA; and Washington, DC.

26136 ■ Yield/Revenue Management: New Strategies for Boosting Profits
American Management Association
1601 Broadway
New York, NY 10019
Ph:(212)586-8100
Free: 800-262-9699
Fax: (212)903-8168
Co. E-mail: customerservice@amanet.org
URL: http://www.amanet.org
Price: $1,995.00 for non-members; $1,895.00 for AMA members. **Description:** Covers different market segments, differentiating products and services to different customers, and selling through a variety of distribution channels. **Locations:** New York, NY.

REFERENCE WORKS

26137 ■ "20 Steps for Pricing a Patent: To Value an Invention You Have to Understand It" in *Journal of Accountancy* **(Vol. 198, November 2004)**
Pub: American Institute of Certified Public Accountants
Ed: J. Timothy Cromley. **Description:** Twenty steps to help certified public accounts and valuators determine the value of a patent are explained.

26138 ■ "Abandoned by Your Accountants" in *Inc.* **(August 2005, pp. 19-21)**
Pub: Inc. Magazine
Ed: Amy Gunderson. **Description:** The Sarbanes-Oxley Act has overwhelmed accountants to the point that companies are finding it difficult to have their books audited. Statistical data included.

26139 ■ "Accountants on the Move" in *Rough Notes* **(Vol. 146, No. 3, March 2003, pp. 30)**
Pub: Rough Notes
Ed: Gene Mason. **Description:** In the light of recent accounting scandals, many accountants are on the move and taking clients with them. Asset/professional liability policies needed by these workers are being carefully underwritten and provided by insurers.

26140 ■ "Accounting for the Budget" in *Law Firm Inc.* **(December 2004)**
Pub: American Lawyer Media LP
Ed: Joanne Sammer. **Description:** It is important for law firms to implement a strong budget and budgeting process in order to set priorities, direct resources, and guide business development. Ways to keep a budget current and to use it as a management tool are explained.

26141 ■ *Accounting the Business Environment*
Pub: Trans-Atlantic Publications, Inc.
Ed: John Watts. **Released:** 1995. **Price:** $67.50.

26142 ■ *The Accounting Cycle*
Pub: Crisp Publications, Inc.
Ed: Jay Jacquet and William C. Miller, Jr. **Price:** $10.95. **Description:** Guide to the accounting cycle, from balance sheets and income statements to closing entries, written for the beginner.

26143 ■ "Accounting Education; Response to Corporate Scandals: Helping the Profession Find Opportunity in Crisis" in *Journal of Accountancy*
Pub: American Institute of Certified Public Accountants
Ed: Pierre L. Titard, Robert L. Braun, Michael J. Meyer. **Description:** Since the recent corporate scandals caused by large corporations, colleges and universities across the nation have changed course offerings of their accounting programs to better prepare students to cope with the ethics of accounting.

26144 ■ *Accounting and Finance for Your Small Business*
Pub: John Wiley & Sons, Incorporated
Ed: Steven M. Bragg; E. James Burton. **Released:** April 2006. **Price:** $49.00. **Description:** Financial procedures and techniques for establishing and maintaining a profitable small company are outlined.

26145 ■ "Accounting Firms" in *San Diego Business Journal* **(Vol. 28, January 15, 2007, No. 3, pp. 20)**
Pub: San Diego Business Journal Associates
Ed: Liz Wiedemann. **Description:** Directory of accounting firms listed by rank, contact information, number of employees.

26146 ■ "The Accounting Fraud Squads" in *Atlanta Business Chronicle* **(Vol. 25, November 15, 2002, No. 23 pp. SS1)**
Pub: American City Business Publications, Inc.
Ed: Lee Hall. **Description:** Following recent corporate scandals, more businesses are seeking fraud investigation and forensic accounting services. Businesses in the U.S. are expected to lose about $600 billion due to fraud in 2002, or $4,500 per employee. Details about the field of forensic accounting are included.

26147 ■ "Accounting Has Record of Trustworthiness" in *Crain's Detroit Business* **(Vol. 18, No. 15, April 15, 2002, pp. 9)**
Pub: Crain Communications Inc. - Detroit
Ed: Leslie Murphy. **Description:** The recent Enron scandal has obscured the accounting industry's reputation for dependability.

26148 ■ "Accumulated Earnings Tax: Deductibility of Paid But Contested Liabilities" in *Journal of Accountancy* **(January 2005)**
Pub: American Institute of Certified Public Accountants
Ed: Ronald R. Hiner. **Description:** Under IRC Section 531, the accumulated earnings tax imposes a penalty tax on earnings accumulated beyond the reasonable needs of a business.

26149 ■ *Activity-Based Costing for Small and Mid-sized Businesses: An Implementation Guide*
Pub: John Wiley & Sons, Inc.
Ed: Douglas T. Hicks. **Released:** 1992. **Price:** $79.95. **Description:** Analyzes activity-based costing (ABC) in regards to small and medium-sized businesses.

26150 ■ "Amortization of Certain Intangible Assets" in *Journal of Accountancy*
Pub: American Institute of Certified Public Accountants
Ed: Jennifer M. Mueller. **Description:** Intangible assets that are the result of contractual or legal rights are explained, including patents, licenses, trademarks, franchise and servicing rights.

26151 ■ "An Option to Do Nothing" in *Forbes* **(Vol. 170, No. 4, September 2, 2002, pp. 45)**
Pub: Forbes Magazine
Ed: Description: Plans for expensing employee options are discussed. Statistical data included.

26152 ■ "Anadarko Laying Off 400 Workers to Cut Costs" in *Houston Business Journal* **(Vol. 34, No. 13, August 8, 2003, pp. 3)**
Pub: American City Business Journals
Description: Anadarko Petroleum announced it will layoff 400 employees; topics include cost control programs, debt management, and business losses.

26153 ■ "Anadarko Seeks Bidders for Possible Buyout" in *Houston Business Journal* **(Vol. 34, No. 14, August 15, 2003, pp. 3)**
Pub: American City Business Journals
Description: Anadarko Petroleum to pursue opportunities to be acquired by a larger company. Topics include business losses, economic conditions and the implementation of cost control measures.

26154 ■ *Annual Register of Certified Public Accountants and Public Accountants of Nevada*
Pub: Nevada State Board of Accountancy
Released: Annual. **Price:** $25. **Covers:** Members of the Nevada State Board of Public Accountants. **Entries Include:** name, address, phone and business associations.

26155 ■ "Apache on the Rise, Anadarko in Decline" in *Houston Business Journal* **(Vol. 34, No. 13, August 8, 2003, pp. 1)**
Pub: American City Business Journals
Ed: Monica Perin. **Description:** Business and management styles of Apache Corporation and Anadarko Petroleum Company are compared, including strategic planning and profit margins.

26156 ■ "Ask Inc." in *Inc.* **(Volume 28, January 2006, No. 1, pp. 51-52)**
Pub: Inc. Magazine
Description: Advice is offered regarding noncompete agreements, factoring companies that pay businesses up-front for outstanding bills and collect payments from customers, and a pet accessory business.

26157 ■ "At Senate Finance, membership has its privilege" in *Tax Notes* **(Vol. 96, No. 14, September 30, 2002, pp. 1802-1806)**
Pub: Tax Notes International
Ed: Martin A. Sullivan. Description: Members of the Senate Finance Committee are working on the draft Small Business and Farm Economic Recovery Act of 2002. The bill proposes tax breaks for economic sectors that already have a relatively light tax burden. It also contains many special provisions which would be politically beneficial to various members of the committee.

26158 ■ "Automate Excel Functions: Easy-to-Create Macros Can Take Over Many Manual Processes" in *Journal of Accountancy* **(January 2005)**
Pub: American Institute of Certified Public Accountants
Ed: Jeff Lenning. Description: Macros can help accounts customize worksheets as well as export journal entries in Microsoft Excel into an accounting package and creating reports in Word.

26159 ■ "Avoid Audits: Take Precautions to Prevent a Visit from the IRS" in *My Business* **(February/March 2003, pp. 45)**
Pub: My Business Magazine
Ed: Alan Breznick. Description: Ways to avoid an audit of a small business tax return are discussed.

26160 ■ "Avoid the Payroll Tax Trap: Using Withheld Payroll Taxes for Other Purposes Can be a Dangerous and Expensive Game" in *Journal of Accountancy*
Pub: American Institute of Certified Public Accountants
Ed: Howard Godfrey. Description: Penalties imposed on businesses using withheld payroll taxes for other purposes are discussed.

26161 ■ "Avoid the Tax Trap When Repaying Shareholder Loans" in *Journal of Accountancy*
Pub: American Institute of Certified Public Accountants
Ed: Brian K. Howell. Description: Certified public accountants can help clients avoid unnecessary taxes when repaying shareholder loans.

26162 ■ "Avoiding a Cash Flow Crunch: Accurate Projections Are Key To Your Business' Survival" in *Black Enterprise* **(Vol. 34, July 2004)**
Pub: Earl G. Graves Publishing Co. Inc.
Ed: Nicole Lewis. Description: According to small business financial experts, it is critical for businesses to pay attention to cash flow when engaging financial commitments that have a scheduled payback time.

26163 ■ "Back to the Future" in *Inc.* **(July 1, 2003)**
Pub: Gruner & Jahr USA Publishing
Description: Analysis of President George W. Bush's tax cut and what it will mean to the economy.

26164 ■ *Beat the Taxman: Easy Ways to Tax Save in Your Small Business*
Pub: John Wiley & Sons, Incorporated
Ed: Stephen Thompson. Released: January 2005. Price: $26.99 (Canadian). Description: Concise tax planner to help entrepreneurs take advantage of current tax laws.

26165 ■ "The Best of Technology Q&A: Answers to Readers' Most-Asked Questions" in *Journal of Accountancy* **(Vol. 198, December 2004, No. 6)**
Pub: American Institute of Certified Public Accountants

Ed: Stanley Zarowin. Description: In depth analysis of various accounting software programs are presented, including Microsoft's Excel 2000.

26166 ■ "Bethpage-based Cablevision Systems to Complete an Internal Accounting Review" in *Long Island Business News* **(March 5, 2004)**
Pub: Dolan Media Newswires
Description: Cablevision Systems launched an internal audit of accounting procedures after uncovering improper recording of contracts in its Rainbow Media unit, prompting a government investigation. The firm hopes to complete the review by the second quarter in order to spin off its Voom satellite television business.

26167 ■ "Big Mistake: How to Avoid Common Tax Mistakes" in *My Business* **(February/March 2003, pp. 46)**
Pub: My Business Magazine
Ed: Tamara Holmes. Description: Small business owners should do tax planning before the end of the year in order to be prepared for April 15. Information is also provided for the IRS' free Electronic Federal Tax Payment System used for employee withholding taxes.

26168 ■ "Bill Would Let Biz Keep Unclaimed $100 Paychecks" in *Crain's Detroit Business* **(Vol. 18, No. 18, May 6, 2002, pp. 24)**
Pub: Crain Communications Inc. - Detroit
Ed: Amy Lane. Description: Many businesses may not know that they are supposed to give the state any unclaimed employee payroll checks, but a bill, if passed, would allow the employer the ability to keep unclaimed checks of $100 or less.

26169 ■ "Billing Bad Debt" in *Hispanic Business* **(October 2003, pp. 102)**
Pub: Hispanic Business
Ed: Milton Zall. Description: Financial managers have several options when it comes to accounting for unpaid receivables, including negotiating a reduced payoff, going to court, or hiring a collection service.

26170 ■ "Black Ink brings dollars into the data-flow equation" in *Boston Business Journal* **(Vol. 22, No. 16, May 24, 2002, pp. 17)**
Pub: MCP, Inc.
Ed: Phil Sweeney. Description: Black Ink Systems is developing a product to assist telecommunications services firms to keep track of their financial information. This product will aid telecommunications services companies to make better decisions.

26171 ■ *Bookkeeping & Administration for the Smaller Business*
Pub: Etta Publishing Company
Ed: Elvira Bellogoni. Released: 1998. Price: $12.95 (trade paper)

26172 ■ *Bookkeeping for a Small Business*
Pub: D B A Books
Ed: Diana Bellavance. Released: 6th ed. 1998. Price: $4.25.

26173 ■ "Bookless Bookkeeping" in *PC Magazine*
Pub: Ziff-Davis Publishing Company
Ed: Richard Morochove. Description: An overview of seven inexpensive accounting programs for small businesses.

26174 ■ "Breaking Free from Budgets" in *Inc.* **(October 1, 2003)**
Pub: Gruner & Jahr USA Publishing
Ed: Suzanne McGee. Description: Exasperated by budgets that muzzle creativity, a growing number of small businesses are breaking free from financial constraints while conserving spending.

26175 ■ "The Buddy System: These Longtime Friends Formed a Growing CPA Firm" in *Black Enterprise* **(Vol. 35, August 2004, No. 1, pp. 47)**
Pub: Earl G. Graves Publishing Co. Inc.
Ed: Robert Janis. Description: Profile of three friends who formed a full-service certified public accounting firm in 1996. Benford Brown & Associates performs audits, accounting services, tax services, and business consulting.

26176 ■ "Bush talks up small business tax relief" in *Tax Notes* **(Vol. 97, No. 9, December 2, 2002, pp. 1135-1136)**
Pub: Tax Notes International
Ed: Patti Mohr. Description: President George W. Bush urged lawmakers to lessen the tax burden on small businesses and make the relevant regulations simpler. Bush said that tax cuts would boost the economy and add more jobs.

26177 ■ "Business ethics issues cross all boundaries" in *Colorado Springs Business Journal* **(March 7, 2003)**
Pub: Dolan Media Newswires
Ed: Lance Gurwell. Description: Ethics issues of concern to chief executives of companies are discussed.

26178 ■ *Business Finance for the Numerically Challenged*
Pub: Career Press, Inc.
Ed: Career Press, Inc. Staff. Released: 1997. Price: $11.99.

26179 ■ *Business Owner's Guide to Accounting & Bookkeeping*
Pub: PSI Research
Ed: Jose F. Placenicia, Bruce Welge and Don Oliver. Released: 2nd ed. 1997. Price: $19.95 (paper).

26180 ■ "Calculating Profits" in *Black Enterprise* **(Vol. 34, No. 6, January 2004, pp. 36)**
Pub: Earl Graves Publishing Co.
Ed: Alan Hughes. Description: An explanation of profit margins and ways to calculate a profit margin are investigated.

26181 ■ "Capital Versus Talent: The Battle That's Reshaping Business" in *Harvard Business Review* **(Vol. 81, No. 7, July 2003, pp. 36)**
Pub: Harvard Business School Press
Ed: Roger L. Martin, Mihnea C. Moldoveanu. Description: Profit allocation is discussed.

26182 ■ "Capturing the Potential: How CPA Firms are Building Successful Financial Services Practices" in *Journal of Accountancy* **(Vol. 198)**
Pub: American Institute of Certified Public Accountants
Ed: Patricia J. Abram, John J. Bowen Jr., Russ Alan Prince, Jeffrey A. Roush. Description: Certified public accounting firms are increasing profits by expanding into the financial services sector.

26183 ■ "The case of the obsolete inventory" in *Red Herring* **(March 2003, pp. 34)**
Pub: Herring Communications Inc.
Ed: Justin Hibbard. Description: In February 2002, Solectron, an electronics manufacturer pressured an employee to write off outdated company inventory. The employee was fired seven months later, now his lawsuit could benefit honest employees throughout the U.S.

26184 ■ "Cash in, cash out" in *Entrepreneur* **(Vol. 31, No. 6, June 2003, pp. 53)**
Pub: Entrepreneur Media Inc.
Ed: Crystal Detamore-Rodman. Description: The management of payables plays a critical role in cash-flow management. The article offers advise for small businesses to gain the best benefit from payment terms.

26185 ■ "Caveats to Selling Financial Services" in *Journal of Accountancy* (Vol. 199, January 2005, No. 1, pp. 29)
Pub: American Institute of Certified Public Accountants
Ed: Bart H. Siegel. **Description:** Certified Public Accounts will face new challenges when offering separately managed accounts, customized bond portfolio services, mutual funds, insurance or other investment products and services.

26186 ■ "Chief concern" in *Entrepreneur* (Vol. 31, No. 4, April 2003, pp. 51)
Pub: Entrepreneur Media Inc.
Ed: David Lipschultz. **Description:** The need for hiring a chief financial officer for companies is examined; one question to ask in making a determination is whether the bill from an accounting firm is higher than the salary of a seasoned financial manager.

26187 ■ "Chop, chop: Bush's plan changes all: tax planning" in *Barron's* (Vol. 82, No. 57, February 10, 2003, pp. 21)
Pub: Barron's
Ed: Karen Hube. **Description:** A detailed analysis of the President's proposed new dividend tax cut, lifetime savings account, retirement savings accounts, and employer retirement savings accounts is provided, with an emphasis on the impacts on individuals.

26188 ■ "A Class Act" in *Entrepreneur* (Vol. 32, December 2004, No. 12, pp. 61)
Pub: Entrepreneur Media Inc.
Ed: C.J. Prince. **Description:** Increasingly, entrepreneurs are taking courses designed to assist in running a business, including leadership, finance, accounting and economics.

26189 ■ "Class-Based Pensions: A Cost-Saving Alternative for Companies of All Sizes" in *Journal of Accountancy* (Vol. 199, January 2005)
Pub: American Institute of Certified Public Accountants
Ed: Mark Papalia. **Description:** Ways small businesses can establish a class-based pension program for their company are discussed, including a plan that places each employee in a separate class.

26190 ■ *College Accounting: A Small Business Approach*
Pub: Richard D. Irwin, Inc.
Ed: Eleanor Schrader. **Released:** 1994. PRICE $40.00.

26191 ■ "Commuting Expenses: What is a 'Metropolitan Area'?" in *Journal of Accountancy* (Vol. 199, January 2005, No. 1, pp. 75)
Pub: American Institute of Certified Public Accountants
Ed: Vinay S. Navani. **Description:** Under revenue ruling 1999-7, costs for traveling from one's residence to a fixed work location, costs can be deducted if they fall under certain criteria.

26192 ■ "A conceptual mistake in the calculation of social security taxes" in *Tax Notes* (Vol. 97, No. 2, October 14, 2002, pp. 283-285)
Pub: Tax Notes International
Ed: M. Hayden Brown. **Description:** The Social Security Agency wants a self-employed person to pay the same amount of social security tax as paid by an employee of identical income combined with his employer. However, due to a mistake in Form 1040, a self-employed person actually has a lesser tax burden than an employed person and employer.

26193 ■ "Conflict of interest" in *Red Herring* (January 2003, pp. 23)
Pub: Herring Communications Inc.
Ed: Stacy Lawrence. **Description:** Most large U.S. firms still pay two-thirds of the money to auditors on non-audit services, however there is a shift toward spending their IT consulting budget elsewhere.

26194 ■ "Congress Scores One For Your Portfolio" in *Fortuneit* (Vol. 146, No. 4, September 2, 2002, pp. 184)
Pub: Time Inc.
Ed: Jeffrey H. Birnbaum. **Description:** Information about the Sarbanes-Oxley bill on corporate governance and accounting reform is presented.

26195 ■ "Cool Tools" in *My Business* (October/November 2003, pp. 25)
Pub: My Business Magazine
Description: Profiles of new office equipment geared towards small business use are given, including Frontgate's Automatic Bill Counter which quickly and accurately counts 1,000 bills per minute saving time and losses due to human error; iPen, a combination ballpoint pen, viewfinder digital camera, Web cam, and stylus for a PDA; Targus' DEFCON Authenticator Suite, a computer security device; and iPod, a digital music player.

26196 ■ "Corporate Image-Maker Sees Hope for Symbol, Pain for Computer Associates" in *Long Island Business News* (March 5, 2004)
Pub: Dolan Media Newswires
Ed: Ken Schachter. **Description:** Ann Stephenson, chief executive of Stephenson Group, a corporate image-maker specializing in technology companies, discusses ways she would rehabilitate the images of Symbol Technologies and Computer Associates. Both firms are facing government investigations into accounting procedures and the sudden departure of high-ranking executives.

26197 ■ "A Corrupt Calculus: The Line Between 'Making the Numbers' and Making Them Up Remains Blurry" in *Barron's* (July 7, 2003, pp. 24)
Pub: Barron's
Ed: Michael Niemira, Bill Alpert, Jay Palmer. **Description:** Two books about corporate accounting and fraud are reviewed, "The Number" book, and "Born to Steal: When the Mafia Hit Wall Street".

26198 ■ "Court Review of IRS Abuse of Discretion" in *Journal of Accountancy* (Vol. 198, December 2004, No. 6, pp. 93)
Pub: American Institute of Certified Public Accountants
Ed: Edward J. Schnee. **Description:** Under numerous code sections, the Internal Revenue Service is allowed to reduce or eliminate a tax liability for equity or hardship reasons at its discretion.

26199 ■ "Cracking the Code" in *Entrepreneur* (Vol. 32, August 2004, No. 8, pp. 48)
Pub: Entrepreneur Media Inc.
Ed: Jennifer Pellet. **Description:** Profile of the Taxpayer Education Communication Small Business/Self-Employed Operating Division provides information and resources to help small business owners understand tax codes.

26200 ■ "Crafting a Web presence" in *Accounting Technology* (Vol. 19, No. 1, January-February 2003, pp. 16)
Pub: Thomson Financial Inc.
Ed: Richard McCausland. **Description:** Jim Schaefer, founder of Schaefer & Company, an 18-year old tax and accounting practice believes that a Web site keeps a business competitive.

26201 ■ "Creative Accounting? Don't laugh!" in *Success from Failure* (August 2000)
Pub: Vision Quest Publishing, Inc.
Ed: Harvey Mackay. **Description:** Recently, the American Management Association polled 500 CEOs across the nation. The survey posed the question: "What must one do to survive in the 21st century?"

26202 ■ "Criminal records" in *Entrepreneur* (Vol. 31, No. 5, May 2003, pp. 72)
Pub: Entrepreneur Media Inc.
Ed: Steven C. Bahls, Jane Easter Bahls. **Description:** Under the Sarbanes-Oxley Act it is a federal crime for businesses to intentionally destroy documents that might be evidence in a federal investigation.

26203 ■ "Crooks and Books" in *The Economist* (Vol. 376, July 30-August 5, 2005, No. 8437, pp. 14)
Pub: The Economist Newspaper Ltd.
Description: Account reform is creating as many problems as it is solving.

26204 ■ "Cutting-Edge Accountant" in *Crain's New York Business* (Vol. 23, January 29, 2007, No. 5, pp. F22)
Pub: Crain Communications, Inc.
Ed: Barbara Benson. **Description:** Profile of Vice President of Corporate Development for Health Insurance Plan of Greater New York, Steve Zeng. HIP plans to go public after a merger with Group Health Incorporated.

26205 ■ "Damages Aren't Always Patently Obvious" in *Journal of Accountancy*
Pub: American Institute of Certified Public Accountants
Ed: Glenn Newman, Richard J. Gering. **Description:** CPA litigation consultants assist patent holders in patent infringement disputes; quantifying damages in these cases can be the focus of a forensic and litigation services practice.

26206 ■ "The Dangers of a Lack of Accountability" in *Automotive News* (Vol. 20, October 4, 2004, No. 40, pp. 8)
Pub: Crain Communications Inc.
Ed: Keith Crain. **Description:** Plans for developing a downtown district, called African Town, in Detroit that would fund money to black-owned businesses is discussed. Many individuals claim the plan is both discriminatory and illegal.

26207 ■ "D.C. Gets It Almost Right" in *Fortuneit* (Vol. 146, No. 4, September 2, 2002, pp. 38)
Pub: Time Inc.
Ed: Cait Murphy. **Description:** The Sarbanes-Oxley bill on corporate governance and accounting reform is profiled.

26208 ■ "Debit Cards Ease FSA Administration Burden" in *Rough Notes* (Vol. 145, No. 9, September 2002, pp. 34)
Pub: Rough Notes
Ed: Len Strazewski. **Description:** Flexible spending accounts are not popular with employers nor employees owing to the heavy paperwork involved, but Congress may introduce legislation that will ease the administrative aspect so as to facilitate usage of the program.

26209 ■ "Debt Allocation and LLCs" in *Journal of Accountancy* (Vol. 198, September 2004, No. 3, pp. 80)
Pub: American Institute of Certified Public Accountants
Ed: Edward J. Schnee. **Description:** An overview of regulations that apply to limited liability companies (LLCs) that apply to the allocation of liabilities to LLC members.

26210 ■ *Deduct It!: Lower Your Small Business Taxes*
Pub: NOLO
Ed: Stephen Fishman. **Released:** September 2005. **Price:** $34.99. **Description:** Ways to maximize business tax deductions for any type of small business owner (sole proprietor, partnership, LLC, corporation).

26211 ■ "Deducting the Cost of Laser Eye Surgery" in *Journal of Accountancy* (Vol. 198, December 2004, No. 6, pp. 92)
Pub: American Institute of Certified Public Accountants
Ed: W. Terry Dancer. **Description:** The Internal Revenue Service has issued a letter ruling that addresses whether surgical procedures to correct nearsightedness, farsightedness and astigmatism can be used as a tax deduction.

26212 ■ "Deemed Substantiation of Business Travel Expenses" in *Journal of Accountancy* **(Vol. 198, October 2004, No. 4, pp. 102)**
Pub: American Institute of Certified Public Accountants
Ed: Charles J. Reichert. Description: The 'deemed-substantiation' method for deducting business travel is discussed.

26213 ■ "Deloitte unit gets 1st woman" in *Crain's Detroit Business* **(Vol. 19, No. 17, April 28, 2003, pp. 3)**
Pub: Crain Communications Inc., Detroit
Ed: Katie Merx. Description: Deloitte & Touche LLP has named Sally Buckles, age 42, as the first woman to head its Detroit office and Great Lakes region. Buckles is the first woman to head one of the Big Four accounting firms.

26214 ■ "Detecting accounting fraud can be tricky" in *Atlanta Business Chronicle* **(Vol. 25, November 15, 2002, No. 23 pp. SS2)**
Pub: American City Business Publications, Inc.
Ed: Tonya Layman. Description: Fraudulent accounting can occur through fraudulent financial reporting or misappropriation of assets. To protect themselves, accountants should follow the Statement of Auditing Standards, take their time during an audit, and identify the kinds of firms they want to work with.

26215 ■ "Digital Rx" in *Fast Company* **(May 2001, pp. 183)**
Pub: Fast Company
Ed: Scott Kirsner. Description: Ways the Detroit Medical Center is using digital technology to repair its fiscal condition are presented.

26216 ■ "Directory of AICPA Selected Services" in *Journal of Accountancy* **(Vol. 199, February 2005, No. 2, pp. 89)**
Pub: American Institute of Certified Public Accountants
Description: The American Institute of Certified Public Accounts' Directory of selected services is provided; contact numbers and Web addresses are included.

26217 ■ "Does New Watchdog Have Teeth?" in *Business Journal-Portland* **(Vol. 20, No. 23, August 8, 2003, pp. 1)**
Pub: American City Business Journals, Inc.
Ed: Aliza Earnshaw. Description: The passage of the federal Sarbanes-Oxley Act of 2002 resulted in the formation of the Public Companies Accounting Oversight Board (PCAOB). The PCAOB will attempt to restore investor confidence in corporations by monitoring financial reports.

26218 ■ "Easy Math" in *Entrepreneur* **(Vol. 31, No. 5, May 2003, pp. 38)**
Pub: Entrepreneur Media Inc.
Ed: Liane Cassavoy. Description: Profile of Simply Accounting 2003 software from ACCPAC International, offering a complete accounting system including payroll and departmental accounting for $169 for the basic version.

26219 ■ "11th Hour" in *Entrepreneur* **(Vol. 27, No. 12, December 1999, pp. 20)**
Pub: Entrepreneur Media Inc.
Ed: Cynthia E. Griffin. Description: A bill in Congress could fundamentally change the way small business bankruptcies are handled. Information about the Bankruptcy Reform Act of 1998 is covered.

26220 ■ "Employer-Provided Education Benefits: Section 132(d) is Worth a Second Look" in *Journal of Accountancy* **(Vol. 198, September 2004)**
Pub: American Institute of Certified Public Accountants
Ed: Edmund D. Fenton, Jr. Description: An overview of the various ways employers are helping their employees with tax-free education benefits, including scholarships and grants under IRC Section 117 and education assistance programs under Section 127, as well as IRC Section 132(d).

26221 ■ "Encourage General Ledger Efficiency" in *Journal of Accountancy* **(Vol. 198, September 2004, No. 3, pp.)**
Pub: American Institute of Certified Public Accountants
Ed: Steven Bragg. Description: Best practices offered by certified public accountants to help keep a general ledger both current and accurate are listed.

26222 ■ "Entrepreneur Column" in *Entrepreneur.com* **(December 21, 2007)**
Pub: Entrepreneur Media Inc.
Ed: Tamara Monosoff. Description: Covers the basic relationships of pricing, costing, profit margins, and other necessary tools for successful business management.

26223 ■ "Everyone's a CFO" in *Inc.* **(September 2005, pp. 42, 45)**
Pub: Inc. Magazine
Ed: Nadine Heintz. Description: DCI CEO, Andrew Levine, assigns employees to present monthly financial reports, teaches them to spot trends and anomalies in the numbers, and has them focus on accounting basics.

26224 ■ "Expensing stock options in not inevitable" in *Red Herring* **(January 2003, pp. 14)**
Pub: Herring Communications Inc.
Ed: John Doerr. Description: The expensing of employee stock options is discussed.

26225 ■ "Expensing Stock Options: A Fair-Value Approach" in *Harvard Business Review* **(Vol. 81, No. 12, December 2003, pp. 105)**
Pub: Harvard Business School Press
Ed: Robert S. Kaplan, Krishna G. Palepu. Description: An examination of methods for fair-value expensing employee stock options, thus eliminating measurement and forecasting errors over time. Estimated option prices, amortized expenses, adjustment to paid-in capital, and total end-of-year reported expenses are calculated in two theoretical scenarios over a four-year period.

26226 ■ "Explore the Art of Consultative Selling" in *Journal of Accountancy* **(Vol. 199, January 2005)**
Pub: American Institute of Certified Public Accountants
Ed: John E. Graziano, Patrick J. Flanagan. Description: Traditional selling vs. consultative selling techniques when integrating financial planning into an accounting practice are explored.

26227 ■ *Finance & Accounting*
Pub: Kendall Hunt Publishing Co.
Ed: Henry Beam. Released: 1995. Price: $1 8.95.

26228 ■ *Finance & Accounting: How to Keep Your Books and Manage Your Finances with an MBA, a CPA, or a Ph.D*
Pub: Adams Media Corporation
Ed: Suzanne Caplan. Price: $19.95.

26229 ■ *Financial Accounting: Guide*
Pub: Kendall Hunt Publishing Co.
Ed: Mohamed Ibrahim. Released: 1995. Price: $19.95.

26230 ■ *Financial Accounting & Reporting*
Pub: South-Western Publishing Co.
Released: 1995. Price: $48.95.

26231 ■ *Financial Essentials for Small Business Success: Accounting, Planning & Recordkeeping Techniques for a Healthy Bottom Line*
Pub: Upstart Publishing Co., Inc.
Ed: Joe Tabet. Released: 1994. Price: $19.95 (paper).

26232 ■ *Financial Management 101: Get a Grip on Your Business Numbers*
Pub: Self-Counsel Press, Incorporated

Ed: Angie Mohr. Released: September 2004. Price: $14.95. Description: An overview of business planning, financial statements, budgeting and advertising for small businesses. s.

26233 ■ "Financial Reporting Goes Global: International Standards Affect U.S. Companies and GAAP" in *Journal of Accountancy* **(Vol. 198)**
Pub: American Institute of Certified Public Accountants
Ed: D.J. Gannon, Alex Ashwal. Description: Summary of the international standards affecting U.S. companies and GAAP (generally accepted accounting principles).

26234 ■ *Financial Times Guide to Business Start Up 2007*
Pub: Pearson Education, Limited
Ed: Sara Williams; Jonquil Lowe. Released: November 2006. Price: $52.50. Description: Guide for starting and running a new business is presented. Sections include ways to get started, direct marketing, customer relations, management and accounting.

26235 ■ "Fit and Trim" in *Entrepreneur* **(Vol. 31, No. 7, July 2003, pp. 74)**
Pub: Entrepreneur Media, Inc.
Ed: Joanne Cleaver. Description: It is necessary for small business owners to examine where overhead is out of control in order to trim expenses.

26236 ■ "Five Checking Account Mistakes to Avoid" in *Black Enterprise* **(Vol. 34, No. 5, December 2003, pp. S11)**
Pub: Earl Graves Publishing Co.
Ed: Tamekia Reece. Description: Five tips to help small businesses avoid accounting mistakes with the firm's checking account.

26237 ■ "The Flaw of averages" in *Harvard Business Review* **(Vol. 80, No. 11, November 2002, pp. 20)**
Pub: Harvard Business School Press
Ed: Sam Savage. Description: The use of an average figure to represent an uncertain quantity can lead to a wrong answer in accounting, investment and sales. Software exists that can fix this flaw.

26238 ■ "Food For Thought" in *Entrepreneur* **(Vol. 32, September 2004, No. 9, pp. 50)**
Pub: Entrepreneur Media Inc.
Ed: Jennifer Pellet. Description: Bills to return the meal and entertainment deduction to 80 percent are pending in both the House and Senate. This increase would help small businesses more than large corporations.

26239 ■ "For Auditors, Gain From All That Pain" in *Long Island Business News* **(May 7, 2004)**
Pub: Dolan Media Newswires
Ed: Ken Schachter. Description: Results of companies required to comply with Section 404 of the Sarbanes-Oxley Act of 2002, which requires management to maintain an adequate internal control structure and procedures for financial reporting, and to assess effectiveness of the company's internal control structure and procedures for reporting financial information, are discussed.

26240 ■ "For the Last Time: Stock Options Are an Expense" in *Harvard Business Review* **(Vol. 81, No. 3, March 2003, pp. 63)**
Pub: Harvard Business School Press
Ed: Zvi Bodie, Robert S. Kaplan, Robert C. Merton. Description: The practice of expensing stock options is discussed.

26241 ■ "Former B.E. 100s Clerk Faces Prison Time" in *Black Enterprise* **(Vol. 35, September 2004, No. 2, pp. 30)**
Pub: Earl G. Graves Publishing Co. Inc.
Ed: Tamara E. Holmes. Description: Joanna L. Cook, former accounts payable clerk for TeleCommunication Systems Inc., pleaded guilty to one count of bank fraud for stealing more than $1 million from the company between 2000 and 2003. An assistant controller and accounting supervisor discovered her fraudulent activity.

26242 ■ "Former Computer Associates Executive Pleads Guilty in U.S. District Court in Brooklyn" in *Long Island Business News* **(Jan. 30, 2004)**
Pub: Dolan Media Newswires
Description: Former senior vice president, Lloyd Silverstein, of Computer Associates International, pleaded guilty to charges of obstruction of justice in the federal investigation of the software maker's accounting practices. The company has also received notice that it will be the target of civil charges by the Securities and Exchange Commission.

26243 ■ "Fraud Risk: Are You Prepared? The Mission: To Create Stronger Support for an Ethically Sound Business Environment" in *Journal of Accountancy*
Pub: American Institute of Certified Public Accountants
Ed: Steven E. Sacks. Description: Incentives that reward individuals for short term results can sometimes result in fraud and abuse; ways this fraud is affecting the certified public accounting profession is examined.

26244 ■ "From Fifth Hire to Top Exec, New CEO to Lead SurePayroll" in *Crain's Chicago Business* **(Vol. 26, No. 50, December 15, 2003, pp. 12)**
Pub: Crain Communications, Inc.
Ed: Julie Johnsson. Description: Profile of Michael Alter, newly appointed CEO of SurePayroll. The firm, started in 1999, provides payroll checks to companies with fewer than 100 employees. The process is simpler than traditional payroll services with everything done online, and costs 30-50 percent less than competitors.

26245 ■ "Fulfill the Promise of Electronic Billing" in *E-business Advisor* **(Vol. 18, No. 7, July 2000, pp. 26)**
Pub: Advisor Media, Inc.
Ed: Jim Flynn. Description: Electronic bill payment and presentment (EBPP) has not taken off as expected due to such problems as poor implementation of the technology for the consumer market and bill consolidation technology is still in the embryonic stage.

26246 ■ "The Future is Here: The Modernizing of IRS e-File" in *Journal of Accountancy* **(Vol. 198, December 2004, No. 6, pp. 89)**
Pub: American Institute of Certified Public Accountants
Ed: Bert DuMars. Description: Ways the Internal Revenue Service is updating and modernizing electronic returns are listed.

26247 ■ "Get the Raise You Deserve: A Step-by-Step Guide to Negotiating the Right Pay Package" in *Journal of Accountancy* **(October 2004)**
Pub: American Institute of Certified Public Accountants
Ed: Anita Dennis. Description: According to experts, there are several steps that certified public accountants can take to receive the pay they feel they are worth.

26248 ■ "Global accounting is coming" in *Harvard Business Review* **(Vol. 81, No. 4, April 2003, pp. 24)**
Pub: Harvard Business School Press
Ed: Richard G. Barker. Description: The recent accounting scandals have led to international influence on U.S. financial reporting. Under the emerging global standards, income statements will reveal more than has been the custom with U.S. firms.

26249 ■ "Granting Options Like It's 1999" in *Inc.* **(October 2005, pp. 34)**
Pub: Inc. Magazine
Description: Private firms will be required to expense the value of outstanding employee stock options, beginning 2006.

26250 ■ "Grice, Lund & Tarkington Merges with Oregon Firm" in *San Diego Business Journal* **(Vol. 28, January 15, 2007, No. 3, pp. 19)**
Pub: San Diego Business Journal Associates
Ed: Andy Killion. Description: Accounting firm, Grice, Lund & Tarkington has merged with Aldrich Kilbride & Tatone. The two firms will operate under the Aldrich Kilbride & Tatone name. The merger will improve the company's ability to address client needs in the changing world of accounting and financial services.

26251 ■ "A Gross Tax Proposal" in *Inc.* **(July 1, 2003)**
Pub: Gruner & Jahr USA Publishing
Description: A business activity tax stands to change the way taxes are calculated in the state of Kentucky.

26252 ■ "Hiring an Accountant" in *Crain's Detroit Business* **(Vol. 19, No. 49, December 8, 2003, pp. 14)**
Pub: Crain Communications Inc., Detroit
Description: Questions an employer should ask when hiring an accountant are listed.

26253 ■ "Home, Sweet Office" in *Entrepreneur* **(Vol. 31, No. 11, November 2003, pp. 72)**
Pub: Entrepreneur Media, Inc.
Ed: Jennifer Pellet. Description: Internal Revenue Service tax laws regarding the sale of a home that is also used as a home business are explained.

26254 ■ "Hot Disks" in *Entrepreneur* **(Vol. 31, No. 11, November 2003, pp. 58)**
Pub: Entrepreneur Media, Inc.
Ed: Liane Cassavoy. Description: Profiles of new software for small businesses, including Zone Labs firewall products, Nero recording tools, Bill Quick 2003, and LinkFixerPlus.

26255 ■ "Houston-based GC Services Adds 100 Jobs in Oklahoma City" in *Journal Record* **(February 5, 2004)**
Pub: Dolan Media Company
Ed: Darren Currin. Description: GC Services plans to expand the Oklahoma City national service center with an immediate addition of 100 new employees, and ultimately 200 new employees after completion. The firm works with corporation and state agencies managing accounts receivables and customer service needs.

26256 ■ *How to Start an Internet Sales Business*
Pub: Lulu.com
Ed: Dan Davis. Released: August 2005. Price: $19.95. Description: Small business guide for launching an Internet sales company. Topics include business structure, licenses, and taxes.

26257 ■ "Hunting Season: Feds Try to Protect the Little Guy From Payroll Tax Predators" in *Entrepreneur* **(Vol. 32, September 2004, No. 9)**
Pub: Entrepreneur Media Inc.
Ed: Stephen Barlas. Description: The Tax Administration Good Government Act gives the Internal Revenue Service tools to go after payroll/accounting firms that steal a client's employment tax payments, while protecting small businesses that hire the services.

26258 ■ "I Can't Seem to Hire the Right Bookkeeper. Should I Try Using a Personality Test?" in *Inc.* **(October 2005, pp. 62)**
Pub: Inc. Magazine
Description: Personality tests that screen job applicants for traits like reliability and dishonesty have become commonplace in most industries.

26259 ■ "I was greedy, too" in *Harvard Business Review* **(Vol. 81, No. 2, February 2003, pp. 38)**
Pub: Harvard Business School Press
Ed: Diane L. Coutu. Description: Although greed has become an integral part of the U.S. psyche, the psychology of greed has not been studied well. Greed has ebbed and crested throughout this country's history, and most recently with the collapse of Internet companies, corporate malfeasance. However, business schools continue to graduate a high number of students.

26260 ■ "IAEM Commission To Oversee Audits: Exhibitors To Constitute a Majority; Body Will Enforce Audit Standards" in *Tradeshow Week* **(Vol. 34)**
Pub: Reed Business Information
Ed: Margo McCall. Description: Event and Exhibition Audit Commission will begin certifying procedures used by tradeshow auditing firms in 2005. Auditors that successfully undergo a review by the commission will be entitled to use a seal of certification.

26261 ■ "I'm Game: What Hot, New Pastime is Inspiring Entrepreneurs to Launch Businesses?" in *Entrepreneur* **(Vol. 32, September 2004)**
Pub: Entrepreneur Media Inc.
Ed: Nichole L. Torres. Description: Cashflow 101 is the new business board game that teaches financial principles for accounting and investing. Profiles of entrepreneurs who launched a business after playing the game are included.

26262 ■ "Impact of Self-Employment Loss on Earned Income" in *Journal of Accountancy* **(Vol. 198, September 2004, No. 3, pp.)**
Pub: American Institute of Certified Public Accountants
Ed: Claire Y. Nash. Description: Information about the various tax code sections defined as 'earned income' are explored.

26263 ■ "In Accounting, Number of Registered Sole Practitioners Decreasing" in *Long Island Business News* **(March 5, 2004)**
Pub: Dolan Media Newswires
Ed: David Reich-Hale. Description: The number of registered accounting sole practitioners in New York has decreased 25 percent since 2000, according to a public relations manager at the New York State Society of Certified Public Accountants.

26264 ■ "Increasing Transparency in Peer Review: Members Speak Out" in *Journal of Accountancy* **(Vol. 198, December 2004, No. 6, pp. 22)**
Pub: American Institute of Certified Public Accountants
Ed: Adam Snyder. Description: The results of a survey of small accounting firms practicing in ten states about increasing transparency by making peer review information a part of public record, are presented.

26265 ■ "Install Your Own Wireless Networks" in *Journal of Accountancy* **(Vol. 198)**
Pub: American Institute of Certified Public Accountants
Ed: Bryce H. Peterson, William G. Heninger, Craig J. Lindstrom, Marshall B. Romney. Description: Information is presented to help network computer systems using a wireless local area network (WLAN).

26266 ■ "Interest Paid as an Administrative Expense" in *Journal of Accountancy* **(Vol. 198, December 2004, No. 6, pp. 95)**
Pub: American Institute of Certified Public Accountants
Ed: Michael H. Brown. Description: Tax laws regarding deductions used for interest paid by an estate are discussed.

26267 ■ "Internet Banking Can Improve Your Cash Management" in *Ingram's* **(Vol. 28, No. 1, January 2002, pp. 42)**
Pub: Show Me Publishing, Inc.
Ed: Gary Wilcutt. Description: The benefits of using Internet banking services for a small business are investigated.

26268 ■ **"Internet or Desktop" in** *PC Magazine* **(February 20, 2001, pp. 145)**
Pub: Ziff-Davis Publishing Company
Ed: Wayne Kawamoto. **Description:** Reviews of accounting software packages that are available for the desktop or online.

26269 ■ **"Intuit launches small business marketplace" in** *Network World* **(September 18, 2000, pp. NA)**
Pub: Network World Inc.
Ed: Sam Costello. **Description:** A profile of Quick-Books Shopping Source, targeted at small businesses. The service will provide discounts on business supplies and services, ranging from computer to clothing, and even janitorial services.

26270 ■ **"Investor: Boarding School" in** *Red Herring* **(No. 99, June 15 & July 1, 2001, pp. 130, 132)**
Pub: Herring Communications
Ed: Beverly Goodman. **Description:** An overview of the new audit committee rules adopted by the stock exchanges is presented. The volatility of today's market is discussed.

26271 ■ **"IRS Agrees to Pursue Legislative Changes to Section 6103" in** *Tax Notes* **(Vol. 102, No. 3, January 19, 2004, pp. 295-298)**
Pub: Tax Notes International
Ed: Heather Bennett, Timothy Catts. **Description:** The issue of using taxpayer identification numbers in conflict with immigrations laws is examined.

26272 ■ **"IRS Allows Statistical Sampling for M&E Costs: New Procedure May Increase Taxpayer Deductions" in** *Journal of Accountancy* **(Vol. 198)**
Pub: American Institute of Certified Public Accountants
Ed: Lesli S. Laffie. **Description:** The Internal Revenue Service now permits the use of statistical sampling to account for allowable expense deductions for meals and entertainment.

26273 ■ **"Is 'Equitable Remedy' Settlement Excludable from Gross Income?" in** *Journal of Accountancy* **(Vol. 198, December 2004, No. 6, pp. 94)**
Pub: American Institute of Certified Public Accountants
Description: A case testing the definition of personal physical injury or physical sickness in an equitable remedy is discussed.

26274 ■ **"It's Important to Be Proactive about Risk Issues" in** *Atlanta Business Chronicle* **(Vol. 24, No. 9, August 3, 2001, pp. 9B)**
Pub: American City Business Journals Inc.
Description: Major factors resulting in business failure include customer demand shortage, irregularities in accounting, issues concerning supply chain and competitive pressures. In protecting a business from risk of failure, in addition to purchasing insurance, a culture and organizational structure where risk management is seen as everyone's job, is essential.

26275 ■ **"Jump-Start Success: How to Set Up a World-Class Internal Audit Function" in** *Journal of Accountancy* **(Vol. 199, February 2005, No. 2)**
Pub: American Institute of Certified Public Accountants
Ed: Bruce Caplain. **Description:** Advice is offered for setting up a successful internal audit function for a company.

26276 ■ *Keeping the Books: Basic Recordkeeping and Accounting for the Small Business*
Pub: Upstart Publishing Co., Inc.
Ed: Linda Pinson and Jerry A. Jinnett. **Released:** 4th ed., 1998. **Price:** $22.95 (paper). **Description:** Guide to recordkeeping for small businesses, covering accounts receivable and accounts payable, petty cash, travel/entertainment records, budgeting, profit and loss statements, and cash flow.

26277 ■ **"Law of the Land" in** *Entrepreneur* **(Vol. 33, October 2005, No. 10, pp. 89)**
Pub: Entrepreneur Media Inc.
Ed: Marc Diener. **Description:** Six rules to make the most of a company's money are listed.

26278 ■ **"Lawmaker in Okla. Seeks to Discourage Fines for Tax Preparers" in** *Journal Record (Oklahoma City, OK)* **(February 6, 2007)**
Pub: Journal Record
Ed: Janice Francis-Smith. **Description:** Representative Charles Key, R-Oklahoma, plans to introduce a House Concurrent Resolution that would discourage state regulators from imposing fines on tax preparers that offer refund anticipation loans.

26279 ■ **"Learn Your ABC" in** *Hispanic Business* **(December 2001, pp. 68)**
Pub: Hispanic Business
Ed: Milton Zall. **Description:** The method of activity-based accounting (ABC) is discussed. ABC is a valuable tool for assessing operating expenses.

26280 ■ **"Lease on Life?" in** *Entrepreneur* **(Vol. 32, November 2004, No. 11, pp. 98)**
Pub: Entrepreneur Media Inc.
Ed: Jane Easter Bahls. **Description:** According to the National Association of Professional Employer Organizations, 2 to 3 million Americans are co-employed in professional employer organizations (PEO) arrangements. The employer and the PEO are both legally responsible for payment of payroll taxes and workers' compensation, and compliance with government regulations.

26281 ■ **"Let Them Eat Cake: When It Comes to Small Business, a New Tax-Cut Bill is Half-Baked" in** *Entrepreneur* **(Vol. 32, November 2004)**
Pub: Entrepreneur Media Inc.
Ed: Stephen Barlas. **Description:** New tax incentives for U.S. manufacturers are discussed.

26282 ■ **"Look before you lay off" in** *Harvard Business Review* **(Vol. 80, No. 4, April 2002, pp. 20)**
Pub: Harvard Business School Press
Ed: Darrell Rigby. **Description:** An examination of the pitfalls inherent in layoffs during an economic downturn. Research shows that shareholders punish companies that use layoffs solely to cut costs. Graphs are included.

26283 ■ **"Make Driving Less Taxing" in** *My Business* **(April/May 2003, pp. 10)**
Pub: My Business Magazine
Ed: Alan Breznick. **Description:** Entrepreneurs can deduct up to $25,000 of a Sport Utility Vehicle's purchase price from income taxes if the SUV is heavy enough and as long as it is used mainly for business.

26284 ■ **"Make the Most of Buy-Sell Agreements: These Complex Contracts Solve Many Problems" in** *Journal of Accountancy* **(Vol. 198, October 2004)**
Pub: American Institute of Certified Public Accountants
Ed: Thomas F. Burrage, Chad Hoekstra. **Description:** A Summary of buy-sell agreements is highlighted.

26285 ■ **"Make your layoff list and check it twice" in** *BlackEnterprise* **(Vol. 32, No. 3, October 2001, pp. 70)**
Pub: Earl Graves Publishing Co.
Ed: Robyn D. Clarke. **Description:** David A. Branch, an employment and civil rights attorney in Washington DC, provides four important points for businesses to consider when planning a pre-layoff checklist.

26286 ■ **"Making Book" in** *Entrepreneur* **(Vol. 33, February 2005, No. 2, pp. 37)**
Pub: Entrepreneur Media Inc.
Ed: Mike Hogan. **Description:** Microsoft Office 2003 has designed a new Office Small Business Accounting program that offers ease in connecting to other Office applications.

26287 ■ **"Making Pro Formas Perform" in** *Harvard Business Review* **(Vol. 81, No. 10, October 2003, pp. 24)**
Pub: Harvard Business School Press
Ed: Stephen Bryan, Steven Lilien. **Description:** Quarterly earnings reports from the Dow 30 during 2001 are analyzed to show that pro forma earnings deviated sometimes considerably from generally accepted accounting principles.

26288 ■ **"Manager in a box" in** *Hispanic Business* **(Vol. 22, No. 10, October 2000, pp. 114)**
Pub: Hispanic Business
Ed: Roger Harris. **Description:** The Tenant Pro 5.0 property management software system is evaluated. The package is an easy to use product, combining an accounting program and a useful database management program, and is suitable for either small or very large numbers of properties.

26289 ■ *Managing by the Numbers: Financial Essentials for the Growing Business*
Pub: Upstart Publishing Co., Inc.
Ed: David H. Bangs, Jr. **Released:** 1992. **Price:** $19.95 (paper). **Description:** Discusses accounting help, balance sheets and P&L statements, cash flow and outflow, and financial projections.

26290 ■ *Mergers and Acquisitions from A to Z*
Pub: Amacom
Ed: Andrew J. Sherman, Milledge A. Hart. **Released:** December 2005. **Price:** $47.00. **Description:** Guide for the entire process of mergers and acquisitions, including taxes, accounting, laws, and projected financial gain.

26291 ■ *Microfinance*
Pub: Palgrave Macmillan
Ed: Mario La Torre; Gianfranco A. Vento; Philip Molyneux. **Released:** October 2006. **Price:** $80.00. **Description:** Microfinance involves the analysis of operational, managerial and financial aspects of a small business.

26292 ■ **"Microsoft Money 2004 Small Business: www.microsoft.com/money/business" in** *Entrepreneur* **(Vol. 31, No. 12, December 2003, pp. 8)**
Pub: Entrepreneur Media Inc.
Ed: Steve Cooper. **Description:** Profile of Microsoft's latest money management software that allows businesses to download information for various financial institutions.

26293 ■ **"Minimum Wage Hikes Eyed Nationwide" in** *Inc.* **(October 1, 2004)**
Pub: Inc. Magazine
Ed: Jess McCuan. **Description:** New York may become the 13th state to raise its minimum wage above the federal level now set at $5.15 per hour.

26294 ■ *Money Smart Secrets for the Self-Employed*
Pub: Random House, Inc.
Ed: Linda Stern. **Released:** 1997. **Price:** $20.00.

26295 ■ **"Mortgage Warehouse in Melville Announces Staffing Changes" in** *Long Island Business News* **(March 5, 2004)**
Pub: Dolan Media Newswires
Ed: Ryan McCormick. **Description:** Jonathan Foxx and Stephen Mayer have been appointed by Mortgage Warehouse in Melville, New York. Foxx will work as compliance management consultant, while Mayer will be responsible for managing and reviewing every facet of Mortgage Warehouse's financial and accounting records as controller.

26296 ■ **"Move to expense stock options get mixed results" in** *Atlanta Business Chronicle* **(Vol. 25, November 15, 2002, No. 23 pp. SS4)**
Pub: American City Business Publications, Inc.
Ed: Paige Bowers. **Description:** Due to the difficulty of accurately measuring the value of stock options,

some disagree with the trend of expensing stock options, following recent corporate accounting scandals. Others point out that stock options now account for 15 percent of compensation, up from 5 percent, and expensing options may encourage companies to be more selective in how many options are granted. Many believe new regulation is likely in the near future.

26297 ■ "MyPayNet" in *Entrepreneur.com* **(Vol. 34, January 2006, No. 1, pp. 6)**
Pub: Entrepreneur Media Inc.
Ed: Steve Cooper. **Description:** MyPayNet is an electronic invoicing and payment service designed to help small companies send and receive payments electronically.

26298 ■ "National Association of Black Accountants" in *Black Enterprise* **(Vol. 35, December 2004, No. 5, pp. 86)**
Pub: Earl G. Graves Publishing Co. Inc.
Description: Norman Jenkins, vice president of Marriott International Inc., was inducted as present and CEO of the National Association of Black Accounts.

26299 ■ "The Need for Separate Accounts" in *Black Enterprise* **(Vol. 35, October 2004, No. 3, pp. 48)**
Pub: Earl G. Graves Publishing Co. Inc.
Ed: Erin Straker. **Description:** Federal regulations require that corporations and LLCs keep business activities separate from personal activities. Steps to keep personal and business records separated are described.

26300 ■ "A New Abacus for Pensions" in *Business Week* **(January 9, 2006, No. 3966, pp. 91)**
Pub: McGraw-Hill Companies
Description: New Financial Accounting Standards Board rules on post-retirement accounting will change how companies account for pensions and other employee benefits, especially retiree health insurance.

26301 ■ "New 'corporate sheriff' starts touch talk" in *Atlanta Business Chronicle* **(Vol. 25, No. 21, November 1, 2002, pp. 3A)**
Pub: American City Business Publications, Inc.
Ed: Walter Woods. **Description:** U.S. Attorney General, William Duffey, vows to take action against corporate crooks. He is warning Atlanta, Georgia businesses their conduct will be eyed by his office.

26302 ■ "New Laws Tighten Rules, Penalties for Accountants" in *Crain's Detroit Business* **(Vol. 22, January 16, 2006, No. 3, pp. 23)**
Pub: Crain Communications Inc. - Detroit
Ed: Amy Lane. **Description:** Under Michigan's new Public Acts 277-279 laws, all of the state's certified public accounting firms that perform audits, reviews and compilations will have work reviewed by a team of peer accountants.

26303 ■ "No More Postdating: New Bill Allows Banks to Process Your Checks at Warp Speed" in *Black Enterprise* **(Vol. 35, January 2005, No. 6)**
Pub: Earl G. Graves Publishing Co. Inc.
Ed: Tamara E. Holmes. **Description:** A new federal law will allow banks to process checks in one day instead of the traditional two to four grace period. The Check Clearing for the 21st Century Act allows banks to transmit electronic images of a check speeding the processes.

26304 ■ "Nonindividual QTP Contributions: How Employers Can Help Workers Save for College" in *Journal of Accountancy* **(Vol. 198, November 2004)**
Pub: American Institute of Certified Public Accountants
Ed: Lesli S. Laffie. **Description:** Issues involved in an employer using qualified tuition programs for employees are examined.

26305 ■ "Northeast's Largest Independent Accounting Firm Comes to Long Island" in *Long Island Business News* **(February 6, 2004)**
Pub: Dolan Media Newswires
Ed: Ben Abelson. **Description:** Profile of J.H. Cohn, the accounting firm that recently acquired Levine, Levine & Meyrowitz CPAs. Cohn is the largest independent accounting firm in the nation's Northeast area. Profile of the company is included.

26306 ■ "Now You See It: Payroll Tax is Likely the Tax You Most Want to Have Cut, But Will It Ever Happen?" in *Entrepreneur* **(Vol. 31, Aug.2003)**
Pub: Entrepreneur Media, Inc.
Ed: Chris Penttila. **Description:** Payroll taxes make up 34.9 percent of federal revenues and are expected to grow to 36.3 by 2004, thus making it the least-likely tax cut Americans will see take place.

26307 ■ "Numbers Prove Accountants Are On a Roll" in *The Record* **(November 10, 2005)**
Pub: New Jersey Media Group
Ed: Richard Newman. **Description:** In an interview with Scott Levy, partner at Grant Thornton International, he answers questions about the firm's New Jersey operation. The company works for firms in 11 countries with annual revenue of more than $2 billion.

26308 ■ "Office Space: It's better to rent than own" in *Red Herring* **(No. 103, September 1, 2001, pp. 85)**
Pub: Herring Communications
Ed: Duff McDonald. **Description:** More technology firms are using the sale-leaseback transaction as an alternative to monetizing real estate assets.

26309 ■ "Ohio Investment Tax Credit Struck Down" in *Journal of Accountancy* **(Vol. 199, January 2005, No. 1, pp. 76)**
Pub: American Institute of Certified Public Accountants
Ed: Laura Lee Mannino. **Description:** It is important for small businesses to fully understand any tax credits offered by states designed to lure new business to their state.

26310 ■ "An old-fashioned fate: it takes the tax collector to really ruin somebody" in *Barron's* **(Vol. 82, No. 58, February 17, 2003, pp. 31)**
Pub: Barron's
Ed: Thomas G. Donlan. **Description:** Former Sprint CEO, William T. Esprey, was doubly unethical in formulating the tax evasion scam that ruined him; he also leaned on the company auditors, Ernst & Young, to form an illicit tax shelter.

26311 ■ "The Ones That Get Away" in *The Economist* **(Vol. 376, July 30-August 5, 2005, No. 8437, pp. 65-66)**
Pub: The Economist Newspaper Ltd.
Description: The art and science of recruiting and retaining business accounts is examined.

26312 ■ *Open Source Solutions for Small Business Problems*
Pub: Charles River Media
Ed: John Locke. **Released:** May 2004. **Price:** $39.95 (US), $55.95 (Canadian). **Description:** Open source software provides solutions to many small business problems such as tracking electronic documents, scheduling, accounting functions, managing contact lists, and reducing spam.

26313 ■ "Operation no safe haven: there's $400 billion in unregulated money stashed in offshore hedge accounts" in *Red Herring* **(Jan. 2003)**
Pub: Herring Communications Inc.
Ed: Christopher Byron. **Description:** Offshore hedge funds provide an end run around the crackdown on U.S. companies. These accounts allow money to be moved anonymously in and out of the U.S. without going through a U.S. bank.

26314 ■ "Out of Sight: Stock Options Can Stay Off Your Balance Sheet-For Now" in *Entrepreneur* **(Vol. 32, August 2004, No. 8, pp. 31)**
Pub: Entrepreneur Media Inc.
Ed: Stephen Barlas. **Description:** The Financial Accounting Standards Board has proposed reform that would let entrepreneurs measure compensation costs using a simpler 'intrinsic value method' rather than a fair-value-based method.

26315 ■ *Outfoxing the Small Business Owner*
Pub: Adams Media Corporation
Ed: Gene Marks. **Released:** January 2005. **Price:** $12.95 (US), $18.95 (Canadian). **Description:** Special skill sets are required to sell, service or deal with small business customers.

26316 ■ "Papers Away: Tax Records Weighing You Down? Switch to Electronic Storage" in *Entrepreneur* **(Vol. 32, October 2004, No. 10, pp. 60)**
Pub: Entrepreneur Media Inc.
Ed: Joan Szabo. **Description:** Electronic tax records allow a small business to electronically store the documents involved in tax preparation. The method not only saves times, but also cuts expenses on paper and office space, improves security and access to documents.

26317 ■ "Partnership Terminations" in *Journal of Accountancy* **(Vol. 199, January 2005, No. 1, pp. 73)**
Pub: American Institute of Certified Public Accountants
Ed: Edward J. Schnee. **Description:** The Internal Revenue Code as it pertains to partnership terminations is discussed.

26318 ■ "Passing Marks?" in *Entrepreneur* **(Vol. 31, No. 11, November 2003, pp. 70)**
Pub: Entrepreneur Media, Inc.
Ed: Joan Szabo. **Description:** Information on the Regulatory Flexibility Act (RFA) is presented. The RFA is a law designed to make sure federal agencies address the needs of small business when issuing rules and regulations.

26319 ■ "Past due, and getting soaked" in *Crain's Detroit Business* **(Vol. 17, No. 43, October 15, 2001, pp. 1)**
Pub: Crain Communications, Inc.
Ed: Laura Bailey, Terry Kosdrosky. **Description:** According to the U.S. Small Business Administration, 75-80 percent of small businesses suffer from either slow paying customers or customers who don't pay at all. Advice is offered to help small businesses develop effective collections policies.

26320 ■ "Pay Dirt! Finally Making a Profit? Put It Where It Belongs-Back in Your Business" in *Entrepreneur* **(Vol. 31, No. 11, November 2003)**
Pub: Entrepreneur Media, Inc.
Ed: Geoff Williams. **Description:** Small businesses should invest profits back into the company.

26321 ■ "The PCAOB and the Future of Oversight" in *Journal Of Accountancy*
Pub: American Institute of Certified Public Accountants
Ed: Patrick J. McDonnell. **Description:** Review of the Sarbanes-Oxley Act of 2002 created by the Public Company Accounting Oversight Board (PCAOB) is presented. The role of the PCAOB is discussed.

26322 ■ "Penny wise, pound foolish" in *Black Enterprise* **(Vol. 32, No. 10, May 2002, pp. 44)**
Pub: Earl Graves Publishing Co.
Ed: Alan Hughes. **Description:** The importance of maintaining separate personal and business accounts is discussed.

26323 ■ "Pension Pain" in *Forbes* **(Vol. 170, No. 4, September 2, 2002, pp. 144)**
Pub: Forbes Magazine

Ed: A. Gary Shilling. **Description:** Companies will no longer be allowed to boost earnings by including pension plans.

26324 ■ "The Perfect Storm? Employers Need Navigation Tools For The Newest Set of Health Cost Waves" in *Employee Benefit Plan Review* **(Vol. 55)**
Pub: Charles D. Spencer & Associates, Inc.
Ed: Stephen A. Huth. **Description:** Reports from the Department of Labor show that, for the year ended September 30, 2000, benefits costs for private industry workers rose to 6 percent. The largest portion was for health care, and employers will try many strategies to reduce costs, including passing some on to their employees.

26325 ■ "Perquest Brings Payroll Industry Into 21st Century; PayPal Founder Seeds Silicon Valley Startups" in *PR Newswire* **(Nov. 17, 2003)**
Pub: PR Newswire Association, Inc.
Description: Online payroll services are now available online; profile of Perquest's payroll service is provided.

26326 ■ "Pick Your Startup Tool" in *Black Enterprise* **(Vol. 36, November 2005, No. 4, pp. 74)**
Pub: Earl G. Graves Publishing Co. Inc.
Ed: Sonya Donaldson. **Description:** Besides being a good business plan, financial management tools are an asset for planning a marketing strategy. Business Plan Pro Standard, QuickBooks, Peachtree, and Business Resource Software can help startups write business plans that include pricing strategy, advertising, and budgeting.

26327 ■ *PPC's Guide to Audits of Small Businesses, Vol. 3*
Pub: Practitioners Publishing Company
Released: April 2004. **Description:** Technical guide for developing an auditing system for small business. Audit programs, correspondence and checklists included.

26328 ■ "Predictable surprises: The disasters you should have seen coming" in *Harvard Business Review* **(Vol. 81, No. 3, March 2003, pp. 72)**
Pub: Harvard Business School Press
Ed: Michael Watkins, Max Bazerman. **Description:** Many unexpected events that turn into disasters, such as financial scandals and product failures, can be foreseen and avoided, using the RPM approach: recognizing, prioritizing, and mobilizing.

26329 ■ "Price Equals Value Plus Terms" in *Journal of Accountancy*
Pub: American Institute of Certified Public Accountants
Ed: Joel Sinkin. **Description:** Business valuations, succession planning, and buy-sell agreements are discussed, focusing on the certified public accountants role in reviewing the interrelationship of five key variables: the down payment at closing, the length of the payout period on the balance due, the profitability of the deal, the duration of the post-closing retention period with adjustments for lost clients, and the multiple (preferred price based on a multiple of the gross billings).

26330 ■ "Process Online Payments Quickly and Effectively" in *E-business Advisor* **(Vol. 18, No. 6, June 2000, pp. 34)**
Pub: Advisor Media, Inc.
Ed: Glenn T. Shesney. **Description:** Assessment Systems Inc. (ASI), a purveyor of electronically administered tests, has deployed Payment Plus' LiveProcessor electronic commerce software, greatly boosting the number of payments the company can transact per hour. LiveProcessor, a Linux-based system, can process hundreds of transactions per minute during periods of high volume, with per-transaction response time averaging less than three seconds.

26331 ■ *QuickBooks All-in-One Desk Reference for Dummies*
Pub: John Wiley & Sons, Incorporated
Ed: Stephen L. Nelson. **Released:** January 2005. **Price:** $29.99 (US), $42.99 (Canadian). **Description:** Compilation of nine self-contained minibooks to get the most from QuickBooks accounting software. Companion Web site with sample business plan workbook and downloadable profit-volume cost analysis workbook included.

26332 ■ *QuickBooks for the New Bean Counter: Business Owner's Guide 2006*
Pub: Wheatmark
Ed: Joseph L. Catallini. **Released:** July 2006. **Price:** $21.95. **Description:** Profile of QuickBooks software, offering insight into using the software's accounting and bookkeeping functions.

26333 ■ *QuickBooks Simple Start for Dummies*
Pub: John Wiley & Sons, Incorporated
Ed: Stephen L. Nelson. **Released:** September 2004. **Price:** $28.99. **Description:** Profile of Intuits new accounting software geared to micro businesses. Advice is offered on daily, monthly, and yearly accounting activities covering records, sales tax, and reports.

26334 ■ *QuickBooks X on Demand*
Pub: Que
Ed: Gail Perry. **Released:** December 2006. **Price:** $34.99. **Description:** Step-by-step training for using various small business financial software programs; includes illustrated, full color explanations.

26335 ■ *QuickBooks X for Dummies*
Pub: John Wiley & Sons, Incorporated
Ed: Stephen L. Nelson. **Released:** November 2006. **Price:** $21.99. **Description:** Key features of QuickBooks software for small business are introduced. Invoicing and credit memos, recoding sales receipts, accounting, budgeting, taxes, payroll, financial reports, job estimating, billing, tracking, data backup, are among the features.

26336 ■ "Radio Frequency Identification" in *Journal of Accountancy*
Pub: American Institute of Certified Public Accountants
Ed: Harold E. Davis, Michael S. Luehlfing. **Description:** Radio frequency identification (RFID) consists of tags, transceivers and a computer system that share the characteristics, location, arrival/shipment time and other information about inventories. RFID is expected to reduce costs and improve efficiency for managing and accounting inventory.

26337 ■ "Raise Your Voice: A New Committee Promises to Give Small Businesses a Say in Accounting Standards. But Will It Help?" in *Entrepreneur*
Pub: Entrepreneur Media Inc.
Ed: C.J. Prince. **Description:** The Financial Accounting Standards Board (FASB) created the Small Business Advisory Committee in March 2005. The new committee gives entrepreneurs a voice in regulations that affect small business. The committee, which will meet semiannually, consists of a group of 24 lenders, investors and analysts, auditors, and preparers of financial statements.

26338 ■ "Reaching the Small Business Accounting Market" in *Accounting Today* **(Vol. 14, No. 12, July 10, 2000, pp. 41)**
Pub: Faulkner & Gray, Inc.
Ed: Tracey Miller-Segarra. **Description:** There is a new crop of dot-coms seeking to stake their claims in the lucrative small business accounting software market by developing products designed exclusively for the Internet. A profile of three of these software products is presented.

26339 ■ "Renewing a Great Profession: Esteemed Professions Initiate Change - For Their Own Good" in *Journal of Accountancy* **(January 2005)**
Pub: American Institute of Certified Public Accountants

Ed: Robert L. Bunting. **Description:** Qualities required to create a good profession, focusing on the accounting sector, are discussed.

26340 ■ "Repaying the Loan Isn't Enough" in *Business Week* **(No. 3779, April 22, 2002, pp. 16)**
Pub: McGraw-Hill Inc.
Description: Banks are pressuring small companies in need of short-term credit to also use other banking services such as checking, savings and investment accounts for loans less than one year.

26341 ■ "Review process series of checks and balances" in *Atlanta Business Chronicle* **(Vol. 25, November 15, 2002, No. 23 pp. SS5)**
Pub: American City Business Publications, Inc.
Ed: Leslie Williams Johnson. **Description:** Certified public accounting firms perform peer reviews every three years. The three methods, systems, engagement, and report are summarized. The reviews aim to check that professional standards are being followed.

26342 ■ "Sage unveils big plans for small business" in *Accounting Today* **(Vol. 14, No. 13, July 24, 2000, pp. 29)**
Pub: Faulkner & Gray, Inc.
Description: Accounting software development group Sage, announced plans to make several e-commerce innovations this year tied to its new accounting software product, BusinessWorks Gold. Sage said that the product, designed for companies of 50 or fewer employees, will be "the foundation for delivering e-commerce and e-management capabilities to the small business marketplace."

26343 ■ *Schaum's Outline Financial Management, Third Edition*
Pub: McGraw-Hill
Ed: Jae K. Shim; Joel G. Siegel. **Released:** May 2007. **Price:** $22.95 (CND). **Description:** Rules and regulations governing corporate finance, including the Sarbanes-Oxley Act are discussed.

26344 ■ "SEC Acts to Curb Cash Flow Shenanigans" in *Inc.* **(Volume 27, June 2005, No. 6, pp. 26)**
Pub: Inc. Magazine
Description: According to a new study by Georgia Tech's business school cash flow statements need to be scrutinized. Companies regularly wrongly categorize money due from venders, such as members of their distribution network.

26345 ■ "Second Base: Getting the Right Accountant Can Pay Big Dividends" in *Crain's Detroit Business* **(Vol. 19, No. 49, December 8, 2003)**
Pub: Crain Communications Inc., Detroit
Ed: Mike Scott. **Description:** A good accountant can add to a small firm's bottom line. According to Gadis Dillon, an accounting professor, small business owners should network to compare experiences with accounting firms.

26346 ■ "Section 404 Compliance in the Annual Report" in *Journal of Accountancy*
Pub: American Institute of Certified Public Accountants
Ed: Michael Ramos. **Description:** Most publicly traded companies in the U.S. will be required to comply with SEC rules by reporting the effectiveness of internal controls in the annual report. The content required in this report is covered.

26347 ■ "Selling to Audit Committees" in *Journal of Accountancy*
Pub: American Institute of Certified Public Accountants
Ed: Gale Crosley. **Description:** Suggestions to help certified public accounting firms approach and obtain committee boards in each of the three target markets for auditing services: publicly held companies, large private and public-interest entities, and smaller private and public-interest entities.

26348 ■ "Senators Call for Small-Biz Refunds" in *Inc.* (August 1, 2003)
Pub: Gruner & Jahr USA Publishing
Ed: Nadine Heintz. Description: Small businesses may be eligible for a refund of alternative minimum taxes paid. Statistical data included.

26349 ■ "7 Questions to Ask Before You Hire an Accountant" in *My Business* (February/March 2003, pp. 44)
Pub: My Business Magazine
Ed: Julie Bawden Davis. Description: David Stevens, CPA in Santa Fe Springs, California offers 7 questions for small business owners to ask before hiring an accountant for their firm.

26350 ■ "Shred of evidence: learn a lesson from Arthur Anderson" in *Entrepreneur* (Vol. 30, No. 12, December 2002, pp. 106)
Pub: Entrepreneur Media Inc.
Ed: Steven C. Bahls, Jane Easter Bahls. Description: The importance of working with an attorney to ensure compliance with all laws on length of time to retain company documents is discussed.

26351 ■ *Six SIGMA for Small Business*
Pub: Entrepreneur Press
Ed: Greg Brue. Released: October 2005. Price: $19.95 (US), $26.95 (Canadian). Description: Jack Welch's Six SIGMA approach to business covers accounting, finance, sales and marketing, buying a business, human resource development, and new product development.

26352 ■ "Smack Down! Show Those Numbers Who's Boss With a New Accounting Software Program" in *Entrepreneur* (Vol. 31, No. 10, October 2003)
Pub: Entrepreneur Media, Inc.
Ed: Michael Gros, Mario Morejon. Description: Profiles of new accounting software packages to help small firms manage business the way large corporations do, including MyBooks Pro and QuickBooks.

26353 ■ *Small Business Accountant*
Pub: South-Western Publishing Co.
Ed: Hamilton. Released: 1994. Price: $48.95 (paper).

26354 ■ *The Small Business Bible: Everything You Need to Know to Succeed in Your Small Business*
Pub: John Wiley & Sons, Incorporated
Ed: Steven D. Strauss. Released: December 2004. Price: $19.95 (US), $28.99 (Canadian). Description: Comprehensive guide to starting and running a successful small business. Topics include bookkeeping and financial management, marketing, publicity, and advertising.

26355 ■ "Small Business, Big Losses" in *Journal of Accountancy* (Vol. 19)
Pub: American Institute of Certified Public Accountants
Ed: Joseph T. Wells. Description: Occupational fraud is becoming increasingly more prevalent and affects nearly every business. A summary of the key findings of certified frauds examiners (CFEs) in cases of financial statement fraud is highlighted.

26356 ■ "Small Business: Crunching numbers via the Internet" in *Crain's Detroit Business* (Vol. 16, May 29, 2000, pp. 54)
Pub: Crain Communications, Inc.
Ed: Joanne Cleaver. Description: With the growing acceptance of the Internet as a place to conduct business operations, Intuit Company's Quickbooks market position is being challenged.

26357 ■ *Small Business Desk Reference*
Pub: Penguin Books (USA) Incorporated
Ed: Gene Marks. Released: December 2004. Price: $29.95 (US), $44.00 (Canadian). Description: Comprehensive guide for starting or running a successful small business, focusing on buying a business or franchise, writing a business plan, financial management, accounting, legal issues, human resources management, operations, marketing, sales, customer service, taxes, insurance, and ethics. Information for launching a restaurant, property management firm, retail outlet, consulting firm, and service business is included.

26358 ■ *The Small Business Owner's Manual: Everything You Need to Know to Start Up and Run Your Business*
Pub: Career Press, Incorporated
Ed: Joe Kennedy. Released: June 2005. Price: $19.99 (US), $26.95 (Canadian). Description: Comprehensive guide for starting a small business, focusing on twelve ways to obtain financing, business plans, selling and advertising products and services, hiring and firing employees, setting up a Web site, business law, accounting issues, insurance, equipment, computers, banks, financing, customer credit and collection, leasing, and more.

26359 ■ *Small Business Survival Guide: Starting, Protecting, and Securing Your Business for Long-Term Success*
Pub: Adams Media Corporation
Ed: Cliff Ennico. Released: October 2005. Price: $12.95 (US), $17.95 (Canadian). Description: Entrepreneurship in the new millennium. Topics include creditors, taxes, competition, business law, and accounting.

26360 ■ "Small Business and the Use of Accrual Accounting" in *Accounting Today* (Vol. 14, No. 16, September 4, 2000, pp. 10)
Pub: Faulkner & Gray, Inc.
Ed: George G. Jones, Mark A. Luscombe. Description: After the Tax Relief Extension Act of 1999 repealed the use of the installment method by accrual basis taxpayers, a very active lobby campaign immediately emerged to reverse the repeal.

26361 ■ "Small Firms Flock to Remote Deposit Service" in *American Banker* (Vol. 172, January 16, 2006, No. 10, pp. 6A)
Pub: SourceMedia, Inc.
Ed: Johanna Knapschaefer. Description: Nevada State Bank offers remote deposit services for small businesses. The service allows business customers to convert check into digital images and transmit them to a bank for deposit.

26362 ■ "Small Firms Turn to Financial Futures for Fuel" in *Wall Street Journal* (November 3, 2003, pp. A2)
Pub: Dow Jones & Co. Inc.
Ed: Russell Gold. Description: Many small- and medium-sized businesses are switching from utilities to deregulated energy markets for energy needs.

26363 ■ "Small Is Big" in *Forbes* (May 27, 2002, p. 88)
Pub: Forbes Magazine
Ed: Erika Brown. Description: Profile of Intuit's accounting software package QuickBooks Enterprise being marketed to small businesses.

26364 ■ *Small Time Operator: How to Start Your Own Small Business, Keep Your Books, Pay Your Taxes, & Stay out of Trouble!*
Pub: Bell Springs Publishing
Ed: Bernard Kamoroff. Released: 22nd ed. 1998. Price: $16.95.

26365 ■ "Smart inventory: start electing superior filing options now" in *Barron's* (Vol. 82, No. 59, February 24, 2003, pp. 23)
Pub: Barron's
Ed: Joseph F. Gelband. Description: The use of laws from Section 475 of the tax code is one way in which investors can reduce capital gains tax on the sales of securities as long as an investor is considered a securities trader. Use of the provision allows losses to be fully deducted. An explanation of ways an S company can benefit on taxes by changing status to a C company is offered.

26366 ■ "Sorting out Enron mess pumps up Plante & Moran" in *Crain's Detroit Business* (Vol. 19, No. 17, April 28, 2003, pp. 30)
Pub: Crain Communications Inc., Detroit
Description: According to partners at Plante & Moran LLP, the company has made $5.3 million in billable hours investigating Enron Corporation's collapse. The firm has been investigating Enron since July 2002.

26367 ■ "Spring cleaning: tips to get fiscal house in order" in *Atlanta Business Chronicle* (Vol. 23, No. 49, May 11, 2001, pp. 12B)
Pub: American City Business Journals Inc.
Ed: Paula Moore. Description: Businesses need to periodically re-evaluate their business plan and their current position. Spring is a good time to do this, once taxes have been filed. Various options should also be explored, dealing with items such as selling the company, allocating resources, managing succession plans, etc. Business tax planning is also needed.

26368 ■ "Staffing Woes: The 404 Talent War" in *Journal of Accountancy* (Vol. 198, December 2004, No. 6, pp. 62)
Pub: American Institute of Certified Public Accountants
Ed: Barbara Vigilante. Description: Section 404 of the Sarbanes-Oxley Act is discussed. Rule 404 requires companies to hire more certified public accountants to implement and manage these new internal controls.

26369 ■ "Stay In Touch" in *Entrepreneur* (Vol. 33, September 2005, No. 9, pp. 44)
Pub: Entrepreneur Media Inc.
Ed: Description: Quickbooks, Peachtree, and Netsuite software offer complete accounting functions necessary for any growing small business.

26370 ■ *Step-by-Step Bookkeeping: The Complete Handbook for the Small Business*
Pub: Sterling Publishing Co., Inc.
Ed: Robert C. Ragan. Released: Revised edition, 1992. Price: $7.95 (paper). Description: Guide to financial management for small businesses. Provides information on keeping accounts-receivable and -payable records, producing and analyzing profit-and-loss statements, and preparing monthly financial statements.

26371 ■ *Streetwise Finance and Accounting for Entrepreneurs: Set Budgets, Manage Costs, Keep Your Business Profitable*
Pub: Adams Media Corporation
Ed: Suzanne Caplan. Released: November 2006. Price: $25.95. Description: Book offers a basic understanding of accounting and finance for small businesses, including financial statements, credits and debits, as well as establishing a budget. Strategies for small companies in financial distress are included.

26372 ■ *Streetwise Small Business Book of Lists: Hundreds of Lists to Help You Reduce Costs, Increase Revenues, and Boost Your Profits!*
Pub: Adams Media Corporation
Ed: Gene Marks. Released: September 2006. Price: $25.95. Description: Strategies to help small business owners locate services, increase sales, and lower expenses.

26373 ■ "Successful IT practices know their clients well" in *Accounting Today* (Vol. 14, No. 7, April 17, 2000, pp. 26)
Pub: Faulkner & Gray, Inc.
Ed: James C. Metzler. Description: Small businesses make up the largest market in America and claim the client base of the majority of accounting firms. Recognizing key characteristics of the small business market is important to information technology (IT) firms and their professionals. This market choice has the potential to give an IT professional a tremendous sense of satisfaction because of the profound improvements that can take place in the business.

26374 ■ *Successfully Self-Employed: How to Sell What You Do, Do What You Sell, Manage Your Cash in Between*
Pub: Upstart Publishing Company, Inc.
Ed: Gregory Brennan. Released: 1996. Price: $16.95.

26375 ■ **"Succession-Planning Do's and Don'ts: Who Will Take Over When You're Ready to Retire?" in** *Journal of Accountancy* **(February 2005)**
Pub: American Institute of Certified Public Accountants
Ed: Anita Dennis. **Description:** Few certified public accounting firms have set a succession plan into place for selling their firm or passing it down to the next generation.

26376 ■ **"Summerford, Dixon Odom Cite Sarbanes in Breakup" in** *Birmingham Business Journal* **(Vol. 20, No. 31, August 1, 2003, pp. 1)**
Pub: American City Business Journals, Inc.
Ed: Leslie Zganjar. **Description:** A forensic account unit of Dixon Odom has declared independence from its parent firm. Ralph Summerford, the top executive at the new accounting company, attributed the breakup of the company to the new Sarbanes-Oxley Act.

26377 ■ **"SWARM Online services seek small biz through CPAs" in** *Accounting Today* **(Vol. 14, No. 6, April 3, 2000, pp. 1)**
Pub: Faulkner & Gray, Inc.
Ed: John M. Covaleski. **Description:** Internet entrepreneurs are seeking to leverage local tax and accounting firms to electronically deliver business products and services to small and mid-sized businesses.

26378 ■ **"Take a hard look, and do the right thing" in** *Crain's Detroit Business* **(Vol. 19, No. 5, February 3, 2003, pp. 9)**
Pub: Crain Communications Inc., Detroit
Ed: Frank Hennessey. **Description:** The ethical aspects and regulation of business and accounting practices are investigated.

26379 ■ **"Taking Care of Business: Downloadable Programs For Your Enterprise" in** *Black Enterprise* **(Vol. 34, July 2004, No. 12, pp. 145)**
Pub: Earl G. Graves Publishing Co. Inc.
Ed: Jennifer L. Smith. **Description:** Websites offering free, downloadable small business software are presented. Everything from accounting, computer security, as well as investment programs is available from these sites.

26380 ■ **"Taking the Pain Out of Payday" in** *Inc.* **(January 1, 2005)**
Pub: Inc. Magazine
Ed: Nicole Gull. **Description:** Payroll debit cards can be cheaper than traditional payroll systems.

26381 ■ **"Tastes great? Less taxing?" in** *Barron's* **(Vol. 82, No. 57, February 10, 2003, pp. T4)**
Pub: Barron's
Ed: Randall W. Forsyth, Theresa W. Carey, Kathy Yakal. **Description:** Reviews of tax preparation software, including Intuit Turbo Tax Premier, TaxCut Platinum, and TaxACT Online.

26382 ■ **"Tax time is approaching" in** *Black Enterprise* **(Vol. 33, No. 7, February 2003, pp. 6)**
Pub: Earl Graves Publishing Co.
Description: Black Enterprise's Website provides a tax center offering tax advice for individuals and small businesses.

26383 ■ *Tax Planning & Preparation Made Easy for the Self-Employed*
Pub: John Wiley & Sons, Inc.
Ed: Gregory L. Dent. **Released:** 1995. **Price:** $15.95.

26384 ■ **"Tax Season Defanged" in** *Journal of Accountancy* **(Vol. 199)**
Pub: American Institute of Certified Public Accountants
Ed: Edward Mendlowitz. **Description:** Ways to help accounting firms create a successful tax season are examined, including fostering high morale among employees.

26385 ■ **"There are no magic words to alter tax law" in** *Crain's Detroit Business* **(Vol. 19, No. 11, March 17, 2003, pp. 9)**
Pub: Crain Communications Inc., Detroit
Ed: James Jenkins. **Description:** The double taxation of corporate profits is destructive to the American economy, according to Alan Greenspan, Federal Reserve Chairman, as well as leading academics.

26386 ■ **"Think Fast: Take Advantage of Faster Depreciation" in** *Entrepreneur* **(Vol. 32, December 2004, No. 12, pp. 62)**
Pub: Entrepreneur Media Inc.
Ed: Joan Szabo. **Description:** Entrepreneurs who own business real estate might want to perform a cost segregation study (CSS) on their property to review all costs associated with the purchase or construction of a building because of the Internal Revenue Service' willingness to allow business owners to accelerate depreciation on existing buildings or those being built.

26387 ■ **"A thousand bottles of beer on the wall" in** *Washington Business Journal* **(Vol. 22, No. 3, May 23, 2003, pp. 31)**
Pub: Washington Business Journal
Ed: Sean Madigan. **Description:** Profile of the management of a Washington, DC area tavern called the Brickskeller. Topics include management styles, product lines, and financial management.

26388 ■ **"The time for talk is over" in** *Rough Notes* **(Vol. 146, No. 4, April 2003, pp. 16)**
Pub: Rough Notes
Ed: Michael J. Moody. **Description:** After Enron's collapse, enterprise risk management has become more important in corporate governance. Pricewaterhouse-Coopers Inc.'s research indicates that consumer trust can be regained by financial institutions through checks and balances in top managers.

26389 ■ **"Time's Up: New Laws Tell You Who Gets Overtime-And Who Doesn't" in** *Entrepreneur* **(Vol. 32, October 2004, No. 10, pp. 40)**
Pub: Entrepreneur Media Inc.
Ed: Chris Penttila. **Description:** New U.S. Department of Labor rules state that employees earning over $100,000 annually in executive, administrative and professional positions are no longer eligible for overtime, workers earning less than $23,660 annually are.

26390 ■ **"Top-drawer advice: new software tells you how much your charitable contributions are worth" in** *Barron's* **(Vol.82, Feb.17, 2003, pp.T7)**
Pub: Barron's
Ed: Randall W. Forsyth, Theresa W. Carey. **Description:** Two programs that help value donations of used clothing and other goods and work well, include H & R Block Deduction Pro and Income Dynamics ItsDeductible tax preparation software.

26391 ■ **"Training as a Retention Tool" in** *Internal Auditor* **(Vol. 58, No. 5, October 2001, pp. 47)**
Pub: Institute of Internal Auditors, Inc.
Ed: Diane Sears Campbell. **Description:** Many employers are introducing innovative ways to keep their internal auditors professionally challenged in order to retain them.

26392 ■ **"Turning Receivables Into Received" in** *Black Enterprise* **(Vol. 34, No. 7, February 2004, pp. 46)**
Pub: Earl Graves Publishing Co.
Ed: Bridget McCrea. **Description:** Profile of Sweet Survival, a business consulting firm. The company has developed an accounts receivable policy suited to serving small business needs.

26393 ■ **"Turning Receivables Into Received: Don't Let Your Collections Process Fall Through the Cracks" in** *Black Enterprise* **(Vol. 34, No. 7)**
Pub: Earl Graves Publishing Co.
Ed: Bridget McCrea. **Description:** Profile of Sweet Survival, a business consulting firm. The company has developed an accounts receivable policy suited to serving small business needs.

26394 ■ **"Users Size Up Tax Software: Product Ratings Gain, But Vendor Support Slips" in** *Journal of Accountancy* **(Vol. 198, October 2004)**
Pub: American Institute of Certified Public Accountants
Ed: Stanley Zarowin. **Description:** Results of a survey covering tax-preparation software are discussed. Statistical data included.

26395 ■ **"VEBAs and 412(i)s: Maximize client deductions" in** *Accounting Today* **(Vol. 14, No. 11, June 26, 2000, pp. 20)**
Pub: Faulkner & Gray, Inc.
Ed: Lance Wallach. **Description:** There are two programs that, when properly constructed, can substantially reduce taxes for any type of business entity, including a sole proprietorship, partnership, S corporation, C corporation or limited liability partnership: The IRC Section 412(i) plan and the 501(c)(9) tax-exempt trust, which is commonly referred to as the voluntary employees beneficiary association (VEBA). Both programs are outlined.

26396 ■ **"Warning: Credit Crunch" in** *Forbes* **(Vol. 170, No. 3, August 12, 2002, pp. 62)**
Pub: Forbes Magazine
Ed: Robert Lenzner, Matthew Swibel. **Description:** It is predicted that accounting reform on scrutinized lending could harm the U.S. economy.

26397 ■ **"Watch your step" in** *Entrepreneur* **(Vol. 31, No. 6, June 2003, pp. 55)**
Pub: Entrepreneur Media Inc.
Ed: Joan Szabo. **Description:** The IRS is promising to crack down on small business owners not reporting business income, focusing on abusive tax shelters, offshore credit card abuse, high-income nonfilers, and high-income taxpayers engaged in partnerships, trusts or S corporations, as well as selecting 50,000 random returns from 2001.

26398 ■ **"Web-based Accounting" in** *Home Office Computing* **(Vol. 18, No. 11, November 2000, pp. 71)**
Pub: Scholastic Inc.
Ed: Wayne Kawamoto. **Description:** A software buyer's guide featuring integrated accounting software packages and Web-based services of value to the home office user. Among the featured products are BAport Accounting from BAport, the eLedger 2.0 application from Application Service Provider (ASP) eLedger, Peachtree Software's ePeachtree 2.0, Intacct, an online service that offers general ledger, accounts payable, accounts receivable, and human resources functions, NetLedger 4.0, and Bizfinity.

26399 ■ **"West L.A. CPA Firm Opening Valley Office" in** *San Fernando Valley Business Journal* **(Vol. 11, December 2006, No. 25, pp. 1)**
Pub: San Fernando Valley Business Journal Associates
Ed: Shelly Garcia. **Description:** Singer Lewak Greenbaum & Goldstein LLP will open a Warner Center office in hopes of keeping workers in what has become a fiercely competitive employment market and capturing larger ground in the growing financial services market.

26400 ■ **"What a Governance Referee Thinks" in** *Journal of Accountancy* **(Vol. 199, February 2005, No. 2, pp. 43)**
Pub: American Institute of Certified Public Accountants
Ed: Michael Hayes. **Description:** Rules for obtaining a certified public accounting firm are changing as the Sarbanes-Oxley Act is implemented. Experts believe the Sarbanes-Oxley Act is requiring accounting firms to do the things they should have been doing all along.

26401 ■ **"What's Your Project's Real Price Tag?" in** *Harvard Business Review* **(Vol. 81, No. 9, September 2003, pp. 20)**
Pub: Harvard Business School Press
Ed: Quentin W. Fleming, Joel M. Koppelman. **Description:** Fundamental business management accounting techniques, such as CPI earned-value management and EVM, are explored, as well as their usage.

26402 ■ "Who Needs Budgets?" in *Harvard Business Review* (Vol. 81, No. 2, February 2003, pp. 108)
Pub: Harvard Business School Press
Ed: Jeremy Hope, Robin Fraser. **Description:** The article advocates for the abolishment of budgeting within corporations using hypothetical scenarios and real situations to show that budgets can be detrimental to companies.

26403 ■ "Who Needs The Aggravation?" in *Forbes* (Vol. 170, No. 8, October 14, 2002, pp. 56)
Pub: Forbes Magazine
Ed: Carrie Coolidge. **Description:** With the new tough accounting rules, some small companies are deciding that it is better to not be a publicly traded firm.

26404 ■ "Why good accountants do bad audits" in *Harvard Business Review* (Vol. 80, No. 11, November 2002, pp. 96)
Pub: Harvard Business School Press
Ed: Don A. George, Max H. Moore, Bazerman Lowenstein. **Description:** Ways self-serving biases cause bad audits are discussed, advocating fundamental changes in the way the accounting industry operates. The authors suggest that full divestiture of consulting and tax services, rotation of auditing firms, and fixed-term contracts that keep companies from firing auditors.

26405 ■ "Work Like an Insurance Company to Save Money" in *Journal of Accountancy*
Pub: American Institute of Certified Public Accountants
Ed: Joseph A. Gerber, Elliott R. Feldman. **Description:** Financial managers can use the same practices and procedures to recover lost profits as insurance companies use: subrogation, the legal process that permits an insurance company, after paying a policyholder's claim, to sue one or more third parties responsible for causing the damage or injury to the policyholder.

26406 ■ "Worth the Drive? Your Company Cars Could Be Gulping More than Just Gas if You Don't Know What Your Ownership Costs Are" in *Entrepreneur*
Pub: Entrepreneur Media Inc.
Ed: Jill Amadio. **Description:** Four major fixed cost factors are involved when determining the cost of owning a company car: depreciation, state fees, financing and insurance.

26407 ■ "XBRL Revisited: Grasp the Fundamentals to See How Businesses Use XBRL Today" in *Journal of Accountancy* (Vol. 199, February 2005)
Pub: American Institute of Certified Public Accountants
Ed: Neal J. Hannon, Robert J. Gold. **Description:** Extensible Business Reporting Language (XBRL) is increasing in popularity with investors, analysts, public companies and other securities market firms, including certified public accounting businesses. XBRL basics for use are presented.

26408 ■ "You Are What You Charge" in *Journal of Accountancy* (Vol. 198, November 2004, No. 5, pp. 20)
Pub: American Institute of Certified Public Accountants
Ed: Ron Baker, Paul Dunn. **Description:** The four P's of marketing include price, place, promotion, and product, of these pricing is the most complicated.

26409 ■ "You paid that bill with a single click. Or did you?" in *The New York Times* (July 2, 2000, pp. BU10)
Pub: The New York Times Company
Ed: Nancy Lloyd. **Description:** The problems with electronic bill paying are examined.

26410 ■ "Your Best Interest" in *Entrepreneur* (Vol. 32, July 2004, No. 7, pp. 52)
Pub: Entrepreneur Media Inc.
Ed: Jennifer Pellet. **Description:** The Business Checking Freedom Act passed in 2004 will allow banking institutions to offer small businesses interest-paying checking accounts.

26411 ■ "Zalenko and Virchow Krause Join; Firm Wants 'Critical Mass' Locally" in *Crain's Detroit Business* (Vol. 21, January 3, 2005, No. 1)
Pub: Crain Communications Inc. - Detroit
Ed: Katie Merx. **Description:** Zalenko & Associates PC has merged with Virchow Krause & Company LLP, making it a leader in the accounting sector in Michigan. The merge will place the firm as eighth-largest in the state with 105 employees.

TRADE PERIODICALS

26412 ■ *Executive's Tax and Management Report*
Pub: Aspen Publishers Inc.
Ed: Sara Vine, Editor, sara.vine@aspenpublishers.com. **Released:** 2/month. **Price:** $255. **Description:** Supplies information on how to obtain more tax-free cash from a company or business, cut a company's tax bill, increase personal deductions, and deal with new tax crackdowns.

26413 ■ *Keep Up to Date on Accounts Payable*
Pub: Progressive Business Publications
Ed: Nathan Hall, Editor, nhall@pbp.com. **Released:** Semimonthly. **Price:** $299, individuals. **Description:** Supplies updates on state and local sales use taxes, plus IRS 1099 regulations and best practices in accounts payable. Recurring features include interviews, news of research, a calendar of events, and a column titled Sharpen Your Judgment.

VIDEOCASSETTES/ AUDIOCASSETTES

26414 ■ *CPE Network: Accounting and Auditing Report*
Bisk Education
9417 Princess Palm Ave.
Tampa, FL 33619
Free: 800-874-7877
Co. E-mail: info@bisk.com
URL: http://www.bisk.com
Released: 1994. **Price:** $799.00. **Description:** Outlines informaton on current industry issues, pronouncements, new standards, recent decisions, insider reports on exposure drafts, and other early indicators of upcoming changes in the accounting and auditing areas. Video newsletter published 11 times per year. **Availability:** VHS.

26415 ■ *Small Business Accounting Systems*
Instructional Video
2219 C St.
Lincoln, NE 68502
Ph:(402)475-6570
Free: 800-228-0164
Fax: (402)475-6500
Co. E-mail: feedback@insvideo.com
URL: http://www.insvideo.com
Price: $19.95. **Description:** Illustrates basic small business accounting, providing instruction on recording transactions, the balance sheet, and the income statement. **Availability:** VHS.

TRADE SHOWS AND CONVENTIONS

26416 ■ National Society of Public Accountants Annual Convention
National Society of Public Accountants
1010 N. Fairfax St.
Alexandria, VA 22314-1574
Ph:(703)549-6400
Free: 800-966-6679
Fax: (703)549-2984
Co. E-mail: NSA@wizard.net
URL: http://www.nsa.org

Released: Annual. **Principal Exhibits:** Exhibits related to public accounting.

CONSULTANTS

26417 ■ Larry J. Anderson
4021 76th St.
Urbandale, IA 50322
Ph:(515)270-8548
Fax: (515)278-0916
Co. E-mail: Andy4021@aol.com

E-mail: Andy4021@aol.com
Scope: Offers business consulting including temporary technical aid in accounting, turnaround and cash management, and bail-out assistance. Also provides operations research, models, forecasting, project scheduling, and economic forecasting. Provide assistance in group health insurance in both fully insured groups and self-funded groups.

26418 ■ Avery, Cooper & Co.
4918-50th St.
PO Box 1620
Yellowknife, NT, Canada X1A 2P2
Ph:(867)873-3441
Fax: (867)873-2353
Co. E-mail: gerry@averyco.nt.ca
URL: http://www.averyco.nt.ca

E-mail: gerry@averyco.nt.ca
Scope: Accounting and management consulting firm.

26419 ■ Business Learning Center
2206 SE Washington St.
Portland, OR 97222
Ph:(503)653-7108
Fax: (503)786-6064
Co. E-mail: blcmay19@msn.com

E-mail: blcmay19@msn.com
Scope: Provides every type of business service for small businesses, including accounting and tax services, business forms and systems, and investment counseling.

26420 ■ CBIZ Inc.
6050 Oak Tree, Blvd. S, Ste. 500
Cleveland, OH 44131
Ph:(216)447-9000
Fax: (216)447-9007
Co. E-mail: info@cbiz.com
URL: http://www.cbiz.com

E-mail: info@cbiz.com
Scope: A business consulting and tax services firm providing financial, consulting, tax and business services through seven groups: financial management, tax advisory, construction and real estate, healthcare, litigation support, capital resource, and CEO outsource.

26421 ■ Checkmark Software Inc.
724 Whalers Way, Bldg. H, Ste. 101
Fort Collins, CO 80525
Ph:(970)225-0522
Free: 800-444-9922
Fax: (970)225-0611
Co. E-mail: info@checkmark.com
URL: http://www.checkmark.com

E-mail: info@checkmark.com
Scope: Developer of accounting software tools for small businesses. **Special Services:** MultiLedger™

26422 ■ Comprehensive Professional Management Inc.
222 E Dundee Rd.
Wheeling, IL 60090-3009
Ph:(847)520-0101
Fax: (847)520-0372
Co. E-mail: bob@cpmincfs.com

E-mail: bob@cpmincfs.com
Scope: Services include accounting, financial planning, litigation support, pension profit sharing adminis-

tration, practice surveys, professional corporation issues, retirement and estate planning, and tax advice.

26423 ■ DacEasy Inc.
17950 Preston Rd., Ste. 800
Dallas, TX 75252
Ph:(972)732-7500
Free: 800-322-3279
Fax: (972)713-6331
Co. E-mail: sales@daceasy.com
URL: http://www.daceasy.com

E-mail: sales@daceasy.com
Scope: Develops an accounting system for small businesses that integrates accounting, invoicing, payroll, communications, and management software into a single package. **Special Services:** DacEasy.

26424 ■ Dennis M. Dengel
17 Peckham Rd.
Poughkeepsie, NY 12603
Ph:(845)452-2126
Scope: Offers data processing and custom programming in RPG and COBOL for IBM computers. Provides applications for accounts payable/receivable, payroll, general ledger, and inventory. Also repairs and upgrades PCs.

26425 ■ Dorn & Associates Inc.
8506 Bass Lake Rd., Ste. 140
New Hope, MN 55428
Ph:(763)533-7689
Fax: (763)533-1143
Scope: Services include accounting, marketing, employment/partnership, new doctor agreements, personnel issues and human resources assessment, practice management, practice merger/acquisition/sale and/or liquidation, practice surveys and valuation, staff development and training.

26426 ■ Doyle & Dulaney
2124 Kittredge St., Ste. 22
Berkeley, CA 94704-1436
Ph:(510)644-2055
Scope: Business and financial consultants specializing in manual and computer bookkeeping and accounting systems. Expertise in fund accounting, business methods and procedures, reports and other written communications, such as manuals, handbooks, and procedure guides. Also skilled in forms design, records management, and instructional material development. Serving nonprofit organizations, the professions, and smaller service-oriented businesses.

26427 ■ Frankel and Topche P.C.
1700 Galloping Hill Rd.
Kenilworth, NJ 07033
Ph:(908)298-7700
Fax: (908)298-7701
Co. E-mail: info@frankelandtopche.com
URL: http://www.frankelandtopche.com

E-mail: info@frankelandtopche.com
Scope: Offers financial consulting for closely held businesses. Assists in mergers and acquisitions, tax planning, strategic business planning, family succession planning, accounting, auditing, and obtaining financing. The firm serves small businesses in the service, retail, wholesale, and manufacturing industries. Specializes in real estate, lumber and building materials, and service businesses.

26428 ■ Gates, Moore & Co.
3340 Peachtree Rd. NE, Tower Pl. 100, Ste. 600
Atlanta, GA 30326
Ph:(404)266-9876
Fax: (404)266-2669
Co. E-mail: postmaster@gatesmoore.com
URL: http://www.gatesmoore.com

E-mail: postmaster@gatesmoore.com
Scope: Firm provides management consulting and accounting services to medical practices, hospital owned practices, staff model managed care organizations, IPAs, MSOs, PO, and PHOs. Services include

comprehensive operational assessments, managed care negotiations, practice start-ups and expansion, development of MSOs, strategic planning, mergers, cost accounting analysis, practice valuations, income division plans, medical record documentation and coding reviews, expert witness testimony, patient satisfaction surveys and corporate compliance planning. **Publications:** Physicians, Dentists and Veterinarians; Insurance Portability and Accountability Act Privacy Manual; How To Guide for your Medical Practice and Health Insurance Portability and Accountability Act Security Manual; A How To Guide for your Medical Practice; Cost Analysis Made Simple: A Step by Step Guide to Using Cost Accounting to Ensure Practice Profitability; Cost Cutting Strategies for Medical Practices. **Seminars:** Implementing a Cost Accounting Analysis to Monitor Practice Profitability, Georgia Chapter-American Academy of Pediatrics, Jun, 2006; NPI Update, Saint Josephs Hospital, Jun, 2006.

26429 ■ Arnold S. Goldin & Associates Inc.
5030 Champion Blvd., Ste. G-6231
Boca Raton, FL 33496
Ph:(561)994-5810
Fax: (561)994-5860
Co. E-mail: arnold@goldin.com
URL: http://www.goldin.com

E-mail: arnold@goldin.com
Scope: An accounting and management consulting firm. Serves clients worldwide. Provides management services. Handles monthly write-ups and tax returns.

26430 ■ Horwath International Association
420 Lexington Ave., Ste. 526
New York, NY 10170
Ph:(212)808-2000
Fax: (212)808-2020
Co. E-mail: contactus@horwath.com
URL: http://www.horwath.com

E-mail: contactus@horwath.com
Scope: Services include accounting, auditing, tax and management consulting. Provides innovative business solutions in the area of assurance, business services, consulting, corporate finance, risk management, tax and technology. **Seminars:** Demand Creation Training, Dec, 2006; Marketing, Dec, 2006.

26431 ■ Kroll Zolfo Cooper L.L.C.
900 3rd Ave., 6th Fl.
New York, NY 10022
Ph:(212)561-4000
Fax: (212)213-1749
URL: http://www.krollzolfocooper.com
Scope: Firm provides accounting consulting services to businesses.

26432 ■ Charles A. Krueger
1908 Innsbrooke Dr.
Sun Prairie, WI 53590
Ph:(608)837-5247
Fax: (608)825-7538
Co. E-mail: ckrueger@bus.wisc.edu

E-mail: ckrueger@bus.wisc.edu
Scope: Financial management consultant specializing in professional education programs for managers and executives. Programs include: finance and accounting for nonfinancial executives, financial management for executives, and developing and using financial information for decision making. Major industries served include manufacturing, service, healthcare and insurance. **Publications:** "Monitoring Financial Results, chapter in Corporate Controllers Manual", Warren Gorham and Lamont **Seminars:** Finance and Accounting for Nonfinancial Executives; Financial Management for Health Care Executives; Financial Management for Insurance Executives; Direct Costing; Flexible Budgeting; Contribution Reporting; Building Value and Driving Profits - A Business Simulation.

26433 ■ Mitchell & Titus L.L.P.
1 Battery Park Plz., 27th Fl.
New York, NY 10004

Ph:(212)709-4500
Fax: (212)709-4680
Co. E-mail: newyork.office@mitchelltitus.com
URL: http://www.mitchelltitus.com

E-mail: newyork.office@mitchelltitus.com
Scope: Minority-controlled certified public accounting and management consulting firm audit and accounting services tax planning and preparation services management and business advisory services.

26434 ■ Penny & Associates Inc.
16100 Old Simcoe Rd.
Port Perry, ON, Canada L9L 1P3
Ph:(905)985-0712
Free: 800-699-6190
Fax: (905)985-9461
Co. E-mail: mail@pennyinc.com
URL: http://www.pennyinc.com

E-mail: mail@pennyinc.com
Scope: Develops financial reports by providing outsourced accounting and management support services.

26435 ■ Priority Process Associates Inc.
1236 E Horseshoe Bend Ct.
Rochester Hills, MI 48306
Ph:(248)608-8966
Fax: (248)608-8966
Scope: A management consulting firm with expertise in computer technology, telecommunications, and information services. Provides the following specific services: business process re-engineering-establishes correctly implemented, computer technologies that empower and accelerate work groups to act autonomously but in concert with corporate goals, document work-flow analysis-models and simulates the flow of documents through selected organizational processes, enterprise metrics-identifies unique metrics for enterprises to evaluate their continuous improvement of business processes, cost justification-identifies value using Activity Based Costing and innovative approaches to quantify time-to-market reductions, project profitability, and reduce and manage costs, proposal development-generates Requests for Proposals to solicit competitive quotations for cost effective off-the-shelf software, computer hardware, and communication products, implementation planning-negotiates implementation plans for clients through qualified software vendors, custom software integrators, and hardware, communication, and outsource suppliers, project auditing-audits the integration, installation and use of on-time, quality enterprise multi-vendor software, hardware and communications systems on computer networks, training-expands value knowledge through information sources, and client-specific management seminars and skill building workshops. Serves manufacturing industries in the United States.

26436 ■ Marion S. Rice
5281 Pinnacle Rd.
Dayton, OH 45418
Ph:(937)847-1733
Fax: (937)847-0046
Scope: Provides consultation to individuals and small businesses on tax management and bookkeeping activities. **Special Services:** Tax preparation, electronic filing, and refund anticipation loans.

26437 ■ Earl Rodney
5787 W Sunrise Blvd.
Plantation, FL 33313-6269
Ph:(954)583-3635
Fax: (954)321-0532
Co. E-mail: earl3@usa.com

E-mail: earl3@usa.com
Scope: Business and finance consultant serving all industries, nonprofit, and government in Florida. Activities include public accounting, auditing, taxation, expert witness, management advisory services, governmental audits, nonprofit audits, and financial statement disclosures. Also conducts peer reviews of CPA firms. **Publications:** Article on depreciation in

the Practical Accountant. **Seminars:** Off-site Peer Reviews; Classes in accounting disclosures and in how to audit non-profit organizations.

26438 ■ The Stillwater Group
920 E Shore Dr.
PO Box 168
Stillwater, NJ 07875
Ph:(973)579-7080
Fax: (973)579-7970
Co. E-mail: education@stillwater.com
URL: http://www.stillwater.com

E-mail: education@stillwater.com
Scope: Provides strategic planning, budget and financial management, process improvement, organizational design and assessment, and college student services operations.

26439 ■ Donald C. Wright
3906 Lawndale Ln. N
Minneapolis, MN 55446-2940
Ph:(763)478-5595
Co. E-mail: donaldwright@compuserve.com

E-mail: donaldwright@compuserve.com
Scope: Consultant offers expertise in accounting and taxes, personal financial planning, strategic planning, pension/profit sharing planning and administration, professional practice management and surveys. Surveys and consultations performed worldwide. **Seminars:** Qualified pension plans and employee welfare benefit plans.

COMPUTERIZED DATABASES

26440 ■ e-JEP
American Economic Association
2014 Broadway, Ste. 305
Nashville, TN 37203
Ph:(615)322-2595
Fax: (615)343-7590
Co. E-mail: aeainfo@vanderbilt.edu
URL: http://www.vanderbilt.edu/AEA
Description: Contains the full text of the *Journal of Economic Perspectives*. Includes articles, reports, and other material for economists and economics professionals. Features analysis and critiques of recent research findings and developments in public policy.

Includes coverage of global economics issues and developments. Features articles on education in economics, employment issues for economists, and other issues of concern to professional economists. **Availability:** Online: American Economic Association, Thomson West; CD-ROM: American Economic Association. **Type:** Full text.

COMPUTER SYSTEMS/ SOFTWARE

26441 ■ Aatrix Top Pay
Aatrix Software
2100 Library Cir.
Grand Forks, ND 58201
Ph:(701)746-7202
Free: 800-426-0854
Fax: (701)787-0594
URL: http://www.aatrix.com
Price: Contact Aatrix. **Description:** Handles payroll calculations and tax deductions for both salaried and hourly employees.

26442 ■ Argos Software–ABECAS Insight
Argos Computers
5737 N Fresno St.
Fresno, CA 93710
Ph:(559)227-1000
Fax: (559)227-9644
Co. E-mail: info@argosoftware.com
URL: http://www.argosoftware.com
Description: Available for MS-DOS operating system. Payroll system for agricultural employees.

LIBRARIES

26443 ■ Buffalo & Erie County Public Library–Business, Science & Technology
1 Lafayette Sq.
Buffalo, NY 14203
Ph:(716)858-8900
Fax: (716)858-7237
Co. E-mail: bst@buffalolib.org
URL: http://www.buffalolib.org
Contact: Kate Weeks, Div.Mgr.
Scope: Investments, real estate, economics, marketing, engineering, computer science, technology, medical information for laymen, consumer information,

automotive repair. **Services:** Interlibrary loan; copying; Library open to the public. **Holdings:** 312,916 books; 60,516 bound periodical volumes. **Subscriptions:** 2908 journals and other serials; 4 newspapers.

26444 ■ Carnegie Library of Pittsburgh–Library Center
Business Dept.
612 Smithfield St.
Pittsburgh, PA 15222
Ph:(412)281-7141
Fax: (412)471-1724
Co. E-mail: wernerr@carnegielibrary.org
URL: http://www.clpgh.org/locations/business/
Contact: Roye Werner, Dept.Hd.
Scope: Investments, small business, entrepreneurship, management, marketing, insurance, advertising, personal finance, accounting, real estate, job and career, international business. **Services:** Interlibrary loan; Library open to the public. **Holdings:** 14,000 business volumes; VF materials; microfilm; looseleaf services; AV cassettes. **Subscriptions:** 350 business journals, serials, and newspapers.

26445 ■ Nichols College–Conant Library
Center Rd.
Dudley, MA 01571
Ph:(508)213-2222
Free: 877-266-2681
Co. E-mail: reference@nichols.edu
URL: http://www.nichols.edu/library/
Contact: Jim Douglas, Lib.Dir.
Scope: Management, advertising, finance and accounting, small business, marketing, taxation, economics, International trade, humanities. **Services:** Interlibrary loan; copying; information service to groups; document delivery; Library open to Dudley and Webster residents. **Holdings:** 48,000 volumes; 1677 audio/visual titles; 3804 reels of microfilm. **Subscriptions:** 278 journals and electronic subscriptions.

26446 ■ University of Kentucky–Business & Economics Information Center
B&E Info. Ctr., Rm. 116
100 W. Gatton College of Business
Lexington, KY 40406-0093
Ph:(859)257-5868
Fax: (859)323-9496
Co. E-mail: mrazeeq@pop.uk.edu
URL: http://www.uky.edu/~BEIC
Contact: Michael A. Razeeq, Bus.Ref.Libn.
Scope: Business, economics, business management, marketing, finance, accounting. **Services:** Library open to the public for reference use only.

START-UP INFORMATION

26447 ■ "Natural Instinct" in *Entrepreneur* (Vol. 31, No. 8, August 2003, pp. 90)
Pub: Entrepreneur Media, Inc.
Ed: Nichole L. Torres. **Description:** According to the Organic Trade Association, the organic market is growing 20 percent annually. All areas of the industry are experiencing this growth, especially spices, yogurt, coffee and meats.

26448 ■ "Seed Capital for Farm Communities" in *Inc.* (October 1, 2004)
Pub: Inc. Magazine
Ed: Jess McCuan. **Description:** In June, 2004, the U.S. Department of Agriculture along with the Small Business Administration, launched the Rural Business Investment Program, providing $60 million in early stage funding to companies in small rural communities.

ASSOCIATIONS AND OTHER ORGANIZATIONS

26449 ■ ACDI/VOCA
50 F St. NW, Ste. 1075
Washington, DC 20001
Ph:(202)383-4961
Fax: (202)783-7204
Co. E-mail: webmaster@acdivoca.org
URL: http://www.acdivoca.org
Contact: Carl H. Leonard, Pres./CEO
Description: Agricultural cooperatives, agribusinesses, farmers' organizations, and farm credit banks in the United States. Assists in organizing and providing technical assistance for cooperatives and agribusinesses in developing countries, usually under contract with the Agency for International Development. Advises governmental and other agencies in agricultural marketing, supply, and credit; carries out feasibility studies for specific agribusiness ventures; arranges formal and on-the-job training in cooperative practices for government officials, cooperative functionaries, and rural leaders; conducts short- and long-term technical assistance programs. Conducts extensive global volunteer programs that introduce American agricultural and financial know-how to developing economies, an exchange that furthers international cooperation and fellowship and promotes global business. Invites resumes of U.S. agriculture, business, and finance experts who are willing to serve overseas on short-term assignments. **Publications:** *World Report* (quarterly); Annual Report (annual). **Telecommunication Services:** electronic mail, cleonard@acdivoca.org.

26450 ■ Agri-Energy Roundtable
1312 18th St. NW, Ste. 300
Washington, DC 20036
Ph:(202)887-0528
Fax: (202)887-9178
Co. E-mail: agenergy@aol.com
URL: http://www.agribusinesscouncil.org/aer.htm
Contact: Nicholas E. Hollis, Exec. Dir.
Description: International association that includes oil company executives and leaders of international agribusinesses. Serves as an information clearinghouse to improve dialogue on cooperative energy-agricultural development among the industrialized and developing nations. Attempts to bridge the gap on food and energy issues through cooperation between the oil exporting countries and western technology in the private sector. Sponsors trade missions. **Publications:** *Agri-Energy Report* (quarterly); *Agri-Enterprise in Development: New Leadership and Technology for Food Security*; *Beyond Food and Energy Security: New Agribusiness Markets and Technologies*; *Conference Proceedings* (annual); *Food and Energy Security: Managing the New Technologies*; *Managing Agro-Economic Peacekeeping: Trade and Development Realities for Food Security*; *Regional Africa Bulletin*.

26451 ■ Agribusiness Council
1312 18th St. NW, Ste. 300
Washington, DC 20036
Ph:(202)296-4563
Fax: (202)887-9178
Co. E-mail: info@agribusinesscouncil.org
URL: http://www.agribusinesscouncil.org
Contact: Nicholas E. Hollis, Pres./CEO
Description: Business organizations, universities and foundations, and individuals interested in stimulating and encouraging agribusiness in cooperation with the public sector, both domestic and international. Seeks to aid in relieving the problems of world food supply. Supports coordinated agribusiness in the developing nations by identifying opportunities for investment of U.S. private-sector technology management and financial resources. Advises agribusiness leaders about selected developing countries with good investment climates; brings potential investment opportunities to the attention of U.S. agribusiness firms; coordinates informal network of state agribusiness councils and grassroots organization; encourages companies to make investment feasibility studies in agribusiness; provides liaison and information exchange between agribusiness firms, governments, international organizations, universities, foundations, and other groups with the objective of identifying areas of cooperation and mutual interest; encourages projects geared to the conversion of subsistence farming to intensive, higher income agriculture in order to bring the world's rural populations, wherever feasible, into the market economy. **Publications:** Reports (periodic).

26452 ■ Agricultural Groups Concerned About Resources and the Environment
100 Stone Rd. W, Ste. 106
Guelph, ON, Canada N1G 5L3
Ph:(519)837-1326
Fax: (519)837-3209
Co. E-mail: agcare@agcare.org
URL: http://www.agcare.org
Contact: Brian Besley, Chm.
Membership: Farmers and agricultural industries. **Purpose:** Promotes environmentally sustainable food production. Facilitates communication among members; serves as a clearinghouse on sustainable agriculture. **Publications:** *AGCare Update* (quarterly); *Project Report* (periodic); Newsletter (monthly).

26453 ■ Agricultural Products Marketing Board
PO Box 8700
St. John's, NL, Canada A1B 4J6
Ph:(709)729-6758
Fax: (709)729-0205
Co. E-mail: info@gov.nl.ca
URL: http://www.gov.nl.ca/agric/contact/APMarkboard.stm
Contact: Graham Flight
Membership: Marketing agency representing food producers and agricultural industries. **Purpose:** Seeks to increase demand for agricultural products. Conducts publicity campaigns. **Publications:** *The New Farm* (biweekly).

26454 ■ American Brahmousin Council
PO Box 88
Whitesboro, TX 76273
Ph:(903)564-3995
Co. E-mail: info@brahmousin.org
URL: http://www.brahmousin.org
Contact: Bob Cummins, Interim Dir.
Description: Breeders of Brahmousin cattle. **Publications:** *Brahmousin Connection* (quarterly).

26455 ■ American Society of Agricultural Consultants
950 S Cherry St., Ste. 508
Denver, CO 80246-2664
Ph:(303)759-5091
Fax: (303)758-0190
Co. E-mail: asac@agri-associations.org
URL: http://www.agconsultants.org
Contact: Sam N. Bartee CAC, Pres.
Description: Members are independent, full-time consultants in many specialty areas serving agribusiness interests throughout the world. Strives to maintain high standards of ethics and competence in the consulting field. Provides referral service to agribusiness interests seeking consultants having specific knowledge, experience, and expertise. Maintains liaison with governmental agencies utilizing consultants and with legislative and administrative acts affecting consultants. **Publications:** *ASAC Membership Directory* (annual); *ASAC News* (quarterly).

26456 ■ Canadian Agri-Food Research Council–Conseil de recherches agro-alimentaires du Canada
Central Experimental Farm
Heritage House, Bldg. 60
Ottawa, ON, Canada K1A 0C6
Ph:(613)234-2325
Fax: (613)234-2330
Co. E-mail: carc@carc-crac.ca
URL: http://www.carc-crac.ca
Contact: Colleen Campbell, Admin. Asst.
Description: Provides leadership and coordination and networking of agriculture and food research and technology transfer and is a catalyst for building consensus on research prioritization in Canada.

26457 ■ Canadian Consulting Agrologists Association
502-45th St. W, 2nd Fl.
Saskatoon, SK, Canada S7L 6H2
Ph:(306)933-2974
Fax: (306)244-4497
Co. E-mail: info@ccaa.bz
URL: http://www.ccaa.bz
Contact: Adele Buettner, Exec. Dir.
Membership: Agrologists and other agricultural consultants. **Purpose:** Seeks to advance the science and practice of agriculture; promotes professional development of members. Makes available support and services to farmers; conducts research and educational programs. **Publications:** *Professional Papers.*

26458 ■ Canadian Society for Bioengineering
PO Box 23101
RPO McGillivray
Winnipeg, MB, Canada R3T 5S3
Ph:(204)233-1881
Fax: (204)231-8282
Co. E-mail: bioeng@shaw.ca
URL: http://www.bioeng.ca
Contact: James S. Townsend PEng, Sec. Mgr.
Membership: Individuals engaged in the practice of agricultural and biosystems engineering; agricultural and biosystems engineering educators and students. **Purpose:** Seeks to advance the study and practice of agricultural engineering and bioengineering. Conducts research; makes available continuing professional development programs for members. **Publications:** *Canadian Biosystems Engineering*; *Perspectives* (quarterly).

26459 ■ Coalition for a Competitive Food and Agricultural System
1300 L St. NW
Washington, DC 20005
Ph:(202)842-0400
Co. E-mail: bpetersen@ccfas.org
Contact: Bob Petersen, Coord.
Description: Represents interested working for market-based policies designed to benefit people working in the U.S. food and agricultural system.

26460 ■ Communicating for Agriculture and the Self Employed
112 E Lincoln Ave.
Fergus Falls, MN 56537
Ph:(218)739-3241
Free: 800-432-3276
Fax: (218)739-3832
URL: http://www.selfemployedcountry.org
Contact: Milt E. Smedsrud, Founder/Chm.
Description: Promotes the general health, well being and advancement of people in agriculture and agribusiness. Participates in federal and state issues that affect the quality of life in rural America and provides members with a variety of money-saving benefit programs. Conducts grants program, research on rural issues, and international exchange programs with an agricultural focus. **Publications:** *CA Highlights* (monthly); *CAEP In Touch* (quarterly).

26461 ■ IRI Research Institute
PO Box 1276
169 Greenwich Ave.
Stamford, CT 06904-1276
Ph:(203)327-5985
Fax: (203)359-1595
Co. E-mail: iriresrch@aol.com
URL: http://www.dizons.com/johnnyczar/IRI
Contact: Jerome F. Harrington, Pres.
Membership: International technical specialists working in agricultural and agribusiness development. Provides projects such as: development and management of pasture seed industry in Venezuela; livestock improvement in Belize; nontraditional crop improvement program in the Dominican Republic; roadside vegetation and rice production in Brazil; food crops extension program in Indonesia; rice production and management in Guyana; a crop diversification program in Peru, including the Amazon region; coffee production, El Salvador feasibility and evaluation studies, most recently in Costa Rica, Ecuador, Egypt,

Honduras, Kenya, Paraguay, Guyana, Saudi Arabia, and the Yemen Arab Republic. Incorporates a training program for academic credit or practical on-the-job training. Convention/Meeting: none. **Publications:** Bulletin (periodic). Also publishes progress reports.

26462 ■ National Council of Agricultural Employers
1112 16th St. NW, Ste. 920
Washington, DC 20036
Ph:(202)728-0300
Fax: (202)728-0303
Co. E-mail: hughes@ncaeonline.org
URL: http://www.ncaeonline.org
Contact: Sharon M. Hughes CAE, Exec.VP
Description: Growers of agricultural commodities who employ hand labor for field crops; processors and handlers, farm and commodity organizations, and others whose business is related to labor - intensive farming in the U.S. Aims to improve the position and image of U.S. agriculture as an employer of labor and to facilitate and encourage the establishment and maintenance of an adequate force of agricultural employees. Serves as clearinghouse for exchange of information on labor supply, length of employment, and other conditions of work. Does not engage in recruitment, housing, supplying, or employment of agricultural workers, and does not represent its members or others in negotiating with labor unions or other organizations, or in agreeing to any contract relating to hours, wages, or working conditions. Keeps members abreast of national legislation affecting agricultural labor. **Publications:** Newsletter (monthly).

26463 ■ Northwest Farm Managers Association
PO Box 5437
Fargo, ND 58105
Ph:(701)231-7393
Fax: (701)231-1059
Co. E-mail: daakre@ndsuext.nodak.edu
Contact: Dwight Aakre, Exec. Sec.
Description: Manager-operators of commercial farms and agriculturists interested in research in farm management, marketing, and agribusiness. **Publications:** *Northwest Farm Managers Association Membership Directory* (annual); *Plowshares to Printouts.*

26464 ■ Organization for Competitive Markets
PO Box 6486
Lincoln, NE 68506
Ph:(402)817-4443
Fax: (208)441-5092
Co. E-mail: ocm@competitivemarkets.com
URL: http://www.competitivemarkets.com
Contact: Keith Mudd, Pres.
Description: Works for increased competition and protection for the agricultural marketplace. Works against "abuse of corporate power and consolidation of the agricultural market". **Publications:** *A Food and Agricultural Policy for the 21st Century*; *OCM Newsletter.*

26465 ■ United Agribusiness League
54 Corporate Park
Irvine, CA 92606-5105
Ph:(949)975-1424
Free: 800-223-4590
Fax: (949)975-1671
Co. E-mail: bgoodrich@ual.org
URL: http://www.ual.org
Contact: Bill Goodrich, Pres./CEO
Membership: Agricultural industries and businesses. **Purpose:** Promotes "the development and common interest of the agricultural industry". Works to coordinate members' activities to advance agribusiness in general; provides services and benefits to enable members to realize greater productive efficiency. Serves as a clearinghouse on international agribusiness. Provides employee health care plans and other insurance to agribusinesses. **Publications:** *Ag Crime Prevention Brochures*; *Ag News and Views* (monthly); *Crime Prevention* (quarterly); *Healthy Times* (monthly); Membership Directory (annual).

26466 ■ Women in Agribusiness
PO Box 986
Kearney, MO 64060
Contact: Dolores Hamelin, Pres.
Description: Women in agribusiness. Provides a forum for the discussion of ideas and information related to agribusiness. Offers placement, networking, and peer/mentor support services. **Publications:** *Women in Agribusiness Bulletin* (quarterly).

REFERENCE WORKS

26467 ■ "2 Lawsuits Challenge State's Canker Policy" in *Tampa Tribune* (December 22, 2005)
Pub: Media General, Inc.
Ed: Cheryl N. Schmidt. **Description:** Two lawsuits filed by Florida citrus growers challenge the legality of Florida's citrus canker eradication program, mainly due to the recent hurricanes making it impossible to eradicate the canker. Canker does not harm humans but can cause fruit trees to loose nearly half their yields.

26468 ■ *Ag Equipment Power*
Pub: Clintron Publishers
Ed: Clint Withers, Editor. **Released:** Monthly. **Publication Includes:** Featuring news agricultural equipment and technology for growers in Washington, Idaho, and Oregon. List of about 750 manufacturers, distributors, dealers, and suppliers of new and used farm machinery and chemicals; coverage limited to Washington, Oregon, and Idaho. **Entries Include:** Company name, address, product lines. **Arrangement:** Classified by for subscribers.

26469 ■ "AgraQuest Fumigant OK'd" in *Sacramento Bee* (November 18, 2005)
Pub: The Sacramento Bee
Ed: Jim Wasserman. **Description:** AgraQuest Inc. announced approval by both federal and state agencies for its natural soil fumigant that could help replace methyl bromide, the chemical soil sterilizer. AgraQuest is based in Davis, California and reports revenues at $4.2 million for 2005. The firm's products are based on naturally occurring fungus.

26470 ■ *Agri Marketing—Farm Show Issue*
Pub: Doane Agricultural Services
Contact: Sarah Vacek, Mng. Ed.
E-mail: svacek@agrimarketing.com
Released: Annual, July/August; latest edition 2004 edition. **Publication Includes:** List of about 200 agricultural trade shows, expositions, and fairs; coverage limited to the United States and Canada. **Entries Include:** Name of show, exhibit contact person, address, description of show, attendance at most recent show, number of agricultural booth spaces, dates of shows for next two years. **Arrangement:** Alphabetical.

26471 ■ *Agri Marketing—Marketing Services Guide Issue*
Pub: Doane Agricultural Services
Contact: William Schuermann, VP, Ag Svcs.
E-mail: bschuermann@doane.com
Released: Annual, latest edition Oct 2004. **Publication Includes:** Lists over 1400 top agricultural companies in the United States, leading agricultural advertisers (for past five years), marketing services firms (including public relations, photography, editorial, art and graphics, audiovisual, marketing research, marketing consultants), and United States and Canadian radio and television broadcasting stations, advertising and public relations agencies, network programming, and publications. Agriculture-related associations are included. **Entries Include:** For leading companies—Logo, name, address, phone, names of key personnel, products, marketing area, fiscal year, name and city of advertising and/or public relations agency handling account. For leading print advertisers—Company name, address, phone, key personnel, publication unit, sales representative firm, full-page space and cost for advertising. For agen-

cies—Company name, address, name and phone of contact, year established, total agency billings, breakdown of billings by type of activity fo **Arrangement:** Alphabetical. **Indexes:** Service company's service, publication location.

26472 ■ *Agri Marketing—The Top 50*
Pub: Doane Agricultural Services
Contact: Bill Schuermann, Editorial Dir., Publisher
Released: Annual, April or May. **Publication Includes:** List of the top 50 U.S. and Canadian advertising agencies and public relations firms, chosen on the basis of agricultural business income. **Entries Include:** Agency name, location, income for agricultural accounts in most recent year, branch offices, major clients served. **Arrangement:** Alphabetical.

26473 ■ *Agribusiness*
Pub: Van Nostrand Reinhold Co., Inc.
Released: 1997. **Price:** $36.95.

26474 ■ *Agribusiness: An Entrepreneurial Approach*
Pub: Delmar Publishers
Ed: William H. Hamilton. **Released:** 1991. **Price:** $28.50; $10.00 (instructor's guide).

26475 ■ *Agricultural & Industrial Manufacturers Representatives Association—Membership Directory*
Pub: Agricultural & Industrial Manufacturers
   Representatives Association
Contact: Jim Manke Cae, Exec. Dir.
E-mail: jrmanke@aol.com
Released: Annual, October. **Covers:** 120 members; coverage includes Canada. **Entries Include:** Company name, address, phone, name of principal executive, territory covered. **Arrangement:** Alphabetical.

26476 ■ *Alfalfa Processors Council Membership Directory*
Pub: American Feed Industry Association/Alfalfa
   Processors Council (AFIA/APC)
Contact: Wanda L. Cobb
Ed: Wanda L. Cobb, Editor. **Released:** Annual, July. **Covers:** 100 alfalfa processors, firms, and suppliers. **Entries Include:** Company name, address, phone, telex, name and title of contact. **Arrangement:** Geographical by state. **Indexes:** Company name.

26477 ■ *"Alternative Energy Attracts Big Money"* in *Altanta Journal-Constitution* (January 24, 2007)
Pub: Cox Newspapers, Inc.
Ed: Dan Chapman. **Description:** Major corporations, venture capitalists, investment banks, hedge funds and farmers spent $71 billion globally on renewable energy research.

26478 ■ *"Alternative Energy Powers Up In Michigan - Part 1 of 2"* in *Crain's Detroit Business* (Vol. 22, February 6, 2006, No. 6, pp. 10)
Pub: Crain Communications Inc. - Detroit
Ed: Amy Lane. **Description:** McKenzie Bay International Ltd. Located in Farmington Hills, Michigan is launching a commercial wind-energy system that generates and distributes electricity at customer locations, and supplements power from a conventional utility.

26479 ■ *"Alternative Energy Powers Up In Michigan - Part 2 of 2"* in *Crain's Detroit Business* (Vol. 22, February 6, 2006, No. 6, pp. 10)
Pub: Crain Communications Inc. - Detroit
Ed: Amy Lane. **Description:** Michigan is pushing to become the nations' epicenter for research and development into new technology for biodiesel fuels made from renewable resources such as vegetable oil recycled from restaurants or produced from sunflowers, soybeans and canola plants.

26480 ■ *"Aquaculture Becoming Big Business in Rhode Island"* in *Providence Business News* (Vol. 18, No. 16, August 4, 2003, pp. 3)
Pub: Providence Business News, Inc.

Ed: Laura Rickstson. **Description:** The growing aquaculture industry in Rhode Island is examined, including market share of fish industry, market development, and industry forecasts.

26481 ■ *Arkansas Agribusiness Directory*
Pub: Arkansas Department Economic Development
Released: Triennial. **Price:** Free. **Covers:** Producers of agriculturally related products available for export. **Entries Include:** Name, address, phone, and telex numbers. **Arrangement:** Alphabetically and by product categories.

26482 ■ *"At Senate Finance, membership has its privilege"* in *Tax Notes* (Vol. 96, No. 14, September 30, 2002, pp. 1802-1806)
Pub: Tax Notes International
Ed: Martin A. Sullivan. **Description:** Members of the Senate Finance Committee are working on the draft Small Business and Farm Economic Recovery Act of 2002. The bill proposes tax breaks for economic sectors that already have a relatively light tax burden. It also contains many special provisions which would be politically beneficial to various members of the committee.

26483 ■ *"Betting the Farm"* in *Business 2.0* (Vol. 6, September 2005, No. 8, pp. 108)
Pub: Time, Inc.
Ed: Erick Schonfeld. **Description:** The continual advancement of genetically modified crops is paying off for Monsanto after the company took the big risk on biotechnology.

26484 ■ *"Bio Solutions Acquisition"* in *Mississippi Business Journal* (Vol. 29, January 2007, No. 2, pp. 9)
Pub: Venture Publications, Inc.
Ed: Wally Northway **Description:** Bio Solutions Manufacturing Inc. acquired an oil and grease extraction technology for the removal of fat, oil and grease from organic waste effluent.

26485 ■ *"Biotech Crops Turn into Growing Field"* in *Altanta Journal-Constitution* (January 20, 2007)
Pub: Cox Newspapers, Inc.
Ed: Mike Toner. **Description:** According to industry experts, farmers planed genetically modified crops on millions of acres in 2006.

26486 ■ *"Black Farmers Sue USDA for $20.5 Billion"* in *Black Enterprise* (Vol. 35, December 2004, No. 5, pp. 36)
Pub: Earl G. Graves Publishing Co. Inc.
Ed: Tamara E. Holmes. **Description:** A class action lawsuit charging the U.S. Department of Agriculture with denying fair loans and farm programs to 25,000 black farmers is discussed. The Black Farmers and Agriculturist Association and 11 other plaintiffs have filed the suit.

26487 ■ *"Blue Bag Site Faces Scrutiny"* in *Chicago Tribune* (February 17, 2005)
Pub: Knight-Ridder/Tribune Business News
Description: Authorities are investigating an Indiana farmer who allegedly accepted more than six times the amount of waste from blue bag recycling centers than he reported spreading on his fields. Officials are trying to determine whether the farm's operator is dumping more material than allowed on his fields.

26488 ■ *"A Bumper Crop of Worries"* in *Tampa Tribune* (November 30, 2005)
Pub: Media General, Inc.
Ed: Will Rodgers. **Description:** Florida citrus growers face challenges of disease, development, hurricanes, and competition, hurting profits and land use.

26489 ■ *"Business Briefs"* in *St. Louis Post-Dispatch* (December 8, 2004)
Pub: Knight-Ridder/Tribune Business News
Description: Orion Genomics LLC, based at the Center for Emerging Technologies incubator, received a federal grant to research the genetic code of the agricultural pest roundworm. Research is directed at finding alternative ways to destroy or ward off the pest that are more effective than chemical pesticides now used. The company and researchers at North Carolina State University will share the $1.59 million grant.

26490 ■ *"Can't Save the Farm"* in *Black Enterprise* (Vol. 31, No. 5, December 2000, pp. 34)
Pub: Earl Graves Publishing Co.
Ed: Hamil R. Harris. **Description:** Legal relief arrives too late to harvest benefits for black farmers.

26491 ■ *"Carlsbad: Weevil Bugs $900M Nursery Industry"* in *San Diego Business Journal* (Vol. 28, January 8, 2007, No. 2, pp. 27)
Pub: San Diego Business Journal Associates
Ed: Connie Lewis. **Description:** Department of Food and Agriculture has quarantined three nurseries in San Diego County due to infestation of a beetle. It is predicted it could take three to five years to eradicate the root weevil that threatens San Diego County and parts of Orange and Los Angeles Counties.

26492 ■ *"Cod Limits Worry Maine Fishermen"* in *Portland Press Herald* (November 15, 2005)
Pub: Blethen Maine Newspapers, Inc.
Ed: Tom Bell. **Description:** The New England Fishery Management Council is planning regulatory options regarding the new federal regulations limiting the number of cod that can be caught in the Gulf of Maine. The new set of restrictions would go into effect May 1, 2006.

26493 ■ *"The Competition has Nuttin' on this Business"* in *Providence Business News* (Vol. 18, No. 18, August 25, 2003, pp. 10)
Pub: Providence Business News, Inc.
Ed: David Ortiz. **Description:** Profile of Virginia & Spanish Peanut Company and ways they are competing in the industry.

26494 ■ *"Congress Debates Fate of U.S. Agriculture"* in *U.S. Farm News* (Vol. 25, No. 3, Autumn 2001, pp. 7)
Pub: U.S. Farmers Association
Ed: Lem Harris. **Description:** Both Houses of Congress and both major parties are conducting hearings and holding grassroots sessions in farm regions in order to prepare the new Farm Act due in 2002.

26495 ■ *"Controversial Ruling on Cuban Trade"* in *Hispanic Business* (April 2005, pp. 12)
Pub: Hispanic Business
Ed: Patricia Guadalupe. **Description:** A ruling by the U.S. Treasury Department requires all agricultural goods sent to Cuba to paid for in cash by the Cuban government before they can be shipped.

26496 ■ *"Cornucopia"* in *Forbes* (Vol. 175, January 10, 2005, No. 1, pp. 145)
Pub: Forbes Magazine Inc.
Ed: William Heuslein. **Description:** Profile of Corn Products International, producer of refined corn products like sweeteners, starches and corn oil. Investment information is included.

26497 ■ *"Cottage industry pays off for Eskimo women"* in *Alaska Business Monthly* (Vol. 18, No. 10, Oct. 2002, pp. 82)
Pub: Alaska Business Publishing Company, Inc.
Ed: Gerry Watkins. **Description:** Profile of explorer/anthropologist, John J. Teal, Jr. Teal, a Harvard/Yale anthropologist, has established the Institute of Northern Agricultural Research. Through the domestication of the musk ox, Teal not only conducts research on the animal, his work has enabled Alaskan women to use the wool to make hand knitted items that are sold to a co-op, thus providing income for their families.

26498 ■ *"Cropping Up"* in *Hispanic Business* (May 2005, pp. 14)
Pub: Hispanic Business
Description: Pennsylvania State University established the new Latino Agricultural Center that will work to develop agricultural educational resources and offer a Spanish class for agricultural professionals.

26499 ■ "Dairy Co-Op Targets R.I. Consumers" in *Providence Business News* (Vol. 18, No. 19, August 25, 2003, pp. 1)
Pub: Providence Business News, Inc.
Ed: Laura Ricketson. Description: The operations of the Rhode Island Dairy Farm Co-Op are discussed.

26500 ■ "D&PL Reports Loss" in *Mississippi Business Journal* (Vol. 29, January 2007, No. 2, pp. 8)
Pub: Venture Publications, Inc.
Ed: Wally Northway Description: Delta and Pine Land Company reported a net loss during the first quarter ended November 2006. Due to the seasonal nature of the seed business, D&PL typically incurs sizeable losses during the first and fourth fiscal quarters. Statistical data included.

26501 ■ "Developer Buys Moores Farm for $8.66 Million" in *Bradenton Herald* (February 12, 2005)
Pub: Bradenton Herald
Ed: Melissa Followell. Description: Heritage Harbour Development LLC purchased the Moores Dairy Farm in order to expand the Heritage Harbour Community. The land was appraised at $1.08 million, but the competition for land development in the area increased the property's value.

26502 ■ *Directory of American Agriculture*
Pub: Agricultural Resources & Communications Inc.
Contact: Chris Wilson, Publisher
Released: Irregular, Previous edition May 1998. Covers: national and state agricultural organizations; federal and state agricultural departments, agencies, and programs; colleges of agriculture at land grant universities, state 4-H leaders, farm broadcastors and publications, farm credit councils, agricultural information services and other agricultural organizations, agencies and institutions. Entries Include: Organization name, address, phone, fax, name and title of contact. National organization entries include additional information. Arrangement: Alphabetical. Indexes: Categorical, by type of organization.

26503 ■ "Ethanol Push Has Roots from Early 1990s, Support from Farmers" in *Altanta Journal-Constitution* (February 4, 2007)
Pub: Cox Newspapers, Inc.
Ed: Jeff Nesmith. Description: National Farmers Union discusses renewable and alternative energy issues and the food vs. fuel debate.

26504 ■ "Experts Say California Wine Harvest is 'A Perfect Vintage'" in *Sacramento Bee* (October 16, 2005)
Pub: The Sacramento Bee
Ed: Jim Wasserman. Description: Experts are reporting California's 2005 wine harvest the best for quality, price and yield. The wine grape harvest is expected to be 10 percent to 20 percent higher than the previous two years. California accounts for 90 percent of domestic wine production and 10 percent worldwide.

26505 ■ "Failure of Genius" in *Inc.* (August 1, 2003)
Pub: Gruner & Jahr USA Publishing
Ed: Jess McCuan. Description: Profile of Future Beef. The founders of Future Beef were the smartest, most forward-thinking individuals in the beef business, yet the company did not succeed.

26506 ■ "Farmers Faithful to Their Fields" in *Tampa Tribune* (November 28, 2005)
Pub: Media General, Inc.
Ed: Jim Tunstall. Description: Farmers discuss the challenges faced running their farms, where profits can be small or nonexistent. These landowners are now faced with the decision to sell their land to developers for high prices or continue farming.

26507 ■ "Farmers' Livelihood Dried Up by Federal Regs" in *My Business* (September/October 2001, pp. 19)
Pub: My Business Magazine
Description: Brief discussion involving the EPA's move to protect suckerfish by shutting the headgates

of the Upper Klamath Lake Dam in Oregon, cutting water off to 1,500 farms. The owner of a fertilizer company testified before Congress that his business is in jeopardy.

26508 ■ "Farmingdale-based THM Scientific Introduces Product Line Based on Sustainable Agriculture" in *Long Island Business News* (Feb.6, 2004)
Pub: Dolan Media Newswires
Ed: Adina Genn. Description: Profile of Peter Felix and James Sottilo, two arborists who have partnered to develop and produce Rootgrow, a line of organic-compost tea, brewers and related products and services that will preserve the soil. The partners are targeting homeowners, corporate parks, golf courses, and municipalities.

26509 ■ "Federal File: News & Developments in the Business of Government" in *Hispanic Business* (December 2001, pp. FG4, FG6, FG14, FG16)
Pub: Hispanic Business
Description: The Department of Agriculture has an Outreach Office that helps socially disadvantaged farmers and farm workers gain access to federal programs. Federal government employment opportunities for minorities are presented with a listing of internship opportunities. Hispanic entrepreneurs owning 8(a) firms secured 14.4 percent of federal contracts for fiscal year 2000.

26510 ■ "Fishermen's Days Numbered; New Regs Would Cut Time at Sea" in *Providence Business News* (Vol. 18, No. 23, September 22, 2003, pp. 1)
Pub: Providence Business News, Inc.
Ed: Laura Ricketson. Description: New government regulations that take effect May 2004, will reduce the number of fishing days, thus reducing fishermen's catch by 65 percent; the regulations will affect both Canadian and New England fisheries.

26511 ■ "Fresh-Produce Prices Set to Rise in Wake of Crop Freeze" in *Altanta Journal-Constitution* (January 28, 2007)
Pub: Cox Newspapers, Inc.
Ed: Bob Keefe. Description: Record breaking cold temperatures will cause fresh fruit and vegetable prices to rise in 2007.

26512 ■ "Grants for Rural Biz" in *Inc.* (September 1, 2003)
Pub: Gruner & Jahr USA Publishing
Ed: Amy Gunderson. Description: States with a number of farms and fields are making more grants available to small businesses. The program, EPSCor, is funded mostly by the National Science Foundation and fosters scientific research in rural areas.

26513 ■ "Hawaii's Growers Wake Up and Sell the Coffee" in *Pacific Business News* (Vol. 41, No. 19, July 18, 2003, pp. 23)
Pub: American City Business Journals
Ed: Howard Dicus. Description: The success that Hawaii Coffee is experiencing with the sale of specialty coffees using celebrity endorsements is discussed. Topics include strategic planning, advertising, and market development.

26514 ■ "History Bears Fruit for Maine Family's Apple Orchard" in *Portland Press Herald* (October 7, 2005)
Pub: Blethen Maine Newspapers, Inc.
Ed: Matt Wickenheiser. Description: Family-owned Sweetser's Apple Barrel & Orchards of Cumberland, Maine, grows 37 varieties of apples. The company distributes its apples, cider and other products through a roadside stand.

26515 ■ *A History of Small Business in America*
Pub: University of North Carolina Press
Ed: Mansel G. Blackford. Released: January 2003. Price: $18.95. Description: History of American small business from the colonial era to present, showing how it has played a role in the nation's economic, political, and cultural development across manufacturing, sales, services and farming.

26516 ■ "In Brief: Grassley Offers a Bankruptcy Bill" in *American Banker* (Vol. 170, February 4, 2005, No. 24, pp. 3)
Pub: Thomson Financial Media Inc.
Ed: Hannah Bergman. Description: Finance Committee Chairman, Senator Charles Grassley, has introduced a bill that would revamp bankruptcy laws. The bill would require credit card companies to disclose the risks of minimum payment, ban deceptive advertising of low introductory rates, and require the companies to establish a toll-free number for consumers. It would also make permanent the Chapter 12 protections to help farmers from going bankrupt.

26517 ■ "In the Right Field" in *Home Business* (Vol. 13, January/February 2006, No. 1, pp. 92)
Pub: Home Business Magazine
Ed: Sandy Larson. Description: Profile of Gena Nonini, former commodity trader turned farmer. Gena plans to expand her farm's distilled spirits business in 2006, start a second food company, and launch a teaching program for biodynamic production farming.

26518 ■ "John Deere Named In Discrimination Suit" in *Black Enterprise* (Vol. 35, August 2004, No. 1, pp. 30)
Pub: Earl G. Graves Publishing Co. Inc.
Ed: Aisha Jefferson. Description: After working for John Deere for 30 years, Kenny Edwards wanted to become an entrepreneur by purchasing his own John Deere agricultural dealership. Edwards has sued the company for discrimination when it turned down his bid for ownership. Of the 1,400 John Deere agricultural dealerships in the U.S. non are African-American owned, and only 5 percent of owners include women, Hispanics, and Asians.

26519 ■ "Late Buying Boosts Crops" in *Kansas City Star* (March 11, 2005)
Pub: Knight-Ridder/Tribune Business News
Ed: Katie Lindmark. Description: Late buying of futures drove the prices of wheat, soybean and corns futures higher in early March. Statistical data included.

26520 ■ "Living the Lifestyle of the Successful Businessperson" in *Hispanic Business* (March 2005, pp. 62)
Pub: Hispanic Business
Ed: Leslie A. Westbrook. Description: Profile of Watsonville Mayor, Ana Ventura Phares. Her father is the former vice-president of harvesting at Dole.

26521 ■ "Maine Fishermen Welcome Amendment to Preserve Wharf Tax Rates" in *Portland Press Herald* (November 10, 2005)
Pub: Blethen Maine Newspapers, Inc.
Ed: Dennis Hoey. Description: Maine voters overwhelmingly approved a constitutional amendment that allows waterfront land use for commercial fishing activities to remain at its current tax rate.

26522 ■ *MetroFarm: The Guide to Growing for Big Profit on a Small Parcel of Land*
Pub: T S Books
Ed: Michael Olson. Released: 1994. Price: $29.95 (paper).

26523 ■ "Mussel Farmer's Expansion Plan Worries Island Lobster Fishermen" in *Portland Press Herald* (October 11, 2005)
Pub: Blethen Maine Newspapers, Inc.
Ed: Tom Bell. Description: Aqua Farms LLC is seeking to obtain a 10-year lease from the State of Maine for two acres of ocean bottom near Hope Island. The expansion would hurt lobster fishermen in the area.

26524 ■ *National Agri-Marketing Association—Directory of Members*
Pub: National Agri-Marketing Association
Ed: Jennifer Pickett, Editor. Released: Annual, January. Price: $150. Covers: 2,500 persons active in agricultural advertising and marketing for manufacturers, advertising agencies, and media. Published as part of the Agri-Marketing Marketing Services Guide. Entries Include: Member name and position, company name, address, phone. Arrangement: Geographical, alphabetical.

26525 ■ "NLRB Finds California Almond Growers Engaged in Anti-Union Activity" in *Sacramento Bee* **(November 1, 2005)**
Pub: The Sacramento Bee
Ed: Rachel Osterman. **Description:** The National Labor Relations Board has filed a complaint against Blue Diamond Growers for illegally threatening, interrogating and firing workers wishing to unionize the cooperative's downtown almond plant. Details of the complaint are outlined.

26526 ■ "Panel Seeks to Put Organic Loophole Out to Pasture" in *Chicago Tribune* **(March 3, 2005)**
Pub: Knight-Ridder/Tribune Business News
Ed: Andrew Martin. **Description:** An advisory board has recommended that the U.S. Department of Agriculture strengthen existing rules requiring organic livestock to be raised and fed on open pasture rather than confined pens. The move would most directly affect the dairy business.

26527 ■ "Parrish, Fla. Farmland Sells for $6.5 Million" in *Bradenton Herald* **(January 20, 2005)**
Pub: Bradenton Herald
Ed: Matt Griswold. **Description:** Griffin Properties has purchased 195 acres of Parrish farmland for a planned residential housing development. The project will be called the Parrish Plantation. A Michigan man purchased 10 acres of farmland in the area for $1 million, with no plans for development. Eslinger Homes and Visions Southwest Florida Inc. also purchased land in the area to build 33 homes in the $500,000 price range.

26528 ■ "Peanut Growers to Ramp Up Research Work" in *Kiplinger Letter* **(Vol. 78, January 19, 2007, No. 2)**
Pub: Kiplinger
Description: Peanut Foundation will fund $9.5 million in USDA and industry for research to improve the flavor and nutrient content of peanuts, while boosting their oil content.

26529 ■ "Plan Would Share Wealth From $1B Fund" in *Crain's Detroit Business* **(Vol. 21, October 24, 2005, No. 43, pp. 26)**
Pub: Crain Communications Inc. - Detroit
Ed: Amy Lane. **Description:** Life-sciences, technology, tourism, manufacturing, agriculture, film-production, and defense companies will all benefit from $101 million in government funds to support growing or technology-oriented businesses.

26530 ■ "Rainfall Helps Growers" in *Tribune* **(March 2, 2005)**
Pub: Knight-Ridder/Tribune Business News
Description: Central Coast growers and cattle ranchers have benefited from the heavy rainfall this season.

26531 ■ "Ranch Project Hailed as Farmland Preservation Model" in *Sacramento Bee* **(December 8, 2005)**
Pub: The Sacramento Bee
Ed: Jim Wasserman. **Description:** The 300-acre McConeghy Ranch in Solano County is being acclaimed as a national model for preserving farmland. The ranch prevents land within sight of the University of California, Davis, from becoming auto malls, shopping centers and housing subdivisions.

26532 ■ "The Remote Control CEO" in *Inc.* **(October 2005, pp. 96-101, 144, 146)**
Pub: Inc. Magazine
Ed: Donna Fenn. **Description:** CEO, Stephen McConnell believes a major reason for his organic meat company's success is because he works from home four days a week. The success of his firm, Applegate Farms, reinforces this strategy.

26533 ■ "Research Funding New Uses for Eggs, Prune Juice" in *Kiplinger Letter* **(Vol. 78, January 19, 2007, No. 2)**
Pub: Kiplinger
Description: Researchers are placing genes that can produce therapeutic proteins into the genes of hens that create human interferon b-1a, an antiviral drug as well as an antibody that fights melanoma. The oxidants in prune juice are proving to retard oxidation of fatty acids in meat, thus keeping meat fresher for longer periods of time.

26534 ■ "Rise of China's Consumer Class Excites California Ag Industry" in *Sacramento Bee* **(December 19, 2005)**
Pub: The Sacramento Bee
Ed: Jim Wasserman. **Description:** China's recent growth in the world's food markets may pose the largest challenge to California's agricultural industry. Statistical data included.

26535 ■ "Risk Management on the Farm" in *Hispanic Business* **(November 2002, pp. 33)**
Pub: Hispanic Business
Ed: Scott Williams. **Description:** Profile of Jim Baldonado, CEO of The Home Agency of Elwood, Nebraska. Baldonado sells crop insurance, particularly crop revenue coverage to rural farmers in the area.

26536 ■ "Sacramento, Calif.-Area Rice Growers May Reap Benefits of Highest Value Harvest" in *Sacramento Bee* **(October 27, 2005)**
Pub: The Sacramento Bee
Ed: Jim Wasserman. **Description:** Sacramento Valley, California rice growers are predicting their highest value harvest despite a smaller crop than 2004's. These smaller crops are valued at $435 million due to a strong market price.

26537 ■ "SciTech Developments to Watch" in *Business Week* **(January 16, 2006, No. 3967, pp. 87)**
Pub: McGraw-Hill Companies
Description: Scientific and technological developments discussed include a pain-free alternative to pricking fingers for blood sugar readings for diabetics through the use of infrared light bounced off the white of an individual's eye; carbon nanotubes for electronic components; and information about tree farms.

26538 ■ "Senate Finance Committee tries to codify economic substance doctrine" in *Tax Notes* **(Vol. 96, No. 13, Sept. 23, 2002, pp. 1665-1667)**
Pub: Tax Notes International
Ed: Patti Mohr. **Description:** The Small Business and Farm Economic Recovery Act, a draft bill in the U.S. Senate Finance Committee, would provide tax breaks for small businesses and farms. It would be funded by a codification of the 'economic substance' doctrine governing business transactions resulting in tax savings.

26539 ■ "Senator Urges 'Measurable Standard' for Awarding Farm Subsidies" in *Chicago Tribune* **(February 16, 2005)**
Pub: Knight-Ridder/Tribune Business News
Ed: Andrew Martin. **Description:** Although an individual must be actively engaged in a farm in order to received federal farm subsidies, the U.S. Department of Agriculture has paid out millions of dollars to dead farmers and wealthy businessmen who did nothing more than participate in conference calls.

26540 ■ "Sonoma County, Calif., Voters Set to Decide Whether to Ban Biotech Crops" in *Sacramento Bee* **(November 2, 2005)**
Pub: The Sacramento Bee
Ed: Jim Wasserman. **Description:** Sonoma County voters will decide whether to ban biotech crops. If passed, the county will be included among Mendocino, Marin and Trinity counties banning these crops that are used to repel insects and chemical weed killers. In 2004 growers in the county produced $526 million from wine grapes, dairy cows and poultry.

26541 ■ "South Florida Farmers Attempt to Broaden Market for Tropical Fruits" in *Miami Herald* **(June 28, 2004)**
Pub: Knight-Ridder/Tribune Business News
Ed: Christina Hoag. **Description:** South Florida farmers are growing exotic fruits such as lychee and longan, mamey sapote and sapodilla and dragonfruit because of increased interest by consumers in the U.S.

26542 ■ "State's Independent Wineries Are Facing Tough Road" in *Sacramento Bee* **(September 30, 2005)**
Pub: The Sacramento Bee
Ed: Doug Rutsch. **Description:** According to Robert Smiley, a wine industry consultant and management professor at University of California, Davis, small independent wine growers in California are facing difficult challenges in the future. As larger wineries gain market share, smaller companies will find it difficult to compete.

26543 ■ "Stone to Run Hickory Farmer's Market" in *Charlotte Observer* **(January 31, 2007)**
Pub: Knight-Ridder/Tribune Business News
Ed: Jen Aronoff. **Description:** Betty Stone has been hired to manage the Downtown Hickory Farmers Market. The market will run from May 5 through October 6, 2007.

26544 ■ "Study Says Change Tax Laws to Help Forest Products Industry Stay Competitive" in *Portland Press Herald* **(March 25, 2005)**
Pub: Blethen Maine Newspapers, Inc.
Ed: Tux Turkel. **Description:** A recent state-sponsored report, called Maine Future Forest Economy Project, showed a change in the state's tax laws would help the forest industry remain competitive, while encouraging private investment, increase cooperative among state government and industry, and increase the transfer of university sponsored research into next generation commercial products and applications.

26545 ■ *Successful Small-Scale Farming: An Organic Approach*
Pub: Storey Communications, Inc.
Ed: Karl Schwenke. **Released:** Revised edition, 1991. **Price:** $12.95 (paper). **Description:** Provides information for cash crop growers on finding a market.

26546 ■ "Sugar Shortage Affects Sacramento, Calif.-Area Businesses" in *Sacramento Bee* **(October 15, 2005)**
Pub: The Sacramento Bee
Description: Bakery owners can expect at least 5 percent increase in sugar prices due to hurricane damage to the Gulf Coast. Domestic sugarcane accounts for nearly 45 percent of the nation's $10 billion annual refined sugar industry.

26547 ■ "Task Force Recommends Strategies to Improve Maine's Forest Products Industry" in *Portland Press Herald* **(April 6, 2005)**
Pub: Blethen Maine Newspapers, Inc.
Ed: Tux Turkel. **Description:** Maine's Governor John Baldacci created a task force to address the state's forest products industry. The report outlines eight specific initiatives for the Governor to consider for improving the industry.

26548 ■ "Tomato Shortage Is Now a Glut In Florida" in *Bradenton Herald* **(January 19, 2005)**
Pub: Bradenton Herald
Ed: Richard Dymond. **Description:** Jay Taylor, of Palmetto's Taylor-Fulton Packing House, is joining other Florida growers who are dumping thousands of ripe tomatoes rather lose money in a low market.

26549 ■ "A Tough Row to Hoe" in *Hispanic Business* **(October 2002, pp. 26, 28)**
Pub: Hispanic Business
Ed: Lou Gallegos. **Description:** An increasing number of Hispanics in the U.S. are taking up farming. Lou Gallegos, a U.S. Department of Agriculture official, discusses current trends and offers policy recommendations to promote Hispanic farming owner and prosperity.

26550 ■ "Trainers of Racing Horses Face New Drug Fine" in *Chicago Tribune* **(February 18, 2005)**
Pub: Knight-Ridder/Tribune Business News
Ed: Michael Higgins. **Description:** Racing Board officials in Illinois voted to fine trainers whose horses test

positive for drugs, but are letting them keep prize money for wins. The board voted to impose a $250 fine for the first offense, $500 for the second, and $1,000 for all subsequent offenses.

26551 ■ "Twenty Nine Percent of State's Farmers are Female" in *Journal Record* **(February 4, 2004)**
Pub: Dolan Media Company
Description: According to a report by the U.S. Department of Agriculture's National Agricultural Statistics Service, 29 percent of Oklahoma's agriculture producers are women. Statistical data included.

26552 ■ "Udder Irony" in *Forbes* **(Vol. 174, December 27, 2004, No. 13, pp. 54)**
Pub: Forbes Magazine Inc.
Ed: Bernard Condon. **Description:** The U.S. Department of Justice has launched an investigation into the Dairy Farmers of America (DFA) cooperative. The government is looking into whether the DFA has used processing plants it controls to force farmers into joining the cooperative and to pay below-market prices for milk. The State of Florida has also begun its own investigation.

26553 ■ "Uncommon Enterprise: Sweet Dreams" in *My Business* **(April/May 2002, pp. 54)**
Pub: My Business Magazine
Ed: Shannon Scully. **Description:** Profile of Dean Throndsen, owner of Relative Products, in Reedsburg, Wisconsin. Throndsen sells waterbeds for cows to area farmers, which keeps the cows producing more milk.

26554 ■ "U.S.-Canada Agricultural Trade to Get Stickier in 2007" in *Kiplinger Letter* **(Vol. 78, January 19, 2007, No. 2)**
Pub: Kiplinger
Description: Border security, U.S. corn subsidies, USDA proposed fees and inspections of farm goods from Canada along with country-of-origin rules on meat products are expected to make trade between the U.S. and Canada more difficult.

26555 ■ "U.S. Cotton Farmers Waiting Out the Market for Better Prices" in *Kiplinger Letter* **(Vol. 78, January 19, 2007, No. 4)**
Pub: Kiplinger
Description: U.S. cotton exports fell nearly 45 percent in 2006. China and India are expected to turn to U.S. cotton suppliers due to depletion of their crops.

26556 ■ "The Upside and Downside of Outsourcing" in *Business Week* **(February 20, 2006, No. 3972, pp. 18)**
Pub: McGraw-Hill Companies
Description: Foreign companies are outsourcing jobs to the U.S. at record rates. Eight percent of U.S. workers are employed in the service industry, 19 percent in manufacturing, and only 1 percent in farming.

26557 ■ "Vacaville, Calif.-Based Biotech Firm Ends Operations" in *Sacramento Bee* **(December 23, 2005)**
Pub: The Sacramento Bee
Ed: Jim Wasserman. **Description:** Large Scale Biology Corporation, manufacturer of proteins and vaccines for tobacco plants closed its operations in Vacaville, California as well as its site in Kentucky, due to lack of funds. The firm went public five years ago.

26558 ■ "Washington a Leader in Organic Cereal Market" in *Business Journal-Portland* **(Vol. 20, No. 24, August 15, 2003, pp. 14)**
Pub: American City Business Journals, Inc.
Ed: Steve Wilhelm. **Description:** Efforts of Cascadian Farms, Nature's Path Foods Inc., and Small Planet Foods Inc. and their successful marketing of organic cereals in Canada and the U.S. are profiled.

26559 ■ "Washington State Apple Commission Shuts Down Soon after Ruling on Fees" in *News Tribune* **(April 11, 2003)**
Pub: Knight-Ridder/Tribune Business News
Ed: C.R. Roberts. **Description:** The Washington State Apple Commission closed its doors after a fed-eral court decided the commission's collection of mandatory fees from growers was unconstitutional. The Commission was in charge of promoting the state's apple industry.

26560 ■ "Watch That Bird's Rear" in *The Economist* **(Vol. 376, July 16-22, 2005, No. 8435, pp. 30)**
Pub: The Economist Newspaper Ltd.
Description: Oklahoma, home to some of the country's largest poultry businesses, has filed a lawsuit against 14 Arkansas poultry producers, claiming violations of federal and state environmental nuisance laws.

26561 ■ "Will Congress Act to Preserve Family Type Farming?" in *U.S. Farm News* **(Vol. 25, No. 3, Autumn 2001, pp. 6-7)**
Pub: U.S. Farmers Association
Ed: Lem Harris. **Description:** An overview of the new Farm Act being written by Congress is presented.

26562 ■ "Wine Pest Fight Could Get Funds" in *Sacramento Bee* **(November 4, 2005)**
Pub: The Sacramento Bee
Ed: Jim Wasserman. **Description:** President Bush approved $83 billion in agriculture spending that could help California's wine industry. The bill contains $24.2 million to stop the spread of Pierce's disease. The disease occurs when bacterium clogs the circulatory systems of grape vines and is spread by an insect. The disease threatens the entire $15 billion wine industry in California.

26563 ■ "York, Pa.-Based Company Plans to Build Ethanol Plant in Northeast" in *Patriot-News* **(April 11, 2003)**
Pub: Knight-Ridder/Tribune Business News
Ed: Mary Klaus. **Description:** Penn-Mar Ethanol LLC plans to build the first ethanol plant in the Northeast and use corn to make ethanol for fuel, dry distillers grain for cattle and carbon dioxide for soft drinks.

STATISTICAL SOURCES

26564 ■ *Almanac of Business and Industrial Financial Ratios*
Pub: Pearson Education Corp.
Ed: Leo Troy. **Released:** Annual. **Price:** $99.95 (1999 edition—book and CD-ROM). **Description:** Profiles corporate performance in two analytical tables for a variety of industries: one-table reports operating and financial information for corporations with and without net income; the second table provides the same information but only for those corporations that operated at a profit. Includes an appendix that cross-references each industry in the *Almanac* and each industry in the Standard Industry Classification (SIC). Also offers a selected number of ratios displayed graphically, in bar chart form.

TRADE PERIODICALS

26565 ■ *Agri Marketing*
Pub: Doane Agricultural Services
Released: Monthly, 10/year. **Price:** $40 U.S. and Canada; $52 U.S. and Canada two years; $62 other countries; $110 other countries two years. **Description:** Magazine covering marketing, sales, and communications news for agribusiness professionals.

26566 ■ *Agribusiness*
Pub: John Wiley & Sons Inc.
Contact: Michael W. Woolverton, Managing Editor
Ed: Ronald W. Cotterill, Editor, fmpc@canr.cag. uconn.edu. **Released:** 4/year. **Price:** $255 U.S.; $255 Canada and Mexico in Canada, add 7% GST; $279 other countries; $1,235 institutions print, U.S.; $1,275 institutions, Canada and Mexico print & in Canada, add 7% GST; $1,309 institutions, other countries print; $1,359 institutions print & online, U.S.; $1,399 institutions, Canada and Mexico print & online; $1,433 institutions, other countries print & online. **Description:** Publication focusing on applied research in agribusiness, including agricultural inputs, agricultural production, commodity processing, food manufacturing, and food distribution.

26567 ■ *American Journal of Agricultural Economics*
Pub: Blackwell Publishing Inc.
Ed: Paul V. Preckel, Editor. **Released:** 5/yr. **Price:** $261 institutions; $237 institutions; $225 institutions. **Description:** Journal of agricultural and resource economics.

26568 ■ *Arizona Farm Bureau News*
Pub: Arizona Farm Bureau Federation
Released: Semimonthly. **Price:** $25, U.S.. **Description:** Covers the agricultural industry with an emphasis on Arizona. Specializes in issue specific and regulatory news.

26569 ■ *The Business Journal Serving Greater Milwaukee*
Pub: The Business Journal Serving Greater Milwaukee
Contact: Rich Kirchen, Managing Editor
Released: Weekly. **Price:** $92.95 per year; $144.95 two years. **Description:** Tabloid business publication covering the greater Milwaukee, WI, area.

26570 ■ *Canola Digest*
Pub: Canola Council of Canada
Contact: Kelly Funke, Assoc. Ed.
E-mail: funkek@canola-council.org
Ed: Dave Wilkins, Editor, wilkinsd@canola-council. org. **Released:** 6x/yr. **Price:** $35, U.S. and Canada. **Description:** Provides information on canola and related interests. Recurring features include on farm articles, market reports analysis, news of research, a calendar of events, reports of meetings, and news of educational opportunities, industry news and issues.

26571 ■ *Composting News*
Pub: McEntee Media Corp.
Ed: Ken McEntee, Editor, ken@recycle.cc. **Released:** Monthly. **Price:** $83, individuals; $93, Canada and Mexico; $105, other countries. **Description:** Covers news and trends in the composting industry. Also reports on compost product prices. Recurring features include letters to the editor, interviews, news of research, a calendar of events, reports of meetings, and notices of publications available.

26572 ■ *The Davlin Report*
Pub: The Davlin Report Inc.
Ed: Andrew Davlin, Jr., Editor, aquaandy@aol.com. **Released:** Periodic. **Price:** $39.95, U.S. 4 issues; $59.95, U.S. 8 issues. **Description:** Reports on the aquaculture industry & companies, oil & gas companies & attractive common stocks.

26573 ■ *Farm Bureau News*
Pub: American Farm Bureau Federation
Contact: Phyllis Brown
Ed: Lynne Finnerty, Editor, lynnef@fb.org. **Released:** Bimonthly, except monthly in August & December. **Price:** $10, individuals $10/year; $30, individuals first class delivery; $48, elsewhere surface mail; $63, elsewhere airmail. **Description:** Discusses current legislation, court decisions, trade issues, and the use of innovative production methods. Recurring features include editorials, commentaries and the President's Column.

26574 ■ *Farm Industry News*
Pub: Southwest Farm Press
Contact: Ron Sorensen, Publisher
E-mail: rsorensen@primediabusiness.com
Ed: Karen McMahon, Editor, kmc-mahon@primediabusiness.com. **Released:** 12/year. **Price:** $28. **Description:** Agriculture trade magazine covering new products and technology.

26575 ■ *Farm and Ranch News*
Pub: Farm & Ranch News
Contact: George Parker Jr., Publisher
E-mail: fla.best@aol.com
Released: Monthly. **Price:** $12.50 in Florida; $15 out of state. **Description:** Trade publication covering agribusiness issues for commercial farmers and ranchers.

26576 ■ *Farm and Ranch Tax Letter*
Pub: Ag Executive Inc.

Ed: Darrell L. Dunteman, Editor, darrellld@aol.com. **Released:** Monthly. **Price:** $38; $5, single issue. **Description:** Provides information on agricultural taxation.

26577 ■ *Farming Uncle*
Pub: TORO
Contact: Louis Toro III, Editor & Publisher
Released: Quarterly. **Price:** $10; $18 two years; $15 other countries; $3 single issue. **Description:** Agricultural magazine.

26578 ■ *Fastline—Illinois Farm Edition*
Pub: Fastline
Contact: Rick McKay, Sales Mgr
Released: Monthly. **Price:** $12; $18 two years; $36 Canada and Mexico; $85 other countries. **Description:** Illustrated buying guide for the farming industry.

26579 ■ *Fastline—Indiana Farm Edition*
Pub: Fastline
Contact: Rick McKay, Sales Mgr
Released: Monthly. **Price:** $12; $18 two years; $36 Canada and Mexico; $85 other countries. **Description:** Illustrated buying guide for the farming industry.

26580 ■ *Fastline—Iowa Farm Edition*
Pub: Fastline
Contact: Jim Strause, Sales Mgr
E-mail: jstrause@fastline.com
Released: Monthly. **Price:** $12; $18 two years; $36 Canada and Mexico; $85 other countries. **Description:** Illustrated buying guide for the farming industry.

26581 ■ *Fastline—Kansas Farm Edition*
Pub: Fastline
Contact: Heather Baumgardner, Sales Mgr
E-mail: hbaumgardner@fastline.com
Released: Monthly. **Price:** $12; $18 two years; $36 Canada and Mexico; $85 other countries. **Description:** Illustrated buying guide for the farming industry.

26582 ■ *Fastline—Kentucky Farm Edition*
Pub: Fastline
Contact: Jim Cheyne, Sales Mgr
E-mail: jcheyne@fastline.com
Released: Monthly. **Price:** $12; $18 two years; $36 Canada and Mexico; $85 other countries. **Description:** Illustrated buying guide for the farming industry.

26583 ■ *Fastline—Mid-Atlantic Farm Edition*
Pub: Fastline
Contact: William G. Howard, Sales Mgr
Released: Monthly. **Price:** $12; $18 two years; $36 Canada and Mexico; $85 other countries. **Description:** Illustrated buying guide for the farming industry.

26584 ■ *Fastline—Mid-South Farm Edition*
Pub: Fastline
Contact: Heather Baumgardner, Sales Mgr
Released: Monthly. **Price:** $12; $18 two years; $36 Canada and Mexico; $85 other countries. **Description:** Illustrated buying guide for the farming industry.

26585 ■ *Fastline—Minnesota Farm Edition*
Pub: Fastline
Contact: Jim Strause, Sales Mgr
E-mail: jstrause@fastline.com
Released: Monthly. **Price:** $12; $18 two years; $36 Canada and Mexico; $85 other countries. **Description:** Illustrated buying guide for the farming industry.

26586 ■ *Fastline Missouri Farm Edition*
Pub: Fastline
Contact: Jim Cheyne, Sales Mgr
Released: Monthly. **Price:** $12; $18 two years; $36 Canada and Mexico; $85 other countries. **Description:** Illustrated buying guide for the farming industry.

26587 ■ *Fastline—Nebraska Farm Edition*
Pub: Fastline
Contact: Jim Strause, Sales Mgr
E-mail: jstrause@fastline.com
Released: Monthly. **Price:** $12; $18 two years; $36 Canada and Mexico; $85 other countries. **Description:** Illustrated buying guide for the farming industry.

26588 ■ *Fastline—Northeast Farm Edition*
Pub: Fastline
Contact: Jim Cheyne, Sales Mgr
Released: Monthly. **Price:** $12 ; $18 two years; $36 Canada and Mexico; $85 other countries. **Description:** Illustrated buying guide for the farming industry.

26589 ■ *Fastline Ohio Farm Edition*
Pub: Fastline
Contact: Jim Cheyne, Sales Mgr
Released: Monthly. **Price:** $12; $18 two years; $36 Canada and Mexico; $85 other countries. **Description:** Illustrated buying guide for the farming industry.

26590 ■ *Fastline—Oklahoma Farm Edition*
Pub: Fastline
Contact: Heather Baumgardner, Sales Mgr
Released: Monthly. **Price:** $12; $18 two years; $36 Canada and Mexico; $85 other countries. **Description:** Illustrated buying guide for the farming industry.

26591 ■ *Fastline—Rocky Mountain Farm Edition*
Pub: Fastline
Contact: Jim Strause, Sales Mgr
Released: Monthly. **Price:** $12; $18 two years; $36 Canada and Mexico; $85 other countries. **Description:** Illustrated buying guide for the farming industry.

26592 ■ *Fastline—Southeast Farm Edition*
Pub: Fastline
Contact: Jim Cheyne, Sales Mgr
Released: Monthly. **Price:** $12; $18 two years Edition 36; $36 Canada and Mexico; $85 other countries. **Description:** Illustrated buying guide for the farming industry.

26593 ■ *Fastline—Tennessee Farm Edition*
Pub: Fastline
Contact: Jim Cheyne, Sales Mgr
Released: Monthly. **Price:** $12; $18 two years; $36 Canada and Mexico; $85 other countries. **Description:** Illustrated buying guide for the farming industry.

26594 ■ *Fastline—Texas Farm Edition*
Pub: Fastline
Contact: Heather Baumgardner, Sales Mgr
E-mail: hbaumgardner@fastline.com
Released: Monthly. **Price:** $12; $18 two years; $36 Canada and Mexico; $85 other countries. **Description:** Illustrated buying guide for the farming industry.

26595 ■ *Fastline—Wisconsin Farm Edition*
Pub: Fastline
Contact: Rick McKay, Sales Mgr
Released: Monthly. **Price:** $12; $18 two years; $36 Canada and Mexico; $85 other countries. **Description:** Illustrated buying guide for the farming industry.

26596 ■ *Grainews*
Pub: Agricore United
Contact: Andy Sirski, Editorial Dir.
E-mail: andy@fbcpublishing.com
Released: 17/year (plus specials). **Price:** $33.50 Canadian farmers/retired farmers; $30.50 U.S. farmers; $79 outside Canada and U.S. **Description:** A "how-to" paper for Western Canadian farmers and their families.

26597 ■ *Journal of International Food and Agribusiness Marketing*
Pub: The Haworth Press Inc.
Contact: Erdener Kaynak Ph.D., Editor-in-Chief
E-mail: k9x@psu.edu
Released: Bimonthly. **Price:** $75 USA; $150 institutions USA; $320 libraries agencies, USA; $101 Canada; $203 institutions, Canada Canada; $432 libraries agencies, Canada; $109 other countries; $218 institutions, other countries Canada; $464 libraries agencies, other countries. **Description:** Journal studying food and agribusiness marketing systems in a variety of socioeconomic and political systems around the world.

26598 ■ *Journal of Vegetable Crop Production*
Pub: The Haworth Press Inc.

Contact: Bill Cohen Ph.D., Publisher
E-mail: vrusso-usda@lane-ag.org
Ed: Vincent M. Russo, PhD, Editor, vrusso-usda@lane-ag.org. **Released:** Biannual (2 issues per volume). **Description:** Journal of research about the production of vegetable crops.

26599 ■ *The Leader for Agriculture*
Pub: NYFEA—The Association for Educating Agricultural Leaders
Ed: Gordon Stone, Editor, gordonstone@nyfea.org. **Released:** Semiannual. **Price:** $15, individuals. **Description:** Serves as a communications link between state associations. Provides information on state and national educational programs, activities, and meetings. Recurring features include interviews, reports of meetings, and news of educational opportunities.

26600 ■ *Pulse Newsletter*
Pub: Saskatchewan Pulse Corp.
Contact: Donald Jaques, Administrator
Released: Bimonthly. **Price:** $10.70, U.S. and Canada. **Description:** Provides information on the Saskatchewan pulse crop development board, as well as research and marketing of pulses. Recurring features include news of research, a calendar of events, and reports of meetings.

26601 ■ *Weekly Outlook*
Pub: University of Illinois at Urbana-Champaign
Contact: Darrel Good, Coordinator
Released: Weekly (Mon.), 50/year. **Price:** $50. **Description:** Anticipates, reports, and interprets current market information, supply, demand, and price outlook for agricultural products, including corn, soybeans, wheat, cattle, and hogs.

VIDEOCASSETTES/AUDIOCASSETTES

26602 ■ *The Agricultural Marketplace*
Modern Education Services
3645 Crooks
Troy, MI 48084
Ph:(248)816-5050
Free: 800-243-6877
Fax: (248)816-9119
Description: Provides information on livestock futures and options in an easily understood language. **Availability:** VHS.

TRADE SHOWS AND CONVENTIONS

26603 ■ Kansas Agri-Business Expo
Kansas Grain and Feed Association
816 SW Tyler
Topeka, KS 66612
Ph:(785)234-0461
Fax: (785)234-2930
URL: http://www.kansasag.org
Released: Annual. **Audience:** Grain elevator owners and managers, fertilizer and chemical dealers, grain brokers, and commodity merchants. **Principal Exhibits:** Fertilizer and chemical manufacturers equipment, distributors, grain and feed related equipment, related service firms, and agriculture software companies.

26604 ■ Mid-South Farm and Gin Supply Exhibit
Southern Cotton Ginners Association
874 Cotton Gin Pl.
Memphis, TN 38106
Ph:(901)947-3104
Fax: (901)947-3103
Co. E-mail: carmen.griffin@southerncottonginners.org
URL: http://www.southerncottonginners.org
Released: Annual. **Audience:** Agribusiness professionals. **Principal Exhibits:** Agricultural equipment, supplies and services.

26605 ■ National Custom Applicator Exposition

Agribusiness Association of Iowa
900 Des Moines St.
Des Moines, IA 50309
Ph:(515)262-8323
Free: 800-383-1682
Fax: (515)262-8960
URL: http://www.agribiz.org
Released: Annual. **Audience:** Custom applicators of agricultural fertilizers and agrichemicals. **Principal Exhibits:** Agrichemicals, fertilizers, spray equipment tanks, agriplanes, and agricomputer and flotation equipment.

26606 ■ Spokane Ag Expo

Spokane Regional Chamber of Commerce
AG Bureau
801 W. Riverside, Ste. 100
Spokane, WA 99201
Ph:(509)624-1393
Fax: (509)747-0077
Co. E-mail: info@chamber.spokane.net
URL: http://www.spokanechamber.org
Released: Annual. **Audience:** Farmers, ranchers, agribusiness professionals, and general public. **Principal Exhibits:** Farm machinery, technology, and services.

26607 ■ VIV Poultry Yutav

Royal Dutch Jaarbeurs
Jaarbeursplein 6
NL-3521 AL Utrecht, Netherlands
Ph:31 30 2955911
Fax: 31 30 2940379
Co. E-mail: info@jaarbeursutrecht.nl
URL: http://www.jaarbeursutrecht.nl
Released: Annual. **Principal Exhibits:** Poultry farming, breeding, feed, and processing.

26608 ■ World AgExpo

International Agri-Center, Inc.
4450 S Laspine St.
PO Box 1475
Tulare, CA 93274-9539
Ph:(559)688-1751
Free: 800-999-9186
Fax: (559)686-5065
Co. E-mail: info@farmshow.org
URL: http://www.farmshow.org
Released: Annual. **Audience:** Farmers, dairymen and international buyers. **Principal Exhibits:** Agricultural equipment, supplies, and services. **Dates and Locations:** 2007 Feb 13-15, Tulare, CA.

CONSULTANTS

26609 ■ Agland Investment Services Inc.

900 Larkspur Landing Cir., Ste. 205
Larkspur, CA 94939
Ph:(415)461-5820
Fax: (415)461-5821
Co. E-mail: agland@aglandinvest.com
URL: http://www.aglandinvest.com

E-mail: agland@aglandinvest.com
Scope: An agribusiness consulting and investment company which provides a wide range of economic, marketing, technical and investment consultation to agricultural producers, agribusiness companies and government agencies in the Western United States and in many countries around the world. The firm tends to concentrate on high-value specialty crops, including fruits, vegetables and cut flowers.

26610 ■ Agpro Inc.

859 FM 1508
PO Box 100
Paris, TX 75462
Ph:(903)785-5531
Free: 800-527-1030
Fax: (903)784-7895
Co. E-mail: agpro@neto.com
URL: http://www.agprousa.com

E-mail: agpro@neto.com
Scope: Offers agricultural engineering design consultation for animal raising facilities including dairies, beef feedlots, swine operations and embryo transplant facilities. Services include land utilization, plot plans, building design, equipment selection, integration with other farm and commercial activities, pollution control systems, genetic engineering systems and computer applications. Also offers computer control and automation consultation, as well as consultation for waste management and control for food processing plants. Expertise in dairy, swine manure handling and their processing needs. **Special Services:** Agpro®.

26611 ■ Agri-Business Consultants Inc.

911 Edison Ave.
Lansing, MI 48910-3339
Ph:(517)482-7506
Fax: (517)482-7506
Co. E-mail: maotto@ameritech.net

E-mail: maotto@ameritech.net
Scope: Agricultural consultants providing fertilizer recommendations, crop protection recommendations, soil fertility and crop protection consulting, irrigation scheduling, educational sessions, contract research, and expert witness services. Industries served: farmers and ag chemical companies.

26612 ■ Agri Business Group Inc.

3905 Vincennes Rd., Ste. 402
Indianapolis, IN 46268
Ph:(317)415-0500
Free: 800-285-8859
Fax: (317)415-0501
Co. E-mail: information@abginc.com
URL: http://www.abginc.com

E-mail: information@abginc.com
Scope: Provides custom-designed training programs in the following areas: sales, sales management, coaching, market research, strategic planning, and mergers and acquisition consulting. Also provides technical training and product launch support in the areas of agricultural inputs, equipment, distribution, and technology.

26613 ■ Agri-Personnel

5120 Old Bill Cook Rd.
Atlanta, GA 30349-0319
Ph:(404)768-5701
Fax: (404)768-5705
Scope: Agribusiness consultants active in executive/professional/technical recruitment and placement, and in mergers, acquisitions, and divestitures in various industries including dairy, feed, food, fertilizer, farm chemicals, poultry and egg, animal health, and pulp and paper.

26614 ■ AgriCapital Corp.

1410 Broadway, Ste. 1802
New York, NY 10018
Ph:(212)944-9500
Fax: (212)944-9525
Co. E-mail: info@agricapital.com
URL: http://www.agricapital.com

E-mail: info@agricapital.com
Scope: Provides investment banking services for agribusiness clients in the United States and abroad, including financial consulting, debt and equity placements and joint ventures, and mergers and acquisitions. Industries served: agribusiness and food companies. **Publications:** "Seedworld".

26615 ■ Agricultural Consulting Services Inc.

1634 Monroe Ave.
Rochester, NY 14618-9769
Free: 877-310-1100
Fax: 717-315-2200
Co. E-mail: acs@acsoffice.com
URL: http://www.acsoffice.com

E-mail: acs@acsoffice.com
Scope: Provides farm business management services including business and economic analysis, computer hardware and software installation and training, and enterprise budgets and analysis. Also offers crop production management, monitoring, and advises in the areas of crop nutrition, pest management, weed control, tillage practices, and irrigation scheduling. Environmental work includes complete analytical and monitoring services for soil, waste-water, sludge, and groundwater. Serves farms and agribusiness. **Publications:** "Forage - Timing of First Cutting".

26616 ■ Agricultural Engineering Associates

1000 Promontory Dr.
PO Box 4
Uniontown, KS 66779
Ph:(620)756-1000
Free: 800-499-5893
Fax: (620)756-4600
URL: http://www.agengineering.com
Scope: Agricultural engineering consultants offering guidance on the design of swine production facilities, beef feedlots, dairy facilities, waste management systems, soil and water conservation design and resource development including watershed planning, dam design and irrigation supply dam design, grain and feed storage, drying and processing facilities, irrigation system evaluation and design, rural water district system design, land leveling design for irrigation and drainage and land surveying. Industries served: production and commercial agriculture, research, demonstration and test facilities, government agencies and in-house materials testing laboratories.

26617 ■ Agricultural Investment Associates Inc.

1000 Skokie Blvd., Ste. 358
Wilmette, IL 60091
Ph:(847)251-8822
Fax: (847)251-8876
Co. E-mail: johncottingham@att.net

E-mail: johncottingham@att.net
Scope: Investment consultant to domestic and foreign institutions, corporations and individuals covering investments in farms, ranches and agribusinesses. Services include feasibility studies, appraisals, management, analysis and negotiations.

26618 ■ AgriSolutions Inc.

31832 Delhi Rd.
Brighton, IL 62012-9900
Ph:(618)372-3000
Free: 800-829-5555
Fax: (618)372-4000
Co. E-mail: internetmail@agrisolutions.com
URL: http://www.agrisolutions.com

E-mail: internetmail@agrisolutions.com
Scope: Offers a broad range of services in the business of asset management, consulting, investment acquisition, marketing, planning, financial analysis, resource analysis, accounting, recordkeeping, tax preparation, tax consulting and software. Offers opportunities to all facets of the agricultural spectrum including farmers, non-farm entrepreneurs, financial institutions and agribusinesses. Clients range from local farmers to multinational agribusinesses. **Seminars:** Top Producers, Best Managed Farms Conference, 2004. **Special Services:** AgriSolutions®.

26619 ■ AgriTech Inc.

2775 Oakridge Ct.
Columbus, OH 43221
Ph:(614)488-0841
Co. E-mail: agritech@iwaynet.net

E-mail: agritech@iwaynet.net
Scope: A consulting research organization dedicated to serving agribusiness; food, beverage, and dairy processing industries; and government agencies. The client's technology base is used to identify new markets, improve existing markets, develop targeted business and technology plans, and improve operational activities. Specializes in market research, value-added market assessments, feasibility studies, and the evaluation of business and technology plans and strategies. In addition, the firm matches agricultural resources with potential markets to identify value-added products that can promote economic growth.

26620 ■ AGVISE Laboratories Inc.
Hwy. 15
PO Box 510
Northwood, ND 58267
Ph:(701)587-6010
Fax: (701)587-6013
Co. E-mail: agvise@polarcomm.com
URL: http://www.agviselabs.com

E-mail: agvise@polarcomm.com
Scope: Offers analytical services to agriculture and related support companies in crop production, and pest management. Other Agvise services include GLP compliant soil and water characterization. Serves private industries as well as government agencies. **Seminars:** Soil Fertility Seminars. **Special Services:** Maintains AGVISOR(C), a computer delivery system of analytical data that transmits and stores analytical data and has soil fertility recommendations for the North Central region of the U.S. and Central Canada.

26621 ■ Ascheman Associates Inc.
2921 Beverly Dr.
Des Moines, IA 50322
Ph:(515)276-7371
Fax: (515)276-8707
Co. E-mail: rascheman@aol.com

E-mail: rascheman@aol.com
Scope: Provides consulting, expert witness and related agribusiness services to agricultural-oriented businesses including: producers; agrochemical; fertilizer, seed and equipment companies; the insurance industry; the legal profession and government agencies. **Seminars:** Value of Grid Soil Sampling; Liming by the Grid System; Integrated Crop Management Services.

26622 ■ C.C. Canada Forestry Co.
819 Mill St.
PO Box 337
Camden, SC 29020
Ph:(803)432-9780
Fax: (803)432-0232
Co. E-mail: cclandman@aol.com

E-mail: cclandman@aol.com
Scope: Provides consulting services in forest management and appraisal. Services include financial counsel especially in the agricultural field and timberland; and aid in securing loans with major insurance companies for agricultural and agri-business loans. Also advises large corporations, as well as individuals, on real estate investments and acquisitions. Works with government agencies. **Seminars:** Attended continuing education workshops for appraisers in 2000 as well as real estate and forestry.

26623 ■ Chilson's Management Controls Inc.
9645 Arrow Rte., Ste. L
Rancho Cucamonga, CA 91730
Ph:(909)980-5338
Fax: (909)987-3154
Co. E-mail: sales@chilson.com
URL: http://www.chilson.com

E-mail: sales@chilson.com
Scope: Active in egg production, processing, and marketing management consulting. Provides turnkey computer systems for the poultry industry and agribusiness, including hardware, software, installation, training, and continuing support. Software includes flock records, egg processing, perishable distribution, feed mill, and all accounting packages (20 systems). Industries served: poultry, feed, and perishable distribution. **Seminars:** Offers a semi-annual computer workshop. **Special Services:** Largest database for egg production (performance and costs) available in world (over 50,000,000 layers); perishable distribution, poultry processing, feed mill accounting software and flock records software. Softwares on Distribution/ Processing, General Accounting & Production also provided.

26624 ■ Clark Consulting International Inc.
435 Root St.
PO Box 68
Park Ridge, IL 60068-0068

Ph:(847)836-5100
Fax: (847)792-7565
Co. E-mail: warren.clark@ccimarketing.com
URL: http://www.ccimarketing.com

E-mail: warren.clark@ccimarketing.com
Scope: Multipurposed agrimarketing communications consulting firm including public relations, market research, advertising and direct mail expertise. Serves the seed, chemical, machinery, computer and agricultural futures industries. Internet promotion and product marketing in agriculture. **Publications:** W.E. Clark, et al, have had more than 1,000 technical/ product publicity articles published in the major agricultural magazines. **Seminars:** Managing Your Consulting Practice Using Computers; Winning Ag PR Programs That Produce Results; Ag Targeted Direct Mail Niche Marketing. **Special Services:** Maintains a comprehensive agricultural database for magazine editors, farm newspaper editors and farm broadcasters, and a demographically profiled farmer database of 90,000 computer owners.

26625 ■ Custom Forestry
16798 Claridon Troy Rd.
Burton, OH 44021-9606
Ph:(440)834-1680
Fax: (440)834-1680
Scope: Offers forestry consulting services that include forest management, timber sales, valuations, timber trespass valuations and litigation, advice on federal assistance programs, Christmas tree plantation management, multiple use land management, shelter-belts, silviculture, and insect management.

26626 ■ DPRA Inc.
200 Research Dr.
Manhattan, KS 66503
Ph:(785)539-3565
Fax: (785)539-5353
Co. E-mail: info@dpra.com
URL: http://www.dpra.com

E-mail: info@dpra.com
Scope: Consultants on a variety of environmental problems and situations. Experience includes agriculture, agribusiness, water pollution control, and hazardous and municipal waste management. Activities emphasize litigation support, data management, and information services, as well as international programs. Serves private industries as well as government agencies.

26627 ■ Eastern Laboratory Service Associates
517 N George St.
York, PA 17404-2765
Ph:(717)846-4953
Fax: (717)846-4986
Scope: Provides technical counsel on chemical and microbiological testing, evaluation and quality control services primarily for environmental, agribusiness, feed industry and food manufacturing. Offers consultation, advisory services, research and development on technical problems, new product formulation, and product or process improvement. Also performs general testing of refrigerants, food products, solid waste, water and wastewater for compliance with EPA, DER, FDA and other governmental agencies.

26628 ■ Ben Felt & Associates
120 N Elm St.
Escondido, CA 92025
Ph:(760)480-0785
Scope: Advises lenders, owners and managers of agricultural enterprises on matters of financial administration. Also provides expertise in structuring international merger and acquisition opportunities. Concentrates in the following areas: investment capital; expert witness testimony; general financial management advice; preparation of cash flow projections and budgets; provides problem loan administration and negotiates debt restructure; and analyzes the financial impact that economic and political trends may have upon the enterprise. **Special Services:** Custom designed analytical software for agribusinesses; development of agricultural templates for lenders; development of investment analysis programs for clients.

26629 ■ J.H. Hare & Associates Ltd.
1-270 Roslyn Rd.
Winnipeg, MB, Canada R3L 0H3
Ph:(204)477-0066
Free: 800-661-4273
Fax: (204)477-8301
Co. E-mail: info@hareman.com
URL: http://www.hareman.com

E-mail: info@hareman.com
Scope: Agribusiness management consultants with extensive experience in: animal nutrition and feed formulation, agrimarketing, technical services to agribusiness, agricultural promotion, and sales and sales training. Serves the agriculture and food and beverage industries, as well as government agencies.

26630 ■ Indiana Design Consortium Inc.
416 Main St.
PO Box 180
Lafayette, IN 47902-0180
Ph:(765)423-5469
Fax: (765)423-4440
Co. E-mail: idc@idc-marketing.com
URL: http://www.idc-marketing.com

E-mail: idc@idc-marketing.com
Scope: Provides marketing and marketing communications services for industrial, service oriented, and agribusiness clients. Also involved in industrial product design for industry and agribusiness.

26631 ■ INTRANCO Inc.
1825 I St. NW, Ste. 400
Washington, DC 20006-5403
Ph:(202)429-6820
Fax: (703)978-8335
Scope: Provides management consulting for agribusinesses, primarily enterprises in the Third World. Works with private entrepreneurs and government-sponsored institutions. Has experience with livestock, fruits, vegetables, field crops, small animals, fisheries and poultry. Engages in the international trade of agricultural equipment, machinery and raw products. Industries served: food and feed industries and government agencies. **Seminars:** Mold Inhibitors in the 1990 Decade; Agribusiness in West Africa- Is It Possible?; Poultry in Nigeria- The Challenge.

26632 ■ Arden Kashishian
5044 B N Wishon
Fresno, CA 93704
Ph:(559)226-4253
Fax: (559)226-5376
Co. E-mail: ardenkash@aol.com

E-mail: ardenkash@aol.com
Scope: Agricultural consultant offering on-site feasibility and development studies as well as advice on basic farm practices, primarily for production agriculture. Industries served: all agriculture and agricultural exports/imports. **Seminars:** Table Grape Workshop, Egypt, 1995; Dried Fruit Workshop, Macedonia and Armenia, 1993; Cherry Production Workshop, Bulgaria, 1993; and Tomato Post-Harvest Workshop, Egypt, 1993; Tomato Production in Argentina-Onions in Uruguay, Melons in Brazil.

26633 ■ Keck & Co.
410 Walsh Rd.
Atherton, CA 94027
Ph:(650)854-9588
Fax: (650)854-7240
Co. E-mail: info@kecko.com
URL: http://www.keckco.com

E-mail: info@kecko.com
Scope: Conducts management services nationally, focusing on strategic research, marketing, and planning for businesses involved in the packaging container- and equipment industry, food processing, and related technology suppliers. Develops feasibility studies to assess the possible success or failure of entering a new market, introducing a new product or product line extension, or starting a new venture; primary market research to determine what motivates

consumers/buyers, and best "positioning" for product in the marketplace; business development programs; promotional programs to differentiate client company from competitors; vertical/horizontal marketing audits; technology acceptance assessments; due diligence for investors; and management assistance with investment issues. **Seminars:** Taking the Failure Factors Out of New Product Introductions; Introduction to Marketing for Food Manufacturing Personnel; New Product Development Workshop: Plans and Elements; Starting Your Own Consulting Business; The Marketing Plan. **Special Services:** Conducts database searches for venture and expansion capital for packaging companies and companies introducing packaging functional foods. Maintains 1600-record proprietary database of international and North American magazines available to clients for public relations placements. Serves as basis of customized press lists and analysis of media for market entry and promotional purpose.

26634 ■ Daniel F. Mayer
5206 Pear Butte
Yakima, WA 98901
Ph:(509)452-6555
Fax: (509)452-6555
Co. E-mail: bugoff95@aol.com

E-mail: bugoff95@aol.com
Scope: Provides consultant services dealing with entomology (insects). Activities include providing pest control recommendations, research with new pesticides and chemical testing and expert witness services. Industries served are growers, agribusiness firms, chemical companies developing pesticides for agriculture, government agencies, and attorneys. **Publications:** Pollinator Protection: A Bee and Pesticide Handbook, Wicwas Press. **Seminars:** Conducts seminars on insect pests of agriculture.

26635 ■ McKinnon, Allen & Associates Western Ltd.
1115 46th Ave. SE
Calgary, AB, Canada T2G 2A5
Ph:(403)228-4345
Fax: (403)228-3767
Scope: The firms multidisciplinary work team provides independent opinions and practical solutions to a variety of problems in the areas of agribusiness, farm and ranch management, agricultural environmental consulting and rural land use. Specific areas of expertise are as follows: financial advisory consulting, agricultural environmental monitoring, general agricultural management consulting, economic evaluation, land use planning, land valuation, surface rights disputes and expropriations, farm management for absentee owners, and damage claims.

26636 ■ Micro-Macro International Inc.
183 Paradise Blvd., Ste. 108
Athens, GA 30607
Ph:(706)548-4557
Free: 800-837-8664
Fax: (706)548-4891
URL: http://www.mmilabs.com
Scope: Offers consultation on agricultural production field, container, greenhouse and hydroponic systems. Provides analytical services for the analysis of water, waste water, soil, plant tissue and other biological substances for their element content. Industries served: agricultural producers, research institutes and individuals, fertilizer manufacturers and government agencies. **Publications:** Plant Analysis Handbook III: A Practical Sampling, Preparation, Analysis and Interpretation Guide; Kjeldahl Method for Nitrogen (N) Determination; Plant Nutrition Manual. **Seminars:** Offers seminars on techniques of soil testing and plant analysis and laboratory instruction on methods of analysis.

26637 ■ Miller Agricultural Consulting Services
10967 County Rd. 19
Lawton, ND 58345
Ph:(701)655-3591
Co. E-mail: jd7020@polarcomm.com

E-mail: jd7020@polarcomm.com

Scope: Agricultural consultant works with clients in the area of machine design and safety as it pertains to machines used in the production of agricultural crops. Crops include wheat, barley, corn, sunflowers, sugar beets, and potatoes. Special emphasis on farm safety issues, crop drying sysems, and forensic evaluation.

26638 ■ J. Stewart Murray
639 Borebank St.
Winnipeg, MB, Canada R3N 1G1
Ph:(204)488-3885
Fax: (204)489-0129
Scope: Marketing and sales consultants for agriindustrial automotive. Industries served: agriculture-agribusiness, industrial supply trades, and government agencies in Canada.

26639 ■ G.V. Olsen Associates
123 Picketts Ridge Rd.
Redding, CT 06896
Ph:(203)938-4188
Fax: (203)938-4186
Scope: Provides agribusiness research, analysis, and report writing services, focusing on farm input products such as seed, fertilizer, chemicals, and machinery, as well as production, storage, transportation, and marketing of food and fiber products. Also identifies and evaluates new market and product opportunities. Industries served: agribusiness, biotechnology, food, and agriculture. **Publications:** Olsen's Agribusiness Report, a newsletter; other special reports on food testing technology and competitive intelligence systems. **Seminars:** Conducts seminars on food safety.

26640 ■ Pest Pros Inc.
10086 1st St.
PO Box 188
Plainfield, WI 54966-0188
Ph:(715)335-4046
Fax: (715)335-4746
Co. E-mail: consulting@pestprosinc.com
URL: http://www.pestprosinc.com

E-mail: consulting@pestprosinc.com
Scope: Offers agricultural consulting involving fertility and pesticide recommendations, soil microbe assay and contract research.

26641 ■ SEA-ARM Consulting Associates
640 Line St.
Hollister, CA 95023
Ph:(831)637-1468
Fax: (831)637-4377
Scope: Offers expertise regarding financial restructuring (including start-ups and spin-offs) and technology transfer, relating to agriculture production, processing, and marketing. Special emphasis on cooperatives. Industries served: agriculture, agribusiness, cooperatives, and government. **Seminars:** Starting a New Business; Strawberry Production, Organic farm productions, marketing. **Special Services:** All marketing services.

26642 ■ Sobek Engineering
51492 Sobek Rd., E
PO Box 7
Edwall, WA 99008-9703
Ph:(509)236-2371
Fax: (509)236-2426
Co. E-mail: sobekeng@aol.com

E-mail: sobekeng@aol.com
Scope: Provides consulting engineering service in the food processing field and associated agribusiness areas. Has served in the frozen food, flour milling, and freeze-drying areas, as well as agricultural and industrial accident investigation. Also conducts noise surveys and noise abatement engineering.

26643 ■ Southern Plantations Group Inc.
2410 Westgate Dr., Ste. 101
PO Box 70967
Albany, GA 31708
Ph:(229)439-0012
Fax: (229)883-8881

Co. E-mail: spg@splantations.com
URL: http://www.splantations.com

E-mail: spg@splantations.com
Scope: Provides appraisal and counseling services for investors and lenders in farm land, timberland and agribusiness projects across the Southern U.S.; and farm planning, budgeting, management, and accounting services for farmers near its area of activity. Specific services include establishing and reviewing investment criteria, investment selection and negotiation, alternative investment analysis and review, management and operations audits, appraisals, problem investments, and management of property investment and divestment. Industries served: investors, lenders, government agencies, agribusinesses in production, agriculture, input, and marketing sectors. U.S., southeast Asia and Latin America.

26644 ■ Sterling Executive Counselors Inc.
501 S Pokegama Ave.
Grand Rapids, MN 55744-3820
Free: 888-326-4421
Fax: (218)326-4430
Scope: Public affairs and management consultants offering reputation and issue management, issue management, public relations, and government relations counsel. Industries served: agribusiness, pet, gaming, forest products, natural resources, and energy.

26645 ■ Trenna R. Grabowski CPA Ltd.
Twelfth and Broadway
PO Box 38
Du Bois, IL 62831
Ph:(618)787-4430
Fax: (618)787-4460
Co. E-mail: trenna@theagcpa.com
URL: http://www.theagcpa.com

E-mail: trenna@theagcpa.com
Scope: Taxation and general business consultant offering financial management, strategic planning, and budgeting for agribusiness and small and family-owned firms. Heavily involved in tax planning and research. Consulting on choosing hardware and software for agribusiness. Related experience in personal financial planning, tax planning, and projections. Speaking and teaching a speciality, seminars, workshops, and conference presentations available. **Seminars:** Agribusiness Tax Seminar; Tax Planning; Incorporating the Farm; Alternative Forms of Business Organization; Estate and Financial Planning; The Farm Business Plan.

26646 ■ Kenneth D. Weiss
7823 Mystic View Ct.
Derwood, MD 20855-2275
Ph:(301)947-8150
Fax: (301)869-8992
Co. E-mail: Plansolv@aol.com
URL: http://www.plans-and-solutions.com

E-mail: Plansolv@aol.com
Scope: International trade and business consultant specializing in agribusiness, organizing import/export businesses, import procurement, export marketing, import/export procedures, international trade policies, and international licensing and investment. Serves small and large clients including American and foreign importers, exporters, investors and governments. **Publications:** Building an import/export business, 3rd Edition, 2002. **Seminars:** Exporting to the United States.

26647 ■ Ralph E. Williams & Associates
2940 State Rd. 25 N
Lafayette, IN 47905-8804
Ph:(765)429-5576
Co. E-mail: rewjmw@insightbb.com

E-mail: rewjmw@insightbb.com
Scope: Offers services in forensic entomology, use of insects in crime scene investigations. Serves prosecuting attorneys, law enforcement agencies, state and local coroners and medical examiners. Also provides

training and consulting services in livestock and poultry pest control and public health pest control. Serves agribusiness, local and state public health agencies, and individuals. **Seminars:** Forensic Entomology Training Session; Livestock and Poultry Pest Management.

COMPUTERIZED DATABASES

26648 ■ *AGRICOLA Database*
U.S. National Agricultural Library
Abraham Lincoln Bldg.
10301 Baltimore Ave.
Beltsville, MD 20705
Ph:(301)504-5755
Fax: (301)504-6927
Co. E-mail: webmaster@nal.usda.gov
URL: http://www.nalusda.gov
Description: Contains more than 3.5 million records from journal literature, government reports, serials, monographs, theses, patents, audiovisual resources, and technical reports in agriculture and related areas that have been acquired by the National Agricultural Library (NAL) as well as citations contributed by cooperating institutions. Includes agricultural economics and rural sociology, agricultural production, animal sciences, chemistry, entomology, food and human nutrition, forestry, natural resources, pesticides, plant science, soils and fertilizers, and water resources. Also covers related areas such as biology and biotechnology, botany, ecology, and natural history. Contributing agencies include land grant institutions, the NAL Food and Nutrition Information Center (abstracts available from 1973 to date), and the Arid Lands Information Center. Corresponds in part to *Bibliography of Agriculture.* **Availability:** Online: Thomson Dialog, DIMDI (Deutsches Institut fuer Medizinische Dokumentation und Information), Online Computer Library Center Inc. (OCLC), STN International, NISC International Inc., Ovid Technologies Inc., CSA, Community of Science Inc., Thomson Dialog, EBSCO Publishing; CD-ROM: Ovid Technologies Inc;Magnetic Tape: Ovid Technologies Inc;Batch: Nerac Inc. **Type:** Bibliographic.

26649 ■ *CID Service*
U.S. Department of Agriculture (USDA)
1400 Independence Ave. SW
Washington, DC 20250
Ph:(202)720-2791
Fax: (202)690-2164
URL: http://www.usda.gov
Description: Contains 467 categories of information prepared by the U.S. Department of Agriculture and its agencies. Includes national and state agricultural statistics from *Crop and Livestock Reports*; reports on world agricultural trade from the Foreign Agricultural Service; *Outlook and Situation Summaries* from the Economic Research Service; commodity analyses from the Cooperative Extension Services; synopses of USDA-sponsored research; daily market news reports; buy and sell information from the Commodity Credit Corporation; various newsletters; and individual state weekly crop weather reports. Provides a calendar of meetings, conferences, and exhibitions of interest to the USDA, agricultural agencies, and related organizations (e.g., the American Farm Bureau, land-grant universities with agricultural extension services). Includes the name of the event, sponsoring organization, date, location, and speakers. Also provides a directory of food and nutrition experts (e.g., dieticians, nutritionists) with USDA, land-grant universities, or state extension services; a bibliography of U.S. government publications on food and nutrition; the complete text of national and regional press releases; transcripts of press conferences; testimony from Congressional hearings; and speeches by the Secretary of Agriculture. Contains citations, with abstracts, to more than 28,000 social science publications on contemporary North Africa. Covers books, theses, reports, and journal articles. Includes country, time span, and names of important people cited. **Availability:** Online: Martin Worldwide Inc. **Type:** Full text; Directory; Bibliographic.

26650 ■ *Farm Bureau ACRES*
American Farm Bureau
600 Maryland Ave. SW, Ste. 800
Washington, DC 20024
Ph:(202)406-3600
Fax: (202)406-3604
URL: http://www.fb.org
Description: Covers agricultural marketing and related topics. Comprises the following nine files:; Commodity Futures Quotes—updated every 10 minutes.; ACRES Market Analysis—daily and weekly reports on major markets.; Marketing advice—specific ACRES recommendations.; Daily Executive News Watch—daily brief news digests covering national and international events.; USDA Market Wire Reports—more than 800 daily and/or weekly reports released by USDA.; Market Advisory Service—optional advisory service focusing on grain and livestock; produced by AgriVisor Services, Inc.; Smith Barney Market Information—market commentaries on grain, livestock,and other commodities.; Other ACRES reports on trends in the financial and fuel markets; daily weather reports for each agricultural crop and foreign weather; grain and livestock price forecasts; local cash markets information; and general information. **Type:** Full text; Numeric.

COMPUTER SYSTEMS/ SOFTWARE

26651 ■ Red Hen Farming Systems, LLC
Farmer's Software Association (FSA)
425 John Deere Rd., 1 Upstairs
Ft. Collins, CO 80525
Ph:(970)484-9100
Fax: (970)484-9960
Co. E-mail: info@farmgis.com
URL: http://www.farmgis.com
Price: Contact Red Hen for product and Pricing. **Description:** Available for IBM computers and compatibles. System performs agricultural accounting and management functions.

LIBRARIES

26652 ■ Albany Historical Society, Inc. –Library/Special Collections
c/o Doyle Bechtelheimer
415 Grant
Sabetha, KS 66534
Ph:(913)284-3446.
URL: http://www.albanydays.org
Contact: Daryl Bechtelheimer, Pres.
Scope: Agricultural equipment, railroads one-room schools. **Services:** Library open to the public. **Holdings:** 200 books.

26653 ■ Alberta - Agriculture, Food and Rural Development–Business Management Innovations Branch–Library (5030)
5030 50th St., Ste. 201
Olds, AB, Canada T4H 1S1
Ph:(403)556-4240
Fax: (403)556-7545
URL: http://www.agric.gov.ab.ca/app21/rtw/index.jsp
Scope: Agriculture, economics, technology, agricultural economics, farm management, finance, computer. **Services:** Interlibrary loan. **Holdings:** Figures not available.

26654 ■ Alberta - Agriculture, Food and Rural Development–Crop Diversification Centre - South–Branch Library (SS 4)
SS 4
Brooks, AB, Canada T1R 1E6
Ph:(403)362-1300
Fax: (403)362-1306
Co. E-mail: shelley.barkley@gov.ab.ca
Scope: Plants, pathology, horticulture, entomology, special crops. **Services:** Interlibrary loan; copying; Library open to the public at librarian's discretion. **Holdings:** Figures not available.

26655 ■ Booz, Allen & Hamilton, Inc. –Research Services and Information Center
225 W. Wacker Dr., 17th Fl.
Chicago, IL 60606
Ph:(312)346-1900
Fax: (312)578-4615
URL: http://www.boozallen.com
Scope: Management, agribusiness, finance, marketing, manufacturing, retailing, information management, consumer products, health care, telecommunications, food retailing, consulting, electronic commerce. **Services:** Interlibrary loan; center not open to the public. **Holdings:** 5000 books; client reports; company Annual reports. **Subscriptions:** 300 serials.

26656 ■ Canada–Canadian Grain Commission–Library (303 M)
303 Main St., Rm. 801
Winnipeg, MB, Canada R3C 3G8
Ph:(204)983-0878
Fax: (204)983-6098
Co. E-mail: library@grainscanada.gc.ca
URL: http://www.grainscanada.gc.ca
Contact: Sean O'Hara, Libn.
Scope: Cereal chemistry, cereals, oilseeds, grain industry and trade, baking, brewing, milling. **Services:** Interlibrary loan; Reference; copying; SDI; Library open to the public for reference use only. **Holdings:** 5000 books; 10,000 bound periodical volumes; 1000 pamphlets; 1500 reports. **Subscriptions:** 300 journals and other serials; 10 newspapers.

26657 ■ Canada - Agriculture and Agri-Food Canada–Dairy and Swine Research and Development Centre Lennoxville–Library (2000)
2000 Rte. 108 E.
CP 90
Lennoxville, QC, Canada J1M 1Z3
Ph:(819)565-9174
Fax: (819)564-5507
Co. E-mail: gagnegigueres@em.agr.ca
Scope: Dairy cattle, pigs. **Services:** Interlibrary loan; Library provides limited on-site consultation to the public. **Holdings:** 5000 books. **Subscriptions:** 200 journals and other serials.

26658 ■ Cargill, Incorporated–Information Center
PO Box 9300
Minneapolis, MN 55440
Ph:(952)742-6498
Fax: (952)742-6062
Co. E-mail: peter_sidney@cargill.com
Contact: Peter Sidney, Asst. VP
Scope: Grain storage and handling, commodity trading, agribusiness, finance, marketing, biochemistry, hybrid corn breeding and genetics, animal feeding and nutrition, vegetable oil processing and chemistry, agricultural and food products, market research. **Services:** Center not open to the public. **Holdings:** 20,000 books; 500 bound periodical volumes; 250 other cataloged items; 10,000 internal research reports; 2000 general information files; 16,000 documents. **Subscriptions:** 1000 journals and other serials; 20 newspapers.

26659 ■ Delaware Valley College of Science and Agriculture–Joseph Krauskopf Memorial Library
700 E. Butler Ave.
Doylestown, PA 18901-2697
Ph:(215)489-2953
Fax: (215)230-2967
Co. E-mail: kupersmith@devalcol.edu
URL: http://www.devalcol.edu
Contact: Peter Kupersmith, Lib.Dir.
Scope: Agribusiness, agronomy, animal science, computer information systems management, dairy science, English literature, equine science, food industry, horticulture, ornamental horticulture, poultry husbandry, biology, chemistry, business administration. **Services:** Interlibrary loan; copying; Library open to the public for reference use only. **Holdings:** 58,000 volumes; 5652 bound periodical volumes; 2337 reels of microfilm; 90,532 microfiche. **Subscriptions:** 693 journals.

26660 ■ Illinois Agricultural Association–Illinois Farm Bureau Information Research Center
1701 Towanda Ave.
Box 2901
Bloomington, IL 61701
Ph:(309)557-2552
Fax: (309)557-3185
URL: http://www.ilfb.org/
Contact: Vince L. Sampson, Res.Mgr.
Scope: Agriculture - economics, marketing, cooperatives, management, insurance, environment. **Services:** Interlibrary loan; copying; subscriptions; Internet training; abstracting; Library open to the public for reference use only. **Holdings:** 5000 volumes; 100 microforms; 500 audio/visual materials. **Subscriptions:** 500 journals and other serials; 7 newspapers.

26661 ■ International Fertilizer Development Center–Travis P. Hignett Memorial Library
PO Box 2040
Muscle Shoals, AL 35662
Ph:(256)381-6600
Fax: (256)381-7408
Co. E-mail: jriley@ifdc.org
URL: http://www.ifdc.org/Library_Information/
Contact: Jean S. Riley, Sr.Libn.
Scope: Fertilizers, agricultural economics, nutrient management, agribusiness, training. **Services:** Interlibrary loan; literature searching; Library not open to the public. **Holdings:** 20,000 books; 4365 bound periodical volumes; 468 pamphlets; 337 AV programs; 20,000 patents. **Subscriptions:** 200 journals and other serials.

26662 ■ International Food Policy Research Institute–Library
2033 K St., NW
Washington, DC 20006
Ph:(202)862-5614
Fax: (202)467-4439
Co. E-mail: ifpri-library@cgiar.org
URL: http://www.ifpri.org/library/library_menu.asp
Contact: Luz Marina Alvare
Scope: Food policy and research, developmental economics, international trade, food security, agricultural economics and statistics, food safety. **Services:** Interlibrary loan; copying; Library open to the public by appointment. **Holdings:** 3000 books; 4000 research reports. **Subscriptions:** 120 journals and other serials.

26663 ■ Mississippi State University–Agricultural & Forestry Experiment Station–Delta Research and Extension Center (82 St)
82 Stoneville Rd.
PO Box 197
Stoneville, MS 38776
Ph:(662)686-3261
Fax: (662)686-7336
Co. E-mail: rhwatson@drec.msstate.edu
URL: http://www.msstate.edu/dept/drec
Contact: Rhonda H. Watson, Libn.
Scope: Agriculture, botany, agricultural economics, mathematics, agricultural engineering, meteorology. **Services:** Interlibrary loan; Library open to the public. **Holdings:** 14,500 books; 6000 bound periodical volumes; 348 reels of microfilm; 50,000 pamphlets. **Subscriptions:** 225 journals and other serials; 10 newspapers.

26664 ■ Pioneer Hi-Bred International, Inc. –Library Resources Group
7300 NW 62nd Ave.
PO Box 1004
Johnston, IA 50131-1004
Ph:(515)270-4199
Fax: (515)253-2184
Co. E-mail: Dana.Smith@pioneer.com
URL: http://www.pioneer.com
Contact: Dana Smith, Corp.Libn.
Scope: Agriculture, agribusiness, law, taxation, business. **Services:** Interlibrary loan; Library not open to the public. **Holdings:** 1430 books. **Subscriptions:** 299 journals and other serials.

26665 ■ Purdue University Libraries– KRAN–Management and Economics Library
504 W. State St.
West Lafayette, IN 47907-2058
Ph:(765)494-2920
Fax: (765)494-9658
Co. E-mail: kranlib@purdue.edu
URL: http://www.lib.purdue.edu/mel
Contact: Judith M. Nixon, Interim Dir.
Scope: Business organization and management; economics - applied, history, principles, theory, systems; industrial relations; agricultural economics; business statistics and mathematics; marketing; taxation; real estate; finance; accounting. **Services:** Interlibrary loan; copying; Library open to the public. **Holdings:** 115,485 volumes; 5067 bound Annual reports to stockholders; 112,953 microforms; newspaper clippings. **Subscriptions:** 1028 journals and other serials.

26666 ■ Sandoz Agro, Inc.–Corporate Library
1100 E Woodfield Rd., No. 500
Schaumburg, IL 60173-5116
Ph:(847)390-3600
Fax: (847)390-3945
Contact: Candy J. Ortman, Libn./Archv.
Scope: Pesticides, herbicides, organic chemistry, entomology, botany, agribusiness. **Services:** Interlibrary loan. **Holdings:** 7500 books; 7000 bound periodical volumes; 7000 reels of microfilm. **Subscriptions:** 180 journals and other serials.

26667 ■ Tennessee Valley Authority–TVA Environmental Research Center–TVA Research Library (PO Bo)
PO Box 1010 (CTR 1E)
Muscle Shoals, AL 35662-1010
Ph:(256)386-2872
Fax: (256)386-2453
Co. E-mail: dsgambre@tva.gov
Contact: Kelley Murray, Mgr., Info.Mgt.
Scope: Environmental sciences, biomass, chemistry, chemical engineering, competitive business marketing, environmental sciences, waste management. **Services:** Interlibrary loan. **Holdings:** 600 volumes; government documents. **Subscriptions:** 6 journals and other serials.

26668 ■ U.S.D.A.–Economic Research Service–ERS Reference Center (1800)
1800 M St. NW, Rm. 3050
Washington, DC 20036-5831
Ph:(202)694-5058
Fax: (202)694-5689
Co. E-mail: mgraham@ers.usda.gov
URL: http://www.ers.usda.gov
Contact: Marilynn Graham, Dir.
Scope: Agricultural economics. **Services:** Copying (limited); Center open to the public by appointment. **Holdings:** 16,000 monographs; 10,000 microforms; microfiche; archives. **Subscriptions:** 318 journals and other serials.

26669 ■ University of California, Berkeley–Giannini Foundation of Agricultural Economics–Research Library (248 G)
248 Giannini Hall, No. 3310
Berkeley, CA 94720-3310
Ph:(510)642-7121
Fax: (510)643-8911
Co. E-mail: susang@are.berkeley.edu
URL: http://are.berkeley.edu/library/
Contact: Susan Garbarino, Hd.Libn.
Scope: Agriculture - economics, labor, land utilization, valuation and tenure, marketing and transportation problems, cost of production and marketing studies; agricultural economic developments in Lesser Developed Countries; environmental economics; water resources economics; conservation of natural resources. **Services:** Copying; Library open to qualified researchers for reference use only. **Holdings:** 21,000 volumes; 152,000 pamphlets; 3900 microforms; 149 maps. **Subscriptions:** 3000 journals and other serials.

26670 ■ University of California, Davis–Agricultural and Resource Economics Library
One Shields Ave.
Davis, CA 95616-8512
Ph:(530)752-1540
Fax: (530)752-5614
Co. E-mail: barbara@primal.ucdavis.edu
URL: http://www.agecon.ucdavis.edu/arelibrary/library.htm
Contact: Barbara Hegenbart, Libn.
Scope: Agricultural economics; agricultural business; land, resource, and consumer economics. **Services:** Copying; Library open to the public for reference use only. **Holdings:** 9203 volumes; 265,622 pamphlets. **Subscriptions:** 874 journals and other serials.

26671 ■ University of Illinois–Funk Library of Agricultural, Consumer and Environmental Sciences Library
1101 S. Goodwin, MC-633
200 ACES Library, Information and Alumni Center
Urbana, IL 61801
Ph:(217)333-2416
Fax: (217)333-0558
Co. E-mail: aceslib@library.uiuc.edu
URL: http://www.library.uiuc.edu/agx/
Contact: Robert S. Allen, Hd.Libn.
Scope: Agricultural economics, animal science, agricultural engineering, crops, biotechnology, family and consumer economics, foods and nutrition, human development and family ecology, textiles, horticulture, food science and technology, environmental science, agricultural history, forestry, soils. **Services:** Interlibrary loan; copying; Library open to the public. **Holdings:** 97,000 volumes; 12,000 microforms; CD-ROMs; reports; patents; microfiche. **Subscriptions:** 3200 journals and other serials.

26672 ■ University of Minnesota, St. Paul–Magrath Library
1984 Buford Ave.
St. Paul, MN 55108
Ph:(612)624-2233
Fax: (612)625-3134
Co. E-mail: magrath@umn.edu
URL: http://agecon.lib.umn.edu
Scope: Agricultural and applied economics; agricultural engineering; agricultural education; home economics; agronomy and plant genetics; animal science; horticultural sciences; biological sciences; food science and nutrition; plant pathology; soil science; biochemistry; family social science; adult education; social work; votech education; design; housing; apparel. **Services:** Interlibrary loan; copying; Library open to the public for reference use only. **Holdings:** 441,420 volumes; 437,283 documents; 208 AV programs; 977 CD-ROMs; 55,367 microfiche; 1937 microfilm; 3111 maps. **Subscriptions:** 3208 journals and other serials.

26673 ■ University of Wisconsin– Madison–Land Tenure Collection
Steenbock Memorial Library
550 Babcock Dr.
Madison, WI 53706
Ph:(608)262-8029
Fax: (608)262-2141
Co. E-mail: brphilli@facstaff.wisc.edu
URL: http://www.ies.wisc.edu/ltc/library.html
Contact: Beverly R. Phillips, Sr.Libn.
Scope: Land tenure, agrarian reform, agricultural economics, Latin America, Asia, Africa, Eastern Europe, rural development, developing countries. **Services:** Interlibrary loan; copying; Library open to the public. **Holdings:** 30,000 books; 1200 bound periodical volumes; 36,000 unbound reports, manuscripts, clippings, pamphlets, documents; 8 VF drawers of microfilm and microfiche; 100 titles of Economic Development Plans; 250 titles of dissertations. **Subscriptions:** 350 journals and other serials.

26674 ■ University of Wisconsin– Madison–Steenbock Memorial Library
550 Babcock Dr.
Madison, WI 53706-1293
Ph:(608)262-9635

Fax: (608)263-3221
Co. E-mail: jgilbertson@library.wisc.edu
URL: http://steenbock.library.wisc.edu
Contact: Jean Gilbertson, Dir.
Scope: Life sciences, agriculture, veterinary medicine, biotechnology, food and dairy science, family studies, consumer science, agricultural economics. **Services:** Interlibrary loan; copying; document delivery; Library open to the public. **Holdings:** 124,000 books; 121,582 monographs; 73,607 bound periodical volumes; 472,556 documents; 90,221 microforms; 765 AV programs. **Subscriptions:** 2503 journals and other serials.

26675 ■ Vermont Community and Technical Colleges Library
Hartness Library System
Main St.
Randolph Center, VT 05061
Ph:(802)728-1237
Fax: (802)728-1506
Co. E-mail: library@vtc.edu
URL: http://hartness.vsc.edu
Contact: Thomas Raffensperger, Lib.Dir.
Scope: Dairy management; agribusiness; engineering technologies - architectural, civil, computer, electrical, electronics, mechanical,; architecture and building technology; automotive technology; business technology; construction management; landscape development; semi-conductor processing; veterinary technology; nursing; science fiction. **Services:** Copying; workstations; Library open to the public with restrictions. **Holdings:** 56,000 books; 5000 e-books. **Subscriptions:** 400 journals and other serials; 8 newspapers.

26676 ■ Western Maryland Public Libraries–Regional Library
100 S. Potomac St.
Hagerstown, MD 21740
Ph:(301)739-3250
Fax: (301)739-5839
Co. E-mail: jvenditta@washcolibrary.org
URL: http://www.wmpl.net
Contact: John C. Venditta, Assoc.Dir.
Scope: Small business; antiques and collectibles; Civil Service and vocational tests; small scale farming. **Services:** Interlibrary loan; copying; Library open to the public with restrictions. **Holdings:** 62,000 books; 2500 audiovisuals. **Subscriptions:** 3 newspapers.

RESEARCH CENTERS

26677 ■ Agricultural Utilization Research Institute
PO Box 599
Crookston, MN 56716-0599
Ph:(218)281-7600
Free: 800—279-5010
Fax: (218)281-3759
Co. E-mail: eolson@auri.org
URL: http://www.auri.org
Contact: Edgar Olson, Exec.Dir.
E-mail: eolson@auri.org
Scope: Agriculture products from state, including research projects to convert corn to ethanol and biodegradable plastics, and to pelletize soybeans for export. Seeks to identify and create new markets and expand existing markets for new or existing commodities, ingredients, and products; develop energy efficient, natural resource-saving production practice; and develop alternative crops and products for emerging markets. **Services:** Technical assistance to farmers, agribusinesses, and producer groups (daily), New product development, feasibility testing, technology development. **Publications:** Ag Innovation News (quarterly).

26678 ■ Agriculture and Agri-Food Canada–Atlantic Cool Climate Crop Research Centre
308 Brookfield Rd.
PO Box 39088
St. John's, NL, Canada A1E 5Y7
Ph:(709)772-4619

Fax: (709)772-6064
Co. E-mail: Todds@agr.gc.ca
URL: http://res.agr.ca/stjohns/index_e.htm
Contact: Sandy Todd
E-mail: Todds@agr.gc.ca
Scope: Sustainable use of agricultural soils in cool summer agri-ecosystems through land improvement and nutrient management, cool summer forage production and utilization systems, feed grain systems for cool climates, low input production and protection systems for vegetable crops grown in cool agri-ecosystems, wild berry production and protection in cool climates, development of small wild fruits suitable for cultivation in cool climates, and rural technology development in cool summer agriecosystems. **Educational Activities:** Farm Field Day.

26679 ■ Agriculture and Agri-Food Canada–Brandon Research Centre
RR 3
PO Box 1000A
Brandon, MB, Canada R7A 5Y3
Ph:(204)726-7650
Fax: (204)728-3858
Co. E-mail: brc-admin@agr.gc.ca
URL: http://res2.agr.gc.ca/brandon/
Contact: R.M.N. Kucey PhD, Dir.
E-mail: brc-admin@agr.gc.ca
Scope: Advancement of scientific knowledge of sustainable crop and livestock production systems for the Parkland, a vast agro-ecological region of the Canadian Prairies, and development and transfer of innovative technologies in beef cattle production systems, barley breeding, and land resource management. **Services:** Agriculture Research Information Service, research, indentify and deliver relevant information retrieved from electronic databases, journals, technical reports, and other specialized resources; Research and Development Investment Opportunities, collaborative research and development agreements, material transfer agreements, variety licenses, requests for research proposals, government services contracts, and evaluation of intellectual property. **Educational Activities:** Federal Student Work Experience Program (FSWEP), paid student employment programs (Government of Canada), post-secondary co-op education and internship, research affiliate, International exchange programs; Non-paid Student Assignments (Government of Canada), secondary school co-op education program and general assignments such as, work experience programs offered by accredited institutions.

26680 ■ Agriculture and Agri-Food Canada–Lethbridge Research Centre
5403 1st Ave.
PO Box 3000
Lethbridge, AB, Canada T1J 4B1
Ph:(403)327-4561
Fax: (403)382-3156
Co. E-mail: lethbridge@agr.gc.ca
URL: http://res2.agr.gc.ca/lethbridge/
Contact: Dr. Zahir Mir, Actg.Dir.
E-mail: lethbridge@agr.gc.ca
Scope: Beef production and quality. **Publications:** Advance (biweekly); Annual report; Directory of Research Chapters (annually). **Educational Activities:** Conferences, seminars; Congresses; Diagnostic plots; Tours, TV features.

26681 ■ American Seed Research Foundation
225 Reinekers Ln., Ste. 650
Alexandria, VA 22314-2875
Ph:(703)837-8140
Fax: (703)837-9365
URL: http://www.amseed.com/asrf/index.html
Contact: Suzanne Nicolas, Dir.
Scope: Seeds, including technology advancement in the seed industry.

26682 ■ Arizona State University–Sustainable Technologies, Agribusiness Resource Center
Mail Code 0180
Bldg. 340, EAP Rm. 121 & 123
Mesa, AZ 85212

Ph:(480)727-1240
Fax: (480)727-1801
Co. E-mail: john.brock@asu.edu
URL: http://www.poly.asu.edu/star
Contact: Dr. John H. Brock, Coord.
E-mail: john.brock@asu.edu
Scope: Agribusiness policy studies, including research and development related to arid zone requirements, including projects in emerging democracies, economic development, technology, high valued products or industrial product potential, biomass utilization, and specialized instrument development. **Services:** Transfers technology from the University to start-up companies, Biotechnology electronics and other materials. **Publications:** Working Treatise Series. **Educational Activities:** Graduate training.

26683 ■ California Institute for Rural Studies
221 G St., Ste. 204
Davis, CA 95616
Ph:(530)756-6555
Fax: (530)756-7429
Co. E-mail: info@cirsinc.org
URL: http://www.cirsinc.org
Contact: Ron Strochlic, Dir.
E-mail: info@cirsinc.org
Scope: Rural community ethnography and demographics; rural poverty; hired farm labor; labor contractors; pesticide use and sustainable agriculture; land ownership and farm structure; water law, transfers, and distribution; various agricultural health and safety topics. **Services:** Consulting, on a contract basis. **Publications:** Reports and Working Papers; Rural California Report (quarterly). **Educational Activities:** Leadership and liaison training.

26684 ■ California State University, Fresno–Center for Agricultural Business
2910 E Barstow Ave., MS 115
Fresno, CA 93740-0115
Ph:(559)278-4405
Fax: (559)278-6032
Co. E-mail: mpaggi@csufresno.edu
URL: http://cati.csufresno.edu/cab
Contact: Mechel Paggi, Dir.
E-mail: mpaggi@csufresno.edu
Scope: Agribusiness in California, especially the San Joaquin Valley. Studies concentrate on farm business planning and other related labor issues, labor supply and demand (migrant workers and immigration law), computer applications in agriculture, water supply and its environmental consequences, agricultural exports, enhancement of markets and alternatives to traditional export markets, food and fiber industry management, and agricultural process, including processing, brokerage, wholesaling, and agricultural safety issues. **Publications:** Conference proceedings (annually). **Educational Activities:** Safety and human resources workshops; Seminars in computer applications in agriculture and management techniques; Seminars in personnel management and labor laws, in English and Spanish; Seminars in business planning and agricultural trade.

26685 ■ George Morris Centre
Research Park Centre
150 Research Ln., Ste. 225
Guelph, ON, Canada N1G 4T2
Ph:(519)822-3929
Fax: (519)837-8721
Co. E-mail: info@georgemorris.org
URL: http://www.georgemorris.org
Contact: Larry Martin, CEO
E-mail: info@georgemorris.org
Scope: Agricultural policies and marketing strategies, including policy positions and alternatives, agricultural and agrifood industry competitiveness, international trade policies, product standards regulation, marketing boards, and commodity value versus income stabilization. **Publications:** Market reports; Newsletter; Research reports. **Educational Activities:** Canadian Agri-Food Executive Development Program; Canadian Total Excellence in Agricultural Management Program (CTEAM); Courses, on futures and options trading.

26686 ■ Indiana Agricultural Leadership Institute
72 1/2 W Main St.
Danville, IN 46122
Ph:(317)745-0947
Fax: (317)745-0956
Co. E-mail: beth@iali.org
URL: http://www.iali.org
Contact: Beth Archer, Exec.Dir.
E-mail: beth@iali.org
Scope: Agribusiness development. **Services:** Agricultural Leadership Development Program; Resource for Developing Community Leadership Program. **Publications:** Newsletter (bimonthly). **Educational Activities:** Indiana Agricultural Forum; Indiana Agricultural Leadership Program.

26687 ■ Institute for Agriculture and Trade Policy
2105 1st Ave. S
Minneapolis, MN 55404
Ph:(612)870-0453
Fax: (612)870-4846
Co. E-mail: iatp@iatp.org
URL: http://www.iatp.org/iatp
Contact: Mark Ritchie, Pres.
E-mail: iatp@iatp.org
Scope: Food, trade, agriculture, land, rural affairs, environmental issues, and sustainable development.

26688 ■ Iowa State University of Science and Technology–Midwest Agribusiness Trade Research and Information Center
578 Heady Hall
Ames, IA 50011-1070
Ph:(515)294-1183
Fax: (515)294-6336
Co. E-mail: babcock@iastate.edu
URL: http://www.matric.iastate.edu
Contact: Prof. Bruce Babcock, Exec.Dir.
E-mail: babcock@iastate.edu
Scope: Expands international trade in agribusiness products produced in the Midwest by small and medium sized businesses. Focuses on export markets, market impediments, trade agreements, trade policies, and technologies that improve competitiveness in international markets. Market studies focus on geographical markets and value-added and niche markets for non-commodity products. **Services:** Consulting with non-university organizations and agribusinesses to discover and fulfill research and informational needs. **Publications:** Working papers and research papers. **Educational Activities:** Conferences, seminars, on policy and trade issues for agricultural products.

26689 ■ Jubilee Centre for Agricultural Research
22 Glasgow St. N
Guelph, ON, Canada N1H 4V5
Ph:(519)763-2589
Fax: (519)763-6480
Co. E-mail: elbert@terracoeur.com
Contact: Elbert van Donkersgoed
E-mail: elbert@terracoeur.com
Scope: Agricultural and environmental issues, rural families, rural sociology, alternative agriculture, plant and animal biotechnology, stewardship, plant bioengineering, animal rights and welfare, soil and water conservation, acid rain, farm crisis, pollution, recycling, and agriculture policy development.

26690 ■ Maharishi University of Management–Agriculture Institute
1000 N 4th St.
Fairfield, IA 52557
Ph:(641)472-7000
Fax: (641)472-1164
Co. E-mail: smclaskey@mum.edu
Contact: Steve McLaskey PhD, Dir.
E-mail: smclaskey@mum.edu
Scope: Agriculture and environmental science, including the functions of soil animals in maintaining soil structure and fertility, effects of soil algae on agricultural productivity, and testing of various techniques of nontoxic agriculture and horticulture.

26691 ■ New Mexico State University–Agricultural Experiment Station
PO Box 30003, MSC 3BF
Las Cruces, NM 88003-8003
Ph:(505)646-3125
Fax: (505)646-5975
Co. E-mail: ldaugher@nmsu.edu
URL: http://www.cahe.nmsu.edu/aes/
Contact: Dr. LeRoy A. Daugherty, Assoc.Dir.
E-mail: ldaugher@nmsu.edu
Scope: New Mexico and western U.S. agriculture; natural and human resources, especially as it applies to livestock, crops, soils, and improvement of rural living. Conducts studies in agricultural economics, agricultural business, agricultural and extension education, agronomy, animal sciences, clothing/textile/fashion marketing, entomology, environmental science, family and consumer science, fishery and wildlife sciences, forestry, human nutrition and food science, hotel and restaurant management, horticulture, molecular biology, plant breeding, plant pathology, plant physiology, range science, recreational areas management, soil science, and weed science. **Services:** Science-based information service, to citizens of New Mexico, via the Cooperative Extension Service. **Publications:** Annual report; Bulletins (annually); Project reports. **Educational Activities:** Conferences, workshops, short courses, field days (annually), for farmers, cattlemen, conservationists, and homemakers of the state; Technology transfer (annually), for producers, consumers, and environmentalists of the state.

26692 ■ North Carolina State University–Research Stations Division
2 W Edenton St.
Raleigh, NC 27601
Ph:(919)733-3236
Fax: (919)733-1754
Co. E-mail: sandy.maddox@ncmail.net
URL: http://www.ncagr.com/research/
Contact: Dr. Sandra J. Maddox, Dir.
E-mail: sandy.maddox@ncmail.net
Scope: Crops, forestry, aquaculture, livestock, and poultry.

26693 ■ North Dakota Agriculture Department–Research, Information and Policy Development
600 E Boulevard Ave., Dept. 602
Bismarck, ND 58505-0020
Ph:(701)328-2231
Free: 800–242-7535
Fax: (701)328-4567
Co. E-mail: plahlum@state.nd.us
Contact: Patricia Lahlum
E-mail: plahlum@state.nd.us
Scope: Agriculture.

26694 ■ Prairie Agricultural Machinery Institute
Hwy. 5 W
PO Box 1150
Humboldt, SK, Canada S0K 2A0
Ph:(306)682-2555
Free: 800–567-7264
Fax: (306)682-5080
Co. E-mail: humboldt@pami.ca
URL: http://www.pami.ca
Contact: Sharon Doepker, Dir.
E-mail: humboldt@pami.ca
Scope: Component machinery testing. **Publications:** Research reports (occasionally).

26695 ■ Purdue University–Center for Food and Agricultural Business
Krannert Bldg., Rm. 781
403 W State St.
West Lafayette, IN 47907-2056
Ph:(765)494-4247
Fax: (765)494-4333
Co. E-mail: akridge@purdue.edu
URL: http://www.agecon.purdue.edu/cab/index.html
Contact: Dr. Jay T. Akridge, Dir.
E-mail: akridge@purdue.edu
Scope: Agribusiness, including the use of operations research techniques for solving agribusiness prob-

lems; analysis of the specialized marketing, management and finance problems of agricultural businesses; buying behaviors of agricultural producers; risk management strategies of food and agribusiness firms; and evaluation of agribusiness marketing strategies. **Educational Activities:** Food and agribusiness management education programs, including programs that focus on specific functional management areas such as marketing, finance, personnel management, sales management, and relationship marketing.

26696 ■ University of Arkansas at Pine Bluff–Agriculture Research Center
Mail Slot 4990
1200 N University Dr.
Pine Bluff, AR 71601
Ph:(870)575-8529
Fax: (870)575-4678
Co. E-mail: mccray_j@uapb.edu
Contact: Dr. Jacquelyn McCray, Dir.
E-mail: mccray_j@uapb.edu
Scope: Medicinal crops, agriculture biotechnology, crop protection systems, alternative crop production, water quality, small ruminant management, catfish and baitfish production, recreational fishing, human nutrition and development, and family studies. **Services:** Fish diagnostics; Small Farm Program. **Publications:** Arkansas Agriculture and Rural Development Research Journal. **Educational Activities:** Agriculture Field Day; Aquaculture Field Day; Lonoke Farm Field Day; Rural Life Conference.

26697 ■ University of Delaware–Halophyte Biotechnology Center
College of Marine Studies
700 Pilottown Rd.
Lewes, DE 19958
Ph:(302)645-4264
Fax: (302)645-4028
Co. E-mail: jackg@udel.edu
URL: http://www.ocean.udel.edu/halophyte/hbc.htm
Contact: Dr. John Gallagher, Co-Dir.
E-mail: jackg@udel.edu
Scope: Sustainable saline agriculture and wetlands restoration, including improvement of salt-tolerant crops and development of plants that will drive high productivity ecosystems without continual human input. **Publications:** Newsletter. **Educational Activities:** Degree and non-degree programs, in halophyte agronomy and biology, comparative wetland ecology, plant nutrition in saline soils, and salt tolerance mechanisms.

26698 ■ University of Florida–Institute of Food and Agricultural Sciences
1008 McCarty Hall
PO Box 110180
Gainesville, FL 32611-0180
Ph:(352)392-1971
Fax: (352)265-6932
Co. E-mail: jgcheek@ufl.edu
URL: http://www.ifas.ufl.edu
Contact: Dr. Jimmy G. Cheek
E-mail: jgcheek@ufl.edu
Scope: Food and agriculture sciences, natural resources, and renewable resources. **Publications:** Faculty Directory (semiannually); Impact Magazine (quarterly); Inside IFAS Newsletter (monthly); Newsline Newsletter (quarterly).

26699 ■ Western Canada Testing
390 River Rd.
PO Box 1050
Portage la Prairie, MB, Canada R1N 3C5
Ph:(204)857-4811
Fax: (204)239-7124
Co. E-mail: rschott.westest@pami.ca
URL: http://www.westest.ca
Contact: Ryan Schott
E-mail: rschott.westest@pami.ca
Scope: Vibration testing, load simulation testing, data collection services.

START-UP INFORMATION

26700 ■ "Barter's latest comeback" in *The Economist* **(Vol. 357, No. 8, October 21, 2000, pp. 78)**
Pub: Economist Newspaper Ltd.
Description: Most people know barter only from the playground, but a raft of American start-ups are trying to turn swapping into big business on the Internet.

26701 ■ "Does cutting costs sound like a good start-up idea?" in *Entrepreneur* **(Vol. 30, No. 10, October 2002, pp. 134)**
Pub: Entrepreneur Media Inc.
Description: Bob Meyer, publisher of BarterNews Magazine offers five tips for entrepreneurs to use the practice of bartering to reduce startup costs.

26702 ■ "A Fistful of Hours" in *Inc.* **(October 2000, pp. 58)**
Pub: The Goldhirsh Group
Description: Start-up barter exchanges hope to make the world their oyster.

26703 ■ "Five Ways to Finance Your Business" in *Black Enterprise* **(Vol. 31, No. 3, October 2000, pp. 43)**
Pub: Earl Graves Publishing Co.
Ed: Glenn Townes. **Description:** The five best ways to find the cash to make your dream a reality are identified as: personal savings, trade credit, commercial banks, second mortgages, and angel investors.

26704 ■ "Forget About Bartering. For Start-Ups, It's All About the Freebies" in *Inc.* **(May 1, 2005)**
Pub: Inc. Magazine
Ed: Stephanie Clifford. **Description:** Dave Morgan, founder of the Internet marketing firm Real Media shares ideas for starting a company with a minimal cash investment by offering employees benefits for working for him for free. Morgan recruited two recent college graduates to work unpaid for six months.

ASSOCIATIONS AND OTHER ORGANIZATIONS

26705 ■ International Reciprocal Trade Association
140 Metro Park Dr.
Rochester, NY 14623
Ph:(585)424-2940
Fax: (585)424-2964
Co. E-mail: krista@irta.com
URL: http://www.irta.com
Contact: Krista Vardabash, Exec.Dir.
Description: Individuals, partnerships, corporations, and firms that engage in the commercial barter industry worldwide, including local trade exchanges which act as clearinghouses, and corporate trade companies which arrange domestic and international barter

transactions. Works to foster and promote the interests of the commercial barter industry through the establishment of ethical standards and self-regulation; to represent members before government agencies in matters affecting the industry; to introduce firms engaged in bartering activities; to resolve disputes between members; influence public laws and regulations affecting the industry; disseminate information and conduct public relations programs. Serves as a clearinghouse for industry and public inquiries. Compiles statistics on the segment of commercial barter accounted for by organized trade exchanges and corporate trade companies. Conducts consumer protection, educational, and training programs. Operates Corporate Barter Council as a self-governing body for the corporate trade sector. Awards professional accreditation; operates referral and placement services; maintains speakers' bureau; supports charitable programs. **Publications:** *IRTA Dialogue* (quarterly).

26706 ■ The Waterfront Center
1622 Wisconsin Ave. NW
Washington, DC 20007
Ph:(202)337-0356
Fax: (202)986-0448
Co. E-mail: mail@waterfrontcenter.org
URL: http://www.waterfrontcenter.org
Contact: Ann Breen, Co-Dir.
Description: State and local governments; architectural, engineering, and design firms; developers; educational institutions; persons in the boating industry; interested others. Helps communities develop waterfronts that facilitate economic growth while providing for public access and recreation. Conducts forums which address problems and opportunities in a particular community; provides on-site analyses and consulting; offers slide presentations; conducts research. **Publications:** *Caution: Working Waterfront: The Impact of Change on Marine Businesses*; *Fishing Piers: What Cities Can Do*; *Urban Waterfront Resource List* (periodic); *The Waterfront: A Worldwide Urban Success Story* (annual); *Waterfront World Spotlight* (quarterly); *Waterfronts: Cities Reclaim Their Edge*.

REFERENCE WORKS

26707 ■ "Barter systems put the 'trade' in trade group" in *Crain's Detroit Business* **(Vol. 19, No. 16, April 21, 2003, pp. 16)**
Pub: Crain Communications Inc., Detroit
Ed: Laura Bailey. **Description:** Barter exchanges, trade association and Chambers of Commerce help small businesses enjoy bulk-buying discounts and to buy and sell goods and services.

26708 ■ "Business 101" in *Inc.* **(November 2000, pp. 129)**
Pub: The Goldhirsh Group
Description: A checklist of things to consider before receiving equity as pay for services, including tax consequences, due diligence, and timing.

26709 ■ "Cashless customers" in *WorkingWoman* **(Vol. 25, No. 2, February 2000, pp. 69)**
Pub: Lang Communications Inc.
Ed: Lisa Lee Freeman. **Description:** New business may be pulled in through barter networks. Business owners may establish reciprocal trading agreements.

26710 ■ "A Fair Trade" in *Entrepreneur* **(Vol. 31, October 2003)**
Pub: Entrepreneur Media, Inc.
Ed: C.J. Prince. **Description:** The ongoing battle between Qwest Communications International Inc. and the SEC about the firm's reportedly recognizing $2 billion in revenue from "swap" sales dating back to 1999.

26711 ■ "Group thinking" in *Crain's Detroit Business* **(Vol. 19, No. 16, April 21, 2003, pp. 16)**
Pub: Crain Communications Inc., Detroit
Description: Information about bartering and exchanges for small businesses is presented.

26712 ■ "If Members Think Items are Overpriced, They'll Blame Barter Trust's Economy, says CEO Mike Edelhart" in *Inc.* **(October 2000, pp. 58)**
Pub: The Goldhirsh Group
Description: Although exchange customers display some ambivalence about barter, the latest generation of Web-enabled exchange operators is predictability bullish.

26713 ■ "I'll Trade You..." in *Home Office Computing* **(Vol. 18, No. 9, September 2000, pp. 87)**
Pub: Scholastic Inc.
Ed: Steven Van Yoder. **Description:** An overview of Internet sites such as BarterTrust.com, Big-Vine and Ubarter have brought back the ancient concept of barter by linking members with trading networks to create mini-economies.

26714 ■ "Quid Pro Quo: Bartering Is a Cashless Alternative to Conducting Business" in *Black Enterprise* **(Vol. 35, September 2004, No. 2)**
Pub: Earl G. Graves Publishing Co. Inc.
Ed: Zakiyyah El-Amin. **Description:** Bartering has become a popular way for small businesses with a surplus of inventory, unsold goods, and unused labor to do business. Advice is offered for small business owners wishing to join a barter exchange group.

26715 ■ "Skinnyguy.com Rekindles America's Love to Barter" in *PR Newswire* **(January 6, 2003)**
Pub: PR Newswire Association, Inc.
Description: Profile of Skinnyguy.com, retailer of used and new DVC, CD, and VHS products via the Internet.

26716 ■ "Sweat rewards" in *Entrepreneur* **(Vol. 30, No. 3, Marc)**
Pub: Entrepreneur Media Inc.
Ed: Amanda C. Kooser, Geoff Williams. **Description:** Predictions for hot business trends in 2002 are pres-

ented, including online learning, kiosks, online games, bartering, alternative health for pets, managing outsourcing, maternity clothing, life coaches, alternative energy, e-books, plus-size clothing, ethnic foods, personalization themes, boomer menopause, luxury products and services for middle income consumers, technology, marketing, money and management.

26717 ■ "Tip Clubbing" in *Fortune* (Vol. 142, No. 9, October 16, 2000, pp. 312)
Pub: Time Inc.
Ed: Jennifer Pendleton. **Description:** Old-fashioned "leads" clubs are back in vogue where a firm handshake and a winning pitch can land you a few good business leads.

26718 ■ "Trade Ya This" in *PC Magazine* (June 6, 2000, pp. 88)
Pub: Ziff-Davis Publishing Company
Ed: Sebastian Rupley. **Description:** Proponents of the bartering model for online commerce are quick to point out that there is a big difference between a haggling model and a bartering model, because often bartering is a cashless transaction.

26719 ■ "Uncle Same Eases Up on Barter" in *Business Week* (March 27, 2000, pp. F6)
Pub: McGraw-Hill, Inc.
Description: The IRS recently ruled that businesses are no longer required report barter transactions worth less than $1, which covers much of the free and low-cost banner-ad swaps popular among small companies.

FRANCHISES AND BUSINESS OPPORTUNITIES

26720 ■ Itex Corp.
2880 Meade Ave., Ste. 204
Las Vegas, NV 89102
Free: (866)839-4839
Fax: (916)679-1057
Co. E-mail: franchises@itex.com
URL: http://www.itex.com
No. of Company-Owned Units: 4. **Founded:** 1992. **Franchised:** 2002. **Description:** ITEX is a leading retail trade and barter exchange center. **Equity Capital Needed:** PC compatible computer with internet access, 2 incoming phone lines, fax line. **Franchise Fee:** $10,000. **Financial Assistance:** No. **Training:** Support begins with a week of intensive training in California on barter and how to run a successful brokerage and continues with optional quarterly sales training classes around the country and at the annual convention.

Benefits

START-UP INFORMATION

26721 ■ "Healthcare Options" in *Small Business Opportunities* (Vol. 12, No. 3, May 2000, pp. 10, 130)
Pub: Harris Publications, Inc.
Ed: Marie Sherlock. **Description:** As a new business owner, the question of availability and cost of health insurance is vital. This article examines affordable, quality options.

ASSOCIATIONS AND OTHER ORGANIZATIONS

26722 ■ American Mutual Life Association
19424 S Waterloo Rd.
Cleveland, OH 44119
Ph:(216)531-1900
Fax: (216)531-8123
Co. E-mail: amla-ara@earthlink.net
Contact: Albert R. Amigoni, Pres.
Description: Fraternal benefit life insurance society. Maintains recreation center. **Publications:** *Our Voice* (biweekly).

26723 ■ American Society of Pension Professionals and Actuaries
4245 N Fairfax Dr., Ste. 750
Arlington, VA 22203
Ph:(703)516-9300
Fax: (703)516-9308
Co. E-mail: asppa@asppa.org
URL: http://www.aspa.org
Contact: Brian H. Graff Esq., Exec. Dir./CEO
Description: Aims to educate pension actuaries, consultants, administrators, and other benefits professionals. Seeks to preserve and enhance the private pension system as part of the development of a cohesive and coherent national retirement income policy. **Publications:** *ASSPA Journal* (bimonthly); *The Candidate Connection* (3/year); Yearbook (annual).

26724 ■ Council on Employee Benefits
4910 Moorland Ln.
Bethesda, MD 20814
Ph:(301)664-5940
Fax: (301)664-5944
Co. E-mail: scanfield@ceb.org
URL: http://www.ceb.org
Contact: Shane Canfield, Exec. Dir.
Description: Employers seeking informal exchange of experiences and information on the design, financing, and administration of employee benefit programs, both domestic and international. Provides a medium for the exchange of ideas, information, and statistics; sponsors or conducts research projects on benefits; makes known its views on legislative matters affecting employee benefits. Conducts research.

26725 ■ Employee Benefit Research Institute
2121 K St. NW, Ste. 600
Washington, DC 20037-1896
Ph:(202)659-0670
Fax: (202)775-6312
Co. E-mail: info@ebri.org
URL: http://www.ebri.org
Contact: Dallas L. Salisbury, Pres./CEO
Description: Corporations, consulting firms, banks, insurance companies, unions, and others with an interest in the future of employee benefit programs. Purpose is to contribute to the development of effective and responsible public policy in the field of employee benefits through research, publications, educational programs, seminars, and direct communication. Sponsors a broad range of studies on retirement income, health, disability, and other benefit programs; disseminates study results. Maintains research library with information on employee benefit programs. **Publications:** *EBRI Databook on Employee Benefits* (periodic); *EBRI Issue Brief* (monthly); *EBRI Notes* (monthly); *EBRI Pension Investment Report* (periodic); *EBRI Policy Forums* (semiannual); *Washington Bulletin* (biweekly). Also publishes consumer education series and policy studies.

26726 ■ Employers Council on Flexible Compensation
927 15th St. NW, Ste. 1000
Washington, DC 20005
Ph:(202)659-4300
Fax: (202)371-1467
Co. E-mail: info@ecfc.org
URL: http://www.ecfc.org
Contact: Lewis Freeman, Pres.
Description: Represents employers and service providers who have implemented or are interested in flexible compensation plans allowing employees to choose from a variety of benefits packages. Promotes flexible compensation plans including cafeteria plans, health reimbursement arrangements, cash-or-deferred plans, and other defined contribution plans. Monitors legislation and represents members' interests before Congress. Lobbies to preserve and simplify the flexible compensation provisions of the Internal Revenue Code. **Publications:** *ECFC Flex Reporter* (quarterly).

26727 ■ ERISA Industry Committee
1400 L St. NW, Ste. 350
Washington, DC 20005
Ph:(202)789-1400
Fax: (202)789-1120
Co. E-mail: eric@eric.org
URL: http://www.eric.org
Contact: Mark J. Ugoretz, Pres.
Description: Large corporations that sponsor employee pension, health, and other benefit programs. Represents the concerns of major employers regarding policy, legislative, judicial, and regulatory matters involving the administration of private retirement, health, and other employee benefit plans. Issues briefings to members' congressional representatives. Operates speakers' bureau. (ERISA is an acronym for the Employee Retirement Income Security Act of 1974.) **Publications:** *ERIC Executive Report* (bimonthly).

26728 ■ International Foundation of Employee Benefit Plans
PO Box 69
Brookfield, WI 53008-0069
Ph:(262)786-6700
Free: 888-334-3327
Fax: (262)786-8670
Co. E-mail: membership@ifebp.org
URL: http://www.ifebp.org
Contact: Joseph A. Brislin, Pres./Chm.
Description: Provides sources for employee benefits and compensation information and education, including seminars and conferences, books, and an information center, CEBS, and Certificate Series. Conducts more than 100 educational programs. Provides internet job and resume posting service. **Publications:** *Benefits & Compensation Digest* (monthly); *Employee Benefits Legal-Legislative Reporter* (monthly).

26729 ■ International Society of Certified Employee Benefit Specialists
PO Box 209
Brookfield, WI 53008-0209
Ph:(262)786-8771
Fax: (262)786-8650
Co. E-mail: iscebs@iscebs.org
URL: http://www.iscebs.org
Contact: Daniel W. Graham, Exec. Dir.
Description: Graduates of the Certified Employee Benefit Specialist Program, co-sponsored by the International Foundation of Employee Benefit Plans and the Wharton School of the University of Pennsylvania. Promotes continuing education and professional development of employee benefit practitioners through courses and seminars. **Publications:** *Benefits Quarterly* (quarterly); *International Society of Certified Employee Benefit Specialists—Membership Directory* (annual); *International Society of Certified Employee Benefit Specialists—Newsbriefs* (bimonthly). **Telecommunication Services:** electronic mail, dang@iscebs.org.

26730 ■ National Coordinating Committee for Multiemployer Plans
815 16th St. NW
Washington, DC 20006
Ph:(202)737-5315
Fax: (202)737-1308
Co. E-mail: nccmp@nccmp.org
URL: http://www.nccmp.org
Contact: Randy G. DeFrehn, Exec.Dir.
Description: International trade unions and jointly administered employee benefit trust funds. Promotes the interests of organizations that provide retirement security, health, and other welfare benefits to individuals working in industries that, due to their structure, would not otherwise provide sufficient pension and welfare benefits. Lobbies before Congress and federal regulatory agencies and participates in judicial proceedings effecting multiemployer plans and participants.

26731 ■ National Institute of Pension Administrators
401 N Michigan Ave., Ste. 2200
Chicago, IL 60611

Free: 800-999-6472
Fax: (312)245-1085
Co. E-mail: nipa@nipa.org
URL: http://www.nipa.org
Contact: Laura J. Rudzinski, Exec. Dir.
Description: Individuals with at least a year of experience in pension administration, full-time pension administration employees, and interested individuals. Sponsors educational program for the accreditation of pension administrators and a series of regional programs relative to pension/profit-sharing programs and administration. **Publications:** *PLAN Horizons* (quarterly).

26732 ■ Woman's Life Insurance Society
PO Box 5020
Port Huron, MI 48061-5020
Ph:(810)985-5191
Free: 800-521-9292
Fax: (810)985-6970
URL: http://www.womanslifeins.com
Contact: Janice U. Whipple, Natl. Pres./Chm. of the Board
Description: Fraternal benefit life insurance society focusing on the needs of women. Each review or local club engages in local charitable community projects. **Publications:** *The Sales Update* (monthly); *Woman's Life* (quarterly).

26733 ■ Workmen's Benefit Fund of the U. S.A.
99 N Broadway
Hicksville, NY 11801-2905
Ph:(516)938-6060
Fax: (516)938-6882
Co. E-mail: info@wbfusa.org
URL: http://www.wbfusa.com
Contact: Charles L. Grossman, CEO
Description: Serves as a fraternal benefit life insurance society. **Publications:** *WBF in Action* (quarterly). Also publishes WBF Youth In Action.

REFERENCE WORKS

26734 ■ "Abuse-awareness initiative lets employers help parents" in *Business First Columbus* (Vol. 18, No. 26, February 15, 2002, pp. B7)
Pub: Business First Columbus, Inc.
Ed: Betsy Butler. **Description:** A new government initiative is allowing employers to assist employees in abuse cases.

26735 ■ "Account Balances Indicate That 401(k) Participants Have Heard The Long-Term Investor Message" in *Employee Benefit Plan Review* (Vol. 55)
Pub: Charles D. Spencer & Associates, Inc.
Ed: Sue Burzawa. **Description:** Lincolnshire, Illinois-based Hewitt Associates LLC, the health benefit plan consulting company, tracks pension fund activity through its 401(k) Index. Industry analysts said that institutional investors are remaining calm as the country suffers from a period of economic upheaval.

26736 ■ *Advanced Benefits Planning*
Pub: Professional Publications, Inc.
Released: 1996. **Price:** $49.00.

26737 ■ "Age Rage: Younger Employees are Crying Age Discrimination" in *Entrepreneur* (Vol. 32, No. 4, April 2004, pp. 24)
Pub: Entrepreneur Media, Inc.
Ed: Chris Penttila. **Description:** Employees in the forty-something age bracket are filing discrimination suits against employers charging they are being excluded from particular retirement health benefits older employees receive.

26738 ■ "Aid package" in *Entrepreneur* (Vol. 30, No. 12, December 2002, pp. 27)
Pub: Entrepreneur Media Inc.
Ed: Julie Monahan. **Description:** Many business owners are assisting employees to get the most out of their 401(k)s and other retirement plans.

26739 ■ "AIG Plans to Cut 27 Jobs at Neptune, N.J., Offices" in *The Record* (November 8, 2005)
Pub: New Jersey Media Group
Ed: Dennis P. Carmody. **Description:** AIG American General will cut a total of 250 employees from its group benefits workforce over the next 18 months. The group benefits division administers health insurance plans sponsored by employers.

26740 ■ "All About Me" in *My Business* (February/March 2004, pp. 41)
Pub: My Business Magazine
Ed: Melany Klinck. **Description:** The new 401(k), called the Solo 401(k) may be a tax-deferral tool for entrepreneurs, allowing them to defer more income.

26741 ■ "Are American workers vacation deprived?" in *Incentive* (Vol. 174, No. 9, September 2000, pp. 7)
Pub: Bill Communications
Ed: Jeanie Casison. **Description:** Behind the booming economy lies the reality of over-worked and burned out employees working an average 50 hours per week. An initiative to make three week vacations mandatory is discussed, listing a website where readers can sign a petition.

26742 ■ "Arris trades road shows for online presentations" in *Atlanta Business Chronicle* (Vol. 25, No. 19, October 18, 2002, pp. 8B)
Pub: American City Business Publications, Inc.
Ed: Lee Hall. **Description:** Arris Group Inc., in Duluth, Georgia, has shifted most of its employee benefits education efforts onto the Internet, and away from putting its executives on the road. Initially intended to save the company money, the program also proved to be very effective and more popular with employees who found that they did not need to attend meetings. In addition, the program has encouraged employees to participate, due to the confidentiality afforded by the program.

26743 ■ "Ask Inc. Profit Sharing" in *Inc.* (September 2006, pp. 53)
Pub: Gruner & Jahr USA Publishing
Description: Profit sharing plans can be changed without upsetting your employees. Numerous hints and strategies are provided to address this question

26744 ■ "ASPA President Shares Regulatory Outlook, Plans New Association Initiatives" in *Employee Benefit Plan Review* (Vol. 55, No. 7, Jan.2001)
Pub: Charles D. Spencer & Associates, Inc.
Ed: Seymour LaRock. **Description:** George Taylor, president of the American Society of Pension Actuaries, is critical of President Bush's Social Security proposals. He feels the Social Security system must provide all Americans with a floor retirement benefit in conjunction with a healthy private retirement system.

26745 ■ "Attention to Nonmedical Factors Can Facilitate Return-To-Work For Workers' Comp Claimants" in *Employee Benefit Plan Review* (Vol. 55)
Pub: Charles D. Spencer & Associates, Inc.
Ed: Jay E. Betz. **Description:** Workers' compensation insurance is the focus of an interview with Jay E. Betz, an executive at Milwaukee, Wisconsin-based CareNetwork Inc. The goal of workers' compensation services is to return the injured employee to work in a safe and timely manner.

26746 ■ "Attracting the talent you need now" in *Incentive* (Vol. 174, No. 9, September 2000, pp. 98)
Pub: Bill Communications
Ed: Bruce Tulgan. **Description:** Advice for developing a compelling recruiting message and eight factors workers of the future look for in employment offers.

26747 ■ "Balancing act" in *Entrepreneur* (Vol. 31, No. 5, May 2003, pp. 19)
Pub: Entrepreneur Media Inc.
Ed: Chris Penttila. **Description:** The proposed new pension rules by President Bush will make it easier for employers to implement cash-balance pension plans, a type of defined-benefit plan that looks like a 401(k), but accumulate at the same rate regardless of how long an employee stays with the company.

26748 ■ "Benefits to Attract & Retain Key Employees" in *Ingram's* (Vol. 27, No. 5, May 2001, pp. 35)
Pub: Show Me Publishing, Inc.
Ed: Mike Searcy. **Description:** Businesses need to attract and retain employees with good, competitive compensation packages, including flexible spending accounts and retirement packages.

26749 ■ "Benefits Costs Averaged 36.8 Percent Of Payroll In 1999" in *Employee Benefit Plan Review* (Vol. 55, No. 10, April 2001 pp. 14)
Pub: Charles D. Spencer & Associates, Inc.
Description: The U.S. Chamber of Commerce annual survey, "The 2000 Employee Benefits Study", shows the most costly company benefit in 1999 was still paid time off at 30 percent. The second most expensive was medical benefits, which accounted for 26 percent of the benefit dollar.

26750 ■ "Benefits of Old" in *My Business* (February/March 2004, pp. 39)
Pub: My Business Magazine
Ed: Mardy Fones. **Description:** Because of extension IRS reporting and administration requirements, many small businesses do not offer retirement benefits to employees.

26751 ■ "Blue Cross to cut benefits for its workers" in *Crain's Detroit Business* (Vol. 19, No. 16, April 21, 2003, pp. 1)
Pub: Crain Communications Inc., Detroit
Ed: Katie Merx. **Description:** Blue Cross Blue Shield of Michigan plans to cut health benefits for salaried workers and retirees in order to cut costs.

26752 ■ "Blues losses decline for small-group business coverage" in *Crain's Detroit Business* (Vol. 18, No. 17, April 29, 2002, pp. 22)
Pub: Crain Communications Inc. - Detroit
Ed: David Barkholz. **Description:** Blue Cross and Blue Shield of Michigan has cut underwriting losses in its troubled small-group business at a time when legislation is aimed at changing Blues governance and health insurance in Michigan.

26753 ■ "Boosting Morale with Work/Life Benefits" in *Rough Notes* (Vol. 145, No. 12, December 2002, pp. 110)
Pub: Rough Notes
Ed: Len Strazewski. **Description:** Insurance agents can deepen business relations with clients by offering and explaining the issues that occupy them regarding health care benefits to employees.

26754 ■ "Breaking Away" in *Inc.* (October 1, 2004)
Pub: Inc. Magazine
Ed: Nadine Heintz. **Description:** Companies are offering employees paid sabbaticals as a new benefit for long-term workers.

26755 ■ "Brent Bannerman" in *Entrepreneur* (Vol. 31, No. 6, June 2003, pp. 23)
Pub: Entrepreneur Media Inc.
Ed: April Y. Pennington. **Description:** Profile of Brent Bannerman, founder of IE-Engine, the Waltham, Massachusetts business insurance and benefits software developer; Bannerman has projected 2003 sales of $10 million for his company that was founded in 2000.

26756 ■ "Buck's Annual 401(k) Survey Shows Dramatic Growth In Web Administration" in *Employee Benefit Plan Review* (Vol. 55, No. 7, Jan. 2001)
Pub: Charles D. Spencer & Associates, Inc.
Description: Buck Consultant's 11th annual survey reports a dramatic increase in the number of employers who make use of Web technology to administer 401(k) plans.

26757 ■ "Building the Mommy Track" in *Inc.* (September 1, 2003)
Pub: Gruner & Jahr USA Publishing
Description: Ways for small companies to handle maternity leave, small business acquisitions, and commercial leases are discussed.

26758 ■ "Bush Signs HSAs Into Law" in *Tax Notes* **(Vol. 101, No. 11, December 15, 2003, pp. 1250-1251)**
Pub: Tax Notes International
Ed: Patti Mohr. Description: An overview of the health savings accounts President Bush signed into law.

26759 ■ "Business groups urge caution on pension law changes" in *Business First Columbus* **(Vol. 18, No. 25, February 8, 2002, pp. A5)**
Pub: Business First Columbus, Inc.
Description: Brief review of potential changes to pension laws, including the concerns expressed by business groups.

26760 ■ *Business Insurance—Employee Benefit Consultants Issue*
Pub: Crain Communications Inc.
Contact: Martin J. Ross, Publisher
E-mail: mross@businessinsurance.com
Released: Annual, March. Publication Includes: List of about 130 firms that offer employee benefit consulting services. Entries Include: Name, address, phone, fax, year services began, location of U.S. and foreign offices, number of employees, number of clients, fees, services, parent company, gross revenues (if available), names of principals. Arrangement: Alphabetical, by company.

26761 ■ "Businesses Hope to Limit Lawsuits, Expand Health-Care Access" in *Atlanta Business Chronicle* **(Vol. 24, No. 7, July 20, 2001, pp. 3A)**
Pub: American City Business Journals Inc.
Ed: Kent Hoover. Description: A managed-care reform bill sponsored by Rep. Ernest Fletcher would allow patients to file lawsuits over medical coverage decisions, but only after they go through an administrative review. The bill would require most of the lawsuits to be filed in federal court and would cap punitive damages at $500,000. By comparison, the Patients' Bill of Rights, would cap the damages at $5 million.

26762 ■ "Businesses Oppose Family Leave Change" in *Crain's Detroit Business* **(Vol. 16, No. 4, January 24, 2000, pp. 4)**
Pub: Crain Communications, Inc.
Ed: Amy Lane. Description: Michigan's small business community is concerned about the impending federal rule that would allow workers to receive unemployment benefits if they take time off to care for newly born or adopted children.

26763 ■ "California Offers Paid Leave for All Workers" in *Inc.* **(October 1, 2004)**
Pub: Inc. Magazine
Ed: Burt Helm. Description: Information is presented regarding California's new paid family leave benefit and its affect on the state's economy.

26764 ■ "Capitol Coverage" in *My Business* **(December/January 2004, pp. 16-17)**
Pub: My Business Magazine
Ed: Description: The National Federation of Independent Business (NFIB) addresses current issues of importance to small businesses in the U.S., including unemployment insurance benefits, unfair trade regulation, health insurance, and taxes.

26765 ■ "Captives Should Broaden their Focus" in *Rough Notes* **(Vol. 146, No. 9, September 2003, pp. 16)**
Pub: Rough Notes
Ed: Michael J. Moody. Description: Overview of past and current trends in the captive insurance industry, including risk management, employee benefits, and funding programs.

26766 ■ "Cataloging the web" in *Incentive* **(Vol. 174, No. 10, October 2000, pp. 99)**
Pub: Bill Communications
Ed: Emily Hodnett. Description: Online award catalogs have a lot to offer, but before you follow this trend, don't forget the benefits of print copy.

26767 ■ "Central Perks" in *Entrepreneur* **(Vol. 33, September 2005, No. 9, pp. 34)**
Pub: Entrepreneur Media Inc.
Ed: Aliza Pilar Sherman. Description: Most business women owners offer benefits that balances business needs with the needs of her employees.

26768 ■ "Chamber Puts Spotlight on Small-Business Issues" in *Crain's Detroit Business* **(Vol. 19, No. 42, October 20, 2003, pp. 31)**
Pub: Crain Communications Inc., Detroit
Ed: Laura Bailey. Description: The Detroit Regional Chamber is offering several new programs for companies with less than 50 employees, about 96 percent of the Chamber's 20,000-plus membership, including the Small Business Central program.

26769 ■ "Class-Based Pensions: A Cost-Saving Alternative for Companies of All Sizes" in *Journal of Accountancy* **(Vol. 199, January 2005)**
Pub: American Institute of Certified Public Accountants
Ed: Mark Papalia. Description: Ways small businesses can establish a class-based pension program for their company are discussed, including a plan that places each employee in a separate class.

26770 ■ "Clearer Regs on Wellness Programs in the Workplace" in *Kiplinger Letter* **(Vol. 78, January 19, 2007, No. 2)**
Pub: Kiplinger
Description: Employers are creating employee incentives through wellness programs in order cut healthcare costs. Such programs can give employees rewards in the form of a discount or rebate in premiums; a waiver of deductibles, copays or coinsurance; or perhaps a gym membership.

26771 ■ "Commuter Gains" in *Entrepreneur* **(Vol. 33, September 2005, No. 9, pp. 93)**
Pub: Entrepreneur Media Inc.
Ed: Mark Henricks. Description: Bob Begle, owner of a design firm in Atlanta, Georgia, offers free monthly transit passes to his workers in order to attract and retain them.

26772 ■ "Companies don't have to be large to offer big benefits" in *Business First Columbus* **(Vol. 18, No. 40, May 24, 2002, pp. B10)**
Pub: Business First Columbus, Inc.
Ed: Crystal Faulkner. Description: Tax advantages can help defray the cost of employee benefits, these benefits include health care, childcare, life insurance, etc.

26773 ■ "Companies Increasingly Turn to Perks to Retain, Lure Quality Employees" in *Altanta Journal-Constitution* **(February 3, 2007)**
Pub: Cox Newspapers, Inc.
Ed: Tammy Joyner. Description: Various perks provided by different companies are shared; Chick-fil-A offers free lunch to its employees.

26774 ■ "Congress considers legislation on 401(k)s after Enron scandal" in *Crain's Detroit Business* **(Vol. 18, No. 18, May 6, 2002, pp. 13)**
Pub: Crain Communications Inc. - Detroit
Ed: Laura Bailey. Description: There is pending federal legislation to regulate everything from 401(k) plans to accounting practices as a result of the collapse of Enron Corp. in 2001.

26775 ■ "Consultant Outlines Steps For Measuring Effectiveness Of Communications Program" in *Employee Benefit Plan Review* **(Vol. 55, No. 12)**
Pub: Charles D. Spencer & Associates, Inc.
Description: Detroit, Michigan-based Aon Consulting Inc., a management consulting services firm, has developed an employee communication program that allows employers to measure the effectiveness of their program. The program, which is aimed at assessing employee job satisfaction, contains twelve key performance indicators.

26776 ■ "Convenience pushes pendulum back to PPO coverage" in *Crain's Detroit Business* **(Vol. 18, No. 16, April 22)**
Pub: Crain Communications Inc. - Detroit
Ed: David Barkholz. Description: An interview with Kay Farnell, vice president of the family-owned Farnell Equipment Co. Farnell tells how her company's experiment with a health maintenance organization lasted only a year, only to return to a PPO.

26777 ■ "Court Sides With Biz on Disability" in *Inc.* **(August 1, 2003)**
Pub: Gruner & Jahr USA Publishing
Description: The Supreme Court ruled that businesses can reject employee disability benefits when the employer's doctor disagrees with the treating physician. A case involving a Black & Decker employee is cited.

26778 ■ "Crain's seeks benefits vendors for buyer's guide" in *Crain's Detroit Business* **(Vol. 19, No. 15, April 14, 2003, pp. 12)**
Pub: Crain Communications Inc., Detroit
Description: Crain's Detroit Business publication is looking for companies to list in its Employee Benefits Buyers Guide, including employee-benefit consultants; 401(k) plan sellers, administrators, providers; group health care providers; health insurance carriers; dental insurance carriers; and third-party administrators of health care.

26779 ■ *Create Your Own Employee Handbook: A Legal and Practical Guide*
Pub: NOLO
Ed: Amy DelPo, Lisa Guerin. Released: May 2005. Price: $49.99. Description: Information for business owners to develop an employee handbook that covers company benefits, policies, procedures, and more.

26780 ■ *Creative Suggestions on Obtaining Company Benefits for a Small Business: A Workbook*
Pub: Center for Self-Sufficiency Publishing
Ed: Center for Self-Sufficiency staff. Released: Revised edition, 1992. Price: $29.95.

26781 ■ "CyberStarts backs new benefits administrator" in *Atlanta Business Chronicle* **(Vol. 24, No. 11, August 17, 2001, pp. 5A)**
Pub: American City Business Journals Inc.
Ed: Mary Jane Credeur. Description: CyberStats, which has become a holding company, is spinning off Sunaro Inc., a small health-care services company that can reduce the benefits administration fees for small- and mid-sized businesses. Sunaro plans to introduce new software that will cross-reference a patient's benefits coverage with payroll accounts, insurance policies and medical records to find the correct errors.

26782 ■ "Death and taxes" in *Crain's Chicago Business*
Pub: Crain Communications, Inc. Crain Communications, Inc.
Ed: Mary Ellen Podmolik. Description: Along with health care affordability, the federal death tax and President Clinton's recent veto of legislation passed by both the House and Senate to repeal it tops the list of hot-button issues facing small business owners as they head to the polls.

26783 ■ "Delphi looks to fund pension plan by spinning off real estate holdings" in *Crain's Detroit Business* **(Vol. 19, No. 17, Apr. 28, 2003)**
Pub: Crain Communications Inc., Detroit
Ed: Terry Kosdrosky. Description: Delphi Corporation, based in Troy, Michigan is proposing to establish a publicly traded real estate investment trust, or REIT, that would allow the firm to raise nearly $300 million through the sale of preferred stock in exchange for real estate transferred for Delphi to the REIT.

26784 ■ "Dental, vision plan vendors use the Web to administer, communicate, market benefits" in *Employee Benefit Plan Review* **(Vol. 55, No. 6)**
Pub: Charles D. Spencer & Associates, Inc.

Ed: Robert Pruter. **Description:** Dental and vision insurance plan providers are redesigning their Web sites to offer better services to employers and to better market themselves to small businesses.

26785 ■ "Design Innovation Brings Communications Challenges" in *Employee Benefit Plan Review* **(Vol. 55, No. 7, January 2001, pp. 27)**
Pub: Charles D. Spencer & Associates, Inc.
Ed: Sue Burzawa. **Description:** The 401(k) plan design evolved rapidly in the late 1990s, and that trend is continuing. Recent innovations, including automatic enrollment and Web access for information and transactions of plans, are expected to soon be common practice.

26786 ■ "Desperate Pension Funds Plan To Put up to $1B into Private Equity" in *Venture Capital Journal* **(Vol. 42, No. 10, Oct. 2002)**
Pub: Thomas Venture Economics
Ed: Carolina Braunschweig. **Description:** The Missouri legislature has directed its state teachers' pension fund to invest in young companies to stimulate innovation and create jobs. Ted Dintersmith of Charles River Ventures, warns that any LP contemplating entering the private equity or venture capital market should do so with caution.

26787 ■ "Despite Stability in Fuel Prices, Airfares Predicted to Climb this Year" in *San Diego Business Journal* **(Vol. pp.)**
Pub: San Diego Business Journal Associates
Ed: Connie Lewis. **Description:** Business trips will cost travelers an average of 4.5 percent more in 2007 than 2006.

26788 ■ "Does an FSA Make Sense for your Company?" in *Inc.* **(March 2000, pp. 123)**
Pub: The Goldhirsh Group
Ed: Description: Unless your company is so cash rich that it can afford to pay 100 percent of the costs for a top-quality health insurance package for its employees, a flexible spending account — especially the POP variety — will probably make sense. Some of the exceptions are pointed out.

26789 ■ "Domestic Dispute: The Debate Over Benefits For Same-Sex Couples Heats Up" in *Entrepreneur* **(Vol. 32, September 2004, No. 9, pp. 34)**
Pub: Entrepreneur Media Inc.
Ed: Chris Penttila. **Description:** The issues involved for providing benefits to same-sex couples is discussed.

26790 ■ "Don't Bet Your Life On It" in *Inc.* **(August 2005, pp. 24-25)**
Pub: Inc. Magazine
Description: The Internal Revenue Service is cracking down on split-dollar insurance, a common benefit given to company executives.

26791 ■ *Employee Benefits with Cost Control*
Pub: Crisp Publications, Inc.
Ed: Rebecca R. Luhn. **Price:** $10.95.

26792 ■ "Employee Health Costs Rose 6.1 Percent" in *Tampa Tribune* **(November 22, 2005)**
Pub: Media General, Inc.
Ed: Dave Simanoff. **Description:** According to a survey conducted by Mercer Health & Benefits LLC, annual health care costs rose to $7,089 for American employees, up 6.1 percent over 2004.

26793 ■ "Employee Need, Distribution Strategies, Drive Growth in Group Legal" in *Employee Benefit Plan Review* **(Vol. 55, No. 10, April 2001)**
Pub: Charles D. Spencer & Associates, Inc.
Ed: Sue Burzawa. **Description:** Group Legal continues to grow in popularity as an employee benefit. Hyatt Legal Plans has close to 450 employer-sponsored plans that cover 1.5 million employees and dependents, while LegalWise covers 1.4 million people using 300 employer groups.

26794 ■ "Employees still rate health care No. 1 benefit" in *Atlanta Business Chronicle* **(Vol. 25, No. 19, October 18, 2002, pp. 13C)**
Pub: American City Business Publications, Inc.
Ed: Tom Barry. **Description:** Employees still consider health care coverage as the most important benefit, according to a national study conducted by the Employee Benefit Research Institute. Statistical data included.

26795 ■ "Employer-Provided Education Benefits: Section 132(d) is Worth a Second Look" in *Journal of Accountancy* **(Vol. 198, September 2004)**
Pub: American Institute of Certified Public
    Accountants
Ed: Edmund D. Fenton, Jr. **Description:** An overview of the various ways employers are helping their employees with tax-free education benefits, including scholarships and grants under IRC Section 117 and education assistance programs under Section 127, as well as IRC Section 132(d).

26796 ■ "Employers Can Use State Programs to Help Employees Save for College Education" in *Employee Benefit Plan Review* **(Vol. 55, No. 6)**
Pub: Charles D. Spencer & Associates, Inc.
Ed: Sue Burzawa. **Description:** Most states offer either prepaid tuition programs or college savings plans, which allow workers to set aside tax deferred income to pay for college.

26797 ■ "Employers Finding Low-Cost Ways to Motivate, Reward Staff" in *San Diego Business Journal* **(Vol. 22, No. 41, October 8, 2001, pp. 13)**
Pub: San Diego Business Journal
Ed: Mandy Jackson. **Description:** Information is offered to help small businesses retain employees during economic downturns, with benefits playing a major role.

26798 ■ "Employers Get Personal with Doctors in Push for More Generic Use" in *Crain's Detroit Business* **(Vol. 19, No. 15, April 14, 2003)**
Pub: Crain Communications Inc., Detroit
Ed: Roberto Ceniceros. **Description:** In an effort to cut costs, large employers and health plans are trying to persuade doctors to prescribe generic drugs whenever possible, while drug company's have their salespeople persuading doctors to prescribe brand name drugs.

26799 ■ "Enrolling online is No. 1 choice among workers, survey finds" in *Crain's Detroit Business* **(Vol. 18, No. 18, May 6, 2002, pp. 12)**
Pub: Crain Communications Inc. - Detroit
Ed: Jerry Geisel. **Description:** The Internet has become the dominant way for workers to enroll into benefits programs offered by employers.

26800 ■ "ESOPs largely a positive tool, survey finds" in *Employee Benefit Plan Review* **(Vol. 56, No. 1, July 2001, pp. 42)**
Pub: Charles D. Spencer & Associates, Inc.
Description: A survey of 500 companies which offer employee stock ownership plans found that 75 percent of those surveyed reported employee productivity and motivation increased as a result of having the stock ownership program. Statistical data included.

26801 ■ "Executive pay off?" in *Washington Business Journal* **(Vol. 22, No. 3, May 23, 2003, pp. 23)**
Pub: Washington Business Journal
Ed: Roger Hughlett. **Description:** The results of a salary survey of executive compensation of companies in the greater Washington, DC area, including bonuses and stock options are presented.

26802 ■ "Expensing Stock Options: A Fair-Value Approach" in *Harvard Business Review* **(Vol. 81, No. 12, December 2003, pp. 105)**
Pub: Harvard Business School Press

Ed: Robert S. Kaplan, Krishna G. Palepu. **Description:** An examination of methods for fair-value expensing employee stock options, thus eliminating measurement and forecasting errors over time. Estimated option prices, amortized expenses, adjustment to paid-in capital, and total end-of-year reported expenses are calculated in two theoretical scenarios over a four-year period.

26803 ■ "Family matters" in *Entrepreneur* **(Vol. 31, No. 5, May 2003, pp. 30)**
Pub: Entrepreneur Media Inc.
Ed: Geoff Williams. **Description:** In an interview with Marie C. Wilson, president of the Ms. Foundation for Women, Wilson stresses the benefits of providing paid family leave to employees. Entrepreneurs are wondering how they will afford the benefit.

26804 ■ "Family values: companies are catering to the needs of dad, mom and kids" in *Incentive* **(Vol. 174, No. 10, October 2000, pp. 9)**
Pub: Bill Communications
Ed: Libby Estell. **Description:** Family-friendly benefits continue to be a strong retention tool for employers. Workers are putting greater emphasis on family, expecting shorter work hours at the office, and thanks to a strong economy and tight labor market, employers have been accommodating.

26805 ■ "Firms Seek Tonic for Labor-Pool Headaches" in *Crain's Chicago Business* **(Vol. 23, September 11, 2000, pp. 4)**
Pub: Crain Communications, Inc.
Ed: Sarah A. Klein. **Description:** These days employees are looking for coverage for everything from acupuncture to chiropractic treatments to aromatherapy, and more insurers are offering those benefits to them.

26806 ■ "Firms Turn to Perks in Lieu of Bonus Checks" in *Inc.* **(December 1, 2004)**
Pub: Inc. Magazine
Ed: Rod Kurtz. **Description:** According to a recent study, more employees are offering non-monetary awards rather than cash bonuses.

26807 ■ "FMLA Needs to be Fixed to Stop Abuse" in *Crain's Detroit Business* **(Vol. 21, January 10, 2005, No. 2, pp. 9)**
Pub: Crain Communications Inc. - Detroit
Ed: Nancy McKeague. **Description:** Sixty-eight federal lawsuits have been filed challenging the validity of the Family and Medical Leave Act. Managers and business owners struggle to provide these benefits because federal rules make it difficult to administer them.

26808 ■ "Focus on Prohibitive Health-Care Costs: Government help may be on the way" in *Time Inc.* **(Vol. 156, No. 3, July 17, 2000, pp. B13)**
Pub: Time & Life Bldg., Rockefeller Center
Ed: Daniel Kadlec. **Description:** Some 44 million Americans are without health insurance and 60 percent of them work in businesses employing fewer than 500 people or are family members of those who do.

26809 ■ "For the Last Time: Stock Options Are an Expense" in *Harvard Business Review* **(Vol. 81, No. 3, March 2003, pp. 63)**
Pub: Harvard Business School Press
Ed: Zvi Bodie, Robert S. Kaplan, Robert C. Merton. **Description:** The practice of expensing stock options is discussed.

26810 ■ "401 Ok?" in *Entrepreneur* **(Vol. 30, N pp. 81)**
Pub: Entrepreneur Media Inc.
Ed: Jennifer Pellet. **Description:** The growing dissatisfaction with 401(k) investment plans is explored.

26811 ■ "401(k) Becomes Benefit of Choice to Woo Employees" *Crain's Detroit Business* **(Vol.16, No.13, Mar. 27, 2000)**
Pub: Crain Communications, Inc.
Ed: Jennie Phipps. **Description:** One of the first things many managers talk about when interviewing a prospective new employee is the company's 401(k) plan.

26812 ■ **"401(k) Loans: Borrowing against the Future"** in *Atlanta Business Chronicle* (V. 25, No. 19, Oct. 18, 2002, pp. 9C)
Pub: American City Business Publications, Inc.
Ed: Sonny Lufrano. **Description:** The increasing tendency of employees to borrow against 401(k) accounts has raised the issue of the results of non-repayment of those loans. The ability to allow employees to borrow against the accounts was intended to stimulate employee participation in the accounts.

26813 ■ **"GEICO Pays 24.2 Percent In Worker Bonuses"** in *Ledger* (February 26, 2005)
Pub: Knight-Ridder/Tribune Business News
Ed: Kyle Kennedy. **Description:** GEICO, the nation's fifth largest auto insurer, handed employees annual profit-sharing checks at 24.2 percent, up from 17.7 percent in 2004. An employee earning $30,000 collected $7,260 in bonus. Statistical data included.

26814 ■ **"Generation next"** in *San Francisco Business Times* (Vol. 16, No. 42, May 24, 2002, pp. S4)
Pub: San Francisco Business Times Inc.
Ed: Kristen Bole. **Description:** Changes in society which impact women executives and opportunities for women in business are discussed along with employee benefits. Women in the Bay Area are highlighted.

26815 ■ **"Get Used to the Pain"** in *Business Week* (No. 3854, October 20, 2003, pp. 42)
Pub: McGraw-Hill Inc.
Ed: William C. Symonds, Brian Grow, Carol Marie Cropper, Diane Brady. **Description:** Health insurance costs for employers are expected to rise by 16 percent in 2004.

26816 ■ **"Getting Clocked"** in *Entrepreneur* (Vol. 33, October 2005, No. 10, pp. 88)
Pub: Entrepreneur Media Inc.
Ed: Chris Penttila. **Description:** The U.S. Department of Labor is investigating off-the-clock work. Employers should set rules for on-the-clock and off-the-clock working. It is important to record all time worked and to allot a small window for tasks that may need to be done off the clock.

26817 ■ **"Getting Their Slice: Save Money, and Keep Employees Happy With Stock Ownership Plans"** in *Entrepreneur* (Vol. 32, September 2004)
Pub: Entrepreneur Media Inc.
Ed: Joan Szabo. **Description:** Employee stock ownership plans and their tax-deferral benefits are examined.

26818 ■ **"Gone Fishin'"** in *Entrepreneur* (Vol. 28, No. 3, March 2000, pp. 86)
Pub: Entrepreneur Media Inc.
Ed: Brian O'Connell. **Description:** Using the right bait while recruiting top executives for your business.

26819 ■ **"GOOD business and good BUSINESS"** in *Harvard Business Review* (Vol. 81, No. 3, March 2003, pp. 10)
Pub: Harvard Business School Press
Ed: Thomas A. Stewart. **Description:** The editor of Harvard Business Review discusses stock options as too much of a good thing. Originally intended to link managers' interest with those of owners, they now create a means for executives to maximize their profit at the owners' expense.

26820 ■ **"Granting Options Like It's 1999"** in *Inc.* (October 2005, pp. 34)
Pub: Inc. Magazine
Description: Private firms will be required to expense the value of outstanding employee stock options, beginning 2006.

26821 ■ **"HAP boosts employee-pay plans"** in *Crain's Detroit Business* (Vol. 19, No. 6, Feb. 10, 2003, pp. 3)
Pub: Crain Communications Inc., Detroit
Ed: Katie Merx. **Description:** Henry Ford Health System's insurance sector is promoting its product line that will help cut the increasing costs of health care to employers.

26822 ■ **"Harvard Pilgrim Purchases Medical Benefits Company"** in *Boston Globe* (March 8, 2005)
Pub: New York Times Company
Ed: Liz Kowalczyk. **Description:** Health Plans Inc. has been purchased by Harvard Pilgrim Health Care. The move will help position Harvard Pilgrim, the second-largest health insurer in Massachusetts, to compete with Blue Cross and Blue Shield of Massachusetts. Harvard Pilgrim is also considering a move into the self-insured market.

26823 ■ **"Have Your Job and Leave It, Too"** in *Kiplinger's Personal Finance Magazine* (Vol. 54, No. 10, October 2000, pp. 96)
Pub: The Kiplinger Washington Editors, Inc.
Ed: Courtney McGrath. **Description:** A summary of the Family Medical Leave Act.

26824 ■ **"Health-care foundation awards its first grants"** in *Atlanta Business Chronicle* (Vol. 25, January 10, 2003, No. 31, pp. 7A)
Pub: American City Business Publications, Inc.
Ed: Julie Bryant. **Description:** The Healthcare Georgia Foundation has finalized its first round of grants. The foundation, its genesis brought about as part of a judgment against Blue Cross and Blue Shield of Georgia, awarded grants totaling $4.3 million. Serologicals Corporation's CEO, David Dodd, assumes the duties of Georgia Biomedical Partnership chairman.

26825 ■ **"Hit the Mark"** in *My Business* (August/September 2002, pp. 28-35)
Pub: My Business Magazine
Description: Seven small business trends that will position a company for success are profiled. These trends include mentoring programs, e-mail marketing, customer service, personalized products and services, employee stock ownership plans, targeting markets, and automation.

26826 ■ **"Holiday Headache"** in *The Record* (November 14, 2005)
Pub: New Jersey Media Group
Ed: David P. Willis. **Description:** As workers plan vacations around the holiday season from Thanksgiving through New Years, employers scramble to hire replacements.

26827 ■ **"Home Office vs. the Field"** in *Sales & Marketing Management*
Pub: VNU Business Media
Description: Incentives for sales teams are debated by a salesperson and sales manager.

26828 ■ **"Hot Fiscal Issues"** in *Small Business Opportunities* (Vol. 16, November 2004, No. 6, pp. 70-71)
Pub: Harris Publications Inc.
Ed: Gerry Murak. **Description:** Planning for compensation in a family business is critical. Seven signs to consider when planning a long-term compensation strategy are investigated.

26829 ■ **"How to Cover America's Uninsured"** in *Business Week* (No. 3694, August 14, 2000, pp. 72)
Pub: McGraw-Hill, Inc.
Description: The failure of the country's health system is discussed at length.

26830 ■ **"How to Tame a COBRA"** in *Home Office Computing* (Vol. 19, No. 1, January 2001, pp. 94)
Pub: Scholastic Inc.
Ed: Holly Aguirre. **Description:** Those changing jobs or starting a solo business can continue to benefit from group health insurance under the Consolidated Omnibus Recognition Act of 1985 (COBRA). COBRA gives employees and covered dependents the right to continuing medical and dental coverage, including flexible spending accounts, if benefits are lost after leaving a company roster. An in-depth analysis of these benefits is provided.

26831 ■ **"HSAs-A Growing Trend In Health Benefits for Businesses and Individuals"** in *Entrepreneur* (Vol. 32, December 2004, No. 12, pp. 67)
Pub: Entrepreneur Media Inc.
Description: Health savings accounts (HSAs) allow individuals with high-deductible health plans to put pre-tax money aside, spend it tax-free on qualified health expenses, earn interest tax-free and also save the money for health-care expenses in retirement. HSAs may be a way for small companies to manage health benefits costs by exchanging higher deductibles for lower premiums and tax advantages.

26832 ■ **"Humana battles for growth"** in *Atlanta Business Chronicle* (Vol. 25, January 3, 2003, No. 30, pp. 3A)
Pub: American City Business Publications, Inc.
Ed: Julie Bryant. **Description:** Alan Guzzino is the new Georgia market president of Humana Inc. Guzzino was retained to manage the introduction of the company's consumer-driver health benefit plans. This rollout aims to increase the company's competitive edge in the market place.

26833 ■ **"Illinois Gov. Pushes More Pension Reform"** in *Venture Capital Journal* (October 1, 2005)
Pub: Thomason Financial Inc.
Description: Illinois Governor Rod Blagojevich has announced new rules to eliminate contingency fees paid to placement agents and require board of trustee members to disclose more financial information in order to reform pension systems within the state.

26834 ■ **"Internet Facilities Defined Contribution Model For Employer-Sponsored Health Benefits"** in *Employee Benefit Plan Review* (Vol. 55, No.12)
Pub: Charles D. Spencer & Associates, Inc.
Ed: Miriam Basch Scott. **Description:** Defined contribution health benefits plans have been transformed through the advent of the Internet. Regence Blue Cross Blue Shield of Oregon, working with Portland, Oregon-based Myhealthbank Inc., offers self-directed health benefit services.

26835 ■ **"IRS changes and finalizes 2000 cafeteria plan rules"** in *Employee Benefit Plan Review* (Vol. 55, No. 8, February 2001, pp. 13)
Pub: Charles D. Spencer & Associates, Inc.
Description: The changes made by the Internal Revenue Service regarding the status change, cost and coverage rules for cafeteria plans, and published in March 2000, are covered. These changes will be effective for cafeteria plan years beginning on or after January 1, 2001.

26836 ■ **"Is Employer-Sponsored Health Insurance On Its Way Out?"** in *Kiplinger Letter* (Vol. 84, January 26, 2007, No. 4)
Pub: Kiplinger
Description: Congress is not expected to pass a bill that would count employer-provided health benefits as income, making them subject to taxes.

26837 ■ **"Jobless benefits on family leave? Not here"** in *Crain's Detroit Business* (Vol. 16, No. 32, August 7, 2000, pp. 7)
Pub: Crain Communications, Inc.
Ed: Amy Lane. **Description:** Workers throughout the country could become eligible for unemployment benefits if they take time off to care for newly born or adopted children.

26838 ■ **"Jobs Are Back; Too Bad Wages Aren't"** in *Fortune* (Vol. 149, No. 9, May 3, 2004, pp. 40)
Pub: Time Inc.
Ed: Anna Bernasek. **Description:** Despite the number of newly created jobs, wages are remaining the same. One factor accounting for this is the benefits workers receive, which increase costs for employers. Insurance premiums have risen 32 percent over the past five years.

26839 ■ **"Labor Department Seeks Repeal of Regulation Threatening UI Reserves" in** *My Business* **(February/March 2003, pp. 19)**
Pub: My Business Magazine
Description: Many states have been using state unemployment compensation reserves to fund Baby UI for employees following the birth or adoption of a child under the Birth and Adoption Unemployment Compensation Rule. Now small businesses fear that larger taxes will be needed to increase UI funds.

26840 ■ **"Laws Mandating Paid Sick Leave Will Pass in Several States" in** *Kiplinger Letter* **(Vol. 78, January 19, 2007, No. 2)**
Pub: Kiplinger
Description: Massachusetts, Wisconsin, Washington, Main, Montana, Vermont, and Maryland are among the states considering a law to mandate paid sick leave to employees.

26841 ■ **"Less than Half of Small Firms Offer Health Plans" in** *Wall Street Journal* **(November 4, 2003, pp. B9)**
Pub: Dow Jones & Co. Inc.
Ed: Richard C. Breeden. **Description:** It is estimated that less than half of all small businesses are able to offer health care plans to employees.

26842 ■ **"Lifestyle, research drugs cloud benefit decisions" in** *Business First Columbus* **(Vol. 18, No. 40, May 24, 2002, pp. B8)**
Pub: Business First Columbus, Inc.
Ed: Michael Nikunen, Timothy Dickman. **Description:** Companies will continue to find challenges with offering medical coverage to their employees.

26843 ■ **"Linking 'Em Up" in** *Incentive* **(Vol. 174, No. 10, October 2000, pp. 109)**
Pub: Bill Communications
Ed: Joan M. Steinauer. **Description:** Golf professionals like Tiger Woods make the sport of golf a sought-after reward by employees, keeping the sport the top-requested award nationwide.

26844 ■ **"LP's Loans to Executives Raises Issues" in** *Business Journal-Portland* **(Vol. 20, No. 27, September 5, 2003, pp. 1)**
Pub: American City Business Journals, Inc.
Ed: Shelly Strom. **Description:** In a policy that runs counter to efforts to reduce a $1 billion debt, Louisiana Pacific Corporation, a timber products company, continues to increase benefits to its top executives, critics point to the company's loan program for these executives.

26845 ■ **"Making Family Leave Family-Friendly; California is considering subsidizing parental leave" in** *Business Week Online* **(Sept. 20, 2002)**
Pub: McGraw-Hill Inc.
Ed: Aaron Bernstein, Ronald Grover, Cliff Edwards. **Description:** Small business owners share growing concern over the California legislation calling for a paid-family-leave law that would be too costly for small firms to handle. Massachusetts is also considering similar legislation.

26846 ■ **"Managed Care's Poor Health" in** *Rough Notes* **(Vol. 145, No. 2, February 2002, pp. 36)**
Pub: Rough Notes
Ed: Phil Zinkewicz. **Description:** According to surveys by Weiss Ratings Inc., 40.9 percent of health maintenance organizations, 16 percent of banks and financial industries, 25.9 percent of life and health insurers and 18.4 percent of financial industries are in a financially weakened condition. The threat of bioterrorism has had a serious impact on the problem to which no constructive solution has yet been devised.

26847 ■ **"Management commitment to innovation and ESOP stock concentration" in** *Journal of Business Venturing* **(Vol. 15, No. 5-6, Sept.-Nov. 2000)**
Pub: Elsevier Science, Inc.
Ed: John E. Gamble. **Description:** A new study investigates the ability of managers to use employee stock ownership plans to aid managerial decision control.

26848 ■ *Managing Health Benefits in Small and Mid-Sized Organizations*
Pub: Amacom
Ed: Patricia Halo. **Released:** July 1999. **Price:** $35.00. **Description:** Comprehensive guide for developing health care plans for companies employing between 50 and 5,000 employees in order to provide employees with better health care at lower prices.

26849 ■ **"Many small firms are unaware of pension-plan options" in** *Wall Street Journal* **(May 30, 2000, pp. B2)**
Pub: Dow Jones & Co., Inc.
Ed: Eleena de Lisser. **Description:** An update on pension plan options for small businesses is covered.

26850 ■ **"A Market-Driven Approach to Retaining Talent" in** *Harvard Business Review* **(Vol. 78, No. 1, January 2000, pp. 103)**
Pub: Harvard Business School Publishing Corp.
Ed: Peter Cappelli. **Description:** Companies today are employing different strategies for retaining employees through incentive programs such as stock options and lucrative compensation packages. By designing and promoting longterm career employee development, the companies can win back the loyalty of their workforce.

26851 ■ **"Medicaid HMOs seek cure for what ails them" in** *Crain's Detroit Business* **(Vol. 19, No. 15, April 14, 2003, pp. 13)**
Pub: Crain Communications Inc., Detroit
Ed: Katie Merx. **Description:** Although most of Michigan's Medicaid HMO's are reporting profits, the largest are struggling. Information about The Wellness Plan, Great Lakes Health Plan Inc., and OmniCare Health Plan is covered. Statistical data included.

26852 ■ **"Metro firms maintain pay for called-up reservists" in** *Crain's Detroit Business* **(Vol. 19, No. 14, April 7, 2003, pp. 1)**
Pub: Crain Communications Inc., Detroit
Ed: Robert Sherefkin, Robert Ankeny. **Description:** Major Detroit area firms, including auto suppliers and DTE Energy are paying salary differences for employees called up for active military duty. Many are also maintaining medical, dental and life insurance for several months, and some for years.

26853 ■ **"The Mini-K Advantage" in** *Rough Notes* **(Vol. 144, No. 12, December 2001, pp. 80)**
Pub: Rough Notes
Description: Information about the new tax laws that benefit small business 401(k) retirement plans is given. Under the new tax laws, an individual making $100,000 per year can contribute $28,000 to a 401(k) plan.

26854 ■ **"Money-Preneuring" in** *Small Business Opportunities* **(Vol. 17, September 2005, No. 5, pp. 68, 128)**
Pub: Harris Publications Inc.
Ed: Robert A. Adelson. **Description:** Three strategies to give non-family executives a share in the rewards of ownership without transferring any company stock are shared: offering a non-voting stock plan, a non-qualified deferred compensation plan, or a phantom stock plan.

26855 ■ **"Monthly Report - June 2000" in** *Small Business Economic Trends* **(June 2000, pp. 1)**
Pub: National Federation of Independent Business
Description: Small firms' compensation for employees increased for 34 percent of the firms surveyed, while a definite skilled labor shortage was a problem for 24 percent of firms surveyed.

26856 ■ **"MSA Withdrawals: Rules on Tax Exclusion" in** *Employee Benefit Plan Review* **(Vol. 55, No. 12, June 2001, pp. 8)**
Pub: Charles D. Spencer & Associates, Inc.
Description: Questions and answers focus on Cobra rules and tax rules for employee health plans. Employees are advised that they may pay medical bills by using an employer's medical savings account, which are known as Archer MSAs.

26857 ■ **"A New Abacus for Pensions" in** *Business Week* **(January 9, 2006, No. 3966, pp. 91)**
Pub: McGraw-Hill Companies
Description: New Financial Accounting Standards Board rules on post-retirement accounting will change how companies account for pensions and other employee benefits, especially retiree health insurance.

26858 ■ **"New Group Plan Offers 'Free-Agent' Workers Affordable Health Benefits" in** *Boston Globe* **(March 3, 2005)**
Pub: New York Times Company
Ed: Diane E. Lewis. **Description:** National Health Access is offering a program that provides lower cost health insurance to part-time, temporary, seasonal, and contract workers.

26859 ■ **"The New Roth 401(k)" in** *Black Enterprise* **(Vol. 36, December 2005, No. 5, pp. 50)**
Pub: Earl G. Graves Publishing Co. Inc.
Ed: Rene Brinkley. **Description:** Both Roth IRA and the Roth 401(k) plans will allow workers to save money for retirement after taxes have been paid and pay no taxes on the money invested when withdrawn from the account in retirement. Suggestions are made for determining the use of a 401(k) versus a Roth 401(k).

26860 ■ **"News from the Small Business Front" in** *My Business* **(June/July 2002, pp. 14)**
Pub: My Business Magazine
Description: Plans for using wireless technology for small businesses to develop a global wireless Internet network are discussed. Information on the Family and Medical Leave Act is presented.

26861 ■ **"No coddling? Work-site day care, once the rage, falls under pressures" in** *Wall Street Journal* **(April 2, 2002, pp. A1)**
Pub: Wall Street Journal
Ed: Carlos Tejada. **Description:** Issues faced by companies offering on-site day care for employees and their children are discussed.

26862 ■ **"Nobody's Fool? Health Insurance Scams Target Entrepreneurs" in** *Entrepreneur* **(Vol. 32, August 2004, No. 8, pp. 21)**
Pub: Entrepreneur Media Inc.
Ed: Joan Szabo. **Description:** Phony health insurance plan promoters are preying on entrepreneurs promising coverage at premiums below charges by licensed insurers. These fraudulent plans escape state regulators with false claims of federally regulated plans under the Employee Retirement Income Security Act (ERISA), a law that pre-empts states from regulating ERISA-covered employee benefit plans sponsored by private employers.

26863 ■ **"Nonindividual QTP Contributions: How Employers Can Help Workers Save for College" in** *Journal of Accountancy* **(Vol. 198, November 2004)**
Pub: American Institute of Certified Public Accountants
Ed: Lesli S. Laffie. **Description:** Issues involved in an employer using qualified tuition programs for employees are examined.

26864 ■ **"Northside ends exclusive insurer contracts" in** *Atlanta Business Chronicle* **(Vol. 24, No. 15, September 14, 2001, pp. 14A)**
Pub: American City Business Journals Inc.
Description: Northside Hospital has ended its managed care exclusive contracts after giving in to Aetna U.S. Healthcare's non-exclusive contract arrangement. Northside had required that all patients that lived within certain areas go there for care, however, made the changes to continue to represent its consumers and patients and responding to the marketplace.

26865 ■ "On the Disabled List? Save Employees (and Your Business) a World of Hurt With Disability Insurance" in *Entrepreneur* **(Vol. 32)**
Pub: Entrepreneur Media Inc.
Ed: Jacquelyn Lynn. **Description:** Because the average American worker stands a 1 in 3 chance of becoming disabled for 90 days or more, it is important to include disability insurance as an employee benefit.

26866 ■ "One size doesn't fit all" in *Hispanic Business* **(Vol. 22, No. 10, October 2000, pp. 100)**
Pub: Hispanic Business
Ed: Janet Perez. **Description:** The variety of employee benefits available are discussed. The effects of a tight labor market, leading to more choices for employees, are examined and new benefits such as telecommuting, family leave, stock options, and other perks are described.

26867 ■ "Optional benefits aren't always a positive" in *Rough Notes* **(Vol. 146, No. 4, April 2003, pp. 126)**
Pub: Rough Notes
Ed: Len Strazewski. **Description:** In the prevailing competition and struggling economy, employers can hardly afford a broad package of benefits to employees. Brokers and agents should survey the client's employees and ascertain the interest and need for voluntary supplemental benefits, offering the most-needed and valuable coverage.

26868 ■ "Other People's Money: A Pension Fund Learns About Soft Dollars-the Hard Way" in *Barron's* **(July 7, 2003, pp. L7)**
Pub: Barron's
Ed: Erin E. Arvedlund. **Description:** The increasing influence wielded over pension funds by Wall Street, including which portfolio managers they hire and what companies they invest in, is a troubling trend, as evidenced in the case of the Nashville Municipal fund and consultant, William Keith Phillips.

26869 ■ "Paid family leave better if voluntary" in *Crain's Detroit Business* **(Vol. 16, No. 5, January 31, 2000, pp. 8)**
Pub: Crain Communications, Inc.
Description: Information regarding a proposed federal rule to allow employees on unpaid family leave to apply for jobless benefits while taking care of newborns or newly adopted children.

26870 ■ "Pay you back: your employees may be better off driving their own cars" in *Entrepreneur* **(Vol. 30, No. 10, October 2002, pp. 38)**
Pub: Entrepreneur Media Inc.
Ed: Jill Amadio. **Description:** The use of a company reimbursement program for employees using their own automobiles for business, versus driving company cars is investigated.

26871 ■ "The Pay-for-Performance Fallacy" in *Business 2.0* **(Vol. 6, July 2005, No. 6, pp. 64)**
Pub: Time, Inc.
Ed: Jeffrey Pfeffer. **Description:** CEO pay and work performance are covered.

26872 ■ "Pension Funds Prod Firms to Show Management Compensation Packages" in *Sacramento Bee* **(December 22, 2005)**
Pub: The Sacramento Bee
Ed: Gilbert Chan. **Description:** Securities and Exchange Commission Chairman, Christopher Cox, is planning to perform the first changes in executive compensations rules since 1992 by ordering companies to define details of their management compensation packages.

26873 ■ "Pension Liabilities Threaten Suppliers' Credit Ratings" in *Crain's Detroit Business* **(Vol. 19, No. 17, April 28, 2003, pp. 27)**
Pub: Crain Communications Inc., Detroit
Ed: Robert Sherefkin. **Description:** Unfunded pensions and retiree medical liabilities are hurting the four large auto parts makers, Delphi Corporation, Visteon Corporation, Cummins Engine Company Inc., and Eaton Corporation, prompting lower credit ratings for each.

26874 ■ "Pension Pain" in *Forbes* **(Vol. 170, No. 4, September 2, 2002, pp. 144)**
Pub: Forbes Magazine
Ed: A. Gary Shilling. **Description:** Companies will no longer be allowed to boost earnings by including pension plans.

26875 ■ "Pension Performer" in *Hispanic Business* **(April 2005, pp. 26, 28)**
Pub: Hispanic Business
Ed: Joel Russell. **Description:** Profile of Deborah E. Gallegos, CIO for New York City. Gallegos manages five retirement funds for city employees.

26876 ■ "Pension Reform Enhances Sponsored Retirement Plans" in *San Diego Business Journal* **(Vol. 22, No. 41, October 8, 2001, pp. 16)**
Pub: San Diego Business Journal
Ed: Laura Just. **Description:** A listing of the new pension revisions effective in 2002 by the Economic Growth and Tax Relief Reconciliation Act of 2001 are presented.

26877 ■ "The Perfect Storm? Employers Need Navigation Tools For The Newest Set of Health Cost Waves" in *Employee Benefit Plan Review* **(Vol. 55)**
Pub: Charles D. Spencer & Associates, Inc.
Ed: Stephen A. Huth. **Description:** Reports from the Department of Labor show that, for the year ended September 30, 2000, benefits costs for private industry workers rose to 6 percent. The largest portion was for health care, and employers will try many strategies to reduce costs, including passing some on to their employees.

26878 ■ "A perilous chopping block" in *Crain's Detroit Business* **(Vol. 18, No. 18, May 6, 2002, pp. 11)**
Pub: Crain Communications Inc. - Detroit
Ed: Laura Bailey. **Description:** More companies are cutting such employee benefits, as health care, retirement plans, or retiree's health insurance.

26879 ■ "Perks for interns" in *Incentive* **(Vol. 174, No. 10, October 2000, pp. 10)**
Pub: Bill Communications
Ed: Jeanie Casison. **Description:** Forget about the guy in the next cube—companies are trying to make an impression on the workforce of the future.

26880 ■ "Picking a 529 College Savings Plan" in *Black Enterprise* **(Vol. 37, February 2007, No. 7, pp. 46)**
Pub: Earl G. Graves Publishing Co. Inc.
Ed: Carolyn M. Brown. **Description:** Advice is given to help choose the right college savings plan.

26881 ■ "Planning Made Easy" in *Incentive* **(Vol. 174, No. 10, October 2000, pp. 150)**
Pub: Bill Communications
Description: The video entitled Business at Sea, produced by Landry & Kling, specialists in meetings at sea, is profiled. The video provides insights from three corporate and three independent meeting planners, as well as eight cruise line executives, to help accomplish business objectives using a cruise ship.

26882 ■ "Pocketbook Issues: The 2000 election brings some of small business's biggest issues to the forefront" in *Time Inc.* **(Vol.155, May 2000)**
Pub: Time & Life Bldg., Rockefeller Center
Ed: Edward Robinson. **Description:** For the first time in years, the nation's 25 million small business owners feel they have a stake in the election outcome.

26883 ■ *PPC's Guide to Choosing Retirement Plans for Small Businesses*
Pub: Practitioners Publishing Company
Released: June 2004. **Price:** $104.00. **Description:** Guide to evaluate and select retirement plans for small business.

26884 ■ *PPC's Guide to Compensation Planning for Small Business*
Pub: Practitioners Publishing Company
Released: September 2004. **Price:** $104.00. **Description:** Technical guide for developing a compensation system for small business. Forms and letters included.

26885 ■ "Premium RX? Consumer-driven health plans" in *Atlanta Business Chronicle* **(Vol. 25, No. 19, October 18, 2002, pp. 5C)**
Pub: American City Business Publications, Inc.
Ed: Tom Barry. **Description:** Consumer-driven health plans are increasingly being considered by companies as a means to counter the effects of double-digit health insurance premium rates, by trimming the demand for healthcare services. These plans are the other side of the managed care health plan which attempts to control health care costs through the supply side. The consumer-driven health care plans establish medical savings accounts, creating an inducement by the user to consider cost-saving options.

26886 ■ "Premiums to climb at double-digit rate—again" in *Atlanta Business Chronicle* **(Vol. 24, No. 13, August 31, 2001, pp. 14A)**
Pub: American City Business Journals Inc.
Ed: Julie Bryant. **Description:** Health insurance premiums are estimated to continue to rise along with the steady rise of healthcare costs. Small businesses, those with 10 employees or less, are projected to be the most at risk as premiums continue to rise. The Segal Company has predicted that medical costs will increase from 12 to 16 percent in the next year.

26887 ■ "Prescription Drug Cost Containment" in *Rough Notes* **(Vol. 145, No. 2, February 2003, pp. 76)**
Pub: Rough Notes
Ed: Len Strazewski. **Description:** As employer health care costs overwhelm small to medium-sized businesses, they can turn to pharmacy benefits management companies, such as AdvancePCS Inc., Caremark Rx Inc., and Express Scripts, Inc.

26888 ■ "President signs tax cut bill with pension reform" in *Employee Benefit Plan Review* **(Vol. 56, No. 1, July 2001, pp. 10)**
Pub: Charles D. Spencer & Associates, Inc.
Description: President George W. Bush signed the Economic Growth and Tax Relief Reconciliation Act of 2001. Changes in the pension law were made in vesting provisions and compensation limits.

26889 ■ "Producer compensation linked to agency size" in *Rough Notes* **(Vol. 146, No. 3, March 2003, pp. 16)**
Pub: Rough Notes
Ed: Phil Zinkewicz. **Description:** The Business Management Group has released its 2002 Owner, Executive and Producer Compensation Survey. The survey shows that the level of compensation for producers is related to agency size and individual production.

26890 ■ "Protecting the Dream" in *Ingram's* **(Vol. 28, No. 5, May 2002, pp. 28)**
Pub: Show Me Publishing, Inc.
Ed: Cynthia Grimes. **Description:** Legal advice is given to protect small businesses from bankruptcy, lawyers, accounting, cash flow planning, employee benefits and estate planning.

26891 ■ "Protecting What's Yours" in *Hispanic Business* **(Vol. 23, No. 7/8, July/ August 2001, pp. 110)**
Pub: Hispanic Business
Ed: Milton Zall. **Description:** Under deferred compensation plans, key employees are promised future rewards, bankruptcy insurance may be the best insurance to protect deferred compensation plans.

26892 ■ "Rabbi trusts give execs a false sense of security" in *Atlanta Business Chronicle* **(Vol. 25, No. 20, October 25, 2002, pp. 2C)**
Pub: American City Business Publications, Inc.
Ed: Tom Barry. **Description:** The rabbi trust is a non-qualified retirement plan that provides deferred com-

pensation for middle and high level executives. In 1981, a synagogue in Brooklyn, New York wanted to reward a rabbi and established the first trust of its kind. The pros and cons of this type of trust are presented.

26893 ■ **"Raleigh, N.C.-Area Employers Decline to Offer Dating Service as Perk" in** *News & Observer* **(February 1, 2004)**
Pub: News & Observer
Ed: Karin Rives. **Description:** Owners of the William Ashley Agency, Lisa and Bill Horst, approached several Triangle North Carolina companies to offer their matchmaking service as a benefit to employees. The husband and wife team ran into issues such as employer concern about meddling in the personal life of employees, and the liability of matches that did not work out.

26894 ■ **"The Real Pepsi Challenge" in** *New York Times* **(February 4, 2007, pp. 7)**
Pub: New York Times Company
Ed: Stephanie Capparell. **Description:** Special-markets sales staff of the Pepsi-Cola Company is profiled. Walter S. Mack, Jr. took over the company in 1938; Mack strengthened the company by marketing to the African American population.

26895 ■ **"Redefining Sick Days" in** *Sales & Marketing Management* **(Vol. 157)**
Pub: VNU Business Media
Ed: Kathryn Droullard. **Description:** Many companies are now offering flexible time-off policies whereby an employee can use sick time for reasons other than personal illness, such as family issues, personal needs, and stress. Allowing a workforce flexible time off not only motivates a staff, but can also lead to stronger management capabilities.

26896 ■ **"A Refreshing Way to Make a Living" in** *The Record* **(November 6, 2005)**
Pub: New Jersey Media Group
Ed: Teresa M. McAleavy. **Description:** Profile of Judson Kleinman, owner of Corporate Essentials, located in Fairfield, New Jersey. Kleinman sells coffee, tea and other refreshments to employers, who for less than a dollar a day per worker, give to their employees for free as an employee motivation benefit. He also provides clients with the equipment needed for making hot water and brewing gourmet coffee.

26897 ■ **"Reining in activist funds" in** *Harvard Business Review* **(Vol. 81, No. 3, March 2003, pp. 22)**
Pub: Harvard Business School Press
Ed: Tracie Woidtke, Leonard Bierman, Christopher Tuggle. **Description:** Pension fund activism, the practice among public pension funds to promote political causes, is discussed. The argument to de-politicize funds and boards of trustees should be dominated by fund beneficiaries and members with investment expertise rather than by elected government officials is addressed.

26898 ■ **"Report recommends path to foster equity ownership" in** *Employee Benefit Plan Review* **(Vol. 56, No. 1, July 2001, pp. 46)**
Pub: Charles D. Spencer & Associates, Inc.
Description: Employee equity was found to be positive for employers and employees, according to a report by the American Benefits Council.

26899 ■ **"Retirees face waning insurance contributions" in** *Atlanta Business Chronicle* **(Vol. 25, No. 19, October 18, 2002, pp. 7C)**
Pub: American City Business Publications, Inc.
Ed: Tom Barry. **Description:** Retirees in the future are seen as taking over a greater portion of the costs associated with healthcare benefits. By the year 2031, support by employers for retiree health benefits are forecast to shrink to less than 10 percent versus the more than 50 percent that is currently typical for larger companies. According to the study conducted by Watson Wyatt Worldwide, many companies have already eliminated or cut retiree health benefits, and the most vulnerable group targeted are those between the ages of 55 and 64.

26900 ■ **"Retirement Benefits More Important to Workers" in** *Wall Street Journal* **(January 14, 2003, pp. B5)**
Pub: Dow Jones & Co. Inc.
Ed: Richard C. Breeden. **Description:** A new survey shows that employers are unaware of the fact that their employees prefer to have an employee-funded retirement.

26901 ■ **"Retirement Plans: Choosing from the Alphabet Soup" in** *My Business* **(December/January 2003, pp. 16)**
Pub: My Business Magazine
Ed: Karen M. Kroll. **Description:** Less than half small business owners are familiar with retirement accounts. A listing of several plans that are geared to small businesses with one to a few hundred employees are listed, including Simplified Employee Pension (SEP), Savings Incentive Match for Employees IRA (SIMPLE), 401(k), and 401(k) Safe Harbor.

26902 ■ **"Retirement Plans for Small Business" in** *Ingram's* **(Vol. 28, No. 5, May 2002, pp. 31)**
Pub: Show Me Publishing, Inc.
Ed: Michael Searcy. **Description:** Retirement plans for small business owners are presented, including Individual Retirement Arrangement, Simplified Employee Pension IRA and 401(k)Profit Sharing.

26903 ■ **"Revamped Retiring Plans" in** *My Business* **(April/May 2002, pp. 15)**
Pub: My Business Magazine
Ed: Milt Zall. **Description:** Tax legislation signed into law by President Bush in 2001 made significant changes to retirement plans, including loans allowed, limit on annual additions raised, employer's tax deduction increase, increased limit for defined benefit plans, increased compensation limits, and small business tax credits.

26904 ■ **"Rewards For Recruiting: Incentivize Your Reps For Bringing In New Hires" in** *Sales & Marketing Management* **(Vol. 157, February 2005)**
Pub: VNU Business Media
Ed: Julia Chang. **Description:** Referrals from current sales staff help attract top sales people. Some companies are using incentives to encourage salespeople to bring qualified candidates on board.

26905 ■ **"The right rewards" in** *WorkingWoman* **(Vol. 25, No. 7, August 2000, pp. 40)**
Pub: Lang Communications Inc.
Ed: Carol Leonetti Dannhauser. **Description:** Issues concerning the motivation and retention of employees through means and other pay raises are discussed.

26906 ■ **"Rising health premiums mean more uninsured" in** *Atlanta Business Chronicle* **(Vol. 25, No. 19, October 18, 2002, pp. 10C)**
Pub: American City Business Publications, Inc.
Ed: Anya Martin. **Description:** The number of individuals in the state of Georgia without health care insurance is expected to rise because small businesses are having a harder time finding affordable coverage and the slowing economy has forced many small firms to eliminate or cut back coverage.

26907 ■ **"Save It For Later" in** *Entrepreneur* **(Vol. 32, December 2004, No. 12, pp. 68)**
Pub: Entrepreneur Media Inc.
Description: Studies indicate that more than one-third of the eligible work force does not participate in 401(k) retirement plans. Employers might automatically enroll employees into a plan with the option of their opting out.

26908 ■ **"Saving Will Get Sweeter" in** *Kiplinger's Personal Finance Magazine* **(Vol. 54, No. 12, January, 2001, pp. 25)**
Pub: The Kiplinger Washington Editors, Inc.
Ed: Melynda Dovel Wilcox. **Description:** Watch for big changes to retirement plans that are aimed at attracting more employers and workers.

26909 ■ **"Sharebuilder 401(k)" in** *Entrepreneur.com* **(Vol. 34, February 2006, No. 2, pp. 60)**
Pub: Entrepreneur Media Inc.
Description: ShareBuilder 401(K) helps employers deliver retirement plans for a monthly fee of $15 per participant. The software merges with existing payroll and offers online payroll service.

26910 ■ **"Should you take the money...and run?" in** *Women in Business* **(Vol. 54, No. 3, May-June 2002, pp. 40)**
Pub: The ABWA Co Inc.
Ed: Mia Katz. **Description:** Negotiating the salary and benefits for a new job are discussed.

26911 ■ **"A Simple Choice for Small Firms" in** *Kiplinger's Personal Finance Magazine* **(Vol. 54, No. 10, October 2000, pp. 106)**
Pub: The Kiplinger Washington Editors, Inc.
Ed: Mary Beth Franklin. **Description:** The pros and cons of the Simple IRA, which allows participants to defer up to $6,000 annually, are scrutinized.

26912 ■ **"Sleeping On the Job" in** *Incentive* **(Vol. 174, No. 10, October 2000, pp. 1S8)**
Pub: Bill Communications
Ed: Rachel L. Fox. **Description:** In the book Power Sleep (Harper Collins, 1999), author Dr. James B. Maas explores ways that employees can enjoy the benefits of taking naps at work, suggesting improved performance may be just a snooze away!

26913 ■ **"Small-Biz Leaders Mixed on Retirement Proposal" in** *Crain's Detroit Business* **(Vol. 22, January 30, 2006, No. 5, pp. 6)**
Pub: Crain Communications Inc. - Detroit
Ed: Amy Lane. **Description:** Michigan's Governor Jennifer Granholm seeks to create a new retirement-savings program for small business employee working for firms not offering pension coverage. Details of the plan are included.

26914 ■ **"Small Firms, Consumers Have PWBA Health Care Benefit Tools" in** *Employee Benefit Plan Review* **(Vol. 55, No. 8, February 2001, pp. 40)**
Pub: Charles D. Spencer & Associates, Inc.
Description: A discussion regarding online and paper publications of the Pension and Welfare Benefits Administration of the Department of Labor. These tools for helping individuals and small businesses in making decisions about health care benefits have resulted from the Health Benefits Education Campaign.

26915 ■ **"Soaring Salaries: It's Payback Time" in** *Business Week* **(No. 3702, October 9, 2000, pp. F24)**
Pub: McGraw-Hill, Inc.
Description: Executive salaries are reaching record levels. Entrepreneurs are forced to offer as much as 40%-60% increases for new hires and better expand benefits for those already on the payroll. Statistical data included.

26916 ■ **"Spitzer's Stand" in** *Entrepreneur* **(Vol. 33, September 2005, No. 9, pp. 64)**
Pub: Entrepreneur Media Inc.
Ed: Jacquelyn Lynn. **Description:** Eliot Spitzer, New York state attorney general, recommends employers in all states to scrutinize 401(k) plan providers to ensure employees are not being overcharged for benefits, otherwise they may face legal action.

26917 ■ **"Stock answers: Workers need 401(K) advice? Too bad! You can't give it!" in** *Entrepreneur* **(Vol. 30, No. 3, March 2002, pp. 28)**
Pub: Entrepreneur Media Inc.
Ed: Stephen Barlas. **Description:** An overview of the proposed Retirement Security Advice Act, which is opposed by labor and some Democrats, is presented.

26918 ■ "Stock option communications evolve; challenges remain" in *Employee Benefit Plan Review* **(Vol. 56, No. 1, July 2001, pp. 36)**
Pub: Charles D. Spencer & Associates, Inc.
Ed: Sue Burzawa. **Description:** Stock ownership plans should be discussed when the plan is introduced and when transactions take place. Employees should also be reminded that the program is in existence periodically. Supervisors and managers should receive more information so they can provide their employees with correct information about the program.

26919 ■ "Survey Finds Workers Confident of Living Comfortable Retirement" in *Baltimore Sun* **(April 11, 2003)**
Pub: Knight-Ridder/Tribune Business News
Ed: Eileen Ambrose. **Description:** The majority of employees feel optimistic about retirement, according to the 13th Annual Retirement Confidence Survey, conducted in January 2003, for the Employee Benefit Research Institute and its affiliate, the American Savings Education Council.

26920 ■ "Sweet taste of success" in *WorkingWoman* **(Vol. 25, No. 2, February 2000, pp. 34)**
Pub: Lang Communications Inc.
Ed: Amanda Walmac. **Description:** Rena Pocrass of Chocolates a la Carte helps her employees by offering a stock plan.

26921 ■ "Take your pick" in *Entrepreneur* **(Vol. 31, No. 5, May 2003, pp. 69)**
Pub: Entrepreneur Media Inc.
Ed: Mark Henricks. **Description:** Cafeteria health insurance plans let employees preset an amount to pay for selections from various insurances and other benefit providers. Employers prefer cafeteria-style packages because they shift some of the healthcare costs onto employees.

26922 ■ "Taking Care of Baby?" in *Entrepreneur* **(Vol. 32, July 2004, No. 7, pp. 78)**
Pub: Entrepreneur Media Inc.
Ed: Joanne Cleaver. **Description:** According to the Society for Human Resource Management, fewer companies have parental leave policies than in the past. A good family leave policy can give a small business an advantage over big companies with confusing corporate policies, along with offering employees a benefit they want.

26923 ■ "Taking a Dive: A Federally Chartered Insurer of Pensions has Fallen on Hard Times. Taxpayers, Beware" in *Barron's* **(July 21, 2003)**
Pub: Barron's
Ed: Jim McTague. **Description:** The government-run Pension Benefit Guaranty Corporation, which insures more than 30,000 defined-benefit plan payments comprising more than 40 million workers, could be bankrupt in ten years, according to Congress. A bailout would tax citizens in the tens of billions.

26924 ■ "Tax Benefit is Worth Keeping" in *Crain's New York Business* **(Vol. 23, November 20, 2006, No. 47, pp. 10)**
Pub: Crain Communications, Inc.
Description: New York City was desperate to spur housing construction in the 1970's so it created the 421-a program offering ten to twenty-five year reductions in property taxes. The Bloomberg administration wants to overhaul the tax break due to the strong housing market.

26925 ■ "Tax Cut Bill Includes Pension Reform, Other Provisions Affecting Employee Benefits" in *Employee Benefit Plan Review* **(Vol. 55, No. 12)**
Pub: Charles D. Spencer & Associates, Inc.
Description: The Economic Growth and Tax Relief Reconciliation Act of 2001 represents a major advance in pension reform. The new law, which President George W. Bush expects to sign, includes an increase of the annual dollar limit for defined benefit plans.

26926 ■ "Tax-Free College Savings" in *My Business* **(August/September 2002, pp. 15)**
Pub: My Business Magazine
Ed: Phillip L. Pennartz. **Description:** An overview of the 529 Plan that allows individuals to invest in mutual funds for a child's or grandchild's education with tax-free earnings.

26927 ■ "Tax Law Changes Mean Money for Education and Retirement" in *Ingram's* **(Vol. 29, No. 1, January 2003, pp. 19)**
Pub: Show Me Publishing, Inc.
Ed: Jackie Perlman. **Description:** The benefits granted under the Economic Growth and Tax Relief Reconciliation Act of 2001, allows incentives for education and retirement.

26928 ■ "Telecommuter Denied Jobless Benefits" in *Inc.* **(October 1, 2003)**
Pub: Gruner & Jahr USA Publishing
Ed: Patrick J. Sauer. **Description:** An unemployed Florida telecommuter was denied unemployment benefits from the New York company she worked for.

26929 ■ "Termination reasons key to workers' comp claims" in *Business First Columbus* **(Vol. 18, No. 40, May 24, 2002, pp. B6)**
Pub: Business First Columbus, Inc.
Ed: Brent Wilder. **Description:** The Ohio Supreme Court ruled in four cases regarding workers compensation and termination. If an employee is fired for reasons that were well documented prior to a worker being injured, the employee will receive nothing.

26930 ■ "That Bites" in *Entrepreneur* **(Vol. 33, January 2005, No. 1, pp. 69)**
Pub: Entrepreneur Media Inc.
Ed: Joshua Kurlantzick. **Description:** Ninety percent of small companies are not compliant with new COBRA regulations. Employers with more than 20 employees must now give written notice explaining COBRA. Brokers can assist small business owners with COBRA compliance.

26931 ■ "The Solution's So Obvious, Yet So Hard to Follow Sometimes" in *St. Louis Post-Dispatch* **(February 27, 2005)**
Pub: Knight-Ridder/Tribune Business News
Ed: Repps Hudson. **Description:** Some companies are providing employees with laptops and BlackBerry's in order to stay in touch with the office, even when home sick allowing them to work from home.

26932 ■ "There's No Perk Like Home" in *Inc.* **(December 1, 2003)**
Pub: Gruner & Jahr USA Publishing
Ed: Nadine Heintze. **Description:** Some small companies are offering assistance to home purchases to employees. ArchivesOne awards two low interest homes to employees annually.

26933 ■ "Thinking Ahead" in *Entrepreneur* **(Vol. 33, September 2005, No. 9, pp. 62)**
Pub: Entrepreneur Media Inc.
Ed: Jacquelyn Lynn. **Description:** Long term care insurance may be the most important insurance product on the market today. The coverage offers advantages to both the employer and employee, because they are usually tax-deductible, benefits are tax-free, and employees can take their coverage with them if they retire or leave the firm.

26934 ■ *This Is Not Your Parents' Retirement: A Revolutionary Guide for a Revolutionary Generation*
Pub: Entrepreneur Press
Ed: Patrick P. Astre. **Released:** July 2005. **Price:** $19.95 (US), $26.95 (Canadian). **Description:** Mutual funds, stocks, bonds, insurance products, and tax strategies for retirement planning.

26935 ■ "Throwing money away" in *Incentive* **(Vol. 174, No. 9, September 2000, pp. 8)**
Pub: Bill Communications
Ed: Vincent Alonzo. **Description:** Two new surveys prove cash rewards, though popular, don't stick with employees.

26936 ■ "Throwing a Line to Uninsured Workers" in *Business Week* **(No. 3853, October 13, 2003, pp. 88)**
Pub: McGraw-Hill Inc.
Ed: Kimberly Weisul. **Description:** The biggest problem facing small companies is the cost and availability of health insurance for employees. An overview of initiatives offering help for small firms is presented.

26937 ■ "Tight buyout financing may boost use of employee stock plans" in *Wall Street Journal* **(April 30, 2002, pp. B6)**
Pub: Wall Street Journal
Ed: Jeff Bailey. **Description:** Employee stock ownership plans are helping small businesses to resolve succession issues while winning more backing from banks. Statistical data included.

26938 ■ "Time on Their Side" in *Entrepreneur* **(Vol. 32, November 2004, No. 11, pp. 98)**
Pub: Entrepreneur Media Inc.
Ed: Chris Penttila. **Description:** Giving employees an extra hour or two of flexible time or the option to telecommute occasionally, compressed workweeks, closing early on Fridays, are all ways to motivate employees.

26939 ■ "Tips to Keep Your Medical Renewal Cost Under Control" in *Ingram's* **(Vol. 29, No. 9, September 2003, pp. 52)**
Pub: Show Me Publishing, Inc.
Ed: Matt Krull. **Description:** Ways to reduce insurance costs for small businesses in the Greater Kansas City, Missouri area are covered. Topics include employment practices liability insurance, employee medical coverage, and long-term planning.

26940 ■ "Tips on managing older workers" in *Crain's Detroit Business* **(Vol. 17, No. 44, October 22, 2001, pp. 11)**
Pub: Crain Communications, Inc.
Description: Tips for managing an older workforce are covered. Topics covered include compensation benefits, ergonomic equipment, stress management, flexible schedules, conflict resolution, and training.

26941 ■ "To Your Health" in *Entrepreneur* **(Vol. 32, July 2004, No. 7, pp. 35)**
Pub: Entrepreneur Media Inc.
Description: Thirty-seven percent of U.S. entrepreneurs are taking steps to minimize health care costs. Statistical data included.

26942 ■ "TPA business for self-funded plans balanced in 2000" in *Employee Benefit Plan Review* **(Vol. 56, No. 1, July 2001, pp. 18)**
Pub: Charles D. Spencer & Associates, Inc.
Description: The use of third party administrators for self-funded health insurance programs is discussed, including such topics as fees paid and programs provided.

26943 ■ "Tripped up" in *Atlanta Business Chronicle* **(Vol. 25, No. 19, October 18, 2002, pp. 1C)**
Pub: American City Business Publications, Inc.
Ed: Charles Davidson. **Description:** Rising worker's compensation rates are up and company assessments by insurers are getting tougher.

26944 ■ "The Ultimate Employee Buy-In" in *Inc.* **(Volume 27, December 2005, No. 12, pp. 107-111, 114-116)**
Pub: Inc. Magazine
Ed: John Case. **Description:** Employee stock ownership plans, or ESOPs, are becoming a trend among small companies, an alternative to entrepreneurs rather than selling their firm.

26945 ■ *Understanding Workers Compensation*
Pub: Government Institutes
Contact: Kenneth Wolff DC, Medical Examiner/ Disability Evaluator
Released: latest edition 1995. **Price:** $65, individuals softcover. **Publication Includes:** Listing of state and provincial workers compensation administrators. **Entries Include:** Name, address, phone. Principal content of publication is explanation of the Workers Compensation System.

26946 ■ "Uninsured: a Vexing Problem" in *Crain's New York Business* **(Vol. 23, January 15, 2007, No.3, pp. 12)**
Pub: Crain Communications, Inc.
Description: Health insurance costs are so high that many employers cannot afford to insure their employees. A major hospital group and New York's leading insurer proposed modest plans to expand existing programs.

26947 ■ "Union Paychecks Could Be Bigger in 2005, But At a Cost" in *Kansas City Star* **(February 22, 2005)**
Pub: Knight-Ridder/Tribune Business News
Ed: Randolph Heaster. **Description:** Employers that are willing to raise wages during union negotiations will most likely cut health benefits at the same time. According to a recent survey, 60 percent of employers would consider wage hikes, while 69 percent reported health insurance and related benefits were top priority in concession gains.

26948 ■ "Unleash the Power of Leasing" in *Success* **(Vol. 47, No. 4, September 2000, pp. 76)**
Pub: Success Publishing, Inc.
Ed: Tara Baukus Mello. **Description:** Leasing has a whole new twist, it can help stretch finances, reward employees, and find money to grow a business.

26949 ■ "A Virtual, Personal HR" in *PC Magazine* **(December 19, 2000, pp. 7a)**
Pub: Ziff-Davis Publishing Company
Ed: Sarah L. Roberts-Witt. **Description:** A preview of Authoria's software services that uses the Web to answer employees questions concerning their benefits. Authoria claims to save on average $1,700 annually per employee by cutting Human Resource time on benefits administration.

26950 ■ "Web-based services provide easy access to no-cost employer-sponsored discount programs" in *Employee Benefit Plan Review* **(Vol.55, No. 6)**
Pub: Charles D. Spencer & Associates, Inc.
Ed: Miriam Basch Scott. **Description:** Internet companies exist which offer employee discount programs on products and services to businesses that wish to give their workers incentives outside of the workplace.

26951 ■ "Wellness programs" in *Rough Notes* **(Vol. 146, No. 3, March 2003, pp. 134)**
Pub: Rough Notes
Ed: Len Strazewski. **Description:** The benefits of providing physical fitness programs to employees are seen in increased productivity as well as savings to the employer.

26952 ■ "What Eliot Spitzer's Investigations Mean For You" in *Inc.* **(May 1, 2005)**
Pub: Inc. Magazine
Ed: Stephanie Clifford. **Description:** If a 401(k) provider or insurance company overcharges employees, a small business owner may be held liable. It is recommended that employers check fees, commission structures, and overrides with health care providers carefully.

26953 ■ "What You Need to Know About Stock Options" in *Harvard Business Review* **(Vol. 78, No. 2, March 2000, pp. 121)**
Pub: Harvard Business School Publishing Corp.
Ed: Brian J. Hall. **Description:** Despite what critics say, stock option grants are the best form of executive compensation ever devised. But, just having an option plan isn't enough. You have to have the right plan.

26954 ■ "What's the Plan? How President Bush's Second-Term Agenda Will Affect You" in *Entrepreneur* **(Vol. 33, January 2005, No. 1, pp. 24)**
Pub: Entrepreneur Media Inc.
Ed: Crystal Detamore-Rodman. **Description:** President Bush is expected to carryover his first term agenda of making his income tax cuts permanent, a permanent repeal of estate tax, and an expansion of health savings accounts.

26955 ■ "What's Wrong with Executive Compensation" in *Harvard Business Review* **(Vol. 81, No. 1, January 2003, pp. 69)**
Pub: Harvard Business School Press
Ed: Charles Elson. **Description:** Harvard Business Review and the University of Delaware's Center for Corporate Governance convened a roundtable to discuss executive compensation. The twelve panelists discussed ways to align the interests of executives with long-term company interests and the broader questions of corporate governance and company values.

26956 ■ "When Life Happens: A New Trend In Employee Benefits" in *Rough Notes* **(Vol. 145, No. 1, January 2003, pp. 46)**
Pub: Rough Notes
Ed: Elisabeth Boone. **Description:** Fortis Benefits Insurance Company and Work and Family Benefits, are the two companies dealing with broadened benefits packages that help employees balance their work and family responsibilities since 47 percent of them have a dependent care need.

26957 ■ "When You Speak, Lawmakers Listen" in *My Business* **(June/July 2004, pp. 41)**
Pub: My Business Magazine
Description: Lawmakers are interested in small business. The National Federation of Independent Business (NFIB) advocates for small business through its Member Ballot, the largest opinion-gathering effort of its type. Results are given to lawmakers. Currently issues revolved around employer retirement savings accounts, postal rates, debit cards, project labor agreements, and OSHA regulations.

26958 ■ "When You Want a Low Share Price" in *Inc.* **(May 2000, pp. 171)**
Pub: The Goldhirsh Group
Description: One of the most common reasons that business owners knock down their share price is to avoid payroll and other taxes tied to stock gifts for employees. The benefits for doing this are explained.

26959 ■ "Where Everyone's a Winner: Sure, the Annual Trip to Hawaii Is a Great Reward For Your Top Performers" in *Sales & Marketing Management*
Pub: VNU Business Media
Ed: Julia Chang. **Description:** Motivational strategies that benefit an entire sales team, rather than rewarding only the top few salespeople, can provide greater success. In a recent survey, 68 percent of workers stated that more award opportunities would further motivate them in their jobs.

26960 ■ "While I'm Gone: Transitioning Into- and Back From-Family and Medical Leave" in *Black Enterprise* **(Vol. 35, September 2004, No. 2)**
Pub: Earl G. Graves Publishing Co. Inc.
Ed: Carla Thompson. **Description:** According to the 2000 Family and Medical Leave Act (FMLA) survey, conducted by the U.S. Department of Labor, 75 percent of workers took some form of family leave in 1999.

26961 ■ "Workers' Con" in *Forbes* **(Vol. 175, February 28, 2005, No. 4, pp. 34)**
Pub: Forbes Magazine Inc.
Ed: Nathan Vardi. **Description:** American businesses are cheating on workers' compensation, costing billions in added premiums and leaving employees at risk.

26962 ■ "Working at Home" in *Kiplinger's Personal Finance Magazine* **(Vol. 54, No. 10, October 2000, pp. 32)**
Pub: The Kiplinger Washington Editors, Inc.
Description: Chances are you are entitled to family leave, and chances are getting better that you may someday get paid for it. A Web site giving a summary of state laws is included.

26963 ■ "Workplace Column" in *Kansas City Star* **(January 20, 2005)**
Pub: Knight-Ridder/Tribune Business News

Ed: Diane Stafford. **Description:** Eddy Watkins ask his workers to help save the printing company, Watkins Lithographic, from bankruptcy. His employees worked hard to save the business and Watkins rewarded all 31 of them, plus a guest, to a 3-day, all-expense-paid vacation at a Florida resort.

26964 ■ "Year-End Bonus Points" in *Inc.* **(November 1, 2003)**
Pub: Gruner & Jahr USA Publishing
Ed: Jess McCuan. **Description:** Employees prefer trips to cash as bonuses, with Mexico ranking the number one destination for incentive and Las Vegas as the first choice domestically.

TRADE PERIODICALS

26965 ■ *Benefits Law Journal*
Pub: Aspen Publishers Inc.
Contact: Dianne C. Scent
Released: Quarterly. **Price:** $345 list price. **Description:** Journal covering the welfare benefits field, including new types, delivery methods, and legal requirements.

26966 ■ *Benefits Quarterly*
Pub: International Society of Certified Employee Benefit Specialists
Contact: Jack L. VanDerhei PhD
Released: Quarterly. **Price:** $125; $95 students. **Description:** Journal for human resources professionals.

26967 ■ *BNA Pension & Benefits Reporter*
Pub: Bureau of National Affairs Inc.
Contact: D. Sayre
Ed: David A. Sayre, Editor. **Released:** Weekly. **Price:** $940. **Description:** Covers pension developments stemming from the passage of the Employee Retirement Income Security Act of 1974 (ERISA) and its amendments. Discusses pension and welfare benefit regulations, standards, enforcement actions, court decisions, legislative and administrative actions, agency options, and employee benefit trust fund requirements.

26968 ■ *Compensation*
Pub: Bureau of National Affairs Inc.
Contact: Jeff Day, Managing Editor
Released: Weekly. **Price:** $683. **Description:** Offers legal clarification and practical advice on employers' pay and benefit policies. Discusses such topics as health care cost containment, payroll laws and taxes, workers compensation laws, pension law (ERISA), job evaluation, benefit plans, compensation administration, incentive systems, and independent contractors. Compensation is part of the BNA Policy and Practice Series, and can be purchased separately or in any combination with other binder sets entitled Fair Employment Practices, Labor Relations, Personnel Management, or Wages and Hours.

26969 ■ *Compensation & Benefits Management*
Pub: Aspen Publishers Inc.
Released: Quarterly. **Description:** Journal covering issues for compensation and benefits management professionals.

26970 ■ *Compensation & Benefits Review*
Pub: American Management Association
Ed: Fay Hansen, Editor. **Released:** Bimonthly. **Price:** $408 institutions print & online; $387.60 institutions online; $391.68 institutions print only; $394 print only; $85 single issue; $72 institutions single issue. **Description:** Journal on employee compensation and benefits.

26971 ■ *EAP Digest*
Pub: Performance Resource Press Inc.
Contact: Brent Chartier, Managing Editor
Released: Quarterly. **Price:** $36; $45 Canada, Hawaii, and Alaska; $55 other countries; $65 air mail, other countries; $60 two years; $10 single issue. **Description:** Magazine covering planning, development, and administration of employee assistance programs.

26972 ■ EBRI Issue Brief
Pub: Employee Benefit Research Institute
Contact: Steve Blakely
E-mail: blakely@ebri.org
Ed: Dallas Salisbury, Editor, salisbury@ebri.org. **Released:** Monthly. **Price:** Included in membership; $224, nonmembers; $25, single issue. **Description:** Examines, analyzes, and interprets key issues and trends in the employee benefits field. Covers one topic in-depth in each issue. Remarks: Price includes subscription to the newsletter Employee Benefit Notes.

26973 ■ EBRI Pension Investment Report
Pub: Employee Benefit Research Institute
Contact: Dallas L. Salisbury, President
E-mail: salisbury@ebri.org
Released: Irregular. **Price:** $500 single issue. **Description:** Report on private and public pension funds and pension investment perrformance.

26974 ■ Employee Benefit Notes
Pub: Employee Benefit Research Institute
Contact: Steve Blakely
E-mail: blakely@ebri.org
Ed: Dallas Salisbury, Editor, salisbury@ebri.org. **Released:** Monthly. **Price:** Included in membership; $224, nonmembers. **Description:** "Analyzes and discusses newly released employee benefits data and reviews a wide range of policy issues, research and publications." Recurring features include news of research, legal analysis, legislative updates. Remarks: Subscription includes EBRI Issue Brief.

26975 ■ Employee Benefit Plan Review
Pub: Aspen Publishing Inc.
Contact: Barbara Williams, Advertising Mgr
Ed: Bruce F. Spencer, Editor. **Released:** Monthly. **Price:** $85. **Description:** Magazine serving decision-makers who administer, design, install, and service employee benefit plans.

26976 ■ Employee Benefits Cases
Pub: Bureau of National Affairs Inc.
Contact: David A. Sayre, Managing Editor
Released: Weekly, 50/year. **Price:** $1,141. **Description:** Reports full text of federal and state court opinions and selected decisions of arbitrators and the National Labor Relations Board on employee benefits issues. Recurring features include a cumulative index digest, tables of cases, a topical index, and a classification guide.

26977 ■ Employee Benefits Management Directions
Pub: CCH Inc.
Released: Semimonthly. **Price:** $235. **Description:** Considers new trends in employee benefits management, including 401k plans, family leave programs, health insurance, retirement plans, and relocation assistance. Provides tax information and news of legislation and court cases. Recurring features include news of educational opportunities and conferences. Remarks: Included with subscription to Employee Benefits Management.

26978 ■ Employee Compensation
Pub: Business & Legal Reports Inc.
Contact: Stephen Fouvnier J.D., Managing Editor
Released: Monthly. **Price:** $395, Included in membership. **Description:** News, comment, and prognostication on employee compension, and benefits.

26979 ■ Employee Relations Law Journal
Pub: Aspen Publishers Inc.
Released: Quarterly. **Description:** Journal for employers and legal advisors covering problems with equal employment opportunity, occupational health and safety, labor-management relations, and employee benefits and compensation.

26980 ■ Employee Services Management
Pub: ESM Association
Contact: Patrick B. Stinson, Publisher
Ed: Renee M. Mula, Editor. **Released:** Bimonthly. **Price:** $52; $74 two years 2 years. **Description:** Trade magazine focusing on employee services, fitness, and recreation programming.

26981 ■ Employment Relations Today
Pub: John Wiley & Sons Inc.
Contact: Jo-Ann Wasserman, Managing Editor
Ed: Carol Di Paola, Editor. **Released:** 4/year. **Price:** $545 print, U.S.; $545 Canada and Mexico print, for Canada add 7% GST; $569 other countries print; $545 institutions print, U.S.; $545 institutions, Canada and Mexico print, for Canada add 7% GST; $569 institutions, other countries print; $600 institutions print & online, U.S.; $600 institutions, Canada and Mexico print & online, for Canada add 7% GST; $624 institutions, other countries print & online. **Description:** Journal for senior human resources executives covering HR strategies and best practices.

26982 ■ Flexible Benefits
Pub: Aspen Publishers Inc.
Ed: Gregory E. Matthews, Editor. **Released:** Monthly. **Price:** $265, individuals. **Description:** Features news and research of interest to benefit managers and consultants. Focus is on employee benefits that involve choice. Recurring features include news of research, reports of meetings, news of educational opportunities, and original analysis of regulations affecting benefits.

26983 ■ International Personnel Management Association—Agency Issues
Pub: International Personnel Management Association
Contact: Karen D. Smith
Ed: Karen D. Smith, Editor, ksmith@ipma-hr.org. **Released:** 20/year. **Price:** Included in membership. **Description:** Presents news and information on human resources legislation, compensation and benefits, personnel policies, and other areas of interest to public sector human resource departments

26984 ■ Journal of Compensation and Benefits
Pub: RIA Group
Contact: Blanca M. Duque, Advertising Mgr
Ed: Jeffrey D. Mamorsky, Editor. **Released:** Bimonthly. **Price:** $335. **Description:** Magazine offering practical guidance on compensation and employee benefits issues.

26985 ■ Journal of Deferred Compensation
Pub: Aspen Publishers Inc.
Released: Quarterly, 4/yr. **Price:** $259. **Description:** Journal covering analysis, strategies, and advice for executive retirement and compensation professionals.

26986 ■ Journal of Pension Benefits
Pub: Aspen Publishers Inc.
Ed: Ilene Ferenczy, Editor. **Released:** Quarterly. **Price:** $225. **Description:** Journal covering pension issues for pension professionals.

26987 ■ Journal of Pension Planning and Compliance
Pub: Aspen Publishers Inc.
Contact: Bruce J. McNeil, Editor-in-Chief
Released: Quarterly, 4/yr. **Price:** $289 list price. **Description:** Journal covering pension compliance and design issues for professionals.

26988 ■ Medical Benefits
Pub: Aspen Publishers Inc.
Ed: Margaret Mucklo, Editor. **Released:** Semimonthly. **Price:** $275. **Description:** Focuses on key developments, statistics, and studies relating to the health care system. Covers eight major topic areas: cost containment, employee benefits, employee health/wellness, quality of care, delivery systems, government in health care, legal issues, and health care expenditure data.

26989 ■ Pension Plan Guide
Pub: CCH Inc.
Contact: Jan Gerstein, Managing Editor
E-mail: jan.gerstein@wolterskluwer.com
Released: Weekly. **Price:** $1,699 interent; $1,629 print or CD. **Description:** Loose leaf series on pension plans.

26990 ■ Pension Plan Guide—Summary
Pub: CCH Inc.
Contact: Theodore Simons
Ed: Theodore Simons, Editor. **Released:** Weekly. **Price:** $195. **Description:** Focuses on pension non-discrimination rules, benefit trends, court decisions, IRS and ERISA regulation and releases, withdrawal liability, and Supreme Court actions regarding pension plans.

26991 ■ Tax Management Compensation Planning
Pub: Tax Management Inc.
Contact: Glenn B. Davis, Managing Editor
E-mail: gdavis@bna.com
Released: Monthly. **Price:** $462. **Description:** Covers tax planning problems involving employee benefits and executive compensation. Recurring features include detailed analyses, working papers, and bibliographies.

26992 ■ What's New in Benefits & Compensation
Pub: Progressive Business Publications
Ed: John T. Hiatt, Editor. **Released:** Semimonthly. **Price:** $299, individuals. **Description:** Communicates the latest legal, tax and policy developments that help benefits executives address cost concerns while meeting complex needs of employees. Recurring features include interviews, news of research, and a column titled Sharpen Your Judgment.

26993 ■ Work/Life Today
Pub: National Institute of Business Management
Ed: Sharon O'Malley, Editor. **Released:** Monthly. **Price:** $355, individuals. **Description:** Provides information on "family-friendly" benefit programs.

26994 ■ Work Span
Pub: WorldatWork
Ed: Jean Christ-Offerson, Editor, jchristofferson@worldatwork.org. **Released:** 10/year. **Description:** Concentrates on issues in the fields of compensation and benefits and human resource management. Includes legislative updates, resources, and case studies.

26995 ■ WorldatWork Journal
Pub: WorldatWork
Ed: Dan Cafaro, Editor, dcafaro@worldatwork.org. **Released:** 4/year. **Price:** $210, Included in membership; $85, nonmembers U.S. and U.S. territories; $120, nonmembers other countries. **Description:** Offers strategic-focused articles dealing with topics such as compensation, benefits, and human resources management.

CONSULTANTS

26996 ■ A Friend of the Family
1071 Founders Blvd., Ste. A
Athens, GA 30606
Ph:(770)725-2748
Fax: (706)354-1902
Co. E-mail: afriendofthefamily@hotmail.com
URL: http://www.afriend.com

E-mail: afriendofthefamily@hotmail.com
Scope: Human resource development consultants for personal care services as part of employee benefit programs. Programs include: childcare, elder care, home secretaries, shopping and errand services. Serves private industries as well as government agencies. **Special Services:** Maintains a proprietary "friend" software system for telemarketing, tracking, billing, and managing personal referrals.

26997 ■ Abacus Benefit Consultants Inc.
55 Stamp Farm Rd.
Cranston, RI 02921-3401
Ph:(401)942-4900
Fax: (401)942-8989
Co. E-mail: info@abacusbci.com
URL: http://www.abacusbci.com

E-mail: info@abacusbci.com
Scope: Administrators and consultants for employee benefit plans. Offers clients a menu of services in the traditional full service approach and coordinate with insurance companies and/or mutual fund companies with our unbundled service package for 401(k) plans.

26998 ■ Acordia Employers Service Marketing Inc.
426 Leon Sullivan Way
Charleston, WV 25301
Ph:(304)556-1161
Fax: (304)556-1165
Co. E-mail: aesmarketing@acordiaservices.com
URL: http://interact.acordiaservices.com

E-mail: aesmarketing@acordiaservices.com
Scope: Offers specialized cost control and claims administration in the areas of unemployment compensation, workers' compensation, federal black lung, and loss control, and short/long term disability programs.

26999 ■ Administrative Management Group Inc.
3800 N Wilke Rd., Ste. 250
Arlington Heights, IL 60004-1247
Ph:(847)577-6000
Fax: (847)870-9200
Co. E-mail: amgmarketing@amgusa.com
URL: http://www.amgusa.com

E-mail: amgmarketing@amgusa.com
Scope: Offers services in retirement, savings and flexible benefits (including design), recordkeeping and administration for defined benefit, defined contribution and flexible benefit programs, and plan/trust legal documentation drafting. Specialties include communication programs and the preparation of benefit statements, booklets, and audiovisual programs.

27000 ■ Advanced Benefits & Human Resources
9350-F Snowden River Pky., Ste. 222
Columbia, MD 21045
Ph:(410)290-9037
Fax: (410)740-2568
Co. E-mail: hrb@abhr.com

E-mail: hrb@abhr.com
Scope: Provides human resource consulting to high technology businesses. Offers services in the areas of human resources, benefits, and training. Creates, maintains, or updates current human resource functions.

27001 ■ Aldrich & Cox Inc.
3075 Southwestern Blvd., Ste. 202
Orchard Park, NY 14127-1287
Ph:(716)675-6300
Fax: (716)675-2098
Co. E-mail: consult@aldrichandcox.com
URL: http://www.aldrichandcox.com

E-mail: consult@aldrichandcox.com
Scope: Offers insurance and risk management counseling for all lines of insurance and self-insurance to business, industry, institutions, political subdivisions, and utilities. Serves on a continuing basis but is also available for special projects, such as risk management audits in the Eastern United States and Canada.

27002 ■ AmeriFlex Financial Services
3700 State St., Ste.310
Santa Barbara, CA 93101
Ph:(805)898-0893
Free: 800-425-1522
Fax: (805)898-0759
Co. E-mail: abc.service@ameriflex.com
URL: http://www.ameriflex.com

E-mail: abc.service@ameriflex.com
Scope: An independent financial consulting firm. Develops and markets retirement and employee benefit programs to businesses, school districts, hospitals, non-profit organizations, and individual investors.

27003 ■ Aurora Administrative Solutions Ltd.
26 W Nottingham Dr., Ste. 205
PO Box 5818
Dayton, OH 45405
Ph:(937)275-6280
Fax: (937)275-6065
Co. E-mail: benefits@aurorasolutions.com
URL: http://www.aurorasolutions.com

E-mail: benefits@aurorasolutions.com
Scope: Provides employee benefit administrative services to the outsourcing marketplace. Concentrates resources on the administration and compliance of employee benefit plans. Practice limited to flexible benefits plan administration, COBRA administration, employee enrollment and eligibility administration, direct/retiree billing services, hour bank administration, and full benefits outsourcing administration services.

27004 ■ Franklin F. Beach & Co.
5478 N Rolling Oaks Dr.
Memphis, TN 38119-4957
Ph:(901)763-4082
Fax: (901)767-1533
Scope: The firm offers counseling, estate planning and employee benefit planning including pension planning, profit sharing, executive compensation, health and welfare plans, business organization and management expertise.

27005 ■ Benefit Communications Inc.
2126 21st Ave. S
PO Box 120789
Nashville, TN 37212
Ph:(615)292-3786
Free: 800-489-3786
Fax: (615)383-7917
Co. E-mail: info@benefitcommunications.com
URL: http://www.benefitcommunications.com

E-mail: info@benefitcommunications.com
Scope: An employee benefit communications and servicing company that specializes in three areas voluntary products, employee communications and open enrollment outsourcing.

27006 ■ Benefit Dynamics Inc.
8 Ranoldo Ter.
Cherry Hill, NJ 08034
Ph:(856)616-1400
Fax: (856)616-1401
Co. E-mail: benefit@benefitdynamics.com
URL: http://www.benefitdynamics.com

E-mail: benefit@benefitdynamics.com
Scope: A full service employee benefit, record keeping consultant and outsourcing organization. provides pension consulting, administration and actuarial services, cafeteria and flexible benefit plans, human resource systems outsourcing, interactive voice-response systems, electronic employee benefit enrollment, transportation plans.

27007 ■ Benefit Partners Inc.
363 Falconbridge Rd.
Sudbury, ON, Canada P3A 5K5
Ph:(705)524-1559
Free: 800-461-6326
Fax: (705)524-5553
Co. E-mail: info@benefitpartners.com
URL: http://www.benefitpartners.com

E-mail: info@benefitpartners.com
Scope: Services include Employee Benefits, Pension, Executive Compensation, Human Resources and Finacial Management.

27008 ■ Benefit Sources & Solutions
1952 Rte. 22 E
Bound Brook, NJ 08805
Ph:(732)560-1010
Fax: (732)560-1049
Co. E-mail: srappoport@benefitsource.com
URL: http://www.benefitsource.com

E-mail: srappoport@benefitsource.com
Scope: Employee benefit brokers and consultants that designs, implements and administers employee

benefit plans that are integrated an employer's compensation package.

27009 ■ Benetech Inc.
3947 Lennane Dr., Ste. 250
Sacramento, CA 95834
Ph:(916)484-6811
Fax: (916)488-1743
Co. E-mail: info@benetechinc.com
URL: http://www.benetechinc.com

E-mail: info@benetechinc.com
Scope: Consulting firm provides employee benefit planning services, focusing on pension plans and 401-K plans.

27010 ■ Larry W. Buck & Associates Inc.
820 Gessner, Ste. 1355
Houston, TX 77024
Ph:(713)278-0200
Fax: (713)278-0202
Co. E-mail: lbuck@houston.rr.com

E-mail: lbuck@houston.rr.com
Scope: Consulting firm active in risk management and employee benefit planning.

27011 ■ C F Services Group Inc.
9083 Shady Grove Ct.
Gaithersburg, MD 20877
Ph:(301)963-8820
Fax: (301)963-3733
Co. E-mail: contactus@cfservicesgroup.com
URL: http://www.cfservicesgroup.com

E-mail: contactus@cfservicesgroup.com
Scope: Provides advice, information and comparisons regarding life insurance, mutual funds, limited partnerships, and other securities. Emphasis is on employee benefit planning and financial advice for businesses and key executives. Industries served: small businesses and professional practices.

27012 ■ Canadian Work/Family Directions Co.
155 Gordon Baker Rd., Ste. 212
North York, ON, Canada M2H 3N5
Ph:(416)492-3475
Fax: (416)492-8258
Co. E-mail: info@wfdcanada.com

E-mail: info@wfdcanada.com
Scope: A consulting firm focusing on work/family issues including needs assessments, policy reviews, program audits, research and development of products and services, management training, communicating Work/Family programs that specialize in family care, alternative work arrangements, benefits and compensation, and preventive health promotion initiatives. A woman-owned firm providing services to the corporate and government sectors, families, non-governmental organizations, and labor unions in Canada. Operates a branch office in Montreal, PQ, conducts seminars, and publishes Work/Family-Travail et Famille (newsletters). Firm has developed customized software and maintains comprehensive databases.

27013 ■ CCA Strategies L.L.C.
216 S Jefferson St., Ste. 600
Chicago, IL 60661
Ph:(312)454-3222
Fax: (312)454-1213
Co. E-mail: info@ccastrategies.com
URL: http://www.ccastrategies.com

E-mail: info@ccastrategies.com
Scope: Offers counsel to business owners in planning employee benefit programs and in estate planning. Provides retirement and health plan services. Also serves government agencies. **Seminars:** Computershare The Source 2006: Inspiration and Insight; The PDP Advantage for Public Sector plans; National Municipal OPEB Liabilities Conference; Fourth Annual New England Public Finance Conference. Computershare The Source 2006: Inspiration and Insight; The PDP Advantage for Public Sector plans; National Municipal OPEB Liabilities Conference; Fourth Annual New England Public Finance Conference.

27014 ■ Chernoff Diamond & Company L. L.C.
990 Stewart Ave., Ste. 520
Garden City, NY 11530
Ph:(516)683-6100
Fax: (516)683-6163
Co. E-mail: mail@chernoffdiamond.com
URL: http://www.chernoffdiamond.com

E-mail: mail@chernoffdiamond.com
Scope: A benefits advisory firm. Provides comprehensive services and design, implementation and administration of employee benefit plans, pension, profit sharing and 401(k) plans, programs of executive and deferred compensation and sophisticated life insurance plans. **Publications:** Insights Newsletter.

27015 ■ John Chute & Associates
150 Consumers Rd., Ste. 508
Toronto, ON, Canada M2J 1P9
Ph:(416)250-8600
Free: 800-565-2488
Fax: (416)250-8605
Co. E-mail: postmaster@jchute.com
URL: http://www.jchute.com

E-mail: postmaster@jchute.com
Scope: Provides counsel in the design, costing and communication of all forms of employee benefit plans. Also provides professional advice in corporate human resource and organizational development matters.

27016 ■ CMG Consulting Inc.
101 Metro Dr., Ste. 550
San Jose, CA 95110
Ph:(408)452-0422
Free: 800-847-5347
Fax: (408)452-0210
Scope: Provides corporate benefits administration and consulting services, including comprehensive financial and retirement planning services for corporations and individuals. **Special Services:** D-ACCESS.

27017 ■ Compliance Consulting Corp.
406 Marquis St.
PO Box 13673
Jackson, MS 39206-4345
Ph:(601)982-1219
Free: 800-435-1266
Fax: (601)982-1220
Co. E-mail: admin@cobracompliance.com
URL: http://www.cobracompliance.com

E-mail: admin@cobracompliance.com
Scope: A full-service COBRA and HIPAA administration company.

27018 ■ Comprehensive Professional Management Inc.
222 E Dundee Rd.
Wheeling, IL 60090-3009
Ph:(847)520-0101
Fax: (847)520-0372
Co. E-mail: bob@cpmincfs.com

E-mail: bob@cpmincfs.com
Scope: Services include accounting, financial planning, litigation support, pension profit sharing administration, practice surveys, professional corporation issues, retirement and estate planning, and tax advice.

27019 ■ CONEXIS
6191 N State Hwy. 161, Ste. 400
Irving, TX 75038
Free: 877-266-3947
Fax: 877-353-2948
Co. E-mail: customerdelivery@conexis.com
URL: http://www.conexis.org

E-mail: customerdelivery@conexis.com
Scope: Provides web-based COBRA/HIPAA/FSA/Direct Bill compliance and administration services. Texas-based outsourcing solution offers automated benefit administration for all-sized type of business. **Publications:** CompLink. **Seminars:** COBRA/HPAA Compliance.

27020 ■ Counts Benefit Services Inc.
11629 Paramus Dr.
North Potomac, MD 20878-4278
Ph:(301)424-0100
Fax: (301)424-0309
Co. E-mail: jcounts@countsbenefits.us

E-mail: jcounts@countsbenefits.us
Scope: Consulting services include evaluation of employer's benefit plans as to cost vs. benefits, self insured benefits as well as fully insured welfare plans, and defined contribution/defined benefit plans. Also designs executive compensation programs and salary continuation benefits. Active with wide variety of industries. **Seminars:** The Financial Alternative to Success Seminar.

27021 ■ Aaron Deitsch, F.S.A.
107-23 71st Rd., Ste. 231
Forest Hills, NY 11375-0366
Ph:(718)793-9885
Fax: (718)793-9888
Co. E-mail: ad@pensionconsultant.com
URL: http://www.pensionconsultant.com

E-mail: ad@pensionconsultant.com
Scope: Pension consultant and actuary providing consulting services in the employee benefits field, specializing in retirement plans.

27022 ■ Dorn & Associates Inc.
8506 Bass Lake Rd., Ste. 140
New Hope, MN 55428
Ph:(763)533-7689
Fax: (763)533-1143
Scope: Services include accounting, marketing, employment/partnership, new doctor agreements, personnel issues and human resources assessment, practice management, practice merger/acquisition/sale and/or liquidation, practice surveys and valuation, staff development and training.

27023 ■ Employee Benefit Research Institute
2121 K St. NW, Ste. 600
Washington, DC 20037-1896
Ph:(202)659-0670
Fax: (202)775-6312
Co. E-mail: info@ebri.org
URL: http://www.ebri.org

E-mail: info@ebri.org
Scope: A public policy research organization serving as an employee benefits information source on health, welfare and retirement issues. Services include: basic benefit program descriptions, legislation analysis, media coverage and interpretation and long-range planning. Specific areas of expertise are: pensions, Social Security, healthcare, Medicare, long-term care, and flexible benefits. Serves government, academic consumers, consultants, banks, insurance companies, investment managers, law and accounting firms, corporations, and individuals. **Publications:** EBRI Issue Briefs, EBRI Notes, Pension Investment Report (PIR), EBRI Databook on Employee Benefits (4th edition); Fundamentals of Employee Benefits Programs (5th edition). **Seminars:** Policy Forums, Congressional Briefings.

27024 ■ Employee Benefits Of St Cloud Inc.
940 Industrial Dr. S, Ste. 111
Sauk Rapids, MN 56379-1272
Ph:(320)251-0034
Fax: (320)251-0340
Co. E-mail: info@ebsc-online.org
URL: http://www.ebsc-online.org

E-mail: info@ebsc-online.org
Scope: Consulting firm offers employee benefit planning services.

27025 ■ Employee Services Management Association
568 Spring Rd., Ste. D
Elmhurst, IL 60126-3896
Ph:(630)559-0020
Fax: (630)559-0025
Co. E-mail: esmahq@esmassn.org

URL: http://www.esmassn.org

E-mail: esmahq@esmassn.org
Scope: Offers counsel on employee recreation/leisure activities and services for industry, business and government agencies. Provides an information and communication center for persons responsible for administering employee services, recreation and fitness programs. **Publications:** "Employee Services Management (monthly)"; " A Strategic Component of Business".

27026 ■ The Epler Co.
450 B St., Ste. 750
San Diego, CA 92101
Ph:(619)239-0831
Fax: (619)239-0807
Co. E-mail: consultants@eplercompany.com
URL: http://www.eplercompany.com

E-mail: consultants@eplercompany.com
Scope: Offers actuarial and consulting services for employee benefits specializing in retirement plans, health, life, accidental death and dismemberment, long-term disability insurance plans, and executive compensation. Administers retiree health studies, AB1200 studies for schools, and merger studies on benefits. Conducts base pay, bonus and benefit surveys. Designs total compensation programs. Industries Served: United States.

27027 ■ First Health
2180 S 1300 E Ste. 620
Salt Lake City, UT 84106-2813
Ph:(801)488-2634
Fax: (801)568-5652
Scope: Consultants active in the areas of retirement and savings plan design and administration, welfare plan design, and employee benefit communication.

27028 ■ Flex-Plan Services Inc.
11400 SE 6th St., Ste. 125
PO Box 70366
Bellevue, WA 98004
Ph:(425)452-3500
Free: 800-669-3539
Fax: (425)451-7002
Co. E-mail: flexplan@flex-plan.com
URL: http://www.flex-plan.com

E-mail: flexplan@flex-plan.com
Scope: Flexible benefit plan design and administration for cafeteria-type plans, form 5500 preparation and employee benefit statements. Also assists with the design and administration of retirement plans. Offers customized Windows-based software systems that allow employers to communicate with and to enroll employees electronically for all employee benefit plans. Provides employee self service via internet and/or intranet. Industries served: all. **Special Services:** Internet/intranet capable.

27029 ■ Frontiers Benefit Services
1833 W March Ln., Ste. 7
PO Box 7509
Stockton, CA 95207
Ph:(209)956-8686
Free: 800-723-4664
Fax: (209)956-8699
Co. E-mail: info@fbservices.com
URL: http://www.fbservices.com

E-mail: info@fbservices.com
Scope: A consulting and brokerage firm that deals primarily with employee benefit programs, employer education and regulatory compliance.

27030 ■ Gallagher Benefit Services Inc.
Two Pierce Pl.
Itasca, IL 60143
Ph:(630)773-3800
Fax: (630)285-4000
URL: http://www.gallagherbenefits.com
Scope: Offers expertise and guidance in every ara of benefits planning, delivery, and adminstration for a broad range of benefit services.

27031 ■ Health Insurance Specialists Inc.
17620A Redland Rd.
Rockville, MD 20855
Ph:(301)590-0006
Fax: (301)590-0661
Co. E-mail: info@his-inc.com
URL: http://www.his-inc.com

E-mail: info@his-inc.com
Scope: Serves a wide variety of businesses and individuals by designing comprehensive insurance packages and benefit plans, full service insurance and financial services firm, third party administration, human resources outsourcing.

27032 ■ HealthChoice
583 D'Onofrio Dr., Ste. 103
Madison, WI 53719
Ph:(608)833-7988
Free: 800-334-7988
Fax: (608)833-7540
Co. E-mail: info@healthchoice.com
URL: http://www.healthchoice.com/who.cfm

E-mail: info@healthchoice.com
Scope: Firm provides employee assistance program which concentrates on to reduce employer productivity loses. **Publications:** "Graduating From Child Care to Elder Care". **Special Services:** HealthChoice™ & CareQuest® used to reduce employer productivity loses.

27033 ■ Healy & Associates Inc.
3033 W Jefferson St.
Joliet, IL 60435-6449
Ph:(815)741-0102
Fax: (815)744-5412
Scope: Personal development consultant with experience in alcoholism and family treatment; employee assistance program consultation and implementation; health promotion programming on stress, smoking cessation, weight control; alcohol and drug related prevention and educational programming; and individual, group and family counseling. Serves private industries as well as government agencies. **Seminars:** Assertive Communication; Alcohol and Drug Problems in the Workplace; Chemical Dependency: Enabling vs. Intervention; Stress Management; Employee Assistance Programs; Smoking Cessation in the Workplace; Eating and Weight Issues; Cultural Diversity Training; Adapting to Change in the Workplace; Adapting to Shift Work.

27034 ■ Hewitt Associates L.L.C.
100 Half Day Rd.
Lincolnshire, IL 60069-3342
Ph:(847)295-5000
Free: 800-332-2111
Fax: (847)295-7634
Co. E-mail: info@hewittassociates.com
URL: http://www.hewittassociates.com

E-mail: info@hewittassociates.com
Scope: Offers services covering human resources, employee benefits, compensation, financial management and administration. **Publications:** "Lessons Uncovered: It Makes a Difference: Change Management and HR BPO"; "What Makes a Sourcing Advisor a Good Sourcing Advisor?". **Seminars:** How Do You Prepare and Educate Plan Participants, Nov, 2006.

27035 ■ Hooker & Holcombe Inc.
65 LaSalle Rd.
West Hartford, CT 06107-2397
Ph:(860)521-8400
Free: 800-457-1245
Fax: (860)521-3742
Co. E-mail: info@hhconsultants.com
URL: http://www.hhconsultants.com/HH

E-mail: info@hhconsultants.com
Scope: Offers employee benefit services in the areas of pension plans, 401(k) plans, profit sharing, ESOP, thrift and savings plans, retirement plan outsourcing services and actuarial consulting.

27036 ■ In Plain English
14501 Antigone Dr.
PO Box 3300
North Potomac, MD 20878
Ph:(301)340-2821
Free: 800-274-9645
Fax: (301)279-0115
Co. E-mail: rwohl@inplainenglish.com
URL: http://www.inplainenglish.com

E-mail: rwohl@inplainenglish.com
Scope: Management consultants helping government and businesses research, design, write and produce user-oriented management information for human resources, employee benefits, business process, corporate and marketing needs. Employee benefits services include summary plan descriptions, employee benefit booklets, plan documents, communication of employee benefit highlights, pay for performance systems, and Section 125 cafeteria benefit enrollment. Human resources services include producing employee handbooks, employee handbook audits, training manuals, writing training, and personnel policy and policy audits. Consultants also assist clients to re-humanize their business, human resource department, recruitment, and employee benefit program. **Publications:** The Benefits Communication Edge newsletter; The Employee Benefits Communication ToolKit, published by Commerce Clearinghouse. Benefits Communicat ion; a guide published by business & legal reports. **Seminars:** Plain English Writing Training; Summary Plan Description Compliance workshops; Re-Humanizing the Corporation, Human Resources and Employee Benefits Communication Workshop. **Special Services:** Electronic materials; Electronic summary plan descriptions; electronic reference manuals.

27037 ■ Managing Work and Family Inc.
1625 Sheridan Rd.
Wilmette, IL 60091
Ph:(847)308-0919
Fax: (847)475-2021
Co. E-mail: mwfam@aol.com
URL: http://www.mwfam.com

E-mail: mwfam@aol.com
Scope: The firm was designed for employers interested in creating a culture and work environment conducive to loyalty and productivity from employees with family responsibilities. The firm offers consulting, organizational assessments, flexible work option design, training for managers and employees, child and elder care services, videos, books and family days. Representative client industries include: advertising, banking and finance, electronic communications, data processing, education, government, healthcare, hospitality, manufacturing, pharmaceutical and service industries. **Publications:** "Managing Work and Family Kopykit"; "Solving the Work/Family Puzzle". **Seminars:** Workshop on family licensing program, Manager and Employee; Managing Work and Family Core Training; Fathering; Parenting; Career and Personal Life Management.

27038 ■ Money Source Financial Services Inc.
1328 S Main St.
Ann Arbor, MI 48104
Ph:(734)213-0300
Fax: (734)213-5900
Co. E-mail: tpmc@aol.com
URL: http://www.msfs.com

E-mail: tpmc@aol.com
Scope: Provides clients with access to employee benefit programs. Offers access to nearly any investment or insurance products. Provides experience in the design, implementation, and funding of 401(k) plans, Simplified Employee Pension Plan (SEP), profit sharing plans, money purchase plans, and IRA's and rollover plans.

27039 ■ Ralph Moss Ltd.
200 Town Centre Blvd., Ste. 102
Markham, ON, Canada L3R 8G5
Free: 888-667-7583

Fax: (905)513-9893
Co. E-mail: info@ralphmossltd.on.ca
URL: http://www.acelink.com/rmib

E-mail: info@ralphmossltd.on.ca
Scope: Acts as benefit consultants on projects, reviewing and making recommendations, not only on existing benefit programs, but also commenting on the taxability of benefits, legal issues and industry standards, as well as financial underwriting arrangements and other various cost factors. **Publications:** "Financial Planning Report".

27040 ■ New England Human Resource Group
35 Belver Ave., Ste. 107
North Kingstown, RI 02852
Ph:(401)295-2754
Fax: (401)295-2619
Co. E-mail: info@nehrg.com
URL: http://www.nehrg.com

E-mail: info@nehrg.com
Scope: Firm specializes in compensation systems, benefits, legal compliance, personnel policies and resources, employee relations law, safety and risk management, training and development, continuous improvement, career management, organizational change, strategic planning, human resource audits, ISO 9000 & QS 9000, professional development, financial planning, staffing, and executive development.

27041 ■ New Ways to Work Inc.
103 Morris St., Ste. A
Sebastopol, CA 95472-3858
Ph:(707)824-4000
Fax: (707)824-4410
Co. E-mail: info@nww.org
URL: http://www.nww.org

E-mail: info@nww.org
Scope: Focusses on improving the lives of the nation's youth. helps communities build systems that connect schools, community organizations and businesses, and improve the services, educational programs and support the community provides for its youth. creates the environment and guides a process that brings the right people together with customized tools for powerful learning and dramatic change. **Seminars:** Career pathways; building local intermediary organizations; strengthening youth councils; increasing youth involvement; creating quality work-based learning systems.

27042 ■ PAR Enterprises Inc.
1845 Summer St.
Stamford, CT 06905
Ph:(203)973-0366
Free: 888-333-5727
Co. E-mail: par@par-ent.com
URL: http://par-ent.com

E-mail: par@par-ent.com
Scope: Assists in the design or implementation of retirement and health care benefit programs. **Publications:** "Official Compendium Of Inner City Street Games".

27043 ■ Pension Consultants & Administrators Inc.
13510 Lamplight Village Ave.
Austin, TX 78727
Ph:(512)248-2968
Free: 800-982-8151
Fax: (512)707-5303
Scope: Offers design, installation, and communication of employee benefit plans. Specializes in combination 125/401(K) plans as well as 403(b) plans. Provides administration systems and services. Serves private industries as well as government agencies in the U.S. **Seminars:** Offers educational seminars on qualified retirement plans. **Special Services:** Flex-Direct-Automated handling of all 401(K) investments by download from client payroll system. System drafts clients plan/trust account, leaving clients in control of funds until invested according to trustee and for participant direction.

27044 ■ Kevin L. Pohle
5820 Main St., Ste. 316-317
Buffalo, NY 14221
Ph:(716)565-0565
Scope: Firm specializes in business strategic planning services, compensation and benefits consulting, special projects management, cost and productivity analysis, and business crisis management. Industries served: manufacturing, retail, healthcare facilities, educational institutions, and local government and municipalities.

27045 ■ Princeton Health Systems Inc.
9 Mercer St.
Princeton, NJ 08540
Ph:(609)924-7799
Free: 800-437-6668
Fax: (609)497-0739
URL: http://www.princetonhealthsystems.com
Scope: Offers consulting services in the evaluation, planning, implementation and assessment of medical care services to employees, including cost containment strategies and health and fitness programs.

27046 ■ A.E. Roberts Co.
11490 Xeon St. NW, Ste. 200
Coon Rapids, MN 55448
Ph:(763)757-5119
Free: 800-486-4585
Fax: (413)215-6877
Co. E-mail: info@aeroberts.com
URL: http://www.aeroberts.com

E-mail: info@aeroberts.com
Scope: A human resource and employee benefits consultant. Specializes in compliance training, focusing on regulatory compliance and human resource management issues.

27047 ■ The Segal Co.
1 Park Ave.
New York, NY 10016-5895
Ph:(212)251-5900
Fax: (212)251-5290
URL: http://www.segalco.com
Scope: The Segal Company is a leading, independent firm of benefit, compensation and human resources consultants. In January 2002, Segal acquired Sibson Consulting, a human capital consulting firm. The combined organization, with more than 1,000 employees is headquartered in New York and has offices throughout the United States, in Canada and the United Kingdom. Clients include corporations, non-profit organizations, professional service firms, state and local governments and joint boards of trustees administering pension, health and welfare plans under the Taft-Hartley Act. **Publications:** Executive Letter (monthly); Newsletter (periodic U.S. and Canadian versions); and Bulletins (periodic); also surveys on multiemployer pension plans, state employee health insurance, and other employee benefits subjects. **Seminars:** Periodic seminars on subjects of interest to clients. **Special Services:** Strategic HR consulting; Administration and Technology Consulting; Benefits Consulting; Personalized Communications (Intergrated Benefit Statements).

27048 ■ Siebrand-Wilton Associates Inc.
PO Box 337
Marlboro, NJ 07746-0337
Ph:(732)972-1456
Fax: (732)972-0214
Co. E-mail: clientsvcs@s-wa.com
URL: http://www.swausa.com

E-mail: clientsvcs@s-wa.com
Scope: Firm assesses, plans and implements human resources aspects of mergers/acquisitions. Offers human resources consulting in compensation and benefit plan design, mergers and acquisitions (HR aspects), business ethics assessment and development, editing, writing and association management services, and contract professionals and interim executives. **Publications:** "Should Government or Business Try to Save Medicare?," HR News; "Executive Temping," HR Horizons; "When is an Employee Truly an Employee?," HR Magazine; "Examining Your Insurance Carrier," HR Magazine.

27049 ■ The Stoller Co.
190 N Wiget Ln., Ste. 110
Walnut Creek, CA 94598
Ph:(925)932-1800
Free: 800-207-3674
Fax: (925)932-1869
Co. E-mail: info@stollerco.com
URL: http://www.stollerco.com

E-mail: info@stollerco.com
Scope: Specializes in retirement and 401K plans, human resources, compensation, systems consulting, and workplace compliance.

27050 ■ Swartzbaugh-Farber & Associates Inc.
1015 N 98th St., Ste. 221
Omaha, NE 68114-2357
Ph:(402)397-5800
Fax: (402)397-5424
Co. E-mail: securefuture@swartzbaugh.com
URL: http://www.swartzbaugh.com

E-mail: securefuture@swartzbaugh.com
Scope: Specializes in group employee benefits and executive benefits compensation. **Seminars:** Understanding HIPAA Seminar, Mar, 2006; HR - Developing a Profit Center, Nov, 2005.

27051 ■ TRI-AD Actuaries Inc.
221 W Crest St., Ste. 300
Escondido, CA 92025-1737
Ph:(760)743-7555
Free: 800-733-7555
Fax: (760)489-9343
Co. E-mail: info@tri-ad.com
URL: http://www.tri-ad.com

E-mail: info@tri-ad.com
Scope: A full service human resources consulting and administration firm. Specializes in outsourcing benefit administration, designing comprehensive compensation and benefit programs, automating the HR department, reshaping your corporate culture and employee communication. Services include 401k Choice daily record keeping, actuarial services, COBRA Administration, Flexible spending, account administration, health and welfare benefit consulting, human resources effectiveness, organization effectiveness and retirement plans. **Publications:** Check the Rollover Chart to see which types of plans will accept your rollover, Aug, 2006; A Complete Chart of the 2006 Cost of Living Adjustments, Jan, 2006; Valerie Gieseke in Compensation & Benefits Review: Automating Benefits Administration, Nov, 2005. **Seminars:** Preparing for COBRA Open Enrollment, Oct, 2006.

27052 ■ Donald C. Wright
3906 Lawndale Ln. N
Minneapolis, MN 55446-2940
Ph:(763)478-5595
Co. E-mail: donaldwright@compuserve.com

E-mail: donaldwright@compuserve.com
Scope: Consultant offers expertise in accounting and taxes, personal financial planning, strategic planning, pension/profit sharing planning and administration, professional practice management and surveys. Surveys and consultations performed worldwide. **Seminars:** Qualified pension plans and employee welfare benefit plans.

COMPUTERIZED DATABASES

27053 ■ *ABI/INFORM*
ProQuest
300 N Zeeb Rd.
PO Box 1346
Ann Arbor, MI 48106
Ph:(734)761-4700
Free: 800-521-0600
Fax: (734)761-6450
Co. E-mail: info@il.proquest.com

URL: http://www.proquest.com
Description: Provides full text access or bibliographic citations to articles in publications in business and management information worldwide. Includes 2.7 million indexes and abstracts. Comprised of three editions on CD-ROM:; ABI/INFORM Global covers more than 1600 sources, including more than 350 titles from outside the United States.; ABI/INFORM Research covers more than 700 sources.; ABI/INFORM Select covers about 350 sources with coverage beginning in 1991. **Availability:** Online: Ovid Technologies Inc., ProQuest, Thomson Dialog, Questel; Orbit, Gesellschaft fur Betriebswirtschaftliche Information mbH, STN International, Colorado Alliance of Research Libraries, Financial Times, Online Computer Library Center Inc. (OCLC), LexisNexis, EINS - European Information Network Services, Thomson Dialog; Batch: Nerac Inc. **Type:** Full text; Bibliographic; Image.

27054 ■ *Business Insurance*
Crain Communications Inc.
1155 Gratiot Ave.
Detroit, MI 48207
Ph:(313)446-6000
Free: 800-678-2427
Fax: (313)446-0361
Co. E-mail: info@crain.com
URL: http://www.crain.com
Description: Contains the complete text of *Business Insurance*, a newspaper providing information on the purchase and administration of corporate insurance and self-insurance programs, including property and liability insurance, reinsurance, and employee benefit and risk management programs. Includes reports on major commercial insurance claim settlements, legal and regulatory developments affecting the industry, and major losses resulting from fires, explosions, natural disasters, and litigation. Also includes analyses of industry issues and state, national, and international news. **Availability:** Online: Crain Communications Inc., LexisNexis, Dow Jones & Co. Inc., ProQuest, Thomson Dialog, Reuters Group PLC. **Type:** Full text.

27055 ■ *Compliance Guide for Plan Administrators*
CCH Inc.
2700 Lake Cook Rd.
Riverwoods, IL 60015
Ph:(847)267-7000
Free: 800-525-3335
Fax: (773)866-3095
URL: http://www.cch.com
Description: Contains detailed instructions and guidance for pension plan administrators. Includes information on complying with pension and welfare benefit law reporting and disclosure requirements. Focuses on retirement plans subject to ERISA and the Internal Revenue Code. Covers numerous types of retirement plans, fiduciary rules, compliance with the terms of a plan, and plan termination. Includes step-by-step procedures for complying with pension plan laws and regulations. **Availability:** Online: Thomson West; CD-ROM: CCH Inc. **Type:** Full text.

27056 ■ *Employee Benefits Cases*
The Bureau of National Affairs Inc.
1231 25th St. NW
Washington, DC 20037
Ph:(202)452-4200
Free: 800-372-1033
Fax: (202)452-4226
Co. E-mail: customercare@bna.com
URL: http://www.bna.com
Description: Contains the complete text of more than 6000 precedent-setting federal and state court decisions and significant employee benefits rulings of arbitrators. Subjects include reporting and disclosure, funding, participation, deductibility of contributions, preemption of state laws, qualification of employee benefits, plans, taxation of participants, vesting, collective bargaining, fiduciary responsibility, veterans rights, public employee plans, and termination insurance. Listings are arranged in alphabetical order by subject. Also includes a classification guide, topical index, and cumulative digest and index. **Availability:** Online: The Bureau of National Affairs Inc., Thomson West. **Type:** Full text.

27057 ■ *Employee Benefits Infosource*
International Foundation of Employee Benefit Plans
18700 W Bluemound Rd.
PO Box 69
Brookfield, WI 53008-0069
Ph:(262)786-6710
Free: 888-334-3327
Fax: (262)786-8670
Co. E-mail: ebinfo@ifebp.org
URL: http://www.ifebp.org
Description: Contains more than 70,000 citations, with abstracts, to the worldwide literature on employee benefit plans. Covers surveys, statistics, trends, and background information in these areas: corporate, union, and public employee benefit plans, group insurance, international benefits, pension investments, health care, compensation, human resources, and benefit plan service providers. Sources include some 250 periodicals, newsletters, books, research reports, news releases, and proceedings. **Availability:** Online: International Foundation of Employee Benefit Plans, Thomson Dialog. **Type:** Bibliographic.

27058 ■ *Pension & Benefits Daily*
The Bureau of National Affairs Inc.
1231 25th St. NW
Washington, DC 20037
Ph:(202)452-4200
Free: 800-372-1033
Fax: (202)452-4226
Co. E-mail: customercare@bna.com
URL: http://www.bna.com
Description: Contains current information on significant judicial, legislative, and regulatory developments affecting employee benefits and pension planning. Covers federal and state court decisions, legislation, and regulations relating to health insurance, tax reform, benefits, and pensions. Covers such topics as age discrimination, employee stock options, collective bargaining, executive compensation, investments, tax policies and guidance, Social Security, and more. **Availability:** Online: Thomson West, The Bureau of National Affairs Inc. **Type:** Full text.

27059 ■ *Pension & Benefits Reporter*
The Bureau of National Affairs Inc.
1231 25th St. NW
Washington, DC 20037
Ph:(202)452-4200
Free: 800-372-1033
Fax: (202)452-4226
Co. E-mail: customercare@bna.com
URL: http://www.bna.com
Description: Contains up-to-date reporting and coverage of state and federal legislative, regulatory, and judicial activities related to pensions and benefits. Includes coverage of IRS and Labor Department regulations and enforcement issues, tax legislation, health care reform, and developments within industry. Includes taxation of benefits, individual retirement accounts, and fringe benefits. **Availability:** Online: Thomson West, The Bureau of National Affairs Inc. **Type:** Full text.

LIBRARIES

27060 ■ AIAS, Inc.–Library
PO Box 521
Logandale, NV 89021
Ph:(702)398-3701
Fax: (702)398-3700
Contact: D.K. Smith, Libn.
Scope: Employee stock ownership plans. **Services:** Library open to members only. **Holdings:** 2955 books; 2006 reports; 54 manuscripts. **Subscriptions:** 205 journals and other serials; 13 newspapers.

27061 ■ Aon Consulting–Research & Technical Services–Information Center (222 M)
222 Merrimac St.
Box 926
Newburyport, MA 01950
Ph:(978)465-5374
Fax: (978)463-3450
Co. E-mail: David_Maslen@aoncons.com
Contact: David Maslen
Scope: Employee benefits, human resources management, insurance law. **Services:** Interlibrary loan; Library not open to the public. **Holdings:** 300 books; 150 bound periodical volumes; vertical files; model documents; 300 surveys; legislative histories. **Subscriptions:** 163 journals and other serials.

27062 ■ Employee Services Management Association–Information Center
568 Spring Rd., Ste. D
Elmhurst, IL 60126-3896
Ph:(630)559-0020
Fax: (630)559-0025
Co. E-mail: esmahq@esmassn.org
URL: http://www.esmassn.org
Contact: Patrick B. Stinson, Exec.Dir.
Scope: Employees - activities, sports, recreation, facilities, travel, fitness, wellness, preretirement planning, assistance programs, productivity, day care, eldercare. **Services:** Center open to the public for reference use only. **Holdings:** 50 volumes; archives.

27063 ■ Ivins, Phillips, Barker–Library
1700 Pennsylvania Ave. NW, Ste. 600
Washington, DC 20006
Ph:(202)662-3443
Co. E-mail: jefff@ipbtax.com
URL: http://ipbtax.com
Contact: Jeffrey T. Freilich, Libn.
Scope: Pensions, taxation. **Services:** Interlibrary loan; copying; Library not open to the public. **Holdings:** 1000 volumes; technical reports; CD-ROMs.

27064 ■ Towers Perrin–Information Centre
1100 Melville St., Ste. 1600
Vancouver, BC, Canada V6E 4A6
Ph:(604)691-1034
Fax: (604)691-1062
Scope: Actuarial science, employee benefits, compensation, human resources. **Holdings:** Figures not available.

27065 ■ Towers Perrin–Western Canada Information Centre
3700, 150 - 6 Ave., SW
Calgary, AB, Canada T2P 3Y7
Ph:(403)261-1432
Fax: (403)237-6733
Co. E-mail: val.ward@towers.com
Contact: Val Ward
Scope: Human resource management, total rewards, pensions, employee benefits, executive compensation, employee communications, pension and benefits administration services, pension fund asset management. **Services:** Interlibrary loan. **Holdings:** 1000 books. **Subscriptions:** 100 journals and other serials; 4 newspapers.

RESEARCH CENTERS

27066 ■ Pennsylvania State University–Risk Management Research Center
310F Smeal College of Business
University Park, PA 16802
Ph:(814)865-3961
Fax: (814)865-6284

Co. E-mail: afs1@psu.edu
URL: http://www.smeal.psu.edu/rmrc/index.html
Contact: Dr. Arnold F. Shapiro, Dir.
E-mail: afs1@psu.edu
Scope: Encourages and conducts research on the design and funding of employee benefit plans, including pensions and group health insurance, and actuarial studies.

27067 ■ University of North Carolina at Chapel Hill–Cecil G. Sheps Center for Health Services Research
CB No. 7590
725 Martin Luther King Blvd.
Chapel Hill, NC 27599-7590
Ph:(919)966-5011
Fax: (919)966-5764
Co. E-mail: timothy_carey@med.unc.edu
URL: http://www.shepscenter.unc.edu
Contact: Timothy S. Carey MD, Dir.
E-mail: timothy_carey@med.unc.edu
Scope: Aging, disability, and long-term care; child health services; health care economics and finance; health care organization; medical practice; mental health and substance abuse services and systems research; health professions and primary care; preventive health services; rural health research; women's health research; and minority health disparity research. **Services:** Technical assistance, for a number of state agencies. **Publications:** Consensus in DHHS Region IV: Women and Infant Health Indicators for Planning and Evaluation; North Carolina Health Professions Data Book; North Carolina Health Professions Fact Sheet. **Educational Activities:** Annual DHHS Region IV Conference on Maternal and Child Health, Family Planning, and Services for Children With Special Health Needs; Annual DHHS Region IV Workshop on the Collection and Use of Data for MCH and Women's Health Planning and Evaluation; Seminars and training programs.

27068 ■ University of Pennsylvania–Pension Research Council
3620 Locust Walk
3000 Steinberg Hall - Dietrich Hall
Philadelphia, PA 19104-6302
Ph:(215)898-7620
Fax: (215)573-3418
Co. E-mail: mitchelo@wharton.upenn.edu
URL: http://prc.wharton.upenn.edu/prc/prc.html
Contact: Olivia S. Mitchell PhD, Exec.Dir.
E-mail: mitchelo@wharton.upenn.edu
Scope: Private sector and public employee pension and benefits plans and social insurance to the extent to which it influences employer-sponsored arrangements. Seeks to strengthen institutional arrangements designed to provide financial resources for a secure old age through basic research into their social, economic, legal, actuarial, and financial foundations. **Publications:** Newsletter; Working paper series. **Educational Activities:** Symposium (annually).

27069 ■ West Virginia University–Institute for Labor Studies and Research
PO Box 6031
Morgantown, WV 26506-6031
Ph:(304)293-3323
Free: 800—626-4748
Fax: (304)293-3395
Co. E-mail: scbonanno@mail.wvu.edu
URL: http://www.wvu.edu/~exten/depts/ilsr/ilsr.htm
Contact: Steve Bonanno, Interim Dir./Prog.Ldr.
E-mail: scbonanno@mail.wvu.edu
Scope: Labor, including studies on employee benefits, labor-management cooperation, and industrial safety. **Educational Activities:** Residential programs and conferences.

Budgets/Budgeting

START-UP INFORMATION

27070 ■ "Balancing the Books - by the Book" in *Business Week Online* (February 4, 2002)
Pub: McGraw-Hill, Inc.
Description: Small business accounting practice and procedures for entrepreneurs are discussed, including the use of software such as QuickBooks and Peachtree.

27071 ■ "Business Budgeting Basics" in *Home Business* (Vol. 12, October 2005, No. 5, pp. 72)
Pub: Home Business Magazine
Ed: Nora Caley. **Description:** The importance of setting up a budget before launching a new business is stressed. Budgeting will assist in seeing how a business will look in its first six to twelve months.

ASSOCIATIONS AND OTHER ORGANIZATIONS

27072 ■ American Association for Budget and Program Analysis
PO Box 1157
Falls Church, VA 22041
Ph:(703)941-4300
Fax: (703)941-1535
Co. E-mail: aabpa@aol.com
URL: http://www.aabpa.org
Contact: Christine Lawson, Exec.Sec.
Membership: Professionals in budgeting, policy analysis, and program & management analysis evaluation who are employed by the federal government, state and local agencies, private companies, and academic institutions. **Purpose:** Seeks to advance knowledge in budgeting management and program analysis. Promotes the exchange of ideas and information. Conducts monthly program with guest speakers from government agencies, Congress, and institutions. **Publications:** *The Bottom Line* (bimonthly); *Journal of Public Budgeting and Finance* (quarterly).

27073 ■ International Budget Project of the Center on Budget and Policy Priorities
820 1st St. NE, Ste. 510
Washington, DC 20002
Ph:(202)408-1080
Fax: (202)408-8173
Co. E-mail: info@internationalbudget.org
URL: http://www.internationalbudget.org
Contact: Warren Krafchik, Proj. Dir.
Description: Works to assist civil society organizations globally to improve budget policies and decision-making processes. **Publications:** *A Guide to Budget Work for NGOs*; *A Taste of Success: Examples of the Budget Work of NGOs*; *Can Civil Society Add Value to Budget Decision-Making?*; *IBP Newsletter* (bimonthly); *Reports on Budget Transparency*.

REFERENCE WORKS

27074 ■ "20 Steps for Pricing a Patent: To Value an Invention You Have to Understand It" in *Journal of Accountancy* (Vol. 198, November 2004)
Pub: American Institute of Certified Public Accountants
Ed: J. Timothy Cromley. **Description:** Twenty steps to help certified public accounts and valuators determine the value of a patent are explained.

27075 ■ "About My Raise...How To Ask For and Get More Money" in *Black Enterprise* (Vol. 34, July 2004, No. 12, pp. 65)
Pub: Earl G. Graves Publishing Co. Inc.
Ed: Carla Thompson. **Description:** In order to get an overview of wages for a particular position, research must be done into companies within an industry sector, taking into consideration a firm's size and location.

27076 ■ "Accounting for the Budget" in *Law Firm Inc.* (December 2004)
Pub: American Lawyer Media LP
Ed: Joanne Sammer. **Description:** It is important for law firms to implement a strong budget and budgeting process in order to set priorities, direct resources, and guide business development. Ways to keep a budget current and to use it as a management tool are explained.

27077 ■ "Accounting Education; Response to Corporate Scandals: Helping the Profession Find Opportunity in Crisis" in *Journal of Accountancy*
Pub: American Institute of Certified Public Accountants
Ed: Pierre L. Titard, Robert L. Braun, Michael J. Meyer. **Description:** Since the recent corporate scandals caused by large corporations, colleges and universities across the nation have changed course offerings of their accounting programs to better prepare students to cope with the ethics of accounting.

27078 ■ "Accumulated Earnings Tax: Deductibility of Paid But Contested Liabilities" in *Journal of Accountancy* (January 2005)
Pub: American Institute of Certified Public Accountants
Ed: Ronald R. Hiner. **Description:** Under IRC Section 531, the accumulated earnings tax imposes a penalty tax on earnings accumulated beyond the reasonable needs of a business.

27079 ■ "Amortization of Certain Intangible Assets" in *Journal of Accountancy*
Pub: American Institute of Certified Public Accountants
Ed: Jennifer M. Mueller. **Description:** Intangible assets that are the result of contractual or legal rights are explained, including patents, licenses, trademarks, franchise and servicing rights.

27080 ■ "As economy softens, firms trimming travel budgets" in *Atlanta Business Chronicle* (Vol. 24, No. 8, July 27, 2001, pp. NA)
Pub: American City Business Journals Inc.
Ed: Leslie Williams Johnson. **Description:** Companies are reducing the numbers and costs of business trips in an effort to deal with the sagging economy. CEOs are staying in less expensive hotels, business travel accounts are scrutinized for waste, and only the most necessary of trips are taken. Business travelers are searching the Internet for frugal travel opportunities, such as taking cheaper flights that may involve a layover in other cities, rather than taking a more expensive direct flight.

27081 ■ "Automate Excel Functions: Easy-to-Create Macros Can Take Over Many Manual Processes" in *Journal of Accountancy* (January 2005)
Pub: American Institute of Certified Public Accountants
Ed: Jeff Lenning. **Description:** Macros can help accounts customize worksheets as well as export journal entries in Microsoft Excel into an accounting package and creating reports in Word.

27082 ■ "Avoid the Payroll Tax Trap: Using Withheld Payroll Taxes for Other Purposes Can be a Dangerous and Expensive Game" in *Journal of Accountancy*
Pub: American Institute of Certified Public Accountants
Ed: Howard Godfrey. **Description:** Penalties imposed on businesses using withheld payroll taxes for other purposes are discussed.

27083 ■ "Avoid the Tax Trap When Repaying Shareholder Loans" in *Journal of Accountancy*
Pub: American Institute of Certified Public Accountants
Ed: Brian K. Howell. **Description:** Certified public accountants can help clients avoid unnecessary taxes when repaying shareholder loans.

27084 ■ "Avoiding a Cash Flow Crunch: Accurate Projections Are Key To Your Business' Survival" in *Black Enterprise* (Vol. 34, July 2004)
Pub: Earl G. Graves Publishing Co. Inc.
Ed: Nicole Lewis. **Description:** According to small business financial experts, it is critical for businesses to pay attention to cash flow when engaging financial commitments that have a scheduled payback time.

27085 ■ *Basics of Budgeting, Purchasing & Financial Statements*
Pub: Amacom New Media, Inc.
Ed: Robert G. Finney. **Released:** 1999. **Price:** $39.95.

27086 ■ "Be Reasonable" in *Entrepreneur* (Vol. 32, November 2004, No. 11, pp. 24)
Pub: Entrepreneur Media Inc.
Ed: Jill Amadio. **Description:** Profiles of three midsize sedans that are both businesslike and affordable in-

clude the Dodge Stratus sedan, $19,595; the Mazda6, $18,995; and the Subaru Legacy 2.5i, $22,570.

27087 ■ "Beating the Cash Flow Blues" in *Home Business* **(Vol. 12, October 2005, No. 5, pp. 76)**
Pub: Home Business Magazine
Description: Caroline Jordan, small business coach and author, offers seven tips to help small companies avoid cash flow problems.

27088 ■ "Become Famous for What You Do" in *Journal of Accountancy* **(Vol. 198, December 2004, No. 6, pp. 30)**
Pub: American Institute of Certified Public Accountants
Description: A guide to help certified public accounts and/or financial planners become successful is highlighted.

27089 ■ "The Best of Technology Q&A: Answers to Readers' Most-Asked Questions" in *Journal of Accountancy* **(Vol. 198, December 2004, No. 6)**
Pub: American Institute of Certified Public Accountants
Ed: Stanley Zarowin. **Description:** In depth analysis of various accounting software programs are presented, including Microsoft's Excel 2000.

27090 ■ "Blues reforms raise cost worries" in *Crain's Detroit Business* **(Vol. 18, No. 19, May 13, 2002,)**
Pub: Crain Communications Inc. - Detroit
Ed: David Barkholz. **Description:** Rising healthcare costs worry area small businesses.

27091 ■ "Boomer Women Need Financial Advisors" in *Marketing to Women* **(Vol. 19, October 2006, No. 10, pp. 8)**
Pub: EPM Communications, Inc.
Description: Although most financially successful Boomer women don't have financial advisors, The Wall Street Journal reports, they need them. Financial services firms are eager to reach this market as they tend to give referrals.

27092 ■ "Breaking Free from Budgets" in *Inc.* **(October 1, 2003)**
Pub: Gruner & Jahr USA Publishing
Ed: Suzanne McGee. **Description:** Exasperated by budgets that muzzle creativity, a growing number of small businesses are breaking free from financial constraints while conserving spending.

27093 ■ "Budget cuts target cities with living-wage laws" in *Crain's Detroit Business* **(Vol. 18, No. 24,)**
Pub: Crain Communications Inc. - Detroit
Ed: Amy Lane. **Description:** Detroit and other communities in Southeast Michigan with living-wage ordinances have become targets of state budget cuts, endangering millions in revenue-sharing payments.

27094 ■ *Budgeting for a Small Business*
Pub: Crisp Publications, Inc.
Ed: Terry Dickey. **Released:** 1993. **Price:** $15.95 (paper). **Description:** Part of the Small Business & Entrepreneurship Series.

27095 ■ "Capturing the Potential: How CPA Firms are Building Successful Financial Services Practices" in *Journal of Accountancy* **(Vol. 198)**
Pub: American Institute of Certified Public Accountants
Ed: Patricia J. Abram, John J. Bowen Jr., Russ Alan Prince, Jeffrey A. Roush. **Description:** Certified public accounting firms are increasing profits by expanding into the financial services sector.

27096 ■ "The Cash Flow Crunch" in *Home Office Computing* **(Vol. 19, No. 1, January 2001, pp. 88)**
Pub: Scholastic Inc.
Ed: Barbara Axelson. **Description:** Cash flow can become problematic when a small business is faced with an unexpected expense on top of normal monthly or yearly operating costs. Expert recommendations are offered for small businesses, including having cash reserves of up to three to six months available at all times.

27097 ■ *Cash Traps: Small Business Secrets for Reducing Costs and Improving Cash Flow*
Pub: John Wiley & Sons, Inc.
Ed: Jeffrey P. Davidson and Charles W. Dean. **Released:** 1992. **Price:** $59.95; $14.95 (paper).

27098 ■ "Caveats to Selling Financial Services" in *Journal of Accountancy* **(Vol. 199, January 2005, No. 1, pp. 29)**
Pub: American Institute of Certified Public Accountants
Ed: Bart H. Siegel. **Description:** Certified Public Accounts will face new challenges when offering separately managed accounts, customized bond portfolio services, mutual funds, insurance or other investment products and services.

27099 ■ "Class-Based Pensions: A Cost-Saving Alternative for Companies of All Sizes" in *Journal of Accountancy* **(Vol. 199, January 2005)**
Pub: American Institute of Certified Public Accountants
Ed: Mark Papalia. **Description:** Ways small businesses can establish a class-based pension program for their company are discussed, including a plan that places each employee in a separate class.

27100 ■ "Clicking against the Current" in *Crain's Detroit Business* **(Vol. 19, No. 9, March 3, 2003, pp. 3)**
Pub: Crain Communications Inc., Detroit
Ed: Andrew Dietderich. **Description:** Despite reports that technology spending is down and won't increase until 2004, local area technology firms are growing.

27101 ■ "Coming of age" in *Boston Business Journal* **(Vol. 22,)**
Pub: MCP, Inc.
Ed: Phil Sweeney. **Description:** Online retailers are learning ways to survive in a slowing economy.

27102 ■ "Coming Up Short" in *Entrepreneur* **(Vol. 32, December 2004, No. 12, pp. 64)**
Pub: Entrepreneur Media Inc.
Ed: Crystal Detamore-Rodman. **Description:** A major benefit of short-term financing is the flexibility it allows for a small business owner.

27103 ■ "Commuting Expenses: What is a 'Metropolitan Area'?" in *Journal of Accountancy* **(Vol. 199, January 2005, No. 1, pp. 75)**
Pub: American Institute of Certified Public Accountants
Ed: Vinay S. Navani. **Description:** Under revenue ruling 1999-7, costs for traveling from one's residence to a fixed work location, costs can be deducted if they fall under certain criteria.

27104 ■ "Consequences of Information Technology on Work in the Twenty-First Century" in *Employment Relations Today* **(Vol.26, No. 4, Winter 2000)**
Pub: John Wiley & Sons, Inc.
Ed: Joseph F. Coates. **Description:** The implications of information technology advances for human resource management are discussed. Topics addressed include globalization and employee wages, job automation and the management of the labor supply, and training workers in computer skills.

27105 ■ "Cooperation Needed for Budget Priorities" in *Crain's Detroit Business* **(Vol. 21, January 31, 2005, No. 5, pp. 8)**
Pub: Crain Communications Inc. - Detroit
Description: Michigan Association of Realtors and the Michigan Chamber Foundations will pay up to $700,000 to retain Peter Hutchinson to work with the state's legislative leadership on Michigan's budget issues. Hutchinson co-authored the book, The Price of Government.

27106 ■ "Court Review of IRS Abuse of Discretion" in *Journal of Accountancy* **(Vol. 198, December 2004, No. 6, pp. 93)**
Pub: American Institute of Certified Public Accountants

Ed: Edward J. Schnee. **Description:** Under numerous code sections, the Internal Revenue Service is allowed to reduce or eliminate a tax liability for equity or hardship reasons at its discretion.

27107 ■ "Cutting the Corporate Purse Strings" in *Ingram's* **(Vol. 27, No. 7, July 2001, pp. 20)**
Pub: Show Me Publishing, Inc.
Description: Techniques and management theory for women small business owners is outlined. Topics include clarifying objectives, refining business ideas, research ideas, budgeting, concept testing, developing a business plan, and securing financing.

27108 ■ "Cutting Costs Without Drawing Blood" in *Harvard Business Review* **(Vol. 78, No. 5, September-October 2000, pp. 155)**
Pub: Harvard Business School Publishing Corp.
Ed: Tom Copeland. **Description:** The author argues that cutting costs need not be a bloody process involving massive layoffs. Reduction of capital expenditures is another way with a solid evaluation of small ticket budget items particularly effective. The article contains graphs.

27109 ■ "Damages Aren't Always Patently Obvious" in *Journal of Accountancy*
Pub: American Institute of Certified Public Accountants
Ed: Glenn Newman, Richard J. Gering. **Description:** CPA litigation consultants assist patent holders in patent infringement disputes; quantifying damages in these cases can be the focus of a forensic and litigation services practice.

27110 ■ "Debt Allocation and LLCs" in *Journal of Accountancy* **(Vol. 198, September 2004, No. 3, pp. 80)**
Pub: American Institute of Certified Public Accountants
Ed: Edward J. Schnee. **Description:** An overview of regulations that apply to limited liability companies (LLCs) that apply to the allocation of liabilities to LLC members.

27111 ■ "Deducting the Cost of Laser Eye Surgery" in *Journal of Accountancy* **(Vol. 198, December 2004, No. 6, pp. 92)**
Pub: American Institute of Certified Public Accountants
Ed: W. Terry Dancer. **Description:** The Internal Revenue Service has issued a letter ruling that addresses whether surgical procedures to correct nearsightedness, farsightedness and astigmatism can be used as a tax deduction.

27112 ■ "Deemed Substantiation of Business Travel Expenses" in *Journal of Accountancy* **(Vol. 198, October 2004, No. 4, pp. 102)**
Pub: American Institute of Certified Public Accountants
Ed: Charles J. Reichert. **Description:** The 'deemed-substantiation' method for deducting business travel is discussed.

27113 ■ "Directory of AICPA Selected Services" in *Journal of Accountancy* **(Vol. 199, February 2005, No. 2, pp. 89)**
Pub: American Institute of Certified Public Accountants
Description: The American Institute of Certified Public Accounts' Directory of selected services is provided; contact numbers and Web addresses are included.

27114 ■ "Downturn brings opportunities along with risks" in *Atlanta Business Chronicle* **(Vol. 23, No. 49, May 11, 2001, pp. 3B)**
Pub: American City Business Journals Inc.
Ed: Alf Nucifora. **Description:** If a recession does occur, small businesses should be aware of the opportunities, as well as the risks that will come along. Cutting marketing budgets can hurt a firm during and for some years after a recession, according to several studies. Ways to maintain effective marketing with minimal outlays are discussed.

27115 ■ "Employer-Provided Education Benefits: Section 132(d) is Worth a Second Look" in *Journal of Accountancy* **(Vol. 198, September 2004)**
Pub: American Institute of Certified Public Accountants
Ed: Edmund D. Fenton, Jr. **Description:** An overview of the various ways employers are helping their employees with tax-free education benefits, including scholarships and grants under IRC Section 117 and education assistance programs under Section 127, as well as IRC Section 132(d).

27116 ■ "Encourage General Ledger Efficiency" in *Journal of Accountancy* **(Vol. 198, September 2004, No. 3, pp.)**
Pub: American Institute of Certified Public Accountants
Ed: Steven Bragg. **Description:** Best practices offered by certified public accountants to help keep a general ledger both current and accurate are listed.

27117 ■ "The energy roller coaster" in *Red Herring* **(No. 103, September 1, 2001, pp. 42-43)**
Pub: Herring Communications
Ed: Peter Schwartz. **Description:** Advice is given to aid in understanding the future of energy markets, what drives them and how they work, is discussed.

27118 ■ *Entrepreneurial Finance*
Pub: Pearson Education, Limited
Ed: Philip J. Adelman; Alan M. Marks. **Released:** July 2006. **Price:** $87.35. **Description:** Financial aspects of running a small business are covered; topics include sole proprietorships, partnerships, limited liability companies, and private corporations.

27119 ■ "Explore the Art of Consultative Selling" in *Journal of Accountancy* **(Vol. 199, January 2005)**
Pub: American Institute of Certified Public Accountants
Ed: John E. Graziano, Patrick J. Flanagan. **Description:** Traditional selling vs. consultative selling techniques when integrating financial planning into an accounting practice are explored.

27120 ■ *Financial Essentials for Small Business Success: Accounting, Planning & Recordkeeping Techniques for a Healthy Bottom Line*
Pub: Upstart Publishing Co., Inc.
Ed: Joe Tabet. **Released:** 1994. **Price:** $19.95 (paper).

27121 ■ *Financial Management 101: Get a Grip on Your Business Numbers*
Pub: Self-Counsel Press, Incorporated
Ed: Angie Mohr. **Released:** September 2004. **Price:** $14.95. **Description:** An overview of business planning, financial statements, budgeting and advertising for small businesses. s.

27122 ■ "Financial Reporting Goes Global: International Standards Affect U.S. Companies and GAAP" in *Journal of Accountancy* **(Vol. 198)**
Pub: American Institute of Certified Public Accountants
Ed: D.J. Gannon, Alex Ashwal. **Description:** Summary of the international standards affecting U.S. companies and GAAP (generally accepted accounting principles).

27123 ■ "Fleeting Moment" in *Entrepreneur* **(Vol. 32, December 2004, No. 12, pp. 39)**
Pub: Entrepreneur Media Inc.
Ed: Jill Amadio. **Description:** Auto manufacturers, particularly the Big Three in Detroit, provide incentives to small companies to fleet lease from them. The advantages of fleet leasing include tax deductions for interest, ability to hold on to more capital, vehicles are always under warranty, and more.

27124 ■ "Fraud Risk: Are You Prepared? The Mission: To Create Stronger Support for an Ethically Sound Business Environment" in *Journal of Accountancy*
Pub: American Institute of Certified Public Accountants
Ed: Steven E. Sacks. **Description:** Incentives that reward individuals for short term results can sometimes result in fraud and abuse; ways this fraud is affecting the certified public accounting profession is examined.

27125 ■ "The Freeland Conundrum" in *Inc.* **(December 1, 2004)**
Pub: Inc. Magazine
Ed: Mike Brewster. **Description:** Contract workers can save small business money, but there could be hidden costs in an office full of temporary workers.

27126 ■ "The Future is Here: The Modernizing of IRS e-File" in *Journal of Accountancy* **(Vol. 198, December 2004, No. 6, pp. 89)**
Pub: American Institute of Certified Public Accountants
Ed: Bert DuMars. **Description:** Ways the Internal Revenue Service is updating and modernizing electronic returns are listed.

27127 ■ "Get carded" in *Entrepreneur* **(Vol. 30, No. 2, February 2002, pp. 61)**
Pub: Entrepreneur Media Inc.
Ed: Chris Sandlund. **Description:** Creative ways to boost profits for small businesses are explored.

27128 ■ "Get fiscally fit" in *BlackEnterprise* **(Vol. 31, No. 6, January 2001, pp. 102)**
Pub: Earl Graves Publishing Co.
Ed: Monique R. Brown. **Description:** The first chapter in a series of exercises designed to teach effective money management and consumer empowerment is presented.

27129 ■ "Get the Raise You Deserve: A Step-by-Step Guide to Negotiating the Right Pay Package" in *Journal of Accountancy* **(October 2004)**
Pub: American Institute of Certified Public Accountants
Ed: Anita Dennis. **Description:** According to experts, there are several steps that certified public accountants can take to receive the pay they feel they are worth.

27130 ■ "Go With the Flow" in *Small Business Opportunities* **(Vol. 13, No. 6, November 2001, pp. 114)**
Pub: Harris Publications, Inc.
Ed: Jim Schabarum II, Michael Strahan. **Description:** Proper cash flow management can help a small business generate income and also plan for slower times.

27131 ■ "HAP boosts employee-pay plans" in *Crain's Detroit Business* **(Vol. 19, No. 6, Feb. 10, 2003, pp. 3)**
Pub: Crain Communications Inc., Detroit
Ed: Katie Merx. **Description:** Henry Ford Health System's insurance sector is promoting its product line that will help cut the increasing costs of health care to employers.

27132 ■ "Health care needs some strong medicine" in *Crain's Detroit Business* **(Vol. 18, No. 19, May 13, 2002, pp. 9)**
Pub: Crain Communications Inc. - Detroit
Ed: Gail Warden. **Description:** Issues facing the health care and insurance industries are discussed.

27133 ■ "Hedge Fund Investing: Current Advice for Financial Advisers and Planners" in *Journal of Accountancy* **(Vol. 199, February 2005, No. 2)**
Pub: American Institute of Certified Public Accountants
Ed: Thomas G. Evans, Stan Atkinson, Charles H. Cho. **Description:** Nature of hedge funds and the latest news of interest to investors, brokerage firms, and certified public accounts is covered.

27134 ■ "Help! I Need a Job" in *Crain's New York Business* **(Vol. 23, January 8, 2007, No. 2, pp. 23)**
Pub: Crain Communications, Inc.
Description: January is the best time to search for a new job. Companies bring in new management, have gotten their budgets and know the amount of staff that is required to meet their goals.

27135 ■ "Highway Robbery? You Can Make Renting a Car Easier on the Company Budget" in *Entrepreneur* **(Vol. 31, No. 10, October 2003, pp. 26)**
Pub: Entrepreneur Media, Inc.
Description: Tips for renting vehicles to cut company expenses are listed, including resources to compare rental prices, last-minute rates and add-in fees.

27136 ■ "Hit the Road: Itching to Throw Your Business Into High Gear?" in *Entrepreneur* **(Vol. 32, December 2004, No. 12, pp. 37)**
Pub: Entrepreneur Media Inc.
Ed: Jill Amadio. **Description:** Whether choosing crew cabs with short or long beds, passenger or cargo vans, an SUV or car for a small business, thirty new vehicles will be available for 2005.

27137 ■ "Impact of Self-Employment Loss on Earned Income" in *Journal of Accountancy* **(Vol. 198, September 2004, No. 3, pp.)**
Pub: American Institute of Certified Public Accountants
Ed: Claire Y. Nash. **Description:** Information about the various tax code sections defined as 'earned income' are explored.

27138 ■ "In Brief: Grassley Offers a Bankruptcy Bill" in *American Banker* **(Vol. 170, February 4, 2005, No. 24, pp. 3)**
Pub: Thomson Financial Media Inc.
Ed: Hannah Bergman. **Description:** Finance Committee Chairman, Senator Charles Grassley, has introduced a bill that would revamp bankruptcy laws. The bill would require credit card companies to disclose the risks of minimum payment, ban deceptive advertising of low introductory rates, and require the companies to establish a toll-free number for consumers. It would also make permanent the Chapter 12 protections to help farmers from going bankrupt.

27139 ■ "Increasing Transparency in Peer Review: Members Speak Out" in *Journal of Accountancy* **(Vol. 198, December 2004, No. 6, pp. 22)**
Pub: American Institute of Certified Public Accountants
Ed: Adam Snyder. **Description:** The results of a survey of small accounting firms practicing in ten states about increasing transparency by making peer review information a part of public record, are presented.

27140 ■ "Install Your Own Wireless Networks" in *Journal of Accountancy* **(Vol. 198)**
Pub: American Institute of Certified Public Accountants
Ed: Bryce H. Peterson, William G. Heninger, Craig J. Lindstrom, Marshall B. Romney. **Description:** Information is presented to help network computer systems using a wireless local area network (WLAN).

27141 ■ "Interest Paid as an Administrative Expense" in *Journal of Accountancy* **(Vol. 198, December 2004, No. 6, pp. 95)**
Pub: American Institute of Certified Public Accountants
Ed: Michael H. Brown. **Description:** Tax laws regarding deductions used for interest paid by an estate are discussed.

27142 ■ "Investor: Boarding School" in *Red Herring* **(No. 99, June 15 & July 1, 2001, pp. 130, 132)**
Pub: Herring Communications
Ed: Beverly Goodman. **Description:** An overview of the new audit committee rules adopted by the stock exchanges is presented. The volatility of today's market is discussed.

27143 ■ **"IRS Allows Statistical Sampling for M&E Costs: New Procedure May Increase Taxpayer Deductions"** in *Journal of Accountancy* (Vol. 198)
Pub: American Institute of Certified Public Accountants
Ed: Lesli S. Laffie. **Description:** The Internal Revenue Service now permits the use of statistical sampling to account for allowable expense deductions for meals and entertainment.

27144 ■ **"Is 'Equitable Remedy' Settlement Excludable from Gross Income?"** in *Journal of Accountancy* (Vol. 198, December 2004, No. 6, pp. 94)
Pub: American Institute of Certified Public Accountants
Description: A case testing the definition of personal physical injury or physical sickness in an equitable remedy is discussed.

27145 ■ **"It'll Cost Ya: Know How Your Lawyer Tallies Up Your Legal Tab"** in *Entrepreneur* (Vol. 32, July 2004, No. 7, pp. 76)
Pub: Entrepreneur Media Inc.
Ed: Marc Diener. **Description:** Many attorneys will adjust fees for small businesses that know how to ask. Billing information included should explain hourly or daily rates, minimum billing unit, double billing, padded bills, bills that are too general, percentages, flat fees, retainers, and more.

27146 ■ **"It's All Coming Together: A Hybrid Cradle Saves You Wireless Phone Minutes"** in *Entrepreneur* (Vol. 32, No. 2, February 2004, pp. 38)
Pub: Entrepreneur Media, Inc.
Description: Small business can cut costs by bundling land line and wireless phone services together, using the FastForward service. FastForward is currently compatible with Nokia, Motorola, Siemens and Sony Ericsson phones.

27147 ■ **"Jump-Start Success: How to Set Up a World-Class Internal Audit Function"** in *Journal of Accountancy* (Vol. 199, February 2005, No. 2)
Pub: American Institute of Certified Public Accountants
Ed: Bruce Caplain. **Description:** Advice is offered for setting up a successful internal audit function for a company.

27148 ■ **"Keeping It Simple"** in *Entrepreneur* (Vol. 28, No. 8, August 2000, pp. 94)
Pub: Entrepreneur Media Inc.
Ed: Mark Henricks. **Description:** There are three important ways to make your company more efficient and cost-effective: simple beginnings, simplifying simplified, and knowing your limits. These issues are covered in detail.

27149 ■ **"Make the Most of Buy-Sell Agreements: These Complex Contracts Solve Many Problems"** in *Journal of Accountancy* (Vol. 198, October 2004)
Pub: American Institute of Certified Public Accountants
Ed: Thomas F. Burrage, Chad Hoekstra. **Description:** A Summary of buy-sell agreements is highlighted.

27150 ■ **"The Maw of the Law"** in *Success* (Vol. 47, No. 5, October 2000, pp. 42)
Pub: Success Publishing, Inc.
Ed: Michael Barrier. **Description:** With good legal advice more important, and more expensive than ever, how do you afford it?

27151 ■ **"More bang"** in *Entrepreneur* (Vol. 30, No. 2, February)
Pub: Entrepreneur Media Inc.
Ed: Chris Penttila. **Description:** Presentation of twenty-five tips for under $1,000 that will make a business better, from marketing to sales, and employees to equipment.

27152 ■ **"More Checks in the Mail"** in *Hispanic Business* (Vol. 23, No. 7/8, July/August 2001, pp. 30)
Pub: Hispanic Business
Ed: Vivienne Heines. **Description:** According to Tirso Del Junco, member of the Board of Governors of the U.S Postal Service, in order to meet rising labor costs, the postal system will be forced to raise rates again.

27153 ■ **"The Mutual Fund Trading Scandals: Implications for CPAs and Their Clients"** in *Journal of Accountancy* (Vol. 198, December 2004)
Pub: American Institute of Certified Public Accountants
Ed: Brian Carroll. **Description:** An overview of mutual funds and their structure, as well as ways certified public accounts and investment advisors can reassure clients in an unsure climate of corporate scandals.

27154 ■ **"Natural Gas Prices Pinch Businesses"** in *Tampa Tribune* (October 28, 2005)
Pub: Media General, Inc.
Ed: Will Rodgers. **Description:** Natural gas prices are driving the cost of running a small business; the price of natural gas for commercial use rose nearly 41 percent between 2000 and 2004.

27155 ■ **"9 Ways to be More Frugal"** in *My Business* (September/October 2001, pp. 43)
Pub: My Business Magazine
Ed: Shannon Scully. **Description:** Nine easy steps are provided to lower small business costs and improve the bottom line.

27156 ■ **"No Train, No Gain?"** in *Entrepreneur* (Vol. 32, October 2004, No. 10, pp. 96)
Pub: Entrepreneur Media Inc.
Ed: Chris Penttila. **Description:** It is sometimes hard to get a direct payback from costs incurred in training employees. Many entrepreneurs rely on four levels that measure training impact.

27157 ■ **"Nonindividual QTP Contributions: How Employers Can Help Workers Save for College"** in *Journal of Accountancy* (Vol. 198, November 2004)
Pub: American Institute of Certified Public Accountants
Ed: Lesli S. Laffie. **Description:** Issues involved in an employer using qualified tuition programs for employees are examined.

27158 ■ **"Office Space: It's better to rent than own"** in *Red Herring* (No. 103, September 1, 2001, pp. 85)
Pub: Herring Communications
Ed: Duff McDonald. **Description:** More technology firms are using the sale-leaseback transaction as an alternative to monetizing real estate assets.

27159 ■ **"Ohio Investment Tax Credit Struck Down"** in *Journal of Accountancy* (Vol. 199, January 2005, No. 1, pp. 76)
Pub: American Institute of Certified Public Accountants
Ed: Laura Lee Mannino. **Description:** It is important for small businesses to fully understand any tax credits offered by states designed to lure new business to their state.

27160 ■ **"Out Of Pocket, Out Of Mind"** in *Law Firm Inc.* (August 2004)
Pub: American Lawyer Media LP
Ed: Tamara Loomis. **Description:** Cost recovery systems are of major concern to law firms. Many firms are considering whether to absorb costs for copies, laser printouts, faxes, scanning and telephone calls or pass the expense on to clients in order to recover out-of-pocket expenses incurred on the client's behalf.

27161 ■ **"Partnership Terminations"** in *Journal of Accountancy* (Vol. 199, January 2005, No. 1, pp. 73)
Pub: American Institute of Certified Public Accountants

Ed: Edward J. Schnee. **Description:** The Internal Revenue Code as it pertains to partnership terminations is discussed.

27162 ■ **"The PCAOB and the Future of Oversight"** in *Journal Of Accountancy*
Pub: American Institute of Certified Public Accountants
Ed: Patrick J. McDonnell. **Description:** Review of the Sarbanes-Oxley Act of 2002 created by the Public Company Accounting Oversight Board (PCAOB) is presented. The role of the PCAOB is discussed.

27163 ■ **"Port Adopts 2007 Strategic Budget"** in *Bellingham Business Journal* (December 2006, pp. A3)
Pub: Sun News Inc.
Description: 2007 Strategic Budget adopted by the Port of Bellingham Board of Commissioners projects a 5 percent growth of operating revenues and no increase in the number of port employees. The entire Strategic Budget will be available on the Web at portofbellingham.com.

27164 ■ **"Postcard perfect"** in *Incentive* (Vol. 174, No. 10, October 2000, pp. 146)
Pub: Bill Communications
Ed: Lorena Mongelli. **Description:** All types of businesses are discovering postcards and saving money. A website is listed offering tips and ideas for using postcards for your company, including reminder notices, meeting confirmations, thank you notes, and more.

27165 ■ **"Price Equals Value Plus Terms"** in *Journal of Accountancy*
Pub: American Institute of Certified Public Accountants
Ed: Joel Sinkin. **Description:** Business valuations, succession planning, and buy-sell agreements are discussed, focusing on the certified public accountants role in reviewing the interrelationship of five key variables: the down payment at closing, the length of the payout period on the balance due, the profitability of the deal, the duration of the post-closing retention period with adjustments for lost clients, and the multiple (preferred price based on a multiple of the gross billings).

27166 ■ *QuickBooks X for Dummies*
Pub: John Wiley & Sons, Incorporated
Ed: Stephen L. Nelson. **Released:** November 2006. **Price:** $21.99. **Description:** Key features of QuickBooks software for small business are introduced. Invoicing and credit memos, recoding sales receipts, accounting, budgeting, taxes, payroll, financial reports, job estimating, billing, tracking, data backup, are among the features.

27167 ■ **"Radio Frequency Identification"** in *Journal of Accountancy*
Pub: American Institute of Certified Public Accountants
Ed: Harold E. Davis, Michael S. Luehlfing. **Description:** Radio frequency identification (RFID) consists of tags, transceivers and a computer system that share the characteristics, location, arrival/shipment time and other information about inventories. RFID is expected to reduce costs and improve efficiency for managing and accounting inventory.

27168 ■ **"Renewing a Great Profession: Esteemed Professions Initiate Change - For Their Own Good"** in *Journal of Accountancy* (January 2005)
Pub: American Institute of Certified Public Accountants
Ed: Robert L. Bunting. **Description:** Qualities required to create a good profession, focusing on the accounting sector, are discussed.

27169 ■ **"Ringing Up Profits"** in *Small Business Opportunities* (Vol. 16, No. 3, May 2004, pp. 12)
Pub: Harris Publications, Inc.
Ed: Missy Mastel. **Description:** Ways to cut business telecommunications costs, the second highest business expense faced by American small businesses.

27170 ■ "Sales & Marketing: Why Advertise Anyway?" in *Ingram's* (Vol. 27, No. 5, May 2001, pp. 28)
Pub: Show Me Publishing, Inc.
Ed: Rob Pearcy. **Description:** Business plans need to include a marketing budget for advertising in order to be successful.

27171 ■ "The Secret Life of a Tightwad" in *My Business* (April/May 2004, pp. 28-34)
Pub: My Business Magazine
Ed: Shannon Scully. **Description:** Smart tips to help small business owners save on business expenses are shared.

27172 ■ "Section 404 Compliance in the Annual Report" in *Journal of Accountancy*
Pub: American Institute of Certified Public Accountants
Ed: Michael Ramos. **Description:** Most publicly traded companies in the U.S. will be required to comply with SEC rules by reporting the effectiveness of internal controls in the annual report. The content required in this report is covered.

27173 ■ "Selling to Audit Committees" in *Journal of Accountancy*
Pub: American Institute of Certified Public Accountants
Ed: Gale Crosley. **Description:** Suggestions to help certified public accounting firms approach and obtain committee boards in each of the three target markets for auditing services: publicly held companies, large private and public-interest entities, and smaller private and public-interest entities.

27174 ■ "Small Business, Big Losses" in *Journal of Accountancy* (Vol. 19)
Pub: American Institute of Certified Public Accountants
Ed: Joseph T. Wells. **Description:** Occupational fraud is becoming increasingly more prevalent and affects nearly every business. A summary of the key findings of certified frauds examiners (CFEs) in cases of financial statement fraud is highlighted.

27175 ■ *Small Business Cash Flow: Strategies for Making Your Business a Financial Success*
Pub: John Wiley & Sons, Incorporated
Ed: Denise O'Berry. **Released:** October 2006. **Price:** $19.95. **Description:** Tips to help small businesses manage money are given.

27176 ■ *Small Business Clustering Technology: Applications in Marketing, Management, Finance, and IT*
Pub: Idea Group Publishing
Ed: Robert C. MacGregor; Ann Hodgkinson. **Released:** June 2006. **Description:** An overview of the development and role of small business clusters in disciplines that include economics, marketing, management and information systems.

27177 ■ *Small Business Management*
Pub: John Wiley & Sons, Incorporated
Ed: Margaret Burlingame. **Released:** March 2007. **Price:** $44.95. **Description:** Advice for starting and running a small business as well as information on the value and appeal of small businesses, is given. Topics include budgets, taxes, inventory, ethics, e-commerce, and current laws.

27178 ■ *The Small Business Savings Plan: 101 Tactics for Controlling Costs and Boosting the Bottom Line*
Pub: Kaplan Books
Ed: Timothy R. Gase. **Released:** May 2007. **Price:** $28.00. **Description:** Strategies for small business owners to develop a savings plan and increase profits are outlined.

27179 ■ "Smart Tech Solutions For Small Businesses" in *Black Enterprise* (Vol. 35, August 2004, No. 1, pp. 61)
Pub: Earl G. Graves Publishing Co. Inc.
Ed: Schuyler K. Esprit. **Description:** Ramon Ray's Technology Solutions for Growing Businesses is reviewed. Finding the right products for a small business can maximize productivity while minimizing costs.

27180 ■ "Soaring Salaries: It's Payback Time" in *Business Week* (No. 3702, October 9, 2000, pp. F24)
Pub: McGraw-Hill, Inc.
Description: Executive salaries are reaching record levels. Entrepreneurs are forced to offer as much as 40%-60% increases for new hires and better expand benefits for those already on the payroll. Statistical data included.

27181 ■ "Staffing Woes: The 404 Talent War" in *Journal of Accountancy* (Vol. 198, December 2004, No. 6, pp. 62)
Pub: American Institute of Certified Public Accountants
Ed: Barbara Vigilante. **Description:** Section 404 of the Sarbanes-Oxley Act is discussed. Rule 404 requires companies to hire more certified public accountants to implement and manage these new internal controls.

27182 ■ "State biz bankruptcies rise despite national fall" in *Crain's Detroit Business* (Vol. 19, No. 10, March 10, 2003, pp. 18)
Pub: Crain Communications Inc., Detroit
Ed: Michael Strong. **Description:** Nationally, business bankruptcies fell 3.9 percent, however they rose 20 percent in Southeast Michigan.

27183 ■ "Stealing the Show: Exhibitors and Show Managers Fight Suitcasing" in *Tradeshow Week* (Vol. 34, December 6, 2004, No. 49, pp. S3)
Pub: Reed Business Information
Ed: Gary Tufel. **Description:** In a tough economy, exhibitors are upset with sales people who walk the aisles of a tradeshow marketing without paying for booth space, called suitcasing. Suitcasers are able to take buyers away from the show to a hotel or restaurant. Industrial espionage is another problem for exhibitors.

27184 ■ "Street Smarts: Pennies From Heaven" in *Inc.* (December 1, 2004)
Pub: Inc. Magazine
Ed: Norm Brodsky. **Description:** Employee participation in cost control can actually motivate workers.

27185 ■ *Streetwise Finance and Accounting for Entrepreneurs: Set Budgets, Manage Costs, Keep Your Business Profitable*
Pub: Adams Media Corporation
Ed: Suzanne Caplan. **Released:** November 2006. **Price:** $25.95. **Description:** Book offers a basic understanding of accounting and finance for small businesses, including financial statements, credits and debits, as well as establishing a budget. Strategies for small companies in financial distress are included.

27186 ■ *Streetwise Small Business Book of Lists: Hundreds of Lists to Help You Reduce Costs, Increase Revenues, and Boost Your Profits!*
Pub: Adams Media Corporation
Ed: Gene Marks. **Released:** September 2006. **Price:** $25.95. **Description:** Strategies to help small business owners locate services, increase sales, and lower expenses.

27187 ■ "Succession-Planning Do's and Don'ts: Who Will Take Over When You're Ready to Retire?" in *Journal of Accountancy* (February 2005)
Pub: American Institute of Certified Public Accountants
Ed: Anita Dennis. **Description:** Few certified public accounting firms have set a succession plan into place for selling their firm or passing it down to the next generation.

27188 ■ "Taking On the Energy Crunch" in *Fortune* (Vol. 151, February 7, 2005, No. 3, pp. 97)
Pub: Time Inc.
Ed: Marc Gunther. **Description:** The appeal of wind power, because of zero fuel costs, is discussed along with other alternatives to oil and gas. General Motors,

BMW, and S.C. Johnson are buying landfill gas to save money and to help clean the air; the aluminum industry spends $750 for recycled cans; environmentally designed 'green' buildings are another alternative.

27189 ■ "Taking the Pain Out of Payday" in *Inc.* (January 1, 2005)
Pub: Inc. Magazine
Ed: Nicole Gull. **Description:** Payroll debit cards can be cheaper than traditional payroll systems.

27190 ■ "Tax Season Defanged" in *Journal of Accountancy* (Vol. 199)
Pub: American Institute of Certified Public Accountants
Ed: Edward Mendlowitz. **Description:** Ways to help accounting firms create a successful tax season are examined, including fostering high morale among employees.

27191 ■ "This Is a Test" in *Entrepreneur* (Vol. 32, December 2004, No. 12, pp. 97)
Pub: Entrepreneur Media Inc.
Ed: Mark Henricks. **Description:** According to the Small Business Administration, return on investment (ROI) is the single most important measure of a company's financial status. ROI reveals overall profitability, and is calculated by dividing net profit by total assets, and can be easily misinterpreted.

27192 ■ "To say the leased: Smart Moves: Ownership is overrated" in *Entrepreneur* (Vol. 30, No. 2, February 2002, pp. 61)
Pub: Entrepreneur Media Inc.
Ed: Mark Henricks. **Description:** According to a survey of small businesses conducted by the Equipment Leasing Association, 70 percent of owners expect business to slow, and most expect to increase use of equipment leasing to help deal with the slowdown.

27193 ■ "Unleash the Power of Leasing" in *Success* (Vol. 47, No. 4, September 2000, pp. 76)
Pub: Success Publishing, Inc.
Ed: Tara Baukus Mello. **Description:** Leasing has a whole new twist, it can help stretch finances, reward employees, and find money to grow a business.

27194 ■ "Users Size Up Tax Software: Product Ratings Gain, But Vendor Support Slips" in *Journal of Accountancy* (Vol. 198, October 2004)
Pub: American Institute of Certified Public Accountants
Ed: Stanley Zarowin. **Description:** Results of a survey covering tax-preparation software are discussed. Statistical data included.

27195 ■ "Valuation" in *Inc.* (November 2000, pp. 125)
Pub: The Goldhirsh Group
Description: Debt management for entrepreneurs and the question whether to leverage or not to leverage to finance company growth are discussed.

27196 ■ *Valuing the Closely Held Firm*
Pub: Oxford University Press
Ed: Michael S. Long; Thomas A. Bryant. **Released:** March 2007. **Price:** $65.00. **Description:** The differences between a large and small firm and their ability to generate future cash flow are discussed.

27197 ■ "We Must Lose the Entitlement Mentality" in *Crain's Detroit Business* (Vol. 21, October 17, 2005, No. 43, pp. 9)
Pub: Crain Communications Inc. - Detroit
Ed: Mary Kramer. **Description:** Thomas Friedman, New York Times columnist, has written a book that identifies ten trends that are making the global economic playing field more level. Friedman offers advice, although not specifically focused on Michigan manufacturing, in the areas of outsourcing, offshoring and new supply-chain systems.

27198 ■ "What CPAs Need to Know About Separately Managed Accounts" in *Journal of Accountancy*
Pub: American Institute of Certified Public Accountants
Ed: Len Reinhart. **Description:** Certified public accounts are expanding their services to include investment advice along with the traditional tax and accounting services.

27199 ■ "What a Deal! You Can Keep Hotel Costs Down-If You Know What To Look For" in *Entrepreneur* **(Vol. 33, January 2005, No. 1, pp. 22)**
Pub: Entrepreneur Media Inc.
Ed: Chris McGinnis. **Description:** Pricewaterhouse-Coopers predicts the rates businesses pay for hotels will rise by an average of 4 percent this year. Ways to keep hotel expenses at a minimum are examined.

27200 ■ "What a Governance Referee Thinks" in *Journal of Accountancy* **(Vol. 199, February 2005, No. 2, pp. 43)**
Pub: American Institute of Certified Public Accountants
Ed: Michael Hayes. **Description:** Rules for obtaining a certified public accounting firm are changing as the Sarbanes-Oxley Act is implemented. Experts believe the Sarbanes-Oxley Act is requiring accounting firms to do the things they should have been doing all along.

27201 ■ "When Investor Trust is Shaken: Retaining Client Confidence in a Time of Investment Scandals" in *Journal of Accountancy* **(Vol. 198)**
Pub: American Institute of Certified Public Accountants
Ed: Maureen Nevin Duffy. **Description:** Five investment advisers offer techniques certified public accounts and investment advisors can use for dealing with client concerns over the mutual fund trading scandals.

27202 ■ "Work Like an Insurance Company to Save Money" in *Journal of Accountancy*
Pub: American Institute of Certified Public Accountants
Ed: Joseph A. Gerber, Elliott R. Feldman. **Description:** Financial managers can use the same practices and procedures to recover lost profits as insurance companies use: subrogation, the legal process that permits an insurance company, after paying a policyholder's claim, to sue one or more third parties responsible for causing the damage or injury to the policyholder.

27203 ■ "Worth the Drive? Your Company Cars Could Be Gulping More than Just Gas if You Don't Know What Your Ownership Costs Are" in *Entrepreneur*
Pub: Entrepreneur Media Inc.
Ed: Jill Amadio. **Description:** Four major fixed cost factors are involved when determining the cost of owning a company car: depreciation, state fees, financing and insurance.

27204 ■ "XBRL Revisited: Grasp the Fundamentals to See How Businesses Use XBRL Today" in *Journal of Accountancy* **(Vol. 199, February 2005)**
Pub: American Institute of Certified Public Accountants
Ed: Neal J. Hannon, Robert J. Gold. **Description:** Extensible Business Reporting Language (XBRL) is increasing in popularity with investors, analysts, public companies and other securities market firms, including certified public accounting businesses. XBRL basics for use are presented.

27205 ■ "You Are What You Charge" in *Journal of Accountancy* **(Vol. 198, November 2004, No. 5, pp. 20)**
Pub: American Institute of Certified Public Accountants
Ed: Ron Baker, Paul Dunn. **Description:** The four P's of marketing include price, place, promotion, and product, of these pricing is the most complicated.

TRADE PERIODICALS

27206 ■ *Debt-Free and Prosperous Living*
Pub: Debt-Free & Prosperous Living Inc.
Contact: Tony Manganiello, Editor & Publisher
E-mail: anthony@getdebtfree.com
Released: Monthly, 12/year. **Price:** $69, U.S.. **Description:** Provides personal finance information. Includes tips on paying off debts, investing, retirement, and cash-only living.

27207 ■ *Dollars & Cents*
Pub: Finance and Administration Section
Contact: Brenda Luper C.P.A., Section Manager
Ed: Joseph S. Cavarretta, Editor. **Released:** Monthly. **Price:** Included in membership. **Description:** Addresses topics of interest to association specialists in the areas of finance, human resources, technology applications, and staff administration; including changing tax laws, getting the most from a CPA firm, budgeting and resource allocation, office automation, office services administration, personnel management, financial management, and accounting software.

27208 ■ *OMB Watcher*
Pub: OMB Watch
Ed: Patrick Lester, Editor. **Released:** Bimonthly. **Price:** individuals. **Description:** Summarizes initiatives and other administrative issues of the White House Office of Management and Budget (OMB). Frequently includes short analyses of the federal budget and regulatory processes as well as related issues.

27209 ■ *Public Budgeting and Finance*
Pub: North-South Center Press at the University of Miami
Contact: John L. Mikesell, Editor-in-Chief
E-mail: mikesell@indiana.edu
Released: Quarterly. **Price:** $77 print & online; $114 Europe, print & online; $76 out of country print & online; $61 members Americas, print & online; $92 members Europe, print & online; $61 members other countries, print & online; $284 institutions print and premium online; $204 other countries print and premium online; $224 institutions Europe, print and premium online. **Description:** Journal exploring theory and practice in financial management and budgeting at all levels of public sector government.

VIDEOCASSETTES/ AUDIOCASSETTES

27210 ■ *Budgeting*
Video Arts, Inc.
c/o Aim Learning Group
8238-40 Lehigh
Morton Grove, IL 60053-2615
Free: 877-444-2230
Fax: (416)252-2155
Co. E-mail: service@aimlearninggroup.com
URL: http://www.aimlearninggroup.com
Released: 1986. **Price:** $790.00. **Description:** An illustrative program for the business owner in how to balance the company's budget so as to move onto an upward course. **Availability:** VHS; 8mm; 3/4U; Special order formats.

27211 ■ *Doing More with Less*
J. Miller Associates
15669 Live Oak Springs Rd.
Santa Clarita, CA 91351-4712
Ph:(805)251-9310
Fax: (805)251-9192
Price: $99.00. **Description:** Part of the Management Speaks Series. Discusses ways to maximize business resources without increasing costs. **Availability:** VHS.

27212 ■ *FASB 95: Statement of Cash Flows*
Bisk Education
9417 Princess Palm Ave.
Tampa, FL 33619
Free: 800-874-7877
Co. E-mail: info@bisk.com
URL: http://www.bisk.com
Price: $199.00. **Description:** Profiles accounting techniques centering on the assessment of current and future cash inflows, outflows, and cash flow problems that lead to business failure. Includes workbook and quizzer. **Availability:** VHS.

CONSULTANTS

27213 ■ AMC International Inc.
PO Box 11292
Beverly Hills, CA 90213-4292
Ph:(310)652-5620
Fax: (310)652-6709
Co. E-mail: inquiry@amcusa.com
URL: http://www.amcusa.com

E-mail: inquiry@amcusa.com
Scope: Offers day-to-day business management, business turnaround, marketing strategies, development/refinement of corporate mission, and merger and acquisition evaluations. Industries served: all.

27214 ■ Larry J. Anderson
4021 76th St.
Urbandale, IA 50322
Ph:(515)270-8548
Fax: (515)278-0916
Co. E-mail: Andy4021@aol.com

E-mail: Andy4021@aol.com
Scope: Offers business consulting including temporary technical aid in accounting, turnaround and cash management, and bail-out assistance. Also provides operations research, models, forecasting, project scheduling, and economic forecasting. Provide assistance in group health insurance in both fully insured groups and self-funded groups.

27215 ■ Automated Accounting
13800 Heacock St.
Moreno Valley, CA 92553
Ph:(951)653-5053
Co. E-mail: autoacc@earthlink.net

E-mail: autoacc@earthlink.net
Scope: A business management consulting firm that caters to small businesses. Services include part-time chief, financial officer services. Also offers software installation services, tax preparation services and business plan advisory services.

27216 ■ Business Methods Corp.
503 State Rte. 10 E
Randolph, NJ 07869
Ph:(973)328-0086
Fax: (973)328-0091
Co. E-mail: BusinessABC@aol.com
URL: http://www.bmclogo.com

E-mail: BusinessABC@aol.com
Scope: Specialty advertising business which includes custom imprinted promotional product promotions. **Seminars:** Marketing For Small Business; Starting A Home Based Business; Business -Wise Fun.

27217 ■ Expenses Limited Inc.
2204 Morris Ave., Ste. 104
Union, NJ 07083-5914
Ph:(908)688-9080
Fax: (908)688-5045
Scope: Expense reduction services for general and administrative expense areas. Focuses on all industries in the New York City, Philadelphia, and New Jersey areas.

27218 ■ Priority Process Associates Inc.
1236 E Horseshoe Bend Ct.
Rochester Hills, MI 48306
Ph:(248)608-8966
Fax: (248)608-8966
Scope: A management consulting firm with expertise in computer technology, telecommunications, and in-

formation services. Provides the following specific services: business process re-engineering-establishes correctly implemented, computer technologies that empower and accelerate work groups to act autonomously but in concert with corporate goals, document work-flow analysis-models and simulates the flow of documents through selected organizational processes, enterprise metrics-identifies unique metrics for enterprises to evaluate their continuous improvement of business processes, cost justification-identifies value using Activity Based Costing and innovative approaches to quantify time-to-market reductions, project profitability, and reduce and manage costs, proposal development-generates Requests for Proposals to solicit competitive quotations for cost effective off-the-shelf software, computer hardware, and communication products, implementation planning-negotiates implementation plans for clients through qualified software vendors, custom software integrators, and hardware, communication, and outsource suppliers, project auditing-audits the integration, installation and use of on-time, quality enterprise multi-vendor software, hardware and communications systems on computer networks, training-expands clients knowledge through information sources, and client-specific management seminars and skill building workshops. Serves manufacturing industries in the United States.

27219 ■ Harvey C. Skoog
3737 N Robert Rd., No. 'A
Prescott Valley, AZ 86314
Ph:(928)772-1448

Scope: Firm has expertise in taxes, payroll, financial planning, budgeting, buy/sell planning, business start-up, fraud detection, troubled business consulting, acquisition, and marketing. Serves the manufacturing, construction, and retailing industries in Arizona.

27220 ■ Mark Vanderstelt
9831 Gulfstream Ct.
Fishers, IN 46038
Ph:(317)576-9328
Fax: (317)576-9328
Scope: Consulting services include financial planning and analysis, inventory control, cash management, return on investment, budgeting, pricing, system design and analysis, mergers and acquisitions, feasibility studies, data processing, cost systems and controls, and performance measurement. Also performs operational and financial reviews.

FRANCHISES AND BUSINESS OPPORTUNITIES

27221 ■ Leadership Management, Inc.
4567 Lake Shore Dr.
Waco, TX 76710
Ph:(254)776-2060
Free: 800-568-1241
Fax: (254)757-4600
No. of Franchise Units: 227. **Founded:** 1967. **Franchised:** 1967. **Description:** The franchise provides

business aids and services. **Equity Capital Needed:** $30,000. **Franchise Fee:** $30,000. **Financial Assistance:** Yes. **Training:** Yes.

COMPUTER SYSTEMS/ SOFTWARE

27222 ■ Aatrix Top Pay
Aatrix Software
2100 Library Cir.
Grand Forks, ND 58201
Ph:(701)746-7202
Free: 800-426-0854
Fax: (701)787-0594
URL: http://www.aatrix.com
Price: Contact Aatrix. **Description:** Handles payroll calculations and tax deductions for both salaried and hourly employees.

27223 ■ Argos Software–ABECAS Insight
Argos Computers
5737 N Fresno St.
Fresno, CA 93710
Ph:(559)227-1000
Fax: (559)227-9644
Co. E-mail: info@argosoftware.com
URL: http://www.argosoftware.com
Description: Available for MS-DOS operating system. Payroll system for agricultural employees.

START-UP INFORMATION

27224 ■ "Personality Test" in *Entrepreneur.*
com **(Vol. 34, February 2006, No. 2, pp. 122)**
Pub: Entrepreneur Media Inc.
Ed: Romanus Wolter. **Description:** Business interactions must leave a positive impression as well as provide exceptional results.

ASSOCIATIONS AND OTHER ORGANIZATIONS

27225 ■ Association for Business
Communication
Baruch College
Communication Studies
One Bernard Baruch Way
New York, NY 10010
Ph:(646)312-3726
Fax: (646)349-5297
Co. E-mail: myers@businesscommunication.org
URL: http://www.businesscommunication.org
Contact: Dr. Robert J. Myers, Exec. Dir.
Description: College teachers of business communication; management consultants in business communications; training directors and correspondence supervisors of business firms, direct mail copywriters, public relations writers, and others interested in communication for business. **Publications:** *Business Communication Quarterly* (quarterly); *Journal of Business Communication* (quarterly); *Making Communication Requirements More Explicit in the AACSB Standards for MBA Programs.*

27226 ■ International Association of
Business Communicators
1 Hallidie Plz., Ste. 600
San Francisco, CA 94102-2818
Ph:(415)544-4700
Free: 800-776-4222
Fax: (415)544-4747
Co. E-mail: service_centre@iabc.com
URL: http://www.iabc.com
Contact: Julie Freeman, Pres.
Description: Represents Communication managers, public relations directors, writers, editors, audiovisual specialists, and others in the public relations and organizational communication field that use a variety of media to communicate with internal audiences (employees, management, association members, and leaders) and external audiences (media, customers, dealers, investors, and government). Conducts research in the communication field and encourages establishment of college-level programs in organizational communication. Offers accreditation program; conducts surveys on employee communication effectiveness and media trends. **Publications:** *Communication World* (bimonthly).

27227 ■ Society for Technical
Communication
901 N Stuart St., Ste. 904
Arlington, VA 22203-1822
Ph:(703)522-4114
Fax: (703)522-2075
Co. E-mail: stc@stc.org
URL: http://www.stc.org
Contact: Robert H. Moran, Interim Exec. Dir.
Membership: Writers, editors, educators, scientists, engineers, artists, publishers, and others professionally engaged in or interested in the field of technical communication; companies, corporations, organizations, and agencies interested in the aims of the society. **Purpose:** Seeks to advance the theory and practice of technical communication in all media. Sponsors high school writing contests. **Publications:** *Intercom* (10/year); *Technical Communication* (quarterly); Proceedings (annual).

EDUCATIONAL PROGRAMS

27228 ■ Advanced Editing
EEI Communications
66 Canal Center Plaza, Ste. 200
Alexandria, VA 22314
Ph:(703)683-0683
Fax: (703)683-4915
Co. E-mail: info@eeicommunications.com
URL: http://www.eeicommunications.com
Price: $695.00. **Description:** Covers advanced editing techniques, including copyediting, substantive editing, style sheets, English grammar, and query lists. **Locations:** Washington, DC; Silver Spring, MD; and Alexandria, VA.

27229 ■ Advanced Negotiating Skills:
Beyond Win-Win Results (Canada)
Canadian Management Centre
150 York St., 5th Fl.
Toronto, ON, Canada M5H 3S5
Ph:(416)214-5678
Free: 800-262-9699
Fax: (416)313-4985
Co. E-mail: cmcinfo@cmctraining.org
URL: http://cmcamai.org
Price: $1,695.00 Canadian. **Description:** Covers best practices for negotiation, including bargaining, cross-cultural negotiations, resolving conflict, and choosing appropriate language. **Locations:** Toronto, ON.

27230 ■ Assertiveness Training for Managers
(Canada)
Canadian Management Centre
150 York St., 5th Fl.
Toronto, ON, Canada M5H 3S5
Ph:(416)214-5678
Free: 800-262-9699
Fax: (416)313-4985
Co. E-mail: cmcinfo@cmctraining.org
URL: http://cmcamai.org
Price: $1,750.00 Canadian. **Description:** Covers using assertive behavior professionally, requesting change, managing conflict, and defining objectives. **Locations:** Toronto, ON.

27231 ■ Assertiveness Training for Women
in Business
American Management Association
1601 Broadway
New York, NY 10019
Ph:(212)586-8100
Free: 800-262-9699
Fax: (212)903-8168
Co. E-mail: customerservice@amanet.org
URL: http://www.amanet.org
Price: $1.595.00 for non-members; $1,495.00 for AMA members. **Description:** Covers self-image, stress management, various communication techniques for assertiveness, and male and female workplace attitudes. **Locations:** San Francisco, CA; Washington, DC; Atlanta, GA; Chicago, IL; and New York, NY.

27232 ■ Assertiveness Training for Women
in Business (Canada)
Canadian Management Centre
150 York St., 5th Fl.
Toronto, ON, Canada M5H 3S5
Ph:(416)214-5678
Free: 800-262-9699
Fax: (416)313-4985
Co. E-mail: cmcinfo@cmctraining.org
URL: http://cmcamai.org
Price: $1,750.00 Canadian. **Description:** Covers self-image, stress management, various communication techniques for assertiveness, and male and female workplace attitudes. **Locations:** Toronto, ON.

27233 ■ Bias-Free Communications
EEI Communications
66 Canal Center Plaza, Ste. 200
Alexandria, VA 22314
Ph:(703)683-0683
Fax: (703)683-4915
Co. E-mail: info@eeicommunications.com
URL: http://www.eeicommunications.com
Price: $395.00 **Description:** Covers awareness of words that can be offensive, and ensuring that communication is nondiscriminatory and not open for misunderstanding. **Locations:** Silver Spring, MD; and Alexandria, VA.

27234 ■ Building Better Work Relationships:
New Techniques for Results-Oriented
Communication (Canada)
Canadian Management Centre
150 York St., 5th Fl.
Toronto, ON, Canada M5H 3S5
Ph:(416)214-5678
Free: 800-262-9699
Fax: (416)313-4985
Co. E-mail: cmcinfo@cmctraining.org
URL: http://cmcamai.org
Price: $1,750.00 Canadian. **Description:** Seminar for managers; covers the characteristics of effective communication, patterns of behavior, and non-verbal communication. **Locations:** Toronto, ON.

27235 ■ Business Conversation Skills When English Is a Second Language
American Management Association
1601 Broadway
New York, NY 10019
Ph:(212)586-8100
Free: 800-262-9699
Fax: (212)903-8168
Co. E-mail: customerservice@amanet.org
URL: http://www.amanet.org
Price: $1,495 for non-members; $1,295 for AMA members. **Description:** Covers communication skills, including oral and written in today's global market. **Locations:** New York, NY.

27236 ■ Coaching Skills for Managers and Supervisors
Fred Pryor Seminars
9757 Metcalf Ave.
Overland Park, KS 66212
Free: 800-944-8503
Fax: (913)967-8849
Co. E-mail: customerservice@pryor.com
URL: http://www.careertrack.com
Description: Covers developing and using coaching to motivate and inspire your team. **Locations:** Cities throughout the United States.

27237 ■ Communicating Up, Down and Across the Organization
American Management Association
1601 Broadway
New York, NY 10019
Ph:(212)586-8100
Free: 800-262-9699
Fax: (212)903-8168
Co. E-mail: customerservice@amanet.org
URL: http://www.amanet.org
Price: $1,695 for non-members; $1,495 for AMA members. **Description:** Covers the necessary skills to build confidence, effective communication, and productivity within the organization. **Locations:** Washington, DC; and Chicago, IL.

27238 ■ Communication and Interpersonal Skills for Technical Professionals (Canada)
Canadian Management Centre
150 York St., 5th Fl.
Toronto, ON, Canada M5H 3S5
Ph:(416)214-5678
Free: 800-262-9699
Fax: (416)313-4985
Co. E-mail: cmcinfo@cmctraining.org
URL: http://cmc.amai.org
Price: $1,750.00 Canadian. **Description:** Covers effective communication skills, prioritizing, and dealing with various types of communication styles. **Locations:** Toronto, ON.

27239 ■ Communication, Up, Down and Across the Organization
American Management Association
1601 Broadway
New York, NY 10019
Ph:(212)586-8100
Free: 800-262-9699
Fax: (212)903-8168
Co. E-mail: customerservice@amanet.org
URL: http://www.amanet.org
Price: $1,695 for non-members; $1,495 for AMA members. **Description:** Covers the building of confidence to communicate effectively, and increase productivity. **Locations:** New York, NY; Washington, DC; Chicago, IL; and Atlanta, GA.

27240 ■ Comprehensive Proofreading
EEI Communications
66 Canal Center Plaza, Ste. 200
Alexandria, VA 22314
Ph:(703)683-0683
Fax: (703)683-4915
Co. E-mail: info@eeicommunications.com
URL: http://www.eeicommunications.com
Price: $695.00. **Description:** Covers creating proofreading checklists, using style guides, and proofreading electronic documents. **Locations:** Washington, DC; and Alexandria, VA. .

27241 ■ Cross-Functional Communication: Strategies for Workplace Effectiveness
American Management Association
1601 Broadway
New York, NY 10019
Ph:(212)586-8100
Free: 800-262-9699
Fax: (212)903-8168
Co. E-mail: customerservice@amanet.org
URL: http://www.amanet.org
Price: $1,795.00 for non-members; $1,595.00 for AMA members. **Description:** Covers conflict resolution, building positive workplace relationships, increasing morale, and improving interdepartmental communication. **Locations:** San Francisco, CA; Atlanta, GA; and New York, NY.

27242 ■ Developing and Delivering Briefings
EEI Communications
66 Canal Center Plaza, Ste. 200
Alexandria, VA 22314
Ph:(703)683-0683
Fax: (703)683-4915
Co. E-mail: info@eeicommunications.com
URL: http://www.eeicommunications.com
Price: $995.00. **Description:** Covers basic skills for developing and presenting effective and enjoyable briefings and presentations. **Locations:** Silver Spring, MD; and Alexandria, VA.

27243 ■ Developing Effective Business Conversation Skills
American Management Association
1601 Broadway
New York, NY 10019
Ph:(212)586-8100
Free: 800-262-9699
Fax: (212)903-8168
Co. E-mail: customerservice@amanet.org
URL: http://www.amanet.org
Price: $1,695 for non-members; $1,495 for AMA members. **Description:** Covers effective conversational skills, including directing the flow, self-confidence to gain trust, and be able to express yourself clearly in order to be more productive. **Locations:** New York, NY; Washington, DC; and Chicago, IL.

27244 ■ Editorial Skills for Non-Editors
EEI Communications
66 Canal Center Plaza, Ste. 200
Alexandria, VA 22314
Ph:(703)683-0683
Fax: (703)683-4915
Co. E-mail: info@eeicommunications.com
URL: http://www.eeicommunications.com
Price: $395.00. **Description:** Covers punctuation and grammar, usage, and proofreading marks. **Locations:** Washington, DC; Silver Spring, MD; and Alexandria, VA.

27245 ■ Effective Business Writing
EEI Communications
66 Canal Center Plaza, Ste. 200
Alexandria, VA 22314
Ph:(703)683-0683
Fax: (703)683-4915
Co. E-mail: info@eeicommunications.com
URL: http://www.eeicommunications.com
Price: $395.00. **Description:** Covers the basic elements of writing effective business letters, e-mails, and memos, including grammar, audience analysis, persuasion, and usage problems. **Locations:** Washington, DC; Silver Spring, MD; and Alexandria, VA.

27246 ■ Effective Executive Speaking (Canada)
Canadian Management Centre
150 York St., 5th Fl.
Toronto, ON, Canada M5H 3S5
Ph:(416)214-5678
Free: 800-262-9699
Fax: (416)313-4985
Co. E-mail: cmcinfo@cmctraining.org
URL: http://cmcamai.org
Price: $2,195.00 Canadian. **Description:** Covers the basics of writing speeches and presentations, gaining confidence in public speaking, and dealing with audience questions and challenges. **Locations:** Toronto, ON.

27247 ■ Effective Presentation Techniques
EEI Communications
66 Canal Center Plaza, Ste. 200
Alexandria, VA 22314
Ph:(703)683-0683
Fax: (703)683-4915
Co. E-mail: info@eeicommunications.com
URL: http://www.eeicommunications.com
Price: $395.00. **Description:** Covers assessing the audience, organizational skills, and effective delivery styles. **Locations:** Alexandria, VA; and Silver Spring, MD.

27248 ■ Effective Technical Writing
American Management Association
1601 Broadway
New York, NY 10019
Ph:(212)586-8100
Free: 800-262-9699
Fax: (212)903-8168
Co. E-mail: customerservice@amanet.org
URL: http://www.amanet.org
Price: $1,795.00 for non-members; $1,595.00 for AMA members. **Description:** Covers the basics of writing technical documents such as reports, manuals, specifications, proposals, and instructions. **Locations:** Atlanta, GA; Chicago, IL; and New York, NY.

27249 ■ Essentials of Technical Writing and Information Design
EEI Communications
66 Canal Center Plaza, Ste. 200
Alexandria, VA 22314
Ph:(703)683-0683
Fax: (703)683-4915
Co. E-mail: info@eeicommunications.com
URL: http://www.eeicommunications.com
Price: $695.00. **Description:** Covers creating training programs, technical manuals, instructions, and using software to improve documentation. **Locations:** Silver Spring, MD.

27250 ■ The Grammar Course (Canada)
Canadian Management Centre
150 York St., 5th Fl.
Toronto, ON, Canada M5H 3S5
Ph:(866)400-4941 ext. 2252
Free: 877-CMC-2500
Fax: (416)313-4985
Co. E-mail: cmcinfo@cmctraining.org
URL: http://www.cmcamai.org
Price: $995 Canadian. **Description:** Covers basic grammar, spelling and punctuation, proper usage, editing and proofreading. **Locations:** Toronto, ON.

27251 ■ High-Impact Communication Skills for Women
Fred Pryor Seminars
9757 Metcalf Ave.
Overland Park, KS 66212
Free: 800-944-8503
Fax: (913)967-8849
Co. E-mail: customerservice@pryor.com
URL: http://www.careertrack.com
Description: Covers controlling emotions, using influence and persuasion, overcoming public speaking fears, and gaining confidence. **Locations:** Cities throughout the United States.

27252 ■ High Performance Business Plan (Canada)
Canadian Management Centre
150 York St., 5th Fl.
Toronto, ON, Canada M5H 3S5
Ph:(416)214-5678
Free: 800-262-9699
Fax: (416)313-4985
Co. E-mail: cmcinfo@cmctraining.org
URL: http://cmcamai.org
Price: $1,695.00 Canadian. **Description:** Covers developing a business plan to meet organizational objectives and key elements of a business plan. **Locations:** Toronto, ON.

27253 ■ High Performance Business Writing (Canada)
Canadian Management Centre
150 York St., 5th Fl.
Toronto, ON, Canada M5H 3S5

Ph:(416)214-5678
Free: 800-262-9699
Fax: (416)313-4985
Co. E-mail: cmcinfo@cmctraining.org
URL: http://cmcamai.org
Price: $1,650.00 Canadian. **Description:** Covers improving business writing skills, focusing on documents, letters, e-mails, reports, and memos. **Locations:** Toronto, ON.

27254 ■ How to Communicate with Diplomacy, Tact and Credibility
American Management Association
1601 Broadway
New York, NY 10019
Ph:(212)586-8100
Free: 800-262-9699
Fax: (212)903-8168
Co. E-mail: customerservice@amanet.org
URL: http://www.amanet.org
Price: $1,695 for non-members; $1,495 for AMA members. **Description:** Covers effective strategies of communication through listening, including gaining team support that increases productivity. **Locations:** San Francisco, CA; and Atlanta GA.

27255 ■ How to Communicate Effectively When You Can't Be Face-To-Face
American Management Association
1601 Broadway
New York, NY 10019
Ph:(212)586-8100
Free: 800-262-9699
Fax: (212)903-8168
Co. E-mail: customerservice@amanet.org
URL: http://www.amanet.org
Price: $1,395.00 for non-members; $1,295.00 for AMA members. **Description:** Covers work relationships among telecommuters, remote teams, and geographically scattered teams; includes trust issues, best communication channels, and maintaining a team feeling. **Locations:** San Francisco, CA; and Washington, DC.

27256 ■ How to Design Eye-Catching Brochures, Newspapers, Ads, Reports
Fred Pryor Seminars
9757 Metcalf Ave.
Overland Park, KS 66212
Free: 800-944-8503
Fax: (913)967-8849
Co. E-mail: customerservice@pryor.com
URL: http://www.careertrack.com
Description: Covers basic design and layout skills for headlines, text, and graphics for printed documents. **Locations:** Cities throughout the United States.

27257 ■ How to Use a Balanced Scorecard to Implement a Strategic Plan
American Management Association
1601 Broadway
New York, NY 10019
Ph:(212)586-8100
Free: 800-262-9699
Fax: (212)903-8168
Co. E-mail: customerservice@amanet.org
URL: http://www.amanet.org
Price: $2,295.00; $2,095.00 for AMA members. **Description:** Three-day seminar for senior executives; covers different aspects of the scorecard, the implementation of a balanced scorecard, and strategic planning benefits. **Locations:** San Francisco, CA; Chicago, IL; and New York, NY.

27258 ■ How to Work Most Effectively with Your Boss
American Management Association
1601 Broadway
New York, NY 10019
Ph:(212)586-8100
Free: 800-262-9699
Fax: (212)903-8168
Co. E-mail: customerservice@amanet.org
URL: http://www.amanet.org
Price: $1,695.00 for non-members; $1,495.00 for AMA members. **Description:** Covers improving working relationships with management, and increasing productivity and career success as a result. **Locations:** Atlanta, GA; San Francisco; and New York, NY.

27259 ■ Improving Editing Skills
EEI Communications
66 Canal Center Plaza, Ste. 200
Alexandria, VA 22314
Ph:(703)683-0683
Fax: (703)683-4915
Co. E-mail: info@eeicommunications.com
URL: http://www.eeicommunications.com
Price: $395.00. **Description:** Covers the editorial issues such as active and passive voice, lists, redundancy, and sentence construction. **Locations:** Silver Spring, MD; and Alexandria, VA.

27260 ■ Indexing I
EEI Communications
66 Canal Center Plaza, Ste. 200
Alexandria, VA 22314
Ph:(703)683-0683
Fax: (703)683-4915
Co. E-mail: info@eeicommunications.com
URL: http://www.eeicommunications.com
Price: $695.00. **Description:** Covers indexing for websites and books, including determining key words, categorizing information, and using cross-references. **Locations:** Alexandria, VA.

27261 ■ Indexing II
EEI Communications
66 Canal Center Plaza, Ste. 200
Alexandria, VA 22314
Ph:(703)683-0683
Fax: (703)683-4915
Co. E-mail: info@eeicommunications.com
URL: http://www.eeicommunications.com
Price: $395.00. **Description:** Covers editing and evaluating indices. **Locations:** Alexandria, VA.

27262 ■ Interpersonal Skills
American Management Association
1601 Broadway
New York, NY 10019
Ph:(212)586-8100
Free: 800-262-9699
Fax: (212)903-8168
Co. E-mail: customerservice@amanet.org
URL: http://www.amanet.org
Price: $1,795.00 for non-members; $1,595.00 for AMA members. **Description:** Covers problem solving, negotiation, motivating and creating enthusiasm, dealing with conflict, and tactics for working with difficult employees. **Locations:** Cities throughout the United States.

27263 ■ Interpersonal Skills (Canada)
Canadian Management Centre
150 York St., 5th Fl.
Toronto, ON, Canada M5H 3S5
Ph:(416)214-5678
Free: 800-262-9699
Fax: (416)313-4985
Co. E-mail: cmcinfo@cmctraining.org
URL: http://cmcamai.org
Price: $1,750.00 Canadian. **Description:** Covers problem solving, negotiation, motivating and creating enthusiasm, dealing with conflict, and tactics for working with difficult employees. **Locations:** Toronto, ON.

27264 ■ Introduction to Information Design
EEI Communications
66 Canal Center Plaza, Ste. 200
Alexandria, VA 22314
Ph:(703)683-0683
Fax: (703)683-4915
Co. E-mail: info@eeicommunications.com
URL: http://www.eeicommunications.com
Price: $695.00. **Description:** Topics include defining information design, understanding how users process information, techniques for information design, information graphics, and presenting Web information. **Locations:** Silver Spring, MD; and Alexandria, VA.

27265 ■ Listening and Writing: Building a Better Foundation for Better Communication
American Management Association
1601 Broadway
New York, NY 10019
Ph:(212)586-8100

Free: 800-262-9699
Fax: (212)903-8168
Co. E-mail: customerservice@amanet.org
URL: http://www.amanet.org
Price: $1,445.00 for non-members; $1,295.00 for AMA members. **Description:** Covers deciding between oral and written communication, sending a clear message, and various forms of written communication. **Locations:** San Francisco, CA; and Chicago, IL.

27266 ■ Macromedia Captivate
EEI Communications
66 Canal Ctr. Plz., Ste. 200
Alexandria, VA 22314-5507
Ph:(703)683-7453
Free: 888-253-2762
Fax: (703)683-7310
Co. E-mail: train@eeicommunications.com
URL: http://www.eeicommunications.com/training
Price: $695. **Description:** Seminar that teaches how to create professional quality, interactive simulations and software demonstrations without any programming or multimedia knowledge, including basics, captions and timelines, images, pointer paths, buttons, and highlight boxes, movies, rollover captions and rollover images, slide labels and notes, audio, animation, and question slides. **Locations:** Alexandria, VA; Silver Spring, MD; and Washington, DC.

27267 ■ Managing Emotions in the Workplace: Strategies for Success
American Management Association
1601 Broadway
New York, NY 10019
Ph:(212)586-8100
Free: 800-262-9699
Fax: (212)903-8168
Co. E-mail: customerservice@amanet.org
URL: http://www.amanet.org
Price: $1,495.00 for non-members; $1,395.00 for AMA members. **Description:** Covers methods for effectively and professionally communicating emotion, creating positive work environments, and emotional control. **Locations:** San Diego, CA; San Francisco, CA; Washington, DC; Chicago, IL; New York, NY; and Dallas, TX.

27268 ■ Managing Emotions in the Workplace Strategies for Success (Canada)
Canadian Management Centre
150 York St., 5th Fl.
Toronto, ON, Canada M5H 3S5
Ph:(416)214-5678
Free: 800-262-9699
Fax: (416)313-4985
Co. E-mail: cmcinfo@cmctraining.org
URL: http://cmcamai.org
Price: $1,650.00 Canadian. **Description:** Covers methods for effectively and professionally communicating emotion, creating positive work environments, and emotional control. **Locations:** Toronto, ON.

27269 ■ Mistake-Free Grammar & Proofreading
Fred Pryor Seminars
9757 Metcalf Ave.
Overland Park, KS 66212
Free: 800-944-8503
Fax: (913)967-8849
Co. E-mail: customerservice@pryor.com
URL: http://www.careertrack.com
Description: Covers grammar and usage in business writing, including punctuation, capitalization, quotations, spelling, sentence structure, and related topics. **Locations:** Cities throughout the United States.

27270 ■ Negotiating to Win
American Management Association
1601 Broadway
New York, NY 10019
Ph:(212)586-8100
Free: 800-262-9699
Fax: (212)903-8168
Co. E-mail: customerservice@amanet.org
URL: http://www.amanet.org
Price: $1,675.00 for non-members; $1,575.00 for AMA members. **Description:** Covers appropriate

scenarios for negotiation, persuasion skills, and strategies for oral and written negotiations. **Locations:** San Francisco, CA; Washington, DC; Atlanta, GA; Chicago, IL; New York, NY; and Dallas, TX.

27271 ■ Negotiating to Win (Canada)

Canadian Management Centre
150 York St., 5th Fl.
Toronto, ON, Canada M5H 3S5
Ph:(416)214-5678
Free: 800-262-9699
Fax: (416)313-4985
Co. E-mail: cmcinfo@cmctraining.org
URL: http://cmcamai.org
Price: $1,995.00 Canadian. **Description:** Covers techniques for successful negotiations, in every industry and at every level; includes the negotiation process, overcoming people problems, and improving negotiation strategies. **Locations:** Vancouver, BC; Mississauga, ON; and Toronto, ON.

27272 ■ Powerful Persuasion Skills for Technical Professionals

American Management Association
1601 Broadway
New York, NY 10019
Ph:(212)586-8100
Free: 800-262-9699
Fax: (212)903-8168
Co. E-mail: customerservice@amanet.org
URL: http://www.amanet.org
Price: $1,695 for non-members; $1,495 for AMA members. **Description:** Covers the skills needed to motivate others of your ideas, and communicate in a way that others understand. **Locations:** New York, NY; Washington, DC; Chicago, IL.

27273 ■ Professional Presentations with Confidence and Control (Canada)

Canadian Management Centre
150 York St., 5th Fl.
Toronto, ON, Canada M5H 3S5
Free: 877-CMC-2500
Fax: (416)313-4985
Co. E-mail: cmcinfo@cmctraining.org
URL: http://www.cma.org
Price: $1,095 Canadian. **Description:** Seminar covers strategies for developing effective presentation skills, including access empowering states of mind and body, 5 steps to focus the room, change the way you see yourself and others, and how to shift your beliefs to change your expectations. **Locations:** Toronto, ON.

27274 ■ Projecting a Positive Professional Image (Canada)

Canadian Management Centre
150 York St., 5th Fl.
Toronto, ON, Canada M5H 3S5
Ph:(416)214-5678
Free: 800-262-9699
Fax: (416)313-4985
Co. E-mail: cmcinfo@cmctraining.org
URL: http://cmcamai.org
Price: $1,995.00 Canadian. **Description:** Covers an evaluation of your current image, and improving your image, including presentation and communication skills, business etiquette, and executive speech. **Locations:** Toronto, ON.

27275 ■ Responding to Conflict: Strategies for Improved Communication

American Management Association
1601 Broadway
New York, NY 10019
Ph:(212)586-8100
Free: 800-262-9699
Fax: (212)903-8168
Co. E-mail: customerservice@amanet.org
URL: http://www.amanet.org
Price: $1,595.00 for non-members; $1,495.00 for AMA members. **Description:** Covers effective communication, diffusing misunderstanding, creating open and honest work environments, dealing with conflict, and improving listening skills. **Locations:** San Francisco, CA; Washington, DC; Chicago, IL; and New York, NY.

27276 ■ Responding to Conflict: Strategies for Improved Communication (Canada)

Canadian Management Centre
150 York St., 5th Fl.
Toronto, ON, Canada M5H 3S5
Ph:(416)214-5678
Free: 800-262-9699
Fax: (416)313-4985
Co. E-mail: cmcinfo@cmctraining.org
URL: http://cmcamai.org
Price: $1,750.00 Canadian. **Description:** Covers effective communication, diffusing misunderstanding, creating open and honest work environments, dealing with conflict, and improving listening skills. **Locations:** Toronto, ON.

27277 ■ Strategies for Developing Effective Presentation Skills

American Management Association
1601 Broadway
New York, NY 10019
Ph:(212)586-8100
Free: 800-262-9699
Fax: (212)903-8168
Co. E-mail: customerservice@amanet.org
URL: http://www.amanet.org
Price: $1,595.00 for non-members; $1,495.00 for AMA members. **Description:** Covers overcoming stage fright, various types of presentations, developing a full presentation, and techniques for delivering a presentation, including answering questions and interacting with the audience. **Locations:** San Francisco, CA; Washington, DC; Atlanta, GA; Chicago, IL; and New York, NY.

27278 ■ Strategies for Developing Effective Presentation Skills (Canada)

Canadian Management Centre
150 York St., 5th Fl.
Toronto, ON, Canada M5H 3S5
Ph:(416)214-5678
Free: 800-262-9699
Fax: (416)313-4985
Co. E-mail: cmcinfo@cmctraining.org
URL: http://cmcamai.org
Price: $1,750.00 Canadian. **Description:** Covers overcoming stage fright, various types of presentations, developing a full presentation, and techniques for delivering a presentation, including answering questions and interacting with the audience. **Locations:** Toronto, ON.

27279 ■ Strategies of Effective Writing

EEI Communications
66 Canal Center Plaza, Ste. 200
Alexandria, VA 22314
Ph:(703)683-0683
Fax: (703)683-4915
Co. E-mail: info@eeicommunications.com
URL: http://www.eeicommunications.com
Price: $695.00. **Description:** Covers basic writing skills, including effective planning as a means of saving time, generating ideas, organizing ideas, writing concisely and clearly, and attracting and holding readers' interest. **Locations:** Washington, DC; Silver Spring, MD; and Alexandria, VA.

27280 ■ Style Summit

EEI Communications
66 Canal Center Plaza, Ste. 200
Alexandria, VA 22314
Ph:(703)683-0683
Fax: (703)683-4915
Co. E-mail: info@eeicommunications.com
URL: http://www.eeicommunications.com
Price: $695.00. **Description:** Covers style and usage, particularly in regards to e-mail and web communication. **Locations:** Alexandria, VA.

27281 ■ Substantive Editing I

EEI Communications
66 Canal Center Plaza, Ste. 200
Alexandria, VA 22314
Ph:(703)683-0683
Fax: (703)683-4915
Co. E-mail: info@eeicommunications.com
URL: http://www.eeicommunications.com

Price: $395.00. **Description:** Covers editing for clarity and meaning, including reworking vague or inappropriate phrases, untangling muddled language, posing effective questions to the author, and revising with a purpose. **Locations:** Washington, DC; Silver Spring, MD; and Alexandria, VA.

27282 ■ Substantive Editing II

EEI Communications
66 Canal Center Plaza, Ste. 200
Alexandria, VA 22314
Ph:(703)683-0683
Fax: (703)683-4915
Co. E-mail: info@eeicommunications.com
URL: http://www.eeicommunications.com
Price: $395.00. **Description:** Covers editing documents without losing the author's voice; includes determining accuracy, organizing, and revising and rewriting. **Locations:** Washington, DC; Silver Spring, MD; and Alexandria, VA.

27283 ■ Successful Meeting Planning

American Management Association
1601 Broadway
New York, NY 10019
Ph:(212)586-8100
Free: 800-262-9699
Fax: (212)903-8168
Co. E-mail: customerservice@amanet.org
URL: http://www.amanet.org
Price: $1,445.00 for non-members; $1,295.00 for AMA members. **Description:** Covers all aspects of successfully planning a meeting, including objectives, budget, site selection, and working with vendors. **Locations:** Washington, DC; Orlando, FL; Chicago, IL; and New York, NY.

27284 ■ Successful Meeting Planning (Canada)

Canadian Management Centre
150 York St., 5th Fl.
Toronto, ON, Canada M5H 3S5
Ph:(416)214-5678
Free: 800-262-9699
Fax: (416)313-4985
Co. E-mail: cmcinfo@cmctraining.org
URL: http://cmcamai.org
Price: $1,495.00 Canadian. **Description:** Covers all aspects of successfully planning a meeting, including objectives, budget, site selection, and working with vendors. **Locations:** Toronto, ON.

27285 ■ Technical Writing

EEI Communications
66 Canal Center Plaza, Ste. 200
Alexandria, VA 22314
Ph:(703)683-0683
Fax: (703)683-4915
Co. E-mail: info@eeicommunications.com
URL: http://www.eeicommunications.com
Price: $695.00. **Description:** Covers the technical writing process from analyzing an audience and developing a purpose to laying out a document with both text and graphics. **Locations:** Washington, DC; Silver Spring, MD; and Alexandria, VA.

27286 ■ Using a Balanced Scorecard to Implement a Strategic Plan (Canada)

Canadian Management Centre
150 York St., 5th Fl.
Toronto, ON, Canada M5H 3S5
Ph:(416)214-5678
Free: 800-262-9699
Fax: (416)313-4985
Co. E-mail: cmcinfo@cmctraining.org
URL: http://cmcamai.org
Price: $1,795.00 Canadian. **Description:** Three-day seminar for senior executives; covers different aspects of the scorecard, the implementation of a balanced scorecard, and strategic planning benefits. **Locations:** Toronto, ON.

27287 ■ Writing for the Web II

EEI Communications
66 Canal Ctr. Plz., Ste. 200
Alexandria, VA 22314-5507
Ph:(703)683-7453

Free: 888-253-2762
Fax: (703)683-7310
Co. E-mail: train@eeicommunications.com
URL: http://www.eeicommunications.com/training
Price: $695. **Description:** Seminar for persons with 3-5 years' experience as a Web writer or editor, or have completed Writing for the Web I, covering how to define your genre and audience, develop a structure for your Web content, working with subject matter experts who aren't writers, making the most of your writing project, giving and getting feedback, writing links that work for your client, how to write menus so clients can use them, and recasting a print article for the Web. **Locations:** Alexandria, VA; Silver Spring, MD; and Washington, DC.

REFERENCE WORKS

27288 ■ "20 Words That Sell" in *Small Business Opportunities* **(Vol. 16, November 2004, No. 6, pp. 12, 20)**
Pub: Harris Publications Inc.
Ed: Dawn Josephson. **Description:** Communication expert shares insight into the twenty words that can increase sales and profits.

27289 ■ "AAA celebrates 75 years" in *Dispute Resolution Journal* **(Vol. 56, No. 1, February-April 2001, pp. 45)**
Pub: American Arbitration Association
Description: Excerpts from articles published by the American Arbitration Association between 1937 and 1977 on ADR, in celebration of the association's 75th anniversary, are presented.

27290 ■ "ADR: new challenges, new roles and new opportunities" in *Dispute Resolution Journal* **(Vol. 56, No. 1, February-April 2001, pp. 20)**
Pub: American Arbitration Association
Ed: Bennett G. Picker. **Description:** An overview of the changing role of attorneys and their work with the increased use of ADR, which is changing clients' expectations.

27291 ■ "Alcatel Draws Contract" in *San Fernando Valley Business Journal* **(Vol. 11, December 2006, No. 25, pp. 28)**
Pub: San Fernando Valley Business Journal Associates
Description: Alcatel, a company that provides innovative products that allow for seamless communication by integrating data and voice networks, signed a $300 million deal to provide an integrated phone system for over 400 medical facilities in Pennsylvania.

27292 ■ "Arbitration in public sector labor disputes" in *Dispute Resolution Journal* **(Vol. 56, No. 1, February-April 2001, pp. 64)**
Pub: American Arbitration Association
Ed: Richard M. Gaba. **Description:** A discussion about the New York Court of Appeals decisions in Watertown City School District v. Watertown Education Association and Indian River Central School District v. Passino, in which the court permitted arbitrators to handle public sector labor disputes, reversing years of judicial control over such disputes.

27293 ■ *The Art of Communicating: Achieving Interpersonal Impact in Business*
Pub: Crisp Publications, Inc.
Ed: Bert Decker. **Price:** $9.95. **Description:** Uses the nationally known Decker system to improve communication skills.

27294 ■ "Arts Group Adopts New Name, Look, Enhanced Agenda" in *Mississippi Business Journal* **(Vol. 28, September 2006, No. 36, pp. 28)**
Pub: Venture Publications, Inc.
Ed: Wally Northway **Description:** Profile of the Greater Jackson Arts Council. With a new look, name, and logo to add to their enhanced agenda, the Greater Jackson Arts Council boasts a higher degree of professionalism in the portrayal of the arts in the Jackson community. Statistical data included.

27295 ■ "Ask the attorney" in *Red Herring* **(March 2003, pp. 73)**
Pub: Herring Communications Inc.
Description: Legal issues are addressed that include the following topics, pharmaceutical patents, government support for research and development, global commerce, intellectual property rights, the transfer of customer lists from European subsidiary to its U.S. parent company, trademark dilution, venture financing, selling a business, stock options, corporate tax deductions, small business patent methods, and employee use of Instant Messaging with clients.

27296 ■ "Ask the Etiquette Doctor" in *Sales and Marketing.com* **(Vol. 153, No. 3, March 2004, pp. 52)**
Pub: VNU eMedia, Inc.
Description: When giving a presentation at a client's office it is best to arrive ten minutes earlier than the scheduled appointment.

27297 ■ "Ask yourself this" in *Entrepreneur* **(Vol.)**
Pub: Entrepreneur Media Inc.
Ed: Marc Diener. **Description:** Creative thinking can pay big dividends when making business deals. Many entrepreneurs often overlook creative ways to negotiate in business.

27298 ■ "At Your Service" in *Kansas City Star* **(February 6, 2005)**
Pub: Knight-Ridder/Tribune Business News
Ed: Angela D. Curry. **Description:** Important steps to take when receiving an email, supposedly from your banking institution, requesting account information.

27299 ■ "Attacking Anxiety" in *Working Woman* **(Vol. 25, No. 5, May 2000, pp. 40)**
Pub: Lang Communications Inc.
Ed: Carol Leonetti Dannhauser. **Description:** Stress causes tension in workers, which in turn has an effect on productivity and efficiency, and often results in sickness and time off work. Companies such as HLB Communications and the Eliassen Group are finding methods to reduce stress levels in the workplace including massages, health club membership, play breaks and the use of communication consultants.

27300 ■ "Avoiding a Communication Breakdown: Keeping Employees Informed Benefits Business" in *Black Enterprise* **(Vol. 34, September 2003)**
Pub: Earl Graves Publishing Co.
Ed: John G. Clemons. **Description:** Profile of Ariel Capital Management Inc., an investment management company in the Chicago, Illinois area. The firm was rated Number One on Black Enterprise's Asset Managers list. The firm conducts a weekly Breakfast Club for employees to help them learn about the company's operations and services portfolio, honing presentation skills, and building professional skills. Ariel employs 67 people.

27301 ■ "The bargaining table: check your ego at the door." in *Atlanta Business Chronicle* **(Vol. 25, Jan. 10, 2003, No. 31, pp. 1B)**
Pub: American City Business Publications, Inc.
Ed: Tom Barry. **Description:** Negotiation skills are very valuable in today's business world; qualities of an effective negotiator, as well as how to negotiate effectively, as discussed.

27302 ■ "The Bargaining Table" in *Small Business Opportunities* **(Vol. 17, November 2005, No. 6, pp. 12, 20)**
Pub: Harris Publications Inc.
Ed: John Patrick Dolan. **Description:** Ways for salespersons to prepare when negotiating a deal are presented. An inventory of three items to help establish your position is outlined along with a list of a counterpart's position.

27303 ■ "BEA Ships Platform for Deploying Advanced Telecom Services" in *eWeek* **(February 7, 2005)**
Pub: Ziff Davis Media Inc.
Description: BEA Systems Inc. launched a suite of Java-based application development tools to make it easier for telecommunications companies to build advanced voice over Internet Protocol (VOIP), multimedia, and wireless services.

27304 ■ "Black Enterprise's 2000 Business Entertaining Guide" in *Black Enterprise* **(Vol. 31, No. 5, December 2000, pp. 153)**
Pub: Earl Graves Publishing Co.
Ed: Ray Isle. **Description:** How you handle a business dinner can make the difference between success or failure.

27305 ■ "Briefing: Internet Infrastructure" in *Red Herring* **(No. 102, August 15, 2001, pp. 66-67)**
Pub: Herring Communications
Ed: Lee Bruno. **Description:** An overview of next-generation communications.

27306 ■ "Bright lights" in *Entrepreneur* **(Vol. 30, No. 2, Feb)**
Pub: Entrepreneur Media Inc.
Ed: Amanda C. Kooser. **Description:** Information about various portable projectors to help with presentations is offered, including a shopping list for Epson PowerLite 600p, Hitachi CP-X270W, InFocus LP280, Optoma ExPro750, and Sharp PG-C20XU.

27307 ■ "Bronto Email Marketing Toolkit" in *Entrepreneur.com* **(Vol. 34, February 2006, No. 2, pp. 6)**
Pub: Entrepreneur Media Inc.
Description: Free guide offered by Bronto software focuses on email marketing for small business.

27308 ■ "The "Build-the-Box" Lesson" in *Business Communication Quarterly* **(Vol. 63, No. 3, September 2000, pp. 60)**
Pub: Association for Business Communication
Ed: John M. Penrose. **Description:** An exercise in writing clear and concise product manuals for your products.

27309 ■ "Building visibility" in *Women in Business* **(Vol. 54, No. 2, March-April 2002, pp. 32)**
Pub: The ABWA Co Inc.
Ed: Liz Hughes. **Description:** Techniques for building visibility and creating business success are provided, including the avoidance of gossip and increased communication skills.

27310 ■ *Business Communication*
Pub: South-Western Publishing Co.
Ed: Jules Harcourt. **Released:** 1996. **Price:** $59.95.

27311 ■ *Business Communication Strategies*
Pub: Delmar Publishers
Released: 1997. **Price:** $62.95.

27312 ■ *Business Communication That Really Works*
Pub: N T C Contemporary Publishing Co.
Ed: Bonnie Lund. **Released:** 1995. **Price:** $13.95 (paper).

27313 ■ *Business Communication That Really Works!: Technology for Business*
Pub: Affinity Publishing
Ed: Bonnie Lund. **Released:** 1995. **Price:** $13.95 (paper).

27314 ■ "Business Dining Etiquette: Beat Your Competition With Winning Table Manners" in *Black Enterprise* **(Vol. 35, August 2004, No. 1)**
Pub: Earl G. Graves Publishing Co. Inc.
Ed: Kimberly J. Hamilton-Wright. **Description:** Because nearly 50 percent of all business transactions are concluded over a meal, good table manners are critical to image.

27315 ■ "Business Groups Look for Next Generation's Leaders" in *San Fernando Valley Business Journal* **(Vol. 12, January 2007, No. 2, pp. 1)**
Pub: San Fernando Valley Business Journal Associates

Ed: Mark R. Madler. **Description:** A number of business groups in the San Fernando Valley area are reaching out to embrace the younger generation by helping young business professionals make connections and learn leadership skills.

27316 ■ "C-DHP: Where Is The Movement Headed" in *Rough Notes* **(Vol. 145, No. 1, January 2003, pp. 108)**
Pub: Rough Notes
Ed: Michael J. Moody. **Description:** The Consumer-Driven Healthcare Congress held a Winter Symposium on health care planning. The conference brought out communications and education as two major aspects required for employers and employees.

27317 ■ "Cardwell's at the Plaza is on the Plus Side of Ledger" in *St. Louis Post-Dispatch* **(September 17, 2004)**
Pub: Knight-Ridder/Tribune Business News
Ed: Chauncia A. Boyd. **Description:** Profile of Cardwell's at the Plaza, catering to the business lunch crowd. The restaurant offers a variety of items including, ribs, pizza, and seafood.

27318 ■ "The CEO's Secret Handbook" in *Business 2.0* **(Vol. 6, July 2005, No. 6, pp. 68-74)**
Pub: Time, Inc.
Ed: Paul Kaihla. **Description:** Accidental guru, Bill Swanson, CEO at Raython shares a lifetime's worth of executive wisdom in his 760-page spiral-bound guidebook, Swanson's Unwritten Rules of Management.

27319 ■ "The Chinese Negotiation" in *Harvard Business Review* **(Vol. 81, No. 10, October 2003, pp. 82)**
Pub: Harvard Business School Press
Ed: John L. Graham, N. Mark Lam. **Description:** Suggestions for multinational firms looking to conduct negotiations in China are presented. Cultural differences are a critical factor that can make or break an effective negotiation.

27320 ■ "Commentary: For Women in Management, Communication is King" in *Long Island Business News* **(March 12, 2004)**
Pub: Dolan Media Newswires
Ed: Natalie Canavor. **Description:** Reasoning behind women's management skills versus men's are discussed; research studies are used to document opinions.

27321 ■ *Common Sense Purchasing: Hard Knock Lessons Learned from a Purchasing Pro*
Pub: Booksurge, LLC
Ed: Tom DePaoli. **Released:** September 2004. **Price:** $10.95. **Description:** Guide to purchasing and negotiating deals.

27322 ■ *Communicate with Confidence!: How to Say It Right the First Time and Every Time*
Pub: The McGraw-Hill Companies
Ed: Dianna Booher. **Released:** 1995. **Price:** $39.95. **Description:** Contains over 600 speaking and listening tips to improve communication skills, from constructive criticism and conflict resolution to saying "no" without guilt and talking across gender lines.

27323 ■ "Communication Training in Two Companies" in *Business Communication Quarterly* **(Vol. 63, No. 3, September 2000, pp. 104)**
Pub: Association for Business Communication
Ed: Roberta H. Krapels and Barbara D. Davis. **Description:** The implications of survey results for teaching of business communication are discussed. Statistical data is included.

27324 ■ "Communications initiatives vital for small business" in *Atlanta Business Chronicle* **(Vol. 24, No. 14, September 7, 2001, pp. 4B)**
Pub: American City Business Journals Inc.
Ed: Melissa Goehring. **Description:** Melissa Goehring, executive producer at Mountain View Productions

Ltd., discusses communications initiatives. These are both external and internal communications that focus on the company vision and bolster company branding. Goehring says that this method is especially important to small businesses, and outlines ways for which corporations can develop successful communications initiatives.

27325 ■ "The Conflict and Culture Reader" in *Dispute Resolution Journal* **(Vol. 56, No. 2, May-July 2001, pp. 85)**
Pub: American Arbitration Association
Ed: Cindy Fazzi. **Description:** Review of the book, "The Conflict and Culture Reader", is presented.

27326 ■ "Conflict resolution, made simple" in *New York Times* **(March 25, 2001, pp. BU13)**
Pub: The New York Times
Ed: Lawrence VanGelder. **Description:** Three examples of conflict with solutions to resolve the issues are presented.

27327 ■ "Conflict Resolution Using Cognitive Analysis Approach" in *Project Management Journal* **(Vol. 32, No. 2, June 2001, pp. 4)**
Pub: Project Management Institute
Ed: Hashem Al-Tabtabai, Alex P. Alex, Ahmed Aboualfotouh. **Description:** Within the field of project management, research in the subject of conflict analysis and resolution has received considerable attention. This paper presents the application of cognitive analysis, based on the workings of "human judgment theorists", to the resolution of representative conflict situations.

27328 ■ "Conflicts and Conflict Resolution in International Anti-trust: Do We Need International Competition Rules?" in *World Economy* **(Vol. 24)**
Pub: Blackwell Publishers, Inc.
Ed: Henning Klodt. **Description:** The wave of company mergers and acquisitions in the world which are driven by globalization and deregulation could lead to oligopolies in national markets and the world. This paper looks into solutions such as national anti-trust laws applying internationally, or establishing an international competition policy.

27329 ■ "Consorting with Competitors" in *Harvard Business Review* **(Vol. 80, No. 1, January 2002, pp. 21)**
Pub: Harvard Business School Press
Ed: Christopher Kurt. **Description:** Personal insight is given into forming industry consortia, using specifications called Universal Description, Discover, and Integration (UDDI). UDDI allows for integrations of ideas electronically via a directory, and keeps the consortia on track.

27330 ■ "Consultant Outlines Steps For Measuring Effectiveness Of Communications Program" in *Employee Benefit Plan Review* **(Vol. 55, No. 12)**
Pub: Charles D. Spencer & Associates, Inc.
Description: Detroit, Michigan-based Aon Consulting Inc., a management consulting services firm, has developed an employee communication program that allows employers to measure the effectiveness of their program. The program, which is aimed at assessing employee job satisfaction, contains twelve key performance indicators.

27331 ■ "Contact Sport" in *Entrepreneur* **(Vol. 28, No. 2, February 2000, pp. 54)**
Pub: Entrepreneur Media Inc.
Ed: Cassandra Cavanah. **Description:** Tackling customer relationships takes more than just a few friendly phone calls.

27332 ■ "Contact sport: now that's how you play the networking game" in *Entrepreneur* **(Vol. 31, No. 6, June 2003, pp. 28)**
Pub: Entrepreneur Media Inc.
Ed: Joshua Kurlantzick. **Description:** The Ultimate Frisbee Game has become one of the fastest-growing participant sports, according to the Ultimate Players Association. The games popularity has attracted entrepreneurs, making it a great place for business networking.

27333 ■ "Contractual expansion & limitation of judicial review of arbitral awards (Part 2)" in *Dispute Resolution Journal* **(Vol. 56, No. 1)**
Pub: American Arbitration Association
Ed: Kenneth M. Curtin. **Description:** In part two of this two-part article, the author examines court decisions regarding the judicial review of arbitral awards and argues that courts should adhere strictly to the freedom of contract principle to best respect the arbitration process.

27334 ■ "Cool Tools" in *My Business* **(February/March 2004, pp. 18-19)**
Pub: My Business Magazine
Description: Profiles of new devices of interest to the small business owner, including Lingo Talking Translator, which translates nine languages aloud and/or onscreen, and includes a calculator, world clock, currency and metric converters, and an address book; the Auravision EluminX illuminated computer keyboard for working in dark or low-lit spaces; RedEnvelope's messaging pens; and Radio YourWay AM/FM Radio Recorder.

27335 ■ "The cost center that paid its way" in *Harvard Business Review* **(Vol. 80, No. 4, April 2002, pp. 31)**
Pub: Harvard Business School Press
Ed: Julia Kirby. **Description:** A case study where four commentators review the workings of a fictional company's marketing communications department. Advice is offered on how its leader could have avoided the discontent within other departments.

27336 ■ "Costs in international commercial arbitration" in *Dispute Resolution Journal* **(Vol. 56, No. 1, February-April 2001, pp. 30)**
Pub: American Arbitration Association
Ed: Murray L. Smith. **Description:** Questions regarding legal costs in commercial arbitration when practice and laws vary depending on countries involved, are addressed.

27337 ■ "Cracking Wise" in *Entrepreneur* **(Vol. 28, No. 4, April 2000, pp. 150)**
Pub: Entrepreneur Media Inc.
Ed: Marc Diener. **Description:** A sense of humor is a tremendous asset to any dealmaker.

27338 ■ "Crashing Past the Gatekeepers-Part Two" in *Business Week Online* **(April 24, 2002)**
Pub: McGraw-Hill, Inc.
Ed: Michelle Nichols. **Description:** Various approaches are discussed to get passed the barriers, such as secretaries and switchboards, preventing salespersons from reaching potential clients.

27339 ■ *The Creative Communicator: 399 Tools to Communicate Commitment without Boring People to Death!*
Pub: Irwin Professional Publishing
Ed: Barbara A. Glanz. **Released:** 1993. **Price:** $22.00. **Description:** Guide to improving written, oral, and electronic communication. Includes techniques and real-life examples.

27340 ■ "CSDA creates a new Web site" in *Masonry Construction* **(Vol. 16, No. 1, January 2003, pp. 17)**
Pub: Hanley-Wood, Inc.
Ed: Ron Holzhauer. **Description:** The Concrete Sawing and Drilling Association (CSDA) has launched a new Web site that will offer up-to-date information about the industry, membership and upcoming events; as well as a searchable membership database of contractors and manufacturers. The Web site is designed to improve collaboration and communication among members, prospective members, architects, engineers, general contractors, and the government.

27341 ■ "Culture Shock" in *Entrepreneur* **(Vol. 31, No. 9, July 2003, pp. 77)**
Pub: Entrepreneur Media, Inc.
Ed: Marc Diener. **Description:** With increasing numbers of international, multinational and transnational corporations, culture is playing a major role in negotiations.

27342 ■ "Cut the Cord: Presentations Don't Have to Be a Hassle" in *Entrepreneur* (Vol. 32, December 2004, No. 12, pp. 50)
Pub: Entrepreneur Media Inc.
Ed: Amanda C. Kooser. **Description:** Wireless technology enables entrepreneurs to give presentations using the D-Link Wireless Presentation Gate that allows users to connect to VGA-compatible machines like projectors, LCD panels or monitors wirelessly.

27343 ■ "Cyber-Sign" in *PC Magazine* (February 6, 2001, pp. 26)
Pub: Ziff-Davis Publishing Company
Ed: Sally Wiener Grotta. **Description:** Cyber-Sign Electronic Signature Verification Plug-In for Adobe Acrobat is able to verify that a signature is authentic and can establish intent, the two requirements for using e-signatures. The Cyber-Sign products are invaluable for online business communications, making an electronic signature more secure than a traditional paper signature.

27344 ■ "Dairy Queen phasing out frozen yogurt" in (Vol. 14, No. 9, August 29, 2001, pp. 1)
Pub: Howard Waxman
Description: Due to waning sales, Dairy Queen International will no longer sell frozen yogurt at its shops. Dairy Queen has hired Dimension Data/Proxicom to develop an extranet for the company's franchises in the hopes that better communications and information sharing will increase efficiency.

27345 ■ "Deals Unplugged" in *Entrepreneur* (Vol. 31, No. 8, August 2003, pp. 69)
Pub: Entrepreneur Media, Inc.
Ed: Marc Diener. **Description:** When negotiating deals it is time to leave the table when the other side's last best offer isn't good enough, there's a better alternative, or it is discovered that the opponent is unethical, however there are also more subtle signs to look for, such as a difficult opponent or the fact that transactional costs will be too expensive.

27346 ■ "Design Innovation Brings Communications Challenges" in *Employee Benefit Plan Review* (Vol. 55, No. 7, January 2001, pp. 27)
Pub: Charles D. Spencer & Associates, Inc.
Ed: Sue Burzawa. **Description:** The 401(k) plan design evolved rapidly in the late 1990s, and that trend is continuing. Recent innovations, including automatic enrollment and Web access for information and transactions of plans, are expected to soon be common practice.

27347 ■ "Developing Your Leadership Pipeline" in *Harvard Business Review* (Vol. 81, No. 12, December 2003, pp. 76)
Pub: Harvard Business School Press
Ed: Jay A conger, Robert M. Fulmer. **Description:** Key guidelines for effective leadership communication in succession management are examined, including identification of linchpin positions, making the transition process transparent, assessment of progress on a regular basis, and maintaining flexibility.

27348 ■ "Discrimination in the workplace: how mediation can help" in *Dispute Resolution Journal* (Vol. 56, No. 1, February-April 2001, pp. 35)
Pub: American Arbitration Association
Ed: Lamont E. Stallworth, Thomas McPherson, Larry Rute. **Description:** Discussion on ways mediation can help to resolve conflict arising from subtle or unconscious discriminatory acts in the workplace, noting key features of the U.S. Postal Services REDRESS program and the need for national legislation.

27349 ■ "Do You Work for Free?" in *My Business* (February/March 2004, pp. 50)
Pub: My Business Magazine
Ed: Susan Palmquist. **Description:** When negotiating with potential clients, it is important to let a client have only a sampling of your expertise and to remain professional.

27350 ■ "Don't subject those around you to cell hell" in *Atlanta Business Chronicle* (Vol. 25, January 10, 2003, No. 31, pp. 3B)
Pub: American City Business Publications, Inc.
Ed: Connie Glaser. **Description:** A relatively recent phenomenon is the explosion of cellular phone use, and on that also demands its own rules of etiquette, including the workplace. While cell phone use has increased rapidly, polite habits surrounding cell phone use has not. Cellular usage guidelines for the 21st century are discussed.

27351 ■ "E-Mail Alternative" in *Entrepreneur* (Vol. 32, No. 1, January 2004, pp. 47)
Pub: Entrepreneur Media, Inc.
Ed: Liane Cassavoy. **Description:** Eudora 6.0s new SpamWatch feature sends spam to a junk mail folder, making it an alternative to Outlook Express for email.

27352 ■ "An E-Mail from the IRS? Don't Believe It" in *Long Island Business News* (May 7, 2004)
Pub: Dolan Media Newswires
Ed: David Reich-Hale. **Description:** The U.S. Internal Revenue Service has posted a warning to taxpayers about an email scam that tries to trick taxpayers into giving personal information. The email appears to be an official memo from the IRS.

27353 ■ "E-mail Offers a Little Wit with Your News" in *Crain's Detroit Business* (Vol. 19, No. 6, February 10, 2003, pp. 9)
Pub: Crain Communications Inc., Detroit
Ed: Mary Kramer. **Description:** Crain's Detroit offers a free daily e-mail news service providing an online news summary by 3:30 p.m. daily. The service started in January and already has 16,000 people signed up.

27354 ■ *Effective Meeting Skills*
Pub: Crisp Publications, Inc.
Ed: Marion E. Haynes. **Price:** $12.95.

27355 ■ *Effective Presentation Skills*
Pub: Crisp Publications, Inc.
Ed: Steve Mandel. **Released:** Revised edition. **Price:** $9.95.

27356 ■ "Elbows Off the Table" in *My Business* (February/March 2004, pp. 14)
Pub: My Business Magazine
Ed: Julie Bawden Davis. **Description:** Rules of etiquette that still apply to be successful are listed. Manners are critical to business success.

27357 ■ "The Electronic Negotiator" in *Harvard Business Review* (Vol. 78, No. 1, January 2000, pp. 16)
Pub: Harvard Business School Publishing Corp.
Description: Negotiations conducted over e-mail often go nowhere. The article shows what you can do to improve your company's odds of success.

27358 ■ "The electronic personality and digital self" in *Dispute Resolution Journal* (Vol. 56, No. 1, February-April 2001, pp. 8)
Pub: American Arbitration Association
Ed: Robert Gordon. **Description:** A discussion involving the possible uses of the Internet as a venue for dispute resolution, and possible innovations and negatives in using this venue, is highlighted.

27359 ■ "Enjoy the Silence" in *Black Enterprise* (Vol. 36, November 2005, No. 4, pp. 162)
Pub: Earl G. Graves Publishing Co. Inc.
Ed: Robyn D. Clarke. **Description:** Silence can be used as a useful communication tool. Gestures, nods and smiles can also communicate a point in business communications.

27360 ■ "Entrepreneur Column" in *Entrepreneur* (August 18, 2005)
Pub: Entrepreneur Media Inc.
Ed: Gail F. Goodman. **Description:** Electronic newsletters can be a great marketing tool if done properly. Email marketing solutions should include data that allows a firm to analyze and optimize any e-newsletter campaign.

27361 ■ "Entrepreneur Column" in *Entrepreneur.com* (September 7, 2005)
Pub: Entrepreneur Media Inc.
Ed: David Javitch. **Description:** Good communication is the key to any successful company. When communication is positive and effective, employees feel secure, leading to increased productivity along with job satisfaction.

27362 ■ *Essentials of Business Communication*
Pub: South-Westrn Publishing Co.
EDR Mary E. Guffey. **Released:** 1995. **Price:** $53.95.

27363 ■ "Ethics in negotiation: does getting to yes require candor?" in *Dispute Resolution Journal* (Vol. 56, No. 2, May-July 2001, pp. 8)
Pub: American Arbitration Association
Ed: Anne M. Burr. **Description:** The benefits and difficulties derived from being candid during business negotiations are covered.

27364 ■ "Everything You Ever Wanted to Know About Email" in *Inc.* (October 2005, pp. 113-117, 119, 122)
Pub: Inc. Magazine
Ed: John Fried. **Description:** Guide to using email as an important business tool is presented. Tips to keep a system secure, efficient, and affordable are also included.

27365 ■ "The Evolution of E-Mail" in *Ingram's* (Vol. 28, No. 9, September 2002, pp. 62)
Pub: Show Me Publishing, Inc.
Ed: Tom Peterman. **Description:** E-mail is the most popular activity on the Internet and is being used in many ways, such as messaging, online teaching and learning, conferencing, and communication.

27366 ■ *Excellence in Business Communication*
Pub: The McGraw-Hill Companies
Ed: John V. Thill. **Released:** 1995. **Price:** $17.50.

27367 ■ "Eye to Eye" in *Entrepreneur* (Vol. 32, October 2004, No. 10, pp. 89)
Pub: Entrepreneur Media Inc.
Ed: Barry Farber. **Description:** Benefits to meeting business contact in person are listed. When looking into customers' eyes, an entrepreneur can communicate honesty and sincerity as well as confidence.

27368 ■ "Ezsupport Life" in *Entrepreneur.com* (Vol. 34, February 2006, No. 2, pp. 6)
Pub: Entrepreneur Media Inc.
Description: Profile of EzSupport Life, a free, automated online customer-support solution for small businesses.

27369 ■ "Face to face" in *Incentive* (Vol. 174, No. 9, September 2000, pp. 102)
Pub: Bill Communications
Ed: Andrea Nierenberg. **Description:** Tips for sales communication in the electronic age where less face-to-face meetings occur.

27370 ■ "Face Up" in *Entrepreneur* (Vol. 28, No. 9, September 2000, pp. 56)
Pub: Entrepreneur Media Inc.
Ed: Gwen Moran. **Description:** In-person meetings are the best way to make amends for problems with products or services.

27371 ■ "The fast track to fortitude - Helping harried tech pros confront adversity" in *eWeek* (April 2, 2001, pp. 49)
Pub: ZDNet
Ed: Lisa Kosan. **Description:** Employers can address adversity on the job by offering retreats or conflict resolution programs, or both, and by training managers to better listen to staff and pick up on stress-laden body language. Peak Learning Inc. offers adversity training to corporations. Its president and CEO, Paul Stoltz, has coined the term adversity quotient (AQ) to

describe how people respond to adversity. Stoltz cites research studies that show people with a higher AQ make more money, have a higher level of innovation and are better problem solvers. Persons who score at the top take responsibility for fixing a problem, see problems as a result of circumstances (not their own personal flaws) and perceive problems as limited in scope.

27372 ■ "Fax Attack: This Entrepreneur's Fighting Mad About Junk Faxes" in *Entrepreneur* **(Vol. 32, No. 1, January 2004, pp. 34)**
Pub: Entrepreneur Media, Inc.
Ed: Geoff Williams. **Description:** Steve Kirsch, owner of a software company in San Jose, California, has filed a $2.2 trillion class-action lawsuit against Fax. com, in the hopes of ending junk fax mail.

27373 ■ "Feeding Frenzy" in *Entrepreneur. com* **(Vol. 34, February 2006, No. 2, pp. 77)**
Pub: Entrepreneur Media Inc.
Ed: Catherine Seda. **Description:** Creative marketers are using RSS feed in order to send successful marketing email. RSS is 100 percent opt-in. Users subscribe to a reader such as Bloglines, Newsgator, or Pluck and choose the feeds they wish to receive, no spam allowed. The number of RSS users is growing quickly making it an opportunity to market products and services for small companies.

27374 ■ *50 One-Minute Tips to Better Communication*
Pub: Crisp Publications, Inc.
Ed: Phillip Bozek. **Price:** $10.95.

27375 ■ "First Impressions" in *Black Enterprise* **(Vol. 36, December 2005, No. 5, pp. 62)**
Pub: Earl G. Graves Publishing Co. Inc.
Description: Sonya Lowerey, author of The Secret Language of Business Cards, discusses the eight common business card mistakes made by small companies.

27376 ■ "Five Ways to Get People to Listen" in *Folio: the Magazine for Magazine Management* **(Vol. 30, No. 1, January 2001, pp. 9)**
Pub: Intertec Publishing Corp.
Description: Five important principles to use for getting your message across are addressed by Anne Miller, a sales and communications seminar leader, speaker and author.

27377 ■ "Full Esteem Ahead: Act Like an Executive-And Get the Respect You Deserve" in *Entrepreneur* **(Vol. 31, No. 9, September 2003, pp. 104)**
Pub: Entrepreneur Media, Inc.
Description: Ways new entrepreneurs can learn to have the presence of a seasoned pro are listed, including the technique of talking slowly, standing with confidence, body language, and more.

27378 ■ "Game On!" in *Entrepreneur* **(Vol. 32, November 2004, No. 11, pp. 28)**
Pub: Entrepreneur Media Inc.
Ed: Mark Hendricks. **Description:** Some experts believe that employees who grew up playing video games such as Quake and Simcity are better at group communication, creative problem solving and risk taking than non-gamers.

27379 ■ "Generation Gap at the Office" in *Hispanic Business* **(November 2002, pp. 58, 60, 62)**
Pub: Hispanic Business
Ed: Rosa Antonia Carrillo, Rachel Michelson. **Description:** Ways in which communication and a comprehensive transition plan can help family-owned businesses survive into the second generation and beyond.

27380 ■ "Getting Noticed at Work" in *Women in Business* **(Vol. 53, No. 1, January-February, 2001, pp. 22)**
Pub: The ABWA Co. Inc.

Ed: Mary-Lane Kamberg. **Description:** Ways of getting noticed at work, such as communicating, remaining flexible, dressing appropriately, taking pride in work and keeping a positive attitude are discussed.

27381 ■ "Getting to Yes: Negotiating Agreement Without Giving In
Pub: Penguin Books (USA) Incorporated
Ed: Roger Fisher, William L. Ury, Bruce Patton. **Released:** December 1991. **Price:** $15.00. **Description:** Strategies for negotiating mutually acceptable agreements in all types of conflict.

27382 ■ "Go Live: They've Got Questions, You've Got Answers." in *Entrepreneur* **(Vol. 33, March 2005, No. 3, pp. 90)**
Pub: Entrepreneur Media Inc.
Ed: Catherine Seda. **Description:** When designing a Website, consider offering a live chat that helps customers with any frustrations navigating the site, while taking customer service to a higher level.

27383 ■ "Grist: A Passport to America" in *Inc.* **(October 1, 2004)**
Pub: Inc. Magazine
Ed: Adam Hanft. **Description:** Ways blue states and red states are learning to communicate and do business are highlighted.

27384 ■ "Ground Control" in *Entrepreneur* **(Vol. 32, August 2004, No. 8, pp. 34)**
Pub: Entrepreneur Media Inc.
Ed: Gisela M. Pedroza. **Description:** One-Touch NAP 2500 is a mobile satellite system that is mounted to the top of a vehicle. The wireless device can launch a high-speed network for up to five local computers, making it perfect for construction or field-service businesses whose employees are always changing job sites but need to be connected to the company network, Internet or IP phone service.

27385 ■ *Groups in Context: Leadership and Participation in Small Groups*
Pub: McGraw-Hill Companies
Ed: Gerald L. Wilson. **Released:** June 2004. **Price:** $70.00 (US), $105.95 (Canadian). **Description:** Small group communication skills for the workplace, in churches, social groups, or civic organizations.

27386 ■ "Groups Working on Conflict Resolution for Stock Analysts, Investment Bankers" in *Knight-Ridder/Tribune Business News* **(July 29, 2001)**
Pub: Knight-Ridder/Tribune Business News
Description: Congress has held hearings to look at the relationship between Wall Street and securities analysts to try to build trust between firms.

27387 ■ "A Growing Market for Talk" in *Hispanic Business* **(Vol. 24, No. 4, April 2002, pp. 22)**
Pub: Hispanic Business Inc.
Ed: Rick Laezman. **Description:** The Hispanic public-speaking industry has entered a growth mode, and Hispanic motivational speakers are finding corporations, associations and schools eager to hire them.

27388 ■ "Guardian of the Past" in *Crain's Detroit Business* **(Vol. 21, January 3, 2005, No. 1, pp. 19)**
Pub: Crain Communications Inc. - Detroit
Ed: Jennette Smith. **Description:** The Guardian Building is experiencing an increase in tenants after being purchased by the Sterling Group, led by Gary Torgow. Since $1 million in renovations, the building's occupancy rate rose from 6 percent in 2003 to 43 percent in 2004.

27389 ■ *Guide to Business Information on Central and Eastern Europe*
Pub: Taylor and Francis Group LLC
Contact: Tania Koon, Author
Released: Latest edition June 2000. **Price:** $60, individuals. **Covers:** Twelve countries of Central and Eastern Europe. **Entries Include:** Country overview; current developments; company name, address, phone, fax; names and titles of key personnel; industries and services; legislation; and organizations.

27390 ■ *Guide to Business Information on Russia, the NIS, and the Baltic States*
Pub: Taylor and Francis Group LLC
Contact: Tania Koon, Author
Released: Latest edition June 2000. **Price:** $60, individuals. **Covers:** Fifteen countries of Russia, the NIS, and the Baltic States. **Entries Include:** Current developments; company name, address, phone, fax; industries and services; legislation; and organizations.

27391 ■ "Hands On" in *Inc.* **(September 2005, pp. 37-38)**
Pub: Inc. Magazine
Ed: Alison Stein Wellner. **Description:** Email, Blackberrys, and text messaging are replacing face-to-face business communication. Facial expression and body language, voice inflection, and words can help derive meaning to business discussions.

27392 ■ "Hangin' Tough: How to Beef Up Your Negotiating Game" in *Entrepreneur* **(Vol. 32, August 2004, No. 8, pp. 72)**
Pub: Entrepreneur Media Inc.
Ed: Marc Diener. **Description:** Negotiating skills out outlined, focusing on technique, not just game face. If you must give something, be sure to get something back in return.

27393 ■ "Head to Head: How to Deal With Difficult Opponents" in *Entrepreneur* **(Vol. 32, October 2004, No. 10, pp. 96)**
Pub: Entrepreneur Media Inc.
Ed: Marc Diener. **Description:** Building trust is essential when dealing with difficult people in business. Speak to an opponent's interests and make easy concessions in the beginning.

27394 ■ "Here's what I'm thinking: you'll get your best deal if prospects see things your way" in *Entrepreneur* **(Vol. 30, No. 10, Oct. 2002)**
Pub: Entrepreneur Media Inc.
Ed: Marc Diener. **Description:** Preparation is the key to the power of persuasion when negotiating a business deal. Three important tips are offered by speaker and attorney, Marc Diener, author of the book, Deal Power.

27395 ■ "Here's a Late Resolution, But One to Be Taken Seriously" in *St. Louis Post-Dispatch* **(January 9, 2005)**
Pub: Knight-Ridder/Tribune Business News
Ed: Repps Hudson. **Description:** A discussion involving politeness and consideration in the workplace is examined. Consideration of others in the work environment might improve business, boost morale and help with promotion opportunities.

27396 ■ "High resolution" in *Entrepreneur* **(Vol. 30, No. 2, February 2002, pp. 35)**
Pub: Entrepreneur Media Inc.
Ed: Amanda C. Kooser. **Description:** Profile of Dispute Resolution Directory which offers online help in resolving business problems without using court action.

27397 ■ *High Trust Selling: Make More Money, in Less Time, with Less Stress*
Pub: Nelson Business
Ed: Todd Duncan. **Released:** January 2003. **Price:** $22.99. **Description:** Laws governing salesmanship are divided into two sections. The first deals with attitudes, aptitudes, and abilities required for successful selling; the second with communication, courtship, camaraderie and commitments between salespeople and their clients.

27398 ■ "Hoover's Introduces Competitive Intelligence and Media Monitoring Service" in *Information Today* **(Vol. 17, No. 11, Dec. 2000, pp. 31)**
Pub: Information Today, Inc.
Description: Hoover's announces its Intelligence Monitor, a Web service for businesses that need timely market and competitive intelligence information.

27399 ■ "Host a Virtual Meeting: Collaborate with a Video Link and a Whiteboard" in *Journal of Accountancy* (Vol. 199, February 2005, No. 2)
Pub: American Institute of Certified Public Accountants
Ed: Nancy B. Nichols, Stephanie M. Bryant. **Description:** Microsoft offers software that lets a small business host a virtual meeting by computer, allowing participants to talk, share files, and see each other in real time.

27400 ■ *How to Be a Great Communicator: The Complete Guide to Mastering Internal Communications*
Pub: Trans-Atlantic Publications, Inc.
Ed: David Martin. **Released:** 1995. **Price:** $43.50.

27401 ■ *How to Get People to Do Things Your Way*
Pub: N T C Contemporary Publishing Co.
Ed: J. Robert Parkinson. **Released:** 1995. **Price:** $12.95.

27402 ■ "How Good Are Google's Extras?" in *Business Week* (January 16, 2006, No. 3967, pp. 88-90)
Pub: McGraw-Hill Companies
Ed: **Description:** An overview of Froogle, Maps, Gmail, and Picasa 2, Google's added services is presented. These extras offer shopping information, satellite and road maps, photo editing software, and email at no charge to users.

27403 ■ *How to Present Like a Pro: Getting People to See Things Your Way*
Pub: The McGraw-Hill Companies
Ed: Lani Arredondo. **Price:** $21.95. **Description:** Provides instruction on how to improve your communication skills to effectively present your ideas, handle objections and interruptions, and overcome group anxiety. Includes worksheets for preparing presentations.

27404 ■ "If BlackBerry Gets Smushed..." in *Business Week* (January 9, 2006, No. 3966, pp. 16)
Pub: McGraw-Hill Companies
Ed: Stephen H. Wildstrom. **Description:** Alternatives to using BlackBerry email services are discussed in the event of the service being shut down by patent infringement charges. GoodLink from Good Technology offers similar services as does Microsoft with its Exchange email system which is being upgraded.

27405 ■ "If you want something done right, delegate it" in *Women in Business* (Vol. 53, No. 7, January-February 2002, pp. 13)
Pub: The ABWA Co Inc.
Ed: Liz Hughes. **Description:** Delegation can provide a manager with an opportunity to trust their staff and evaluate their own communication skills. Delegation allows a manager additional time for strategic planning.

27406 ■ "IM: When Time Matters" in *Hispanic Business* (November 2002, pp. 34)
Pub: Hispanic Business
Ed: Roger Harris. **Description:** Instant Messaging software is the perfect solution to emergencies and conferencing for small businesses; more than 20 million people worldwide use Instant Messaging in business, and it is predicted by International Data Corp. that more than 300 million will be using the method by 2005.

27407 ■ "In Praise of the 'Thank You' Note: Want to make an impression?" in *Business Week Online* (March 7, 2002)
Pub: McGraw-Hill, Inc.
Description: Handwritten thank you notes can be used as a sales and marketing tool for small businesses. A thank you note displays an attitude of gratitude no ad slogan or coffee mug can match.

27408 ■ "Inbox 101: How to Manage the E-mail Avalanche" in *My Business* (December/January 2004, pp. 40)
Pub: My Business Magazine
Ed: Lena Basha. **Description:** Tips to improve email communication skills are presented, including ways to prevent spam.

27409 ■ *Information Technology for the Small Business: How to Make IT Work For Your Company*
Pub: TAB Computer Systems, Incorporated
Ed: T.J. Benoit. **Released:** June 2006. **Price:** $17.95. **Description:** Basics of information technology to help small companies maximize benefits are covered. Topics include pitfalls to avoid, email and Internet use, data backup, recovery and overall IT organization.

27410 ■ "It's 2006! Whatcha Gonna Do About It?" in *Inc.* (Volume 28, January 2006, No. 1, pp. 78-85, 113)
Pub: Inc. Magazine
Ed: Stephanie Clifford. **Description:** Various entrepreneurs give advice to help small businesses face new challenges in 2006. Topics include investments, the economy, small business trends, logistics, business communication such as blogs, energy issues, consumer products, real estate, interest rates and outsourcing.

27411 ■ "It's the Sound Bite, Stupid" in *Inc.* (Volume 27, June 2005, No. 6, pp. 128)
Pub: Inc. Magazine
Ed: Adam Hanft. **Description:** Business leaders must understand the importance of good communications skills when conducting business.

27412 ■ "Keep in Touch: Be Sure to Reconnect with Your Key Clients" in *Entrepreneur* (Vol. 32, No. 1, January 2004, pp. 79)
Pub: Entrepreneur Media, Inc.
Ed: Nancy Michaels. **Description:** The importance of staying in touch with customers and their needs is stressed.

27413 ■ "Keys to Communication" in *Small Business Opportunities* (Vol. 16, November 2004, No. 6, pp. 10)
Pub: Harris Publications Inc.
Ed: Lydia Ramsey. **Description:** Studies show that words account for only 7 percent of a message, 93 percent is non-verbal. In a business setting, body language must match your words in order to effectively communicate.

27414 ■ "The Language of Business" in *My Business* (November/December 2001, pp. 17)
Pub: My Business Magazine
Ed: Linda Formichelli. **Description:** Translation options for small businesses targeting international customers are covered, including free online translation services, business translation software, and translator/translation agencies.

27415 ■ "Language Is a Virus" in *PC Computing* (March 2000, pp. 62)
Pub: Ziff-Davis Inc.
Ed: Wendy M. Grossman. **Description:** English is the cultural operating system of the Internet and the fragile common thread of global trade. But as trade barriers fall, cultural barriers are on the rise, and the Net is going to be multilingual.

27416 ■ "Leadership" in *Harvard Business Review* (Vol. 79, No. 11, December 2001, pp. 121)
Pub: Harvard Business School Press
Ed: Thomas J. Peters. **Description:** The sloppiness of an executive's workday is discussed, stating that the sad facts of leadership such as endless interruptions can be turned into opportunities to communicate values and persuade.

27417 ■ "Leadership in a combat zone" in *Harvard Business Review* (Vol. 79, No. 11, December 2001, pp. 107)
Pub: Harvard Business School Press

Description: The similarities between leadership in the military and in business are presented. The author, a lieutenant general in the U.S. Army argues that to lead successfully a person must demonstrate both expertise and empathy, know your stuff and listen hard.

27418 ■ "Learn Your Lines" in *Entrepreneur*
Pub: Entrepreneur Media Inc.
Ed: Kimberly L. McCall. **Description:** Eight steps to help sales reps improve selling techniques over the phone.

27419 ■ "Let's Do Lunch: Giving New Meaning to the Term 'Power Lunch'" in *Entrepreneur* (Vol. 32, November 2004, No. 11, pp. 34)
Pub: Entrepreneur Media Inc.
Ed: Nichole L. Torres. **Description:** In Good Company, founded by Nancy Michaels, accepts bids from entrepreneurs. The winners enjoy lunch with a powerful business owner or corporate CEO.

27420 ■ "The Lid On Spam Is Still Loose" in *Business Week* (February 7, 2005, No. 3919, pp. 10)
Pub: McGraw-Hill Companies
Ed: Erin Chambers, Ira Sager. **Description:** Profile of the CAN-SPAM Act, passed by Congress in 2004. The Act sets restrictions on unsolicited email, but has done little to eliminate junk messages. According to MX Logic, 97 percent of unsolicited commercial email defies the law.

27421 ■ *Life's a Game So Fix the Odds: How to Be More Persuasive and Influential in Your Personal and Business*
Pub: John Wiley & Sons, Incorporated
Ed: Philip Hesketh. **Released:** September 2005. **Price:** $24.95 (US), $31.00 (Canadian). **Description:** Seven psychological reasons behind why and how people are persuaded and how to use these reasons to your advantage in both your personal and business life.

27422 ■ "Living High on the Blog" in *Entrepreneur* (Vol. 33, February 2005, No. 2, pp. 65)
Pub: Entrepreneur Media Inc.
Ed: Gwen Moran. **Description:** Reach Communications Consulting founder, William Arruda, discovered an 800 percent hike in traffic on his firm's Website after being mentioned on an Internet blog; ways to add blogs to a public relations campaign are investigated.

27423 ■ "Low-Cost Teleconferencing" in *My Business* (February/March 2004, pp. 17)
Pub: My Business Magazine
Description: Profile of Apple's new iSight, a cylindrical camera and microphone that connects to a Macintosh computer via high-speed firewire and Apple's proprietary multimedia Internet messaging software iCath-AV, providing always-on videoconferencing.

27424 ■ "M-commerce: does 'streaming media' give you the screaming meemies?" in *The New York Times Magazine* (March 19, 2000, pp. 32)
Pub: The New York Times Company
Ed: William Safire. **Description:** New language is being developed around m-commerce which is e-commerce done over mobile phones and hand-held devices.

27425 ■ "Mad skills" in *Entrepreneur* (Vol. 31, No. 4, April 2003, pp. 79)
Pub: Entrepreneur Media Inc.
Ed: Marc Diener. **Description:** Anger can be used as another weapon in the negotiation process, but the proper use of anger is key.

27426 ■ "Making a Clean Break" in *Atlanta Business Chronicle* (Vol. 25, December 6, 2002, No. 26, pp. 1B)
Pub: American City Business Publications, Inc.
Ed: Lee Hall. **Description:** When a business determines that it must terminate a client, being honest and sharing blame are important elements of the process. Business relationships can become strained to the point that they no longer work.

27427 ■ "The Making of a Mediator: Developing Artistry in Practice" in *Dispute Resolution Journal* (Vol. 56, No. 1, February-April 2001, pp. 88)
Pub: American Arbitration Association
Ed: Cindy Fazzi. Description: Review of the book titled, "The Making of a Mediator: Developing Artistry in Practice."

27428 ■ "Marketing" in *Entrepreneur* (Vol. 27, No. 12, December 1999, pp. 40)
Pub: Entrepreneur Media Inc.
Ed: Gwen Moran. Description: The rules of thumb for sending proper business correspondence.

27429 ■ "The Master Negotiator: How To Use the Power of Persuasion to Raise Dollars" in *Black Enterprise* (Vol. 34, No. 2, September 2003)
Pub: Earl Graves Publishing Co.
Ed: Sonya Kimble-Ellis. Description: Profile of 17-year-old Amelia Landreth, who negotiated funds to pay for varsity and junior high basketball teams. Landreths power of persuasion can help all entrepreneurs to raise money.

27430 ■ "McMullouch Has Had Busy Telecommunications Career" in *Mississippi Business Journal* (Vol. 29, January 2007, No. 4, pp. 10)
Pub: Venture Publications, Inc.
Ed: Lynn Lofton Description: Interview and profile of John McCullouch. McCullouch has served as Bell-South's president of operations.

27431 ■ "Mediation for Small Business: Cheaper and Faster Than The Courts" in *My Business* (February/March 2003, pp. 16)
Pub: My Business Magazine
Ed: Alvin M. Hattal. Description: Rather than using the court system, more small businesses are resolving disputes through mediation. Two online mediation services are also listed. Statistical data included.

27432 ■ "Mediation Year 2051?" in *Dispute Resolution Journal* (Vol. 56, No. 1, February-April 2001, pp. 24)
Pub: American Arbitration Association
Ed: Luis Miguel Diaz. Description: Given the advances in high technology, the author imagines what might happen to mediators in the future if a software program is developed to replace the need for their services.

27433 ■ "Meet Market" in *Entrepreneur* (Vol. 28, No. 11, Njovember 2000, pp. 36)
Pub: Entrepreneur Media Inc.
Ed: Eric Brown. Description: Web-based conferencing services are discussed. According to a management consulting firm based in San Francisco, the data-conferencing market will grow from $550 million in 1999 to $1.2 billion in 2000.

27434 ■ "Meet Me at the PC" in *Entrepreneur* (Vol. 28, No. 11, November 2000, pp. 44)
Pub: Entrepreneur Media Inc.
Ed: Ellen Paris. Description: The use of the Internet for business meetings is explored.

27435 ■ "MeetingBridge" in *Entrepreneur* (Vol. 33, September 2005, No. 9, pp. 6)
Pub: Entrepreneur Media Inc.
Ed: Steve Cooper. Description: MeetingBridge offers teleconferencing, Web-conferencing and Webinar needs using a dial-in number and entry code. Web conferencing charges start at 12 cents per minute, teleconferencing at 15 center per minute (29 cents per minute with operation assistance), and Webinar tools and registration services are free.

27436 ■ "Meetings & Clubs" in *Bellingham Business Journal* (January 2007, pp. C3)
Pub: Sun News Inc.
Description: Calendar of clubs and meetings in the Bellingham area targeting business-minded individuals.

27437 ■ "Microsoft to Unveil Product to Manage Net Communications" in *Boston Globe* (March 7, 2005)
Pub: New York Times Company
Ed: Hiawatha Bray. Description: Microsoft announced a new product that will allow businesses to manage telephones, instant messaging, email and video conferencing through a single system.

27438 ■ "MIMlist Draws Eclectic Crowd: Online Forums" in *Tradeshow Week* (Vol. 34, November 29, 2004, No. 48, pp. 52)
Pub: Reed Business Information
Ed: Rachelle Crum. Description: Exhibition industry associations provide a listserve or other online forum exclusively for its members. Profile of MIMlist, a forum of more than 4,000 members is profiled.

27439 ■ "Mind over manners" in *Entrepreneur* (Vol. 31, No. 5, May 2003, pp. 118)
Pub: Entrepreneur Media Inc.
Ed: Nichole L. Torres. Description: Proper business etiquette is discussed to help make a good impression at a dinner business meeting.

27440 ■ "Mind Your Manners" in *Inc.* (September 2005, pp. 51)
Pub: Inc. Magazine
Ed: Allen P. Roberts Jr. Description: Norine Dresser has re-released her book, Multicultural Manners, which offers tips for American companies when negotiating with overseas firms.

27441 ■ "Mind Your Manners" in *Sales & Marketing Management*
Pub: VNU Business Media
Ed: Kathryn Droullard. Description: With new technologies, business communications are becoming less personal as a result of email messages and high-tech devices. A guide to help sales reps avoid 25 common mistakes when corresponding with clients is presented.

27442 ■ "Mind Your P's and Q's" in *Rough Notes* (Vol. 145, No. 2, February 2003, pp. 43)
Pub: Rough Notes
Ed: Emily Huling. Description: Business etiquette is important to observe whether in or out of the office, and when meeting people. The article provides a few do's and don'ts.

27443 ■ "Mississippi Children's Home Services" in *Mississippi Business Journal* (Vol. 29, January 2007, No. 4, pp. 6)
Pub: Venture Publications, Inc.
Description: Profile of Kelly Shannon, Development Coordinator of Mississippi Children's Home Services. She was previously Special Projects Officer of the Mississippi Department of Health's Communications Office.

27444 ■ "Money & Manners" in *Small Business Opportunities* (Vol. 17, September 2005, No. 5, pp. 12)
Pub: Harris Publications Inc.
Ed: Lydia Ramsey. Description: Rudeness can cost a small business sales and revenue. A true/false quiz is offered to judge a company's business etiquette.

27445 ■ "More Than Smart Talk" in *Hispanic Business* (June 2002, pp. 76)
Pub: Hispanic Business
Ed: Scott Williams. Description: Effective communication begins with good listening skills, this is especially important among top management.

27446 ■ "More Women Than Men Have Home Offices" in *Marketing to Women* (Vol. 19, October 2006, No. 10, pp. 12)
Pub: EPM Communications, Inc.
Description: A survey of business professionals by Intellicontact reflects that women are more likely than men to have home offices. The survey also shows that while men and women both check their e-mail frequently, the two sexes manage their inboxes differently.

27447 ■ "Myms, pings and vortals" in *The New York Times* (March 27, 2000, pp. D4, H4)
Pub: The New York Times Company
Ed: David Kirby, Henry Fountain. Description: The article covers computer jargon and how it is transferred to business conversation. Statistical data included.

27448 ■ "Need to Boost Morale? Try Good Food, Fitness and Communication" in *Wall Street Journal* (May 28, 2002, pp. B1)
Pub: Wall Street Journal
Ed: Carol Hymowitz. Description: Suggestions are offered to help boost employee moral in the workplace.

27449 ■ "Negotiate from Strength" in *Success* (Vol. 47, No. 3, July 2000, pp. 74)
Pub: Success Publishing, Inc.
Ed: Scott Smith. Description: Successful deal-making depends largely on preparation.

27450 ■ "Negotiating the spirit of a deal" in *Harvard Business Review* (Vol. 81, No. 2, February 2003, pp. 66)
Pub: Harvard Business School Press
Ed: Ron S. Fortgang, David A. Lax, James K. Sebenius. Description: Negotiating a deal can succeed or fail based upon a complete understanding by all parties of issues that are implied, such as expectations and social issues, as well as what is written down.

27451 ■ "Negotiating without a net. A conversation with the NYPD's Dominick J. Misino" in *Harvard Business Review* (Vol. 80, Oct. 2002, pp. 49)
Pub: Harvard Business School Press
Ed: Diane L. Coutu. Description: Dominick J. Misino answers questions about management techniques used to run the New York City Police Department.

27452 ■ "Network for a greater good in 2002" in *Women in Business* (Vol. 54, No. 2, March-April 2002, pp. 33)
Pub: The ABWA Co Inc.
Ed: Donna Fisher. Description: Networking tools for businesswomen are provided; maintaining networks and using business cards are discussed.

27453 ■ "Networking for Success" in *Hispanic Business* (Vol. 24, No. 4, April 2002, pp. 26)
Pub: Hispanic Business Inc.
Ed: Scott Williams. Description: Advanced interpersonal communication skills enable women executives to climb the career ladder. Interviews with successful Hispanic women include Patricia Romero Cronin, VP at IBM; Cari Dominguez, EEOC Chair; and Rebeca Johnson, VP of ethnic and urban marketing at Frito-Lay Inc.

27454 ■ "The New Kid: Another Wireless Technology is Moving into the Neighborhood" in *Entrepreneur* (Vol. 32, July 2004, No. 7, pp. 25)
Pub: Entrepreneur Media Inc.
Ed: Steve Cooper. Description: Ultra Wide Band (UWB) wireless communication technology transmits data in short, low-powered pulses over a wide range of frequency spectrums. The new technology could help entrepreneurs to use UWB as wireless backup drives, transferring data from a scanner or connecting with a camera for videoconferencing wirelessly.

27455 ■ "News Blog Highlights Women's Careers" in *Marketing to Women* (Vol. 19, November 2006, No. 11, pp. 5)
Pub: EPM Communications, Inc.
Description: NewsonWomen.com, a news blog for businesswomen and their career achievements, has added executive job postings to its content.

27456 ■ "Nice meeting you!" in *Entrepreneur* (Vol. 30, No. 12, December 2002, pp. 111)
Pub: Entrepreneur Media Inc.
Ed: Nichole L. Torres. Description: Ideas for business networking to help grow a business are presented.

27457 ■ "9/11 Calls: Wireless Devices in the Post-Attacks Era" in *Entrepeneur* (Vol. 30, No. 1, January 2002, pp. 39)
Pub: Entrepreneur Media Inc.
Ed: Mike Hogan. **Description:** After 9/11, Americans learned that wireless communications will be important in future emergencies.

27458 ■ "Nothing Personal" in *Entrepreneur* (Vol. 31, No. 10, October 2003, pp. 85)
Pub: Entrepreneur Media, Inc.
Ed: Marc Diener. **Description:** The art of negotiation to make better business deals is discussed.

27459 ■ "Now you've done it! Real deal" in *Entrepreneur* (Vol. 30, No. 3, March 2002, pp.)
Pub: Entrepreneur Media Inc.
Ed: Marc Diener. **Description:** Five basic principles to avoid during negotiations are presented.

27460 ■ "On the Business of Life" in *Forbes* (Vol. 175, January 31, 2005, No. 2, pp. 156)
Pub: Forbes Magazine Inc.
Description: It is proper business etiquette to call when people who accept business invitations to luncheons, dinners or other functions that involve planning of food, seating souvenirs, or other amenities cannot attend the event.

27461 ■ "On Her Best Behavior" in *Home Business* (Vol. 12, October 2005, No. 5, pp. 41)
Pub: Home Business Magazine
Ed: Sandy Larson. **Description:** Syndi Seid, founder of San-Francisco-based Advanced Etiquette, stresses the importance of using proper table manners while dining with clients.

27462 ■ "Once Upon A Time: Use stories to perk up your presentations" in *My Business* (June/July 2002, pp. 15)
Pub: My Business Magazine
Ed: Ivan Sylvester. **Description:** Three ways to make storytelling perk up a presentation are outlined.

27463 ■ "Online Education: Global Questions, Local Answers" in *Journal of Business Communication* (Vol. 44, January 2007, No. 1, pp. 96)
Pub: Association for Business Communication
Ed: Christopher Lam. **Description:** A collection of essays entitled, Online Education: Global Questions, Local Answers looks at professional communication and the effect of online education. Although the focus is mainly on technical communication, business communication scholars and practitioners will also find this collection a valuable read.

27464 ■ "Online Office" in *Entrepreneur* (Vol. 32, No. 1, January 2004, pp. 47)
Pub: Entrepreneur Media, Inc.
Ed: Liane Cassovoy. **Description:** Profile of Microsoft's Web conferencing with Office Live Meeting, which includes tools for application viewing and sharing, attendance reposing and recording.

27465 ■ *Open Source Solutions for Small Business Problems*
Pub: Charles River Media
Ed: John Locke. **Released:** May 2004. **Price:** $39.95 (US), $55.95 (Canadian). **Description:** Open source software provides solutions to many small business problems such as tracking electronic documents, scheduling, accounting functions, managing contact lists, and reducing spam.

27466 ■ "Opening the Kimono" in *Inc.* (September 1, 2003)
Pub: Gruner & Jahr USA Publishing
Ed: Bobbie Gossage. **Description:** How much information should be revealed when negotiating with potential partners? Tips for successful negotiating are revealed.

27467 ■ "Over their heads" in *Black Enterprise* (Vol. 31, No. 5, December 2000, pp. 79)
Pub: Earl Graves Publishing Co.
Ed: Robyn D. Clarke. **Description:** The topic of office politics and ways to bypass the chain of command in certain situations are covered.

27468 ■ *The Owners Manual for Small Business*
Pub: Planning Shop
Ed: Rhonda Abrams. **Released:** December 2005. **Price:** $19.95. **Description:** Reference book offering tips for starting a small business, low-cost marketing, and communicating effectively.

27469 ■ "Paulson Changes Name of Business" in *Bellingham Business Journal* (January 2007, pp. A19)
Pub: Sun News Inc.
Description: Judith Paulson, certified financial planner, changed the name of her business from Financial Counseling Services to Paulson Financial Services. With the change of the name also comes a new focus in which she plans to provide insurance and tax planning, financial education, and retirement planning.

27470 ■ "Personal, Thoughtful Ways to Stay in Touch" in *Rough Notes* (Vol. 145, No. 2, February 2003, pp. 32)
Pub: Rough Notes
Description: Staying in touch with business contacts and customers is very important in marketing. This can be done with phone calls, cards, a newsletter, or a personal note.

27471 ■ "Politics as Usual?" in *Sales and Marketing.com* (Vol. 156, No. 3, March 2004, pp. 14)
Pub: VNU eMedia, Inc.
Ed: Amy Moerke. **Description:** Guidelines for discussing politics with clients are presented. The course of conversation will be determined by the relationship between salesperson and client.

27472 ■ "Postcard perfect" in *Incentive* (Vol. 174, No. 10, October 2000, pp. 146)
Pub: Bill Communications
Ed: Lorena Mongelli. **Description:** All types of businesses are discovering postcards and saving money. A website is listed offering tips and ideas for using postcards for your company, including reminder notices, meeting confirmations, thank you notes, and more.

27473 ■ "Power Lunch" in *St. Louis Post-Dispatch* (August 13, 2004)
Pub: Knight-Ridder/Tribune Business News
Ed: Christopher Carey. **Description:** Profile of Arcelia's, the family owned restaurant, which attracts the business community. Tom Townsend shares how he planned his advertising agency while lunching at the popular spot.

27474 ■ *PPC's Guide to Small Business Consulting Engagements*
Pub: Practitioners Publishing Company
Released: March 2004. **Description:** Technical guide for conducting consulting engagements for small business.

27475 ■ "Press Conference: You've Worked Hard to Land That Media Interview-So Don't Blow Your Opportunity" in *Entrepreneur*
Pub: Entrepreneur Media Inc.
Ed: Kim T. Gordon. **Description:** Techniques for handling print, radio and television interviews are offered. Preparation is stressed as a key to a successful interview.

27476 ■ "Professionals and Professors: Substance or Style?" in *Business Communication Quarterly* (Vol. 63, No. 3, September 2000, pp. 9)
Pub: Association for Business Communication
Ed: Srivatsa Seshandri and Larry D. Theye. **Description:** The article gives an overall assessment of communication skills, standards of good writing, and writing style.

27477 ■ "Pushing the Right Buttons" in *Crain's Detroit Business* (Vol. 23, January 15,2007, No. 3, pp. 11)
Pub: Crain Communications Inc. - Detroit
Ed: Amy Lane. **Description:** Speed, flexibility, and time compression advantages are driving wireless companies to expand networks and facilities in Southeastern Michigan to further serve small business needs. Significant cost savings can be realized when converting from land-based fax and phone lines.

27478 ■ "Put Some Wow In Your Website" in *Inc.* (September 2006, pp. 44-45)
Pub: Gruner & Jahr USA Publishing
Ed: Michael Fitzgerald. **Description:** Websites get stale quickly and need constant changes to continue to attract attention to your message and products. New graphics, sounds, and more are provided as examples of techniques to accomplish this.

27479 ■ "Q&A" in *Home Office Computing* (Vol. 18, No. 12, December 2000, pp. 15)
Pub: Scholastic Inc.
Ed: Marilyn Zelinsky Syarto. **Description:** June Cline, a professional speaker and humorist, based in Kennesaw, Georgia, talks about how to get over a bad public-speaking experience.

27480 ■ "Quality Time: Not Getting What You Want Out of Your Sales Meeting? Here are 5 Tips to Point You in the Right Direction" in *Entrepreneur*
Pub: Entrepreneur Media Inc.
Ed: Kimberly L. McCall. **Description:** Besides confidence building, information dissemination, and company strategies, sales meetings can also be used to inspire a sales team to produce. Steps to changing dull sales meetings into creative sales meetings are listed.

27481 ■ "Rapport & Revenue" in *Small Business Opportunities* (July 2005)
Pub: Harris Publications Inc.
Description: Three Customer Relationship Management systems are outlined to help a small business choose the best one. According to recent studies only 30 percent of customer relationship management programs are successful.

27482 ■ "Reality TV for Business" in *Hispanic Business* (September 2003, pp. 74)
Pub: Hispanic Business
Ed: Roger Harris. **Description:** Profile of the new lower priced and higher quality videoconferencing devices affordable for all small companies.

27483 ■ "A Reason for Ranting" in *Black Enterprise* (Vol. 36, November 2005, No. 4, pp. 161)
Pub: Earl G. Graves Publishing Co. Inc.
Ed: Robyn D. Clarke. **Description:** Three tips to vent constructively in order to resolve a problem or concern are listed.

27484 ■ "Recipe for success in construction mediation" in *Dispute Resolution Journal* (Vol. 56, No. 2, May-July 2001, pp. 16)
Pub: American Arbitration Association
Ed: John P. Madden. **Description:** Tips to enhance the mediation process when used to resolve construction disputes are listed.

27485 ■ "Repackage Your Words" in *Sales & Marketing Management* (Vol. 159, January-February 2007, No. 1, pp. 45)
Pub: VNU Business Media
Description: Tips for presenting a PowerPoint slideshow are presented by Jerry Weissman, author of Presenting to Win: The Art of Telling Your Story.

27486 ■ "Resolving Owner Conflicts" in *Rough Notes* (Vol. 145, No. 9, September 2002, pp. 26)
Pub: Rough Notes
Ed: Paul J. DiStefano. **Description:** Lack of communications between owners of the insurance agency often results in disagreements. Unresolved conflict among owners can impede the future of an agency, whether the issue relates to money or operating philosophy.

27487 ■ "Resolving Personal and Organizational Conflict" in *Dispute Resolution Journal* **(Vol. 56,No. 2)**
Pub: American Arbitration Association
Ed: Cindy Fazzi. **Description:** Review of the publication titled, "Resolving Personal and Organizational Conflict: Stories of Transformation and Forgiveness", is presented.

27488 ■ "The Revised Uniform Arbitration Act: an overview" in *Dispute Resolution Journal* **(Vol. 56, No. 2, May-July 2001, pp. 28)**
Pub: American Arbitration Association
Ed: Timothy J. Heinsz. **Description:** An outline of the changes made under the Revised Uniform Arbitration Act and the need for Congress to revise the Federal Arbitration Act.

27489 ■ "Sage Advice" in *Entrepreneur* **(Vol. 33, September 2005, No. 9, pp. 86)**
Pub: Entrepreneur Media Inc.
Ed: Kirsten Osolind. **Description:** Three mediation tools to help create a B2B marketing program are explained.

27490 ■ "Sales Strategies" in *Small Business Opportunities* **(Vol. 17, November 2005, No. 6, pp. 64)**
Pub: Harris Publications Inc.
Ed: Steve Bookbinder. **Description:** Seven things every business owner must do in order to prepare for a first meeting with a client.

27491 ■ "S&MM Pulse" in *Sales & Marketing Management* **(Vol. 158, November-December 2006, No. 11, pp. 16)**
Pub: VNU Business Media
Description: Customer service is stressed, including improved communication skills.

27492 ■ "Say It and Sell It" in *Sales & Marketing Management* **(Vol. 158, October 2006, No. 10, pp. 15)**
Pub: VNU Business Media
Description: A voice coach offers insight in giving sales presentations. The coach recommends pacing yourself and practicing your pitch in order to have a better vocal impact.

27493 ■ "Security: Messaging Gets Serious" in *Red Herring* **(No. 103, September 1, 2001, pp. 25-26)**
Pub: Herring Communications
Ed: Mark Chediak. **Description:** The use of Internet Instant Messaging (IM) applications is discussed, with an emphasis on security.

27494 ■ "Seeing is Believing: Will VoIP Technology Finally Make Videoconferencing a Reality?" in *Entrepreneur* **(Vol. 32, November 2004, No. 11)**
Pub: Entrepreneur Media Inc.
Ed: Mike Hogan. **Description:** Profile of the Packet8 Desktop VideoPhone that allows users to not only hear, but see calling partners. The calling plan starts at $29.95 per month and offers voice mail, three-way conferencing, and call forwarding.

27495 ■ "Self-Service" in *Inc.* **(October 2005, pp. 124-125, 128)**
Pub: Inc. Magazine
Description: When choosing software to manage email it is important to consider four basic questions: what you want the email to do, an access point, security, and costs. Comparisons of Microsoft Outlook 2003, IBM Lotus Notes 7.0, Qualcomm Eudora 6.2, and Mozilla Thunderbird 1.0 software are shown.

27496 ■ "Sending the Right Messages: How to Make Staff Meetings More Effective" in *Black Enterprise* **(Vol. 35, November 2004, No. 4, pp. 74)**
Pub: Earl G. Graves Publishing Co. Inc.
Ed: Carla Thompson. **Description:** Ways to make staff meetings more effectiive are discussed using the strategy of Maria Tajil Battle, senior vice president of public affairs and marketing. Battle sees meetings as an opportunity to discern information to report to bosses about her division's activities.

27497 ■ "Shattered Magazine: A Monthly for the Global Businesswoman" in *Marketing to Women* **(Vol. 19, December 2006, No. 2, pp. 6)**
Pub: EPM Communications, Inc.
Ed: Julie Ros. **Description:** Shattered is a glossy magazine distributed monthly and run by veteran financial journalist, Julie Ros. Shattered concentrates its focus on the business world and puts special emphasis on the global impact women are having in the leadership roles of the business community.

27498 ■ "Singing the blues?" in *Entrepreneur* **(Vol. 31, No. 4, April 2003, pp. 20)**
Pub: Entrepreneur Media Inc.
Ed: Nichole L. Torres. **Description:** Profile of the band Face the Music. This blues band goes into companies to energize the workforce, increase teamwork, reduce stress, and improve communication.

27499 ■ "6 Second Strategist" in *Atlanta Business Chronicle* **(Vol. 25, No. 21, November 1, 2002, pp. 9B)**
Pub: American City Business Publications, Inc.
Ed: Chad Shultz. **Description:** Ways to communicate a firm's policies are discussed. Companies are urged not to rely on handbooks.

27500 ■ "So Long, Stage Fright" in *Success* **(Vol. 47, No. 2, June 2000, pp. 70)**
Pub: Success Publishing, Inc.
Ed: Azriela Jaffe. **Description:** Banish public speaking jitters with ten top strategies.

27501 ■ "Socialtext Update Knots Closer Enterprise Ties" in *eWeek* **(February 7, 2005)**
Pub: Ziff Davis Media Inc.
Description: Profile of Socialtext Workspace 1.5, which integrates the wiki service with enterprise directories based on lightweight directory access protocol and Microsoft Active Directory. Socialtext develops enterprise social software that allows people and companies to use the Web to communicate more effectively.

27502 ■ "SpamCheck http://spamcheck. sitesell.com" in *Entrepreneur* **(Vol. 32, No. 1, January 2004, pp. 10)**
Pub: Entrepreneur Media, Inc.
Ed: Steve Cooper. **Description:** SpamCheck will check a small businesses email and inform them with a spam score and recommend ways to decrease spam email.

27503 ■ "Speak Up: Hate to Negotiate? That's Still No Excuse to Avoid Learning This Skill" in *Entrepreneur* **(Vol. 32, September 2004)**
Pub: Entrepreneur Media Inc.
Ed: Marc Diener. **Description:** The art of negotiating is investigated. Tips are offered to entrepreneurs to improve their skills at the bargaining table.

27504 ■ "Speak up!" in *Women in Business* **(Vol. 54, No. 2, March-April 2002, pp. 38)**
Pub: The ABWA Co Inc.
Ed: Renee Grant-Williams. **Description:** Public speaking techniques are presented, including the techniques of practicing before an audience and combating stage fright.

27505 ■ "Specs & the single arbitration clause" in *Dispute Resolution Journal* **(Vol. 56, No. 2, May-July 2001, pp. 58)**
Pub: American Arbitration Association
Ed: Thomas W. Lyons. **Description:** The problems which can arise from unilateral arbitration clauses in standardized contracts are outlined.

27506 ■ "SPIM Infests" in *St. Louis Post-Dispatch* **(February 26, 2005)**
Pub: Knight-Ridder/Tribune Business News
Ed: David Sheets. **Description:** Nearly 17 million Americans report unsolicited ads during real-time online conversations and more is expected as instant messaging becomes more popular in the workplace. Spim, is spam hitting instant messages.

27507 ■ "Staying Interactive: Web Presentation Success Requires More Than Just Technical Skills" in *Sales & Marketing Management* **(Vol. 157)**
Pub: VNU Business Media
Ed: Julia Chang. **Description:** According to a study performed by Wainhouse Research, a market research firm in Massachusetts, forty percent of companies are expected to increased spending on Web conferencing in 2005. Webinar provides training in the technical skills required for Web conferencing, but also emphasizes ways to use voice to emphasize points and captivate an audience.

27508 ■ "Stockholders in Cyberspace: Weick's Sensemaking Online" in *Journal of Business Communication* **(Vol. 44, January 2007, No. 1, pp. 13)**
Pub: Association for Business Communication
Ed: Andrew F. Herrmann. **Description:** Stockholders are using the Internet's discussion boards to make sense of their financial holdings.

27509 ■ "Support the Advocate!" in *Bellingham Business Journal* **(December 2006, pp. 3)**
Pub: Sun News Inc.
Ed: Drew Graham. **Description:** The Whatcom Business Advocate is now a pull-out section of the Business Journal. One of the premier news publications the newsletter reaches more than 30,000 individual readers each month. The newsletter and journal are excellent sources for advertisers.

27510 ■ "Take It Or Leave It: The Only Guide to Negotiating You Will Ever Need" in *Inc.* **(August 1, 2003)**
Pub: Gruner & Jahr USA Publishing
Ed: Rob Walker. **Description:** In order to become a good negotiator it is important to change your mindset and your behavior. A guide to becoming a better negotiator is presented.

27511 ■ "Talk Direct" in *PC Magazine* **(February 6, 2001, pp. 26)**
Pub: Ziff-Davis Publishing Company
Ed: Sally Wiener Grotta. **Description:** Review of Veritel's Talk Direct, that allows dialing into your company's toll-free phone line and speaking your name to access all the telephony tools at the office. This software helps the company tighten control over costs while improving communication among employees.

27512 ■ "Talking the Talk" in *Inc.* **(December 1, 2003)**
Pub: Gruner & Jahr USA Publishing
Ed: Bobbie Gossage. **Description:** This fall, Webster released its first guide to business terms.

27513 ■ "Textron Fastening adds to efforts in mobile phoning" in *Crain's Detroit Business* **(Vol. 16, No. 46, November 13, 2000, pp. 25)**
Pub: Crain Communications, Inc.
Ed: Roger Renstrom. **Description:** Textron Fastening Systems, based in Troy, Michigan, has moved to acquire injection molding, decorating, and assembly capabilities to support the mobile phone market. Details of the deal are included.

27514 ■ "The Champagne Group Launches 'Manager Makeover' Program" in *Bellingham Business Journal* **(January 2007, pp. 4)**
Pub: Sun News Inc.
Description: Twelve-year-old business and leadership coaching company, The Champagne Group, is launching their new Manager Makeover Program. The five-step, customized program equips managers with techniques on becoming leaders who can resolve conflicts and increase performance.

27515 ■ "A theory of mediation" in *Dispute Resolution Journal* **(Vol. 56, No. 2, May-July 2001, pp. 78)**
Pub: American Arbitration Association
Ed: Douglas E. Noll. **Description:** A theoretical framework for mediation is provided to incorporate mediation's various styles and outcomes to help practitioners and clients determine appropriate approaches in various circumstances.

27516 ■ "Through the grapevine: E-mail newsletter has owners tasting profits" in *Entrepreneur* (Vol. 31, No. 6, June 2003, pp. 81)
Pub: Entrepreneur Media Inc.
Ed: April Y. Pennington. Description: Customer relations depend on communication and many companies are using email newsletters to stay in touch with customers.

27517 ■ "Tips on managing older workers" in *Crain's Detroit Business* (Vol. 17, No. 44, October 22, 2001, pp. 11)
Pub: Crain Communications, Inc.
Description: Tips for managing an older workforce are covered. Topics covered include compensation benefits, ergonomic equipment, stress management, flexible schedules, conflict resolution, and training.

27518 ■ "Tough Talk" in *Entrepreneur.com* (Vol. 34, February 2006, No. 2, pp. 100)
Pub: Entrepreneur Media Inc.
Ed: Nichole L. Torres. Description: Barbara Pachter, author of The Power of Positive Confrontation: The Skills You Need to Know to Handle Conflicts at Work, Home, and in Life, offers five tips for successful business conversations.

27519 ■ "Training Managers to be Better Communicators" in *Employment Relations Today* (Vol. 27, No. 1, Spring 2000, pp. 73)
Pub: John Wiley & Sons, Inc.
Ed: Merna Skinner. Description: Covers ways to train managers in effective business communication, focusing on the mistakes managers often make when communicating with their subordinates. Topics addressed include human resource management, self-awareness, and developing interpersonal skills.

27520 ■ "A Tug of War: Real Deal: You Can't Have It All." in *Entrepreneur* (Vol. 31, No. 9, September 2003, pp. 81)
Pub: Entrepreneur Media, Inc.
Ed: Marc Diener. Description: When negotiating deals, it is important to understand two critical tools: concession and the condition. A concession is what is given, the condition the "if" clause.

27521 ■ "United Front" in *Entrepreneur* (Vol. 33, January 2005, No. 1, pp. 47)
Pub: Entrepreneur Media Inc.
Ed: Mike Hogan. Description: Unified messaging (UM) or unified communications (UC) will allow voice mail, email, and instant messaging to be delivered to the same inbox.

27522 ■ "Up in Arms: Prepare for Litigation With These Weapons of Mass Discussion" in *Entrepreneur* (Vol. 33, January 2005, No. 1, pp. 70)
Pub: Entrepreneur Media Inc.
Ed: Marc Diener. Description: Business negotiation skills are discussed for planning possible litigation.

27523 ■ "Video To Go" in *Entrepreneur* (Vol. 31, No. 9, September 2003, pp. 32)
Pub: Entrepreneur Media, Inc.
Ed: Gisela M. Pedroza. Description: Profile of the Blue Thunder Mini Cam from Digital Integrated Systems; the system can be used for video mail and videoconferencing while traveling.

27524 ■ "Viewer's Choice" in *Entrepreneur* (Vol. 30, No. 3, March 2002, pp. 44)
Pub: Entrepreneur Media Inc.
Ed: Amanda C. Kooser. Description: Videoconferencing is offering entrepreneurs, as well as established small businesses, a safe, timesaving and economical choice to decrease the amount of business travel the would otherwise have to do. A resource guide for choosing the proper Web cam is included.

27525 ■ "Voices carry" in *Entrepreneur* (Vol. 31, No. 6, June 2003, pp. 80)
Pub: Entrepreneur Media Inc.
Ed: Elizabeth J. Goodgold. Description: Ways to improve vocal skills are listed, including improving elocution, slowing down speech, finding a perfect pitch, and using a tape recorder.

27526 ■ "VoIP; After Years of Hype, a Real Market has Emerged for Voice Over IP." in *Venture Capital Journal* (December 1, 2004)
Pub: Thomason Financial Inc.
Ed: Michael Fitzgerald. Description: Voice over Internet Protocol (VoIP) will create new ways to handle music, videos, video-conferencing and other types of multimedia. Venture capitalists are prepared to ramp up VoIP investments for the next year. In 2004 VCs invested $355 million for 18 companies. Statistical data included.

27527 ■ "Waterfront, Airport on Top of List For Port" in *Bellingham Business Journal* (January 2007, pp. B5)
Pub: Sun News Inc.
Ed: Dan Hiestand. Description: New Whatcom redevelopment for the former Georgia-Pacific waterfront property is in the works. The city and port have been working to create a cohesive plan for the site. Sixty-eight percent of the property leaves ownership in the public's hands.

27528 ■ "Web Site" in *Entrepreneur* (Vol. 28, No. 2, February 2000, pp. 38)
Pub: Entrepreneur Media Inc.
Ed: Robert McGarvey. Description: The Right Answer, a company that bills itself as "the customer service finessing center", offers four online quizzes that test a company's service skills.

27529 ■ "Web.Preneuring" in *Small Business Opportunities* (Vol. 16, No. 3, May 2004, pp. 50)
Pub: Harris Publications, Inc.
Ed: Corey Rudl. Description: Brightmail reports that 41 percent of all email is spam, and will cost U.S. businesses $10 billion in 2004. Ways to determine the difference between opt-in email and spam are presented.

27530 ■ "Weigh your opt-ins" in *Entrepreneur* (Vol. 30, No. 10, October 2002, pp. 96)
Pub: Entrepreneur Media Inc.
Ed: Kim T. Gordon. Description: Much less costly than paper newsletters, e-mail letters can be a successful communication tool for marketing a product or service.

27531 ■ "What arbitration agreement? Compelling non-signatories to arbitrate" in *Dispute Resolution Journal* (Vol. 56, May-July 2001, pp. 40)
Pub: American Arbitration Association
Ed: Charles Lee Eisen. Description: The legal principles and theory which can bind non-signatory parties to arbitration agreements are discussed.

27532 ■ "What makes great boards great." in *Harvard Business Review* (Vol. 80, No. 9, Sept. 2002, pp. 106)
Pub: Harvard Business School Press
Ed: Jeffrey A. Sonnenfeld. Description: An overview of the basic traits required to establish a good board of directors is presented.

27533 ■ "What a Smile Means" in *Inc.* (October 1, 2003)
Pub: Gruner & Jahr USA Publishing
Ed: Bobbie Gossage. Description: A smile can mean a lot to a small business when negotiating deals. Smiles and frowns reflect a consumer's opinion more accurately, according to facial coding research studies.

27534 ■ "Whatcom E-View Moving to New Space" in *Bellingham Business Journal* (December 2006, pp. A3)
Pub: Sun News Inc.
Description: Eview.com, an Internet-based community which serves as a consumer ratings site and local search engine, recently moved its offices to a new five-acre property.

27535 ■ "What's the Deal?" in *Entrepreneur* (Vol. 31, No. 10, October 2003, pp. 34)
Pub: Entrepreneur Media, Inc.

Ed: Mark Hendricks. Description: Book review of, "The Only Negotiating Guide You'll Ever Need", written by Peter B. Stark and Jane Flaherty. Stark and Flaherty, both business consultants, stress that negotiators must always consider the other side's needs in order to win repeat customers and develop strong vendor relationships.

27536 ■ "What's Next? Mistakes Were Made" in *Inc.* (November 2006, pp. 65-66)
Pub: Gruner & Jahr USA Publishing
Ed: David H. Friedman. Description: Never hide mistakes made by a company. Communicate the event in order to develop an atmosphere of openness and of learning by mistakes, rather than that mistakes are shameful and attempts are made to cover them up.

27537 ■ "Whipping up a great meeting" in *Black Enterprise* (Vol. 31, No. 5, December 2000, pp. 82)
Pub: Earl Graves Publishing Co.
Ed: Robyn D. Clarke. Description: The ten essential ingredients for meetings that get results are explained.

27538 ■ "Who's Talking Behind Your Back?" in *Crain's Chicago Business* (Vol. 30, January 2007, No. 3, pp. 18)
Pub: Crain Communications, Inc.
Ed: Steve Hendershot. Description: Chicago's Word of Mouth Marketing Association, Womma, cultivates, studies, and celebrates consumers telling others about a company or its products or services. Success stories included.

27539 ■ "Why Small Business is Important" in *Bellingham Business Journal* (January 2007, pp. 1)
Pub: Sun News Inc.
Description: While large companies are facing cutbacks, small business are becoming the job creation machine of the future. Small companies have the benefits of being flexible while enjoying the increased economies of scale from the industry as a whole.

27540 ■ "Women's Talk Radio Network Launches" in *Marketing to Women* (Vol. 19, October 2006, No. 10, pp. 5)
Pub: EPM Communications, Inc.
Description: GreenStone Media launches a new talk radio network just for women. It will feature four weekday programs including a show for working moms hosted by author Lisa Birnbach. Healthcare, education, and work-family balance are among the topics covered.

27541 ■ "Word Menu" in *Entrepreneur* (Vol. 31, No. 8, August 2003, pp. 6)
Pub: Entrepreneur Media, Inc.
Ed: Steve Cooper. Description: Profile of Write Brothers' reference software that helps entrepreneurs improve business communications. The software includes a reverse dictionary, an almanac and more.

27542 ■ "Work with Me! Resolving Everyday Conflicts in Your Organization" in *Dispute Resolution Journal* (Vol. 56, No. 1, February-April 2001)
Pub: American Arbitration Association
Ed: Cindy Fazzi. Description: Book review of the recent publication, "Work with Me! Resolving Everyday Conflicts in Your Organization", which helps management deal with problems arising with employees in small companies.

27543 ■ "Write On" in *Entrepreneur* (Vol. 33, March 2005, No. 3, pp. 94)
Pub: Entrepreneur Media Inc.
Ed: Chris Penttila. Description: Deborah Dumaine, author of Write to the Top: Writing for Corporate Success and founder of Better Communications, helps employees improve writing skills.

27544 ■ "Yes, No, Maybe So" in *Inc.* (August 1, 2003)
Pub: Gruner & Jahr USA Publishing
Ed: John Koten. Description: The silent treatment is one of the oldest tactics in journalism, but can also be used in business negotiations.

27545 ■ "You Don't Say" in *Entrepreneur*
(Vol. 31, No. 10, October 2003, pp. 81)
Pub: Entrepreneur Media, Inc.
Ed: Joanne Cleaver. **Description:** Information about
the jargon screener, "Bullfighter", which cleans documents to increase readability, and runs in Windows
2000 and XP environments.

27546 ■ "You think that's funny?" in
Entrepreneur **(Vol. 30, No. 12, December
2002, pp. 101)**
Pub: Entrepreneur Media Inc.
Ed: Chris Sandlund. **Description:** Humor can become a distraction during business communication,
and it is important to know when humor can and cannot be considered appropriate.

TRADE PERIODICALS

27547 ■ *China Weekly Fax Bulletin*
Pub: Orbis Publications L.L.C.
Ed: Derek Scissors, Editor, dscissors@orbispub.com.
Released: Weekly. **Price:** $495, U.S. and Canada;
$595, elsewhere. **Description:** Reports on political,
economic and business events in China via fax. Re-
marks: Also available via e-mail.

27548 ■ *Communication Bulletin for*
Managers and Supervisors
Pub: Progressive Business Publications
Ed: Jim Giuliano, Editor. **Released:** Monthly. **Price:**
$94.56. **Description:** Spotlights the latest highlights
on the art of communicaiton.

27549 ■ *Communications Business &*
Finance
Pub: Telecommunications Reports International Inc.
Ed: Tom Leithauser, Editor, tleithause@tr.com. **Released:** Biweekly. **Price:** $695, U.S. and Canada;
$775, elsewhere. **Description:** Provides timely news
and in-depth analysis on the financial and investment
aspects of the multi billion dollar communications
business. Covers opportunities, business actions and
reactions, as well as the impact of regulation on the financial health of competing companies. Also focuses
on wireless, cable, and satellites. Recurring features
include interviews, reports of meetings, and columns
titled Investment Notes, Telecom IPO Scoreboard.

27550 ■ *Corporate Writer and Editor*
Pub: Lawrence Ragan Communications Inc.
Released: Monthly. **Price:** $209, U.S.; $239, other
countries. **Description:** Presents information designed to help corporate writers and editors create
successful company publications. Topics include writing, design, finding the right outside designers and
freelancers, and others.

27551 ■ *Exclamation Point*
Pub: Robinson Kurtin Communications
Contact: Sondra Kurtin, Publisher
E-mail: skurtin@robinsonkurtin.com
Ed: James Schulman, Editor, jschul-
man@robinsonkurtin.com. **Released:** Quarterly.
Price: Free. **Description:** Features articles on com-
munication topics.

27552 ■ *The Facilitator*
Pub: Nurre Ink
Contact: Susan M. Nurre, Editor & Publisher
E-mail: snurre@thefacilitator.com
Released: Quarterly. **Price:** $35, U.S.; $35, institutions; $40, out of country. **Description:** Provides arti-
cles written by facilitators that are designed to link
facilitators from around the world in a forum of sharing,
networking, and communicating. Includes updates on
training, automated meeting tools, and resources. Recurring features include tips and techniques, a calendar of events, reports of meetings, news of
educational opportunities, book reviews, and notices
of publications available.

27553 ■ *The Gauge*
Pub: Delahaye Medialink
Contact: Katharine Delahaye Paine, Publisher

E-mail: kpaine@delahaye.com
Ed: William Teunis Paarlberg, Editor, wpaarl-
berg@aol.com. **Released:** Bimonthly. **Price:** $75. **De-
scription:** Provides information on and evaluates
marketing communications activities of companies.
Recurring features include interviews, news of research, and a calendar of events.

27554 ■ *Harvard Management*
Communication Letter
Pub: Harvard Business School Publishing
Ed: Nick Morgan, Editor, nmorgan@hbsp.harvard.
edu. **Released:** Monthly. **Price:** $99, U.S.; $119, Can-
ada and Mexico; $139, elsewhere; $169, two years in
USA. **Description:** Provides information and tech-
niques for managers on effective communication.

27555 ■ *Intelligent Enterprise featuring*
Transform
Pub: CMP Media L.L.C.
Contact: Pauline Beall, National Sales Mgr.
E-mail: pbeall@cmp.com
Released: Monthly. **Description:** Trade magazine
covering imaging and document solutions in business.

27556 ■ *Journal of Employee*
Communication Management
Pub: Lawrence Ragan Communications Inc.
Ed: David Murray, Editor, dmurrayil@earthlink.net.
Released: Bimonthly. **Price:** $249, U.S.; $279, other
countries. **Description:** Covers corporate communications issues, such as increasing retention, developing measurement tools, and addressing issues such
as mergers, downsizing, and branding.

27557 ■ *Mexico Watch*
Pub: Orbis Publications L.L.C.
Ed: Stephen Foster, Editor, sfoster@orbispub.com.
Released: Monthly. **Price:** $595. **Description:** Re-
ports on political, economic and business events in
Mexico.

27558 ■ *The Nash & Cibinic Report*
Pub: West Group
Ed: Ralph Nash, Editor. **Released:** Monthly. **Price:**
$1,300. **Description:** Discusses government con-
tracts analysis and reporting. Topics include procurement management, contractor claims, and
competition and awards.

27559 ■ *The Retort*
Pub: The Chemists' Club Library
Released: Bimonthly. **Description:** Highlights the
Club's services and resources about chemistry and
the chemical business, as well as membership news
and events. Recurring features include a collection
and a column titled President's Message.

27560 ■ *Telecom Asia*
Pub: Advanstar Communications
Ed: Robert Poe, Editor. **Released:** Monthly. **Price:**
$480 Hong Kong only; $86 U.S. (within Asia); $96
U.S. (outside Asia). **Description:** Trade magazine for
planning, engineering, and operational managers responsible for the design, installation, marketing, and
maintenance of public and private telecom systems
and networks in Asia and the Pacific Rim.

27561 ■ *Women Chemists*
Pub: American Chemical Society
Ed: Teri Quinn Gray, Editor. **Released:** Semiannual.
Description: Aims "to be leaders in attracting, developing, and promoting women in the chemical sciences." Reports on women's achievements in the
chemical sciences, as well as grants available, symposiums, and current events.

VIDEOCASSETTES/
AUDIOCASSETTES

27562 ■ *The Art of Telecommunication*
Bennu Productions, Inc.
350 5th Ave.
New York, NY 10118-0110

Ph:(212)563-8020
Fax: (212)563-8006
Price: $49.95. **Description:** Describes the telephone
skills that are an integral part of the business world
today. Also discusses office protocol, basic telecommunications equipment, and the facsimile machine.
Availability: VHS.

27563 ■ *Be Prepared to Speak*
Instructional Video
2219 C St.
Lincoln, NE 68502
Ph:(402)475-6570
Free: 800-228-0164
Fax: (402)475-6500
Co. E-mail: feedback@insvideo.com
URL: http://www.insvideo.com
Price: $79.95. **Description:** Comprehensive training
program that furnishes information on various aspects
of public speaking, including speech writing, mental
preparation, and speech-giving exercises. **Availabili-
ty:** VHS.

27564 ■ *Communicate!*
Crisp Learning
Thomson Course Technology
25 Thomson Pl.
Boston, MA 02210
Free: 800-442-7477
URL: http://www.courseilt.com
Price: $98. **Description:** This video helps you and
your associates learn what good communication is,
analyze your own communication skills, and add to
your existing skills. **Availability:** VHS.

27565 ■ *Communication*
American Media, Inc.
4621 121st St.
Urbandale, IA 50323-2311
Ph:(515)224-0919
Free: 888-776-8268
Fax: (515)327-2555
Co. E-mail: custsvc@ammedia.com
URL: http://www.ammedia.com
Released: 1989. **Price:** $1485.00. **Description:**
Communication, in the form of memos, phone calls,
and presentations are essentia! to business success.
Availability: VHS; 3/4U.

27566 ■ *Effective Presentations: How to*
Make Powerhouse Presentations That Get
the Results You Want
Instructional Video
2219 C St.
Lincoln, NE 68502
Ph:(402)475-6570
Free: 800-228-0164
Fax: (402)475-6500
Co. E-mail: feedback@insvideo.com
URL: http://www.insvideo.com
Price: $69.95. **Description:** Describes effective pre-
sentation methods, including how to understand and
evaluate your listeners' expectations, how to organize
your ideas and make them interesting, and how to
create your own style. Includes guidebook. **Availabili-
ty:** VHS.

27567 ■ *How to Deal with the Foreign*
Accent: Diversity on the Phone
Excellence in Training Corp.
1303 Marsh Ln.
Carrollton, TX 75006
Free: 800-747-6569
Released: 1991. **Price:** $375.00. **Description:** A
guide to communicating with people whose first lan-
guage is other than English. **Availability:** VHS; 3/4U;
Special order formats.

27568 ■ *Introduction to Technical and*
Business Communication
GPN Educational Media
Box 80669
Lincoln, NE 68501-0669
Ph:(402)472-2007
Free: 800-228-4630
Fax: 800-306-2330
URL: http://gpn.unl.edu

Released: 1983. **Price:** $300.00. **Description:** This course teaches businessmen the fundamentals of technical writing and business communication. **Availability:** VHS; 3/4U; Special order formats.

27569 ■ *Listening Skills*
Video Arts, Inc.
c/o Aim Learning Group
8238-40 Lehigh
Morton Grove, IL 60053-2615
Free: 877-444-2230
Fax: (416)252-2155
Co. E-mail: service@aimlearninggroup.com
URL: http://www.aimlearninggroup.com
Released: 1991. **Price:** $200.00. **Description:** The skill of listening is demonstrated using clips that show how people feel when they are not listened to. **Availability:** VHS; 8mm; 3/4U; Special order formats.

27570 ■ *Manners at Work*
American Media, Inc.
4621 121st St.
Urbandale, IA 50323-2311
Ph:(515)224-0919
Free: 888-776-8268
Fax: (515)327-2555
Co. E-mail: custsvc@ammedia.com
URL: http://www.ammedia.com
Released: 1990. **Price:** $395.00. **Description:** The basics of corporate etiquette, including introductions, handshakes, and professional conduct, are covered. **Availability:** VHS; 3/4U; 8mm.

TRADE SHOWS AND CONVENTIONS

27571 ■ Alliance Texas
Showorks Inc.
1325 W. 1st Ave., Ste. 312
Spokane, WA 99201
Ph:(509)838-8755
Fax: (509)838-2838
Co. E-mail: showorks@showorksinc.com
URL: http://www.showorksinc.com
Audience: Buyers and contracting officers from military bases. **Principal Exhibits:** Small business procurement opportunities.

27572 ■ Association for Business Communication Annual Convention
Association for Business Communication
Baruch College, CUNY
Box B8-240
One Bernard Baruch Way
New York, NY 10010
Ph:(646)312-3726
Fax: (646)349-5297
Co. E-mail: myers@businesscommunication.org
URL: http://www.businesscommunication.org
Released: Annual. **Audience:** College business communication teachers. **Principal Exhibits:** Books and communication technology products.

27573 ■ Texas Press Association Annual Midwinter Conference and Trade Show
Texas Press Association
718 W. 5th St.
Austin, TX 78701
Ph:(512)477-6755
Fax: (512)477-6759
URL: http://www.texaspress.com
Released: Annual. **Audience:** Newspaper publishers, editors, and members of corporate communications departments. **Principal Exhibits:** Equipment, supplies, and services for newspapers and corporate communication departments. **Dates and Locations:** 2007 Jan 18-20, Houston, TX; 2008 Jan 17-19, Dallas, TX.

CONSULTANTS

27574 ■ American English Academy
111 N Atlantic Blvd., Ste. 112
Monterey Park, CA 91754
Ph:(626)457-2800
Fax: (626)457-2808
Co. E-mail: admission@aea-usa.com
URL: http://www.aea-usa.com

E-mail: admission@aea-usa.com
Scope: Specializes in providing on-site English language and communication development for corporations and individuals. Also develops and delivers training in speaking, writing, pronunciation, grammar, and idioms with an emphasis on business communication. Offers individual, small group, intensive, and long-distance learning. All programs are tailor-made for each client. **Seminars:** Offers seminars on all aspects of English and cultural awareness.

27575 ■ Blackmon Roberts Group Inc.
902 S South Florida, Ste. 205
Lakeland, FL 33803
Ph:(863)802-1280
Fax: (863)802-1290
Co. E-mail: dbeinformation@blackmonroberts.com
URL: http://www.blackmonroberts.com

E-mail: dbeinformation@blackmonroberts.com
Scope: Technical support consultant in technical writing, planning, research, needs analysis, marketing and training, offers training programs from cultural sensitivity issues to effective listening skills.

27576 ■ Kay Britten Communications Inc.
6057 Waterview Ct.
West Bloomfield, MI 48322
Ph:(248)592-0507
Scope: Business communication master coach and motivator.

27577 ■ Casino, Hotel & Resort Consultants L.L.C.
8100 Via Del Cerro Ct.
Las Vegas, NV 89117
Ph:(702)646-7200
Fax: (702)646-6680
Co. E-mail: info@hraba.com
URL: http://www.hraba.com

E-mail: info@hraba.com
Scope: Casino and hospitality industry consultants. Firm specializes in developing and implementing customized forecast and labor management control systems that deliver immediate, positive impact to the company's bottom line. We are involved in production planning, emply surveys and communication, inventory management, business process reviews, audits, development and implementation of key management reports. **Seminars:** Payroll Cost Control and Effective Staff Scheduling

27578 ■ Charismedia
610 W End Ave.
New York, NY 10001
Ph:(212)362-6808
Fax: (212)362-6809
Co. E-mail: info@Charismedia.net
URL: http://www.charismedia.net

E-mail: info@Charismedia.net
Scope: Offers speech and image training as well as speech writing services for effective presentation skills. **Publications:** "The New Secrets of Charisma," McGraw-Hill. **Seminars:** Charisma Skills Training-The best investment for successful careers and relationships; Three-stage Anti-Stagefright Breathing.

27579 ■ Communispond Inc.
52 Vanderbilt Ave., Fl. 7
New York, NY 10017
Ph:(212)972-4899
Free: 800-529-5925
Fax: (212)972-4855
URL: http://www.communispond.com

Scope: Firm is a comprehensive communications and sales training resource. It partners with its clients to help them reach their strategic goals. The business communication curriculum includes executive presentation skills, senior executive, speaking on paper, communicating for improved performance, interviewing skills, and media skills. The socratic sales curriculum includes socratic selling skills, sales presentation skills, socratic negotiating skills, communicating for improved sales performance, selling on paper, hiring the right salesperson, and strategic account management. Delivery options include open enrollment programs, tailored corporate programs, train-the-trainer, and custom design and delivery for unique organizational goals. Special techniques include methods for handling confrontational situations, conferences, meetings, news briefings, media interviews, sales proposals, and speaker's bureaus. **Publications:** "*Socratic Selling*".

27580 ■ COMsciences Inc.
6210 Wilshire Blvd., Ste. 200
Los Angeles, CA 90048
Ph:(323)937-7607
Fax: (323)937-0160
Co. E-mail: info@comsciences.com
URL: http://www.comsciences.com

E-mail: info@comsciences.com
Scope: Firm offers research services to support public relations, corporate advertising, impact of new communications media, communication entertainment, and iternet/web development. Also provides strategic management consulting on communications, marketing, opinion surveys, and organizational development and assessment. The company specializes in media campaigns and evaluation tools. Also conducts government sponsored and media sponsored surveys. Serves all industry sectors, especially .com, wireless telecommunications, interactive media, and consumer electronics. **Publications:** "Wanted: Radical Thinking," PMG World Magazine, Mar, 2003. **Special Services:** Spin™; Event™; NewsMaker Polling™; TradeShow™; mPoll™; mVote™; iMAP™; wForum; mCRM™.

27581 ■ Consulting Partners Inc.
14911 Quorum Dr., Ste. 120
Dallas, TX 75254
Ph:(972)386-7858
Fax: (972)386-8667
Co. E-mail: info@consultingpartners.com
URL: http://www.consultingpartners.com

E-mail: info@consultingpartners.com
Scope: We are a Modis company, specializing in technical communications, technical writing, custom instructor-led training, computer-based training, web-based training, language translation, documentation, and editing.

27582 ■ Development Resource Consultants
PO Box 118
Rancho Cucamonga, CA 91729
Ph:(909)902-7655
Fax: (909)476-6942
Co. E-mail: info@gotodrc.com

E-mail: info@gotodrc.com
Scope: A small business advisory service specializing in office re-organization, employee training in office organization, communication skills, sales training and career counseling.

27583 ■ Full Voice
11130 Holmes Rd.
Kansas City, MO 64101
Ph:(816)941-0011
Fax: (816)444-0505
Scope: Formalizes a program of proven techniques into a practical method of helping individuals improve their ability to better present themselves when speaking in a professional situation. Industries Served: all. **Publications:** You Can Sound Like You Know What Youre Saying. **Seminars:** You Can Sound Like You Know What Youre Saying; How to Make Yours a

Championship Team; Functional English for Foreign Trade; The Effective Voice for Customer Service Enhancement; The Psychology of Vocal Performance; You Can Speak With Conviction.

27584 ■ Germuska Communications
441 N Brockway St.
PO Box 426
Palatine, IL 60067
Ph:(847)934-1984
Co. E-mail: tom@germuska.com

E-mail: tom@germuska.com
Scope: Offers public relations and business communications consulting and services for corporations, organizations and individuals. Additional expertise in crisis communications; speech writing; grant writing annual report and newsletter production; as well as developing and executing successful print and broadcast public relations programs. Industries served: advertising, consumer products, entertainment, recreation and travel, hospitality, individuals, manufacturing, nonprofit organizations and associations, service industries, and transportation. **Seminars:** Crisis Communications Planning; Newsletter Production; Public Relations for Not-for-Profit Organizations.

27585 ■ Great Western Association Management Inc.
7995 E Prentice Ave., Ste. 100
Greenwood Village, CO 80111
Ph:(303)770-2220
Fax: (303)770-1614
Co. E-mail: info83@gwami.com
URL: http://www.gwami.com

E-mail: info83@gwami.com
Scope: Expertise in managing not for-profit organizations. Clients select from a menu of services including association development and public relations, conferences and seminars, financial management, membership communications, and governance. Expertise also includes association strategic planning, compliance, lobbying, meeting planning, fundraising, marketing and communications.

27586 ■ The Handler Group Inc.
425 W End Ave.
New York, NY 10024
Ph:(212)595-6697
Fax: (212)627-1124
Scope: Provides marketing, communication planning, and design services, specializing in development of internal and external business communications. Develops corporate identity, corporate literature, employee communications, sales promotion materials, consumer product packaging and information, brochures, annual reports, and presentation materials. Industries served: cable/television, technology software, business information, hospitality, and banking.

27587 ■ Tim W. Hrastar Associates
184 Abbey Dr.
Springboro, OH 45066
Ph:(937)886-0186
Fax: (937)886-0186
Co. E-mail: twh@rapportmarketing.com
URL: http://www.rapportmarketing.com

E-mail: twh@rapportmarketing.com
Scope: Specializes in helping the accounting and legal professions improve their communications and client relations. Offers communications expertise with emphasis on interpersonal and organizational communications. Experienced in presentation skills coaching, meeting dynamics, counseling in marketing, and client relations communications for professional services field. Clients include Fortune 500 companies as well as small businesses, government agencies, and other organizations in such diverse fields as food service, finance, health-care, travel, and consumer and industrial products. **Publications:** How to Make Persuasive Presentations with Confidence; Returning Phone Calls, Why Its Important; Five Tips on Thinking Ahead of Your Clients. **Seminars:** Business Development for Lawyers; Persuasive Communications in the Courtroom. **Special Services:** Rapport Marketing®.

27588 ■ Beverly Hyman and Associates
420 Madison Ave., Ste. 905
New York, NY 10017
Ph:(212)983-6250
Fax: (212)983-6342
Co. E-mail: bevhyman@aol.com
URL: http://www.beverlyhyman.com

E-mail: bevhyman@aol.com
Scope: Communication and training consultants offering such programs as training the trainer, communications skills, business (or technical) writing, public speaking, management skills or supervisory skills, negotiations, direct communication (assertiveness training), women in management, time management, and sales training. Serves private industries as well as government agencies. **Seminars:** Training the Trainer; Advanced Training the Trainer; Coaching and Counseling; Constructive Feedback; Supervisory Skills; Writing Skills; Interpersonal Communications; Leadership Skills; Presentation Skills; Customer Service; Communication Skills; Public Speaking; Negotiating Skills; Women in Management; Time Management; Sales Training Skills; Assertiveness Skills. **Special Services:** Intranet and Internet based training packages; video scripting and production; publication assessment; motivational speeches; curriculum design; facilitation.

27589 ■ In Plain English
14501 Antigone Dr.
PO Box 3300
North Potomac, MD 20878
Ph:(301)340-2821
Free: 800-274-9645
Fax: (301)279-0115
Co. E-mail: rwohl@inplainenglish.com
URL: http://www.inplainenglish.com

E-mail: rwohl@inplainenglish.com
Scope: Management consultants helping government and businesses research, design, write and produce user-oriented management information for human resources, employee benefits, business process, corporate and marketing needs. Employee benefits services include summary plan descriptions, employee benefit booklets, plan documents, communication of employee benefit highlights, pay for performance systems, and Section 125 cafeteria benefit enrollment. Human resources services include producing employee handbooks, employee handbook audits, training manuals, writing training, and personnel policy and policy audits. Consultants also assist clients to re-humanize their business, human resource department, recruitment, and employee benefit program. **Publications:** The Benefits Communication Edge newsletter; The Employee Benefits Communication ToolKit, published by Commerce Clearinghouse. Benefits Communicat ion; a guide published by business & legal reports. **Seminars:** Plain English Writing Training; Summary Plan Description Compliance workshops; Re-Humanizing the Corporation, Human Resources and Employee Benefits Communication Workshop. **Special Services:** Electronic materials; Electronic summary plan descriptions; electronic reference manuals.

27590 ■ Komei Inc.
8910 Purdue Rd., Ste. 480
Indianapolis, IN 46268-1197
Ph:(317)616-1810
Fax: (317)616-1811
Co. E-mail: solutions@komei.com
URL: http://www.komei.com

E-mail: solutions@komei.com
Scope: Global corporation dedicated to helping people and organizations "change together," and reach their goals, through better communication. Offers customized in-house seminars, workshops, and coaching in writing, presentation skills, international and intercultural communication, and team and community building. **Publications:** Written Communication Profiler. **Seminars:** Writing; Presentation Skills; International and Intercultural Communication.

27591 ■ Miller, Hellwig Associates
150 W End Ave.
New York, NY 10023-5713
Ph:(212)799-0471
Fax: (212)877-0186
Co. E-mail: millerhelwig@earthlink.net

E-mail: millerhelwig@earthlink.net
Scope: Consulting services in the areas of start-up businesses; small business management; employee surveys and communication; performance appraisals; executive searches; team building; personnel policies and procedures; market research. Also involved in improving cross-cultural and multi-cultural relationships, particularly with Japanese clients. **Seminars:** Objectives and standards/recruiting for boards of directors.

27592 ■ Organization Counselors Inc.
44 W Broadway, Ste. 1102
PO Box 987
Salt Lake City, UT 84101
Ph:(801)363-2900
Fax: (801)363-0861
Co. E-mail: jpanos@xmission.com

E-mail: jpanos@xmission.com
Scope: Firm specializes in organizational development; employee surveys and communication; outplacement; team building; total quality management (TQM) and continuous improvement. **Seminars:** Correcting Performance Problems; Total Quality Management; Employee Selection; Performance Management.

27593 ■ James G. Patterson - The Cogent Communicator
9571 E Caldwell Dr.
Tucson, AZ 85747-9218
Ph:(520)574-9353
Fax: (520)574-0620
Co. E-mail: cogent@indirect.com
URL: http://home.flash.net/~cogent

E-mail: cogent@indirect.com
Scope: Trainer and consultant in quality and communication. Specialties include ISO 9000, TQM, quality audits, communication audits, effective writing, presentation skills and negotiating. Actively promotes speaking and consulting to association groups. Serves corporate and government audiences worldwide. **Publications:** "Benchmarking Basics Crisp", 1995; "Supervisory Communication AMI", 1995; "Negotiating AMACOM worksmart series" 1995; "Intro to ISO 9000", Crisp Publications, 1994; "Leadership Development", ASTD Info-line 1994. **Seminars:** Intro to ISO 9000; Implementing an Effective TQM Program; Teambuilding; Leadership Development; Effective Writing; Presentation Skills for Executives; Negotiation Skills; Customer Service. **Special Services:** Maintains ISO 9000 "Nicodemus" software.

27594 ■ Roger S. Peterson Marketing & Communications
3090 Union St.
Rocklin, CA 95677-1837
Ph:(916)624-1894
Fax: (916)624-3069
Co. E-mail: peterson@market-strategy.com
URL: http://www.market-strategy.com

E-mail: peterson@market-strategy.com
Scope: Specializes in business to business marketing communications, marketing diagnostics and market strategy for small to mid-sized firms. Peterson is also an experienced business writer, having published more than 70 articles, one book and many corporate pieces. **Publications:** "AMA Handbook for: Managing Business-to-Business Marketing Communications". **Seminars:** Essentials of Marketing; The Communications Audit; Survival Training for Product Managers; Marketing Positioning & Promotion; Marketing Tools and How to Use Them; Marketing for Small Business, various American Management Association Courses.

27595 ■ ProActive English
1001 Pine St., Ste. 1004
San Francisco, CA 94109

Ph:(415)752-2270
Co. E-mail: infopae@proactive-english.com
URL: http://www.proactive-english.com

E-mail: infopae@proactive-english.com
Scope: Offers on-site individual and small group language and communication training. Sets up learning plans tailored to the needs and schedules of managers and executives who are non-native English speakers. Serves all industries. **Seminars:** Communicating in Business Situations; Presentations and Pronunciation.

27596 ■ Tom Shillock Consulting
5545 SW Windsor Ct.
Portland, OR 97221-2150
Ph:(503)291-7928
Fax: (503)221-2052
Co. E-mail: shillock@ee.pdx.edu

E-mail: shillock@ee.pdx.edu
Scope: Offers consulting services in marketing and communications including public relations and advertising. Industries served: high technology.

27597 ■ Trendzitions Inc.
310 Goddard, Ste. 100
Irvine, CA 92618
Ph:(949)727-9100
Free: 800-266-2767
Fax: (949)851-8444
Co. E-mail: bgeer@trendzitions.com
URL: http://www.trendzitions.com

E-mail: bgeer@trendzitions.com
Scope: Provides services in the areas of communications consulting, project management, construction management, and furniture procurement. Offers information on spatial uses, building codes, ADA compliance, and city ordinances. Also offers budget projections.

27598 ■ Walcoff & Associates
12015 Lee Jackson Hwy., Ste. 500
Fairfax, VA 22033
Ph:(703)934-9848

Fax: (703)934-9866
Scope: Provides technical services in the core services of the Defense core provides reengineering, defense reinvestment and technology transfer; test and evaluation engineering; analysis support; software test and evaluation; and information management services. Transportation core provides logistics and analysis; public outreach; team and consensus building; program assessment and restructuring; and information clearinghouse services. Health core provides technical information; training and organizational development; health-related research; disability research and management; and policy analysis services. Energy core provides technology transfer, modeling and simulation; reengineering; and information management services. Environment core provides environmental program support; environmental communications; and environmental technology. Also provides communications services, including conference design and management and technical documentation, program logistics and analysis; motion picture and videotape production, and other outreach initiatives. Services provided to all cabinet-level agencies.

27599 ■ The Watts Corp.
22117 161st Ave. SE
Monroe, WA 98272-9171
Ph:(425)941-6781
Fax: (360)805-5873
Co. E-mail: info@wattslink.com
URL: http://www.wattslink.com

E-mail: info@wattslink.com
Scope: A profit coach with expertise in sales & profitabilty, general operations. Available as seminar presenter and venture turn-arounds. **Seminars:** Customized programs to address specific needs of your company. **Special Services:** IT services available.

27600 ■ Ann Welsh Communications Inc.
1110 Yonge St., Ste. 301
Toronto, ON, Canada M4W 2L6
Ph:(416)972-1930
Fax: (416)972-6494

Co. E-mail: ann@annwelsh.com
URL: http://annwelsh.com

E-mail: ann@annwelsh.com
Scope: Change management facilitation and communications, executive writing services.

27601 ■ WorkTalk Communications
1022 Indiana Ct.
Venice, CA 90291
Ph:(310)396-8303
Free: 888-967-5825
Fax: (310)399-5828
Co. E-mail: consulting@worktalk.com
URL: http://www.worktalk.com

E-mail: consulting@worktalk.com
Scope: Editing services in the areas of sales and marketing letters, core client correspondence, manuals and procedures, and proposals. Writing services include employee communications, core correspondence, manuals and procedures documents, and corporate speech-writing. **Publications:** "Get to the Point! Painless Advice on Writing Memos, Letters, Reports and E-mails Your Clients and Colleagues Will Understand," Three Rivers Press, 2001. **Seminars:** Get to the Point When You Date; Cut Your Writing Time in Half. **Special Services:** Writamins™.

FRANCHISES AND BUSINESS OPPORTUNITIES

27602 ■ Allegra Print & Imaging
21680 Haggerty Rd.
Northville, MI 48167
Free: 888-258-2730
Fax: (248)596-8601
URL: http://www.allegranetwork.com
No. of Franchise Units: 400+. **Founded:** 1976. **Franchised:** 1977. **Description:** Full service printing centers. **Equity Capital Needed:** $155,600-$279,000. **Franchise Fee:** $30,000. **Financial Assistance:** Yes. **Training:** Yes.

Business Correspondence

ASSOCIATIONS AND OTHER ORGANIZATIONS

27603 ■ Association for Business Communication
Baruch College
Communication Studies
One Bernard Baruch Way
New York, NY 10010
Ph:(646)312-3726
Fax: (646)349-5297
Co. E-mail: myers@businesscommunication.org
URL: http://www.businesscommunication.org
Contact: Dr. Robert J. Myers, Exec. Dir.
Description: College teachers of business communication; management consultants in business communications; training directors and correspondence supervisors of business firms, direct mail copywriters, public relations writers, and others interested in communication for business. **Publications:** *Business Communication Quarterly* (quarterly); *Journal of Business Communication* (quarterly); *Making Communication Requirements More Explicit in the AACSB Standards for MBA Programs.*

27604 ■ International Association of Business Communicators
1 Hallidie Plz., Ste. 600
San Francisco, CA 94102-2818
Ph:(415)544-4700
Free: 800-776-4222
Fax: (415)544-4747
Co. E-mail: service_centre@iabc.com
URL: http://www.iabc.com
Contact: Julie Freeman, Pres.
Description: Represents Communication managers, public relations directors, writers, editors, audiovisual specialists, and others in the public relations and organizational communication field that use a variety of media to communicate with internal audiences (employees, management, association members, and leaders) and external audiences (media, customers, dealers, investors, and government). Conducts research in the communication field and encourages establishment of college-level programs in organizational communication. Offers accreditation program; conducts surveys on employee communication effectiveness and media trends. **Publications:** *Communication World* (bimonthly).

EDUCATIONAL PROGRAMS

27605 ■ Business English and Grammar Review
Arizona Government Training Center
621 S. 48th St., Ste. 103
Tempe, AZ 85281
Ph:(480)967-7544
Free: 800-970-1270
Fax: (480)966-6325
Co. E-mail: help@agts.com
URL: http://www.agts.com

Price: $219.00 for non-members; $179.00 for AGTS members. **Description:** Covers grammatical errors, punctuation, sentence structure, spelling, and plurals and possessives. **Locations:** Tempe, AZ.

27606 ■ Communicating Up, Down and Across the Organization (Canada)
Canadian Management Centre
150 York St., 5th Fl.
Toronto, ON, Canada M5H 3S5
Free: 877-CMC-2500
Fax: (416)313-4985
Co. E-mail: cmcinfo@cmctraining.org
URL: http://www.cma.org
Price: $1,695. **Description:** Seminar that encourages dialogue throughout the organization and between different departments, including gaining self-esteem, targeting your message by knowing your audience, building team commitment, develop interpersonal techniques for influencing, build persuasive business cases, and constructing an informative, attention getting project update. **Locations:** Toronto, ON.

27607 ■ Effective Technical Writing
1601 Broadway
New York, NY 12983
Ph:(518)891-1500
Free: 800-262-9699
Fax: (518)891-0368
Co. E-mail: customerservice@amanet.org
URL: http://www.amanet.org
Price: $1895.00 ($1695.00 for AMA members). **Description:** Seminar for business professionals who communicate technical information. Topics covered include basics of good technical writing, planning and organizing, selecting format, editing and revising techniques, and using graphs, charts, and tables. **Locations:** Cities throughout the United States.

27608 ■ Fundamentals of Business Writing (Canada)
Canadian Management Centre
150 York St., 5th Fl.
Toronto, ON, Canada M5H 3S5
Free: 877-CMC-2500
Fax: (416)313-4985
Co. E-mail: cmcinfo@cmctraining.org
URL: http://www.cma.org
Price: $1,495 Canadian. **Description:** Seminar that covers effective communication through the written word to increase your writing confidence, including differences between academic and business writing, 4 steps for effective writing, 3 formats for letters, 3 techniques to get e-mails read and acted upon, what to include and what to ignore, and powerful opening and closing lines. **Locations:** Toronto, ON.

27609 ■ How to Communicate with Diplomacy, Tact and Credibility (Canada)
Canadian Management Centre
150 York St., 5th Fl.
Toronto, ON, Canada M5H 3S5
Free: 877-CMC-2500
Fax: (416)313-4985
Co. E-mail: cmcinfo@cmctraining.org

URL: http://www.cma.org
Price: $1,695 Canadian. **Description:** Seminar covering how to mold your communication style to meet the needs of individual situations, develop active listening and questioning strategies, gain cooperation and respect by promoting and modeling tolerance with politically correct attitudes and communication, break through communication gridlock, expand the communication network, and turn communication conflicts into opportunities for cooperation and growth. **Locations:** Toronto, ON.

27610 ■ How to Sharpen Your Business Writing Skills
American Management Association
1601 Broadway
New York, NY 10019
Ph:(212)586-8100
Free: 800-262-9699
Fax: (212)903-8168
Co. E-mail: customerservice@amanet.org
URL: http://www.amanet.org
Price: $1,745.00; $1,645 for AMA members. **Description:** Covers how to solve common writing problems, various writing concepts, and how to write effective letters, memos, reports, and business proposals. **Locations:** San Francisco, CA; Washington, DC; Atlanta, GA; Chicago, IL; and New York, NY.

27611 ■ Introduction to Emotional Intelligence (Canada)
Canadian Management Centre
150 York St., 5th Fl.
Toronto, ON, Canada M5H 3S5
Free: 877-CMC-2500
Fax: (416)313-4985
Co. E-mail: cmcinfo@cmctraining.org
URL: http://www.cma.org
Price: $995 Canadian. **Description:** Seminar that covers the 3 domains of competence, definition of emotional intelligence and its core competencies, the science behind emotional intelligence, and personal action plans for the application of emotional intelligence in the workplace. **Locations:** Toronto, ON.

27612 ■ Powerful Persuasion Skills for Technical Professionals (Canada)
Canadian Management Centre
150 York St., 5th Fl.
Toronto, ON, Canada M5H 3S5
Free: 877-CMC-2500
Fax: (416)313-4985
Co. E-mail: cmcinfo@cmctraining.org
URL: http://www.cma.org
Price: $1,595 Canadian. **Description:** Seminar for technical professionals who want to distinguish negotiation from persuasion, translate difficult information into simple terms, utilize thinking styles to influence and gain support, apply techniques for direct and indirect influence, interpersonal influence to develop strong communication, and how to reframe ideas to effectively motivate non-technical professionals. **Locations:** Toronto, ON.

27613 ■ Win-Win Negotiations: An Overview (Canada)
Canadian Management Centre
150 York St., 5th Fl.
Toronto, ON, Canada M5H 3S5
Free: 877-CMC-2500
Fax: (416)313-4985
Co. E-mail: cmcinfo@cmctraining.org
URL: http://www.cma.org
Price: $995 Canadian. **Description:** Seminar that covers the best practices to transform negotiations into a positive experience for both parties, including plan for negotiation, determine your purpose, identify and prioritize issues, design a strategy to achieve desired outcome, and meet the challenge. **Locations:** Toronto, ON.

27614 ■ Writing the Perfect Business E-Mail
EEI Communications
66 Canal Ctr. Plz., Ste. 200
Alexandria, VA 22314-5507
Ph:(703)683-7453
Free: 888-253-2762
Fax: (703)683-7310
Co. E-mail: train@eeicommunications.com
URL: http://www.eeicommunications.com/training
Price: $395. **Description:** Seminar that covers e-mails that get read and are understood, including keeping it short and simple, make it useful, spelling, grammar, and other problems, controlling emotion, writing attachments that get read, progress reports, instructions, and evaluations and recommendations. **Locations:** Alexandria, VA; Silver Spring, MD; and Washington, DC.

REFERENCE WORKS

27615 ■ "Appearances Count" in *Small Business Opportunities* **(Vol. 12, No. 2, March 2000, pp. 12)**
Pub: Harris Publications, Inc.
Ed: Lin Grensing-Pophal. **Description:** Ways to produce revenue-generating sales letters from a home computer are explored.

27616 ■ "Ask the attorney" in *Red Herring* **(March 2003, pp. 73)**
Pub: Herring Communications Inc.
Description: Legal issues are addressed that include the following topics, pharmaceutical patents, government support for research and development, global commerce, intellectual property rights, the transfer of customer lists from European subsidiary to its U.S. parent company, trademark dilution, venture financing, selling a business, stock options, corporate tax deductions, small business patent methods, and employee use of Instant Messaging with clients.

27617 ■ "At Your Service" in *Kansas City Star* **(February 6, 2005)**
Pub: Knight-Ridder/Tribune Business News
Ed: Angela D. Curry. **Description:** Important steps to take when receiving an email, supposedly from your banking institution, requesting account information.

27618 ■ *The Basics of Business Writing*
Pub: AMACOM
Ed: Marty Stuckey. **Released:** 1992. **Price:** $10.95 (paper); ($9.85 for AMA members). **Description:** Part of the WorkSmart series of do-it-yourself guides to skill-building and personal improvement.

27619 ■ *Better Business Writing*
Pub: Crisp Publications, Inc.
Ed: Susan L. Brock. **Price:** $9.95.

27620 ■ "Big Bucks" in *Entrepreneur* **(Vol. 28, No. 2, February 2000, pp. 28)**
Pub: Entrepreneur Media Inc.
Description: The business-to-business e-commerce marketplace is expected to reach $1.5 trillion in 2004, according to investment bankers Goldman, Sachs & Co.

27621 ■ "Bronto Email Marketing Toolkit" in *Entrepreneur.com* **(Vol. 34, February 2006, No. 2, pp. 6)**
Pub: Entrepreneur Media Inc.
Description: Free guide offered by Bronto software focuses on email marketing for small business.

27622 ■ *The Building Blocks of Business Writing*
Pub: Crisp Publications, Inc.
Ed: Jack Swenson. **Price:** $9.95.

27623 ■ *Business Writing the Modular Way*
Pub: Books on Demand
Ed: Harley Bjelland. **Released:** 1992. **Price:** $80.70. **Description:** Introduces the modular approach to writing memos, letters, articles, reports, proposals, manuals, specifications, and books.

27624 ■ *Complete Book of Business Forms*
Pub: Oasis Press
Ed: Richard G. Stuart. **Price:** $49.95 (ringbound); $19.95 (paper). **Description:** Contains 197 business forms for various business needs, including personnel, finance, operations, sales and marketing, and order entry.

27625 ■ *The Complete Book of Business Forms and Agreements*
Pub: The McGraw-Hill Companies
Ed: Cliff Roberson. **Released:** 1993. **Price:** $79.95. **Description:** Contains business agreements, contracts, and ready-to-use forms for various business transactions. Includes diskette.

27626 ■ *The Creative Communicator: 399 Tools to Communicate Commitment without Boring People to Death!*
Pub: Irwin Professional Publishing
Ed: Barbara A. Glanz. **Released:** 1993. **Price:** $22.00. **Description:** Guide to improving written, oral, and electronic communication. Includes techniques and real-life examples.

27627 ■ "An E-Mail from the IRS? Don't Believe It" in *Long Island Business News* **(May 7, 2004)**
Pub: Dolan Media Newswires
Ed: David Reich-Hale. **Description:** The U.S. Internal Revenue Service has posted a warning to taxpayers about an email scam that tries to trick taxpayers into giving personal information. The email appears to be an official memo from the IRS.

27628 ■ "E-mail Offers a Little Wit with Your News" in *Crain's Detroit Business* **(Vol. 19, No. 6, February 10, 2003, pp. 9)**
Pub: Crain Communications Inc., Detroit
Ed: Mary Kramer. **Description:** Crain's Detroit offers a free daily e-mail news service providing an online news summary by 3:30 p.m. daily. The service started in January and already has 16,000 people signed up.

27629 ■ "E-mail Security Firm is Chaudry's Last Start-up" in *Atlanta Business Chronicle* **(Vol. 24, No. 13, August 24, 2001, pp. 5A)**
Pub: American City Business Journals Inc.
Ed: Mary Jane Credeur. **Description:** CipherTrust is a new company that offers IronMail, a security appliance that acts as a firewall to protect e-mail from hackers and viruses. Founder Jay Chaudry, who has started six companies, says that this will be his last start-up for the foreseeable future, since he wants to be able to focus, rather than spreading himself too thin.

27630 ■ *Effective Business Communications*
Pub: The McGraw-Hill Companies
Ed: Herta A. Murphy. **Released:** 1991. **Price:** $59.50. **Description:** Covers commercial correspondence, business reportwriting, and the essential role of business communications in business.

27631 ■ "The Electronic Negotiator" in *Harvard Business Review* **(Vol. 78, No. 1, January 2000, pp. 16)**
Pub: Harvard Business School Publishing Corp.

Description: Negotiations conducted over e-mail often go nowhere. The article shows what you can do to improve your company's odds of success.

27632 ■ *The Elements of Business Writing: A Guide to Writing Clear, Concise Letters, Memos, Reports, Proposals, and Other Business Documents*
Pub: Macmillan Publishing Co., Inc.
Ed: Gary Blake. **Released:** 1992. **Price:** $9.95.

27633 ■ *The Elements of Technical Writing*
Pub: Macmillan Publishing Co., Inc.
Ed: Robert W. Bly and Gary Blake. **Released:** 1993. **Price:** $9.95.

27634 ■ "Entrepreneur Column" in *Entrepreneur* **(August 18, 2005)**
Pub: Entrepreneur Media Inc.
Ed: Gail F. Goodman. **Description:** Electronic newsletters can be a great marketing tool if done properly. Email marketing solutions should include data that allows a firm to analyze and optimize any e-newsletter campaign.

27635 ■ "Equal Time? Legal" in *Entrepreneur* **(Vol. 31, No. 9, September 2003, pp. 80)**
Pub: Entrepreneur Media, Inc.
Ed: Jane Easter Bahls. **Description:** Labor unions may be able to use company email systems in order to communicate with members. A discussion regarding a recent decision by an administrative judge for the National Labor Relations Board involving Prudential Insurance's Office & Professional Employees International Union is cited.

27636 ■ "Everything You Ever Wanted to Know About Email" in *Inc.* **(October 2005, pp. 113-117, 119, 122)**
Pub: Inc. Magazine
Ed: John Fried. **Description:** Guide to using email as an important business tool is presented. Tips to keep a system secure, efficient, and affordable are also included.

27637 ■ *The Executive's Business Letter Book: Ready-to-Use Business Letters for Business Owners and Executives*
Pub: Dearborn Financial Publishing, Inc.
Ed: Ted Nicholas. **Released:** Revised edition, 1992. **Price:** $69.95 (paper). **Description:** Provides information on writing clear, effective business letters. Includes more than 150 letters.

27638 ■ "Ezsupport Life" in *Entrepreneur. com* **(Vol. 34, February 2006, No. 2, pp. 6)**
Pub: Entrepreneur Media Inc.
Description: Profile of EzSupport Life, a free, automated online customer-support solution for small businesses.

27639 ■ "Feeding Frenzy" in *Entrepreneur. com* **(Vol. 34, February 2006, No. 2, pp. 77)**
Pub: Entrepreneur Media Inc.
Ed: Catherine Seda. **Description:** Creative marketers are using RSS feed in order to send successful marketing email. RSS is 100 percent opt-in. Users subscribe to a reader such as Bloglines, Newsgator, or Pluck and choose the feeds they wish to receive, no spam allowed. The number of RSS users is growing quickly making it an opportunity to market products and services for small companies.

27640 ■ "Getting the Dish; Blogs Allow Everyone to be a Critic" in *Crain's New York Business* **(Vol. 23, January 29, 2007, No. 5, pp. 48)**
Pub: Crain Communications, Inc.
Description: Blogs are changing the landscape of the dining scene. Everyone can be a critic on such blogs as Chowmaster.com, Mouthfulsfood.com, or Thestrongbuzz.com among hosts of others.

27641 ■ *Handbook of Business Letters*
Pub: Prentice Hall
Ed: Lester E. Frailey. **Released:** Third edition, 1991. **Price:** $39.95 (paper). **Description:** Includes 720

model letters that reflect current business situations, trends in letterhead design, letter formality, and terms of address. Letters cover such topics as sales, requests, credit, collections, reminders, adjustments, appreciation, refusals, sympathy, follow-up, applications, explanations, commendations, reprimands, inspiration, congratulations, sales management, price increases, employee motivation, overcoming objections, recovering lost customers, soothing irate customers, and correcting misunderstandings.

27642 ■ *Handbook for Business Writing*
Pub: NTC Business Books
Ed: L. Sue Baugh, Maridell Fryar, and David A. Thomas. **Price:** $19.95. **Description:** Covers writing reports, memos, proposals, and letters.

27643 ■ "Hands On" in *Inc.* (September 2005, pp. 37-38)
Pub: Inc. Magazine
Ed: Alison Stein Wellner. **Description:** Email, Blackberrys, and text messaging are replacing face-to-face business communication. Facial expression and body language, voice inflection, and words can help derive meaning to business discussions.

27644 ■ "How Good Are Google's Extras?" in *Business Week* (January 16, 2006, No. 3967, pp. 88-90)
Pub: McGraw-Hill Companies
Ed: **Description:** An overview of Froogle, Maps, Gmail, and Picasa 2, Google's added services is presented. These extras offer shopping information, satellite and road maps, photo editing software, and email at no charge to users.

27645 ■ "If BlackBerry Gets Smushed..." in *Business Week* (January 9, 2006, No. 3966, pp. 16)
Pub: McGraw-Hill Companies
Ed: Stephen H. Wildstrom. **Description:** Alternatives to using BlackBerry email services are discussed in the event of the service being shut down by patent infringement charges. GoodLink from Good Technology offers similar services as does Microsoft with its Exchange email system which is being upgraded.

27646 ■ "In Praise of the 'Thank You' Note: Want to make an impression?" in *Business Week Online* (March 7, 2002)
Pub: McGraw-Hill, Inc.
Description: Handwritten thank you notes can be used as a sales and marketing tool for small businesses. A thank you note displays an attitude of gratitude no ad slogan or coffee mug can match.

27647 ■ "Inbox 101: How to Manage the E-mail Avalanche" in *My Business* (December/January 2004, pp. 40)
Pub: My Business Magazine
Ed: Lena Basha. **Description:** Tips to improve email communication skills are presented, including ways to prevent spam.

27648 ■ *Information Technology for the Small Business: How to Make IT Work For Your Company*
Pub: TAB Computer Systems, Incorporated
Ed: T.J. Benoit. **Released:** June 2006. **Price:** $17.95. **Description:** Basics of information technology to help small companies maximize benefits are covered. Topics include pitfalls to avoid, email and Internet use, data backup, recovery and overall IT organization.

27649 ■ "It's the Sound Bite, Stupid" in *Inc.* (Volume 27, June 2005, No. 6, pp. 128)
Pub: Inc. Magazine
Ed: Adam Hanft. **Description:** Business leaders must understand the importance of good communications skills when conducting business.

27650 ■ "It's a Trap! Watch Your Step-Pharming Scams Are Lurking Around Every Corner" in *Entrepreneur* (Vol. 33, August 2005, No. 8, pp. 40)
Pub: Entrepreneur Media Inc.
Ed: Mike Hogan. **Description:** Netcraft, a network security company, identifies phishing emails that try to scam customers into giving up personal financial information. Ways to avoid these scams are listed.

27651 ■ "Jet Stream E-Mail" in *Inc.* (September 1, 2003)
Pub: Gruner & Jahr USA Publishing
Ed: Anton Piech. **Description:** Business travelers will now be able to access and send email while traveling on airplanes. No software downloading will be necessary to use this service.

27652 ■ "Just Ask: Use e-mail to start a conversation with online buyers" in *My Business* (October/November 2002, pp. 17)
Pub: My Business Magazine
Description: Customer emails can be a good tool to target customers for online purchases.

27653 ■ "Keep in Touch: Be Sure to Reconnect with Your Key Clients" in *Entrepreneur* (Vol. 32, No. 1, January 2004, pp. 79)
Pub: Entrepreneur Media, Inc.
Ed: Nancy Michaels. **Description:** The importance of staying in touch with customers and their needs is stressed.

27654 ■ "Little things mean a lot" in *Rough Notes* (Vol. 146, No. 3, March 2003, pp. 118)
Pub: Rough Notes
Ed: Robert L. Bailey. **Description:** The song, "Little Things Mean a Lot" translates into a valuable lesson in business leadership. Customers never forget the small courtesies or notes of appreciation from staff, however they never forget negative treatment either.

27655 ■ "Making E-Mail Work" in *Sales and Marketing.com* (Vol. 156, No. 3, March 2004, pp. 18)
Pub: VNU eMedia, Inc.
Ed: Ellen Neuborne. **Description:** Marketers are adjusting online newsletters sent to customers with the newly established spam laws. Four ways to send successful emails to customers that will help a small business grow are examined.

27656 ■ "MeetingBridge" in *Entrepreneur* (Vol. 33, September 2005, No. 9, pp. 6)
Pub: Entrepreneur Media Inc.
Ed: Steve Cooper. **Description:** MeetingBridge offers teleconferencing, Web-conferencing and Webinar needs using a dial-in number and entry code. Web conferencing charges start at 12 cents per minute, teleconferencing at 15 center per minute (29 cents per minute with operation assistance), and Webinar tools and registration services are free.

27657 ■ "Mind Your Manners" in *Sales & Marketing Management*
Pub: VNU Business Media
Ed: Kathryn Droullard. **Description:** With new technologies, business communications are becoming less personal as a result of email messages and high-tech devices. A guide to help sales reps avoid 25 common mistakes when corresponding with clients is presented.

27658 ■ "Mind Your P's and Q's" in *Entrepreneur* (Vol. 32, September 2004, No. 9, pp. 77)
Pub: Entrepreneur Media Inc.
Ed: Joanne Cleaver. **Description:** Misspelled words can destroy a small business' credibility, not to mention the costs involved in misspelling in an advertisement or business contract.

27659 ■ "Mind Your P's and Q's" in *Rough Notes* (Vol. 145, No. 2, February 2003, pp. 43)
Pub: Rough Notes
Ed: Emily Huling. **Description:** Business etiquette is important to observe whether in or out of the office, and when meeting people. The article provides a few do's and don'ts.

27660 ■ "More Women Than Men Have Home Offices" in *Marketing to Women* (Vol. 19, October 2006, No. 10, pp. 12)
Pub: EPM Communications, Inc.
Description: A survey of business professionals by Intellicontact reflects that women are more likely than men to have home offices. The survey also shows that while men and women both check their e-mail frequently, the two sexes manage their inboxes differently.

27661 ■ "My Gadget" in *My Business* (February/March 2004, pp. 17)
Pub: My Business Magazine
Ed: Lena Basha. **Description:** Profile of AccuCard, a self-updating address book designed for use with Microsoft Outlook. The service will send personalized quarterly emails to every small business contact, requesting updated or confirmation of correct contact information and automatically updates information every three months.

27662 ■ "New Growth in the Garden State" in *Fast Company* (August 2001, pp. 36)
Pub: Fast Company
Ed: Heath Row. **Description:** In March 2001, two longtime members of the Fast Company community launched a CoF cell in Morristown, New Jersey, with more than 75 people joining within two months. Cell members have established a set of design principles for their organization, principles that any networking group, team or company should take seriously.

27663 ■ "News Blog Highlights Women's Careers" in *Marketing to Women* (Vol. 19, November 2006, No. 11, pp. 5)
Pub: EPM Communications, Inc.
Description: NewsonWomen.com, a news blog for businesswomen and their career achievements, has added executive job postings to its content.

27664 ■ "Nonprofits shift strategy to personal appeals" in *Atlanta Business Chronicle* (Vol. 25, December 6, 2002, No. 26, pp. 5A)
Pub: American City Business Publications, Inc.
Ed: Wendy Bowman-Litter. **Description:** In the Atlanta, Georgia area, non-profit organizations are using personal phone calls to longtime donors to thank them for past support. A simple thank-you call that doesn't include a request for additional financial support can be an effective way of keeping long-time donors.

27665 ■ "Oceanside: Chamber Gets in Networking Fast Lane" in *San Diego Business Journal* (Vol. 28, January 15, 2007, No. 3, pp. 16)
Pub: San Diego Business Journal Associates
Ed: Pat Broderick. **Description:** The Oceanside Chamber of Commerce is offering five-minute networking sessions to members.

27666 ■ "On the Business of Life" in *Forbes* (Vol. 175, January 31, 2005, No. 2, pp. 156)
Pub: Forbes Magazine Inc.
Description: It is proper business etiquette to call when people who accept business invitations to luncheons, dinners or other functions that involve planning of food, seating souvenirs, or other amenities cannot attend the event.

27667 ■ "The Paper Chase" in *Small Business Opportunities* (Vol. 12, No. 5, September 2000, pp. 66)
Pub: Harris Publications, Inc.
Ed: Marie Sherlock. **Description:** Simple solutions to keep from getting overwhelmed by mail and paperwork are offered by a professional organizer.

27668 ■ "Personal, Thoughtful Ways to Stay in Touch" in *Rough Notes* (Vol. 145, No. 2, February 2003, pp. 32)
Pub: Rough Notes
Description: Staying in touch with business contacts and customers is very important in marketing. This can be done with phone calls, cards, a newsletter, or a personal note.

27669 ■ "Postal Rate Hikes" in *Kiplinger Letter* (Vol. 78, January 5, 2007, No. 1)
Pub: Kiplinger
Description: Postal rates are expected to rise from 39 cents to 42 cents for first-class stamps. Business mailers will increase by 9 percent for invoices and ad mailings.

27670 ■ "Q&A" in *Home Office Computing* (Vol. 18, No. 8, August 2000, pp. 15)
Pub: Scholastic Inc.

Ed: Marilyn Zelinsky Syarto. **Description:** Debra Koontz Traverso, author of Outsmarting Goliath, addresses e-mail etiquette.

27671 ■ *The Random House Guide to Business Writing*
Pub: The McGraw-Hill Companies
Ed: J. Forman. **Released:** 1990. **Price:** $14.95 (paper).

27672 ■ "Recover Deleted E-Mail" in *PC World* (Vol. 23, April 2005, No. 4, pp. 150)
Pub: PC World Communications, Inc.
Description: DTI Data Recovery's E-Recovery for Outlook Express allows users to recover email messages for a fee.

27673 ■ "Resolving Owner Conflicts" in *Rough Notes* (Vol. 145, No. 9, September 2002, pp. 26)
Pub: Rough Notes
Ed: Paul J. DiStefano. **Description:** Lack of communications between owners of the insurance agency often results in disagreements. Unresolved conflict among owners can impede the future of an agency, whether the issue relates to money or operating philosophy.

27674 ■ "The Rules of E-etiquette" in *Incentive* (Vol. 174, No. 10, October 2000, pp. 140)
Pub: Bill Communications
Ed: Dana May Casperson. **Description:** Today more businesses are using E-mail communication to help turn prospects into clients. Some of the advantages to this are listed.

27675 ■ "Self-Service" in *Inc.* (October 2005, pp. 124-125, 128)
Pub: Inc. Magazine
Description: When choosing software to manage email it is important to consider four basic questions: what you want the email to do, an access point, security, and costs. Comparisons of Microsoft Outlook 2003, IBM Lotus Notes 7.0, Qualcomm Eudora 6.2, and Mozilla Thunderbird 1.0 software are shown.

27676 ■ *Send Me a Memo: A Handbook of Model Memos*
Pub: Facts on File, Inc.
Ed: Dianna Booher. **Price:** $19.95. **Description:** Includes advice on office politics and tact.

27677 ■ "Sign of the Times: Are You Missing Out on This Simple, Inexpensive Marketing Tool?" in *Entrepreneur* (Vol. 33, January 2005, No. 1)
Pub: Entrepreneur Media Inc.
Ed: Catherine Seda. **Description:** Tactics to use email messages as an inexpensive marketing tool are given.

27678 ■ "Spread the News: Communicate with Customers" in *My Business* (October/November 2003, pp. 46)
Pub: My Business Magazine
Ed: Julie Bawden Davis. **Description:** In order to create a successful newsletter for a small company the owner must know the purpose for creating the newsletter, identify the audience, determine frequency of publishing, consider outsourcing or designing it in-house, and most importantly have the newsletter be a professional extension of the business.

27679 ■ "Spreading Viruses Can be a Good Thing" in *Crain's Chicago Business* (Vol. 30, January 2007, No. 3, pp. 18)
Pub: Crain Communications, Inc.
Ed: Steve Hendershot. **Description:** Viral Marketing, spreading a company's message by email which directs consumers to the company's website, is another of the creative new marketing techniques finding success online. Downsides of this powerful tool are explored.

27680 ■ "Talking the Talk" in *Inc.* (December 1, 2003)
Pub: Gruner & Jahr USA Publishing
Ed: Bobbie Gossage. **Description:** This fall, Webster released its first guide to business terms.

27681 ■ "Thanks for the Biz" in *Small Business Opportunities* (Vol. 12, No. 2, March 2000, pp. 10)
Pub: Harris Publications, Inc.
Ed: Andrea Nierenberg. **Description:** Eight ways to say thanks to customers are presented.

27682 ■ "Through the grapevine: E-mail newsletter has owners tasting profits" in *Entrepreneur* (Vol. 31, No. 6, June 2003, pp. 81)
Pub: Entrepreneur Media Inc.
Ed: April Y. Pennington. **Description:** Customer relations depend on communication and many companies are using email newsletters to stay in touch with customers.

27683 ■ "Weigh your opt-ins" in *Entrepreneur* (Vol. 30, No. 10, October 2002, pp. 96)
Pub: Entrepreneur Media Inc.
Ed: Kim T. Gordon. **Description:** Much less costly than paper newsletters, e-mail letters can be a successful communication tool for marketing a product or service.

27684 ■ "What's Next: Data Disasters" in *Inc.* (November 1, 2003)
Pub: Gruner & Jahr USA Publishing
Ed: Robert X. Cringely. **Description:** Litigation may require a small business to produce every email employees have written.

27685 ■ *Winning Proposals: How to Write Them and Get Results*
Pub: Self-Counsel Press, Inc.
Ed: Hans Tammemagi. **Released:** 1995. **Price:** $13.95 (paper).

27686 ■ *Would You Put That in Writing?*
Pub: Facts on File, Inc.
Ed: Dianna Booher. **Released:** Revised edition 1992. **Price:** $18.95. **Description:** Business writing handbook.

27687 ■ "Write On" in *Entrepreneur* (Vol. 33, March 2005, No. 3, pp. 94)
Pub: Entrepreneur Media Inc.
Ed: Chris Penttila. **Description:** Deborah Dumaine, author of Write to the Top: Writing for Corporate Success and founder of Better Communications, helps employees improve writing skills.

27688 ■ *Writing Business Proposals and Reports*
Pub: Crisp Publications, Inc.
Ed: Susan L. Brock. **Price:** $10.95.

27689 ■ *Writing Effectively in Business*
Pub: HarperCollins College
Ed: Beth S. Neman and Sandra Smythe. **Released:** 1991. **Price:** $45.95.

27690 ■ "You Don't Say" in *Entrepreneur* (Vol. 31, No. 10, October 2003, pp. 81)
Pub: Entrepreneur Media, Inc.
Ed: Joanne Cleaver. **Description:** Information about the jargon screener, "Bullfighter", which cleans documents to increase readability, and runs in Windows 2000 and XP environments.

27691 ■ "You think that's funny?" in *Entrepreneur* (Vol. 30, No. 12, December 2002, pp. 101)
Pub: Entrepreneur Media Inc.
Ed: Chris Sandlund. **Description:** Humor can become a distraction during business communication, and it is important to know when humor can and cannot be considered appropriate.

27692 ■ "Your Own Style" in *Entrepreneur* (Vol. 33, January 2005, No. 1, pp. 43)
Pub: Entrepreneur Media Inc.
Ed: Liane Cassavoy. **Description:** Profile of High-Logic's Font Creator Program 4.5, users can select and edit any TrueType font and convert scanned images to TrueType fonts, including a font that looks like your own handwriting.

TRADE PERIODICALS

27693 ■ *Business Communications Review*
Pub: MediaLive BCR Events Inc.
Contact: Joanne Bonaminio, Mktg. Mgr.
E-mail: jbonaminio@bcr.com
Released: Monthly. **Price:** $45; $15 single issue. **Description:** Magazine covering telecommunications management, networking, and technology.

27694 ■ *Copy Editor*
Pub: Barbara Wallraff
Ed: Barbara Wallraff, Editor, barbaraw@copyeditor.com. **Released:** Bimonthly. **Price:** $69; $74, Canada and Mexico; $128, two years; $138, Canada and Mexico 2 years. **Description:** Covers new words, changes in usage, and reference books for editors.

27695 ■ *Sid Cato's Newsletter on Annual Reports*
Pub: Cato Communications Inc.
Contact: Sid Cato
Ed: Sid Cato, Editor, sidcato@sidcato.com. **Released:** Monthly. **Price:** $197, individuals $197/year; $315.20, two years. **Description:** Provides comment and criticism of the corporate annual report to shareholders. Discusses trends and reviews annual reports. Offers advice on better report writing, Recurring features include findings and news of research, and interviews with key figures in the field.

27696 ■ *Writing That Works*
Pub: Communications Concepts Inc.
Contact: John De Lellis, Editor & Publisher
Released: Monthly. **Price:** $119 U.S., Canada and Mexico. **Description:** Advises corporate, nonprofit, agency and independent communicators on business writing and publishing. Also covers writing techniques, style matters, publication management, and online publishing. Publisher also sponsors annual APEX Awards for Publication Excellence.

VIDEOCASSETTES/ AUDIOCASSETTES

27697 ■ *Basic Steps for Better Business Writing*
Encyclopedia Britannica
331 N. LaSalle St.
Chicago, IL 60610
Ph:(312)347-7159
Free: 800-323-1229
Fax: (312)294-2104
URL: http://www.britannica.com
Released: 1988. **Price:** $1995.00. **Description:** This package of five video-cassettes, including a Leader's Guide, shows employees how to cut their writing time in half while generating written communications that sell ideas, stimulate action and reduce confusion. **Availability:** VHS; 3/4U.

27698 ■ *Better Business Grammar*
Briefings Publishing Group
300 N Washington St., Ste. 605
Alexandria, VA 22314
Ph:(703)684-2318
Free: 800-722-9221
Fax: (703)684-2136
Co. E-mail: customerservice@douglaspublications.com
URL: http://www.briefings.com
Released: 1991. **Price:** $79.00. **Description:** Basic tips for managers on how to get over common stumbling blocks of the English language when writing. **Availability:** VHS.

27699 ■ *Business Writing: Quick, Clear,*
Concise
American Media, Inc.
4621 121st St.
Urbandale, IA 50323-2311
Ph:(515)224-0919
Free: 888-776-8268
Fax: (515)327-2555
Co. E-mail: custsvc@ammedia.com
URL: http://www.ammedia.com
Released: 1992. **Price:** $695.00. **Description:** Features tips on reducing writing time, improving clarity, and organizing ideas using a five-step method. Includes an instructor's guide, participant workbooks, an erase-board, and overhead transparencies. **Availability:** VHS; 3/4U; 8mm.

27700 ■ *Business Writing Skills Series*
Cambridge Educational
c/o Films Media Group
PO Box 2053
Princeton, NJ 08843-2053
Free: 800-257-5126
Fax: (609)671-0266
Co. E-mail: custserve@filmsmediagroup.com
URL: http://www.cambridgeol.com
Released: 199?. **Price:** $149.95. **Description:** Two tape series offers practical tips for organizing your thoughts effectively for written business communication. Includes advice on breaking writer's block, creating a strong opening and closing, choosing a formal versus an informal style, and more. **Availability:** VHS.

27701 ■ *Communication*
American Media, Inc.
4621 121st St.
Urbandale, IA 50323-2311
Ph:(515)224-0919
Free: 888-776-8268
Fax: (515)327-2555
Co. E-mail: custsvc@ammedia.com
URL: http://www.ammedia.com
Released: 1989. **Price:** $1485.00. **Description:** Communication, in the form of memos, phone calls, and presentations are essential to business success. **Availability:** VHS; 3/4U.

27702 ■ *Techniques to Improve Your*
Writing: Practical G/T Business Writing
Instructional Video
2219 C St.
Lincoln, NE 68502
Ph:(402)475-6570
Free: 800-228-0164
Fax: (402)475-6500
Co. E-mail: feedback@insvideo.com
URL: http://www.insvideo.com
Price: $79.95. **Description:** Outlines techniques on how to write reports, memos, and letters more clearly. Also covers tough punctuation and grammar questions. Includes handbook. **Availability:** VHS.

CONSULTANTS

27703 ■ Alliance Management International
Ltd.
PO Box 470691
Cleveland, OH 44147-0691
Ph:(440)838-1922
Fax: (928)752-5728
Co. E-mail: bgruss@cox.net
URL: http://www.members.cox.net/bgruss

E-mail: bgruss@cox.net
Scope: A consulting company that helps to form national and international strategic alliances. Handles alliances between companies forming joint ventures. Staff specialized in small company-large company alliance, alliance assessment and analysis, and alliance strategic planning. **Seminars:** Joint Business Planning; Developing a Shared Vision; Current and New/ Prospective Partner Assessment; Customer Service; Sales Training; Leader and Management Skills.

27704 ■ American English Academy
111 N Atlantic Blvd., Ste. 112
Monterey Park, CA 91754
Ph:(626)457-2800
Fax: (626)457-2808
Co. E-mail: admission@aea-usa.com
URL: http://www.aea-usa.com

E-mail: admission@aea-usa.com
Scope: Specializes in providing on-site English language and communication development for corporations and individuals. Also develops and delivers training in speaking, writing, pronunciation, grammar, and idioms with an emphasis on business communication. Offers individual, small group, intensive, and long-distance learning. All programs are tailor-made for each client. **Seminars:** Offers seminars on all aspects of English and cultural awareness.

27705 ■ Consulting Partners Inc.
14911 Quorum Dr., Ste. 120
Dallas, TX 75254
Ph:(972)386-7858
Fax: (972)386-8667
Co. E-mail: info@consultingpartners.com
URL: http://www.consultingpartners.com

E-mail: info@consultingpartners.com
Scope: We are a Modis company, specializing in technical communications, technical writing, custom instructor-led training, computer-based training, web-based training, language translation, documentation, and editing.

27706 ■ The Handler Group Inc.
425 W End Ave.
New York, NY 10024
Ph:(212)595-6697
Fax: (212)627-1124
Scope: Provides marketing, communication planning, and design services, specializing in development of internal and external business communications. Develops corporate identity, corporate literature, employee communications, sales promotion materials, consumer product packaging and information, brochures, annual reports, and presentation materials. Industries served: cable/television, technology software, business information, hospitality, and banking.

27707 ■ Navarro, Kim & Associates
529 N Charles St., Ste. 202
Baltimore, MD 21201-5043
Ph:(410)837-6317
Fax: (410)837-6294
Co. E-mail: bnavarro@sprynet.com

E-mail: bnavarro@sprynet.com
Scope: Firm specializes in bridging the gap between firms and non-traditional ethnic communities, especially in community development and institutional building.

27708 ■ Turn of Phrase
2529 Meade Ct.
Ann Arbor, MI 48105
Ph:(734)995-1579
Fax: (734)995-1321
Scope: Offers professional writing and editing on business topics. For example, prepares reference manuals, user guides, learning guides, Microsoft Windows help systems, reports, white papers, and other types of documents. Specializes in writing about computer software, especially for non-technical readers. Industries served: engineering, computer, manufacturing. **Publications:** A library of user manuals for a giant accounting database system; a user guide for a document retrieval database; a learning guide and a Windows help system for a knowledge-based system; an installation, operation, and maintenance guide for a line of pneumatic ground water sampling pumps; a book for manufacturing managers introducing the goals, concepts, and challenges of moving toward precision manufacturing; a Windows help system for a system that navigates through the Dow/Jones Retrieval service; articles for a newsletter for a recycling consulting company; a report describing an open inte-

grated architecture for manufacturing computer systems being explored and developed by a national consortium; user/reference manuals and Windows help systems for both modules of a client-service based healthcare analysis and reporting tool designed for large healthcare plans; manuals for various components of a large client-server based retail planning sysem.

27709 ■ WorkTalk Communications
1022 Indiana Ct.
Venice, CA 90291
Ph:(310)396-8303
Free: 888-967-5825
Fax: (310)399-5828
Co. E-mail: consulting@worktalk.com
URL: http://www.worktalk.com

E-mail: consulting@worktalk.com
Scope: Editing services in the areas of sales and marketing letters, core client correspondence, manuals and procedures, and proposals. Writing services include employee communications, core correspondence, manuals and procedures documents, and corporate speech-writing. **Publications:** "Get to the Point! Painless Advice on Writing Memos, Letters, Reports and E-mails Your Clients and Colleagues Will Understand," Three Rivers Press, 2001. **Seminars:** Get to the Point When You Date; Cut Your Writing Time in Half. **Special Services:** Writamins™.

27710 ■ Write It Well
PO Box 13098
Oakland, CA 94601
Ph:(415)459-3563
Fax: (415)459-8618
Co. E-mail: info@writeitwell.com
URL: http://www.writeitwell.com

E-mail: info@writeitwell.com
Scope: Develops training programs, instructional materials, and procedures manuals; conduct customized in-house classes in communications skills and performance management. Offers Training for Letter Communication. **Publications:** "Professional Writing Skills: A Self-Paced Training Program"; "Grammar for Grownups: A Self-Paced Training Program"; "Writing Performance Documentation: A Self-Paced Training Program"; "Report and Proposal Writing for Environmental Professionals: A Self-Paced Training Program"; "How To Write Reports and Proposals: A Self-Paced Training Program"; "Just Commas: 9 Basic Rules to Master Comma Usage"; "E-mail - a Write It a Well Guide".

COMPUTER SYSTEMS/
SOFTWARE

27711 ■ *Better Business Writing–Crisp*
Learning
Chris Learning
PO Box 6900
Florence, KY 41022
Ph:800-442-7477
Free: 800-442-7477
Fax: (859)647-5963
Co. E-mail: courseiltcrisp@thomaslearning.com
URL: http://www.courseilt.com
Price: $99.00 (VCI CD-ROM). **Description:** Based on the *Better Business Writing* video and book. Includes book and user's guide.

RESEARCH CENTERS

27712 ■ Colorado State University–Center for
Research on Communication and
Technologies
C-223 Clark Bldg.
Fort Collins, CO 80523-1785
Ph:(970)491-5674
Fax: (970)491-2908
Co. E-mail: Don.Zimmerman@ColoState.Edu
URL: http://www.colostate.edu/Depts/CROWACT/

Contact: Prof. Don Zimmerman
E-mail: Don.Zimmerman@ColoState.Edu
Scope: Health communication, risk communication, usability testing, diffusion of innovations, Web design, human factors, human computer interactions, interface design, writing, writing processes, online writing centers, technology transfer, science communication, legibility, tobacco and alcohol warnings, digital television, communicating risk of sexually transmitted diseases, communication history.

27713 ■ University of Notre Dame–Fanning Center for Business Communication
234 Mendoza College of Business
Notre Dame, IN 46556
Ph:(574)631-8397
Fax: (574)631-5255
Co. E-mail: jorourke@nd.edu
URL: http://www.nd.edu/~fanning
Contact: Prof. James S. O'Rourke IV
E-mail: jorourke@nd.edu
Scope: Business communication, including writing, speaking, listening, persuasion and other communica-

tion behaviors in the workplace; corporate communication, including the production of case studies designed to support instruction; intercultural communication, including the production of books and learning materials designed to support instruction. **Services:** Instruction, counseling, and guidance, in management and corporate communication. **Publications:** Management and Corporate Communication Case Studies (semiannually). **Educational Activities:** Conference on Corporate Communication (annually); Management Development Seminars; Workshops. **Awards:** E.D. Fanning Award; L.B. Pilkinton Award.

START-UP INFORMATION

27714 ■ "Building a Better Skunk Works" in *Fast Company* (March 2005, No. 92, pp. 68)
Pub: Gruner & Jahr USA Publishing
Ed: Alan Deutschman. **Description:** Rod Adkins talks about IBM's move in 2000 to put him in charge of its new venture called, emerging-business opportunities, and the challenges he faced. The new technology applies wireless technology to extend computing beyond the home and office to such places as the car (with voice-command navigation systems). By 2003, Adkins had revved up annual sales of $2.4 billion.

27715 ■ "Burn, babay, Burn" in *Entrepreneur* (Vol. 28, No. 6, June 2000, pp. 76)
Pub: Entrepreneur Media Inc.
Description: Presenting Entrepreneur and Dun & Bradstreet's Sixth Annual Hot 100 list of the fastest growing entrepreneurial businesses in America.

27716 ■ "The Disruptive Startup" in *Inc.* (February 1, 2002)
Pub: Inc. Magazine
Ed: Nancy Lyons. **Description:** Interview with Harvard Business School professor and author, Clayton M. Christensen. Christensen helps identify strategies that allow new growth companies succeed.

27717 ■ *Entrepreneurship Strategy: Changing Patterns in New Venture Creation, Growth, and Reinvention*
Pub: SAGE Publications, Incorporated
Ed: Lisa K. Gundry; Jill R. Kickul. **Released:** August 2006. **Price:** $69.95. **Description:** Entrepreneurial strategies that incorporate new venture emergence, early growth, and reinvention and innovation are examined.

27718 ■ "Explosive Success" in *Small Business Opportunities* (Vol. 14, No. 1, January 2002, pp. 62-64)
Pub: Harris Publications, Inc.
Ed: Annette Wood. **Description:** Profile of Sandy Faust, who launched her circuit board company from her back porch, and has turned the business into a $1 million a year enterprise. Faust has won numerous business awards and plans to grow the business for her family then retire.

27719 ■ "Finding the Fault Line Where A New Business Can Grow" in *Fortune* (Vol. 142, No. 10, October 30, 2000, pp. 294+)
Pub: Time Inc.
Ed: Thomas A. Stewart. **Description:** The new company, 12 Entrepreneuring, an operating company whose mission is to reinvent business, is profiled.

27720 ■ "A Fortune From Home" in *Small Business Opportunities* (Vol. 13, No. 5, September 2001, pp. 22-24, 26, 28, 30, 32, 34, 36, 40)
Pub: Harris Publications, Inc.
Description: Helpful information is provided to start a mail order business for less than $25. The article contains ideas, tips and pointers on how to find a product, market it, and bankroll the profits.

27721 ■ "Franchising" in *Black Enterprise* (Vol. 32, No. 10, May 2002, pp. 101)
Pub: Earl Graves Publishing Co.
Ed: Carolyn M. Brown. **Description:** Franchising is one of the fastest growing segments of American business and is seen as an ideal partnership for an independent entrepreneur. More minorities are discovering franchising opportunities by increased recruiting by companies like Wendy's, Merry Maids, Jan Pro, Subway, Church's Chicken (TM), and Interim Healthcare. Profile of aforementioned franchise opportunities are included.

27722 ■ "Get 'em while they're hot" in *Entrepreneur* (Vol. 30, No. 12, December 2002, pp. 85)
Pub: Entrepreneur Media Inc.
Ed: Steve Cooper, Mark Henricks, Gisela M. Pedroza, April Y. Pennington, Chris Penttila, Chris Sandlund, Devlin Smith, Nichole L. Torres. **Description:** The hottest business opportunities for entrepreneurs in 2003 are listed, including online learning, outsourcing, home entertainment installation, health care technology, medi-spas, Instant Messaging-related services and products, sleep-related products, singles-related products and services, yoga studios, food supplements, online gaming, bankruptcy services, pet accessories, security, large-size clothing, online auction aftermarket services, scheduling software, and specialty ice cream shops.

27723 ■ *Going Solo: Developing a Home-Based Consulting Business from the Ground Up*
Pub: McGraw-Hill Companies Incorporated
Ed: William J. Bond. **Released:** January 1997. **Price:** $14.95. **Description:** Ways to turn specialized knowledge into a home-based successful consulting firm, focusing on targeting client needs, business plans, and growth.

27724 ■ "Growth Strategies" in *Inc.* (November 2000, pp. 78)
Pub: The Goldhirsh Group
Description: Chris Zane's bike shop was healthy and profitable, but he needed the skills of a CEO to make it grow.

27725 ■ "Hot 100" in *Entrepreneur* (Vol. 31, No. 6, June 2003, pp. 64)
Pub: Entrepreneur Media Inc.
Ed: Amanda C. Kooser. **Description:** Twenty-five of the 100 companies hitting the year's hottest industry for 2003 come from the business services sector, nine providing logistics services (such as freight-handling, trucking and transportation) and six providing marketing and advertising services.

27726 ■ "Marketing Know-How" in *Black Enterprise* (Vol. 30, No. 5, December 1999, pp. 42)
Pub: Earl Graves Publishing Co.
Ed: Gerda Gallop-Goodman. **Description:** Advice is given to an entrepreneur who wants to expand a small African American ceramic statues business.

27727 ■ "The Messenger" in *Black Enterprise* (Vol. 30, No. 12, July 2000, pp. 55)
Pub: Earl Graves Publishing Co.
Ed: Rebecca Rohan. **Description:** Build your customer base with an electric newsletter.

27728 ■ "Milwaukee Mayor Says Federal Business Development Program Will Create Jobs" in *Milwaukee Journal Sentinel* (December 8, 2005)
Pub: Journal Sentinel, Inc.
Ed: Tom Daykin. **Description:** The Federal government is expanding its Renewal Community program in Milwaukee, Wisconsin. The program gives subsidies to new business development in poor neighborhoods.

27729 ■ "New Owners Cook Up Redo of Clarkston Cafe" in *Crain's Detroit Business* (Vol. 22, December 4, 2006, No. 29, pp. 24)
Pub: Crain Communications Inc. - Detroit
Ed: Brent Snavely. **Description:** Renown French restaurant is reopening with new menu and many renovations. Clarkston Cafe was the site of Kid Rock and Pamela Anderson's wedding ceremonies.

27730 ■ "New Stratford, Conn., Needlework Quickly Gains Fans" in *Connecticut Post* (January 31, 2003)
Pub: Knight-Ridder/Tribune Business News
Ed: Stephania H. Davis. **Description:** Profile of Janet Kemp Fine Yarns and Needlework. Kemp tells how she and her husband obtained a second mortgage on their home in order to start her business. The store features high quality yarns, patterns, and accessories for the crafts of knitting, embroidering and needlepoint.

27731 ■ "Priority packets pay to fly first class" in *Red Herring* (No. 87, December 18, 2000, pp. 44, 46)
Pub: Herring Communications, Inc.
Ed: Scott Tyler Shafer. **Description:** A profile of Village Networks, the New Jersey high-tech start-up and its founder Kai Eng.

27732 ■ "Read Smart, Grow Smart" in *Fast Company* (May 2001, pp. 202)
Pub: Fast Company
Ed: Amy Wilson Sheldon. **Description:** Profile of Gil Elbaz, co-founder and CIO of Oingo, a search-technology firm based in Los Angeles, California. Elbaz shows how to create a company that's built to last when others are failing.

27733 ■ "Reeling In the Big One" in *Inc.* (August 1, 2004)
Pub: Inc. Magazine
Ed: Jess McCuan. **Description:** Ways a startup business can land a large, brand name client are examined.

27734 ■ "Shoestring Start-Ups" in *Small Business Opportunities* (Vol. 13, No. 6, November 2001, pp. 22-24, 26, 28, 30, 32, 34, 36, 116)
Pub: Harris Publications, Inc.

Description: The top 50 small business that can be started with little or no capital are previewed, some as little as $100 or less, including the ten steps to follow when starting a new business.

27735 ■ "Told You So" in *Entrepreneur* **(Vol. 28, No. 6, June 2000, pp. 90)**
Pub: Entrepreneur Media Inc.
Ed: Laura Tiffany. **Description:** A directory of the Hot 100 businesses that proves there is life after recognition in Entrepreneur magazine. Statistical data is included.

27736 ■ "Urban Legend: Do 90 Percent of Startups Really Fail to Make It Past Their First Year?" in *Entrepreneur* **(Vol. 31, No. 8, Aug., 2003)**
Pub: Entrepreneur Media, Inc.
Ed: Karen E. Spaeder. **Description:** According to an economist with the Small Business Administration's Office of Advocacy, a business closure does not necessarily mean failure; exit strategies for businesses are discussed.

27737 ■ "You Don't Know Jackalope" in *Success* **(Vol. 47, No. 4, September 2000, pp. 18)**
Pub: Success Publishing, Inc.
Ed: Michael Barrier. **Description:** Darby McQuade, founder of a store called Jackalope in Santa Fe, New Mexico, has discovered a way to maintain a growing business while sharing his love for animals with his customers.

ASSOCIATIONS AND OTHER ORGANIZATIONS

27738 ■ Association for Corporate Growth - Toronto Chapter
390 Bay St., Ste. 2701
Toronto, ON, Canada M5H 2Y2
Ph:(416)868-1881
Fax: (416)860-0580
Co. E-mail: acgtoronto@baystco.com
URL: http://www.acg.org/toronto
Contact: Ms. Sue Anderson, Chapter Administrator
Membership: Professionals with a leadership role in strategic corporate growth. **Purpose:** Seeks to facilitate the professional advancement of members, and the practice of corporate growth management. Fosters communication and cooperation among members; conducts continuing professional education programs. **Publications:** *Mergers & Acquisitions - The Dealmaker's Journal* (monthly).

EDUCATIONAL PROGRAMS

27739 ■ Developing and Executing a Customer-centric Strategy
American Management Association
1601 Broadway
New York, NY 10019
Ph:(212)586-8100
Free: 800-262-9699
Fax: (212)903-8168
Co. E-mail: customerservice@amanet.org
URL: http://www.amanet.org
Price: $1,895 for non-members; $1,695 for AMA members. **Description:** Covers developing a strong customer base that guarantees increased revenue. **Locations:** New York, NY; Washington, DC; Chicago, IL; Atlanta, GA; and San Francisco, CA.

REFERENCE WORKS

27740 ■ "3Q a good one for local firms, if you ignore auto industry" in *Crain's Detroit Business* **(Vol. 22, November 13, 2006, No. 46, pp. 3)**
Pub: Crain Communications Inc. - Detroit
Ed: Tom Henderson **Description:** Although the difficulties of the auto industry dominate the news, non-

automotive businesses are doing very well with double digit growth. Michigan still lags the S & P because of the size of the auto industry and the depth of the associated troubles.

27741 ■ "'04 Was Good Year for Show Managers" in *Tradeshow Week* **(Vol. 34)**
Pub: Reed Business Information
Ed: Rachelle Crum. **Description:** According to Tradeshow Week's 2004 Show Management Salary Survey, salaries rose 3.6 percent more in 2004 over 2003 and are expected to increase by the same amount in 2005. Show managers averaged $58,822 in the U.S. and Canada for 2004, perks and bonuses were up 32 percent worth $14,159.

27742 ■ *The 7 Irrefutable Rules of Small Business Growth*
Pub: John Wiley & Sons, Incorporated
Ed: Steven S. Little. **Released:** February 2005. **Price:** $18.95. **Description:** Proven strategies to maintain small business growth are outlined, covering topics such as technology, business plans, hiring, and more.

27743 ■ "10 Local Companies Make Inc. List of Fastest-Growing" in *Crain's Detroit Business* **(Vol. 21, October 31, 2005, No. 44, pp. 32)**
Pub: Crain Communications Inc. - Detroit
Ed: Laura Bommarito. **Description:** Ten local companies made the Inc. magazine's annual list of the 500 fastest-growing businesses in the U.S. The three top rankings include, Arbor Networks, seller of network security and software equipment, ranked No. 9; Commodity Sourcing Group, No. 22, buys and distributes goods and services for health care organizations; and BullsEye Telecom, provider of telephone and Internet services to businesses ranked No. 82.

27744 ■ "75 Reasons to Be Glad You're an American Entrepreneur Right Now" in *Inc.* **(October 2005, pp. 88-95)**
Pub: Inc. Magazine
Ed: Michael S. Hopkins. **Description:** The diverse ways in which the culture, the economy, and entrepreneurship are making this the best time in history to build a business in America.

27745 ■ "100th Bank" in *San Fernando Valley Business Journal* **(Vol. 12, January 2007, No. 2, pp. 37)**
Pub: San Fernando Valley Business Journal Associates
Ed: Vanessa Herman. **Description:** Countrywide Bank, a unit of Countrywide Financial Corp., has opened its 100th financial center in Smithtown, New York. The company now has financial centers in thirteen states and assets have grown to over $88 billion.

27746 ■ "2005: A Quiet, But Critical Year for Venture Capital" in *Venture Capital Journal* **(January 1, 2005)**
Pub: Thomason Financial Inc.
Description: Some industry experts are predicting a transformation in the venture capital industry for 2005, with a shift toward seed and early stage investing.

27747 ■ "2005 Outlook: Low Growth Is OK" in *Tradeshow Week* **(Vol. 34, December 20, 2004, No. 51, pp. 8)**
Pub: Reed Business Information
Ed: Michael Hughes. **Description:** The exhibition industry is predicting an increase in companies participating in shows. Fifty-six percent of show managers are predicting total gross revenue growth between 1 and 10 percent for 2005.

27748 ■ "A 35-Year Old Downtown Shop is Expanding" in *Bellingham Business Journal* **(December 2006, pp. A5)**
Pub: Sun News Inc.
Description: The Stamp & Coin Place, a store that buys and sells stamps and coins as well as offers bullion transactions, is expanding its store to offer more space for storage and offices.

27749 ■ "About this report" in *Crain's Detroit Business* **(Vol. 19, No. 17, April 28, 2003, pp. 14)**
Pub: Crain Communications Inc., Detroit
Description: Crain's Business Detroit sent surveys to six leadership organizations' alumni in the State of Michigan, including Leadership Detroit, Leadership Oakland, Leadership Macomb, Leadership Ann Arbor, the Detroit Orientation Institute at Wayne State University and Leadership Windsor/Essex.

27750 ■ "Accessing Minority Markets" in *Hispanic Business* **(Vol. 24, No. 5, May 2002, pp. 14)**
Pub: Hispanic Business Inc.
Ed: Holly Ocasio Rizzo. **Description:** The U.S. Chamber of Commerce has launched a new program called, Access America, in order to gain a foothold with Hispanics and other minorities.

27751 ■ "Acquisitions helped increase offerings" in *Crain's Detroit Business* **(Vol. 19, No. 13, March 31, 2003, pp. 12)**
Pub: Crain Communications Inc., Detroit
Description: Special report on Integration Projects Inc., now called Dewpoint Inc. after acquisition the company modified service offerings in order to cope with the market.

27752 ■ *Action Plans for the Small Business: Growth Strategies for Businesses Wondering Where to Go Next*
Pub: DBM Publishing
Ed: Shailendra Vyakarnam. **Released:** 1995. **Price:** $25.00.

27753 ■ "The Activist Ingredient" in *Inc.* **(July 1, 2003)**
Pub: Gruner & Jahr USA Publishing
Ed: Bobbie Gossage. **Description:** Paul Osterman of the Sloan School of Management at MIT suggests that managers take lessons from grassroots political groups to avoid employee burnout while maintaining growth.

27754 ■ "Ad Sales Growth to Slow in 2001" in *Folio: the Magazine for Magazine Management* **(Vol. 30, No. 1, January 2001, pp. 15)**
Pub: Intertec Publishing Corp.
Ed: Dale Buss. **Description:** Barring an outright recession, advertising growth will remain healthy as manufacturers introduce new products and sophisticated marketers realize that advertising is never expendable.

27755 ■ "Ad Time Firm Expands" in *San Fernando Valley Business Journal* **(Vol. 11, December 2006, No. 25, pp. 28)**
Pub: San Fernando Valley Business Journal Associates
Description: Bid4Spots.com, an online advertising firm, will expand its unique reverse auction method of selling unused radio ad time to independent online radio. Bid4Spots has a patent pending for this unique advertising method.

27756 ■ "Aether Systems Unveils $125M Venture Arm" in *Venture Capital Journal* **(Vol. 40, No. 10, October 2000, pp. 6)**
Pub: Venture Economics
Description: In order to expand its markets, Aether Systems Inc., provider of wireless data products and services, launched Aether Capital as its venture capital arm.

27757 ■ "After Bitter Dot-Com Pill, Market Sweetens for Office Suite Operators" in *Long Island Business News* **(March 12, 2004)**
Pub: Dolan Media Newswires
Ed: Claude Solnik. **Description:** Office suite occupancy is on the rise on Long Island, New York as well as nationwide. Office suite operators will also rent space on temporary basis to clients seeking an infrastructure offering high-tech services.

27758 ■ "Against the Grain" in *Fast Company* (May 2001, pp. 201)
Pub: Fast Company
Ed: Cathy Olofson. **Description:** Taking a diversified company to the Web is no easy task, but Monica Morse, a managing director of Cargill's Eventures team, believes that the agribusiness company has what it takes to move B2B to a profit.

27759 ■ "AIG Plans to Cut 27 Jobs at Neptune, N.J., Offices" in *The Record* (November 8, 2005)
Pub: New Jersey Media Group
Ed: Dennis P. Carmody. **Description:** AIG American General will cut a total of 250 employees from its group benefits workforce over the next 18 months. The group benefits division administers health insurance plans sponsored by employers.

27760 ■ "Airport Industrial Sites in Demand" in *Milwaukee Journal Sentinel* (December 19, 2005)
Pub: Journal Sentinel, Inc.
Ed: Tom Daykin. **Description:** Several light large industrial buildings are being developed near Mitchell International Airport. New interest in such space used for storing and distributing products, as well as manufacturers, holds hope for the economy.

27761 ■ "All Systems Grow: You Don't Have to be a Rocket Scientist to Grow Your Business." in *Entrepreneur* (Vol. 33, March 2005, No. 3)
Pub: Entrepreneur Media Inc.
Ed: Julie Monahan. **Description:** Seven strategies to develop and grow a small business are presented.

27762 ■ "Allegiant Files Statement for IPO of Common Stock" in *Bellingham Business Journal* (December 2006, pp. A3)
Pub: Sun News Inc.
Description: Las Vegas-based Allegiant Travel Company announced its plans for a public offering of its common stock. The company plans to list its shares on the NASDAQ stock market under the ticker symbol ALGT.

27763 ■ "Allen Tate Expanding to Research Triangle Park: Firm Expects Raleigh Market to Grow Faster" in *Charlotte Observer* (January 31, 2007)
Pub: Knight-Ridder/Tribune Business News
Ed: Doug Smith; Dudley Price. **Description:** Allen Tate Realtors expanded its operations to the Research Triangle area. The firm is predicting a strong market and growth in Charlotte, North Carolina.

27764 ■ "Allsbrook Predicts Economic Pickup in Months Ahead" in *Birmingham Business Journal* (Vol. 20, No. 33, August 15, 2003, pp. 6)
Pub: American City Business Journals, Inc.
Ed: Leslie Zganjar. **Description:** Bob Allsbrook of AmSouth Bancorp shares his economic forecast, focusing on economic conditions, interest rates, and recessions.

27765 ■ "Alternative Energy Powers Up In Michigan - Part 1 of 2" in *Crain's Detroit Business* (Vol. 22, February 6, 2006, No. 6, pp. 10)
Pub: Crain Communications Inc. - Detroit
Ed: Amy Lane. **Description:** McKenzie Bay International Ltd. Located in Farmington Hills, Michigan is launching a commercial wind-energy system that generates and distributes electricity at customer locations, and supplements power from a conventional utility.

27766 ■ "Alternative Energy Powers Up In Michigan - Part 2 of 2" in *Crain's Detroit Business* (Vol. 22, February 6, 2006, No. 6, pp. 10)
Pub: Crain Communications Inc. - Detroit
Ed: Amy Lane. **Description:** Michigan is pushing to become the nations' epicenter for research and development into new technology for biodiesel fuels made from renewable resources such as vegetable oil recycled from restaurants or produced from sunflowers, soybeans and canola plants.

27767 ■ "Am. Axle Plans China, Europe Plants" in *Crain's Detroit Business* (Vol. 21, October 31, 2005, No. 44, pp. 4)
Pub: Crain Communications Inc. - Detroit
Ed: Terry Kosdrosky. **Description:** American Axle & Manufacturing Holdings Inc. will open its first manufacturing plant in China in late 2007 or early 2008, followed by a new plant in Central or Eastern Europe soon after.

27768 ■ "Ameribank Plans Branch in Palm Beach Gardens" in *South Florida Business Journal* (Vol. 23, No. 47, June 27, 2003, pp. 2)
Pub: American City Business Journals
Ed: Jim Freer. **Description:** Plans by Ameribank to open a branch office in Palm Beach, Florida are discussed.

27769 ■ "American Outcast" in *Entrepreneur.com* (Vol. 34, February 2006, No. 2, pp. 81)
Pub: Entrepreneur Media Inc.
Ed: Laurel Delaney. **Description:** In order to compete in a global market, small American companies must position their brands as local in order market a good brand strategy, as well as to promote a new brand with cultural sensitivity.

27770 ■ "Amgen's Profit Up 58 Percent in 2nd Quarter" in *Providence Business News* (Vol. 18, No. 15, July 28, 2003, pp. 1)
Pub: Providence Business News, Inc.
Ed: Mike Colias. **Description:** A presentation of second-quarter profits in 2003 reported by Amgen Inc. Topics include market share, market development, and business strategy.

27771 ■ "Amount raised by venture funds plunged to $6.9 billion in 2002" in *Wall Street Journal* (February 11, 2003, pp. C5)
Pub: Dow Jones & Co. Inc.
Ed: Raymond Hennessey. **Description:** Reports from Thomson Venture Economics and National Venture Capital Association show venture capital fell to $6.9 billion in 2002.

27772 ■ "Another Wave of HQ Job Cuts at Sears" in *Crain's Chicago Business* (Vol. 26, No. 50, December 15, 2003, pp. 1)
Pub: Crain Communications, Inc.
Ed: Sandra Jones. **Description:** Sears, Roebuck and Company employed 5,300 workers at its Hoffman Estates headquarters in Illinois at the first of 2003, and the staff was cut to 4,800 by December, with further cuts predicted. After Sears sold its 94-year-old credit card division, the company's stores could not generate enough income to make up for the loss of credit card profits. Statistical data included.

27773 ■ "Answering the call" in *Crain's Detroit Business* (Vol. 19, No. 11, March 17, 2003, pp. 13)
Pub: Crain Communications Inc., Detroit
Description: Answering Service Inc., the telephone answering service located in Southfield, Michigan has revamped its infrastructure and wired its offices together, a move that should save the firm $150,000 annually.

27774 ■ "Answering the call: security firm is expanding as demand increases" in *Black Enterprise* (Vol. 32, No. 8, March 2002, pp. 52)
Pub: Earl Graves Publishing Co.
Ed: Alan Hughes. **Description:** Profile of Protection Corporations of America, a security company that hopes to answer the nation's call for increased security for business.

27775 ■ "AOL and Time Warner promise to broaden the Internet's horizons" in *Red Herring* (No. 87, December 18, 2000, pp. 38, 40)
Pub: Herring Communications, Inc.
Ed: Cara Cunningham. **Description:** It is predicted that by 2003, only one-third of residential Internet users will have broadband access.

27776 ■ "Apex Property Management Moves" in *Bellingham Business Journal* (January 2007, pp. A6)
Pub: Sun News Inc.
Description: Apex Property Management has moved to a new location in order to increase their workspace. The company works with condominium and homeowners associations, as well as commercial property owners.

27777 ■ "Apex Venture Partners Preps for Fifth Vehicle" in *Venture Capital Journal* (Vol. 40, No. 10, November 2000, pp. 16)
Pub: Venture Economics
Description: Apex Venture Partners began raising its fifth fund in January 2001. The new fund will invest in about 25-35 companies with initial investments in the $2 million range. Apex mainly backs telecommunications, software, information technology, and consumer-related companies in the U.S.

27778 ◪ "Apocalypse Net" in *Red Herring* (No. 102, August 15, 2001, pp. 54-56)
Pub: Herring Communications
Ed: John Geirland. **Description:** In the 1990's, Hollywood executives launched two waves of attack on the Internet, with plenty of casualties. Now, these Web-shocked vets are heading back to the hills.

27779 ■ "The Appellation Trail" in *Forbes* (Vol. 170, No. 5, September 16, 2002, pp. 103)
Pub: Forbes Magazine
Ed: Quentin Hardy. **Description:** Profile of winegrower, Andy Beckstoffer of Beckstoffer Family Vineyards, located in Napa Valley, California. Beckstoffer is expanding the company to nearby Lake County.

27780 ■ "Apple, Goodyear Each Climb 4.9 Percent" in *Wall Street Journal* (Vol. 248, December 2006, No. 153, pp. B3)
Pub: Dow Jones & Co. Inc.
Ed: Anjali Cordeiro **Description:** With the Dow Jones averages at a steady decline, Apple Computers and Goodyear Tire and Rubber put up their best performances in over three years. This will have a positive impact on their perspective suppliers and subsidiaries

27781 ■ "Applebee's to open in Lancaster" in *Business First of Buffalo* (Vol. 18, No. 46, August 12, 2002, pp. 15)
Pub: Knight-Ridder/Tribune Business News
Ed: James Fink. **Description:** Applebee's Neighborhood Grill and Bar is expected to open in early fall of 2002 at the Gateway Center shopping center in Lancaster, New York.

27782 ■ "Appleseed's distribution center expands" in *Boston Business Journal* (Vol. 22, No. 12, April 26, 2002, pp. 5)
Pub: MCP, Inc.
Ed: Donna L. Goodison. **Description:** Appleseed's Inc. is expanding its distribution center due to growth.

27783 ■ "Applying Old Ideals to Crain's New Tasks" in *Crain's New York Business* (Vol. 23, January 8, 2007, No. 2, pp. 11)
Pub: Crain Communications, Inc.
Ed: Greg David. **Description:** Crain's New York Business announces its plans for the coming year which include a comprehensive website that will provide readers with daily news stories.

27784 ■ "Arbor Realty Provides $35M in Financing" in *Long Island Business News* (February 27, 2004)
Pub: Dolan Media Newswires
Ed: Nick Anastasi. **Description:** Arbor Realty Limited Partnership has provided $35 million in financing to assist Prime Outlets Acquisition Company for the acquisition of 36 major outlet centers in the U.S. and Puerto Rico from Prime Retail Inc.

27785 ■ "An Army of Moms and Pops" in *Business Week* (No. 3799, Sept. 16, 2002, pp. 18)
Pub: McGraw-Hill Inc.
Ed: Michael J. Mandel. **Description:** According to the U.S. Census Bureau's study called County Business

Patterns, the average number of employees per business establishment in America was 16.1 in 2000 and the number of small businesses has risen 9 percent since 1993. Statistical data included.

27786 ■ "Around ground zero, an effort to rescue mom-and-pop shops" in *Wall Street Journal* **(February 8, 2002, pp. A1)**
Pub: Wall Street Journal
Ed: Lucette Lagnado. **Description:** The article asks the question: Is the microlender's program merely delaying layoffs by small businesses near the former World Trade Center after 9-11?

27787 ■ "Arson Charges Spotlight Downtown Bergenfield, N.J., Business Slump" in *The Record* **(February 17, 2004)**
Pub: Knight-Ridder/Tribune Business News
Ed: Catherine Holahan. **Description:** Profile of Osiris Tejeda, owner of Tropical Billiards Cafe, who is charged with aggravated arson with his wife.

27788 ■ "The Art of Business Judo" in *Fast Company* **(August 2001, pp. 116)**
Pub: Fast Company
Ed: Jill Rosenfeld. **Description:** It's the essence of competition: big versus little, strong versus slight, heavy versus light; ways for small companies to compete with larger corporations are presented by former Judo champion, Jimmy Pedro.

27789 ■ "Artists Can Help Draw Tourists to Detroit" in *Crain's Detroit Business* **(Vol. 19, No. 49, December 8, 2003, pp. 9)**
Pub: Crain Communications Inc., Detroit
Ed: Description: Ideas to maintain and attract young people to the City of Detroit are discussed.

27790 ■ "Ashley Capital branches out into new kind of development" in *Crain's Detroit Business* **(Vol. 19, No. 17, April 28, 2003, pp. 3)**
Pub: Crain Communications Inc., Detroit
Ed: Jennette Smith. **Description:** Ashley Capital is showing confidence in the Detroit metropolitan area's eventual market rebound by constructing a build-to-suit building for Transfreight Ltd. and leased land to client ASW Services for a building. The new projects equal nearly 300,000 square feet and $9 million in investment. Ashley Capital is best known for speculative big box distribution centers.

27791 ■ "Asia Rising" in *Black Enterprise* **(Vol. 35, October 2004, No. 3, pp. 46)**
Pub: Earl G. Graves Publishing Co. Inc.
Ed: Donald Jay Korn. **Description:** China and India are two emerging global economies making them attractive for investing. Manufacturing and high tech jobs are being outsourced to both countries. It is important to research before investing in China and India, as well as any international funds.

27792 ■ "Assist2Sell Expands to Service Home Buyers" in *Bellingham Business Journal* **(January 2007, pp. 3)**
Pub: Sun News Inc.
Description: Exclusive Buyer Agency is a new service provided by Assist2Sell Home Buyers & Sellers Advantage, Whatcom County's leading discount real estate agency.

27793 ■ "At Deadline" in *Crain's New York Business* **(Vol. 20, No. 12, March 22, 2004, pp. 1)**
Pub: Crain Communications, Inc.
Description: Miscellaneous business briefs are cited, including information showing sixteen percent of New York City employers plan to hire more staff in the second quarter of 2004; Quickdrop International has been given state approval to begin selling franchises in New York for eBay drop-off centers.

27794 ■ "At a Glance: The Inner City 100 CEOs" in *Inc.* **(May 2000, pp. 78)**
Pub: The Goldhirsh Group
Description: A comprehensive listing of statistical data about the Inner City 100 companies.

27795 ■ "At Last, Stirrings in the PC Market" in *Barron's* **(August 25, 2003, pp. T3)**
Pub: Barron's
Ed: Mark Veverka. **Description:** Personal computer sales, long expected to benefit from the need for consumers to replace aging systems, have finally begun to increase, according to reports from market leaders at Hewlett-Packard and Dell.

27796 ■ "At Top Speed" in *Hispanic Business* **(July/August 2004, pp. 26)**
Pub: Hispanic Business
Description: Hispanic-owned companies grew at the same rate as the U.S. economy in 2004; statistical composites of the top 100 Hispanic companies picked by Hispanic Business, along with company performance by industry are highlighted.

27797 ■ "Atlanta Life to manage investments" in *BlackEnterprise* **(Vol. 32, No. 2, September 2001, pp. 22)**
Pub: Earl Graves Publishing Co.
Ed: Matthew S. Scott. **Description:** Recognizing the need for progressive growth and expansion, Atlanta Life Insurance Company has formed the Atlanta Life Financial Group Inc., a new holding company that allows the nation's second largest black-owned life insurance company to become a full-service financial services organization. The firm will begin operation by the end of 2001.

27798 ■ "Atlanta's top telephone system suppliers" in *Atlanta Business Chronicle* **(Vol. 25, Nov. 15, 2002, No. 23 pp. 13C)**
Pub: American City Business Publications, Inc.
Description: The top ten telephone system suppliers in Atlanta, Georgia are ranked by the number of systems installed in 2001. The listing includes number of new systems and other systems, number of lines installed, company-wide revenue, number of technicians, employees in Atlanta, affiliated carriers, other services, target markets, chief officer in Atlanta, company headquarters, and year of establishment.

27799 ■ "Atlanta's Top Commercial Developers" in *Atlanta Business Chronicle* **(Vol. 24, No. 14, September 7, 2001, pp. 16C)**
Pub: American City Business Journals Inc.
Description: The top commercial developers in Atlanta are listed in ranking by the square feet developed. The top three are Carter & Associates, with 5,074,700 square feet, Holder Properties Inc., with 1,350,800 square feet, and Pope & Land Enterprises Inc., with 1,340,000 square feet. Statistical data included.

27800 ■ "August, Ga., Lacks Demographics to Draw Upscale Retailers" in *Augusta Chronicle* **(February 17, 2004)**
Pub: Knight-Ridder/Tribune Business News
Ed: James Gallagher. **Description:** Profile of HiFi Buys, a high-end electronics retailer expanding in the Atlanta, Georgia area.

27801 ■ "Auto show also an engine for small-business growth" in *Crain's Detroit Business* **(Vol. 19, No. 2, January 20, 2003, pp. 1)**
Pub: Crain Communications Inc., Detroit
Ed: Robert Ankeny. **Description:** The North American International Auto Show brought more than $300 million to Detroit small businesses in January 2003. It is estimated that nearly every type of business in the area benefited from the show.

27802 ■ "Automotive Dealers Move Wheels" in *Hispanic Business* **(Vol. 22, No. 6, June 2000, pp. 100)**
Pub: Hispanic Business
Ed: Christopher D. Lancette, Scott Williams, Joel Russell. **Description:** Paul Young Auto Mall in Laredo, Texas, is one of the top ten Hispanic-owned auto dealerships in the United States, with revenues of $95.97 million. Paul Young, Jr., owner of the company, says that the firm's growth is partially due to the town's population increase.

27803 ■ "Avoid the Supply Chain Squeeze" in *E-business Advisor* **(Vol. 18, No. 7, July 2000, pp. 18)**
Pub: Advisor Media, Inc.
Ed: Ben Chen, Lara Kass. **Description:** The next wave of e-commerce may result in significant disintermediation in select industry supply chains. It will be driven by the concurrent development of advanced computing technologies, such as high-definition text, with the implementation of new broadband Internet technologies that will redistribute the power within the supply chain to suppliers/manufacturers and consumers in certain industries. The article tells how these trends are transforming the book industry, home video industry and the music industry.

27804 ■ "Axion CEO heads in new, profitable direction" in *Atlanta Business Chronicle* **(Vol. 24, No. 11, August 17, 2001, pp. 40A)**
Pub: American City Business Journals Inc.
Ed: Mary Jane Credeur. **Description:** Axiom Solutions International is now focused on software integration, with the bulk of its business involving linking software via several satellite offices to a central network server for clients. The company became profitable in July and is expected to report revenue of $2.5 million by end-2001. The company and Hansjoerg Beha's management strategy are discussed.

27805 ■ "B2B Exchanges Survival Guide" in *Internet World* **(Vol. 7, No. 1, January 15, 2001, pp. 48)**
Pub: Mecklermedia Corporation
Ed: Ruhan Memishi. **Description:** It is estimated that the use and success of business-to-business exchanges will continue to grow and that by 2004 seven percent of the global economy could be fueled by these exchanges. An outline of the important steps a company needs to take in order to succeed in e-commerce.

27806 ■ "B2G Supplies Revenue Gains" in *Hispanic Business* **(July/August 2002, pp. 32, 34)**
Pub: Hispanic Business
Ed: U. S. defense spending boosts revenues for the Hispanic Business High-Tech 50, the nation's largest Hispanic-owned high-tech businesses. A list of the 2002 High-Tech 50 is included, featuring ranking for 2002 and 2001, company/location, CEO, product/service, number of employees, and revenue for 2001.

27807 ■ "Back to business with Staples: new chief works to reclaim the chain's roots" in *Barron's* **(Vol. 82, No. 59, Feb. 24, 2003, pp. T8)**
Pub: Barron's
Ed: Lawrence Strauss. **Description:** Profile of Ronald L. Sargent, newly appointed CEO of Staples. Sargent is refocusing the retailer on its original vision, the small business customer, and is committed to raising earnings as the best way to raising share prices.

27808 ■ "The Balancing Act: How Busy Executives Make Their Lives Work" in *Black Enterprise* **(Vol. 37, February 2007, No. 7, pp. 118)**
Pub: Earl G. Graves Publishing Co. Inc.
Ed: Marcia A. Reed-Woodard. **Description:** More than 70 percent of women with children work outside the home, according to a 2005 survey conducted by the U.S. Department of Labor Bureau. One of the biggest struggles these women face is balancing family with career aspirations and climbing the corporate ranks.

27809 ■ "Bank CEO Aims to Compound Marketshare" in *Crain's Chicago Business* **(Vol. 30, January 2007, No. 3, pp. 6)**
Pub: Crain Communications, Inc.
Ed: Lorene Yue. **Description:** Profile of Bruce Taylor, CEO of Taylor Capital Group Inc., who aims to increase the bank's marketshare, expand the bank's financial management business and get more business from their existing customers.

27810 ■ "Bankers' Gaze Turns Northward" in *South Florida Business Journal* **(Vol. 23, No. 53, August 8, 2003, pp. 1A)**
Pub: American City Business Journals
Ed: Jim Freer. **Description:** The introduction of new bank branches in West Palm Beach, Florida, including an industry overview, is discussed.

27811 ■ "Banking on California" in *San Francisco Business Times* **(Vol. 18, No. 6, September 19, 2003, pp. 19)**
Pub: American City Business Journals
Ed: Mark Calvey. **Description:** Citibank's purchase of California Federal Bank last year has gone smoothly, the next task is to attract customers from other large competitors.

27812 ■ "Bankruptcies" in *Crain's Detroit Business* **(Vol. 18, No. 24, 2002, pp. 6)**
Pub: Crain Communications Inc. - Detroit
Description: A listing of local businesses filing for Chapter 7 or 11 protection in the U.S. Bankruptcy Court in Detroit is presented.

27813 ■ "Bankruptcy Could Cost Firm $310M" in *Atlanta Business Chronicle* **(Vol. 26, No. 9, August 8, 2003, pp. 1A)**
Pub: American City Business Publications, Inc.
Ed: Mary Jane Credeur. **Description:** Atlanta, George-based Global Payments Inc., a transaction processing company, may lose about $310 million if financially-troubled Air Canada does not pay its debts. Global Payments is the primary processor of the airline's tickets that are purchased with credit cards and debit cards.

27814 ■ "Bankruptcy filings grow. Ohio stats among leaders" in *Business First Columbus* **(Vol. 18, No. 40, May 24, 2002, pp. A1)**
Pub: Business First Columbus, Inc.
Ed: Kathy Hoke. **Description:** Ohio consumers are filing personal bankruptcies at rates that exceed most of the U.S. Reasons given include personal illness, divorce, and job loss. In the Columbus area, bankruptcies have increased by 20 percent.

27815 ■ "Bank's branch-a-year strategy gets trimmed back by circumstances" in *Crain's Detroit Business* **(Vol. 16, No. 49, Dec. 4, 2000, pp. 32)**
Pub: Crain Communications, Inc.
Ed: Katie Merx. **Description:** Clarkston State Bank did not reach its branch-opening goal this year, but expects catch up next year.

27816 ■ "Banner Year" in *Entrepreneur* **(Vol. 32, September 2004, No. 9, pp. 34)**
Pub: Entrepreneur Media Inc.
Description: Online advertising has seen a dramatic increase in 2004. Statistical data included.

27817 ■ *Basic Business Statistics*
Pub: Prentice Hall
Released: 1995.

27818 ■ "Bay State VC pace falls to 1999 level" in *Boston Business Journal* **(Vol. 22, No. 16, May 24, 2002, pp. 1)**
Pub: MCP, Inc.
Ed: Edward Mason. **Description:** Massachusetts venture capital investments declined by 44 percent during first quarter 2002, when compared with same quarter of 2001. A total about $734 million in investments for first quarter 2002 versus a total of $1.3 billion in investments in first quarter 2001 were tabulated.

27819 ■ "Bayou Boycott Spurs Buying" in *Inc.* **(July 1, 2003)**
Pub: Gruner & Jahr USA Publishing
Description: Louisiana small businesses are profiting from anti-French sentiment following issues between Jacques Chirac and George W. Bush.

27820 ■ "Beall's Push to Expand Existing Florida Stores Reaps Dividends On Grand Scale" in *Bradenton Herald* **(January 20, 2005)**
Pub: Bradenton Herald

Ed: Dana Sanchez. **Description:** Beall's Inc. plans to expand all of its Florida outlet stores that are smaller than 20,000 square feet in size. The firm has 258 outlet stores in the state. With the increases space, the stores will begin selling books, multimedia and children's items along with more clothing.

27821 ■ "Bean Counter" in *San Francisco Business Times* **(Vol. 17, No. 53, August 8, 2003, pp. 27)**
Pub: American City Business Journals
Ed: Steven E.F. Brown. **Description:** An overview and history of JBR Gourmet Foods, Inc., a family-owned company that has earnings of $25 million annually roasting and distributing its own blend of coffee beans.

27822 ■ "Bean Enjoys Expanding Eat With Us Restaurants, Franchises" in *Mississippi Business Journal* **(Vol. 28, January 2007, No. 36, pp. 34)**
Pub: Venture Publications, Inc.
Ed: Lynn Lofton **Description:** Profile of John Bean who started family business Eat With Us, a fast-growing Columbus-based company with several popular dining brands and several restaurants.

27823 ■ *Beans: Four Principles for Running a Business in Good Times or Bad*
Pub: John Wiley & Sons, Incorporated
Ed: Leslie Yerkes, Charles Decker, Bob Nelson **Released:** June 2003. **Price:** $19.95. **Description:** Profile of Monorail Espresso, the popular Seattle coffee company that has become prosperous by intentionally staying small and building a strong customer service program.

27824 ■ "Beauty's new age" in *WWD* **(Vol. 184, No. 59, September 20, 2002, pp. S1)**
Pub: Fairchild Publications, Inc.
Description: The growing market for anti-aging products and anti-aging ingredients in other products like facial moisturizers is examined. Retail sales of age specialist products rose to $400 million in 2001.

27825 ■ "Behind the Numbers" in *Forbes* **(October 30, 2000, pp. 222)**
Pub: Forbes Magazine
Ed: Lisa McDonald. **Description:** The criteria used to rank small companies are listed.

27826 ■ "" in *Bellingham Business Journal* **(January 2007, pp.)**
Pub: Sun News Inc.
Description: Profile of Christian bikers Mike and Pam Melland, owners of Biker's Oasis. The shop sells motorcycle parts and accessories, helmets, leather clothing, chrome accessories, intercom systems, and radio headsets.

27827 ■ "Belt-Tightening at Pfizer?" in *Business Week Online* **(February 9, 2005)**
Pub: McGraw-Hill Companies
Ed: Amy Barrett. **Description:** Pfizer is expected to announce a major restructuring of the company in order to cut costs, but its sales force is believed to be safe from cuts.

27828 ■ "Bennett Pursues Public Input On Growth Issues" in *Bradenton Herald* **(February 2, 2005)**
Pub: Bradenton Herald
Ed: Stephen Majors. **Description:** Florida Senator Mike Bennett will not make a decision on the state's impending state-growth-management legislation until more planning experts and the public have had input. Senator Bennett will hold workshops throughout the state to explore better ways to plan business growth.

27829 ■ "Bereinga Starts $150M Fund, Opens China Office" in *Crain's Detroit Business* **(Vol. 23, February 5, 2007, No. 6, pp. 25)**
Pub: Crain Communications Inc. - Detroit
Ed: Tom Henderson **Description:** Tier one auto supplier acquisition or venture with Chinese is early project justifying Shanghai office; firm also hopes to help keep Southeast Michigan out front of new investments in not only auto-related commerce.

27830 ■ "Best Practices" in *Entrepreneur* **(Vol. 32, October 2004, No. 10, pp. 84)**
Pub: Entrepreneur Media Inc.
Ed: Mark Henricks. **Description:** Doctors, lawyers and other professionals are taking the lead from entrepreneurs when running and building their businesses. Innovative solutions to grow a professional practice like an entrepreneur are shared.

27831 ■ "Bets are off at state racetracks" in *Crain's Detroit Business* **(Vol. 18, No. 21, May 27, 2002, pp. 18)**
Pub: Crain Communications Inc. - Detroit
Ed: Andrew Dietderich. **Description:** Horse-racing bets in Michigan have dropped nearly $25 million in 2001, forcing metro Detroit tracks to try to win back gamblers they've lost to the areas casinos.

27832 ■ "Better Luck Next Year?" in *Black Enterprise* **(Vol. 32, No. 8, March 2002, pp. 33)**
Pub: Earl Graves Publishing Co.
Ed: Alan Hughes. **Description:** According to the National Bureau of Economic Research, consumer psychology is key to the timing of an economic recovery. Forecasts are predicted for the four quarters of 2002 and beyond.

27833 ■ "The Better Mousetrap: Detroit holds its own nationally in gaining new patents" in *Crain's Detroit Business* **(Vol. 16, Mar. 20, 2000)**
Pub: Crain Communications, Inc.
Ed: Matt Roush. **Description:** Although auto companies still hold the most patents in Michigan, the Detroit area innovation is getting more diverse.

27834 ■ "Betting on Growth" in *Hispanic Business* **(June 2005, pp. 98)**
Pub: Hispanic Business
Ed: Joel Russell. **Description:** Top Hispanic finance companies are counting on strong demand and cash to grow their sector in 2005. Statistical data included.

27835 ■ "Biddeford, Maine, Cord Business Weathers Trials of Domestic Textile Industry" in *Portland Press Herald* **(November 18, 2005)**
Pub: Blethen Maine Newspapers, Inc.
Ed: Seth Harkenss. **Description:** Bob Rice, entrepreneur and owner of Spurwink Cordage, discusses his success in an industry that is rapidly shrinking in the U.S. Spurwink Cordage reported nearly $1 million in annual sales, mostly to saddle manufacturers in western states.

27836 ■ "Big Boy Plans Big Growth in Franchises; Deals Signed for 23 Diners, One for 60 in Works" in *Crain's Detroit Business* **(Vol. 21)**
Pub: Crain Communications Inc. - Detroit
Ed: Brent Snavely. **Description:** Big Boy Restaurants International LLC will expand its operations with about 23 new restaurants over the next six years. The company is also close to closing a deal for 60 restaurants in southern California. Brief history of the company is included.

27837 ■ "Big Clients Push Construction Boom" in *Hispanic Business* **(Vol. 22, No. 6, June 2000, pp. 102)**
Pub: Hispanic Business
Ed: Christopher D. Lancette, Scott Williams, Joel Russell. **Description:** Hispanic-owned construction and steel company, Ideal Group, is ranked 52nd in the Hispanic Business 500 with revenues of $73.26 million in 1999. CEO, Frank Venegas, Jr., says that the company's growth has been encouraged by clients such as Chrysler and Ford who support the development.

27838 ■ "Big Deal: Landing a Large Account Doesn't Have to Be Out of Your Reach" in *Entrepreneur*
Pub: Entrepreneur Media Inc.
Ed: Barry Farber. **Description:** Five strategies to increase sales, and land large accounts, are examined.

27839 ■ **"The Big Disconnect"** in *Barron's* (Vol. 82, No. 59, February 24, 2003, pp. T1)
Pub: Barron's
Ed: Eric J. Savitz. Description: The technology industry is fundamentally weak, and a recent rally is not likely to provide long-term relief to the industry. Several inventions introduced at a February 2003 Demo conference are described.

27840 ■ **"Big Gulp"** in *Forbes* (Vol. 175, January 10, 2005, No. 1, pp. 68)
Pub: Forbes Magazine Inc.
Ed: Lea Goldman. Description: Profile of Richard Sands, CEO of Constellation Brands, the largest producer of wine worldwide. Sands grew the company to $3.8 billion in sales of wine and spirits. Statistical data included.

27841 ■ **"Big Ideas for Small Biz"** in *Small Business Opportunities* (Vol. 16, No. 1, January 2004, pp. 92)
Pub: Harris Publications, Inc.
Ed: James Feldman. Description: Four ways to be innovative and creative with a small business include fostering a business climate, becoming number one with clients, creating a partnership with clients, and a partnership with employees.

27842 ■ **"The Big Picture"** in *Fast Company* (November 2001, pp. 134)
Pub: Fast Company
Ed: George Anders. Description: The five technologies that are gaining universal acceptance and massive impact are profiled.

27843 ■ **"Big Plans on the Drawing Board"** in *Boston Business Journal* (Vol. 22, No. 16, May 24, 200)
Pub: MCP, Inc.
Ed: Bill Archambeault. Description: Profile of Steffian Bradley, CEO of Kurt Rockstroh, who is managing the company's international expansion.

27844 ■ **"Big Plans"** in *Entrepreneur* (Vol. 30, No. 2, February 2002, p)
Pub: Entrepreneur Media Inc.
Ed: Aliza Pilar Sherman. Description: A report released in late 2001 by the Center for Women's Business Research (formerly the National Foundation for Women Business Owners), states that women-owned firms formed in the last decade are more growth-oriented than their predecessors.

27845 ■ **"The Big Squeeze Part II: How VC Firms Are Coping"** in *Venture Capital Journal* (Vol. 42, No. 5, May 2002, pp. 27, 29-31)
Pub: Thomas Venture Economics
Ed: Dan Primack. Description: Venture capitalists have been advising fiscal discipline to portfolio companies for two years, and now see they need to take their own advice for their firms.

27846 ■ **"The Big Squeeze"** in *Venture Capital Journal* (Vol. 42, No. 5, May 2002, pp. 20-26)
Pub: Thomas Venture Economics
Ed: Dan Primack. Description: Market pressures have forced most banks, venture firms, technology companies to scale back and slow growth.

27847 ■ *Bigger Isn't Always Better*
Pub: AMACOM
Ed: Robert M. Tomasko. Price: $24.95.

27848 ■ **"Biotech Crops Turn into Growing Field"** in *Altanta Journal-Constitution* (January 20, 2007)
Pub: Cox Newspapers, Inc.
Ed: Mike Toner. Description: According to industry experts, farmers planed genetically modified crops on millions of acres in 2006.

27849 ■ **"Blazing New Trails"** in *Black Enterprise* (Vol. 35, October 2004, No. 3, pp. 145)
Pub: Earl G. Graves Publishing Co. Inc.

Ed: Nkechi I. Olisemeka. Description: Winners of the 2004 Black Enterprise Small Business Awards are profiled. These entrepreneurs help redefine small business excellence for black companies.

27850 ■ **"The Bleeding-Heart Rationalist: William Morris b. 1911"** in *New York Times* (December 31, 2006, pp. 14)
Pub: New York Times Company
Ed: Walter Kirn. Description: Profile of William Norris, founder of Control Data Corporation, now defunct, but at one time, one of the nation's largest computer manufacturing companies. Norris also founded an institute that promoted education and small business growth.

27851 ■ **"Blight Busters puts $1.6M into theater plan"** in *Crain's Detroit Business* (Vol. 19, No. 6, February 10, 2003, pp. 25)
Pub: Crain Communications Inc., Detroit
Ed: Robert Ankeny. Description: Redford Township, Michigan will soon enjoy a 350-seat community auditorium, part of major restoration being done to a city landmark.

27852 ■ **"Blip in auto sales could spell doom for suppliers"** in *Crain's Detroit Business* (Vol. 19, No. 3, January 20, 2003, pp. 1)
Pub: Crain Communications Inc., Detroit
Ed: Amy Wilson. Description: Analysts predict a drop in new car sales by 1 million or more vehicles in 2003, resulting in the loss of nearly 6 percent of parts suppliers, with some of the industry's larger suppliers among those businesses failing.

27853 ■ **"The Blush Is Off As Consumers Pick Variety in Flowers for Valentine's Day"** in *Boston Globe* (February 11, 2005)
Pub: New York Times Company
Ed: Chris Reidy. Description: Roses are no longer the first choice for Valentine's Day flowers. Consumers are choosing tulips, orchids, or mixed arrangements in favorite colors. Imports account for 70 percent of fresh flowers sold in the U.S. and account for the new choices.

27854 ■ **"Boat Gambling"** in *Forbes* (Vol. 174, December 27, 2004, No. 13, pp. 90)
Pub: Forbes Magazine Inc.
Ed: Andrew T. Gillies. Description: Net income for ship owners is expected to rise in 2005. A steady growth in demand for oil tankers is expected. Investors predict cargo hauling operations to grow in the next few years.

27855 ■ **"Bob Mathews sees reduced activity, but steady demand"** in *Atlanta Business Chronicle* (Vol. 24, No. 14, September 7, 2001, pp. 5C)
Pub: American City Business Journals Inc.
Description: Bob Mathews, executive vice president of Colliers Cauble & Company, talks about his career and changes he has seen in the market. Various questions asked deal with his career in real estate, changes in financing, and sub-market activity. Mathews is also the Atlanta Commercial Board of Realtors' president.

27856 ■ **"BofA Cutting 70 Charlotte Tech Jobs"** in *Charlotte Observer* (January 31, 2007)
Pub: Knight-Ridder/Tribune Business News
Ed: Rick Rothacker. Description: Bank of America announced the elimination of 70 technology positions at their Charlotte, North Carolina facility. The move is part of the company's effort to increase efficiency.

27857 ■ **"Boise fitness centers brace for challenge from Gold's Gym"** in *Vancouver Business Journal* (December 2, 2002)
Pub: Dolan Media Newswires
Ed: Steve Martin. Description: Profile of Gold's Gyms, and its expansion, particularly in the Boise, Idaho area. Gold's Gyms are working to stay current with workout trends, including not only free-weights and workout machines, but martial arts, tanning and massage, child-care, Pilates, yoga, even specific exercise regimens for golfers, etc.

27858 ■ **"Boldness and prudence can accelerate business growth"** in *Ingram's* (Vol. 28, No. 3, March 2002, pp. 21)
Pub: Show Me Publishing, Inc.
Ed: J. Chris Snedeker. Description: Small business owners are challenged daily to balance boldness with prudence; when taking bold marketing initiatives, the company's bottom line should be kept in mind.

27859 ■ **"Boom: Marketing to the Ultimate Power Consumer"** in *Marketing to Women* (Vol. 20, January 2007, No. 1, pp. 6)
Pub: EPM Communications, Inc.
Ed: Mary Brown; Carol Osborn. Description: The Baby Boomer woman has emerged as a leader in driving the marketplace. Carol Osborn, the co-author of Boom explains this phenomenon.

27860 ■ **"Borders: New stores, efficiencies help improve financial picture"** in *Crain's Detroit Business* (Vol. 19, No. 11, March 17, 2003)
Pub: Crain Communications Inc., Detroit
Ed: Brent Snavely. Description: Borders Group Inc. announced an increase in net income in the fourth quarter 2002. Borders credits new stores and efficient management for the increase.

27861 ■ **"Born Leaders? Learn to be the leader of your pack"** in *My Business* (April/May 2003, pp. 42)
Pub: My Business Magazine
Ed: Mardy Fones. Description: The success of any small business is directly related to its owner.

27862 ■ **"Bosch posts sales spike but expects tighter 2003"** in *Crain's Detroit Business* (Vol. 19, No. 12, March 24, 2003, pp. 14)
Pub: Crain Communications Inc., Detroit
Ed: Julie Cantwell. Description: The Robert Bosch Corporation saw a 7.1 percent increase in its automotive sales due to customer incentives in the last quarter of 2002. The automotive supplier expects to see a slowdown in 2003.

27863 ■ **"The Boston Globe Downtown Column"** in *Boston Globe* (April 11, 2003)
Pub: Knight-Ridder/Tribune Business News
Ed: Steve Bailey. Description: Profile of the Massachusetts Convention Center Authority and its planned development.

27864 ■ **"Bottom feeding for blockbuster businesses"** in *Harvard Business Review* (Vol. 81, No. 3, March 2003, pp. 52)
Pub: Harvard Business School Press
Ed: David Rosenblum, Doug Tomlinson, Larry Scott. Description: Research shows that companies can make profits from customers that are momentarily unprofitable and executives should ask themselves how they can make money from customers shunned by others, such as by serving small businesses that can't afford expensive services.

27865 ■ **"Boudin Rises, Again; Bakery Restaurant Set for Suburban Return"** in *Crain's Chicago Business* (Vol. 30, January 2007, No. 4, pp. 13)
Pub: Crain Communications, Inc.
Ed: H. Lee Murphy. Description: Boudin Bakery is returning to Chicago after a five-year absence. The company is expanding to include a sister Italian chain, Go Roma.

27866 ■ **"Bound by the Long View"** in *Business Journal-Milwaukee* (Vol. 20, No. 48, August 15, 2003, pp. A25)
Pub: American City Business Journals, Inc.
Ed: Becca Mader. Description: A children's bookbinder and distributor, Demco Media Ltd., has moved to a new facility as part of its expansion plan. Demco Media, led by Brendan Wall, has leased a small part of a new $3 million, 200,000-square foot warehouse and manufacturing complex.

27867 ■ "Bradenton Central CRA To Launch New Business Development Center" in *Bradenton Herald* (January 29, 2005)
Pub: Bradenton Herald
Ed: Tim W. McCann. **Description:** The Bradenton Central Community Redevelopment Agency is working to grow the economy of the area. The Agency will create a small business center with a professional counselor to assist small business owners in applying for a business loan, advertising, marketing and legal issues.

27868 ■ "A Brand to Unify the Region" in *Milwaukee Journal Sentinel* (December 15, 2005)
Pub: Journal Sentinel, Inc.
Ed: Rick Romell. **Description:** Newly formed Milwaukee Regional Economic Development Council has designated the seven area counties as "Milwaukee 7" in order to unite the communities into an economic unit that will attract and retain business growth in the region.

27869 ■ "Breadth of World Housing Boom Stuns Analysts" in *Milwaukee Journal Sentinel* (December 4, 2005)
Pub: Journal Sentinel, Inc.
Ed: Michele Derus. **Description:** According to the Organization for Economic Cooperation and Development, 18 regions in the world are experiencing a ten-year housing boom, setting a record. Statistical details included.

27870 ■ "Breakfast Yogurt" in *Dairy Foods* (Vol. 103, No. 10, October 2002, pp. 12)
Pub: Business News Publishing Co.
Description: Profile of Dean Foods Company, Dallas, Texas, and their new yogurt sticks for breakfast and snacks.

27871 ■ "Breaking out" in *Barron's* (Vol. 82, No. 58, February 17, 2003, pp. 23)
Pub: Barron's
Ed: Rhonda Brammer. **Description:** Lifetime Hoan's household wares is enjoying steady sales growth and improving margins, making its share of $5 a good value. The only stock sector to enjoy a positive mark in January 2003 was high tech.

27872 ■ "Breakthroughs for black-owned agencies" in *BlackEnterprise* (Vol. 32, No. 2, September 2001, pp. 21)
Pub: Earl Graves Publishing Co.
Ed: Lloyd Gite. **Description:** Don Coleman and Burrell, two of the nation's largest black-owned advertising agencies made breakthroughs in the advertising industry by scoring major contracts with Kmart and General Mills, respectively.

27873 ■ "Brick by brick" in *Crain's Detroit Business* (Vol. 19, No. 12, March 24, 2003, pp. 3)
Pub: Crain Communications Inc., Detroit
Ed: Robert Ankeny. **Description:** In order to pick up the slack from lagging government funding for redevelopment projects in the city of Detroit, foundations and corporations are increasing support.

27874 ■ "Briefing: Semiconductors" in *Red Herring* (No. 99, June 15 & July 1, 2001, pp. 100-101)
Pub: Herring Communications
Ed: Dean Takahashi. **Description:** An overview of the downturn in the high tech sector.

27875 ■ "Bright Signs for 2004" in *My Business* (February/March 2004, pp. 44)
Pub: My Business Magazine
Ed: Bill Dunkelberg. **Description:** The National Federation of Independent Business' (NFIBs) Small Business Optimism Index reached its highest levels in third and fourth quarters of 2003. Real output in the economy grew at an 8 percent annual rate in third quarter, attributed to child tax credits that were probably spent in that quarter.

27876 ■ "Brighton, Howell Hope Plans Boost Retail" in *Crain's Detroit Business* (Vol. 21, January 17, 2005, No. 3, pp. 28)
Pub: Crain Communications Inc. - Detroit
Ed: Sheena Harrison. **Description:** Plans by Livingston County Communities, Brighton and Howell, are underway to attract new businesses. Road construction, new signs, and beautification projects are some of the improvements planned for retail growth in the area.

27877 ■ "Broadband Access" in *Hispanic Business* (March 2005, pp. 14)
Pub: Hispanic Business
Description: According to a study by the Tomas Rivera Policy Institute, increasing broadband access to African Americans and Hispanics could equate to as much as $74 million in monthly revenue for technology providers.

27878 ■ "Broadband Internet access" in *Red Herring* (No. 105, October 1, 2001, pp. 34)
Pub: Herring Communications
Ed: Mark A. Mowrey. **Description:** According to a report by the Federal Communications Commission in August 2001, 96 percent of the U.S. population lives in the 75 percent of zip codes where at least one broadband provider offers service. Statistical data included.

27879 ■ "Bryson Buys Two Agencies" in *Mississippi Business Journal* (Vol. 29, January 2007, No. 2, pp. 8)
Pub: Venture Publications, Inc.
Ed: Wally Northway **Description:** Bryson Insurance acquires Banks Insurance and Shackleford Brothers & Fortenberry.

27880 ■ "Buckle up" in *Atlanta Business Chronicle* (Vol. 23, No. 30, December 29, 2000, pp. 27A)
Pub: American City Business Journals Inc.
Ed: Chaundra Frierson. **Description:** Economic forecasts and trends in consumer spending show that the economy is approaching a slowdown which will test newer businesses. Some strategies in order to survive tough times include using a conservative budget and keeping inventories low.

27881 ■ "The Bucks Start Here" in *Business Week* (No. 3658, December 6, 1999, pp. F10)
Pub: McGraw-Hill, Inc.
Description: Small, fast growing companies are investing in their businesses without taking out new bank loans to do it. As bank rates rise and profit margins remain strong, these companies are choosing to finance growth from their own cash flow.

27882 ■ "Build a Better Business" in *Black Enterprise* (Vol. 35, October 2004, No. 3, pp. 136)
Pub: Earl G. Graves Publishing Co. Inc.
Ed: Robert Anthony, Sonya A. Donaldson. **Description:** Emerging new technologies can help small businesses seem larger than they really are. Co-founder of Krazy Kickz, Sam Robinson, tells how upgrading the company's phone system led to a better customer service system.

27883 ■ "Build Your Business with eBay" in *Home Business* (Vol. 13, January/February 2006, No. 1, pp. 58, 60)
Pub: Home Business Magazine
Description: According to the American Business Association, consumers are using online markets as a convenient way to buy products. Small companies should diversify into the online sector as a means to grow a business. Tips for opening an online shop are outlined.

27884 ■ "Builder plans $80M in homes; Majority are proposed for Macomb County" in *Crain's Detroit Business* (Vol. 19, Jan. 13, 2003, pp. 3)
Pub: Crain Communications Inc., Detroit
Ed: Jennette Smith. **Description:** Profile of Lombardo Company, a developer planning to launch several home construction and condominium projects in Macomb County, Michigan.

27885 ■ "Building Boom Hits Homestead" in *South Florida Business Journal* (Vol. 23, No. 48, July 4, 2003, pp. 1)
Pub: American City Business Journals
Ed: Paola Iuspa-Abbott. **Description:** The Homestead, Florida area is experiencing a land rush. Former groves and vegetable fields are being replaced with tract homes. Land values have doubled in the last few years. Lennar Corporation plans to build about 1,500 homes in the area.

27886 ■ "Building a collection" in *Crain's Detroit Business* (Vol. 19, No. 6, February 10, 2003, pp. 1)
Pub: Crain Communications Inc., Detroit
Ed: Brent Snavely. **Description:** The Suburban Collection's auto dealerships now comprise the largest privately held dealership chain in Michigan.

27887 ■ "Building vital region requires teamwork" in *Crain's Detroit Business* (Vol. 19, No. 17, April 28, 2003, pp. 9)
Pub: Crain Communications Inc., Detroit
Ed: Richard Rassel. **Description:** The necessary upgrades needed to establish the Detroit region as a competitive economic region are discussed, including the importance for lawmakers to work together for a common goal.

27888 ■ "Building Your Business" in *Small Business Opportunities* (Vol. 17, May 2005, No. 3, pp. 12)
Pub: Harris Publications Inc.
Ed: Carla Longley Vincent. **Description:** Seven ways for a small business to tap into customers and increase profits include the development of alliances, franchising, adding wholesale clients, sell to the government, work with nonprofits, market yourself, and create new goods or services.

27889 ■ "Bullish on minority business: MBDA director sees better days ahead" in *Black Enterprise* (Vol. 32, No. 8, March 2002, pp. 28)
Pub: Earl Graves Publishing Co.
Description: Despite the slow economy, Ronald N. Langston, national director of the Minority Business Development Agency, states that minority businesses across the board have been expanding and growing.

27890 ■ "Bunny Money" in *Entrepreneur* (Vol. 30, No. 3, March 2002)
Pub: Entrepreneur Media Inc.
Ed: Michelle Prather. **Description:** Gift basket retailers, as well as gift shops, are expecting higher profits on Easter sales this year.

27891 ■ "Burst of Energy" in *Entrepreneur. com* (Vol. 34, February 2006, No. 2, pp. 46)
Pub: Entrepreneur Media Inc.
Ed: Kristin Ohlson. **Description:** Renewable, clean energy is a growing sector. Liquid Resources produces nearly 3 million gallons of ethanol annually, with water as its only waste product.

27892 ■ "Busch Gardens Sees 2005 Attendance Grow" in *Tampa Tribune* (December 28, 2005)
Pub: Media General, Inc.
Ed: Randy Diamond. **Description:** Busch Gardens amusement park is crediting its new SheiKra roller coaster for a 4.9 percent increase in attendance in 2005. Overall, the top amusement parks in North America reported increases for 2005 at 4.1 percent. These increases are the first seen since the September 11 terrorist attacks.

27893 ■ "Bush Growth Package Boost for Main Street" in *My Business* (April/May 2003, pp. 19)
Pub: My Business Magazine
Description: President Bush's recently unveiled growth package could offer tax relief to small business owners by increasing expensing limits and reducing individual income taxes.

27894 ■ "Bush talks up small business tax relief" in *Tax Notes* **(Vol. 97, No. 9, December 2, 2002, pp. 1135-1136)**
Pub: Tax Notes International
Ed: Patti Mohr. **Description:** President George W. Bush urged lawmakers to lessen the tax burden on small businesses and make the relevant regulations simpler. Bush said that tax cuts would boost the economy and add more jobs.

27895 ■ "Business Buzz" in *Tribune* **(March 11, 2005)**
Pub: Knight-Ridder/Tribune Business News
Description: America West Airlines added another regional flight to Phoenix, Arizona, making business travel to the city more accessible.

27896 ■ "Business Development through Philanthropy" in *Ingram's* **(Vol. 27, No. 12, December 2001, pp. 23)**
Pub: Show Me Publishing, Inc.
Description: The use of philanthropy for business development is discussed. As a business owner, this activity will improve company image and expand networking opportunities.

27897 ■ "Business Diary" in *Crain's Detroit Business* **(Vol. 19, No. 15, April 14, 2003, pp. 20)**
Pub: Crain Communications Inc., Detroit
Description: Recent acquisitions, nominations for the United Way Volunteer Center of Oakland County's Home Town Business Champion Award, and area contracts are topics covered.

27898 ■ "Business Digest" in *Salt Lake Tribune* **(February 24, 2005)**
Pub: Knight-Ridder/Tribune Business News
Ed: Mike Gorrell. **Description:** Utah hotels are experiencing record numbers with 57.6 percent occupancy rates reported for January 2005, nearly 4 percent higher than last year; Salt Lake City hotels were higher at 64.7 percent in January.

27899 ■ "The Business of Fitness" in *Birmingham Business Journal* **(Vol. 20, No. 31, August 1, 2003, pp. 11)**
Pub: American City Business Journals, Inc.
Ed: Lauren Bishop. **Description:** Fitness Together, a personal training company, is expanding its franchise in Alabama and North Carolina under the leadership of Forrest Walden and Aaron Crocker. Fitness Together is owned by Castlerock, the Colorado-based Fitness for Life Franchise Corporation.

27900 ■ "Business Groups Divided Over Cuts to MEDC Funding" in *Crain's Detroit Business* **(Vol. 19, No. 17, April 28, 2003, pp. 6)**
Pub: Crain Communications Inc., Detroit
Description: The Michigan Manufacturers Association, the Detroit Regional Chamber and eight other local chambers have formed a new coalition to urge lawmakers to not go beyond Governor Granholm's recommended reductions in the budget of the Michigan Economic Development Corporation because it would damage the state's ability to compete for business investments and jobs.

27901 ■ "Business Integrator Entrepreneur Marries Technology and Advertising to Grow Business" in *Black Enterprise* **(Vol. 35, Jan. 2005, No. 6)**
Pub: Earl G. Graves Publishing Co. Inc.
Ed: Nichole Lewis. **Description:** Interactive marketing strategies have helped POWERi to grow in the travel and tourism industry despite a slowdown since the terrorist attacks of 9-11. The firm operates three lines of business: technology within an advertising agency that could also provide marketing strategy and graphic design services. The firm reported revenues of $1 million in 2003.

27902 ■ "Business Is Booming - How Do You Keep up?" in *Women In Business* **(Vol. 52, No. 2, March 2000, pp. 42)**
Pub: The ABWA Co., Inc.
Ed: Jane Thomas. **Description:** Businesses need to plan in order to manage expansion successfully. There are various sources of information on this topic.

27903 ■ "Business Models: SSPs adapt to market change" in *Red Herring* **(No. 105, October 1, 2001, pp. 84)**
Pub: Herring Communications
Ed: Jennifer Lewis. **Description:** Global growth for the storage utility market is expected to grow to over $6 billion in the U.S., around $9 billion in Europe, over $12 billion in Canada, and more than $14 billion in the rest of the world by the year 2005.

27904 ■ "The Business of Nanotech" in *Business Week* **(February 14, 2005, No. 3920, pp. 64)**
Pub: McGraw-Hill Companies
Ed: Stephen Baker, Adam Aston. **Description:** Soon cars, chips and even golf balls will be produced using new materials engineered down to the level of individual atoms. Some 1,200 nano startups have emerged globally.

27905 ■ "Business Owners Frown on Economic Ills" in *Pittsburgh Business Times* **(Vol. 22, No. 4, August 16, 2002, pp. 3)**
Pub: Pittsburgh Business Times
Ed: Kent Bernhard, Jr. **Description:** A new survey on small businesses, which was conducted by American City Business Journal, has found that the national economic downturn is influencing expansion planning.

27906 ■ *Business Statistics*
Pub: Mosby Year Book, Inc.
Released: 1996. **Price:** $46.95.

27907 ■ *Business Statistics of the United States*
Pub: Bernan Press
Ed: Courtenay M. Slater. **Released:** 1995. **Price:** $49.00.

27908 ■ "The Business Week News You Need to Know" in *Business Week* **(January 23, 2006, No. 3968, pp. 30-31)**
Pub: McGraw-Hill Companies
Ed: Harry Maurer. **Description:** News about the Detroit Auto Show, job growth, Home Depot's expansion plans, Internet search engines, new executive pay rules, the stock market, and more.

27909 ■ "Businesses Assessing Granholm's Plans for SBT Overhaul" in *Crain's Detroit Business* **(Vol. 21, January 31, 2005, No. 5, pp. 6)**
Pub: Crain Communications Inc. - Detroit
Ed: Amy Lane. **Description:** Under a business-tax proposal, Michigan's single-business tax will not expire at the end of 2009. The pros and cons of this move are discussed with business experts from the state.

27910 ■ "Businesses Have Faith in the Economy's Resiliency" in *Kiplinger Letter* **(Vol. 78, January 5, 2007, No. 1)**
Pub: Kiplinger
Description: Businesses added an additional 167,000 workers in December 2006, and unemployment at a low 4.5 percent. The Federal Reserve is expected to keep interest rates steady most of 2007.

27911 ■ "Businesses push better public transit" in *Crain's Detroit Business* **(Vol. 19, No. 17, April 28, 2003, pp. 18)**
Pub: Crain Communications Inc., Detroit
Ed: Terry Kosdrosky. **Description:** Detroit area businesses are pushing for legislation to establish an authority to oversee the Detroit and suburban bus systems.

27912 ■ "Butler, Wis., Printing Plant Expands Operations" in *Milwaukee Journal Sentinel* **(December 17, 2005)**
Pub: Journal Sentinel, Inc.
Ed: Joel Dresang. **Description:** Ries Graphics expanded its printing plant in Butler, Wisconsin by adding new equipment and employees in the hopes of increasing sales. The family-owned business is celebrating its 90th year with the $5 million expansion.

27913 ■ "Buy, buy biotech?" in *Entrepreneur* **(Vol. 30, No. 3, March 2002, pp. 72)**
Pub: Entrepreneur Media Inc.
Ed: Jennifer Pellet. **Description:** Despite the warnings about bioterrorism, experts warn that biotech firms are difficult to evaluate before investing.

27914 ■ "Buyers Gain Upper Hand as House Sales Decline" in *Sacramento Bee* **(November 18, 2005)**
Pub: The Sacramento Bee
Ed: Andrew Lepage. **Description:** With sales falling to 2,801 in October, Sacramento's housing sector is truly a buyer's market. The decline, the lowest in four years, cuts across homes in all price categories.

27915 ■ "Cabela's reels in local developer to Dundee" in *Crain's Detroit Business* **(Vol. 19, No. 15, April 14, 2003, pp. 1)**
Pub: Crain Communications Inc., Detroit
Ed: Jennette Smith. **Description:** Cabela's, the outdoor outfitter, specializing in hunting, fishing and outdoor gear opened in 2000 in the city of Dundee, Michigan. The store is attracting hotels, restaurants and a new Daimler-Chrysler AG plant.

27916 ■ "Cable Networks Help Boost First-Quarter Profit for E.W. Scripps Co." in *Denver Post* **(April 11, 2003)**
Pub: Knight-Ridder/Tribune Business News
Ed: Aldo Svaldi. **Description:** E.W. Scripps Company, parent of the Rocky Mountain News, saw a 32 percent rise in the first quarter 2003, despite a slow growth at the Cincinnati media company's newspapers.

27917 ■ "Cablevision Systems Corp. Tops 1M Interactive Optimum Customers" in *Long Island Business News* **(March 12, 2004)**
Pub: Dolan Media Newswires
Description: Cablevision Systems Corporation began offering digital cable services in 2003; the service, called Interactive Optimum, or iO, currently has one million customers.

27918 ■ "California Lost Jobs in September" in *Sacramento Bee* **(October 22, 2005)**
Pub: The Sacramento Bee
Ed: Dale Kasler. **Description:** Californians saw the first job decline for 2005 in September with unemployment rates falling to 5.1 percent, only a tenth of a point. Economists believe the drop was due mainly from some schools opening earlier than usual.

27919 ■ "California based Robeks Fruit Smoothies Sets Expansion in NY Metro..." in *Long Island Business News* **(Feb.27,2004)**
Pub: Dolan Media Newswires
Ed: Nick Anastasi. **Description:** Profile of Robeks Fruit Smoothies & Healthy Treats, a franchise eatery based in Manhattan Beach, California. Founded in 1995, the franchise currently has 45 stores in three states and expects to expand into 26 metropolitan areas in the U.S.

27920 ■ "Camas, Vancouver advance toward boundary compromise" in *Vancouver, WA Business Journal* **(February 28, 2003)**
Pub: Dolan Media Newswires
Ed: Cami Joner. **Description:** Vancouver and Camas officials are gearing towards a compromise on boundary issues. Both communities wish to expand urban growth boundaries by the same 12 square miles of reserve land. Vancouver officials target the area for job creation with a new industrial base, while Camas officials envision a mix of commercial, industrial and residential use for the land.

27921 ■ "Can Productivity Keep Up the Good Work?" in *Business Week* **(December 19, 2005, No. 3964, pp. 25-26)**
Pub: McGraw-Hill Companies
Ed: James C. Cooper, Kathleen Madigan. **Description:** U.S. productivity is critical to keeping inflation under control. Statistical data included.

27922 ■ "Can the Profit Boom Last? Businesses Have Been Churning Out Earnings" in *Fortune* **(Vol. 152, October 17, 2005, No. 8, pp. 215)**
Pub: Time Inc.
Ed: David Stires. Description: With rising costs in energy and interest rates, coupled with falling consumer confidence, tough times may be ahead for small businesses.

27923 ■ "Can This Duo be Saved? Renovating 2 Tallest Edifices Downtown Will Be Costly, Owner Says" in *Charlotte Observer* **(February 4, 2007)**
Pub: Knight-Ridder/Tribune Business News
Ed: Jefferson George. Description: Gastonia, North Carolina city leaders are making plans to renovate the Lawyers Building and the Commercial Building in an effort to revitalize the downtown area.

27924 ■ "Can This Really Be Hewlett-Packard?" in *Business Week* **(December 19, 2005, No. 3964, pp. 49-50)**
Pub: McGraw-Hill Companies
Ed: Peter Burrows. Description: Hewlett-Packard is running on all cylinders thanks to the reorganization and cost-cutting measures taking by its CEO, Mark V. Hurd. The company can now focus on growth and expansion.

27925 ■ "C&S Marketing to be CoreLogic" in *Sacramento Bee* **(October 25, 2005)**
Pub: The Sacramento Bee
Ed: Dale Kasler. Description: C&S Marketing recently changed its name to CoreLogic. The software maker, located in Sacramento, California, helps mortgage lenders detect fraud and estimate property values and was recently named one of the nation's 500 fastest growing private companies by Inc. magazine.

27926 ■ "Capital City Bank & Trust Co. expands to Albany" in *Atlanta Business Chronicle* **(Vol. 24, No. 8, July 27, 2001, pp. 16A)**
Pub: American City Business Journals Inc.
Ed: Meredith Jordan. Description: Capitol City Bank and Trust Co., an African American bank that promotes small business, will open a branch in Albany. The new Capital City branch, the fifth, will provide jobs for about ten people.

27927 ■ "Capital Crunch" in *Hispanic Business* **(March 2002, pp. 44, 46, 48, 50, 52)**
Pub: Hispanic Business
Ed: Joel Russell. Description: After September 11, federal funds have been shifted from community development to emergency response. A listing of Hispanic nonprofit organizations, located in all 50 states and the District of Columbia, is presented.

27928 ■ "Capital Spending" in *Business Week* **(January 16, 2006, No. 3967, pp. 24)**
Pub: McGraw-Hill Companies
Ed: Description: Recent trends in the industrial sector show that industrial output is growing faster than the rate at which companies are adding to their production capacity, signaling an acceleration in capital spending.

27929 ■ "Caribbean Connection: This Shipping Professional is Taking His Company Overseas" in *Black Enterprise* **(Vol. 34, July 2004, No. 12)**
Pub: Earl G. Graves Publishing Co. Inc.
Ed: Arlene McKanic. Description: Franklin Vieira, CEO of minority owned Caribbean Cargo & Package Services, a shipping firm headquartered at John F. Kennedy International Airport in New York City, is expanding his company overseas. The company's Brooklyn, New York branch also helps individuals and small businesses shipping merchandise to the Caribbean.

27930 ■ "Case Study. Anatomy of a Business Decision" in *Inc.* **(September 2006, pp. 47-48, 50)**
Pub: Gruner & Jahr USA Publishing
Ed: Phaedra Hise. Description: Review and analysis of a downmarketing strategy is detailed in this article.

Small business growth typically moves to higher end customers that are increasingly difficult to please. If it isn't cost effective, going back to the basics of the success of the growth may expand the business and increase profitability.

27931 ■ "Cash is King" in *Fast Company* **(May 2001, pp. 80)**
Pub: Fast Company
Ed: Walter Wriston. Description: Interview with Walter Wriston, former CEO of Citicorp/Citibank. Wriston advises that during economic hard times small businesses need to get back to the basics: inventory control, receivables, payables, and cash flow, the things forgotten during the new economy. Focus on generating cash, and a company will be positioned to take advantage of opportunities that the cash-strapped firms can't afford.

27932 ■ "Catch of the Day: Next up: distributed networks" in *Red Herring* **(No. 103, September 1, 2001, pp. 18)**
Pub: Herring Communications
Ed: Rafe Needleman. Description: The trend of distributed computing is covered. The distributed computing concept can be applied to scarce networking resources, particularly wireless bandwidth, in ways that could drive revenue by encouraging sales of devices for the end user.

27933 ■ "Catch 'Em If You Can" in *Entrepreneur.com* **(Vol. 34, February 2006, No. 2, pp. 90)**
Pub: Entrepreneur Media Inc.
Description: Rankings of the fastest growing 100 U.S. and Canadian franchise opportunities are presented along with contact information.

27934 ■ "Catering Company Expands Operations" in *Bellingham Business Journal* **(December 2006, pp. A6)**
Pub: Sun News Inc.
Description: Ciao Thyme, a catering company owned by Jessica and Mataio Gillis, will be moving to a larger space in March 2007. They plan to add an event space, a small private dining facility and will be offering cooking classes.

27935 ■ "Caution: Merger Ahead" in *Ingram's* **(Vol. 28, No. 9, September 2002, pp. 20)**
Pub: Show Me Publishing, Inc.
Ed: James M. Selle. Description: A guide for considerations when small businesses consider a merger are presented, including issues such as expansion, additional products and/or services, new markets, and a competitor's customers base.

27936 ■ "Centerpoint is sidelined" in *Red Herring* **(March 2003, pp. 67)**
Pub: Herring Communications Inc.
Ed: Om Malik. Description: The demise of Centerpoint Broadband Technologies, a high-profile startup, developing wireless technologies and a new optical-transport mechanism, is chronicled.

27937 ■ "CEO Confidence on the Rise" in *Hispanic Business* **(November 2003, pp. 22)**
Pub: Hispanic Business
Description: CEO's confidence grew significantly in the third quarter 2003, according to the latest TEC Confidence Index, a quarterly survey of chief executives across the nation. The survey covers current economic trends and issues affecting small to medium-sized companies.

27938 ■ "CEO of Fort Lauderdale, Fla., Women's Fitness Chain Creates Smaller Outlets" in *Miami Herald* **(November 11, 2002)**
Pub: Knight Ridder/Tribune Business News
Description: Profile of Roger Wittenberns, the man behind Lady of America fitness centers for women. Wittenberns opened his first women-only fitness center in Houston in 1984, and has expanded to 290 franchise locations to date.

27939 ■ "CEO sells IT company to help it grow" in *Crain's Detroit Business* **(Vol. 18, No.)**
Pub: Crain Communications Inc. - Detroit
Ed: Andrew Dietderich. Description: Ciber Inc. has purchased Southfield, Michigan's Decision Consultants Inc., an information technology services company.

27940 ■ "Chairman Sees T. Rowe Price Group Positioned for Economic Rebound" in *Baltimore Sun* **(April 11, 2003)**
Pub: Knight-Ridder/Tribune Business News
Ed: William Patalon, III. Description: T. Rowe Price, the financial investment firm, is positioned for an economic rebound by the end of 2003. The company's broad mutual fund lineup and diversified business base contributes to the firm's success.

27941 ■ "Change Without Pain" in *Harvard Business Review* **(Vol. 78, No. 4, July 2000, pp. 75)**
Pub: Harvard Business School Publishing Corp.
Ed: Eric Abrahamson. Description: Research shows companies should intersperse major change with smaller, organic change. Cases cited include New York City-based law firm Finley, Kumble, Wagner, Heine, Underberg, Manley, Myerson and Casey and General Electric.

27942 ■ "Charted Territory: Candy Crosses the Border to Open New Doors" in *Entrepreneur* **(Vol. 31, No. 9, September 2003, pp. 85)**
Pub: Entrepreneur Media, Inc.
Ed: April Y. Pennington. Description: Profile of Krave's Candy Company, a Winnipeg, Manitoba, Canada-based candy maker. Wal-Mart USA tested the product, Clodhoppers, during Christmas 2000 and Clodhoppers can now be found in all 2,700 Wal-Mart stores.

27943 ■ "Charter Service Gets OK To Build Hangar At SRQ" in *Bradenton Herald* **(January 25, 2005)**
Pub: Bradenton Herald
Ed: Dana Sanchez. Description: Rectrix Aerodrome Center Inc., a charter and jet management company, will build a hangar at the Sarasota-Bradenton International Airport in Florida. The project is expected to create new jobs, enhance the firm's image, and increase the number of corporate jets managed.

27944 ■ "The chemistry of super-growth" in *Hispanic Business* **(Vol. 21, No. 12, December 1999, pp. 26)**
Pub: Hispanic Business
Ed: Scott Williams. Description: It is becoming increasingly common for firms to focus on what they do best, according to Plaza Group Inc.'s CEO, Randy Velerde. He won the 1999 Hispanic Business Magazine Entrepreneur of the Year Award.

27945 ■ "China" in *Business Week* **(January 23, 2006, No. 3968, pp. 44-45)**
Pub: McGraw-Hill Companies
Ed: Brian Bremner. Description: Citibank has been out-hustled by rivals HSBC, Bank of America, and Goldman Sachs in making deals with large Chinese banking firms. Acquisitions, consumer banking, and corporate clients could help Citi compete.

27946 ■ "China Route Hinges on Biz vs Politics" in *Crain's Detroit Business* **(Vol. 22, September 25-October 1, 2006, No. 39, pp. 1, 40)**
Pub: Crain Communications Inc. - Detroit
Ed: Michelle Martinez. Description: Competition for non-stop airline travel from US to China between four major carriers depends upon a combination of business and politics. Location of connection is in four different cities.

27947 ■ "Chrysler Deal Has SET Looking at Opening New Plant In Ohio" in *Crain's Detroit Business* **(Vol. 21, October 10, 2005, No. 43, pp. 42)**
Pub: Crain Communications Inc. - Detroit

Ed: Terry Kosdrosky. **Description:** After winning a big contract from the Chrysler Group, SET Enterprises Inc. is planning to open a new plant in Cleveland, Ohio. SET is a Warren, Michigan metal processor. The deal will supply steel blanks for the Dodge Durango SUV and Dodge Caravan and Chrysler Town & Country minivans.

27948 ■ **"Chula Vista: Dobson's Has Designs on Eastlake"** in *San Diego Business Journal* **(Vol. 28, January 8, 2007, No. 2, pp. 27)**
Pub: San Diego Business Journal Associates
Ed: Mike Allen. **Description:** Dobson's restaurant is planning to open a new location in the Eastlake Design District in 2007. The upscale restaurant will seat 120 patrons, making it double the size of the original eatery.

27949 ▨ **"Cineplex Galaxy Income Fund Reports Fourth Quarter and Year End Results"** in *Canadian Corporate News* **(February 7, 2007)**
Pub: Comtex News Network, Inc.
Description: Financial results for fourth quarter 2006 were announced by Cineplex Galaxy Income Fund. The fund reported $195 million in revenue, up nearly $2 million for 2005. Statistical data included.

27950 ■ **"Circulation losses continue at most state newspapers"** in *Atlanta Business Chronicle* **(Vol. 25, November 15, 2002, No. 23 pp. 3A)**
Pub: American City Business Publications, Inc.
Ed: Jim Lovel. **Description:** Over the past six months, ten of the sixteen Georgia newspapers reporting to the Audit Bureau of Circulation have lost circulation. For the past ten years, newspaper sales have dropped more than one percent per year, and the trend continues.

27951 ■ **"City Bank Expands as Merger Bid Threatens Branches"** in *Pacific Business News* **(Vol. 41, No. 16, June 27, 2003, pp. 12)**
Pub: American City Business Journals
Ed: Eddy Conway. **Description:** City Bank is fighting a hostile takeover by Central Pacific Bank by opening new branches on Oahu and the big island. If Central Pacific Bank's offer of an exchange of stocks and $70 per share is a success, it plans to shut many of City Banks' branches.

27952 ■ **"Clarion Partners buys 36 buildings in Atlanta"** in *Atlanta Business Chronicle* **(Vol. 25, December 20, 2002, No. 28, pp. 14A)**
Pub: American City Business Publications, Inc.
Ed: Jarred Schenke. **Description:** Clarion Partners has acquired a total of 36 buildings in the Atlanta, Georgia area from Crow Holdings Industrial Trust, as part of a larger, nationwide purchase of 287 industrial properties valued at $1.6 million from Crow. The total purchase covers more than 320 acres of land zoned for industry, covering over 35 million square feet.

27953 ■ **"Clean-Water Company Begins a Growth Spurt"** in *Portland Press Herald* **(April 22, 2005)**
Pub: Blethen Maine Newspapers, Inc.
Ed: Matt Wickenheiser. **Description:** Vortechnics acquired Stormwater Management Inc. a competitor located in Portland, Oregon. Vortechnics makes systems that clean storm water runoff from parking lots, roads and other surfaces. Vortechnics CEO, David Miley, believes the company is a good example of how small businesses can grow.

27954 ■ **"Cleanup Delays Lessens Katrina's Economic Toll, Economist Says"** in *Milwaukee Journal Sentinel* **(December 21, 2005)**
Pub: Journal Sentinel, Inc.
Ed: Michele Derus. **Description:** According to experts, the longer the recovery from Hurricane Katrina takes the less impact it will have on the U.S. economy. These delays will help U.S. markets to absorb the huge reconstruction needs, including the construction of nearly 300,000 homes. It is predicted that 2006 Gross Domestic Product will increase 3.8 to 4.3 percent.

27955 ■ **"Clear Sailing"** in *Refrigerated & Frozen Foods* **(Vol. 14, No. 7, July 2003, pp. 19)**
Pub: Stagnito Communications
Ed: Bob Garrison. **Description:** Profile of Kahiki Foods, covering the company's history and success at becoming one of the nation's largest frozen Asian food processors.

27956 ▨ **"Clicking for Cash"** in *Business Week* **(No. 3698, September 11, 2000, pp. F37)**
Pub: McGraw-Hill, Inc.
Description: Small businesses turn to online finance companies for loans and credit.

27957 ■ **"Clicks to Bricks"** in *Entrepreneur* **(Vol. 33, August 2005, No. 8, pp. 44)**
Pub: Entrepreneur Media Inc.
Ed: Melissa Campanelli. **Description:** Following a current trend, more e-tailers are opening brick-and-mortar stores. This move will strengthen brand-name recognition, give local customers a place to shop or return merchandise, lower promotional fees, and expand a customer base.

27958 ▨ **"Close the Loop"** in *Entrepreneur* **(Vol. 31, No. 10, October 2003, pp. 82)**
Pub: Entrepreneur Media, Inc.
Ed: Chris Penttila. **Description:** Today companies can outsource most types of work, a trend entrepreneurs are using to grow their business.

27959 ▨ **"Closing Raises Loan Questions"** in *Pittsburgh Business Times* **(Vol. 23, No. 3, August 8, 2003, pp. 1)**
Pub: Pittsburgh Business Times
Ed: Tim Schooley, Suzanne Elliott. **Description:** May Department Stores Company announced the closing of its Lord and Taylor store in downtown Pittsburgh, Pennsylvania. The city council has accepted that it will not be repaid the $11.75 million loan it made to the May Company upon the store's opening three years ago.

27960 ■ **"CMGI Ventures Streamlines Operations"** in *Venture Capital Journa l* **(Vol. 40, No. 10, October 2000, pp. 5-6)**
Pub: Venture Economics
Description: The Internet operating and development company CMGI Inc., outlines its plans to overhaul its 17 majority-owned operating companies and Ventures investing affiliate into six official business lines.

27961 ■ **"Coming Back to Life"** in *Fortune* **(Vol. 152, October 3, 2005, No. 7, pp. 64)**
Pub: Time Inc.
Ed: Description: The resiliency of the U.S. economy is explored, along with the recovery efforts in the Gulf Coast region after Hurricane Katrina.

27962 ▨ **"Coming Up Short on Nonfinancial Performance Measurement"** in *Harvard Business Review* **(Vol. 81, No. 11, November 2003, pp. 88)**
Pub: Harvard Business School Press
Ed: Christopher D. Ittner, David F. Larcker. **Description:** The influence of non-financial performance criteria, such as customer loyalty and corporate profits is examined.

27963 ▨ *Common Sense Business: Starting, Operating, and Growing Your Small Business-In Any Economy!*
Pub: HarperCollins Publishers, Inc.
Ed: Steve Gottry. **Released:** July 2006. **Price:** $13.95. **Description:** Ideas are offered to help entrepreneurs start and manage a company.

27964 ■ **"Common Sense Still Rules in the Heartland"** in *Ingram's* **(Vol. 28, No. 5, May 2002, pp. 37)**
Pub: Show Me Publishing, Inc.
Ed: Jack Cashill. **Description:** Profile of Pat McCown and Brett Gordon, who build McCown Gordon Construction LLC, a company based not on project but relationships. McCown Gordon is now one of the top 20 construction companies in Kansas City.

27965 ■ **"The Companies"** in *Inc.* **(October 17, 1999, pp. 57)**
Pub: The Goldhirsh Group
Description: A listing of the top employers in the United States, with statistics including the number of full-time employees, company benchmarks for the year, HR policies, customer information, and global trends. Also listed are the number of companies that made the Inc. 500 last year, those that broke $100 million in sales, and which ones are only five years old.

27966 ■ **"Compare Your Clicks: www. compareyourclicks.com"** in *Entrepreneur* **(Vol. 32, November 2004, No. 11, pp. 6)**
Pub: Entrepreneur Media Inc.
Ed: Steve Cooper. **Description:** Profile of Compare Your Clicks, an online resource that lets marketers run live comparisons of keyword bid prices at multiple search engines.

27967 ▨ *The Complete Demographic Reference Guide*
Pub: Urban Decision Systems
Released: 1992. **Price:** $195.00. **Description:** Guide providing demographic information for evaluating potential sites and determining target markets. Includes income, households, population, race, male/female ratio, occupation, and ranking tables for every U.S. ZIP code.

27968 ■ **"Confidence is key: economist cites the importance of business outlook to recovery"** in *Black Enterprise* **(Vol. 33, No. 6, Jan. 2003)**
Pub: Earl Graves Publishing Co.
Ed: Thomas Boston. **Description:** The Gazelle Index, a survey of 350 of the nation's fastest growing black-owned businesses, measured by workforce growth rates, took a sharp plunge, from 67.7 to 49.5 during second and third quarters. Business owners become more negative about economic conditions when readings fall below 50.

27969 ■ **"Connecting Firms with Needed Funds; Financial Assistance"** in *Crain's New York Business* **(Vol. 22, November 13, 2006, No. 46, pp. 32)**
Pub: Crain Communications, Inc.
Description: Listing of organizations that provide incentives or financial assistance to firms that are based in New York or are relocating to the area.

27970 ■ **"Connections for Business"** in *Black Enterprise* **(Vol. 35, November 2004, No. 4, pp. 81)**
Pub: Earl G. Graves Publishing Co. Inc.
Ed: Matthew S. Scott. **Description:** Profile of Hamet Watt, former partner in a North Carolina venture capital firm called New Africa Opportunity Fund, that helps black and minority-owned companies secure funding. Four years later Watt joined NextMedium, but is also committed to mentoring minority entrepreneurs.

27971 ■ **"Consensus forecasts of financial institutions"** in *Journal of Business Forecasting* **(Vol. 19, No. 2, Summer 2000, pp. 37)**
Pub: Graceway Publishing Co., Inc.
Ed: Dennis F. Ellis. **Description:** Forecasts for the U.S. economy for the last quarter of 2000 and the first three quarters of 2001 are presented. It is predicted that the growth of the economy will slow down during this period.

27972 ■ **"Consider the recession over"** in *My Business* **(April/May 2002, pp. 49)**
Pub: My Business Magazine
Ed: Bill Dunkelberg. **Description:** Fourth quarter 2001 Gross Domestic Product results showed a 1.4 percent annual rate of growth. Statistical information on small business optimism, inventory plans, and sales expectations are included.

27973 ■ **"Consorting with Competitors"** in *Harvard Business Review* **(Vol. 80, No. 1, January 2002, pp. 21)**
Pub: Harvard Business School Press
Ed: Christopher Kurt. **Description:** Personal insight is given into forming industry consortia, using specifica-

tions called Universal Description, Discover, and Integration (UDDI). UDDI allows for integrations of ideas electronically via a directory, and keeps the consortia on track.

27974 ■ "Construction in the Fast Mode" in *Hispanic Business* **(Vol. 23, No. 7/8, July/August 2001, pp. 44, 46, 48, 50, 52, 54, 56)**
Pub: Hispanic Business
Ed: Joel Russell. **Description:** Aggressive builders gain momentum during good times and keep it going when the economy slows. Statistical data included.

27975 ■ "Continental Airlines' Deb Rating Suffers Another Blow" in *Houston Chronicle* **(April 11, 2003)**
Pub: Knight-Ridder/Tribune Business News
Ed: Bill Hensel. **Description:** A discussion into Continental Airline's credit rating being lowered in April 2003, by Moody's Investors Service is presented. The move cited weak air travel demand and falling revenues.

27976 ■ "The Contrarian: Want a hot tip? Avoid JagNotes.com" in *Red Herring* **(No. 102, August 15, 2001, pp. 88)**
Pub: Herring Communications
Ed: Christopher Byron. **Description:** Profile of JagNotes.com, the Web-based streaming-video service.

27977 ■ "Control Your Content" in *E-business Advisor* **(Vol. 18, No. 10, October 2000, pp. 42)**
Pub: Advisor Media, Inc.
Ed: Andre McMillan. **Description:** As a business Web site grows, so does the need for managing the content of the site. This article explores content management and how it differs from document management. The author strongly urges that before products are purchased, there be an advisory board for continuing management and operational committees that can help determine need.

27978 ■ "A Conversation With Steve Cassin, Macomb County Director of Planning and Economic Development" in *Crain's Detroit Business* **(Vol. 21)**
Pub: Crain Communications Inc. - Detroit
Ed: Anjali Fluker. **Description:** In an interview with Steve Cassin, director of planning and economic development for Macomb County, Michigan, he talks about the challenges and initiatives his county is taking on in a move to attract new business to the area.

27979 ■ "Corporate Coffers Full of Cash" in *Kansas City Star* **(March 8, 2005)**
Pub: Knight-Ridder/Tribune Business News
Ed: Chris Lester. **Description:** Corporate finances are at their best, and what companies do with that money will determine economics on Wall Street and in general. If spent wisely, it could be positive for both financial markets and economic growth.

27980 ■ *Corporate Entrepreneurship: Top Managers and New Business Creation*
Pub: Cambridge University Press
Ed: Vijay Sathe. **Released:** February 2007. **Price:** $35.00. **Description:** Studies covering entrepreneurship and business growth are examined.

27981 ■ "CPI Aerostructures Wins $3M Contract for Assemblies" in *Long Island Business News* **(March 12, 2004)**
Pub: Dolan Media Newswires
Description: CPI Aerostructures Inc. announced the procurement of a new contract worth approximately $3 million to build aircraft structural assemblies. CPI reports this contract as one of its largest ever from a non-governmental or military entity.

27982 ■ "Cracking the Code of Change" in *Harvard Business Review* **(Vol. 78, No. 3, May 2000, pp. 133)**
Pub: Harvard Business School Publishing Corp.
Ed: Michael Beer, Nitin Nohria. **Description:** New research indicates that combining "hard" and "soft" approaches to changing businesses can radically transform the way companies do change.

27983 ■ "Crafts Americana Group to Expand Presence in Vancouver, Wash." in *The Columbian* **(February 22, 2003)**
Pub: Knight-Ridder/Tribune Business News
Ed: Gretchen Fehrenbacher. **Description:** Profile of Crafts American Group, the company specializing in catalog and Web sales of craft supplies, is planning to expand with 40,000 square foot of new space, which includes retail space. The new building will offer a larger area for crafts classes and products, including quilting, tole painting, and knitting.

27984 ■ "Crash Course" in *Entrepreneur* **(Vol. 28, No. 1, January 2000, pp. 89)**
Pub: Entrepreneur Media Inc.
Ed: Geoff Williams. **Description:** When your business is growing so fast it's out of control, here's how to pull the entrepreneurial equivalent of steering into the skid.

27985 ■ "A Crash Diet for Dot-Coms" in *Kiplinger's Personal Finance Magazine* **(Vol. 54, No. 8, August 2000, pp. 21)**
Pub: The Kiplinger Washington Editors, Inc.
Ed: Melynda Dovel Wilcox. **Description:** With Web downsizing, the Internet superhighway is no longer the road to riches. But, high-tech employees still have a ticket to ride.

27986 ■ "Cream of the crop" in *BlackEnterprise* **(Vol. 31, No. 10, May 2001, pp. 47)**
Pub: Earl Graves Publishing Co.
Ed: Paula McCoy-Pinderhughes, Roger Barnes. **Description:** The theme of the sixth annual Black Enterprise/Bank of America Entrepreneurs Conference is "Leading in a Changing Economy: Innovation, Transformation, Growth". The Black Enterprise Small Business Awards categories include Emerging Company of the Year, Business Innovator of the Year, the Rising Star Award, and the Kidpreneurs Award. Statistical data included.

27987 ■ "Creaming up the competition" in *Atlanta Business Chronicle* **(Vol. 24, No. 13, August 31, 2001, pp. 3A)**
Pub: American City Business Journals Inc.
Ed: Jarred Schenke. **Description:** Cold Stone Creamer, a Scottsdale, Arizona-based ice cream parlor, is planning to open 30 stores in Atlanta during the next three to four years, according to Stone's co-owner of the region franchise rights, Brad Spratte. Ice cream with the normal levels of butter fat, which Stone sells, has increases in sales by 6 percent from 2000. Although Cold Stone is doing well, Baskin-Robbins, the largest chain of ice cream parlors, has been successful in the Atlanta area.

27988 ■ "Creating a Recipe for an Empire" in *Crain's New York Business* **(Vol. 23, January 29, 2007, No. 5, pp. F22)**
Pub: Crain Communications, Inc.
Ed: **Description:** Profile of Kenny Lao, co-founder of Rickshaw Dumpling Bar, whose business plan for the casual Chelsea eatery won a contest at Stern and attracted the school's dean, Thomas Cooley, as an investor. Rickshaw's revenues in fiscal 2005 reached $1.3 million and are on track to rise another 12 percent in 2006. He intends to open six more Rickshaw bars within the next few years.

27989 ■ "Creative Accounting? Don't laugh!" in *Success from Failure* **(August 2000)**
Pub: Vision Quest Publishing, Inc.
Ed: Harvey Mackay. **Description:** Recently, the American Management Association polled 500 CEOs across the nation. The survey posed the question: "What must one do to survive in the 21st century?"

27990 ■ "Crossroads of Growth" in *Crain's Detroit Business*
Pub: Crain Communications Inc. - Detroit
Ed: Brent Snavely. **Description:** Ray Township officials are working with developers on the township's first proposed shopping center. Officials have made it clear they will not approve anything resembling big-box retail, like Wal-Mart or Meijer at the site.

27991 ■ "Crucial triad" in *Daily Business Review* **(Vol. 77, No. 198, March 24, 2003, pp. AA4)**
Pub: American Lawyer Media LP
Ed: David Geyer, Elizabeth Lampert. **Description:** Ways in which law firm partners can use the triad of business development, marketing and media relations to better serve clients is explained.

27992 ■ "Cuba's prosperous future" in *Hispanic Business* **(Vol. 22, No. 4, April 2000, pp. 38)**
Pub: Hispanic Business
Ed: Christopher D. Lancette. **Description:** The eventual total opening of the Cuban market will result in large profits for many U.S. businesses. Certain industries are already open to U.S. companies and the U.S.-Cuba Trade & Economic Council estimate the $750 million of business was completed between 1994 and 1999.

27993 ■ "CultureScape and the Redemption of Kansas City" in *Ingram's* **(Vol. 29, No. 8, August 2003, pp. 13)**
Pub: Show Me Publishing, Inc.
Ed: Jack Cashill. **Description:** An unidentified architect is planning to redevelop an area of Kansas City, Missouri. The plan is called, The Bush Creek CultureScape, and will include the Irish Museum and Cultural Center and parks.

27994 ■ "Curves for Women Fitness Centers Power Up by Going Lean, Not Mean" in *Chicago Tribune* **(October 27, 2002)**
Pub: Knight Ridder/Tribune Business News
Ed: Wendy Navratil. **Description:** Profile of Curves For Women, the women-only fitness centers. Statistical data included.

27995 ■ "Curves for Women's Salmon Creek branch expands into new space" in *Vancouver Business Journal* **(November 1, 2002)**
Pub: Dolan Media Newswires
Ed: Charlie Devereux. **Description:** The Salmon Creek, Washington's branch of the women's health club, Curves For Women, has expanded to a new location. The new center is twice the size of the previous space, allowing more room for patrons to workout. A profile of Beth Hamilton is provided. Statistical information included.

27996 ■ "The Customer Loyalty Puzzle" in *E-business Advisor* **(Vol. 17, No. 12, December 1999, pp. 10)**
Pub: Advisor Media, Inc.
Ed: Laurie Windham. **Description:** E-business owners can offer excellent customer service on the Web by linking marketing, sales, delivery, and support into one rewarding experience. E-business owners should include fulfillment and support among customer services to build customer confidence and to reduce operating expenses. Developing trust is important to e-business relationships because the Web does not offer face-to-face contact.

27997 ■ "Cutbacks at another consultant" in *The New York Times* **(December 8, 2000, pp. C3)**
Pub: The New York Times Company
Ed: Matt Richtel. **Description:** E-commerce consultant Viant to layoff 125 employees.

27998 ■ "Cutbacks mean less on table for, and from, caterers" in *Crain's Detroit Business* **(Vol. 18, No. 22, June 3, 2002, pp. 33)**
Pub: Crain Communications Inc. - Detroit
Ed: Michael Strong. **Description:** The downturn in the economy has affected catering businesses and event-oriented businesses, as well as the increase in more companies offering these services.

27999 ■ *Cute Little Store: Between the Entrepreneurial Dream and Business Reality*
Pub: Outskirts Press, Incorporated
Ed: Adeena Mignogna. **Released:** May 2006. **Price:** $11.95. **Description:** Challenges of starting and growing a retail business are profiled.

28000 ■ "Cuts in Retail, Manufacturing Hurt Northern New Jersey's Job Growth" in *The Record* (November 9, 2005)
Pub: New Jersey Media Group
Ed: Kathleen Lynn. **Description:** According to the federal Bureau of Labor Statistics, northern New Jersey firms are not hiring new employees. Statistical data included.

28001 ■ "Cutting the layoff line" in *Black Enterprise* (Vol. 32, No. 5, December 2001, pp. 22)
Pub: Earl Graves Publishing Co.
Ed: K. Terrell Reed. **Description:** An overview of black-owned broadcasting companies and how they have avoided the mass layoffs and hiring freezes plaguing other media companies.

28002 ■ "Cyber contracting" in *Hispanic Business* (Vol. 22, No. 6, June 2000, pp. 122)
Pub: Hispanic Business
Ed: Janet Perez. **Description:** Two Internet sites are in the vanguard of the fast-growing area of online contracting. Guru.com, begun in 1999, and MonsterTalent Market, an offshoot of Monster.com, both specialize in finding contract staff. They see their growth as a sign of the rapidly changing economy in the United States.

28003 ■ "Cybersecurity: Opportunities for Agents" in *Rough Notes* (Vol. 145, No. 1, January 2003, pp. 110)
Pub: Rough Notes
Ed: G. Edward Kalbaugh. **Description:** Any product or action to secure a wired or wireless work constitutes CyberSecurity, such as virus protection for computers, risk identification, insurance, risk assessment, and liability insurance. CyberSecurity promises to be one of the fastest growing businesses of the future, as more than $330 billion have been earmarked for the Department of Homeland Security.

28004 ■ "The cycle turns for technology in 2003" in *Red Herring* (January 2003, pp. 70)
Pub: Herring Communications Inc.
Ed: Arnie Berman. **Description:** The economic future for the technology industry is examined.

28005 ■ "Cymfony: www.cymfony.com" in *Entrepreneur* (Vol. 33, February 2005, No. 2, pp. 8)
Pub: Entrepreneur Media Inc.
Description: Cymfony is an online application that monitors business trends by scanning all online and offline media, broadcast mentions, message-board postings, blogs and more, capturing what journalists and consumers think about a company.

28006 ■ "Dairy Market Trends: Milk's Downturn Trend Continues, Other Segments Grow" in *Dairy Foods* (Vol. 103, No. 10, October 2002, pp. 19)
Pub: Business News Publishing Co.
Description: Yogurt and frozen novelties continue to build market share, while milk and cheese products continue to decline. Historical sales data for milk, frozen novelties, yogurt and yogurt drinks, and cheese are included.

28007 ■ "D&PL Reports Loss" in *Mississippi Business Journal* (Vol. 29, January 2007, No. 2, pp. 8)
Pub: Venture Publications, Inc.
Ed: Wally Northway **Description:** Delta and Pine Land Company reported a net loss during the first quarter ended November 2006. Due to the seasonal nature of the seed business, D&PL typically incurs sizeable losses during the first and fourth fiscal quarters. Statistical data included.

28008 ■ "De-Vine Tragedy" in *Forbes* (Vol. 175, February 14, 2005, No. 3, pp. 56)
Pub: Forbes Magazine Inc.
Ed: Dirk Smillie. **Description:** Interview with filmmaker, Jonathan Nossiter, where he speaks about his new wine documentary that attacks the globalization of the wine trade and defends small wine producers.

28009 ■ "Deal Volume Remains Steady in Q2 But How Bout Some Exits?" in *Venture Capital Journal* (September 1, 2005)
Pub: Thomason Financial Inc.
Description: Second earnings for venture capital firms are reported. Nearly $5.82 billion was invested in 751 deals in second quarter 2005, up from the first quarter, according to The MoneyTree Survey.

28010 ■ "Dealflop: Good night, sweetheart" in *Red Herring* (No. 103, September 1, 2001, pp. 33)
Pub: Herring Communications
Ed: Julie Landry. **Description:** The demise of Tradia, a consumer-to-consumer e-commerce and swapping site, cost Accel Partners, Sequoia Capital, and angels Roger Sippl and Ron Conway $14 million.

28011 ■ "Deer Park-Based Cannillo Motorsports Sells High-End Cars for the Masses" in *Long Island Business News* (February 27, 2004)
Pub: Dolan Media Newswires
Ed: Nick Anastasi. **Description:** Profile of Cannillo Motorsports, a new car dealer offering pre-owned luxury automobiles, specializing in British, German and Italian models priced from $20,000 to $35,000. Cars are found through auctions, car shows and sales sheets across the country.

28012 ■ "Deficits" in *Business Week* (February 20, 2006, No. 3972, pp. 30)
Pub: McGraw-Hill Companies
Ed: James Mehring. **Description:** According to the U.S. Congressional Budget Office (CBO), recent budget deficits are beginning to shrink. The CBO expects a $337 billion deficit for fiscal year ending September 30, 2006, falling to $270 billion next year, with an expected balanced budget by 2012.

28013 ■ "Dekor faces challenges" in *Atlanta Business Chronicle* (Vol. 24, No. 14, September 7, 2001, pp. 3A)
Pub: American City Business Journals Inc.
Ed: Jarred Schenke. **Description:** Dekor Inc., an Atlanta, Georgia home furnishings retailer, is waiting to achieve profit goals when it succeeds in opening eleven stores. Jim Inglis, Dekor's CEO, believes the company will be able to achieve its goal despite the low economy.

28014 ■ "Delta may lose $1 billion again" in *Atlanta Business Chronicle* (Vol. 25, January 10, 2003, No. 31, pp. 3A)
Pub: American City Business Publications, Inc.
Ed: Walter Woods. **Description:** Delta Air Lines is expected to announce a loss of $1 billion for the second straight year, according to industry analysts. The fourth quarter net loss of the embattled carrier is expected to be between $250 million and $300 million. Insiders warn that the airline industry is in grave danger.

28015 ■ "Dentist Office to Anchor New Sarasota County, Fla., Office Park" in *Bradenton Herald* (April 11 2003)
Pub: Knight-Ridder/Tribune Business News
Ed: Matt Griswold. **Description:** Sarasota attorney David Band is heading the development of a 12,800 square-foot professional office complex for Ranch Lake Plaza, which will feature a dentist office, accountants, law firms, insurance offices, and other professional business tenants.

28016 ■ "Department-Store Chain Boosts N.J. Index" in *The Record* (November 13, 2005)
Pub: New Jersey Media Group
Ed: William Conroy. **Description:** Federated Department Stores Inc. pushed the Asbury Park Press/ Bloomberg 75 index to a 2.48 percent gain in November 2005. Statistical data included for the index, which is made up of 75 companies.

28017 ■ "Designer Babies" in *Entrepreneur* (Vol. 33, September 2005, No. 9, pp. 24)
Pub: Entrepreneur Media Inc.
Ed: April Y. Pennington. **Description:** According to the NPD Group, the children's clothing market grew to

$29 billion in the U.S. in 2004. Major designers are adding children's collections to their lines to satisfy trend-setting parents.

28018 ■ "Desire-more than need-builds a business" in *Wall Street Journal* (May 21, 2002, pp. B4)
Pub: Wall Street Journal
Ed: Jeff Bailey. **Description:** A survey conducted by Global Entrepreneurship Monitor showed that the most successful entrepreneurs started their business by choice, not necessity.

28019 ■ "DeSoto County Lures Bonanza of New Banks" in *Memphis Business Journal* (Vol. 25, No. 19, September 5, 2003, pp. 1)
Pub: American City Business Journals
Ed: Rob Robertson. **Description:** DeSoto County, Tennessee continues to experience economic growth and population expansion. To meet the growth, the banking and financial services industry continues to expand in the area.

28020 ■ "Despite Smaller Loans, SBA Breaks Records" in *Inc.* (November 1, 2004)
Pub: Inc. Magazine
Ed: Darren Dahl. **Description:** The U. S. Small Business Administration backed a record number of loans in 2004, providing $15 billion in loans to businesses. These loans have helped small and family-owned small business to create 1.5 million jobs.

28021 ■ "Detroit ballot to feature $130M in bond proposals" in *Crain's Detroit Business* (Vol. 19, No. 16, April 21, 2003, pp. 23)
Pub: Crain Communications Inc., Detroit
Ed: Robert Ankeny. **Description:** Detroit voters will decide on $130 million in bond issues to finance building and development projects in the city in April 2003. These proposals are for renovation or expansion at the Charles Wright Museum of African-American History; improvements to Cobo Center and the People Mover; revitalization of the east riverfront, including housing and other redevelopment; and a public-safety mall, a new police precinct, and new fire stations.

28022 ■ "Detroit construction slowed in 2002; Number of permits rose, but dollar value fell" in *Crain's Detroit Business* (Jan. 20, 2003, pp.20)
Pub: Crain Communications Inc., Detroit
Ed: Robert Ankeny. **Description:** New construction permits issued by the City of Detroit fell by more than 26 percent in 2002 after 586 permits being issued in 2001. Statistical data included.

28023 ■ "Detroit falls on list of best places for biz" in *Crain's Detroit Business* (Vol. 18, No. 24, June 17, 2002, pp. 29)
Pub: Crain Communications Inc. - Detroit
Ed: Eric Morath. **Description:** According to Forbes magazine and the Milken Institute, Detroit fell further on the list of best places to do business and advance a career in 2001, falling 29 spots to 91. The ranking was based on three factors: job creation, growth in average wages, and growth in technology industries.

28024 ■ "Detroit Free Press Small Business Column" in *Detroit Free Press* (July 7, 2005)
Pub: Knight-Ridder/Tribune Business News
Ed: Carol Cain. **Description:** Halo Group offers information technology services to Fortune 1000 firms, providing contract staffing and recruiting. The firm was started when three co-workers left another company and together started the business.

28025 ■ "Detroit Free Press Tom Walsh Column" in *Detroit Free Press* (April 11, 2003)
Pub: Knight-Ridder/Tribune Business News
Ed: Tom Walsh. **Description:** Residential development and business growth for the Detroit and surrounding areas of Michigan are addressed.

28026 ■ "Detroit looks for retail to follow housing growth" in *Crain's Detroit Business* (Vol. 18, No. 45, November 11, 2002, pp. 16)
Pub: Crain Communications Inc., Detroit

Ed: Robert Ankeny. **Description:** Officials from the City of Detroit, along with private-sector leaders, predict a growth in retail in 2003, following the growth trend in new housing development. Statistical data included.

28027 ■ "Detroit Lawyers Pick Up Extra Work" in *Crain's Detroit Business* (Vol. 21, October 17, 2005, No. 43, pp. 32)
Pub: Crain Communications Inc. - Detroit
Ed: Robert Ankeny. **Description:** Due to Delphi Corporation's Chapter 11 filing, Detroit area law firms are representing some of the companies involved, including tier-two and smaller suppliers.

28028 ■ "Detroit: No vacancy; New hotels may not bring enough rooms" in *Crain's Detroit Business* (Vol. 19, No. 6, February 10, 2003, pp. 15)
Pub: Crain Communications Inc., Detroit
Ed: Robert Ankeny. **Description:** The Book Cadillac Hotel is planning a $150 million renovation, creating 500 new rooms for Detroit visitors, but it still may not be enough new rooms for the city.

28029 ■ "Detroit Renaissance Goal" in *Crain's Detroit Business* (Vol. 22, January 23, 2006, No. 4, pp. 3)
Pub: Crain Communications Inc. - Detroit
Ed: Robert Ankeny. **Description:** Detroit Renaissance Inc. plans to develop five or six specific strategies to spur economic growth and development in the City of Detroit, Michigan.

28030 ■ "Developer Sees a Bright Future for Downtown St. Louis" in *St. Louis Post-Dispatch* (November 19, 2004)
Pub: Knight-Ridder/Tribune Business News
Ed: Mary Jo Feldstein. **Description:** Richard Baron has been committed to rebuilding and enriching parts of St. Louis for more than 25 years. Baron co-founded the Center of Creative Arts, and along with his business, McCormack Baron Salazar Inc, he is able to merge business interests with philanthropy and civic work.

28031 ■ "Developer Sets His Sights On the East Side" in *Milwaukee Journal Sentinel* (December 12, 2005)
Pub: Journal Sentinel, Inc.
Ed: Tom Daykin. **Description:** Warren Barr of Renaissant Development Group LLC, is planning to build a new high-rise in Milwaukee. The project calls for two 20-story towers and will have more than 300 units.

28032 ■ "Developers Jockey for Retail at Trade Center" in *Crain's New York Business* (Vol. 20, No. 12, March 22, 2004, pp. 1)
Pub: Crain Communications, Inc.
Ed: Christine Haughney. **Description:** The Port Authority of New York and New Jersey is making plans for retail space to be built on the World Trade Center site. Developers are lobbying to manage the projects, with The Related Companies the leading contender.

28033 ■ "Development to Add $1M Homes to Washtenaw" in *Crain's Detroit Business* (Vol. 19, No. 43, October 27, 2003, pp. 3)
Pub: Crain Communications Inc., Detroit
Ed: Laura Bailey. **Description:** Profile of Wexford Builders Inc.'s plans to build Three Arch Bay, a 27-home development of $1.2-$3 million homes in Lodi Township, Michigan.

28034 ■ "Dialing Up Market Share" in *Hispanic Business* (October 2002, pp. 14)
Pub: Hispanic Business
Description: It is predicted that Hispanics will spend more than $21.3 billion on local, long distance, wireless, and Internet services in 2002.

28035 ■ "Differentiating Legal Issues by Business Type" in *Journal of Small Business Management* (Vol. 44, October 2006, No. 4, pp. 563)
Pub: Blackwell Publishing, Inc.
Ed: Sandra Malach; Peter Robinson; Tannis Radcliffe. **Description:** A fundamental issue when form-

ing a business and its strategic operation is developing legal strategies to better protect the assets of the business and entrepreneur. An analysis of data indicated that certain legal issues are relevant to specific types of new ventures while certain legal issues are important to all new ventures. Depending on the category of business, the relevancy of individual legal issues will vary. Statistical data included.

28036 ■ "Digging Deeper and Keeping Up" in *Employment Relations Today* (Vol. 26, No. 4, Winter 2000, pp. 95)
Pub: John Wiley & Sons, Inc.
Description: A bibliography of books that deal with the future of work and employment is presented. Topics include the Internet, unemployment, and employee relations.

28037 ■ "Digital Detroit gathering helps build new economy in Motown" in *Crain's Detroit Business* (Vol. 16, No. 49, December 4, 2000, pp. 42)
Pub: Crain Communications, Inc.
Ed: Katie Merx. **Description:** The Digital Detroit L. L.C. conference provided the much-needed jumpstart for Detroit's high tech industry. Internet startup gurus, tech-side workers from traditional businesses, lawyers and economic development officials were in attendance.

28038 ■ "Digital Entertainment" in *Business 2.0* (Vol. 6, September 2005, No. 8, pp. 30)
Pub: Time, Inc.
Ed: Matthew Maier. **Description:** Wireless phone carriers such as Verizon Wireless will launch third-generation music services that allow users to download full-length songs. It is predicted that the mobile music industry will reach $9 billion by year 2010.

28039 ■ "Digital Rx" in *Fast Company* (May 2001, pp. 183)
Pub: Fast Company
Ed: Scott Kirsner. **Description:** Ways the Detroit Medical Center is using digital technology to repair its fiscal condition are presented.

28040 ■ "Discovering a Spin-Off Business" in *Home Business* (Vol. 12, March/April 2005, No. 2, pp. 40, 42-43)
Pub: Home Business Magazine
Ed: Priscilla Y. Huff. **Description:** Entrepreneurs share ways they used spin-off ventures to attract new customers and revitalize old ones.

28041 ■ "Diversification, Efficiency Boosts Firm" in *San Fernando Valley Business Journal* (Vol. 11, November 2006, No. 24, pp. 23)
Pub: San Fernando Valley Business Journal Associates
Ed: Chris Coates. **Description:** Profile of Systech Solutions, a professional services firm that specializes in the Internet. The company's client list includes Wal-Mart.com, Disney, IHOP Corp., American Express Co., and a host of other Fortune 500 and 1000 companies.

28042 ■ "A Diversity Plan Turns 100" in *Hispanic Business* (September 2003, pp. 30, 32)
Pub: Hispanic Business
Ed: Gina Binole. **Description:** Ford Motor Company has prospered for 100 years by marketing to the Hispanic market. James Padilla, president of Ford's North American production, discusses the fact that Ford Motor Company understands the power of the Hispanic consumer and the importance of the Hispanic business owner.

28043 ■ "Diving In; New Owner Plans to Use PPOM as Platform for National Network, Fast Growth" in *Crain's Detroit Business* (January 10, 2005)
Pub: Crain Communications Inc. - Detroit
Ed: Katie Merx. **Description:** Plans to double PPOM's market share in Michigan are discussed with president and CEO, Jeffrey Connolly. The move would more than triple the health care provider network's membership.

28044 ■ "Dixie Queen Plans to Grow by 200 Units" in *Memphis Business Journal* (Vol. 25, No. 17, August 22, 2003, pp. 1)
Pub: American City Business Journals
Ed: Michael Sheffield. **Description:** Dixie Queen plans to franchise its fast food restaurants outside the Memphis, Tennessee area. Owner, David Raffanty, has hired UrbanArch Associates PC to remodel the company's existing buildings.

28045 ■ "Do you have a well-designed organization?" in *Harvard Business Review* (Vol. 80, No. 3, March 2002, pp. 117)
Pub: Harvard Business School Press
Ed: Michael Goold, Andrew Campbell. **Description:** An executive's job of creating a new organizational design and the nine tests of organization design, which can either evaluate an existing structure or create a new one are discussed.

28046 ■ "Does the Franchisor Provide Value to Franchisees?" in *Journal of Small Business Management* (Vol. 41, No. 4, October 2003, pp. 366)
Pub: International Council of Small Business
Ed: Marko Grunhagen, Michael J. Dorsch. **Description:** The degree to which a franchise system penetrates a target market over time is often influenced by the rate its individual franchisees expand.

28047 ■ "Doing Your Part?" in *Entrepreneur* (Vol. 31, No. 9, September 2003)
Pub: Entrepreneur Media, Inc.
Ed: Geoff Williams. **Description:** An interview with Liz Cohen, author of "A Consumers' Republic: The Politics of Mass Consumption in Postwar America"; the book argues that shopping has long been a form of patriotism.

28048 ■ "Dollar signs get attention as cost of growth starts to weigh" in *Crain's Detroit Business* (Vol. 19, No. 17, April 28, 2003, pp. 18)
Pub: Crain Communications Inc., Detroit
Ed: Terry Kosdrosky. **Description:** Southeast Michigan will need $41 billion dollars in the next 22 years for roads and public transportation, but will receive only $24 billion from gas taxes and local general-fund money for projects.

28049 ■ "Dollars in the Deals" in *Hispanic Business* (Vol. 23, No. 11, November 2001, pp. 52, 54)
Pub: Hispanic Business Inc.
Ed: Jonathan J. Higuera. **Description:** The top 50 exporters in the United States realize that a strong dollar hurts markets overseas and focus on marketing strategies to overcome it. Uncertainties faced by various exporters are discussed.

28050 ■ "The domino effect: ripples from September 11 spread FAR and WIDE" in *Black Enterprise* (Vol. 32, No. 6, January 2002, pp. 53)
Pub: Earl Graves Publishing Co.
Ed: Sonya A. Donaldson, Alan Hughes, Terrell Reed. **Description:** The impacts on business after the September 11 terrorist attacks, including consumer reaction, are discussed with an optimistic outlook for the future.

28051 ■ "Don't Be a Stranger" in *Inc.* (January 1, 2005)
Pub: Inc. Magazine
Ed: Laura Rich. **Description:** Alumni programs can be a great way to network and increase business for small companies.

28052 ■ "Don't Be Thrown by the Yield Curve" in *Business Week* (January 16, 2006, No. 3967, pp. 40)
Pub: McGraw-Hill Companies
Ed: Roben Farzad, Justin Hibbard. **Description:** The latest inversion curve does not necessarily signal a recession and might benefit some industries, while hurting others. Those sectors expected to benefit include capital equipment and energy services, while mortgage lenders and homebuilders stand to lose.

28053 ■ *Don't Bitch, Just Get Rich*
Pub: Simon and Schuster Incorporated
Ed: Toney Fitzgerald. **Released:** June 2006. **Price:** $16.00. **Description:** Advice is given to business leaders to help them shift from the position whereby money has power over you to taking responsibility for life choices in order to meet new challenges.

28054 ■ **"Don't Get Mad, Get Practical"** in *My Business* (April/May 2004, pp. 39)
Pub: My Business Magazine
Description: Ways to diffuse any difficult situation are listed in order to use conflict as a means for business growth.

28055 ■ **"Don't Go Changing"** in *Entrepreneur* (Vol. 28, No. 3, March 2000, pp. 122)
Pub: Entrepreneur Media Inc.
Description: Limiting change in business is the topic of this discussion.

28056 ■ **"Don't Shrink from Ambitious Detroit Plans"** in *Crain's Detroit Business* (Vol. 19, No. 4, January 27, 2003, pp. 9)
Pub: Crain Communications Inc., Detroit
Ed: Mary Kramer. **Description:** The City of Detroit intends to use some of its assets to boost travel and tourism to the city.

28057 ■ **"Dot-com Bust Fallout"** in *Hispanic Business* (November 2002, pp. 14)
Pub: Hispanic Business
Description: Startups that received venture-backed funding in 1999 and 2000 are failing at a faster rate than startups initially funded between 1992 and 1998. Statistical data included.

28058 ■ **"Dot-Com Distress"** in *PC Magazine* (February 20, 2001, pp. 67)
Pub: Ziff-Davis Publishing Company
Ed: Sebastian Rupley. **Description:** A concise history of the dot-com industry is presented, including some optimism for the future of those e-tailers that survive.

28059 ■ **"Dot-com Seeks Firm Footing"** in *Boston Business Journal* (Vol. 22, No. 11, April 19, 2002, pp. 11)
Pub: MCP, Inc.
Ed: Scott Savitz. **Description:** Shoebuy.com Inc. has 10,000 products with 220 brands and increasing numbers of customers. By sticking to a disciplined marketing style, this dot.com online retailer has been able to grow steadily.

28060 ■ **"Dov Charney, Like It Or Not"** in *Inc.* (September 2005, pp. 124-131)
Pub: Inc. Magazine
Ed: Josh Dean. **Description:** Profile of Dov Charney, founder and CEO of American Apparel; Charney shares his management style that has made the $250 million firm so successful.

28061 ■ **"Down, not out"** in *Black Enterprise* (Vol. 32, No. 7, February 2002, pp. 184)
Pub: Earl Graves Publishing Co.
Description: Technology is hoping to make a comeback.

28062 ■ **"Drink tank"** in *Entrepreneur* (Vol. 30, No. 1, January 20)
Pub: Entrepreneur Media Inc.
Ed: Michelle Prather. **Description:** According to Beverage Marketing Corporation of New York City, water is the fastest-growing major U.S. beverage category, expected to surpass coffee and milk and take second place in volume to soft drinks by year 2004. Four companies dominate the water market: Pepsi, Danone, Coke and Perrier Group of America.

28063 ■ **"Drugmaker Ups Dosage; Acquisition Expected to Double Revenue"** in *Crain's New York Business* (Vol. 23, January 22, 2007, No. 4, pp. 4)
Pub: Crain Communications, Inc.
Description: Barr Pharmaceuticals Inc. won a bidding war to acquire Pliva for $2.5 billion. The acquisition is expected to double Barr's revenue which had been falling over the last two years.

28064 ■ **"DTE aims to spark growth beyond electricity"** in *Crain's Detroit Business* (Vol. 19, No. 15, April 14, 2003, pp. 3)
Pub: Crain Communications Inc., Detroit
Ed: Amy Lane. **Description:** DTE Energy Company is expecting to see growth in 2003 through its non-regulated business' areas of coal reclamation and methane-gas extraction from coal beds.

28065 ■ **"E-Commerce Market Heats Up"** in *Hispanic Business* (October 2003, pp. 98, 100)
Pub: Hispanic Business
Ed: Andrea Siedsma. **Description:** New studies indicate Hispanics are ready to buy online if merchants carry the right products, a strong brand, and financial security. A listing of the top sites for Hispanic online shoppers is included. Statistical data included.

28066 ■ **"E-mail Marketer Looks for More Clout"** in *Atlanta Business Chronicle* (Vol. 25, December 13, 2002, No. 27, pp. A3)
Pub: American City Business Publications, Inc.
Ed: Mary Jane Credeur. **Description:** Silverpop Systems Inc. has acquired Epigraphx LLC, Redwood, California. The acquisition took place in December 2002, as part of Silverpop's initiative to grow in the e-mail marketing industry. The deal will increase staff to 55 and will triple Silverpop's revenues, which remain undisclosed. The deal also expands Silverpop's client roster and increased profits are discussed by Silverpop CEO, Bill Nussey.

28067 ■ **"E-Marketplaces: Opportunity or Threat?"** in *E-business Advisor* (Vol. 18, No. 7, July 2000, pp. 32)
Pub: Advisor Media, Inc.
Ed: Elizabeth Sara. **Description:** Businesses in the e-marketplace arena are obliged, not only to adapt their existing business processes to take advantage of the Web's inherent benefits, but also to keep their relatively new e-commerce solutions functionally current and flexible to keep in step with the market. Participating in private business-to-business (B2B) sales channels offer the advantage of enhanced contractual relationships with business partners. Price structures for products are included.

28068 ■ *E-Myth Mastery: The Seven Essential Disciplines for Building a World Class Company*
Pub: HarperCollins Publishers Inc.
Ed: Michael E. Gerber. **Released:** March 2007. **Price:** $16.95. **Description:** Leadership, marketing, money, management, lead conversion, lead generation, client fulfillment are the seven keys to successful entrepreneurship.

28069 ■ *The E-Myth Revisited: Why Most Small Businesses Don't Work and What to Do About It*
Pub: HarperInformation
Ed: Michael E. Gerber. **Released:** April 1995. **Price:** $16.00. **Description:** Keys for developing a prosperous small business is presented in an updated version of the author's best-seller published in the nineties.

28070 ■ **"E-signing law seen as a boon to e-business"** in *The New York Times* (July 4, 2000, pp. C1)
Pub: The New York Times Company
Ed: Barnaby J. Feder. **Description:** Analysts expect that the new law letting businesses and consumers sign legally binding accords with electronic signatures will increase the speed at which electronic businesses develop. The new process, called 'e-signing', will likely give rise to many personal identification technologies that can serve as alternatives to writing one's name on paper.

28071 ■ **"Early warning"** in *Black Enterprise* (Vol. 32, No. 8, March 2002, pp.)
Pub: Earl Graves Publishing Co.
Ed: Alan Hughes. **Description:** An interview with Ray Wilkins, president and CEO of SBC Pacific Bell, about last year's dotcom meltdown.

28072 ■ **"Earnings up 18 Percent for '02; 4Q Totals Rise 141 Percent from '01"** in *Crain's Detroit Business* (V. 19, No. 8, 2/24/03)
Pub: Crain Communications Inc., Detroit
Ed: Katie Merx. **Description:** Southeast Michigan companies saw profits rise in the second half of 2002, spurred on by automotive sales and business spending.

28073 ■ **"Earnings Improve, but Overall Picture Isn't Exactly Rosy"** in *Crain's Detroit Business* (Vol. 18, No. 21, May 27, 2002, pp. 1)
Pub: Crain Communications Inc. - Detroit
Ed: Katie Merx. **Description:** Metro Detroit firms showed improved earnings for the first quarter 2002 compared to same quarter last year, but the economic rebound is going more slowly than analysts originally predicted.

28074 ■ **"Earnings Rise Is 3rd Straight; Analysts See a Recovery"** in *Crain's Detroit Business* (Vol. 18, No. 50, December 16, 2002, pp. 1)
Pub: Crain Communications Inc., Detroit
Ed: Katie Merx. **Description:** Detroit-area public companies report increased profits for the third straight quarter in the period ending September 30, 2002. Strengths and weaknesses in various sectors are discussed.

28075 ■ **"EarthLink Posts Loss for Fourth Quarter"** in *Altanta Journal-Constitution* (February 7, 2007)
Pub: Cox Newspapers, Inc.
Ed: Scott Leith. **Description:** EarthLink expects to post losses in 2007; the firm reported nearly $25 million in losses for fourth quarter 2006. Statistical data included.

28076 ■ **"Easter Is Big Business for Pennsylvania Candy Companies"** in *Knight-Ridder/Tribune Business News* (March 30, 2002, pp. ITEM02089101)
Pub: Knight-Ridder Inc.
Ed: Jane Haseldine. **Description:** Profile of candy makers located in Pennsylvania, one of the nation's leaders in chocolate production.

28077 ■ **"EastGroup Buys Buildings in Mississippi Business Journal* (Vol. 29, January 2007, No. 4, pp. 9)
Pub: Venture Publications, Inc.
Ed: Wally Northway **Description:** EastGroup Properties acquired three business distribution buildings in Charlotte, NC, for $9.3 million. This increases EastGroup's total portfolio to almost 24 million square feet of properties in the Charlotte area under development.

28078 ■ **"Eastland Future Unclear: Local Merchants Say They're OK Amid Closings of 4 More Stores"** in *Charlotte Observer* (February 8, 2007)
Pub: Knight-Ridder/Tribune Business News
Ed: Nichole Monroe Bell. **Description:** Retailers in the Eastland Mall that market goods to shoppers looking for the urban, hip-hop look are most successful.

28079 ■ **"Easy Does It"** in *Entrepreneur* (Vol. 33, October 2005, No. 10, pp. 122)
Pub: Entrepreneur Media Inc.
Ed: Romanus Wolter. **Description:** In order to be successful, entrepreneurs must learn to balance work time with their personal life as a small business grows. A good rule to follow: success is not about the number of hours worked, but the outcome of the efforts involved.

28080 ■ **"Eateries team up for clout"** in *Black Enterprise* (Vol. 31, No. 5, December 2000, pp. 170)
Pub: Earl Graves Publishing Co.
Ed: Ann Brown. **Description:** Black restaurant association wants to help owners grow their businesses.

28081 ■ **"Eating Up Profits"** in *Hispanic Business* (June 2005, pp. 94)
Pub: Hispanic Business

Ed: Keith Rosenblum. **Description:** Rising costs deter an otherwise strong 2004 for manufacturers in the U.S. Statistical data included.

28082 ■ "Ebank gains altitude after midflight change" in *Atlanta Business Chronicle* **(Vol. 24, No. 9, August 3, 2001, pp. 19A)**
Pub: American City Business Journals Inc.
Ed: Meredith Jordan. **Description:** Ebank.com Inc., based in Atlanta, Georgia, was headed for certain disaster as a dot-com bank. According to Jim Box, the new president and CEO, has turned the company around 100 percent, and the company is growing financially and considering acquisitions and still enjoys a presence on the Web.

28083 ■ "Economic Developers Expect a Busier Year in '03" in *Atlanta Business Chronicle* **(Vol. 25, December 6, 2002, No. 26, pp. 8A)**
Pub: American City Business Publications, Inc.
Ed: Jarred Schenke. **Description:** The Georgia Department of Industry, Trade and Tourism and Georgia Power Company, Georgia's largest economic development organizations, are working to attract more companies to the state. This trend could generate business for industrial real estate planners.

28084 ■ "Economic and Financial Indicators" in *The Economist* **(Vol. 377, October 1-7, 2005, No. 8446, pp. 96-97)**
Pub: The Economist Newspaper Ltd.
Description: Statistics involving fifteen developed economies are presented, along with a look at competitiveness and the world's largest companies.

28085 ■ "Economic Outlook" in *Business 2.0* **(Vol. 6, July 2005, No. 6, pp. 32)**
Pub: Time, Inc.
Description: Chief forecasting economist at Global Insight, Nariman Behravesh, predicts American corporations will begin spending in the coming year.

28086 ■ "Economist Offers 2005 Outlook For 2 Florida Counties" in *Bradenton Herald* **(January 13, 2005)**
Pub: Bradenton Herald
Description: Economist Henry Fishkind predicts the first half of 2005 will show excellent growth for both Manatee and Sarasota Counties in Florida. Local tourism, condominium conversions, residential and non-residential construction are sited for the areas growth.

28087 ■ "Economists Divided Over Downturn" in *Hispanic Business* **(Vol. 23, No. 11, November 2001, pp. 16)**
Pub: Hispanic Business Inc.
Ed: Derek Reveron. **Description:** Economists struggle to take terrorist attacks into account in making recession forecasts. A listing of economic conditions after critical events in American history are cited.

28088 ■ "Economy Adds 262,000 Jobs" in *Boston Globe* **(March 5, 2005)**
Pub: New York Times Company
Ed: Charles Stein. **Description:** The government reported 262,000 new jobs in February 2005, supporting predictions of a strong economic job market.

28089 ■ "Economy Expands Modestly, but Unemployment Rate Rises" in *Atlanta Journal-Constitution* **(February 3, 2007)**
Pub: Cox Newspapers, Inc.
Ed: Michael E. Kanell. **Description:** Despite a modest jump in the economy, unemployment numbers rose, according to the U.S. Department of Labor Statistics.

28090 ■ "Economy Refuses to Fall" in *Atlanta Journal-Constitution* **(February 1, 2007)**
Pub: Cox Newspapers, Inc.
Ed: Michael E. Kanell. **Description:** Fourth quarter 2006 showed a solid 3.5 percent growth in the U.S. economy; however residential spending fell 19.2 percent.

28091 ■ "Economy: So much for technology's third-quarter save" in *Red Herring* **(No. 103, September 1, 2001, pp. 24)**
Pub: Herring Communications
Ed: Dan Briody. **Description:** A bleak forecast for the third quarter 2001 in the technology sector is discussed.

28092 ■ "Educational-software concern is cutting work force by 20 percent" in *Wall Street Journal* **(May 20, 2002, pp. C9)**
Pub: Wall Street Journal
Description: Docent Inc, the educational software company, is planning to cut its workforce by 20 percent this year.

28093 ■ "Electrical-Wiring Company is Moving to Ferndale" in *Bellingham Business Journal* **(December 2006, pp. A4)**
Pub: Sun News Inc.
Description: With its move to a larger facility in Ferndale, Express Electric, a fifteen-year old company specializing in wiring buildings and homes, will expand to include a showroom for retail sales of home theater systems.

28094 ■ "Electricity, natural gas facing uncertain future" in *Atlanta Business Chronicle* **(Vol. 25, January 10, 2003, No. 31, pp. 24A)**
Pub: American City Business Publications, Inc.
Ed: Don Reichardt. **Description:** According to the Georgia Economic Outlook 2003 survey, electric utilities are positioned for growth while natural gas utilities will have to deal with the effects of deregulation and volatile prices.

28095 ■ "Elephants on a chip" in *Barron's* **(Vol. 82, No. 58, February 17, 2003, pp. T1)**
Pub: Barron's
Ed: Bill Alpert. **Description:** Smaller 'point solution' semiconductor firms may be pushed aside in the Texas Instruments vs. Intel battle for market share, including Broadcom, Marvell, and Intersill.

28096 ■ "Eliminate Fulfillment Problems" in *E-business Advisor* **(Vol. 18, No. 3, March 2000, pp. 28)**
Pub: Advisor Media, Inc.
Ed: Patrick Rigney. **Description:** The best ways to integrate an online system with an existing business is to establish a separate order fulfillment center, or to outsource order processing. Orders are then sent directly to the company's warehouse.

28097 ■ "Elk Grove Village, Ill. Officials Wary of O'Hare Airport Expansion" in *Chicago Tribune* **(April 11, 2003)**
Pub: Knight-Ridder/Tribune Business News
Ed: John Keilman. **Description:** The Mayor of Elk Grove Village, Illinois is concerned that O'Hare Airport expansion plans could tear down industrial park buildings in the Village.

28098 ■ *Email Marketing by the Numbers: How to Use the World's Greatest Marketing Tool to Take Any Organization to the Next Level*
Pub: John Wiley and Sons Inc.
Ed: Chris Baggott. **Released:** April 2007. **Price:** $29.99 (CND). **Description:** Tips for using email to market small business products and services are provided.

28099 ■ "Eminem" in *Crain's Detroit Business* **(Vol. 19, No. 1, January 6, 2003, pp. 11)**
Pub: Crain Communications Inc., Detroit
Ed: Andrew Dietderich. **Description:** Marshall Mathers, aka Eminem, created new opportunities for Detroit area businesses, including Cranbrook Schools, Detroit Motor Company, Pure Detroit, Inc., and the Detroit Metro Convention and Visitors Bureau, with his movie 8 Mile.

28100 ■ "Employment Will Be Stable, Survey Says" in *Milwaukee Journal Sentinel* **(December 13, 2005)**
Pub: Journal Sentinel, Inc.

Ed: Joel Dresang. **Description:** According to the Manpower Employment Outlook Survey, 23 percent of 16,000 employers will add employees in first quarter 2006, while 10 percent report plans to downsize.

28101 ■ "The End of Detroit: How the Big Three Lost Their Grip on the American Car Market" in *Harvard Business Review* **(Vol.81, No.11, Nov. 2003)**
Pub: Harvard Business School Press
Ed: John T. Landry. **Description:** Review of the book, The End of Detroit: How the Big Three Lost Their Grip on the American Car Market.

28102 ■ "The end of the PC world as we know it" in *Red Herring* **(No. 106, October 15, 2001, pp. 16)**
Pub: Herring Communications
Ed: Anthony B. Perkins. **Description:** A discussion of reasons for the slowing market in PC sales, including Internet-enabled cell phones, handheld organizers, and email devices. The result of price wars has forced the larger makers to not only merge, but also diversify their companies.

28103 ■ "Energy: The changing balance of power" in *Red Herring* **(No. 103, September 1, 2001, pp. 66)**
Pub: Herring Communications
Ed: Lee Bruno. **Description:** A discussion regarding the need for standards to ensure that alternative power sources, such as micropower, can easily plug into the grid, which is critical for deregulated markets to move forward.

28104 ■ "Engineering a Culture" in *Crain's Detroit Business* **(Vol. 19, No. 45, November 10, 2003, pp. 41)**
Pub: Crain Communications Inc., Detroit
Ed: Andrew Dietderich. **Description:** Profile of Troy, Michigan-based Altair Engineering Inc. The firm was started in 1985 by three ex-General Motors Corporation employees and now employs 700 employees in 11 countries, with revenue expected to reach $75 in 2003.

28105 ■ *Enterprise, Entrepreneurship and Innovation: Concepts, Context and Commercialization*
Pub: Elsevier Science and Technology Books
Ed: Robin Lowe, Sue Marriott. **Released:** June 2006. **Price:** $39.95. **Description:** Application of enterprise, innovation and entrepreneurship are discussed to help companies grow.

28106 ■ "Enterprising Moves" in *MEDIAWEEK* **(Vol. 11, No. 4, January 22, 2001, pp. 65)**
Pub: BPI Communications
Ed: Lori Lefevre. **Description:** Major publishers are building up their small-business books in a big way. Despite the large number of mergers in recent years, some 5.8 million small businesses continue to thrive, and several leading publishers hope to increase their coverage to win over new readers and ads.

28107 ■ "Entravision Acquires Three L.A. Stations" in *Hispanic Business* **(March 2003, pp. 20)**
Pub: Hispanic Business
Description: Entravision, upon regulatory approval, will acquire three radio stations in the greater Los Angeles area serving the Hispanic market. Statistical data included.

28108 ■ "Entrepreneur Column" in *Entrepreneur.com* **(Jan. 2006)**
Pub: Entrepreneur Media Inc.
Ed: Kim Gordon. **Description:** A step-by-step guide to successfully grow a small business while staying ahead of inflation.

28109 ■ *The Entrepreneurial Process: Economic Growth, Men, Women & Minorities*
Pub: Greenwood Publishing Group, Inc.
Ed: Paul D. Reynolds and Sammis B. White. **Released:** 1997. **Price:** $59.95 (cloth).

28110 ■ *Entrepreneurial Strategies: New Technologies and Emerging Markets*
Pub: Blackwell Publishing Limited
Ed: Arnold Cooper; Sharon Alvarez; Alejandro Carrera; Luiz Mesquita; Robert Vassolo. **Released:** August 2006. **Price:** $69.95. **Description:** Ideas to help a small business expand into emerging market economies (EMEs) are discussed. Despite the high failure rate, this book helps a small firm develop a successful plan.

28111 ■ *Entrepreneurial Strategy Emerging Businesses in Declining Industries*
Pub: Edward Elgar Publishing, Incorporated
Ed: Cassia. **Released:** July 2006. **Price:** $110.00. **Description:** Role of entrepreneurship in context of older and declining industries is explored. The book offers insight into entrepreneurial dynamics behind emerging businesses in declining industries, especially the roles of resources processes and people.

28112 ■ *The Entrepreneur's Guide to Growing Up: Taking Your Small Company to the Next Level*
Pub: Self-Counsel Press, Inc.
Ed: Edna Sheedy. **Released:** 1993. **Price:** $8.95. **Description:** Guide to managing small business growth after start-up.

28113 ■ *Entrepreneurship: A Process Perspective*
Pub: Thomson South-Western
Ed: Robert A. Baron; Scott A. Shane. **Released:** February 2007. **Price:** $137.95. **Description:** Entrepreneurial process covering team building, finances, business plan, legal issues, marketing, growth and exit strategies.

28114 ■ *Entrepreneurship and Economic Growth*
Pub: Edward Elgar Publishing, Incorporated
Ed: Carree. **Released:** October 2006. **Price:** $195.00. **Description:** Historic and country-specific studies and articles regarding entrepreneurship and innovation, growth models, competition and productivity, and empirical evidence.

28115 ■ *Entrepreneurship and the Financial Community Starting Up and Growing New Businesses*
Pub: Edward Elgar Publishing, Incorporated
Ed: Clarysse. **Released:** November 2006. **Price:** $75.00. **Description:** Understanding the role of private equity providers in the development and growth processes of small business.

28116 ■ *Entrepreneurship and the Growth of Firms*
Pub: Edward Elgar Publishing, Incorporated
Ed: Davidsson. **Released:** December 2006. **Price:** $100.00. **Description:** Relationships between entrepreneurial skills and business growth are explored.

28117 ■ *Entrepreneurship, Innovation and Economic Growth*
Pub: Edward Elgar Publishing, Incorporated
Ed: David B. Audretsch. **Released:** July 2006. **Price:** $145.00. **Description:** Links between entrepreneurship, innovation and economic growth are examined.

28118 ■ *Entrepreneurship, Innovation and the Growth Mechanism of the Free-Enterprise Economies*
Pub: Princeton University Press
Ed: Eytan Sheshinski; William J. Baumol. **Released:** January 2007. **Price:** $65.00. **Description:** Scholars address the free-enterprise Western economies.

28119 ■ *Entrepreneurship: The Engine of Growth*
Pub: Greenwood Publishing Group, Incorporated
Ed: Maria Minniti; Andrew Zacharakis; Stephen Spinelli; Mark P. Rice; Timothy G. Habbershon. **Released:** November 2006. **Price:** $300.00. **Description:** Dynamics of entrepreneurship are examined.

28120 ■ *Entrepreneurship in the U.S.: The 2005 Assessment*
Pub: Springer
Ed: Paul Reynolds. **Released:** March 2007. **Price:** $79.95. **Description:** Entrepreneurship and its role in the U.S. economy is discussed, examining new business creation and its impact on job growth, productivity enhancements, innovation, and social mobility.

28121 ■ "Environmental technology firm files bankruptcy" in *Atlanta Business Chronicle* (Vol. 25, December 20, 2002, No. 28, pp. 8A)
Pub: American City Business Publications, Inc.
Ed: Mary Jane Credeur. **Description:** Apyron Technologies Inc., a manufacturer of commercial water, air and emissions purification and detoxification products, has filed for Chapter 7 bankruptcy in the U.S. Bankruptcy Court, Atlanta, Georgia. The eight-year-old firm has raised nearly $17 million over that same period, and lists for around $2 million in claims.

28122 ■ "Environmental and Ownership Characteristics of Small Businesses and their Impact on Development" in *Journal of Small Business Management*
Pub: West Virginia University
Ed: William B. Gartner, Subodh Bhat. **Description:** This article explores the relationship between the characteristics of a small business's location (crime, neighborhood appearance, and transportation accessibility) and a small business owner's expectations of future firm growth.

28123 ■ "An Evening with the Brain Trust" in *Hispanic Business* (October 2003, pp. 40)
Pub: Hispanic Business
Description: Academics, diplomats, investors, and CEOs come together to discuss public policy at the U.S. Hispanic Economic Summit, hosted at the Organization of American States in the Hall of the Americas.

28124 ■ *Every Business Is a Growth Business: How Your Company Can Prosper Year after Year*
Pub: Random House, Inc.
Ed: N. Tichy and R. Charan. **Released:** 1998. **Price:** $29.95(cloth).

28125 ■ "The evolution of corporate diversity" in *Hispanic Business* (Vol. 22, No. 9, September 2000, pp. 36)
Pub: Hispanic Business
Ed: Janet Perez. **Description:** Issues concerning the positive benefits derived by American corporations through initiatives in the workplace to encourage diversity and employment of minority groups, such as Hispanics, are discussed.

28126 ■ "Ex-burger king teams with Hawkins; Group may be pursuing KFC deal" in *Crain's Detroit Business* (Vol. 18, No.51, Dec. 23, 2002, pp. 1)
Pub: Crain Communications Inc., Detroit
Ed: Michael Strong. **Description:** Profile of La-Van Hawkins, owner of 117 Pizza Hut restaurants in Michigan. Hawkins has hired Robert Lowes, a former CEO of Burger King Inc., and is hoping to acquire KFC Inc., the chicken fast food chain.

28127 ■ "Ex-Tiger adds trucking company to his lineup" in *Crain's Detroit Business* (Vol. 16, No. 9, February 28, 2000, pp. 1)
Pub: Crain Communications, Inc.
Ed: Terry Kosdrosky. **Description:** Former Detroit Tiger Cecil Fielder is moving back to Detroit. Cecil will be in charge of developing new business for minority trucking firm, Betz Trucking.

28128 ■ "Exaggeration Nation" in *Inc.* (Volume 27, July 2005, No. 7, pp. 112)
Pub: Inc. Magazine
Ed: Adam Hanft. **Description:** Few business owners tell the whole truth and inflate a company's revenue. Russell Simmons, hip-hop impresario was humiliated publicly for inflating the revenue of Phat Farm in 2003.

28129 ■ "Exchange Overload" in *Red Herring* (No. 103, September 1, 2001, pp. 46-52)
Pub: Herring Communications
Ed: Christopher Locke, Michael V. Copeland. **Description:** Dominating North America's $400 billion gas and electricity market isn't enough for Enron. Now it wants to be the king of B2B trading. Can it work? A profile of Jeffrey Skilling, CEO and president, is included.

28130 ■ "Exec has Firm Grip on Software Sales" in *Crain's New York Business* (Vol. 23, January 29, 2007, No. 5, pp. F13)
Pub: Crain Communications, Inc.
Ed: Amanda Fung. **Description:** Profile of Amanda Fung and her position as business and marketing officer for Microsoft Corp's New York/New Jersey district. Her precision helped bring in revenues of more than $492 million for her region in 2006 and her team expects this year's revenues to exceed $600 million.

28131 ■ "Executives see trouble spreading" in *The New York Times* (December 4, 2000, pp. C1)
Pub: The New York Times Company
Ed: Andrew Ross Sorkin. **Description:** The high technology industry, particularly the online, software, computer equipment, and semiconductor segments are bracing for a continued slowdown. Telecom and consulting firms are also watching for signs of retrenchment. Some executives said that recent investor-sell off had driven stock prices too low. Others said any problems were limited to particular companies, not whole industries. The computer peripherals area was held up as a bright spot. Presently there are stock bargains out there for investors willing to wait for renewed growth, and the stomach for near term uncertainty. Statistical data included.

28132 ■ "Expanding an Empire" in *Small Business Opportunities* (Vol. 16, November 2004, No. 6, pp. 62, 64, 138)
Pub: Harris Publications Inc.
Description: Profile of franchisor, Martinizing Dry Cleaning, headquartered in Loveland, Ohio. The upscale dry cleaning franchisor targets white collar customers with incomes more than $60,000 and are between the ages of 25 and 59. The company was launched in 1949. Growth strategies and predictions are included.

28133 ■ "Experts: Emotions keep faltering suppliers going" in *Crain's Detroit Business* (Vol. 19, No. 2, January 13, 2003, pp. 12)
Pub: Crain Communications Inc., Detroit
Ed: Terry Kosdrosky. **Description:** An overview of the auto suppliers industry including the prospect of having to sell off companies due to low production by automakers.

28134 ■ "Export Advice" in *Entrepreneur* (Vol. 33, January 2005, No. 1, pp. 72)
Pub: Entrepreneur Media Inc.
Ed: Joshua Kurlantzick. **Description:** Small business exporters are among the fastest-growing sectors of American entrepreneurs in the U.S. The Department of Commerce has developed a new Website geared to assist smaller American export companies.

28135 ■ "The Export Engine Is Shifting Into High Gear" in *Business Week* (January 16, 2006, No. 3967, pp. 23-24)
Pub: McGraw-Hill Companies
Ed: James C. Cooper. **Description:** U. S. exporters are expected to benefit from the growing world economy despite a drop in the U.S. dollar. Recent studies show more balance in the growing global economy. Statistical data included.

28136 ■ "Extreme Pizza eying Atlanta for expansion" in *Atlanta Business Chronicle* (Vol. 25, No. 19, October 18, 2002, pp. 21A)
Pub: American City Business Publications, Inc.
Ed: Mark Chediak. **Description:** Extreme Pizza, headquartered in San Francisco, California, is looking to expand into almost 12 metropolitan areas in 2003,

and may include Atlanta, Georgia. Emboldened by revenue growth of 50 percent in 2002, the pizza parlor chain is hoping to more than double the number of its outlets. The highest level of interest include Arizona, Colorado, and Oregon.

28137 ■ "Eyeing Rivals, Foxwoods Set To Expand" in *Boston Globe* (February 2, 2005)
Pub: New York Times Company
Ed: Ralph Ranalli. Description: Foxwoods, the world's largest casino complex, is planning to expand by adding 2 million square feet to its New England complex. The casino plans to increase marketing to blacks, Hispanics, and Asians.

28138 ■ "Factory Card Gets Back in Party Mood" in *Crain's Chicago Business* (Vol. 26, No. 50, December 15, 2003, pp. 6)
Pub: Crain Communications, Inc.
Ed: H. Lee Murphy. Description: Profile of Factory Card & Party Outlet Corporation is presented. The firm filed Chapter 11 reorganization in April 2002, and investors have seen the stock rise from less than $2 to more than $20 in 2003. The company plans to open ten more stores in 2004.

28139 ■ "Factory Card Gets Back in Party Mood; Judicious Growth, Curtailed Costs Restore Firms Health" in *Crains Chicago Business* (Vol. 26)
Pub: Crain Communications, Inc.
Ed: H. Lee Murphy. Description: Profile of Factory Card & Party Outlet Corporation is presented. The firm filed Chapter 11 reorganization in April 2002, and investors have seen the stock rise from less than $2 to more than $20 in 2003. The company plans to open ten more stores in 2004.

28140 ■ "Failure Rates for Female-Controlled Businesses: Are They Any Different?" in *Journal of Small Business Management* (Vol. 41, July 2003)
Pub: International Council of Small Business
Ed: John Watson. Description: According to studies, female-owned businesses generally under-perform male-owned businesses on various measures such as revenue, profit, growth, and failure rates. Statistical data included.

28141 ■ "Fairhaven Business Owners Open Pottery Production Facility" in *Bellingham Business Journal* (December 2006, pp. A6)
Pub: Sun News Inc.
Description: Fairhaven's Mud In Your Eye Pottery, owned by Cate Howell and husband Jeff McDougall, features dinnerware, mugs, serving and baking dishes, steins, and sushi trays. Due to demand from wholesalers they have opened Cascadia Stoneware USA, Inc., a pottery production facility which wholesales their wares to other businesses.

28142 ■ "Falling Behind" in *Entrepreneur* (Vol. 31, No. 8, August 2003, pp. 53)
Pub: Entrepreneur Media, Inc.
Ed: Joshua Kurlantzick. Description: Over the last six months, U.S. currency rates have fallen, affecting small businesses across the U.S.

28143 ■ "Family Ties" in *Entrepreneur* (Vol. 31, No. 7, July 2003, pp. 30)
Pub: Entrepreneur Media, Inc.
Ed: Nichole L. Torres. Description: Revenues for family run businesses grew by 50 percent from 1997 to 2002, according to a study conducted by the Raymond Institute of Family Business and the Mass Mutual Financial Group. Sixty percent of family owned businesses felt optimistic about their company's future and 50 percent planned to hire new employees in the next year.

28144 ■ "Fantastic Sams To Open Manatee County, Fla. Hair Salon" in *Bradenton Herald* (January 5, 2005)
Pub: Bradenton Herald
Ed: Kurt D. Schultheis. Description: Lee Kline, owner of the new Fantastic Sams hair salon explains reasons for his site selection in the Cortez Commons Plaza in Manatee County, Florida.

28145 ■ "FAQs of Life in the New Economy" in *Fast Company* (September 2001, pp. 22)
Pub: Fast Company
Description: Overview of the economics and the new economy, and the way the new economy keeps changing.

28146 ■ "Fare Cuts Might Signal End to Airlines as We Know Them" in *St. Louis Post-Dispatch* (January 9, 2005)
Pub: Knight-Ridder/Tribune Business News
Ed: David Nicklaus. Description: Economics for air travel have changed permanently. Businesses and individuals are able to find bargain fares using the Internet. Cutting prices may not be the best remedy to restore profitability.

28147 ■ "Farmer Jack plans to add up to 17 stores" in *Crain's Detroit Business* (Vol. 16, No. 50, December 11, 2000, pp. 25)
Pub: Crain Communications, Inc.
Ed: Elizabeth Weigandt. Description: Farmer Jack Supermarkets plans to open 12 to 14 stores next year and expects to purchase three stores owned by Churchill's Super Markets in Toledo during the first quarter.

28148 ■ "Fashion Sense Dictates Where Women Shop" in *Marketing to Women* (Vol. 19, October 2006, No. 10, pp. 7)
Pub: EPM Communications, Inc.
Description: According to BIGresearch, while women overall choose value-priced retailers, fashionistas would rather shop at specialty or department stores.

28149 ■ *Faster Company: Building the World's Nuttiest, Turn-on-a-Dime, Home-Grown, Billion Dollar Business*
Pub: John Wiley & Sons, Inc.
Ed: Patrick Kelly and John Case. Released: 1998.
Price: $24.95.

28150 ■ "Fastest Growth by Revenue Category" in *San Fernando Valley Business Journal* (Vol. 11, November 2006, No. 24, pp. 21)
Pub: San Fernando Valley Business Journal Associates
Description: Listing of statistical data on fifty of the San Fernando Valley area's fastest growing private companies based on revenue.

28151 ■ "Fear Factor" in *Entrepreneur.com* (Vol. 34, February 2006, No. 2, pp. 144)
Pub: Entrepreneur Media Inc.
Ed: Robert Kiyosaki. Description: Fear can keep an entrepreneur from growing a company to its full potential. It is important to have a clear, big vision for your business.

28152 ■ "February sales at Claire's jump 6 percent" in *Daily Business Review* (Vol. 77, No. 187, March 7, 2003)
Pub: American Lawyer Media LP
Ed: AnaMaria Colmenares. Description: Claire's Stores sales rose 6 percent despite a plunge in consumer confidence and a drop in national retail sales. The company currently operates 2,900 stores worldwide and is looking to expand into Spain. Statistical data included.

28153 ■ "February Job Gains Boost Stocks, But Pay Scales Show Decline" in *Atlanta Journal-Constitution* (March 5, 2005)
Pub: Knight-Ridder/Tribune Business News
Ed: Michael E. Kanell. Description: There were 262,000 new jobs added to U.S. payrolls in February 2005. According to the U.S. Bureau of Labor Statistics most incomes are not keeping pace with cost of living.

28154 ■ "Fed Bumps Rate to 4.25 Percent" in *Milwaukee Journal Sentinel* (December 14, 2005)
Pub: Journal Sentinel, Inc.
Ed: Avrum D. Lank. Description: Policy-makers at the Federal Reserve raised interest rates by one-quarter of one percent, to 4.25 percent, with future increases expected. Statistical data included.

28155 ■ "Federal stimulus can ensure recovery" in *Atlanta Business Chronicle* (Vol. 25, January 10, 2003, No. 31, pp. 32A)
Pub: American City Business Publications, Inc.
Ed: Jim Molis. Description: A stimulus package from the Federal Government will go a long way in helping the economy on its way to recovery. However, war with Iraq or North Korea would most certainly bring the economy back down.

28156 ■ "FEI's Strategy for Reaching Big Leagues" in *Business Journal-Portland* (Vol. 20, No. 24, August 15, 2003, pp. 1)
Pub: American City Business Journals, Inc.
Ed: Aliza Earnshaw. Description: Profile of FEI Company, manufacturer of three-dimensional inspection technology used in semiconductor manufacturing. The firm's goal is to have $1 billion in revenue.

28157 ■ "Fever Pitch: Pull Out Your Thermometers, 'Cause Things Are Heating Up!" in *Entrepreneur* (Vol. 32, December 2004, No. 12, pp. 72)
Pub: Entrepreneur Media Inc.
Ed: Karen Axelton, Steve Cooper, Amanda C. Kooser, April Y. Pennington, Karen E. Spaeder, Laura Tiffany, Nichole L. Torres, Sara Wilson, Natalia Olenicoff, Rebecca Villaneda, Jeri Yoshida. Description: Newest trends, hottest markets and business ideas for small companies in 2005 are presented, including the use of borrowing a business model.

28158 ■ "Fields of Dreams" in *Crain's New York Business* (Vol. 23, January 1, 2007, No. 1, pp. 3)
Pub: Crain Communications, Inc.
Description: Overview of planned 18,000 seat basketball arena for the Nets is part of a controversial multi-use development in Brooklyn.

28159 ■ "$55M in redevelopment planned for Livonia sites" in *Detroit Business* (Vol. 19, No. 14, April 7, 2003, pp. 6)
Pub: Crain Communications Inc., Detroit
Ed: Laura Bailey. Description: Phoenix Land Development has plans for 94 ranch condominiums and 45,000 square feet of retail space in the City of Livonia, Michigan. Phoenix will also develop on the site of the former George Burns Theatre with a drug store and a bank.

28160 ■ "A 50-Year Legacy" in *Candy Industry* (Vol. 167, April 2002, pp. 29)
Pub: Stagnito Communications Inc.
Description: Profile of Anthony-Thomas Candy Company. The family owned business is celebrating its 50th anniversary.

28161 ■ "First-Half Disbursements Continue Venture Capital's Record-Setting Pace" in *Venture Capital Journal* (Vol. 40, No. 10, Oct. 2000, pp. 47)
Pub: Venture Economics
Ed: Daniel Primack, Jennifer Strauss. Description: Venture capital money is still flowing into innovative new companies. The article includes investment totals by region and by quarter. Statistical data included.

28162 ■ "Fitness Chain Curves Makes Boston Push" in *Boston Business Journal* (Vol. 23, No. 30, August 29, 2003, pp. 3)
Pub: American City Business Journals
Ed: Jill Lerner. Description: The growing success of Curves for Women locations in the Boston, Massachusetts area is explored. Topics include the franchise company's marketing plans, strategic planning, and market development.

28163 ■ "Five Questions" in *Sales & Marketing Management* (Vol. 157, January 2005, No. 1, pp. 15)
Pub: VNU Business Media
Description: Kim Olson, director of Brand Public Relations, answers five questions regarding marketing strategies for small, growing companies.

28164 ■ "A flat road ahead" in *My Business* (September/October 2001, pp. 47)
Pub: My Business Magazine
Ed: Bill Dunkelberg. **Description:** Findings from a recent NFIB survey suggests that the economy slowed substantially in the second half of 2000. Statistical data included.

28165 ■ "Flexibility drove new revenue source" in *Crain's Detroit Business* (Vol. 19, No. 13, March 31, 2003, pp. 14)
Pub: Crain Communications Inc., Detroit
Description: Founder, Mark Campbell of Stoneage. com, a Troy company, states that flexibility is the key to his successful online used-car database.

28166 ■ "Florida is Fastest-Growing State in U.S." in *Tampa Tribune* (December 22, 2005)
Pub: Media General, Inc.
Ed: Chris Echegaray. **Description:** Florida was ranked as the fastest growing state in the U.S., followed by Texas and California.

28167 ■ "Flowers Foods Profits Rise" in *Altanta Journal-Constitution* (February 2, 2007)
Pub: Cox Newspapers, Inc.
Ed: Robert Luke. **Description:** Flowers Foods, baker of brands such as Nature's Own, Cobblestone Mill, Sunbeam and Mrs. Freshley's, predicts furthers price increases on baked goods due to the rising price of flour and corn-based sweeteners.

28168 ■ "A Focus on Firm Profits" in *Black Enterprise* (Vol. 35, August 2004, No. 1, pp. 40)
Pub: Earl G. Graves Publishing Co. Inc.
Ed: Sakina P. Spruell. **Description:** Trevon Hunt's five stock picks earned a collective return of 29.10 percent from June 5, 2003 to June 4, 2004. Health insurer Aetna and semiconductor manufacturer International Rectifier were the two biggest growth leaders in Hunt's portfolio.

28169 ■ "Focus on emerging markets" in *Black Enterprise* (Vol. 32, No. April 2002, 9, pp. 30)
Pub: Earl Graves Publishing Co.
Ed: Matthew S. Scott. **Description:** Presentation of trends in the minority community, focusing on publicly traded companies pursuing the minority marketplace, are minority-owned, and are southeast-based large- and mid-cap companies.

28170 ■ "Follow the Leader" in *Crain's Detroit Business* (Vol. 18, No. 20, May 2)
Pub: Crain Communications Inc. - Detroit
Ed: Amy Lane. **Description:** A new state agency will offer low-interest loans to spur the development of statewide high-speed Internet access.

28171 ■ "Follow the Market Cues" in *Harvard Business Review* (Vol. 80, No. 5, May 2002, pp. 20)
Pub: Harvard Business School Press
Ed: Peter Navarro. **Description:** Knowledge of stock market cycles can help executives make broad strategic decisions as well as more tactical ones. Companies must be aware of their sector's place in the business cycle.

28172 ■ "Food Industry Veteran Has It His Way" in *Black Enterprise* (Vol. 35, February 2005, No. 7, pp. 36)
Pub: Earl G. Graves Publishing Co. Inc.
Ed: Latif Lewis. **Description:** Charles H. James III became Burger King's largest African American franchise. James now owns 37 stores in the Chicago area. Profile of James is included.

28173 ■ "For Beall's, Bigger Is Always Better" in *Bradenton Herald* (February 14, 2005)
Pub: Bradenton Herald
Ed: Dana Sanchez. **Description:** The growth of Beall's Inc. from a dry-goods store to a national chain, with sales approaching $1 billion, is profiled. Retail experts analyze the key factors to explain the retailer's growth.

28174 ■ "For the People" in *Entrepreneur. com* (Vol. 34, February 2006, No. 2, pp. 68)
Pub: Entrepreneur Media Inc.
Ed: Joshua Kurlantzick. **Description:** The U.S. government's contract budget has grown to $300 billion and is growing due to more outsourcing to contractors. Entrepreneurs share secrets to procuring government contracts.

28175 ■ "Forbes Chocolate" in *Dairy Field* (Vol. 185, No. 2, February 2002, pp. 53)
Pub: Stagnito Communications Inc.
Description: Forbes Chocolate, Cleveland manufacturer of chocolate and other flavor powders for milk, ice cream and frozen yogurt, has celebrated its 100th anniversary. Benjamin P. Forbes started the company in 1901 by making chocolate for candy. After 100 years, the Forbes' plant bears no physical resemblance to the original factory, but its employees remain dedicated to the core principles that brought them through the first century.

28176 ■ "Ford to Mark 100th Anniversary This Year" in *San Jose Mercury News* (April 11, 2003)
Pub: Knight-Ridder/Tribune Business News
Ed: Matt Nauman. **Description:** Ford Motor Company will use its 100th Anniversary as a tool to market its vehicles, through reminders of Ford's impact over the past century.

28177 ■ "Foreign expansion of small firms: the impact of domestic alternatives" in *Journal of Business Venturing* (Vol. 16, No. 6, Nov. 2001)
Pub: Elsevier Science, Inc.
Ed: Rongxin Chen, Marc J. Martin. **Description:** Research investigating factors influencing small foreign expansion plans of small firms is presented. It is concluded that the types of products offered and the domestic size of the small company tend to influence the success of its foreign expansion.

28178 ■ "Forget the Series; St. Louis has Bragging Rights for Job Growth" in *St. Louis Post-Dispatch* (December 19, 2004)
Pub: Knight-Ridder/Tribune Business News
Ed: David Nicklaus. **Description:** St. Louis area reported 42,000 new jobs for the period October 2003 to October 2004, and if the trend continues could be the most jobs added to the region since 1988. St. Louis also saw three initial public offerings in 2004. Las Vegas, Nevada is also reporting high growth for the same time period.

28179 ■ "The Forgotten Strategy" in *Harvard Business Review* (Vol. 81, No. 11, November 2003, pp. 76)
Pub: Harvard Business School Press
Ed: Pankaj Ghemawat. **Description:** Potential changes in business globalization strategies are examined.

28180 ■ "Fortune's 100 Fastest Growing: Who made this years' list?" in *Fortuneit* (Vol. 146, No. 4, September 2, 2002, pp. 161)
Pub: Time Inc.
Ed: Matthew Boyle. **Description:** The 100 Fastest-Growing Companies are listed, with statistics including earnings-per-share growth; net income; revenue, total return; and stock price.

28181 ■ "Forward Thinking" in *PC Magazine* (March 7, 2000, pp. 7)
Pub: Ziff-Davis Publishing Company
Ed: Michael J. Miller. **Description:** The Y2K crisis has passed and companies are now focusing on the task of moving their IT infrastructures into the 21st century. Hardware and software integration should be a great part of this effort as companies move to centralized administration, single log-ons, and a greater reliance on certificates and directories. Microsoft's Windows 2000 has arrived and should be a part of this movement. New applications and Web services will facilitate this integration for smaller organizations. New network infrastructures will provide high-speed connections for both local and remote users, wireless access to data and virtual private networks.

28182 ■ "Found in Yonkers" in *Crain's New York Business* (Vol. 23, January 15, 2007, No. 3, pp. 37)
Pub: Crain Communications, Inc.
Description: Yonkers, Westchester's largest city, has unveiled a master plan of $3.1 billion to redevelop downtown and attract more companies, according to Yonkers Industrial Development Agency.

28183 ■ "Franchise to go: despite a recession some of these businesses are hot" in *Black Enterprise* (Vol. 32, No. 9, April 2002, pp. 46)
Pub: Earl Graves Publishing Co.
Ed: Alan Hughes. **Description:** The advantages of buying a franchise business are examined. Recommendations for choosing a franchise are also discussed.

28184 ■ "Free Agents in the Olde World" in *Fast Company* (May 2001, pp. 136)
Pub: Fast Company
Ed: Jill Rosenfeld. **Description:** Thomas Malone, a professor at MIT's Sloan School of Management and founder of the Center for Coordination Science, takes a look at the future of commerce and at the structure of how work will get done.

28185 ■ "A Fresh Look for Northeast Brookfield" in *Business Journal-Milwaukee* (Vol. 20, No. 51, September 5, 2003, pp. A1)
Pub: American City Business Journals, Inc.
Ed: Mark Kass. **Description:** As part of urban redevelopment, the city of Brookfield, Wisconsin, is considering finding a major retail or office development for the area. One company that was named as a possible candidate is Costco Wholesale Corporation.

28186 ■ "Fresh Sets of Eyes on Detroit" in *Crain's Detroit Business* (Vol. 22, January 30, 2006, No. 5, pp. 1)
Pub: Crain Communications Inc. - Detroit
Ed: Andrew Dietderich. **Description:** Out-of-town investors and developers are seeing the City of Detroit in a new light after Super Bowl XL. Downtown Detroit is overcoming its negative image.

28187 ■ "Friends in High Places" in *Hispanic Business* (Vol. 23, No. 7/8, July/August 2001, pp. 62, 64)
Pub: Hispanic Business
Ed: Scott Williams. **Description:** Profile of the newly formed Hispanic Network of Entrepreneurs. The group hopes to ease the way for a new generation of Hispanic entrepreneurs in the high-tech industry, business development, venture capital financing, recruiting and exchange of ideas.

28188 ■ "From Feast to Famine?" in *Hispanic Business* (Vol. 23, No. 11, November 2001, pp. 42, 44, 46, 48-49)
Pub: Hispanic Business Inc.
Ed: Scott Williams. **Description:** Export revenues for Hispanic companies grew in 2000, but the slowing economy may halt further growth in certain sectors. Statistics on the fastest-growing top 50 exporters, top 50 exporters by state and by sector is included.

28189 ■ "Frontier Could Land Here" in *Pittsburgh Business Times* (Vol. 22, No. 52, July 11, 2003, pp. 1)
Pub: Pittsburgh Business Times
Ed: Christopher Davis. **Description:** Discussions are underway between Denver-based Frontier Airlines and officials of the local airport in Allegheny County, Pennsylvania.

28190 ■ "Fueling tomorrow's growth" in *Harvard Business Review* (Vol. 80, No. 9, September 2002, pp. 51)
Pub: Harvard Business School Press
Ed: Robert McGarvey. **Description:** New sources of oil, new fuels, and conservation are discussed in an overview of future products.

28191 ■ "Full circle" in *Candy Industry* (Vol. 167, No. 4, April 2002, pp. 24)
Pub: Stagnito Communications Inc.

Ed: Carla Zanetos Cully. **Description:** Profile of ways the family-owned Anthony-Thomas Candy Company continues to reinvent itself in order to meet the demands of an ever-changing marketplace.

28192 ■ **"Fund-Raising Falters, VCs Keep Cutting Back" in** *Venture Capital Journal* **(Vol. 42, No. 10, October 2002, pp. 18-20)**
Pub: Thomas Venture Economics
Description: Venture capital firms refunded more money to limited partners than they raised in the second quarter 2002, the first time that has happened.

28193 ■ **"Fund-Raising Soars 78 Percent, Momentum Builds" in** *Venture Capital Journal* **(December 1, 2004)**
Pub: Thomason Financial Inc.
Description: Venture firms raised more capital in the first three quarters of 2004 than all of 2003, with 125 venture funds taking in nearly $11.25 billion in commitments and the number is expected to grow.

28194 ■ **"Furniture.com stages revival, forges ties with non-com allies" in** *Boston Business Journal* **(Vol. 22, No. 11, April 19, 2002, pp. 1)**
Pub: MCP, Inc.
Description: Furniture.com Inc., which went into bankruptcy, is making a comeback by partnering with brick-and-mortar retailers like Levitz Furniture Corporation and Seaman Furniture Company Inc.; Furniture.com is being backed by Resurgence Asset Management LLC.

28195 ■ **"The Future of Franchising: Taking Advantage of the Changing Complexion of the American Economy" in** *Black Enterprise* **(Vol. 32, No. 2)**
Pub: Earl Graves Publishing Co.
Ed: C. Everett Wallace. **Description:** Franchising remains one of the fastest growing segments of the American business economy. The article addresses the potential business franchise opportunity in minority communities with information for the following franchises: Jan-Pro Cleaning Systems, AAMCO Transmissions, SIGN-A-RAMA, Chick-fil-A, Sunoco Inc., Kumon Math and Reading Centers, Choice Hotels, Liberty Tax Service, Dunhill Staffing Systems Inc., The Athlete's Foot, KFC, Meineke, Denny's, Subway, Coverall Cleaning Concepts, Church's Chicken, and Wendy's.

28196 ■ **"Gallery of Growth" in** *Houston Business Journal* **(Vol. 34, No. 7, June 27, 2003, pp. 19A)**
Pub: American City Business Journals
Ed: Mary Ann Azevedo. **Description:** Profile of Ahmad El Naggar, who opened a furniture showroom without air conditioning, but offers lower prices.

28197 ■ **"Gearing Up For Expansion" in** *Fast Company* **(March 2005, No. 92, pp. 90)**
Pub: Gruner & Jahr USA Publishing
Ed: Shonan Noronha. **Description:** Profile of Adobe's Acrobat 7 business software designed to allow users to take total control over the creation and distribution of important documents, as well as making them more accessible to clients, coworkers, and strategic partners.

28198 ■ **"Generate More Revenue with a Bottom-Up Marketing Plan" in** *Home Business* **(Vol. 12, March/April 2005, No. 2, pp. 32, 34-35)**
Pub: Home Business Magazine
Ed: Sonya Carmichael Jones. **Description:** Marketing to grow a home business is discussed using a bottom-up plan.

28199 ■ **"Georgia ringing up new telecom contract" in** *Atlanta Business Chronicle* **(Vol. 25, November 8, 2002, No. 22 pp. 3A)**
Pub: American City Business Publications, Inc.
Ed: Mary Jane Credeur. **Description:** ConnectGeorgia intends to re-bid on the ten-year contract for the $1.8 billion Converged Communications Outsourcing Project in Georgia. ConnectGeorgia is a team that in-

volves BellSouth Corporation, AT&T Corporation, EDS Corporation, and Lockheed Martin Corporation. IBM Corporation and Unisys are leading teams that intend to make bids on the contract, and Northrup Grumman Corporation, Los Angeles, and KPMG LLP may also bid.

28200 ■ **"Georgia medical device business growing" in** *Atlanta Business Chronicle* **(Vol. 25, No. 19, October 18, 2002, pp. 3A)**
Pub: American City Business Publications, Inc.
Ed: Julie Bryant. **Description:** The number of medical device companies operating in the state of Georgia currently totals more than 225, with growth centered in the small- to medium-size category. However, industry leaders in the state contend that the medical device industry has yet to take-off in the state. Many of these firms are divisions of much larger companies.

28201 ■ **"Get In Sync: To Spark Business Growth, Follow the Leader In Your Industry" in** *Entrepreneur* **(Vol. 31, No. 10, October 2003, pp. 38)**
Pub: Entrepreneur Media, Inc.
Ed: David Newton. **Description:** Coordinating business strategy with a wide range of administrative and managerial processes is a major key to growing a company.

28202 ■ **"Get Ready to Grow" in** *My Business* **(April/May 2004, pp. 40)**
Pub: My Business Magazine
Ed: Bill Dunkelberg. **Description:** According to the National Federation of Independent Business, profit trends are the highest since 2000 with capital spending plans also the highest since 2000. Small business are voicing strongest optimism in 20 years.

28203 ■ **"Getting Ahead Of the Weather" in** *Fortune* **(Vol. 151, February 7, 2005, No. 3, pp. 87)**
Pub: Time Inc.
Ed: Abraham Lustgarten. **Description:** The National Oceanic and Atmospheric Administration estimates a third of the U.S. gross domestic product is affected by weather in the form of slowed transportation, inflated energy costs, and interrupted sales. Steps some businesses are taking to protect their firms against the elements are profiled.

28204 ■ **"Getting Paid Faster" in** *Black Enterprise* **(Vol. 36, February 2006, No. 7, pp. 58)**
Pub: Earl G. Graves Publishing Co. Inc.
Ed: Bridget McCrea. **Description:** Large corporations and the government are using credit-card-like accounts through Visa and MasterCard for purchasing products and services. Visa has launched a program to introduce to small businesses in order to setup accounts to accept the purchasing cards in order to grow their businesses.

28205 ■ *Getting to Scale: Growing Your Business Without Selling Out*
Pub: Berrett-Koehler Publishers, Incorporated
Ed: Jill Bamburg. **Released:** July 2006. **Price:** $14.95. **Description:** Ways for entrepreneurs to preserve the value of their company while maintaining growth and competitiveness.

28206 ■ **"The Giant that would be King" in** *Red Herring* **(No. 102, August 15, 2001, pp. 40-45)**
Pub: Herring Communications
Ed: Robert LaFranco. **Description:** Microsoft transformed personal computing, is it about to reinvent entertainment? Streaming media is growing at a fast pace helping to promote new startup companies.

28207 ■ **"Glass Ceiling Persists in the Board Room" in** *Marketing to Women* **(Vol. 19, December 2006, No. 2, pp. 8)**
Pub: EPM Communications, Inc.
Description: A study by search firm Heidrick & Struggles and Women Corporate Directors shows that executive inequality remains high despite the number of women who hold board seats. Although these women

tend to mentor and recommend other women for candidates, only 54 percent say that at least one of the women recommended was actually elected to the board. Despite the meager statistics, 76 percent of women on boards surveyed stated that they oppose a legal quota that would mandate an increase of women occupying board seats.

28208 ■ **"Global Spectrum: Making a Difference in the Convention Center Industry" in** *Tradeshow Week* **(Vol. 34, November 29, 2004, No. 48, pp. S2)**
Pub: Reed Business Information
Description: Profile of Global Spectrum, a private management firm in the tradeshow sector. Global Spectrum is a subsidiary of Comcast-Spectator of Philadelphia, Pennsylvania. The company has increased management contracts for arenas, convention centers, stadiums and ice rinks by more than 500 percent since January 2000 when it was created.

28209 ■ **"GM Hopes Boosting Mileage Will Slow Big Models' Sales Drain" in** *Milwaukee Journal Sentinel* **(December 10, 2005)**
Pub: Journal Sentinel, Inc.
Ed: Thomas Content. **Description:** General Motors Corporation is promoting mileage ratings of its SUV models in the hopes of increasing sales for these vehicles.

28210 ■ **"Go For the Gold" in** *Entrepreneur* **(Vol. 32, October 2004, No. 10, pp. 68)**
Pub: Entrepreneur Media Inc.
Ed: David Worrell. **Description:** Planning for the day an entrepreneur will sell their business is critical. Growth potential is key when determining a company's worth.

28211 ■ **"Go West: Want a Few Business Pointers? Mosey on Over to Deadwood" in** *Entrepreneur* **(Vol. 32, November 2004, No. 11, pp. 22)**
Pub: Entrepreneur Media Inc.
Ed: Steve Cooper. **Description:** HBO's new series Deadwood, based on a real-life town in South Dakota around 1876, offers insight into business leadership, contracts, property rights, marketing, managing and business expansion.

28212 ■ **"Going Global: International Business Tips Make a World of Difference" in** *Entrepreneur* **(Vol. 32, December 2004, No. 12, pp. 34)**
Pub: Entrepreneur Media Inc.
Ed: Aliza Pilar Sherman. **Description:** Tips for women business owners to follow when expanding markets and increasing sales by doing business with overseas vendors and clients.

28213 ■ **"Going Global: Lessons from Late Movers" in** *Harvard Business Review* **(Vol. 78, No. 2, March 2000, pp. 132)**
Pub: Harvard Business School Publishing Corp.
Ed: Christopher A. Bartlett, Sumantra Ghoshal. **Description:** Contrary to popular wisdom, companies from the fringes of the world economy can become global players. What they need is organizational confidence, a clear strategy, a passion for learning, and the leadership to bring these factors together.

28214 ■ **"Going Medium-Tech" in** *Inc.* **(Volume 27, December 2005, No. 12, pp. 77-78)**
Pub: Inc. Magazine
Ed: David H. Freedman. **Description:** Most successful companies place themselves somewhere in the middle of technology.

28215 ■ **"Going Nuclear" in** *Business 2.0* **(Vol. 6, May 2005, No. 4, pp. 90-95)**
Pub: Time, Inc.
Ed: G. Pascal Zachary. **Description:** Randy Edington, troubleshooter for sick nuclear plants, explains how Entergy is making aging atomic power plants successful, fueling the industry's doubtful resurgence.

28216 ■ "Going Public" in *Entrepreneur* (Vol. 31, No. 11, November 2003, pp. 65)
Pub: Entrepreneur Media, Inc.
Ed: C.J. Prince. **Description:** Reverse mergers are investigated. A reverse merger allows private companies to become public by acquiring or merging with a public 'shell' company.

28217 ■ "The Good Fight" in *Entrepreneur* (Vol. 30, No. 3, March 2002, pp. 48)
Pub: Entrepreneur Media Inc.
Ed: Janean Chun. **Description:** The author calls for entrepreneurs to change the corporate way of thinking in America, in other words a call to common sense.

28218 ■ "Good to Great" in *Fast Company* (November 2001, pp. 90)
Pub: Fast Company
Ed: Jim Collins. **Description:** Several myths regarding company performance are explored, focusing on issues that transform a company from good to great.

28219 ■ *Good to Great: Why Some Companies Make the Leap...and Others Don't*
Pub: HarperInformation
Ed: Jim Collins. **Released:** October 2001. **Price:** $27.50. **Description:** Management styles for growing a modern business.

28220 ■ "Good News (Almost) Everywhere You Look" in *My Business* (June/July 2004, pp. 42)
Pub: My Business Magazine
Ed: Bill Dunkelberg. **Description:** Small business owner optimism is at historically strong levels. The Index of Small Business Optimism reported in over 100 for the eleventh month in a row. Statistical data included.

28221 ■ "Good night, sweetheart" in *Red Herring* (No. 106, October 15, 2001, pp. 35)
Pub: Herring Communications
Ed: Julie Landry. **Description:** The failure of Cerulic, the wireless-service provider, will open competition for MobileStart Network and Wayport.

28222 ■ *The Google Story: Inside the Hottest Business, Media, and Technology Success of Our Time*
Pub: Random Housing Publishing Group
Ed: David A. Vise; Mark Malseed. **Price:** $26.00.

28223 ■ "Google World: http://google.indicateur.com" in *Entrepreneur* (Vol. 31, No. 10, October 2003, pp. 6)
Pub: Entrepreneur Media, Inc.
Ed: Steve Cooper. **Description:** Ways the Google search engine can help a small business are discussed.

28224 ■ "Grand Slam" in *Birmingham Business Journal* (Vol. 20, No. 31, August 1, 2003, pp. 15)
Pub: American City Business Journals, Inc.
Ed: Gilbert Nicholson. **Description:** Falling interest rates and rising sales of homes has increased business for home appraisal and inspection services. Jones Appraisal Company has not been able to keep up with demand from real estate companies.

28225 ■ "Grape Expectations: Are You Thinking About Getting Into the Wine Business?" in *Entrepreneur* (Vol. 31, No. 10, October 2003, pp. 106)
Pub: Entrepreneur Media, Inc.
Ed: Nichole L. Torres. **Description:** Winemaking has outpaced the economy in growth, even during recessions, and is expected to be a growth industry for the future.

28226 ■ "Graphiti: Eking out e-commerce" in *Red Herring* (No. 103, September 1, 2001, pp. 28)
Pub: Herring Communications
Ed: Elizabeth Lamb. **Description:** Online retail continues with steady growth; the number of online shoppers has risen by 50 percent worldwide, from 2000. Statistical data included.

28227 ■ "Graphiti: Online demographics" in *Red Herring* (No. 102, August 15, 2001, pp. 26)
Pub: Herring Communications
Ed: Elizabeth Lamb. **Description:** An overview of the growth of online use globally. Charts and graphs are included, featuring adult Internet usage by gender, female Internet users, and teen and adult Internet use.

28228 ■ "Greased Lightning" in *Forbes* (Vol. 170, No. 9, October 28, 2002, pp. 246)
Pub: Forbes Magazine
Ed: Lea Goldman. **Description:** Sonic Corporation, one of Forbes Best Small Companies for 2002, and one-fifth the size of McDonald's, is profiled.

28229 ■ "The Great Comeback" in *My Business* (April/May 2003, pp. 26-28, 30-32)
Pub: My Business Magazine
Ed: Shannon Scully. **Description:** Various business owners discuss their road from business failure and back again to running successful companies.

28230 ■ "Great Time to Go It Alone" in *Kiplinger's Personal Finance Magazine* (Vol. 58, No. 5, May 2004, pp. 20)
Pub: Kiplinger Washington Editors, Inc.
Ed: Melynda Dovel Wilcox. **Description:** Government statistics underestimate the number of jobs being created each month at small and startup companies, and the number of individuals becoming entrepreneurs.

28231 ■ "The great unknown" in *Entrepreneur* (Vol. 31, No. 6, June 2003, pp. 19)
Pub: Entrepreneur Media Inc.
Ed: Chris Penttila. **Description:** The frustrations faced by entrepreneurs during a struggling economy are discussed.

28232 ■ "Green Energy Co. Goes Public" in *Long Island Business News* (May 7, 2004)
Pub: Dolan Media Newswires
Description: New York International Log and Lumber Company started trading on the Nasdaq's Over-the-Counter market at 60 cents per share. The company describes itself as a green, bio-energy supplier of wood chips to utilities and corporation who burn them to produce energy.

28233 ■ "Greenspan in Florida warns home prices are likely to fall this year" in *Daily Business Review* (Vol. 77, March 5, 2003)
Pub: American Lawyer Media LP
Description: Federal Reserve Chairman, Alan Greenspan, warned that housing prices may fall after years of rapid increase, which in turn, will slow recent consumer-spending boom to purchase household goods and services.

28234 ■ "A grim adventure: Amphion Capital's venture fund loses all" in *Barron's* (Vol. 82, No. 58, February 17, 2003, pp. T8)
Pub: Barron's
Ed: Eric J. Savitz. **Description:** Amphion's portfolio of tech stocks all collapsed in the past two years, as the fund's assets under management dropped from $91.8 million January 30, 2000 to below zero at the end of 2002. Major losses were Axcess and Biocentric Solutions.

28235 ■ "Grist: A Passport to America" in *Inc.* (October 1, 2004)
Pub: Inc. Magazine
Ed: Adam Hanft. **Description:** Ways blue states and red states are learning to communicate and do business are highlighted.

28236 ■ "Grist: An Entrepreneurs Resolutions" in *Inc.* (January 1, 2005)
Pub: Inc. Magazine
Ed: Adam Hanft. **Description:** Small business New Year's resolutions are discussed, including recommendations to help grow a business.

28237 ■ "Grow Your Client BASE" in *Home Office Computing* (Vol. 18, No. 8, August 2000, pp. 54)
Pub: Scholastic Inc.
Ed: Jeffery D. Zbar. **Description:** Five simple strategies are provided for finding new customers and generating repeat business for home-based companies.

28238 ■ "Growing for broke" in *Harvard Business Review* (Vol. 80, No. 9, September 2002, pp. 27)
Pub: Harvard Business School Press
Ed: Paul Hemp. **Description:** Experts discuss a hypothetical situation whereby a small firm desires to grow and expand by acquiring another company.

28239 ■ *Growing Business Handbook: Inspirational Advice from Successful Entrepreneurs and Fast-Growing UK Companies*
Pub: Kogan Page, Limited
Ed: Adam Jolly. **Released:** February 2007. **Price:** $49.95. **Description:** Tips for growing and running a successful business are covered, focusing on senior managers in middle market and SME companies.

28240 ■ "Growing a Business" in *Small Business Opportunities* (Vol. 16, No. 3, May 2004, pp. 80, 84)
Pub: Harris Publications, Inc.
Ed: Vicki Gerson. **Description:** Profile of Bill Meadows, who was born in a coal mining camp and now runs a chain of retail nurseries valued at $72 million. The nurseries focus exclusively on plants, shrubs, and trees.

28241 ■ "Growing Concern" in *Pittsburgh Business Times* (Vol. 23, No. 4, August 15, 2003, pp. 19)
Pub: Pittsburgh Business Times
Ed: Patty Tascarella. **Description:** The growing success of Pittsburgh, Pennsylvania-based EZ-FLO Inc. is presented. Topics include managing a small business, marketing strategy, and sales volume.

28242 ■ "Growing From the Middle" in *Hispanic Business* (July/August 2004, pp. 20, 22, 24)
Pub: Hispanic Business
Ed: Joel Russell. **Description:** Medium-sized companies have become a powerful force in economic development. These companies have balanced expansion strategies and financial stability, and many are Hispanic-owned.

28243 ■ *Growing and Managing a Small Business: An Entrepreneurial Perspective*
Pub: Houghton Mifflin College Division
Ed: Kathleen R. Allen. **Released:** July 2006. **Price:** $105.27. **Description:** Introduction to business ownership and management from startup through growth.

28244 ■ "A Growing Market for Talk" in *Hispanic Business* (Vol. 24, No. 4, April 2002, pp. 22)
Pub: Hispanic Business Inc.
Ed: Rick Laezman. **Description:** The Hispanic public-speaking industry has entered a growth mode, and Hispanic motivational speakers are finding corporations, associations and schools eager to hire them.

28245 ■ "Growing Pains" in *Home Business* (Vol. 13, January/February 2006, No. 1, pp. 88, 90-91)
Pub: Home Business Magazine
Ed: Jodi Helmer. **Description:** Home-based business owners can hire employees to help grow a company. Tips to discover if your home-based firm is ready to hire an employee are included.

28246 ■ "Growing Pains" in *Inc.* (October 2000, pp. 20)
Pub: The Goldhirsh Group
Ed: Toby Toler. **Description:** The control of one's company and one's time are investigated, with comments from entrepreneurs about methods they have used in the past.

28247 ■ "Growing Representation?" in *Hispanic Business* **(Vol. 24, No. 1/2, January/February 2002, pp. 28, 30)**
Pub: Hispanic Business Inc.
Description: Corporate boards have more Hispanic members in 2002, but the article questions whether the increase is reflective of a trend or just better survey data used. A listing of the 2002 Hispanic Business Boardroom Elite is presented. Statistical data included.

28248 ■ *Growing Your Business*
Pub: Routledge Inc.
Ed: Burke. **Released:** December 2006. **Price:** $150.00. **Description:** Growth strategies for small businesses are presented.

28249 ■ "Growth Amid Uncertainty" in *Hispanic Business* **(Vol. 23, No. 11, November 2001, pp. 12)**
Pub: Hispanic Business Inc.
Ed: Patricia Guadalupe. **Description:** The theme for the annual MED Week gathering of minority entrepreneurs was: Strategies for Growth in the American Economy. Federal officials discussed ways for minority entrepreneurs to expand their businesses in the aftermath of September 11. Forecasts for various industries were presented.

28250 ■ "Growth Guru: How to Turn Your Business Into a Hot Commodity" in *Entrepreneur* **(Vol. 31, No. 7, July 2003, pp. 27)**
Pub: Entrepreneur Media, Inc.
Ed: Mark Henricks. **Description:** Reviews of the books, "What I Learned Before I Sold to Warren Buffett", which deals with hiring, leading, communicating, decision-making and general management issues; and "What's The Big Idea", which deals with management ideas, are presented.

28251 ■ *Growth/Management of Entrepreneur Businesses*
Pub: Houghton Mifflin Co.
Ed: Allen. **Released:** 1998. **Price:** $52.17.

28252 ■ "The Growth of Minority Car Dealerships" in *Minority Business Journal* **(Vol. 17, No. 5, September/October 2001, pp. 3, 6-7)**
Pub: Minority Business Journal
Ed: Nicholas R. Hunter. **Description:** Today auto manufacturers work to draw not only minority buyers for their vehicles, but also for minorities to buy their dealerships to sell automobiles. Small profiles are given on successful minority dealers throughout the country, as well as information about Ford's Minority Retailer Development Program and the Ford Dealership Office Management Training Program.

28253 ■ "Growth Outside the Core" in *Harvard Business Review* **(Vol. 81, No. 12, December 2003, pp. 66)**
Pub: Harvard Business School Press
Ed: Chris Zook, James Allen. **Description:** Six methods to launch corporate growth into adjacent businesses, using Nike Inc.'s diversification from athletic shoes to golf equipment and apparel is explored. The methods include entering new geographies, using new distribution channels, developing new services and products, and targeting new customer segments.

28254 ■ "Growth Slow But Sure" in *My Business* **(April/May 2003, pp. 48)**
Pub: My Business Magazine
Ed: Bill Dunkelberg. **Description:** According to the University of Michigan Index in February 2003, the real economy is not doing as poorly as the confidence measures are suggesting, the latest GDP growth near 3 percent in real terms, is compared to an average of 3.5 percent over the past few decades.

28255 ■ *The Growth Strategy: How to Build a New Business into a Successful Enterprise*
Pub: Knowledge Exchange
Ed: Peter Engel. **Released:** 1997. **Price:** $22.95 (cloth).

28256 ■ "Growth Tales; Key Strategies Used by Young Firms" in *Crain's New York Business* **(Vol. 22, December 11, 2006, No. 50, pp. 27)**
Pub: Crain Communications, Inc.
Ed: Lisa Goff. **Description:** Profile of businesses who have used innovative marketing campaigns that cost little to no capital.

28257 ■ "Guarded About the Hispanic Economy" in *Hispanic Business* **(Vol. 24, No. 5, May 2002, pp. 18, 20, 22, 25)**
Pub: Hispanic Business Inc.
Description: Although the U.S. economy is expected to continue its slow recovery, some forecast worsening Hispanic joblessness, declining revenues for Hispanic-owned firms, and a drop-off in U.S.-Latin American trade.

28258 ■ *Guerrilla Marketing, 4th Edition: Easy and Inexpensive Strategies for Making Big Profits from Your Small Business*
Pub: Houghton Mifflin Company
Ed: Jay Conrad Levinson. **Released:** May 2007. **Price:** $19.95. **Description:** Marketing strategies for small businesses is designed to revolutionize, expand and grow businesses. .

28259 ■ *Guts & Borrowed Money: Straight Talk for Starting & Growing Your Small Business*
Pub: Bard Press
Ed: Tom S. Gillis. **Released:** 1997. **Price:** $29.95 (cloth); $19.95 (paper).

28260 ■ "Hamtramck DDA OKs Plans for Jos. Campau District" in *Crain's Detroit Business* **(Vol. 22, February 13, 2006, No. 7, pp. 26)**
Pub: Crain Communications Inc. - Detroit
Ed: Robert Ankeny. **Description:** The Joseph Campau Avenue strip in Hamtramck, Michigan has been approved for ten community and development initiatives which will help to recruit and retain businesses, improve the buildings and promote a public safety program for the city's commercial district.

28261 ■ *The Handbook of Financing Growth: Strategies and Capital Structure*
Pub: John Wiley & Sons, Incorporated
Ed: Kenneth H. Marks, John P. Funkhouser, Larry E. Robbins. **Released:** March 2005. **Price:** $79.95 (US), $123.95 (Canadian). **Description:** Using empirical data and actual case studies, strategies are presented to illustrate capital structures and fund raising techniques for emerging growth and middle-market companies.

28262 ■ "Hard Landing for Landlines" in *Crain's New York Business* **(Vol. 22, December 4, 2006, No. 49, pp. 3)**
Pub: Crain Communications, Inc.
Description: More than two million residential landline customers are choosing Internet telephone service and cell phones over their landlines. Verizon is suffering the greatest in this new trend.

28263 ■ "Harley's '06 Models Revving Sales" in *Milwaukee Journal Sentinel* **(December 20, 2005)**
Pub: Journal Sentinel, Inc.
Ed: Rick Barrett. **Description:** Harley-Davidson is expanding their lineup of 2006 touring bikes in hopes of increasing sales. Reports from various dealerships vary, although most are confident the new bikes along with incentives will boost sales.

28264 ■ "Harley's Leadership U-Turn" in *Harvard Business Review* **(Vol. 78, No. 4, July 2000, pp. 43)**
Pub: Harvard Business School Publishing Corp.
Ed: Rich Teerlink. **Description:** Former company executive details how the company was saved from financial disaster.

28265 ■ "Hartford Expands Small Commercial Offerings" in *Rough Notes* **(Vol. 145, No. 6, June 2002, pp. 50)**
Pub: Rough Notes
Ed: Dennis Pillsbury. **Description:** The Hartford, an insurance company, is committed to serve the insurance needs of small commercial businesses. Its share in the market is around 4.2 percent of a $30 billion small business market.

28266 ■ "Hartsfield bracing for choppy '03" in *Atlanta Business Chronicle* **(Vol. 25, January 3, 2003, No. 30, pp. 1A)**
Pub: American City Business Publications, Inc.
Ed: Walter Woods. **Description:** Hartfield Atlanta International Airport is looking for ways to positively impact its revenue stream. According to Ben DeCosta, general manager of the airport, several ideas to effect cost efficient change have been suggested. One idea is to provide wireless Internet access in terminals.

28267 ■ "Has Riverboat Gambling Enhanced Kansas City's River Front?" in *Ingram's* **(Vol. 29, No. 1, January 2003, pp. 6)**
Pub: Show Me Publishing, Inc.
Ed: Kevin P. Mullaly, Greg Hawley. **Description:** Comments and opinions regarding the existing river boat gambling in Kansas City, Missouri are presented.

28268 ■ "Hauppauge-based Spellman High Voltage Electronics Doubles the Size of Its Bohemia Facility" in *Long Island Business News* **(Jan.30,2004)**
Pub: Dolan Media Newswires
Ed: Nick Anastasi. **Description:** The nation's largest independent manufacturer of high-voltage power conversion products, Spellman High Voltage Electronics Corporation, has doubled the size of its Bohemia facility. The expansion will include metal fabrication and machining divisions.

28269 ■ "He knows if you've been naughty, but you can still send him e-mail" in *The New York Times* **(December 13, 2000, pp. D10, H10)**
Pub: The New York Times Company
Ed: James Barron. **Description:** Web sites having to do with Santa Claus see a huge rise in business.

28270 ■ "Heller Family Pays $4.1M for Warehouse" in *Journal Record (Oklahoma City, OK)* **(February 6, 2007)**
Pub: Journal Record
Ed: Kirby Lee Davis. **Description:** Heller Family Investments LLC purchased the Airpark Distribution Center industrial building, the 19th property in the family portfolio. The family is expected to purchase two more properties in 2007.

28271 ■ "Henry Schein Expands Office Space in Melville" in *Long Island Business News* **(February 27, 2004)**
Pub: Dolan Media Newswires
Ed: Nick Anastasi. **Description:** Henry Schein Inc. is relocating to a 150,000-square foot building. The distributor of health care products will also hold the right to expand 80 Bayliss. Schein is the largest distributor of healthcare products and services to office-based healthcare practitioners in the combined North American and European markets and has operations in Australia and New Zealand.

28272 ■ "Heroes Of Small Business" in *Fortune* **(Vol. 142, No. 11, November 13, 2000, pp. F348B+)**
Pub: Time Inc.
Description: Fortune spotlights 15 people they consider to be heroes in the new Fortune Hall of Fame. From Apple's Steve Jobs to Kinko's founder Paul Orfalea to Earl Graves of Black Enterprise, meet some of the most influential entrepreneurs of the past two decades.

28273 ■ "Hey, Listen Up!" in *Entrepreneur* **(Vol. 31, No. 9, July 2003, pp. 124)**
Pub: Entrepreneur Media, Inc.
Ed: Romanus Wolter. **Description:** Steps to help entrepreneurs grow a business and become open to ideas are listed.

28274 ■ "A Hidden Gem? Quebec Looks To Flex Muscle" in *Venture Capital Journal* (Vol. 42, No. 5, May 2002, pp. 44-45)
Pub: Thomas Venture Economics
Ed: Danielle Fugazy. **Description:** American venture capitalists have not invested much in Quebec's industry in the past, but the continuous growth Quebec is seeing in the fields of engineering, transportation, telecommunications, aeronautics and aerospace technology, medical research, computer science and biotechnology, has American VCs taking a second look.

28275 ■ "High-end home sales falter in North Fulton" in *Atlanta Business Chronicle* (Vol. 25, December 6, 2002, No. 26, pp. 3A)
Pub: American City Business Publications, Inc.
Ed: Lisa R. Schoolcraft. **Description:** The inventory of completed, but available homes priced in the $950,000 range in North Fulton County, Georgia is at 52 percent, according to Phillip Rassel, Metrostudy Inc.'s director for the Atlanta market. The preferred inventory level would be less than 40 percent, and it was close to that one year ago. Mr. Rassel states that North Fulton can be used to gauge slowdowns.

28276 ■ "High Hopes: Ralph Mitchell's Picks Have Growth Potential" in *Black Enterprise* (Vol. 37, February 2007, No. 7, pp. 42)
Pub: Earl G. Graves Publishing Co. Inc.
Ed: Carolyn M. Brown. **Description:** Ralph Mitchell, president and senior financial advisor of Braintree-Carthage Financial Group, offers three recommendations: Toll Brothers, Home Depot, and Lowe's.

28277 ■ "High Profit in Play" in *Small Business Opportunities* (Vol. 16, No. 1, January 2004, pp. 62, 64)
Pub: Harris Publications, Inc.
Ed: Stan Roberts. **Description:** Profile of Ron Kaplan who took over his family's toy distribution business, Action Products International in Orlando, Florida, in 1997. Kaplan decided to shift the focus of the company from supplying toys, books and souvenirs to museums, to concentrating on manufacturing educational toys. The company now reports sales of $6 million a year.

28278 ■ "A high-tech domino effect: as dotcoms go, so go the e-commerce consultants" in *The New York Times* (December 16, 2000, pp. B1, C1)
Pub: The New York Times Company
Ed: Jonathan D. Glater. **Description:** All electronic-commerce consultant firms have suffered as a result of the weakness in the online sector. Firms like Scient Corporation and others that grew too rapidly are finding that demand for their services has evaporated, and are now having to lay off employees by the hundreds as they face a capital crunch.

28279 ■ "High Tech's Unwavering Champion" in *Hispanic Business* (March 2002, pp. 24-26)
Pub: Hispanic Business
Ed: Derek Reveron. **Description:** Amerindo's Alberto Vilar predicts that, despite recent setbacks, the world is on the verge of another technology revolution.

28280 ■ "Higher Revenue Boosts Call for Tax Cut" in *Boston Globe* (February 2, 2005)
Pub: New York Times Company
Ed: Scott S. Greenberger. **Description:** Massachusetts Governor Mitt Romney is proposing an income tax cut that would cost the state $225 million in fiscal 2006. The state's tax total for January 2005 was 11.9 percent higher than January 2004, predicting projected revenue of $16.5 billion for fiscal 2005.

28281 ■ "The Hispanic Business 500" in *Hispanic Business* (June 2002, pp. 44, 46, 48, 50, 52, 54, 56, 58, 60, 62, 64)
Pub: Hispanic Business
Description: A listing of the Hispanic Business 500 is presented. Burt Automotive became the largest Hispanic company in the U.S. for 2002, with revenues of almost $1.5 billion.

28282 ■ "Hispanic Business Fastest-Growing 100" in *Hispanic Business* (July/August 2004, pp. 30, 32, 34)
Pub: Hispanic Business
Description: A listing of Hispanic Business' top 100 Hispanic-owned companies. These companies highlight niche-market success in a moderate-growth economy. Statistical data includes sales growth 1999-2003, gross sales, profit range, number of employees, and year founded.

28283 ■ "HispanicBusiness.com Expands" in *Hispanic Business* (Vol. 23, No. 5, May 2001, pp. 18)
Pub: Hispanic Business
Description: HispanicBusiness.com, the official Web site of Hispanic Business magazine, has launched a series of online and offline initiatives designed to reposition the site as a full-service resource center.

28284 ■ "Hispantelligence quarterly" in *Hispanic Business* (March 2003, pp. 10)
Pub: Hispanic Business
Description: The Hispanic Business Stock Index and Stock Market Indexes are compared, as well as a presentation of trade statistics and macroeconomic statistics.

28285 ■ "Hispantelligence Report" in *Hispanic Business* (October 2003, pp. 14, 16, 20)
Pub: Hispanic Business
Description: Stock market indexes compared to Hispanic companies, homeownership among minorities, wealth by asset category for Hispanics and non-Hispanics, Hispanic asset portfolio, educational achievements and income levels, distribution of households by household income bracket and education level, educational attainment of household heads, and number of income earners per household of Hispanics and non-Hispanics.

28286 ■ "Hispantelligence Reports" in *Hispanic Business* (June 2005, pp. 12)
Pub: Hispanic Business
Description: Presentation of the Hispanic Business Stock Index shows the current value of thirteen Hispanic companies from January 3 through April 21, 2005. Growth for Hispanic-owned businesses is reflected in a graph showing numbers from years 1987 through 2010.

28287 ■ "Hit the Mark" in *My Business* (August/September 2002, pp. 28-35)
Pub: My Business Magazine
Description: Seven small business trends that will position a company for success are profiled. These trends include mentoring programs, e-mail marketing, customer service, personalized products and services, employee stock ownership plans, targeting markets, and automation.

28288 ■ "Hollister wins business praise" in *Crain's Detroit Business* (Vol. 18, No. 51, December 23, 2002, pp. 7)
Pub: Crain Communications Inc., Detroit
Ed: Amy Lane. **Description:** Business representatives are encouraged by the appointment of David Hollister as the State of Michigan's next economic development chief.

28289 ■ "Hollywood Opens Ahead Of Schedule" in *Mississippi Business Journal* (Vol. 28, September 2006, No. 36, pp. 20)
Pub: Venture Publications, Inc.
Description: Former Bay St. Louis Casino, Casino Magic reopened early despite severe storm damage. Now called Hollywood Casino, the casino has more than 75 percent of the original employees and many upgrades.

28290 ■ "Home-building firms post double-digit profits, but Wall Street remains unimpressed" in *Daily Business Review* (Vol. 77, Jan. 7, 2003)
Pub: American Lawyer Media LP
Description: Fourth quarter 2002, showed double-digit earnings for homebuilders, but the industry's stocks continue to under-perform.

28291 ■ "Home Building at Record High" in *Tampa Tribune* (October 27, 2005)
Pub: Media General, Inc.
Ed: Shannon Behnken. **Description:** According to the newly released Metrostudy, new home builders may face a shortage of land in 2006. The study focused on Hillsborough, Pasco, Pinnellas, Hernando and Citrus, Florida counties.

28292 ■ "Homewood Gets a $7M Hilton" in *Birmingham Business Journal* (Vol. 20, No. 29, July 18, 2003, pp. 1)
Pub: American City Business Journals, Inc.
Ed: Gilbert Nicholson. **Description:** HP Hotels, Inc. in Birmingham, Alabama, is in the early phase of constructing a $7 million, 95-room Hilton Hotel in Wildwood North. Chiman Patel and Mike Hines began the company a year ago and now own or manage 15 hotels.

28293 ■ "Hospitality in Kansas City" in *Ingram's* (Vol. 28, No. 2, February 2002, pp. 25)
Pub: Show Me Publishing, Inc.
Description: A review of the past and current state of the hospitality industry in Kansas City is provided. In 1986, Kansas City ranked just under New York City, Chicago and Atlanta; San Antonio, Denver and Indianapolis now surpass Kansas City.

28294 ■ "Hot Shots: 200 Up And Coming Companies" in *Forbes* (Vol. 172, No. 9, October 27, 2003, pp. 139)
Pub: Forbes Magazine
Ed: Cecily J. Fluke, Lesley Kump. **Description:** Share prices of 200 entrepreneurial firms are up an average of 58 percent over the last years, earnings per share increased 19 percent and return on equity rose 15 percent. Statistical data showing the companies recent performance is included.

28295 ■ "Hot Shots: U.S. Top 15" in *Forbes* (Vol. 6, No. 20, October 27, 2003, pp. 53)
Pub: Forbes Magazine
Description: A ranking of America's top small companies (under $500 million in revenues, but otherwise according to criteria similar to those ranked under $1 billion).

28296 ■ "Hot Spots" in *Entrepreneur* (Vol. 33, October 2005, No. 10, pp. 68)
Pub: Entrepreneur Media Inc.
Ed: Mark Henricks. **Description:** Top twenty large cities, ten med-size cities, and the top ten states for starting or relocating an existing business are listed. Also included is the Entrepreneurial Activity Index to help measure the best spots to start or expand a business.

28297 ■ "Housing Program Breaks Mortgage Lending Record" in *Milwaukee Journal Sentinel* (December 2, 2005)
Pub: Journal Sentinel, Inc.
Ed: Leonard Sykes, Jr. **Description:** Wisconsin Housing and Economic Development Authority reported a record in mortgage lending for the third year in a row. First-time home buyers are the agency's primary market.

28298 ■ "Housing market at high risk" in *Atlanta Business Chronicle* (Vol. 25, January 10, 2003, No. 31, pp. 1A)
Pub: American City Business Publications, Inc.
Ed: Lisa R. Schoolcraft. **Description:** The troubled economy has led to an increase in home foreclosures. Atlanta, Georgia has the highest housing market risk based on the change in the rate of economic growth, construction lending trends and levels, and the divergence of housing prices and income growth. In December 2002, there were 2,884 homes scheduled for foreclosure in metro Atlanta.

28299 ■ "Houston-Based ChaseCom L.P." in *Black Enterprise* (Vol. 35, December 2004, No. 5, pp. 38)
Pub: Earl G. Graves Publishing Co. Inc.
Ed: Malik Singleton. **Description:** ChaseCom LP in Houston, Texas has opened a new call center in Fort Smith, Arkansas creating 140 jobs paying $8 to $12 per hour. The firm provides telecom services and customer support.

28300 ■ "Houston-based GC Services Adds 100 Jobs in Oklahoma City" in *Journal Record* (February 5, 2004)
Pub: Dolan Media Company
Ed: Darren Currin. Description: GC Services plans to expand the Oklahoma City national service center with an immediate addition of 100 new employees, and ultimately 200 new employees after completion. The firm works with corporation and state agencies managing accounts receivables and customer service needs.

28301 ■ "How Blue Will Christmas Be? As sales keep plunging, retailers are panicking" in *Fortuneit* (Vol. 146, No. 9, Nov. 11, 2002, pp. 127)
Pub: Time Inc.
Ed: Cora Daniels. Description: Predictions regarding the retail conditions for Christmas 2002 are discussed. Since retail accounts for 23 percent of the U.S. gross domestic product, the holiday season is crucial.

28302 ■ "How EDS Got Its Groove Back" in *Fast Company* (November 2001, pp. 106)
Pub: Fast Company
Ed: Bill Breen. Description: Profile of Electronic Data Systems Corporation (EDS), and how Dick Brown turned the company around. Financial information included.

28303 ■ "How I Did It" in *Inc.* (Volume 28, January 2006, No. 1, pp. 86-88)
Pub: Inc. Magazine
Ed: Sasha Issenberg. Description: In an interview, Joe Sitt, explains how he has lured the nation's top retail chains into inner cities and yuppie downtown communities.

28304 ■ "How IBM Builds New Businesses" in *Fast Company* (March 2005, No. 92, pp. 72)
Pub: Gruner & Jahr USA Publishing
Description: IBM is used as an example to help small business grow. It is important to tap into senior leaders at a company who are secure and willing to take risks.

28305 ■ "How to Improve Georgia's Economy" in *Atlanta Business Chronicle* (Vol. 25, December 6, 2002, No. 26, pp. 35A)
Pub: American City Business Publications, Inc.
Ed: Georgia Description: Governor-elect, Sonny Perdue, should back the Metro Atlanta Chamber of Commerce's attempts to attract the secretariat of the Free Trade Area of the Americas to the city. He should also consider opening field offices of the Georgia Department of Industry, Trade and Tourism in Latin American cities.

28306 ■ "How Killer B-to-B's Slid to the Endangered List" in *The New York Times* (May 7, 2000, pp. BU1)
Pub: The New York Times Company
Ed: Bob Tedeschi. Description: Business-to-business Internet stocks plunge in value.

28307 ■ *How to Make Big Money in Your Own Small Business: Unexpected Rules Every Small Business Owner Needs to Know*
Pub: Hyperion Press
Ed: Jeffrey J. Fox. Released: May 2004. Price: $16.95. Description: Former sales and marketing pro offers advice on growing a small business.

28308 ■ "How to Survive When You've Lost Your Monopoly" in *Success from Failure* (August 2000)
Pub: Vision Quest Publishing, Inc.
Ed: Terry Brock. Description: At some point in time a small business will suffer a setback. Doug Wolford, general manager at Network Solutions, shares important lessons that will help a company thrive from any setback encountered.

28309 ■ "How They Did It" in *Crain's Detroit Business* (Vol. 19, No. 13, March 31, 2003, pp. 20)
Pub: Crain Communications Inc., Detroit
Ed: Laura Bailey. Description: The Detroit Public School system was able to get minority-owned and Detroit-based businesses to invest in its $1.5 billion building program.

28310 ■ "How To Crack Big-Box Retail" in *Inc.* (October 1, 2004)
Pub: Inc. Magazine
Ed: Rod Kurtz. Description: Ways to land a small business' product on the shelves of big-box retailers are explored.

28311 ■ "How To Stay on a Winning Streak" in *Inc.* (October 1, 2004)
Pub: Inc. Magazine
Ed: Nadine Heintz. Description: The four commandments created by Rosabeth Moss Kanater of the Harvard Business School are shared. Thou shalt not: panic, be rigid, deny change; thou shalt: celebrate success.

28312 ■ "How to Vitalize a Home-Based Operation" in *Home Business* (Vol. 12, October 2005, No. 5, pp. 32, 34, 95)
Pub: Home Business Magazine
Ed: Alan Stewart. Description: In order to be successful, home-based business owners must continue to refine and improve operations, be ready to take on new projects, new customers and new marketplaces.

28313 ■ "HR Battles to Conquer" in *Hispanic Business* (June 2002, pp. 72)
Pub: Hispanic Business
Ed: Derek Reveron. Description: Human resource managers are facing several issues since the terrorist attacks against the U.S. Despite these issues, Hispanic Business 500 firms grew at a 4.9 percent rate last year.

28314 ■ "HTVN Files for Bankruptcy" in *Hispanic Business* (March 2002, pp. 12)
Pub: Hispanic Business
Description: Hispanic Television Network has filed for Chapter 11 bankruptcy protection.

28315 ■ "Humana battles for growth" in *Atlanta Business Chronicle* (Vol. 25, January 3, 2003, No. 30, pp. 3A)
Pub: American City Business Publications, Inc.
Ed: Julie Bryant. Description: Alan Guzzino is the new Georgia market president of Humana Inc. Guzzino was retained to manage the introduction of the company's consumer-driver health benefit plans. This rollout aims to increase the company's competitive edge in the market place.

28316 ■ "Huron to Announce $25M Deal, Eyes New $250M Fund" in *Crain's Detroit Business* (Vol. 23, No. 3, January 15, 2007, pp. 26)
Pub: Crain Communications Inc. - Detroit
Ed: Tom Henderson. Description: Huron Capital Partners L.L.C. is coming off a record year for deal volume. A new $25M deal was announced, two more under letters of intent, and has begun raising funds for large $250M fund by the end of 2007.

28317 ■ "Hurricane Won't Blow Down State Economy" in *Crain's Detroit Business* (Vol. 21, October 3, 2005, No. 43, pp. 48)
Pub: Crain Communications Inc. - Detroit
Ed: Tom Henderson. Description: According to the Michigan Business Activity Index, Michigan's economy rose 2 points in August to 111, making it stronger to fend off the consequences of the hurricanes hitting the Gulf Coast in 2005.

28318 ■ "IGT: In Search of the Next Jackpot" in *Business Week* (February 14, 2005, No. 3920, pp. 58)
Pub: McGraw-Hill Companies
Ed: Christopher Palmeri. Description: Profile of International Game Technology, responsible for the 800,000 slot machines seen in U.S. and Canadian casinos. Domestic slot machine sales have tumbled 35 percent in first quarter 2005, and the company expects sales to be flat the rest of the year. Thomas Matthews, the firm's chairman and CEO, will focus on new types of games, international sales, and expanding beyond traditional slots.

28319 ■ "In Brief: Small-Business Poll: Economy Worsening" in *American Banker* (Vol. 170, September 5, 2006, No. 170, pp. 9)
Pub: SourceMedia, Inc.
Description: According to a survey conducted by Discover Financial Services, most small business owners are pessimistic about the economy. Statistical data included.

28320 ■ "In Entertainment Men Out-Earn Women" in *Marketing to Women* (Vol. 20, January 2007, No. 1, pp. 4)
Pub: EPM Communications, Inc.
Ed: Susan Nunziata. Description: Particularly among the upper ranks of the entertainment industry executives, females are paid less than male counterparts. Statistical data included.

28321 ■ "In Helen's good graces" in *Candy Industry* (Vol. 167, No. 3, March 2002, pp. 34)
Pub: Stagnito Communications Inc.
Ed: Bernard Pacyniak. Description: Recently acquired Helen Grace Chocolates finds itself focused on what founder Bill Grace always intended, producing good chocolates. The new owners, Robert and David Worth, are focusing on national expansion for the company.

28322 ■ "In with the New" in *Entrepreneur* (Vol. 28, No. 10, October 2000, pp. 102)
Pub: Entrepreneur Media Inc.
Ed: Mark Henricks. Description: The key to fast growth lies is not only treating your existing customers well, but also in seeking new customers.

28323 ■ "The Incredibly Unproductive Shareholder" in *Harvard Business Review* (Vol. 80, No. 1, January 2002, pp. 18)
Pub: Harvard Business School Press
Ed: Marjorie Kelly. Description: Stock-market investors' interests have often been put above that of the company, which has resulted in decisions that have been counterproductive.

28324 ■ "Incubators that actually work? You won't find them only in Internet space" in *Inc.* (November 2000, pp. 64)
Pub: The Goldhirsh Group
Description: In an Inc. survey of more than 30 incubator-savvy CEOs and experts in the field, eight nonprofit incubators throughout the nation stood out.

28325 ■ "Indian Retail Reform" in *The Economist* (Vol. 376, July 16-22, 2005, No. 8435, pp. 39-40)
Pub: The Economist Newspaper Ltd.
Description: Wal-Mart and other American companies are working to break into India's retail sector, which has been closed to outsiders for a long time. Many large retailers are using India as a significant source of supplies to support their efforts.

28326 ■ "Industrial Metamorphosis" in *The Economist* (Vol. 377, October 1-7, 2005, No. 8446, pp. 69-70)
Pub: The Economist Newspaper Ltd.
Description: Despite the drop in manufacturing jobs in America, manufacturing real output has been growing by nearly 4 percent annually since 1991, faster than overall GDP growth. Statistical data included.

28327 ■ "Information Technology" in *Ingram's* (Vol. 27, No. 7, July 2001, pp. 76)
Pub: Show Me Publishing, Inc.
Description: Review of Kansas City's growing information technology industry is outlined. Local business professionals have put together a Technology Panel to address the needs of the growing industry.

28328 ■ "Innotrac tries to get back on track after telecom woes" in *Atlanta Business Chronicle* (Vol. 25, November 29, 2002, No. 25, pp. 3A)
Pub: American City Business Publications, Inc.
Ed: Mary Jane Credeur. Description: Innotrac Corporation has suffered financially as telecommunications firms cut costs to make up for reduced demand in services. The company posted a 36 percent decline in revenue for the first nine months of 2002 compared to the same period in 2001.

28329 ■ "The Innovation Conversation" in *Fast Company* **(July 2001, pp. 70)**
Pub: Fast Company
Description: Fast Company gathered ten business leaders for a 90-minute roundtable discussion in San Francisco, California. The following questions were addressed: What is the state of innovation? How are leaders competing on innovation?

28330 ■ "Inside Microsoft. Balancing Creativity and Discipline" in *Harvard Business Review* **(Vol. 80, No. 1, January 2002, pp. 73)**
Pub: Harvard Business School Press
Ed: Robert Herbold. **Description:** Microsoft's hands-off management approach began to interfere with productivity; this required rethinking the company, better integration of information, and general operations while maintaining the company's need for creative thinking.

28331 ■ *Instant Cashflow: Hundreds of Proven Strategies to Win Customers, Boost Margins and Take More Money Home*
Pub: McGraw-Hill Companies
Ed: Bradley J. Sugars. **Released:** December 2005. **Price:** $16.95 (US), $22.95 (Canadian). **Description:** Nearly 300 proven marketing and sales strategies are shared by the author, a self-made millionaire. Advice on creating the proper mindset, generating new leads, boosting the conversion rate of leads to sales, maximizing the value of the average sale, and measuring results is included.

28332 ■ *Instant Profit: Successful Strategies to Boost Your Margin and Increase the Profitability of Your Business*
Pub: McGraw-Hill Companies
Ed: Bradley J. Sugars. **Released:** December 2005. **Price:** $16.95 (US), $22.95 (Canadian). **Description:** Advice on management, money, marketing, and merchandising a successful small business is offered.

28333 ■ "Insurance Firms Forecast Profitable Year" in *Pacific Business News* **(Vol. 41, No. 19, July 18, 2003, pp. 12)**
Pub: American City Business Journals
Ed: Eddy Conway. **Description:** Profile and forecasts of Hawaii's insurance industry are presented. Topics include economic conditions, profits and losses, and business forecasts.

28334 ■ "Insurer State Farm Closes Buffalo, N.Y.-Area Claims Offices; 30 Jobs to Be Cut" in *Buffalo News* **(February 17, 2004)**
Pub: Knight-Ridder/Tribune Business News
Ed: Jonathan D. Epstein. **Description:** Although State Farm Mutual Insurance Company is expanding its injury claims central office in Rochester, New York, it is closing four offices in the Buffalo, New York area.

28335 ■ "Intel Inside: The Chips Get Hot" in *Barron's* **(August 25, 2003, pp. T1)**
Pub: Barron's
Ed: Bill Alpert. **Description:** Growing demand for Intel's market-leading Pentium microprocessors has moved the company to project an 11-percent increase for third quarter sales. Investors welcomed the news by bidding Intel's share price up a dollar, or nearly 4 percent, to more than $27/share.

28336 ■ "Interiors By Design" in *Black Enterprise* **(Vol. 35, October 2004, No. 3, pp. 54)**
Pub: Earl G. Graves Publishing Co. Inc.
Ed: Virginia Myers Kelly. **Description:** Profile of Dennese Guadeloupe Rojas, a laid off direct mail worker, who earned a degree in interior design and is now the successful owner of Interiors By Design. Rojas offers interior and exterior design as well as home accessories to her clients. She started out working from home, but soon found she needed more space.

28337 ■ *International Entrepreneurship in Small and Medium Size Enterprises: Orientation, Environment and Strategy*
Pub: Edward Elgar Publishing, Incorporated
Ed: Hamid Etemad. **Released:** November 2004. **Price:** $110.00. **Description:** Issues involved in inter-

nationalizing small and medium sized (SME) businesses. Topics include an investigation into the emerging patterns of SME growth and international expansion in response to the changing competitive environment, dynamics of competitive behavior, entrepreneurial processes and a formulation of strategy.

28338 ■ *Introduction to Business Statistics*
Pub: Harcourt Brace College Publishers
Released: 1996. **Price:** $55.25.

28339 ■ "Intuitively clear: the king of personal-finance software sets sights on small business" in *Barron's* **(Vol. 82, Feb. 24, 2003, pp.17)**
Pub: Barron's
Ed: Jay Palmer. **Description:** Demand for software products by Intuit Inc. is likely to continue to increase, thereby positively affecting the company's stock price. One analyst predicts that the new company's earnings growth will exceed 50 percent in 2003, as more small businesses buy the new software packages.

28340 ■ "Investment continues to drop" in *Crain's Detroit Business* **(Vol. 19, No. 12, March 24, 2003, pp. 11)**
Pub: Crain Communications Inc., Detroit
Ed: Katie Merx. **Description:** Despite the fact that venture capital investment fell to 1998 levels in 2002, Michigan investors expect the VC market to improve in 2003.

28341 ■ "Investment Pace Starts To Return to Normal" in *Venture Capital Journal*
Pub: Thomason Financial Inc.
Description: New Enterprise Associates was the most active investor in 2004, doing 70 deals, followed by Draper Fisher Jurvetson, with 55 deals. A listing of the top ten VCs for 2004 is provided.

28342 ■ "Investor: Earnings projections for technology are still too lofty" in *Red Herring* **(No. 103, September 1, 2001, pp. 82-83)**
Pub: Herring Communications
Ed: J.P. Vicente. **Description:** Predictions that technology earnings will not return to the high levels seen in 2000 until 2004, at the earliest.

28343 ■ "Investors still in the game, looking beyond the slump" in *Business First Columbus* **(Vol. 18, No. 28, March 1, pp. B12)**
Pub: Business First Columbus, Inc.
Ed: David F. Webb, Andrew C. McAllister. **Description:** Information regarding real estate development investment opportunities is presented.

28344 ■ "Invisible Inc." in *Crain's Detroit Business* **(Vol. 19, No. 3, January 20, 2003, pp. 10)**
Pub: Crain Communications Inc., Detroit
Description: A list of printing companies that went out of business in the Detroit area in years 2001 and 2002 is presented.

28345 ■ "IPOs Take a Break After a Big Year" in *Venture Capital Journal* **(January 1, 2005)**
Pub: Thomason Financial Inc.
Ed: Lawrence Aragon. **Description:** Five venture-backed companies went public November 2004, causing the IPO market to slow some for the month; average deals for 2004 was $110 million, an increase of $38 million from same period 2003.

28346 ■ "IPOs: Things of the Past" in *Crain's New York Business* **(Vol. 23, January 1, 2007, No. 1, pp. 14)**
Pub: Crain Communications, Inc.
Description: Relegence Corp., a Manhattan-based company that gathers business information from around the globe and allows people to personalize the news delivered to their desktops, was acquired by AOL. The new trend in the business realm is to slowly grow then be acquired by a larger company instead of going public.

28347 ■ "Is the Internet Second Nature" in *Fast Company* **(July 2001, pp. 145)**
Pub: Fast Company
Ed: Cheryl Dahle. **Description:** Ways to tap the real power of the Internet to transform small business are investigated.

28348 ■ "It figures" in *Entrepreneur* **(Vol. 30, No. 3, March 2002, pp. 34)**
Pub: Entrepreneur Media Inc.
Description: A presentation of how companies are managing during the economic slowdown; other business-related statistics are included.

28349 ■ "It looks as if they got it right this time" in *Crain's Detroit Business* **(Vol. 18, No. 50, December 16, 2002, pp. 8)**
Pub: Crain Communications Inc., Detroit
Ed: Keith Crane. **Description:** The redevelopment of Detroit's riverfront property is discussed.

28350 ■ "It's All In Your Head" in *Entrepreneur* **(Vol. 33, January 2005, No. 1, pp. 58)**
Pub: Entrepreneur Media Inc.
Ed: Chris Penttila. **Description:** Ways for small business owners to cope with the ever changing economy.

28351 ■ "It's Fall, And The Shopping Is Easy" in *Fortune* **(Vol. 142, No. 10, October 30, 2000, pp. 208)**
Pub: Time Inc.
Ed: Joel Dreyfuss. **Description:** When the office computers are more than three years old, it's probably time to consider some new hardware. And now is a great opportunity.

28352 ■ "It's a Stretch" in *Entrepreneur* **(Vol. 30, No. 1, January 2002, pp. 48)**
Pub: Entrepreneur Media Inc.
Ed: Mark Henricks. **Description:** The difficulty for small businesses to bridge the gap between a good product and enough capacity to fulfill the needs of big customers who can help grow a business. Expansion loans are difficult to procure for small businesses, especially in new technologies areas.

28353 ■ "It's Time For Venture Capital Firms To Grow Up" in *Venture Capital Journal* **(Vol. 42, No. 8, August 2002, pp. 38-39)**
Pub: Thomas Venture Economics
Ed: R. David Spreng. **Description:** Venture capital is moving from its beginnings as a cottage industry to a more mainstreamed asset class. The five traits of a next-generation venture capitalist are listed.

28354 ■ "Jamul Plans $200 Million Facility" in *San Diego Business Journal* **(Vol. 28, January 1, 2007, No. 1, pp. 8)**
Pub: San Diego Business Journal Associates
Ed: Brad Graves. **Description:** Urban Design Group Inc. plans to build Native American casino in Jamul, California. The complex would fit on the six-acre American Indian reservation off Route 94.

28355 ■ "J.C. Watts First Black John Deere Dealer" in *Black Enterprise* **(Vol. 37, November 2006, No. 4, pp. 36)**
Pub: Earl G. Graves Publishing Co. Inc.
Ed: Kiara Ashanti. **Description:** Profile of former Congressman J.C. Watts Jr., a man who grew up in rural America and is the first African American to own a John Deere Dealership.

28356 ■ "Jetblue Outlines Massive Logan Expansion" in *Boston Globe* **(February 3, 2005)**
Pub: New York Times Company
Ed: Keith Reed. **Description:** JetBlue's plans for expansion at Logan International Airport in Boston are outlined. The expansion could make JetBlue one of the largest airlines operating out of Logan and calls for the hiring of about 500 new employees.

28357 ■ "Job Growth Encouraging in Silicon Valley, Nationwide" in *San Jose Mercury News* **(March 5, 2005)**
Pub: Knight-Ridder/Tribune Business News

Ed: Nicole C. Wong. **Description:** Nearly 169,400 new manufacturing jobs were created in Silicon Valley in January 2005, offering hope for a recovering economy in the area.

28358 ■ **"Job Growth in State Catching Up to Nation"** in *San Jose Mercury News* **(February 26, 2005)**
Pub: Knight-Ridder/Tribune Business News
Ed: Nicole C. Wong. **Description:** Twenty thousand new jobs were added to California's economy in January 2005. Total jobs are up 1.6 percent in the state and 1.7 percent nationally.

28359 ■ **"Job Outlook Stays Bright in Florida"** in *Tampa Tribune* **(December 16, 2005)**
Pub: Media General, Inc.
Ed: Dave Simanoff. **Description:** Tampa, Florida is seeing an increase in job growth, leading the nation by adding 255,100 jobs in the last year.

28360 ■ **"Jobless Claims Data Not As Bad As Feared by Economists"** in *Atlanta Journal-Constitution* **(April 11, 2003)**
Pub: Knight-Ridder/Tribune Business News
Ed: Michael E. Kanell. **Description:** Nearly 20,000 fewer people applied for unemployment in the nation for the month of March 2003, lower than predicted by analysts. The current jobless rate in America stands at 5.8 percent. Statistical data included.

28361 ■ **"Jobs Increase in Milwaukee Area"** in *Milwaukee Journal Sentinel* **(December 22, 2005)**
Pub: Journal Sentinel, Inc.
Ed: Joel Dresang. **Description:** According to the Wisconsin Department of Workforce Development, Milwaukee showed an increase in jobs over the last year, including the manufacturing sector. From November 2004 to November 2005, 1,300 new factory jobs were created paying an average of $17.37 an hour.

28362 ■ **"Johnson County, Missouri"** in *Ingram's* **(Vol. 29, No. 9, September 2003, pp. 34)**
Pub: Show Me Publishing, Inc.
Description: Profile of Johnson County, Missouri. Topics include economic conditions and development, industrialization, and local colleges and universities.

28363 ■ **"Joining Forces"** in *Home Business* **(Vol. 12, October 2005, No. 5, pp. 64, 66)**
Pub: Home Business Magazine
Ed: Priscilla Y. Huff. **Description:** Through the use of the Internet and affordable technology, home-based business owners are forming virtual alliances to help one another grow their businesses.

28364 ■ **"Jordanian delegation looks to expand business ties"** in *Crain's Detroit Business* **(Vol. 18, No. 50, December 16, 2002, pp. 22)**
Pub: Crain Communications Inc., Detroit
Ed: Robert Ankeny. **Description:** A Jordanian delegation arrived in Detroit in December 2002 in an attempt to expand business relations with Jordan and Southeast Michigan.

28365 ■ **"Joyless recovery based on Georgia Economic Outlook"** in *Atlanta Business Chronicle* **(Vol. 25, January 10, 2003, No. 31, pp. 23A)**
Pub: American City Business Publications, Inc.
Ed: Deirdre Gregg. **Description:** The outlook for Georgia's economy is bleak, according to University of Georgia's Georgia Economic Outlook 2003. Economic indicators for the region are discussed. Statistical data included.

28366 ■ **"JPMorgan Chase Regional Economist Forecasts Long Island Growth for 2004"** in *Long Island Business News* **(January 30, 2004)**
Pub: Dolan Media Newswires
Description: Marc Goloven, an economist for JPMorgan Chase predicts economic growth of about 4 per-

cent nationwide and in the Long Island, New York region. Goloven attributes this in part to the fact that many small businesses suffered less economic damage in the last few years. Long Island has shifted away from the manufacturing sector to the services industry, helping the area.

28367 ■ **"'JR still starts with W; Ratings up and Smith's re-upped"** in *Crain's Detroit Business* **(Vol. 19, No. 4, January 27, 2003, pp. 1)**
Pub: Crain Communications Inc., Detroit
Ed: Jennette Smith. **Description:** Paul W. Smith has signed a new, long-term contract with radio station WJR AM 760. Smith, along with format changes, has helped bring ratings back up to the top.

28368 ■ **"The Juggling Act"** in *My Business* **(October/November 2003, pp. 36-39)**
Pub: My Business Magazine
Ed: Nancy Mann Jackson. **Description:** Owning one business is not as difficult as it seems; tips to help entrepreneurs handle the operations of more than one business are given, including good organization skills.

28369 ■ **"The Juice is Loose"** in *My Business* **(April/May 2004, pp. 16)**
Pub: My Business Magazine
Ed: Gwen Moran. **Description:** Creative solutions can help a small business grow.

28370 ■ *Jump Start Your Business Brain: Ideas, Advice and Insights for Immediate Marketing and Innovation Success*
Pub: Emmis Books
Ed: Doug Hall. **Released:** April 2005. **Price:** $23.99. **Description:** Strategies to improve sales, marketing, and business development.

28371 ■ **"Just the Tiqit"** in *Red Herring* **(January 2003, pp. 26)**
Pub: Herring Communications Inc.
Ed: Dean Takahashi. **Description:** Profile of Tiqit Computers, a Silicon Valley startup, developing a PC into a device that could fit into a pants pocket.

28372 ■ **"Ka-Boom! Looks Like the Economy is Finally Growing-And Guess What's Leading the Way?"** in *Entrepreneur* **(Vol. 32, August 2004)**
Pub: Entrepreneur Media Inc.
Ed: Mike Hogan. **Description:** Technology is being credited as the catalyst for the growing economy in the U.S., which averaged 5.5 percent growth over the last two years. The U.S. Bureau of Labor Statistics expects continued growth in the economy at the rate of about 4 percent or more in 2005.

28373 ■ **"Kar Nut Products Gets New HQ; Snack-Maker Cites Growth for Need for Space"** in *Crain's Detroit Business* **(Vol. 21, January 10, 2005)**
Pub: Crain Communications Inc. - Detroit
Ed: Anjali Fluker. **Description:** Kar Nut Products Company moved its headquarters from Ferndale to Madison Heights, Michigan. The relocation is the result of company growth for the maker of snacks and trail mixes. Details of the new facility and statistical data is included.

28374 ■ **"KCBS-KCAL Studio Center Complex"** in *San Fernando Valley Business Journal* **(Vol. 12, January 2007, No. 1, pp. 12)**
Pub: San Fernando Valley Business Journal Associates
Description: KCBS-KCAL Studio Center Complex opens in March on the back lot of the CBS Studio Center, which means business growth for the businesses and eateries nearby.

28375 ■ **"Keep it Simple"** in *Entrepreneur. com* **(Vol. 34, February 2006, No. 2, pp. 60)**
Pub: Entrepreneur Media Inc.
Ed: Chris Penttila. **Description:** Twenty-five tips for fine tuning a small business are outlined, focusing on technology, money, banking, taxes, credit and collection, accounting systems, mergers, management, and marketing ideas.

28376 ■ **"Keeping It Positive"** in *Small Business Opportunities* **(Vol. 17, May 2005, No. 3, pp. 18, 20)**
Pub: Harris Publications Inc.
Ed: Dave Anderson. **Description:** Small business owners can increase profits when boosting employee morale. Positive reinforcement should be given verbally or tangibly and should be as specific as possible.

28377 ■ **"Kelly Thinks Globally and Earns Locally; International Sales Up 50 Percent Over 2 Years"** in *Crain's Detroit Business* **(Vol. 21)**
Pub: Crain Communications Inc. - Detroit
Ed: Brent Snavely. **Description:** Kelly Services Inc. reports a 50 percent rise in sales over the last two years, mainly due to the implementation of its international growth strategy. Net income from international sales increased to $12.8 million in 2004.

28378 ■ **"Key is getting region's leaders at one table"** in *Crain's Detroit Business* **(Vol. 19, No. 17, April 28, 2003, pp. 8)**
Pub: Crain Communications Inc., Detroit
Description: According to a recent survey conducted by the Metropolitan Affairs Coalition, a majority of metro Detroit residents would favor regional cooperation to help move Detroit forward into a stronger economic region.

28379 ■ **"Keys to Successful Multiple-Unit Franchising"** in *Black Enterprise* **(Vol. 34, No. 4, November 2003, pp. 157)**
Pub: Earl Graves Publishing Co.
Description: Multi-unit franchising has increased over the last few years. According to FRANdata, a franchise firm located in Washington, reports 27,000 franchisees own and operate two or more franchises in the U.S. Statistical data included.

28380 ■ **"King of the Hill"** in *Houston Business Journal* **(Vol. 34, No. 15, August 22, 2003, pp. 17)**
Pub: American City Business Journals
Ed: Allison Wollam. **Description:** Profile of Berryhill Baja Grill's operations and growth plans is presented.

28381 ■ **"Kirkland's, Gap Will Close At Leases' End"** in *Bradenton Herald* **(January 22, 2005)**
Pub: Bradenton Herald
Ed: Kurt D. Schultheis. **Description:** Both Kirkland's and the Gap plan to close stores in the DeSoto Square Mall when their leases expire; a spokesperson for the Gap declined comment; Wendy Scott, district manager for Kirkland's reports that the company is in no danger.

28382 ■ **"Kmart closings to take another slice from Little Caesar"** in *Crain's Detroit Business* **(Vol. 19, No. 4, January 27, 2003, pp. 7)**
Pub: Crain Communications Inc., Detroit
Ed: Brent Snavely. **Description:** The proposed closing of 326 Kmart stores will also close 101 Little Caesar Pizza Stations located inside the retail stores. Contracts between the two companies lapsed in August 2002 and the two companies have been in negotiations for at least six months.

28383 ■ **"Knowledge helped company bounce back"** in *Crain's Detroit Business* **(Vol. 19, No. 11, March 17, 2003, pp. 14)**
Pub: Crain Communications Inc., Detroit
Ed: Laura Bailey. **Description:** Robert Verdun, head of CFI, a company specializing in software and consulting to help large companies control real estate costs, is profiled.

28384 ■ **"Kohl's Announces Plans to Open Its First Baltimore County, Md. Store"** in *Baltimore Sun* **(April 11, 2003)**
Pub: Knight-Ridder/Tribune Business News
Ed: Lorraine Mirabella. **Description:** Kohl's Corporation plans to open its first store in Baltimore Country, Maryland to anchor the redeveloped Yorkridge Shopping Center in Lutherville.

28385 ■ "Labor and delivery" in *WorkingWoman* (Vol. 25, No. 2, February 2000, pp. 28)
Pub: Lang Communications Inc.
Ed: Patti Wolter. Description: Secretary of Labor, Alexis Herman, wants all workers to participate in the expanding economy.

28386 ■ "Lakeland, Fla.-Based Health Club Chain Survives 20 Years in Changing Business" in *Lakeland Ledger* (August 15, 2002)
Pub: Knight Ridder/Tribune Business News
Ed: Michael Sasso. Description: Owner of Lifestyle Family Fitness, Geoff Dyer, explains how his business has survived twenty years in the ever-changing fitness industry. Dyer has 13 clubs in the region, and plans to open a fourteenth center in the Orlando area.

28387 ■ "Lakeway Inn Gets $1.5 M Remodel" in *Bellingham Business Journal* (January 2007, pp. A1)
Pub: Sun News Inc.
Ed: Dan Hiestand. Description: Profile of Lakeway Inn & Conference Center that began a $1.5 million renovation that will dramatically upgrade 132 guest rooms, common areas, and its indoor pool.

28388 ■ "Land use requires regional cooperation" in *Crain's Detroit Business* (Vol. 19, No. 14, April 7, 2003, pp. 9)
Pub: Crain Communications Inc., Detroit
Ed: Mary Kramer. Description: Agenda Ann Arbor held its annual meeting to discuss the city's public policy issues, such as regional land use planning.

28389 ■ "Large industrial gas companies setting sights on Detroit" in *Crain's Detroit Business* (Vol. 19, No. 4, January 27, 2003, pp. 21)
Pub: Crain Communications Inc., Detroit
Ed: Michael Strong. Description: Welding equipment suppliers and independent industrial gas suppliers in the metro Detroit, Michigan area are consolidating to improve product offerings and tap into new customer bases.

28390 ■ "Las Vegas Hotel Revenues Surge as Casino Earnings Slump" in *Las Vegas Review-Journal* (February 17, 2004)
Pub: Knight-Ridder/Tribune Business News
Ed: Rod Smith. Description: Top nine hotels in Las Vegas, Nevada are seeing increased revenues from rooms, food and beverages, however casino revenues are low.

28391 ■ "Last-Minute Shoppers Boost Holiday Retail Sales" in *Sacramento Bee* (December 29, 2005)
Pub: The Sacramento Bee
Ed: Jon Ortiz. Description: Last minute shoppers increased sales for many retailers in the Sacramento area, setting a strong finish to the 2005 shopping season. Chain store sales were reported up by 2.8 percent for the week before Christmas Day.

28392 ■ "Late Buying Boosts Crops" in *Kansas City Star* (March 11, 2005)
Pub: Knight-Ridder/Tribune Business News
Ed: Katie Lindmark. Description: Late buying of futures drove the prices of wheat, soybean and corns futures higher in early March. Statistical data included.

28393 ■ "Later Easter, War Crimp March Retail Sales" in *Atlanta Journal-Constitution* (April 11, 2003)
Pub: Knight-Ridder/Tribune Business News
Ed: Renee DeGross. Description: Cooler weather concerns, the Iraqi War, and a late Easter all contributed to lower retail sales for March 2003. Statistical data included.

28394 ■ "Latinas' Businesses and Earnings are Seeing Major Growth" in *Marketing to Women* (Vol. 19, October 2006, No. 10, pp. 2)
Pub: EPM Communications, Inc.
Description: According to Hispanic Business Inc., Hispanic woman-owned businesses grew 64 percent between 1997 and 2004. Latinas' median incomes also grew. Statistical data included.

28395 ■ "The Launch" in *Inc.* (October 17, 2000, pp. 57)
Pub: The Goldhirsh Group
Description: This article sites statistics including the Inc. 500 by sector, initial start-up capital, how CEOs raised that start-up capital, and the Top 10 fastest growing companies that were formed in 1995.

28396 ■ *Law for the Small and Growing Business*
Pub: Jordans Publishing Limited
Ed: P. Bohm. Released: February 2007. Price: $59. 98. Description: Legal and regulatory issues facing small businesses, including employment law, health and safety, commercial property, company law and finance are covered.

28397 ■ "Layoffs, no tax hike in city's proposed budget" in *Atlanta Business Chronicle* (Vol. 25, No. 21, November 1, 2002, pp. 2A)
Pub: American City Business Publications, Inc.
Ed: Sarah Rubenstein. Description: Atlanta Mayor, Shirley Frankin, will submit a 2003 budget to the Atlanta City Council seeking layoffs totaling a maximum of 300 employees, although tax increases will be excluded, according to Atlanta Chief Financial Officer, Rick Anderson.

28398 ■ "LBA event draws a crowd" in *Hispanic Business* (Vol. 22, No. 11, November 2000, pp. 14)
Pub: Hispanic Business
Ed: Andrea Siedsma. Description: A presentation of events at the Latino Business Expo in September 2000, organized by the Latin Business Association, showing the growth of Hispanic American businesses.

28399 ■ "Lead Generator: Quick Ideas For Better Sales Leads" in *Sales & Marketing Management* (Vol. 157, January 2005, No. 1, pp. 11)
Pub: VNU Business Media
Description: Three techniques that general leads for a sales team are listed.

28400 ■ "Leaders Prepare for Lean Times" in *Hispanic Business* (Vol. 23, No. 11, November 2001, pp. 14)
Pub: Hispanic Business Inc.
Ed: Mark Hagland. Description: Terrorism and business development were the topics at the 19th Annual United States Hispanic Leadership Institute (USHLI) conference, held September 27-30 in Chicago, Illinois. Juan Andrade, President of the USHLI, feels that the focus on terrorism will interfere with effective business development growth.

28401 ■ "Leading Indicators: Continued Growth" in *My Business* (December/January 2004, pp. 50)
Pub: My Business Magazine
Description: National Federation of Independent Business' Small Business Optimism Index hit 104.6, the highest reading since the early 1980s, signaling economic growth. The economy grew 7.2 percent in third quarter 2003, the fastest growth rate in 19 years. Statistical data included.

28402 ■ "Leading Indicators; Slow (But Steady) Growth" in *My Business* (December/January 2003, pp. 48)
Pub: My Business Magazine
Ed: Bill Dunkelberg. Description: Small business optimism, small business hiring plans, and inventory plans are among the items discussed. Growth in real gross domestic product averaged 3 percent in the 12 months following the September 11 tragedy, down only by one-half percent of the average trend.

28403 ■ "Learning Curves: How to Avoid 3 First-Time Mistakes" in *My Business* (December/January 2004, pp. 48)
Pub: My Business Magazine
Ed: Jamie Roberts. Description: Profile of Gary Heavin, founder and CEO of Curves International, the 30-minute strength and exercise club for women. It is estimated that a new Curves location opens every four hours.

28404 ■ "Lender forecloses on historic hotel" in *Houston Business Journal* (Vol. 33, No. 51, May 2, 2003, pp. 1A)
Pub: Houston Business Journal
Ed: Nancy Sarnoff. Description: On April 1, 2003, Southwest Bank of Texas foreclosed on the Tennison Hotel after One Bayou Park Ltd. defaulted on a construction loan. One Bayou Park had tried various ways to redevelop the property.

28405 ■ "Lending Tree earns first profit, branches out" in *Atlanta Business Chronicle* (Vol. 25, No. 22, November 8, 2002, pp. 8A)
Pub: American City Business Publications, Inc.
Ed: Jen Zoghby. Description: Lending Tree Inc. anticipates generating a profit in fourth quarter 2002 and all of 2003 when revenue is expected to total $131 million. Lending Tree has been increasing business from realty services offerings and is considering various ideas for 2003 to aid its growth efforts. The firm will continue its free membership program that offers discounts on various services.

28406 ■ "Lennar Corp. Expands With Five Polk Projects" in *Ledger* (February 24, 2005)
Pub: Knight-Ridder/Tribune Business News
Ed: Rachel Pleasant. Description: Lennar Corporation, the Miami-based home builder, is expanding into Polk County with five new housing developments.

28407 ■ "Let the games begin" in *Red Herring* (No. 106, October 15, 2001, pp. 30)
Pub: Herring Communications
Ed: Mark A. Mowrey. Description: It is predicted that the electronic-gaming industry will see a growth spurt, stemming from the introduction of two game machines in November 2001. According to an IDC survey, 25 percent of U.S. online gamers spend five or more hours per week playing online games. Statistical data included.

28408 ■ "Let it rain" in *Ingram's* (Vol. 28, No. 3, March 2002, pp. 35)
Pub: Show Me Publishing, Inc.
Ed: Jack Cashill. Description: Lawyers discuss the necessary attributes for "rainmaking", the ability of lawyers to generate revenue.

28409 ■ *Let's Buy a Company: How to Accelerate Growth Through Acquisitions*
Pub: Career Press, Incorporated
Ed: H. Lee Rust. Released: December 2005. Price: $18.90 (US), $25.95 (Canadian). Description: Advice for negotiating terms and pricing as well as other aspects of mergers and acquisitions in small companies.

28410 ■ "Let's Hang Together" in *Ingram's* (Vol. 29, No. 7, July 2003, pp. 83)
Pub: Show Me Publishing, Inc.
Ed: Dick King. Description: Difficulties encountered when Kansas City, Missouri sought cooperation with surrounding areas in and out of the state to develop the region.

28411 ■ "Let's roll up our sleeves" in *Crain's Detroit Business* (Vol. 18, No. 50, December 16, 2002, pp. 6)
Pub: Crain Communications Inc., Detroit
Description: Two hundred million dollars worth of redevelopment projects for Detroit's riverfront are discussed.

28412 ■ "Leveraged growth. Expanding sales without sacrificing profits" in *Harvard Business Review* (Vol. 80, No. 10, October 2002, pp. 68)
Pub: Harvard Business School Press
Ed: John Hagel. Description: The concept of leveraged growth, where growth does not occur by acquisitions, rather relying upon skills and assets that a firm already has available.

28413 ■ "The Life Sciences Building Boom" in *Boston Globe* (January 31, 2005)
Pub: New York Times Company
Ed: Jeffrey Krasner. Description: Boston, Massachusetts has experienced growth in the life sciences sector since 2003 and this growth is expected to continue through 2007. More than 24 life-sciences projects are underway, including laboratories, hospital expansions, academic centers and housing for scientists.

28414 ■ "LifeSecure Goes National" in *Crain's Detroit Business* **(Vol. 23, January 29, 2007, No. 5, pp. 17)**
Pub: Crain Communications Inc. - Detroit
Ed: Tom Henderson. **Description:** Small Brighton firm that specializes in long term insurance care Purchased a Dallas company to get licenses to sell in 41 states. Acquisition was the key to success in growing nationally and rapidly.

28415 ■ "The Little Guys Spy a Slowdown" in *Business Week* **(No. 3691, July 24, 2000, pp. 26)**
Pub: McGraw-Hill, Inc.
Description: Recent reports of sluggish hiring gains, flat vehicle sales and weak consumer spending confirm the findings from the National Federation of Independent Business' month survey of members, that small business optimism fell to 97.9 in June, its lowest level since the fall of 1993.

28416 ■ "Loan Will Go To Help Old Area" in *Sacramento Bee* **(December 20, 2005)**
Pub: The Sacramento Bee
Ed: Gilbert Chan. **Description:** One of Sacramento's oldest business districts has received a $4 million loan from the California Infrastructure and Economic Development Bank. The loan will help boost the economy and revitalize the area.

28417 ■ "Local Business Bankruptcies Outpace Nation" in *Boston Business Journal* **(Vol. 22, No. 16, May 24, 2002, pp. 1)**
Pub: MCP, Inc.
Ed: Edward Mason. **Description:** Business failures increased in Massachusetts by 24 percent for first quarter 2002, the first increase since 1999. Business failures increased throughout the U.S. by 11 percent for same quarter. Statistical data included.

28418 ■ "Local Business Changes Name" in *Bellingham Business Journal* **(January 2007, pp. 3)**
Pub: Sun News Inc.
Description: Profile of bridal self-help e-commerce website, TheSimplyOrganizedBride.com. The business name was changed from Weddings by Deborah to better reflect the nature of the business. Advertising opportunities for local wedding vendors, free tips and wedding articles, and a category for local bridal shows are now included in the content of the site.

28419 ■ "Local Businesses Discover There's No Place Like Home" in *Bradenton Herald* **(February 7, 2005)**
Pub: Bradenton Herald
Ed: Kurt D. Schultheis. **Description:** Profile of individuals who leave their hometowns, but return to raise their families and develop successful small businesses.

28420 ■ "Local Courses Try to Stay Chipper after Weak Year" in *Crain's Detroit Business* **(Vol. 19, No. 14, April 7, 2003, pp. 14)**
Pub: Crain Communications Inc., Detroit
Ed: Jason Deegan. **Description:** Report on the status of Michigan golf courses after a weak year in 2002. Renewed confidence was seen at the annual golf show held at the Novi Expo Center.

28421 ■ "Local Economy to Do Better Than State, Nation in '07" in *San Diego Business Journal* **(Vol. 28, January 1, 2007, No. 1, pp. 1)**
Pub: San Diego Business Journal Associates
Ed: Michelle Mowad. **Description:** San Diego County's economy predicted to fare better than that of the state or nation, despite a slowing of business activities.

28422 ■ *Local Enterprises in the Global Economy: Issues of Governance and Upgrading*
Pub: Edward Elgar Publishing, Incorporated
Ed: Hubert Schmitz. **Released:** April 2004. **Price:** $35.00 (soft cover), $110.00 (hard bound). **Description:** Examination of the relationships between globalization, corporate governance, and the economic performance of small businesses and local enterprises.

28423 ■ "Local Gelato King is Getting Ready to Expand His Empire" in *Bellingham Business Journal* **(January 2007, pp. A4)**
Pub: Sun News Inc.
Description: Profile Sirena Gelato, owned by Fahri Ugurlu, who has decided to expand the business by adding a wholesale component.

28424 ■ "Local Paradox" in *Atlanta Business Chronicle* **(Vol. 23, No. 40, March 9, 2001, pp. 1B)**
Pub: American City Business Journals Inc.
Ed: Chaundra Frierson. **Description:** The Network of City Business in Atlanta, surveyed 700 small businesses in the year 2000, and discovered that 70 percent received 100 percent of their revenues from their home base. For small business owners in Atlanta, deriving the major portion of their sales from the home base has proven to be challenging. The article discusses the ways small business owners in Atlanta are searching for ways to thrive in this particular market.

28425 ■ "Local Realty Firm's Owner Confident In Strength of Real Estate Market" in *Bradenton Herald* **(January 28, 2005)**
Pub: Bradenton Herald
Ed: Melissa Followell. **Description:** Michael Saunders, owner of a real estate firm by the same name, describes the current real estate market in Lakewood Ranch, Florida as the fastest pace seen in more than 30 years.

28426 ■ "Local Restaurants Report Sales Decline since Sept. 11" in *Crain's Detroit Business* **(Vol. 18, No. 17, April 29, 2002, pp. 16)**
Pub: Crain Communications Inc. - Detroit
Ed: Michael Strong. **Description:** Sales at metro Detroit restaurants have been down since the terrorist attacks of September 11, 2001, and trail restaurants across the nation which have seen sales increases since December.

28427 ■ "Local Truckers Cheer an Upsurge in Business" in *Birmingham Business Journal* **(Vol. 20, No. 28, July 11, 2003, pp. 15)**
Pub: American City Business Journals, Inc.
Ed: Gilbert Nicholson. **Description:** Birmingham, Alabama trucking firms have seen business increase 15-25 percent during the period January-June 2003, compared to same period 2002.

28428 ■ "Location, Location, Location" in *Inc.* **(October 17, 2000, pp. 57)**
Pub: The Goldhirsh Group
Description: Small business statistics covering the state with the biggest gain in companies since 1999, the biggest drop in companies since 1999, the top five metro areas by number of companies, and the top five states by number of companies per million residents.

28429 ■ "Lockport Tops Eastern Niagara List" in *Business First Buffalo* **(Vol. 19, No. 44, July 25, 2003, pp. 1)**
Pub: American City Business Journals, Inc.
Ed: G. Scott Thomas. **Description:** A ranking of neighborhoods in Erie and Niagara Counties, New York revealed Lockport, located in Eastern Niagara County, has a good reputation among residents and was rated the seventh fastest-growing town in western New York.

28430 ■ "Loehmann's New Owner Keeps the Faith" in *Fortune* **(Vol. 151, February 7, 2005, No. 3, pp. 26)**
Pub: Time Inc.
Ed: Barney Gimbel. **Description:** Profile of Bahrain's First Islamic Investment Bank, a Middle East-based investment firm located in the U.S. Through its American subsidiary, Crescent Capital Investment, the company has invested $2 billion into the U.S. market, particularly businesses that don't sell alcohol, charge interest, or allow gambling, produce tobacco, make unwholesome entertainment, or deal with pork.

28431 ■ "Logged on; Moon Valley Furniture's New Owner Expanding Biz." in *Crain's Detroit Business* **(Vol. 23, January 29, 2007, No. 5, pp. 3)**
Pub: Crain Communications Inc. - Detroit
Ed: Sheena Harrison. **Description:** New business oriented owner sees growth potential in rustic furniture market by aligning with log-home builders. Growth forecast to triple in the next five years.

28432 ■ "Long Island's Industrial Agencies Spend $733 Million in 2003 on Economic Incentives" in *Long Island Business News* **(February 20, 2004)**
Pub: Dolan Media Newswires
Ed: Nick Anastasi. **Description:** Eight industrial development agencies in Long Island spent more than $733 million in economic incentives to draw and retain companies in the area.

28433 ■ "Long Island's Patent Production Falls Nearly 20 Percent Since 1988" in *Long Island Business News* **(March 5, 2004)**
Pub: Dolan Media Newswires
Ed: Ken Schachter. **Description:** Long Island's future economic health is tied to industries such as life sciences, software development and defense-industry prototyping and design rather than large-scale manufacturing. Patent growth is used to gauge the economic progress of the area.

28434 ■ "Long in the Tooth" in *Red Herring* **(January 2003, pp. 72)**
Pub: Herring Communications Inc.
Ed: Duff McDonald. **Description:** Statistical information regarding the November 2001 rally, especially in the tech sector, is presented.

28435 ■ "Look to the Future" in *Atlanta Business Chronicle* **(Vol. 25, No. 20, October 25, 2002, pp. 1)**
Pub: American City Business Publications, Inc.
Ed: Tonya Layman. **Description:** Phase 1 of the High Museum of Art expansion in Atlanta, Georgia's Midtown corridor will be completed in 2005. This expansion will join Georgia Tech's new Technology Square, along with the new Centergy office development, slated to be completed in August 2003.

28436 ■ "Look for the Pony" in *Forbes* **(May 29, 2000, pp. 104)**
Pub: Forbes Magazine
Ed: John Rutledge. **Description:** The article helps to explore the hidden assets in a business.

28437 ■ "Lord and Taylor Exit Leave Hole" in *Pittsburgh Business Times* **(Vol. 23, No. 2, August 1, 2003, pp. 1)**
Pub: Pittsburgh Business Times
Ed: Tim Schooley. **Description:** Lord and Taylor, owned by May Department Stores Company, will close its store in downtown Pittsburgh, Pennsylvania; the 125,000 square foot store opened only three years ago.

28438 ■ "Los Angeles Redevelopment Agency Will See Major Restructuring" in *Daily News* **(April 11, 2003)**
Pub: Knight-Ridder/Tribune Business News
Ed: Harrison Sheppard. **Description:** The Community Redevelopment Agency in Burbank, California announced a restructuring plan designed to make the agency more efficient in the face of budget cuts and layoffs.

28439 ■ "Low-key expansion expected for manufacturers" in *Atlanta Business Chronicle* **(Vol. 25, January 10, 2003, No. 31, pp. 24A)**
Pub: American City Business Publications, Inc.
Ed: Tony Heffernan. **Description:** Even though Georgia's manufacturing sector has been in a slump since 2002, the Georgia Economic Outlook 2003 survey indicated that capacity, production, and utilization will expand slightly in 2003.

28440 ■ "Loyal Clients Boost Revenue" in *Home Business* (Vol. 12, October 2005, No. 5, pp. 48, 50-51)
Pub: Home Business Magazine
Ed: Jim Kleidon. Description: Ten pointers to improve customer satisfaction are listed, and must be executed before, during and after a service takes place.

28441 ■ "Luxury for the masses" in *Harvard Business Review* (Vol. 81, No. 4, April 2003, pp. 48)
Pub: Harvard Business School Press
Ed: Michael J. Silverstien, Neil Fiske. Description: A description of the new products called new luxury. New luxury is the result of America's middle market consumers moving to higher levels of quality and taste than ever before. These new luxury products generate high sales volumes and bring companies providing them levels of profitability beyond those of conventional competitors.

28442 ■ "Lyon Twp. apple orchard eyed for $70M development" in *Crain's Detroit Business* (Vol. 19, No. 13, March 31, 2003, pp. 6)
Pub: Crain Communications Inc., Detroit
Ed: Andrew Dietderich. Description: Plans to clear a popular 191-acre apple orchard in Lyon Township, Michigan are underway. The plans call for single-family homes and attached condominiums and nearly 120,000 square feet of retail space.

28443 ■ "Madison, Wis., University Research Park Expands Again" in *Milwaukee Journal Sentinel* (December 1, 2005)
Pub: Journal Sentinel, Inc.
Ed: Kathleen Gallagher. Description: University Research Park in Madison is expanding in order to accommodate 20 incubator suites for young companies being spun out of research findings at the University of Wisconsin-Madison.

28444 ■ "Magazines Snare More Dot-Com Ad Dollars" in *Folio: the Magazine for Magazine Management* (Vol. 30, No. 1, January 2001, pp. 7)
Pub: Intertec Publishing Corp.
Ed: Dale Buss. Description: As advertisers redirect their money to more targeted media, the magazine industry is reaping the benefits and enjoying a healthy gain over last year's share of the dot-com ad dollar distribution.

28445 ■ "The Magic Number" in *Inc.* (September 1, 2003)
Pub: Gruner & Jahr USA Publishing
Ed: Norm Brodsky. Description: Small businesses all have key numbers to track on a daily or weekly basis. These numbers are an essential part of running a successful enterprise. Key numbers give financial information needed to take timely action. Tips to help small companies forecast critical issues are shared.

28446 ■ "Magna Rating Adjusted" in *Mississippi Business Journal* (Vol. 29, January 2007, No. 2, pp. 8)
Pub: Venture Publications, Inc.
Ed: Wally Northway Description: Magna Insurance Company has had its financial strength rating downgraded from B to B by A.M. Best Co.

28447 ■ "Maine Faces Slow Population Growth, Aging Workforce" in *Portland Press Herald* (May 6, 2005)
Pub: Blethen Maine Newspapers, Inc.
Ed: Tux Turkel. Description: Maine is experiencing slow population growth coupled with an aging workforce, making the state's ability to expand its economy over the next ten years a challenge.

28448 ■ "Maine Thing: Camden Tries New Approach" in *American Banker* (Vol. 172, January 18, 2007, No. 12, pp. 1)
Pub: SourceMedia, Inc.
Ed: Bonnie McGeer. Description: Camden National Bank, located in Maine, is offering small business financial centers in order to expand business. The centers target small and medium-sized firms, relying on referrals from accountants and attorneys. Statistical data included.

28449 ■ "Maintenance-Free Condos Offer Stunning Views" in *Bradenton Herald* (February 3, 2005)
Pub: Bradenton Herald
Ed: Melissa Followell. Description: Many people in the Bradenton, Florida area are trading traffic and higher taxes for the convenience and pleasure of living in maintenance free condominiums.

28450 ■ *Make Your Business Survive and Thrive! 100+ Proven Marketing Methods to Help You Beat the Odds*
Pub: John Wiley & Sons, Incorporated
Ed: Priscilla Y. Huff. Released: December 2006. Price: $19.95. Description: Small business and entrepreneurial expert gives information to help small and home-based businesses grow.

28451 ■ "Making Dough: Warren Brown is Baking His Way to Success" in *Black Enterprise* (Vol. 35, September 2004, No. 2, pp. 45)
Pub: Earl G. Graves Publishing Co. Inc.
Ed: Virginia Myers Kelly. Description: Profile of Warren Brown, founder of a bakery called Cake Love, which earned $529,000 in revenues in 2003. Brown shares his experiences which began by baking in his small apartment after coming home from a full time job. Specialty cake shops are growing in popularity in the U.S.

28452 ■ "Managed Care's Poor Health" in *Rough Notes* (Vol. 145, No. 2, February 2002, pp. 36)
Pub: Rough Notes
Ed: Phil Zinkewicz. Description: According to surveys by Weiss Ratings Inc., 40.9 percent of health maintenance organizations, 16 percent of banks and financial industries, 25.9 percent of life and health insurers and 18.4 percent of financial industries are in a financially weakened condition. The threat of bioterrorism has had a serious impact on the problem to which no constructive solution has yet been devised.

28453 ■ *Managing Business Growth: Get a Grip on the Numbers That Count*
Pub: Self-Counsel Press, Incorporated
Ed: Angie Mohr. Released: September 2004. Price: $14.95. Description: Fourth book in the Numbers 101 for Small Business Series, teaches how small company owners can expand their businesses using sound financial planning.

28454 ■ "Manatee Boat Makers Are Hiring, But Workers Aren't Plentiful" in *Bradenton Herald* (February 4, 2005)
Pub: Bradenton Herald
Ed: Tilde Herrera. Description: Growth of the boating industry has increased significantly, with Chris-Craft reporting above 15 percent increase in sales for 2004. However, companies are having difficulty finding skilled labor to produce the growing demand.

28455 ■ "Manatee County, Fla. New Home Permits Up 13 Percent in 2004" in *Bradenton Herald* (January 5, 2005)
Pub: Bradenton Herald
Ed: Melissa Followell. Description: Manatee County, Florida is reporting a boom in new residential construction. The areas experienced a 13 percent rise in residential permits in 2004, due to the increase in property values and influx of new residents. Manatee County is becoming a bedroom community for the large urban areas.

28456 ■ "Manufacturing Sector Expects Improvement After Slow January" in *Journal Record (Oklahoma City, OK)* (February 1, 2007)
Pub: Journal Record
Ed: Jerry Shottenkirk. Description: Oklahoma manufacturing numbers fell in January 2007, but is expected to recover shortly.

28457 ■ "Manufacturing Sector Strengthening" in *Milwaukee Journal Sentinel* (December 1, 2005)
Pub: Journal Sentinel, Inc.

Ed: Thomas Content, Rick Barrett. Description: According to two recent reports, the manufacturing sector is seeing an increase in production while the economy in the Milwaukee, Wisconsin area rose 10 points from October to November 2005.

28458 ■ "Mapping the World of Customer Satisfaction" in *Harvard Business Review* (Vol. 78, No. 3, May 2000, pp. 30)
Pub: Harvard Business School Publishing Corp.
Ed: Regina Fazio Maruca. Description: Traditional satisfaction surveys often obscure the differences among customers in different regions of the country and different areas of the world.

28459 ■ "March Is National Craft Month" in *PR Newswire* (March 7, 2003)
Pub: PR Newswire Association, Inc.
Description: While other industries are experiencing a slowdown, the crafting industry is flourishing, due in large part, to its strong emotional appeal.

28460 ■ "Mark Hoffman" in *Internet World* (Vol. 7, No. 1, January 15, 2001, pp. 41)
Pub: Mecklermedia Corporation
Ed: Ruhan Memishi. Description: Mark Hoffman, chairman and CEO of Commerce One is interviewed about his views on business exchanges and his company. Hoffman believes there will be an increase in both business-to-business exchanges and growth in services for a competitive edge.

28461 ■ "Market Watch" in *Entrepreneur* (Vol. 28, No. 1, January 2000, pp. 46)
Pub: Entrepreneur Media Inc.
Ed: Melissa Campanelli. Description: The new Web-marketing service, eAnalytics from Adknowledge, is profiled.

28462 ■ "Marketing and sales" in *Boston Business Journal* (Vol. 22, No. 14, May 10, 2002, pp. 22)
Pub: MCP, Inc.
Ed: Ken Cook. Description: The difference between marketing and sales, and how each is important and supports the other for sustainable growth, is discussed.

28463 ■ "Marketing Your Consulting Service by Elaine Biech: www.josseybass.com" in *Entrepreneur* (Vol. 31, No. 10, October 2003, pp. 6)
Pub: Entrepreneur Media, Inc.
Ed: Steve Cooper. Description: Marketing tactics to help grow a business are presented.

28464 ■ "Marysville, Calif., Downtown Building Gets New Look, New Name" in *Marysville Appeal-Democrat* (January 26, 2003)
Pub: Knight Ridder/Tribune Business News
Ed: Scott Bransford. Description: The Library Square building, renamed Downtown Plaza in Marysville, California, has been renovated to attract new businesses. Shops at the building now include a Pizza Guys franchise, and Curves women's fitness and weight loss center. Rental prices are included.

28465 ■ "Masco Corp. (NYSE:MAS)" in *Crain's Detroit Business* (Vol. 16, No. 46, November 13, 2000, pp. 4)
Pub: Crain Communications, Inc.
Ed: Leslie Green. Description: Taylor-based Masco has reported a disappointing dip in their company's performance, although Wall Street hasn't lowered its "buy" rating. Masco Corporation is the country's largest maker of cabinets, faucets, locks and other home-improvement products.

28466 ■ "Masco hopes Home Depot deals, new product line build growth" in *Crain's Detroit Business* (Vol. 19, No. 7, Feb. 17, 2003, pp. 4)
Pub: Crain Communications Inc., Detroit
Ed: Michael Strong. Description: Taylor-based Masco Corporation expects to report a 40 percent increase in earnings for 2003 because of two new acquisitions, new products and more exposure in Home Depot stores.

28467 ■ "Massachusetts Jobless Insurance Trust Fund May Need Federal Help" in *Boston Globe* **(April 11, 2003)**
Pub: Knight-Ridder/Tribune Business News
Ed: Matthew Brelis. **Description:** The State of Massachusetts' unemployment insurance trust fund is facing insolvency after two years of rising unemployment rates and will require federal loans to pay benefits in 2003.

28468 ■ *Mastering Business Growth and Change Made Easy*
Pub: Entrepreneur Press
Ed: Jeffrey A. Hansen. **Released:** October 2005.
Price: $19.95 (US), $26.95 (Canadian). **Description:** Tips for growing a small business, regardless of state or environment.

28469 ■ "Mavericks" in *Success* **(Vol. 47, No. 2, June 2000, pp. 18)**
Pub: Success Publishing, Inc.
Ed: Russell Wild. **Description:** A profile of Jack Barringer's Cactus Jack line of cleaning products.

28470 ■ *Maximum Marketing, Minimum Dollars: The Top 50 Ways to Grow Your Small Business*
Pub: Kaplan Books
Ed: Kim Gordon. **Released:** April 2006. **Price:** $24.00. **Description:** Marketing tips to increase sales are presented. Small business owners will learn to maximize marketing with 50 innovative and affordable methods, including online marketing.

28471 ■ "MBDA's new horizons" in *Hispanic Business* **(Vol. 22, No. 11, November 2000, pp. 18)**
Pub: Hispanic Business
Ed: Patricia Guadalupe. **Description:** Issues are presented concerning the report by the Minority Business Development Agency in 2000, which revealed rapid growth in the expansion of Hispanic American businesses to $1-trillion in 1998 from $700-billion in 1990.

28472 ■ "M.D. Hodges changes strategy" in *Atlanta Business Chronicle* **(Vol. 25, December 6, 2002, No. 26, pp. 7C)**
Pub: American City Business Publications, Inc.
Ed: Anya Martin. **Description:** Development and lease management company, M.D. Hodges Enterprises Inc., Atlanta, Georgia, has won the 2002 Developer of the Year Award from the Georgia Chapter of the National Association of Industrial and Office Properties, according to NAIOP judge, Bo Jackson. Jackson is the executive vice president of the office division of Colonial Properties Trust. The firm was chosen for its creativity.

28473 ■ "MDC Homes expanding in North Carolina" in *Atlanta Business Chronicle* **(Vol. 25, No. 22, November 8, 2002, pp. 25A)**
Pub: American City Business Publications, Inc.
Ed: Jennifer Boyd Sidden. **Description:** MDC Homes, Atlanta, Georgia, is entering the Triad area of North Carolina. The firm will be involved in setting up single-family homes as well as two-story executive homes. MDC set up 1,100 homes in Georgia and the Carolina's in 2001.

28474 ■ *Medium Sized Firms and Economics Growth*
Pub: Nova Science Publishers, Incorporated
Ed: Janez Prasniker. **Released:** February 2005.
Price: $79.00. **Description:** Medium sized companies should have a more definitive presence in modern microeconomic theory, the theory of entrepreneurship, and the theory of financial markets.

28475 ■ "The Mentoring Advantage (Dearborn Trade) www.dearborn.com" in *Entrepreneur* **(Vol. 33, February 2005, No. 2, pp. 8)**
Pub: Entrepreneur Media Inc.
Description: Florence Stone addresses selecting mentors and implementing business mentoring programs.

28476 ■ "Merger with Advo May Mean Shift in Business for Valassis" in *Crain's Detroit Business* **(Vol. 232, January 8, 2007, No. 2, pp. 4)**
Pub: Crain Communications Inc. - Detroit
Ed: Bill Shea. **Description:** The merger of Valassis and Advo is a long term strategy to grow the business into direct mailing. Valassis has been limited solely to the insert mailings in periodicals.

28477 ■ "Metro homes become harder to sell" in *Atlanta Business Chronicle* **(Vol. 25, January 10, 2003, No. 31, pp. 1A)**
Pub: American City Business Publications, Inc.
Ed: Lisa R. Schoolcraft. **Description:** Homes sales are down in several Atlanta communities, including Flowery Branch, down 26 percent; Norcross, down 26.6 percent; Snellville, down 22.9 percent; and Powder Springs, down 22.6 percent. Housing sales are up in several Atlanta communities, including Jonesboro, up 266.7 percent; Adairsville, up 107.1 percent; Braselton, up 93.8 percent; and Winston, up 87.5 percent.

28478 ■ "MHV Opens 100th SONIC" in *Mississippi Business Journal* **(Vol. 28, September 2006, No. 36, pp. 8)**
Pub: Venture Publications, Inc.
Description: Profile of McClain, Harvey, Vaughn (MHV), SONICS's third largest franchise group. The group has just opened its 100th SONIC drive in. Statistical data included.

28479 ■ "Miami strikes back in bid for trade capital" in *Atlanta Business Chronicle* **(Vol. 25, No. 19, October 18, 2002)**
Pub: American City Business Publications, Inc.
Description: Miami, Florida business leaders are initiating a new lobbying effort to become the headquarters for the Free Trade Area of the Americas (FTAA) trade federation. The move has been sparked by a similar move by the city of Atlanta, Georgia to become the headquarters for the FTAA. Other cities competing for the honor include cities in Panama and Mexico.

28480 ■ "Miami Upstart Goes National" in *Hispanic Business* **(October 2002, pp. 86)**
Pub: Hispanic Business
Ed: Roger Harris. **Description:** Profile of Nextrox, an Internet service provider based in Miami, Florida, has grown into a national information technology company in less than seven years.

28481 ■ "Michael Witt Hired as Long Island Partnership 'Concierge'" in *Long Island Business News* **(February 20, 2004)**
Pub: Dolan Media Newswires
Ed: Ken Schachter. **Description:** Plans to attract and retain companies in the Long Island, New York region are discussed with newly appointed executive director of the Long Island Partnership, Michael Watt. Watt describes his position as being a corporate concierge.

28482 ■ "Michigan Bank Finally Gets Georgia Toehold" in *American Banker* **(Vol. 170, February 3, 2005, No. 23, pp. 1)**
Pub: Thomson Financial Media Inc.
Ed: John Reosti. **Description:** Capitol Bancorp Ltd. of Michigan has acquired Peoples State Bank in Jeffersonville, Georgia. The acquisition will qualify Capitol as a Georgia holding company, enabling them to charter banks and open branches in the state.

28483 ■ "Michigan Firm Buys Signs Now" in *Bradenton Herald* **(February 11, 2005)**
Pub: Bradenton Herald
Ed: Matt Griswold. **Description:** Allegra Network LLC, a Michigan-based sign company has purchased Signs Now Corporation's assets and franchise agreements. The sale will have little impact on local stores. Allegra is the franchisor for six various printing brands in the U.S., Canada and Japan; leading brands include Allegra Print & Imaging, American Speedy Printing Centers, and Insty-Prints.

28484 ■ "Microeconomics" in *Red Herring* **(No. 103, September 1, 2001, pp. 73)**
Pub: Herring Communications
Ed: Ronald Recinto. **Description:** Although compatibility issues have slowed the adoption of microturbines in the United States, growth in the global markets looks promising.

28485 ■ "Microsoft and market expect slower start for Windows 2000 sales" in *Wall Street Journal* **(February 14, 2000, pp. B8)**
Pub: Dow Jones & Co., Inc.
Ed: David Bank. **Description:** Microsoft Corporation's Windows 2000 is a server software package designed for small business and corporate computing networks. Analysts and Microsoft itself expect few NT users to upgrade at first, but by the end of next year 50 percent will have done so. Generally, systems operators for the first batch of bug fixes are to come out before purchasing new software. Nevertheless, Windows 2000 should add $3.5 billion to Microsoft's projected $25 billion revenue for fiscal year 2000.

28486 ■ "Milford DDA to Redevelop Former TRW Plant" in *Crain's Detroit Business* **(Vol. 21, November 7, 2005, No. 45, pp. 36)**
Pub: Crain Communications Inc. - Detroit
Ed: Andrew Dieterich. **Description:** A developer is planning to convert the former TRW Automotive Inc. plant building into a development that includes a hotel and residential homes.

28487 ■ "Minnesota-Based Developer Seeks Funds for Shingle Springs, Calif., Casino" in *Sacramento Bee* **(December 25, 2005)**
Pub: The Sacramento Bee
Ed: Dale Kasler. **Description:** Minnesota-based Lakes Entertainment Inc., a casino development company, is having difficulties launchings its proposed Indian casino in Shingle Springs, California. The company is facing growing losses due to development costs at the site.

28488 ■ "Minority Businesses Look For a Boost From Super Bowl and Beyond" in *Crain's Detroit Business* **(Vol. 21, October 10, 2005, No. 43)**
Pub: Crain Communications Inc. - Detroit
Ed: Sheena Harrison. **Description:** Minority and women business owners are capitalizing on the opportunities presented by the Super Bowl XL coming to Detroit, Michigan. More than 1,100 of these companies have applied or are participating in the Super Bowl's Emerging Business Program open to any certified minority- or woman-owned firm in the state. It also provides training and networking to help compete in contracts.

28489 ■ "Minority Certification Needs Examination" in *Crain's Detroit Business* **(Vol. 18, No. 20, May 20, 2002, pp. 8)**
Pub: Crain Communications Inc. - Detroit
Description: Commitments by automakers and large suppliers from minority-owned firms has helped them to grow and to get some of that business, the smaller minority-owned businesses have often formed partnerships or joint ventures with larger, non-minority firms, thus helping the smaller to grow.

28490 ■ "Minority-Owned Businesses Up" in *Inc.* **(April 2000, pp. 145)**
Pub: The Goldhirsh Group
Ed: Christopher Caggiano. **Description:** The rising economic tide of the 1990s helped minority-owned business in America. The U.S. Small Business Administration estimates that the number of minority-owned businesses more than doubled from 1987 to 1997, from a quarter million to a half million businesses, and that the revenues they collectively generated grew more than fourfold.

28491 ■ "A Misleading Predictor of Inflation" in *Business Week* **(January 23, 2006, No. 3968, pp. 28)**
Pub: McGraw-Hill Companies
Ed: James Mehring. **Description:** Wage growth is slowing; private sector wages and salaries grew 2.2 percent over last year but down from a 3 percent pace two years ago.

28492 ■ "Mississippi-Corporate Partnership Boosts Shipyards" in *Sun Herald* **(April 11, 2003)**
Pub: Knight-Ridder/Tribune Business News
Ed: David Tortorano. **Description:** The planned three-year expansion at two Mississippi shipyards will add 2,000 new jobs to the area.

28493 ■ **"Mixed Fate for Black Law Firms"** in *Black Enterprise* **(Vol. 34, No. 4, November 2003, pp. 27)**
Pub: Earl Graves Publishing Co.
Ed: Cliff Hocker. **Description:** Of the 12 original law firms highlighted in an August 1993 issue of Black Enterprise, only one-fourth are still operating. Profiles of the existing firms are included.

28494 ■ **"A Mixed Forecast for 2002"** in *Hispanic Business* **(Vol. 24, No. 1/2, January/February 2002, pp. 14, 16)**
Pub: Hispanic Business Inc.
Ed: Scott Williams. **Description:** Experts make forecasts on an economic recovery in 2002, and the ramifications for Hispanic business and consumers. Statistical data included.

28495 ■ *Modern Business Statistics*
Pub: Wadsworth Publishing Co.
Ed: George C. Canova. **Released:** 1995. **Price:** $19.95.

28496 ■ **"Mohr, Davidow Names New Partner, East Coast Presence"** in *Venture Capital Journal* **(Vol. 40, No. 10, October 2000, pp. 34)**
Pub: Venture Economics
Description: The article includes the announcement from Mohr, Davidow Ventures that the firm hired Partner Michael Sheridan to lead the company's effort to establish an East Coast presence.

28497 ■ **"Moms Have Their Own Generation Gap"** in *Marketing to Women* **(Vol. 20, January 2007, No. 1, pp. 5)**
Pub: EPM Communications, Inc.
Description: A Johnson & Johnson study compares the mothers of today with the mothers of 1967. Statistical data included.

28498 ■ **"Moms Say Missing Their Babies is Hardest Part of Returning to Work"** in *Marketing to Women* **(Vol. 19, November 2006, No. 11, pp. 3)**
Pub: EPM Communications, Inc.
Description: According to a survey by Modern Mom, the hardest thing about going to work outside the home for mothers is the separation anxiety they experience with their children. This leads to problems like getting to the office on time and getting back to speed with projects.

28499 ■ **"Money that Binds from Afar"** in *Hispanic Business* **(November 2003, pp. 60, 62, 64)**
Pub: Hispanic Business
Ed: Derek Reveron. **Description:** Remittances and direct investment connect the U.S. Hispanic economy to hemispheric financial development. Statistical data included, along with average transfer costs for $200 and Latin American remittances.

28500 ■ **"Money & Manners"** in *Small Business Opportunities* **(Vol. 17, September 2005, No. 5, pp. 12)**
Pub: Harris Publications Inc.
Ed: Lydia Ramsey. **Description:** Rudeness can cost a small business sales and revenue. A true/false quiz is offered to judge a company's business etiquette.

28501 ■ **"Money Talks; Here's Message to Michigan"** in *Crain's Detroit Business* **(Vol. 22, November 20, 2006, No. 47, pp. 9)**
Pub: Crain Communications Inc. - Detroit
Ed: William Watch **Description:** Capital moves quickly away from troubled areas. International markets such as Mexico and Brazil are more attractive to investors than Detroit.

28502 ■ **"Monthly report-December 2001"** in *Small Business Economic Trends* **(December 2001, pp. 1)**
Pub: National Federation of Independent Business Foundation
Description: A survey of the small business owners/members of the National Federation of Independent

Business is presented. Topics summarized include optimism index and outlook, earnings, sales, prices, employment, credit conditions, interest rates, inventories, capital investments, and important issues facing small business.

28503 ■ **"Monthly report-January 2002"** in *Small Business Economic Trends* **(January 2002, pp. 1)**
Pub: National Federation of Independent Business Foundation
Description: A survey conducted by the National Federation of Independent Business in December 2001 found that the Small Business Optimism Index rose from 99.4 in November to 100.4 in December. Topics covered include optimism index, prices, sales, compensation, credit conditions, interest rates, inventories, capital outlays, and more.

28504 ■ **"More Cell Phone Providers Using Stealthy Approach to Erecting Towers"** in *Chicago Tribune* **(March 4, 2005)**
Pub: Knight-Ridder/Tribune Business News
Ed: Lisa Black. **Description:** Many communities are resisting the construction of cell towers for the ever-expanding telecommunications network. In a move to address concerns, wireless companies are trying to conceal the towers within grain silos, affixing them to street lights or chimneys, or disguising them as flag poles, large boulders, or even palm trees.

28505 ■ **"More steady growth: Hispanic ad expenditures increase 11 percent to reach nearly $1.9 billion"** in *Hispanic Business* **(Dec. 1999, pp.56)**
Pub: Hispanic Business
Ed: Tim Dougherty. **Description:** Expansion in Hispanic advertising expenditures slowed to 11 percent in 1999, from 21 percent in 1998. However, the Top 50 Advertiser total rose 30 percent to $545.97 million. The impact of the Internet on Hispanic advertising is discussed.

28506 ■ **"More dealers may signal end of mobile-phone boom"** in *Crain's Detroit Business* **(Vol. 18, No. 49, December 9, 2002, pp. 25)**
Pub: Crain Communications Inc., Detroit
Ed: Andrew Dietderich. **Description:** Wireless Toyz aims to continue growing and become the next Blockbuster Video.

28507 ■ **"More than luck was required to remake San Diego's economy"** in *Wall Street Journal* **(June 13, 2000, pp. B4)**
Pub: Dow Jones & Co., Inc.
Ed: Jeffrey Tannenbaum. **Description:** A report showing that the San Diego area became an incubator for high-tech firms thanks to superb cooperation between government, entrepreneurs and academics.

28508 ■ **"More Shrinkage: Digest Readers Cut and Run"** in *Barron's* **(August 25, 2003, pp. 10)**
Pub: Barron's
Ed: Leslie P. Norton. **Description:** Periodical publisher Reader's Digest reported magazine sales down nearly 20 percent from the previous year, following earlier disclosures of depressed fourth-quarter earnings and low projections for 2004.

28509 ■ **"More Women Than Men Have Home Offices"** in *Marketing to Women* **(Vol. 19, October 2006, No. 10, pp. 12)**
Pub: EPM Communications, Inc.
Description: A survey of business professionals by Intellicontact reflects that women are more likely than men to have home offices. The survey also shows that while men and women both check their e-mail frequently, the two sexes manage their inboxes differently.

28510 ■ **"Mortgage Lenders Post Record Years, Expect Slowdown"** in *Atlanta Business Chronicle* **(Vol. 25, December 20, 2002, No. 28, pp. 3A)**
Pub: American City Business Publications, Inc.
Ed: Lisa R. Schoolcraft. **Description:** Mortgage lenders in the Atlanta, Georgia area do not anticipate that

the record pace of mortgage volume in 2002 will be repeated in 2003. This reflects the view of the Mortgage Bankers Association of America, located in Washington, DC. According to the Association, banks across the U.S. will see mortgage volume reach $2.42 trillion in 2002, but that number will shrink to $1.77 trillion in 2003. The reason for the fall-off will be due to modest increases in mortgage rates over the upcoming 18-month period, as well as a fall-off in the number of people able to refinance mortgages.

28511 ■ **"Most Likely to Succeed"** in *Inc.* **(Volume 28, January 2006, No. 1, pp. 26)**
Pub: Inc. Magazine
Ed: Jim Melloan. **Description:** Innovative technology companies are launching new products in 2006.

28512 ■ **"Most Women Make Electronics Buying Choices"** in *Marketing to Women* **(Vol. 19, November 2006, No. 11, pp. 11)**
Pub: EPM Communications, Inc.
Description: According to the Vertis 2006 Customer Focus Home Electronics Study, more than nine in ten women in the 35-49 age group say they are chief or equal decision-makers when shopping for home electronics. Statistical data included.

28513 ■ **"Motorola's Cell Slide Resumes"** in *Crain's Chicago Business* **(Vol. 26, No. 50, December 15, 2003, pp. 3)**
Pub: Crain Communications, Inc.
Ed: Julie Johnsson. **Description:** Motorola Inc. is seeing a drop in sales, mostly due to consumers desire to own cellular phones equipped with cameras and color screens. The firm hopes to recapture some marketshare lost in Europe, however Motorola's marketshare in the U.S. is expected to fall further in fourth quarter 2003.

28514 ■ **"Motorola's Cell Slide Resumes; Rivals with Camera Phones Steal Marketshare"** in *Crains Chicago Business* **(Vol. 26, No. 50)**
Pub: Crain Communications, Inc.
Ed: Julie Johnsson. **Description:** Motorola Inc. is seeing a drop in sales, mostly due to consumers desire to own cellular phones equipped with cameras and color screens. The firm hopes to recapture some marketshare lost in Europe, however Motorola's marketshare in the U.S. is expected to fall further in fourth quarter 2003.

28515 ■ **"Move over, Charlotte"** in *Atlanta Business Chronicle* **(Vol. 25, December 6, 2002, No. 26, pp. 1A)**
Pub: American City Business Publications, Inc.
Ed: Meredith Jordan. **Description:** Federal Deposit Insurance Corporation data indicates that the deposits of FDIC-insured institutions in Atlanta, Georgia area were greater than all other Southeastern metropolitan areas. As of June 2002, deposits of FDIC-insured institutions in the Atlanta area were $62 billion.

28516 ■ **"Move Over"** in *Entrepreneur* **(Vol. 33, September 2005, No. 9, pp. 55)**
Pub: Entrepreneur Media Inc.
Ed: David Worrell. **Description:** John Jansheski, founder and CEO of DenTek Oral Care, found that moving his company closer to his largest customers saved his business $1 million in shipping costs in 2004.

28517 ■ **"Moving from one product was their prize"** in *Crain's Detroit Business* **(Vol. 19, No. 13, March 31, 2003, pp. 13)**
Pub: Crain Communications Inc., Detroit
Description: Profile of EPrize LLC, the company offers Web-based sweepstakes designed to draw Internet surfers with prizes and has expanded the enterprise in order to stay in business.

28518 ■ **"Mr. Pita legal woes haven't put a wrap on expansion"** in *Crain's Detroit Business* **(Vol. 18, No. 24, June 17, 2002, pp. 22)**
Pub: Crain Communications Inc. - Detroit
Ed: Michael Strong. **Description:** Shelby Township-based Mr. Pita, plans to open eight more locations, despite internal legal problems that could hinder the company's expansion.

28519 ■ **"Mr. Pita Wagons Rolling Along"** in *Crain's Detroit Business* (Vol. 22, February 6, 2006, No. 6, pp. 21)
Pub: Crain Communications Inc. - Detroit
Ed: Brent Snavely. Description: Mr. Pita Franchise Corporation is using three lunch wagons to deliver both hot and cold lunches to workers at various locations. Mr. Pita has 37 franchised locations in Michigan with plans to expand in Florida, Tennessee, Ohio and Illinois.

28520 ■ **"Mr. Prime Time"** in *Hispanic Business* (Vol. 23, No. 7/8, July/August 2001, pp. 74, 76, 78)
Pub: Hispanic Business
Ed: Tim Dougherty. Description: Profile of actor, Esai Morales, as well as an overview of the Hispanic film-making industry. Statistical data included.

28521 ■ **"MSCI-Red Herring Index"** in *Red Herring* (January 2003, pp. 72)
Pub: Herring Communications Inc.
Description: An index comparison is presented, highlighting the following industries: communications equipment, Internet software & services, semiconductor equipment and products, wireless telecom services, electronic equipment and instruments, IT consulting and services, computers and peripherals, broadcasting and cable TV, software, diversified telecom services, and publishing.

28522 ■ *Multiply Your Profits: A Common-Sense Approach for Small to Midsize Businesses*
Pub: Inverness Publishing
Ed: Richard Peelo. Released: 1998.

28523 ■ **"NAIAS Spotlight Shines on Design"** in *Crain's Detroit Business* (Vol. 23, January 1, 2007, No. 1, pp. 1)
Pub: Crain Communications Inc. - Detroit
Ed: Jennette Smith. Description: Differentiation in design and styling are getting the most attention at the Auto Show in Detroit this year. All brands are about equal in quality and reliability due to engineering advances, so differentiation in styling has moved back to the forefront. Industry cutbacks and layoffs have not affected the design areas.

28524 ■ **"Nanotech Grows"** in *Red Herring* (No. 99, June 15 & July 1, 2001, pp. 46-47)
Pub: Herring Communications
Description: A brief chronology of nanotechnology. Nanotechnology is the science of the extremely small, nano meaning one-billionth.

28525 ■ **"Nanotechnology sector analysis"** in *Red Herring* (March 2003, pp. 62)
Pub: Herring Communications Inc.
Description: An overview of the nanotechnology industry is presented, including information nano-based devices that can change electronics one atom at a time.

28526 ■ **"National Survey Finds More Small-Business Owners Planning to Increase Their Staffs"** in *Long Island Business News* (January 30, 2004)
Pub: Dolan Media Newswires
Ed: Ben Abelson. Description: According to a study done by the National Federation of Independent Business, 20 percent of U.S. small businesses plan to increase staff this year, a number higher than at any other point in the past 3-1/2 years. The financial services sector is leading the way in this trend.

28527 ■ **"National Urban League: State of Black America"** in *Black Enterprise* (Vol. 34, July 2004, No. 12, pp. 28)
Pub: Earl G. Graves Publishing Co. Inc.
Ed: Marcia A. Wade. Description: Disparities between black and white Americans are reported showing that in order to level the playing field an additional 23,698 black students would need to earn bachelor's degrees from four-year colleges annually. It would also require 751,000 blacks to find employment and that three white businesses fold for every black startup company.

28528 ■ **"Nature Brings Uncertainty and Opportunity"** in *Venture Capital Journal* (October 1, 2005)
Pub: Thomason Financial Inc.
Description: Impacts of Hurricane Katrina and the passing of Chief Justice William Rehnquist on the venture capital sector are discussed. In the first half of 2005, VCs had already invested $239.6 million in alternative energy companies up nearly $40 million over last year.

28529 ■ **"Neighborhood Mortgage Announces Office Expansion"** in *Bellingham Business Journal* (December 2006, pp. 2)
Pub: Sun News Inc.
Description: Neighborhood Mortgage plans to expand and relocate its home office by Spring 2007. The move will help accommodate the company's rapid growth by tripling the square footage of the building and offer convenient access to and from the freeway.

28530 ■ **"The New Atlantic Century"** in *Harvard Business Review* (Vol. 78, No. 1, January 2000, pp. 17)
Pub: Harvard Business School Publishing Corp.
Ed: Hermann Simon, Max Otte. Description: The economic relationship between the United States and Europe is about to enter its strongest period ever.

28531 ■ **"New Beginnings for VIBE"** in *Black Enterprise* (Vol. 37, November 2006, No. 4, pp. 34)
Pub: Earl G. Graves Publishing Co. Inc.
Ed: Mashaun D. Simon. Description: Danyel Smith replaced Mimi Valdes as editor-in-chief of VIBE magazine after the Wicks Group, private equity firm focused on selected segments of the media, communications, and information industries, purchased the magazine.

28532 ■ **"New Biscotti Company Gets Cooking"** in *Bellingham Business Journal* (December 2006, pp. A5)
Pub: Sun News Inc.
Description: Profile of Kyoung Croft, owner of Rainy Days Kitchen, a company that produces non-traditional biscotti,

28533 ■ **"New Business on Champion Street Uncorks a New Trend"** in *Bellingham Business Journal* (January 2007, pp. A4)
Pub: Sun News Inc.
Description: Overview of Whatcom Winemakers which has developed a fresh new concept for the wine industry, do-it-yourself winemaking. The winemaking shop is slated to open in February.

28534 ■ **"New Business Owners Learn the Ropes in 2006"** in *Bellingham Business Journal* (January 2007, pp.)
Pub: Sun News Inc.
Ed: Dan Hiestand. Description: Local business owners say that the biggest challenge of the business is getting one's name out there.

28535 ■ **"The New Economic World Order"** in *Red Herring* (No. 102, August 15, 2001, pp. 16)
Pub: Herring Communications
Ed: Anthony B. Perkins. Description: The principles that nations must embrace in order to compete successfully in and share the rewards of the new economic order are addressed.

28536 ■ **"New Economy Creates New Markets"** in *Hispanic Business* (Vol. 22, No. 1/2, January/February, pp. 24, 26)
Pub: Hispanic Business
Description: Marketers share strategies at the Se Habla Expanol Market and Media Expo.

28537 ■ **"The new economy's currency is stock, stock, and stock"** in *The New York Times* (March 27, 2000, pp. D12, H12)
Pub: The New York Times Company
Ed: Martha Baer. Description: An investigation into equity reimbursements for all Web business contractors.

28538 ■ **"The New Edition"** in *Internet World* (Vol. 7, No. 2, January 15, 2001, pp. 20)
Pub: Mecklermedia Corporation
Ed: Anastasia M. Ashman. Description: Electronic books currently represent a publishing segment so miniscule as to be virtually invisible, were it not receiving disproportionate media coverage. Market researchers, nevertheless, expect the market for E-books to reach $2.3 billion by 2005. E-publishing could dramatically transform the centuries-old industry and even revolutionize the way consumers use information, but the biggest obstacle may be publishers themselves, who have vast investments in the status quo.

28539 ■ **"The new fact of HACR"** in *Hispanic Business* (Vol. 21, No. 12, December 1999, pp. 22)
Pub: Hispanic Business
Ed: Patricia Guadalupe. Description: The role of the Hispanic Association on Corporate Responsibility (HACR), will collaborate with U.S. firms to identify opportunities which will allow Hispanic business activity to expand, according to Anna Escobeda Cabral, the association's new leader.

28540 ■ **"New Group Seeks Greater Hispanic Influence"** in *Hispanic Business* (Vol. 23, No. 7/8, July/August 2001, pp. 24)
Pub: Hispanic Business
Description: The newly formed National Advancement of Hispanic People (NAAHP) will pursue increased political and economic influence for U.S. Hispanics. The organization will rely on membership dues rather than corporate sponsorship.

28541 ■ **"New Habits Die Hard"** in *Red Herring* (No. 102, August 15, 2001, pp. 48-50, 52-53)
Pub: Herring Communications
Ed: Peter Rojas. Description: College students have grown accustomed to getting online entertainment for free; the article discusses the challenges facing Hollywood in delivery entertainment with today's new technologies.

28542 ■ **"New Home Construction Reaches 21-Year-High Pace in January"** in *Chicago Tribune* (February 17, 2005)
Pub: Knight-Ridder/Tribune Business News
Ed: William Sluis. Description: Despite industry prediction, new home construction rose to a 21-year-high, with record construction of single-family homes. An overview of Chicago-area new home construction is presented.

28543 ■ **"New Jersey-Based Arts, Crafts Chain to Open Store in Erie, Pa"** in *Erie Times-News* (March 4, 2002)
Pub: Knight Ridder/Tribune Business News
Ed: Jim Martin. Description: Profile of A.C. Moore Arts and Crafts Inc., a New Jersey chain of more than 70 craft stores. The company is set to open a new store in the Millcreek Mall and is expected to employ between 35-60 craft enthusiasts, each with their own area of expertise.

28544 ■ **"New Jersey Jobless Rate Down, But Jobs Lost"** in *The Record* (November 18, 2005)
Pub: New Jersey Media Group
Ed: Michael L. Diamond. Description: According to the New Jersey Department of Labor and Workforce Development office, the state's unemployment rate fell to 3.9 percent in October 2005. However, the state's economy lost 4,700 jobs during the month. The pattern shows that New Jersey private-sector firms are hiring workers cautiously.

28545 ■ **"A New Leaf"** in *Entrepreneur* (Vol. 32, November 2004, No. 11, pp. 95)
Pub: Entrepreneur Media Inc.
Ed: Mark Henricks. Description: Consulting firm, McKinsey & Company has designed a four-step process that assists entrepreneurs when making changes to a company. The first step involves convincing people, including employees, that a change is necessary for the firm.

28546 ■ "New Local Bank to Open 2 Sites" in *Sacramento Bee* (November 3, 2005)
Pub: The Sacramento Bee
Ed: Clint Swett. **Description:** Community Business Bank plans to open two new branches in West Sacramento and Lodi, California. The branches will serve small businesses, not-for-profits and professionals.

28547 ■ "New Media Venture Partners" in *Venture Capital Journal* (Vol. 40, No. 10, October 2000, pp. 52-53)
Pub: Venture Economics
Description: Profile of New Media Venture Partners (NMVP), the fast growing digital media holding company focused on investing in and developing core technologies, the next phase of the Internet - the development and distribution of digital media and content. A listing of NMVP's portfolio companies is included.

28548 ■ "New Muscle for Old Strip Malls" in *Business 2.0* (Vol. 6, July 2005, No. 6, pp. 50)
Pub: Time, Inc.
Ed: Nicole Joseph. **Description:** 24 Hour Fitness chain is using abandoned grocery stores to startup new fitness centers. With big-box retailers taking over mid-size grocery stores, the $1 billion fitness chain sees an endless opportunity for expansion.

28549 ■ "New Rochelle-Based Simone Development Increases its Long Island Holdings" in *Long Island Business News* (February 20, 2004)
Pub: Dolan Media Newswires
Ed: Nick Anastasi. **Description:** Simone Development of New Rochelle, New York has purchased 150,000-square foot industrial building on South Oyster Bay Road, increasing the firm's holdings to nearly 1 million square feet of space in 27 buildings.

28550 ■ "New Shopping Centers on Tap in Fast-Growing Livingston County" in *Crain's Detroit Business* (Vol. 22, January 2, 2006, No. 1)
Pub: Crain Communications Inc. - Detroit
Ed: Sheena Harrison. **Description:** Construction on a new shopping center is underway in Green Oaks of Livingston County, Michigan and is expected to be one of the state's top shopping destinations. Another retail center is being planned in Hartland, Township.

28551 ■ "New Site Gives Lipari Foods Room to Continue Growth" in *Crain's Detroit Business* (Vol. 23, January 8, 2007, No. 2, pp. 10)
Pub: Crain Communications Inc. - Detroit
Ed: Brent Snaveley. **Description:** New location doubles size of local wholesale food delivery service. Recent growth with expanded product offerings dictates larger warehouse requirements. Plans are to expand territory to surrounding states in the Midwest.

28552 ■ "The New Skin Trade" in *Business 2.0* (Vol. 7, January/February 2006, No. 1, pp. 48, 50, 52)
Pub: Time, Inc.
Ed: Elizabeth Esfahani. **Description:** Nonsurgical techniques for keeping people looking young with soon be a $20 billion market.

28553 ■ "New Study: County Tourism Taking Off" in *Bellingham Business Journal* (December 2006, pp. A4)
Pub: Sun News Inc.
Description: Washington State Office of Community, Trade and Economic Development released a study showing that Whatcom County ranked fifth of the state's thirty-nine counties in terms tourism and of total visitor spending. Statistical data included.

28554 ■ "New Tacks for Tough Times" in *Business Week Online* (Oct. 17, 2002)
Pub: McGraw-Hill Inc.
Ed: Roger Franklin. **Description:** According to a small business survey, 75 percent of the 5,000 firms responding, have a positive attitude about the future, and predict bottom-line growth. One-third of the companies expect significant expansion.

28555 ■ *New Technology-Based Firms in the New Millennium, Volume 5*
Pub: Elsevier Science and Technology Books
Ed: Ray Oakey; Saleema Kauser; Aard Groen; Peter van der Sijde. **Released:** November 2006. **Price:** $145.00. **Description:** Papers from the Annual High Technology Smal Firms conference are presented. Experts address strategic growth for these small firms.

28556 ■ "A new terminal at National?" in *Washington Business Journal* (Vol. 22, No. 3, May 23, 2003, pp. 1)
Pub: Washington Business Journal
Ed: John Wilen. **Description:** U.S. Airways plans construction of a new airport terminal at Washington's Reagan National Airport. Data covering U.S. Airways growth, design and construction and financial management is included.

28557 ■ "A New View of Downtown. Perceptions Improve; Concerns Remain" in *Business Journal-Milwaukee* (Vol. 20, No. 51, September 5, 2003)
Pub: American City Business Journals, Inc.
Ed: Pete Millard. **Description:** Monica Dignam, president of Monalco Inc., stated recently that because of efforts to improve the image of Milwaukee, Wisconsin, people are more willing to visit, shop and live in the city.

28558 ■ "A new way of business" in *Atlanta Business Chronicle* (Vol. 24, No. 11, August 17, 2001, pp. 1A)
Pub: American City Business Journals Inc.
Ed: Matt Gove. **Description:** The city of Atlanta, Georgia's business culture is being changed by the steady stream of new companies, giving an edge to the city's Southern gentility. The city was once run by a handful of powerful people. The city has been forced to accept other spheres of influences and some of the backlashes are discussed.

28559 ■ "New World Order: the European Union Will Soon be a Bigger Cash Cow" in *Entrepreneur* (Vol. 32, No. 4, April 2004, pp. 19)
Pub: Entrepreneur Media, Inc.
Ed: Joshua Kurlantzick. **Description:** Entrepreneurs should not overlook overseas markets in central and Eastern Europe when expanding international business.

28560 ■ "New Year Brings New Growth" in *My Business* (February/March 2003, pp. 48)
Pub: My Business Magazine
Ed: Bill Dunkelberg. **Description:** Third quarter growth for 2002 came in at 4 percent for Gross Domestic Product, the normal trend would be at 3.5 percent. Statistical data included.

28561 ■ "News on Women" in *Marketing to Women* (Vol. 19, November 2006, No. 22, pp. 8)
Pub: EPM Communications, Inc.
Description: Various excerpts from articles and reports intended to provide information relevant to marketers targeting female consumers.

28562 ■ "Newsday's Weekday, Saturday Circulation Drops 2 Percent" in *Newsday* (March 3, 2005)
Pub: Knight-Ridder/Tribune Business News
Ed: James T. Madore. **Description:** Newsday reports circulation dropped 2 percent in the last six months for weekday and Saturday publications, and Sunday sales were down by 8.4 percent.

28563 ■ "The Next Big Trend: Cutting Mgmt. Fees" in *Venture Capital Journal* (Vol. 42, No. 9, September 2002, pp. 6, 8-9)
Pub: Thomas Venture Economics
Ed: Lawrence Aragon. **Description:** Private equity firms are planning to cut fees or work out new fee arrangements with limited partners. VantagePoint Venture Partners' plans to defer fees for 18 months on its $1.6 billion Fund IV.

28564 ■ "$93M in Development Planned for South Lyon" in *Crain's Detroit Business* (V. 19, No. 7, 2/17/03, pp. 22)
Pub: Crain Communications Inc., Detroit
Ed: Andrew Dietderich. **Description:** Two planned developments worth more than $93 million will add more than 200 new homes to South Lyon, Michigan.

28565 ■ "No More Free Rides: It's the End of the Free Lunch on the Web" in *Black Enterprise* (Vol. 32, No. 6, January 2002, pp. 39)
Pub: Earl Graves Publishing Co.
Ed: Rebecca Rohan. **Description:** Former free service providers know that their customer base is price-sensitive and charge less than fee-based competitors, but worry how their customers will cope with being charged after using free services for so long.

28566 ■ "No Respect: ONI Systems is the ugly stepchild of the networking market" in *Red Herring* (No. 105, October 1, 2001, pp. 92)
Pub: Herring Communications
Ed: Om Malik. **Description:** Profile of ONI Systems, which focuses on metropolitan area networks (MANs) that connect businesses and other commercial enterprises to the optical fibers beneath city streets using metro dense wave division multiplexing (DWDM) equipment. Despite the fact that ONI has stronger fundamentals than many other networking companies, the firm's stock has fallen along with the telecom equipment sector.

28567 ■ "No, They Can't Do It Themselves" in *Inc.* (July 1, 2004)
Pub: Inc. Magazine
Ed: Jess McCuan. **Description:** Founders of the do-it-yourself journal, ReadyMade magazine, partnered with a small Colorado publisher in order to compete with rival Budget Living.

28568 ■ "No Wonder Market Shares are Falling" in *Automotive News* (Vol. 79, February 21, 2005, No. 6135, pp. 12)
Pub: Crain Communications Inc.
Ed: Keith Crain. **Description:** With China, and soon Europe, entering the automobile market with new models, the U.S. automakers need a plan to retain market share.

28569 ■ "North Cobb office market healthier than most" in *Atlanta Business Chronicle* (Vol. 25, December 6, 2002, No. 26, pp. 20C)
Pub: American City Business Publications, Inc.
Ed: Martin Sinderman. **Description:** The office submarket at Atlanta's I-75 North/Marietta/Johnson Ferry Road has seen some increased tenant activity, particularly in the Town Center area. Statistical data included.

28570 ■ "Northwest seeks to cut $1.5B, but little impact felt at Metro for now" in *Crain's Detroit Business* (Vol. 19, No. 7, Feb. 17, 2003)
Pub: Crain Communications Inc., Detroit
Ed: Michael Strong. **Description:** Northwest Airlines is expected to cut $1.5 billion from its operating costs, but little or no impact is expected for the Detroit Metropolitan Airport.

28571 ■ "Northwest may be next with low-cost subsidiary" in *Crain's Detroit Business* (Vol. 19, No. 6, February 10, 2003, pp. 1)
Pub: Crain Communications Inc., Detroit
Ed: Michael Strong. **Description:** Northwest Airlines is considering creating its own low-cost carrier in an effort to improve its financial status.

28572 ■ "Northwest sees friendlier skies; Detroit called key to strategy" in *Crain's Detroit Business* (Vol. 19, No. 1, Jan. 6, 2003, pp. 18)
Pub: Crain Communications Inc., Detroit
Ed: Michael Strong. **Description:** Despite the Chapter 11 filing by United Airlines, Northwest Airlines feels it will survive the tough operating environment, and expects to improve its position at its Detroit hub.

28573 ■ "The Not-So-Golden state? Economic optimism is gathering steam across most of the country" in *Business Week Online* **(April 25, 2002)**
Pub: McGraw-Hill, Inc.
Ed: Roger Franklin. Description: Most small businesses believe the economy is poised to improve, that is, all but the small business community in California. Statistical data included.

28574 ■ "Now Boarding" in *Inc.* **(Volume 28, January 2006, No. 1, pp. 66)**
Pub: Inc. Magazine
Ed: Larry Olmsted. Description: More than 100 discount airlines have been launched globally since 2004. A few of the best budget carriers are listed for the business traveler going overseas to India, the Mediterranean, Southeast Asia, South America, and Eastern Europe.

28575 ■ "No. 1 Company Succeeds in Rehabilitating Malls" in *San Fernando Valley Business Journal* **(Vol. 11, November 2006, No. 24, pp. 22)**
Pub: San Fernando Valley Business Journal Associates
Ed: Chris Coates. Description: Profile of NewMark Merrill Cos., a mall developer and shopping center real estate firm, which redevelops underperforming malls by building new ones. The company's revenue increased from $15.9 million in 2004 to $37.2 million in 2005, a rise of $133.68 percent.

28576 ■ "The Numbers" in *Fortune* **(Vol. 140, No. 12, December 20, 1999 pp. 52)**
Pub: Time Inc.
Description: An executive survey on U.S. economic growth and the Y2K bug. Polling and statistical data include such issues as economic growth, budgets, and advertising.

28577 ■ "NY Metro Gets $388M in Fourth-Quarter Venture Funds, Survey Says" in *Long Island Business News* **(February 20, 2004)**
Pub: Dolan Media Newswires
Ed: Ken Schachter. Description: The Money Tree survey conducted by PricewaterhouseCoopers, Venture Economics and the National Venture Capital Association, reported companies received $388 million fourth quarter 2003, up 9 percent over same period 2002. Statistical data included.

28578 ■ "NYC Hotels Register Gains; Occupancy Hits 85-Percent for March" in *Crain's New York Business* **(Vol. 20, No. 16, April 19, 2004, pp. 4)**
Pub: Crain Communications, Inc.
Ed: Lisa Fickenscher. Description: New York City hotel occupancies are reported at 85 percent for March 2004, the highest level since 1969, showing signs of economic recovery.

28579 ■ "O2 Interactive Realizes Profits as it Builds Relationships" in *San Diego Business Journal* **(Vol. 28, January 8, 2007, No. 2, pp. 9)**
Pub: San Diego Business Journal Associates
Ed: Amy Yarnall. Description: O2 Interactive, seven-employee firm, that creates customer relation software for the homebuilding industry, doubled its sales in 2006.

28580 ■ "Oakland cities try to reinvigorate neglected areas" in *Crain's Detroit Business* **(Vol. 19, No. 1, Jan. 6, 2003, pp. 7)**
Pub: Crain Communications Inc., Detroit
Ed: Andrew Dietderich. Description: A listing of vacant or blighted properties in Oakland County, Michigan communities are promoting redevelopment, amounting to nearly $57 million in projects.

28581 ■ "Office vacancies, lease perks pile up" in *Crain's Detroit Business* **(Vol. 19, No. 4, January 27, 2003, pp. 3)**
Pub: Crain Communications Inc., Detroit
Ed: Jennette Smith. Description: In an effort to fill vacancies, Detroit-area landlords are offering free rent, money for improvement, and perks for real estate brokers.

28582 ■ "OKC-based Dobson Communications Subscribers Up 14,400" in *Journal Record* **(February 4, 2004)**
Pub: Dolan Media Company
Description: Dobson Communications reported an increase of 14,400 net subscribers for fourth quarter 2003 to its 1.55 million total subscribers. Dobson owns wireless operations in 16 states.

28583 ■ "OKC Chamber of Commerce Finds Many Firms Interested in City" in *Journal Record* **(February 4, 2004)**
Pub: Dolan Media Company
Ed: Darren Currin. Description: The Greater Oklahoma City Chamber of Commerce is seeing increased interest from companies looking to relocate to the area, as well as existing local firms looking to expand.

28584 ■ "The Old Economy Meets the New Economy" in *Fast Company* **(November 2001, pp. 70)**
Pub: Fast Company
Description: Fast Company recently convened a session in Chicago with experts from the world's strongest and oldest brands with the objective of finding new insights on emerging best practices when it comes to customers, technology and business.

28585 ■ "Old King Coal Comes Back: Actually, It Never Really Left" in *Fortune* **(Vol. 151, February 21, 2005, No. 4, pp. 114)**
Pub: Time Inc.
Ed: Jeremy Main. Description: Profile of Peabody Energy, owner of the largest coalmine in the world, the North Antelope-Rochelle Mine. The coal industry is working to improve the mining, transporting, and burning of coal in order to increase production.

28586 ■ "On the Lookout" in *Entrepreneur* **(Vol. 33, October 2005, No. 10, pp. 82)**
Pub: Entrepreneur Media Inc.
Ed: Gwen Moran. Description: Watching current events and celebrity styles help retailers predict trends.

28587 ■ "On the mend" in *Business First Columbus* **(Vol. 18, No. 40, March 24, 2002, pp. A1)**
Pub: Business First Columbus, Inc.
Ed: David Mildenberg. Description: Ohio's small businesses see slight economic improvements. According to a small business survey by InSight Poll, 506 small businesses nationally are expanding.

28588 ■ "On the Radar" in *E-business Advisor* **(Vol. 18, No. 5, May 2000, pp. 8)**
Pub: Advisor Media, Inc.
Description: According to an international survey taken among major firms in manufacturing, financial services, transportation and other various industries, revenues from electronic commerce accounted for less than 5 percent of revenues in 79 percent of the companies surveyed. In addition, over 60 percent of companies surveyed still do not have extranets to link with key suppliers and financial partners.

28589 ■ "One Big Reason to Expect a Decent Year for Jobs" in *Business Week* **(January 23, 2006, No. 3968, pp. 27-28)**
Pub: McGraw-Hill Companies
Ed: James C. Cooper. Description: Companies can no longer meet the demand with existing workers. The Labor Department reported a 4.9 percent jobless rate. Statistical data included.

28590 ■ "One D's Big Challenge: Shaking Myopia" in *Crain's Detroit Business* **(Vol. 22, November 20, 2006, No. 47, pp. 1)**
Pub: Crain Communications Inc. - Detroit
Ed: Sherri Begin. Description: One D was formed to focus on what's good for the community or region and not just any one organization or community. Six groups have been formed with objectives to form six action plans to achieve the desired results and prioritize the resources.

28591 ■ "One Final Note: Why Your Last Impression Is As Important As Your First" in *Black Enterprise* **(Vol. 35, November 2004, No. 4, pp. 76)**
Pub: Earl G. Graves Publishing Co. Inc.
Ed: Erin Straker. Description: Final impressions in business are as important as first impressions. Show appreciation for time spent at a business meeting.

28592 ■ "$160M plan pushed for NE Ann Arbor" in *Crain's Detroit Business* **(Vol. 19, No. 1, Jan. 6, 2003, pp. 1)**
Pub: Crain Communications Inc., Detroit
Ed: Laura Bailey. Description: A proposed new development in Ann Arbor, Michigan is facing expensive environmental clean up on the site before development can begin. Neighbors in the area are concerned about the plans for development, as are existing businesses. The $160 million project would include offices, a health center, housing and retail space.

28593 ■ "The One Number You Need to Grow" in *Harvard Business Review* **(Vol. 81, No. 12, December 2003, pp. 46)**
Pub: Harvard Business School Press
Ed: Frederick F. Reichheld. Description: The power of customer word-of-mouth communication and corporate growth are examined. Loyal customers promote growth by personally endorsing to friends the businesses they patronize. Means for measuring the effects of these promoters are described.

28594 ■ "Online Retail Sales Jumper 13.1 Percent in Fourth Quarter" in *Wall Street Journal* **(February 21, 2002, pp. B6)**
Pub: Wall Street Journal
Description: Statistics showing a 13.1 increase in online retail sales is presented.

28595 ■ "Online Sales Booming; Retailers Rethink Web Biz as Sales Increase" in *Crain's Detroit Business* **(Vol. 19, No. 1, Jan. 6, 2003, pp. 3)**
Pub: Crain Communications Inc., Detroit
Ed: Brent Snavely. Description: Total consumer online sales were up 29 percent during the period November 1 and December 20, 2002. This increase has many retailers rethinking their online sales potential. Tips for developing successful Web sites are presented.

28596 ■ "Online Sales Continue To Climb at L.L. Bean, Other Retailers" in *Portland Press Herald* **(December 13, 2005)**
Pub: Blethen Maine Newspapers, Inc.
Ed: Edward D. Murphy. Description: L.L. Bean reports a 47 percent rise in sales over 2004. Other online retailers are also experiencing increased sales in 2004.

28597 ■ "Open Your Books To Grow Your Business" in *My Business* **(November/December 2001, pp. 42)**
Pub: My Business Magazine
Ed: Shannon Scully. Description: Open book management (OBM), is described by its originator, Victor Ornelas owner of a Latino marketing firm in Dallas, Texas. Open book management is a company policy that requires the business owner to share the company's financial information with its employees.

28598 ■ "Optics' Second Wave: Test-and-measurement stocks burn brightly" in *Red Herring* **(No. 102, August 15, 2001, pp. 86)**
Pub: Herring Communications
Ed: Stephen Lucey. Description: Profiles of three optical equipment and testing companies that have solid growth prospects, including Acterna, Digital Lightwave, and EXFO, are presented.

28599 ■ "Optimism takes a dip" in *My Business* **(November/December 2001, pp. 49)**
Pub: My Business Magazine
Ed: Bill Dunkelberg. Description: Changes in small business optimism, before and after the September 11, 2001, attack are discussed. Statistical data included.

28600 ■ "Or you could call it schadenfreude.com" in *The New York Times* (December 13, 2000, pp. D8, H8)
Pub: The New York Times Company
Ed: Jane Fritsch. **Description:** Philip Kaplan's dotcom deathwatch Web site mockingly tracks business failures in the world of electronic commerce.

28601 ■ "Orchestrating Assistance; Chambers of Commerce" in *Crain's New York Business* (Vol. 22, November 13, 2006, No. 46, pp. 38)
Pub: Crain Communications, Inc.
Description: Listing of local chapters of New York's chambers of commerce. These organizations serve as sources of information and representation for local business interest provide a number of services and a wide variety of programs for small businesses.

28602 ■ "Our So-Called Economic Recovery" in *Hispanic Business* (May 2005, pp. 6)
Pub: Hispanic Business
Ed: Jesus Chavarria. **Description:** Despite the 4.4 expanded GDP and the addition of 1.7 million jobs, many have yet to feel the economic recovery of 2004.

28603 ■ "Out of stock" in *Entrepreneur* (Vol. 30, No. 3, March 2002, pp. 65)
Pub: Entrepreneur Media Inc.
Ed: Jennifer Pellet. **Description:** In the right circumstances, going private might be the best solution for a company. The special circumstances involved in going private are discussed.

28604 ■ "The outlook for United States corporate earnings" in *Journal of Business Forecasting* (Vol. 19, No. 2, Summer 2000, pp. 41)
Pub: Graceway Publishing Co., Inc.
Ed: Joseph S. Kalinowksi. **Description:** Forecasts are presented for the earnings of U.S. industries for the second half of 2000 and into 2001. Growth is expected to slow down during this period, compared with the dramatic growth of earnings in the first part of 2000.

28605 ■ "Outsourced e-mail" in *PC Computing* (April 2000, pp. 117)
Pub: Ziff-Davis Inc.
Ed: Bonny L. Georgia. **Description:** Ferris Research predicts that within one year, e-mail traffic will increase three to five times, and storage requirements could more than double. The article shows how to outsource e-mail in order to increase business.

28606 ■ "Overcome E-Business Barriers" in *E-business Advisor* (Vol. 18, No. 1, January 2000, pp. 10)
Pub: Advisor Media, Inc.
Ed: Laurie Windham. **Description:** Today's e-business environment challenges managers to respond with effective online business strategies. Customers have already demonstrated their preference to do business over the Web, especially for routine tasks, and businesses that offer online services early are rewarded with customer loyalty and marketshare. Understanding how an e-business strategy influences time-to-market considerations is crucial to success.

28607 ■ "Overview: The List" in *Inc.* (October 17, 2000, pp. 115)
Pub: The Goldhirsh Group
Ed: Edward O. Welles. **Description:** An overview of the Inc. 500 companies for the year.

28608 ■ "Pa. comes in at No. 24 in small business study" in *Philadelphia Business Journal* (Vol. 19, No. 36, October 13, 2000, pp. 6)
Pub: Philadelphia Business Journal
Ed: Natalie Kostelni. **Description:** As a consequence of its high tax rates, Pennsylvania ranked 24th among the 50 states and the District of Columbia in the latest survey of the state's small business climate.

28609 ■ "Pacific Growth, Others Bank on Emerging Firms" in *San Francisco Business Times* (Vol. 17, No. 50, July 18, 2003, pp. 1)
Pub: American City Business Journals
Ed: Mark Calvey. **Description:** Reasons behind Pacific Growth Equities relocation of its headquarters to larger facilities in downtown San Francisco, California.

28610 ■ "Package deal" in *Entrepreneur* (Vol. 31, No. 4, April 2003, pp. 22)
Pub: Entrepreneur Media Inc.
Ed: Stephen Barlas. **Description:** The new economic stimulus package proposed by President George W. Bush would increase the annual allowance for expensing of capital investments from $25,000 to $75,000 for small businesses, and tie the ceiling in the future to inflation.

28611 ■ "Paper Mountain" in *Boston Business Journal* (Vol. 22, No. 15, May 17, 2002)
Pub: MCP, Inc.
Ed: Tom Witkowski. **Description:** Iron Mountain's growth has made it Boston Business Journal's Company of the Year. Acquisitions and diversification have aided the company in its growth.

28612 ■ "Partners in Style" in *Hispanic Business* (May 2005, pp. 64, 66)
Pub: Hispanic Business
Ed: Jaime Adame. **Description:** Luis Delgado, cofounder and CEO of Samy Salon Collections, the top-selling hair care brand on the Home Shopping Network, discusses his plan to fund his company's expansion.

28613 ■ "Patriot Ford in Copiague Driven to Bankruptcy Protection" in *Long Island Business News* (February 6, 2004)
Pub: Dolan Media Newswires
Ed: Claude Solnik. **Description:** Patriot Ford in Copiague, New York has filed for bankruptcy protection, along with McDaniel Ford Inc., and Harbor Lincoln Mercury. The auto dealers blame competition, sales drops, and a troubled automotive industry for the filings. Ford Motor Company, located in Dearborn, Michigan, saw revenue fall to $83.6 billion in 2003 from $87.1 in 2002.

28614 ■ "Paulson Changes Name of Business" in *Bellingham Business Journal* (January 2007, pp. A19)
Pub: Sun News Inc.
Description: Judith Paulson, certified financial planner, changed the name of her business from Financial Counseling Services to Paulson Financial Services. With the change of the name also comes a new focus in which she plans to provide insurance and tax planning, financial education, and retirement planning.

28615 ■ "Pay as You Click" in *Crain's New York Business* (Vol. 22, December 11, 2006, No. 50, pp. 19)
Pub: Crain Communications, Inc.
Description: Google Inc. started an online payment service, Google Checkout. It developed the service at its New York office. Google Checkout, which launched in June 2006, aims to compete with PayPal.

28616 ■ "Peek ahead" in *Entrepreneur* (Vol. 30, No. 1, January 2002, pp. 10)
Pub: Entrepreneur Media Inc.
Ed: Rieva Lesonsky. **Description:** An interview with Elaine S. Peck, who shares her insights as well as those of business consultant colleagues Georgia Hunt and Carroll Aieleen, on the economic outlook for 2002.

28617 ■ "A Penchant for Profits" in *Entrepreneur* (Vol. 33, August 2005, No. 8, pp. 53)
Pub: Entrepreneur Media Inc.
Ed: David Worrell. **Description:** Profile of co-founder and CEO of Avidian Technologies, Bellevue, Washington is presented. James Wong's firm has grown 400 percent annually since 2003, with more than 7,000 registers users of its software.

28618 ■ "Peninsula Alliance for Economic Development Place Information Kiosk in Airport" in *Dolan's Virginia Business Observer* (June 30, 2003)
Pub: Dolan Media Newswires
Description: In an effort to promote the Peninsula to business, the Peninsula Alliance for Economic Development has placed a kiosk with information on the regions workforce, technology assets and quality of life at the Newport News/Williamsburg International Airport.

28619 ■ "Penney" in *Business Week* (January 9, 2006, No. 3966, pp. 82, 84)
Pub: McGraw-Hill Companies
Ed: Robert Berner. **Description:** Profile of Myron "Mike" Ullman III, chief executive for J.C. Penney's, who has launched new brand management techniques to boost the retailer's sales and earnings.

28620 ■ "Pennsylvania Governor Says Business Taxes May Aid City of Pittsburgh Bailout" in *Pittsburgh Post-Gazette* (April 11, 2003)
Pub: Knight-Ridder/Tribune Business News
Ed: Johanna A. Pro. **Description:** According to Pennsylvania Governor Ed Rendell, a new plan to save the City of Pittsburgh from financial disaster could include a new tax on business.

28621 ■ "Perfecting the Growth Spurt" in *Hispanic Business* (Vol. 23, No. 11, November 2001, pp. 24-25, 28)
Pub: Hispanic Business Inc.
Ed: James E. Garcia. **Description:** Profile of Juan Mencia, CEO of The Cube Corporation. The Cube Corporation provides facility management services to the federal government. Mencia was the winner of the Hispanic Business Entrepreneur of the Year 2001 Award. Brief profiles of runners up are included.

28622 ■ "Personal Business" in *Business Week* (January 9, 2006, No. 3966, pp.)
Pub: McGraw-Hill Companies
Description: Stock and mutual fund figures for the week of January 1-8, 2005, as well as interest rates and forecasts for the week ahead.

28623 ■ "Pharmed Wins for Innovation" in *Hispanic Business* (Vol. 23, No. 7/8, July/August 2001, pp. 6)
Pub: Hispanic Business
Description: The Pharmed Group, ranked 24th on the Hispanic Business 500, won the 2001 Cutting Edge Award from the Greater Miami Chamber of Commerce, for exceptional innovative business techniques.

28624 ■ "Phoenix tops list of fertile areas for small companies" in *Wall Street Journal* (December 7, 1999, pp. B2)
Pub: Dow Jones & Co., Inc.
Ed: Jeffrey A. Tannenbaum. **Description:** Statistical data citing Phoenix, Arizona as the number one spot to run a small business.

28625 ■ "Phoenix" in *Sales & Marketing Management* (Vol. 159, January-February 2007, No. 1, pp. 41)
Pub: VNU Business Media
Description: Phoenix, Arizona is the nation's fastest growing city, making it a top choice for conventions and seminars.

28626 ■ "Pines Tract Plans Unveiled" in *Miami Herald* (March 9, 2005)
Pub: Knight-Ridder/Tribune Business News
Ed: Patrick Danner. **Description:** Real estate investment trust, Duke Realty Corporation, announced plans to develop 40 acres in Pembroke Pines. The retail development will include 400,000 square feet of space, and eight office buildings may also be built.

28627 ■ "Pittsburgh Region Sees Largest '00-'02 Population Drop" in *Pittsburgh Business Times* (Vol. 23, No. 1, July 25, 2003, pp. 1)
Pub: Pittsburgh Business Times

Ed: Christopher Davis. **Description:** Industry analysts report that the Pittsburgh, Pennsylvania region experienced a larger decline in population among the country's 729 statistical areas. Pittsburgh lost over 13,000 residents between 2000 and 2002.

28628 ■ **"Pizza Schmizza Ready to Take on Puget Sound" in** *Business Journal-Portland* **(Vol. 20, No. 22, August 1, 2003, pp. 7)**
Pub: American City Business Journals, Inc.
Ed: Robert Goldfield. **Description:** An overview of the growing success and expansion plans of Portland, Oregon-based Pizza Schmizza. Topics include management styles, competition, and long-term goals.

28629 ■ **"Plan May Need Overhaul to Maintain Growth" in** *Crain's Detroit Business* **(Vol. 21, January 17, 2005, No. 3, pp. 18)**
Pub: Crain Communications Inc. - Detroit
Ed: Sheena Harrison. **Description:** Quality Cable has seen growth since achieving ISO 9001: 2000 certification. The company produces medical cables. William Connors discussed the firm's plans for growth.

28630 ■ **"Planning in Pittsburgh, Chicago has produced results" in** *Crain's Detroit Business* **(Vol. 19, No. 17, April 28, 2003, pp. 19)**
Pub: Crain Communications Inc., Detroit
Ed: Terry Kosdrosky. **Description:** Detroit regional planners are looking at programs in Chicago, Illinois and Pittsburgh, Pennsylvania that promote regional planning.

28631 ■ **"Playbook" in** *Business 2.0* **(Vol. 6, May 2005, No. 4, pp. 121-122, 126-127)**
Pub: Time, Inc.
Ed: Damon Darlin. **Description:** Leadership is the difference between enterprises that flourish and those that fail. Ways to turn a company into a thriving business are examined.

28632 ■ **"Plumbing Business Moves to Hannegan" in** *Bellingham Business Journal* **(December 2006, pp. A6)**
Pub: Sun News Inc.
Description: Professional Plumbing LLC is moving to a new location to expand the business. The space will allow Professional Plumbing to be more open to the public.

28633 ■ **"Plunkett's E-Commerce & Internet Business Almanac 2001-2002" in** *Business Information Alert* **(Vol. 14, No. 9, October 2002, pp. 9)**
Pub: Alert Publications
Ed: Marther Jo Sani. **Description:** Profile of "Plunkett's E-Commerce & Internet Business Almanac 2001-2002" is presented. The publication serves as a general source of information that contributes to market research, strategic planning, and career building.

28634 ■ **"Polk Job Growth Boomed in 2004" in** *Ledger* **(February 19, 2005)**
Pub: Knight-Ridder/Tribune Business News
Ed: Kyle Kennedy. **Description:** Polk County, Florida reports job growth nearly double that of the national average. Statistical data included.

28635 ■ **"Pomona, Calif., Aftermarket Auto Firm Goes After Markets in Midwest" in** *Business Press* **(September 3, 2003)**
Pub: Knight Ridder/Tribune Business News
Ed: Joseph Ascenzi. **Description:** Keystone Industries Inc., the world's largest distributor of aftermarket auto parts, has acquired Kansas Bumper and Body Parts and Mo-Kan Auto Body Supply.

28636 ■ **"Port Adopts 2007 Strategic Budget" in** *Bellingham Business Journal* **(December 2006, pp. A3)**
Pub: Sun News Inc.
Description: 2007 Strategic Budget adopted by the Port of Bellingham Board of Commissioners projects a 5 percent growth of operating revenues and no increase in the number of port employees. The entire Strategic Budget will be available on the Web at portofbellingham.com.

28637 ■ **"Portland Seeks Biotech Park to Stimulate New Business" in** *Portland Press Herald* **(December 13, 2005)**
Pub: Blethen Maine Newspapers, Inc.
Ed: Kelley Bouchard. **Description:** Portland, Maine officials are proposing the development of a biotechnology park in order to compete for tenants seeking similar locations in the Boston, Massachusetts area.

28638 ■ **"Positioning properties: Top office owners map plans for 2003" in** *Atlanta Business Chronicle* **(Vol. 25, No. 21, Nov. 1, 2002, pp. 1C)**
Pub: American City Business Publications, Inc.
Ed: Martin Sinderman. **Description:** The 2003 plans of leading Atlanta, Georgia area office owners are discussed. The leaders are Cousins Properties Inc., Equity Office Properties Trust, Hines Interests LP, Trizec Properties Inc., and Highwood's Properties Inc.

28639 ■ **"Post It and They Will Come" in** *Home Office Computing* **(Vol. 18, No. 11, November 2000, pp. 40)**
Pub: Scholastic Inc.
Ed: Eileen Bien Calabro. **Description:** Ways to use message boards to expand your business are highlighted.

28640 ■ **"Power Up!" in** *Entrepreneur* **(Vol. 31, No. 9, September 2003, pp. 20)**
Pub: Entrepreneur Media, Inc.
Description: Steps to take a company to the next level are examined.

28641 ■ **"PR Exec: Agencies Share Blame for Crash" in** *Atlanta Business Chronicle* **(Vol. 24, No. 13, August 31, 2001, pp. 3A)**
Pub: American City Business Journals Inc.
Ed: Jim Lovel. **Description:** Richard Edelman, CEO and president of Edelman Public Relations Worldwide, believes that public relations companies were largely involved in the crash of the dot-coms. Revenue for PR agencies rose 34 percent last year.

28642 ■ **"Practical Ideas for Improving Your Business" in** *Journal of Accountancy* **(Vol. 199, February 2005, No. 2, pp. 108)**
Pub: American Institute of Certified Public Accountants
Ed: Stanley Zarowin. **Description:** Computers are playing a vital role in business growth. Should business managers or information technology staff be in charge of choosing the technical products and services for a company?

28643 ■ **"Preoccupied with what's working— or what's not—many CEOs see only linear paths to growth" in** *Inc.* **(November 2000, pp. 78)**
Pub: The Goldhirsh Group
Description: A profile of a bike shop owner and the lessons he learned while trying to expand his existing business.

28644 ■ **"Printers producing plenty of red ink" in** *Crain's Detroit Business* **(Vol. 19, No. 3, January 20, 2003, pp. 10)**
Pub: Crain Communications Inc., Detroit
Ed: Michael Strong. **Description:** The financial status of Detroit's printing companies is examined. A slowing economy has led to company failures and huge sales declines for commercial printers in the Detroit area.

28645 ■ **"Private firms surviving downturn" in** *Atlanta Business Chronicle* **(Vol. 25, November 8, 2002, No. 22 pp. 3A)**
Pub: American City Business Publications, Inc.
Ed: Jim Lovel. **Description:** Private firms in the Atlanta, Georgia area are succeeding during the existing economic downturn, especially Hooters of America Inc., which generated revenue at $526 million in 2001 and John Wieland Homes and Neighborhoods Inc., generating revenue of nearly $440 million in 2001 with a total of 20,000 house sales as of November 2002.

28646 ■ **"Prized Package: DHL Hub Could Deliver 500 Jobs" in** *South Florida Business Journal* **(Vol. 23, No. 52, August 1, 2003, pp. 1)**
Pub: American City Business Journals
Ed: Darcie Lunsford. **Description:** DHL plans to build its new headquarters in south Florida.

28647 ■ **"Production Co. Enters Familiar Chapter: 11" in** *Washington Business Journal* **(Vol. 22, No. 17, August 29, 2003, pp. 1)**
Pub: Washington Business Journal
Ed: Greg A. Lohr. **Description:** Reasons behind Roland House's filing for Chapter 11 bankruptcy protection is examined. Topics include economic conditions, debt management, and long term planning.

28648 ■ **"Profit is no accident" in** *Crain's Detroit Business* **(Vol. 18, No.)**
Pub: Crain Communications Inc. - Detroit
Ed: David Barkholz. **Description:** Profile of James Epolito, CEO of the Lansing, Michigan-based Accident Fund Co.

28649 ■ **"Profit Comes Harder: WD-40 Co." in** *San Diego Business Journal* **(Vol. 28, January 15, 2007, No. 3, pp. 38)**
Pub: San Diego Business Journal Associates
Ed: Andy Killion. **Description:** Lubricant and cleaning product manufacturer, WD-40 Company, posted first-quarter earnings up 7.1 percent.

28650 ■ **"Profit Globally, Give Globally" in** *Harvard Business Review* **(Vol. 81, No. 12, December 2003, pp. 16)**
Pub: Harvard Business School Press
Ed: John Quelch, V. Kasturi Rangan. **Description:** An overview of ways corporations can and should increase non-domestic philanthropic aid is presented. Topics include sensitivity and diplomacy involved in international economic relations, and issues such as tax breaks and local law.

28651 ■ *Profit Zone: How Strategic Business Design Will Lead You to Tomorrow's Profits*
Pub: John Wiley & Sons, Inc.
Ed: Adrian J. Slywotsky. **Released:** 1998. **Price:** $29.95 (cloth).

28652 ■ **"A profitable year for Aaron Rents" in** *Atlanta Business Chronicle* **(Vol. 25, November 29, 2002, No. 25, pp. 3A)**
Pub: American City Business Publications, Inc.
Ed: Lisa R. Schoolcraft. **Description:** Aaron Rents Inc. posted $10.3 million in net earnings for the first nine months of 2002, an 87 percent increase from the same period in 2001. However, the company anticipates less growth in the next few years due to the high number of new store openings in 2001. New stores generally take a few years to show substantial gains.

28653 ■ **"Profiting in a Sideways Market" in** *Hispanic Business* **(March 2005, pp. 20, 22, 24)**
Pub: Hispanic Business
Ed: Joel Russell. **Description:** Financial experts are not predicting a raging bull market any time soon, but investors can still make gains if they invest wisely. Top twelve Latin funds are presented showing their 2004 rates of return.

28654 ■ **"Program Off To A Great Start Providing Capital for Gazelles" in** *Mississippi Business Journal* **(Vol. 29, January 2007, No. 2, pp. 21)**
Pub: Venture Publications, Inc.
Ed: Becky Gillette **Description:** High-performance emerging technology companies known as gazelles are getting seed and growth capitol from the newly established Mississippi Angel Network.

28655 ■ **"Promoting their own" in** *Crain's Detroit Business* **(Vol. 16, No. 49, December 4, 2000, pp. 25)**
Pub: Crain Communications, Inc.
Ed: David Barkholz. **Description:** Championing doctors has become a popular tool in a hot year for local hospital advertising.

28656 ■ **"Prospects improve for toolmakers, but cash crunch may hurt"** in *Crain's Detroit Business* (Vol. 19, No. 9, March 3, 2003, pp. 26)
Pub: Crain Communications Inc., Detroit
Ed: Terry Kosdrosky. **Description:** Tool and equipment makers in the Detroit area are seeing an increase in orders, but past lack of work has left many with cash flow problems.

28657 ■ **"Publix chief leads quietly"** in *Atlanta Business Chronicle* (Vol. 24, No. 13, August 31, 2001, pp. 3A)
Pub: American City Business Journals Inc.
Ed: Jarred Schenke. **Description:** Bob Moore is the president of Publix Super Markets Inc., an Atlanta company that has opened 97 stores after entering the market a decade ago. Moore, who started at Publix as a stock boy, has moved up the ranks, and has seen Publix grab 27.4 percent of the metro grocery market share. Publix has future plans of launching an online site and acquiring a grocery chain to promote further growth.

28658 ■ **"Pueblo Economic Development Corp. names operations director"** in *Pueblo Business Journal* (February 28, 2003)
Pub: Dolan Media Newswires
Ed: William Dagendesh. **Description:** Joan Acosta has been named operations director for the Pueblo Economic Development Corporation. Established in 1981, the corporation promotes Pueblo to other communities.

28659 ■ **"Pulling together"** in *Crain's Detroit Business* (Vol. 19, No. 17, April 28, 2003, pp. 14)
Pub: Crain Communications Inc., Detroit
Ed: Terry Kosdrosky. **Description:** Business leaders in the Detroit, Michigan area are promoting regional approaches to transportation, land use, Detroit development and arts funding.

28660 ■ **"Push Your Plans Through"** in *PC Computing* (April 2000, pp. 100)
Pub: Ziff-Davis Inc.
Ed: Jason Compton. **Description:** When a business wants to build a new corporate campus, but needs the approval of local zoning commissions, it is vital to put together a winning presentation showing the benefits of the project.

28661 ■ **"Putting Focus on 4 Famed Firms"** in *Crain's New York Business* (Vol. 22, November 27, 2006, No. 48, pp. 17)
Pub: Crain Communications, Inc.
Ed: Aaron Elstein. **Description:** Crain's spotlight on key statistics of four well-known businesses in the New York area includes information on Eileen Fisher Inc., Key Food Stores Co-Operative Inc., Ziff Davis Holdings Inc., and Publishers Clearing House.

28662 ■ **"Q&A: Jack Bamberger"** in *Folio: the Magazine for Magazine Management* (Vol. 30, No. 1, January 2001, pp. 18)
Pub: Intertec Publishing Corp.
Ed: Caroline Jenkins. **Description:** An interview with Jack Bamberger addressing Folio's IdustryClick Web site, the company's ongoing integration with Intertec, and his view of the future of vertical online communities.

28663 ■ **"Q401 Will it Matter?"** in *Red Herring* (No. 105, October 1, 2001, pp. 58-59)
Pub: Herring Communications
Ed: Eric Moskowitz. **Description:** An overview of the history of fourth quarter statistics, including tech earnings estimates, change in information technology spending growth, venture capital by sector, value of global M&A activity, and global IPOs.

28664 ■ **"Quarterly report-February 2002"** in *Small Business Economic Trends* (February 2002, pp. 1)
Pub: National Federation of Independent Business Foundation
Description: The National Federation of Independent Business's survey of small business owners/members conducted January 2002, showed the Small Business Optimism Index rose from 100.4 in December to 103.5 in January, the highest reading since first quarter 2000. The results of the survey cover expansion, earnings, sales, prices, compensation, credit conditions, interest rates, capital outlays, and important issues are discussed, graphed and tabulated.

28665 ■ **"The Quest for Resilience"** in *Harvard Business Review* (Vol. 81, No. 9, September 2003, pp. 52)
Pub: Harvard Business School Press
Ed: Gary Hamel, Lisa Valikangas. **Description:** Once-successful billion dollar companies are now finding it increasingly difficult to return the same level of profits as in the past. Companies that continue to perform well are able to quickly adapt to changes often by introducing new and/or unconventional ideas.

28666 ■ **"A Quickened Pace; Lender Powers through Rapid Growth"** in *Crain's Detroit Business* (Vol. 19, No. 42, October 20, 2003, pp. 1)
Pub: Crain Communications Inc., Detroit
Ed: Katie Merx. **Description:** Profile of Quicken Loans Inc., which operates Rock Financial in Michigan. The firm has more than tripled its business in the past two years, growing from $4.6 billion to $15 billion in loans.

28667 ■ **"A Quickened Pace; Lender Powers through Rapid Growth, Prepares for Interest Rates to Rise"** in *Crain's Detroit Business* (Vol. 19)
Pub: Crain Communications Inc., Detroit
Ed: Katie Merx. **Description:** Profile of Quicken Loans Inc., which operates Rock Financial in Michigan. The firm has more than tripled its business in the past two years, growing from $4.6 billion to $15 billion in loans.

28668 ■ **"QuickSeek"** in *Entrepreneur* (Vol. 33, September 2005, No. 9, pp. 6)
Pub: Entrepreneur Media Inc.
Ed: Steve Cooper. **Description:** Online directory, QuickSeek, lists more than 16 million businesses in a database. Information includes operating hours, business descriptions, email addresses, directions and links to corporate sites. Preferred listings, which include full-page design with graphics, photos and images, run $99 per year.

28669 ■ **"Racial divisions still hang over efforts to foster cooperation"** in *Crain's Detroit Business* (Vol. 19, No. 17, April 28, 2003)
Pub: Crain Communications Inc., Detroit
Ed: Terry Kosdrosky. **Description:** Issues of segregation and racism in the Detroit metropolitan and surrounding areas are discussed. Business leaders are hoping to attract new residents to Detroit and to change the tone of political discourse.

28670 ■ **"Racing for growth: an interview with Perkin Elmer's Greg Summe"** in *Harvard Business Review* (Vol. 78, No. 6, Nov. - Dec. 2000, pp. 14)
Pub: Harvard Business School Publishing Corp.
Description: An interview with Greg Summe, chairman and CEO of Perkin Elmer.

28671 ■ **"The Rat Pack"** in *Forbes* (Vol. 170, No. 9, October 28, 2002, pp. 228)
Pub: Forbes Magazine
Ed: Nathan Vardi. **Description:** Profile of James Foster who breeds and maintains rodents for pharmaceutical and biotechnology companies researching genes and drugs, at the cost of $10 per animal per month.

28672 ■ **"Real Estate Company Expands, Changes Name"** in *Bellingham Business Journal* (January 2007, pp. 3)
Pub: Sun News Inc.
Description: Phil Dyer & Associates, Inc. Realtors has changed its name to Sterling Real Estate Group. The company has expanded and recently opened a second office to compliment its existing office.

28673 ■ **"Real Estate Insiders to Reveal Forecasts for the Coming Year"** in *Crain's Detroit Business* (Vol. 19, No. 1, January 6, 2003, pp. 6)
Pub: Crain Communications Inc., Detroit
Ed: Jennette Smith. **Description:** The Commercial Real Estate Trends and Forecasts Seminar will be held January 17, 2003. The seminar will highlight keynote speaker, Bradley Olsen, president of Atlantic Partners Ltd.; Bradley will discuss the impact international capital markets will have on the Motor City in 2003.

28674 ■ **"Rearrangement: Sellers of office furniture go through changes"** in *Crain's Detroit Business* (Vol. 18, No. 19, May 13, 2002, pp. 13)
Pub: Crain Communications Inc. - Detroit
Ed: Brent Snavely. **Description:** The impact from the sales of local office furniture firms, Workplace Integrators LLC, and University Business Interiors Inc., is discussed.

28675 ■ **"(Re)Born To Be Wild"** in *Inc.* (Volume 28, January 2006, No. 1, pp. 70-77)
Pub: Inc. Magazine
Ed: Donna Fenn. **Description:** Profile of Mike Schwartz who took over a failing Harley Davidson dealership in New Castle, Delaware. The store was selling only 153 motorcycles a year and now boasts 1,700 sales annually. Schwartz tells how he cleaned the place up and moved it to a new building.

28676 ■ **"Rebound Continues"** in *My Business* (October/November 2003, pp. 50)
Pub: My Business Magazine
Ed: Bill Dunkelberg. **Description:** The National Federation of Independent Business' (NFIBs) Small Business Optimism Index hit a record high for the monthly surveys that began in 1986. Nine of ten components advanced, with the only decline shown in expected credit market conditions, meaning owners believe financing customer purchases will be more difficult in the coming months. Statistical data included.

28677 ■ **"Rebuilding Your Business With Former and Current Customers"** in *Ingram's* (Vol. 27, No. 8, August 2001, pp. 19)
Pub: Show Me Publishing, Inc.
Ed: Tom Sight. **Description:** Advice for motivating employees and improving customer service within a small business is given.

28678 ■ **"Recession session"** in *Entrepreneur* (Vol. 30, No. 3, March 2002, pp.)
Pub: Entrepreneur Media Inc.
Ed: Mark Henricks. **Description:** An interview with various experts and entrepreneurs to learn how and when they recommend aggressive or defensive positions in the areas of money management, people management, marketing, and technology.

28679 ■ **"Recession takes its toll"** in *Black Enterprise* (Vol. 33, No. 6, Jan. 2003, pp. 26)
Pub: Earl Graves Publishing Co.
Ed: Cliff Hocker. **Description:** According to the U.S. Census Bureau, poverty among Americans rose from 11.3 percent to 11.7 percent. Statistical data included.

28680 ■ **"Recipe for Growth"** in *Fast Company* (November 2001, pp. 40)
Pub: Fast Company
Ed: Fara Warner. **Description:** How does Whirlpool cook up great ideas to get back on the fast track? By turning people loose on the challenge of innovation, and then turning up the heat on their best ideas.

28681 ■ **"Record Profits Lead to Record Bonus for Goldman Sachs CEO"** in *San Diego Business Journal* (Vol. 28, January 15, 2007, No. 3, pp. 10)
Pub: San Diego Business Journal Associates
Ed: Mike Allen. **Description:** Profile of Lloyd Blankfein, chief executive at Goldman Sachs; Blankfein pushed the company to 58 percent increase in profits since taking over.

28682 ■ "Recovery Continues" in *My Business* **(June/July 2002, pp. 49)**
Pub: My Business Magazine
Ed: Bill Dunkelberg. Description: First quarter 2001 economic growth surged with Gross Domestic Product growing at the rate of 5.8 percent. Small business optimism, hiring plans and sales statistics are presented.

28683 ■ "Recovery for Some; Chicago's Economy Will Lag the State and Nation Next Year" in *Crains Chicago Business* **(Vol. 26, No. 51)**
Pub: Crain Communications, Inc.
Ed: Sandra Jones. Description: Chicago's economy is expected to see a 2.96 percent rise in 2004, with the warehousing and distribution, financial services, and hospitality sectors feeling strongest growth with an increase in business travel to the area. However, Chicago's economy is expected to grow at a slower pace than the state or the nation.

28684 ■ "Recovery driving shaky growth in transportation" in *Atlanta Business Chronicle* **(Vol. 25, January 10, 2003, No. 31, pp. 20A)**
Pub: American City Business Publications, Inc.
Ed: Charles Davidson. Description: The Georgia Economic Outlook 2003 indicates that, since the transportation sector is integral to the overall economy, the transportation sector will remain sluggish as the overall economy struggles to move out of its slump. Of the trucking, airline, and railroad sectors, airlines seem to have the toughest road ahead for recovery.

28685 ■ "Recovery Will Probably Take a While Yet" in *Crain's Detroit Business* **(Vol. 19, No. 42, October 20, 2003, pp. 8)**
Pub: Crain Communications Inc., Detroit
Ed: Keith Crain. Description: The economic process involved in a jobless recovery is explored.

28686 ■ "Recreational/Personal Watercraft Market" in *Rough Notes* **(Vol. 145, No. 2, February 2003, pp. 48)**
Pub: Rough Notes
Ed: Larry G. France. Description: The watercraft insurance market has been declining as it is an industry that depends largely on the economy. Boat insurance is provided by agencies listed, including American Modern Insurance Group, American Reliable Insurance Company, and BAT Insurance Corporation.

28687 ■ "The Red Herring Portfolio: Another market false start" in *Red Herring* **(No. 105, October 1, 2001, pp. 102)**
Pub: Herring Communications
Description: Presentation of the Red Herring Portfolio, including stock profiles of AOL Time Warner, Applied Materials, Atmel, Cisco Systems, Comcast, Electronic Data Systems, EMC, Immunex, Nokia, Oracle, and Peregrine Systems, and Stellent.

28688 ■ "The Red Herring Portfolio: Going nowhere fast" in *Red Herring* **(No. 103, September 1, 2001, pp. 96)**
Pub: Herring Communications
Description: Presentation of the Red Herring Portfolio, including stock profiles of AOL Time Warner, Atmel, Cisco Systems, Comcast, Electronic Data Systems, EMC, Immunex, Integrated Circuit Systems, IntraNet Solutions, Nokia, Oracle, and Peregrine Systems.

28689 ■ "The Red Herring Portfolio: Not a stellar performance" in *Red Herring* **(No. 105, October 1, 2001, pp. 104)**
Pub: Herring Communications
Description: Presentation of the Red Herring Portfolio, including stock profiles of AOL Time Warner, Applied Materials, Atmel, Cisco Systems, Comcast, Electronic Data Systems, EMC, Immunex, Nokia, Oracle, and Peregrine Systems, and Stellent.

28690 ■ "The Red Herring Portfolio" in *Red Herring* **(No. 99, June 15 & July 1, 2001, pp. 146)**
Pub: Herring Communications
Description: Presentation of the Red Herring portfolio, presenting the companies, number of shares, price in May 2001, and more.

28691 ■ "The Red Herring Portfolio: Stuck inside a sideways pattern with the market" in *Red Herring* **(No. 102, August 15, 2001, pp. 96)**
Pub: Herring Communications
Description: Presentation of the Red Herring Portfolio, including stock profiles of AOL Time Warner, Atmel, Cisco Systems, Comcast, Electronic Data Systems, EMC, Immunex, Integrated Circuit Systems, IntraNet Solutions, Nokia, Oracle, and Peregrine Systems.

28692 ■ "Reed Jumps Onto the Medical Bandwagon " in *Tradeshow Week* **(Vol. 3)**
Pub: Reed Business Information
Ed: Rachelle Crum. Description: Reed Exhibitions has launched a new show division along with its sister company, publisher Elsevier Health Sciences. The new division will focus on continuing medical education. Reed Medical Education is committed to improving health care delivery.

28693 ■ "Regional Insurers Thrive" in *Rough Notes* **(Vol. 145, No. 2, February 2003, pp. 78)**
Pub: Rough Notes
Ed: Phil Zinkewicz. Description: Despite predictions of observers, experts and analysts, small and regional insurers increased direct written premiums nearly twice the growth achieved by large insurers between 1996-2000.

28694 ■ "Regulation Nation" in *Entrepreneur* **(Vol. 32, October 2004, No. 10, pp. 32)**
Pub: Entrepreneur Media Inc.
Ed: Joshua Kurlantzick. Description: Federal regulations are limiting the growth of small business in America. The Small Business Administration's Office of Advocacy estimates small firms with less than 20 employees pay nearly $7,000 per employee in regulatory costs.

28695 ■ "Reimagining Union Station" in *Ingram's* **(Vol. 29, No. 1, January 2003, pp. 13)**
Pub: Show Me Publishing, Inc.
Ed: Jack Cashill. Description: A presentation of the history of Union Station, Kansas City, Missouri is given, along with the names of those linked to that history. The author suggests the dramatization of the stories would make the building embraceable by the public.

28696 ■ "Residential, commercial builders see more decline" in *Atlanta Business Chronicle* **(Vol. 25, January 10, 2003, No. 31, pp. 22A)**
Pub: American City Business Publications, Inc.
Ed: Randy Southerland. Description: The Georgia Economic Outlook 2003 survey indicates that commercial real estate construction companies will face tough times in the coming months. Residential construction companies will also likely face a slowdown.

28697 ■ "Resources: Web Sites, Organizations, Events and More to Grow Your Business" in *Entrepreneur* **(Vol. 32, October 2004, No. 10, pp. 8)**
Pub: Entrepreneur Media Inc.
Ed: Steve Cooper. Description: Resources to help small business is featured. Loopnet.com, an online commercial real estate services offers more than 250,000 commercial lease and sales listings; Cybersource.com manages online payments; American FactFinder offers U.S. Census Bureau data sets; ContentFinder.com helps small businesses find syndicated content sources for Websites, newsletters and other Intranets.

28698 ■ "Resources: Web Sites, Organizations, Events and More To Grow Your Business" in *Entrepreneur* **(Vol. 32, September 2004, No. 9, pp. 8)**
Pub: Entrepreneur Media Inc.
Ed: Steve Cooper. Description: Resources to help small business are featured including the Small Business Administration's effort to help teen entrepreneurs launch a business; KnockNow an online community of entrepreneurs, executives, venture capitalists, angel investors, service sector companies, and government; the SBA's business Website offering information on small business development, financial assistance, taxes, laws and regulations, international trade, workplace issues, buying and selling and federal forms.

28699 ■ "Restart: Network Engines Finds Profits After the Tech Bubble Burst" in *Boston Business Journal* **(Vol. 23, No. 27, August 8, 2003)**
Pub: American City Business Journals
Ed: Tom Witkowski. Description: The operations and growth of Canton, Massachusetts-based Network Engines are discussed.

28700 ■ "Restaurant Depot Expanding in Bohemia" in *Long Island Business News* **(March 5, 2004)**
Pub: Dolan Media Newswires
Ed: Nick Anastasi. Description: The Restaurant Depot in Bohemia, New York is expanding its facilities by more than 8,000 square feet. The restaurant was deliberately built small in order to gauge market demand.

28701 ■ "Restaurants are Hiring Workers Faster than Other Economic Sectors" in *The Record* **(November 19, 2005)**
Pub: New Jersey Media Group
Ed: Kathleen Lynn. Description: New Jersey-based restaurants are hiring new workers three times the rate of the overall job market. The state reported 215,000 restaurants in October 2005, up nearly 3 percent of same time last year. Statistical data included.

28702 ■ "Restaurants, retail attracted by neighborhood" in *Atlanta Business Chronicle* **(Vol. 25, No. 20, October 25, 2002, pp. 3)**
Pub: American City Business Publications, Inc.
Ed: Phillip Nutman. Description: Smaller boutique-like restaurants are thriving in the Midtown district of Atlanta, Georgia.

28703 ■ "Retail Exec Stays in Style" in *Crain's New York Business* **(Vol. 23, January 29, 2007, No. 5, pp. F3)**
Pub: Crain Communications, Inc.
Ed: Elisabeth Butler. Description: Profile of Adrienne Lazarus and her position as President of Ann Taylor Stores Corp. The executive was brought in to revitalize the fashion chain.

28704 ■ "Retailers Beginning to Get Holiday Spirit" in *Crain's Detroit Business* **(Vol. 19, No. 42, October 20, 2003, pp. 1)**
Pub: Crain Communications Inc., Detroit
Ed: Brent Snavely. Description: Metropolitan Detroit retailers expect sales increases for the holidays in 2003, and have ordered more inventory than 2002.

28705 ■ "Retailers Beginning to Get Holiday Spirit; Many Boost Inventory in Hopes of Strong Sales" in *Crain's Detroit Business* **(Vol. 19)**
Pub: Crain Communications Inc., Detroit
Ed: Brent Snavely. Description: Metropolitan Detroit retailers expect sales increases for the holidays in 2003, and have ordered more inventory than 2002.

28706 ■ "Retailers Have Disappointing March" in *Baltimore Sun* **(April 11, 2003)**
Pub: Knight-Ridder/Tribune Business News
Ed: Lorraine Mirabella. Description: March 2003 saw disappointing retail sales for both outlet as well as upscale chains. The war and a weakened economy continue to put a crimp on consumer spending.

28707 ■ "Retailers' Outlook 'Rosy'" in *Milwaukee Journal Sentinel* **(December 14, 2005)**
Pub: Journal Sentinel, Inc.
Ed: Doris Hajewski. Description: Retail experts are predicting a profitable holiday season. The International Council of Shopping Centers' retail chain index reported this week a 0.9 percent rise over the previous week.

28708 ■ "The Return of the Black Entrepreneur" in *Business Week Online* **(Oct. 8, 2002)**
Pub: McGraw-Hill Inc.
Ed: Kimberly Weisul. Description: A recent study conducted by the Ewing Marion Kauffman Foundation shows that the number of African American entrepreneurs in the U.S. is on the rise. A second phase of the study will be published sometime in 2003.

28709 ■ "The Return of the Global Brand" in *Harvard Business Review* **(Vol. 81, No. 8, August 2003, pp. 22)**
Pub: Harvard Business School Press
Ed: John Quelch. Description: Since Theordore Levitt published The Globalization of Markets in the Harvard Business Review twenty years ago, the world's economic development has adapted accordingly. International companies are finding that standardized products marketed globally have been widely accepted. This is contrary to previous efforts to develop products for regional markets. Today, China is poised to duplicate Japan's global branding successes, cutting into U.S. business sales.

28710 ■ "Return To Me" in *Entrepreneur* **(Vol. 33, September 2005, No. 9, pp. 28)**
Pub: Entrepreneur Media Inc.
Ed: Mark Henricks. Description: Authors Don Peppers and Martha Rogers help small business owners capitalize on return customers for sales. They recommend a focus on assessing and tracking customer equity, lifetime customer value and specific measure to maximize those values.

28711 ■ "Revving in the Motor City: Michelle Sherman Chauffeurs Us through Detroit" in *Black Enterprise* **(Vol. 34, No. 4, Nov. 2003, pp. 176)**
Pub: Earl Graves Publishing Co.
Ed: Sonia Alleyne. Description: Empowerment Zone funding has attributed to new construction for both business and entertainment in Detroit, Michigan; new jobs have grown at the rate of 1.77 percent since 1998 and are forecasted to grow to an annual rate of 9.1 percent through 2010.

28712 ■ "The Rich Get Richer" in *Hispanic Business* **(June 2005, pp. 26, 28, 30)**
Pub: Hispanic Business
Description: Although the 500 largest Hispanic-owned U.S. businesses reported strong growth in 2004, only a few of the companies accounted for most of the new revenues. Statistical data included.

28713 ■ "Riding Out the Crash" in *Hispanic Business* **(Vol. 23, No. 5, May 2001, pp. 42, 44-45)**
Pub: Hispanic Business
Ed: Derek Reveron. Description: Hispanic-themed Web sites that focus on niche markets stand the best chance of long-term survival. An interview with Fernando Espuelas, CEO of StarMedia is presented.

28714 ■ "Riding the Telecom-Computer Convergence" in *Hispanic Business* **(Vol. 23, No. 7/8, July/August 2001, pp. 60)**
Pub: Hispanic Business
Ed: Joel Russell. Description: An overview of the fast-growth, high-tech Hispanic firms specializing in networking and system integration. Statistical data included.

28715 ■ "Right Place, Right Time; Small Businesses Aren't Just Surviving." in *Business Week* **(No. 3853, Oct. 13, 2003, pp. 82)**
Pub: McGraw-Hill Inc.

Ed: Peter Coy. Description: Small business is becoming a strong force in the economy, especially since the Bush tax-cut program helps small companies.

28716 ■ "Road-money halt slows $172.5M Oakland plan" in *Crain's Detroit Business* **(Vol. 19, No. 17, April 28, 2003, pp. 1)**
Pub: Crain Communications Inc., Detroit
Ed: Andrew Dietderich. Description: A proposed road project in Oakland County could yield nearly $16 million in annual tax revenue to the state, county and city. Plans call for at least 15 buildings totaling 1.6 million square feet on 107 acres and will be developed by Grand/Sakwa Properties LLC of Farmington Hills, Michigan.

28717 ■ "Rofin-Sinar sales rise 61 percent" in *Crain's Detroit Business* **(Vol. 16, No. 46, November 13, 2000, pp. 4)**
Pub: Crain Communications, Inc.
Ed: Leslie Green. Description: An overview of Rofin-Sinar Technologies, the Plymouth, Michigan-based maker of laser processing systems that sells to the machine-tool, automotive and semiconductor industries.

28718 ■ "Roll On: Davin Enjoys Just Spinning Your Wheels" in *Black Enterprise* **(Vol. 34, No. 4, November 2003, pp. 180)**
Pub: Earl Graves Publishing Co.
Ed: Linda S. Lawson. Description: Profile of Ian Hardman, CEO of Davin Wheels in Rhode Island. The company's patented chrome rims adorn the cars of executives and celebrities alike, ranging in price from $12,000-$14,000, with custom rims costing more.

28719 ■ "Room Glut Has Hotels Unsettled" in *Atlanta Business Chronicle* **(Vol. 25, December 6, 2002, No. 26, pp. 1)**
Pub: American City Business Publications, Inc.
Ed: Walter Woods. Description: There are over 86,000 hotel rooms in the metro Atlanta, Georgia area, making the impact of the recent recession in the travel sector even harder on hoteliers there. During the travel recession, the number of visitors to trade shows, and the like have, fallen significantly.

28720 ■ "Room to Grow: yes, even in the most stagnant economy, it's possible to expand" in *Entrepreneur* **(Vol. 31, No. 6, June 2003, pp. 28)**
Pub: Entrepreneur Media Inc.
Ed: Mark Henricks. Description: Management consultants Adrian Slywotzky and Richard Wise offer a strategy that demands innovation in a slow or no-growth market or economy.

28721 ■ "Room for Growth in the Big Apple" in *Black Enterprise* **(Vol. 31, No. 5, December 2000, pp. 64)**
Pub: Earl Graves Publishing Co.
Ed: Robyn D. Clarke. Description: The qualities that set Esystems Inc apart from the competition are discussed with owner Glenwood Elam Jr.

28722 ■ "Roomier Recreational Trailers Becoming More Popular" in *Providence Business News* **(Vol. 18, No. 17, August 11, 2003, pp. 2)**
Pub: Providence Business News, Inc.
Ed: Laura Ricketson. Description: Sales of luxury versions of recreational trailers, comparable to a traditional mobile home, are on the rise. Currently, there are about 8,000 such vehicles produced annually.

28723 ■ "RosettaNet: The Key to Supply Chain Efficiency?" in *E-business Advisor* **(Vol. 17, No. 12, December 1999, pp. 16)**
Pub: Advisor Media, Inc.
Ed: Rik Drummond. Description: The RosettaNet consortium, established in 1998 by Fadi Chehade, aims to create a single software standard throughout the IT supply chain, thus standardizing e-business operations. RosettaNet is presently defining open interfaces among supply chain manufacturers, distributors, resellers, and customers. RosettaNet's goal is to help computer makers and distributors defend their business against Dell and other Web-based made-to-order computer sellers.

28724 ■ "Rough-Cut Dimon" in *Forbes* **(May 13, 2002, p. 64)**
Pub: Forbes Magazine
Ed: Mark Tatge. Description: Profile of James Dimon. Dimon rescued Bank One back from the brink after leaving Citigroup four years ago.

28725 ■ "Rumbo Continues Rollout" in *Hispanic Business* **(October 2004, pp. 24)**
Pub: Hispanic Business
Description: Meximerica Media has launched it second Spanish-language daily newspaper called, Rumbo de Houston. Rumbo is aimed at Hispanic readers between the ages of 21 and 54.

28726 ■ "Running Hot-and Cold-on the Web" in *Business Week Online* **(Nov. 15, 2002)**
Pub: McGraw-Hill Inc.
Ed: Karen E. Klein. Description: With the inception of annual search engine fees and a drop in Internet sales, a small retail business selling heating pads and ice packs online and wholesale to gift shops, is questioning the value of selling online.

28727 ■ "Running Into Profits" in *My Business* **(June/July 2004, pp. 16)**
Pub: My Business Magazine
Description: Jogging sessions fit into tight schedules may actually improve a company's profits.

28728 ■ "Ruth's Chris Steak House Opens in Sacramento" in *Sacramento Bee* **(December 20, 2005)**
Pub: The Sacramento Bee
Ed: Jon Ortiz. Description: Ruth's Chris Steakhouse Inc. opened a new restaurant in Sacramento, California in December 2005. The firm received criticism when it moved it headquarters from New Orleans to Orlando, Florida.

28729 ■ "Saco's Downtown Merchants Say Big-Box Retailers Are Hurting Businesses" in *Portland Press Herald* **(April 19, 2005)**
Pub: Blethen Maine Newspapers, Inc.
Ed: Seth Harkness. Description: Slow growth in downtown districts can be attributed to big-box stores and supermarkets. A recent study showed that Saco, Maine businesses reported 5.9 percent annual increase in sales since 1996, however some merchants refuse to work together effectively to compete with large retailers.

28730 ■ "Sacramento, Calif.-Area Rice Growers May Reap Benefits of Highest Value Harvest" in *Sacramento Bee* **(October 27, 2005)**
Pub: The Sacramento Bee
Ed: Jim Wasserman. Description: Sacramento Valley, California rice growers are predicting their highest value harvest despite a smaller crop than 2004's. These smaller crops are valued at $435 million due to a strong market price.

28731 ■ "Sacramento, Calif.-Area Small Businesses Remain Optimistic for Year Ahead" in *Sacramento Bee* **(October 21, 2005)**
Pub: The Sacramento Bee
Ed: Thuy-Doan Le. Description: Despite the recent hurricanes and rising gas prices, local small businesses remain optimistic for 2006. According to a recent survey conducted by American Express, 59 percent of West Coast small business owners said they will hire new employees within the next six months.

28732 ■ "Sacramento, Calif., Housing Market Offers Mixed Signals" in *Sacramento Bee* **(December 20, 2005)**
Pub: The Sacramento Bee
Ed: Andrew Lepage. Description: Home sales fell by 21 percent in November 2005 for the Sacramento, California region, making for a buyers market. The region saw its first decline in number of homes for sale since February 2005.

28733 ■ "Sacrificing a profitable account in favor of growth" in *Atlanta Business Chronicle* (Vol. 24, No. 13, August 31, 2001, pp. 40A)
Pub: American City Business Journals Inc.
Ed: Christina Breda. Description: Protocall Communications Inc.'s co-founders and owners, Ellen and Scott Kleinknecht, discuss the way they manage their company. Statistical data included.

28734 ■ "St. Charles Builders React to Steel Crisis" in *St. Charles Business Record* (May 3, 2004)
Pub: Dolan Media Company
Ed: Rachel Brown. Description: Construction contractors, subcontractors, and suppliers of steel-based products in St. Charles County, Missouri, were caught off-guard by the more than 90 percent rise in steel prices.

28735 ■ "A Sales Channel They Can't Resist" in *Business 2.0* (Vol. 6, September 2005, No. 8, pp. 90)
Pub: Time, Inc.
Ed: Elizabeth Esfahani. Description: The secret to cable television's QVC network is discussed. QVC has the ability to capitalize on the art and science of television retailing through real-time lighting, camera angles, and dialogue to maximize sales and profits.

28736 ■ "Sales & Marketing Employment Market Remains Strong" in *Hispanic Business* (Vol. 23, No. 5, May 2001, pp. 80)
Pub: Hispanic Business
Description: According to a recent survey by a national recruitment firm, sales and marketing positions remain strong, particularly in the telecommunications industry, pharmaceuticals, transportation, and information technology.

28737 ■ "Sales Picture Brightens for Sparks Exhibits and Environments" in *Tradeshow Week* (Vol. 34, December 6, 2004, No. 49, pp. 2)
Pub: Reed Business Information
Description: Sparks Exhibits and Environments attributes its growth in revenue to sales from new and existing customers; Marlton reported a $6 million rise in revenue; Exhibitgroup/Giltspur reported a 5.8 percent third quarter revenue gain.

28738 ■ "Sales, Profits Surge for Jabil" in *Tampa Tribune* (December 21, 2005)
Pub: Media General, Inc.
Ed: Richard Mullins. Description: Jabil Circuit Inc. of St. Petersburg, Florida reported a 31 percent increase in sales in the first quarter ending November 30 for fiscal year 2006. Jabil employs nearly 50,000 people in 19 countries, 2,000 of which are in the Tampa Bay area.

28739 ■ "Sales Secrets" in *Atlanta Business Chronicle* (Vol. 25, Nov. 8, 2002, No. 22 pp. 2B)
Pub: American City Business Publications, Inc.
Ed: Jeffrey Gitomer. Description: A list of elements that businesses may need in order to maintain a stellar sales team is given. Businesses are urged to focus on the sales cycle, not the salesperson.

28740 ■ "San Diego: Stone Makes Rock-Solid Impression" in *San Diego Business Journal* (Vol. 28, January 15, 2007, No. 3, pp. 16)
Pub: San Diego Business Journal Associates
Ed: Amy Yarnall. Description: Profile of San Diego-based StoneImpressions and its Make-Mine-a-Million, a program that helps women entrepreneurs develop million dollar businesses.

28741 ■ "Sandy, Ore., Candy Farm Produces All Things Chocolate" in *Knight-Ridder/ Tribune Business News* (Melissa L. Jones, pp. ITEM02087067)
Pub: Knight-Ridder Inc.
Ed: Melissa L. Jones. Description: Profile of the Oregon Candy Farm, located in Sandy, Oregon. For thirty years customers have come to watch chocolate being made at the store.

28742 ■ "SAP AG Starting Unit to Target Small, Medium-Sized Firms" in *Philadelphia Inquirer* (November 13, 2006)
Pub: Philadelphia Newspapers LLC
Ed: Akweli Parker. Description: SAP AG is launching a new office that will offer software to small and medium-sized businesses. The move will help to spur growth. Statistical data included.

28743 ■ "Save the Founder" in *Inc.* (October 2005, pp. 156)
Pub: Inc. Magazine
Ed: Adam Hanft. Description: No matter how large or successful a business becomes, it is necessary for its founder to remain its leader.

28744 ■ "School Is In for Entrepreneurs: Continuing Education Courses Abound." in *Black Enterprise* (Vol. 35, October 2004, No. 3)
Pub: Earl G. Graves Publishing Co. Inc.
Ed: Bridget McCrea. Description: A growing number of small business owners are taking courses to help them better manage company growth, employees, financial operations, and other key issues.

28745 ■ "School Overcrowding Concerns Businesses" in *Bradenton Herald* (February 11, 2005)
Pub: Bradenton Herald
Ed: Description: Small businesses in the Lakewood Ranch district are worried that school overcrowding will discourage prospective employees from moving to the area. A Manatee County commissioner addressed the Lakewood Ranch Business Alliance discussing possible tax increases to help remedy the situation.

28746 ■ "School's out; Working Moms are Worried" in *Marketing to Women* (Vol. 20, January 2007, No. 1, pp. 5)
Pub: EPM Communications, Inc.
Description: Catalyst, a non-profit research firm dedicated to expanding workplace opportunities to women, has discovered that work productivity tends to be drained by concern over their children's after-school time activities.

28747 ■ "Searching for Signs of Intelligent Life" in *Barron's* (August 11, 2003, pp. T1)
Pub: Barron's
Ed: Eric C. Fleming. Description: Internet search engine services, forecasted to profit from the growing use of the Web to find jobs, dates, information, and more are welcoming a stock bubble of sorts. LookSmart's 3.5 share price is four times its October 2002 low, while FindWhat has grown fivefold to more than 17. The competition for the paid search market, primarily between Overture and privately-held Google is detailed.

28748 ■ "Season's Ho! Ho! Turns No! No! No!" in *Atlanta Business Chronicle* (Vol. 25, January 3, 2003, No. 30, pp. 3B)
Pub: American City Business Publications, Inc.
Ed: Alf Nucifora. Description: Retailing over the holidays was not impressive. Internet sales were positive, posting double-digit, year-to-year, seasonal increases around 30-70 percent for various categories. Statistical data included.

28749 ■ "Secondaries Ready For The Big Leagues" in *Venture Capital Journal* (July 1, 2003)
Pub: Thomson Financial Inc.
Description: The lack of corporate buying and a weak IPO market are leaving funds with little or no opportunity to improve returns. Statistical data included.

28750 ■ "Security Companies Expect War to Increase Business" in *Crain's Detroit Business* (Vol. 19, No. 12, March 24, 2003, pp. 24)
Pub: Crain Communications Inc., Detroit
Ed: Andrew Dietderich. Description: Raj Patel, manager of Plante & Moran LLP, the Southfield, Michigan-based security consulting firm, expects a rise in business due to the war in Iraq.

28751 ■ "The Security-Industrial Complex" in *Forbes* (Vol. 174, November 29, 2004, No. 11, pp. 44)
Pub: Forbes Magazine Inc.
Ed: Mark P. Mills. Description: Security is a growing technology business in the U.S. The money flowing into the military and homeland infrastructure will revolutionize technologies and materials. Terror-sensing tools will expand to applications in medicine, industry, transportation, telecommunications and entertainment driving a tech boom.

28752 ■ "Seeing the Light" in *Entrepreneur* (Vol. 33, September 2005, No. 9, pp. 92)
Pub: Entrepreneur Media Inc.
Ed: Chris Penttila. Description: It is predicted that a move to extend daylight savings time would be an economic boom to small businesses. Consumers would spend the extra daylight time shopping, dining at restaurants, working out at fitness centers, etc.

28753 ■ "Semiconductor Industry's Growth Will Slow" in *Kiplinger Letter* (Vol. 78, January 19, 2007, No. 2)
Pub: Kiplinger
Description: Semiconductor manufacturers are expecting a 3 percent drop in sales worldwide in 2007.

28754 ■ *Send 'Em One White Sock: 67 Outrageously Simple Ideas from Around the World for Building Your Business*
Pub: The McGraw-Hill Companies
Ed: Stan Rapp and Thomas L. Collins. Released: 1998. Price: $18.00.

28755 ■ "Sense & Sensibility" in *Small Business Opportunities* (Vol. 12, No. 2, March 2000, pp. 18)
Pub: Harris Publications, Inc.
Ed: Carla Goodman. Description: Advice to find, hire and work with a consultant to help build a small business is presented. A checklist of information for evaluating a consultant before hiring, is also included.

28756 ■ "Several restaurants to be added to Boston's menu" in *Boston Business Journal* (Vol. 22, No. 16, May 24, 2002, pp. 10)
Pub: MCP, Inc.
Ed: Donna L. Goodison. Description: Several new restaurants are opening in Boston, MA, while others are expanding their businesses.

28757 ■ "S.F. Slashes Economic Development" in *San Francisco Business Times* (Vol. 17, No. 53, August 8, 2003, pp. 1)
Pub: American City Business Journals
Ed: Eric Young. Description: San Francisco, California officials have decided that, because of a budget shortfall, the city will discontinue its economic development department as of July 1, 2003. Funding was cut by 90 percent, staffing reduced 66 percent.

28758 ■ "Shattered Magazine: A Monthly for the Global Businesswoman" in *Marketing to Women* (Vol. 19, December 2006, No. 2, pp. 6)
Pub: EPM Communications, Inc.
Ed: Julie Ros. Description: Shattered is a glossy magazine distributed monthly and run by veteran financial journalist, Julie Ros. Shattered concentrates its focus on the business world and puts special emphasis on the global impact women are having in the leadership roles of the business community.

28759 ■ "Shelby Supervisor Hopes Township Plan Can Spur More Growth" in *Crain's Detroit Business* (Vol. 21, January 31, 2005, No. 5, pp. 35)
Pub: Crain Communications Inc. - Detroit
Ed: Anjali Fluker. Description: Plans for new buildings and upgrades to older buildings along Shelby Township, Michigan's Van Dyke corridor are highlighted. The master plan would create a center of activity for shopping, entertainment, recreation and municipal buildings.

28760 ■ "Shifting Into Growth Mode" in *Sales and Marketing.com* (Vol. 156, No. 3, March 2004, pp. 12)
Pub: VNU eMedia, Inc.
Ed: Michele Marchetti. **Description:** Managers will be required to makes changes to maximize productivity of sales teams as firms shift from survival mode to growth mode. Several management tactics are outlined.

28761 ■ "Short and Sweet" in *Entrepreneur* (Vol. 32, No. 2, February 2004, pp. 74)
Pub: Entrepreneur Media, Inc.
Ed: Kimberly L. McCall. **Description:** Tactics that can be used to shorten a sales cycle in order to increase profits are explained.

28762 ■ "Show Me the Money" in *Sales and Marketing.com* (Vol. 156, No. 3, March 2004, pp. 16)
Pub: VNU eMedia, Inc.
Ed: Julia Chang. **Description:** As companies transfer from cost cutting to growth strategies, sales commission plans will also change. Salespersons will have higher quotas and underperformers will most likely receive lower commissions than top performers.

28763 ■ "Signs of Life? You'll Need Plenty of Patience to Profit from M-Commerce" in *Entrepreneur* (Vol. 31, No. 10, October 2003, pp. 28)
Pub: Entrepreneur Media, Inc.
Ed: Amanda C. Kooser. **Description:** M-Commerce, or mobile commerce, is discussed. The sector has seen disappointing early experiences, but many entrepreneurs are looking forward to a full-blown m-commerce future.

28764 ■ "Silicon Still Matters" in *Forbes* (March 25, 2002, p. 60)
Pub: Forbes Magazine
Ed: Edward Clendaniel. **Description:** The ups and downs of the high tech industry are highlighted showing how the leaders are able to cope during the down times.

28765 ■ "Sink or Swim" in *My Business* (February/March 2004, pp. 20-25)
Pub: My Business Magazine
Ed: Shannon Scully. **Description:** The importance of e-commerce to small business marketing is discussed. The process of building a Website in order to improve a brick-and-mortar business is critical. A Website should be easy for a customer to surf; it is suggested to stay away from fancy Flash products.

28766 ■ "The Sinking of the Dot-Com Fleet" in *Information Today* (Vol. 17, No. 11, December 2000, pp. 42)
Pub: Information Today, Inc.
Ed: Robin Peek. **Description:** With the Web's golden era over, 2001 will be a saner year.

28767 ■ "Skokie Taxed by School-Business Rift" in *Chicago Tribune* (March 9, 2005)
Pub: Knight-Ridder/Tribune Business News
Ed: M. Daniel Gibbard. **Description:** School officials and Skokie business leaders are debating the end of a special tax that finances downtown redevelopment. The Skokie Village board is trying to negotiate a compromise acceptable to both sides.

28768 ■ "Sleepy Little Towns Turn High Tech" in *Home Office Computing* (Vol. 19, No. 1, January 2001, pp. 17)
Pub: Scholastic Inc.
Ed: Lisa Roberts. **Description:** The agricultural town of Petaluma, California suddenly found itself a high-tech center when local firm Ceret Corp was acquired by networking giant Cisco Systems and 40 other telecom firms established facilities in the area. Petaluma has become a model for many other rural areas whose economies are disappearing. Tazwell County, Virginia has adopted a similar strategy in an effort to attract high-technology companies to an area where population has been declining.

28769 ■ "Slump wipes 228 eateries off S.F. menu" in *San Francisco Business Times* (Vol. 16, No. 42, May 24, 2002, pp. 3)
Pub: San Francisco Business Times Inc.
Ed: Jessica Materna. **Description:** A report from the Golden Gate Restaurant Association states that San Francisco, California lost 7 percent of its eating places in the six months from June to December 2001. Rising city fees for services such as water and garbage are discussed along with drops in income for restaurants which managed to stay open.

28770 ■ "Small-Biz Owners' Wild Mood Swings" in *Inc.* (July 1, 2003)
Pub: Gruner & Jahr USA Publishing
Description: The National Federation of Independent Businesses monthly index measuring small business optimism hit a 10-year low in March 2003.

28771 ■ "Small Business Advisor: A pressing matter" in *Crain's Chicago Businesss*
Pub: Crain Communications, Inc. Crain Communications, Inc.
Ed: Barbara B. Buchholz. **Description:** Twenty years ago, when Robert and Lynne Pascal were seeking a challenge, they started a printing company and are now moving their business to the Internet.

28772 ■ "Small Business Advisor: Choose kids' or collectors' market" in *Crain's Chicago Business* (Vol. 23, November 13, 2000, pp. SB17)
Pub: Crain Communications, Inc. Crain Communications, Inc.
Ed: Warren Denniston. **Description:** Checkerboard Toys Inc. faces numerous challenges, including business focus and capital funding.

28773 ■ "Small Business Advisor: Identify and protect your niches" in *Crain's Chicago Business* (Vol. 23, October 9, 2000, pp. SB15)
Pub: Crain Communications, Inc. Crain Communications, Inc.
Ed: Lisa Kieres. **Description:** Unlike most printers, Robert and Lynne Pascal are in an enviable position, with great growth trends and outlook.

28774 ■ *Small Business Cash Flow: Strategies for Making Your Business a Financial Success*
Pub: John Wiley & Sons, Incorporated
Ed: Denise O'Berry. **Released:** October 2006. **Price:** $19.95. **Description:** Tips to help small businesses manage money are given.

28775 ■ "Small business" in *Crain's Detroit Business* (Vol. 18, No. 45, November 11, 2002, pp. 23)
Pub: Crain Communications Inc., Detroit
Description: Ways to improve profits for various types of small businesses are presented, including marketing ideas and pricing.

28776 ■ "Small-Business Exports Show Big Growth" in *Hispanic Business* (Vol. 22, No. 1/2, January/February, pp. 16)
Pub: Hispanic Business
Description: Capsule of data from the Small Business Administration (SBA) showing small businesses with strong growth in exports. A Website with information on SBA positions and programs is also listed.

28777 ■ "Small Business Growth: Intention, Ability, and Opportunity" in *Journal of Small Business Management* (Vol. 41, No. 4, October 2003)
Pub: International Council of Small Business
Ed: Alison Morrison, John Breen, Shameem Ali. **Description:** Small businesses are recognized as vital contributors to economic development, job creation, and general health and welfare of economies, representing a significant proportion of the world economy.

28778 ■ "Small Business Index Falls as Sales Growth Slows" in *Wall Street Journal* (July 17, 2000, pp. A2)
Pub: Dow Jones & Co., Inc.

Ed: Rodney Ho. **Description:** Statistical information regarding the falling business index.

28779 ■ "Small Business Owners are Less Optimistic" in *Milwaukee Journal Sentinel* (December 2, 2005)
Pub: Journal Sentinel, Inc.
Ed: Rick Romell. **Description:** A survey released by the National Federation of Independent Business reported 59.5 percent of small business owners had a positive economic outlook in November, down 6 percent from September 2005.

28780 ■ "Small Business Resource Guide: Service Providers: Part 1 of 2" in *Crain's Detroit Business* (Vol. 15, No. 50, Dec. 13, 1999, pp. E-11)
Pub: Crain Communications, Inc.
Description: The Michigan Economic Development Corporation is the State of Michigan's one-stop resource for businesses seeking growth in the state. Includes a listing of the SBA's programs and contact information.

28781 ■ "Small Business Resource Guide: Service Providers: Part 2 of 2" in *Crain's Detroit Business* (Vol. 15, No. 50, Dec. 13, 1999, pp. E-13)
Pub: Crain Communications, Inc.
Description: More contact information for small and start-up business in the State of Michigan, including information about Michigan State University Extension Service, the public library systems, organizations, IRS publications, regulators, Michigan Unemployment Agency, and the Michigan Department of Environmental Quality.

28782 ■ *Small Business Sourcebook*
Pub: Gale Group
Released: July 2005. **Price:** $430.00. **Description:** Two-volume guide to more than 27,300 listings of live and print sources for small business startups as well as small business growth and development. Over 30,500 topics are included.

28783 ■ *Small Business Turnaround*
Pub: Adams Media Corporation
Ed: Marc Kramer. **Price:** $17.95 paperback.

28784 ■ "Small Businesses Are Engine to American Economy" in *Atlanta Business Chronicle* (Vol. 24, No. 9, August 3, 2001, pp. 10B)
Pub: American City Business Journals Inc.
Ed: Paige Bowers. **Description:** Senator Max Cleland discusses what he has done in support of small business in America. The Senator's support includes reducing taxes on small businesses, broadening health care options and boosting the opportunities for minority and women-owned enterprises.

28785 ■ "Small Businesses Fuel Growth" in *Success* (Vol. 47, No. 3, July 2000, pp. 16)
Pub: Success Publishing, Inc.
Description: A study showing that small businesses are getting a boost from ever-cheaper information technology and easier access to financial assistance, and are helping to fuel the U.S. economy's record expansion. The study also predicts that this segment of the American economy will see a shift in management as well as the labor force over the next 15 years. Entrepreneurs will no longer be predominately young, white men. They will be older women, many of whom will also be Hispanic and African-American, reflecting the same shift in the U.S. population as a whole.

28786 ■ "Small Deals, Big Business" in *Washington Business Journal* (Vol. 22, No. 17, August 29, 2003, pp. 17)
Pub: Washington Business Journal
Description: The growing role of small business in the software industry is discussed. Topics include growing sales, marketing strategy, and market adaptability.

28787 ■ "Small Firm Bankruptcy" in *Journal of Small Business Management* (Vol. 44, October 2006, No. 4, pp. 493)
Pub: Blackwell Publishing, Inc.
Ed: Richard Carter; Howard Van Auken. **Description:** Results of a survey attempt to identify the root causes of bankruptcy in firms. Statistical data included.

28788 ■ "Small Firms Still Strain for Space: Outlook Brighter for Companies in Need of More Room" in *Crain's Chicago Business* (Vol.23, Dec. 11)
Pub: Crain Communications, Inc. Crain Communications, Inc.
Ed: H. Lee Murphy. **Description:** Small companies in the Chicago area are looking for larger offices because of business growth.

28789 ■ "The Small Picture: How Does the Federal Deficit Affect Your Business?" in *Entrepreneur* (Vol. 31, No. 6, June 2003, pp. 26)
Pub: Entrepreneur Media Inc.
Ed: Joshua Kurlantzick. **Description:** The impact of the national deficit and ways it affects small businesses is examined.

28790 ■ "Small Town Car Dealers Survive" in *Business First Buffalo* (Vol. 19, No. 46, August 8, 2003, pp. 1B)
Pub: American City Business Journals, Inc.
Ed: Tom Hartley. **Description:** Spacc Pontiac-GMC, led by owner and president Larry Spacciapolli, is trying to survive in a market dominated by national car dealers. The National Automobile Dealers Association reports the number of existing car dealers decline annually.

28791 ■ "Small, Yes-But With A Big Back Office" in *Business Week* (No. 3853, October 13, 2003, pp. 86)
Pub: McGraw-Hill Inc.
Ed: Charles Haddad. **Description:** Information technology is helping small firms compete with large corporations. Web-based software allows small businesses to perform all functions electronically.

28792 ■ "Smaller, greener jobs dominate remodeling" in *Atlanta Business Chronicle* (Vol. 24, No. 13, August 31, 2001, pp. 5B)
Pub: American City Business Journals Inc.
Ed: Matthew Slater. **Description:** The downturn in the economy has led to fewer large demands for remodeling, but it has also led to many demands for small remodeling jobs, such as kitchens and bathrooms.

28793 ■ "Smart growth advocates push for change" in *Atlanta Business Chronicle* (Vol. 24, No. 14, September 7, 2001, pp. 10C)
Pub: American City Business Journals Inc.
Description: Several participants from various organizations took part in a discussion by Atlanta Business Chronicle focusing on Smart Growth. Those present were Steve Macauley, Dough Spohn, Dan Reuter, Billy Mitchell, Jim Durrett, Kevin Green, Egbert Perry, Sam Williams, Larry Frank, M. von Nkosi, Hattie Dorsey, Gregg T. Logan, and Ron Terwilliger.

28794 ■ "Software Company Makes List of Country's 500 Fastest-Growing Private Firms" in *Sacramento Bee* (October 19, 2005)
Pub: The Sacramento Bee
Ed: Dale Kasler. **Description:** C&S Marketing was listed as one of Inc. magazine's top 500 fastest growing companies. Firms were ranked according to percent sales growth from 2001 to 2004. The firm provides software to mortgage companies that help estimate property values and eliminate fraud.

28795 ■ "Some Local Firms Find Opportunity in Telecom" in *Atlanta Business Chronicle* (Vol. 25, November 15, 2002, No. 23 pp. 11C)
Pub: American City Business Publications, Inc.
Ed: Jan R. Costello. **Description:** Information is included regarding Cbeyond Communications LLC, Movaz Networks Inc., and Wave7 Optics Inc. and their CEOs. All three Atlanta-based, small telecommunications companies are relatively new and are seeing growth, despite the industry collapse.

28796 ■ "Some Service-Related Businesses Surge Ahead" in *Atlanta Business Chronicle* (Vol. 25, January 10, 2003, No. 31, pp. 21A)
Pub: American City Business Publications, Inc.
Ed: Leslie Williams Johnson. **Description:** According to the Georgia Economic Outlook 2003 report, the service business sector will grow despite the fact that some areas will face difficult times. The forecasts for specific types of services are discussed.

28797 ■ "Some Suppliers Expanding Biz" in *Crain's Detroit Business* (Vol. 22, January 16, 2006, No. 3, pp. 3)
Pub: Crain Communications Inc. - Detroit
Ed: Brent Snavely. **Description:** More than six local automotive suppliers are planning to spend millions in capital expenditures in 2006. A listing of announced initiatives is included.

28798 ■ "Sour forecasts reach fruition; Local companies' 3Q profits fall 26.8 percent from '99" in *Crain's Detroit Business* (Vol. 16, No. 47)
Pub: Crain Communications, Inc.
Ed: Katie Merx. **Description:** The slowdown economists predicted for Michigan emerged during the third quarter of 1999.

28799 ■ "South Florida Farmers Attempt to Broaden Market for Tropical Fruits" in *Miami Herald* (June 28, 2004)
Pub: Knight-Ridder/Tribune Business News
Ed: Christina Hoag. **Description:** South Florida farmers are growing exotic fruits such as lychee and longan, mamey sapote and sapodilla and dragonfruit because of increased interest by consumers in the U.S.

28800 ■ "Southampton Town Board Approves a $20 Million Affordable Housing Development Plan" in *Long Island Business News* (March 5, 2004)
Pub: Dolan Media Newswires
Ed: Nick Anastasi. **Description:** A $20 million residential unit has been approved by the Southampton Town Board. The new development will bring affordable housing to the East End municipality with a 50-unit condominium complex; prices will range from $185,000 to $500,000.

28801 ■ "Southern gentleman sparks downtown growth" in *Atlanta Business Chronicle* (Vol. 25, No. 22, November 8, 2002, pp. 5C)
Pub: American City Business Publications, Inc.
Ed: Anya Martin. **Description:** Aderhold Properties Inc.'s former chairman, John E. Aberhold, has been inducted into the Atlanta Convention and Visitors Bureau Hospitality Hall of Fame. Aberhold was instrumental in the rehabilitation of downtown Atlanta, Georgia.

28802 ■ "Southwest Adds Chicago Flight" in *Sacramento Bee* (October 28, 2005)
Pub: The Sacramento Bee
Ed: Clint Swett. **Description:** Southwest Airlines added a second nonstop flight from Sacramento, California to Chicago, Illinois' Midway Airport. The flights will begin in early 2006. Southwest Airlines is reporting record travel rates for 2005.

28803 ■ "Spectacular growth forces Accident Fund to limit new biz" in *Crain's Detroit Business* (Vol. 18, No. 22, June 3, 2002, pp. 37)
Pub: Crain Communications Inc. - Detroit
Ed: David Barkholz. **Description:** The Accident Fund Company grew so fast in the first quarter of 2002, the management of workers' compensation insurer, has struggled to keep independent agents from writing new business.

28804 ■ "Speculations" in *Forbes* (October 30, 2000, pp. 266)
Pub: Forbes Magazine
Ed: Lisa McDonald. **Description:** An overview of small companies poised to be successful, based upon their stock values.

28805 ■ "Spend cycle" in *Entrepreneur* (Vol. 30, No. 2, February 2002, pp. 28)
Pub: Entrepreneur Media Inc.
Ed: Steve Cooper. **Description:** Consumer spending as a percentage of Gross Domestic Product (GDP) has remained relatively unchanged for the last 50 years. Statistical data included.

28806 ■ "Spot-condemnation law better for neighborhoods, leaders say" in *Crain's Detroit Business* (Vol. 18, No. 21, May 27, 2002, pp. 40)
Pub: Crain Communications Inc. - Detroit
Ed: Robert Ankeny. **Description:** A new anti-blight law aimed at redeveloping deteriorating property will probably be more useful in Detroit's neighborhoods than downtown, according to many city and business leaders.

28807 ■ "Spotlight Rick Chesley; Chairman Builds Law Office From Ground Up" in *Crain's Chicago Business* (Vol. 30, January 2007, No. 2, pp. 5)
Pub: Crain Communications, Inc.
Ed: Lorene Yue. **Description:** Profile of Rick Chesley, office chair for law firm, Paul Hastings Janofsky & Walker LLP's at the new Chicago location. Hastings' goal is to establish a strong Chicago presence for the firm.

28808 ■ "Sprucing Up Riverwalk: Ceremony Celebrates Groundbreaking of Offices, Artworks" in *Bradenton Herald* (January 29, 2005)
Pub: Bradenton Herald
Ed: Kurt D. Schultheis. **Description:** City officials and business leaders of the Manatee Riverwalk area in Bradenton and Palmetto, Florida, celebrated the construction of an $8 million office building and three sculptures.

28809 ■ "Stand by NASA research" in *Red Herring* (March 2003, pp. 17)
Pub: Herring Communications Inc.
Description: NASA research and development has resulted in growth in technology sectors such as communications, energy and the robotics industry.

28810 ■ *The Starbucks Experience: 5 Principles for Turing Ordinary into Extraordinary*
Pub: McGraw-Hill
Ed: Joseph A. Michelli. **Released:** November 2006.

28811 ■ *Start, Run & Grow a Successful Small Business*
Pub: C C H, Inc.
Ed: Susan Jacksach; designed by Tim Kaage; contribution by Martin Bush. **Released:** 2nd ed. 1998. **Price:** $24.95.

28812 ■ *Start, Run, and Grow a Successful Small Business, 2nd Edition*
Pub: CCH, Inc.
Ed: Susan M. Jacksack. **Price:** $24.95.

28813 ■ *Start Small, Finish Big*
Pub: Warner Business Books
Ed: Fred DeLuca. **Price:** $14.95.

28814 ■ "Starting From Zero: Entrepreneur Reaps Success During Rocky Tech Times" in *Black Enterprise* (Vol. 34, July 2004, No. 12, pp. 53)
Pub: Earl G. Graves Publishing Co. Inc.
Ed: Bridget McCrea. **Description:** Profile of Glenn Davis, owner of Virginia-based BranCore Technologies. Working from home, Davis borrowed $15,000 from his 401(k) to launch his minority-owned firm that provides project management and e-commerce consulting.

28815 ■ "State Dept. of Economic Development Reports Strong Growth" in *St. Charles Business Record* (May 7, 2004)
Pub: Dolan Media Company
Description: State of Missouri's Department of Economic Growth reported 6,100 new jobs were added in the state, first quarter 2004, 16th in the country. New business formations were at 14,930 in 2003 in approximately 100 various industries. Statistical data included.

28816 ■ "State biz bankruptcies rise despite national fall" in *Crain's Detroit Business* (Vol. 19, No. 10, March 10, 2003, pp. 18)
Pub: Crain Communications Inc., Detroit
Ed: Michael Strong. Description: Nationally, business bankruptcies fell 3.9 percent, however they rose 20 percent in Southeast Michigan.

28817 ■ *The State of Small Business*
Pub: Gordon Press Publishers
Released: 1997. Price: $600.95 (library binding; 2 vols.).

28818 ■ "The State of Small Business: Confident, yet cautious, in 2001" in *Crain's Chicago Business* (Vol. 23, December 11, 2000, pp. SB1)
Pub: Crain Communications, Inc.
Ed: H. Lee Murphy. Description: Despite the slowing economy, small firms still look for growth.

28819 ■ "State, U.S. Housing Sales Hit New Highs in 2004" in *Boston Globe* (January 26, 2005)
Pub: New York Times Company
Ed: Chris Reidy. Description: Lower mortgage rates are credited for housing sales to hit record highs nationally. Real estate experts do not expect the trend to continue because mortgage rates are supposed to climb in 2005. Statistical data for the Massachusetts housing industry are included.

28820 ■ "State's Jobs Up 1.7 Percent" in *Sacramento Bee* (October 5, 2005)
Pub: The Sacramento Bee
Ed: Rachel Osterman. Description: California reported job growth at 1.7 percent in the second quarter, 2005, making the state's economy 16th strongest in the nation. Statistical data included.

28821 ■ "Stats of the Month" in *Business Week* (No. 3761, December 10, 2001, pp. SB9)
Pub: McGraw-Hill Inc.
Description: Statistical data regarding issues facing small business growth is presented.

28822 ■ "Staying Afloat: VCs Raise Annex Funds to Buoy Waning Portfolios" in *Venture Capital Journal* (Vol. 41, No. 8, August 2000, pp. 27-30)
Pub: Venture Economics
Ed: Carolina Braunschweig. Description: In an effort to sustain troubled portfolios and reverse negative returns, a few venture capitalists are going back to their LPs to raise annex funds. This latest breed of venture fund, also known as bailout funds, has put some of the nation's largest VC firms in the same predicament as their struggling startups - asking for more funds after recently losing money.

28823 ■ "Steady Economic Growth" in *My Business* (October/November 2002, pp. 39)
Pub: My Business Magazine
Ed: Bill Dunkelberg. Description: Small business optimism, hiring and sales prices are profiled from 2000-2002. Statistical data included.

28824 ■ "Stepping On It: Will New Measures Really Rev Up U.S. Manufacturers' Engines?" in *Entrepreneur* (Vol. 32, July 2004, No. 7, pp. 35)
Pub: Entrepreneur Media Inc.
Ed: Stephen Barlas. Description: Under Executive Order by President Bush, federal agencies are to emphasize manufacturing in the Small Business Innovation Research (SBIR) and Small Business Technology Transfer (STTR) programs.

28825 ■ "Stock Watch: Aeropostale Flies Past Competitors" in *Crain's New York Business* (Vol. 20, No. 12, March 22, 2004, pp. 3)
Pub: Crain Communications, Inc.
Ed: Tommy Fernandez. Description: Stock prices for Aeropostale, Inc., the teen clothing retailer, have tripled in one year. Statistical data included.

28826 ■ "Stock uncertainty treats state better than nation as a whole" in *Crain's Detroit Business* (Vol. 19, No. 1, January 6, 2003, pp. 4)
Pub: Crain Communications Inc., Detroit
Ed: Katie Merx. Description: The four key reasons why Michigan stocks fared better than the Standard & Poors 500 are listed. Experts project that the state will finish 2003 flat or slightly up.

28827 ■ "Stockholders in Cyberspace: Weick's Sensemaking Online" in *Journal of Business Communication* (Vol. 44, January 2007, No. 1, pp. 13)
Pub: Association for Business Communication
Ed: Andrew F. Herrmann. Description: Stockholders are using the Internet's discussion boards to make sense of their financial holdings.

28828 ■ "Stockton, Calif., Chocolate Company Recognized for Quick Growth" in *Knight-Ridder/Tribune Business News* (October 29, 2001)
Pub: Knight-Ridder/Tribune Business News
Ed: Liz Benston. Description: Profile of Chocoholics Divine Desserts, the manufacturer of chocolates treats. The company's sales have grown more than 600 percent since 1996.

28829 ■ "Storage: With the dumb dot-com money gone, the space race begins in earnest" in *Red Herring* (No. 105, October 1, 2001, pp. 76-77)
Pub: Herring Communications
Ed: Tim Devaney, Scott Tyler Shafer. Description: Storage companies must confront the obstacles once overlooked, including costs and network-based solutions. Statistical data is offered showing data-storage revenue forecast for 2003, customer expectations for growth of storage budget during 2001, median storage capacity of Global 2000 companies, total global capacity of installed networked storage, and average cost of storage system capacity.

28830 ■ *Straight Talk About Small Business Success in New Jersey: How to Maximize the Growth, Cash Flow and Profitability of Your Small Business*
Pub: Business Success Systems, Incorporated
Ed: Salim Omar. Released: April 2004. Price: $18.95. Description: Small business information geared to new and existing small businesses in New Jersey.

28831 ■ *Strategies for Growth in SMEs: The Role of Information and Information Systems*
Pub: Elsevier Science & Technology Books
Ed: Margi Levy, Philip Powell. Released: November 2004. Price: $49.95. Description: Role of information and information systems in the growth of small and medium-sized enterprises in the U.S.

28832 ■ "Strategies Keep Business Warm When Weather Cools" in *Crain's Detroit Business* (Vol. 21, December 19, 2005, No. 51, pp. 15)
Pub: Crain Communications Inc. - Detroit
Ed: Sheena Harrison. Description: Great Lakes Landscape Design Inc. of Oak Park, Michigan, offers snow removal services during the winter months. Ninety percent of the company's revenue comes from landscaping, planting, pruning and other horticultural work during the warmer months.

28833 ■ "Straub's Doesn't Fill its Baskets With a Lot of Gimmicks" in *St. Louis Post-Dispatch* (October 29, 2004)
Pub: Knight-Ridder/Tribune Business News
Ed: Linda Tucci. Description: Profile of Straub's Markets Inc., the 103 year-old-old family grocer. In an interview with Trip Straub, son of President Jack Straub, the fourth generation running the firm, he shares how he reinvented the stores through diversification of product line and remodeling shops. These steps have doubled total sales over an eight-year period.

28834 ■ *Streetwise Small Business Book of Lists: Hundreds of Lists to Help You Reduce Costs, Increase Revenues, and Boost Your Profits!*
Pub: Adams Media Corporation
Ed: Gene Marks. Released: September 2006. Price: $25.95. Description: Strategies to help small business owners locate services, increase sales, and lower expenses.

28835 ■ "Strength in numbers" in *Washington Business Journal* (Vol. 22, No. 3, May 23, 2003, pp. 3)
Pub: Washington Business Journal
Ed: John Wilen. Description: The economic outlook for the Washington, DC area is discussed, including employment levels, layoffs, and growth within the computer industry.

28836 ■ "Strong Demand Is Firing Up U.S. Factories" in *Business Week* (January 31, 2005, pp. 23)
Pub: McGraw-Hill Companies
Ed: James C. Cooper, Kathleen Madigan. Description: Spending by U.S. consumers, businesses, and governments for all goods and services grew 4.9 percent in the third quarter of 2004 and is expected to grow at the same rate for the fourth quarter.

28837 ■ "The Struggle for Sales Overseas" in *Hispanic Business* (November 2002, pp. 36)
Pub: Hispanic Business
Ed: Joel Russell. Description: Statistics are shared regarding Hispanic companies exporting products are featured. Overall exports for the first seven months of 2002 were down 8 percent from same period in 2001.

28838 ■ "Student Loan Firm Will Add 170 Jobs" in *Tampa Tribune* (November 29, 2005)
Pub: Media General, Inc.
Ed: Dave Simanoff. Description: Academic Financial Services in Tampa Bay, Florida is hiring 170 more workers for its new office space. The firm will receive $510,000 in tax rebates, $3,000 for each new job created and maintained.

28839 ■ "Study shows businesses are slow to embrace e-commerce" in *Black Enterprise* (Vol. 32)
Pub: Earl Graves Publishing Co.
Ed: Bevolyn Williams-Harold. Description: The Minority Business Development Agency is urging minority-owned businesses to use e-commerce to help grow their companies. Statistical data included.

28840 ■ "Study Foresees End of Boeing's Commercial Work; Company Calls Report Flawed" in *News Tribune* (April 11, 2003)
Pub: Knight-Ridder/Tribune Business News
Ed: John Gillie. Description: According to a study written by two State University of New York at Buffalo researchers, the growing expertise of overseas aerospace companies along with the demand for higher profits could prompt Boeing to leave the commercial airplane business within the next ten years.

28841 ■ "Successful Expo! Expo! Mirrors Greater Optimism" in *Tradeshow Week* (Vol. 34, December 13, 2004, No. 50, pp. 1)
Pub: Reed Business Information
Ed: Margo McCall. Description: The International Association for Exhibition Management reported increased attendance for its annual Expo! Expo! Meeting, showing optimism for the industry.

28842 ■ "Sunshine State Summit" in *Hispanic Business* (March 2003, pp. 26, 28)
Pub: Hispanic Business
Ed: Abel Magana. Description: The Florida State Hispanic Chamber of Commerce Conference is highlighted. The event, held January 22-23, 2003, announced a series of 15 regional seminars organized through the cooperation of the U.S. Chamber of Commerce, the Small Business Administration, and the newly formed National Coalition of Hispanic Chambers of Commerce.

28843 ■ "Supplier Innovation Key to Industry Future, Exec Says" in *Crain's Detroit Business* (Vol. 21, January 24, 2005, No. 4, pp. 5)

Pub: Crain Communications Inc. - Detroit

Ed: Terry Kosdrosky. Description: According to Paul Wilbur, president of ASC Inc., suppliers need to bring the latest and best technology to automakers in order to survive, despite added costs.

28844 ■ "Supply Chain Challenges: Building Relationships" in *Harvard Business Review* (Vol. 81, No. 7, July 2003, pp. 64)

Pub: Harvard Business School Press

Ed: Julia Kirby. Description: The development of business logistics systems is discussed.

28845 ■ "Support for Rapid-Growth Firms" in *Journal of Small Business Management* (Vol. 41, No. 4, October 2003, pp. 346)

Pub: International Council of Small Business

Ed: Eileen Fischer, A. Rebecca Reuber. Description: Perspectives of small business owners, government policymakers, and external resource providers on ways rapid-growth firms should be supported.

28846 ■ "Survey finds optimism up at businesses" in *Pittsburgh Business Times* (Vol. 22, No. 46, May 30, 2003, pp. 3)

Pub: Pittsburgh Business Times

Ed: Kent Bernhard, Jr. Description: The results of a business survey of small businesses in the Pittsburgh, Pennsylvania area is presented, including economic conditions, capital investment planning, and economic forecasts.

28847 ■ "Survey: economy will continue to affect growth" in *Atlanta Business Chronicle* (Vol. 25, November 15, 2002, No. 23 pp. SS12)

Pub: American City Business Publications, Inc.

Description: Members of Atlanta's legal community were surveyed by the Atlanta Business Chronicle about expectations for business in 2003, the biggest challenges expected in Atlanta for the next year, and expectations for their practices. Responses from eight professionals are included.

28848 ■ "Survey: Tech Spending Likely to Stabilize, but Not Show Big Increase This Year" in *Daily Business Review* (Vol. 77, March 12, 2003)

Pub: American Lawyer Media LP

Description: Goldman Sachs polled technology buyers in February 2003 and found that many executives expect information technology spending to increase in 2003. Further results of the survey are discussed.

28849 ■ "Survival of the Fittest: As Your Business Grows, So Do the Challenges." in *Entrepreneur* (Vol. 32, December 2004, No. 12)

Pub: Entrepreneur Media Inc.

Ed: Romanus Wolter. Description: Four steps to help entrepreneurs face new business challenges with confidence are featured.

28850 ■ *Sustainable Growth and Performance in East Asia, Book III*

Pub: Edward Elgar Publishing, Incorporated

Released: June 2005. Price: $145.00. Description: Ways small and medium sized enterprises contribute to achieving and sustaining growth and performance in their particular economies along with ways in which governments can assist and enhance that contribution.

28851 ■ "Switching Gears Pays Off" in *Crain's Detroit Business* (Vol. 21, October 10, 2005, No. 43, pp. 21)

Pub: Crain Communications Inc. - Detroit

Ed: Terry Kosdrosky. Description: Porsche Engineering Services Inc. has changed its strategy to working on engineering design, testing, clay modeling, computer modeling, vehicle launches, and supplier management rather than focusing on high-tech projects.

28852 ■ "Sycuan" in *San Diego Business Journal* (Vol. 28, January 1, 2007, No. 1, pp. 8)

Pub: San Diego Business Journal Associates

Ed: Brad Graves. Description: Sycuan Resort, formerly known as Singing Hills County Club, may become the site of a new casino with 5,000 slot machines.

28853 ■ "Systemax Pares U.S., LI Staff" in *Long Island Business News* (February 20, 2004)

Pub: Dolan Media Newswires

Description: Computer supplier, Systemax Inc., plans to lay 200 employees off in the U.S., along with the elimination of 50 jobs in the U.K.

28854 ■ "Tactics: Semiconductors will lead the tech recovery" in *Red Herring* (No. 105, October 1, 2001, pp. 102)

Pub: Herring Communications

Ed: Arnold Berman. Description: Economic indicators suggest that the technology sector is beginning to recover from the technology downturn, and the chip industry will remain at the leading edge of the recovery.

28855 ■ "Tactics: Technology's earnings riddle" in *Red Herring* (No. 103, September 1, 2001, pp. 88)

Pub: Herring Communications

Ed: Pip Coburn. Description: For the last four years, the technology sector experienced either the largest or second-largest gains in earnings. However, for 2001, it's on track to come in dead last.

28856 ■ "Tactics: Will better be good enough?" in *Red Herring* (No. 102, August 15, 2001, pp. 94)

Pub: Herring Communications

Ed: Arnold Berman. Description: In 2002, the questions about technology stocks will have more to do with valuation, rather than the broad spending environment.

28857 ■ "Take it from me" in *Entrepreneur* (Vol. 31, No. 4, April 2003, pp. 26)

Pub: Entrepreneur Media Inc.

Ed: Aliza Pilar Sherman. Description: An interview with two women business owners offering advice in management, business growth, and business downsizing.

28858 ■ "Taking Off" in *Washington Business Journal* (Vol. 22, No. 20, September 19, 2003, pp. 34)

Pub: Washington Business Journal

Ed: Tania Anderson. Description: Atlantic Coast Airlines Inc., formerly a regional feeder airline for United Airlines, wants to become a major carrier. Atlantic Coast expects its contract with United to cease during United's bankruptcy reorganization.

28859 ■ "Taking stock" in *Harvard Business Review* (Vol. 81, No. 1, January 2003, pp. 19)

Pub: Harvard Business School Press

Ed: Roger L. Martin. Description: The Dean of Rotman School of Management at the University of Toronto disputes the theory that managers should be compensated with company stock or options; he suggests bonuses based on real earnings growth.

28860 ■ "Talk America Plans $40M State Expansion" in *Crain's Detroit Business* (Vol. 21, January 24, 2005, No. 4, pp. 12)

Pub: Crain Communications Inc. - Detroit

Ed: Amy Lane. Description: By using discount elements of SBC Communications Inc.'s network, Talk America has built a successful telephone company. The $200 million company is planning a $40 million expansion in Michigan.

28861 ■ "The Talk of the Inc. 500" in *Inc.* (October, 2000, pp. 13)

Pub: The Goldhirsh Group

Description: Attendees at the Inc. 500 conference contended that the biggest problems facing America's

fastest growing companies in 2000 were related to financing business growth. Nearly 75 percent of attendees said they would consider a merger if the right offer came along and nearly two-thirds expressed difficulty implementing e-commerce solutions and many plan to spend more money on Internet marketing than on more traditional marketing media.

28862 ■ "Tampa, Fla.-Based Fitness Club Company Expands Manatee County Operations" in *Bradenton Herald* (September 12, 2002)

Pub: Knight Ridder/Tribune Business News

Ed: Matt Griswold. Description: Profile of Tampa-based Shapes Family Fitness, Inc., owner and operator of Total Fitness women's health clubs and the co-ed Southside Athletic Clubs along the Gulf coast from Tampa to Venice, Florida.

28863 ■ "Target plans superstores" in *Crain's Detroit Business* (Vol. 19, No. 14, April 7, 2003, pp. 48)

Pub: Crain Communications Inc., Detroit

Ed: Brent Snavely. Description: Target Corporation has announced plans to build 30-35 grocery and merchandise stores per year, calling them SuperTarget.

28864 ■ "Targeting Options Threatens Innovation and Growth" in *Venture Capital Journal* (Vol. 42, No. 5, May 2002, pp. 42)

Pub: Thomas Venture Economics

Ed: Craig A.T. Jones. Description: Stock options are critical in fostering innovation and entrepreneurship; the mandatory expensing of these options would make them too expensive to issue for most organizations.

28865 ■ "Tattoo Shop Moves to Cornwall Avenue" in *Bellingham Business Journal* (January 2007, pp. A5)

Pub: Sun News Inc.

Description: Tattoo shop, The Inkwell, owned by Brandon Bradshaw has moved to a spacious new location.

28866 ■ "Tech and the City: What Cities Are Rising Fast on the High-Tech Horizon?" in *Entrepreneur* (Vol. 32, October 2004, No. 10, pp. 36)

Pub: Entrepreneur Media Inc.

Ed: Melissa Campanelli. Description: U.S. cities offering opportunity for high-tech companies include Camden, New Jersey where the New Jersey Economic Development Authority is developing the Camden Waterfront Technology Center; Madison, Wisconsin's economic development initiative, Technology Zone Program; Tucson, Arizona, with area companies working with the SBA SBIR and SBTT federal grant programs to attract high tech companies; and South Lafayette, Louisiana's Acadiana Technology Immersion Center.

28867 ■ "Tech firms uncertain about tech forecast" in *Atlanta Business Chronicle* (Vol. 25, November 15, 2002, No. 23 pp. 2C)

Pub: American City Business Publications, Inc.

Ed: Charles Davidson. Description: Many technology executives in Atlanta expect customers to buy more business products or services during the first or second quarter of 2003, and IDC expects the global information technology market to grow 9 percent to $1 trillion during 2003. Details on technology spending for various companies are included.

28868 ■ "Tech firms like Granholm's economic plan" in *Crain's Detroit Business* (Vol. 18, No. 22, June 3, 2002, pp. 53)

Pub: Crain Communications Inc. - Detroit

Ed: Andrew Dietderich. Description: The Michigan State Attorney General has called for the creation of the Michigan Technology Tri-Corridor, which would expand the state's $40 million Life Sciences Corridor and promote automotive technology and homeland security research and development programs.

28869 ■ **"Tech Jobs Look Up" in** *Crain's Detroit Business* **(Vol. 22, September 25-October 1, 2006, No. 39, pp. 1, 39)**
Pub: Crain Communications Inc. - Detroit
Ed: Andrew Dietderich. Description: New Products and recent retirements have resulted in a shortage in Information Technology and other high tech areas. Significant percentage of growth is in Southeastern Michigan.

28870 ■ **"The Tech Track" in** *Hispanic Business* **(January/February 2005, pp. 56, 58)**
Pub: Hispanic Business
Ed: Anthony Limon. Description: The Information Technology Association of America reports a 2 percent increase in employment for first quarter periods of 2003 and 2004. The technology sector is slowly re-absorbing displaced workers, however banking, finance, manufacturing, food service and transportation accounted for 89 percent of new IT jobs. Statistical data included.

28871 ■ **"Tech-wreck survivors" in** *Crain's Detroit Business* **(Vol. 19, No. 13, March 31, 2003, pp. 11)**
Pub: Crain Communications Inc., Detroit
Ed: Andrew Dietderich. Description: Information on seven metro Detroit area high tech companies that have prospered while others have gone out of business is discussed. The CEOs of Clarity LLC, Dewpoint Inc., ePrize LLC, Fry Inc., The Menlo Institute LLC, New World Systems, and Stoneage.com are interviewed.

28872 ■ **"Technology's Growth Champs" in** *Forbes* **(Vol. 175, February 14, 2005, No. 3, pp. 100)**
Pub: Forbes Magazine Inc.
Ed: Jody Yen. Description: Profiles of the 25 fastest growing technology companies in the U.S. are presented. AtRoad of Fremont, California is number one in five-year sales growth.

28873 ■ **"Telecom: As companies go bankrupt, buyout firms lick their chops" in** *Red Herring* **(No. 105, October 1, 2001, pp. 24-25)**
Pub: Herring Communications
Ed: Om Malik. Description: Interview with Arun Sarin, who sees the current problems faced by the telecom industry as an opportunity to make money.

28874 ■ **"Telecom recession may have hit bottom" in** *Atlanta Business Chronicle* **(Vol. 25, January 3, 2003, No. 30, pp. 3A)**
Pub: American City Business Publications, Inc.
Ed: Mary Jane Credeur. Description: In the year 2003, a slight recovery in the telecom recession could be in the making. Already BellSouth Corporation and other Baby Bells have experienced a rise in stock prices. In the fourth quarter 2002, BellSouth reported a shares' gain of 43.2 percent.

28875 ■ **"Telecom's transformation continues in Georgia" in** *Atlanta Business Chronicle* **(Vol. 25, January 10, 2003, No. 31, pp. 17A)**
Pub: American City Business Publications, Inc.
Ed: Charles Davidson. Description: In the midst of a drastic recession, the communications industry is poised for recovery, even though full recovery may be a long way off. Trends in telecommunications like bundling - offering an array of communications services in one package with one price - are here to stay. Wireless device usage will continue to increase.

28876 ■ **"10 Names that Drive the Game" in** *Crain's Detroit Business* **(Vol. 19, No. 14, April 7, 2003, pp. 11)**
Pub: Crain Communications Inc., Detroit
Ed: Jason Deegan. Description: With 800 courses, the state of Michigan has the most golf courses of any state in the nation. Challenges faced by course owners, including a short playing season and golf-related jobs, long working hours, and other issues are discussed.

28877 ■ **"10 Rules for Bouncing Back" in** *My Business* **(April/May 2003, pp. 32)**
Pub: My Business Magazine
Description: A list of the top ten truths to motivate small business owners, compiled from motivational books, is presented.

28878 ■ *$10,000 -a-Day Business Opportunities: Seminars, Newsletters, Cassettes, Software & More*
Pub: New Ventures Publishing Group
Ed: J. Stephen Lanning. Released: 1998.

28879 ■ **"Tewksbury Firm Cashes in as Internet Calling Grows" in** *Boston Globe* **(March 7, 2005)**
Pub: New York Times Company
Ed: Peter J. Howe. Description: Starent Networks Corporation is handling the delivery of Verizon's VCast video-on-cellphone service on its Broadband Access network. Verizon will spend more than $1 billion to expand its network in 2005.

28880 ■ **"TGIFridays to Open Restaurant at Islip MacArthur Airport" in** *Long Island Business News* **(February 6, 2004)**
Pub: Dolan Media Newswires
Description: TGIFridays will open a new restaurant in the food court at Islip MacArthur Airport, part of the airports expansion.

28881 ■ **"That Clicking Sound: Grandma's favorite hobby hooks a new generation of young, urban go-getters" in** *Time* **(Vol. 155, Jan. 31, 2000)**
Pub: Time Inc.
Description: Nearly four million women started knitting in 1999, and most were between the ages of 20 and 30. These women are seeing the craft as a means for relaxation and are boosting profits for the industry.

28882 ■ **"That Trade Deficit Is No Debacle" in** *Business Week* **(January 31, 2005, pp. 30)**
Pub: McGraw-Hill Companies
Ed: Peter Coy. Description: Imports exceeded exports in November 2004 by a record $60 billion, the trade deficit now stands at around 6 percent of gross domestic product, the highest level in history.

28883 ■ **"The AdStop Inc.: www.theadstop.com" in** *Entrepreneur* **(Vol. 31, No. 12, December 2003, pp. 8)**
Pub: Entrepreneur Media Inc.
Ed: Steve Cooper. Description: Profile of The AdStop Inc. Web site that offers resources for Internet advertising to help grow a business.

28884 ■ **"The Champagne Group Launches 'Manager Makeover' Program" in** *Bellingham Business Journal* **(January 2007, pp. 4)**
Pub: Sun News Inc.
Description: Twelve-year-old business and leadership coaching company, The Champagne Group, is launching its new Manager Makeover Program. The five-step, customized program equips managers with techniques on becoming leaders who can resolve conflicts and increase performance.

28885 ■ **"The Easy Entree Expands Service to Accommodate Walk-In Customers" in** *Bellingham Business Journal* **(December 2006, pp. 2)**
Pub: Sun News Inc.
Description: Evelyn Turner, owner of The Easy Entree, has expanded her business to now offer a walk-in service for customers. Patrons can create their own entrees or pick up pre-made entrees to take home and cook or freeze.

28886 ■ **"The Individual Investor And The Power Of Research" in** *Wall Street Journal* **(Vol. 248, December 2006, No. 142, pp. S1)**
Pub: Dow Jones & Co. Inc.
Ed: Associated Press Description: Profile of UBS Wealth Management Research (WMR). WMR crafts strategic, actionable investment for UBS investor clients and their financial advisors. Statistical data included.

28887 ■ **"The 'IT' Factor" in** *Hispanic Business* **(November 2006, pp. 26, 28, 30)**
Pub: Hispanic Business
Ed: Keith Rosenblum. Description: Profile of Abba Tech, the New Mexico information technology firm that is competing with large companies through service and knowledge.

28888 ■ **"The Pantry Expands Presence" in** *Mississippi Business Journal* **(Vol. 29, January 2007, No. 2, pp. 8)**
Pub: Venture Publications, Inc.
Ed: Wally Northway Description: Eight convenience stores in Mississippi and Florida have been acquired by The Pantry Inc. Statistical data included.

28889 ■ **"The U.S. Commercial Service: www.export.gov/comm_svc" in** *Entrepreneur* **(Vol. 32, November 2004, No. 11, pp. 6)**
Pub: Entrepreneur Media Inc.
Ed: Steve Cooper. Description: U.S. Commercial Service offers global business solutions in the areas of market research, trade events to promote businesses and services, introductions between buyers and distributors, and export counseling.

28890 ■ **"They Want You" in** *Inc.* **(Volume 27, June 2005, No. 6, pp. 32)**
Pub: Inc. Magazine
Ed: Michelle Leder. Description: To encourage growth, states are offering incentives to court entrepreneurs.

28891 ■ **"Think Happy Thoughts" in** *My Business* **(September/October 2001, pp. 50)**
Pub: My Business Magazine
Ed: Harvey King. Description: The article offers the optimist words of the writer regarding the nation's economy, and one way to help it improve.

28892 ■ **"Think Tech; Automation Alley" in** *Crain's Detroit Business* **(Vol. 21, October 3, 2005, No. 43, pp. 1)**
Pub: Crain Communications Inc. - Detroit
Ed: Andrew Dietderich, Sheena Harrison. Description: Two technology companies are working to keep and attract technology companies and jobs to Southeastern Michigan. The state lost 17,600 tech jobs between 2002 and 2003. Automation Alley of Troy and Sparks of Ann Arbor hope to double the number of tech companies and triple the number of tech workers by 2010.

28893 ■ **"This Biz is Growing by Leaps and Bounds" in** *Small Business Opportunities* **(Vol. 16, November 2004, No. 6, pp. 90)**
Pub: Harris Publications Inc.
Description: Firehouse Subs has announced a new program, American Dream, that will convert its 30 corporate stores where managers can become equity partners or owners. The program provides financing.

28894 ■ **"This Just In" in** *Crain's Detroit Business* **(Vol. 16, No. 46, November 13, 2000, pp. 1)**
Pub: Crain Communications, Inc.
Ed: Katie Merx. Description: Various news items from Detroit-area businesses, including information about the Society of Automotive Engineers (SAE), service grants, Costco Wholesale Corporation, and Teligent Inc. Statistical data is included.

28895 ■ **"This Week: Raising the Roof at North Pier?" in** *Crain's Chicago Business* **(Vol. 29, December 2006, No. 51, pp. 1)**
Pub: Crain Communications, Inc.
Ed: Thomas A. Corfman. Description: Chicago developer, Dan McLean, has expanded a proposed partial residential conversion of the former North Pier terminal.

28896 ■ *301 Great Ideas for Using Technology to Grow Your Business*
Pub: Inc. Publishing
Ed: Phaedra Hise. Released: 1998. Price: $14.95.

28897 ■ "365-day forecast" in *Entrepreneur*
(Vol. 30, No. 1, January 2000)
Pub: Entrepreneur Media Inc.
Ed: Steve Cooper. **Description:** Various economic experts make forecasts and offer insight concerning the economic future during 2002.

28898 ■ "Three Scary Words: Buy it Used"
in *Inc.* **(September 2006, pp. 29-31)**
Pub: Gruner & Jahr USA Publishing
Ed: Max Chafkin. **Description:** Secondhand items have become more attractive to consumers. Internet auctions like eBay or listings on Crain's list have given rise to tremendous growth of these items. Manufacturers are rethinking their product life strategies as the consequences could be serious.

28899 ■ "Thrift: working at home or hardly
working?" in *Red Herring* **(January 2003, pp.**
67)
Pub: Herring Communications Inc.
Ed: Sarah Fallon. **Description:** According to a Forrester Research Report conducted by its IT consultancy, 15 percent of recession-affected consumers are more likely to purchase a laptop computer than those unaffected.

28900 ■ "Thrifts adrift? Mortgage slowdown
would hurt the industry" in *Barron's* **(Vol. 82,**
No. 59, February 24, 2003, pp. T6)
Pub: Barron's
Ed: Allison Krampf. **Description:** Mortgage rates are not expected to remain at 40-year lows much longer, and an increase in rates will likely adversely affect the stock prices of thrifts that finance home purchases. The effects that a change in the market will create are examined.

28901 ■ "Thriving Locally in the Global
Economy" in *Harvard Business Review* **(Vol.**
81, No. 8, August 2003, pp. 119)
Pub: Harvard Business School Press
Ed: Rosabeth Moss Kanter. **Description:** Economic development in five towns in the U.S. dispel the belief that globalization will adversely impact local communities.

28902 ■ "Tips for collecting performance
numbers" in *Crain's Detroit Business* **(Vol.**
19, No. 3, January 20, 2003, pp. 14)
Pub: Crain Communications Inc., Detroit
Description: Key indicators for checking small business performance are listed. It is advised that the indicators be reported regularly, and the use of software programs, called dashboard products, can help track performance numbers.

28903 ■ "To Fill A Widening Niche" in
Hispanic Business **(July/August 2002, pp. 36,**
38, 42, 44, 46, 48)
Pub: Hispanic Business
Ed: Description: The companies listed on the Hispanic Business Fastest-Growing 100 all rely on core competencies and specific niche markets to create growth, resulting in 62.6 percent per year. Statistics data included.

28904 ■ "To Join Or Not To Join? Trade
Groups Can Boost Business-If You Pick the
Right One" in *Black Enterprise* **(Vol. 34, No.**
3, October 2003)
Pub: Earl Graves Publishing Co.
Ed: Bridget McCrea. **Description:** Issues to keep in mind before joining a trade group are presented, including the ways trade groups provide networking opportunities for entrepreneurs to help grow a small business.

28905 ■ "To Manage Growth, Embrace
Change" in *Ingram's* **(Vol. 29, No. 7, July**
2003, pp. 24)
Pub: Show Me Publishing, Inc.
Ed: Bob Gould. **Description:** Guidance for companies looking to grow and retain the corporate vision while tapping into new talents is given.

28906 ■ "Too Much Too Soon?" in *Inc.*
(November 1, 2003)
Pub: Gruner & Jahr USA Publishing
Description: Perils of franchising are investigated.

28907 ■ "The Top 25" in *Entrepreneur* **(Vol.**
31, No. 10, October 2003, pp. 22)
Pub: Entrepreneur Media, Inc.
Description: The top 25 cities for entrepreneurs are ranked, with Las Vegas, Nevada leading the way for entrepreneurial activity and job growth.

28908 ■ "Top 25 Cities" in *Entrepreneur*
(Vol. 30, No, 10, October 2002, pp. 30)
Pub: Entrepreneur Media Inc.
Description: The top 25 cities to start or move an existing business to are listed, with Washington, DC ranking first with highest small-business growth.

28909 ■ "The Top 25 VC Firms of 2000" in
Red Herring **(No. 99, June 15 & July 1, 2001,**
pp. 68, 70)
Pub: Herring Communications
Ed: Kate McKinley. **Description:** Venture capital investments in the tech sector fell 41 percent from the third to fourth quarter 2000. A listing of the top 25 venture capital firms is presented, ranked by the average equi-return performance of their IPOs in 2000.

28910 ■ "Tough times force banks to own
other businesses" in *Crain's Detroit*
Business **(Vol. 18, No. 22, June 3, 2002, pp.**
1)
Pub: Crain Communications Inc. - Detroit
Ed: Katie Merx. **Description:** Faced with numerous turnaround and bankruptcy reorganizations, banks and corporate bondholders are left with equity stakes in businesses on the brink.

28911 ■ "Tower Automotive Plans to Cut
More Jobs, Close More Plants" in *Crain's*
Detroit Business **(Vol. 22, January 16, 2006,**
No. 4, pp.)
Pub: Crain Communications Inc. - Detroit
Ed: Greg Migliore. **Description:** Tower Automotive Inc. filed documents to emerge from Chapter 11 reorganization. The automotive supplier plans to reduce the number of North American plants from 24 to about 15.

28912 ■ "Toyota's Plans Get Suppliers
Worked Up; U.S. Expansion Drives Scramble
for Business" in *Crain's Detroit Business*
(Vol. 21)
Pub: Crain Communications Inc. - Detroit
Ed: Terry Kosdrosky. **Description:** Automotive suppliers are working to secure new contracts with Toyota Motor Manufacturing after it announced expansion plans.

28913 ■ "Tracking the Hispanic Traveler" in
Hispanic Business **(Vol. 23, No. 10, October,**
2001, pp. 40)
Pub: Hispanic Business
Ed: Derek Reveron. **Description:** Travel among Hispanics has increased 11 percent between 1997 and 1999, according to a survey by the Travel Industry Association (TIA), with future growth predicted. Much of the growth can be attributed to better marketing to reach the minority traveler through targeted advertising, minority travel guides, and special ethnic programs.

28914 ■ *Trading Places: SMEs in the Global*
Economy, A Critical Research Handbook
Pub: Edward Elgar Publishing, Incorporated
Ed: Lloyd-Reason. **Released:** September 2006.
Price: $110.00. **Description:** An overview of international research for small and medium-sized companies wishing to expand in the global economy.

28915 ■ "Trading Takes a Breather" in *Red*
Herring **(No. 105, October 1, 2001, pp. 30)**
Pub: Herring Communications
Ed: Elizabeth Lamb. **Description:** The volume of daily stock trading executed online during the second and third quarters has fallen, with about 5 percent of the 1.2 billion shares traded on the New York Stock Exchange (NYSE) being transacted through its wireless trading system. Statistical data included.

28916 ■ "Trends" in *E-business Advisor*
(Vol. 17, No. 12, December 1999, pp. 8)
Pub: Advisor Media, Inc.
Description: New business-to-business "e-market makers" are "reintermediaries" that enter supply chains and introduce new efficiencies and ways of buying and selling products and services. According to Dataquest, a unit of Gartner Group Inc., an e-market maker is an organization that develops a business-to-business, Internet Protocol (IP) network-based e-marketplace of buyers and sellers within a particular industry, geographic region, or affinity group.

28917 ■ "Trickle Up: Small Companies
Slowly Build Momentum in the Job Market"
in *Wall Street Journal* **(December 4, 2003, pp.**
A1)
Pub: Dow Jones & Co. Inc.
Ed: Clare Ansberry. **Description:** As the economy improves, more small companies are hiring new employees, health care and construction sectors are improving.

28918 ■ "Trouble Ahead For Stocks" in
Fortune **(Vol. 151, February 21, 2005, No. 4,**
pp. 124)
Pub: Time Inc.
Ed: David Stires. **Description:** Major U.S. equity indexes finished negative in January 2005, however Wall Street is expecting high single-digits gains for the year.

28919 ■ "The Trouble With Lifestyle
Entrepreneurs" in *Inc.* **(Volume 27, July 2005,**
No. 7, pp. 21-23)
Pub: Inc. Magazine
Ed: Daniel McGinn. **Description:** New Zealand business owners are able to enjoy a work-life balance, but this trend is becoming a national crisis. American entrepreneurs can take note that growing a business in the U.S. requires a fast-paced, stressed lifestyle. The American economy is fueled by small business.

28920 ■ "Troy plan draws interest from big-
name developers" in *Crain's Detroit*
Business **(Vol. 19, No. 9, March 3, 2003, pp.**
3)
Pub: Crain Communications Inc., Detroit
Ed: Andrew Dietderich. **Description:** Plans for a proposed 500-room hotel and 200,000 square foot convention center at I-75 and Big Beaver Road in Troy is drawing attention from major real estate developers.

28921 ■ *True to Yourself: Leading a Values-*
Based Business
Pub: Berrett-Koehler Publishers, Incorporated
Ed: Mark S. Albion. **Released:** June 2006. **Price:**
$14.95. **Description:** Pressures faced by entrepreneurs running small companies are discussed. Advice is offered to help grow and maintain a profitable business.

28922 ■ "Tulsa-based SpiritBank
Reconsiders Future of Branching" in *Journal*
Record (Oklahoma City, OK) **(February 8,**
2007)
Pub: Journal Record
Ed: Kirby Lee Davis. **Description:** SpiritBank will not add any new branches to its banking system in 2007. Details are discussed with chief executive, Albert Kelly.

28923 ■ "Tulsa Home Sales See Another
Record Year" in *Journal Record (Oklahoma*
City, OK) **(February 1, 2007)**
Pub: Journal Record
Ed: Kirby Lee Davis. **Description:** Greater Tulsa Association of Realtors reported record years in 2005 and 2006; they expect to see continuing growth in 2007.

28924 ■ "Turn Customer Input into
Innovation" in *Harvard Business Review*
(Vol. 80, No. 1, January 2002, pp. 91)
Pub: Harvard Business School Press
Ed: Anthony W. Ulwick. **Description:** A new methodology is proposed for more effectively capturing cus-

tomer input for new products and services that should minimize failure when the product or service is introduced. Previous methods often failed to correctly understand customer feedback.

28925 ■ **"The Turning of Atlanta" in** *Harvard Business Review* **(Vol. 81, No. 12, December 2003, pp. 18)**
Pub: Harvard Business School Press
Description: Atlanta, Georgia Mayor Shirley Franklin addresses questions regarding layoffs and work performance, prioritization, maintaining communication with the public, measurement of achievement, and remaining challenges for the city.

28926 ■ **"Turning South; Sterling Heights Pushes Redevelopment of Older Areas as Vacant Land Dries Up" in** *Crain's Detroit Business* **(Vol. 21)**
Pub: Crain Communications Inc. - Detroit
Ed: Anjali Fluker. **Description:** Many areas in the city of Sterling Heights, Michigan are zoned for mixed-use projects. The city is seeking developers to renovate vacant sites to bring a lifestyle center that combines retail, commercial and residential space.

28927 ■ **"Two projects worth $27M planned for Royal Oak" in** *Crain's Detroit Business* **(Vol. 19, No. 16, April 21, 2003, pp. 3)**
Pub: Crain Communications Inc., Detroit
Ed: Andrew Dietderich. **Description:** Two new development projects for the city of Royal Oak, Michigan will be worth nearly $27 million. The sites combined will bring 72 new residential units, nearly 20,000 square feet of office space, and nearly 200 public parking spots in the downtown area.

28928 ■ **"Two Growing Hispanic Radio Companies Broadcast Expansion Plans" in** *Hispanic Business* **(October 2006, pp. 16)**
Pub: Hispanic Business
Description: Border Media Partners purchased two CBS-owned radio stations in San Antonio, Texas. Details of the transaction are included.

28929 ■ **"$200 million is key to riverfront plan" in** *Crain's Detroit Business* **(Vol. 18, No. 50, December 16, 2002, pp. 1)**
Pub: Crain Communications Inc., Detroit
Ed: Robert Ankeny. **Description:** Future plans for the Detroit riverfront are presented. Statistical data included.

28930 ■ **"Two $10,000 Questions for Small Business" in** *The New York Times* **(November 12, 2000, pp. BU14)**
Pub: The New York Times Company
Ed: Mickey Meece. **Description:** A survey conducted by Willard & Shullman on the financial status of small businesses.

28931 ■ **"2002 BE Banks" in** *Black Enterprise* **(Vol. 33, No. 6, January 2003, pp. 24)**
Pub: Earl Graves Publishing Co.
Ed: Alan Hughes. **Description:** Harbor Bankshares Corporation, parent company of The Harbor Bank of Maryland, had formed two new subsidiaries designed to spur economic development in the greater Baltimore-Washington DC metropolitan area.

28932 ■ **"Two Views on 2003" in** *Rough Notes* **(Vol. 145, No. 1, January 2003, pp. 204)**
Pub: Rough Notes
Ed: Samuel Schiff. **Description:** The Conning Research and Consulting's Jack Gohsler believes the insurance industry's outlook will improve slightly in 2003. Dr. Robert Hartwig of the Insurance Information Institute says that credit information will now be used in insurance underwriting.

28933 ■ **"Tying a Lucrative Knot - WeddingNetwork.com sits on the brink of database-sharing bliss" in** *PC Magazine* **(February 20, 2001, pp. 17a)**
Pub: Ziff-Davis Publishing Company
Ed: Judy DeYoung. **Description:** WeddingNetwork. com, a Web site that has sold wedding products and services since 1998, had to reinvent its business model when sales proved slow and developed extensive personalization capabilities.

28934 ■ **"The Ultimate 12-Step in Business" in** *Fast Company* **(August 2001, pp. 196)**
Pub: Fast Company
Description: A tutorial for the twelve steps needed to return to the old economy are highlighted.

28935 ■ *Ultimate Homebased Business Handbook: How to Start, Run, and Grow Your Own Profitable Business*
Pub: Entrepreneur Press
Ed: James Stephenson. **Released:** July 2004. **Price:** $23.95 (US), $34.95 (Canadian). **Description:** Detailed information for anyone wanting to start a home-based business. Topics include how-to tips, ideas, tools, and print and online resources.

28936 ■ **"Understanding Women is Key to Biz Success, Author Says" in** *Crain's Detroit Business* **(Vol. 22, November 20, 2006, No. 47, pp. 6)**
Pub: Crain Communications Inc. - Detroit
Ed: Bill Shea. **Description:** Successful companies recognize that women make 80% of all buying decisions. Author also has advice for women-owned businesses with trend and specifics provided.

28937 ■ **"Unemployment higher in 2002, but rate of job loss slowed" in** *Crain's Detroit Business* **(Vol. 19, No. 9, March 3, 2003, pp. 1)**
Pub: Crain Communications Inc., Detroit
Ed: Amy Lane. **Description:** Unemployment rates rose in the Detroit area from half a percentage point in Washtenaw County to 1.1 point in Wayne County according to data from the Michigan Department of Career Development.

28938 ■ **"U.S. Exports in 2007" in** *Kiplinger Letter* **(Vol. 78, January 5, 2007, No. 1)**
Pub: Kiplinger
Description: U.S. export growth is expected to drop by nearly 5 percent in 2007, reflective of slow growth in countries such as Canada, Mexico, parts of Europe, China, Japan, and South Korea.

28939 ■ **"The U.S. Is In Decline-And That's a Good Thing" in** *Fortune* **(Vol. 151, February 21, 2005, No. 4, pp. 58)**
Pub: Time Inc.
Ed: Geoffrey Colvin. **Description:** Reasons for America's declining economy in the global market is examined. Statistical data included.

28940 ■ **"UnitedAuto seeks $250M for more acquisitions" in** *Crain's Detroit Business* **(Vol. 16, No. 50, December 11, 2000, pp. 4)**
Pub: Crain Communications, Inc.
Ed: Jim Henry. **Description:** UnitedAuto Group Inc. is quietly positioning itself for a round of car dealership Pac-Man. The Detroit-based dealership group operates more than 100 dealerships.

28941 ■ **"Unleash the Power of Leasing" in** *Success* **(Vol. 47, No. 4, September 2000, pp. 76)**
Pub: Success Publishing, Inc.
Ed: Tara Baukus Mello. **Description:** Leasing has a whole new twist, it can help stretch finances, reward employees, and find money to grow a business.

28942 ■ **"Unselfish Teamwork Helps Gibson Insurance Agency Grow" in** *Rough Notes* **(Vol. 146, No. 9, September 2003, pp. 18)**
Pub: Rough Notes
Ed: Dennis H. Pillsbury. **Description:** Profile of Gibson Insurance Agency; topics include teamwork, management styles, and market share.

28943 ■ **"Up in the Air: Dotcom Stocks Could be Poised for a Comeback" in** *Entrepreneur* **(Vol. 31, No. 10, October 2003, pp. 38)**
Pub: Entrepreneur Media, Inc.
Ed: Julie Monahan. **Description:** Internet stocks seem to be climbing out of the dotcom doldrums; the first half 2003 showed the first real gains in three years.

28944 ■ **"Up Front: Thinking Outside the Box" in** *My Business* **(April/May 2003, pp. 8-9)**
Pub: My Business Magazine
Ed: Kathleen Landis. **Description:** One of the best ways to build a business is to ask clients for referrals; author Maribeth Kuzmeski, business consultant and author refers to client referrals as "strategic alliances", which allow two companies to create an advantage over competitors.

28945 ■ **"Up To the Challenge" in** *Entrepreneur.com* **(Vol. 34, February 2006, No. 2, pp. 64)**
Pub: Entrepreneur Media Inc.
Ed: Mark Henricks. **Description:** Three company founders discuss the obstacles that prevented them from reaching the next level of business. The companies represent three different industries at three different sales levels.

28946 ■ **"Uplifting" in** *Pittsburgh Business Times* **(Vol. 23, No. 5, August 22, 2003, pp. 1)**
Pub: Pittsburgh Business Times
Ed: Christopher Davis. **Description:** Rock Ferrone, owner of Rockpointe Business Airpark, is planning a $10 million expansion of the airport's runway. The small airport, located in West Deer Township, Pennsylvania, may also become the new home of a large, unspecified firm.

28947 ■ **"Urban Renewal May Hire Contractor to Evaluate Skirvin Proposals" in** *Journal Record* **(June 24, 2003)**
Pub: Dolan Media Company
Ed: Matt Maile. **Description:** Five developers have stepped forward with offers to reopen the Skirvin as a hotel or residential development. The Oklahoma City Urban Renewal Authority may hire an independent consultant to evaluate proposals for the site.

28948 ■ **"An Urban Survivor Poised for Better Times" in** *Crain's Chicago Business* **(Vol. 26, No. 50, December 15, 2003, pp. 8)**
Pub: Crain Communications, Inc.
Ed: Joe Cappo. **Description:** A new study conducted by CEOs for Cities, reports that large urban cities like Chicago, Illinois are seeing a new economic success rate because these cities are becoming more diverse. The study was based on five categories, such as educational levels of the population, diversity and specialties of businesses, population and per-capita income growth, and property values.

28949 ■ **"The Urge to Merge" in** *Black Enterprise* **(Vol. 35, August 2004, No. 1, pp. 50)**
Pub: Earl G. Graves Publishing Co. Inc.
Ed: Bridget McCrea. **Description:** According to a recent survey, 20 percent of more than 400 CEOs of high-growth small businesses plan to use mergers and acquisitions to generate new business growth.

28950 ■ **"The Urge to Merge" in** *Fortune* **(Vol. 151, February 21, 2005, No. 4, pp. 21)**
Pub: Time Inc.
Ed: Shawn Tully. **Description:** Corporate American has launched new mergers after three years of avoiding new deals. Forty-eight new deals equaling $1 billion or more were announced between November 2004 and January 2005. Experts warn that historically, big deals produce twice as many failures as winners.

28951 ■ **"U.S." in** *Business Week* **(February 20, 2006, No. 3972, pp. 29)**
Pub: McGraw-Hill Companies
Ed: James C. Cooper. **Description:** The question is asked: When should U.S. lawmakers and investors start to worry about the inflation implications of tight labor markets? Statistical data included.

28952 ■ **"U.S.: The Fed: Trying To Shift Into Neutral" in** *Business Week* **(February 14, 2005, No. 3920, pp. 23)**
Pub: McGraw-Hill Companies
Ed: James C. Cooper, Kathleen Madigan. **Description:** The Federal Reserve raised interest rates on February 2, 2005, hiking rates by a quarter-point at each of the next three meetings scheduled for the first half of the year. Two questions the Fed will also need to confront on monetary policy are discussed.

28953 ■ "Utilities Boost Companies; Utility Services" in *Crain's New York Business* (Vol. 22, November 13, 2006, No. 46, pp. 36)
Pub: Crain Communications, Inc.
Description: Listing of companies that provide utility programs, incentives and benefits to small businesses looking to relocate within the five boroughs of New York City or expand their businesses in the area.

28954 ■ "Vacancy Squeeze" in *San Fernando Valley Business Journal* (Vol. 12, January 2007, No. 2, pp. 32)
Pub: San Fernando Valley Business Journal Associates
Ed: Shelly Garcia. Description: San Fernando Valley office vacancy rates continued to fall in the fourth quarter of the year. This is causing an increase in rents for most submarkets.

28955 ■ "The Value of Networking" in *Home Business* (Vol. 13, January/February 2006, No. 1, pp. 42, 44-45)
Pub: Home Business Magazine
Ed: Christopher J. Bachler. Description: Networking skills to market and grow a business, including a list of prospects, are discussed.

28956 ■ "Vancouver Vanguard" in *Fast Company* (September 2001, pp. 36)
Pub: Fast Company
Description: Fast Company's Heath Row will embark on the third-annual CoF Roadshow through North America. While spending time in Vancouver, British Columbia, Canada, Row will address ways Canada is competing in the global market.

28957 ■ "VC Company to Double One Fund, Add $40M Fund." in *Crain's Detroit Business* (Vol. 23, January 15,2007, No. 3, pp. 26)
Pub: Crain Communications Inc. - Detroit
Ed: Tom Henderson. Description: Local Venture Capital firm adds personnel and expands funds to increase business. First fund is doubled to $20M and began raising money for a second fund of $40M.

28958 ■ "VC Whispers: Glowing optimism" in *Red Herring* (No. 103, September 1, 2001, pp. 78)
Pub: Herring Communications
Ed: Lawrence Aragon. Description: Despite the fact that venture deals in energy-related companies have slowed, venture capitalists predict a bright future for the sector. Statistical data included.

28959 ■ "VCs Born in the Bubble Start To Go Pop!" in *Venture Capital Journal* (Vol. 42, No. 10, October 2002, pp. 14, 16)
Pub: Thomas Venture Economics
Ed: Michael V. Copeland. Description: It is estimated that new firms launched two years ago could shrink by one-third. Four first-time venture funds raised during the Internet bubble have stopped doing business, which include Seattle-based Incepta a Bechtel Enterprises Holdings-backed firm; New York City firms Starting-Point Venture Partners and Metropolis Venture Partners; and White Plains, New York iCentennial Ventures.

28960 ■ "Veltri, Edgcomb to close Macomb plants" in *Crain's Detroit Business* (Vol. 19, No. 15, April 14, 2003, pp. 30)
Pub: Crain Communications Inc., Detroit
Ed: Terry Kosdrosky. Description: Veltri Metal Products Inc. and Edgcomb Metals Company, both located in Macomb County, Michigan will close their plants. The closing will add 149 to the unemployment list in Michigan.

28961 ■ "Venture-backed IPOs Rebound from Q2 Slump" in *Venture Capital Journal* (Vol. 40, No. 10, November 2000, pp. 10, 12, 14)
Pub: Venture Economics
Description: Venture-backed companies raised more than $7.57 billion in the third quarter of 2000. Statistical data included.

28962 ■ "Venture Capital: First-round investments: now for the small and the brave" in *Red Herring* (No. 105, October 1, 2001, pp. 38-39)
Pub: Herring Communications
Ed: Lawrence Aragon, Julie Landry. Description: Venture capitalists are taking more time before investing in new investments and spending more time trying to raise follow-on rounds for their existing companies. Statistical data included.

28963 ■ "Venture-capital investing fell to five-year low in 1st quarter" in *Wall Street Journal* (April 29, 2003, pp. C5)
Pub: Dow Jones & Co. Inc.
Ed: Ann Grimes. Description: According to the MoneyTree Survey prepared by National Venture Capital Association, Thomson Venture Economics and PricewaterhouseCoopers, venture capital investing fell to a five year low in first quarter 2003.

28964 ■ "Venture Michigan Makes First Investment Commitments" in *Crain's Detroit Business* (Vol. 23, January 29, 2007, No. 5, pp. 17)
Pub: Crain Communications Inc. - Detroit
Ed: Amy Lane. Description: First investment commitments to smaller venture capital fund providers is made by state venture group. Investments are in capital funds that support start-up firms with a Michigan presence that engage in new product development, research, and technology in non-manufacturing sectors.

28965 ■ "Ventures' valuations decline" in *Wall Street Journal* (June 3, 2003, pp. C5)
Pub: Dow Jones & Co. Inc.
Description: Profile of venture-capital backed companies is presented.

28966 ■ "Venturing Forward?" in *Boston Business Journal* (Vol. 23, No. 33, September 19, 2003, pp. 40)
Pub: American City Business Journals
Ed: Edward Mason. Description: Business for venture capital companies is returning after a long dry spell since the stock market crash of 2000. Boston Millennia Partners has recently made four deals.

28967 ■ "Verizon Told to Widen Service" in *The Record* (November 17, 2005)
Pub: New Jersey Media Group
Ed: Martha McKay. Description: New Jersey legislation required Verizon to build its new high-speed fiber network in all 526 towns where the company currently offers phone service.

28968 ■ "Visteon's new HQ to start rising in April" in *Crain's Detroit Business* (Vol. 19, No. 7, February 17, 2003, pp. 23)
Pub: Crain Communications Inc., Detroit
Ed: Jennette Smith, Terry Kosdrosky. Description: The new headquarters for Visteon Corporation will begin construction in April 2003. The new site is located in Van Buren Township, Michigan.

28969 ■ "Voters will be asked to expand industrial park" in *Atlanta Business Chronicle* (Vol. 25, January 10, 2003, No. 31, pp. 4A)
Pub: American City Business Publications, Inc.
Ed: Charles E. Arnold. Description: Voters will be asked to vote on a 1-cent special local sales tax that will finance the preparation of a proposed $29.4 million, 842-acre industrial park expansion in Spalding County, Georgia. The expansion entails adding to an existing park ($21.7 million/652 acres) and creating another ($7.7. million/190 acres).

28970 ■ "Waking Up IBM: How a Gang of Unlikely Rebels Transformed Big Blue" in *Harvard Business Review* (Vol. 78, No. 4, July 2000, pp. 137)
Pub: Harvard Business School Publishing Corp.
Ed: Gary Hamel. Description: The article reviews how IBM avoided insolvency by introducing new ideas for business development.

28971 ■ "Wal-Mart Said to Be Weighing Bid for Massachusetts-Based BJ's Wholesale Club" in *Boston Globe* (April 11, 2003)
Pub: Knight-Ridder/Tribune Business News
Ed: Chris Reidy. Description: Wal-Mart Stores Inc. is considering a bid to purchase BJ's Wholesale Club Inc., located in Natick, Massachusetts. The chain operates about 140 club stores with sales of nearly $5.9 billion in 2002.

28972 ■ "Wanted: stimulus: report says GOP is not doing all it can for small business" in *Black Enterprise* (Vol. 33, No. 7, Feb. 2003)
Pub: Earl Graves Publishing Co.
Ed: Joyce Jones. Description: Federal funding and legislation important to small business is discussed.

28973 ■ "War Earnings" in *Forbes* (Vol. 175, January 10, 2005, No. 1, pp. 140)
Pub: Forbes Magazine Inc.
Ed: David Serchuk. Description: Profile of Perini Corporation, the company rebuilding power stations in Iraq and installing new military bases in Afghanistan. The firm has seen revenues grow 71.2 percent in the last year and average three-year earnings-per-share is up 63.7 percent.

28974 ■ "War takes toll on local economy" in *Crain's Detroit Business* (Vol. 19, No. 14, April 7, 2003, pp. 39)
Pub: Crain Communications Inc., Detroit
Ed: Katie Merx. Description: Local economists report that the war is depressing the already soft economy in southeast Michigan, but report good news amid all of the gloom.

28975 ■ "Watching baby grow" in *WorkingWoman* (Vol. 25, No. 4, April 2000, pp. 32)
Pub: Lang Communications Inc.
Ed: Eilene Zimmerman. Description: Advice is given to O. Robin Sweet, founder of Well Fed Baby.

28976 ■ "Waterfront, Airport on Top of List For Port" in *Bellingham Business Journal* (January 2007, pp. B5)
Pub: Sun News Inc.
Ed: Dan Hiestand. Description: New Whatcom redevelopment for the former Georgia-Pacific waterfront property is in the works. The city and port have been working to create a cohesive plan for the site. Sixty-eight percent of the property leaves ownership in the public's hands.

28977 ■ "We, the entrepreneurs" in *Entrepreneur* (Vol. 30, No. 2, February 2002, pp. 8)
Pub: Entrepreneur Media Inc.
Ed: Rieva Lesonsky. Description: A discussion on the role entrepreneurs play in the United States economy.

28978 ■ "Weathering the Storm; True, things have been better for the nation's entrepreneurs" in *Business Week Online* (November 18, 2002)
Pub: McGraw-Hill Inc.
Ed: Alison Ogden. Description: According to a new survey conducted by the National Federation of Independent Businesses, small businesses are holding their own in the slow economy, and have defied the uncertain trends from the threats of terrorism and corporate scandals.

28979 ■ "Websites and Beyond" in *Entrepreneur* (Vol. 33, October 2005, No. 10, pp. 42)
Pub: Entrepreneur Media Inc.
Description: Five tips for choosing a Web solutions provider to help grow a business are listed.

28980 ■ "Webvan, Microsoft, and the second-mover advantage" in *Red Herring* (No. 102, August 15, 2001, pp. 100)
Pub: Herring Communications
Ed: Jason Pontin. Description: Discussion regarding the second-mover advantage. The rule of the second-

mover advantage states that, market dominance rarely goes to the pluck startup that first releases a product, but to the second company, sometimes an established business, that most effectively markets and sells the products, and which then gives the best customer service.

28981 ■ **"West Dearborn Rising"** in *Crain's Detroit Business* **(Vol. 21, October 31, 2005, No. 44, pp. 11)**
Pub: Crain Communications Inc. - Detroit
Ed: Brent Snavely. **Description:** In the past three years, the City of Dearborn has emerged as a thriving entertainment district. New restaurants, sports bars and clubs have city officials developing plans to expand parking.

28982 ■ **"West L.A. CPA Firm Opening Valley Office"** in *San Fernando Valley Business Journal* **(Vol. 11, December 2006, No. 25, pp. 1)**
Pub: San Fernando Valley Business Journal Associates
Ed: Shelly Garcia. **Description:** Singer Lewak Greenbaum & Goldstein LLP will open a Warner Center office in hopes of keeping workers in what has become a fiercely competitive employment market and capturing larger ground in the growing financial services market.

28983 ■ **"Western Airlines Announces Inaugural Flight Schedule"** in *Bellingham Business Journal* **(January 2006, pp. A5)**
Pub: Sun News Inc.
Description: Western Airlines begins direct-flight service between Bellingham International Airport and four West Coast cities. This will double the number of destination sites for flying out of Bellingham.

28984 ■ **"What Ales You?"** in *Entrepreneur.com* **(Vol. 34, February 2006, No. 2, pp. 73)**
Pub: Entrepreneur Media Inc.
Ed: John W. Ellis IV. **Description:** Profile of Vic Gumper and Daniel Rogers, expert microbrewers and owners of Lanesplitter Pizza & Pub in California. The partners attribute their success to the 20 unique brews offered on their menu.

28985 ■ **"What Drives Inspiration?"** in *Entrepreneur* **(Vol. 32, October 2004, No. 10, pp. 22)**
Pub: Entrepreneur Media Inc.
Description: Tips to help entrepreneurs to be creative and successful are featured.

28986 ■ **"What Goes Up: Now There's a New Way to Track Small Business's Ups and Downs"** in *Entrepreneur* **(Vol. 32, No. 1, January 2004, pp. 30)**
Pub: Entrepreneur Media, Inc.
Description: The Small Business Index (SBI) will help entrepreneurs track 19 economic indicators affecting small businesses. The indicators are grouped in four categories: costs factors, credit conditions, industry metrics, and trade competitiveness.

28987 ■ **"What It Takes to be a Successful Intrapreneur"** in *Black Enterprise* **(Vol. 36, December 2005, No. 5, pp.)**
Pub: Earl G. Graves Publishing Co. Inc.
Ed: Nicole Marie Richardson. **Description:** Enterprising and innovative corporate professionals are being called intrapreneurs, or corporate entrepreneurship and corporate renewal professionals.

28988 ■ **"What I've Learned About Women"** in *Marketing to Women* **(Vol. 19, November 2006, No. 1, pp. 2)**
Pub: EPM Communications, Inc.
Ed: Lisa Finn. **Description:** Over the years the women's marketing landscape has changed a great deal. Companies are more open to testing their ideas and doing research and women are helping marketers do their job better by expressing their opinions to companies.

28989 ■ **"What Office?"** in *Entrepreneur* **(Vol. 33, October 2005, No. 10, pp. 94)**
Pub: Entrepreneur Media Inc.
Ed: Nichole L. Torres. **Description:** Building a virtual network of employees who communicate via phone, email and fax could be just the ticket to higher profits and business growth.

28990 ■ **"What Should I Do? Last Year's Poor Performance Can Push This Year's Quotas Higher"** in *Sales & Marketing Management*
Pub: VNU Business Media
Description: Strategies to pacify a sales team faced with higher quotas are presented.

28991 ■ **"What the Titans Can Teach Us"** in *Harvard Business Review* **(Vol. 79, No. 11, December 2001, pp. 70)**
Pub: Harvard Business School Press
Ed: Richard S. Tedlow. **Description:** Profile of legendary leaders of American business such as Andrew Carnegie, Henry Ford and Sam Walton of Wal-Mart. While some of their traits should not be emulated, the author argues that we can all learn from them. These people had the courage to bet on their vision of market potential, they shaped their vision into a mission for the company and they delivered more than they promised.

28992 ■ **"What Took You So Long To Call?"** in *Fast Company* **(November 2001, pp. 165)**
Pub: Fast Company
Ed: George Anders. **Description:** Profile of Internet telephony, and the ways it is transforming the business market.

28993 ■ **"What Women Want at Work"** in *Marketing to Women* **(Vol. 20, January 2007, No. 1, pp. 5)**
Pub: EPM Communications, Inc.
Description: Men and women at different ages want different things from their workplace. According to a study by The American Business Collaboration, employers may want to factor in these differences when trying to attract and retain top female talent.

28994 ■ **"What's Brewing at Starbucks?"** in *Black Enterprise* **(Vol. 35, August 2004, No. 1, pp. 25)**
Pub: Earl G. Graves Publishing Co. Inc.
Ed: Ann Brown. **Description:** Starbucks Coffee Company is using entertainment as a vehicle to take the company to the next level. Starbucks acquired the music company Hear-Music in 1999 and is offering five songs for $6.99 with the purchase of any beverage.

28995 ■ **"What's Next"** in *Inc.* **(Volume 27, March 2005, No. 3, pp. 59-60)**
Pub: Inc. Magazine
Ed: David H. Freedman. **Description:** High tech companies expand in pieces and turn fast-growth units into stand-alone entities. Tips to develop a successful fractural approach to business growth are shared.

28996 ■ **"What's Next for The Internet"** in *Venture Capital Journal* **(July 1, 2003)**
Pub: Thomson Financial Inc.
Description: The future of the Internet is discussed. The value of the Philadelphia Internet Index has doubled since late 2002. One industry expert estimates that so far, the Internet revolution is less than 3 percent complete.

28997 ■ **"When company values backfire"** in *Harvard Business Review* **(Vol. 80, No. 11, November 2002, pp. 18)**
Pub: Harvard Business School Press
Ed: Amy C. Edmondson. **Description:** Ways the CEO of a company attempted to promote strong values but had his intentions misinterpreted by employees is described. The staff considered his decision to grow the company to be motivated by greed. The author advises leaders to work diligently to invite discussion and seek honest feedback.

28998 ■ **"When a turnaround stalls"** in *Harvard Business Review* **(Vol. 80, No. 2, February 2002, pp. 45)**
Pub: Harvard Business School Press
Ed: Robert A.F. Reisner. **Description:** An investigation into the story of how the U.S. Postal Service transformed itself into a competitive business and holds lessons for any company attempting to keep a change initiative form failing.

28999 ■ **"Where Are You Going?"** in *My Business* **(April/May 2003, pp. 46)**
Pub: My Business Magazine
Ed: Karen J. Bannan. **Description:** Business visions require identifying a target market, as well as the services and products a small business intends to supply.

29000 ■ **"Where to Find Business Answers; Advice and Education"** in *Crain's New York Business* **(Vol. 22, November 13, 2006, No. 46, pp. 24)**
Pub: Crain Communications, Inc.
Description: Listing of organizations and agencies that provide training, financial and managerial advice, and technical expertise to current or would-be business owners.

29001 ■ **"Where Have the Leaders Gone?"** in *Ingram's* **(Vol. 29, No. 1, January 2003, pp. 4)**
Pub: Show Me Publishing, Inc.
Ed: J. Sweney. **Description:** The policy of Mayor Kay Barnes' investment in buildings and facilities is questioned. Ideas on issues involving infrastructure and leadership for Kansas City, Missouri are also discussed.

29002 ■ **"Where the Jobs Are"** in *Black Enterprise* **(Vol. 32, No. 7, February 2002, pp. 95)**
Pub: Earl Graves Publishing Co.
Ed: Winifred DeSouza, Sonya A. Donaldson. **Description:** The article predicts that although the economy appears bleak and jobs seem scarce, over the next six years, 5.8 million employment opportunities will be open in several fields nationwide. Statistical data included.

29003 ■ *Where to Make Money: A Rating Guide to Opportunities in America's Metro Areas*
Pub: Prometheus Books
Ed: G. Scott Thomas. **Released:** 1993. **Price:** $38.95; $20.95 (paper). **Description:** Ranks the 73 largest metropolitan areas in the U.S. according to the economic opportunities they offer. Includes information on unemployment rates, local employment by sectors, housing prices, growth potential, business opportunities, and openness to women and minorities.

29004 ■ **"Where's the Beef? Has Your Business Lost Momentum?"** in *Entrepreneur* **(Vol. 31, No. 11, November 2003, pp. 92)**
Pub: Entrepreneur Media, Inc.
Ed: Chris Penttila. **Description:** Many small businesses have the opportunity to beat larger companies because of the maneuverability of being small, but many times entrepreneurs 'sacred cows' prevent them from acting fast.

29005 ■ **"Who has the next big idea?"** in *Fast Company* **(September 2001, pp. 108)**
Pub: Fast Company
Ed: Daniel H. Pink. **Description:** Michael Hammer, consultant, author, evangelical business revolutionary, unleashed re-engineering on an unsuspecting public in the early 1990s, now he's back with a new book, a new agenda, and a bunch of new ideas.

29006 ■ **"Who's Working in Our Interest"** in *Crain's Detroit Business* **(Vol. 23, January 15, 2007, No. 3, pp. 8)**
Pub: Crain Communications Inc. - Detroit
Ed: Christopher Crain. **Description:** Northwest loses bid for direct flight to Shanghai; $200M business potential lost. Decision may have adverse affect on expansion and growth in the Chinese market for local businesses.

29007 ■ "Why Kansas City Needs a New Downtown Arena" in *Ingram's* (Vol. 29, No. 1, January 2003, pp. 15)
Pub: Show Me Publishing, Inc.
Ed: William R. Worley. **Description:** Bill Worley, chairman of Kingston Environmental, explains why Kansas City, Missouri needs a new downtown area, despite objections from others.

29008 ■ "Why Small Business is Important" in *Bellingham Business Journal* (January 2007, pp. 1)
Pub: Sun News Inc.
Description: While large companies are facing cutbacks, small businesses are becoming the job creation machine of the future. Small companies have the benefits of being flexible while enjoying the increased economies of scale from the industry as a whole.

29009 ■ "Why the Street Isn't Hip to Electronic Arts' Game" in *Fortune* (Vol. 151, February 21, 2005, No. 4, pp. 53)
Pub: Time Inc.
Ed: Andy Serwer. **Description:** Electronic Arts stock has tripled in the last five years. As the world's largest video game publisher for computers and handheld devices, the company has produced Madden football, the Sims, and Need for Speed, with market share of 57.5 percent in North America.

29010 ■ "A Wild Ride: The Twists and Turns of Running Your Own Business Can Throw You for a Loop" in *Entrepreneur* (Vol. 31, October 2003)
Pub: Entrepreneur Media, Inc.
Ed: Romanus Wolter. **Description:** Four tips to get a small business back on track are presented.

29011 ■ "Will disruptive innovations cure health care?" in *Harvard Business Review* (Vol. 78, No. 5, September-October 2000, pp. 102)
Pub: Harvard Business School Publishing Corp.
Ed: John Richard, Clayton M. Kenagy, Christensen Bohmer. **Description:** This article discusses the need for "disruptive" technological innovations in the health care industry. The authors argue that technology that ultimately improves an industry will at first be disruptive and appear to threaten the profits of companies in the industry. Graphs are included.

29012 ■ "'Will He Be a Friend or Foe?'" in *Fortune* (Vol. 142, No. 11, November 13, 2000, pp. F384V+)
Pub: Time Inc.
Ed: Jay Branegan. **Description:** Both Vice President Al Gore and Texas Governor George W. Bush favor small business' contribution to growth, jobs and innovation, making small business a winner no matter which candidate wins the election.

29013 ■ "Williams-Sonoma Tries a New Recipe: Pottery Barn Kids is a hit" in *Business Week* (May 6, 2002, pp. 36)
Pub: McGraw-Hill Inc.
Ed: Louise Lee. **Description:** Profile of the San Francisco-based specialty retailer that is aggressively pushing into new retail sectors including the kids market and a furniture catalog.

29014 ■ "Wine country's pinot push is bearing fruit" in *San Francisco Business Times* (Vol. 16, No. 43, May 31, 2002, pp. 3)
Pub: San Francisco Business Times Inc.
Ed: Meg Walker. **Description:** Shipments of California pinot noir wines increased from $132 million in 2000 to $200 million in 2001. Success for the industry and marketing of the wine is discussed.

29015 ■ "Winston-Salem, N.C. Area Attracts $567 Million in Venture Capital" in *Winston-Salem Journal* (April 11, 2003)
Pub: Knight-Ridder/Tribune Business News
Ed: Kristi E. Swartz. **Description:** Local investments in the Winston-Salem area helped place North Carolina in the ninth spot for venture capital investments nationally, according to a report by the Council for Entrepreneurial Development.

29016 ■ "Wired Right: Ian Kery Is Ready To Take Freeman's New Electrical Division To the West Coast and Beyond" in *Tradeshow Week* (Vol. 34)
Pub: Reed Business Information
Ed: Heidi Genoist. **Description:** An interview with Ian Kery, owner of Toronto, Canada's largest electrical firm. Kery is selling that firm and moving to Anaheim, California to launch its West Coast Electrical Division. Kery provides tradeshow electrical services.

29017 ■ "Wireless Poised to Explode, but Problems Remain, Panel Says" in *Daily Camera* (April 11, 2003)
Pub: Knight-Ridder/Tribune Business News
Ed: Erika Stutzman. **Description:** The future of wireless technology is discussed.

29018 ■ "Wisconsin Economic Development Programs Could be Hurt by Tax Fight" in *Milwaukee Journal Sentinel* (December 8, 2005)
Pub: Journal Sentinel, Inc.
Ed: Rick Barrett. **Description:** Due to a court battle, state-sponsored tax incentive programs for businesses could actually undermine these programs designed to attract and retain businesses. Details of the lawsuit are discussed.

29019 ■ "Wisconsin Grants Economic Assistance to Four Companies, One Technical College" in *Milwaukee Journal Sentinel* (December 1, 2005)
Pub: Journal Sentinel, Inc.
Ed: Rick Barrett. **Description:** MCL Industries, Moraine Park Technical College, Burns Best Company, ABC Computers, and SMT Engineering will receive nearly $2 million in state assistance for employee training and expansion projects.

29020 ■ "Wisconsin Job Market Continues to Grow Despite Shrinking Labor Force" in *Milwaukee Journal Sentinel* (December 16, 2005)
Pub: Journal Sentinel, Inc.
Ed: Joel Dresang. **Description:** Continued job growth, despite a shrinking labor force, is reported by a Wisconsin labor analyst. Statistical data from Wisconsin's Department of Workforce Labor is included.

29021 ■ "With the Big Dogs" in *Crain's Detroit Business* (Vol. 21, December 19, 2005, No. 51, pp. 3)
Pub: Crain Communications Inc. - Detroit
Ed: Brent Snavely. **Description:** Profile of Pet Supplies 'Plus' franchises. The pet food retailer's expansion makes it the third-largest pet food retailers in the nation. Statistical data included.

29022 ■ "With large chains and specialty stores looking to expand their markets, Detroit becomes a Grocery Battleground" in *Crain's Detroit Business*
Pub: Crain Communications, Inc.
Ed: Joseph Serwach. **Description:** 'While Michigan's major grocery chains have tried to consolidate by opening stores and buying smaller independents, a host of new rivals from major retailers to smaller chains have been eyeing the Detroit area, each seeking a niche of their own.

29023 ■ "Women Business Owners Get Credit Easily" in *Marketing to Women* (Vol. 19, November 2006, No. 11, pp. 12)
Pub: EPM Communications, Inc.
Description: According to a Gallup study commissioned by Wells Fargo, women find it easier to obtain credit than men. Statistical data included.

29024 ■ "Women Favor Discounters for Back-to-School" in *Marketing to Women* (Vol. 19, October 2006, No. 10, pp. 11)
Pub: EPM Communications, Inc.
Description: When back-to-school shopping men are more likely to shop at specialty and department stores, while women are more likely to shop at drugstores and discounters, according to BIGresearch and the National Retail Federation. Statistical data included.

29025 ■ "Women Want More Info on Wellness" in *Marketing to Women* (Vol. 19, December 2006, No. 2, pp. 8)
Pub: EPM Communications, Inc.
Description: IVilliage.com reports that although women consider wellness a top priority in their lives, studies show that two-thirds of women surveyed feel that their lives are out of balance. Statistical data included.

29026 ■ "Women's Firms Reach Nearly $2 Trillion in Sales" in *Marketing to Women* (Vol. 19, October 2006, No. 10, pp. 12)
Pub: EPM Communications, Inc.
Description: According to the Center for Women's Business Research, women own a half or majority stake in 40 percent of all businesses in the U.S. and employ 12.8 million people. Statistical data included.

29027 ■ "Women's Fitness Chains Pour on 24 More Stores" in *Sacramento Business Journal* (Vol. 19, No. 25, August 30, 2002, pp. 1)
Pub: American City Business Journals, Inc.
Ed: Kelly Johnson. **Description:** Health fitness centers, Contours Express and Curves for Women, plan to expand in the Sacramento, California area. Contours Express will open its first four centers in the area, and Curves for Women will open 20 additional centers.

29028 ■ "Workforce Board Seeks To Improve Jobs" in *Bradenton Herald* (January 28, 2005)
Pub: Bradenton Herald
Ed: Matt Griswold. **Description:** The Suncoast Workforce Board is working to improve the Manatee-Sarasota business climate through education of employees. After a study of the region's economy, the area benefits from its desirable geography and is among the nation's top performing regions, but has issues with its workforce.

29029 ■ "Working With Developers Aids Washington Twp." in *Crain's Detroit Business* (Vol. 21, January 17, 2005, No. 3, pp. 12)
Pub: Crain Communications Inc. - Detroit
Ed: Brent Snavely. **Description:** Washington Township, Michigan's population is expected to grow to 33,187 by 2030, according to the Southeast Michigan Council of Governments. The township is meeting with developers to plan properties that preserve mature trees. Upcoming projects are outlined.

29030 ■ "World Cities Alliance: www.worldcitiesalliance.com" in *Entrepreneur* (Vol. 31, No. 12, December 2003, pp. 8)
Pub: Entrepreneur Media Inc.
Ed: Steve Cooper. **Description:** Ways to expand a small business internationally are highlighted using a Web site that covers information on labor costs, site location, taxation, start-up assistance, employee orientation and more.

29031 ■ "World Savings Bank Opens First LI Location" in *Long Island Business News* (February 6, 2004)
Pub: Dolan Media Newswires
Ed: Ben Abelson. **Description:** World Savings Bank, a retail-oriented bank, is expanding from Oakland, California into Long Island, New York. Another branch is expected to open in the summer of 2004. Other banks in the area are welcoming the new competition.

29032 ■ "World Wide Technology Expands" in *Black Enterprise* (Vol. 37, December 2006, No. 5, pp. 34)
Pub: Earl G. Graves Publishing Co. Inc.
Ed: Marcia A. Wade. **Description:** World Wide Technology Inc. opened a streamlined, higher capacity 12,000-square-foot Integration Technology Center near its corporate headquarters in St. Louis. The new venture will transfer lower costs to customers.

29033 ■ "The Year 2000 Top Inc. 500" in *Inc.* (October 17, 2000 pp. 57)
Pub: The Goldhirsh Group

Description: The 2000 Inc. 500 Almanac, listing their top 500 pick companies by state.

29034 ■ "The Year Ahead" in *Hispanic Business* (January/February 2005, pp. 60, 62)
Pub: Hispanic Business
Ed: Juan Solana. **Description:** Slower growth, higher interest rates and moderate inflation is expected for 2005. U.S. economic forecasts are included.

29035 ■ "Yielding to Yoga" in *Crain's Chicago Business* (Vol. 25, No. 49, Dec. 9, 2002, pp. SB1)
Pub: Crain Communications, Inc.
Ed: H. Lee Murphy. **Description:** It is estimated that there are nearly 300 yoga studios in the Chicago, Illinois area alone, but analysts worry how long American interest will hold in yoga.

29036 ■ *Your Business, Your Future: How to Predict and Harness Growth*
Pub: Allen and Unwin Pty., Limited
Ed: Linda Hailey. **Released:** January 2007. **Price:** $16.95. **Description:** Four distinct phases every small companies faces during growth are profiled.

29037 ■ *Your First Business Plan: A Simple Question-and-Answer Format Designed to Help You Write Your Own Plan*
Pub: Sourcebooks, Incorporated
Ed: Joseph A. Covello. **Released:** May 2005. **Price:** $14.95. **Description:** Writing a good first business plan outlines successful business growth.

29038 ■ "Your career can still thrive in an age of flux" in *Black Enterprise* (Vol. 33, No. 3, October 2002, pp. 163)
Pub: Earl Graves Publishing Co.
Description: Despite reports of layoffs, corporate bankruptcies, and stagnant raises along with a volatile stock market, this can also be an exciting time in the labor market. Companies are competing for the best talent available, with the proper skills, opportunities abound.

29039 ■ "Your New Neighborhood" in *Small Business Opportunities* (Vol. 17, May 2005, No. 3, pp. 10)
Pub: Harris Publications Inc.
Ed: Hector Orci. **Description:** Ways small businesses can attract a diverse clientele are discussed.

TRADE PERIODICALS

29040 ■ *China Weekly Fax Bulletin*
Pub: Orbis Publications L.L.C.
Ed: Derek Scissors, Editor, dscissors@orbispub.com. **Released:** Weekly. **Price:** $495, U.S. and Canada; $595, elsewhere. **Description:** Reports on political, economic and business events in China via fax. Remarks: Also available via e-mail.

29041 ■ *Expansion Management*
Pub: Penton Media Inc.
Contact: Michael Keating, Publisher
E-mail: mkeating@penton.com
Released: Monthly, 7 issues. **Price:** $49.50 Canada; $67.50 international. **Description:** Magazine assisting executives and managers worldwide in planning and overseeing their companies' facilities development and other expansion and relocation activities.

29042 ■ *Mexico Watch*
Pub: Orbis Publications L.L.C.
Ed: Stephen Foster, Editor, sfoster@orbispub.com. **Released:** Monthly. **Price:** $595. **Description:** Reports on political, economic and business events in Mexico.

29043 ■ *NACOMEX Insider*
Pub: NACOMEX USA Inc.
Contact: Robert Zises
Ed: Robert Zises, Editor, zises@nacomex.com. **Released:** Quarterly. **Price:** $199, U.S.. **Description:** Provides information on historical values, current tactics, and residual value forecasting for ad valorem tax, bankruptcy, loss compensation, and related purposes. Recurring features include news of research and a column titled Industry Round-up.

29044 ■ *Recon For Investors (RFI)*
Pub: Echo 4 Communications
Ed: Robert K. Morgan, Editor, rkm-echo4@worldnet.att.net. **Released:** Daily. **Price:** $449, U.S.. **Description:** Provides updates on financial, investment, political and other "Recon" that has the potential to impact the financial markets and the economy. Also highlights "hazards and opportunities."

VIDEOCASSETTES/ AUDIOCASSETTES

29045 ■ *Growing Your Company*
Instructional Video
2219 C St.
Lincoln, NE 68502
Ph:(402)475-6570
Free: 800-228-0164
Fax: (402)475-6500
Co. E-mail: feedback@insvideo.com
URL: http://www.insvideo.com
Price: $99.00. **Description:** Offers advise on issues affecting business owners and managers, such as financial strategy, employee motivation, outselling the competition, and quality. **Availability:** VHS.

29046 ■ *The Ten Commandments of Networking*
TomKat Productions
2537 S. Gessner, Ste. 114
Houston, TX 77063
Fax: (713)975-0532
Co. E-mail: tom@tomkatpro.com
URL: http://www.tomkatpro.com/index.html
Released: 1994. **Price:** $39.95. **Description:** One-part seminar and one-part live demonstration of various networking situations, geared toward the entrepreneur who wants to expand and cultivate personal and business relationships. **Availability:** VHS.

CONSULTANTS

29047 ■ BPT Consulting Associates Ltd.
12 Parmenter Rd., Ste. B6
Londonderry, NH 03053
Ph:(603)437-8484
Co. E-mail: bptcons@tiac.net
URL: http://www.bptconsulting.com

E-mail: bptcons@tiac.net
Scope: Provides management consulting expertise and resources to cross-industry clients with services for: Business Management consulting, People/Human Resources Transition and Training programs, and a full cadre of multi-disciplined Technology Computer experts. Virtual consultants with expertise in e-commerce, supply chain management, organizational development, and business application development consulting. **Seminars:** Business: MRPII, DRPII, JIT/TQC. Business Requirements Analysis, Small Business Start-Up, Strategic Planning. People: Team Building, Performance Evaluation, Career Transition and Counseling Seminars. Technology: User Training for Customized Software, Internet, Full array of application development, i.e., C, Java, website development. **Special Services:** Provides a full array of computer and related user training services. Resources include application developers, database developers and managers, project management experts for a full array of industries (manufacturing, software, defense, healthcare, pharmaceutical, and small business).

29048 ■ Flor & Associates
179 Schan Dr.
Churchville, PA 18966
Ph:(215)355-7466
Fax: (215)355-7464
Co. E-mail: fredflor@msn.com

E-mail: fredflor@msn.com
Scope: Business Development Consulting helping companies increase the value of their businesses.

Services include: market development for technologies and products; product positioning strategies; technology assessment; competitive intelligence and analysis; team augmentation and facilitation; business growth strategies including acquisitions, licensing, and partnerships.

29049 ■ Herpers Gowling L.L.P.
4 Hughson St., Ste. 300
Hamilton, ON, Canada L8N 3Z1
Ph:(905)529-3328
Free: 888-735-9909
Fax: (905)529-3980
Co. E-mail: dgowling@herpersgowling.com
URL: http://www.herpersgowling.com

E-mail: dgowling@herpersgowling.com
Scope: Provides services to small and medium size businesses in the areas of financial management, strategic planning, mergers and acquisitions and re-engineering/restructuring.

29050 ■ Plans and Solutions Inc.
PO Box 8905
Gaithersburg, MD 20898-8905
Ph:(301)947-8150
Fax: (240)525-5601
Co. E-mail: info@plansandsolutions.com
URL: http://www.plansandsolutions.com

E-mail: info@plansandsolutions.com
Scope: Business and strategic planning, market research and development. Most clients are minority-owned businesses in the USA and companies overseas that want to begin or increase exports to the United States and Canada. **Publications:** "Building an Import/Export Business," John Wiley & Sons, 2002.

29051 ■ Ransford
Niels Esperson Bldg., 12th Fl.
808 Travis St., Ste. 1200
Houston, TX 77002-5706
Ph:(713)722-7281
Free: 800-782-2838
Fax: (713)722-0950
Co. E-mail: info@ransford.com
URL: http://ransford.com

E-mail: info@ransford.com
Scope: Strategic business growth for professional services organizations. Researches and analyzes business practices to provide critical information and insight in the areas of strategy, market intelligence, mergers and acquisitions, talent, acquisition, training and change management.

29052 ■ Norman A. Robins Consulting
5127 S Cornell Ave.
Chicago, IL 60615
Ph:(773)667-6463
Scope: Helps companies develop strategic plans that will improve profits, reduce costs, and accelerate growth.

29053 ■ The Sanderson Group Inc.
219 Manahan Ct.
East Brunswick, NJ 08816
Ph:(732)254-8440
Fax: (732)254-8450
Co. E-mail: tsgrobin@aol.com
URL: http://thesandersongroup.com

E-mail: tsgrobin@aol.com
Scope: Provides innovative marketing and sales solutions tailored to each client's individual business needs. Helps clients grow and manage their businesses. Services provided include strategic and marketing planning, target marketing with expertise in college/teen markets, integrated marketing programs, sampling, event marketing, new product development, corporate communications, strategic alliance formation, web site strategic partnerships, Web site development and marketing, new business development, market research, sales and field force creation and management, and customer acquisition.

29054 ■ Herbert Stillman
21405 Woodchuck Ln.
Boca Raton, FL 33428
Ph:(561)483-0624
Co. E-mail: herb616@aol.com

E-mail: herb616@aol.com
Scope: Offers consulting services in the following areas: management, start-ups, profit maximization, world wide negotiating, interim management, corporate debt resolution.

LIBRARIES

29055 ■ Buffalo & Erie County Public Library–Business, Science & Technology
1 Lafayette Sq.
Buffalo, NY 14203
Ph:(716)858-8900
Fax: (716)858-7237
Co. E-mail: bst@buffalolib.org
URL: http://www.buffalolib.org
Contact: Kate Weeks, Div.Mgr.
Scope: Investments, real estate, economics, marketing, engineering, computer science, technology, medical information for laymen, consumer information, automotive repair. **Services:** Interlibrary loan; copying; Library open to the public. **Holdings:** 312,916 books; 60,516 bound periodical volumes. **Subscriptions:** 2908 journals and other serials; 4 newspapers.

29056 ■ U.S. Dept. of Commerce–Library & Information Services
1401 Constitution Ave., NW
Washington, DC 20230
Ph:(202)482-5511
Fax: (202)482-5685
Co. E-mail: vwhisenton@doc.gov
URL: http://www.osec.doc.gov/lib/
Contact: Vera E. Whisenton, Dir.
Scope: Economics, export-import, foreign trade, business, economic theory, economic conditions, statistics, marketing, industry, finance, management, telecommunications. **Services:** Interlibrary loan; copying; Library open to the public for reference use only. **Holdings:** 45,000 books and bound periodical volumes; 4300 reels of microfilm; 250,000 volumes of microfiche. **Subscriptions:** 625 journals and other serials.

29057 ■ University of South Carolina–The Moore School of Business–Elliot White Springs Business Library (Franc)
Francis M. Hipp Bldg., 2nd Fl.
1705 College St.
Columbia, SC 29208
Ph:(803)777-6032
Fax: (803)777-6876
Co. E-mail: gardnerd@gwm.sc.edu
URL: http://www.sc.edu/library/pubserv/business.html
Contact: Dwight Gardner, Dept.Hd.
Scope: Corporations. **Services:** Interlibrary loan; copying; Library open to the public with restrictions.

Holdings: 30,000 books; 4000 bound periodical volumes. **Subscriptions:** 350 journals and other serials; 5 newspapers.

RESEARCH CENTERS

29058 ■ Iowa Human Services Department–Research, Analysis and Statistics Bureau
Hoover Bldg.
1305 E Walnut St.
Des Moines, IA 50319
Ph:(515)281-5780
Fax: (515)281-4342
Co. E-mail: whoshaw@dhs.state.ia.us
Contact: Walt Hoshaw, Ch.
E-mail: whoshaw@dhs.state.ia.us
Scope: Human services statistics, program evaluation, needs analyses.

29059 ■ Minnesota Labor and Industry Department–Research and Statistics Office
443 Lafayette Rd. N.
St. Paul, MN 55155
Ph:(651)284-5025
Free: 800–342-5354
Fax: (651)284-5726
Co. E-mail: dli.research@state.mn.us
URL: http://www.doli.state.mn.us/research.html
Contact: Dr. Theresa Van Hoomissen, Dir.
E-mail: dli.research@state.mn.us
Scope: Workers' compensation, safety, occupational illness and injury.

START-UP INFORMATION

29060 ■ *Becoming a Personal Trainer for Dummies*
Pub: John Wiley & Sons, Incorporated
Ed: Melyssa Michael, Linda Formichelli. **Released:** October 2004. **Price:** $19.99 (US), $25.99 (Canadian). **Description:** Legal and tax issues involved in starting and running a personal trainer firm. The book offers suggestions for incorporating massage and nutritional services.

29061 ■ "Buying a Small Business? Beware!" in *Business Week Online* (December 4, 2002)
Pub: McGraw-Hill Inc.
Description: An interview with attorney Mitchell Stern, explains pitfalls that entrepreneurs must avoid before purchasing a new business. Stern suggests that the perspective buyer also look at the historical analysis and financial records of a company and project their income when going forward with the firm.

29062 ■ "Documenting Profit" in *Small Business Opportunities* (Vol. 16, No. 3, May 2004, pp. 58, 120)
Pub: Harris Publications, Inc.
Ed: Jan Fields. **Description:** Profile of Ira and Linda Distenfield, the couple behind We The People, a franchised legal document processing service. Currently there are 120 open or under construction franchises in 26 states. Total investment ranges between $139,500 to $151,500.

29063 ■ *Enterprise Planning and Development: Small Business and Enterprise Start-Up Survival and Growth*
Pub: Elsevier Science and Technology Books
Ed: David Butler. **Released:** August 2006. **Price:** $42.95. **Description:** Innovation, intellectual property, and exit strategies are among the issues discussed in this book involving current entrepreneurship.

29064 ■ "The Four Questions" in *Home Business* (Vol. 12, March/April 2005, No. 2, pp. 64)
Pub: Home Business Magazine
Ed: Dr. Paul E. Adams. **Description:** Four questions to ask before applying to a bank for a new small business loan. It is important for entrepreneurs to understand their customer base.

29065 ■ "Hands On" in *Inc.* (September 2000, pp. 107)
Pub: The Goldhirsh Group
Ed: Mike Hoffman. **Description:** Small-fry entrepreneurs who can't afford top legal or Human Resource advice may be confused by arcane federal rules. A thorough rundown on regulations covering small companies is included.

29066 ■ *How to Start, Operate and Market a Freelance Notary Signing Agent Business*
Pub: Gom Publishing, LLC
Ed: Victoria Ring. **Released:** September 2004. **Price:** $19.99. **Description:** Due to the changes in the 2001

Uniform Commercial Code allowing notary public agents to serve as a witness to mortgage loan closings (eliminating the 2-witness requirement under the old code), notaries are working directly for mortgage, title and signing companies as mobile notaries.

29067 ■ "Is My Partnership Fair?" in *Inc.* (July 1, 2004)
Pub: Inc. Magazine
Description: A small business entrepreneur of a 50-50 partnership talks about protecting ideas and the pros and cons of leasing versus purchasing new technology.

29068 ■ "Learning the Ropes" in *Entrepreneur* (Vol. 33, October 2005, No. 10, pp. 99)
Pub: Entrepreneur Media Inc.
Description: A.D. Banker & Company helps individuals wishing to buy a franchise obtain licenses in the insurance, security, legal and accounting industries through classroom, online and self-study courses.

29069 ■ *Legal Guide for Starting and Running a Small Business*
Pub: NOLO
Ed: Fred Steingold, Lisa Guerin. **Released:** March 2005. **Price:** $34.99. **Description:** Information for starting a new business focusing on choosing a business structure, taxes, employees and independent contractors, trademark and service marks, licensing and permits, leasing and improvement of commercial space, buying and selling a business, and more.

29070 ■ "License to Bill?" in *Black Enterprise* (Vol. 34, No. 4, November 2003, pp. 48)
Pub: Earl Graves Publishing Co.
Ed: Alan Hughes. **Description:** Information for starting a home-based business and licensing processes are discussed.

29071 ■ "Master of your domain" in *WorkingWoman* (Vol. 25, No. 4, April 2000, pp. 54)
Pub: Lang Communications Inc.
Ed: Parry Aftab. **Description:** Legal advice for setting up a web site on the Internet and choosing and registering a domain name is explained.

29072 ■ *Partnership: Small Business Start-Up Kit*
Pub: Nova Publishing Company
Ed: Daniel Sitarz. **Released:** November 2005. **Price:** $29.95. **Description:** Guidebook detailing partnership law by state covering the formation and use of partnerships as a business form. Information on filing requirements, property laws, legal liability, standards, and the new Revised Uniform Partnership Act is covered.

29073 ■ *Small Business Legal Tool Kit*
Pub: Entrepreneur Press
Ed: Ira Nottonson; Theresa A. Pickner. **Released:** May 2007. **Price:** $36.95. **Description:** Legal expertise is provided by two leading entrepreneurial attorneys. Issues covered include forming and operating a business: taxes, contracts, leases, bylaws, trademarks, small claims court, etc.

29074 ■ *The Small Business Owner's Manual: Everything You Need to Know to Start Up and Run Your Business*
Pub: Career Press, Incorporated
Ed: Joe Kennedy. **Released:** June 2005. **Price:** $19.99 (US), $26.95 (Canadian). **Description:** Comprehensive guide for starting a small business, focusing on twelve ways to obtain financing, business plans, selling and advertising products and services, hiring and firing employees, setting up a Web site, business law, accounting issues, insurance, equipment, computers, banks, financing, customer credit and collection, leasing, and more.

29075 ■ "Small or Not, It's the Law" in *Inc.* (September 2000, pp. 107)
Pub: The Goldhirsh Group
Ed: Ilan Mochari. **Description:** Frequent legal consultations add up, but many small business owners believe the cost is worth it for peace of mind and avoided litigation.

29076 ■ "Street Smarts: Don't Sign Anything Yet" in *Inc.* (January 1, 2005)
Pub: Inc. Magazine
Ed: Norm Brodsky. **Description:** When starting a new business, it is important for entrepreneurs to beware of commitments made in the process.

29077 ■ "Street Smarts: The Myths About Niches" in *Inc.* (August 1, 2004)
Pub: Inc. Magazine
Ed: Norm Brodsky. **Description:** For a small business starting out, finding its niche is key, being prepared for it to change and keep on changing is essential.

29078 ■ "Uncle Sam, Paralegal" in *Hispanic Business* (June 2002, pp. 22)
Pub: Hispanic Business
Ed: Teresa Talerico. **Description:** The Small Business Administration has launched a new Web site that assists entrepreneurs with legal questions. Since Hispanic entrepreneurs are eligible for a number of federal and state programs that are subject to changing regulations, the site will be very beneficial.

29079 ■ *Working for Yourself: An Entrepreneur's Guide to the Basics*
Pub: Kogan Page, Limited
Ed: Jonathan Reuvid. **Released:** September 2006. **Description:** Guide for starting a new business venture, focusing on raising financing, legal and tax issues, marketing, information technology, and site location.

29080 ■ "You need to know" in *BlackEnterprise* (Vol. 31, No. 12, July 2001, pp. 45)
Pub: Earl Graves Publishing Co.
Ed: Bridget McCrea. **Description:** It is very common for small start-up companies to overlook simple issues and its not until they get sued or are penalized that the owner realizes that his or her personal life savings are tied up in the business and they should have taken different steps in the process of their early business plans. Ways for small businesses to find affordable legal advice is outlined.

29081 ■ *Your First Business Plan: A Simple Question-and-Answer Format Designed to Help You Write Your Own Plan*
Pub: Sourcebooks, Incorporated
Ed: Joseph A. Covello. **Released:** May 2005. **Price:** $14.95. **Description:** Writing a good first business plan outlines successful business growth.

EDUCATIONAL PROGRAMS

29082 ■ Issues in Employment Law (Canada)
Canadian Management Centre
150 York St., 5th Fl.
Toronto, ON, Canada M5H 3S5
Ph:(866)400-4941 ext. 2252
Free: 877-CMC-2500
Fax: (416)313-4985
Co. E-mail: cmcinfo@cmctraining.org
URL: http://www.cmcamai.org
Price: $1,650 Canadian. **Description:** Covers employment laws within the human resource department.
Locations: Toronto, ON.

29083 ■ The Legal Aspects of Purchasing and Supply Chain Management
American Management Association
1601 Broadway
New York, NY 10019
Ph:(212)586-8100
Free: 800-262-9699
Fax: (212)903-8168
Co. E-mail: customerservice@amanet.org
URL: http://www.amanet.org
Price: $1,995 for non-members; $1,795 for AMA members. **Description:** Covers contract laws, including government antitrust regulations, the Uniform Commercial Code, and The Federal Bankruptcy Act as they relate to your organization, as well as negotiating the terms and conditions to avoid disputes with suppliers. **Locations:** New York, NY; Las Vegas, NV; Chicago, IL; and San Francisco, CA.

29084 ■ Purchasing Contract Management: How to Avoid Legal Pitfalls
American Management Association
1601 Broadway
New York, NY 10019
Ph:(212)586-8100
Free: 800-262-9699
Fax: (212)903-8168
Co. E-mail: customerservice@amanet.org
URL: http://www.amanet.org
Price: $1,995 for non-members; $1,795 for AMA members. **Description:** Covers the complete drafting of a binding contract, and how to avoid any legal consequences later. **Locations:** New York, NY; Atlanta, GA; Chicago, IL; Scottsdale, AZ; Las Vegas, NV; Washington, DC; and San Francisco, CA.

29085 ■ Understanding the New Security and Compliance Regulations for Export/Import: What Every Supply Chain manager Needs to Know
American Management Association
1601 Broadway
New York, NY 10019
Ph:(212)586-8100
Free: 800-262-9699
Fax: (212)903-8168
Co. E-mail: customerservice@amanet.org
URL: http://www.amanet.org
Price: $1,895 for non-members; $1,695 for AMA members. **Description:** Covers the current rules and regulations of U.S. Customs, including the newly formed Office of Homeland Security, and form effective strategic partnerships with government agencies and supply chains. **Locations:** New York, NY; Atlanta, GA; Chicago, IL; and San Francisco, CA.

DIRECTORIES OF EDUCATIONAL PROGRAMS

29086 ■ *Neal-Schuman Guide to Finding Legal and Regulatory Information on the Internet*
Pub: Neal-Schuman Publishers Inc.
Ed: Yvonne J. Chandler, Editor. **Released:** new edition expected 2005. **Price:** $135, individuals. **Covers:** 947 Internet sites offering local, state, and federal legal and government information. **Entries Include:** Title, publishing agency, URL, brief description of the site.

REFERENCE WORKS

29087 ■ *365 Answers about Human Resources for the Small Business Owner: What Every Manager Needs to Know about Work Place Law*
Pub: Atlantic Publishing Company
Ed: Mary Holihan. **Released:** June 2006. **Price:** $21.95. **Description:** Common questions employers ask about employees and the law are answered.

29088 ■ "Access Now...Or Lawsuit Later" in *Birmingham Business Journal* (Vol. 20, No. 40, October 3, 2003, pp. 1)
Pub: American City Business Journals, Inc.
Ed: Ryan Mahoney. **Description:** Access Now Inc., a disability advocacy group, has filed 66 cases with violations of the Americans with Disabilities Act against businesses in Birmingham, Alabama.

29089 ■ "Action Sacked" in *Entrepreneur* (Vol. 33, August 2005, No. 8, pp. 18)
Pub: Entrepreneur Media Inc.
Ed: Jane Easter Bahls. **Description:** President Bush signed the Class Action Fairness Act of 2005 in February. The new law is expected to protect small businesses from class-action lawsuits.

29090 ■ "ADR: new challenges, new roles and new opportunities" in *Dispute Resolution Journal* (Vol. 56, No. 1, February-April 2001, pp. 20)
Pub: American Arbitration Association
Ed: Bennett G. Picker. **Description:** An overview of the changing role of attorneys and their work with the increased use of ADR, which is changing clients' expectations.

29091 ■ "Affirmative Action Upheld" in *Black Enterprise* (Vol. 34, No. 2, September 2003, pp. 23)
Pub: Earl Graves Publishing Co.
Ed: Cliff Hocker. **Description:** The U.S. Supreme Court upheld the race-conscious admission practices of the University of Michigan Law School in June 2003. William B. Harvey, vice president and director of the Office of Minorities in Higher Education at the American Council on Education (ACE) discusses the issues centering on affirmative action.

29092 ■ "Age On Your Side" in *Black Enterprise* (Vol. 36, February 2006, No. 7, pp. 74)
Pub: Earl G. Graves Publishing Co. Inc.
Ed: L. Taylor. **Description:** The Age Discrimination Act of 1967 is examined.

29093 ■ "Ahead of the Law" in *Adweek* (Vol. 46, January 17, 2005, No. 3, pp. 16)
Pub: VNU Business Media
Ed: Wendy Melillo. **Description:** Laws and regulations involving television advertising are examined.

29094 ■ "Ambulance Chasing, Web-Style" in *Forbes* (Vol. 174, December 27, 2004, No. 13, pp. 56)
Pub: Forbes Magazine Inc.
Ed: David Whelan. **Description:** Law firms are paying large sums to place pay-per-click ads on Internet sites. The ads take the user to a law firm's Web site or a middleman, and a lawyer pays up to $160 to the Internet service provider.

29095 ■ *American Bar Association Small Business*
Pub: Random House, Inc.
Released: 1998. **Price:** $13.00.

29096 ■ "America's Top Black Lawyers" in *Black Enterprise* (Vol. 34, No. 4, November 2003, pp. 120)
Pub: Earl Graves Publishing Co.
Description: Profiles of America's top black lawyers are presented. In the 1970's there were about 3,000 African American lawyers, today more than 20,000.

29097 ■ "Andrews & Kurth goes high-tech with ex-Brobeck attorneys" in *Houston Business Journal* (Vol. 33, No. 49, April 18, 2003, pp. 2A)
Pub: Houston Business Journal
Ed: Jim Greer. **Description:** The law firm of Andrews & Kurth has hired three attorneys specializing in securities law.

29098 ■ "Apple Squares Off Against Resellers" in *Inc.* (September 1, 2004)
Pub: Inc. Magazine
Ed: Cara Cannella. **Description:** The legal battle between Apple and its resellers that began four years ago is examined. The battle started when resellers concluded that Apple was mistreating them by opening outlets near their businesses.

29099 ■ "Appleton, Wis.-Based Construction Company Settles Racial Harassment Suit" in *Milwaukee Journal Sentinel* (December 1, 2005)
Pub: Journal Sentinel, Inc.
Ed: Tom Daykin. **Description:** Details of the racial harassment complaint filed by an employee of Wisconsin's largest construction firm are outlined. The suit claimed that the company created a hostile work environment for African-American employees of a subcontractor hired by the firm.

29100 ■ *Are Government Purchasing Policies Failing Small Business?: Congressional Hearing*
Pub: DIANE Publishing Company
Ed: John F. Kerry. **Released:** November 2004. **Price:** $35.00. **Description:** Covers Congressional hearing: Steven App, Treasury Department; Fred Armendariz and Major Clark, Small Business Administration; Susan Allen, Pan Asian American Chamber of Commerce; Stephen Denlinger, Latin American Management Association; Charles Henry, National Veteran's Business Development Corporation; Morris Hudson, MO Procurement Technology Assistance Centers; Bar Kasoff, Women Impact, Public Policy; Pam Mazza, Piliero, Massa and Pargament; Ron Newlan, HubZone Contract National Council; Pat Parker, Native American Management Service; Joann Payne, Women First National Legislative Commission; Mike Robinson, MA Small Business Development Centers; Ramon Rodriguez, Hispanic Chamber of Commerce; Angela Styles, Office of Management and Budget; Ralph Thomas, NASA; John Turner, MN Business Enterprise Legal Defense Fund; James Turpin, American Subcontractor's Association, Inc.; and Henry Wilfong, National Association of Small Disadvantaged Business.

29101 ■ "Arm yourself for the coming battle over social security" in *Harvard Business Review* (Vol. 80, No. 11, November 2002, pp. 52)
Pub: Harvard Business School Press
Description: A visiting professor at Harvard Law School and a former member of the President's Committee to Strengthen Social Security describes the problems ahead for the Social Security system. He outlines three alternatives to reforming the system, including increasing contributions, decreasing growth of benefits for the affluent, and increasing returns on Social Security assets.

29102 ■ "ArvinMeritor Rival Files New Patent Suit" in *Crain's Detroit Business* (Vol. 19, No. 49, December 8, 2003, pp. 4)
Pub: Crain Communications Inc., Detroit

Ed: Terry Kosdrosky. **Description:** Overview of a patent-infringement lawsuit against ArvinMeritor Inc. regarding a truck transmission is presented.

29103 ■ "Ask the attorney" in *Red Herring* (March 2003, pp. 73)
Pub: Herring Communications Inc.
Description: Legal issues are addressed that include the following topics, pharmaceutical patents, government support for research and development, global commerce, intellectual property rights, the transfer of customer lists from European subsidiary to its U.S. parent company, trademark dilution, venture financing, selling a business, stock options, corporate tax deductions, small business patent methods, and employee use of Instant Messaging with clients.

29104 ■ "Ask Inc." in *Inc.* (Volume 28, January 2006, No. 1, pp. 51-52)
Pub: Inc. Magazine
Description: Advice is offered regarding noncompete agreements, factoring companies that pay businesses up-front for outstanding bills and collect payments from customers, and a pet accessory business.

29105 ■ "AT&T Sues eBay and PayPal" in *Cardline* (Vol. 3, No. 48, November 28, 2003, pp. 1)
Pub: Thomson Media
Description: AT&T Corporation has filed a patent infringement lawsuit against eBay and its subsidiary PayPal Inc over failure to reach a licensing agreement. EBAY PRODUCT/EBAY SERVICE

29106 ■ "Attorney General to offer olive branch to Silicon Valley" in *The New York Times* (April 5, 2000, pp. C2)
Pub: The New York Times Company
Ed: John Markoff. **Description:** Janet Reno to fight computer crime and strengthen network security.

29107 ■ *The Attorney's Handbook on Small Business Reorganization Under Chapter 11*
Pub: Argyle Publishing Co.
Ed: John H. Williamson. **Released:** Third edition, 1992. **Price:** $27.95; $20.00 (paper).

29108 ■ "Avoid litigation" in *Black Enterprise* (Vol. 32, No. 8, March 2002, pp. 49)
Pub: Earl Graves Publishing Co.
Ed: Bridget McCrea. **Description:** Entrepreneurs cannot afford the financial and emotional stress that comes with legal litigation. Key areas to help small business avoid lawsuits are examined.

29109 ■ "Bad credit and employment" in *Black Enterprise* (Vol. 31, No. 5, December 2000, pp. 172)
Pub: Earl Graves Publishing Co.
Ed: Bevolyn Williams-Harold. **Description:** The issue of screening job applicants based on credit history is discussed.

29110 ■ "Bad Judgment? Even Top Execs Can Make Mistakes" in *Entrepreneur* (Vol. 31, No. 9, September 2003, pp. 79)
Pub: Entrepreneur Media, Inc.
Ed: Jacquelyn Lynn. **Description:** The importance of carrying directors and officers (D&O) liability insurance for a small business is emphasized. This insurance covers directors and officers against wrongful acts typically described as bad business judgment.

29111 ■ "Baker, Donelson, Bearman, Caldwell & Berkowitz, PC" in *Mississippi Business Journal* (Vol. 29, January 2007, No. 4, pp. 6)
Pub: Venture Publications, Inc.
Description: Profile of William S. Painter of law firm Baker, Donelson, Bearman, Caldwell & Berkowitz, PC, who concentrates his practice in the areas of corporate, tax and healthcare restructuring.

29112 ■ "Bank deals draw fines" in *Business First of Buffalo* (Vol. 18, No. 46, August 12, 2002, pp. 1)
Pub: Knight-Ridder/Tribune Business News

Ed: Tom Hartley. **Description:** HSBC Bank USA, located in Buffalo, New York, has been fined more than $71,000 for violating a law that prevents business dealings with nations on so-called U.S. enemies' lists, including dealings with the Taliban in Afghanistan, and Cuba, Kosovo, Iraq and Libya.

29113 ■ *Bankruptcy Basics for Small Business*
Pub: Clark Boardman Callaghan
Ed: S. Suzanne Walsh. **Released:** 1994. **Price:** $75.00.

29114 ■ "Bankruptcy Law Would Mean Tougher Consequences for Consumers" in *Chicago Tribune* (March 11, 2005)
Pub: Knight-Ridder/Tribune Business News
Ed: Lorene Yue. **Description:** The newly created federal Bankruptcy Abuse Prevention and Consumer Protection Act of 2005 is outlined.

29115 ■ "Bankruptcy Reform Trying to Scale Final Hurdle" in *Atlanta Business Chronicle* (Vol. 24, No. 8, July 27, 2001, pp. 4A)
Pub: American City Business Journals Inc.
Ed: Kent Hoover. **Description:** A bill crafted by creditors and designed to change the laws regarding bankruptcy may be signed into law before Labor Day. Because wealthy debtors may abuse the current system by shielding their assets in states such as Florida that keep homes from the reach of creditors, the new law will allow debtors to only protect $125,000 of home equity. Analysts predict that if the bill becomes law, bankruptcies will increase dramatically in the months before it goes into effect.

29116 ■ "Bankruptcy Reform Will Punish Debtors" in *Atlanta Business Chronicle* (Vol. 25, No. 20, October 25, 2002, pp. 38A)
Pub: American City Business Publications, Inc.
Ed: Mark Meltzer. **Description:** The lame-duck session of Congress will likely decide whether to reform the nation's bankruptcy laws. At issue is the reduction of the number of bankruptcies by making filing more difficult. Currently, Atlanta, Georgia is among the leading major metropolitan regions in bankruptcy filings.

29117 ■ *Basic Legal Forms for Business*
Pub: John Wiley & Sons, Inc.
Ed: Morris A. Nunes. **Released:** 1993. **Price:** $37.50 (paper). **Description:** Contains 110 legal forms for business. Includes diskette.

29118 ■ "Battle between Compuware, IBM escalates in counterclaim" in *Crain's Detroit Business* (Vol. 19, No. 14, April 7, 2003, pp. 4)
Pub: Crain Communications Inc., Detroit
Ed: Andrew Dietderich. **Description:** The legal battle between Compuware and IBM has ensued for more than thirteen months. The two software companies are battling over Compuware's accusation that IBM has misappropriated trade secrets, committed antitrust law violations and unfair competition practices.

29119 ■ "Battle brews against tort reform" in *Atlanta Business Chronicle* (Vol. 25, Dec. 13, 2002, No. 27, pp. A1)
Pub: American City Business Publications, Inc.
Ed: Julie Bryant. **Description:** As political move towards tort reform in Georgia gathers strength with the election of Sonny Perdue, trial attorneys and the victims they represent are presenting data indicating that such reforms do not halt medical malpractice insurance premium hikes. Caps on jury awards are, however, sought by physicians as they face mounting insurance premiums.

29120 ■ "Be a complete lawyer" in *Daily Business Review* (Vol. 77, No. 198, March 24, 2003, pp. A6)
Pub: American Lawyer Media LP
Ed: Vance Salter. **Description:** The topic of pro bono work done by successful attorneys is discussed. The Supreme Court and the Florida Bar recognized the best performers with service awards at the Supreme Court of Florida.

29121 ■ "Before You Sign on the Dotted Line..." in *Black Enterprise* (Vol. 35, October 2004, No. 3, pp. 200)
Pub: Earl G. Graves Publishing Co. Inc.
Ed: Tamara Holmes. **Description:** Before hiring any company, it is imperative to check with the Better Business Bureau and your state attorney general's office. Web sites are also featured for checking a company before signing a contract.

29122 ■ "Best Practices" in *Entrepreneur* (Vol. 32, October 2004, No. 10, pp. 84)
Pub: Entrepreneur Media Inc.
Ed: Mark Henricks. **Description:** Doctors, lawyers and other professionals are taking the lead from entrepreneurs when running and building their businesses. Innovative solutions to grow a professional practice like an entrepreneur are shared.

29123 ■ "Better Safe: Does Your Product Need a Warning Label?" in *Entrepreneur* (Vol. 31, No. 9, July 2003, pp. 76)
Pub: Entrepreneur Media, Inc.
Ed: Jane Easter Bahls. **Description:** When injured, a consumer can sue not only the manufacturer, but also the supplier, dealer, distributor or rental yard.

29124 ■ "Beware the Dotted Line" in *Hispanic Business* (December 2002, pp. 55)
Pub: Hispanic Business
Ed: Francisco Ramos, Jr. **Description:** The importance of reading the fine print before signing a contract is stressed. Ten traps to beware when signing a contract are outlined.

29125 ■ "Billion-Dollar Plan in Limbo" in *Pacific Business News* (Vol. 41, No. 20, July 25, 2003, pp. 1)
Pub: American City Business Journals
Ed: Terrence Sing. **Description:** A law suit has been filed in the 3rd Circuit Court trying to prevent 1250 Oceanside Partners from developing a track of agricultural land into a $1 billion residential complex.

29126 ■ "Biloxi, Miss., Bed, Breakfast Law Upheld" in *Sun Herald* (January 7, 2004)
Pub: Knight-Ridder/Tribune Business News
Ed: Tom Wilemon. **Description:** Supreme Court Justice Oliver Diaz Jr. and former wife Jennifer, founders of Green Oaks LLC, dispute the city of Biloxi's law that would prohibit weddings at bed-and-breakfast inns in residential areas. The Diazes were indicted in July 2003 on federal fraud and bribery charges along with lawyer Paul Minor, who was also charged with racketeering.

29127 ■ "Black Farmers Sue USDA for $20.5 Billion" in *Black Enterprise* (Vol. 35, December 2004, No. 5, pp. 36)
Pub: Earl G. Graves Publishing Co. Inc.
Ed: Tamara E. Holmes. **Description:** A class action lawsuit charging the U.S. Department of Agriculture with denying fair loans and farm programs to 25,000 black farmers is discussed. The Black Farmers and Agriculturist Association and 11 other plaintiffs have filed the suit.

29128 ■ "Black Firm Sues SBA, Alleges Funding Bias" in *Boston Business Journal* (Vol. 23, No. 30, August 29, 2003, pp. 18)
Pub: American City Business Journals
Ed: Kent Hoover. **Description:** The racial discrimination lawsuit filed by minority-owned Small Business Investment Corporation against the U.S. Small Business Administration is addressed. Topics include management teams, funding of minority business, and business start-up loans.

29129 ■ "Bradenton Central CRA To Launch New Business Development Center" in *Bradenton Herald* (January 29, 2005)
Pub: Bradenton Herald
Ed: Tim W. McCann. **Description:** The Bradenton Central Community Redevelopment Agency is working to grow the economy of the area. The Agency will create a small business center with a professional counselor to assist small business owners in applying for a business loan, advertising, marketing and legal issues.

29130 ■ "Briefly" in *Crain's Detroit Business* **(Vol. 21, December 19, 2005, No. 51, pp. 14)**
Pub: Crain Communications Inc. - Detroit
Ed: Anjali Fluker, Michelle Martinez, Brent Snavely.
Description: Auction-It-Today Inc. opens a new franchise; new laws governing false Medicaid claims; and Talon Building Company opens a new medical office building.

29131 ■ "Bruce Sunstein: Inventor Defender" in *Boston Business Journal* **(Vol. 23, No. 27, August 8, 2003, pp. 1)**
Pub: American City Business Journals
Ed: Sheri Qualters. Description: Interview with intellectual property attorney, Bruce Sunstein, in which he discusses his practice.

29132 ■ "Burger King Franchisees, Parent Squabble Over Firm's Declining Fortunes" in *Portland Press Herald* **(November 8, 2005)**
Pub: Blethen Maine Newspapers, Inc.
Ed: Edward D. Murphy. Description: Burger King franchisees contend that the company's corporate headquarters' bad management has left them with declining profits. Continual turnover in leadership, quick changes in promotional strategies, and the change of the company's logo have all cost franchisees large sums of money, especially changing signs and restaurant supplies to reflect the new logo.

29133 ■ "Burrell CEO Steps Down" in *Black Enterprise* **(Vol. 35, August 2004, No. 1, pp. 23)**
Pub: Earl G. Graves Publishing Co. Inc.
Ed: Dahna M. Chandler. Description: Thomas J. Burrell, founder of a black-owned advertising firm, is stepping down as chairman and CEO of his Chicago, Illinois-based company. Burrell is credited with redefining the advertising industry.

29134 ■ "Business Briefs" in *News Tribune* **(March 10, 2005)**
Pub: News Tribune
Description: Mega Life and Health Insurance Company of Oklahoma has been ordered to stop selling health insurance that violates Washington law. Washington state law requires group insurance policies to include emergency services, mammograms, maternity care stays, newborn coverage and reconstruction breast surgery.

29135 ■ "Business groups urge caution on pension law changes" in *Business First Columbus* **(Vol. 18, No. 25, February 8, 2002, pp. A5)**
Pub: Business First Columbus, Inc.
Description: Brief review of potential changes to pension laws, including the concerns expressed by business groups.

29136 ■ *Business Law Made Simple*
Pub: Doubleday & Co., Inc.
Ed: Stephen G. Christianson. Released: 1995. Price: $12.00.

29137 ■ "Business Services" in *Entrepreneur* **(Vol. 31, No. 5, May 2003, pp. 8)**
Pub: Entrepreneur Media Inc.
Description: A directory of business services is presented, listing such services as franchise consultation, attorneys, entrepreneurial information radio shows, sales and marketing plans, business startup information, home-based businesses, raising business capital, e-businesses, B2B sales leads, and software.

29138 ■ "Buy, Sell & Rent" in *Black Enterprise* **(Vol. 34, July 2004, No. 12, pp. 116)**
Pub: Earl G. Graves Publishing Co. Inc.
Ed: Donald Jay Korn. Description: Real estate investors must be aware of and understand the housing laws and regulations when buying, selling and renting properties.

29139 ■ "Can you trust your law firm?" in *Harvard Business Review* **(Vol. 80, No. 11, November 2002, pp. 22)**
Pub: Harvard Business School Press
Ed: Bronwyn Fryer. Description: A Boston University law professor and legal ethics expert advises managers to get legal advice in writing, record all oral communications, and seek second opinions.

29140 ■ "Can Firms Ban Weapons?" in *St. Louis Post-Dispatch* **(December 6, 2004)**
Pub: Knight-Ridder/Tribune Business News
Ed: Repps Hudson. Description: Potential for workforce violence and the fight over whether employees should have the right to carry firearms at work is examined.

29141 ■ "Can You Judge a Biz by Its Color?" in *Inc.* **(August 1, 2004)**
Pub: Inc. Magazine
Ed: Lora Kolodny. Description: A Federal Court recently determined that corporations, which have the same legal status as individuals, can now sue for racial discrimination.

29142 ■ *Canadian Small Business Kit for Dummies*
Pub: John Wiley & Sons, Incorporated
Ed: Margaret Kerr; JoAnn Kurtz. Released: May 2006. Price: $28.99. Description: Resources include information on changes to laws and taxes for small businesses in Canada.

29143 ■ "Can't We All Get Along?" in *Inc.* **(Volume 27, June 2005, No. 6, pp. 34, 36)**
Pub: Inc. Magazine
Ed: Dimitra Kessenides. Description: As litigation costs rise, arbitration can be a good strategy for both employees and employers in cases. Statistical data included.

29144 ■ "Captive Agents Face Off Against Their Captors" in *Rough Notes* **(Vol. 145, No. 1, January 2003, pp. 78)**
Pub: Rough Notes
Ed: Phil Zinkewicz. Description: Captive insurance agents who either remained as independent agents or released by Allstate Insurance Company or State Farm Insurance Company, are involved in litigation with former companies.

29145 ■ "The Case of A Lifetime" in *Hispanic Business* **(April 2005, pp. 22, 24-25)**
Pub: Hispanic Business
Ed: Joel Russell. Description: Profile of Brigida Benitez whose affirmative action suit put her in the winning circle. She was voted 2005 Woman of the Year by Hispanic Magazine. Benitz' well-publicized case involving three white college applicants who filed discrimination suits because race was considered in the application processes is discussed.

29146 ■ "Casino Case Hits Legal Jackpot" in *Inc.* **(August 1, 2003)**
Pub: Gruner & Jahr USA Publishing
Ed: Bobbie Gossage. Description: A new ruling against Caesars Palace in Las Vegas, Nevada, will affect all companies when firing employees. The Supreme Court affirmed that circumstantial evidence in the casino's firing of an employee would suffice for a female warehouse worker fired for brawling with a coworker.

29147 ■ "The Chamber Steps Up Its War On the SEC" in *Business Week* **(February 14, 2005, No. 3920, pp. 45)**
Pub: McGraw-Hill Companies
Ed: Richard S. Dunham. Description: The U.S. Chamber of Commerce is continuing its battle with the Securities & Exchange Commission by filing a brief in support of Siebel Systems, which the SEC has charged with violating a 2000 rule that bars businesses from selectively disclosing material information.

29148 ■ "Change Without Pain" in *Harvard Business Review* **(Vol. 78, No. 4, July 2000, pp. 75)**
Pub: Harvard Business School Publishing Corp.
Ed: Eric Abrahamson. Description: Research shows companies should intersperse major change with smaller, organic change. Cases cited include New York City-based law firm Finley, Kumble, Wagner, Heine, Underberg, Manley, Myerson and Casey and General Electric.

29149 ■ "Changing Course" in *Pittsburgh Business Times* **(Vol. 23, No. 5, August 22, 2003, pp. 13)**
Pub: Pittsburgh Business Times
Ed: Patty Tascarella. Description: Edwin Grinberg, president at Lionshead Financial Planning Company, will continue his role as counsel at Feldstein Grinberg Stein & McKee. Mr. Grinberg launched Lionshead to provide additional services to his law firm's clients.

29150 ■ "Chapman Charged with Fraud" in *Black Enterprise* **(Vol. 34, No. 2, September 2003, pp. 26)**
Pub: Earl Graves Publishing Co.
Ed: Joyce Jones. Description: Nathan A. Chapman, Jr. was indicted by a federal grand jury on the charge of scheming to defraud the State Retirement & Pension System of Maryland, shareholders and his companies, and the public. The investment banker was charged on 39-counts with mail fraud, wire fraud, securities fraud and conspiracy.

29151 ■ "ChoicePoint's Actions Could be Damaging, Experts Say" in *Atlanta Journal-Constitution* **(March 5, 2005)**
Pub: Knight-Ridder/Tribune Business News
Ed: Matt Kempner. Description: State and federal investigators are looking into ChoicePoint's steps since the discovery of its selling at least 145,000 Americans' personal information to a bogus company. This data is normally sold to insurance companies, law enforcement agencies, companies screening potential employees and landlords considering renters.

29152 ■ *Clicking Through: A Survival Guide for Bringing Your Company Online*
Pub: Bloomberg Press
Ed: Jonathan I. Ezor. Released: January 2000. Price: $19.95. Description: Summary of legal compliance issues faced by small companies doing business on the Internet, including copyright and patent laws.

29153 ■ "Client Surveys Slow to Catch on as a Legal Marketing Tool" in *Journal Record* **(Oklahoma City, OK) (February 8, 2007)**
Pub: Journal Record
Ed: Dick Dahl. Description: Client surveys are not as successful a marketing tool for attorneys as other industries.

29154 ■ "Closing the Book on Public Records" in *Kiplinger's Personal Finance Magazine* **(Vol. 55, No. 1, January, 2001, pp. 26)**
Pub: The Kiplinger Washington Editors, Inc.
Ed: Kathy Jones. Description: Thirty-one states have enacted, or are considering laws to keep personal information off the Internet, but these laws could end up limiting consumer access to important information.

29155 ■ "Cochran Firm Wins Record $1.62 Billion Insurance Fraud Case" in *Black Enterprise* **(Vol. 34, July 2004, No. 12, pp. 21)**
Pub: Earl G. Graves Publishing Co. Inc.
Ed: Carolyn M. Brown. Description: The Cochran Firm's record winning insurance fraud case could help bring about reform in the insurance industry. The verdict has impacted the way insurance agents are being hired and trained.

29156 ■ "Cold Remedy Control has Pharmacies on Hot Seat" in *Milwaukee Journal Sentinel* **(December 6, 2005)**
Pub: Journal Sentinel, Inc.
Ed: Doris Hajewski. Description: A new Wisconsin law classifies cold remedies with pseudoephedrine a

controlled substance. A controlled substance can be sold only by a licensed pharmacist in the state. Grocers, convenience stores and other retail outlets can no longer sell any cold remedies containing pseudoephedrine.

29157 ■ "Commentary: Real Estate Binders: Are They Enforceable?" in *Long Island Business News* **(February 20, 2004)**
Pub: Dolan Media Newswires
Description: The rights and obligations to parties involved in a residential real estate binder are explained.

29158 ■ "Commercial Fraud Insight" in *Entrepreneur.com* **(Vol. 34, January 2006, No. 1, pp. 6)**
Pub: Entrepreneur Media Inc.
Ed: Steve Cooper. **Description:** Experian offers commercial fraud and authentication software to help small businesses verify addresses, tax ID numbers, phone numbers, DBA names and more. The database represents more than 16 million U.S. businesses.

29159 ■ "Companies Still Evaluating Blackout Toll" in *Pittsburgh Business Times* **(Vol. 23, No. 5, August 22, 2003, pp. 1)**
Pub: Pittsburgh Business Times
Ed: Christopher Davis. **Description:** The recent power failure on the East Coast had a significant impact on many businesses in the greater Pittsburgh, Pennsylvania area. But companies, such as financial services and legal service firms did not suffer as great a hardship.

29160 ■ "Companies Team to Help Small Law Firms" in *Crain's Detroit Business* **(Vol. 19, No. 45, November 10, 2003, pp. 41)**
Pub: Crain Communications Inc., Detroit
Ed: Robert Ankeny. **Description:** Professional Human Capital LLC offers administrative and human-resource services to small law firms and solo practitioners in the Metropolitan Detroit area. The new company will handle tasks specific to law firms, including payroll, taxes and health insurance.

29161 ■ *The Complete Book of Business Forms and Agreements*
Pub: The McGraw-Hill Companies
Ed: Cliff Roberson. **Released:** 1993. **Price:** $79.95. **Description:** Contains business agreements, contracts, and ready-to-use forms for various business transactions. Includes diskette.

29162 ■ *Complete Employee Handbook: A Step-by-Step Guide to Create a Custom Handbook That Protects Both the Employer and the Employee*
Pub: Moyer Bell
Ed: Michael A. Holzschu. **Released:** August 2007. **Price:** $39.95. **Description:** Comprehensive guide for employers deal with personnel issues; CD-ROM contains sample employee handbooks, federal regulations and laws, forms for complying with government programs and worksheets for assessing personnel needs and goals.

29163 ■ "Construction Defect Bill Is Progressing in Nevada, Lobbyist Says" in *Las Vegas Review-Journal* **(April 11, 2003)**
Pub: Knight-Ridder/Tribune Business News
Ed: Hubble Smith. **Description:** According to a lobbyist for the construction industry in Nevada, legislation aimed at reforming construction defect laws could help lower liability insurance rates.

29164 ■ *Contemporary Business Law*
Pub: West Publishing Co.
Ed: Richard A. Mann. **Released:** 1995.

29165 ■ "Contractual expansion & limitation of judicial review of arbitral awards (Part 2)" in *Dispute Resolution Journal* **(Vol. 56, No. 1)**
Pub: American Arbitration Association
Ed: Kenneth M. Curtin. **Description:** In part two of this two-part article, the author examines court decisions regarding the judicial review of arbitral awards and argues that courts should adhere strictly to the freedom of contract principle to best respect the arbitration process.

29166 ■ "A Conversation With Robin Asher, Clark Hill, LLC" in *Crain's Detroit Business* **(Vol. 23, February 5, 2007, No. 6, pp. 11)**
Pub: Crain Communications Inc. - Detroit
Ed: Tom Henderson. **Description:** Patent attorney discusses new patent process rules expected to be in effect later this year that would streamline the patent process. Supreme Court decision could help define what makes an idea obvious and not rely on technicalities and fine print.

29167 ■ "Corporate Cases" in *Business Week* **(January 23, 2006, No. 3968, pp. 37-38)**
Pub: McGraw-Hill Companies
Ed: Lorraine Woellert. **Description:** The backlash against prosecutors coaxing companies to waive attorney-client privilege is discussed. Statistical data included.

29168 ■ "Corporate Scandals Inspire Texas Fraud Bill" in *Houston Chronicle* **(April 11, 2003)**
Pub: Knight-Ridder/Tribune Business News
Ed: Janet Elliott. **Description:** In response to recent corporate scandals, the Senate unanimously approved a bill to crack down on business fraud. Senate Bill 1059 would create a corporate integrity unit in the Texas attorney general's office. Details of the bill are examined.

29169 ■ "Corporate Versus Individual Moral Responsibility" in *Journal of Business Ethics* **(Vol. 46, No. 2, August 15, 2003, pp. 143)**
Pub: Kluwer Academic Publishers Group
Ed: C. Soares. **Description:** There is a clear tendency in contemporary political/legal thought to limit agency to individual agents, thereby denying the existence and relevance of collective moral agency in general, and corporate agency in particular.

29170 ■ *Corporation & Business Associations, Statutes, Rules, Materials, & Forms*
Pub: Foundation Press, Inc.
Ed: Melvin A. Eisenberg. **Released:** 1995. PRC $20.95.

29171 ■ "A Corrupt Calculus: The Line Between 'Making the Numbers' and Making Them Up Remains Blurry" in *Barron's* **(July 7, 2003, pp. 24)**
Pub: Barron's
Ed: Michael Niemira, Bill Alpert, Jay Palmer. **Description:** Two books about corporate accounting and fraud are reviewed, "The Number" book, and "Born to Steal: When the Mafia Hit Wall Street".

29172 ■ "Court Battle Pits Fridge Pack vs. FridgeMaster" in *Atlanta Business Chronicle* **(Vol. 26, No. 10, August 15, 2003, pp. 1)**
Pub: American City Business Publications, Inc.
Ed: Charles Davidson. **Description:** Lawsuit filed by Riverwood International Corporation against Mead-Westvaco Corporation for patent infringement over the use of the terms FridgeMaster and Fridge Pack in advertising is examined.

29173 ■ "Court Battles" in *Business Week* **(December 19, 2005, No. 3964, pp. 33-34)**
Pub: McGraw-Hill Companies
Ed: Catherine Yang. **Description:** A settlement of the patent fight could net $1 billion for the late Tom Campana's NTP.

29174 ■ "Court Decisions - Privacy coverage differs from patent infringement" in *Rough Notes* **(Vol. 145, No. 1, January 2003, pp. 10)**
Pub: Rough Notes
Description: In a suit for breach of contract filed by Konami (America) Inc. against Hartford Insurance Company of Illinois, the Appellate Court of Illinois, held that piracy differed from, and that the case did not involve, patent infringement.

29175 ■ "Court OKs Meridian Ch. 11 Plan" in *Crain's Detroit Business* **(Vol. 22, December 11, 2006, No. 50, pp. 6)**
Pub: Crain Communications Inc. - Detroit
Ed: Bill Shea. **Description:** U.S. bankruptcy court approved reorganization plan to emerge from Chapter Eleven bankruptcy for local auto parts supplier. Management reorganization, reduced workforce, and price negotiations were part of plan filed last May.

29176 ■ "Court Sides With Biz on Disability" in *Inc.* **(August 1, 2003)**
Pub: Gruner & Jahr USA Publishing
Description: The Supreme Court ruled that businesses can reject employee disability benefits when the employer's doctor disagrees with the treating physician. A case involving a Black & Decker employee is cited.

29177 ■ "Courting the future" in *Crain's Detroit Business* **(Vol. 19, No. 14, April 7, 2003, pp. 1)**
Pub: Crain Communications Inc., Detroit
Ed: Robert Ankeny. **Description:** Profile of Reginald Turner, president of the State Bar of Michigan is presented. Turner's successful career includes partnerships at two prestigious Detroit law firms, presidencies of two major Michigan bar associations and significant roles in city, county and state affairs and in the Democratic Party.

29178 ■ "Courting Trouble" in *Inc.* **(October 1, 2003)**
Pub: Gruner & Jahr USA Publishing
Ed: Nadine Heintz. **Description:** Profile of an entrepreneur facing mail fraud charges engaged in a fraudulent scheme to obtain certification as a disadvantaged small business in 2000, in order to procure government road-construction contracts set aside for minorities and women.

29179 ■ "Cover Me: How to Spread the Risk of a Deal Around" in *Entrepreneur* **(Vol. 33, February 2005, No. 2, pp. 73)**
Pub: Entrepreneur Media Inc.
Ed: Marc Diener. **Description:** Standards to be set by an attorney when a small business is making a large deal. These standards will help balance risks.

29180 ■ "Crackdown on Mutual Fund Abuse" in *Black Enterprise* **(Vol. 34, No. 5, December 2003, pp. 22)**
Pub: Earl Graves Publishing Co.
Ed: Jeffrey McKinney. **Description:** The Securities and Exchange Commission is cracking down on U.S. firms improperly trading mutual funds. So far, 80 of the nation's largest mutual funds operations have received letters requesting information about ways they buy and sell mutual funds.

29181 ■ "Cracker Barrel Pays $8.7M to Settle Race Case" in *Black Enterprise* **(Vol. 35, December 2004, No. 5, pp. 38)**
Pub: Earl G. Graves Publishing Co. Inc.
Ed: Nicole Richardson. **Description:** In lawsuits filed by employees and customers, Cracker Barrel restaurant chain has agreed to pay $8.7 million to settle allegations of discrimination.

29182 ■ "Cracking Down On Copycats" in *Milwaukee Journal Sentinel* **(December 6, 2005)**
Pub: Journal Sentinel, Inc.
Ed: Rick Barrett. **Description:** Wisconsin marine manufacturers fear a new law that prohibits competitors from building unauthorized copies of a hull design will not be enough to stop them from hull splashing because it is not strong enough and is difficult for manufacturers to use.

29183 ■ "Cream of the Crop" in *Hispanic Business* **(March 2002, pp. 36)**
Pub: Hispanic Business
Description: Advice is given for choosing a business or law school, with information geared toward Hispanic students.

29184 ■ "Creditor sues to wring money from former Code-Alarm" in *Crain's Detroit Business* (Vol. 18, No. 24, June 17, 2002, pp. 29)
Pub: Crain Communications Inc. - Detroit
Ed: Michael Strong. **Description:** Old CA Inc., formerly Code-Alarm Inc., faces a lawsuit from one former vendor, while others are trying to secure payments three months after the firm was sold.

29185 ■ "Criminal records" in *Entrepreneur* (Vol. 31, No. 5, May 2003, pp. 72)
Pub: Entrepreneur Media Inc.
Ed: Steven C. Bahls, Jane Easter Bahls. **Description:** Under the Sarbanes-Oxley Act it is a federal crime for businesses to intentionally destroy documents that might be evidence in a federal investigation.

29186 ■ "Crucial triad" in *Daily Business Review* (Vol. 77, No. 198, March 24, 2003, pp. AA4)
Pub: American Lawyer Media LP
Ed: David Geyer, Elizabeth Lampert. **Description:** Ways in which law firm partners can use the triad of business development, marketing and media relations to better serve clients is explained.

29187 ■ "Current Events" in *Forbes* (January 21, 2002, p. 29)
Pub: Forbes Magazine
Ed: Paul Johnson. **Description:** Information is presented regarding the antitrust case against Microsoft; legal information is discussed about the equality for businesses, regardless of size, under the law.

29188 ■ "Cybercrime: Interpol for the Internet" in *Red Herring* (No. 103, September 1, 2001, p. 27)
Pub: Herring Communications
Ed: Julia Lawlor. **Description:** An overview of the European Cybercrime Treaty, which includes 43 European members, the U.S., Japan, Canada, and South Africa. The treaty would make unauthorized computer-system break-ins a criminal offense, punishable by prison.

29189 ■ "The Dangers of a Lack of Accountability" in *Automotive News* (Vol. 20, October 4, 2004, No. 40, pp. 8)
Pub: Crain Communications Inc.
Ed: Keith Crain. **Description:** Plans for developing a downtown district, called African Town, in Detroit that would fund money to black-owned businesses is discussed. Many individuals claim the plan is both discriminatory and illegal.

29190 ■ "DCT sues Detroit Edison over fuel cell technology" in *Crain's Detroit Business* (Vol. 16, No. 49, December 4, 2000, pp. 42)
Pub: Crain Communications, Inc.
Ed: Leslie Green. **Description:** Family-owned auto supplier DCT Inc. is taking on energy giant DTE Energy Company in Wayne County Circuit Court, claiming three DTE affiliates deprived it of profits from the emerging fuel cell market by stealing trade secrets and disclosing proprietary information.

29191 ■ "Declaring War On Wal-Mart" in *Business Week* (February 7, 2005, No. 3919, pp. 31)
Pub: McGraw-Hill Companies
Ed: Aaron Bernstein. **Description:** Wal-Mart has launched an ad campaign in January with the message: Wal-Mart is working for everyone. The retailer is fighting back against allegations of sex discrimination, poverty-level wages, and non-union workforce.

29192 ■ "Delta Agrees to Settle Potential Allegations of Employee-Fund Misuse" in *Altanta Journal-Constitution* (February 7, 2007)
Pub: Cox Newspapers, Inc.
Ed: Russell Grantham. **Description:** Delta Airlines will pay $70 million into a fund for disabled employees and surviving relatives of retired employees in order to settle allegations that the airline used the fund after 9/11 for other expenses.

29193 ■ "Dentist Office to Anchor New Sarasota County, Fla., Office Park" in *Bradenton Herald* (April 11 2003)
Pub: Knight-Ridder/Tribune Business News
Ed: Matt Griswold. **Description:** Sarasota attorney David Band is heading the development of a 12,800 square-foot professional office complex for Ranch Lake Plaza, which will feature a dentist office, accountants, law firms, insurance offices, and other professional business tenants.

29194 ■ "Detroit Free Press Small Business Column" in *Detroit Free Press* (May 16, 2005)
Pub: Knight-Ridder/Tribune Business News
Ed: Carol Cain. **Description:** Denise Ilitch is joining Clark Hill PLC in order to assist the Detroit law firm with its business customers.

29195 ■ "Detroit Lawyers Pick Up Extra Work" in *Crain's Detroit Business* (Vol. 21, October 17, 2005, No. 43, pp. 32)
Pub: Crain Communications Inc. - Detroit
Ed: Robert Ankeny. **Description:** Due to Delphi Corporation's Chapter 11 filing, Detroit area law firms are representing some of the companies involved, including tier-two and smaller suppliers.

29196 ■ *Dictionary of Real Estate Terms*
Pub: Barron's Educational Series, Incorporated
Ed: Jack P. Friedman, Jack C. Harris. **Released:** March 2004. **Price:** $13.95. **Description:** More than 2,500 real estate terms relating to mortgages and financing, brokerage law, architecture, rentals and leases, property insurance, and more.

29197 ■ "Differentiating Legal Issues by Business Type" in *Journal of Small Business Management* (Vol. 44, October 2006, No. 4, pp. 563)
Pub: Blackwell Publishing, Inc.
Ed: Sandra Malach; Peter Robinson; Tannis Radcliffe. **Description:** A fundamental issue when forming a business and its strategic operation is developing legal strategies to better protect the assets of the business and entrepreneur. An analysis of data indicated that certain legal issues are relevant to specific types of new ventures while certain legal issues are important to all new ventures. Depending on the category of business, the relevancy of individual legal issues will vary. Statistical data included.

29198 ■ "Digital Signatures vs. Electronic Signatures" in *E-business Advisor* (Vol. 18, No. 4, April 2000, pp. 48)
Pub: Advisor Media, Inc.
Ed: Tom Melling. **Description:** Confusion between the definitions of digital signatures and electronic signatures could result in poorly constructed legislation that may create barriers to e-commerce and make electronic contracts unenforceable.

29199 ■ "Diversity in the Workplace" in *My Business* (February/March 2004, pp. 15)
Pub: My Business Magazine
Ed: Dennis McCafferty. **Description:** Legal experts offer advice on workplace practices involving ethnic diversity.

29200 ■ "Do-Not-Call Suit Gets $500" in *Sacramento Bee* (November 30, 2005)
Pub: The Sacramento Bee
Ed: Dale Kasler. **Description:** California officials fined a $500 penalty against a Florida mortgage company, LMA Marketing Inc., accused of violating the state's do-not-call telemarketing ban.

29201 ■ "Do the Right Thing - Or Else" in *Inc.* (November 1, 2004)
Pub: Inc. Magazine
Ed: Darren Dahl. **Description:** New Federal ethics rules apply to all companies, regardless of size.

29202 ■ "Does New Watchdog Have Teeth?" in *Business Journal-Portland* (Vol. 20, No. 23, August 8, 2003, pp. 1)
Pub: American City Business Journals, Inc.
Ed: Aliza Earnshaw. **Description:** The passage of the federal Sarbanes-Oxley Act of 2002 resulted in the formation of the Public Companies Accounting Oversight Board (PCAOB). The PCAOB will attempt to restore investor confidence in corporations by monitoring financial reports.

29203 ■ "Dollars for Scholars" in *Hispanic Business* (September 2003, pp. 64, 66, 68)
Pub: Hispanic Business
Description: A select guide to scholarships for the study of business or law is presented.

29204 ■ "Don Quixote In Court" in *Forbes* (Vol. 170, No. 8, October 14, 2002, pp. 97)
Pub: Forbes Magazine
Ed: Ashlea Ebeling. **Description:** Jeff Abraham won a $15 million verdict for blowing the whistle on his employer, South Korea's Hyundai Group. Abraham reflects on his experience and questions whether he would do the same thing again.

29205 ■ "Don't Junk Property Rights" in *Forbes* (Vol. 174, December 27, 2004, No. 13, pp. 25)
Pub: Forbes Magazine Inc.
Ed: Steve Forbes. **Description:** The U.S. Supreme Court will issue two critical rulings on property rights in the next few months.

29206 ■ "Down the chute" in *Daily Business Review* (Vol. 77, No. 198, March 24, 2003, pp. A8)
Pub: American Lawyer Media LP
Ed: Laurie Cunningham. **Description:** The Florida Supreme Court has ruled that out-of-state lawyers could not represent clients in securities arbitration.

29207 ■ "E-Cognita founders to lead group at Miller, Canfield" in *Crain's Detroit Business* (Vol. 19, No. 15, April 14, 2003, pp. 25)
Pub: Crain Communications Inc., Detroit
Ed: Jennette Smith. **Description:** Founders of the technology company E-Cognita, will be working with the newly formed capital-markets lending group at the Detroit law firm Miller, Canfield, Paddock and Stone PLC. E-Cognita Technologies Inc. developed software called StreamLoaner and Lexicon to manage transactions and automate documents and is used by lenders, lawyers, and other parties involved in loan closings.

29208 ■ "E-commerce can pose legal risks for businesses" in *Crain's Detroit Business* (Vol. 16, No. 16, April 17, 2000, pp. 17)
Pub: Crain Communications, Inc.
Ed: Tim Moran. **Description:** The potential of legal risk when doing business on the Internet is examined.

29209 ■ "E-Commerce: When You Put Your 'John Hancock' on the Web Form!" in *Ingram's* (Vol. 27, No. 5, May 2001, pp. 33)
Pub: Show Me Publishing, Inc.
Ed: Arthur L. Smith. **Description:** Businesses are still finding ample opportunities from the electronic marketplace. Contracts made electronically are just as binding as the traditional paper contract.

29210 ■ "E-signing law seen as a boon to e-business" in *The New York Times* (July 4, 2000, pp. C1)
Pub: The New York Times Company
Ed: Barnaby J. Feder. **Description:** Analysts expect that the new law letting businesses and consumers sign legally binding accords with electronic signatures will increase the speed at which electronic businesses develop. The new process, called 'e-signing', will likely give rise to many personal identification technologies that can serve as alternatives to writing one's name on paper.

29211 ■ "Ease up on us, one industry that finances small firms asks the U.S." in *Wall Street Journal* (July 18, 2000, pp. B2)
Pub: Dow Jones & Co., Inc.
Ed: Jeffrey A. Tannenbaum. **Description:** Investment firms request an easing of regulations on financing small business.

29212 ■ "Eateries Shut In Raids Over Labor Laws" in *Sacramento Bee* **(November 15, 2005)**
Pub: The Sacramento Bee
Ed: Rachel Osterman. Description: State officials temporarily closed more than a dozen restaurants in the Sacramento, California area. Of 20 establishments inspected, 16 were in violation of labor laws, including workers' compensation, overtime, meal breaks, and minimum wage rules.

29213 ■ "Eco-Radicals Target Growth in Sierra Hills" in *San Jose Mercury News* **(March 9, 2005)**
Pub: Knight-Ridder/Tribune Business News
Ed: Dana Hull. Description: The Earth Liberation Front, an underground environmental network is attacking the foothill towns and fast-growing communities in the Bay Area of San Francisco, California.

29214 ■ "The Economics" in *Law Firm Inc.* **(August 2004)**
Pub: American Lawyer Media LP
Ed: Sam Collier. Description: Law firms should compare costs when planning to outsource technology services based on combination of capacity (the number of users and workstations), complexity and features, and service level.

29215 ■ "EEOC Sues Charlotte-Based Lebo's" in *Charlotte Observer* **(February 7, 2007)**
Pub: Knight-Ridder/Tribune Business News
Ed: Mike Drummond. Description: The U.S. Equal Employment Opportunity Commission filed a pregnancy discrimination lawsuit against Lebo's Shoe Stores, located in Charlotte, North Carolina. The suit alleges the store withdrew an offer to hire a woman after finding out she was pregnant.

29216 ■ *Effect of the Overvalued Dollar on Small Exporters: Congressional Hearing*
Pub: DIANE Publishing Company
Ed: Donald Manzullo. Released: October 2004. Price: $30.00. Description: Congressional hearing: Witnesses: Dr. Lawrence Chimerine, Economist; Tony Raimondo, President and CEO, Behlen Manufacturing Company; Robert J. Weskamp, President, Wes-Tech, Inc.; Wayne Dollar, President, Georgia Farm Bureau; and Vargese George, President and CEO, Westex International, Inc. Appendix includes correspondence sent to committee on the overvalued dollar.

29217 ■ "11th Hour" in *Entrepreneur* **(Vol. 27, No. 12, December 1999, pp. 20)**
Pub: Entrepreneur Media Inc.
Ed: Cynthia E. Griffin. Description: A bill in Congress could fundamentally change the way small business bankruptcies are handled. Information about the Bankruptcy Reform Act of 1998 is covered.

29218 ■ "Emerging Threat: Human Rights Claims" in *Harvard Business Review* **(Vol. 81, No. 8, August 2003, pp. 16)**
Pub: Harvard Business School Press
Ed: Elliot Schrage. Description: In this historical overview, U.S. courts are accepting an increasing number of human rights cases against companies involving the Alien Tort Statute (ATS) enacted in 1789. This act grants original jurisdiction to the U.S. federal courts for civil actions brought by an alien for a tort committed in violation of international law. In 1980, the first significant civil rights case was brought using ATS.

29219 ■ "Employees Sue Best Buy for Race, Gender Discrimination" in *Sacramento Bee* **(December 9, 2005)**
Pub: The Sacramento Bee
Ed: Rachel Osterman. Description: Retailer, Best Buy is being sued for race and gender discrimination for alleged lower wages than those paid to white males and for steering women employees away from high-paying sales jobs.

29220 ■ "Employers Can Expect More Legal Challenges from Workers" in *Kiplinger Letter* **(Vol. 84, January 26, 2007, No. 4)**
Pub: Kiplinger
Description: Employers may be faced will legal challenges concerning issues of overtime and The Family and Medical Leave Act since the Supreme Court broadened the definition of retaliation to include words and actions by supervisors outside the workplace.

29221 ■ "Employing Her Literary Skills" in *San Diego Business Journal* **(Vol. 28, January 8, 2007, No. 2, pp. 10)**
Pub: San Diego Business Journal Associates
Ed: Michelle Mowad. Description: Profile of Professor Susan Bisom-Rapp, author of a new book on international and comparative employment law. The book covers laws in nine countries, including labor and employment law regulations.

29222 ■ "Employment Law at the Dawn of the New Millennium" in *Employment Relations Today* **(Vol. 26, No. 4, Winter 2000, pp. 109)**
Pub: John Wiley & Sons, Inc.
Ed: William C. Martucci and Jeffrey M. Place. Description: The interpretation and construction of employment law at the turn of the 21st century are described. Topics addressed include protection for employees under anti-discrimination laws, employee privacy rights, and flexible working environments.

29223 ■ *Enabling Environments for Jobs and Entrepreneurship: The Role of Policy and Law in Small Enterprise Employment*
Pub: International Labour Office
Ed: Gerhard Reinecke, Simon White. Released: February 2004. Price: $22.95. Description: National policies, laws and regulations governing workplace safety.

29224 ■ *Entrepreneurship: A Process Perspective*
Pub: Thomson South-Western
Ed: Robert A. Baron; Scott A. Shane. Released: February 2007. Price: $137.95. Description: Entrepreneurial process covering team building, finances, business plan, legal issues, marketing, growth and exit strategies.

29225 ■ *The Essential Corporation Handbook*
Pub: Oasis Press
Ed: Carl R. Sniffen. Released: 1992. Price: $21.95 (paper).

29226 ■ "Ethics of Justice and Care in Corporate Crisis Management" in *Journal of Business Ethics* **(Vol. 46, No. 4, Sept. 15, 2003, pp. 351)**
Pub: Kluwer Academic Publishers Group
Ed: Sheldene Simola. Description: The importance of ethics in corporate crisis management is discussed.

29227 ■ "Ex-Breed exec sues automakers, suppliers over sensor patent" in *Crain's Detroit Business* **(Vol. 19, No. 9, March 3, 2003, pp. 28)**
Pub: Crain Communications Inc., Detroit
Ed: Terry Kosdrosky. Description: David Breed, inventor and former executive at Breed Technologies Inc., is suing global automakers and several parts suppliers over a patent-infringement for a side-impact airbag sensor.

29228 ■ "Ex-TV Exec Sues Over Lentek Deal" in *Orlando Business Journal* **(Vol. 20, No. 2, June 27, 2003, pp. 1)**
Pub: American City Business Journals, Inc.
Ed: Chad Eric Watt. Description: Information is provided regarding a lawsuit filed by majority stockholder Roy M. Speer, against Lentek International Inc. Topics include allegations of fraud, poor financial management and questionable accounting procedures.

29229 ■ "Facing the Online Music" in *Inc.* **(July 1, 2003)**
Pub: Gruner & Jahr USA Publishing

Description: Entrepreneurs have a stake in the debate over downloading online music and are skeptical of the recording industry's attempts to rewrite intellectual property law.

29230 ■ "Fact and Comment" in *Forbes Global* **(Vol. 7, December 20, 2004, No. 22, pp. 9)**
Pub: Forbes Magazine Inc.
Ed: Steve Forbes. Description: Two critical issues on property rights will be addressed by the U.S. Supreme Court.

29231 ■ "Faster Tech Transfer" in *Inc.* **(July 1, 2003)**
Pub: Gruner & Jahr USA Publishing
Description: Technology transfer from colleges to private sector is discussed, using examples of universities tech transfer that fueled 450 business and 4,000 licenses in 2002. Transferring innovation from college laboratories to the private sector has startups and schools arguing over licensing and royalty deals.

29232 ■ "Fax Attack: This Entrepreneur's Fighting Mad About Junk Faxes" in *Entrepreneur* **(Vol. 32, No. 1, January 2004, pp. 34)**
Pub: Entrepreneur Media, Inc.
Ed: Geoff Williams. Description: Steve Kirsch, owner of a software company in San Jose, California, has filed a $2.2 trillion class-action lawsuit against Fax.com, in the hopes of ending junk fax mail.

29233 ■ "Fax Regs Rethought" in *Inc.* **(December 1, 2004)**
Pub: Inc. Magazine
Ed: Darren Dahl. Description: Federal regulations regarding mass faxes could hurt small businesses. The new law would allow businesses to fax any customer they have done businesses with in the last seven years.

29234 ■ "Federal Contracts Draw New Scrutiny" in *Inc.* **(August 2005, pp. 24)**
Pub: Inc. Magazine
Ed: Darren Dahl. Description: The Small Business Administration reported ways that large companies are erroneously categorized in order to procure federal government contracts.

29235 ■ "Federal suit alleges MVM overbilled" in *Washington Business Journal* **(Vol. 21, No. 50, April 11, 2003, pp. 1)**
Pub: Washington Business Journal
Ed: Sean Madigan. Description: A civil suit has been filed against MVM Inc. by the U.S. Department of Justice, alleging that MVM submitted 44 false invoices on a security services contract. MVM is alleged to have invoiced for 4 security guards in supervisory positions, before they were actually trained.

29236 ■ "Federal Trade Comm. Report Says Long Island a Favorite of Scam Artists" in *Long Island Business News* **(January 30, 2004)**
Pub: Dolan Media Newswires
Ed: Ken Schachter. Description: According to a new federal ranking of metro-area populations, Long Island, New York ranked 12th as a favorite target of scam artists. Statistical data included.

29237 ■ "Feds Accuse Sacramento, Calif.-Based Restaurant of Sex Discrimination" in *Sacramento Bee* **(September 30, 2005)**
Pub: The Sacramento Bee
Ed: Dale Kasler. Description: U.S. Equal Employment Opportunity Commission is suing Randy Paragary's restaurant chain for alleged unfair treatment of women, especially those of Mexican descent. According to the claim, Mexican women were not allowed to take work breaks or vacations and were required to perform tasks other female workers were not asked to do.

29238 ■ "Fee Bargain: Law Firm Mergers May Give You More Room to Negotiate Legal Fees" in *Entrepreneur* (Vol. 31, No. 7, July 2003, pp. 27)
Pub: Entrepreneur Media, Inc.
Ed: Chris Penttila. Description: In the soft economy, law firms are struggling to stay afloat with fewer clients and increasing operational costs, therefore some firms are merging offering lower fees and more services.

29239 ■ "A Fight for Rights" in *Hispanic Business* (October 2004, pp. 50, 52, 54)
Pub: Hispanic Business
Ed: Jonathan J. Higuera. Description: Profile of Ann Marie Tallman, leader at the Mexican American Legal Defense and Educational Fund. Tallman is committed to adding economic rights to the group's agenda.

29240 ■ "Firm-and-Fixed-Plan Rule Reaffirmed" in *Journal of Accountancy* (Vol. 199, February 2005, No. 2, pp. 75)
Pub: American Institute of Certified Public Accountants
Ed: Edward J. Schnee. Description: Case of Merrill & Lynch Co. v. Commissioner is examined. The case involved the firm-and-fixed-plan rule.

29241 ■ "Firms Paid $1.6 Million in Penalties, California Pesticide Regulators Report" in *Sacramento Bee* (December 28, 2005)
Pub: The Sacramento Bee
Ed: Jim Wasserman. Description: Firms illegally selling pesticides in the State of California were fined a combined total of $1.6 million by the California Department of Pesticide Control. Most of the penalties incurred were due to chemical products that were not approved for sale in the state, while others were to firms not paying mandatory environmental fees.

29242 ■ "Firms maintain strong pro bono presence" in *Atlanta Business Chronicle* (Vol. 25, November 15, 2002, No. 23 pp. SS10)
Pub: American City Business Publications, Inc.
Ed: Tonya Layman. Description: Law firms, such as Kilpatrick Stockton LLP; Troutman Sanders LLP; Smith, Gambrell & Russell LLP; and Hunton & Williams are increasing pro bono activities. Often, pro bono work energizes lawyers at these firms and improves morale, and in some cases, months with the highest number of pro bono hours are also the months with the highest billable hours.

29243 ■ "FMLA Needs to be Fixed to Stop Abuse" in *Crain's Detroit Business* (Vol. 21, January 10, 2005, No. 2, pp. 9)
Pub: Crain Communications Inc. - Detroit
Ed: Nancy McKeague. Description: Sixty-eight federal lawsuits have been filed challenging the validity of the Family and Medical Leave Act. Managers and business owners struggle to provide these benefits because federal rules make it difficult to administer them.

29244 ■ "Following the Leader: Learn these Laws, and Employees Won't Be Far Behind You" in *Entrepreneur* (Vol. 32, July 2004, No. 7, pp. 34)
Pub: Entrepreneur Media Inc.
Description: Review of Michael Feiner's book, The Feiner Points of Leadership. The book offers insight into motivating employees and creating loyalty.

29245 ■ "Food Fight! How Should Restaurateurs Deal With the Weighty Problem of Customer's Obesity?" in *Entrepreneur* (Vol. 31, July 2003)
Pub: Entrepreneur Media, Inc.
Ed: Julie Monahan. Description: Should restaurants be held liable for customer's weight problems? Industry associations are developing consumer education campaigns emphasizing a balanced diet and exercise to lose or maintain weight and stay healthy.

29246 ■ "Form finder" in *Entrepreneur* (Vol. 30, No. 3, March 2002, pp. 40)
Pub: Entrepreneur Media Inc.

Ed: Liane Gouthro. Description: Profile of Cosmi Swift Ware Personal and Business Legal Forms to Go software; this software will create more than 200 legal documents including bankruptcies, wills and leases; basic legal help is also included.

29247 ■ "Former B.E. 100s CEO Convicted" in *Black Enterprise* (Vol. 35, October 2004, No. 3, pp. 33)
Pub: Earl G. Graves Publishing Co. Inc.
Ed: K. Terrell Reed. Description: Nathan A. Chapman, former investment banker, has been convicted of fraud. Chapman was convicted of 15 counts of wire fraud, two counts of mail fraud, three counts of investment advisory fraud, one count of making false statements to Securities and Exchange Commission, and two counts of making false statements on tax returns.

29248 ■ "Former B.E. 100s Clerk Faces Prison Time" in *Black Enterprise* (Vol. 35, September 2004, No. 2, pp. 30)
Pub: Earl G. Graves Publishing Co. Inc.
Ed: Tamara E. Holmes. Description: Joanna L. Cook, former accounts payable clerk for TeleCommunication Systems Inc., pleaded guilty to one count of bank fraud for stealing more than $1 million from the company between 2000 and 2003. An assistant controller and accounting supervisor discovered her fraudulent activity.

29249 ■ "Former Collection Attorney Needs Consultants to Offer Bulletproof Asset Protection" in *Success* (Vol. 47, No. 2, June 2000, pp. 88)
Pub: Success Publishing, Inc.
Description: Bill Reed, former collection attorney and author, tells how he changed his career to start a consultant agency to help people protect their assets. Mr. Reed trains Asset Protection Consultants nationwide to work with clients in their own areas.

29250 ■ "Former Computer Associates Executive Pleads Guilty in U.S. District Court in Brooklyn" in *Long Island Business News* (Jan. 30, 2004)
Pub: Dolan Media Newswires
Description: Former senior vice president, Lloyd Silverstein, of Computer Associates International, pleaded guilty to charges of obstruction of justice in the federal investigation of the software maker's accounting practices. The company has also received notice that it will be the target of civil charges by the Securities and Exchange Commission.

29251 ■ "Former Couch Street Figure Heads to Prison" in *Business Journal-Portland* (Vol. 20, No. 24, August 15, 2003, pp. 8)
Pub: American City Business Journals, Inc.
Ed: Shelly Strom. Description: Cleburne Jr. Brigham has been sentenced to 37 years in prison for alleged falsification of a loan application, making false statements to the U.S. Small Business Administration, misuse of social security number, and using the Couch Street Fish House illegally.

29252 ■ "Former Manager Files Suit Against OKC-based Hudiburg Auto Group" in *Journal Record (Oklahoma City, OK)* (February 6, 2007)
Pub: Journal Record
Ed: Marie Price. Description: Details of a lawsuit filed by a former manager at Hudiburg Auto Suit are explored. The suit alleges a breached oral contract that would allow the general manager to purchase shares of Big Red Sports/Imports.

29253 ■ "Forward: Patents" in *Red Herring* (No. 99, June 15 & July 1, 2001, pp. 34-35)
Pub: Herring Communications
Ed: Stephan Herrera. Description: Overview of the biotech legal case, Festo, a recent patent-infringement decision that has fundamentally changed the balance of power that has long favored patent holders over those who deliberately or incidentally design products based on similar science.

29254 ■ "Fraud Alert" in *Small Business Opportunities* (Vol. 17, May 2005, No. 3, pp. 80, 84)
Pub: Harris Publications Inc.
Ed: Carla Longley Vincent. Description: Ways to avoid small business fraud is investigated. According to the Association for Certified Fraud Examiners (ACFE) small firms are more vulnerable to fraud and employees with 100 or less employees suffered an average loss of $127,500, while larger firms reported $97,000.

29255 ■ "Fraud Risk: Are You Prepared? The Mission: To Create Stronger Support for an Ethically Sound Business Environment" in *Journal of Accountancy*
Pub: American Institute of Certified Public Accountants
Ed: Steven E. Sacks. Description: Incentives that reward individuals for short term results can sometimes result in fraud and abuse; ways this fraud is affecting the certified public accounting profession is examined.

29256 ■ "Funds Face Unexpected Antitrust Problem" in *Venture Capital Journal* (January 1, 2005)
Pub: Thomason Financial Inc.
Description: Profile of the Clayton Act Section 8 of federal antitrust law is examined. The Act, antitrust law, which prohibits an end-run around the Sherman Act's ban on monopolization and agreements in restraint of trade by prohibiting the same person from serving on boards of competitive companies, has rarely been enforced by either private litigants or by the federal government.

29257 ■ "Ga. Chamber seeking 'civil justice' reform" in *Atlanta Business Chronicle* (Vol. 25, November 29, 2002, No. 25 pp. 28A)
Pub: American City Business Publications, Inc.
Ed: David Allison. Description: The main objective of the Georgia Chamber of Commerce in the next session of state legislature is to amend civil justice in Georgia. Chamber leaders have outlined nine reforms they hope to introduce into law.

29258 ■ "Gas Station Owners May Be Pumping Red Ink" in *Business Week* (No. 3699, September 18, 2000, pp. 156)
Pub: McGraw-Hill, Inc.
Description: Owners of service stations face upgrades of diesel tanks to accommodate law changes, but the pace of this change causes concerns.

29259 ■ "Georgia Insurer Riles Its Rivals" in *Crain's Detroit Business* (Vol. 19, No. 43, October 27, 2003, pp. 3)
Pub: Crain Communications Inc., Detroit
Ed: Katie Merx. Description: Palmer and Cay Inc., based in Savannah, Georgia, has expanded into the Detroit, Michigan market. The firm hired 22 area insurance professionals as part of the expansion. These hirings have prompted Marsh, the parent company, to sue Palmer and Cay Inc.

29260 ■ "Georgia Insurer Riles Its Rivals; Palmer & Cay's Moves In Detroit Prompt Marsh USA to Sue" in *Crain's Detroit Business* (Vol. 19)
Pub: Crain Communications Inc., Detroit
Ed: Katie Merx. Description: Palmer and Cay Inc., based in Savannah, Georgia, has expanded into the Detroit, Michigan market. The firm hired 22 area insurance professionals as part of the expansion. These hirings have prompted Marsh, the parent company, to sue Palmer and Cay Inc.

29261 ■ "Georgia Senate Panel Approves Right to Buy, Sell Water Permits" in *Atlanta Journal-Constitution* (April 11, 2003)
Pub: Knight-Ridder/Tribune Business News
Ed: Stacy Shelton. Description: A committee voted in April 2003, allowing industries, cities, and farmers the right to buy and sell water permits they obtained free. The practice is called "permit trading" and is opposed by various environmental groups, while economists say it will help mold state water policy.

29262 ■ "Getting Out of an IRS Mess" in *Black Enterprise* **(Vol. 37, December 2006, No. 5, pp. 53)**
Pub: Earl G. Graves Publishing Co. Inc.
Ed: Carolyn M. Brown. **Description:** Owing back taxes to the IRS can lead to huge penalties and interest. Here are some tips on how to handle paying the IRS what you owe them.

29263 ■ "Give Advice? Get Protected!" in *Small Business Opportunities* **(Vol. 13, No. 5, September 2001, pp. 18)**
Pub: Harris Publications, Inc.
Ed: Carla Vincent. **Description:** Concise information regarding professional liability insurance is presented. A brief profile of Nolo Press, a provider of self-help legal solutions for consumers and small businesses is also included.

29264 ■ "Giving mergers a head start" in *Harvard Business Review* **(Vol. 80, No. 10, October 2002, pp. 20)**
Pub: Harvard Business School Press
Ed: Randy Croyle, Patrick Kager. **Description:** Advice is given for managing the process of merging two companies. Relying on former company employees can help ameliorate difficulties to antitrust laws, and smooth the merger process.

29265 ■ "Go West: Want a Few Business Pointers? Mosey on Over to Deadwood" in *Entrepreneur* **(Vol. 32, November 2004, No. 11, pp. 22)**
Pub: Entrepreneur Media Inc.
Ed: Steve Cooper. **Description:** HBO's new series Deadwood, based on a real-life town in South Dakota around 1876, offers insight into business leadership, contracts, property rights, marketing, managing and business expansion.

29266 ■ "Going Private: How VCs Can Get in the Game" in *Venture Capital Journal* **(Vol. 42, No. 10, October 2002, pp. 49)**
Pub: Thomas Venture Economics
Ed: Jonathan Bell. **Description:** A trend towards venture capital firms to reverse course and help companies go private is examined. To minimize the risk that the transaction may be questionable as being unfair to minority shareholders, an independent and disinterested committee of the company's board should handle negotiations.

29267 ■ "Going Separate Ways: In a Law Suit; You and an Employee Could Be Sent Down Different Paths" in *Entrepreneur* **(Vol. 32, August 2004)**
Pub: Entrepreneur Media Inc.
Ed: Jacquelyn Lynn. **Description:** Business owners need to analyze insurance coverage in the event of a law suit that includes multiple defendants.

29268 ■ "Good Libations?" in *Entrepreneur* **(Vol. 32, December 2004, No. 12, pp. 100)**
Pub: Entrepreneur Media Inc.
Ed: Jane Easter Bahls. **Description:** When planning a company party or event, it is essential to consider what could happen if alcohol was served and an employee drove home drunk.

29269 ■ "Good Vibes: Socially Responsible Investing is Gaining Fans...and Clout" in *Barron's* **(July 7, 2003, pp. L3)**
Pub: Barron's
Ed: Robin Goldwyn Blumenthal. **Description:** High profile corporate corruption scandals, such as Enron and WorldCom, have helped strengthen the position of socially responsible investing advocates, even in the Wall Street community, where they were most widely derided. A review of the increasing influence of socially responsible investing is provided.

29270 ■ "Goodwill for Your Ex" in *Inc.* **(September 1, 2003)**
Pub: Gruner & Jahr USA Publishing
Ed: Mike Hofman. **Description:** Should 'goodwill' be considered divisible property for small business owners in divorce cases?

29271 ■ "Got milked?" in *BlackEnterprise* **(Vol. 32, No. 3, October 2001, pp. 168)**
Pub: Earl Graves Publishing Co.
Ed: Sonia Alleyne. **Description:** Brief article listing a Web site that offers free legal advice for issues such as accidents, bankruptcy, and taxes to intellectual property, immigration, and estate planning.

29272 ■ "Government Hooks Man for Phishing" in *Cardline* **(Vol. 4, No. 13, March 26, 2004, pp. 1)**
Pub: Thomson Media Inc.
Description: An identity-theft scam has been shut down. Zachary Keith Hill used the logos of Internet service provider America Online (AOL) and the online payment service, PayPal to scam consumers into revealing credit card numbers and other confidential information.

29273 ■ "Granholm wants to scrap workers' comp appeal board" in *Crain's Detroit Business* **(Vol. 19, No. 11, March 17, 2003, pp. 6)**
Pub: Crain Communications Inc., Detroit
Ed: Amy Lane. **Description:** Michigan Governor Jennifer Granholm wants to eliminate the Workers' Compensation Appellate Commission; manufacturers feel they would lose an important place to adjudicate claims for disability benefits outside of court.

29274 ■ "Grave Matters" in *Crain's Detroit Business* **(Vol. 22, January 16, 2006, No. 3, pp. 3)**
Pub: Crain Communications Inc. - Detroit
Ed: Andrew Dieterich. **Description:** Monument sellers in Michigan have filed a complaint against cemeteries citing the cemeteries are tying services such as burial and grave site maintenance with sales of grave markers. Simpson Granite and Arnet's Inc. are leading the class action lawsuit.

29275 ■ "Greed Is Bad" in *Red Herring* **(No. 106, October 15, 2001, pp. 92)**
Pub: Herring Communications
Ed: Dan Briody. **Description:** The entire semiconductor has slumped over the past 12 months, but shares of Rambus have been hit particularly hard due to critical losses in patent litigation lawsuits. Rambus, a semiconductor designer, depends on the aggressive pursuit and defense of its patented intellectual property.

29276 ■ "Greener pastures" in *Atlanta Business Chronicle* **(Vol. 25, No. 20, October 25, 2002, pp. 1C)**
Pub: American City Business Publications, Inc.
Ed: Don Reichart. **Description:** The Georgia Fair Lending Act has been in effect for a very short period of time. This law was enacted to prevent home mortgage abuses and carries strict penalties for non-compliance.

29277 ■ "Greener Pastures: Exodus from Fidelity Continues as Another Hot Manager Heads to a Hedge Fund" in *Barron's* **(July 21, 2003, pp. F2)**
Pub: Barron's
Ed: Erin E. Arvedlund. **Description:** David Glancy is one of a growing number of fund managers leaving Fidelity to start their own funds. Some analysts are encouraging investors to follow their fund managers, posing a graver threat to Fidelity. Investigations by state attorneys general and an investor lawsuit are among the plagues afflicting Morgan Stanley.

29278 ■ "The Greens Bite Back" in *The Economist* **(Vol. 377, October 22-28, 2005, No. 8449, pp. 35)**
Pub: The Economist Newspaper Ltd.
Description: Oregon's strict land-use laws protect the area's rural character, but in November 2004 a new initiative was placed on the ballot, Measure 37, which gave landowners previously banned from turning rural land into houses the right to develop.

29279 ■ "Growth of home health products industry brings liability issues" in *Pittsburgh Business Times* **(Vol. 22, No. 39, April 11, 2003)**
Pub: Pittsburgh Business Times
Ed: Christopher Davis. **Description:** Medical equipment manufacturers must remain aware of liability issues when allowing devices to be operated in patient homes.

29280 ■ "A Guide through the Garnishment Jungle" in *Employment Relations Today* **(Vol. 27, No. 1, Spring 2000, pp. 117)**
Pub: John Wiley & Sons, Inc.
Ed: Marilyn E. Culp, Deanna R. Lindquist, Chaton Turner Williams, Tamila V. Lee, and Charles M. Rice. **Description:** Accounting of federal and state garnishment laws that impact the ability of employers to withhold an employees pay because of financial obligations of the employee to his or her creditor. Federal limits on garnishment laws due to the Consumer Credit Protection Act are addressed. Statistical data included.

29281 ■ "The Hague: Laws without Borders" in *Red Herring* **(No. 106, October 15, 2001, pp. 25-26)**
Pub: Herring Communications
Ed: Julia Lawlor. **Description:** Important information regarding the Hague Convention on Jurisdiction and Foreign Judgments in Civil Matters is covered. The Hague treaty would deal with civil lawsuits and would require that laws regarding matters like libel, copyright, patents, and trademarks - which differ among countries - be enforced uniformly in the 53 nations participating in treaty talks.

29282 ■ "Hallandale Beach, Fla., City Leaders Criticize Dating Service Company" in *Miami Herald* **(December 2, 2003)**
Pub: Knight Ridder/Business Tribune News
Ed: Hector Florin. **Description:** Hallandale Beach, Florida city leaders are questioning the ethics of the dating service, Great Expectations.

29283 ■ "Harris Beach Will Move Law Offices to Main Street" in *Business First Buffalo* **(Vol. 19, No. 47, August 15, 2003, pp. 1)**
Pub: American City Business Journals, Inc.
Ed: James Fink. **Description:** Plans by the law firm of Harris Beach LLP to open a new office in the heart of Buffalo, New York are examined.

29284 ■ "Harris Teeter sued by black employees" in *Atlanta Business Chronicle* **(Vol. 24, No. 14, September 7, 2001, pp. 1A)**
Pub: American City Business Journals Inc.
Ed: Matt Gove. **Description:** Harris Teeter Inc. and Ruddick Corporation, its parent, are both being sued by nine African-Americans for racial discrimination. Gordon, Silberman, Wiggins, & Childs, the law firm handling the case, sought class-action status following the original suit.

29285 ■ "Helping Victims Unravel Identity Theft" in *Business Journal-Portland* **(Vol. 20, No. 29, September 19, 2003, pp. 1)**
Pub: American City Business Journals, Inc.
Ed: Robin J. Moody. **Description:** Identity Safeguards, located in Tualatin, Oregon, offers protection against identity theft. The startup company provides educational and credit report monitoring services to consumers victimized by identity theft.

29286 ■ "Hey, you can't do that!" in *BlackEnterprise* **(Vol. 31, No. 7, February 2001, pp. 57)**
Pub: Earl Graves Publishing Co.
Ed: Bridget McCrea. **Description:** Profile of Edward Russell and Nicholas Stracick, partners in the company All Pro Sports Camps, Inc. After two years of presentations to the Walt Disney Company, Disney rejected the partners plans for a multi-use sports complex to be built in Orlando, Florida. The article shows how this small business went up against Disney and won.

29287 ■ "High Court Hears Case Pitting Property Rights Against Redevelopment" in *Chicago Tribune* **(February 23, 2005)**
Pub: Knight-Ridder/Tribune Business News
Ed: Jan Crawford Greenburg. **Description:** Supreme Court justices are deciding whether local governments should be allowed to condemn an individual's home or business in order to redevelop the property for more lucrative reasons. This case could limit the government's ability to condemn property for economic redevelopment under current power of eminent domain.

29288 ■ "High resolution" in *Entrepreneur* **(Vol. 30, No. 2, February 2002, pp. 35)**
Pub: Entrepreneur Media Inc.
Ed: Amanda C. Kooser. **Description:** Profile of Dispute Resolution Directory which offers online help in resolving business problems without using court action.

29289 ■ "The Hispanic Business Top 10 Law Schools" in *Hispanic Business* **(March 2002, pp. 44, 46, 48)**
Pub: Hispanic Business
Description: The top 10 law schools recommended for Hispanic students is presented, with University of Texas at Austin leading the list.

29290 ■ "Home Builder Falls Under SEC Scrutiny" in *Orlando Business Journal* **(Vol. 20, No. 10, August 22, 2003, pp. 1)**
Pub: American City Business Journals, Inc.
Ed: Jill Krueger. **Description:** The merger with a Colorado petroleum company gave Whitemark Homes Inc. an entry to the stock exchange. Whitemark also purchased a consulting firm, which collapsed and was brought under investigation.

29291 ■ "Houston-Based Restaurant Chain Uses Mystery Shoppers to Ensure Quality" in *Beaumont Enterprise* **(January 24, 2005)**
Pub: Beaumont Enterprise
Ed: Rachel Stone. **Description:** Restaurants, department stores, movie theaters, hotels, apartment complexes, banks, law firms, and many other businesses are using mystery shoppers to evaluate their businesses.

29292 ■ *How to Form Your Own Corporation without a Lawyer for Under $75.00*
Pub: Dearborn Trade Publishing Inc.
Ed: Ted Nicholas; Sean P. Melvin. **Price:** $19.95.

29293 ■ *How to Start a Bankruptcy Forms Processing Service*
Pub: Graphico Publishing Company
Ed: Victoria Ring. **Released:** September 2004. **Price:** $59.99. **Description:** Due to the increase in bankruptcy filings, attorneys are outsourcing related jobs in order to reduce overhead.

29294 ■ *How and When to Be Your Own Lawyer: A Step-by-Step Guide to Effectively Using Our Legal System*
Pub: Avery Publishing Group
Ed: Robert V. Schachner with Marvin Quittner. **Released:** 1993. **Price:** $14.95 (paper). **Description:** Provides information on using the legal system, including filing papers, drawing up complaints, using a law library, and preparing for a trial.

29295 ■ "Hunting Season: Feds Try to Protect the Little Guy From Payroll Tax Predators" in *Entrepreneur* **(Vol. 32, September 2004, No. 9)**
Pub: Entrepreneur Media Inc.
Ed: Stephen Barlas. **Description:** The Tax Administration Good Government Act gives the Internal Revenue Service tools to go after payroll/accounting firms that steal a client's employment tax payments, while protecting small businesses that hire the services.

29296 ■ "I'd Like to Buy Machinery From China" in *Inc.* **(September 2005, pp. 53)**
Pub: Inc. Magazine
Description: When purchasing equipment from China, can American businesses hold Chinese manufacturers responsible if machines violate patent laws?

29297 ■ "Identity Theft Still Top Fraud Complaint" in *Kansas City Star* **(February 2, 2005)**
Pub: Knight-Ridder/Tribune Business News
Ed: Paul Wenske. **Description:** According to the Federal Trade Commission (FTC), identity theft continues to be the number one complaint from consumers for the fifth consecutive year. Identity theft accounted for 39 percent of the fraud complaints filed with the FTC in 2004.

29298 ■ "Ideology, Politics & the Bench" in *Hispanic Business* **(June 2002, pp. 18)**
Pub: Hispanic Business
Ed: Joel Russell. **Description:** Issues and ethnicity shape support and criticism of Miguel Estrada's judicial nomination. The question of Estrada's stand on affirmative action is discussed.

29299 ■ "If I had had more experience, if I was more careful, if I was more competent" in *Fast Company* **(June 2001, pp. 161)**
Pub: Fast Company
Ed: Michael Saylor. **Description:** Profile of MicroStrategy Inc., and the ongoing investigation of the company, by the U.S. Securities and Exchange Commission.

29300 ■ "Illicit Affairs?" in *Entrepreneur* **(Vol. 32)**
Pub: Entrepreneur Media Inc.
Ed: Jane Easter Bahls. **Description:** The Foreign Corrupt Practice Act (FCPA), enacted by Congress in 1977, prohibits the use of bribery of officials in other countries in order to do business overseas. It is illegal to make payments, promises, or offers of anything of value to foreign officials to obtain or retain business, or to make payments to a third party.

29301 ■ "The Importance of Well-Crafted Terms" in *Law Firm Inc.* **(August 2004)**
Pub: American Lawyer Media LP
Ed: Mark Hanchet, Edward Hansen. **Description:** Agreements involving complex technology relationships should be negotiated and drafted with the idea of avoiding future litigation because of the long-term partnerships they create. These contracts cover such issues as outsourcing and enterprise resources planning (ERP) licensing and implementation agreements; risk avoidance, scope of services, service levels and cost need to be agreed upon before the contract is signed.

29302 ■ "In Brief: Firms Eager to Avoid Illegal Workers" in *American Banker* **(Vol. 171, November 2, 2006, No. 211, pp. 17)**
Pub: SourceMedia, Inc.
Ed: H. Michael Jalili. **Description:** According to a survey conducted by Discover Financial Services, most small businesses and their customers are willing to pay more for services and goods if such costs would help curb illegal immigration.

29303 ■ "In Brief: Grassley Offers a Bankruptcy Bill" in *American Banker* **(Vol. 170, February 4, 2005, No. 24, pp. 3)**
Pub: Thomson Financial Media Inc.
Ed: Hannah Bergman. **Description:** Finance Committee Chairman, Senator Charles Grassley, has introduced a bill that would revamp bankruptcy laws. The bill would require credit card companies to disclose the risks of minimum payment, ban deceptive advertising of low introductory rates, and require the companies to establish a toll-free number for consumers. It would also make permanent the Chapter 12 protections to help farmers from going bankrupt.

29304 ■ "In Corporate-Fraud Cases, Lawyer's Approval Can Let Client Avoid Charges" in *Houston Chronicle* **(April 11, 2003)**
Pub: Knight-Ridder/Tribune Business News
Ed: Mary Flood. **Description:** The ramifications of an attorney's approval of a business deal are explored.

29305 ■ "In Hot Water? Take a Closer Look at Your Marketing Materials, Or You May Get Burned" in *Entrepreneur* **(Vol. 32, September 2004)**
Pub: Entrepreneur Media Inc.
Ed: Catherine Seda. **Description:** Although not illegal, using another company's trademark or logo on a Website, banner ad, or newsletter could get a small company into legal trouble. Internet marketing law includes copyrights, privacy rights, trademark usage and order fulfillment and more aggressive legal action to protect brands is taking place.

29306 ■ "In Praise of the Paper Trail" in *Hispanic Business* **(June 2002, pp. 92)**
Pub: Hispanic Business
Description: The importance of documenting meetings, conversations, and agreements to protect a CEO when a deal goes array is stressed. Tips for documenting events is included.

29307 ■ *Incorporate Your Business: A 50 State Legal Guide to Forming a Corporation*
Pub: Nolo
Ed: Anthony Mancuso. **Released:** August 2001. **Price:** $50.00. **Description:** Legal guide to incorporating a business in the U.S., covering all 50 states.

29308 ■ *Incorporating Form Samples or Information for the Fifty States*
Pub: Data Notes Publishing Co.
Contact: A. C. Doyle
Ed: A. C. Doyle, Editor. **Released:** Irregular, Latest edition 1999. **Price:** $49.95. **Description:** Microfiche. Includes a list of state agencies that handle incorporation applications and actual forms. **Entries Include:** Agency name, address. **Arrangement:** Geographical.

29309 ■ "Independent's Day" in *Entrepreneur* **(Vol. 32, December 2004, No. 12, pp. 62)**
Pub: Entrepreneur Media Inc.
Ed: Jennifer Pellet. **Description:** Large investment firms like Citigroup, Merrill Lynch and Morgan Stanley must now provide clients with an independent source of research along with their own analysts' reports. Reports can be gotten from the firm's Website or a toll-free number.

29310 ■ "Industry Fights Law on Violent Video Games" in *Crain's Detroit Business* **(Vol. 21, October 24, 2005, No. 43, pp. 1)**
Pub: Crain Communications Inc. - Detroit
Ed: Andrew Dietderich. **Description:** If passed, a new law would limit the sale or rental of certain violent video games to individuals under the age of 17. Retailers could be fined up to $5,000 for each offense.

29311 ■ "Influence-Peddling" in *Business Week* **(January 16, 2006, No. 3967, pp. 32)**
Pub: McGraw-Hill Companies
Ed: Description: A guilty plea by Jack Abramoff could mean tighter rules for corporate lobbyists. Abramoff plead guilty to charges of conspiracy, mail fraud and tax evasion. Senator John McCain has proposed a bill that would require lobbyists to disclose all fees, report who's giving to charities, and make gifts to lawmakers illegal.

29312 ■ "International E-Commerce: The Time is Now" in *E-business Advisor* **(Vol. 18, No. 10, October 2000, pp. 28)**
Pub: Advisor Media, Inc.
Ed: Donald DePalma. **Description:** Internet usage is not just limited to the United States. It is exploding worldwide, and therefore, offers the opportunity to gain international customers. It is important for Web sites to be designed to entice these international "visitors", while being aware of customs, laws and politics specific to the potential customer's country.

29313 ■ "Internet Law Arena Marked by Issues About Spam, Pop-Up Ads, Domain Names, and File Sharing" in *Long Island Business News* **(Feb.6, 2004)**
Pub: Dolan Media Newswires
Ed: Rosmaria Mancini. **Description:** Microsoft and New York's State Attorney General have partnered

and filed lawsuits against a spamming ring allegedly responsible for sending billions of deceptive and illegal emails. CAN-SPAM (Controlling the Assault of Non-Solicited Pornography and Marketing Act), is federal legislation that would require marketers to provide return addresses in emails so consumers can request being removed from mailing lists.

29314 ■ "Investigations" in *Business Week* **(January 16, 2006, No. 3967, pp. 34, 36, 38)**
Pub: McGraw-Hill Companies
Ed: Arlene Weintraub, Amy Barrett. **Description:** A radical dental treatment spurs a lawsuit brought about by Aetna Insurance, while raising questions about the insurance and the Federal Drug Administrations' device-clearance process. Statistical data included.

29315 ■ "IPO Scandal Means Venture Capitalists Need To Be More Vigilant" in *Venture Capital Journal* **(Vol. 42, No. 10, October 2002, pp. 50)**
Pub: Thomas Venture Economics
Ed: Thomas C. McConnell. **Description:** Initial Public Offering practices are the latest business practices to come under regulatory, Congressional and media scrutiny.

29316 ■ "Is 'Equitable Remedy' Settlement Excludable from Gross Income?" in *Journal of Accountancy* **(Vol. 198, December 2004, No. 6, pp. 94)**
Pub: American Institute of Certified Public Accountants
Description: A case testing the definition of personal physical injury or physical sickness in an equitable remedy is discussed.

29317 ■ "It'll Cost Ya: Know How Your Lawyer Tallies Up Your Legal Tab" in *Entrepreneur* **(Vol. 32, July 2004, No. 7, pp. 76)**
Pub: Entrepreneur Media Inc.
Ed: Marc Diener. **Description:** Many attorneys will adjust fees for small businesses that know how to ask. Billing information included should explain hourly or daily rates, minimum billing unit, double billing, padded bills, bills that are too general, percentages, flat fees, retainers, and more.

29318 ■ "It's All Talk" in *Entrepreneur* **(Vol. 31, No. 5, May 2003, pp. 73)**
Pub: Entrepreneur Media Inc.
Ed: Marc Diener. **Description:** Rules to follow when contracts must be read without the aid of an attorney are cited. It is important to read the contract slowly, reading every word.

29319 ■ "It's the Law" in *Entrepreneur* **(Vol. 30, No. 3, March 2002, pp. 42)**
Pub: Entrepreneur Media Inc.
Ed: Amanda C. Kooser. **Description:** The Small Business Administration has created a Web site designed to help small business stay informed of laws and regulations.

29320 ■ "It's Settled: A New Law Makes it Easier to Reach Settlements" in *Entrepreneur* **(Vol. 33, February 2005, No. 2, pp. 74)**
Pub: Entrepreneur Media Inc.
Ed: Jane Easter Bahls. **Description:** American Jobs Creation Act of 2004, Section 703, the Civil Rights Tax Relief Acts overturns a tax rule that no longer requires the winner of wrongful termination or workplace discrimination to pay taxes on any money awarded in the lawsuit.

29321 ■ "It's a Trap! Watch Your Step-Pharming Scams Are Lurking Around Every Corner" in *Entrepreneur* **(Vol. 33, August 2005, No. 8, pp. 40)**
Pub: Entrepreneur Media Inc.
Ed: Mike Hogan. **Description:** Netcraft, a network security company, identifies phishing emails that try to scam customers into giving up personal financial information. Ways to avoid these scams are listed.

29322 ■ "John Deere Named In Discrimination Suit" in *Black Enterprise* **(Vol. 35, August 2004, No. 1, pp. 30)**
Pub: Earl G. Graves Publishing Co. Inc.
Ed: Aisha Jefferson. **Description:** After working for John Deere for 30 years, Kenny Edwards wanted to become an entrepreneur by purchasing his own John Deere agricultural dealership. Edwards has sued the company for discrimination when it turned down his bid for ownership. Of the 1,400 John Deere agricultural dealerships in the U.S. non are African-American owned, and only 5 percent of owners include women, Hispanics, and Asians.

29323 ■ "Jonathan Hoffman Was Sure a Former Staffer Had Stolen His Company's Ideas" in *Inc.* **(September 2005, pp. 55-56)**
Pub: Inc. Magazine
Ed: Lora Kolodny. **Description:** Jonathan Hoffman, CEO of School Zone Publishing, maker of educational media; Hoffman discusses the way the family business handled litigation when a former employee stole his company's ideas.

29324 ■ "Judge Rejects Effort to Keep Billing Records for Boston's Big Dig a Secret" in *Boston Globe* **(April 11, 2003)**
Pub: Knight-Ridder/Tribune Business News
Ed: Sean P. Murphy. **Description:** Release of the records pertaining to Boston's Big Dig and the millions of dollars paid to private sector managers is discussed.

29325 ■ "Jury Finds 2 Guilty of Scamming Investors" in *St. Louis Post-Dispatch* **(February 3, 2005)**
Pub: St. Louis Post-Dispatch
Ed: Peter Shinkle. **Description:** Two St. Louis men were found guilty of defrauding investors in the area by telling them that eBay.com was going to purchase their startup company.

29326 ■ "Jury is still out: Is the bar ready for virtual law firms?" in *Boston Business Journal* **(Vol. 22, No. 3, February 22, 2002, pp. 27)**
Pub: MCP, Inc.
Ed: Sheri Qualters. **Description:** An investigation into the possibility of law firms using the Internet for legal services.

29327 ■ "Kansas Investigators Target Wichita Dating Service in Credit-Card Fraud Probe" in *Wichita Eagle* **(February 13, 2004)**
Pub: Knight-Ridder/Tribune Business News
Ed: Tim Potter. **Description:** State of Kansas attorney general's office filed a civil lawsuit seeking $1.2 million from a dating service's franchises in Wichita and Overland Park. The lawsuit claims Great Expectations of violating Kansas Consumer Protection Act through deceptive and unconscionable practices, charging the business knowingly targeted vulnerable individuals and charged thousands of dollars on credit cards of certain clients.

29328 ■ "Keeping It Legal" in *Small Business Opportunities* **(Vol. 12, No. 2, March 2000, pp. 76)**
Pub: Harris Publications, Inc.
Ed: Lin Grensing-Pophal. **Description:** Guidelines for creating advertising to stay on the right side of the law are presented.

29329 ■ "Kiss Privacy Goodbye" in *Fortune* **(Vol. 151, January 10, 2005, No. 1, pp. 55)**
Pub: Time Inc.
Ed: Peter H. Lewis. **Description:** Surveillance devices aimed at humans are being developed at historical rates. These devices can be anything ranging from lasers that monitor members of a crowd for abnormal vital signs, to biometric scanners that find individual travelers from a distance and link them to commercial or governmental databases. The Biometric Group, a consulting company, predicts worldwide sales and licensing of fingerprinting, facial recognition, and other biometic devices to increase to more than $1.8 billion in 2005 and $4.8 billion by 2008.

29330 ■ "Kmart scurries to tie loose ends as approval of Ch. 11 plan nears" in *Crain's Detroit Business* **(Vol. 19, No. 15, April 14, 2003)**
Pub: Crain Communications Inc., Detroit
Ed: Brent Snavely. **Description:** Information regarding Kmart Corporation's bankruptcy is discussed, including bids for 64 leases from retailers including Lowe's Companies Inc., J.C. Penney Company Inc. and Target Corporation.

29331 ■ "Know your limits" in *Entrepreneur* **(Vol. 31, No. 6, June 2003, pp. 73)**
Pub: Entrepreneur Media Inc.
Ed: Joanne Cleaver. **Description:** The U.S. Circuit Court of Appeals in California ruled that failure to fulfill a contract is just that and no more, fueling an emerging national precedent.

29332 ■ "Know the Rules" in *Black Enterprise* **(Vol. 35, December 2004, No. 5, pp. 56)**
Pub: Earl G. Graves Publishing Co. Inc.
Ed: Arlene McKanic. **Description:** Rules and regulations governing home-based businesses have become more complex, especially tax laws. The Internal Revenue Service is unfair to home-based companies when it comes to deductions, while zoning codes create other barriers.

29333 ■ "La-Van Hawkins Linked to Philadelphia Corruption Probe" in *Black Enterprise* **(Vol. 35, September 2004, No. 2)**
Pub: Earl G. Graves Publishing Co. Inc.
Ed: Alan Hughes. **Description:** CEO of La-Van Hawkins Food & Entertainment Group LLC, La-Van Hawkins, has been connected to a Philadelphia corruption case where people have been charged for paying off former Philadelphia treasurer in a scandal in which 12 people have been indicted. Hawkins is charged with conspiring to commit honest services fraud, four counts of wire fraud, and four counts of perjuring himself before the Grand Jury investigating the case.

29334 ■ "Labor pains: if immigration laws tighten, all entrepreneurs could feel the squeeze" in *Entrepreneur* **(Vol. 31, No. 5, May 2003)**
Pub: Entrepreneur Media Inc.
Ed: Mark Henricks. **Description:** According to an analysis of Census data by the Center for Labor Market Studies, the American economic boom of the 1990s was fueled from laborers coming from foreign countries. With immigration laws being tightened in the wake of 9/11, many entrepreneurs are concerned about a reduced flow of immigrant workers.

29335 ■ "Labor Relations" in *Inc.* **(Volume 27, December 2005, No. 12, pp. 34)**
Pub: Inc. Magazine
Description: Union members have been banned from installing giant inflatable rats in front of businesses and construction sites employing non-union workers.

29336 ■ "Laterals keep coming" in *Black Enterprise* **(Vol. 33, No. 198, March 24, 2003, pp. AA2)**
Pub: Earl Graves Publishing Co.
Ed: Matthew Haggman. **Description:** The slowing economy has forced partners in law firms to look to the state of Florida.

29337 ■ "Laterals keep coming" in *Daily Business Review* **(Vol. 77, No. 198, March 24, 2003, pp. AA2)**
Pub: American Lawyer Media LP
Ed: Matthew Haggman. **Description:** Law firms are becoming increasingly dependent upon hiring laterals for growing their business rather than promoting from within.

29338 ■ "Laterals? Pass" in *Daily Business Review* **(Vol. 77, No. 146, Jan. 7, 2003, pp. A8)**
Pub: American Lawyer Media LP
Ed: Anthony Lin. **Description:** Many of the nation's top law firms poach partners from each other in order to provide more services.

29339 ■ **"Law Firm Recruiters Face Hurdles in Pay, Local Economy"** in *Crain's Detroit Business* (Vol. 22, November 27, 2006, No. 48, pp. 18)
Pub: Crain Communications Inc. - Detroit
Ed: Robert Ankeny. Description: Recruitment and retention of new lawyers continues to be difficult for law firms in the Detroit area. Negative image of the area and the climate are major factors making recruitment from other areas difficult.

29340 ■ **"Law Firms Beef Up Extranets to Handle Complex Deals"** in *Crain's Detroit Business* (Vol. 23, January 29, 2007, No. 5, pp. 26)
Pub: Crain Communications Inc. - Detroit
Ed: Robert Ankeny. Description: Virtual private computer networks eliminate multiple copies and shipping in complex legal and real estate deals. Documents can be displayed in War rooms with multiple parties exchanging information simultaneously. Huge savings in copying and shipping of paper copies are realized.

29341 ■ *Law (in Plain English) for Small Business*
Pub: Sourcebooks, Incorporated
Ed: Leonard D. DuBoff. Released: November 2006. Description: Small business law is described in easy to read format.

29342 ■ **"Law-Less Approach"** in *Pittsburgh Business Times* (Vol. 23, No. 9, September 19, 2003, pp. 1)
Pub: Pittsburgh Business Times
Ed: Christopher Davis, Patty Tascarella. Description: Eckert Seamonas Cherin and Mellott LLC has assigned Arnie Silverman to head up the intellectual property team charged with handling the law firm's Alcoa contract. Eckert Seamans is the fourth largest law firm in the Pittsburgh, Pennsylvania area.

29343 ■ *Law for the Small Business Owner*
Pub: Oceana Publications, Inc.
Ed: Margaret C. Jasper. Released: 1994. Price: $22.50 (library binding).

29344 ■ *Law for the Small and Growing Business*
Pub: Jordans Publishing Limited
Ed: P. Bohm. Released: February 2007. Price: $59.98. Description: Legal and regulatory issues facing small businesses, including employment law, health and safety, commercial property, company law and finance are covered.

29345 ■ **"Law Talent"** in *Entrepreneur* (Vol. 32, October 2004, No. 10, pp. 98)
Pub: Entrepreneur Media Inc.
Ed: Jane Easter Bahls. Description: Smart entrepreneurs understand the concept that lawyers can offer more than the knowledge of law to a company, they can help decision makers in terms of transitions, of what might happen in relationships.

29346 ■ **"Law provides more protection for whistle-blowers"** in *Atlanta Business Chronicle* (Vol. 25, November 15, 2002, No. 23 pp. SS3)
Pub: American City Business Publications, Inc.
Ed: Leslie Williams Johnson. Description: The federal Sarbanes-Oxley Act of 2002 provides additional protection to employees at publicly traded companies who report fraud committed by employees. Details of the act and steps to be taken by companies to avoid litigation are included.

29347 ■ **"Lawmakers take aim at living-wage laws"** in *Crain's Detroit Business* (Vol. 19, No. 8, February 24, 2003, pp. 7)
Pub: Crain Communications Inc., Detroit
Ed: Amy Lane. Description: Republican lawmakers are working on ordinances that would allow local governments to require higher minimum wage from businesses that are vendors or receive other forms of local government assistance; Governor Granholm opposes the bill.

29348 ■ **"Laws Mandating Paid Sick Leave Will Pass in Several States"** in *Kiplinger Letter* (Vol. 78, January 19, 2007, No. 2)
Pub: Kiplinger
Description: Massachusetts, Wisconsin, Washington, Main, Montana, Vermont, and Maryland are among the states considering a law to mandate paid sick leave to employees.

29349 ■ **"Lawsuit: EPA ignored impact of lead regulation"** in *Atlanta Business Chronicle* (Vol. 23, No. 46, April 20, 2001, pp. 11A)
Pub: American City Business Journals Inc.
Ed: Kent Hoover. Description: The Small Business Regulatory Enforcement Fairness Act will be sued to challenge a recent Environmental Protection Agency regulation that requires reports from any company that makes or uses at least 100 pounds of lead per year. A lawsuit filed by a coalition of 36 trade associations says that the EPA did not consider the effect of the regulation on small businesses. The National Federation of Independent Business will also file suit.

29350 ■ **"Lawsuit against Masco alleges predatory pricing"** in *Crain's Detroit Business* (Vol. 19, No. 10, March 10, 2003, pp. 32)
Pub: Crain Communications Inc., Detroit
Ed: Michael Strong. Description: Wilson Insulation Group Inc. has filed a lawsuit against Masco Corporation for predatory pricing and monopolizing in an attempt to drive Wilson out of the Augusta, Georgia market.

29351 ■ **"Lawsuit, Tax Lien Plague Post-Bankruptcy Orbcomm"** in *Washington Business Journal* (Vol. 22, No. 9, July 4, 2003, pp. 5)
Pub: Washington Business Journal
Ed: Roger Hughlett. Description: Orbcomm's post-bankruptcy battles to survive in light of the recent lawsuits and tax liens are discussed.

29352 ■ **"Lawyering Up"** in *Boston Business Journal* (Vol. 23, No. 30, August 29, 2003, pp. 1)
Pub: American City Business Journals
Ed: Sheri Qualters. Description: Forecasts by officers of Boston, Massachusetts-based Legal Staffing Solutions regarding the state of employment in the legal services market. Topics include levels of employee recruitment, economic conditions, and effects of past layoffs.

29353 ■ **"Lawyers on War-Path Filing Wage and Hour Lawsuits"** in *Kiplinger Letter* (Vol. 78, January 19, 2007, No. 2)
Pub: Kiplinger
Description: Attorneys are targeting clients with the use of Websites to looking for disgruntled employees. Major settlements are discussed.

29354 ■ **"Lease on Life?"** in *Entrepreneur* (Vol. 32, November 2004, No. 11, pp. 98)
Pub: Entrepreneur Media Inc.
Ed: Jane Easter Bahls. Description: According to the National Association of Professional Employer Organizations, 2 to 3 million Americans are co-employed in professional employer organizations (PEO) arrangements. The employer and the PEO are both legally responsible for payment of payroll taxes and workers' compensation, and compliance with government regulations.

29355 ■ **"Leave It To Them: Make Sure Your Family Gets What It Needs by Including a Disclaimer Provision in Your Estate Plan"** in *Entrepreneur*
Pub: Entrepreneur Media Inc.
Ed: Scott Bernard Nelson. Description: With federal estate laws changing nearly every year, it is important to include a disclaimer provision when planning an estate, which would allow a couple to take advantage of the estate-tax exemption.

29356 ■ **"A Leg Up on Legal Fees"** in *My Business* (October/November 2002, pp. 52)
Pub: My Business Magazine
Description: Web sites offering advice for writing simple legal documents, such as employment contracts and real estate leases, are listed.

29357 ■ **"Legal Aid: Sample Legal Documents can Lower Your Attorney Fees"** in *Black Enterprise* (Vol. 37, October 2006, No. 3, pp. 210)
Pub: Earl G. Graves Publishing Co. Inc.
Ed: Tamara E. Holmes. Description: FreeLegalForms.net provides thousands of free legal forms. These forms are not a substitute for consultation with an attorney but the sample documents can help save you time and money.

29358 ■ *Legal & Corporate Forms for Small Business*
Pub: Prentice Hall General Reference & Travel
Ed: J. K. Lasser staff. Released: 1994. Price: $34.95 (paper).

29359 ■ **"Legal Eagle?"** in *Entrepreneur* (Vol. 32, October 2004, No. 10, pp. 89)
Pub: Entrepreneur Media Inc.
Ed: Gwen Moran. Description: Important updates on marketing law are shared, including an amendment to telemarketing sales rules, Internet spam, and security software.

29360 ■ **"Legal Ease"** in *My Business* (December/January 2004, pp. 53)
Pub: My Business Magazine
Ed: Lena Basha. Description: Profile of Legalzoom.com, an online legal document and resource center for small businesses.

29361 ■ *Legal Help for Your Business*
Pub: Bell Springs Publishing
Ed: Mead Hedglon. Price: $16.95. Description: Save both your money and your sanity in dealing with legal matters: when you don't need lawyers, how to avoid litigation, and if necessary, how to get the best legal help at the lowest possible cost.

29362 ■ **"Legal News Publisher Sells His Interest in Company"** in *Crain's Detroit Business* (Vol. 22, February 13, 2006, No. 7, pp. 26)
Pub: Crain Communications Inc. - Detroit
Ed: Tom Henderson. Description: John Parks sold his minority interest in Detroit Legal News Publishing LLC to the Minneapolis-based Dolan Media Company. The move came after Parks retired from the firm. Parks will continue to serve as a consultant through 2006.

29363 ■ **"Legally bound"** in *Crain's Detroit Business* (Vol. 19, No. 17, April 28, 2003, pp. 3)
Pub: Crain Communications Inc., Detroit
Ed: Laura Bailey. Description: Michigan law schools are reporting applications for enrollment up as much as 100 percent in the last two years, following a national trend.

29364 ■ **"Lentek Lands in Chapter 11"** in *Orlando Business Journal* (Vol. 20, No. 5, July 18, 2003, pp. 1)
Pub: American City Business Journals, Inc.
Ed: Chad Eric Watt. Description: Reasons behind Lentek International's filing for Chapter 11 bankruptcy protection are listed. Topics include business losses, economic conditions, and business management.

29365 ■ **"Let the (Political) Games Begin"** in *Inc.* (Volume 27, June 2005, No. 6, pp. 51-52, 54, 56)
Pub: Inc. Magazine
Ed: Description: Information to assist companies who are faced with the government wanting to take their land.

29366 ■ "Let it rain" in *Ingram's* (Vol. 28, No. 3, March 2002, pp. 35)
Pub: Show Me Publishing, Inc.
Ed: Jack Cashill. Description: Lawyers discuss the necessary attributes for "rainmaking", the ability of lawyers to generate revenue.

29367 ■ "Liar, Liar: In the Race to Make Money, Some American Businesses Have Been Lying Their Pants Off" in *Entrepreneur* (Vol. 31, Oct. 2003)
Pub: Entrepreneur Media, Inc.
Ed: Joshua Kurlantzick. Description: Despite the business scandals and legislation of 2002, lies and dishonesty are a more acceptable part of business in America.

29368 ■ "The Lid On Spam Is Still Loose" in *Business Week* (February 7, 2005, No. 3919, pp. 10)
Pub: McGraw-Hill Companies
Ed: Erin Chambers, Ira Sager. Description: Profile of the CAN-SPAM Act, passed by Congress in 2004. The Act sets restrictions on unsolicited email, but has done little to eliminate junk messages. According to MX Logic, 97 percent of unsolicited commercial email defies the law.

29369 ■ "Life after bankruptcy: there are still pitfalls in folding a business" in *Black Enterprise* (Vol. 33, No. 3, October 2002, pp. 58)
Pub: Earl Graves Publishing Co.
Ed: Bridget McCrea. Description: When filing for bankruptcy, small business owners have two choices: Chapter 7 or Chapter 11. The process for filing for bankruptcy is described, along with tips to make the processes easier.

29370 ■ "A line in the sand" in *InfoWorld* (Vol. 23, No. 5, January 29, 2001, pp. 1)
Pub: InfoWorld
Ed: Tom Sullivan, Ed Scannell. Description: Sun and Microsoft have settled a three-year lawsuit over the latter's use of Java, drawing a line that eliminates true standards and forces developers to sacrifice either tight integration with Windows applications or true portability. Microsoft immediately began offering Java User Migration Path (JUMP), a set of development tools for migrating products from Java to its .NET platform. Both companies claim victory in the settlement, which analysts say is not a surprise.

29371 ■ "Litigation's price boosts arbitration's appeal" in *Atlanta Business Chronicle* (Vol. 25, November 15, 2002, No. 23 pp. SS15)
Pub: American City Business Publications, Inc.
Ed: Linda Goodspeed. Description: The number of arbitration cases has increased to 218,032 in 2001, from 60,808 in 1990, as litigation costs continue to rise. Arbitration is used to settle a variety of disputes. Employment contracts represent a newer and more controversial use for arbitration, and some pros and cons are discussed.

29372 ■ "LoanGiant.com Files for Chapter 11" in *Crain's Detroit Business* (Vol. 21, October 10, 2005, No. 43, pp. 3)
Pub: Crain Communications Inc. - Detroit
Ed: Description: LoanGiant, based in Southfield, Michigan, has filed for Chapter 11 bankruptcy protection. The firm has been accused of fraudulent mortgage loan and documentation practices.

29373 ■ "Long Island Law Firm Takes Steps To Increase Pro Bono Work" in *Long Island Business News* (February 6, 2004)
Pub: Dolan Media Newswires
Ed: Claude Solnik. Description: Long Island law firms are stepping up efforts to offer pro bono services to those in need in the area.

29374 ■ "Lop Legal Costs" in *My Business* (April/May 2002, pp. 16)
Pub: My Business Magazine
Ed: Deborah L. Jacobs. Description: Ten ways to reduce legal fees are listed.

29375 ■ "Madame chairman" in *WorkingWoman* (Vol. 25, No. 5, May 2000, pp. 30)
Pub: Lang Communications Inc.
Ed: Karen Bennett. Description: Christine Lagarde holds the top position of one of the world's biggest law firms, Baker and McKenzie. Issues concerning her attitudes towards the firm, law, cultural differences and balancing family needs with the demands of work, are presented.

29376 ■ "Making Lemonade" in *Entrepreneur* (Vol. 33, October 2005, No. 10, pp. 83)
Pub: Entrepreneur Media Inc.
Ed: Gwen Moran. Description: When the owner of a bird-cage and accessories company suffers from a legal battle, she found a way to turn adversity into opportunity.

29377 ■ "Making Pro Formas Perform" in *Harvard Business Review* (Vol. 81, No. 10, October 2003, pp. 24)
Pub: Harvard Business School Press
Ed: Stephen Bryan, Steven Lilien. Description: Quarterly earnings reports from the Dow 30 during 2001 are analyzed to show that pro forma earnings deviated sometimes considerably from generally accepted accounting principles.

29378 ■ "Marsh Mac Settles Up" in *Business Week* (February 14, 2005, No. 3920, pp. 42)
Pub: McGraw-Hill Companies
Ed: Monica Gagnier. Description: Marsh & McLennan, the largest insurance broker in the world, settled civil fraud charges brought on by New York Attorney General Eliot Spitzer. Marsh will ban 'contingency fees' and other practices such as 'tying' as part of the settlement.

29379 ■ "The Maw of the Law" in *Success* (Vol. 47, No. 5, October 2000, pp. 42)
Pub: Success Publishing, Inc.
Ed: Michael Barrier. Description: With good legal advice more important, and more expensive than ever, how do you afford it?

29380 ■ "McClatchy-Owned Minneapolis Newspaper Settles Advertiser Lawsuit" in *Sacramento Bee* (December 21, 2005)
Pub: The Sacramento Bee
Ed: Gilbert Chan. Description: The Star Tribune has settled an advertiser lawsuit accusing the newspaper of inflating circulation figures. The Minneapolis publication, owned by Sacramento, California-based McClatchy Company, agreed to pay $55,000 to two employment agencies located in the Twin Cities area after their charges were validated by an independent auditor.

29381 ■ "Melville-Based DealerTrack Inc. Sue Rival Mich.-Based RouteOne" in *Long Island Business News* (February 6, 2004)
Pub: Dolan Media Newswires
Ed: Ken Schachter. Description: DealerTrack Inc. has filed a patent lawsuit against Michigan-based RouteOne, a joint venture between DaimlerChrysler Service, Ford Motor Credit Company, General Motors Acceptance Corporation, and Toyota Financial Services. The lawsuit charges RouteOne of infringing on two patents related to a routing system, method and computer program for analyzing credit applications.

29382 ■ "Mending Fences" in *Entrepreneur* (Vol. 33, October 2005, No. 10, pp. 90)
Pub: Entrepreneur Media Inc.
Ed: Jane Easter Bahls. Description: Processes to help settle a conflict with a neighboring business are discussed. To avoid a legal battle, mediation may help find a mutually agreeable solution.

29383 ■ *Mergers and Acquisitions from A to Z*
Pub: Amacom
Ed: Andrew J. Sherman, Milledge A. Hart. Released: December 2005. Price: $47.00. Description: Guide for the entire process of mergers and acquisitions, including taxes, accounting, laws, and projected financial gain.

29384 ■ "MGM Taking Bids for Two Casinos in Detroit" in *Crain's Detroit Business* (Vol. 21, February 7, 2005, No. 6, pp. 3)
Pub: Crain Communications Inc. - Detroit
Ed: Robert Ankeny. Description: MGM Mirage Inc. announced plans for a buyout in spring 2004, but under Michigan law, no casino owner can have more than 10 percent interest in more than one casino.

29385 ■ "Microsoft Lawyer Makes Living Hunting Down Pirates" in *Altanta Journal-Constitution* (January 28, 2007)
Pub: Cox Newspapers, Inc.
Ed: Bill Husted. Description: Mary Jo Schrade works to combat software piracy for Microsoft; Schrade uses leads from the public and secret shoppers buying computers and software that is then tested for legitimacy.

29386 ■ "Minimize Your Legal Risks" in *Folio: the Magazine for Magazine Management* (Vol. 30, No. 1, January 2001, pp. 25)
Pub: Intertec Publishing Corp.
Ed: Lawrence Savell, Deborah J. Schwab. Description: To avoid spending a great deal of time and money defending against a lawsuit, it is better to ask "Am I defaming anyone with the material I am about to print or post?" Eight key questions that can help avoid litigation are discussed.

29387 ■ "Mixed Fate for Black Law Firms" in *Black Enterprise* (Vol. 34, No. 4, November 2003, pp. 27)
Pub: Earl Graves Publishing Co.
Ed: Cliff Hocker. Description: Of the 12 original law firms highlighted in an August 1993 issue of Black Enterprise, only one-fourth are still operating. Profiles of the existing firms are included.

29388 ■ "More protection means less worry over suits" in *Wall Street Journal* (October 8, 2002, pp. B4)
Pub: Dow Jones & Co. Inc.
Ed: Richard Breeden. Description: An examination of tort reform for small business is presented.

29389 ■ "Moving Daze" in *Law Firm Inc.* (October 2004)
Pub: American Lawyer Media LP
Ed: Kristin Eliasberg. Description: Things to consider when a law firm is relocating the business. Many firms consult a real estate professional to help with planning the move, as well as finding the right space and negotiating the deal.

29390 ■ "Mr. Pita legal woes haven't put a wrap on expansion" in *Crain's Detroit Business* (Vol. 18, No. 24, June 17, 2002, pp. 22)
Pub: Crain Communications Inc. - Detroit
Ed: Michael Strong. Description: Shelby Township-based Mr. Pita, plans to open eight more locations, despite internal legal problems that could hinder the company's expansion.

29391 ■ "Musical cases" in *Crain's Detroit Business* (Vol. 19, No. 10, March 10, 2003, pp. 34)
Pub: Crain Communications Inc., Detroit
Description: Information on two pending lawsuits faced by Luck's Music Library regarding copyright laws affecting all works of authorship and not just music is examined.

29392 ■ "The Myth of the Superstar CEO" in *Venture Capital Journal* (November 1, 2004)
Pub: Thomason Financial Inc.
Ed: Ravi Chiruvolu. Description: PeopleSoft, the enterprise software company, replaced its CEO Craig Conway with founder and chairman, Dave Duffield. Whether a superstar CEO is worth the time, effort and additional equity required to retain him or her is addressed.

29393 ■ "The Name Game" in *Entrepreneur* (Vol. 33, January 2005, No. 1, pp. 72)
Pub: Entrepreneur Media Inc.

Ed: Jane Easter Bahls. **Description:** Under the legal doctrine, reverse confusion, small companies can file lawsuits against large corporations over trademark infringement.

29394 ■ "Name Grab-Cybersquaters, once a mere nuisance, now can go to prison for violating your trademark" in *PC Computing* **(April 2000, pp. 40)**
Pub: Ziff-Davis Inc.
Ed: Christopher Null. **Description:** The U.S. Anti-Cybersquatting Consumer Protection Act (ACPA), which was signed into law on November 29, 1999, has triggered a rash of lawsuits targeting cybersquatters. The most notable filing so far is the Coalition to Advance the Protection of Sports logos' (CAPS) case against FlairMail.com, which offers free e-mail addresses from sports domains like goavalanche.net and mightyducks1.com. Domain names have become very expensive commodities, as evidenced by the $7.5 million Business.com domain name.

29395 ■ "The Need for Tort Reform" in *My Business* **(October/November 2002, pp. 49)**
Pub: My Business Magazine
Ed: Hilda Bankston. **Description:** The former owner of a Fayette, Mississippi family-owned drug store tells how her and her pharmacist husband were named in a class action lawsuit over the prescription drug Fen-Phen. The lawsuit has devastated the family as well as the community and its small businesses.

29396 ■ "Net Data Seller Can Be Sued in Stalking-Murder Case" in *Daily Business Review* **(Vol. 77, No. 190, March 12, 2003, pp. A7)**
Pub: American Lawyer Media LP
Ed: Peter Page. **Description:** The New Hampshire Supreme Court ruled that the family of a woman killed by a stalker can sue the Internet data broker hired by the stalker to locate his victim.

29397 ■ "Network Marketing or Pyramid Scheme?" in *Black Enterprise* **(Vol. 35, November 2004, No. 4, pp. 102)**
Pub: Earl G. Graves Publishing Co. Inc.
Ed: Wendy Harris. **Description:** When Cameron Brickey signed up to be an independent associate for Pre-Paid Legal Services Inc., a network marketing company, he thought he would earn an easy living. The company provides affordable legal services targeted to low- and middle-income individuals and families. While many multilevel marketing companies are legitimate, also known as pyramid schemes, they can be risky.

29398 ■ "A New Abacus for Pensions" in *Business Week* **(January 9, 2006, No. 3966, pp. 91)**
Pub: McGraw-Hill Companies
Description: New Financial Accounting Standards Board rules on post-retirement accounting will change how companies account for pensions and other employee benefits, especially retiree health insurance.

29399 ■ "New EEOC and OFCCP Issues for the Year 2000 and Beyond" in *Employment Relations Today* **(Vol. 26, No. 4, Winter 2000, pp. 99)**
Pub: John Wiley & Sons, Inc.
Ed: Morgan D. Hodgson, Ronald S. Cooper, and Lloyd C. Loomis. **Description:** Reviews federal regulations regarding employment discrimination, focusing on the policies enacted by the US Equal Opportunity Commission and the Office of Federal Contract Compliance Programs. Topics addressed include the interpretation of the Americans with Disabilities Act of 1990, immigration and work policies, and enforcing discrimination law compliance within government organizations.

29400 ■ "New dean has expensive plans for Emory Law" in *Atlanta Business Chronicle* **(Vol. 25, November 15, 2002, No. 23 pp. SS7)**
Pub: American City Business Publications, Inc.
Ed: Lee Hall. **Description:** Tom Arthur aims to increase the endowment of Emory University's School

of Law and plans to enlist help from alumni and Atlanta's business community in development of a strategic plan for the school's future. Arthur believes the school needs a unique selling feature to attract prospective students. Biographical information included.

29401 ■ "New Hampshire Attorney General Probes Mall's Ouster of Diamond Kiosk" in *The Telegraph* **(December 18, 2003)**
Pub: Knight Ridder/Tribune Business News
Ed: Karen Spiller. **Description:** An antitrust and price-fixing investigation is being carried out by the New Hampshire Attorney General's office into the owners of a diamond kiosk at the Pheasant Lane Mall.

29402 ■ "New Law Reduced Liability for Architects, Engineers" in *Crain's Detroit Business* **(Vol. 21, January 10, 2005, No. 2, pp. 22)**
Pub: Crain Communications Inc. - Detroit
Ed: Amy Lane. **Description:** Michigan Governor Jennifer Granholm signed into law a small bill that will reduce the liability architects and engineers face on state construction projects.

29403 ■ "New Laws Take On Delaware Subsidiaries" in *Inc.* **(January 1, 2005)**
Pub: Inc. Magazine
Ed: Lora Kolodny. **Description:** New York Tax Courts have imposed taxes on revenue derived from intellectual property.

29404 ■ "A New Pain in the Neck-OSHA lays down ergonomic standards for businesses great and small" in *PC Computing* **(April 2000, pp. 44)**
Pub: Ziff-Davis Inc.
Ed: Jennifer Powell. **Description:** The Occupational Safety and Health Administration's (OSHA) move to protect knowledge workers from workplace injuries caused by musculoskeletal disorders (MSD) is facing stiff opposition from businesses and some members of Congress. OSHA estimates that more than 600,000 people suffer from lost-workday MSDs each year and that MSDs account for more than one-third of all occupational injuries. Opponents of the regulations argue that there is not enough scientific data to know what causes injuries due to MSD or what workplace changes will stop them.

29405 ■ "New Rules for Corporate Counsel" in *Inc.* **(September 1, 2003)**
Pub: Gruner & Jahr USA Publishing
Ed: Anton Piech. **Description:** Specific steps attorneys should take to become more independent of a client company's executive team are outlined.

29406 ■ "New SEC Rule Means Business" in *Business Journal-Milwaukee* **(Vol. 20, No. 47, August 8, 2003, pp. A13)**
Pub: American City Business Journals, Inc.
Ed: Michael Muckian. **Description:** An examination of how Vista 360 Inc. regulatory compliance services for investment advisors is booming following new reporting rules by the U.S. Securities and Exchange Commission.

29407 ■ "New SEC Rules Regarding Selective Disclosure and Insider Trading Increase Risks" in *Venture Capital Journal* **(Vol.40, No.10, Oct. 2000)**
Pub: Venture Economics
Description: In depth report examining the Regulation Fair Disclosure (FD), issued by the Securities and Exchange Commission, and two new insider trading rules.

29408 ■ *New Technology-Based Firms in the New Millennium, Volume 3*
Pub: Elsevier Science & Technology Books
Ed: Ray Oakey, Wim During, Seleema Kauser. **Released:** June 2004. **Price:** $110.00. **Description:** Collection of papers from the Annual International High Technology Firms (HTSFs) Conference covering issues of importance to governments as they develop technological program. Papers are grouped into three sections: strategy, spin-off firms, clusters, networking, and global issues.

29409 ■ *New Technology-Based Firms in the New Millennium, Volume 4*
Pub: Elsevier Science & Technology Books
Ed: Ray Oakey, Wim During, Seleema Kauser. **Released:** December 2005. **Price:** $135.00. **Description:** Collection of papers from the Annual International High Technology Firms (HTSFs) Conference cover issues of importance to governments as they develop technological program. Papers are grouped into three sections: theory, strategy and clustering, and spin-off firms.

29410 ■ "A New Wrinkle On Age Bias" in *Inc.* **(Volume 27, July 2005, No. 7, pp. 36)**
Pub: Inc. Magazine
Ed: Darren Dahl. **Description:** The Supreme Court made it easier to file age discrimination claims in federal court. There were 8,000 age discrimination cases filed in the U.S. in 2004 against companies with less than 500 employees.

29411 ■ "New Year, New Laws" in *Inc.* **(Volume 28, January 2006, No. 1, pp. 24)**
Pub: Inc. Magazine
Description: An entrepreneur's guide to new state policies taking effect in 2006, along with their positive, negative, mixed and uncertain impacts.

29412 ■ "News from the Small Business Front" in *My Business* **(June/July 2002, pp. 14)**
Pub: My Business Magazine
Description: Plans for using wireless technology for small businesses to develop a global wireless Internet network are discussed. Information on the Family and Medical Leave Act is presented.

29413 ■ "Newsday Suit Lawyer Enlists 'Big Firms'" in *Long Island Business News* **(February 27, 2004)**
Pub: Dolan Media Newswires
Ed: Ken Schachter. **Description:** A $100 million racketeering lawsuit has been filed by Joseph Giaimo, alleging inflated circulation figures. Giaimo's firm, Giaimo & Vreeburg of Forest Hills, has recruited larger legal firms to assist in the lawsuit.

29414 ■ "Newsstand" in *Home Business* **(Vol. 12, October 2005, No. 5, pp. 38-39)**
Pub: Home Business Magazine
Description: Various topics are covered, including information about home-based business tax deductions, the link between home computers and entrepreneurship, income gaps, demographics of home-based business owners, creation of more home-based businesses due to merger-related job cuts, and frivolous lawsuits against home-based entrepreneurs.

29415 ■ "NFIB Report From The State Capitals" in *My Business* **(August/September 2002, pp. 20-22)**
Pub: My Business Magazine
Description: Issues important to small businesses are listed by state.

29416 ■ "NFIB Report from the State Capitals" in *My Business* **(April/May 2002, pp. 22-25)**
Pub: My Business Magazine
Description: Current small business issues are presented in a listing by state.

29417 ■ "Nip It In the Bud" in *Entrepreneur* **(Vol. 32, November 2004, No. 11, pp. 95)**
Pub: Entrepreneur Media Inc.
Ed: Chris Penttila. **Description:** An ombudsman program can act like an insurance policy by providing a confidential resource for employees.

29418 ■ "NMAC Settles Suit" in *Hispanic Business* **(September 2003, pp. 20)**
Pub: Hispanic Business
Description: Nissan Motor Acceptance Corporation (NMAC) has finalized the settlement of a lawsuit with minority car buyers, where African Americans and Hispanics were charged higher interest rates than whites.

29419 ■ **"No Bankruptcy Break for Hurricane Victims"** in *Credit Union Journal* **(Vol. 9, October 3, 2005, No. 39, pp. 12)**
Pub: SourceMedia, Inc.
Description: An overview of the new consumer bankruptcy law is presented. The new law takes effect October 17, 2005.

29420 ■ **"Not hiring"** in *Entrepreneur* **(Vol. 30, No. 12, December 2002, pp. 103)**
Pub: Entrepreneur Media Inc.
Ed: Chris Penttila. **Description:** Simple steps to follow to develop a rejection process for job candidates are listed. The importance of putting closure to rejected resumes is stressed.

29421 ■ **"NW Miss. Firms Merge To Meet Growing Needs Of Region"** in *Mississippi Business Journal* **(Vol. 28, September 2006, No. 37, pp. 20)**
Pub: Venture Publications, Inc.
Ed: Wally Northway **Description:** Law firm Smith Phillips Mitchell & Scott has merged with law firm Nowak & Neyman to create Smith Phillips Mitchell Scott & Nowak, LLP. The firm now covers most of the Northwest Mississippi region.

29422 ■ **"NY Bankruptcy Courts Shift to Online Filing"** in *Long Island Business News* **(February 6, 2004)**
Pub: Dolan Media Newswires
Ed: Claude Solnik. **Description:** U.S. Bankruptcy Court for the Southern District of New York has begun accepting electronic Chapter 11 filing; the Eastern District has followed suit. Electronic filing for both nonbankruptcy and bankruptcy cases has also been accepted nationwide.

29423 ■ **"Oil Slicks"** in *Inc.* **(October 1, 2003)**
Pub: Gruner & Jahr USA Publishing
Ed: Tahl Raz. **Description:** Tim Marquez and Rod Eson were on their way to revolutionizing the oil industry until they ran into legal issues that tore them apart.

29424 ■ **"OKC Man Charged in Connection With Identity Theft Ring"** in *Journal Record (Oklahoma City, OK)* **(February 5, 2007)**
Pub: Journal Record
Ed: Marie Price. **Description:** Oklahoma City man is charged with identity theft. The man is part of a group stealing credit cards in order to open accounts and purchase good from Advance Auto Parts in Oklahoma City.

29425 ■ **"On the Internet, a Second Act"** in *Barron's* **(July 28, 2003, pp. T1)**
Pub: Barron's
Ed: Bill Alpert. **Description:** Michael Wachs, who conducts online interviews of executives for CEOcast, also spent nearly a year in federal prison for swindling Chase Manhattan Bank out of nearly $21 million. Questions are raised about the legality of his role with CEOcast on the provisions of his settlement with Chase.

29426 ■ **"One More For the Road"** in *Sales & Marketing Management* **(January 2005)**
Pub: VNU Business Media
Ed: Denis Jensen. **Description:** Sales executives, as well as management, should avoid the pitfalls of drinking when entertaining business clients. One accident involving an employee under the influence will cause insurance rates to go up.

29427 ■ **"The Online Lawyer"** in *Hispanic Business* **(October 2002, pp. 90)**
Pub: Hispanic Business
Ed: Derek Reveron. **Description:** Caution is advised when seeking legal services online, however small businesses are finding reliable legal services online. A listing of Web site offering legal services is included.

29428 ■ **"Online Publisher Seeks Dismissal of Apple's Trade-Secret Lawsuit"** in *San Jose Mercury News* **(March 8, 2005)**
Pub: Knight-Ridder/Tribune Business News
Ed: Dawn C. Chmielewski. **Description:** Website Think Secret has requested the court dismiss the computer company's trade-secret lawsuit with online publishers and Apple Computer. Apple sued Think Secret's creator of misappropriating trade secrets in his online posts about some of Apple's products.

29429 ■ **"Operation no safe haven: there's $400 billion in unregulated money stashed in offshore hedge accounts"** in *Red Herring* **(Jan. 2003)**
Pub: Herring Communications Inc.
Ed: Christopher Byron. **Description:** Offshore hedge funds provide an end run around the crackdown on U.S. companies. These accounts allow money to be moved anonymously in and out of the U.S. without going through a U.S. bank.

29430 ■ **"Out Of Pocket, Out Of Mind"** in *Law Firm Inc.* **(August 2004)**
Pub: American Lawyer Media LP
Ed: Tamara Loomis. **Description:** Cost recovery systems are of major concern to law firms. Many firms are considering whether to absorb costs for copies, laser printouts, faxes, scanning and telephone calls or pass the expense on to clients in order to recover out-of-pocket expenses incurred on the client's behalf.

29431 ■ **"Overtime Reform Overdoses on Politics"** in *Inc.* **(July 1, 2004)**
Pub: Inc. Magazine
Ed: Jess McCuan. **Description:** New rules governing overtime will be part of the overhauling of the Fair Labor Standards Act in 2004, but politics are leaving rules unclear.

29432 ■ **"Overwhelmed nurses leaving medicine to help lawyers"** in *Atlanta Business Chronicle* **(Vol. 25, No. 20, October 25, 2002, pp. 3A)**
Pub: American City Business Publications, Inc.
Ed: Julie Bryant. **Description:** There is currently a growing shortage of nurses because many of these professionals are tired of the low wages, demanding hours and minimal staff levels and are turning to the field of law to assist attorneys.

29433 ■ **"The Patent Epidemic"** in *Business Week* **(January 9, 2006, No. 3966, pp. 60-62)**
Pub: McGraw-Hill Companies
Ed: Michael Orey. **Description:** Defeating suspicious patents can take years, cost millions, and slow innovation, however, the Supreme Court may reshape patent law.

29434 ■ **"Patent Pending"** in *Entrepreneur* **(Vol. 33, October 2005, No. 10, pp. 28)**
Pub: Entrepreneur Media Inc.
Ed: Chris Penttila. **Description:** The U.S. Federal Trade Commission is recommending stiffer qualification standards for patents, allowing competitors to challenge patents early in the application process, to make is simpler for competitors to review each other's patents, and to limit damage awards in cases of willful infringement.

29435 ■ *Patent Reexamination and Small Business Innovation: Congressional Hearing*
Pub: DIANE Publishing Company
Ed: Howard Coble. **Released:** February 2004. **Price:** $25.00. **Description:** Congressional hearing: Witness: Peter Theis, President, Theis Research, Inc.; Paul Heckel, Independent Inventor; Nancy Linck, Senior Vice President, General Counsel and Secretary, Guilford Pharmaceuticals, Inc.; and Mark H. Webbink, Senior Vice President and General Counsel, Red Hat, Inc.

29436 ■ **"Patrick Tisdale, Chief Information Officer"** in *Law Firm Inc.* **(August 2004)**
Pub: American Lawyer Media LP
Description: Patrick Tisdale, chief information officer of Orrick explains how e-learning tools were made available to staff to improve skills. Tisdale also focused on increasing the help desk's level of expertise and instill the important role they play in the law firm, using a week long course in customer service skills.

29437 ■ **"Pattern Behavior"** in *Entrepreneur* **(Vol. 28, No. 11, November 2000, pp. 22)**
Pub: Entrepreneur Media Inc.
Ed: Geoff Williams. **Description:** Cross-stitch companies plan legal action to halt online sharing of patterns.

29438 ■ **"Payroll Piggy Bank?"** in *Entrepreneur* **(Vol. 31, No. 9, September 2003, pp. 61)**
Pub: Entrepreneur Media, Inc.
Ed: Joan Szabo. **Description:** Borrowing money withheld from employee paychecks to pay federal income, social security and Medicare taxes, as well as state and local taxes, is illegal and should never be considered.

29439 ■ **"Philly Firm Launches Lawsuit over 'Space'"** in *Orlando Business Journal* **(Vol. 20, No. 7, August 1, 2003, No. pp. 1)**
Pub: American City Business Journals, Inc.
Ed: Bob Mervine. **Description:** An overview of a lawsuit filed by Environmental Tectonics against Walt Disney World for breach of contract following a dispute over installation of a new thrill ride in the Florida theme park.

29440 ■ **"A Phony Cure; Shifting Class Actions to Federal Courts Is No Reform"** in *Business Week* **(February 7, 2005, No. 3919, pp. 33)**
Pub: McGraw-Hill Companies
Ed: Lorraine Woellert. **Description:** New legislation would require class action lawsuits to be filed in Federal Courts rather than in rural areas that have strong consumer-protection laws, anti-business jurors, and judges who help the local plaintiffs' bar.

29441 ■ **"A Pluralistic Account of Intellectual Property"** in *Journal of Business Ethics* **(Vol. 46, No. 4, September 15, 2003, pp. 319)**
Pub: Kluwer Academic Publishers Group
Ed: David B. Resnik. **Description:** Reviews of six different approaches to intellectual property are presented.

29442 ■ **"Point, Click, File a Lawsuit"** in *Sacramento Bee* **(December 11, 2005)**
Pub: The Sacramento Bee
Ed: Jim Wasserman. **Description:** LegalZoom.com will handle legal complaints online. The firm employs 120 workers to prepare legal complaints, send them to court, and even serve defendants.

29443 ■ **"Power Broker Gets 7 1/2 Years in Prison"** in *Black Enterprise* **(Vol. 35, January 2005, No. 6, pp. 28)**
Pub: Earl G. Graves Publishing Co. Inc.
Ed: Carolyn M. Brown. **Description:** Nathan Chapman Jr. has been sentenced to 7-1/2 years in prison and fined for defrauding Maryland's retirement system and stealing from his own firm.

29444 ■ *PPC's Small Business Tax Guide*
Pub: Practitioners Publishing Company
Ed: Douglas L. Weinbrenner, Virginia R. Bergman, Toni M. Greenwall, James A. Keller, Scott Mayfield, Linda A. Markwood. **Released:** January 2005. **Price:** $135.00. **Description:** Business tax laws are covered in an easy to understand format.

29445 ■ *PPC's Small Business Tax Guide, Vol. 2*
Pub: Practitioners Publishing Company
Ed: Douglas L. Weinbrenner, Virginia R. Bergman, Toni M. Greenwall, James A. Keller, Scott Mayfield, Linda A. Markwood. **Released:** January 2005. **Price:** $135.00. **Description:** Second volume containing technical guide covering business tax laws.

29446 ■ **"Predatory Towing"** in *San Fernando Valley Business Journal* **(Vol. 12, January 2007, No. 2, pp. 37)**
Pub: San Fernando Valley Business Journal Associates
Ed: Vanessa Herman. **Description:** State Towing Inc. and the company's owner, Reza Nowrooz, was found guilty of two counts of unlawfully taking vehicles and one count of attempted extortion.

29447 ■ "Pregnancy Claim Settlements Rise" in *Inc.* (September 2005, pp. 30)
Pub: Inc. Magazine
Description: Pregnancy discrimination lawsuits are on the rise. The Equal Employment Opportunity Commission received 4,512 complaints in 2004.

29448 ■ "Prepare for Y2K Litigation" in *E-business Advisor* (Vol. 17, No. 12, December 1999, pp. 36)
Pub: Advisor Media, Inc.
Ed: Sean P. Melvin. **Description:** Leaders of e-businesses should anticipate some lawsuits triggered by Y2K, so they should consider lawsuit defense strategies and start preventative maintenance measures.

29449 ■ "Private Matters: Retail Alert: Keep an Eye on New RFID Privacy Legislation" in *Entrepreneur* (Vol. 32, October 2004, No. 10, pp. 38)
Pub: Entrepreneur Media Inc.
Ed: Amanda C. Kooser. **Description:** Wireless capabilities that track products as they move through the supply chain, known as radio frequency identification (RFID) are growing in popularity with retailers. Several states are considering privacy legislation to regulate RFID so companies could not collect and use data collected regarding customers.

29450 ■ "Private-to-Private Corruption" in *Journal of Business Ethics* (Vol. 47, No. 3, October 15, 2003, pp. 253)
Pub: Kluwer Academic Publishers Group
Ed: Antonio Argandona. **Description:** Private-to-private corruption has been neglected and only recently receiving coverage by the media.

29451 ■ "Profit Globally, Give Globally" in *Harvard Business Review* (Vol. 81, No. 12, December 2003, pp. 16)
Pub: Harvard Business School Press
Ed: John Quelch, V. Kasturi Rangan. **Description:** An overview of ways corporations can and should increase non-domestic philanthropic aid is presented. Topics include sensitivity and diplomacy involved in international economic relations, and issues such as tax breaks and local law.

29452 ■ "Profiting from Copyrighted Materials" in *Rough Notes* (Vol. 146, No. 3, March 2003, pp. 104)
Pub: Rough Notes
Ed: G. Edward Kalbaugh. **Description:** Owners of Internet sites with public access should understand copyright laws to protect information and themselves.

29453 ■ "Protect Company Info" in *Small Business Opportunities* (Vol. 16, No. 2, March 2004, pp. 86)
Pub: Harris Publications, Inc.
Ed: John DiFrances. **Description:** Ways to protect a small business' proprietary information while remaining within the U.S. law. Three written policies to protect information include one regarding the exchange of technical data between an organization's U.S. and offshore company owned or representative offices and personnel; another regarding employees taking technical and business data, both hard copy and electronic, home or downloading it remotely after company hours; and lastly one regarding what types of technical and business data may be carried on laptop computers and/or downloaded when outside the U.S.

29454 ■ "Protect Yourself From Lawsuits" in *My Business* (November/December 2001, pp. 42)
Pub: My Business Magazine
Ed: Milton Zall. **Description:** Three legal requirements to follow in order to augment employee severance packages with "no-suit" agreements are covered.

29455 ■ "Protecting the Dream" in *Ingram's* (Vol. 28, No. 5, May 2002, pp. 28)
Pub: Show Me Publishing, Inc.
Ed: Cynthia Grimes. **Description:** Legal advice is given to protect small businesses from bankruptcy, lawyers, accounting, cash flow planning, employee benefits and estate planning.

29456 ■ "Q&A" in *Home Office Computing* (Vol. 18, No. 7, July 2000, pp. 13)
Pub: Scholastic Inc.
Ed: Cristina Gair. **Description:** Jay Westermeier, attorney at Piper, Maybury, Rudnick & Wolfe, in Washington, D.C., discusses ways to avoid legal problems when selling goods and services online.

29457 ■ "Raines Stays Cool Under Fire" in *Black Enterprise* (Vol. 35, December 2004, No. 5, pp. 34)
Pub: Earl G. Graves Publishing Co. Inc.
Ed: Hamil Harris. **Description:** Overview of the case against Franklin Raines, CEO of Fannie Mae, the nation's largest source of financing for home mortgages. Franklin has been charged with engaging in accounting violations.

29458 ■ "Raising the Bar" in *Hispanic Business* (June 2005, pp. 104, 106)
Pub: Hispanic Business
Ed: Anthony Limon. **Description:** Hispanics benefit as law firms bid to reflect a more diversified clientele. Profile of Salomon Chiquiar-Rabinovich is included.

29459 ■ "Rate Increases Nail Homebuilding Sector" in *Business Journal-Portland* (Vol. 20, No. 26, August 29, 2003, pp. 18)
Pub: American City Business Journals, Inc.
Ed: Robert Goldfield. **Description:** Insurance companies have doubled or tripled premiums for building contracts for various reasons, including the appearance of toxic mold in homes and resulting lawsuits.

29460 ■ "Rating the Governors" in *Inc.* (November 2006, pp. 95-98, 100, 102, 104, 106)
Pub: Gruner & Jahr USA Publishing
Ed: Mike Hofman. **Description:** Best governors for business are the least partisan. Governors of various states are discussed and rated on several criteria: tax and fiscal policy, health care, education, regulation, and work force and economic development.

29461 ■ "Raw Deal: Avoid These Consumer Scams at all Costs" in *Black Enterprise* (Vol. 35, September 2004, No. 2, pp. 185)
Pub: Earl G. Graves Publishing Co. Inc.
Ed: Tanisha A. Sykes. **Description:** A listing of generic scams for consumers to beware of are offered by The Identity Theft Resource Center, including free credit report emails, the Nigerian 419 scam, Visa/MasterCard alerts, email chain letters, and in-store security scams.

29462 ■ "Read fine print yearly to avoid costly contractual obligations" in *Boston Business Journal* (Vol. 22, No. 14, May 10, 2002, pp. 42)
Pub: MCP, Inc.
Ed: Sari Ann Strassburg. **Description:** There are bound to be disputes wherever there are contracts, advice is given on the importance of reading all fine print on the purchase order and invoice, which are the basis of contracts.

29463 ■ "Reading, writing, and protection" in *Black Enterprise* (Vol. 32, No. 5,)
Pub: Earl Graves Publishing Co.
Ed: Roger Barnes. **Description:** Three commonly overlooked provisions when a small business enters a contract, ways to construct a contract, and finding legal help are highlighted.

29464 ■ "The Real Deal" in *Entrepreneur* (Vol. 33, September 2005, No. 9, pp. 74)
Pub: Entrepreneur Media Inc.
Ed: April Y. Pennington, Nichole L. Torres, Geoff Williams, Sara Wilson. **Description:** Entrepreneurs discuss the highs and lows of business ownership, from embezzlement, international trade, and selling a product to Target.

29465 ■ "Reality check: threat of lawsuit changes discriminatory payment practices" in *Black Enterprise* (Vol. 33, No. 3, Oct. 2002, pp. 178)
Pub: Earl Graves Publishing Co.

Ed: Lee Anna Jackson. **Description:** Lawyers in Washington, DC have filed a lawsuit against retailers that are refusing to accept out-of-state checks from African American customers. Patterns of discrimination are surfacing through the use of testers from The Equal Rights Center (TERC) attempting to purchase items with checks at various retail establishments.

29466 ■ "Reforming pro forma" in *Entrepreneur* (Vol. 31, No. 5, May 2003, pp. 50)
Pub: Entrepreneur Media Inc.
Ed: Jennifer Pellet. **Description:** The issue of pro forma financial reports used by small businesses in the past is discussed. The SEC is working to bring pro forma reporting under control.

29467 ■ "Regulation Nation" in *Entrepreneur* (Vol. 32, October 2004, No. 10, pp. 32)
Pub: Entrepreneur Media Inc.
Ed: Joshua Kurlantzick. **Description:** Federal regulations are limiting the growth of small business in America. The Small Business Administration's Office of Advocacy estimates small firms with less than 20 employees pay nearly $7,000 per employee in regulatory costs.

29468 ■ "Reporters' Notebook; Weighing Fed's Tough-guy Tactics" in *Crain's Detroit Business* (Vol. 22, December 11, 2006, No. 50, pp. 11)
Pub: Crain Communications Inc. - Detroit
Ed: Robert Ankeny. **Description:** U.S. Justice Department Thompson Memorandum demands that corporations under investigation waive the attorney-client privilege and also pressures those companies to stop paying attorney fees for employees facing charges.

29469 ■ "The Revised Uniform Arbitration Act: an overview" in *Dispute Resolution Journal* (Vol. 56, No. 2, May-July 2001, pp. 28)
Pub: American Arbitration Association
Ed: Timothy J. Heinsz. **Description:** An outline of the changes made under the Revised Uniform Arbitration Act and the need for Congress to revise the Federal Arbitration Act.

29470 ■ "Robert Wagner Hosts The Litigation Explosion" in *Entrepreneur* (Vol. 33, January 2005, No. 1, pp. 104)
Pub: Entrepreneur Media Inc.
Description: The rewards of high income and owning your own business as a consultant providing asset protection, financial privacy and tax reduction are highlighted.

29471 ■ "Round Two: Microsoft Appeals $140M Judgment For Local Inventor" in *Crain's Detroit Business* (Vol. 23, January 8, 2007, No. 2, pp. 1)
Pub: Crain Communications Inc. - Detroit
Ed: Tom Henderson. **Description:** Local Inventor prepares for appeal of judgment against Microsoft for $140M. Patent infringement for a process to combat software piracy is the central issue.

29472 ■ "Rule Book: Does Your Small Business Need an Employee Manual?" in *My Business* (June/July 2004, pp. 14)
Pub: My Business Magazine
Description: Review of the book, Create Your Own Employee Handbook: A Legal and Practical Guide, which teaches a company to express its culture and beliefs, ensure consistency for all employees, and clearly explain expectations of each employee in the form of an employee manual.

29473 ■ "Ruling on Tax Incentives May Head to High Court" in *Crain's Detroit Business* (Vol. 21, January 31, 2005, No. 5, pp. 33)
Pub: Crain Communications Inc. - Detroit
Ed: Amy Lane. **Description:** A legal dispute in Ohio could have an impact of Michigan's main business-tax incentive, the Michigan Economic Growth Authority program whereby Michigan grants single-business-tax credits for incentives for corporate investment.

29474 ■ **"Rumblings"** in *Crain's Detroit Business* **(Vol. 19, No. 1, January 6, 2003, pp. 22)**
Pub: Crain Communications Inc., Detroit
Description: Crain's Detroit Business and WJR AM 760 radio station along with the Rehabilitation Institute of Michigan have launched a competition to find the '50 Fittest CEOs' in metropolitan Detroit. According to an investment banker, Compuware Corporation is being targeted for acquisition. A listing of the top six law firms in the Detroit area making The National Law Journal 250 for 2002 is presented.

29475 ■ **"A Run of Luck"** in *Entrepreneur* **(Vol. 33, March 2005, No. 3, pp. 55)**
Pub: Entrepreneur Media Inc.
Ed: David Worrell. **Description:** Profile of Client Profiles Inc., a legal software company. CEO White McIsaac, tells how he wanted to sell his business, while maintaining control of the company's direction.

29476 ■ **"St. Catherine of Siena Medical Center Seeks to Block LIRR"** in *Long Island Business News* **(March 12, 2004)**
Pub: Dolan Media Newswires
Ed: Claude Solnik. **Description:** The Long Island Rail Road is being asked by St. Catherine of Siena Medical Center to remove a site adjacent to the hospital from its list of potential locations for a new rail yard. The Medical Center is citing potential health risks as their reason to halt the rail road's plans.

29477 ■ **"Sales"** in *Inc.* **(Volume 27, March 2005, No. 3, pp. 38)**
Pub: Inc. Magazine
Ed: Mike Brewster. **Description:** Large corporations require a request for proposal when purchasing products or services in order to comply with corporate governance standards.

29478 ■ **"Say What? Decipher Common Contract Legalese"** in *Entrepreneur* **(Vol. 32, December 2004, No. 12, pp. 98)**
Pub: Entrepreneur Media Inc.
Ed: Marc Diener. **Description:** Common clauses to beware of when entering into legal contracts are examined.

29479 ■ **"Scammers Have Been Downloading Software From My Website Using Stolen PayPal Accounts. What Can I Do?"** in *Inc.* **(Vol. 27, July 2005)**
Pub: Inc. Magazine
Description: PayPal accounts are being swiped with the identity-theft technique known as phishing. PayPal's seller-protection policy covers only physical goods, rendering dealers responsible for refunding any scammed customers.

29480 ■ **"SEC, FBI Bring Fraud Charges Against Former Brocade Management"** in *Hispanic Business* **(September 2006, pp. 12)**
Pub: Hispanic Business
Description: Top executives are facing 20 years in prison, $5 million in fines along with restitution for allegedly backdating stock options grants, concealing millions of dollars in expenses.

29481 ■ **"SEC Opens Inquiry Linked to Newsday Circulation"** in *Long Island Business News* **(February 27, 2004)**
Pub: Dolan Media Newswires
Description: An inquiry by the Securities and Exchange Commission into the inflated circulation figures by Newsday is discussed. Newsday denies all charges.

29482 ■ **"Security Breach? New Laws Could Change How You Handle Customer Info"** in *Entrepreneur* **(Vol. 33, October 2005, No. 10, pp. 24)**
Pub: Entrepreneur Media Inc.
Ed: Amanda C. Kooser. **Description:** New federal laws to protect customer privacy will apply to all firms that collect confidential or personal information from consumers.

29483 ■ **"Seeing Red Over Big Blue's China Deal"** in *Business Week* **(February 14, 2005, No. 3920, pp. 45)**
Pub: McGraw-Hill Companies
Ed: Stan Crock, Richard S. Dunham. **Description:** U.S. Homeland Security Department and the FBI are concerned over the sale of IBM's PC business that could help China's military. Issues involved include the possible transfer of encryption technology and the higher-end IBM operations in Research Triangle Park, North Carolina, which could make industrial espionage easier. China has an estimated $400 billion in dollar reserves, which could start a strategic buying spree by China.

29484 ■ **"Senate Targets Payroll Tax Scam"** in *Inc.* **(August 1, 2004)**
Pub: Inc. Magazine
Ed: Nadine Heintz. **Description:** Roger Cyr, owner of Lily Moon Cafe in Saco, Maine alleges that his payroll tax accountant stole tax payments from dozens of companies, including his own.

29485 ■ **"Service with a smile"** in *Entrepreneur* **(Vol. 30, No. 2, February 2002, pp. 66)**
Pub: Entrepreneur Media Inc.
Ed: Steven C. Bahls, Jane Easter Bahls. **Description:** The legal aspects for managing employees who are signed up with the armed forces reserves are discussed.

29486 ■ **"Several Queen's Advertisers File $100M Lawsuit Against Newsday"** in *Long Island Business News* **(February 13, 2004)**
Pub: Dolan Media Newswires
Description: Advertisers in Queens, New York have filed a lawsuit against Newsday, alleging that the paper manipulated circulation numbers to increase advertising rates.

29487 ■ **"Severed Ties"** in *Entrepreneur* **(Vol. 33, October 2005, No. 10, pp. 30)**
Pub: Entrepreneur Media Inc.
Ed: Crystal Detamore-Rodman. **Description:** New laws aimed at reforming the bankruptcy system will slow the growth of new companies as well expansion of existing companies.

29488 ■ **"Shh...It's a Secret"** in *Entrepreneur.com* **(Vol. 34, February 2006, No. 2, pp. 82)**
Pub: Entrepreneur Media Inc.
Ed: Jane Easter Bahls. **Description:** When employees leave to work for a competitor, it is essential they understand the confidentiality of your company's trade secrets. Steps to ensure legal protection of company knowledge are covered.

29489 ■ **"Shielding Your Home from Lawsuits"** in *Hispanic Business* **(October 2003, pp. 90)**
Pub: Hispanic Business
Ed: Glen M. Terrones, Christopher Jarvis, David Mandell. **Description:** Tools to help small business owners protect their homes from lawsuits are given, including the formation of limited liability companies and family limited partnerships.

29490 ■ **"Shred of evidence: learn a lesson from Arthur Anderson"** in *Entrepreneur* **(Vol. 30, No. 12, December 2002, pp. 106)**
Pub: Entrepreneur Media Inc.
Ed: Steven C. Bahls, Jane Easter Bahls. **Description:** The importance of working with an attorney to ensure compliance with all laws on length of time to retain company documents is discussed.

29491 ■ **"Sign right here"** in *The New York Times* **(October 8, 2000, pp. WK2)**
Pub: The New York Times Company
Ed: John Schwartz. **Description:** An overview of electronic signatures in the Global Commerce Act.

29492 ■ **"Slick Tricks"** in *Entrepreneur* **(Vol. 31, No. 7, July 2003, pp. 73)**
Pub: Entrepreneur Media, Inc.
Ed: Joanne Cleaver. **Description:** Telecommunications scams continue with newer attacks of hijacked

phone accounts (slamming), unauthorized add-on charges (cramming). It is important for small business owners to warn employees of such scams to avoid problems.

29493 ■ **"Small businesses fret over delays in eliminating an unpopular 1999 law"** in *Wall Street Journal* **(July 19, 2000, pp. A1)**
Pub: Dow Jones & Co., Inc.
Ed: Tom Herman. **Description:** A discussion regarding the law that governs small businesses selling part or whole on an installment plan.

29494 ■ *Small Business Access to Health Care: Congressional Hearing*
Pub: DIANE Publishing Company
Ed: Donald A. Manzullo. **Released:** August 2004. **Price:** $25.00. **Description:** Congressional hearing held at Crystal Lake, Illinois. Witnesses: Mary Blankenbaker, Co-Owner, Benjamin's Restaurant; Ryan Brauns, Senior Vice President, Rockford Consulting and Brokerage; Scott Shalek, RHU, Shalek Financial Services; Brad Close, National Federation of Independent Businesses; Ken Koehler, Flowerwood, Inc.; Brad Buxton, Vice President of Networks and Medical Management, Blue Cross and Blue Shield of Illinois; Isabella Wilson, Chief Financial Office, Illinois Blower, Inc.; and James Milam, Illinois State Medical Society.

29495 ■ **"Small Business, Big Losses"** in *Journal of Accountancy* **(Vol. 19)**
Pub: American Institute of Certified Public Accountants
Ed: Joseph T. Wells. **Description:** Occupational fraud is becoming increasingly more prevalent and affects nearly every business. A summary of the key findings of certified frauds examiners (CFEs) in cases of financial statement fraud is highlighted.

29496 ■ *Small Business Desk Reference*
Pub: Penguin Books (USA) Incorporated
Ed: Gene Marks. **Released:** December 2004. **Price:** $29.95 (US), $44.00 (Canadian). **Description:** Comprehensive guide for starting or running a successful small business, focusing on buying a business or franchise, writing a business plan, financial management, accounting, legal issues, human resources management, operations, marketing, sales, customer service, taxes, insurance, and ethics. Information for launching a restaurant, property management firm, retail outlet, consulting firm, and service business is included.

29497 ■ **"Small Business Groups Intensify Efforts to Repeal a Recently Enacted Law"** in *Wall Street Journal* **(January 19, 2000, pp. A1)**
Pub: Dow Jones & Co., Inc.
Ed: Tom Herman. **Description:** An overview of a tax law related to the accrual method.

29498 ■ **"Small Business Groups and Lawyers Step Up Efforts to Erase a 1999 law"** in *Wall Street Journal* **(April 12, 2000, pp. A1)**
Pub: Dow Jones & Co., Inc.
Ed: Tom Herman. **Description:** The law on taxation of installment-plan business sales is covered.

29499 ■ *The Small Business Legal Kit*
Pub: Adams Media Corporation
Ed: J. W. Dicks. **Released:** 1997. **Price:** $16.95 (cloth); $19.95 (w/disk).

29500 ■ *Small Business Legal Smarts*
Pub: Bloomberg Press
Ed: Deborah L. Jacobs. **Released:** 1998. **Price:** $16.95.

29501 ■ *Small Business Legal Strategies*
Pub: Aspatore Books, Incorporated
Released: July 2004. **Price:** $37.95. **Description:** Corporate Chairs and Partners from top firms in the U.S. offering insight into selecting, engaging, employing, and benefiting from external corporate counsel for the small business owner or executive.

29502 ■ *Small Business Management*
Pub: John Wiley & Sons, Incorporated
Ed: Margaret Burlingame. **Released:** March 2007.
Price: $44.95. **Description:** Advice for starting and running a small business as well as information on the value and appeal of small businesses, is given. Topics include budgets, taxes, inventory, ethics, e-commerce, and current laws.

29503 ■ *Small Business Survival Guide: Starting, Protecting, and Securing Your Business for Long-Term Success*
Pub: Adams Media Corporation
Ed: Cliff Ennico. **Released:** October 2005. **Price:** $12.95 (US), $17.95 (Canadian). **Description:** Entrepreneurship in the new millennium. Topics include creditors, taxes, competition, business law, and accounting.

29504 ■ *Small Business Taxation*
Pub: CCH Incorporated
Ed: Gary Maydew. **Released:** February 2005. **Price:** $99.00. **Description:** Tax laws governing small business are outlined.

29505 ■ *Small Time Operator: How to Start Your Own Business, Keep Your Books, Pay Your Taxes, and Stay Out of Trouble*
Pub: Bell Springs Publishing
Ed: Bernard B. Kamoroff. **Released:** February 2005. **Price:** $17.95. **Description:** Comprehensive guide for starting any kind of business.

29506 ■ "Smart inventory: start electing superior filing options now" in *Barron's* (Vol. 82, No. 59, February 24, 2003, pp. 23)
Pub: Barron's
Ed: Joseph F. Gelband. **Description:** The use of laws from Section 475 of the tax code is one way in which investors can reduce capital gains tax on the sales of securities as long as an investor is considered a securities trader. Use of the provision allows losses to be fully deducted. An explanation of ways an S company can benefit on taxes by changing status to a C company is offered.

29507 ■ "Smart patents" in *Harvard Business Review* (Vol. 80, No. 4, April 2002, pp. 18)
Pub: Harvard Business School Press
Ed: Robert Maxwell. **Description:** Information is presented about the little-used legal device known as the continuation patent. This 'child' patent allows a company to extend the examination period and make changes in the language of the 'parent' patent.

29508 ■ "Snow, rain and sleet lead to weather delay claims" in *Business First Columbus* (Vol. 18, No. 25, February 8, 2002, pp. 17)
Pub: Business First Columbus, Inc.
Ed: Michael S. Holman, Gregory T. Parks. **Description:** An examination of construction law, particularly in cases of weather delays.

29509 ■ "The Social Cost of Fraud and Bankruptcy" in *Harvard Business Review* (Vol. 81, No. 12, December 2003, pp. 20)
Pub: Harvard Business School Press
Ed: Joseph Bower, Stuart Gilson. **Description:** The unfair advantage Chapter 11 bankruptcy law provides to companies that have operated outside the legally sanctioned business practices to which other firms have subscribed is addressed. Discussions focus on how firms obeying the laws are penalized, using the WorldCom Inc. case as an example.

29510 ■ "Spam Could Be a Scam: Internet Tricks Are Becoming High Crimes" in *Black Enterprise* (Vol. 35, August 2004, No. 1, pp. 30)
Pub: Earl G. Graves Publishing Co. Inc.
Ed: Siobhan Benet. **Description:** Internet crime, also called cybercrime, is the third priority after counterterrorism and counterintelligence for the Federal Bureau of Investigation.

29511 ■ "Spotlight Rick Chesley; Chairman Builds Law Office From Ground Up" in *Crain's Chicago Business* (Vol. 30, January 2007, No. 2, pp. 5)
Pub: Crain Communications, Inc.
Ed: Lorene Yue. **Description:** Profile of Rick Chesley, office chair for law firm, Paul Hastings Janofsky & Walker LLP's at the new Chicago location. Hastings' goal is to establish a strong Chicago presence for the firm.

29512 ■ "Star Attorney" in *Black Enterprise* (Vol. 34, No. 4, November 2003, pp. 60)
Pub: Earl Graves Publishing Co.
Ed: Sonia Alleyne. **Description:** Advice is offered to a law school student regarding a career in entertainment and/or sports law.

29513 ■ "State Coughs as Firms Seek Millions" in *Atlanta Business Chronicle* (Vol. 25, December 13, 2002, No. 27, pp. A3)
Pub: American City Business Publications, Inc.
Ed: Sara Rubenstein. **Description:** A group of some 130 Atlanta, Georgia area companies are suing the Georgia Environmental Protection Division and Department of Revenue in January 2003, seeking payment of over $9 million in fees for auto emissions tests that were allegedly collected illegally. The state contends that refunds would lead to cuts in the emissions inspection program, which is designed to help the metropolitan Atlanta region meet federal air quality standards. Georgia's Supreme Court ruled in 2001 that the fees were collected illegally.

29514 ■ "State Franchise Laws and the Small Business Franchise Act of 1999" in (Vol. 55, No. 4, August 2000, pp. 1699)
Pub: American Bar Association
Ed: Thomas J. Collin. **Description:** Unless a business sells to customers directly or through factory branches, they will need to take a close account of state franchise laws as they make decisions about distribution changes, and they may find that these laws raise significant barriers to change.

29515 ■ "State Investigates 'Tribal Coverage" in *San Francisco Business Times* (Vol. 18, No. 6, September 19, 2003, pp. 1)
Pub: American City Business Journals
Ed: Daniel S. Levine. **Description:** Native Americans are being hired and leased back to avoid workers compensation costs to employers, which may be against California law.

29516 ■ "States Target Outsourcing" in *Inc.* (July 1, 2004)
Pub: Inc. Magazine
Ed: Darren Dahl. **Description:** Several states hope legislation efforts will help curb the trend toward outsourcing to companies overseas.

29517 ■ "Status Woe: Contractors' Illegal Workers Could Put You in a Legal Pickle" in *Entrepreneur* (Vol. 32, No. 4, April 2004, pp. 23)
Pub: Entrepreneur Media, Inc.
Ed: Chris Penttila. **Description:** Small businesses can face lawsuits and fines up to $10,000 per illegal alien employee for every day worked on-site. It is important for small firms, when outsourcing, to review contracts with vendors supplying contract workers.

29518 ■ "Staying Out of Court" in *Business Week* (No. 3702, October 9, 2000, pp. F16)
Pub: McGraw-Hill, Inc.
Description: Alternatives to a courtroom battle are covered, including mediation, where a neutral party helps negotiate a settlement, and arbitration, where the neutral's decision is binding.

29519 ■ "Strategies" in *Business Week* (December 19, 2005, No. 3964, pp. 44-45)
Pub: McGraw-Hill Companies
Ed: Kenji Hall, Peter Burrows. **Description:** Toshiba Corporation is able to keep innovations out of the hands of competitors.

29520 ■ "Street Smarts: Presumed Guilty" in *Inc.* (October 1, 2004)
Pub: Inc. Magazine
Ed: Norm Brodsky. **Description:** Experts recommend that small businesses let lawyers make legal decision, but to keep business decisions with company management.

29521 ■ "Stressed Out" in *PC Computing* (April 2000, pp. 44)
Pub: Ziff-Davis Inc.
Ed: Jennifer Powell. **Description:** The seriousness of musculoskeletal disorders and their impact is covered. Musculoskeletal disorders (MSDs), also known as repetitive strain injuries (RSIs), can begin whenever a part of the body is used in the same way repeatedly, especially when twisting or lifting.

29522 ■ "Striving for 'Critical Mass'" in *Hispanic Business* (Vol. 23, No. 10, October, 2001, pp. 16)
Pub: Hispanic Business
Ed: Rick Laezman. **Description:** The LaRaza Lawyers Association of California is working to strengthen Hispanic legal influence. Despite the fact that Hispanics account for more than 30 percent of California's population, only 4 percent are attorneys.

29523 ■ "Study: Insurance Fraud Thriving" in *Orlando Business Journal* (Vol. 20, No. 13, September 12, 2003, pp. 1)
Pub: American City Business Journals, Inc.
Ed: Susan Lundine. **Description:** Researchers at the Health Policy Institute of Georgetown University reported that Florida has a disproportionate number of health insurance fraud cases. Nearly 30,000 Florida residents have been left with $6 million in unpaid medical bills by fraudulent companies.

29524 ■ "Sued Over the Dress Code" in *Inc.* (October 1, 2003)
Pub: Gruner & Jahr USA Publishing
Ed: Cara Cannella. **Description:** Abercrombie and Fitch has been sued for not supplying the costly apparel it requires employees to wear. Workers won a $2.2 million settlement.

29525 ■ "Sued Over an Employee's Cell Phone" in *Inc.* (July 1, 2004)
Pub: Inc. Magazine
Ed: Jess McCuan. **Description:** Liability for car accidents involving employees using a company cell phone is investigated.

29526 ■ "Suit May Cost Post Unit its Trademark" in *Washington Business Journal* (Vol. 22, No. 15, August 15, 2003, pp. 3)
Pub: Washington Business Journal
Ed: Greg A. Lohr. **Description:** Information regarding the Washington Post's lawsuit against PRIMEDIA Inc. for trademark infringement. Topics include trademark law and competition.

29527 ■ "Suit May Force SBC Refunds" in *Atlanta Journal-Constitution* (February 17, 2004)
Pub: Knight-Ridder/Tribune Business News
Ed: Purva Patel. **Description:** SBC business customers have filed a class-action suit against the phone company for overcharging them.

29528 ■ "Supreme Court Rules Regal Entertainment's Style is Unfair to Disabled Customers" in *Miami Herald* (June 29, 2004)
Pub: Knight-Ridder/Tribune Business News
Ed: Gillian Wee. **Description:** U.S. Supreme Court has ruled Regal Entertainment Group's theaters discriminate against disabled customers. The stadium-style seating in the theater requires handicapped guests to sit in seats located at the front of the show, and they claim these seats are uncomfortable.

29529 ■ "Survey: economy will continue to affect growth" in *Atlanta Business Chronicle* (Vol. 25, November 15, 2002, No. 23 pp. SS12)
Pub: American City Business Publications, Inc.
Description: Members of Atlanta's legal community were surveyed by the Atlanta Business Chronicle

about expectations for business in 2003, the biggest challenges expected in Atlanta for the next year, and expectations for their practices. Responses from eight professionals are included.

29530 ■ "Surviving Legal Adversity" in
Success **(Vol. 47, No. 3, July 2000, pp. 63)**
Pub: Success Publishing, Inc.
Ed: Michael Zinn. **Description:** Ideas to help deal with unexpected litigation in business.

29531 ■ "Surviving Sarbanes-Oxley" in *Inc.*
(September 2005, pp. 132-138)
Pub: Inc. Magazine
Ed: Amy Feldman. **Description:** The Sarbanes-Oxley Act was intended to crack down on large public companies, but the Act has created a burden for many smaller, private firms. Policymakers are looking into ways to undo damages. Five ways companies can comply to the Sarbanes-Oxley Act are listed.

29532 ■ "Susan McMillan Appointed Executive Director of the Long Island Better Business Bureau" in *Long Island Business News* **(Feb. 6, 2004)**
Pub: Dolan Media Newswires
Ed: Ryan McCormick. **Description:** Profile of Susan McMillan, newly appointed executive director of the Long Island Better Business Bureau. McMillan also serves on the Consumer Affairs Committee of the Bar Association of the City of New York and is an active member of the Small Business Advisory Committee.

29533 ■ "The Sweet Smell of a Settlement"
in *Inc.* **(December 1, 2003)**
Pub: Gruner & Jahr USA Publishing
Ed: Bo Burlingham. **Description:** After an epic battle of perfume brands, Terri Williamson and Jennifer Lopez both end up winners.

29534 ■ "Symbol Technologies Wins Landmark Lawsuit in Nevada Federal Court" in *Long Island Business News* **(January 30, 2004)**
Pub: Dolan Media Newswires
Description: A federal judge in Nevada has ruled that a coalition of bar code companies did not infringe on patents of the Lemelson Foundation, saving retail chains hundreds of millions in royalties.

29535 ■ "Symbolism with a Bottom Line" in *Hispanic Business* **(Vol. 23, No. 7/8, July/August 2001, pp. 16)**
Pub: Hispanic Business
Ed: Leigh Miller. **Description:** In April 2001, Georgia Governor Roy Barnes signed a state law designating Hispanics as an official minority group. Hispanic businesses will now qualify as minority-owned firms.

29536 ■ "Take a hard look, and do the right thing" in *Crain's Detroit Business* **(Vol. 19, No. 5, February 3, 2003, pp. 9)**
Pub: Crain Communications Inc., Detroit
Ed: Frank Hennessey. **Description:** The ethical aspects and regulation of business and accounting practices are investigated.

29537 ■ "Take Note: Document Incidents Now, and Avoid Lawsuits Later" in *Entrepreneur* **(Vol. 32, October 2004, No. 10, pp. 64)**
Pub: Entrepreneur Media Inc.
Ed: Jacquelyn Lynn. **Description:** Proper documentation at the time of an injury or property damage occurring at a small company will give the firm a stronger position in litigation. If possible, take photographs, save security tapes and store documents in a safe place.

29538 ■ "Taking License: It Pays to Do Your Homework Before Signing a Licensing Agreement" in *Entrepreneur* **(Vol. 32, December 2004, No. 12)**
Pub: Entrepreneur Media Inc.
Ed: Don Debelak. **Description:** Kevin O'Rourke chronicles his journey from product development to achieving $10 million in projected sales in 2004. O'Rourke licensed the ElectraTrac, an extension cord with electric plugs located at every eight feet, used by consumers, creators of lighting shows, and electrical and construction contractors.

29539 ■ "Taubman-Simon battle employs an army of high-priced advisers" in *Crain's Detroit Business* **(Vol. 19, No. 17, April 28, 2003, pp. 4)**
Pub: Crain Communications Inc., Detroit
Ed: Brent Snavely. **Description:** An overview of information regarding Taubman Centers Inc.'s battle to defeat a hostile takeover by rival mall developer Simon Property Group Inc. Today lawyers, accountants and lobbyists tend to be the weapons of choice on the corporate-takeover battlefield.

29540 ■ *Tax Savvy for Small Business: Year-Round Tax Strategies to Save You Money*
Pub: NOLO
Ed: Frederick W. Daily, Bethany K. Laurence. **Released:** September 2005. **Price:** $36.99. **Description:** Tax strategies for small business. Includes the latest tax numbers and laws as well as current Internal Revenue Service forms and publications.

29541 ■ "Tech Talk" in *St. Louis Post-Dispatch* **(December 11, 2004)**
Pub: Knight-Ridder/Tribune Business News
Ed: David Sheets. **Description:** In November, several mall kiosks were found to be selling counterfeit Nintendo video games and game players in the St. Louis, Missouri area. Among the games are Donkey Kong and Mario Bros. titles.

29542 ■ "Telecommuter Denied Jobless Benefits" in *Inc.* **(October 1, 2003)**
Pub: Gruner & Jahr USA Publishing
Ed: Patrick J. Sauer. **Description:** An unemployed Florida telecommuter was denied unemployment benefits from the New York company she worked for.

29543 ■ "Terrorism Backup Legislation Raises Many Questions" in *Rough Notes* **(Vol. 145, No. 2, February 2003, pp. 34)**
Pub: Rough Notes
Ed: Phil Zinkewicz. **Description:** Terrorism insurance, its back up legislation, and obligations of agents and insurance companies in regard to disclosure requirements has turned out to be so complex it raises serious questions on compliance.

29544 ■ "Texas Doctors Take Pains to Follow Privacy Rules" in *Houston Chronicle* **(April 11, 2003)**
Pub: Knight-Ridder/Tribune Business News
Description: Measures to protect patient's privacy are being taken by doctors at medical facilities in the Houston, Texas area. These rules will comply with the new federal privacy standards.

29545 ■ "The Supreme Court" in *Business Week* **(December 19, 2005, No. 3964, pp. 42)**
Pub: McGraw-Hill Companies
Description: Stock holdings of justices can keep corporate cases off the docket.

29546 ■ "There's More Than One Way to Bust a Trust" in *Inc.* **(Volume 27, December 2005, No. 12, pp. 24)**
Pub: Inc. Magazine
Ed: Robert Litan. **Description:** The Federal Government failed to break Microsoft's monopoly; details of Microsoft's case are investigated.

29547 ■ "Ties That Bind" in *Entrepreneur* **(Vol. 31, No. 10, October 2003)**
Pub: Entrepreneur Media, Inc.
Ed: Jane Easter Bahls. **Description:** Many companies require employees to sign an agreement waiving their right to sue over employment disputes, rather using a panel of arbitrators.

29548 ■ "Time Right To Let Sun Shine On AG, Outside Attorneys" in *Mississippi Business Journal* **(Vol. 29, January 2007 , No. 29, pp. 4)**
Pub: Venture Publications, Inc.
Ed: Joe D. Jones **Description:** Mississippi Open Lawyer Fees Act has been written and introduced to the Legislature to bring added openness, oversight and accountability to the Attorney General's Office when outside lawyers are hired to work on behalf of the state.

29549 ■ "Time's Up: New Laws Tell You Who Gets Overtime-And Who Doesn't" in *Entrepreneur* **(Vol. 32, October 2004, No. 10, pp. 40)**
Pub: Entrepreneur Media Inc.
Ed: Chris Penttila. **Description:** New U.S. Department of Labor rules state that employees earning over $100,000 annually in executive, administrative and professional positions are no longer eligible for overtime, workers earning less than $23,660 annually are.

29550 ■ "Tobacco Sales to Minors Decline In Oklahoma" in *Journal Record (Oklahoma City, OK)* **(February 7, 2007)**
Pub: Journal Record
Description: For the third consecutive year, tobacco sales to minors had dropped; the drop also lowers the rate in which the state is fined by the Federal government.

29551 ■ "Top 10 Law Schools for Hispanics" in *Hispanic Business* **(September 2004, pp. 70, 72, 74, 76)**
Pub: Hispanic Business
Description: The top ten law schools for Hispanics are reviewed. University of Texas at Austin's School of Law scored number one, followed by the University of Miami. Statistical data included.

29552 ■ "Tougher Test for Bankruptcy" in *Black Enterprise* **(Vol. 36, November 2005, No. 4, pp. 56)**
Pub: Earl G. Graves Publishing Co. Inc.
Ed: Melissa S. Monroe. **Description:** The new Bankruptcy Abuse Prevention and Consumer Protection Act of 2005 was made law October 17, 2005. The Act forces many who intended to file for Chapter 7 bankruptcy to file for Chapter 13 bankruptcy instead, and commit to a payment plan.

29553 ■ "Trademarks: A Primer" in *Small Business Opportunities* **(Vol. 16, No. 1, January 2004, pp. 10)**
Pub: Harris Publications, Inc.
Ed: Therese B. Varndell, Esq. **Description:** Because trademarks are important assets to businesses, it is critical to avoid pitfalls when developing a trademark. Trademarks can be registered prior to starting a business based on an "intent-to-use".

29554 ■ "Trainers of Racing Horses Face New Drug Fine" in *Chicago Tribune* **(February 18, 2005)**
Pub: Knight-Ridder/Tribune Business News
Ed: Michael Higgins. **Description:** Racing Board officials in Illinois voted to fine trainers whose horses test positive for drugs, but are letting them keep prize money for wins. The board voted to impose a $250 fine for the first offense, $500 for the second, and $1,000 for all subsequent offenses.

29555 ■ "A Treasury move fails to defuse small business anger over a 1999 law" in *Wall Street Journal* **(March 1, 2000, pp. A1)**
Pub: Dow Jones & Co., Inc.
Ed: Tom Herman. **Description:** Taxes on proceeds from a business sale must be paid all at once, in most cases.

29556 ■ "Tulsa Insurance Company Sues Kansas-based Bank" in *Journal Record (Oklahoma City, OK)* **(February 8, 2007)**
Pub: Journal Record
Ed: Ginger Shepherd. **Description:** Details of International Insurance Brokers Ltd. lawsuit against Team Bank NA, Team Financial Inc., and Mystic Capital Advisors Group LLC are profiled. The suit alleges conspiracy, fraud, misrepresentation and breach of contract relating to the same of Team Insurance Group.

29557 ■ "Two Identity-Theft Bills Filed In Oklahoma House of Representatives" in *Journal Record* **(February 5, 2004)**
Pub: Dolan Media Company
Description: Two bills filed in the Oklahoma House of Representatives would tighten state laws against identity theft.

29558 ■ Ultimate Guide to Project Management
Pub: Entrepreneurial Press
Ed: Sid Kemp. Released: October 2005. Price: $29.95 (US), $39.95 (Canadian). Description: Project management strategies including writing a business plan and developing a good advertising campaign.

29559 ■ Ultimate Small Business Advisor
Pub: Entrepreneur Press
Ed: Andi Axman. Released: May 2007. Price: $30.95. Description: Tip for starting and running a small business, including new tax rulings and laws affecting small business, are shared.

29560 ■ Ultimate Startup Directory: Expert Advice and 1,500 Great Startup Ideas
Pub: Entrepreneur Press
Ed: James Stephenson. Released: February 2007. Price: $30.95 (CND). Description: Startup opportunities in over 30 industries are given, along with information on investment, earning potential, skills, legal requirements and more.

29561 ■ "Under Pressure: If an Employee Feels Forced to Quit, It Could Be Trouble" in Entrepreneur
Pub: Entrepreneur Media Inc.
Ed: Jane Easter Bahls. Description: Constructive discharge is the legal concept that means conditions at work had become so intolerable that any reasonable employee would have quit. An employee can sue under these conditions and an employer can be held liable.

29562 ■ Understanding Small Business
Pub: Tate Publishing and Enterprises, LLC
Ed: Edward McMahon. Released: May 2006. Price: $20.95. Description: Three step process to help an entrepreneur build a basic business plan and an effective cash flow statement to minimize risk.

29563 ■ "U.S. District Court of Appeals Sides with Baby Bells Over 1996 Telecommunications Act" in Long Island Business News (March 12, 2004)
Pub: Dolan Media Newswires
Ed: Claude Solnik. Description: Small local telecommunications carriers worry about the new court ruling that they feel will undo the Telecommunications Act of 1996. The small firms worry the new ruling will take away ability to lease infrastructure at a wholesale rate from Baby Bells, thus inhibiting them from remaining competitive in the industry.

29564 ■ "U.S. District Court Issues Injunction to Prevent Hi-Tech Pharmacal..." in Long Island Business News (March 5, 2004)
Pub: Dolan Media Newswires
Description: A preliminary injunction has been issued against Hi-Tech Pharmacal Company Inc. for selling Tannate 12d S, a generic form of MedPoint's Tussi-12d S cough medication. MedPoint claims Hi-Tech is violating its patent on the cough drug.

29565 ■ "UnitedAuto Dealerships Sued" in Crain's Detroit Business (Vol. 19, No. 45, November 10, 2003, pp. 4)
Pub: Crain Communications Inc., Detroit
Ed: Brent Snavely. Description: UnitedAuto Groups Inc. was named in a lawsuit alleging failure to pay sales employees properly, by bilking sales staff of commission compensation due them.

29566 ■ "Up in Arms: Prepare for Litigation With These Weapons of Mass Discussion" in Entrepreneur (Vol. 33, January 2005, No. 1, pp. 70)
Pub: Entrepreneur Media Inc.
Ed: Marc Diener. Description: Business negotiation skills are discussed for planning possible litigation.

29567 ■ The Upstart Small Business Legal Guide: How to Understand Legal Issues & Protect Your Small Business Complete with Forms
Pub: Upstart Publishing Co., Inc.

Ed: Robert Firedman. Released: 2nd ed. 1998. Price: $29.95.

29568 ■ "Value system" in Entrepreneur (Vol. 30, No. 3, March)
Pub: Entrepreneur Media Inc.
Ed: Steven C. Bahls, Jane Easter Bahls. Description: Under Title VII of the Civil Rights Act of 1964, employers must make reasonable accommodations for employees' religious practices, unless doing so would impose an undue hardship on the company.

29569 ■ "Walk the Line" in Entrepreneur.com (Vol. 34, February 2006, No. 2, pp. 80)
Pub: Entrepreneur Media Inc.
Ed: Chris Penttila. Description: The Supreme Court ruled in November 2005 that workers must be paid for time spent between locker rooms and workstations as well as time spent waiting in line to turn in or receive work equipment.

29570 ■ "Wall Street Rogues: Fast Cars, Women, and Cash. These Financial Whizzes Had It All" in Black Enterprise (Vol. 35, August 2004, No. 1)
Pub: Earl G. Graves Publishing Co. Inc.
Ed: Alan Hughes. Description: Alan Brian Bond, one time Wall Street all-star, conspired with a broker to inflate client fees from 1993 to 1998. Bonds clients, mostly African Americans, lost nearly $57 million.

29571 ■ "Washington gridlock worries small business groups" in Wall Street Journal (November 1, 2000, pp. A1)
Pub: Dow Jones & Co., Inc.
Ed: Tom Herman. Description: Groups want repeal of 1999 law that says businesses that sell operations at a profit must pay a lump-sum capital gains tax.

29572 ■ "Watch That Bird's Rear" in The Economist (Vol. 376, July 16-22, 2005, No. 8435, pp. 30)
Pub: The Economist Newspaper Ltd.
Description: Oklahoma, home to some of the country's largest poultry businesses, has filed a lawsuit against 14 Arkansas poultry producers, claiming violations of federal and state environmental nuisance laws.

29573 ■ "A Web Wake-Up; Posting of OU Student's Paper Turns Into Lesson That Helps Define Defamation in a New Medium" in Crain's Detroit Business
Pub: Crain Communications Inc. - Detroit
Ed: Andrew Dietderich. Description: Posting of student papers on the Internet can be a wake-up call for small businesses. An Oakland University professor posted an essay written by a student that contained statements about the student's former employer, who sued the school, student and professor when it discovered the paper through an Internet search.

29574 ■ "What arbitration agreement? Compelling non-signatories to arbitrate" in Dispute Resolution Journal (Vol. 56, May-July 2001, pp. 40)
Pub: American Arbitration Association
Ed: Charles Lee Eisen. Description: The legal principles and theory which can bind non-signatory parties to arbitration agreements are discussed.

29575 ■ "What a Governance Referee Thinks" in Journal of Accountancy (Vol. 199, February 2005, No. 2, pp. 43)
Pub: American Institute of Certified Public Accountants
Ed: Michael Hayes. Description: Rules for obtaining a certified public accounting firm are changing as the Sarbanes-Oxley Act is implemented. Experts believe the Sarbanes-Oxley Act is requiring accounting firms to do the things they should have been doing all along.

29576 ■ "What's Cookin'?" in Entrepreneur (Vol. 32, December 2004, No. 12, pp. 30)
Pub: Entrepreneur Media Inc.
Ed: Stephen Barlas. Description: The Federal Trade Commission's amendments to its Franchise Rule may ban post-sale encroachment on franchisees, market territory and restrictions on suppliers.

29577 ■ "What's Next: Data Disasters" in Inc. (November 1, 2003)
Pub: Gruner & Jahr USA Publishing
Ed: Robert X. Cringely. Description: Litigation may require a small business to produce every email employees have written.

29578 ■ "What's Next: They've Got Your Number" in Inc. (August 1, 2003)
Pub: Gruner & Jahr USA Publishing
Ed: Robert X. Cringely. Description: Identity theft using a combination of computer technology and government information is a major crime just waiting to happen.

29579 ■ "When Leadership Means Letting Go" in Law Firm Inc. (October 2004)
Pub: American Lawyer Media LP
Description: In law firms, it is important for the chief marketing officer to report to the firm's top leader in order for the position to be taken seriously. The chief marketing leader's expertise to handle marketing and sales efforts is critical.

29580 ■ "When You Speak, Lawmakers Listen" in My Business (June/July 2004, pp. 41)
Pub: My Business Magazine
Description: Lawmakers are interested in small business. The National Federation of Independent Business (NFIB) advocates for small business through its Member Ballot, the largest opinion-gathering effort of its type. Results are given to lawmakers. Currently issues revolved around employer retirement savings accounts, postal rates, debit cards, project labor agreements, and OSHA regulations.

29581 ■ "Which School is Right?" in Hispanic Business (September 2003, pp. 46)
Pub: Hispanic Business
Ed: Joel Russell. Description: For Hispanic students, selecting an MBA or a law school program involves academic, social, personal, and financial considerations.

29582 ■ "Whose drug is it, anyway?" in Washington Business Journal (Vol. 21, No. 44, Feb. 28, 2003, pp. 2,6)
Pub: Washington Business Journal
Ed: Jennifer Taylor. Description: Alleged legal loopholes abound keeping generic drug companies from getting their products to market faster. President Bush has proposed new rules that might fix one of those loopholes. Large companies with costly employee benefit plans are getting involved also. Drug companies with blockbuster drugs try to keep patents in effect as long as possible, claiming that research and development costs are astronomical.

29583 ■ "Why Businesses Should Have Judge Dread" in Inc. (Volume 27, June 2005, No. 6, pp. 24)
Pub: Inc. Magazine
Ed: Allen P. Roberts Jr. Description: Because of increasing business-related cases moving from state to federal district courts on issues of interstate commerce, as well as employment law and intellectual property disputes, it is important for federal judge nominees to be scrutinized on business law.

29584 ■ "Why I Love My Lawyer" in My Business (October/November 2003, pp. 55)
Pub: My Business Magazine
Ed: Harvey King. Description: The importance for small businesses to rely on good legal advise is stressed.

29585 ■ "With Revenue Flattening, David Galbenski Needed a Bold New Plan" in Inc. (Volume 28, January 2006, No. 1, pp. 44-46)
Pub: Inc. Magazine
Ed: Darren Dahl. Description: David Galbenski, owner of a temporary, contract legal firm discusses whether outsourcing to India was a smart move for his firm located in Royal Oak, Michigan.

29586 ■ "Witness protection" in
Entrepreneur **(Vol. 31, No. 4, April 2003, pp. 78)**
Pub: Entrepreneur Media Inc.
Ed: Steven C. Bahls, Jane Easter Bahls. **Description:** Profile of the Sarbanes-Oxley Act of 2002, which protects whistle-blowers reporting corporate wrong doing is presented, along with its impact on business.

29587 ■ "Word games" in *Entrepreneur* **(Vol. 31, No. 6, June 2003, pp. 76)**
Pub: Entrepreneur Media Inc.
Ed: Steven C. Bahls, Jane Easter Bahls. **Description:** The importance of making sure that contracts are clear and unambiguous is stressed. Franchise owners of Carvel Ice Cream in East Coast states discovered the franchisor Carvel Corporation could sell its ice cream in supermarkets for less money because of ambiguous language in their contracts.

29588 ■ *Working for Yourself: Law and Taxes for Independent Contractors, Freelancers and Consultants*
Pub: NOLO
Ed: Stephen Fishman. **Released:** October 2004. **Price:** $39.99. **Description:** Laws and tax rules governing independent contractors, freelancers and consultants.

29589 ■ "Worried on Woodward; Police Caucus on Robbers of Oakland Businesses" in *Crain's Detroit Business* **(Vol. 21, January 31, 2005, No. 5)**
Pub: Crain Communications Inc. - Detroit
Ed: Sheena Harrison, Anjali Fluker. **Description:** Royal Oak, Birmingham and Farmington Hills, Michigan police departments are joining forces in an attempt to share strategies and information to find suspects who are committing armed robbery against area businesses. One robbery resulted in the shooting of two employees.

29590 ■ "You Know My Name (Don't Call My Number)" in *Inc.* **(July 1, 2003)**
Pub: Gruner & Jahr USA Publishing
Description: The legal status of the no-call list for telemarketers is presented.

29591 ■ *Your Lawyer: An Owner's Manual*
Pub: Agate Publishing, Incorporated
Ed: Henry C. Krasnow. **Released:** November 2005. **Price:** $14.00. **Description:** Small business guide that assists owners and managers to find, work with, and inspire attorneys. Includes an overview of the legal processes involved in running a small company.

29592 ■ "You're Deposing Me?" in *Hispanic Business* **(March 2003, p. 57)**
Pub: Hispanic Business
Ed: Francisco Ramos, Jr. **Description:** Advice is offered to employees when faced with a legal deposition while working for a company that is being sued. Five steps to follow are presented, including contacting a lawyer, reviewing relevant documents, allowing time for preparation, going through a practice run, and finding out why you were deposed by the other side.

TRADE PERIODICALS

29593 ■ *Association Law and Policy*
Pub: American Society of Association Executives
Price: Included in membership. **Description:** Internet newsletter providing information on antitrust, tax, employment, and other legal issue affecting associations and association executives.

29594 ■ *Bank & Corporate Governance Law Reporter*
Pub: Bank & Corporate Governance Law Reporter
Released: Monthly. **Price:** $2,525. **Description:** Professional journal covering corporate governance and securities law. Available in print format or via e-mail.

29595 ■ *The Business Torts Reporter*
Pub: Aspen Law & Business

Ed: Richard E. Kaye, Editor. **Released:** Monthly. **Price:** $410. **Description:** Journal covering business tort law for legal professionals.

29596 ■ *California Business Law Practitioner*
Pub: Continuing Education of the Bar
Ed: Marie Editor. **Released:** Quarterly. **Price:** $219, individuals. **Description:** Features articles focusing on how-to aspects of specific business transactions, with detailed forms and checklists. Also contains a reader's forum.

29597 ■ *California Labor and Employment ALERT Newsletter*
Pub: Castle Publications Ltd.
Contact: Richard Simmons, President
Released: Bimonthly. **Price:** $75; $85 includes 3-ring binder. **Description:** Reports on current developments in California and federal laws concerning personnel and employment issues. Recurring features include notices of publications available.

29598 ■ *Employment Law Strategist*
Pub: Law Journal Newsletter
Contact: Stephen L. Sheinfeld, Editor-in-Chief
Released: Monthly. **Price:** $279, individuals for print version per year; $299, individuals for electronic version per year; $349, individuals for print and electronic version per year. **Description:** Covers employment law topics, including immigration laws, repetitive stress claims, workplace violence, liability of actions of intoxicated employees, record keeping, liability for fetal injury, independent contractor, and employee issues.

29599 ■ *Insights*
Pub: Aspen Law & Business
Contact: Amy L. Goodman, Principle Author
Released: Monthly. **Price:** $515. **Description:** Journal covering legal developments in corporate and securities law on the state, national and worldwide levels.

29600 ■ *International Journal of Franchising and Distribution Law*
Pub: Kluwer Academic/Plenum Publishing Corp.
Ed: Martin Mendelsohn, Editor. **Released:** Quarterly. **Description:** Journal covering franchise law worldwide.

29601 ■ *Laborwatch*
Pub: Berens & Tate, P.C.
Ed: Mark McQueen, Editor. **Released:** Monthly. **Price:** $167; $277, two years. **Description:** Monthly report on the developments in labor relations, employment litigation, and human resource management.

29602 ■ *Legislative Watch*
Pub: American Tort Reform Association
Ed: Lissa Astilla, Editor, lastilla@atra.org. **Released:** Weekly. **Price:** Included in membership. **Description:** Membership newsletter of the American Tort Reform Association.

29603 ■ *RICO Law Reporter*
Pub: RICO Law Reporter
Released: Monthly. **Description:** Professional journal covering securities law. Available in print format or via e-mail.

29604 ■ *You & the Law*
Pub: National Institute of Business Management
Ed: Amy Beth Miller, Editor. **Released:** 12/year. **Price:** $192. **Description:** Covers the employment law area. Provides information for managers and business owners interested in the relationship between the law and their business.

VIDEOCASSETTES/ AUDIOCASSETTES

29605 ■ *Annual Spring Pension Law and Practice Update*
American Law Institute
American Bar Association Committee on Continuing Education
4025 Chestnut St.
Philadelphia, PA 19104

Ph:(215)243-1600
Free: 800-CLE-NEWS
Fax: (215)243-1664
Co. E-mail: PHunt@ali.org
URL: http://www.ali.org
Released: 1991. **Price:** $210. **Description:** Series introducing pension and profit-sharing plan drafters and designers to I.R.C. Section 401(a)(4) and the determination letter process, executive compensation, fiduciary responsibility and more. Complete with study materials. **Availability:** VHS.

29606 ■ *Business Litigation*
National Institute for Trial Advocacy (NITA)
53550 Generations Drive
PO Box 6500
South Bend, IN 46635-1570
Ph:(574)271-8370
Free: 800-225-6482
Fax: (574)271-8375
Co. E-mail: Gagnon.4@nd.edu
URL: http://www.nita.org/
Released: 1987. **Price:** $1995.00. **Description:** Provides a practical primer to business litigation with an emphasis on the prevention of disputes, the effect they have on the client's business, and alternatives to going to court. Since many disputes do end up in civil court, the series covers pretrial and trial strategies, the examining of friendly and hostile witnesses, and closing statements. **Availability:** VHS; 3/4U.

CONSULTANTS

29607 ■ *Law Offices of David Bow Woo*
700 S Flower St., Ste. 1100
Los Angeles, CA 90017-4113
Ph:(213)892-6309
Fax: (213)892-2215
Scope: Experienced attorney who specializes in business litigation and transactions. Emphasis is on financial motivation and import and export trade financing.

29608 ■ Comprehensive Professional Management Inc.
222 E Dundee Rd.
Wheeling, IL 60090-3009
Ph:(847)520-0101
Fax: (847)520-0372
Co. E-mail: bob@cpmincfs.com

E-mail: bob@cpmincfs.com
Scope: Services include accounting, financial planning, litigation support, pension profit sharing administration, practice surveys, professional corporation issues, retirement and estate planning, and tax advice.

29609 ■ donphin.com Inc.
5713 Corporate Way, Ste. 101
West Palm Beach, FL 33407
Ph:(561)688-1000
Free: 800-234-3304
Fax: (561)688-1142
Co. E-mail: inquiry@donphin.com
URL: http://www.donphin.com

E-mail: inquiry@donphin.com
Scope: Offers a comprehensive approach to understanding and applying a broad range of business principles: legal compliance issues, management concerns, health and safety, customer service, marketing, information management. Industries served: all developing small businesses. **Publications:** "Doing Business Right!". **Seminars:** Doing Business Right!; HR That Works!.

29610 ■ Equity Partners Of America Ltd.
1450 W Long Lake Rd., Ste. 340
Troy, MI 48098
Ph:(248)952-0300
Fax: (248)952-0314
Co. E-mail: equitypartners@email.msn.com

E-mail: equitypartners@email.msn.com
Scope: Private investment bank specializes in debt and equity capital procurement; buying and selling

businesses; shareholder value enhancement strategies; and litigation and alternative dispute resolution assistance; including expert witness assistance. Serves manufacturing, distribution and service industries. **Seminars:** Preparation of a business plan; Use of financial statements in damage claims; Determining the value of a business; When to sell a family business.

29611 ■ Invent Resources Inc.
PO Box 548
Lexington, MA 02420-0005
Ph:(781)862-0200
Fax: (781)721-2300
Co. E-mail: rsilver@world.std.com
URL: http://www.inventresources.com

E-mail: rsilver@world.std.com
Scope: An organization comprised of four scientists and engineers that have helped to develop more than 200 products for their clients. After accepting a request for an invention, Invent Resources offers a license to the intellectual property and negotiates a royalty arrangement. Provides support in developing and prototyping the product.

FRANCHISES AND BUSINESS OPPORTUNITIES

29612 ■ AAA Franchise Legal Help Hotline
Franchise Foundations
4157 23rd St.
San Francisco, CA 94114
Free: 800-942-4402
Founded: 1980. **Description:** Advice on franchise legal issues.

29613 ■ Baum Fallenbaum, Attorneys
5415 Queen Mary Rd., Ste. 2
Montreal, QC, Canada H3X 1V1
Ph:(514)486-2003
Free: 888-LAW-5850
Description: Counseling franchise business regulations.

29614 ■ Bellavia & Kassel, PC
Attorneys at Law
200 Old Country Rd.
Mineola, NY 11501
Ph:(516)873-1900
Fax: (516)873-9032
Description: Full service franchise attorneys.

29615 ■ Bundy & Morrill
12351 Lake City Way NE, Ste. 202
Seattle, WA 98125-5437
Ph:(206)367-4640
Fax: (206)367-5507
Founded: 1981. **Description:** Franchise lawyers.

29616 ■ Carter & Tani
402 E Roosevelt Rd., Ste. 206
Wheaton, IL 60187
Ph:(630)668-2135
Founded: 1977. **Description:** Assist start-up franchisees and franchisors.

29617 ■ Chandler, Franklin & O'Bryan
2564 Ivy Rd.
Charlottesville, VA 22903
Ph:(804)971-7273
Free: 800-572-2099
Founded: 1982. **Description:** Franchise litigation services.

29618 ■ Decker Simone
Symphony Towers
750 B St., Ste. 2560
San Diego, CA 92101
Ph:(619)233-0900
Fax: (619)233-0939
Description: Franchise attorney.

29619 ■ Dickinson, Wheelock & FFrench, P.C.
952 Echo Ln., Ste. 420
Houston, TX 77024
Free: 800-727-3458
Fax: (713)722-9688
Description: Franchise and business attorneys.

29620 ■ Franchise Esq
PO Box 450
Lincolnshire, IL 60069
Ph:(847)634-4877
Fax: (847)634-4877
Description: Attorney / Consultant/ Real Estate Broker.

29621 ■ Franchise Law Team
30021 Tomas, Ste. 260
Rancho Santa Margarita, CA 92688
Ph:(949)459-7474
Free: 888-276-2976
Fax: (949)459-7772
Founded: 1985. **Description:** Registration, advice, and dispute resolution.

29622 ■ Friedman, Rosenwasser & Goldbaum, P.A.
5355 Town Center Rd., Ste. 801
The Plaza
Boca Raton, FL 33486
Ph:(561)395-5511
Fax: (561)395-2648
Founded: 1986. **Description:** International and domestic franchise services.

29623 ■ Gowling Lafleur Henderson LLP
1055 Dunsmuir St., Ste. 2300
PO Box 49122
Vancouver, BC, Canada V7X 1J1
Ph:(604)683-6498
Fax: (604)683-3558
Founded: 1877. **Description:** Full service law firm for franchisors.

29624 ■ Greenspan & Greenspan
150 Grand St., No. 605
White Plains, NY 10601-4821
Ph:(914)946-2500
Free: 800-553-6009
Founded: 1959. **Description:** Full service law firm.

29625 ■ Gregory J. Ellis & Associates, Ltd.
999 Plz. Dr., Ste.777
Schaumburg, IL 60173
Ph:(847)413-0999
Fax: (847)413-0959
Founded: 1980. **Description:** Provides full range of legal services.

29626 ■ Harold L. Kestenbaum, Esq.
1320 Reckson P12
Uniondale, NY 11556
Ph:(516)745-0099
Fax: (516)745-0293
Founded: 1977. **Description:** Franchise attorney and consultant.

29627 ■ iFranchise Group
905 W 175th St., Ste. 2-N
Homewood, IL 60430
Ph:(708)957-2300
Fax: (708)957-2395
Co. E-mail: info@ifranchise.net
URL: http://www.ifranchise.com
Description: Offers services on strategic planning, franchise law, operations documentation, marketing and sales, and executive recruiting for franchisors.

29628 ■ James B. Sheets, Attorney at Law
One Summit Ave., Ste. 304
Fort Worth, TX 76102
Ph:(817)335-6040
Fax: (817)335-2503
Description: Legal services.

29629 ■ John R. Mohr
7545 Winding Wy.
Tipp City, OH 45371-9240

Ph:(937)824-2808
Description: Franchise attorney.

29630 ■ Joseph J. Walczak, P.C.
14045 S 88th Ave.
Orland Park, IL 60462
Ph:(708)349-6908
Fax: (708)349-2438
Founded: 1988. **Description:** Franchise and trademark law.

29631 ■ Kanouse & Walker, P.A.
2255 Glades Rd.
Boca Raton, FL 33431
Ph:(561)451-8090
Fax: (561)451-8089
Founded: 1974. **Description:** Represents franchisees in buying a franchise.

29632 ■ Kidzone
1 Gunton Pl.
Staten Island, NY 10309
Ph:(718)948-6710
No. of Company-Owned Units: 4. **Founded:** 1998. **Franchised:** 2004. **Description:** Private birthday party and play place. **Equity Capital Needed:** $96,000-$139,000. **Franchise Fee:** $30,000. **Financial Assistance:** No. **Training:** Yes.

29633 ■ Law Office of James F. McLaughlin
4 Victory St.
Shelton, CT 06484
Ph:(203)924-9669
Fax: (203)924-9669
Founded: 1993. **Description:** Legal services, franchising operations.

29634 ■ Law Office of Suzanne C. Cummings & Associates, P.C.
23 Walkers Brook Dr.
Reading, MA 01867
Ph:(781)481-9090
Free: 800-982-9636
Fax: (781)481-9191
Description: Franchise law and business advisors.

29635 ■ Lawrence Krieger, Attorney at Law
The Wilder Bldg.
8 Exchange Blvd., Ste. 400
Rochester, NY 14614
Ph:(585)325-2640
Free: 800-719-3260
Fax: (585)325-1946
Founded: 1991. **Description:** Western New York franchisee law practice.

29636 ■ Lopatka Franchise Services
1824 W Stewart Ave.
Park Ridge, IL 60068
Ph:(847)692-9585
Fax: (847)692-6809
Description: Franchisee legal and real estate services.

29637 ■ Marks & Associates, Attorneys-at-Law
63 Riverside Ave.
Red Bank, NJ 07701
Ph:(732)747-7100
Fax: (732)219-0625
Founded: 1971. **Description:** Franchisee and franchisor representation.

29638 ■ Mcdermott, Will & Emery
600 13th St., NW
Washington, DC 20005
Ph:(202)756-8610
Fax: (202)756-8087
Description: The franchise consists mainly of attorneys.

29639 ■ Miller Thomson LLP
Barristers & Solicitors
20 Queen St. W, Ste. 2500
Toronto, ON, Canada M5H 3S1
Ph:(416)595-2639
Fax: (416)595-8695

Founded: 1957. **Description:** Full service law firm with franchise group.

29640 ■ Mitchell J. Kassoff, Esq. (Attorney)
2 Foster Ct.
South Orange, NJ 07079-1002
Ph:(973)762-1776
Founded: 1979. **Description:** Nationwide legal representation.

29641 ■ Nord & Demand
228 Main St.
Toms River, NJ 08753
Ph:(732)240-9960
Founded: 1995. **Description:** Franchise attorney.

29642 ■ Paul Jones, Barrister, Solicitor, & Trademark Agent
One First Canadian Pl., Ste. 840
PO Box 489
Toronto, ON, Canada M5X 1E5
Ph:(416)703-5716
Fax: (416)703-6180
Founded: 2004. **Description:** Law firm experienced in franchising & distribution.

29643 ■ Peter C. Lagarias, Esq.
The Legal Solutions Group, L.L.P.
1629 Fifth Ave.
San Rafael, CA 94901-1828
Ph:(415)460-0100
Fax: (415)460-1099
Description: Franchise litigation and service.

29644 ■ Zarco Einhorn & Salkowski, P.A.
International Pl.
100 SE 2nd St., 27th Fl.
Miami, FL 33131
Ph:(305)374-5418
Fax: (305)374-5428
Founded: 1992. **Description:** Franchise and commercial litigation.

COMPUTERIZED DATABASES

29645 ■ ABA/BNA Lawyers' Manual on Professional Conduct
The Bureau of National Affairs Inc.
1231 25th St. NW
Washington, DC 20037
Ph:(202)452-4200
Free: 800-372-1033
Fax: (202)452-4226
Co. E-mail: customercare@bna.com
URL: http://www.bna.com
Description: Contains news and advice on attorney conduct. Contains full text of the ABA Model Rules of Professional Conduct and Responsibility, ABA ethics opinions, state ethics rule comparisons with ABA models, and other relevant model standards. Includes issues relating to conflicts of interest, client confidences, advertising, fees, discipline, malpractice and related topics. Also includes biweekly reports on recent court decisions, ethics opinions, disciplinary actions and news. **Availability:** Online: The Bureau of National Affairs Inc., Thomson West. **Type:** Full text.

29646 ■ American Journey: The Constitution and Supreme Court
Thomson Gale
27500 Drake Rd.
Farmington Hills, MI 48331-3535
Ph:(248)699-4253
Free: 800-877-GALE
Fax: (248)699-8069
Co. E-mail: gale.galeord@thomson.com
URL: http://www.gale.com
Description: Contains Supreme Court decisions that interpreted it and the enduring issues that contribute to the public debate in America. Major themes include: the Constitutional Convention and James Madison's detailed debate notes, the role of the Supreme Court,

including complete decisions and dissenting opinions on a wide range of constitutional questions, state's rights, original intent, separation of powers, and republican government and a hyperlinked version of the Constitution. **Availability:** Online: Thomson Gale; CD-ROM: Thomson Gale. **Type:** Full text; Audio; Image.

29647 ■ Atlantic Provinces Reports
Maritime Law Book Ltd.
PO Box 302
Fredericton, NB, Canada E3B 4Y9
Ph:(506)453-9921
Free: 800-561-0220
Fax: (506)453-9525
Co. E-mail: help@mlb.nb.ca
URL: http://www.mlb.nb.ca
Description: Contains headnotes of selected judicial decisions of the courts of New Brunswick, Nova Scotia, Newfoundland, and Prince Edward Island. Also includes decisions of the Supreme Court of Canada on appeals from these provincial courts. Corresponds to *New Brunswick Reports* (2d Series), *Nova Scotia Reports* (2d Series), and *Newfoundland and Prince Edward Island Reports*. **Availability:** Online: LexisNexis Quicklaw; CD-ROM: Maritime Law Book Ltd.; Diskette: Maritime Law Book Ltd. **Type:** Bibliographic.

29648 ■ Bankruptcy Law Reporter
The Bureau of National Affairs Inc.
1231 25th St. NW
Washington, DC 20037
Ph:(202)452-4200
Free: 800-372-1033
Fax: (202)452-4226
Co. E-mail: customercare@bna.com
URL: http://www.bna.com
Description: Contains coverage of every aspect of bankruptcy law. Subjects encompass bankruptcy jury trials, bankruptcy fraud and abuse, bad faith filings, exemptions, executory contracts, home mortgage cramdowns, judicial liens, lender liability, lien stripping, trustees' duties, and related topics. **Availability:** Online: The Bureau of National Affairs Inc., Thomson West. **Type:** Full text.

29649 ■ The Bar Register of Preeminent Lawyers
Martindale-Hubbell
Reed Reference Publishing Group
121 Chanlon Rd.
New Providence, NJ 07974
Ph:(908)464-6800
Free: 800-526-4902
Fax: (908)771-8704
Co. E-mail: info@martindale.com
URL: http://www.martindale.com
Description: Contains information on more than 10,000 law practices rated in the *Martindale-Hubbell Law Directory*. Includes names of members of the firm; names of associates and "of counsel"; full contact information, including address, telephone numbers and email; representative clients; and additional branch office locations. Listings are arranged by state and city under 66 areas of practice—from administrative law and general practice to transportation and tax law. Also contains an index by firm name. **Availability:** Online: LexisNexis. **Type:** Directory.

29650 ■ Canadian Law List
Canada Law Book Inc.
240 Edward St.
Aurora, ON, Canada L4G 3S9
Ph:(905)841-6472
Free: 800-263-3269
Fax: (905)841-5085
Co. E-mail: sales@canadalawbook.ca
URL: http://www.canadalawbook.ca
Description: Contains a listing of 55,000 lawyers and 18,000 legal firms, judges and government offices in Canada. Includes law firm profiles, world-wide affiliations, personal biographical information and listings of government departments, plus related legal services. Searchable by title, year called to the bar, law firm, telephone and fax numbers, and email addresses. **Availability:** CD-ROM: Canada Law Book Inc. **Type:** Directory.

29651 ■ CCH PROTOS
CCH Inc.
2700 Lake Cook Rd.
Riverwoods, IL 60015
Ph:(847)267-7000
Free: 800-525-3335
Fax: (773)866-3095
URL: http://www.cch.com
Description: Contains information on taxes in Canada. Includes interpretation bulletins, circulars, rulings, Department of Finance releases, Revenue Canada releases, court cases, Internal Revenue Canada documents, draft legislation and explanatory notes, CCH Tax newsletters, and more. **Type:** Bulletin board.

29652 ■ Class Action Litigation Report
The Bureau of National Affairs Inc.
1231 25th St. NW
Washington, DC 20037
Ph:(202)452-4200
Free: 800-372-1033
Fax: (202)452-4226
Co. E-mail: customercare@bna.com
URL: http://www.bna.com
Description: Contains information on all aspects of class action litigation. Subjects include class certification, class actions filed, antitrust, consumer issues, rule reform, verdicts and settlements, attorney fees, employment and discrimination, health care, mass torts, securities, and products issues. Includes highlights of the top reports, brief descriptions of other prominent developments, summaries of case filings, new reports, conference reports, analysis and perspective, and practice tips. Arranged by topical list, litigation subjects, and alphabetical table of cases. **Availability:** Online: The Bureau of National Affairs Inc., Thomson West. **Type:** Full text.

29653 ■ Computer Technology Law Report
The Bureau of National Affairs Inc.
1231 25th St. NW
Washington, DC 20037
Ph:(202)452-4200
Free: 800-372-1033
Fax: (202)452-4226
Co. E-mail: customercare@bna.com
URL: http://www.bna.com
Description: Contains news and developments in the field of computer technology law. Subjects include antitrust issues; computer technology exports; contract liability; design patents; digital assets; network security; "open source" software licensing and development; patent protection; reverse engineering; tort liability; trademark protection; the Uniform Computer Transaction Act; liability for defective computer hardware and software products; insurance coverage for computer-related liabilities; patent protection for software and computer-related products and services; software licensing and piracy; and software copyright protection. Includes summaries of the most important developments in the field; brief descriptions of other important issues; court proceedings of related cases and decision; news of non-judicial developments; lists of conferences, seminars and related events; and a list of related websites. Enables users to access by alphabetical list of topics and by issue date. **Availability:** Online: The Bureau of National Affairs Inc., Thomson West. **Type:** Full text.

29654 ■ Corporate Law Daily
The Bureau of National Affairs Inc.
1231 25th St. NW
Washington, DC 20037
Ph:(202)452-4200
Free: 800-372-1033
Fax: (202)452-4226
Co. E-mail: customercare@bna.com
URL: http://www.bna.com
Description: Contains the full spectrum of judicial, legislative, regulatory, and tax issues that affect corporate practice. Subjects include antitrust, corporate criminal liability, international trade, litigation, occupational safety and health, product liability, professional responsibility, securities, corporate law, corporate governance, employment discrimination, environmental enforcement, and intellectual property. **Availability:** Online: The Bureau of National Affairs Inc., Thomson West. **Type:** Full text.

29655 ■ *Criminal Law Reporter*
The Bureau of National Affairs Inc.
1231 25th St. NW
Washington, DC 20037
Ph:(202)452-4200
Free: 800-372-1033
Fax: (202)452-4226
Co. E-mail: customercare@bna.com
URL: http://www.bna.com
Description: Contains reports on news and court proceedings in the field of criminal law. Subjects include appeals, arrest, capital punishment, civil liability, civil rights, confrontation and cross-examination, defenses, double jeopardy, drugs, driving, electronic surveillance and wiretapping, police misconduct, prisons and jails, racketeering, representation by counsel, search and seizure, self-incrimination, sentencing, sex offenses, state constitutional law, statutory interpretation, witnesses, entrapment, evidence, firearms, forfeiture, fraud, grand juries, guilty pleas, habeas corpus, immunity, interrogation and confessions, jury trial, money laundering, and obscenity. Sections include Highlights, In This Issue, Table of Cases, Court Decision, In Brief, News, Conference Reports, Special Reports, Circuit Split Roundup, Supreme Court Proceedings, and Index and Table of Cases. **Availability:** Online: The Bureau of National Affairs Inc., Thomson West. **Type:** Full text.

29656 ■ *DART: British Columbia Labour Decisions*
Canada Law Book Inc.
240 Edward St.
Aurora, ON, Canada L4G 3S9
Ph:(905)841-6472
Free: 800-263-3269
Fax: (905)841-5085
Co. E-mail: sales@canadalawbook.ca
URL: http://www.canadalawbook.ca
Description: Covers British Columbia Decisions and Labour Arbitration since 1982, British Columbia Labour Relations Board/Industrial Relations Council Decisions since 1979, Federal Labour Arbitration Decisions 1997/98, and Canadian Labour Arbitration Summaries from 1999 to the present. Updates are available online. **Availability:** CD-ROM: Canada Law Book Inc. **Type:** Full text.

29657 ■ *DART: British Columbia Statute Service*
Canada Law Book Inc.
240 Edward St.
Aurora, ON, Canada L4G 3S9
Ph:(905)841-6472
Free: 800-263-3269
Fax: (905)841-5085
Co. E-mail: sales@canadalawbook.ca
URL: http://www.canadalawbook.ca
Description: Contains all British Columbia Statutes from the 1996 consolidation, including all new Acts, the British Columbia Statute Citator, and the Annotations of British Columbia and Supreme Court of Canada Decisions reported in the *British Columbia Decisions Statute Citator*. Includes complete amendment history for each statute, including amendments that have received Royal Assent but are not yet in force. **Availability:** Online: Canada Law Book Inc; CD-ROM: Canada Law Book Inc. **Type:** Full text.

29658 ■ *DART: Western Decisions*
Canada Law Book Inc.
240 Edward St.
Aurora, ON, Canada L4G 3S9
Ph:(905)841-6472
Free: 800-263-3269
Fax: (905)841-5085
Co. E-mail: sales@canadalawbook.ca
URL: http://www.canadalawbook.ca
Description: Covers British Columbia decisions, civil and criminal cases since 1979; Manitoba decisions, civil and criminal cases since 1980; Saskatchewan decisions, civil and criminal cases since 1980; and Alberta decisions, civil and criminal cases since 1980. **Availability:** CD-ROM: Canada Law Book Inc. **Type:** Full text.

29659 ■ *EIU ViewsWire*
The Economist Group
26 Red Lion Sq.
London WC1R 4HQ, United Kingdom
Ph:44 20 75768181
Fax: 44 20 75768476
Co. E-mail: london@eiu.com
URL: http://www.eiu.com
Description: Provides up to 150 articles daily covering practical business intelligence, including key events, market issues, impending crises, and the business and regulatory environment in emerging and International markets. Covers information from more than 195 countries. Includes: Briefings: critical political, economic, and business changes around the world organized by the topics of company, economy, finance, politics, regulations, and industry. Forecasts:; Country updates-continuously updated overviews of GDP, inflation, demand, investment, fiscal policy, interest rates, currency, external accounts, and the political scene in more than 190 countries.; Consensus forecasts-monthly currency, interest rate, and equity market short-term outlooks provided by multinational companies and investment banks.; Country risk summary-political and credit risk ratings and analysis for 100 countries.; Five-year forecasts—quarterly growth, inflation, and trade indicators for 60 countries.; Forecast summaries—quarterly key economic indicators and business watchlist. Background: facts and figures on current conditions in more than 190 countries.; Key economic indicators—quarterly statistics on growth, trade, reserves, and currencies.; Basic data and country fact sheet-population data, per capita GDP, political structure, taxes, foreign trade and policy issues.; Trade, tax and forex regulations-Connecticut updated full regulatory profiles on 60 countries. **Availability:** Online: The Economist Group, Thomson Financial, Financial Times, LexisNexis. **Type:** Full text; Numeric.

29660 ■ *Electronic Commerce & Law Report*
The Bureau of National Affairs Inc.
1231 25th St. NW
Washington, DC 20037
Ph:(202)452-4200
Free: 800-372-1033
Fax: (202)452-4226
Co. E-mail: customercare@bna.com
URL: http://www.bna.com
Description: Contains news and developments in the field of electronic commerce law. Topics include consumer protection laws, copyright and trademark issues, cryptography, database protection, defamation, domain name disputes, electronic signatures, free speech/First Amendment issues, information licensing, Internet governance, Internet-related telecommunications regulation, jurisdiction, network security, online contracting, online gambling, online marketing, privacy, and trade regulation. Covers summaries of the most significant developments in e-commerce law; e-commerce news from legislatures, agencies, and industry; and court proceedings. Enables users to search by topic, state, company and medium. **Availability:** Online: The Bureau of National Affairs Inc., Thomson West. **Type:** Full text.

29661 ■ *Family Law Reporter*
The Bureau of National Affairs Inc.
1231 25th St. NW
Washington, DC 20037
Ph:(202)452-4200
Free: 800-372-1033
Fax: (202)452-4226
Co. E-mail: customercare@bna.com
URL: http://www.bna.com
Description: Contains information on family law. Includes new state and federal legislative developments, appellate court family cases, and monitors new trends and issues. Subjects include adoption, alimony, child custody, bankruptcy and marital debts, child abduction, domestic partnership and non-marital relationships, domestic torts, equitable distribution, grandparents' rights, joint tenancy, military benefits, prenuptial agreements, joint tenancy, paternity, visitation rights, child support, domestic torts, IRS rulings, separation agreemtns, surrogate parenthood and assisted conception, taxes and divorce planning, Uni-

form Child Custody Jurisdiction Enforcement Act, Uniform Interstate Family Support Act, visitation, pensions, and property rights. Information is organized by topic or by state. **Availability:** Online: The Bureau of National Affairs Inc., Thomson West. **Type:** Full text.

29662 ■ *Florida Jurisprudence on Westlaw*
Thomson West
610 Opperman Dr.
Eagan, MN 55123
Ph:(651)687-7000
Free: 800-344-5008
Fax: (651)687-5827
Co. E-mail: west.customer.service@thomson.com
URL: http://www.westlaw.com
Description: Contains the complete text of the multi-volume encyclopedia of Florida law, *Florida Jurisprudence, Second Edition*. Includes supplementary materials as part of updated documents. Organized into 220 topics including Table of statutes and Table of Cases. **Availability:** Online: Thomson West; CD-ROM: Thomson West. **Type:** Full text.

29663 ■ *Grey Areas Newsletter*
LexisNexis Quicklaw
2 Gore St.
PO Box 2080
Kingston, ON, Canada K7L 5J8
Ph:(613)549-4611
Free: 800-267-9470
Fax: (613)548-4260
Co. E-mail: sales@quicklaw.com
URL: http://www.quicklaw.com
Description: Provides access to the newsletter by the Toronto law firm of Steinecke, Martinand Maciura. Covers the regulation of professional groups and self-management of specific industries. **Availability:** Online: LexisNexis Quicklaw. **Type:** Full text.

29664 ■ *A Guide to Federal Sector Equal Employment Law and Practice*
Dewey Publications Inc.
2009 N 14th St., Ste. 705
Arlington, VA 22201
Ph:(703)524-1355
Fax: (703)524-1463
Co. E-mail: info@deweypub.com
URL: http://www.deweypub.com
Description: Provides references to thousands of decisions of the EEOC Office of Federal Operations, along with procedural and practice guidance. Integrates the new civil rights laws and updated EEOC Part 1614 regulations for Federal sector employees. Corresponds to the print version of *A Guide to Federal Sector Equal Employment Law and Practice*. **Availability:** CD-ROM: Dewey Publications Inc. **Type:** Full text.

29665 ■ *A Guide to Merit Systems Protection Board Law and Practice*
Dewey Publications Inc.
2009 N 14th St., Ste. 705
Arlington, VA 22201
Ph:(703)524-1355
Fax: (703)524-1463
Co. E-mail: info@deweypub.com
URL: http://www.deweypub.com
Description: Analyzes thousands of published decisions of the MSPB, the courts, and nonprecedential decisions of the U.S. Court of Appeals for the Federal Court. Includes the latest revisions in statutes, regulations, and case decisions. Corresponds to the print version of *A Guide to Merit Systems Protection Board Law and Practice*. **Availability:** CD-ROM: Dewey Publications Inc. **Type:** Full text.

29666 ■ *Industrial Patent Activity in the United States Parts 1 and 2, 1974-1998*
U.S. Patent and Trademark Office (PTO)
Crystal Plaza 3, Rm. 2C02
600 Dulany St.
PO Box 1450
Alexandria, VA 22313-1450
Ph:(703)308-4357
Free: 800-786-9199
Fax: (703)306-2737
Co. E-mail: usptoinfo@uspto.gov

URL: http://www.uspto.gov

Description: Provides information on the activity, ownership, and National origin of utility Patents granted by the U.S. Patent and Trademark Office. Part 1, Time Series Profile by Company and Country of Origin, 1974-1998, covers ownership and national origin of patents granted by U.S. Patent Office between 1974 and 1998. Includes list of more than 8500 corporations, universities, Government agencies,and other businesses that received patents, ranked by degree of activity. Part 2, Alphabetical Listing by Company, 1974-1998, contains alphabetical list of every U.S. and foreign organization that was granted five or more U.S. patents between 1974 and 1998. **Availability:** CD-ROM: U.S. Department of Commerce. **Type:** Patents/Trademarks.

29667 ■ *IRS Publication 334: Tax Guide for Small Business*
U.S. Internal Revenue Service (IRS)
1111 Constitution Ave. NW
Washington, DC 20224
Ph:(202)622-2000
Free: 800-829-3676
Fax: (202)622-6642
URL: http://www.irs.ustreas.gov
Description: Contains the complete text of the 2004 edition of *IRS Publication 334 (Tax Guide for Small Business)*, covering information on U.S. federal tax law and tax return preparation for small businesses. Enables the user to search by topic and to retrieve IRS listings of technical authorities. **Availability:** Online: U.S. Internal Revenue Service (IRS). **Type:** Full text; Directory.

29668 ■ *Judicial News*
LexisNexis Quicklaw
2 Gore St.
PO Box 2080
Kingston, ON, Canada K7L 5J8
Ph:(613)549-4611
Free: 800-267-9470
Fax: (613)548-4260
Co. E-mail: sales@quicklaw.com
URL: http://www.quicklaw.com
Description: Provides press releases from Canada Justice and provincial governments on judicial appointments. Includes Information on courts throughout Canada. **Type:** Full text.

29669 ■ *KeyCite*
Thomson West
610 Opperman Dr.
Eagan, MN 55123
Ph:(651)687-7000
Free: 800-344-5008
Fax: (651)687-5827
Co. E-mail: west.customer.service@thomson.com
URL: http://www.westlaw.com
Description: Contains citing references, including case law and secondary law. Provides direct history, negative indirect history, and related references to the history of a case. **Availability:** Online: Thomson West. **Type:** Bibliographic; Full text.

29670 ■ *Labor and Employment Law Library*
The Bureau of National Affairs Inc.
1231 25th St. NW
Washington, DC 20037
Ph:(202)452-4200
Free: 800-372-1033
Fax: (202)452-4226
Co. E-mail: customercare@bna.com
URL: http://www.bna.com
Description: Contains information on all aspects of labor and employment law. Includes news summaries and analysis of developments; full text of federal and summaries of state statutes, regulations, and policy statements regarding fair employment practices; full text of significant federal and state decisions regarding fair employment practices from 1965 to the present; full text of federal and summaries of state statutes, regulations, and policy statements regarding individual employment rights; full text of significant federal and state decisions regarding individual employment rights from 1986 to the present; full text of

federal and summaries of state statutes, regulations, and policy statements regarding wages and hours; full text of significant federal and state decisions regarding wages and hours from 1959 to the present; full text of federal and summaries of state statutes, regulations, and policy statements regarding Americans with Disabilities Act cases; full text of significant federal and state decisions regarding Americans with Disabilities Act cases from 1974 to the present; full text of labor arbitration and dispute decisions, arbitration rules and procedures; full text of significant federal and state decisions regarding labor-management decisions from 1984 to the present; and state laws. Subjects include discrimination, wages and hours, sexual harassment, absenteeism and turnover, affirmative action/diversity, age bias and compulsory retirement, Americans with disabilities, benefit plans, collective bargaining, contract negotiation and enforcement, drug and alcohol testing, employment-at-will, employment testing, fair employment practices, family and medical leave, fetal protection, handling grievances, hiring, hours of work, independent contractors, individual employment rights, jurisdiction and procedure, labor arbitration, labor-management relations, layoffs and shutdowns, leave rights, overtime pay, pay equity, workers' compensation, work rules and discipline, wages and hours, union organizing, termination, temporary and leased workers, strikes and slowdowns, smoking in the workplace, safety and health, right to information, privacy, political activies, pension law/ERISA, and minimum wage. **Availability:** Online: The Bureau of National Affairs Inc; CD-ROM: The Bureau of National Affairs Inc. **Type:** Full text.

29671 ■ *The Law Digest*
Martindale-Hubbell
Reed Reference Publishing Group
121 Chanlon Rd.
New Providence, NJ 07974
Ph:(908)464-6800
Free: 800-526-4902
Fax: (908)771-8704
Co. E-mail: info@martindale.com
URL: http://www.martindale.com
Description: Contains summaries of statutory law worldwide. Includes up-to-date digests of laws of the 50 states, the District of Columbia, Puerto Rico and the U.S. Virgin Islands; English-language summaries of the laws of 80 countries, including new sections on Vietnam, the Slovak Republic, the Republic of Latvia, and the Island of Guernsey; complete texts of over 50 Uniform and Model Acts and International Conventions; and information on the Federal Judiciary and the Rules of Conduct of the American Bar Association. Listings are classified under more than 100 topics and 700 subheadings, including Absentees, Frauds, Motor Vehicles, Trade Secrets and Witnesses. **Availability:** Online: LexisNexis. **Type:** Full text.

29672 ■ *Lawyer Locator*
Martindale-Hubbell
Reed Reference Publishing Group
121 Chanlon Rd.
New Providence, NJ 07974
Ph:(908)464-6800
Free: 800-526-4902
Fax: (908)771-8704
Co. E-mail: info@martindale.com
URL: http://www.martindale.com
Description: Contains information on more than one million lawyers and law firms in 160 countries. Enables the user to search by name, geographic location, area of practice, firm size and languages. **Availability:** Online: LexisNexis. **Type:** Directory.

29673 ■ *Manitoba Automobile Injury Compensation Appeal Commission Decisions*
LexisNexis Quicklaw
2 Gore St.
PO Box 2080
Kingston, ON, Canada K7L 5J8
Ph:(613)549-4611
Free: 800-267-9470
Fax: (613)548-4260
Co. E-mail: sales@quicklaw.com
URL: http://www.quicklaw.com

Description: Provides access to rulings on appeals from Manitoba Public Insurance Officers involving compensation for auto accident injuries. **Type:** Full text.

29674 ■ *Mergers & Acquisitions Reports*
Thomson Financial
195 Broadway
New York, NY 10007
Ph:(646)822-2000
Co. E-mail: TFOnlineRequests@thomson.com
URL: http://www.thomson.com
Description: Contains the complete text of *Mergers & Acquisitions Report*, a weekly newsletter covering corporate acquisition finance strategies, planned acquisitions and divestitures, current deals, risk arbitrage trends, and laws and regulations. **Availability:** Online: LexisNexis. **Type:** Full text.

29675 ■ *The National Law Journal*
American Lawyer Media Inc.
105 Madison Ave., 7th Fl.
New York, NY 10016
Ph:(212)779-9200
Free: 800-888-8300
Fax: (212)481-8255
Co. E-mail: editorial@amlaw.com
URL: http://www.americanlawyer.com
Description: Contains the complete text of *The National Law Journal*, a weekly newspaper for the legal profession. Feature articles cover trends in case law, employment, criminal investigations, and law office management techniques. Also covers major legal events and personalities, with analyses of their social and legal impact. **Availability:** Online: American Lawyer Media Inc., LexisNexis, Thomson West. **Type:** Full text.

29676 ■ *New York Jurisprudence, 2d, LawDesk CD-ROM*
Thomson West
610 Opperman Dr.
Eagan, MN 55123
Ph:(651)687-7000
Free: 800-344-5008
Fax: (651)687-5827
Co. E-mail: west.customer.service@thomson.com
URL: http://www.westlaw.com
Description: Provides the full text of the multi-volume encyclopedia of New York law, *New York Jurisprudence, Second Edition*. Supplementary materials are included as part of any updated document. **Availability:** CD-ROM: Thomson West. **Type:** Full text.

29677 ■ *Ohio Jurisprudence on Westlaw*
Thomson West
610 Opperman Dr.
Eagan, MN 55123
Ph:(651)687-7000
Free: 800-344-5008
Fax: (651)687-5827
Co. E-mail: west.customer.service@thomson.com
URL: http://www.westlaw.com
Description: Contains a comprehensive encyclopedia of civil and criminal Ohio law, substantive and procedural. Organized into 400 topics, including: Table of Statutes and Table of Cases with Annotation References to specific provisions of the Ohio Constitution, statutes, and regulations. Also includes references to other Westlaw sources; Indexing by descriptions or legal concept for fast referencing; and Footnotes citing cases, statutes, and law review articles. **Availability:** Online: Thomson West; CD-ROM: Thomson West. **Type:** Full text.

29678 ■ *OneDisc*
Tax Analysts
510 N Washington St., Ste. 400
Falls Church, VA 22046
Ph:(703)533-4400
Free: 800-955-2444
Co. E-mail: cservice@tax.org
URL: http://www.taxanalysts.com
Description: Contains many of the basic IRS documents including the Internal Revenue Code, the IRS Regulations, IRS Tax Information Publications, IRS

Revenue Rulings, IRS Revenue Procedures, IRS Letter Rulings, and IRS Announcements. Features Tax Analysts' More Understandable Code and a Federal TaxGuide to make it easier to work with the Internal Revenue Code and related IRS regulations. **Availability:** CD-ROM: Tax Analysts. **Type:** Full text.

29679 ■ *Ontario Regulations and Rules of Court*

LexisNexis Quicklaw
2 Gore St.
PO Box 2080
Kingston, ON, Canada K7L 5J8
Ph:(613)549-4611
Free: 800-267-9470
Fax: (613)548-4260
Co. E-mail: sales@quicklaw.com
URL: http://www.quicklaw.com
Description: Provides a consolidation of Ontario Regulations provided by the Ontario government. Each regulation is a single document. Includes a menu for easy searching. **Type:** Full text.

29680 ■ *Payne's Publications on Family Law*

LexisNexis Quicklaw
2 Gore St.
PO Box 2080
Kingston, ON, Canada K7L 5J8
Ph:(613)549-4611
Free: 800-267-9470
Fax: (613)548-4260
Co. E-mail: sales@quicklaw.com
URL: http://www.quicklaw.com
Description: Provides searchable access to texts, journal articles and unpublished papers on all aspects of family law written by Julien D. Payne, University of Ottawa. **Type:** Full text.

29681 ■ *Pharmaceutical Law & Industry Report*

The Bureau of National Affairs Inc.
1231 25th St. NW
Washington, DC 20037
Ph:(202)452-4200
Free: 800-372-1033
Fax: (202)452-4226
Co. E-mail: customercare@bna.com
URL: http://www.bna.com
Description: Contains news on federal and state laws and regulations regarding the pharmaceutical and biotech industries. Also includes federal and state legislative, regulatory, and legal developments that affect drug costs, pharmaceutical pricing and reimbursement. Topics include antitrust enforcement actions, fraud and abuse investigations, drug formularies, state discount/rebate programs, generics vs. brand name drugs, reforms to the Hatch Waxman Act governing generic drugs, pharmacy benefit management regulation, lawsuits involving patent issues or Food and Drug Administration regulations, health insurance plans, patents on drugs, manufacturing costs, pricing, regulation of drug company advertising, International price regulation, and product liability of drug manufacturers. Sections include Highlights, Index, Lead Report, News, Analysis & Perspective, and Regulatory Calendar. **Availability:** Online: The Bureau of National Affairs Inc. **Type:** Full text.

29682 ■ *Robertson Personal Injury NetLetter*

LexisNexis Quicklaw
2 Gore St.
PO Box 2080
Kingston, ON, Canada K7L 5J8
Ph:(613)549-4611
Free: 800-267-9470
Fax: (613)548-4260
Co. E-mail: sales@quicklaw.com
URL: http://www.quicklaw.com
Description: Provides access to the newsletter by Professor Gerald Robertson, University of Alberta. **Availability:** Online: LexisNexis Quicklaw. **Type:** Full text.

29683 ■ *State Research Library*

Tax Analysts
510 N Washington St., Ste. 400
Falls Church, VA 22046

Ph:(703)533-4400
Free: 800-955-2444
Co. E-mail: cservice@tax.org
URL: http://www.taxanalysts.com
Description: Provides a complete set of statutes and regulations from all 50 states, the District of Columbia, and U.S. possessions. Also includes a quick reference tax rate chart for each state for sales, use, income, estate, inheritance, gift, and gasoline taxes. **Availability:** Online: Thomson West. **Type:** Full text.

29684 ■ *State Tax Notes*

Tax Analysts
510 N Washington St., Ste. 400
Falls Church, VA 22046
Ph:(703)533-4400
Free: 800-955-2444
Co. E-mail: cservice@tax.org
URL: http://www.taxanalysts.com
Description: Follows tax developments in every state, and keeps track of interstate trends. Covers multi-state Organizations, state tax conferences, tax decisions from courts nationwide, rulings and regulations from revenue departments, and legislation from all 50 states each week. **Availability:** Online: LexisNexis. **Type:** Full text.

29685 ■ *The State Tax OneDisc*

Tax Analysts
510 N Washington St., Ste. 400
Falls Church, VA 22046
Ph:(703)533-4400
Free: 800-955-2444
Co. E-mail: cservice@tax.org
URL: http://www.taxanalysts.com
Description: Contains tax statutes, regulations, and court cases for all 50 states and the District of Columbia and governing territories.Includes directory information for all state revenue officials, state supreme court clerks, and state attorney generals. Also includes the U.S. tax code and pertinent regulations, State Supreme Court cases and U.S. Supreme Court cases dealing with taxes. **Availability:** CD-ROM: Tax Analysts. **Type:** Full text.

29686 ■ *State Tax Today*

Tax Analysts
510 N Washington St., Ste. 400
Falls Church, VA 22046
Ph:(703)533-4400
Free: 800-955-2444
Co. E-mail: cservice@tax.org
URL: http://www.taxanalysts.com
Description: Covers tax news and documents from every state, the District of Columbia, and all U.S. possessions, complete with summaries and full text of legislation. Includes proposed and finalized regulations, *Revenue Rulings & Procedures*, supreme, appellate, and tax court opinions, and private letter rulings. **Availability:** Online: Tax Analysts. **Type:** Full text.

29687 ■ *Tax Directory*

Tax Analysts
510 N Washington St., Ste. 400
Falls Church, VA 22046
Ph:(703)533-4400
Free: 800-955-2444
Co. E-mail: cservice@tax.org
URL: http://www.taxanalysts.com
Description: Contains information on more than 20,00 tax professionals. Vol. One Government Officials Worldwide including state and federal officials, including taxwriting committees U.S. Department of Treasury and IRS, Tax Court Judges, International Financial Specialists, Tax and Business Journalists, Professional Associations, and Tax Groups and Coalitions. Vol. Two Corporate Tax Managers including names and contact information for tax managers in largest U.S corporations. Entries including industry description derived from the Securities and Exchange Commission's four-digit Standard Industry Classification code used by the listed companies for filing purposes. **Availability:** Online: LexisNexis; CD-ROM: Tax Analysts. **Type:** Directory.

29688 ■ *Tax Notes*

Tax Analysts
510 N Washington St., Ste. 400
Falls Church, VA 22046
Ph:(703)533-4400
Free: 800-955-2444
Co. E-mail: cservice@tax.org
URL: http://www.taxanalysts.com
Description: Contains the complete text of *Tax Notes Magazine*, covering all aspects of U.S. federal taxation. Includes news items and feature articles on tax developments, tax policy issues, and congressional developments. Also provides summaries of Internal Revenue Service (IRS) regulations, relevant court opinions, tax-related correspondence between the U.S. Treasury and the tax bar, IRS letter rulings and Technical Advice Memorandums, *Congressional Record* items, IRS manual changes, and IRS proposed and final regulations (with public comments). Also provides summaries of such documents as the IRS General Counsel Memorandums, Supreme Court tax-related opinions, and Actions on Decisions; IRS revenue rulings and revenue procedures; and tax-related reports from congressional tax-writing committees, the Joint Committee on Taxation, the IRS, U.S. Treasury, General Accounting Office, Congressional Budget Office, and other sources. **Availability:** Online: LexisNexis; CD-ROM: Tax Analysts. **Type:** Full text.

29689 ■ *Tax Notes International*

Tax Analysts
510 N Washington St., Ste. 400
Falls Church, VA 22046
Ph:(703)533-4400
Free: 800-955-2444
Co. E-mail: cservice@tax.org
URL: http://www.taxanalysts.com
Description: Covers tax news, digests, commentary, and documents at the International level. Provides updates on statutes, regulations, new court decisions, and a tax calendar covering important international tax events and conferences. **Availability:** Online: Tax Analysts, LexisNexis. **Type:** Full text.

29690 ■ *TaxPractice*

Tax Analysts
510 N Washington St., Ste. 400
Falls Church, VA 22046
Ph:(703)533-4400
Free: 800-955-2444
Co. E-mail: cservice@tax.org
URL: http://www.taxanalysts.com
Description: Covers all federal tax News related to tax practice and litigation. Reports on the most important new IRS rulings and regulations, and tax developments in Congress and the courts, and significant tax cases. Included with the Complete Federal Research Library. **Availability:** Online: LexisNexis. **Type:** Full text.

29691 ■ *Texas Jurisprudence on Westlaw*

Thomson West
610 Opperman Dr.
Eagan, MN 55123
Ph:(651)687-7000
Free: 800-344-5008
Fax: (651)687-5827
Co. E-mail: west.customer.service@thomson.com
URL: http://www.westlaw.com
Description: Provides the full text of *Texas Jurisprudence, Third Edition*. Contains a comprehensive encyclopedia of Texas law. **Availability:** Online: Thomson West; CD-ROM: Thomson West. **Type:** Full text.

29692 ■ *TOMES Plus System*

Thomson Microdex
6200 S Syracuse Way, Ste. 300
Greenwood Village, CO 80111-4740
Ph:(303)486-6400
Free: 800-525-9083
Fax: (303)486-6464
Co. E-mail: mdx.info@thomson.com
URL: http://www.micromedex.com
Description: Contains chemical, medical, and toxicological information for the industrial and occupational

medicine markets. Covers clinical effects, range of toxicity, workplace standards, kinetics, and physio-chemical standards. Comprises 16 files:; MEDITEXT Medical Managements—contains protocols on the evaluation, medical response, and treatment of individuals acutely exposed to industrial chemicals. Includes Occupational Safety and Health Administration (OSHA) occupational exposure standards.; HAZARDTEXT Hazard Managements—contains initial response protocols to incidents involving hazardous materials (e.g., fires, spills, leaks). Includes Occupational Safety and Health Administration (OSHA) occupational exposure standards.; Hazardous Substances Data Bank (HSDB)—contains data on more than 4200 chemical substances that are of known or potential toxicity and to which substantial populations are exposed.; OHM/TADS (Oil and Hazardous Materials/ Technical Assistance Data System)—contains data gathered from published literature on 1402 materials that have been designated oil or hazardous materials. Provides technical support for dealing with potential or actual dangers resulting from the discharge of oil or hazardous substances. Up to 126 data fields, some textual and some numeric, may be present for each record (i.e., one material). A record includes identification of the substance (CAS Registry Number, common and trade names, and chemical formula), physical properties, uses, toxicity, handling procedures, and suggested methods for disposing of spilled materials. Produced by the U.S. Environmental Protection Agency (EPA). Corresponds to the OHM-TADS online database.; Chemical Hazards Response Information System (CHRIS)—contains information on approximately 1200 chemical substances for use in spill situations. Includes chemical names and synonyms, molecular formula, biological and fire hazard potential, and chemical and physical properties. Also includes information on water pollution and toxicity of chemicals to aquatic life. Produced by the U.S. Coast Guard. Corresponds to the Chemical Hazards Response Information System (CHRIS) online database.; IRIS (Integrated Risk Information System)—contains information on the health risk assessment of more than 450 hazardous substances. Covers toxicity, carcinogenicity, chemical and physical properties, and applicable regulations. Includes reference doses (i.e., concentrations of substances below which adverse health effects are not expected to occur), and carcinogenic risk assessment of varying concentrations of substances in air and drinking water. Also includes summaries of EPA regulatory actions. Produced by the U.S. Environmental Protection Agency (EPA). Corresponds to the IRIS online database.; INFOTEXT Documents—provides general health and safety data on nonchemical-specific topics such as ergonomics and human health risk assessments.; Registry of Toxic Effects of Chemical Substances (RTECS)—offers toxicity data on more than 135,000 substances, extracted from scientific literature worldwide, includes specifics on mutagenicity, carcinogenicity, reproductive hazards, and acute and chronic toxicity of hazardous substances.; 1996 North American Emergency Response Guidebook (NAERG).; NIOSH (National Institute for Occupational Safety and Health) Pocket Guide—contains critical industrial hygiene data for approximately 675 chemicals with information on exposure limits, U.S. IDLH concentrations, incompatibilities and reactivities, personal protection, and recommendations for respirator selection.; New Jersey Fact Sheets from the N.J. Department of Health—offers employee-oriented exposure risk information useful when addressing worker right-to-know issues and developing training programs. Includes generic, non-technical worker safety and training information, frequently asked questions & answers, and a glossary of terms for more than 700 hazardous substances. **Availability:** Online: Thomson Microdex. **Type:** Bibliographic; Full text; Numeric.

29693 ■ Toxics Law Reporter
The Bureau of National Affairs Inc.
1231 25th St. NW
Washington, DC 20037
Ph:(202)452-4200
Free: 800-372-1033
Fax:(202)452-4226
Co. E-mail: customercare@bna.com

URL: http://www.bna.com
Description: Contains news, developments, and federal and state actions in the field of toxic tort, hazardous waste, and related insurance litigation. Subjects include allocation issues, business and real estate transactions, CERCLA/superfund, contribution protection, cost recovery and cleanup litigation, due diligence, environmental exposure, government enforcement actions, hazardous waste law, liability insurance, occupational exposure, parent/subsidiary petroleum exclusion, personal injury, product liability, property damage, RCRA citizen suits, residential exposure, spills, state suits, and tort reform. Includes highlights of the week's most significant developments in the field; list of reports grouped by subject; reports on pending litigation, court decisions, verdicts and settlements and procedural developments; lists of meetings and conferences related to the field; table of cases in alphabetical order, and cumulative index of articles and cases. **Availability:** Online: Thomson West, The Bureau of National Affairs Inc. **Type:** Full text.

LIBRARIES

29694 ■ Alberta Securities Commission–Resource Centre
300-5th Ave. SW, 4th Fl.
Calgary, AB, Canada T2P 3C4
Ph:(403)297-6454
Fax:(403)297-6156
Co. E-mail: yanming.fei@seccom.ab.ca
URL: http://www.albertasecurities.com
Contact: Yanming Fei, Libn.
Scope: Securities legislation, corporate law. **Services:** Library open to the public by appointment. **Holdings:** Figures not available.

29695 ■ Arnold & Porter–Library
399 Park Ave.
New York, NY 10022-4690
Ph:(212)715-1382
Fax:(212)715-1399
Co. E-mail: kim.fenty@aporter.com
Contact: Kim R. Fenty, Lib.Mgr.
Scope: Litigation; law - tax, corporate, and environmental. **Services:** Interlibrary loan; Library not open to the public. **Holdings:** 20,000 books; 400 bound periodical volumes. **Subscriptions:** 205 journals and other serials; 15 newspapers.

29696 ■ Bryan Cave LLP–Law Library
700 13th St. NW, Ste. 600
Washington, DC 20005-3960
Ph:(202)508-6000
Fax:(202)508-6200
Co. E-mail: laura.green@bryancave.com
Contact: Laurie Green, Mgr., Lib. & Res.Svcs.
Scope: Government and politics; law - commercial, corporate, environmental, intellectual property, taxation. **Services:** Interlibrary loan; copying; faxing; Library open to the public with restrictions. **Holdings:** 11,000 volumes. **Subscriptions:** 200 journals and other serials.

29697 ■ Hewlett-Packard Company–Legal/ Tax Library
3000 Hanover St.
M/S 1069
Palo Alto, CA 94304-1185
Ph:(650)857-6001
Fax:(650)857-2732
URL: http://www.hp.com
Contact: Emily Morris, Info.Anl.
Scope: Legal topics, intellectual property, taxation. **Services:** Library not open to the public. **Holdings:** 2000 books. **Subscriptions:** 160 journals and other serials; 6 newspapers.

29698 ■ Lang Michener LLP–Library
1500-1055 W. Georgia St.
PO Box 11117
Vancouver, BC, Canada V6E 4N7
Ph:(604)689-9111
Fax:(604)685-7084

Co. E-mail: library@lmls.com
URL: http://www.langmichener.ca/
Contact: Anne Ikeda
Scope: Law - tax, mining; litigation; corporate securities. **Services:** Library not open to the public. **Holdings:** Figures not available.

29699 ■ LECG, LLC–Library
2000 Powell St., Ste. 600
Emeryville, CA 94608
Ph:(510)653-9800
Fax:(510)653-9898
Co. E-mail: nancy_adams@lecg.com
URL: http://www.lecg.com
Contact: Nancy Adams
Scope: Economics, business, antitrust. **Services:** Library not open to the public. **Holdings:** 2500 books. **Subscriptions:** 50 journals and other serials; 4 newspapers.

29700 ■ Long & Levit–Library
601 Montgomery St., Ste. 900
San Francisco, CA 94111
Ph:(415)397-2222
Fax:(415)397-6392
Contact: Holly Mohler, Libn.
Scope: Insurance, environmental, professional liability, construction. **Services:** Interlibrary loan; copying; Library open to the public at librarian's discretion. **Holdings:** 10,000 books. **Subscriptions:** 75 journals and other serials; 4 newspapers.

29701 ■ McCarthy Tetrault–Library
PO Box 10424, Pacific Centre
777 Dunsmuir St., Ste. 1300
Vancouver, BC, Canada V7Y 1K2
Ph:(604)643-7931
Fax:(604)643-7900
Co. E-mail: scrysler@van.mccarthy.ca
URL: http://www.mccarthy.ca
Contact: Susan Crysler
Scope: Law, corporate law, securities. **Services:** Library not open to the public. **Holdings:** Figures not available.

29702 ■ Miller Thomson–Library
20 Queen St. W, Ste. 2700
PO Box 27
Toronto, ON, Canada M5H 3S1
Ph:(416)595-8537
Fax:(416)595-8695
Co. E-mail: ifreeman@millerthomson.com
URL: http://www.millerthomson.com
Contact: Ines Freeman, Libn.
Scope: Law - labor, estate, tax, corporate, commercial, environmental. **Services:** Interlibrary loan; copying; Library not open to the public. **Holdings:** 2000 books. **Subscriptions:** 20 journals and other serials; 6 newspapers.

RESEARCH CENTERS

29703 ■ Boston University–Center for Law and Technology
765 Commonwealth Ave., 8th Fl.
Boston, MA 02215
Ph:(617)353-5294
Fax:(617)353-3077
Co. E-mail: mbaram@bu.edu
URL: http://www.bu.edu/law
Contact: Prof. Michael Baram, Dir.
E-mail: mbaram@bu.edu
Scope: Law and technology issues, with recent focus on new biotechnology products for gene therapy and transgenic agriculture, and other applications. Other subjects include expert systems software and legal and professional responsibility issues, corporate management of environmental risk and self-auditing, multinational corporations and environmental protection, chemical industry initiatives for preventing accident hazards, right-to-know as a regulatory alternative for protecting health, safety, and environment, and telecom/internet legal issues. **Educational Activities:** Seminars, symposia, conferences and speakers.

Business Plans

START-UP INFORMATION

29704 ■ "And on your Left" in *Entrepreneur* (Vol. 28, No. 9, September 2000, pp. 48)
Pub: Entrepreneur Media Inc.
Ed: Cynthia E. Griffin. **Description:** The things investors are looking at when touring a business are examined.

29705 ■ "The art of making a plan and making it happen" in *The New York Times* (December 18, 2000, pp. C16)
Pub: The New York Times Company
Ed: Lisa Belkin. **Description:** Business plans for the self-employed are discussed.

29706 ■ "Association is adjusting image of chiropractors" in *Washington Business Journal* (Vol. 18, No. 47, March 24, 2000, pp. 53)
Pub: American City Business Journals, Inc.
Ed: Jane Cys. **Description:** The national trend toward large group practices has other health care professionals team up with chiropractors, thus helping to change the image of chiropractors as a more respectable profession.

29707 ■ "Battle of the Business Plans: a new march madness" in *Fortune* (Vol. 141, No. 2, January 24, 2000, pp. 128)
Pub: Time Inc.
Ed: Eric Nee. **Description:** Some of the most successful technology companies were started by university students. To this end, venture capitals have been scouring college campuses looking for the next big thing.

29708 ■ "Beating the odds: remembering the basics of business can help" in *Black Enterprise* (Vol. 32, No. 6, January 2002, pp. 35)
Pub: Earl Graves Publishing Co.
Ed: Glenn Townes. **Description:** The key to starting and sustaining a small business is to have a strong, basic understanding of business practices. Advice is given to manage small businesses.

29709 ■ *Becoming a Personal Trainer for Dummies*
Pub: John Wiley & Sons, Incorporated
Ed: Melyssa Michael, Linda Formichelli. **Released:** October 2004. **Price:** $19.99 (US), $25.99 (Canadian). **Description:** Legal and tax issues involved in starting and running a personal trainer firm. The book offers suggestions for incorporating massage and nutritional services.

29710 ■ "Bizdom U. Set to Teach Next Gen of Startups" in *Crain's Detroit Business* (Vol. 22, November 13, 2006, No. 46, pp. 1)
Pub: Crain Communications Inc. - Detroit
Ed: Sheena Harrison. **Description:** Local businessman invests $10M to form Bizdom U. that teaches entrepreneurs based on experience from other entrepreneurs' successes and failures. Focus will be on developing business plans for their own businesses on a two year program taught by actual local entrepreneurs.

29711 ■ "Blending In Family" in *Ingram's* (Vol. 28, No. 5, May 2002, pp. 35)
Pub: Show Me Publishing, Inc.
Ed: Chuck Vogt, Sr. **Description:** One of the challenges facing the owner of a startup small business is recruiting the right employees. Four objectives are listed to help a firm be successful.

29712 ■ "Bouncing back" in *Entrepreneur* (Vol. 30, No. 3, March 2002, pp. 134)
Pub: Entrepreneur Media Inc.
Ed: Nichole L. Torres. **Description:** Valuable information for entrepreneurs starting a new business after losing a job is offered.

29713 ■ "Bright Idea" in *My Business* (February/March 2004, pp. 48)
Pub: My Business Magazine
Ed: Lena Basha. **Description:** Profile of IdeaCafe.com, offering resources on building a business plan to information on ways to de-stress.

29714 ■ "Build Your Dream Home Business" in *Home Business* (Vol. 12, October 2005, No. 5, pp. 16, 18-22, 102, 104)
Pub: Home Business Magazine
Ed: Sandy Larson. **Description:** Ten steps to starting a home-based business, starting from the initial planning phase to financing a venture as well as marketing strategies.

29715 ■ "Building vs. buying" in *BlackEnterprise* (Vol. 31, No. 6, January 2001, pp. 39)
Pub: Earl Graves Publishing Co.
Ed: Glenn Townes. **Description:** Ideas are presented to would-be entrepreneurs on the advantages and disadvantages to buying an existing business or building one from scratch.

29716 ■ "Business information centers" in *BlackEnterprise* (Vol. 31, No. 12, July 2001, pp. 48)
Pub: Earl Graves Publishing Co.
Ed: Roger Barnes. **Description:** Profile of the Small Business Administration's (SBA) Business Information Center (BIC), the government-funded business resource with more than 65 BIC offices in more than 35 states. BICs provide a one-stop location for information, education, workshops, and training designed to address a broad variety of business start-up and development issues.

29717 ■ "Business plan pro" in *Black Enterprise* (Vol. 33, No. 6, January 2003, pp. 10)
Pub: Earl Graves Publishing Co.
Description: The tools needed to write a successful business plan are provided at blackenterprise.com. The site helps entrepreneurs to write a plan, figure startup costs, find financing, along with tips on launching a Website for a new or existing small business.

29718 ■ "Careful planning" in *BlackEnterprise* (Vol. 32, No. 2, September 2001, pp. 50)
Pub: Earl Graves Publishing Co.
Ed: Paul McCoy-Pinderhughes. **Description:** Information offered to start a travel/meeting and event planning business.

29719 ■ *Complete Business Management Guide for Kitchen & Bathroom Professionals: Starting & Staying in Business*
Pub: National Kitchen & Bath Association
Ed: Hank Darlington. **Released:** 1997. **Price:** $30.00 (cloth).

29720 ■ *The Complete Small Business Start-up Guide*
Pub: John Wiley & Sons, Incorporated
Ed: Lisa Rogak. **Released:** November 2004. **Price:** $14.95. **Description:** Guide to starting a small company, focusing on development of a business plan, organizational structure, advertising, hiring, selection of suppliers, and using the Internet to market your firm.

29721 ■ "Cover Story" in *Inc.* (September 2000, pp. 70)
Pub: The Goldhirsh Group
Description: Ways to avoid pitfalls when filling a term sheet for a venture capitalist are explained.

29722 ■ "The Design of an Ideal Business" in *Home Business* (Vol. 12, October 2005, No. 5, pp. 58, 60)
Pub: Home Business Magazine
Ed: Brad DeHaven. **Description:** Ten steps for starting a successful new business are outlined, including low start-up costs.

29723 ■ "Detroit Free Press Small Business Column" in *Detroit Free Press* (September 12, 2005)
Pub: Knight-Ridder/Tribune Business News
Ed: Carol Cain. **Description:** Jeff Williams runs Bizstarters.com, a company that helps people over the age of 50 start new businesses. Williams offers a booklet that outlines ten tips to having fun while making money after age 50.

29724 ■ "The Disruptive Startup" in *Inc.* (February 1, 2002)
Pub: Inc. Magazine
Ed: Nancy Lyons. **Description:** Interview with Harvard Business School professor and author, Clayton M. Christensen. Christensen helps identify strategies that allow new growth companies succeed.

29725 ■ "Doing Your Homework" in *Home Business* (Vol. 12, October 2005, No. 5, pp. 62)
Pub: Home Business Magazine
Ed: Kurt English, Esq. **Description:** Questions to ask before starting a home-based business are discussed. The importance of researching key issues is stressed.

29726 ■ "Don't get bogged down with futile procedures" in *Atlanta Business Chronicle* (Vol. 23, No. 46, April 20, 2001, pp. 66A)
Pub: American City Business Journals Inc.
Ed: Donna Chambers. **Description:** A small company should define its procedures from the start in order to provide for any circumstances that could arise, in both the short-term and the long-term for every department within the business.

29727 ■ *The Elements of Small Business*
Pub: Silver Lake Publishing
Ed: John Thaler. **Released:** October 2004. **Price:** $24.95. **Description:** Concepts, markets, worksheets, letters, business plans, and sample legal forms for starting and running a small business are included.

29728 ■ "Entrepreneur Column" in *Entrepreneur.com* (November 16, 2006)
Pub: Entrepreneur Media Inc.
Ed: Tim Berry. **Description:** Sticking to a business plan is critical in the launch of a new business. If one element is missing, do not proceed without amending that or altering the plan.

29729 ■ *Entrepreneurial Itch: What No One Tells You About Starting Your Own Business*
Pub: Self-Counsel Press Inc.
Ed: David Trahair. **Released:** December 2006. **Price:** $13.95. **Description:** Small business accountant shares a plan for starting a business.

29730 ■ *Entrepreneurship*
Pub: John Wiley and Sons Inc.
Ed: William D. Bygrave; Andrew Zacharakis. **Released:** March 2007. **Price:** $115.95. **Description:** Information for starting a new business is shared, focusing on marketing and financing a product or service.

29731 ■ *Entrepreneurship Strategy: Changing Patterns in New Venture Creation, Growth, and Reinvention*
Pub: SAGE Publications, Incorporated
Ed: Lisa K. Gundry; Jill R. Kickul. **Released:** August 2006. **Price:** $69.95. **Description:** Entrepreneurial strategies that incorporate new venture emergence, early growth, and reinvention and innovation are examined.

29732 ■ "Entrepreneurship, too, has its economic limits" in *Wall Street Journal* (October 1, 2002, pp. B4)
Pub: Dow Jones & Co. Inc.
Ed: Jeff Bailey. **Description:** Economic factors for entrepreneurs is presented. Statistical data included.

29733 ■ "Fly Solo: How to Build a Profitable Enterprise" in *Black Enterprise* (Vol. 30, No. 6, January 2000, pp. 72)
Pub: Earl Graves Publishing Co.
Ed: Millicent Lownes-Jackson and Gerda Gallop-Goodman. **Description:** Ways to assess your entrepreneurial sills are explored. Do you have the skills, abilities and knowledge required for the business you'd like to start? Do you have the ability to nurture and grow a business? Are you prepared to make sacrifices? Are you self-motivated? Do you like being in charge? Do you have the financial means to start a business? These questions must be answered truthfully before you move into self-employment.

29734 ■ "Flying Solo" in *Small Business Opportunities* (Vol. 12, No. 3, May 2000, pp. 20)
Pub: Harris Publications, Inc.
Ed: Lin Grensing-Pophal. **Description:** Going it alone when starting a new business requires some adjusting. The article addresses ways of coping.

29735 ■ "A Fortune From Home" in *Small Business Opportunities* (Vol. 13, No. 5, September 2001, pp. 22-24, 26, 28, 30, 32, 34, 36, 40)
Pub: Harris Publications, Inc.
Description: Helpful information is provided to start a mail order business for less than $25. The article contains ideas, tips and pointers on how to find a product, market it, and bankroll the profits.

29736 ■ "From idea to inspiration" in *Entrepreneur* (Vol. 30, No. 3, March 2002, pp. 29)
Pub: Entrepreneur Media Inc.
Ed: Mark Henricks. **Description:** Book review of 'The Big Idea', written by attorney Steven D. Strauss. The books tells how many products came to exist.

29737 ■ "Get On The Plan" in *Entrepreneur* (Vol. 33, October 2005, No. 10, pp. 14)
Pub: Entrepreneur Media Inc.
Description: Review of the book, "The Idiot's Guide to Business Plans", which explains the process of writing a business plan.

29738 ■ "Getting off to the Right Start" in *Venture Capital Journal* (Vol. 40, No. 10, November 2000, pp. 40-41)
Pub: Venture Economics
Ed: Jay K. Hachigian. **Description:** Advice for entrepreneurs to avoid start-up problems, including ways to lay a proper foundation - setting up a common sense capital structure; ways to protect intellectual property; and good operating procedures.

29739 ■ "Getting Set for Success with Your Own Small Business" in *Small Business Opportunities* (Vol. 12, No. 3, May 2000, pp. 110)
Pub: Harris Publications, Inc.
Description: Statistics regarding new business startups presented by the Small Business Administration (SBA) and Richard E. Irwin Research, Inc., along with advice for entrepreneurs, is provided.

29740 ■ "Goal for Entrepreneurs who have more equipment or employees than business demands" in *Business First Columbus* (Vol. 18, No. 25)
Pub: Business First Columbus, Inc.
Ed: Lisa Hooker. **Description:** Business plans for entrepreneurs with more equipment and employees than required to run their businesses.

29741 ■ *Going Solo: Developing a Home-Based Consulting Business from the Ground Up*
Pub: McGraw-Hill Companies Incorporated
Ed: William J. Bond. **Released:** January 1997. **Price:** $14.95. **Description:** Ways to turn specialized knowledge into a home-based successful consulting firm, focusing on targeting client needs, business plans, and growth.

29742 ■ "Gray Might be a Geek, thought DeVeau, but he was a Geek with Vision" in *Inc.* (May 2000, pp. 94)
Pub: The Goldhirsh Group
Ed: David H. Freedman. **Description:** An internet company finds its niche in an unlikely place, a depressed factory town in Lynn, Massachusetts. The article tells of its success.

29743 ■ *The Harvard Entrepreneurs Club Guide to Starting Your Own Business*
Pub: John Wiley & Sons, Inc.
Ed: Sharma. **Released:** 1999. **Price:** $14.95.

29744 ■ *How to Get the Financing for Your New Small Business: Innovative Solutions from the Experts Who Do It Every Day*
Pub: Atlantic Publishing Company
Ed: Sharon L. Fullen. **Released:** August 2005. **Price:** $39.95, includes companion CD-Rom. **Description:** Ready capital is essential for starting and expanding a small business. Topics include traditional financing methods, financial statements, and a good business plan.

29745 ■ "How to Get Started in Business" in *Crain's Detroit Business* (Vol. 16, No. 50, December 11, 2000, pp. E-6)
Pub: Crain Communications, Inc.
Description: The U.S. Small Business Administration provides the first steps an entrepreneur should take toward starting a business. Questions are provided to help create a focused, well-researched business plan that can serve as a blueprint for your business.

29746 ■ "How to Stay on the Move...When the World is Slowing Down" in *Fast Company* (July 2001, pp. 113)
Pub: Fast Company
Ed: Scott Kirsner. **Description:** It is hard to remember a less-inviting time to have a great idea for a new company or to champion new ideas to change a big company. Leaders who think big aren't willing to downsize their ambitions they just work a little harder and smarter. Some battle-tested advice on how to stay fast in slow times is offered.

29747 ■ "I Did It My Way" in *Entrepreneur* (Vol. 31, No. 8, August 2003, pp. 112)
Pub: Entrepreneur Media, Inc.
Ed: Romanus Wolter. **Description:** The secret to entrepreneurial success is to discover what works for you by taking action according to your personality and instincts. A method to help create a business plan is presented.

29748 ■ "Identify All Possible Exits" in *Business Week Online* (Dec. 6, 2002)
Pub: McGraw-Hill Inc.
Ed: William J. Link. **Description:** Advice for entrepreneurs to keep exit strategies in mind when planning a start up company is given.

29749 ■ "Love Story" in *Entrepreneur* (Vol. 28, No. 8, August 2000, pp. 142)
Pub: Entrepreneur Media Inc.
Ed: Paul Edwards and Sarah Edwards. **Description:** Help in finding a small business that fulfills personal passions.

29750 ■ "Market Planning 101" in *Home Business* (Vol. 12, October 2005, No. 5, pp. 42, 44-45)
Pub: Home Business Magazine
Ed: Christopher J. Bachler. **Description:** A quick marketing plan for any small business is presented and includes all the basic information required to attract loans, partners, business services and even Small Business Administration assistance.

29751 ■ "Needbucks.com" in *Forbes* (January 10, 2000, pp. 188)
Pub: Forbes Magazine
Ed: Guy Kawasaki. **Description:** There is plenty of money for raising capital out there, but there are also a lot of bad business plans. Ten tips to improve the odds that your plan is read, and possibly funded, are provided.

29752 ■ "A New Century for Start-ups" in *Hispanic Business* (Vol. 22, No. 3, March 2000, pp. 54)
Pub: Hispanic Business
Ed: Christopher D. Lancette. **Description:** The importance of a comprehensive business plan to the successful winning of venture capital backing are explored. The calculation of required start-up capital is often underestimated and often results in business failure.

29753 ■ "The perils of starting a service firm" in *Wall Street Journal* (May 28, 2002, pp. B5)
Pub: Wall Street Journal
Ed: Jeff Bailey. **Description:** Must-know advice is offered for would-be entrepreneurs wishing to start a service firm, is presented. Statistical data included.

29754 ■ "Pick Your Startup Tool" in *Black Enterprise* (Vol. 36, November 2005, No. 4, pp. 74)
Pub: Earl G. Graves Publishing Co. Inc.
Ed: Sonya Donaldson. **Description:** Besides being a good business plan, financial management tools are an asset for planning a marketing strategy. Business Plan Pro Standard, QuickBooks, Peachtree, and Business Resource Software can help startups write business plans that include pricing strategy, advertising, and budgeting.

29755 ■ "A Plan for Today's Money Market" in Hispanic Business (March 2003, pp. 42, 44)
Pub: Hispanic Business
Ed: Andrea Siedsma. Description: A well-crafted business plan is essential for an entrepreneur to obtain capital. The plan must emphasize honesty, credibility, and the details of marketing. Sandra Delarosa, a California female entrepreneur, outlines the details of her business plan for procuring capital. Web sites to assist in writing a business plan are included.

29756 ■ "Planning for Gold" in Entrepreneur (Vol. 32, November 2004, No. 11, pp. 112)
Pub: Entrepreneur Media Inc.
Ed: Nichole L. Torres. Description: Business plan competitions are growing in popularity. In order for entrepreneurs to cash in and win cash, services or venture capital they must understand the process. Many of the competitions are associated with university MBA programs, but there are also those produced by communities, which are open to anyone in the local area or a particular business sector.

29757 ■ "Shape Up!" in Entrepreneur (Vol. 31, No. 10, October 2003, pp. 100)
Pub: Entrepreneur Media, Inc.
Ed: Chris Penttila. Description: Three entrepreneurial fitness tests are offered to entrepreneurs to see if they have what it takes to endure the startup phase.

29758 ■ "A Sharp Focus on Fuzzy Thinking" in Business Week Online (February 2)
Pub: McGraw-Hill, Inc.
Description: Advice for targeting a market for its services is offered to a new business consulting firm. The firm prepares business plans, writes proposals, assists recording artists and actors with PR and industry agreements, as well as outsourcing registration and licensing for insurance and securities brokers, and prepares trademark and copyright applications.

29759 ■ The Small Business Owner's Manual: Everything You Need to Know to Start Up and Run Your Business
Pub: Career Press, Incorporated
Ed: Joe Kennedy. Released: June 2005. Price: $19.99 (US) $26.95 (Canadian). Description: Comprehensive guide for starting a small business, focusing on twelve ways to obtain financing, business plans, selling and advertising products and services, hiring and firing employees, setting up a Web site, business law, accounting issues, insurance, equipment, computers, banks, financing, customer credit and collection, leasing, and more.

29760 ■ "Smart Business Tools" in Black Enterprise (Vol. 32, No. 9, April 2002, pp. 54)
Pub: Earl Graves Publishing Co.
Ed: Sonya A. Donaldson. Description: A profile of business plan authorship software called Plan Write Expert Edition for Business, produced by Business Resource Software.

29761 ■ So You're Thinking about Starting a Business: A Comprehensive General Start Up Manual
Pub: Business of Your Own
Ed: Millicent G. Lownes. Released: 1998. Price: $49.95.

29762 ■ "Stake Your Claim: Contrary to Popular Belief, There's No Need to Ante Up a Fortune When You're Playing the Startup Game" in Entrepreneur
Pub: Entrepreneur Media Inc.
Ed: Karen E. Spaeder. Description: Three entrepreneurs share ways they started their high-cost businesses without large sums of money: Steve Bandovich, owner of Cloud 9 Specialty Car Rentals; Chi Conley, who started up with one hotel and now owns 31 hospitality businesses in Northern California; and Tom Hatten, who started Mountainside Fitness in 1991.

29763 ■ "Start a Business at Home? You've Got to be Kidding" in Inc. (December 1999, pp. 92)
Pub: The Goldhirsh Group
Description: After running his business from home for two weeks, the owner of a $65 million a year business argues against running a home-based business.

29764 ■ "Start with Nothing" in Inc. (February 1, 2002)
Pub: Inc. Magazine
Ed: Emily Barker. Description: Greg Gianforte, founder of the software company Brightwork Development Inc., shares his secrets for launching a successful new company, with a focus on sales.

29765 ■ "Starting a business? Then get with the plan" in Crain's Detroit Business (Vol. 18, No. 49, December 9, 2002, pp. 17)
Pub: Crain Communications Inc., Detroit
Ed: Laura Bailey. Description: When starting a new company, it is imperative to have a good business plan.

29766 ■ "Street Smarts: Don't Sign Anything Yet" in Inc. (January 1, 2005)
Pub: Inc. Magazine
Ed: Norm Brodsky. Description: When starting a new business, it is important for entrepreneurs to beware of commitments made in the process.

29767 ■ "Street Smarts" in Inc. (August 2000, pp. 37)
Pub: The Goldhirsh Group
Ed: Norm Brodsky and Bo Burlingham. Description: Sometimes the hardest part of starting a business is figuring out where to begin. Those beginning a business should remain focused on the primary goals, and not get lost in details.

29768 ■ "Strong Structure" in Black Enterprise (Vol. 34, July 2004, No. 12, pp. 48)
Pub: Earl G. Graves Publishing Co. Inc.
Ed: Alan Hughes. Description: Advice is given for launching a small business. The entrepreneur needs information for choosing the business structure that is right for his new firm. Guidelines for choosing a sole proprietorship, partnership, limited liability company, C corporation, and S corporation are outlined.

29769 ■ "Stump the slump" in Entrepreneur (Vol. 30, No. 2, February 2002, pp. 90)
Pub: Entrepreneur Media Inc.
Ed: Michele Marrinan. Description: Many entrepreneurs are taking advantage of the economic downturn to start new businesses. Ways to work the economy to find financing are discussed, including the importance of a solid business plan.

29770 ■ Swimming Against the Stream: Launching Your Business and Making Your Life
Pub: Macmillan Publishers Limited
Ed: Tim Waterstone. Released: March 2007. Price: $17.99. Description: Ten rules for launching a new business are outlined using real-life experiences.

29771 ■ The Unofficial Guide to Starting a Small Business
Pub: John Wiley & Sons, Incorporated
Ed: Marcia Layton Turner. Released: October 2004. Price: $16.99. Description: Information and tools for starting a small business, covering the start-up process, from market research, to business plans, to marketing programs.

29772 ■ "The Village Vanguard: Two new-economy entrepreneurs aim to jump-start businesses in college towns" in Fortune (July 10, 2000, pp.154)
Pub: Time Inc.
Ed: Andy Serwer. Description: Village Ventures wants to build businesses in places that are brainy and bucolic, and overlooked by venture capitalists.

29773 ■ What No Ever Tells You About Starting Your Own Business: Real-Life Start-Up Advice from 101 Successful Entrepreneurs
Pub: Kaplan Publishing
Ed: Jan Norman. Released: July 2004. Price: $18.95 (US); $28.95 (Canadian). Description: From planning to marketing, advice is given to entrepreneurs starting new companies. s.

29774 ■ What No One Ever Tells You about Starting Your Own Business: Real Life Start-Up Advice from 101 Successful Entrepreneurs
Pub: Upstart Publishing Co., Inc.
Ed: Jan Norman. Released: 1999. Price: $17.95.

29775 ■ "What's In a Name? Often Overlooked, Choosing the Right Business Moniker is Key" in Black Enterprise (Vol. 34, No. 4, Nov. 2003)
Pub: Earl Graves Publishing Co.
Ed: Marcia A. Wade. Description: Both private and practical issues involved in naming a new business are explored. The importance of finding a name that does not require extensive advertising to communicate a company's function is stressed.

29776 ■ "Yes, you can" in Black Enterprise (Vol. 31, No. 5, December 2000, pp. 64)
Pub: Earl Graves Publishing Co.
Ed: Feona Huff. Description: How to start, operate and grow a business while developing yourself and pursuing your personal goals.

29777 ■ "You need to know" in BlackEnterprise (Vol. 31, No. 12, July 2001, pp. 45)
Pub: Earl Graves Publishing Co.
Ed: Bridget McCrea. Description: It is very common for small start-up companies to overlook simple issues and its not until they get sued or are penalized that the owner realizes that his or her personal life savings are tied up in the business and they should have taken different steps in the process of their early business plans. Ways for small businesses to find affordable legal advice is outlined.

ASSOCIATIONS AND OTHER ORGANIZATIONS

29778 ■ Auto Suppliers Benchmarking Association
4606 FM 1960 W, Ste. 250
Houston, TX 77069-9949
Ph:(281)440-5044
Fax: (281)440-6677
URL: http://www.asbabenchmarking.com
Contact: Mark T. Czarnecki, Pres.
Membership: Automotive supplier firms with an interest in benchmarking. Purpose: Promotes the use of benchmarking, wherein businesses compare their processes with those of their competitors, as a means of improving corporate efficiency and profitability. Facilitates exchange of information among members; conducts target operations, procurement, development, and maintenance studies; identifies model business practices.

REFERENCE WORKS

29779 ■ "3-D Negotiation: Playing the Whole Game" in Harvard Business Review (Vol. 81, No. 11, November 2003, pp. 64)
Pub: Harvard Business School Press
Ed: David A. Lax, James K. Sebenius. Description: Business negotiations require thorough planning and development in order to be successful.

29780 ■ The 7 Irrefutable Rules of Small Business Growth
Pub: John Wiley & Sons, Incorporated
Ed: Steven S. Little. Released: February 2005. Price: $18.95. Description: Proven strategies to maintain small business growth are outlined, covering topics such as technology, business plans, hiring, and more.

29781 ■ **"The '42 Formula' For Success"** in *Inc.* **(August 1, 2003)**
Pub: Gruner & Jahr USA Publishing
Ed: Tahl Raz. **Description:** Author Nitin Nohria offers information and advice on why some small business owners succeed and others fail.

29782 ■ *101 Internet Businesses You Can Start from Home: How to Choose and Build Your Own Successful E-Business*
Pub: Maximum Press
Ed: Susan Sweeney. **Released:** June 2006. **Price:** $29.95. **Description:** Guide for starting and growing an Internet business; information for developing a business plan, risk levels, and promotional techniques are included.

29783 ■ **"A Market for Ideas"** in *The Economist* **(Vol. 377, October 22-28, 2005, No. 8449, pp. 3-6, 8-10, 12-18)**
Pub: The Economist Newspaper Ltd.
Description: The magazine presents information collected from a survey conducted on issues of patents and technology. Protection of intellectual property can be good for both the technology industry and its customers. The patent system, companies preparing for intellectual-property battles, a new intellectual-property business model, sharing intellectual property, Indian and Chinese competition in innovation, and new markets for intellectual property are among issues investigated.

29784 ■ *Adams Streetwise Complete Business Plan: Create a Business Plan to Finance & Run a New or Existing Business*
Pub: Adams Media Corporation
Ed: Bob Adams. **Released:** 1998. **Price:** $16.95.

29785 ■ **"All Systems Grow: You Don't Have to be a Rocket Scientist to Grow Your Business."** in *Entrepreneur* **(Vol. 33, March 2005, No. 3)**
Pub: Entrepreneur Media Inc.
Ed: Julie Monahan. **Description:** Seven strategies to develop and grow a small business are presented.

29786 ■ **"American Outcast"** in *Entrepreneur.com* **(Vol. 34, February 2006, No. 2, pp. 81)**
Pub: Entrepreneur Media Inc.
Ed: Laurel Delaney. **Description:** In order to compete in a global market, small American companies must position their brands as local in order market a good brand strategy, as well as to promote a new brand with cultural sensitivity.

29787 ■ *Anatomy of a Business Plan: A Step-by-Step Guide to Starting Smart, Building the Business, & Securing Your Companies Future*
Pub: Upstart Publishing Co., Inc.
Ed: Linda Pinson. **Released:** 1999.

29788 ■ **"Anatomy of a Merger"** in *Rough Notes* **(Vol. 145, No. 2, February 2003, pp. 66)**
Pub: Rough Notes
Ed: Paul J. DiStefano. **Description:** When insurance agencies merge, the principals should address the issues of equity allocation, compensations, and the assumption of roles and responsibilities.

29789 ■ **"Apache on the Rise, Anadarko in Decline"** in *Houston Business Journal* **(Vol. 34, No. 13, August 8, 2003, pp. 1)**
Pub: American City Business Journals
Ed: Monica Perin. **Description:** Business and management styles of Apache Corporation and Anadarko Petroleum Company are compared, including strategic planning and profit margins.

29790 ■ **"Art of Business"** in *Entrepreneur.com* **(Vol. 34, February 2006, No. 2, pp. 46)**
Pub: Entrepreneur Media Inc.
Ed: Sara Wilson. **Description:** The MacDowell Colony serves not only as an inspiration to artists of all disciplines, but the Colony's methods for fostering creativity can be used to teach entrepreneurs the value of time and space in order to generate ideas.

29791 ■ **"Arvin Meritor Says It's Done Selling"** in *Crain's Detroit Business* **(Vol. 23, February 5, 2007, No. 6, pp. 29)**
Pub: Crain Communications Inc. - Detroit
Ed: Brent Snaveley. **Description:** Auto Supplier Arvin Meritor, Inc. has completed selling off its non-core businesses and will now concentrate on growing those globally. $200M capital was raised in the sale of its last non core businesses in 2006.

29792 ■ **"As Clock Ticks on 2006, Tax Debate Continues"** in *Crain's Detroit Business* **(Vol. 22, December 11, 2006, No. 50, pp. 7)**
Pub: Crain Communications Inc. - Detroit
Ed: Amy Lane. **Description:** State Legislature postpones action on state's business tax until 2007. Decision was made to wait until January due to the upcoming break for the Holidays and the complexity of the issues.

29793 ■ **"Ask Inc: Dividing the Corporate Pie"** in *Inc.* **(July 1, 2003)**
Pub: Gruner & Jahr USA Publishing
Description: Two business partners grapple over who's entitled to what; plus ways to update a business plan.

29794 ■ **"The Authority of Ideas"** in *Harvard Business Review* **(Vol. 81, No. 8, August 2003, pp. 144)**
Pub: Harvard Business School Press
Ed: Lawrence Summers. **Description:** How good ideas are, and how fast a company can find/implement will be a significant factor in the company's earnings. Business can gain insight into managing this asset by looking at research universities.

29795 ■ **"Auto Consolidation Likely to Speed Up"** in *Crain's Detroit Business* **(Vol. 23, January 8, 2007, No. 2, pp. 15)**
Pub: Crain Communications Inc. - Detroit
Ed: Brent Snaveley. **Description:** Further consolidations and bankruptcies in the auto supply business are increasing. Industry is in the midst of a major restructuring.

29796 ■ **"Avis Ford Owner Passes Reins of Dealerships to Sons"** in *Crain's Detroit Business* **(Vol. 21, January 24, 2005, No. 4, pp. 19)**
Pub: Crain Communications Inc. - Detroit
Ed: Brent Snavely. **Description:** Walter Douglas Sr. has passed the day-to-day management over to his son Mark Douglas and is helping son Edmund Douglas to open a Jaguar-Land Rover dealership in Sylvania. Ohio. Walter Douglas will remain Avis' chairman.

29797 ■ **"B2B Exchanges Survival Guide"** in *Internet World* **(Vol. 7, No. 1, January 15, 2001, pp. 48)**
Pub: Mecklermedia Corporation
Ed: Ruhan Memishi. **Description:** It is estimated that the use and success of business-to-business exchanges will continue to grow and that by 2004 seven percent of the global economy could be fueled by these exchanges. An outline of the important steps a company needs to take in order to succeed in e-commerce.

29798 ■ **"Banker Right on the Money with Financial Powerhouse"** in *Houston Business Journal* **(Vol. 34, No. 13, August 8, 2003, pp. 2)**
Pub: American City Business Journals
Ed: Jim Greer. **Description:** The growing success of Southwest Bank of Texas is presented. Topics include market development, strategic planning, and management styles.

29799 ■ **"Be Prepared"** in *Harvard Business Review* **(Vol. 81, No. 11, November 2003, pp. 20)**
Pub: Harvard Business School Press
Ed: Leonard Fuld. **Description:** Utilization of business intelligence tools can aid companies in planning for the future.

29800 ■ **"Beating Strong"** in *Houston Business Journal* **(Vol. 34, No. 14, August 15, 2003, pp. 17)**
Pub: American City Business Journals
Ed: Allison Wollam. **Description:** Profile of American Medical Equipment, Houston, Texas, as it prepares to move into new facilities in the Texas Medical Center. Topics include business planning, management styles, and medical equipment product lines.

29801 ■ **"Biz Leaders Want Quick Action on SBT replacement"** in *Crain's Detroit Business* **(Vol. 22, November 13, 2006, No. 46, pp. 1)**
Pub: Crain Communications Inc. - Detroit
Ed: Amy Lane. **Description:** Business leaders are looking to Lansing for quick action to alleviate the business uncertainty quickly. Recent election results should clear the way for action between the governor and the House to act decisively to establish the new business tax structure to replace the single business tax.

29802 ■ **"Biz Plan Competition"** in *Black Enterprise* **(Vol. 34, No. 2, September 2003, pp. 12)**
Pub: Earl Graves Publishing Co.
Description: Blackenterprise.com is offering $1,000 or a copy of Business Plan Pro software to winners of its best business plan competition.

29803 ■ **"Bloopers & Blunders"** in *Small Business Opportunities* **(Vol. 16, November 2004, No. 6, pp. 72)**
Pub: Harris Publications Inc.
Ed: Joanne G. Sujansky. **Description:** Seven mistakes made by company leaders and ways to avoid them are explained: lack of trust, failure to shape and share vision, unclear expectations, insufficient modeling of desire behaviors, too little partnering, failure to retain top talent, and too little celebration of success.

29804 ■ *Blue Ocean Strategy: How to Create Uncontested Market Space and Make Competition Irrelevant*
Pub: Harvard Business School Publishing
Ed: W. Chan Kim. **Released:** January 2005. **Price:** $29.95.

29805 ■ **"Brainstorming"** in *Small Business Opportunities* **(Vol. 12, No. 2, March 2000, pp. 120)**
Pub: Harris Publications, Inc.
Ed: Robert Spiegel. **Description:** Six ways to generate big ideas for small business are presented, including inviting friends, professionals, and relatives to brainstorm.

29806 ■ **"Brainy Is As Brainy Does"** in *BlackEnterprise* **(Vol. 31, No. 7, February 2001, pp. 134)**
Pub: Earl Graves Publishing Co.
Ed: Mary H. McCormack. **Description:** The article suggests that sometimes putting too much thought in a business plan can actually undermine the company. Tips to keep small business on track are presented.

29807 ■ **"Building an Innovation Factory"** in *Harvard Business Review* **(Vol. 78, No. 3, May 2000, pp. 157)**
Pub: Harvard Business School Publishing Corp.
Ed: Andrew Hargadon, Robert I. Sutton. **Description:** The best innovators are not lone geniuses. They are people who can take an idea that's obvious in one context and apply it in a not-so-obvious way to a different context. The best companies have learned to systematize that process.

29808 ■ **"Business planning practices in small companies: survey results"** in *Journal of Business Forecasting* **(Vol. 19, No. 2, Summer 2000, pp. 3)**
Pub: Graceway Publishing Co., Inc.
Ed: Surendra S. Singhvi. **Description:** The results of a survey on the planning practices of 24 small businesses in the U.S. are presented, with focus on the reasons for planning, the length of time the plan is for and if it has been successful.

29809 ■ **"Business Intelligence" in** *E-business Advisor* **(Vol. 18, No. 8, August 2000, pp. 22)**
Pub: Advisor Media, Inc.
Ed: Claudia Imhoff. **Description:** A description of the concept of Corporate Information Factory (CIF), which provides a high-level guide to developing an e-business plan.

29810 ■ *A Business of My Own? 21 Steps to Successfully Starting and Running a Small Business*
Pub: Enfield Publishing
Ed: Marjorie Cleveland Fisher. **Released:** January 2005. **Price:** $24.95. **Description:** New ideas to start or grow a small business, including ideas for writing business plans with examples, adopting a business structure, and setting goals and objectives.

29811 ■ **"Business Plan Basics" in** *Crain's Detroit Business* **(Vol. 19, No. 49, December 8, 2003, pp. 12)**
Pub: Crain Communications Inc., Detroit
Description: Four questions to consider when writing a business plan are offered by the U.S. Small Business Association.

29812 ■ *Business Plan Handbook*
Pub: Rector Press, Ltd.
Released: 1995. **Price:** $115.00.

29813 ■ **"Business Plan Helps Set Goals, Draw Investors" in** *Crain's Detroit Business* **(Vol. 22, November 20, 2006, No. 47, pp. 18)**
Pub: Crain Communications Inc. - Detroit
Ed: Sheena Harrison. **Description:** Financial investors always require a business plan before they will commit to investment in new or expanding ventures. Sound business planning and management also include a good business plan with time phased measurable goals to monitor progress and indicate need for adjustments of the plan.

29814 ■ *The Business Planner: A Complete Guide to Raising Finances for Your Business*
Pub: Butterworth-Heinemann
Ed: Iain Maitland. **Released:** 1992. **Price:** $36.95 (paper). **Description:** Covers the writing of business plans, including writing the commercial section, drawing up the financial section, adding the appendices, and putting it together.

29815 ■ *Business Planning in Four Steps & a Leap*
Pub: Northern Economic Initiatives Corp.
Ed: Scott Sporte. **Released:** 1995. **Price:** $24.00.

29816 ■ *The Business Planning Guide: Creating a Plan for Success in Your Own Business*
Pub: Upstart Publishing Co., Inc.
Ed: David H. Bangs, Jr. **Released:** Sixth edition, 1992. **Price:** $22.95 (paper). **Description:** Provides information for creating a business plan and financial proposal. Includes sample business plan, checklists, and worksheets.

29817 ■ *Business Plans Handbook*
Pub: Thomson Gale
Contact: Deborah J. Baker
Released: Annual, latest edition 10, published July, 2004; new edition expected November, 2005. **Price:** $160. **Publication Includes:** 20-25 actual business plans, including executive summaries, market profiles and analyses, product and production information, and management, personnel, and financial data. Appendix includes a sample business plan template; two fictional plans; listings of small business associations, consultants, venture capital/finance companies; SBA and SBDC offices; SCORE offices; small business term glossary; and a cumulative index.

29818 ■ *Business Plans Kit for Dummies, 2nd Edition*
Pub: John Wiley and Sons Inc.
Released: September 2005.

29819 ■ *Business Plans to Manage Day-to-Day Operations: Real-life Results for Small Business Owners and Operators*
Pub: John Wiley & Sons, Inc.
Ed: Christopher R. Malburg. **Released:** 1993. **Price:** $39.95 (paper). **Description:** Guide to long-term business planning, covering goal setting, financial planning, and motivation.

29820 ■ *Business Plans That Work: A Guide for Small Business*
Pub: McGraw-Hill Companies
Ed: Jeffry A. Timmons, Stephen Spinelli, Andrew Zacharakis. **Released:** May 2004. **Price:** $16.95 (US), $24.95 (Canadian). **Description:** Guide for preparing a small business plan along with an analysis of potential business opportunities.

29821 ■ *Business Plans That Work for Your Small Business*
Pub: C C H, Inc.
Ed: Susan M. Jacksacke. **Released:** 1998. **Price:** $19.95.

29822 ■ **"Calling in Sick" in** *Fortune* **(Vol. 152, August 8, 2005, No. 3, pp. 96H)**
Pub: Time Inc.
Ed: Kevin Kelly. **Description:** The importance for a company to have a backup plan in the event the CEO is too ill to report to work is stressed.

29823 ■ **"Case Study. Anatomy of a Business Decision" in** *Inc.* **(September 2006, pp. 47-48, 50)**
Pub: Gruner & Jahr USA Publishing
Ed: Phaedra Hise. **Description:** Review and analysis of a downmarketing strategy is detailed in this article. Small business growth typically moves to higher end customers that are increasingly difficult to please. If it isn't cost effective, going back to the basics of the success of the growth may expand the business and increase profitability.

29824 ■ **"Caught in the 'Net" in** *Journal of Business Strategies* **(Vol. 21, No. 5, September 2000, pp. 4)**
Pub: Center for Business and Economic Research
Description: The Internet has become an obsession that's affecting the global economy, businesses of all sizes, and lifestyles. Statistical data included.

29825 ■ **"Chicago" in** *Entrepreneur* **(Vol. 28, No. 17, July 2000, pp. 142)**
Pub: Entrepreneur Media Inc.
Ed: Cynthia E. Griffin. **Description:** DePaul University students offer free services to small business start-ups.

29826 ■ **"Co-opting Customer Competence" in** *Harvard Business Review* **(Vol. 78, No. 1, January 2000, pp. 79)**
Pub: Harvard Business School Publishing Corp.
Ed: C.K. Prahalad, Venkatram Ramaswamy. **Description:** In the new economy, companies must incorporate customer experience into their business models, in ways up until now were untapped. The challenges for doing that are addressed.

29827 ■ *The Company We Keep: Reinventing Small Business for People, Community, and Place*
Pub: Chelsea Green Publishing
Ed: John Abrams. **Released:** May 2005. **Price:** $27.50 (US); $31.50 (Canadian). **Description:** The new business trend in social entrepreneurship as a business plan enables small business owners to meet the triple bottom line of profits for people (employees and owners), community, and the environment.

29828 ■ *The Complete Book of Business Plans: Simple Steps to Writing a Powerful Business Plan*
Pub: Sourcebooks, Inc.
Ed: Joseph A. Covello and Brian J. Hazelgreen. **Released:** 1994. **Price:** $29.95; $19.95 (paper). **Description:** Part of the Small Business series.

29829 ■ *Computer Applications for Business Planning: A Practical Hands-On Text*
Pub: Tangent Publishing
Ed: Andrew J. Batchelor. **Released:** 1995. **Price:** $55.00.

29830 ■ **"Computer-Assisted Consulting" in** *Hispanic Business* **(Vol. 24, No. 5, May 2002, pp. 50)**
Pub: Hispanic Business Inc.
Ed: Roger Harris. **Description:** BRS software products will help business consultants to become more successful. The software packages offer solid advice on everything from writing business and marketing plans to development of pricing and sales strategies.

29831 ■ **"Compuware to Buy Back up to 34 Million Shares" in** *Crain's Detroit Business* **(Vol. 22, December 18, 2006, No. 51 pp. 4)**
Pub: Crain Communications Inc. - Detroit
Ed: Tom Henderson. **Description:** Stock buyback approved by board for 34 million shares of company stock. This will start immediately and continue through June 30.Also approved was the purchase of $200M in additional stock at management's discretion with no timing specified.

29832 ■ **"Construction Delayed on Tower Project" in** *Bellingham Business Journal* **(December 2006, pp. A1)**
Pub: Sun News Inc.
Ed: Heidi Schiller. **Description:** Bay View Tower developers have postponed breaking ground until spring on 2007 on their condominium project. Due to overbuilding in cities across the country financers are apprehensive about the housing market.

29833 ■ *Contingency Planning and Disaster Recovery: A Small Business Guide*
Pub: John Wiley & Sons, Incorporated
Ed: Donna R. Childs. **Released:** October 2002. **Price:** $59.00. **Description:** Four keys issues to help a business plan for disasters include: preparation, response, recovery, and sample IT solutions in order to secure property and confidential data files and covers the six types of disasters: human errors, equipment failures, third-party failures, environmental hazards, fires and other structural catastrophes, and terrorism and sabotage.

29834 ■ **"Control Your Content" in** *E-business Advisor* **(Vol. 18, No. 10, October 2000, pp. 42)**
Pub: Advisor Media, Inc.
Ed: Andre McMillan. **Description:** As a business Web site grows, so does the need for managing the content of the site. This article explores content management and how it differs from document management. The author strongly urges that before products are purchased, there be an advisory board for continuing management and operational committees that can help determine need.

29835 ■ **"Corporate Diversity" in** *Hispanic Business* **(January/February 2005, pp. 50, 52, 54)**
Pub: Hispanic Business
Description: In response to the ever-changing consumer and workforce demographics, corporate diversity means creating programs that integrate with core company values and accountability measures. Ways to measure the return on investment for these practices are presented.

29836 ■ *Crafting the Successful Business Plan*
Pub: Prentice Hall
Ed: Erik Hyypia. **Released:** 1992. **Price:** $12.95 (paper).

29837 ■ **"Craig Rosebraugh's War" in** *Inc.* **(October 2005, pp. 136-139, 141-142)**
Pub: Inc. Magazine
Ed: Bill Donahue. **Description:** Profile of Craig Rosebraugh, owner of an Oregon restaurant. Rosebraugh discusses his determination to make his business a success and is already working on his exit strategy.

29838 ■ "Creative Control" in *Washington Business Journal* **(Vol. 22, No. 9, July 4, 2003, pp. 16)**
Pub: Washington Business Journal
Ed: Chris Silva. **Description:** Management style, marketing and strategic planning of Washington, DC-based Healthcare Ventures LLC is discussed.

29839 ■ "Crisis Mode" in *Entrepreneur* **(Vol. 32, December 2004, No. 12, pp. 32)**
Pub: Entrepreneur Media Inc.
Ed: Geoff Williams. **Description:** When a personal crisis hits a small business owner, experts recommend giving full disclosure to employees.

29840 ■ "A Crisis Waiting to Happen?" in *My Business* **(August/September 2002, pp. 16)**
Pub: My Business Magazine
Ed: Ivan Sylvester. **Description:** The top 15 crises that can happen in a business are listed, along with seven steps to prepare for and manage any small business crisis.

29841 ■ "Curtain Call?" in *Entrepreneur* **(Vol. 32, October 2004, No. 10, pp. 72)**
Pub: Entrepreneur Media Inc.
Ed: David Worrell. **Description:** Profile of Chuck Hawkes, executive coach with DreamsFulfilled in Charlotte, North Carolina. Hawkes helps executives and entrepreneurs discover what they want to do after selling a business or retiring.

29842 ■ "Cutting to the chase" in *Crain's Detroit Business* **(Vol. 18, No. 32, Aug. 12, 2002, pp. 11)**
Pub: Crain Communications Inc., Detroit
Ed: Laura Bailey. **Description:** Tips are offered for small businesses to put in place a business plan that determines expenses in order to set pricing for products and services.

29843 ■ "Cutting the Corporate Purse Strings" in *Ingram's* **(Vol. 27, No. 7, July 2001, pp. 20)**
Pub: Show Me Publishing, Inc.
Description: Techniques and management theory for women small business owners is outlined. Topics include clarifying objectives, refining business ideas, research ideas, budgeting, concept testing, developing a business plan, and securing financing.

29844 ■ "Cutting Costs Without Drawing Blood" in *Harvard Business Review* **(Vol. 78, No. 5, September-October 2000, pp. 155)**
Pub: Harvard Business School Publishing Corp.
Ed: Tom Copeland. **Description:** The author argues that cutting costs need not be a bloody process involving massive layoffs. Reduction of capital expenditures is another way with a solid evaluation of small ticket budget items particularly effective. The article contains graphs.

29845 ■ "Debt End Ahead? Don't Let Debt Put Your Business in a Tight Spot-Learn How to Use Leverage to Your Advantage" in *Entrepreneur* **(Vol.32)**
Pub: Entrepreneur Media Inc.
Ed: David Worrell. **Description:** Entrepreneurs must be wary of using family homes, credit cards and personal guarantees as leverage for solving financial business problems.

29846 ■ "Deciding Which Shares to Share" in *Inc.* **(May 2000, pp. 171)**
Pub: The Goldhirsh Group
Description: An overview for small businesses thinking of selling shares of their company.

29847 ■ "Detroit Free Press Small Business Column" in *Detroit Free Press* **(June 20, 2005)**
Pub: Knight-Ridder/Tribune Business News
Ed: Carol Cain. **Description:** According to the Small Business Administration, four out of five new small businesses fail within five years of starting up. Minesh Baxi offers a listing of the ten most common mistakes small and mid-size companies make.

29848 ■ "Develop a Mission Statement for Your Business" in *Home Business* **(Vol. 13, January/February 2006, No. 1, pp. 64)**
Pub: Home Business Magazine
Ed: Steven D. Strauss. **Description:** Mission statements help keep a business on track and the best time for an entrepreneur to reflect on a business is during the New Year period.

29849 ■ "Differentiating Legal Issues by Business Type" in *Journal of Small Business Management* **(Vol. 44, October 2006, No. 4, pp. 563)**
Pub: Blackwell Publishing, Inc.
Ed: Sandra Malach; Peter Robinson; Tannis Radcliffe. **Description:** A fundamental issue when forming a business and its strategic operation is developing legal strategies to better protect the assets of the business and entrepreneur. An analysis of data indicated that certain legal issues are relevant to specific types of new ventures while certain legal issues are important to all new ventures. Depending on the category of business, the relevancy of individual legal issues will vary. Statistical data included.

29850 ■ "Do you have a well-designed organization?" in *Harvard Business Review* **(Vol. 80, No. 3, March 2002, pp. 117)**
Pub: Harvard Business School Press
Ed: Michael Goold, Andrew Campbell. **Description:** An executive's job of creating a new organizational design and the nine tests of organization design, which can either evaluate an existing structure or create a new one are discussed.

29851 ■ "Don't Go Changing" in *Entrepreneur* **(Vol. 28, No. 3, March 2000, pp. 122)**
Pub: Entrepreneur Media Inc.
Description: Limiting change in business is the topic of this discussion.

29852 ■ "Don't Just Dream—Plan" in *Black Enterprise* **(Vol. 35, January 2005, No. 6, pp. 97)**
Pub: Earl G. Graves Publishing Co. Inc.
Ed: Alfred A. Edmond Jr. **Description:** Principles of goal-setting and techniques used to achieve goals are discussed, including a listing of books designed to motivate individuals and would-be entrepreneurs.

29853 ■ *Dreams with a Deadline: How to Turn a Strategy for Tomorrow Into a Plan for Today*
Pub: Pearson Education, Limited
Ed: Jacques Horovitz; Anne-Valerie Ohlsson-Corboz. **Released:** November 2006. **Price:** $54.00. **Description:** Tips for successful entrepreneurship are covered.

29854 ■ "Elements of a business plan" in *Crain's Detroit Business* **(Vol. 16, No. 50, December 11, 2000, pp. E-2)**
Pub: Crain Communications, Inc.
Description: The elements of a comprehensive business plan are appraised.

29855 ■ *Emergency Procedures for the Small Business & Shop: A Guide & Disaster Plan Framework*
Pub: Ritchie Unlimited Publications
Ed: Ralph W. Ritchie. **Released:** 1997. **Price:** $19.95.

29856 ■ "Engineering a Structure that's Lasted Generations" in *San Francisco Business Times* **(Vol. 17, No. 48, July 4, 2003, pp. 18)**
Pub: American City Business Journals
Ed: James Temple. **Description:** History of Bechtel and how it has managed to survive four generations, while many family-owned businesses fail after the third generation, is examined.

29857 ■ "Entrepreneur Column" in *Entrepreneur* **(August 11, 2005)**
Pub: Entrepreneur Media Inc.
Ed: Tim Berry. **Description:** Effective business plans include at least three vital pro forma statements based on three main accounting statements. These statements are outlined in detail.

29858 ■ "Entrepreneur Column" in *Entrepreneur.com* **(Jan. 2006)**
Pub: Entrepreneur Media Inc.
Ed: Kim Gordon. **Description:** A step-by-step guide to successfully grow a small business while staying ahead of inflation.

29859 ■ *The Entrepreneur's Guide to Building a Better Business Plan: A Step-by-Step Approach*
Pub: John Wiley & Sons, Inc.
Ed: Harold J. McLaughlin. **Released:** 1992. **Price:** $85.00 (paper).

29860 ■ *The Entrepreneur's Guide to Preparing a Winning Business Plan and Raising Venture Capital*
Pub: Prentice Hall
Ed: Keith W. Schilit. **Released:** 1990. **Price:** $32.95 (paper). **Description:** Workbook for developing a business plan. Includes appendix of state-by-state listings of venture capital firms.

29861 ■ *The Entrepreneur's Strategy Guide: Ten Keys for Achieving Marketplace Leadership*
Pub: Greenwood Publishing Group, Incorporated
Ed: Tom Cannon. **Released:** September 2006. **Price:** $44.95. **Description:** Ten principles of marketplace leadership are explored. The book provides a plan for small businesses, including diagnostics, checklists, and other interactive exercises to study both external and internal principles.

29862 ■ *Entrepreneurship*
Pub: McGraw-Hill Higher Education
Ed: Robert D. Hisrich; Michael P. Peters; Dean A. Shepherd. **Released:** October 2006. **Price:** $106.50. **Description:** Advice is offered to entrepreneurs in formulating, planning, and implementing a business plan.

29863 ■ *Entrepreneurship: A Process Perspective*
Pub: Thomson South-Western
Ed: Robert A. Baron; Scott A. Shane. **Released:** February 2007. **Price:** $137.95. **Description:** Entrepreneurial process covering team building, finances, business plan, legal issues, marketing, growth and exit strategies.

29864 ■ "Environmental and Ownership Characteristics of Small Businesses and their Impact on Development" in *Journal of Small Business Management*
Pub: West Virginia University
Ed: William B. Gartner, Subodh Bhat. **Description:** This article explores the relationship between the characteristics of a small business's location (crime, neighborhood appearance, and transportation accessibility) and a small business owner's expectations of future firm growth.

29865 ■ *The Ernst and Young Business Plan Guide*
Pub: John Wiley & Sons, Inc.
Ed: Compiled by Ernst & Young staff. **Released:** Second edition, 1993. **Price:** $49.95; $14.95 (paper). **Description:** Guide to researching, writing, and presenting a winning business plan. Explores planning and development, using a sample plan; discussion ranges from defining a business conceptually to developing strategy and understanding the financial rewards that strategy will produce.

29866 ■ *Essentials of Entrepreneurship and Small Business Management*
Pub: Prentice Hall PTR
Ed: Thomas W. Zimmerer; Norman M. Scarborough; Doug Wilson. **Released:** February 2007. **Price:** $106.67. **Description:** New venture creation and the knowledge required to start a new business are shared. The challenges of entrepreneurship, business plans, marketing, e-commerce, and financial considerations are explored.

29867 ■ "An Executive Risk Handbook" in *Fortune* (Vol. 152, October 3, 2005, No. 7, pp. 69)
Pub: Time Inc.
Ed: Geoffrey Colvin. **Description:** Contingency planning for natural disasters is covered. Understanding corporate risk has companies adopting risk management programs that include the appointment of a chief risk officer.

29868 ■ "Executive Training" in *Black Enterprise* (Vol. 37, December 2006, No. 5, pp. 70)
Pub: Earl G. Graves Publishing Co. Inc.
Ed: Marcia A. Reed-Woodard. **Description:** Roy N. Gundy Jr. was preparing to introduce a new strategic plan within his division and understood that his plan may fail if not executed properly. He discusses his experience in the Wharton School's executive education workshop Implementing Strategy, at the University of Pennsylvania and gives tips on putting strategy into action.

29869 ■ "Exit Strategy" in *Inc.* (October 2005, pp. 80-81)
Pub: Inc. Magazine
Ed: Allen P. Roberts Jr. **Description:** Mike Canney sold his defense company for $42.5 million. Canney now spends his time driving race cars.

29870 ■ "The Extra Mile: Going Above and Beyond May Be Your Winning Business Strategy" in *Entrepreneur* (Vol. 32, No. 1, January 2004, pp. 27)
Pub: Entrepreneur Media, Inc.
Ed: Mark Henricks. **Description:** Profile of Todd Skinner, motivation speaker and author of Beyond the Summit: Setting and Surpassing Extraordinary Business Goals.

29871 ■ "A family affair" in *Black Enterprise* (Vol. 33, No. 3, October 2002, pp. 154)
Pub: Earl Graves Publishing Co.
Ed: George Alexander. **Description:** The largest part of American wealth lies in the family-owned businesses that make up 80-90 percent of all business enterprises in North America. The importance of a succession plan for family-owned firms is discussed. A survey by the Family Firm Institute of 800 family-owned businesses showed that insufficient estate planning, failure to prepare for the inevitable transition, and lack of funds to pay estate taxes are the leading causes for most family-owned business failures.

29872 ■ "Family-Biz Circle" in *Business Week Online* (February 17, 2006)
Pub: McGraw-Hill Companies
Description: Entrepreneurs must develop a business plan to pass the family-owned business to the next generation. Consultants at the Family Business Institute can help small business owners construct a plan designed for their small business.

29873 ■ *Faster Company: Building the World's Nuttiest, Turn-on-a-Dime, Home-Grown, Billion Dollar Business*
Pub: John Wiley & Sons, Inc.
Ed: Patrick Kelly and John Case. **Released:** 1998. **Price:** $24.95.

29874 ■ "Faurecia May Buy to Grow, but Only If It Fits Plan" in *Crain's Detroit Business* (Vol.23, January 15, 2007, No.3, pp. 1)
Pub: Crain Communications Inc. - Detroit
Ed: Brent Snaveley. **Description:** European interiors supplier may enter domestic supply market by purchasing acquisitions in U.S. market if they match their business plan. A global giant, but currently not in the U.S. domestic market, Faurecia was invited in by General Motors since nearly 40 percent of domestic competition is bankrupt or struggling financially.

29875 ■ "Fear Factor" in *Entrepreneur.com* (Vol. 34, February 2006, No. 2, pp. 144)
Pub: Entrepreneur Media Inc.
Ed: Robert Kiyosaki. **Description:** Fear can keep an entrepreneur from growing a company to its full potential. It is important to have a clear, big vision for your business.

29876 ■ "Fever Pitch: Pull Out Your Thermometers, 'Cause Things Are Heating Up!" in *Entrepreneur* (Vol. 32, December 2004, No. 12, pp. 72)
Pub: Entrepreneur Media Inc.
Ed: Karen Axelton, Steve Cooper, Amanda C. Kooser, April Y. Pennington, Karen E. Spaeder, Laura Tiffany, Nichole L. Torres, Sara Wilson, Natalia Olenicoff, Rebecca Villaneda, Jeri Yoshida. **Description:** Newest trends, hottest markets and business ideas for small companies in 2005 are presented, including the use of borrowing a business model.

29877 ■ "Fields of Dreams" in *Crain's New York Business* (Vol. 23, January 1, 2007, No. 1, pp. 3)
Pub: Crain Communications, Inc.
Description: Overview of planned 18,000 seat basketball arena for the Nets is part of a controversial multi-use development in Brooklyn.

29878 ■ "Financing First Steps" in *Entrepreneur* (Vol. 33, October 2005, No. 10, pp. 94)
Pub: Entrepreneur Media Inc.
Ed: Nichole L. Torres. **Description:** The importance of writing a good business plan before seeking startup financing is stressed.

29879 ■ "Finding a Niche Within a Niche" in *Black Enterprise* (Vol. 36, February 2006, No. 7, pp. 93)
Pub: Earl G. Graves Publishing Co. Inc.
Ed: Layton Turner. **Description:** Choosing a niche is a good strategy for businesses with fewer resources than larger competitors.

29880 ■ "Fire in the belly" in *WorkingWoman* (Vol. 25, No. 2, February 2000, pp. 48)
Pub: Lang Communications Inc.
Ed: Russell Wild. **Description:** Successful women give secrets for staying motivated, including patting oneself on the back and taking the long view.

29881 ■ "For Small Businesses, Future of Biz Taxes Will be Crucial" in *Crain's Detroit Business* (Vol. 22, November 27, 2006, No. 48, pp. 15)
Pub: Crain Communications Inc. - Detroit
Ed: Sheena Harrison. **Description:** With the cancellation of the Single Business Tax, small businesses will be central in the talks and discussions on changes necessary to replace revenue losses. Also of concern is the difficulty of hiring qualified employees with affordable wages and benefits.

29882 ■ "Ford Motor Company Is Sponsoring the Ford BEST Business Plan Contest..." in *Black Enterprise* (Vol. 34, No. 7, February 2004)
Pub: Earl Graves Publishing Co.
Ed: Carolyn M. Brown. **Description:** Ford Motor Company, in association with SCORE "Counselors to America's Small Business" and Diversity Inc., is sponsoring the BEST Business Plan contest. Prospective entrepreneurs submit a business plan to be reviewed by counselors at SCORE. The grand prize of $50,000 and two runner-up prizes of $25,000 each, will help the winners startup their businesses.

29883 ■ "From Wish to Goal" in *Black Enterprise* (Vol. 35, January 2005, No. 6, pp. 97)
Pub: Earl G. Graves Publishing Co. Inc.
Description: Gadsden's tips for setting and achieving goals are listed. These goals will help inspiring entrepreneurs follow their vision. Rev. Nathaniel Gadsden founded the Writers Wordshop, a not-for-profit agency that helps poets develop their writing skills.

29884 ■ "The Fruitful Flaws of Strategy Metaphors" in *Harvard Business Review* (Vol. 81, No. 9, September 2003, pp. 86)
Pub: Harvard Business School Press
Ed: Tihamer von Ghyczy. **Description:** Companies looking for parallels outside of business need to look at differences, not similarities.

29885 ■ "Fuel Efficiency Becomes Grail" in *Crain's Detroit Business* (Vol. 23, January 8, 2007, No. 2, pp. 11)
Pub: Crain Communications Inc. - Detroit
Ed: Brent Snaveley. **Description:** Fuel efficiency, quality, and safety are primary customer concerns for vehicle and subsystems development. Many suppliers are shifting capital expenditures toward smaller fuel efficient vehicles.

29886 ■ "Get In Sync: To Spark Business Growth, Follow the Leader In Your Industry" in *Entrepreneur* (Vol. 31, No. 10, October 2003, pp. 38)
Pub: Entrepreneur Media, Inc.
Ed: David Newton. **Description:** Coordinating business strategy with a wide range of administrative and managerial processes is a major key to growing a company.

29887 ■ *Getting Ready*
Pub: Self-Counsel Press, Inc.
Ed: Dan Kennedy. **Released:** 1991. **Price:** $16.95 (paper). **Description:** Guide to preparing a business plan, deciding the best small business to start, and determining your own strengths and weaknesses.

29888 ■ "Go For the Gold" in *Entrepreneur* (Vol. 32, October 2004, No. 10, pp. 68)
Pub: Entrepreneur Media Inc.
Ed: David Worrell. **Description:** Planning for the day an entrepreneur will sell their business is critical. Growth potential is key when determining a company's worth.

29889 ■ "Goal Tending" in *Small Business Opportunities* (Fall 2005)
Pub: Harris Publications Inc.
Ed: Lonnie Pacelli. **Description:** Five tips to help a small business owner face challenges are outlined, including a good business plan.

29890 ■ "Got Game?" in *Entrepreneur* (Vol. 32, October 2004, No. 10, pp. 95)
Pub: Entrepreneur Media Inc.
Ed: Chris Penttila. **Description:** Entrepreneurial introspection is a growing trend in small business. Strategic plans implemented inside a company help give employees and managers a realistic look at the business and its goals.

29891 ■ "Groups Push Forward on Mass Transit Proposals" in *Crain's Detroit Business* (Vol. 23, February 5, 2007, No. 6, pp. 1)
Pub: Crain Communications Inc. - Detroit
Ed: Andrew Dietderich. **Description:** Fast transit study proposals from Ann Arbor to Detroit are being backed by Amtrak and state and local governments. Three year trial to be undertaken patterned after other successful systems in other cities.

29892 ■ "Guide Advises Would-Be Entrepreneurs" in *Marketing to Women* (Vol. 20, January 2007, No. 1, pp. 8)
Pub: EPM Communications, Inc.
Description: Smart Women and Small Business: How to Make the Leap from Corporate Careers to the Right Small Enterprise, a new how-to guide book for women looking to leave their corporate careers and join the entrepreneurial workforce, offers tips on getting loans, starting a business, working with business partners, and finding and closing the right deals.

29893 ■ "Hand Off" in *My Business* (October/November 2002, pp. 26-31, 33)
Pub: My Business Magazine
Ed: Shannon Scully. **Description:** Information for passing a family-owned business down to children is presented. According to the Small Business Administration, more than 70 percent of family businesses don't survive through a second generation, and only about 10 percent will survive a third.

29894 ■ "Handing it over: businesses need a plan for passing the torch" in *Black Enterprise* (Vol. 32, No. 8, March 2002, pp. 50)

Pub: Earl Graves Publishing Co.

Ed: Alan Hughes. **Description:** A listing of things a sole proprietor should consider before having a succession plan drawn up for a business is presented. According to the U.S. Census Bureau, nearly 90 percent of the 823,500 African American-owned businesses in 1997, were sole proprietorships.

29895 ■ "Hard Sell" in *Entrepreneur* (Vol. 28, No. 11, November 2000, pp. 40)

Pub: Entrepreneur Media Inc.

Ed: Doug Hood. **Description:** A business owners asks for advice in liquidating assets after closing his business.

29896 ■ "Having trouble with your strategy? Then map it" in *Harvard Business Review* (Vol. 78, No. 5, September-October 2000, pp. 167)

Pub: Harvard Business School Publishing Corp.

Ed: David P., Robert S., Norton Kaplan. **Description:** The authors demonstrate with graphs the advantages of using strategy maps. Such maps, by giving a visual representation of a company's objectives, help employees see more clearly their place in the plan.

29897 ■ "Healthy Transition" in *Success* (Vol. 47, No. 2, June 2000, pp. 52)

Pub: Success Publishing, Inc.

Ed: Karen Fuller. **Description:** A profile of Molina Health Care showing how the lack of a succession plan could have cost the family their business. Instead, revenue is expected to reach $300 million this year.

29898 ■ "Heir Raising" in *Entrepreneur* (Vol. 33, February 2005, No. 2, pp. 82)

Pub: Entrepreneur Media Inc.

Ed: Sara Wilson. **Description:** Profile of Dave and Ellie Woodruff who purchased a Meineke Car Care Center franchise for their son, Michael. The couple has plans to open two more franchises for their two daughters. The family discusses their business plans intended to secure their children's future.

29899 ■ "How to Plan as a Small Scale Business Owner" in *Journal of Small Business Management* (Vol. 38, No. 38, April 2000, pp. 1)

Pub: West Virginia University

Ed: Michael Frese, Marco van Gelderen, Michael Ombach. **Description:** This study takes a psychological approach to investigate the process characteristics of action strategies used by small business owners; these strategy characteristics are then related to the firms' success. The objective of the research is to deepen the understanding of how strategies are used and how the owner's strategy-relevant behavior is related to the business' success.

29900 ■ *How to Prepare and Present a Business Plan*

Pub: Simon & Schuster, Inc.

Ed: Joseph R. Mancuso. **Released:** 1992. **Price:** $15.00 (paper), **Description:** Includes plans based on actual businesses.

29901 ■ *How to Prepare a Results-Driven Business Plan*

Pub: AMACOM

Ed: Gregory J. Massarella, Patrick D. Zorsch, Daniel D. Jacobson, and Marc J. Rittenhouse. **Released:** 1993. **Price:** $65.00 ($58.50 for AMA members). **Description:** Workbook covering how to write a business plan. Contains examples, worksheets, a computer template, and an appendix with a completed business plan.

29902 ■ "How to Prepare Your Home Business for a Natural Disaster" in *Home Business* (Vol. 13, January/February 2006, No. 1, pp. 82, 84)

Pub: Home Business Magazine

Ed: William J. Lynott. **Description:** Keys to reducing risk in the event of a natural disaster include a prepa-

ration and recovery plan, off-site back-up records, insurance coverage, backup power sources, and customer contact.

29903 ■ *How to Really Create a Successful Business Plan*

Pub: Inc. Publishing

Ed: David E. Gumpert. **Released:** Revised edition, 1994. **Price:** $19.95. **Description:** Guide to preparing a business plan.

29904 ■ *How to Start a Home-Based Craft Business, 5th Edition*

Pub: Globe Pequot Press

Ed: Kenn Oberrecht. **Released:** July 2007. **Price:** $18.95. **Description:** Advice for starting a home-based craft business is given, including sources for finding supplies on the Internet, writing a business plan, publicity, zoning ordinances, and more.

29905 ■ "How To Assemble a Board of Directors" in *Inc.* (October 1, 2004)

Pub: Inc. Magazine

Ed: Nicole Gull. **Description:** Advice for putting together a Board of Directors that will best serve a small business is given.

29906 ■ "How To Groom a No. 2 (Or, Gasp, a Successor)" in *Inc.* (October 1, 2004)

Pub: Inc. Magazine

Ed: Patrick J. Sauer. **Description:** Ways to handle choosing a successor, or second-in-command are examined, along with the decision to stay within the company or to look outside.

29907 ■ "The How-Tos of Writing a Strong Business Plan" in *Atlanta Business Chronicle* (Vol. 24, No. 9, August 3, 2001, pp. 6B)

Pub: American City Business Journals Inc.

Ed: Dan Kolber. **Description:** The recommendations for writing a strong business plan include knowing your audience, finding your voice and editing. Additionally, it is recommended that a business plan be brief and interesting and that naming the plan something other than a plan might be a good idea.

29908 ■ "How to Vitalize a Home-Based Operation" in *Home Business* (Vol. 12, October 2005, No. 5, pp. 32, 34, 95)

Pub: Home Business Magazine

Ed: Alan Stewart. **Description:** In order to be successful, home-based business owners must continue to refine and improve operations, be ready to take on new projects, new customers and new marketplaces.

29909 ■ "How We're Fixing Up Tyco" in *Harvard Business Review* (Vol. 81, No. 12, December 2003, pp. 96)

Pub: Harvard Business School Press

Ed: Eric M. Pillmore. **Description:** An overview is presented on the management reform processes underway at Tyco International Ltd. These include aligning corporate divisions with company objectives, launching a new yearly bonus plan, capping stock-option-equity awards and severance payments, and adjusting director compensations.

29910 ■ "How to Win Big and Get Ahead Fast" in *Inc.* (September 1, 2003)

Pub: Gruner & Jahr USA Publishing

Description: College business-plan contests offer competitors the chance to win money to launch a startup.

29911 ■ *How to Write a Business Plan*

Pub: NOLO

Ed: Mike McKeever. **Released:** January 2007. **Price:** $34.99. **Description:** Author, teacher and financial manager shows how to write an effective business plan. Examples and worksheets are included.

29912 ■ *How to Write a Business Plan 4.4*

Pub: Nolo Press

Ed: Mike McKeever edited by Peri Pakroo. **Released:** 4th ed. 1997. **Price:** $21.95.

29913 ■ *How to Write a Great Business Plan for Your Small Business in 60 Minutes or Less*

Pub: Atlantic Publishing

Ed: Sharon L. Fullen. **Released:** September 2005. **Price:** $39.95 includes CD-Rom. **Description:** A good business plan outlines goals and works as a company's resume to obtain funding, credit from suppliers, management of the operations and finances, promotion and marketing, and more.

29914 ■ *How to Write a Successful Business Plan: Step-by-Step Guide to Business Success*

Pub: Lewis & Renn Associates, Inc.

Ed: Jerre G. Lewis. **Released:** 1995. **Price:** $14.95.

29915 ■ *How to Write a Winning Business Plan*

Pub: Prentice Hall

Ed: Joseph Mancuso. **Released:** 1990. **Price:** $15.00 (paper).

29916 ■ "In care of emergency" in *Entrepreneur* (Vol. 31, No. 4, April 2003, pp. 58)

Pub: Entrepreneur Media Inc.

Ed: Daniel Tynan. **Description:** Lonnie Lehrer, CEO of Leros Point to Point, a New York City limousine service, tells how he saved his company in the aftermath of September 11, 2001.

29917 ■ "The Incredibly Unproductive Shareholder" in *Harvard Business Review* (Vol. 80, No. 1, January 2002, pp. 18)

Pub: Harvard Business School Press

Ed: Marjorie Kelly. **Description:** Stock-market investors' interests have often been put above that of the company, which has resulted in decisions that have been counterproductive.

29918 ■ "Ingram's Industry Outlook" in *Ingram's* (Vol. 29, No. 7, July 2003, pp. 73)

Pub: Show Me Publishing, Inc.

Description: Twenty-eight prominent attorneys met to discuss the role of law firms in the Kansas City, Missouri area.

29919 ■ "Inside Microsoft. Balancing Creativity and Discipline" in *Harvard Business Review* (Vol. 80, No. 1, January 2002, pp. 73)

Pub: Harvard Business School Press

Ed: Robert Herbold. **Description:** Microsoft's hands-off management approach began to interfere with productivity; this required rethinking the company, better integration of information, and general operations while maintaining the company's need for creative thinking.

29920 ■ "Inside Out" in *Houston Business Journal* (Vol. 34, No. 11, July 25, pp. 19)

Pub: American City Business Journals

Ed: Catherine Spaulding. **Description:** Profile of the design firm Batsche Design; topics include management style, business strategy, and competition.

29921 ■ *Instinct: Tapping Your Entrepreneurial DNA to Achieve Your Business Goals*

Pub: Warner Books, Incorporated

Ed: Mary H. Frakes; Thomas L. Harrison. **Released:** September 2006. **Price:** $15.99. **Description:** Research shows that entrepreneurs may attribute their success to genetics.

29922 ■ "It's Business...and Personal" in *Black Enterprise* (Vol. 34, July 2004, No. 12, pp. 38)

Pub: Earl G. Graves Publishing Co. Inc.

Ed: Aissatou Sidime. **Description:** Anthony Harris, owner of Popular Demand clothing store and Popular Demand Unisex Salon in Cleveland, Ohio, reports how he has formed a retirement savings account by investing in mutual funds and government bonds through a financial advisor who also helped Harris find personal medical coverage and life insurance.

29923 ■ "It's a Snap" in *Houston Business Journal* (Vol. 34, No. 18, September 12, 2003, pp. 17)
Pub: American City Business Journals
Ed: Allison Wollam. **Description:** Alvin Gee, owner of Alvin Gee Photography, has thrived during the economic downturn by leasing space to other businesses.

29924 ■ "It's The Business Model, Stupid!" in *Fortune* (Vol. 143, No. 1, January 8, 2001, pp. 54)
Pub: Time Inc.
Ed: Geoffrey Colvin. **Description:** An investigation into the reasons businesses fail. Fortune's Dot-Com Deathwatch is up to 135 failed companies in the past year, mostly startups with bad business models.

29925 ■ "Keep It Simple" in *Forbes* (Vol. 171, No. 2, January 20, 2003, pp. 108)
Pub: Forbes Magazine
Ed: John W. Rogers, Jr. **Description:** It is best to present a straightforward business plan in order to procure investments. Information about companies with clear missions, and straightforward business models is presented.

29926 ■ "Keep it Simple" in *Entrepreneur.com* (Vol. 34, February 2006, No. 2, pp. 60)
Pub: Entrepreneur Media Inc.
Ed: Chris Penttila. **Description:** Twenty-five tips for fine tuning a small business are outlined, focusing on technology, money, banking, taxes, credit and collection, accounting systems, mergers, management, and marketing ideas.

29927 ■ "The last thing you should do is panic" in *Fast Company* (May 2001, pp. 90)
Pub: Fast Company
Ed: William F. Miller. **Description:** Profile of William F. Miller, chairman of Borland Software Corporation and Sentius Corporation, and is president and CEO of emeritus of SRI International. Miller offers advice that during a slow economy small businesses should put resources into the strongest areas of the company.

29928 ■ *Launching New Ventures*
Pub: Upstart Publishing Co., Inc.
Released: 1995. **Price:** $63.95.

29929 ■ "Local Daily Papers Hit Hard by Declining Circulation" in *Crain's Detroit Business* (Vol. 22, December 4, 2006, No. 49, pp. 3)
Pub: Crain Communications Inc. - Detroit
Ed: Tom Henderson. **Description:** Subscription cancellations continue exceed lead national trend of declining reliance for information from printed sources. National and local statistics are included in this summary.

29930 ■ "Logged on; Moon Valley Furniture's New Owner Expanding Biz." in *Crain's Detroit Business* (Vol. 23, January 29, 2007, No. 5, pp. 3)
Pub: Crain Communications Inc. - Detroit
Ed: Sheena Harrison. **Description:** New business oriented owner sees growth potential in rustic furniture market by aligning with log-home builders. Growth forecast to triple in the next five years.

29931 ■ "Man With a Plan" in *My Business* (December/January 2004, pp. 56)
Pub: My Business Magazine
Ed: N.C. Tognazzini. **Description:** Profile of a business owner who named his business plan Earl because he felt it was such an integral part of his success it deserved a name.

29932 ■ "Managing Creativity in a Progressive Home Business" in *Home Business* (Vol. 13, January/February 2006, No. 1, pp. 28, 30-31, 95)
Pub: Home Business Magazine
Ed: Alan Stewart. **Description:** Identification and solutions to solving home-based business issues is examined.

29933 ■ "Manufacturing Job Losses Hit Other Sectors" in *Crain's Detroit Business* (Vol. 22, November 20, 2006, No. 47, pp. 3)
Pub: Crain Communications Inc. - Detroit
Ed: Amy Lane. **Description:** Detroit area service industry job market is flat as a result of the decline in manufacturing job. Service sector jobs are still growing in the rest of the state, however.

29934 ■ *The Market Planning Guide: Creating a Plan to Successfully Market Your Business, Products or Service*
Pub: Upstart Publishing Co., Inc.
Ed: David H. Bangs. **Released:** 5th ed. 1998. **Price:** $22.95 (cloth).

29935 ■ "Methodology" in *Inc.* (May 2000, pp. 61)
Pub: The Goldhirsh Group
Ed: Stephen Adams. **Description:** A listing of the Inner City 100 and the qualifications used in their selection.

29936 ■ "Model behavior" in *Entrepreneur* (Vol. 30, No. 3, March 2002, pp. 68)
Pub: Entrepreneur Media Inc.
Ed: David Newton. **Description:** Raising money for a growing company has taken a turn back to basics, opportunity and market share are no longer enough to secure capital; the business model, once again, plays a major role.

29937 ■ "Mom and Pop Psychology" in *Inc.* (December 1, 2003)
Pub: Gruner & Jahr USA Publishing
Ed: Bobbie Gossage. **Description:** Every small business has a personality all its own. Ways to help find that out are presented.

29938 ■ "A More Perfect Business" in *Inc.* (August 1, 2003)
Pub: Gruner & Jahr USA Publishing
Ed: Matthew Fogel. **Description:** A family-business constitution could help direct a company through crisis and change. The constitution would consist of a statement of principles designed to guide issues of ownership, performance, accountability, and compensation, though would not be legally binding.

29939 ■ "NAIAS Spotlight Shines on Design" in *Crain's Detroit Business* (Vol. 23, January 1, 2007, No. 1, pp. 1)
Pub: Crain Communications Inc. - Detroit
Ed: Jennette Smith. **Description:** Differentiation in design and styling are getting the most attention at the Auto Show in Detroit this year. All brands are about equal in quality and reliability due to engineering advances, so differentiation in styling has moved back to the forefront. Industry cutbacks and layoffs have not affected the design areas.

29940 ■ "NCR Spinoff Hits Home" in *San Diego Business Journal* (Vol. 28, January 15, 2007, No. 3, pp. 38)
Pub: San Diego Business Journal Associates
Ed: Brad Graves. **Description:** NCR Corporation will spin off its Teradata Data Warehousing business to shareholders to help both companies focus on customer base, business strategy and operational needs.

29941 ■ "New Business on Champion Street Uncorks a New Trend" in *Bellingham Business Journal* (January 2007, pp. A4)
Pub: Sun News Inc.
Description: Overview of Whatcom Winemakers which has developed a fresh new concept for the wine industry, do-it-yourself winemaking. The winemaking shop is slated to open in February.

29942 ■ "New Site Gives Lipari Foods Room to Continue Growth" in *Crain's Detroit Business* (Vol. 23, January 8, 2007, No. 2, pp. 10)
Pub: Crain Communications Inc. - Detroit
Ed: Brent Snaveley. **Description:** New location doubles size of local wholesale food delivery service. Recent growth with expanded product offerings dictates larger warehouse requirements. Plans are to expand territory to surrounding states in the Midwest.

29943 ■ "The Next Generation. Planning Ahead" in *San Francisco Business Times* (Vol. 17, No. 48, July 4, 2003, pp. 15)
Pub: American City Business Journals
Ed: Jessica Materna. **Description:** Sugarbowl Baker, owned and operated by Andrew Ly, is an example of a family-owned business that is trying to buck the trend of effectively passing on the company to the next generation. A recent study by the University of Connecticut's Family Business Program has found that only 30 percent of such companies can achieve this goal, and only 10 percent can survive a third generation change of ownership. Family rivalries are the given reason for such high failure rates.

29944 ■ "No Slowdown Likely for Rising Health Costs" in *Crain's Detroit Business* (Vol. 22, November 27, 2006, No. 48, pp. 21)
Pub: Crain Communications Inc. - Detroit
Ed: Andrew Dietderich. **Description:** Double digit increases in health care are forecast for 2007. Health carriers say too many people who can afford to pay for medical treatment are leaving Michigan. This leaves a more indigent population behind. Governor is proposing assistance for access to universal health care.

29945 ■ "Note to Staff" in *My Business* (April/May 2004, pp. 44)
Pub: My Business Magazine
Ed: Lee Gimpel. **Description:** Small business owners should create a business manual for employees, allowing the owner time away from the company.

29946 ■ "On a Mission" in *Black Enterprise* (Vol. 34, No. 5, December 2003, pp. 50)
Pub: Earl Graves Publishing Co.
Ed: Alan Hughes. **Description:** Concepts to consider when creating a mission statement for a small company are highlighted.

29947 ■ "On the Radar" in *E-business Advisor* (Vol. 18, No. 4, April 2000, pp. 8)
Pub: Advisor Media, Inc.
Description: Several vendors have come up with products and services to help companies with e-business strategy. Bolero.net is aimed at helping multinational companies with international commerce. RadView Software's WebLoad Resource Manager and WebLoad Workstation electronic commerce software products are designed to test, analyze, and verify e-business applications. Other companies offering products and services are Primix Solutions, IBM and CyberTrust.

29948 ■ "On Your Mind" in *Forbes* (February 19, 2001, pp. 34)
Pub: Forbes Magazine
Ed: Katarzyna Moreno. **Description:** The pros and cons of using a personal name as the name of a business are investigated.

29949 ■ "One D's Big Challenge: Shaking Myopia" in *Crain's Detroit Business* (Vol. 22, November 20, 2006, No. 47, pp. 1)
Pub: Crain Communications Inc. - Detroit
Ed: Sherri Begin. **Description:** One D was formed to focus on what's good for the community or region and not just any one organization or community. Six groups have been formed with objectives to form six action plans to achieve the desired results and prioritize the resources.

29950 ■ *The One Page Business Plan: Start with a Vision, Build a Company!*
Pub: Rent.A.CFO
Ed: James T. Horan, Jr., edited by Rebecca S. Shaw, illustrated by Ruthie Petty, foreword by Tom Peters. **Released:** 1998. **Price:** $19.95.

29951 ■ "Opening Pitch: Developing a Business Plan" in *Crain's Detroit Business* (Vol. 19, No. 49, December 8, 2003, pp. 11)
Pub: Crain Communications Inc., Detroit
Ed: Mike Scott. **Description:** A good business plan should be kept up-to-date and shared with employees and lenders, in order to help small business owners understand their company.

29952 ■ "Openings Balance Closings" in *Crain's Detroit Business* **(Vol. 23, February 5, 2007, No. 6, pp. 23)**
Pub: Crain Communications Inc. - Detroit
Ed: Brent Snaveley. **Description:** Numerous restaurant closings are offset by new openings as the population and business shift away from the automotive based market in certain locations. Some businesses are relocating whereas others are closing entirely. New ones reflect new business and population concentrations.

29953 ■ "Plan to Avoid Confusion When Passing the Torch" in *Atlanta Business Chronicle* **(Vol. 23, No. 49, May 11, 2001, pp. 10B)**
Pub: American City Business Journals Inc.
Ed: James Lea. **Description:** Family-owned businesses must make careful plans for passing on of ownership and management, especially when divorce has complicated the family dynamics. Co-owners must also be aware that they will not necessarily want to retire at the same time, and offspring may or may not want to continue in the family business. The economics of multiple ownership can also be complicated, especially if a business cannot support two or more families.

29954 ■ "Plan a legacy for your business and your family" in *Black Enterprise* **(Vol. 33, No. 3, October 2002, pp. 104)**
Pub: Earl Graves Publishing Co.
Description: Case studies for small, family-owned business planning are presented, including business planning, estate planning, and financial security.

29955 ■ "Plan May Need Overhaul to Maintain Growth" in *Crain's Detroit Business* **(Vol. 21, January 17, 2005, No. 3, pp. 18)**
Pub: Crain Communications Inc. - Detroit
Ed: Sheena Harrison. **Description:** Quality Cable has seen growth since achieving ISO 9001: 2000 certification. The company produces medical cables. William Connors discussed the firm's plans for growth.

29956 ■ "Planned transition" in *Business First Columbus* **(Vol. 1)**
Pub: Business First Columbus, Inc.
Ed: Drew Bracken. **Description:** Profile of family-owned business, Velvet Ice Cream, and how, together with a consultant, developed a flexible transition plan for the firm.

29957 ■ *Planning for Business Owners & Professionals*
Pub: American College, The
Ed: Theodore T. Kurlowicz, James F. Ivers, John J. McFadden. **Released:** 1999. **Price:** $46.00

29958 ■ "Planning Your Exit Strategy: Three Ways To Go" in *My Business* **(October/ November 2003, pp. 30-35)**
Pub: My Business Magazine
Ed: Shannon Scully, Steve Becker. **Description:** Exit strategy plans help small businesses not only decide ways to get out of the company, but they also lay the groundwork for getting ahead. Profiles of small business owners and their exit strategies are investigated.

29959 ■ "Posecai's To Open" in *Mississippi Business Journal* **(Vol. 29, January 2007, No. 4, pp. 9)**
Pub: Venture Publications, Inc.
Ed: Wally Northway **Description:** Ted Posecai has purchased former home of The Willows Restaurant on Trailwood Drive in Greenville. Posecai plans to open a new upscale restaurant to be called Posecai's.

29960 ■ "The Power of Touch" in *Entrepreneur* **(Vol. 28, No. 9, September 2000, pp. 26)**
Pub: Entrepreneur Media Inc.
Ed: Watts Wacker. **Description:** The cost is nothing. The potential is limitless. The future of the "touch" economy is investigated.

29961 ■ "The Power of Your Reputation Equals Profits Can Be a Tangible Business Strategy" in *Black Enterprise* **(Vol. 35, August 2004, No. 1)**
Pub: Earl G. Graves Publishing Co. Inc.
Ed: **Description:** Ways a woman used her reputation to promote her graphic design business are outlined.

29962 ■ "Pre-Nups for Small Business" in *Black Enterprise* **(Vol. 30, No. 7, February 2000, pp. 65)**
Pub: Earl Graves Publishing Co.
Ed: Michael S. Mullman. **Description:** Plan your exit before you open the door. By writing a comprehensive shareholder agreement concerning such issues, shareholders simplify estate planning, reduce some of the risk and uncertainty inherent in any business and ensure an orderly continuation of their firm's work.

29963 ■ *Preparing a Successful Business Plan: A Practical Guide for Small Business*
Pub: Self-Counsel Press, Inc.
Ed: Rodger Touchie. **Released:** Second edition, 1993. **Price:** $14.95 (paper). **Description:** Book and worksheets focusing on how to prepare a business plan. A sample plan is included.

29964 ■ "Proquest's Slimdown Has Little Effect on Local Jobs" in *Crain's Detroit Business* **(Vol. 23, January 29, 2007, No. 5, pp. 13)**
Pub: Crain Communications Inc. - Detroit
Ed: Bill Shea. **Description:** Proquest's realignment of business objectives will shift the emphasis of its operations to Dallas, but will not result in significant local job losses. A merger between the spun-off Information and Learning unit and Cambridge Information Group has been formed to continue that business and lease the current Ann Arbor facilities.

29965 ■ "Protecting the Dream" in *Ingram's* **(Vol. 28, No. 5, May 2002, pp. 28)**
Pub: Show Me Publishing, Inc.
Ed: Cynthia Grimes. **Description:** Legal advice is given to protect small businesses from bankruptcy, lawyers, accounting, cash flow planning, employee benefits and estate planning.

29966 ■ "Prove Your Worth: Forget the Stock Market." in *Entrepreneur* **(Vol. 31, No. 7, July 2003, pp. 64)**
Pub: Entrepreneur Media, Inc.
Ed: Mark Henricks. **Description:** It is recommended that entrepreneurs invest in their own companies, rather than the stock market as a good investment.

29967 ■ "The Pump-and-Dump Economy" in *Wall Street Journal* **(Vol. 248, January 2007, No. 146, pp. A16)**
Pub: Dow Jones & Co. Inc.
Ed: Michael S. Malone **Description:** Start-ups are not aiming for an IPo in their business plan these days. Instead most newly-formed private companies set goals to be acquired by an established company which could lead to a radical shift in the U.S. economy.

29968 ■ "Push Your Plans Through" in *PC Computing* **(April 2000, pp. 100)**
Pub: Ziff-Davis Inc.
Ed: Jason Compton. **Description:** When a business wants to build a new corporate campus, but needs the approval of local zoning commissions, it is vital to put together a winning presentation showing the benefits of the project.

29969 ■ "The Quest for Resilience" in *Harvard Business Review* **(Vol. 81, No. 9, September 2003, pp. 52)**
Pub: Harvard Business School Press
Ed: Gary Hamel, Lisa Valikangas. **Description:** Once-successful billion dollar companies are now finding it increasingly difficult to return the same level of profits as in the past. Companies that continue to perform well are able to quickly adapt to changes often by introducing new and/or unconventional ideas.

29970 ■ "Quick Pick" in *Entrepreneur* **(Vol. 32, September 2004, No. 9, pp. 72)**
Pub: Entrepreneur Media Inc.
Description: Resources at CapturePlanning.com assist small companies to craft business proposals.

29971 ■ "R-E-S-P-E-C-T: The Changing Attitudes Toward Home-Based Businesses" in *My Business* **(October/November 2002, pp. 45)**
Pub: My Business Magazine
Ed: Mardy Fornes. **Description:** The importance of developing a strong business plan is key to running a successful home business. Some of the obstacles faced by those operating a home-based company are discussed.

29972 ■ "Reaching for less than the sky: as boldest fall, modest dreamers fly on" in *The New York Times* **(December 13, 2000, pp. D1, H1)**
Pub: The New York Times Company
Ed: Saul Hansell. **Description:** Lessons on what works and what doesn't work for Internet-based businesses.

29973 ■ "Ready, Set Strategize" in *Inc.* **(October 2005, pp. 41-42, 44, 46)**
Pub: Inc. Magazine
Ed: Darren Dahl. **Description:** Strategic planning can be time-consuming and labor-intensive. Advice for developing a new strategic business plan in 48 hours is outlined.

29974 ■ "The Real Deal" in *Entrepreneur* **(Vol. 33, January 2005, No. 1, pp. 28)**
Pub: Entrepreneur Media Inc.
Ed: Mark Henricks. **Description:** Review of the book, Confronting Reality: The Discipline of Getting Things Right, by Larry Bossidy and Ram Charan. The book offers a program to help entrepreneurs understand if their businesses are positioned to make profits and how to set the right future direction.

29975 ■ "Reality Check: Even the Best Execs Can Blow It When They Lose Tough" in *Entrepreneur* **(Vol. 31, No. 8, August 2003, pp. 25)**
Pub: Entrepreneur Media, Inc.
Ed: Mark Henricks. **Description:** Review of the book, "Why Smart Executives Fail", written by Sydney Finkelstein is presented. The author, a Dartmouth College professor, and his students studied over 50 commercial business failures and cite what went wrong to cause each company's demise.

29976 ■ "Reality Check" in *InfoWorld* **(Vol. 27, May 16, 2005, No. 20, pp. 22)**
Pub: InfoWorld Media Group, Inc.
Ed: Ephraim Schwartz. **Description:** Ways to create a data recovery plan after a natural disaster or an attack on the U.S. telecommunications infrastructure are discussed.

29977 ■ "Regrets" in *Inc.* **(October 17, 2000, pp. 98)**
Pub: The Goldhirsh Group
Description: Seven Inc. 500 company founders talk about their past business regrets.

29978 ■ "Remember Y2K threat at small firms? Forget it" in *Wall Street Journal* **(January 4, 2000, pp. A4)**
Pub: Dow Jones & Co., Inc.
Ed: Rodney Ho, Jeffrey A. Tannenbaum, and Dan Morse. **Description:** The article observes that small businesses appear unaffected by the Year 2000 computer transition.

29979 ■ "Reporter's Notebook; The Question of Private Equity" in *Crain's Detroit Business* **(Vol. 23, January 29, 2007, No. 5, pp. 11)**
Pub: Crain Communications Inc. - Detroit
Ed: Brent Snaveley. **Description:** Many smaller auto suppliers have been purchased by private equity and hedge funds. This may not be in the best interests of the supplier company or the customer, but may be necessary for survival.

29980 ■ "Required Reading" in *Entrepreneur* **(Vol. 31, No. 7, July 2003, pp. 32)**
Pub: Entrepreneur Media, Inc.
Ed: Aliza Pilar Sherman. **Description:** Reviews of books recommended for aspiring and current women entrepreneurs are shared. Many of these successful women are using the wisdom found in these books to improve business strategies.

29981 ■ "Restaurateur's Answer to Construction is a Second Eatery" in *Houston Business Journal* **(Vol. 34, No. 7, June 27, 2003, pp. 2A)**
Pub: American City Business Journals
Ed: Allison Wollam. **Description:** Restaurateur Youssef Nafaa kept his downtown restaurant open during light rail construction, while using his other restaurant for finance.

29982 ■ "The right place for a bottleneck" in *IIE Solutions* **(Vol. 34, No. 12, Dec. 2002, pp. 34)**
Pub: Institute of Industrial Engineers, Inc.
Ed: D. Bergin, Peter H. Davidoff, F.C. Weston, Jr. **Description:** Business planning for a microbrewery include capacity planning and constraints analysis. Simulation is a good tool for analyzing the impact of marginal changes in the physical composition of a microbrewery.

29983 ■ "Safeguard your financial legacy" in *BlackEnterprise* **(Vol. 32, No. 3, October 2001, pp. 75)**
Pub: Earl Graves Publishing Co.
Ed: Carolyn M. Brown. **Description:** In small business, the transferring of wealth requires solid tax and estate planning. The article lists safeguards to secure a family legacy. Ten steps to financial empowerment are included.

29984 ■ "Sales & Marketing: Why Advertise Anyway?" in *Ingram's* **(Vol. 27, No. 5, May 2001, pp. 28)**
Pub: Show Me Publishing, Inc.
Ed: Rob Pearcy. **Description:** Business plans need to include a marketing budget for advertising in order to be successful.

29985 ■ "Sample business plans" in *Crain's Detroit Business* **(Vol. 18, No. 49, December 9, 2002, pp. 17)**
Pub: Crain Communications Inc., Detroit
Description: The Small Business Administration provides examples of business plans for small companies.

29986 ■ "Screen Test" in *Success* **(Vol. 47, No. 1, January 2000, pp. 18)**
Pub: Success Publishing, Inc.
Ed: Jeffrey Adduci. **Description:** Four questions to determine if a business should go public.

29987 ■ "Second Time Around" in *Small Business Opportunities* **(Vol. 12, No. 3, May 2000, pp. 18)**
Pub: Harris Publications, Inc.
Ed: Sandy Weinberg. **Description:** Failing to properly plan for business succession can lead to a company's downfall. Three things that can help preserve a family business are examined.

29988 ■ "Self-Help for Small-Business Planners" in *Hispanic Business* **(Vol. 23, No. 11, November 2001, pp. 6)**
Pub: Hispanic Business Inc.
Ed: Jesus Chavarria. **Description:** After the September 11 terrorists attacks, many business planners looked to the federal government for direction, but business planners should not depend on politically motivated stimuli.

29989 ■ "Service Providers" in *Crain's Detroit Business* **(Vol. 16, No. 50, December 11, 2000, pp. E-13)**
Pub: Crain Communications, Inc.
Description: An extensive listing of services provided in Michigan that help startups and existing businesses get access to programs available to them.

29990 ■ "Shielding Your Home from Lawsuits" in *Hispanic Business* **(October 2003, pp. 90)**
Pub: Hispanic Business
Ed: Glen M. Terrones, Christopher Jarvis, David Mandell. **Description:** Tools to help small business owners protect their homes from lawsuits are given, including the formation of limited liability companies and family limited partnerships.

29991 ■ "Show Me the Money!" in *Success* **(Vol. 47, No. 6, November 2000, pp. 60)**
Pub: Success Publishing, Inc.
Ed: Phil Garfinkle. **Description:** Many companies are unable to secure financing, not because of a flaw in their business, but because of flaws in how they approach the capital formation process. A listing of some of the most common gaffes, and the steps entrepreneurs should take to avoid them.

29992 ■ "Sizing Up the Market" in *Boston Business Journal* **(Vol. 23, No. 25, July 25, 2003, pp. 3)**
Pub: American City Business Journals
Ed: Paul T. Gannon. **Description:** Profile of Boston, Massachusetts-based Shaw's Supermarkets Inc. Topics include competition, strategic business planning, and market development.

29993 ■ *Small Business: An Entrepreneur's Business Plan*
Pub: South-Western
Ed: J.D Ryan, Gail P. Hiduke. **Released:** June 2005. **Price:** $90.95. **Description:** Assistance in preparing a business plan that identifies opportunities and ways to target a customer market.

29994 ■ *Small Business Desk Reference*
Pub: Penguin Books (USA) Incorporated
Ed: Gene Marks. **Released:** December 2004. **Price:** $29.95 (US), $44.00 (Canadian). **Description:** Comprehensive guide for starting or running a successful small business, focusing on buying a business or franchise, writing a business plan, financial management, accounting, legal issues, human resources management, operations, marketing, sales, customer service, taxes, insurance, and ethics. Information for launching a restaurant, property management firm, retail outlet, consulting firm, and service business is included.

29995 ■ *Small Business Management*
Pub: John Wiley and Sons Inc.
Ed: Margaret Burlingame; Don Gulbrandsen; Richard M. Hodgetts; Donald F. Kuratko. **Released:** March 2007. **Price:** $44.95. **Description:** Tips for starting and running a successful small business are given, including advice on writing a business plan, financing, and the law.

29996 ■ "Small firms cut hires, inventory, capital plans" in *Wall Street Journal* **(November 15, 2000, pp. B17)**
Pub: Dow Jones & Co., Inc.
Description: A survey by the National Federation of Independent Business is examined.

29997 ■ "Smaller Shopping Centers Adopt Larger Style" in *Crain's Detroit Business* **(Vol. 22, December 4, 2006, No. 49, pp. 33)**
Pub: Crain Communications Inc. - Detroit
Ed: Anjali Fluker. **Description:** Fancy landscaping, public gathering areas, and more attractive architecture are no longer limited to only high-end restaurants and stores. Smaller proposed developments in the suburbs are including similar features to attract more customers and improve the shopping experience.

29998 ■ "Smart Answers" in *Business Week* **(No. 3694, August 14, 2000, pp. F14)**
Pub: McGraw-Hill, Inc.
Description: The owner of a family-owned travel agency asks how to legally close the business.

29999 ■ "Something Different" in *Entrepreneur* **(Vol. 28, No. 2, February 2000, pp. 40)**
Pub: Entrepreneur Media Inc.

Ed: Gwen Moran. **Description:** Most conventional marketing wisdom emphasizes the importance of setting goals for your business and working tirelessly toward them. However, it's sometimes just as important to change course when opportunities arise.

30000 ■ "Sonic Shifts Momentum With Purchase of 12 Car Dealerships" in *Houston Business Journal* **(Vol. 34, No. 14, August 15, 2003, pp. 7)**
Pub: American City Business Journals
Ed: Allison Wollam. **Description:** Sonic Automotive, Houston, Texas, acquired 12 Houston-area car dealerships. Topics include market share, market development, and strategic planning.

30001 ■ "Soup's On" in *San Francisco Business Times* **(Vol. 18, No. 2, August 22, 2003, pp. 38)**
Pub: American City Business Journals
Ed: Jessica Materna. **Description:** The growing success of the San Francisco Soup Company is examined, including sales levels, management styles, and long term plans.

30002 ■ "Speed Kills: Supply Chain Lessons From the War in Iraq" in *Harvard Business Review* **(Vol. 81, No. 11, November 2003, pp. 16)**
Pub: Harvard Business School Press
Ed: Diane K. Morales, Steve Geary. **Description:** The supply chain management system utilized by the U.S. during the Iraq War is discussed in context to business supply chain management.

30003 ■ "Spilling the Beans?" in *Entrepreneur* **(Vol. 31, No. 11, November 2003, pp. 136)**
Pub: Entrepreneur Media, Inc.
Ed: Romanus Wolter. **Description:** Secrets for entrepreneurs to share an idea while protecting their business is discussed. Tips for revealing only the most necessary details are listed.

30004 ■ "The Spirit of Independence" in *Home Office Computing* **(Vol. 18, No. 7, July 2000, pp. 42)**
Pub: Scholastic Inc.
Ed: Dave Johnson. **Description:** An annotated list of 76 home-office Web site-based resources is presented. Categories include the following: Application Service Providers (ASP), finding clients, your business, your business plans, communications, education, finance/banking, finance/taxes, government, home networking, home office, Internet, legal, marketing, mobile, online storage, online support, reference library, shipping, shopping, telecommuting, tools, travel, and bookmarks.

30005 ■ "Spring cleaning: tips to get fiscal house in order" in *Atlanta Business Chronicle* **(Vol. 23, No. 49, May 11, 2001, pp. 12B)**
Pub: American City Business Journals Inc.
Ed: Paula Moore. **Description:** Businesses need to periodically re-evaluate their business plan and their current position. Spring is a good time to do this, once taxes have been filed. Various options should also be explored, dealing with items such as selling the company, allocating resources, managing succession plans, etc. Business tax planning is also needed.

30006 ■ "Stakes High For Region as Big Three, UAW Sit Down to Talk." in *Crain's Detroit Business* **(Vol. 23, January 1, 2007, No. 1, pp. 3)**
Pub: Crain Communications Inc. - Detroit
Ed: Brent Snaveley. **Description:** Major conflicts loom as contracts expire and must be renegotiated. Financial distress of the North American auto industry is pitted against the declining Union membership and Jobs Bank program. Strikes are possible on these major issues.

30007 ■ "State Turns Up Heat on Green" in *Crain's Detroit Business* **(Vol. 22, November 20, 2006, No. 47, pp. 11)**
Pub: Crain Communications Inc. - Detroit

Ed: Amy Lane. **Description:** Governor Granholm has issued a directive that requires that all new construction and renovation for not only state agencies, but also that universities and colleges achieve the standards for green LEED (Leadership in Energy and Environmental Design) certification. It is hoped that this will spread into the private sector also.

30008 ■ "Stock of Ages" in *Entrepreneur* (Vol. 28, No. 8, August 2000, pp. 102)
Pub: Entrepreneur Media Inc.
Ed: Patricia Schiff Estess. **Description:** Every relative seems to want a piece of the family business pie, and the author offers insight in preventing your business from becoming a casualty of shareholding squabbles.

30009 ■ *Strategic Planning for New & Emerging Businesses*
Pub: Dearborn Trade
Ed: Fred Fly, Charles Stoner, Laurence Weinzimmer. **Released:** 1999. **Price:** $35.00

30010 ■ *Strategic Planning for the New & Small Business*
Pub: Upstart Publishing Co., Inc.
Ed: Fred L. Fry. **Released:** 1995. **Price:** $47.95 (paper).

30011 ■ "The Strategic Planning Payoff" in *Hispanic Business* (June 2002, pp. 66)
Pub: Hispanic Business
Ed: Scott Williams. **Description:** The importance of writing a good business plan is stressed. Eighty-two percent of Hispanic Business 500 companies have all written successful business plans.

30012 ■ *Strategic Planning for the Small Business: Situations, Weapons, Objectives & Tactics*
Pub: Adams Publishing
Ed: Craig Rice. **Released:** 1990. **Price:** $10.95 (paper).

30013 ■ *Strategizing, Disequilibrium, and Profit*
Pub: Stanford University Press
Ed: John A. Mathews. **Released:** June 2006. **Price:** $24.95. **Description:** Author proposes the use of a conceptual framework that is consistent with real economies instead of equilibrium-based foundations when creating a business strategy.

30014 ■ *The Successful Business Plan: Secrets and Strategies*
Pub: PSI Research
Ed: Rhonda M. Abrams. **Released:** 1993. **Price:** $49.95 (looseleaf binder); $21.95 (paper). **Description:** Provides information on preparing a business plan. Includes tips from venture capitalists and bankers, and a method of flow-through financials for fundable proposals. Contains sample plan and worksheets.

30015 ■ "Succession-Planning Do's and Don'ts: Who Will Take Over When You're Ready to Retire?" in *Journal of Accountancy* (February 2005)
Pub: American Institute of Certified Public Accountants
Ed: Anita Dennis. **Description:** Few certified public accounting firms have set a succession plan into place for selling their firm or passing it down to the next generation.

30016 ■ "Supplier Takes Care to Shield Business" in *Crain's Detroit Business* (Vol. 21, October 17, 2005, No. 43, pp. 33)
Pub: Crain Communications Inc. - Detroit
Description: Rcik Hecker, owner of Eifel Inc. is taking steps to protect his mold-making company after Delphi Corporation filed for Chapter 11 bankruptcy.

30017 ■ "Take It to the Bank" in *Washington Business Journal* (Vol. 22, No. 15, August 15, 2003, pp. 3)
Pub: Washington Business Journal
Ed: Tim Mazzucca. **Description:** Profile of Washington's newest bank, Congressional Bank, examining management goals and plans, including long term planning, market development, and management styles.

30018 ■ "A tale of 25 Cities" in *Entrepreneur* (Vol. 28, No. 10, October 2000, pp. 86)
Pub: Entrepreneur Media Inc.
Ed: Mark Henricks. **Description:** A listing of the cities in the top 10 large U.S. metropolitan areas in Entrepreneur and Dun & Bradstreet's Seventh Annual Ranking of the Best Cities in the Nation for Entrepreneurship.

30019 ■ "Tap into Expert Input" in *Black Enterprise* (Vol. 30, No. 12, July 2000, pp. 47)
Pub: Earl Graves Publishing Co.
Ed: Craig Owen White. **Description:** Learn how a board of advisors can benefit your firm with regard to employment policies, insurance coverage and strategic alliances.

30020 ■ "Taxing Concerns" in *Small Business Opportunities* (Vol. 12, No. 2, March 2000, pp. 98)
Pub: Harris Publications, Inc.
Description: By being pro-active about taxes, small businesses can fine-tune outcomes, anticipate cash flow needs, and reduce accountant's fees.

30021 ■ "Tee Off Online" in *Black Enterprise* (Vol. 37, January 2007, No. 6, pp. 52)
Pub: Earl G. Graves Publishing Co. Inc.
Ed: James C. Johnson. **Description:** The E-Com Resource Center is one of many resources that are available for those interested in starting an e-commerce business. One of the first steps is to create a business plan, of which there are free samples available at BPlans.com.

30022 ■ "Tell me no secrets" in *Entrepreneur* (Vol. 31, No. 5, May 2003, pp. 48)
Pub: Entrepreneur Media Inc.
Ed: David Worrell. **Description:** The topic of nondisclosure agreements is discussed in the context of venture capital as well as other business negotiations.

30023 ■ "The Individual Investor And The Power Of Research" in *Wall Street Journal* (Vol. 248, December 2006, No. 142, pp. S1)
Pub: Dow Jones & Co. Inc.
Ed: Associated Press **Description:** Profile of UBS Wealth Management Research (WMR). WMR crafts strategic, actionable investment for UBS investor clients and their financial advisors. Statistical data included.

30024 ■ "Think Ahead" in *Entrepreneur* (Vol. 32, October 2004, No. 10, pp. 40)
Pub: Entrepreneur Media Inc.
Ed: Mark Henricks. **Description:** Review of Seeing What's Next, written by Clayton M. Christensen, Scott D. Anthony, and Erik A. Roth. The book shows entrepreneurs ways to spot upcoming disruptive innovations that could threaten a company's success. A three-step process for predicting industry change is presented.

30025 ■ "Tips for Tough Transitions" in *Business Week Online* (February 16, 2006)
Pub: McGraw-Hill Companies
Description: Options are offered to family members not interested in continuing a family business include selling the business or working with an investment firm.

30026 ■ "To Achieve It, Write It Down" in *Black Enterprise* (Vol. 35, January 2005, No. 6, pp. 96)
Pub: Earl G. Graves Publishing Co. Inc.
Ed: Marcia A. Wade. **Description:** The Small Business Administration recommends that entrepreneurs write down their visions and goals and offers a Website designed to give information for starting a new business. Rev. Nathaniel Gadsden, founder of the Writers Wordshop, suggests writing a business plan before embarking on a new career path.

30027 ■ "To L.L.C. or not to L.L.C.? That can be sticky question" in *Crain's Detroit Business* (Vol. 18, No. 49, December 9, 2002, pp. 14)
Pub: Crain Communications Inc., Detroit
Ed: Laura Bailey. **Description:** Important issues to be considered by all entrepreneurs regarding planning the structure of a new or existing small business are examined.

30028 ■ "To Manage Growth, Embrace Change" in *Ingram's* (Vol. 29, No. 7, July 2003, pp. 24)
Pub: Show Me Publishing, Inc.
Ed: Bob Gould. **Description:** Guidance for companies looking to grow and retain the corporate vision while tapping into new talents is given.

30029 ■ *The Total Business Plan: How to Write, Rewrite, and Revise*
Pub: John Wiley & Sons, Inc.
Ed: Patrick D. O'Hara. **Released:** 1994, second edition. **Price:** $49.95. **Description:** A step-by-step book for writing a business plan. Shows how to modify and tailor a business plan using spread sheet analysis, a word processor, and computer graphics. Available on diskette.

30030 ■ "Transforming Life, Transforming Business: The Life-Science Revolution" in *Harvard Business Review* (Vol. 78, No. 2, March 2000, pp. 96)
Pub: Harvard Business School Publishing Corp.
Ed: Juan Enriquez, Ray A. Goldberg. **Description:** Advances in genetic research are setting off an industrial convergence that will have profound implications for the global economy. Farmers, computer companies, drug makers, chemical processors, and health care providers will all be drawn into the new life-science industry. This article will help show how companies can change the way they think about their businesses in order to make a successful transition.

30031 ■ "Two Marketing Firms Called Momentum Was One Too Many" in *Inc.* (Volume 27, June 2005, No. 6, pp. 41-42)
Pub: Inc. Magazine
Ed: Nicole Gull. **Description:** Brad Nierenberg discusses the risks he took when changing his business name from Momentum Marketing to Red Peg. The article also examines the way the firm marketed its new name.

30032 ■ "The Ultimate Business Plan" in *Success* (Vol. 47, No. 1, January 2000, pp. 44)
Pub: Success Publishing, Inc.
Ed: C.J. Prince. **Description:** Miles Spencer, co-founder of MoneyHunt Properties in Norwalk, Connecticut, and a member of the venture fund Capital Express, advises no one write your business plan but you. Included are informative tips including: The Executive Summary, Management: Who's Running This Thing?, Marketing, Financials, and Your Tone.

30033 ■ *Ultimate Guide to Buying or Selling Your Business*
Pub: Entrepreneur Press
Ed: Ira N. Nottonson. **Released:** September 2004. **Price:** $24.95 (US), $35.95 (Canadian). **Description:** Proven strategies to evaluate, negotiate, and buy or sell a small business. Franchise and family business succession planning is included.

30034 ■ "Understanding Women is Key to Biz Success, Author Says" in *Crain's Detroit Business* (Vol. 22, November 20, 2006, No. 47, pp. 6)
Pub: Crain Communications Inc. - Detroit
Ed: Bill Shea. **Description:** Successful companies recognize that women make 80% of all buying decisions. Author also has advice for women-owned businesses with trend and specifics provided.

30035 ■ "Upfront: Be Flexible or Fold" in *My Business* (June/July 2002, pp. 13-14)
Pub: My Business Magazine
Ed: Karen E. Klein. **Description:** Sometimes a small firm needs to steer away from original business plans

in order to grow. Martha C. de al Torre, Hispanic Business Woman of the Year 2000, tells how she learned to be flexible and creative with her business plan.

30036 ■ "Waterfront, Airport on Top of List For Port" in *Bellingham Business Journal* **(January 2007, pp. B5)**
Pub: Sun News Inc.
Ed: Dan Hiestand. **Description:** New Whatcom redevelopment for the former Georgia-Pacific waterfront property is in the works. The city and port have been working to create a cohesive plan for the site. Sixty-eight percent of the property leaves ownership in the public's hands.

30037 ■ "Welcome to the Valley of the Damned.Com" in *Fortune* **(Vol. 143, No. 1, January 8, 2001, pp. 52)**
Pub: Time Inc.
Description: A listing of the 135 dot-coms that went bankrupt or shut down operations in 2000.

30038 ■ *What Self-Made Millionaires Really Think, Know and Do: A Straight-Talking Guide to Business Success and Personal Riches*
Pub: John Wiley & Sons, Incorporated
Ed: Richard Dobbins; Barrie Pettman. **Released:** September 2006. **Price:** $24.95. **Description:** Guide for understanding the concepts of entrepreneurial success; the book offers insight into bringing an idea into reality, marketing, time management, leadership skills, and setting clear goals.

30039 ■ "What's your real cost of capital?" in *Harvard Business Review* **(Vol. 80, No. 10, October 2002, pp. 114)**
Pub: Harvard Business School Press
Ed: James J. McNulty. **Description:** The article suggests that corporate capital asset pricing models are flawed and provides a new analysis technique.

30040 ■ "What's in a Domain Name?" in *Home Office Computing* **(Vol. 18, No. 8, August 2000, pp. 81)**
Pub: Scholastic Inc.
Ed: William Van Winkle. **Description:** The task of selecting the right domain name is a critical one for a small business. The first step in the process is to settle on a name that is appropriate for the business, then searching the various domain registration sites to determine if the name is still available. Alternative strategies using Web services to select a domain name are also discussed.

30041 ■ "What's In a Name?" in *Inc.* **(July 1, 2004)**
Pub: Inc. Magazine
Ed: Bobbie Gossage. **Description:** Choosing a company or brand name is critical to success. Ways to get the name your small company deserves are outlined.

30042 ■ "What's Your Problem?" in *Entrepreneur* **(Vol. 31, No. 9, September 2003, pp. 106)**
Pub: Entrepreneur Media, Inc.
Description: Registering a business name varies from state to state. It is recommended to log onto the state's Web site to find the requirements.

30043 ■ "When it's time to retire, who will mind the gay-owned store?" in *Wall Street Journal* **(February 16, 2000, pp. B1)**
Pub: Dow Jones & Co., Inc.
Ed: Pui-Wing Tam. **Description:** Tours run by Michael Parkin and Frederick Rappart are described.

30044 ■ "Where Are You Going?" in *My Business* **(April/May 2003, pp. 46)**
Pub: My Business Magazine
Ed: Karen J. Bannan. **Description:** Business visions require identifying a target market, as well as the services and products a small business intends to supply.

30045 ■ "Where to Find Business Answers; Advice and Education" in *Crain's New York Business* **(Vol. 22, November 13, 2006, No. 46, pp. 24)**
Pub: Crain Communications, Inc.
Description: Listing of organizations and agencies that provide training, financial and managerial advice, and technical expertise to current or would-be business owners.

30046 ■ "Who's the Boss? Business isn't a democracy" in *Fortune* **(Vol. 141, No. 5, March 6, 2000, pp. 432A+)**
Pub: Time Inc.
Description: Every company needs an absolute ruler. This article helps you decide if you have what it takes to be a leader.

30047 ■ "Who's Next? Smart Moves" in *Entrepreneur* **(Vol. 30, No. 3, March 2002, pp. 77)**
Pub: Entrepreneur Media Inc.
Ed: Mark Henricks. **Description:** The importance of having a plan for succession is stressed for all businesses.

30048 ■ "Who's No. 1?" in *Entrepreneur* **(Vol. 32, December 2004, No. 12, pp. 26)**
Pub: Entrepreneur Media Inc.
Ed: Judith Potwora. **Description:** According to experts, city rankings are targeted to large corporations, small business owners should choose location based on how well-suited an area is to a particular product or service.

30049 ■ "Why Good Projects Fail Anyway" in *Harvard Business Review* **(Vol. 81, No. 9, September 2003, pp. 109)**
Pub: Harvard Business School Press
Ed: Nadim F. Matta; Ronald N. Ashkenas. **Description:** Suggestions for designing projects, including business plans that have a greater chance of success than most are provided.

30050 ■ "Why Hard-Nosed Executives Should Care About Management Theory" in *Harvard Business Review* **(Vol. 81, No. 9, September 2003, pp. 66)**
Pub: Harvard Business School Press
Ed: Clayton M. Christensen, Michael E. Raynor. **Description:** Often, business executives use generic business plans that are in vogue at the moment; creating a sound business theory, as described, is more likely to provide the desired goals.

30051 ■ "Why business models matter" in *Harvard Business Review* **(Vol. 80, No. 5, May 2002, pp. 86)**
Pub: Harvard Business School Press
Ed: Joan Magretta. **Description:** The concepts of business models and strategy are clarified; the business model is a story which explains how an enterprise works, it complements strategy which deals with competition.

30052 ■ "Worst-case scenario" in *Entrepreneur* **(Vol. 30, No. 2, February 2)**
Pub: Entrepreneur Media Inc.
Ed: Chris Penttila. **Description:** Tips that may save employees lives in a crisis are examined.

30053 ■ "Writing a Business Plan" in *Crain's Detroit Business* **(Vol. 15, No. 50, December 13, 1999, pp. E-7)**
Pub: Crain Communications, Inc.
Description: A concise outline for writing a business plan is described.

30054 ■ *Writing a Convincing Business Plan*
Pub: Barron's Educational Series, Inc.
Ed: Art DeThomas. **Released:** 1995.

30055 ■ *Your First Business Plan: Learn the Critical Steps to Writing a Winning Business Plan*
Pub: Sourcebooks, Inc.
Ed: Joseph A. Covello. **Released:** 1995. **Price:** $12.95 (paper).

30056 ■ "Your space is the place" in *Fast Company* **(May 2001, pp. 60)**
Pub: Fast Company
Ed: Alison Wellner. **Description:** According to Stephen Roulac, founder and CEO of the Roulac Group Inc., a consulting firm based in San Rafael, California that specializes in real estate, states that people are now selecting where they want to live, then seeking employment, whereas in the past it was the opposite.

TRADE PERIODICALS

30057 ■ *Enrich!*
Pub: National Chamber of Commerce for Women
Contact: Jay Orson, Ad.Mgr.
Ed: R. Wright, Editor. **Released:** Bimonthly. **Price:** $96. **Description:** Strives to assist readers on business-plan, career-path, and pay-comparison goals.

VIDEOCASSETTES/ AUDIOCASSETTES

30058 ■ *Managing the Emerging Company*
Leslie T. McClure
PO Box 1223
Pebble Beach, CA 93953
Ph:(831)647-0680
Fax: (831)647-0682
Released: 1997. **Price:** $990.00. **Description:** Ten-volume set deals with the functions of developing and running a business. **Availability:** VHS.

30059 ■ *Product Strategy: All the Right Moves*
RMI Media
1365 N. Winchester
Olathe, KS 66061
Ph:(913)768-1696
Fax: (913)768-0184
Co. E-mail: actmedia@act.org
URL: http://www.rmimedia.com
Released: 1991. **Price:** $89.95. **Description:** Presents a case study of Carushka, a dance and exercise wear manufacturer, to demonstrate successful methods for increasing product use and customers; finding new uses for existing products; and broadening the product appeal to old and new markets. **Availability:** VHS.

CONSULTANTS

30060 ■ Ameriwest Business Consultants Inc.
PO Box 26266
Colorado Springs, CO 80936
Ph:(719)380-7096
Fax: (719)380-7096
Co. E-mail: email@abchelp.com
URL: http://www.abchelp.com

E-mail: email@abchelp.com
Scope: Specializes in assisting start-up businesses and those with sales of 5 million dollars or less and/or those who have 50 employees or less. Services and products offered include written business plans; do-it-yourself business plan kits; business valuations; do-it-yourself business start-up kits; written loan packages; do-it-yourself loan packaging guides; business analysis; do-it-yourself financial projections software; do-it-yourself complete financial analysis; web site development assistance; general consulting.

30061 ■ Beacon Management Group Inc.
1000 W McNab Rd.
Pompano Beach, FL 33069
Ph:(954)782-1119
Free: 800-771-8721
Fax: (954)969-2566
Co. E-mail: md@beaconmgmt.com
URL: http://www.beaconmgmt.com

E-mail: md@beaconmgmt.com
Scope: Provides entrepreneurial companies with managerial and financial expertise. Services include strategic and business planning; corporate finance; franchise development services; information management; turnaround management and consulting; and joint venture, strategic alliances and acquisition services, including due diligence, market intelligence, targeted searches, valuation, negotiation, and deal structure. Provides assistance for financially-troubled companies, not-for-profits and the public sector

30062 ■ Biomedical Management Resources
PO Box 521125
Salt Lake City, UT 84152-1125
Ph:(801)272-4668
Fax: (801)277-3290
Co. E-mail: SeniorManagement@
  BiomedicalManagement.com
URL: http://www.biomedicalmanagement.com

E-mail: SeniorManagement@
  BiomedicalManagement.com
Scope: Provides business development, interim management, and executive search services. Assists companies in strategic alliances, corporate partnering, business acquisition. Demonstrated success in identifying recruiting, and placing key managers in difficult to hire positions.

30063 ■ BPT Consulting Associates Ltd.
12 Parmenter Rd., Ste. B6
Londonderry, NH 03053
Ph:(603)437-8484
Co. E-mail: bptcons@tiac.net
URL: http://www.bptconsulting.com

E-mail: bptcons@tiac.net
Scope: Provides management consulting expertise and resources to cross-industry clients with services for: Business Management consulting, People/Human Resources Transition and Training programs, and a full cadre of multi-disciplined Technology Computer experts. Virtual consultants with expertise in e-commerce, supply chain management, organizational development, and business application development consulting. **Seminars:** Business: MRPII, DRPII, JIT/TQC. Business Requirements Analysis, Small Business Start-Up, Strategic Planning. People: Team Building, Performance Evaluation, Career Transition and Counseling Seminars. Technology: User Training for Customized Software, Internet, Full array of application development, i.e., C, Java, website development. **Special Services:** Provides a full array of computer and related user training services. Resources include application developers, database developers and managers, project management experts for a full array of industries (manufacturing, software, defense, healthcare, pharmaceutical, and small business).

30064 ■ Bran Management Services Inc.
7116 Lupton Dr., Ste. 100
Dallas, TX 75225-1735
Ph:(214)739-2340
Fax: (214)739-2360
Scope: Offers management consulting services to companies in manufacturing, distribution and services to help them cope with growth and change. Helps small businesses create and identify product strategies. Services include developing international business opportunities; turnaround management; sales and marketing development; business planning; acquisitions and mergers.

30065 ■ Business Development Group Inc.
220 E Huron, Ste. 250
Ann Arbor, MI 48104
Ph:(248)552-0821
Fax: (248)552-1924
Co. E-mail: info@busdevgroup.com
URL: http://www.busdevgroup.com

E-mail: info@busdevgroup.com
Scope: Consulting firm expertise in leadership development; strategic thinking; organizational transforma-

tion; team-based work systems; organizational learning; rapid change; knowledge management; competitive intelligence; crisis management; merger and acquisition integration; product integration and new product development. **Publications:** "Navigating in the Sea of Change," Competitive Intelligence Review Journal; "The Influence of Cultural Aspects of Strategic Information, Analysis, and Delivery"; "What Leadership Needs From Competitive Intelligence Professionals," Journal of Association for Global and Strategic Information. **Seminars:** Process of Self-Design for the Evolving Organization; Large System Change Intervention; Self Assessment and the Transformational Process; The Knowledge Exchange - Shared Practices Workshop.

30066 ■ Business Resource Software Inc.
2013 Wells Branch Pky., Ste. 206
Austin, TX 78728
Ph:(512)251-7541
Free: 800-423-1228
Fax: (512)251-4401
Co. E-mail: sales@brs-inc.com
URL: http://www.brs-inc.com

E-mail: sales@brs-inc.com
Scope: Provides 'Expert System' software for strategy, planning and marketing in business planning and operation with the emerging personal computer technologies of spreadsheet and word processing to create a product which would assist in the development and evaluation of marketing strategies. **Special Services:** Insight for Sales Strategy applies expert system technology to analysis of complex sales. Plan Write Expert Edition is a business plan software.

30067 ■ BusinessPlanWorld.com
PO Box 1322
Mississauga, ON, Canada L4Y 4B6
Ph:(709)643-8544
Co. E-mail: theboss@businessplanworld.com
URL: http://www.businessplanworld.com

E-mail: theboss@businessplanworld.com
Scope: Services include business plan creation, complete website development services and educational software development. **Publications:** How to open a Bed and Breakfast; How to open a Bookstore; How to open a Restaurant; How to open a Youth Centre; How to open a Rough Collie Kennel; How to open a Video Store; How to open a Confectionary.

30068 ■ Elizabeth Capen
27 E 95th St.
New York, NY 10128-0805
Ph:(212)427-7654
Fax: (212)876-3190
Scope: Focuses on strategic marketing planning and positioning. Identifies effective marketing tools; plans and reviews advertising and collateral materials; writes business plans; and performs secondary research and competitive analysis. Industries served: services, small businesses, and entrepreneurial ventures in northeastern and middle Atlantic regions. **Seminars:** Handling Issues of Growth; Using Published Information as a Marketing Tool.

30069 ■ CAST Management Consultants Inc.
700 S Flower St., Ste. 1900
Los Angeles, CA 90017
Ph:(213)614-8066
Fax: (213)614-0760
Co. E-mail: info@castconsultants.com
URL: http://www.castconsultants.com

E-mail: info@castconsultants.com
Scope: Management consultants active in the following areas: business strategy formulation, market analysis, business plan formulation, competitive advantage analysis, information technology development, organizational development, financial analysis and planning, strategic planning, entry strategies into new markets, implementation of strategy, international strategic planning, international marketing, and international joint venture. Serves private industries as well as government agencies. **Seminars:** Seminar on Overseas Growth Strategies for High Technology Companies.

30070 ■ CEA Investments Corp.
301-2210 W 40th Ave.
Vancouver, BC, Canada V6M 1W6
Ph:(604)689-5547
Fax: (604)689-5567
Co. E-mail: info@ceainvestment.com
URL: http://www.ceainvestment.com

E-mail: info@ceainvestment.com
Scope: Specializes in strategic planning, mergers and acquisitions, and operations consulting, to mid-sized corporations. Areas of expertise include corporate planning, financial engineering, joint venture structuring, international corporate networking, identifying acquisition opportunities, locating investment partners, corporate evaluations, negotiating buy/sell agreements, business planning, markets studies and products evaluation, and outsourcing.

30071 ■ CFO Service
112 Chester Ave.
Saint Louis, MO 63122
Ph:(314)757-2940
Co. E-mail: jskae@cfoservice.com
URL: http://www.cfoservice.com

E-mail: jskae@cfoservice.com
Scope: A group of professional executives that provide upper management services to companies that cannot support a full time COO or CFO. Provides clients in the areas of business planning, company policies, contract negotiations, safety policies, product and service pricing, loans management, taxes, cost analysis, loss control and budgeting.

30072 ■ Chamberlain & Cansler Inc.
2251 Perimeter Park Dr.
Atlanta, GA 30341
Ph:(770)457-5699
Scope: Firm specializes in strategic planning; profit enhancement; small business management; interim management; crisis management; turnarounds.

30073 ■ Clayton/Curtis/Cottrell
1722 Madison Ct.
Louisville, CO 80027
Ph:(303)665-2005
Fax: (303)665-2276
Scope: Firm specializes packaged goods, telecommunications, direct marketing & printing, & packaging industries. Services include strategic planning; profit enhancement; start-up businesses; mergers and acquisitions; joint ventures; divestitures; interim management; crisis management; turnarounds; market size, segmentation and rates of growth; competitor intelligence; image & reputation, & competitive analysis.

30074 ■ John Alan Cohan
415 N Camden Dr., Ste. 100
Beverly Hills, CA 90210
Ph:(310)557-9900
Free: 800-255-1529
Fax: (310)859-8656
Co. E-mail: johnalancohan@aol.com

E-mail: johnalancohan@aol.com
Scope: Development of business plans for startups in the fields of livestock, horses, farming, or aviation. Tax consultations and tax opinion letters to support deductions.

30075 ■ Comprehensive Planning Services
3201 Lucas Cir.
Lafayette, CA 94549
Ph:(925)283-8272
Fax: (925)283-8272
Scope: Business/financial consultants with related experience in marketing, finance, organization, business planning, and profit development. Industries served include construction, manufacturing, and wholesale.

30076 ■ CRO Engineering Ltd.
1895 William Hodgins Ln.
Carp, ON, Canada K0A 1L0
Ph:(613)839-1108
Fax: (613)839-1406

Co. E-mail: grefford@ieee.org
URL: http://www.croengineering.com

E-mail: grefford@ieee.org
Scope: Specializes in management services, contract R and D, risk analysis, business services. technology assessment, independent engineering verification and validation, audit services, project or program management, engineering cost analysis, technology research. Engineering review, business plan analysis/development.

30077 ■ DRI Consulting
2 Otter Ln.
North Oaks, MN 55127-6436
Ph:(651)415-1400
Free: (866)276-4600
Fax: (651)415-9968
Co. E-mail: dric@dric.com
URL: http://www.dric.com

E-mail: dric@dric.com
Scope: Licensed psychologists providing organization and management consulting. developing leaders, managers and individuals through coaching, business strategy, career development, crisis management, policy consultation and technology optimization.

30078 ■ Entrepreneurial Strategies
107 S Yellowstone Ave., Ste. C
Bozeman, MT 59718
Ph:(406)587-5664
Fax: (406)586-0396
Scope: Academic consultants helping organizations become more entrepreneurial; helping communities become more entrepreneurial; market assessments for 'really new' products/technologies; strategic planning and marketing planning.

30079 ■ FCP Consulting
500 Sutter St., Ste. 507
San Francisco, CA 94102
Ph:(415)956-5558
Fax: (415)956-5722
Co. E-mail: cox@coxcmc.com
URL: http://www.coxcmc.com

E-mail: cox@coxcmc.com
Scope: Management consulting in Business-To-Business sales.

30080 ■ Fogg Management Consulting
80 Shadow Farm Way
Wakefield, RI 02879
Ph:(401)789-9511
Fax: (401)789-8544
Co. E-mail: davis.fogg@foggmgt.com
URL: http://www.foggmgt

E-mail: davis.fogg@foggmgt.com
Scope: Provides strategic planning and implementation services. Serves all industries in the United States Coaches CEOs and senior executives. **Publications:** Team-Based Strategic Planning; Diagnostic Marketing; Implementing Your Strategic Plan. **Seminars:** Key notes on vision, leadership and implementation.

30081 ■ Frankel and Topche P.C.
1700 Galloping Hill Rd.
Kenilworth, NJ 07033
Ph:(908)298-7700
Fax: (908)298-7701
Co. E-mail: info@frankelandtopche.com
URL: http://www.frankelandtopche.com

E-mail: info@frankelandtopche.com
Scope: Offers financial consulting for closely held businesses. Assists in mergers and acquisitions, tax planning, strategic business planning, family succession planning, accounting, auditing, and obtaining financing. The firm serves small businesses in the service, retail, wholesale, and manufacturing industries. Specializes in real estate, lumber and building materials, and service businesses.

30082 ■ Gerson Goodson Inc.
2451 McMullen Booth Rd., Ste. 216
Clearwater, FL 33759

Ph:(727)726-7619
Free: 888-237-7424
Fax: (727)726-2406
Co. E-mail: getrich@richgerson.com
URL: http://www.richgerson.com

E-mail: getrich@richgerson.com
Scope: Firm provides performance management consulting services to improve performance, maximize productivity and turn ordinary performers into extraordinary performers. Conducts a systematic needs analysis of the entire marketing, sales and customer service operations of the company. Identifies hidden, neglected and underutilized marketing, sales and customer service assets. Creates customized and unique breakthrough marketing, sales and customer service programs for them. Develops feedback, measurement and tracking systems to determine the effectiveness of programs and services. Also provides systematic follow-ups to ensure complete satisfaction with work. **Publications:** "Beyond Customer Service"; "Winning The Inner Game Of Selling"; "Marketing Strategies for Small Businesses". **Seminars:** The Marketing Difference That Makes The Difference: How To Position Your Company For Rapid Growth Regardless Of The Economy Or The Competition; Growing Your Business With What You Already Have: How To Identify And Profit From The Hidden Marketing Assets That Are Currently Costing You Money; The R Factor In Customer Service: 5 Ways To Grow Your Business For Little Or No Cost.

30083 ■ Great Lakes Consulting Group Inc.
1217 S Walnut St.
South Bend, IN 46619-4305
Ph:(574)287-4500
Fax: (574)234-8207
Scope: Provides consulting services in the areas of strategic planning; feasibility studies; start-up businesses; small business management; mergers and acquisitions; joint ventures; divestitures; interim management; crisis management; turnarounds; business process re-engineering; venture capital; and international trade.

30084 ■ The Greystone Group Inc.
678 Front St., Ste. 159
Grand Rapids, MI 49504
Ph:(616)451-8880
Fax: (616)451-9180
Co. E-mail: consult@greystonegp.com
URL: http://www.greystonegp.com

E-mail: consult@greystonegp.com
Scope: Firm specializes in strategic planning and communications; organizational development; start-up businesses; business management; mergers and acquisitions; joint ventures; divestitures; business process re-engineering.

30085 ■ Grimmick Consulting Services
455 Donner Way
San Ramon, CA 94583
Ph:(925)735-9090
Fax: (925)735-1100
Co. E-mail: grimmick@pacbell.net

E-mail: grimmick@pacbell.net
Scope: Provides consulting services in the areas of strategic planning; organizational assessment; organizational development; leadership development and Baldridge Criteria.

30086 ■ Health Strategy Group Inc.
46 River Rd.
Chatham, NY 12037
Ph:(518)392-6770
Scope: Provides consulting services in the areas of strategic planning, feasibility studies, start-up businesses, organizational development, market research, customer service audits, new product development, marketing, public relations.

30087 ■ Healthscope Inc.
60 Chestnut Ave.
Wayne, PA 19087
Ph:(610)687-6199

Fax: (610)687-6376
Co. E-mail: health@voicenet.com

E-mail: health@voicenet.com
Scope: An independent health care management and consulting firm. Provides business planning, decision making and implementation support. Specialties include strategic business consulting, business plan development focused on bottom-line improvement, revenue enhancement/expense reduction planning and implementation, practice expansion/consolidation, feasibility studies and decision making, new site/service start-up planning and implementation practice valuation and transition, physician group mergers and affiliations, joint ventures, MSO planning, start-up and management, IPA/PO development support, physician network reengineering, medical practice management, baseline operational and financial assessment, managed care contracting support, personnel management, physician compensation planning, fee schedule development, day-to-day operations management supervision, financial management, clinical protocols development, customized management report development, physician and staff education; performance monitoring, billing system evaluation, planning and selection, interim or ongoing management support, practice reorganization, patient accounts management, practice marketing.

30088 ■ Hewitt Development Enterprises
1717 N Bayshore Dr., Ste. 2154
Miami, FL 33132
Ph:(305)372-0941
Free: 800-631-3098
Fax: (305)372-0941
Co. E-mail: info@hewittdevelopment.com
URL: http://www.hewittdevelopment.com

E-mail: info@hewittdevelopment.com
Scope: A manufacturing management consulting firm. Specializes in strategic planning; profit enhancement; start-up businesses; interim management; crisis management; turnarounds; production planning; Just-in-Time inventory management; and project management.

30089 ■ Horizon Consulting Services
1315 Garthwick Dr.
Los Altos, CA 94024-6147
Ph:(650)967-0906
Fax: (650)967-0906
Scope: Assists start-up to mid-sized businesses to grow and increase profits through effective business plans and operational programs. Areas of expertise include business plans and strategies; market evaluations; competitive analysis; pricing; financial plans and budgets; financial management; marketing strategies; product positioning and introduction, forecasting and analysis; and business policies and procedures. Concentrates on providing practical results, customized to the needs and budget of its clients. Industries served: high-technology industries including computers, software, communications, other electronic products and components, and other manufacturing and service industries.

30090 ■ K & T Training
103 Greenville St.
Newnan, GA 30263-2630
Ph:(770)253-5870
Fax: (770)253-8866
Scope: Specializes in strategic planning; profit enhancement; organizational development; start-up businesses; interim management; crisis management; turnarounds; business process re-engineering; team building; cost controls.

30091 ■ Keck & Co.
410 Walsh Rd.
Atherton, CA 94027
Ph:(650)854-9588
Fax: (650)854-7240
Co. E-mail: info@kecko.com
URL: http://www.keckco.com

E-mail: info@kecko.com
Scope: Conducts management services nationally, focusing on strategic research, marketing, and plan-

ning for businesses involved in the packaging container and equipment industry, food processing, and related technology suppliers. Develops feasibility studies to assess the possible success or failure of entering a new market, introducing a new product or product line extension, or starting a new venture; primary market research to determine what motivates consumers/buyers, and best "positioning" for product in the marketplace; business development programs; promotional programs to differentiate client company from competitors; vertical/horizontal marketing audits; technology acceptance assessments; due diligence for investors; and management assistance with investment issues. **Seminars:** Taking the Failure Factors Out of New Product Introductions; Introduction to Marketing for Food Manufacturing Personnel; New Product Development Workshop: Plans and Elements; Starting Your Own Consulting Business; The Marketing Plan. **Special Services:** Conducts database searches for venture and expansion capital for packaging companies and companies introducing packaging functional foods. Maintains 1600-record proprietary database of international and North American magazines available to clients for public relations placements. Serves as basis of customized press lists and analysis of media for market entry and promotional purpose.

30092 ■ Keiei Senryaku Corp.
19191 S Vermont Ave., Ste. 530
Torrance, CA 90502
Ph:(310)366-3331
Free: 800-951-8780
Fax: (310)366-3330
Co. E-mail: takenakaes@earthlink.net

E-mail: takenakaes@earthlink.net
Scope: Consulting services in the areas of strategic planning; feasibility studies; profit enhancement; organizational development; start-up businesses; mergers and acquisitions; joint ventures; divestitures; executive searches; sales management; competitive analysis. Entering Japanese market.

30093 ■ Key Communications Group Inc.
5617 Warwick Pl.
Chevy Chase, MD 20815-5503
Ph:(301)656-0450
Free: 800-705-5353
Fax: (301)656-4554
Co. E-mail: mr.dm@verizon.net

E-mail: mr.dm@verizon.net
Scope: Direct marketing and publishing consultants specializing in subscriber and member acquisition for newsletters and other niche B2B publications, organizations and associations. Specialties: small and start-up businesses; mergers and acquisitions; joint ventures; divestitures; product development; employee surveys and communication; market research; customer service audits; new product development; direct marketing; and competitive intelligence.

30094 ■ Management Strategies
1000 S Old Woodward, Ste. 105
Birmingham, MI 48009
Ph:(248)258-2756
Fax: (248)258-3407
Co. E-mail: bob@hois.com

E-mail: bob@hois.com
Scope: Firm specializes in strategic planning; feasibility studies; profit enhancement; organizational studies; start-up businesses; turnarounds; business process re-engineering; industrial engineering; marketing; ecommerce.

30095 ■ Market Focus
12 Maryland Rd.
PO Box 402
Maplewood, NJ 07040
Ph:(973)378-2470
Fax: (973)378-2470
Co. E-mail: mcss66@marketfocus.com

E-mail: mcss66@marketfocus.com
Scope: Offers advisory services to executives of corporate business units and mid-sized companies in the

development and implementation of corporate and market strategies. Studies relate to business planning, new market/product entry, acquisitions and industry/competitive profiles for firms in advanced technology, business and financial services and basic industry. Projects focus on practical, effective approaches to maximizing the potential of existing operations and exploiting future growth opportunities. Practice philosophy emphasizes close client relationships, active management participation and senior consultant involvement. **Publications:** "Are Your Customers Buying What You're Selling", Constructive Strategy Newsletter; "Improving Productivity: Now More Than Ever", Constructive Strategy Newsletter; "Surviving in Hard Times", NJ Contractor. **Seminars:** Charting a Course for Future Company Growth; Marketing Planning; Construction Marketing in the 90's; Marketing and The CFO.

30096 ■ Marketing Leverage Inc.
180 Glastonbury Blvd.
Glastonbury, CT 06033
Ph:(860)633-1422
Free: 800-633-1422
Fax: (860)659-8664
Co. E-mail: office@marketingleverage.com
URL: http://www.marketingleverage.com

E-mail: office@marketingleverage.com
Scope: Consults with senior management at leading corporations to improve performance by maximizing customer value. We specialize in the targeting, retention and satisfaction of customers for companies in services industries with particular expertise in insurance, financial services, health care and technology services. Most clients belong to the Fortune 1000 group. Specific services include customer research, analysis of lifetime value, development of customer retention strategies, evaluation of web strategies, working with client teams.

30097 ■ McCreight & Company Inc.
36 Grove St.
New Canaan, CT 06840
Ph:(203)801-5000
Fax: (203)801-5013
Co. E-mail: roc@implementstrategy.com
URL: http://www.implementstrategy.com

E-mail: roc@implementstrategy.com
Scope: We assist our global clients with strategy implementation involving large-scale change, including mergers, divestitures, alliances, and new business launches. Along with our alliance partners, we focus on issues that energize or constrain strategic change including: plans and goals; transition design; management competence; organization structure, effectiveness, and staffing; roles and responsibilities; management processes; information management and technology; and change management effectiveness. **Publications:** Strategy Implementation Insights; ePerspective; Board Effectiveness Insights; and Information Technology Insights. **Seminars:** Successful Mergers and Acquisitions - An Implementation Guide; Global 100 - One-Face-to-the-Customer; Implementation of Strategic Change.

30098 ■ McDonald Consulting Group Inc.
7701 France Ave. S, Ste. 200
Edina, MN 55435
Ph:(952)841-6357
Fax: (507)664-9389
Co. E-mail: rmcdonald@mcdonaldconsultinggroup. com
URL: http://www.mcdonaldconsultinggroup.com

E-mail: rmcdonald@mcdonaldconsultinggroup.com
Scope: A management consulting firm specializing in assisting insurance companies improve operations. Provides services in the areas of strategic planning; profit enhancement; organizational development; interim management; crisis management; turnarounds; business process re-engineering; benefits and compensation planning and total quality management (TQM).

30099 ■ Jerome W. McGee & Associates
7826 Eastern Ave. NW, Ste. 30
Washington, DC 20012-1324
Ph:(202)726-7272
Fax: (202)726-2946
Scope: Business consultants experienced in office automation, small business management, invention and patent counseling, technology commercialization, loan packaging and business plan development. **Seminars:** Marketing Research for the High-Technology Business; Introduction to Microcomputers; Marketing Technological Products to Industry; How to Evaluate Your Technical Idea; Patenting Your Own Invention.

30100 ■ McShane Group Inc.
2345 York Rd.
Timonium, MD 21093
Ph:(410)560-0077
Fax: (410)560-2718
Co. E-mail: tmcshane@mcshanegroup.com
URL: http://www.mcshanegroup.com

E-mail: tmcshane@mcshanegroup.com
Scope: Management consulting firm specializing in helping financially troubled companies. All senior level business executives with strong operations backgrounds. Focuses on turnarounds, interim management, crisis management, debt restructuring, organizational restructuring, operating business and asset sales.

30101 ■ Mefford, Knutson & Associates Inc.
6437 Lyndale Ave. S
Richfield, MN 55423-1465
Ph:(612)869-8011
Free: 800-831-0228
Fax: (612)893-1806
Co. E-mail: don@mkaonline.net
URL: http://www.mkaonline.net

E-mail: don@mkaonline.net
Scope: Firm specializes in start-up businesses; strategic planning; mergers and acquisitions; joint ventures; divestitures; business process re-engineering; personnel policies and procedures; market research; new product development and cost controls.

30102 ■ Milestone Inc.
PO Box 630
Dedham, MA 02027
Ph:(781)467-1200
Fax: (781)467-0299
Co. E-mail: bob@milestoneideas.com
URL: http://www.milestoneideas.com

E-mail: bob@milestoneideas.com
Scope: Specialized group of business creativity and innovation facilitators who are passionately connected to the overt and covert motivations and values that enrich and complicate brands, the people who buy them, and the people who make them interesting, surprising and unique. Facilitates 100 business creativity and innovation growth sessions per year. Many established and emerging organizations have found the organizational learning focus helps them prosper when using the facilitation services to: Discover new strategic growth strategies and planning options; Create new ideas, new promises, value propositions, products and programs; Identify and integrate customer passions in new and surprising ways; realize higher returns on involvement, interest and investment; refine processes, accelerate innovative growth and build better teams. **Seminars:** Ideas in Action; Double-Gesturing; Growth in a period of no growth; Strike while the iron is cold; Natural Creative Strategies. **Special Services:** Milestone®; IMMERgENT®; Immersion®.

30103 ■ Moneysoft Inc.
1 E Camelback Rd., Ste. 550
Phoenix, AZ 85012
Ph:(602)266-7270
Free: 800-966-7797
Co. E-mail: info@moneysoft.com
URL: http://www.moneysoft.com

E-mail: info@moneysoft.com

Scope: Specializes in the publication of software for the corporate acquisition and development community. Assists businesses develop acquisition goals and criteria that build shareholder value; determine whether an acquisition candidate meets their criteria, conduct analysis of the candidate's historic performance and position; estimate the candidate's future earnings capacity; prepare professional-quality valuations and appraisal reports for tax, business planning or litigation related matters; determine purchase price and optimal terms. Prepare a detailed plan to finance the acquisition; estimate the future earnings of the candidate after the acquisition; generate fact-filled acquisition proposals for presentation to management and funding sources; and manage and track fixed assets and depreciation. **Special Services:** Corporate Valuation Professional™; DealSense®; Buy-Out Plan®; Corporate Valuation™; Lightning Deal Reviewer®; Fixed Asset Pro™.

30104 ■ Mykytyn Consulting Group Inc.
185 N Redwood Dr., Ste. 200
San Rafael, CA 94903
Ph:(415)491-1770
Fax: (415)491-1251
Co. E-mail: info@mcgi.com

E-mail: info@mcgi.com

Scope: Develops structural models of new businesses and industries. Provides an interim CEO and management team at the start-up of a new business. Experienced in computer science and operations research.

30105 ■ The Nelson Group Ltd.
5 Milk St., Ste. 4
Portland, ME 04101
Ph:(207)775-1199
Fax: (207)775-0141
URL: http://www.nelsonltd.com

Scope: Consulting services in the areas of strategic planning; organizational development; small business management; mergers and acquisitions; joint ventures; divestitures; interim management; crisis management; turnarounds; performance appraisals; executive searches; outplacement; and team building.

30106 ■ Nightingale Associates
7445 Setting Sun Way
Columbia, MD 21046-1261
Ph:(410)381-4280
Fax: (410)381-4280
Co. E-mail: fcnight@aol.com
URL: http://www.members.aol.com/fcnight

E-mail: fcnight@aol.com

Scope: Nightingale Associates is an international management training and consulting firm. Their concentration is on improving operational performance through the utilization of the most effective modern management techniques, executive and organizational assessment, reengineering of business processes, creative strategic thinking and focusing of the energies of all organizational participants. In addition they also work in the area of supply chain management and cost reduction through the utilization of the optimum purchasing, inventory management and distribution practices. **Seminars:** Advanced Management; Business Process Reengineering; Strategic Thinking; Creative Problem Solving; Customer Service; International Purchasing and Materials Management; Fundamentals of Purchasing.

30107 ■ Organizational Futures
56 Pine St., Ste. 2b
Providence, RI 02903
Ph:(401)351-7110
Fax: (401)351-7158
Scope: Builder of agile human networks to champion innovation and mobilize change; to pursue business opportunities; to custom design agile organizations and communities, to foster civic engagement. **Seminars:** Facilitating for Results.

30108 ■ P2C2 Group Inc.
4101 Denfeld Ave.
Kensington, MD 20895-1514

Ph:(301)942-7985
Fax: (301)942-7986
Co. E-mail: info@p2c2group.com
URL: http://www.p2c2group.com

E-mail: info@p2c2group.com

Scope: Firm specializes in federal information technology management including capital investment management, strategic plans, policy, enterprise architecture, information security, documentation and knowledge management, OMB and NIST compliance, and IT program management. **Publications:** "How to Work with Proposal Consultants"; "Outside Reviewers for Proposals"; "The High Cost of Federal Information Technology".

30109 ■ PCS Laboratory Services Group Inc.
4750 Venture Dr., Ste. 400
Ann Arbor, MI 48108
Ph:(734)662-6363
Free: 800-860-5454
Fax: (734)662-7118
Co. E-mail: root@chilab.com

E-mail: root@chilab.com

Scope: Park City Solutions/Laboratory Services Group offers a comprehensive set of solutions to today's laboratory management challenges, such as: recruitment support, clinical laboratory operations improvement (identification and quantification of non-value added activities, workstation comparative cost analysis, etc.), advanced benchmarking methodology, multi-lab consolidation feasibility assessment, laboratory sales and marketing, regulatory compliance reviews and training, lab billing and collections consulting, and pathology staffing and compensation consulting.

30110 ■ Performance Consulting Associates Inc.
3700 Crestwood Pky., Ste. 100
Duluth, GA 30096
Ph:(770)717-2737
Fax: (770)717-7014
Co. E-mail: info@pcaconsulting.com
URL: http://www.pcaconsulting.com

E-mail: info@pcaconsulting.com

Scope: Maintenance consulting and engineering firm specializing in production planning, project management, team building, and re-engineering maintenance. **Publications:** "Asset Reliability Coordinator," Maintenance Technology; "Does Planning Pay," Plant Services; "Know What It Is You Have To Maintain," Maintenance Technology.

30111 ■ Performance Consulting Group
8535 Baymeadows Rd., Ste. 143-3
Jacksonville, FL 32202
Ph:(904)448-4473
Fax: (904)287-1244
Scope: Consulting services in the areas of strategic planning; profit enhancement; product development; production planning.

30112 ■ Pioneer Business Consultants
9042 Garfield Ave., Ste. 312
Huntington Beach, CA 92646
Ph:(714)964-7600
Fax: (714)962-6585
Scope: Offers general management consulting specializing in business acquisitions, tax and business planning, cash flow analyses, business valuations and business sales and expert witness court testimony regarding business sales, valuations and accounting.

30113 ■ Plans and Solutions Inc.
PO Box 8905
Gaithersburg, MD 20898-8905
Ph:(301)947-8150
Fax: (240)525-5601
Co. E-mail: info@plansandsolutions.com
URL: http://www.plansandsolutions.com

E-mail: info@plansandsolutions.com

Scope: Business and strategic planning, market research and development. Most clients are minority-

owned businesses in the USA and companies overseas that want to begin or increase exports to the United States and Canada. **Publications:** "Building an Import/Export Business," John Wiley & Sons, 2002.

30114 ■ Rothschild Strategies Unlimited L.L.C.
PO Box 7568
Wilton, CT 06897-7568
Ph:(203)846-6898
Fax: (203)847-1426
Co. E-mail: bill@strategyleader.com
URL: http://www.strategyleader.com

E-mail: bill@strategyleader.com

Scope: Consults with senior management and business level strategy teams to develop overall strategic direction, set priorities and creates sustainable competitive advantages and differentiators. Enables organizations to enhance their own strategic thinking and leadership skills so that they can continue to develop and implement profitable growth strategies. **Publications:** "Putting It All Together-a guide to strategic thinking"; "Competitive Advantage"; "Ristaker, Caretaker, Surgeon & Undertaker-four faces of strategic leadership". **Special Services:** StrategyLeader®.

30115 ■ Sklar & Associates
1101 S Arlington Ridge Rd. Ste. 511
Arlington, VA 22202-1925
Ph:(202)257-5061
Fax: (202)828-4130
Co. E-mail: sklarincdc@aol.com
URL: http://www.sklarinc.com

E-mail: sklarincdc@aol.com

Scope: Provides Audit Oversight services to listed corporations on Sarbanes-Oxley compliance. **Seminars:** Financial Analysis in MBA; Emerging Company Finance; Due Diligence in Business Acquisition; Business Valuation. **Special Services:** Financial Modeling. Course titled *Understanding and Detecting Deceptive Creative Accounting Practices.*

30116 ■ Staubs Business Services
23320 S Vermont Ave.
Torrance, CA 90502-2940
Ph:(310)830-9128
Fax: (310)830-9128
Co. E-mail: harry_l_staubs@lamg.com

E-mail: harry_l_staubs@lamg.com

Scope: Business consulting support to new product development and business plans.

30117 ■ R.F. Stengel & Company Inc.
780 Yellow Springs Rd.
Paoli, PA 19301
Ph:(610)296-8950
Fax: (610)296-8991
Scope: A management consulting and crisis management firm providing services to financially and operationally troubled companies. Develops and implements business recovery programs.

30118 ■ Strategic Mangement Services
3126 Duval St.
Austin, TX 78705
Ph:(512)477-4094
Fax: (512)478-8301
Scope: Devlops business and strategic plans for beginning or established companies. Provides management and leadership consulting and training. Industries served: insurance, health care, restaurant, small manufacturing.

30119 ■ Strategic MindShare Consulting
1401 Brickell Ave., Ste. 640
Miami, FL 33131
Ph:(305)377-2220
Fax: (305)377-2280
Co. E-mail: dee@strategicmindshare.com
URL: http://www.strategicmindshare.com

E-mail: dee@strategicmindshare.com

Scope: Firm specializes in strategic planning; feasibility studies; profit enhancement; organizational development; start-up businesses; mergers and acquisitions; joint ventures; divestitures; interim management; crisis management; turnarounds; new product development and competitive analysis. **Publications:** "Top Ten CEO Burning Issues for 2005"; "Top Ten Consumer Behavioral Trends for 2005"; "The Influence Factors".

30120 ■ Tamayo Consulting Inc.
169 Saxony Rd., Ste. 112
Encinitas, CA 92024-6779
Free: 800-580-9606
Fax: (760)479-1465
Co. E-mail: info@tamayoconsulting.com
URL: http://www.tamayoconsulting.com

E-mail: info@tamayoconsulting.com
Scope: Training and consulting firm specializing in: leadership and team development. Industries served: private, non-profit, government, educational.

30121 ■ ValueNomics Value Specialists
10 Almaden Blvd., Ste. 1450
San Jose, CA 95113-2226
Ph:(408)257-8521
Fax: (408)257-1146
Co. E-mail: value@valuenomics.com
URL: http://www.valuenomics.com

E-mail: value@valuenomics.com
Scope: Specializes in valuations; appraisals; strategic planning; feasibility studies; mergers and acquisitions; joint ventures; divestitures; competitive intelligence; and due diligence. Acts as an expert witness. Offers litigation support. **Publications:** "The Business of Business Valuation and the CPA as an expert witness". **Special Services:** ValueNomics®.

30122 ■ VenturEdge Corp.
4711 Yonge St., Ste. 1105
Toronto, ON, Canada M2N 6K8
Ph:(416)224-2000
Fax: (416)224-2376
Co. E-mail: info@venturedge.com
URL: http://www.venturedge.com

E-mail: info@venturedge.com
Scope: Services include strategy formulation; performance improvement; business coaching; competitive intelligence; business planning; acquiring capital; financial management; and succession planning in mergers and acquisitions.

30123 ■ Vision Management
149 Meadows Rd.
Lafayette, NJ 07848-3120

Ph:(973)702-1116
Fax: (201)702-8311
Scope: Firm specializes in profit enhancement; strategic planning; business process re-engineering; industrial engineering; facilities planning; team building; inventory management; and Total Quality Management (TQM).

30124 ■ Weich & Bilotti Inc.
74 Main St.
Framingham, MA 01702
Ph:(508)879-8007
Fax: (508)879-7811
Co. E-mail: info@weich-bilotti.com
URL: http://www.weich.com

E-mail: info@weich-bilotti.com
Scope: Specializes in business plans, venture capital, computer information systems, turnaround/interim management, retail consulting, start-up process, college recruiting, and IS and IT personnel.

30125 ■ Western Capital Holdings Inc.
10050 E Applwood Dr.
Parker, CO 80138
Ph:(303)841-1022
Fax: (303)770-1945
Scope: Specialists in all phases of financial and management consulting. Provide strong emphasis in strategic planning and corporate development, financial analysis, acquisitions, investment banking and corporate finance. Projects range in size and duration to fit clients needs. Services can be applied to many diverse financial projects that may include the following: business plan development, budgeting and forecasting, strategic planning, cash flow analysis, cash flow management, corporate development, banking relations, asset management, and financial analysis. Industries served: food industry, manufacturing, distribution, retailing, computer services, agribusiness, financial services, insurance, and government agencies. **Seminars:** Buy Low, Sell High, Collect Early and Pay Late; Preparing Your Company for Sale; Venture Capital - Finding an Angel.

COMPUTER SYSTEMS/ SOFTWARE

30126 ■ Automate Your Business Plan 12.0
Out of Your Mind ... and Into the Marketplace
13381 White Sand Dr.
Tustin, CA 92780-4565

Ph:(714)544-0248
Free: 800-419-1513
Fax: (714)730-1414
Co. E-mail: lpinson@business-plan.com
URL: http://www.business-plan.com
Price: $95.00. **Description:** A computer program designed to help prepare a business plan.

RESEARCH CENTERS

30127 ■ Chadron State College–Nebraska Business Development Center
354 Admin. Bldg.
1000 Main St.
Chadron, NE 69337
Ph:(308)432-6286
Fax: (308)432-6430
Co. E-mail: chanson@csc,edu
URL: http://www.csc.edu/n/nbdc/default.htm
Contact: Cliff Hanson, Dir.
E-mail: chanson@csc.edu
Scope: Management education, market research, marketing plans, strategic planning, financial planning, cash flow budgeting, capital budgeting, loan packaging, rural development, and business plans. **Services:** Consulting. **Publications:** NBDC Business Calendar (annually). **Educational Activities:** Continuing education programs.

30128 ■ University of Nebraska at Omaha–Nebraska Business Development Center
6001 Dodge St.
Omaha, NE 68182
Ph:(402)554-2521
Fax: (402)554-3473
Co. E-mail: rbernier@mail.unomaha.edu
URL: http://nbdc.unomaha.edu
Contact: Robert Bernier, Dep.Dir.
E-mail: rbernier@mail.unomaha.edu
Scope: Management education, market research, marketing plans, strategic planning, financial planning, cash flow budgeting, capital budgeting, loan packaging, and rural development. **Services:** Business consulting; Government procurement assistance; Manufacturing assistance. **Publications:** Keys to Successful Business Start-Up in Nebraska; NBDC Business Calendar (annually). **Educational Activities:** Computer training and business education programs.

Business Relocation

START-UP INFORMATION

30129 ■ "Separation Anxiety" in
Entrepreneur (Vol. 28, No. 6, June 2000, pp.
170)
Pub: Entrepreneur Media Inc.
Ed: Paul Edwards and Sarah Edwards. **Description:**
Should a photography studio and home be in different
structures? Editors probe that question.

REFERENCE WORKS

30130 ■ "Aftermarket Technology to Move
150 N.J. Jobs to OKC" in *Journal Record*
(June 24, 2003)
Pub: Dolan Media Company
Ed: Janice Francis-Smith. **Description:** Aftermarket
Technology Corporation, a remanufacturer of transmissions and recovering of other auto parts, will consolidate its New Jersey facility into its Oklahoma City
plant.

30131 ■ "Amendment to Thwart Scavengers
Could Hurt Scrap Dealers" in *Crain's Detroit
Business* (Vol. 22, December 4, 2006, No. 49,
pp. 27)
Pub: Crain Communications Inc. - Detroit
Ed: Anjali Fluker. **Description:** New city ordinance
may drive legitimate scrap dealers out of the city limits.
Intent was to prevent theft and stripping of copper
from residences and businesses.

30132 ■ "Apex Property Management
Moves" in *Bellingham Business Journal*
(January 2007, pp. A6)
Pub: Sun News Inc.
Description: Apex Property Management has moved
to a new location in order to increase their workspace.
The company works with condominium and home-
owners associations, as well as commercial property
owners.

30133 ■ "At close range" in *WorkingWoman*
(Vol. 25, No. 6, June 2000, pp. 32)
Pub: Lang Communications Inc.
Ed: Danielle Svetcov. **Description:** A freelance writer
describes the communication difficulties she encountered with her parents when she returned to live near
them in San Francisco, California, after living a distance for seven years.

30134 ■ "Bald is Beautiful. Concierge Makes
Any Wish Come True" in *South Florida
Business Journal* (Vol. 23, No. 48, July 4,
2003, pp. 31)
Pub: American City Business Journals
Ed: John T. Fakler. **Description:** Steve Sims, owner
of BlueFish Concierge, has moved to Delray Beach
from Geneva and plans to move the company's headquarters from Europe to South Florida to better cater
to rich clientele.

30135 ■ "Beating Strong" in *Houston
Business Journal* (Vol. 34, No. 14, August 15,
2003, pp. 17)
Pub: American City Business Journals
Ed: Allison Wollam. **Description:** Profile of American
Medical Equipment, Houston, Texas, as it prepares to
move into new facilities in the Texas Medical Center.
Topics include business planning, management
styles, and medical equipment product lines.

30136 ■ "Brentwood's Blue Light Special" in
Washington Business Journal (Vol. 22, No.
15, August 15, 2003, pp. 1)
Pub: Washington Business Journal
Ed: Eleni Kretikos. **Description:** The move by Kmart
Corporation to put one of its Washington, DC's stores
up for sale is discussed. Topics include business losses, business relocation, and corporation reorganizations.

30137 ■ "Catering Company Expands
Operations" in *Bellingham Business Journal*
(December 2006, pp. A6)
Pub: Sun News Inc.
Description: Ciao Thyme, a catering company
owned by Jessica and Mataio Gillis, will be moving to
a larger space in March 2007. They plan to add an
event space, a small private dining facility and will be
offering cooking classes.

30138 ■ "Citgo Mulls Relocation to Houston"
in *Houston Business Journal* (Vol. 34, No.
14, August 15, 2003, pp. 1)
Pub: American City Business Journals
Ed: Monica Perin. **Description:** Citgo Petroleum Corporation announced plans to move corporate headquarters from Tulsa, Oklahoma to Houston, Texas.
Topics include tax incentives, business incentives,
and economic conditions.

30139 ■ "Citizens Bank To Lend Low-Interest
Loans to Firms Relocating to
Massachusetts" in *Boston Globe* (February
4, 2005)
Pub: New York Times Company
Ed: Sasha Talcott. **Description:** A partnership between Citizens Bank and the State of Massachusetts
will offer loans to companies expanding or relocating
to the state. The loans will be set at a fixed rate of 3.5
percent and for every $400,000 borrowed, the compa-
ny will be required to create one new job.

30140 ■ "Clybourn Ave.'s PMD Corridor
Leads Nowhere" in *Crain's Chicago
Business* (Vol. 30, January 2007, No. 1, pp. 8)
Pub: Crain Communications, Inc.
Description: In an effort to stem the loss of manufacturing jobs the city created planned manufacturing districts. A. Finkl & Sons Co. is moving its manufacturing
plant to a new location and real estate developers are
clamoring to turn the site into one of Chicago's hottest
neighborhoods but are not able to make the purchase
since the plant sits in a PMD.

30141 ■ *Company Relocation Handbook:
Making the Right Move*
Pub: Oasis Press
Ed: Sharon K. Ward and William G. Ward. **Released:**
1991. **Price:** $39.95 (ringbound); $19.95 (paper). **Description:** Provides information on business relocation, including making the right choice and handling
the logistics of moving. Part of the successful in Business library.

30142 ■ "Connecticut's Biggest Bank
Heading to Long Island" in *Long Island
Business News* (March 12, 2004)
Pub: Dolan Media Newswires
Ed: David Reich-Hale. **Description:** Webster Financial Corporation of Waterbury, Connecticut, will open
branches in Long Island, New York. Webster also
branched out into Massachusetts and Rhode Island in
2003 when it acquired Firstfed America Bancorp.

30143 ■ "Connecting Firms with Needed
Funds; Financial Assistance" in *Crain's New
York Business* (Vol. 22, November 13, 2006,
No. 46, pp. 32)
Pub: Crain Communications, Inc.
Description: Listing of organizations that provide in-
centives or financial assistance to firms that are based
in New York or are relocating to the area.

30144 ■ "Electrical-Wiring Company is
Moving to Ferndale" in *Bellingham Business
Journal* (December 2006, pp. A4)
Pub: Sun News Inc.
Description: With its move to a larger facility in Ferndale, Express Electric, a fifteen-year old company
specializing in wiring buildings and homes, will expand
to include a showroom for retail sales of home theater
systems.

30145 ■ "Environmental and Ownership
Characteristics of Small Businesses and
their Impact on Development" in *Journal of
Small Business Management*
Pub: West Virginia University
Ed: William B. Gartner, Subodh Bhat. **Description:**
This article explores the relationship between the
characteristics of a small business's location (crime,
neighborhood appearance, and transportation accessibility) and a small business owner's expectations of
future firm growth.

30146 ■ "Falling in Gov" in *Entrepreneur*
(Vol. 30, No. 3, March 200)
Pub: Entrepreneur Media Inc.
Ed: Amanda C. Kooser. **Description:** E-government
is the next fertile, immense market space on which
young entrepreneurs should set their focus. E-
government is businesses that provide technical services to state agencies.

30147 ■ "Four Starrs Moves, Doubles Size"
in *Bellingham Business Journal* (January
2007, pp. A6)
Pub: Sun News Inc.
Description: Danielle Starr, owner of Four Starrs
Boutique is moving to a location double the size of the
original. The women's boutique sells cosmetics and
clothing lines not readily available to the area.

30148 ■ "Good for Business: Houston is a Hot Spot for Economic Growth" in *Black Enterprise* (Vol. 37, October 2006, No. 3, pp. 216)
Pub: Earl G. Graves Publishing Co. Inc.
Ed: Jeanette Valentine. **Description:** Fast-growing sectors in the biotechnology and healthcare industries are among the driving forces of Houston's economic growth. More than 76,000 small businesses in the area employ about one in four area workers, according to the Small Business Administration. Housing and business costs are 26 and 11 percent below the national average, respectively, garnering the attention of corporate giants.

30149 ■ "Harris Beach Will Move Law Offices to Main Street" in *Business First Buffalo* (Vol. 19, No. 47, August 15, 2003, pp. 1)
Pub: American City Business Journals, Inc.
Ed: James Fink. **Description:** Plans by the law firm of Harris Beach LLP to open a new office in the heart of Buffalo, New York are examined.

30150 ■ "Hot Spots" in *Entrepreneur* (Vol. 33, October 2005, No. 10, pp. 68)
Pub: Entrepreneur Media Inc.
Ed: Mark Henricks. **Description:** Top twenty large cities, ten med-size cities, and the top ten states for starting or relocating an existing business are listed. Also included is the Entrepreneurial Activity Index to help measure the best spots to start or expand a business.

30151 ■ "In Demand" in *Entrepreneur* (Vol. 32, November 2004, No. 11, pp. 89)
Pub: Entrepreneur Media Inc.
Ed: Gwen Moran. **Description:** Brother filmmakers, Gregg and Evan Spiridellis, share ways to handle overnight success with a product. After producing an animated political film on their Website Jibjab, the entrepreneurs were not prepared for the number of phone calls, emails and national media appearances that followed. Hiring temp help and including an email contact on their Website could have helped.

30152 ■ "Kar Nut Products Gets New HQ; Snack-Maker Cites Growth for Need for Space" in *Crain's Detroit Business* (Vol. 21, January 10, 2005)
Pub: Crain Communications Inc. - Detroit
Ed: Anjali Fluker. **Description:** Kar Nut Products Company moved its headquarters from Ferndale to Madison Heights, Michigan. The relocation is the result of company growth for the maker of snacks and trail mixes. Details of the new facility and statistical data is included.

30153 ■ "Large industrial gas companies setting sights on Detroit" in *Crain's Detroit Business* (Vol. 19, No. 4, January 27, 2003, pp. 21)
Pub: Crain Communications Inc., Detroit
Ed: Michael Strong. **Description:** Welding equipment suppliers and independent industrial gas suppliers in the metro Detroit, Michigan area are consolidating to improve product offerings and tap into new customer bases.

30154 ■ "Lawn Tractor Manufacturer Relocates From Wisconsin to Portland, Maine" in *Portland Press Herald* (August 17, 2005)
Pub: Blethen Maine Newspapers, Inc.
Ed: Edward D. Murphy. **Description:** Eastman Industries is moving its lawn and garden tractor plant from Wisconsin to Portland, Maine. The new plant will add about a dozen new manufacturing jobs to the area. Details of the move are included.

30155 ■ "Macromedia Inc. Strikes Gold Worth $55M HQ Buy" in *San Francisco Business Times* (Vol. 18, No. 2, August 22, 2003, pp. 1)
Pub: American City Business Journals
Ed: James Temple. **Description:** Macromedia, provider of business Web and software applications, is moving its corporate headquarters to a group of San Francisco office buildings.

30156 ■ *Membership Directory/Relocation Guide*
Pub: Catawba County Chamber of Commerce
Covers: Chamber members. **Entries Include:** Contact details.

30157 ■ "More Retail Chains Heading this Way" in *Crain's Chicago Business* (Vol. 26, No. 51, December 22, 2003, pp. 6)
Pub: Crain Communications, Inc.
Ed: H. Lee Murphy. **Description:** Staples Inc., Dick's Sporting Goods, Ross Stores Inc. (apparel), National Wholesale Liquidators Inc., Home Now Furniture LLC, and Anna's Linens Inc., are among the retailers looking to enter the Chicago, Illinois retail market. The new trend is prompted by the upswing in the economy, along with the closing of Montgomery Ward & Company and Service Merchandise.

30158 ■ "More Retail Chains Heading this Way; Drawn by Vacant Sites, Competitive Considerations" in *Crains Chicago Business* (Vol. 26, No. 51)
Pub: Crain Communications, Inc.
Ed: H. Lee Murphy. **Description:** Staples Inc., Dick's Sporting Goods, Ross Stores Inc. (apparel), National Wholesale Liquidators Inc., Home Now Furniture LLC, and Anna's Linens Inc., are among the retailers looking to enter the Chicago, Illinois retail market. The new trend is prompted by the upswing in the economy, along with the closing of Montgomery Ward & Company and Service Merchandise.

30159 ■ "Move Over" in *Entrepreneur* (Vol. 33, September 2005, No. 9, pp. 55)
Pub: Entrepreneur Media Inc.
Ed: David Worrell. **Description:** John Jansheski, founder and CEO of DenTek Oral Care, found that moving his company closer to his largest customers saved his business $1 million in shipping costs in 2004.

30160 ■ "Moving Daze" in *Law Firm Inc.* (October 2004)
Pub: American Lawyer Media LP
Ed: Kristin Eliasberg. **Description:** Things to consider when a law firm is relocating the business. Many firms consult a real estate professional to help with planning the move, as well as finding the right space and negotiating the deal.

30161 ■ "Nassau County Executive Tom Suozzi Proposes Empire Zone" in *Long Island Business News* (March 5, 2004)
Pub: Dolan Media Newswires
Ed: Rosmaria Mancini. **Description:** Tom Suozzi, Nassau County Executive, would like to see the County included in the currently established 72 empire zones in the state of New York. These zones offer incentives, such as property tax abatements and utility rate reductions for companies within its boundaries, and encourages other businesses outside of New York to relocate or current firms to remain in the area.

30162 ■ "Neighborhood Mortgage Announces Office Expansion" in *Bellingham Business Journal* (December 2006, pp. 2)
Pub: Sun News Inc.
Description: Neighborhood Mortgage plans to expand and relocate its home office by Spring 2007. The move will help accommodate the company's rapid growth by tripling the square footage of the building and offer convenient access to and from the freeway.

30163 ■ "New Site Gives Lipari Foods Room to Continue Growth" in *Crain's Detroit Business* (Vol. 23, January 8, 2007, No. 2, pp. 10)
Pub: Crain Communications Inc. - Detroit
Ed: Brent Snavely. **Description:** New location doubles size of local wholesale food delivery service. Recent growth with expanded product offerings dictates larger warehouse requirements. Plans are to expand territory to surrounding states in the Midwest.

30164 ■ "Newspaper Relocates" in *Bellingham Business Journal* (January 2007, pp. A5)
Pub: Sun News Inc.
Description: Local publication Cascadia Weekly recently moved into new offices.

30165 ■ "Pacific Growth, Others Bank on Emerging Firms" in *San Francisco Business Times* (Vol. 17, No. 50, July 18, 2003, pp. 1)
Pub: American City Business Journals
Ed: Mark Calvey. **Description:** Reasons behind Pacific Growth Equities relocation of its headquarters to larger facilities in downtown San Francisco, California.

30166 ■ "Phoenix tops list of fertile areas for small companies" in *Wall Street Journal* (December 7, 1999, pp. B2)
Pub: Dow Jones & Co., Inc.
Ed: Jeffrey A. Tannenbaum. **Description:** Statistical data citing Phoenix, Arizona as the number one spot to run a small business.

30167 ■ "Plumbing Business Moves to Hannegan" in *Bellingham Business Journal* (December 2006, pp. A6)
Pub: Sun News Inc.
Description: Professional Plumbing LLC is moving to a new location to expand the business. The space will allow Professional Plumbing to be more open to the public.

30168 ■ "Profile: Chicago Native on the Front Lines of WaMu's Local Push" in *Crain's Chicago Business* (Vol. 26, No. 50, December 15, 2003)
Pub: Crain Communications, Inc.
Ed: Steve Daniels. **Description:** Profile of Anthony R. Manisco, who expanded Washington Mutual Inc. from Seattle, Washington into the Chicago, Illinois market. The difficulty merging into the Chicago market is discussed.

30169 ■ "Real Estate Company Expands, Changes Name" in *Bellingham Business Journal* (January 2007, pp. 3)
Pub: Sun News Inc.
Description: Phil Dyer & Associates, Inc. Realtors has changed its name to Sterling Real Estate Group. The company has expanded and recently opened a second office to compliment its existing office.

30170 ■ *Relocating Your Workplace*
Pub: Crisp Publications, Inc.
Ed: Wadman Daly. **Price:** $19.95. **Description:** Guide for the moving process, including site selection, hiring an architect, and planning your move.

30171 ■ "Relocation Tools: What You Need To Know About Moving To a New Town" in *Black Enterprise* (Vol. 35, August 2004, No. 1, pp. 68)
Pub: Earl G. Graves Publishing Co. Inc.
Ed: Keisha-Gay Anderson. **Description:** Challenges faced with business relocation are discussed.

30172 ■ "A San Francisco Chronicle: George Dewey's View of the Bay" in *Black Enterprise* (Vol. 34, No. 3, October 2003, pp. 142)
Pub: Earl Graves Publishing Co.
Ed: Sonia Alleyne. **Description:** George Dewey, an investment banking director for Citigroup Global Markets Inc., relocated to the San Francisco Bay area two years ago, and recommends the city as one of the best cities because it is a thriving business center.

30173 ■ "Setting Sail" in *Crain's New York Business* (Vol. 23, January 15, 2007, No. 3, pp. 25)
Pub: Crain Communications, Inc.
Description: Small business tenants are finding that they are able to move their firms a short distance away and avoid renewing leases that are demanding up to double the rent for the next lease cycle.

30174 ■ "Several buildings may change hands in coming months" in *Crain's Detroit Business* **(Dec. 16, 2002, pp. 17)**
Pub: Crain Communications Inc., Detroit
Ed: Jennette Smith. Description: A number of metropolitan Detroit office buildings are for sale. Negotiations are underway for some high-profile properties, such as Motorola Inc. in Farmington Hills and Compuware Corporation's headquarters, also located in Farmington Hills.

30175 ■ "Sleepy Little Towns Turn High Tech" in *Home Office Computing* **(Vol. 19, No. 1, January 2001, pp. 17)**
Pub: Scholastic Inc.
Ed: Lisa Roberts. Description: The agricultural town of Petaluma, California suddenly found itself a high-tech center when local firm Ceret Corp was acquired by networking giant Cisco Systems and 40 other telecom firms established facilities in the area. Petaluma has become a model for many other rural areas whose economies are disappearing. Tazwell County, Virginia has adopted a similar strategy in an effort to attract high-technology companies to an area where population has been declining.

30176 ■ "Smart Set" in *Inc.* **(November 1, 2003)**
Pub: Gruner & Jahr USA Publishing
Ed: Bobbie Gossage. Description: Hiring incentives and tax abatements are attracting new business to the Lawrence, Kansas area, especially in the area of bio-technology.

30177 ■ "South Texas Builders Head for Houston's Border" in *Houston Business Journal* **(Vol. 34, No. 8, July 4, 2003, pp. 1)**
Pub: American City Business Journals
Ed: Jennifer Dawson. Description: Armadillo Homes (San Antonio, Texas) and Obra Homes (McAllen, Texas) have both opened offices in Houston and are expected to begin building homes in the area.

30178 ■ "Spanish Firm Hopes U.S. Is In the Bag" in *Crain's Chicago Business* **(Vol. 26, No. 51, December 22, 2003, pp. 14)**
Pub: Crain Communications, Inc.
Ed: Sandra Jones. Description: Profile of Frag Comercio Internacional, one of Spain's biggest handbag makers. The firm has opened a store in Chicago, Illinois and hopes to expand retail operations to 100 stores across the nation. The store offers an ever-changing choice of purses and totes, all priced at $32. The handbags will be displayed museum-style, using a minimalist concept.

30179 ■ "Study Says Corporate Relocations Don't Impact California Economy" in *Sacramento Bee* **(October 26, 2005)**
Pub: The Sacramento Bee
Ed: Dale Kasler. Description: A study conducted by the Public Policy Institute of California reports corporate relocations do not effect the economy in California due to the small percentage of job losses.

30180 ■ "Tattoo Shop Moves to Cornwall Avenue" in *Bellingham Business Journal* **(January 2007, pp. A5)**
Pub: Sun News Inc.
Description: Tattoo shop, The Inkwell, owned by Brandon Bradshaw has moved to a spacious new location.

30181 ■ "Trading Places" in *Small Business Opportunities* **(Vol. 12, No. 3, May 2000, pp. 12, 58)**
Pub: Harris Publications, Inc.
Description: To secure good office space at favorable lease terms, the small business owner needs to be savvy and ask the right questions. Tips from a pro are offered.

30182 ■ "UDM Hopes Move Will Help Renew Detroit Neighborhood" in *Crain's Detroit Business* **(Vol. 22, December 11, 2006, No.50, pp. 3)**
Pub: Crain Communications Inc. - Detroit
Ed: Sheena Harrison Description: University of Detroit plans to move its dental school to Detroit's Core

City neighborhood in January, 2008. Developers hope it has the effect of attracting other small businesses around and further aid in the restructuring of that area.

30183 ■ "Utilities Boost Companies; Utility Services" in *Crain's New York Business* **(Vol. 22, November 13, 2006, No. 46, pp. 36)**
Pub: Crain Communications, Inc.
Description: Listing of companies that provide utility programs, incentives and benefits to small businesses looking to relocate within the five boroughs of New York City or expand their businesses in the area.

30184 ■ "Whatcom E-View Moving to New Space" in *Bellingham Business Journal* **(December 2006, pp. A3)**
Pub: Sun News Inc.
Description: Eview.com, an Internet-based community which serves as a consumer ratings site and local search engine, recently moved its offices to a new five-acre property.

30185 ■ "What's Your Problem?" in *Entrepreneur* **(Vol. 32, October 2004, No. 10, pp. 104)**
Pub: Entrepreneur Media Inc.
Ed: Paul Edwards, Sarah Edwards. Description: Entrepreneur relocating to new town seeks advice for starting his sports-related business in the new area.

30186 ■ "Who's No. 1?" in *Entrepreneur* **(Vol. 32, December 2004, No. 12, pp. 26)**
Pub: Entrepreneur Media Inc.
Ed: Judith Potwora. Description: According to experts, city rankings are targeted to large corporations, small business owners should choose location based on how well-suited an area is to a particular product or service.

30187 ■ "Wired Right: Ian Kery Is Ready To Take Freeman's New Electrical Division To the West Coast and Beyond" in *Tradeshow Week* **(Vol. 34)**
Pub: Reed Business Information
Ed: Heidi Genoist. Description: An interview with Ian Kery, owner of Toronto, Canada's largest electrical firm. Kery is selling that firm and moving to Anaheim, California to launch its West Coast Electrical Division. Kery provides tradeshow electrical services.

TRADE PERIODICALS

30188 ■ *Expansion Management*
Pub: Penton Media Inc.
Contact: Michael Keating, Publisher
E-mail: mkeating@penton.com
Released: Monthly, 7 issues. Price: $49.50 Canada; $67.50 international. Description: Magazine assisting executives and managers worldwide in planning and overseeing their companies' facilities development and other expansion and relocation activities.

30189 ■ *Plants Sites & Parks*
Pub: Reed Business Information
Contact: Lisa Bouchey
E-mail: lbouchey@reedbusiness.com
Released: Bimonthly. Price: Free to qualified subscribers; $36 others; $5 single issue. Description: Magazine for corporations and manufacturers planning to expand or relocate.

CONSULTANTS

30190 ■ AOS-USA
7000 Central Pky., Ste. 1500
Atlanta, GA 30328
Ph:(770)393-4700
Fax: (770)698-0461
Co. E-mail: info@aos-usa.com
URL: http://www.facilityres.com

E-mail: info@aos-usa.com

30191 ■ Daniel Bloom and Associates Inc.
11517 128th Ave. N
PO Box 1233
Largo, FL 33779-1233
Ph:(727)581-6216
Co. E-mail: dan@dbalconsulting.com
URL: http://www.dbaiconsulting.com

E-mail: dan@dbalconsulting.com
Scope: Human resources management consultant with a specialization in corporate relocation. Offers clients a turn key service aimed at meeting the unique relocation needs of their employees. Develops and implements training programs within the relocation industry. Publications: "Recoup Your Hiring Investment," Brainbuzz.com, Aug, 2000.

30192 ■ Boyd Company Inc.
301 N Harrison St., Ste. 415
Princeton, NJ 08540
Ph:(609)890-0726
Fax: (609)588-0518
Co. E-mail: contact@theboydcompany.com
URL: http://www.theboydcompany.com

E-mail: contact@theboydcompany.com
Scope: Provides site selection services to corporate clients expanding or relocating manufacturing, office, and distribution warehousing facilities. Provides corporate management with objective and authoritative analyses of all geographically-variable costs and other quantitative and qualitative location factors affecting optimum site selection. Firm works throughout the 50 states on behalf of leading United States corporations and overseas companies planning direct investment in the United States. Special Services: BizCosts®.

30193 ■ Christopher N. Carson CRE
12 Chelsea Ct.
Hillsdale, NJ 07642-1227
Ph:(201)664-4451
Fax: (201)664-1267
Co. E-mail: cncarson@msn.com

E-mail: cncarson@msn.com
Scope: Construction Consulting, Construction Management, Building Management Consulting, Provide Expert Witness Testimony in Dispute Matters. Arbitrator for Alternate Dispute Resolution cases.

30194 ■ C.D.S. Building Movers
8 Sweetman Dr.
Stittsville, ON, Canada K2S 1G2
Ph:(613)836-1215
Free: 800-267-5516
Fax: (613)831-0240
Co. E-mail: info@cdsmovers.com
URL: http://www.cdsmovers.com

E-mail: info@cdsmovers.com
Scope: Structural engineering and building relocation consultants providing appraisals and feasibility studies for the relocation of large buildings and structures. Specializing in Historic and Heritage Masonry Buildings.

30195 ■ The Foster Group
13321 Purple Sage Rd.
Dallas, TX 75240
Ph:(972)690-4041
Fax: (972)692-7042
Scope: Leadership development/team building/appreciative inquiry/conflict resolution for managers and executive. Fundraising, grantuniting for nonprofits. Publications: Move It! Relocating Your Business with No Downtime, 120-page manual available from the firm. Seminars: One-, two- and three-day seminars for leadership and productivity. Special Services: Development of coursework, publishing.

30196 ■ Hartford Despatch International
225 Prospect St.
PO Box 280271
East Hartford, CT 06128
Ph:(860)528-9551
Free: 800-678-9000

Fax: (860)282-1224
Co. E-mail: custsvc@hartforddespatch.com
URL: http://www.hartforddespatch.com

E-mail: custsvc@hartforddespatch.com
Scope: Domestic and international relocation services company. An independent provider of worldwide moving and storage services.

30197 ■ International Management Consulting Group Inc.
1309 Harlan Dr., Ste. 205
Bellevue, NE 68005-6604
Ph:(402)291-4545
Free: 800-665-4624
Fax: (402)291-4343
Co. E-mail: imcg@neonramp.com

E-mail: imcg@neonramp.com
Scope: Offers the following operational effectiveness programs: productivity improvement programs directed toward any sized business; business and strategic planning for executives; executive and employee seminars; work measurement and performance accounting; relocation planning and management services; job design, job analysis and human resources selection consulting; executive out placement services; and total quality management business processes re-engineering, procurement and purchasing practices. Also provides analysis of business problems faced by entrepreneurs and small business owners. Consultants seek cost savings for clients while expanding into new markets and managed growth opportunities for any sized businesses. Industries served: nearly all; but specialize in the following: insurance, transportation (passenger), family-owned businesses, and light manufacturing heavy production environment and wholesale/retail. **Publications:** "Why Every Executive Needs a Coach™," 1997; "The Professional Job Finding System™," 1997; "Why Small Business Is Where It's AT in the 1990's"; "It's All in the Plan," Small Business Reports, Jun, 1994; "Six Tips for Picking a Consultant," Small Business Reports, Jan, 1994. **Seminars:** Why Every Executive Needs a Coach; Strategic Planning for the 21st Century Executive; Mistakes Managers Make: And How to Avoid Them; Entrepreneurship in the 1990's; How to Start a Small Business and Survive; Time Management for Business Owners; Stress Management: How to Live With Stress; How to Select a Consultant in the 1990's; Total Quality Management: What's It All About; Business Process Reengineering; Activity-Based Learning™. **Special Services:** Activity-based learning™.

30198 ■ NRI Relocation Inc.
195 Arlington Heights Rd., Ste. 101
Buffalo Grove, IL 60089
Ph:(847)215-5000
Free: 800-598-8887

Fax: (847)215-7633
Co. E-mail: nri@nrirelocation.com
URL: http://www.nrirelocation.com

E-mail: nri@nrirelocation.com
Scope: A full service relocation management company. Assists corporations in the creation and execution of relocation programs. Services include developing, updating and implementing relocation policies for employees, new hires and special group moves; design and implementation of in-house or modified in-house relocation management; appraisal, marketing and acquisition of residential property; homefinding; temporary living; household goods transportation; policy counseling and spouse assistance. International services include language and cultural training; freight forwarding; destination services; Visa; repatriation and spouse assistance.

30199 ■ Overland, Pacific & Cutler Inc.
100 W Broadway, Ste. 500
Long Beach, CA 90802-4432
Ph:(562)304-2000
Free: 800-400-7356
Fax: (562)304-2000
Co. E-mail: info@pacrelo.com
URL: http://www.opcservices.com

E-mail: info@pacrelo.com
Scope: A full-service relocation assistance, inspection, and property management firm providing services to Redevelopment Agencies, School Districts, Housing Authorities, Transportation Authorities, other public agencies and private sector clients. Demonstrated consistent on-time, on-budget performance in hundreds of successful residential tenant, homeowner, commercial, industrial and mobile home park projects using federal (HUD, FAA, DOT, CDBG, HOME) or state relocation guidelines. Specific services include: on-site project administration with bilingual staff, comprehensive initial project planning, analysis and budgeting, preparation of Relocation and Replacement Housing Plans, administration of temporary moves for housing rehabilitation projects, public housing/Section 8 HQS inspection services, liaison work with community groups, social service agencies and legislative bodies, and support in eminent domain litigation and expert witness testimony.

30200 ■ Project Advantage Inc.
24 Frank Lloyd Write Dr., Lobby M
PO Box 325
Ann Arbor, MI 48106
Ph:(734)930-4300
Free: 800-320-3328
Fax: (734)930-4299
Co. E-mail: info@projectadvantage.com

E-mail: info@projectadvantage.com

Scope: A relocation services consultancy that helps corporations and organizations plan and implement major facility re-locations. The firm assists its clients in four areas: strategic relocation planning, master planning, relocation implementation planning, and specialized relocation training programs for the relocation teams. Serves large corporations in all industries, as well as organizations and government entities. **Publications:** "Systematic Management of Government Re-locations"; "Systematic Management of Business Re-locations".

30201 ■ Prudential Relocation Intercultural Services
2555 55th St., Ste. 201D
Boulder, CO 80301
Ph:(303)449-8440
Free: 800-622-6722
Fax: (303)449-1064
Scope: Senior level consulting specializing in the cross-cultural aspects of international business. Client assignments focus on areas such as corporate image overseas, foreign business practices and structures, multicultural management teambuilding, development of off-shore joint ventures, alliances and supplier networks, intercultural negotiations, global strategic planning, analysis of power structures in foreign business communities, and coaching of top level international business travelers. **Publications:** Workbook programs available on Japan, Mexico, U.K., France, and Germany (videos). **Seminars:** Custom tailored seminars on over 90 countries available for expatriates and international business travelers.

30202 ■ The Wadley-Donovan Group L.L.C.
505 Morris Ave., Ste. 102
Springfield, NJ 07081
Ph:(973)379-7700
Free: 800-929-5622
Fax: (973)379-7771
Co. E-mail: wfedrick@wadley-donovan.com
URL: http://www.wadley-donovan.com

E-mail: wfedrick@wadley-donovan.com
Scope: Business location/relocation specialists, from strategic planning through decision and implementation. Services include: definition of strategic issues for the geographic deployment of people and facilities; delineating alternatives to the current geographic configuration; relocation feasibility analyses; identification and evaluation of locations for new facilities, or relocating operations; site identification and evaluation; economic development incentive negotiations; and relocation implementation services. Services extend to detailed planning, employee surveys, attrition management, and recruitment and training strategies at the new location. **Seminars:** Corporate Location Trends in the Mid 1990s; Labor Challenges Facing Corporate America; Labor Quality Challenges and Employment Growth Opportunities for Center Cities.

Business Scams (How to Avoid)

ASSOCIATIONS AND OTHER ORGANIZATIONS

30203 ■ BBB Wise Giving Alliance
4200 Wilson Blvd., Ste. 800
Arlington, VA 22203-1838
Ph:(703)276-0100
Fax: (703)525-8277
Co. E-mail: give@cbbb.bbb.org
URL: http://www.give.org
Contact: Herman A. Taylor, Pres./CEO
Membership: Supported by companies and local Better Business Bureaus operated autonomously in the United States and Puerto Rico, which are in turn supported by 270,000 local business members. **Purpose:** Seeks to promote and foster the highest ethical relationship between businesses and the public through voluntary self-regulation, consumer and business education, and service excellence. Provides support to local Better Business Bureaus. Administers the advertising industry's self-regulatory program that monitors and investigates the truth and accuracy of national advertising claims; monitors and pre-screens advertising directed towards children. Develops information on national charitable organizations and whether they meet voluntary ethical standards for soliciting organizations. Provides information to help consumers and businesses make informed purchasing decisions and avoid costly scams and frauds; and settles consumer complaints through arbitration and other means. Operates BBB AUTO LINE, a national mediation and arbitration service providing an independent forum to resolve consumer complaints involving 32 participating auto manufacturers; Local Better Business Bureaus respond to more than 23 million requests for service annually, fielding 20 million pre-purchase inquiries and 3 million complaints. **Publications:** *BBB Wise Giving Guide* (quarterly); Annual Report (annual). Also publishes arbitration forms and pamphlets, consumer education leaflets, and parent guides for advertising aimed at children.

REFERENCE WORKS

30204 ■ "Avoiding Invention Scams" in *Black Enterprise* (Vol. 37, January 2007, No. 6, pp. 46)
Pub: Earl G. Graves Publishing Co. Inc.
Ed: James C. Johnson. **Description:** Invention promotion firms provide inventors assistance in developing a prototype for product development. It is important to research these companies before making a commitment to work with them because there are a number of these firms that are not legitimate and have caused independent inventors to lose thousands of dollars by making false claims as to the market potential of the inventions.

30205 ■ "Bad Policy" in *Forbes* (Vol. 171, No. 1, January 6, 2003, pp. 150)
Pub: Forbes Magazine

Ed: Carrie Coolidge. **Description:** Five important tips for individuals purchasing insurance in order to avoid becoming a victim of fraud are presented.

30206 ■ "Bar the door; New threats from viruses" in *Crain's Detroit Business* (Vol. 19, No. 3, Jan. 20, 2003, pp. 11)
Pub: Crain Communications Inc., Detroit
Ed: Andrew Dietderich. **Description:** The importance of data security is discussed. An interview with Ken Farmer, president of DataManagement Inc., is expecting a 40 percent increase in business in 2003 as firms are increasing data security efforts. Various methods to protect computers from hackers and viruses are examined, including alternative lines, firewall systems, disaster-recovery plans, anti-virus software.

30207 ■ "Card Tricks" in *Entrepreneur* (Vol. 30, No. 2, February 2002, pp)
Pub: Entrepreneur Media Inc.
Ed: Amanda C. Kooser. **Description:** The biggest problem for online retailers comes with accepting credit cards because of chargebacks when a customer disputes a charge on their bill, often due to unreceived merchandise or lack of quality in the product. The strict rules and dispute processes designed to protect consumers actually aids some people to use chargebacks as a vehicle for defrauding Internet businesses.

30208 ■ "Con Artists Target Collision Industry" in *Automotive Body Repair*
Pub: Advanstar Communications Inc.
Ed: Tim Sramcik. **Description:** Autobody scam artists are offering cut-rate services or free windshield replacements at parking lots, and sometimes a potential victim's home. Consumers are advised to contact the Better Business Bureau to be sure a company is reputable.

30209 ■ "Corporate Scandals Inspire Texas Fraud Bill" in *Houston Chronicle* (April 11, 2003)
Pub: Knight-Ridder/Tribune Business News
Ed: Janet Elliott. **Description:** In response to recent corporate scandals, the Senate unanimously approved a bill to crack down on business fraud. Senate Bill 1059 would create a corporate integrity unit in the Texas attorney general's office. Details of the bill are examined.

30210 ■ "Customers Must Look Out for Themselves in 'Phishing' E-mail Situations" in *The Record* (February 12, 2005)
Pub: The Record
Ed: Joe Goldeen. **Description:** Phishing scams are email messages sent to individuals asking for personal information. Washington Mutual Bank, eBay, AOL, Citibank, PayPal and others have asked customers to beware of phishing scams.

30211 ■ "Customers Wary of Online Banking Security Breeches" in *Providence Business News* (Vol. 18, No. 13, July 14, 2003, pp. 3)
Pub: Providence Business News, Inc.
Ed: Patricia Resende. **Description:** Safety precautions undertaken by Rhode Island banks to protect online banking customers are discussed.

30212 ■ "Cybercrime: Interpol for the Internet" in *Red Herring* (No. 103, September 1, 2001, pp. 27)
Pub: Herring Communications
Ed: Julia Lawlor. **Description:** An overview of the European Cybercrime Treaty, which includes 43 European members, the U.S., Japan, Canada, and South Africa. The treaty would make unauthorized computer-system break-ins a criminal offense, punishable by prison.

30213 ■ "Digital Scammer" in *Entrepreneur* (Vol. 30, No. 2, February 2002, pp. 28)
Pub: Entrepreneur Media Inc.
Description: The ten most common online scams according to the National Consumer League are presented. Statistical data included.

30214 ■ *Directory of Better Business Bureaus*
Pub: Council of Better Business Bureaus Inc.
Contact: Steve Davis, CON
Released: Irregular, latest edition May 1997. **Price:** Free. **Covers:** about 185 Better Business Bureaus in the United States and Canada. **Entries Include:** Name, address, phone. **Arrangement:** Geographical.

30215 ■ "Don't Fall for these Numbers" in *Kiplinger's Personal Finance Magazine* (Vol. 55, No. 1, January, 2001, pp. 28)
Pub: The Kiplinger Washington Editors, Inc.
Description: Investigators are cracking down on work-at-home schemes that cost consumers more than they'll ever earn.

30216 ■ "Don't Get Scammed" in *Entrepreneur* (Vol. 28, No. 4, April 2000, pp. 42)
Pub: Entrepreneur Media Inc.
Ed: Robert McGarvey. **Description:** It is estimated that as many as one million small businesses have been a victim of fraud on the Internet.

30217 ■ "An E-Mail from the IRS? Don't Believe It" in *Long Island Business News* (May 7, 2004)
Pub: Dolan Media Newswires
Ed: David Reich-Hale. **Description:** The U.S. Internal Revenue Service has posted a warning to taxpayers about an email scam that tries to trick taxpayers into giving personal information. The email appears to be an official memo from the IRS.

30218 ■ "Eight Tips to Spot Bad Checks" in *My Business* (February/March 2003, pp. 15)
Pub: My Business Magazine
Description: According to the Nilson Report, nearly 1.2 million bad checks are written daily in the U.S., equating to approximately $55.8 million in losses to retailers. Eight tips to spot a bad check are listed.

30219 ■ "Fake Microsoft Mail Is Sypware Phishing Attack" in *eWeek* (February 7, 2005)
Pub: Ziff Davis Media Inc.
Description: Microsoft plans to make its 'Windows Genuine Advantage' anti-piracy initiative mandatory in

2005. The plan will protect users from Internet scammers sending out emails that arrive with a subject line: Microsoft Windows Update.

30220 ■ "Federal Trade Comm. Report Says Long Island a Favorite of Scam Artists" in *Long Island Business News* **(January 30, 2004)**
Pub: Dolan Media Newswires
Ed: Ken Schachter. **Description:** According to a new federal ranking of metro-area populations, Long Island, New York ranked 12th as a favorite target of scam artists. Statistical data included.

30221 ■ "First Was Phishing, Next Is Pharming" in *eWeek* **(February 2, 2005)**
Pub: Ziff Davis Media Inc.
Description: Security threats known as phishing and pharming are covered. Pharming is a new application of well-known security weaknesses, requiring banks and other institutions to upgrade their DNS systems and domain registrations in order to protect customers from attack when using their Websites.

30222 ■ *Fleeced: Telemarketing Rip-offs & How to Avoid Them*
Pub: Prometheus Books
Ed: Fred Shulte. **Released:** 1995. **Price:** $24.95.

30223 ■ "Fly By Night? Don't Fall for a Scam-Use These Tips Before You Buy Health Insurance" in *Entrepreneur* **(Vol. 31, No. 10, October 2003)**
Pub: Entrepreneur Media, Inc.
Ed: Jacquelyn Lynn. **Description:** Health insurance scams targeting small businesses and their employees often collect millions of dollars before vanishing when claims start coming in. Tips to avoid fraudulent insurance companies are listed.

30224 ■ "Fraud Alert" in *Small Business Opportunities* **(Vol. 17, May 2005, No. 3, pp. 80, 84)**
Pub: Harris Publications Inc.
Ed: Carla Longley Vincent. **Description:** Ways to avoid small business fraud is investigated. According to the Association for Certified Fraud Examiners (ACFE) small firms are more vulnerable to fraud and employees with 100 or less employees suffered an average loss of $127,500, while larger firms reported $97,000.

30225 ■ "Fraud Risk: Are You Prepared? The Mission: To Create Stronger Support for an Ethically Sound Business Environment" in *Journal of Accountancy*
Pub: American Institute of Certified Public
        Accountants
Ed: Steven E. Sacks. **Description:** Incentives that reward individuals for short term results can sometimes result in fraud and abuse; ways this fraud is affecting the certified public accounting profession is examined.

30226 ■ "Funny Money: Counterfeit Money Scams Persist" in *Black Enterprise* **(Vol. 34, No. 3, October 2003, pp. 135)**
Pub: Earl Graves Publishing Co.
Ed: Kimberly J. Hamilton-Wright. **Description:** Ways to handle a situation where you are passed counterfeit money are discussed by William Byrd, a detective with the Atlanta Police Department's Fraud Unit.

30227 ■ "Hacker 'Mudge' Returns to BBN" in *eWeek* **(February 2, 2005)**
Pub: Ziff Davis Media Inc.
Description: Profile of Peiter Zatko, security specialist, who rejoined Internet firm BBN Technologies Inc. in February 2005.

30228 ■ "Hewlett-Packard Was Far From First To Try 'PreTexting'" in *Wall Street Journal* **(Vol. 248, December 2006, No. 149, pp. A1)**
Pub: Dow Jones & Co. Inc.
Ed: John A. Emshwiller **Description:** Hewlett-Packard Co. as well as all the major lenders can no longer use 'Pretexting'- the practice of impersonating people in order to receive phone or financial records, as it is now being federally prohibited.

30229 ■ "The High Cost of Penny-Ante Scams" in *Business Week Online* **(September 25, 2003)**
Pub: McGraw-Hill Inc.
Ed: Karen E. Klein. **Description:** Small business owners tend to be easy marks for con men and embezzlers. Robert Silbering, whose firm specializes in corporate fraud, asset-tracing and recover due to diligence, and global intelligence answers questions to help small businesses avoid business scams.

30230 ■ "How to Avoid Auction Scams" in *New York Times* **(March 20, 2004, pp. C2)**
Pub: New York Times Company
Ed: Katie Hafner. **Description:** Tips to avoid scams on eBay and other online auction sites. Issues covered include price, payment, the seller, photos and descriptions, location, off-site sales, private auctions and more.

30231 ■ "Identity Theft Still Top Fraud Complaint" in *Kansas City Star* **(February 2, 2005)**
Pub: Knight-Ridder/Tribune Business News
Ed: Paul Wenske. **Description:** According to the Federal Trade Commission (FTC), identity theft continues to be the number one complaint from consumers for the fifth consecutive year. Identity theft accounted for 39 percent of the fraud complaints filed with the FTC in 2004.

30232 ■ "Internet Auctions Rank High in U.S. Complaints about Online Fraud" in *Atlanta Journal-Constitution* **(April 11, 2003)**
Pub: Knight-Ridder/Tribune Business News
Ed: Tasgola Karla Bruner. **Description:** The number of complaints about online auction fraud tripled from 2001 to 2002, according to a report by the Internet Fraud Complaint Center. The dollar loss from cases reported in 2002 equaled $54 million.

30233 ■ "Investment Chat Rooms Can Be Hazardous" in *Women in Business* **(Vol. 53, No. 2, March-April, 2001, pp. 26)**
Pub: The ABWA Co. Inc.
Ed: Edward Jones. **Description:** Issues concerning the use of Internet chat rooms are discussed. The potential risks involved in following unsound investment tips or falling for scams are explored and the need to conduct independent advice, is stressed.

30234 ■ "ISPs Need To Keep Moving Against Spam" in *eWeek* **(February 3, 2005)**
Pub: Ziff Davis Media Inc.
Description: Internet service providers need to provide better security against spammers in order to protect customers on the Internet.

30235 ■ "Jury Finds 2 Guilty of Scamming Investors" in *St. Louis Post-Dispatch* **(February 3, 2005)**
Pub: St. Louis Post-Dispatch
Ed: Peter Shinkle. **Description:** Two St. Louis men were found guilty of defrauding investors in the area by telling them that eBay.com was going to purchase their startup company.

30236 ■ "Kansas Investigators Target Wichita Dating Service in Credit-Card Fraud Probe" in *Wichita Eagle* **(February 13, 2004)**
Pub: Knight-Ridder/Tribune Business News
Ed: Tim Potter. **Description:** State of Kansas attorney general's office filed a civil lawsuit seeking $1.2 million from a dating service's franchises in Wichita and Overland Park. The lawsuit claims Great Expectations of violating Kansas Consumer Protection Act through deceptive and unconscionable practices, charging the business knowingly targeted vulnerable individuals and charged thousands of dollars on credit cards of certain clients.

30237 ■ "Knowing the Score About False Notes" in *Business Week* **(Sept. 11, 2002)**
Pub: McGraw-Hill Inc.
Ed: Karen E. Klein. **Description:** A guide to spotting counterfeit money is offered to small business owners. The police or U.S. Secret Service should be notified as soon as possible after collecting suspicious currency.

30238 ■ "Let The Buyer Beware" in *Small Business Opportunities* **(Vol. 13, No. 6, November 2001, pp. 20)**
Pub: Harris Publications, Inc.
Description: The Imaging Supplies Coalition (ISC), offers information on Telemarketing Fraud and Piracy, including the principal ways to spot a phone scam.

30239 ■ "Many Ways to Lose" in *Kiplinger's Personal Finance Magazine* **(Vol. 54, No. 11, November 2000, pp. 98)**
Pub: The Kiplinger Washington Editors, Inc.
Ed: Kimberly Lankford. **Description:** Federal and state investigators are working overtime to combat fraud in deals that let investors collect on a stranger's life insurance policy.

30240 ■ "Net Profits" in *Entrepreneur* **(Vol. 27, No. 12, December 1999, pp. 48)**
Pub: Entrepreneur Media Inc.
Ed: Melissa Campanelli. **Description:** If you sell on the Web, you know that fraud is part of the e-commerce game. Helpful hints to avoid online thieves.

30241 ■ "Network Marketing or Pyramid Scheme?" in *Black Enterprise* **(Vol. 35, November 2004, No. 4, pp. 102)**
Pub: Earl G. Graves Publishing Co. Inc.
Ed: Wendy Harris. **Description:** When Cameron Brickey signed up to be an independent associate for Pre-Paid Legal Services Inc., a network marketing company, he thought he would earn an easy living. The company provides affordable legal services targeted to low- and middle-income individuals and families. While many multilevel marketing companies are legitimate, also known as pyramid schemes, they can be risky.

30242 ■ "New Campaign Aims to Educate Californians About Fake Insurance Policies" in *Sacramento Bee* **(October 1, 2005)**
Pub: The Sacramento Bee
Ed: Andrew McIntosh. **Description:** California's insurance commissioner has started a statewide campaign to educate the state's businesses and consumers about fraudulent insurance policies. Commissioner John Garamendi recommends that consumers contact his office before purchasing business insurance, or personal car, health or life insurance policies.

30243 ■ "Nobody's Fool? Health Insurance Scams Target Entrepreneurs" in *Entrepreneur* **(Vol. 32, August 2004, No. 8, pp. 21)**
Pub: Entrepreneur Media Inc.
Ed: Joan Szabo. **Description:** Phony health insurance plan promoters are preying on entrepreneurs promising coverage at premiums below charges by licensed insurers. These fraudulent plans escape state regulators with false claims of federally regulated plans under the Employee Retirement Income Security Act (ERISA), a law that pre-empts states from regulating ERISA-covered employee benefit plans sponsored by private employers.

30244 ■ "Of Two Minds: Is Consumer fraud a serious threat to online auctions?" in *Internet World* **(Vol. 7, No. 1, January 15, 2001, pp. 28)**
Pub: Mecklermedia Corporation
Ed: Phillip McKee, Brian Fitzgerald. **Description:** If left unchecked, fraud can undermine consumer confidence. The larger auction Web sites are attempting to take action to prevent it, but frequently the smaller sites are giving the entire category a bad name. There are some precautions consumers can follow to protect themselves against fraud, such as asking questions, using an escrow service, insisting on insurance, and never paying with cash.

30245 ■ "Popular Lance Armstrong Wristbands Spawn Counterfits" in *Boston Globe* **(January 28, 2005)**
Pub: New York Times Company
Ed: Carolyn Shapiro. **Description:** The Lance Armstrong Foundation is taking steps to stop the sale of

counterfit LiveStrong wristbands. The bracelets are sold for $1 each and raise money to support cancer survivors and cancer research. Nike has joined the Foundation with its Wear Yellow, Live Strong campaign to help support breast cancer survivors.

30246 ■ "Protect Yourself" in *PC Computing* (April 2000, pp. 35)
Pub: Ziff-Davis Inc.
Ed: Paul Somerson. **Description:** The importance of network security for small businesses, home-based businesses, and teleworkers is the topic of this article.

30247 ■ "Raw Deal: Avoid These Consumer Scams at all Costs" in *Black Enterprise* (Vol. 35, September 2004, No. 2, pp. 185)
Pub: Earl G. Graves Publishing Co. Inc.
Ed: Tanisha A. Sykes. **Description:** A listing of generic scams for consumers to beware of are offered by The Identity Theft Resource Center, including free credit report emails, the Nigerian 419 scam, Visa/ MasterCard alerts, email chain letters, and in-store security scams.

30248 ■ "Real Estate Horrors" in *Black Enterprise* (Vol. 32, No. 6, January 2002, pp. 86)
Pub: Earl Graves Publishing Co.
Ed: Danielle Langford. **Description:** 'Bait and switch' tactics used in the mortgage industry are examined. Helpful resources are listed. It is important for consumers to research because factors vary from state to state and from person to person.

30249 ■ "A real steal" in *Entrepreneur* (Vol. 31, No. 5, May 2003, pp. 45)
Pub: Entrepreneur Media Inc.
Ed: Jennifer Pellet. **Description:** According to market research firm Gartner Inc., one in twenty online consumers were victims of credit card fraud in 2001. The single-use credit card numbers being used for shopping online is explained.

30250 ■ "Right Tone Separates Reliable Post-Disaster Vendors from Bottom Feeders" in *South Florida Sun-Sentinel* (October 24, 2004)
Pub: South Florida Sun-Sentinel
Ed: Ian Katz. **Description:** The State of Florida is warning both consumers and businesses to beware of vendor terrorists who capitalize on a client's fears and insecurities after natural disasters occur.

30251 ■ "Scam Alert" in *Kiplinger's Personal Finance Magazine* (Vol. 58, No. 5, May 2004, pp. 21)
Pub: Kiplinger Washington Editors, Inc.
Description: A bogus Web site mimicking the National Do Not Call Registry site, is being used to collect personal data for spammers and identity thieves.

30252 ■ "Scammers Have Been Downloading Software From My Website Using Stolen PayPal Accounts. What Can I Do?" in *Inc.* (Vol. 27, July 2005)
Pub: Inc. Magazine
Description: PayPal accounts are being swiped with the identity-theft technique known as phishing. PayPal's seller-protection policy covers only physical goods, rendering dealers responsible for refunding any scammed customers.

30253 ■ "Spam Could Be a Scam: Internet Tricks Are Becoming High Crimes" in *Black Enterprise* (Vol. 35, August 2004, No. 1, pp. 30)
Pub: Earl G. Graves Publishing Co. Inc.
Ed: Siobhan Benet. **Description:** Internet crime, also called cybercrime, is the third priority after counterterrorism and counterintelligence for the Federal Bureau of Investigation.

30254 ■ "A Spam Law That Slams Small Business" in *Business Week Online* (November 5, 2003)
Pub: McGraw-Hill Inc.
Ed: Christopher Kenton. **Description:** The impact of new California legislation that makes it a crime to send any unsolicited commercial email from or to any email account accessed from or billed to a California address is examined.

30255 ■ "Spam Uncanned: Why the Recent Anti-Spam Legislation Isn't Protecting You" in *Entrepreneur* (Vol. 32, July 2004, No. 7, pp. 72)
Pub: Entrepreneur Media Inc.
Ed: Catherine Seda. **Description:** Can-Spam, the new legislation designed to protect Internet email users, does not prevent spam, it only attempts to regulate the way it is sent. Steps to help protect privacy while using a computer online are shared.

30256 ■ "Spot a fake" in *Entrepreneur* (Vol. 30, No. 10, October 2002, pp. 55)
Pub: Entrepreneur Media Inc.
Ed: Jennifer Pellet. **Description:** Ways to detect counterfeit currency are defined.

30257 ■ "Stamp It Out: A New Proposal Aims to Bring Spam Under Control" in *Entrepreneur* (Vol. 32, July 2004, No. 7, pp. 28)
Pub: Entrepreneur Media Inc.
Ed: Amanda C. Kooser. **Description:** Two proposals to help eliminated unwanted spam email are being considered. E-postage is an idea to attach a virtual stamp in email in order to reduce unwanted bulk email. Hashcash would require a sender's computer to solve a computational problem as proof of good faith. Good legislation will be required to alleviate the problem of spam.

30258 ■ "Stop, e-Thief!" in *Entrepreneur* (Vol. 28, No. 11, November 2000, pp. 30)
Pub: Entrepreneur Media Inc.
Ed: Robert McGarvey. **Description:** Web resources for stopping Internet fraud are investigated. Suggestions to protect your business are offered.

30259 ■ "Survey: Residents think scandal will shape up business behavior" in *Crain's Detroit Business* (Vol. 18, No. 22, June 3, 2002, pp. 1)
Pub: Crain Communications Inc. - Detroit
Ed: Brent Snavely. **Description:** Following the collapse of Enron Corporation, most Michigan residents think that the financial and accounting scandal will cause Michigan-based companies to act more responsibly and ethically than in the past.

30260 ■ "Tech Talk" in *St. Louis Post-Dispatch* (December 31, 2004)
Pub: Knight-Ridder/Tribune Business News
Ed: David Sheets. **Description:** Joseph E. Walsh Jr., patent attorney, explains how he nearly fell prey to techno-fraud in the form of an email that appeared to be from his bank. Phishing, carding or spoofing are techniques that try to extract important information from individuals using fake emails that appear to be authentic.

30261 ■ "The Villians of Currency" in *Wall Street Journal* (Vol. 249, January 2007, No. 5, pp. B1-B2)
Pub: Dow Jones & Co. Inc.
Ed: Joanna Slater. **Description:** Increasingly scam artists are using currency-trading schemes to take advantage of both novice and experienced investors.

30262 ■ "Watch Out For Career Scams" in *Black Enterprise* (Vol. 34, No. 3, October 2003, pp. 53)
Pub: Earl Graves Publishing Co.
Ed: Laura Egodigwe. **Description:** Ways to distinguish a career counselor when seeking professional career advice is explained. Career counselors must meet a minimum education requirement of a master's degrees and be licensed by the state in which they practice. Many also seek certification from professional bodies.

30263 ■ "Wayne County chief creates post to watch ethics and efficiency" in *Crain's Detroit Business* (Vol. 19, No. 15, April 14, 2003)
Pub: Crain Communications Inc., Detroit
Ed: Robert Ankeny. **Description:** David Esper has been appointed by Wayne County Executive Robert Ficano to work as the county's ethics watchdog and efficiency expert. Esper feels the existing ethics ordinance in Wayne County, Michigan is limited in scope and may need to be expanded.

30264 ■ "The Web: Land of Opportunists" in *Home Office Computing* (Vol. 18, No. 10, October 2000, pp. 11)
Pub: Scholastic Inc.
Ed: Lisa Roberts. **Description:** The Internet has become fertile ground for scams, many of them long in use before the new technology was available to spread ideas faster. E-mails and Web sites advertising fraudulent pyramid schemes abound. The FTC says online auctions account for 50 percent of all complaints about Internet scams; sellers routinely do not deliver what they promised. Offering a free Web site for 30 days is another scam.

30265 ■ "What's Next: They've Got Your Number" in *Inc.* (August 1, 2003)
Pub: Gruner & Jahr USA Publishing
Ed: Robert X. Cringely. **Description:** Identity theft using a combination of computer technology and government information is a major crime just waiting to happen.

30266 ■ "Why business ethics is worthy of discussion" in *Atlanta Business Chronicle* (Vol. 25, November 15, 2002, No. 23 pp. 6B)
Pub: American City Business Publications, Inc.
Ed: John C. Knapp. **Description:** Business ethics is often associated with the aftermath of a scandal or fraud and is often thought of as negative. Businesses that embrace daily discussions tend to be the exception, but tremendous value can result from such discussions.

30267 ■ "The Work-At-Home Diaries" in *Inc.* (February 1, 2002)
Pub: Inc. Magazine
Ed: Joseph Rosenbloom. **Description:** Chronicle of what happened when the author tried to take advantage of an advertised work-at-home money-making opportunity. At the end of nearly two months of work, Rosenbloom calculated that instead of earning the $2,400 promised in the advertising, he was out $261. 55.

30268 ■ "Work-At-Home Scheme" in *Black Enterprise* (Vol. 35, October 2004, No. 3, pp. 200)
Pub: Earl G. Graves Publishing Co. Inc.
Ed: Tanisha A. Sykes. **Description:** Before committing to a work-at-home operation, it is important to investigate the company by requesting written materials by mail which include product and service information and information about the company. Information to file a complaint with the Federal Trade Commission is provided.

TRADE PERIODICALS

30269 ■ *Alliance Against Fraud in Telemarketing and Electronic Commerce Focus on Fraud*
Pub: National Consumers League
Contact: Susan Grant
Ed: Susan Grant, Editor. **Released:** Quarterly. **Price:** $9, U.S.; $12, elsewhere. **Description:** Provides information about latest trends in telemarketing and Internet fraud, enforcement actions, industry fraud-fighting efforts, and educational resources.

30270 ■ *Business Crimes*
Pub: Law Journal Newsletter
Contact: James Niss, Editor-in-Chief
Released: Monthly. **Price:** $289, individuals for print version per year; $349, individuals for electronic version; $399, individuals for print and electronic version. **Description:** Covers latest developments in foreign corrupt practices, mail and wire fraud, RICO, organizational sentencing guidelines. Recurring features include columns titled "Business Crimes Hotline," "The Money Laundering Monitor," and "The Professional Newswire."

30271 ■ *Consumer Protection Report*
Pub: National Association of Attorneys General
Ed: Sarah Reznek, Editor, sreznek@naag.org. **Released:** Bimonthly. **Description:** Seeks to protect citi-

zens from consumer frauds. Reports on legislation, regulations, the Federal Trade Commission, and on state activities such as consumer information and complaint programs. Examines consumer fraud lawsuits throughout the country, covering cases involving such matters as false advertising, fraudulent billing, and regulation of charitable trusts and organizations. Recurring features include announcements and news of publications.

30272 ■ E Securities
Pub: Law Journal Newsletter
Contact: Sarah Hewitt, Editor-in-Chief
Price: $369. **Description:** Covers topics in Internet security, including the Blue Sky Law, securities fraud online, Internet Roadshows, and others. Recurring features include columns titled "Web Site of the month," "Enforcement Update," "Regulatory Round-up," "Dispatch from Europe," and "Dispatch from Asia."

30273 ■ Homecare Administrative HORIZONS
Pub: Beacon Health Corp.
Contact: Diane J. Omdahl RN, MS, Editor-in-Chief
Released: Monthly. **Price:** $249, individuals. **Description:** Provides homecare agency management

information on all kinds of business and personnel topics. Incorporates comprehensive how-to information, current regulatory requirements, and documentation strategies. Runs a series of articles, including how to move into managed care, how to manage and measure outcomes, how to survive scrutiny by medicare's fraud squad, strengthening agency/physician relationships, and personnel issues. Recurring features include columns titled Peaks & Valleys, Fine-tuning the Fundamentals, Clearing the Fog, and Higher Ground.

VIDEOCASSETTES/ AUDIOCASSETTES

30274 ■ LBOs and Fraudulent Conveyances
Practicing Law Institute
810 7th Ave.
New York, NY 10019
Ph:(212)824-5710
Free: 800-260-4PLI
Co. E-mail: info@pli.edu
URL: http://www.pli.edu
Released: 1988. **Price:** $24.95. **Description:** Defines state and federal laws regarding fraudulent con-

veyances following a leverage buy-out. **Availability:** VHS.

RESEARCH CENTERS

30275 ■ Babson College–Board of Research
Babson Hall 204
Babson Park, MA 02457-0310
Ph:(781)239-5339
Fax: (781)239-6416
Co. E-mail: chern@babson.edu
URL: http://www.babson.edu/bor/
Contact: Susan Chern, Coord.
E-mail: chern@babson.edu
Scope: Encourage and support the research activities of the college. **Publications:** Research at Babson College (quarterly); Working papers (annually). **Educational Activities:** Research forums, featuring research related topics; Research Chats (10/year), featuring faculty research projects. **Awards:** Babson faculty summer stipends; Grants, for research related expenses.

ASSOCIATIONS AND OTHER ORGANIZATIONS

30276 ■ Caribbean-Central American Action
1818 N St. NW, Ste. 310
Washington, DC 20036
Ph:(202)466-7464
Fax: (202)822-0075
Co. E-mail: info@c-caa.org
URL: http://www.c-caa.org
Contact: Federico Sacasa, Pres.
Description: Promotes private-sector-led economic development in the Caribbean Basin and throughout the hemisphere; facilitates trade and investment in the region by stimulating a constructive dialogue between the private and public sectors to improve the policy and regulatory environments for business on both international and local levels; conducts policy-oriented programs in sectors such as financial services, transportation, energy, agriculture, textiles, intellectual property rights, tourism, telecommunications, and information technology. **Publications:** *Caribbean Basin Profile* (annual); *CCAA Quarterly* (quarterly).

30277 ■ European Travel Commission
50 W 23rd St., 11th Fl.
New York, NY 10010
Co. E-mail: etc@spring-obrien.com
URL: http://www.VisitEurope.com
Contact: Robert K. Franklin, Exec.Dir.
Purpose: Represents government tourism organizations cooperating to promote travel to Europe and further international goodwill and economic prosperity. **Publications:** *VisitEurope* (monthly).

30278 ■ International Business Aviation Council
999 Rue University, Ste. 16-33
Montreal, QC, Canada H3C 5J9
Ph:(514)954-8054
Fax: (514)954-6161
Co. E-mail: info@ibac.org
URL: http://www.ibac.org
Contact: Donald D. Spruston, Dir. Gen.
Description: International business aircraft associations; national and regional business aviation organizations or subgroups. Aims to: provide information on all aspects of international business aircraft operations; ensure that the interests of international business aviation are brought to the attention of and understood by authorities; improve the safety, efficiency and economic use of business aircraft operating internationally. Stresses the importance of business aviation to the economy and to the well-being of all nations. Maintains liaison with international aviation organizations to ensure safe and orderly growth of international business aviation throughout the world. Compiles statistics. **Publications:** *IBAC Update* (quarterly); *International Business Aviation Council—News Release* (periodic); *What is IBAC* (periodic); Journal (quarterly); Annual Report (annual). **Telecommunication Services:** electronic mail, dspruston@ibac.org.

30279 ■ National Business Travel Association
110 N Royal, 4th Fl.
Alexandria, VA 22314
Ph:(703)684-0836
Fax: (703)684-0263
Co. E-mail: info@nbta.org
URL: http://www.nbta.org
Contact: Caleb Tiller, Senior Mgr., Public Relations
Membership: Travel managers and providers. **Purpose:** Works to enhance the educational advancement and image of the profession and membership; enhance the value of the travel manager in meeting corporate travel needs and financial goals; provide education to members about industry matters, issues, and technology; cultivate a positive public image of the corporate travel industry; advocate and protect the interests of members and their corporations on legislative and regulatory matters; promote safety, security, efficiency and quality travel; and enhance professionalism and recognition of the industry and individual members. Provides a forum for the constructive exchange of information and ideas among members. **Publications:** *Conference Journal* (annual); Membership Directory (annual).

REFERENCE WORKS

30280 ■ "2007's Trends in Travel and Tourism" in *Bellingham Business Journal* (January 2007, pp. C15)
Pub: Sun News Inc.
Ed: John Cooper. **Description:** Trends in travel for 2007 are explored.

30281 ■ "A Little Lost? Get Directions at Your Fingertips" in *Entrepreneur* (Vol. 31, No. 10, October 2003, pp. 46)
Pub: Entrepreneur Media, Inc.
Ed: Mike Hogan. **Description:** Profile of Mapopolis.com's ClearRoute service, offering traffic flow and other real-time street data, is presented.

30282 ■ "An African American in Paris: Ricki Stevenson's Entree to the City of Light" in *Black Enterprise* (Vol. 35, January 2005, No. 6)
Pub: Earl G. Graves Publishing Co. Inc.
Ed: Maureen Jenkins. **Description:** Profile of Paris as a city that attracts African Americans for business and pleasure. Many black entrepreneurs are enjoying Paris as a great place to grow their business.

30283 ■ "Air Campaign: Think Wireless Devices and Air Travel Don't Mix?" in *Entrepreneur* (Vol. 32, November 2004, No. 11, pp. 60)
Pub: Entrepreneur Media Inc.
Ed: Amanda C. Kooser. **Description:** Entrepreneurs and other business travelers prefer taking care of business in-flight and American Airlines and Qualcomm have teamed to offer an in-cabin cellular station to send and receive calls and text messages.

30284 ■ "Air-Tight Technology For the Business Traveler" in *My Business* (April/May 2004, pp. 20)
Pub: My Business Magazine
Description: Profile of Eagle Creek, offering packing systems for the business traveler.

30285 ■ "Airfares Increase Amid High Demand" in *Tampa Tribune* (November 30, 2005)
Pub: Media General, Inc.
Ed: Ted Jackovics. **Description:** Airline fares rose an average of 10 percent according to a representative at Travelocity.com.

30286 ■ "Airlines to match United offer" in *Wall Street Journal* (June 9, 2003, pp. A6)
Pub: Dow Jones & Co. Inc.
Ed: Susan Carey. **Description:** Major airlines will match United Airline's offer for frequent flier miles, U.S. round trip ticket with purchase of three round trip business fares in September 2003.

30287 ■ "American Airlines' Future Hangs Union Votes" in *Dallas Morning News* (April 11, 2003)
Pub: Knight-Ridder/Tribune Business News
Ed: Eric Torbenson. **Description:** American Airlines and its three major unions reached last-minute deals on March 31, 2003 for $1.62 billion in annual concessions. Details of the negotiations are included.

30288 ■ "An Oasis of Luxury" in *Hispanic Business* (Vol. 23, No. 5, May 2001, pp. 74)
Pub: Hispanic Business
Ed: Barbara Beckley. **Description:** A sampling of Las Vegas hotels catering to executives is presented, including the Aladdin Resort & Casino, Bellagio, Four Seasons Hotel Las Vegas, Mandalay Bay Resort, and Venetian Las Vegas.

30289 ■ "Around Town: Paris" in *Black Enterprise* (Vol. 35, January 2005, No. 6, pp. 104)
Pub: Earl G. Graves Publishing Co. Inc.
Description: When traveling to Paris, France for business or leisure, the city offers a variety of accommodations, restaurants, and nightspots. Currency information is also explained.

30290 ■ "As economy softens, firms trimming travel budgets" in *Atlanta Business Chronicle* (Vol. 24, No. 8, July 27, 2001, pp. NA)
Pub: American City Business Journals Inc.
Ed: Leslie Williams Johnson. **Description:** Companies are reducing the numbers and costs of business trips in an effort to deal with the sagging economy. CEOs are staying in less expensive hotels, business travel accounts are scrutinized for waste, and only the most necessary of trips are taken. Business travelers are searching the Internet for frugal travel opportunities, such as taking cheaper flights that may involve a layover in other cities, rather than taking a more expensive direct flight.

30291 ■ **"Bargain Season Begins" in** *Hispanic Business* **(Vol. 24, No. 4, April 2002, pp. 62)**
Pub: Hispanic Business Inc.
Ed: Barbara Beckley. **Description:** As the airline industry recovers, it will take initiative and patience to find special promotions that will make business travel, as well as vacation travel, less expensive.

30292 ■ **"Beantown Flavor: Columnist Adrian Walker Gives Us a Taste of Boston" in** *Black Enterprise* **(Vol. 34, No. 5, December 2003, pp. 152)**
Pub: Earl Graves Publishing Co.
Ed: Adrian Walker. **Description:** Brief overview of the city of Boston through the eyes of Boston Globe columnist Adrian Walker, who sees the town as one of the most intellectually stimulating centers in the country.

30293 ■ **"Beating Travel Stress" in** *Small Business Opportunities* **(Vol. 16, November 2004, No. 6, pp. 100, 104)**
Pub: Harris Publications Inc.
Ed: Jerry Teplitz. **Description:** Ten ways to handle stress whether vacationing or traveling for business, including beating jet lag.

30294 ■ *Being Self-Employed: How to Run a Business Out of Your Home, Claim Travel and Depreciation and Earn a Good Income Well into Your 70s or 80s*
Pub: Allyear Tax Guides
Ed: Holmes F. Crouch, Irma Jean Crouch, Barbara J. MacRae. **Released:** September 2004. **Price:** $24.95 (US), $37.95 (Canadian). **Description:** Guide for small business to keep accurate tax records.

30295 ■ **"Best Travel Web Site: Hotwire. com" in** *Entrepreneur* **(Vol. 32, No. 4, April 2004, pp. 47)**
Pub: Entrepreneur Media, Inc.
Description: Profile of Hotwire.com, which can save money for small business owners who are able to plan business travel on short notice.

30296 ■ **"Betting on Business" in** *Hispanic Business* **(December 2002, pp. 57)**
Pub: Hispanic Business
Ed: Barbara Beckley. **Description:** The city of Las Vegas offers more than 6 million square feet of meeting and exhibit space. A listing of the top hotels selected by businesses is presented.

30297 ■ **"Bits and Bytes" in** *Kansas City Star* **(February 1, 2005)**
Pub: Knight-Ridder/Tribune Business News
Ed: David Hayes. **Description:** Weathernews offers current weather reports, forecasts, color radar, airport weather, travel forecasts and local photos on its mobile phone service.

30298 ■ **"Board the Linux love boat" in** *San Francisco Business Times* **(Vol. 16, No. 43, May 31, 2002, pp. 19)**
Pub: San Francisco Business Times Inc.
Ed: Lizette Wilson. **Description:** Firms like Palo Alto, California's Geekcruises.com offer technical training on trips. The firms' cruises are organized around the training courses; clients and marketing are also discussed.

30299 ■ **"Book It! Using an Online Travel Site has its Advantages for Small Companies" in** *Entrepreneur* **(Vol. 32, No. 1, January 2004, pp. 22)**
Pub: Entrepreneur Media, Inc.
Description: Expedia, Orbitz, and Travelocity are the three top online travel services offering products to help small business save money on business travel. All three offer a small firm a private booking site ranging around $150 to startup and lower transaction costs.

30300 ■ **"Boston Around Town" in** *Black Enterprise* **(Vol. 34, No. 5, December 2003, pp. 153)**
Pub: Earl Graves Publishing Co.

Ed: Linda S. Lawson. **Description:** Directory of accommodations, restaurants, bars for conducting business, nightlife, parking, hair salons, and shopping geared to both business travelers as well as vacationers is presented.

30301 ■ **"The buddy system" in** *WorkingWoman* **(Vol. 25, No. 5, May 2000, pp. 84)**
Pub: Lang Communications Inc.
Ed: JoBeth McDaniel. **Description:** There is a simple set of rules that enables business travel with a colleague to go smoothly. These rules include avoiding office gossip, flying separately, sharing dinner but not accommodation, and not hold meetings in hotel rooms.

30302 ■ **"Business Buzz" in** *Tribune* **(March 11, 2005)**
Pub: Knight-Ridder/Tribune Business News
Description: America West Airlines added another regional flight to Phoenix, Arizona, making business travel to the city more accessible.

30303 ■ **"The Business Traveler: Taking Advantage of Bargains on the Road" in** *Black Enterprise* **(Vol. 35, November 2004, No. 4, pp. 191)**
Pub: Earl G. Graves Publishing Co. Inc.
Ed: Lee Anna Jackson. **Description:** African American business travel increased by 20 percent between 2000 and 2002, accounting for 8.4 to 10.8 million business trips per year for that time period.

30304 ■ **"By Land, Air, and Sea: New Passport Rules in Effect" in** *Black Enterprise* **(Vol. 37, January 2007, No. 6., pp. 101)**
Pub: Earl G. Graves Publishing Co. Inc.
Ed: Stephanie Young. **Description:** As part of a new security measure by the Western Hemisphere Travel Initiative, a passport will now be required for U.S. citizens traveling by air between Mexico, Canada, South and Central America, and the Caribbean. This initiative, designed to easily identify travelers and enforce border security, will most likely extend to land or sea travel no later than January 1, 2008.

30305 ■ **"B.Y.O. GPS" in** *Business 2.0* **(Vol. 6, September 2005, No. 8, pp. 132)**
Pub: Time, Inc.
Ed: Matthew Maier. **Description:** Owning your own portable GPS system is a wiser choice than the renting the costly units offered by car rental companies. Reviews of the Magellan RoadMate 760, Palm GPS Navigator, Microsoft Streets & Trips 2005 are included.

30306 ■ **"Bystrom Providing In-Room Massages at Lakeway Inn & Convention Center" in** *Bellingham Business Journal* **(January 2007, pp. A17)**
Pub: Sun News Inc.
Description: Profile of Charisma Bystrom who has been selected as the exclusive massage practitioner for the guests of Bellingham's Lakeway Inn & Convention Center. Bystrom collaborates with her husband, Scott MacGregor, on tandem massages.

30307 ■ **"Caribbean Charisma" in** *Hispanic Business* **(October 2003, pp. 104, 106)**
Pub: Hispanic Business
Ed: Barbara Beckley. **Description:** Puerto Rico offers a unique mix of business amenities and coastal attractions.

30308 ■ **"CEO Buyer's Guide: Travel" in** *Hispanic Business* **(November 2002, pp. BG14)**
Pub: Hispanic Business
Description: Short profiles of Marriott Hotels, Avis Rent A Car System Inc., and American Airlines AAdvantage programs that cater to business travelers.

30309 ■ **"Charter Service Suspends Use of Plane After Crash" in** *San Fernando Valley Business Journal* **(Vol. 12, January 2007, No. 2, pp. 6)**
Pub: San Fernando Valley Business Journal Associates

Ed: Mark R. Madler. **Description:** Sun Quest Executive Air Charter, a Van Nuys-based company, has suspended flying its Cessna Citation jets in the wake of a plane crash that killed Frank Kratzer, the company's founder.

30310 ■ **"Checking In: Chicago: Cheryl Burton Whirls Through the Windy City" in** *Black Enterprise* **(Vol. 34, July 2004, No. 12, pp. 150)**
Pub: Earl G. Graves Publishing Co. Inc.
Ed: Description: Chicago, Illinois is presented as a city that welcomes entrepreneurial spirit. A tour of the city is also offered showcasing hotels and restaurants of interest to the business or vacationing traveler.

30311 ■ **"China Route Hinges on Biz vs Politics" in** *Crain's Detroit Business* **(Vol. 22, September 25-October 1, 2006, No. 39, pp. 1, 40)**
Pub: Crain Communications Inc. - Detroit
Ed: Michelle Martinez. **Description:** Competition for non-stop airline travel from US to China between four major carriers depends upon a combination of business and politics. Location of connection is in four different cities.

30312 ■ **"City of Angels" in** *Hispanic Business* **(Vol. 23, No. 10, October, 2001, pp. 96)**
Pub: Hispanic Business
Ed: Barbara Beckley. **Description:** Profile of Los Angeles, California, as a site to mix business and pleasure is explored.

30313 ■ **"Come Fly With Me" in** *Black Enterprise* **(Vol. 35, September 2004, No. 2, pp. 54)**
Pub: Earl G. Graves Publishing Co. Inc.
Ed: Tariq Muhammad. **Description:** Although online travel booking may offer great deals for domestic travel, for international travel, multiple destinations, or other special trips, a travel agent is recommended.

30314 ■ **"Cut Travel Expenses" in** *Inc.* **(July 1, 2003)**
Pub: Gruner & Jahr USA Publishing
Description: Big travel Websites are scrambling to help small companies cut business travel costs. Statistical data included.

30315 ■ **"Cutbacks manifesting as lower hotel occupancy" in** *Atlanta Business Chronicle* **(Vol. 24, No. 14, September 7, 2001, pp. S5)**
Pub: American City Business Journals Inc.
Ed: Erica Stephens. **Description:** Atlanta hotels are suffering from cutbacks in business travel budgets. The National Business Travel Association conducted a recent survey which reported the number of travel managers using only necessary travel services is 61 percent. Hotel occupancy during a large amount of 2001's first two quarters was down 0.7 percent in metro Atlanta.

30316 ■ **"Dare to Disconnect" in** *Home Office Computing* **(Vol. 19, No. 1, January 2001, pp. 92)**
Pub: Scholastic Inc.
Ed: Jeffery D. Zbar. **Description:** The article explores the fact that most teleworkers take their offices with them when traveling.

30317 ■ **"Deemed Substantiation of Business Travel Expenses" in** *Journal of Accountancy* **(Vol. 198, October 2004, No. 4, pp. 102)**
Pub: American Institute of Certified Public Accountants
Ed: Charles J. Reichert. **Description:** The 'deemed-substantiation' method for deducting business travel is discussed.

30318 ■ **"Delta may lose $1 billion again" in** *Atlanta Business Chronicle* **(Vol. 25, January 10, 2003, pp. 3A)**
Pub: American City Business Publications, Inc.
Ed: Walter Woods. **Description:** Delta Air Lines is expected to announce a loss of $1 billion for the second

straight year, according to industry analysts. The fourth quarter net loss of the embattled carrier is expected to be between $250 million and $300 million. Insiders warn that the airline industry is in grave danger.

30319 ■ **"Delta compromises on new $100 standby fee"** in *Atlanta Business Chronicle* (Vol. 25, No. 22, November 8, 2002, pp. 7A)
Pub: American City Business Publications, Inc.
Ed: Chris McGinnis. **Description:** Delta Air Lines Inc. is instituting a standby fee, but customer criticism has pressured the airline into making concessions. AirTran Airways is beginning its "AirTran JetConnect" regional jet service.

30320 ■ **"Do the locomotive"** in *WorkingWoman* (Vol. 25, No. 2, February 2000, pp. 76)
Pub: Lang Communications Inc.
Ed: Bob Woods. **Description:** Business travel on new high-speed trains may be faster by up to 50 percent on Amtrak's Acela service.

30321 ■ **"Effects of SARS Hit Colorado Firms' Dealings with Asia"** in *Denver Post* (April 11, 2003)
Pub: Knight-Ridder/Tribune Business News
Ed: Marsha Austin. **Description:** The SARS epidemic hitting China has caused many Colorado companies to ban business travel to China, Hong Kong and other Asian countries.

30322 ■ **"El Commuters Brace for Cuts"** in *Crain's Chicago Business* (Vol. 30, January 2007, No. 3, pp. 12)
Pub: Crain Communications, Inc.
Description: CTA will begin building new tracks to accommodate wider platforms at Belmont and Fullerton and finish modernization of the Brown Line. During this two-year time frame rush-hour service will be cut on the Red, Purple and Brown el lines. Rush-hour capacity will be reduced by about 20 percent.

30323 ■ **"Extra Special: Booking Sites Offer More Bang for Your Buck-And Then Some"** in *Entrepreneur* (Vol. 32, November 2004, No. 11, pp. 22)
Pub: Entrepreneur Media Inc.
Ed: Chris McGinnis. **Description:** Low-fare airlines offer online booking sites for companies willing to book directly with them rather than using a travel agent. Airtran-A2B Corporate Travel, Jetblue-Companyblue, and Southwest-SWABIZ, are featured.

30324 ■ **"Fare Cuts Might Signal End to Airlines as We Know Them"** in *St. Louis Post-Dispatch* (January 9, 2005)
Pub: Knight-Ridder/Tribune Business News
Ed: David Nicklaus. **Description:** Economics for air travel have changed permanently. Businesses and individuals are able to find bargain fares using the Internet. Cutting prices may not be the best remedy to restore profitability.

30325 ■ **"Fare Game"** in *Success* (Vol. 47, No. 1, January 2000, pp. 26)
Pub: Success Publishing, Inc.
Ed: George Hobica. **Description:** Play your cards right, and you can save a bundle on air travel.

30326 ■ **"The Fast Track: How to Jet Through the Airport and Get On Your Way"** in *Entrepreneur* (Vol. 31, No. 7, July 2003, pp. 24)
Pub: Entrepreneur Media, Inc.
Ed: Christopher McGinnis. **Description:** Steps to speed the business traveler's journey from the airport to the plane are listed.

30327 ■ **"Flying From the Computer"** in *The Economist* (Vol. 377, October 1-7, 2005, No. 8446, pp. 65-67)
Pub: The Economist Newspaper Ltd.
Description: The Internet has created intense competition among travel providers. Statistical data included.

30328 ■ **"Flying solo: pay more for a travel agent? Why not just go online?"** in *Entrepreneur* (Vol. 30, No. 9, September 2002, pp. 24)
Pub: Entrepreneur Media Inc.
Ed: Christopher Elliott. **Description:** According to the National Business Travel Association, more companies are using the Internet to book business travel in order to save booking fees for airline tickets.

30329 ■ **"For Want of a Nail...The War Was Lost"** in *E-business Advisor* (Vol. 18, No. 12, December 2000, pp. 6)
Pub: Advisor Media, Inc.
Ed: John L. Hawkins. **Description:** Tips for e-commerce users include the use of the Sprint digital network for cell phone use when traveling. Sprint's voice mail and text messaging features are useless, taking days or even weeks for the notification of a message. IBM ThinkPad notebooks are good machines, but spare parts are in short supply. A battery replacement can take up to a year to receive. A Compaq desktop's automatic system for communicating with the company about updates occupies so much processing power, it slows the system's performance.

30330 ■ **"Forecasts Call for More Green"** in *Hispanic Business* (December 2003, pp. 60)
Pub: Hispanic Business
Ed: Barbara Beckley. **Description:** Corporate travel costs are forecast to increase slightly in 2004, but hotel and car rental expenses will remain flat.

30331 ■ **"Fraction action: can't afford an entire jet? Try winging it with a piece of one"** in *Entrepreneur* (Vol. 31, No. 4, April 2003)
Pub: Entrepreneur Media Inc.
Ed: Christopher Elliott. **Description:** Fractional-ownership options, or the equivalent of owning a timeshare in a plane, are a unique strategy for small businesses with smaller travel budgets.

30332 ■ **"Frontier Could Land Here"** in *Pittsburgh Business Times* (Vol. 22, No. 52, July 11, 2003, pp. 1)
Pub: Pittsburgh Business Times
Ed: Christopher Davis. **Description:** Discussions are underway between Denver-based Frontier Airlines and officials of the local airport in Allegheny County, Pennsylvania.

30333 ■ **"Fun Money: Mixing Business and Pleasure Can Pay Off"** in *Entrepreneur* (Vol. 32, August 2004, No. 8, pp. 48)
Pub: Entrepreneur Media Inc.
Ed: Joan Szabo. **Description:** Tax rules regarding business travel write-offs are examined.

30334 ■ **"Get Smart! When Using Wi-Fi Hot Spots, Don't Throw Caution to the Wind"** in *Entrepreneur* (Vol. 32, July 2004, No. 7, pp. 45)
Pub: Entrepreneur Media Inc.
Ed: Amanda C. Kooser. **Description:** Security is stressed for business travelers while using Wi-Fi connections.

30335 ■ **"Getting Around"** in *PC Magazine* (February 20, 2001, pp. 67)
Pub: Ziff-Davis Publishing Company
Ed: Walaika Haskins. **Description:** New Web services and software are attempting to make life easier for business travelers. Offerings from companies such as i-tinerary Travel Solutions and SideStep seek to provide hassle-free travel.

30336 ■ **"Getting Away and Meaning It"** in *Inc.* (July 1, 2003)
Pub: Gruner & Jahr USA Publishing
Description: Ways to make business a part of a vacation trip and avoid ruining please by keeping work distractions to a minimum.

30337 ■ **"Give Me Mylanta"** in *Fast Company* (September 2001, pp. 74)
Pub: Fast Company
Ed: Erika Germer. **Description:** A presentation of things to do while staying in Atlanta, Georgia on a business trip.

30338 ■ **"Going Local for Travel"** in *Ingram's* (Vol. 29, No. 7, July 2003, pp. 41)
Pub: Show Me Publishing, Inc.
Description: All About Travel Inc., is a locally owned Kansas City, Missouri, $51 million travel agency. Brent Blake, CEO, stated that the company has become the largest travel agency in the area by concentrating on business travelers.

30339 ■ **"The Good Life by the Bay"** in *Hispanic Business* (Vol. 24, No. 1/2, January/February 2002, pp. 64)
Pub: Hispanic Business Inc.
Ed: Barbara Beckley. **Description:** San Francisco offers memorable cuisine and lodging as well as traditional attractions. Information for corporate stays of 30 days or longer is offered.

30340 ■ **"Groups Push Forward on Mass Transit Proposals"** in *Crain's Detroit Business* (Vol. 23, February 5, 2007, No. 6, pp. 1)
Pub: Crain Communications Inc. - Detroit
Ed: Andrew Dietderich. **Description:** Fast transit study proposals from Ann Arbor to Detroit are being backed by Amtrak and state and local governments. Three year trial to be undertaken patterned after other successful systems in other cities.

30341 ■ **"Guarding gizmos"** in *Atlanta Business Chronicle* (Vol. 24, No. 8, July 27, 2001, pp. 1C)
Pub: American City Business Journals Inc.
Ed: Mary Jane Credeur. **Description:** Since more and more business persons rely on digital datebooks, laptops, and cellular phones, there is an increased risk of losing important information by theft or loss. According to the National Business Travelers Association, nearly 400,000 laptops were taken from their owners in 2000. Disastrous scenarios involving lost planners and laptops and ways to reduce the risk of losing important devices are discussed.

30342 ■ **"Half Pints: Wireless Routers Have the Size Advantage"** in *Entrepreneur* (Vol. 33, January 2005, No. 1, pp. 42)
Pub: Entrepreneur Media Inc.
Ed: Amanda C. Kooser. **Description:** Business travelers can now access the Internet in hotel rooms via a wireless travel router. These devices are manufactured by D-Link, Netgear, SMC and 3Com.

30343 ■ **"Hartsfield bracing for choppy '03"** in *Atlanta Business Chronicle* (Vol. 25, January 3, 2003, No. 30, pp. 1A)
Pub: American City Business Publications, Inc.
Ed: Walter Woods. **Description:** Hartfield Atlanta International Airport is looking for ways to positively impact its revenue stream. According to Ben DeCosta, general manager of the airport, several ideas to effect cost efficient change have been suggested. One idea is to provide wireless Internet access in terminals.

30344 ■ **"Have Kid, Won't Travel"** in *Fast Company* (November 2001, pp. 48)
Pub: Fast Company
Ed: Christine Canabou. **Description:** Profile of David Peterson, cofounder, CEO and chairman of the Atlanta-based North Highland Company, the management and technology consulting firm. Mr. Peterson's work force is able to drive to their client's site, rather than having to spend much of their time away from their homes and families.

30345 ■ **"Have Kudos, Will Travel"** in *Hispanic Business* (July/August 2002, pp. 80)
Pub: Hispanic Business
Ed: Barbara Beckley. **Description:** The SITE Foundation released a report that states travel incentives to employees can increase work productivity by as much as 22 percent.

30346 ■ **"Here Comes the Sun"** in *Entrepreneur* (Vol. 32, December 2004, No. 12, pp. 16)
Pub: Entrepreneur Media Inc.
Ed: Gisela M. Pedroza. **Description:** Profile of the Luxury Atomic Solar G-Shock Watch, geared to the international business traveler. The watch features local time for 30 cities around the world.

30347 ■ "Home Office vs. the Field" in *Sales & Marketing Management*
Pub: VNU Business Media
Description: Incentives for sales teams are debated by a salesperson and sales manager.

30348 ■ "Hospitality Industry Continues Rough Ride in 2003" in *Atlanta Business Chronicle* (Vol. 25, January 10, 2003, No. 31, pp. 16A)
Pub: American City Business Publications, Inc.
Ed: Tom Barry. **Description:** Insiders indicated that the hospitality industry, hit hard by the terror attacks of 9/11, will not likely recover fully until 2004. Atlanta, Georgia will be sensitive to the slow recovery process since the city relies on the business traveler. Business travel, which is enabled by corporate profits and sales, will slowly recover as will the larger market.

30349 ■ "Hotels With a Sweaty Twist On Room Service" in *Inc.* (May 1, 2005)
Pub: Inc. Magazine
Ed: Stephanie Clifford. **Description:** Upscale hotel chains are providing in-room fitness facilities to business travelers.

30350 ■ "How To Love Your Layover" in *Business 2.0* (Vol. 6, September 2005, No. 8, pp. 130)
Pub: Time, Inc.
Ed: Georgia Flight. **Description:** Airports are offering business travelers creative ways to pass time while waiting for departures. Dallas/Fort Worth International Airport has opened a $1.2 billion Terminal D which highlights live music on the mezzanine level above the food court, as well as displaying artwork throughout the terminal.

30351 ■ "I'd Rather Be Flying (Myself)" in *Inc.* (January 1, 2002)
Pub: Inc. Magazine
Ed: Phaedra Hise. **Description:** Business owners have always been more likely than most people to be private pilots, and this practice is becoming more popular.

30352 ■ "If the spirit moves you" in *Fast Company* (May 2001, pp. 54)
Pub: Fast Company
Ed: Jill Rosenfield. **Description:** An overview of the executive retreats that have become a staple of corporate life.

30353 ■ "Import an Income" in *Small Business Opportunities* (Vol. 12, No. 5, September 2000, pp. 100)
Pub: Harris Publications, Inc.
Ed: Marie Sherlock. **Description:** Love to travel? Consider starting an import business that requires trips around the world.

30354 ■ "The Internet vs. the travel agent" in *Hispanic Business* (Vol. 22, No. 6, June 2000, pp. 146)
Pub: Hispanic Business
Ed: Barbara Beckley. **Description:** The World Wide Web offers many bargains for business travelers, but some businesspeople prefer a good travel agent. Around 3 percent of travel, valued at $4 billion, is booked via the Internet and this is set to rise to over $30 billion by 2004.

30355 ■ "Investment in Transit System the First Step in Pursuit of Games" in *Crain's Chicago Business* (Vol. 30, January 2007, No. 1, pp. 8)
Pub: Crain Communications, Inc.
Ed: MarySue Barrett. **Description:** Chicago is one of the cities that are attempting to win the 2016 Olympics bid. State lawmakers must decide whether to shrink or expand the region's public transit system. Chicago must also continue to develop mixed-income communities to attract consumers from a wide range of income levels that would be expected to come to Chicago for the games.

30356 ■ "It's On Us: On Your Next Trip, Let Your Hotel Pick Up the Tab For Extras" in *Entrepreneur* (Vol. 31, No. 8, August 2003, pp. 20)
Pub: Entrepreneur Media, Inc.
Ed: Christopher McGinnis. **Description:** Because of increased competition, many hotels are offering extras to business travelers, including free meals, high speed internet service, and more.

30357 ■ *The Itty Bitty Guide to Business Travel*
Pub: Chronicle Books LLC
Ed: Stacie Krajchir, Carrie Rosten. **Released:** February 2004. **Price:** $6.95. **Description:** Advice on all aspects of business travel, including low-price airfare, packing and coping with stress.

30358 ■ "Jet Stream E-Mail" in *Inc.* (September 1, 2003)
Pub: Gruner & Jahr USA Publishing
Ed: Anton Piech. **Description:** Business travelers will now be able to access and send email while traveling on airplanes. No software downloading will be necessary to use this service.

30359 ■ "Jetblue Outlines Massive Logan Expansion" in *Boston Globe* (February 3, 2005)
Pub: New York Times Company
Ed: Keith Reed. **Description:** JetBlue's plans for expansion at Logan International Airport in Boston are outlined. The expansion could make JetBlue one of the largest airlines operating out of Logan and calls for the hiring of about 500 new employees.

30360 ■ "Just for Her" in *Inc.* (April 1, 2005)
Pub: Inc. Magazine
Ed: Bobbie Gossage. **Description:** Mobile Edge has created fashionable laptop bags geared towards traveling businesswomen.

30361 ■ "Keep in Touch...Even in the Air. These New Tech Features Are Ready for Takeoff" in *Entrepreneur* (Vol. 32, December 2004, No. 12)
Pub: Entrepreneur Media Inc.
Ed: Chris McGinnis. **Description:** In-flight cell phones, Internet and satellite television are now available for the business traveler.

30362 ■ "Ken Chenault: Dealing Out the Cards" in *Business Week* (February 14, 2005, No. 3920, pp. 42)
Pub: McGraw-Hill Companies
Ed: Mara der Hvanesian. **Description:** American Express is returning to its core card and payments business, credit cards, corporate travel and entertainment cards, as well as reloadable traveler's checks.

30363 ■ "Lack of Lease Could Cost US Airways" in *Pittsburgh Business Times* (Vol. 23, No. 5, August 22, 2003, pp. 3)
Pub: Pittsburgh Business Times
Ed: Christopher Davis. **Description:** US Airway's future at Pittsburgh International Airport is in jeopardy following the airline's decision to reject its leases. The airline, led by CEO David Siegel, has been offered a $264 million financial incentive package by the City of Pittsburgh.

30364 ■ "Lagging behind? Get ahead of jet lag before it gets the best of you" in *Entrepreneur* (Vol. 31, No. 6, June 2003, pp. 24)
Pub: Entrepreneur Media Inc.
Ed: Christopher Elliott. **Description:** Several new remedies and regimens designed to treat jet lag for the weary business traveler are explored.

30365 ■ "Lakeway Inn Gets $1.5 M Remodel" in *Bellingham Business Journal* (January 2007, pp. A1)
Pub: Sun News Inc.
Ed: Dan Hiestand. **Description:** Profile of Lakeway Inn & Conference Center that began a $1.5 million renovation that will dramatically upgrade 132 guest rooms, common areas, and its indoor pool.

30366 ■ "Lakewood Hotel Draws Lofty Rating From Chain" in *Bradenton Herald* (February 3, 2005)
Pub: Bradenton Herald
Ed: Matt Griswold. **Description:** Holiday Inn at Lakewood Ranch is rated as one of the top performing properties catering to business travelers. The hotel boasts an 81 percent average occupancy, 20 points higher than the industry average of 61 percent.

30367 ■ "Lemon Aid" in *WorkingWoman* (Vol. 25, No. 8, September 2000, pp. 94)
Pub: Lang Communications Inc.
Ed: JoBeth McDaniel. **Description:** Advice for travelers for getting a good quality hotel room, a safe hire car and a comfortable seat on an aircraft is presented.

30368 ■ "Less Bang For Your Buck" in *Black Enterprise* (Vol. 36, November 2005, No. 4, pp. 168)
Pub: Earl G. Graves Publishing Co. Inc.
Ed: Siobhan Benet. **Description:** With careful planning, traveling abroad has become very affordable. Tips to plan a trip overseas are included.

30369 ■ "Life after business" in *Women in Business* (Vol. 53, No. 2, March-April, 2001, pp. 38)
Pub: The ABWA Co. Inc.
Ed: Melissa Will. **Description:** Advice and information on participating in group travel are discussed. The advantages of being part of a group and the opportunities available on a cruise sponsored by the American Business Women's Association are discussed.

30370 ■ "The Limo Jet: Its Time is Coming" in *Business Week* (December 11, 2000, pp. 5)
Pub: McGraw-Hill, Inc.
Description: Fast, efficient, and safe point-to-point transportation at unheard-of-pricing will explode demand.

30371 ■ "Living the Lifestyle of the Successful Businessperson" in *Hispanic Business* (January/February 2005, pp. 63, 64)
Pub: Hispanic Business
Ed: Leslie A. Westbrook. **Description:** Victor Lopez, senior vice president at Hyatt Hotels Corporation believes balance is the key to a successful executive lifestyle. Profile of X9 GPS that allows users to map a route and upload the information onto a watch is included.

30372 ■ "Looting Luggage: Safeguarding Your Valuables Against Airport Employee Theft" in *Black Enterprise* (Vol. 34, No. 6, January 2004)
Pub: Earl Graves Publishing Co.
Ed: Leslie E. Royal. **Description:** According to the Transportation Security Administration, 400 million pieces of baggage were checked in at airports in the first half of 2003, and 11,000 lost, damaged, stolen or delayed luggage claims were made. Ways to protect valuables while traveling for business or leisure are listed.

30373 ■ "Making the upgrade" in *Working Woman* (Vol. 25, No. 6, June 2000, pp. 114)
Pub: Lang Communications Inc.
Ed: JoBeth McDaniel. **Description:** Advice on upgrading your air ticket from coach class to first class is offered, including always using the same airline, searching for seats on the Internet and plan your business trips well in advance.

30374 ■ "Maps on Tap" in *Entrepreneur.com* (Vol. 34, February 2006, No. 2, pp. 38)
Pub: Entrepreneur Media Inc.
Description: Profile of TomTom Navigator 5 Bluetooth GPS receiver that turns your PDA or smartphone into a GPS navigation system.

30375 ■ "Maryland-based Hotel Chains Step Up Efforts in Pursuit of Business Travelers" in *Daily Record* (January 28, 2005)
Pub: Dolan Media Newswires
Ed: Kara Kridler. **Description:** With the expected increase in business travel, hoteliers in Maryland are

hoping to attract professionals to their properties with new offerings. Marriott offers a virtual concierge service that allows guests to make online requests before check-in.

30376 ■ "Meeting and Greeting" in *PC Magazine* **(February 20, 2001, pp. 129)**
Pub: Ziff-Davis Publishing Company
Ed: Walaika Haskins. **Description:** A profile of CoolE-mail.com, that offers traveling professionals wireless access to e-mail, faxes and voice mail at a central location.

30377 ■ "Mile-High Vacation" in *Hispanic Business* **(Vol. 23, No. 7/8, July/August 2001, pp. 108)**
Pub: Hispanic Business
Ed: Barbara Beckley. **Description:** Profile of Denver, Colorado and its cultural and social attractions, area hotels are highlighted.

30378 ■ "Miles to go: when an airline goes bust, do your points take flight?" in *Entrepreneur* **(Vol. 31, No. 5, May 2003, pp. 22)**
Pub: Entrepreneur Media Inc.
Ed: Christopher Elliott. **Description:** United Airlines and U.S. Airways have assured customers that their points are fine, although the companies have filed for Chapter 11 bankruptcy protection. Most airline companies will honor miles from other airlines that have gone out of business.

30379 ■ "More fly charter, wing it themselves" in *Crain's Detroit Business* **(Vol. 19, No. 9, March 3, 2003, pp. 18)**
Pub: Crain Communications Inc., Detroit
Ed: Michael Strong. **Description:** Many high-level executives are chartering or purchasing the own planes for business travel.

30380 ■ "My, Oh, Miami" in *Entrepreneur* **(Vol. 30, No. 2, February 2002, pp. 20)**
Pub: Entrepreneur Media Inc.
Ed: Christopher Elliott. **Description:** Information for planning a business trip to Miami, Florida is furnished.

30381 ■ "My Own Private Way to Go" in *Working Woman* **(Vol. 25, No. 7, August 2000, pp. 86)**
Pub: Lang Communications Inc.
Ed: Bob Woods. **Description:** The price and accessibility of private charter flying is making it a more practical way for business people to travel.

30382 ■ "Nation's busiest airports expand to ease delays" in *Atlanta Business Chronicle* **(Vol. 25, No. 22, November 8, 2002, pp. 13C)**
Pub: American City Business Publications, Inc.
Ed: Jan R. Costello. **Description:** Hartsfield Atlanta International Airport and nearly all other major U.S. airports are presently carrying out enhancement projects. Hartsfield intends to spend $5.4 million on its effort.

30383 ■ "The need for privacy" in *Crain's Detroit Business* **(Vol. 18, No. 24, June)**
Pub: Crain Communications Inc. - Detroit
Ed: Michael Strong. **Description:** With long lines at airport security, local executives are purchasing small planes for business travel. Sales of small planes and fractional ownership of jets are rising.

30384 ■ "New 'Heads in Beds' in Suburban Hotels" in *Boston Business Journal* **(Vol. 23, No. 21, June 27, 2003, pp. 1)**
Pub: American City Business Journals
Ed: Jill Lerner. **Description:** Occupancy rates in hotels outside of Boston, Massachusetts are down 50 percent, while downtown Boston hotels are reporting 63.5 percent occupancy rates. Revenues have declined for Boston properties by 13.9 percent between January and May 2003. Experts predict the decline is due to a reduction in corporate travel.

30385 ■ "New SkyMiles rules penalize low-fare fliers" in *Atlanta Business Chronicle* **(Vol. 25, December 20, 2002, No. 28, pp. 9A)**
Pub: American City Business Publications, Inc.
Ed: Chris McGinnis. **Description:** Delta Air Lines Inc. will use a multiplier based on how much a customer spends for tickets to determine the reward status of its customers. The most expensive fares will receive a multiplier of two, while the least expensive fairs will be given a 0.5 multiplier. Delta's Platinum members will not be affected by these changes.

30386 ■ "New Study: County Tourism Taking Off" in *Bellingham Business Journal* **(December 2006, pp. A4)**
Pub: Sun News Inc.
Description: Washington State Office of Community, Trade and Economic Development released a study showing that Whatcom County ranked fifth of the state's thirty-nine counties in terms tourism and of total visitor spending. Statistical data included.

30387 ■ "A new terminal at National?" in *Washington Business Journal* **(Vol. 22, No. 3, May 23, 2003, pp. 1)**
Pub: Washington Business Journal
Ed: John Wilen. **Description:** U.S. Airways plans construction of a new airport terminal at Washington's Reagan National Airport. Data covering U.S. Airways growth, design and construction and financial management is included.

30388 ■ "A Night's Sleep, Ultracheap" in *Business Week* **(January 23, 2006, No. 3968, pp. 73)**
Pub: McGraw-Hill Companies
Ed: Pete Engardio. **Description:** Bangalore's indiOne hotel offers rooms for business travels for $22 per night.

30389 ■ "Northwest seeks to cut $1.5B, but little impact felt at Metro for now" in *Crain's Detroit Business* **(Vol. 19, No. 7, Feb. 17, 2003)**
Pub: Crain Communications Inc., Detroit
Ed: Michael Strong. **Description:** Northwest Airlines is expected to cut $1.5 billion from its operating costs, but little or no impact is expected for the Detroit Metropolitan Airport.

30390 ■ "Northwest Bounty" in *Hispanic Business* **(Vol. 24, No. 5, May 2002, pp. 56)**
Pub: Hispanic Business Inc.
Ed: Barbara Beckley. **Description:** Seattle, the city that birthed industry giants such as Boeing, Microsoft, Nordstrom, Starbuck's and Princess Cruises all started by entrepreneurs, is also a good choice for travel.

30391 ■ "Northwest may be next with low-cost subsidiary" in *Crain's Detroit Business* **(Vol. 19, No. 6, February 10, 2003, pp. 1)**
Pub: Crain Communications Inc., Detroit
Ed: Michael Strong. **Description:** Northwest Airlines is considering creating its own low-cost carrier in an effort to improve its financial status.

30392 ■ "Now Boarding" in *Inc.* **(Volume 28, January 2006, No. 1, pp. 66)**
Pub: Inc. Magazine
Ed: Larry Olmsted. **Description:** More than 100 discount airlines have been launched globally since 2004. A few of the best budget carriers are listed for the business traveler going overseas to India, the Mediterranean, Southeast Asia, South America, and Eastern Europe.

30393 ■ "Now Boarding: Small Business" in *Business Week* **(May 22, 2000, pp. F54)**
Pub: McGraw-Hill, Inc.
Description: Information and statistical data are included in this overview of business travel for small-business persons.

30394 ■ "On the road to fitness" in *Women in Business* **(Vol. 54, No. 2, March-April 2002, pp. 30)**
Pub: The ABWA Co Inc.
Ed: Mary-Lane Kamberg. **Description:** Businesswomen should maintain their physical fitness routines and business travel should not interfere.

30395 ■ "On the Fly: Try These Money-Saving Tricks for Last-Minute Travel Plans" in *Entrepreneur* **(Vol. 32, October 2004, No. 10, pp. 28)**
Pub: Entrepreneur Media Inc.
Ed: Chris McGinnis. **Description:** Planning business travel ahead of time will cut travel expenses and trip stresses. Tips to assist the business traveler are presented.

30396 ■ "On the Go! Winning travel tips for small business owners" in *My Business* **(April/May 2002, pp. 28-35)**
Pub: My Business Magazine
Ed: Shannon Scully, Lisa Waddle. **Description:** The best ways to save time and money for business travel, while staying connected to the company are explored. Laptops, cell phones, software, email, video conferencing, Web cams, airlines, hotels, car rental companies, credit cards are among the topics covered.

30397 ■ "On the Road to Records" in *Business Journal-Milwaukee* **(Vol. 20, No. 52, September 12, 2003, pp. A1)**
Pub: American City Business Journals, Inc.
Ed: Pete Millard. **Description:** Amtrak train service between Chicago, Illinois and Milwaukee, Wisconsin has risen in passenger traffic due to increased business ridership. The Amtrak route, operated with Hiawatha trains, reported a 13.4 percent rise in riders with 40,124 total passengers in July 2003.

30398 ■ "One Site Does Not Fit All" in *Business 2.0* **(Vol. 6, July 2005, No. 6, pp. 110-111)**
Pub: Time, Inc.
Ed: Tom Price. **Description:** To get the most out of a business team's next retreat, the article recommends sparing no expense and to tailor the destination to the manager's goal. Sites geared to team building, leadership retreats, brainstorming, and strategy sessions are highlighted.

30399 ■ "Palmdale, Calif., Hampton Inn to House Business Travelers to Sports Fans" in *Daily News* **(February 17, 2004)**
Pub: Knight-Ridder/Tribune Business News
Ed: Jim Skeen. **Description:** Hampton Inn is building a new hotel in Palmdale, California that will cater to business travelers as well as those attending sports tournaments.

30400 ■ "Pearl by the Sea" in *Hispanic Business* **(March 2002, pp. 64)**
Pub: Hispanic Business
Ed: Barbara Beckley. **Description:** Hispanic business executives are enjoying the luxury and authentic Mexican charm of Manzanillo.

30401 ■ "Perked-Up Flyers" in *Hispanic Business* **(March 2003, pp. 64)**
Pub: Hispanic Business
Ed: Barbara Beckley. **Description:** A listing of the amenities and services being offered by airlines to executives is presented. American Airlines, Continental Airlines, Delta Air Lines, Northwest Airlines and United Airlines are among the airlines profiled.

30402 ■ "Playing It Safe: Security on the Road is in Your Own Hands" in *Sales and Marketing.com* **(Vol. 156, No. 3, February 2004, pp. 53)**
Pub: VNU eMedia, Inc.
Description: Security while traveling for business is discussed. John Fannin, CEO of Wilmington, Delaware's SafePlace, shows hotels how to improve security.

30403 ■ "Please stay! You have the hotels rights where you want them" in *Entrepreneur* **(Vol. 30, No. 10, October 2002, pp. 34)**
Pub: Entrepreneur Media Inc.
Ed: Christopher Elliott. **Description:** With the slow down in the economy, hotels are offering various perks to business travelers. Offerings from hotels catering to the business traveler include Hilton, Marriott, Starwood, Wyndham, as well as smaller properties and bed-and-breakfast inns.

30404 ■ "Power Play" in *Entrepreneur* (Vol. 32, August 2004, No. 8, pp. 42)
Pub: Entrepreneur Media Inc.
Ed: Gisela M. Pedroza. **Description:** Belkin's Universal Power Adapter can recharge all electronic devices in a car, plane or from any standard AC wall outlet, making it a good choice for business travel.

30405 ■ "Present Perfect" in *Fast Company* (September 2001, pp. 164)
Pub: Fast Company
Ed: Alison Overholt. **Description:** Profile of Westin Hotels and Resorts, San Francisco airport restaurants, and Virgin Atlantic Airways for the business traveler.

30406 ■ "Printing in the Privacy of Your Hotel Room" in *Law Firm Inc.* (October 2004)
Pub: American Lawyer Media LP
Ed: John Bringardner. **Description:** Small, lightweight computer printers that fit into a business traveler's carry-on luggage are profiled, including HP DeskJet 450wbt, Canon i80, and the Brother MW-140BT.

30407 ■ "Ready to land" in *Crain's Detroit Business* (Vol. 19, No. 16, April 21, 2003, pp. 11)
Pub: Crain Communications Inc., Detroit
Ed: Amy Lane. **Description:** Detroit Metropolitan Airport will offer wireless high-speed Internet access to passengers waiting in the airport's terminals. Concourse Communications Group LLC, Springfield, Massachusetts, has an airport contract that includes providing the wireless access known as Wi-Fi in the new Midfield Terminal.

30408 ■ "Recovery for Some; Chicago's Economy Will Lag the State and Nation Next Year" in *Crain's Chicago Business* (December 22, 2003)
Pub: Crain Communications, Inc.
Ed: Sandra Jones. **Description:** Chicago's economy is expected to see a 2.96 percent rise in 2004, with the warehousing and distribution, financial services, and hospitality sectors feeling strongest growth with an increase in business travel to the area. However, Chicago's economy is expected to grow at a slower pace than the state or the nation.

30409 ■ "Relaxed fit: Tailor your travel for less stress and maximum chill" in *Entrepreneur* (Vol. 30, No. 3, March 2002, pp. 24)
Pub: Entrepreneur Media Inc.
Ed: Christopher Elliott. **Description:** Airports are offering amenities for travels to help them distress, including movie and DVD rentals, bookstores, massage therapists, and more.

30410 ■ "Return of the Agent" in *Entrepreneur.com* (Vol. 34, January 2006, No. 1, pp. 19)
Pub: Entrepreneur Media Inc.
Ed: Chris McGinnis. **Description:** Although 65 percent of all business travel is booked online, if a trip is complex, it is best to consult a travel expert.

30411 ■ "Road Warriors" in *BlackEnterprise* (Vol. 32, No. 2, September 2001, pp. 106)
Pub: Earl Graves Publishing Co.
Ed: Marilyn Zelinsky Syarto. **Description:** Telecommunications equipment and use of technology during business travel are explained.

30412 ■ "Room Glut Has Hotels Unsettled" in *Atlanta Business Chronicle* (Vol. 25, December 6, 2002, No. 26, pp. 1)
Pub: American City Business Publications, Inc.
Ed: Walter Woods. **Description:** There are over 86,000 hotel rooms in the metro Atlanta, Georgia area, making the impact of the recent recession in the travel sector even harder on hoteliers there. During the travel recession, the number of visitors to trade shows, and the like have, fallen significantly.

30413 ■ "Rout and About" in *Entrepreneur* (Vol. 32, December 2004, No. 12, pp. 54)
Pub: Entrepreneur Media Inc.
Ed: Gisela M. Pedroza. **Description:** Profile of Netgear's WGR101 wireless travel router that allows users to deploy a wireless network and share a single, fast Internet connection in any conference room, hotel room or other Wi-Fi sport with Internet Access, making it a good choice for the business traveler.

30414 ■ "Safety Measures" in *Washington Business Journal* (Vol. 22, No. 16, August 22, 2003, pp. 18)
Pub: Washington Business Journal
Ed: Tim Pappa. **Description:** Gary Noesner, from Control Risks Groups, points out the importance of travel information. Control Risks offers software and services to make data acquisition easier. Such information can result in saving the lives of employees of international businesses or government officials in the field.

30415 ■ "Seeing Stars" in *Entrepreneur* (Vol. 33, August 2005, No. 8, pp. 18)
Pub: Entrepreneur Media Inc.
Ed: Chris McGinnis. **Description:** Tripadvisor.com, Hotelchatter.com, Hotelshark.com, travel.yahoo.com, and citysearch.com offer hotel reviews from real travelers.

30416 ■ "Shop Around: This Technology Can Help You Comparison Shop for Low Fares" in *Entrepreneur* (Vol. 32, July 2004, No. 7, pp. 28)
Pub: Entrepreneur Media Inc.
Ed: Chris McGinnis. **Description:** Web-scraping sites and software allow users to search multiple sites and prices in easy-to-read charts for comparison shopping travel fares. SideStep, ITA Software, and TravelAxe are profiled.

30417 ■ "Sleep tight" in *Entrepreneur* (Vol. 30, No. 2, February 2002, pp. 20)
Pub: Entrepreneur Media Inc.
Ed: Christopher Elliott. **Description:** Hotels are upgrading mattresses, pillows and linens in order to draw travelers.

30418 ■ "Southwest Adds Chicago Flight" in *Sacramento Bee* (October 28, 2005)
Pub: The Sacramento Bee
Ed: Clint Swett. **Description:** Southwest Airlines added a second nonstop flight from Sacramento, California to Chicago, Illinois' Midway Airport. The flights will begin in early 2006. Southwest Airlines is reporting record travel rates for 2005.

30419 ■ "T & E Report" in *Sales & Marketing Management* (Vol. 157, January 2005, No. 1, pp. 54)
Pub: VNU Business Media
Description: Rent-A-Wreck, headquartered in Owing, Maryland, is marketing price advantage to attract business travelers with low-cost rentals ten to twenty percent lower than larger car rental agencies.

30420 ■ "Taking Off" in *Washington Business Journal* (Vol. 22, No. 20, September 19, 2003, pp. 34)
Pub: Washington Business Journal
Ed: Tania Anderson. **Description:** Atlantic Coast Airlines Inc., formerly a regional feeder airline for United Airlines, wants to become a major carrier. Atlantic Coast expects its contract with United to cease during United's bankruptcy reorganization.

30421 ■ "T&E Report" in *Sales and Marketing.com* (Vol. 156, No. 3, March 2004, pp. 68)
Pub: VNU eMedia, Inc.
Description: Profiles of carry-on luggage to help make business travel easier.

30422 ■ "A Tasty Blend of the Old and New" in *Hispanic Business* (June 2002, pp. 104)
Pub: Hispanic Business
Ed: Barbara Beckley. **Description:** San Antonio, Texas is the perfect city to mix business with pleasure. Information for contacting the San Antonio Convention and Visitors Bureau is listed.

30423 ■ "Technology Column" in *Tampa Tribune* (February 28, 2005)
Pub: Knight-Ridder/Tribune Business News
Ed: Doug Stanley. **Description:** Yahoo is offering a new service that sends driving directions to a cell phone or other mobile device.

30424 ■ "That'll be extra: fees, fees and more fees-don't pay what you don't have to" in *Entrepreneur* (Vol. 30, No. 12, Dec. 2002, pp. 26)
Pub: Entrepreneur Media Inc.
Ed: Christopher Elliott. **Description:** As a means to attract more business, travel companies have cut rates on services.

30425 ■ "Therapy Island" in *Hispanic Business* (Vol. 23, No. 11, November 2001, pp. 66)
Pub: Hispanic Business Inc.
Ed: Barbara Beckley. **Description:** Hawaiian resorts are placing a new focus on culture and history, along with traditional healing methods, resulting in a new wave of spas and treatments said to offer mind and body rejuvenation.

30426 ■ "3.5 Trillion Miles...and Counting" in *Fast Company* (September 2001, pp. 166)
Pub: Fast Company
Ed: Ron Lieber. **Description:** They are the world's most powerful promotional currency, a medium of exchange that people manage almost as carefully as cash. So, what does the future hold for frequent-flier miles? Answers to seven high-flying questions are presented.

30427 ■ "TomTom GO910: On the Road Again" in *Black Enterprise* (Vol. 37, January 2007, No. 6, pp. 52)
Pub: Earl G. Graves Publishing Co. Inc.
Ed: Stephanie Young. **Description:** TomTom GO 910 is a GPS navigator that offers detailed maps of the U.S., Canada, and Europe. Consumers view their routes by a customizable LCD screen showing everything from the quickest to the shortest routes available or how to avoid toll roads. Business travelers may find this product invaluable as it also functions as a cell phone and connects to a variety of other multi-media devices.

30428 ■ "Tracking T&E deductions" in *Hispanic Business* (Vol. 22, No. 4, April 2000, pp. 77)
Pub: Hispanic Business
Ed: Milton Zall. **Description:** The Internal Revenue Service has revised its regulations concerning the claiming of travel and entertaining cost allowances. Documentary evidence is only required for individual bills or daily expenditure totals of over $75.

30429 ■ "Tracking a trend" in *Entrepreneur* (Vol. 30, No. 1, January 2002, pp. 24)
Pub: Entrepreneur Media Inc.
Ed: Christopher Elliott. **Description:** More business travelers are using trains as an alternative to air travel because of their convenience and amenities never found on an airplane, while also providing great networking opportunities.

30430 ■ "Travel Plans Gone Awry; How to Prepare for Emergencies" in *Black Enterprise* (Vol. 35, February 2005, No. 7, pp. 161)
Pub: Earl G. Graves Publishing Co. Inc.
Ed: Jennifer L. Smith. **Description:** Whether traveling for business or vacation, travel insurance will protect individuals in case of emergency.

30431 ■ "Travel Web sites reaching out to business" in *Atlanta Business Chronicle* (Vol. 25, January 3, 2003, No. 30, pp. 2A)
Pub: American City Business Publications, Inc.
Ed: Robert Mullins. **Description:** Business travelers are being sought after more frequently by the online travel Web sites. New services and features are cropping up in order to cater to business travelers. One such new service is called SideStep, which began in July 2002.

30432 ■ "Traveling Right" in *Small Business Opportunities* **(Vol. 12, No. 5, September 2000, pp. 17)**
Pub: Harris Publications, Inc.
Description: Merger creates full-service travel company to help small businesses get where they are going. Biztravel@myCompany is the first travel management offering to provide smaller businesses with the full service and travel options that larger businesses usually receive.

30433 ■ "Travel...More and Less" in *Fast Company* **(September 2001, pp. 170)**
Pub: Fast Company
Ed: Ron Lieber. **Description:** In response to the economic downturn, small companies are cutting back on business travel.

30434 ■ "Truly Personal Entertainment" in *Sales & Marketing Management* **(Vol. 158, October 2006, No. 10, pp. 52)**
Pub: VNU Business Media
Ed: Tali Arbel. **Description:** DVD/VCD players or a video iPod can help business travelers pass time on airlines or buses.

30435 ■ "UAL to open fourth club at O'Hare" in *Travel Weekly* **(Vol. 61, No. 34, August 26, 2002, pp. 32)**
Pub: NorthStar Travel Media, LLC
Description: United airlines opened its fourth Red Carpet Club at Chicago's O'Hare airport. The private-membership club offers work carrels with business equipment, television, bar service and morning and late-afternoon snacks.

30436 ■ *The Unofficial Business Traveler's Pocket Guide: 249 Tips Even the Best Business Traveler May Not Know*
Pub: The McGraw-Hill Companies
Ed: Christopher J. McGinnis. **Released:** 1998. **Price:** $10.95.

30437 ■ "Up and away to better health" in *BlackEnterprise* **(Vol. 32, No. 3, October 2001, pp. 168)**
Pub: Earl Graves Publishing Co.
Ed: Ann Brown. **Description:** According to Diana Fairechild, a former flight attendant who logged more than 10 million miles before authoring Jet Smarter: The Air Traveler's Rx, 90 percent of airline passengers get sick after flying. Tips for frequent flyers to avoid problems are cited.

30438 ■ "Uplifting" in *Pittsburgh Business Times* **(Vol. 23, No. 5, August 22, 2003, pp. 1)**
Pub: Pittsburgh Business Times
Ed: Christopher Davis. **Description:** Rock Ferrone, owner of Rockpointe Business Airpark, is planning a $10 million expansion of the airport's runway. The small airport, located in West Deer Township, Pennsylvania, may also become the new home of a large, unspecified firm.

30439 ■ "Vacation Research Made Easy" in *Black Enterprise* **(Vol. 36, November 2005, No. 4, pp. 168)**
Pub: Earl G. Graves Publishing Co. Inc.
Ed: Leslie E. Royal. **Description:** Travel Brochure Center offers free travel brochures, guides, maps, and planning kits for arranging travel to the U.S. and Canada.

30440 ■ "Vonage V-Phone: Use Your Laptop to Make Calls Via the Internet" in *Black Enterprise* **(Vol. 37, January 2007, No. 6, pp. 52)**
Pub: Earl G. Graves Publishing Co. Inc.
Ed: James C. Johnson. **Description:** Overview of the Vonage V-Phone, which is small flash drive device that lets you make phone calls through a high-speed Internet connection and plugs into any computer's USB port. Business travels may find this product to be a wonderful solution as it includes 250MB of memory and can store files, digital photos, MP3s, and more.

30441 ■ "Wanted: Road warrior queen" in *Incentive* **(Vol. 174, No. 8, August 2000, pp. 8)**
Pub: Bill Communications
Ed: Jeanie Casison. **Description:** Wyndham Hotels and Resorts recognizes women business travelers.

30442 ■ "West L.A. CPA Firm Opening Valley Office" in *San Fernando Valley Business Journal* **(Vol. 11, December 2006, No. 25, pp. 1)**
Pub: San Fernando Valley Business Journal Associates
Ed: Shelly Garcia. **Description:** Singer Lewak Greenbaum & Goldstein LLP will open a Warner Center office in hopes of keeping workers in what has become a fiercely competitive employment market and capturing larger ground in the growing financial services market.

30443 ■ "Western Airlines Announces Inaugural Flight Schedule" in *Bellingham Business Journal* **(January 2006, pp. A5)**
Pub: Sun News Inc.
Description: Western Airlines begins direct-flight service between Bellingham International Airport and four West Coast cities. This will double the number of destination sites for flying out of Bellingham.

30444 ■ "What a Deal! You Can Keep Hotel Costs Down-If You Know What To Look For" in *Entrepreneur* **(Vol. 33, January 2005, No. 1, pp. 22)**
Pub: Entrepreneur Media Inc.
Ed: Chris McGinnis. **Description:** Pricewaterhouse-Coopers predicts the rates businesses pay for hotels will rise by an average of 4 percent this year. Ways to keep hotel expenses at a minimum are examined.

30445 ■ "The Wheel Deal" in *Fast Company* **(September 2001, pp. 168)**
Pub: Fast Company
Ed: Christine Canabou. **Description:** Profile of the latest trends in the luggage industry, focusing on the business traveler.

30446 ■ "Who's the Boss?" in *Entrepreneur* **(Vol. 33, September 2005, No. 9, pp. 23)**
Pub: Entrepreneur Media Inc.
Ed: Chris McGinnis. **Description:** A list of four ways to keep travel expenses at a minimum are explained, including the review of expense reports, writing a travel policy, choosing a single travel agency, and creation of a standardized form for employees to track reimbursable expenses.

30447 ■ "Who's Working in Our Interest" in *Crain's Detroit Business* **(Vol. 23, January 15, 2007, No. 3, pp. 8)**
Pub: Crain Communications Inc. - Detroit
Ed: Christopher Crain. **Description:** Northwest loses bid for direct flight to Shanghai; $200M business potential lost. Decision may have adverse affect on expansion and growth in the Chinese market for local businesses.

30448 ■ "Wi-Fi, Where Are You? Where to Find the Nearest Free Hot Spot" in *Entrepreneur.com* **(Vol. 34, February 2006, No. 2, pp. 19)**
Pub: Entrepreneur Media Inc.
Ed: Chris McGinnis. **Description:** Business travelers are increasingly depending on fast and easy wireless Internet connections when on the road. Hotel chains often offer free Wi-Fi.

30449 ■ "Wingate Inn, the Preferred Hotel of the Company of Friends" in *Fast Company* **(March 2005, No. 92, pp. 94)**
Pub: Gruner & Jahr USA Publishing
Description: Profile of Wingate Inn, with 150 hotels nationwide, and its partnership with the Company of Friends; membership in the Company of Friends guarantees the best available rate when staying at a Wingate Inn. The hotel chain offers business travelers free high speed wired and wireless Internet access.

30450 ■ "The winner's circle" in *Entrepreneur* **(Vol. 31, No. 4, April 2003, pp. 33)**
Pub: Entrepreneur Media Inc.
Ed: Christopher Elliott, Christopher McGinnis. **Description:** A listing of the latest Business Travel Award winners selected by the magazine is presented, and include airlines, hotels, and major rental car companies.

30451 ■ "Winner's Circle: Kudos to these Web Sites for Offering Terrific Travel Tips" in *Entrepreneur* **(Vol. 32, No. 4, April 2004, pp. 24)**
Pub: Entrepreneur Media, Inc.
Ed: Chris McGinnis. **Description:** Advice for the experienced business traveler is offered, along with Web addresses to sites offering specialized assistance.

30452 ■ "Work Gear" in *St. Louis Post-Dispatch* **(November 5, 2004)**
Pub: Knight-Ridder/Tribune Business News
Ed: Jo Krummrich. **Description:** Perfect Solutions Digital Map Distance Finder calculates the miles and travel times between destinations, making it a good device for field reps.

30453 ■ "Work It! Score Great Deals With the Best-Kept Travel Secrets Around" in *Entrepreneur* **(Vol. 32, August 2004, No. 8, pp. 28)**
Pub: Entrepreneur Media Inc.
Ed: Chris McGinnis. **Description:** Tips for saving money on business trips is offered by a former corporate traveler, turned author and consultant.

30454 ■ "Working on Thin Air" in *Hispanic Business* **(October 2004, pp. 116, 118)**
Pub: Hispanic Business
Ed: Scott Williams. **Description:** Wireless electronic devices are being used increasingly by business travelers. Profiles of Sandisk Cruzer Titanium high-speed flash drive, Garmin iQue 3200 Global Positioning System, Sony's TR3A computer notebook, Mirra personal computer server, Kensington WiFi Detector, and HP iPAQ H6315 Pocket PC are included.

30455 ■ "You Can Take It With You: Use Your Mobile Phone Even While Abroad" in *Entrepreneur* **(Vol. 32, July 2004, No. 7, pp. 43)**
Pub: Entrepreneur Media Inc.
Ed: Amanda C. Kooser. **Description:** Entrepreneurs who travel outside of the U.S. are able to use their mobile phones while abroad. Dual-network phones work over both CDMA and GMS networks so a personal phone can be used with an international calling plan.

30456 ■ "You Need a Break" in *Success* **(Vol. 47, No. 1, January 2000, pp. 14)**
Pub: Success Publishing, Inc.
Description: Ways to write off expenses for time spent working on your vacation are discussed. Jan Zobel, author of "Minding Her Own Business: The Self-Employed Woman's Guide to Taxes and Record-keeping" (Easthill Press, 1998), gives advice for deducting your family vacation as a business trip.

30457 ■ "Your Loss? Don't Risk Losing Your Laptop (or PDA or Phone) on Your Next Flight" in *Entrepreneur* **(Vol. 31, No. 9, September 2003)**
Pub: Entrepreneur Media, Inc.
Ed: Christopher McGinnis. **Description:** Thousands of laptops, mobile phones, PDAs and other devices are left behind at airports by business travelers; tips to help avoid loss, including labeling, are included.

TRADE PERIODICALS

30458 ■ *21st Century Adventures*
Pub: 21st Century Adventures
Contact: Peter R. Madsen, Mktg. Dir.
Ed: Jennifer M. Tenney, Editor, jen@10e-design.com. **Description:** Travel magazine for those seeking adventure. Articles, written by freelance travelers, offer detailed information on specific destinations.

30459 ■ *Better Business Traveling*
Pub: Traveling Times Inc.
Ed: Mirko A. Ilich, Editor. **Released:** Monthly. **Description:** Provides news and information of interest to business travelers.

30460 ■ *Business Travel News*
Pub: VNU Business Media USA
Contact: Chris Davis, Managing Editor
E-mail: cdavis@btnonline.com
Released: Weekly. **Price:** $171.35. **Description:** Tabloid newspaper covering business travel.

30461 ■ *Consumer Reports Travel Letter*
Pub: Consumers Union of U.S. Inc.
Ed: Laurie Berger, Editor, lberger@crtl.com. **Released:** 12/year. **Description:** Provides travelers with information and advice on travel goods and services. Discusses such topics as air and rail passes, air fare, hotel rates, car rental fees, and techniques for optimizing foreign exchange rates.

30462 ■ *Corporate Meetings & Incentives*
Pub: Primedia Business Magazines & Media
Contact: Melissa Fromento, Publisher
E-mail: mfromento@primediabusiness.com
Ed: Barbara Scofidio, Editor, bscofidio@primediabusiness.com. **Released:** Monthly. **Price:** $97 Canada per year; Free to qualified subscribers; $123 other countries. **Description:** Magazine for executives and travel professionals responsible for choosing sites and destinations for meeting and incentive travel programs.

30463 ■ *Runzheimer Reports on Travel Management*
Pub: Runzheimer International
Ed: Phyllis Schumann, Sr., Editor, ps@runzheimer.com. **Released:** Monthly. **Price:** $295 print; $250 e-mail. **Description:** Intended to help control business travel costs. Covers travel budgets, corporate arrangements with travel agencies, in-house travel departments, and travel policies for business firms. Also discusses negotiation of special rates/services with travel suppliers. Recurring features include a profile of a major city, with information on car rentals, hotels, and special attractions. Remarks: Also available via e-mail.

30464 ■ *Southern Festivals*
Pub: Southern Festivals
Released: Bimonthly. **Description:** A statewide newspaper covering travel and tourism.

30465 ■ *ThriftyTraveling.com*
Pub: ThriftyTravelPortal

Contact: Mary Van Meer
Ed: Mary Van Meer, Editor. **Released:** Bimonthly. **Price:** $29.95, individuals U.S.. **Description:** Aims to help you "stretch your travel dollar." Filled with tips, resources, and late-breaking travel news. Includes a detailed annual index. Remarks: Also includes special sections for over-50 travelers and those looking for travel bargains on the Internet.

30466 ■ *Travel Manager's Executive Briefing*
Pub: American Business Publishing
Contact: Beth-Ann Kerber, Managing Editor
E-mail: bkerber@healthrespubs.com
Description: Follows developments in the field of travel and expense cost control. Recurring features include news of discounted air fares, car rentals, and hotel bills; case histories of other companies cutting costs; travel alternatives, phone savings, planning for meetings; and trends in government legislation affecting business travel costs.

CONSULTANTS

30467 ■ CM Uberman Enterprises
1370 Piccard Dr., Ste. 200
Rockville, MD 20850-4304
Ph:(301)417-0030
Fax: (301)417-0507
Scope: Conference and meeting management assistance offered to nonprofit institutions and agencies. Maintains a discount travel network covering hotels, airline flights, and care rentals. Serves all travelers: corporate, nonprofit and personal.

30468 ■ Off the Beaten Path L.L.C.
7 E Beall St.
Bozeman, MT 59715
Ph:(406)586-1311
Free: 800-445-2995
Fax: (406)587-4147
Co. E-mail: travel@offthebeatenpath.com
URL: http://www.offthebeatenpath.com

E-mail: travel@offthebeatenpath.com
Scope: A travel planning services consultancy and consulting on ecotourism; positioning of one's lodge/business in the marketplace, pricing, marketing plans and strategic planning.

30469 ■ Total Travel Management
1441 E Maple Rd.
Troy, MI 48083
Ph:(248)528-8000
Free: 888-886-8864

Fax: (248)528-3696
Co. E-mail: sales@ttm.com

E-mail: sales@ttm.com
Scope: Travel consultant in developing and renewing corporate travel policies, as well as negotiating special air, hotel, and car rental rates.

30470 ■ Trans-Research International Inc.
2320 Clifftops Ave.
PO Box 1178
Monteagle, TN 37356-1178
Ph:(931)924-7280
Fax: (931)924-7279
Scope: Transportation consultant in corporate transportation cost reduction and management, third party logistics evaluations and private fleet anaylsis. **Seminars:** Negotiating for Profit.

LIBRARIES

30471 ■ Maritz Travel Company–Resource Center
1395 N. Highway Dr.
Fenton, MO 63026
Ph:800-253-7562
Co. E-mail: hamiltsa@maritz.com
URL: http://www.maritztravel.com/
Contact: Sue Hamilton, Supv.
Scope: Travel data - hotels, restaurants, sightseeing, steamships, countries and cities. **Services:** Interlibrary loan; Library not open to the public. **Holdings:** 300 books; 177 bound periodical volumes; 95 VF drawers of travel-related brochures and reports; 2200 videotapes. **Subscriptions:** 35 journals and other serials.

30472 ■ Nadasdy Ferenc Museum–Library
Var-u 1
H-9600 Sarvar, Hungary
Scope: Regional history. **Services:** Library open to the public with restrictions. **Holdings:** 4000 volumes.

30473 ■ Travel Industry Association of America–Library
1100 New York Ave. NW, Ste. 450
Washington, DC 20005-3934
Ph:(202)408-8422
Fax: (202)408-1255
URL: http://www.tia.org
Contact: Suzanne D. Cook, Sr.VP, Res.
Scope: Travel and tourism. **Services:** Library not open to the public. **Holdings:** 3000 research documents; 3800 government documents; 250 unpublished travel research reports; 15,000 clippings; 20 tapes. **Subscriptions:** 27 journals and other serials.

Business Vision/Goals

START-UP INFORMATION

30474 ■ **"Beating the odds: remembering the basics of business can help"** in *Black Enterprise* (Vol. 32, No. 6, January 2002, pp. 35)
Pub: Earl Graves Publishing Co.
Ed: Glenn Townes. **Description:** The key to starting and sustaining a small business is to have a strong, basic understanding of business practices. Advice is given to manage small businesses.

30475 ■ *A Business of My Own? 21 Steps to Successfully Starting and Running a Small Business*
Pub: Enfield Publishing
Ed: Marjorie Cleveland Fisher. **Released:** January 2005. **Price:** $24.95. **Description:** New ideas to start or grow a small business, including ideas for writing business plans with examples, adopting a business structure, and setting goals and objectives.

30476 ■ **"The Disruptive Startup"** in *Inc.* (February 1, 2002)
Pub: Inc. Magazine
Ed: Nancy Lyons. **Description:** Interview with Harvard Business School professor and author, Clayton M. Christensen. Christensen helps identify strategies that allow new growth companies succeed.

30477 ■ **"Entrepreneur Column"** in *Entrepreneur.com* (November 16, 2006)
Pub: Entrepreneur Media Inc.
Ed: Tim Berry. **Description:** Sticking to a business plan is critical in the launch of a new business. If one element is missing, do not proceed without amending that or altering the plan.

30478 ■ **"Entrepreneur in Residence"** in *Red Herring* (No. 87, December 18, 2000, pp. 212)
Pub: Herring Communications, Inc.
Ed: Desh Deshpande. **Description:** Desh Deshpande, cofounder and chairman of Sycamore Networks, offers advice to entrepreneurs on finding the right niche.

30479 ■ **"Fly Solo: How to Build a Profitable Enterprise"** in *Black Enterprise* (Vol. 30, No. 6, January 2000, pp. 72)
Pub: Earl Graves Publishing Co.
Ed: Millicent Lownes-Jackson and Gerda Gallop-Goodman. **Description:** Ways to assess your entrepreneurial sills are explored. Do you have the skills, abilities and knowledge required for the business you'd like to start? Do you have the ability to nurture and grow a business? Are you prepared to make sacrifices? Are you self-motivated? Do you like being in charge? Do you have the financial means to start a business? These questions must be answered truthfully before you move into self-employment.

30480 ■ **"From idea to inspiration"** in *Entrepreneur* (Vol. 30, No. 3, March 2002, pp. 29)
Pub: Entrepreneur Media Inc.

Ed: Mark Henricks. **Description:** Book review of 'The Big Idea', written by attorney Steven D. Strauss. The books tells how many products came to exist.

30481 ■ **"Get On The Plan"** in *Entrepreneur* (Vol. 33, October 2005, No. 10, pp. 14)
Pub: Entrepreneur Media Inc.
Description: Review of the book, "The Idiot's Guide to Business Plans", which explains the process of writing a business plan.

30482 ■ **"Getting Set for Success with Your Own Small Business"** in *Small Business Opportunities* (Vol. 12, No. 3, May 2000, pp. 110)
Pub: Harris Publications, Inc.
Description: Statistics regarding new business start-ups presented by the Small Business Administration (SBA) and Richard E. Irwin Research, Inc., along with advice for entrepreneurs, is provided.

30483 ■ **"Hall of Mirrors"** in *Small Business Opportunities* (Vol. 12, No. 3, May 2000, pp. 44)
Pub: Harris Publications, Inc.
Ed: Stan Roberts. **Description:** A profile of Tom Levine and how he worked part-time installing mirrors, before starting his own mirror business that now earns $300,000 annually.

30484 ■ **"How to Stay on the Move...When the World is Slowing Down"** in *Fast Company* (July 2001, pp. 113)
Pub: Fast Company
Ed: Scott Kirsner. **Description:** It is hard to remember a less-inviting time to have a great idea for a new company or to champion new ideas to change a big company. Leaders who think big aren't willing to downsize their ambitions they just work a little harder and smarter. Some battle-tested advice on how to stay fast in slow times is offered.

30485 ■ **"Identify All Possible Exits"** in *Business Week Online* (Dec. 6, 2002)
Pub: McGraw-Hill Inc.
Ed: William J. Link. **Description:** Advice for entrepreneurs to keep exit strategies in mind when planning a start up company is given.

30486 ■ **"Is My Partnership Fair?"** in *Inc.* (July 1, 2004)
Pub: Inc. Magazine
Description: A small business entrepreneur of a 50-50 partnership talks about protecting ideas and the pros and cons of leasing versus purchasing new technology.

30487 ■ **"Just Desserts"** in *Small Business Opportunities* (Vol. 12, No. 3, May 2000, pp. 54)
Pub: Harris Publications, Inc.
Ed: Jerilyn Kaufman. **Description:** Alicia Dargan, the mastermind behind AMK Specialty Gourmet, Inc., chronicles the family dessert shop from start-up to their current success, with earnings at $300,000 a year.

30488 ■ **"Luck of the Draw: A Windfall Helps One Man's Small Business Dream Come True"** in *Entrepreneur* (Vol. 31, No. 10, October 2003)
Pub: Entrepreneur Media, Inc.
Ed: Devlin Smith. **Description:** Profile of Timothy Tuttle, who won $1.9 million on a quarter slot machine in Las Vegas, Nevada, and started his own quick-service chain specializing in Orleans fare like gumbo and beignets.

30489 ■ **"Minneapolis"** in *Entrepreneur* (Vol. 28, No. 4, April 2000, pp. 162)
Pub: Entrepreneur Media, Inc.
Ed: Cynthia E. Griffin. **Description:** Use this incubator to hatch your business in 90 days or less. Entrenaut, a Minneapolis incubator is profiled.

30490 ■ **"New Owners Cook Up Redo of Clarkston Cafe"** in *Crain's Detroit Business* (Vol. 22, December 4, 2006, No. 29, pp. 24)
Pub: Crain Communications Inc. - Detroit
Ed: Brent Snavely. **Description:** Renown French restaurant is reopening with new menu and many renovations. Clarkston Cafe was the site of Kid Rock and Pamela Anderson's wedding ceremonies.

30491 ■ **"Shoestring Start-Ups"** in *Small Business Opportunities* (Vol. 13, No. 6, November 2001, pp. 22-24, 26, 28, 30, 32, 34, 36, 116)
Pub: Harris Publications, Inc.
Description: The top 50 small business that can be started with little or no capital are previewed, some as little as $100 or less, including the ten steps to follow when starting a new business.

30492 ■ **"Shop for Success"** in *Small Business Opportunities* (Vol. 12, No. 3, May 2000, pp. 46-48)
Pub: Harris Publications, Inc.
Ed: Marie Sherlock. **Description:** To cash in on used sports equipment, this second-hand shop owner tells how he makes $500,000 a year selling used sporting goods.

30493 ■ **"Starting a business? Then get with the plan"** in *Crain's Detroit Business* (Vol. 18, No. 49, December 9, 2002, pp. 17)
Pub: Crain Communications Inc., Detroit
Ed: Laura Bailey. **Description:** When starting a new company, it is imperative to have a good business plan.

30494 ■ **"Street Smarts"** in *Inc.* (August 2000, pp. 37)
Pub: The Goldhirsh Group
Ed: Norm Brodsky and Bo Burlingham. **Description:** Sometimes the hardest part of starting a business is figuring out where to begin. Those beginning a business should remain focused on the primary goals, and not get lost in details.

30495 ■ **"Yes, you can"** in *Black Enterprise* (Vol. 31, No. 5, December 2000, pp. 64)
Pub: Earl Graves Publishing Co.

Ed: Feona Huff. Description: How to start, operate and grow a business while developing yourself and pursuing your personal goals.

30496 ■ "You Don't Know Jackalope" in *Success* **(Vol. 47, No. 4, September 2000, pp. 18)**
Pub: Success Publishing, Inc.
Ed: Michael Barrier. Description: Darby McQuade, founder of a store called Jackalope in Santa Fe, New Mexico, has discovered a way to maintain a growing business while sharing his love for animals with his customers.

ASSOCIATIONS AND OTHER ORGANIZATIONS

30497 ■ Agile Manufacturing Benchmarking Consortium
4606 FM 1960 W, Ste. 250
Houston, TX 77069
Ph:(281)440-5044
Fax: (281)440-6677
URL: http://www.ambcbenchmarking.org
Description: Promotes the use of benchmarking to facilitate process improvement and to achieve total quality. Facilitates exchange of information among members, conducts target operations, procurement, development and maintenance studies, and identifies model business practices.

EDUCATIONAL PROGRAMS

30498 ■ Aligning IT with Corporate Strategy
American Management Association
1601 Broadway
New York, NY 10019
Ph:(212)586-8100
Free: 800-262-9699
Fax: (212)903-8168
Co. E-mail: customerservice@amanet.org
URL: http://www.amanet.org
Price: $1,695.00; $1,595.00 for AMA members. Description: Three-day seminar for senior executives and IT managers; covers aligning business and IT goals, choosing hardware and software, enterprise strategy, and implementing and monitoring an IT Alignment Plan. Locations: San Francisco, CA; Chicago, IL; New York, NY.

30499 ■ Small Project/Task Management for Team Members (Canada)
Canadian Management Centre
150 York St., 5th Fl.
Toronto, ON, Canada M5H 3S5
Free: 877-CMC-2500
Fax: (416)313-4985
Co. E-mail: cmcinfo@cmctraining.org
URL: http://www.cma.org
Price: $995 Canadian. Description: Seminar that covers how to work with project managers and senior managers, including ways to contribute to the overall work plan, ways to develop task plans, and how to effectively communicate with project managers. Locations: Toronto, ON.

REFERENCE WORKS

30500 ■ "The '42 Formula' For Success" in *Inc.* **(August 1, 2003)**
Pub: Gruner & Jahr USA Publishing
Ed: Tahl Raz. Description: Author Nitin Nohria offers information and advice on why some small business owners succeed and others fail.

30501 ■ "ABN Amro To Cut 900 Positions In North America" in *Wall Street Journal* **(Vol. 248, December 2006, No. 152, pp. A7)**
Pub: Dow Jones & Co. Inc.
Ed: Reuters News Service Description: ABN Amro Holding NV., Parent of Chicago-based LaSalle Bank plans to cut 900 more North American Jobs to reduce costs amid growing competition.

30502 ■ "All in a day's work" in *Harvard Business Review* **(Vol. 79, No. 11, December 2001, pp. 54)**
Pub: Harvard Business School Press
Description: A roundtable discussion with six experts from the corporate world, the nonprofit sector, and academia on tough questions about leadership is presented. Three common themes emerged: the need for a leader to formulate and communicate a vision for the organization, the need for the leader to add value to an enterprise and the organizational imperative for the leader to motivate followers.

30503 ■ "Allegiant Files Statement for IPO of Common Stock" in *Bellingham Business Journal* **(December 2006, pp. A3)**
Pub: Sun News Inc.
Description: Las Vegas-based Allegiant Travel Company announced its plans for a public offering of its common stock. The company plans to list its shares on the NASDAQ stock market under the ticker symbol ALGT.

30504 ■ "Applying Old Ideals to Crain's New Tasks" in *Crain's New York Business* **(Vol. 23, January 8, 2007, No. 2, pp. 11)**
Pub: Crain Communications, Inc.
Ed: Greg David. Description: Crain's New York Business announces its plans for the coming year which include a comprehensive website that will provide readers with daily news stories.

30505 ■ "Arvin Meritor Says It's Done Selling" in *Crain's Detroit Business* **(Vol. 23, February 5, 2007, No. 6, pp. 29)**
Pub: Crain Communications Inc. - Detroit
Ed: Brent Snaveley. Description: Auto Supplier Arvin Meritor, Inc. has completed selling off its non-core businesses and will now concentrate on growing those globally. $200M capital was raised in the sale of its last non core businesses in 2006.

30506 ■ "Banking on Tomorrow" in *Fast Company* **(November 2001, pp. 50)**
Pub: Fast Company
Ed: Scott Kirsner. Description: The best way to prepare for the future is to see it come to life before your eyes. That's why executives from the financial services companies come play at the Merlin Center, an idea fun factory for the financial industry.

30507 ■ "Banners Tout Development" in *Mississippi Business Journal* **(Vol. 29, January 2007, No. 4, pp. 11)**
Pub: Venture Publications, Inc.
Ed: Wally Northway Description: Flashy banners have been erected all over downtown Jackson's business district. The banner idea, originated by a local restaurateur, is designed to bring visual attention to many unnoticed development projects and businesses in the area.

30508 ■ "Beating the Dream-Busters: Don't Let Loved Ones Keep You From Living Your Dream" in *Black Enterprise* **(Vol. 34, No. 5, December 2003)**
Pub: Earl Graves Publishing Co.
Description: Tips to help individuals avoid negativity and criticism from loved ones when trying to fulfill career/business visions and goals.

30509 ■ "Being Small, Looking Big" in *Boston Business Journal* **(Vol. 23, No. 21, June 27, 2003, pp. 24)**
Pub: American City Business Journals
Ed: Chelsea Lowe. Description: Nancy Michaels of Impression Impact, Inc. discusses ways small companies can market themselves in a way that makes them look large, without spending large amounts of money to do so.

30510 ■ *Benchmarking for Best Practices: How to Define, Locate, and Emulate the Best in the Business*
Pub: The McGraw-Hill Companies
Ed: Christopher E. Bogan and Michael M. English. Released: 1995. Price: $29.95. Description: Guides businesses through the 9-step benchmarking model. Includes tips, charts, case studies, ethics guidelines, and other benchmarking advice.

30511 ■ "Beyond the exchange: the future of B2B" in *Harvard Business Review* **(Vol. 78, No. 6, November-December 2000, pp. 86)**
Pub: Harvard Business School Publishing Corp.
Description: The evolution of business-to-business commerce on the Internet, and how it has been influenced by such revolutionary changes as an influx of specialists, a proliferation of creative business models, and new challenges for buyers and sellers. The article also forecasts the future of B2B on the Internet.

30512 ■ "Bloopers & Blunders" in *Small Business Opportunities* **(Vol. 16, November 2004, No. 6, pp. 72)**
Pub: Harris Publications Inc.
Ed: Joanne G. Sujansky. Description: Seven mistakes made by company leaders and ways to avoid them are explained: lack of trust, failure to shape and share vision, unclear expectations, insufficient modeling of desire behaviors, too little partnering, failure to retain top talent, and too little celebration of success.

30513 ■ "Boudin Rises, Again; Bakery Restaurant Set for Suburban Return" in *Crain's Chicago Business* **(Vol. 30, January 2007, No. 4, pp. 13)**
Pub: Crain Communications, Inc.
Ed: H. Lee Murphy. Description: Boudin Bakery is returning to Chicago after a five-year absence. The company is expanding to include a sister Italian chain, Go Roma.

30514 ■ "Brainstorming" in *Small Business Opportunities* **(Vol. 12, No. 2, March 2000, pp. 120)**
Pub: Harris Publications, Inc.
Ed: Robert Spiegel. Description: Six ways to generate big ideas for small business are presented, including inviting friends, professionals, and relatives to brainstorm.

30515 ■ *Building a Business the Buddhist Way*
Pub: Celestial Arts Publishing Company
Ed: Geri Larkin. Released: September 2004. Price: $18.95 (Canadian). Description: Principles of entrepreneurship for starting and growing a business while maintaining a balance between business goals and spiritual goals.

30516 ■ "Building an Innovation Factory" in *Harvard Business Review* **(Vol. 78, No. 3, May 2000, pp. 157)**
Pub: Harvard Business School Publishing Corp.
Ed: Andrew Hargadon, Robert I. Sutton. Description: The best innovators are not lone geniuses. They are people who can take an idea that's obvious in one context and apply it in a not-so-obvious way to a different context. The best companies have learned to systematize that process.

30517 ■ "Business Plan Helps Set Goals, Draw Investors" in *Crain's Detroit Business* **(Vol. 22, November 20, 2006, No. 47, pp. 18)**
Pub: Crain Communications Inc. - Detroit
Ed: Sheena Harrison. Description: Financial investors always require a business plan before they will commit to investment in new or expanding ventures. Sound business planning and management also include a good business plan with time phased measurable goals to monitor progress and indicate need for adjustments of the plan.

30518 ■ "C & A Says Company Will Be Sold" in *Crain's Detroit Business* **(Vol. 22, November 20, 2006, No. 47, pp. 4)**
Pub: Crain Communications Inc. - Detroit
Ed: Brent Snaveley. Description: Southfield based interior supplier has decided to go out of business in wake of reduced sales volume and difficulty in emerging from bankruptcy. Entire company or individual assets are available for sale and will be consolidated and closed as the business winds down.

30519 ■ "Chocolate Maker Plans New Plant in Pauls Valley, Okla" in *Knight-Ridder/Tribune Business News* (April 11, 2002, pp. ITEM02101008)
Pub: Knight-Ridder Inc.
Ed: Ed Godfrey. **Description:** Jerry Couch, general manager of Ada-based Bedre Chocolates, owned by the Chickasaw Nation, hopes to make Pauls valley a tourist stop for his candy store.

30520 ■ "Clear leadership" in *Women in Business* (Vol. 54, No. 5, September-October 2002, pp. 41)
Pub: The ABWA Company, Inc.
Ed: Andrew Harvey. **Description:** Leadership requires a vision of where an organization will be taken.

30521 ■ "Close to Finding RedZone's Niche" in *Pittsburgh Business Times* (Vol. 4, August 15, 2003, pp. 14)
Pub: Pittsburgh Business Times
Ed: Maria Guzzo. **Description:** Profile of Pittsburgh, Pennsylvania-based RedZone Robotics Inc.; topics include market development, management styles, and management of small business.

30522 ■ "Coevolving At Last, a Way to Make Synergies Work" in *Harvard Business Review* (Vol. 78, No. 1, January 2000, pp. 91)
Pub: Harvard Business School Publishing Corp.
Ed: Kathleen M. Eisenhardt, D. Charles Galunic. **Description:** Cross-business synergies as a strategy is the challenge most companies are trying to capture. The process of coevolution, whereby companies collaborate to achieve a specific goal, is one that can help managers direct the company.

30523 ■ "Composite forecasting: combining forecasts for improved accuracy" in *Journal of Business Forecasting* (Vol.19,No. 2,Summer 2000, pp. 2)
Pub: Graceway Publishing Co., Inc.
Ed: Charles W. Chase, Jr. **Description:** The practice of composite forecasting, combining several business forecasts prepared in different ways, is described, together with a history of this method. Ex-post forecasts are also explained.

30524 ■ "Consensus forecasts of financial institutions" in *Journal of Business Forecasting* (Vol. 19, No. 2, Summer 2000, pp. 37)
Pub: Graceway Publishing Co., Inc.
Ed: Dennis F. Ellis. **Description:** Forecasts for the U.S. economy for the last quarter of 2000 and the first three quarters of 2001 are presented. It is predicted that the growth of the economy will slow down during this period.

30525 ■ "Corporate Venture Capital: Moving to the Head of the Class" in *Venture Capital Journal* (Vol. 40, No. 10, November 2000, pp. 43-46)
Pub: Venture Economics
Ed: Alistair Christopher. **Description:** Ways established venture capital firms are working to differentiate themselves from their competitors are highlighted.

30526 ■ "Creating a Recipe for an Empire" in *Crain's New York Business* (Vol. 23, January 29, 2007, No. 5, pp. F22)
Pub: Crain Communications, Inc.
Ed: Description: Profile of Kenny Lao, co-founder of Rickshaw Dumpling Bar, whose business plan for the casual Chelsea eatery won a contest at Stern and attracted the school's dean, Thomas Cooley, as an investor. Rickshaw's revenues in fiscal 2005 reached $1.3 million and are on track to rise another 12 percent in 2006. He intends to open six more Rickshaw bars within the next few years.

30527 ■ "Creativity Regained" in *Inc.* (September 1, 2003)
Pub: Gruner & Jahr USA Publishing
Ed: Stephen H. Zades. **Description:** Actor, Robert Redford, founded the Sundance Institute, and in the process changed an industry. His theories of innovation and creativity will inspire any entrepreneur to improve his or her business.

30528 ■ "A delicate balance" in *Red Herring* (March 2003, pp. 44)
Pub: Herring Communications Inc.
Ed: John Micklethwait, Adrian Wooldridge. **Description:** A review of the book, "The Company: A Short History of a Revolutionary Idea", by John Micklethwait and Adrian Wooldridge.

30529 ■ "Delusions of Success: How Optimism Undermines Executives' Decisions" in *Harvard Business Review* (Vol. 81, No. 7, July 2003, pp. 56)
Pub: Harvard Business School Press
Ed: Dan Lovallo, Daniel Kahneman. **Description:** Realistic business forecasting is discussed.

30530 ■ "Detroit Free Press Small Business Column" in *Detroit Free Press* (June 20, 2005)
Pub: Knight-Ridder/Tribune Business News
Ed: Carol Cain. **Description:** According to the Small Business Administration, four out of five new small businesses fail within five years of starting up. Minesh Baxi offers a listing of the ten most common mistakes small and mid-size companies make.

30531 ■ "Don't Just Dream—Plan" in *Black Enterprise* (Vol. 35, January 2005, No. 6, pp. 97)
Pub: Earl G. Graves Publishing Co. Inc.
Ed: Alfred A. Edmond Jr. **Description:** Principles of goal-setting and techniques used to achieve goals are discussed, including a listing of books designed to motivate individuals and would-be entrepreneurs.

30532 ■ "Dream Your Way to Success: Think Visualization Is Easier Said than Done?" in *Black Enterprise* (Vol. 33, No. 6, January 2003, pp. 84)
Pub: Earl Graves Publishing Co.
Ed: Caroline V. Clarke. **Description:** A technique for achieving success through creative visualization is presented.

30533 ■ "Drugmaker Ups Dosage; Acquisition Expected to Double Revenue" in *Crain's New York Business* (Vol. 23, January 22, 2007, No. 4, pp. 4)
Pub: Crain Communications, Inc.
Description: Barr Pharmaceuticals Inc. won a bidding war to acquire Pliva for $2.5 billion. The acquisition is expected to double Barr's revenue which had been falling over the last two years.

30534 ■ "Easy Does It" in *Entrepreneur* (Vol. 33, October 2005, No. 10, pp. 122)
Pub: Entrepreneur Media Inc.
Ed: Romanus Wolter. **Description:** In order to be successful, entrepreneurs must learn to balance work time with their personal life as a small business grows. A good rule to follow: success is not about the number of hours worked, but the outcome of the efforts involved.

30535 ■ "The empire strikes back; Counterrevolutionary strategies for industry leaders" in *Harvard Business Review* (Vol. 80, Nov. 2002, pp. 66)
Pub: Harvard Business School Press
Ed: Richard D'Aveni. **Description:** Five ways that industry leaders can respond to revolutionary business models or disruptive technologies. The strategies are containment, shaping, absorption, neutralization and annulment.

30536 ■ "Entrepreneur Column" in *Entrepreneur.com* (December 28, 2006)
Pub: Entrepreneur Media Inc.
Ed: Paige Arnof-Fenn. **Description:** Reflections and insight into setting practical business goals of a home-based business, including office relocation and organization.

30537 ■ "Environmental and Ownership Characteristics of Small Businesses and their Impact on Development" in *Journal of Small Business Management*
Pub: West Virginia University

Ed: William B. Gartner, Subodh Bhat. **Description:** This article explores the relationship between the characteristics of a small business's location (crime, neighborhood appearance, and transportation accessibility) and a small business owner's expectations of future firm growth.

30538 ■ "Everything In Its Place" in *San Fernando Valley Business Journal* (Vol. 8, No. 12, June 9, 2003, pp. 23)
Pub: San Fernando Business Journal
Ed: Rosanna Mah. **Description:** Profile of Dorothy Breininger, owner of Canoga Park, California-based Center for Organization and Goal Planning. Breininger provides professional organization services to large and small companies.

30539 ■ "A family affair" in *Black Enterprise* (Vol. 33, No. 3, October 2002, pp. 154)
Pub: Earl Graves Publishing Co.
Ed: George Alexander. **Description:** The largest part of American wealth lies in the family-owned businesses that make up 80-90 percent of all business enterprises in North America. The importance of a succession plan for family-owned firms is discussed. A survey by the Family Firm Institute of 800 family-owned businesses showed that insufficient estate planning, failure to prepare for the inevitable transition, and lack of funds to pay estate taxes are the leading causes for most family-owned business failures.

30540 ■ "Fear of feedback" in *Harvard Business Review* (Vol. 81, No. 4, April 2003, pp. 101)
Pub: Harvard Business School Press
Ed: Jay M. Jackman, Myra H. Strober. **Description:** The negative effects of the fear of feedback for workers and bosses are addressed. Ways to overcome that fear so employees can bring work into better alignment with organizational goals are discussed.

30541 ■ "FEI's Strategy for Reaching Big Leagues" in *Business Journal-Portland* (Vol. 20, No. 24, August 15, 2003, pp. 1)
Pub: American City Business Journals, Inc.
Ed: Aliza Earnshaw. **Description:** Profile of FEI Company, manufacturer of three-dimensional inspection technology used in semiconductor manufacturing. The firm's goal is to have $1 billion in revenue.

30542 ■ "Found in Yonkers" in *Crain's New York Business* (Vol. 23, January 15, 2007, No. 3, pp. 37)
Pub: Crain Communications, Inc.
Description: Yonkers, Westchester's largest city, has unveiled a master plan of $3.1 billion to redevelop downtown and attract more companies, according to Yonkers Industrial Development Agency.

30543 ■ "Four Starrs Moves, Doubles Size" in *Bellingham Business Journal* (January 2007, pp. A6)
Pub: Sun News Inc.
Description: Danielle Starr, owner of Four Starrs Boutique is moving to a location double the size of the original. The women's boutique sells cosmetics and clothing lines not readily available to the area.

30544 ■ "From Wish to Goal" in *Black Enterprise* (Vol. 35, January 2005, No. 6, pp. 97)
Pub: Earl G. Graves Publishing Co. Inc.
Description: Gadsden's tips for setting and achieving goals are listed. These goals will help inspiring entrepreneurs follow their vision. Rev. Nathaniel Gadsden founded the Writers Wordshop, a not-for-profit agency that helps poets develop their writing skills.

30545 ■ "The Fruitful Flaws of Strategy Metaphors" in *Harvard Business Review* (Vol. 81, No. 9, September 2003, pp. 86)
Pub: Harvard Business School Press
Ed: Tihamer von Ghyczy. **Description:** Companies looking for parallels outside of business need to look at differences, not similarities.

30546 ■ "Fuel Efficiency Becomes Grail" in *Crain's Detroit Business* **(Vol. 23, January 8, 2007, No. 2, pp. 11)**
Pub: Crain Communications Inc. - Detroit
Ed: Brent Snaveley. **Description:** Fuel efficiency, quality, and safety are primary customer concerns for vehicle and subsystems development. Many suppliers are shifting capital expenditures toward smaller fuel efficient vehicles.

30547 ■ "Get Smart" in *Entrepreneur* **(Vol. 32, July 2004, No. 7, pp. 34)**
Pub: Entrepreneur Media Inc.
Ed: Mark Henricks. **Description:** Review of the book, MBA In a Box, which offers practical ideas from top business leaders.

30548 ■ "Getting It Right the Second Time" in *Harvard Business Review* **(Vol. 80, No. 1, January 2002, pp. 62)**
Pub: Harvard Business School Press
Ed: Gabriel Szulanski, Sidney Winter. **Description:** Research has shown the difficulty with which businesses have had in transferring management successes from one division to another. Effective knowledge management transfer is critical, as is understanding why a procedure initially succeeded.

30549 ■ "Glass Ceiling Persists in the Board Room" in *Marketing to Women* **(Vol. 19, December 2006, No. 2, pp. 8)**
Pub: EPM Communications, Inc.
Description: A study by search firm Heidrick & Struggles and Women Corporate Directors shows that executive inequality remains high despite the number of women who hold board seats. Although these women tend to mentor and recommend other women for candidates, only 54 percent say that at least one of the women recommended was actually elected to the board. Despite the meager statistics, 76 percent of women on boards surveyed stated that they oppose a legal quota that would mandate an increase of women occupying board seats.

30550 ■ *Goals and Goal Setting*
Pub: Crisp Publications, Inc.
Ed: Larrie Rouillard. **Price:** $10.95. **Description:** Teaches the fundamentals of goal setting in both business and personal lives. Includes exercises and activities to help set, manage and achieve goals.

30551 ■ "Got Game?" in *Entrepreneur* **(Vol. 32, October 2004, No. 10, pp. 95)**
Pub: Entrepreneur Media Inc.
Ed: Chris Penttila. **Description:** Entrepreneurial introspection is a growing trend in small business. Strategic plans implemented inside a company help give employees and managers a realistic look at the business and its goals.

30552 ■ "Group Therapy" in *Forbes* **(April 3, 2000, pp. 138)**
Pub: Forbes Magazine
Ed: Leigh Gallagher. **Description:** The Young Entrepreneurs Association, the global association for small business operators under the age of 40, is profiled.

30553 ■ "Growth Tales; Key Strategies Used by Young Firms" in *Crain's New York Business* **(Vol. 22, December 11, 2006, No. 50, pp. 27)**
Pub: Crain Communications, Inc.
Ed: Lisa Goff. **Description:** Profile of businesses who have used innovative marketing campaigns that cost little to no capital.

30554 ■ "Guide Advises Would-Be Entrepreneurs" in *Marketing to Women* **(Vol. 20, January 2007, No. 1, pp. 8)**
Pub: EPM Communications, Inc.
Description: Smart Women and Small Business: How to Make the Leap from Corporate Careers to the Right Small Enterprise, a new how-to guide book for women looking to leave their corporate careers and join the entrepreneurial workforce, offers tips on getting loans, starting a business, working with business partners, and finding and closing the right deals.

30555 ■ "Having trouble with your strategy? Then map it" in *Harvard Business Review* **(Vol. 78, No. 5, September-October 2000, pp. 167)**
Pub: Harvard Business School Publishing Corp.
Ed: David P., Robert S., Norton Kaplan. **Description:** The authors demonstrate with graphs the advantages of using strategy maps. Such maps, by giving a visual representation of a company's objectives, help employees see more clearly their place in the plan.

30556 ■ "Home Depot Offers Expensive Lesson in Curbing Execs' Pay" in *Crain's Chicago Business* **(Vol. 30, January 2007, No. 3, pp. 13)**
Pub: Crain Communications, Inc.
Ed: Description: Linking executive pay to performance is becoming a top priority for the board of directors as part of their role is compensation watchdogs. Recent departure of Home Depot's CEO, Robert Nardelli left him with a $210 million compensation package. Profile of the Home Depot debacle included.

30557 ■ "How to Plan as a Small Scale Business Owner" in *Journal of Small Business Management* **(Vol. 38, No. 38, April 2000, pp. 1)**
Pub: West Virginia University
Ed: Michael Frese, Marco van Gelderen, Michael Ombach. **Description:** This study takes a psychological approach to investigate the process characteristics of action strategies used by small business owners; these strategy characteristics are then related to the firms' success. The objective of the research is to deepen the understanding of how strategies are used and how the owner's strategy-relevant behavior is related to the business' success.

30558 ■ "The Imagination Gap" in *Internet World* **(Vol. 7, No. 1, January 15, 2001, pp. 8)**
Pub: Mecklermedia Corporation
Ed: Tony Rizzo. **Description:** The so-called 'imagination gap', a concept noted by author Bob Crowley, is a growing issue as the technology and business strategy curves fail to keep pace with one another amid the growing importance of E-commerce. Internet and Web technology grew at a substantial rate between 1994 and 1999, but only a tiny percentage of traditional businesses took advantage of it effectively, and a few pure Internet businesses, such as Amazon.com, developed entirely new strategies. Companies often fail to adjust their business strategies to leverage new technology and fall behind as the economy moves to E-business.

30559 ■ "In Helen's good graces" in *Candy Industry* **(Vol. 167, No. 3, March 2002, pp. 34)**
Pub: Stagnito Communications Inc.
Ed: Bernard Pacyniak. **Description:** Recently acquired Helen Grace Chocolates finds itself focused on what founder Bill Grace always intended, producing good chocolates. The new owners, Robert and David Worth, are focusing on national expansion for the company.

30560 ■ "IPOs: Things of the Past" in *Crain's New York Business* **(Vol. 23, January 1, 2007, No. 1, pp. 14)**
Pub: Crain Communications, Inc.
Description: Relegence Corp., a Manhattan-based company that gathers business information from around the globe and allows people to personalize the news delivered to their desktops, was acquired by AOL. The new trend in the business realm is to slowly grow then be acquired by a larger company instead of going public.

30561 ■ "It's Business...and Personal" in *Black Enterprise* **(Vol. 34, July 2004, No. 12, pp. 38)**
Pub: Earl G. Graves Publishing Co. Inc.
Ed: Aissatou Sidime. **Description:** Anthony Harris, owner of Popular Demand clothing store and Popular Demand Unisex Salon in Cleveland, Ohio, reports how he has formed a retirement savings account by investing in mutual funds and government bonds through a financial advisor who also helped Harris find personal medical coverage and life insurance.

30562 ■ "J.C. Watts First Black John Deere Dealer" in *Black Enterprise* **(Vol. 37, November 2006, No. 4, pp. 36)**
Pub: Earl G. Graves Publishing Co. Inc.
Ed: Kiara Ashanti. **Description:** Profile of former Congressman J.C. Watts Jr., a man who grew up in rural America and is the first African American to own a John Deere Dealership.

30563 ■ "Jerry's Diner is One Man's Business Vision Come True" in *Miami Herald* **(March 10, 2005)**
Pub: Knight-Ridder/Tribune Business News
Ed: Brighton Watambwa. **Description:** Profile of Darcy Jenkins, owner of Jerry's Diner and Catering. Jenkins left his job as national trainer for Rainforest Cafe to open his own restaurant and shares how his skills help him run his own business.

30564 ■ "King of the Hill" in *Houston Business Journal* **(Vol. 34, No. 15, August 22, 2003, pp. 17)**
Pub: American City Business Journals
Ed: Allison Wollam. **Description:** Profile of Berryhill Baja Grill's operations and growth plans is presented.

30565 ■ "A Labor of Love: Have You Lost That Lovin' Feeling For Your Business?" in *Entrepreneur* **(Vol. 32, November 2004, No. 11, pp. 130)**
Pub: Entrepreneur Media Inc.
Ed: Romanus Wolter. **Description:** Four ways to renew entrepreneurial passion are designed to bring happiness back into day-to-day business activities.

30566 ■ *Leadership 101: What Every Leader Needs to Know*
Pub: Nelson Business
Ed: John C. Maxwell. **Released:** September 2002. **Price:** $9.99. **Description:** Ways to enhance leadership skills focusing on following a vision and bringing others along.

30567 ■ "Local Gelato King is Getting Ready to Expand His Empire" in *Bellingham Business Journal* **(January 2007, pp. A4)**
Pub: Sun News Inc.
Description: Profile Sirena Gelato, owned by Fahri Ugurlu, who has decided to expand the business by adding a wholesale component.

30568 ■ "Mega Wal-Marts Crush Business Diversity" in *Bellingham Business Journal* **(January 2007, pp. C14)**
Pub: Sun News Inc.
Description: Small businesses are the backbone of the Bellingham economy. Wal-Mart threatens the economic diversity by flattening competition and erasing longtime family-owned businesses.

30569 ■ "Money Talks; Here's Message to Michigan" in *Crain's Detroit Business* **(Vol. 22, November 20, 2006, No. 47, pp. 9)**
Pub: Crain Communications Inc. - Detroit
Ed: William Watch **Description:** Capital moves quickly away from troubled areas. International markets such as Mexico and Brazil are more attractive to investors than Detroit.

30570 ■ "More dealers may signal end of mobile-phone boom" in *Crain's Detroit Business* **(Vol. 18, No. 49, December 9, 2002, pp. 25)**
Pub: Crain Communications Inc., Detroit
Ed: Andrew Dietderich. **Description:** Wireless Toyz aims to continue growing and become the next Blockbuster Video.

30571 ■ "Neighborhood Mortgage Announces Office Expansion" in *Bellingham Business Journal* **(December 2006, pp. 2)**
Pub: Sun News Inc.
Description: Neighborhood Mortgage plans to expand and relocate its home office by Spring 2007. The move will help accommodate the company's rapid growth by tripling the square footage of the building and offer convenient access to and from the freeway.

30572 ■ "New Beginnings for VIBE" in *Black Enterprise* (Vol. 37, November 2006, No. 4, pp. 34)
Pub: Earl G. Graves Publishing Co. Inc.
Ed: Mashaun D. Simon. **Description:** Danyel Smith replaced Mimi Valdes as editor-in-chief of VIBE magazine after the Wicks Group, private equity firm focused on selected segments of the media, communications, and information industries, purchased the magazine.

30573 ■ *The New Business Landscape: Taking Your Business into the Twenty-First Century*
Pub: The Potlatch Group, Inc.
Ed: Susan E. Mehrtens. **Released:** 1997. **Price:** $15.95.

30574 ■ "New developments in business forecasting: debunking executive conventional wisdom" in *Journal of Business Forecasting* (Vol. 19, No. 2)
Pub: Graceway Publishing Co., Inc.
Ed: Larry Lapide. **Description:** A selection of opinions widely held by executives on the subject of business forecasting are discussed, with reasons why they are accurate. The importance of demand forecasting is emphasized.

30575 ■ "Not so fast!: Studies show many of you aren't looking before you leap" in *Entrepreneur* (Vol. 31, No. 6, June 2003, pp. 30)
Pub: Entrepreneur Media Inc.
Ed: David Newton. **Description:** The topic of risk assessment for entrepreneurs is highlighted, stating that vision alone isn't enough to ensure success.

30576 ■ "The Old Economy Meets the New Economy" in *Fast Company* (November 2001, pp. 70)
Pub: Fast Company
Description: Fast Company recently convened a session in Chicago with experts from the world's strongest and oldest brands with the objective of finding new insights on emerging best practices when it comes to customers, technology and business.

30577 ■ "On a Mission" in *Black Enterprise* (Vol. 34, No. 5, December 2003, pp. 50)
Pub: Earl Graves Publishing Co.
Ed: Alan Hughes. **Description:** Concepts to consider when creating a mission statement for a small company are highlighted.

30578 ■ "Opening Pitch: Developing a Business Plan" in *Crain's Detroit Business* (Vol. 19, No. 49, December 8, 2003, pp. 11)
Pub: Crain Communications Inc., Detroit
Ed: Mike Scott. **Description:** A good business plan should be kept up-to-date and shared with employees and lenders, in order to help small business owners understand their company.

30579 ■ "The outlook for United States corporate earnings" in *Journal of Business Forecasting* (Vol. 19, No. 2, Summer 2000, pp. 41)
Pub: Graceway Publishing Co., Inc.
Ed: Joseph S. Kalinowksi. **Description:** Forecasts are presented for the earnings of U.S. industries for the second half of 2000 and into 2001. Growth is expected to slow down during this period, compared with the dramatic growth of earnings in the first part of 2000.

30580 ■ "Paving the Cow Path" in *Rough Notes* (Vol. 146, No. 9, September 2003, pp. 40)
Pub: Rough Notes
Ed: John Ashenburst. **Description:** Overview of changes and future trends in the insurance industry. Topics covered include risk management services, Internet marketing of services, and insurance services offered through banks.

30581 ■ "A Perfect Brainstorm" in *Inc.* (October 1, 2003)
Pub: Gruner & Jahr USA Publishing

Ed: Alison Stein Wellner. **Description:** New scientific research suggests that brainstorming can help an entrepreneur attain business visions and goals.

30582 ■ "Pizza Schmizza Ready to Take on Puget Sound" in *Business Journal-Portland* (Vol. 20, No. 22, August 1, 2003, pp. 7)
Pub: American City Business Journals, Inc.
Ed: Robert Goldfield. **Description:** An overview of the growing success and expansion plans of Portland, Oregon-based Pizza Schmizza. Topics include management styles, competition, and long-term goals.

30583 ■ "Plan a legacy for your business and your family" in *Black Enterprise* (Vol. 33, No. 3, October 2002, pp. 104)
Pub: Earl Graves Publishing Co.
Description: Case studies for small, family-owned business planning are presented, including business planning, estate planning, and financial security.

30584 ■ "Planning Your Exit Strategy: Three Ways To Go" in *My Business* (October/November 2003, pp. 30-35)
Pub: My Business Magazine
Ed: Shannon Scully, Steve Becker. **Description:** Exit strategy plans help small businesses not only decide ways to get out of the company, but they also lay the groundwork for getting ahead. Profiles of small business owners and their exit strategies are investigated.

30585 ■ "Port Adopts 2007 Strategic Budget" in *Bellingham Business Journal* (December 2006, pp. A3)
Pub: Sun News Inc.
Description: 2007 Strategic Budget adopted by the Port of Bellingham Board of Commissioners projects a 5 percent growth of operating revenues and no increase in the number of port employees. The entire Strategic Budget will be available on the Web at portofbellingham.com.

30586 ■ "Prepare for takeoff" in *Entrepreneur* (Vol. 31, No. 6, June 2003, pp. 124)
Pub: Entrepreneur Media Inc.
Ed: Romanus Wolter. **Description:** Advice is offered for would-be entrepreneurs to use when preparing a business plan.

30587 ■ "The Pump-and-Dump Economy" in *Wall Street Journal* (Vol. 248, January 2007, No. 146, pp. A16)
Pub: Dow Jones & Co. Inc.
Ed: Michael S. Malone **Description:** Start-ups are not aiming for an IPo in their business plan these days. Instead most newly-formed private companies set goals to be acquired by an established company which could lead to a radical shift in the U.S. economy.

30588 ■ "The Race to Reach Critical Mass" in *Hispanic Business* (Vol. 22, No. 1/2, January/February, pp. 18, 20, 22)
Pub: Hispanic Business
Ed: Derek Reveron. **Description:** By forming an alliance with his competitors, Manuel Chavez creates a new model for winning business from large corporations.

30589 ■ "Rating reasonable risks" in *Women in Business* (Vol. 53, No. 4, July-August, 2001, pp. 18)
Pub: The ABWA Co. Inc.
Ed: Melissa Will. **Description:** Issues concerning strategies of identifying, setting, managing and analyzing the effects of risks in everyday life are discussed. Particular attention is given to techniques of coping with risks, including considering in advance the ways in which they may affect the risk taker.

30590 ■ "The Real Deal" in *Entrepreneur* (Vol. 33, January 2005, No. 1, pp. 28)
Pub: Entrepreneur Media Inc.
Ed: Mark Henricks. **Description:** Review of the book, Confronting Reality: The Discipline of Getting Things Right, by Larry Bossidy and Ram Charan. The book offers a program to help entrepreneurs understand if their businesses are positioned to make profits and how to set the right future direction.

30591 ■ "Regrets" in *Inc.* (October 17, 2000, pp. 98)
Pub: The Goldhirsh Group
Description: Seven Inc. 500 company founders talk about their past business regrets.

30592 ■ "Report From Las Vegas: Inside the Home Office Of the Future" in *Fortune* (Vol. 141, No. 3, February 7, 2000, pp. 56)
Pub: Time Inc.
Ed: Joel Dreyfuss. **Description:** Information from the Consumer Electronics Show held each year in Las Vegas tell that the use of high technology in the home has extended into the creation of the home office.

30593 ■ "Retail Exec Stays in Style" in *Crain's New York Business* (Vol. 23, January 29, 2007, No. 5, pp. F3)
Pub: Crain Communications, Inc.
Ed: Elisabeth Butler. **Description:** Profile of Adrienne Lazarus and her position as President of Ann Taylor Stores Corp. The executive was brought in to revitalize the fashion chain.

30594 ■ "Sample business plans" in *Crain's Detroit Business* (Vol. 18, No. 49, December 9, 2002, pp. 17)
Pub: Crain Communications Inc., Detroit
Description: The Small Business Administration provides examples of business plans for small companies.

30595 ■ "Say Cheese, Fairhaven" in *Bellingham Business Journal* (December 2006, pp. A3)
Pub: Sun News Inc.
Description: Profile of Rachel Riggs, a lover of artisan cheeses, who opened a new shop in Fairhaven named Quel Fromage. The store will supply restaurants and offers retail customers over 125 varieties of cheese and other specialty items not available locally to customers. It will also feature wine pairings, guest cheesemakers, and more.

30596 ■ "Seeing Is Believing: Creating a Vision To Guide Your Team To Success" in *Black Enterprise* (Vol. 35, September 2004, No. 2, pp. 181)
Pub: Earl G. Graves Publishing Co. Inc.
Ed: Kimberly J. Hamilton-Wright. **Description:** Small business success can be attributed to setting a vision of excellence for the entire team to follow.

30597 ■ "Sense & Sensibility" in *Small Business Opportunities* (Vol. 12, No. 2, March 2000, pp. 18)
Pub: Harris Publications, Inc.
Ed: Carla Goodman. **Description:** Advice to find, hire and work with a consultant to help build a small business is presented. A checklist of information for evaluating a consultant before hiring, is also included.

30598 ■ "Shattered Magazine: A Monthly for the Global Businesswoman" in *Marketing to Women* (Vol. 19, December 2006, No. 2, pp. 6)
Pub: EPM Communications, Inc.
Ed: Julie Ros. **Description:** Shattered is a glossy magazine distributed monthly and run by veteran financial journalist, Julie Ros. Shattered concentrates its focus on the business world and puts special emphasis on the global impact women are having in the leadership roles of the business community.

30599 ■ "Sleep-state visualization in five easy steps" in *Black Enterprise* (Vol. 33, No. 6, January 2003, pp. 84)
Pub: Earl Graves Publishing Co.
Description: Five steps for creative visualization are presented, from formulating a question during the day to finding the answer while asleep; persistence is the key.

30600 ■ "Small businesses are starting to sweat a little about the future" in *Wall Street Journal* (April 4, 2000, pp. B2)
Pub: Dow Jones & Co., Inc.
Ed: Joshua Harris Prager. **Description:** A recent survey shows optimism is down regarding the economic future.

30601 ■ " Small business owners' outlook soars on sales prospects " in *Wall Street Journal* (February 29, 2000, pp. B2)
Pub: Dow Jones & Co., Inc.
Ed: Rodney Ho. **Description:** An update on small business shows that small business owners are optimistic about sales.

30602 ■ "Something Different" in *Entrepreneur* (Vol. 28, No. 2, February 2000, pp. 40)
Pub: Entrepreneur Media Inc.
Ed: Gwen Moran. **Description:** Most conventional marketing wisdom emphasizes the importance of setting goals for your business and working tirelessly toward them. However, it's sometimes just as important to change course when opportunities arise.

30603 ■ "Space Trade" in *Crain's New York Business* (Vol. 22, November 27, 2006, No. 48, pp. 33)
Pub: Crain Communications, Inc.
Description: US Airways' $8 million bid for a hostile takeover of Delta Air Lines would form a merger that would free up 10 percent of the airport slots on the East Coast and create the nation's largest airline.

30604 ■ "Spilling the Beans?" in *Entrepreneur* (Vol. 31, No. 11, November 2003, pp. 136)
Pub: Entrepreneur Media, Inc.
Ed: Romanus Wolter. **Description:** Secrets for entrepreneurs to share an idea while protecting their business is discussed. Tips for revealing only the most necessary details are listed.

30605 ■ "Spotlight Rick Chesley; Chairman Builds Law Office From Ground Up" in *Crain's Chicago Business* (Vol. 30, January 2007, No. 2, pp. 5)
Pub: Crain Communications, Inc.
Ed: Lorene Yue. **Description:** Profile of Rick Chesley, office chair for law firm, Paul Hastings Janofsky & Walker LLP's at the new Chicago location. Hastings' goal is to establish a strong Chicago presence for the firm.

30606 ■ "Stick-to-itiveness will always lead you to success" in *Atlanta Business Chronicle* (Vol. 24, No. 9, August 3, 2001, pp. 3B)
Pub: American City Business Journals Inc.
Ed: Jeffrey Gitomer. **Description:** The article outlines recommendations for the development of persistence, according to Napoleon Hill, author of 'Think and Grow Rich'. Four steps toward developing the habit of persistence are having a definite purpose, a definite plan, closing the mind to negative influences, and forming friendly alliances.

30607 ■ "Succession-Planning Do's and Don'ts: Who Will Take Over When You're Ready to Retire?" in *Journal of Accountancy* (February 2005)
Pub: American Institute of Certified Public Accountants
Ed: Anita Dennis. **Description:** Few certified public accounting firms have set a succession plan into place for selling their firm or passing it down to the next generation.

30608 ■ "Surviving the ups and downs of corporate restructuring" in *Women In Business* (Vol. 52, No. 3, May 2000, pp. 14)
Pub: The ABWA Co., Inc.
Ed: Mary-Lane Kamberg. **Description:** Advice on how to foresee the possibility of downsizing occurring in a company and information on how to find support and a new job is discussed.

30609 ■ "Takeover Offer Is Accepted By Parent Of Argo-Tech" in *Wall Street Journal* (Vol. 248, December 2006, No. 152, pp. A7)
Pub: Dow Jones & Co. Inc.
Ed: Reuters News Service **Description:** Eaton Corp., is to acquire AT Holdings Corp., parent of Argo-Tech Corp. Argo-Tech makers of military and aerospace

fuel pumps as well as numerous non-aerospace businesses provides 60% of all commercial airliner fuel pumps, yet these non-aerospace businesses won't be included in the transaction, leaving this vital area of commercial airliner manufacture with an uncertain future.

30610 ■ "Taking the Emotions out of Business Decisions" in *Success from Failure* (August 2000)
Pub: Vision Quest Publishing, Inc.
Ed: Charles K. Oppenheimer, Jr. **Description:** When you become emotionally involved in your business to the point it becomes a part of you, you are then unable to separate your emotional self from your logical and practical self. Without keeping your emotional self in check, you are unable to make the important decisions that are best for you, your company and your family.

30611 ■ "Taking Spiritual E-Path" in *Crain's New York Business* (Vol. 23, November 20, 2006, No. 47, pp. 29)
Pub: Crain Communications, Inc.
Ed: Description: Profile of Cathy O'Brien and her position at Beliefnet, a website which combines blogs, news and videos, and a free e-mail newsletter on subjects of faith, spirituality and religion. O'Brien hopes to attract advertisers to the popular eight-year-old site.

30612 ■ "Targeting Options Threatens Innovation and Growth" in *Venture Capital Journal* (Vol. 42, No. 5, May 2002, pp. 42)
Pub: Thomas Venture Economics
Ed: Craig A.T. Jones. **Description:** Stock options are critical in fostering innovation and entrepreneurship; the mandatory expensing of these options would make them too expensive to issue for most organizations.

30613 ■ "Tech Firm CEO's Solution: Unify Segments" in *Crain's Chicago Business* (Vol. 30, January 2007, No. 5, pp. 6)
Pub: Crain Communications, Inc.
Description: Profile of Brandon Glenn, CEO of Technology Solutions Co., a Chicago-based information technology firm that is publicly traded. Although Glenn has never before served as a CEO, but feels he will be able to return Tech Solutions to the black by creating a unifying theme between the company's three business segments.

30614 ■ "The Easy Entree Expands Service to Accommodate Walk-In Customers" in *Bellingham Business Journal* (December 2006, pp. 2)
Pub: Sun News Inc.
Description: Evelyn Turner, owner of The Easy Entree, has expanded her business to now offer a walk-in service for customers. Patrons can create their own entrees or pick up pre-made entrees to take home and cook or freeze.

30615 ■ "Thinking Outside the Box" in *E-business Advisor* (Vol. 18, No. 10, October 2000, pp. 8)
Pub: Advisor Media, Inc.
Ed: Jane Falla. **Description:** The only thing we can count on is change. The trick is to make the opportunities outweigh the obstacles. The challenge is to achieve the often delicate balance of risks and rewards.

30616 ■ "This Is Not About Charity" in *Forbes* (August 21, 2000, pp. 70)
Pub: Forbes Magazine
Ed: Ann Marsh. **Description:** Academy of Business Leadership teaches teenagers to reach for their dreams.

30617 ■ "To Achieve It, Write It Down" in *Black Enterprise* (Vol. 35, January 2005, No. 6, pp. 96)
Pub: Earl G. Graves Publishing Co. Inc.
Ed: Marcia A. Wade. **Description:** The Small Business Administration recommends that entrepreneurs write down their visions and goals and offers a Website designed to give information for starting a new business. Rev. Nathaniel Gadsden, founder of the Writers Wordshop, suggests writing a business plan before embarking on a new career path.

30618 ■ "To Manage Growth, Embrace Change" in *Ingram's* (Vol. 29, No. 7, July 2003, pp. 24)
Pub: Show Me Publishing, Inc.
Ed: Bob Gould. **Description:** Guidance for companies looking to grow and retain the corporate vision while tapping into new talents is given.

30619 ■ "Transforming Life, Transforming Business: The Life-Science Revolution" in *Harvard Business Review* (Vol. 78, No. 2, March 2000, pp. 96)
Pub: Harvard Business School Publishing Corp.
Ed: Juan Enriquez, Ray A. Goldberg. **Description:** Advances in genetic research are setting off an industrial convergence that will have profound implications for the global economy. Farmers, computer companies, drug makers, chemical processors, and health care providers will all be drawn into the new life-science industry. This article will help show how companies can change the way they think about their businesses in order to make a successful transition.

30620 ■ "Uncharted Territory" in *Entrepreneur* (Vol. 32, No. 1, January 2004, pp. 27)
Pub: Entrepreneur Media, Inc.
Ed: Don Nichols. **Description:** Profile of Bill Davidson, author of Breakthrough: How Great Companies Set Outrageous Objectives-and Achieve Them. Davidson advises entrepreneurs to set outrageous objectives and to use creative thinking about customer care, cost reduction, and other issues to reach customers.

30621 ■ "Valley Record Label Goes Back to Future" in *San Fernando Valley Business Journal* (Vol. 11, November 2006, No. 24, pp. 1)
Pub: San Fernando Valley Business Journal Associates
Ed: Mark R. Madler. **Description:** Profile of independent record label, Your Music America.

30622 ■ *Vision: How Leaders Develop It, Share It, & Sustain It*
Pub: The McGraw-Hill Companies
Ed: Joseph V. Quigley. **Released:** 1993. **Price:** $14. 95. **Description:** Provides an explanation of vision and describes how to implement it.

30623 ■ "Waterfront, Airport on Top of List For Port" in *Bellingham Business Journal* (January 2007, pp. B5)
Pub: Sun News Inc.
Ed: Dan Hiestand. **Description:** New Whatcom redevelopment for the former Georgia-Pacific waterfront property is in the works. The city and port have been working to create a cohesive plan for the site. Sixty-eight percent of the property leaves ownership in the public's hands.

30624 ■ "What dreams may come" in *Entrepreneur* (Vol. 31, No. 6, June 2003, pp. 32)
Pub: Entrepreneur Media Inc.
Ed: Aliza Pilar Sherman. **Description:** According to dream analyst, Layne Dalfen, dreams can create scenarios that mirror the feelings and events we are experiencing in our lives and can be used to find solutions to issues.

30625 ■ "What Drives Inspiration?" in *Entrepreneur* (Vol. 32, July 2004, No. 7, pp. 26)
Pub: Entrepreneur Media Inc.
Description: Tips to inspire entrepreneurs are given: keep dreaming, believe in yourself, get a tune-up, mind the details, enjoy the ride.

30626 ■ "What the Titans Can Teach Us" in *Harvard Business Review* (Vol. 79, No. 11, December 2001, pp. 70)
Pub: Harvard Business School Press
Ed: Richard S. Tedlow. **Description:** Profile of legendary leaders of American business such as Andrew Carnegie, Henry Ford and Sam Walton of Wal-Mart.

While some of their traits should not be emulated, the author argues that we can all learn from them. These people had the courage to bet on their vision of market potential, they shaped their vision into a mission for the company and they delivered more than they promised.

30627 ■ "When company values backfire" in
Harvard Business Review **(Vol. 80, No. 11, November 2002, pp. 18)**
Pub: Harvard Business School Press
Ed: Amy C. Edmondson. **Description:** Ways the CEO of a company attempted to promote strong values but had his intentions misinterpreted by employees is described. The staff considered his decision to grow the company to be motivated by greed. The author advises leaders to work diligently to invite discussion and seek honest feedback.

30628 ■ "Where Are You Going?" in *My Business* **(April/May 2003, pp. 46)**
Pub: My Business Magazine
Ed: Karen J. Bannan. **Description:** Business visions require identifying a target market, as well as the services and products a small business intends to supply.

30629 ■ "Where's the Love?" in
Entrepreneur **(Vol. 31, No. 10, October 2003)**
Pub: Entrepreneur Media, Inc.
Ed: Nichole L. Torres. **Description:** When entrepreneurs lose interest in their business, it is time for them to rediscover the passion they once had for their company.

30630 ■ "Why business models matter" in
Harvard Business Review **(Vol. 80, No. 5, May 2002, pp. 86)**
Pub: Harvard Business School Press
Ed: Joan Magretta. **Description:** The concepts of business models and strategy are clarified; the business model is a story which explains how an enterprise works, it complements strategy which deals with competition.

30631 ■ "Women Business Owners Seek Financing" in *Marketing to Women* **(Vol. 19, December 2006, No. 2, pp. 8)**
Pub: EPM Communications, Inc.
Description: A study by the Center for Women's Business Research shows that women business owners have become more savvy when seeking financial support for their business ventures. Statistical data included.

30632 ■ "Would You Recommend Us? Perfect Your Service By Asking The Only Question That Matters." in *Inc.* **(September 2006, pp. 40, 42)**
Pub: Gruner & Jahr USA Publishing
Ed: Darren Dahl. **Description:** The most important question to ask in measuring your customer service is for a referral. If sales are stagnant or edging downward, many strategies can be costly and not address the real problem of how you're perceived by your customers.

30633 ■ "Yes, You Can!" in *Entrepreneur* **(Vol. 32, No. 1, January 2004, pp. 32)**
Pub: Entrepreneur Media, Inc.
Ed: Aliza Pilar Sherman. **Description:** Entrepreneurs share visions and goals for their businesses.

30634 ■ "Your Annual Business Tune-Up" in
Business Week **(December 28, 2006)**
Pub: McGraw-Hill Companies
Ed: Karen E. Klein. **Description:** Interview with entrepreneurial expert, Ty Freyvogel, founder of EntrpreneursLab.com. Freyvogel gives tips on how a thorough review of existing systems, vendors, customers, and employees could help keep an entrepreneur's business not only safe but highly successful in the upcoming year.

VIDEOCASSETTES/ AUDIOCASSETTES

30635 ■ *Action Plans for Implementing Quality and Productivity*
Massachusetts Institute of Technology (MIT)
Center for Advanced Educational Services
77 Massachusetts Ave., Rm. 9-234
Cambridge, MA 02139-4307
Ph:(617)253-7408
Fax: (617)253-8301
Co. E-mail: caes-courses@mit.edu
URL: http://www-caes.mit.edu
Released: 1988. **Price:** $1400.00. **Description:** Dr. Myron Tribus suggests that American companies start planning ahead for the future instead of just shooting for the "quick fix." **Availability:** VHS; 3/4U.

30636 ■ *Goal Setting*
1st Financial Training Services
1515 E. Woodfield Rd., Ste. 345
Schaumburg, IL 60173
Ph:(847)969-0900
Free: 800-442-8662
Fax: (847)969-0521
Co. E-mail: sales@1stfinancialtraining.com
URL: http://www.1stfinancialtraining.com
Released: 1987. **Price:** $150.00. **Description:** The importance of goals is discussed as well as types of goals, and characteristics of effective goals. **Availability:** VHS; 3/4U.

30637 ■ *Goals and Objectives*
1st Financial Training Services
1515 E. Woodfield Rd., Ste. 345
Schaumburg, IL 60173
Ph:(847)969-0900
Free: 800-442-8662
Fax: (847)969-0521
Co. E-mail: sales@1stfinancialtraining.com
URL: http://www.1stfinancialtraining.com
Released: 1987. **Price:** $150.00. **Description:** Supervisors are the ones who have to tell the workers just what it is exactly that the top brass wants from them. **Availability:** VHS; 3/4U.

30638 ■ *Goals: Setting and Achieving Them on Schedule*
Cambridge Educational
c/o Films Media Group
PO Box 2053
Princeton, NJ 08843-2053
Free: 800-257-5126
Fax: (609)671-0266
Co. E-mail: custserve@filmsmediagroup.com
URL: http://www.cambridgeol.com
Released: 1986. **Price:** $49.95. **Description:** Setting realistic goals is one way for a person to get ahead, in either business or school. Ziglar shows you how. **Availability:** VHS.

30639 ■ *Make More Money by Setting Goals/ Rick Barrera*
Instructional Video
2219 C St.
Lincoln, NE 68502
Ph:(402)475-6570
Free: 800-228-0164
Fax: (402)475-6500
Co. E-mail: feedback@insvideo.com
URL: http://www.insvideo.com
Price: $95.00. **Description:** Rick Barrera offers his program developing the proper goals to increase business and income. Available only in the U.S. **Availability:** VHS.

CONSULTANTS

30640 ■ Adventure Learning Associates Inc.
567 Hale Rd.
PO Box 6062
Brattleboro, VT 05302
Ph:(802)254-6160

Free: 800-551-3210
Fax: (802)254-3582
Co. E-mail: info@alrna.com
URL: http://www.alrna.com

E-mail: info@alrna.com
Scope: Provides consulting services and training in experiential training and development. Specifically provides teambuilding, communications skills, and empowerment skill sessions. Also focuses on needs analysis, strategic planning, and visioning for newly developing groups. Firm specializes in training trainers in experiential outdoor programming. Industries served: all including government and can work with intact groups at all levels from line staff to boards and executive committees. **Seminars:** Train the Adventure Trainer.

30641 ■ Persephone C. Agrafiotis
302 N Bay St.
Manchester, NH 03104-2324
Ph:(603)625-8446
Fax: (603)625-8446
Co. E-mail: persephonea@webtv.com

E-mail: persephonea@webtv.com
Scope: Provides Record Review and Medical Expert Witness for Medical Legal cases in Medical Case Review, Nursing, Health Administration, Gerontology, Pediatrics and other clinical areas. Offers Health Care Management Consultation in Home Care, Long Term Care and General Management. Provides expertise in Preferred Provider Contracting Negotiations, Accrediting Processed to include JCAHO, Operations Review, Operations Auditing, Strategic Planning, Business Ethics Review and Implementation. Policy and Procedure, Strategies for the Future Planning, Review/Revision/Implementation, and Educational Programming. Industries Served: health care, human services, government and educational institutions. **Publications:** Contributing columnist in regional monthly publication "Health Care Review", column on Pediatric Home Care; Contributing columnist in regional publication "Hospital News", column on Key Notes for Managers; Contributing author to several text books published by Mosby Co. and professional journals as "Inservice Education and Training" and "The American Journal of Nursing"; Published Doctoral Dissertation at Boston College, "An Analysis of the Curriculum of Moral Education of Baccalaureate Nursing Students in New England". **Seminars:** Organizational Development; Group Dynamics; Leadership; Motivation; Assertiveness and Change; Performance Appraisals; Principles of Management; Marketing Educational Programs; etc.

30642 ■ AMC International Inc.
PO Box 11292
Beverly Hills, CA 90213-4292
Ph:(310)652-5620
Fax: (310)652-6709
Co. E-mail: inquiry@amcusa.com
URL: http://www.amcusa.com

E-mail: inquiry@amcusa.com
Scope: Offers day-to-day business management, business turnaround, marketing strategies, development/refinement of corporate mission, and merger and acquisition evaluations. Industries served: all.

30643 ■ Ameriwest Business Consultants Inc.
PO Box 26266
Colorado Springs, CO 80936
Ph:(719)380-7096
Fax: (719)380-7096
Co. E-mail: email@abchelp.com
URL: http://www.abchelp.com

E-mail: email@abchelp.com
Scope: Specializes in assisting start-up businesses and those with sales of 5 million dollars or less and/or those who have 50 employees or less. Services and products offered include written business plans; do-it-yourself business plan kits; business valuations; doit-yourself business start-up kits; written loan packages;

do-it-yourself loan packaging guides; business analysis; do-it-yourself financial projections software; do-it-yourself complete financial analysis; web site development assistance; general consulting.

30644 ■ BroadVision Inc.
585 Broadway
Redwood City, CA 94063
Ph:(650)542-5100
Free: (866)287-6669
Fax: (650)542-5900
Co. E-mail: info@broadvision.com
URL: http://www.broadvision.com

E-mail: info@broadvision.com
Scope: Areas of expertise include strategic services, interactive services, content and creative services and client services. Services include business planning, application strategy, ROI analysis, organization and business process consulting, building and deploying applications, content management, sourcing and workflow processes. **Special Services:** BroadVision Process; BroadVision Commerce; BroadVision Portal; BroadVision Content Services; BroadVision eMarketing; BroadVision QuickSilver; BroadVision Deployment; BroadVision Multi-Touchpoint; BroadVision Search.

30645 ■ CFO Service
112 Chester Ave.
Saint Louis, MO 63122
Ph:(314)757-2940
Co. E-mail: jskae@cfoservice.com
URL: http://www.cfoservice.com

E-mail: jskae@cfoservice.com
Scope: A group of professional executives that provide upper management services to companies that cannot support a full time COO or CFO. Provides clients in the areas of business planning, company policies, contract negotiations, safety policies, product and service pricing, loans management, taxes, cost analysis, loss control and budgeting.

30646 ■ Flor & Associates
179 Schan Dr.
Churchville, PA 18966
Ph:(215)355-7466
Fax: (215)355-7464
Co. E-mail: fredflor@msn.com

E-mail: fredflor@msn.com
Scope: Business Development Consulting helping companies increase the value of their businesses. Services include: market development for technologies and products; product positioning strategies; technology assessment; competitive intelligence and analysis; team augmentation and facilitation; business growth strategies including acquisitions, licensing, and partnerships.

30647 ■ J.B. Geller Consulting Inc.
9 Ridgedale Ln.
West Dennis, MA 02670-2545
Ph:(508)760-0044
Fax: (508)943-4122
Co. E-mail: jbgeller@capecod.net

E-mail: jbgeller@capecod.net
Scope: A full service human resources consulting firm whose purpose is to empower leaders, managers and employees to welcome changes created by internal and external forces such as employment laws, mergers, acquisition, re-engineering, change in management, etc. Specific services include: management development, organizational development, visioning, personnel policy development and communication, recruitment, employee relations, team building, and career development. Recent emphasis on prevention of sexual harassment, the Americans with Disabilities Act, disability awareness, and visioning. Industries served: financial services, manufacturing, high-tech, healthcare, retail services, and government agencies. Certified as a women business enterprise. **Publications:** Making Diversity Work; A Managers Guide to Human Behavior, American Management Association, 1994; How to Comply with the Americans with Disabilities Act, American Management Association, 1992. **Seminars:** Visioning for Leaders: how to create and communicate a vision, purpose and mission; Training Needs Assessment; How to Conduct Focus Groups; Interviewing Skills for Supervisors; Employment Laws for Supervisors; Disability Awareness Training; Prevention of Sexual Harassment; How to Comply with the Americans with Disabilities Act; Fearless Firing; Performance Management.

30648 ■ Claude Hayes & Associates
5115 Maryland Way Frnt.
Brentwood, TN 37027-7556
Ph:(615)377-0743
Fax: (615)370-8106
Scope: Turnarounds, Re-engineering, Re-Structuring, Re-Organization, Start-ups, High profile growth, Acquisitions, Divestures, Due Diligence, Strategic/Business (Marketing/Sales) Plans, Inventory Control and Management, Cost Pricing and Control. Market Management, Demand Forecasting.

30649 ■ Jarlett Consulting
3634 Tierra De Dios
Escondido, CA 92025
Fax: (760)741-2863
Co. E-mail: jarlett@earthlink.net

E-mail: jarlett@earthlink.net
Scope: Offers a comprehensive, integrated approach to "successfully managing the future" by understanding trends, setting goals, evaluating options, planning and managing. Includes analysis of global, national, state and local trends on technological, social, political and management issues. Selection of advanced products and services that meet future business goals, management of research and development, evaluating customers and competition, and writing winning proposals. **Publications:** Mastering Your Future (15 minute demo video available free); Making the Right Choices of Future Change and Growth (book available free). **Seminars:** Offers seminars and workshops for businesses, government agencies, educational institutions and other public/private organizations.

30650 ■ ReCourses Inc.
Nashville, TN 37211-6271
Ph:(615)831-2212
Free: 888-476-5884
Fax: 888-648-5884
Co. E-mail: info@recourses.com
URL: http://www.recourses.com

E-mail: info@recourses.com
Scope: A management consulting firm that works exclusively with small service providers in the communications industry, including public relations firms, advertising agencies, interactive companies and design studios. Services include Total Business Review, a complete examination of your business starting with an on-site examination/discussion, followed by written recommendations and then supplemented with six months of implementation guidance. Areas reviewed include positioning, marketing, management, personnel, structure, finance, retirement, technology and specific growth issues. **Special Services:** ReCourses®.

LIBRARIES

30651 ■ University of South Carolina–The Moore School of Business–Elliot White Springs Business Library (Franc)
Francis M. Hipp Bldg., 2nd Fl.
1705 College St.
Columbia, SC 29208
Ph:(803)777-6032
Fax: (803)777-6876
Co. E-mail: gardnerd@gwm.sc.edu
URL: http://www.sc.edu/library/pubserv/business.html
Contact: Dwight Gardner, Dept.Hd.
Scope: Corporations. **Services:** Interlibrary loan; copying; Library open to the public with restrictions. **Holdings:** 30,000 books; 4000 bound periodical volumes. **Subscriptions:** 350 journals and other serials; 5 newspapers.

START-UP INFORMATION

30652 ■ **"Building vs. buying"** in *BlackEnterprise* **(Vol. 31, No. 6, January 2001, pp. 39)**
Pub: Earl Graves Publishing Co.
Ed: Glenn Townes. **Description:** Ideas are presented to would-be entrepreneurs on the advantages and disadvantages to buying an existing business or building one from scratch.

30653 ■ **"Cracking the Code"** in *My Business* **(October/November 2003, pp. 49)**
Pub: My Business Magazine
Description: The top ten franchising industries are listed in the following order: fast food, retail, service, automotive, restaurants, maintenance, building and construction, retail-food, business services, and lodging. It is advised to seek legal advice before purchasing a franchise business.

30654 ■ **"Find the Perfect Biz"** in *Small Business Opportunities* **(Vol. 13, No. 5, September 2001, pp. 20)**
Pub: Harris Publications, Inc.
Description: Profile of FranChoice, a network of independent consultants who provide franchises with pre-screened, high quality leads to selected franchisors across the U.S. A list of the top ten franchise industries is provided.

30655 ■ *Legal Guide for Starting and Running a Small Business*
Pub: NOLO
Ed: Fred Steingold, Lisa Guerin. **Released:** March 2005. **Price:** $34.99. **Description:** Information for starting a new business focusing on choosing a business structure, taxes, employees and independent contractors, trademark and service marks, licensing and permits, leasing and improvement of commercial space, buying and selling a business, and more.

30656 ■ **"Less Is More"** in *Entrepreneur* **(Vol. 33, October 2005, No. 10, pp. 100)**
Pub: Entrepreneur Media Inc.
Description: A listing of 107 franchises that cost less than $25,000 to start up are listed, including phone numbers and Websites.

30657 ■ **"So Close...Yet so Far"** in *Entrepreneur* **(Vol. 28, No. 10, October 2000, pp. 38)**
Pub: Entrepreneur Media Inc.
Ed: Doug Hood and Marilea S. Hood. **Description:** You're buying a business, but your banker won't loan you the full amount, this article will help you find capital for your small business.

ASSOCIATIONS AND OTHER ORGANIZATIONS

30658 ■ **Institute of Certified Business Counselors**
18615 Willamette Dr.
West Linn, OR 97068
Free: 877-ICB-CORG
Fax: (503)292-8237
Co. E-mail: inquiry@i-cbc.org
URL: http://www.i-cbc.org
Contact: Jeff Adam, Pres.
Membership: Bankers, consultants, accountants, attorneys, appraisers, merger and acquisition specialists, estate planners, financial consultants, and business brokers active in the continuation, evaluation, financing, or marketing of privately held businesses. Offers training and advice on how to buy or sell a business, including information on what to look for in a prospective deal. Maintains speakers' bureau. **Publications:** *CBC Roster* (annual); *The Certified Business Counselor* (bimonthly).

EDUCATIONAL PROGRAMS

30659 ■ **Valuation of Companies (Canada)**
Canadian Management Centre
150 York St., 5th Fl.
Toronto, ON, Canada M5H 3S5
Ph:(416)214-5678
Free: 800-262-9699
Fax: (416)313-4985
Co. E-mail: cmcinfo@cmctraining.org
URL: http://cmcamai.org
Price: $1,995.00 Canadian. **Description:** Covers valuation methods for buyers and sellers, capitalization rates and multiples, cash flows and book values, and differing processes depending on a company's tax status. **Locations:** Toronto, ON.

30660 ■ **Valuation of Companies: The Practical Aspects**
American Management Association
1601 Broadway
New York, NY 10019
Ph:(212)586-8100
Free: 800-262-9699
Fax: (212)903-8168
Co. E-mail: customerservice@amanet.org
URL: http://www.amanet.org
Price: $3,695.00 for non-members; $3,295.00 for AMA members. **Description:** Covers all aspects of company valuation, including valuation methods, tax considerations, and future predictions. **Locations:** Atlanta, GA; and New York, NY.

REFERENCE WORKS

30661 ■ **"An Acquired Taste"** in *Entrepreneur* **(Vol. 32, October 2004, No. 10, pp. 62)**
Pub: Entrepreneur Media Inc.
Ed: Crystal Detamore-Rodman. **Description:** Tim Johnstone is a former division manager for a large bank working on the due-diligence team that analyzed companies the bank wanted to buy. Johnstone's experience helped him when he decided to purchase the Anywear Shoe Company in Seattle, Washington. The firm manufactures and distributes professional footwear.

30662 ■ **"Ask Inc. Partnerships"** in *Inc.* **(November 2006, pp. 57)**
Pub: Gruner & Jahr USA Publishing
Description: Buyouts of partners that leave the company require accurate assessment of the current value of the stock. That may require hiring a consultant to put a current value on the business to arrive at an amicable settlement.

30663 ■ **"Before You Try To Sell, Make Sure You Know What Buyers Want"** in *Inc.* **(April 1, 2005)**
Pub: Inc. Magazine
Ed: Norm Brodsky. **Description:** Most small business owners have an inflated idea of their company's value. When purchasing a new business, it is important to look at a firm's sales free cash flow, a function of profit, not sales.

30664 ■ *Business Buying Basics*
Pub: Robert Erdmann Publishing
Ed: Martin Bloom. **Released:** 1992. **Price:** $12.95 (paper).

30665 ■ *Buy the Right Business—At the Right Price: The Guide to Small Business Acquisition*
Pub: Upstart Publishing Co., Inc.
Ed: Brian Knight and the associates of Country Business, Inc. **Price:** $18.95 (paper). **Description:** Provides information on buying a business, including establishing how much a business is worth, determining whether a business is well managed, and negotiating for terms that satisfy both buyer and seller. Contains forms and worksheets.

30666 ■ *Buy Your Own Business: The Definitive Guide to Identifying & Purchasing a Business You Can Make*
Pub: Macmillan Publishing Co. Inc.
Ed: Mitchell B. Stern. **Released:** 1999. **Price:** $17.95.

30667 ■ *Buying a Business*
Pub: Crisp Publications, Inc.
Ed: Ronald J. McGregor. **Released:** 1993. **Price:** $15.95 (paper).

30668 ■ *Buying In: A Complete Guide to Acquiring a Business or Professional Practice*
Pub: The McGraw-Hill Companies
Ed: Lawrence W. Tuller. **Released:** 1991. **Price:** $24.95.

30669 ■ *Buying & Selling Small Business*
Pub: Self-Counsel Press, Inc.
Ed: Michael M. Coltman. **Released:** 1994. **Price:** $9.95 (paper).

30670 ■ *Buying Your Own Business*
Pub: Adams Media Corp.
Ed: Russell Robb. **Released:** 1997. **Price:** $9.95.

30671 ■ "CEO Runs a Site with Bite" in *Crain's New York Business* (Vol. 23, January 29, 2007, No. 5, pp. F17)
Pub: Crain Communications, Inc.
Ed: Julie Satow. **Description:** Profile of chief executive, Ryan Slack of PropertyShark.com, a Brookly-based website that has a membership of over 200,000. The site offers users access to property information such as sales prices, code violations, appraisal values and previous owners.

30672 ■ *Complete Idiot's Guide to Buying & Selling a Business*
Pub: Macmillan Publishing Co. Inc.
Ed: Gottlieb. **Released:** 1998. **Price:** $18.95.

30673 ■ "Consulting the Homeland" in *Crain's New York Business* (Vol. 23, January 29, 2007, No. 5, pp. F9)
Pub: Crain Communications, Inc.
Ed: Samantha Marshall. **Description:** Profile of Wendy Cai, director of Chinese Services Group, Deloitte & Touche USA, and one-time owner of e-commerce company Hagglers.com. She is one of the youngest directors in Deloitte's history and advises Fortune 500 companies on China investments ranging from $10 to $50 million.

30674 ■ "ConventionSouth Honors Jackson CVB" in *Mississippi Business Journal* (Vol. 29, January 2007, No. 2, pp. 28)
Pub: Venture Publications, Inc.
Description: Jackson Convention and Visitors Bureau was presented with ConventionSouth Magazine's annual Reader's Choice Award in December.

30675 ■ "Dot-Com for Sale" in *E-business Advisor* (Vol. 18, No. 10, October 2000, pp. 48)
Pub: Advisor Media, Inc.
Ed: Ben Chen. **Description:** Gaining customers, skilled employees, knowledge, and strategic alliances are some of the reasons for the flurry of acquisitions and mergers in the dot.com world. This article examines reasons, and discusses the things to look for when contemplating a business move, including goal compatibility, cost for acquiring a new customer base, and whether the new company would have what the existing company does not have and needs.

30676 ■ *The Entrepreneur's Guide to Buying a Small Business Franchise or NonFranchise*
Pub: Carlyle Publishing Co.
Released: 1997. **Price:** $39.95.

30677 ■ "Environmental and Ownership Characteristics of Small Businesses and their Impact on Development" in *Journal of Small Business Management*
Pub: West Virginia University
Ed: William B. Gartner, Subodh Bhat. **Description:** This article explores the relationship between the characteristics of a small business's location (crime, neighborhood appearance, and transportation accessibility) and a small business owner's expectations of future firm growth.

30678 ■ "Fitness 24 Buys DAC Club" in *Mississippi Business Journal* (Vol. 29, January 2007, No. 2, pp. 8)
Pub: Venture Publications, Inc.

Ed: Wally Northway **Description:** Regional fitness management company DAC sold its fitness club in Olive Branch to Fitness 24. DAC sold this facility in order to increase overall profitability of its existing clubs.

30679 ■ "Godwin Group" in *Mississippi Business Journal* (Vol. 29, January 2007, No. 3, pp. A6)
Pub: Venture Publications, Inc.
Description: Profile of Joey Lee, vice president, coastal region of Godwin Group. Lee has previously served as Godwin Group's account manager, strategic communications.

30680 ■ *Guide to Buying & Selling a Business, Vol. 2*
Pub: Practitioners Publishing Co.
Ed: William R. Bischoff. **Released:** 1995.

30681 ■ *How to Buy and/or Sell a Small Business for Maximum Profit: A Step-by-Step Guide*
Pub: Atlantic Publishing Company
Ed: Rene V. Richards. **Released:** August 2005. **Price:** $24.95. **Description:** Suggestions, insights and techniques for buying and selling small businesses, includes advice on when to buy or sell, how to market the business, explanation of legal and financial documents involved in the sale and closing of a deal.

30682 ■ *How to Buy a Business with No Money Down*
Pub: International Wealth Success, Inc.
Ed: Jeryn W. Calhoun. **Released:** 1st ed. 1999. **Price:** $19.50.

30683 ■ *How to Buy a Great Business with No Cash Down*
Pub: John Wiley & Sons, Inc.
Ed: Arnold S. Goldstein. **Released:** 1991. **Price:** $17.95 (paper). **Description:** Provides "no cash down" techniques, strategies, and formulas for each phase of the buy-sell process; explains how to prospect for no-cash deals, avoid costly errors and common pitfalls, evaluate what a business is worth, and find the right investment partners. Includes checklists, forms, and sample agreements.

30684 ■ *How to Create a Buy-Sell Agreement & Control the Destiny of Your Small Business*
Pub: Nolo Press
Ed: Anthony Mancuso and Bethany K. Laurence. **Released:** 1998. **Price:** $49.95 (diskette). **Description:** Show business owners how to draft a buy-sell agreement, which ensures a smooth transition following the departure of a business partner.

30685 ■ "Knight Ridder's Happy Ending?" in *Business Week* (February 20, 2006, No. 3972, pp. 26)
Pub: McGraw-Hill Companies
Ed: Jon Fine. **Description:** Rumors suggest that The McClatchy Company partnered with The Times Company, may bid to purchase Knight Ridder Inc.

30686 ■ *Let's Buy a Company: How to Accelerate Growth Through Acquisitions*
Pub: Career Press, Incorporated
Ed: H. Lee Rust. **Released:** December 2005. **Price:** $18.99 (US), $25.95 (Canadian). **Description:** Advice for negotiating terms and pricing as well as other aspects of mergers and acquisitions in small companies.

30687 ■ "Measure Twice, Cut Once" in *Milwaukee Journal Sentinel* (December 14, 2005)
Pub: Journal Sentinel, Inc.
Ed: Lawrence Sussman. **Description:** Edward Hines Lumber Company of Buffalo Grove, Illinois has purchased the Cedarburg Lumber Company in Jackson. Details of the sale are included.

30688 ■ *Mergers and Acquisitions from A to Z*
Pub: Amacom

Ed: Andrew J. Sherman, Milledge A. Hart. **Released:** December 2005. **Price:** $47.00. **Description:** Guide for the entire process of mergers and acquisitions, including taxes, accounting, laws, and projected financial gain.

30689 ■ "Murdock Carrousel Sold" in *Charlotte Observer* (January 31, 2007)
Pub: Knight-Ridder/Tribune Business News
Ed: Bob Fliss. **Description:** Details on the sale of the Murdock Carrousel shopping center are highlighted. The deal was reported at $281 million.

30690 ■ *Negotiating the Purchase or Sale of a Business*
Pub: Bell Springs Publishing
Ed: James C. Comiskey. **Price:** $18.95. **Description:** This guide will help the seller determine a fair asking price, prepare for the sale, and deal with prospective buyers. Includes legal and tax aspects of a sale, the contract, and common financing agreements.

30691 ■ "New Jersey Firm Busy Westbrook, Maine, Online Classified Company" in *Portland Press Herald* (December 7, 2005)
Pub: Blethen Maine Newspapers, Inc.
Ed: Matt Wickensheiser. **Description:** The Journal Register has purchased JobsInTheUS, an online employment classifieds company. The Journal Register owns papers in Connecticut, Pennsylvania, Ohio, Rhode Island, New York, and Michigan.

30692 ■ "On the Merge" in *Entrepreneur* (Vol. 33, October 2005, No. 10, pp. 87)
Pub: Entrepreneur Media Inc.
Ed: Sara Wilson. **Description:** Scott D'Entremont, co-founder of a conferencing services provider, shares insight into helping employees feel a sense of unity when merging two companies.

30693 ■ "One of Portland, Maine's Fastest Growing Tech Companies is Sold" in *Portland Press Herald* (December 20, 2005)
Pub: Blethen Maine Newspapers, Inc.
Ed: Matt Wickensheiser. **Description:** IntelliCare Inc., one of Portland, Maine's largest technology companies was recently acquired by PolyMedica Corporation. The firm is a telemedicine company offering telephone-based nursing services and technology.

30694 ■ *Purchase and Sale of Small Businesses: Tax and Legal Aspects*
Pub: John Wiley & Sons, Inc.
Ed: Marc J. Lane. **Released:** Second edition, 1991. **Price:** $137.50.

30695 ■ "Resistance is Futile: EDS has been on a buying binge" in *Red Herring* (No. 102, August 15, 2001, pp. 84-85)
Pub: Herring Communications
Ed: J.P. Vicente. **Description:** Electronics Data Systems' (EDS) acquired Sabre's airline outsourcing unit, Systematics, and Structural Dynamics Research Corporation in 2001, despite the slowing of mergers and acquisitions.

30696 ■ "Roseville, Calif., Gourmet Gift Firm Puts Buyout on Hold" in *Sacramento Bee* (October 21, 2005)
Pub: The Sacramento Bee
Ed: Clint Swett. **Description:** Shari's Berries International, famous for its chocolate-dipped strawberries, has put its management-led buyout on hold in order to concentrate on the holiday season. Unforgettable Gifts Inc. had offered $1.69 million in cash along with $1.26 million in promissory notes as well as assumption of the firm's $2.35 million debt.

30697 ■ *The Secret of Exiting Your Business Under Your Terms!*
Pub: Outskirts Press, Incorporated
Ed: Gene H. Irwin. **Released:** August 2005. **Price:** $29.95. **Description:** Topics include how to sell a business for the highest value, tax laws governing the sale of a business, finding the right buyer, mergers and acquisitions, negotiating the sale, and using a limited auction to increase future value of a business.

30698 ■ Six SIGMA for Small Business
Pub: Entrepreneur Press
Ed: Greg Brue. **Released:** October 2005. **Price:** $19.95 (US), $26.95 (Canadian). **Description:** Jack Welch's Six SIGMA approach to business covers accounting, finance, sales and marketing, buying a business, human resource development, and new product development.

30699 ■ Small Business Desk Reference
Pub: Penguin Books (USA) Incorporated
Ed: Gene Marks. **Released:** December 2004. **Price:** $29.95 (US), $44.00 (Canadian). **Description:** Comprehensive guide for starting or running a successful small business, focusing on buying a business or franchise, writing a business plan, financial management, accounting, legal issues, human resources management, operations, marketing, sales, customer service, taxes, insurance, and ethics. Information for launching a restaurant, property management firm, retail outlet, consulting firm, and service business is included.

30700 ■ "Smooth Selling" in My Business (September/October 2001, pp. 34-37)
Pub: My Business Magazine
Ed: Jamie Clary. **Description:** Insights from former small business owners are offered to help sell a business. In addition to attorneys and brokers, various books and Web sites are given; information for investing the income received from the sale, and the six most costly selling mistakes are summarized.

30701 ■ "Spanish-Language Radio Mogul Buys 24th Station" in Sacramento Bee (October 14, 2005)
Pub: The Sacramento Bee
Ed: Clint Swett. **Description:** Amador Bustos purchased his 24th radio station, with the goal of owning 50 within the next few years. Bustos' company ranks number five among Spanish radio broadcasting firms in the U.S. The new station is the only Spanish language one in a market with a population of over 150,000 Latinos.

30702 ■ "Surviving the New Economy" in Inc. (October 1, 2003)
Pub: Gruner & Jahr USA Publishing
Ed: Nadine Heintz. **Description:** Profile of Data Return and its management. Data Return is a Web-hosting firm sold by Sunny Vanderbeck, who is considering buying his company back.

30703 ■ Ultimate Guide to Buying or Selling Your Business
Pub: Entrepreneur Press
Ed: Ira N. Nottonson. **Released:** September 2004. **Price:** $24.95 (US), $35.95 (Canadian). **Description:** Proven strategies to evaluate, negotiate, and buy or sell a small business. Franchise and family business succession planning is included.

30704 ■ "Utilities Boost Companies; Utility Services" in Crain's New York Business (Vol. 22, November 13, 2006, No. 46, pp. 36)
Pub: Crain Communications, Inc.
Description: Listing of companies that provide utility programs, incentives and benefits to small businesses looking to relocate within the five boroughs of New York City or expand their businesses in the area.

30705 ■ "Verizon Taps Strigl To Become President, Chief Operating Officer" in Wall Street Journal (Vol. 248, December 2006, No. 145, pp. B10)
Pub: Dow Jones & Co. Inc.
Ed: Wallstreet Journal News **Description:** Profile of Denny Strigl, newly appointed president and chief operating officer of Verizon Wireless. Strigl helped propel Verizon Wireless into a leadership position in the cellphone market.

30706 ■ "Women Business Owners Get Credit Easily" in Marketing to Women (Vol. 19, November 2006, No. 11, pp. 12)
Pub: EPM Communications, Inc.
Description: According to a Gallup study commissioned by Wells Fargo, women find it easier to obtain credit than men. Statistical data included.

30707 ■ "Women Business Owners Seek Financing" in Marketing to Women (Vol. 19, December 2006, No. 2, pp. 8)
Pub: EPM Communications, Inc.
Description: A study by the Center for Women's Business Research shows that women business owners have become more savvy when seeking financial support for their business ventures. Statistical data included.

30708 ■ "Would You Like a Franchise With That?" in Entrepreneur (Vol. 33, January 2005, No. 1, pp. 120)
Pub: Entrepreneur Media Inc.
Ed: April Y. Pennington. **Description:** Things to consider when considering a franchise are discussed.

TRADE PERIODICALS

30709 ■ Venture Capital Journal
Pub: Venture Economics Inc.
Contact: Kathleen Devlin, Editor-in-Chief
E-mail: Lawrence.Aragon@thomson.com
Released: Monthly. **Price:** $960, U.S. first year; $1650, elsewhere for combination of print and online edition. **Description:** Hard news, analysis and data on the North American private equity market.

VIDEOCASSETTES/ AUDIOCASSETTES

30710 ■ How to Buy a Good Business with No Cash
Cambridge Educational
c/o Films Media Group
PO Box 2053
Princeton, NJ 08843-2053
Free: 800-257-5126
Fax: (609)671-0266
Co. E-mail: custserve@filmsmediagroup.com
URL: http://www.cambridgeol.com
Released: 1987. **Price:** $39.95. **Description:** Successful venture capitalist Lionel Haines shows how someone can purchase a business without any cash. **Availability:** VHS; 3/4U.

30711 ■ New or Used? Buying a Firm or Starting Your Own
Instructional Video
2219 C St.
Lincoln, NE 68502
Ph:(402)475-6570
Free: 800-228-0164
Fax: (402)475-6500
Co. E-mail: feedback@insvideo.com
URL: http://www.insvideo.com
Price: $99.00. **Description:** Details the different options open to anyone wanting to start or obtain their own business. Discusses the various factors to be considered when putting a value on a company, negotiating price and terms, and closing the deal. **Availability:** VHS.

30712 ■ Understanding Business Valuation
Chesney Communications
2302 Martin St., Ste. 125
Irvine, CA 92612
Ph:(949)263-5500
Free: 800-223-8878
Fax: (949)263-5506
Released: 1987. **Description:** A look for the small businessman at how to plan the future of his company-growth, reinvestment and possible sale. **Availability:** VHS; 3/4U.

CONSULTANTS

30713 ■ BPT Consulting Associates Ltd.
12 Parmenter Rd., Ste. B6
Londonderry, NH 03053

Ph:(603)437-8484
Co. E-mail: bptcons@tiac.net
URL: http://www.bptconsulting.com

E-mail: bptcons@tiac.net
Scope: Provides management consulting expertise and resources to cross-industry clients with services for: Business Management consulting, People/Human Resources Transition and Training programs, and a full cadre of multi-disciplined Technology Computer experts. Virtual consultants with expertise in e-commerce, supply chain management, organizational development, and business application development consulting. **Seminars:** Business: MRPII, DRPII, JIT/TQC. Business Requirements Analysis, Small Business Start-Up, Strategic Planning. People: Team Building, Performance Evaluation, Career Transition and Counseling Seminars. Technology: User Training for Customized Software, Internet, Full array of application development, i.e., C, Java, website development. **Special Services:** Provides a full array of computer and related user training services. Resources include application developers, database developers and managers, project management experts for a full array of industries (manufacturing, software, defense, healthcare, pharmaceutical, and small business).

30714 ■ Business Team
1901 S Bascom Ave., Ste. 400
Campbell, CA 95008
Ph:(408)246-1102
Fax: (408)246-2219
Co. E-mail: sanjose@business-team.com
URL: http://www.business-team.com

E-mail: sanjose@business-team.com
Scope: Business consulting services offered to companies looking for buyers. Specializes in mergers and acquisitions, business brokerage, and valuations. **Seminars:** Business Valuation - Enhancing the Value of Your Company.

30715 ■ Country Squire Inc.
10400 Griffin Rd., Ste. 303B
Fort Lauderdale, FL 33328
Ph:(954)434-0200
Free: 800-887-4867
Fax: (954)434-0200
Co. E-mail: info@thelandpro.com
URL: http://www.thelandpro.com

E-mail: info@thelandpro.com
Scope: Offers services in locating, pricing, and purchase of real property as well as representation of both buyers and/or sellers in real estate transactions and the negotiation of sales or acquisitions of businesses. Strong background and expertise in management and valuation of real estate brokerage operations. **Seminars:** Competitor Intelligence: How to Get It/How to Use It.

30716 ■ Equity Partners Of America Ltd.
1450 W Long Lake Rd., Ste. 340
Troy, MI 48098
Ph:(248)952-0300
Fax: (248)952-0314
Co. E-mail: equitypartners@email.msn.com

E-mail: equitypartners@email.msn.com
Scope: Private investment bank specializes in debt and equity capital procurement; buying and selling businesses; shareholder value enhancement strategies; and litigation and alternative dispute resolution assistance; including expert witness assistance. Serves manufacturing, distribution and service industries. **Seminars:** Preparation of a business plan; Use of financial statements in damage claims; Determining the value of a business; When to sell a family business.

30717 ■ Hampton Group
9110-B Alcosta Blvd., Ste. 238
San Ramon, CA 94583
Ph:(925)830-3447
Free: 800-820-6424
Fax: (925)831-8194

Co. E-mail: dataforpeter@hotmail.com

E-mail: dataforpeter@hotmail.com
Scope: Consults on the buying and selling of small and medium-sized businesses.

30718 ■ Pundmann & Company Inc.
PO Box 446
Saint Charles, MO 63302
Ph:(636)940-1111
Fax: (636)925-0000
Co. E-mail: pundmann@aol.com
URL: http://www.pundmann.com

E-mail: pundmann@aol.com
Scope: Merchant banking firm providing advice to companies concerning mergers and acquisitions, private financing and business strategy. Offers clients expert assistance in a wide range of financial activities, such as asset redeployments, private placements, recapitalizations, strategic financial counseling and venture capital investments. Also provides in-house venture capital to clients. Industries served: general.

30719 ■ Harvey C. Skoog
3737 N Robert Rd., No. A
Prescott Valley, AZ 86314
Ph:(928)772-1448
Scope: Firm has expertise in taxes, payroll, financial planning, budgeting, buy/sell planning, business start-up, fraud detection, troubled business consulting, acquisition, and marketing. Serves the manufacturing, construction, and retailing industries in Arizona.

30720 ■ Venture Economics Inc.
395 Hudson St.
New York, NY 10014
Ph:(212)807-5000
Free: 888-989-8373
Fax: (212)807-5122
Scope: Venture capital and business development specialists providing customized research for industrial and financial corporations. Services include: identification of high-potential companies for investment, alliance or acquisition; assistance in establishing venture capital or strategic alliance programs; and assistance with specific acquisition searches. Services for institutional investors in venture capital include: basic education and due diligence evaluation of venture

capital as an investment; development of venture capital investment strategy; and identification of investment opportunities, portfolio monitoring, analysis, performance; and benchmarking for the venture capital asset class. Serves private industries as well as government agencies. **Seminars:** Venture Capital Forum; Leveraged Buy-out Symposia; Strategic Partnering Symposia; Performance Monitoring Workshop.

FRANCHISES AND BUSINESS OPPORTUNITIES

30721 ■ FranchiseBuyersAgent
Franchise One, Inc.
9463 Hwy 377 S, Ste.111
Fort Worth, TX 76126
Ph:(817)249-2126
Free: 800-505-7380
Fax: (817)249-7524
Co. E-mail: info@franchise-one.com
URL: http://www.franchisebuyersagent.com
Founded: 1992. **Description:** Representing franchise buyers exclusively.

Compensation

ASSOCIATIONS AND OTHER ORGANIZATIONS

30722 ■ Council on Employee Benefits
4910 Moorland Ln.
Bethesda, MD 20814
Ph:(301)664-5940
Fax: (301)664-5944
Co. E-mail: scanfield@ceb.org
URL: http://www.ceb.org
Contact: Shane Canfield, Exec. Dir.
Description: Employers seeking informal exchange of experiences and information on the design, financing, and administration of employee benefit programs, both domestic and international. Provides a medium for the exchange of ideas, information, and statistics; sponsors or conducts research projects on benefits; makes known its views on legislative matters affecting employee benefits. Conducts research.

30723 ■ Employee Benefit Research Institute
2121 K St. NW, Ste. 600
Washington, DC 20037-1896
Ph:(202)659-0670
Fax: (202)775-6312
Co. E-mail: info@ebri.org
URL: http://www.ebri.org
Contact: Dallas L. Salisbury, Pres./CEO
Description: Corporations, consulting firms, banks, insurance companies, unions, and others with an interest in the future of employee benefit programs. Purpose is to contribute to the development of effective and responsible public policy in the field of employee benefits through research, publications, educational programs, seminars, and direct communication. Sponsors a broad range of studies on retirement income, health, disability, and other benefit programs; disseminates study results. Maintains research library with information on employee benefit programs. **Publications:** *EBRI Databook on Employee Benefits* (periodic); *EBRI Issue Brief* (monthly); *EBRI Notes* (monthly); *EBRI Pension Investment Report* (periodic); *EBRI Policy Forums* (semiannual); *Washington Bulletin* (biweekly). Also publishes consumer education series and policy studies.

30724 ■ Employers Council on Flexible Compensation
927 15th St. NW, Ste. 1000
Washington, DC 20005
Ph:(202)659-4300
Fax: (202)371-1467
Co. E-mail: info@ecfc.org
URL: http://www.ecfc.org
Contact: Lewis Freeman, Pres.
Description: Represents employers and service providers who have implemented or are interested in flexible compensation plans allowing employees to choose from a variety of benefits packages. Promotes flexible compensation plans including cafeteria plans, health reimbursement arrangements, cash-or-deferred plans, and other defined contribution plans. Monitors legislation and represents members' inter-

ests before Congress. Lobbies to preserve and simplify the flexible compensation provisions of the Internal Revenue Code. **Publications:** *ECFC Flex Reporter* (quarterly).

30725 ■ International Foundation of Employee Benefit Plans
PO Box 69
Brookfield, WI 53008-0069
Ph:(262)786-6700
Free: 888-334-3327
Fax: (262)786-8670
Co. E-mail: membership@ifebp.org
URL: http://www.ifebp.org
Contact: Joseph A. Brislin, Pres./Chm.
Description: Provides sources for employee benefits and compensation information and education, including seminars and conferences, books, and an information center, CEBS, and Certificate Series. Conducts more than 100 educational programs. Provides internet job and resume posting service. **Publications:** *Benefits & Compensation Digest* (monthly); *Employee Benefits Legal-Legislative Reporter* (monthly).

30726 ■ UWC - Strategic Services on Unemployment and Workers' Compensation
1331 Pennsylvania Ave. NW, Ste. 600
Washington, DC 20004
Ph:(202)637-3464
Fax: (202)783-1616
Co. E-mail: oxfelde@uwcstrategy.org
URL: http://www.uwcstrategy.org
Contact: Eric Oxfeld, Pres.
Description: Works to serve the business community by promoting Unemployment Insurance (UI) and Workers' Compensation (WC) programs that provide fair benefits to workers at affordable cost to employers and the community. **Publications:** *Highlights of State Unemployment Compensation Laws* (annual).

30727 ■ WorldatWork
14040 N Northsight Blvd.
Scottsdale, AZ 85260
Ph:(480)951-9191
Free: 877-951-9191
Fax: (480)483-8352
Co. E-mail: customerrelations@worldatwork.org
URL: http://www.worldatwork.org
Contact: Anne C. Ruddy CPCU, Pres.
Description: Dedicated to knowledge leadership in compensation, benefits and total rewards, focusing on disciplines associated with attracting, retaining and motivating employees. Offers CCP, CBP, and GRP certification and education programs, conducts surveys, research and provides networking opportunities. **Publications:** *The Conference Insider*; *Salary Budget Survey*; *Workspan* (monthly); *Workspan Weekly* (weekly); *WorldatWork Journal* (quarterly); *Annual Report* (annual). Numerous additional publications, surveys and reports available. See Web site for details.

REFERENCE WORKS

30728 ■ *Business Insurance—Employee Benefit Consultants Issue*
Pub: Crain Communications Inc.
Contact: Martin J. Ross, Publisher
E-mail: mross@businessinsurance.com
Released: Annual, March. **Publication Includes:** List of about 130 firms that offer employee benefit consulting services. **Entries Include:** Name, address, phone, fax, year services began, location of U.S. and foreign offices, number of employees, number of clients, fees, services, parent company, gross revenues (if available), names of principals. **Arrangement:** Alphabetical, by company.

30729 ■ "Can't Pay Like the Big Guys? Think Creatively." in *Crain's Detroit Business* (Vol. 23, January 15, 2007, No. 3, pp. 18)
Pub: Crain Communications Inc. - Detroit
Ed: Sheena Harrison. **Description:** Smaller firms have an advantage in being flexible with non-monetary perks to attract high caliber recruits; this is sometimes necessary in order to compete against the larger companies offering higher salaries but are less flexible in their benefits and perks. Be creative, but within the law. Additional vacation, equity in the company, bonuses, and profit sharing are among the benefits suggested.

30730 ■ *Commissions, Bonuses & Beyond: Sales & Marketing Management's Guide to Sales Compensation*
Pub: Probus Publishing Co., Inc.
Ed: William Keenan, Jr., editor. **Released:** 1994. **Price:** $50.00; $61.50 (Canada). **Description:** Provides information for small business owners and sales and marketing executives on sales compensation planning. Covers developing compensation plans that match strategic plans, benchmarking compensation plans, modeling plan to drive corporate goals, and implementing a plan design. Also contains survey data and a glossary of sales compensation terms.

30731 ■ *Compensation and Motivation: Maximizing Employee Performance with Behavior-Based Incentive Plans*
Pub: AMACOM
Ed: Thomas J. McCoy. **Released:** 1992. **Price:** $65.00 ($65.00 for AMA members). **Description:** Guide to maximizing employee performance with Behavior-Based Incentive Compensation (BBIC) plans. Explains how compensation can no longer be viewed as a financial cost, but as an organizational tool for performance improvement. Covers identifying an organization's needs, choosing the right mix of cash and non-cash compensation to answer those needs, and creating a plan to maximize performance.

30732 ■ *Compensation: Nonqualified Deferred Compensation Answer Book: Forms and Checklists*
Pub: Rector Press, Ltd.
Released: 1995. **Price:** $118.00.

30733 ■ *Compensation for Teams: How to Design and Implement Team-Based Reward Programs*
Pub: AMACOM
Ed: Steven E. Gross. **Released:** 1995. **Price:** $65.00.

30734 ■ *Directory of Worker's Compensation*
Pub: Capitol Publications
Released: 1995. **Price:** $179.00.

30735 ■ *Employee Benefits*
Pub: Dearborn Financial Publishing, Inc.
Ed: Burton T. Beam, Jr. **Released:** 1995. **Price:** $55.95.

30736 ■ *Innovative Reward Systems for the Changing Workplace*
Pub: The McGraw-Hill Companies
Ed: Thomas B. Wilson. **Released:** 1995. **Price:** $32.95. **Description:** Guide for businesses undergoing re-organization, downsizing, etc. Provides information and instruction on developing reward/compensation systems that motivate people to change.

30737 ■ *Just Compensation*
Pub: NAL Dutton
Ed: Robert N. Charrette. **Released:** 1996. **Price:** $4.99.

30738 ■ *"A Market-Driven Approach to Retaining Talent"* in *Harvard Business Review* (Vol. 78, No. 1, January 2000, pp. 103)
Pub: Harvard Business School Publishing Corp.
Ed: Peter Cappelli. **Description:** Companies today are employing different strategies for retaining employees through incentive programs such as stock options and lucrative compensation packages. By designing and promoting longterm career employee development, the companies can win back the loyalty of their workforce.

30739 ■ *"Pay you back: your employees may be better off driving their own cars"* in *Entrepreneur* (Vol. 30, No. 10, October 2002, pp. 38)
Pub: Entrepreneur Media Inc.
Ed: Jill Amadio. **Description:** The use of a company reimbursement program for employees using their own automobiles for business, versus driving company cars is investigated.

30740 ■ *People, Performance & Pay: Dynamic Compensation for Changing Organizations*
Pub: The Free Press
Ed: Thomas P. Flannery. **Released:** 1995. **Price:** $27.00.

30741 ■ *Strategic Pay: Aligning Organizational Strategies and Pay Systems*
Pub: Jossey-Bass, Inc.
Ed: Edward E. Lawler III. **Released:** 1990. **Price:** $30.95. **Description:** Provides information on compensation, covering pay for performance, profit sharing, gain sharing, stock-option plans, and determining the right compensation mix.

30742 ■ *Understanding Workers' Compensation: A Guide for Safety & Health Professionals*
Pub: Government Institutes, Inc.
Ed: Kenneth Wolff. **Released:** 1995. **Price:** $49.00.

30743 ■ *Unemployment Compensation: A Cost You Can Cut*
Pub: American Chamber of Commerce Publishers
Ed: Frick Company staff. **Released:** 1995. **Price:** $75.00.

30744 ■ *Worker's Compensation Insurance: The Survival Guide for Business*
Pub: LEXIS Law Publishing
Ed: Joseph P. Bacarro. **Released:** 1997. **Price:** $85.00 (ringbound); Vol. Issue 6.

TRADE PERIODICALS

30745 ■ *BNA Pension & Benefits Reporter*
Pub: Bureau of National Affairs Inc.
Contact: D. Sayre
Ed: David A. Sayre, Editor. **Released:** Weekly. **Price:** $940. **Description:** Covers pension developments stemming from the passage of the Employee Retirement Income Security Act of 1974 (ERISA) and its amendments. Discusses pension and welfare benefit regulations, standards, enforcement actions, court decisions, legislative and administrative actions, agency options, and employee benefit trust fund requirements.

30746 ■ *Compensation*
Pub: Bureau of National Affairs Inc.
Contact: Jeff Day, Managing Editor
Released: Weekly. **Price:** $683. **Description:** Offers legal clarification and practical advice on employers' pay and benefit policies. Discusses such topics as health care cost containment, payroll laws and taxes, workers compensation laws, pension law (ERISA), job evaluation, benefit plans, compensation administration, incentive systems, and independent contractors. Compensation is part of the BNA Policy and Practice Series, and can be purchased separately or in any combination with other binder sets entitled Fair Employment Practices, Labor Relations, Personnel Management, or Wages and Hours.

30747 ■ *Compensation & Benefits Report*
Pub: Aspen Publishers Inc.
Contact: Michele Rubin, Senior Editor
E-mail: michele.rubin@aspenpubl.com
Released: Semimonthly. **Price:** $219. **Description:** Provides legislative news concerning benefits and compensation. Reports and explains consequences of recent court cases. Indicates what companies are doing to keep their compensation and benefits competitive. Recurring features include interviews.

30748 ■ *EBRI Issue Brief*
Pub: Employee Benefit Research Institute
Contact: Steve Blakely
E-mail: blakely@ebri.org
Ed: Dallas Salisbury, Editor, salisbury@ebri.org. **Released:** Monthly. **Price:** Included in membership; $224, nonmembers; $25, single issue. **Description:** Examines, analyzes, and interprets key issues and trends in the employee benefits field. Covers one topic in-depth in each issue. Remarks: Price includes subscription to the newsletter Employee Benefit Notes.

30749 ■ *Employee Benefit Notes*
Pub: Employee Benefit Research Institute
Contact: Steve Blakely
E-mail: blakely@ebri.org
Ed: Dallas Salisbury, Editor, salisbury@ebri.org. **Released:** Monthly. **Price:** Included in membership; $224, nonmembers. **Description:** "Analyzes and discusses newly released employee benefits data and reviews a wide range of policy issues, research and publications." Recurring features include news of research, legal analysis, legislative updates. Remarks: Subscription includes EBRI Issue Brief.

30750 ■ *Employee Benefits Cases*
Pub: Bureau of National Affairs Inc.
Contact: David A. Sayre, Managing Editor
Released: Weekly, 50/year. **Price:** $1,141. **Description:** Reports full text of federal and state court opinions and selected decisions of arbitrators and the National Labor Relations Board on employee benefits issues. Recurring features include a cumulative index digest, tables of cases, a topical index, and a classification guide.

30751 ■ *Employee Benefits Digest*
Pub: International Foundation of Employee Benefit Plans
Contact: Ronaelle Carlson
E-mail: ronaellec@ifebp.org
Released: Monthly. **Price:** $100. **Description:** Covers the field of employee benefits. Recurring features include notices of publications and educational opportunities, news and announcements for members, and a review of current literature.

30752 ■ *Employee Benefits Review*
Pub: S. Harman & Associates Inc.
Ed: Saundra K. Harman, Editor. **Released:** Monthly, 12/year. **Description:** Covers labor, personnel, and technical issues in the federal personnel area. Lists upcoming conferences, workshops, and training seminars. Remarks: Also available via e-mail.

30753 ■ *Employee Compensation*
Pub: Business & Legal Reports Inc.
Contact: Stephen Fouvnier J.D., Managing Editor
Released: Monthly. **Price:** $395, Included in membership. **Description:** News, comment, and prognostication on employee compension, and benefits.

30754 ■ *Executive Compensation Reports*
Pub: Harcourt Inc.
Ed: Carol Bowie, Editor. **Released:** 24/year. **Price:** $475, U.S.; $499, elsewhere. **Description:** Provides executive compensation information and data.

30755 ■ *Legal-Legislative Reporter*
Pub: International Foundation of Employee Benefit Plans
Contact: Mary Jo Brzezinski
Ed: Harry W. Burton, Editor. **Released:** Monthly. **Price:** $110 as part of publication package. **Description:** Presents news of court and legislative actions pertinent to employee benefit plans.

30756 ■ *Retirement Plans Report*
Pub: Western League of Savings Institutions
Ed: Gloria Sewell-Hacko, Editor. **Released:** Quarterly. **Description:** Reports on tax reform laws affecting retirement plan benefits. Covers IRAs (Individual Retirement Accounts) as well as the Basic Plan. Includes a question-and-answer column.

30757 ■ *Tax Management Compensation Planning*
Pub: Tax Management Inc.
Contact: Glenn B. Davis, Managing Editor
E-mail: gdavis@bna.com
Released: Monthly. **Price:** $462. **Description:** Covers tax planning problems involving employee benefits and executive compensation. Recurring features include detailed analyses, working papers, and bibliographies.

30758 ■ *Wages and Hours*
Pub: Bureau of National Affairs Inc.
Contact: Nancy J. Sedmak, Managing Editor
Released: Weekly. **Price:** $611. **Description:** Provides a guide to compliance with federal and state regulation of wages, hours, and child labor. Covers such topics as hours of work; minimum wage and overtime pay; equal pay; motice posting, reporting, and record-keeping; enforcement and administration; exemptions; home work rules; public contracts; and industry and occupation checklists. Part of the BNA Policy and Practice Series, Wages and Hours can be purchased separately or in any combination with other binder publications entitled Compensation, Fair Employment Practices, Labor Relations, or Personnel Management.

30759 ■ *Work Span*
Pub: WorldatWork
Ed: Jean Christ-Offerson, Editor, jchristofferson@worldatwork.org. **Released:** 10/year. **Description:** Concentrates on issues in the fields of compensation and benefits and human resource management. Includes legislative updates, resources, and case studies.

30760 ■ *Workers' Compensation Monitor*
Pub: LRP Publications
Ed: Gary Mogel, Editor. **Released:** Monthly. **Price:** $210, individuals plus $22 s/h. **Description:** Suggests ways to reduce workers' compensation costs and improve your return-to-work programs. Provides proven solutions your colleagues have implemented to resolve their challenges. Keeps readers up-to-date on the latest developments in national workers' compensation issues including benefits, insurance coverage, legislative reform and costs.

CONSULTANTS

30761 ■ The Epler Co.
450 B St., Ste. 750
San Diego, CA 92101
Ph:(619)239-0831
Fax: (619)239-0807
Co. E-mail: consultants@eplercompany.com
URL: http://www.eplercompany.com

E-mail: consultants@eplercompany.com
Scope: Offers actuarial and consulting services for employee benefits specializing in retirement plans, health, life, accidental death and dismemberment, long-term disability insurance plans, and executive compensation. Administers retiree health studies, AB1200 studies for schools, and merger studies on benefits. Conducts base pay, bonus and benefit surveys. Designs total compensation programs. Industries Served: United States.

30762 ■ Fox Lawson & Associates L.L.C.
1335 County Rd. D E
Saint Paul, MN 55109-5260
Ph:(651)635-0976
Free: 800-383-0976
Fax: (651)635-0980
URL: http://www.foxlawson.com
Scope: A compensation and human resources consulting firm. Provides services to businesses of all sizes including finance, manufacturing, high tech, software development, food, retail, wholesale trade, communications, transportation, service, not-for-profit and education. **Publications:** "Effective Bonus Plans," Ventures Magazine, Feb, 2000; "Split Dollar Insurance," Ventures Magazine, Jan, 2000; "Compensating Contractors and Vendors," Ventures Magazine, Dec, 1999. **Seminars:** Compensation Strategies - Not Having a Plan Could Break the Bank.

30763 ■ Kevin L. Pohle
5820 Main St., Ste. 316-317
Buffalo, NY 14221
Ph:(716)565-0565
Scope: Firm specializes in business strategic planning services, compensation and benefits consulting, special projects management, cost and productivity analysis, and business crisis management. Industries served: manufacturing, retail, healthcare facilities, educational institutions, and local government and municipalities.

30764 ■ Harvey C. Skoog
3737 N Robert Rd., No. A
Prescott Valley, AZ 86314
Ph:(928)772-1448
Scope: Firm has expertise in taxes, payroll, financial planning, budgeting, buy/sell planning, business start-up, fraud detection, troubled business consulting, acquisition, and marketing. Serves the manufacturing, construction, and retailing industries in Arizona.

COMPUTERIZED DATABASES

30765 ■ *Manitoba Automobile Injury Compensation Appeal Commission Decisions*
LexisNexis Quicklaw
2 Gore St.
PO Box 2080
Kingston, ON, Canada K7L 5J8
Ph:(613)549-4611
Free: 800-267-9470
Fax: (613)548-4260
Co. E-mail: sales@quicklaw.com
URL: http://www.quicklaw.com
Description: Provides access to rulings on appeals from Manitoba Public Insurance Officers involving compensation for auto accident injuries. **Type:** Full text.

30766 ■ *Pension & Benefits Reporter*
The Bureau of National Affairs Inc.
1231 25th St. NW
Washington, DC 20037
Ph:(202)452-4200
Free: 800-372-1033
Fax: (202)452-4226
Co. E-mail: customercare@bna.com
URL: http://www.bna.com
Description: Contains up-to-date reporting and coverage of state and federal legislative, regulatory, and judicial activities related to pensions and benefits. Includes coverage of IRS and Labor Department regulations and enforcement issues, tax legislation, health care reform, and developments within industry. Includes taxation of benefits, individual retirement accounts, and fringe benefits. **Availability:** Online: Thomson West, The Bureau of National Affairs Inc. **Type:** Full text.

30767 ■ *Robertson Personal Injury NetLetter*
LexisNexis Quicklaw
2 Gore St.
PO Box 2080
Kingston, ON, Canada K7L 5J8
Ph:(613)549-4611
Free: 800-267-9470
Fax: (613)548-4260
Co. E-mail: sales@quicklaw.com
URL: http://www.quicklaw.com
Description: Provides access to the newsletter by Professor Gerald Robertson, University of Alberta. **Availability:** Online: LexisNexis Quicklaw. **Type:** Full text.

30768 ■ *State Health Care Regulatory Developments*
The Bureau of National Affairs Inc.
1231 25th St. NW
Washington, DC 20037
Ph:(202)452-4200
Free: 800-372-1033
Fax: (202)452-4226
Co. E-mail: customercare@bna.com
URL: http://www.bna.com
Description: Contains information on health care regulatory news and developments in the United States. Subjects include community-based care, home care, emergency care, infectious diseases, managed care, insurance, laboratories, Medicaid, mental health, medical waste, nursing homes, pharmaceuticals, physician services, professional licensing, provider relationships, worker protection and compensation. Entries are organized by state, topic, and register citation. **Availability:** Online: The Bureau of National Affairs Inc., Thomson West. **Type:** Full text.

30769 ■ *Tax Management Compensation Planning Journal*
BNA Tax Management, Inc.
1250 23rd St. NW
Washington, DC 20037-1166
Ph:(202)833-7240
Free: 800-372-1033
Fax: (202)294-6760
Co. E-mail: tm@bna.com
URL: http://www.taxmanagement.bna.com
Description: Reviews news developments which affect tax planning in major areas of specialized tax practice. Includes professional practitioners' commentary as well as reviews of actual or model benefit plans. Provides information on compensation related matters in Congress, the U.S. Treasury, Internal Revenue Serivice (IRS), the U.S. Labor Department, and the Pension Benefit Guaranty Corporation (PBGC). **Availability:** Online: BNA Tax Management, Inc. **Type:** Full text.

LIBRARIES

30770 ■ Towers Perrin–Information Centre
1100 Melville St., Ste. 1600
Vancouver, BC, Canada V6E 4A6
Ph:(604)691-1034
Fax: (604)691-1062
Scope: Actuarial science, employee benefits, compensation, human resources. **Holdings:** Figures not available.

RESEARCH CENTERS

30771 ■ Miami University–Center for Pension and Retirement Research
208E Laws Hall
Department of Economics
Oxford, OH 45056
Ph:(513)529-2836
Fax: (513)529-3308
Contact: William Even, Dir.
Scope: Historical origin of pensions, factors influencing the availability and type of pension plans offered, and the incentive effects of pensions on labor turnover and retirement decisions. Also conducts a panel study of income dynamics, retirement history survey, current population survey, and newly entitled beneficiary survey. **Publications:** CPRR Conference Book.

30772 ■ University of Waterloo–Institute of Insurance and Pension Research
Department of Statistics & Actuarial Science
Waterloo, ON, Canada N2L 3G1
Ph:(519)888-4767
Fax: (519)746-1875
Co. E-mail: rlbrown@uwaterloo.ca
URL: http://www.stats.uwaterloo.ca/stats_navigation/IIPR/IIPR.shtml
Contact: Dr. R.L. Brown, Dir.
E-mail: rlbrown@uwaterloo.ca
Scope: Insurance and pension research. **Services:** Contract research. **Educational Activities:** Seminars and colloquia.

START-UP INFORMATION

30773 ■ *The Art of the Start: The Time-Tested, Battle-Hardened Guide for Anyone Starting Anything*
Pub: Penguin Books (USA) Incorporated
Ed: Guy Kawasaki **Released:** September 2004. **Price:** $26.95. **Description:** Advice for someone starting a new business covering topics such as hiring employees, building a brand, business competition, and management.

30774 ■ "My Best Practices: Sell smarter. Streamline your office. Work better. Crush competition" in *FSB* (Vol. 10, No. 9, Dec. 1, 2000, pp. 54)
Pub: Time Inc.
Description: If you really want to outdistance competitors, the author recommends using today's new technology as powerfully as possible to run your business.

30775 ■ "Quebec's Competitive Edge" in *Venture Capital Journal* (Vol. 42, No. 5, May 2002, pp. 51-52)
Pub: Thomas Venture Economics
Description: U.S. venture capital firms that invest in Quebec, Canada may have a head start on the competition. Statistical data included.

REFERENCE WORKS

30776 ■ "ABN Amro To Cut 900 Positions In North America" in *Wall Street Journal* (Vol. 248, December 2006, No. 152, pp. A7)
Pub: Dow Jones & Co. Inc.
Ed: Reuters News Service **Description:** ABN Amro Holding NV., Parent of Chicago-based LaSalle Bank plans to cut 900 more North American Jobs to reduce costs amid growing competition.

30777 ■ "Advocate or Competitor?" in *Hispanic Business* (Vol. 24, No. 1/2, January/ February 2002, pp. 18-20, 22)
Pub: Hispanic Business Inc.
Description: A summary of the United States Hispanic Chamber of Commerce (USHCC) making a business decision to publish a new magazine called Hispanic Trends and the controversy arising from this publication.

30778 ■ "The Age of the Choiceboard" in *Harvard Business Review* (Vol. 78, No. 1, January 2000, pp. 40)
Pub: Harvard Business School Publishing Corp.
Ed: Adrian J. Slywotzky. **Description:** As customers gain control over the design of products, competition within and among industries will take on a whole new shape.

30779 ■ "Almost Famous: Market Yourself as an Expert" in *My Business* (October/ November 2003, pp. 45)
Pub: My Business Magazine

Ed: Nancy Mann Jackson. **Description:** The importance of establishing one's self as an expert in the particular field in which you are selling will help a salesperson stand out from competitors. Tips includes speaking at conferences, creating informational products, the use of newspapers and magazines or business publications, writing articles, or doing guest spots on television or radio shows.

30780 ■ *Alpha Dogs: How Your Small Business Can Become a Leader of the Pack*
Pub: HarperInformation
Ed: Donna Fenn. **Released:** December 2005. **Price:** $24.95. **Description:** Ways for an entrepreneur to outsmart competitors in the marketplace, to generate higher sales, and earn lasting customer and employee loyalty.

30781 ■ "The Art of Business Judo" in *Fast Company* (August 2001, pp. 116)
Pub: Fast Company
Ed: Jill Rosenfeld. **Description:** It's the essence of competition: big versus little, strong versus slight, heavy versus light; ways for small companies to compete with larger corporations are presented by former Judo champion, Jimmy Pedro.

30782 ■ "AT & T Heads Into TV Fray With Passage of Video Bill" in *Crain's Detroit Business* (Vol. 22, December 18, 2006, No. 51, pp. 5)
Pub: Crain Communications Inc. - Detroit
Ed: Amy Lane. **Description:** AT&T is making a large investment in Michigan as a result of the new bill passed last week to open competition amongst high tech cable suppliers; franchising process is revised opening the doors to a new video battle amongst Comcast and AT&T.

30783 ■ "AT&T Set To Take On Cable As Purchase is Cleared" in *Wall Street Journal* (Vol. 248, December 2006, No. 153, pp. A3)
Pub: Dow Jones & Co. Inc.
Ed: Amol Sharma, Corey Boles **Description:** FCC approved the largest deal in the U.S. telecommunications industry between AT&T and BellSouth Corp. The merger places new pressure on its considerably smaller competitors like Verizon and Vonage.

30784 ■ "Baby Bells must accept competition" in *Red Herring* (January 2003, pp. 17)
Pub: Herring Communications Inc.
Description: The four remaining Baby Bells must improve their businesses in order to remain competitive.

30785 ■ *Balls!: 6 Rules for Winning Today's Business Game*
Pub: John Wiley & Sons, Incorporated
Ed: Alexi Venneri. **Released:** January 2005. **Price:** $19.95. **Description:** In order to be successful business leaders must be brave, authentic, loud, lovable, and spunky and they need to lead their competition.

30786 ■ "A Bank, At Your Service" in *Inc.* (Volume 28, January 2006, No. 1, pp. 21-23)
Pub: Inc. Magazine
Ed: Dan Ackman. **Description:** In order to compete with larger banks, local bankers are focusing efforts on business owners.

30787 ■ "Banking on California" in *San Francisco Business Times* (Vol. 18, No. 6, September 19, 2003, pp. 19)
Pub: American City Business Journals
Ed: Mark Calvey. **Description:** Citibank's purchase of California Federal Bank last year has gone smoothly, the next task is to attract customers from other large competitors.

30788 ■ "Bartech and Nucon Win Staffing Deals" in *Black Enterprise* (Vol. 35, November 2004, No. 4, pp. 32)
Pub: Earl G. Graves Publishing Co. Inc.
Ed: Erin Straker. **Description:** Bartech Workforce Management secured a multi-year contract with Eaton Corporation to manage all temporary staffing and vendor services for Eaton nationwide, including all information technology, industrial and technical staffing.

30789 ■ "Battle between Compuware, IBM escalates in counterclaim" in *Crain's Detroit Business* (Vol. 19, No. 14, April 7, 2003, pp. 4)
Pub: Crain Communications Inc., Detroit
Ed: Andrew Dietderich. **Description:** The legal battle between Compuware and IBM has ensued for more than thirteen months. The two software companies are battling over Compuware's accusation that IBM has misappropriated trade secrets, committed antitrust law violations and unfair competition practices.

30790 ■ "Be Prepared" in *Inc.* (Volume 28, January 2006, No. 1, pp. 53-54)
Pub: Inc. Magazine
Ed: Norm Brodsky. **Description:** The greatest competitive edge a company can have, is to know more than your competitor knows when a longtime client's contract is due to expire.

30791 ■ *Beating the Competition: A Practical Guide to Benchmarking*
Pub: Washington Researchers, Ltd.
Released: 1992. **Price:** $155.00. **Description:** Describes the benchmarking process, from identifying successful companies and measuring their performance, to designing ways to surpass them. Includes real-life examples.

30792 ■ *Beating the Competition: 150 Ways to Win New Customers for Your Small Business*
Pub: Madison Books
Ed: Tait Trussell. **Released:** 1992. **Price:** $10.95 (paper). **Description:** Discusses how to attract new customers and the importance of public relations. Includes sample press releases and communication plans.

30793 ■ "Bells want to raise rates of competitors" in *Atlanta Business Chronicle* (Vol. 25, December 6, 2002, No. 26, pp. 1)
Pub: American City Business Publications, Inc.
Ed: Mary Jane Credeur. Description: Bell companies are trying to get Federal regulators to reduce or eliminate discounts they must pay to competitors that use Bell networks. This move comes as the Bell companies have entered the long-distance markets in several states. BellSouth Corporation asserts that the discounts are unfair.

30794 ■ "Better Rivals" in *My Business* (June/July 2004, pp. 47)
Pub: My Business Magazine
Ed: Dennis McCafferty. Description: Customer service is key to beating competition when running a small business.

30795 ■ "Big Deal" in *Entrepreneur* (Vol. 33, January 2005, No. 1, pp. 63)
Pub: Entrepreneur Media Inc.
Ed: Gwen Moran. Description: Tips for growing companies to consider when partnering with a competitor.

30796 ■ "The Big Guns' Next Target: eBay" in *Business 2.0* (Vol. 7, January/February 2006, No. 1, pp. 21-22)
Pub: Time, Inc.
Ed: Michael V. Copeland. Description: eBay's lucrative auctions are being targeted by Google and Microsoft to move into classified advertising.

30797 ■ "Biz Schools Find 'Flat is the New Up' for MBA Enrollment" in *Crain's Detroit Business* (Vol. 21, October 17, 2005, No. 43, pp. 17)
Pub: Crain Communications Inc. - Detroit
Ed: Nancy Nall Derringer. Description: Southeastern Michigan business schools are seeing a slowdown in applicants for full-time programs and a larger demand for part-time or executive programs, creating a more competitive market for these schools.

30798 ■ *Blue Ocean Strategy: How to Create Uncontested Market Space and Make Competition Irrelevant*
Pub: Harvard Business School Publishing
Ed: W. Chan Kim. Released: January 2005. Price: $29.95.

30799 ■ "Boise fitness centers brace for challenge from Gold's Gym" in *Vancouver Business Journal* (December 2, 2002)
Pub: Dolan Media Newswires
Ed: Steve Martin. Description: Profile of Gold's Gyms, and its expansion, particularly in the Boise, Idaho area. Gold's Gyms are working to stay current with workout trends, including not only free-weights and workout machines, but martial arts, tanning and massage, child-care, Pilates, yoga, even specific exercise regimens for golfers, etc.

30800 ■ "Boosting Corporate Diversity" in *Hispanic Business* (April 2005, pp. 14)
Pub: Hispanic Business
Description: Many corporate managers believe that diversity programs provide a competitive edge because they improve a company's performance and leadership. The University of Texas, Austin started a program to expand the number of diverse students for their MBA program.

30801 ■ "Bored Meeting" in *Entrepreneur* (Vol. 31, No. 9, September 2003, pp. 78)
Pub: Entrepreneur Media, Inc.
Description: Business owners serving on commissions quickly find out it is not a way to gather intelligence about competitors, rather they should cultivate relationships with commercial real estate brokers and landlords.

30802 ■ "Bovine Blues?" in *Entrepreneur* (Vol. 31, No. 8, August 2003, pp. 25)
Pub: Entrepreneur Media, Inc.
Ed: Mark Henricks. Description: Review of the book, "Purple Cow: Transform Your Business by Being Remarkable", written by Seth Godin. Godin believes every company needs something phenomenal, counterintuitive and exciting in order to take attention away from competitors.

30803 ■ "Breakthrough Performance: Sales Success" in *Entrepreneur* (Vol. 31, No. 9, September 2003, pp. 84)
Pub: Entrepreneur Media, Inc.
Ed: Barry Farber. Description: Five proven strategies to excel at breakthrough selling are examined. A breakthrough is defined as any significant advance or development that removes a barrier to progress.

30804 ■ "Bridging the On-the-Road Blues" in *Business Journal-Milwaukee* (Vol. 20, No. 50, August 29, 2003, pp. A30)
Pub: American City Business Journals, Inc.
Ed: Becca Mader. Description: An examination of services offered by Milwaukee, Wisconsin-based BridgeStreet Accommodations Inc. Topics covered include employee housing, cost control advantages, and area competition.

30805 ■ "Builder Bandits" in *Tampa Tribune* (December 12, 2005)
Pub: Media General, Inc.
Ed: Shannon Behnken. Description: Florida's booming economy and hurricane damage has forced building trade subcontractors to compete over workers by raising hourly wages by $3-$5.

30806 ■ "A Bumper Crop of Worries" in *Tampa Tribune* (November 30, 2005)
Pub: Media General, Inc.
Ed: Will Rodgers. Description: Florida citrus growers face challenges of disease, development, hurricanes, and competition, hurting profits and land use.

30807 ■ "Business Dining Etiquette: Beat Your Competition With Winning Table Manners" in *Black Enterprise* (Vol. 35, August 2004, No. 1)
Pub: Earl G. Graves Publishing Co. Inc.
Ed: Kimberly J. Hamilton-Wright. Description: Because nearly 50 percent of all business transactions are concluded over a meal, good table manners are critical to image.

30808 ■ *Business Warrior: Strategy for Entrepreneurs*
Pub: Clearbridge Publishing
Ed: Sun Tzu. Released: September 2006. Price: $19.95. Description: Advice to help entrepreneurs understand competitive strategies in order to succeed, focusing on sales, marketing, and personnel management.

30809 ■ "By Gum!...It Is Possible to Beat Everyone-Even Big Companies-To Market..." in *Entrepreneur* (Vol. 32, November 2004, No. 11, pp. 26)
Pub: Entrepreneur Media Inc.
Ed: Geoff Williams. Description: Profile of Art Baer, who invested $20,000 of his own money to launch Impress Gum. Baer recognized the opportunity when Singapore lifted its ban on chewing gum, where residents chew gum for medicinal purposes.

30810 ■ "Can This Really Be Hewlett-Packard?" in *Business Week* (December 19, 2005, No. 3964, pp. 49-50)
Pub: McGraw-Hill Companies
Ed: Peter Burrows. Description: Hewlett-Packard is running on all cylinders thanks to the reorganization and cost-cutting measures taking by its CEO, Mark V. Hurd. The company can now focus on growth and expansion.

30811 ■ "Carrying Coffee to Seattle" in *The Economist* (Vol. 377, October 1-7, 2005, No. 8446, pp. 37)
Pub: The Economist Newspaper Ltd.
Description: Colombia's National Federation of Coffee Growers have opened coffee shops in New York, Washington DC, and Seattle, competing with Starbucks. The move is to launch the federation's global expansion. The federation acts as buyer, marketer, technical advisor and banker to Colombian coffee farmers.

30812 ■ "Carver vs. OneUnited" in *Black Enterprise* (Vol. 35, December 2004, No. 5, pp. 96)
Pub: Earl G. Graves Publishing Co. Inc.
Ed: Sakina P. Spruell. Description: Profile of Deborah Wright, who has set her sights on making her firm a billion dollar giant. Carver was involved in a failed attempt in a takeover bid for Independence Federal Savings Bank.

30813 ■ "Case Study" in *Inc.* (December 1, 2004)
Pub: Inc. Magazine
Ed: Lora Kolodny. Description: Intellinitiative's board games were selling fast until a giant brand took over and pushed them out of the store.

30814 ■ "Catch-22: Are Small Companies that Buy from Giant Retailers Sleeping with the Enemy" in *Entrepreneur* (Vol. 31, No. 9, September 2003)
Pub: Entrepreneur Media, Inc.
Ed: Joshua Kurlantzick. Description: Small retailers have to compete with megastores such as Sam's Club, Target, Wal-Mart and others, with main suppliers, putting more stress on small businesses.

30815 ■ "Chatting With the Enemy" in *My Business* (April/May 2004, pp. 49)
Pub: My Business Magazine
Ed: Michael Helfand. Description: Profile of Michael Helfand, co-founder of www.FindGreatLawyers.com, an online attorney-referral business. Helfand discusses information management.

30816 ■ "China" in *Business Week* (January 23, 2006, No. 3968, pp. 44-45)
Pub: McGraw-Hill Companies
Ed: Brian Bremner. Description: Citibank has been out-hustled by rivals HSBC, Bank of America, and Goldman Sachs in making deals with large Chinese banking firms. Acquisitions, consumer banking, and corporate clients could help Citi compete.

30817 ■ "China's cheap labor is next threat to suppliers" in *Crain's Detroit Business* (Vol. 19, No. 2, January 13, 2003, pp. 13)
Pub: Crain Communications Inc., Detroit
Ed: Terry Kosdrosky. Description: U.S. auto suppliers are facing yet another threat, the growing Chinese economy. China's large supply of educated workers earning low incomes threaten the security of small to mid-size manufacturers in the U.S., especially the tool and die industry.

30818 ■ "The coach who got poached" in *Harvard Business Review* (Vol. 80, No. 3, March 2002, pp. 31)
Pub: Harvard Business School Press
Ed: Idalene F. Kesner. Description: A case study about a manager who develops excellent people only to see them stolen away by other divisions.

30819 ■ "Coca-Cola Bottler Up for Sale: CEO J. Bruce Llewellyn Seeks Retirement" in *Black Enterprise* (Vol. 37, December 2006, No. 5, pp. 31)
Pub: Earl G. Graves Publishing Co. Inc.
Ed: Marcia A. Wade. Description: J. Bruce Llewellyn of Brucephil Inc., the parent company of the Philadelphia Coca-Cola Bottling Co. has agreed to sell its remaining shares to Coca-Cola Co., which previously owned 31 percent of Philly Coke. Analysts believe that Coca-Cola will eventually sell its shares to another bottler.

30820 ■ "Competing with the Big Guys" in *Home Business* (Vol. 13, January/February 2006, No. 1, pp. 71)
Pub: Home Business Magazine
Ed: Sandy Larson. Description: Profile of Seema Matia who runs a marketing research firm from her home in Calabasas, California. Matia offers services to small and medium-sized businesses.

30821 ■ **"Competition Forces Malls to Redefine Marketing"** in *Atlanta Business Chronicle* (Vol. 26, No. 11, August 22, 2003, pp. 3A)
Pub: American City Business Publications, Inc.
Ed: Jim Lovel. **Description:** Small shopping centers have a larger customer base than larger regional malls in the Atlanta, Georgia area.

30822 ■ **"Competition to Heat Up Among Health Insurers"** in *Pittsburgh Business Times* (Vol. 23, No. 1, July 25, 2003, pp. 1)
Pub: Pittsburgh Business Times
Ed: Lynne Glover. **Description:** United Healthcare, the largest health insurance company in the U.S., will expand to the Sacramento area.

30823 ■ **"Competition Keeps Athletic Execs Stoked"** in *Crain's Detroit Business* (Vol. 21, October 3, 2005, No. 43, pp. 27)
Pub: Crain Communications Inc. - Detroit
Ed: Scott Cendrowski. **Description:** Clubs and competitive sports leagues contribute to keeping executives competitive.

30824 ■ **"The Competition has Nuttin' on this Business"** in *Providence Business News* (Vol. 18, No. 18, August 25, 2003, pp. 10)
Pub: Providence Business News, Inc.
Ed: David Ortiz. **Description:** Profile of Virginia & Spanish Peanut Company and ways they are competing in the industry.

30825 ■ **"The Competitiveness of Small and Medium Enterprises"** in *Journal of Business Venturing* (Vol. 17, No. 2, March 2002, pp. 123)
Pub: Elsevier Science, Inc.
Ed: Thomas W.Y. Man, Theresa Lau, K.F. Chan. **Description:** The development of a conceptual model, patterned after the notion of competitiveness and the competency approach, is discussed. This conceptual model was developed to connect the performance of the traits small and medium-sized enterprises (SME), owner-managers and their companies have in common.

30826 ■ **"Consorting with Competitors"** in *Harvard Business Review* (Vol. 80, No. 1, January 2002, pp. 21)
Pub: Harvard Business School Press
Ed: Christopher Kurt. **Description:** Personal insight is given into forming industry consortia, using specifications called Universal Description, Discover, and Integration (UDDI). UDDI allows for integrations of ideas electronically via a directory, and keeps the consortia on track.

30827 ■ **"Contest Challenges Teens to Consider Entrepreneurship"** in *Kansas City Star* (March 8, 2005)
Pub: Knight-Ridder/Tribune Business News
Ed: Donna Vestal. **Description:** The National Association of Women Business Owners and Adams-Gabbert & Associates Inc. in Kansas City have announced a contest for senior girls to enter. The competition is meant to promote entrepreneurship among young women.

30828 ■ **"Copy Cop Fights Back, Takes the Digital Plunge"** in *Boston Business Journal* (Vol. 23, No. 30, August 29, 2003, pp. 4)
Pub: American City Business Journals
Ed: Jill Lerner. **Description:** Efforts by Boston, Massachusetts-based Copy Cop to recapture lost market share is examined. Topics include making capital investments in the company, developing new markets, and taking on competition.

30829 ■ *Corporate Entrepreneurship & Innovation*
Pub: Thomson South-Western
Ed: Michael H. Morris; Donald F. Kuratko. **Released:** January 2007. **Price:** $104.95. **Description:** Innovation is the key to running a successful small business. The book helps entrepreneurs to develop the skills and business savvy to sustain a competitive edge.

30830 ■ **"A Corporate Science Project"** in *Business Week* (December 19, 2005, No. 3964, pp. 108)
Pub: McGraw-Hill Companies
Ed: Craig R. Barrett. **Description:** U.S. businesses need to help turn out more mat and science graduates in order to stay competitive in a global economy.

30831 ■ **"The costs of e-commerce"** in *Hispanic Business* (Vol. 22, No. 4, April 2000, pp. 78)
Pub: Hispanic Business
Ed: Vaughn Hagerty. **Description:** The rapidly changing composition of businesses on the Internet makes it difficult for Internet-based companies to keep track of their competitors. The effects on business success of a lack of knowledge of competitors are discussed.

30832 ■ **"Crafting a Web presence"** in *Accounting Technology* (Vol. 19, No. 1, January-February 2003, pp. 16)
Pub: Thomson Financial Inc.
Ed: Richard McCausland. **Description:** Jim Schaefer, founder of Schaefer & Company, an 18-year old tax and accounting practice believes that a Web site keeps a business competitive.

30833 ■ **"Credit Unions Share Branches to Compete with Bigger, National Banks"** in *Portland Press Herald* (May 17, 2005)
Pub: Blethen Maine Newspapers, Inc.
Ed: Edward D. Murphy. **Description:** A new trend shows credit unions sharing branches in order to compete with larger banking institutions which control about 80 percent of the market.

30834 ■ **"Damariscotta, Maine, Merchants Worry About Wal-Mart"** in *Portland Press Herald* (December 1, 2005)
Pub: Blethen Maine Newspapers, Inc.
Ed: Dennis Hoey. **Description:** Plans for a new Wal-Mart in Damariscotta, Maine has small business retailers concerned about competition. Many downtown merchants believe a Wal-Mart store will detract from the downtown area and force many out of business.

30835 ■ **"Dare to Compare."** in *Entrepreneur* (Vol. 33, January 2005, No. 1, pp. 43)
Pub: Entrepreneur Media Inc.
Ed: Melissa Campanelli. **Description:** Online merchants wishing to grow their business might consider placing products on comparison shopping Websites. These sites display product information in a simple format and lets buyers compare and choose the best product from a list of different retailers.

30836 ■ **"Dear Air Over America"** in *Red Herring* (No. 105, October 1, 2001, pp. 42-46, 48)
Pub: Herring Communications
Ed: Dan Briody. **Description:** Without 3G spectrum, the U.S. wireless industry will fall further behind its international competitors. The article addresses the government's unwillingness to make the spectrum available in the U.S.

30837 ■ **"Demolition derby: two guys, plus slurs, lies and videotape"** in *Wall Street Journal* (July 21, 2000, pp. A1)
Pub: Dow Jones & Co., Inc.
Ed: Barbara Martinez. **Description:** The article covers information about a decades-old St. Louis business feud.

30838 ■ **"The DHL EuroCup: Shots on Goal"** in *Harvard Business Review* (Vol. 81, No. 11, November 2003, pp. 43)
Pub: Harvard Business School Press
Ed: Paul Hemp. **Description:** Increasing teamwork through competition in the business setting is shown in an examination of the DHL EuroCup soccer tournament.

30839 ■ **"Do I Have a Choice?"** in *Inc.* (September 2005, pp. 40)
Pub: Inc. Magazine
Ed: Stephanie Clifford. **Description:** Greg Roderick's firm offers three health plans to his employees, which encourages competition among providers. Statistical data included.

30840 ■ **"Do-It-Yourself Insurance"** in *Inc.* (Volume 27, December 2005, No. 12, pp. 39-40, 42)
Pub: Inc. Magazine
Ed: Alison Stein Wellner. **Description:** Individual insurance policies are becoming more popular, but premiums vary from state to state. The pros of cons of a small business replacing group health plans in favor for individual policies are discussed.

30841 ■ **"Dream Machines"** in *Business Week* (January 16, 2006, No. 3967, pp. 52-56, 58)
Pub: McGraw-Hill Companies
Ed: Lee Walczak, David Welch. **Description:** The automobile industry is taking advantage of the competitive pressure it faces by offering new designs, technology-driven innovation, safety features, and more choices to customize vehicles.

30842 ■ **"Dry Cleaning Dons a Corporate Veneer"** in *Tampa Tribune* (December 9, 2005)
Pub: Media General, Inc.
Ed: Mary Shedden. **Description:** Independently run dry cleaning stores are facing stiff competition from national franchise chains. Dryclean USA is expanding into the Florida market and boasts nearly 400 shops in the U.S., Caribbean, Mexico, and Brazil.

30843 ■ **"Economic and Financial Indicators"** in *The Economist* (Vol. 377, October 1-7, 2005, No. 8446, pp. 96-97)
Pub: The Economist Newspaper Ltd.
Description: Statistics involving fifteen developed economies are presented, along with a look at competitiveness and the world's largest companies.

30844 ■ **"Elephants on a chip"** in *Barron's* (Vol. 82, No. 58, February 17, 2003, pp. T1)
Pub: Barron's
Ed: Bill Alpert. **Description:** Smaller 'point solution' semiconductor firms may be pushed aside in the Texas Instruments vs. Intel battle for market share, including Broadcom, Marvell, and Intersill.

30845 ■ **"The Endangered Department Store"** in *Boston Globe* (February 13, 2005)
Pub: New York Times Company
Ed: Keith Reed. **Description:** The merger between Macy's and Filene's is causing experts to question whether mass-market department stores are on the decline. Many department stores are reinventing themselves in order to stay competitive with the luxury high-end and low-cost discount stores.

30846 ■ **"Enemy Mine: Learning to Live with the Competitors You Love to Hate"** in *Entrepreneur* (Vol. 31, No. 10, October 2003, pp. 34)
Pub: Entrepreneur Media, Inc.
Ed: Michael D. Alter. **Description:** Profile of SurePayroll (ranked Number 6 in the country) and ways it is able to compete with rivals, ADP and Paychex, ranked number one and two, respectively.

30847 ■ **"Entrepreneur Column"** in *Entrepreneur* (August 4, 2005)
Pub: Entrepreneur Media Inc.
Ed: Tom Hopkins. **Description:** The meaning behind a customer's desire to shop around before purchasing a product or service is examined. It is important for small business owners to research their competition.

30848 ■ *Entrepreneurship and Economic Growth*
Pub: Edward Elgar Publishing, Incorporated
Ed: Carree. **Released:** October 2006. **Price:** $195.00. **Description:** Historic and country-specific studies and articles regarding entrepreneurship and innovation, growth models, competition and productivity, and empirical evidence.

30849 ■ **"The Ethics of Consumer Sovereignty in an Age of High Tech"** in *Journal of Business Ethics* (Vol. 28, No. 1, November 1, 2000, pp. 1)
Pub: Kluwer Academic Publishers

Ed: M. Joseph Sirgy, Chenting Su. **Description:** The world of high tech is increasingly responsible for changes in the opportunity, ability, and motivation of business firms to compete. Furthermore, it is also increasingly responsible for the same motivation of consumers to engage in rational decision-making.

30850 ■ **"Excluded Taxi Groups Aren't Hailing Rival's Airport Deal" in** *Sacramento Bee* **(November 16, 2005)**
Pub: The Sacramento Bee
Ed: Judy Lin. **Description:** Sacramento County officials approved a three-year pact with the Sacramento Independent Taxi Owners Association for exclusive pickup privileges at the Sacramento International Airport. The three other taxi groups competed for the contract charge the County is imposing a monopoly of services, thus hurting the taxi industry and denying airport passengers cheaper fares.

30851 ■ **"Expanding Your Network of Contacts" in** *Black Enterprise* **(Vol. 35, January 2005, No. 6, pp. 111)**
Pub: Earl G. Graves Publishing Co. Inc.
Ed: Lisa Downer. **Description:** Invitation to business owners, entrepreneurs and corporate executives is extended for the 2005 Black Enterprise/General Motors Entrepreneurs Conference to be held in May 2005 in Dallas, Texas. The conference theme is, Seasons of Change, and explores the role that change management plays in gaining or retaining a competitive advantage.

30852 ■ **"FC Shortlist" in** *Fast Company* **(October 2001, pp. 46)**
Pub: Fast Company
Description: Review of the book "Gonzo Marketing: Winning Through Worst Practices" by Christopher Locke. The author describes micro-audiences and micro-markets as the new units of growth and competitive advantage. The book by Barbara Waugh, "The Soul in the Computer: The Story of a Corporate Revolutionary" is also reviewed. Ms. Waugh is the worldwide change manager at Hewlett-Packard and cofounder of HP's World e-Inclusion unit.

30853 ■ **"Fierce Competition in Security Field" in** *San Jose Mercury News* **(February 16, 2005)**
Pub: Knight-Ridder/Tribune Business News
Ed: Dan Lee. **Description:** Microsoft's new anti-virus software service will be available at the end of 2005; the firm is also releasing an updated version of its Internet Explorer browser that will block Internet attacks and other cyber-scams.

30854 ■ **"Fight Brews in Senate Over Bill to Change TV Franchises" in** *Crain's Detroit Business* **(Vol. 22, November 20, 2006, No. 47, pp. 25)**
Pub: Crain Communications Inc. - Detroit
Ed: Amy Lane. **Description:** State issuing guideline template to communities to permit more competition in the video provider market. Currently awarding franchises is a city by city function without any clear guidelines for standardization from one community to another. AT and T is making a major investment in Michigan and challenging existing cable franchises in local communities.

30855 ■ **"Fighting Back" in** *Business Week* **(No. 3678, April 24, 2000, pp. F36)**
Pub: McGraw-Hill, Inc.
Description: Ways small companies can fight back against larger companies.

30856 ■ **"Finding a Niche Within a Niche" in** *Black Enterprise* **(Vol. 36, February 2006, No. 7, pp. 93)**
Pub: Earl G. Graves Publishing Co. Inc.
Ed: Layton Turner. **Description:** Choosing a niche is a good strategy for businesses with fewer resources than larger competitors.

30857 ■ **"Finishing Touches - The Web is crowded and intensely competitive" in** *PC Magazine* **(February 20, 2001, pp. 133)**
Pub: Ziff-Davis Publishing Company

Ed: Neil Randall. **Description:** BeautyQ.com's Web site is designed to attract teen-age girls by offering health and style advice. The site enjoyed brisk traffic, but lacked repeat visitors until the organization added a bulletin board. The typical visitor now spends more than ten minutes on the site and many of them make repeat visits.

30858 ■ **"Finning the Flames" in** *Entrepreneur* **(Vol. 31, No. 9, July 2003, pp. 126)**
Pub: Entrepreneur Media, Inc.
Ed: Don Debelak. **Description:** Profile of Bob Evans, founder of Bob Evans Designs Inc. in Santa Barbara, California. Evans' company designed swimming fins designed to propel swimmers through water faster with less effort. Evans discusses how he stays ahead of a market where competitors sell lower-priced, more traditional products.

30859 ■ **"FIOS TV" in** *Crain's New York Business* **(Vol. 22, November 27, 2006, No. 48, pp. 33)**
Pub: Crain Communications, Inc.
Description: FiOs TV is a television service offered by Verizon and is currently available in small cities and suburban areas in seven states. The company won a statewide TV franchise in New Jersey and is doing business in forty Long Island communities.

30860 ■ **"Flip the Competition" in** *Fast Company* **(August 2001, pp. 10)**
Pub: Fast Company
Ed: Jennifer Reingold. **Description:** Review of the book, "The Art of Business Judo" is highlighted. The author, David B. Yoffie, is a master at decoding high-tech strategies.

30861 ■ **"Flying From the Computer" in** *The Economist* **(Vol. 377, October 1-7, 2005, No. 8446, pp. 65-67)**
Pub: The Economist Newspaper Ltd.
Description: The Internet has created intense competition among travel providers. Statistical data included.

30862 ■ **"Foreign Targets" in** *Hispanic Business* **(July/August 2004, pp. 48)**
Pub: Hispanic Business
Ed: Michael Caplinger. **Description:** Wholesalers and manufactures share insight into winning in a competitive global market. Statistical data included.

30863 ■ **"Funny Business: No Ifs, Ands or Buts" in** *Entrepreneur* **(Vol. 32, October 2004, No. 10, pp. 93)**
Pub: Entrepreneur Media Inc.
Ed: Jerry Fisher. **Description:** Individuals can promote a product or service and help it to stand out from competition.

30864 ■ **"The Game of War" in** *Red Herring* **(No. 106, October 15, 2001, pp. 54-58, 60)**
Pub: Herring Communications
Ed: Dean Takahashi. **Description:** This November, Microsoft, Sony, and Nintendo will face off in a battle for the video console market. Profiles of PlayStation character Crash Bandicoot, Nintendo's Mario, and Xbox siren Raven are key players in the struggle for control of the video console market.

30865 ■ **"Geography is Destiny" in** *Inc.* **(September 1, 2004)**
Pub: Inc. Magazine
Ed: Darren Dahl. **Description:** How three company builders gained competitive advantage by thinking smartly about commercial real estate is discussed.

30866 ■ *Get Better or Get Beaten: Thirty-One Leadership Secrets from GE's Jack Welch*
Pub: Irwin Professional Publishing
Ed: Robert Slater. **Released:** 1995. **Price:** $16.95.

30867 ■ **"Get the Scoop" in** *Entrepreneur* **(Vol. 28, No. 2, February 2000, pp. 142)**
Pub: Entrepreneur Media Inc.
Ed: Gwen Moran. **Description:** When it comes to promoting your business, knowledge is power. The more you know about your market, customers, competition and prospects, the more likely you are to make smart decisions.

30868 ■ **"Get Tough: No More Mr. Nice Guy."** **in** *Entrepreneur* **(Vol. 33, January 2005, No. 1, pp. 28)**
Pub: Entrepreneur Media Inc.
Ed: Mark Henricks. **Description:** Review of the book, Hardball: Are You Playing to Play or Playing to Win?, by George Stalk and Rob Lachenauer. The authors explain how to gain and maintain a competitive advantage by enticing competitors into retreat.

30869 ■ **"Getting the Dish; Blogs Allow Everyone to be a Critic" in** *Crain's New York Business* **(Vol. 23, January 29, 2007, No. 5, pp. 48)**
Pub: Crain Communications, Inc.
Description: Blogs are changing the landscape of the dining scene. Everyone can be a critic on such blogs as Chowmaster.com, Mouthfulsfood.com, or Thestrongbuzz.com among hosts of others.

30870 ■ *Getting to Scale: Growing Your Business Without Selling Out*
Pub: Berrett-Koehler Publishers, Incorporated
Ed: Jill Bamburg. **Released:** July 2006. **Price:** $14.95. **Description:** Ways for entrepreneurs to preserve the value of their company while maintaining growth and competitiveness.

30871 ■ **"GlitzyShow, Worry Galore" in** *Wall Street Journal* **(Vol. 249 January 2007, No. 5, pp. A2)**
Pub: Dow Jones & Co. Inc.
Ed: Associated Press. **Description:** Despite the glitzy displays of the North American Auto Show, auto-industry executives worry that 2007 may be one of the weakest years in more than a decade. Emerging markets in India and Eastern Europe are still relatively small and in the case of China, increasingly competitive.

30872 ■ **"Guarding your turf: how the small guy can fend off big biz encroachment" in** *Black Enterprise* **(Vol. 33, No. 3, October 2002, pp. 56)**
Pub: Earl Graves Publishing Co.
Ed: Bridget McCrea. **Description:** Strategies to help small business owners compete and successfully win contracts over larger firms are presented. Emphasis is given on the use of electronic commerce as a priority for doing business.

30873 ■ **"Has eBay Finally Gone Too Far? EBay's Arrogance Paves the Way for the Competition" in** *PR Newswire* **(January 20, 2005)**
Pub: PR Newswire Association LLC
Description: eBay sellers are searching for an alternative online auction because of increased fees imposed by the online auction giant. Chris Fain, founder and CEO of OnlineAuction.com, has created his site after many sellers refused to pay the increased fees imposed by eBay. Information on MyPoAss.com, another newly formed auction website is also included.

30874 ■ **"Health Care Battle Heats Up" in** *San Francisco Business Times* **(Vol. 17, No. 50, July 18, 2003, pp. 1)**
Pub: American City Business Journals
Ed: Meg Walker. **Description:** Growing competition between Sutter Health and Kaiser Permanente in Marin, California is examined. Topics include marketing strategy, membership prices and rates, and market share.

30875 ■ **"Help Wanted" in** *Entrepreneur.com* **(Vol. 34, February 2006, No. 2, pp. 80)**
Pub: Entrepreneur Media Inc.
Ed: Chris Penttila. **Description:** Globalization, outsourcing and competition for capital are putting pressure on small companies to operate more like large businesses. Ideas for hiring CEOs for a small firm are included.

30876 ■ **"The Hidden Dragon" in** *Harvard Business Review* **(Vol. 81, No. 10, October 2003, pp. 92)**
Pub: Harvard Business School Press
Ed: Ming Zeng, Peter J. Williamson. **Description:** Multinational corporations should give up precon-

ceived notions about China and Chinese products and being prepared for exports of consumer goods from China that are already competing in the U.S. and globally, to the disadvantage of many multinationals and taking away market share.

30877 ■ "The Hidden Value of Slow Sellers" in *Inc.* (October 2005, pp. 36)
Pub: Inc. Magazine
Description: According to a recent study that tracked sales at an online grocery store, a reduced choice of products led to a drop in sales, and fewer customers.

30878 ■ "High-Wired Competition" in *Inc.* (November 15, 2000, pp. 26)
Pub: The Goldhirsh Group
Description: The articles tells how high-tech competitors are setting up shop in a 400,000 square-foot renovated building in New York City.

30879 ■ "Hoover's Introduces Competitive Intelligence and Media Monitoring Service" in *Information Today* (Vol. 17, No. 11, Dec. 2000, pp. 31)
Pub: Information Today, Inc.
Description: Hoover's announces its Intelligence Monitor, a Web service for businesses that need timely market and competitive intelligence information.

30880 ■ *How Competitors Learn Your Company's Secrets*
Pub: Washington Researchers, Ltd.
Released: 1991. **Price:** $125.00. **Description:** Step-by-step guide on how to protect company secrets from inquisitive competitors. Leads one through the process of preparing the entire company to resist incursions by outside information-gatherers. Includes revealing case studies detailing how actual executives obtained precious company secrets from competitors, and how their efforts could have been thwarted.

30881 ■ *How to Drive Your Competition Crazy: Creating Disruption for Fun & Profit*
Pub: Hyperion
Ed: Guy Kawasaki. **Released:** 1996. **Price:** $12.95.

30882 ■ *How to Find Information about Companies*
Pub: Washington Researchers, Ltd.
Ed: Washington Researchers. **Released:** 1994. **Price:** $395.00 (each volume); $885.00 (three-volume set). **Description:** Volume 1 lists 9,000 information resources. Volume 2 and Volume 3 provide guidance for researching companies.

30883 ■ "How to Lose Customers" in *Inc.* (Volume 27, July 2005, No. 7, pp. 49, 51)
Pub: Inc. Magazine
Ed: Norm Brodsky. **Description:** A commitment to customer service can help a small business attract customers away from competitors.

30884 ■ "How To Beat WalMart" in *Business 2.0* (Vol. 6, May 2005, No. 4, pp. 108-114)
Pub: Time, Inc.
Ed: Matthew Maier. **Description:** Four rules to help companies to compete with a nearby WalMart store, along with ways to not compete.

30885 ■ *How to Win at Everything: Experts Reveal the Fine Art of Beating the Competition*
Pub: Bantam Books, Inc.
Ed: Dan Bensimhon. **Released:** 1996. **Price:** $10.95.

30886 ■ "Humana battles for growth" in *Atlanta Business Chronicle* (Vol. 25, January 3, 2003, No. 30, pp. 3A)
Pub: American City Business Publications, Inc.
Ed: Julie Bryant. **Description:** Alan Guzzino is the new Georgia market president of Humana Inc. Guzzino was retained to manage the introduction of the company's consumer-driver health benefit plans. This rollout aims to increase the company's competitive edge in the market place.

30887 ■ "If I knew then what I know now" in *WorkingWoman* (Vol. 25, No. 7, August 2000, pp. 48)
Pub: Lang Communications Inc.
Ed: Jeanne McDowell. **Description:** The views of seven successful American business women are shared, covering early working experience, combining family and work and competing in a male dominated sector.

30888 ■ "In Search of...Can Customers Search Your Website-And Actually Find What They Need?" in *Entrepreneur* (Vol. 32, November 2004, No. 11)
Pub: Entrepreneur Media Inc.
Ed: Melissa Campanelli. **Description:** Netpreneurs are improving search functions in order to compete with the success of Google. Options for upgrading Web sites are offered.

30889 ■ "Innovation drain" in *Crain's Detroit Business* (Vol. 19, No. 1, Jan. 6, 2003, pp. 3)
Pub: Crain Communications Inc., Detroit
Ed: Terry Kosdrosky. **Description:** Automotive industry analysts are predicting that cost reductions demanded by the Big Three on suppliers could result in business going to foreign competitors.

30890 ■ "Inside Out" in *Houston Business Journal* (Vol. 34, No. 11, July 25, pp. 19)
Pub: American City Business Journals
Ed: Catherine Spaulding. **Description:** Profile of the design firm Batsche Design; topics include management style, business strategy, and competition.

30891 ■ *International Entrepreneurship in Small and Medium Size Enterprises: Orientation, Environment and Strategy*
Pub: Edward Elgar Publishing, Incorporated
Ed: Hamid Etemad. **Released:** November 2004. **Price:** $110.00. **Description:** Issues involved in internationalizing small and medium sized (SME) businesses. Topics include an investigation into the emerging patterns of SME growth and international expansion in response to the changing competitive environment, dynamics of competitive behavior, entrepreneurial processes and a formulation of strategy.

30892 ■ "Investing in Training Will Yield a Powerful ROI" in *Venture Capital Journal* (November 1, 2004)
Pub: Thomason Financial Inc.
Description: Venture capital firms implementing training programs see a return on that investment by creating a competitive advantage as well as improved performance.

30893 ■ "Investment in Transit System the First Step in Pursuit of Games" in *Crain's Chicago Business* (Vol. 30, January 2007, No. 1, pp. 8)
Pub: Crain Communications, Inc.
Ed: MarySue Barrett. **Description:** Chicago is one of the cities that are attempting to win the 2016 Olympics bid. State lawmakers must decide whether to shrink or expand the region's public transit system. Chicago must also continue to develop mixed-income communities to attract consumers from a wide range of income levels that would be expected to come to Chicago for the games.

30894 ■ "It's Important to Be Proactive about Risk Issues" in *Atlanta Business Chronicle* (Vol. 24, No. 9, August 3, 2001, pp. 9B)
Pub: American City Business Journals Inc.
Description: Major factors resulting in business failure include customer demand shortage, irregularities in accounting, issues concerning supply chain and competitive pressures. In protecting a business from risk of failure, in addition to purchasing insurance, a culture and organizational structure where risk management is seen as everyone's job, is essential.

30895 ■ "It's Son of NAFTA" in *Inc.* (Volume 27, July 2005, No. 7, pp. 26-27)
Pub: Inc. Magazine
Ed: Darren Dahl. **Description:** Will the new Central America Free Trade Agreement (CAFTA), which eliminates duties on trade between the U.S. and six Central American countries, help American businesses stay competitive?

30896 ■ "Jump-starting broadband" in *Barron's* (Vol. 82, No. 54, January 20, 2003, pp. T1)
Pub: Barron's
Ed: Bill Alpert. **Description:** Federal Communications Commissioners disagreed with FCC Chairman Michael K. Powell's planned broadband deregulation of local Bell lines in Congressional testimony. However, the future of competition in broadband is likely to be 802.11/Wi-Fi networks.

30897 ■ "Just Say Om" in *Inc.* (July 1, 2003)
Pub: Gruner & Jahr USA Publishing
Ed: Nicole Gull. **Description:** Profile of Sara Chambers, who started her yoga company long before yoga was considered chic. Chambers now faces stiff competition from rivals such as Nike and Reebok.

30898 ■ "Keeping Their Options Open" in *Boston Business Journal* (Vol. 23, No. 26, August 1, 2003, pp. 3)
Pub: American City Business Journals
Description: Profile of Boston, Massachusetts-based Progressive Software Inc., including an examination of Boston-area technology companies as highlighted by the plight of Progressive Software Inc. Topics include economic conditions, competition, and financial management.

30899 ■ "King of the Hill" in *Houston Business Journal* (Vol. 34, No. 15, August 22, 2003, pp. 17)
Pub: American City Business Journals
Ed: Allison Wollam. **Description:** Profile of Berryhill Baja Grill's operations and growth plans is presented.

30900 ■ "King Kullen Freshening Up Image" in *Long Island Business News* (May 7, 2004)
Pub: Dolan Media Newswires
Ed: David Reich-Hale. **Description:** Profile of King Kullen, America's first supermarket. The company is revamping stores as it faces competition from Stop & Shop and Waldbaum's.

30901 ■ *Knock Your Socks Off Selling*
Pub: Amacom
Ed: Jeffrey Gitomer. **Released:** May 1999. **Price:** $17.95. **Description:** Tips for salespeople to succeed in a competitive sales environment.

30902 ■ "The Lark" in *Crain's Detroit Business* (Vol. 21, November 7, 2005, No. 45, pp. 16)
Pub: Crain Communications Inc. - Detroit
Ed: Brent Snavely. **Description:** Profile of James and Mary Lark, husband and wife owners of West Bloomfield Michigan restaurant, The Lark. The Larks opened their European country inn twenty-five years ago and credit their long-term success to offering customers ambiance, service and quality.

30903 ■ "Lawsuit against Masco alleges predatory pricing" in *Crain's Detroit Business* (Vol. 19, No. 10, March 10, 2003, pp. 32)
Pub: Crain Communications Inc., Detroit
Ed: Michael Strong. **Description:** Wilson Insulation Group Inc. has filed a lawsuit against Masco Corporation for predatory pricing and monopolizing in an attempt to drive Wilson out of the Augusta, Georgia market.

30904 ■ "The Laziness Factor in Loyalty" in *American Banker* (Vol. 170, September 5, 2006, No. 170, pp. 4A)
Pub: SourceMedia, Inc.
Ed: Katie Kuehner-Hebert. **Description:** According to a recent survey conducted by the National Federation of Independent Business Research Foundation, most small business owners were satisfied with their banking services and had no plans to switch to another financial institution.

30905 ■ "Level Playing Field" in *Entrepreneur* (Vol. 32, No. 2, February 2004, pp. 28)
Pub: Entrepreneur Media, Inc.

Ed: Stephen Barlas. **Description:** U.S. Small Business Administration has created new rules that will prohibit the bundling of small contracts, thus enabling more small businesses to compete with larger firms.

30906 ■ "Life in the slow lane" in *Entrepreneur* **(Vol. 30, No. 3, March 2002,)**
Pub: Entrepreneur Media Inc.
Ed: Joshua Kurlantzick. **Description:** With Internet usage by businesses increasing, the United States Postal Service is seeing a decline in services. Several small private delivery courier services have developed in the past few years to compete with the USPS Priority Mail service. The new services the USPS now offers online are discussed.

30907 ■ "Local Motion: For a Competitive Edge, Offer Items Made Locally" in *Entrepreneur* **(Vol. 32, November 2004, No. 11, pp. 90)**
Pub: Entrepreneur Media Inc.
Ed: Gwen Moran. **Description:** Trade shows, farmers markets, festivals, local events, as well as local business associations are good sources for locating manufacturers.

30908 ■ "Luxury for the masses" in *Harvard Business Review* **(Vol. 81, No. 4, April 2003, pp. 48)**
Pub: Harvard Business School Press
Ed: Michael J. Silverstien, Neil Fiske. **Description:** A description of the new products called new luxury. New luxury is the result of America's middle market consumers moving to higher levels of quality and taste than ever before. These new luxury products generate high sales volumes and bring companies providing them levels of profitability beyond those of conventional competitors.

30909 ■ "Main Street Moves Online" in *Business Week* **(No. 3678, April 24, 2000, pp. F10)**
Pub: McGraw-Hill, Inc.
Description: In a recent survey by the National Trust for Historic Preservation, 84 percent of small businesses located in historic downtown shopping districts said they had increased their Internet usage in 1999.

30910 ■ "Managing a Multicultural Workforce" in *BlackEnterprise* **(Vol. 31, No. 12, July 2001, pp. 120)**
Pub: Earl Graves Publishing Co.
Description: In order to maintain a competitive edge, it has become critical that company's use appropriate management of their multicultural workforce in order to remain competitive in the marketplace.

30911 ■ "Maneuver warfare: Can modern military strategy lead you to victory?" in *Harvard Business Review* **(Vol. 80, No. 4, April 2002, pp. 57)**
Pub: Harvard Business School Press
Ed: Jason A. Clemons, Eric K. Clemons, Santamaria Clemons. **Description:** Warfare as a metaphor for business is examined by presenting the theory of maneuver warfare by which a company, rather than destroying a competitor, renders that adversary unable to fight as an effective, coordinated whole.

30912 ■ *Mastering the Complex Sales: How to Compete and Win When the Stakes Are High!*
Pub: John Wiley & Sons, Incorporated
Ed: Jeff Thull. **Released:** May 2003. **Price:** $24.95.
Description: Guide to compete for and win in complex selling, the business-to-business transactions involving multiple decisions by multiple people from multiple perspectives.

30913 ■ "Microchip Delays Start in Gresham" in *Business Journal-Portland* **(Vol. 20, No. 22, August 1, 2003, pp. 1)**
Pub: American City Business Journals, Inc.
Ed: Aliza Earnshaw. **Description:** Profile of Microchip Technology Inc. and production delays being encountered, as well as competition, production management, and market conditions.

30914 ■ "Mobilize! These Businesses Get Moving" in *My Business* **(August/September 2002, pp. 38-41)**
Pub: My Business Magazine
Ed: Kathleen Landis. **Description:** Many small business are now delivering services directly to the customer's front door as a means of better serving clients and setting themselves apart from competitors. Profiled in the article is a traveling dentist, veterinarian, car detailer, and a paper shredding firm.

30915 ■ "The More, the Merrier" in *Inc.* **(September 2005, pp. 65-66)**
Pub: Inc. Magazine
Ed: Norm Brodsky. **Description:** The new privacy laws have encouraged more entrepreneurs to launch document-destruction firms. The author addresses why competition is good for any industry.

30916 ■ "More Retail Chains Heading this Way" in *Crain's Chicago Business* **(Vol. 26, No. 51, December 22, 2003, pp. 6)**
Pub: Crain Communications, Inc.
Ed: H. Lee Murphy. **Description:** Staples Inc., Dick's Sporting Goods, Ross Stores Inc. (apparel), National Wholesale Liquidators Inc., Home Now Furniture LLC, and Anna's Linens Inc., are among the retailers looking to enter the Chicago, Illinois retail market. The new trend is prompted by the upswing in the economy, along with the closing of Montgomery Ward & Company and Service Merchandise.

30917 ■ "More Retail Chains Heading this Way; Drawn by Vacant Sites, Competitive Considerations" in *Crains Chicago Business* **(Vol. 26, No. 51)**
Pub: Crain Communications, Inc.
Ed: H. Lee Murphy. **Description:** Staples Inc., Dick's Sporting Goods, Ross Stores Inc. (apparel), National Wholesale Liquidators Inc., Home Now Furniture LLC, and Anna's Linens Inc., are among the retailers looking to enter the Chicago, Illinois retail market. The new trend is prompted by the upswing in the economy, along with the closing of Montgomery Ward & Company and Service Merchandise.

30918 ■ "NASA Training Program" in *Black Enterprise* **(Vol. 30, No. 10, May 2000, pp. 52)**
Pub: Earl Graves Publishing Co.
Ed: Gerda Gallop-Goodman. **Description:** Small, disadvantaged businesses learn how to vie for contracts.

30919 ■ "Needs Toner: Facing Rivals, Lexmark Shares Could Go Lower" in *Barron's* **(July 28, 2003, pp. 15)**
Pub: Barron's
Ed: Sandra Ward. **Description:** Printer manufacturer Lexmark's recent net loss of nearly 20 percent from its share price was occasioned by third-quarter earnings that were shy of estimates by only one penny. The market's extreme reaction to the near-miss betrays deeper-seated misgivings about Lexmark's competitiveness in the sector.

30920 ■ "No Line At 6 a.m. Black Friday" in *Tampa Tribune* **(December 7, 2005)**
Pub: Media General, Inc.
Ed: Michael Sasso. **Description:** A group of independent retailers share marketing ideas they use to increase sales during the holidays, especially on Black Friday, the day after Thanksgiving.

30921 ■ "No, They Can't Do It Themselves" in *Inc.* **(July 1, 2004)**
Pub: Inc. Magazine
Ed: Jess McCuan. **Description:** Founders of the do-it-yourself journal, ReadyMade magazine, partnered with a small Colorado publisher in order to compete with rival Budget Living.

30922 ■ "Omniplex on the Case" in *Black Enterprise* **(Vol. 37, December 2006, No. 5, pp. 38)**
Pub: Earl G. Graves Publishing Co. Inc.
Ed: Glenn Townes. **Description:** Office of Personnel Management in Washington D.C. recently awarded a service contract to Omniplex World Services Corp. Virginia-based, The Chantilly, will perform security investigations and background checks on current and prospective federal employees and military personnel and contractors.

30923 ■ "On the Same Page: Gain Competitive Edge With a Company-Wide Focus on Customers" in *Sales & Marketing Management* **(Vol. 157, Jan. 2005)**
Pub: VNU Business Media
Ed: Sara Calabro. **Description:** Customer touchpoint management (CTM) is the understanding that a company's relationship with customers is not just about sales, but is the responsibility of the entire business.

30924 ■ "OnlineAuction.com Makes Bid for Outraged eBay Sellers" in *PR Newswire* **(January 18, 2005)**
Pub: PR Newswire Association LLC
Description: Chris Fain, a disgruntled eBay seller, created OnlineAuction.com to compete with the online auction. OnlineAuction.com allows the client to sell unlimited items at an $8 fee per month, with no individual listing or final value fees.

30925 ■ "OnlineAuction.com Ready for Return, Rematch With eBay" in *Mail Tribune* **(February 2, 2005)**
Pub: Mail Tribune
Ed: Greg Stiles. **Description:** Profile of Chris Fain, who has re-launched the eBay competitor, OnlineAuction.com. Fain is committed to providing a more convenient online auction with lower fees than eBay.

30926 ■ "Oreo Woes Bringing Kraft Down" in *Crain's Chicago Business* **(Vol. 26, No. 50, December 15, 2003, pp. 4)**
Pub: Crain Communications, Inc.
Ed: James B. Arndorfer. **Description:** Sales of the popular Oreo cookie are falling, hurting Kraft Foods Inc. Consumer concerns over weight, increased prices, and private-label cookie competitors are contributing to the 91-year-old brand's decline. Statistical data regarding the biscuit, snack and confectionery sector is included.

30927 ■ "Oreo Woes Bringing Kraft Down; Fat Fears, Price Hikes, Private-Label Brands Sap Sales" in *Crains Chicago Business* **(Vol. 26, No. 50)**
Pub: Crain Communications, Inc.
Ed: James B. Arndorfer. **Description:** Sales of the popular Oreo cookie are falling, hurting Kraft Foods Inc. Consumer concerns over weight, increased prices, and private-label cookie competitors are contributing to the 91-year-old brand's decline. Statistical data regarding the biscuit, snack and confectionery sector is included.

30928 ■ "Out there in never-Bell land, where phone service is way above average, and competitive" in *The New York Times* **(March 9, 2000, pp. C1)**
Pub: The New York Times Company
Ed: Julie Flaherty. **Description:** Informative article featuring community telephone companies.

30929 ■ "Partners in Branding" in *Sales and Marketing.com* **(Vol. 156, No. 3, March 2004, pp. 10)**
Pub: VNU eMedia, Inc.
Ed: Jennifer Gilbert. **Description:** Marketing partnerships would be formed for brand-building as much as they are formed for increasing sales. The three main reasons for companies to partner is to bring new customers to current target markets, to extend a brand to a new product or service, and to preempt competition.

30930 ■ "Pay as You Click" in *Crain's New York Business* **(Vol. 22, December 11, 2006, No. 50, pp. 19)**
Pub: Crain Communications, Inc.
Description: Google Inc. started an online payment service, Google Checkout. It developed the service at its New York office. Google Checkout, which launched in June 2006, aims to compete with PayPal.

30931 ■ *Peak Your Profits: How to Outsell, Outmarket & Outnegotiate Your Competition*
Pub: Career Press, Inc.
Ed: Jeff Blackman. **Released:** 1996. **Price:** $22.95.

30932 ■ **"Pizza Schmizza Ready to Take on Puget Sound"** in *Business Journal-Portland* (Vol. 20, No. 22, August 1, 2003, pp. 7)
Pub: American City Business Journals, Inc.
Ed: Robert Goldfield. Description: An overview of the growing success and expansion plans of Portland, Oregon-based Pizza Schmizza. Topics include management styles, competition, and long-term goals.

30933 ■ **"Planning for Gold"** in *Entrepreneur* (Vol. 32, November 2004, No. 11, pp. 112)
Pub: Entrepreneur Media Inc.
Ed: Nichole L. Torres. Description: Business plan competitions are growing in popularity. In order for entrepreneurs to cash in and win cash, services or venture capital they must understand the process. Many of the competitions are associated with university MBA programs, but there are also those produced by communities, which are open to anyone in the local area or a particular business sector.

30934 ■ **"Qcorps Scores Military Coup"** in *Houston Business Journal* (Vol. 34, No. 17, September 5, 2003, pp. 1)
Pub: American City Business Journals
Ed: Jennifer Dawson. Description: Examination of the U.S. Army contract awarded to Houston, Texas-based Qcorps Residential Inc. Topics include other defense contracts held by the company, limiting competition, and managing moving services for military personnel.

30935 ■ **"Rabbit on a Run"** in *Business 2.0* (Vol. 7, January/February 2006, No. 1, pp. 69)
Pub: Time, Inc.
Ed: Monica Khemsurov. Description: Metrokane used the existing design of a popular corkscrew to jump past a competitor and sell 200,000 units in 2005. Statistical data included.

30936 ■ *Researching Company Financial Information*
Pub: Washington Researchers
Released: Edition V. Price: $59, individuals. Description: Helps readers learn how to research and understand financial data from companies, as well as compile in-depth financial data on competitors in order to get a better picture of the competition. Publication Includes: A directory of corporate financial info sources.

30937 ■ **"Retailers Optimistic They Can Compete for Slice of Macomb"** in *Crain's Detroit Business* (Vol. 21, October 31, 2005, No. 44, pp. 3)
Pub: Crain Communications Inc. - Detroit
Ed: Brent Snavely. Description: Retail development, housing growth and the shopping mall in Clinton Township are among the factors for Parisian building a store that will anchor the new mall called Partridge Creek.

30938 ■ **"Rivaling a Giant"** in *Boston Business Journal* (Vol. 23, No. 30, August 29, 2003, pp. 3)
Pub: American City Business Journals
Ed: Tom Witkowski. Description: Profile of Enterasys Networks efforts to capture market share away from rival giant Cisco Systems Inc. Topics include market development, product development, and competition.

30939 ■ **"Saco's Downtown Merchants Say Big-Box Retailers Are Hurting Businesses"** in *Portland Press Herald* (April 19, 2005)
Pub: Blethen Maine Newspapers, Inc.
Ed: Seth Harkness. Description: Slow growth in downtown districts can be attributed to big-box stores and supermarkets. A recent study showed that Saco, Maine businesses reported 5.9 percent annual increase in sales since 1996, however some merchants refuse to work together effectively to compete with large retailers.

30940 ■ **"Safeway gets in shape for food fight"** in *San Francisco Business Times* (Vol. 16, No. 42, May 24, 2002, pp. 1)
Pub: San Francisco Business Times Inc.
Ed: Mark Calvey. Description: Safeway Inc. is preparing for increased competition in the grocery industry since Wal-Mart plans to sell groceries at 40 California stores in the next few years. Safeway's consolidated purchasing and other efforts to reduce expenses are discussed along with forecasts about pricing.

30941 ■ **"San Jose, Calif., Woman is Secret Shopper Evaluating Quality of Business"** in *San Jose Mercury News* (August 10, 2004)
Pub: San Jose Mercury News
Ed: Michele Chandler. Description: Mystery shoppers routinely snoop around stores and restaurants at the request of business owners in order to survey the quality of their products, pricing, and services.

30942 ■ **"Sara Lee's Apparel Biz Bind"** in *Crain's Chicago Business* (Vol. 26, No. 50, December 15, 2003, pp. 4)
Pub: Crain Communications, Inc.
Ed: James B. Arndorfer. Description: Large retailers like Wal-Mart, Target, and K-Mart are marketing brands that directly compete with Sara Lee's apparel brands, such as Hanes and Champion. Statistical data included.

30943 ■ **"SBC, Other Providers Spar on Phone Rules"** in *Crain's Detroit Business* (Vol. 21, October 3, 2005, No. 43, pp. 6)
Pub: Crain Communications Inc. - Detroit
Ed: Amy Lane. Description: Competitive land-line systems in Michigan are important for small businesses. The Michigan Alliance for Competitive Telecommunications wants to see provisions that ensure competition at the basic calling level.

30944 ■ **"Searching for Signs of Intelligent Life"** in *Barron's* (August 11, 2003, pp. T1)
Pub: Barron's
Ed: Eric C. Fleming. Description: Internet search engine services, forecasted to profit from the growing use of the Web to find jobs, dates, information, and more are welcoming a stock bubble of sorts. LookSmart's 3.5 share price is four times its October 2002 low, while FindWhat has grown fivefold to more than 17. The competition for the paid search market, primarily between Overture and privately-held Google is detailed.

30945 ■ **"Second 'Mix-In' Ice Cream Shop Comes to Stockton, Calif."** in *The Record* (November 5, 2002)
Pub: Knight Ridder/Tribune Business News
Ed: Reed Fujii. Description: The competition in ice cream retailing in the Stockton, California area is discussed. Shops profiled include Cold Stone Creamery and Maggie Moo's International LLC.

30946 ■ *The Secret Language of Competitive Intelligence: How to See Through and Stay Ahead of Business Disruptions, Distortions, Rumors, and Smoke*
Pub: Crown Publishing Group
Ed: Leonard M. Fuld. Released: May 2006. Price: $24.95.

30947 ■ **"Seeing the light"** in *Boston Business Journal* (Vol. 22, No. 15, May 17, 2002)
Pub: MCP, Inc.
Ed: Sean McFadden. Description: Profile of Rhonda Kallman, founder of New Century Brewing Co. Kallman introduced Edison Light Beer in September 2001 locally, and it will enter the national market by late 2003.

30948 ■ **"Send in the Clones"** in *Entrepreneur* (Vol. 31, No. 9, September 2003, pp. 128)
Pub: Entrepreneur Media, Inc.
Ed: Don Debelak. Description: Developing an innovative produce is the dream of every entrepreneur, but being able to market a new product is key. Jay Sorenson, founder of Java Jacket in Portland, Oregon patented the Jay Jacket, an insulating sleeve designed to keep beverages in a paper cup warm, shares advice on marketing an invention.

30949 ■ **"Setting Sights on the Hispanic Buyer"** in *Hispanic Business* (November 2002, pp. 49, 52, 54)
Pub: Hispanic Business
Ed: Paul A. Eisenstein. Description: Hispanics as a target market for the automobile industry is discussed. Statistical data covering Hispanic new and used car and truck purchases from 1994 through 2000 is presented.

30950 ■ **"Shh...It's a Secret"** in *Entrepreneur. com* (Vol. 34, February 2006, No. 2, pp. 82)
Pub: Entrepreneur Media Inc.
Ed: Jane Easter Bahls. Description: When employees leave to work for a competitor, it is essential they understand the confidentiality of your company's trade secrets. Steps to ensure legal protection of company knowledge are covered.

30951 ■ **"Sizing Up the Market"** in *Boston Business Journal* (Vol. 23, No. 25, July 25, 2003, pp. 3)
Pub: American City Business Journals
Ed: Paul T. Gannon. Description: Profile of Boston, Massachusetts-based Shaw's Supermarkets Inc. Topics include competition, strategic business planning, and market development.

30952 ■ **"Small Business Gets Big Squeeze From Property Insurance Rates"** in *Tampa Tribune* (February 6, 2007)
Pub: Media General Inc.
Ed: Dave Simanoff. Description: Rising costs for property insurance is making it harder for small companies to remain competitive.

30953 ■ *Small Business Survival Guide: Starting, Protecting, and Securing Your Business for Long-Term Success*
Pub: Adams Media Corporation
Ed: Cliff Ennico. Released: October 2005. Price: $12.95 (US), $17.95 (Canadian). Description: Entrepreneurship in the new millennium. Topics include creditors, taxes, competition, business law, and accounting.

30954 ■ **"Small Exporters in a Big World"** in *Hispanic Business* (November 2003, pp. 42-43, 46, 48, 50)
Pub: Hispanic Business
Ed: Jennifer Riley. Description: Hispanic firms that have succeeded abroad show they can compete in the large and profitable markets of the global economy. Statistical data included.

30955 ■ **"Small Firms Emphasize Trade-Show Marketing"** in *Crain's Detroit Business* (Vol. 21, February 7, 2005, No. 6, pp. 24)
Pub: Crain Communications Inc. - Detroit
Ed: DeAnna Belger. Description: According to a recent survey, more small companies in Michigan rely on trade shows than their larger competitors. Most respondents reported attending trade shows to generate sales leads, increase visibility, and to network.

30956 ■ *Small Firms in Global Competition*
Pub: Oxford University Press, Inc.
Ed: Tamir Agmon, editor. Released: 1993. Price: $45.00.

30957 ■ **"Small, Yes-But With A Big Back Office"** in *Business Week* (No. 3853, October 13, 2003, pp. 86)
Pub: McGraw-Hill Inc.
Ed: Charles Haddad. Description: Information technology is helping small firms compete with large corporations. Web-based software allows small businesses to perform all functions electronically.

30958 ■ **"A smarter way to sell commodities"** in *Harvard Business Review* (Vol. 80, No. 4, April 2002, pp. 24)
Pub: Harvard Business School Press
Ed: Ajay Kohli, Robert S. Lurie. Description: Commodities sellers can differentiate their products from those of the competition by reducing risk for their customers according to marketing experts, Robert Lurie and Ajay Kohli.

30959 ■ "Spies in the Boardroom?" in
Forbes **(Vol. 170, No. 5, September 16, 2002, pp. 45)**
Pub: Forbes Magazine
Ed: Luisa Kroll. **Description:** CCBN.com's founder Jeffrey Parker filed a law suit against the Canadian information services corporation, Thomas Corporation in July 2002.

30960 ■ "Status Quota? Without Trade Quotas, U.S. Textile-Makers Struggle" in *Entrepreneur* **(Vol. 33, September 2005, No. 9, pp. 23)**
Pub: Entrepreneur Media Inc.
Ed: Scott Bernard Nelson. **Description:** When a global system of trade quotas expired in 2004, Chinese imports flooded the U.S. market, as high as 1,000 percent increase in some markets. In May 2005, the U.S. imposed a new quota limiting year-over-year increases in China's textile imports to 7.5 percent, providing only temporary relief. The U.S. textile industry must find new ways in which to compete with foreign competitors.

30961 ■ "Storage Showdown: Hitachi is now a big thorn in EMC's side" in *Red Herring* **(No. 105, October 1, 2001, pp. 100-101)**
Pub: Herring Communications
Ed: Beverly Goodman. **Description:** The competition between Hitachi and EMC is discussed. EMC is still ahead of Hitachi in market share, but Hitachi's storage revenue is growing faster. Statistical data included showing first quarter revenues for EMC, Compaq Computer, Hewlett-Packard, Sun Microsystems, IBM, and Hitachi Data Systems.

30962 ■ "Strategies, Let's Be Friends" in *Inc.* **(Volume 27, March 2005, No. 3, pp. 33-34)**
Pub: Inc. Magazine
Ed: Allison Stein Wellner. **Description:** New research shows that CEOs who become friendly with competitors achieve more success than others.

30963 ■ "Street Smarts: The Capacity Trap II" in *Inc.* **(December 1, 2003)**
Pub: Gruner & Jahr USA Publishing
Ed: Norm Brodsky. **Description:** Sometimes its better to let unused capacity remain unused rather than win a contract that will be too costly to meet.

30964 ■ "Strength in Numbers" in *Home Office Computing* **(Vol. 18, No. 11, November 2000, pp. 58)**
Pub: Scholastic Inc.
Ed: Jeffrey D. Zbar. **Description:** When competing with bigger companies, small businesses need to develop partnerships to help snag the big projects.

30965 ■ "Study Says Change Tax Laws to Help Forest Products Industry Stay Competitive" in *Portland Press Herald* **(March 25, 2005)**
Pub: Blethen Maine Newspapers, Inc.
Ed: Tux Turkel. **Description:** A recent state-sponsored report, called Maine Future Forest Economy Project, showed a change in the state's tax laws would help the forest industry remain competitive, while encouraging private investment, increase cooperative among state government and industry, and increase the transfer of university sponsored research into next generation commercial products and applications.

30966 ■ "Suit May Cost Post Unit its Trademark" in *Washington Business Journal* **(Vol. 22, No. 15, August 15, 2003, pp. 3)**
Pub: Washington Business Journal
Ed: Greg A. Lohr. **Description:** Information regarding the Washington Post's lawsuit against PRIMEDIA Inc. for trademark infringement. Topics include trademark law and competition.

30967 ■ "Syndication: The Emerging Model for Business in the Internet Era" in *Harvard Business Review* **(Vol. 78, No. 3, May 2000, pp. 85)**
Pub: Harvard Business School Publishing Corp.
Ed: Kevin Werbach. **Description:** Many of the new rules about competition and strategy can be found in the concept of syndication, a way of doing business that has its origins in the entertainment world, but is now expanding to define the structure of e-business.

30968 ■ "Tackling the Competition" in *Home Business* **(Vol. 12, March/April 2005, No. 2, pp. 80)**
Pub: Home Business Magazine
Ed: Sandy Larson. **Description:** Profile of Stan Webber, creator of football coaching software.

30969 ■ "Taming of the Crew: What Lion Tamers Teach Us About Team Management" in *Entrepreneur* **(Vol. 33, January 2005, No. 1, pp. 26)**
Pub: Entrepreneur Media Inc.
Ed: Geoff Williams. **Description:** In his book, Lion Taming: Working Successfully With Leaders, Bosses and Other Tough Customers, Steve Katz gathers insights from professional lion tamers to help entrepreneurs learn to tame suppliers, customers and competitors.

30970 ■ "Tea, anyone? Competition is brewing for coffee bars" in *Wall Street Journal* **(July 18, 2000, pp. B2)**
Pub: Dow Jones & Co., Inc.
Ed: Jeffrey A. Tannenbaum. **Description:** An update on the growing number of coffee bars and the competition they face in order to stay in business.

30971 ■ "The 'IT' Factor" in *Hispanic Business* **(November 2006, pp. 26, 28, 30)**
Pub: Hispanic Business
Ed: Keith Rosenblum. **Description:** Profile of Abba Tech, the New Mexico information technology firm that is competing with large companies through service and knowledge.

30972 ■ "This Week: McD's Tests Trans-Free Oil in 1,200 Locations" in *Crain's Chicago Business* **(Vol. 29, December 2006, No. 50, pp. 1)**
Pub: Crain Communications, Inc.
Ed: Julie Jargon. **Description:** Just under ten percent of McDonald's U.S. outlets are performing initial tests with trans fat-free oil in their foods. Pressure is high as rival fast food restaurants have already introduced these trans fat-free foods and New York passed the ban which takes place in July.

30973 ■ "Three questions you need to ask about your brand" in *Harvard Business Review* **(Vol. 80, No. 9, September 2002, pp. 80)**
Pub: Harvard Business School Press
Ed: Kevin Lane Keller, Brian Sternthal, Alice Tybout. **Description:** Successful brand positioning is not so much about differentiating a product from competitors as it is in understanding the frame of reference in which the product must compete for attention. Various companies' efforts are explored.

30974 ■ "Ticket Resellers Aim to Be Top Draws" in *Business Week Online* **(February 3, 2005)**
Pub: McGraw-Hill Companies
Ed: Sarah Lacey. **Description:** Secondary-ticket companies are competing for customers. Profiles of industry leaders and companies are provided.

30975 ■ "A Tough Sell" in *Hispanic Business* **(December 2006, pp. 48)**
Pub: Hispanic Business
Ed: Hildy Medina. **Description:** Television networks are competing for young Hispanic viewers for both Spanish and English speaking shows.

30976 ■ "Toward the Development of Measures of Distinctive Competencies among Small Independent Retailers" in *Journal of Small Business Management*
Pub: West Virginia University
Ed: Jeffrey E. McGee, Mark Peterson. **Description:** To remain competitive in markets increasingly dominated by large discount chains, "category killers", and other mass-merchandisers, small independent retailers need to develop distinctive competencies. A study providing insight into the multidimensional character of distinctive competencies by measuring the resources and capabilities possessed by 255 independent drug stores is presented.

30977 ■ "Transforming Business Structures to Hyborg" in *Employment Relations Today* **(Vol. 26, No. 4, Winter 2000, pp. 5)**
Pub: John Wiley & Sons, Inc.
Ed: Arnold Brown. **Description:** The organizational structure and corporate culture at the turn of the 21st century are studied. Topics addressed include international economic relations, competition, corporate values, employer-employee relations, and human resource management.

30978 ■ "Twin Picks" in *Entrepreneur* **(Vol. 32, December 2004, No. 12, pp. 95)**
Pub: Entrepreneur Media Inc.
Ed: Jerry Fisher. **Description:** Side-by-side comparison marketing is presented using a soluble, natural health supplement as an example.

30979 ■ "U.S. District Court of Appeals Sides with Baby Bells Over 1996 Telecommunications Act" in *Long Island Business News* **(March 12, 2004)**
Pub: Dolan Media Newswires
Ed: Claude Solnik. **Description:** Small local telecommunications carriers worry about the new court ruling that they feel will undo the Telecommunications Act of 1996. The small firms worry the new ruling will take away ability to lease infrastructure at a wholesale rate from Baby Bells, thus inhibiting them from remaining competitive in the industry.

30980 ■ "U.S. Postal Service Offers Free At-Home Pickups for eBay Sellers" in *Portland Press Herald* **(March 29, 2005)**
Pub: Blethen Maine Newspapers, Inc.
Ed: Edward D. Murphy. **Description:** The U.S. Postal Service is offering free at-home pickup service to individuals selling items on eBay's auction site. The move will help the government agency compete with United Parcel Service, FedEx and other shippers.

30981 ■ "Up Front" in *Business Week* **(January 16, 2006, No. 3967, pp. 11-12, 14)**
Pub: McGraw-Hill Companies
Ed: Dan Beucke. **Description:** Information regarding construction wages in the U.S., Chrysler's new Baby Bentley sedan, teen trends, online sales taxes, and airline competition are among the topics discussed.

30982 ■ "U.S.: Signs That Inflation Is Losing Its Fangs" in *Business Week* **(February 7, 2005, No. 3919, pp. 25)**
Pub: McGraw-Hill Companies
Ed: James C. Cooper, Kathleen Madigan. **Description:** Global competition and information technology should help curb inflation in 2005. Statistical data included.

30983 ■ "Use It or Lose It: Is Your Business Usable-or Disposable? Figure It Out Before Your Competitors Gain an Edge" in *Entrepreneur* **(Vol.32)**
Pub: Entrepreneur Media Inc.
Ed: Mark Henricks. **Description:** Geoffrey Hart explains his concerns of usability when setting out to develop a medical device for soothing and entertaining children during the process of anesthetizing them for medial or dental procedures.

30984 ■ "Vancouver Vanguard" in *Fast Company* **(September 2001, pp. 36)**
Pub: Fast Company
Description: Fast Company's Heath Row will embark on the third-annual CoF Roadshow through North America. While spending time in Vancouver, British Columbia, Canada, Row will address ways Canada is competing in the global market.

30985 ■ **"Wal-Mart Expansion Plans Feed Grocery Competition"** in *Crain's Detroit Business* (Vol. 19, No. 45, November 10, 2003, pp. 26)
Pub: Crain Communications Inc., Detroit
Ed: Brent Snavely. **Description:** Wal-Mart Stores Inc. plans to expand operations, putting pressure on profits and market share of the top grocery chains.

30986 ■ **"Wanted"** in *Milwaukee Journal Sentinel* (December 11, 2005)
Pub: Journal Sentinel, Inc.
Description: Manufacturers are facing a shortage of skilled workers. Pay and global competition are among the issues facing manufacturers and the National Association of Manufacturers reports the human capital performance gap as a threat to U.S. competitiveness and the nation's most critical business issue.

30987 ■ **"The War of the Wires"** in *The Economist* (Vol. 376, July 30-August 5, 2005, No. 8437, pp. 53-54)
Pub: The Economist Newspaper Ltd.
Description: Established telecommunications companies are battling against innovative competitors.

30988 ■ **"Ward off Competitors"** in *PC Computing* (April 2000, pp. 95)
Pub: Ziff-Davis Inc.
Ed: Jason Compton. **Description:** Microsoft MapPoint 2000 will help a retail store use customer zip code and sales amount information to see how the proximity of a competitor will affect sales volumes.

30989 ■ **"The Wegman's Way"** in *Fortune* (Vol. 151, January 24, 2005, No. 2, pp. 62)
Pub: Time Inc.
Ed: Matthew Boyle, Ellen Florian Kratz. **Description:** Profile of Wegmans, voted the best company to work for in America by its employees. The supermarket is also beating competitors in the tough grocery business.

30990 ■ **"Welcome to the Valley of the Damned.Com"** in *Fortune* (Vol. 143, No. 1, January 8, 2001, pp. 52)
Pub: Time Inc.
Description: A listing of the 135 dot-coms that went bankrupt or shut down operations in 2000.

30991 ■ **"What Leaders Really Do"** in *Harvard Business Review* (Vol. 79, No. 11, December 2001, pp. 85)
Pub: Harvard Business School Press
Ed: John P. Kotter. **Description:** Leadership is different from management. Leadership and management are two complementary systems. While management copes with complexity, leadership copes with change. Because the business world has become more competitive and demands more change, it also demands more leadership.

30992 ■ **"When a turnaround stalls"** in *Harvard Business Review* (Vol. 80, No. 2, February 2002, pp. 45)
Pub: Harvard Business School Press
Ed: Robert A.F. Reisner. **Description:** An investigation into the story of how the U.S. Postal Service transformed itself into a competitive business and holds lessons for any company attempting to keep a change initiative form failing.

30993 ■ **"Why business models matter"** in *Harvard Business Review* (Vol. 80, No. 5, May 2002, pp. 86)
Pub: Harvard Business School Press
Ed: Joan Magretta. **Description:** The concepts of business models and strategy are clarified; the business model is a story which explains how an enterprise works, it complements strategy which deals with competition.

30994 ■ **"Will I Lose If I Beat the Boss At Racquetball?"** in *Fortune* (Vol. 151, January 24, 2005, No. 2, pp. 36)
Pub: Time Inc.
Ed: Anne Fisher. **Description:** A manager may not respect the employee that lets him win at sports. Research shows that people like those who are most like them, so the rule would be to play to win. Many managers report learning more about colleagues and bosses playing a sport with them, than ever learned in a business meeting.

30995 ■ **Win Government Contracts for Your Small Business**
Pub: CCH Incorporated
Ed: John Digiacomo, James Kleckner. **Released:** May 2005. **Price:** $24.95 (US), $34.95 (Canadian). **Description:** Strategies to find, negotiate, and win government contracts, including the latest information for competing for these contracts. Tips for using the Internet, finding government buyers, and writing a winning proposal are included.

30996 ■ **"Your Father's Bank"** in *Inc.* (September 1, 2004)
Pub: Inc. Magazine
Ed: Ed Welles. **Description:** Citigroup is feeling competition from smaller, traditional community banks such as Burke & Herbert.

TRADE PERIODICALS

30997 ■ **Journal of Industry, Competition and Trade**
Pub: Kluwer Academic/Plenum Publishing Corp.
Contact: Karl Aiginger, Editor-in-Chief
Released: 4/year. **Price:** $267 institutions print or online ed., add 20% for both together; $66 print ed. **Description:** Journal covering research on industry, competition and trade.

VIDEOCASSETTES/ AUDIOCASSETTES

30998 ■ **Building Strategic Relationships**
J. Miller Associates
15669 Live Oak Springs Rd.
Santa Clarita, CA 91351-4712
Ph:(805)251-9310
Fax: (805)251-9192
Price: $99.00. **Description:** Part of the Management Speaks Series. Details ways in which businesses can make use of their competition to help them better their chances for success. **Availability:** VHS.

30999 ■ **Competing for Customers**
J. Miller Associates
15669 Live Oak Springs Rd.
Santa Clarita, CA 91351-4712
Ph:(805)251-9310
Fax: (805)251-9192
Price: $99.00. **Description:** Part of the Management Speaks Series. Outlines how to win over the customer, customer relationships, new strategy for building customer loyalty, unsatisfied consumers, and the importance of customer service. **Availability:** VHS.

31000 ■ **Concerns Quarterly with Footage from CBS News: General Business**
Harcourt Brace College Publishers
301 Commerce, Ste. 3700
Fort Worth, TX 76102
Ph:(817)334-7500
Free: 800-237-2665
Fax: (817)334-0947
Co. E-mail: info@harcourt.com
URL: http://www.harcourt.com
Released: 1995. **Price:** $80.00. **Description:** Video newsletter containing footage from such CBS programs as CBS Evening News, 48 Hours, Street Stories, and CBS This Morning. Provides information on such topics as ethical responsibilities in business, people in business, competition, manufacturing, and marketing. Comes with instructor's guide. Available at an annual subscription rate of $300.00. **Availability:** VHS.

31001 ■ **Michael Porter on Competitive Strategy**
Harvard Business School
60 Harvard Way
Boston, MA 02163
Ph:(617)783-7500
Free: 800-988-0886
URL: http://hbs.edu
Released: 1989. **Price:** $1000.00. **Description:** The professor at Harvard Business School gives a few tips that will keep your business on top of its competition. **Availability:** VHS.

31002 ■ **Swim with the Sharks without Being Eaten Alive**
Instructional Video
2219 C St.
Lincoln, NE 68502
Ph:(402)475-6570
Free: 800-228-0164
Fax: (402)475-6500
Co. E-mail: feedback@insvideo.com
URL: http://www.insvideo.com
Price: $595.00. **Description:** Based on Harvey Mackay's best-selling book of the same name. Offers training advice on how to beat your competition, make the crucial sale, open the closed door, and swing the million-dollar deal at the last minute. **Availability:** VHS.

CONSULTANTS

31003 ■ **ARDITO Information & Research Inc.**
1019 Sedwick Dr., Ste. G
Wilmington, DE 19803
Ph:(302)479-5373
Free: 800-836-9068
Fax: (302)479-5375
Co. E-mail: sardito@ardito.com
URL: http://www.ardito.com

E-mail: sardito@ardito.com
Scope: A full-service information and research firm. Provides information in area of financial data, published research, demographic data, industry-specific publications, competitor data, marketing and sales trends, new product developments, government relations, bibliographies. Industries served are pharmaceutical, health, publishing, and environment, and business.

31004 ■ **Conor Environmental Services Inc.**
4 Shoppers Ln., Ste. 202
Turnersville, NJ 08012-1400
Ph:(609)589-5475
Fax: (609)589-6037
Co. E-mail: consultces@usa.net

E-mail: consultces@usa.net
Scope: Firm provides a full range of environmental and engineering consulting services for both public and private organizations. Environmental company provides assessment, engineering, and remediation services, specializing in industrial and hazardous waste management. The integrated approach-combining scientific, engineering, and management services-provides cost-effective solutions to the complex scope of environmental problems. Offers expertise in the following areas: complete engineering and environmental turnkey services; groundwater and underground storage tank services; water and wastewater treatment services; environmental review and audit services; site investigation and remediation services; risk assessment and audit programs; and spill response management and planning services. Industries served: manufacturing, petroleum, power plants, utilities, wastewater treatment facilities, pipelines, landfills, banks, financial institutions, real estate developers, law firms, insurance companies, and government. **Seminars:** Beating the Competition: Winning with Better Information. **Special Services:** Company uses more than 4,000 world-class, restricted access databases to offer exhaustive coverage of business and marketing.

31005 ■ Queens Business Consulting
Queens School of Business, Goodes Hall, 143
   Union St.
Kingston, ON, Canada K7L 3N6
Ph:(613)533-2309
Fax: (613)533-2370
Co. E-mail: qbc@business.queensu.ca
URL: http://www.business.queensu.ca/qbc

E-mail: qbc@business.queensu.ca
Scope: Provides business plans, feasibility studies, financial planning, competitor analysis, market research, marketing strategies, production planning, and systems implementation.

RESEARCH CENTERS

31006 ■ University of California, Los Angeles–Research Program in Takeovers and Corporate Restructuring
258 Tavistock Ave.
Los Angeles, CA 90049-3229
Ph:(310)472-5110
Fax: (310)472-9471
Co. E-mail: jweston@anderson.ucla.edu
URL: http://www.anderson.ucla.edu/faculty/john.
   weston
Contact: Prof. J. Fred Weston, Dir.

E-mail: jweston@anderson.ucla.edu
Scope: Diversification studies, pricing policies, economic implications of management of decentralized firms, industrial structure, regulated industries, corporate power, corporate governance, measurement of business risk, advertising and profits, concentration and inflation, mergers and acquisitions, corporate control, restructuring, antitrust, and case studies of individual industries and firms. **Publications:** Working papers; Journal articles. **Educational Activities:** Presentations to congressional committees.

START-UP INFORMATION

31007 ■ **"Delivering a New (Business) Life"** in *Ingram's* (Vol. 28, No. 5, May 2002, pp. 32)
Pub: Show Me Publishing, Inc.
Description: Profile of George Guile and Rob Waetzig, who have started a small delivery services firm named Plaza Couriers. Guile and Waetzig say their pricing and the fact that they are locals help to differentiate them from their competitors.

REFERENCE WORKS

31008 ■ **"Amid Customer Backlash, eBay Reduces Some Fees"** in *eWeek* (February 7, 2005)
Pub: Ziff Davis Media Inc.
Description: Online auction eBay has reduced some of its fees in response to customer complaints of price hikes imposed in January 2005.

31009 ■ **"Analysts: Pricing, Material Costs to Spur Supplier Mergers"** in *Crain's Detroit Business* (Vol. 21, January 10, 2005, No. 2, pp. 19)
Pub: Crain Communications Inc. - Detroit
Ed: Julie Armstrong. **Description:** Consolidation of automotive suppliers will rise in 2005 because of high raw-material prices and pricing pressures from automakers.

31010 ■ **"Automaker pullback blamed for Detroit stamper's closing"** in *Crain's Detroit Business* (Vol. 19, No. 8, February 24, 2003, pp. 6)
Pub: Crain Communications Inc., Detroit
Ed: Terry Kosdrosky. **Description:** Davis Tool & Engineering Company will close its doors after being open for 65 years. The Detroit stamping plant is closing as the result of price competition and the automaker's recent trend to push component production back in-house.

31011 ■ **"Bells want to raise rates of competitors"** in *Atlanta Business Chronicle* (Vol. 25, December 6, 2002, No. 26, pp. 1)
Pub: American City Business Publications, Inc.
Ed: Mary Jane Credeur. **Description:** Bell companies are trying to get Federal regulators to reduce or eliminate discounts they must pay to competitors that use Bell networks. This move comes as the Bell companies have entered the long-distance markets in several states. BellSouth Corporation asserts that the discounts are unfair.

31012 ■ **"Big Box vs. Online"** in *Hispanic Business* (March 2003, pp. 25)
Pub: Hispanic Business
Ed: Roger Harris. **Description:** Internet shoppers are finding very competitive pricing between purchasing online versus going to a brick and mortar store. An online shopping checklist is provided to assist consumers when making purchases online.

31013 ■ **"Bill Would Ease Rules on Store Price Tags"** in *Crain's Detroit Business* (Vol. 22, December 4, 2006, No. 49, pp. 6)
Pub: Crain Communications Inc. - Detroit
Ed: Amy Lane. **Description:** New bill will aid attraction of new members of the retailing industry to come to Michigan. Video scanning is now permissible to replace individual pricing tags or labels if certain conditions are met.

31014 ■ **"Boost Your Bottom Line By Taking the Guesswork Out of Pricing"** in *Inc.* (Volume 27, June 2005, No. 6, pp. 72-76, 78, 80, 82)
Pub: Inc. Magazine
Ed: Alison Stein Wellner. **Description:** Many business owners trust their instinct with pricing products and services. A better approach might be to ask what that product or service is really worth.

31015 ■ **"Build a Strong Customer-Brand Relationship"** in *E-business Advisor* (Vol. 18, No. 4, April 2000, pp. 34)
Pub: Advisor Media, Inc.
Ed: Doug Barton. **Description:** The article shows how the Internet is changing marketing practices as companies focus on developing customer loyalty instead of building brand images through advertising and traditional distribution channels. The two main factors driving sales are now customer loyalty and price.

31016 ■ **"Cablevision Plans Faster Internet Service Without Raising Price"** in *The Record* (November 8, 2005)
Pub: New Jersey Media Group
Ed: Martha McKay. **Description:** New York-based Cablevision plans to sell a higher-speed service for less money than those offered by Verizon. Details of the plan are disclosed.

31017 ■ **"Canada Rx offers access to Canadian pharmacies"** in *Atlanta Business Chronicle* (Vol. 25, January 10, 2003, No. 31, pp. 17A)
Pub: American City Business Publications, Inc.
Ed: Melissa Fowler. **Description:** Canada Rx Shop is described as an entity that supplies a Web-based ordering connection between clients in the U.S. and the pharmaceutical market in Canada. Tom Connell, owner of the company, stated that he and his wife became Rx affiliates to offer clients another way to manage their finances. Increasing prescription costs in the U.S. have sent many Americans, though primarily senior citizens, north of the border seeking cheaper drug prices. The article provides information on the service, the risks and the legal implications.

31018 ■ **"Caution: Merger Ahead"** in *Ingram's* (Vol. 28, No. 9, September 2002, pp. 20)
Pub: Show Me Publishing, Inc.
Ed: James M. Selle. **Description:** A guide for considerations when small businesses consider a merger are presented, including issues such as expansion, additional products and/or services, new markets, and a competitor's customers base.

31019 ■ ***Complete Idiot's Guide to Starting an Ebay Business***
Pub: Penguin Books (USA) Incorporated
Ed: Barbara Weltman, Kara Gordon, Shirley Muse. **Released:** February 2005. **Price:** $19.95 (US), $29.00 (Canadian). **Description:** Guide for starting an eBay business includes information on products to sell, how to price merchandise, and details for working with services like PayPal, and how to organize fulfillment services.

31020 ■ **"Cost Transparency: The Net's Real Threat to Prices and Brands"** in *Harvard Business Review* (Vol. 78, No. 2, March 2000, pp. 43)
Pub: Harvard Business School Publishing Corp.
Ed: Indrajit Sinha. **Description:** The vast sea of information about prices, competitors, and features that is readily available on the Internet helps buyers "see through" the costs of products and services. That's bad news for manufacturers and retailers, and there are ways to fight back.

31021 ■ **"Cutting to the chase"** in *Crain's Detroit Business* (Vol. 18, No. 32, Aug. 12, 2002, pp. 11)
Pub: Crain Communications Inc., Detroit
Ed: Laura Bailey. **Description:** Tips are offered for small businesses to put in place a business plan that determines expenses in order to set pricing for products and services.

31022 ■ **"Dare to Compare."** in *Entrepreneur* (Vol. 33, January 2005, No. 1, pp. 43)
Pub: Entrepreneur Media Inc.
Ed: Melissa Campanelli. **Description:** Online merchants wishing to grow their business might consider placing products on comparison shopping Websites. These sites display product information in a simple format and lets buyers compare and choose the best product from a list of different retailers.

31023 ■ **"Dealing With Cost Hikes"** in *Inc.* (August 2005, pp. 49-50)
Pub: Inc. Magazine
Ed: Description: Although conventional wisdom dictates that now is the time to raise prices, it may be precisely the reason to hold off. Cutting the middleperson could be an alternative to price increases.

31024 ■ **"Do-It-Yourself Insurance"** in *Inc.* (Volume 27, December 2005, No. 12, pp. 39-40, 42)
Pub: Inc. Magazine
Ed: Alison Stein Wellner. **Description:** Individual insurance policies are becoming more popular, but premiums vary from state to state. The pros of cons of a small business replacing group health plans in favor for individual policies are discussed.

31025 ■ **"E-Tailers Pay a High Price for Free Shipping"** in *Business Week Online* (December 6, 2001)
Pub: McGraw-Hill, Inc.
Description: The cost of offering free shipping by online retailers is discussed.

31026 ■ **"Entrepreneur Column"** in *Entrepreneur* **(August 4, 2005)**
Pub: Entrepreneur Media Inc.
Ed: Tom Hopkins. **Description:** The meaning behind a customer's desire to shop around before purchasing a product or service is examined. It is important for small business owners to research their competition.

31027 ■ **"The fabric of consumer reality"** in *Red Herring* **(March 2003, pp. 54)**
Pub: Herring Communications Inc.
Ed: Alan Zeichick. **Description:** The economics of nanotechnology are discussed. In order for a particular consumer good to be priced competitively, the nano-scale components required must be manufactured in bulk, using techniques similar to those used in making larger-scale products.

31028 ■ **"Fee Bargain: Law Firm Mergers May Give You More Room to Negotiate Legal Fees"** in *Entrepreneur* **(Vol. 31, No. 7, July 2003, pp. 27)**
Pub: Entrepreneur Media, Inc.
Ed: Chris Penttila. **Description:** In the soft economy, law firms are struggling to stay afloat with fewer clients and increasing operational costs, therefore some firms are merging offering lower fees and more services.

31029 ■ **"Finning the Flames"** in *Entrepreneur* **(Vol. 31, No. 9, July 2003, pp. 126)**
Pub: Entrepreneur Media, Inc.
Ed: Don Debelak. **Description:** Profile of Bob Evans, founder of Bob Evans Designs Inc. in Santa Barbara, California. Evans' company designed swimming fins designed to propel swimmers through water faster with less effort. Evans discusses how he stays ahead of a market where competitors sell lower-priced, more traditional products.

31030 ■ **"FIOS TV"** in *Crain's New York Business* **(Vol. 22, November 27, 2006, No. 48, pp. 33)**
Pub: Crain Communications, Inc.
Description: FiOs TV is a television service offered by Verizon and is currently available in small cities and suburban areas in seven states. The company won a statewide TV franchise in New Jersey and is doing business in forty Long Island communities.

31031 ■ **"Free Agents in the Olde World"** in *Fast Company* **(May 2001, pp. 136)**
Pub: Fast Company
Ed: Jill Rosenfeld. **Description:** Thomas Malone, a professor at MIT's Sloan School of Management and founder of the Center for Coordination Science, takes a look at the future of commerce and at the structure of how work will get done.

31032 ■ **"From Fifth Hire to Top Exec, New CEO to Lead SurePayroll"** in *Crain's Chicago Business* **(Vol. 26, No. 50, December 15, 2003, pp. 12)**
Pub: Crain Communications, Inc.
Ed: Julie Johnsson. **Description:** Profile of Michael Alter, newly appointed CEO of SurePayroll. The firm, started in 1999, provides payroll checks to companies with fewer than 100 employees. The process is simpler than traditional payroll services with everything done online, and costs 30-50 percent less than competitors.

31033 ■ **"Get your fix: had enough of auctions?"** in *Entrepreneur* **(Vol. 31, No. 4, April 2003, pp. 75)**
Pub: Entrepreneur Media Inc.
Ed: Mark Henricks. **Description:** An overview of the fixed-price marketplace is presented. The fixed-price marketplace is where pre-owned, overstocked and clearance items are listed and sold by prices set by the seller and make it easy to put large inventories of goods online for sale.

31034 ■ **"Getting Personal"** in *Entrepreneur* **(Vol. 33, October 2005, No. 10, pp. 44)**
Pub: Entrepreneur Media Inc.
Ed: Melissa Campanelli. **Description:** Personalized pricing allows electronic retailers to charge different customers different prices for the same products based on information about the particular customer. The pros and cons of this practice are examined.

31035 ■ **"Houston-Based Restaurant Chain Uses Mystery Shoppers to Ensure Quality"** in *Beaumont Enterprise* **(January 24, 2005)**
Pub: Beaumont Enterprise
Ed: Rachel Stone. **Description:** Restaurants, department stores, movie theaters, hotels, apartment complexes, banks, law firms, and many other businesses are using mystery shoppers to evaluate their businesses.

31036 ■ **"How to Fight a Price War"** in *Harvard Business Review* **(Vol. 78, No. 2, March 2000, pp. 107)**
Pub: Harvard Business School Publishing Corp.
Ed: Akshay R. Rao, Mark E. Bergen, Scott Davis. **Description:** If you find yourself facing a price war, you'll need to understand how it started in order to respond effectively. Often, the best counter attack does not have to involve a retaliatory price cut.

31037 ■ **"How to Price Your E-Book"** in *Web Marketing Today* **(No. 121, February 5, 2003)**
Pub: Wilson Internet Services
Ed: Ralph F. Wilson. **Description:** The main factors to consider when determining pricing for an electronic book are explained, including value and market analysis, fame and reputation, cost analysis, and the reader's budget.

31038 ■ **"Illicit Affairs?"** in *Entrepreneur* **(Vol. 32)**
Pub: Entrepreneur Media Inc.
Ed: Jane Easter Bahls. **Description:** The Foreign Corrupt Practice Act (FCPA), enacted by Congress in 1977, prohibits the use of bribery of officials in other countries in order to do business overseas. It is illegal to make payments, promises, or offers of anything of value to foreign officials to obtain or retain business, or to make payments to a third party.

31039 ■ **"In retail, discounters beat out high-end stores"** in *Atlanta Business Chronicle* **(Vol. 25, January 10, 2003, No. 31, pp. 23A)**
Pub: American City Business Publications, Inc.
Ed: Tom Barry. **Description:** The Georgia Economic Outlook 2003 survey indicates that in the coming months, inexpensive goods will fare better than luxury items in the retail sector.

31040 ■ **"Innovation drain"** in *Crain's Detroit Business* **(Vol. 19, No. 1, Jan. 6, 2003, pp. 3)**
Pub: Crain Communications Inc., Detroit
Ed: Terry Kosdrosky. **Description:** Automotive industry analysts are predicting that cost reductions demanded by the Big Three on suppliers could result in business going to foreign competitors.

31041 ■ **"Is your price right?"** in *Atlanta Business Chronicle* **(Vol. 24, No. 13, August 31, 2001, pp. 41A)**
Pub: American City Business Journals Inc.
Ed: Chaundra Frierson. **Description:** Various executives from companies and universities talk about product pricing and how companies can evaluate their costs.

31042 ■ **"It's all about the profits (you're the boss)"** in *Black Enterprise* **(Vol. 33, No. 3, October 2002, pp. S3)**
Pub: Earl Graves Publishing Co.
Ed: Carolyn M. Brown. **Description:** Financial management advice is given for student-owned businesses. A formula is provided for pricing services or products.

31043 ■ **"Keep 'Em Clicking"** in *Home Office Computing* **(Vol. 19, No. 2, February 2001, pp. 73)**
Pub: Scholastic Inc.
Ed: Mark Kakkuri. **Description:** Small business Web sites often lose out to competitors who can sell products for less. In order to achieve customer loyalty, a business must offer superior customer services and interaction. By personalizing customer services, a relationship will result that will bring customers back. One way to learn what customers want out of service is by conducting surveys and instant polls.

31044 ■ **"Lawsuit against Masco alleges predatory pricing"** in *Crain's Detroit Business* **(Vol. 19, No. 10, March 10, 2003, pp. 32)**
Pub: Crain Communications Inc., Detroit
Ed: Michael Strong. **Description:** Wilson Insulation Group Inc. has filed a lawsuit against Masco Corporation for predatory pricing and monopolizing in an attempt to drive Wilson out of the Augusta, Georgia market.

31045 ■ **"Made in America?"** in *Entrepreneur* **(Vol. 31, No. 10, October 2003, pp. 72)**
Pub: Entrepreneur Media, Inc.
Ed: Joshua Kurlantzick. **Description:** The consequences of U.S. businesses using overseas labor to produce products and reduce costs to small U.S. manufacturers are examined.

31046 ■ **"Most valuable players"** in *Entrepreneur* **(Vol. 31, No. 6, June 2003, pp. 68)**
Pub: Entrepreneur Media Inc.
Ed: Joshua Kurlantzick. **Description:** Rather than cutting prices to compete with large chains, small businesses should continue to offer customers value-added services.

31047 ■ **"Music"** in *Business Week* **(December 19, 2005, No. 3964, pp. 40)**
Pub: McGraw-Hill Companies
Ed: Peter Burrows. **Description:** Critics say iTunes-only downloads and inflexible pricing are hurting song sales.

31048 ■ **"Mystery Shoppers Enjoy Being Spies"** in *Atlanta Journal-Constitution* **(January 29, 2005)**
Pub: Atlanta Journal-Constitution
Ed: Renee DeGross. **Description:** Department stores and other retailers are using mystery shoppers to see their stores the way their customers see them; hotels and restaurants chains have begun using mystery shoppers also.

31049 ■ **"Name Your Price"** in *Entrepreneur* **(Vol. 33, September 2005, No. 9, pp. 108)**
Pub: Entrepreneur Media Inc.
Ed: Geoff Williams. **Description:** Professional Pricing Society located in Marietta, Georgia offers advice to small business owners for setting prices for products and services.

31050 ■ **"OnlineAuction.com Ready for Return, Rematch With eBay"** in *Mail Tribune* **(February 2, 2005)**
Pub: Mail Tribune
Ed: Greg Stiles. **Description:** Profile of Chris Fain, who has re-launched the eBay competitor, OnlineAuction.com. Fain is committed to providing a more convenient online auction with lower fees than eBay.

31051 ■ **"Oreo Woes Bringing Kraft Down"** in *Crain's Chicago Business* **(Vol. 26, No. 50, December 15, 2003, pp. 4)**
Pub: Crain Communications, Inc.
Ed: James B. Arndorfer. **Description:** Sales of the popular Oreo cookie are falling, hurting Kraft Foods Inc. Consumer concerns over weight, increased prices, and private-label cookie competitors are contributing to the 91-year-old brand's decline. Statistical data regarding the biscuit, snack and confectionery sector is included.

31052 ■ **"Oreo Woes Bringing Kraft Down; Fat Fears, Price Hikes, Private-Label Brands Sap Sales"** in *Crains Chicago Business* **(Vol. 26, No. 50)**
Pub: Crain Communications, Inc.
Ed: James B. Arndorfer. **Description:** Sales of the popular Oreo cookie are falling, hurting Kraft Foods Inc. Consumer concerns over weight, increased prices, and private-label cookie competitors are contributing to the 91-year-old brand's decline. Statistical data regarding the biscuit, snack and confectionery sector is included.

31053 ■ **"Out Of Pocket, Out Of Mind" in** *Law Firm Inc.* **(August 2004)**
Pub: American Lawyer Media LP
Ed: Tamara Loomis. Description: Cost recovery systems are of major concern to law firms. Many firms are considering whether to absorb costs for copies, laser printouts, faxes, scanning and telephone calls or pass the expense on to clients in order to recover out-of-pocket expenses incurred on the client's behalf.

31054 ■ **"Paper, Printing & Profit" in** *Small Business Opportunities* **(Vol. 16, No. 2, March 2004, pp. 70)**
Pub: Harris Publications, Inc.
Ed: Annette Wood. Description: Profile of Eric Jacobsen and Mahlon Regier, owners of Timber Creek Paper of Wichita, Kansas. The owners stay competitive by focusing on customer service, catering to smaller accounts such as churches, small businesses and local printers.

31055 ■ **"Pick Your Startup Tool" in** *Black Enterprise* **(Vol. 36, November 2005, No. 4, pp. 74)**
Pub: Earl G. Graves Publishing Co. Inc.
Ed: Sonya Donaldson. Description: Besides being a good business plan, financial management tools are an asset for planning a marketing strategy. Business Plan Pro Standard, QuickBooks, Peachtree, and Business Resource Software can help startups write business plans that include pricing strategy, advertising, and budgeting.

31056 ■ **"Price Fix" in** *Entrepreneur* **(Vol. 33, September 2005, No. 9, pp. 56)**
Pub: Entrepreneur Media Inc.
Ed: C.J. Prince. Description: Small business owners are watching their industries larger retailers and manufacturers for insight into pricing goods.

31057 ■ **"The Price is Right" in** *Inc.* **(July 1, 2003)**
Pub: Gruner & Jahr USA Publishing
Description: Profiles of profit-analyzing software to help small businesses set pricing for products and services are investigated.

31058 ■ **"The price slice" in** *Crain's Detroit Business* **(Vol. 18, No. 49, Dec. 9, 2002, pp. 11)**
Pub: Crain Communications Inc., Detroit
Ed: Laura Bailey. Description: Items for small businesses to consider when setting prices for products or services are outlined.

31059 ■ **"Priced to Sell" in** *Entrepreneur.com* **(Vol. 34, February 2006, No. 2, pp. 100)**
Pub: Entrepreneur Media Inc.
Ed: Nichole L. Torres. Description: Ways to market products based on selling price are presented. It is essential to know where your band fits in the marketplace.

31060 ■ **"Pricing and the psychology of consumption" in** *Harvard Business Review* **(Vol. 80, No. 9, September 2002, pp. 90)**
Pub: Harvard Business School Press
Ed: John Gourville, Dilip Soman. Description: Consumer psychology is a critical factor in pricing goods and services, and one that is often ignored by executives when determining price.

31061 ■ **"Ready? Set? Search! Rev Up Your Sales With Comparison-Shopping Engines" in** *Entrepreneur* **(Vol. 31, No. 9, September 2003, pp. 87)**
Pub: Entrepreneur Media, Inc.
Ed: Catherine Seda. Description: According to a survey conducted in January 2003, more than 50 percent of shoppers believe comparison-shopping search engines save time and money. The sites offer product descriptions, prices, and customer testimonials.

31062 ■ **"Renters Gloat Over Housing Slump" in** *Wall Street Journal* **(Vol. 248, December 2006, No. 149, pp. D1-D3)**
Pub: Dow Jones & Co. Inc.
Ed: James R. Hagerty George Anders Description: Renters were ridiculed for not purchasing homes dur-

ing the housing boom, but are now feeling some satisfaction due to the slump in the market. Profile of economist Dean Baker and his recent condo sale and new rental situation.

31063 ■ **"Rewarding Rebates" in** *Black Enterprise* **(Vol. 36, November 2005, No. 4, pp. 166)**
Pub: Earl G. Graves Publishing Co. Inc.
Ed: Stephanie Young. Description: The National Retail Federation reports that online rebate offers from stores provide ease in use while avoiding the hassle of finding serial numbers and product codes, filling out paperwork, and mailing in paperwork.

31064 ■ **"San Jose, Calif., Woman is Secret Shopper Evaluating Quality of Business" in** *San Jose Mercury News* **(August 10, 2004)**
Pub: San Jose Mercury News
Ed: Michele Chandler. Description: Mystery shoppers routinely snoop around stores and restaurants at the request of business owners in order to survey the quality of their products, pricing, and services.

31065 ■ **"Sara Lee's Apparel Biz Bind" in** *Crain's Chicago Business* **(Vol. 26, No. 50, December 15, 2003, pp. 4)**
Pub: Crain Communications, Inc.
Ed: James B. Arndorfer. Description: Large retailers like Wal-Mart, Target, and K-Mart are marketing brands that directly compete with Sara Lee's apparel brands, such as Hanes and Champion. Statistical data included.

31066 ■ **"Shift in business strategy helps Littlearth turn around financials" in** *Pittsburgh Business Times* **(Vol. 22, No. 42, May 2, 2003)**
Pub: Pittsburgh Business Times
Ed: Tim Schooley. Description: Littlearth increased the prices of recycled handbags and belts by 30 percent and increased sales by 20 percent.

31067 ■ **"Shipping out" in** *Entrepreneur* **(Vol. 31, No. 6, June 2003, pp. 42)**
Pub: Entrepreneur Media Inc.
Ed: Melissa Campanelli. Description: Many online retailers have followed Amazon.com and have begun offering free shipping with purchases. The advantages and downside to providing this service are discussed.

31068 ■ **"Shop Around: This Technology Can Help You Comparison Shop for Low Fares" in** *Entrepreneur* **(Vol. 32, July 2004, No. 7, pp. 28)**
Pub: Entrepreneur Media Inc.
Ed: Chris McGinnis. Description: Web-scraping sites and software allow users to search multiple sites and prices in easy-to-read charts for comparison shopping travel fares. SideStep, ITA Software, and TravelAxe are profiled.

31069 ■ **"Shopping Spies Help Retail Businesses Keep Eye on Service" in** *Charlotte Observer* **(October 10, 2004)**
Pub: Charlotte Observer
Ed: Leigh Dyer. Description: Charlotte, North Carolina-based Belk Department Stores is using mystery shoppers in order to enforce store policies. The store managers' annual bonus is based on this program.

31070 ■ **"The Skinflint Goes Shopping" in** *Forbes* **(December 24, 2001, p. 100)**
Pub: Forbes Magazine
Ed: Stephen Manes. Description: The article explores shopping bargains online. Price-comparison Web sites are great places to gather information, but many often miss the best deals.

31071 ■ **"Small business" in** *Crain's Detroit Business* **(Vol. 18, No. 45, November 11, 2002, pp. 23)**
Pub: Crain Communications Inc., Detroit
Description: Ways to improve profits for various types of small businesses are presented, including marketing ideas and pricing.

31072 ■ **"A smarter way to sell commodities" in** *Harvard Business Review* **(Vol. 80, No. 4, April 2002, pp. 24)**
Pub: Harvard Business School Press
Ed: Ajay Kohli, Robert S. Lurie. Description: Commodities sellers can differentiate their products from those of the competition by reducing risk for their customers according to marketing experts, Robert Lurie and Ajay Kohli.

31073 ■ **"Stop on a Dime" in** *Entrepreneur. com* **(Vol. 34, January 2006, No. 1, pp. 27)**
Pub: Entrepreneur Media Inc.
Ed: Mark Henricks. Description: In the book The Art of Pricing, author Raft Mohammed offers expert advice on pricing products and services. Mohammed suggests offering discounts to some customers, while charging premiums to others and to bundle to create high-priced packages to those who value them and bare bones packages to bargain shoppers.

31074 ■ **"Street Smarts" in** *Inc.* **(May 2000, pp. 33)**
Pub: The Goldhirsh Group
Ed: Norm Brodsky. Description: It's harder than ever to get customers to accept price increases, but you're making a mistake if you don't raise prices on a regular basis.

31075 ■ **"Tiered pricing plans have benefits and disadvantages" in** *Business First Columbus* **(Vol. 18, No. 40, May 24, 2002, pp. B11)**
Pub: Business First Columbus, Inc.
Ed: David Miller. Description: Tiered pricing is a new idea within the health insurance industry that allows customers to pay a fixed price for services regardless of the actual cost of the service.

31076 ■ **"The true believer" in** *Red Herring* **(March 2003, pp. 56)**
Pub: Herring Communications Inc.
Ed: Lee Bruno. Description: Scientific developments that are transforming nanotechnology from science fiction to reality are explored, including challenges facing the nanotechnology industry and the talents and skills needed for newcomers to the industry.

31077 ■ **"What's It Worth? Get Your Prices Right, Or It'll Cost You" in** *Entrepreneur* **(Vol. 32, December 2004, No. 12, pp. 92)**
Pub: Entrepreneur Media Inc.
Ed: Gwen Moran. Description: Retail experts advise independent retailers to know their margins in order to master higher sales volumes. Buy one get one free offers can backfire, and it might be wiser to use longer-term loyalty programs.

31078 ■ **"When Is the Price Right?" in** *Black Enterprise* **(Vol. 34, July 2004, No. 12, pp. 42)**
Pub: Earl G. Graves Publishing Co. Inc.
Ed: Bridget McCrea. Description: When a small business is forced to cut prices to maintain market share and reduce inventory, it is important to reduce prices enough to attract customers without cutting too deeply into the company's profit margin.

31079 ■ **"Who benefits from price promotions?" in** *Harvard Business Review* **(Vol. 80, No. 9, September 2002, pp. 22)**
Pub: Harvard Business School Press
Ed: Shuba Srinivasan. Description: Research has shown that reducing prices temporarily as part of a marketing campaign can adversely affect a retail company.

31080 ■ **"Why Haven't You Called" in** *Atlanta Business Chronicle* **(Vol. 25, November 29, 2002, No. 25, pp. 1B)**
Pub: American City Business Publications, Inc.
Ed: Don Reichardt. Description: Business leaders have the tendency to blame slumping sales on the economy, but many factors contribute to lower sales. A company's future and success depends partly on the ability to confront other possible causes of declining sales, such as altered consumer behavior, pricing changes, sales force difficulties, and new competitive pressure.

31081 ■ "You Are What You Charge" in
Journal of Accountancy (Vol. 198, November
2004, No. 5, pp. 20)
Pub: American Institute of Certified Public
    Accountants
Ed: Ron Baker, Paul Dunn. **Description:** The four P's
of marketing include price, place, promotion, and
product, of these pricing is the most complicated.

VIDEOCASSETTES/
AUDIOCASSETTES

31082 ■ *Product Costs: What's In Them*
Phoenix Learning Group
2349 Chaffee Dr.
St. Louis, MO 63146
Ph:(314)569-0211
Free: 800-221-1274
Fax: (314)569-2834
URL: http://www.phoenixlearninggroup.com
Released: 1979. **Description:** This show presents
the factors that effect the final price of a product.
Availability: VHS; 3/4U.

31083 ■ *Swim with the Sharks without Being
Eaten Alive*
Instructional Video
2219 C St.
Lincoln, NE 68502
Ph:(402)475-6570
Free: 800-228-0164
Fax: (402)475-6500
Co. E-mail: feedback@insvideo.com
URL: http://www.insvideo.com
Price: $595.00. **Description:** Based on Harvey
Mackay's best-selling book of the same name. Offers
training advice on how to beat your competition, make
the crucial sale, open the closed door, and swing the
million-dollar deal at the last minute. **Availability:**
VHS.

CONSULTANTS

31084 ■ Mark Vanderstelt
9831 Gulfstream Ct.
Fishers, IN 46038
Ph:(317)576-9328
Fax: (317)576-9328
Scope: Consulting services include financial planning
and analysis, inventory control, cash management,
return on investment, budgeting, pricing, system de-

sign and analysis, mergers and acquisitions, feasibility studies, data processing, cost systems and
controls, and performance measurement. Also performs operational and financial reviews.

RESEARCH CENTERS

**31085 ■ Weber State University–Center for
Business and Economic Development**
3815 University Cir.
Ogden, UT 84408-3815
Ph:(801)626-7232
Fax: (801)626-7423
Co. E-mail: bking1@weber.edu
URL: http://weber.edu/sbdc
Contact: Beverly King, Dir.
E-mail: bking1@weber.edu
Scope: Business development activities, market research, survey research, focus groups, and government feasibility studies. **Services:** Provides
consulting and technical assistance for small businesses and contractual work for government and
large businesses; Incubator program (semimonthly),
technical assistance. **Educational Activities:**
Courses on business planning and entrepreneurship
and 40 annual training events; Scholarship (semiannually), for successful completion of entrepreneurship
courses. **Awards:** Coleman Foundation Grant, for entrepreneurial outreach and education.

START-UP INFORMATION

31086 ■ "Actioncoaching.com" in *Entrepreneur.com* (Vol. 34, January 2006, No. 1, pp. 6)
Pub: Entrepreneur Media Inc.
Ed: Steve Cooper. **Description:** The Business Coaching Franchise has launched its new Action-Coaching.com, a franchise offering small business owners topics for growing a business, marketing, and selling products and services.

31087 ■ "An agent for change" in *BlackEnterprise* (Vol. 31, No. 6, January 2001, pp. 99)
Pub: Earl Graves Publishing Co.
Ed: Robyn D. Clarke. **Description:** Profile of Sanyu Barnicoat, owner of the consulting firm, The Change Agents Group in West Orange, New Jersey. Ms. Barnicoat trains and coaches individuals, small groups, and major corporations on ways to make changes in an organization, and how to cope with those changes in the workplace.

31088 ■ "All the Rage: Wondering What Everyone Will Be Crazy About in the Coming Year?" in *Entrepreneur* (Vol. 33, January 2005, No. 1, pp. 84)
Pub: Entrepreneur Media Inc.
Ed: Sara Wilson. **Description:** Fitness and weight-loss, technical consulting, eBay drop-off stores, child tutoring/enrichment programs and senior care are among the top franchises for 2005.

31089 ■ "Bandy Resigns As President of TSEA: Six-Year Head To Start Association Management Firm With Wife in April" in *Tradeshow Week* (Vol. 34)
Pub: Reed Business Information
Ed: Heidi Genoist. **Description:** Michael Bandy resigned as president of the Trade Show Exhibitors Association in order to launch an independent association management and consulting firm with his wife Dee Dee.

31090 ■ "Bouncing back" in *Entrepreneur* (Vol. 30, No. 3, March 2002, pp. 134)
Pub: Entrepreneur Media Inc.
Ed: Nichole L. Torres. **Description:** Valuable information for entrepreneurs starting a new business after losing a job is offered.

31091 ■ "Conference Helps Moms Jumpstart Home-Based Business Careers" in *Orange County Register* (January 28, 2005)
Pub: Freedom Communications Inc.
Ed: Nancy Luna. **Description:** The top ten home-based businesses are listed: Internet sales and marketing, Web and graphic design, online research, technical support, virtual assistant, business coach, event planner, children's product development, home services, and direct sales.

31092 ■ "Eco-Preneuring" in *Small Business Opportunities* (Vol. 13, No. 6, November 2001, pp. 42, 44)
Pub: Harris Publications, Inc.
Ed: John Marshall. **Description:** Profile of Eric Floyd, president and owner of EDF Associates, a Southern California-based environmental consulting firm.

31093 ■ *Going Solo: Developing a Home-Based Consulting Business from the Ground Up*
Pub: McGraw-Hill Companies Incorporated
Ed: William J. Bond. **Released:** January 1997. **Price:** $14.95. **Description:** Ways to turn specialized knowledge into a home-based successful consulting firm, focusing on targeting client needs, business plans, and growth.

31094 ■ *How to Get Started in Your Own Consulting Practice*
Pub: New Ventures Publishing Group
Ed: Herman R. Holtz. **Released:** 1998.

31095 ■ "Inside the Customer-Focused Company" in *Harvard Business Review* (Vol. 78, No. 3, May 2000, pp. S20)
Pub: Harvard Business School Publishing Corp.
Ed: Cary Jehl Broussard. **Description:** The article shows how a change agent, or type of business consultant, and vocal consumers help structure an entire organization.

31096 ■ "A launching point to the next step" in *Hispanic Business* (Vol. 22, No. 6, June 2000, pp. 42)
Pub: Hispanic Business
Ed: Derek Reveron. **Description:** Potomac Management Group Inc., founded as a part-time information technology and logistics consultancy by Dennis Garcia in 1992, has won a $22 million, 5-year contract from the U.S. Coast Guard. The company expects revenues to reach over $8 million in 2000.

31097 ■ "Peer to peer" in *Harvard Business Review* (Vol. 78, No. 5, September-October 2000, pp. 32)
Pub: Harvard Business School Publishing Corp.
Ed: Roberta Fusaro. **Description:** Two peer groups for CEOs, offered in the Boston area, and conducted by the Catlin Group and the Commonwealth Institute, help CEOs of start-up high tech companies deal with the challenges of their new position.

31098 ■ "Silver (and Gold) in Senior Services" in *Home Business* (Vol. 13, January/February 2006, No. 1, pp. 32, 34, 66, 68)
Pub: Home Business Magazine
Ed: Priscilla Y. Huff. **Description:** Fifteen home-based businesses targeting senior citizens include medical claims assistance, senior care consulting, nutrition, in-home care, money managers, seamstress/tailoring, handyman services, financial planning, home business consulting, home delivery, exercise, computer consulting, antique appraisals, lawn and garden services, and transcription and/or video services.

31099 ■ *The Six Figure Consultant: How to Start (or Jump-Start) Your Consulting Career & Earn $100,000+ a Year*
Pub: Upstart Publishing Co., Inc.
Ed: Robert W. Bly. **Released:** 1998. **Price:** $29.95. **Description:** Presents a collection of proven strategies & effective methods for revving up any consulting career.

31100 ■ *Small Business Desk Reference*
Pub: Penguin Books (USA) Incorporated
Ed: Gene Marks. **Released:** December 2004. **Price:** $29.95 (US), $44.00 (Canadian). **Description:** Comprehensive guide for starting or running a successful small business, focusing on buying a business or franchise, writing a business plan, financial management, accounting, legal issues, human resources management, operations, marketing, sales, customer service, taxes, insurance, and ethics. Information for launching a restaurant, property management firm, retail outlet, consulting firm, and service business is included.

31101 ■ "The Urge to Unbundle" in *Fast Company* (February 2005, No. 91, pp. 23)
Pub: Gruner & Jahr USA Publishing
Ed: George Mannes. **Description:** Profile of Courtney Lynch and Angie Morgan, founders of the newly formed Lead Star leadership consulting firm. Their public relations company is committed to providing national media exposure to clients.

ASSOCIATIONS AND OTHER ORGANIZATIONS

31102 ■ **Association of Independent Consultants**
15 Wilson St.
Markham, ON, Canada L3P 1M9
Ph:(416)410-8163
Fax: (905)294-9435
Co. E-mail: info1@aiconsult.ca
URL: http://www.aiconsult.ca
Contact: Keith Thirgood, Pres.
Membership: Independent consultants. **Purpose:** Promotes professional advancement of members. Facilitates communication and cooperation among members; makes available volume discounts to members. Conducts business education courses; maintains speakers' bureau. **Publications:** *Thrive-on-Line.* **Telecommunication Services:** electronic mail, president1@aiconsult.ca.

31103 ■ **Association of Management Consulting Firms**
380 Lexington Ave., Ste. 1700
New York, NY 10168
Ph:(212)551-7887
Fax: (212)551-7934
Co. E-mail: info@amcf.org
URL: http://www.amcf.org
Contact: Elizabeth Ann Kovacs, Pres./CEO
Description: Trade association for consulting organizations that provide a broad range of managerial ser-

vices to commercial, industrial, governmental, and other organizations and individuals. Seeks to unite management-consulting firms in order to develop and improve professional standards and practice in the field. Offers information and referral services on management consultants; administers public relations program. Conducts research. Monitors regulatory environment. **Publications:** *15th Annual Operating Ratios for Management Consulting Firms: A Resource for Benchmarking* (annual); *Research Findings* (annual).

31104 ■ Association of Professional Computer Consultants

2323 Yonge St., Ste. 400
Toronto, ON, Canada M4P 2C9
Ph:(416)545-5275
Free: 888-487-2722
Co. E-mail: info@apcconline.com
URL: http://www.apcconline.com
Contact: Ms. Tamara Der-Ohanian, Exec. Dir.
Description: Promotes the interests of Independent Computer Consultants. **Publications:** *Gateway* (periodic).

31105 ■ Association of Proposal Management Professionals

300 Smelter Ave. NE, Ste. 1
PMB 383
Great Falls, MT 59404-1958
Ph:(406)454-0090
Fax: (406)454-0090
Co. E-mail: apmpmemserv@msn.com
URL: http://www.apmp.org
Contact: David L. Winton, Exec. Dir.
Membership: Proposal managers, proposal planners, proposal writers, consultants, desktop publishers, and marketing managers. **Purpose:** Encourages unity and cooperation among industry professionals. Seeks to broaden member knowledge and skills through developmental, educational, and social activities. Maintains speakers' bureau. Provides current information and developments in the field. **Publications:** *APMP Professional Journal* (semiannual); *Perspective* (quarterly); Proceedings (annual).

31106 ■ Canadian Association of International Development Consultants–Regroupement des consultants canadiens en developpement internationale

PO Box 1139
Sta. B
Ottawa, ON, Canada K1P 5R2
Ph:(613)746-2554
Co. E-mail: mail@caidc-rccdi.ca
URL: http://www.caidc-rccdi.ca
Contact: Amitav Rath, Treas.
Purpose: Aims to provide services for, and to represent the interests of, Canadian international development consultants.

EDUCATIONAL PROGRAMS

31107 ■ Successful Internal Consulting for IS Professionals: How to Meet Your Client's Needs

American Management Association
1601 Broadway
New York, NY 10019
Ph:(212)586-8100
Free: 800-262-9699
Fax: (212)903-8168
Co. E-mail: customerservice@amanet.org
URL: http://www.amanet.org
Price: $1,595.00 for non-members; $1,495.00 for AMA members. **Description:** Three-day seminar for systems analysts and information specialists; covers communicating with clients, developing written and oral presentations, determining project requirements, and managing project scope. **Locations:** Atlanta, GA; and New York, NY.

REFERENCE WORKS

31108 ■ "Account Balances Indicate That 401(k) Participants Have Heard The Long-Term Investor Message" in *Employee Benefit Plan Review* (Vol. 55)

Pub: Charles D. Spencer & Associates, Inc.
Ed: Sue Burzawa. **Description:** Lincolnshire, Illinois-based Hewitt Associates LLC, the health benefit plan consulting company, tracks pension fund activity through its 401(k) Index. Industry analysts said that institutional investors are remaining calm as the country suffers from a period of economic upheaval.

31109 ■ "Advice on Advisors: Fed up with bad advise?" in *FSB* (Vol. 10, No. 9, December 1, 2000, pp. 98)

Pub: Time Inc.
Ed: Description: An approach for finding the right advisors for your business is covered.

31110 ■ "Ask Inc." in *Inc.* (September 1, 2004)

Pub: Inc. Magazine
Description: A small stationery shop in Kansas is looking for new investors and the vice president of a residential mortgage brokerage wants to hire a coach or trainer to work with the firm's CEO.

31111 ■ "Ask Inc. Partnerships" in *Inc.* (November 2006, pp. 57)

Pub: Gruner & Jahr USA Publishing
Description: Buyouts of partners that leave the company require accurate assessment of the current value of the stock. That may require hiring a consultant to put a current value on the business to arrive at an amicable settlement.

31112 ■ "Back in the Saddle" in *Home Business* (Vol. 12, March/April 2005, No. 2, pp. 48)

Pub: Home Business Magazine
Ed: Sandy Larson. **Description:** Profile of Jim Stewart who runs his strategic project management business from his home.

31113 ■ "Blogger's Block: Sick of Blogging? Here's How to Deal with Business Blog Burnout" in *Entrepreneur* (Vol. 32, December 2004, No. 12)

Pub: Entrepreneur Media Inc.
Ed: Steve Cooper. **Description:** Debbie Well, a business blogging consultant founded WordBiz Report. Wells' publishing and consulting firm offers services in the area of e-newsletters and other Web content, including blogging.

31114 ■ "Broaddus Opens Office" in *Mississippi Business Journal* (Vol. 28, September 2006, No. 36, pp. 23)

Pub: Venture Publications, Inc.
Description: Profile of Broaddus & Associates, construction planning and management firm. Broaddus & Associates has opened an office in the Mississippi Gulf Coast area, its first office outside of Texas, to aid in the vast need in rebuilding management and planning.

31115 ■ "The Buddy System: These Longtime Friends Formed a Growing CPA Firm" in *Black Enterprise* (Vol. 35, August 2004, No. 1, pp. 47)

Pub: Earl G. Graves Publishing Co. Inc.
Ed: Robert Janis. **Description:** Profile of three friends who formed a full-service certified public accounting firm in 1996. Benford Brown & Associates performs audits, accounting services, tax services, and business consulting.

31116 ■ *Budgeting for a Small Business*

Pub: Crisp Publications, Inc.
Ed: Terry Dickey. **Released:** 1993. **Price:** $15.95 (paper). **Description:** Part of the Small Business & Entrepreneurship Series.

31117 ■ "Built For Speed: Baba Garba Looks to Take His Broadband Business Abroad" in *Black Enterprise* (Vol. 34, No. 5, December 2003, pp. 50)

Pub: Earl Graves Publishing Co.
Ed: Zakiyyah El-Amin. **Description:** Profile of Baba Garba, founder of Infonit LLC, launched in 2000 and located in Niles, Michigan. The firm provides broadband installation and information technology consulting.

31118 ■ *The Business of Consulting: The Basics & Beyond*

Pub: Jossey-Bass, Inc. Publishers
Ed: Elaine Biech. **Released:** 1998. **Price:** $39.95 (cloth).

31119 ■ "Business Near You: Beverly Hills Franchise Offers Directors for Smaller Firms" in *Detroit Free Press* (January 21, 2007)

Pub: Knight-Ridder/Tribune Business News
Ed: Carol Cain. **Description:** Profile of Carl Ammaccapane, president of The Alternative Board in Beverly Hills. The firm assists small to mid-sized businesses organize an outside board of directors consisting of owners of companies of similar size.

31120 ■ "Business On Her Own Terms" in *Black Enterprise* (Vol. 35, August 2004, No. 1, pp. 57)

Pub: Earl G. Graves Publishing Co. Inc.
Ed: Bridget McCrea. **Description:** Profile of Fay Coleman, president and CEO of her Silver Spring, Maryland firm, Westover Consultants Inc. Coleman started her business in the basement of her home and began developing educational training programs, planning events, creating public outreach programs, and conducting surveys for government agencies. Today, the firm comprises three divisions: Health and Behavior Sciences, Management Support Services, and Information Technology Services.

31121 ■ "Can C.K. Prahalad Pass the Test?" in *Fast Company* (August 2001, pp. 108)

Pub: Fast Company
Ed: Jennifer Reingold. **Description:** Profile of C.K. Prahalad, one of the business world's most influential professors and consultants, has left the University of Michigan and invested millions of dollars of his own money to put himself to the test. He wants to build a company around the ideas and principles he's been teaching others, and hopes to change the world in the process.

31122 ■ *Client-Centered Consulting: A Practical Guide for Internal Advisers and Trainers*

Pub: The McGraw-Hill Companies
Ed: Peter Cockman. **Released:** 1992.

31123 ■ "Clutter Busters: From Closets to Cabinets to Garages, Americans' Clutter is Piling Up Like Never Before" in *Entrepreneur*

Pub: Entrepreneur Media Inc.
Ed: Nichole L. Torres. **Description:** According to the National Association of Professional Organizers, the increased public interest in organizing their lives, professional organizers have doubled in number in the last two years. Some of these entrepreneurs are manufacturing organizing products, while others are becoming professional consultants.

31124 ■ "Company Looks to Link Rural Firms with City Buyers" in *St. Louis Post-Dispatch* (February 17, 2005)

Pub: Knight-Ridder/Tribune Business News
Ed: Martin Van Der Werf. **Description:** Profile of Rural Business Consultants, led by Robert Fowler. The firm links interested buyers with rural companies, mostly manufacturers. Many of the buyers will be able to take advantage of a federal program that guarantees loans for businesses in rural areas.

31125 ■ *The Complete Guide to Consulting Success*

Pub: Dearborn Financial Publishing, Inc.
Ed: Howard L. Shenson. **Released:** 3rd ed. 1997. **Price:** $69.95 (ringbound); $29.95 (paper).

31126 ■ **"Consultant Outlines Steps For Measuring Effectiveness Of Communications Program" in** *Employee Benefit Plan Review* **(Vol. 55, No. 12)**
Pub: Charles D. Spencer & Associates, Inc.
Description: Detroit, Michigan-based Aon Consulting Inc., a management consulting services firm, has developed an employee communication program that allows employers to measure the effectiveness of their program. The program, which is aimed at assessing employee job satisfaction, contains twelve key performance indicators.

31127 ■ *The Consultant's Calling: Bringing Who You Are to What You Do*
Pub: Jossey-Bass, Inc.
Ed: Geoffrey M. Bellman. **Released:** 1992. **Price:** $33.95 (cloth); $19.00 (paper).

31128 ■ **"A consultant's comeuppance" in** *Harvard Business Review* **(Vol. 81, No. 2, February 2003, pp. 26)**
Pub: Harvard Business School Press
Ed: Robert Buday. **Description:** Experts discuss how a fictitious company might better manage its relations with business consultancy.

31129 ■ *Consultants and Consulting Organizations Directory*
Pub: Thomson Gale
Ed: Deborah J. Baker, Editor. **Released:** Annual, latest edition 29th, Published April 2006. **Price:** $985, individuals. **Covers:** over 25,000 firms, individuals, and and organizations active in consulting. **Entries Include:** Individual or organization name, address, phone, fax, e-mail, URL, specialties, founding date, branch offices, names and titles of key personnel, number of employees, financial data, publications, seminars and workshops. **Arrangement:** By broad subject categories. **Indexes:** Subject, geographical, organization name.

31130 ■ **"Consultants on their own" in** *Atlanta Business Chronicle* **(Vol. 24, No. 10, August 10, 2001, pp. 3A)**
Pub: American City Business Journals Inc.
Ed: Jim Lovel. **Description:** An increasing number of marketing consultants are becoming independent for various reasons. As their numbers increase, the consultants have found new ways to boost their business, including formal alliances setting up a Web site devoted to independents.

31131 ■ *The Contract and Fee-Setting Guide for Consultants and Professionals*
Pub: John Wiley & Sons, Inc.
Ed: Howard L. Shenson. **Released:** 1990. **Price:** $75.00; $29.95 (paper). **Description:** Provides information for consultants on writing proposals and setting fees.

31132 ■ **"Corporate Image-Maker Sees Hope for Symbol, Pain for Computer Associates" in** *Long Island Business News* **(March 5, 2004)**
Pub: Dolan Media Newswires
Ed: Ken Schachter. **Description:** Ann Stephenson, chief executive of Stephenson Group, a corporate image-maker specializing in technology companies, discusses ways she would rehabilitate the images of Symbol Technologies and Computer Associates. Both firms are facing government investigations into accounting procedures and the sudden departure of high-ranking executives.

31133 ■ **"Cracking Wise" in** *Entrepreneur* **(Vol. 28, No. 4, April 2000, pp. 150)**
Pub: Entrepreneur Media Inc.
Ed: Marc Diener. **Description:** A sense of humor is a tremendous asset to any dealmaker.

31134 ■ **"Cultural Access Moves into Medical Research" in** *Hispanic Business* **(Vol. 23, No. 5, May 2001, pp. 6)**
Pub: Hispanic Business
Description: Cultural Access Group, a multicultural marketing firm, hired Raul Lopez to manage its new Miami office.

31135 ■ **"Curtain Call?" in** *Entrepreneur* **(Vol. 32, October 2004, No. 10, pp. 72)**
Pub: Entrepreneur Media Inc.
Ed: David Worrell. **Description:** Profile of Chuck Hawkes, executive coach with DreamsFulfilled in Charlotte, North Carolina. Hawkes helps executives and entrepreneurs discover what they want to do after selling a business or retiring.

31136 ■ **"Cutbacks at another consultant" in** *The New York Times* **(December 8, 2000, pp. C3)**
Pub: The New York Times Company
Ed: Matt Richtel. **Description:** E-commerce consultant Viant to layoff 125 employees.

31137 ■ *D & B Consultants Directory*
Pub: Dun & Bradstreet Corp.
Contact: Allan Z. Loren, Chm. & Ceo
Released: Annual. **Covers:** top 30,000 U.S. consulting firms in more than 200 areas of specialization. **Entries Include:** Firm name, address, phone, sales, number of employees, year established, description of service, other locations, names and titles of key personnel, reference to parent company, D&B DUNS number, trade name, consulting activity, owned companies clientele, territory served, number of accounts, stock exchange symbol and indicator for publicly owned companies. **Arrangement:** Complete consultants profiles appear in the consultants alphabetical section. Companies are cross-referenced geographically and by activity. **Indexes:** All companies with a primary or secondary Standard Industrial Classification (SIC) code of 8748 "Business Consulting Services," as well as those companies whose type of business description includes the word "consult." All companies must have a phone number and be either a headquarters or single location.

31138 ■ **"Designs on Success" in** *Small Business Opportunities* **(Vol. 17, November 2005, No. 6, pp. 72, 106)**
Pub: Harris Publications Inc.
Ed: Rob Marsh. **Description:** Rob Marsh from LogoWorks.com offers advice on ways to create or improve a company logo that will help brand a service or product and draw new clients.

31139 ■ **"Detroit Free Press Oakland Small Business Column" in** *Detroit Free Press* **(May 26, 2005)**
Pub: Knight-Ridder/Tribune Business News
Ed: Carol Cain. **Description:** Stephen Wiesman worked as a firefighter until being injured in 2002. Wiesman plans to introduce a new product he developed that will make stoves safer to use. Also featured: David Moncur's marketing, creative and technology consulting company.

31140 ■ **"Detroit Free Press Small Business Column" in** *Detroit Free Press* **(May 16, 2005)**
Pub: Knight-Ridder/Tribune Business News
Ed: Carol Cain. **Description:** Denise Ilitch is joining Clark Hill PLC in order to assist the Detroit law firm with its business customers.

31141 ■ **"Do You Love What You Do?" in** *Fast Company* **(March 2005, No. 92, pp. 88)**
Pub: Gruner & Jahr USA Publishing
Ed: Marshall Goldsmith. **Description:** Profile of Warren Bennis, founding chairman of the Leadership Institute at the University of Southern California. Bennis discusses job satisfaction.

31142 ■ **"Don't Just Listen Connect" in** *Fast Company* **(August 2001, pp. 140)**
Pub: Fast Company
Ed: Paul C. Judge. **Description:** An interview with John I. Sviokla, vice chairman and leader of the digital-strategy practice at DiamondCluster International Inc., a consulting firm in Chicago. Sviokla makes a series of connections when interacting with customers and compares technology today to where it must be in the future.

31143 ■ **"The education of Clint Reilly" in** *San Francisco Business Times* **(Vol. 16, No. 43, May 21, 2002, pp. 3)**
Pub: San Francisco Business Times Inc.
Ed: Steve Ginsberg. **Description:** Political consultant Clint Reilly, began to invest in San Francisco real estate by purchasing the Merchants Exchange Building in 1995. Problems with that $17.5 million purchase and Reilly's mayoral campaign in 1999 are discussed.

31144 ■ **"Ex-BBDO Exec Forms New Agency" in** *Crain's Detroit Business* **(Vol. 21, January 24, 2005, No. 4, pp. 18)**
Pub: Crain Communications Inc. - Detroit
Ed: Jean Halliday. **Description:** Profile of Mike Vogel, former CEO of Omnicom Group's BBDO Detroit has left that firm in order to form RTV Communications Group. Vogel's new firm will consist of RTV Consulting, Consolidated Purchasing Partners and Vineyard Group, all located in Auburn Hills, Michigan. RTV offers marketing, strategy, consulting, creative, public relations, advertising, media, events and printing services.

31145 ■ **"The Excellence Group Helping Good Schools Become Great." in** *Mississippi Business Journal* **(Vol. 28, September 2006, No. 37, pp. 18)**
Pub: Venture Publications, Inc.
Ed: Wally Northway **Description:** Profile of new educational consulting firm, The Excellence Group, LLC. The firm offers a unique blend of seasoned educators, administrators and an attorney who specializes in school law.

31146 ■ **"Executives see trouble spreading" in** *The New York Times* **(December 4, 2000, pp. C1)**
Pub: The New York Times Company
Ed: Andrew Ross Sorkin. **Description:** The high technology industry, particularly the online, software, computer equipment, and semiconductor segments are bracing for a continued slowdown. Telecom and consulting firms are also watching for signs of retrenchment. Some executives said that recent investor-sell off had driven stock prices too low. Others said any problems were limited to particular companies, not whole industries. The computer peripherals area was held up as a bright spot. Presently there are stock bargains out there for investors willing to wait for renewed growth, and the stomach for near term uncertainty. Statistical data included.

31147 ■ **"Explore the Art of Consultative Selling" in** *Journal of Accountancy* **(Vol. 199, January 2005)**
Pub: American Institute of Certified Public Accountants
Ed: John E. Graziano, Patrick J. Flanagan. **Description:** Traditional selling vs. consultative selling techniques when integrating financial planning into an accounting practice are explored.

31148 ■ **"Failure is not an option" in** *Fast Company* **(June 2001, pp. 44)**
Pub: Fast Company
Ed: Jennifer Reingold. **Description:** Unveiled in January 2001 by Plural Inc., the Wall Street Solutions Center (WSSC) was designed to help companies make big technology bets, without betting the future of the company in the process. Plural Inc. is an e-business consulting firm.

31149 ■ **"Family-Business Psychology" in** *Forbes* **(December 25, 2000, pp. 134)**
Pub: Forbes Magazine
Ed: Brigid McMenamin. **Description:** Over the past few years a large number of family-business experts, including lawyers, MBAs, accountants, and psychologists, have sprung up, all promising to help families prosper along with their businesses for generations to come.

31150 ■ **"Find the Perfect Biz" in** *Small Business Opportunities* **(Vol. 13, No. 5, September 2001, pp. 20)**
Pub: Harris Publications Inc.
Description: Profile of FranChoice, a network of independent consultants who provide franchises with pre-

screened, high quality leads to selected franchisors across the U.S. A list of the top ten franchise industries is provided.

31151 ■ "Finding Millions in the Trash" in *Small Business Opportunities* **(Vol. 13, No. 5, September 2001, pp. 52-54)**
Pub: Harris Publications, Inc.
Description: Profile of Environmental Waste Solutions, the waste management consulting firm. Owners Darwyn Williams and Steve Ellis have developed an Affiliate Program to help small businesses start their own waste management consulting business.

31152 ■ "Five Ways to Avoid Disaster" in *Fast Company* **(June 2001, pp. 46)**
Pub: Fast Company
Description: Neil Isford, president and CEO of Plural, the e-business consulting firm, outlines five ways to avoid technology-enabled disasters.

31153 ■ "For the Love of the Game: How One Woman Scores in the Sports Entertainment Industry" in *Black Enterprise* **(Vol. 35, August 2004)**
Pub: Earl G. Graves Publishing Co. Inc.
Ed: Zakiyyah El-Amin. **Description:** Profile of Cydni Bickerstaff, founder of Bickerstaff Sports & Entertainment. Bickerstaff is a full-service sports marketing, managing, and event production company, specializing in marketing and promotions, sporting events, athlete appearances, and sponsorships.

31154 ■ "Former Collection Attorney Needs Consultants to Offer Bulletproof Asset Protection" in *Success* **(Vol. 47, No. 2, June 2000, pp. 88)**
Pub: Success Publishing, Inc.
Description: Bill Reed, former collection attorney and author, tells how he changed his career to start a consultant agency to help people protect their assets. Mr. Reed trains Asset Protection Consultants nationwide to work with clients in their own areas.

31155 ■ *Get Clients Now!, 2nd Edition: A 28-Day Marketing Program for Professionals, Consultants, and Coaches*
Pub: American Management Association
Ed: C.J. Hayden. **Released:** 2006. **Price:** $19.95.

31156 ■ "Get It Straight" in *Black Enterprise* **(Vol. 34, No. 2, September 2003, pp. 62)**
Pub: Earl Graves Publishing Co.
Ed: Sonia Alleyne. **Description:** A career counselor can assist individuals wishing to discover a talent or purpose in life, and developing them into a career or an entrepreneurial venture.

31157 ■ "A Gift is a Reward is an Incentive" in *Incentive* **(Vol. 174, No. 8, August 2000, pp. S8)**
Pub: Bill Communications
Description: While many in the incentive industry tend to use the terms gift, reward and incentive interchangeably, management consultant and author, Alexander Hiam, who wrote the book Motivating & Rewarding Employees—New and Better Ways to Inspire Your People, claims these words should not be synonymous.

31158 ■ "Global Spectrum: Making a Difference in the Convention Center Industry" in *Tradeshow Week* **(Vol. 34, November 29, 2004, No. 48, pp. S2)**
Pub: Reed Business Information
Description: Profile of Global Spectrum, a private management firm in the tradeshow sector. Global Spectrum is a subsidiary of Comcast-Spectator of Philadelphia, Pennsylvania. The company has increased management contracts for arenas, convention centers, stadiums and ice rinks by more than 500 percent since January 2000 when it was created.

31159 ■ "Going outside for expert help: Family businesses have options to get objective advice" in *Crain's Chicago Business* **(Vol.23,Nov.13,2000)**
Pub: Crain Communications, Inc. Crain Communications, Inc.

Ed: Barbara B. Buchholz. **Description:** How William Lane re-structured his family's 52-year-old manufacturing company around his family's needs.

31160 ■ *Guide to Small Business Consulting Engagements*
Pub: Practitioners Publishing Co.
Ed: Douglas R. Carmichael, Don Pallais, Cherie W. Shipp, Glenn J. Vice and Sharon Armendariz. **Released:** 3 vols. 1998. **Price:** $164.00 (ringbound).

31161 ■ "Gurus in the garage" in *Harvard Business Review* **(Vol. 78, No. 6, November-December 2000, pp. 71)**
Pub: Harvard Business School Publishing Corp.
Description: Description of a special type of advisor who helps entrepreneurs with a variety of tasks, including recruiting staff and negotiating seed money.

31162 ■ "Harrison, Maine, Homeland Security Consultant Telecommutes Around the Globe" in *Portland Press Herald* **(May 20, 2005)**
Pub: Blethen Maine Newspapers, Inc.
Ed: Matt Wickenheiser. **Description:** Profile of Clifford A. Lewis, CEO of Strategy X, a new homeland security company. Lewis is committed to the idea of running a global business successfully from his hometown through the use of the Internet. Strategy X offers consulting services to assess and advise on security systems and processes of military bases, dams, power plants, and other facilities.

31163 ■ "Have Kid, Won't Travel" in *Fast Company* **(November 2001, pp. 48)**
Pub: Fast Company
Ed: Christine Canabou. **Description:** Profile of David Peterson, cofounder, CEO and chairman of the Atlanta-based North Highland Company, the management and technology consulting firm. Mr. Peterson's work force is able to drive to their client's site, rather than having to spend much of their time away from their homes and families.

31164 ■ "Have a Talent for Sales?" in *Black Enterprise* **(Vol. 36, November 2005, No. 4, pp. 60)**
Pub: Earl G. Graves Publishing Co. Inc.
Ed: Eve Tahmincioglu. **Description:** African American women are looking towards direct-selling as a means of empowerment and selling products targeted to African Americans. Our Own Image is a firm that sells Afrocentric products ranging from decor items to cosmetics.

31165 ■ "A Head Start: Need Some Help Thinking More Clearly Under Pressure" in *Entrepreneur* **(Vol. 31, No. 7, July 2003, pp. 73)**
Pub: Entrepreneur Media, Inc.
Ed: Mark Henricks. **Description:** Profile of Kevin Cashman, CEO of Leader-Source, a leadership consulting firm in Minneapolis, Minnesota. Cashman spends 30 minutes each morning and at the end of each workday in meditation to bring clarity and focus to his life.

31166 ■ "Here's What You Can Do" in *Crain's Chicago Business* **(Vol. 30, January 2007, No. 1, pp. 15)**
Pub: Crain Communications, Inc.
Ed: Sarah A. Klein. **Description:** Many developers want to be energy-efficient but good information is not available and most tips are put together by those not familiar with building science. Interview with John Porterfield, co-founder of Informed Energy Decisions LLC, a consulting firm that helps improve the energy performance of structures, talks about common defects in buildings which keep them from being efficient.

31167 ■ *High Income Consulting: How to Build & Market Your Professional Practice*
Pub: Nicholas Brealey Publishing
Ed: Tom Lambert. **Released:** 2nd ed. 1997. **Price:** $19.95 (paper); $40.00 (cloth).

31168 ■ "High-Quality Relationships Succeed Where Incentives Fall Short" in *Incentive* **(Vol. 174, No. 9, September 2000, pp. 76)**
Pub: Bill Communications
Ed: Jim Ryan. **Description:** With today's increasingly complex marketplace, businesses have reason to be concerned about selling products and services. Warnings about consultants offering relationships, but are really selling incentive programs are investigated.

31169 ■ "A high-tech domino effect: as dot-coms go, so go the e-commerce consultants" in *The New York Times* **(December 16, 2000, pp. B1, C1)**
Pub: The New York Times Company
Ed: Jonathan D. Glater. **Description:** All electronic-commerce consultant firms have suffered as a result of the weakness in the online sector. Firms like Scient Corporation and others that grew too rapidly are finding that demand for their services has evaporated, and are now having to lay off employees by the hundreds as they face a capital crunch.

31170 ■ "Hiring a guide just to find the camp" in *The New York Times* **(February 20, 2000, pp. A39)**
Pub: The New York Times Company
Ed: Matthew Purdy. **Description:** Profile of Camp Connection, the new company that helps parents choose summer camps for their children.

31171 ■ "Home Depot Offers Expensive Lesson in Curbing Execs' Pay" in *Crain's Chicago Business* **(Vol. 30, January 2007, No. 3, pp. 13)**
Pub: Crain Communications, Inc.
Ed: Description: Linking executive pay to performance is becoming a top priority for the board of directors as part of their role in compensation watchdogs. Recent departure of Home Depot's CEO, Robert Nardelli left him with a $210 million compensation package. Profile of the Home Depot debacle included.

31172 ■ "Hotel Consultant Finds Room at the Top" in *Crain's New York Business* **(Vol. 21, January 31, 2005, No. 5, pp. 18)**
Pub: Crain Communications Inc.
Ed: Lisa Fickenscher. **Description:** Profile of Cheryl Boyer, consultant to the hospitality and leisure industry.

31173 ■ *How to Become a Successful Consultant in Your Own Field*
Pub: Prima Publishing & Communications
Ed: Hubert Bermont. **Released:** 1991, third edition. **Price:** $21.95; 12.95 (paper). **Description:** Step-by-step guide to starting a consulting business.

31174 ■ *How to Make It Big as a Consultant*
Pub: AMACOM
Ed: William A. Cohen. **Released:** Second edition, 1993. **Price:** $17.95 (paper). **Description:** Covers finding and interviewing clients; using direct and indirect marketing; writing proposals; pricing fairly; solving clients' problems; handling ethical issues. Also covers negotiating, planning, and scheduling contracts.

31175 ■ *How to Make at Least $100,000 Every Year as a Successful Consultant in Your Own Field*
Pub: JLA Publications
Ed: Jeffrey Lant. **Released:** 1992. **Price:** $35.00 (paper).

31176 ■ *How to Select and Use Consultants: A Client's Guide*
Pub: International Labor Office
Ed: Milan Kubr. **Released:** 1993. **Price:** $27.00 (paper). **Description:** Guide for managers and entrepreneurs.

31177 ■ *Inside the Technical Consulting Business: Launching & Building Your Independent Practice*
Pub: John Wiley & Sons, Inc.
Ed: Harvey Kaye. **Released:** 3rd ed. 1997. **Price:** $49.95 (cloth).

31178 ■ "Integration managers: special leaders for special times" in *Harvard Business Review* (Vol. 78, No. 6, November-December 2000, pp. 108)
Pub: Harvard Business School Publishing Corp.
Description: In order to figure out the best way to merge with other businesses, companies are appointing a new and unique kind of manager. This is important, since last year companies globally invested $3.3 trillion on mergers and acquisitions, 32 percent more than was spent in 1998.

31179 ■ "It's All About the Image" in *Crain's New York Business* (Vol. 22, December 11, 2006, No. 50, pp. 26)
Pub: Crain Communications, Inc.
Description: Advantage Consulting Services, a Los Angeles-based Internet marketing consultancy, offers businesses the service of creating and maintaining their MySpace pages.

31180 ■ "JBHM Education Group, LLC" in *Mississippi Business Journal* (Vol. 29, January 2007, No. 4, pp. 6)
Pub: Venture Publications, Inc.
Description: Profile of Pat Whitlock, who recently joined JBHM Education Group as human resources director. She most recently worked as a human resources manager at Time Warner Cable. JBHM Education Group provides educational management consulting to over 200 schools in Alabama, Arkansas, Louisiana and Mississippi.

31181 ■ "Keep It Up! Need Some Motivation? Someone To Show You the Ropes?" in *Entrepreneur.com* (Vol. 34, February 2006, No. 2, pp. 98)
Pub: Entrepreneur Media Inc.
Ed: Nichole L. Torres. **Description:** Business coaches can help entrepreneurs work through issues when starting a new company. These coaches offer an outside perspective to entrepreneurs in order to succeed.

31182 ■ "Know Thy Worth" in *Entrepreneur. com* (Vol. 34, February 2006, No. 2, pp. 50)
Pub: Entrepreneur Media Inc.
Ed: C.J. Prince. **Description:** A business valuation can help an owner put a precise number on the company's present and future value. It will help when choosing to sell the business, gifting the business to heirs, recruiting new investors, or bringing employees into ownership.

31183 ■ "Living High on the Blog" in *Entrepreneur* (Vol. 33, February 2005, No. 2, pp. 65)
Pub: Entrepreneur Media Inc.
Ed: Gwen Moran. **Description:** Reach Communications Consulting founder, William Arruda, discovered an 800 percent hike in traffic on his firm's Website after being mentioned on an Internet blog; ways to add blogs to a public relations campaign are investigated.

31184 ■ "Looking for Leverage" in *Hispanic Business* (Vol. 23, No. 5, May 2001, pp. 32, 34, 36)
Pub: Hispanic Business
Ed: Scott Williams. **Description:** Companies looking to grow have a variety of high-tech options. Advice is given from Omni/Strat, a Miami-based consulting firm that helps companies leverage technology to improve customer relationships, business intelligence, and e-commerce. The Web Head Group, located in San Antonio, Texas, also offers technology advice to small businesses.

31185 ■ "Making a Comeback" in *Entrepreneur* (Vol. 32, August 2004, No. 8, pp. 71)
Pub: Entrepreneur Media Inc.
Ed: Joanne Cleaver. **Description:** Advantages as well as disadvantages to rehiring an employee to serve as a consultant are explored.

31186 ■ *Management Consulting: Theory & Tools for Small Business Interventions*
Pub: Dame Publications, Inc.
Ed: Porth and Saltis. **Released:** 1998. **Price:** $32.95.

31187 ■ "Managing in the Cappuccino Economy" in *Harvard Business Review* (Vol. 78, No. 2, March 2000, pp. 177)
Pub: Harvard Business School Publishing Corp.
Ed: Eileen C. Shapiro. **Description:** Chris Argyris offers an insightful diagnosis of why traditional companies don't empower their people.

31188 ■ *Managing India's Small Industrial Economy: The Catalytic Role of Industrial Counselors and Policy Makers*
Pub: Sage Publications, Incorporated
Ed: V. Padmanand, V.G. Patel. **Released:** June 2004. **Price:** $28.95. **Description:** Case studies and methodology are used to discuss the areas where industrial consultants are influencing sustainability and growth of small businesses in India's industrial economy.

31189 ■ "Marcus Buckingham Thinks Your Boss Has an Attitude Problem" in *Fast Company* (August 2001, pp. 88)
Pub: Fast Company
Ed: Polly LaBarre. **Description:** Marcus Buckingham is a consultant who teaches CEOs how to get the most from their employees. Buckingham has authored two books to help managers lead their employees.

31190 ■ "Marketers, a Lawyer, And a Techie—Cheap" in *FSB* (Vol. 10, No. 9, December 1, 2000, pp. 118)
Pub: Time Inc.
Ed: Maggie Overfelt. **Description:** A compilation of Web sites offering affordable advice for small businesses, with a brief description of each site.

31191 ■ *Marketing for Dummies*
Pub: John Wiley & Sons Inc.
Ed: Alexander Hiam, Editor. **Released:** latest edition 2. **Price:** $21.99, individuals. **Publication Includes:** Marketing web sites, marketing consultants, trade associations, market researchers, and other experts. **Entries Include:** Individual or company name, address, phone number, web site address (where applicable). Principal content of publication is articles on marketing strategies.

31192 ■ "Master of Disaster" in *Fast Company* (November 2001, pp. 46)
Pub: Fast Company
Ed: Annie F. Pyatak. **Description:** Profile of Gordon Ballinger, of MapInfo Corporation. Mr. Ballinger helps federal, state, and local authorities access the information they need to recover from disasters.

31193 ■ "MomandPop.com" in *PC Magazine* (January 16, 2001, pp. 131)
Pub: Ziff-Davis Publishing Company
Ed: Alan Cohen. **Description:** Scouring the Web for handy resources is a luxury small business owners often don't have. A bevy of portals has simplified matters, bringing information, advice, and services to one place. Dozens of small business sites have popped up in the past year, but the best of the lot is AllBusiness. This site provides access to 250 business forms and agreements and how-to guides on everything from protecting trademarks to terminating an employee.

31194 ■ "Motivator Vehicles" in *Sacramento Bee* (October 31, 2005)
Pub: The Sacramento Bee
Ed: Rachel Osterman. **Description:** Experts recommend small companies reward hardworking employees with items used daily rather than a large company dinner or the like. Gift certificates to popular coffee houses or retailers motivate workers.

31195 ■ "A New Leaf" in *Entrepreneur* (Vol. 32, November 2004, No. 11, pp. 95)
Pub: Entrepreneur Media Inc.
Ed: Mark Henricks. **Description:** Consulting firm, McKinsey & Company has designed a four-step process that assists entrepreneurs when making changes to a company. The first step involves convincing people, including employees, that a change is necessary for the firm.

31196 ■ "Office Optional" in *Inc.* (Volume 27, December 2005, No. 12, pp. 42, 44)
Pub: Inc. Magazine
Ed: Darren Dahl. **Description:** Profile of Point B, a consulting firm employee 223 workers. Co-founders Tim Jenkins and Darran Littlefield run their virtually with employees in Seattle, Denver, Phoenix, and Portland, Oregon, and each consultant works with clients locally. Three tips for running a virtual office are outlined.

31197 ■ "Perfect Proposals" in *Sales & Marketing Management* (Vol. 159, January-February 2007, No. 1, pp. 9)
Pub: VNU Business Media
Description: Michael McLaughlin, principal at MindShare Consulting LLC, offers tips for developing sales proposals, and stresses keeping it simple.

31198 ■ "Planning Made Easy" in *Incentive* (Vol. 174, No. 10, October 2000, pp. 150)
Pub: Bill Communications
Description: The video entitled Business at Sea, produced by Landry & Kling, specialists in meetings at sea, is profiled. The video provides insights from three corporate and three independent meeting planners, as well as eight cruise line executives, to help accomplish business objectives using a cruise ship.

31199 ■ "Pop Quiz: A Quick Test of Your Managerial Skills" in *Sales & Marketing Management* (Vol. 158, November-December 2006, No. 11, pp. 17)
Pub: VNU Business Media
Description: Leadership and sales coaching consultant shares tips for sales managers.

31200 ■ "The Power of the Pack" in *Sales & Marketing Management* (Vol. 159, January-February 2007, No. 1, pp. 45)
Pub: VNU Business Media
Description: Root Learning, a learning solutions company, informs applicants of the firm's sense of hierarchy. Prospective employees are informed about the policy whereby employees are called roosters or rootizens.

31201 ■ *PPC's Guide to Small Business Consulting Engagements*
Pub: Practitioners Publishing Company
Released: March 2004. **Description:** Technical guide for conducting consulting engagements for small business.

31202 ■ *PPC's Guide to Small Business Consulting Engagements, Vol. 2*
Pub: Practitioners Publishing Company
Released: March 2004. **Description:** Second volume of the technical guide for conducting consulting engagements for small business.

31203 ■ *PPC's Guide to Small Business Consulting Engagements, Vol. 3*
Pub: Practitioners Publishing Company
Released: March 2004. **Description:** Third volume of the technical guide for conducting consulting engagements for small business.

31204 ■ "Present Perfect" in *Incentive* (Vol. 174, No. 9, September 2000, pp. 65)
Pub: Bill Communications
Ed: Joan M. Steinauer. **Description:** Buying holiday gifts for employees gets easier when you enlist the help of a gift service company.

31205 ■ "Prioritizing a Hectic Schedule" in *Sales & Marketing Management* (Vol. 157, January 2005, No. 1, pp. 52)
Pub: VNU Business Media
Ed: Kathryn Droullard. **Description:** Profile of Brian O'Neill, marketing and communications director at Circadian Technologies in Lexington, Massachusetts; O'Neill assists managers of extended-hour, shift-work operations to build time-management skills.

31206 ■ "Q&A" in *Home Office Computing* (Vol. 18, No. 11, November 2000, pp. 15)
Pub: Scholastic Inc.
Ed: Marilyn Zelinsky Syarto. **Description:** Are you drowning in e-mail? David Ferris, president of Ferris Research, a San Francisco-based consulting firm specializing in messaging and collaborative technology, discusses how to manage e-mail overload.

31207 ■ "Reality Checker" in *Forbes* (February 19, 2001, pp. 95)
Pub: Forbes Magazine
Ed: Jennifer Godwin. **Description:** A profile of Joseph W. Goodman, a retired electrical engineer, who has become a consultant for venture capital firms.

31208 ■ "Resources: Web Sites, Organizations, Events and More to Grow Your Business" in *Entrepreneur* (Vol. 32, October 2004, No. 10, pp. 8)
Pub: Entrepreneur Media Inc.
Ed: Steve Cooper. **Description:** Resources to help small business is featured. Loopnet.com, an online commercial real estate services offers more than 250,000 commercial lease and sales listings; Cybersource.com manages online payments; American FactFinder offers U.S. Census Bureau data sets; ContentFinder.com helps small businesses find syndicated content sources for Websites, newsletters and other Intranets.

31209 ■ "Robert Wagner Hosts The Litigation Explosion" in *Entrepreneur* (Vol. 33, January 2005, No. 1, pp. 104)
Pub: Entrepreneur Media Inc.
Description: The rewards of high income and owning your own business as a consultant providing asset protection, financial privacy and tax reduction are highlighted.

31210 ■ "Said The Spider" in *Entrepreneur* (Vol. 28, No. 4, April 2000, pp. 149)
Pub: Entrepreneur Media Inc.
Ed: Barry Farber. **Description:** Learn to win sales from our eight-legged friend's greatest architectural accomplishment, the spider web. It can help you to allocate at a glance, make connections, think on the road, and look into the future.

31211 ■ "Searching for Relief" in *My Business* (April/May 2003, pp. 49)
Pub: My Business Magazine
Ed: Charlotte Franck. **Description:** The importance of defining goals when choosing a business consultant is stressed. One small business owner tells how she used bartering as a strategy for acquiring consulting services.

31212 ■ Selecting and Working with Consultants
Pub: Crisp Publications, Inc.
Ed: Thomas J. Ucko. **Price:** $9.95. **Description:** Shows how to locate, interview, select and evaluate the best consultant for any job.

31213 ■ "Sense & Sensibility" in *Small Business Opportunities* (Vol. 12, No. 2, March 2000, pp. 18)
Pub: Harris Publications, Inc.
Ed: Carla Goodman. **Description:** Advice to find, hire and work with a consultant to help build a small business is presented. A checklist of information for evaluating a consultant before hiring, is also included.

31214 ■ "Service To A Tee" in *Entrepreneur* (Vol. 28, No. 4, April 2000, pp. 172)
Pub: Entrepreneur Media Inc.
Ed: Paul Edward and Sarah Edward. **Description:** Marketing tips for consultants.

31215 ■ "Sharpening the Saw When You Work as a Consultant" in *Home Business* (Vol. 12, March/April 2005, No. 2, pp. 66)
Pub: Home Business Magazine
Ed: Steven D. Strauss. **Description:** Ways for consultants to increase revenue are addressed.

31216 ■ "Signal Strength" in *Entrepreneur* (Vol. 33, March 2005, No. 3, pp. 18)
Pub: Entrepreneur Media Inc.
Ed: John F. Ince. **Description:** Venture capital firms are ramping up marketing efforts by hiring public relations firms to promote their portfolio companies and full-time marketing consultants to introduce their names to prospective entrepreneurs.

31217 ■ "Slack Off" in *Fast Company* (August 2001, pp. 27)
Pub: Fast Company
Ed: George Anders. **Description:** Who says being productive always means being busy? Not high-tech consultant Tom Demaro, who shares his reasons for being so up on downtime.

31218 ■ "Small Business Advisor: Dialing for dollars" in *Crain's Chicago Business* (Vol. 23, December 11, 2000, pp. SB16)
Pub: Crain Communications, Inc. Crain Communications, Inc.
Ed: Barbara B. Buchholz. **Description:** A profile of Jeffery L. Furst and his company, FurstPerson Inc. that recruits and trains personnel for corporate telemarketing firms. Advice is given for growth, including statistical data and an industry overview.

31219 ■ "Small-Business Services" in *PC Magazine* (February 8, 2000, pp. 156)
Pub: Ziff-Davis Publishing Company
Ed: Don Willmott. **Description:** A compilation of service sites geared to serve small businesses, including CenterBeam, eFax.com, myTalk, Stamps.com, and Zkey.com.

31220 ■ "Special Opps" in *Entrepreneur* (Vol. 32, October 2004, No. 10, pp. 38)
Pub: Entrepreneur Media Inc.
Ed: Geoff Williams. **Description:** Profile of Mark Wilson, former Marine, who has restructured his company in order to tap into a new market in Iraq. Wilson is a franchisee of The Growth Coach, which works with self-employed and small business owners. He has created a Web site for entrepreneurs who are military reservists searching for strategies to keep their businesses operating while deployed in Iraq. Chris Exline, CEO of Home Essentials, generated $3.5 billion in revenue for 2003, by renting home essentials to individuals working in foreign countries.

31221 ■ "Starting From Zero: Entrepreneur Reaps Success During Rocky Tech Times" in *Black Enterprise* (Vol. 34, July 2004, No. 12, pp. 53)
Pub: Earl G. Graves Publishing Co. Inc.
Ed: Bridget McCrea. **Description:** Profile of Glenn Davis, owner of Virginia-based BranCore Technologies. Working from home, Davis borrowed $15,000 from his 401(k) to launch his minority-owned firm that provides project management and e-commerce consulting.

31222 ■ "Sticking to what she knows" in *BlackEnterprise* (Vol. 32, No. 2, September 2001, pp. 46)
Pub: Earl Graves Publishing Co.
Ed: Quincy Lewis. **Description:** Profile of Sheri Huguely, president of entertainment consulting firm Glue Inc. In 2000, the company had revenues of $252,000 with a goal of $350,000 for 2001.

31223 ■ "Street Smarts. Are You Listening to Me?" in *Inc.* (November 2006, pp. 61-62)
Pub: Gruner & Jahr USA Publishing
Ed: Norm Brodsky. **Description:** As an entrepreneur, you ultimately need to make the final decisions. Sometimes too much advice from the wrong persons on the right things or the right person on the wrong things clouds the issue and can lead to a bad final decision you may have to live with.

31224 ■ "Successful IT practices know their clients well" in *Accounting Today* (Vol. 14, No. 7, April 17, 2000, pp. 26)
Pub: Faulkner & Gray, Inc.
Ed: James C. Metzler. **Description:** Small businesses make up the largest market in America and claim

the client base of the majority of accounting firms. Recognizing key characteristics of the small business market is important to information technology (IT) firms and their professionals. This market choice has the potential to give an IT professional a tremendous sense of satisfaction because of the profound improvements that can take place in the business.

31225 ■ "Take No For an Answer: Don't Dismiss Naysayers-Ask For Advice, and Turn It Into a Tool for Success" in *Entrepreneur* (October 2004)
Pub: Entrepreneur Media Inc.
Ed: Romanus Wolter. **Description:** Entrepreneurs can ask the people who offer negative comments to also offer advice and not take comments personally.

31226 ■ "Team-Building Outings Heat Up" in *Crain's Chicago Business* (Vol. 30, January 2007, No. 3, pp. 23)
Pub: Crain Communications, Inc.
Ed: Kevin Davis. **Description:** Team-building skills are often an important key to a successful business. Chicago-area cooking schools provide programs that bring corporate employees into the kitchen to prepare meals, working in teams.

31227 ■ "Team-Building Remains Essential in Downturn" in *Atlanta Business Chronicle* (Vol. 24, No. 14, September 7, 2001, pp. S11)
Pub: American City Business Journals Inc.
Ed: Judith Potwora. **Description:** Executives from team-building corporations discuss team-building and the services each company offers to small businesses.

31228 ■ "The Telework Puzzle" in *Home Office Computing* (Vol. 19, No. 1, January 2001, pp. 90)
Pub: Scholastic Inc.
Ed: Lisa Roberts. **Description:** TManage Inc founder and CEO, Glenn Lovelace, discusses the factors that make telecommuting programs succeed or fail. Lovelace was director of telecommuting for Nortel Networks before starting his own consulting firm to outsource telework programs.

31229 ■ "That Bites" in *Entrepreneur* (Vol. 33, January 2005, No. 1, pp. 69)
Pub: Entrepreneur Media Inc.
Ed: Joshua Kurlantzick. **Description:** Ninety percent of small companies are not compliant with new COBRA regulations. Employers with more than 20 employees must now give written notice explaining COBRA. Brokers can assist small business owners with COBRA compliance.

31230 ■ "Threat Level" in *Entrepreneur* (Vol. 31, No. 8, August 2003, pp. 28)
Pub: Entrepreneur Media, Inc.
Ed: Michael Miora, Geoff Williams. **Description:** Michael Miora, CEO and founder of ContingenZ Corporation in Playa del Rey, California, discusses the threat of cyberterrorism and business. Miora's incident management and planning firm offers expertise to the National Reconnaissance Office, the government agency that builds America's spy satellites.

31231 ■ "Tony Thompson Believes in Playing the Cards He Was Dealt" in *St. Louis Post-Dispatch* (March 4, 2005)
Pub: Knight-Ridder/Tribune Business News
Ed: Maring Van Der Werf. **Description:** Profile of the Kwame Building Group, one of the 100 largest construction management firms in the U.S. Tony Thompson, owner, discusses the growth of his firm.

31232 ■ "Tough Sell" in *Black Enterprise* (Vol. 37, October 2006, No. 3, pp. 92)
Pub: Earl G. Graves Publishing Co. Inc.
Ed: Sonia Alleyne. **Description:** Career coaches can evaluate your talents and skills. In an era where more companies are downsizing a coach can help you decide if you are suited for your industry or should try switching careers.

31233 ■ **"Tracking Tech Time"** in *Inc.* **(November 15, 2000, pp. 26)**
Pub: The Goldhirsh Group
Description: Profile of the professional services automation (PSA) software that helps Internet consultants figure prices and track their services.

31234 ■ **"Training Day: Need a Sales Trainer to Whip Your Staff Into Shape?"** in *Entrepreneur* **(Vol. 32, October 2004, No. 10, pp. 90)**
Pub: Entrepreneur Media Inc.
Ed: Kimberly L. McCall. **Description:** Sales trainers can rev up a sales team by teaching closing skills. Tips for finding the right sales coach are presented.

31235 ■ **"Trying to Reach a Senior Level Executive?"** in *Sales & Marketing Management* **(Vol. 159, January-February 2007, No. 1, pp. 9)**
Pub: VNU Business Media
Description: Ernest Nicastro, principal of Positive Response LLC, offers advice for reaching the attention of top level executives when trying to sell products or services.

31236 ■ **"Turning Receivables Into Received"** in *Black Enterprise* **(Vol. 34, No. 7, February 2004, pp. 46)**
Pub: Earl Graves Publishing Co.
Ed: Bridget McCrea. **Description:** Profile of Sweet Survival, a business consulting firm. The company has developed an accounts receivable policy suited to serving small business needs.

31237 ■ **"Turning Receivables Into Received: Don't Let Your Collections Process Fall Through the Cracks"** in *Black Enterprise* **(Vol. 34, No. 7)**
Pub: Earl Graves Publishing Co.
Ed: Bridget McCrea. **Description:** Profile of Sweet Survival, a business consulting firm. The company has developed an accounts receivable policy suited to serving small business needs.

31238 ■ **"Turning Your Services Into a Product"** in *Home Business* **(Vol. 13, January/February 2006, No. 1, pp. 62)**
Pub: Home Business Magazine
Ed: C.J. Hayden. **Description:** Consultants can grow a business by offering tangible services that a client can trust will produce the result they are expecting.

31239 ■ **"Up Against the Ropes: A Professional Coach May Help"** in *Black Enterprise* **(Vol. 37, December 2006, No. 5, pp. 72)**
Pub: Earl G. Graves Publishing Co. Inc.
Ed: Description: Executive coaching is now a $1 billion industry. The coaching process itself and traits to look for in a coach are discussed.

31240 ■ **"Using Security Consultants is Playing It Safe"** in *San Antonio Express-News* **(January 23, 2005)**
Pub: San Antonio Express-News
Ed: Aissatou Sidime. **Description:** Security consultants provide assessments of potential dangers and analyze physical structures for lighting, security camera or sensor placement, entrance and exit locations, and crime in the area.

31241 ■ **"View Master"** in *Fast Company* **(September 2001, pp. 72)**
Pub: Fast Company
Ed: Paul C. Judge. **Description:** Profile of Adam Cohen, cofounder of Urban Data solutions. An architect by training, Cohen is able to master details from dozens of sources and apply them to the maps made by his company.

31242 ■ **"Virtual Assistants Become Real Help as more U.S. Firms Use Outsourced Aides"** in *Chicago Tribune* **(October 3, 2004)**
Pub: Chicago Tribune
Ed: Barbara Rose. **Description:** Profile of Kelly Kalmes, corporate trainer and consultant working from her home office in Evanston, Illinois. Kalmes' secretary moved to Paris and now works as her personal assistant using email, shared computer files, and an Internet phone service to take care of business from her new home in Europe.

31243 ■ **"Virtual Company Achieves Actual Savings"** in *Home Business* **(Vol. 12, March/April 2005, No. 2, pp. 48)**
Pub: Home Business Magazine
Ed: Sandy Larson. **Description:** Profile of Karlin Sloan, who runs her executive coaching firm from her home using a telecommuting program.

31244 ■ **"Warp Speed"** in *Sales & Marketing Management* **(Vol. 157, Jan. 20, 2005)**
Pub: VNU Business Media
Ed: Michele Marchetti. **Description:** According to Patricia Gardner, founder of Maximum Sales, sales and management consulting firm in Sparks, Maryland, the most important thing small companies neglect during a high-growth period, is to write job descriptions for its sales staff and other employees.

31245 ■ **"Watch Out For Career Scams"** in *Black Enterprise* **(Vol. 34, No. 3, October 2003, pp. 53)**
Pub: Earl Graves Publishing Co.
Ed: Laura Egodigwe. **Description:** Ways to distinguish a career counselor when seeking professional career advice is explained. Career counselors must meet a minimum education requirement of a master's degrees and be licensed by the state in which they practice. Many also seek certification from professional bodies.

31246 ■ **"Websites"** in *Black Enterprise* **(Vol. 34, No. 5, December 2003, pp. S8)**
Pub: Earl Graves Publishing Co.
Ed: Sonya Kimble-Ellis. **Description:** A listing of three Web sites offering startup advice to young entrepreneurs is presented.

31247 ■ **"What Price Time?"** in *Home Office Computing* **(Vol. 18, No. 10, October 2000, pp. 14)**
Pub: Scholastic Inc.
Ed: William Van Winkle. **Description:** A list of new companies bringing service providers and users together to help save time is provided.

31248 ■ **"When Your Job Really Makes You Sick"** in *Black Enterprise* **(Vol. 34, No. 5, December 2003, pp. 63)**
Pub: Earl Graves Publishing Co.
Ed: Lee Anna Jackson. **Description:** Profile of Erica Benson, owner of A-Solution, her home-based consulting service offering job coaching among professional and business services.

31249 ■ **"When Your Job Really Makes You Sick: Why You Need to Develop a High Adversity Quotient"** in *Black Enterprise* **(Vol. 34, December 2003)**
Pub: Earl Graves Publishing Co.
Ed: Lee Anna Jackson. **Description:** Profile of Erica Benson, owner of A-Solution, her home-based consulting service offering job coaching among professional and business services.

31250 ■ **"Whistle Shop: Turn Your Store Into a Destination by Making Shopping an Event"** in *Entrepreneur* **(Vol. 33, March 2005, No. 3, pp. 86)**
Pub: Entrepreneur Media Inc.
Ed: Gwen Moran. **Description:** Ways to create more entertaining shopping experiences are offered by Debbie Allen, a retail consultant and author of Confessions of Shameless Self Promoters.

31251 ■ **"Who has the next big idea?"** in *Fast Company* **(September 2001, pp. 108)**
Pub: Fast Company
Ed: Daniel H. Pink. **Description:** Michael Hammer, consultant, author, evangelical business revolutionary, unleashed re-engineering on an unsuspecting public in the early 1990s, now he's back with a new book, a new agenda, and a bunch of new ideas.

31252 ■ **"Who Wants to be an Expert?"** in *Home Office Computing* **(Vol. 18, No. 8, August 2000, pp. 22)**
Pub: Scholastic Inc.
Ed: Sonya Donaldson. **Description:** An explanation of Web sites offering consulting services to small business is provided, with advice for choosing the right firm.

31253 ■ **"Why You're Hiring All Wrong"** in *Inc.* **(February 1, 2002)**
Pub: Inc. Magazine
Ed: Kate O'Sullivan. **Description:** Advice is offered for creating a long-range career plan for every employee hired, including the use of a consulting firm to review these plans annually.

31254 ■ **"Work Area Clutter is Not a Problem Unless It's a Problem"** in *St. Louis Post-Dispatch* **(January 30, 2005)**
Pub: Knight-Ridder/Tribune Business News
Ed: Repps Hudson. **Description:** David Munz, a professor of organizational psychology at St. Louis University and also a business consultant, discusses workplace clutter issues.

31255 ■ *Working for Yourself: Law and Taxes for Independent Contractors, Freelancers and Consultants*
Pub: NOLO
Ed: Stephen Fishman. **Released:** October 2004. **Price:** $39.99. **Description:** Laws and tax rules governing independent contractors, freelancers and consultants.

31256 ■ **"WSJ Honors Economist"** in *Hispanic Business* **(June 2005, pp. 18)**
Pub: Hispanic Business
Description: Maria Fiorini Ramierez, president and CEO of her global economic and financial consulting firm of the same name, was named one of the top two economists in the U.S. in forecasting the actual rate of inflation during the last three years by The Wall Street Journal.

31257 ■ **"You hire them to do the tough work, but how easy is it to work with them?"** in *E-business Advisor* **(Vol. 18, No. 10, Oct. 2000, pp. 12)**
Pub: Advisor Media, Inc.
Description: Market researcher and consulting firm the Aberdeen Group predicts that IT firms' spending on professional service automation will grow from $100 million to $1.3 billion by 2003.

31258 ■ **"You're Fired!"** in *Forbes* **(Vol. 174, December 13, 2004, No. 12, pp. 89)**
Pub: Forbes Magazine Inc.
Ed: Christopher Steiner. **Description:** Profile of Achilles Group, a firm that assists businesses with personnel matters such as firings, discrimination suits, personality conflicts, threatened lawsuits, EEOC claims, and hiring.

TRADE PERIODICALS

31259 ■ *California Special Education Alert*
Pub: LRP Publications
Contact: Steve Bevilacquar, Editorial Dir.
Released: Monthly. **Price:** $240 plus $22 s/h. **Description:** Assists California special education administrators comply with changing special education laws, regulations, and policies on the state and federal level to avoid litigation. Recurring features include letters to the editor, interviews, and reports of meetings.

31260 ■ *SoloDining.com*
Pub: SoloDining.com
Contact: Marya Charles Alexander
Ed: Marya Charles Alexander, Editor. **Released:** Quarterly. **Price:** $25; $25, Canada plus $5 postage. **Description:** Provides strategies and tips on how to increase one's comfort and options when dining alone. Presents information on notable solo-friendly restaurants in the US and other countries. Describes solo-dining amenities to look for or suggest to restaurants. Now includes tips on solo travel.

31261 ■ *Team Management Briefings*
Pub: Briefings Publishing Group
Contact: Deirdre Hackett, Managing Editor
E-mail: dhackett@briefings.com
Released: Monthly. **Price:** $138, U.S.; $158, Canada; $258, other countries. **Description:** Practical tips and tactics on running work teams. Covers topics such as communication, group dynamics, empowerment, coaching, and improving meetings.

VIDEOCASSETTES/ AUDIOCASSETTES

31262 ■ *How to Build a Profitable Consulting Practice 1 & 2*
Chesney Communications
2302 Martin St., Ste. 125
Irvine, CA 92612
Ph:(949)263-5500
Free: 800-223-8878
Fax: (949)263-5506
Released: 1987. **Price:** $59.95. **Description:** An entire Howard Shenson seminar about setting up a consulting practice, condensed into two hours. **Availability:** VHS; 3/4U.

CONSULTANTS

31263 ■ 2010 Fund 5
24351 Spartan St., Ste. 120
Mission Viejo, CA 92691
Ph:(949)583-1992
Scope: Funds in formation that will invest in technologies licensed from 30 universities. **Seminars:** Chair, Corporate Investment and Strategic Alliance Conferences.

31264 ■ ADG Group
4261 Northside Dr., Ste. 200
Atlanta, GA 30327
Ph:(404)264-9301
Fax: (404)261-3439
Scope: Corporate finance advisory firm specializing in arranging venture capital financing for emerging companies. Assists with mergers, acquisitions, and divestitures. Offers balance sheet restructuring services for bankrupt and financially troubled companies. Also offers independent due diligence investigations.

31265 ■ Advanced Benefits & Human Resources
9350-F Snowden River Pky., Ste. 222
Columbia, MD 21045
Ph:(410)290-9037
Fax: (410)740-2568
Co. E-mail: hrb@abhr.com

E-mail: hrb@abhr.com
Scope: Provides human resource consulting to high technology businesses. Offers services in the areas of human resources, benefits, and training. Creates, maintains, or updates current human resource functions.

31266 ■ The Advantage Group Inc.
38 Wellington St. E, Ste. 200
Toronto, ON, Canada M5E 1C7
Ph:(416)863-0685
Free: 800-671-1048
Fax: (416)863-0787
Co. E-mail: answers@advantagegroup.com
URL: http://www.advantagegroup.com

E-mail: answers@advantagegroup.com
Scope: Specializes in two key areas: performance benchmarking and pricing strategy. Each stream has developed a wide variety of customizable proprietary research tools to meet the needs of the clients. **Publications:** "7 Steps to building better customer relationships"; "How to Add Value to Customer Relationships"; "Top 10 Key Benefits of Building Business Relationships"; "Tips for Creating Better Relationships".

31267 ■ Advisory Management Services Inc.
9600 E 129th St., Ste. B
Kansas City, MO 64149-1025
Ph:(816)765-9611
Fax: (816)765-7447
Co. E-mail: amsi1@mindspring.com

E-mail: amsi1@mindspring.com
Scope: A management consulting and training firm specializing in employee relations, management and staff training, organizational development, strategic planning, and continuous quality improvement.

31268 ■ Aegis Communications Inc.
2 Greenwich Plz., Ste. 100
Greenwich, CT 06830
Ph:(203)622-4944
Scope: Marketing firm specializing in using visualization tools to help clients define communication needs and develop communication strategies and plans.

31269 ■ The Alliance Management Group Inc.
38 Old Chester Rd., Ste. 300
Gladstone, NJ 07934
Ph:(908)234-2344
Fax: (908)234-0638
Co. E-mail: Kathy@strategicalliance.com
URL: http://www.strategicalliance.com

E-mail: Kathy@strategicalliance.com
Publications: Allocating Patent Rights in Collaborative Research Agreements; Protecting Know-how and Trade Secrets in Collaborative Research Agreements, Aug, 2006; Sourcing External Technology for Innovation, Jun, 2006.

31270 ■ Alliance Management International Ltd.
PO Box 470691
Cleveland, OH 44147-0691
Ph:(440)838-1922
Fax: (928)752-5728
Co. E-mail: bgruss@cox.net
URL: http://www.members.cox.net/bgruss

E-mail: bgruss@cox.net
Scope: A consulting company that helps to form national and international strategic alliances. Handles alliances between companies forming joint ventures. Staff specialized in small company-large company alliance, alliance assessment and analysis, and alliance strategic planning. **Seminars:** Joint Business Planning; Developing a Shared Vision; Current and New/ Prospective Partner Assessment; Customer Service; Sales Training; Leader and Management Skills.

31271 ■ Alternative Services Inc.
32625 7 Mile Rd., Ste. 10
Livonia, MI 48152-4269
Ph:(248)471-4880
Fax: (248)471-5230
Scope: Provides social services management support to group homes for the mentally disabled. Also offers marketing, training, and financial services to businesses and nonprofit organizations.

31272 ■ Ambler Growth Strategy Consultants Inc.
3432 Reading Ave.
Hammonton, NJ 08037-8008
Ph:(609)567-9669
Free: 888-253-6662
Fax: (609)567-3810
Co. E-mail: ambler@ambler.com
URL: http://www.aldonna.com

E-mail: ambler@ambler.com
Scope: Growth strategies, strategic assessments, CEO coaching. **Publications:** "Celebrate Selling: The Consultative-Relationship Way". **Seminars:** Strategic Leadership; Managing Innovation; Breaking Through Classic Barriers to Growth; Energize Your Enterprise; Capture Your Competitive Advantage; Four Entrepreneurial Styles; Perservance and Resilience; Real-Time Strategic Planning/RO1. **Special Services:** The Growth Strategist™.

31273 ■ American English Academy
111 N Atlantic Blvd., Ste. 112
Monterey Park, CA 91754
Ph:(626)457-2800
Fax: (626)457-2808
Co. E-mail: admission@aea-usa.com
URL: http://www.aea-usa.com

E-mail: admission@aea-usa.com
Scope: Specializes in providing on-site English language and communication development for corporations and individuals. Also develops and delivers training in speaking, writing, pronunciation, grammar, and idioms with an emphasis on business communication. Offers individual, small group, intensive, and long-distance learning. All programs are tailor-made for each client. **Seminars:** Offers seminars on all aspects of English and cultural awareness.

31274 ■ Anderson/Roethle Inc.
700 N Water St., Ste. 1100
Milwaukee, WI 53202
Ph:(414)276-0070
Fax: (414)276-4364
Co. E-mail: info@anderson-roethle.com
URL: http://www.anderson-roethle.com

E-mail: info@anderson-roethle.com
Scope: Provides merger, acquisition and divestiture advisory services. Offers strategic planning, valuations and specialized M&A advisory services.

31275 ■ L.G. Anthony, Food Service Consultant
40 Wellington Blvd.
Reading, PA 19610
Ph:(610)670-0477
Scope: Provides food service facility planning, layout and design, including equipment selection and specification. Also offers management systems and operations analysis, such as the development of operating policies and procedures. Firm can design menu planning and recipe development, food selection and specification, work simplification, service, and quality control around current concepts in the field. Industries served: hospital, nursing home, restaurant, group homes; commercial and institutional food service industries. **Seminars:** Food Service Sanitation; Menu Planning; Work Simplification; Quality Control in Food Service.

31276 ■ Apex Innovations Inc.
14830 W 117th St., Ste. 200
PO Box 15208
Olathe, KS 66062
Ph:(816)561-7787
Fax: (913)254-0320
URL: http://www.apex-innovations.com
Scope: A firm of business operations and technology professionals providing solutions nationwide for business needs. Provides a bridge between operations and technology for clients in manufacturing, insurance, banking, and government. Offers services in business planning, assessment, education, business performance improvement, change management, and the planning, and implementation management of solutions. **Special Services:** i-INFO.

31277 ■ Scott Ashby Teleselling Inc.
1102 Ben Franklin Dr., Ste. 309
Sarasota, FL 34236
Ph:(941)388-4283
Fax: (941)388-5240
Co. E-mail: rscottashby@netscape.net
URL: http://www.scottashbyteleselling.com

E-mail: rscottashby@netscape.net
Scope: Provides consulting services and customized training programs that emphasize consultative telephone selling techniques. **Publications:** "How Will The Internet Affect Teleselling Programs?"; "When is Telemarketing Really Not Telemarketing?"; "The Future of Account Management Telesales".

31278 ■ Association of Home-Based Women Entrepreneurs
11330 Olive Blvd., Ste. 106
Saint Louis, MO 63141-7161

Ph:(314)995-1455
Fax: (314)909-8179
Co. E-mail: aschaefer@advbizsol.com
URL: http://www.hbwe.org

E-mail: aschaefer@advbizsol.com
Scope: A non-profit womens organization who target the needs of women entrepreneurs/business owners working from home based offices. **Seminars:** Twenty Five Key Steps To Maintaining A Successful Home-Based Business, Nov, 2006; Pyro Marketing, Jan, 2007.

31279 ■ Aurora Management Partners Inc.
4485 Tench Rd., Ste. 340A
Suwanee, GA 30024
Ph:(770)904-5207
Co. E-mail: rturcotte@auroramp.com
URL: http://www.auroramp.com

E-mail: rturcotte@auroramp.com
Scope: Firm specializes in turnaround management and reorganization consulting. **Publications:** Back From The Brink - Bland Farms; New Breed of Turnaround Managers; Key Performance Drivers - Bland Farms; The Missing Element in Corporate Governance Ratings.

31280 ■ Automated Accounting
13800 Heacock St.
Moreno Valley, CA 92553
Ph:(951)653-5053
Co. E-mail: autoacc@earthlink.net

E-mail: autoacc@earthlink.net
Scope: A business management consulting firm that caters to small businesses. Services include part-time chief, financial officer services. Also offers software installation services, tax preparation services and business plan advisory services.

31281 ■ Bahr International Inc.
PO Box 795
Gainesville, TX 76241
Ph:(940)665-2344
Fax: (940)665-2359
Co. E-mail: info@bahrintl.com
URL: http://www.bahrintl.com

E-mail: info@bahrintl.com
Scope: Offers consulting in general management, corporate polices and culture, and strategic and long-range planning. Provides management audits and reports and profit improvement programs. High level strategic marketing, advertising strategy/tactics, turnaround consulting and management.

31282 ■ Beacon Management Group Inc.
1000 W McNab Rd.
Pompano Beach, FL 33069
Ph:(954)782-1119
Free: 800-771-8721
Fax: (954)969-2566
Co. E-mail: md@beaconmgmt.com
URL: http://www.beaconmgmt.com

E-mail: md@beaconmgmt.com
Scope: Provides entrepreneurial companies with managerial and financial expertise. Services include strategic and business planning; corporate finance; franchise development services; information management; turnaround management and consulting; and joint venture, strategic alliances and acquisition services, including due diligence, market intelligence, targeted searches, valuation, negotiation, and deal structure. Provides assistance for financially-troubled companies, not-for-profits and the public sector

31283 ■ Benchmark Consulting Group Inc.
110 Broad St.
Boston, MA 02110-3030
Ph:(617)482-7661
Fax: (617)423-2158
Scope: Provides financial and management services to companies. Helps companies grow through debt and equity sourcing and restructuring, business valuation, acquisition/divestiture, computer information systems, and improved operation profitability.

31284 ■ Bio-Technical Resources
1035 S 7th St.
Manitowoc, WI 54220
Ph:(920)684-5518
Fax: (920)684-5519
Co. E-mail: info@biotechresources.com
URL: http://www.biotechresources.com

E-mail: info@biotechresources.com
Scope: Provides innovative solutions for the development of biotechnology products and processes through contract services in research and development, bioprocess scale-up, pilot scale manufacturing, technology and economic assessments. **Publications:** "Reduction of Background Interference in the Spectrophotometric Assay of Mevalonate Kinase," 2006; "A Soluble Form of Phosphatase in Saccharomyces cerevisiae Capable of Converting Farnesyl Diphosphate to E, E-Farnesol," 2006; "Ascorbate Biosynthesis: A Diversity of Pathways," BIOS Scientific Publishers, 2004; "The Biotechnology of Ascorbic Acid Manufacture," BIOS Scientific Publishers, 2004; "Detection of Farnesyl Diphosphate Accumulation in Yeast ERG9 Mutants," 2003; "Reverse Two-Hybrid System: Detecting Critical Interaction Domains and Screening for Inhibitors," Eaton Publishing, 2000. **Seminars:** Metabolic Engineering for Industrial Production of Glucosamine and N-Acetylglucosamine, Soc. Ind. Micro. Annual Meeting, Aug, 2003; Metabolic Engineering of E. coli for the Industrial Production of Glucosamine, Seventh Annual Symposium on Industrial and Fermentation Microbiology, Apr, 2003.

31285 ■ BioChem Technology Inc.
100 Ross Rd., Ste. 201
King of Prussia, PA 19406
Ph:(610)768-9360
Fax: (610)768-9363
Co. E-mail: sales@biochemtech.com
URL: http://www.biochemtech.com

E-mail: sales@biochemtech.com
Scope: Consultants in wastewater treatment processes specializing in evaluation and optimization of biological nutrient removal facilities. On-line process monitoring and control of wastewater treatment processes as well as yeast, bacterial or fungal fermentation. Experience in biochemical process development, wastewater treatment process design, fermentation system design, process and plant design, biochemical engineering research and a variety of engineering specialties. Undertakes a wide variety of projects which range from preliminary feasibility studies to the development and optimization of a biological process. **Special Services:** BioGuide®; BioChem®.

31286 ■ BioSciCon Inc.
14905 Forest Landing Cir.
Rockville, MD 20850
Ph:(301)610-9130
Fax: (301)610-7662
Co. E-mail: info@BioSciCon.com
URL: http://www.bioscicon.com

E-mail: info@BioSciCon.com
Scope: Sponsoring development of the technology of the Pap test accuracy via introduction of a new biomarker that enhances visibility of abnormal cells on Pap smears or monolayers of cervical cells obtained in solution. Conducts clinical trials for assessment of the test efficacy and safety, manufactures research tools for conduct of trials, and markets IP to license manufacturing, marketing, sales and distribution rights of the new technology line of products. **Publications:** "Cervical acid phosphatase: A biomarker of cervical dysplasia and potential surrogate endpoint for colposcopy," 2004; "Journal of Clinical Oncology," 2004. **Special Services:** MarkPap®.

31287 ■ Birchfield Jacobs Foodsystems Inc.
519 N Charles St., Ste. 350A
Baltimore, MD 21201
Ph:(410)528-8700
Fax: (410)528-6060
Co. E-mail: marketing@birchfieldjacobs.com
URL: http://www.birchfieldjacobs.com

E-mail: marketing@birchfieldjacobs.com
Scope: Food facilities design consultants for colleges, universities, schools, healthcare facilities, government, military, correctional, country clubs, and restaurants. Services include facilities design, feasibility studies, operations analysis, and master planning.

31288 ■ Blankinship & Associates Inc.
322 C St.
Davis, CA 95616
Ph:(530)757-0941
Fax: (530)757-0940
Co. E-mail: blankinship@envtox.com
URL: http://www.envtox.com

E-mail: blankinship@envtox.com
Scope: A human resource management and development consulting firm specializing in small to medium size businesses.

31289 ■ C. Clint Bolte & Associates
809 Philadelphia Ave.
Chambersburg, PA 17201
Ph:(717)263-5768
Fax: (717)263-8945
Co. E-mail: clint@clintbolte.com
URL: http://www.clintbolte.com

E-mail: clint@clintbolte.com
Scope: Provides management consulting services to firms involved with the printing industry. Services include outsourcing studies, graphics supply chain management studies, company and equipment valuations, plant layout services, litigation support, fulfillment warehouse consulting and product development services. **Publications:** "Time to Break Through the Glass Ceiling," The Seybold Report, May, 2006; "Challenges & Opportunities Presented by Postal Rate Increases," The Seybold Report, May, 2006; "Packaging Roll Sheeting Comes of Age," The Seybold Report, May, 2006; "Diversifying With Mailing & Fulfillment Services," The Seybold Report, Jan, 2006.

31290 ■ BPT Consulting Associates Ltd.
12 Parmenter Rd., Ste. B6
Londonderry, NH 03053
Ph:(603)437-8484
Co. E-mail: bptcons@tiac.net
URL: http://www.bptconsulting.com

E-mail: bptcons@tiac.net
Scope: Provides management consulting expertise and resources to cross-industry clients with services for: Business Management consulting, People/Human Resources Transition and Training programs, and a full cadre of multi-disciplined Technology Computer experts. Virtual consultants with expertise in e-commerce, supply chain management, organizational development, and business application development consulting. **Seminars:** Business: MRPII, DRPII, JIT/TQC. Business Requirements Analysis, Small Business Start-Up, Strategic Planning. People: Team Building, Performance Evaluation, Career Transition and Counseling Seminars. Technology: User Training for Customized Software, Internet, Full array of application development, i.e., C, Java, website development. **Special Services:** Provides a full array of computer and related user training services. Resources include application developers, database developers and managers, project management experts for a full array of industries (manufacturing, software, defense, healthcare, pharmaceutical, and small business).

31291 ■ Bran Management Services Inc.
7116 Lupton Dr., Ste. 100
Dallas, TX 75225-1735
Ph:(214)739-2340
Fax: (214)739-2360
Scope: Offers management consulting services to companies in manufacturing, distribution and services to help them cope with growth and change. Helps small businesses create and identify product strategies. Services include developing international business opportunities; turnaround management; sales and marketing development; business planning; acquisitions and mergers.

31292 ■ Business Consulting Services
PO Box 431
Swarthmore, PA 19081
Ph:(610)328-9806
Co. E-mail: bcs@consultbiz.com
URL: http://www.consultbiz.com

E-mail: bcs@consultbiz.com
Scope: Specializes in the improvement of business operations and the planning and implementation of information technology strategies. **Publications:** "If You Fail To Plan"; "The True Cost Of Technology"; "Why Projects Fail"; "Planning For A Business Disruption". **Seminars:** How To Select, Manage and Contract Consultants, and Other Resources; How To Market Professional Services.

31293 ■ Business Education Associates
PO Box 4
Bethel, CT 06801
Ph:(203)798-6035
Co. E-mail: bob@ashfordgrp.com
URL: http://www.ashfordgrp.com

E-mail: bob@ashfordgrp.com
Scope: Offers tailored management education programs. Has been designed to meet the business education needs of companies implementing new systems and companies to re-educate users of existing systems. **Publications:** "The Ashford Group and TQuist Partner to Provide High Impact Manufacturing Solutions"; "The Future of ERP".

31294 ■ Business Improvement Architects
33 Riderwood Dr.
Toronto, ON, Canada M2L 2X4
Ph:(416)444-8225
Free: (866)346-3242
Fax: (416)444-6743
Co. E-mail: info@bia.ca
URL: http://www.bia.ca

E-mail: info@bia.ca
Scope: Specializes in management training, project management, marketing planning, promotions and incentives.

31295 ■ ByrneMRG
22 Isle of Pines Dr.
Hilton Head Island, SC 29928
Ph:(215)630-7411
Free: 888-816-8080
Co. E-mail: info@byrnemrg.com
URL: http://www.byrnemrg.com

E-mail: info@byrnemrg.com
Scope: Firm specializes in management consulting, including department management, equipment evaluation and selection, project management, R and D planning, and database design and management. **Publications:** "Implementing Solutions to Everyday Issues".

31296 ■ Capell & Associates
2038 18th St. NW, Ste. 403
Washington, DC 20009
Ph:(202)332-6272
Fax: (202)332-7478
Co. E-mail: dan_capell@att.net

E-mail: dan_capell@att.net
Scope: Consultant for magazine publishing industry, particularly in the area of circulation.

31297 ■ Casino, Hotel & Resort Consultants L.L.C.
8100 Via Del Cerro Ct.
Las Vegas, NV 89117
Ph:(702)646-7200
Fax: (702)646-6680
Co. E-mail: info@hraba.com
URL: http://www.hraba.com

E-mail: info@hraba.com
Scope: Casino and hospitality industry consultants. Firm specializes in developing and implementing cus-

tomized forecast and labor management control systems that deliver immediate, positive impact to the company's bottom line. We are involved in production planning, emply surveys and communication, inventory management, business process reviews, audits, development and implementation of key management reports. **Seminars:** Payroll Cost Control and Effective Staff Scheduling

31298 ■ CBIZ Inc.
6050 Oak Tree, Blvd. S, Ste. 500
Cleveland, OH 44131
Ph:(216)447-9000
Fax: (216)447-9007
Co. E-mail: info@cbiz.com
URL: http://www.cbiz.com

E-mail: info@cbiz.com
Scope: A business consulting and tax services firm providing financial, consulting, tax and business services through seven groups: financial management, tax advisory, construction and real estate, healthcare, litigation support, capital resource, and CEO outsource.

31299 ■ Center for Lifestyle Enhancement - Columbia Medical Center of Plano
Medical Center of Plano, 3901 W 15th St.
Plano, TX 75075
Ph:(972)596-6800
Fax: (972)519-1299
Co. E-mail: mcp.cle@hcahealthcare.com
URL: http://www.medicalcenterofplano.com

E-mail: mcp.cle@hcahealthcare.com
Scope: Provides professional health counseling in the areas of general nutrition for weight management, eating disorders, diabetic education, cholesterol reduction, and adolescent weight management. Offers work site health promotion and preventive services. Also coordinates speaker's bureau, cooking classes, and physician referrals. Industries served: education, insurance, healthcare, retail/wholesale, data processing, and manufacturing in Dallas, Ft. Worth, and Collin County, Texas. **Seminars:** Rx Diet and Exercise; Smoking Cessation; Stress Management; Health Fairs; Fitness Screenings; Body Composition; Nutrition Analysis; Exercise Classes; Prenatal Nutrition; SHAPEDOWN; Successfully Managing Diabetes.

31300 ■ The Center for Organizational Excellence
15200 Shady Grove Rd., Ste. 400
Rockville, MD 20850
Ph:(301)948-1922
Free: 877-674-3923
Fax: (301)948-2158
Co. E-mail: results@center4oe.com
URL: http://www.center4oe.com

E-mail: results@center4oe.com
Scope: An organizational effectiveness consulting firm specializing in helping organizations achieve results through people, process, and performance. Service areas include organizational performance systems, leadership systems, customer systems, and learning systems.

31301 ■ Center for Personal Empowerment
102 N Main St.
Columbia, IL 62236-1702
Ph:(618)281-3565
Fax: (618)476-7083
Co. E-mail: personalempowerment@wholenet.net

E-mail: personalempowerment@wholenet.net
Scope: Private consultations and trainings to educate on how to determine which emotions, events, beliefs from the past prevent you from achieving success. Methods used include Time Line Therapy, News Linguistic Programming and hypnosis. Behavior Modification through NLP trainings. **Seminars:** NLP Practitioner Training, Hypnosis Certification Training, Lifemap Seminars.

31302 ■ CEO Advisors
848 Brickell Ave., Ste. 603
Miami, FL 33131

Ph:(305)371-8560
Fax: (305)371-8563
Co. E-mail: info@ceoadvisors.us
URL: http://www.ceoadvisors.us

E-mail: info@ceoadvisors.us
Scope: Specializes in strategic planning; profit enhancement; start-up businesses; venture capital; appraisals and valuations. **Seminars:** Innovation and High Performance Organizations.

31303 ■ CFI Group USA L.L.C.
625 Avis Dr.
Ann Arbor, MI 48108
Ph:(734)930-9090
Fax: (734)930-0911
Co. E-mail: contactcfi@cfigroup.com
URL: http://www.cfigroup.com

E-mail: contactcfi@cfigroup.com
Scope: Management consulting firm that helps its clients worldwide to maximize shareholder value by optimizing customer and employee satisfaction. **Publications:** "Consumers Rate the Post-Boom Industry," Mortgage Banking, Jan, 2005"; "Interview with a Customer Satisfaction Guru," Rotman Magazine, 2005".

31304 ■ CFO Service
112 Chester Ave.
Saint Louis, MO 63122
Ph:(314)757-2940
Co. E-mail: jskae@cfoservice.com
URL: http://www.cfoservice.com

E-mail: jskae@cfoservice.com
Scope: A group of professional executives that provide upper management services to companies that cannot support a full time COO or CFO. Provides clients in the areas of business planning, company policies, contract negotiations, safety policies, product and service pricing, loans management, taxes, cost analysis, loss control and budgeting.

31305 ■ Chamberlain & Cansler Inc.
2251 Perimeter Park Dr.
Atlanta, GA 30341
Ph:(770)457-5699
Scope: Firm specializes in strategic planning; profit enhancement; small business management; interim management; crisis management; turnarounds.

31306 ■ Charismedia
610 W End Ave.
New York, NY 10001
Ph:(212)362-6808
Fax: (212)362-6809
Co. E-mail: info@Charismedia.net
URL: http://www.charismedia.net

E-mail: info@Charismedia.net
Scope: Offers speech and image training as well as speech writing services for effective presentation skills. **Publications:** "The New Secrets of Charisma," McGraw-Hill. **Seminars:** Charisma Skills Training-The best investment for successful careers and relationships; Three-stage Anti-Stagefright Breathing.

31307 ■ Chartered Management Co.
125 S Wacker Dr., Ste. 300
Chicago, IL 60606-4402
Ph:(312)214-2575
Scope: Operations improvement consultants. Specializes in strategic planning; feasibility studies; management audits and reports; profit enhancement; start-up businesses; mergers and acquisitions; joint ventures; divestitures; interim management; crisis management; turnarounds; business process re-engineering; venture capital; and due diligence.

31308 ■ The Children's Psychological Trauma Center
31 Clara Ave.
South San Francisco, CA 94080
Ph:(650)589-7989
Fax: (650)589-7989
Co. E-mail: gil.kliman@cphc-sf.org

URL: http://www.expertchildpsychiatry.org

E-mail: gil.kliman@cphc-sf.org

Scope: Treats those with psychological trauma claimed from stressors including institutional negligence, vehicular and aviation accidents, wrongful death in the family, rape, molestation, fire, explosion, flood, earthquake, loss of parents, terrorism, kidnapping, disfiguring events, emotional damage from social work, medical malpractice or defective products. Provides evaluation and reports to referring professionals. Experienced in forensic consultation and testimony. **Publications:** "The practice of behavioural treatment in the acute rehabilitation setting"

31309 ■ Claremont Consulting Group
4525 Castle Ln.
La Canada, CA 91011-1436
Ph:(818)249-0584
Fax: (818)249-5811
Scope: Consulting, coaching, training, & litigation support in project management, engineering management, system engineering & cost estimating. **Publications:** Over 85 publications, including, "What Every Engineer Should Know About Project Management." **Seminars:** Project Management, System Engineering & Cost Estimating.

31310 ■ Clayton/Curtis/Cottrell
1722 Madison Ct.
Louisville, CO 80027
Ph:(303)665-2005
Fax: (303)665-2276
Scope: Firm specializes packaged goods, telecommunications, direct marketing & printing, & packaging industries. Services include strategic planning; profit enhancement; start-up businesses; mergers and acquisitions; joint ventures; divestitures; interim management; crisis management; turnarounds; market size, segmentation and rates of growth; competitor intelligence; image & reputation, & competitive analysis.

31311 ■ Columbia Consultants
5010 Dorsey Hall Dr., Ste. 202
Ellicott City, MD 21042-7860
Ph:(410)992-4700
Fax: (410)992-4910
Scope: A complete personnel service offering placement of both permanent and temporary employees.

31312 ■ Comer & Associates L.L.C.
5255 Holmes Pl.
Boulder, CO 80303
Ph:(303)786-7986
Free: 888-950-3190
Fax: (303)473-9830
URL: http://www.comerassociates.com
Scope: Specialize in developing markets & businesses. Marketing support includes: developing & writing strategic & tactical business plans; developing & writing focused, effective market plans; researching market potential & competition; implementing targeted marketing tactics to achieve company objectives; conducting customer surveys to determine satisfaction & attitudes toward client. Maintains a network of database research specialists, market communications providers, public relations firms, internet resources, focus group facilitators, technical writers & executive recruiters to assist with any project. Organization development support includes: executive/management training programs; executive coaching; team building; developing effective organization structures & proscesses; management of change in dynamic & competitive environments; individual coaching for management & leadership effectiveness. **Seminars:** Developing a strategic market plan; market research: defining your opportunity; management & leadership effectiveness; team building; developing a business plan.

31313 ■ C.C. Comfort Consulting
3370 N Hayden Rd.
Scottsdale, AZ 85251
Ph:(602)483-8364
Co. E-mail: cccomfortcfe@martindalemail.com

E-mail: cccomfortcfe@martindalemail.com

Scope: Evaluates, develops and implements financial, operational and compliance management systems' strategies, programs and practices. Professional recognition as Certified Public Accountant, Internal Auditor, Cost Analyst and Fraud Examiner plus investigatory, law enforcement, and court experience ensure confidential handling of sensitive and legal matters. Works with management, audit, legal, security and outside personnel to evaluate and improve compliance, efficiency and effectiveness.

31314 ■ Consultants National Resource Center
27-A Big Spring Rd.
PO Box 430
Clear Spring, MD 21722
Ph:(301)791-9332
Free: 800-290-3196
Fax: (301)582-3639
Scope: Provides marketing and strategic planning services for consultants. Also serves as membership center for the professional management institute. Industries served: all consulting disciplines. **Publications:** "Consulting Opportunities Journal"; "How to Master Continuous Learning". **Seminars:** how to series on starting and building a consulting practice; Introduction to the Professional Management Institute; Consulting Bootcamp; Planagement®.

31315 ■ Consulting & Conciliation Service
3405 I St., Ste. 2
Sacramento, CA 95816
Ph:(916)396-0480
Free: 888-898-9780
Co. E-mail: peace@conciliation.org
URL: http://www.conciliation.org

E-mail: peace@conciliation.org
Scope: Offers consulting and conciliation services. Provides pre-mediation counseling, training and research on preparing for a peaceful society, mediation and facilitation, and preparation for shifts in structure, policy and personnel. Offers sliding scale business rates and free individual consultation.

31316 ■ The Consulting Exchange
1770 Mass Ave., Ste. 288
Cambridge, MA 02140
Ph:(617)576-2100
Free: 800-824-4828
Co. E-mail: gday@cx.com
URL: http://www.cx.com

E-mail: gday@cx.com
Scope: A consultant referral service for management and technical consultants. Serves a local, regional, and international client base. **Publications:** "Getting Full Value From Consulting is in Your Hands", May 25, 1998; "Looking for a Consultant?", June 2, 2001.

31317 ■ Consulting Partners Inc.
14911 Quorum Dr., Ste. 120
Dallas, TX 75254
Ph:(972)386-7858
Fax: (972)386-8667
Co. E-mail: info@consultingpartners.com
URL: http://www.consultingpartners.com

E-mail: info@consultingpartners.com
Scope: We are a Modis company, specializing in technical communications, technical writing, custom instructor-led training, computer-based training, web-based training, language translation, documentation, and editing.

31318 ■ The Consulting Source Inc.
1403 S Addison Ct.
Aurora, CO 80018-6003
Ph:(303)366-4800
Free: 800-520-1998
Fax: (303)366-4801
Co. E-mail: info@consultingsource.com
URL: http://www.consultingsource.com

E-mail: info@consultingsource.com
Scope: A consultant search and referral service, this firm has more than 25 years experience helping companies identify the best professional expertise to meet their consulting requirements. Will find the most effective match from within its own database or will search national, regional and local consulting firms for the right fit. Services are provided free of charge to client companies in all industries in the US Fee-based services provided for RFP development, reference checks and selection assistance.

31319 ■ The Corlund Group L.L.C.
101 Federal St., Ste. 310
Boston, MA 02110
Ph:(617)423-9364
Fax: (617)423-9371
Co. E-mail: info@corlundgroup.com
URL: http://www.corlundgroup.com

E-mail: info@corlundgroup.com
Scope: Boutique firms offers services in the areas of leadership, governance, and change, with a particular focus on CEO and senior executive succession planning, including assessment, development, and orchestrating succession processes with management and Boards of Directors. Also Board governance effectiveness. **Publications:** "Leadership Due Diligence: The Neglected Governance Frontier," Directorship, Sep, 2001; "Leadership Due Diligence: Managing the Risks," The Corporate Board, Aug, 2001; "Succession: The need for detailed insight," Directors and Boards, 2001; "CEO Succession: Who's Doing Due Diligence?," 2001.

31320 ■ Donna Cornell Enterprises Inc.
68 N Plank Rd., Ste. 204
Newburgh, NY 12550-2122
Ph:(845)565-0088
Fax: (845)565-0084
Co. E-mail: rc@cornellcareercenter.com
URL: http://www.dce.com

E-mail: rc@cornellcareercenter.com
Scope: Offers services in career consultant, professional search, job placement, and national professional search. **Publications:** "The Power of the Woman Within".

31321 ■ Corporate Consulting Inc.
3333 Belcaro Dr.
Denver, CO 80209
Ph:(303)698-9292
Fax: (303)698-9292
Co. E-mail: corpcons@compuserve.com

E-mail: corpcons@compuserve.com
Scope: Specializes in feasibility studies; organizational development; small business management; mergers and acquisitions; joint ventures; divestitures; interim management; crisis management; turnarounds; financing; appraisals and valuations; and due diligence studies.

31322 ■ COTC Technologies Inc.
44 E Spaulding Ste. 1A
Pueblo West, CO 81007
Ph:(719)547-0938
Free: 888-547-0938
Fax: (719)547-1105
Co. E-mail: info@cotc-consulting.com
URL: http://www.cotc-consulting.com

E-mail: info@cotc-consulting.com
Scope: Provides software consulting services to organizations that require assistance with their HP3000 Computer System. Provides systems analysis, programming, operations support, system management, and performance specialists. Also provides PC software and hardware support and consulting. Additionally, they provide various training for the HP3000 computer system. Industries served: healthcare, aerospace procurement, aerospace proposal activities, HP3000 computer systems. **Special Services:** HP3000 MPE, MPE/IX, MPE/IX, Turbo Image DBMS, Image/SQL DAMS, COBOL, DBA Activities, AMISYS, JCL, Utilities, PC DOS, Windows 3.1, Windows 98, Windows 95, SQL, and Systems Administration.

31323 ■ Coyne Associates
4010 E Lake St.
Minneapolis, MN 55406
Ph:(612)724-1188
Fax: (612)722-1379
Scope: A marketing and public relations consulting firm specializing in assisting architectural, engineering, and contractor/developer firms. Services include marketing plains and audits, strategic planning, corporate identity, turnarounds, and sales training.

31324 ■ Creative Computer Resources Inc.
5001 Horizons Dr., Ste. 200
Columbus, OH 43220
Ph:(614)384-7557
Fax: (614)573-6331
Co. E-mail: team@Planet-CCR.com
URL: http://www.planet-ccr.com

E-mail: team@Planet-CCR.com
Scope: Offers information systems support, custom software development, web site design, development and implementation. Provides information technology support and management services to small and mid-size businesses.

31325 ■ Crystal Clear Communications Inc.
8989 N Port Washington Rd., Ste. 210
Milwaukee, WI 53217-1667
Ph:(414)228-8799
Scope: Specializes in strategic planning; organizational development; small business management; mergers and acquisitions; joint ventures; divestitures; strategy implementation; executive coaching.

31326 ■ Development Resource Consultants
PO Box 118
Rancho Cucamonga, CA 91729
Ph:(909)902-7655
Fax: (909)476-6942
Co. E-mail: info@gotodrc.com

E-mail: info@gotodrc.com
Scope: A small business advisory service specializing in office re-organization, employee training in office organization, communication skills, sales training and career counseling.

31327 ■ The Devine Group Inc.
10200 Alliance Rd., Ste. 310
Cincinnati, OH 45242
Ph:(513)792-7500
Free: (866)792-7500
Fax: (513)793-8535
Co. E-mail: sales@devinegroup.com
URL: http://www.devinegroup.com

E-mail: sales@devinegroup.com
Scope: A human resource consulting company devoted to providing reliable and responsive information focusing on performance issues and answers. Dedicated to analyzing and enhancing job performance. Custom design and implement programs and workshops that will result in demonstrable behavior change on the job. Assist clients enhance their productivity via behavior analysis. **Seminars:** The Devine Inventory™ Level One Training, Feb, 2006. **Special Services:** Devine Inventory®.

31328 ■ DiamondCluster International Inc.
875 N Michigan Ave., Ste. 3000
John Hancock Ctr.
Chicago, IL 60611
Ph:(312)255-5000
Fax: (312)255-6000
Co. E-mail: info@diamondcluster.com
URL: http://www.diamondcluster.com

E-mail: info@diamondcluster.com
Scope: Provides business consulting services to help companies develop business strategies. Bridges the gap between strategy definition and the implementation of that strategy. **Publications:** *Context* Magazine.

31329 ■ Dimond Hospitality Consulting Group Inc.
5710 Stoneway Trl.
Nashville, TN 37209

Ph:(615)353-0033
Fax: (615)352-5290
Co. E-mail: dimond@dimondconsultinggroup.com
URL: http://www.dimondconsultinggroup.com

E-mail: dimond@dimondconsultinggroup.com
Scope: Specializes in strategic planning; start-up businesses; business process re-engineering; team building; competitive analysis; venture capital; competitive intelligence; and due diligence. Offers litigation support. Comprehensive hospitality consulting firm that serves as an adviser to leading hotel companies, independent hotels, lending institutions, trustees, law firms, investment companies and municipalities in the areas of:Asset management, Acquisition due diligence, Arbitration ,Disposition advisory services, Exit strategies, Financial review and analysis, Impact studies, Mediation.

31330 ■ Diversified Health Resources Inc.
875 N Michigan Ave., Ste. 3250
Chicago, IL 60611-1901
Ph:(312)266-0466
Fax: (312)266-0715
URL: http://www.diversifiedhealth.net
Scope: Offers healthcare consulting for hospitals, nursing homes (including homes for the aged), and other health-related facilities and companies. Specializes in planning and marketing. Also conducts executive searches for top level healthcare administrative positions. Serves private industries as well as government agencies.

31331 ■ DRI Consulting
2 Otter Ln.
North Oaks, MN 55127-6436
Ph:(651)415-1400
Free: (866)276-4600
Fax: (651)415-9968
Co. E-mail: dric@dric.com
URL: http://www.dric.com

E-mail: dric@dric.com
Scope: Licensed psychologists providing organization and management consulting. developing leaders, managers and individuals through coaching, business strategy, career development, crisis management, policy consultation and technology optimization.

31332 ■ Dropkin & Co.
390 George St.
New Brunswick, NJ 08901
Ph:(732)828-3211
Fax: (732)828-4118
Co. E-mail: murray@dropkin.com
URL: http://www.dropkin.com

E-mail: murray@dropkin.com
Scope: Firm specializes in feasibility studies; business management; business process re-engineering; and team building, healthcare and housing. **Publications:** "Guide to Auditing Nonprofit Organizations"; "The Cash Flow Management Book for Nonprofits"

31333 ■ Dubuc Lucke & Co.
414 Walnut St., Ste607
Cincinnati, OH 45202
Ph:(513)579-8330
Fax: (513)241-6669
Scope: Consulting services in the areas of profit enhancement; small business management; mergers and acquisitions; joint ventures; divestitures; interim management; crisis management; turnarounds; appraisals; valuations; due diligence; and international trade.

31334 ■ The DuMond Group
5282 Princeton Ave.
Westminster, CA 92683-2753
Ph:(714)373-0610
Scope: Firm specializes in organizational development; small business management; employee surveys and communication; performance appraisals; and team building.

31335 ■ Dunelm International
14 S Bryn Mawr Ave., Ste. 206
Bryn Mawr, PA 19010-3216

Ph:(610)520-4491
Fax: (610)520-4492
Scope: Firm specializes in feasibility studies; start-up businesses; interim management; crisis management; turnarounds; business process re-engineering; sales forecasting; supply chain solution and project management.

31336 ■ Eastern Point Consulting Group Inc.
75 Oak St.
Newton, MA 02464
Ph:(617)965-4141
Fax: (617)965-4172
Co. E-mail: info@eastpt.com
URL: http://www.eastpt.com

E-mail: info@eastpt.com
Scope: Specializes in bringing practical solutions to complex challenges. Provides consultation and training in managing diversity; comprehensive sexual-harassment policies and programs; organizational development; benchmarks 360 skills assessment; executive coaching; strategic human resource planning; team building; leadership development for women; mentoring programs; and gender issues in the workplace. **Seminars:** Leadership Development for Women.

31337 ■ Education Development Center
55 Chapel St.
Newton, MA 02458-1060
Ph:(617)969-7100
Free: 800-225-4276
Fax: (617)969-5979
Co. E-mail: comment@edc.org
URL: http://www.edc.org

E-mail: comment@edc.org
Scope: Non-profit organization; Health and Human Development Programs division specializes in promoting health and justice across the life cycle in many settings. HHD conducts research, evaluation, program development and professional development activities.

31338 ■ Effective Compensation Inc.
3609 S Wadsworth Blvd., Ste. 260
Lakewood, CO 80235
Ph:(303)854-1000
Free: 877-746-4324
Fax: (303)854-1030
Co. E-mail: eci@effectivecompensation.com
URL: http://www.effectivecompensation.com

E-mail: eci@effectivecompensation.com
Scope: Helps organizations determine how to competitively pay their employees. Provides quality, culture sensitive, compensation consulting assistance to all types of employers. **Publications:** Industry Compensation Surveys.

31339 ■ Effective Resources Inc.
2803 Southfield Ct.
Holiday, FL 34691-2505
Ph:(727)944-2507
Free: 800-288-6044
Fax: (727)944-2607
Co. E-mail: customerservice@effectiveresources.com
URL: http://www.effectiveresources.com

E-mail: customerservice@effectiveresources.com
Scope: Concerned with technical aspects of human resource management. Specializes in compensation and incentive plans; performance appraisals; team building; and personnel policies and procedures; affirmative action plan preparation.

31340 ■ Effectiveness Resource Group Inc.
PO Box 7149
Bellevue, WA 98008-1149
Ph:(206)949-4171
Fax: (425)957-9186
Co. E-mail: don@consultdon.com
URL: http://www.consultdon.com

E-mail: don@consultdon.com

Scope: Provides problem-solving help to client organizations in public and private sectors so they can release and mobilize the full potential of their personnel to achieve productive and satisfying results. Emphasis is on technical/human productivity improvement projects and systems, total human resource systems design and implementation, and a whole systems approach to organizational change design and implementation. Serves private industries as well as government agencies. Consults with both internal and external consultants via e-mail and phone. Also offers executive coaching. **Seminars:** Life/Work Goals Exploration; Influencing Change Thru Consultation; Designing and Leading Participative Meetings; Designing, Leading and Managing Change; Project Management and Leadership; Performance Management; Productive Management of Differences; Performance Correction.

31341 ■ Environmental Health Science Inc.
418 Wall St.
Princeton, NJ 08540
Ph:(609)924-7616
Free: 800-841-8923
Fax: (609)924-0793
Co. E-mail: info@speechgeneratingdevices.com
URL: http://www.speechgeneratingdevices.com

E-mail: info@speechgeneratingdevices.com
Scope: Specialists in rehabilitation technology for speech disorder and physically disabled persons. Offers demonstrations, evaluations and sales of the following types of equipment: augmentative speech communication systems, adaptive switches and specialty controls, and computer access devices. Industries served: hospitals and rehabilitation centers, schools, and special service organizations such as United Cerebral Palsy Association, Department of Human Services, etc. **Seminars:** Augmentative Communication and Assistive Devices.

31342 ■ Everest Marketing
957 Ashland Ave.
Saint Paul, MN 55104
Ph:(612)581-1333
Fax: (651)221-1978
Co. E-mail: aistrup@aistrup.com
URL: http://www.aistrup.com

E-mail: aistrup@aistrup.com
Scope: Provides business-to-business marketing services including marketing plan development, marketing communications, market research and business intelligence. **Publications:** "Finding and Using Local Market Research To Improve Your Sales"; "Marketing to the Right People at the Right Time"; "Marketing in a Sales-Driven Environment"; "Money Well Spent! (Eight Steps to a successful consulting project)"; "Does this sound like you?"; "Marketing Quickies". **Seminars:** Market Research Basics for Managers; Profiting from Your Customer Database; Developing Your Strategic Marketing Plan from the Ground Up; A Team Process for Developing Your Marketing Plan; Developing a Commercialization Plan for Your SBIR (Small Business Innovation Research) Proposal; Using Marketing Strategies to Jump-Start Your Sales; Marketing in a Sales-Driven Environment & Marketing in a Technology-Driven Environment.

31343 ■ Everett & Co.
3126 S Franklin St.
Englewood, CO 80113
Ph:(303)761-7999
Fax: (303)781-8296
Co. E-mail: everettco@qwest.net
URL: http://www.everettco.com

E-mail: everettco@qwest.net
Scope: Management and financial consultants provide business planning, start-up assistance as well as in-depth financial and project analysis. Helps plan for increased cash flow and working capital reduction. Industries served: manufacturing, wholesaling, service and technological. Corporate United States subsidiary creation and maintenance services for international firms.

31344 ■ Facility Directions Inc.
PO Box 761
Manchester, MO 63011
Ph:(636)256-4400
Free: 800-536-0044
Fax: (636)227-2868
Co. E-mail: info@facilitydirections.com
URL: http://www.facilitydirections.com

E-mail: walty@facilitydirections.com
Scope: Firm specializes in service to financial institutions; strategic planning; feasibility studies; facility and space planning; attitude surveys; site selection. **Publications:** Newsletter — "Directions".

31345 ■ Family Resource Center on Disabilities
20 E Jackson Blvd., Rm. 300
Chicago, IL 60604
Ph:(312)939-3513
Free: 800-952-4199
Fax: (312)939-7297
Co. E-mail: contact@frcd.org
URL: http://www.frcd.org

E-mail: contact@frcd.org
Scope: Provides consulting services to advocacy groups and individuals seeking support for children with disabilities. **Publications:** "How to Get Services by Being Assertive"; "How to Organize an Effective Parent/Advocacy Group and Move Bureaucracies"; "MAINROADS Travel to Tomorrow - a Road Map for the Future". **Seminars:** How to Support Parents as Effective Advocates; How to Get Services by Being Assertive; How to Develop an Awareness Program for Nondisabled Children; How to Organize a Parent Support Group; How to Move Bureaucratic Mountains; How to Raise Money Painlessly through Publishing; How to Use Humor in Public Presentations.

31346 ■ FCP Consulting
500 Sutter St., Ste. 507
San Francisco, CA 94102
Ph:(415)956-5558
Fax: (415)956-5722
Co. E-mail: cox@coxcmc.com
URL: http://www.coxcmc.com

E-mail: cox@coxcmc.com
Scope: Management consulting in Business-To-Business sales.

31347 ■ Federer Resources Inc.
106 E 6th St.
Austin, TX 78701-3659
Ph:(512)476-8800
Scope: Firm specializes in feasibility studies; start-up businesses; small business management; mergers and acquisitions; joint ventures; divestitures; interim management; crisis management; turnarounds; production planning; team building; appraisals and valuations.

31348 ■ First Strike Management Consulting Inc.
401 Loblolly Ave.
PO Box 1188
Little River, SC 29566-1188
Ph:(843)385-6338
Fax: (843)390-1004
Co. E-mail: fsmc.hq@fsmc.com
URL: http://www.fsmc.com

E-mail: fsmc.hq@fsmc.com
Scope: A management consulting firm that provides services such as proposals, enterprise systems, management systems, and staff augmentation. Specializes in new business proposals, project management support and training. **Publications:** Project Management for Executives, Project Risk Management, Project Communications Management, Winning Proposals, Four Computer Based Training (CBT) courses. **Seminars:** Preparing Winning Proposals in Response to Government RFPs.

31349 ■ Flett Research Ltd.
440 DeSalaberry Ave.
Winnipeg, MB, Canada R2L 0Y7
Ph:(204)667-2505
Fax: (204)667-2505
Co. E-mail: flett@flettresearch.ca
URL: http://www.flettresearch.ca

E-mail: flett@flettresearch.ca
Scope: Provides environmental audits and assessments. Offers contract research and consultation on environmental topics, specializing in limnology, with emphasis in microbiology, bio-geochemistry and radio-chemistry. Performs dating of sediments via Pb-210 and CS-137 methods, to determine sediment accumulation rates in lakes. One of a handful of labs in the world able to carry out total mercury and methyl mercury analyses at the sub-nanogram and L concentration in water.

31350 ■ Focus Performance Systems Inc.
13911 Ridgedale Dr., Ste. 430
Minnetonka, MN 55305
Ph:(952)595-8000
Fax: (952)595-0679
Co. E-mail: info@focustools.com
URL: http://www.focustools.com

E-mail: info@focustools.com
Scope: Consultants specializing in the development and implementation of problem-solving, decision-making, and team processes for managers/supervisors and key people in a variety of organizations. Industries served: manufacturing, industrial, insurance/banking, healthcare and government. **Seminars:** How To Create Innovative Solutions On Demand, Jul, 2006; Essential tools to solve problems, make decisions and execute plans, faster and more effectively, Jul, 2006. **Special Services:** Decision Focus®; Team Focus™.

31351 ■ Freese & Associates Inc.
PO Box 814
Chagrin Falls, OH 44022-0814
Ph:(440)564-9183
Fax: (440)564-7339
Co. E-mail: tfreese@freeseinc.com
URL: http://www.freeseinc.com

E-mail: tfreese@freeseinc.com
Scope: A management consulting firm offering advice in all forms of business logistics. Consulting services are in the areas of strategic planning; network analysis, site selection, facility layout and design, outsourcing, warehousing, transportation and customer service. Typical projects include 3PL marketing surveys; third party outsourcing selection; operational audits; competitive analysis; inventory management; due diligence; and implementation project management. **Publications:** "Building Relationships is Key to Motivation," Distribution Center Management, Apr, 2006; "Getting Maximum Results from Performance Reviews," WERCSheet, Oct, 2003; "SCM: Making the Vision a Reality," Supply Chain Management Review, Oct, 2003; "Contents Under Pressure," DCVelocity, Aug, 2003; "When Considering Outsourcing, It's Really a Financial Decision," Inventory Management Report, Mar, 2003. **Seminars:** Keys to Retaining & Motivating Your Associates, Mar, 2006; The Value and Challenges of Supply Chain Management, Global Supply Chain & Logistics Conference, Feb, 2006; Best Practices in Logistics in China, Jun, 2005; Keys to Motivating Associates, WERC Annual Conference, May, 2005; The Goal and the Way of International Cooperation in Logistics, Apr, 2005.

31352 ■ Full Voice
11130 Holmes Rd.
Kansas City, MO 64101
Ph:(816)941-0011
Fax: (816)444-0505
Scope: Formalizes a program of proven techniques into a practical method of helping individuals improve their ability to better present themselves when speaking in a professional situation. Industries Served: all. **Publications:** You Can Sound Like You Know What Youre Saying. **Seminars:** You Can Sound Like You Know What Youre Saying; How to Make Yours a Championship Team; Functional English for Foreign

Trade; The Effective Voice for Customer Service Enhancement; The Psychology of Vocal Performance; You Can Speak With Conviction.

31353 ■ GEC Consultants Inc.
4604 Birchwood Ave.
Skokie, IL 60076
Ph:(847)674-6310
Fax: (847)674-3946
Co. E-mail: gec@gecconsultants.com
URL: http://www.gecconsultants.com

E-mail: gec@gecconsultants.com
Scope: Consulting in all areas of bar and restaurant operations. Restaurant manager development appraises existing locations or sites. Studies the feasibility of projects. Develop new concepts. Assist in expanding, existing food operations, marketing, expert witness (legal) for hospitality/restaurant industry. **Publications:** Marketing For The 21st Century; Profitability In The Banquet Industry; Starting a Restaurant, Bar or Catering Business. **Seminars:** Member MSPC Speakers Bureau. How to increase restaurant profit. **Special Services:** Chef's menu, recipe, and inventory program.

31354 ■ Gerson Goodson Inc.
2451 McMullen Booth Rd., Ste. 216
Clearwater, FL 33759
Ph:(727)726-7619
Free: 888-237-7424
Fax: (727)726-2406
Co. E-mail: getrich@richgerson.com
URL: http://www.richgerson.com

E-mail: getrich@richgerson.com
Scope: Firm provides performance management consulting services to improve performance, maximize productivity and turn ordinary performers into extraordinary performers. Conducts a systematic needs analysis of the entire marketing, sales and customer service operations of the company. Identifies hidden, neglected and underutilized marketing, sales and customer service assets. Creates customized and unique breakthrough marketing, sales and customer service programs for them. Develops feedback, measurement and tracking systems to determine the effectiveness of programs and services. Also provides systematic follow-ups to ensure complete satisfaction with work. **Publications:** "Beyond Customer Service"; "Winning The Inner Game Of Selling"; "Marketing Strategies for Small Businesses". **Seminars:** The Marketing Difference That Makes The Difference: How To Position Your Company For Rapid Growth Regardless Of The Economy Or The Competition; Growing Your Business With What You Already Have: How To Identify And Profit From The Hidden Marketing Assets That Are Currently Costing You Money; The R Factor In Customer Service: 5 Ways To Grow Your Business For Little Or No Cost.

31355 ■ Glass & Associates Inc.
623 5th Ave., Fl. 15
New York, NY 10022
Ph:(212)223-2002
Free: (866)452-7716
Fax: (212)223-5477
Co. E-mail: jmansell@glass-consulting.com
URL: http://www.glass-consulting.com

E-mail: jmansell@glass-consulting.com
Scope: Works with troubled companies, functioning as agents of change to help organizations deal with extraordinary needs in situations ranging from the early stages of financial decline to "life-or-death" crisis conditions. Provides in-depth analysis and strategic planning, backed up by leadership and decisive action to help under-performing companies change the way they operate and survive crisis situations. Assists management, creditors, lenders and other "parties in interest" involved with financially troubled companies; crisis management services include on-site interim crisis management, including direction of the Chapter 11 process, for insolvent companies; human resources services include personnel for temporary senior-level management and professional staff

assignments; executive search, selection and placement; specialized advisory services in human resource areas such as worker's compensation and health benefits.

31356 ■ Global Business Consultants
120 Market Sq.
PO Box 776
Pinehurst, NC 28374-0776
Ph:(910)295-5991
Free: 800-991-4990
Fax: (910)295-5908
Co. E-mail: info@yourculturecoach.com

E-mail: info@yourculturecoach.com
Scope: Firm specializes in human resources management; project management; software development; and international trade. Offers litigation support.

31357 ■ Global Technology Transfer
1500 Dixie Hwy.
Covington, KY 41011
Ph:(859)431-1262
Fax: (859)431-5148
Co. E-mail: arzembrodt@worldnet.att.net

E-mail: arzembrodt@worldnet.att.net
Scope: Firm specializes in product development; quality assurance; new product development; and total quality management focusing on household chemical specialties, especially air fresheners. Utilizes latest technology from global resources. Specializes in enhancement products for home and automobile.

31358 ■ Arnold S. Goldin & Associates Inc.
5030 Champion Blvd., Ste. G-6231
Boca Raton, FL 33496
Ph:(561)994-5810
Fax: (561)994-5860
Co. E-mail: arnold@goldin.com
URL: http://www.goldin.com

E-mail: arnold@goldin.com
Scope: An accounting and management consulting firm. Serves clients worldwide. Provides management services. Handles monthly write-ups and tax returns.

31359 ■ Goldore Consulting Inc.
120-5 St. NW
PO Box 590
Linden, AB, Canada T0M 1J0
Ph:(403)546-4208
Fax: (403)546-4208
Co. E-mail: goldore@leadershipessentials.com

E-mail: goldore@leadershipessentials.com
Scope: Provides consulting service in Leadership and management skills. Industries served: primarily charities, non-profits; some businesses. **Seminars:** O Desafio de Lideranca; The Challenge Of Leadership; Le Challenge du Leadership; El Desafio de Liderazgo; Tantangan Kipeminpinan.

31360 ■ Great Lakes Consulting Group Inc.
1217 S Walnut St.
South Bend, IN 46619-4305
Ph:(574)287-4500
Fax: (574)234-8207
Scope: Provides consulting services in the areas of strategic planning; feasibility studies; start-up businesses; small business management; mergers and acquisitions; joint ventures; divestitures; interim management; crisis management; turnarounds; business process re-engineering; venture capital; and international trade.

31361 ■ Great Western Association Management Inc.
7995 E Prentice Ave., Ste. 100
Greenwood Village, CO 80111
Ph:(303)770-2220
Fax: (303)770-1614
Co. E-mail: info83@gwami.com
URL: http://www.gwami.com

E-mail: info83@gwami.com

Scope: Expertise in managing not for-profit organizations. Clients select from a menu of services including association development and public relations, conferences and seminars, financial management, membership communications, and governance. Expertise also includes association strategic planning, compliance, lobbying, meeting planning, fundraising, marketing and communications.

31362 ■ Joel Greenstein & Associates
6212 Nethercombe Ct.
McLean, VA 22101
Ph:(703)893-1888
Co. E-mail: jgreenstein@contractmasters.com

E-mail: jgreenstein@contractmasters.com
Scope: Provides services to minority and women-owned businesses and government agencies. Experienced in interpreting federal and agency-specific acquisition regulations and contract terms and conditions. Offers assistance with preparing technical and cost proposals and sealed bids.

31363 ■ The Greystone Group Inc.
678 Front St., Ste. 159
Grand Rapids, MI 49504
Ph:(616)451-8880
Fax: (616)451-9180
Co. E-mail: consult@greystonegp.com
URL: http://www.greystonegp.com

E-mail: consult@greystonegp.com
Scope: Firm specializes in strategic planning and communications; organizational development; start-up businesses; business management; mergers and acquisitions; joint ventures; divestitures; business process re-engineering.

31364 ■ Grief Counseling & Support Services
8600 W Chester Pke., Ste. 304
Upper Darby, PA 19082
Ph:(610)789-7707
Fax: (610)469-9499
Scope: Specializing in consulting and training services for organizations dealing with loss, trauma and grief issues. These services may include management consultations, crisis intervention, educational programming, policy development, program design, group process work, individual counseling or other support services. Training and support services also provided for loss issues for mental retardation service providers. Serves private industries as well as government agencies. **Seminars:** Seminars on grief, mourning, Drug, alcohol, sex addiction, loss designed to meet individual situations. All seminars tailor-made to specific organizational needs.

31365 ■ Grimmick Consulting Services
455 Donner Way
San Ramon, CA 94583
Ph:(925)735-9090
Fax: (925)735-1100
Co. E-mail: grimmick@pacbell.net

E-mail: grimmick@pacbell.net
Scope: Provides consulting services in the areas of strategic planning; organizational assessment; organizational development; leadership development and Baldrige Criteria.

31366 ■ Harding & Co.
9 Sommer Ave.
Maplewood, NJ 07040
Ph:(973)763-9284
Fax: (973)763-9347
Co. E-mail: fharding@hardingco.com
URL: http://www.hardingco.com

E-mail: fharding@hardingco.com
Scope: Firm specializes in sales management, client development, and employee training. **Publications:** "Rain Making: The Professional's Guide to Attracting New Clients"; "Creating Rainmakers: The Managers Guide to Training Professionals to Attract New Clients"; "Cross-Selling Success: A Rainmakers Guide to Professional Account Development".

31367 ■ Harris Advertising
4162 Fenton Rd.
Flint, MI 48507-2473
Ph:(810)232-4120
Scope: Conducts leadership training seminars for businesses and organizations. Participants learn problem solving techniques, communications skills, conflict resolution, leadership styles, dynamics of group development and participation, time management, and successful meeting management. Serves private industries as well as government agencies.

31368 ■ Health Information Referral System
RR1 Box 850
Woodstock, VT 05091
Ph:(802)457-3455

31369 ■ Health Strategy Group Inc.
46 River Rd.
Chatham, NY 12037
Ph:(518)392-6770
Scope: Provides consulting services in the areas of strategic planning, feasibility studies, start-up businesses, organizational development, market research, customer service audits, new product development, marketing, public relations.

31370 ■ Hewitt Development Enterprises
1717 N Bayshore Dr., Ste. 2154
Miami, FL 33132
Ph:(305)372-0941
Free: 800-631-3098
Fax: (305)372-0941
Co. E-mail: info@hewittdevelopment.com
URL: http://www.hewittdevelopment.com

E-mail: info@hewittdevelopment.com
Scope: A manufacturing management consulting firm. Specializes in strategic planning; profit enhancement; start-up businesses; interim management; crisis management; turnarounds; production planning; Just-in-Time inventory management; and project management.

31371 ■ Hickey & Hill Inc.
1009 Oak Hill Rd., Ste. 201
Lafayette, CA 94549
Ph:(925)283-7802
Fax: (925)283-4259
Scope: Firm provides management consulting services to companies in financial distress. Expertise area: corporate restructuring and turnaround.

31372 ■ hightechbiz.com
4209 Santa Monica Blvd., Ste. 201
Los Angeles, CA 90029-3027
Ph:(818)216-9356
Free: 877-648-4753
Fax: (323)913-3355
Co. E-mail: info@hightechbiz.com
URL: http://www.hightechbiz.com

E-mail: info@hightechbiz.com
Scope: Business development, strategic planning and investing in high tech companies. Turnaround consulting and financial sort our of distressed business and start up companies with strong emphasis on technology. A full service marketing agency specializing in integrated marketing solutions. Products and services include marketing surveys; positioning surveys; strategic & tactical plans; implementation plans; management consulting; product brochures; product catalogs; product packaging; product data sheets; direct mail programs; media research; competitive research; complete creative; production and film; media placement; corporate identity; in-house creative; public relations; logos & stationary; annual reports; publications; corporate brochures; corporate videos; trade show booth graphics; concept & design; copywriting; computerized production; illustration/cartoons; computer graphics; Internet home page design; media relations; financial relations; news releases; feature length stories; new product releases; and tracking and clipping.

31373 ■ Hills Consulting Group Inc.
6 Partridge Ct.
Novato, CA 94945

Ph:(415)898-3944
Scope: Strategic marketing consulting and training firm. Specializes in strategic planning; marketing surveys; market research; customer service audits; new product development; competitive analysis; and sales forecasting.

31374 ■ Holt Capital
1100 Dexter Ave. N
Seattle, WA 98109
Ph:(206)676-3822
Fax: (206)789-8034
Co. E-mail: info@holtcapital.com
URL: http://www.holtcapital.com

E-mail: info@holtcapital.com
Scope: Connects companies with capital. Mergers and acquisitions, finance through debt and leasing, private equity and venture capital. Is a registered Investment Advisor. **Publications:** "Is Your First Paragraph a Turn-off?"; "Bubble Rubble: Bridging the Price Gapfor an Early-Stage Business"; "Are You Ready For The New New Economy?"; "Could I Get Money or Jail Time With That? The Sarbanes-Oxley Act Of 2002 gives early-stage companies More Risks". **Seminars:** Attracting Private Investors; Five Proven Ways to Finance Your Company.

31375 ■ Hornberger & Associates
1966 Lombard St., Ste. 200
San Francisco, CA 94123
Ph:(415)346-2106
Fax: (415)346-9993
Co. E-mail: info@hornbergerassociates.com
URL: http://www.hornbergerassociates.com

E-mail: info@hornbergerassociates.com
Scope: Firm specializes in Internet marketing, strategic planning; new product development; client acquisition and retention; helping banks and brokerage firms do more business with affluent clients. **Seminars:** Building a Marketing Plan Directed at Emerging Wealth Baby Boomers.

31376 ■ Human Resource Specialties Inc.
3 Monroe Pky., Ste. 900
PO Box 1733
Lake Oswego, OR 97035
Ph:(503)697-3329
Free: 800-354-3512
Fax: (503)636-1594
Co. E-mail: info@hrspecialties.com
URL: http://www.hrspecialties.com

E-mail: info@hrspecialties.com
Scope: Provides human resources assistance to organizations. Offers preparation of affirmative action plans, support documents, and adverse impact studies of personnel activities. Also offers customized consultations in small business services, diversity and discrimination, and investigations, complaints and grievances.

31377 ■ Idi-Supply Inc.
3866 N Fratney St.
PO Box 12050
Milwaukee, WI 53212
Ph:(414)961-2365
Fax: (414)961-1582
Scope: Firm specializes in start-up businesses; small business management; mergers and acquisitions; joint ventures; divestitures; venture capital; appraisals; valuations; and international trade.

31378 ■ I.H.R. Solutions
3333 E Bayaud Ave., Ste. 219
Denver, CO 80209
Ph:(303)588-4243
Fax: (303)978-0473
Co. E-mail: dhollands@ihrsolutions.com
URL: http://www.ihrsolutions.com

E-mail: dhollands@ihrsolutions.com
Scope: Provides joint-venture and start-up human resource consulting services as well as advice on organization development for international human capital. Industries Served: high-tech and telecommunications.

31379 ■ IMC Consulting & Training
901 McHenry Ave., Ste. A
Modesto, CA 95350
Ph:(209)572-2271
Fax: (209)572-2862
Co. E-mail: michael@imc-1.net
URL: http://www.imc-1.net

E-mail: michael@imc-1.net
Scope: Firm helps businesses and professionals identify, develop and market their selling proposition to increase profits. Services include B-to-B surveys, direct marketing, media relations, planning and strategy, sales management, training and leadership coaching. **Publications:** "Adapting to Change - The New Competitive Advantage," Business Journal, Jul, 2004; "Consultant Earns Advanced Certificate," HCCSC Business Review, Dec, 2004. **Seminars:** Winning the 2nd Half: A 6-month Plan to Score New Customers and Profits.

31380 ■ In Plain English
14501 Antigone Dr.
PO Box 3300
North Potomac, MD 20878
Ph:(301)340-2821
Free: 800-274-9645
Fax: (301)279-0115
Co. E-mail: rwohl@inplainenglish.com
URL: http://www.inplainenglish.com

E-mail: rwohl@inplainenglish.com
Scope: Management consultants helping government and businesses research, design, write and produce user-oriented management information for human resources, employee benefits, business process, corporate and marketing needs. Employee benefits services include summary plan descriptions, employee benefit booklets, plan documents, communication of employee benefit highlights, pay for performance systems, and Section 125 cafeteria benefit enrollment. Human resources services include producing employee handbooks, employee handbook audits, training manuals, writing training, and personnel policy and policy audits. Consultants also assist clients to re-humanize their business, human resource department, recruitment, and employee benefit program. **Publications:** The Benefits Communication Edge newsletter; The Employee Benefits Communication ToolKit, published by Commerce Clearinghouse. Benefits Communicat ion; a guide published by business & legal reports. **Seminars:** Plain English Writing Training; Summary Plan Description Compliance workshops; Re-Humanizing the Corporation, Human Resources and Employee Benefits Communication Workshop. **Special Services:** Electronic materials; Electronic summary plan descriptions; electronic reference manuals.

31381 ■ Innovative Scientific Analysis & Computing
Flagstaff Rd.
PO Box 1636
Boulder, CO 80306-1636
Ph:(303)440-7673
Fax: (303)545-6674
Co. E-mail: ros5e@isaac.com
URL: http://www.isaac.com

E-mail: ros5e@isaac.com
Scope: Engineering services includes mathematical analysis (specializing in optimal estimation), scientific programming, and database design and development, data encryption and security.

31382 ■ Institute for Management Excellence
PO Box 5459
Lacey, WA 98509-5459
Ph:(360)412-0404
URL: http://www.itstime.com
Scope: Management consulting and training focuses on improving productivity, using "best practices" and creative techniques. Practices based on company's theme, "It's time for new ways of doing business." Industries Served: Public Sector, Law Enforcement, Finance/Banking,   Non-Profit,   Computers/High

Technology, Education, Human Resources, Utilities. **Publications:** "The Other Side of Midnight, 2000: An Executive Guide to the Year 2000 Problem" ISBN: 0-9643853-9-2, Authors: Barbara Taylor and Martha Daniel. **Seminars:** The Personality Game, Team Building and Communication Skills, Sexual Harassment and Discrimination Prevention. **Special Services:** Project management for computer systems implementations, including web/internet consulting.

31383 ■ Institute of Public Administration
411 Lafayette St., Ste. 303
New York, NY 10003
Ph:(212)992-9899
Free: 800-258-1102
Fax: (212)995-4876
Co. E-mail: info@theipa.org
URL: http://www.theipa.org

E-mail: info@theipa.org
Scope: A private nonprofit consulting, research and education organization experienced in management of governments and public enterprises. Firm's activities are directed toward the solution of emerging problems of government, organization, financial management and policies, and public enterprises in the United States and abroad. Emphasizes innovation, demonstration of new techniques, and communication among governments and between the public and private sectors. Programs are financed chiefly by contracts with local, state and federal governments, international aid agencies and foreign governments, public enterprises, and by foundation grants. Areas of concentration include personnel administration, structures and resources of local legislative bodies, training, structure and financing of public enterprises, public finance, financial management and anti-corruption systems, urban and regional planning, organization and management, city/county charter revision, urban transportation, public sector ethics and citizenship, and management of government procurement systems. **Seminars:** Offers a range of seminars and training workshops tailored to the needs of participants.

31384 ■ Interpersonal Coaching & Consulting
1516 W Lake St., Ste. 2000S
Minneapolis, MN 55408
Ph:(612)381-2494
Fax: (612)381-2494
Co. E-mail: mail@interpersonal-coaching.com
URL: http://www.interpersonal-coaching.com

E-mail: mail@interpersonal-coaching.com
Scope: Provides coaching and consulting to businesses and organizations. Assesses the interpersonal workplace through interviews, assessment instruments and individual group settings. Experienced as a therapist for over a decade.

31385 ■ Invent Resources Inc.
PO Box 548
Lexington, MA 02420-0005
Ph:(781)862-0200
Fax: (781)721-2300
Co. E-mail: rsilver@world.std.com
URL: http://www.inventresources.com

E-mail: rsilver@world.std.com
Scope: An organization comprised of four scientists and engineers that have helped to develop more than 200 products for their clients. After accepting a request for an invention, Invent Resources offers a license to the intellectual property and negotiates a royalty arrangement. Provides support in developing and prototyping the product.

31386 ■ Jest for the Health of It Services
PO Box 8484
Santa Cruz, CA 95061-8484
Ph:(831)425-8436
Fax: (831)425-8437
Co. E-mail: pwooten@jesthealth.com
URL: http://www.jesthealth.com

E-mail: pwooten@jesthealth.com

Scope: Develops and presents seminars, keynotes, and skill shops about the power of humor. Provides consulting services for development of humor rooms and comedy carts in hospitals. Conducts training for clowns to make visits in hospitals and nursing homes. Industries served: health professionals and businesses wishing to educate staff about healthy lifestyle choices. **Publications:** "Heart Humor and Healing and Compassionate Laughter:Jest for your Health"; "The Hospital Clown: A Closer Look". **Seminars:** Professional Survival-You Can Laugh or Cry: Stress Control; Choosing the Amusing-Humor Techniques for Work and Home; What's So Funny-What Humor Is, Isn't and Should Be; You've Got To Be Kidding Learning to Laugh at Life's Upsets and Setbacks; Tickle While You Teach-Learning with Laughter.

31387 ■ Jim Castello Marketing Consultants
PO Box 950492
Osteen, FL 32764
Ph:(407)321-6322
Scope: Consultant will develop creative ideas and marketing strategies, including collateral programs, public relations, advertising, and brochures. Industries served: all golf related industry/business, golf manufacturers, golf resorts, golf residential developments, golf professionals, golf clothing, golf accessories, golf associations, and golf travel. **Seminars:** How To Seminar for Family Fun Center Entrepreneurs; How To Seminar for Creativity in Golf Marketing; The Golf Business on the Internet.

31388 ■ Johnston Co.
1646 Massachusetts Ave., Ste. 22
Lexington, MA 02420
Ph:(781)862-7595
Fax: (781)862-9066
Co. E-mail: info@johnstoncompany.com
URL: http://www.johnstoncompany.com

E-mail: info@johnstoncompany.com
Scope: Firm specializes in management audits and reports; start-up businesses; small business management; mergers and acquisitions; joint ventures; divestitures; interim management; crisis management; turnarounds; cost controls; financing; venture capital.

31389 ■ K & T Training
103 Greenville St.
Newnan, GA 30263-2630
Ph:(770)253-5870
Fax: (770)253-8866
Scope: Specializes in strategic planning; profit enhancement; organizational development; start-up businesses; interim management; crisis management; turnarounds; business process re-engineering; team building; cost controls.

31390 ■ Keck & Co.
410 Walsh Rd.
Atherton, CA 94027
Ph:(650)854-9588
Fax: (650)854-7240
Co. E-mail: info@kecko.com
URL: http://www.keckco.com

E-mail: info@kecko.com
Scope: Conducts management services nationally, focusing on strategic research, marketing, and planning for businesses involved in the packaging container and equipment industry, food processing, and related technology suppliers. Develops feasibility studies to assess the possible success or failure of entering a new market, introducing a new product or product line extension, or starting a new venture; primary market research to determine what motivates consumers/buyers, and best "positioning" for product in the marketplace; business development programs; promotional programs to differentiate client company from competitors; vertical/horizontal marketing audits; technology acceptance assessments; due diligence for investors; and management assistance with investment issues. **Seminars:** Taking the Failure Factors Out of New Product Introductions; Introduction to Marketing for Food Manufacturing Personnel; New Product Development Workshop: Plans and Ele-

ments; Starting Your Own Consulting Business; The Marketing Plan. **Special Services:** Conducts database searches for venture and expansion capital for packaging companies and companies introducing packaging functional foods. Maintains 1600-record proprietary database of international and North American magazines available to clients for public relations placements. Serves as basis of customized press lists and analysis of media for market entry and promotional purpose.

31391 ■ Keiei Senryaku Corp.
19191 S Vermont Ave., Ste. 530
Torrance, CA 90502
Ph:(310)366-3331
Free: 800-951-8780
Fax: (310)366-3330
Co. E-mail: takenakaes@earthlink.net

E-mail: takenakaes@earthlink.net
Scope: Consulting services in the areas of strategic planning; feasibility studies; profit enhancement; organizational development; start-up businesses; mergers and acquisitions; joint ventures; divestitures; executive searches; sales management; competitive analysis. Entering Japanese market.

31392 ■ Key Communications Group Inc.
5617 Warwick Pl.
Chevy Chase, MD 20815-5503
Ph:(301)656-0450
Free: 800-705-5353
Fax: (301)656-4554
Co. E-mail: mr.dm@verizon.net

E-mail: mr.dm@verizon.net
Scope: Direct marketing and publishing consultants specializing in subscriber and member acquisition for newsletters and other niche B2B publications, organizations and associations. Specialties: small and start-up businesses; mergers and acquisitions; joint ventures; divestitures; product development; employee surveys and communication; market research; customer service audits; new product development; direct marketing; and competitive intelligence.

31393 ■ Koch Group Inc.
240 E Lake St., Ste. 300
Addison, IL 60101
Ph:(630)941-1100
Free: 800-470-7845
Fax: (630)941-3865
Co. E-mail: info@kochgroup.com
URL: http://www.kochgroup.com

E-mail: info@kochgroup.com
Scope: Provides industrial marketing consulting services to small to mid-sized manufacturers. Primary assistance includes industrial market research and analysis, identification of potential markets, strategic planning and plan implementation. Most project activities focus on increasing profitable sales to existing markets, new markets or geographic areas previously unserved. Specializes in assisting manufacturers identify, recruit, and manage manufacturers agents and reps. Also develops industrial websites that generate excellent opportunities for increased sales. **Seminars:** Niche Marketing; Regional Industrial Association Recruiting; Strategic Marketing for Manufacturers; Strategic Marketing; How To Identify, Screen, Interview and Select High Quality Agents; Basics of Industrial Market Research; Elements of Industrial Marketing.

31394 ■ Kostka & Company Inc.
2114 Town Pl.
Middletown, CT 06457
Co. E-mail: mail@mmgnet.com
URL: http://www.mmgnet.com

E-mail: mail@mmgnet.com
Scope: Management consulting firm that specializes in business process re-engineering, risk management, and information technology.

31395 ■ Kroll Zolfo Cooper L.L.C.
900 3rd Ave., 6th Fl.
New York, NY 10022

Ph:(212)561-4000
Fax: (212)213-1749
URL: http://www.krollzolfocooper.com
Scope: Firm provides accounting consulting services to businesses.

31396 ■ Kubba Consultants Inc.
801 Glendale Rd.
Glenview, IL 60025
Ph:(847)729-0051
Fax: (847)729-8765
Co. E-mail: edkubba@aol.com
URL: http://www.kubbainc.com

E-mail: edkubba@aol.com
Scope: Industrial and business-to-business marketing research and consulting. Services include new product research, new market evaluation, competitor analysis and customer value analysis.

31397 ■ William E. Kuhn & Associates
234 Cook St.
Denver, CO 80206-5305
Ph:(303)322-8233
Fax: (303)322-9032
Co. E-mail: billkuhn1@cs.com

E-mail: billkuhn1@cs.com
Scope: Firm specializes in strategic planning; profit enhancement; small business management; mergers and acquisitions; joint ventures; divestitures; human resources management; performance appraisals; team building; sales management; appraisals and valuations.

31398 ■ Liberty Business Strategies Ltd.
The Times Bldg., Ste. 400, Suburban Sq.
Ardmore, PA 19003
Ph:(610)649-3800
Fax: (610)649-0408
Co. E-mail: info@libertystrategies.com
URL: http://www.libertystrategies.com

E-mail: info@libertystrategies.com
Scope: Management consulting firm working with clients to gain speed and agility in driving their business strategy. The consulting model builds the alignment of strategy, organization commitment, and technology.

31399 ■ Linda Lipsky Restaurant Consultants Inc.
216 Foxcroft Rd.
Broomall, PA 19008
Ph:(610)325-3663
Free: 877-425-3663
Fax: (610)325-3329
Co. E-mail: lipsky@restaurantconsult.com
URL: http://www.restaurantconsult.com

E-mail: lipsky@restaurantconsult.com
Scope: Helps food and beverage operations achieve their highest level of profits, product consistency and service quality. Concentrates on implementing cost-cutting measures, developing training programs for both front and heart of the house employees, engineering menus, performing Spotter's reports and creating organizational manuals and procedures for restaurant, bar, hotel, banquet facility, country clubs, or caterer. Key areas of specialization include on-site operations evaluations to identify ineffective cost controls, flaws in the organizational structure and inadequacies of management systems, policies and procedures; profit enhancement as a result of implementing cost-cutting measures in all prime cost areas; server training, sales incentive training, and management training and evaluation programs; recipe documentation, cost analysis, menu pricing and menu copy writing; competitive market surveys and market positioning analysis, and bridge management. **Seminars:** Designing Menus for Maximum Sales and Profits; How to Maximize Your Check Average; Going Beyond Your Customer's Expectations; Making the Best First and Last Impression; Make Every Labor Dollar Count; Conducting Your Own In-House Inspection. **Special Services:** T.I.P.S®.

31400 ■ May Toy Lukens
3226 NE 26th Ct.
Renton, WA 98056
Ph:(425)891-3226
Scope: Provide training to teach people to think of ways to improve their operations continuously by changing the way they think, and how they are motivated. Industries served: all, particularly financial. Operational analysis and training. **Seminars:** Seminars and workshops in maximizing resource utilization and staff potential.

31401 ■ Lupfer & Associates
92 Glen St.
South Natick, MA 01760
Ph:(508)655-3950
Fax: (508)655-7826
Co. E-mail: donlupfer@aol.com
URL: http://www.lupferassociates.com

E-mail: donlupfer@aol.com
Scope: Assists off shore hi-tech companies in entering United States markets and specializes in channel development for all sorts of products. Perform MARCOM support for hi-tech United States clients. **Publications:** "What's Next For Distribution-Feast or Famine?"; "The Changing Global Marketplace"; "Making Global Distribution Work". **Seminars:** How to do Business in the United States.

31402 ■ Management Resource Partners
181 2nd Ave., Ste. 542
San Mateo, CA 94401-3813
Ph:(650)401-5850
Fax: (650)401-5850
Scope: Firm specializes in strategic planning; small business management; mergers and acquisitions; joint ventures; divestitures; interim management; crisis management; turnarounds; venture capital; appraisals and valuations.

31403 ■ Management Strategies
1000 S Old Woodward, Ste. 105
Birmingham, MI 48009
Ph:(248)258-2756
Fax: (248)258-3407
Co. E-mail: bob@hois.com

E-mail: bob@hois.com
Scope: Firm specializes in strategic planning; feasibility studies; profit enhancement; organizational studies; start-up businesses; turnarounds; business process re-engineering; industrial engineering; marketing; ecommerce.

31404 ■ Mankind Research Foundation
1315 Apple Ave.
Silver Spring, MD 20910-3614
Ph:(301)587-8686
Fax: (301)585-8959
Scope: Firm provide an organization for scientific development and application of technology that could have positive impact on the health, education, and welfare of mankind. Provide solution to seek and apply futuristic solutions to current problems. Provides services in the areas of advanced sciences, biotechnical, bionic, biocybernetic, biomedical, holistic health, bioimmunology, solar energy, accelerated learning, and sensory aids for handicapped. Current specific activities involve research in AIDS, drug abuse, affordable housing, food for the hungry, and literacy and remedial education.

31405 ■ Marketing Leverage Inc.
180 Glastonbury Blvd.
Glastonbury, CT 06033
Ph:(860)633-1422
Free: 800-633-1422
Fax: (860)659-8664
Co. E-mail: office@marketingleverage.com
URL: http://www.marketingleverage.com

E-mail: office@marketingleverage.com
Scope: Consults with senior management at leading corporations to improve performance by maximizing customer value. We specialize in the targeting, reten-tion and satisfaction of customers for companies in services industries with particular expertise in insurance, financial services, health care and technology services. Most clients belong to the Fortune 1000 group. Specific services include customer research, analysis of lifetime value, development of customer retention strategies, evaluation of web strategies, working with client teams.

31406 ■ McCreight & Company Inc.
36 Grove St.
New Canaan, CT 06840
Ph:(203)801-5000
Fax: (203)801-5013
Co. E-mail: roc@implementstrategy.com
URL: http://www.implementstrategy.com

E-mail: roc@implementstrategy.com
Scope: We assist our global clients with strategy implementation involving large-scale change, including mergers, divestitures, alliances, and new business launches. Along with our alliance partners, we focus on issues that energize or constrain strategic change including: plans and goals; transition design; management competence; organization structure, effectiveness, and staffing; roles and responsibilities; management processes; information management and technology; and change management effectiveness. **Publications:** Strategy Implementation Insights; ePerspective; Board Effectiveness Insights; and Information Technology Insights. **Seminars:** Successful Mergers and Acquisitions - An Implementation Guide; Global 100 - One-Face-to-the-Customer; Implementation of Strategic Change.

31407 ■ McDonald Consulting Group Inc.
7701 France Ave. S, Ste. 200
Edina, MN 55435
Ph:(952)841-6357
Fax: (507)664-9389
Co. E-mail: rmcdonald@mcdonaldconsultinggroup.
  com
URL: http://www.mcdonaldconsultinggroup.com

E-mail: rmcdonald@mcdonaldconsultinggroup.com
Scope: A management consulting firm specializing in assisting insurance companies improve operations. Provides services in the areas of strategic planning; profit enhancement; organizational development; interim management; crisis management; turnarounds; business process re-engineering; benefits and compensation planning and total quality management (TQM).

31408 ■ McShane Group Inc.
2345 York Rd.
Timonium, MD 21093
Ph:(410)560-0077
Fax: (410)560-2718
Co. E-mail: tmcshane@mcshanegroup.com
URL: http://www.mcshanegroup.com

E-mail: tmcshane@mcshanegroup.com
Scope: Management consulting firm specializing in helping financially troubled companies. All senior level business executives with strong operations backgrounds. Focuses on turnarounds, interim management, crisis management, debt restructuring, organizational restructuring, operating business and asset sales.

31409 ■ Medical Imaging Consultants Inc.
1037 Rte. 46 E G-2
Clifton, NJ 07013-2445
Ph:(973)574-8000
Free: 800-589-5685
Fax: (973)574-8001
Co. E-mail: info@micinfo.com
URL: http://www.micinfo.com

E-mail: info@micinfo.com
Scope: Provides management consulting services to hospitals, imaging centers, health-care companies and insurance companies. Firm specializes in interim management; crisis management; turnarounds; market research; and new product development. **Semi-**

nars: Sectional Anatomy & Imaging Strategies; CT Cross-Trainer; CT Registry Review Program; MR Cross-Trainer; Digital Mammography Essentials for Technologists; Radiology Trends for Technologists.

31410 ■ Medical Outcomes Management Inc.
Central Street Office Pk., 132 Central St., Ste. 215
Foxborough, MA 02035-2422
Ph:(508)543-0050
Fax: (508)543-1919
Co. E-mail: info@mom-inc.com
URL: http://www.mom-inc.com

E-mail: info@mom-inc.com
Scope: A health-care management and technology consulting firm providing a specially focused group of services, such as disease management programs, pharmaco-economic studies and medical writing. Physician educational outreach. **Publications:** "Treatment of acute exacerbation's of chronic bronchitis in patients with chronic obstructive pulmonary disease: A retrospective cohort analysis or Clarithromycin extended release vs. Azithromycin," 2003; "A retrospective analysis of cyclooxygenase-II inhibitor response patterns," 2002; "The formulary management system and decision-making process at Horizon Blue Cross Blue Shield of New Jersey," Pharmacotherapy, 2001. **Seminars:** Economic Modeling as a Disease Management Tool, Academy of Managed Care Pharmacy, Apr, 2005; Integrating Disease State Management and Economics, Academy of Managed Care Pharmacy, Oct, 2004; Clinical and economic outcomes in the treatment of peripheral occlusive diseases, Mar, 2003.

31411 ■ Mefford, Knutson & Associates Inc.
6437 Lyndale Ave. S
Richfield, MN 55423-1465
Ph:(612)869-8011
Free: 800-831-0228
Fax: (612)893-1806
Co. E-mail: don@mkaonline.net
URL: http://www.mkaonline.net

E-mail: don@mkaonline.net
Scope: Firm specializes in start-up businesses; strategic planning; mergers and acquisitions; joint ventures; divestitures; business process re-engineering; personnel policies and procedures; market research; new product development and cost controls.

31412 ■ Harvey A. Meier Co.
9 S Washington, Ste. 512, The Hutton Bldg.
Spokane, WA 99201-3709
Ph:(509)458-3210
Fax: (509)458-3216
Co. E-mail: hamco@harveymeier.com
URL: http://www.harveymeier.com

E-mail: hamco@harveymeier.com
Scope: Consulting firm specializes in Interim Management, Strategic Planning, Financial Planning and Organization Governance.

31413 ■ Colmen Menard Company Inc.
The Woods, 994 Old Eagle School Rd., Ste. 1000
Wayne, PA 19087
Ph:(484)367-0300
Fax: (484)367-0305
Co. E-mail: cmci@colmenmenard.com
URL: http://www.colmenmenard.com

E-mail: cmci@colmenmenard.com
Scope: Merger and acquisition corporate finance and business advisory services for public and private companies located in North America.

31414 ■ Richard Meyerhoff
110 Sutter St.
San Francisco, CA 94104
Ph:(415)668-6698

31415 ■ Midwest Computer Group L.L.C.
6060 Franks Rd.
House Springs, MO 63051-1101
Ph:(636)677-0287
Fax: (636)677-0287

Co. E-mail: consulting@mcgcomputer.com
URL: http://www.mcgcomputer.com

E-mail: consulting@mcgcomputer.com
Scope: Firm specializes in helping businesses create accounting, marketing and business information systems; software development; and database design and management.

31416 ■ Midwest Research Institute
425 Volker Blvd.
Kansas City, MO 64110
Ph:(816)753-7600
Fax: (816)753-8420
Co. E-mail: info@mriresearch.org
URL: http://www.mriresearch.org

E-mail: info@mriresearch.org
Scope: An independent, not-for-profit organization that performs research and development under contract with industry, government, and other private and public groups. Areas of current research and development include: chemistry, biological sciences, toxicology, health research, management sciences, environmental sciences, hazardous waste, renewable energy, materials sciences, pharmaceutical product development, and national security and defense. Has operated and managed the National Renewable Energy Laboratory (NREL) in Golden, Colorado for the U.S. Department of Energy since its inception in 1977. **Publications:** Annual Report (May).

31417 ■ Miller, Hellwig Associates
150 W End Ave.
New York, NY 10023-5713
Ph:(212)799-0471
Fax: (212)877-0186
Co. E-mail: millerhelwig@earthlink.net

E-mail: millerhelwig@earthlink.net
Scope: Consulting services in the areas of start-up businesses; small business management; employee surveys and communication; performance appraisals; executive searches; team building; personnel policies and procedures; market research. Also involved in improving cross-cultural and multi-cultural relationships, particularly with Japanese clients. **Seminars:** Objectives and standards/recruiting for boards of directors.

31418 ■ R.E. Moulton Inc.
50 Doaks Ln.
Marblehead, MA 01945
Ph:(781)631-1325
Fax: (781)631-2165
Co. E-mail: mike_lee@remoultoninc.com
URL: http://www.remoultoninc.com

E-mail: mike_lee@remoultoninc.com
Scope: Health Risk Management for employees with 20 or more employees. Specialize in Plan Design and Third Party Administration Services.

31419 ■ Mykytyn Consulting Group Inc.
185 N Redwood Dr., Ste. 200
San Rafael, CA 94903
Ph:(415)491-1770
Fax: (415)491-1251
Co. E-mail: info@mcgi.com

E-mail: info@mcgi.com
Scope: Develops structural models of new businesses and industries. Provides an interim CEO and management team at the start-up of a new business. Experienced in computer science and operations research.

31420 ■ National Bureau of Certified Consultants Inc.
1850 5th Ave.
San Diego, CA 92101
Ph:(619)239-7076
Free: 888-543-1114
Fax: (619)296-3580
Co. E-mail: nationalbureau@att.net

E-mail: nationalbureau@att.net
Scope: Referral services available to companies seeking Certified Professional Consultants to Man-

agement. These services are on a no fee basis. Industries served: Manufacturing and Services Industries. **Publications:** Consultants Bulletin published six times per year. **Seminars:** Annual conference for management consultants.

31421 ■ National Center for Public Policy Research
501 Capitol Ct. NE
Washington, DC 20002
Ph:(202)543-4110
Fax: (202)543-5975
Co. E-mail: info@nationalcenter.org
URL: http://www.nationalcenter.org

E-mail: info@nationalcenter.org
Scope: Nonprofit organization offers advice and information on international affairs and United States domestic affairs. Sponsors Project 21. Has a special emphasis an environmental and regulatory issues and civil rights issues. **Publications:** National Policy Analysis; Legal Briefs; White Paper, National Policy Analysis 523.

31422 ■ Navarro, Kim & Associates
529 N Charles St., Ste. 202
Baltimore, MD 21201-5043
Ph:(410)837-6317
Fax: (410)837-6294
Co. E-mail: bnavarro@sprynet.com

E-mail: bnavarro@sprynet.com
Scope: Firm specializes in bridging the gap between firms and non-traditional ethnic communities, especially in community development and institutional building.

31423 ■ The Nelson Group Ltd.
5 Milk St., Ste. 4
Portland, ME 04101
Ph:(207)775-1199
Fax: (207)775-0141
URL: http://www.nelsonltd.com
Scope: Consulting services in the areas of strategic planning; organizational development; small business management; mergers and acquisitions; joint ventures; divestitures; interim management; crisis management; turnarounds; performance appraisals; executive searches; outplacement; and team building.

31424 ■ The New Marketing Network Inc.
405 N Wabash Ave., Fl. 48
Chicago, IL 60611
Ph:(312)670-0096
Fax: (312)670-0126
Co. E-mail: info@newmarketingnetwork.com
URL: http://www.newmarketingnetwork.com

E-mail: info@newmarketingnetwork.com
Scope: Firm specializes in new product development; business and brand franchise expansion; Strategic planning and positioning; qualitative and quantitative Research; value added focus group moderating.

31425 ■ Nightingale Associates
7445 Setting Sun Way
Columbia, MD 21046-1261
Ph:(410)381-4280
Fax: (410)381-4280
Co. E-mail: fcnight@aol.com
URL: http://www.members.aol.com/fcnight

E-mail: fcnight@aol.com
Scope: Nightingale Associates is an international management training and consulting firm. Their concentration is on improving operational performance through the utilization of the most effective modern management techniques, executive and organizational assessment, reengineering of business processes, creative strategic thinking and focusing of the energies of all organizational participants. In addition they also work in the area of supply chain management and cost reduction through the utilization of the optimum purchasing, inventory management and distribution practices. **Seminars:** Advanced Management; Business Process Reengineering; Strategic Thinking; Creative Problem Solving; Customer Service; International Purchasing and Materials Management; Fundamentals of Purchasing.

31426 ■ North Carolina Fair Share
530 N Person St.
PO Box 12543
Raleigh, NC 27605
Ph:(919)832-7130
Fax: (919)832-4635
Co. E-mail: ncfslrw@aol.com

E-mail: ncfslrw@aol.com
Scope: Social services firm consults on community organizing and lobbying for health issues.

31427 ■ Occupational & Environmental Health Consulting Services
635 Harding Rd.
Hinsdale, IL 60521-4814
Ph:(630)325-2083
Fax: (630)325-2098
URL: http://www.safety-epa.com
Scope: Provides consulting to industry on safety program development and implementation, industrial hygiene monitoring programs, occupational health nursing, wellness programs, medical monitoring, accident trending and statistics, emergency response planning, multilingual training, right-to-know compliance and training, hazardous waste management, radon monitoring and mitigation, asbestos school inspection, and project management. Also offers indoor air quality, expert witnessing service. **Publications:** "Global Occupational Exposure Limits for over 5,000 Specific Chemicals"; "Post-Remediation Verification and Clearance Testing for Mold and Bacteria Risk Based Levels of Cleanliness". **Seminars:** Right-To-Know Compliance; Setting Internal Exposure Standards; Hospital Right-to-Know and Contingency Response; Ethylene Oxide Control; Industrial Hygiene Training; Asbestos Worker Training; Biosafety; Asbestos Operations and Maintenance. **Special Services:** Firm offers Safety Software Program.

31428 ■ Organization Counselors Inc.
44 W Broadway, Ste. 1102
PO Box 987
Salt Lake City, UT 84101
Ph:(801)363-2900
Fax: (801)363-0861
Co. E-mail: jpanos@xmission.com

E-mail: jpanos@xmission.com
Scope: Firm specializes in organizational development; employee surveys and communication; outplacement; team building; total quality management (TQM) and continuous improvement. **Seminars:** Correcting Performance Problems; Total Quality Management; Employee Selection; Performance Management.

31429 ■ Organizational Futures
56 Pine St., Ste. 2b
Providence, RI 02903
Ph:(401)351-7110
Fax: (401)351-7158
Scope: Builder of agile human networks to champion innovation and mobilize change; to pursue business opportunities; to custom design agile organizations and communities, to foster civic engagement. **Seminars:** Facilitating for Results.

31430 ■ Organizational Improvement Associates
15 Princeton Ln.
New Fairfield, CT 06812
Ph:(203)746-8687
Fax: (203)746-8687
Co. E-mail: daveknibbe@earthlink.net

E-mail: daveknibbe@earthlink.net
Scope: Specializes in high-performance team development, executive coaching, employee development programs, performance management and reward systems, and dispute mediation. Industries served: consumer products, telecommunications, finance, healthcare, amusement/leisure, hospitality/lodging, retail, and pharmaceuticals worldwide.

31431 ■ P2C2 Group Inc.
4101 Denfeld Ave.
Kensington, MD 20895-1514

Ph:(301)942-7985
Fax: (301)942-7986
Co. E-mail: info@p2c2group.com
URL: http://www.p2c2group.com

E-mail: info@p2c2group.com
Scope: Firm specializes in federal information technology management including capital investment management, strategic plans, policy, enterprise architecture, information security, documentation and knowledge management, OMB and NIST compliance, and IT program management. **Publications:** "How to Work with Proposal Consultants"; "Outside Reviewers for Proposals"; "The High Cost of Federal Information Technology".

31432 ■ Papa & Associates Inc.
200 Consumers Rd., Ste. 305
Toronto, ON, Canada M2J 4R4
Ph:(416)512-7272
Fax: (416)512-2016
Co. E-mail: ppapa@papa-associates.com
URL: http://www.papa-associates.com

E-mail: ppapa@papa-associates.com
Scope: Firm provides broad based management consulting services in the areas of quality assurance, environmental, health and safety and integrated management systems.

31433 ■ Parker Consultants Inc.
67 Mason St.
Greenwich, CT 06830
Ph:(203)869-9400
Scope: Firm specializes in strategic planning; organizational development; small business management; performance appraisals; executive searches; team building; and customer service audits.

31434 ■ Partners for Market Leadership Inc.
400 Galleria Pky., Ste. 1500
Atlanta, GA 30339
Ph:(770)850-1409
Free: 800-984-1110
Co. E-mail: dcarpenter@market-leadership.com
URL: http://www.market-leadership.com

E-mail: dcarpenter@market-leadership.com
Scope: Change management firm. Provides consulting services in the areas of strategic planning, start-up businesses, mergers and acquisitions, joint ventures, divestitures, interim management, crisis management, turnarounds, new product development, sales management and competitive analysis.

31435 ■ Pathways To Wellness
13845 Flintlock Dr.
Corpus Christi, TX 78418
Ph:(361)949-4790
Fax: (361)949-4627
Co. E-mail: path2wellness@earthlink.net
URL: http://www.path2wellness.com

E-mail: path2wellness@earthlink.net
Scope: Offer natural holistic health counseling, yoga classes and teachers training programs for individuals and companies. R.Y.T.500 and R.Y.Training Center through the Yoga Alliance. Hatha Yoga style is traditional and includes all aspects of yoga from jnana, bhakti, karma, and hatha for all levels of student. Health counseling includes nutritional guidance, kinesiology, iridology, reflexology, energy healing, massage therapy and reflexology, herbal and supplemental direction, creative visualization and meditation. Teachers training program will qualify students for registry with the Yoga Alliance. **Publications:** Is It You Holding You Back?; Is Yoga For Everyone?; The Balancing Act for Staying Healthy; Spring Housecleaning for your Body; Who Needs Nutritional Support...What are the Indicators?; Get Quality work from Healthy Employees!; Creating a Healthy Work Environment. **Seminars:** Is It You Holding You Back?; Introduction to Natural Health and Healthy Living; Introduction to Yoga and Meditation; Creative Visualization for Creating a Healthy Life; Mind/Body Connections for a Wealth of Health; The Eyes Are the

Windows to the Soul: Explanations of non-invasive ways to get and stay healthy through Iris interpretations.

31436 ■ PCS Laboratory Services Group Inc.
4750 Venture Dr., Ste. 400
Ann Arbor, MI 48108
Ph:(734)662-6363
Free: 800-860-5454
Fax: (734)662-7118
Co. E-mail: root@chilab.com

E-mail: root@chilab.com
Scope: Park City Solutions/Laboratory Services Group offers a comprehensive set of solutions to today's laboratory management challenges, such as: recruitment support, clinical laboratory operations improvement (identification and quantification of non-value added activities, workstation comparative cost analysis, etc.), advanced benchmarking methodology, multi-lab consolidation feasibility assessment, laboratory sales and marketing, regulatory compliance reviews and training, lab billing and collections consulting, and pathology staffing and compensation consulting.

31437 ■ The Performance Builders Publishing
PO Box 160150
Nashville, TN 37216
Free: (866)222-2606
Fax: (931)526-8376
Co. E-mail: customersfirst@pbbooks.org
URL: http://www.pbbooks.org

E-mail: customersfirst@pbbooks.org

31438 ■ Performance Consulting Associates Inc.
3700 Crestwood Pky., Ste. 100
Duluth, GA 30096
Ph:(770)717-2737
Fax: (770)717-7014
Co. E-mail: info@pcaconsulting.com
URL: http://www.pcaconsulting.com

E-mail: info@pcaconsulting.com
Scope: Maintenance consulting and engineering firm specializing in production planning, project management, team building, and re-engineering maintenance. **Publications:** "Asset Reliability Coordinator," Maintenance Technology; "Does Planning Pay," Plant Services; "Know What It Is You Have To Maintain," Maintenance Technology.

31439 ■ Performance Consulting Group
8535 Baymeadows Rd., Ste. 143-3
Jacksonville, FL 32202
Ph:(904)448-4473
Fax: (904)287-1244
Scope: Consulting services in the areas of strategic planning; profit enhancement; product development; production planning.

31440 ■ Performance Dynamics Group
1400 N Sam Houston Pky. E, Ste. 130
Houston, TX 77032
Ph:(281)987-8875
Fax: (281)987-2153
Co. E-mail: ingram@pdq.net

E-mail: ingram@pdq.net
Scope: An organizational consulting group whose approach to learning and employee empowerment is designed to be both effective and efficient in achieving the specific knowledge and skill goals of a given program, and also to foster and develop initiative, self confidence, creative problem-solving ability and interpersonal effectiveness of all participants. **Seminars:** Programs for organizations include: Accelerated Approach to Change (2 days); Commitment to Quality (1 day); Managing Cultural Diversity (2 days); The Corporate Energizer (1/2 day); The Power Pole Experience (1/2 day); Team Assessment (1/2 day); and Self-Directed Work Teams (2 days).

31441 ■ Plans and Solutions Inc.
PO Box 8905
Gaithersburg, MD 20898-8905
Ph:(301)947-8150
Fax: (240)525-5601
Co. E-mail: info@plansandsolutions.com
URL: http://www.plansandsolutions.com

E-mail: info@plansandsolutions.com
Scope: Business and strategic planning, market research and development. Most clients are minority-owned businesses in the USA and companies overseas that want to begin or increase exports to the United States and Canada. **Publications:** "Building an Import/Export Business," John Wiley & Sons, 2002.

31442 ■ Practice Development Counsel
60 Sutton Pl. S
New York, NY 10022
Ph:(212)593-1549
Fax: (212)980-7940
Co. E-mail: pwhaserot@pdcounsel.com
URL: http://www.pdcounsel.com

E-mail: pwhaserot@pdcounsel.com
Scope: Specializes in business development, service quality, retention, organizational development work/life excellence, and conflict resolution for professional firms. Provides coaching, client relationship management and quality service programs; strategic marketing planning/implementation; ancillary businesses/diversification; market research, trend watching, benchmarking; facilitation and planning for retreats and creative decision making; new business proposals and presentations; marketing communications and public relations; and business development training, coaching, and materials. Also offers speaker's services - engagements, publicity, etc. Industries served: law, accounting, and financial services, executive search, design, architecture, real estate, and management consultants worldwide. **Publications:** "The Rainmaking Machine: Marketing Planning, Strategy and Management For Law Firms"; "The Marketer's Handbook of Tips & Checklists"; "Venturesome Questions: The Law Firms Guide to Developing a New Business Venture". **Seminars:** Managing Work Expectations; Effective Coaching Skills; Service Quality; End-Running the Resistance Professionals Have to Getting Client Input; Ancillary Business Activities; Marketing for Professional Firms; Marketing Ethics; Business Development Training; Trends in Professional Services Marketing; Client Relationship Management; Collaborative Culture; Reaching Consensus; Conflict Resolution; Worklife Balance; Generaltional Issues; Preparing New Partners; Becoming the Employer of Choice; A Marketing Approach to Recruiting; Implementing Workplace Flexibility; The Business Case for Flexible Work Arrangements. **Special Services:** The Flexible Firm™; AuthenticWorks™; Coach-for-the-Coach™.

31443 ■ Praxis Media Inc.
48 Harbourview Ave.
South Norwalk, CT 06854-4822
Ph:(203)866-6666
Fax: (203)853-8299
Co. E-mail: aldo@praxismediainc.com

E-mail: aldo@praxismediainc.com
Scope: Media needs analysis and project planning specialists provide services in product introductions, communications planning, technology application, promotion and marketing communications. Also assists with focus groups, research, concept development, creative development, scripting and executive speech coaching/training. Industries served: financial services, high-tech, travel and leisure, health and pharmaceutical and telecommunications.

31444 ■ ProActive English
1001 Pine St., Ste. 1004
San Francisco, CA 94109
Ph:(415)752-2270
Co. E-mail: infopae@proactive-english.com
URL: http://www.proactive-english.com

E-mail: infopae@proactive-english.com
Scope: Offers on-site individual and small group language and communication training. Sets up learning plans tailored to the needs and schedules of managers and executives who are non-native English speakers. Serves all industries. **Seminars:** Communicating in Business Situations; Presentations and Pronunciation.

31445 ■ Professional Counseling Centers of Indiana
543 Coventry Way
Noblesville, IN 46060-9024
Ph:(317)846-7999
Fax: (317)574-5063
Scope: Business counselors offer expertise in the following areas: employee assistance, managed care, alcohol and drug treatment, labor and union consultation, and industrial mental health.

31446 ■ Public Administration Service
7927 Jones Branch Dr., Ste. 100 S
McLean, VA 22102-3322
Ph:(703)734-8970
Fax: (703)734-4965
Co. E-mail: postmaster@pashq.org
URL: http://www.pashq.org

E-mail: postmaster@pashq.org
Scope: Performs a variety of consulting and research work in serving the special needs of governments and other public service institutions. Services range from technical studies of central management problems to analyses of public policy issues, and in development administration water sewerage management and systems, rural development, and small farmer organization privatization, and management. Devoted exclusively to improving the conduct of public activities. Consulting services in the United States include organization and management, data processing and automation plans, position classification and compensation plans, police and fire service studies, public works and utilities studies, and parks management studies.

31447 ■ Public Policy Communications
4163 Dingman Dr.
Sanibel, FL 33957
Ph:(941)395-6773
Fax: (941)395-6779
Scope: Provides strategic communications for progressive causes, candidates, and socially-responsible businesses. These include public relations strategies, political campaign planning, organizational development, and training. Substantial work in report writing, editing and design as well as production of a full range of media materials. Industries served: nonprofit, social change organizations, foundations, political campaigns, environmentally and consumer-oriented businesses, and government agencies. **Publications:** "Winning Local and State Elections," Free Press MacMillan; "Giving the Media Your Message, and The News Media and the Big Lie". **Seminars:** Giving the Media Your Message; Effective Public Relations Practices; Winning Your Election; Understanding the Government Budget Process; How to Be an Effective Advocate; Strategic Planning for Non-Profits.

31448 ■ Public Sector Consultants Inc.
600 W St. Joseph St., Ste. 10
Lansing, MI 48933-2267
Ph:(517)484-4954
Fax: (517)484-6549
Co. E-mail: psc@pscinc.com
URL: http://www.pscinc.com

E-mail: psc@pscinc.com
Scope: Offers policy research expertise, specializing in opinion polling, public relations, conference planning, and legislative and economic analysis. Industries served: associations, education, environment, health-care, and public finance in Michigan.

31449 ■ The Purchasing Department
34 Claremont Ave.
Maplewood, NJ 07040-2118
Ph:(973)275-1188

Fax: (973)275-0749
Co. E-mail: eostpd@aol.com

E-mail: eostpd@aol.com
Scope: Provides state-of-the-art procurement arrangements, process re-engineering and outsourcing assistance to any business wishing to achieve purchasing savings and efficiencies to improve bottom-line results. Available to provide contract services to businesses requiring specialized supplemental assistance to back up own personnel on special projects. **Seminars:** Green Purchasing: Buying Recycled Products; Ethics; Measuring Purchasing Performance; Supplier Teaming and Quality; Preparing for ISO 9000 in the Purchasing Department.

31450 ■ Reed Royalty Public Affairs Inc.
30205 Hillside Ter.
San Juan Capistrano, CA 92675-1542
Ph:(949)240-2022
Fax: (949)240-0304
Scope: A governmental relations consultant who provides lobbying for changes in laws and government regulations, helps in obtaining licenses and permits, provides corporate training in governmental relations and assistance in winning government contracts. Services includ crisis management, business association management and issue-specific community and media relations.

31451 ■ Rental Relocation Inc.
281 S Atlanta St.
Roswell, GA 30075
Ph:(770)641-8393
Free: 800-641-7368
Fax: (770)641-8607
Co. E-mail: ahlsinfo@rentalrelocation.com
URL: http://www.rentalrelocation.com

E-mail: ahlsinfo@rentalrelocation.com
Scope: Relocation firm offering services in corporate housing, rentals, free metro Atlanta apartment locating service, property management, house and condo rental relocation tours.

31452 ■ Rose & Crangle Ltd.
117 N 4th St.
PO Box 285
Lincoln, KS 67455-0285
Ph:(785)524-5050
Fax: (785)524-3130
Co. E-mail: rcltd@nckcn.com

E-mail: rcltd@nckcn.com
Scope: Firm provides evaluation, planning and policy analyses for universities, associations, foundations, governmental agencies and private companies engaged in scientific, technological or educational activities. Special expertise in the development of new institutions. Special skills in providing planning and related group facilitation workshops.

31453 ■ Rothschild Strategies Unlimited L.L.C.
PO Box 7568
Wilton, CT 06897-7568
Ph:(203)846-6898
Fax: (203)847-1426
Co. E-mail: bill@strategyleader.com
URL: http://www.strategyleader.com

E-mail: bill@strategyleader.com
Scope: Consults with senior management and business level strategy teams to develop overall strategic direction, set priorities and creates sustainable competitive advantages and differentiators. Enables organizations to enhance their own strategic thinking and leadership skills so that they can continue to develop and implement profitable growth strategies. **Publications:** "Putting It All Together-a guide to strategic thinking"; "Competitive Advantage"; "Ristaker, Caretaker, Surgeon & Undertaker-four faces of strategic leadership". **Special Services:** StrategyLeader®.

31454 ■ Sanford Consulting
52 Perry Corners Rd.
Amenia, NY 12501

Ph:(845)373-8960
Fax: (845)373-8961
Co. E-mail: sanford@mohawk.com

E-mail: sanford@mohawk.com
Scope: Helps businesses find, sell, (to), and keep customers. Provides management and marketing services, including problem analysis and solution design for new business development, market analysis and segmentation, departmental organization, and administrative policies and procedures. Industries served: small business, telecommunications, professional services, healthcare, and nonprofits in the continental United States. **Seminars:** Trade show succes; Finding customers; Business attitudes at not for profit and others.

31455 ■ SBR Global
3 - 14 College St.
Toronto, ON, Canada M5G 1K2
Ph:(416)962-7500
Fax: (416)962-7505
Co. E-mail: bizdev@sbr-global.com
URL: http://www.sbr-global.com

E-mail: bizdev@sbr-global.com
Scope: Specializes in the leasing of multidisciplinary, high-performance work teams at customer in-house cost, under a mixed military/general contracting model. Engagements include BPR, IE, SA, market and competitor intelligence, logistics, strategy, audit, workouts/turnarounds, M&A support/targeting, statistics and microeconomic modeling, PMO support. **Seminars:** Electronic counter measures; Strategic planning; Project management.

31456 ■ David G. Schantz & Associates
29 Wood Run Cir.
Rochester, NY 14612-2271
Ph:(716)723-0760
Fax: (716)723-8724
Co. E-mail: daveschantz@yahoo.com
URL: http://www.daveschantz.freeservers.com

E-mail: daveschantz@yahoo.com
Scope: Consultant provides industrial engineering services for photofinishing labs, including amateur-wholesale, professional, commercial, school, and package.

31457 ■ Schneider Consulting Group Inc.
50 S Steele St., Ste. 390
Denver, CO 80209
Ph:(303)320-4413
Fax: (303)320-5795
Co. E-mail: info@scgfambus.com
URL: http://www.schneiderconsultinggroup.com

E-mail: info@scgfambus.com
Scope: Assists family-owned and privately-held business transition to the next generation and/or to a more professionally managed company, turnaround consulting for small and medium size companies.

31458 ■ Sklar & Associates
1101 S Arlington Ridge Rd. Ste. 511
Arlington, VA 22202-1925
Ph:(202)257-5061
Fax: (202)828-4130
Co. E-mail: sklarincdc@aol.com
URL: http://www.sklarinc.com

E-mail: sklarincdc@aol.com
Scope: Provides Audit Oversight services to listed corporations on Sarbanes-Oxley compliance. **Seminars:** Financial Analysis in MBA; Emerging Company Finance; Due Diligence in Business Acquisition; Business Valuation. **Special Services:** Financial Modeling. Course titled *Understanding and Detecting Deceptive Creative Accounting Practices.*

31459 ■ Harvey C. Skoog
3737 N Robert Rd., No. A
Prescott Valley, AZ 86314
Ph:(928)772-1448
Scope: Firm has expertise in taxes, payroll, financial planning, budgeting, buy/sell planning, business start-

up, fraud detection, troubled business consulting, acquisition, construction, and retailing industries in Arizona.

31460 ■ R.F. Stengel & Company Inc.
780 Yellow Springs Rd.
Paoli, PA 19301
Ph:(610)296-8950
Fax: (610)296-8991
Scope: A management consulting and crisis management firm providing services to financially and operationally troubled companies. Develops and implements business recovery programs.

31461 ■ Straightline Services Inc.
11 Centre St., Ste. 10
Salem, CT 06420
Ph:(860)889-7929
Fax: (860)885-1894
Co. E-mail: straitln@aol.com

E-mail: straitln@aol.com
Scope: Design and implementation of organizational infrastructure, business plans and troubleshooting. Emphasis on operations with a central and field or satellite offices. Industries Served: Construction, resorts, Indian tribes, academies, small-medium sized business- mostly privately held. **Publications:** Photos published in "Engineering News Record," "New England Construction News." **Seminars:** Start up, Troubleshooting seminars. **Special Services:** Commercial/Industrial Photography - Member of CIPNE (Comm/Ind Photographers of New England). Also member of the National Bureau of Professional Management Consultants is a CPCM or Certified Professional Consultant to Management.

31462 ■ Strategic Mangement Services
3126 Duval St.
Austin, TX 78705
Ph:(512)477-4094
Fax: (512)478-8301
Scope: Devlops business and strategic plans for beginning or established companies. Provides management and leadership consulting and training. Industries served: insurance, health care, restaurant, small manufacturing.

31463 ■ Strategic MindShare Consulting
1401 Brickell Ave., Ste. 640
Miami, FL 33131
Ph:(305)377-2220
Fax: (305)377-2280
Co. E-mail: dee@strategicmindshare.com
URL: http://www.strategicmindshare.com

E-mail: dee@strategicmindshare.com
Scope: Firm specializes in strategic planning; feasibility studies; profit enhancement; organizational development; start-up businesses; mergers and acquisitions; joint ventures; divestitures; interim management; crisis management; turnarounds; new product development and competitive analysis. **Publications:** "Top Ten CEO Burning Issues for 2005"; "Top Ten Consumer Behavioral Trends for 2005"; "The Influence Factors".

31464 ■ TC International Marketing Inc.
18 Blooms Corners Rd.
Warwick, NY 10990-2401
Ph:(845)258-7482
Fax: (845)986-2130
Co. E-mail: tcintl@warwick.net
URL: http://www.tcintlmarketing.com

E-mail: tcintl@warwick.net
Scope: Business expansion consulting, including feasibility studies, mergers and acquisitions, divestments, market research, and strategizing.

31465 ■ Technology Management Group
3 Penny Ln.
PO Box 3260
Woodbridge, CT 06525-1531
Ph:(203)387-1430
Fax: (203)387-1470
Co. E-mail: info@commtechsoftware.com

E-mail: info@commtechsoftware.com
Scope: Consulting services include analysis of market opportunities; product introductions; new ventures; acquisitions analysis; licensing, joint ventures, and OEM arrangements. Emphasis on polymers, medical devices, biotechnology, pharmaceuticals, and chemicals.

31466 ■ Trendzitions Inc.
310 Goddard, Ste. 100
Irvine, CA 92618
Ph:(949)727-9100
Free: 800-266-2767
Fax: (949)851-8444
Co. E-mail: bgeer@trendzitions.com
URL: http://www.trendzitions.com

E-mail: bgeer@trendzitions.com
Scope: Provides services in the areas of communications consulting, project management, construction management, and furniture procurement. Offers information on spatial uses, building codes, ADA compliance, and city ordinances. Also offers budget projections.

31467 ■ Turnaround Inc.
3415 A St. NW
Gig Harbor, WA 98335
Ph:(253)857-6730
Fax: (253)857-6344
Co. E-mail: info@turnround-inc.com
URL: http://www.turnaround-inc.com

E-mail: info@turnround-inc.com
Scope: Firm provides interim executive management assistance and management advisory to small, medium and family-owned businesses that are not meeting their goals. Services include acting as an interim executive or on-site manager. Extensive practices in arena of bankruptcy management. **Publications:** "How to Identify Problem and Promising Management"; "How to Tell if Your Company is a Bankruptcy Candidate"; "Signs that Your Company is in Trouble"; "The Turnaround Specialist: How to File a Petition Under 11 USC 11". **Seminars:** Competitive Intelligence Gathering.

31468 ■ ValueNomics Value Specialists
10 Almaden Blvd., Ste. 1450
San Jose, CA 95113-2226
Ph:(408)257-8521
Fax: (408)257-1146
Co. E-mail: value@valuenomics.com
URL: http://www.valuenomics.com

E-mail: value@valuenomics.com
Scope: Specializes in valuations; appraisals; strategic planning; feasibility studies; mergers and acquisitions; joint ventures; divestitures; competitive intelligence; and due diligence. Acts as an expert witness. Offers litigation support. **Publications:** "The Business of Business Valuation and the CPA as an expert witness". **Special Services:** ValueNomics®.

31469 ■ Via Nova Consulting
1228 Winburn Dr.
Atlanta, GA 30344
Ph:(404)761-7484
Fax: (404)762-7123
Scope: Consulting services in the areas of strategic planning; privatization; executive searches; market research; customer service audits; new product development; competitive intelligence; and Total Quality Management (TQM).

31470 ■ Vision Management
149 Meadows Rd.
Lafayette, NJ 07848-3120
Ph:(973)702-1116
Fax: (201)702-8311
Scope: Firm specializes in profit enhancement; strategic planning; business process re-engineering; industrial engineering; facilities planning; team building; inventory management; and Total Quality Management (TQM).

31471 ■ The Walk The Talk Co.
2925 LBJ Fwy., Ste. 201
Dallas, TX 75234
Ph:(972)243-8863
Free: 800-888-2811
Fax: (972)243-0815
Co. E-mail: info@walkthetalk.com
URL: http://www.walkthetalk.com

E-mail: info@walkthetalk.com
Scope: Assists a wide variety of organizations in implementing POSITIVE DISCIPLINE®, the proprietary performance management system developed by the firm which concentrates on individual responsibility and decision making instead of disciplinary penalties. Helps organizations develop and implement PEER REVIEW, a proven system that helps solve employee problems in a remarkable way-through employees; and MULTISOURCE360®, an evaluation process whereby feedback is compiled from a full-range of sources, including a self-evaluation, leadership development workshops and keynote presentations and publications. **Publications:** "Positive Discipline"; "Leadership Secrets of Santa Claus"; "Start Right-Stay Right"; "Walk Awhile In MY Shoes"; "Listen Up, Leader!"; "Five Star Teamwork"; "Ethics4Everyone"; "Leadership Courage"; "The Manager's Communication Handbook"; "180 Ways To Walk The Recognition Talk"; "The Manager's Coaching Handbook". **Seminars:** Walk the Talk; Coaching for Continuous Improvement; Managing Employee Performance; Customized Management Development Forums; Keynote presentations; Leadership Development Workshops; Consulting Services and Publications; Customer service training; Ethics & Values training.

31472 ■ Weich & Bilotti Inc.
74 Main St.
Framingham, MA 01702
Ph:(508)879-8007
Fax: (508)879-7811
Co. E-mail: info@weich-bilotti.com
URL: http://www.weich.com

E-mail: info@weich-bilotti.com
Scope: Specializes in business plans, venture capital, computer information systems, turnaround/interim management, retail consulting, start-up process, college recruiting, and IS and IT personnel.

31473 ■ Wheeler and Young Inc.
33 Peter St.
Markham, ON, Canada L3P 2A5
Ph:(905)471-9064
Fax: (905)471-9989
Co. E-mail: wheeler@ericwheeler.ca

E-mail: wheeler@ericwheeler.ca
Scope: Business management services, including ISO 9000 implementation, software development process, and knowledge-management in organizations. Industries Served: Knowledge-based industries, including software and hardware development, medical and legal professionals, information service providers. **Seminars:** The Web, Software, and Getting it Right.

31474 ■ ZS Engineering P.C.
99 Tulip Ave.
Floral Park, NY 11001
Ph:(516)328-3200
Fax: (516)328-6195
Co. E-mail: office@zsengineering.com
URL: http://www.zsengineering.com

E-mail: office@zsengineering.com
Scope: Offers engineering consulting services to building owners, building managers and contractors. Speciallizes in design and inspections of fire alarm systems, sprinkler systems, smoke control systems, building evaluations for fire code compliance, violations removal. **Seminars:** Fire protection courses for contractors and building management.

FRANCHISES AND BUSINESS OPPORTUNITIES

31475 ■ ABX-Associates Business Xchange
7604 Oak St.
Frisco, TX 75034
Ph:(214)850-6131
Fax: (866)462-7229
Founded: 1971. **Description:** Nationwide franchise brokers network.

31476 ■ American Franchise Consultants
520 W Gleneagles Dr.
Phoenix, AZ 85023
Free: 800-424-0749
Founded: 1995. **Description:** Business consultants.

31477 ■ Benchmark Group
121 W Walnut St.
Rogers, AR 72756
Ph:(479)636-5004
Free: 800-321-8721
Fax: (479)621-0318
Founded: 1978. **Description:** Building design and rollout services.

31478 ■ Biga & Associates, Inc.
200 E Evergreen, Ste. 123
Mount Prospect, IL 60004
Ph:(847)870-7521
Fax: (847)870-7553
Founded: 1989. **Description:** Franchise consultants.

31479 ■ Cummings Business Development Corp.
23 Walkers Brook Dr.
Reading, MA 01867
Ph:(771)942-9220
Free: 800-982-9636
Fax: (781)942-0924
Founded: 1992. **Description:** Full service franchise consulting firm.

31480 ■ Fortune Management
9888 Carroll Center Rd., No. 100
San Diego, CA 92126
Ph:(858)535-6203
Free: 800-628-1052
Fax: (858)535-6375
No. of Franchise Units: 37. **Founded:** 1990. **Franchised:** 1990. **Description:** Dental consulting company. **Equity Capital Needed:** $32,000 minimum in liquidity. **Franchise Fee:** $42,000. **Financial Assistance:** Yes. **Training:** Yes.

31481 ■ Franchise Development International, LLC
370 SE 15 Ave.
Pompano Beach, FL 33060
Ph:(954)942-9424
Fax: (954)783-5177
Founded: 1991. **Description:** Franchise development and marketing.

31482 ■ Franchise Developments, Inc.
4730 Centre Ave.
Pittsburgh, PA 15213
Ph:(412)521-4988
Fax: (412)687-0541
Founded: 1970. **Description:** Develop, implement and launch franchise programs.

31483 ■ Franchise Foundations
4157 23rd St.
San Francisco, CA 94114
Free: 800-942-4402
Founded: 1980. **Description:** Franchise consulting.

31484 ■ Franchise Masters International
8301 Golden Valley Rd., Ste. 230
Minneapolis, MN 55427
Ph:(763)541-0832
Free: 800-541-1385
Fax: (763)542-2246
Founded: 1980. **Description:** Planning, legal, manuals, advertising and marketing.

31485 ■ Franchise Specialists, Inc.
1234 Maple St. Ext.
Moon Twp, PA 15108
Free: 800-261-5055
Founded: 1978. **Description:** Professional franchise development and sales.

31486 ■ Franchisee Financialine
American Association of Franchisees and Dealers
PO Box 81887
San Diego, CA 92138-1887
Ph:(619)209-3775
Free: 800-733-9858
Fax: (619)209-3777
Founded: 1992. **Description:** Accounting services for franchisees.

31487 ■ Francorp, Inc.
20200 Governors Dr.
Olympia Fields, IL 60461
Ph:(708)481-2900
Free: 800-372-6244
Co. E-mail: info@francorp.com
URL: http://www.francorp.com
Founded: 1976. **Description:** Offers consultancy on franchising business. Consultants have provided full development programs, including feasibility studies, business plans, legal documents, operations manuals, and marketing materials for clients since 1976. **Training:** Provides post-development services for establishing franchisors, including lead generation programs, brochures, videotapes, international brokerage, PR, and expert witness service.

31488 ■ Franquest
Douglas Matheson & Co., Inc.
PO Box 2038
Pismo Beach, CA 93448
Ph:(805)773-5377
Free: 800-794-0117
Fax: (805)773-5687
Founded: 1978. **Description:** Offers consultancy on franchising issues.

31489 ■ Fransearch, Inc.
450 E 1000 N, Ste. 101
North Salt Lake, UT 84054-1925
Ph:(801)397-3726
Description: Franchise executive recruiting.

31490 ■ Franstaff, Inc.
73 S Palm Ave., Ste. 219
Sarasota, FL 34236
Ph:(941)952-9555
Description: Provides consultancy on franchising matters.

31491 ■ HRX
574 Prairie Ctr. Dr., No. 135/285
Eden Prairie, MN 55344
Ph:(952)996-0975
Fax: (952)996-0976
Founded: 1992. **Description:** Human resource consulting and training firm.

31492 ■ Information Services Inc.
2811 NE 46th St.
Lighthouse Pt., FL 33064
Ph:(954)942-0242
Fax: (954)783-2570
Founded: 1982. **Description:** Sell franchise and business opportunities.

31493 ■ Intel Marketing Associates, Inc.
227 Bellevue Way NE, Ste. 178
Bellevue, WA 98004
Ph:(206)781-1047
Description: Franchise marketing and consulting firm.

31494 ■ International Franchise Dev./Frannet Div. LLC
29125 Chargrin Blvd., No. 200
Cleveland, OH 44122
Ph:(216)831-2610
Fax: (216)765-7118
Founded: 1990. **Description:** Franchise selection advice and development.

31495 ■ L. Michael Schwartz, P.A.
10561 Barkley Pl., Ste. 510
Overland Park, KS 66212-1860
Ph:(913)341-1919
Fax: (913)341-0007
Description: Franchise consulting and full legal services.

**31496 ■ Leon Gottlieb USA/Int'l Franchise/
Restaurant Consultants**
Leon Gottlieb & Associates
4601 Sendero Pl.
Tarzana, CA 91356-4821
Ph:(818)757-1131
Fax: (818)757-1816
Founded: 1960. **Description:** Consultant, expert witness, arbitrator.

31497 ■ Lite For Life
Lite for Life Franchise Corp., Inc.
388 Second St.
Los Altos, CA 94022
Ph:(650)941-3200
Fax: (650)559-3111
No. of Franchise Units: 2 **No. of Company-Owned
Units:** 4. **Founded:** 1978. **Franchised:** 2003. **Description:** Weight loss and nutritional consulting. **Equity Capital Needed:** $75,000+. **Franchise Fee:**
$20,000. **Financial Assistance:** No. **Training:** Yes.

31498 ■ Market Potential Mapping
PO Box 1602
Lake Junaluska, NC 28745-1602
Free: 888-627-2770
Fax: (828)627-1525
Founded: 1997. **Description:** Location strategy/site selection.

31499 ■ Marketing Resources Group
71-58 Austin St.
Forest Hills, NY 11375
Ph:(718)261-8882
Description: Franchise development, marketing, and sales.

31500 ■ McGrow Consulting
30 N St.
Hingham, MA 02043
Ph:(781)740-2211
Free: 800-358-8011
Founded: 1980. **Description:** Franchise consulting firm.

31501 ■ Seaboard Franchise Services Co.
3000 Weslayan Dr., Ste. 108
Houston, TX 77027
Ph:(713)621-6200
Fax: (713)621-8200
Founded: 1992. **Description:** Franchise consultants.

31502 ■ Thirteen-One, Inc.
2221 Westcreek Ln., 15F
Houston, TX 77027
Ph:(713)622-7209
Fax: (713)629-7618
Founded: 1980. **Description:** Franchise consultants.

31503 ■ TPMC Realty Services Group
1412 Main St., No. 19Fl.
Dallas, TX 75202-4018
Ph:(214)416-5225
Fax: (214)416-7919
Founded: 1987. **Description:** Offers franchise consultants.

31504 ■ WLH & Associates
5622 Dumfries Ct. W
Dublin, OH 43017
Ph:(614)764-1644
Founded: 1984. **Description:** Consulting in franchise sales and marketing.

31505 ■ World Franchise Consultants
15965 Jeanette
Southfield, MI 48075
Ph:(248)559-1415
Founded: 1973. **Description:** Franchise consulting and referral.

Credit and Collection

START-UP INFORMATION

31506 ■ "Helping Victims Unravel Identity Theft" in *Business Journal-Portland* (Vol. 20, No. 29, September 19, 2003, pp. 1)
Pub: American City Business Journals, Inc.
Ed: Robin J. Moody. **Description:** Identity Safeguards, located in Tualatin, Oregon, offers protection against identity theft. The startup company provides educational and credit report monitoring services to consumers victimized by identity theft.

31507 ■ *How to Start a Bankruptcy Forms Processing Service*
Pub: Graphico Publishing Company
Ed: Victoria Ring. **Released:** September 2004. **Price:** $59.99. **Description:** Due to the increase in bankruptcy filings, attorneys are outsourcing related jobs in order to reduce overhead.

31508 ■ "What's your problem?" in *Entrepreneur* (Vol. 30, No. 12, Dec. 2002)
Pub: Entrepreneur Media Inc.
Ed: Paul Edwards, Sarah Edwards. **Description:** Advice for starting a new business for persons with bad credit history is offered.

ASSOCIATIONS AND OTHER ORGANIZATIONS

31509 ■ **National Association of Credit Management**
8840 Columbia 100 Pkwy.
Columbia, MD 21045
Ph:(410)740-5560
Free: 800-955-8815
Fax: (410)740-5574
Co. E-mail: robins@nacm.org
URL: http://www.nacm.org
Contact: Robin D. Schauseil CAE, Pres./COO
Description: Credit and financial executives representing manufacturers, wholesalers, financial institutions, insurance companies, utilities, and other businesses interested in business credit. Promotes sound credit practices and legislation. Conducts Graduate School of Credit and Financial Management at Dartmouth College, Hanover, NH. **Publications:** *Business Credit* (10/year); *Credit Executives Handbook*; *Digest of Commercial Laws*; *Manual of Credit and Commercial Laws* (annual).

REFERENCE WORKS

31510 ■ "Access to Capital and Terms of Credit: A Comparison of Men- and Women-Owned Small Businesses" in *Journal of Small Business Management*
Pub: West Virginia University
Ed: Susan Coleman. **Description:** A comparison of access to capital for men- and women-owned small businesses. The study uses data from the 1993 National Survey of Small Business Finances.

31511 ■ *All About Credit*
Pub: Kaplan Publishing
Ed: Deborah McNaughton **Released:** April 1999. **Price:** $15.95. **Description:** Debt solution to specific credit problems for individuals denied credit, trying to mortgage a home, problems with creditors, and bankruptcy.

31512 ■ "Ask Inc." in *Inc.* (Volume 28, January 2006, No. 1, pp. 51-52)
Pub: Inc. Magazine
Description: Advice is offered regarding noncompete agreements, factoring companies that pay businesses up-front for outstanding bills and collect payments from customers, and a pet accessory business.

31513 ■ "Beat Those Bouncing Checks" in *Hispanic Business* (December 2003, pp. 58)
Pub: Hispanic Business
Ed: Roger Harris. **Description:** Profile of Justchex, the online service that can help a small business receive payment for about 80 percent of returned checks.

31514 ■ "Beware of credit card offers ($s and sense)" in *Black Enterprise* (Vol. 33, No. 3, October 2002, pp. S4)
Pub: Earl Graves Publishing Co.
Ed: Carolyn M. Brown. **Description:** Advice is offered about the responsible use of credit and credit cards, especially for teens. Contact information is provided for the National Consumers League, and information for establishing and maintaining a clean credit report.

31515 ■ "Billing Bad Debt" in *Hispanic Business* (October 2003, pp. 102)
Pub: Hispanic Business
Ed: Milton Zall. **Description:** Financial managers have several options when it comes to accounting for unpaid receivables, including negotiating a reduced payoff, going to court, or hiring a collection service.

31516 ■ "The Bill's In the Mail"Bill Me Later" Payment Option" in *Entrepreneur.com* (Vol. 34, February 2006, No. 2, pp. 36)
Pub: Entrepreneur Media Inc.
Ed: Melissa Campanelli. **Description:** I4 Commerce's Bill Me Later Service provides payment options for Web customers, eliminating the need for clients to post their credit card numbers on the Internet.

31517 ■ "Can you be a merchant vendor?" in *Home Office Computing* (Vol. 18, No. 11, November 2000, pp. 20)
Pub: Scholastic Inc.
Ed: William Van Winkle. **Description:** A description of effective, online person-to-person (P2P) payment systems is provided.

31518 ■ *Cash Flow, Credit and Collection: Over 100 Proven Techniques for Protecting and Strengthening Your Balance Sheet*
Pub: Probus Publishing Co., Inc.
Ed: Basil P. Mavrovitis. **Released:** Revised edition, 1993. **Price:** $32.50. **Description:** Provides informa-

tion on cash management. Contains checklists, tips, examples, illustrations, and case studies. Also includes cash management ideas for credit practitioners and guidelines for cash management practices.

31519 ■ "Cashing In on Bad Debts" in *Hispanic Business* (Vol. 24, No. 5, May 2002, pp. 52)
Pub: Hispanic Business Inc.
Ed: Milton Zall. **Description:** Ways to claim bad debts as tax deductions are discussed.

31520 ■ "The Check's in the E-Mail" in *Entrepreneur* (Vol. 32, October 2004, No. 10, pp. 66)
Pub: Entrepreneur Media Inc.
Description: Banking law, Check 21, allows an electronic facsimile of a paper check to have the same legal standing of the original paper check it represents. This process will have a profound affect on the way businesses make and receive check payments.

31521 ■ "The Check's in the Mail" in *Home Office Computing* (Vol. 18, No. 11, November 2000, pp. 98)
Pub: Scholastic Inc.
Ed: Holly Aguirre. **Description:** Rules for ensuring timely and error-free billing and payment are covered.

31522 ■ "Click Here For Credit Info" in *Business Week* (No. 3761, December 10, 2001, pp.SB4)
Pub: McGraw-Hill Inc.
Description: Profile of QuickBooks Pro, the software that gives direct access to credit reports from Dun & Bradstreet for a mere $10 per report.

31523 ■ "A Collect Calling" in *Entrepreneur* (Vol. 28, No. 10, October 2000, pp. 156)
Pub: Entrepreneur Media Inc.
Ed: Paul Edwards and Sarah Edwards. **Description:** The duties of a judgment recovery specialist are outlined.

31524 ■ *Collect Those Debts!*
Pub: Self-Counsel Press, Inc.
Ed: Timothy R. Paulsen. **Released:** 1992. **Price:** $8.95 (paper). **Description:** Presents methods of debt management.

31525 ■ "Collecting Pesky Past Due Debts" in *My Business* (September/October 2001, pp. 39)
Pub: My Business Magazine
Ed: Ted Tate. **Description:** Richard L. Christopher, president of All-Star Limousine in Cleveland, Ohio, provides strategies for dealing with slow paying accounts.

31526 ■ *Collection Techniques for Small Business*
Pub: Oasis Press
Ed: Gini G. Scott. **Released:** 1994. **Price:** $19.95 (paper); $39.95 (ringbound).

31527 ∎ *The Complete Book of Collection Letters, Telephone Collection Scripts, and Faxes*
Pub: The McGraw-Hill Companies
Ed: Cecil J. Bond. **Released:** 1995. **Price:** $69.95. **Description:** Provides information on how to effectively handle delinquent accounts using letters, phones, and faxes. Includes 400 examples of effective letters and phone scripts plus information on how to employ skip tracing, liens, and holding orders to legally collect on outstanding accounts.

31528 ∎ *The Complete Credits and Collection Starter Success Kit*
Pub: International Wealth Success, Inc.
Ed: James V. Scalo. **Released:** 1996. **Price:** $29.50.

31529 ∎ *Complete Idiot's Guide to Starting an Ebay Business*
Pub: Penguin Books (USA) Incorporated
Ed: Barbara Weltman, Kara Gordon, Shirley Muse. **Released:** February 2005. **Price:** $19.95 (US), $29.00 (Canadian). **Description:** Guide for starting an eBay business includes information on products to sell, how to price merchandise, and details for working with services like PayPal, and how to organize fulfillment services.

31530 ∎ "Consumer Finance" in *Business Week* (January 16, 2006, No. 3967, pp. 38)
Pub: McGraw-Hill Companies
Ed: Peter Burrows. **Description:** A new trend shows online brands offering shoppers Bill Me later payment options in order to spur sales growth and offer a billing method to consumers uneasy about using their credit cards on the Internet. So far 230 e-commerce sites offer this service.

31531 ∎ "Credit Checkup" in *Black Enterprise* (Vol. 36, February 2006, No. 7, pp. 169)
Pub: Earl G. Graves Publishing Co. Inc.
Ed: Tanisha A. Sykes. **Description:** TrueCredit lists five ways to maintain or improve a credit standing rating.

31532 ∎ "Credit Denied: Dot-Coms Feel the Squeeze" in *Fortune* (Vol. 142, No. 3, July 24, 2000, pp. 336+)
Pub: Time Inc.
Ed: Tyler Maroney. **Description:** As more and more Internet startups stumble, and vendors are left holding the bag, companies that do business with the Net newcomers are losing faith in their clients' financial stability.

31533 ∎ "Credit Score Providers Address Concerns" in *Rough Notes* (Vol. 145, No. 2, February 2003, pp. 90)
Pub: Rough Notes
Ed: Bruce Hicks. **Description:** A panel discussion on credit scoring was held by the Society of CPCU's consisting of William T. Atkins, Lamont D. Boyd, Gary Skerl, John B. Wilson, and Gregg L. Antenen.

31534 ∎ "Credit Use Strangles Wealth" in *Black Enterprise* (Vol. 35, November 2004, No. 4, pp. 38)
Pub: Earl G. Graves Publishing Co. Inc.
Ed: Aissatou Sidime. **Description:** Minorities are most at risk of damaging financial futures due to poor credit card management, according to the U.S. Federal Reserve.

31535 ∎ "Creditor sues to wring money from former Code-Alarm" in *Crain's Detroit Business* (Vol. 18, No. 24, June 17, 2002, pp. 29)
Pub: Crain Communications Inc. - Detroit
Ed: Michael Strong. **Description:** Old CA Inc., formerly Code-Alarm Inc., faces a lawsuit from one former vendor, while others are trying to secure payments three months after the firm was sold.

31536 ∎ *Credits and Collections: Techniques for Improving Your Cash Flow*
Pub: Crisp Publications, Inc.
Ed: Candace Mondello. **Price:** $9.95.

31537 ∎ "Dealing with slow-paying customers" in *Crain's Detroit Business* (Vol. 19, No. 7, February 17, 2003, pp. 14)
Pub: Crain Communications Inc., Detroit
Description: Five tips for dealing with slow paying customers are listed.

31538 ∎ "Debate Over Credit Scoring May Head to Court" in *Crain's Detroit Business* (Vol. 21, January 24, 2005, No. 4, pp. 6)
Pub: Crain Communications Inc. - Detroit
Ed: Amy Lane. **Description:** A proposed new law in Michigan would prohibit insurance companies from using credit scores for setting insurance rates.

31539 ∎ "Debt Collection" in *Black Enterprise* (Vol. 34, No. 3, October 2003, pp. 136)
Pub: Earl Graves Publishing Co.
Ed: Tanisha A. Sykes. **Description:** According to a member activity report by the National Foundation for Credit Counseling, the average debt management client is 35 years of age, and 95 percent of his or her income is debt. The NCFF offers free and affordable financial advice to consumers. A plan for negotiating with a lender is presented.

31540 ∎ "Discrimination in the Small-Business Credit Market" in *Review of Economics and Statistics* (Vol. 85, No. 4, November 2003, pp. 930)
Pub: MIT Press Journals
Ed: David G. Blanchflower, Philip B. Levine, David J. Zimmerman. **Description:** Using data from the 1993 and 1998 National Surveys of Small Business Finances to examine the existence of racial discrimination in the small-business credit market, an econometric analysis of loan outcomes by race was conducted. The study found that black-owned small businesses are about twice as likely to be denied credit, even after controlling the differences in credit-worthiness and other factors. A series of specification checks indicates that this gap is unlikely to be explained by omitted variable bias. These results indicate that the racial disparity in credit availability is likely caused by discrimination.

31541 ∎ "Do You Rate?" in *Entrepreneur* (Vol. 31, No. 10, October 2003, pp. 59)
Pub: Entrepreneur Media, Inc.
Ed: Joshua Kurlantzick. **Description:** Many small companies are struggling to maintain good credit ratings because of the continued weak economy.

31542 ∎ "Eight Tips to Spot Bad Checks" in *My Business* (February/March 2003, pp. 15)
Pub: My Business Magazine
Description: According to the Nilson Report, nearly 1.2 million bad checks are written daily in the U.S., equating to approximately $55.8 million in losses to retailers. Eight tips to spot a bad check are listed.

31543 ∎ *Extending Credit and Collecting Cash*
Pub: Crisp Publications, Inc.
Ed: Lynn Harrison. **Released:** 1993. **Price:** $15.95. **Description:** Part of the Small Business & Entrepreneurship Series.

31544 ∎ "The Factoring Factor" in *Inc.* (February 1, 2002)
Pub: Inc. Magazine
Ed: Jane Salodof MacNeil. **Description:** Slow-paying customers got you in a cash-flow crisis? A listing of sites that can help collect is offered.

31545 ∎ "Fantastic Plastic" in *Entrepreneur* (Vol. 33, January 2005, No. 1, pp. 49)
Pub: Entrepreneur Media Inc.
Ed: C.J. Prince. **Description:** Paying by credit card allows a small business to maximize cash flow, offers rewards, and provides an accurate accounting for expenses.

31546 ∎ "Federal Legislation Lays Groundwork for Electronic Check Exchange" in *Long Island Business News* (February 13, 2004)
Pub: Dolan Media Newswires
Ed: Claude Solnik. **Description:** Federal legislation will allow banks to process checks using electronic transfers of scanned checks, making deposits almost immediate. The new system will cut costs for financial institutions.

31547 ∎ "Final Chapter" in *Entrepreneur* (Vol. 28, No. 4, April 2000, pp. 130)
Pub: Entrepreneur Media Inc.
Ed: Jacquelyn Lynn. **Description:** Steps to take when a customer goes bankrupt, the legal notice every business owner dreads.

31548 ∎ "For-Your-Own-Good Innovation" in *Inc.* (September 1, 2003)
Pub: Gruner & Jahr USA Publishing
Ed: Rod Kurtz. **Description:** The California firm, Payment Protection Systems, sells a dashboard device called On Time to used car dealers. The device disables a vehicle if the owner does not make a scheduled payment. Flexplay Technologies in New York has invented a disc to curb software and copyright piracy.

31549 ∎ "Forgive Us Our Debts...The Creditor May, But the IRS Won't" in *Black Enterprise* (Vol. 34, July 2004, No. 12, pp. 143)
Pub: Earl G. Graves Publishing Co. Inc.
Ed: Leslie E. Royal. **Description:** While some mortgage lenders, car financiers, and credit card issuers may forgive debt when an individual agrees to pay a certain amount off the balance, the Internal Revenue Service will never write-off taxes owed.

31550 ∎ "Fulfill the Promise of Electronic Billing" in *E-business Advisor* (Vol. 18, No. 7, July 2000, pp. 26)
Pub: Advisor Media, Inc.
Ed: Jim Flynn. **Description:** Electronic bill payment and presentment (EBPP) has not taken off as expected due to such problems as poor implementation of the technology for the consumer market and bill consolidation technology is still in the embryonic stage.

31551 ∎ "Getting tough on slow payers can pay off" in *Crain's Detroit Business* (Vol. 19, No. 7, February 17, 2003, pp. 14)
Pub: Crain Communications Inc., Detroit
Ed: Laura Bailey. **Description:** Bad debt and slow paying customers are one of the biggest issues faced by small businesses, and problems are worse in a tight economy.

31552 ∎ "Getting Paid: Collection Tips for Handling Slow- or Non-Paying Clients" in *Black Enterprise* (Vol. 35, December 2004, No. 5, pp. 65)
Pub: Earl G. Graves Publishing Co. Inc.
Ed: Carolyn M. Brown. **Description:** Bilateral Credit Corporation, a commercial collection agency, recommends negotiating terms in advance with clients, separating collection and business functions, and keeping internal accounting systems in order.

31553 ∎ "Getting Paid Faster" in *Black Enterprise* (Vol. 36, February 2006, No. 7, pp. 58)
Pub: Earl G. Graves Publishing Co. Inc.
Ed: Bridget McCrea. **Description:** Large corporations and the government are using credit-card-like accounts through Visa and MasterCard for purchasing products and services. Visa has launched a program to introduce to small businesses in order to setup accounts to accept the purchasing cards in order to grow their businesses.

31554 ∎ "Gold Rush" in *Business Week* (January 9, 2006, No. 3966, pp. 68-72, 74, 76)
Pub: McGraw-Hill Companies
Ed: Brian Grow. **Description:** Online payment systems are facing security issues because online hackers are able to steal bank and credit card information. E-Gold is digital currency and customers using the service can enter false information in order to steal from an account.

31555 ■ "Her Line of Credit Was in Default. Her Partnership With Her Mom Was Faltering" in *Inc.* (Volume 27, December 2005, No. 12, pp. 59-60)
Pub: Inc. Magazine
Ed: Nadine Heintz. **Description:** Heather Antonelli, CEO of Eminence Style, a furniture wholesaling business, tells why she decided to close her business and declare bankruptcy.

31556 ■ *How to Collect Debts (And Still Keep Your Customers)*
Pub: Amacom
Ed: David Sher, Martin Sher. **Released:** May 1999. **Price:** $24.95. **Description:** Suggestions for collecting as much money as possible, as quickly as possible, while maintaining customer goodwill, along with strategies for eliminating bad debt.

31557 ■ *How to Write a Great Business Plan for Your Small Business in 60 Minutes or Less*
Pub: Atlantic Publishing
Ed: Sharon L. Fullen. **Released:** September 2005. **Price:** $39.95 includes CD-Rom. **Description:** A good business plan outlines goals and works as a company's resume to obtain funding, credit from suppliers, management of the operations and finances, promotion and marketing, and more.

31558 ■ "In Brief: Discover Touting Gas Rewards" in *American Banker* (Vol. 172, January 31, 2007, No. 21, pp. 16)
Pub: SourceMedia, Inc.
Ed: H. Michael Jalili. **Description:** Discover Financial Services LLC reported a direct correlation between energy prices and small business confidence. Discover's small business program that offers cash back on gasoline purchases has been successful. Statistical data included.

31559 ■ "In Brief: MBNA Issuing eBay Product in Canada" in *American Banker Newsletter* (Vol. 168, No. 208, October 29, 2003, pp. 9)
Pub: Thomson Media
Description: MBNA Corporation and eBay Inc. offers a Canadian version of the eBay Anything Points Master Card, a credit card product that allows individuals to earn points towards discounts when purchasing eBay auction items.

31560 ■ "Kansas Investigators Target Wichita Dating Service in Credit-Card Fraud Probe" in *Wichita Eagle* (February 13, 2004)
Pub: Knight-Ridder/Tribune Business News
Ed: Tim Potter. **Description:** State of Kansas attorney general's office filed a civil lawsuit seeking $1.2 million from a dating service's franchises in Wichita and Overland Park. The lawsuit claims Great Expectations of violating Kansas Consumer Protection Act through deceptive and unconscionable practices, charging the business knowingly targeted vulnerable individuals and charged thousands of dollars on credit cards of certain clients.

31561 ■ "Keep it Simple" in *Entrepreneur. com* (Vol. 34, February 2006, No. 2, pp. 60)
Pub: Entrepreneur Media Inc.
Ed: Chris Penttila. **Description:** Twenty-five tips for fine tuning a small business are outlined, focusing on technology, money, banking, taxes, credit and collection, accounting systems, mergers, management, and marketing ideas.

31562 ■ "Lessons From Katrina on Prepaid Cards" in *American Banker* (Vol. 170, September 30, 2005, No. 189, pp. 11)
Pub: SourceMedia, Inc.
Description: Prepaid payroll cards and debit cards offer advantages in times of disaster because funds can be delivered electronically. The federal government agency, FEMA, is working to distribute relief payments through the use of cards. Risk management guidelines for the process are discussed.

31563 ■ "Make Them Pay!" in *Inc.* (August 1, 2003)
Pub: Gruner & Jahr USA Publishing
Description: Dealing with a deadbeat client, the good and bad for small firms operating in Mexico, and a twist on the personal asset loan guarantee are among the issues discussed.

31564 ■ "Melville-Based DealerTrack Inc. Sue Rival Mich.-Based RouteOne" in *Long Island Business News* (February 6, 2004)
Pub: Dolan Media Newswires
Ed: Ken Schachter. **Description:** DealerTrack Inc. has filed a patent lawsuit against Michigan-based RouteOne, a joint venture between DaimlerChrysler Service, Ford Motor Credit Company, General Motors Acceptance Corporation, and Toyota Financial Services. The lawsuit charges RouteOne of infringing on two patents related to a routing system, method and computer program for analyzing credit applications.

31565 ■ "More credit card bills past due in fourth quarter" in *Daily Business Review* (Vol. 77, No. 201, March 27, 2003, pp. A6)
Pub: American Lawyer Media LP
Description: Delinquent credit card accounts soared to record levels in the fourth quarter 2002. Statistical data included.

31566 ■ "Moving On: Ex-Apprentices Find Life After 'The Donald' is All Business" in *Entrepreneur* (Vol. 32, October 2004, No. 10, pp. 28)
Pub: Entrepreneur Media Inc.
Ed: April Y. Pennington. **Description:** Many of the runner-up contestants competing on The Apprentice television show are becoming entrepreneurs. Kwame Jackson and a friend started Legacy Communications Group, an entertainment financing company; Troy McClain co-Founded Solution Source Media, offering information and products related to credit and real estate; Sam Solovey founded an auctioneering business; Omarosa Manigault-Stallworth is working on a clothing line; Jessie Conners created an interactive real estate and investment resource firm; Katrina Campin, a residential and commercial full-service real estate brokerage company.

31567 ■ "MyPayNet" in *Entrepreneur.com* (Vol. 34, January 2006, No. 1, pp. 6)
Pub: Entrepreneur Media Inc.
Ed: Steve Cooper. **Description:** MyPayNet is an electronic invoicing and payment service designed to help small companies send and receive payments electronically.

31568 ■ "No Bankruptcy Break for Hurricane Victims" in *Credit Union Journal* (Vol. 9, October 3, 2005, No. 39, pp. 12)
Pub: SourceMedia, Inc.
Description: An overview of the new consumer bankruptcy law is presented. The new law takes effect October 17, 2005.

31569 ■ "No Credit? No Problem! Here's How to Get Good Credit If You Don't Have Any" in *Black Enterprise* (Vol. 35, February 2005, No. 7)
Pub: Earl G. Graves Publishing Co. Inc.
Ed: Siobhan Leftwich. **Description:** Ways to establish or rebuild credit are explored. Things to be aware of when applying for credit are listed.

31570 ■ "No More Debt" in *Black Enterprise* (Vol. 37, November 2006, No. 4, pp. 159)
Pub: Earl G. Graves Publishing Co. Inc.
Ed: Tanisha A. Sykes. **Description:** Eliminating debt is not necessarily easy and can be overwhelming. Here are some tips for reducing and eventually getting out of debt.

31571 ■ "NY State Attorney General Cracks Down on Auto and Credit Complaints" in *Long Island Business News* (February 13, 2004)
Pub: Dolan Media Newswires
Ed: Rosmaria Mancini. **Description:** New York State Attorney General, Eliot Spitzer, lists automobile prob-

lems and credit and banking issues a top priority for his office. Spitzer's Long Island regional office has handled more than 3,700 customer complaints on these issues. The Attorney General has released a report outlining actions taken by his office on behalf of the complainants.

31572 ■ "Olddebts.com: www.olddebts.com" in *Entrepreneur* (Vol. 31, No. 10, October 2003, pp. 6)
Pub: Entrepreneur Media, Inc.
Ed: Steve Cooper. **Description:** Website OldDebts. com will assist a small business to send a series of customized collection letters to debtors and report them to credit bureaus.

31573 ■ "Overplayed Hand: Portfolio Recovery Associates, a Credit-Card Debt Collector, May be Flying too High" in *Barron's* (July 7, 2003)
Pub: Barron's
Ed: Gene Epstein. **Description:** Portfolio Recovery Associates went public in November 2002, and has seen valuation nearly twice the average of the debt-collection industry it services. Reasons are detailed for expecting a present, if not precipitous, decline in the company's share price.

31574 ■ "Owners find credit a bit harder to get" in *Wall Street Journal* (April 30, 2002, pp. B6)
Pub: Wall Street Journal
Description: Small business owners are having more difficulty procuring loans. Statistical data included.

31575 ■ "Past due, and getting soaked" in *Crain's Detroit Business* (Vol. 17, No. 43, October 15, 2001, pp. 1)
Pub: Crain Communications, Inc.
Ed: Laura Bailey, Terry Kosdrosky. **Description:** According to the U.S. Small Business Administration, 75-80 percent of small businesses suffer from either slow paying customers or customers who don't pay at all. Advice is offered to help small businesses develop effective collections policies.

31576 ■ "Pay Up" in *PC Computing* (April 2000, pp. 37)
Pub: Ziff-Davis Inc.
Description: Electronic bill paying is the next e-commerce industry trend to be tapped. It is predicted that the Web could cut the cost of transactions in half and creditors would be paid more promptly, and checks would not bounce.

31577 ■ "Personal Business" in *Business Week* (January 9, 2006, No. 3966, pp. 94)
Pub: McGraw-Hill Companies
Ed: Mara der Hovanesian. **Description:** Topics include a takeover of auto lender Americredit, overseas shipping, and retail shopping in China.

31578 ■ *Practical Debt Collecting for Small Companies and Traders*
Pub: Meadow Books
Ed: Robin Evelegh. **Released:** December 2006. **Price:** $12.99. **Description:** Credit and collection guide for small companies.

31579 ■ "Prepaid Card Benefits Breast Cancer Research" in *Marketing to Women* (Vol. 19, November 2006, No. 11, pp. 5)
Pub: EPM Communications, Inc.
Description: NetSpend prepaid card marketer and financial services company, ACE Cash Express partner to launch a reloadable prepaid debit card for breast cancer research. A portion of all purchases made with the pink All-Access Visa Card through October 2007 will be donated to breast cancer research and educational charities.

31580 ■ "Process Online Payments Quickly and Effectively" in *E-business Advisor* (Vol. 18, No. 6, June 2000, pp. 34)
Pub: Advisor Media, Inc.
Ed: Glenn T. Shesney. **Description:** Assessment Systems Inc. (ASI), a purveyor of electronically admin-

istered tests, has deployed Payment Plus' Live-Processor electronic commerce software, greatly boosting the number of payments the company can transact per hour. LiveProcessor, a Linux-based system, can process hundreds of transactions per minute during periods of high volume, with per-transaction response time averaging less than three seconds.

31581 ■ **"A real steal" in** *Entrepreneur* **(Vol. 31, No. 5, May 2003, pp. 45)**
Pub: Entrepreneur Media Inc.
Ed: Jennifer Pellet. **Description:** According to market research firm Gartner Inc., one in twenty online consumers were victims of credit card fraud in 2001. The single-use credit card numbers being used for shopping online is explained.

31582 ■ **"Risky Business: Staff Smarts" in** *Entrepreneur* **(Vol. 31, No. 9, September 2003, pp. 78)**
Pub: Entrepreneur Media, Inc.
Ed: Chris Penttila. **Description:** Employers are running credit checks on job applicants, and can by law, reject prospective employees on the basis of personal credit history. Information to assess a credit report is included.

31583 ■ **"Score Savvy: Business Credit Scores are on the Horizon" in** *Entrepreneur* **(Vol. 31, Oct. 2003)**
Pub: Entrepreneur Media, Inc.
Ed: Joanne Cleaver. **Description:** Lenders will begin using credit scores, similar to those assigned to most consumers, by summer 2004, making the loan process difficult for businesses with complicated credit histories.

31584 ■ **"Sensing the System Is Being Abused, Congress Passed a Bill in March to Help Creditors Recover More Debt From Businesses That Have Filed Bankruptcy" i**
Pub: Inc. Magazine
Ed: Mike Hoffman. **Description:** Congress passed a bill in March 2005 that will help creditors recover more debt from businesses filing bankruptcy.

31585 ■ **"Simon Group Offers Cobranded Giftcard" in** *Marketing to Women* **(Vol. 19, October 2006, No. 10, pp. 9)**
Pub: EPM Communications, Inc.
Description: Komen Foundation partners with Simon Property Group to produce a cobranded Simon Pink Ribbon Giftcard. This Visa debit card issued by Meta-Bank are sold at Simon malls nationwide and online at Simon.com. One dollar from every card purchased will be donated to the Komen Foundation.

31586 ■ *The Small Business Credit & Collection Guide*
Pub: Carol Publishing Group
Ed: Gini G. Scott. **Released:** 1995. **Price:** $9.95.

31587 ■ *The Small Business Owner's Manual: Everything You Need to Know to Start Up and Run Your Business*
Pub: Career Press, Incorporated
Ed: Joe Kennedy. **Released:** June 2005. **Price:** $19.99 (US), $26.95 (Canadian). **Description:** Comprehensive guide for starting a small business, focusing on twelve ways to obtain financing, business plans, selling and advertising products and services, hiring and firing employees, setting up a Web site, business law, accounting issues, insurance, equipment, computers, banks, financing, customer credit and collection, leasing, and more.

31588 ■ *Small Business Survival Guide: Starting, Protecting, and Securing Your Business for Long-Term Success*
Pub: Adams Media Corporation
Ed: Cliff Ennico. **Released:** October 2005. **Price:** $12.95 (US), $17.95 (Canadian). **Description:** Entrepreneurship in the new millennium. Topics include creditors, taxes, competition, business law, and accounting.

31589 ■ **"Stop payment" in** *Crain's Detroit Business* **(Vol. 19, No. 16, April 21, 2003, pp. 1)**
Pub: Crain Communications Inc., Detroit
Ed: Brent Snavely. **Description:** Information is given on a ruling in the Kmart Corporation bankruptcy case on the $327 million in payments by Kmart to suppliers, the ruling could impact bankruptcy cases in the future.

31590 ■ **"Stressed Industries Drive Demand for Temporary Execs" in** *Crain's Detroit Business* **(Vol. 22, January 2, 2006, No. 1, pp. 22)**
Pub: Crain Communications Inc. - Detroit
Ed: Terry Kosdrosky, Brent Snavely. **Description:** Due to changes in bankruptcy laws and private-equity buyers, as well as issues facing the auto industry, local firms are hiring temporary executives.

31591 ■ **"Taking credit" in** *Entrepreneur* **(Vol. 30, No)**
Pub: Entrepreneur Media Inc.
Ed: Jennifer Pellet. **Description:** American Express, MasterCard and Visa are aggressively offering low introductory rates and perks like vendor discounts, reward programs and consulting services to small businesses.

31592 ■ **"Taking Credit" in** *Small Business Opportunities* **(Vol. 13, No. 5, September 2001, pp. 68)**
Pub: Harris Publications, Inc.
Ed: Lin Grensing-Pophal. **Description:** Three categories of choices that small businesses face when processing credit card payments online are addressed, including e-mail processing, contracting with a middle person, or processing credit cards on-site.

31593 ■ **"Too Much Information?" in** *Black Enterprise* **(Vol. 37, December 2006, No. 5, pp. 59)**
Pub: Earl G. Graves Publishing Co. Inc.
Ed: James C. Johnson. **Description:** African American business owners often face the dilemma of whether or not to divulge their minority status when soliciting new customers and financial institutions. The quality of the products or services is always the key factor and race should never define one's business; however, it is appropriate to market oneself as a minority or women-owned business, especially if the company is in an industry where those clients are offered top-tier contracts.

31594 ■ **"Trusting Credit Counselors" in** *Black Enterprise* **(Vol. 34, No. 7, February 2004, pp. 140)**
Pub: Earl Graves Publishing Co.
Ed: Tanisha A. Sykes. **Description:** The Federal Trade Commission has listed questions to ask when applying for credit counseling, as well as companies to avoid when pursing credit counseling.

31595 ■ **"Turning Receivables Into Received" in** *Black Enterprise* **(Vol. 34, No. 7, February 2004, pp. 46)**
Pub: Earl Graves Publishing Co.
Ed: Bridget McCrea. **Description:** Profile of Sweet Survival, a business consulting firm. The company has developed an accounts receivable policy suited to serving small business needs.

31596 ■ **"Turning Receivables Into Received: Don't Let Your Collections Process Fall Through the Cracks" in** *Black Enterprise* **(Vol. 34, No. 7)**
Pub: Earl Graves Publishing Co.
Ed: Bridget McCrea. **Description:** Profile of Sweet Survival, a business consulting firm. The company has developed an accounts receivable policy suited to serving small business needs.

31597 ■ **"Two Views on 2003" in** *Rough Notes* **(Vol. 145, No. 1, January 2003, pp. 204)**
Pub: Rough Notes
Ed: Samuel Schiff. **Description:** The Conning Research and Consulting's Jack Gohsler believes the insurance industry's outlook will improve slightly in 2003. Dr. Robert Hartwig of the Insurance Information Institute says that credit information will now be used in insurance underwriting.

31598 ■ *Ultimate Credit and Collection Handbook*
Pub: Entrepreneur Press
Ed: Michelle Dunn. **Released:** August 2006. **Price:** $36.95. **Description:** Entrepreneurial experts offer advice for successful credit and collection procedures.

31599 ■ *The Visa Approval Backlog and Its Impact on American Small Business: Congressional Hearing*
Pub: DIANE Publishing Company
Ed: Donald A. Manzullo. **Released:** July 2006. **Price:** $30.00. **Description:** Information regarding the Congressional hearing involving the Visa approval backlog is discussed.

31600 ■ **"Visa Rolls Out Business Card" in** *American Banker* **(Vol. 171, September 27, 2006, No. 186, pp. 7)**
Pub: SourceMedia, Inc.
Ed: Kate Berry. **Description:** Visa USA announced its new small business credit card that is aimed at business owners with annual household incomes over $125,000.

31601 ■ **"Visteon's 'pay to play' is the wrong strategy" in** *Crain's Detroit Business* **(Vol. 19, No. 9, March 3, 2003, pp. 8)**
Pub: Crain Communications Inc., Detroit
Description: Visteon Corporation is asking automotive suppliers for prepayment of at least 10 percent of contract values and price reductions.

31602 ■ **"Weblining" in** *Business Week* **(No. 3675, April 3, 2000, pp. EB22)**
Pub: McGraw-Hill, Inc.
Description: Tracking personal information using Web technology is discussed.

31603 ■ **"What Goes Up: Now There's a New Way to Track Small Business's Ups and Downs" in** *Entrepreneur* **(Vol. 32, No. 1, January 2004, pp. 30)**
Pub: Entrepreneur Media, Inc.
Description: The Small Business Index (SBI) will help entrepreneurs track 19 economic indicators affecting small businesses. The indicators are grouped in four categories: costs factors, credit conditions, industry metrics, and trade competitiveness.

31604 ■ **"What To Do When Your Client Declares Bankruptcy" in** *Home Business* **(Vol. 13, January/February 2006, No. 1, pp. 76)**
Pub: Home Business Magazine
Ed: Kurt English, Esq. **Description:** In a slow economy, small and home-based businesses should collect money in advance from clients whenever possible. Legal steps to take when accounts become delinquent are discussed.

31605 ■ **"What's Your Problem?" in** *Entrepreneur* **(Vol. 33, October 2005, No. 10, pp. 97)**
Pub: Entrepreneur Media Inc.
Ed: Nichole L. Torres. **Description:** Three ways to determine a new customers credit history are examined.

31606 ■ **"When You Speak, Lawmakers Listen" in** *My Business* **(June/July 2004, pp. 41)**
Pub: My Business Magazine
Description: Lawmakers are interested in small business. The National Federation of Independent Business (NFIB) advocates for small business through its Member Ballot, the largest opinion-gathering effort of its type. Results are given to lawmakers. Currently issues revolved around employer retirement savings accounts, postal rates, debit cards, project labor agreements, and OSHA regulations.

31607 ■ **"Women Business Owners Get Credit Easily" in** *Marketing to Women* **(Vol. 19, November 2006, No. 11, pp. 12)**
Pub: EPM Communications, Inc.
Description: According to a Gallup study commissioned by Wells Fargo, women find it easier to obtain credit than men. Statistical data included.

31608 ■ "Women Business Owners Seek Financing" in *Marketing to Women* **(Vol. 19, December 2006, No. 2, pp. 8)**
Pub: EPM Communications, Inc.
Description: A study by the Center for Women's Business Research shows that women business owners have become more savvy when seeking financial support for their business ventures. Statistical data included.

31609 ■ "Xign's Order-to-Pay Service Aims to Save Time, Money" in *eWeek* **(February 2, 2005)**
Pub: Ziff Davis Media Inc.
Description: Profile of Xign Payment Services Network (XPSN), an electronic order delivery system that also processes invoices and payment services for business-to-business commerce.

31610 ■ "Your Recovery Rights" in *Small Business Opportunities* **(Vol. 12, No. 2, March 2000, pp. 90)**
Pub: Harris Publications, Inc.
Ed: Robert C. Meier. **Description:** Tips are offered to reclaim merchandise from an insolvent customer.

TRADE PERIODICALS

31611 ■ *Collections & Credit Risk*
Pub: SourceMedia Inc.
Contact: John Stewart, VP and Group Publisher
Released: Monthly. **Price:** $199 U.S. 1 year (12 issues); $148 Canada 1 year (12 issues); $213 U.S. 2 year (24 issues); $276 Canada 2 year (24 issues). **Description:** Business publication tracking trends in the credit and collections industry.

31612 ■ *CreditWeek*
Pub: Standard & Poor's
Contact: Grace Schalkwyk, Publisher
Ed: Marguerite Nugent, Editor. **Released:** Weekly. **Price:** $3,050. **Description:** Information and news weekly serving the global credit markets.

31613 ■ *Profitable Lending Strategies*
Pub: Siefer Consultants Inc.
Contact: Joan Currie
Ed: Dana Siefer, Editor. **Released:** Monthly. **Price:** $349, U.S.; $279 charter rate. **Description:** Focuses on "what financial institutions are doing to increase their loan portfolios and reduce delinquencies and chargeoffs." Other topics include home equity loans, student loans, credit cards, direct and in-direct auto loans, collections, promotions, credit insurance, credit screening and processing.

31614 ■ *What's Working in Credit & Collections*
Pub: Progressive Business Publications
Ed: Russell Case, Editor. **Released:** Semimonthly. **Price:** $253, individuals. **Description:** Teaches successful credit and collection techniques to build credit sales while avoiding losses. Recurring features include interviews, news of research, a calendar of events, and a column titled Sharpen Your Judgment.

VIDEOCASSETTES/ AUDIOCASSETTES

31615 ■ *It's in the Mail: Techniques for Collecting Debts*
Video Arts, Inc.
c/o Aim Learning Group
8238-40 Lehigh
Morton Grove, IL 60053-2615
Free: 877-444-2230
Fax: (416)252-2155
Co. E-mail: service@aimlearninggroup.com
URL: http://www.aimlearninggroup.com
Released: 1989. **Price:** $755.00. **Description:** A business guide to pressuring and applying legal leans on outstanding debtors. **Availability:** VHS; 3/4U.

CONSULTANTS

31616 ■ FinTrace Inc.
130 E 59th St., Ste. 1300
New York, NY 10022
Ph:(212)759-1688
Fax: (212)826-7019
Co. E-mail: info@fintrace.com
URL: http://www.fintrace.com

E-mail: info@fintrace.com
Scope: Firm conducts financial investigations. Specializes in locating missing property owners, unclaimed property, and assets, such as stocks, bonds, dividends, life insurance proceeds, mutual fund shares, bank accounts, oil and mineral royalties, and other tangible and financial instruments. Also purchases uncollected judicial judgments, investigates telecommunications and utility billing for surcharges, and obtains refunds. Industries served: all. **Special Services:** FinTrace®.

31617 ■ NetKnowledge Technologies L.L.C.
300 Pistachio Cir.
Irving, TX 75063
Ph:(214)213-6226
Fax: (972)910-0059
Co. E-mail: info@dassnagar.com
URL: http://www.nktllc.com

E-mail: info@dassnagar.com
Scope: Works with executives worldwide to solve pressing business problems through the integration of business strategy and operations; information technology; and change management. **Special Services:** An application that allows users to receive and pay all utility bills online using the web, corporate Intranets, or Extranets as well as broadcast the bills using push technology.

LIBRARIES

31618 ■ Loan Brokers Association–Information Services
917 S. Park St.
Owosso, MI 48867-4422
Contact: Ben Campbell, Dir.
Scope: Loan brokers, loan consulting, credit repair, lending, credit cards, venture capital. **Services:** Copying; SDI; Library to members or by permission.

START-UP INFORMATION

31619 ■ "Ask Yourself What the Hell Really Works Here?" in *Fast Company* **(May 2001, pp. 82)**
Pub: Fast Company
Ed: Lee A. Iacocca. **Description:** Lee Iacocca, currently founder and chairman of EV Global Motors Inc., Los Angeles, California, offers advice to entrepreneurs, including the importance of customer service and standing behind products and service.

31620 ■ "Balancing Act" in *Entrepreneur*
Pub: Entrepreneur Media Inc.
Ed: Nichole L. Torres. **Description:** Art of finding new customers, while maintaining existing ones for a new company is outlined.

31621 ■ "Blazing Profit" in *Small Business Opportunities* **(Vol. 14, No. 1, January 2002, pp. 52-53)**
Pub: Harris Publications, Inc.
Ed: Annette Wood. **Description:** Profile of Fireplaces Plus, Inc., which sells traditional wood burning stoves, fireplaces and gas models, as well as accessories. After one year in business Fire Places Plus projects sales up to $320,000 and co-owner, Jerry Malcom, attributes customer service to the company's success.

31622 ■ "Eco-Preneuring" in *Small Business Opportunities* **(Vol. 14, No. 1, January 2002, pp. 72, 74)**
Pub: Harris Publications, Inc.
Ed: Marie Sherlock. **Description:** Profile of Matt Walstatter and Ryan Sanders, who launched an organic food delivery service called Organic Harvest Home Delivery. The co-owners hope to expand the business, including a Web site. The business places emphasis on customer service and the delivery of quality produce.

31623 ■ "Inside the Customer-Focused Company" in *Harvard Business Review* **(Vol. 78, No. 3, May 2000, pp. S20)**
Pub: Harvard Business School Publishing Corp.
Ed: Cary Jehl Broussard. **Description:** The article shows how a change agent, or type of business consultant, and vocal consumers help structure an entire organization.

ASSOCIATIONS AND OTHER ORGANIZATIONS

31624 ■ Help Desk Institute
102 S Tejon, Ste. 1200
Colorado Springs, CO 80903
Ph:(719)268-0174
Free: 800-248-5667
Fax: (719)268-0184
Co. E-mail: support@thinkhdi.com
URL: http://www.helpdeskinst.com
Contact: Sophie Klossner, Board Admin.

Membership: Corporations, organizations, and agencies offering help desks or other customer or user information services. **Purpose:** Promotes effective operation of help desks and related services. Facilitates exchange of information among members; evaluates and certifies support centers; conducts research and educational programs. **Publications:** *Focus Book Series*; *HDI Industry Insider* (biweekly); *Support and Service Suppliers Directory* (periodic); *SupportWorld*; Reports (annual).

31625 ■ International Customer Service Association
401 N Michigan Ave.
Chicago, IL 60611
Ph:(312)321-6800
Free: 800-360-ICSA
Co. E-mail: icsa@smithbucklin.com
URL: http://www.icsa.com
Contact: Kimberly Mims, Pres.
Description: Customer service professionals in public and private sectors united to develop the theory and understanding of customer service and management. Goals are to: promote professional development; standardize terminology and phrases; provide career counseling and placement services; establish hiring guidelines, performance standards, and job descriptions. Provides a forum for shared problems and solutions. Compiles statistics. **Publications:** *Customer Service Management Guide*; *ICSA Journal* (semiannual); *ICSA News* (bimonthly); *1995 Compensation Study*; *1996 Benchmarking Study*; Membership Directory (annual).

EDUCATIONAL PROGRAMS

31626 ■ Customer Satisfaction Measurement
American Management Association
1601 Broadway
New York, NY 10019
Ph:(212)586-8100
Free: 800-262-9699
Fax: (212)903-8168
Co. E-mail: customerservice@amanet.org
URL: http://www.amanet.org
Price: $1,495.00 for non-members; $1,395.00 for AMA members. **Description:** Covers the tools and strategies for measuring customer service satisfaction, and using the information effectively. **Locations:** New York, NY.

31627 ■ Customer Service Excellence for Front-Line Staff—Level 2 (Canada)
Canadian Management Centre
150 York St., 5th Fl.
Toronto, ON, Canada M5H 3S5
Ph:(866)400-4941 ext. 2252
Free: 877-CMC-2500
Fax: (416)313-4985
Co. E-mail: cmcinfo@cmctraining.org
URL: http://www.cmcamai.org
Price: $995 Canadian. **Description:** Covers the four styles of customer communication, including the six

steps to recover from customer dissatisfaction, and the five-steps that guarantee customer loyalty. **Locations:** Toronto, ON.

31628 ■ Customer Service Excellence: How to Win and Keep Customers
American Management Association
1601 Broadway
New York, NY 10019
Ph:(212)586-8100
Free: 800-262-9699
Fax: (212)903-8168
Co. E-mail: customerservice@amanet.org
URL: http://www.amanet.org
Price: $1,695.00 for non-members; $1,495.00 for AMA members. **Description:** Covers the skills needed to communicate professionalism, gain respect, improve customer relationships, and secure competitive advantage. **Locations:** Washington, DC; and Chicago, IL.

31629 ■ Customer Service Management— Delivering Satisfaction and Profit
American Management Association
1601 Broadway
New York, NY 10019
Ph:(212)586-8100
Free: 800-262-9699
Fax: (212)903-8168
Co. E-mail: customerservice@amanet.org
URL: http://www.amanet.org
Price: $1,895 for non-members; $1,695 for AMA members. **Description:** Covers the basics of customer service, including motivating customer service associates, and maintaining a successful recruiting staff. **Locations:** Las Vegas, NV.

31630 ■ Customer Service Managing: Delivering Satisfaction and Profit
American Management Association
1601 Broadway
New York, NY 10019
Ph:(212)586-8100
Free: 800-262-9699
Fax: (212)903-8168
Co. E-mail: customerservice@amanet.org
URL: http://www.amanet.org
Price: $1,695.00 for non-members; $1,595.00 for AMA members. **Description:** Covers motivating customer service associates to deliver satisfying customer experiences in order to assure repeat business; includes involving the entire organization, using technology, recruiting staff, and measuring success. **Locations:** Washington, DC; and Las Vegas, NV.

31631 ■ Delivering Superior Customer Service (for Front Line Staff) (Canada)
Canadian Management Centre
150 York St., 5th Fl.
Toronto, ON, Canada M5H 3S5
Ph:(416)214-5678
Free: 800-262-9699
Fax: (416)313-4985
Co. E-mail: cmcinfo@cmctraining.org
URL: http://www.cmcamai.org
Price: $1,495.00 Canadian. **Description:** Covers communication skills for improving customer rela-

tions, turning dissatisfied customers into loyal clients, and keeping a positive frame of mind while working. **Locations:** Toronto, ON.

31632 ■ Delivering Superior Customer Service for Supervisors and Managers (Canada)
Canadian Management Centre
150 York St., 5th Fl.
Toronto, ON, Canada M5H 3S5
Ph:(416)214-5678
Free: 800-262-9699
Fax: (416)313-4985
Co. E-mail: cmcinfo@cmctraining.org
URL: http://cmcamai.org
Price: $1,695.00 Canadian. **Description:** Covers building a supportive, creative environment, improving team morale and motivation, different customer types, and handling difficult customers. **Locations:** Toronto, ON.

REFERENCE WORKS

31633 ■ *101 Ways to Really Satisfy Your Customers: How to Keep Your Customers and Attract New Ones*
Pub: Allen & Unwin Pty., Limited
Ed: Andrew Griffiths. **Released:** April 2007. **Price:** $14.95. **Description:** Tips for providing excellent customer service that ensure loyalty and interest to a small business are examined.

31634 ■ "Advisory Board Members Help Students Understand Market and Customers" in *Long Island Business News* **(February 13, 2004)**
Pub: Dolan Media Newswires
Ed: Adina Genn. **Description:** Suggestions for choosing people to serve on an advisory board are offered. It is important to consider the board's mission and to appoint individuals who will help the firm beyond the boardroom.

31635 ■ *Alpha Dogs: How Your Small Business Can Become a Leader of the Pack*
Pub: HarperCollins Publishers, Inc.
Ed: Donna Fenn. **Released:** May 2007. **Price:** $14.95. **Description:** Profiles of eight successful entrepreneurs along with information for developing customer service, technology and competition.

31636 ■ *AMA Customer Satisfaction Research*
Pub: N T C Comtemporary Publishing Co.
Ed: Alan Dutka. **Released:** 1994. **Price:** $49.95. **Description:** Step-by-step guide to customer satisfaction research. Includes questionnaires.

31637 ■ "Amid Customer Backlash, eBay Reduces Some Fees" in *eWeek* **(February 7, 2005)**
Pub: Ziff Davis Media Inc.
Description: Online auction eBay has reduced some of its fees in response to customer complaints of price hikes imposed in January 2005.

31638 ■ "Angling for workplace fun" in *Incentive* **(Vol. 174, No. 10, October 2000, pp. 135)**
Pub: Bill Communications
Ed: Phil Strand. **Description:** A motivational video shown to customer service employees, helped Sprint surpass employee retention goals and improve its customer service rating. The video was produced by ChartHouse Learning Video, and is called FISH! It was filmed at a Seattle world-famous fish market.

31639 ■ "At Their Service" in *Entrepreneur* **(Vol. 31, No. 7, July 2003, pp. 40)**
Pub: Entrepreneur Media, Inc.
Ed: Melissa Campanelli. **Description:** Online retailers should never abandoned good customer services, even during a slower economy. Online shoppers have grown to expect excellent customer service from the Web sites in which they purchase.

31640 ■ "At Your Service: Is Your Service Center Living Up to its Potential?" in *Entrepreneur* **(Vol. 31, No. 10, October 2003, pp. 81)**
Pub: Entrepreneur Media, Inc.
Ed: Mark Henricks. **Description:** Profile of Doug Hass, co-founder and head of the factory service center for ImageStream Internet Solutions. Hass describes how the factory's customer service sets it apart from most manufacturers' centers.

31641 ■ "ATMs Keep Evolving as Part of Customers' Everyday Life" in *Pacific Business News* **(Vol. 41, No. 24, August 22, 2003, pp. 10)**
Pub: American City Business Journals
Ed: Terri Inefuku. **Description:** Industry analysts state that the number of automated teller machines (ATMs) is rising in Hawaii. Bank of Hawaii has 475 ATMs, while First Hawaiian Bank has 184 ATMs in the state.

31642 ■ "Avoid the four perils of CRM" in *Harvard Business Review* **(Vol. 80, No. 2, February 2002, pp. 101)**
Pub: Harvard Business School Press
Ed: Darrell K. Rigby, Frederick F. Reichheld, Phil Schefter. **Description:** Advice is given to companies on how they can have successful customer relationship management (CRM) programs.

31643 ■ "Back Office" in *Forbes* **(Vol. 175, February 14, 2005, No. 3, pp. 130)**
Pub: Forbes Magazine Inc.
Ed: Daniel Kruger. **Description:** Profile of Marshall & Ilsley, a small bank with 240 branches. The bank offers customers wire transfers and check-imaging.

31644 ■ *Benchmarking Customer Service*
Pub: Trans-Atlantic Publications, Inc.
Ed: Glen Peters. **Released:** 1995. **Price:** $42.50.

31645 ■ "The best-laid incentive plans" in *Harvard Business Review* **(Vol. 81, No. 1, January 2003, pp. 27)**
Pub: Harvard Business School Press
Ed: Steve Kerr. **Description:** A case study is presented where a CFO and chief administrative officer of a consumer durables manufacturer has instituted a performance management system that seemed successful to him, but had negative results for employee morale and customer service. Four experts offer advice on ways the company should proceed.

31646 ■ "Better Rivals" in *My Business* **(June/July 2004, pp. 47)**
Pub: My Business Magazine
Ed: Dennis McCafferty. **Description:** Customer service is key to beating competition when running a small business.

31647 ■ *Beyond Customer Service*
Pub: Crisp Publications, Inc.
Ed: Richard F. Gerson. **Price:** $9.95. **Description:** Provides information on retaining and satisfying established customers.

31648 ■ "Big Ideas for Small Biz" in *Small Business Opportunities* **(Vol. 16, No. 1, January 2004, pp. 92)**
Pub: Harris Publications, Inc.
Ed: James Feldman. **Description:** Four ways to be innovative and creative with a small business include fostering a business climate, becoming number one with clients, creating a partnership with clients, and a partnership with employees.

31649 ■ "Broker In a Rival's Branch? Your Bank Can Do It Too" in *American Banker* **(Vol. 170, February 2, 2005, No. 22, pp. 5)**
Pub: Thomson Financial Media Inc.
Ed: Paul Nadler. **Description:** Small banks are concerned that larger banks will entice their customers with more complex services; however an experiment showed that large banks are now providing the same quality customer service as community banks, one of their strongest assets.

31650 ■ "Bugged out" in *Entrepreneur* **(Vol. 31, No. 5, May 2003, pp. 38)**
Pub: Entrepreneur Media Inc.
Ed: Melissa Campanelli. **Description:** Information about Web bugs as a means to gather data on visitors to Web sites is presented. Most Web bugs are used through products and services from firms offering site analysis services or products.

31651 ■ "Build a Better Business" in *Black Enterprise* **(Vol. 35, October 2004, No. 3, pp. 136)**
Pub: Earl G. Graves Publishing Co. Inc.
Ed: Robert Anthony, Sonya A. Donaldson. **Description:** Emerging new technologies can help small businesses seem larger than they really are. Co-founder of Krazy Kickz, Sam Robinson, tells how upgrading the company's phone system led to a better customer service system.

31652 ■ *Building Bridges to Customers*
Pub: Productivity Press
Ed: Gerald A. Michaelson. **Released:** 1995. **Price:** $12.95.

31653 ■ "Bull in a China Shop? If That's How Parents Feel Bringing Kids Into Your Store, They'll Pass You By" in *Entrepreneur* **(Vol. 32)**
Pub: Entrepreneur Media Inc.
Description: Many retail operations are setting up an area for children to play while parents shop.

31654 ■ "Business Gone Wild" in *Entrepreneur* **(Vol. 32, July 2004, No. 7, pp. 69)**
Pub: Entrepreneur Media Inc.
Ed: Gwen Moran. **Description:** Profile of California Tortilla restaurants in the Washington DC area; partner Pam Felix, who also co-owns a comedy club, suggested customers do silly things in order to get free food. The marketing technique has increased profits for the restaurants.

31655 ■ "By Special Request: Pleasing One Client Pays Off in the Long Run" in *Entrepreneur* **(Vol. 31, No. 8, August 2003, pp. 73)**
Pub: Entrepreneur Media, Inc.
Ed: April Y. Pennington. **Description:** Profile of Sugar Film Production, Dallas, Texas, and owners Chris Smith and Tony Miglini, who pride themselves on creating large budget-quality film projects on small budgets.

31656 ■ "Card Tricks" in *Entrepreneur* **(Vol. 30, No. 2, February 2002, pp)**
Pub: Entrepreneur Media Inc.
Ed: Amanda C. Kooser. **Description:** The biggest problem for online retailers comes with accepting credit cards because of chargebacks when a customer disputes a charge on their bill, often due to unreceived merchandise or lack of quality in the product. The strict rules and dispute processes designed to protect consumers actually aids some people to use chargebacks as a vehicle for defrauding Internet businesses.

31657 ■ "CELLIT Technologies Empowers CB Richard Ellis to Deliver Superior Customer Service" in *PR Newswire* **(October 29, 2001, pp. NA)**
Pub: PR Newswire Association, Inc.
Description: Real estate services provider, CB Richard Ellis has implemented a combined solution from CELLLIT and Siebel Systems to execute a Customer Demand Strategy (CDS).

31658 ■ "Changing Times Require Changes in Recruiting Styles" in *Rough Notes* **(Vol. 145, No. 2, February 2003, pp. 65)**
Pub: Rough Notes
Ed: Troy Korsgaden. **Description:** The insurance and financial services industry must create deliberate recruitment processes to maintain seamless and expert service to customers.

31659 ■ *Cisco Network Design Solutions for Small-Medium Businesses*
Pub: Pearson Technology Group Canada
Ed: Peter Rybaczyk. **Released:** August 2004. **Price:** $73.00. **Description:** Solutions for computer networking professionals using computer networks within a small to medium-sized business. Topics cover not only core networking issues and solutions, but security, IP telephony, unified communications, customer relations management, wireless LANs, and more.

31660 ■ "Clicks, not licks, as Green Stamps go digital" in *The New York Times* (March 9, 2000, pp. D1, G1)
Pub: The New York Times Company
Ed: Michelle Slatella. **Description:** S&H Green Stamps are back with green points, an online form of Green Stamps, given out as rewards for shopping online.

31661 ■ "Clueing in customers." in *Harvard Business Review* (Vol. 81, No. 2, February 2003, pp. 100)
Pub: Harvard Business School Press
Ed: Leonard L. Berry, Neeli Bendapudi. **Description:** Evidence management is discussed by examining how the Mayo Clinic has continually worked to provide as positive an experience as possible to its patients. As a result, word of mouth about the hospital is quite positive, along with strong customer loyalty.

31662 ■ "Co-opting Customer Competence" in *Harvard Business Review* (Vol. 78, No. 1, January 2000, pp. 79)
Pub: Harvard Business School Publishing Corp.
Ed: C.K. Prahalad, Venkatram Ramaswamy. **Description:** In the new economy, companies must incorporate customer experience into their business models, in ways up until now were untapped. The challenges for doing that are addressed.

31663 ■ "Commentary: Good customer service-a ghost of retail's past?" in *Colorado Springs Business Journal* (March 7, 2003)
Pub: Dolan Media Newswires
Ed: Marylou Doehrman. **Description:** The importance of a good customer service policy for retail stores is stressed, citing that a good policy will keep customers coming back.

31664 ■ "Commentary: Testimonials-Let Your Customers Do the Talking" in *Long Island Business News* (March 12, 2004)
Pub: Dolan Media Newswires
Ed: Adina Genn. **Description:** Long Island businesses are cultivating customer testimonials on the Web, in brochures and on site. Tips for using customer praise to promote a business are included.

31665 ■ "Commentary: Testimonials-Let Your Customers Do the Talking" in *Long Island Business News* (March 12, 2004)
Pub: Dolan Media Newswires
Ed: Adina Genn. **Description:** Long Island businesses are cultivating customer testimonials on the Web, in brochures and on site. Tips for using customer praise to promote a business are included.

31666 ■ *The Complete Customer Service Letter Book*
Pub: The McGraw-Hill Companies
Ed: Edward W. Werz. **Released:** 1995. **Price:** $14.99 (includes disk). **Description:** Manual for writing various types of letters to current and potential customers. Sample letters contained on 3 1/2 inch disk that can be customized and printed out on IBM-compatible word processor.

31667 ■ *Consumer Middle East*
Pub: Euromonitor International
Released: Published February, 2004. **Price:** $995, individuals U.S.D. **Publication Includes:** List of 10 countries in the Middle East. Principal content of publication is Information regarding the Middle East including regional marketing perimeters, consumer markets, demographics, economic indicators, standards of living, household characteristics, consumer expenditures, and service industries.

31668 ■ "Consumers Ethics: The Role of Religiosity" in *Journal of Business Ethics* (Vol. 46, No. 2, August 15, 2003, pp. 151)
Pub: Kluwer Academic Publishers Group
Ed: Scott J. Vitell, Joseph G.P. Paolillo. **Description:** Results of a study investigating the role that religiosity plays in determining consumer attitudes/beliefs regarding various questionable consumer practice, along with other personal factors are offered.

31669 ■ "Contact Sport" in *Entrepreneur* (Vol. 28, No. 2, February 2000, pp. 54)
Pub: Entrepreneur Media Inc.
Ed: Cassandra Cavanah. **Description:** Tackling customer relationships takes more than just a few friendly phone calls.

31670 ■ "Conversation with Martha Rogers" in *Inc.* (November 15, 2000, pp. 69)
Pub: The Goldhirsh Group
Description: Ways to improve customer service are discussed.

31671 ■ "Cooperation vs. conflict" in *Incentive* (Vol. 174, No. 7, July 2000, pp. 78)
Pub: Bill Communications
Ed: John Farrell. **Description:** Selling should never be viewed as a winner-take-all game. Collaboration between channel relationships is necessary to solve customer-business issues.

31672 ■ "Corporate Present-Giving Looking Up After Slow Stretch" in *Milwaukee Journal Sentinel* (December 3, 2005)
Pub: Journal Sentinel, Inc.
Ed: Rick Romell. **Description:** According to a survey conducted by American Express, 71 percent of small businesses plan to give holiday gifts to clients and customers in 2005.

31673 ■ "Corporate Ties" in *Black Enterprise* (Vol. 34, July 2004, No. 12, pp. 41)
Pub: Earl G. Graves Publishing Co. Inc.
Ed: Nicole Lewis. **Description:** Profile of Alice Turner Byrd, owner of Turner Training USA. Byrd's firm provides corporate training to management and staff in CIGNA Corporation's customer service division.

31674 ■ "Cream of the Crop" in *Entrepreneur.com* (Vol. 34, January 2006, No. 1, pp. 25)
Pub: Entrepreneur Media Inc.
Ed: April Y. Pennington. **Description:** Profile of Cold Stone Creamery's founder, Doug Ducey, who discusses the firm's emphasis on customer service. The company is offering franchising opportunities throughout the country.

31675 ■ "Create a Client Loyalty Program" in *Rough Notes* (Vol. 146, No. 3, March 2003, pp. 52)
Pub: Rough Notes
Ed: Steve Andersen. **Description:** Pareto's Principle, the 80/20 Rule, can be used in managing an insurance agency by focusing 80 percent of time and energy on 20 percent of its clients.

31676 ■ "Create Compelling Web Content" in *E-business Advisor* (Vol. 18, No. 2, February 2000, pp. 24)
Pub: Advisor Media, Inc.
Ed: Laurie Windham. **Description:** Compelling content is an essential aspect of successful e-commerce Web sites. Updated and relevant content retains customer interest in the site and increases customer satisfaction. An infrastructure that supports the development of collaborative content publishing enables the Web master to focus on other issues, such as quality control. Good content, which personalizes, informs, supports, directs, sells and fulfills, is essential for solidifying customer relationships.

31677 ■ "Create Customer-Effective E-Services" in *E-business Advisor* (Vol. 18, No. 12, December 2000, pp. 26)
Pub: Advisor Media, Inc.
Ed: Jodie Dalgleish. **Description:** Effective customer services are essential for successful e-commerce op-

erations. An e-commerce Web site must communicate clearly with the customers and make it easy for them to negotiate the site and make purchases. The site should make it simple to compare products within the site and across multiple sites, and be guided immediately to the more important parts of the site.

31678 ■ *Creating a Customer Focused Company: 25 Proven Customer Service Strategies*
Pub: Trans-Atlantic Publications, Inc.
Ed: Ian Linton. **Released:** 1995. **Price:** $72.50.

31679 ■ *Creating Customer Value: The Path to Sustainable Competitive Advantage*
Pub: South-Western Publishing Co.
Ed: Earl Naumann. **Released:** 1995. **Price:** $24.95.

31680 ■ *Creating Customers for Life*
Pub: Productivity Press
Ed: Eberhard E. Scheuing. **Released:** 1995. **Price:** $12.95.

31681 ■ "CRM: Buy or Rent?" in *Sales and Marketing.com* (Vol. 156, No. 3, March 2004, pp. 40)
Pub: VNU eMedia, Inc.
Ed: Daniel Tynan. **Description:** An analyst with Aberdeen Group in Boston, Massachusetts, discusses issues facing small companies when choosing a customer relation management system (CRM). There are two types of systems available: traditional CRM software that can be purchased, or renting off-the-shelf CRM applications at Web sites like Salesforce.com or Salesnet.

31682 ■ "CRM providers fighting for market share" in *Atlanta Business Chronicle* (Vol. 25, November 15, 2002, No. 23 pp. 13C)
Pub: American City Business Publications, Inc.
Ed: Tony Heffernan. **Description:** Profile of customer relationship software produced by Firstwave Technologies Inc. Since the recession, many companies have postponed investments in the software, creating hard times for Firstwave and other software firms.

31683 ■ "Crowd Control" in *Entrepreneur* (Vol. 31, No. 8, August 2003, pp. 33)
Pub: Entrepreneur Media, Inc.
Ed: Amanda C. Kooser. **Description:** Customer relations management (CRM) is a philosophy and way of doing business. Advice is shared for developing the right CRM for businesses.

31684 ■ "CSFB Repositions Top Exec" in *Black Enterprise* (Vol. 35, November 2004, No. 4, pp. 30)
Pub: Earl G. Graves Publishing Co. Inc.
Ed: K. Terrell Reed. **Description:** Credit Suisse First Boston has appointed Adebayo Bayo Ogunlesi as its newly created chief client officer and executive vice chairman. Qgunlesi will devote his time working with clients.

31685 ■ *Customer-Centered Growth*
Pub: Addison Wesley Longman
Ed: Whiteley. **Released:** 1997. PRC $25.00.

31686 ■ "Customer-Centric CRM Requires Perspective in 360 degrees" in *Microsoft Executive Circle* (Vol. 1, No. 2, Q2 2001, pp. 22-24, 27)
Pub: Putman Media
Ed: Ronni T. Marshak. **Description:** Customer Relationship Management tools must monitor sales processes, marketing campaigns, customer service, and customer behavior in order to be successful.

31687 ■ *The Customer Comes Second: And Other Secrets of Exceptional Service*
Pub: William Morrow & Co., Inc.
Ed: Hal F. Rosenbluth. **Released:** 1994. **Price:** $12.95 (paper).

31688 ■ *Customer Driven Strategy: Winning Through Operational Excellence*
Pub: John Wiley & Sons, Inc.
Ed: Thomas E. Wallace. **Released:** 1995. **Price:** $39.95.

31689 ■ "The Customer Has Escaped" in *Harvard Business Review* **(Vol. 81, No. 11, November 2003, pp. 96)**
Pub: Harvard Business School Press
Ed: Paul F. Nunes, Frank V. Cespedes. **Description:** Consumer behavior and the economic benefits of the wise use of available distribution channels are discussed.

31690 ■ "Customer Loyalty Keeps Funeral Homes Family Run" in *Business First Columbus* **(Vol. 18, No. 25, February 8, 2002, pp. B7)**
Pub: Business First Columbus, Inc.
Ed: Craig Lovelace. **Description:** Profile of Schoedinger Funeral Home and Cremation Service, located in the Columbus area, and ways they retain customer loyalty.

31691 ■ "The Customer Loyalty Puzzle" in *E-business Advisor* **(Vol. 17, No. 12, December 1999, pp. 10)**
Pub: Advisor Media, Inc.
Ed: Laurie Windham. **Description:** E-business owners can offer excellent customer service on the Web by linking marketing, sales, delivery, and support into one rewarding experience. E-business owners should include fulfillment and support among customer services to build customer confidence and to reduce operating expenses. Developing trust is important to e-business relationships because the Web does not offer face-to-face contact.

31692 ■ *Customer Service: A Practical Approach*
Pub: Prentice Hall
Ed: Elaine K. Harris. **Released:** 1996. PRC $34.80

31693 ■ "Customer Service Center Will Rise in Indian Land" in *Charlotte Observer* **(February 4, 2007)**
Pub: Knight-Ridder/Tribune Business News
Ed: Taylor Bright. **Description:** Kennametal is building a new customer service center in Lancaster County, North Carolina. Kennametal makes metal tools and parts, specializing in metals highly resistant to heat.

31694 ■ *Customer Service for Dummies*
Pub: I D G Books Worldwide
Ed: Karen Dunn. **Released:** 1995. **Price:** $19.99.

31695 ■ "Customerretention.com: www.customerretention.com" in *Entrepreneur* **(Vol. 31, No. 10, October 2003, pp. 6)**
Pub: Entrepreneur Media, Inc.
Ed: Steve Cooper. **Description:** Website that provides consulting services to small and large companies on customer retention strategies.

31696 ■ "Customers as Innovators" in *Harvard Business Review* **(Vol. 80, No. 4, April 2002, pp. 74)**
Pub: Harvard Business School Press
Ed: Eric Stefan, von Hippel Thomke. **Description:** A radically new approach to research and development is described. Companies are now encouraging customers to design and develop their own products and advice is given on how this can be achieved.

31697 ■ *Cute Little Store: Between the Entrepreneurial Dream and Business Reality*
Pub: Outskirts Press, Incorporated
Ed: Adeena Mignogna. **Released:** May 2006. **Price:** $11.95. **Description:** Challenges of starting and growing a retail business are profiled.

31698 ■ *Delivering Customer Value: It's Everyone's Job*
Pub: Productivity Press
Ed: Karl Albrecht. **Released:** 1995. **Price:** $12.95.

31699 ■ *Delivering Knock Your Socks off Service*
Pub: AMACOM
Ed: Kristin Anderson and Ron Zemke. **Released:** 1991. **Price:** $16.95 (paper); ($14.35 for AMA members).

31700 ■ "Dell NFIB The Voice of Small Business" in *My Business* **(June/July 2004, pp. 26-27)**
Pub: My Business Magazine
Description: Ten finalists chosen for the Small Business Excellence in Customer Experience Award are profiled. Winners were selected by members of the Herb Kelleher Center for Entrepreneurship at the University of Texas at Austin.

31701 ■ "Detroit Free Press Macomb Small Business Column" in *Detroit Free Press* **(September 8, 2005)**
Pub: Knight-Ridder/Tribune Business News
Ed: Carol Cain. **Description:** Sandra Wowk uses the philosophy of customer comfort to run her successful jewelry and watch store.

31702 ■ "Don't Just Listen Connect" in *Fast Company* **(August 2001, pp. 140)**
Pub: Fast Company
Ed: Paul C. Judge. **Description:** An interview with John I. Sviokla, vice chairman and leader of the digital-strategy practice at DiamondCluster International Inc., a consulting firm in Chicago. Sviokla makes a series of connections when interacting with customers and compares technology today to where it must be in the future.

31703 ■ "Drawing the Line: The Right Way To Do Business With Friends" in *Sales & Marketing Management* **(Vol. 157, February 2005, No. 2, pp. 18)**
Pub: VNU Business Media
Ed: Sara Calabro. **Description:** The best way to handle business relationships with friends is to use the same client-customer principles of other deals, including putting everything in writing.

31704 ■ *The Dynamics of Service: Reflections on the Changing Nature of Customer-Provider Interactions*
Pub: Jossey-Bass, Inc.
Ed: Barbara A. Gutek. **Released:** 1995. **Price:** $29.95.

31705 ■ "e-Biz Buzz" in *E-business Advisor* **(Vol. 18, No. 3, March 2000, pp. 50)**
Pub: Advisor Media, Inc.
Ed: Buzz Hunter. **Description:** Tips for running a successful e-commerce Web site are offered.

31706 ■ "E-Commerce Complaints" in *Small Business Opportunities* **(Vol. 14, No. 1, January 2002, pp. 16)**
Pub: Harris Publications, Inc.
Description: Ten tips for dealing with customer complaints online offered by Karen Leland and Keith Bailey, authors of Online Customer Service For Dummies are investigated.

31707 ■ "E-Loyalty" in *Harvard Business Review* **(Vol. 78, No. 4, July 2000, pp. 105)**
Pub: Harvard Business School Publishing Corp.
Ed: Frederick F. Reichheld, Phil Schefter. **Description:** Bain and Company Inc. is studying the strategies and practices of top Internet companies. They have surveyed thousands of their customers to assess e-loyalty.

31708 ■ "Eliminate Fulfillment Problems" in *E-business Advisor* **(Vol. 18, No. 3, March 2000, pp. 28)**
Pub: Advisor Media, Inc.
Ed: Patrick Rigney. **Description:** The best ways to integrate an online system with an existing business is to establish a separate order fulfillment center, or to outsource order processing. Orders are then sent directly to the company's warehouse.

31709 ■ *Employee Incentive Contests: For Improved Marketing, Customer Service, and Morale*
Pub: Silverpoint Press
Ed: Dave Marley. **Released:** 1995. **Price:** $19.95.

31710 ■ "The enemies of trust" in *Harvard Business Review* **(Vol. 81, No. 2, February 2003, pp. 88)**
Pub: Harvard Business School Press
Ed: Robert Galford, Ann Siebold Drapeau. **Description:** The relationship between a business and its client and a company's relationship with its employees is contrasted showing that the business/client relationship allows for trust to develop easier than that of the company/managers/employees relationships.

31711 ■ "Enterprise Software: An industry finds order in the madness" in *Red Herring* **(No. 105, October 1, 2001, pp. 74-75)**
Pub: Herring Communications
Ed: Justin Hibbard. **Description:** An overview of the enterprise software industry, which represents nearly 80 percent of the packaged application market, is presented. High market potential seems to exist with customer relationship management, supply chain management, and e-commerce software.

31712 ■ "Entrepreneur Column" in *Entrepreneur.com* **(September 7, 2006)**
Pub: Entrepreneur Media Inc.
Ed: Gail Goodman. **Description:** Website design is critical to convert curious online visitors to new customers. Special consideration should be given to the persons who found you through paid searches. A special Web page, offering free benefits to these potential customers, is one of many suggestions to serve these special customers.

31713 ■ "Everything designed with the customer in mind" in *Rough Notes* **(Vol. 146, No. 3, March 2003, pp. 18)**
Pub: Rough Notes
Ed: Dennis Pillsbury. **Description:** Roach Howard Smith and Hunter of Dallas/Fort Worth, Texas, is an insurance agency founded by Richard Roach in 1955 that specializes in commercial lines. The firm is now run by Karen K. Farris, who says the firm employs a customer-focused staff.

31714 ■ "Exploding the Self-Service Myth" in *Harvard Business Review* **(Vol. 78, No. 3, May 2000, pp. 26)**
Pub: Harvard Business School Publishing Corp.
Ed: Youngme Moon, Frances X. Frei. **Description:** Instead of forcing customers to do all the work, the most successful e-commerce sites are taking over many aspects of the shopping process.

31715 ■ "The Extra Mile: Customer Service That's a Step Beyond" in *Sales & Marketing Management* **(Vol. 158, October 2006, No. 10, pp. 14)**
Pub: VNU Business Media
Description: An independent knife distributor shares the story of gifting a hunting knife to a client, resulting in increased orders.

31716 ■ "Ezsupport Life" in *Entrepreneur.com* **(Vol. 34, February 2006, No. 2, pp. 6)**
Pub: Entrepreneur Media Inc.
Description: Profile of EzSupport Life, a free, automated online customer-support solution for small businesses.

31717 ■ "Fast Talk" in *Fast Company* **(September 2001, pp. 80)**
Pub: Fast Company
Description: The state of the customer economy is addressed, focusing on customer-relationship management.

31718 ■ *Financial Times Guide to Business Start Up 2007*
Pub: Pearson Education, Limited
Ed: Sara Williams; Jonquil Lowe. **Released:** November 2006. **Price:** $52.50. **Description:** Guide for starting and running a new business is presented. Sections include ways to get started, direct marketing, customer relations, management and accounting.

31719 ■ *Find & Keep Customers for Your Small Business*
Pub: CCH, Inc.
Ed: Joanne Y. Cleaver. **Released:** 1999.

31720 ■ *"Find Your Niche-and Stick with It"* in *Business Week Online* (March 22, 2002)
Pub: McGraw-Hill, Inc.
Description: An interview with Leslie Godwin, a career and life-transition coach located in Calabas, California, explains how narrowing focus can help small businesses to attract good customers and while better-serving that customer base.

31721 ■ *"First Person"* in *Entrepreneur* (Vol. 28, No. 3, March 2000, pp. 146)
Pub: Entrepreneur Media Inc.
Ed: Barry Farber. **Description:** If you want to know what customers want, all you need is to ask them.

31722 ■ *"Get the Current View of Your Customers"* in *E-business Advisor* (Vol. 18, No. 12, December 2000, pp. 42)
Pub: Advisor Media, Inc.
Ed: Claudia Imhoff. **Description:** Successful e-commerce businesses employ analytical and tactical customer relationship management (CRM) applications to offer personalized and current information to their customers. CRM applications are not easy to implement because they involve so many departments and require a significant change in business practices. The system must offer instant access to customer information from anywhere and quick analysis of the data.

31723 ■ *"Get the Scoop"* in *Entrepreneur* (Vol. 28, No. 2, February 2000, pp. 142)
Pub: Entrepreneur Media Inc.
Ed: Gwen Moran. **Description:** When it comes to promoting your business, knowledge is power. The more you know about your market, customers, competition and prospects, the more likely you are to make smart decisions.

31724 ■ *"Getting Connected"* in *Incentive* (Vol. 174, No. 10, October 2000, pp. 1S3)
Pub: Bill Communications
Ed: Emily Hodnett. **Description:** Motivating customer service representatives may mean the difference between service with a smile and half-hearted help.

31725 ■ *"Getting Personal"* in *Home Office Computing* (Vol. 18, No. 11, November 2000, pp. 88)
Pub: Scholastic Inc.
Ed: Jeffery D. Zbar. **Description:** The three biggest mistakes business owners make regarding customer service are examined.

31726 ■ *"Going the Extra Mile"* in *Black Enterprise* (Vol. 35, November 2004, No. 4, pp. 58)
Pub: Earl G. Graves Publishing Co. Inc.
Ed: Bridget McCrea. **Description:** Profile of Cheryl Hudson-Jackson co-founder of Rubynesque, an intimate apparel store catering to plus-size women.

31727 ■ *Great Customer Service on the Telephone*
Pub: AMACOM
Ed: Kristin Anderson. **Released:** 1992. **Price:** $10.95 (paper); ($9.85 for AMA members). **Description:** Step-by-step guide to improving telephone techniques, covering taking messages, screening calls, and dealing with telephone fraud.

31728 ■ *"Happy Returns"* in *Entrepreneur* (Vol. 32, No. 1, January 2004, pp. 39)
Pub: Entrepreneur Media, Inc.
Ed: Melissa Campanelli. **Description:** The importance of repeat business from customers, for both online retailers and brick-and-mortar businesses is discussed.

31729 ■ *"Happy Returns"* in *Entrepreneur.com* (Vol. 34, January 2006, No. 1, pp. 40)
Pub: Entrepreneur Media Inc.

Ed: Melissa Campanelli. **Description:** Online retailers should make the return process as easy as possible for customers by using a prepaid return label or box, give a longer time for returns, and to look at returns as an opportunity by providing good customer service.

31730 ■ *"Healthcare: Information Systems Help Patients and Providers Breathe Easier"* in *Microsoft Executive Circle* (Vol. 1, No. 2, Q2 2001)
Pub: Putman Media
Ed: Craig A. Shutt. **Description:** New technology is trimming costs while improving patient-physician interaction in the healthcare industry.

31731 ■ *"HelpStar"* in *Sales & Marketing Management* (Vol. 157, February 2005, No. 2, pp. 22)
Pub: VNU Business Media
Description: Profile of HelpStar, the help-desk request-tracking and request management system. The system supports sales calls, follows up on customer problems, creates a history of customer contacts, and prioritizes customer requests for businesses.

31732 ■ *"Hit the Mark"* in *My Business* (August/September 2002, pp. 28-35)
Pub: My Business Magazine
Description: Seven small business trends that will position a company for success are profiled. These trends include mentoring programs, e-mail marketing, customer service, personalized products and services, employee stock ownership plans, targeting markets, and automation.

31733 ■ *"Houston-Based ChaseCom L.P."* in *Black Enterprise* (Vol. 35, December 2004, No. 5, pp. 38)
Pub: Earl G. Graves Publishing Co. Inc.
Ed: Malik Singleton. **Description:** ChaseCom LP in Houston, Texas has opened a new call center in Fort Smith, Arkansas creating 140 jobs paying $8 to $12 per hour. The firm provides telecom services and customer support.

31734 ■ *"Houston-based GC Services Adds 100 Jobs in Oklahoma City"* in *Journal Record* (February 5, 2004)
Pub: Dolan Media Company
Ed: Darren Currin. **Description:** GC Services plans to expand the Oklahoma City national service center with an immediate addition of 100 new employees, and ultimately 200 new employees after completion. The firm works with corporation and state agencies managing accounts receivables and customer service needs.

31735 ■ *"Houston-Based Restaurant Chain Uses Mystery Shoppers to Ensure Quality"* in *Beaumont Enterprise* (January 24, 2005)
Pub: Beaumont Enterprise
Ed: Rachel Stone. **Description:** Restaurants, department stores, movie theaters, hotels, apartment complexes, banks, law firms, and many other businesses are using mystery shoppers to evaluate their businesses.

31736 ■ *"Houston Microbrewery Has Cult Following"* in *Houston Chronicle* (October 6, 2002)
Pub: Knight Ridder/Tribune Business News
Ed: David Kaplan. **Description:** Customer loyalty is uncommonly high for microbreweries; a discussion regarding this loyalty is covered by various microbrewery owners.

31737 ■ *How to Collect Debts (And Still Keep Your Customers)*
Pub: Amacom
Ed: David Sher, Martin Sher. **Released:** May 1999. **Price:** $24.95. **Description:** Suggestions for collecting as much money as possible, as quickly as possible, while maintaining customer goodwill, along with strategies for eliminating bad debt.

31738 ■ *"How Data Mining Makes Businesses Smarter"* in *Red Herring* (No. 105, October 1, 2001, pp. 78-79)
Pub: Herring Communications
Ed: Alan Zeichick. **Description:** Data warehouses and data-mining software enable any business to collect and interpret transaction information and use it to predict customer's reactions.

31739 ■ *"How to Lose Customers"* in *Inc.* (Volume 27, July 2005, No. 7, pp. 49, 51)
Pub: Inc. Magazine
Ed: Norm Brodsky. **Description:** A commitment to customer service can help a small business attract customers away from competitors.

31740 ■ *"How Surveys Influence Customers"* in *Harvard Business Review* (Vol. 80, No. 5, May 2002, pp. 18)
Pub: Harvard Business School Press
Ed: Vicki G. Morwitz, Paul M. Dholakia. **Description:** New research indicates that a customer survey can enhance the loyalty and profitability of already satisfied customers. Surveys seem to crystallize existing opinions and focus attention on them.

31741 ■ *"Humanize Your Web Customer Service"* in *E-business Advisor* (Vol. 18, No. 8, August 2000, pp. 12)
Pub: Advisor Media, Inc.
Ed: Kim M. Bayne. **Description:** The article tells how Lands' End chose WebLine Communications' applications to provide online customers with services similar to those of live sales clerks in a store.

31742 ■ *"If You Want Business, Answer Your Phone"* in *Crain's Detroit Business* (Vol. 19, No. 45, November 10, 2003, pp. 8)
Pub: Crain Communications Inc., Detroit
Ed: Keith Crain. **Description:** Customers prefer to do business with a human being when ordering a product or service.

31743 ■ *"Imaging: Changing the Way We Do Business"* in *Rough Notes* (Vol. 146, No. 3, March 2003, pp. 56)
Pub: Rough Notes
Ed: Robert E. Dunn. **Description:** Hotchkiss Insurance Agency Inc. reduced paper workload by using imaging or digital scanning of documents. This process enables the firm to focus on customer services and communications.

31744 ■ *"In with the New"* in *Entrepreneur* (Vol. 28, No. 10, October 2000, pp. 102)
Pub: Entrepreneur Media Inc.
Ed: Mark Henricks. **Description:** The key to fast growth lies is not only treating your existing customers well, but also in seeking new customers.

31745 ■ *"In Search of the Operator"* in *Wall Street Journal* (May 8, 2002, pp. D1)
Pub: Wall Street Journal
Ed: Jane Spencer. **Description:** An overview of automated customer service systems. Statistical data included.

31746 ■ *Instant Cashflow: Hundreds of Proven Strategies to Win Customers, Boost Margins and Take More Money Home*
Pub: McGraw-Hill Companies
Ed: Bradley J. Sugars. **Released:** December 2005. **Price:** $16.95 (US), $22.95 (Canadian). **Description:** Nearly 300 proven marketing and sales strategies are shared by the author, a self-made millionaire. Advice on creating the proper mindset, generating new leads, boosting the conversion rate of leads to sales, maximizing the value of the average sale, and measuring results is included.

31747 ■ *"It's a Matter of Style"* in *Rough Notes* (Vol. 146, No. 9, September 2003, pp. 60)
Pub: Rough Notes
Ed: Sharon S. Denzler. **Description:** Developing and maintaining outstanding customer service for insurance agents, including customer relations, interpersonal relations, and personality traits are presented.

31748 ■ "It's the Service, Stupid! Want Repeat Business?" in *Sales and Marketing.com* (Vol. 156, No. 3, March 2004, pp. 8)
Pub: VNU eMedia, Inc.
Ed: Betsy Cummings. **Description:** Customer service is critical to saving existing clients.

31749 ■ "Keep 'Em Clicking" in *Home Office Computing* (Vol. 19, No. 2, February 2001, pp. 73)
Pub: Scholastic Inc.
Ed: Mark Kakkuri. **Description:** Small business Web sites often lose out to competitors who can sell products for less. In order to achieve customer loyalty, a business must offer superior customer services and interaction. By personalizing customer services, a relationship will result that will bring customers back. One way to learn what customers want out of service is by conducting surveys and instant polls.

31750 ■ "Keeping Customers Clueless?" in *Home Office Computing* (Vol. 18, No. 8, August 2000, pp. 22)
Pub: Scholastic Inc.
Ed: Laura Turley. **Description:** A recent report by Jupiter Communications states that as e-commerce continues to grow, so does customer dissatisfaction. Results of the report are examined.

31751 ■ *Keeping Customers Happy*
Pub: Self-Counsel Press, Inc.
Ed: Jacqueline Dunckel and Brian Taylor. **Released:** Third edition, 1994. **Price:** $9.95 (paper).

31752 ■ *The Kindess Revolution: The Company-Wide Culture Shift That Inspires Phenomenal Customer Service*
Pub: American Management Association
Ed: Ed Horrell. **Released:** 2006. **Price:** $23.00.

31753 ■ "Know Thy Customer: How CRM Software Helps One Company Deliver" in *My Business* (October/November 2003, pp. 46)
Pub: My Business Magazine
Ed: Karen J. Bannan. **Description:** The cost savings and benefits for small businesses using customer relationship management software to improve service, increase efficiency, reduce customer service calls, automate marketing, and retain existing customers are examined.

31754 ■ "Knowing What Customers Want" in *Inc.* (August 2005, pp. 22-23)
Pub: Inc. Magazine
Ed: Description: The 'sense and response' supply chain process is outlined, focusing on why it works so fast.

31755 ■ "Knowledge Networks: Making the Brand" in *Venture Capital Journal* (Vol. 41, No. 8, August 2000, pp. 18)
Pub: Venture Economics
Ed: Alistair Christopher. **Description:** Profile of Knowledge Networks, a marketing intelligence system firm, claims they offer an exclusive service to businesses that shows a concise view of consumers and their behavior toward advertising, brands, and buying.

31756 ■ "Labor for Love" in *Entrepreneur* (Vol. 33, February 2005, No. 2, pp. 68)
Pub: Entrepreneur Media Inc.
Ed: Kirsten Osolind. **Description:** Three steps for entrepreneurs that help increase client base are listed, using love as the topic. Listening to customers, then initiating two-way dialogue is essential.

31757 ■ "Leave Me Alone!" in *Entrepreneur* (Vol. 32, August 2004, No. 8, pp. 31)
Pub: Entrepreneur Media Inc.
Description: Sixty-percent of consumers have a negative opinion of marketing and advertising than in the past, with 69 percent interested in products and services that help block or skip marketing promotions.

31758 ■ *Lip Service vs. Customer Service: Making Customer Cents for Customer Sense*
Pub: Kendall Hunt Publishing Co.

Ed: Lynda Jeppesen. **Released:** 1995. **Price:** $14.95.

31759 ■ "Little things mean a lot" in *Rough Notes* (Vol. 146, No. 3, March 2003, pp. 118)
Pub: Rough Notes
Ed: Robert L. Bailey. **Description:** The song, "Little Things Mean a Lot" translates into a valuable lesson in business leadership. Customers never forget the small courtesies or notes of appreciation from staff, however they never forget negative treatment either.

31760 ■ "Long Island Banks Compete for Customers by Offering 'Pay Less' ATMs" in *Long Island Business News* (February 13, 2004)
Pub: Dolan Media Newswires
Ed: Claude Solnik. **Description:** Many banks are offering free or low-cost ATM services in order to attract new customers.

31761 ■ "Long Island Banks Upgrade IT to Improve Service, Sales" in *Long Island Business News* (February 13, 2004)
Pub: Dolan Media Newswires
Ed: Claude Solnik. **Description:** Many banks, including Astoria, have redesigned computer hardware and software to create a single system whereby tellers and customer services representatives can obtain a customer's complete profile. The new system will improve a company's ability to cross-sell products and make follow-up calls.

31762 ■ "Long Island's Newsday Fields Post-Redesign Reactions" in *Long Island Business News* (March 12, 2004)
Pub: Dolan Media Newswires
Ed: Claude Solnik. **Description:** Long Island's Newsday received thousands of calls, letters and emails since implementing its new design. Management will listen to the feedback before making any changes in layout or the look of the paper. Newsday has a daily circulation of about 580,000, reaching 1 million readers.

31763 ■ "Looking for Leverage" in *Hispanic Business* (Vol. 23, No. 5, May 2001, pp. 32, 34, 36)
Pub: Hispanic Business
Ed: Scott Williams. **Description:** Companies looking to grow have a variety of high-tech options. Advice is given from Omni/Strat, a Miami-based consulting firm that helps companies leverage technology to improve customer relationships, business intelligence, and e-commerce. The Web Head Group, located in San Antonio, Texas, also offers technology advice to small businesses.

31764 ■ "Loyal Clients Boost Revenue" in *Home Business* (Vol. 12, October 2005, No. 5, pp. 48, 50-51)
Pub: Home Business Magazine
Ed: Jim Kleidon. **Description:** Ten pointers to improve customer satisfaction are listed, and must be executed before, during and after a service takes place.

31765 ■ "Loyal Customers can't be Strangers" in *Microsoft Executive Circle* (Vol. 1, No. 2, Q2 2001, pp. 8-10)
Pub: Putman Media
Ed: Claudio Marcus. **Description:** The importance of customer service as a tool to build lasting client relationships is stressed. Three steps to deploy customer relationship management are listed.

31766 ■ "Make Corporate America Work for You" in *Inc.* (July 1, 2003)
Pub: Gruner & Jahr USA Publishing
Ed: Alison Stein Wellner. **Description:** Corporate America wants your business, but whom can you trust? Information is provided to sort out responsible vendors.

31767 ■ "Making Your Case: Think Client Testimonials are Just Icing on the Cake?" in *Entrepreneur* (Vol. 33, January 2005, No. 1, pp. 64)
Pub: Entrepreneur Media Inc.

Ed: Kimberly L. McCall. **Description:** Customer testimonials can act as a case study for increasing sales.

31768 ■ *Managing to Keep the Customer: How to Achieve and Maintain Superior Customer Service Throughout the Organization*
Pub: Jossey-Bass, Inc.
Ed: Robert L. Desatnick and Denis H. Detzel. **Released:** Revised edition, 1993. **Price:** $24.95.

31769 ■ *Managing Knock Your Socks Off Service*
Pub: Pfeiffer & Co.
Ed: Chip R. Bell and Ron Zemke. **Price:** $17.95 (paper).

31770 ■ *Managing Quality Customer Service*
Pub: Crisp Publications, Inc.
Ed: William B. Martin. **Price:** $12.95.

31771 ■ *Managing a Small Business Made Easy*
Pub: Entrepreneur Press
Ed: Martin E. Davis. **Released:** September 2005. **Price:** $19.95 (US), $26.95 (Canadian). **Description:** Examination of the essential elements for an entrepreneur running a business, including advice on leadership, customer service, financials, and more.

31772 ■ "Manners Matter" in *Home Office Computing* (Vol. 18, No. 9, September 2000, pp. 40)
Pub: Scholastic Inc.
Description: Marjorie Brody, owner of Brody Communications Ltd. a communications consulting firm, states that people are getting ruder and technology hasn't helped. Brody offers suggestions for being more courteous to others.

31773 ■ "Many unhappy returns" in *Entrepreneur* (Vol. 31, No. 6, June 2003, pp. 74)
Pub: Entrepreneur Media Inc.
Ed: Joanne Cleaver. **Description:** Jim Dion, retail consultant, advises his clients to add a complaint and returns section to a customer database in order to track customer services.

31774 ■ "MAPICS Implements Web-based Self Service Tool to Enhance Customer Service For High Tech Manufacturers" in *PR Newswire* (Oct. 29, 2001)
Pub: PR Newswire Association, Inc.
Description: New solutions database offers on-demand support for MAPICS' ERP for extended systems customers. MAPICS is a leading provider of collaborative, extended enterprise applications for manufacturers.

31775 ■ "Mapping the World of Customer Satisfaction" in *Harvard Business Review* (Vol. 78, No. 3, May 2000, pp. 30)
Pub: Harvard Business School Publishing Corp.
Ed: Regina Fazio Maruca. **Description:** Traditional satisfaction surveys often obscure the differences among customers in different regions of the country and different areas of the world.

31776 ■ "A Matter of Opinion" in *Entrepreneur* (Vol. 31, No. 8, August 2003, pp. 72)
Pub: Entrepreneur Media, Inc.
Ed: Elizabeth Goodgold. **Description:** According to Jeffrey G. Jordan, market researcher for 1-on-One Marketing Associates, mystery shopping, customer comment cards, on-site intercepting, Web site evaluation and toll-free telephone numbers are great ways to get customer feedback.

31777 ■ *Measuring Customer Satisfaction*
Pub: Crisp Publications, Inc.
Ed: Richard F. Gerson. **Price:** $19.95.

31778 ■ *Meeting Customer Needs*
Pub: Butterworth-Heinemann
Ed: Ian Smith. **Released:** 1994. **Price:** $34.95. **Description:** Describes how to meet customer needs through marketing planning.

31779 ■ "Memphis, Tenn., Entrepreneurs Urged to Stay Close to Customers" in *Commercial Appeal* (October 27, 2004)
Pub: The Commercial Appeal
Ed: Maria Burnham. **Description:** Maria Fischer, owner of a virtual assistant business, found inspiration from L.D. Beard, founder of Biotechnology Inc. when he spoke to entrepreneurs about the importance of staying in close contact with customers.

31780 ■ "Middays of Thunder" in *Inc.* (January 1, 2002)
Pub: Inc. Magazine
Ed: Rebecca Dorr. **Description:** Robert River, founder of Spectrum Communications Cabling Services Inc., tells how he took his top customers and some employees to a race track to race cars, rather than dinner or a ball game.

31781 ■ "Mobilize! These Businesses Get Moving" in *My Business* (August/September 2002, pp. 38-41)
Pub: My Business Magazine
Ed: Kathleen Landis. **Description:** Many small business are now delivering services directly to the customer's front door as a means of better serving clients and setting themselves apart from competitors. Profiled in the article is a traveling dentist, veterinarian, car detailer, and a paper shredding firm.

31782 ■ "Most valuable players" in *Entrepreneur* (Vol. 31, No. 6, June 2003, pp. 68)
Pub: Entrepreneur Media Inc.
Ed: Joshua Kurlantzick. **Description:** Rather than cutting prices to compete with large chains, small businesses should continue to offer customers value-added services.

31783 ■ *Multicultural Customer Service*
Pub: Irwin Professional Publishing
Ed: Leslie Aguilar. **Released:** 1995. **Price:** $10.00.

31784 ■ "My Business Manual: Due Diligence" in *My Business* (December/January 2003, pp. 44)
Pub: My Business Magazine
Ed: Julie Bawden Davis. **Description:** A good customer service program ensures repeat business. Five easy ways to gain new customers are also listed.

31785 ■ "My Business Manual: One Step Ahead" in *My Business* (December/January 2003, pp. 43)
Pub: My Business Magazine
Ed: Alan S. Horowitz. **Description:** Customer loyalty programs are discussed, including tips on starting a frequent buyer program.

31786 ■ "My Business Manual: Open Up" in *My Business* (December/January 2003, pp. 41-42)
Pub: My Business Magazine
Ed: John Rubino. **Description:** Five ways to grow a business by targeting new customers are highlighted, including identification of the new target market, becoming part of the community, know the limitations of a business, getting clients interested in a product, and ways to market a new product.

31787 ■ "My Business Manual: The First Line of Defense" in *My Business* (December/January 2003, pp. 45)
Pub: My Business Magazine
Ed: Gina Binole. **Description:** According to the U.S. Office of Consumer Affairs, 91 percent of dissatisfied customers will not return to a business. The importance of educating a workforce on customer service is stressed.

31788 ■ "My Gadget" in *My Business* (June/July 2004, pp. 22)
Pub: My Business Magazine
Description: Jason Knief, owner of a beer, wine and spirits store, uses the gadget called, Whispering Windows. The device attaches to a window or other flat surface and produces smooth and steady musical sounds that attract customers.

31789 ■ "Mystery Shopper Reports Lead to Several Firings at Roanoke, Va., Theater" in *Roanoke Times* (July 13, 2004)
Pub: Roanoke Times
Ed: Ryan Basen. **Description:** Carmike, one of three major movie theater companies in Southwest Virginia, fired several of its employees based on reports from mystery shoppers sent into their movie theaters.

31790 ■ "Mystery Shoppers Enjoy Being Spies" in *Atlanta Journal-Constitution* (January 29, 2005)
Pub: Atlanta Journal-Constitution
Ed: Renee DeGross. **Description:** Department stores and other retailers are using mystery shoppers to see their stores the way their customers see them; hotels and restaurants chains have begun using mystery shoppers also.

31791 ■ "Mystery Shoppers Help Provide Certainty for Several Major Companies" in *Chicago Tribune* (July 4, 2004)
Pub: Chicago Tribune
Ed: Becky Yerak. **Description:** Mystery shoppers assist businesses to improve customer service. Profile of Barb Bullock, a certified mystery shopper, is included.

31792 ■ "Mystery Shoppers Keep Eye on Customer Service" in *Washington Times* (July 8, 2004)
Pub: Washington Times
Ed: Donna DeMarco. **Description:** Profile of Max Jakeman, mystery shopper in Alexandria, Virginia. According to the National Center for Professional Mystery Shoppers and Merchandisers, $400-$600 million is spent annually in this field. Statistical data included.

31793 ■ "Mystery Shoppers Take a Second Glance at Customer Service" in *Business Record* (Vol. 22, August 30, 2004, No. 35, pp. 1)
Pub: Business Publication Corporation
Ed: Erin Morain. **Description:** Prairie Life Health & Fitness center in West Des Moines, Iowa uses mystery shoppers to conduct market research.

31794 ■ "National Shopping Service Announces 150,000th Mystery Shopper" in *Internet Wire* (October 26, 2004)
Pub: COMTEX News Network Inc.
Description: National Shopping Service provides evaluation and feedback to its customers through a mystery shopper program. The firm has more than 150,000 registered mystery shoppers performing over 30,000 client visits per month.

31795 ■ "Need Help? Don't Call Us" in *Inc.* (August 2005, pp. 36)
Pub: Inc. Magazine
Ed: Etelka Lehoczky. **Description:** Online forums are turning clients into a low-cost support staff. Nick Bradbury tells how he built a Web forum with 2,000 users.

31796 ■ "Net Company: Don't Shout, Listen" in *Fast Company* (August 2001, pp. 129)
Pub: Fast Company
Ed: Fara Warner. **Description:** The article shows how the Proctor & Gamble company has turned the Internet into a device for listening to customers, and also experiment with their brands.

31797 ■ "Never say 'NO'" in *Women in Business* (Vol. 54, No. 2, March-April 2002, pp. 27)
Pub: The ABWA Co Inc.
Ed: Barton Goldsmith. **Description:** Customer service representatives should provide alternatives for their clients; the word NO should never be an option.

31798 ■ "The New Net CEO" in *Harvard Business Review* (Vol. 78, No. 3, May 2000, pp. S10)
Pub: Harvard Business School Publishing Corp.
Ed: Chuck Martin. **Description:** Executives in electronic commerce must understand the way in which the industry operates and must focus on the customer.

31799 ■ "The New You" in *Entrepreneur* (Vol. 32, October 2004, No. 10, pp. 100)
Pub: Entrepreneur Media Inc.
Ed: Nichole L. Torres. **Description:** According to market strategists, entrepreneurs should take a long look at their brand and focus on services or products that fit the overall brand.

31800 ■ "1999 McKinsey Awards" in *Harvard Business* (Vol. 78, No. 1, January 2000, pp. 137)
Pub: Harvard Business School Publishing Corp.
Description: This article defines the three types of businesses companies are engaged in: customer service, operations, and product development.

31801 ■ "No Room for Mediocrity" in *Fast Company* (September 2001, pp. 160)
Pub: Fast Company
Ed: Jill Rosenfeld. **Description:** Do you want to check out the future of hotels? Then check into the Peninsula Beverly Hills, where Ali Kasikci is creating rooms with incomparable service, built around unconventional ideas.

31802 ■ "Not for sale" in *BlackEnterprise* (Vol. 32, No. 3, October 2001, pp. 165)
Pub: Earl Graves Publishing Co.
Ed: Leslie E. Royal. **Description:** Profile of the Gramm-Leach-Bliley Financial Services Modernization Act signed into law by President Clinton in 1999. The bill requires all financial institutions to inform their current and former customers how their personal and financial information is to be disclosed, shared, and sold to its affiliates and other companies.

31803 ■ "The Old Economy Meets the New Economy" in *Fast Company* (November 2001, pp. 70)
Pub: Fast Company
Description: Fast Company recently convened a session in Chicago with experts from the world's strongest and oldest brands with the objective of finding new insights on emerging best practices when it comes to customers, technology and business.

31804 ■ "On the Same Page: Gain Competitive Edge With a Company-Wide Focus on Customers" in *Sales & Marketing Management* (Vol. 157, Jan. 2005)
Pub: VNU Business Media
Ed: Sara Calabro. **Description:** Customer touchpoint management (CTM) is the understanding that a company's relationship with customers is not just about sales, but is the responsibility of the entire business.

31805 ■ "On a Shoestring" in *Entrepreneur* (Vol. 32, September 2004, No. 9, pp. 107)
Pub: Entrepreneur Media Inc.
Description: Profile of Rick Kushel and Ed Vogelsong, who built their document storage company based on customer service. With $5,000 of startup money the two built a storage system that includes both hard copies and electronic copies, and currently consists of more than 400,000 square feet of storage space.

31806 ■ "The One Number You Need to Grow" in *Harvard Business Review* (Vol. 81, No. 12, December 2003, pp. 46)
Pub: Harvard Business School Press
Ed: Frederick F. Reichheld. **Description:** The power of customer word-of-mouth communication and corporate growth are examined. Loyal customers promote growth by personally endorsing to friends the businesses they patronize. Means for measuring the effects of these promoters are described.

31807 ■ "One Smart Customer" in *Fast Company* (September 2001, pp. 68)
Pub: Fast Company
Description: The CEO of NetSolve addresses the importance of customer service and ways to avoid problems.

31808 ■ **"The Only Question That Matters"** in *Business 2.0* (Vol. 6, September 2005, No. 8, pp. 50)
Pub: Time, Inc.
Ed: Description: Companies using the net promoter technique are listed. This technique asks customers whether they would recommend a product, subtracts positive responses from neutral and negative ones giving a barometer of customer satisfaction.

31809 ■ **"...Or Your Money Back"** in *Inc.* (September 2005, pp. 46)
Pub: Inc. Magazine
Ed: Dee Gill. **Description:** Money-back guaranties will entice customers, thus increase sales.

31810 ■ **"Out Of Pocket, Out Of Mind"** in *Law Firm Inc.* (August 2004)
Pub: American Lawyer Media LP
Ed: Tamara Loomis. **Description:** Cost recovery systems are of major concern to law firms. Many firms are considering whether to absorb costs for copies, laser printouts, faxes, scanning and telephone calls or pass the expense on to clients in order to recover out-of-pocket expenses incurred on the client's behalf.

31811 ■ *Outfoxing the Small Business Owner*
Pub: Adams Media Corporation
Ed: Gene Marks. **Released:** January 2005. **Price:** $12.95 (US), $18.95 (Canadian). **Description:** Special skill sets are required to sell, service or deal with small business customers.

31812 ■ **"Paper, Printing & Profit"** in *Small Business Opportunities* (Vol. 16, No. 2, March 2004, pp. 70)
Pub: Harris Publications, Inc.
Ed: Annette Wood. **Description:** Profile of Eric Jacobsen and Mahlon Regier, owners of Timber Creek Paper of Wichita, Kansas. The owners stay competitive by focusing on customer service, catering to smaller accounts such as churches, small businesses and local printers.

31813 ■ **"Paying in Kind"** in *Entrepreneur.com* (Vol. 34, February 2006, No. 2, pp. 82)
Pub: Entrepreneur Media Inc.
Ed: Mark Henricks. **Description:** Some companies send surveys to customers in order to determine the quality of customer service provided by employees.

31814 ■ **"The Perfect Connection"** in *Small Business Opportunities* (Vol. 16, No. 3, May 2004, pp. 72)
Pub: Harris Publications, Inc.
Ed: Chuck Green. **Description:** Profile of Jeff Liggett, ANET Internet Solutions, a bandwidth supplier. Liggett suggests it is important to expand gradually.

31815 ■ **"The Perfect System"** in *Small Business Opportunities* (Vol. 14, No. 1, January 2002, pp. 70, 104)
Pub: Harris Publications, Inc.
Ed: Paul Soltoff. **Description:** Tips on selecting the right email marketing system for small business are explored, including profitability, permission issues, and customer affinity.

31816 ■ **"Personal issues"** in *Entrepreneur* (Vol. 30, No. 2, February 2002, pp. 22)
Pub: Entrepreneur Media Inc.
Ed: Mark Henricks. **Description:** Review of the book entitled, "Making It Personal", by personalization and privacy expert Bruce Kasanoff. The books explores personalization and privacy issues, including technical complexity, ethical uncertainty and still-evolving legal oversight when customers share information.

31817 ■ **"Personal, Thoughtful Ways to Stay in Touch"** in *Rough Notes* (Vol. 145, No. 2, February 2003, pp. 32)
Pub: Rough Notes
Description: Staying in touch with business contacts and customers is very important in marketing. This can be done with phone calls, cards, a newsletter, or a personal note.

31818 ■ **"Perspective"** in *Harvard Business Review* (Vol. 78, No. 3, May 2000, pp. S3)
Pub: Harvard Business School Publishing Corp.
Description: How are corporate executives handling the new business focus: customer centricity? If you're not already focused on the customer, you may be prodded to change.

31819 ■ **"The Pivotal roles of Customer Service Professionals"** in *Rough Notes* (Vol. 145, No. 2, February 2003, pp. 88)
Pub: Rough Notes
Ed: Jim Cuprisin. **Description:** The role of the insurance customer service professional is the most customer critical in an insurance agency because the position plays a vital role in the company's growth and profitability.

31820 ■ **"Portland, Maine-Based L.L. Bean Ranks High In Customer Loyalty"** in *Portland Press Herald* (April 8, 2005)
Pub: Blethen Maine Newspapers, Inc.
Ed: Edward D. Murphy. **Description:** According to a recent survey conducted by Brand Keys Fashion Index, L.L. Bean ranked six. The survey measures brand importance to consumers and sales growth.

31821 ■ **"Power to the Buyer With Group Buying Sites"** in *E-business Advisor* (Vol. 18, No. 2, February 2000, pp. 10)
Pub: Advisor Media, Inc.
Ed: Erica Rugullies. **Description:** Group buying practices that enable customers to lower their acquisition costs and allow the vendor to reach new audiences, test new promotions and sell excess inventory are discussed.

31822 ■ **"Present Perfect"** in *Fast Company* (September 2001, pp. 164)
Pub: Fast Company
Ed: Alison Overholt. **Description:** Profile of Westin Hotels and Resorts, San Francisco airport restaurants, and Virgin Atlantic Airways for the business traveler.

31823 ■ **"Pricing and the psychology of consumption"** in *Harvard Business Review* (Vol. 80, No. 9, September 2002, pp. 90)
Pub: Harvard Business School Press
Ed: John Gourville, Dilip Soman. **Description:** Consumer psychology is a critical factor in pricing goods and services, and one that is often ignored by executives when determining price.

31824 ■ **"Priority Mail"** in *Entrepreneur* (Vol. 28, No. 1, January 2000, pp. 38)
Pub: Entrepreneur Media Inc.
Ed: Gwen Moran. **Description:** If you think it's okay to wait a few days before returning e-mail inquiries, you could be committing customer service suicide.

31825 ■ **"Promoting Praise: Incorporating Client Feedback Into Your Motivation Efforts"** in *Sales & Marketing Management* (Vol. 157, Jan. 2005)
Pub: VNU Business Media
Ed: Kathryn Droullard. **Description:** Positive customer feedback can be used as a tool to motivate sales teams.

31826 ■ *Quality Customer Service*
Pub: Crisp Publications, Inc.
Ed: William B. Martin. **Released:** Third edition. **Price:** $10.95.

31827 ■ *The Quest for Quality: Prescriptions for Service Excellence*
Pub: St. Martin's Press, Inc.
Ed: Phillip S. Wexler. **Released:** 1996. **Price:** $13.95.

31828 ■ **"Rapport & Revenue"** in *Small Business Opportunities* (July 2005)
Pub: Harris Publications Inc.
Description: Three Customer Relationship Management systems are outlined to help a small business choose the best one. According to recent studies only 30 percent of customer relationship management programs are successful.

31829 ■ *Raving Fans: A Revolutionary Approach to Customer Service*
Pub: William Morrow & Co., Inc.
Ed: Ken Blanchard and Sheldon Bowles. **Released:** 1993. **Price:** $12.00. **Description:** Provides customer-driven strategies for custom service, focusing on deciding on company vision, discovering who the customer is, and delivering what is promised.

31830 ■ **"Rebuilding Your Business With Former and Current Customers"** in *Ingram's* (Vol. 27, No. 8, August 2001, pp. 19)
Pub: Show Me Publishing, Inc.
Ed: Tom Sight. **Description:** Advice for motivating employees and improving customer service within a small business is given.

31831 ■ **"A Recipe for Perfection"** in *Inc.* (July 1, 2003)
Pub: Gruner & Jahr USA Publishing
Description: America's most luxurious inn, Inn at Little Washington located in Virginia, reveals its secrets for satisfying the world's toughest customers.

31832 ■ **"Recreation"** in *Inc.* (Volume 27, July 2005, No. 7, pp. 57-58)
Pub: Inc. Magazine
Ed: Patrick J. Sauer. **Description:** A well-planned company barbeque can be used as a business opportunity for recruitment, marketing, worker and customer loyalty, employee motivation, and finding new customers. Barbeque sauce recipe included.

31833 ■ **"Relationship Advice"** in *Entrepreneur* (Vol. 32, No. 1, January 2004, pp. 47)
Pub: Entrepreneur Media, Inc.
Ed: Liane Cassavoy. **Description:** Profile of Salesnet's online Customer Relation Management application that includes tools for managing accounts and contacts.

31834 ■ **"Remember Service With a Smile?"** in *Microsoft Executive Circle* (Vol. 1, No. 2, Q2 2001, pp. 16-18, 21)
Pub: Putman Media
Ed: Keith Larson. **Description:** Today's technology can assist companies to respond more rapidly and accurately to ensure customer satisfaction.

31835 ■ **"Retail/Hospitality"** in *Microsoft Executive Circle* (Vol. 1, No. 2, Q2 2001, pp. 34-37)
Pub: Putman Media
Ed: Craig A. Shutt. **Description:** New technology is providing consumers faster, more personalized service at restaurants, while cutting costs for restaurant owners.

31836 ■ **"Retailers, Beware"** in *Entrepreneur* (Vol. 28, No. 4, April 2000, pp. 58)
Pub: Entrepreneur Media Inc.
Description: A recent study by Harte-Hanks Market Research found that 69 percent of consumers are dissatisfied with the service they receive and, therefore, don't feel a need to be loyal to the stores in which they shop.

31837 ■ **"Retailing Your Personal Lines Accounts"** in *Rough Notes* (Vol. 146, No. 9, September 2003, pp. 56)
Pub: Rough Notes
Ed: Troy Korsgaden. **Description:** Ways for insurance agents to increase personal insurance lines; topics include strategic marketing, techniques in selling, and tips on improving customer service.

31838 ■ **"Retention Rate Can Be Enhanced"** in *Morgage Servicing News* (Vol. 5, No. 10, November 2001, pp. 4)
Pub: Thompson Financial Publishing
Ed: Steve Kropper. **Description:** Interview with Steven Kropper, co-founder and CEO of Domania Inc., a Boston-based financial and marketing services software company that provides customer acquisition and retention products, shares insight into retaining customers.

31839 ■ **"A rewarding experience" in** *Incentive* **(Vol. 174, No. 8, August 2000, pp. 12)**
Pub: Bill Communications
Ed: Don Mogelefsky. **Description:** Inspiring a sales force, rewarding a customer, or recognizing an employee can all be done easily and efficiently online.

31840 ■ **"Righting the Digital Ship" in** *Black Enterprise* **(Vol. 36, February 2006, No. 7, pp. 63)**
Pub: Earl G. Graves Publishing Co. Inc.
Ed: Bridget McCrea. **Description:** Champ Mitchell, CEO and chairman of Network Solutions in Virginia, created a customer service program that replaced nearly 70 percent of its current employees, and setup a six-week intensive training program to ensure newly hired employees are highly skilled.

31841 ■ **"Sales & Marketing: The Power of Brand" in** *Ingram's* **(Vol. 27, No. 6, June 2001, pp. 23)**
Pub: Show Me Publishing, Inc.
Ed: Jean Hughes. **Description:** The answer to increasing product usage is to leverage the company's brand and to strengthen account relationships.

31842 ■ **"S&MM Pulse" in** *Sales & Marketing Management* **(Vol. 158, November-December 2006, No. 11, pp. 16)**
Pub: VNU Business Media
Description: Customer service is stressed, including improved communication skills.

31843 ■ **"Telecommunications: 'Press ' for Satisfied Users" in** *Microsoft Executive Circle* **(Vol. 1, No. 2, Q2 2001, pp. 42-44)**
Pub: Putman Media
Ed: Marty Weil. **Description:** New telecommunication programs could generate 30 percent of revenue for companies within five years and improve customer satisfaction and loyalty.

31844 ■ **"A Second Act for CRM" in** *Inc.* **(Volume 27, March 2005, No. 3, pp. 40, 42)**
Pub: Inc. Magazine
Ed: Ellen Neuborne. **Description:** Customer relationship management software will manage customer databases. A recent study found that 60 percent of midsize companies will adopt or expand CRM usage over the next two years.

31845 ■ **"Secret Shopper" in** *Home Office Computing* **(Vol. 18, No. 11, November 2000, pp. 12)**
Pub: Scholastic Inc.
Description: Catalogs and Web sites can save time when purchasing, but getting help can prove much more challenging. Two resellers, pcconnection.com and CDW.com, were tested for customer service. While buying products was made easy, there was some difficulty in obtaining basic information about products from service representatives.

31846 ■ **Serves You Right!**
Pub: Serves You Right!, Incorporated
Ed: Susan Brooks. **Released:** May 2004. **Price:** $15.95. **Description:** Profile of excellence in customer service.

31847 ■ **"Service that truly makes a difference" in** *Rough Notes* **(Vol. 146, No. 4, April 2003, pp. 114)**
Pub: Rough Notes
Ed: Suellyn Boastick. **Description:** Customer satisfaction and customer relationships require anticipation of needs, communication with clients and outreach services to the community.

31848 ■ **The Service Edge: 101 Companies That Profit from Customer Care**
Pub: Plume
Ed: Ron Zemke and Dick Schaaf. **Price:** $16.95. **Description:** Profiles 101 companies that the author feels has turned outstanding customer service into a competitive edge.

31849 ■ *Service, Service, Service...The Key to Winning and Keeping Customers for Life*
Pub: National Press Publications
Ed: Marian Thomas. **Released:** 1992. **Price:** $7.95.
Description: Published by National Seminars.

31850 ■ **"Service With a Smile" in** *Inc.* **(October 2005, pp. 75-76)**
Pub: Inc. Magazine
Ed: David H. Freedman. **Description:** The article exams the ways in which technology has harmed customer service and ways three startup companies plan to rescue it. According to one study, 37 percent of callers who reach an automated voice system press zero in the hopes of speaking to an actual person.

31851 ■ **"Serving Your Client-And Yourself" in** *Sales and Marketing.com* **(Vol. 156, No. 3, March 2004, pp. 20)**
Pub: VNU eMedia, Inc.
Ed: Daniel Tynan. **Description:** Profile of Craig Elias, founder of InnerSell, a firm through which salespeople can locate services for their customers, make referrals, and earn a percentage of the deal.

31852 ■ **"Shopping For Good Health: Perception Strategies Adds 'Mystery' to Medicine" in** *Indianapolis Business Journal* **(September 27, 2004)**
Pub: Indianapolis Business Journal Corp.
Ed: Shelley Swift. **Description:** Mystery shoppers are helping to shape the standard for patient satisfaction at health care facilities nationwide. Kevin Billingsley, founder of Perception Strategies Inc., applies the mystery shopping technique to the field of health care.

31853 ■ **"Shopping Spies Help Retail Businesses Keep Eye on Service" in** *Charlotte Observer* **(October 10, 2004)**
Pub: Charlotte Observer
Ed: Leigh Dyer. **Description:** Charlotte, North Carolina-based Belk Department Stores is using mystery shoppers in order to enforce store policies. The store managers' annual bonus is based on this program.

31854 ■ **"Six Sigma: New Opportunites for HR, New Career Growth for Employees" in** *Employment Relations Today* **(Vol. 27,No. 2, Summer 2000, pp. 1)**
Pub: John Wiley & Sons, Inc.
Ed: Joseph A. DeFeo. **Description:** It is essential that Human Resources managers understand their role in improving efficiency and competitiveness with regard to products and all customer services. The six sigma quality concept for measuring the effectiveness of business processes is described.

31855 ■ **"Small Business Advisor: A Customer for All Seasons" in** *Ingram's* **(Vol. 27, No. 5, May 2001, pp. 25)**
Pub: Show Me Publishing, Inc.
Ed: Jeff Yowell. **Description:** In order to retain customers, customer relationship management needs to be part of a company's marketing plan.

31856 ■ **"Small Business Advisor: Dialing for dollars" in** *Crain's Chicago Business* **(Vol. 23, December 11, 2000, pp. SB16)**
Pub: Crain Communications, Inc. Crain Communications, Inc.
Ed: Barbara B. Buchholz. **Description:** A profile of Jeffery L. Furst and his company, FurstPerson Inc. that recruits and trains personnel for corporate telemarketing firms. Advice is given for growth, including statistical data and an industry overview.

31857 ■ *Small Business Desk Reference*
Pub: Penguin Books (USA) Incorporated
Ed: Gene Marks. **Released:** December 2004. **Price:** $29.95 (US), $44.00 (Canadian). **Description:** Comprehensive guide for starting or running a successful small business, focusing on buying a business or franchise, writing a business plan, financial management, accounting, legal issues, human resources management, operations, marketing, sales, customer service, taxes, insurance, and ethics. Information for launching a restaurant, property management firm, retail outlet, consulting service, and service business is included.

31858 ■ **"Smile: Your Company's Under Attack" in** *PC Computing* **(March 2000, pp. 42)**
Pub: Ziff-Davis Inc.
Ed: Jamais Cascio. **Description:** Online consumer complaint sites, which are increasing in popularity, result in bad publicity for companies, and, the means by which the company chooses to handle the sites can be detrimental for company public relations. Companies have launched high-profile lawsuits and directly threatened the owner of the complaint domain. The reaction by the companies to the sites brings much more attention to the complaints than the original site. The best way to handle complaints is to respond to customers and work to resolve issues rather than ignoring them. Customer support sites are very easy to establish, and it is an easy way to keep in contact with customers.

31859 ■ **"Software-Maker Bulks up with $20 Million VC Deal" in** *Atlanta Business Chronicle* **(Vol. 25, No. 21, November 1, 2002, pp. 3A)**
Pub: American City Business Publications, Inc.
Ed: Mary Jane Credeur. **Description:** WebTone Technologies Inc. of Georgia, a customer relationship management software producer, has received $20 million in venture capital. Technology Crossover Ventures was the leader of the funding round.

31860 ■ **"Sports Scenario: There's No Room for Ball Hogs on Your Team" in** *Small Business Opportunities* **(Vol. 16, No. 1, January 2004, pp. 54)**
Pub: Harris Publications, Inc.
Ed: Pam Mitchell. **Description:** Teamwork is imperative in order for a small business to succeed. The four major issues that cause sub-optimal teamwork are investigated. Customer value programs can become strategic planning sessions.

31861 ■ **"Spread the Word: Get Customers Talking and They'll Do Your Advertising For You" in** *Entrepreneur* **(Vol. 33, February 2005, No. 2)**
Pub: Entrepreneur Media Inc.
Ed: Jerry Fisher. **Description:** Co-authors of Creating Customer Evangelists, Ben McConnell and Jackie Huba suggest that word-of-mouth advertising is an important component to any sales program.

31862 ■ **"Steal This Customer" in** *Internet World* **(Vol. 7, No. 1, January 15, 2001, pp. 32)**
Pub: Mecklermedia Corporation
Ed: Jason Black. **Description:** Acquiring and retaining customers is a major problem for online retailers, but need not be insurmountable. Many consumers use the Web for the online equivalent of window-shopping and price comparison; competing retailers have the opportunity to lure buyers with better offers, and Internet technology can greatly speed the process. Advertisements can be sent directly to the screen of a user browsing a competitor's site with the aid of Dash.com, Gator.com and other browser add-ons.

31863 ■ **"Stocks" in** *Business Week* **(January 9, 2006, No. 3966, pp. 92)**
Pub: McGraw-Hill Companies
Ed: Lauren Young. **Description:** According to new studies, companies with high customer service satisfaction ratings deliver a stronger market share. Apple, Yahoo!, VF Corporation and Toyota top the list of 200 companies compiled by the University of Michigan's Ross School of Business.

31864 ■ **"Straight talking: to tell or not to tell?" in** *Entrepreneur* **(Vol. 30, No. 10, October 2002, pp. 47)**
Pub: Entrepreneur Media Inc.
Ed: Melissa Campanelli. **Description:** A study conducted by the Consumer Web Watch shows that less than 30 percent of respondents trust information on Web sites that sell products and services.

31865 ■ "Strategic and Ethical Considerations in Managing Digital Privacy" in *Journal of Business Ethics* (Vol. 46, No. 2, Aug. 15, 2003)
Pub: Kluwer Academic Publishers Group
Ed: Ravi Sarathy, Chrisopher J. Robertson. **Description:** Individualized customer information is at the heart of online commerce. Using increasing amounts of customer-specific data enhances the success and value of one-to-one online marketing, but the extensive gathering and use of data specific to individuals also causes alarm over the loss of digital privacy.

31866 ■ "Street Smarts. Keep Your Customers" in *Inc.* (September 2006, pp. 57-58)
Pub: Gruner & Jahr USA Publishing
Ed: Norm Brodsky. **Description:** Keeping customers is as important as recruiting new ones and much more economical. Listen to your customers input and react to their requests, complaints, and maybe even their demands, if reasonable; if that's what it takes to keep them.

31867 ■ "Super Sales in Service" in *Small Business Opportunities* (Vol. 17, September 2005, No. 5, pp. 76, 86)
Pub: Harris Publications, Inc.
Ed: Chuck Green. **Description:** Jenny Cooper, owner of a boutique offering bath and body products attributes her success to knowing how to treat her customers. Her boutique also offers a variety of accessories.

31868 ■ "Survey Your Customers" in *Home Business* (Vol. 12, March/April 2005, No. 2, pp. 50, 52-53)
Pub: Home Business Magazine
Ed: Christopher J. Bachler. **Description:** A customer survey provides important information to improve customer service as well as how to market wisely.

31869 ■ *Sustaining Knock Your Socks Off Service*
Pub: AMACOM
Ed: Ron Zemke and Thomas K. Connellan. **Released:** 1993. **Price:** $17.95 (paper); ($16.15 for AMA members).

31870 ■ "Sweet Rewards" in *Entrepreneur* (Vol. 31, No. 8, August 2003, pp. 75)
Pub: Entrepreneur Media, Inc.
Ed: Kim T. Gordon. **Description:** Win over existing customers with a customer loyalty program and increase sales at the same time.

31871 ■ "Sweet Victory" in *My Business* (December/January 2004, pp. 12)
Pub: My Business Magazine
Ed: Jamie Roberts. **Description:** Profile of Mike and Carol Hamilton, owners of Carol Hamilton's Chutters General Store, offering 650 glass jars filled with candy, making the store the home of the largest candy counter in the world. The Littleton, New Hampshire store is one in a trend of small companies restoring and maintaining the main streets of towns in America. These small firms believe they can compete against large chains by offering unique customer service and products.

31872 ■ "Swimgear Web Site Crosses Oceans" in *My Business* (June/July 2002, pp. 46)
Pub: My Business Magazine
Ed: Shannon Scully. **Description:** Profile of Terry Gill Hammond, who began selling swimwear from her home. With five retail stores in the Atlanta area, Hammond decided to start selling her products online and discovered that Web customers require different service than in-store customers.

31873 ■ "Taking the Hospitality Test" in *Crain's Detroit Business* (Vol. 21, October 10, 2005, No. 43, pp. 11)
Pub: Crain Communications Inc. - Detroit
Ed: Robert Ankeny. **Description:** According to Service Advantage International, limo drivers, hotel help, waitresses and store clerks are friendly, courteous, neat and professional, but few service workers were able to recommend any Detroit attractions to visitors.

31874 ■ "Talking Shop: Wonder What Makes Shoppers Tick?" in *Entrepreneur* (Vol. 31, No. 9, September 2003, pp. 62)
Pub: Entrepreneur Media, Inc.
Ed: Elizabeth Goodgold. **Description:** ESPN Zone, Hot Topic, Starbucks, Anthropologie and Build-A-Bear Workshop share tips to target customers, develop an enduring brand, create a destination, sell a lifestyle and build a relationship with customers.

31875 ■ "Taming of the Crew: What Lion Tamers Teach Us About Team Management" in *Entrepreneur* (Vol. 33, January 2005, No. 1, pp. 26)
Pub: Entrepreneur Media Inc.
Ed: Geoff Williams. **Description:** In his book, Lion Taming: Working Successfully With Leaders, Bosses and Other Tough Customers, Steve Katz gathers insights from professional lion tamers to help entrepreneurs learn to tame suppliers, customers and competitors.

31876 ■ "Teacher in Chief" in *Fast Company* (September 2001, pp. 66)
Pub: Fast Company
Ed: Jennifer Reingold. **Description:** Why would a CEO of a fast-growing company take time out every month to teach his new hires? He does this because he wants them to take customer service as seriously as he does.

31877 ■ "Team Up for Riches" in *Small Business Opportunities* (Vol. 16, No. 2, March 2004, pp. 154, 170)
Pub: Harris Publications, Inc.
Ed: Brian Tracy. **Description:** Review of Brian Tracy's book, Goals: New Book Shows How! The book offers 21 ways to set and achieve goals in every area of life. Tracy suggests putting the customer on your team to build sales and increase your bottom line.

31878 ■ *Telephone Terrific! Facts, Fun and 103 "How-To" Tips for Phone Success*
Pub: Dartnell Corp.
Ed: David Dee. **Released:** 1994. **Price:** $10.95 (paper); $12.95 (Canada). **Description:** Guide for small business owners and professionals who conduct business over the phone. Includes tips for making and placing calls, time management techniques, and insight into serving customers courteously and efficiently.

31879 ■ "Thanks for the Biz" in *Small Business Opportunities* (Vol. 12, No. 2, March 2000, pp. 10)
Pub: Harris Publications, Inc.
Ed: Andrea Nierenberg. **Description:** Eight ways to say thanks to customers are presented.

31880 ■ "Their Life's Work" in *Tampa Tribune* (November 25, 2005)
Pub: Media General, Inc.
Ed: Dave Simanoff. **Description:** Employees with long tenure become an integral part of any small business, creating a bond and trust between management and employee as well as customer satisfaction.

31881 ■ "They Bought In. Now They Want to Bail Out" in *Harvard Business Review* (Vol. 81, No. 12, December 2003, pp. 28)
Pub: Harvard Business School Press
Ed: Eric McNulty. **Description:** A hypothetical case is presented in which a chief technology officer is required to justify a potential investment in customer relationship management software. Teaching highlights include evaluating whether the fictional company needs the software, techniques for selling an idea or project, and the importance of widespread support for the success of such ventures.

31882 ■ "This Call May Be Monitored" in *Inc.* (Volume 27, June 2005, No. 6, pp. 29-30)
Pub: Inc. Magazine
Ed: Jennifer Gill. **Description:** Companies are hiring professional snoops in order to improve customer satisfaction for their firm. Call center etiquette is examined.

31883 ■ "Through the grapevine: E-mail newsletter has owners tasting profits" in *Entrepreneur* (Vol. 31, No. 6, June 2003, pp. 81)
Pub: Entrepreneur Media Inc.
Ed: April Y. Pennington. **Description:** Customer relations depend on communication and many companies are using email newsletters to stay in touch with customers.

31884 ■ "Treat me well when I visit" in *Crain's Detroit Business* (Vol. 18, No. 23, June 10, 20)
Pub: Crain Communications Inc. - Detroit
Ed: Joe Novak. **Description:** When creating a Web site, the developer has to walk a fine line to create something functional, while also being aesthetically pleasing.

31885 ■ "Trends Tips Ideas" in *Success* (Vol. 47, No. 6, November 2000, pp. 12)
Pub: Success Publishing, Inc.
Description: Inadequate customer service costs sales and goodwill. On the Internet, customer service can be particularly bad. A recent report estimated that more than $6 billion in online sales was lost last year due to inadequate customer service. The recent Web entry ServiceEngine allows e-commerce businesses to offer customer service over its platform, which automates the entire customer service process.

31886 ■ "Trinity Potter celebrates 15th anniversary behind strong commitment to quality" in *Gifts & Decorative Accessories* (Jan. 2003, pp.190)
Pub: Reed Business Information
Description: The family owned Trinity Pottery is profiled. Each Trinity Pottery piece is handcrafted, and the company offers competitive pricing. The company prides itself on its reputation for offering great customer service to its clientele.

31887 ■ "Trying Times: Every Once in a While, You'll Meet Difficult Customers" in *Entrepreneur* (Vol. 31, No. 9, July 2003, pp. 80)
Pub: Entrepreneur Media, Inc.
Ed: Barry Farber. **Description:** Ways to deal with difficult customers for salespeople are discussed, including the know-it-all customer, the silent type, and the indecisive prospect.

31888 ■ "Tulsa-Based Dollar Thrifty Automotive Group Inc. to Outsource Call Center" in *Journal Record (Oklahoma City, OK)* (February 8, 2007)
Pub: Journal Record
Description: Dollar Thrifty Automotive Group Inc. shares plans to outsource its call center services, including reservations and customer support services, to PRC in Plantation, Florida.

31889 ■ "Turn Customer Input into Innovation" in *Harvard Business Review* (Vol. 80, No. 1, January 2002, pp. 91)
Pub: Harvard Business School Press
Ed: Anthony W. Ulwick. **Description:** A new methodology is proposed for more effectively capturing customer input for new products and services that should minimize failure when the product or service is introduced. Previous methods often failed to correctly understand customer feedback.

31890 ■ *Twenty-Five Tips for Customer Service: An Action Plan for Service Success*
Pub: Trans-Atlantic Publications, Inc.
Ed: Ian Linton. **Released:** 1995. **Price:** $47.50.

31891 ■ *Twenty Ways to Improve Customer Service*
Pub: Crisp Publications, Inc.
Ed: Lloyd Finch. **Price:** $12.95.

31892 ■ "Uncharted Territory" in *Entrepreneur* (Vol. 32, No. 1, January 2004, pp. 27)
Pub: Entrepreneur Media, Inc.
Ed: Don Nichols. **Description:** Profile of Bill Davidson, author of Breakthrough: How Great Companies

Set Outrageous Objectives-and Achieve Them. Davidson advises entrepreneurs to set outrageous objectives and to use creative thinking about customer care, cost reduction, and other issues to reach customers.

31893 ■ "U.S. Postal Service Business Reply Mail" in *Entrepreneur* **(Vol. 33, August 2005, No. 8, pp. 4)**
Pub: Entrepreneur Media Inc.
Ed: Steve Cooper. **Description:** Offering customers a postage-free reply can prove to be an effective marketing tool. The U.S. Postal Service charges only for those pieces of mail returned.

31894 ■ "Unlock Information, Unleash the Future" in *Microsoft Executive Circle* **(Vol. 1, No. 2, Q2 2001, pp. 14-15)**
Pub: Putman Media
Description: Businesses must integrate information from a wide range of sources in order to deliver customized and personalized customer service.

31895 ■ "Upfront: Saddle Up" in *My Business* **(October/November 2002, pp. 13-14)**
Pub: My Business Magazine
Ed: Alan Joch. **Description:** Profile of Robert Ferrand, owner of SaddleTech.com in Woodside, California. Ferrand sends his customers email greetings that are signed by his horse, Ace, and the customers love it. Tips for good customer relationship management are highlighted.

31896 ■ *Value Added Customer Service: The Employees Guide to Creating Satisfied Customer*
Pub: Contemporary Books, Inc.
Ed: Tom Reilly. **Released:** 1996. **Price:** $11.95.

31897 ■ "Web Site" in *Entrepreneur* **(Vol. 28, No. 2, February 2000, pp. 38)**
Pub: Entrepreneur Media Inc.
Ed: Robert McGarvey. **Description:** The Right Answer, a company that bills itself as "the customer service finessing center", offers four online quizzes that test a company's service skills.

31898 ■ "Web.Preneuring" in *Small Business Opportunities* **(Vol. 14, No. 1, January 2002, pp. 88)**
Pub: Harris Publications, Inc.
Ed: Marie Sherlock. **Description:** Ways to jumpstart an online business with a customer loyalty program are presented, including a reward system.

31899 ■ "Weigh your opt-ins" in *Entrepreneur* **(Vol. 30, No. 10, October 2002, pp. 96)**
Pub: Entrepreneur Media Inc.
Ed: Kim T. Gordon. **Description:** Much less costly than paper newsletters, e-mail letters can be a successful communication tool for marketing a product or service.

31900 ■ "What Customer Relationship?" in *Sales & Marketing Management* **(Vol. 159, January-February 2007, No. 1, pp. 11)**
Pub: VNU Business Media
Ed: Scott Horstein. **Description:** Customer relationship management is explained; marketing strategies using this concept are included.

31901 ■ "What Drives Inspiration?" in *Entrepreneur* **(Vol. 32, December 2004, No. 12, pp. 20)**
Pub: Entrepreneur Media Inc.
Description: Four tips for entrepreneurs to remain flexible in managing their business include: being realistic, updating technology, customer satisfaction, and being a good boss.

31902 ■ "What Makes a High Quality Customer Service Team?" in *Rough Notes* **(Vol. 146, No. 9, September 2003, pp. 74)**
Pub: Rough Notes
Ed: Thomas A. McCoy. **Description:** Information on the way insurance agents can improve customer service skills is shared. Topics include customer satisfaction, customer loyalty, and maintaining high levels of customer relations.

31903 ■ "What's the Secret to Successful CRM?" in *E-business Advisor* **(Vol. 18, No. 8, August 2000, pp. 41)**
Pub: Advisor Media, Inc.
Ed: Renee Sommer. **Description:** New technologies are offering effective customer relationship management (CRM), employing interactive, two-way communications that will provide new dimensions of customer satisfaction.

31904 ■ "When Business is Personal" in *Home Office Computing* **(Vol. 18, No. 9, September 2000, pp. 18)**
Pub: Scholastic Inc.
Ed: Toni Kistner. **Description:** The customer/vendor relationship is explored.

31905 ■ "When a Customer Believes in You...They'll Stick with You Almost No Matter What" in *Fast Company* **(June 2001, pp. 138)**
Pub: Fast Company
Ed: Mike Ruettgers. **Description:** Profile of EMC Corporation, located in Hopkinton, Massachusetts. The article tells how the company was able to avoid bankruptcy by initiating a change-control process.

31906 ■ "When You Really Lose Customers" in *Entrepreneur* **(Vol. 30, No. 1)**
Pub: Entrepreneur Media Inc.
Ed: Melissa Campanelli. **Description:** A recent study shows that less than one-third of consumers notify regularly visited Web sites, online newsletters and discussion lists with new email addresses. Statistical data included.

31907 ■ "Why There's No Escaping the Blog" in *Fortune* **(Vol. 151, January 10, 2005, No. 1, pp. 44)**
Pub: Time Inc.
Ed: David Kirkpatrick, Daniel Roth, Oliver Ryan. **Description:** Microsoft has unveiled a plan to develop a new service called MSN Spaces, an online software that allows users to easily create and maintain blogs on the Internet. The power of blogs and bloggers to make or break a product or service is examined.

31908 ■ "Windows 98 Lives" in *Black Enterprise* **(Vol. 34, No. 3, October 2003, pp. 51)**
Pub: Earl Graves Publishing Co.
Ed: Sonya A. Donaldson. **Description:** Support information for users with Windows 98 on their PC is provided.

31909 ■ "Winds of Change" in *Entrepreneur* **(Vol. 33, October 2005, No. 10, pp. 82)**
Pub: Entrepreneur Media Inc.
Ed: Barry Farber. **Description:** Ten ways to help customers adjust to changes in your firm's products or services are outlined, focusing on how the changes will help them.

31910 ■ "Winning the paper chase" in *Incentive* **(Vol. 174, No. 10, October 2000, pp. 123)**
Pub: Bill Communications
Ed: Libby Estell. **Description:** Profile of the Kelly Paper Company, that has locked in its customer base and boosted sales by using a points-based loyalty program that allows customers to choose from among a variety of rewards.

31911 ■ "Works Great! Sales success" in *Entrepreneur* **(Vol. 30, No. 2, February 2002,)**
Pub: Entrepreneur Media Inc.
Ed: Barry Farber. **Description:** The use of customer testimonials to increase sales is examined.

31912 ■ "Would You Recommend Us? Perfect Your Service By Asking The Only Question That Matters." in *Inc.* **(September 2006, pp. 40, 42)**
Pub: Gruner & Jahr USA Publishing
Ed: Darren Dahl. **Description:** The most important question to ask in measuring your customer service is for a referral. If sales are stagnant or edging downward, many strategies can be costly and not address the real problem of how you're perceived by your customers.

31913 ■ "Yourshop@Black Enterprise.com" in *Black Enterprise* **(Vol. 31, No. 2, September 2000, pp. 215)**
Pub: Earl Graves Publishing Co.
Ed: Dorett Smith. **Description:** Small business can join the e-commerce revolution. If you are considering a Web presence to sell your company's products online, you'll need to weigh a number of factors related to e-business planning, such as productivity and functionality, advertising, sales, and service.

TRADE PERIODICALS

31914 ■ *Customer Service Advantage*
Pub: Progressive Business Publications
Ed: Michele McGovern, Editor. **Released:** Semimonthly. **Price:** $253, individuals. **Description:** Presents practical methods for quantifying customer service benefits and motivating employees day in and day out. Recurring features include interviews, news of research, a calendar of events, news of educational opportunities, and a column titled Sharpen Your Judgment.

31915 ■ *First-Rate Customer Service*
Pub: Briefings Publishing Group
Ed: John McDonnel, Editor, edit@epinc.com. **Released:** Biweekly. **Description:** Offers customer contact personnel advice on enthusiasm and a service-oriented attitude on the job. Recurring features include feature titled A Case in Point. **Remarks:** Also available in Spanish.

31916 ■ *Journal of Relationship Marketing*
Pub: The Haworth Press Inc.
Contact: Bill Cohen Ph.D., Publisher
Released: Quarterly, 4 issues/volume. **Price:** $60 U.S.; $81; $87 other countries; $140 institutions U.S.; $189 institutions, Canada; $203 institutions, other countries; $340 libraries agencies, U.S.; $459 libraries agencies, Canada; $493 libraries agencies, other countries. **Description:** Journal on marketing.

31917 ■ *Smart Customer Service*
Pub: Clement Communications Inc.
Contact: Mike Johnson, Sr. Editor
Released: Biweekly. **Price:** $195. **Description:** Provides managers and supervisors with techniques and strategies to improve customer service and employee satisfaction. Includes information on recruiting higher quality employees.

VIDEOCASSETTES/ AUDIOCASSETTES

31918 ■ *Beyond Close to the Customer*
Phoenix Learning Group
2349 Chaffee Dr.
St. Louis, MO 63146
Ph:(314)569-0211
Free: 800-221-1274
Fax: (314)569-2834
URL: http://www.phoenixlearninggroup.com
Released: 1989. **Price:** $895.00. **Description:** This is a three-part customer service enhancement program. **Availability:** VHS; 3/4U.

31919 ■ *Competing for Customers*
J. Miller Associates
15669 Live Oak Springs Rd.
Santa Clarita, CA 91351-4712
Ph:(805)251-9310
Fax: (805)251-9192
Price: $99.00. **Description:** Part of the Management Speaks Series. Outlines how to win over the customer, customer relationships, new strategy for building customer loyalty, unsatisfied consumers, and the importance of customer service. **Availability:** VHS.

31920 ■ *Competing Through Customer Service*
Video Arts, Inc.
c/o Aim Learning Group
8238-40 Lehigh
Morton Grove, IL 60053-2615

Free: 877-444-2230
Fax: (416)252-2155
Co. E-mail: service@aimlearninggroup.com
URL: http://www.aimlearninggroup.com
Released: 1989. **Price:** $730.00. **Description:** This video shows sure-fire methods for improving customer service by understanding and responding effectively to customer needs. **Availability:** VHS; 8mm; 3/4U; Special order formats.

31921 ■ *Customer Care Classic Moments*
Video Arts, Inc.
c/o Aim Learning Group
8238-40 Lehigh
Morton Grove, IL 60053-2615
Free: 877-444-2230
Fax: (416)252-2155
Co. E-mail: service@aimlearninggroup.com
URL: http://www.aimlearninggroup.com
Released: 1991. **Price:** $200.00. **Description:** Dealing with difficult customers is the focus of this video. Can be used to inject humor into a meeting, or as a meaningful exercise. **Availability:** VHS; 8mm; 3/4U; Special order formats.

31922 ■ *Customer Expectations*
1st Financial Training Services
1515 E. Woodfield Rd., Ste. 345
Schaumburg, IL 60173
Ph:(847)969-0900
Free: 800-442-8662
Fax: (847)969-0521
Co. E-mail: sales@1stfinancialtraining.com
URL: http://www.1stfinancialtraining.com
Released: 1987. **Price:** $299.00. **Description:** Companies have to know what customers want before they can give it to them. **Availability:** VHS; 3/4U.

31923 ■ *Customer Retention/Service Quality*
1st Financial Training Services
1515 E. Woodfield Rd., Ste. 345
Schaumburg, IL 60173
Ph:(847)969-0900
Free: 800-442-8662
Fax: (847)969-0521
Co. E-mail: sales@1stfinancialtraining.com
URL: http://www.1stfinancialtraining.com
Released: 1987. **Price:** $250.00. **Description:** Pope tells businesses how to keep their customers coming back. **Availability:** VHS; 3/4U.

31924 ■ *Customer Service or Else*
Enterprise Media
91 Harvey St.
Cambridge, MA 02140
Ph:(617)354-0017
Free: 800-423-6021
Fax: (617)354-1637
Co. E-mail: stewart@enterprisemedia.com
URL: http://www.enterprisemedia.com
Price: $795.00. **Description:** Peter Glen lectures on customer service issues. Full of funny, entertaining stories about customer service successes and nightmares. Comes with guide. **Availability:** VHS.

31925 ■ *Customer Service: It Pays to Please*
AIMS Multimedia
20765 Superior St.
Chatsworth, CA 91311-4409
Ph:(818)773-4300
Free: 800-367-2467
Fax: (818)341-6700
Co. E-mail: info@aims.multimedia.com
URL: http://www.aimsmultimedia.com
Released: 1985. **Description:** An instructional program that reveals the benefits and good business sense implicit in useful customer service. **Availability:** VHS; 3/4U.

31926 ■ *Customer Service: It's Good Business & It's Everybody's Business*
1st Financial Training Services
1515 E. Woodfield Rd., Ste. 345
Schaumburg, IL 60173
Ph:(847)969-0900
Free: 800-442-8662
Fax: (847)969-0521

Co. E-mail: sales@1stfinancialtraining.com
URL: http://www.1stfinancialtraining.com
Released: 1987. **Price:** $325.00. **Description:** A demonstration of what some good workers have in common-good customer service skills. **Availability:** VHS; 3/4U.

31927 ■ *Dealing with the Irate Customer*
Advantage Media
c/o Kantola Productions
55 Sunnyside Ave.
Mill Valley, CA 94941
Ph:(415)381-9363
Free: 800-989-8273
Fax: (415)381-9801
Co. E-mail: info@kantola.com
URL: http://www.kantola.com/d/advantage.htm
Released: 1988. **Price:** $495.00. **Description:** Features role play as a model for dealing with the three types of anger. Good visual reinforcement. **Availability:** VHS.

31928 ■ *Doesn't Anybody Care?*
Salenger Films, Inc.
1635 12th St.
Santa Monica, CA 90404-9988
Ph:(310)450-1300
Free: 800-775-5025
Fax: (310)450-1010
Co. E-mail: salenger@aol.com
URL: http://salengerfilms.visualnet.com
Released: 1985. **Price:** $485.00. **Description:** A primer on customer service training. **Availability:** 3/4U; Special order formats.

31929 ■ *Don't Mind Him—He's Only a Customer*
Video Arts, Inc.
c/o Aim Learning Group
8238-40 Lehigh
Morton Grove, IL 60053-2615
Free: 877-444-2230
Fax: (416)252-2155
Co. E-mail: service@aimlearninggroup.com
URL: http://www.aimlearninggroup.com
Released: 1989. **Price:** $415.00. **Description:** Ideas are given as to how customers can be treated better. **Availability:** VHS; 3/4U.

31930 ■ *Effective Telephone Calling*
Encyclopedia Britannica
331 N. LaSalle St.
Chicago, IL 60610
Ph:(312)347-7159
Free: 800-323-1229
Fax: (312)294-2104
URL: http://www.britannica.com
Released: 1989. **Description:** This program demonstrates an easy-to-follow procedure for placing outgoing calls to reduce telephone cost, avoid misunderstandings and project a courteous, business-like image. **Availability:** VHS; 3/4U.

31931 ■ *The End of the Line*
American Media, Inc.
4621 121st St.
Urbandale, IA 50323-2311
Ph:(515)224-0919
Free: 888-776-8268
Fax: (515)327-2555
Co. E-mail: custsvc@ammedia.com
URL: http://www.ammedia.com
Released: 1992. **Price:** $495.00. **Description:** Teaches employees how to effectively deal with angry customers over the telephone. Includes a leader's guide. **Availability:** VHS; 3/4U; 8mm.

31932 ■ *The Good Old Days of Quality Service*
American Media, Inc.
4621 121st St.
Urbandale, IA 50323-2311
Ph:(515)224-0919
Free: 888-776-8268
Fax: (515)327-2555
Co. E-mail: custsvc@ammedia.com
URL: http://www.ammedia.com

Released: 1992. **Price:** $350.00. **Description:** A motivational program to teach employees about quality customer service through narrated musical vignettes. **Availability:** VHS; 3/4U; 8mm.

31933 ■ *Hot Under the Collar: Dealing with Angry Customers*
American Media, Inc.
4621 121st St.
Urbandale, IA 50323-2311
Ph:(515)224-0919
Free: 888-776-8268
Fax: (515)327-2555
Co. E-mail: custsvc@ammedia.com
URL: http://www.ammedia.com
Released: 1989. **Price:** $495.00. **Description:** Employees are taught how to properly deal with customers who are not happy. A leader's guide and reminder cards are available. **Availability:** VHS; 3/4U; Special order formats.

31934 ■ *How to Deliver Superior Customer Service*
Instructional Video
2219 C St.
Lincoln, NE 68502
Ph:(402)475-6570
Free: 800-228-0164
Fax: (402)475-6500
Co. E-mail: feedback@insvideo.com
URL: http://www.insvideo.com
Price: $99.00. **Description:** Offers advice from 15 experts on how to improve customer service, including how to perceive what the customer wants and motivating employees. **Availability:** VHS.

31935 ■ *How to Lose Customers without Really Trying (Attack & Defend)*
Video Arts, Inc.
c/o Aim Learning Group
8238-40 Lehigh
Morton Grove, IL 60053-2615
Free: 877-444-2230
Fax: (416)252-2155
Co. E-mail: service@aimlearninggroup.com
URL: http://www.aimlearninggroup.com
Released: 1988. **Price:** $790.00. **Description:** A two-pronged approach to customer service that helps to identify and eliminate the most common pitfalls in dealing with customers when things go wrong. **Availability:** VHS; 8mm; 3/4U; Special order formats.

31936 ■ *I Love People...It's Customers I Can't Stand*
Instructional Video
2219 C St.
Lincoln, NE 68502
Ph:(402)475-6570
Free: 800-228-0164
Fax: (402)475-6500
Co. E-mail: feedback@insvideo.com
URL: http://www.insvideo.com
Price: $98.00. **Description:** Discusses five different types of problem customers and procedures for dealing with them. **Availability:** VHS.

31937 ■ *It's Your Choice*
American Media, Inc.
4621 121st St.
Urbandale, IA 50323-2311
Ph:(515)224-0919
Free: 888-776-8268
Fax: (515)327-2555
Co. E-mail: custsvc@ammedia.com
URL: http://www.ammedia.com
Released: 1988. **Price:** $495.00. **Description:** A service manager is told that he can either change his attitude or find another job. The importance of treating customers politely is stressed. **Availability:** VHS; 3/4U.

31938 ■ *Managing for Customer Care*
American Media, Inc.
4621 121st St.
Urbandale, IA 50323-2311
Ph:(515)224-0919
Free: 888-776-8268

Fax: (515)327-2555
Co. E-mail: custsvc@ammedia.com
URL: http://www.ammedia.com
Released: 1990. **Price:** $495.00. **Description:** Aimed at managers and supervisors, this video tells how to deal with day-to-day customer service situations. Includes a trainer's guide, six overhead transparencies, and masters for photocopying. **Availability:** VHS; 3/4U; 8mm.

31939 ■ *Managing Difficult Customers 1...2...3*
Salenger Films, Inc.
1635 12th St.
Santa Monica, CA 90404-9988
Ph:(310)450-1300
Free: 800-775-5025
Fax: (310)450-1010
Co. E-mail: salenger@aol.com
URL: http://salengerfilms.visualnet.com
Released: 1990. **Price:** $495.00. **Description:** Gives tips on telephone skills as well as ideas for handling angry, talkative, and demanding customers. Skits show how to take charge of the situation. **Availability:** VHS; 3/4U.

31940 ■ *Objection Handling: Overcoming the Hurdles*
Aspen Publishers
7201 McKinney Circ.
Frederick, MD 21704
Ph:(301)644-3599
Free: 800-638-8437
Fax: (301)644-3550
URL: http://www.aspenpublishers.com
Price: $495.00. **Description:** Suggests a five-step strategy to overcoming common customer objections. Unfortunately, the stiff actors provide poor examples. **Availability:** VHS.

31941 ■ *Oops! Time for Service Recovery*
Salenger Films, Inc.
1635 12th St.
Santa Monica, CA 90404-9988
Ph:(310)450-1300
Free: 800-775-5025
Fax: (310)450-1010
Co. E-mail: salenger@aol.com
URL: http://salengerfilms.visualnet.com
Released: 1991. **Price:** $650.00. **Description:** Discusses what to do when there is a service breakdown, disappointment, or misunderstanding with a customer. Available in two versions—one with stopping places with questions for dicussion and one with no stops. **Availability:** VHS; 3/4U.

31942 ■ *Partnering: The Heart of Selling Today*
American Media, Inc.
4621 121st St.
Urbandale, IA 50323-2311
Ph:(515)224-0919
Free: 888-776-8268
Fax: (515)327-2555
Co. E-mail: custsvc@ammedia.com
URL: http://www.ammedia.com
Price: $475.00. **Description:** Focuses on building lasting relationships with customers through partnering, a technique that helps customers solve their problems and questions. **Availability:** VHS; 3/4U; 8mm.

31943 ■ *The Power of Customer Service*
Nightingale-Conant Corp.
6245 W. Howard St.
Niles, IL 60714
Ph:(847)647-0300
Free: 800-560-6081
URL: http://www.nightingale.com
Released: 1991. **Price:** $95.00. **Description:** Customer-oriented service can be the greatest asset for any business. This video discusses the training and building of a service-oriented team. Includes an audio cassette and book. **Availability:** VHS.

31944 ■ *Quality Service: Frontline Commitment*
Phoenix Learning Group
2349 Chaffee Dr.
St. Louis, MO 63146

Ph:(314)569-0211
Free: 800-221-1274
Fax: (314)569-2834
URL: http://www.phoenixlearninggroup.com
Price: $495.00. **Description:** Focuses on customer service breakdowns and the necessary skills to remedy the situation. One in a pair of videos using the same scenarios to illustrate different points. **Availability:** VHS.

31945 ■ *Quality Service: The Three R's for Managers*
Phoenix Learning Group
2349 Chaffee Dr.
St. Louis, MO 63146
Ph:(314)569-0211
Free: 800-221-1274
Fax: (314)569-2834
URL: http://www.phoenixlearninggroup.com
Price: $495.00. **Description:** Focuses on customer service breakdowns and the necessary skills to remedy the situation. One of a pair of videos using the same scenarios to illustrate different points. **Availability:** VHS.

31946 ■ *Service Excellence*
Video Arts, Inc.
c/o Aim Learning Group
8238-40 Lehigh
Morton Grove, IL 60053-2615
Free: 877-444-2230
Fax: (416)252-2155
Co. E-mail: service@aimlearninggroup.com
URL: http://www.aimlearninggroup.com
Released: 1989. **Price:** $730.00. **Description:** This two-part video shows how your company can increase its profits by improving the three principal areas of customer service. At the end of the program is an opportunity to develop a customized strategy for customer service. **Availability:** VHS; 8mm; 3/4U; Special order formats.

31947 ■ *Service Sells/Phil Wexler*
Instructional Video
2219 C St.
Lincoln, NE 68502
Ph:(402)475-6570
Free: 800-228-0164
Fax: (402)475-6500
Co. E-mail: feedback@insvideo.com
URL: http://www.insvideo.com
Price: $395.00. **Description:** Phil Wexler offers tips on customer service and its effects on the success of the business. He covers the difference between operations-based thinking and market-based thinking, how the right choices can have an immediate impact on your business, targeting the needs of the customer, and minimizing customer complaints and objections. **Availability:** VHS.

31948 ■ *Service That Sells*
International Dairy-Deli-Bakery Association (IDDBA)
313 Price Pl., Ste. 202
PO Box 5528
Madison, WI 53705-0528
Ph:(608)238-7908
Fax: (608)238-6330
Co. E-mail: iddba@iddba.org
Price: $160.00. **Description:** Bakery customer service training video. **Availability:** VHS.

31949 ■ *Take a Minute: The Organized Call*
Salenger Films, Inc.
1635 12th St.
Santa Monica, CA 90404-9988
Ph:(310)450-1300
Free: 800-775-5025
Fax: (310)450-1010
Co. E-mail: salenger@aol.com
URL: http://salengerfilms.visualnet.com
Price: $395.00. **Description:** Presents a four-step method to help employees prepare for and organize their outgoing calls. Creates a favorable impression with customers. **Availability:** VHS; 3/4U.

31950 ■ *Tony Alessandra, Ph.D.: On Customer-Driven Service*
Instructional Video
2219 C St.
Lincoln, NE 68502
Ph:(402)475-6570
Free: 800-228-0164
Fax: (402)475-6500
Co. E-mail: feedback@insvideo.com
URL: http://www.insvideo.com
Price: $95.00. **Description:** Part of the Tony Alessandra, Ph.D. Series. Outlines techniques to identify and exceed customer expectations and build strong, long-term customer relationships. **Availability:** VHS.

31951 ■ *Twelve Steps to Superior Customer Service*
Aspen Publishers
7201 McKinney Circ.
Frederick, MD 21704
Ph:(301)644-3599
Free: 800-638-8437
Fax: (301)644-3550
URL: http://www.aspenpublishers.com
Released: 1986. **Price:** $495.00. **Description:** A manager's step-by-step guide to effective customer service. **Availability:** VHS; 3/4U; Special order formats.

31952 ■ *What Customers Want*
Salenger Films, Inc.
1635 12th St.
Santa Monica, CA 90404-9988
Ph:(310)450-1300
Free: 800-775-5025
Fax: (310)450-1010
Co. E-mail: salenger@aol.com
URL: http://salengerfilms.visualnet.com
Price: $525.00. **Description:** Six customers describe the kind of service they prefer so employees will have a better understanding of their customers' expectations. Includes skits to illustrate positive customer service. **Availability:** VHS; 3/4U.

31953 ■ *Who Killed Service?*
American Media, Inc.
4621 121st St.
Urbandale, IA 50323-2311
Ph:(515)224-0919
Free: 888-776-8268
Fax: (515)327-2555
Co. E-mail: custsvc@ammedia.com
URL: http://www.ammedia.com
Price: $1495.00. **Description:** Two programs, one for employees of all levels and one for management, discuss ways to provide top-notch customer service through a motivating and humorous video about a detective searching for the person who committed "servicide" at a company. **Availability:** VHS; 3/4U; 8mm.

CONSULTANTS

31954 ■ The Advantage Group Inc.
38 Wellington St. E, Ste. 200
Toronto, ON, Canada M5E 1C7
Ph:(416)863-0685
Free: 800-671-1048
Fax: (416)863-0787
Co. E-mail: answers@advantagegroup.com
URL: http://www.advantagegroup.com

E-mail: answers@advantagegroup.com
Scope: Specializes in two key areas: performance benchmarking and pricing strategy. Each stream has developed a wide variety of customizable proprietary research tools to meet the needs of the clients. **Publications:** "7 Steps to building better customer relationships"; "How to Add Value to Customer Relationships"; "Top 10 Key Benefits of Building Business Relationships"; "Tips for Creating Better Relationships".

31955 ■ Ann Arbor Consulting Associates Inc.
5204 Jackson Rd.
Ann Arbor, MI 48103

Ph:(734)995-2404
Fax: (734)930-2018
Co. E-mail: philalexander@b2badvantage.net
URL: http://www.annarborconsulting.b2badvantage.
net/

E-mail: philalexander@b2badvantage.net
Scope: Offers coaching and consulting to CEOs and top managers of smaller businesses in the areas of human resources development, total quality management, JP&R performance management systems, employee surveys, team building and strategic planning. **Publications:** JP&R System Manuals and Forms.

31956 ■ Asset Development Group
74 Blue Heron Dr.
Toms River, NJ 08753
Ph:(732)255-7855
Scope: A human resource consulting firm whose mission is twofold: to help people and their organizations to achieve their full potential and to help companies expand their strategic and financial perspectives. To this end, ADG develops programs that make significant and measurable improvements in productivity, profitability, customer satisfaction, operations, and in most areas of an organization. Specific areas include: sales and marketing, leadership and management development, customer service, critical thinking, strategic thinking and planning/selecting/assessing human resources, career management, and continuous process (quality) improvement.

31957 ■ Barclay Consulting Associates
PO Box 1040
Larchmont, NY 10538
Ph:(914)698-8100
Fax: (914)834-9428
Co. E-mail: mjmargol@aol.com

E-mail: mjmargol@aol.com
Scope: Specializes in helping companies improve their logistics operations. The firm provides assistance in strategic planning, operations planning and productivity improvement in the following areas: customer service, order processing, transportation, warehousing, inventory management, facilities network planning, procurement, and forecasting. Serves private industries as well as government agencies.

31958 ■ Barker & Associates
1974 Wexford Cir.
Wheaton, IL 60187-6166
Ph:(630)260-9927
Fax: (630)260-9928
Scope: Consulting, training, and coaching firm specializing in providing human resource assessment, selection and development services focused primarily on people skills. Serves small, mid, and large-size organizations in both private industry and not-for-profit associations. **Seminars:** Offers numerous seminars and workshops in the field of professional development, such as Strategic Marketing; Consultative Selling and Customer Service; From Hiring to Appraising - Developing Your Employees; Increased Productivity Through Managed Stress; Producing People Results Through Teambuilding; Conflict Management; Communications, Managing Transition and Change; and Creative Problem Solving.

31959 ■ The Benchmarking Network Inc.
4606 FM 1960 W, Ste. 300
Houston, TX 77069-9949
Ph:(281)440-5044
Fax: (281)440-6677
Co. E-mail: Additional@benchmarkingnetwork.com
URL: http://www.benchmarkingnetwork.com

E-mail: Additional@benchmarkingnetwork.com
Scope: Firm leads benchmarking studies worldwide, as well as providing measures and metrics expertise, training, research, and implementation in support of process improvement, reengineering efforts and six sigma programs. Industries served: service, manufacturing, financial, retail, telecommunications, utilities, insurance, information systems, and healthcare. **Publications:** M. Czarnecki, *Benchmarking Strategies for*

Healthcare Management, Aspen Publishers (1994); M. Czarnecki, *Benchmarking Strategies in Accounting & Finance*, AICPA (1993); M. Czarnecki and B. Hager, *Total Quality Management in Accounting & Finance*, AICPA (1995); M. Czarnecki, *Managing by Measuring*, Amacom Books (1999). **Seminars:** Benchmarking - Introduction; Benchmarking - Advanced Topics; Customer Satisfaction Measurement; Total Quality Management; New Product Development as well as others. Over a dozen annual networking meetings targeting various industries or business processes. **Special Services:** The Benchmarking Network On-Line Bulletin Board of Benchmarking Activities; The Benchmarking Network Database of Corporate Performance Statistics; The Benchmarking Network Best Practices Database; The Benchmarking Network Database of Performance Measures.

31960 ■ Business Ventures Inc.
1650 Oakbrook Dr., Ste. 440
Norcross, GA 30093-1881
Ph:(770)729-8000
Fax: (770)729-8028
Scope: Business development consultants specializing in construction industry. Works with HVAC, plumbing, and electrical contraction who need assistance in marketing, sales and promotion, operations management or finance. Also plan, execute, and monitor the marketing, sales, and promotional activities for new product introductions. Firm also writes business plans, monitors financial health of businesses, and performs operations management. **Publications:** How to Write a Business Plan, Atlanta Business Chronicle; Ask 10 Questions Before You Begin Your Business, Income Opportunities. **Seminars:** The Seven Rules for Business Success; The Seven Greatest Lies of Small Business; Understanding the Financial Side of Business; Small Business Marketing; Strategic Business Planning.

31961 ■ Creative Communications International
676 Germantown Pky., Ste. 538
Cordova, TN 38018
Ph:(901)755-2013
Free: 800-989-2013
Fax: (901)755-2228
Scope: A communication consulting, training and publishing company. Trains customer service, teleservice, order fulfillment and reservation call center personnel on "developing a dynamic phone personality." **Publications:** Becoming An Effective Storyteller.

31962 ■ Creative Concepts International Inc.
108 Eagle Glen Dr.
Woodstock, GA 30189
Ph:(770)926-1395
Free: 877-815-8666
Fax: (770)926-1806
Co. E-mail: gene@geneswindell.com
URL: http://www.geneswindell.com

E-mail: gene@geneswindell.com
Scope: Gene Swindell's Optimal Resource Systems. Topics covered include leadership; team dynamics; effective customer service; coach management; interpersonal skills; personal development skills. Industries served: government, healthcare, manufacturing, banking/financial, and professional firms. **Publications:** The ABC's of Success (handbook for personal development and achievement); Customer Service Excellence (video series); Drive Time Tapes (audio training tapes). **Seminars:** Leadership to Master Change; Quality Customer Service; Teambuilding That Works; Coach Management.

31963 ■ Creative Training
1621 N 50th Pl.
Milwaukee, WI 53208-2206
Ph:(414)771-3372
Fax: (414)771-8224
Co. E-mail: jschill12@aol.com

E-mail: jschill12@aol.com
Scope: Training consulting firm offers management research and training. Specializes in personal devel-

opment programs, management and supervisory skills development. Focuses on performance, improvement, time strategies, mastering work skills, teambuilding, leadership, and effective communications. Systems used include: Performax Systems programs, profiles and assessment instruments. Serves corporate, nonprofit, and federal, state, and local government employee audiences. **Seminars:** Time Management Strategies; Effective Listening; Improving Group Relationships; Innovation Seminar; Effective Management Strategies.

31964 ■ Cusato Ray & Associates Inc.
5676 Spinnaker Bay Dr.
Long Beach, CA 90802
Fax: (562)494-3403
Scope: Provides training materials to all industries in the areas of team building, customer service/contact, sales management, time management, and people selection. General Management Consultants. **Seminars:** Offers In-House seminars on team building & people skills.

31965 ■ donphin.com Inc.
5713 Corporate Way, Ste. 101
West Palm Beach, FL 33407
Ph:(561)688-1000
Free: 800-234-3304
Fax: (561)688-1142
Co. E-mail: inquiry@donphin.com
URL: http://www.donphin.com

E-mail: inquiry@donphin.com
Scope: Offers a comprehensive approach to understanding and applying a broad range of business principles: legal compliance issues, management concerns, health and safety, customer service, marketing, information management. Industries served: all developing small businesses. **Publications:** "Doing Business Right!". **Seminars:** Doing Business Right!; HR That Works!.

31966 ■ Dynamic Development
11 Bel Aire Dr.
Stamford, CT 06905
Ph:(203)329-0695
Fax: (203)329-1062
Scope: Offers a wide variety of customized training programs in management/supervisory, communication, interpersonal, customer service, and sales skills. Special services include design of unique training, team building and other interactive learning solutions to organizational problems. DD will also provide assessment services to diagnose training needs and organizational problems. Clients served to date include major corporations in a wide range of industries, small companies, governmental and educational institutions. **Publications:** G. Dangot-Simpkin, "The Dangers of Goals Setting," Supervisory Management (Spring 1992); "Are You Stifling Your Employees?" Supervisory Management (Spring 1992); "7 Ways Managers Undermine Teamwork," Supervisory Management (Spring 1992). **Seminars:** Offers both public seminars and custom designed programs on: Appraising Performance; Communicating Effectively; Cross-cultural Communication; Conducting Productive Meetings; Conflict Resolution; Customer Service Techniques; Decision Making; Delegating; Group Decision-Making; Interviewing Skills; Leadership Styles & Selection; Legal Issues in Human Resources; Listening Skills; Motivating & Rewarding Performance; Managing Change; Negotiation Skills; Networking Skills; Non-Verbal Communication; Problem-Solving; Proposal Writing; Public Speaking & Presentations; Sales Techniques; Supervising Employees; Stress Management; Team Building; Time Management; Training Trainers.

31967 ■ Enterprise Consulting Inc.
151 Fulton St.
Norwood, MA 02062
Ph:(781)762-4680
Co. E-mail: sales@eci-soft.com
URL: http://www.eci-soft.com

E-mail: sales@eci-soft.com
Scope: An independent consulting firm specializing in telecommunications analysis and design. Company is

divided into two divisions, a Business Consulting Division providing consulting to businesses, colleges and universities, healthcare and municipal clients; and a Strategic Services Division specializing in industry trends, marketing strategies and other industry related subjects. Consulting Division services include: voice and data network analysis and design, PBX system analysis and design, voice processing system design, customer service/ACD design, development of in-house management teams, policy and procedures manuals, radio paging systems, healthcare communications systems design, long distance optimization studies, development of strategic telecommunications plans, cable plant engineering analysis and design including fiberoptic backbone design, Local Area Network design and interconnection, CCTV and CATV network design, and development of cable plant Schematico via AutoCad. Industries served: healthcare, college and university, manufacturing, financial services, state and municipal government agencies, utilities and professional service firms. **Seminars:** Voice Processing Systems Design; Basic Telecommunications for New Managers; Information Transport Network Design.

31968 ■ Golden Eagle Business Services Inc.
PO Box 43447
Atlanta, GA 30336-0447
Ph:(404)881-6777
Fax: (770)944-9495
Co. E-mail: ivorydorsey@ivorydorsey.com
URL: http://www.ivorydorsey.com

E-mail: ivorydorsey@ivorydorsey.com
Scope: Provides sales, management, customer service change management and motivational training and consulting programs. Also public speaking engagements and special business projects. Serves private industries as well as government agencies. **Publications:** "Universal Appeal: The Bottom Line Benefit of Diversity". **Seminars:** The Art of Delegation; The Winds of Change; Employee Motivation; Managing Diversity: Perception, Performance and Power; Developing a Sales Mentality in Customer Service.

31969 ■ Donald Harmon
4 Clark St.
Cresskill, NJ 07626
Ph:(201)567-3743
Fax: (201)567-8892

31970 ■ Richard M. Harris Associates
255 Carlton Ter.
Teaneck, NJ 07666-3403
Ph:(201)692-0488
Fax: (201)801-0092
Co. E-mail: rmharassoc@aol.com

E-mail: rmharassoc@aol.com
Scope: Offers small-group, customized workshops as well as one-on-one training in speaking skills and listening skills. Applications include: leadership development, management and sales presentation, meeting management, customer service, coaching and counseling and teambuilding. Industries served: drug and pharmaceutical, telecommunications, newspaper publishing, chemicals, advertising, printing and the military. **Publications:** The Listening Leader: Powerful New Strategies for Becoming an Influential Communicator, Praeger Publishers, Apr, 2006. **Seminars:** Persuasive Speaking Seminar; Selling Communications Skills; Listening to Lead; Executive Presentation Skills; Professional Communications Skills (PCS); A Practical Telephone-Skills Enhancement Workshop.

31971 ■ Health Strategy Group Inc.
46 River Rd.
Chatham, NY 12037
Ph:(518)392-6770
Scope: Provides consulting services in the areas of strategic planning, feasibility studies, start-up businesses, organizational development, market research, customer service audits, new product development, marketing, public relations.

31972 ■ David Herson Associates
524 Baldwin St.
Virginia Beach, VA 23452-7104
Ph:(757)463-7424
Fax: (757)463-7424
Scope: Provides programs for organizations to increase understanding in various human resources areas. Specialty is customized training, that is, researching and developing programs with the purpose of meeting the program needs of the client. Industries served: clients of all sizes in businesses, government agencies and associations. **Seminars:** Diversity; Sexual Harassment; Stress Management; SelfEsteem; Conflict Management.

31973 ■ Hills Consulting Group Inc.
6 Partridge Ct.
Novato, CA 94945
Ph:(415)898-3944
Scope: Strategic marketing consulting and training firm. Specializes in strategic planning; marketing surveys; market research; customer service audits; new product development; competitive analysis; and sales forecasting.

31974 ■ Hissong Associates Inc.
2335 Riviera Dr.
Vienna, VA 22181-3117
Ph:(703)281-2817
Fax: (703)242-8055
Scope: Training consultants offering applied programs for organizational effectiveness, human resources development, and sales. Provides customized programs aimed at improving management, productivity, sales and harmony in the workplace. Primary focus is management and supervisory training, sales training and customer service training, team innovation, as well as consultation and personnel screening. Also offers a full range of videos, audio albums, training manuals, computer software and assessment instruments on many business subjects. Serves private industries, associations and government agencies. **Seminars:** Reading the Customer: A Differential Approach to Increased Sales; Teambuilding; The Empowered Manager; Presentation Excellence: People-Reading Secrets; Quality Customer Service; Customer Focused Selling; Time Management; Transcending the Recession on the Bridge of Eagles; Managing with Style; Interpersonal Excellence; and customized seminars designed to meet the needs of specific organizations. **Special Services:** SPQ Gold Assessment Instrument for screening and developing salespeople; Profiles Evaluation Program (PEP) for employee screening and professional development.

31975 ■ Howick Associates
111 N Fairchild St.
Madison, WI 53703
Ph:(608)233-3377
Free: 800-236-3370
Fax: (608)233-1194
Co. E-mail: info@howickassociates.com
URL: http://www.howickassociates.com

E-mail: info@howickassociates.com
Scope: Organizational development and training firm committed to helping organizations meet the demand for greater productivity by enhancing individual, team, and organizational effectiveness. Practice is focused on large Wisconsin-based companies and organizations. **Publications:** "The Compleat Facilitator: A Guide" **Seminars:** Enhancing Your Presentation Style; Perceptive Communications; Listening; Effective Meeting Skills; Strategic Thinking & Planning; Performance Measurement; Facilitation Skills.

31976 ■ Impact Training Associates Inc.
320 Arden Ave., Ste. 240
Glendale, CA 91203
Ph:(818)241-3537
Free: 800-848-4333
Fax: (818)241-4416
Scope: Provides customized training that strengthens both individuals and organizations. This enables clients to better meet the changing requirements in the

competitive marketplace of the 21st century. Focuses on accelerated learning and action-oriented training that can be applied immediately. Certified Woman Business Enterprise. **Seminars:** List of public seminars and in-house workshops available from firm upon request.

31977 ■ Key Communications Group Inc.
5617 Warwick Pl.
Chevy Chase, MD 20815-5503
Ph:(301)656-0450
Free: 800-705-5353
Fax: (301)656-4554
Co. E-mail: mr.dm@verizon.net

E-mail: mr.dm@verizon.net
Scope: Direct marketing and publishing consultants specializing in subscriber and member acquisition for newsletters and other niche B2B publications, organizations and associations. Specialties: small and start-up businesses; mergers and acquisitions; joint ventures; divestitures; product development; employee surveys and communication; market research; customer service audits; new product development; direct marketing; and competitive intelligence.

31978 ■ Key Management Strategies
871 North Easton Rd.
Glenside, PA 19038-5239
Ph:(215)887-8775
Fax: (215)887-9121
Scope: Human resource consultants specializing in organization development and training to improve quality of customer service. Industries served: service, retail, hospitality, manufacturing, insurance, non-profit agencies, and the public sector. **Seminars:** The Service Enthusiast (customer contact training); Enthusiastic Supervision (service supervision and management); Enthusiastic Leadership: Building a Service Culture From the Top Down; Front Line Solutions: Employee Involvement to Enhance Service; Game Simulations, Including Pirate's Cove and Rocket Science.

31979 ■ Kutler Consultants
1420 Locust St., Ste. 35Q
Philadelphia, PA 19102
Ph:(215)735-7385
Scope: Merchandise operations management consultants whose focus is on maximizing customer service and profitability through effective inventory management -assuring that quality merchandise, properly packaged, is in the right place at the right time, and to fill customer orders immediately. Specific areas of consulting include forecasting, inventory control, quality assurance and packaging, transportation and distribution, management information, order processing and fulfillment, statistical analysis, operations research and systems development. Industries served: catalog, direct mail, television shopping, and home party plan.

31980 ■ Lieber & Associates
3740 N Lake Shore Dr., Ste. 15B-2
Chicago, IL 60613-4202
Ph:(773)325-9400
Fax: (773)325-0621
Co. E-mail: info@lieberandassociates.com
URL: http://www.lieberandassociates.com

E-mail: info@lieberandassociates.com
Scope: Provides telephone marketing (inbound and outbound); database marketing; and telecommunications technology services for sales, customer service, and order departments. Also upgrades existing operations and start-ups. Performs strategic planning, facility design, equipment specification, network (telephone line) design, software recommendations, staff planning, database design, management systems development, program design, scripting, and project management to meet client requirements. Projects 800 number call volumes. Industries served: direct marketing, catalog order, customer service, utilities, cable television, travel and hospitality, advertising, broadcasting, general business and government in the United States and Worldwide. **Publications:**

"How to Integrate Telephone and Direct Marketing," 1993 **Seminars:** How to Integrate Telephone and Direct Marketing; Outsourcing Nuts and Bolts; How to Measure and Manage Telemarketing. **Special Services:** Maintains proprietary databases of telemarketing information software, and telephone systems. Also develops custom telecommunications devices for clients to meet special needs.

31981 ■ Management 21 Inc.
111 10th Ave. S, Ste. 401
Nashville, TN 37203
Ph:(615)871-4321
Free: 800-899-0021
Fax: (615)871-9821
Co. E-mail: info@management21.com
URL: http://www.management21.com

E-mail: info@management21.com
Scope: Training and consulting firm providing tested models for improving organizational and individual performance. Offers an architecture for organizational transformation that can involve a wide scope of dimensions, including assessment of organizational effectiveness, strategic planning, assessment and development of leadership and consulting skills, role clarification, continuous improvement and customer satisfaction, and non-traditional selling. **Seminars:** Organizational Transformation Architecturem System; Design Your Future system; The Lifetime Customer Process; Creating and Leading High Performance Teams; Role Clarification, Partnership Selling system.

31982 ■ Marketing Leverage Inc.
180 Glastonbury Blvd.
Glastonbury, CT 06033
Ph:(860)633-1422
Free: 800-633-1422
Fax: (860)659-8664
Co. E-mail: office@marketingleverage.com
URL: http://www.marketingleverage.com

E-mail: office@marketingleverage.com
Scope: Consults with senior management at leading corporations to improve performance by maximizing customer value. We specialize in the targeting, retention and satisfaction of customers for companies in services industries with particular expertise in insurance, financial services, health care and technology services. Most clients belong to the Fortune 1000 group. Specific services include customer research, analysis of lifetime value, development of customer retention strategies, evaluation of web strategies, working with client teams.

31983 ■ McDargh Communications
33465 Dosinia Dr.
Dana Point, CA 92629-4488
Ph:(949)496-8640
Free: 877-477-4718
Fax: (949)248-7805
Co. E-mail: bonnie@eileenmcdargh.com
URL: http://www.eileenmcdargh.com

E-mail: bonnie@eileenmcdargh.com
Scope: Provides management communications consulting for team building, management communication and training in a variety of communication-related skills. facilitates management retreats. **Publications:** "The Spirit of Nurse Leadership"; "Burnout, Balance & Bounty"; "Books: Work For a Living and Still be Free to Live"; "The Resilient Spirit"; "Off the Chart Results"; "A Woman's Way to Incredible Success"; "Meditations for the Road Warrior".

31984 ■ Parker Consultants Inc.
67 Mason St.
Greenwich, CT 06830
Ph:(203)869-9400
Scope: Firm specializes in strategic planning; organizational development; small business management; performance appraisals; executive searches; team building; and customer service audits.

31985 ■ Personal Achievement Institute
1 Speaking Success Rd.
Kingman, AZ 86402-6543

Ph:(928)753-7546
Free: 800-321-1225
Fax: (928)753-7554
Co. E-mail: info@speakingbizsuccess.com
URL: http://www.dubinspeak.com

E-mail: info@speakingbizsuccess.com
Scope: Consulting firm serves professional speakers, offering expertise in such areas as positioning, packaging, promotion, and presentation. **Publications:** Speaking Success System: Professional Speakers Profit Letter; Burt Dubin Private Letter; Inner Circle Letter; Mission Possible!; Positioning Magic. **Seminars:** Speaking Success Boot Camps; Boot Camps-at-Sea, Inner Circle Retreats. **Special Services:** Developing the Professional Speaker's Mission Statement.

31986 ■ The Plotkin Group
5650 El Camino Real, Ste. 215
Carlsbad, CA 92008
Ph:(760)603-8791
Free: 800-877-5685
Fax: (760)603-8570
Co. E-mail: buytests@plotkingroup.com
URL: http://www.plotkingroup.com

E-mail: buytests@plotkingroup.com
Scope: Employee testing and training organization offering pre-employment honesty, altitude, aptitude and skills tests; and past employment, 360 degree assessments, behavior, style and communication tests by phone, paper and pencil, computers, the web, employee attitude surveys, customer service, sales, and management training. **Publications:** "Above and Beyond". **Seminars:** Building a Winning Team; Above and Beyond Customer Service Training; Taking the Guess Work Out of Hiring and Promoting.

31987 ■ Retail Management Consultants
1635 S Rancho Santa Fe Rd., Ste. 206
San Marcos, CA 92078-5158
Ph:(760)471-0207
Free: 800-766-1908
Fax: (760)471-0263
Co. E-mail: info@whalinonretail.com
URL: http://www.whalinonretail.com

E-mail: info@whalinonretail.com
Scope: Specializes in helping retail organizations become more efficient, productive, and profitable. Consulting services include advertising and marketing, employee training programs, customer service improvement, and customer research. Industries served: all segments of the retail industry. **Publications:** "Treasure Hunt: Inside the Mind of the New Consumer"; "The Bear Necessities of Business: Building a Company with Heart". **Seminars:** Retail Success!; Great Store Managers Make Great Stores!; Competition: Powerful trends that are changing what people buy, how they buy, and where they buy!; Stop, Look, Touch, and Buy: The Dynamics of Merchandising; Double Your Sales and Triple Your Profits with High-Impact Marketing and Promotions!; Every Customer Every Day.

31988 ■ Service Quality Institute
9201 E Bloomington Fwy.
Minneapolis, MN 55420-3437
Ph:(952)884-3311
Free: 800-548-0538
Fax: (952)884-8901
Co. E-mail: quality@servicequality.com
URL: http://www.customer-service.com

E-mail: quality@servicequality.com
Scope: Helps organizations keep customers, build market share, and improve the performance of the entire work force to develop a culture of delivering superior customer service. **Publications:** Published, "Achieving Excellence Through Customer Service," Bestsellers Publishers; "Ca$hing In: Get Promoted, Make More Money, Love Your Job," Bestsellers Publishing; "The Spirit of Excellence,"; "Servicio Al Cliente". **Seminars:** E-Service; Achieving Excellence Through Customer Service; Cashing In Feelings;

Leading Empowered Teams for Service Quality; Exceptional Service; Attaining Excellence by Keeping More Customers; Customer Service Excellence; Five Star Service; Creating a Service Culture Strategy; Leading Empowered Teams. **Special Services:** "Buck-A-Day," and "Good Idea," two Idea Campaigns on cost reduction, quality, and customer satisfaction.

31989 ■ Joe Turner
3525 Sandybrook Ln., 2nd Fl.
Napa, CA 94558
Ph:(707)224-6344
Free: 888-754-6900
Fax: (707)224-6392
Co. E-mail: jmt@joeturner.com
URL: http://www.joeturner.com

E-mail: jmt@joeturner.com
Scope: Provides customer service consulting, materials, software and training for the new home industry. Specializes in construction defect litigation. Specific problem solving, including recruiting, validating employment information, meeting with homeowners and strategic assessment are available. Produces homeowner manuals for builders and developers. **Seminars:** Training seminars for customer service and corporate staff, custom-designed for each client.

31990 ■ Western Connection
1118 E Orangewood Ave.
Phoenix, AZ 85020-5029
Ph:(602)870-3333
Fax: (602)997-1676
Co. E-mail: bill@billjohnson.com
URL: http://www.billjohnson.com

E-mail: bill@billjohnson.com
Scope: Advises in the areas of sales and sales management, focusing on customer service and telephone courtesy. Presents seminars on team-building, management, sales and organization assessments, including retail/distributor sales of tangibles; managing priorities; handling stress; and time management. Also offers individual consulting. Industries served: hospitality, automotive, banking and finance, entertainment, legal, nonprofit and retail/wholesale in public and private sector. **Publications:** "Customer Service and Telephone Courtesy, a seven module video program for one-on-one or group workshop"; "The seven modules are available individually or on one cassette complete"; "Time Management and Customer Service, mini-seminars on video". **Seminars:** Sales Skills Workshops; Managing and Selling Different People Differently; Customer Relations and Telephone Courtesy; Speaking and Presentation Skills; Managing Priorities and Stress; Taming the Meeting Time Killers, Team Building. **Special Services:** Internet-based instant organization climate, management, personnel surveys, web based sales course.

31991 ■ Your Writing Partner
2137 Mount Vernon Rd.
Atlanta, GA 30338
Ph:(770)395-7483
Free: 800-745-0494
Fax: (770)395-1931
Co. E-mail: kay@yourwritingpartner.net
URL: http://www.yourwritingpartner.net

E-mail: kay@yourwritingpartner.net
Scope: Human resource consultants who provide custom-designed and generic programs for clients. Services include customer analysis, instructional design, and training program design. Also provide performance improvement, editing, proofing, and rewriting services; meeting emceeing, planning and facilitation; conflict resolution; executive coaching. Industries served: banking, healthcare, hospitality, utilities, credit unions, insurance, food, and associations. **Publications:** "Don't Let Your Participles Dangle in Public," 2005; "Business Etiquette and Professionalism"; "Handling Diversity in the Workplace: Communication is the Key"; "How to Provide Excellent Service in any Organization". **Seminars:** Business Etiquette and Professionalism; Understanding and Communi-

cating With Others; Politically Correct and Profitable Writing Skills; Setting the Stage for Excellent Service; The Art of Successful Presentations; Friendly Fire: How Being Your Own Sweet Self Can Burn Others; Ideas Into Action: How to Keep All Those Good Conference Ideas From Going to Waste; Management and Supervisory Skills.

31992 ■ **Ziglar**
15303 Dallas Pky., Ste. 550
Addison, TX 75001
Ph:(972)233-9191
Free: 800-527-0306
Fax: (972)991-1853
Co. E-mail: info@ziglar.com
URL: http://www.ziglartraining.com

E-mail: info@ziglar.com
Scope: Offers management planning, strategic planning, teambuilding, skills assessment, and custom training to provide clients with the tools to build their business. **Publications:** Ziglar On Selling; Over the Top; Qualities of Success; Z. Ziglar Changing the Picture; One Step At a Time. **Seminars:** Born to win; Get Motivated; Ziglar Sales System; Essential Presentation Skills: Custom Curricula.

COMPUTER SYSTEMS/SOFTWARE

31993 ■ **Measuring Customer Satisfaction–Crisp Learning–Thomson Learning (10650)**
Chris Learning
10650 Toebben Dr.
Independence, KY 41051
Ph:800-442-7477
Free: 800-442-7477
Fax: (859)647-5963
URL: http://www.courseilt.com
Price: Description: Based on the *Measuring Customer Satisfaction* video and book. Includes book and user's guide.

31994 ■ **Telephone Courtesy and Customer Service–Crisp Learning–Thomson Learning (10650)**
Chris Learning
10650 Toebben Dr.
Independence, KY 41051
Ph:800-442-7477
Free: 800-442-7477
Fax: (859)647-5963

URL: http://www.courseilt.com
Price: Description: Based on the *Telephone Courtesy and Customer Service* video and book. Includes book and user's guide.

RESEARCH CENTERS

31995 ■ **Purdue University–Center for Customer-Driven Quality**
1262 Matthews Hall, Ste. 118
West Lafayette, IN 47907-1262
Ph:(765)494-9933
Fax: (765)494-0287
Co. E-mail: xdj1@cfs.purdue.edu
URL: http://www.ccdq.com
Contact: Dr. Richard Feinberg, Dir.
E-mail: xdj1@cfs.purdue.edu
Scope: Customer research, including basic design and implementation of inbound customer call-centers, customer privacy, complaint demographics, and customer satisfaction. **Educational Activities:** Call Center Certification Program; Courses and guest lectures; Quality customer service video training.

Discrimination/Sexual Harassment

ASSOCIATIONS AND OTHER ORGANIZATIONS

31996 ■ Americans With Disabilities Act
9841 SW 100 Ave.
Miami, FL 33176
Ph:(305)271-0012
Fax: (305)273-1221
Co. E-mail: ergobob@consultant.com
URL: http://www.rehabserv.com
Contact: Robert L. Lessne PhD
Membership: Individuals and organizations united to ensure compliance with the Americans With Disabilities Act of 1992. Compiles statistics; sponsors competitions; maintains speakers' bureau; and operates a museum with cones for visually impaired individuals. **Publications:** *ADA Compliance Kit*; *ADA Compliance Sourcebook*.

31997 ■ Common Destiny Alliance
CODA EDPL Benjamin Bldg.
University of Maryland
College Park, MD 20742
Ph:(301)405-0639
Fax: (301)405-3573
Co. E-mail: mh267@umail.umd.edu
URL: http://www.education.umd.edu/CODA/index.
html
Contact: Walter Allen, Scholar
Membership: Organizations and scholars interested in working to end prejudice. **Purpose:** Fosters the viewpoint that cultural diversity is "a resource that can help the nation attain goals such as improving economic productivity and the academic achievement of all children." Seeks to end racial isolation in schools, neighborhoods, and the work force. Promotes social policies, especially those related to education, that encourage racial and ethnic understanding and cooperation. Conducts research to identify the causes of racism and means to overcome racism. **Publications:** *Toward a Common Destiny: Improving Race and Ethnic Relations in America*; *Tracking, Diversity, and Educational Equity: What's New in the Research?*.

REFERENCE WORKS

31998 ■ *Academic and Workplace Sexual Harassment: A Resource Manual*
Pub: State University of New York Press
Ed: Michele A. Paludi and Richard B. Barickman. **Released:** 1991. **Price:** $64.50; $19.95 (paper). **Description:** Includes index.

31999 ■ "Access Now...Or Lawsuit Later" in *Birmingham Business Journal* (Vol. 20, No. 40, October 3, 2003, pp. 1)
Pub: American City Business Journals, Inc.
Ed: Ryan Mahoney. **Description:** Access Now Inc., a disability advocacy group, has filed 66 cases with violations of the Americans with Disabilities Act against businesses in Birmingham, Alabama.

32000 ■ *ADA Handbook: Employment and Construction Issues Affecting Your Business*
Pub: Dearborn Financial Publishing, Inc.
Ed: Martha R. Williams and Marcia L. Russell. **Price:** $29.95 (paper).

32001 ■ *Addressing Sexual Harassment in the Workplace: Trainer's Package*
Pub: Pfeiffer & Co.
Price: $99.95 (trainer's package, looseleaf); $4.95 (*The Woman and the Sailor*, paper); $4.95 (*The Promotion*, paper); $5.95 (*Tina Carlan*, paper); $2.95 (Sexual-Harassment Awareness Test, paper); $9.95 (Sexual-Harassment Readings, paper). **Description:** Trainer's package contains one of each of the following: Trainer's Materials, *The Woman and the Sailor*, *The Promotion*, *Tina Carlan*, the Sexual-Harassment Awareness Test, and Readings Section; additional copies may be purchased separately. Interactive workshop designed to increase awareness of sexual harassment, techniques to deal with it, and strategies to end it.

32002 ■ "Affirmative Action Upheld" in *Black Enterprise* (Vol. 34, No. 2, September 2003, pp. 23)
Pub: Earl Graves Publishing Co.
Ed: Cliff Hocker. **Description:** The U.S. Supreme Court upheld the race-conscious admission practices of the University of Michigan Law School in June 2003. William B. Harvey, vice president and director of the Office of Minorities in Higher Education at the American Council on Education (ACE) discusses the issues centering on affirmative action.

32003 ■ "Age Rage: Younger Employees are Crying Age Discrimination" in *Entrepreneur* (Vol. 32, No. 4, April 2004, pp. 24)
Pub: Entrepreneur Media, Inc.
Ed: Chris Penttila. **Description:** Employees in the forty-something age bracket are filing discrimination suits against employers charging they are being excluded from particular retirement health benefits older employees receive.

32004 ■ *The Americans with Disabilities Act Handbook*
Pub: DIANE Publishing Co.
Released: 1993. **Price:** $29.95 (paper). **Description:** Handbook providing information on the Americans with Disabilities Act (ADA). Includes the full text of the ADA and a list of sources and resources, with addresses and phone numbers.

32005 ■ *The Americans with Disabilities Act: Hiring, Accommodating and Supervising Employees with Disabilities*
Pub: Crisp Publications, Inc.
Ed: Mary B. Dickson. **Released:** 1995. **Price:** $15.95.

32006 ■ "Appleton, Wis.-Based Construction Company Settles Racial Harassment Suit" in *Milwaukee Journal Sentinel* (December 1, 2005)
Pub: Journal Sentinel, Inc.
Ed: Tom Daykin. **Description:** Details of the racial harassment complaint filed by an employee of Wiscon-

sin's largest construction firm are outlined. The suit claimed that the company created a hostile work environment for African-American employees of a subcontractor hired by the firm.

32007 ■ *Bridging the Age Gap*
Pub: Pfeiffer & Co.
Ed: Catherine D. Fyock. **Price:** $75.00 (leader's guide, looseleaf); $9.95 (participant's workbook, paper). **Description:** Part of the Managing Diversity Workshop Series.

32008 ■ "Can You Judge a Biz by Its Color?" in *Inc.* (August 1, 2004)
Pub: Inc. Magazine
Ed: Lora Kolodny. **Description:** A Federal Court recently determined that corporations, which have the same legal status as individuals, can now sue for racial discrimination.

32009 ■ *Complying with the ADA: A Small Business Guide to Hiring and Employing the Disabled*
Pub: John Wiley & Sons, Inc.
Ed: Jeffrey G. Allen. **Released:** 1993. **Price:** $55.00; $17.95 (paper). **Description:** Guide to the American with Disabilities Act (ADA), covering hiring and employing the disabled, construction requirements, and economic implications of the ADA.

32010 ■ *Complying with the Americans with Disabilities Act: A Guidebook for Management and People with Disabilities*
Pub: Greenwood Publishing Group, Inc.
Ed: Don Fersh and Peter W. Thomas. **Released:** 1993. **Price:** $52.95.

32011 ■ "Construction workers charge bias" in *BlackEnterprise* (Vol. 32, No. 3, October 2001, pp. 26)
Pub: Earl Graves Publishing Co.
Ed: Curtis Simmons. **Description:** The Equal Employment Opportunity Commission (EEOC) launched a major lawsuit against The Industrial Company (TIC), charging racial discrimination in its construction business. The lawsuit is considered to be the largest discrimination case in twenty years. When the EEOC began to investigate the group's charges, it found a pattern of nationwide discrimination at TIC.

32012 ■ "Cracker Barrel Faces More Racial Bias Charges" in *Black Enterprise* (Vol. 34, No. 4, November 2003, pp. 28)
Pub: Earl Graves Publishing Co.
Ed: Carolyn M. Brown. **Description:** Cracker Barrel Restaurants are once again hit with allegations of racial discrimination by twenty-three African American customers in Bryant and North Little Rock, Arkansas.

32013 ■ "Cracker Barrel Pays $8.7M to Settle Race Case" in *Black Enterprise* (Vol. 35, December 2004, No. 5, pp. 38)
Pub: Earl G. Graves Publishing Co. Inc.
Ed: Nicole Richardson. **Description:** In lawsuits filed by employees and customers, Cracker Barrel restaurant chain has agreed to pay $8.7 million to settle allegations of discrimination.

32014 ■ **"The Dangers of a Lack of Accountability"** in *Automotive News* (Vol. 20, October 4, 2004, No. 40, pp. 8)
Pub: Crain Communications Inc.
Ed: Keith Crain. **Description:** Plans for developing a downtown district, called African Town, in Detroit that would fund money to black-owned businesses is discussed. Many individuals claim the plan is both discriminatory and illegal.

32015 ■ **"Declaring War On Wal-Mart"** in *Business Week* (February 7, 2005, No. 3919, pp. 31)
Pub: McGraw-Hill Companies
Ed: Aaron Bernstein. **Description:** Wal-Mart has launched an ad campaign in January with the message: Wal-Mart is working for everyone. The retailer is fighting back against allegations of sex discrimination, poverty-level wages, and non-union workforce.

32016 ■ *Discrimination*
Pub: Facts on File, Inc.
Released: 1997. **Price:** $35.00.

32017 ■ **"Discrimination in the Small-Business Credit Market"** in *Review of Economics and Statistics* (Vol. 85, No. 4, November 2003, pp. 930)
Pub: MIT Press Journals
Ed: David G. Blanchflower, Philip B. Levine, David J. Zimmerman. **Description:** Using data from the 1993 and 1998 National Surveys of Small Business Finances to examine the existence of racial discrimination in the small-business credit market, an econometric analysis of loan outcomes by race was conducted. The study found that black-owned small businesses are about twice as likely to be denied credit, even after controlling the differences in creditworthiness and other factors. A series of specification checks indicates that this gap is unlikely to be explained by omitted variable bias. These results indicate that the racial disparity in credit availability is likely caused by discrimination.

32018 ■ **"Discrimination in the workplace: how mediation can help"** in *Dispute Resolution Journal* (Vol. 56, No. 1, February-April 2001, pp. 35)
Pub: American Arbitration Association
Ed: Lamont E. Stallworth, Thomas McPherson, Larry Rute. **Description:** Discussion on ways mediation can help to resolve conflict arising from subtle or unconscious discriminatory acts in the workplace, noting key features of the U.S. Postal Services REDRESS program and the need for national legislation.

32019 ■ **"EEOC Sues Charlotte-Based Lebo's"** in *Charlotte Observer* (February 7, 2007)
Pub: Knight-Ridder/Tribune Business News
Ed: Mike Drummond. **Description:** The U.S. Equal Employment Opportunity Commission filed a pregnancy discrimination lawsuit against Lebo's Shoe Stores, located in Charlotte, North Carolina. The suit alleges the store withdrew an offer to hire a woman after finding out she was pregnant.

32020 ■ **"Embracing Diversity, Not Division"** in *Black Enterprise* (Vol. 34, No. 7, February 2004, pp. 14)
Pub: Earl Graves Publishing Co.
Ed: Earl G. Graves, Sr. **Description:** Diversity, whether corporate or otherwise, is not only respecting and honoring the differences between cultures, it also means recognizing the cultural variety that exists within and among minority groups, including language, heritage, or skin color.

32021 ■ **"Employees Sue Best Buy for Race, Gender Discrimination"** in *Sacramento Bee* (December 9, 2005)
Pub: The Sacramento Bee
Ed: Rachel Osterman. **Description:** Retailer, Best Buy is being sued for race and gender discrimination for alleged lower wages than those paid to white males and for steering women employees away from high-paying sales jobs.

32022 ■ *Employing People with Capabilities: Responding to the Americans with Disabilities Act*
Pub: Pfeiffer & Co.
Ed: Catherine D. Fyock. **Price:** $79.95 (leader's guide, looseleaf); $9.95 (participant's workbook, paper). **Description:** Part of the Managing Diversity Workshop Series.

32023 ■ *Employment Law: A Guide to the Workplace Rights of Managers and Workers*
Pub: Blackwell Publishers
Ed: Benjamin W. Wolkinson. **Released:** 1995. **Price:** $31.95.

32024 ■ **"Employment Law at the Dawn of the New Millennium"** in *Employment Relations Today* (Vol. 26, No. 4, Winter 2000, pp. 109)
Pub: John Wiley & Sons, Inc.
Ed: William C. Martucci and Jeffrey M. Place. **Description:** The interpretation and construction of employment law at the turn of the 21st century are described. Topics addressed include protection for employees under anti-discrimination laws, employee privacy rights, and flexible working environments.

32025 ■ **"Feds Accuse Sacramento, Calif.-Based Restaurant of Sex Discrimination"** in *Sacramento Bee* (September 30, 2005)
Pub: The Sacramento Bee
Ed: Dale Kasler. **Description:** U.S. Equal Employment Opportunity Commission is suing Randy Paragary's restaurant chain for alleged unfair treatment of women, especially those of Mexican descent. According to the claim, Mexican women were not allowed to take work breaks or vacations and were required to perform tasks other female workers were not asked to do.

32026 ■ **"Fighting an Age-Old Scourge"** in *Hispanic Business* (October 2002, pp. 82)
Pub: Hispanic Business
Ed: Nancie Hudson. **Description:** An increasing number of companies are instituting corporate diversity training programs to combat workplace discrimination.

32027 ■ *Gender and Racial Inequality at Work: The Sources and Consequences of Employment Segregation*
Pub: ILR Press
Ed: Donald Tomaskovic-Devey. **Released:** 1993. **Price:** $38.00; $16.95 (paper).

32028 ■ *Guide to Affirmative Action*
Pub: Crisp Publications, Inc.
Ed: Pamela J. Conrad and Robert B. Maddux. **Price:** $9.95.

32029 ■ *Harassed: 100 Women Define Inappropriate Behavior in the Workplace*
Pub: Irwin Professional Publishing
Ed: Nancy Dodd McCann and Thomas A. McGinn. **Released:** 1992. **Price:** $17.00. **Description:** Guide for men to sexual harassment in the workplace. Includes responses of 100 women surveyed regarding 50 examples of harassment.

32030 ■ **"Harris Teeter sued by black employees"** in *Atlanta Business Chronicle* (Vol. 24, No. 14, September 7, 2001, pp. 1A)
Pub: American City Business Journals Inc.
Ed: Matt Gove. **Description:** Harris Teeter Inc. and Ruddick Corporation, its parent, are both being sued by nine African-Americans for racial discrimination. Gordon, Silberman, Wiggins, & Childs, the law firm handling the case, sought class-action status following the original suit.

32031 ■ **"Hit Discriminators Where it Hurts"** in *Black Enterprise* (Vol. 34, No. 4, November 2003, pp. 28)
Pub: Earl Graves Publishing Co.
Ed: Darrell Williams. **Description:** African American consumers account for 5 percent of all U.S. consumer spending and 4 percent of Gross Domestic Product, making them a powerful force in the U.S. economy. However, black consumers believe they are still greeted with suspicion about intentions and skepticism about ability to pay.

32032 ■ *How to Combat Sexual Harassment at Work: A Guide to Implementing the European Commission Code of Practice*
Pub: DIANE Publishing Co.
Ed: Ineke M. De Vries. **Released:** 1995. **Price:** $35.00.

32033 ■ *Human Resource Executive's Survival Guide to the Americans with Disabilities Act*
Pub: LRP Publications
Ed: Patricia A. Morrissey. **Released:** 1992. **Price:** $135.00. **Description:** Provides information on American with Disabilities Act (ADA) requirements, including implications for employers, strategies for compliance, and required accommodations. Contains list of resources and text of the act.

32034 ■ **"Ideology, Politics & the Bench"** in *Hispanic Business* (June 2002, pp. 18)
Pub: Hispanic Business
Ed: Joel Russell. **Description:** Issues and ethnicity shape support and criticism of Miguel Estrada's judicial nomination. The question of Estrada's stand on affirmative action is discussed.

32035 ■ **"In the Hot Seat"** in *Entrepreneur. com* (Vol. 34, January 2006, No. 1, pp. 19)
Pub: Entrepreneur Media Inc.
Ed: Chris Penttila. **Description:** According to a 2005 survey conducted by CareerBuilder.com, more than 56 percent of workers stated they have dated a co-worker. These office romances are becoming the stuff new legal battles are made of in the workplace. Sexual harassment suits are arising after workers lose promotions to those dating supervisors.

32036 ■ **"In Praise of Boundaries: A Conversation with Miss Manners"** in *Harvard Business Review* (Vol. 81, No. 12, December 2003, pp. 41)
Pub: Harvard Business School Press
Ed: Diane L. Coutu. **Description:** Judith Martin, known as the syndicated columnist Miss Manners, argues in favor of establishing formal limits to govern behavior in the office, as the personalization of business relations interferes with efficiency and in some cases, can have legal repercussions, such as sexual harassment.

32037 ■ **"It's Settled: A New Law Makes it Easier to Reach Settlements"** in *Entrepreneur* (Vol. 33, February 2005, No. 2, pp. 74)
Pub: Entrepreneur Media Inc.
Ed: Jane Easter Bahls. **Description:** American Jobs Creation Act of 2004, Section 703, the Civil Rights Tax Relief Acts overturns a tax rule that no longer requires the winner of wrongful termination or workplace discrimination to pay taxes on any money awarded in the lawsuit.

32038 ■ **"John Deere Named In Discrimination Suit"** in *Black Enterprise* (Vol. 35, August 2004, No. 1, pp. 30)
Pub: Earl G. Graves Publishing Co. Inc.
Ed: Aisha Jefferson. **Description:** After working for John Deere for 30 years, Kenny Edwards wanted to become an entrepreneur by purchasing his own John Deere agricultural dealership. Edwards has sued the company for discrimination when it turned down his bid for ownership. Of the 1,400 John Deere agricultural dealerships in the U.S. non are African-American owned, and only 5 percent of owners include women, Hispanics, and Asians.

32039 ■ **"Let's Talk About Sexism: Do Sexist Attitudes Still Exist in Business? Women Sound Off"** in *Entrepreneur* (Vol. 32, No. 4, April 2004)
Pub: Entrepreneur Media, Inc.
Ed: Aliza Pilar Sherman. **Description:** Women entrepreneurs discuss the issues of sexism in business, comparing issues today with those of the past. The article is divided with interviews with these women in each decade starting in the 1970s.

32040 ■ *Library in a Book—Sexual Harassment*
Pub: Facts On File Inc.
Released: Irregular. **Publication Includes:** Lists of organizations, associations, and individuals dealing with sexual harassment. **Entries Include:** For companies—Contact information. For individuals—Biographical data. Principal content of publication is introductory history and overview, chronology of major events, glossary of important terms, discussion of major issues, and excerpts.

32041 ■ "Locker Room Tactics" in *Hispanic Business* (October 2002, pp. 76)
Pub: Hispanic Business
Ed: Teresa Talerico. **Description:** Professional coaching is used to help individuals and companies obtain results and reach goals. Corporate diversity training can work to combat workplace discrimination.

32042 ■ "Make sure that employee ranking systems are effective" in *Atlanta Business Chronicle* (Vol. 24, No. 13, August 24, 2001, pp. 6B)
Pub: American City Business Journals Inc.
Ed: Emory Mulling. **Description:** Employee ranking schemes can be used to determine which employees should be the first to be laid off and how to administer raises, but such programs must be carefully designed and managed to prevent charges of discrimination. For example, an employee who has just been promoted because of effectiveness might not achieve the same high ranking immediately in the new position, and so might be unfairly punished. Also systems that force ranking employees on a bell curve might punish some employees, while some managers might inflate the ranking of their employees to make themselves look good.

32043 ■ *Making Advances: What You Can Do about Sexual Harassment at Work*
Pub: Parkwest Publications, Inc.
Ed: Liz Curtis. **Released:** 1995. **Price:** $7.95.

32044 ■ *Managing Older Workers*
Pub: Crisp Publications, Inc.
Ed: Gordon F. Shea. **Price:** $9.95.

32045 ■ "Minority Banks are Called to Account" in *Inc.* (October 1, 2003)
Pub: Gruner & Jahr USA Publishing
Ed: Patrick J. Sauer. **Description:** California's Chinese banks come under fire for discrimination. These banks help immigrants to become entrepreneurs, but do not lend enough to African Americans or Latinos.

32046 ■ "More Minority Portfolio Managers Sought" in *Sacramento Bee* (November 13, 2005)
Pub: The Sacramento Bee
Ed: Gilbert Chan. **Description:** Most private equity senior staff are white males from Ivy League schools; women and minorities continue to be ignored by money management companies. Many of the major money manager firms have paid millions in damages to settle sex-discrimination cases.

32047 ■ "New EEOC and OFCCP Issues for the Year 2000 and Beyond" in *Employment Relations Today* (Vol. 26, No. 4, Winter 2000, pp. 99)
Pub: John Wiley & Sons, Inc.
Ed: Morgan D. Hodgson, Ronald S. Cooper, and Lloyd C. Loomis. **Description:** Reviews federal regulations regarding employment discrimination, focusing on the policies enacted by the US Equal Opportunity Commission and the Office of Federal Contract Compliance Programs. Topics addressed include the interpretation of the Americans with Disabilities Act of 1990, immigration and work policies, and enforcing discrimination law compliance within government organizations.

32048 ■ "A New Wrinkle On Age Bias" in *Inc.* (Volume 27, July 2005, No. 7, pp. 36)
Pub: Inc. Magazine
Ed: Darren Dahl. **Description:** The Supreme Court made it easier to file age discrimination claims in federal court. There were 8,000 age discrimination cases filed in the U.S. in 2004 against companies with less than 500 employees.

32049 ■ *The 9to5 Guide to Combating Sexual Harassment: Candid Advice from 9to5, the National Association of Working Women*
Pub: John Wiley & Sons, Inc.
Ed: Ellen Bravo and Ellen Cassedy. **Released:** 1992. **Price:** $12.95 (paper).

32050 ■ "NMAC Settles Suit" in *Hispanic Business* (September 2003, pp. 20)
Pub: Hispanic Business
Description: Nissan Motor Acceptance Corporation (NMAC) has finalized the settlement of a lawsuit with minority car buyers, where African Americans and Hispanics were charged higher interest rates than whites.

32051 ■ "OFCCP Contractor Survey; New Worker Economic Opportunity Law" in *Employment Relations Today* (Vol. 27, No. 2, Summer 2000, pp. 81)
Pub: John Wiley & Sons, Inc.
Ed: Morgan D. Hodgson and Ronald S. Cooper. **Description:** The Labor Department's office of Federal Contract Compliance's proposed rule to revise its affirmative action regulations contains a survey requesting detailed information concerning the employee pay policies of federal contractors. The Equal Employment Opportunity Commission's manual offers guidelines for pursuing charges of discrimination in the workplace.

32052 ■ "Pregnancy Claim Settlements Rise" in *Inc.* (September 2005, pp. 30)
Pub: Inc. Magazine
Description: Pregnancy discrimination lawsuits are on the rise. The Equal Employment Opportunity Commission received 4,512 complaints in 2004.

32053 ■ "The Problem of Perceptions: Reasons for Outsourcing the Sexual Harassment Investigation" in *Employment Relations Today* (Vol.27, No.1)
Pub: John Wiley & Sons, Inc.
Ed: Jonathan Day. **Description:** Management of sexual harassment allegations by human resource departments are explored. Topics addressed include employee perceptions of harassment cases, and the outsourcing of an investigation to an independent third party.

32054 ■ "Race Matters: Studies Show Race, Even Black-Sounding Names, Causes Doors To Shut" in *Black Enterprise* (Vol. 34, February 2004)
Pub: Earl Graves Publishing Co.
Ed: Marie Evan. **Description:** According to a study conducted by a sociologist at Northwestern University in Evanston, Illinois, 17 percent of white ex-cons were called back for job interviews from applications filed, while only 14 percent of crime-free Blacks were called. A study by the University of Chicago on hiring discrimination is also cited. Statistical data included.

32055 ■ "Reality check: threat of lawsuit changes discriminatory payment practices" in *Black Enterprise* (Vol. 33, No. 3, Oct. 2002, pp. 178)
Pub: Earl Graves Publishing Co.
Ed: Lee Anna Jackson. **Description:** Lawyers in Washington, DC have filed a lawsuit against retailers that are refusing to accept out-of-state checks from African American customers. Patterns of discrimination are surfacing through the use of testers from The Equal Rights Center (TERC) attempting to purchase items with checks at various retail establishments.

32056 ■ "Recent State Legislative Developments Concerning Employment Discrimination..." in *Employment Relations Today* (Summer 2000, pp. 89)
Pub: John Wiley & Sons, Inc.
Ed: William C. Martucci and Eric W. Smith. **Description:** A summary of recent state legislative activity regarding employment discrimination and whistleblower protections is presented. The legislation is of importance to multi-state employees who must ensure their operations comply with state laws and regulations.

32057 ■ *Remedies in Employment Discrimination Law*
Pub: John Wiley & Sons, Inc.
Ed: Robert Belton. **Released:** 1992. **Price:** $150.00. **Description:** Covers monetary and nonmonetary remedies to employment discrimination.

32058 ■ *Rights and Respect: What You Need to Know about Gender Bias and Sexual Harassment*
Pub: Millbrook Press, Inc.
Ed: Kathlyn Gay. **Released:** 1995. **Price:** $16.90.

32059 ■ "Sacramento, Calif., Minorities Pay More for Mortgages, Report Says" in *Sacramento Bee* (December 16, 2005)
Pub: The Sacramento Bee
Ed: Andrew McIntosh. **Description:** According to a new report released by the California Reinvestment Coalition, African Americans and Latinos in Sacramento, California pay more for mortgages than others, especially lower income minorities.

32060 ■ *Sex-Based Employment Discrimination*
Pub: Clark Boardman Callaghan
Ed: Susan M. Omilian. **Released:** 1990; updated annually. **Price:** $130.00. **Description:** Provides information on sexual discrimination. Covers such topics as compensation, harassment, and pregnancy.

32061 ■ *Sexual Harassment*
Pub: ABC-CLIO
Ed: Lynn Eisaguirre, Editor. **Released:** Dec 1997. **Price:** $25, individuals eBook. **Publication Includes:** List of agencies and organizations in the U.S. Concerned with sexual harassment. **Entries Include:** Organization name, address, phone. Principal content of publication is information on the history, social context, legal precedent, and legislative background of sexual harassment issues. Part of "Contemporary World Issues Series. ". **Arrangement:** Directory of organizations, selected print resources, film, internet resources.

32062 ■ *Sexual Harassment on the Job*
Pub: Nolo Press
Ed: Bill Petrocelli. **Released:** 1992. **Price:** $18.95 (paper).

32063 ■ *Sexual Harassment: What You Need to Know*
Pub: Crisp Publications, Inc.
Ed: Susan B. Benton-Powers and Lee T. Paterson. **Released:** 1995. **Price:** $15.95.

32064 ■ *Sexual Harassment in the Workplace*
Pub: Crisp Publications, Inc.
Ed: Juliana Lightle and Elizabeth H. Doucet. **Price:** $10.95. **Description:** Explains the legal, professional and personal aspects of sexual harassment, how to handle complaints, and how to prevent it from happening in your business.

32065 ■ "The Social Movement That Grew Up" in *Hispanic Business* (March 2004, pp. 20, 22)
Pub: Hispanic Business
Ed: Joel Russell. **Description:** When civil rights fervor turned to economic empowerment, new companies grew, including Hispanic Business magazine. Profile of the magazine is included.

32066 ■ *Supervising Employees with Disabilities*
Pub: Crisp Publications, Inc.
Ed: Mary B. Dickson. **Price:** $10.95.

32067 ■ *Take Back Your Power: A Working Woman's Response to Sexual Harassment*
Pub: Ism Press, Inc.
Ed: Jennifer Coburn. **Released:** 1995. **Price:** $10.00.

32068 ■ "US Supreme Court Rules on Punitive Damages in Title VII Discrimination Cases" in *Employment Relations Today* (Vol. 27, No.1, Spring2000)
Pub: John Wiley & Sons, Inc.
Ed: Arthur F. Silbergeld and Tracy L. Turner. **Description:** A study of punitive damages under Title VII of the Civil Rights Act of 1964, focusing on employer liability in the US Supreme Court case of Kolstad v. American Dental Association. Topics addressed include employer liability for discrimination, and the influence of the Kolstad case on the amount of punitive damages awarded.

32069 ■ *What Business Must Know about the ADA: 1992 Compliance Guide*
Pub: Chamber of Commerce of the U.S.
Ed: Compiled by U.S. Chamber of Commerce staff; Cheryl Nikos, editor. **Released:** Revised edition, 1992. **Price:** $21.00.

32070 ■ "When Will 'Content of Character' Count?" in *Black Enterprise* (Vol. 34, No. 6, January 2004, pp. 12)
Pub: Earl Graves Publishing Co.
Ed: Earl G. Graves, Sr. **Description:** Despite the good news on the economic front, diversity remains a priority in the upper echelons of major corporations, however the large majority of black Americans still face racism in the pursuit of employment.

32071 ■ *Women in the Workplace: Eliminating Sexual Harassment and Improving Cross-Gender Communication*
Pub: Pfeiffer & Co.
Ed: Catherine D. Fyock. **Price:** $75.00 (leader's guide, looseleaf); $9.95 (participant's workbook, paper). **Description:** Part of the Managing Diversity Workshop Series.

32072 ■ *Working Woman's Guide to Her Job Rights*
Pub: Gordon Press Publishers
Released: 1995. **Price:** $253.95.

32073 ■ "You're Fired!" in *Forbes* (Vol. 174, December 13, 2004, No. 12, pp. 89)
Pub: Forbes Magazine Inc.
Ed: Christopher Steiner. **Description:** Profile of Achilles Group, a firm that assists businesses with personnel matters such as firings, discrimination suits, personality conflicts, threatened lawsuits, EEOC claims, and hiring.

TRADE PERIODICALS

32074 ■ *The Columbus Times*
Pub: Columbus Times
Contact: Ophelia Devore Mitchell, CEO
Released: Weekly (Wed.). **Description:** Black community newspaper.

32075 ■ *Manager's Legal Bulletin*
Pub: Alexander Hamilton Institute Inc.
Ed: Gloria Ju, Editor. **Released:** Semimonthly. **Price:** $66, individuals; $2.75, single issue. **Description:** Shows managers how to handle problems in the workplace without provoking lawsuits for illegal discrimination in hiring, firing, promotions, sexual harassment, or discipline decisions.

32076 ■ *Mealey's Emerging Insurance Disputes*
Pub: Mealey Publications
Contact: A. Spencer
Ed: Steve Berstler, Editor. **Released:** Semimonthly. **Price:** $900, U.S.; $1,020 foreign. **Description:** Finds and tracks new areas of insurance litigation as they arise. Follows coverage actions involving underlying claims of sexual harassment and discrimination; sexual molestation and assault; attorney liability; patent and trademark infringement; construction defects, directors and officers claims; emotional distress; and intentional acts.

32077 ■ *The Webb Report*
Pub: Pacific Resource Development Group, Inc.
Ed: Susan L. Webb, Editor. **Released:** Monthly. **Price:** Free; $10, single issue subscribers; $15, single issue non-subscribers. **Description:** Provides information on court cases and issues involving sexual harassment and guidelines concerning what is and what is not considered to be harassment and what to do about it. Recurring features include news of research and notices of publications available.

VIDEOCASSETTES/ AUDIOCASSETTES

32078 ■ *ADA: Commonsense Compliance*
Audio Graphics Training Systems
503 Gabbettville Rd.
Lagrange, GA 30240
Ph:(706)883-6366
Free: 800-814-9792
Fax: (706)882-3004
Price: $695.00. **Description:** Illustrates the legal issues of the ADA through well-acted vignettes. Designed to be viewed in conjunction with "ADA: Understanding the Law." **Availability:** VHS.

32079 ■ *The ADA Maze: What You Can Do*
Commonwealth Films, Inc.
223 Commonwealth Ave.
Boston, MA 02116
Ph:(617)262-5634
Fax: (617)262-6948
Co. E-mail: info@commonwealthfilms.com
URL: http://www.commonwealthfilms.com
Released: 1991. **Price:** $425.00. **Description:** Defines the legal aspects of hiring according to the ADA through a combination of interviews and graphics. Aimed at managers, topics include the intent of the ADA, writing job descriptions, interviewing guidelines and more. **Availability:** VHS.

32080 ■ *ADA: Understanding the Law*
Audio Graphics Training Systems
503 Gabbettville Rd.
Lagrange, GA 30240
Ph:(706)883-6366
Free: 800-814-9792
Fax: (706)882-3004
Price: $695.00. **Description:** Discusses the new ADA laws in a conference room setting. Confronts typical objections from management and gives clear information on legal requirements and ramifications. Designed to be viewed in conjunction with "ADA: Commonsense Compliance." **Availability:** VHS.

32081 ■ *Adjust Your Set: The Static Is Real*
University of Toronto
Media Commons
Robarts Library
130 St. George St., 3rd Fl.
Toronto, ON, Canada M5S 1A5
Ph:(416)978-6520
Fax: (416)978-8707
Co. E-mail: luke.dellcese@utoronto.ca
URL: http://www.utoronto.ca
Price: $79.95. **Description:** Addresses the issues that exist between men and women on the subject of sexual harassment. Contains vignettes on emotional manipulation, subtle threats of violence, heterosexism, feminist backlash in the classroom, harassment of disabled women, and battering in heterosexual relationships. Written and presented by students. **Availability:** VHS.

32082 ■ *The Americans with Disabilities Act: New Access to the Workplace*
Phoenix Learning Group
2349 Chaffee Dr.
St. Louis, MO 63146
Ph:(314)569-0211
Free: 800-221-1274
Fax: (314)569-2834
URL: http://www.phoenixlearninggroup.com
Price: $495.00. **Description:** Covers a broad scope of information through interviews with government officials. Intended mainly for employers. **Availability:** VHS.

32083 ■ *Bridges: Skills to Manage a Diverse Workforce*
LearnCom HR Consulting and Training
38 Discovery, Ste. 250
Irvine, CA 92618
Ph:(515)440-0890
Free: 800-698-8263
Fax: (515)221-3149
Co. E-mail: nhartline@learncom.com
URL: http://www.learncomhr.com
Released: 1990. **Price:** $175.00. **Description:** An eight-part series designed to train supervisors and managers to deal with a culturally diverse workforce. The tapes are available individually or as a set. Trainer's manuals and participants manuals are included. **Availability:** VHS; 3/4U.

32084 ■ *Choices*
LearnCom HR Consulting and Training
38 Discovery, Ste. 250
Irvine, CA 92618
Ph:(515)440-0890
Free: 800-698-8263
Fax: (515)221-3149
Co. E-mail: nhartline@learncom.com
URL: http://www.learncomhr.com
Released: 1990. **Price:** $175.00. **Description:** A 12-part training course, designed to help train managers in EEO and affirmative action. Tapes are available as a set or individually. Trainer and participant manuals are included. **Availability:** VHS; 3/4U.

32085 ■ *Crossing the Line*
CA Working Group/We Do the Work
PO Box 10326
Oakland, CA 94610
Ph:(510)268-9675
Fax: (510)268-3606
Co. E-mail: wedothework@igc.org
URL: http://www.pbs.org/livelyhood
Price: $795.00. **Description:** Seven-part sexual harassment prevention training program that combines informed discussion of the legalities with seven real-life vignettes. Covers tips on how to identify behaviors that would be considered sexual harassment, how to differentiate between quid pro quo and hostile environments, and how to encourage environments that prevent sexual harassment. Includes participant and instructor's guides. **Availability:** VHS.

32086 ■ *Expanding Equal Opportunities— Implementing the Americans with Disabilities Act*
National Audiovisual Center
5285 Port Royal Rd.
Springfield, VA 22161
Ph:(703)605-4603
Free: 800-553-6847
Fax: (703)321-8547
Co. E-mail: orders@ntis.fedworld.gov
URL: http://www.ntis.gov/products/nac/index.asp
Released: 1991. **Price:** $35.00. **Description:** Explains aspects of the Americans with Disabilities Act and how it affects the workplace. **Availability:** VHS.

32087 ■ *The Fairer Sex?*
corVISION Media, Inc.
872 S Milwaukee Ave., Ste. 295
Libertyville, IL 60048
Ph:(847)549-7860
Free: 877-364-7485
Fax: (847)549-7861
Co. E-mail: corvision@aol.com
URL: http://www.corvision.com
Price: $295.00. **Description:** Tests whether women are truly discriminated in job market and in consumer purchasing situations. Intended to modify discriminatory behavior. **Availability:** VHS.

32088 ■ *Gateway to Opportunity: Interviewing Job Applicants with Disabilities*
Advantage Media
c/o Kantola Productions
55 Sunnyside Ave.
Mill Valley, CA 94941
Ph:(415)381-9363
Free: 800-989-8273

Fax: (415)381-9801
Co. E-mail: info@kantola.com
URL: http://www.kantola.com/d/advantage.htm
Released: 1992. **Price:** $495.00. **Description:** Illustrates detailed guidelines for interviewing according to the ADA through a combination of short scenarios and interviews. Note, however, that the guidelines don't necessarily address the legal issues per se. **Availability:** VHS.

32089 ■ Given the Opportunity: Interacting with Individuals with Disabilities
American Media, Inc.
4621 121st St.
Urbandale, IA 50323-2311
Ph:(515)224-0919
Free: 888-776-8268
Fax: (515)327-2555
Co. E-mail: custsvc@ammedia.com
URL: http://www.ammedia.com
Released: 1992. **Price:** $450.00. **Description:** A guide to interaction with the disabled in the workplace. Focuses primarily on four disabilities: hearing, sight, immobility, and the developmentally challenged, and the means of overcoming awkwardness when confronted with the disabled. **Availability:** VHS.

32090 ■ Handling the Sexual Harassment Complaint
Excellence in Training Corp.
1303 Marsh Ln.
Carrollton, TX 75006
Free: 800-747-6569
Released: 1991. **Price:** $495.00. **Description:** A program designed to train managers and supervisors how to avoid problems by the handling sexual harassment complaints correctly and legally. Includes a leader's guide and desk reminder cards. **Availability:** VHS; 3/4U; Special order formats.

32091 ■ Intent vs. Impact
LearnCom HR Consulting and Training
38 Discovery, Ste. 250
Irvine, CA 92618
Ph:(515)440-0890
Free: 800-698-8263
Fax: (515)221-3149
Co. E-mail: nhartline@learncom.com
URL: http://www.learncomhr.com
Released: 1991. **Price:** $175.00. **Description:** Two complete video training programs designed to help identify subtle forms of sexual harassment in the workplace. A trainer's manual and participants' manuals are included. **Availability:** VHS; 3/4U.

32092 ■ Is It Sexual Harassment?
Cambridge Educational
c/o Films Media Group
PO Box 2053
Princeton, NJ 08843-2053
Free: 800-257-5126
Fax: (609)671-0266
Co. E-mail: custserve@filmsmediagroup.com
URL: http://www.cambridgeol.com
Released: 1994. **Price:** $39.95. **Description:** Sexual harassment scenarios to educate groups. Includes workbook. **Availability:** VHS.

32093 ■ It's Not Just Courtesy—It's the Law
Excellence in Training Corp.
1303 Marsh Ln.
Carrollton, TX 75006
Free: 800-747-6569
Released: 1991. **Price:** $495.00. **Description:** A training program to raise awareness of sexual harassment among employees and teach them how to handle it. A leader's guide is included. **Availability:** VHS; 3/4U; Special order formats.

32094 ■ Making the ADA Work for You
American Media, Inc.
4621 121st St.
Urbandale, IA 50323-2311
Ph:(515)224-0919
Free: 888-776-8268
Fax: (515)327-2555
Co. E-mail: custsvc@ammedia.com

URL: http://www.ammedia.com
Released: 1992. **Price:** $595.00. **Description:** Aimed at supervisors and managers, this program features five narrators, each with a different disability, who present various scenarios. Interviewing, the definition of marginal functions, customer and employee reactions, and other topics are addressed. **Availability:** VHS.

32095 ■ Preventing Sexual Harassment: A Management Responsibility
LearnCom HR Consulting and Training
38 Discovery, Ste. 250
Irvine, CA 92618
Ph:(515)440-0890
Free: 800-698-8263
Fax: (515)221-3149
Co. E-mail: nhartline@learncom.com
URL: http://www.learncomhr.com
Released: 1992. **Description:** Training program consisting of two videotapes designed to show managers how to identify and prevent sexual harassement in the workplace and minimize liability. Defines sexual harassment, shows managers and supervisors how they can be held personally liable, presents practical steps to prevent harassment, details the elements of effective remedial action, and examines case studies. **Availability:** VHS; 3/4U.

32096 ■ Preventing Sexual Harassment: A Shared Responsibility
LearnCom HR Consulting and Training
38 Discovery, Ste. 250
Irvine, CA 92618
Ph:(515)440-0890
Free: 800-698-8263
Fax: (515)221-3149
Co. E-mail: nhartline@learncom.com
URL: http://www.learncomhr.com
Released: 1992. **Description:** Training program designed to prevent sexual harassment by employees and to minimize liability. Demonstrates the employer's prohibition against sexual harassment, highlights the availability of internal procedures for the resolution of complaints, and encourages employees to use internal procedures. **Availability:** VHS; 3/4U.

32097 ■ Putting the ADA to Work for You
American Occupational Therapy Association
4720 Montgomery Ln.
PO Box 31220
Bethesda, MD 20824-1220
Ph:(301)652-2682
Free: 800-377-8555
Fax: (301)652-7711
Co. E-mail: products@aota.org
URL: http://www.aota.org
Released: 1992. **Price:** $50.00. **Description:** A real bargain for its low price and straight-forward approach. Combines interviews and short vignettes to suggest approaches to "reasonable accommodations." **Availability:** VHS.

32098 ■ Sexual Harassment: Crossing the Line
Cambridge Educational
c/o Films Media Group
PO Box 2053
Princeton, NJ 08843-2053
Free: 800-257-5126
Fax: (609)671-0266
Co. E-mail: custserve@filmsmediagroup.com
URL: http://www.cambridgeol.com
Released: 1993. **Price:** $89.95. **Description:** Sexual harassment in schools and in the workplace is discussed. **Availability:** VHS.

32099 ■ Sexual Harassment: Handling the Complaint
Audio Graphics Training Systems
503 Gabbettville Rd.
Lagrange, GA 30240
Ph:(706)883-6366
Free: 800-814-9792
Fax: (706)882-3004
Price: $1295.00. **Description:** Part two in a two-part series addressing the behavioral and legal issues sur-

rounding sexual harassment. Directly confronts sensitive material in a constructive manner through well-acted vignettes. **Availability:** VHS.

32100 ■ Sexual Harassment: It's Hurting People
Sunburst Technology
400 Columbus Ave, Ste 160E
Valhalla, NY 10595-1349
Ph:(914)747-3310
Fax: (914)747-4109
Co. E-mail: webmaster@snysunburst.com
URL: http://www.sunburst.com
Price: $179. **Description:** Defines sexual harassment as any unwelcome sexual behavior and illustrates its demeaning and hurtful effects. Includes teacher's guide. **Availability:** VHS.

32101 ■ Sexual Harassment: Serious Business
American Management Association
9 Galen St.
PO Box 9119
Watertown, MA 02472
Ph:(617)926-4600
Free: 800-225-3215
Fax: (617)923-1875
URL: http://www.amanet.org
Price: $495.00. **Description:** Provides information on how to recognize and prevent sexual harassment in the workplace. **Availability:** VHS; CC.

32102 ■ Sexual Harassment: Walking the Corporate Fine Line
Salenger Films, Inc.
1635 12th St.
Santa Monica, CA 90404-9988
Ph:(310)450-1300
Free: 800-775-5025
Fax: (310)450-1010
Co. E-mail: salenger@aol.com
URL: http://salengerfilms.visualnet.com
Price: $495.00. **Description:** Examines what constitutes sexual harassment and how it can be prevented. **Availability:** VHS.

32103 ■ Sexual Harassment in the Workplace...Identify. Stop. Prevent.
Excellence in Training Corp.
1303 Marsh Ln.
Carrollton, TX 75006
Free: 800-747-6569
Released: 1991. **Price:** $575.00. **Description:** A training program in the prevention and/or eliminating of sexual harassment in the workplace. A leader's guide and desk reminder cards are included. **Availability:** VHS; 3/4U; Special order formats.

32104 ■ Welcome to the Team: Disability Etiquette in the Workplace
Advantage Media
c/o Kantola Productions
55 Sunnyside Ave.
Mill Valley, CA 94941
Ph:(415)381-9363
Free: 800-989-8273
Fax: (415)381-9801
Co. E-mail: info@kantola.com
URL: http://www.kantola.com/d/advantage.htm
Released: 1992. **Price:** $495.00. **Description:** Illustrates the concept of "reasonable accommodations," through various examples and practical suggestions. Recommended for both managers and employees. Part one of a two part program. **Availability:** VHS.

CONSULTANTS

32105 ■ AIDS Partnership Michigan
2751 E Jefferson Ave., Ste. 301
Detroit, MI 48207
Ph:(313)446-9800
Free: 800-872-2437
Fax: (313)446-9839
Co. E-mail: info@aidspartnership.org
URL: http://www.aidspartnership.org

E-mail: info@aidspartnership.org
Scope: Offers advice to corporations on the effects of HIV & AIDS in the workplace. Focus is on infected employee rights, co-worker rights, and employer responsibilities. Serves all industries.

32106 ■ Applied Personnel Research
27 Judith Rd.
Newton, MA 02459
Ph:(617)244-8859
Fax: (617)244-8904
Co. E-mail: Inquiry@appliedpersonnelresearch.com
URL: http://www.appliedpersonnelresearch.com

E-mail: Inquiry@appliedpersonnelresearch.com
Scope: Industrial psychology consulting services in the areas of personnel assessment and selection, and solution-oriented applied personnel research involving data collection and data analysis. Customized Consulting solutions can be provided.

32107 ■ D.R. Bennett & Associates
11846 Balboa Blvd., No. 298
Granada Hills, CA 91344
Ph:(818)360-2375
Fax: (818)366-7593
Co. E-mail: dbennett69@aol.com

E-mail: dbennett69@aol.com
Scope: Human resources consultant who writes all human resources forms including employee handbooks and job descriptions; sets up employment applications, employee files and procedures to comply with regulations affecting employers; and finds and screens applicants and does the initial interviewing. Also offers management training in the areas of interviewing, employee evaluations, how to handle sexual harassment claims and progressive discipline and documentation. All services are tailored to meet EEOC and INS regulations as well as labor laws, to reduce exposure to worker's compensation stress claims, unemployment claims and wrongful termination suits. Industries served: small businesses with 25-100 employees. **Seminars:** Interviewing Skills Seminar; Performance Appraisal Seminar.

32108 ■ Dr. John A. Berger & Associates
2021 Midwest Rd., Ste. 200
Oak Brook, IL 60523-1370
Ph:(630)953-8638
Fax: (630)953-8687
Scope: Full service human resources consulting firm specializing in the practice of industrial/organizational psychology. Specializes in the areas of recruitment and selection; management continuity, development and succession planning; capability and performance testing and evaluation; organizational analysis and design, performance management; outplacement and terminations; turnarounds and crisis management; compensation; family owned business counseling - conflict resolution, management succession, and career planning for family members. Has developed structured hiring guides and selection systems; Has designed, developed and implemented a variety of performance appraisal systems both as part of total compensation projects and stand alone systems. Has served as an expert witness in a number of wrongful discharge and EEO discrimination cases. Industries served: manufacturing, financial services, high-tech, insurance, utilities, construction, retail, professional services, government, healthcare, publishing, leisure and food services.

32109 ■ CoastalAMI
4621 121st St.
Urbandale, IA 50323-2311
Ph:(515)224-0919
Free: 888-776-8268
Fax: (515)327-2555
URL: http://www.coastalhr.com
Scope: Provides consulting services and seminars on all aspects of management, human resources, and business, including customer relations and sexual harassment, works with managers one-on-one, implements programs, and presents seminars for entire

departments. Serves private industries as well as government agencies. **Seminars:** Legal Issues; Stress Management; Change; Communication; Team Building; Leadership; Management; Supervision; Conflict Resolution; Performance Appraisal; Train-the-Trainer. **Special Services:** LMS systems, custom e-learning content development and enterprise wide systems implementations.

32110 ■ DiversityWorks
1924 Franklin St., Ste. 201
Oakland, CA 94612
Ph:(510)763-9300
Fax: (510)763-9311
Co. E-mail: mail@diversityworks.org
URL: http://www.diversityworks.org

E-mail: mail@diversityworks.org
Scope: Two main focus areas include (1)Working with young people directly, training and empowering them to become peer to peer diversity trainers and (2)Working with schools, community groups and progressive corporations to increase diversity awareness. Offers workshops, staff trainings, focus group facilitation and diversity program management. **Publications:** "DiversityWords".

32111 ■ DJT Consulting Group L.L.C.
2900 Sonoma Blvd., Ste. C
PO Box 6652
Vallejo, CA 94591
Ph:(707)674-0174
Fax: (707)638-0499
Co. E-mail: info@djtconsulting.com
URL: http://www.djtconsulting.com

E-mail: info@djtconsulting.com
Scope: Offers a range of grant management services including contract monitoring, research, grant writing, evaluation and project management. **Seminars:** Finding and Winning Government Grants.

32112 ■ Eastern Point Consulting Group Inc.
75 Oak St.
Newton, MA 02464
Ph:(617)965-4141
Fax: (617)965-4172
Co. E-mail: info@eastpt.com
URL: http://www.eastpt.com

E-mail: info@eastpt.com
Scope: Specializes in bringing practical solutions to complex challenges. Provides consultation and training in managing diversity; comprehensive sexual-harassment policies and programs; organizational development; benchmarks 360 skills assessment; executive coaching; strategic human resource planning; team building; leadership development for women; mentoring programs; and gender issues in the workplace. **Seminars:** Leadership Development for Women.

32113 ■ FW Consultants Ltd.
1025 W Glen Oaks Ln., Ste. 105
Mequon, WI 53092
Ph:(262)241-8234
Fax: (262)241-8340
Co. E-mail: evelyn_freemanwalker@ameritech.net
URL: http://www.fwcons.com

E-mail: evelyn_freemanwalker@ameritech.net
Scope: Human resources consultants specializing in equal employment ppportunity and affirmative action programs, and statistical analyses to defend discrimination charges. Serves private industries as well as government agencies. **Seminars:** Affirmative Action Program Development.

32114 ■ Catherine Gaffigan
400 W 43rd St., Ste. 44L
New York, NY 10036
Ph:(212)586-6300
Co. E-mail: catherig@touro.edu
URL: http://www.catherinegaffigan.com

E-mail: catherig@touro.edu
Scope: Offers services towards the art of acting with the intention of making a career in the business. Provides consulting services for the art of acting.

32115 ■ Haight Consulting
1726 Palisades Dr.
Pacific Palisades, CA 90272-9867
Ph:(310)454-2988
Fax: (310)454-4516
Co. E-mail: haightcnsl@yahoo.com

E-mail: haightcnsl@yahoo.com
Scope: Human Resources compliance: helping employers prevent and resolve issues on sexual harassment, disability discrimination, other forms of discrimination and harassment, retaliation, FMLA, and employee safety. Training (management, HR staff and internal investigators); policies and procedures; compliance program audits; expert witness/litigation consulting; and on-call consultation on individual issues and investigations. **Publications:** "The Federal Leave Compliance Kit"; "Disability discrimination Administration Package"; "Disability discrimination Reasonable Accommodation Kit"; "The Sexual Harassment Investigator's Kit"; "The California Sexual Harassment Compliance Kit"; "California Employee Safety Compliance Checklists"; "The CA Disability Leave Kit". **Seminars:** Management and HR training on disability discrimination; sexual harassment; discrimination and harassment laws; FMLA; retaliation; recruiting and selection; preventing and resolving performance issues. **Special Services:** Audits of existing compliance programs for discrimination and harassment laws; Litigation consulting and expert witness; On-call consultations on individual issues and investigations.

32116 ■ Human Resources Group Ltd.
16781 Torrence Ave., Ste. 305
Lansing, IL 60438-6025
Ph:(708)672-3370
Fax: (708)672-3467
Co. E-mail: rorr@humanresourcesgroupltd.com
URL: http://www.humanresourcesgroupltd.com

E-mail: rorr@humanresourcesgroupltd.com
Scope: Offers human resource consulting to small or medium-sized companies with limited human resource staffs. Areas of expertise include sales and management training/development, employee opinion surveys, employee retention programs, customer service, communication strategies, and performance evaluation programs. Development of policies/procedures, employee handbooks, jobs compendium, and turnover reduction strategies. Provides training in legal compliance, i.e. Americans with Disabilities Act, sexual harassment, etc. Industries served: retail, casino gaming (including Indian gaming) and hospitality. **Publications:** "Employee Surveys: Being a 'Mind Reader" Was never So Easy"; "Getting Over The Underachievers"; "Employee Retention? No Problem!"; "Is Your Company The Employer Of Choice?" **Seminars:** Effective Sales Management; Basics of Supervisory Management; Human Resource Educational Program; Human Resources and the Small Business; Customer Service.

32117 ■ The Kaleel Jamison Consulting Group Inc.
279 River St., Ste. 401
Troy, NY 12180
Ph:(518)271-7000
Free: 888-552-4662
Fax: (518)271-4400
Co. E-mail: info@kjcg.com
URL: http://www.kjcg.com

E-mail: info@kjcg.com
Scope: The firm creates high performing, worthy organizations through its unique brand of management consulting and strategic culture change, also assists organizations to become places where all people can do their best work by shifting focus to business cultures that integrate individual and organizational needs and competencies, which improve productivity, product/service quality and bottom line performance. **Publications:** "The Inclusion Breakthrough: Unleashing the Real Power of Diversity," Berrett-Koehler, 2002; "Eight Essential Axioms for Rapid Culture Change". **Seminars:** D/Ops: Developing The Organi-

zational And Personal Self; Dealing with Covert Processes.

32118 ■ Litigation Management & Training Services Inc.
301 E Ocean Blvd., Ste. 520
Long Beach, CA 90802-4862
Ph:(562)495-0098
Free: 800-548-6468
Fax: (562)495-1786
Co. E-mail: info@preventlitigation.com
URL: http://www.preventlitigation.com

E-mail: info@preventlitigation.com
Scope: Consults with private industry employers and government agencies on proactive legal management of the workplace, including sexual harassment prevention, legal aspects of human resources management, how to hire, fire and manage employees legally. Special programs for adopting and enforcing e-mail and internet abuse policies. Also trains on avoiding liabilities for design and delivery of training programs, health and safety regulatory compliance issues and legal aspects of violence prevention and workplace security. Personnel policy development, internal discrimination and misconduct investigations. **Seminars:** Personnel Policies - Adoption and Enforcement; How to Hire and Fire Legally; Avoiding Wrongful Discharge Claims; Avoid Liability for Design and Delivery of Training Programs; How to Adopt and Enforce Defensible E-mail and Internet Policies, The Americans with Disabilities Act, and the Family Medical Leave Act; Legal Issues of the 21st century; Prevention of Sexual Harassment; Legal Employment Policies; Equal Employment Opportunities Compliance; How to Conduct a Defensible Internal Misconduct Investigation; Creating an Atmosphere of Respect. **Special Services:** Mediation Services.

32119 ■ Pacific Resource Development Group Inc.
1651 NE 185th St.
Shoreline, WA 98155
Ph:(206)367-1418
Free: 800-767-3062
Fax: (206)367-1418
Co. E-mail: pacres@shadesofgray.com
URL: http://www.shadesofgray.com

E-mail: pacres@shadesofgray.com
Scope: A consulting firm specializing in sexual harassment. Firm provides consulting and training services for managers, supervisors, general employees and individuals. Services include training, investigations, expert witness, and training products materials such as videos and books. **Publications:** Shockwaves: The Global Impact of Sexual Harassment! Master Media Ltd., March 1994; Step Forward, MasterMedia, 1991; Training Investigator Manuals, 2002; Video Program, 1998. **Seminars:** Sexual Harassment. **Special Services:** Investigations and expert witness.

32120 ■ John Smithkey, III, RN
1271 Overland Ave. NE
North Canton, OH 44720-1731
Ph:(330)494-3729
Scope: Specializes in public and occupational health, HIV/AIDS education and prevention programs, grant and proposal writing, and programs for businesses and employees.

32121 ■ Stier Associates
4 Dunellen
Cromwell, CT 06416-2702
Ph:(860)635-1590
Fax: (860)635-1591
Co. E-mail: s.stier@worldnet.att.net

E-mail: s.stier@worldnet.att.net
Scope: Personal development consulting. Subspecialty in Family-Owned businesses. Services include succession planning, executive coaching, strategic management, team building, board development. Consulting services for public companies include process consulting, team building, executive coaching, diversity management, and strategic management. Consulting to religious institutions.

32122 ■ The Training Station
PO Box 170536
Arlington, TX 76003
Ph:(817)683-2650
Free: 800-594-8181
Fax: 888-448-2237
URL: http://www.thetrainers.com
Scope: Training, human resource development, and marketing services consultants. Conducts needs analysis, program develoment, design, writing, execution, follow-up and assessment. Provides speaking engagements and seminars for all personnel. Specialize in sales and marketing, sexual harassment, recruiting, interviewing, selection and management skills. Management assessment tools and programs available. Standard or generic programs are available for immediate tailoring or modification, as well as custom developed materials and programs. Train-the-trainer methodology is also an option. Consulting on human resource issues are available upon request. Industries served: chemical, food service, manufacturing, banking, medical, pharmaceutical, optical, and hard goods; also serve the electrical utility, retail, and power goods markets. **Seminars:** Management Forum Series (9 topics offered in 1-day each presentations); R.I.S.K.; S.H.A.M.E. (Sexual Harassment Awareness Managed Effectively), a 1/2 day workshop; M.U.S.T. (Management Understanding of Sales and Training), a 4-5 day orientation to sales management process; Power Sales Management; Stress Management Training; Show Selling Seminar. **Special Services:** Sales and management need analysis software; Management Audit Profile, and Sales Opinion Survey.

32123 ■ Vaccari & Associates Inc.
17 Cypress St.
Marblehead, MA 01945
Ph:(781)639-0946
Fax: (781)639-0946
Co. E-mail: rvaccari1@verizon.net
URL: http://www.vaccari-associates.com

E-mail: rvaccari1@verizon.net
Scope: A provider of appraisals for primary and secondary mortgages; mortgage refinancing; employee relocation; private mortgage insurance removal; estate planning and divorce settlement.

COMPUTERIZED DATABASES

32124 ■ *Employment Discrimination Report*
The Bureau of National Affairs Inc.
1231 25th St. NW
Washington, DC 20037
Ph:(202)452-4200
Free: 800-372-1033
Fax: (202)452-4226
Co. E-mail: customercare@bna.com
URL: http://www.bna.com
Description: Contains legislative, judicial and regulatory developments and news in the field of equal employment opportunity. Subjects cover age-based

discrimination, appearance-based discrimination, class actions, damages and remedies, disabilities-based discrimination, national origin-based discrimination, race-based discrimination, religion-based discrimination, retaliation, rules of evidence, sexual harassment, sexual orientation-based discrimination, taxation, testers, discovery, employment practices liability insurance, family and medical leave, gender-based discrimination, glass ceiling, and jury practice. Sections include Highlights, Table of Contents, State Index, News, Table of Cases, Court Decisions, Verdicts & Settlements, State News, Arbitration, Interviews, Text, and Calendar of Events. **Availability:** Online: The Bureau of National Affairs Inc., Thomson West. **Type:** Full text.

LIBRARIES

32125 ■ Tennessee (State) Human Rights Commission–Resource Library
Cornerstone Sq. Bldg., Ste. 400
530 Church St.
Nashville, TN 37243-0745
Ph:(615)741-5825
Fax: (615)532-2197
Scope: Race relations; discrimination in employment, housing, and public accommodations; legislation and decisions rendered in discrimination cases. **Services:** Library open to the public with restrictions. **Holdings:** 75 books; 500 bound periodical volumes; commission-related materials. **Subscriptions:** 10 journals and other serials.

32126 ■ U.S. Equal Employment Opportunity Commission–Library
1801 L St. NW, Rm. 6502
Washington, DC 20507
Ph:(202)663-4630
Fax: (202)663-4629
URL: http://www.eeoc.gov/
Contact: Susan D. Taylor, Lib.Dir.
Scope: Employment discrimination, minorities, women, aged, persons with disabilities, labor law, civil rights. **Services:** Interlibrary loan; copying; Library open to the public by appointment. **Holdings:** 25,000 books. **Subscriptions:** 300 journals and other serials; 8 newspapers.

RESEARCH CENTERS

32127 ■ Center for Women Policy Studies
1776 Massachusetts Ave. NW, Ste. 450
Washington, DC 20036
Ph:(202)872-1770
Fax: (202)296-8962
Co. E-mail: cwps@centerwomenpolicy.org
URL: http://www.centerwomenpolicy.org
Contact: Leslie R. Wolfe, Pres.
E-mail: cwps@centerwomenpolicy.org
Scope: Public policy (federal, state, and global) that promotes women's human rights. Current key policy issues include access to education for low income women, the women's HIV/AIDS epidemic in the USA and worldwide, violence against women and girls, international trafficking of women and girls, work/family and workplace diversity, reproductive rights and justice, and the impact of US foreign policy on women worldwide. Designs model legislation and develops and disseminates research reports and policy papers. **Publications:** News from the Center for Women Policy Studies (quarterly). **Educational Activities:** Foreign policy institute (annually), for state legislators; Policy seminars.

ASSOCIATIONS AND OTHER ORGANIZATIONS

32128 ■ Allied Distribution, Inc.
PO Box 607
Eagle River, WI 54521
Ph:(715)479-3530
Fax: (715)479-3551
Co. E-mail: info@warehousenetwork.com
URL: http://www.warehousenetwork.com
Contact: Ernest B. Brunswick, Pres.
Description: Represents public and contract warehouses and distribution centers. Maintains an associated network of public warehouse and distribution centers throughout the U.S., Canada, Mexico, and other areas. Not affiliated with Allied Van Lines. Convention/Meeting: none. **Publications:** *Warehousing and Distribution Centers Membership Directory* (biennial).

32129 ■ Canadian Association of Chemical Distributors–L'Association Canadienne des Distributeurs de Produits Chimiques
627 Lyons Ln., Ste. 301
Oakville, ON, Canada L6J 5Z7
Ph:(905)844-9140
Fax: (905)844-5706
Co. E-mail: cacd@cacd.ca
URL: http://www.cacd.ca
Contact: Cathy Campbell, Managing Dir.
Membership: Chemical distributors in Canada. **Purpose:** Represents members to governments, allied associations, and the public. **Publications:** *The Chemunicator* (quarterly).

32130 ■ Distribution Business Management Association
2938 Columbia Ave., Ste. 1102
Lancaster, PA 17603
Ph:(717)295-0033
Fax: (717)299-2154
Co. E-mail: dbminfo@dbm-assoc.com
URL: http://www.dcenter.com
Contact: Amy Z. Thorn, Exec. Dir.
Membership: Management personnel in the wholesale distribution industries. **Purpose:** Promotes education and continuing professional development in the materials handling, distribution, and supply chain industries. Conducts educational programs. **Publications:** *Distribution Business Management Journal* (semiannual).

32131 ■ Distribution Research and Education Foundation
1725 K St. NW, Ste. 300
Washington, DC 20006
Ph:(202)872-0885
Fax: (202)785-0586
Co. E-mail: rschreibman@nawd.org
URL: http://www.naw.org/Template.
    cfm?section=DREF
Contact: Ron Schreibman, Exec.Dir.
Description: Firms that are members of the National Association of Wholesaler-Distributors , wholesalers,

and trade associations. Seeks to advance knowledge in the field of wholesale distribution by means of long-range research projects. **Publications:** *The Acquisitive Distributor*; *Connect with Your Suppliers: A Wholesaler-Distributor's Guide to Electronic Communications Systems*; *Facing the Forces of Change: The Road to Opportunity* (triennial); *Price for Success: A Practical Guide for Improving Margins in Wholesale Distribution*.

32132 ■ General Merchandise Distributors Council
1275 Lake Plaza Dr.
Colorado Springs, CO 80906
Ph:(719)576-4260
Fax: (719)576-2661
Co. E-mail: info@gmdc.org
URL: http://gmdc.org
Contact: David T. McConnell Jr., Pres./CEO
Membership: General merchandise (nonfood) units of wholesale grocers, cooperatives, and voluntaries (110); chain food stores, service merchandisers, drug chains, mass merchandisers, wholesale drug companies, and wholesale clubs; manufacturers or suppliers of general merchandise (540) and health and beauty care products. **Purpose:** Works to improve management operations, marketing programs, sales techniques, merchandising, and distribution functions of members; furthers management education and employee training; and promotes understanding and cooperation among members, the public, and government. Conducts research and compiles statistics. **Publications:** *Conference Chronicles* (semiannual); *Focus* (quarterly); *Legislative Advisory* (monthly); *Marketing Conference Transcripts* (semiannual); *Off the Shelf* (quarterly); *Seminar Educational Transcripts* (semiannual); *White Paper*; Membership Directory (annual).

32133 ■ LTD Shippers Association
1230 Pottstown Pike, Ste. 6
Glenmoore, PA 19343
Ph:(610)458-3636
Fax: (610)458-8039
URL: http://www.ltdmgmt.com
Contact: Tom Craig, Pres.
Description: Works to leverage the buying power of the members for lower ocean freight prices. Has scope that includes ocean rates from Asia to United States, to Canada, Mexico, Puerto Rico and many other destinations; also rates to the US and Canada from Brazil, the Mediterranean, India and other origins. Aims to design, develop, negotiate, implement and manage logistics or transportation programs for members.

32134 ■ National Association of Wholesaler-Distributors
1725 K St. NW, Ste. 300
Washington, DC 20006-1419
Ph:(202)872-0885
Fax: (202)785-0586
Co. E-mail: naw@nawd.org
URL: http://www.naw.org
Contact: Dirk Van Dongen, Pres.

Description: Federation of national, state, and regional associations, and individual wholesaler-distributor firms. Represents industry's views to the federal government. Analyzes current and proposed legislation and government regulations affecting the industry. Maintains public relations and media programs and a research foundation. Conducts wholesale executive management courses. **Publications:** *NAW Report* (bimonthly); *SmartBrief*. **Telecommunication Services:** electronic mail, dvandongen@nawd.org.

32135 ■ National Convenience Store Distributors Association–Association nationale des distributeurs aux petites surfaces alimentaires
1695 Laval Blvd., Ste. 410
Laval, QC, Canada H7S 2M2
Ph:(450)967-3858
Free: 888-686-2823
Fax: (450)967-8839
Co. E-mail: nacda@nacda.ca
URL: http://www.nacda.ca
Contact: Bill Allen, Chm.
Description: Assists members in providing dependable distribution of convenience products between suppliers and retailers. Represents member's interests with the government and other industry key players. Conducts educational seminars and programs relevant to member's business needs, thus contributing to the improvement of the convenience supply chain. **Publications:** *Distribution Management in the New Economy: A Blueprint for Success*; *Electronic-Commerce for Distribution Channels*; *Values Shift*; *Winning Strategies for a Consolidating Wholesale Distribution Industry*.

REFERENCE WORKS

32136 ■ "10 Local Companies Make Inc. List of Fastest-Growing" in *Crain's Detroit Business* (Vol. 21, October 31, 2005, No. 44, pp. 32)
Pub: Crain Communications Inc. - Detroit
Ed: Laura Bommarito. **Description:** Ten local companies made the Inc. magazine's annual list of the 500 fastest-growing businesses in the U.S. The three top rankings include, Arbor Networks, seller of network security and software equipment, ranked No. 9; Commodity Sourcing Group, No. 22, buys and distributes goods and services for health care organizations; and BullsEye Telecom, provider of telephone and Internet services to businesses ranked No. 82.

32137 ■ "Aftermarket Auto Parts Alliance" in *Motor Age* (Vol. 122, No. 11, November 2003, pp. 86)
Pub: Advanstar Communications, Inc.
Description: Aftermarket Auto Parts Alliance has added three new warehouse distributors to its membership.

32138 ■ **"Airport Industrial Sites in Demand"** in *Milwaukee Journal Sentinel* (December 19, 2005)

Pub: Journal Sentinel, Inc.

Ed: Tom Daykin. **Description:** Several light large industrial buildings are being developed near Mitchell International Airport. New interest in such space used for storing and distributing products, as well as manufacturers, holds hope for the economy.

32139 ■ *American Wholesalers and Distributors Directory*

Pub: Thomson Gale

Contact: Deborah J. Baker

Released: Annual, latest edition 13, published September, 2004; next edition September, 2005. **Price:** $305, individuals. **Covers:** more than 28,000 wholesalers and distributors of consumer products in the U.S. **Entries Include:** Company name, address, phone, fax, e-mail, URLs, names and titles of key personnel, personal e-mail addresses, number of employees, financial data, product line, Standard Industrial Classification (SIC) code, and date established. **Arrangement:** Classified by subject, then alphabetical by company name. **Indexes:** SIC, geographical, alphabetical.

32140 ■ **"Appleseed's distribution center expands"** in *Boston Business Journal* (Vol. 22, No. 12, April 26, 2002, pp. 5)

Pub: MCP, Inc.

Ed: Donna L. Goodison. **Description:** Appleseed's Inc. is expanding its distribution center due to growth.

32141 ■ **"Ashley Capital branches out into new kind of development"** in *Crain's Detroit Business* (Vol. 19, No. 17, April 28, 2003, pp. 3)

Pub: Crain Communications Inc., Detroit

Ed: Jennette Smith. **Description:** Ashley Capital is showing confidence in the Detroit metropolitan area's eventual market rebound by constructing a build-to-suit building for Transfreight Ltd. and leased land to client ASW Services for a building. The new projects equal nearly 300,000 square feet and $9 million in investment. Ashley Capital is best known for speculative big box distribution centers.

32142 ■ *Associated Equipment Distributors—Membership Directory*

Pub: Associated Equipment Distributors Inc.

Released: Annual, May, Latest edition 2004-2005. **Price:** $50, members single copy; $100, nonmembers single copy. **Covers:** Fifteen hundred U.S. and Canadian distributors. Available as a special issue of Construction Equipment Distribution magazine. **Entries Include:** Information on each company's branches, manufacturer members, banks, finance companies, specialized service firms and trade press, and AED contact person.

32143 ■ **"Backward Thinking: Reverse Auctions Could Help You Get More Contracts"** in *Entrepreneur* (Vol. 32, November 2004, No. 11, pp. 32)

Pub: Entrepreneur Media Inc.

Ed: Chris Penttila. **Description:** Reverse auctions let suppliers and distributors to underbid each other online in real time until a contract price drops as low as it will go.

32144 ■ **"Better Safe: Does Your Product Need a Warning Label?"** in *Entrepreneur* (Vol. 31, No. 9, July 2003, pp. 76)

Pub: Entrepreneur Media, Inc.

Ed: Jane Easter Bahls. **Description:** When injured, a consumer can sue not only the manufacturer, but also the supplier, dealer, distributor or rental yard.

32145 ■ **"Bulking up; Dollar Castle's ruler plans retailing, distribution kingdom"** in *Crain's Detroit Business* (Dec. 9, 2002, pp. 3)

Pub: Crain Communications Inc., Detroit

Ed: Laura Bailey. **Description:** Profile of Dollar Castle's owner Eddie Denha and his successful management style.

32146 ■ **"Calif. Company snaps up Texas Winn-Dixie center"** in *Atlanta Business Chronicle* (Vol. 25, December 6, 2002, No. 26, pp. 32C)

Pub: American City Business Publications, Inc.

Ed: Michael Whiteley. **Description:** Industrial Realty Group (IRG), Torrance, California, has acquired the South Fort Worth, Texas distribution center of Winn-Dixie Stores Inc. The grocer had pulled out of the Texas and Oklahoma markets five months earlier. The deal closed on 11/15/02; the purchase is part of IRG's strategy of acquiring buildings at low costs in order to offer low lease rates.

32147 ■ **"Capital City Beverage To Distribute Energy Drink"** in *Mississippi Business Journal* (Vol. 29, January 2007, No. 2, pp. 30)

Pub: Venture Publications, Inc.

Description: Capital City Beverage Company has created a distribution deal with Who's Your Daddy Inc. CCBC will distribute the entire line of Who's Your Daddy "King of Energy" drinks in 18 counties of Central Mississippi.

32148 ■ **"Champagne Toasts: Brian Nembhard Schools Us On the Best of the Bubbly"** in *Black Enterprise* (Vol. 34, July 2004, No. 12, pp. 138)

Pub: Earl G. Graves Publishing Co. Inc.

Ed: Sean Drakes. **Description:** Brian Nembhard, president and CEO of Nembo Imports Ltd., a New York and Caribbean-based importer and distributor of fine wines and champagne, has been commissioned by the Ritz Carleton Hotel in Montego Bay, Jamaica to reconstruct the resort's wine list.

32149 ■ **"Culture Cash"** in *Hispanic Business* (June 2005, pp. 86)

Pub: Hispanic Business

Ed: Keith Rosenblum. **Description:** Distributors are using ethnicity as a means to grow their businesses.

32150 ■ **"The Customer Has Escaped"** in *Harvard Business Review* (Vol. 81, No. 11, November 2003, pp. 96)

Pub: Harvard Business School Press

Ed: Paul F. Nunes, Frank V. Cespedes. **Description:** Consumer behavior and the economic benefits of the wise use of available distribution channels are discussed.

32151 ■ **"A different kind of service"** in *BlackEnterprise* (Vol. 32, No. 3, October 2001, pp. 54)

Pub: Earl Graves Publishing Co.

Ed: Quincy L. Lewis. **Description:** Profile of Reginald Ball, who served as a Secret Service agent for the U.S. Treasury Department. Ball has created RB Industries, a general-line industrial products distribution company based in Sterling Heights, Michigan.

32152 ■ **"eBay"** in *DSN Retail Fax* (Vol. 10, No. 26, June 30, 2003)

Pub: Lebhar-Friedman Inc.

Description: UPS and eBay have extended their partnership and introduced a new line of shipping tools for eBay customers.

32153 ■ **"Feeling Loaded Down? Use Partnerships to Bag New Customers"** in *My Business* (October/November 2003, pp. 44)

Pub: My Business Magazine

Ed: Paige Orr. **Description:** Michael Hess, president and chief executive of Road Wired, a technology travel accessory firm, partnered with Travelpro International, a luggage manufacturer and distributor. This partnership has helped Hess to grow his business.

32154 ■ **"The Film Biz Goes Filmless"** in *Business 2.0* (Vol. 6, July 2005, No. 6, pp. 30)

Pub: Time, Inc.

Description: A move to distribute movies to theater houses digitally could save Hollywood up to $1 billion annually.

32155 ■ **"Growth Outside the Core"** in *Harvard Business Review* (Vol. 81, No. 12, December 2003, pp. 66)

Pub: Harvard Business School Press

Ed: Chris Zook, James Allen. **Description:** Six methods to launch corporate growth into adjacent businesses, using Nike Inc.'s diversification from athletic shoes to golf equipment and apparel is explored. The methods include entering new geographies, using new distribution channels, developing new services and products, and targeting new customer segments.

32156 ■ **"High Profit in Play"** in *Small Business Opportunities* (Vol. 16, No. 1, January 2004, pp. 62, 64)

Pub: Harris Publications, Inc.

Ed: Stan Roberts. **Description:** Profile of Ron Kaplan who took over his family's toy distribution business, Action Products International in Orlando, Florida, in 1997. Kaplan decided to shift the focus of the company from supplying toys, books and souvenirs to museums, to concentrating on manufacturing educational toys. The company now reports sales of $6 million a year.

32157 ■ **"Hiring the Right People to Rep Your Products"** in *Black Enterprise* (Vol. 35, November 2004, No. 4, pp. 54)

Pub: Earl G. Graves Publishing Co. Inc.

Ed: Robert Janis. **Description:** Tips for finding the right salesperson for a new product are presented.

32158 ■ **"Image Feels Tower's Pain"** in *San Fernando Valley Business Journal* (Vol. 11, November 2006, No. 24, pp. 10)

Pub: San Fernando Valley Business Journal Associates

Ed: Chris Coates. **Description:** Revenues of Image Entertainment Inc., a distributor of entertainment products such as DVDs and CDs, have decreased 4 percent to $22.8 million. The demise of Tower Records plus a downturn in the sales of DVDs are the largest factors contributing to this decline.

32159 ■ **"Looking ahead"** in *Black Enterprise* (Vol. 32, No. , , pp.)

Pub: Earl Graves Publishing Co.

Description: A discussion exploring the future of Glory Foods Inc. since the death of its co-founder and president, William F. Williams. Glory Foods is a distributor of prepackaged soul food.

32160 ■ **"Nall Launches Video Game Co."** in *San Fernando Valley Business Journal* (Vol. 11, December 2006, No. 25, pp. 27)

Pub: San Fernando Valley Business Journal Associates

Description: Special effects veteran, Roger Nall has launched Red Rover Games, a web-based business that develops and distributes games to download and play.

32161 ■ **"Recovery for Some; Chicago's Economy Will Lag the State and Nation Next Year"** in *Crain's Chicago Business* (December 22, 2003)

Pub: Crain Communications, Inc.

Ed: Sandra Jones. **Description:** Chicago's economy is expected to see a 2.96 percent rise in 2004, with the warehousing and distribution, financial services, and hospitality sectors feeling strongest growth with an increase in business travel to the area. However, Chicago's economy is expected to grow at a slower pace than the state or the nation.

32162 ■ **"Source Interlink, Batanga Ink Distribution Pact"** in *Hispanic Business* (March 2003, pp. 24)

Pub: Hispanic Business

Description: Source Interlink's International Periodical Distributors division will distribute Batanga magazine to U.S. retailers. Batanga magazine is geared to Hispanics ages 12-34 and covers the Latin music sector.

32163 ■ "The U.S. Commercial Service: www.export.gov/comm_svc" in *Entrepreneur* (Vol. 32, November 2004, No. 11, pp. 6)
Pub: Entrepreneur Media Inc.
Ed: Steve Cooper. **Description:** U.S. Commercial Service offers global business solutions in the areas of market research, trade events to promote businesses and services, introductions between buyers and distributors, and export counseling.

32164 ■ *To Your Door Directory*
Pub: To Your Door Enterprises, Inc.
Price: Free. **Covers:** Chicagoland businesses that deliver products/services to homes. **Entries Include:** Company or service name, address, phone.

32165 ■ "The U.S. Postal Service and eBay Are Offering a Delivery Tracking Service" in *Traffic World* (Vol. 267, Oct. 27, 2003)
Pub: Traffic World
Description: The U.S. Postal service and eBay have partnered to offer shipment tracking and other postal-related services.

32166 ■ "Valley Record Label Goes Back to Future" in *San Fernando Valley Business Journal* (Vol. 11, November 2006, No. 24, pp. 1)
Pub: San Fernando Valley Business Journal Associates
Ed: Mark R. Madler. **Description:** Profile of independent record label, Your Music America.

32167 ■ "Why Bright Star Shines" in *Hispanic Business* (January/February 2004, pp. 14-16, 18)
Pub: Hispanic Business
Ed: Joel Russell. **Description:** Profile of Marcelo Claure, CEO of Brightstar and winner of the Hispanic Business Entrepreneur of the Year Award. Brightstar Corporation, a cellular phone distributor, reported double-digit growth for six years. Claure attributes the firm's success to smart use of technology and an aggressive approach to training.

32168 ■ "Year's biggest industrial deal months in making" in *Atlanta Business Chronicle* (Vol. 25, December 13, 2002, No. 27, pp. A3)
Pub: American City Business Publications, Inc.
Ed: Jarred Schenko. **Description:** APL Logistics Inc., will build a 992,000 square foot warehouse distribution complex in Douglas County, Georgia. The complex will be developed by Catellus Development Corporation and is expected to be completed in 2004. The Douglas County site was chosen over one in Cobb County because of access to Hartsfield Atlanta International Airport and a highway.

TRADE PERIODICALS

32169 ■ *Davis Database*
Pub: Herbert W. Davis and Co.
Contact: William H. Drumm, President
E-mail: william.drumm@establishinc.com
Released: Annual. **Price:** Free. **Description:** Discusses current topics in physical distribution and customer service and provides ideas to improve customer service and increase productivity. Offers results of service performance and cost surveys by industry. Recurring features include news of research and survey questionnaires.

32170 ■ *Distribution Center Management*
Pub: Alexander Research & Communications Inc.
Contact: Margaret DeWitt, Publisher
Ed: Troy Reynolds, Editor. **Released:** Monthly. **Price:** $199, individuals. **Description:** The monthly newsletter for distribution centers and warehouse managers with ideas and information on how to run their facilities more productively.

32171 ■ *The Distributor's & Wholesaler's Advisor*
Pub: Whitaker Newsletters Inc.

Ed: Susan M. Dyckman, Editor, dwaeditor@aol.com.
Released: Semiannual. **Description:** Provides case studies, how-to-do-it reports, and industry news of interest to wholesalers and distributors. Covers management strategies, working with manufacturers, logistics and warehousing, finance, personnel issues, sales management, technology, customer service, and law and regulation.

32172 ■ *Drop Shipping Marketing Methods*
Pub: Consolidated Marketing Services, Inc.
Ed: Nicholas T. Scheel, Editor, nscheel@drop-shipping-news.com. **Released:** Monthly. **Price:** $18, U.S. $25/year. **Description:** Supplies data on firms that drop ship their products as a means of distribution. Contains information on sources of consumer and industrial products, formulation of marketing policy, and on the pricing, ordering, packaging, and handling of drop shipments. Includes articles on uses of direct mail and direct-response advertising.

32173 ■ *Profiles in PDM*
Pub: Hunt Personnel Ltd.
Ed: Alex Metz, Editor. **Released:** Bimonthly. **Price:** Free. **Description:** Published as a series of bulletins on basic principles of physical distribution management. Carries articles written to "highlight trends, provoke ideas or provide general information."

TRADE SHOWS AND CONVENTIONS

32174 ■ **Distribution Computer Expo**
C.S. Report, Inc.
101 Fellowship Rd., Ste. 101
PO Box 696
Uwchland, PA 19480
Ph:(610)458-6410
Free: 800-338-4112
Fax: (610)458-6415
URL: http://www.logistar.com
Released: Annual. **Audience:** Distribution, transportation, logistics, and warehouse professionals. **Principal Exhibits:** Computer programs and computerized services for the logistics, distribution, transportation, and truck fleet operation and warehousing industries and supply chain management, e-commerce, B to B, and B to C. **Dates and Locations:** 2007.

32175 ■ **Food Industry Productivity Convention & Exposition**
Food Distributors International
201 Park Washington Ct.
Falls Church, VA 22046-4521
Ph:(703)532-9400
Fax: (703)538-4673
Released: Annual. **Audience:** Wholesale grocers, foodservice distributors, food industry executives, retail chains, and grocery manufacturers. **Principal Exhibits:** Material handling equipment, trucks, fork lifts, trailers, trucks, racks and pallets, computers and software, warehouse and fleet consultants and other services and equipment related to warehousing, distribution, human resources, information technology, logistics and transportation. **Dates and Locations:** 2007 Oct.

CONSULTANTS

32176 ■ **Bavier, Bulger & Goodyear Inc.**
270 Amity Rd., Ste. 222
Woodbridge, CT 06525-2236
Ph:(203)389-1534
Fax: (203)387-8558
Scope: Firm specializes in all areas of manufacturing and distribution operations starting with facility planning, staffing and startup activities, and extending through organization, methods, processes and systems. Focuses on turnaround and improved management, performance measurement, controls, and disciplines. Specialized services include operational

due diligence of target companies in merger and acquisition transactions, as well as operations audits. Reports focus on identification of issues and solutions, heavy emphasis on controls, measurements, and profit improvement through cost reductions. Serves manufacturing and distribution clients; automotive primary, precious, and fabricated metals; rubber; plastics; electrical; electromechanical; electronic; ceramic; assembly; glass; chemical; synthetic materials; china; and printing industries. **Seminars:** Develops and produces video training and orientation programs for clients. **Special Services:** Maintains proprietary labor control software. Also has expertise in variety of integrated software packages for materials, business management and warehousing/distribution management control.

32177 ■ **Myron I. Blumenfeld & Associates**
303 E 83rd St., Ste. 16B
New York, NY 10028
Ph:(212)706-2112
Fax: (212)706-2118
Co. E-mail: mikeblumenfeld@myroniblumenfeld.com
URL: http://www.myroniblumenfeld.com

E-mail: mikeblumenfeld@myroniblumenfeld.com
Scope: Management specialists for consumer goods manufactures, wholesalers and retail in the areas of inventory management, strategic planning, logistics, merchandise planning, merchandise distribution and organization structure and development. **Seminars:** Starting Your Own Business; Business Planning; Inventory Management; New Innovations in Retail Distribution Technology; Bar Coding and Quick Response; Merchandise Planning for Quick Response; Global Marketing.

32178 ■ **Clear Light Books**
823 Don Diego Ave.
Santa Fe, NM 87505
Ph:(505)989-9590
Free: 800-253-2747
Fax: (505)989-9519
Co. E-mail: clpublish@aol.com
URL: http://www.clearlightbooks.com

E-mail: clpublish@aol.com
Scope: Business management consulting specifically in the area of profit planning, as well as warehouse and distribution assistance. Additional expertise in computer system design. Industries served: small/medium-sized businesses and warehouse/distribution. **Publications:** "Warehouse or Wherehouse, A New Frontier in Manufacturing Systems Integration and Automation" **Special Services:** Developed Warestudy™an in-depth analysis of warehouse and distribution automation requirements; developed Profit Planning™, an in-depth analysis designed to improve the profitability and effectiveness of small to medium-sized businesses.

32179 ■ **Compliance Systems Inc.**
Hamilton House, 26 E Bryan St.
PO Box 9981
Savannah, GA 31412
Ph:(912)233-8181
Fax: (912)231-2938
Co. E-mail: csi@colonialmarine.com

E-mail: csi@colonialmarine.com
Scope: Marine consultants specializing in all areas of shipping and marine safety, including Port State Control Compliance, ISM Code Internal Auditing, and OPA 90 Compliance and Maritime Security.

32180 ■ **General Business Consultants Inc.**
1502 Elmwood Ave.
Wilmette, IL 60091-1653
Ph:(847)256-3260
Fax: (847)256-1410
Co. E-mail: dick@genbuscon.com
URL: http://www.genbuscon.com

E-mail: dick@genbuscon.com
Scope: Specializes in helping wholesalers, distributors, supply houses and manufacturers acquire and

use information technology more profitably. Firm services help avoid the pitfalls and problems of complex, confusing things such as: long range business/systems planning; system selection, contract negotiation and installation management (of complete systems and warehouse management systems); do it yourself warehouse management systems. Business Improvement Services involve advanced recommendations for improving: profits and customer service; inventory management and warehouse operations; gross margins; business/systems continuity; e-commerce. **Publications:** "Do you really need a new system?"; "New Warehouse Management Technologies Beat The Old Ones"; "How To Avoid A Warehouse Management System Horror Story". **Seminars:** Tech Trends That Can Hurt Distributors And Wholesalers; Do you really need a new system?; Warehouse Management Systems (WMS).

32181 ■ Irving Shaw and Associates
417 Andover Dr., Ste. C
Monroe Township, NJ 08831-4304
Ph:(609)860-1122
Fax: (609)860-0996
Scope: Management consultants specializing in facilities design for factories and distribution centers. Consulting includes, but is not limited to, factory layout, distribution center planning, materials handling improvement, organization, planning, scheduling, and controls. Active with a variety of manufacturers and distribution companies.

32182 ■ Wesley-Kind Associates Inc.
200 Old Country Rd., Ste. 364
Mineola, NY 11501-4240
Ph:(516)747-3434
Fax: (516)248-2728
Scope: Material handling and distribution consultants offering advice on plant and warehouse layouts and operating systems for the movement, storage and control of materials and products. Expertise includes materials and production management, advanced handling/storage systems, packaging and unitizing systems, capacity, productivity and customer service audits, order filling systems, data processing control systems, transportation systems, site location analysis, facilities planning, and implementation. Industries served: manufacturing, distribution and retail corporations and state and U.S. government agencies. **Publications:** How to Reengineer the Storage Function, Penton Publishing - 1995.

FRANCHISES AND BUSINESS OPPORTUNITIES

32183 ■ 1st Propane
1st Propane Franchising, Inc.
14670 Cantova Way, Ste. 208
Rancho Murieta, CA 95683
Free: 877-977-6726
Fax: (916)354-1533
Co. E-mail: info@1st-propane.com
URL: http://www.1st-propane.com
No. of Franchise Units: 7. **Founded:** 1990. **Franchised:** 1998. **Description:** Distribution of propane gas for home and business use. Tanks from 100 to 1000 gallons in size are rented for use in homes and business. **Equity Capital Needed:** $100,000. **Franchise Fee:** $30,000. **Financial Assistance:** Third party financing is available for equipment. **Training:** 5-weeks of initial training. Active ongoing training and support.

32184 ■ Matrix System Automotive Finishes, Inc.
Matrix Franchise Sales, LLC
850 Ladd Rd., Bldg. E
Walled Lake, MI 48390
Ph:(248)668-8135
Free: 800-735-0303
Fax: (248)668-8134
Founded: 1983. **Franchised:** 2002. **Description:** Auto refinish paint distributor/store. **Equity Capital Needed:** $50,000 minimum cash; $170,000-$259,000, including franchise and working capital. **Franchise Fee:** $10,000-$25,000. **Financial Assistance:** No. **Training:** Yes.

32185 ■ Multi-Menu
3200 1ere Rue Local 510
Longueuil, QC, Canada J3Y 8Y5
Ph:(450)462-0056
Free: 877-462-0056
Fax: (450)462-0206
Co. E-mail: multimenu@multimenu.ca
URL: http://www.multimenu.ca
No. of Franchise Units: 100. **No. of Company-Owned Units:** 1. **Founded:** 1996. **Description:** Home distribution of cat, dog food, and accessories. Looking for master franchisors, master distributors and franchisees throughout Canada and the U.S. **Eq-**uity Capital Needed: $13,500. **Franchise Fee:** $9,500. **Training:** Monthly seminars.

RESEARCH CENTERS

32186 ■ National Association of Wholesaler-Distributors–Distribution Research and Education Foundation
1725 K St. NW
Washington, DC 20006
Ph:(202)872-0885
Fax: (202)785-0586
Co. E-mail: rschreibman@nawd.org
URL: http://www.naw.org/Template.cfm?section=DREF
Contact: Ron Schreibman, Exec.Dir.
E-mail: rschreibman@nawd.org
Scope: Wholesale distribution, focusing on long-range projects to advance knowledge in the field.

32187 ■ Texas A&M University–Thomas and Joan Read Center for Distribution Research and Education
3367 TAMU
College Station, TX 77843-3367
Ph:(979)845-4984
Fax: (979)845-4980
Co. E-mail: lawrence@entc.tamu.edu
URL: http://readcenter.tamu.edu
Contact: Barry Lawrence, Dir.
E-mail: lawrence@entc.tamu.edu
Scope: Industrial distribution, sales force issues, quality assessment, logistics process design, e-commerce, distribution information systems interface, inventory management, supply chain management, financial analysis, organizational change, organizational culture, implementation of strategic plans, team building, benchmarking and gap analysis, developing core competencies, manufacturer-distributor relations, distributor profitability, purchasing, negotiations, distributor's asset management, financial transactions of the wholesaler-distributor, improving distributor return on investment, distribution operations management, product line profitability, trends, high-tech marketing, strategic alliances, strategic planning, market. **Publications:** E-newsletter (3/year). **Educational Activities:** Certificate in Distribution Management program; Continuing education programs for distributors and manufacturers; Distributor Management Development Seminars.

START-UP INFORMATION

32188 ■ *How to Start a Home-Based Mail Order Business*
Pub: Globe Pequot Press
Ed: Georganne Fiumara. **Released:** January 2005.
Price: $17.95. **Description:** Step-by-step guide for starting and growing a home-based mail order business. Information about equipment, pricing, online marketing, are included along with worksheets and checklists for planning.

32189 ■ *"New Economy"* in *Inc.* (November 2000, pp. 37)
Pub: The Goldhirsh Group
Description: Profile of Dave Bell, a senior at Nashua High School, in Nashua, New Hampshire who is hard at work building his new company.

ASSOCIATIONS AND OTHER ORGANIZATIONS

32190 ■ Action for Enterprise
2009 N 14th St., Ste. 301
Arlington, VA 22201
Ph:(703)243-9172
Fax: (703)243-9123
Co. E-mail: info@actionforenterprise.org
URL: http://www.actionforenterprise.org
Contact: Frank Lusby, Exec. Dir./Founder
Description: Seeks to design and implement small enterprise development programs, based on a comprehensive analysis of business sectors and the interrelationships of enterprises that function with them. Initiates efforts to develop sustainable business development service providers at the local level.

32191 ■ American Woman's Economic Development Corporation
216 E 45th St., 10th Fl.
New York, NY 10017
Ph:(917)368-6100
Co. E-mail: info@awed.org
URL: http://www.awed.org
Contact: Roseanne Antonucci, Exec.Dir.
Description: Entrepreneurs and executives from the private sector. Seeks to help entrepreneurial women start and grow their own businesses. Provides formal course instruction, one-on-one business counseling, seminars, special events, and peer group support. Seeks to increase the start-up, survival and expansion rates of small businesses. Represents women from all socio-economic levels, including formerly employed women and women from low-income communities.
Publications: *AWED's in Business* (bimonthly).

32192 ■ Asia Pacific Foundation of Canada–Fondation Asie Pacifique du Canada
890 W Pender St., Ste. 220
Vancouver, BC, Canada V6C 1J9
Ph:(604)684-5986
Fax: (604)681-1370
Co. E-mail: info@asiapacific.ca
URL: http://www.asiapacific.ca
Contact: Mr. Yuen Pau Woo, Pres./Co-CEO
Purpose: Seeks to remove barriers to international trade between Canada and Asia. Conducts applied research and policy analysis for issues related to Canada-Asia relations. Maintains network of study and research centers; works to improve access to information on Asian cultures and trade within Canada. **Publications:** *Asia Pacific Papers* (periodic); *Canada Asia Review* (annual); *Country Backgrounders*; *Pacific Rim Profiles*.

32193 ■ Brazil-Canada Chamber of Commerce
438 University Ave., Ste. 1618
Box 60
Toronto, ON, Canada M5G 2K8
Ph:(416)364-3555
Fax: (416)595-8226
Co. E-mail: bccc@caie.ca
URL: http://www.ccacanada.com/bccc
Contact: Mary Anderson, Pres.
Membership: Canadian corporations doing business in Brazil. **Purpose:** Promotes increased trade between Canada and Brazil. Provides assistance to companies wishing to trade with Brazil. Represents members before international trade organizations and government agencies and lobbies for removal of statutory barriers to commerce.

32194 ■ British Canadian Chamber of Trade and Commerce–La Chambre de Commerce Canada - Grande Bretagne
PO Box 423
Beaconsfield, QC, Canada H9W 5T9
Ph:(514)841-6664
Fax: (514)630-0280
Co. E-mail: east@bcctc.ca
URL: http://www.bcctc.ca
Contact: Philip Gorick, Exec. Dir.
Membership: Canadian corporations doing business in the United Kingdom. **Purpose:** Promotes increased trade between Britain and Canada. Represents members' interests; lobbies for removal of statutory impediments to trade. **Publications:** *Connections* (quarterly).

32195 ■ Canada-Czech Republic Chamber of Commerce
909 Bay St., Ste. 1006
Toronto, ON, Canada M5S 3G2
Ph:(416)929-3432
Fax: (416)929-3432
Co. E-mail: trade@ccrcc.net
URL: http://www.ccrcc.net
Contact: Mr. Lubomir Novotny, Exec. Dir.
Membership: Businesses in Canada and the Czech Republic. **Purpose:** Promotes increased trade and investment between Canada and the Czech Republic. Promotes the Czech Republic as a gateway to Central and Eastern Europe, and Canada as a gateway to the North American Free Trade Agreement countries. Conducts educational programs.

32196 ■ Canada-Finland Chamber of Commerce
1200 Bay St., Ste. 604
Toronto, ON, Canada M5R 2A5
Ph:(416)964-7400
Fax: (416)921-0318
URL: http://www.finnishcanadian.com/cfcc
Contact: Tommi Korhonen, Pres.
Membership: Canadian and Finnish businesses.
Purpose: Promotes increased trade between Canada and Finland. Provides information, assistance, and services to Finnish and Canadian corporations wishing to participate in international trade.

32197 ■ Canada-India Business Council–Conseil de Commerce Canada-Inde
1 St. Clair Ave. E, Ste. 804
Toronto, ON, Canada M4T 2V7
Ph:(416)214-5947
Fax: (416)214-9081
Co. E-mail: info@canada-indiabusiness.ca
URL: http://www.canada-indiabusiness.ca
Contact: Kam Rathee, Pres./Exec. Dir.
Membership: Canadian businesses trading with India. **Purpose:** Promotes increased trade between Canada and India. Advocates for legislation conducive to trade; represents members before trade and industrial organizations and the public.

32198 ■ Canada-Pakistan Business Council
7825 Bayview Ave., Ste. 1311
Thornhill, ON, Canada L3T 7N2
Ph:(905)763-8281
Co. E-mail: cpbc@rogers.com
URL: http://www.cpbc.info
Contact: Anwar Merchant, Pres.
Membership: Businesses and service providers.
Purpose: Promotes increased trade between Canada and Pakistan. Facilitates mutual economic development through transfer of technology; encourages and assists in the formation of joint ventures involving Canadian and Pakistani companies. Conducts educational programs. **Publications:** *Canada Pakistan Bulletin* (quarterly).

32199 ■ Canada Taiwan Trade Association
300-5687 Yew St.
Vancouver, BC, Canada V6M 3Y2
Ph:(604)263-1021
Fax: (604)263-2737
Co. E-mail: ctta@uniserve.com
Contact: Garth Edgar, Pres.
Membership: Corporations and trade organizations.
Purpose: Promotes increased trade between Canada and Taiwan. Conducts research; serves as a clearinghouse on trade with and between Canada and Taiwan; lobbies for removal of statutory and regulatory barriers to trade.

32200 ■ Canadian Association of Importers and Exporters–Association canadienne des importateurs et expotateurs
438 University Ave., Ste. 1618
PO Box 60
Toronto, ON, Canada M5G 2K8
Ph:(416)595-5333

Fax: (416)595-8226
Co. E-mail: info@iecanada.com
URL: http://www.caie.ca
Contact: Mrs. Mary Anderson CITP, Pres.
Membership: Individuals and firms with an interest in Canada's international trade. **Purpose:** Promotes increased participation by Canada in the global economy; seeks to maintain a business climate conducive to increased international trade. Represents members' interests before government agencies; prepares model trade programs, regulations, and policies. Provides advice and assistance to members; serves as a clearinghouse on international trade. **Publications:** *I.E. Global* (semiannual); *ImportWeek* (weekly); *Tradeweek* (semimonthly); Membership Directory (annual).

32201 ■ Canadian Association of Regulated Importers–Association Canadienne des Importateurs Reglementes
2525 St. Laurent Blvd., Ste. 203
Ottawa, ON, Canada K1H 8P5
Ph:(613)738-1729
Fax: (613)733-9501
Co. E-mail: devalkc@magma.ca
URL: http://www.cariimport.org
Contact: Ian Hesketh, Chm.
Membership: Companies engaged in the importation of goods into Canada. **Purpose:** Promotes removal of international and domestic barriers to trade. Represents members before government agencies and international trade organizations.

32202 ■ Canadian Chamber of Commerce–Chambre de Commerce du Canada
350 Sparks St., Ste. 501
Delta Office Tower
Ottawa, ON, Canada K1R 7S8
Ph:(613)238-4000
Fax: (613)238-7643
Co. E-mail: info@chamber.ca
URL: http://www.chamber.ca
Contact: Nancy Hughes Anthony, Pres./CEO
Description: Businesses, business and trade promotion organizations, and individuals with an interest in promoting trade and commerce in Canada. Seeks to improve domestic business conditions and increase foreign trade. Facilitates communication among members; functions as liaison between members and government agencies and international business organizations. Gathers and disseminates business and trade information; compiles statistics.

32203 ■ Canadian Committee for Pacific Economic Cooperation–Comite National pour la Cooperation Economique avec la Region du Pacifique
890 W Pender St., Ste. 220
Vancouver, BC, Canada V6C 1J9
Ph:(604)684-5986
Fax: (604)681-1370
Co. E-mail: info@asiapacific.ca
URL: http://www.asiapacificbusiness.ca
Contact: Paul Irwin, Dir.
Membership: Representatives of Canadian businesses, government agencies, and trade organizations. **Purpose:** Promotes increased and more profitable participation by Canada in Asian and Pacific trade. Represents Canada's interests in the Pacific Economic Cooperation Council. **Publications:** *Canada Asia Review* (annual).

32204 ■ Canadian Council for Aboriginal Business–Le Conseil Canadien pour le Commerce Autochtone
Coach House, Main Fl.
204A St. George St.
Toronto, ON, Canada M5R 2N5
Ph:(416)961-8663
Fax: (416)961-3995
Co. E-mail: jsoulodre@ccab.com
URL: http://www.ccab.com
Contact: Jocelyne Soulodre, Pres./CEO
Description: Promotes the full participation of aboriginal people in the Canadian economy. Seeks to con-

nect aboriginal and non-aboriginal people and companies with the opportunities required to achieve personal and business success. Develops and operates the Progressive Aboriginal Relations (PAR) benchmarking and hallmarking program. Administers the Canadian Aboriginal Business Hall of Fame.

32205 ■ Canadian Council of Chief Executives–Conseil Canadien des Chefs d'Enterprise
99 Bank St., Ste. 1001
Ottawa, ON, Canada K1P 6B9
Ph:(613)238-3727
Fax: (613)236-8679
Co. E-mail: leaders@ceocouncil.ca
URL: http://www.ceocouncil.ca
Contact: Thomas d'Aquino, Pres./CEO
Membership: Businesses and trade organizations. **Purpose:** Promotes a healthy national economy. Conducts research; lobbies for legislation favorable to business; represents members' interests.

32206 ■ Canadian Council for International Business–Conseil Canadien pour le Commerce International
Delta Office Tower
350 Sparks St., Ste. 501
Ottawa, ON, Canada K1R 7S8
Ph:(613)230-5462
Fax: (613)230-7087
Co. E-mail: bkeyes@chamber.ca
URL: http://www.ccib.org
Contact: Robert J. Keyes, CEO/Pres.
Membership: Businesses engaged in international trade or operations. **Purpose:** Seeks to remove statutory and regulatory barriers to international commerce. Facilitates communication and cooperation among members; represents members' interests before industrial and trade organizations and government agencies. **Publications:** Annual Report (annual).

32207 ■ Canadian Federation of Independent Business–Federation Canadienne de l'Entreprise Independante
4141 Yonge St., Ste. 401
Willowdale, ON, Canada M2P 2A6
Ph:(416)222-8022
Fax: (416)222-7593
Co. E-mail: cfib@cfib.ca
URL: http://www.cfib.ca
Contact: Catherine Swift, Pres./CEO
Membership: Independent businesses. **Purpose:** Promotes economic well-being of members and seeks to maintain a healthy domestic business climate. Represents members' interests before government agencies, labor and industrial organizations, and the public.

32208 ■ Canadian German Chamber of Industry and Commerce–La Chambre Canadienne Allemande de l'Industrie et du Commerce
480 University Ave., Ste. 1410
Toronto, ON, Canada M5G 1V2
Ph:(416)598-3355
Fax: (416)598-1840
Co. E-mail: info@germanchamber.ca
URL: http://www.germanchamber.ca
Contact: Thomas Beck, Pres./CEO
Membership: Canadian and German corporations and trade and industrial organizations. **Purpose:** Promotes increased trade between Canada and Germany. Lobbies for removal of barriers to trade; represents the interests of business before government agencies, international trade organizations, and the public.
Publications: *Canadian German Trade* (bimonthly).

32209 ■ Canadian Labour Congress–Congres du travail du Canada
2841 Riverside Dr.
Ottawa, ON, Canada K1V 8X7
Ph:(613)521-3400
Fax: (613)521-4655
Co. E-mail: president@clc-ctc.ca
URL: http://www.clc-ctc.ca
Contact: Ken Georgetti, Pres.
Description: Works to ensure that all Canadians are able to find employment at fair wages, with union rep-

resentation and the right to collective bargaining, in a safe environment. Seeks to create a just and equitable society. Joins with other organizations for advocacy and action on behalf of working Canadians. Facilitates establishment of grass roots organizations. Conducts research and educational programs; maintains speakers' bureau; compiles statistics. **Publications:** *C.L.C. Fax-Press* (weekly); *Sweatshop Alert* (periodic); *UI Bulletin* (periodic).

32210 ■ Canadian Netherlands Business and Professional Association
PO Box 5073, Sta. A
Toronto, ON, Canada M5W 1N4
Ph:(416)537-1128
Fax: (416)537-8781
Co. E-mail: putnam@sympatico.ca
URL: http://www.cnbpa.ca
Contact: Kevin Putnam, Sec.
Membership: Business people and professionals in Canada and the Netherlands. **Purpose:** Promotes increased trade and communication between Canada and the Netherlands. Serves as a forum for the exchange of information among members.

32211 ■ Committee for Economic Development
2000 L St. NW, Ste. 700
Washington, DC 20036
Ph:(202)296-5860
Free: 800-676-7353
Fax: (202)223-0776
Co. E-mail: info@ced.org
URL: http://www.ced.org
Contact: Charles E.M. Kolb, Pres.
Description: Trustees are heads of major corporations or university presidents. Works with expert advisers. Conducts research and formulates policy recommendations on national and international economic issues, including education, trade policy, U.S.-Japan economic relations, and problems of the inner city. Seeks to contribute to full employment, higher living standards, and increased opportunities for all through its studies and reports; promote economic growth and stability; strengthen the concepts and institutions essential to progress in a free society. **Publications:** *Statements on National Policy*. **Telecommunication Services:** electronic mail, charles.kolb@ced.org.

32212 ■ Corporation for Enterprise Development
777 N Capital St. NE, Ste. 800
Washington, DC 20002
Ph:(202)408-9788
Fax: (202)408-9793
Co. E-mail: info-dc@cfed.org
URL: http://www.cfed.org
Contact: Andrea Levere, Pres.
Description: Provides assistance to public and private organizations concerned with increasing economic opportunity of individuals through the encouragement and support of enterprise development; serves as a forum for the exchange of ideas. Strives to research, develop, and disseminate entrepreneurial policy initiatives at the local, state, and federal levels. Conducts consulting services and compiles statistics. **Publications:** *Accountability Newsletter* (monthly); *Assets* (quarterly); *The Development Report Card for the States* (annual); *Effective State Policy and Practice* (quarterly). Also publishes books and monographs. **Telecommunication Services:** electronic mail, alevere@cfed.org.

32213 ■ Council of Development Finance Agencies
815 Superior Ave., Ste. 1301
Cleveland, OH 44114
Ph:(216)920-3073
Fax: (216)771-4938
Co. E-mail: info@cdfa.net
URL: http://www.cdfa.net
Contact: Toby Rittner, Exec.Dir.
Description: Works for the advancement of development finance concerns and interests. Represents the nation's leading and most knowledgeable members of the development finance community from the public, private and non-profit sectors. **Publications:** *CDFA Update* (monthly).

32214 ■ Dialogue on Diversity
1000 Connecticut Ave. NW, Ste. 600
Washington, DC 20036
Ph:(703)631-0650
Fax: (703)631-0617
Co. E-mail: dialog.div@prodigy.net
URL: http://www.dialogueondiversity.org
Contact: Ma. Cristina C. Caballero, Pres./CEO
Description: Promotes social and political advancement of women and men from diverse ethnic and national traditions; fosters increased economic empowerment; aims to promote and develop entrepreneurial excellence, technology, networking, and education.

32215 ■ Edmonton Chamber of Commerce/World Trade Center Edmonton
Ste. 700-9990, Jasper Ave.
Edmonton, AB, Canada T5J 1P7
Ph:(780)426-4620
Fax: (780)424-7946
Co. E-mail: info@edmontonchamber.com
URL: http://www.edmontonchamber.com
Contact: Ms. Kimberly Nishikaze, Communications Mgr.
Description: Serves as the official voice of business in the Edmonton area. Provides networking opportunities via special events held during the year. Provides discount and affinity programs, business referrals and business resources. Owns and operates the World Trade Center Edmonton (WTCE), which is a member of the World Trade Centers Organization, a network of 300 centers in almost 100 countries worldwide. Assists businesses, professionals, and interested individuals in developing national and international trade by providing information and advice on new markets and products. Organizes trade missions to World Trade Centers and facilitates contact with government agencies. Offers research and information gathering on trade opportunities, educational programs, and consumer and business assistance. **Publications:** *Commerce News* (monthly); *Edmonton Commerce Directory* (annual).

32216 ■ International Economic Development Council
734 15th St. NW, Ste. 900
Washington, DC 20005
Ph:(202)223-7800
Fax: (202)223-4745
Co. E-mail: jfinkle@iedconline.org
URL: http://www.iedconline.org
Contact: Jeff Finkle, Pres./CEO
Description: Works to help economic development professionals improve the quality of life in their communities. Represents all levels of government, academia, and private industry; provides a broad range of member services including research, advisory services, conferences, professional certification, professional development, publications, legislative tracking and more. **Publications:** *Annual Federal Review and Budget Overview* (annual); *Economic Development Journal* (quarterly); *Economic Development Now* (bimonthly); *Federal Review* (annual).

32217 ■ International Finance Corporation
2121 Pennsylvania Ave. NW
Washington, DC 20433
Ph:(202)473-1000
Fax: (202)974-4384
Co. E-mail: webmaster@ifc.org
URL: http://www.ifc.org
Contact: Lars Thunell, Exec. VP
Description: Promotes sustainable private sector investments in developing countries, as a way to reduce poverty and improve people's lives.

32218 ■ National Association of Development Organizations Research Foundation
400 N Capitol St. NW, Ste. 390
Washington, DC 20001
Ph:(202)624-7806
Fax: (202)624-8813
Co. E-mail: info@nado.org
URL: http://www.nado.org
Contact: Laurie Thompson, Dir. of Programs

Description: Identifies, studies and promotes regional solutions and approaches to improving local prosperity and services through the nationwide network of regional development organizations. Shares best practices and offer professional development training, analyzes the impact of federal policies and programs on regional development organizations, and examines the latest developments and trends in small metro and rural America. Provides federal advocacy, informative research, special reports and training to the nation's rural regional development organizations.

32219 ■ National Development Council
708 Third Ave., Ste. 710
New York, NY 10017
Ph:(212)682-1106
Fax: (212)573-6118
Co. E-mail: training@nationaldevelopmentcouncil.org
URL: http://www.nationaldevelopmentcouncil.org
Contact: Robert W. Davenport, Pres.
Description: Brings innovative economic development financing programs to urban and rural communities interested in local business and industrial growth, commercial revitalization, and permanent job creation. Finances professionals' work with cities, counties, and states to: build permanent systems for developing financing; train local staff; structure and negotiate financing for development projects, local business development, and industrial expansion. Conducts intensive training program for economic development professionals with courses in business credit analysis, real estate financing, loan packaging, federal financing, and program management and implementation; has provided advice to Congress and federal agencies that has helped create lending programs for job creation and small business investment; has initiated and managed presidential programs for Presidents Nixon, Ford, Carter, and Reagan. **Publications:** *Developments Newsletter* (quarterly).

32220 ■ National Economic Development and Law Center
2201 Broadway, Ste. 815
Oakland, CA 94612
Ph:(510)251-2600
Fax: (510)251-0600
Co. E-mail: roger@nedlc.org
URL: http://www.nedlc.org
Contact: Roger A. Clay Jr., Pres.
Description: Offers assistance to Community Development Corporations (CDCs), other community organizations, state and local governments, co-ops, and legal services attorneys working in the field of economic development. Provides counseling and representation in connection with: establishment and financing of activities; business, corporate, and commercial transactions; tax exemptions; security offerings; comprehensive planning assistance related to economic and community development. Seeks to create a uniform and comprehensive community economic development policy through continuing planning assistance and training and legal education, with special emphasis on integrating development of business, jobs, health care, and housing interests. Acts as liaison in counseling research and representation; recommends administrative, legal, and legislative solutions on economic development issues to federal agencies, and state and local governments and agencies. Sponsors seminars and workshops on legal and tax issues. **Publications:** *Economic Development Law Center Report* (quarterly).

32221 ■ Pacific Basin Economic Council - Canadian Committee
890 W Pender St., Ste. 220
Vancouver, BC, Canada V6C 1J9
Ph:(604)684-5986
Fax: (604)681-1370
Co. E-mail: info@asiapacific.ca
URL: http://www.asiapacific.ca
Contact: Paul Irwin, Dir.
Membership: Canadian corporations. **Purpose:** Promotes increased trade between the countries bordering the Pacific Ocean. Gathers and disseminates information on international trade issues. **Publications:** *PBEC Report* (periodic).

32222 ■ Sustainable Development Technology Canada–Technologies du Developpement Durable du Canada
45 O'Connor St., Ste. 1850
Ottawa, ON, Canada K1P 1A4
Ph:(613)234-6313
Fax: (613)234-0303
Co. E-mail: info@sdtc.ca
URL: http://www.sdtc.ca
Contact: Vicky J. Sharpe, Pres./CEO
Description: Seeks to promote a sustainable development technology infrastructure in Canada. **Publications:** Annual Report (annual).

32223 ■ Swedish-Canadian Chamber of Commerce
2 Bloor St. W, Ste. 504
Toronto, ON, Canada M4W 3E2
Ph:(416)925-8661
Fax: (416)929-8639
Co. E-mail: mglindmark@sccc.ca
URL: http://www.sccc.ca
Contact: Monika G. Lindmark, Exec. Dir.
Description: Facilitates business and cultural development between Sweden and Canada. Provides knowledge about both countries and promotes trade and business opportunities. Serves as a forum allowing Swedes and Canadians with mutual interests to connect at various levels, affords members' business and finds cultural and social opportunities. **Publications:** Directory (periodic).

32224 ■ USA Engage
1625 K St. NW
Washington, DC 20006
Ph:(202)464-2025
Co. E-mail: jcolvin@nftc.org
URL: http://www.usaengage.org
Contact: Jake Colvin, Dir.
Description: Promotes economic strength in America as integral to the nation's security and worldwide leadership.

32225 ■ World Trade Centre Montreal
380 St. Antoine St. W, Ste. 6000
Montreal, QC, Canada H2Y 3X7
Ph:(514)871-4002
Free: 877-590-4040
Fax: (514)849-3813
Co. E-mail: wtcmontreal@ccmm.qc.ca
URL: http://www.wtcmontreal.com
Contact: Jack Chadirdjian, Dir.
Description: Businesses, professionals, and interested individuals. Seeks to foster the export of products and services by supporting, training and advising companies, associations and economic development institutions and organizations on certain activities on international markets through an integrated programme of export solutions.

32226 ■ World Trade Centre Vancouver
Vancouver Bd. of Trade
999 Canada Pl., Ste. 400
Vancouver, BC, Canada V6C 3E1
Ph:(604)681-2111
Fax: (604)681-0437
Co. E-mail: contactus@boardoftrade.com
URL: http://www.boardoftrade.com
Contact: Mr. Blair Qualey, Exec. Dir.
Description: Businesses, professionals, and interested individuals. Facilitates the development of national and international trade by providing traders and investors with information and advice on new markets and products. Organizes trade missions to World Trade Centers and facilitates contact with government agencies. Offers research and information gathering on trade opportunities, educational programs, and consumer and business assistance. **Publications:** *Sounding Board* (monthly).

32227 ■ World Trade and Convention Centre Halifax
1800 Argyle St.
PO Box 955
Halifax, NS, Canada B3J 2V9
Ph:(902)421-1302
Fax: (902)422-2922

Co. E-mail: pcody@wtcchmc.com
URL: http://www.wtcchalifax.com
Contact: Paul Cody
Description: Businesses, professionals, and interested individuals. Facilitates the development of national and international trade by providing traders and investors with information and advice on new markets and products. Organizes trade missions to World Trade Centers and facilitates contact with government agencies. Offers services such as: research and information gathering on trade opportunities, educational programs, and consumer and business assistance.

DIRECTORIES OF EDUCATIONAL PROGRAMS

32228 ■ *City Government Economic Program Administration Directory*
Pub: infoUSA Inc.
Released: Annual. **Entries Include:** Name, address, phone (including area code), size of advertisement, year first in "Yellow Pages," name of owner or manager, number of employees. Compiled from telephone company "Yellow Pages," nationwide.

32229 ■ *Industrial Property Directory*
Pub: infoUSA Inc.
Released: Annual. **Entries Include:** Name, address, phone (including area code), size of advertisement, year first in "Yellow Pages," name of owner or manager, number of employees. Compiled from telephone company "Yellow Pages," nationwide.

REFERENCE WORKS

32230 ■ "3Q a good one for local firms, if you ignore auto industry" in *Crain's Detroit Business* (Vol. 22, November 13, 2006, No. 46, pp. 3)
Pub: Crain Communications Inc. - Detroit
Ed: Tom Henderson **Description:** Although the difficulties of the auto industry dominate the news, non-automotive businesses are doing very well with double digit growth. Michigan still lags the S & P because of the size of the auto industry and the depth of the associated troubles.

32231 ■ "8 Detroit Projects Get More Than $170M in Tax Breaks" in *Crain's Detroit Business* (Vol. 23, January 8, 2007, No. 2, pp. 10)
Pub: Crain Communications Inc. - Detroit
Ed: Robert Ankeny. **Description:** Brownfield state tax credits and state and local tax capture involve $839M in private investment and creation of 1,320 jobs.

32232 ■ "About this report" in *Crain's Detroit Business* (Vol. 19, No. 17, April 28, 2003, pp. 14)
Pub: Crain Communications Inc., Detroit
Description: Crain's Business Detroit sent surveys to six leadership organizations' alumni in the State of Michigan, including Leadership Detroit, Leadership Oakland, Leadership Macomb, Leadership Ann Arbor, the Detroit Orientation Institute at Wayne State University and Leadership Windsor/Essex.

32233 ■ "Abraham Lincoln and the Global Economy" in *Harvard Business Review* (Vol. 81, No. 8, August 2003, pp. 58)
Pub: Harvard Business School Press
Ed: Robert D. Hormats. **Description:** Ways the economic developments during the early 1800s helped the U.S. develop a national economy, and might be a possible blueprint for globalization.

32234 ■ "Account Balances Indicate That 401(k) Participants Have Heard The Long-Term Investor Message" in *Employee Benefit Plan Review* (Vol. 55)
Pub: Charles D. Spencer & Associates, Inc.
Ed: Sue Burzawa. **Description:** Lincolnshire, Illinois-based Hewitt Associates LLC, the health benefit plan consulting company, tracks pension fund activity through its 401(k) Index. Industry analysts said that institutional investors are remaining calm as the country suffers from a period of economic upheaval.

32235 ■ "Affluence in Two Cultures" in *Hispanic Business* (December 2003, pp. 30, 32)
Pub: Hispanic Business
Description: English language skills lead to higher income and net worth for American Hispanics. Statistical data included showing income and occupation by language dominance, and more.

32236 ■ "After a Bumpy Period, Local Industry Seems to Be Soaring" in *Ledger* (February 20, 2005)
Pub: Knight-Ridder/Tribune Business News
Ed: Mary Toothman. **Description:** Polk County hotels, restaurants and tourist attractions are reporting an increase in tourism.

32237 ■ "The Age of Disruption" in *Fast Company* (September 2001, pp. 18)
Pub: Fast Company
Description: The ways business and economics are changing are discussed by Harvard's Juan Enriquez, author of the book "As the Future Catches You: How Genomics and Other Forces Are Changing Your Life, Work, Health, and Wealth."

32238 ■ "Agendas Cross in SHCC Boardroom" in *Hispanic Business* (March 2002, pp. 56-58)
Pub: Hispanic Business
Ed: Joel Russell. **Description:** Information regarding the U.S. Hispanic Chamber of Commerce's election of a new chairman is discussed, as well as economic issues.

32239 ■ "AIG Plans to Cut 27 Jobs at Neptune, N.J., Offices" in *The Record* (November 8, 2005)
Pub: New Jersey Media Group
Ed: Dennis P. Carmody. **Description:** AIG American General will cut a total of 250 employees from its group benefits workforce over the next 18 months. The group benefits division administers health insurance plans sponsored by employers.

32240 ■ "Airline Slump Hurts Houston-Based Maker of Tow Tractors" in *Houston Chronicle* (April 11, 2003)
Pub: Knight-Ridder/Tribune Business News
Description: Houston manufacturer, Steward & Stevenson Services, reported a revision in its fourth-quarter earnings report due to the slump in airline travel. The company makes airline-equipment such as tractors that push out and tow aircraft.

32241 ■ "Airport Industrial Sites in Demand" in *Milwaukee Journal Sentinel* (December 19, 2005)
Pub: Journal Sentinel, Inc.
Ed: Tom Daykin. **Description:** Several light large industrial buildings are being developed near Mitchell International Airport. New interest in such space used for storing and distributing products, as well as manufacturers, holds hope for the economy.

32242 ■ "Allsbrook Predicts Economic Pickup in Months Ahead" in *Birmingham Business Journal* (Vol. 20, No. 33, August 15, 2003, pp. 6)
Pub: American City Business Journals, Inc.
Ed: Leslie Zganjar. **Description:** Bob Allsbrook of AmSouth Bancorp shares his economic forecast, focusing on economic conditions, interest rates, and recessions.

32243 ■ "The 'Always On' Economy" in *Inc.* (Volume 27, June 2005, No. 6, pp. 59-60)
Pub: Inc. Magazine
Ed: David H. Freedman. **Description:** New communications systems are able to keep companies in contact with employees and customers 24/7.

32244 ■ "Amex Says MBNA Card Spending is 7 Percent Above Plan" in *American Banker* (Vol. 170, February 4, 2005, No. 24, pp. 5)
Pub: Thomson Financial Media Inc.
Ed: Isabelle Lindenmayer. **Description:** American Express Company reports 7 percent better than expected transactions on its new MBNA American Express card.

32245 ■ "Anadarko Laying Off 400 Workers to Cut Costs" in *Houston Business Journal* (Vol. 34, No. 13, August 8, 2003, pp. 3)
Pub: American City Business Journals
Description: Anadarko Petroleum announced it will layoff 400 employees; topics include cost control programs, debt management, and business losses.

32246 ■ "Anadarko Seeks Bidders for Possible Buyout" in *Houston Business Journal* (Vol. 34, No. 14, August 15, 2003, pp. 3)
Pub: American City Business Journals
Description: Anadarko Petroleum to pursue opportunities to be acquired by a larger company. Topics include business losses, economic conditions and the implementation of cost control measures.

32247 ■ "Analysts Mixed on WNY Economy" in *Business First Buffalo* (Vol. 19, No. 44, July 25, 2003, pp. 1)
Pub: American City Business Journals, Inc.
Ed: Tom Hartley. **Description:** Industry analysts report that economic conditions in western New York remain flat, but are showing some signs of economic revival with stronger financial performance at M and T Bank. The bank reported a 4.4 percent increase in commercial and industrial lending.

32248 ■ "Andrew Lo" in *Business Week* (February 20, 2006, No. 3972, pp. 22)
Pub: McGraw-Hill Companies
Ed: Christopher Farrell. **Description:** Andrew W. Lo, a finance professor at Massachusetts Institute of Technology, along with a group of economists are conducting research in the neurosciences and cognitive psychology to better understand how investors make financial decisions.

32249 ■ "Another Wave of HQ Job Cuts at Sears" in *Crain's Chicago Business* (Vol. 26, No. 50, December 15, 2003, pp. 1)
Pub: Crain Communications, Inc.
Ed: Sandra Jones. **Description:** Sears, Roebuck and Company employed 5,300 workers at its Hoffman Estates headquarters in Illinois at the first of 2003, and the staff was cut to 4,800 by December, with further cuts predicted. After Sears sold its 94-year-old credit card division, the company's stores could not generate enough income to make up for the loss of credit card profits. Statistical data included.

32250 ■ "Anti-Recession Strategies" in *Small Business Opportunities* (Vol. 14, No. 1, January 2002, pp. 10)
Pub: Harris Publications, Inc.
Ed: Jerry Buchs. **Description:** Recession-proof business strategies to help small businesses cope during an economic downturn are presented.

32251 ■ "Apple, Goodyear Each Climb 4.9 Percent" in *Wall Street Journal* (Vol. 248, December 2006, No. 153, pp. B3)
Pub: Dow Jones & Co. Inc.
Ed: Anjali Cordeiro **Description:** With the Dow Jones averages at a steady decline, Apple Computers and Goodyear Tire and Rubber put up their best performances in over three years. This will have a positive impact on their perspective suppliers and subsidiaries

32252 ■ "As economy softens, firms trimming travel budgets" in *Atlanta Business Chronicle* (Vol. 24, No. 8, July 27, 2001, pp. NA)
Pub: American City Business Journals Inc.
Ed: Leslie Williams Johnson. **Description:** Companies are reducing the numbers and costs of business trips in an effort to deal with the sagging economy. CEOs are staying in less expensive hotels, business travel accounts are scrutinized for waste, and only the most necessary of trips are taken. Business travelers are searching the Internet for frugal travel opportunities, such as taking cheaper flights that may involve a layover in other cities, rather than taking a more expensive direct flight.

32253 ■ "At Senate Finance, membership has its privilege" in *Tax Notes* (Vol. 96, No. 14, September 30, 2002, pp. 1802-1806)
Pub: Tax Notes International
Ed: Martin A. Sullivan. Description: Members of the Senate Finance Committee are working on the draft Small Business and Farm Economic Recovery Act of 2002. The bill proposes tax breaks for economic sectors that already have a relatively light tax burden. It also contains many special provisions which would be politically beneficial to various members of the committee.

32254 ■ "At Top Speed" in *Hispanic Business* (July/August 2004, pp. 26)
Pub: Hispanic Business
Description: Hispanic-owned companies grew at the same rate as the U.S. economy in 2004; statistical composites of the top 100 Hispanic companies picked by Hispanic Business, along with company performance by industry are highlighted.

32255 ■ "Atlanta Slips a Notch as Retailers Shop Elsewhere" in *Atlanta Business Chronicle* (Vol. 26, No. 14, September 12, 2003, pp. 5A)
Pub: American City Business Publications, Inc.
Ed: Lisa R. Schoolcraft. Description: The Atlanta, Georgia area has declined as a location for new retail development projects. Industry analysts at North American Properties state that shopping center developers are concerned about the region's lagging economic conditions.

32256 ■ "Automaker-Union Talks Critical to State" in *Crain's Detroit Business* (Vol. 22, November 27, 2006, No. 48, pp. 8)
Pub: Crain Communications Inc. - Detroit
Description: Critical business issue in 2007 for the State of Michigan will be the auto contract talks between the UAW and the Big 3 US automakers. Not only will the results affect the companies themselves, but all the other manufacturers in the region and the ability to draw new manufacturers into the State.

32257 ■ "Back to Business as Usual" in *Atlanta Business Chronicle* (Vol. 26, No. 10, August 15, 2003, pp. 1)
Pub: American City Business Publications, Inc.
Ed: Jim Lovel. Description: The results of a recent economic survey by SunTrust Banks Inc. of the greater Atlanta, Georgia region are presented. Topics include interest rates, unemployment, and real estate sales.

32258 ■ "Back to Technology" in *Black Enterprise* (Vol. 34, No. 6, January 2004)
Pub: Earl Graves Publishing Co.
Ed: Nicole Lewis. Description: Patrick Lyons, associate portfolio manager at NCM Capital Management Group in Durham, North Carolina is predicting a come back for the technology sector. He also expects a 4-5 percent growth in the economy over the next four quarters.

32259 ■ "Back to Technology: Patrick Lyons of NCM Capital Management Says a Tech Binge is Likely" in *Black Enterprise* (Vol. 34, January 2004)
Pub: Earl Graves Publishing Co.
Ed: Nicole Lewis. Description: Patrick Lyons, associate portfolio manager at NCM Capital Management Group in Durham, North Carolina is predicting a come back for the technology sector. He also expects a 4-5 percent growth in the economy over the next four quarters.

32260 ■ "Backing Mike's Pro-Biz Tax Plan" in *Crain's New York Business* (Vol. 23, January 22, 2007, No. 4, pp. 12)
Pub: Crain Communications, Inc.
Ed: Description: New York's Mayor Bloomberg wants to revamp the unincorporated business tax which would help S corporations, since these companies must report profits as income on their personal tax forms, they are effectively taxed twice. Small Companies would benefit from a new credit which would

partially offset that burden. He also wants to eliminate the city's 4 percent sales tax on footwear and clothing purchases to boost the city's economy and would help compete with New Jersey.

32261 ■ "Bank Stock Binge" in *Black Enterprise* (Vol. 35, January 2005, No. 6, pp. 34)
Pub: Earl G. Graves Publishing Co. Inc.
Ed: Nicole Lewis. Description: Bank analyst, Fred Cummings, discusses which banks are likely to survive the current economic conditions affecting the industry. Recent economic and business trends have created an environment for bank mergers and acquisitions in the Midwest, according to Cummings.

32262 ■ "Banker Boosts Community" in *Crain's New York Business* (Vol. 23, January 29, 2007, No. 5, pp. F14)
Pub: Crain Communications, Inc.
Ed: Tom Fredrickson. Description: Profile of Maurice L. Coleman, New York Market Executive for Bank of America. Under his leadership, Bank of America is becoming a major player in community development in New York City, specifically targeting affordable housing and small businesses in low-income areas. Statistical data included.

32263 ■ "Bankruptcies" in *Crain's Detroit Business* (Vol. 18, No. 24, 2002, pp. 6)
Pub: Crain Communications Inc. - Detroit
Description: A listing of local businesses filing for Chapter 7 or 11 protection in the U.S. Bankruptcy Court in Detroit is presented.

32264 ■ "Bankruptcy filings grow. Ohio stats among leaders" in *Business First Columbus* (Vol. 18, No. 40, May 24, 2002, pp. A1)
Pub: Business First Columbus, Inc.
Ed: Kathy Hoke. Description: Ohio consumers are filing personal bankruptcies at rates that exceed most of the U.S. Reasons given include personal illness, divorce, and job loss. In the Columbus area, bankruptcies have increased by 20 percent.

32265 ■ "Banks' distressed loans are on the rise" in *Atlanta Business Chronicle* (Vol. 24, No. 9, August 3, 2001, pp. 3A)
Pub: American City Business Journals Inc.
Ed: Meredith Jordan. Description: Across the nation, large banks are noticing an increase in non-performing loans. From the first quarter of 2000 to the first quarter of 2001, Bank of America, the largest bank in Georgia, has recorded an increase of non-performing loans of 61.4 percent. Non-performing loans are hose that demonstrate signs of negativity that could indicate a strong chance they will not be re-paid in the future.

32266 ■ "Banners Tout Development" in *Mississippi Business Journal* (Vol. 29, January 2007, No. 4, pp. 11)
Pub: Venture Publications, Inc.
Ed: Wally Northway Description: Flashy banners have been erected all over downtown Jackson's business district. The banner idea, originated by a local restaurateur, is designed to bring visual attention to many unnoticed development projects and businesses in the area.

32267 ■ "Bargain Season Begins" in *Hispanic Business* (Vol. 24, No. 4, April 2002, pp. 62)
Pub: Hispanic Business Inc.
Ed: Barbara Beckley. Description: As the airline industry recovers, it will take initiative and patience to find special promotions that will make business travel, as well as vacation travel, less expensive.

32268 ■ "B.E. teams up with CNNfn" in *Black Enterprise* (Vol. 33, No. 6, January 2003, pp. 10)
Pub: Earl Graves Publishing Co.
Description: Blackenterprise.com and CNNfn have partnered to bring "The Economic Divide in America" online. The series reports on race, gender, education, and housing, as well as factors affecting an individual's ability to build wealth.

32269 ■ "Beating Burnout" in *Sales and Marketing.com* (Vol. 153, No. 3, March 2004, pp. 47)
Pub: VNU eMedia, Inc.
Ed: Julia Chang. Description: According to a survey conducted by ComPsych Corporation, located in Chicago, Illinois, 63 percent of employees expect high stress levels in the second half of 2003.

32270 ■ "Beating the Odds" in *Success* (Vol. 47, No. 3, July 2000, pp. 28)
Pub: Success Publishing, Inc.
Ed: Joan Szabo. Description: Alan Greenspan has achieved an important distinction in his 13-year tenure as chairman of the Federal Reserve Board. Under his leadership, the United States has enjoyed the longest economic expansion in its history.

32271 ■ *Best of Both Worlds: Winning Government Funding for Commercial Product Development under the Small Business Innovation Research Program*
Pub: Sphinx Technologies, Inc.
Ed: John H. Sangster. Released: 1994. Price: $64.95; $49.95 (paper).

32272 ■ *Best Practice in Development of Entrepreneurship and SMEs in Countries in Transition: The Belarusian Experience*
Pub: United Nations Publications
Ed: United Nations, Economic Commission for Europe Staff. Released: January 2005. Price: $22.00. Description: Compilation of papers presented at the Forum on Best Practice in the Development of Entrepreneurship and Small and Medium-sized Enterprises (SMEs) in Countries in Transition: The Belarussian Experience, a forum organized by the United Nations Economic Commission for Europe. The book helps to assist Belarus with transitioning to a market economy.

32273 ■ "The Best Sunset Provision Ever" in *Inc.* (October 2005, pp. 34)
Pub: Inc. Magazine
Ed: Lora Kolodny. Description: It is expected that all companies, regardless of size and industry, will benefit from the new Energy Act that extends daylight-savings time by four weeks, beginning March 2007. The Journal of Banking and Finance reports daylight-savings time will promote a healthier economy and higher stock market returns because exposure to full-spectrum light early in the day improves mood and concentration of employees.

32274 ■ "Better Luck Next Year?" in *Black Enterprise* (Vol. 32, No. 8, March 2002, pp. 33)
Pub: Earl Graves Publishing Co.
Ed: Alan Hughes. Description: According to the National Bureau of Economic Research, consumer psychology is key to the timing of an economic recovery. Forecasts are predicted for the four quarters of 2002 and beyond.

32275 ■ "The Big Bang: How Franchising Became an Economic Powerhouse the World Over" in *Entrepreneur* (Vol. 32, No. 1, January 2004, pp. 86)
Pub: Entrepreneur Media, Inc.
Ed: David J. Kaufmann. Description: David J. Kaufmann offers a perspective on the ways franchising has change the economy and opportunity for entrepreneurs during the last 25 years.

32276 ■ "Big Religious Meetings Hold Promise of Big Payoffs for Local Economy" in *Crain's Detroit Business* (Vol. 22, February 13, 2006, No. 7)
Pub: Crain Communications Inc. - Detroit
Ed: Anjali Fluker. Description: Progressive National Baptist Convention and the National Baptist Convention USA Inc., are among the big events scheduled for the City of Detroit in the next few years. These religious conventions are expected to boost the economy of Southeast Michigan.

32277 ■ **"Big Success Can Start With a Few Steps"** in *Mississippi Business Journal* (Vol. 29, January 2007, No. 4, pp. 5)
Pub: Venture Publications, Inc.
Ed: Phil Hardwick. **Description:** "ABC Volume One", published by the Boomtown Institute, is a new successful manual for many people in the world of economic and community development in small towns. Best used as a discussion guide in community development organizations, it is an offspring of Jack Schultz' "Boomtown USA- The 7-1/2 Keys to Big Success in Small Towns".

32278 ■ **"Bio-Layoffs Cool Once-Booking Job Market"** in *Boston Business Journal* (Vol. 23, No. 21, June 27, 2003, pp. 1)
Pub: American City Business Journals
Ed: Allison Connolly. **Description:** Massachusetts' biotechnology industry has suffered 1,000 job losses in the past six months. Though expectations are that the industry will play a significant role in improving the state's economy, experts predict that in the short-term, the industry will continue to decline.

32279 ■ **"Blip in auto sales could spell doom for suppliers"** in *Crain's Detroit Business* (Vol. 19, No. 3, January 20, 2003, pp. 1)
Pub: Crain Communications Inc., Detroit
Ed: Amy Wilson. **Description:** Analysts predict a drop in new car sales by 1 million or more vehicles in 2003, resulting in the loss of nearly 6 percent of parts suppliers, with some of the industry's larger suppliers among those businesses failing.

32280 ■ **"Blown Away By Katrina"** in *Black Enterprise* (Vol. 36, November 2005, No. 4, pp. 148)
Pub: Earl G. Graves Publishing Co. Inc.
Ed: Alan Hughes. **Description:** More than 60,000 African American businesses were destroyed by Hurricane Katrina. Rebuilding costs are estimated to reach at least $100 billion and jobs could be created and Black entrepreneurs in construction and other sectors could benefit.

32281 ■ **"A Brand to Unify the Region"** in *Milwaukee Journal Sentinel* (December 15, 2005)
Pub: Journal Sentinel, Inc.
Ed: Rick Romell. **Description:** Newly formed Milwaukee Regional Economic Development Council has designated the seven area counties as "Milwaukee 7" in order to unite the communities into an economic unit that will attract and retain business growth in the region.

32282 ■ **"Bright Signs for 2004"** in *My Business* (February/March 2004, pp. 44)
Pub: My Business Magazine
Ed: Bill Dunkelberg. **Description:** The National Federation of Independent Business' (NFIBs) Small Business Optimism Index reached its highest levels in third and fourth quarters of 2003. Real output in the economy grew at an 8 percent annual rate in third quarter, attributed to child tax credits that were probably spent in that quarter.

32283 ■ **"Bring the New Economy Home"** in *Home Office Computing* (Vol. 18, No. 12, December 2000, pp. 66)
Pub: Scholastic Inc.
Ed: William Van Winkle. **Description:** A guide to so-called New Economy concepts that can benefit a small business is presented. Small and home-based firms can seldom afford in-house expert help, and outsourcing is a viable option for a variety of business processors. Experts recommend that companies outsource to providers with other clients in the same line of business.

32284 ■ **"Buckle up"** in *Atlanta Business Chronicle* (Vol. 23, No. 30, December 29, 2000, pp. 27A)
Pub: American City Business Journals Inc.
Ed: Chaundra Frierson. **Description:** Economic forecasts and trends in consumer spending show that the economy is approaching a slowdown which will test newer businesses. Some strategies in order to survive tough times include using a conservative budget and keeping inventories low.

32285 ■ **"Builder Bandits"** in *Tampa Tribune* (December 12, 2005)
Pub: Media General, Inc.
Ed: Shannon Behnken. **Description:** Florida's booming economy and hurricane damage has forced building trade subcontractors to compete over workers by raising hourly wages by $3-$5.

32286 ■ **"Building vital region requires teamwork"** in *Crain's Detroit Business* (Vol. 19, No. 17, April 28, 2003, pp. 9)
Pub: Crain Communications Inc., Detroit
Ed: Richard Rassel. **Description:** The necessary upgrades needed to establish the Detroit region as a competitive economic region are discussed, including the importance for lawmakers to work together for a common goal.

32287 ■ **"The Bulls are Back"** in *My Business* (June/July 2004, pp. 13)
Pub: My Business Magazine
Description: Privately held companies are predicting increased value and planning more mergers and acquisitions in the growing economy.

32288 ■ **"Bumpy Ride"** in *Hispanic Business* (October 2006, pp. 24, 26)
Pub: Hispanic Business
Ed: Juan Solana. **Description:** Rising gas prices are expected to slow the U.S. economy even further; the housing market continues to fall. Statistical data included.

32289 ■ **"Bush talks up small business tax relief"** in *Tax Notes* (Vol. 97, No. 9, December 2, 2002, pp. 1135-1136)
Pub: Tax Notes International
Ed: Patti Mohr. **Description:** President George W. Bush urged lawmakers to lessen the tax burden on small businesses and make the relevant regulations simpler. Bush said that tax cuts would boost the economy and add more jobs.

32290 ■ **"The Business of Base Closures"** in *Inc.* (September 2005, pp. 34)
Pub: Inc. Magazine
Description: Economic impact of the Pentagon's announcement to close as many as 150 military bases across the country is examined.

32291 ■ **"Business Bookshelf"** in *Small Business Opportunities* (Vol. 16, No. 1, January 2004, pp. 126)
Pub: Harris Publications, Inc.
Description: Reviews of the books, "Beans: Four Principles For Running a Business In Good Times or Bad", by Leslie A. Yerkes and Charles Decker; and "Business Lessons with Sharkmaster, Jr.", by Randy Clay.

32292 ■ **"Business Groups Divided Over Cuts to MEDC Funding"** in *Crain's Detroit Business* (Vol. 19, No. 17, April 28, 2003, pp. 6)
Pub: Crain Communications Inc., Detroit
Description: The Michigan Manufacturers Association, the Detroit Regional Chamber and eight other local chambers have formed a new coalition to urge lawmakers to not go beyond Governor Granholm's recommended reductions in the budget of the Michigan Economic Development Corporation because it would damage the state's ability to compete for business investments and jobs.

32293 ■ **"Business Owners Frown on Economic Ills"** in *Pittsburgh Business Times* (Vol. 22, No. 4, August 16, 2002, pp. 3)
Pub: Pittsburgh Business Times
Ed: Kent Bernhard, Jr. **Description:** A new survey on small businesses, which was conducted by American City Business Journal, has found that the national economic downturn is influencing expansion planning.

32294 ■ **"The Business Week"** in *Business Week* (December 19, 2005, No. 3964, pp. 28-29)
Pub: McGraw-Hill Companies
Ed: Harry Maurer. **Description:** Stocks, tax reform, a weak Japanese economy, wages, international investment, and airplane orders are among issues discussed.

32295 ■ **"Businesses Have Faith in the Economy's Resiliency"** in *Kiplinger Letter* (Vol. 78, January 5, 2007, No. 1)
Pub: Kiplinger
Description: Businesses added an additional 167,000 workers in December 2006, and unemployment at a low 4.5 percent. The Federal Reserve is expected to keep interest rates steady most of 2007.

32296 ■ **"Businesses push better public transit"** in *Crain's Detroit Business* (Vol. 19, No. 17, April 28, 2003, pp. 18)
Pub: Crain Communications Inc., Detroit
Ed: Terry Kosdrosky. **Description:** Detroit area businesses are pushing for legislation to establish an authority to oversee the Detroit and suburban bus systems.

32297 ■ **"Businesses Warn State: Don't Hurt Economy to Fix Budget"** in *Crain's Detroit Business* (Vol. 19, No. 42, October 20, 2003, pp. 29)
Pub: Crain Communications Inc., Detroit
Ed: Amy Lane. **Description:** Business officials are warning Michigan's governor that any new or increased taxes or fees could increase job losses in the state.

32298 ■ **"By the Numbers: Hopes are pinned on a second-half recovery"** in *Red Herring* (No. 99, June 15 & July 1, 2001, pp. 136)
Pub: Herring Communications
Ed: J.P. Vicente. **Description:** An overview of the current economic conditions, including charts and graphs, showing top gainers and losers.

32299 ■ **"California Job Growth Slows"** in *Sacramento Bee* (November 19, 2005)
Pub: The Sacramento Bee
Ed: Rachel Osterman. **Description:** Job growth in California is slowing down. As of July 2005, employer payrolls were up by an average of 20,900 positions per month, but have slowed to around 10,000.

32300 ■ **"California Lost Jobs in September"** in *Sacramento Bee* (October 22, 2005)
Pub: The Sacramento Bee
Ed: Dale Kasler. **Description:** Californians saw the first job decline for 2005 in September with unemployment rates falling to 5.1 percent, only a tenth of a point. Economists believe the drop was due mainly from some schools opening earlier than usual.

32301 ■ **"Cameco Reports Record Revenue, Earnings and Cash Flows for 2006"** in *Canadian Corporate News* (February 7, 2007)
Pub: Comtex News Network, Inc.
Description: Cameco Corporation recorded record revenue, earnings and cash flow for 2006. Statistical details included.

32302 ■ **"Can everyone contribute?"** in *Black Enterprise* (Vol. 33, No. 3, Oct. 2002, pp. 71)
Pub: Earl Graves Publishing Co.
Ed: Christina Morgan. **Description:** Management strategies are covered by Tony Manning, business consultant and author; Manning suggests that managers need to do more than concentrate on the bottom line during a down economy and pay attention to the future needs of the company when the economy changes as well.

32303 ■ **"Can the Fed Keep Things Cooking At a Low Boil?"** in *Business Week* (January 9, 2006, No. 3966, pp. 21)
Pub: McGraw-Hill Companies
Ed: James C. Cooper. **Description:** The Federal Reserve is committed to lifting interest rates to a neutral level that will not stimulate or restrict economic growth, while keeping inflation under control.

32304 ■ **"Can Productivity Keep Up the Good Work?"** in *Business Week* (December 19, 2005, No. 3964, pp. 25-26)
Pub: McGraw-Hill Companies
Ed: James C. Cooper, Kathleen Madigan. **Description:** U.S. productivity is critical to keeping inflation under control. Statistical data included.

32305 ■ "Can the Profit Boom Last? Businesses Have Been Churning Out Earnings" in *Fortune* **(Vol. 152, October 17, 2005, No. 8, pp. 215)**
Pub: Time Inc.
Ed: David Stires. **Description:** With rising costs in energy and interest rates, coupled with falling consumer confidence, tough times may be ahead for small businesses.

32306 ■ "Capital Spending" in *Business Week* **(January 16, 2006, No. 3967, pp. 24)**
Pub: McGraw-Hill Companies
Ed: Description: Recent trends in the industrial sector show that industrial output is growing faster than the rate at which companies are adding to their production capacity, signaling an acceleration in capital spending.

32307 ■ "Capitol Coverage: A Report on Politics and Policy from NFIB" in *My Business* **(October/November 2003, pp. 16-17)**
Pub: My Business Magazine
Description: The National Federation of Independent Business (NFIB) addresses current issues of importance to small businesses in the U.S., including economic impact of policies, white collar overtime, health insurance, and the 2004 NFIB Summit, to be held in Washington, DC in June 2004.

32308 ■ "Careful planning can ease stress of layoffs" in *Atlanta Business Chronicle* **(Vol. 25, No. 19, October 18, 2002, pp. 4B)**
Pub: American City Business Publications, Inc.
Ed: Emory Mulling. **Description:** Slow economies bring with them the prospect of employee layoffs. A stressful situation, companies can take steps to mitigate the impact on all concerned by implementing a well thought out plan that takes into account those who will and will not be affected.

32309 ■ "Cash is King" in *Fast Company* **(May 2001, pp. 80)**
Pub: Fast Company
Ed: Walter Wriston. **Description:** Interview with Walter Wriston, former CEO of Citicorp/Citibank. Wriston advises that during economic hard times small businesses need to get back to the basics: inventory control, receivables, payables, and cash flow, the things forgotten during the new economy. Focus on generating cash, and a company will be positioned to take advantage of opportunities that the cash-strapped firms can't afford.

32310 ■ "A Cautious Optimism" in *Forbes* **(Vol. 175, February 14, 2005, No. 3, pp. 132)**
Pub: Forbes Magazine Inc.
Ed: Laszlo Birinyi, Jr. **Description:** An overview of the stock market for 2004 is presented.

32311 ■ "CBC and Chrysler Strike Deal" in *Black Enterprise* **(Vol. 37, December 2006, No. 5, pp. 36)**
Pub: Earl G. Graves Publishing Co. Inc.
Ed: Kiara Ashanti. **Description:** Congressional Black Foundation and Chrysler Financial have partnered to provide financial education to students at historically black colleges and universities. The prime objective of the program is to reduce the number of college students that graduate with poor credit scores and high debt.

32312 ■ "Celebrate Success. Embrace Innovation" in *Black Enterprise* **(Vol. 37, February 2007, No. 7, pp. 145)**
Pub: Earl G. Graves Publishing Co. Inc.
Description: 2007 Women of Power Summit provides networking opportunities, empowerment sessions, and nightly entertainment. More than 500 executive women of color are expected to attend this inspiring summit in Phoenix, February 7-10.

32313 ■ "CEO Confidence on the Rise" in *Hispanic Business* **(November 2003, pp. 22)**
Pub: Hispanic Business
Description: CEO's confidence grew significantly in the third quarter 2003, according to the latest TEC

Confidence Index, a quarterly survey of chief executives across the nation. The survey covers current economic trends and issues affecting small to medium-sized companies.

32314 ■ "Chicago Tribune Business Agenda" in *Chicago Tribune* **(February 28, 2005)**
Pub: Knight-Ridder/Tribune Business News
Description: Economic predictions, unemployment rates, and manufacturing are issues discussed.

32315 ■ "Citgo Mulls Relocation to Houston" in *Houston Business Journal* **(Vol. 34, No. 14, August 15, 2003, pp. 1)**
Pub: American City Business Journals
Ed: Monica Perin. **Description:** Citgo Petroleum Corporation announced plans to move corporate headquarters from Tulsa, Oklahoma to Houston, Texas. Topics include tax incentives, business incentives, and economic conditions.

32316 ■ "A Class Act" in *Entrepreneur* **(Vol. 32, December 2004, No. 12, pp. 61)**
Pub: Entrepreneur Media Inc.
Ed: C.J. Prince. **Description:** Increasingly, entrepreneurs are taking courses designed to assist in running a business, including leadership, finance, accounting and economics.

32317 ■ "Cleanup Delays Lessens Katrina's Economic Toll, Economist Says" in *Milwaukee Journal Sentinel* **(December 21, 2005)**
Pub: Journal Sentinel, Inc.
Ed: Michele Derus. **Description:** According to experts, the longer the recovery from Hurricane Katrina takes the less impact it will have on the U.S. economy. These delays will help U.S. markets to absorb the huge reconstruction needs, including the construction of nearly 300,000 homes. It is predicted that 2006 Gross Domestic Product will increase 3.8 to 4.3 percent.

32318 ■ "Clybourn Ave.'s PMD Corridor Leads Nowhere" in *Crain's Chicago Business* **(Vol. 30, January 2007, No. 1, pp. 8)**
Pub: Crain Communications, Inc.
Description: In an effort to stem the loss of manufacturing jobs the city created planned manufacturing districts. A. Finkl & Sons Co. is moving its manufacturing plant to a new location and real estate developers are clamoring to turn the site into one of Chicago's hottest neighborhoods but are not able to make the purchase since the plant sits in a PMD.

32319 ■ *Code of Federal Regulations: Title 13: Business Credit and Assistance*
Pub: United States Government Printing Office
Ed: Department of Commerce Staff. **Released:** April 2005. **Price:** $55.00. **Description:** Title 13 covers regulations governing the activities of the Small Business Administration and the Department of Commerce. Book covers information on business credit, finance, and economic development.

32320 ■ "Coming Back to Life" in *Fortune* **(Vol. 152, October 3, 2005, No. 7, pp. 64)**
Pub: Time Inc.
Ed: Description: The resiliency of the U.S. economy is explored, along with the recovery efforts in the Gulf Coast region after Hurricane Katrina.

32321 ■ "Commentary: Departure of Jobs Hurts National Security" in *Long Island Business News* **(February 6, 2004)**
Pub: Dolan Media Newswires
Ed: John Kiernan. **Description:** The trend to send jobs overseas not only hurts America's economy, but also jeopardizes national security in the long term. National policy must be created to encourage and keep manufacturing jobs and capacity in the U.S.

32322 ■ "Commentary: Is America III Positioned for Global Economy?" in *Long Island Business News* **(February 6, 2004)**
Pub: Dolan Media Newswires
Ed: Jerry Kremer. **Description:** Two million jobs have been lost to overseas workers since 2000. Many of

these positions went overseas to countries such as China, India, Japan, as well as others. Major American corporations are able to save money by outsourcing to these countries.

32323 ■ *Common Sense Business: Starting, Operating, and Growing Your Small Business-In Any Economy!*
Pub: HarperInformation
Ed: Steve Gottry. **Released:** August 2005. **Price:** $19.95 (US), $26.95 (Canadian). **Description:** Strategies for starting, operating and growing a small business in any economy. .

32324 ■ "Communities push ambitious SmartZone plans" in *Crain's Detroit Business* **(Vol. 16, No. 46, November 13, 2000, pp. 42)**
Pub: Crain Communications, Inc.
Ed: Amy Lane. **Description:** The Michigan Economic Development Corporation will choose sites for state-designated clusters of businesses, research, training and support in the states' technology-oriented Smart-Zones.

32325 ■ "Companies spiff up dress codes in recession" in *Atlanta Business Chronicle* **(Vol. 25, No. 19, October 18, 2002, pp. 4C)**
Pub: American City Business Publications, Inc.
Ed: Ray Glier. **Description:** Casual dress codes at companies are becoming a casualty of the current economic recession, as businesses become more serious about doing business.

32326 ■ "Companies Still Evaluating Blackout Toll" in *Pittsburgh Business Times* **(Vol. 23, No. 5, August 22, 2003, pp. 1)**
Pub: Pittsburgh Business Times
Ed: Christopher Davis. **Description:** The recent power failure on the East Coast had a significant impact on many businesses in the greater Pittsburgh, Pennsylvania area. But companies, such as financial services and legal service firms did not suffer as great a hardship.

32327 ■ "Confidence is key: economist cites the importance of business outlook to recovery" in *Black Enterprise* **(Vol. 33, No. 6, Jan. 2003)**
Pub: Earl Graves Publishing Co.
Ed: Thomas Boston. **Description:** The Gazelle Index, a survey of 350 of the nation's fastest growing black-owned businesses, measured by workforce growth rates, took a sharp plunge, from 67.7 to 49.5 during second and third quarters. Business owners become more negative about economic conditions when readings fall below 50.

32328 ■ "Consider the recession over" in *My Business* **(April/May 2002, pp. 49)**
Pub: My Business Magazine
Ed: Bill Dunkelberg. **Description:** Fourth quarter 2001 Gross Domestic Product results showed a 1.4 percent annual rate of growth. Statistical information on small business optimism, inventory plans, and sales expectations are included.

32329 ■ "Construction Delayed on Tower Project" in *Bellingham Business Journal* **(December 2006, pp. A1)**
Pub: Sun News Inc.
Ed: Heidi Schiller. **Description:** Bay View Tower developers have postponed breaking ground until spring on 2007 on their condominium project. Due to over-building in cities across the country financers are apprehensive about the housing market.

32330 ■ "Continental Airlines' Deb Rating Suffers Another Blow" in *Houston Chronicle* **(April 11, 2003)**
Pub: Knight-Ridder/Tribune Business News
Ed: Bill Hensel. **Description:** A discussion into Continental Airline's credit rating being lowered in April 2003, by Moody's Investors Service is presented. The move cited weak air travel demand and falling revenues.

32331 ■ "A Conversation with George Jackson, Detroit Economic Growth Corp." in *Crain's Detroit Business* **(Vol. 21, January 3, 2005, No. 1)**
Pub: Crain Communications Inc. - Detroit
Ed: Robert Ankeny. **Description:** In an interview with George Jackson, president of the Detroit Economic Growth Corporation, plans to prepare for baseball's All-Star Game as well as NFL Super Bowl XL are discussed.

32332 ■ "A Conversation With Michael Beauregard, Huron Capital Partners" in *Crain's Detroit Business* **(Vol. 21, January 31, 2005, No. 5)**
Pub: Crain Communications Inc. - Detroit
Ed: Michelle Martinez. **Description:** The outlook for non-automotive mergers and acquisitions are discussed with Michael Beauregard, a partner with Huron Capital Partners. Beauregard predicts a strong economic climate for 2005.

32333 ■ "A Conversation With Steve Cassin, Macomb County Director of Planning and Economic Development" in *Crain's Detroit Business* **(Vol. 21)**
Pub: Crain Communications Inc. - Detroit
Ed: Anjali Fluker. **Description:** In an interview with Steve Cassin, director of planning and economic development for Macomb County, Michigan, he talks about the challenges and initiatives his county is taking on in a move to attract new business to the area.

32334 ■ "Cooperation Needed for Budget Priorities" in *Crain's Detroit Business* **(Vol. 21, January 31, 2005, No. 5, pp. 8)**
Pub: Crain Communications Inc. - Detroit
Description: Michigan Association of Realtors and the Michigan Chamber Foundations will pay up to $700,000 to retain Peter Hutchinson to work with the state's legislative leadership on Michigan's budget issues. Hutchinson co-authored the book, The Price of Government.

32335 ■ "Corporate Coffers Full of Cash" in *Kansas City Star* **(March 8, 2005)**
Pub: Knight-Ridder/Tribune Business News
Ed: Chris Lester. **Description:** Corporate finances are at their best, and what companies do with that money will determine economics on Wall Street and in general. If spent wisely, it could be positive for both financial markets and economic growth.

32336 ■ "Council Promotes Banners, Tours to Publicize Super Bowl" in *Crain's Detroit Business* **(Vol. 21, October 10, 2005, No. 43, pp. 33)**
Pub: Crain Communications Inc. - Detroit
Ed: Jennette Smith. **Description:** Detroit's Tourism Economic Development Councils is recommending the use of banners on businesses and downtown tours as a means to publicize and market Super Bowl XL. The move is expected to help businesses after the game has departed.

32337 ■ *Council for Urban Economic Development—Membership Directory*
Pub: International Economic Development Council
Contact: Jeffrey A. Finkle, Pres./CEO
Released: Irregular, latest edition 2000-2001; previous edition July 1998. **Covers:** Approximately 2,700 economic development professionals working in local and state governments; private sector professionals and corporations; local and community development corporations; neighborhood and manpower groups. **Entries Include:** For individual members—Name, address, phone. For corporations and community groups—Organization name, address, phone, fax, name and title of contact. **Arrangement:** Personal. **Indexes:** Geographical, Organizational.

32338 ■ "A crafty Christmas: with people cutting spending, more gifts are homemade" in *Wall Street Journal* **(Dec. 20, 2002, pp. W14)**
Pub: Dow Jones & Co. Inc.
Ed: Danielle Reed. **Description:** The slow economy has turned people towards making homemade gifts for loved ones, particularly hand-knitted items.

32339 ■ "The Crash of 2006" in *Home Business* **(Vol. 13, January/February 2006, No. 1, pp. 16, 18-22, 102, 104)**
Pub: Home Business Magazine
Ed: Richard Henderson. **Description:** Home business owners can find opportunity in bad economic times. The home-based advantage in a touch economy is discussed.

32340 ■ "Credit Use Strangles Wealth" in *Black Enterprise* **(Vol. 35, November 2004, No. 4, pp. 38)**
Pub: Earl G. Graves Publishing Co. Inc.
Ed: Aissatou Sidime. **Description:** Minorities are most at risk of damaging financial futures due to poor credit card management, according to the U.S. Federal Reserve.

32341 ■ "Crisis Mode: Economic Crises are Trickling Down to Entrepreneurs. How Are They Fighting Back?" in *Entrepreneur* **(Vol. 32, August 2004)**
Pub: Entrepreneur Media Inc.
Ed: Chris Penttila. **Description:** Costs for running a small business are hurting entrepreneurs bottom line.

32342 ■ "The Cure for What Ails You" in *Black Enterprise* **(Vol. 34, No. 6, January 2004, pp. 69)**
Pub: Earl Graves Publishing Co.
Ed: Donald Jay Korn. **Description:** Profile of Joseph Williams, whose firm builds high-end custom made staircases for upscale homes. Williams expects to see annual sales for 2004 at $8.4 with a rising economy.

32343 ■ "Cutbacks mean less on table for, and from, caterers" in *Crain's Detroit Business* **(Vol. 18, No. 22, June 3, 2002, pp. 33)**
Pub: Crain Communications Inc. - Detroit
Ed: Michael Strong. **Description:** The downturn in the economy has affected catering businesses and event-oriented businesses, as well as the increase in more companies offering these services.

32344 ■ "Cycles teach you patience" in *Fast Company* **(May 2001, pp. 88)**
Pub: Fast Company
Ed: Warren Bennis. **Description:** Leadership guru Warren Bennis, discusses economic cycles and how these cycles teach patience to business owners.

32345 ■ "Dark Dollar Signs" in *Hispanic Business* **(June 2005, pp. 22, 24)**
Pub: Hispanic Business
Ed: Andrea Lehman. **Description:** Signs of a struggling economy continue through mid-2005. U.S. currency is on the decline amid troubling financial indicators. U.S. economic forecasts are cited. Statistical data included.

32346 ■ "David Nicklaus Column" in *St. Louis Post-Dispatch* **(August 22, 2004)**
Pub: Knight-Ridder/Tribune Business News
Ed: David Nicklaus. **Description:** When the Federal Reserve recently raised the prime interest rate, other rates began to fall. Home mortgage loan rates are down half a percent from early summer, fueling the housing market. Despite high oil prices, bad economic news has been good for the home buyers.

32347 ■ "Deal Volume Remains Steady in Q2 But How Bout Some Exits?" in *Venture Capital Journal* **(September 1, 2005)**
Pub: Thomason Financial Inc.
Description: Second earnings for venture capital firms are reported. Nearly $5.82 billion was invested in 751 deals in second quarter 2005, up from the first quarter, according to The MoneyTree Survey.

32348 ■ "Dealing With Cost Hikes" in *Inc.* **(August 2005, pp. 49-50)**
Pub: Inc. Magazine
Ed: Description: Although conventional wisdom dictates that now is the time to raise prices, it may be precisely the reason to hold off. Cutting the middleperson could be an alternative to price increases.

32349 ■ "Deficits" in *Business Week* **(February 20, 2006, No. 3972, pp. 30)**
Pub: McGraw-Hill Companies
Ed: James Mehring. **Description:** According to the U.S. Congressional Budget Office (CBO), recent budget deficits are beginning to shrink. The CBO expects a $337 billion deficit for fiscal year ending September 30, 2006, falling to $270 billion next year, with an expected balanced budget by 2012.

32350 ■ "DeSoto County Lures Bonanza of New Banks" in *Memphis Business Journal* **(Vol. 25, No. 19, September 5, 2003, pp. 1)**
Pub: American City Business Journals
Ed: Rob Robertson. **Description:** DeSoto County, Tennessee continues to experience economic growth and population expansion. To meet the growth, the banking and financial services industry continues to expand in the area.

32351 ■ "Detroit office vacancies at 18 percent" in *Crain's Detroit Business* **(Vol. 16, No. 46, November 12, 2000, pp. 3)**
Pub: Crain Communications, Inc.
Ed: Robert Ankeny. **Description:** Downtown Detroit's office space will increase due to the merger of two major corporations. Details are included.

32352 ■ "Detroit ballot to feature $130M in bond proposals" in *Crain's Detroit Business* **(Vol. 19, No. 16, April 21, 2003, pp. 23)**
Pub: Crain Communications Inc., Detroit
Ed: Robert Ankeny. **Description:** Detroit voters will decide on $130 million in bond issues to finance building and development projects in the city in April 2003. These proposals are for renovation or expansion at the Charles Wright Museum of African-American History; improvements to Cobo Center and the People Mover; revitalization of the east riverfront, including housing and other redevelopment; and a public-safety mall, a new police precinct, and new fire stations.

32353 ■ "Detroit Free Press Wayne Small Business Column" in *Detroit Free Press* **(July 21, 2005)**
Pub: Knight-Ridder/Tribune Business News
Ed: Carol Cain. **Description:** Mark Slagle, owner of Mr. Handyman of Southeastern Wayne County franchise, discusses growing a small business in a tough economy. Mr. Handyman offers full-service repair and maintenance for homeowners.

32354 ■ "Detroit Renaissance Goal" in *Crain's Detroit Business* **(Vol. 22, January 23, 2006, No. 4, pp. 3)**
Pub: Crain Communications Inc. - Detroit
Ed: Robert Ankeny. **Description:** Detroit Renaissance Inc. plans to develop five or six specific strategies to spur economic growth and development in the City of Detroit, Michigan.

32355 ■ *Developmental Entrepreneurship: Adversity, Risk, and Isolation*
Pub: Elsevier Science and Technology Books
Ed: Craig Galbraith. **Released:** August 2006. **Price:** $99.95. **Description:** Volume five of the series, this book focuses on the fields of entrepreneurship, sociology, and economics. Fifteen articles related to entrepreneurship and small business development within a global environment are included.

32356 ■ *Directory of Incentives for Business Investment and Development in the United States*
Pub: National Association of State Development Agencies
Released: Latest edition 1998. **Covers:** about 750 state business location and expansion direct financial incentive programs. **Entries Include:** Program title; name, address, and phone of contact; description of incentive, terms and conditions, eligibility criteria, application procedure, volume or level of program activity.

32357 ■ "Do You Rate?" in *Entrepreneur* **(Vol. 31, No. 10, October 2003, pp. 59)**
Pub: Entrepreneur Media, Inc.

Ed: Joshua Kurlantzick. **Description:** Many small companies are struggling to maintain good credit ratings because of the continued weak economy.

32358 ■ "Doing business in a dangerous world" in *Harvard Business Review* (Vol. 80, No. 4, April 2002, pp. 22)

Pub: Harvard Business School Press

Ed: Gardiner Morse. **Description:** A discussion with former chairman of the National Commission on Terrorism, L. Paul Bremer, about the risks to American businesses from terrorism and the resentment in developing economies toward the dominant position of the U.S. in the world.

32359 ■ "Doing Your Part?" in *Entrepreneur* (Vol. 31, No. 9, September 2003)

Pub: Entrepreneur Media, Inc.

Ed: Geoff Williams. **Description:** An interview with Liz Cohen, author of "A Consumers' Republic: The Politics of Mass Consumption in Postwar America"; the book argues that shopping has long been a form of patriotism.

32360 ■ "Dollar signs get attention as cost of growth starts to weigh" in *Crain's Detroit Business* (Vol. 19, No. 17, April 28, 2003, pp. 18)

Pub: Crain Communications Inc., Detroit

Ed: Terry Kosdrosky. **Description:** Southeast Michigan will need $41 billion dollars in the next 22 years for roads and public transportation, but will receive only $24 billion from gas taxes and local general-fund money for projects.

32361 ■ "Don't Be Thrown by the Yield Curve" in *Business Week* (January 16, 2006, No. 3967, pp. 40)

Pub: McGraw-Hill Companies

Ed: Roben Farzad, Justin Hibbard. **Description:** The latest inversion curve does not necessarily signal a recession and might benefit some industries, while hurting others. Those sectors expected to benefit include capital equipment and energy services, while mortgage lenders and homebuilders stand to lose.

32362 ■ "Don't Watch This Curve Too Closely" in *Business Week* (January 9, 2006, No. 3966, pp. 22)

Pub: McGraw-Hill Companies

Description: A description of the inverted yield curve is presented. The yield curve is a graph of interest rate levels across all the various maturities, from the overnight federal funds rate to the 10-year Treasury note. The current curve inverted yield curve, which occurs when short rates are higher than long rates, no longer appears ominous to economists.

32363 ■ "Don't throw out the old economy yet" in *Crain's Detroit Business* (Vol. 16, No. 17, April 24, 2000, pp. 8)

Pub: Crain Communications, Inc.

Ed: Keith Crain. **Description:** This may not be the new economy, but it sure has a lot to do with new Internet businesses.

32364 ■ "Down Economy Helps Incubate Small Businesses" in *Crain's Detroit Business* (Vol. 19, No. 45, November 10, 2003, pp. 11)

Pub: Crain Communications Inc., Detroit

Ed: Laura Bailey. **Description:** The State of Michigan reported 8,432 new business entities in 2003, and expects the trend to grow in 2004.

32365 ■ "The downside of good times" in *Journal of Accountancy* (Vol. 190, No. 5, November 2000, pp. 53)

Pub: Harborside Financial Center

Ed: Anita Dennis. **Description:** The article shows why it is important for small businesses to remember the basics even during a strong economy.

32366 ■ "Dresser to Close Plant Eliminate 244 Jobs" in *Houston Business Journal* (Vol. 34, No. 14, August 15, 2003, pp. 3)

Pub: American City Business Journals

Description: Dresser Flow Solutions plans to close its manufacturing facility in Houston, Texas as part of a business consolidation effort. Topics include business losses, economic conditions, and layoffs.

32367 ■ "DTE aims to spark growth beyond electricity" in *Crain's Detroit Business* (Vol. 19, No. 15, April 14, 2003, pp. 3)

Pub: Crain Communications Inc., Detroit

Ed: Amy Lane. **Description:** DTE Energy Company is expecting to see growth in 2003 through its non-regulated business areas of coal reclamation and methane-gas extraction from coal beds.

32368 ■ "E-Government Catching On" in *Hispanic Business* (Vol. 23, No. 5, May 2001, pp. 22, 24)

Pub: Hispanic Business

Ed: Patricia Guadalupe. **Description:** The U.S. government is developing programs to access procurement, recruitment, and economic development. The FirstGov.gov links users to more than 20 million federal Web pages.

32369 ■ "Earnings up 18 Percent for '02; 4Q Totals Rise 141 Percent from '01" in *Crain's Detroit Business* (V. 19, No. 8, 2/24/03)

Pub: Crain Communications Inc., Detroit

Ed: Katie Merx. **Description:** Southeast Michigan companies saw profits rise in the second half of 2002, spurred on by automotive sales and business spending.

32370 ■ "Earnings Gain, Wealth Loss" in *Black Enterprise* (Vol. 35, January 2005, No. 6, pp. 30)

Pub: Earl G. Graves Publishing Co. Inc.

Ed: Nadirah Sabir. **Description:** Family income rose in the late 1990s in both black and white families, and at their highest in 2000 for both. Employment rates also rose during the same time period. Statistical data included.

32371 ■ "Earnings Improve, but Overall Picture Isn't Exactly Rosy" in *Crain's Detroit Business* (Vol. 18, No. 21, May 27, 2002, pp. 1)

Pub: Crain Communications Inc. - Detroit

Ed: Katie Merx. **Description:** Metro Detroit firms showed improved earnings for the first quarter 2002 compared to same quarter last year, but the economic rebound is going more slowly than analysts originally predicted.

32372 ■ "Earnings Rise Is 3rd Straight; Analysts See a Recovery" in *Crain's Detroit Business* (Vol. 18, No. 50, December 16, 2002, pp. 1)

Pub: Crain Communications Inc., Detroit

Ed: Katie Merx. **Description:** Detroit-area public companies report increased profits for the third straight quarter in the period ending September 30, 2002. Strengths and weaknesses in various sectors are discussed.

32373 ■ "EastGroup Buys Buildings" in *Mississippi Business Journal* (Vol. 29, January 2007, No. 4, pp. 9)

Pub: Venture Publications, Inc.

Ed: Wally Northway **Description:** EastGroup Properties acquired three business distribution buildings in Charlotte, NC, for $9.3 million. This increases EastGroup's total portfolio to almost 24 million square feet of properties in the Charlotte area under development.

32374 ■ "Eating Up Profits" in *Hispanic Business* (June 2005, pp. 94)

Pub: Hispanic Business

Ed: Keith Rosenblum. **Description:** Rising costs deter an otherwise strong 2004 for manufacturers in the U.S. Statistical data included.

32375 ■ "Economic Developers Expect a Busier Year in '03" in *Atlanta Business Chronicle* (Vol. 25, December 6, 2002, No. 26, pp. 8A)

Pub: American City Business Publications, Inc.

Ed: Jarred Schenke. **Description:** The Georgia Department of Industry, Trade and Tourism and Georgia Power Company, Georgia's largest economic development organizations, are working to attract more companies to the state. This trend could generate business for industrial real estate planners.

32376 ■ *Economic Development Administration—Annual Report*

Pub: U.S. Economic Development Administration

Ed: Juanita L. Toatley, Editor. **Released:** Annual, Latest edition 2004. **Covers:** recipients of grants, grant supplements, and loan guarantees from the Economic Development Administration under the Public Works and Economic Development Act of 1965. Projects funded include public works, business development, research, planning, and disaster recovery. **Entries Include:** Recipient name, location, date of obligation, funds received by type of assistance, type of project, identification number. **Arrangement:** Geographical.

32377 ■ "Economic and Financial Indicators" in *The Economist* (Vol. 376, July 16-22, 2005, No. 8435, pp. 96-97)

Pub: The Economist Newspaper Ltd. .

Description: Statistics on fifteen developed economies, focusing on the banking industry, are presented.

32378 ■ "The Economic Ground War" in *Hispanic Business* (March 2003, pp. 18)

Pub: Hispanic Business

Ed: Joel Russell. **Description:** Small business executives and economic experts are predicting a slowdown for the first half of 2003. It is hoped that spending will increase when global political threats are stabilized.

32379 ■ "Economic Outlook" in *Business 2.0* (Vol. 6, July 2005, No. 6, pp. 32)

Pub: Time, Inc.

Description: Chief forecasting economist at Global Insight, Nariman Behravesh, predicts American corporations will begin spending in the coming year.

32380 ■ *The Economics of Entrepreneurship*

Pub: Edward Elgar Publishing, Incorporated

Ed: Parker. **Released:** April 2006. **Price:** $240.00. **Description:** Previously published articles influencing research into the economic structure of entrepreneurship are examined.

32381 ■ "Economics Focus" in *The Economist* (Vol. 376, July 30-August 5, 2005, No. 8437, pp. 70)

Pub: The Economist Newspaper Ltd.

Description: The strength of the American labor market is examined, focusing on 5.1 million workers missing from the reported unemployment figures.

32382 ■ *The Economics and Management of Small Business: An International Perspective*

Pub: Routledge

Ed: Graham Bannock. **Released:** April 2005. **Price:** $132.00 (US), $190.00 (Canadian). **Description:** International perspectives on the economics and management of small business, featuring case studies and empirical research.

32383 ■ *The Economics of Self-Employment and Entrepreneurship*

Pub: Cambridge University Press

Ed: Simon C. Parker. **Released:** July 2006. **Price:** $50.00. **Description:** The importance of self-employment and entrepreneurship in a modern economy is explored.

32384 ■ *The Economics of Small Firms*

Pub: Routledge Inc.

Ed: Johnson. **Released:** December 2006. **Price:** $41. 95. **Description:** Introduction to the economics of small business, covering both theoretical and empirical issues.

32385 ■ "Economist Offers 2005 Outlook For 2 Florida Counties" in *Bradenton Herald* (January 13, 2005)

Pub: Bradenton Herald

Ed: Dana Sanchez. **Description:** Economist Henry Fishkind predicts the first half of 2005 will show excellent growth for both Manatee and Sarasota Counties in Florida. Local tourism, condominium conversions, residential and non-residential construction are sited for the areas growth.

32386 ■ **"Economist Says Focus on Emerging Markets to Boost Foreign Trade"** in *Portland Press Herald* **(June 17, 2005)**
Pub: Blethen Maine Newspapers, Inc.
Ed: Edward D. Murphy. Description: Emerging economies present the greatest opportunity for businesses looking to increase foreign trade. Maine ranked ninth among states in export growth from 2000 to 2004. Statistical data included.

32387 ■ **"Economist Upbeat About Macomb in 2005 Despite Lagging Recovery"** in *Crain's Detroit Business* **(Vol. 21, January 24, 2005, No. 4, pp. 5)**
Pub: Crain Communications Inc. - Detroit
Ed: Anjali Fluker. Description: Macomb County, Michigan is falling behind the national economic recovery being experienced in other counties. Issues of loss in manufacturing and the domestic automobile industry were sited as factors.

32388 ■ **"Economists Divided Over Downturn"** in *Hispanic Business* **(Vol. 23, No. 11, November 2001, pp. 16)**
Pub: Hispanic Business Inc.
Ed: Derek Reveron. Description: Economists struggle to take terrorist attacks into account in making recession forecasts. A listing of economic conditions after critical events in American history are cited.

32389 ■ **"Economists Raise Concerns about South Carolina Governor's Tax Cut Proposal"** in *The State* **(February 17, 2004)**
Pub: Knight-Ridder/Tribune Business News
Ed: Jennifer Talhelm. Description: Impact of the lower state income tax in South Carolina to schools, local governments and state-supported services. Economists address these issues.

32390 ■ **"Economy Adds 262,000 Jobs"** in *Boston Globe* **(March 5, 2005)**
Pub: New York Times Company
Ed: Charles Stein. Description: The government reported 262,000 new jobs in February 2005, supporting predictions of a strong economic job market.

32391 ■ **"Economy Expands Modestly, but Unemployment Rate Rises"** in *Atlanta Journal-Constitution* **(February 3, 2007)**
Pub: Cox Newspapers, Inc.
Ed: Michael E. Kanell. Description: Despite a modest jump in the economy, unemployment numbers rose, according to the U.S. Department of Labor Statistics.

32392 ■ **"Economy Refuses to Fall"** in *Atlanta Journal-Constitution* **(February 1, 2007)**
Pub: Cox Newspapers, Inc.
Ed: Michael E. Kanell. Description: Fourth quarter 2006 showed a solid 3.5 percent growth in the U.S. economy; however residential spending fell 19.2 percent.

32393 ■ **"Economy: So much for technology's third-quarter save"** in *Red Herring* **(No. 103, September 1, 2001, pp. 24)**
Pub: Herring Communications
Ed: Dan Briody. Description: A bleak forecast for the third quarter 2001 in the technology sector is discussed.

32394 ■ **"Economy Stephen Levy"** in *Venture Capital Journal* **(January 1, 2005)**
Pub: Thomason Financial Inc.
Description: Stephen Levy, director and co-founder of the Center for Continuing Study of the California Economy, believes an export boom would be the best thing for the 2005 economy, and the continued drop in new company formation the worst.

32395 ■ **"Economy's Pain Reaches Office Landlords"** in *Wall Street Journal* **(May 22, 2002, pp. B8)**
Pub: Wall Street Journal
Ed: Peter Grant. Description: Office building owners are experiencing a greater vacancy rate since office tenants are not renewing leases because of downsizing in the slower economy.

32396 ■ **"Economy.sup.2"** in *Entrepreneur* **(Vol. 30, No. 2, February 2002,)**
Pub: Entrepreneur Media Inc.
Ed: Geoff Williams. Description: Profile of and interview with Nathan Myhrvold, CEO of Intellectual Ventures, a private entrepreneurial partnership in Bellevue, Washington.

32397 ■ **"Education, Economy Key for Voters"** in *Hispanic Business* **(September 2004, pp. 16)**
Pub: Hispanic Business
Ed: Patricia Guadalupe. Description: Hispanic voters are focused on education and economic issues when considering how they will vote.

32398 ■ *Effect of the Overvalued Dollar on Small Exporters: Congressional Hearing*
Pub: DIANE Publishing Company
Ed: Donald Manzullo. Released: October 2004. Price: $30.00. Description: Congressional hearing: Witnesses: Dr. Lawrence Chimerine, Economist; Tony Raimondo, President and CEO, Behlen Manufacturing Company; Robert J. Weskamp, President, Wes-Tech, Inc.; Wayne Dollar, President, Georgia Farm Bureau; and Vargese George, President and CEO, Westex International, Inc. Appendix includes correspondence sent to committee on the overvalued dollar.

32399 ■ **"Electricity, natural gas facing uncertain future"** in *Atlanta Business Chronicle* **(Vol. 25, January 10, 2003, No. 31, pp. 24A)**
Pub: American City Business Publications, Inc.
Ed: Don Reichardt. Description: According to the Georgia Economic Outlook 2003 survey, electric utilities are positioned for growth while natural gas utilities will have to deal with the effects of deregulation and volatile prices.

32400 ■ **"Embrace the Deficit"** in *Wall Street Journal* **(Vol. 248, January 2007, No. 146, pp. B1-B3)**
Pub: Dow Jones & Co. Inc.
Ed: David Malpass Description: U.S. trade deficit may not be as weak and unbalanced as it seems at first glance.

32401 ■ **"Emergency care for Detroit's health system"** in *Crain's Detroit Business* **(Vol. 19, No. 15, April 14, 2003, pp. 11)**
Pub: Crain Communications Inc., Detroit
Ed: Katie Merx. Description: Issues involving Detroit's health care system are discussed, including the crises in rising benefit rates for businesses, drug costs, the growing number of working persons without healthcare insurance, and the level of federal and state reimbursement for Medicaid patients.

32402 ■ *The Emerging Digital Economy: Entrepreneurship, Clusters, and Policy*
Pub: Springer
Ed: Borje Johansson; Charlie Karlsson; Roger Stough. Released: August 2006. Price: $119.00. Description: The new economy, or digital economy, and its impact on the way industries and firms choose to locate and cluster geographically.

32403 ■ **"Emerging-Market Indicators"** in *The Economist* **(Vol. 376, July 16-22, 2005, No. 8435, pp. 98)**
Pub: The Economist Newspaper Ltd.
Description: Statistics on 25 emerging economies, along with an investigation into stock markets are presented.

32404 ■ **"Employee Organizations: Tomorrow's Possibilities"** in *Employment Relations Today* **(Vol. 26, No. 4, Winter 2000, pp. 53)**
Pub: John Wiley & Sons, Inc.
Ed: Arthur B. Shostak. Description: An investigation into the future of employees' organizations within corporations, focusing on the structure of corporate culture in the 21st century. The article identifies five factors that will influence employee groups in the future, which include economic expansion, communication systems, artificial intelligence, smart technology, and genetic engineering.

32405 ■ **"Employers Won't Give Big Pay Raises in 2006, Survey Finds"** in *Sacramento Bee* **(December 3, 2005)**
Pub: The Sacramento Bee
Ed: Rachel Osterman. Description: According to a recent survey of more than 1,000 employers across the country, average salary increases will be 3.6 percent in 2006. Companies are expected to offer bonuses and incentive pay based on performance.

32406 ■ **"Employment Will Be Stable, Survey Says"** in *Milwaukee Journal Sentinel* **(December 13, 2005)**
Pub: Journal Sentinel, Inc.
Ed: Joel Dresang. Description: According to the Manpower Employment Outlook Survey, 23 percent of 16,000 employers will add employees in first quarter 2006, while 10 percent report plans to downsize.

32407 ■ **"Entrepreneur Column"** in *Entrepreneur.com* **(Jan. 2006)**
Pub: Entrepreneur Media Inc.
Ed: Kim Gordon. Description: A step-by-step guide to successfully grow a small business while staying ahead of inflation.

32408 ■ *The Entrepreneurial Imperative: How America's Economic Miracle Will Reshape the World (And Change Your Life)*
Pub: HarperCollins Publishers, Inc.
Ed: Carl J. Schramm. Released: October 2006. Price: $24.95. Description: Carl Schramm, president of Kauffman Foundation discusses the secret to America's economy.

32409 ■ *Entrepreneurship and Economic Growth*
Pub: Edward Elgar Publishing, Incorporated
Ed: Carree. Released: October 2006. Price: $195. 00. Description: Historic and country-specific studies and articles regarding entrepreneurship and innovation, growth models, competition and productivity, and empirical evidence.

32410 ■ *Entrepreneurship and Economic Progress*
Pub: Routledge Inc.
Ed: Randall Holcombe. Released: October 2006. Description: Economic models of economic growth and the ways entrepreneurial progress are highlighted.

32411 ■ *Entrepreneurship, Geography, and American Economic Growth*
Pub: Cambridge University Press
Ed: Zoltan Acs; Catherine Armington. Released: June 2006. Price: $70.00. Description: Knowledge among college-educated workers was among the key reasons for economic growth throughout the U.S. in the 1990s.

32412 ■ *Entrepreneurship, Innovation and Economic Growth*
Pub: Edward Elgar Publishing, Incorporated
Ed: David B. Audretsch. Released: July 2006. Price: $145.00. Description: Links between entrepreneurship, innovation and economic growth are examined.

32413 ■ *Entrepreneurship, Innovation and the Growth Mechanism of the Free-Enterprise Economies*
Pub: Princeton University Press
Ed: Eytan Sheshinski; William J. Baumol. Released: January 2007. Price: $65.00. Description: Scholars address the free-enterprise Western economies.

32414 ■ *Entrepreneurship, Investment and Spatial Dynamics Lessons and Implications for an Enlarged EU*
Pub: Edward Elgar Publishing, Incorporated
Ed: Nijkamp. Released: September 2006. Price: $100.00. Description: Understanding the impact and interaction between investment, knowledge and entrepreneurship with an expanding European Union.

32415 ■ *Entrepreneurship in the U.S.: The 2005 Assessment*
Pub: Springer

Ed: Paul Reynolds. **Released:** March 2007. **Price:** $79.95. **Description:** Entrepreneurship and its role in the U.S. economy is discussed, examining new business creation and its impact on job growth, productivity enhancements, innovation, and social mobility.

32416 ■ "Environmental and Ownership Characteristics of Small Businesses and their Impact on Development" in *Journal of Small Business Management*
Pub: West Virginia University
Ed: William B. Gartner, Subodh Bhat. **Description:** This article explores the relationship between the characteristics of a small business's location (crime, neighborhood appearance, and transportation accessibility) and a small business owner's expectations of future firm growth.

32417 ■ "An Era of Downsized Expectations" in *Hispanic Business* **(March 2002, pp. 28, 30-31)**
Pub: Hispanic Business
Ed: Mark Egan. **Description:** Hispanic money managers are using caution against the use of irrational exuberance regarding current investments.

32418 ■ "Execs getting more political: Efforts to influence policy growing" in *Crain's Chicago Business* **(Vol. 23, October 9, 2000, pp. SB2)**
Pub: Crain Communications, Inc. Crain Communications, Inc.
Ed: Mary Ellen Podmolik. **Description:** As small business has grown an economic force, so too, has its collective voice in local, state and national politics, but many small business owners often are too busy running successful companies during a bull market.

32419 ■ "Experimental Games for the Design of Reputation Management Systems" in *IBM Systems Journal* **(Vol. 42, No. 3, September 2003, pp. 498)**
Pub: IBM Technical Journals
Ed: C. Keser. **Description:** Trust between people engaging in economic transactions affects the economic growth of their community. Reputation management systems, such as the Feedback Forum of eBay Inc., can increase the trust level of the participants. The paper shows that experimental economics can be used in a controlled laboratory environment to measure trust and trust enhancement. Emerging issues in the design of reputation management systems are discussed.

32420 ■ "The Export Engine Is Shifting Into High Gear" in *Business Week* **(January 16, 2006, No. 3967, pp. 23-24)**
Pub: McGraw-Hill Companies
Ed: James C. Cooper. **Description:** U. S. exporters are expected to benefit from the growing world economy despite a drop in the U.S. dollar. Recent studies show more balance in the growing global economy. Statistical data included.

32421 ■ "Fallen and Can't Get Up: Even Greenspan Can't Hold Off the Bond Bears" in *Barron's* **(July 21, 2003, pp. MW11)**
Pub: Barron's
Ed: Jennifer Ablan. **Description:** Bond markets continued to unravel, despite mollifying statements from Federal Reserve Chairman Alan Greenspan. Analysts were disheartened by the Federal government's plan to buy long-term treasury securities to keep rates under control, a program similar to Japan's price-keeping operations (PKO) of the early 1990s.

32422 ■ "Falling Behind" in *Entrepreneur* **(Vol. 31, No. 8, August 2003, pp. 53)**
Pub: Entrepreneur Media, Inc.
Ed: Joshua Kurlantzick. **Description:** Over the last six months, U.S. currency rates have fallen, affecting small businesses across the U.S.

32423 ■ "FAQs of Life in the New Economy" in *Fast Company* **(September 2001, pp. 22)**
Pub: Fast Company
Description: Overview of the economics and the new economy, and the way the new economy keeps changing.

32424 ■ "February Job Gains Boost Stocks, But Pay Scales Show Decline" in *Atlanta Journal-Constitution* **(March 5, 2005)**
Pub: Knight-Ridder/Tribune Business News
Ed: Michael E. Kanell. **Description:** There were 262,000 new jobs added to U.S. payrolls in February 2005. According to the U.S. Bureau of Labor Statistics most incomes are not keeping pace with cost of living.

32425 ■ "Fed Bumps Rate to 4.25 Percent" in *Milwaukee Journal Sentinel* **(December 14, 2005)**
Pub: Journal Sentinel, Inc.
Ed: Avrum D. Lank. **Description:** Policy-makers at the Federal Reserve raised interest rates by one-quarter of one percent, to 4.25 percent, with future increases expected. Statistical data included.

32426 ■ "Federal stimulus can ensure recovery" in *Atlanta Business Chronicle* **(Vol. 25, January 10, 2003, No. 31, pp. 32A)**
Pub: American City Business Publications, Inc.
Ed: Jim Molis. **Description:** A stimulus package from the Federal Government will go a long way in helping the economy on its way to recovery. However, war with Iraq or North Korea would most certainly bring the economy back down.

32427 ■ *Female Enterprise in the New Economy*
Pub: University of Toronto Press
Ed: Karen D. Hughes. **Released:** December 2005. **Price:** $24.95 (US), $29.95 (Canadian). **Description:** Examination of whether the increasingly entrepreneurial economy is offering women more opportunity or increases their risk for poverty and economic insecurity.

32428 ■ "Fields of Dreams" in *Crain's New York Business* **(Vol. 23, January 1, 2007, No. 1, pp. 3)**
Pub: Crain Communications, Inc.
Description: Overview of planned 18,000 seat basketball arena for the Nets is part of a controversial multi-use development in Brooklyn.

32429 ■ "A Fight for Rights" in *Hispanic Business* **(October 2004, pp. 50, 52, 54)**
Pub: Hispanic Business
Ed: Jonathan J. Higuera. **Description:** Profile of Ann Marie Tallman, leader at the Mexican American Legal Defense and Educational Fund. Tallman is committed to adding economic rights to the group's agenda.

32430 ■ "Financial Industry Expects Growth Amid Radical Changes" in *Crain's Detroit Business* **(Vol. 19, No. 45, November 10, 2003, pp. 24)**
Pub: Crain Communications Inc., Detroit
Ed: Katie Merx. **Description:** Southeast Michigan banks are expecting increases across the board in commercial lines of business, credit unions are expected to expand, and mortgage companies and brokers are offering new services to keep business brisk when interest rates rise. Venture capital and mergers-and-acquisition are also projected to do well.

32431 ■ "Financial services firms foresee mixed results" in *Atlanta Business Chronicle* **(Vol. 25, January 10, 2003, No. 31, pp. 18A)**
Pub: American City Business Publications, Inc.
Ed: Tony Heffernan. **Description:** The University of Georgia's Georgia Economic Outlook 2003 indicates that financial services companies will have mixed performances this coming year. One performance issue is that community banks will do better than bigger banks because they are not dependent on venture capital lending.

32432 ■ "Finding the Middle Ground" in *Black Enterprise* **(Vol. 34, No. 6, January 2004)**
Pub: Earl Graves Publishing Co.
Ed: James A. Anderson. **Description:** According to market experts, mid-sized companies offer opportunity in most market conditions and are recommended in 2004. Statistical data included.

32433 ■ "Firms Skid on Rising Oil and Gas Prices" in *Black Enterprise* **(Vol. 36, February 2006, No. 7, pp. 35)**
Pub: Earl G. Graves Publishing Co. Inc.
Ed: Wendy Isom. **Description:** Small businesses across the nation are facing economic difficulties incurred by rising oil and gas prices in the aftermath of Hurricane Katrina.

32434 ■ "Firms Will Spend Less on Buildings and Equipment This Year" in *Kiplinger Letter* **(Vol. 78, January 19, 2007, No. 2)**
Pub: Kiplinger
Description: Small business will spend about 2 percent less in building and equipment purchases in 2007. Industrial equipment, telecommunications and diesel engines will be the hardest hit.

32435 ■ "A flat road ahead" in *My Business* **(September/October 2001, pp. 47)**
Pub: My Business Magazine
Ed: Bill Dunkelberg. **Description:** Findings from a recent NFIB survey suggests that the economy slowed substantially in the second half of 2000. Statistical data included.

32436 ■ "Florida is Fastest-Growing State in U.S." in *Tampa Tribune* **(December 22, 2005)**
Pub: Media General, Inc.
Ed: Chris Echegaray. **Description:** Florida was ranked as the fastest growing state in the U.S., followed by Texas and California.

32437 ■ "The Fog of the Budget; How Bush Will Mask the Biggest National Debt in History" in *Business Week* **(February 14, 2005, No. 3920)**
Pub: McGraw-Hill Companies
Ed: Howard Gleckman. **Description:** The U.S. budget that covers fiscal years 2006 through 2010 will omit certain expenses. Historically, White House budget writers on both sides have used fiscal gimmickry when presenting their budgets to Congress and U.S. citizens.

32438 ■ "Folly and fortitude" in *Harvard Business Review* **(Vol. 80, No. 10, October 2002, pp. 10)**
Pub: Harvard Business School Press
Description: The exuberant spending by companies and consumers in the late 1990s has not produced high inflation; however, corporate corruption has increased, partly due to such spending and other factors.

32439 ■ "Food for thought" in *Black Enterprise* **(Vol. 32, No. 9, Ma rch 2002, pp. 102)**
Pub: Earl Graves Publishing Co.
Ed: James A. Anderson. **Description:** Five funds concentrating on the food industry and consumer staples are highlighted. Statistical data included.

32440 ■ "Fool's Paradise" in *Forbes* **(Vol. 175, February 14, 2005, No. 3, pp. 44)**
Pub: Forbes Magazine Inc.
Ed: Bernard Condon. **Description:** Interest rates are low and America is saturated in money. What happens when the tide turns?

32441 ■ "For U.S. Small Biz, Fertile Soil in Europe" in *Business Week Online* **(April 3, 2002)**
Pub: McGraw-Hill, Inc.
Description: This year 2002 is turning out to be a great year for many small and midsize American companies selling to or operating in Europe, especially high-tech companies.

32442 ■ "Foreclosures Rise; Yuppie Belt Hit Hard as Defaults Climb 10% City wide" in *Crain's Chicago Business* **(December 8, 2003)**
Pub: Crain Communications, Inc.
Ed: Steve Daniels. **Description:** Foreclosures rose in Chicago, Illinois' more affluent neighborhoods in 2003, including such areas as Lakeview, Lincoln Square, and the Near North Side; blame is directed at the current recession that left thousands of white-collar workers without jobs.

32443 ■ **"Foreclosures Rise; Yuppie Belt Hit Hard as Defaults Climb 10 Percent Citywide"** in *Crains Chicago Business* (Vol. 26, No. 49)
Pub: Crain Communications, Inc.
Ed: Steve Daniels. **Description:** Foreclosures rose in Chicago, Illinois' more affluent neighborhoods in 2003, including such areas as Lakeview, Lincoln Square, and the Near North Side; blame is directed at the current recession that left thousands of white-collar workers without jobs.

32444 ■ **"Forget the Series; St. Louis has Bragging Rights for Job Growth"** in *St. Louis Post-Dispatch* (December 19, 2004)
Pub: Knight-Ridder/Tribune Business News
Ed: David Nicklaus. **Description:** St. Louis area reported 42,000 new jobs for the period October 2003 to October 2004, and if the trend continues could be the most jobs added to the region since 1988. St. Louis also saw three initial public offerings in 2004. Las Vegas, Nevada is also reporting high growth for the same time period.

32445 ■ **"Found in Yonkers"** in *Crain's New York Business* (Vol. 23, January 15, 2007, No. 3, pp. 37)
Pub: Crain Communications, Inc.
Description: Yonkers, Westchester's largest city, has unveiled a master plan of $3.1 billion to redevelop downtown and attract more companies, according to Yonkers Industrial Development Agency.

32446 ■ *Freakonomics: A Rogue Economist Explores the Hidden Side of Everything*
Pub: William Morrow
Ed: Steven D. Levitt; Stephen J. Dubner. **Price:** $25.95.

32447 ■ **"Get ready for spikes in gasoline prices, as supplies tighten"** in *Wall Street Journal* (January 24, 2002, pp. A1)
Pub: Wall Street Journal
Ed: Alexei Barrionuevo. **Description:** Small business expenses will see sharp increases as the cost of oil escalates. Statistical data included.

32448 ■ **"Get Ready to Grow"** in *My Business* (April/May 2004, pp. 40)
Pub: My Business Magazine
Ed: Bill Dunkelberg. **Description:** According to the National Federation of Independent Business, profit trends are the highest since 2000 with capital spending plans also the highest since 2000. Small business are voicing strongest optimism in 20 years.

32449 ■ **"Getting on the Road Toward Financial Freedom"** in *Black Enterprise* (Vol. 35, October 2004, No. 3, pp. 125)
Pub: Earl G. Graves Publishing Co. Inc.
Ed: Lynnette Khalfani. **Description:** Three strategies to economically empower individuals are examined. Eliminating debt, setting up a financial record-keeping system, and tossing old records are a few suggestions offered.

32450 ■ **"Global Economy Reaches Into Your Wallet"** in *Hispanic Business* (March 2005, pp. 6)
Pub: Hispanic Business
Ed: Jesus Chavarria. **Description:** Although the U.S. continues to increase its exports the growth of imports remains larger, hurting the U.S. economy.

32451 ■ **"Globalized Economy a Double-Edged Sword for Americans"** in *Altanta Journal-Constitution* (January 18, 2007)
Pub: Cox Newspapers, Inc.
Ed: Michael E. Kanell. **Description:** Foreign investment and trade is impacting Americans in various ways and widening the gap between the rich and middle class.

32452 ■ **"Good for Business: Houston is a Hot Spot for Economic Growth"** in *Black Enterprise* (Vol. 37, October 2006, No. 3, pp. 216)
Pub: Earl G. Graves Publishing Co. Inc.
Ed: Jeanette Valentine. **Description:** Fast-growing sectors in the biotechnology and healthcare industries

are among the driving forces of Houston's economic growth. More than 76,000 small businesses in the area employ about one in four area workers, according to the Small Business Administration. Housing and business costs are 26 and 11 percent below the national average, respectively, garnering the attention of corporate giants.

32453 ■ **"The Good Deflation: Falling Prices Can be Sign of Economic Strength"** in *Barron's* (July 28, 2003, pp. 31)
Pub: Barron's
Ed: Shlomo Maital. **Description:** The deflation harrying the U.S. economy at present is different from that responsible for Japan's lingering economic illness: supply-side, instead of demand-side. Further, fundamental differences between the U.S. and Japan indicate that the formers' problems will not be as severe or long lasting.

32454 ■ **"Good News (Almost) Everywhere You Look"** in *My Business* (June/July 2004, pp. 42)
Pub: My Business Magazine
Ed: Bill Dunkelberg. **Description:** Small business owner optimism is at historically strong levels. The Index of Small Business Optimism reported in over 100 for the eleventh month in a row. Statistical data included.

32455 ■ **"The Great Jobs Switch"** in *The Economist* (Vol. 377, October 1-7, 2005, No. 8446, pp. 13, 16)
Pub: The Economist Newspaper Ltd.
Description: Manufacturing accounts for less than 10 percent of all jobs in the U.S. However, the fall in manufacturing jobs is a sign of economic progress, not decline.

32456 ■ **"Great Time to Go It Alone"** in *Kiplinger's Personal Finance Magazine* (Vol. 58, No. 5, May 2004, pp. 20)
Pub: Kiplinger Washington Editors, Inc.
Ed: Melynda Dovel Wilcox. **Description:** Government statistics underestimate the number of jobs being created each month at small and startup companies, and the number of individuals becoming entrepreneurs.

32457 ■ **"The great unknown"** in *Entrepreneur* (Vol. 31, No. 6, June 2003, pp. 19)
Pub: Entrepreneur Media Inc.
Ed: Chris Penttila. **Description:** The frustrations faced by entrepreneurs during a struggling economy are discussed.

32458 ■ **"Greenspan Floats Sales Tax"** in *Chicago Tribune* (March 4, 2005)
Pub: Knight-Ridder/Tribune Business News
Ed: William Neikirk. **Description:** Alan Greenspan, chairman of the U.S. Federal Reserve, is recommending consideration of a national sales tax as part of the restructuring of the federal tax system.

32459 ■ **"Gridlock Alert; Who is Driving"** in *Crain's New York Business* (Vol. 22, December 11, 2006, No. 50, pp. 14)
Pub: Crain Communications, Inc.
Description: Traffic jams in Manhattan impose enormous costs on the economy, argued The Partnership for New York City. The Business Advocacy Group called for greater study of the issue before establishing congestion pricing fees for cars that enter the most crowded sections of Manhattan.

32460 ■ **"Grist: The Inevitable Rise of the Entrepreneur"** in *Inc.* (October 1, 2003)
Pub: Gruner & Jahr USA Publishing
Ed: Adam Hanft. **Description:** The natural life of the American economy always eventually favors the entrepreneur.

32461 ■ **"Grocery Prices in 2007"** in *Kiplinger Letter* (Vol. 78, January 19, 2007, No. 2)
Pub: Kiplinger
Description: Despite higher prices for livestock feed and energy, prices are expected to remain stable. However, eggs, fish and some fresh fruit and vegetables are expected to rise at least 4 to 5 percent.

32462 ■ **"Growing From the Middle"** in *Hispanic Business* (July/August 2004, pp. 20, 22, 24)
Pub: Hispanic Business
Ed: Joel Russell. **Description:** Medium-sized companies have become a powerful force in economic development. These companies have balanced expansion strategies and financial stability, and many are Hispanic-owned.

32463 ■ **"Growth Slow But Sure"** in *My Business* (April/May 2003, pp. 48)
Pub: My Business Magazine
Ed: Bill Dunkelberg. **Description:** According to the University of Michigan Index in February 2003, the real economy is not doing as poorly as the confidence measures are suggesting, the latest GDP growth near 3 percent in real terms, is compared to an average of 3.5 percent over the past few decades.

32464 ■ **"Guarded About the Hispanic Economy"** in *Hispanic Business* (Vol. 24, No. 5, May 2002, pp. 18, 20, 22, 25)
Pub: Hispanic Business Inc.
Description: Although the U.S. economy is expected to continue its slow recovery, some forecast worsening Hispanic joblessness, declining revenues for Hispanic-owned firms, and a drop-off in U.S.-Latin American trade.

32465 ■ *Guerrilla Marketing During Tough Times*
Pub: Morgan James Publishing, LLC
Ed: Jay Conrad Levinson. **Released:** October 2005. **Price:** $14.00. **Description:** Ways to market a small business during slow economic times.

32466 ■ **"Hamtramck DDA OKs Plans for Jos. Campau District"** in *Crain's Detroit Business* (Vol. 22, February 13, 2006, No. 7, pp. 26)
Pub: Crain Communications Inc. - Detroit
Ed: Robert Ankeny. **Description:** The Joseph Campau Avenue strip in Hamtramck, Michigan has been approved for ten community and development initiatives which will help to recruit and retain businesses, improve the buildings and promote a public safety program for the city's commercial district.

32467 ■ **"Handicapping the Hispanic Economy"** in *Hispanic Business* (November 2002, pp. 18-20)
Pub: Hispanic Business
Description: The future trends in elections, labor, international trade, technology education and banking access to loans are discussed by experts.

32468 ■ **"Hard Landing for Landlines"** in *Crain's New York Business* (Vol. 22, December 4, 2006, No. 49, pp. 3)
Pub: Crain Communications, Inc.
Description: More than two million residential landline customers are choosing Internet telephone service and cell phones over their landlines. Verizon is suffering the greatest in this new trend.

32469 ■ **"Has Riverboat Gambling Enhanced Kansas City's River Front?"** in *Ingram's* (Vol. 29, No. 1, January 2003, pp. 6)
Pub: Show Me Publishing, Inc.
Ed: Kevin P. Mullaly, Greg Hawley. **Description:** Comments and opinions regarding the existing river boat gambling in Kansas City, Missouri are presented.

32470 ■ **"Heading Up in a Down Year"** in *Hispanic Business* (June 2002, pp. 38, 40, 42)
Pub: Hispanic Business
Description: Revenue for the Hispanic Business 500 grew 10.9 percent in 2001, despite an economic slowdown in the U.S. Statistical data included.

32471 ■ **"Hedge Funds Beat S&P 500 Index's Return in January 2004"** in *Long Island Business News* (February 20, 2004)
Pub: Dolan Media Newswires
Ed: Ben Abelson. **Description:** According to Hennessee Hedge Fund Index, the funds produced at 2.1 percent in January 2004, compared to the expected 1.8 percent.

32472 ■ "Hidden treasure" in *Entrepreneur* (Vol. 30, No. 2, February 2002, pp. 56)
Pub: Entrepreneur Media Inc.
Ed: Sean P. Melvin. **Description:** In a tightened economy, entrepreneurs can look for capital in the nooks, crannies, equipment and real estate the business already owns.

32473 ■ "Hiring is Slow Despite Optimism About Economy" in *Wall Street Journal* (August 12, 2003, pp. B9)
Pub: Dow Jones & Co. Inc.
Ed: Richard C. Breeden. **Description:** According to the National Federation of Independent Business survey, companies are slow to hire new employees, despite good news on the economy.

32474 ■ "Hispanic Business Seats 2002 Board of Economists" in *Hispanic Business* (March 2002, pp. 20-23)
Pub: Hispanic Business
Description: The new Hispanic Business magazine's Board of Economists for 2002 have been selected. The members come from leading universities, research organizations, and government agencies and will cover economic issues, particularly those related to Hispanic business. A brief biography of each member is included.

32475 ■ "Hispanic Business Stock Index Debuts" in *Hispanic Business* (March 2003, pp. 12, 14)
Pub: Hispanic Business
Ed: Juan Solana, Joel Russell. **Description:** Hispan-Telligence, a research unit of Hispanic Business Inc. has developed the Hispanic Business Stock Index (HBSI) to track countries or industries to provide a barometer of conditions for firms in the U.S. Hispanic market. Statistical data included.

32476 ■ "The Hispanic Middle Class Comes of Age" in *Hispanic Business* (December 2001, pp. 21-22, 26, 28, 30, 32)
Pub: Hispanic Business
Ed: Robert R. Brischetto. **Description:** U.S. Hispanics are more numerous, and more prosperous. Demographics are presented, along with statistical data.

32477 ■ "Hispantelligence Report" in *Hispanic Business* (December 2003, pp. 10)
Pub: Hispanic Business
Description: Stock market indexes compared to Hispanic companies and annual household food expenditures are presented. Statistical data included.

32478 ■ "Hispantelligence Reports" in *Hispanic Business* (June 2005, pp. 12)
Pub: Hispanic Business
Description: Presentation of the Hispanic Business Stock Index shows the current value of thirteen Hispanic companies from January 3 through April 21, 2005. Growth for Hispanic-owned businesses is reflected in a graph showing numbers from years 1987 through 2010.

32479 ■ *A History of Small Business in America*
Pub: University of North Carolina Press
Ed: Mansel G. Blackford. **Released:** January 2003. **Price:** $18.95. **Description:** History of American small business from the colonial era to present, showing how it has played a role in the nation's economic, political, and cultural development across manufacturing, sales, services and farming.

32480 ■ "Hit Discriminators Where it Hurts" in *Black Enterprise* (Vol. 34, No. 4, November 2003, pp. 28)
Pub: Earl Graves Publishing Co.
Ed: Darrell Williams. **Description:** African American consumers account for 5 percent of all U.S. consumer spending and 4 percent of Gross Domestic Product, making them a powerful force in the U.S. economy. However, black consumers believe they are still greeted with suspicion about intentions and skepticism about ability to pay.

32481 ■ "Holding Pattern" in *Entrepreneur* (Vol. 33, September 2005, No. 9, pp. 26)
Pub: Entrepreneur Media Inc.
Ed: Mark Henricks. **Description:** Small business hiring has been at a standstill in 2005 and small business salaries fell 2.2 percent from January to June. Statistical data included.

32482 ■ "Hollister wins business praise" in *Crain's Detroit Business* (Vol. 18, No. 51, December 23, 2002, pp. 7)
Pub: Crain Communications Inc., Detroit
Ed: Amy Lane. **Description:** Business representatives are encouraged by the appointment of David Hollister as the State of Michigan's next economic development chief.

32483 ■ "A Home of Their Own" in *Hispanic Business* (October 2004, pp. 28)
Pub: Hispanic Business
Description: Homeownership gaps in the Hispanic community represents around 4 million homeowners. Closing the ownership gap is key to boosting economic development.

32484 ■ "Home crafting stimulates togetherness" in *Retail Merchandiser* (Vol. 42, No. 11, Nov. 2002, pp. 33)
Pub: VNU Business Media
Description: The uncertain economic environment has more people spending time at home, which in turn promotes crafting; parents are spending time with children putting together easy craft kits. Chuck Waimon, COO of Fairfield Processing in Danbury, Connecticut shares his views on consumer trends in home crafts.

32485 ■ "Homeownership up, but home equity declining" in *Business First Columbus* (Vol. 18, No. 26, February 15, 2002, pp. 39)
Pub: Business First Columbus, Inc.
Ed: Sonny Lufrano. **Description:** Statistical data on home ownership and equity is presented.

32486 ■ "Honoring the Profit" in *PC Computing* (April, 2000, pp. 58)
Pub: Ziff-Davis Inc.
Ed: Jennifer Brandlon. **Description:** A Princeton University study of American attitudes towards materialism and faith reported that spiritual values still sway economic behavior.

32487 ■ "Hot 100" in *Entrepreneur* (Vol. 31, No. 6, June 2003, pp. 64)
Pub: Entrepreneur Media Inc.
Ed: Amanda C. Kooser. **Description:** Twenty-five of the 100 companies hitting the year's hottest industry for 2003 come from the business services sector, nine providing logistics services (such as freight-handling, trucking and transportation) and six providing marketing and advertising services.

32488 ■ "House of Cards? Home-Equity Borrowing Could be Risky Business as Interest Rates Rise" in *Entrepreneur* (Vol. 31, October 2003)
Pub: Entrepreneur Media, Inc.
Ed: Scott Bernard Nelson. **Description:** Because of lower interest rates, home equity loans have been popular over the last few years; the dangers risked taking home equity loans are discussed.

32489 ■ "House Party Over? High Cost of Living in New Jersey Continues" in *The Record* (November 16, 2005)
Pub: New Jersey Media Group
Ed: Kathleen Lynn. **Description:** New Jersey home prices rose 15 percent over the third quarter of 2004 and rose again in September 2005, a sign that the housing market may be weakening.

32490 ■ "Housing Market Slowdown Will Weaken California Economy, Forecasters Say" in *Sacramento Bee* (December 7, 2005)
Pub: The Sacramento Bee
Ed: Dale Kasler. **Description:** Economic experts from the University of California, Los Angeles, predict the housing slowdown will weaken the state's economy. The university's Anderson Forecast said the downshift in real estate will lead to job losses.

32491 ■ "Housing Pilot Plan Updated" in *Mississippi Business Journal* (Vol. 29, January 2007, No. 4, pp. 8)
Pub: Venture Publications, Inc.
Ed: Wally Northway **Description:** Mississippi has been granted more than $280 million in funding from FEMA for the Alternative Housing Pilot Program. Under this plan some FEMA trailers would be replaced with more sustainable alternative housing. Plan aims to demonstrate that safer, more livable emergency housing can be produced for victims of major natural disasters.

32492 ■ "Housing market at high risk" in *Atlanta Business Chronicle* (Vol. 25, January 10, 2003, No. 31, pp. 1A)
Pub: American City Business Publications, Inc.
Ed: Lisa R. Schoolcraft. **Description:** The troubled economy has led to an increase in home foreclosures. Atlanta, Georgia has the highest housing market risk based on the change in the rate of economic growth, construction lending trends and levels, and the divergence of housing prices and income growth. In December 2002, there were 2,884 homes scheduled for foreclosure in metro Atlanta.

32493 ■ "How Blue Will Christmas Be? As sales keep plunging, retailers are panicking" in *Fortuneit* (Vol. 146, No. 9, Nov. 11, 2002, pp. 127)
Pub: Time Inc.
Ed: Cora Daniels. **Description:** Predictions regarding the retail conditions for Christmas 2002 are discussed. Since retail accounts for 23 percent of the U.S. gross domestic product, the holiday season is crucial.

32494 ■ "How to Calm Workers' Fears" in *Austin Business Journal* (Vol. 21, No. 25, September 7, 2001, pp. 17)
Pub: Austin Business Journal, Inc.
Description: Robert Half International offers tips on motivating employees during an economic slowdown.

32495 ■ "How China Runs the World Economy" in *The Economist* (Vol. 376, July 30-August 5, 2005, No. 8437, pp. 11)
Pub: The Economist Newspaper Ltd.
Description: Global wages, profits, prices and interest rates are influenced by events in China.

32496 ■ "How High Can Low Go Without Adverse Effects on Economy?" in *St. Louis Post-Dispatch* (March 9, 2005)
Pub: Knight-Ridder/Tribune Business News
Ed: David Nicklaus. **Description:** Minimum wage laws are discussed. The Senate rejected two proposals to raise the minimum wage from $5.15 an hour in March.

32497 ■ "How to Improve Georgia's Economy" in *Atlanta Business Chronicle* (Vol. 25, December 6, 2002, No. 26, pp. 35A)
Pub: American City Business Publications, Inc.
Ed: Georgia **Description:** Governor-elect, Sonny Perdue, should back the Metro Atlanta Chamber of Commerce's attempts to attract the secretariat of the Free Trade Area of the Americas to the city. He should also consider opening field offices of the Georgia Department of Industry, Trade and Tourism in Latin American cities.

32498 ■ "How Not to Forecast Price Hikes" in *Business Week* (December 19, 2005, No. 3964, pp. 26)
Pub: McGraw-Hill Companies
Ed: Kathleen Madigan. **Description:** Investors and economists measure success by accurate forecasting of inflation trends, but sometimes what worked in the past no longer holds true.

32499 ■ "How the Quest for Efficiency Corroded the Market" in *Harvard Business Review* (Vol. 81, No. 7, July 2003, pp. 76)
Pub: Harvard Business School Press
Ed: Paul M. Healy, Krishna G. Palepu. **Description:** Analysis of the U.S. financial system is provided.

32500 ■ **"How to Teach Economics" in** *Ingram's* **(Vol. 28, No. 6, June 2002, pp. 28)**
Pub: Show Me Publishing, Inc.
Description: A recent initiative by the Kansas Council on Economic Education trained 700 local teachers on economics and economic principles to ensure that their 50,000 students will acquire a better education in economics.

32501 ■ **"Hurricane Won't Blow Down State Economy" in** *Crain's Detroit Business* **(Vol. 21, October 3, 2005, No. 43, pp. 48)**
Pub: Crain Communications Inc. - Detroit
Ed: Tom Henderson. **Description:** According to the Michigan Business Activity Index, Michigan's economy rose 2 points in August to 111, making it stronger to fend off the consequences of the hurricanes hitting the Gulf Coast in 2005.

32502 ■ **"I-5 Corridor: Nurturing Its Economic Potential" in** *San Fernando Valley Business Journal* **(Vol. 11, December 2006, No. 25, pp. 35)**
Pub: San Fernando Valley Business Journal Associates
Ed: Jason Schaff. **Description:** North Valley area sticks out when compared to the remade cities of Burbank and Gendale due to its lack of industrial diversity and cohesiveness that would make it a larger contributor to the economy of the region. Statistical data included.

32503 ■ **"I'm O.K., You're Not" in** *Business Week* **(No. 3694, August 14, 2000, pp. F10)**
Pub: McGraw-Hill, Inc.
Description: Many entrepreneurs see the dot-com shakeout as an opportunity to recapture some lost business.

32504 ■ **"The Impact of Immigrant Entrepreneurs" in** *Business Week* **(February 7, 2007)**
Pub: McGraw-Hill Companies
Ed: Kerry Miller. **Description:** Overview of immigrant entrepreneur's impact on economic development and their status as a driving force for the U.S. economy.

32505 ■ **"In Brief: Small-Business Poll: Economy Worsening" in** *American Banker* **(Vol. 170, September 5, 2006, No. 170, pp. 9)**
Pub: SourceMedia, Inc.
Description: According to a survey conducted by Discover Financial Services, most small business owners are pessimistic about the economy. Statistical data included.

32506 ■ **"In the Hood" in** *Entrepreneur* **(Vol. 28, No. 8, August 2000, pp. 100)**
Pub: Entrepreneur Media Inc.
Ed: Jacquelyn Lynn. **Description:** The world's growing at Internet speed, but your local economic development agency is still watching out for you.

32507 ■ **"In My Humble Opinion" in** *Fast Company* **(November 2001, pp. 82)**
Pub: Fast Company
Ed: John Ellis, Seth Godin. **Description:** The article uses Gannett and Yahoo to address the differences between the old and new economy. Gannett is the diversified media concern owning USA Today, various local newspapers and 22 television stations. Yahoo is the Internet portal through which nearly 200 million people use monthly.

32508 ■ **"In Search of Global Leaders" in** *Harvard Business Review* **(Vol. 81, No. 8, August 2003, pp. 38)**
Pub: Harvard Business School Press
Description: Stephen Green (CEO of HSBC), Fred Hassan (Chairman and CEO of Shering-Plough), Jeffrey Immelt (Chairman and CEO of General Electric), Michael Marks (CEO of Flextronics), and Daniel Meiland (Executive Chairman of Egon Zdhndr International) all express views about what global means, within an economic framework.

32509 ■ *Innovation and Entrepreneurship*
Pub: HarperInformation
Ed: Peter F. Drucker. **Released:** May 1993. **Price:** $14.50. **Description:** Innovation and entrepreneurship in America's new economy.

32510 ■ **"Insurance Firms Forecast Profitable Year" in** *Pacific Business News* **(Vol. 41, No. 19, July 18, 2003, pp. 12)**
Pub: American City Business Journals
Ed: Eddy Conway. **Description:** Profile and forecasts of Hawaii's insurance industry are presented. Topics include economic conditions, profits and losses, and business forecasts.

32511 ■ **"Interest Rate Speculation May Be Fueling Home Buying in Denver Area" in** *Denver Post* **(January 26, 2005)**
Pub: Knight-Ridder/Tribune Business News
Ed: Christine Tatum. **Description:** Low interest rates are fueling home sales in the Denver, Colorado area. Statistical data included.

32512 ■ **"Investment in Transit System the First Step in Pursuit of Games" in** *Crain's Chicago Business* **(Vol. 30, January 2007, No. 1, pp. 8)**
Pub: Crain Communications, Inc.
Ed: MarySue Barrett. **Description:** Chicago is one of the cities that are attempting to win the 2016 Olympics bid. State lawmakers must decide whether to shrink or expand the region's public transit system. Chicago must also continue to develop mixed-income communities to attract consumers from a wide range of income levels that would be expected to come to Chicago for the games.

32513 ■ **"Investors Likely to be Wary of Suppliers, Analysts Say" in** *Crain's Detroit Business* **(Vol. 21, October 17, 2005, No. 43, pp. 33)**
Pub: Crain Communications Inc. - Detroit
Ed: Terry Kosdrosky. **Description:** Potential investors and analysts grow wearing of suppliers in the wake of Delphi Corporation's Chapter 11 bankruptcy.

32514 ■ **"Investors Retrench with Bond in Shaky Market" in** *Atlanta Business Chronicle* **(Vol. 25, No. 20, October 25, 2002, pp. 3C)**
Pub: American City Business Publications, Inc.
Ed: Tony Heffernan. **Description:** Investors are seeing safety amid a volatile stock market and an uncertain economy. For investors, safety translates to bonds, especially U.S. Treasury securities, rather than corporate securities.

32515 ■ **"Is Pearl Headed for a Fall?" in** *Business Journal-Portland* **(Vol. 20, No. 22, August 1, 2003, pp. 1)**
Pub: American City Business Journals, Inc.
Ed: Heidi J. Stout. **Description:** Profile of the real estate market in the greater Portland, Oregon area, topics include real estate development, interest rates, and the impact of U.S. economic conditions on the market.

32516 ■ **"It figures" in** *Entrepreneur* **(Vol. 30, No. 3, March 2002, pp. 34)**
Pub: Entrepreneur Media Inc.
Description: A presentation of how companies are managing during the economic slowdown; other business-related statistics are included.

32517 ■ **"It's 2006! Whatcha Gonna Do About It?" in** *Inc.* **(Volume 28, January 2006, No. 1, pp. 78-85, 113)**
Pub: Inc. Magazine
Ed: Stephanie Clifford. **Description:** Various entrepreneurs give advice to help small businesses face new challenges in 2006. Topics include investments, the economy, small business trends, logistics, business communication such as blogs, energy issues, consumer products, real estate, interest rates and outsourcing.

32518 ■ **"It's All In Your Head" in** *Entrepreneur* **(Vol. 33, January 2005, No. 1, pp. 58)**
Pub: Entrepreneur Media Inc.
Ed: Chris Penttila. **Description:** Ways for small business owners to cope with the ever changing economy.

32519 ■ **"January Retail Sales Will Exaggerate Consumer Spending Strength" in** *Kiplinger Letter* **(Vol. 78, January 19, 2007, No. 2)**
Pub: Kiplinger
Description: Gift cards sold during the holidays are likely to spur retail sales for January 2007. Retail sales are expected to hit 3.5 percent for 2007, lower than last year's 4 percent.

32520 ■ **"Job Growth in State Catching Up to Nation" in** *San Jose Mercury News* **(February 26, 2005)**
Pub: Knight-Ridder/Tribune Business News
Ed: Nicole C. Wong. **Description:** Twenty thousand new jobs were added to California's economy in January 2005. Total jobs are up 1.6 percent in the state and 1.7 percent nationally.

32521 ■ **"Job Market May Be Turning Around" in** *Hispanic Business* **(October 2003, pp. 111)**
Pub: Hispanic Business
Description: According to a career services Internet company, the job market in North America is stabilizing. Statistical data included.

32522 ■ **"Job Outlook Stays Bright in Florida" in** *Tampa Tribune* **(December 16, 2005)**
Pub: Media General, Inc.
Ed: Dave Simanoff. **Description:** Tampa, Florida is seeing an increase in job growth, leading the nation by adding 255,100 jobs in the last year.

32523 ■ **"Jobless Claims Data Not As Bad As Feared by Economists" in** *Atlanta Journal-Constitution* **(April 11, 2003)**
Pub: Knight-Ridder/Tribune Business News
Ed: Michael E. Kanell. **Description:** Nearly 20,000 fewer people applied for unemployment in the nation for the month of March 2003, lower than predicted by analysts. The current jobless rate in America stands at 5.8 percent. Statistical data included.

32524 ■ **"Jobs Are Back; Too Bad Wages Aren't" in** *Fortune* **(Vol. 149, No. 9, May 3, 2004, pp. 40)**
Pub: Time, Inc.
Ed: Anna Bernasek. **Description:** Despite the number of newly created jobs, wages are remaining the same. One factor accounting for this is the benefits workers receive, which increase costs for employers. Insurance premiums have risen 32 percent over the past five years.

32525 ■ **"Johnson County, Missouri" in** *Ingram's* **(Vol. 29, No. 9, September 2003, pp. 34)**
Pub: Show Me Publishing, Inc.
Description: Profile of Johnson County, Missouri. Topics include economic conditions and development, industrialization, and local colleges and universities.

32526 ■ **"The Joy of Quitting" in** *Fortune* **(Vol. 141, No. 3, February 7, 2000, pp. 199+)**
Pub: Time Inc.
Description: The new economy is changing the way people look at their jobs. The article suggests that leaving a job you are unhappy doing is the right thing to do.

32527 ■ **"Joyless recovery based on Georgia Economic Outlook" in** *Atlanta Business Chronicle* **(Vol. 25, January 10, 2003, No. 31, pp. 23A)**
Pub: American City Business Publications, Inc.
Ed: Deirdre Gregg. **Description:** The outlook for Georgia's economy is bleak, according to University of Georgia's Georgia Economic Outlook 2003. Economic indicators for the region are discussed. Statistical data included.

32528 ■ "JPMorgan Chase Regional Economist Forecasts Long Island Growth for 2004" in *Long Island Business News* **(January 30, 2004)**
Pub: Dolan Media Newswires
Description: Marc Goloven, an economist for JPMorgan Chase predicts economic growth of about 4 percent nationwide and in the Long Island, New York region. Goloven attributes this in part to the fact that many small businesses suffered less economic damage in the last few years. Long Island has shifted away from the manufacturing sector to the services industry, helping the area.

32529 ■ "Justice's warning" in *Black Enterprise* **(Vol. 33, No. 198, March 24, 2003, pp. A3)**
Pub: Earl Graves Publishing Co.
Ed: Laurie Cunningham. **Description:** Florida Supreme Court Justice Raoul Cantero III, warns of inadequate funding for the justice system in his state.

32530 ■ "Ka-Boom! Looks Like the Economy is Finally Growing-And Guess What's Leading the Way?" in *Entrepreneur* **(Vol. 32, August 2004)**
Pub: Entrepreneur Media Inc.
Ed: Mike Hogan. **Description:** Technology is being credited as the catalyst for the growing economy in the U.S., which averaged 5.5 percent growth over the last two years. The U.S. Bureau of Labor Statistics expects continued growth in the economy at the rate of about 4 percent or more in 2005.

32531 ■ "KCBS-KCAL Studio Center Complex" in *San Fernando Valley Business Journal* **(Vol. 12, January 2007, No. 1, pp. 12)**
Pub: San Fernando Valley Business Journal Associates
Description: KCBS-KCAL Studio Center Complex opens in March on the back lot of the CBS Studio Center, which means business growth for the businesses and eateries nearby.

32532 ■ "Keeping Their Options Open" in *Boston Business Journal* **(Vol. 23, No. 26, August 1, 2003, pp. 3)**
Pub: American City Business Journals
Description: Profile of Boston, Massachusetts-based Progressive Software Inc., including an examination of Boston-area technology companies as highlighted by the plight of Progressive Software Inc. Topics include economic conditions, competition, and financial management.

32533 ■ "Key is getting region's leaders at one table" in *Crain's Detroit Business* **(Vol. 19, No. 17, April 28, 2003, pp. 8)**
Pub: Crain Communications Inc., Detroit
Description: According to a recent survey conducted by the Metropolitan Affairs Coalition, a majority of metro Detroit residents would favor regional cooperation to help move Detroit forward into a stronger economic region.

32534 ■ "King: 'It's not a recession. It's a disaster'" in *Atlanta Business Chronicle* **(Vol. 25, No. 21, November 1, 2002, pp. 6C)**
Pub: American City Business Publications, Inc.
Ed: Jarred Schenke. **Description:** King Industrial Realty Inc. head, Charlie King, believes that the industrial real estate recession could be the worst since he began his career. Atlanta industrial sub-markets that have experienced negative absorption of real estate are listed.

32535 ■ "L.A. County Econowatch" in *San Fernando Valley Business Journal* **(Vol. 11, December 2006, No. 25, pp. 25)**
Pub: San Fernando Valley Business Journal Associates
Description: Statistical data included for factors affecting the L.A. County's economy, including numbers of bankruptcies, electricity accounts, tourism activity, real estate figures and others.

32536 ■ "Lake Success Based Astoria Financial Finds Fewer Acquisition Opportunities..." in *Long Island Business News* **(Mar. 5, 2004)**
Pub: Dolan Media Newswires
Description: Astoria Financial Corporation, with $22.5 billion in assets from bank acquisitions, expects to see fewer mergers in the industry.

32537 ■ "Land of the Free" in *Fast Company* **(May 2001, pp. 125)**
Pub: Fast Company
Ed: Daniel H. Pink. **Description:** During an economic downturn, the rules of supply and demand, profit and loss, and the art of value creation remain the same.

32538 ■ "The last thing you should do is panic" in *Fast Company* **(May 2001, pp. 90)**
Pub: Fast Company
Ed: William F. Miller. **Description:** Profile of William F. Miller, chairman of Borland Software Corporation and Sentius Corporation, and is president and CEO of emeritus of SRI International. Miller offers advice that during a slow economy small businesses should put resources into the strongest areas of the company.

32539 ■ "Laterals keep coming" in *Black Enterprise* **(Vol. 33, No. 198, March 24, 2003, pp. AA2)**
Pub: Earl Graves Publishing Co.
Ed: Matthew Haggman. **Description:** The slowing economy has forced partners in law firms to look to the state of Florida.

32540 ■ "Lawyering Up" in *Boston Business Journal* **(Vol. 23, No. 30, August 29, 2003, pp. 1)**
Pub: American City Business Journals
Ed: Sheri Qualters. **Description:** Forecasts by officers of Boston, Massachusetts-based Legal Staffing Solutions regarding the state of employment in the legal services market. Topics include levels of employee recruitment, economic conditions, and effects of past layoffs.

32541 ■ "Leaders Prepare for Lean Times" in *Hispanic Business* **(Vol. 23, No. 11, November 2001, pp. 14)**
Pub: Hispanic Business Inc.
Ed: Mark Hagland. **Description:** Terrorism and business development were the topics at the 19th Annual United States Hispanic Leadership Institute (USHLI) conference, held September 27-30 in Chicago, Illinois. Juan Andrade, President of the USHLI, feels that the focus on terrorism will interfere with effective business development growth.

32542 ■ "Leading Indicators: Continued Growth" in *My Business* **(December/January 2004, pp. 50)**
Pub: My Business Magazine
Description: National Federation of Independent Business' Small Business Optimism Index hit 104.6, the highest reading since the early 1980s, signaling economic growth. The economy grew 7.2 percent in third quarter 2003, the fastest growth rate in 19 years. Statistical data included.

32543 ■ "Leading Lenders Shift as 2006 Activity Slows" in *Crain's New York Business* **(Vol. 22, December 11, 2006, No. 50, pp. 28)**
Pub: Crain Communications, Inc.
Description: HSBC, leader of last year's SBA loans, recorded steep declines in both the value and number of its SBA loans. Bank of America took first place in the number of SBA loans for 2006, while J.P. Morgan Chase captured second place.

32544 ■ "The least lease" in *Entrepreneur* **(Vol. 30, No. 3, March 2002, pp. 65)**
Pub: Entrepreneur Media Inc.
Ed: Jennifer Pellet. **Description:** Because of the economic downturn, commercial real estate has become more affordable and companies are able to bargain for lower priced leases.

32545 ■ "Loan Will Go To Help Old Area" in *Sacramento Bee* **(December 20, 2005)**
Pub: The Sacramento Bee
Ed: Gilbert Chan. **Description:** One of Sacramento's oldest business districts has received a $4 million loan from the California Infrastructure and Economic Development Bank. The loan will help boost the economy and revitalize the area.

32546 ■ "Local Business Bankruptcies Outpace Nation" in *Boston Business Journal* **(Vol. 22, No. 16, May 24, 2002, pp. 1)**
Pub: MCP, Inc.
Ed: Edward Mason. **Description:** Business failures increased in Massachusetts by 24 percent for first quarter 2002, the first increase since 1999. Business failures increased throughout the U.S. by 11 percent for same quarter. Statistical data included.

32547 ■ "Local Courses Try to Stay Chipper after Weak Year" in *Crain's Detroit Business* **(Vol. 19, No. 14, April 7, 2003, pp. 14)**
Pub: Crain Communications Inc., Detroit
Ed: Jason Deegan. **Description:** Report on the status of Michigan golf courses after a weak year in 2002. Renewed confidence was seen at the annual golf show held at the Novi Expo Center.

32548 ■ "Local Economy to Do Better Than State, Nation in '07" in *San Diego Business Journal* **(Vol. 28, January 1, 2007, No. 1, pp. 1)**
Pub: San Diego Business Journal Associates
Ed: Michelle Mowad. **Description:** San Diego County's economy predicted to fare better than that of the state or nation, despite a slowing of business activities.

32549 ■ *Local Enterprises in the Global Economy: Issues of Governance and Upgrading*
Pub: Edward Elgar Publishing, Incorporated
Ed: Hubert Schmitz. **Released:** April 2004. **Price:** $35.00 (soft cover), $110.00 (hard bound). **Description:** Examination of the relationships between globalization, corporate governance, and the economic performance of small businesses and local enterprises.

32550 ■ "Long Island's Patent Production Falls Nearly 20 Percent Since 1988" in *Long Island Business News* **(March 5, 2004)**
Pub: Dolan Media Newswires
Ed: Ken Schachter. **Description:** Long Island's future economic health is tied to industries such as life sciences, software development and defense-industry prototyping and design rather than large-scale manufacturing. Patent growth is used to gauge the economic progress of the area.

32551 ■ "Long-term bunker: Louis A. Holland thinks more turbulence is ahead" in *Black Enterprise* **(Vol. 33, No. 3, Oct. 2002, pp. 48)**
Pub: Earl Graves Publishing Co.
Ed: James A. Anderson. **Description:** Louis A. Holland, money manager, speaks about the state of the stock market in the U.S. Holland makes predictions and stock picks and provides statistical data.

32552 ■ "Long-Term Bunker: Louis A. Holland Thinks More Turbulence Is Ahead" in *Black Enterprise* **(Vol. 33, No. 3, Oct. 2002, pp. 48)**
Pub: Earl Graves Publishing Co.
Ed: James A. Anderson. **Description:** Louis A. Holland, money manager, speaks about the state of the stock market in the U.S. Holland makes predictions and stock picks and provides statistical data.

32553 ■ "Look at the Big Economic Picture." in *Black Enterprise* **(Vol. 35, September 2004, No. 2, pp. 38)**
Pub: Earl G. Graves Publishing Co. Inc.
Ed: Nicole Lewis. **Description:** Experts agree there is more to picking stocks than analyzing a company's balance sheet. Ronald A. Johnson, chief strategist at

Smith, Graham & Company, recommends also looking at macroeconomics indicators such as interest rates and inflation, along with historical performance of sectors and companies, looking for patterns that indicate ways a company performed during various business cycles like recession or economic expansion.

32554 ■ "Look before you lay off" in *Harvard Business Review* **(Vol. 80, No. 4, April 2002, pp. 20)**
Pub: Harvard Business School Press
Ed: Darrell Rigby. **Description:** An examination of the pitfalls inherent in layoffs during an economic downturn. Research shows that shareholders punish companies that use layoffs solely to cut costs. Graphs are included.

32555 ■ "Looking for The Prevailing Wind The bulls and bears are both blowing plenty of hot air these days" in *Fortune* **(May 15, 2000, p. 441)**
Pub: Time Inc.
Ed: Jim Griffin. **Description:** The two sides do agree on one thing, though: the economy is so good, it hurts. A discussion of the ways the good economy is impacting the stock market.

32556 ■ "Maine Executives Give State's Economy 'Worst' Rating" in *Portland Press Herald* **(May 27, 2005)**
Pub: Blethen Maine Newspapers, Inc.
Ed: Edward D. Murphy. **Description:** Market Research Insight surveyed 502 business leaders from Maine and discovered senior managers have a negative view of the economy, the business climate, and the state's ability to handle its economic issues.

32557 ■ "Maine Faces Slow Population Growth, Aging Workforce" in *Portland Press Herald* **(May 6, 2005)**
Pub: Blethen Maine Newspapers, Inc.
Ed: Tux Turkel. **Description:** Maine is experiencing slow population growth coupled with an aging workforce, making the state's ability to expand its economy over the next ten years a challenge.

32558 ■ "Maine Home Sales Fall 4 Percent" in *Portland Press Herald* **(November 30, 2005)**
Pub: Blethen Maine Newspapers, Inc.
Ed: Tux Turkel. **Description:** After nearly five years of growth, home sales in the State of Maine fell by 4 percent in October 2005, due mainly to rising prices.

32559 ■ "Make your layoff list and check it twice" in *BlackEnterprise* **(Vol. 32, No. 3, October 2001, pp. 70)**
Pub: Earl Graves Publishing Co.
Ed: Robyn D. Clarke. **Description:** David A. Branch, an employment and civil rights attorney in Washington DC, provides four important points for businesses to consider when planning a pre-layoff checklist.

32560 ■ "Managed Care's Poor Health" in *Rough Notes* **(Vol. 145, No. 2, February 2002, pp. 36)**
Pub: Rough Notes
Ed: Phil Zinkewicz. **Description:** According to surveys by Weiss Ratings Inc., 40.9 percent of health maintenance organizations, 16 percent of banks and financial industries, 25.9 percent of life and health insurers and 18.4 percent of financial industries are in a financially weakened condition. The threat of bioterrorism has had a serious impact on the problem to which no constructive solution has yet been devised.

32561 ■ *Managing India's Small Industrial Economy: The Catalytic Role of Industrial Counselors and Policy Makers*
Pub: Sage Publications, Incorporated
Ed: V. Padmanand, V.G. Patel. **Released:** June 2004. **Price:** $28.95. **Description:** Case studies and methodology are used to discuss the areas where industrial consultants are influencing sustainability and growth of small businesses in India's industrial economy.

32562 ■ "Manufacturing History: Tales of Turning Points in Factory Jobs are Just That" in *Barron's* **(July 28, 2003, pp. 30)**
Pub: Barron's
Ed: Gene Epstein. **Description:** The continuing erosion of manufacturing jobs in the U.S. may have produced a nearly 40-year low, with less than 15 million factory-related jobs; and its percentage of total private employment, at less than 15 percent, may be nearly 20 percent less than the previous low; but that still does not indicate anything structurally wrong, or any harmful effect of foreign manufacturing.

32563 ■ "Manufacturing Sector Strengthening" in *Milwaukee Journal Sentinel* **(December 1, 2005)**
Pub: Journal Sentinel, Inc.
Ed: Thomas Content, Rick Barrett. **Description:** According to two recent reports, the manufacturing sector is seeing an increase in production while the economy in the Milwaukee, Wisconsin area rose 10 points from October to November 2005.

32564 ■ "Market Drifts While Tech Stocks Wilt" in *Barron's* **(August 11, 2003, pp. MW3)**
Pub: Barron's
Ed: Vito J. Racanelli. **Description:** Stock markets, which seemed willing to rally on the thinnest of premises in the second quarter, now appear resolved to stagnate despite genuinely positive indicators. Factory orders increased nearly 2 percent in June, while labor productivity gained almost 6 percent.

32565 ■ "Massachusetts Jobless Insurance Trust Fund May Need Federal Help" in *Boston Globe* **(April 11, 2003)**
Pub: Knight-Ridder/Tribune Business News
Ed: Matthew Brelis. **Description:** The State of Massachusetts' unemployment insurance trust fund is facing insolvency after two years of rising unemployment rates and will require federal loans to pay benefits in 2003.

32566 ■ "Maybe it's time to batten down the hatches" in *Crain's Detroit Business* **(Vol. 19, No. 11, March 17, 2003, pp. 8)**
Pub: Crain Communications Inc., Detroit
Ed: Keith Crain. **Description:** Detroit-area businesses, as well as charities, fear the economy will not improve in 2003. It is recommended that businesses have a contingency plan if the economy continues to decline.

32567 ■ "M.D. Hodges changes strategy" in *Atlanta Business Chronicle* **(Vol. 25, December 6, 2002, No. 26, pp. 7C)**
Pub: American City Business Publications, Inc.
Ed: Anya Martin. **Description:** Development and lease management company, M.D. Hodges Enterprises Inc., Atlanta, Georgia, has won the 2002 Developer of the Year Award from the Georgia Chapter of the National Association of Industrial and Office Properties, according to NAIOP judge, Bo Jackson. Jackson is the executive vice president of the office division of Colonial Properties Trust. The firm was chosen for its creativity.

32568 ■ "Measuring Progress: A Look at the Economic Strides of African Americans in Recent Decades" in *Black Enterprise* **(December 2003)**
Pub: Earl Graves Publishing Co.
Ed: Latif Lewis. **Description:** Homeownership among African Americans rose in the 1990s to 42.7 percent. Statistical data included.

32569 ■ "MEDC Showcases Michigan's Automotive Brainpower at Auto Show Symposium" in *Crain's Detroit Business* **(Vol. 21, December 19, 2005)**
Pub: Crain Communications Inc. - Detroit
Ed: Terry Kosdrosky. **Description:** Michigan Economic Development Corporation hosted a symposium promoting Michigan's automotive intellectual power.

32570 ■ *Medium Sized Firms and Economics Growth*
Pub: Nova Science Publishers, Incorporated

Ed: Janez Prasniker. **Released:** February 2005. **Price:** $79.00. **Description:** Medium sized companies should have a more definitive presence in modern microeconomic theory, the theory of entrepreneurship, and the theory of financial markets.

32571 ■ "Mega Wal-Marts Crush Business Diversity" in *Bellingham Business Journal* **(January 2007, pp. C14)**
Pub: Sun News Inc.
Description: Small businesses are the backbone of the Bellingham economy. Wal-Mart threatens the economic diversity by flattening competition and erasing longtime family-owned businesses.

32572 ■ "Military Base Closures Could Have Big Impact on California Economy" in *San Jose Mercury News* **(February 17, 2005)**
Pub: Knight-Ridder/Tribune Business News
Ed: Jim Puzzanghera. **Description:** The closing of the U.S. Naval Air Station at Moffett Field, the Presidio in San Francisco, and Fort Ord along Monterey Bay will cost the State of California $9.6 billion in lost revenues annually.

32573 ■ "A Misleading Predictor of Inflation" in *Business Week* **(January 23, 2006, No. 3968, pp. 28)**
Pub: McGraw-Hill Companies
Ed: James Mehring. **Description:** Wage growth is slowing; private sector wages and salaries grew 2.2 percent over last year but down from a 3 percent pace two years ago.

32574 ■ "Missouri's System of Higher Education: the New Rules for the Knowledge Economy" in *Ingram's* **(Vol. 29, No. 8, August 2003, pp. 75)**
Pub: Show Me Publishing, Inc.
Ed: Quentin Wilson. **Description:** The changes Missouri's colleges and universities are offering to meet the demands of potential students are presented.

32575 ■ "A Mixed Forecast for 2002" in *Hispanic Business* **(Vol. 24, No. 1/2, January/ February 2002, pp. 14, 16)**
Pub: Hispanic Business Inc.
Ed: Scott Williams. **Description:** Experts make forecasts on an economic recovery in 2002, and the ramifications for Hispanic business and consumers. Statistical data included.

32576 ■ "Mixed Grill: A Quarter's Menu: Good-and Some Bad—News" in *Barron's* **(July 7, 2003, pp. 22)**
Pub: Barron's
Ed: Shirley A. Lazo. **Description:** Nearly one hundred companies reported dividend increases in June 2003, up 10 percent from 2002, reflecting the influence of reduced taxes on certain corporate dividends. A corresponding and irregular increase in cutback is the negative counter to this trend.

32577 ■ "Mixed Signals" in *Entrepreneur* **(Vol. 33, September 2005, No. 9, pp. 18)**
Pub: Entrepreneur Media Inc.
Ed: Chris Penttila. **Description:** Chris Mazzilli, co-founder of Gotham Comedy Club in New York City is offering comedy packages to corporations as a way to grow his business in a slow economy. Patrick Calello, founder of Automoblox in New Jersey, offers customer referrals and demonstrations of his wooden toy car kits to help sales in the slumping economy.

32578 ■ "Money that Binds from Afar" in *Hispanic Business* **(November 2003, pp. 60, 62, 64)**
Pub: Hispanic Business
Ed: Derek Reveron. **Description:** Remittances and direct investment connect the U.S. Hispanic economy to hemispheric financial development. Statistical data included, along with average transfer costs for $200 and Latin American remittances.

32579 ■ "Monthly report-December 2001" in *Small Business Economic Trends* **(December 2001, pp. 1)**
Pub: National Federation of Independent Business Foundation

Description: A survey of the small business owners/members of the National Federation of Independent Business is presented. Topics summarized include optimism index and outlook, earnings, sales, prices, employment, credit conditions, interest rates, inventories, capital investments, and important issues facing small business.

32580 ■ "Monthly report-January 2002" in *Small Business Economic Trends* (January 2002, pp. 1)
Pub: National Federation of Independent Business Foundation
Description: A survey conducted by the National Federation of Independent Business in December 2001 found that the Small Business Optimism Index rose from 99.4 in November to 100.4 in December. Topics covered include optimism index, prices, sales, compensation, credit conditions, interest rates, inventories, capital outlays, and more.

32581 ■ "Mortgage Lenders Brace for Layoffs" in *Boston Business Journal* (Vol. 23, No. 30, August 29, 2003, pp. 1)
Pub: American City Business Journals
Ed: Edward Mason. **Description:** The economic climate for mortgage lenders in the greater Boston, Massachusetts region are discussed. Topics include economic conditions, high interest rates, and forecasts of industry layoffs.

32582 ■ "Move over, Charlotte" in *Atlanta Business Chronicle* (Vol. 25, December 6, 2002, No. 26, pp. 1A)
Pub: American City Business Publications, Inc.
Ed: Meredith Jordan. **Description:** Federal Deposit Insurance Corporation data indicates that the deposits of FDIC-insured institutions in Atlanta, Georgia area were greater than all other Southeastern metropolitan areas. As of June 2002, deposits of FDIC-insured institutions in the Atlanta area were $62 billion.

32583 ■ "Nassau Democrats Propose Reforms to Prevent Mismanagement" in *Long Island Business News* (March 12, 2004)
Pub: Dolan Media Newswires
Ed: Rosmaria Mancini. **Description:** Nassau County Legislatures have proposed procedural reforms to protect the county from mismanagement scandals in its Department of Economic Development. The Legislature cites serious issues in the personnel management, and purchasing and procurement practices and voice a need for new rules, regulations and policies.

32584 ■ "National Urban League: State of Black America" in *Black Enterprise* (Vol. 34, July 2004, No. 12, pp. 28)
Pub: Earl G. Graves Publishing Co. Inc.
Ed: Marcia A. Wade. **Description:** Disparities between black and white Americans are reported showing that in order to level the playing field an additional 23,698 black students would need to earn bachelor's degrees from four-year colleges annually. It would also require 751,000 blacks to find employment and that three white businesses fold for every black startup company.

32585 ■ "Nearly Three Years Into an Economic Recovery" in *St. Louis Post-Dispatch* (October 15, 2004)
Pub: Knight-Ridder/Tribune Business News
Ed: David Nicklaus. **Description:** Despite the economic recovery of the last three years, small businesses are using profits for savings or to repay debt, rather than upgrades or expansion of the company.

32586 ■ "The network of relationships between the economic environment and the entrepreneurial culture firms" in *Journal of Business Venturing*
Pub: Elsevier Science, Inc.
Ed: Antonio Minguzzi, Renato Passaro. **Description:** A new study theorizes that the entrepreneurial culture in small companies is influenced by their relationships with the economic environment.

32587 ■ "The New Economic World Order" in *Red Herring* (No. 102, August 15, 2001, pp. 16)
Pub: Herring Communications
Ed: Anthony B. Perkins. **Description:** The principles that nations must embrace in order to compete successfully in and share the rewards of the new economic order are addressed.

32588 ■ "New Economy Creates New Markets" in *Hispanic Business* (Vol. 22, No. 1/2, January/February, pp. 24, 26)
Pub: Hispanic Business
Description: Marketers share strategies at the Se Habla Expanol Market and Media Expo.

32589 ■ "New Group Seeks Greater Hispanic Influence" in *Hispanic Business* (Vol. 23, No. 7/8, July/August 2001, pp. 24)
Pub: Hispanic Business
Description: The newly formed National Advancement of Hispanic People (NAAHP) will pursue increased political and economic influence for U.S. Hispanics. The organization will rely on membership dues rather than corporate sponsorship.

32590 ■ "New Group Weighs Solutions" in *Crain's Detroit Business* (Vol. 19, No. 16, April 21, 2003, pp. 25)
Pub: Crain Communications Inc., Detroit
Ed: Katie Merx. **Description:** Governor Jennifer Granholm charges group of state and local health care officials to find a solution to uncompensated medical care in Michigan.

32591 ■ "The New Hispanic Information Economy" in *Hispanic Business* (November 2003, pp. 26, 28, 30)
Pub: Hispanic Business
Ed: Scott Williams. **Description:** A convergence of market demand and capable researchers has created a viable market for numbers on U.S. Hispanics. Within the realm of public policy, Hispanics are gaining attention.

32592 ■ "New-Home Sales Drop 9.2 Percent" in *Atlanta Journal-Constitution* (March 1, 2005)
Pub: Knight-Ridder/Tribune Business News
Ed: Michael E. Kanell. **Description:** Despite new homes sales falling 9.2 percent nationally, the Atlanta areas showed no signs of slowing. The Midwest was hardest hit where sales plunged 40 percent. Statistical data included.

32593 ■ "New Issues: There's a Side Door into the Public Markets" in *Red Herring* (No. 99, June 15 & July 1, 2001, pp. 138)
Pub: Herring Communications
Ed: Stephen Lacey. **Description:** The alternative to an Initial Public Offering (IPO), is coming back into style: Divestiture. Divestiture is when a company simply distributes shares of a subsidiary to its own stockholders, in a one-step spin-off.

32594 ■ "New Study: County Tourism Taking Off" in *Bellingham Business Journal* (December 2006, pp. A4)
Pub: Sun News Inc.
Description: Washington State Office of Community, Trade and Economic Development released a study showing that Whatcom County ranked fifth of the state's thirty-nine counties in terms tourism and of total visitor spending. Statistical data included.

32595 ■ "New World Border" in *Hispanic Business* (Vol. 23, No. 7/8, July/August 2001, pp. 14)
Pub: Hispanic Business
Ed: Scott Williams. **Description:** A group of business representatives from California, Arizona, New Mexico, and Texas have formed the non-profit Southwest Hispanic Economic Alliance (SHEA) to address Mexico/U.S. border and other issues of concern to the region's large Hispanic population.

32596 ■ "The New World Disorder" in *Harvard Business Review* (Vol. 81, No. 8, August 2003, pp. 70)
Pub: Harvard Business School Press
Ed: Nicolas Checa, John Maguire, Jonathan Barney. **Description:** The efforts of U.S. Presidents George Bush, Sr. and Bill Clinton to develop globalization have been largely wiped out by the following: George W. Bush's overriding concern with combating terrorism, the 1997 financial crisis in Thailand, how the IMF responded to the Thailand problem, and how financial industries have responded to the above.

32597 ■ "New Year Brings New Growth" in *My Business* (February/March 2003, pp. 48)
Pub: My Business Magazine
Ed: Bill Dunkelberg. **Description:** Third quarter growth for 2002 came in at 4 percent for Gross Domestic Product, the normal trend would be at 3.5 percent. Statistical data included.

32598 ■ "Newsstand" in *Home Business* (Vol. 13, January/February 2006, No. 1, pp. 38-39)
Pub: Home Business Magazine
Description: Topics include marketing of office supplies and equipment, rising gas prices, toxic office environments, entrepreneurship, and online retailing.

32599 ■ "NFIB Building on Tax Cut Victory for Members" in *My Business* (September/October 2001, pp. 18)
Pub: My Business Magazine
Description: President Bush's tax refund will benefit small business in two ways: it returns money back to small business owners while giving the economy a needed boost.

32600 ■ "90 percent of laid-off hotel workers back on the job" in *Boston Business Journal* (Vol. 22, No. 16, May 24, 2002, pp. 7)
Pub: MCP, Inc.
Ed: Donna L. Goodison. **Description:** Boston hotels rehired 900 workers in May 2002, out of the 1,000 that were laid off after the September 11, 2001, terrorist attacks. Hotel occupancy rates have also rebounded.

32601 ■ "No mercy: are VCs sucking the life out of your business?" in *Entrepreneur* (Vol. 30, No. 12, December 2002, pp. 79)
Pub: Entrepreneur Media Inc.
Ed: C.J. Prince. **Description:** Difficulties small businesses encounter in finding venture capital backing during a poor economy are discussed.

32602 ■ "Nonprofits Eye New Revenue Ideas as Gifts, Grants Dwindle" in *Boston Business Journal* (Vol. 23, No. 31, September 5, 2003, pp. 1)
Pub: American City Business Journals
Ed: Jill Lerner. **Description:** Nonprofit organizations in the Boston, Massachusetts-area are facing a sharp decline in revenues as the national economy continues to drop. Nonprofits, such as the Freedom Trail Foundation, are depending on major annual fundraising events and innovative financing to survive.

32603 ■ "The Not-So-Golden state? Economic optimism is gathering steam across most of the country" in *Business Week Online* (April 25, 2002)
Pub: McGraw-Hill, Inc.
Ed: Roger Franklin. **Description:** Most small businesses believe the economy is poised to improve, that is, all but the small business community in California. Statistical data included.

32604 ■ "Nothing to fear? White House seeks cheerleaders for the economy" in *Wall Street Journal* (May 31, 2002, pp. A4)
Pub: Wall Street Journal
Ed: **Description:** In an effort to boost consumer confidence, the White House is promoting the economy being on the rise.

32605 ■ "The Numbers" in *Fortune* (Vol. 142, No. 9, October 16, 2000, pp. 64)
Pub: Time Inc.

Description: Executive's opinions regarding the future of the U.S. economic conditions. Statistics are shown.

32606 ■ "NYC Hotels Register Gains; Occupancy Hits 85-Percent for March" in *Crain's New York Business* **(Vol. 20, No. 16, April 19, 2004, pp. 4)**
Pub: Crain Communications, Inc.
Ed: Lisa Fickenscher. **Description:** New York City hotel occupancies are reported at 85 percent for March 2004, the highest level since 1969, showing signs of economic recovery.

32607 ■ "Oahu Apartment Inventory Down, Rents Up" in *Pacific Business News* **(Vol. 41, No. 19, July 18, 2003, pp. 1)**
Pub: American City Business Journals
Ed: Eddy Conway. **Description:** Apartment availability on the island of Oahu is discussed, covering apartment prices and rates, economic conditions, and occupancy rates.

32608 ■ "Officials Hope Testing Center Spurs More International Investment" in *Crain's Detroit Business* **(Vol. 21, October 10, 2005, No. 43)**
Pub: Crain Communications Inc. - Detroit
Ed: Sheena Harrison. **Description:** Economic development officials in Livingston County, Michigan are hoping the move by Aisin Holdings of America Inc. to open its first test track and providing ground in the U.S. will attract more foreign investment to the region.

32609 ■ "On the Hunt for High-End Hires" in *Crain's Detroit Business* **(Vol. 21, October 31, 2005, No. 44, pp. 1)**
Pub: Crain Communications Inc. - Detroit
Ed: Andrew Dietderich. **Description:** John Bukowicz, CEO of Corporate Consulting Associates Inc. in Bloomfield Hills, Michigan, reports business is up 15 percent for the executive recruitment and job placement firm.

32610 ■ "On the March: War and Peace Aid General Dynamics" in *Barron's* **(July 7, 2003, pp. 22)**
Pub: Barron's
Ed: Dimitra Defotis. **Description:** Defense contractor, General Dynamics, has yet to profit from the flurry of defense spending as a result of the Iraq war and the Pentagon's restructuring efforts. The firm's $75 share price is 30 percent lower than its 52-week high, but a strengthening economy and diversification of defense offerings stand to profit the firm.

32611 ■ "On the mend" in *Business First Columbus* **(Vol. 18, No. 40, March 24, 2002, pp. A1)**
Pub: Business First Columbus, Inc.
Ed: David Mildenberg. **Description:** Ohio's small businesses see slight economic improvements. According to a small business survey by InSight Poll, 506 small businesses nationally are expanding.

32612 ■ "On the Rise: What Will Expected Interest-Rate Hikes Mean To You?" in *Entrepreneur* **(Vol. 32, September 2004, No. 9, pp. 30)**
Pub: Entrepreneur Media Inc.
Ed: Julie Monahan. **Description:** Interest rates are rising and small business must plan strategies for the changing economy.

32613 ■ "One Big Reason to Expect a Decent Year for Jobs" in *Business Week* **(January 23, 2006, No. 3968, pp. 27-28)**
Pub: McGraw-Hill Companies
Ed: James C. Cooper. **Description:** Companies can no longer meet the demand with existing workers. The Labor Department reported a 4.9 percent jobless rate. Statistical data included.

32614 ■ "One D's Big Challenge: Shaking Myopia" in *Crain's Detroit Business* **(Vol. 22, November 20, 2006, No. 47, pp. 1)**
Pub: Crain Communications Inc. - Detroit
Ed: Sherri Begin. **Description:** One D was formed to focus on what's good for the community or region and

not just any one organization or community. Six groups have been formed with objectives to form six action plans to achieve the desired results and prioritize the resources.

32615 ■ "100 Best Companies to Work for: In Good Times They GoWild with Perks" in *Fortuneit* **(V. 146, No. 1, 1/20/03, pp. 127)**
Pub: Time Inc.
Ed: Christopher Tkaczyk, Ann Harrington, Milton Moskowitz, Robert Levering. **Description:** A listing of Fortune's 100 Best Companies To Work For is presented. Criteria for selection included a sampling of employee opinion from 269 candidate companies regarding their workplaces. Statistics include information on the firm's headquarters; U.S. employees, including minority and women percentages; percent of job growth and number of new jobs; and applicants and voluntary turnover.

32616 ■ "One Man's Alien is Another's Employee" in *Inc.* **(October 2005, pp. 32)**
Pub: Inc. Magazine
Ed: Darren Dahl. **Description:** Iowa reports a 26 percent hike in Hispanics living in the state and reports that these foreign-born workers are vital to its growing economy.

32617 ■ "Optimism takes a dip" in *My Business* **(November/December 2001, pp. 49)**
Pub: My Business Magazine
Ed: Bill Dunkelberg. **Description:** Changes in small business optimism, before and after the September 11, 2001, attack are discussed. Statistical data included.

32618 ■ "Orchestrating Assistance; Chambers of Commerce" in *Crain's New York Business* **(Vol. 22, November 13, 2006, No. 46, pp. 38)**
Pub: Crain Communications, Inc.
Description: Listing of local chapters of New York's chambers of commerce. These organizations serve as sources of information and representation for local business interest provide a number of services and a wide variety of programs for small businesses.

32619 ■ "Orders Up; Jobs Below Forecast" in *Charlotte Observer* **(February 2, 2007)**
Pub: Knight-Ridder/Tribune Business News
Ed: Kerry Hall. **Description:** U.S. Labor Department reported unemployment rates at 4.6 percent, up one-tenth of a percent. Economists had predicted 170,000 new jobs, but only 111,000 were created.

32620 ■ "Other Comments" in *Forbes* **(Vol. 170, No. 6, September 30, 2002, pp. 36)**
Pub: Forbes Magazine
Description: The depression in high technology and telecommunications, as well as telecommunications policies, and other business issues are analyzed.

32621 ■ "Our Rankings Are Derived From 3-Month Rolling Averages of US Bureau of Labor Statistics Unadjusted Employment Data" in *Inc.* **(May1,2006)**
Pub: Inc. Magazine
Ed: Michael A. Shires. **Description:** Data reported September 1994 to September 2004 from the U.S. Bureau of Labor Statistics is presented. Statistical data included.

32622 ■ "Our So-Called Economic Recovery" in *Hispanic Business* **(May 2005, pp. 6)**
Pub: Hispanic Business
Ed: Jesus Chavarria. **Description:** Despite the 4.4 expanded GDP and the addition of 1.7 million jobs, many have yet to feel the economic recovery of 2004.

32623 ■ "Package deal" in *Entrepreneur* **(Vol. 31, No. 4, April 2003, pp. 22)**
Pub: Entrepreneur Media Inc.
Ed: Stephen Barlas. **Description:** The new economic stimulus package proposed by President George W. Bush would increase the annual allowance for expensing of capital investments from $25,000 to $75,000 for small businesses, and tie the ceiling in the future to inflation.

32624 ■ "Peek ahead" in *Entrepreneur* **(Vol. 30, No. 1, January 2002, pp. 10)**
Pub: Entrepreneur Media Inc.
Ed: Rieva Lesonsky. **Description:** An interview with Elaine S. Peck, who shares her insights as well as those of business consultant colleagues Georgia Hunt and Carroll Aieleen, on the economic outlook for 2002.

32625 ■ "A Peek Inside a Public Organization" in *Hispanic Business* **(July/August 2002, pp. 18, 20)**
Pub: Hispanic Business
Ed: Joel Russell. **Description:** A financial analysis of the U. S. Hispanic Chamber of Commerce finds questionable controls and accountability. Statistical data included.

32626 ■ *Petty Capitalists and Globalization: Flexibility, Entrepreneurship, and Economic Development*
Pub: State University of New York Press
Ed: Alan Smart, Josephine Smart. **Released:** March 2005. **Price:** $70.00. **Description:** Investigation into ways small businesses in Europe, Asia, and Latin America are required to operate and compete in the fast-growing transnational economy.

32627 ■ "Pinstriped Populist" in *New York Times* **(November 12, 2006, pp. 15)**
Pub: New York Times Company
Ed: David Sirota. **Description:** Profile of Lou Dobbs, author of How the Government, Big Business, and Special Interest Groups Are Waging War on the American Dream and How to Fight Back. Dobbs, a financial journalist, examines wages, corruption, trade, outsourcing, immigration and health care.

32628 ■ "Pittsburgh Region Sees Largest '00-'02 Population Drop" in *Pittsburgh Business Times* **(Vol. 23, No. 1, July 25, 2003, pp. 1)**
Pub: Pittsburgh Business Times
Ed: Christopher Davis. **Description:** Industry analysts report that the Pittsburgh, Pennsylvania region experienced a larger decline in population among the country's 729 statistical areas. Pittsburgh lost over 13,000 residents between 2000 and 2002.

32629 ■ "Planning in Pittsburgh, Chicago has produced results" in *Crain's Detroit Business* **(Vol. 19, No. 17, April 28, 2003, pp. 19)**
Pub: Crain Communications Inc., Detroit
Ed: Terry Kosdrosky. **Description:** Detroit regional planners are looking at programs in Chicago, Illinois and Pittsburgh, Pennsylvania that promote regional planning.

32630 ■ "Playing the Fuel" in *Hispanic Business* **(June 2005, pp. 88)**
Pub: Hispanic Business
Ed: Kevin Savetz. **Description:** Trucking firms are reporting business growth despite the high price of fuel. Fuel surcharges help increase revenues, but stop trucking companies from raising fees to cover the cost of maintenance, tires and new vehicles.

32631 ■ "Policy Follies: Fiscal and Monetary Levers Lose their Power" in *Barron's* **(August 18, 2003, pp. 28)**
Pub: Barron's
Ed: Gene Epstein. **Description:** The U.S. economic recovery, following the recession of 2000, has been low against historic measures, with a GDP of roughly 2.5 percent trailing its expected recovery rate of 4 percent. Reasons may include the impact of the World Trade Center attacks, but misguided monetary and fiscal policies share the blame as well.

32632 ■ "Polk Job Growth Boomed in 2004" in *Ledger* **(February 19, 2005)**
Pub: Knight-Ridder/Tribune Business News
Ed: Kyle Kennedy. **Description:** Polk County, Florida reports job growth nearly double that of the national average. Statistical data included.

32633 ■ **"Port Adopts 2007 Strategic Budget"** in *Bellingham Business Journal* (December 2006, pp. A3)
Pub: Sun News Inc.
Description: 2007 Strategic Budget adopted by the Port of Bellingham Board of Commissioners projects a 5 percent growth of operating revenues and no increase in the number of port employees. The entire Strategic Budget will be available on the Web at portofbellingham.com.

32634 ■ **"The Power of Touch"** in *Entrepreneur* (Vol. 28, No. 9, September 2000, pp. 26)
Pub: Entrepreneur Media Inc.
Ed: Watts Wacker. **Description:** The cost is nothing. The potential is limitless. The future of the "touch" economy is investigated.

32635 ■ *Prices, Cycles & Growth*
Pub: M I T Press
Ed: Hukukane Nikaido. **Released:** 1995. **Price:** $42.00.

32636 ■ **"Prices, Wages in 2007"** in *Kiplinger Letter* (Vol. 84, January 26, 2007, No. 4)
Pub: Kiplinger
Description: Economic growth is expected to slow to 2.5 percent in 2007, keeping prices level and company profits lower.

32637 ■ **"Printers producing plenty of red ink"** in *Crain's Detroit Business* (Vol. 19, No. 3, January 20, 2003, pp. 10)
Pub: Crain Communications Inc., Detroit
Ed: Michael Strong. **Description:** The financial status of Detroit's printing companies is examined. A slowing economy has led to company failures and huge sales declines for commercial printers in the Detroit area.

32638 ■ **"Priority"** in *Inc.* (Volume 27, March 2005, No. 3, pp. 23-26, 28, 30)
Pub: Inc. Magazine
Description: Business information discussed includes information about the SEC looking into unlicensed investment brokers, the economy, freight coops to help shippers ease costs, hiring, Google, education, SBA assistance to women entrepreneurs, and new inventions.

32639 ■ **"Private firms surviving downturn"** in *Atlanta Business Chronicle* (Vol. 25, November 8, 2002, No. 22 pp. 3A)
Pub: American City Business Publications, Inc.
Ed: Jim Lovel. **Description:** Private firms in the Atlanta, Georgia area are succeeding during the existing economic downturn, especially Hooters of America Inc., which generated revenue at $526 million in 2001 and John Wieland Homes and Neighborhoods Inc., generating revenue of nearly $440 million in 2001 with a total of 20,000 house sales as of November 2002.

32640 ■ **"Production Co. Enters Familiar Chapter: 11"** in *Washington Business Journal* (Vol. 22, No. 17, August 29, 2003, pp. 1)
Pub: Washington Business Journal
Ed: Greg A. Lohr. **Description:** Reasons behind Roland House's filing for Chapter 11 bankruptcy protection is examined. Topics include economic conditions, debt management, and long term planning.

32641 ■ **"Profit Globally, Give Globally"** in *Harvard Business Review* (Vol. 81, No. 12, December 2003, pp. 16)
Pub: Harvard Business School Press
Ed: John Quelch, V. Kasturi Rangan. **Description:** An overview of ways corporations can and should increase non-domestic philanthropic aid is presented. Topics include sensitivity and diplomacy involved in international economic relations, and issues such as tax breaks and local law.

32642 ■ **"Profiting in a Sideways Market"** in *Hispanic Business* (March 2005, pp. 20, 22, 24)
Pub: Hispanic Business
Ed: Joel Russell. **Description:** Financial experts are not predicting a raging bull market any time soon, but

investors can still make gains if they invest wisely. Top twelve Latin funds are presented showing their 2004 rates of return.

32643 ■ **"Pueblo Economic Development Corp. names operations director"** in *Pueblo Business Journal* (February 28, 2003)
Pub: Dolan Media Newswires
Ed: William Dagendesh. **Description:** Joan Acosta has been named operations director for the Pueblo Economic Development Corporation. Established in 1981, the corporation promotes Pueblo to other communities.

32644 ■ **"Pulling together"** in *Crain's Detroit Business* (Vol. 19, No. 17, April 28, 2003, pp. 14)
Pub: Crain Communications Inc., Detroit
Ed: Terry Kosdrosky. **Description:** Business leaders in the Detroit, Michigan area are promoting regional approaches to transportation, land use, Detroit development and arts funding.

32645 ■ **"Q&A: Forecasts from Five New York Real Estate Experts"** in *Crain's New York Business* (Vol. 23, January 15, 2007, No. 3, pp. 40)
Pub: Crain Communications, Inc.
Description: Real estate experts, Peter Riguardi, Ken Krasnow, Joseph R. Harbert, Barry M. Gosin, and Howard Fiddle give their predictions for what lies ahead in 2007 for the real estate industry.

32646 ■ **"Q401 Will it Matter?"** in *Red Herring* (No. 105, October 1, 2001, pp. 58-59)
Pub: Herring Communications
Ed: Eric Moskowitz. **Description:** An overview of the history of fourth quarter statistics, including tech earnings estimates, change in information technology spending growth, venture capital by sector, value of global M&A activity, and global IPOs.

32647 ■ **"Quarterly report-February 2002"** in *Small Business Economic Trends* (February 2002, pp. 1)
Pub: National Federation of Independent Business Foundation
Description: The National Federation of Independent Business's survey of small business owners/members conducted January 2002, showed the Small Business Optimism Index rose from 100.4 in December to 103.5 in January, the highest reading since first quarter 2000. The results of the survey cover expansion, earnings, sales, prices, compensation, credit conditions, interest rates, capital outlays, and important issues are discussed, graphed and tabulated.

32648 ■ **"R and D Spending Jumps as Firms Foresee Recovery"** in *Atlanta Business Chronicle* (Vol. 26, No. 10, August 15, 2003, pp. 1)
Pub: American City Business Publications, Inc.
Ed: Mary Jane Credeur. **Description:** The first signs of economic recovery for the greater Atlanta, Georgia area are in the form of higher research and development spending by local technology firms.

32649 ■ **"Racial divisions still hang over efforts to foster cooperation"** in *Crain's Detroit Business* (Vol. 19, No. 17, April 28, 2003)
Pub: Crain Communications Inc., Detroit
Ed: Terry Kosdrosky. **Description:** Issues of segregation and racism in the Detroit metropolitan and surrounding areas are discussed. Business leaders are hoping to attract new residents to Detroit and to change the tone of political discourse.

32650 ■ **"Real Estate Company Expands, Changes Name"** in *Bellingham Business Journal* (January 2007, pp. 3)
Pub: Sun News Inc.
Description: Phil Dyer & Associates, Inc. Realtors has changed its name to Sterling Real Estate Group. The company has expanded and recently opened a second office to compliment its existing office.

32651 ■ **"Real Estate Niches Continue as Bright Spots"** in *Crain's Detroit Business* (Vol. 22, November 27, 2006, No. 48, pp. 18)
Pub: Crain Communications Inc. - Detroit
Ed: Jennette Smith. **Description:** Five year downward trend and transition period has driven real estate professionals into niche marketing in redevelopment and mixed use projects. Smaller projects are very successful in downtown areas with assistance of the local communities.

32652 ■ **"The Real New Economy"** in *Harvard Business Review* (Vol. 81, No. 10, October 2003, pp. 104)
Pub: Harvard Business School Press
Ed: Diana Farrell. **Description:** Research data gathered in France, Germany, and the U.S. suggests that a new economy did develop in the 1990s. While not being what was expected or predicted, it is based on information technology, increased productivity and competition, and the speed of innovation and change.

32653 ■ **"Rebound Continues"** in *My Business* (October/November 2003, pp. 50)
Pub: My Business Magazine
Ed: Bill Dunkelberg. **Description:** The National Federation of Independent Business' (NFIBs) Small Business Optimism Index hit a record high for the monthly surveys that began in 1986. Nine of ten components advanced, with the only decline shown in expected credit market conditions, meaning owners believe financing customer purchases will be more difficult in the coming months. Statistical data included.

32654 ■ **"Recession session"** in *Entrepreneur* (Vol. 30, No. 3, March 2002, pp.)
Pub: Entrepreneur Media Inc.
Ed: Mark Henricks. **Description:** An interview with various experts and entrepreneurs to learn how and when they recommend aggressive or defensive positions in the areas of money management, people management, marketing, and technology.

32655 ■ **"Recession takes its toll"** in *Black Enterprise* (Vol. 33, No. 6, Jan. 2003, pp. 26)
Pub: Earl Graves Publishing Co.
Ed: Cliff Hocker. **Description:** According to the U.S. Census Bureau, poverty among Americans rose from 11.3 percent to 11.7 percent. Statistical data included.

32656 ■ **"Recovery Continues"** in *My Business* (June/July 2002, pp. 49)
Pub: My Business Magazine
Ed: Bill Dunkelberg. **Description:** First quarter 2001 economic growth surged with Gross Domestic Product growing at the rate of 5.8 percent. Small business optimism, hiring plans and sales statistics are presented.

32657 ■ **"Recovery for Some; Chicago's Economy Will Lag the State and Nation Next Year"** in *Crain's Chicago Business* (December 22, 2003)
Pub: Crain Communications, Inc.
Ed: Sandra Jones. **Description:** Chicago's economy is expected to see a 2.96 percent rise in 2004, with the warehousing and distribution, financial services, and hospitality sectors feeling strongest growth with an increase in business travel to the area. However, Chicago's economy is expected to grow at a slower pace than the state or the nation.

32658 ■ **"Recovery driving shaky growth in transportation"** in *Atlanta Business Chronicle* (Vol. 25, January 10, 2003, No. 31, pp. 20A)
Pub: American City Business Publications, Inc.
Ed: Charles Davidson. **Description:** The Georgia Economic Outlook 2003 indicates that, since the transportation sector is integral to the overall economy, the transportation sector will remain sluggish as the overall economy struggles to move out of its slump. Of the trucking, airline, and railroad sectors, airlines seem to have the toughest road ahead for recovery.

32659 ■ "Recovery Will Have to Wait" in *Washington Business Journal* **(Vol. 22, No. 18, September 5, 2003, pp. 1)**
Pub: Washington Business Journal
Ed: Suzanne White, John Wilen. Description: Industry overview of the commercial real estate market in the Washington, DC Metropolitan area, which may not see a total recovery until 2007.

32660 ■ "Recovery Will Probably Take a While Yet" in *Crain's Detroit Business* **(Vol. 19, No. 42, October 20, 2003, pp. 8)**
Pub: Crain Communications Inc., Detroit
Ed: Keith Crain. Description: The economic process involved in a jobless recovery is explored.

32661 ■ "Recreational/Personal Watercraft Market" in *Rough Notes* **(Vol. 145, No. 2, February 2003, pp. 48)**
Pub: Rough Notes
Ed: Larry G. France. Description: The watercraft insurance market has been declining as it is an industry that depends largely on the economy. Boat insurance is provided by agencies listed, including American Modern Insurance Group, American Reliable Insurance Company, and BAT Insurance Corporation.

32662 ■ "Rental rates down but Midtown still desirable" in *Atlanta Business Chronicle* **(Vol. 25, No. 20, October 25, 2002, pp. 2)**
Pub: American City Business Publications, Inc.
Ed: Tonya Layman. Description: The rental prices in the Midtown corridor section of Atlanta, Georgia have fallen, but Midtown remains a desirable location.

32663 ■ "Reputations built now will outlast downturn" in *Atlanta Business Chronicle* **(Vol. 24, No. 11, August 17, 2001, pp. 9B)**
Pub: American City Business Journals Inc.
Ed: Chuck Johnson. Description: Measures that can be taken by those in the technology community to overcome the economic difficulties are discussed. These include coming to grips with the fact that times are tough and understanding that all industry sectors have been impacted, just not equally.

32664 ■ "Residential, commercial builders see more decline" in *Atlanta Business Chronicle* **(Vol. 25, January 10, 2003, No. 31, pp. 22A)**
Pub: American City Business Publications, Inc.
Ed: Randy Southerland. Description: The Georgia Economic Outlook 2003 survey indicates that commercial real estate construction companies will face tough times in the coming months. Residential construction companies will also likely face a slowdown.

32665 ■ "The Restaurant Business" in *The Economist* **(Vol. 376, July 16-22, 2005, No. 8435, pp. 60)**
Pub: The Economist Newspaper Ltd.
Description: American restaurants, including franchise fast-food stores, are facing a decline in sales due to the slow economy.

32666 ■ "Restaurants stay hot commodities despite downturn" in *Boston Business Journal* **(Vol. 22, No. 15, May 17, 2002, pp. 13)**
Pub: MCP, Inc.
Ed: Donna L. Goodison. Description: Restaurants in the Boston area remain in business despite the economic slowdown.

32667 ■ "Retail Experts Laud Costco's Shopping Strategy" in *Business Journal-Portland* **(Vol. 20, No. 22, August 1, 2003, pp. 11)**
Pub: American City Business Journals, Inc.
Ed: Carol Tice. Description: Marketing strategy used by Costco Companies is examined, including management styles, U.S. economic conditions, and business planning.

32668 ■ "Retailers Helped by Chill, Gas Price Dip" in *The Record* **(November 4, 2005)**
Pub: New Jersey Media Group
Ed: Joan Verdon. Description: Falling gas prices and warmer temperatures boosted New Jersey's retail sales in October 2005. A recent survey shows that consumers are more price-driven in 2005.

32669 ■ "The Return of the Global Brand" in *Harvard Business Review* **(Vol. 81, No. 8, August 2003, pp. 22)**
Pub: Harvard Business School Press
Ed: John Quelch. Description: Since Theordore Levitt published The Globalization of Markets in the Harvard Business Review twenty years ago, the world's economic development has adapted accordingly. International companies are finding that standardized products marketed globally have been widely accepted. This is contrary to previous efforts to develop products for regional markets. Today, China is poised to duplicate Japan's global branding successes, cutting into U.S. business sales.

32670 ■ "Riding with the Currency" in *Black Enterprise* **(Vol. 35, December 2004, No. 5, pp. 109)**
Pub: Earl G. Graves Publishing Co. Inc.
Ed: Rene Brinkley. Description: How businesses can react when the dollar is weak. An examination of what drives cost and money. Statistical data included.

32671 ■ "Riding Out the Crash" in *Hispanic Business* **(Vol. 23, No. 5, May 2001, pp. 42, 44-45)**
Pub: Hispanic Business
Ed: Derek Reveron. Description: Hispanic-themed Web sites that focus on niche markets stand the best chance of long-term survival. An interview with Fernando Espuelas, CEO of StarMedia is presented.

32672 ■ "Rising Drug Costs" in *Venture Capital Journal* **(October 1, 2204)**
Pub: Thomason Financial Inc.
Ed: Alastair Goldfisher. Description: With the rising costs of conducting clinical trials of new drugs, technology companies may choose offshore outsourcing of research and development to save money. However, the cost of new drug development is rising worldwide. Statistical data included.

32673 ■ "Road-money halt slows $172.5M Oakland plan" in *Crain's Detroit Business* **(Vol. 19, No. 17, April 28, 2003, pp. 1)**
Pub: Crain Communications Inc., Detroit
Ed: Andrew Dietderich. Description: A proposed road project in Oakland County could yield nearly $16 million in annual tax revenue to the state, county and city. Plans call for at least 15 buildings totaling 1.6 million square feet on 107 acres and will be developed by Grand/Sakwa Properties LLC of Farmington Hills, Michigan.

32674 ■ "Room Glut Has Hotels Unsettled" in *Atlanta Business Chronicle* **(Vol. 25, December 6, 2002, No. 26, pp. 1)**
Pub: American City Business Publications, Inc.
Ed: Walter Woods. Description: There are over 86,000 hotel rooms in the metro Atlanta, Georgia area, making the impact of the recent recession in the travel sector even harder on hoteliers there. During the travel recession, the number of visitors to trade shows, and the like have, fallen significantly.

32675 ■ "Room to Grow: yes, even in the most stagnant economy, it's possible to expand" in *Entrepreneur* **(Vol. 31, No. 6, June 2003, pp. 28)**
Pub: Entrepreneur Media Inc.
Ed: Mark Henricks. Description: Management consultants Adrian Slywotzky and Richard Wise offer a strategy that demands innovation in a slow or no-growth market or economy.

32676 ■ "Rotary Club Of Jackson Invests In Metro Students" in *Mississippi Business Journal* **(Vol. 28, September 2006, No. 36, pp. 3)**
Pub: Venture Publications, Inc.
Ed: Lynne Jeter Description: Profile of the Rotary Club of Jackson and it's college scholarship program to aid low income potential students of the Jackson community in attending college.

32677 ■ "Sacramento, Calif.-Area Small Businesses Remain Optimistic for Year Ahead" in *Sacramento Bee* **(October 21, 2005)**
Pub: The Sacramento Bee
Ed: Thuy-Doan Le. Description: Despite the recent hurricanes and rising gas prices, local small businesses remain optimistic for 2006. According to a recent survey conducted by American Express, 59 percent of West Coast small business owners said they will hire new employees within the next six months.

32678 ■ "Sales" in *Inc.* **(February 1, 2002)**
Pub: Inc. Magazine
Ed: Susan Greco. Description: An overview of ways smart companies are tackling today's toughest selling challenges in today's economic downturn.

32679 ■ "Same Markets, New Marketplaces" in *Black Enterprise* **(Vol. 35, September 2004, No. 2, pp. 34)**
Pub: Earl G. Graves Publishing Co. Inc.
Ed: Malik Singleton. Description: According to a study performed by the Center for Women's Business Research, African American women entrepreneurs in nontraditional sectors rose between 1997 and 2002. Wisconsin, Delaware, and Oregon were among the top states experiencing the rise, with Wisconsin reporting 453 percent growth in the number of African American women-owned businesses. Statistical data included.

32680 ■ "SBA adjusts revenue standards for inflation" in *Boston Business Journal* **(Vol. 22, No. 3, February 22, 2002, pp. 22)**
Pub: MCP, Inc.
Description: The Small Business Administration adjusted revenue standards for inflation.

32681 ■ "Secondaries Jay Pierrepont" in *Venture Capital Journal* **(January 1, 2005)**
Pub: Thomason Financial Inc.
Description: In an interview, Jay Pierrepont discusses the secondaries market. Pierrepont makes his predictions for the best and worst things that could happen to the consumer market it 2005.

32682 ■ "Seeing the future in real time" in *Red Herring* **(No. 99, June 15 & July 1, 2001, pp. 21-22)**
Pub: Herring Communications
Ed: Anthony B. Perkins. Description: Discussion highlighting a speech made by Vinod Khosla at the recent Venture 2001 conference in reference to the information technology industry. Mr. Khosla, called the most successful venture capitalist on the planet by Red Herring, discussed the impact the Internet is having on the entire model of computing.

32683 ■ "Self-Employed Boost the Economic Recovery" in *Wall Street Journal* **(December 1, 2003, pp. A2)**
Pub: Dow Jones & Co. Inc.
Ed: Jon E. Hilsenrath. Description: Small businesses are aiding in the economic recovery.

32684 ■ "S.F. Slashes Economic Development" in *San Francisco Business Times* **(Vol. 17, No. 53, August 8, 2003, pp. 1)**
Pub: American City Business Journals
Ed: Eric Young. Description: San Francisco, California officials have decided that, because of a budget shortfall, the city will discontinue its economic development department as of July 1, 2003. Funding was cut by 90 percent, staffing reduced 66 percent.

32685 ■ "Shrinking Surplus: George W. Bush, technology CEO?" in *Red Herring* **(No. 105, October 1, 2001, pp. 88-89)**
Pub: Herring Communications
Ed: J.P. Vicente. Description: Due to the deterioration in corporate profits, the U.S. is facing the largest quarterly drop in tax payments since 1992. Statistical data included.

32686 ■ "Slow Economic Recovery Prompts More Firms to Turn to 'Just-in-Time' Employment" in Seattle Times (November 16, 2004)
Pub: The Seattle Times
Ed: Shirleen Holt. Description: Washington State's economic recovery discussed with business owners in the Seattle area. Marlene Wong, specialist in resources consulting and office administration, finds work through community bulletin boards and her own Website where she advertises herself as a virtual assistant.

32687 ■ "Slower, but Still Strong" in Kiplinger's Personal Finance Magazine (Vol. 55, No. 1, January, 2001, pp. 20)
Pub: The Kiplinger Washington Editors, Inc.
Ed: Melynda Dovel Wilcox. Description: Politics aside, the economic growth rate will settle down to a healthy pace. And the budget surpluses are safe for now.

32688 ■ "Small-Biz Owners' Wild Mood Swings" in Inc. (July 1, 2003)
Pub: Gruner & Jahr USA Publishing
Description: The National Federation of Independent Businesses monthly index measuring small business optimism hit a 10-year low in March 2003.

32689 ■ Small Business Clustering Technology: Applications in Marketing, Management, Finance, and IT
Pub: Idea Group Publishing
Ed: Robert C. MacGregor; Ann Hodgkinson. Released: June 2006. Description: An overview of the development and role of small business clusters in disciplines that include economics, marketing, management and information systems.

32690 ■ "Small Business: Just When Hopes Were High" in Business Week (January 8, 2007)
Pub: McGraw-Hill Companies
Ed: James Mehring. Description: Overview of the reasons for a fall in confidence concerning the economy among small businesses and the affect this could have in the coming year.

32691 ■ "Small Business Owners are Less Optimistic" in Milwaukee Journal Sentinel (December 2, 2005)
Pub: Journal Sentinel, Inc.
Ed: Rick Romell. Description: A survey released by the National Federation of Independent Business reported 59.5 percent of small business owners had a positive economic outlook in November, down 6 percent from September 2005.

32692 ■ "Small Businesses Are Engine to American Economy" in Atlanta Business Chronicle (Vol. 24, No. 9, August 3, 2001, pp. 10B)
Pub: American City Business Journals Inc.
Ed: Paige Bowers. Description: Senator Max Cleland discusses what he has done in support of small business in America. The Senator's support includes reducing taxes on small businesses, broadening health care options and boosting the opportunities for minority and women-owned enterprises.

32693 ■ "Small Businesses Fuel Growth" in Success (Vol. 47, No. 3, July 2000, pp. 16)
Pub: Success Publishing, Inc.
Description: A study showing that small businesses are getting a boost from ever-cheaper information technology and easier access to financial assistance, and are helping to fuel the U.S. economy's record expansion. The study also predicts that this segment of the American economy will see a shift in management as well as the labor force over the next 15 years. Entrepreneurs will no longer be predominately young, white men. They will be older women, many of whom will also be Hispanic and African-American, reflecting the same shift in the U.S. population as a whole.

32694 ■ "Small Exporters in a Big World" in Hispanic Business (November 2003, pp. 42-43, 46, 48, 50)
Pub: Hispanic Business
Ed: Jennifer Riley. Description: Hispanic firms that have succeeded abroad show they can compete in the large and profitable markets of the global economy. Statistical data included.

32695 ■ "Small Firm Bankruptcy" in Journal of Small Business Management (Vol. 44, October 2006, No. 4, pp. 493)
Pub: Blackwell Publishing, Inc.
Ed: Richard Carter; Howard Van Auken. Description: Results of a survey attempt to identify the root causes of bankruptcy in firms. Statistical data included.

32696 ■ Small Firms and Economic Growth
Pub: Ashgate Publishing Co., Inc.
Ed: Zoltan J. Acs. Released: 1995. Price: $420.00.

32697 ■ "The Small Picture: How Does the Federal Deficit Affect Your Business?" in Entrepreneur (Vol. 31, No. 6, June 2003, pp. 26)
Pub: Entrepreneur Media Inc.
Ed: Joshua Kurlantzick. Description: The impact of the national deficit and ways it affects small businesses is examined.

32698 ■ "So Many Lenders, So Few Takers" in Business Week (January 9, 2006, No. 3966, pp. 79-80)
Pub: McGraw-Hill Companies
Ed: Justin Hibbard. Description: Companies specializing in risky mortgage loans may face an onslaught of defaults. The leading companies include New Century TRS Holdings, Accredited Home Lenders Holding, Delta Financial, NovaStar Financial, Mortgageit Holdings, IMPAC Mortgage holdings, Aames Investment, Homebanc, and Netbank.

32699 ■ Social Entrepreneurship
Pub: Palgrave Macmillan
Ed: Johanna Mair; Jeffrey Robinson; Kai Hockerts. Released: June 2006. Price: $80.00. Description: Social entrepreneurship is the process involving innovative approaches to solving social problems while creating economic value.

32700 ■ "The Social Movement That Grew Up" in Hispanic Business (March 2004, pp. 20, 22)
Pub: Hispanic Business
Ed: Joel Russell. Description: When civil rights fervor turned to economic empowerment, new companies grew, including Hispanic Business magazine. Profile of the magazine is included.

32701 ■ "Soft Economy Collides With Old Ideas" in Hispanic Business (Vol. 23, No. 5, May 2001, pp. 6)
Pub: Hispanic Business
Ed: Jesus Chavarria. Description: A report by the editor regarding the New Economy and the current slowdown, and ways to turn the economy around.

32702 ■ "Soft Landing Strategy" in Forbes (December 25, 2000, pp. 300)
Pub: Forbes Magazine
Ed: Robert S. Salomon. Description: This is clearly a better time to invest than was the case a year ago. A plan for investing in an economic slow down is discussed.

32703 ■ "Soft Market Stall Apartments" in Houston Business Journal (Vol. 34, No. 11, July 25, pp. 1)
Pub: American City Business Journals
Ed: Nancy Sarnoff. Description: Profile of real estate sales and marketing in the greater Houston area; including real estate development, real estate prices and rates, and poor economic conditions.

32704 ■ "Solving the regional puzzle" in Crain's Detroit Business (Vol. 19, No. 17, April 28, 2003, pp. 1)
Pub: Crain Communications Inc., Detroit

Description: An introduction to a survey conducted by Crain's Detroit Business regarding regional issues affecting business and the economy in the Detroit area.

32705 ■ "Some outplacement firms benefit in down economy" in Boston Business Journal (Vol. 22, No. 14, May 10, 2002, pp. 38)
Pub: MCP, Inc.
Ed: Pam Derringer. Description: Corporate spending for outplacement has declined so there is more competition, but those who have size, reputation and niche have a chance of surviving in the down economy.

32706 ■ "Special Report" in The Economist (Vol. 376, July 30-August 5, 2005, No. 8437, pp. 61-63)
Pub: The Economist Newspaper Ltd.
Description: China is becoming the determiner of issues affecting workers, companies, financial markets and economies worldwide.

32707 ■ "Spend cycle" in Entrepreneur (Vol. 30, No. 2, February 2002, pp. 28)
Pub: Entrepreneur Media Inc.
Ed: Steve Cooper. Description: Consumer spending as a percentage of Gross Domestic Product (GDP) has remained relatively unchanged for the last 50 years. Statistical data included.

32708 ■ "State Dept. of Economic Development Reports Strong Growth" in St. Charles Business Record (May 7, 2004)
Pub: Dolan Media Company
Description: State of Missouri's Department of Economic Growth reported 6,100 new jobs were added in the state, first quarter 2004, 16th in the country. New business formations were at 14,930 in 2003 in approximately 100 various industries. Statistical data included.

32709 ■ "State Needs to Think Big to Retool Economy" in Crain's Detroit Business (Vol. 21, October 17, 2005, No. 43, pp. 8)
Pub: Crain Communications Inc. - Detroit
Description: Michigan state political, civic and business leaders need to create an economic plan that covers both short- and long-term goals to aid in the state's recovery.

32710 ■ "State Officials Waiting to See Impact On Revenue" in Crain's Detroit Business (Vol. 21, October 17, 2005, No. 43, pp. 32)
Pub: Crain Communications Inc. - Detroit
Ed: Amy Lane. Description: Michigan state officials are waiting to see how the Chapter 11 filing by Delphi Corporation will impact the state's economy.

32711 ■ "The State of Small Business: Confident, yet cautious, in 2001" in Crain's Chicago Business (Vol. 23, December 11, 2000, pp. SB1)
Pub: Crain Communications, Inc.
Ed: H. Lee Murphy. Description: Despite the slowing economy, small firms still look for growth.

32712 ■ "State Stocks Show Generally Strong 3Q, Despite Auto Woes" in Crain's Detroit Business (Vol. 21, October 10, 2005, No. 43, pp. 43)
Pub: Crain Communications Inc. - Detroit
Ed: Tom Henderson. Description: Michigan's publicly traded companies reported a good showing for third quarter 2005. David Sowerby, portfolio manager for Loomis Sayles & Co. LP, showed a share-based gain of 3.8 percent, up a bit from Standard & Poor's index.

32713 ■ "State's Economy to Join Recovery by Third Quarter of Next Year" in Crain's Detroit Business (Vol. 19, No. 45, November 10, 2003)
Pub: Crain Communications Inc., Detroit
Ed: Katie Merx. Description: Michigan's economy was down 2.5 percent from 2002, while the national economy recorded a third consecutive year of growth in 2003. According to a report by the University of Michigan Research Seminar, it forecasts local job growth in the fourth quarter 2003 throughout 2004.

32714 ■ "State's Jobs Up 1.7 Percent" in *Sacramento Bee* **(October 5, 2005)**
Pub: The Sacramento Bee
Ed: Rachel Osterman. Description: California reported job growth at 1.7 percent in the second quarter, 2005, making the state's economy 16th strongest in the nation. Statistical data included.

32715 ■ "Steady Economic Growth" in *My Business* **(October/November 2002, pp. 39)**
Pub: My Business Magazine
Ed: Bill Dunkelberg. Description: Small business optimism, hiring and sales prices are profiled from 2000-2002. Statistical data included.

32716 ■ "Stealing the Show: Exhibitors and Show Managers Fight Suitcasing" in *Tradeshow Week* **(Vol. 34, December 6, 2004, No. 49, pp. S3)**
Pub: Reed Business Information
Ed: Gary Tufel. Description: In a tough economy, exhibitors are upset with sales people who walk the aisles of a tradeshow marketing without paying for booth space, called suitcasing. Suitcasers are able to take buyers away from the show to a hotel or restaurant. Industrial espionage is another problem for exhibitors.

32717 ■ "Stepping down" in *Entrepreneur* **(Vol. 30, No. 2, February 2002, pp. 64)**
Pub: Entrepreneur Media Inc.
Ed: Chris Sandlund. Description: Some executives are taking lower positions during the economic slump.

32718 ■ "Stimulus or Bust? Although Bush Touts Tax Cut, the B.E. 100s Have Mixed Feelings" in *Black Enterprise* **(Vol. 34, September 2003)**
Pub: Earl Graves Publishing Co.
Ed: Cliff Hocker. Description: Executives from the Black Enterprises 100 have mixed feeling as to the impact of President Bush's tax cuts on minority, small businesses.

32719 ■ "Stock Index Changes with the Times" in *Hispanic Business* **(March 2004, pp. 10)**
Pub: Hispanic Business
Ed: Juan Solana, Michael Caplinger. Description: Barometer of conditions for companies in the U.S. Hispanic market is presented. Statistical data included.

32720 ■ "Stockholders in Cyberspace: Weick's Sensemaking Online" in *Journal of Business Communication* **(Vol. 44, January 2007, No. 1, pp. 13)**
Pub: Association for Business Communication
Ed: Andrew F. Herrmann. Description: Stockholders are using the Internet's discussion boards to make sense of their financial holdings.

32721 ■ "Stormy Times" in *Crain's Detroit Business* **(Vol. 21, November 7, 2005, No. 45, pp. 25)**
Pub: Crain Communications Inc. - Detroit
Ed: Sherri Begin. Description: Despite the hurricane relief efforts, most nonprofits blame the lagging economy on a drop in fundraising. It is necessary for organizations to cultivate donors who will remain loyal.

32722 ■ "Strength in numbers" in *Washington Business Journal* **(Vol. 22, No. 3, May 23, 2003, pp. 3)**
Pub: Washington Business Journal
Ed: John Wilen. Description: The economic outlook for the Washington, DC area is discussed, including employment levels, layoffs, and growth within the computer industry.

32723 ■ *Strengthening Technology Incubation System for Creating High Technology-Based Enterprises in Asia and the Pacific*
Pub: United Nations Publications
Released: January 2005. Price: $75.00. Description: Report reviewing policy guidelines and practices to establish technology incubators that will help entrepreneurs develop small technology-based enterprises in different national economies.

32724 ■ "The Struggle to Sell the Economy's Sizzle" in *Business Week* **(January 23, 2006, No. 3968, pp. 43)**
Pub: McGraw-Hill Companies
Ed: Richard S. Dunham. Description: The Bush Administration is struggling to promote the nation's economy, despite the 400,000 new jobs posted in the past two months.

32725 ■ *Studies of Entrepreneurship, Business and Government in Hong Kong: The Economic Development of a Small Open Economy*
Pub: Edwin Mellen Press
Ed: Fu-Lai Tony Yu. Released: November 2006. Price: $109.95. Description: Institutional and Austrian theories are used to analyze the transformation taking place in Hong Kong's economy.

32726 ■ "Study Says Corporate Relocations Don't Impact California Economy" in *Sacramento Bee* **(October 26, 2005)**
Pub: The Sacramento Bee
Ed: Dale Kasler. Description: A study conducted by the Public Policy Institute of California reports corporate relocations do not effect the economy in California due to the small percentage of job losses.

32727 ■ "Stump the slump" in *Entrepreneur* **(Vol. 30, No. 2, February 2002, pp. 90)**
Pub: Entrepreneur Media Inc.
Ed: Michele Marrinan. Description: Many entrepreneurs are taking advantage of the economic downturn to start new businesses. Ways to work the economy to find financing are discussed, including the importance of a solid business plan.

32728 ■ "Successful Expo! Expo! Mirrors Greater Optimism" in *Tradeshow Week* **(Vol. 34, December 13, 2004, No. 50, pp. 1)**
Pub: Reed Business Information
Ed: Margo McCall. Description: The International Association for Exhibition Management reported increased attendance for its annual Expo! Expo! Meeting, showing optimism for the industry.

32729 ■ "Suffolk County Executive Names Andrea Lohneiss as Commissioner of Economic Development" in *Long Island Business News* **(March 5, 2004)**
Pub: Dolan Media Newswires
Ed: Rosmaria Mancini. Description: Profile of Andrea Lohneiss, newly appointed commission of economic development in Suffolk County, New York. Lohneiss cites downtown revitalization as a top priority.

32730 ■ "Survey finds optimism up at businesses" in *Pittsburgh Business Times* **(Vol. 22, No. 46, May 30, 2003, pp. 3)**
Pub: Pittsburgh Business Times
Ed: Kent Bernhard, Jr. Description: The results of a business survey of small businesses in the Pittsburgh, Pennsylvania area is presented, including economic conditions, capital investment planning, and economic forecasts.

32731 ■ "Survey: economy will continue to affect growth" in *Atlanta Business Chronicle* **(Vol. 25, November 15, 2002, No. 23 pp. SS12)**
Pub: American City Business Publications, Inc.
Description: Members of Atlanta's legal community were surveyed by the Atlanta Business Chronicle about expectations for business in 2003, the biggest challenges expected in Atlanta for the next year, and expectations for their practices. Responses from eight professionals are included.

32732 ■ "Survey: Small-biz owners seeing better economic outlook ahead" in *Business First Columbus* **(Vol. 18, No. 25, February 8, 2002, pp. A3)**
Pub: Business First Columbus, Inc.
Ed: Kathy Showalter. Description: According to a recent small business survey, owners feel optimistic about the economy.

32733 ■ "Survey: Tech Spending Likely to Stabilize, but Not Show Big Increase This Year" in *Daily Business Review* **(Vol. 77, March 12, 2003)**
Pub: American Lawyer Media LP
Description: Goldman Sachs polled technology buyers in February 2003 and found that many executives expect information technology spending to increase in 2003. Further results of the survey are discussed.

32734 ■ "Surveys: Unhappiness growing in workforce" in *Austin Business Journal* **(Vol. 21, No. 25, September 7, 2001, pp. 21)**
Pub: Austin Business Journal, Inc.
Description: According to two recent surveys, the economic downturn is affecting workers' attitudes towards their employers; the surveys were conducted by CareerBuilder Inc., an online recruiting network, and Peter D. Hart Research.

32735 ■ "Surviving the New Economy" in *Inc.* **(October 1, 2003)**
Pub: Gruner & Jahr USA Publishing
Ed: Nadine Heintz. Description: Profile of Data Return and its management. Data Return is a Web-hosting firm sold by Sunny Vanderbeck, who is considering buying his company back.

32736 ■ "Taking Our Affluence For Granted" in *Black Enterprise* **(Vol. 34, No. 3, October 2003, pp. 12)**
Pub: Earl Graves Publishing Co.
Ed: Earl G. Graves, Sr. Description: The importance of black consumer spending and marketing strategies directed towards African Americans is discussed.

32737 ■ "The Talk of the Inc. 500" in *Inc.* **(October, 2000, pp. 13)**
Pub: The Goldhirsh Group
Description: Attendees at the Inc. 500 conference contended that the biggest problems facing America's fastest growing companies in 2000 were related to financing business growth. Nearly 75 percent of attendees said they would consider a merger if the right offer came along and nearly two-thirds expressed difficulty implementing e-commerce solutions and many plan to spend more money on Internet marketing than on more traditional marketing media.

32738 ■ "Tampa, Fla.-Area Housing Downshifts" in *Tampa Tribune* **(December 24, 2005)**
Pub: Media General, Inc.
Ed: Dave Simanoff. Description: Real estate experts are predicting a slowdown in demand, sales, and price appreciation in 2006, however a growing economy in the area will help to maintain a strong housing market for the Tampa region.

32739 ■ "Tax Law Changes Mean Money for Education and Retirement" in *Ingram's* **(Vol. 29, No. 1, January 2003, pp. 19)**
Pub: Show Me Publishing, Inc.
Ed: Jackie Perlman. Description: The benefits granted under the Economic Growth and Tax Relief Reconciliation Act of 2001, allows incentives for education and retirement.

32740 ■ "Tech firms like Granholm's economic plan" in *Crain's Detroit Business* **(Vol. 18, No. 22, June 3, 2002, pp. 53)**
Pub: Crain Communications Inc. - Detroit
Ed: Andrew Dietderich. Description: The Michigan State Attorney General has called for the creation of the Michigan Technology Tri-Corridor, which would expand the state's $40 million Life Sciences Corridor and promote automotive technology and homeland security research and development programs.

32741 ■ "Temp Hiring Signals Economic Recovery" in *Inc.* **(January 1, 2004)**
Pub: Gruner & Jahr USA Publishing
Ed: Nadine Heintz. Description: Demand for temporary employees, especially in the manufacturing industry, has been a sign of economic recovery in the past. With an increase in demand for temps, agencies may see a double-digit revenue growth for 2004.

32742 ■ **"Think Happy Thoughts" in** *My Business* **(September/October 2001, pp. 50)**
Pub: My Business Magazine
Ed: Harvey King. **Description:** The article offers the optimist words of the writer regarding the nation's economy, and one way to help it improve.

32743 ■ **"This Just In" in** *Crain's Detroit Business* **(Vol. 21, January 24, 2005, No. 4, pp. 1)**
Pub: Crain Communications Inc. - Detroit
Ed: Amy Lane, Sheena Harrison. **Description:** Plans for advertising Michigan as a travel and business destination have been put on hold. The Michigan Economic Development Corporation halted the two-year plan because of budget concerns.

32744 ■ **"Those Weren't the Days?" in** *Inc.* **(August 1, 2003)**
Pub: Gruner & Jahr USA Publishing
Ed: Mike Hofman. **Description:** Joseph E. Stiglitz, economist for the Clinton Administration, ponders his legacy.

32745 ■ **"365-day forecast" in** *Entrepreneur* **(Vol. 30, No. 1, January 2000)**
Pub: Entrepreneur Media Inc.
Ed: Steve Cooper. **Description:** Various economic experts make forecasts and offer insight concerning the economic future during 2002.

32746 ■ **"Thriving Locally in the Global Economy" in** *Harvard Business Review* **(Vol. 81, No. 8, August 2003, pp. 119)**
Pub: Harvard Business School Press
Ed: Rosabeth Moss Kanter. **Description:** Economic development in five towns in the U.S. dispel the belief that globalization will adversely impact local communities.

32747 ■ **"The Time is Now" in** *My Business* **(April/May 2004, pp. 14)**
Pub: My Business Magazine
Ed: Lena Basha. **Description:** With a growing economy, it is important for small businesses to focus on employee retention; flexibility is an important incentive to employees.

32748 ■ **"Tips for cutting costs" in** *Crain's Detroit Business* **(Vol. 18, No. 32, August 12, 2002, pp. 12)**
Pub: Crain Communications Inc., Detroit
Description: The Small Business Administration offers advice to small businesses for cutting business expenses, including inventory, payments, overhead, management compensation, equipment costs, expansion, joint ventures, risk management, and the use of buying groups.

32749 ■ **"To say the leased: Smart Moves: Ownership is overrated" in** *Entrepreneur* **(Vol. 30, No. 2, February 2002, pp. 61)**
Pub: Entrepreneur Media Inc.
Ed: Mark Henricks. **Description:** According to a survey of small businesses conducted by the Equipment Leasing Association, 70 percent of owners expect business to slow, and most expect to increase use of equipment leasing to help deal with the slowdown.

32750 ■ **"Tough times force banks to own other businesses" in** *Crain's Detroit Business* **(Vol. 18, No. 22, June 3, 2002, pp. 1)**
Pub: Crain Communications Inc. - Detroit
Ed: Katie Merx. **Description:** Faced with numerous turnaround and bankruptcy reorganizations, banks and corporate bondholders are left with equity stakes in businesses on the brink.

32751 ■ *Trading Places: SMEs in the Global Economy, A Critical Research Handbook*
Pub: Edward Elgar Publishing, Incorporated
Ed: Lloyd-Reason. **Released:** September 2006. **Price:** $110.00. **Description:** An overview of international research for small and medium-sized companies wishing to expand in the global economy.

32752 ■ **"Transforming Business Structures to Hyborg" in** *Employment Relations Today* **(Vol. 26, No. 4, Winter 2000, pp. 5)**
Pub: John Wiley & Sons, Inc.
Ed: Arnold Brown. **Description:** The organizational structure and corporate culture at the turn of the 21st century are studied. Topics addressed include international economic relations, competition, corporate values, employer-employee relations, and human resource management.

32753 ■ **"Travel Agency Business All Over the Map" in** *Pacific Business News* **(Vol. 41, No. 19, July 18, 2003, pp. 10)**
Pub: American City Business Journals
Ed: Eddy Conway. **Description:** Challenges facing the travel industry, highlighted by the difficulties facing Total Travel Inc., are examined. Topics include economic conditions, Internet use by customers, and business losses.

32754 ■ **"Trickle Up: Small Companies Slowly Build Momentum in the Job Market" in** *Wall Street Journal* **(December 4, 2003, pp. A1)**
Pub: Dow Jones & Co. Inc.
Ed: Clare Ansberry. **Description:** As the economy improves, more small companies are hiring new employees, health care and construction sectors are improving.

32755 ■ **"The Trouble With Lifestyle Entrepreneurs" in** *Inc.* **(Volume 27, July 2005, No. 7, pp. 21-23)**
Pub: Inc. Magazine
Ed: Daniel McGinn. **Description:** New Zealand business owners are able to enjoy a work-life balance, but this trend is becoming a national crisis. American entrepreneurs can take note that growing a business in the U.S. requires a fast-paced, stressed lifestyle. The American economy is fueled by small business.

32756 ■ **"Two Detroit Riverfront Projects Win Tax Breaks" in** *Crain's Detroit Business* **(Vol. 22, November 27, 2006, No. 48, pp. 25)**
Pub: Crain Communications Inc. - Detroit
Ed: Amy Lane. **Description:** Tax credits and other assistance were approved by the Michigan Economic Growth Authority for two brownfield-redevelopment projects. Townhomes and retail space to be built just East of the Renaissance Center.

32757 ■ **"2003 Economic Forecast" in** *Ingram's* **(Vol. 29, No. 1, January 2003, pp. 47)**
Pub: Show Me Publishing, Inc.
Description: Highlights from the annual panel discussion on the 2003 Economic Forecast sponsored by the magazine are presented. The panel was attended by Tom Hoenig, president of the Federal Reserve Bank of Kansas City; honorary chairman, Clyde Wendel, President of American-Kansas City, Bill Greiner of UMB; Frank Lenk of Mid America Regional Council; Ernie Goss of Creighton University; and Doug Houston of the University of Kansas.

32758 ■ **"2002 BE Banks" in** *Black Enterprise* **(Vol. 33, No. 6, January 2003, pp. 24)**
Pub: Earl Graves Publishing Co.
Ed: Alan Hughes. **Description:** Harbor Bankshares Corporation, parent company of The Harbor Bank of Maryland, had formed two new subsidiaries designed to spur economic development in the greater Baltimore-Washington DC metropolitan area.

32759 ■ **"Two Types of Niches" in** *San Diego Business Journal* **(Vol. 28, January 1, 2007, No. 1, pp. 4)**
Pub: San Diego Business Journal Associates
Ed: Pat Broderick. **Description:** Associated General Contractors of America is predicting both soft and solid niches in the commercial building industry for 2007.

32760 ■ **"UDM Hopes Move Will Help Renew Detroit Neighborhood" in** *Crain's Detroit Business* **(Vol. 22, December 11, 2006, No.50, pp. 3)**
Pub: Crain Communications Inc. - Detroit
Ed: Sheena Harrison **Description:** University of Detroit plans to move its dental school to Detroit's Core City neighborhood in January, 2008. Developers hope it has the effect of attracting other small businesses around and further aid in the restructuring of that area.

32761 ■ **"The Ultimate 12-Step in Business" in** *Fast Company* **(August 2001, pp. 196)**
Pub: Fast Company
Description: A tutorial for the twelve steps needed to return to the old economy are highlighted.

32762 ■ **"Unemployment higher in 2002, but rate of job loss slowed" in** *Crain's Detroit Business* **(Vol. 19, No. 9, March 3, 2003, pp. 1)**
Pub: Crain Communications Inc., Detroit
Ed: Amy Lane. **Description:** Unemployment rates rose in the Detroit area from half a percentage point in Washtenaw County to 1.1 point in Wayne County according to data from the Michigan Department of Career Development.

32763 ■ **"U.S. Exports in 2007" in** *Kiplinger Letter* **(Vol. 78, January 5, 2007, No. 1)**
Pub: Kiplinger
Description: U.S. export growth is expected to drop by nearly 5 percent in 2007, reflective of slow growth in countries such as Canada, Mexico, parts of Europe, China, Japan, and South Korea.

32764 ■ **"The U.S. Is In Decline-And That's a Good Thing" in** *Fortune* **(Vol. 151, February 21, 2005, No. 4, pp. 58)**
Pub: Time Inc.
Ed: Geoffrey Colvin. **Description:** Reasons for America's declining economy in the global market is examined. Statistical data included.

32765 ■ **"Unleashing The Millennium" in** *Fortune* **(Vol. 141, No. 5, March 6, 2000, pp. 16+)**
Pub: Time Inc.
Ed: Paul Krugman. **Description:** An inquiry into what went right with the free market system at the turn of the century, and whether this trend will continue.

32766 ■ **"Unpredictable Flight Path" in** *Washington Business Journal* **(Vol. 22, No. 18, September 5, 2003, pp. 3)**
Pub: Washington Business Journal
Ed: John Wilen. **Description:** Forty-nine workers in United Airlines' airfreight operations at Washington Dulles International Airport have been laid off as a result of the airlines' restructuring program.

32767 ■ **"Upping the Minimum Wage: Small Business Bust or Low-Income Boost?" in** *Black Enterprise* **(Vol. 35, October 2004, No. 3, pp. 60)**
Pub: Earl G. Graves Publishing Co. Inc.
Ed: Cliff Hocker. **Description:** Legislation sponsored by Senator Edward M. Kennedy could raise the federal minimum wage from $5.15 per hour to $5.85 within 60 days of the bill's passage. Hikes in the minimum wage could hurt small businesses.

32768 ■ **"Ups & downs" in** *Entrepreneur* **(Vol. 30, No. 2, February 2002, pp. 66)**
Pub: Entrepreneur Media Inc.
Ed: Jacquelyn Lynn. **Description:** Four tips for getting insurance rates on the same tract as the economy are presented.

32769 ■ **"The Upside and Downside of Outsourcing" in** *Business Week* **(February 20, 2006, No. 3972, pp. 18)**
Pub: McGraw-Hill Companies
Description: Foreign companies are outsourcing jobs to the U.S. at record rates. Eight percent of U.S. workers are employed in the service industry, 19 percent in manufacturing, and only 1 percent in farming.

32770 ■ "An Urban Survivor Poised for Better Times" in *Crain's Chicago Business* (Vol. 26, No. 50, December 15, 2003, pp. 8)
Pub: Crain Communications, Inc.
Ed: Joe Cappo. Description: A new study conducted by CEOs for Cities, reports that large urban cities like Chicago, Illinois are seeing a new economic success rate because these cities are becoming more diverse. The study was based on five categories, such as educational levels of the population, diversity and specialties of businesses, population and per-capita income growth, and property values.

32771 ■ "U.S." in *Business Week* (February 20, 2006, No. 3972, pp. 29)
Pub: McGraw-Hill Companies
Ed: James C. Cooper. Description: The question is asked: When should U.S. lawmakers and investors start to worry about the inflation implications of tight labor markets? Statistical data included.

32772 ■ "U.S.: Signs That Inflation Is Losing Its Fangs" in *Business Week* (February 7, 2005, No. 3919, pp. 25)
Pub: McGraw-Hill Companies
Ed: James C. Cooper, Kathleen Madigan. Description: Global competition and information technology should help curb inflation in 2005. Statistical data included.

32773 ■ "U.S.: The Fed: Trying To Shift Into Neutral" in *Business Week* (February 14, 2005, No. 3920, pp. 23)
Pub: McGraw-Hill Companies
Ed: James C. Cooper, Kathleen Madigan. Description: The Federal Reserve raised interest rates on February 2, 2005, hiking rates by a quarter-point at each of the next three meetings scheduled for the first half of the year. Two questions the Fed will also need to confront on monetary policy are discussed.

32774 ■ "Utilities Boost Companies; Utility Services" in *Crain's New York Business* (Vol. 22, November 13, 2006, No. 46, pp. 36)
Pub: Crain Communications, Inc.
Description: Listing of companies that provide utility programs, incentives and benefits to small businesses looking to relocate within the five boroughs of New York City or expand their businesses in the area.

32775 ■ "Vacancy Rates Begin to Ease; Companies' Unused Space Likely to Slow Rebound in Office Market" in *Crain's Detroit Business* (Vol. 19)
Pub: Crain Communications Inc., Detroit
Ed: Jennette Smith. Description: Brokers are predicting gradual declines in unemployment and improved company earnings should help real estate recover and office vacancy rates improve.

32776 ■ "Vacancy Rates Begin to Ease" in *Crain's Detroit Business* (Vol. 19, No. 42, October 20, 2003, pp. 3)
Pub: Crain Communications Inc., Detroit
Ed: Jennette Smith. Description: Brokers are predicting gradual declines in unemployment and improved company earnings should help real estate recover and office vacancy rates improve.

32777 ■ "Valley Econowatch" in *San Fernando Valley Business Journal* (Vol. 11, December 2006, No. 25, pp. 25)
Pub: San Fernando Valley Business Journal Associates
Description: Statistical data included for factors affecting the San Fernando Valley's economy, including numbers of bankruptcies, electricity accounts, tourism activity, real estate figures and others.

32778 ■ "VCs See Bottom, Expect To Do More Deals" in *Venture Capital Journal* (July 1, 2003)
Pub: Thomson Financial Inc.
Description: According to a survey conducted by Venture Capital Journal, VCs are feeling more optimistic, yet cautious, about the industry and are predicting a slow recovery. More startups are experiencing funding, particularly seed- and early-stage rounds, focusing both by industry and region. Life sciences and nanotechnology are receiving the most interest.

32779 ■ "A Venture Capitalist's View of 9-11" in *Venture Capital Journal* (Vol. 42, No. 9, September 2002, pp. 28-29)
Pub: Thomas Venture Economics
Ed: Alan Patricof. Description: Alan Patricof, vice chairman of Apax Partners Inc., an international private equity firm, shares his perspective of New York City after 9-11, including the economic impact of the attacks.

32780 ■ "Voting With Their Pocketbooks" in *Fortune* (Vol. 141, No. 10, May 15, 2000, pp. F372P)
Pub: Time Inc.
Ed: Edward Robinson. Description: A scorecard featuring the issues affecting small business owners in the 2000 election campaign.

32781 ■ "War takes toll on local economy" in *Crain's Detroit Business* (Vol. 19, No. 14, April 7, 2003, pp. 39)
Pub: Crain Communications Inc., Detroit
Ed: Katie Merx. Description: Local economists report that the war is depressing the already soft economy in southeast Michigan, but report good news amid all of the gloom.

32782 ■ "Warning: Credit Crunch" in *Forbes* (Vol. 170, No. 3, August 12, 2002, pp. 62)
Pub: Forbes Magazine
Ed: Robert Lenzner, Matthew Swibel. Description: It is predicted that accounting reform on scrutinized lending could harm the U.S. economy.

32783 ■ "Wary of Economic Instability" in *Hispanic Business* (March 2002, pp. 34)
Pub: Hispanic Business
Description: Results of a survey of financial professionals from the directory of registered money managers, conducted by Hispanic Magazine, are presented. Statistical data included.

32784 ■ "We, the entrepreneurs" in *Entrepreneur* (Vol. 30, No. 2, February 2002, pp. 8)
Pub: Entrepreneur Media Inc.
Ed: Rieva Lesonsky. Description: A discussion on the role entrepreneurs play in the United States economy.

32785 ■ "We Must Discuss Regional Government" in *Crain's Detroit Business* (Vol. 21, January 10, 2005, No. 2, pp. 8)
Pub: Crain Communications Inc. - Detroit
Ed: Keith Crain. Description: The impact of Detroit's dwindling population is discussed. The city's population is expected to be below 1 million, while suburbs continue growing at a rapid pace. Regional government must address how this impacts the city's economy.

32786 ■ "Wealth happens" in *Harvard Business Review* (Vol. 80, No. 4, April 2002, pp. 49)
Pub: Harvard Business School Press
Ed: Mark Buchanan. Description: A discussion into how wealth is distributed in societies by examining the pattern of distribution originally discovered by Vilfredo Pareto, and the ways in which the degree of wealth concentration can be influenced.

32787 ■ "Weathering the Storm; True, things have been better for the nation's entrepreneurs" in *Business Week Online* (November 18, 2002)
Pub: McGraw-Hill Inc.
Ed: Alison Ogden. Description: According to a new survey conducted by the National Federation of Independent Businesses, small businesses are holding their own in the slow economy, and have defied the uncertain trends from the threats of terrorism and corporate scandals.

32788 ■ "What Is the New Economics?" in *Fast Company* (September 2001, pp. 118)
Pub: Fast Company
Ed: John Ellis. Description: Yale economist Robert J. Shiller, wrote the defining book on the Internet bubble: irrational exuberance. Now he's busy rewriting the laws of economics, where emotion and psychology dominate data and numbers.

32789 ■ "What Makes Global Firms Resilient?" in *Harvard Business Review* (Vol. 81, No. 7, July 2003, pp. 14)
Pub: Harvard Business School Press
Ed: Gardiner Morse. Description: The economic importance of globalization is discussed by author, Daniel Yergin.

32790 ■ "What the One Hand Giveth" in *Ingram's* (Vol. 28, No. 9, September 2002, pp. 15)
Pub: Show Me Publishing, Inc.
Ed: Jack Cashill. Description: While being stimulated by local governments, rural economies are being stifled by too many regulations and programs from the federal government, the most oppressive of which is the Hazard Analysis and Critical Control Point, issued by the Food and Drug Administration.

32791 ■ "When the Going Gets Tough...many turn to financial counselors" in *Business Week Online* (November 15, 2002)
Pub: McGraw-Hill Inc.
Ed: Sandra Block. Description: Small business owners often turn to financial counselors for advice on careers, family and security. Nearly 60 percent of all people will consult a financial adviser after a major catastrophe or change in their lives. Since the terrorist attacks of 911, many professionals are seeking ways to leave the corporate life behind, while others are facing changes due to the recession.

32792 ■ "When an Incubator Goes Cold" in *Business Week Online* ()
Pub: McGraw-Hill, Inc.
Description: Investors in Idealab! want to liquidate the Pasadena high tech incubator, but instead feel they are being offered a fraction of what their shares of stock are worth.

32793 ■ "Where Have the Leaders Gone?" in *Ingram's* (Vol. 29, No. 1, January 2003, pp. 4)
Pub: Show Me Publishing, Inc.
Ed: J. Sweney. Description: The policy of Mayor Kay Barnes' investment in buildings and facilities is questioned. Ideas on issues involving infrastructure and leadership for Kansas City, Missouri are also discussed.

32794 ■ "Where the Jobs Are" in *Black Enterprise* (Vol. 32, No. 7, February 2002, pp. 95)
Pub: Earl Graves Publishing Co.
Ed: Winifred DeSouza, Sonya A. Donaldson. Description: The article predicts that although the economy appears bleak and jobs seem scarce, over the next six years, 5.8 million employment opportunities will be open in several fields nationwide. Statistical data included.

32795 ■ "Who Are We?" in *Hispanic Business* (July/August 2004, pp. 16)
Pub: Hispanic Business
Description: Excerpts of Henry Cisneros rebuttal to a Harvard professor's contention that Hispanics are challenging America's identity. However, evidence from successful cities across the nation, population diversity is a driving force in the new economy.

32796 ■ "Why Haven't You Called" in *Atlanta Business Chronicle* (Vol. 25, November 29, 2002, No. 25, pp. 1B)
Pub: American City Business Publications, Inc.
Ed: Don Reichardt. Description: Business leaders have the tendency to blame slumping sales on the economy, but many factors contribute to lower sales. A company's future and success depends partly on the ability to confront other possible causes of declining sales, such as altered consumer behavior, pricing changes, sales force difficulties, and new competitive pressure.

32797 ■ "Why Small Business is Important" in *Bellingham Business Journal* (January 2007, pp. 1)
Pub: Sun News Inc.
Description: While large companies are facing cutbacks, small businesses are becoming the job creation machine of the future. Small companies have the benefits of being flexible while enjoying the increased economies of scale from the industry as a whole.

32798 ■ "Why the Valley Way is Here to Stay" in *Fortune* (Vol. 141, No. 11, May 29, 2000, pp. 36+)
Pub: Time Inc.
Ed: J. Bradford DeLong. **Description:** Despite the bluster about the new economy, not much is actually new. Productivity is at the same rate experienced in the 1960s.

32799 ■ "'Will He Be a Friend or Foe?'" in *Fortune* (Vol. 142, No. 11, November 13, 2000, pp. F384V+)
Pub: Time Inc.
Ed: Jay Branegan. **Description:** Both Vice President Al Gore and Texas Governor George W. Bush favor small business' contribution to growth, jobs and innovation, making small business a winner no matter which candidate wins the election.

32800 ■ "Wisconsin Economic Development Programs Could be Hurt by Tax Fight" in *Milwaukee Journal Sentinel* (December 8, 2005)
Pub: Journal Sentinel, Inc.
Ed: Rick Barrett. **Description:** Due to a court battle, state-sponsored tax incentive programs for businesses could actually undermine these programs designed to attract and retain businesses. Details of the lawsuit are discussed.

32801 ■ *The Wisdom of Crowds: Why the Many Are Smarter Than the Few and How Collective Wisdom Shapes Business, Economies, Societies and Nations*
Pub: Doubleday Canada, Limited
Ed: James Surrowiecki. **Released:** May 2004. **Price:** $24.95. **Description:** The premise that the many are smarter than the few and its impact on business, economics, societies and nations is discussed.

32802 ■ "WSJ Honors Economist" in *Hispanic Business* (June 2005, pp. 18)
Pub: Hispanic Business
Description: Maria Fiorini Ramierez, president and CEO of her global economic and financial consulting firm of the same name, was named one of the top two economists in the U.S. in forecasting the actual rate of inflation during the last three years by The Wall Street Journal.

32803 ■ "Wyandotte County" in *Ingram's* (Vol. 28, No. 9, September 2002, pp. 69)
Pub: Show Me Publishing, Inc.
Description: During a Wyandotte County economic development forum hosted by the magazine, the transformation of Wyandotte County resulting from the unified form of local government was discussed.

32804 ■ "The Year Ahead" in *Hispanic Business* (January/February 2005, pp. 60, 62)
Pub: Hispanic Business
Ed: Juan Solana. **Description:** Slower growth, higher interest rates and moderate inflation is expected for 2005. U.S. economic forecasts are included.

32805 ■ "The Year of the Convertible" in *Forbes* (Vol. 175, February 14, 2005, No. 3, pp. 134)
Pub: Forbes Magazine Inc.
Ed: Richard Lehmann. **Description:** Experts are advising people to invest in convertible preferred stocks in 2005. Convertibles are considered a safe alternative for achieving above-average returns in a growing economy.

32806 ■ "Young Banks Hurting as Nation Celebrates Interest Rate Cuts" in *Washington Business Journal* (Vol. 22, No. 9, July 4, 2003)
Pub: Washington Business Journal
Ed: Tim Mazzucca. **Description:** Problems facing new banks, highlighting the case history of Freedom Bank in Washington, DC, are examined.

32807 ■ "Your Best M&A Strategy" in *Harvard Business Review* (Vol. 81, No. 3, March 2003, pp. 16)
Pub: Harvard Business School Press

Ed: Sam Rovit. **Description:** A director with Bain and Company argues that companies that make frequent acquisitions perform best when they buy throughout the economic cycle. Companies that buy during specific parts of the cycle lag behind the constant buyers.

32808 ■ "Your Career: Take Charge and Find Peace of Mind" in *Atlanta Business Chronicle* (Vol. 25, No. 20, October 25, 2002, pp. 8B)
Pub: American City Business Publications, Inc.
Ed: Emory Mulling. **Description:** The article discusses looking forward and preparing for the future, as it relates to career. Networking and building a skills base are two suggestions.

32809 ■ "Your Loss Is Your Gain" in *Entrepreneur* (Vol. 31, No. 5, May 2003, pp. 50)
Pub: Entrepreneur Media Inc.
Ed: Joan Szabo. **Description:** One of the advantages of an S corporation is the firm's annual income or losses are passed to shareholder; gains are reflected on individual shareholder's tax returns, and losses are deductible. If a small business suffered losses due to a slow economy, it may be able to save taxes from those losses if the firm has Section 1244 stock.

32810 ■ "You've got to keep your nose down and your fanny up" in *Fast Company* (May 2001, pp. 92)
Pub: Fast Company
Ed: Robert L. Crandall. **Description:** Former CEO for American Airlines/AMR Corporation, Robert Crandall, created a number of breakthrough programs including AAdvantage, the industry's first frequent-flier program.

32811 ■ "Yuppie joblessness brings new perk: great deals on yoga" in *Wall Street Journal* (Dec. 5, 2002, pp. A1)
Pub: Dow Jones & Co. Inc.
Ed: Pui-Wing Tam. **Description:** The resulting number of unemployed from the economic downturn has given those without jobs more time to workout, and gyms are offering great deals to increase their membership.

TRADE PERIODICALS

32812 ■ *ACCRA Research in Review*
Pub: American Chamber of Commerce Researchers Association
Ed: Dr. Kenneth E. Poole, Editor. **Released:** Quarterly. **Price:** Included in membership. **Description:** Carries information on research methodology specific to the study of community economic development.

32813 ■ *American Institute for Economic Research—Research Reports*
Pub: American Institute for Economic Research
Ed: Larry Pratt, Editor. **Released:** Semimonthly. **Price:** $59. **Description:** Presents the results of the institute's research, including analyses of significant economic developments and their implications, especially the statistical indications of business-cycle changes.

32814 ■ *Business Facilities*
Pub: Group C Communications Inc.
Contact: Ted Coene, Publisher
E-mail: dgoldstein@groupc.com
Ed: Jennifer Staats, Editor, jstaats@groupc.com. **Released:** Monthly. **Description:** Professional magazine focusing on corporate expansion, commercial/industrial real estate, and economic development.

32815 ■ *Economic Development*
Pub: Wakeman/Walworth Inc.
Ed: Keyes Walworth, Editor. **Released:** Weekly, 48/year. **Price:** $245, U.S. and Canada; $265, elsewhere; $435, two years U.S. and Canada; $480, two years elsewhere. **Description:** Covers state efforts to attract new industry, jobs, commerce, and tourism, in-

cluding such factors as environmental requirements, mass transportation policies, highway construction plans, utility rates, changes in labor laws, tax policies, and enterprise zones. Provides information on urban development programs as affected by growth control legislation, state construction programs, and building codes.

32816 ■ *Economic Development Research Focus*
Pub: Economic Development Institute
Contact: Robert Lann
E-mail: robert.lann@edi.gatech.edu
Ed: Lincoln S. Bates, Editor, lincoln.bates@edi.gatech.edu. **Released:** 3/year. **Price:** Free. **Description:** Reports on the progress and results of studies and activities undertaken by the Center for Economic Development Services. Covers relevant topics, legislation and resources; and presents success stories. Recurring features include notices of publications available, and departments titled Georgia Text, and What Works.

32817 ■ *Entrepreneurship and Regional Development*
Pub: Taylor & Francis
Ed: Edward J. Malecki, Editor, Bengt. Johannisson@ehv.vxu.se. **Released:** Bimonthly, 6/yr. **Price:** $457 institutions online; $219 print; $481 institutions online & print. **Description:** Journal containing information on economic development - entrepreneurial vitality and innovation - as local and regional phenomena.

32818 ■ *Future Economic Trends*
Pub: Conservative Publishing Corp.
Ed: C.J. Jones, Editor. **Released:** Monthly. **Price:** $149 per year; $79 new subscriber. **Description:** Covers economic and political science in an historical perspective. Provides financial survival advice and the destruction of the U.S. economy and the dollar. Recurring features include Feature Article, History Tells Us, Hard Money, and As We Go to Press.

32819 ■ *International Trade Reporter*
Pub: Bureau of National Affairs Inc.
Contact: Linda G. Botsford, Managing Editor
Released: Weekly. **Price:** $1,159. **Description:** Covers current international trade policies of the U.S. and of major U.S. trading partners. Topics include bilateral negotiations, customs, export/import policy, foreign investment, standards, taxation, and other related issues. Recurring features include a calendar of events, reports of meetings, and notices of publications available.

32820 ■ *Internationalist*
Pub: Assist International
Ed: Peter J. Robinson, Jr., Editor. **Released:** 3x/yr. **Price:** $15, individuals. **Description:** Communicates international trade events, conferences, seminars, and trade shows occuring in the New York/Connecticut/New Jersey region. Recurring features include a calendar of events and a listing of international trade resources available in the tri-state region.

32821 ■ *Journal of Economics and Management Strategy*
Pub: MIT Press
Ed: Daniel F. Spulber, Editor. **Released:** Quarterly. **Price:** $53 print & online; $50 online only; $298 institutions print & premium online; $271 institutions print & standard online; $257 institutions premium online. **Description:** Journal providing a forum for research and discussion on competitive strategies of managers and the organizational structure of firms.

32822 ■ *North American Journal of Economics and Finance*
Pub: Elsevier Science B.V.
Contact: Sven W. Arndt, Managing Editor
E-mail: sven.arndt@claremontmckenna.edu
Released: 3/year. **Price:** $99; $427 institutions. **Description:** Scholarly journal sponsored by the North American Economics and Finance Association.

32823 ■ *Quarterly Journal of Business & Economics*
Pub: University of Nebraska
Contact: Margo Young, Managing Editor
E-mail: myoung1@unl.edu
Ed: George M. McCabe, Editor, gmccabe1@unl.edu.
Released: Quarterly. **Price:** $24; $45 institutions; $37 out of country; $55 institutions out of country. **Description:** Journal reporting on finance and economics.

32824 ■ *San Francisco Bulletin*
Pub: San Francisco Chamber of Commerce
Ed: Carol Piasente, Editor. **Released:** Monthly. **Description:** Publishes activities of the San Francisco Chamber of Commerce.

32825 ■ *Utah Department of Workforce Services Workforce Information*
Pub: Utah Department of Workforce Services
Ed: Kenneth Jensen, Editor. **Released:** Monthly. **Price:** Free. **Description:** Offers economic data and analysis for the state of Utah.

VIDEOCASSETTES/ AUDIOCASSETTES

32826 ■ *Small Business in a Big World*
Instructional Video
2219 C St.
Lincoln, NE 68502
Ph:(402)475-6570
Free: 800-228-0164
Fax: (402)475-6500
Co. E-mail: feedback@insvideo.com
URL: http://www.insvideo.com
Price: $99.00. **Description:** Demonstrates how small business has contributed to the overall economy. Includes profiles of small retail, service, manufacturing, professional, high tech, wholesale, and warehousing operations at work. **Availability:** VHS.

TRADE SHOWS AND CONVENTIONS

32827 ■ National Association Business Economics Annual Meeting
National Association for Business Economics
1233 20th St., NW No. 505
Washington, DC 20036
Ph:(202)463-6223
Fax: (202)463-6239
Co. E-mail: nabe@nabe.com
URL: http://www.nabe.com
Released: Annual. **Principal Exhibits:** Business economics products and services.

CONSULTANTS

32828 ■ Consulting, Appraisals & Studies Ltd.
111 W Jackson Blvd., Ste. 1142
Chicago, IL 60604-3886
Ph:(312)939-7775
Scope: Real estate and planning consultants offering economic market analyses, feasibility studies, appraisals, development and investment evaluations, fiscal impact reviews and counseling for private and public sector clients. Projects have involved housing, retail shopping and services, industrial, office, hotels and motels, recreational, institutional and public facilities. Other services include demographic surveys and social and economic impacts, with specialized expertise in rehab and redevelopment, historical preservation and urban planning and zoning. Industries served: business, financial, real estate, developers and government agencies in the U.S. and Canada.

32829 ■ HyettPalma Inc.
1600 Prince St., Ste. 110
Alexandria, VA 22314

Ph:(703)683-5126
Fax: (703)836-5887
Co. E-mail: info@hyettpalma.com
URL: http://www.hyettpalma.com

E-mail: info@hyettpalma.com
Scope: Specializes in economic development in downtown and commercial districts. The firm services feature comprehensive economic enhancement strategies, market analysis, business retention, creation and attraction strategies, business clustering strategies and business district audits. **Publications:** Recruiting Developers: Using Rfps To Package Projects; Focus Groups For Downtown; Business Clustering: How To Leverage Sales. **Seminars:** America Downtown-New Thinking, New Life, Dec, 2005; Americas Downtown Renaissance: Retail Revitalization and More, NYS Tug Hill Commission, 2003.

32830 ■ Organizational Futures
56 Pine St., Ste. 2b
Providence, RI 02903
Ph:(401)351-7110
Fax: (401)351-7158
Scope: Builder of agile human networks to champion innovation and mobilize change; to pursue business opportunities; to custom design agile organizations and communities, to foster civic engagement. **Seminars:** Facilitating for Results.

COMPUTERIZED DATABASES

32831 ■ *ABI/INFORM*
ProQuest
300 N Zeeb Rd.
PO Box 1346
Ann Arbor, MI 48106
Ph:(734)761-4700
Free: 800-521-0600
Fax: (734)761-6450
Co. E-mail: info@il.proquest.com
URL: http://www.proquest.com
Description: Provides full text access or bibliographic citations to articles in publications in business and management information worldwide. Includes 2.7 million indexes and abstracts. Comprised of three editions on CD-ROM:; ABI/INFORM Global covers more than 1600 sources, including more than 350 titles from outside the United States.; ABI/INFORM Research covers more than 700 sources.; ABI/INFORM Select covers about 350 sources with coverage beginning in 1991. **Availability:** Online: Ovid Technologies Inc., ProQuest, Thomson Dialog, Questel; Orbit, Gesellschaft fur Betriebswirtschaftliche Information mbH, STN International, Colorado Alliance of Research Libraries, Financial Times, Online Computer Library Center Inc. (OCLC), LexisNexis, EINS - European Information Network Services, Thomson Dialog; Batch: Nerac Inc. **Type:** Full text; Bibliographic; Image.

32832 ■ *Claritas Demographics - Annual Update*
Claritas Inc.
5375 Mira Sorrento Pl., Ste. 400
San Diego, CA 92121
Free: 800-866-6520
Fax: (858)550-5800
Co. E-mail: info@claritas.com
URL: http://www.claritas.com
Description: Contains 2000 data, current-year estimates, and five-year projections of key demographics, including data on households, populations, families, income, age, and race. **Availability:** CD-ROM: Claritas Inc; Diskette: Claritas Inc;Magnetic Tape: Claritas Inc. **Type:** Statistical.

32833 ■ *County and City Data Book*
U.S. Census Bureau
4700 Silver Hill Rd.
Washington, DC 20233-0001
Ph:(301)457-4100
Fax: (301)457-4714
Co. E-mail: webmaster@census.gov

URL: http://www.census.gov
Description: Contains demographic, economic, and geographic data on U.S. counties and cities. Includes 220 data items for states and counties, 200 data items for cities, and 33 data items for places of 2500 or more. Covers 3141 counties, 1100 incorporated cities of 5000 or more persons, and 11,000 places of 2500 or more persons. Includes detailed information on cities with 25,000 or more inhabitants. Coverage includes land area, population, households, vital statistics, labor force, education, crime, and, for cities, form of government, Moody's bond rating, climate, and residential energy consumption. Address such topics as age, money and personal income, population, housing ownership and value, births and deaths, business, banking, climate, employment, and more. Data are collected from federal agencies and private organizations. Public domain software enables the user to search by states, counties, cities of more than 25,000, and places of more than 2500. Downloadable as PDF file. Corresponds to *County and City Data Book* print edition. **Availability:** Online: U.S. Census Bureau; CD-ROM: U.S. Census Bureau. **Type:** Statistical.

LIBRARIES

32834 ■ Enterprise Newfoundland and Labrador–Business Resource Centre
Viking Bldg.
136 Crosbie Rd.
St. John's, NL, Canada A1B 3K3
Ph:(709)772-6022
Fax: (709)772-6090
Co. E-mail: info@cbsc.ic.gc.ca
URL: http://www.cbsc.org/af
Contact: Beulah Bouzane, Dir.
Scope: Marketing, small business, economic and regional development. **Services:** Copying; SDI; center open to the public. **Holdings:** 10,000 books; 20 VF drawers of subject files; Standard Industrial Classification (SIC) files. **Subscriptions:** 300 journals and other serials.

32835 ■ LECG, LLC–Library
2000 Powell St., Ste. 600
Emeryville, CA 94608
Ph:(510)653-9800
Fax: (510)653-9898
Co. E-mail: nancy_adams@lecg.com
URL: http://www.lecg.com
Contact: Nancy Adams
Scope: Economics, business, antitrust. **Services:** Library not open to the public. **Holdings:** 2500 books. **Subscriptions:** 50 journals and other serials; 4 newspapers.

32836 ■ Ontario Ministry of Economic Development and Trade–InfoSource
900 Bay St.
Hearst Block, 6th Fl.
Toronto, ON, Canada M7A 2E1
Ph:(416)325-6626
Fax: (416)325-6825
Co. E-mail: janice.somers@edt.gov.on.ca
Scope: Trade, industry, small business, technology, management, company information. **Services:** Copying; scanning. **Holdings:** 200 books; microfiche; 20 CD-ROMs.

32837 ■ U.S.D.A.–National Agricultural Library–Rural Information Center (10301)
10301 Baltimore Ave., Rm. 304
Beltsville, MD 20705
Ph:(301)504-5372
Free: 800-633-7701
Fax: (301)504-5181
Co. E-mail: ric@nal.usda.gov
URL: http://www.nal.usda.gov/ric/
Contact: Patricia LaCaille John, Coord.
Scope: Economic development; small business development; city and county government services; government and private grants and funding sources; rural communities; community leadership; natural resources. **Services:** Reference; center open to the public. **Holdings:** Figures not available.

32838 ■ University of Kentucky–Business & Economics Information Center
B&E Info. Ctr., Rm. 116
100 W. Gatton College of Business
Lexington, KY 40406-0093
Ph:(859)257-5868
Fax: (859)323-9496
Co. E-mail: mrazeeq@pop.uk.edu
URL: http://www.uky.edu/~BEIC
Contact: Michael A. Razeeq, Bus.Ref.Libn.
Scope: Business, economics, business management, marketing, finance, accounting. **Services:** Library open to the public for reference use only.

32839 ■ West Virginia University–College of Business and Economics–Bureau of Business and Economic Research (320 B)
320 Business and Economics Bldg.
Box 6025
Morgantown, WV 26506-6025
Ph:(304)293-7831
Fax: (304)293-7061
Co. E-mail: Tom.Witt@mail.wvu.edu
URL: http://bber.wvu.edu
Contact: Tom S. Witt, Assoc. Dean
Scope: Economics, West Virginia economy. **Services:** Library not open to the public. **Holdings:** 300 books; 600 other cataloged items. **Subscriptions:** 12 journals and other serials; 4 newspapers.

RESEARCH CENTERS

32840 ■ Arizona State University–Bank One Economic Outlook Center
W.P. Carey School of Business
PO Box 874011
Tempe, AZ 85287-4011
Ph:(480)965-5543
Free: 800—448-0432
Fax: (480)965-5458
Co. E-mail: wpcareyeoc@asu.edu
URL: http://wpcarey.asu.edu/seid/EOC
Contact: Tracy Clark, Assoc.Dir.
E-mail: wpcareyeoc@asu.edu
Scope: Economic and business climate forecasts for Arizona and the western United States, including California, Utah, Nevada, Oregon, New Mexico, Colorado, Idaho, Washington, and Texas. **Services:** Forecasting newsletters and economic analysis. **Publications:** Bank One Arizona Blue Chip Economic Forecast (monthly); Greater Phoenix Blue Chip Economic Forecast (quarterly); Job Growth Update: Ranking the States & MSA's (monthly); Mexico Consensus Economic Forecast (quarterly); Western Blue Chip Economic Forecast (10/year).

32841 ■ Atlantic Institute for Market Studies
2000 Barrington St., Ste. 1006
Cogswell Tower
Halifax, NS, Canada B3J 3K1
Ph:(902)429-1143
Fax: (902)425-1393
Co. E-mail: aims@aims.ca
URL: http://www.aims.ca/
Contact: Brian Lee Crowley, Pres.
E-mail: aims@aims.ca
Scope: Current and emerging economic and public policy issues facing Atlantic Canadians and Canadians more generally, including the economic and social characteristics and potentials of Atlantic Canada and its four constituent provinces. **Publications:** AIMS On-Line Newsletter; Books; Papers. **Educational Activities:** Conferences, meetings, seminars; Lectures; Training programs.

32842 ■ Atlantic Provinces Economic Council
5121 Sackville St., Ste. 500
Halifax, NS, Canada B3J 1K1
Ph:(902)422-6516
Fax: (902)429-6803
Co. E-mail: info@apec-econ.ca
URL: http://www.apec-econ.ca
Contact: Elizabeth Beale, Pres./CEO
E-mail: info@apec-econ.ca

Scope: Economic development of the Atlantic Region of Canada by monitoring and analyzing current and emerging economic trends and policies. **Services:** Consulting. **Educational Activities:** Business Outlook Conference (annually), held each fall; Forums and dinners.

32843 ■ Ball State University–Bureau of Business Research
Miller College of Business, WB 149
Muncie, IN 47306
Ph:(765)285-5926
Fax: (765)285-8024
Co. E-mail: jlane@bsu.edu
URL: http://www.bsu.edu/cob/bbr/
Contact: Judy A. Lane, Assoc.Dir.
E-mail: jlane@bsu.edu
Scope: Business and economics, including special studies designed to contribute to economic development and growth of eastern Indiana. Compiles and disseminates current economic and business data. **Services:** Word processing and computer statistical services to faculty. **Publications:** Mid-American Journal of Business (semiannually). **Educational Activities:** Staff monograph and paper seminars.

32844 ■ Baylor University–Center for Business and Economic Research
PO Box 98003
Waco, TX 76798
Ph:(254)710-4146
Fax: (254)710-6142
Co. E-mail: tom_kelly@baylor.edu
URL: http://www.baylor.edu/business/economic_research
Contact: Dr. Thomas M. Kelly, Dir.
E-mail: tom_kelly@baylor.edu
Scope: Local business and economic conditions. Conducts community economic base studies and supplies social and economic data to local agencies. Compiles and releases monthly indexes of business activity, indexes of consumer prices, and estimates of retail sales to newspapers. Tabulates and analyzes census and other data as requested by local agencies.

32845 ■ Case Western Reserve University–Center for Regional Economic Issues
11119 Bellflower Rd., No. 250
Cleveland, OH 44106-7235
Ph:(216)368-5534
Free: 800—723-0203
Fax: (216)368-5542
Co. E-mail: ed.morrison@case.edu
Contact: Ed Morrison, Exec.Dir.
E-mail: ed.morrison@case.edu
Scope: Economic conditions of the Great Lakes region, including changing economic base and competition with other regions. Studies include relationship of regional growth to technology base and higher education, methods to reduce poverty in industrial cities, public investments and the fiscal capacity of cities, and enterprise development in older cities. **Publications:** REI Program Papers; REI Working Papers. **Educational Activities:** Annual Conferences; Executive education workshops.

32846 ■ Center for the Study of Economics
1518 Walnut St., Ste. 604
Philadelphia, PA 19102
Ph:(215)545-6004
Fax: (215)545-4929
Co. E-mail: manager@urbantools.net
URL: http://www.urbantools.net
Contact: R. Joshua Vincent, Exec.Dir.
E-mail: manager@urbantools.net
Scope: Property tax reform, land value taxation, also unemployment, recession, and inflation. **Services:** Consulting. **Publications:** Incentive Taxation (8/year).

32847 ■ Centre for the Study of Living Standards–Centre d'étude des niveaux de vie
111 Sparks St., Ste. 500
Ottawa, ON, Canada K1P 5B5
Ph:(613)233-8891

Fax: (613)233-8250
Co. E-mail: csls@csls.ca
URL: http://www.csls.ca/
Contact: Dr. Andrew Sharpe, Exec.Dir.
E-mail: csls@csls.ca
Scope: Trends in and determinants of productivity, living standards and economic and social wellbeing. **Services:** Database development (occasionally). **Publications:** CSLS Research Reports (10/year); International Productivity Monitor (semiannually).

32848 ■ Chapman University–A. Gary Anderson Center for Economic Research
George L. Argyros School of Business & Economics
1 University Dr.
Orange, CA 92866
Ph:(714)997-6693
Fax: (714)997-6601
Co. E-mail: adibi@chapman.edu
URL: http://www.acer.chapman.edu
Contact: Esmael Adibi, Dir.
E-mail: adibi@chapman.edu
Scope: Economics and business in the U.S. and California, as well as in Orange County, Los Angeles County, and the Inland Empire in California. **Services:** Consulting. **Publications:** Economic & Business Review (semiannually); Local business surveys; Newsletter; Working papers. **Educational Activities:** Chapman University Economic Forecast Conference (annually), each December; Workshops, conferences.

32849 ■ East Tennessee State University–Bureau of Business and Economic Research
222 Sam Wilson Hall
PO Box 70700
Johnson City, TN 37614-1710
Ph:(423)439-5677
Fax: (423)439-8381
Co. E-mail: smitjl01@etsu.edu
URL: http://www.etsu.edu/cbat/bureau/
Contact: Jon L. Smith PhD, Dir.
E-mail: smitjl01@etsu.edu
Scope: Regional business conditions and the economic development of northeast Tennessee and the Tri-Cities Metropolitan Statistical Area (MSA) (Johnson City, Kingsport, and Bristol). Assists faculty and students in research efforts. **Services:** Business Development Program; Economic feasibility (impact) studies; Global research; Implementation of pay systems; Regional development information. **Publications:** East Tennessee Business Indicators; Labor Market Report; Tri-Cities Retail Sales Report (quarterly). **Educational Activities:** Business programs; Economic Development Seminars; Workforce Development Seminars.

32850 ■ Fort Lewis College–Office of Economic Analysis and Business Research
Durango, CO 81301
Ph:(970)247-7624
Fax: (970)247-7623
Co. E-mail: walker_d@fortlewis.edu
Contact: Deborah Walker, Dir.
E-mail: walker_d@fortlewis.edu
Scope: Economics and local economic conditions. **Services:** Conducts contract research and serves as a clearinghouse linking college faculty and the business community. **Publications:** Econometer (quarterly).

32851 ■ Georgia Southern University–Bureau of Business Research and Economic Development
PO Box 8151-01
Statesboro, GA 30460-8151
Ph:(912)681-0872
Fax: (912)681-5581
Co. E-mail: pisley@georgiasouthern.edu
URL: http://www.livingoak.org
Contact: Dr. Phyllis Isley, Dir.
E-mail: pisley@georgiasouthern.edu
Scope: Local economic development, economic forecasting, regional economics, and public finance. **Services:** Consulting and assistance for local businesses and communities.

32852 ■ Georgia State University–Economic Forecasting Center
PO Box 3988
Atlanta, GA 30302-3988
Ph:(404)651-3298
Fax: (404)651-3299
Co. E-mail: rdhawan@gsu.edu
URL: http://robinson.gsu.edu/efc/
Contact: Dr. Rajeev Dhawan, Dir.
E-mail: rdhawan@gsu.edu
Scope: National, regional, and state economic analysis and forecasting. Studies include econometric descriptions of the United States, the Southeast, Georgia, and the Atlanta metropolitan area, including short-term interest rates, long-term bond issues, foreign competition, and currency stability. The Center's objective is to provide economic commentary and analysis to the public and to the business community in particular. **Services:** Entitles sponsors to all data collected or produced by the Center and to one or two private meetings yearly with the Center director. **Publications:** Forecast of Georgia and Atlanta (quarterly); Forecast of the Nation (quarterly); Southeast States Indicators (quarterly). **Educational Activities:** Economic Forecasting Conference (quarterly); Facilities for research on forecasting and related topics; Instructs students in applied economics; Sponsors' Seminar (quarterly).

32853 ■ Hawaii Business, Economic Development, and Tourism Department–Research and Economic Analysis Division
Capitol District Bldg.
250 S Hotel St.
PO Box 2359
Honolulu, HI 96804
Ph:(808)586-2423
Fax: (808)587-2790
Co. E-mail: library@dbedt.hawaii.gov
URL: http://www.hawaii.gov/dbedt
Contact: Pearl Imada-Iboshi, Hd.
E-mail: library@dbedt.hawaii.gov
Scope: Business, economic development, tourism. **Services:** Statistical and economic information to the public. **Publications:** Hawaii's Economy (occasionally); Quarterly Statistical and Economic Report; State of Hawaii Data Book (annually). **Educational Activities:** Census data workshops and meetings.

32854 ■ Idaho State University–Center for Business Research
921 S 8th Ave.
PO Box 8044
Pocatello, ID 83209
Ph:(208)282-3050
Fax: (208)236-5960
Co. E-mail: zelupaul@isu.edu
URL: http://www.isu.edu/cbr
Contact: Dr. Paul R. Zelus, Dir.
E-mail: zelupaul@isu.edu
Scope: Business and economic research pertinent to needs of Idaho's business, government, and service organizations, including economic base studies, evaluation of effects of proposed and existing legislation, resource utilization recommendations, and other issues upon request. **Services:** Data information and survey and data analysis consultation. **Publications:** Annual Report; Dataletter (quarterly); Proceedings of Idaho State Annual Tax Institute. **Educational Activities:** Supervisory training and professional development programs, on a continuing basis at irregular intervals.

32855 ■ Indiana University Bloomington–Indiana Business Research Center
Graduate & Executive Education Center, Ste. 3110
Kelley School of Business
1275 E 10th St.
Bloomington, IN 47405-1701
Ph:(812)855-5507
Fax: (812)855-7763
Co. E-mail: conover@indiana.edu
URL: http://www.ibrc.indiana.edu
Contact: Jerry Conover, Dir.
E-mail: conover@indiana.edu

Scope: Indiana's economic development, population trends, state and local economic indicators, and information technology. **Publications:** InContext (monthly); Indiana Business Review (quarterly); Indiana Factbook (biennially). **Educational Activities:** Public presentations and training.

32856 ■ Interuniversity Research Centre on Quantitative Economics
3150, rue Jean-Brillant, Bureau C-6088
C.P. 6128, succursale Centre-ville
Montreal, QC, Canada H3C 3J7
Ph:(514)343-6557
Fax: (514)343-5831
Co. E-mail: emanuela.cardia@umontreal.ca
URL: http://www.cireq.umontreal.ca
Contact: Emanuela Cardia, Dir.
E-mail: emanuela.cardia@umontreal.ca
Scope: Theoretical and applied econometrics, decision theory, macroeconomics policies and financial markets as well as environmental problems. **Publications:** Annual report; Research papers. **Educational Activities:** Conferences; Seminars (periodically); Special lectures.

32857 ■ Jacksonville State University–Center for Economic Development
College of Commerce & Business Administration
Jacksonville, AL 36265-1602
Ph:(256)782-5324
Fax: (256)782-5179
Co. E-mail: pshaddix@jsu.edu
URL: http://www.jsu.edu/depart/ced/
Contact: Pat W. Shaddix, Dir.
E-mail: pshaddix@jsu.edu
Scope: Industrial needs analysis for cities and counties and business research, including retail and service studies. Special projects include economic development strategies for Alabama counties and marketing plan considerations for local governments, including Best Fit Studies. **Services:** Maintains a small business development center; State Data Center affiliate. **Publications:** JSU Economic Update; Monographs. **Educational Activities:** Supervisory training, planning.

32858 ■ New School University–Community Development Research Center
Milano Graduate School of Management & Urban Policy
72 5th Ave.
New York, NY 10011
Ph:(212)229-5400
Fax: (212)229-5354
Co. E-mail: ServonL@newschool.edu
URL: http://www.newschool.edu/milano/cdrc/
Contact: Lisa Servon PhD, Assoc.Dir.
E-mail: ServonL@newschool.edu
Scope: Basic and applied interdisciplinary research on community-based approaches to the economic, social, political, and physical revitalization of poor communities; and the effectiveness of community-based strategies in comparison to other, non community-based approaches. The Center seeks to build a base of knowledge on community-based efforts toward the revitalization of poor neighborhoods, examine current activities and programs and the factors that contribute to or limit their effectiveness, and understand the interaction between community-based efforts and the larger policy context and socio-economic climate in which they operate. **Publications:** Newsletter; Research Reports (periodically); Working Papers (periodically). **Educational Activities:** Conferences (occasionally); Roundtables (occasionally); Seminars (occasionally).

32859 ■ North Dakota State University–Institute for Business and Industry Development
2718 Gateway Ave., Ste. 104
Bismarck, ND 58503
Ph:(701)328-9718
Fax: (701)328-9721
Co. E-mail: kathleen.tweeten@ndsu.nodak.edu
URL: http://www.ag.ndsu.nodak.edu/ibid
Contact: Kathleen Tweeten, Dir.
E-mail: kathleen.tweeten@ndsu.nodak.edu

Scope: Business and community economic development. **Services:** Engineering extension services.

32860 ■ Plattsburgh State University of New York–Technical Assistance Center
Redcay 213
101 Broad St.
Plattsburgh, NY 12901
Ph:(518)564-2214
Fax: (518)564-3220
Co. E-mail: tac@plattsburgh.edu
URL: http://tac.plattsburgh.edu
Contact: Howard Lowe, Dir.
E-mail: tac@plattsburgh.edu
Scope: Regional economic development, project development and implementation for public and private enterprises. Specialties include data/demographic research, tourism studies and seminars, telecommunications, and Geographic Information System - GIS. **Services:** Consulting; Demographic and economic data retrieval; GIS; Grant writing assistance; Needs assessments, economic impact analyses, competitive intelligence; Telecommunications network planning and development; Tourism marketing conversion analyses. **Publications:** A Guide to State, Regional, County, and Local Business Financing Programs for Northern New York (annually); NY County demographic profiles (7/year). **Educational Activities:** Workshops.

32861 ■ Princeton University–Research Program in Development Studies
Wallace Hall
Woodrow Wilson School of Public & International Affairs
Princeton, NJ 08544
Ph:(609)258-6403
Fax: (609)258-5974
Co. E-mail: accase@princeton.edu
URL: http://www.wws.princeton.edu/~rpds
Contact: Anne C. Case, Dir.
E-mail: accase@princeton.edu
Scope: Economic development, particularly in health and microeconomics. **Publications:** Working Paper Series. **Educational Activities:** Research seminars in economic development for staff and graduate students of the School (biweekly).

32862 ■ Simon Fraser University–Centre for Sustainable Community Development
8888 University Dr.
Burnaby, BC, Canada V5A 1S6
Ph:(604)291-5849
Fax: (604)291-5473
Co. E-mail: cedadmin@sfu.ca
URL: http://www.sfu.ca/cedc/
Contact: Mark Roseland PhD, Dir.
E-mail: cedadmin@sfu.ca
Scope: Community economic development through access to knowledge, programs, markets, and funds. **Services:** ced-net, a worldwide discussion group of CED participants.

32863 ■ State University of New York College at Oneonta–Center for Economic and Community Development
Bacon Hall
Morris Conference Center
Oneonta, NY 13820
Ph:(607)436-2792
Fax: (607)436-2786
Co. E-mail: cecd@oneonta.edu
URL: http://www.oneonta.edu/advancement/cecd
Contact: Barry P. Warren PhD, Dir.
E-mail: cecd@oneonta.edu
Scope: Community, government, and marketing surveys; downtown development studies and marketing research, including business start-up consultation, economic impact analysis, community priorities planning, teleconferencing, on-line database searches, evaluation services for drug treatment courts. **Educational Activities:** Industry and government conferences; Leadership Otsego.

32864 ■ Texas A&M International University–Texas Center for Border Economic and Enterprise Development

5201 University Blvd.
Laredo, TX 78041-1900
Ph:(956)326-2546
Fax: (956)326-2544
Co. E-mail: jmpatrick@tamiu.edu
URL: http://texascenter.tamiu.edu
Contact: Dr. J. Michael Patrick, Dir.
E-mail: jmpatrick@tamiu.edu
Scope: International trade and border economic enterprise and development. **Services:** Data accessible by Internet. **Publications:** Border Business Indicators. **Educational Activities:** Internet home pages; Maquila visits; USIA delegations.

32865 ■ University of Alberta–Institute for Public Economics

8-26 Hm Tory
Department of Economics
Edmonton, AB, Canada T6H 2H4
Ph:(780)492-6670
Fax: (780)492-3300
Co. E-mail: IPE@ualberta.ca
URL: http://222.uofaweb.uaberta.ca/ipe/
Contact: Bradford Reid, Dir.
E-mail: IPE@ualberta.ca
Scope: Public economics, including the public sector and its influence on the economy and society. **Educational Activities:** Seminars.

32866 ■ University of Colorado at Boulder–Carl McGuire Center for International Studies

Department of Economics
256 UCB
Boulder, CO 80309-0256
Ph:(303)492-6394
Fax: (303)492-8960
Co. E-mail: wolfgang.keller@colorado.edu
URL: http://www.colorado.edu/Economics/mcguire/
Contact: Wolfgang Keller, Dir.
E-mail: wolfgang.keller@colorado.edu
Scope: Organized within the Economics Department, the Center conducts research and graduate training in a broad range of topics relating to international economics, including international trade and finance, international trade negotiations, monetary theory and policy, economic development, and macroeconomics. Offers students in international economics exposure to interdisciplinary study involving the University's programs in international politics, conflict and peace studies, and international business. **Educational Activities:** Workshop in international economics for graduate students and faculty of the Economics Department.

32867 ■ University of Connecticut–Connecticut Center for Economic Analysis

Monteith Bldg., Box U-1240
341 Mansfield Rd.
Storrs, CT 06269-1240
Ph:(860)486-0485
Fax: (860)486-4463
Co. E-mail: fred.carstensen@uconn.edu
URL: http://ccea.uconn.edu
Contact: Prof. Fred V. Carstensen, Dir.
E-mail: fred.carstensen@uconn.edu
Scope: Economic analysis, including state and local finance, economic impact, policy analysis, cluster analysis, assessment of fiscal structure, dynamic forecasting, econometrics, bench-marketing, labor and health economics. **Services:** Forecasting (monthly). **Publications:** The Connecticut Economy (quarterly). **Educational Activities:** Economic Outlook Conferences (periodically); Releave Event/Press Conference for The Connecticut Economy (quarterly).

32868 ■ University of Maryland at College Park–Center for International Economics

Department of Economics
4118 Tydings Hall
College Park, MD 20742
Ph:(301)405-3550
Fax: (301)405-7835
Co. E-mail: calvo@econ.umd.edu
URL: http://www.bsos.umd.edu/econ/cie/ciehome.html
Contact: Prof. Guillermo Calvo, Dir.
E-mail: calvo@econ.umd.edu
Scope: International economics. **Educational Activities:** Conferences; Graduate Training Program; Professional Training Program in International Economics.

32869 ■ University of North Carolina at Chapel Hill–Institute for Economic Development

CB 3140
Chapel Hill, NC 27599-3140
Ph:(919)962-4767
Fax: (919)962-5206
Co. E-mail: hgold@email.unc.edu
Contact: Prof. Harvey A. Goldstein, Dir.
E-mail: hgold@email.unc.edu
Scope: Economic and industrial development, labor market forcasting, fiscal and economic impact analysis, strategic planning, technology studies, urban and regional development planning. **Services:** Consultation and technical assistance.; Provides economic appraisals and strategy formulation by graduate student analysts to qualified local agencies, and economic development bodies.. **Publications:** Carolina Planning Journal (semiannually). **Educational Activities:** Master's and Ph.D. degrees in regional planning.; UNC (Basic) Economic Development Course, accredited y the American Economic Development Council..

32870 ■ University of North Texas–Center for Economic Development and Research

PO Box 310469
Denton, TX 76203
Ph:(940)565-4049
Fax: (940)565-4658
Co. E-mail: budw@scs.unt.edu
URL: http://www.unt.edu/cedr
Contact: Bernard L. Weinstein, Dir.
E-mail: budw@scs.unt.edu
Scope: Applied economics, business, and public policy, particularly in the areas of economic development, fiscal analysis, energy policy, economic forecasting, and public policy. **Publications:** Perspectives (semiannually).

32871 ■ University of Texas at Austin–Bureau of Business Research

Red McCombs School of Business, B8500
1 University Sta.
Austin, TX 78712-0226
Ph:(512)471-5180
Free: 888–212-4386
Fax: (512)471-1063
Co. E-mail: bruce.kellison@mccombs.utexas.edu
URL: http://bbr.icc.utexas.edu
Contact: Dr. J. Bruce Kellison, Assoc.Dir.
E-mail: bruce.kellison@mccombs.utexas.edu
Scope: Economics and business in Texas, including economic development and planning, natural resources. **Services:** Free information, on the state economy and demography by phone. **Publications:** Research News (bimonthly); Texas Business Review (bimonthly). **Educational Activities:** Conferences and workshops, related to the economy of Texas.

32872 ■ University of Texas—Pan American–Center for Entrepreneurship and Economic Development

ITT Rm. 1.210
1201 W University Dr.
Edinburg, TX 78539-2999
Ph:(956)381-3361
Fax: (956)381-2322
Co. E-mail: ceed@panam.edu
URL: http://coserve1.panam.edu/ceed/
Contact: Roland S. Arriola, VP for Ext.Aff.
E-mail: ceed@panam.edu
Scope: South Texas business assistance and economic research, focusing on business plans, economic area profiles, economic impact studies, economic development planning, market feasibility studies, international trade, urban and rural commercial revitalization, industrial park development and feasibility, geographic information systems, and land use surveys. The center also has a bi-national agreement with Mexico to provide Mexican business and demographic information for U.S. businesses. These services are provided to businesses, local government, economic development organizations, and the community in general. The center has an agreement with the rural empowerment zone to provide management and technical assistance to the communities. **Publications:** Border Chronicle; Red Factbook. **Educational Activities:** Seminars and workshops; Training in economic development.

32873 ■ University of Utah–Bureau of Economic and Business Research

1645 E Campus Center Dr., Rm. 401
Campus Mail KDGB 401
Salt Lake City, UT 84112-9302
Ph:(801)581-6333
Fax: (801)581-3354
Co. E-mail: bureau@business.utah.edu
URL: http://www.business.utah.edu/bebr/
Contact: James A. Wood, Dir.
E-mail: bureau@business.utah.edu
Scope: Economics and business with emphasis on development of economy and resources of the state. **Services:** Inquiry service for individuals and businesses. **Publications:** Utah Construction Report (quarterly); Utah Economic and Business Review (bimonthly).

32874 ■ University of Wisconsin—Superior–Northern Center for Community and Economic Development

Erlanson, 305
PO Box 2000
Superior, WI 54880-2898
Ph:(715)394-8208
Fax: (715)394-8592
Co. E-mail: jhembd@uwsuper.edu
URL: http://www.uwsuper.edu/NCCED
Contact: Jerry Hembd, Dir.
E-mail: jhembd@uwsuper.edu
Scope: Regional and local economic development, including area economic profiles surveys, and statistical analyses. **Services:** Consulting. **Educational Activities:** Training.

32875 ■ Williams College–Center for Development Economics

1065 Main St.
Williamstown, MA 01267
Ph:(413)597-2148
Fax: (413)597-4076
Co. E-mail: cde@williams.edu
URL: http://www.williams.edu/cde/
Contact: Pamela D. Turton, Asst.Dir.
E-mail: cde@williams.edu
Scope: Problems of economic development, emphasizing external trade and finance policies, domestic resource and investment policies, industrialization and technology strategies, and developing countries. **Publications:** Research Memorandum Series. **Educational Activities:** Public seminars (occasionally).

Education and Training

START-UP INFORMATION

32876 ■ "Bizdom U. Set to Teach Next Gen of Startups" in *Crain's Detroit Business* (Vol. 22, November 13, 2006, No. 46, pp. 1)
Pub: Crain Communications Inc. - Detroit
Ed: Sheena Harrison. **Description:** Local businessman invests $10M to form Bizdom U. that teaches entrepreneurs based on experience from other entrepreneurs' successes and failures. Focus will be on developing business plans for their own businesses on a two year program taught by actual local entrepreneurs.

32877 ■ "A Career, Not a Job" in *Forbes* (November 27, 2000, pp. 98)
Pub: Forbes Magazine
Ed: Eileen Glanton. **Description:** Profile of Twin Cities Rise job training program in Minneapolis, Minnesota. Steven Rothschild started the job training program in 1993 in order to help graduates launch substantial careers as computer technicians, accountants, and customer-service employees.

32878 ■ "Dramatic Success" in *Small Business Opportunities* (Vol. 17, November 2005, No. 6, pp. 52, 54)
Pub: Harris Publications Inc.
Description: Profile of Drama Kids, the $10.5 million a year children's after-school drama program. The program offers original lessons with a focus on advancing language, speech and acting skills.

32879 ■ *Entrepreneurship with Online Learning Center Access Card*
Pub: McGraw-Hill Higher Education
Ed: Robert D. Hirich; Michael P. Peters; Dean A. Shepherd. **Released:** October 2006. **Price:** $103.25.
Description: Book instructs students on entrepreneurial processes that include starting a new business.

32880 ■ "Find your working way" in *Black Enterprise* (Vol. 31, No. 5, December 2000, pp. 79)
Pub: Earl Graves Publishing Co.
Description: The question of loans to pay for career improvement is answered.

32881 ■ "Franchise Finds" in *Small Business Opportunities* (Vol. 14, No. 1, January 2002, pp. 126)
Pub: Harris Publications, Inc.
Description: Profile of three franchise opportunities, including Village Inn Restaurants, Primrose School Franchising Company, and Supercuts, Inc.

32882 ■ "Franchisor Contacts" in *Hispanic Business* (October 2004, pp. 114)
Pub: Hispanic Business
Ed: Description: Contact information for franchising opportunities of interest to Hispanic entrepreneurs is presented. Opportunities in the following sectors is presented: automotive, business aids and services, education and training, cleaning and sanitation, employment services, grocery and specialty stores, tutoring and learning aids, packaging and mailing, rentals, restaurants, carry-outs and drive-ins.

32883 ■ "Free Entrepreneurial Workshop" in *Minority Business Journal* (Vol. 17, No. 5, September/October 2001, pp. 2)
Pub: Minority Business Journal
Description: The Workshop in Business Opportunities (WIBO) has offered a free, 16-week intensive educational course for 35 years. The course, comparable to a short-course MBA curriculum, is taught by volunteer New York business owners and senior corporation executives. Alumni are entitled to free lifetime consulting services.

32884 ■ "Guiding Light; Feeling a Little Lost at the Helm of Your Business?" in *Entrepreneur* (Vol. 31, No. 8, August 2003, pp. 84)
Pub: Entrepreneur Media, Inc.
Ed: Geoff Williams. **Description:** Profile of the Build Your Own Business (BYOB) 10-week program that helps entrepreneurs, targeting residents in underserved, urban neighborhoods. Entrepreneurs can receive ongoing free services upon completion of the classes, including financial counseling and tax preparation from BYOB's nonprofit organization, Smart Money Community Services in Cincinnati, Ohio.

32885 ■ "TAMACC Launches Leadership School" in *Hispanic Business* (July/August 2002, pp. 10)
Pub: Hispanic Business
Description: A new initiative undertaken by the Texas Association of Mexican American Chambers of Commerce, called Rules of Engagement: A Leadership Institute, will help Hispanic Texans to develop businesses, reform education, and influence lawmakers.

ASSOCIATIONS AND OTHER ORGANIZATIONS

32886 ■ **AACSB International - Association to Advance Collegiate Schools of Business**
777 S Harbour Island Blvd., Ste. 750
Tampa, FL 33602-5730
Ph:(813)769-6500
Fax: (813)769-6559
Co. E-mail: roxanna@aacsb.edu
URL: http://www.aacsb.edu
Contact: Roxanna Strawn, Asst. VP, Communications
Description: Institutions offering accredited programs of instruction in business administration and accounting at the college level; non-accredited schools; business firms; governmental and professional organizations; educational institutions and organizations outside the U.S. Provides accreditation for bachelor's, master's, and doctoral degree programs in business administration and accounting. Serves as a professional association for management education. Compiles statistics, conducts research, and conducts professional development programs. **Publications:** *AACSB-The International Association for Management Education Membership Directory* (annual); *Achieving Quality and Continuous Improvement Through Self-Evaluation and Peer Review (Standards for Accreditation)* (annual); *BizEd* (bimonthly); *Business and Management Education Funding Alert* (monthly); *eNewsline* (monthly); *Ethics Education in Business Schools*; *Guide to Doctoral Programs in Business and Management* (periodic); *Management Education at Risk*; *Salary Survey* (annual); *Sustaining Scholarship in Business Schools*. Publishes studies, international resource guides, diversity, management of technology, and quality management curriculum guides. Videos are also available.

32887 ■ **American Association of Teachers of Italian**
Dept. of French and Italian
Indiana University
Ballentine 642
Bloomington, IN 47405
Ph:(812)855-2508
Fax: (812)855-8877
Co. E-mail: pgiordano@mail.ucf.edu
URL: http://www.aati-online.org
Contact: Paolo Giordano, Pres.
Description: Professional society of college and secondary school teachers and others interested in Italian language and culture. Promotes study of Italian language, literature, and culture in schools. Maintains speakers' bureau; compiles statistics. Works with Italian government and universities to sponsor special seminars and with Italian-American organizations for the promotion of the Italian language in the K-12 schools. **Publications:** *AATI Newsletter* (semiannual); *Journal Italica* (quarterly).

32888 ■ **American Society for Training and Development**
1640 King St.
Box 1443
Alexandria, VA 22313-2043
Ph:(703)683-8100
Free: 800-628-2783
Fax: (703)683-8103
URL: http://www.astd.org
Contact: Kimo Kippen, Chm.-Elect
Description: Promotes workplace learning and performance; represents the field to U.S. federal and state policymakers through education, policy development, grassroots support and work in coalitions with other national organizations in business, education and labor. Offers the Human Performance Improvement Certificate Program. **Publications:** *ASTD Buyer's Guide and Consultants Directory*; *Infoline Plus* (monthly); *TD Magazine*; Annual Report (annual); Newsletter (monthly).

32889 ■ **Association to Advance Collegiate Schools of Business**
777 S Harbour Island Blvd., Ste. 750
Tampa, FL 33602-5730

Ph:(813)769-6500
Fax: (813)769-6559
Co. E-mail: roxanna@aacsb.edu
URL: http://www.aacsb.edu
Contact: Roxanna Strawn, Asst. VP for
Communications
Description: Promotes advancement of collegiate schools of business. **Publications:** *BizEd* (bimonthly); *eNewsline* (11/year); *Ethics Education in B-Schools*; *Management Education at Risk*; *Sustaining Scholarship in Business Schools*.

32890 ■ ASTD
Box 1443
1640 King St.
Alexandria, VA 22313-2043
Ph:(703)683-8100
Free: 800-628-2783
Fax: (703)683-8103
Co. E-mail: customercare@astd.org
URL: http://www.astd.org
Contact: Tony Bingham, Pres./CEO
Description: Represents workplace learning and performance professionals. **Publications:** *ASTD Buyer's Guide* (annual); *Info-Line: Tips, Tools, and Intelligence for Trainers* (monthly); *T&D Magazine* (monthly).

32891 ■ Canadian Association for Distance Education–Association canadienne de l'education a distance
260 Dalhousie St., Ste. 204
Ottawa, ON, Canada K1N 7E4
Ph:(613)241-0018
Fax: (613)241-0019
Co. E-mail: cade-aced@csse.ca
URL: http://www.cade-aced.ca
Contact: Mr. Tim Howard, Dir. of Administration
Membership: Educators, students, and other individuals with an interest in distance education. **Purpose:** Promotes advancement in the field of distance education. Encourages use of new technologies in distance education. **Publications:** *Asynchronous Learning Networks* (periodic); *Journal of Distance Education* (semiannual).

32892 ■ Canadian Association of Independent Schools
12 Bannockburn Ave.
Toronto, ON, Canada M5M 2M8
Ph:(416)780-1779
Fax: (416)780-9301
Co. E-mail: admin@cais.ca
URL: http://www.cais.ca
Contact: Dr. James Christopher, Exec. Dir.
Membership: Private schools. **Purpose:** Promotes excellence in independent education. Represents members' interests. **Publications:** Membership Directory (biennial).

32893 ■ Canadian Federation of University Women–Federation Canadienne des Femmes Diplomees des Universites
251 Bank St., Ste. 600
Ottawa, ON, Canada K2P 1X3
Ph:(613)234-8252
Fax: (613)234-8221
Co. E-mail: cfuwgen@rogers.com
URL: http://www.cfuw.org
Contact: Susan Russell, Exec. Dir.
Description: Women graduates from accredited universities from around the world. Promotes continuing education for women. Fosters communication and fellowship among members. Advocates for status of women and human rights and equality rights. **Publications:** *The Communicator* (periodic).

32894 ■ A Commitment to Training and Employment for Women
215 Spadina Ave., Ste. 350
Toronto, ON, Canada M5T 2C7
Ph:(416)599-3590
Fax: (416)599-2043
Co. E-mail: info@actew.org
URL: http://www.actew.org
Contact: Jen Liptrot, Exec. Dir.
Description: Serves as umbrella organization of agencies, networks, and groups working on the local

level to support existing education and training opportunities for women (particularly lower income, refugee, and older women). Encourages the creation of new programs. Conducts research, lobbying, and advocacy. **Publications:** Newsletter (monthly).

32895 ■ Community College Business Officers
PO Box 5565
Charlottesville, VA 22905-5565
Ph:(434)293-2825
Fax: (434)245-8453
Co. E-mail: info@ccbo.org
URL: http://www.ccbo.org
Contact: Dr. Bob Hassmiller CAE, Exec. Dir.
Description: Represents business officers. Works to support business officers. **Publications:** *The Bottom Line* (quarterly).

32896 ■ Council for Art Education
PO Box 479
Hanson, MA 02341-0479
Ph:(781)293-4100
Fax: (781)294-0808
Co. E-mail: sarahs@acminet.org
URL: http://www.acminet.org/cfae.htm
Contact: Deborah M. Fanning CAE, Exec. VP
Purpose: Promotes increased public funding for art education; seeks to publicize the value of art education and improve the quality of school art programs. Sponsors National Youth Art Month each March. **Publications:** *YAM News* (quarterly).

32897 ■ Music Notation Modernization Association
PO Box 241
Kirksville, MO 63501
Ph:(660)665-8098
Fax: (660)665-8098
Co. E-mail: scott.reed@mnma.org
URL: http://www.mnma.org
Contact: Mr. Scott B. Reed, Exec. Dir.
Description: Seeks to help modernize the current music notation system. **Publications:** *Music Notation News* (quarterly).

32898 ■ National Association for Industry-Education Cooperation
235 Hendricks Blvd.
Buffalo, NY 14226-3304
Ph:(716)834-7047
Fax: (716)834-7047
Co. E-mail: naiec@pcom.net
URL: http://www2.pcom.net/naiec
Contact: Dr. Donald M. Clark, Pres./CEO
Description: Representatives of business, industry, education, government, labor, and the professions. Fosters industry-education collaboration in continuous school improvement and workforce preparation in order to develop responsive academic and vocational programs which will more effectively serve the needs of both the students and employers as well as further human resources and economic development. Provides technical assistance to schools implementing industry-education councils, high-performance sustainable education systems and business- or industry-sponsored programs. Promotes improved career and entrepreneurship education and supports school-based job placement. Provides staff development programs to improve instruction and curricula and the efficiency and effectiveness of educational management through use of corporate and volunteer services. Acts as national clearinghouse for information on industry involvement in education; serves as liaison between organizations involved in industry-education cooperation, including American Association for Career Education, National Research Center for Career and Technical, and American Society for Training and Development. Conducts research and policy studies. **Publications:** Newsletter (bimonthly).

32899 ■ National Black MBA Association
180 N Michigan Ave., Ste. 1400
Chicago, IL 60601
Ph:(312)236-2622
Fax: (312)236-0390
Co. E-mail: mail@nbmbaa.org

URL: http://www.nbmbaa.org
Contact: Ms. Barbara L. Thomas, Pres./CEO
Description: Business professionals, lawyers, accountants, and engineers concerned with the role of blacks who hold advanced management degrees. Works to create economic and intellectual wealth for the black community. Encourages blacks to pursue continuing business education; assists students preparing to enter the business world. Provides programs for minority youths, students, and professionals, and entrepreneurs including workshops, panel discussions, and Destination MBA seminar. Sponsors job fairs. Works with graduate schools. Operates job placement service. **Publications:** *Black MBA Magazine*; *National Black MBA Association—Newsletter* (monthly); *NBMBAA Program Book* (annual).

32900 ■ National Business Education Association
1914 Association Dr.
Reston, VA 20191-1596
Ph:(703)860-8300
Fax: (703)620-4483
Co. E-mail: nbea@nbea.org
URL: http://www.nbea.org
Contact: Dr. Janet M. Treichel, Exec. Dir.
Membership: Teachers of business subjects in secondary and postsecondary schools and colleges; administrators and research workers in business education; businesspersons interested in business education; teachers in educational institutions training business teachers; high school and college students preparing for careers in business. **Publications:** *Business Education Forum* (quarterly); *Keying In* (quarterly); *NBEA Yearbook* (annual).

EDUCATIONAL PROGRAMS

32901 ■ Adobe Acrobat eForms!
EEI Communications
66 Canal Center Plaza, Ste. 200
Alexandria, VA 22314
Ph:(703)683-0683
Fax: (703)683-4915
Co. E-mail: info@eeicommunications.com
URL: http://www.eeicommunications.com
Price: $695.00. **Description:** Covers developing PDF forms using Adobe Acrobat and JavaScript. **Locations:** Alexandria, VA.

32902 ■ Adobe Acrobat I
EEI Communications
66 Canal Center Plaza, Ste. 200
Alexandria, VA 22314
Ph:(703)683-0683
Fax: (703)683-4915
Co. E-mail: info@eeicommunications.com
URL: http://www.eeicommunications.com
Price: $695.00. **Description:** Covers creating PDF documents, including using hyperlinks, bookmarks, sound clips, and security. **Locations:** Silver Spring, MD; and Alexandria, VA.

32903 ■ Adobe After Effects
EEI Communications
66 Canal Center Plaza, Ste. 200
Alexandria, VA 22314
Ph:(703)683-0683
Fax: (703)683-4915
Co. E-mail: info@eeicommunications.com
URL: http://www.eeicommunications.com
Price: $995.00. **Description:** Covers using After Effects to create digital composites, smooth 2-D animations, and elaborate special effects. **Locations:** Alexandria, VA.

32904 ■ Adobe FrameMaker I
EEI Communications
66 Canal Center Plaza, Ste. 200
Alexandria, VA 22314
Ph:(703)683-0683
Fax: (703)683-4915
Co. E-mail: info@eeicommunications.com
URL: http://www.eeicommunications.com
Price: $995.00. **Description:** Covers paragraph designs, color use, graphics, headers and footers, ta-

bles, and advanced editing techniques. **Locations:** Silver Spring, MD; and Alexandria, VA.

32905 ■ Adobe FrameMaker II
EEI Communications
66 Canal Center Plaza, Ste. 200
Alexandria, VA 22314
Ph:(703)683-0683
Fax: (703)683-4915
Co. E-mail: info@eeicommunications.com
URL: http://www.eeicommunications.com
Price: $695.00. **Description:** Covers cross-references, footnotes, creating a book file, hyperlinks, and exporting to HTML and PDF. **Locations:** Silver Spring, MD; and Alexandria, VA.

32906 ■ Adobe Illustrator I
EEI Communications
66 Canal Center Plaza, Ste. 200
Alexandria, VA 22314
Ph:(703)683-0683
Fax: (703)683-4915
Co. E-mail: info@eeicommunications.com
URL: http://www.eeicommunications.com
Price: $695.00. **Description:** Covers basic graphic design features, including creating geometric shapes and free forms, using type, creating graphs, and using the manipulation tools. **Locations:** Silver Spring, MD; and Alexandria, VA.

32907 ■ Adobe Illustrator II
EEI Communications
66 Canal Center Plaza, Ste. 200
Alexandria, VA 22314
Ph:(703)683-0683
Fax: (703)683-4915
Co. E-mail: info@eeicommunications.com
URL: http://www.eeicommunications.com
Price: $695.00. **Description:** Covers some advanced features of Illustrator, including custom brush patterns, blending modes, effects and styles, and image maps. **Locations:** Silver Spring, MD; and Alexandria, VA.

32908 ■ Adobe Illustrator III: Classic Art Techniques
EEI Communications
66 Canal Center Plaza, Ste. 200
Alexandria, VA 22314
Ph:(703)683-0683
Fax: (703)683-4915
Co. E-mail: info@eeicommunications.com
URL: http://www.eeicommunications.com
Price: $695.00. **Description:** Covers one- and two-point perspective, shadows, geometric depth, and masking and pathfinders. **Locations:** Silver Spring, MD; and Alexandria, VA.

32909 ■ Adobe InDesign I
EEI Communications
66 Canal Center Plaza, Ste. 200
Alexandria, VA 22314
Ph:(703)683-0683
Fax: (703)683-4915
Co. E-mail: info@eeicommunications.com
URL: http://www.eeicommunications.com
Price: $695.00. **Description:** Covers basic techniques for creating graphic-intensive documents including editing master pages, placeholder frames, applying color, and flowing and threading text. **Locations:** Silver Spring, MD; and Alexandria, VA.

32910 ■ Adobe InDesign II
EEI Communications
66 Canal Center Plaza, Ste. 200
Alexandria, VA 22314
Ph:(703)683-0683
Fax: (703)683-4915
Co. E-mail: info@eeicommunications.com
URL: http://www.eeicommunications.com
Price: $695.00. **Description:** Covers techniques for creating graphic-intensive documents including typography, decorative and special font features, exporting documents, importing and linking graphics, drawing straight and curved segments, and advanced frame techniques. **Locations:** Silver Spring, MD; and Alexandria, VA.

32911 ■ Adobe PageMaker I
EEI Communications
66 Canal Center Plaza, Ste. 200
Alexandria, VA 22314
Ph:(703)683-0683
Fax: (703)683-4915
Co. E-mail: info@eeicommunications.com
URL: http://www.eeicommunications.com
Price: $695.00. **Description:** Covers a basic introduction to the page-layout software, including importing text, paragraph formatting, and using graphics. **Locations:** Silver Spring, MD; and Alexandria, VA.

32912 ■ Adobe PageMaker II
EEI Communications
66 Canal Center Plaza, Ste. 200
Alexandria, VA 22314
Ph:(703)683-0683
Fax: (703)683-4915
Co. E-mail: info@eeicommunications.com
URL: http://www.eeicommunications.com
Price: $695.00. **Description:** Covers adding and removing pages from documents, and creating and using styles, master pages, frames, and templates. **Locations:** Silver Spring, MD; and Alexandria, VA.

32913 ■ Adobe PageMaker III
EEI Communications
66 Canal Center Plaza, Ste. 200
Alexandria, VA 22314
Ph:(703)683-0683
Fax: (703)683-4915
Co. E-mail: info@eeicommunications.com
URL: http://www.eeicommunications.com
Price: $395.00. **Description:** Covers working with book features and exporting documents for electronic publishing. **Locations:** Silver Spring, MD; and Alexandria, VA.

32914 ■ Adobe Photoshop: Digital Scanning for Production
EEI Communications
66 Canal Center Plaza, Ste. 200
Alexandria, VA 22314
Ph:(703)683-0683
Fax: (703)683-4915
Co. E-mail: info@eeicommunications.com
URL: http://www.eeicommunications.com
Price: $695.00. **Description:** Seminar covers utilizing Adobe Photoshop with digital scanning to produce camera-ready artwork for print and Web reproduction. **Locations:** Silver Spring, MD; and Alexandria, VA.

32915 ■ Adobe Photoshop I
EEI Communications
66 Canal Center Plaza, Ste. 200
Alexandria, VA 22314
Ph:(703)683-0683
Fax: (703)683-4915
Co. E-mail: info@eeicommunications.com
URL: http://www.eeicommunications.com
Price: $695.00. **Description:** Covers the basic photo manipulation features of Photoshop. **Locations:** Silver Spring, MD; and Alexandria, VA.

32916 ■ Adobe Photoshop II
EEI Communications
66 Canal Center Plaza, Ste. 200
Alexandria, VA 22314
Ph:(703)683-0683
Fax: (703)683-4915
Co. E-mail: info@eeicommunications.com
URL: http://www.eeicommunications.com
Price: $995.00. **Description:** Covers intermediate techniques including channel and masking, paths, layering, spot techniques, proper file formatting, and gamuts and color transition issues. **Locations:** Silver Spring, MD; and Alexandria, VA.

32917 ■ Adobe Photoshop III: Tips and Tricks
EEI Communications
66 Canal Center Plaza, Ste. 200
Alexandria, VA 22314
Ph:(703)683-0683
Fax: (703)683-4915
Co. E-mail: info@eeicommunications.com

URL: http://www.eeicommunications.com
Price: $395.00. **Description:** Covers advanced Photoshop techniques and effects. **Locations:** Silver Spring, MD; and Alexandria, VA.

32918 ■ Adobe Photoshop for Photography
EEI Communications
66 Canal Center Plaza, Ste. 200
Alexandria, VA 22314
Ph:(703)683-0683
Fax: (703)683-4915
Co. E-mail: info@eeicommunications.com
URL: http://www.eeicommunications.com
Price: $695.00. **Description:** Covers the basics of Photoshop's capabilities for working with photographs, including the handling and manipulation of pictures. **Locations:** Silver Spring, MD; and Alexandria, VA.

32919 ■ Adobe Premiere
EEI Communications
66 Canal Center Plaza, Ste. 200
Alexandria, VA 22314
Ph:(703)683-0683
Fax: (703)683-4915
Co. E-mail: info@eeicommunications.com
URL: http://www.eeicommunications.com
Price: $695.00. **Description:** Covers an introduction to video capture and video editing utilizing Premiere. **Locations:** Silver Spring, MD; and Alexandria, VA.

32920 ■ Animation Concepts
EEI Communications
66 Canal Center Plaza, Ste. 200
Alexandria, VA 22314
Ph:(703)683-0683
Fax: (703)683-4915
Co. E-mail: info@eeicommunications.com
URL: http://www.eeicommunications.com
Price: $1,495.00. **Description:** Covers the creation of animation using Photoshop, Illustrator, AfterEffects, Premiere, and StudioPro. **Locations:** Alexandria, VA.

32921 ■ Business Systems Development Process (Canada)
Canadian Management Centre
150 York St., 5th Fl.
Toronto, ON, Canada M5H 3S5
Ph:(416)214-5678
Free: 800-262-9699
Fax: (416)313-4985
Co. E-mail: cmcinfo@cmctraining.org
URL: http://cmcamai.org
Price: $1,850.00 Canadian. **Description:** Four-day seminar for business and IT managers; covers change management, requirements analysis, project management, and the phases of a software development life cycle. **Locations:** Toronto, ON.

32922 ■ Dealing with Competing Demands: Mastering the Managerial Balancing Act
American Management Association
1601 Broadway
New York, NY 10019
Ph:(212)586-8100
Free: 800-262-9699
Fax: (212)903-8168
Co. E-mail: customerservice@amanet.org
URL: http://www.amanet.org
Price: $1,595.00 for non-members; $1,495.00 for AMA members. **Description:** Covers techniques for a more effective workplace; aligning your personal and professional lives, prioritizing and managing tasks and projects, and diffusing stress. **Locations:** Washington, DC; Chicago, IL; and New York, NY.

32923 ■ Dealing with Competing Demands: Mastering the Managerial Balancing Act (Canada)
Canadian Management Centre
150 York St., 5th Fl.
Toronto, ON, Canada M5H 3S5
Ph:(416)214-5678
Free: 800-262-9699
Fax: (416)313-4985
Co. E-mail: cmcinfo@cmctraining.org
URL: http://cmcamai.org

Price: $1,695.00 Canadian. **Description:** Covers managing projects and priorities, organizing work, facilitating meetings, and dealing with stress. **Locations:** Toronto, ON.

32924 ■ Digital Photography Techniques
EEI Communications
66 Canal Center Plaza, Ste. 200
Alexandria, VA 22314
Ph:(703)683-0683
Fax: (703)683-4915
Co. E-mail: info@eeicommunications.com
URL: http://www.eeicommunications.com
Price: $695.00. **Description:** Covers using a digital camera, and manipulating digital pictures with Photoshop. **Locations:** Silver Spring, MD; and Alexandria, VA.

32925 ■ E-mail Marketing, RSS Feeds, and Blogs
EEI Communications
66 Canal Ctr. Plz., Ste. 200
Alexandria, VA 22314-5507
Ph:(703)683-7453
Free: 888-253-2762
Fax: (703)683-7310
Co. E-mail: train@eeicommunications.com
URL: http://www.eeicommunications.com/training
Price: $695. **Description:** Seminar that teaches how to reach customers and prospects by getting around the spam filters without breaking the CAN-SPAM laws by using a mix of e-mail, RSS feeds, and blogs **Locations:** Alexandria, VA; Silver Spring, MD; and Washington, DC.

32926 ■ Editing Stronger Magazines
EEI Communications
66 Canal Ctr. Plz., Ste. 200
Alexandria, VA 22314-5507
Ph:(703)683-7453
Free: 888-253-2762
Fax: (703)683-7310
Co. E-mail: train@eeicommunications.com
URL: http://www.eeicommunications.com/training
Price: $695. **Description:** Seminar that focuses on magazine editing problems, generating new ideas, and an overview of strong editorial practices, including group discussion and critiques of magazine samples, and magazine trends. Includes an informal constructive peer critique of the magazine you are currently working on. **Locations:** Alexandria, VA; Silver Spring, MD; and Washington, DC.

32927 ■ Electronic Editing I
EEI Communications
66 Canal Ctr. Plz., Ste. 200
Alexandria, VA 22314-5507
Ph:(703)683-7453
Free: 888-253-2762
Fax: (703)683-7310
Co. E-mail: train@eeicommunications.com
URL: http://www.eeicommunications.com/training
Price: $395. **Description:** Seminar that covers marking copy using style sheets, tracking changes and comparing documents, using the "search and replace" function, analyzing global changes, writing macros to make repetitive tasks simpler, checking references against citations, and develop a systematic approach to electronic manuscripts. **Locations:** Alexandria, VA; Silver Spring, MD; and Washington, DC.

32928 ■ Electronic Editing II
EEI Communications
66 Canal Ctr. Plz., Ste. 200
Alexandria, VA 22314-5507
Ph:(703)683-7453
Free: 888-253-2762
Fax: (703)683-7310
Co. E-mail: train@eeicommunications.com
URL: http://www.eeicommunications.com/training
Price: $395. **Description:** Covers the creating of more powerful macros in Microsoft Word for global text correction, facilitate the author approval and final correction process, merge multiple reviewers' comments into one file, and create macros in Word for finalizing and cleaning up the document after editing and approval is complete. **Locations:** Alexandria, VA; Silver Spring, MD; and Washington, DC.

32929 ■ Fundamentals of IT Cost Management
American Management Association
1601 Broadway
New York, NY 10019
Ph:(212)586-8100
Free: 800-262-9699
Fax: (212)903-8168
Co. E-mail: customerservice@amanet.org
URL: http://www.amanet.org
Price: $1,795 for non-members; $1,595 for AMA members. **Description:** Covers the strategic development of your IT plan to keep cost down, and meet your financial target. **Locations:** Chicago, IL; and New York, NY.

32930 ■ Get Sharp: Smarter Decision Making and Critical Thinking for Administrative Professionals
American Management Association
1601 Broadway
New York, NY 10019
Ph:(212)586-8100
Free: 800-262-9699
Fax: (212)903-8168
Co. E-mail: customerservice@amanet.org
URL: http://www.amanet.org
Price: $1,445 for non-members; $1,295 for AMA members. **Description:** Covers the skills needed for critical thinking, and stress-free problem solving. **Locations:** New York, NY; Atlanta, GA; Washington, DC; and San Francisco, CA.

32931 ■ How to Design a Web-based Training Course
American Management Association
1601 Broadway
New York, NY 10019
Ph:(212)586-8100
Free: 800-262-9699
Fax: (212)903-8168
Co. E-mail: customerservice@amanet.org
URL: http://www.amanet.org
Price: $1,495.00 for non-members; $1,395.00 for AMA members. **Description:** Covers web training and its benefits, and developing and designing an online course. **Locations:** Washington, DC; and Chicago, IL.

32932 ■ Improving Editing Skills
EEI Communications
66 Canal Ctr. Plz., Ste. 200
Alexandria, VA 22314-5507
Ph:(703)683-7453
Free: 888-253-2762
Fax: (703)683-7310
Co. E-mail: train@eeicommunications.com
URL: http://www.eeicommunications.com/training
Price: $395. **Description:** Covers the main problems that an editor encounters, including lists, active and passive voice, convoluted sentence construction, ambiguity and redundancy, and noun strings. **Locations:** Alexandria, VA; Silver Spring, MD; and Washington, DC.

32933 ■ Instructional Design for Multimedia
EEI Communications
66 Canal Center Plaza, Ste. 200
Alexandria, VA 22314
Ph:(703)683-0683
Fax: (703)683-4915
Co. E-mail: info@eeicommunications.com
URL: http://www.eeicommunications.com
Price: $995.00. **Description:** Seminar that covers how to apply the basics of instructional design, including assessing adult learners and creating measurable learning objectives, and creating interactive multimedia training programs. **Locations:** Alexandria, VA.

32934 ■ Integrating Databases with the Web
EEI Communications
66 Canal Center Plaza, Ste. 200
Alexandria, VA 22314
Ph:(703)683-0683
Fax: (703)683-4915
Co. E-mail: info@eeicommunications.com
URL: http://www.eeicommunications.com

Price: $695.00. **Description:** Covers the basics of integrating a database with the world wide web using a Microsoft Access database, active server pages, or Microsoft's Internet Information Server. **Locations:** Silver Spring, MD; and Alexandria, VA.

32935 ■ Introduction to the Mac
EEI Communications
66 Canal Center Plaza, Ste. 200
Alexandria, VA 22314
Ph:(703)683-0683
Fax: (703)683-4915
Co. E-mail: info@eeicommunications.com
URL: http://www.eeicommunications.com
Price: $395.00. **Description:** Covers an introduction to the Macintosh operating system, file and document management, hardware components, and multiple applications. **Locations:** Silver Spring, MD; and Alexandria, VA.

32936 ■ Introduction to OS X
EEI Communications
66 Canal Ctr. Plz., Ste. 200
Alexandria, VA 22314-5507
Ph:(703)683-7453
Free: 888-253-2762
Fax: (703)683-7310
Co. E-mail: train@eeicommunications.com
URL: http://www.eeicommunications.com/training
Price: $395. **Description:** Seminar for the beginning MAC user, including the foundation for all MAC courses. **Locations:** Alexandria, VA; Silver Spring, MD; and Washington, DC.

32937 ■ Introduction to RoboHELP Classic
EEI Communications
66 Canal Center Plaza, Ste. 200
Alexandria, VA 22314
Ph:(703)683-0683
Fax: (703)683-4915
Co. E-mail: info@eeicommunications.com
URL: http://www.eeicommunications.com
Price: $695.00. **Description:** Covers the basic techniques for creating Windows-based Help systems for Windows 95, Windows 3.1, and Windows NT 4.0 utilizing RoboHELP. **Locations:** Alexandria, VA.

32938 ■ Introduction to RoboHELP HTML Edition
EEI Communications
66 Canal Center Plaza, Ste. 200
Alexandria, VA 22314
Ph:(703)683-0683
Fax: (703)683-4915
Co. E-mail: info@eeicommunications.com
URL: http://www.eeicommunications.com
Price: $695.00. **Description:** Covers the basic techniques for creating HTML Help systems for Windows 98 and Windows NT 5.0 utilizing RoboHELP HTML Edition. **Locations:** Alexandria, VA.

32939 ■ Introduction to Windows
EEI Communications
66 Canal Center Plaza, Ste. 200
Alexandria, VA 22314
Ph:(703)683-0683
Fax: (703)683-4915
Co. E-mail: info@eeicommunications.com
URL: http://www.eeicommunications.com
Price: $395.00. **Description:** Covers introduction to the PC and the basics of Windows. **Locations:** Alexandria, VA.

32940 ■ Java for Non-Programmers
EEI Communications
66 Canal Center Plaza, Ste. 200
Alexandria, VA 22314
Ph:(703)683-0683
Fax: (703)683-4915
Co. E-mail: info@eeicommunications.com
URL: http://www.eeicommunications.com
Price: $995.00. **Description:** Covers the basics of Java and how to use it for developing websites. **Locations:** Alexandria, VA.

32941 ■ Mac Repair and Troubleshooting II
EEI Communications
66 Canal Center Plaza, Ste. 200
Alexandria, VA 22314

Ph:(703)683-0683
Fax: (703)683-4915
Co. E-mail: info@eeicommunications.com
URL: http://www.eeicommunications.com
Price: $395.00. **Description:** Covers an advanced look at Macintosh hardware and operation. **Locations:** Silver Spring, MD; and Alexandria, VA.

32942 ■ Macromedia Authorware I
EEI Communications
66 Canal Center Plaza, Ste. 200
Alexandria, VA 22314
Ph:(703)683-0683
Fax: (703)683-4915
Co. E-mail: info@eeicommunications.com
URL: http://www.eeicommunications.com
Price: $1,695.00. **Description:** Covers how to utilize Authorware to develop presentations, quizzes, interactive hypertext, Help systems, and glossaries. **Locations:** Alexandria, VA.

32943 ■ Macromedia Authorware III
EEI Communications
66 Canal Center Plaza, Ste. 200
Alexandria, VA 22314
Ph:(703)683-0683
Fax: (703)683-4915
Co. E-mail: info@eeicommunications.com
URL: http://www.eeicommunications.com
Price: $1,095.00. **Description:** Covers advanced topics including functions and variables, decision loops, judging, and use of new RTF tools. **Locations:** Alexandria, VA.

32944 ■ Macromedia Director I
EEI Communications
66 Canal Center Plaza, Ste. 200
Alexandria, VA 22314
Ph:(703)683-0683
Fax: (703)683-4915
Co. E-mail: info@eeicommunications.com
URL: http://www.eeicommunications.com
Price: $695.00. **Description:** Covers how to create interactive training applications, electronic marketing pieces, and presentations utilizing Macromedia Director. **Locations:** Silver Spring, MD; and Alexandria, VA.

32945 ■ Macromedia Director II
EEI Communications
66 Canal Center Plaza, Ste. 200
Alexandria, VA 22314
Ph:(703)683-0683
Fax: (703)683-4915
Co. E-mail: info@eeicommunications.com
URL: http://www.eeicommunications.com
Price: $1,095.00. **Description:** Seminar introduces Lingo, Director's programming language. **Locations:** Silver Spring, MD; and Alexandria, VA.

32946 ■ Macromedia Director III: Intensive
EEI Communications
66 Canal Center Plaza, Ste. 200
Alexandria, VA 22314
Ph:(703)683-0683
Fax: (703)683-4915
Co. E-mail: info@eeicommunications.com
URL: http://www.eeicommunications.com
Price: $695.00. **Description:** Advanced seminar covers the planning, artwork, and code phase of creating an actual product. **Locations:** Alexandria, VA.

32947 ■ Macromedia Flash I
EEI Communications
66 Canal Center Plaza, Ste. 200
Alexandria, VA 22314
Ph:(703)683-0683
Fax: (703)683-4915
Co. E-mail: info@eeicommunications.com
URL: http://www.eeicommunications.com
Price: $695.00. **Description:** Covers the basics of Flash including creating animation on the Web that downloads fast and takes up less file space. **Locations:** Silver Spring, MD; and Alexandria, VA.

32948 ■ Macromedia Flash II
EEI Communications
66 Canal Center Plaza, Ste. 200
Alexandria, VA 22314

Ph:(703)683-0683
Fax: (703)683-4915
Co. E-mail: info@eeicommunications.com
URL: http://www.eeicommunications.com
Price: $995.00. **Description:** Covers advanced techniques including planning, organizing, and creating a Flash project. **Locations:** Silver Spring, MD; and Alexandria, VA.

32949 ■ Macromedia HomeSite
EEI Communications
66 Canal Center Plaza, Ste. 200
Alexandria, VA 22314
Ph:(703)683-0683
Fax: (703)683-4915
Co. E-mail: info@eeicommunications.com
URL: http://www.eeicommunications.com
Price: $695.00. **Description:** Covers developing websites using HomeSite. **Locations:** Alexandria, VA.

32950 ■ Marketing Communications for Non-Marketers
EEI Communications
66 Canal Ctr. Plz., Ste. 200
Alexandria, VA 22314-5507
Ph:(703)683-7453
Free: 888-253-2762
Fax: (703)683-7310
Co. E-mail: train@eeicommunications.com
URL: http://www.eeicommunications.com/training
Price: $895. **Description:** Seminar that teaches how to sell products inside or outside the organization, including communications today, the "marketing" in communications, writing basics, the thoughtful way to write, branding, and the marketing communications plan. **Locations:** Alexandria, VA; Silver Spring, MD; and Washington, DC.

32951 ■ Mastering Information Overload: Speed Reading and Memory Skills
American Management Association
1601 Broadway
New York, NY 10019
Ph:(212)586-8100
Free: 800-262-9699
Fax: (212)903-8168
Co. E-mail: customerservice@amanet.org
URL: http://www.amanet.org
Price: $1,595.00 for non-members; $1,495.00 for AMA members. **Description:** Covers following the news and industry trends, note-taking skills, comprehension techniques, and technical reading. **Locations:** New York, NY.

32952 ■ Microsoft Access I
EEI Communications
66 Canal Center Plaza, Ste. 200
Alexandria, VA 22314
Ph:(703)683-0683
Fax: (703)683-4915
Co. E-mail: info@eeicommunications.com
URL: http://www.eeicommunications.com
Price: $695.00. **Description:** Covers basic database concepts using Access. **Locations:** Silver Spring, MD; and Alexandria, VA.

32953 ■ Microsoft Access II
EEI Communications
66 Canal Center Plaza, Ste. 200
Alexandria, VA 22314
Ph:(703)683-0683
Fax: (703)683-4915
Co. E-mail: info@eeicommunications.com
URL: http://www.eeicommunications.com
Price: $395.00. **Description:** Covers database concepts including table design and relationships, advanced query, functions, and form and report techniques. **Locations:** Silver Spring, MD; and Alexandria, VA.

32954 ■ Microsoft Excel I
EEI Communications
66 Canal Center Plaza, Ste. 200
Alexandria, VA 22314
Ph:(703)683-0683
Fax: (703)683-4915

Co. E-mail: info@eeicommunications.com
URL: http://www.eeicommunications.com
Price: $695.00. **Description:** Covers the basics of creating simple and complex spreadsheets, including absolute and relative formulas, formatting cells and cell ranges, control pages, working with multiple sheets, and using templates. **Locations:** Washington, DC; Silver Spring, MD; and Alexandria, VA.

32955 ■ Microsoft FrontPage
EEI Communications
66 Canal Center Plaza, Ste. 200
Alexandria, VA 22314
Ph:(703)683-0683
Fax: (703)683-4915
Co. E-mail: info@eeicommunications.com
URL: http://www.eeicommunications.com
Price: $695.00. **Description:** Covers using FrontPage to develop websites. **Locations:** Alexandria, VA.

32956 ■ Microsoft Office
Fred Pryor Seminars
9757 Metcalf Ave.
Overland Park, KS 66212
Free: 800-944-8503
Fax: (913)967-8849
Co. E-mail: customerservice@pryor.com
URL: http://www.careertrack.com
Description: Covers using Microsoft Office programs to improve work efficiency, create better looking documents, and eliminate repetitive tasks. **Locations:** Cities throughout the United States.

32957 ■ Microsoft PowerPoint
EEI Communications
66 Canal Center Plaza, Ste. 200
Alexandria, VA 22314
Ph:(703)683-0683
Fax: (703)683-4915
Co. E-mail: info@eeicommunications.com
URL: http://www.eeicommunications.com
Price: $695.00. **Description:** Covers creating slides and electronic presentations utilizing PowerPoint. **Locations:** Silver Spring, MD; and Alexandria, VA.

32958 ■ Microsoft Project I
EEI Communications
66 Canal Center Plaza, Ste. 200
Alexandria, VA 22314
Ph:(703)683-0683
Fax: (703)683-4915
Co. E-mail: info@eeicommunications.com
URL: http://www.eeicommunications.com
Price: $695.00. **Description:** Covers using Project to successfully manage projects, including using Gantt charts, resource leveling, and establishing task dependencies. **Locations:** Silver Spring, MD; and Alexandria, VA.

32959 ■ Microsoft Publisher
EEI Communications
66 Canal Center Plaza, Ste. 200
Alexandria, VA 22314
Ph:(703)683-0683
Fax: (703)683-4915
Co. E-mail: info@eeicommunications.com
URL: http://www.eeicommunications.com
Price: $695.00. **Description:** Covers how to use Publisher to create flyers, brochures, and newsletters that are print-ready and viewable on the Web. **Locations:** Silver Spring, MD.

32960 ■ Microsoft Word I
EEI Communications
66 Canal Center Plaza, Ste. 200
Alexandria, VA 22314
Ph:(703)683-0683
Fax: (703)683-4915
Co. E-mail: info@eeicommunications.com
URL: http://www.eeicommunications.com
Price: $395.00. **Description:** Covers how to create basic documents using Word. **Locations:** Silver Spring, MD; and Alexandria, VA.

32961 ■ Microsoft Word II
EEI Communications
66 Canal Center Plaza, Ste. 200
Alexandria, VA 22314

Ph:(703)683-0683
Fax: (703)683-4915
Co. E-mail: info@eeicommunications.com
URL: http://www.eeicommunications.com
Price: $395.00. **Description:** Covers techniques including creating styles and sections, newspaper-style layouts, creating charts, and adding clip art. **Locations:** Silver Spring, MD; and Alexandria, VA.

32962 ■ Microsoft Word III
EEI Communications
66 Canal Center Plaza, Ste. 200
Alexandria, VA 22314
Ph:(703)683-0683
Fax: (703)683-4915
Co. E-mail: info@eeicommunications.com
URL: http://www.eeicommunications.com
Price: $395.00. **Description:** Covers advanced Word skills including running, recording, and running macros, creating custom toolbars, creating online forms, working with master documents, and creating table of contents and indexes. **Locations:** Silver Spring, MD; and Alexandria, VA.

32963 ■ Moving Ahead: Breaking Destructive Behavior Patterns That Hold You Back
American Management Association
1601 Broadway
New York, NY 10019
Ph:(212)586-8100
Free: 800-262-9699
Fax: (212)903-8168
Co. E-mail: customerservice@amanet.org
URL: http://www.amanet.org
Price: $1,695.00 for non-members; $1,495.00 for AMA members. **Description:** Covers resolution techniques for bad workplace behaviors. **Locations:** Washington, DC.

32964 ■ Networking
EEI Communications
66 Canal Center Plaza, Ste. 200
Alexandria, VA 22314
Ph:(703)683-0683
Fax: (703)683-4915
Co. E-mail: info@eeicommunications.com
URL: http://www.eeicommunications.com
Price: $595.00. **Description:** Covers the setup and maintenance of a small-office Local Area Network (LAN). **Locations:** Alexandria, VA.

32965 ■ Online Marketing and Search Engine Optimization
EEI Communications
66 Canal Ctr. Plz., Ste. 200
Alexandria, VA 22314-5507
Ph:(703)683-7453
Free: 888-253-2762
Fax: (703)683-7310
Co. E-mail: train@eeicommunications.com
URL: http://www.eeicommunications.com/training
Price: $695. **Description:** Covers how to increase traffic to your online site to market your products and services using the Web, including creating and implementation of your plan, setting a budget, redesigning Web site for search engine optimization, tips and tricks, promotion hints, tips, and advice, and how to measure your Internet marketing results. **Locations:** Alexandria, VA; Silver Spring, MD; and Washington, DC.

32966 ■ PC Repair and Troubleshooting I
EEI Communications
66 Canal Center Plaza, Ste. 200
Alexandria, VA 22314
Ph:(703)683-0683
Fax: (703)683-4915
Co. E-mail: info@eeicommunications.com
URL: http://www.eeicommunications.com
Price: $395.00. **Description:** Covers disassembling and reassembling a PC, maintaining your PC, adding RAM, recognizing problems, and a review of the operating system. **Locations:** Alexandria, VA.

32967 ■ PC Repair and Troubleshooting II
EEI Communications
66 Canal Center Plaza, Ste. 200
Alexandria, VA 22314

Ph:(703)683-0683
Fax: (703)683-4915
Co. E-mail: info@eeicommunications.com
URL: http://www.eeicommunications.com
Price: $425.00. **Description:** Covers adding RAM, adding a CD-ROM drive, upgrading the hard drive, and peripheral devices. **Locations:** Alexandria, VA.

32968 ■ Programming Boot Camp
EEI Communications
66 Canal Center Plaza, Ste. 200
Alexandria, VA 22314
Ph:(703)683-0683
Fax: (703)683-4915
Co. E-mail: info@eeicommunications.com
URL: http://www.eeicommunications.com
Price: $695.00. **Description:** Covers basic concepts of scripting languages and tools, including JavaScript and Visual Basic. **Locations:** Silver Spring, MD; and Alexandria, VA.

32969 ■ Public Relations-More Than Publicity
EEI Communications
66 Canal Ctr. Plz., Ste. 200
Alexandria, VA 22314-5507
Ph:(703)683-7453
Free: 888-253-2762
Fax: (703)683-7310
Co. E-mail: train@eeicommunications.com
URL: http://www.eeicommunications.com/training
Price: $895. **Description:** Seminar for middle managers, project directors, and mid-level communications professionals, that covers writing a plan and how to create productive relationships with any organization's range of constituencies, from employees to community decision makers, including defining public relations and its components, public relations tools and effective writing, identifying audiences, special public relations functions, and public relations and management. **Locations:** Alexandria, VA; Silver Spring, MD; and Washington, DC.

32970 ■ QuarkXPress I
EEI Communications
66 Canal Center Plaza, Ste. 200
Alexandria, VA 22314
Ph:(703)683-0683
Fax: (703)683-4915
Co. E-mail: info@eeicommunications.com
URL: http://www.eeicommunications.com
Price: $695.00. **Description:** Covers basic desktop publishing skills including creating and saving documents, formatting text and paragraphs, and manipulating graphics. **Locations:** Silver Spring, MD; and Alexandria, VA.

32971 ■ QuarkXPress II
EEI Communications
66 Canal Center Plaza, Ste. 200
Alexandria, VA 22314
Ph:(703)683-0683
Fax: (703)683-4915
Co. E-mail: info@eeicommunications.com
URL: http://www.eeicommunications.com
Price: $695.00. **Description:** Covers desktop publishing skills including paragraph and character style sheets, libraries, master pages, tracking and kerning, and processing colors. **Locations:** Silver Spring, MD; and Alexandria, VA.

32972 ■ QuarkXPress III
EEI Communications
66 Canal Center Plaza, Ste. 200
Alexandria, VA 22314
Ph:(703)683-0683
Fax: (703)683-4915
Co. E-mail: info@eeicommunications.com
URL: http://www.eeicommunications.com
Price: $395.00. **Description:** Covers advanced desktop publishing skills including building table of contents and indexes, creating PostScript files, working with books, and synchronizing documents. **Locations:** Silver Spring, MD; and Alexandria, VA.

32973 ■ Stress Management for Women
Fred Pryor Seminars
9757 Metcalf Ave.
Overland Park, KS 66212

Free: 800-944-8503
Fax: (913)967-8849
Co. E-mail: customerservice@pryor.com
URL: http://www.careertrack.com
Description: Covers the major causes of stress, tips for dealing with stress, and techniques for balancing many commitments. **Locations:** Cities throughout the United States.

32974 ■ Style Summit: Editorial Evolution in the Internet Era
EEI Communications
66 Canal Ctr. Plz., Ste. 200
Alexandria, VA 22314-5507
Ph:(703)683-7453
Free: 888-253-2762
Fax: (703)683-7310
Co. E-mail: train@eeicommunications.com
URL: http://www.eeicommunications.com/training
Price: $695. **Description:** Covers simplifying the editorial process, including issues such as nouns used as verbs (E-mail me), e-jargon and acronyms, and informal usages that seem to break the rules (like vs. such as; more vs. over). **Locations:** Alexandria, VA; Silver Spring, MD; and Washington, DC.

32975 ■ Visual Basic I
EEI Communications
66 Canal Center Plaza, Ste. 200
Alexandria, VA 22314
Ph:(703)683-0683
Fax: (703)683-4915
Co. E-mail: info@eeicommunications.com
URL: http://www.eeicommunications.com
Price: $695.00. **Description:** Covers Visual Basic topics that allow a user to create interactive, user-driven applications for a Windows platform. **Locations:** Alexandria, VA.

32976 ■ Visual Basic II
EEI Communications
66 Canal Center Plaza, Ste. 200
Alexandria, VA 22314
Ph:(703)683-0683
Fax: (703)683-4915
Co. E-mail: info@eeicommunications.com
URL: http://www.eeicommunications.com
Price: $695.00. **Description:** Covers connecting a Visual Basic application to a database, utilizing Visual Data Access Tools and SQL, manipulating databases, and dynamic link libraries. **Locations:** Alexandria, VA.

32977 ■ Web Design for Wider Access: Techniques for Compliance
EEI Communications
66 Canal Center Plaza, Ste. 200
Alexandria, VA 22314
Ph:(703)683-0683
Fax: (703)683-4915
Co. E-mail: info@eeicommunications.com
URL: http://www.eeicommunications.com
Price: $395.00. **Description:** Covers techniques for designing websites that comply with federal guidelines for handicapped access. **Locations:** Silver Spring, MD; and Alexandria, VA.

32978 ■ Web Publishing for Desktop Publishers
EEI Communications
66 Canal Center Plaza, Ste. 200
Alexandria, VA 22314
Ph:(703)683-0683
Fax: (703)683-4915
Co. E-mail: info@eeicommunications.com
URL: http://www.eeicommunications.com
Price: $395.00. **Description:** Covers HTML basics, applying design principles to the Web, using software to publish to the web, and using various types of web publishing. **Locations:** Silver Spring, MD; and Alexandria, VA.

32979 ■ The Women's Conference
Fred Pryor Seminars
9757 Metcalf Ave.
Overland Park, KS 66212
Free: 800-944-8503

Fax: (913)967-8849
Co. E-mail: customerservice@pryor.com
URL: http://www.careertrack.com
Description: Covers the following topics: enhancing your career and professional development; expert communication skills just for women; and the women's professional toolbox. **Locations:** Cities throughout the United States.

32980 ■ Work Improvement Through Redesign and Simplification (Canada)
Canadian Management Centre
150 York St., 5th Fl.
Toronto, ON, Canada M5H 3S5
Ph:(416)214-5678
Free: 800-262-9699
Fax: (416)313-4985
Co. E-mail: cmcinfo@cmctraining.org
URL: http://cmcamai.org
Price: $1,795.00 Canadian. **Description:** Covers the fundamentals of work redesign, techniques to streamline processes, process organization and ownership, analysis of current procedures, and implementing continuous improvement. **Locations:** Toronto, ON.

32981 ■ Writing the Perfect Business E-Mail
EEI Communications
66 Canal Ctr. Plz., Ste. 200
Alexandria, VA 22314-5507
Ph:(703)683-7453
Free: 888-253-2762
Fax: (703)683-7310
Co. E-mail: train@eeicommunications.com
URL: http://www.eeicommunications.com/training
Price: $395. **Description:** Seminar that covers e-mails that get read and are understood, including keeping it short and simple, make it useful, spelling, grammar, and other problems, controlling emotion, writing attachments that get read, progress reports, instructions, and evaluations and recommendations. **Locations:** Alexandria, VA; Silver Spring, MD; and Washington, DC.

32982 ■ XML and Databases
EEI Communications
66 Canal Center Plaza, Ste. 200
Alexandria, VA 22314
Ph:(703)683-0683
Fax: (703)683-4915
Co. E-mail: info@eeicommunications.com
URL: http://www.eeicommunications.com
Price: $995.00. **Description:** Covers translating XML to a relational database structure and related technologies. **Locations:** Silver Spring, MD; and Alexandria, VA.

DIRECTORIES OF EDUCATIONAL PROGRAMS

32983 ■ *American Society Training and Development Buyer's Guide and Consultant Directory*
Pub: American Society for Training & Development
Released: Annual. **Covers:** Over 580 suppliers and consultants in the training and development of employees.

32984 ■ *BusinessWeek Guide to the Best Business Schools*
Pub: McGraw-Hill
Released: 8th edition, April 2003. **Covers:** The top 25 business schools and 25 runners-up, ranked by recent graduates and corporate recruiters. **Entries Include:** School contact information; tips on GMAT prep courses; free application software.

32985 ■ *Complete Book of Business Schools*
Pub: The Princeton Review
Contact: Nedda Gilbert, Author
Released: Latest edition 2002, published October 2001. **Price:** $21.95, individuals. **Covers:** Approximately 372 business schools. **Entries Include:** Institution information, programs, student information, computer and research facilities, expenses and financial aid, admissions information, international students, and employment information.

32986 ■ *The Directory of Computer Assisted Assessment Products and Producers*
Pub: Guildford Educational Services Ltd.
Ed: Mrs. Christine Ward, Editor. **Released:** 1-2 years; new edition 2000. **Price:** $40 CD-ROM plus VAT; $35 printed guide plus VAT. **Covers:** 264 producers of software and 407 software products used in assessment, including computerized tests, software to deliver user-defined tests and recording systems. **Entries Include:** Contact information; details on software products, including functions, main users, hardware requirements, price, and references to published reviews.

REFERENCE WORKS

32987 ■ "ABCS of E-Learning" in *Training* (Vol. 40, No. 1, January 2003, pp. 61)
Pub: VNU Business Media
Ed: Janice Love. **Description:** There are four types of e-learning: leader-led, self-paced, performance tools, and informal learning. The book, 'ABCS of Learning' is a comprehensive and practical book to educate people about e-learning as a solution to training problems.

32988 ■ "Accounting Education; Response to Corporate Scandals: Helping the Profession Find Opportunity in Crisis" in *Journal of Accountancy*
Pub: American Institute of Certified Public Accountants
Ed: Pierre L. Titard, Robert L. Braun, Michael J. Meyer. **Description:** Since the recent corporate scandals caused by large corporations, colleges and universities across the nation have changed course offerings of their accounting programs to better prepare students to cope with the ethics of accounting.

32989 ■ *Active Training: A Handbook of Techniques, Designs, Case Examples, and Tips*
Pub: Pfeiffer & Co.
Ed: Mel Silberman. **Price:** $44.95.

32990 ■ "Adults Fueling Back To School Movement" in *Crain's Detroit Business* (Vol. 23, January 15, 2007, No. 3, pp. 9)
Pub: Crain Communications Inc. - Detroit
Ed: Mary Kramer. **Description:** Dramatic increase in enrollments by older workers. Early retirements and auto worker buyouts, which include substantial tuition assistance, are contributing to the increase in 50-plus age group returning to college for additional education.

32991 ■ "Affirmative Action Front and Center" in *Hispanic Business* (March 2003, pp. 20, 22, 24)
Pub: Hispanic Business
Ed: Tim Dougherty. **Description:** The Supreme Court will consider two related cases with implications for college-bound Hispanic students.

32992 ■ "Affirmative Action on Trial" in *Hispanic Business* (September 2003, pp. 40-42, 44)
Pub: Hispanic Business
Ed: Holly Ocasio Rizzo. **Description:** The nation's law and business schools are struggling to raise minority enrollment, and the new U.S. Supreme Court ruling struck down a plan giving Hispanics and other minorities extra points toward undergraduate admission.

32993 ■ "Affirmative Action Upheld" in *Black Enterprise* (Vol. 34, No. 2, September 2003, pp. 23)
Pub: Earl Graves Publishing Co.
Ed: Cliff Hocker. **Description:** The U.S. Supreme Court upheld the race-conscious admission practices of the University of Michigan Law School in June 2003. William B. Harvey, vice president and director of the Office of Minorities in Higher Education at the American Council on Education (ACE) discusses the issues centering on affirmative action.

32994 ■ "Agent of Change" in *Rough Notes* (Vol. 145, No. 9, September 2002, pp. 38)
Pub: Rough Notes
Ed: Elaine Tolen. **Description:** Dick Fournier, owner of Oregon Insurance Agency, attributes the independent insurance agency's success to former owner Martin K. Bowes, and his staff. He also favors updating the agency with technology and continuing education.

32995 ■ "An Older Sibling In Your Corner Eases Entry Into The Real World" in *Wall Street Journal* (Vol. 248, December 2006, No. 149, pp. B6)
Pub: Dow Jones & Co. Inc.
Ed: Emily Meehan **Description:** Recent college grads often utilize the success, resources and connections of their older siblings while transitioning to life after college and establishing a foothold in their perspective careers.

32996 ■ "The anxiety of learning" in *Harvard Business Review* (Vol. 80, No. 3, March 2002, pp. 100)
Pub: Harvard Business School Press
Ed: Edgar H. Schein. **Description:** An interview with psychologist Edgar H. Schein, who explains why few learning institutions actually exist and the difficulty of transformational learning.

32997 ■ "Are sec. 529 plans a better choice than education IRAs?" in *The Tax Adviser* (Vol. 32, No. 10, October 2001, pp. 668)
Pub: Harborside Financial Center
Ed: Philip E. Moore. **Description:** A comparison is made between Education IRAs and qualified tuition programs (Sec. 529 plans), to help parents identify the best way to save for their children's education.

32998 ■ "Ask Inc.: Do I Have to Go to School?" in *Inc.* (October 1, 2003)
Pub: Gruner & Jahr USA Publishing
Description: Advice is given to individuals considering entrepreneurship, focusing on sales strategies for individuals who hate to sell and the whether an entrepreneur needs a college degree.

32999 ■ "Ask Inc. Education" in *Inc.* (November 2006, pp. 51-52)
Pub: Gruner & Jahr USA Publishing
Ed: John Corsault **Description:** While there are many successful entrepreneurs who didn't attend or finish college, odds for successful businesses still favor those who complete their education seven to one.

33000 ■ "Ask Inc." in *Inc.* (September 1, 2004)
Pub: Inc. Magazine
Description: A small stationery shop in Kansas is looking for new investors and the vice president of a residential mortgage brokerage wants to hire a coach or trainer to work with the firm's CEO.

33001 ■ "Assist2Sell Expands to Service Home Buyers" in *Bellingham Business Journal* (January 2007, pp. 3)
Pub: Sun News Inc.
Description: Exclusive Buyer Agency is a new service provided by Assist2Sell Home Buyers & Sellers Advantage, Whatcom County's leading discount real estate agency.

33002 ■ "B-School Gets Stamp of Approval" in *Black Enterprise* (Vol. 34, July 2004, No. 12, pp. 26)
Pub: Earl G. Graves Publishing Co. Inc.
Ed: Tamara E. Holmes. **Description:** Medgar Evers College School of Business has achieved accreditation. The historically black college plans to contact alumni within a few years of graduation to track the success of its graduates in the business world.

33003 ■ "Back to School" in *Home Office Computing* (Vol. 18, No. 10, October 2000, pp. 94)
Pub: Scholastic Inc.
Ed: Jeffery D. Zbar. **Description:** Michael C. Britt has 22 years of work experience with the U.S. Navy. He's

also the in-house computer trainer and help-desk supervisor for a Norfolk, Virginia-based law firm. What's more, he runs Computer Clown Inc., a home-based computer sales and consulting service. But, Britt has no college degree, and when the subject of career advancement comes up, he's shot down for want of that piece of parchment.

33004 ■ "Back to School" in *Inc.* **(September 1, 2003)**
Pub: Gruner & Jahr USA Publishing
Ed: Nicole Gull. **Description:** At Merkle Direct Marketing, education is not an option for its employees it is a requirement for working there.

33005 ■ "Back to School" in *My Business* **(September/October 2001, pp. 24-25, 28-30)**
Pub: My Business Magazine
Ed: Shannon Scully, Lisa Waddle. **Description:** Small business owners are using boot camps, peer teaching, and e-learning to train their employees. Various small businesses share the unique ways they are training their work force.

33006 ■ "The Balancing Act: How Busy Executives Make Their Lives Work" in *Black Enterprise* **(Vol. 37, February 2007, No. 7, pp. 118)**
Pub: Earl G. Graves Publishing Co. Inc.
Ed: Marcia A. Reed-Woodard. **Description:** More than 70 percent of women with children work outside the home, according to a 2005 survey conducted by the U.S. Department of Labor Bureau. One of the biggest struggles these women face is balancing family with career aspirations and climbing the corporate ranks.

33007 ■ *Barron's Guide to Graduate Business Schools*
Pub: Barron's Educational Series Inc.
Contact: Derrell Buono
Released: Biennial, latest edition 13. **Price:** $16.95 paperback; list price; $15.26 web price. **Covers:** more than 600 colleges offering graduate business degrees, including Master of Business Administration. **Entries Include:** Institution name, address, phone, fax, e-mail, website, enrollment, description of graduate program, admission requirements, availability of financial aid, library and computer facilities, placement programs. Includes information on applications, selection of school, tests, etc. **Arrangement:** Geographical. **Indexes:** Institution name.

33008 ■ "Basic Training" in *Crain's Detroit Business* **(Vol. 21, October 10, 2005, No. 43, pp. 12)**
Pub: Crain Communications Inc. - Detroit
Ed: Robert Ankeny. **Description:** Super Bowl XL Host Committee volunteers, along with waiters, taxi drivers and hotel concierges will be required to take a four-hour service training program that includes learning information about the city of Detroit. The program is designed to help give visitors a good experience.

33009 ■ "Belhaven College" in *Mississippi Business Journal* **(Vol. 28, September 2006, No. 36, pp. 6)**
Pub: Venture Publications, Inc.
Description: Profile of Belhaven College's three newest faculty members: Dr. Donnie Andrews, Dr. Brenda Redfern and Public Manager Randy Russ.

33010 ■ "The Best Jobs That Nobody Wants" in *Inc.* **(September 2005, pp. 30, 32)**
Pub: Inc. Magazine
Ed: Max Chafkin. **Description:** College entrepreneurship departments are having difficulty finding professors to teach classes.

33011 ■ "Best Practices" in *Entrepreneur* **(Vol. 32, October 2004, No. 10, pp. 84)**
Pub: Entrepreneur Media Inc.
Ed: Mark Henricks. **Description:** Doctors, lawyers and other professionals are taking the lead from entrepreneurs when running and building their businesses. Innovative solutions to grow a professional practice like an entrepreneur are shared.

33012 ■ "Big Biz on Campus: Class Is Now In Session For College Entrepreneurs." in *Entrepreneur* **(Vol. 32, December 2004, No. 12, pp. 130)**
Pub: Entrepreneur Media Inc.
Ed: Nichole L. Torres. **Description:** According to the Collegiate Entrepreneurs' Organization and the Institute for Entrepreneurial Studies at the University of Illinois, there has been an increased interest in entrepreneurship at colleges over the last five years, with more than 1,500 colleges and universities offering entrepreneurial training.

33013 ■ "Biotech sector seeks advanced degrees" in *Atlanta Business Chronicle* **(Vol. 24, No. 11, August 17, 2001, pp. 4B)**
Pub: American City Business Journals Inc.
Ed: Erica Stephens. **Description:** Atlanta's biotechnology sector is hiring graduates with advanced degrees as fast as they graduate, but undergraduates are not having the same success. Educators and employers expect that to change as the young biotechnology companies continue to grow. Area research institutions are gearing up to offer undergraduate and high-level degrees in biotechnology and related fields.

33014 ■ "Biz Schools Find 'Flat is the New Up' for MBA Enrollment" in *Crain's Detroit Business* **(Vol. 21, October 17, 2005, No. 43, pp. 17)**
Pub: Crain Communications Inc. - Detroit
Ed: Nancy Nall Derringer. **Description:** Southeastern Michigan business schools are seeing a slowdown in applicants for full-time programs and a larger demand for part-time or executive programs, creating a more competitive market for these schools.

33015 ■ "The Bleeding-Heart Rationalist: William Morris b. 1911" in *New York Times* **(December 31, 2006, pp. 14)**
Pub: New York Times Company
Ed: Walter Kirn. **Description:** Profile of William Norris, founder of Control Data Corporation, now defunct, but at one time, one of the nation's largest computer manufacturing companies. Norris also founded an institute that promoted education and small business growth.

33016 ■ "Blues offer grant to study nurse shortage" in *Crain's Detroit Business* **(Vol. 19, No. 15, April 14, 2003, pp. 14)**
Pub: Crain Communications Inc., Detroit
Ed: Ian McClure. **Description:** Blue Cross Blue Shield of Michigan Foundation, located in Detroit, Michigan, is providing grant opportunities for new programs and research to help ease the nursing shortage facing the state.

33017 ■ "Board the Linux love boat" in *San Francisco Business Times* **(Vol. 16, No. 43, May 31, 2002, pp. 19)**
Pub: San Francisco Business Times Inc.
Ed: Lizette Wilson. **Description:** Firms like Palo Alto, California's Geekcruises.com offer technical training on trips. The firms' cruises are organized around the training courses; clients and marketing are also discussed.

33018 ■ "Boosting Corporate Diversity" in *Hispanic Business* **(April 2005, pp. 14)**
Pub: Hispanic Business
Description: Many corporate managers believe that diversity programs provide a competitive edge because they improve a company's performance and leadership. The University of Texas, Austin started a program to expand the number of diverse students for their MBA program.

33019 ■ "Briefly" in *Crain's Detroit Business* **(Vol. 21, January 17, 2005, No. 3, pp. 29)**
Pub: Crain Communications Inc. - Detroit
Description: Walsh College launched the Walsh Family Business Center, offering lunch and a discussion on running a family-owned business.

33020 ■ "Bristow Car Dealership Owner Receives Education Award" in *Journal Record* **(February 4, 2004)**
Pub: Dolan Media Company
Description: Crown Bristow Chrysler-Dodge-Jeep owner, Henry Primeaux, won the Dealer of the Year Award from Dealer Magazine/Automotive Youth Educational Systems, a mentoring program to encourage young people to consider careers in retail automotive service.

33021 ■ "Build a Better Virus" in *Inc.* **(September 1, 2003)**
Pub: Gruner & Jahr USA Publishing
Ed: Bobbie Gossage. **Description:** University of Calgary teaches students about computer viruses by having them create their own virus. This course has become very controversial because of security concerns.

33022 ■ "Building Character" in *Black Enterprise* **(Vol. 35, January 2005, No. 6, pp. 41)**
Pub: Earl G. Graves Publishing Co. Inc.
Ed: Glenn Townes. **Description:** Mike Jones has launched, Discover Leadership Training, providing weekend training and development seminars designed to develop and improve leadership skills.

33023 ■ "Building a Professional Pipeline" in *Hispanic Business* **(March 2004, pp. 44-45)**
Pub: Hispanic Business
Ed: Janet Perez. **Description:** A new report finds schools need to do more to prepare Hispanics for business careers.

33024 ■ "Business Bookshelf" in *Small Business Opportunities* **(Vol. 13, No. 5, September 2001, pp. 118)**
Pub: Harris Publications, Inc.
Description: Book reviews, including 'The E-Commerce Arsenal, which addresses 12 technologies needed to prevail in the digital arena; 'E-Business To Go', where the author believes now is the best time to start an e-business; and 'Lawn Care & Gardening', a down-to-earth guide to the lawn care business.

33025 ■ "Business Groups Look for Next Generation's Leaders" in *San Fernando Valley Business Journal* **(Vol. 12, January 2007, No. 2, pp. 1)**
Pub: San Fernando Valley Business Journal Associates
Ed: Mark R. Madler. **Description:** A number of business groups in the San Fernando Valley area are reaching out to embrace the younger generation by helping young business professionals make connections and learn leadership skills.

33026 ■ "Business schools vying for professors with Ph.D.s" in *Atlanta Business Chronicle* **(Vol. 24, No. 13, August 31, 2001, pp. 2C)**
Pub: American City Business Journals Inc.
Ed: Anya Martin. **Description:** Business schools are aggressively seeking to hire professors with PhDs for their Business Administration programs. Candidates are able to demand high salaries and many benefits. The shortage is said to be less critical in the Atlanta area than in other regions of the country.

33027 ■ "By Degrees" in *Entrepreneur* **(Vol. 32, December 2004, No. 12, pp. 98)**
Pub: Entrepreneur Media Inc.
Ed: Chris Penttila. **Description:** According to the Bureau of Labor Statistics, the number of jobs filled, between 2000 to 2010, by PhDs will increase by nearly 25 percent. It is important for employers to understand how to meld MBAs and PhDs in the workplace.

33028 ■ "C-DHP: Where Is The Movement Headed" in *Rough Notes* **(Vol. 145, No. 1, January 2003, pp. 108)**
Pub: Rough Notes
Ed: Michael J. Moody. **Description:** The Consumer-Driven Healthcare Congress held a Winter Symposium on health care planning. The conference brought out communications and education as two major aspects required for employers and employees.

33029 ■ "Calendar" in *San Fernando Valley Business Journal* (Vol. 12, January 2007, No. 2, pp. 40)

Pub: San Fernando Valley Business Journal Associates

Description: Listing of events, conferences, and other resources for small business owners and aspiring entrepreneurs.

33030 ■ *The Campus CEO: The Student Entrepreneur's Guide to Launching a Multi-Million Dollar Business*

Pub: Kaplan Books

Ed: Randal Pinkett. **Released:** February 2007. **Price:** $21.00 (CND). **Description:** Tips for generating income, while attending college is presented to students.

33031 ■ "Can Entrepreneurship Be Taught? You Bet It Can" in *Entrepreneur* (Vol. 31, No. 4, April 2003, pp. 62)

Pub: Entrepreneur Media Inc.

Ed: David Newton, Mark Henricks. **Description:** The first Annual Top 100 Entrepreneurial Colleges and Universities lists the top schools teaching entrepreneurial skills in the United States.

33032 ■ "Can Loyalty Be Leased?" in *Harvard Business Review* (Vol. 80, No. 9, Sept. 2002, pp. 24)

Pub: Harvard Business School Press

Ed: Elizabeth Craig, John Kimberly, Hamid Bouchikhi. **Description:** Research involving 400 mid-level executives from various companies throughout the world has shown that executive education that improve an executive's marketable talents, resulted in more executives staying with a company.

33033 ■ "The Case of A Lifetime" in *Hispanic Business* (April 2005, pp. 22, 24-25)

Pub: Hispanic Business

Ed: Joel Russell. **Description:** Profile of Brigida Benitez whose affirmative action suit put her in the winning circle. She was voted 2005 Woman of the Year by Hispanic Magazine. Benitz' well-publicized case involving three white college applicants who filed discrimination suits because race was considered in the application processes is discussed.

33034 ■ "Case In Point" in *Entrepreneur* (Vol. 31, No. 8, August 2003, pp. 66)

Pub: Entrepreneur Media, Inc.

Ed: Joanne Cleaver. **Description:** Allowing a small firm to participate in a local business school's case study or class research project could help a small business become stronger. Faculty members in major metropolitan areas are always looking to do case studies on small companies in the area.

33035 ■ "Case Study" in *Inc.* (January 1, 2005)

Pub: Inc. Magazine

Ed: Patrick J. Sauer. **Description:** Magnetech Industrial Services is considering the implementation of an apprenticeship program in order to triple its work force in a slowing industry.

33036 ■ "CBC and Chrysler Strike Deal" in *Black Enterprise* (Vol. 37, December 2006, No. 5, pp. 36)

Pub: Earl G. Graves Publishing Co. Inc.

Ed: Kiara Ashanti. **Description:** Congressional Black Foundation and Chrysler Financial have partnered to provide financial education to students at historically black colleges and universities. The prime objective of the program is to reduce the number of college students that graduate with poor credit scores and high debt.

33037 ■ "Chefs Show Off at Schoolcraft College Fundraiser" in *Crain's Detroit Business* (Vol. 21, October 3, 2005, No. 43, pp. 20)

Pub: Crain Communications Inc. - Detroit

Ed: Brent Snavely. **Description:** Schoolcraft College's annual Culinary Extravaganza allows forty-six of metropolitan Detroit's best restaurants, wine distributors and wineries to offer sample offerings. The event, which also featured a silent auction, raised about $100,000 to be used for a scholarship fund.

33038 ■ "Children's Products and Services" in *Entrepreneur* (Vol. 32, No. 1, January 2004, pp. 178)

Pub: Entrepreneur Media, Inc.

Description: Franchise opportunities in available for retail children's products and children's services industries.

33039 ■ "Cisco, SBA announce online learning program" in *Network World* (July 24, 2000, pp. NA)

Pub: Network World Inc.

Ed: Margaret Johnston. **Description:** The Small Business Administration and Cisco offer an online training partnership to help small businesses incorporate the Internet into their day-to-day business operations.

33040 ■ "A Class Act" in *Entrepreneur* (Vol. 32, December 2004, No. 12, pp. 61)

Pub: Entrepreneur Media Inc.

Ed: C.J. Prince. **Description:** Increasingly, entrepreneurs are taking courses designed to assist in running a business, including leadership, finance, accounting and economics.

33041 ■ "Clone yourself" in *WorkingWoman* (Vol. 25, No. 5, May 2000, pp. 79)

Pub: Lang Communications Inc.

Ed: Russell Wild. **Description:** Planning for a successor is a good strategy for career development and makes good sense. Issues concerning the training of a replacement and the ability to delegate are presented.

33042 ■ *Coaching for Commitment: Managerial Strategies for Obtaining Superior Performance*

Pub: Pfeiffer & Co.

Ed: Dennis C. Kinlaw. **Price:** $29.95.

33043 ■ *Coaching for Commitment Trainer's Package*

Pub: Pfeiffer & Co.

Ed: Dennis C. Kinlaw. **Price:** $295.00 (trainer's package); $59.95 (participant's packet); $7.95 (PSSQ instrument only). **Description:** Trainer's package contains trainer's guide, participant workbooks 1 and 2, PSSQ, CSI Self, CSI Other, employee effectiveness profile, employee effectiveness profile short form, 20-page bonus supplement, one VHS videocassette, and the *Coaching for Commitment* book. Participant's packet contains participant workbooks 1 and 2, PSSQ, CSI Self, and the *Coaching for Commitment* book.

33044 ■ "Cochran Firm Wins Record $1.62 Billion Insurance Fraud Case" in *Black Enterprise* (Vol. 34, July 2004, No. 12, pp. 21)

Pub: Earl G. Graves Publishing Co. Inc.

Ed: Carolyn M. Brown. **Description:** The Cochran Firm's record winning insurance fraud case could help bring about reform in the insurance industry. The verdict has impacted the way insurance agents are being hired and trained.

33045 ■ "A College Lockout?" in *Hispanic Business* (October 2002, pp. 30-32, 34)

Pub: Hispanic Business

Ed: Scott Williams. **Description:** An investigation into the issues involving the low national average of Hispanics achieving postsecondary degrees. Statistical data included showing degrees earned by Hispanics, including associate's, bachelor's, master's, and doctorate degrees.

33046 ■ "Communication Training in Two Companies" in *Business Communication Quarterly* (Vol. 63, No. 3, September 2000, pp. 104)

Pub: Association for Business Communication

Ed: Roberta H. Krapels and Barbara D. Davis. **Description:** The implications of survey results for teaching of business communication are discussed. Statistical data is included.

33047 ■ "Community Colleges Near Capacity for Retraining Workers" in *Crain's Detroit Business* (Vol. 21, October 17, 2005, No. 43, pp. 15)

Pub: Crain Communications Inc. - Detroit

Ed: Sherri Begin. **Description:** Displaced workers are filling area community colleges for retraining in the areas of nursing, health care services, automotive service technology, digital media, culinary and hospitality programs.

33048 ■ *The Complete Games Trainers Play*

Pub: The McGraw-Hill Companies

Ed: Edward E. Scannell and John W. Newstrom. **Released:** 1995. **Price:** $110.00. **Description:** Complete set of the Games Trainers Play series, including a Master Trainer's Kit.

33049 ■ "Compulsory ethics education and the cognitive moral development of salespeople" in *Journal of Business Ethics* (Vol. 28, No. 3)

Pub: Kluwer Academic Publishers

Ed: George Izzo. **Description:** The results of research conducted on the effect of compulsory ethics education on the moral development of real estate salespeople using comparative statistical measures of ethical reasoning ability.

33050 ■ "A Computer on Every Desk: Online Learning Takes Off" in *Long Island Business News* (February 27, 2004)

Pub: Dolan Media Newswires

Ed: Claude Solnik. **Description:** The Internet's impact on education at universities and colleges across the nation is discussed. Institutions have partnered with Blackboard.com, a company that offers a system for using and managing the Web in educational environments and allows instructors to control content and assignment management, online assessments, student tracking and virtual collaboration.

33051 ■ "Consequences of Information Technology on Work in the Twenty-First Century" in *Employment Relations Today* (Vol.26, No. 4, Winter 2000)

Pub: John Wiley & Sons, Inc.

Ed: Joseph F. Coates. **Description:** The implications of information technology advances for human resource management are discussed. Topics addressed include globalization and employee wages, job automation and the management of the labor supply, and training workers in computer skills.

33052 ■ "Convention Calendar" in *Black Enterprise* (Vol. 37, December 2006, No. 5, pp. 74)

Pub: Earl G. Graves Publishing Co. Inc.

Description: Listing of conferences and summits targeting African American business owners and executives.

33053 ■ "Conventions" in *Crain's Chicago Business* (Vol. 30, January 2007, No. 5, pp. 15)

Pub: Crain Communications, Inc.

Description: Listings of business oriented conferences and conventions through the month of March.

33054 ■ "Coordinating Staff With IT Technology" in *Ingram's* (Vol. 27, No. 8, August 2001, pp. 23)

Pub: Show Me Publishing, Inc.

Ed: Michael May. **Description:** The management of employees use of information technology is discussed. Advice is given on software training and Internet usage monitoring.

33055 ■ "A Corporate Science Project" in *Business Week* (December 19, 2005, No. 3964, pp. 108)

Pub: McGraw-Hill Companies

Ed: Craig R. Barrett. **Description:** U.S. businesses need to help turn out more mat and science graduates in order to stay competitive in a global economy.

33056 ■ "Corporate Ties" in *Black Enterprise* (Vol. 34, July 2004, No. 12, pp. 41)
Pub: Earl G. Graves Publishing Co. Inc.
Ed: Nicole Lewis. Description: Profile of Alice Turner Byrd, owner of Turner Training USA. Byrd's firm provides corporate training to management and staff in CIGNA Corporation's customer service division.

33057 ■ "Cracking the Code" in *Entrepreneur* (Vol. 32, August 2004, No. 8, pp. 48)
Pub: Entrepreneur Media Inc.
Ed: Jennifer Pellet. Description: Profile of the Taxpayer Education Communication Small Business/Self-Employed Operating Division provides information and resources to help small business owners understand tax codes.

33058 ■ "Crain's Co-Sponsoring Sales-Training Seminar" in *Crain's Detroit Business* (Vol. 22, January 2, 2006, No. 1, pp. 17)
Pub: Crain Communications Inc. - Detroit
Ed: Joanne Scharich. Description: Crain's Detroit Business will sponsor a sales-training seminar at Schoolcraft College in Livonia, Michigan. Contact information included.

33059 ■ "Cream of the Crop" in *Hispanic Business* (March 2002, pp. 36)
Pub: Hispanic Business
Description: Advice is given for choosing a business or law school, with information geared toward Hispanic students.

33060 ■ "Creating human links" in *Black Enterprise* (Vol. 33, No. 3, October 2002, pp. 66)
Pub: Earl Graves Publishing Co.
Ed: Shani Smothers. Description: Founder of Youth LINKS USA, Alicia R. Jones, helps to eradicate technical literacy for youth in the Detroit, Michigan area. Jones offers training in software programs and A certification for computer repair up to the Microsoft Certified Engineer Training.

33061 ■ "Crime and Small Business" in *Journal of Small Business Management* (Vol. 38, No. 3, July 2000, pp. 1)
Pub: West Virginia University
Ed: Donald F. Kuratko, Jeffrey S. Hornsby, Douglas W. Naffziger, Richard M. Hodgetts. Description: An examination of levels of crime and the methods of crime prevention in U.S. small business is presented.

33062 ■ "Cropping Up" in *Hispanic Business* (May 2005, pp. 14)
Pub: Hispanic Business
Description: Pennsylvania State University established the new Latino Agricultural Center that will work to develop agricultural educational resources and offer a Spanish class for agricultural professionals.

33063 ■ "The Crying Game" in *Forbes* (Vol. 174, December 27, 2004, No. 13, pp. 182)
Pub: Forbes Magazine Inc.
Ed: Lea Goldman. Description: Profile of the Missouri Auction School that teaches individuals on ways to advertise and promote auctions, manage an auctioneering business and managing paperwork.

33064 ■ "Dealflow: Startup Intelligence" in *Red Herring* (No. 99, June 15 & July 1, 2001, pp. 36)
Pub: Herring Communications
Ed: Julie Landry. Description: A compilation of e-learning companies that were able to raise large amounts of venture capital, including Blackboard, Bigchalk, and Logilent.

33065 ■ "Dean of Boston College Business School Wants to Emphasize Ethics and Values" in *Boston Globe* (March 8, 2005)
Pub: New York Times Company
Ed: Robert Weisman. Description: Boston College's School of Business is stressing ethics and values in its new curriculum.

33066 ■ "A Decade Well Spent" in *Hispanic Business* (October 2003, pp. 42)
Pub: Hispanic Business
Ed: Janet Perez. Description: The Hispanic College Fund celebrates 10 years of helping the best and brightest get an education.

33067 ■ *Delivering Effective Training Sessions*
Pub: Crisp Publications, Inc.
Ed: Geri McArdle. Price: $9.95.

33068 ■ "Detroit Free Press Small Business Column" in *Detroit Free Press* (July 11, 2005)
Pub: Knight-Ridder/Tribune Business News
Ed: Carol Cain. Description: Timothy Faley, managing director of the Samuel Zell and Robert H. Lurie Institute for Entrepreneurial Studies at the University of Michigan Ross School of Business, helps guide startup companies on all aspects of entrepreneurship; contact information is included.

33069 ■ *Developing Managers As Coaches: A Trainer's Guide*
Pub: The McGraw-Hill Companies
Ed: Frank S. Salisbury. Released: 1995. Price: $24.95 (paper). Description: Explains the P.O.W.E.R. model of coaching (Purpose, Objectives, What's happening now, Empowering and Review), and provides instruction on implementing the P.O.W.E.R. model in business.

33070 ■ "Developing the Workforce" in *Ingram's* (Vol. 28, No. 9, September 2002, pp. 61)
Pub: Show Me Publishing, Inc.
Ed: Rick Beasley. Description: Industries complain about a lack of skilled workers therefore educators, business leaders, and policy makers should work together to provide education and training towards a highly skilled workforce.

33071 ■ *Development First: Strategies for Self-Development*
Pub: Personnel Decisions
Ed: David B. Petterson. Released: 1995. Price: $14.95.

33072 ■ "Dialing Up a Degree" in *Crain's Detroit Business* (Vol. 21, October 17, 2005, No. 43, pp. 11)
Pub: Crain Communications Inc. - Detroit
Ed: Sherr Begin. Description: Online college and university courses are growing in popularity because of the convenience they offer.

33073 ■ "Differentiating Legal Issues by Business Type" in *Journal of Small Business Management* (Vol. 44, October 2006, No. 4, pp. 563)
Pub: Blackwell Publishing, Inc.
Ed: Sandra Malach; Peter Robinson; Tannis Radcliffe. Description: A fundamental issue when forming a business and its strategic operation is developing legal strategies to better protect the assets of the business and entrepreneur. An analysis of data indicated that certain legal issues are relevant to specific types of new ventures while certain legal issues are important to all new ventures. Depending on the category of business, the relevancy of individual legal issues will vary. Statistical data included.

33074 ■ "Do You Love What You Do?" in *Fast Company* (March 2005, No. 92, pp. 88)
Pub: Gruner & Jahr USA Publishing
Ed: Marshall Goldsmith. Description: Profile of Warren Bennis, founding chairman of the Leadership Institute at the University of Southern California. Bennis discusses job satisfaction.

33075 ■ "Dollars for Scholars" in *Hispanic Business* (September 2003, pp. 64, 66, 68)
Pub: Hispanic Business
Description: A select guide to scholarships for the study of business or law is presented.

33076 ■ "E-Learning Takes Off!" in *Small Business Opportunities* (Vol. 13, No. 6, November 2001, pp. 92, 94)
Pub: Harris Publications, Inc.
Description: Profile of Walden e-learning programs.

33077 ■ "E-Train" in *Sales & Marketing Management* (Vol. 157, February 2005, No. 2, pp. 20)
Pub: VNU Business Media
Description: Arcadian Software offers software designed to guide users through negotiations by analyzing human interactions and negotiation theory. The program contains four tools: Quick Plan, Full Plan, Problem Solver, and Profiler.

33078 ■ "E-Train" in *Sales and Marketing.com* (Vol. 156, No. 3, March 2004, pp. 19)
Pub: VNU eMedia, Inc.
Description: Profile of Ninth House Inc.'s Instant Advice E-Learning Solution. Using an online library of 500 business topics, users receive coaching from notable management gurus such as Tom Peters and Ken Blanchard.

33079 ■ "The Early Bird Gets the Worm" in *Black Enterprise* (Vol. 37, January 2007, No. 6, pp. 111)
Pub: Earl G. Graves Publishing Co. Inc.
Ed: Tykisha N. Lundy. Description: General Motors hosts the Black Enterprise Conference And Expo: Where Deals Are Made at Walt Disney World's Swan and Dolphin Resort, May 9-12. The conference will offer great information to entrepreneurs.

33080 ■ "Education" in *Business Week* (January 9, 2006, No. 3966, pp. 40-43)
Pub: McGraw-Hill Companies
Ed: Louis Lavelle. Description: China will require 75,000 business executives with international experience by year 2010, 70,000 more than exist today. The country is equipping its schools with programs offering Western management ideas to better serve its growing global economy.

33081 ■ "Education, Economy Key for Voters" in *Hispanic Business* (September 2004, pp. 16)
Pub: Hispanic Business
Ed: Patricia Guadalupe. Description: Hispanic voters are focused on education and economic issues when considering how they will vote.

33082 ■ *The Encyclopedia of Group Activities: 150 Practical Designs for Successful Facilitating*
Pub: Pfeiffer & Co.
Ed: J. William Pfeiffer. Price: $149.00 (looseleaf).

33083 ■ *The Encyclopedia of Icebreakers: Structured Activities That Warm-Up, Motivate, Challenge, Acquaint and Energize*
Pub: Pfeiffer & Co.
Price: $99.95 (looseleaf).

33084 ■ *Enlightened Leadership: Best Practice Guidelines and Timesaving Tools for Easily Implementing Learning Organizations*
Pub: Learning House Publishing, Incorporated
Ed: Alan G. Thomas; Ralph L. LoVuolo; Jeanne C. Hillson. Released: September 2006, printable 3 times/year. Price: $21.00. Description: Book provides the tools required to create a learning organization management model along with a step-by-step guide for team planning and learning. The strategy works as a manager's self-help guide as well as offering continuous learning and improvement for company-wide success.

33085 ■ "Entrepreneur Foundation Retools Its Teaching Model" in *Business First Columbus* (Vol. 18, No. 40, March 24, 2002, pp. A11)
Pub: Business First Columbus, Inc.
Ed: Laura Newpoff. Description: The non-profit Ohio Foundation for Entrepreneurial Education has decided to stop offering business development courses for small businesses, and will instead offer private label custom programs to small businesses.

33086 ■ "Entrepreneurs: Can Detroit Grow Them? :Part 2 of 2" in *Crain's Detroit Business* **(Vol. 22, November 27, 2006, No. 48, pp. 28)**

Pub: Crain Communications Inc. - Detroit

Description: Detroit lags behind other cities in developing entrepreneurs. Advice is provided in this column to address the things that hinder individual development and risk taking.

33087 ■ "Entrepreneurs Learn to Implement Ideas" in *San Fernando Valley Business Journal* **(Vol. 11, November 2006, No. 23, pp. 1)**

Pub: San Fernando Valley Business Journal Associates

Ed: Chris Coates. **Description:** Overview of the Dream and Discover 2006 Entrepreneurs Conference at College of the Canyons. The conference included four seminars ranging from small business practices, growth strategies and the various challenges of starting a business.

33088 ■ "Entrepreneurship Center Receives Gift" in *Hispanic Business* **(March 2005, pp. 14)**

Pub: Hispanic Business

Description: Sergio Pino, chairman and CEO of Century Homebuilders, has given $2 million to Florida International University's Global Entrepreneurship Center.

33089 ■ *Entrepreneurship Education: Current Developments, Future Directions*

Pub: Greenwood Publishing Group, Inc.

Ed: Calvin A. Kent, editor. **Released:** 1990. **Price:** $59.95. **Description:** Surveys and reports on developments in entrepreneurship education at the university, secondary, and elementary levels. Includes a bibliography and an index. Explores successful and unsuccessful strategies, suggests ways to improve current programs, and proposes solutions for areas not adequately covered by existing programs.

33090 ■ "The Entrepreneurship Institute: www.tei.net" in *Entrepreneur* **(Vol. 32, November 2004, No. 11, pp. 6)**

Pub: Entrepreneur Media Inc.

Ed: Steve Cooper. **Description:** The Entrepreneurship Institute offers an online library of more than 100 presentations from 22 cities featuring entrepreneurs and business leaders.

33091 ■ *Even More Games Trainers Play*

Pub: The McGraw-Hill Companies

Ed: Edward E. Scannell and John W. Newstrom. **Released:** Fourth edition, 1995. **Price:** $24.95. **Description:** Provides descriptions of and instructions on games that develop employees' skills. Fourth edition focuses on team building, quality initiatives and quality service.

33092 ■ "The Excellence Group Helping Good Schools Become Great." in *Mississippi Business Journal* **(Vol. 28, September 2006, No. 37, pp. 30)**

Pub: Venture Publications, Inc.

Ed: Wally Northway **Description:** Profile of new educational consulting firm, The Excellence Group, LLC. The firm offers a unique blend of seasoned educators, administrators and an attorney who specializes in school law.

33093 ■ "Excusez moi, parlez-vous francais? Learn Another Language to Increase Your Marketability" in *Black Enterprise* **(December 2004)**

Pub: Earl G. Graves Publishing Co. Inc.

Ed: Kimberly J. Hamilton-Wright. **Description:** Learning a second language can help professionals become more marketable in a global economy.

33094 ■ "Executive Training" in *Black Enterprise* **(Vol. 37, December 2006, No. 5, pp. 70)**

Pub: Earl G. Graves Publishing Co. Inc.

Ed: Marcia A. Reed-Woodard. **Description:** Roy N. Gundy Jr. was preparing to introduce a new strategic plan within his division and understood that his plan may fail if not executed properly. He discusses his experience in the Wharton School's executive education workshop Implementing Strategy, at the University of Pennsylvania and gives tips on putting strategy into action.

33095 ■ "The Fast Track to CE Credits" in *Rough Notes* **(Vol. 145, No. 2, February 2003, pp. 84)**

Pub: Rough Notes

Ed: Barbara Morris. **Description:** Insurance agents can have their continuing education with online CE education, such as WEBCE.com or CEU.com with convenience, flexibility and speed.

33096 ■ "Fighting an Age-Old Scourge" in *Hispanic Business* **(October 2002, pp. 82)**

Pub: Hispanic Business

Ed: Nancie Hudson. **Description:** An increasing number of companies are instituting corporate diversity training programs to combat workplace discrimination.

33097 ■ "Find Online Training That Pays Off" in *Fortune* **(Vol. 151, February 7, 2005, No. 3, pp. 34)**

Pub: Time Inc.

Ed: Anne Fisher. **Description:** Online courses that help employees obtain needed knowledge are discussed. According to Pathlore Software, a firm that designs online curriculums for various companies, suggests a three-stage approach to online employee learning.

33098 ■ "Firms shape students into future workers" in *Atlanta Business Chronicle* **(Vol. 24, No. 11, August 17, 2001, pp. 3B)**

Pub: American City Business Journals Inc.

Ed: Paige Boweres. **Description:** Companies, such as Zcorum Inc., are working with Atlanta-area colleges and universities through the Intellectual Capital Partnership Program, a statewide economic development initiative that teams universities with companies so that companies can meet their immediate information technology staff needs. The initiative and its impact are discussed.

33099 ■ "Free Tuition: Win New Customers With Educational Programs" in *Sales & Marketing Management* **(Vol. 157, February 2005, No. 2, pp. 20)**

Pub: VNU Business Media

Ed: Julia Chang. **Description:** Many companies have begun offering free sales and marketing seminars in their stores to attract small business owners. Office Depot held a series of seminars that incorporated some product pitches, but the real goal was to build a relationship with its small business customers.

33100 ■ "From the Firehouse to the Schoolhouse" in *Black Enterprise* **(Vol. 33, No. 6, Jan. 2003, pp. 32)**

Pub: Earl Graves Publishing Co.

Ed: Glenn Townes. **Description:** Profile of Marco Johnson, former firefighter, founded the Lancaster, California-based Antelope Valley Medical College where Johnson teaches individuals life-saving skills. Johnson outlines his road to entrepreneurship, from college, to football, to firehouse, to entrepreneur.

33101 ■ "Get All Your Work Done in Half the Time, Be the Office Hero...and Go Home Early" in *PC Computing* **(March 2000, pp. 128)**

Pub: Ziff-Davis Inc.

Ed: Leslie Ayers. **Description:** Web-based courses that let people learn at their convenience are discussed. These courses are considered to be the best way to build technology and business skills.

33102 ■ "Getting Beyond a Bachelor's Degree" in *Hispanic Business* **(December 2002, pp. 44, 46, 48)**

Pub: Hispanic Business

Ed: Scott Williams. **Description:** Despite the fact that more Hispanics are attending colleges and universities in record numbers, very few are continuing on to graduate school.

33103 ■ "Getting Girls to the Lab Bench" in *Business Week* **(February 7, 2005, No. 3919, pp. 42)**

Pub: McGraw-Hill Companies

Ed: Catherine Arnst. **Description:** In order to remain competitive in the engineering and science sectors, women must be encouraged to enter these fields.

33104 ■ "Getting To Know the Bull and the Bear" in *Black Enterprise* **(Vol. 34, No. 5, December 2003, pp. S10)**

Pub: Earl Graves Publishing Co.

Ed: Siobhan Benet. **Description:** Profile of Bull & Bear Investment Camp in Kansas City, Missouri. The camp teaches young investors about stocks, bonds, mutual funds, and the importance of saving.

33105 ■ "Global Trade" in *Entrepreneur.com* **(Vol. 34, February 2006, No. 2, pp. 120)**

Pub: Entrepreneur Media Inc.

Ed: Nichole L. Torres. **Description:** Careful research and planning are required to start an international business. Many colleges are offering international business courses to help entrepreneurs understand issues concerning taxes, trade law, currency conversion, language translation and cultural understanding.

33106 ■ "Goldmining for Internships" in *Black Enterprise* **(Vol. 34, No. 5, December 2003, pp. S6)**

Pub: Earl Graves Publishing Co.

Ed: Raelyn C. Johnson. **Description:** Information is provided for individuals wishing to intern at a company in order to get hands-on experience.

33107 ■ "Golf School Caters to Women" in *Marketing to Women* **(Vol. 20, January 2007, No. 1, pp. 8)**

Pub: EPM Communications, Inc.

Description: Golf Made Simple, a golf school program with locations in California and Florida, is targeting businesswomen who would like to acquire skills in the sport. Three, five, or seven-day instruction is followed by e-mail and phone call follow-up with a professional coach.

33108 ■ "Good as Gold" in *Entrepreneur* **(Vol. 32, No. 1, January 2004, pp. 106)**

Pub: Entrepreneur Media, Inc.

Ed: Devlin Smith. **Description:** The hottest franchising trends for 2004 include senior care, child products and services, technology, home improvement, fitness, income tax preparation, business consulting, specialty ice cream and coffee.

33109 ■ "Groom Your Workforce" in *PC Computing* **(March 2000, pp. 137)**

Pub: Ziff-Davis Inc.

Ed: Leslie Ayers. **Description:** Internet training will teach employees the best way to do their jobs more effectively, with the convenience of learning on their own time and at their own pace.

33110 ■ "Grow Your Own Executive Team" in *Journal of Accountancy* **(Vol. 199, January 2005, No. 1, pp. 108)**

Pub: American Institute of Certified Public Accountants

Ed: Stanley Zarowin. **Description:** Experts advise small business to establish a management incubator in order to promote present staff into key positions.

33111 ■ "Helping Victims Unravel Identity Theft" in *Business Journal-Portland* **(Vol. 20, No. 29, September 19, 2003, pp. 1)**

Pub: American City Business Journals, Inc.

Ed: Robin J. Moody. **Description:** Identity Safeguards, located in Tualatin, Oregon, offers protection against identity theft. The startup company provides educational and credit report monitoring services to consumers victimized by identity theft.

33112 ■ "A High ROI Weapon" in *Ingram's* **(Vol. 28, No. 5, May 2002, pp. 29)**

Pub: Show Me Publishing, Inc.

Ed: Richard Delaney. **Description:** A sales development training program can give a high return-on-investment for small businesses. The gains in sales quickly pays for the expenses incurred in training.

33113 ■ "High-tech, low-tech methods can help cut costs for training" in *Crain's Detroit Business* (Vol. 19, No. 17, April 28, 2003, pp. 12)
Pub: Crain Communications Inc., Detroit
Ed: Ian McClure. Description: Employee training can range from using the intranet for in-house training and testing materials, as well as tuition reimbursement for employees to attend classes. Various approaches to effectively and efficiently train employees for different types of companies are discussed.

33114 ■ "Hire Education" in *Hispanic Business* (May 2005, pp. 56)
Pub: Hispanic Business
Ed: Joel Russell. Description: A new job training program SER National helps Hispanic seniors, ages 55 and over, train for jobs. SER National was awarded a $26 million grant from the U.S. Labor Department.

33115 ■ "Hire Learning" in *Entrepreneur* (Vol. 32, November 2004, No. 11, pp. 100)
Pub: Entrepreneur Media Inc.
Ed: Nichole L. Torres. Description: According to Kathleen Miller, founder of Miller Consultants Inc., entrepreneurs who take the time to teach newly hired employees find they become more productive.

33116 ■ "His Brother's Keeper: a Mentor Learns the True Meaning of Leadership" in *Black Enterprise* (Vol. 37, December 2006, No. 5, pp. 69)
Pub: Earl G. Graves Publishing Co. Inc.
Ed: Laura Egodigwe. Description: Interview with Keith R. Wyche of Pitney Bowes Management Services which discusses the relationship between a mentor and mentee as well as sponsorship.

33117 ■ "The Hispanic Business Top 10 Business Schools" in *Hispanic Business* (March 2002, pp. 38, 40, 42)
Pub: Hispanic Business
Description: A listing of the top 10 business schools for Hispanic students across the U.S. is presented, with University of Texas at Austin placing first.

33118 ■ "The Hispanic Business Top 10 Law Schools" in *Hispanic Business* (March 2002, pp. 44, 46, 48)
Pub: Hispanic Business
Description: The top 10 law schools recommended for Hispanic students is presented, with University of Texas at Austin leading the list.

33119 ■ "Home Depot" in *Sales & Marketing Management* (Vol. 159, January-February 2007, No. 1, pp. 15)
Pub: VNU Business Media
Ed: Sarah Boehle. Description: Home Depot's Web-based training program is being used as a successful case study for other firms.

33120 ■ "How to Help Women? Start With an MBA" in *Crain's Detroit Business* (Vol. 22, December 4, 2006, No. 49, pp. 11)
Pub: Crain Communications Inc. - Detroit
Ed: Sheena Harrison. Description: Increased percentage of women in MBA programs will lead to more advancement of women in the work place. Women's Initiative is working to increase the enrollment of women in University of Michigan's Ross School of Business through various student organizations and foundations.

33121 ■ *How to Hire, Train, and Keep the Best Employees for Your Small Business*
Pub: Atlantic Publishing Company
Ed: Dianna Podmoroff. Released: June 2004. Price: $29.95. Description: Costs of hiring, training, and lost productivity costs related to losing employees.

33122 ■ *How to Run Seminars and Workshops: Presentation Skills for Consultants, Trainers, and Teachers*
Pub: Pfeiffer & Co.
Ed: Robert L. Jolles. Price: $55.00.

33123 ■ "How to Teach Economics" in *Ingram's* (Vol. 28, No. 6, June 2002, pp. 28)
Pub: Show Me Publishing, Inc.
Description: A recent initiative by the Kansas Council on Economic Education trained 700 local teachers on economics and economic principles to ensure that their 50,000 students will acquire a better education in economics.

33124 ■ "How They Did It" in *Crain's Detroit Business* (Vol. 19, No. 13, March 31, 2003, pp. 20)
Pub: Crain Communications Inc., Detroit
Ed: Laura Bailey. Description: The Detroit Public School system was able to get minority-owned and Detroit-based businesses to invest in its $1.5 billion building program.

33125 ■ *How to Write Training Materials*
Pub: Pfeiffer & Co.
Ed: Linda Stoneall. Price: $29.95.

33126 ■ "Humanizing Leaders" in *Fast Company* (March 2005, No. 92, pp. 82)
Pub: Gruner & Jahr USA Publishing
Ed: Jennifer Vilaga. Description: Leadership courses are previewed, including a six-day course that allows business leaders to address the larger issues of leadership, innovation and creativity.

33127 ■ "I was greedy, too" in *Harvard Business Review* (Vol. 81, No. 2, February 2003, pp. 38)
Pub: Harvard Business School Press
Ed: Diane L. Coutu. Description: Although greed has become an integral part of the U.S. psyche, the psychology of greed has not been studied well. Greed has ebbed and crested throughout this country's history, and most recently with the collapse of Internet companies, corporate malfeasance. However, business schools continue to graduate a high number of students.

33128 ■ *Imaginative Events for Training*
Pub: The McGraw-Hill Companies
Ed: Ken Jones. Released: 1995. Price: $24.95. Description: Provides instructions and handouts for games, simulations, and role-playing to improve employees' communication and cooperation skills.

33129 ■ "In-house corporate universities growing in popularity" in *Crain's Detroit Business* (Vol. 18, No. 24, June 17, 2002, pp. 15)
Pub: Crain Communications Inc. - Detroit
Ed: Eric Morath. Description: A growing number of businesses are operating their own corporate university to train employees.

33130 ■ "Inspiring a Growth Industry. Inspiration Software Changes Heading and Reaps the Rewards" in *Business Journal-Portland* (Aug. 15, 2003)
Pub: American City Business Journals, Inc.
Ed: Aliza Earnshaw. Description: Profile of Inspiration Software Inc., located in Portland, Oregon. The small firm offers innovative educational software for elementary school students. The company's main clients are cash-strapped schools looking for ways to improve students' test scores.

33131 ■ "Institute for Financial Literacy Thrives Teaching Adults to Manage Money" in *Portland Press Herald* (December 2, 2005)
Pub: Blethen Maine Newspapers, Inc.
Ed: Tux Turkel. Description: Institute for Financial Literacy helps adults learn to manage personal finances. The new federal bankruptcy laws will require the firm to add another 150 workers in late 2006.

33132 ■ "Interest Increases in Wedding Coordinator as Potential Career" in *Daily Record* (June 28, 2004)
Pub: Dolan Media Newswires
Ed: Andrea Cecil. Description: An overview of community college courses aimed at increasing the number of individuals interested in becoming a wedding and event planner.

33133 ■ *International Entrepreneurship Education Issues and Newness*
Pub: Edward Elgar Publishing, Incorporated
Ed: Fayolle. Released: August 2006. Price: $120.00. Description: Entrepreneurial education, focusing on economic, political and social needs of a changing world; ideas for reassessing, redeveloping, and renewing curricula and methods for teaching entrepreneurship are offered.

33134 ■ *International Handbook of Women and Small Business Entrepreneurship*
Pub: Edward Elgar Publishing, Incorporated
Ed: Sandra L. Fielden. Released: June 2005. Price: $165.00. Description: The number of women entrepreneurs is growing at a faster rate than male counterparts worldwide. Insight into the phenomenon is targeted to scholars and students of women in management and entrepreneurship as well as policymakers and small business service providers.

33135 ■ "The Internship Edge" in *Hispanic Business* (Vol. 23, No. 10, October, 2001, pp. 90, 92)
Pub: Hispanic Business
Ed: Janet Perez. Description: For young Hispanics entering the work force, internships can provide an advantage. A profile of Belinda Stubblefield, vice president of global diversity at Delta Airlines, has developed initiatives that enable Delta to attract and leverage a highly skilled, diverse work force.

33136 ■ "Internships" in *Black Enterprise* (Vol. 34, No. 5, December 2003, pp. S11)
Pub: Earl Graves Publishing Co.
Description: Students looking for an internship in the financial industry will find a listing of companies with such programs. Contact information is included.

33137 ■ "Investing in Training Will Yield a Powerful ROI" in *Venture Capital Journal* (November 1, 2004)
Pub: Thomason Financial Inc.
Description: Venture capital firms implementing training programs see a return on that investment by creating a competitive advantage as well as improved performance.

33138 ■ "Investment Camps" in *Black Enterprise* (Vol. 34, No. 5, December 2003, pp. S11)
Pub: Earl Graves Publishing Co.
Ed: Siobhan Benet. Description: Profile of Money Camp for Kids, which teaches middle school and high school students the importance of financial independence.

33139 ■ "IPOs/Recent Issues" in *Venture Capital Journal* (Vol. 41, No. 8, August 2000, pp. 42-45)
Pub: Venture Economics
Description: Profile of seven venture-backed companies that went public during June 2001, including General Maritime Corporation, Monolithic System Technology Inc., MultiLink Technology Corporation, The Princeton Review, Torch Offshore Inc., Unilab Corporation, and United Surgical Partners International.

33140 ■ "JBHM Education Group, LLC" in *Mississippi Business Journal* (Vol. 29, January 2007, No. 4, pp. 6)
Pub: Venture Publications, Inc.
Description: Profile of Pat Whitlock, who recently joined JBHM Education Group as human resources director. She most recently worked as a human resources manager at Time Warner Cable. JBHM Education Group provides educational management consulting to over 200 schools in Alabama, Arkansas, Louisiana and Mississippi.

33141 ■ "JCJC, SMG Partner" in *Mississippi Business Journal* (Vol. 29, January 2007, No. 4, pp. 9)
Pub: Venture Publications, Inc.
Ed: Wally Northway Description: Jones County Junior College began a unique partnership with local

area high-tech business Service Management Group, Inc. SMG will train sophomore computer information systems technology students at JCJC and transition them to full-time SMG employees after graduation from JCJC.

33142 ■ "Job Titles of the Future: Chief Academic Officer" in *Fast Company* **(September 2001, pp. 60)**
Pub: Fast Company
Ed: Erika Germer. **Description:** Profile of Jack Leonard, formerly assistant headmaster for curriculum at Dorchester High School near Boston, Massachusetts, has been assigned the new title of chief academic officer.

33143 ■ "Job Training Serious Play" in *Crain's Detroit Business* **(Vol. 19, No. 17, April 28, 2003, pp. 11)**
Pub: Crain Communications Inc., Detroit
Ed: Laura Bailey. **Description:** Profile of Rachel Evans and Sue Jackson, co-founders of Rochester Hills, Michigan EnteLead Inc. The firm provides professional training based on the science of organizational development, using hands-on activities to teach, including Lego building blocks.

33144 ■ "Joining Forces" in *Washington Business Journal* **(Vol. 22, No. 15, August 15, 2003, pp. 20)**
Pub: Washington Business Journal
Ed: Tania Anderson. **Description:** The development and growth of a public relations trade association in Washington, DC is discussed. Topics include professional associations, professional development, and continuing education.

33145 ■ "Jonathan Hoffman Was Sure a Former Staffer Had Stolen His Company's Ideas" in *Inc.* **(September 2005, pp. 55-56)**
Pub: Inc. Magazine
Ed: Lora Kolodny. **Description:** Jonathan Hoffman, CEO of School Zone Publishing, maker of educational media; Hoffman discusses the way the family business handled litigation when a former employee stole his company's ideas.

33146 ■ "Keeping pace with technology" in *Women in Business* **(Vol. 54, No. 2, March-April 2002, pp. 22)**
Pub: The ABWA Co Inc.
Ed: Mary-Lane Kamberg. **Description:** Businesswomen must take information technology courses to remain computer literate in the 21st century workplace. Online education sites and information technology courses are listed.

33147 ■ "Keller Graduate School of Management of DeVry University" in *Ingram's* **(Vol. 29, No. 8, August 2003, pp. 59)**
Pub: Show Me Publishing, Inc.
Description: Keller Graduate School of Management of DeVry University highlights its management programs.

33148 ■ "Knowledge On Demand" in *PC Computing* **(March 2000, pp. 128)**
Pub: Ziff-Davis Inc.
Ed: Leslie Ayers. **Description:** Companies are finding that it is easier to train employees via the Web, since it can be done from anywhere, anytime. This article focuses on companies that offer this service.

33149 ■ "A labor in progress" in *Hispanic Business* **(Vol. 22, No. 9, September 2000, pp. 20)**
Pub: Hispanic Business
Description: An interview with U.S. Labor Secretary, Alexis Herman, discussing the need for more money to be invested in the American education system to ensure a greater number of skilled workers in the future.

33150 ■ "Leadership Training" in *Black Enterprise* **(Vol. 37, January 2007, No. 6, pp. 56)**
Pub: Earl G. Graves Publishing Co. Inc.
Ed: Sonia Alleyne. **Description:** Profile of Theopolis Holman, Group Vice-President of Duke Energy, who

discusses how he prepared for the merger between Duke Energy and Cinergy. Holman oversees a division of 9,000 service contractors and employees.

33151 ■ "Learn and Grow Rich" in *Black Enterprise* **(Vol. 32, No. 10, May 2002, pp. 106)**
Pub: Earl Graves Publishing Co.
Ed: Dennis P. Kimbro. **Description:** Tips to achieve success in life are presented by Dennis P. Kimbro, management consultant, educator, speaker, and author of the book 'What Makes the Great Great: Strategies for Extraordinary Achievement'.

33152 ■ "Learning Curve" in *Entrepreneur* **(Vol. 33, September 2005, No. 9, pp. 126)**
Pub: Entrepreneur Media Inc.
Ed: Nichole L. Torres. **Description:** University of Washington in Seattle offers students the opportunity to consult for local businesses through its Business and Economic Development Program. The course offers real insight and experience into entrepreneurship.

33153 ■ "Learning across lines. The secret to more efficient factories" in *Harvard Business Review* **(Vol. 80, No. 10, October 2002, pp. 107)**
Pub: Harvard Business School Press
Ed: Michael A. Lapre, Luke N. Van Wassenhove. **Description:** The complexities and pitfalls associated with efforts to boost operating productivity at factories are reviewed. This effort invariably also requires employees learning new skills and transferring those skills to other parts of the factory or company.

33154 ■ "Legally bound" in *Crain's Detroit Business* **(Vol. 19, No. 17, April 28, 2003, pp. 3)**
Pub: Crain Communications Inc., Detroit
Ed: Laura Bailey. **Description:** Michigan law schools are reporting applications for enrollment up as much as 100 percent in the last two years, following a national trend.

33155 ■ "Lending a Helping Hand Even When Off Duty" in *Home Business* **(Vol. 12, March/April 2005, No. 2, pp. 62)**
Pub: Home Business Magazine
Ed: Sandy Larson. **Description:** Profile of Randy Gabel and Scott Mullins, licensed paramedics, who run a home-based company offering emergency training courses.

33156 ■ "Lesson Plan: Cashing in Online" in *Orlando Sentinel* **(February 1, 2005)**
Pub: Orlando Sentinel
Ed: Gary Taylor. **Description:** Profile of the newly created 8-hour class that teaches the ins and outs of the online auction site, eBay. Courses are held at Seminole Community College in Lake County School District of Florida.

33157 ■ "The Life of a Landlord: Acquiring the Building is Just the Beginning." in *Black Enterprise* **(Vol. 35, August 2004, No. 1, pp. 94)**
Pub: Earl G. Graves Publishing Co. Inc.
Ed: Donald Jay Korn. **Description:** Harry Norton II, entrepreneur and real estate investor, offers boot camp seminars for landlords to be sure his properties are being maintained. Norton encourages tenants to inform him of any issues, especially before they become major problems. It is important for all real estate investors to have a strong system in place when buying and leasing property.

33158 ■ "Maine Program Merges On-The-Job Trainings with College Education" in *Portland Press Herald* **(August 30, 2005)**
Pub: Blethen Maine Newspapers, Inc.
Ed: Matt Wickenheiser. **Description:** Maine residents can enroll in apprenticeship programs in the child care, marine trades, construction and other industries. Funding for the program was set at $600,000 for fiscal year 2005.

33159 ■ *Make Training Worth Every Penny: On-Target Evaluation*
Pub: Pfeiffer & Co.
Ed: Jane Holcomb. **Price:** $19.95. **Description:** Shows how to evaluate your training processes and programs to determine if they are fulfilling their purpose, plus advice on how to make training more effective.

33160 ■ "Making a Dent" in *The Record* **(November 7, 2005)**
Pub: New Jersey Media Group
Ed: Dennis P. Carmody. **Description:** Monmouth County Vocational School offers a program that teaches auto body skills to help increase the number of individuals interested in opening auto repair companies.

33161 ■ "Making an Educated Decision" in *Business Week Online* **(February 16, 2006)**
Pub: McGraw-Hill Companies
Description: Business schools are helping entrepreneurs prepare to enter into family enterprises.

33162 ■ "Making Life Easier Overseas; Export Assistance" in *Crain's New York Business* **(Vol. 22, November 13, 2006, No. 46, pp. 22)**
Pub: Crain Communications, Inc.
Description: Listing of agencies that provide financial assistance and technical information for companies that sell goods overseas.

33163 ■ "Making Strides in Building Jobs" in *Milwaukee Journal Sentinel* **(December 3, 2005)**
Pub: Journal Sentinel, Inc.
Ed: Joel Dresang. **Description:** Big Step, also known as the Building Industry Group Skilled Trades Employment Program, shares its plans to train Milwaukee, Wisconsin residents for skilled trades in the construction industry. Statistical and detailed plans are included.

33164 ■ *Managing Learning in Organizations*
Pub: Taylor & Francis, Inc.
Ed: David Casey. **Released:** 1993. **Price:** $79.00; $29.00 (paper).

33165 ■ "Master of Her Retail Space" in *Crain's New York Business* **(Vol. 23, January 29, 2007, No. 5, pp. F11)**
Pub: Crain Communications, Inc.
Ed: Elisabeth Butler. **Description:** Profile of Amira Yunis and her position as executive vice president of Newmark Knight Frank Retail. Ms. Yunis won the Real Estate Board of New York's Retail Deal of the Year award for putting Trader Joe's into Union Square. She brokered $10 million in business last year as well.

33166 ■ "Maximize Your Resources" in *Small Business Opportunities* **(Vol. 13, No. 6, November 2001, pp. 12, 133)**
Pub: Harris Publications, Inc.
Ed: Mike Foster. **Description:** Ideas and suggestions are offered to use more of the software programs on a computer besides word processing, with emphasis on training.

33167 ■ "MBA Programs That Work for the Working Professional" in *Ingram's* **(Vol. 29, No. 8, August 2003, pp. 53)**
Pub: Show Me Publishing, Inc.
Description: The range of business schools in the Kansas City, Missouri areas offering MBA programs is covered.

33168 ■ "MC, MMA Offering Manufacturing Management Program" in *Mississippi Business Journal* **(Vol. 29, January 2007, No. 3, pp. A15)**
Pub: Venture Publications, Inc.
Ed: M.R. Gorringe. **Description:** Mississippi Manufacturers Association and the School of Business at Mississippi College will offer a Certified Manager of Performance Excellence in Manufacturing Program. The program is built around the Baldridge Criteria for Performance Excellence.

33169 ■ "Measurement of Human Potential" in *Employment Relations Today* (Vol. 27, No. 2, Summer 2000, pp. 15)
Pub: John Wiley & Sons, Inc.
Ed: Cabot L. Jaffee, Sr. Description: One of the major challenges facing U.S. companies is the training of a workforce composed of non-traditional employees. Methods of assessing employee's aptitudes are described and the role of efficient and effective testing in quality training programs is discussed.

33170 ■ "Meetings & Clubs" in *Bellingham Business Journal* (January 2007, pp. C3)
Pub: Sun News Inc.
Description: Calendar of clubs and meetings in the Bellingham area targeting business-minded individuals.

33171 ■ "Memories...Are Just That" in *Ingram's* (Vol. 28, No. 9, September 2002, pp. 37)
Pub: Show Me Publishing, Inc.
Ed: Chris Becicka. Description: Schools for higher education are providing students with advantages never before offered by older ones, and that difference is due to the new technologies introduced in education.

33172 ■ "The Mentoring Advantage (Dearborn Trade) www.dearborn.com" in *Entrepreneur* (Vol. 33, February 2005, No. 2, pp. 8)
Pub: Entrepreneur Media Inc.
Description: Florence Stone addresses selecting mentors and implementing business mentoring programs.

33173 ■ "Microsoft Sees 'Untapped Territory'" in *Hispanic Business* (Vol. 23, No. 5, May 2001, pp. 46)
Pub: Hispanic Business
Ed: Jim Medina. Description: Small minority-owned businesses are being offered free technology workshops by Microsoft Corporation, through October 2001.

33174 ■ "Missouri's System of Higher Education: the New Rules for the Knowledge Economy" in *Ingram's* (Vol. 29, No. 8, August 2003, pp. 75)
Pub: Show Me Publishing, Inc.
Ed: Quentin Wilson. Description: The changes Missouri's colleges and universities are offering to meet the demands of potential students are presented.

33175 ■ "Money Is Out There, But Where?" in *Crain's Chicago Business* (Vol. 30, January 2007, No. 1, pp. 12)
Pub: Crain Communications, Inc.
Ed: Dee Gill. Description: Chicago is a great place to start a business and entrepreneurs have a wealth of free help, resources, and information available to them. Unfortunately, most have no idea these services even exist and as a result money set aside for small businesses never gets spent. SourceLink is one such service that can help entrepreneurs find those resources.

33176 ■ "Mrs. D & I are cool (handle your business)" in *Black Enterprise* (Vol. 33, No. 3, October 2002, pp. S9)
Pub: Earl Graves Publishing Co.
Ed: Sheri Holder. Description: The importance of interaction with adults can help students when it is time to begin a career.

33177 ■ "MTDC 'speaks' for itself" in *Women In Business* (Vol. 52, No. 4, July 2000, pp. 35)
Pub: The ABWA Co., Inc.
Ed: Rachel Warbington. Description: The benefit of participating in the American Business Women's Association program of Membership Training & Development Certification are discussed.

33178 ■ "Much Higher Learning: Exploring the Benefits Of an Academic Career" in *Black Enterprise* (Vol. 34, July 2004, No. 12, pp. 61)
Pub: Earl G. Graves Publishing Co. Inc.
Ed: Lee Anna Jackson. Description: Profile of the PhD Project, an organization that is committed to increasing the diversity of business school faculty by focusing minorities in the direction of doctoral programs. The program receives contributions from numerous corporations.

33179 ■ "My Business Manual: The First Line of Defense" in *My Business* (December/January 2003, pp. 45)
Pub: My Business Magazine
Ed: Gina Binole. Description: According to the U.S. Office of Consumer Affairs, 91 percent of dissatisfied customers will not return to a business. The importance of educating a workforce on customer service is stressed.

33180 ■ "NASA Training Program" in *Black Enterprise* (Vol. 30, No. 10, May 2000, pp. 52)
Pub: Earl Graves Publishing Co.
Ed: Gerda Gallop-Goodman. Description: Small, disadvantaged businesses learn how to vie for contracts.

33181 ■ "National Alliance Promotes Professionalism Through Education" in *Rough Notes* (Vol. 145, No. 9, September 2002, pp. 112)
Pub: Rough Notes
Description: The National Alliance of Insurance Education and Research headed by William T. Hold, was formed in Austin, in 1993 and attracted more than 100,000 individuals in almost 2,000 National Alliance programs covering personal lines, commercial casualty, agency management and commercial property.

33182 ■ "National Urban League: State of Black America" in *Black Enterprise* (Vol. 34, July 2004, No. 12, pp. 28)
Pub: Earl G. Graves Publishing Co. Inc.
Ed: Marcia A. Wade. Description: Disparities between black and white Americans are reported showing that in order to level the playing field an additional 23,698 black students would need to earn bachelor's degrees from four-year colleges annually. It would also require 751,000 blacks to find employment and that three white businesses fold for every black startup company.

33183 ■ "Negotiating Tips" in *Black Enterprise* (Vol. 37, December 2006, No. 5, pp. 70)
Pub: Earl G. Graves Publishing Co. Inc.
Description: Sekou Kaalund, head of strategy, mergers & acquisitions at Citigroup Securities & Fund Services, states that "Negotiation skills are paramount to success in a business environment because of client, employee, and shareholder relationships". He discusses how the book by George Kohlrieser, Hostage at the Table: How Leaders Can Overcome Conflict, Influence Others, and Raise Performance, has helped him negotiate more powerfully and enhance his skills at conflict-resolution.

33184 ■ "New Campaign Aims to Educate Californians About Fake Insurance Policies" in *Sacramento Bee* (October 1, 2005)
Pub: The Sacramento Bee
Ed: Andrew McIntosh. Description: California's insurance commissioner has started a statewide campaign to educate the state's businesses and consumers about fraudulent insurance policies. Commissioner John Garamendi recommends that consumers contact his office before purchasing business insurance, or personal car, health or life insurance policies.

33185 ■ "New Career Center Opens at Right Time: Laid-Off Freightliner Workers Will Need Help" in *Charlotte Observer* (February 1, 2007)
Pub: Knight-Ridder/Tribune Business News
Ed: Gail Smith-Arrants. Description: Rowan-Cabarrus Community College announced the opening of its new career development center that will help area workers train for new careers.

33186 ■ "New dean has expensive plans for Emory Law" in *Atlanta Business Chronicle* (Vol. 25, November 15, 2002, No. 23 pp. SS7)
Pub: American City Business Publications, Inc.
Ed: Lee Hall. Description: Tom Arthur aims to increase the endowment of Emory University's School of Law and plans to enlist help from alumni and Atlanta's business community in development of a strategic plan for the school's future. Arthur believes the school needs a unique selling feature to attract prospective students. Biographical information included.

33187 ■ "New Foundation" in *Hispanic Business* (June 2005, pp. 20)
Pub: Hispanic Business
Description: Hispanic Advertising Agencies Foundation was created by the Association of Hispanic Advertising Agencies in an effort to fund and distribute market research related to Hispanic consumers. The foundation will also offer educational opportunities and scholarships to individuals pursuing a career in Hispanic advertising.

33188 ■ "The New School" in *Entrepreneur.com* (Vol. 34, February 2006, No. 2, pp. 28)
Pub: Entrepreneur Media Inc.
Ed: Mark Henricks. Description: The School of the Future, backed by Microsoft Corporation, will give each pupil a PC and teachers will present lessons on interactive whiteboards that are connected to the Internet and equipped with speakers and capable of playing DVDs. Graduates will have digital literacy skills to meet employer demands.

33189 ■ "The New School: What to Expect from Today's MBA Program" in *Black Enterprise* (Vol. 34, No. 4, November 2003, pp. 57)
Pub: Earl Graves Publishing Co.
Ed: Kim Jack Riley. Description: Career specialists are warning against postponing a job search and pursuing a master's degree. Primary concerns of employers in today's market are listed.

33190 ■ "New Wright Museum CEO: Increase Role in Schools" in *Crain's Detroit Business* (Vol. 22, December 11, 2006, No. 50, pp. 13)
Pub: Crain Communications Inc. - Detroit
Ed: Sherri Begin. Description: African American History Museum wants to form more partnerships with schools and businesses to increase the value and quality of education in Detroit history. CEO hopes the museum will become a model for national identity.

33191 ■ "No Fast Cash Class" in *Black Enterprise* (Vol. 37, December 2006, No. 5, pp. 72)
Pub: Earl G. Graves Publishing Co. Inc.
Ed: Description: There are no shortcuts to a obtaining a career as a financial planner. Certified Financial Planner Board of Standards has specific requirements for certification which include having a bachelor's degree from an accredited U.S. school before candidates are even eligible for taking the certification exam. Other criteria and requirements are discussed.

33192 ■ "No Train, No Gain?" in *Entrepreneur* (Vol. 32, October 2004, No. 10, pp. 96)
Pub: Entrepreneur Media Inc.
Ed: Chris Penttila. Description: It is sometimes hard to get a direct payback from costs incurred in training employees. Many entrepreneurs rely on four levels that measure training impact.

33193 ■ "The nontraditional student in you" in *Women In Business* (Vol. 52, No. 4, July 2000, pp. 14)
Pub: The ABWA Co., Inc.
Ed: Michele Compton and Candy Schock. Description: The rising numbers of Americans who return to education as adults are presented. Seventy-six million adults were taking adult education courses in 1995 and this number is expected to rise to 100 million by 2004.

33194 ■ "Northwest Mississippi Community College" in *Mississippi Business Journal* (Vol. 28, September 2006, No. 36, pp. 6)
Pub: Venture Publications, Inc.
Description: Profile of Dr. Chuck Strong, Northwest Mississippi Community College's vice president for educational affairs.

33195 ■ "The Not-So-Talented Tenth" in *Sales & Marketing Management* (Vol. 158, November-December 2006, No. 11, pp. 16)
Pub: VNU Business Media
Ed: Michelle Marchetti. **Description:** New sales staff at Financial Resources of America must complete the company's five-day training program before selling to customers.

33196 ■ "Of Mouse and Men" in *Crain's Detroit Business* (Vol. 18, No. 24, June 17, 2002)
Pub: Crain Communications Inc. - Detroit
Ed: Laura Bailey. **Description:** E-learning is becoming more popular for cash- and time-strapped companies; companies are also designing e-learning courses to fit the client.

33197 ■ "On-line Training Tips" in *Crain's Detroit Business* (Vol. 19, No. 17, April 28, 2003, pp. 12)
Pub: Crain Communications Inc., Detroit
Description: Issues to consider when making a decision to offer online training to employees are listed.

33198 ■ *100 Training Games*
Pub: The McGraw-Hill Companies
Ed: Gary Kroehnert. **Price:** $24.95. **Description:** Contains role playing, simulations, exercises and other games that develop communication, teamwork, stress and time management and conflict resolution among employees. Includes index grid and system of graphic symbols to locate complementary games and games geared for specific situations.

33199 ■ "One Tough Lesson Plan" in *Forbes* (Vol. 170, No. 9, October 28, 2002, pp. 238)
Pub: Forbes Magazine
Ed: Luisa Kroll. **Description:** Chosen as one of the 200 Best Companies by Forbes, co-founder and chief executive of Corinthian Colleges tells how he uses his past military career to oversee 4,800 faculty and staff and more than 34,000 students. Corinthian Colleges is one the country's largest post-secondary education companies.

33200 ■ "Online Education: Global Questions, Local Answers" in *Journal of Business Communication* (Vol. 44, January 2007, No. 1, pp. 96)
Pub: Association for Business Communication
Ed: Christopher Lam. **Description:** A collection of essays entitled, Online Education: Global Questions, Local Answers looks at professional communication and the effect of online education. Although the focus is mainly on technical communication, business communication scholars and practitioners will also find this collection a valuable read.

33201 ■ "Opportunity knocks at Kauffman" in *Ingram's* (Vol. 28, No. 3, March 2002, pp. 17)
Pub: Show Me Publishing, Inc.
Ed: Jack Cashill. **Description:** The Kauffman Foundation offers young people in the Kansas City area an opportunity to acquire real-world business skills.

33202 ■ "Oxymoron 101" in *Forbes* (Vol. 170, No. 12, December 9, 2002, pp. 164)
Pub: Forbes Magazine
Ed: Dan Seligman. **Description:** Despite the increase in business ethics programs being increase at the nation's colleges and universities, there's no sign that the studies will prevent more business scandals such as Enron.

33203 ■ "Partnership: Cisco, SBA team on online learning" in *InfoWorld* (Vol. 22, No. 30, July 24, 2000, pp. 20)
Pub: InfoWorld

Ed: Carolyn A. April. **Description:** The U.S. Small Business Administration (SBA) and Cisco Systems last week announced an online training partnership to help small businesses incorporate the Internet into their day-to-day business operations.

33204 ■ "Patrick Tisdale, Chief Information Officer" in *Law Firm Inc.* (August 2004)
Pub: American Lawyer Media LP
Description: Patrick Tisdale, chief information officer of Orrick explains how e-learning tools were made available to staff to improve skills. Tisdale also focused on increasing the help desk's level of expertise and instill the important role they play in the law firm, using a week long course in customer service skills.

33205 ■ "Personalize your management development" in *Harvard Business Review* (Vol. 81, No. 3, March 2003, pp. 113)
Pub: Harvard Business School Press
Ed: Natalie Shope Griffin. **Description:** The problems organizations have with leadership development are explored. An outline of specific training approaches for various types of prospective leaders, such as reluctant leaders, arrogant leaders, overlooked leaders, and workaholics is presented.

33206 ■ "The Place That Gump Built" in *Hispanic Business* (Vol. 23, No. 7/8, July/August 2001, pp. 94, 96)
Pub: Hispanic Business
Ed: Jeff Favre. **Description:** The University of Southern California (USC) School of Cinema-Television's Robert Zemeckis Center for the Digital Arts exposes students to the latest in filmmaking technology.

33207 ■ "Plan would gut MEDC to fund scholarships" in *Crain's Detroit Business* (Vol. 19, No. 14, April 7, 2003, pp. 1)
Pub: Crain Communications Inc., Detroit
Ed: Robert Ankeny. **Description:** The Michigan Economic Development Corporation could lose operating money if the House Republican proposal to cut $59 million from the business-attraction agency passes; the funds would be shifted to fully restore merit-scholarship funding in the 2004 state budget.

33208 ■ *Planning Your Future*
Pub: AMIDEAST Publications
Released: Irregular. **Price:** $29.95, out of area plus $5 first class mail; $29.95, other countries plus $13 air mail. **Covers:** over 1,000 printed and electronic sources of information on education and training for approximately 150 careers, including accredited programs, nontraditional education, internships, and disabled student services. **Entries Include:** Title name, date of publication, order address. **Arrangement:** Occupation. **Indexes:** Publisher, subject, title.

33209 ■ "The Power of the Pack" in *Sales & Marketing Management* (Vol. 159, January-February 2007, No. 1, pp. 45)
Pub: VNU Business Media
Description: Root Learning, a learning solutions company, informs applicants of the firm's sense of hierarchy. Prospective employees are informed about the policy whereby employees are called roosters or rootizens.

33210 ■ "Pre-Showtime class on the art of selling space" in *Atlanta Business Chronicle* (Vol. 25, No. 21, November 1, 2002, pp. 9C)
Pub: American City Business Publications, Inc.
Ed: Leslie Williams Johnson. **Description:** "Marketing Commercial Real Estate 101-The Experts Talk" is being offered as a class to real estate professionals before they attend the annual Showtime tradeshow. The class, focusing on selling commercial real estate space, is available at no charge for the 1,600 members of the Atlanta Commercial Board of Realtors.

33211 ■ "Predicting Success" in *Hispanic Business* (July/August 2002, pp. 68, 70, 72)
Pub: Hispanic Business
Ed: Scott Williams. **Description:** Studies show that K-12 children who receive regular encouragement are more likely to complete college and go on fulfilling and productive careers. Hispanics from low-income families, and those whose parents did not go to college, are less likely to attend college.

33212 ■ "Priority" in *Inc.* (Volume 27, March 2005, No. 3, pp. 23-26, 28, 30)
Pub: Inc. Magazine
Description: Business information discussed includes information about the SEC looking into unlicensed investment brokers, the economy, freight co-ops to help shippers ease costs, hiring, Google, education, SBA assistance to women entrepreneurs, and new inventions.

33213 ■ "Program reawakens 'Spirit of Delta' in employees" in *Atlanta Business Chronicle* (Vol. 25, No. 19, October 18, 2002, pp. 7B)
Pub: American City Business Publications, Inc.
Ed: Lee Hall. **Description:** Delta Air Lines Inc. has allocated $2 million to a voluntary employee education effort called the Business Literacy Initiative. The effort is designed to foster a sense of ownership among the airline's employees, as well as to inform them on the way business decisions are made.

33214 ■ "Pursuits" in *Inc.* (Volume 27, March 2005, No. 3, pp. 62-63)
Pub: Inc. Magazine
Ed: Jess McCuan. **Description:** Profile of Greg James, founder of Topics Entertainment, an educational software developer. After years of success, James is devoting time to environmental causes and is making changes in his personal life.

33215 ■ "Qualified state tuition programs: EGTRRA update" in *The Tax Adviser* (Vol. 32, No. 10, October 2001, pp. 672)
Pub: Harborside Financial Center
Ed: Philip E. Moore. **Description:** The impact that the Economic Growth and Tax Relief Reconciliation Act (EGTRRA) will have on qualified state tuition programs (Sec. 529 plans) is discussed. The new law, will most likely, make Sec. 29 plans more popular.

33216 ■ "Reading for retention" in *Women in Business* (Vol. 53, No. 4, July-August, 2001, pp. 26)
Pub: The ABWA Co. Inc.
Ed: Ron Fry. **Description:** An excerpt from the book 'Improve Your Memory' is presented, with focus on techniques of memorization, including evaluating the reading material, identifying the essential facts, taking notes, and outlining the text's headlines and keywords.

33217 ■ "Real Estate Ambitions" in *Black Enterprise* (Vol. 37, January 2007, No. 6, pp. 101)
Pub: Earl G. Graves Publishing Co. Inc.
Ed: Description: National Real Estate Investors Association is a nonprofit trade association for both advanced as well as novice real estate investors that offers information on builders to contractors to banks. When looking to become a real estate investor utilize this organization, talk to various investors like the president of your local chapter, let people know your aspirations, and see if you can find a partner who has experience in the field. Resources included.

33218 ■ "Rebuilding Shangri-la" in *Inc.* (September 2005, pp. 154-159)
Pub: Inc. Magazine
Ed: Hillary Johnson. **Description:** When the Ojai Valley Inn was forced to close for renovations, it faced losing most of its workforce. Managers developed a job-retraining program to retain its employees. Details of the Inn and restaurant's renovation are included.

33219 ■ "Reed Jumps Onto the Medical Bandwagon " in *Tradeshow Week* (Vol. 3)
Pub: Reed Business Information
Ed: Rachelle Crum. **Description:** Reed Exhibitions has launched a new show division along with its sister company, publisher Elsevier Health Sciences. The new division will focus on continuing medical education. Reed Medical Education is committed to improving health care delivery.

33220 ■ "Reg Complexity Fuels Demand for ABA Institute" in *American Banker* **(Vol. 170, February 3, 2005, No. 23, pp. 3)**
Pub: Thomson Financial Media Inc.
Ed: Shawna Gamache. **Description:** Profile of the Institute of Certified Bankers, located in Washington, DC. The institute grants certificates in nine different specialties, such as trust advisor and compliance manager. Statistical data included.

33221 ■ "Relative power and influence strategy" in *Journal of Organizational Behavior* **(Vol. 23, No. 2, March 2002, pp. 167)**
Pub: John Wiley & Sons Inc.
Ed: Anit Somech, Anat Drach-Zahavy. **Description:** Management training should provide supervisory personnel with techniques to utilize to influence their subordinates to achieve the desired results. As a result of the training, supervisory personnel should then be able to decide which techniques would work best with each subordinate.

33222 ■ "Resources for employee classes" in *Incentive* **(Vol. 174, No. 9, September 2000, pp. 103)**
Pub: Bill Communications
Ed: Richard G. Einsman. **Description:** How to keep current with the constantly changing knowledge in today's business management and technology, and tips for finding the right sources for training is offered.

33223 ■ "The ROI On Your MBA" in *Business 2.0* **(Vol. 6, September 2005, No. 8, pp. 99)**
Pub: Time, Inc.
Ed: Rob Howe. **Description:** MBA candidates will find an extensive review of the top MBA schools in order to compare their return on investment.

33224 ■ "Role of Coach Critical to Success of New Producer" in *Rough Notes* **(Vol. 145, No. 9, September 2002, pp. 30)**
Pub: Rough Notes
Ed: Bud Antrim. **Description:** Trainees at insurance agencies like Rue Insurance, Trenton, New Jersey; JWF Companies, Indianapolis, Indiana; Johnson, Kendall and Johnson, Langhorne, Pennsylvania, who learn from coaches are able to produce earlier in their career. Mentors serve as models and training has become an important component in the company development program.

33225 ■ "Rotary Club Of Jackson Invests In Metro Students" in *Mississippi Business Journal* **(Vol. 28, September 2006, No. 36, pp. 3)**
Pub: Venture Publications, Inc.
Ed: Lynne Jeter **Description:** Profile of the Rotary Club of Jackson and it's college scholarship program to aid low income potential students of the Jackson community in attending college.

33226 ■ "Running the Gauntlet of Higher Education" in *Hispanic Business* **(Vol. 23, No. 5, May 2001, pp. 62, 64)**
Pub: Hispanic Business
Ed: Janet Perez. **Description:** A study by the American Association of University Women Educational Foundation found that Hispanic girls face many obstacles while pursuing their education.

33227 ■ "Saying Goodbye to the Standardized Test Prep Blues" in *Home Business* **(Vol. 12, October 2005, No. 5, pp. 57)**
Pub: Home Business Magazine
Ed: Sandy Larson. **Description:** Renee Mazer, high school tutor, discusses her non-traditional methods to help prepare students for the S.A.T. test.

33228 ■ "Scandal 101: Lessons From Ken Lay" in *Fortuneit* **(Vol. 146, No. 4, September 2, 2002, pp. 52)**
Pub: Time Inc.
Ed: Julie Schlosser. **Description:** A listing of U.S. universities offering Ethics and Management Courses, starting fall 2002.

33229 ■ "School Career Centers Think Outside the Box" in *Long Island Business News* **(February 27, 2004)**
Pub: Dolan Media Newswires
Ed: Claude Solnik. **Description:** Stony Brook University in New York has created a business etiquette program where potential employers meet with job-seeking students for a three-course meal and networking.

33230 ■ "School Is In for Entrepreneurs: Continuing Education Courses Abound." in *Black Enterprise* **(Vol. 35, October 2004, No. 3)**
Pub: Earl G. Graves Publishing Co. Inc.
Ed: Bridget McCrea. **Description:** A growing number of small business owners are taking courses to help them better manage company growth, employees, financial operations, and other key issues.

33231 ■ *Secrets to Enliven Learning: How to Develop Extraordinary Self-Directed Training Materials*
Pub: Pfeiffer & Co.
Ed: Ann Petit. **Price:** $29.95 (paper).

33232 ■ *Seminars to Build Your Business*
Pub: Self-Counsel Press, Inc.
Ed: Barbara Sisking. **Released:** 1998. **Price:** $11.95.

33233 ■ "Sharpening the Saw When You Work as a Consultant" in *Home Business* **(Vol. 12, March/April 2005, No. 2, pp. 66)**
Pub: Home Business Magazine
Ed: Steven D. Strauss. **Description:** Ways for consultants to increase revenue are addressed.

33234 ■ "Site Attracting Jobseekers" in *Mississippi Business Journal* **(Vol. 28, September 2006, No. 28, pp. 31)**
Pub: Venture Publications, Inc.
Description: Through Hinds Community College's new Web site, area employers and jobseekers are finding each other at an amazing rate. The HCC job placement Web site can be viewed at http://www.hindscc.edu/jobplacement/.

33235 ■ "6 Second Strategist" in *Atlanta Business Chronicle* **(Vol. 25, No. 21, November 1, 2002, pp. 9B)**
Pub: American City Business Publications, Inc.
Ed: Chad Shultz. **Description:** Ways to communicate a firm's policies are discussed. Companies are urged not to rely on handbooks.

33236 ■ "Small Biz Survivors" in *Small Business Opportunities* **(Vol. 13, No. 6, November 2001, pp. 74-76, 80)**
Pub: Harris Publications, Inc.
Description: Profile of Outward Bound, the adventure-based education organization, with more than 35 schools in 19 nations. Outward Bound Professional Development Programs benefit both small and large companies. A list of Outward Bound U.S. locations is provided.

33237 ■ "Small Business Advisor: Dialing for dollars" in *Crain's Chicago Business* **(Vol. 23, December 11, 2000, pp. SB16)**
Pub: Crain Communications, Inc. Crain Communications, Inc.
Ed: Barbara B. Buchholz. **Description:** A profile of Jeffery L. Furst and his company, FurstPerson Inc. that recruits and trains personnel for corporate telemarketing firms. Advice is given for growth, including statistical data and an industry overview.

33238 ■ "Small Firm Bankruptcy" in *Journal of Small Business Management* **(Vol. 44, October 2006, No. 4, pp. 493)**
Pub: Blackwell Publishing, Inc.
Ed: Richard Carter; Howard Van Auken. **Description:** Results of a survey attempt to identify the root causes of bankruptcy in firms. Statistical data included.

33239 ■ "Smart Set" in *Inc.* **(November 1, 2003)**
Pub: Gruner & Jahr USA Publishing

33240 ■ "Star Attorney" in *Black Enterprise* **(Vol. 34, No. 4, November 2003, pp. 60)**
Pub: Earl Graves Publishing Co.
Ed: Sonia Alleyne. **Description:** Advice is offered to a law school student regarding a career in entertainment and/or sports law.

33241 ■ "Star quality" in *WorkingWoman* **(Vol. 28, No. 5, May 2000, pp. 50)**
Pub: Lang Communications Inc.
Ed: Betsy Wiesendanger. **Description:** The stories of the winners in the second annual Entrepreneurial Excellence Awards include women who have exploited the technology boom, used innovative staffing solutions to beat labor problems, and offered free training to help women out of the welfare dependence scenario.

33242 ■ "Staying in the Loop: Continuing Education for Entrepreneurs" in *My Business* **(December/January 2003, pp. 14)**
Pub: My Business Magazine
Ed: Nancy Mann Jackson. **Description:** The importance for small business owners to continue learning is stressed. There are a number of venues for the entrepreneur to stay current, including networking, workshops, professional associations, and independent learning.

33243 ■ "A Step Beyond" in *Entrepreneur* **(Vol. 32, July 2004, No. 7, pp. 44)**
Pub: Entrepreneur Media Inc.
Ed: Steve Cooper. **Description:** Microsoft is sponsoring its Touch Point Series seminars to help small businesses capitalize on all of the features of its Office Suite software. The seminar content is refreshed on a quarterly basis.

33244 ■ "Student teachers" in *Entrepreneur* **(Vol. 30, No. 10, October 2002, pp. 93)**
Pub: Entrepreneur Media Inc.
Ed: Nichole L. Torres. **Description:** Information about small business participation in Emory University's business school competition is provided.

33245 ■ *Successful New-Employee Orientation: Assess, Plan, Conduct, and Evaluate Your Program*
Pub: Pfeiffer & Co.
Ed: Jean Barbazette. **Price:** $79.95 (looseleaf).

33246 ■ "A Super superhighway" in *Incentive* **(Vol. 174, No. 9, September 2000, pp. 14)**
Pub: Bill Communications
Ed: Don Mogelefsky. **Description:** Fulfilling incentive program needs, finding top-notch speakers and training employees can all be done online. A brief overview of three such websites that offer these services to employers is contained in the article.

33247 ■ "Talking tiger, hidden classroom" in *Ingram's* **(Vol. 28, No. 6, June 2002, pp. 53)**
Pub: Show Me Publishing, Inc.
Description: A review of the forthcoming education systems and e-learning technologies that will be available to students in the future is presented. Product developments include synthespians, computer gaming, natural language interfaces, speech recognition, and bio-interfaces.

33248 ■ "Tapping the Potential of Employee Ranks; Human Resources" in *Crain's New York Business* **(Vol. 22, November 13, 2006, No. 46, pp. 32)**
Pub: Crain Communications, Inc.
Description: Listing of organizations that provide counseling and research on human resources issues, as well as offering employee recruitment and training, oftentimes with tax break incentives.

Ed: Bobbie Gossage. **Description:** Hiring incentives and tax abatements are attracting new business to the Lawrence, Kansas area, especially in the area of bio-technology.

33249 ■ "Tax Experts Are Standing By" in Business Week (No. 3702, October 9, 2000, pp. F4)
Pub: McGraw-Hill, Inc.
Description: The IRS has opened a new unit for small business in order to strengthen education regarding the complex tax codes.

33250 ■ Team Training: From Startup to High Performance
Pub: The McGraw-Hill Companies
Ed: Carl Harchman. **Released:** 1995. **Price:** $39.95.

33251 ■ "Tech Training on the Hill" in Hispanic Business (July/August 2004, pp. 14)
Pub: Hispanic Business
Description: The Congressional Hispanic Caucus Institute has launched the CHCI-Dell Technology Center that will train congressional fellows and interns working for Latino leadership.

33252 ■ Technical Trainer's Source Book
Pub: Pfeiffer & Co.
Price: $99.95 (looseleaf).

33253 ■ "Technology" in Fortunet (Vol. 146, No. 12, December 9, 2002, pp. 39)
Pub: Time Inc.
Ed: Grainger David. **Description:** Guidance is given for training technology help desk employees.

33254 ■ "Today's Specialist" in Entrepreneur (Vol. 33, August 2005, No. 8, pp. 28)
Pub: Entrepreneur Media Inc.
Ed: Amanda C. Kooser. **Description:** The Microsoft Partner Program offers providers and resellers certification in specific disciplines and also gives access to Microsoft's support network.

33255 ■ "Too old to learn?" in Harvard Business Review (Vol. 78, No. 6, November-December 2000, pp. 37)
Pub: Harvard Business School Publishing Corp.
Description: Armor Coat Insurance executives share their experiences working with 20-somethings to update their computer and Internet skills.

33256 ■ "Top 10 Business Schools for Hispanics" in Hispanic Business (September 2003, pp. 48, 50, 52, 54)
Pub: Hispanic Business
Description: A listing of the top ten business schools for Hispanic students to consider, with University of Texas at Austin's McCombs School of Business at number one, followed by Yale University's Yale School of Management.

33257 ■ "Top 10 Law Schools for Hispanics" in Hispanic Business (September 2004, pp. 70, 72, 74, 76)
Pub: Hispanic Business
Description: The top ten law schools for Hispanics are reviewed. University of Texas at Austin's School of Law scored number one, followed by the University of Miami. Statistical data included.

33258 ■ "Top MBA Programs (MO&KS)" in Ingram's (Vol. 28, No. 9, September 2002, pp. 42)
Pub: Show Me Publishing, Inc.
Description: A listing of the top Missouri and Kansas universities offerings MBA degree courses ranked according to 2001 enrollment. The top three are Webster University; Baker University, School of Professorial and Graduate Studies; and Rockhurst University.

33259 ■ "Top Ten Program Offers Many Possibilities for Women" in Women in Business (Vol. 53, No. 1, January-February, 2001, pp. 16)
Pub: The ABWA Co. Inc.
Ed: Melissa Will. **Description:** The Top Ten Business Women of the American Business Women's Association (ABWA) program and its opportunities for women in business are discussed.

33260 ■ "Top Ten Schools for Hispanics: Engineering" in Hispanic Business (September 2006, pp. 76, 78, 80)
Pub: Hispanic Business
Description: Top ten universities offering engineering degrees targeted to Hispanic students include, University Texas at El Paso, Purdue University, Georgia Institute of Technology, Massachusetts Institute of Technology, University of California Irvine, Michigan State University, University of Central Florida, Stanford University, University of Texas at Austin, and University of New Mexico.

33261 ■ "Top Ten Schools for Hispanics MBA" in Hispanic Business (September 2006, pp. 70, 72, 74)
Pub: Hispanic Business
Description: Top ten universities offering MBA programs targeted to Hispanic students include, Stanford University; University of California, Berkley; Dartmouth College; University of Texas at Austin; New York University; Yale University; University of Miami; Duke University; Columbia University; and Florida International University.

33262 ■ "Top Ten Schools for Hispanics: Medical" in Hispanic Business (September 2006, pp. 82, 84, 86)
Pub: Hispanic Business
Description: Top ten universities offering medical degrees geared towards Hispanic students include, Stanford University, University of Texas Health Science Center, University of Texas Medical Branch, University of New Mexico, University of Miami, University of Texas Southwestern Medical Center at Dallas, University of Illinois, University of Texas at Houston, University of Arizona, and Texas A&M.

33263 ■ TQM for Training
Pub: The McGraw-Hill Companies
Ed: Elaine Biech. **Released:** 1995. **Price:** $29.95. **Description:** Guide for training employees in the Total Quality Management system. Includes worksheets and case histories.

33264 ■ "Traditional vs. On-Line Learning: It's Not an Either/or Proposition" in Employment Relations Today (Vol.27, No.1, Spring 2000, pp. 47)
Pub: John Wiley & Sons, Inc.
Ed: James H.S. Davis. **Description:** Issues discussed concern the management of corporate training programs, focusing on the use of traditional and online education techniques. Topics addressed include how to most efficiently combine classroom and Internet-based training and methodologies to offer employees the opportunity to advance their skills.

33265 ■ "Training Day: Need a Sales Trainer to Whip Your Staff Into Shape?" in Entrepreneur (Vol. 32, October 2004, No. 10, pp. 90)
Pub: Entrepreneur Media Inc.
Ed: Kimberly L. McCall. **Description:** Sales trainers can rev up a sales team by teaching closing skills. Tips for finding the right sales coach are presented.

33266 ■ Training Methods That Work
Pub: Crisp Publications, Inc.
Ed: Lois B. Hart. **Price:** $10.95.

33267 ■ Training Resources
Pub: American Society for Training & Development
Contact: Christopher Palazio, Advertising Coord.
E-mail: cpalazio@astd.org
Released: Annual, December. **Entries Include:** Company name, contact information and name, profile, list of products and services. **Database Covers:** businesses and individual consultants offering products, services, and equipment for sale to persons in corporate training and human resource development. **Arrangement:** Alphabetical. **Indexes:** Subject, geographical, industry focus.

33268 ■ "Training Trainers and Leaders" in Women in Business (Vol. 53, No. 7, January-February 2002, pp. 30)
Pub: The ABWA Co Inc.
Description: The American Business Women's Association provides the Membership Training and Development Certification Program and the Leadership Certificate Program for developing training and leadership skills. Organization members have used the skills they have learned in the programs at work and in volunteer situations.

33269 ■ Trump University Entrepreneurship 101
Pub: John Wiley & Sons, Incorporated
Ed: Mike Gordon. **Released:** January 2007. **Price:** $21.95. **Description:** Entrepreneurs, past, present or future, will find this book helpful. The book covers three objectives: to energize readers to be courageous when taking steps toward an entrepreneurial goal, works to demystify the entrepreneurial process, and to help individuals improve success.

33270 ■ "Turning Designers Into Managers" in Business Week (No. 3761, December 10, 2001, pp. 60EU1)
Pub: McGraw-Hill Inc.
Description: Richard Koshalek tells how he is rebuilding Pasadena's Art Center College of Design curriculum to include courses on entrepreneurial leadership.

33271 ■ 20 Active Training Programs
Pub: Pfeiffer & Co.
Ed: Mel Silberman. **Price:** $149.00 (each, two volumes). **Description:** Volume I covers such topics as stress management, customer service, creative problem solving, conflict resolution, performance review, and employee motivation. Volume II covers current topics, including goal setting, leadership in a Total Quality organization, ethics and business, sexual harassment, AIDS in the workplace, substance abuse in the workplace, employee literacy problems, and mentoring.

33272 ■ University Associates Training Technologies
Pub: Pfeiffer & Co.
Ed: J. William Pfeiffer and Arlette C. Ballew. **Price:** $139.00 (paper, 7 volumes). **Description:** Boxed set of seven volumes containing techniques for experiential learning in human resources development. Volume 1: Using Structured Experiences in HRD; Volume 2: Using Instruments in HRD; Volume 3: Using Lecturettes, Theory, and Models in HRD; Volume 4: Using Role Plays in HRD; Volume 5: Using Case Studies, Simulations, and Games in HRD; Volume 6: Design Skills in HRD; Volume 7: Presentation and Evaluation Skills in HRD. Includes index to all volumes.

33273 ■ "Up Against the Ropes: A Professional Coach May Help" in Black Enterprise (Vol. 37, December 2006, No. 5, pp. 72)
Pub: Earl G. Graves Publishing Co. Inc.
Ed: Description: Executive coaching is now a $1 billion industry. The coaching process itself and traits to look for in a coach are discussed.

33274 ■ "Video Ventures" in Small Business Opportunities (Vol. 17, September 2005, No. 5, pp. 52, 54)
Pub: Harris Publications Inc.
Ed: Mollie Neal. **Description:** Profile of Tamara Carlisle, founder of a film production company that produces entertainment products for children that also educate.

33275 ■ "Walsh College offers business information-technology degree" in Crain's Detroit Business (Vol. 19, No. 17, April 28, 2003, pp. 13)
Pub: Crain Communications Inc., Detroit
Description: Walsh College, located in Troy, Michigan is offering a Bachelor of Science degree in business information technology to help students develop skills for survival in the information technology world.

33276 ■ **"What Women Want at Work" in** *Marketing to Women* **(Vol. 20, January 2007, No. 1, pp. 5)**
Pub: EPM Communications, Inc.
Description: Men and women at different ages want different things from their workplace. According to a study by The American Business Collaboration, employers may want to factor in these differences when trying to attract and retain top female talent.

33277 ■ **"When to Put the Brakes on Learning." in** *Harvard Business Review* **(Vol. 81, No. 2, February 2003, pp. 20)**
Pub: Harvard Business School Press
Ed: J. Stuart Bunderson, Kathleen M. Sutcliffe. **Description:** Two fortune 100 companies' business units are compared to show that continued learning can reach a point of diminishing returns. Three suggestions are offered to help manage learning within a company.

33278 ■ **"When Wolfe Hires Someone for a Job Working a Cash Register or Cutting Meat, odds are, that Person was a Customer First"in** *Inc.***(May2000)**
Pub: The Goldhirsh Group
Description: The challenges of hiring, retaining, and training employees in the inner city are explored.

33279 ■ **"Where Are the 529 Plans?" in** *Black Enterprise* **(Vol. 34, No. 5, December 2003, pp. 40)**
Pub: Earl Graves Publishing Co.
Ed: Matthew S. Scott. **Description:** Information about the 529 state-sponsored college savings plan, giving individuals the ability to invest money in a pre-selected portfolio of stocks and bonds for future education expenses.

33280 ■ **"Where to Find Business Answers; Advice and Education" in** *Crain's New York Business* **(Vol. 22, November 13, 2006, No. 46, pp. 24)**
Pub: Crain Communications, Inc.
Description: Listing of organizations and agencies that provide training, financial and managerial advice, and technical expertise to current or would-be business owners.

33281 ■ **"Which School is Right?" in** *Hispanic Business* **(September 2003, pp. 46)**
Pub: Hispanic Business
Ed: Joel Russell. **Description:** For Hispanic students, selecting an MBA or a law school program involves academic, social, personal, and financial considerations.

33282 ■ **"Why We Misread Motives" in** *Harvard Business Review* **(Vol. 81, No. 1, January 2003)**
Pub: Harvard Business School Press
Description: Research by Stanford University professor, Chip Heath, suggests that managers tend to have an extrinsic incentives bias by assuming that others are more driven than they are by external rewards for work. Extrinsic rewards are such things as pay and job security, while intrinsic rewards are learning new skills and contributing to an organization.

33283 ■ **"Wisconsin Grants Economic Assistance to Four Companies, One Technical College" in** *Milwaukee Journal Sentinel* **(December 1, 2005)**
Pub: Journal Sentinel, Inc.
Ed: Rick Barrett. **Description:** MCL Industries, Moraine Park Technical College, Burns Best Company, ABC Computers, and SMT Engineering will receive nearly $2 million in state assistance for employee training and expansion projects.

33284 ■ **"Workforce Board Seeks To Improve Jobs" in** *Bradenton Herald* **(January 28, 2005)**
Pub: Bradenton Herald
Ed: Matt Griswold. **Description:** The Suncoast Workforce Board is working to improve the Manatee-Sarasota business climate through education of employees. After a study of the region's economy, the area benefits from its desirable geography and is among the nation's top performing regions, but has issues with its workforce.

33285 ■ **"The workplace: learn to do more with less" in** *Atlanta Business Chronicle* **(Vol. 25, No. 20, October 25, 2002, pp. 12B)**
Pub: American City Business Publications, Inc.
Ed: Emory Mulling. **Description:** Suggestions are given to improve workplace performance in these trying economic times. Training and matching the right person with the right skills for each job is important. Additionally, it is important to recognize that employees want to be developed and to increase their work skills base.

33286 ■ **"Yaknow?" in** *Entrepreneur* **(Vol. 28, No. 10, October 2000, pp. 15)**
Pub: Entrepreneur Media Inc.
Ed: Cynthia Harrington. **Description:** In the quickly evolving e-business world, one of the most important tasks facing netpreneurs is education. The latest changes in technology, marketing trends, evolving business models and financing deals are high priorities.

33287 ■ **"Yes to English, No to Espanol?" in** *Hispanic Business* **(Vol. 23, No. 10, October, 2001, pp. 26)**
Pub: Hispanic Business
Ed: Domenico Maceri. **Description:** According to the article, lower income and a lack of language skills conspire against Hispanic and other immigrant children. These challenges require compensatory education to enable these children to become employable.

33288 ■ **"Young Millionaires: Class of 2004" in** *Entrepreneur* **(Vol. 32, November 2004, No. 11, pp. 77)**
Pub: Entrepreneur Media Inc.
Ed: Amanda C. Kooser, April Y. Pennington, Jonathan Riggs, Nichole L. Torres, Sara Wilson. **Description:** Profiles of successful entrepreneurs include Cristina Bartolucci and Laura Deluisa, manufacturers of specialty makeup and body creams; Ashton Palmer and Kristy Royce, founders of an Internet-based adventure travel company; Bernard Frei, who sells soccer and rugby apparel online; Christopher Faulkner, a Web-hosting and data center infrastructure provider; Marco and Sandra Johnson, who founded an accredited medical college; Shawn Nelson, owner of modular furniture stores; a media advertising company; James P. Funderburk Jr., owner of clothing stores, a private nightclub and real estate company; and a firm that manages online sites for clothing manufacturers.

33289 ■ **"Your Personal/Virtual Mentor" in** *Small Business Opportunities* **(Vol. 12, No. 5, September 2000, pp. 68)**
Pub: Harris Publications, Inc.
Description: A description of the new software, Mentor, that provides just-in-time multimedia desktop training to computer users as an efficient alternative to traditional computer-based training.

TRADE PERIODICALS

33290 ■ *AACE Bonus Briefs*
Pub: American Association for Career Education
Ed: Pat Nellor Wickwire, Editor. **Released:** Quarterly. **Price:** Included in membership. **Description:** Contains brief papers by American Association for Career Education members on current issues in careers, education, and employment.

33291 ■ *AACE Distinguished Member Series*
Pub: American Association for Career Education
Ed: Pat Nellor Wickwire, Editor. **Released:** Periodic. **Price:** Included in membership. **Description:** Publication of the American Association for Career Education. Provides information on careers, education, and employment.

33292 ■ *AACSB Newsline*
Pub: AACSB—American Assembly of Collegiate Schools of Business
Contact: Roxanna Motchan
Ed: Roxanna Motchan, Editor, roxanna@aacsb.edu. **Released:** 4/yr. **Price:** $25 /year; $35 elsewhere. **De-**scription: Covers issues and events affecting management education, and Association projects and activities. Recurring features include notices of publications available and news of educational opportunities.

33293 ■ *California Special Education Alert*
Pub: LRP Publications
Contact: Steve Bevilacquar, Editorial Dir.
Released: Monthly. **Price:** $240 plus $22 s/h. **Description:** Assists California special education administrators comply with changing special education laws, regulations, and policies on the state and federal level to avoid litigation. Recurring features include letters to the editor, interviews, and reports of meetings.

33294 ■ *The Chemical Educator*
Pub: The Chemical Educator
Contact: Clifford LeMaster, Editor-in-Chief
E-mail: tce@chemeducator.org
Ed: Brian P. Coppola, Editor, bcoppola@umich.edu. **Released:** Bimonthly. **Price:** $29.95 print archive edition available separately; $149.95 institutions print ,faculty, students, and staff; $10 single issue hardcopy domestic shipping included. **Description:** Online journal for chemical educators with a print archive version.

33295 ■ *Education Network*
Pub: International Federation of Accountants
Ed: Mr. Julian Freedman, Editor. **Description:** Provides a forum for exchanging information on developments in accountant education. Topics include preaccreditation programs, self-study materials, testing and other assessment methods, continuing professional education, and educating for information technology.

33296 ■ *Education Today*
Pub: Family Education Network
Contact: Lynn McBrien, Editor-in-Chief
Released: 8x/yr. **Price:** $16.95, individuals. **Description:** Designed to help parents with the education of their kids. Covers trends in education, what's working, and parent tips. Spotlights math and science education. Also publishes audio, video, and game reviews. Recurring features include letters to the editor, interviews, news of research, news of educational opportunities, book reviews, and notices of publications available.

33297 ■ *Education Update*
Pub: Education Update Inc.
Contact: Steve Bailey, Advertising Executive
Released: Monthly. **Price:** $30 1 year. **Description:** Newspaper focusing on education nationwide with a concentration on New York City.

33298 ■ *Inclusive Education Programs*
Pub: LRP Publications
Ed: Lisa Lombardo, Editor. **Released:** Monthly. **Price:** $160 plus $22 s/h. **Description:** Presents educators with effective ways to include children with disabilities in the regular education classroom and to help them understand the legal requirements governing inclusion. Recurring features include letters to the editor, interviews, and reports of meetings.

33299 ■ *Infoline*
Pub: American Society for Training & Development
Ed: Stephanie Sussan, Editor. **Released:** Monthly. **Price:** $89 members annual U.S.; $105 members annual Canada/Mexico; $129 members annual international; $129 nonmembers annual U.S.; $115 nonmembers annual Canada/Mexico; $169 nonmembers annual international. **Description:** Magazine offering how-to information for training and development professionals.

33300 ■ *InfoLines*
Pub: Training Resource Network Inc.
Contact: Dale Dileo, Publisher
E-mail: daled@trninc.com
Ed: Dawn Langton, Editor, dawnl@trninc.com. **Released:** 10/year. **Price:** $99, U.S.; $99 e-mail edition; $199, two years; $149, other countries. **Description:** Discusses training and employment opportunities for people with disabilities, techniques and news.

33301 ■ Journal of Developmental and Learning Disorders
Pub: International Universities Press Inc.
Ed: Stanley Greenspan, MD, Editor. **Released:** Semi-annual. **Price:** $42; $70. **Description:** Journal concerned with the identification, prevention, and treatment of disorders that interfere with adaptive developmental and learning processes.

33302 ■ MultiMedia Internetscholarshipools
Pub: Information Today Inc.
Contact: Michael V. Zarrello, Advertising Sales Director
E-mail: mzarrello@infotoday.com
Ed: David Hoffman, Editor, hoffmand@infotoday.com. **Released:** Bimonthly, 6/yr. **Price:** $39.95 U.S.; $54 Canada and Mexico; $63 other countries. **Description:** Consumer guide to high-tech school products. Includes purchasing recommendations, cost-saving tips, and technical advice. Written for and by K-12 school professionals.

33303 ■ NACO Update on Job Training
Pub: National Association of Counties
Ed: Cynthia Kenny, Editor. **Released:** 24/year. **Price:** Included in membership. **Description:** Provides federal, state, and local information on the operation of the Job Training Partnership Act (JTPA). Highlights other issues on employment and training ranging from economic development to welfare. Provides in-depth analysis by focusing on a single topic each issue.

33304 ■ School Scene
Pub: Technology Student Association (TSA)
Contact: Lynda Haitz
Ed: Jane Wright, Editor. **Released:** 3x/yr. **Price:** Included in membership. **Description:** Functions as a member newsletter for the Technology Student Association. Dedicated to preparing membership for the challenges of a dynamic world by promoting personal growth and opportunities. Also provides competitive event news and tips, along with conference news. Recurring features include interviews, a calendar of events, reports of meetings, news of educational opportunities, and notices of publications available.

33305 ■ Teach Magazine
Pub: TEACH Magazine
Contact: Vinicio Scarci
Released: 5/yr. **Description:** Educational publication featuring reproducible teaching units.

33306 ■ Thimband-The Newsletter
Pub: Continuus
Contact: A. Doyle
Ed: A.C. Doyle, Editor. **Released:** Annual. **Price:** $6. **Description:** Provides useful information for homemakers and consumers.

VIDEOCASSETTES/ AUDIOCASSETTES

33307 ■ Adult Learning? You've Got to Be Kidding!
American Society for Training and Development (ASTD)
1640 King St.
Box 1443
Alexandria, VA 22313-2043
Ph:(703)683-8100
Free: 800-628-2783
Fax: (703)683-8103
URL: http://www.astd.org
Released: 1989. **Description:** A look at the seven steps to becoming an all-star trainer in business and industry. Describes how to use the principles of learning theory to improve training sessions. Focuses on the issues of the adult learner, including fear of failure, new technology vs. past experience, and bureaucratic systems. **Availability:** VHS; 3/4U.

33308 ■ Basic Techniques in Practical Chemistry
TMW Media Group
2321 Abbot Kinney Blvd., Ste 101
Venice, CA 90291

Ph:(310)577-8581
Free: 800-262-8862
Fax: (310)574-0886
URL: http://www.tmwmedia.com
Released: 1997. **Price:** $395.00. **Description:** Ten-volume series provide hands on presentations and precise, analytical content that make difficult chemistry understandable for all levels. **Availability:** VHS.

33309 ■ Charley Chapters: Contraction Action
Media, Inc.
PO Box 496
Media, PA 19063
Ph:(610)565-2844
Free: 800-523-0118
Fax: (610)565-3614
Released: 1996. **Price:** $225.00. **Description:** Explains the rules for changing two words into one. **Availability:** VHS.

33310 ■ Charley Chapters: Root Words, Prefixes, and Suffixes
Media, Inc.
PO Box 496
Media, PA 19063
Ph:(610)565-2844
Free: 800-523-0118
Fax: (610)565-3614
Released: 1996. **Price:** $225.00. **Description:** Provides lessons for making spelling easier. **Availability:** VHS.

33311 ■ Charley Chapters: Suffixes and Their Rule Changes
Media, Inc.
PO Box 496
Media, PA 19063
Ph:(610)565-2844
Free: 800-523-0118
Fax: (610)565-3614
Released: 1996. **Price:** $225.00. **Description:** Explains the rules for the ways words change when suffixes are added. **Availability:** VHS.

33312 ■ Charley Chapters: Writing with Synonyms, Antonyms, and the Thesaurus
Media, Inc.
PO Box 496
Media, PA 19063
Ph:(610)565-2844
Free: 800-523-0118
Fax: (610)565-3614
Released: 1995. **Price:** $225.00. **Description:** Explains how to expand vocabulary and writing skills. **Availability:** VHS.

33313 ■ Common Miracles: The New American Revolution in Learning
MPI Home Video
16101 S. 108th Ave.
Orland Park, IL 60467
Ph:(708)460-0555
Free: 800-323-0442
Fax: (708)873-3177
URL: http://www.mpihomevideo.com
Released: 1997. **Price:** $19.98. **Description:** Peter Jennings examines the future of education. **Availability:** VHS.

33314 ■ Disney Presents Bill Nye the Science Guy Sampler III
Buena Vista Home Entertainment
500 S. Buena Vista St.
Burbank, CA 91521-1120
Free: 800-723-4763
URL: http://www.bvhe.com
Price: $199.00. **Description:** Collection of 10 full-length shows featuring lessons in archeology, volcanoes, inventions, animal locomotion, and more. **Availability:** VHS.

33315 ■ The Eisenhower Era, 1940-1960
Buena Vista Home Entertainment
500 S. Buena Vista St.
Burbank, CA 91521-1120
Free: 800-723-4763

URL: http://www.bvhe.com
Price: $699.00. **Description:** Twenty-volume series covers four thematic units: World War II, The Cold War, The Eisenhower Presidency (Domestic Policy), and The Eisenhower Presidency (Foreign Policy). Includes teacher's guide, companion software, and activities. **Availability:** VHS.

33316 ■ Got a Problem? Solve It!
Sunburst Technology
400 Columbus Ave, Ste 160E
Valhalla, NY 10595-1349
Ph:(914)747-3310
Fax: (914)747-4109
Co. E-mail: webmaster@snysunburst.com
URL: http://www.sunburst.com
Released: 1997. **Price:** $59.95. **Description:** Four vignettes present positive strategies for logical thinking and problem solving. On-screen questions promote classroom discussions. **Availability:** VHS.

33317 ■ Helping Your Child Succeed in School
Tapeworm Video Distributors
27833 Hopkins Ave., Unit 6
Valencia, CA 91355
Ph:(661)257-4904
Fax: (661)257-4820
Co. E-mail: sales@tapeworm.com
URL: http://www.tapeworm.com
Price: $18.95. **Description:** Six part video series discussing aspects of all stages of learning and development. **Availability:** VHS.

33318 ■ Hola Amigos Boxed Set
Monterey Home Video
566 St. Charles Dr.
Thousand Oaks, CA 91360-3901
Ph:(805)494-7199
Free: 800-424-2593
Fax: (805)496-6061
Released: 1997. **Price:** $54.95. **Description:** Three-volume set uses songs and games to provide a gentle introduction to the Spanish language. **Availability:** VHS.

33319 ■ How to Be a Better Trainer
Government VideoSource, Inc.
461 Miller Dr.
Elgin, IL 60123-7232
Ph:(847)931-1955
Price: $249.95. **Description:** Three-volume series introduces employers, managers and teachers to the elements and techniques of effective training. **Availability:** VHS.

33320 ■ How to Succeed in the Changing Workplace
Government VideoSource, Inc.
461 Miller Dr.
Elgin, IL 60123-7232
Ph:(847)931-1955
Price: $495. **Description:** Visits various companies to see how employees have adapted to change and new challenges. Offers strategies for dealing with change in the workplace. **Availability:** VHS.

33321 ■ Johnny Tremain
Buena Vista Home Entertainment
500 S. Buena Vista St.
Burbank, CA 91521-1120
Free: 800-723-4763
URL: http://www.bvhe.com
Released: 1997. **Price:** $99.00. **Description:** Presents reenactments of historical figures and events such as the Boston Tea Party, Paul Revere, and Samuel Adams. **Availability:** VHS.

33322 ■ Just the Facts Learning Series: The Great American State Quiz
Goldhil Home Media
5284 Adolfo Rd.
Camarillo, CA 93012
Ph:(805)765-1500
Fax: (805)373-1603
Co. E-mail: customerservice@goldhil.com
URL: http://www.goldhilentertainment.com

Released: 1997. **Price:** $14.95. **Description:** Presents a fun way to learn about the states and capitals. **Availability:** VHS.

33323 ■ *Science in Action*
TMW Media Group
2321 Abbot Kinney Blvd., Ste 101
Venice, CA 90291
Ph:(310)577-8581
Free: 800-262-8862
Fax: (310)574-0886
URL: http://www.tmwmedia.com
Released: 1997. **Price:** $119.00. **Description:** Six-volume series explains basic scientific concepts and principles in an easy-to-understand manner. **Availability:** VHS.

33324 ■ *Something Special*
Educational Activities, Inc.
PO Box 392
Freeport, NY 11520
Ph:(516)223-4666
Free: 800-645-3739
Fax: (516)623-9282
Co. E-mail: learn@edact.com
URL: http://www.edact.com
Released: 1997. **Price:** $19.95. **Description:** Teaches movement vocabulary skills and promotes self-esteem. **Availability:** VHS.

33325 ■ *The Story of Joshua and the Battle of Jericho*
McGraw Hill Book Co.
Continuing Education Program
4401 Connecticut NW
Lower Level
Washington, DC 20008
Ph:(202)244-1600
Free: 800-331-5094
Fax: (202)244-2047
Released: 1997. **Price:** $12.98. **Description:** Animated bible story. **Availability:** VHS.

33326 ■ *Table Time for Tots*
Tapeworm Video Distributors
27833 Hopkins Ave., Unit 6
Valencia, CA 91355
Ph:(661)257-4904
Fax: (661)257-4820
Co. E-mail: sales@tapeworm.com
URL: http://www.tapeworm.com
Released: 1997. **Price:** $14.95. **Description:** Introduces children to the basic food groups using poem and song. **Availability:** VHS.

33327 ■ *Training 101: Principles, Processes and People Every Trainer Should Know*
American Society for Training and Development
   (ASTD)
1640 King St.
Box 1443
Alexandria, VA 22313-2043
Ph:(703)683-8100
Free: 800-628-2783
Fax: (703)683-8103
URL: http://www.astd.org
Released: 1989. **Description:** A video overview of training, designed to give trainers more competence and confidence. Basic processes and concepts are explained and human resource development experts present descriptions of their work. **Availability:** VHS; 3/4U.

33328 ■ *Transformations: Science, Technology, and Society*
Karol Media
Hanover Industrial Estates
375 Stewart Rd.
PO Box 7600
Wilkes Barre, PA 18773-7600
Ph:(570)822-8899
Free: 800-526-4773
Fax: (570)822-8226
Co. E-mail: sales@karolmedia.com
URL: http://www.karolmedia.com
Released: 1997. **Price:** $125.00. **Description:** Eight-volume series designed to motivate learning and enhance science instruction. **Availability:** VHS.

33329 ■ *Volcanoes: Cauldrons of Fury*
MPI Home Video
16101 S. 108th Ave.
Orland Park, IL 60467
Ph:(708)460-0555
Free: 800-323-0442
Fax: (708)873-3177
URL: http://www.mpihomevideo.com
Price: $19.98. **Description:** Examines the causes, history and future of volcanoes. **Availability:** VHS.

TRADE SHOWS AND CONVENTIONS

33330 ■ Michigan Association for Computer Users in Learning Conference
Michigan Association for Computer Users in
   Learning
PO Box 518
Holt, MI 48842-0518
Ph:(517)694-9756
Fax: (517)694-9773
Co. E-mail: macul@macul.org
URL: http://www.macul.org
Released: Annual. **Audience:** Educational technology professionals. **Principal Exhibits:** Computer and educational equipment, supplies, and services. **Dates and Locations:** 2007 Mar 14-16, Detroit, MI; 2008 Mar 05-07, Grand Rapids, MI; 2009 Mar 18-20, Detroit, MI.

33331 ■ National Association for Membership Development
American Chamber of Commerce Executives
4825 Eisenhower Ave., Ste. 250
Alexandria, VA 22304
Ph:(703)998-0072
Free: 800-394-2223
Fax: (703)212-9512
Co. E-mail: events@acce.org
URL: http://www.acce.org
Released: Annual. **Principal Exhibits:** Business education products and services.

CONSULTANTS

33332 ■ AMC International Inc.
PO Box 11292
Beverly Hills, CA 90213-4292
Ph:(310)652-5620
Fax: (310)652-6709
Co. E-mail: inquiry@amcusa.com
URL: http://www.amcusa.com

E-mail: inquiry@amcusa.com
Scope: Offers day-to-day business management, business turnaround, marketing strategies, development/refinement of corporate mission, and merger and acquisition evaluations. Industries served: all.

33333 ■ American English Academy
111 N Atlantic Blvd., Ste. 112
Monterey Park, CA 91754
Ph:(626)457-2800
Fax: (626)457-2808
Co. E-mail: admission@aea-usa.com
URL: http://www.aea-usa.com

E-mail: admission@aea-usa.com
Scope: Specializes in providing on-site English language and communication development for corporations and individuals. Also develops and delivers training in speaking, writing, pronunciation, grammar, and idioms with an emphasis on business communication. Offers individual, small group, intensive, and long-distance learning. All programs are tailor-made for each client. **Seminars:** Offers seminars on all aspects of English and cultural awareness.

33334 ■ Blackmon Roberts Group Inc.
902 S South Florida, Ste. 205
Lakeland, FL 33803

Ph:(863)802-1280
Fax: (863)802-1290
Co. E-mail: dbeinformation@blackmonroberts.com
URL: http://www.blackmonroberts.com

E-mail: dbeinformation@blackmonroberts.com
Scope: Technical support consultant in technical writing, planning, research, needs analysis, marketing and training, offers training programs from cultural sensitivity issues to effective listening skills.

33335 ■ Daniel Bloom and Associates Inc.
11517 128th Ave. N
PO Box 1233
Largo, FL 33779-1233
Ph:(727)581-6216
Co. E-mail: dan@dbalconsulting.com
URL: http://www.dbaiconsulting.com

E-mail: dan@dbalconsulting.com
Scope: Human resources management consultant with a specialization in corporate relocation. Offers clients a turn key service aimed at meeting the unique relocation needs of their employees. Develops and implements training programs within the relocation industry. **Publications:** "Recoup Your Hiring Investment," Brainbuzz.com, Aug, 2000.

33336 ■ Business Education Associates
PO Box 4
Bethel, CT 06801
Ph:(203)798-6035
Co. E-mail: bob@ashfordgrp.com
URL: http://www.ashfordgrp

E-mail: bob@ashfordgrp.com
Scope: Offers tailored management education programs. Has been designed to meet the business education needs of companies implementing new systems and companies to re-educate users of existing systems. **Publications:** "The Ashford Group and TQuist Partner to Provide High Impact Manufacturing Solutions"; "The Future of ERP".

33337 ■ Business Improvement Architects
33 Riderwood Dr.
Toronto, ON, Canada M2L 2X4
Ph:(416)444-8225
Free: (866)346-3242
Fax: (416)444-6743
Co. E-mail: info@bia.ca
URL: http://www.bia.ca

E-mail: info@bia.ca
Scope: Specializes in management training, project management, marketing planning, promotions and incentives.

33338 ■ Carl M. Caplan, D.D.S., M.B.A.
2910 Lightfoot Dr.
Baltimore, MD 21209
Ph:(410)484-3658
Scope: Firm provides business services in the area of employment/partnership/new doctor agreements, practice management and mergers/acquisitions/sales and/or liquidation, practice valuation, and staff development and training.

33339 ■ Center for Personal Empowerment
102 N Main St.
Columbia, IL 62236-1702
Ph:(618)281-3565
Fax: (618)476-7083
Co. E-mail: personalempowerment@wholenet.net

E-mail: personalempowerment@wholenet.net
Scope: Private consultations and trainings to educate on how to determine which emotions, events, beliefs from the past prevent you from achieving success. Methods used include Time Line Therapy, News Linguistic Programming and hypnosis. Behavior Modification through NLP trainings. **Seminars:** NLP Practitioner Training, Hypnosis Certification Training, Lifemap Seminars.

33340 ■ Competitive Edge Inc.
241 E Crestwood Rd.
PO Box 2418
Peachtree City, GA 30269

Ph:(770)487-6460
Fax: (770)487-2919
Co. E-mail: judy@competitiveedgeinc.com
URL: http://www.competitiveedgeinc.com

E-mail: judy@competitiveedgeinc.com
Scope: Human Resources consulting firm providing customized training and software solutions to assist clients in optimizing their human intellectual capital through effective selection, coaching, and training. Works with a network of consultants that are located throughout the United States, Canada, and Europe. **Publications:** "Energizing People: Unleashing The Power of DISC"; "The Ripple Effect: How the Global Model of Endorsement Opens Doors to Success"; "The Journey - Quotes to keep your boat afloat"; "The Universal Language DISC Reference Manual ". **Seminars:** How to Recruit and Retain High Performing Employees; The Importance of Values Matching For Sales Selection; How to Build a High Performance Team; Dynamic Communication Skills; Creating Nurturing Customer Relationships.

33341 ■ Consulting Partners Inc.
14911 Quorum Dr., Ste. 120
Dallas, TX 75254
Ph:(972)386-7858
Fax: (972)386-8667
Co. E-mail: info@consultingpartners.com
URL: http://www.consultingpartners.com

E-mail: info@consultingpartners.com
Scope: We are a Modis company, specializing in technical communications, technical writing, custom instructor-led training, computer-based training, web-based training, language translation, documentation, and editing.

33342 ■ Donna Cornell Enterprises Inc.
68 N Plank Rd., Ste. 204
Newburgh, NY 12550-2122
Ph:(845)565-0088
Fax: (845)565-0084
Co. E-mail: rc@cornellcareercenter.com
URL: http://www.dce.com

E-mail: rc@cornellcareercenter.com
Scope: Offers services in career consultant, professional search, job placement, and national professional search. **Publications:** "The Power of the Woman Within".

33343 ■ donphin.com Inc.
5713 Corporate Way, Ste. 101
West Palm Beach, FL 33407
Ph:(561)688-1000
Free: 800-234-3304
Fax: (561)688-1142
Co. E-mail: inquiry@donphin.com
URL: http://www.donphin.com

E-mail: inquiry@donphin.com
Scope: Offers a comprehensive approach to understanding and applying a broad range of business principles: legal compliance issues, management concerns, health and safety, customer service, marketing, information management. Industries served: all developing small businesses. **Publications:** "Doing Business Right!". **Seminars:** Doing Business Right!; HR That Works!.

33344 ■ Dorn & Associates Inc.
8506 Bass Lake Rd., Ste. 140
New Hope, MN 55428
Ph:(763)533-7689
Fax: (763)533-1143
Scope: Services include accounting, marketing, employment/partnership, new doctor agreements, personnel issues and human resources assessment, practice management, practice merger/acquisition/sale and/or liquidation, practice surveys and valuation, staff development and training.

33345 ■ Full Voice
11130 Holmes Rd.
Kansas City, MO 64101
Ph:(816)941-0011

Fax: (816)444-0505
Scope: Formalizes a program of proven techniques into a practical method of helping individuals improve their ability to better present themselves when speaking in a professional situation. Industries Served: all. **Publications:** You Can Sound Like You Know What Youre Saying. **Seminars:** You Can Sound Like You Know What Youre Saying; How to Make Yours a Championship Team; Functional English for Foreign Trade; The Effective Voice for Customer Service Enhancement; The Psychology of Vocal Performance; You Can Speak With Conviction.

33346 ■ Harding & Co.
9 Sommer Ave.
Maplewood, NJ 07040
Ph:(973)763-9284
Fax: (973)763-9347
Co. E-mail: fharding@hardingco.com
URL: http://www.hardingco.com

E-mail: fharding@hardingco.com
Scope: Firm specializes in sales management, client development, and employee training. **Publications:** "Rain Making: The Professional's Guide to Attracting New Clients"; "Creating Rainmakers: The Managers Guide to Training Professionals to Attract New Clients"; "Cross-Selling Success: A Rainmakers Guide to Professional Account Development".

33347 ■ Hills Consulting Group Inc.
6 Partridge Ct.
Novato, CA 94945
Ph:(415)898-3944
Scope: Strategic marketing consulting and training firm. Specializes in strategic planning; marketing surveys; market research; customer service audits; new product development; competitive analysis; and sales forecasting.

33348 ■ Interpersonal Coaching & Consulting
1516 W Lake St., Ste. 2000S
Minneapolis, MN 55408
Ph:(612)381-2494
Fax: (612)381-2494
Co. E-mail: mail@interpersonal-coaching.com
URL: http://www.interpersonal-coaching.com

E-mail: mail@interpersonal-coaching.com
Scope: Provides coaching and consulting to businesses and organizations. Assesses the interpersonal workplace through interviews, assessment instruments and individual group settings. Experienced as a therapist for over a decade.

33349 ■ Mandalay Associates L.L.C.
3020 El Cerrito Plz.
PMB 226
El Cerrito, CA 94530-4002
Ph:(510)526-4651
Fax: (510)526-5774
Co. E-mail: contact@mandalayassociates.com
URL: http://www.mandalayassociates.com

E-mail: contact@mandalayassociates.com
Scope: Business management firm specializes in conflict resolution, employee relations, employment and placement, organizational analysis and development, human resources program development, program and project management, and staff development and training.

33350 ■ Milestone Inc.
PO Box 630
Dedham, MA 02027
Ph:(781)467-1200
Fax: (781)467-0299
Co. E-mail: bob@milestoneideas.com
URL: http://www.milestoneideas.com

E-mail: bob@milestoneideas.com
Scope: Specialized group of business creativity and innovation facilitators who are passionately connected to the overt and covert motivations and values that enrich and complicate brands, the people who buy them,

and the people who make them interesting, surprising and unique. Facilitates 100 business creativity and innovation growth sessions per year. Many established and emerging organizations have found the organizational learning focus helps them prosper when using the facilitation services to: Discover new strategic growth strategies and planning options; Create new ideas, new promises, value propositions, products and programs; Identify and integrate customer passions in new and surprising ways; realize higher returns on involvement, interest and investment; refine processes, accelerate innovative growth and build better teams. **Seminars:** Ideas in Action; Double-Gesturing; Growth in a period of no growth; Strike while the iron is cold; Natural Creative Strategies. **Special Services:** Milestone®; IMMERgENT®; Immersion®.

33351 ■ National Pediculosis Association Inc.
50 Kearney Rd.
Needham, MA 02494
Ph:(781)449-6487
Free: 800-446-4672
Fax: (781)449-8129
Co. E-mail: npa@headlice.org
URL: http://www.headlice.org

E-mail: npa@headlice.org
Scope: Consultants in head lice and scabies management, treatment, prevention, and education. Specializes in monitoring health policy administration in schools and trends in the treatment of head lice. Emphasis is on educational activities. Industries served: schools, health professionals, medical professionals, child care centers, health departments, hospitals, HMO's, clinics, libraries, parents, PTA's, camps, military bases, and churches. **Publications:** "All out Comb out". **Special Services:** LiceMeister®.

33352 ■ Priority Process Associates Inc.
1236 E Horseshoe Bend Ct.
Rochester Hills, MI 48306
Ph:(248)608-8966
Fax: (248)608-8966
Scope: A management consulting firm with expertise in computer technology, telecommunications, and information services. Provides the following specific services: business process re-engineering-establishes correctly implemented, computer technologies that empower and accelerate work groups to act autonomously but in concert with corporate goals, document work-flow analysis-models and simulates the flow of documents through selected organizational processes, enterprise metrics-identifies unique metrics for enterprises to evaluate their continuous improvement of business processes, cost justification-identifies value using Activity Based Costing and innovative approaches to quantify time-to-market reductions, project profitability, and reduce and manage costs, proposal development-generates Requests for Proposals to solicit competitive quotations for cost effective off-the-shelf software, computer hardware, and communication products, implementation planning-negotiates implementation plans for clients through qualified software vendors, custom software integrators, and hardware, communication, and outsource suppliers, project auditing-audits the integration, installation and use of on-time, quality enterprise multi-vendor software, hardware and communications systems on computer networks, training-expands clients knowledge through information sources, and client-specific management seminars and skill building workshops. Serves manufacturing industries in the United States.

33353 ■ ProActive English
1001 Pine St., Ste. 1004
San Francisco, CA 94109
Ph:(415)752-2270
Co. E-mail: infopae@proactive-english.com
URL: http://www.proactive-english.com

E-mail: infopae@proactive-english.com
Scope: Offers on-site individual and small group language and communication training. Sets up learning

plans tailored to the needs and schedules of managers and executives who are non-native English speakers. Serves all industries. **Seminars:** Communicating in Business Situations; Presentations and Pronunciation.

33354 ■ Professional Psychological Services
4130 Linden Ave., Ste. 309
Dayton, OH 45432
Ph:(513)254-7301
Fax: (513)254-2117
Co. E-mail: ppsdocs@aol.com

E-mail: ppsdocs@aol.com
Scope: Offers clinical services, human relations training, multicultural and pluralistic training, and staff development and training.

33355 ■ Sandy Corp.
1500 W Big Beaver Rd.
Troy, MI 48084-3526
Ph:(248)649-0800
Free: 800-733-4739
Fax: (248)649-3614
Co. E-mail: info@sandycorp.com
URL: http://www.sandycorp.com

E-mail: info@sandycorp.com
Scope: A full-service, publicly held, company specializing in the design, development and production of specific consulting, training, communicating and evaluating programs to help clients improve the capabilities of their people to such a level that consistent performance on the job becomes a visible, valued competitive strength. Emphasis is on performance improvement, process and culture exchange, quality and customer satisfaction, using print, video, slides, film, classroom training, business theatre and satellite television media for sales, service and management training and launching new products, new business methods and even totally new organizations. Industries served: automotive industry, general manufacturing, the hospitality industry and government agencies.

33356 ■ Tamayo Consulting Inc.
169 Saxony Rd., Ste. 112
Encinitas, CA 92024-6779
Free: 800-580-9606
Fax: (760)479-1465
Co. E-mail: info@tamayoconsulting.com
URL: http://www.tamayoconsulting.com

E-mail: info@tamayoconsulting.com
Scope: Training and consulting firm specializing in: leadership and team development. Industries served: private, non-profit, government, educational.

33357 ■ Tel-Advise
2096 Lander Rd.
Mayfield Heights, OH 44124-4100
Ph:(440)646-9861
Fax: (440)646-9851
Co. E-mail: info@teladvise.com
URL: http://www.teladvise.com

E-mail: info@teladvise.com
Scope: Services including training, consulting, implementation, and turn-key solutions. The training programs create a learning curve to ease the migration into effortless manageability of the Internet. Business applications and teaching employees how to utilize them. The consultation services enable a company to reduce the number of hours spent on system requirements and implementation, and to integrate the software and hardware available to suit the needs of a network. Strategic planning, design, information mapping, implementation, and management to any level of network and computing requirements. **Publications:** "Spanning the Globe".

33358 ■ Training Systems Plus
742 Brent Dr.
PO Box 185
Mulvane, KS 67110-1245
Ph:(316)777-1337
Fax: (316)777-0802
Scope: Provides management and training systems to businesses to improve operational profitability as

well as individual management and employee performance. Activities include consultation, job descriptions, evaluation forms, training seminars, training materials, operations manuals, and employee handbooks. **Seminars:** Effective Classroom Instruction; Training System Design; Interviewing and Selecting; Performance Management, Leadership Skills.

FRANCHISES AND BUSINESS OPPORTUNITIES

33359 ■ A.D. Banker & Company - Training Centers
5000 College Blvd., 110
Overland Park, KS 66211
Free: 800-255-0408
Fax: (913)451-1214
No. of Franchise Units: 8. **No. of Company-Owned Units:** 80. **Founded:** 1979. **Franchised:** 2005. **Description:** Exam preparation and continuing education training. **Equity Capital Needed:** $29,000-$97,000. **Franchise Fee:** $8,900-$36,400. **Royalty Fee:** 12%. **Financial Assistance:** Third-party financing available. **Training:** Provides 5 days at headquarters and ongoing support.

33360 ■ Canadian School of Natural Nutrition
10720 Yonge St., Ste. 220
Richmond Hill, ON, Canada L4C 3C9
Ph:(905)737-8729
Free: 800-569-9938
Fax: (905)737-7830
Co. E-mail: hq@csnn.ca
URL: http://www.csnn.ca
No. of Franchise Units: 4. **No. of Company-Owned Units:** 8. **Founded:** 1994. **Franchised:** 1996. **Description:** private vocational school offering adult education leading to professional designations: RHN-Reg. Holistic Nutritionist, and RECP-Reg, ElderCare Practitioner. Franchisees are licensed to distribute CSNN curriculum material to students through classroom education. CSNN offers two programs: Natural Nutrition and Elder Care. CSNN is privately owned, incorporated as 3393291 Canada Inc. **Equity Capital Needed:** $70,000 Canadian Capital. **Franchise Fee:** $12,000. **Training:** Ongoing.

33361 ■ Clay For Kids
512 Canterbury Pl. SW
Calgary, AB, Canada T2W 2G2
Ph:(403)281-4811
Fax: (403)281-4816
Co. E-mail: Maureen@clayforkids.com
URL: http://www.clayforkids.com
No. of Franchise Units: 3. **Founded:** 1981. **Franchised:** 2004. **Description:** School program that runs 1 1/2 hours and starts with a pottery wheel demonstration. Each student then produces one piece of finished work that is fired in a kiln and returned to the school within 21 days. Painting and finishing information will be provided. **Equity Capital Needed:** $600,000-$100,000 **Franchise Fee:** $14,500-$31,500. **Training:** Yes.

33362 ■ Dale Carnegie Training
290 Motor Pky.
Hauppauge, NY 11788
Ph:(631)415-9300
Fax: (631)415-9358
No. of Franchise Units: 120. **No. of Company-Owned Units:** 3. **Founded:** 1912. **Franchised:** 1999. **Description:** Sales & human development training. **Equity Capital Needed:** $32,700-$221,900. **Franchise Fee:** $25,000. **Royalty Fee:** 12%. **Financial Assistance:** No. **Training:** Offers 1 week at headquarters, 10 days on-site with ongoing support.

33363 ■ Drama Kids International, Inc.
3225-B Corporate Ct.
Ellicott City, MD 21042
Ph:(410)480-2015
Fax: (410)480-2026
Co. E-mail: dramakids@starpower.net
URL: http://www.dramakids.com
No. of Franchise Units: 128. **No. of Company-Owned Units:** 2. **Founded:** 1979. **Franchised:** 1989.

Description: After-school developmental drama program. Curriculum uses fun & creative drama activities so kids ages 5-17 act confidently and speak clearly. **Equity Capital Needed:** $35,000-$43,000. **Franchise Fee:** $27,500. **Financial Assistance:** $10,000 in interest-free financing. **Training:** Formal initial training followed up with additional 'in-school' hands-on training, assistance in setting up class locations, pre-opening, post-opening assistance, and site visits. Field support provided on an ongoing basis.

33364 ■ Fastrackids International, Ltd.
6900 E Belleview Ave., 1st Fl.
Greenwood Village, CO 80111
Ph:(303)224-0200
Free: 888-576-6888
Fax: (303)224-0222
Co. E-mail: info@fastrackids.com
URL: http://www.fastrackids.com
No. of Franchise Units: 150+. **Founded:** 1998. **Franchised:** 1998. **Description:** An accelerated learning system for children. **Equity Capital Needed:** $33,800-$183,500. **Franchise Fee:** $22,000. **Financial Assistance:** Company will assist in obtaining financing or in some instances provide limited financing. **Managerial Assistance:** Newsletters, a web site, and a procedures manual. **Training:** Provides initial training, periodic regional seminars, an annual international conference, sales/telemarketing assistance, and classroom facilitation tips.

33365 ■ Frozen Ropes Training Centers
12 Elkay Dr.
Chester, NY 10918
Ph:(845)469-7331
Fax: (845)469-6742
No. of Franchise Units: 9. **No. of Company-Owned Units:** 1. **Founded:** 1994. **Franchised:** 2003. **Description:** Baseball & softball instruction. **Equity Capital Needed:** $219,800-$276,200. **Franchise Fee:** $45,000. **Royalty Fee:** 3-6%. **Financial Assistance:** No.

33366 ■ KidzArt
KidzArt Texas LLC
1902 E Common St., Ste. 400
New Braunfels, TX 78130
Ph:(830)626-1959
Free: 800-379-8302
Fax: (830)626-0260
Co. E-mail: info@kidzart.com
URL: http://www.kidzart.com
No. of Franchise Units: 67. **Founded:** 1997. **Franchised:** 2002. **Description:** Offers children's products and education services. **Equity Capital Needed:** $50,000-$75,000. **Franchise Fee:** $31,900. **Financial Assistance:** Third partySBA registry approved franchisee. **Training:** Offers 1 week business/operations training and cutting edge franchisee support; conferences, monthly training calls, one on one quick start coaching and ongoing support.

33367 ■ Kumon North America, Inc.
Glenpointe Centre E
300 Frank W Burr Blvd., 5th Fl.
Teaneck, NJ 07666
Free: (866)633-0740
Fax: (201)928-0044
Co. E-mail: franchise@kumon.com
URL: http://www.kumon.com
No. of Franchise Units: 25,813. **No. of Company-Owned Units:** 31. **Founded:** 1958. **Franchised:** 1980. **Description:** North America provider of supplemental math and learning material. The learning center caters to all ages and abilities from pre-school through high school. **Franchise Fee:** $1,000. **Training:** Kumon has offices worldwide to provide training, support and on-site consultation to franchisees.

33368 ■ Language Leaders Franchising L. L.C.
Foreign Language Network, L.L.C.
3N503 Townhall Rd.
Elburn, IL 60119
Ph:(630)578-0948
No. of Company-Owned Units: 1. **Founded:** 1998. **Franchised:** 2004. **Description:** Foreign language

education and interpreting. **Equity Capital Needed:** $18,700-$107,000. **Franchise Fee:** $10,000-$90,000. **Royalty Fee:** 15%. **Financial Assistance:** In-house assistance with franchise fee. **Training:** 2 days training at headquarters.

33369 ■ LearningRX Franchise Corp.
LearningRx, Inc.
5085 List Dr., Ste. 201
Colorado Springs, CO 80919
Ph:(719)264-8808
Free: 800-535-5441
No. of Franchise Units: 1. **No. of Company-Owned Units:** 1. **Founded:** 1987. **Franchised:** 2003. **Description:** One on one brain skills and reading training. **Equity Capital Needed:** $26,000-$88,000. **Franchise Fee:** $12,500-$42,500. **Financial Assistance:** No. **Training:** Yes.

33370 ■ Little Dreamers Preschool
114 Hyannis Dr.
Holly Springs, NC 27540
Ph:(919)524-2826
Fax: (919)380-0901
No. of Company-Owned Units: 2. **Founded:** 2001. **Franchised:** 2004. **Description:** Half-day morning educational pre-school. **Equity Capital Needed:** $50,000-$75,000. **Franchise Fee:** $25,000. **Financial Assistance:** No. **Training:** Yes.

33371 ■ The Mad Science Group
8360 Bougainville St., No. 201
Montreal, QC, Canada H4P 2G1
Ph:(514)344-4181
Free: 800-586-5231
Fax: (514)344-6695
Co. E-mail: joel@madscience.org
URL: http://www.madscience.org
No. of Franchise Units: 200. **Founded:** 1985. **Franchised:** 1995. **Description:** Mad Science is a service company specializing in fun hands on educational science for children. We send trained instructors with all required materials and supplies to conduct on-site activities to schools and other organizations dealing with kids. Our franchisees are sales marketing oriented individuals who enjoy a hands-on owner operated business that enriches children and contributes to the community. **Equity Capital Needed:** $10,000-$23,500 franchise fee, $25,000 equipment package; $20,000-$30,000 working capital. **Franchise Fee:** $10,000-$23,500. **Financial Assistance:** $23,500 start-up cash; $60,000-$80,000 total investment required. Work with AT & T to help with financing. **Training:** 6 day training at corporate headquarters followed by 5 day training on-site.

33372 ■ Mathnasium Learning Centers
5120 W Goldleaf Cir., Ste. 130
Los Angeles, CA 90056
Ph:(323)421-8000
Free: 877-531-MATH
Fax: (310)943-2111
Co. E-mail: franchise@mathnasium.com
URL: http://www.mathnasium.com
No. of Franchise Units: 170. **No. of Company-Owned Units:** 2. **Founded:** 2002. **Franchised:** 2003. **Description:** Mathnasium provides the most effective mathematics in education available to grade school children after school, in an attractive neighborhood learning center environment. The Mathnasium Method, developed over 30 years of hands-on experience, is engaging for students and builds confidence as it builds real understanding. Created to address a real need in the market by a team with unparalleled success in the industry, the business model is strong and the opportunity is now. **Equity Capital Needed:** Franchise fee, $15,500; Start-up, $50,000-$70,000; plus capital, $50,000-$70,000. **Franchise Fee:** $15,500. **Training:** Complete initial training at corporate headquarters and ongoing support.

33373 ■ Online Trading Academy
18004 Sky Park Cir., S. No. 140
Irvine, CA 92614
Ph:(949)608-6020
Fax: (949)608-6026
No. of Franchise Units: 5. **Founded:** 1998. **Franchised:** 2004. **Description:** Stock-trading instruction.

Equity Capital Needed: $200,400-$373,000. **Franchise Fee:** $65,000-$190,000. **Royalty Fee:** 10%. **Financial Assistance:** Third party financing available. **Training:** Offers 2 weeks training at headquarters, 1 week at franchisees location and ongoing support.

33374 ■ The Original Woodwork Shop & School
4221-6th St., SE
Calgary, AB, Canada T2G 4E7
Free: 877-955-4192
Fax: (403)995-4192
Co. E-mail: thewoodworkshopandschool@shaw.ca
URL: http://www.theworkshopandschool.com
No. of Franchise Units: 2. **No. of Company-Owned Units:** 1. **Founded:** 1997. **Franchised:** 2002. **Description:** We have a practical approach to teaching woodworking. We teach everyone how to build furniture. We also provide do-it-yourself time shops on building custom furniture. We also sell specialty lumber. **Equity Capital Needed:** $65,000. **Franchise Fee:** $25,000. **Training:** 2 weeks initial and ongoing support.

33375 ■ Oxford Learning Centers
747 Hyde Park Rd., Ste. 230
London, ON, Canada N6H 3S3
Ph:(519)473-1207
Free: 888-559-2212
Fax: (519)473-6086
Co. E-mail: franchise@oxfordlearning.com
URL: http://www.oxfordlearning.com
No. of Franchise Units: 116. **No. of Company-Owned Units:** 1. **Founded:** 1984. **Franchised:** 1991. **Description:** Oxford is an educational franchise in Canada, which provides extensive training in all fields. **Equity Capital Needed:** $140,000-$210,000. **Franchise Fee:** $39,500. **Training:** 1 week at home, 2 weeks at head office, and ongoing support included.

33376 ■ Pathways Education & Training Centers, Inc.
40 N 300 E, Ste. 202
St. George, UT 84770
Ph:(435)674-1331
Free: (866)845-6463
Fax: (435)674-1831
No. of Franchise Units: 6. **No. of Company-Owned Units:** 1. **Founded:** 2000. **Franchised:** 2005. **Description:** Brain integration program. **Equity Capital Needed:** $20,000. **Financial Assistance:** No. **Training:** Yes.

33377 ■ Safekidscard
17100 B-Bear Valley Rd., No. 238
Victorville, CA 92392
Ph:(909)496-9982
Fax: (760)249-5751
No. of Franchise Units: 19. **Founded:** 2002. **Franchised:** 2003. **Description:** Children's products and education services are offered. **Equity Capital Needed:** $11,900, includes 3-in-one turn-key business franchise. **Franchise Fee:** $11,900. **Financial Assistance:** No. **Training:** Yes.

33378 ■ Science Explorers Inc.
1192 Horseshoe Pike
Downingtown, PA 19335
Ph:(610)269-3347
Free: 877-870-9517
Fax: (610)269-3775
No. of Franchise Units: 3. **No. of Company-Owned Units:** 2. **Founded:** 1999. **Franchised:** 2003. **Description:** Hands-on science programs for children. **Equity Capital Needed:** $19,500-$37,500. **Franchise Fee:** $8,000. **Financial Assistance:** No. **Training:** Yes.

33379 ■ Spirit of Math Schools
120A Willowdale Ave., Unit A & B
Toronto, ON, Canada M2N 4Y2
Ph:(416)223-1985
Fax: (416)946-1902
Co. E-mail: franchise@spiritofmath.com
URL: http://www.spititofmath.com
No. of Franchise Units: 3. **No. of Company-Owned Units:** 7. **Founded:** 1992. **Franchised:** 2004. **De-**

scription: Offers an after-school classroom program for high performing students. It develops as skill-based understanding of math focusing on problem solving, co-operation and numeric skills and produces some of the top math students in the nation. **Training:** A comprehensive training and support program is provided.

33380 ■ Swyrich Corporation
Hall Of Names
830 Development Dr.
Kingston, ON, Canada K7M 5V7
Ph:(613)384-2257
Free: 800-265-7099
Fax: (613)384-0606
Co. E-mail: info@swyrich.com
URL: http://www.swyrich.com
No. of Franchise Units: 135. **Founded:** 1991. **Franchised:** 1991. **Description:** Sales of heraldic materials. Coats of arms, surname histories, first name histories, Scottish clan badges and histories, Irish Sept histories and coats of arms. **Equity Capital Needed:** $10,000-$30,000. **Franchise Fee:** $5,000. **Royalty Fee:** Varies. **Financial Assistance:** Direct financial assistance available. **Managerial Assistance:** Regularly updated software that is completely user friendly and fully supported. **Training:** Training includes online and telephone support.

33381 ■ Whizard Academy For Mathematics & English
30 Glen Cameron Rd., No. 200
Thornhill, ON, Canada L3T 1N7
Ph:(905)709-3233
Free: 800-809-5555
Fax: (905)709-3045
Co. E-mail: balti@acadfor.com
URL: http://www.whizardmath.com
No. of Franchise Units: 48. **No. of Company-Owned Units:** 4. **Founded:** 1992. **Franchised:** 1993. **Description:** Licensees provide math, science and English tutoring to school age children from kindergarten to the end of high school. Individualized, self-paced learning is provided in learning centers located in malls and strip plazas, using a unique audiovisual learning program. **Equity Capital Needed:** $100,000-$130,000. **Franchise Fee:** $35,000. **Royalty Fee:** 11%. **Financial Assistance:** No. **Training:** Offers 1 week training.

33382 ■ The Whole Child Learning Co.
921 Belvin St.
San Marcos, TX 78666
Ph:(512)396-2740
Free: 888-317-3535
Fax: (512)392-7820
No. of Franchise Units: 6. **No. of Company-Owned Units:** 4. **Founded:** 1996. **Franchised:** 1999. **Description:** Educational services for children. **Equity Capital Needed:** $7,500. **Franchise Fee:** $15,000. **Financial Assistance:** Yes. **Training:** Yes.

33383 ■ Young Rembrandts, A Children's Drawing Program
Young Rembrandts
23 N Union St.
Elgin, IL 60123
Ph:(847)742-6999
Free: (866)300-6010
Fax: (847)742-7197
Co. E-mail: yr@youngrembrandts.com
URL: http://www.youngrembrandts.com
No. of Franchise Units: 56. **No. of Company-Owned Units:** 3. **Founded:** 1988. **Franchised:** 2001. **Description:** Offers unique drawing program to young children. **Equity Capital Needed:** Liquid $50,000; $100,000 net. **Franchise Fee:** $31,500. **Financial Assistance:** No. **Training:** Yes.

COMPUTERIZED DATABASES

33384 ■ *Health & Wellness InSite*
Thomson Dialog
11000 Regency Pky., Ste. 10
Cary, NC 27511

Ph:(919)462-8600
Free: 800-3-DIALOG
Fax: (919)468-9890
Co. E-mail: intelligence.data@tfn.com
URL: http://www.dialog.com/sources/intelligence_
data

Description: Contains complete information about health, medicine, fitness, and nutrition. Provides access to 170 of the world's leading professional and consumer health publications, including *The Lancet* and *Nutrition Today;* 550 health and medical pamphlets; 200,000 health-related articles from more than 3000 other publications; and 1800 overviews of different diseases and medical conditions published by Clinical Reference Systems, Ltd. Includes six medical reference books: *Columbia University College of Physicians & Surgeons Complete Home Medical Guide; Mosby's Medical, Nursing, and Allied Health Dictionary; Consumer Health Information Source Book; The People's Book of Medical Tests; USP DI-Vol. II Advice for the Patient; Drug Information in Lay Language;* and *The Complete Directory for People With Chronic Illness..* Allows searches by article title, article type, author, company name, person discussed in the article, publication name, publication date range, publication type, target audience, ticker symbol, words in the title, and words that appear anywhere in the article. **Availability:** Online: Thomson Dialog. **Type:** Full text.

33385 ■ *Peterson's Vocational/Technical Schools Database*
Peterson's
Princeton Pike Corporate Ctr.
2000 Lenox Dr.
PO Box 67005
Lawrenceville, NJ 08648
Ph:(609)896-1800
Free: 800-338-3282
Fax: (609)896-4531
Co. E-mail: custsvc@petersons.com
URL: http://www.petersons.com

Description: Contains information on some 6500 accredited schools offering more than 240 vocational and technical training programs. For each school, provides programs offered; courses offered; degrees awarded; admissions requirements and deadlines; tuition costs and available financial aid; available student services such as career placement; enrollment size; program's background and accreditation; and whom to contact. Corresponds to *Peterson's Guide To Vocational and Technical Schools.* **Type:** Directory.

LIBRARIES

33386 ■ American Society for Training and Development (ASTD)–Information Center
1640 King St.
PO Box 1443
Alexandria, VA 22313-2043
Ph:(703)683-8100
Fax: (703)683-1523
Co. E-mail: customercare@astd.org
URL: http://www.astd.org
Contact: Debbie Wise, Proj.Mgr.
Scope: Human resource development - general, management, training, career development, Organization development, consulting skills. **Services:** Library open to national members of the Society. **Holdings:** 3000 bound volumes. **Subscriptions:** 60 journals and other serials.

33387 ■ National Association for Industry-Education Cooperation–Library
235 Hendricks Blvd.
Buffalo, NY 14226-3304
Ph:(716)834-7047
Fax: (716)834-7047
Co. E-mail: naiec@pcom.net
URL: http://www2.pcom.net/naiec/
Contact: Dr. Donald M. Clark, Pres./CEO
Scope: Industry involvement in education to further continuous systemwide school improvement, work force preparation, economic development. **Services:** Library open to members. **Holdings:** 1340 books; 45 bound periodical volumes; 2 AV programs; 89 manuscripts.

RESEARCH CENTERS

33388 ■ Center for Entrepreneurial Studies and Development
College of Engineering & Mineral Research
West Virginia University
1062 Maple Dr., Ste. 2
Morgantown, WV 26505
Ph:(304)293-5551
Fax: (304)293-6707
Co. E-mail: jbyrd@mail.cesd.wvu.edu
URL: http://www.cesd.wvu.edu
Contact: Dr. Jack Byrd Jr., Exec.Dir.
E-mail: jbyrd@mail.cesd.wvu.edu
Scope: Business operations improvement, employee training, management, and systems development. Operations improvement studies focus on quality control, materials handling systems, cost reduction, work standards development, facilities utilization and planning, work methods, inventory control systems, and computer applications. Employee training focuses on supervisory development, quality training, and problem solving. Management studies focus on management development programs, organization development, steering committee development, facilitation, incentives, and small business organizations. Systems studies focus on business plan development. **Services:** Competitive and economic development strategies; Market assessment and development; Operational improvements; Performance management; Provides assistance in new product or service development. **Publications:** Think About.

33389 ■ CORD
PO Box 21689
Waco, TX 76702-1689
Ph:(254)772-8756
Free: 800—972-2766
Fax: (254)772-8972
Co. E-mail: hull@cord.org
URL: http://www.cord.org
Contact: Dan Hull, Pres./CEO
E-mail: hull@cord.org
Scope: Educational research and evaluation; designs and develops instructional materials and curricula for grades 7-14; creates innovative applications of educational technology. **Services:** Consulting and coordination services; Forms networks and partnerships. **Publications:** Newsletter (monthly); White papers. **Educational Activities:** Curricula development; Teacher workshops.

33390 ■ Illinois State Board of Education–Data Analysis and Progress Reporting Division
100 N 1st St.
Springfield, IL 62777
Ph:(217)782-3950
Fax: (217)524-7784
Co. E-mail: cwise@isbe.net
URL: http://www.isbe.net/research/Default.htm
Contact: Connie Wise, Division Admin.
E-mail: cwise@isbe.net
Scope: Education policy.

33391 ■ Indiana University Bloomington–Center for Evaluation and EDU Policy
509 E 3rd St.
Bloomington, IN 47401-3654
Ph:(812)855-4438
Free: 800—511-6575
Fax: (812)856-5890
Co. E-mail: jplucker@indiana.edu
URL: http://ceep.indiana.edu
Contact: Jonathan Plucker PhD, Dir.
E-mail: jplucker@indiana.edu
Scope: Program evaluation and policy research, primarily on education issues but also in health care. **Publications:** Policy Bulletins (monthly); Policy Reports; Special Reports and Technical Studies.

33392 ■ Indiana University Bloomington–Center for Postsecondary Research
Eigenmann Hall, Ste. 419
1900 E 10th St.
Bloomington, IN 47406-7512
Ph:(812)856-5824
Free: (866)-435-6773
Fax: (812)856-5150
Co. E-mail: nsse@indiana.edu
URL: http://www.nsse.iub.edu
Contact: Dr. George Kuh, Dir.
E-mail: nsse@indiana.edu
Scope: Policy issues and issues related to student learning and personal development, including student engagement, student persistence and attrition, institutional advancement, enrollment management and marketing, program evaluation, institutional culture, student learning and personal development, and equity and access in higher education. **Publications:** National Survey of Student Engagement (annually).

33393 ■ Indiana University Bloomington–Center for the Study of Institutions, Population, and Environmental Change
408 N Indiana Ave.
Bloomington, IN 47408-3799
Ph:(812)855-2230
Fax: (812)855-2634
Co. E-mail: cipec@indiana.edu
URL: http://www.cipec.org
Contact: Elinor Ostrom PhD, Co-Dir.
E-mail: cipec@indiana.edu
Scope: Processes of change in forest environments as mediated by institutional arrangements, demographic factors, and other major human driving forces. **Educational Activities:** Summer Institute.

33394 ■ Indiana University-Purdue University at Indianapolis–Center for American Studies
545 Cavanaugh Hall
425 University Blvd.
Indianapolis, IN 46202
Ph:(317)278-3374
Fax: (317)274-2170
Co. E-mail: mwokeck@iupui.edu
Contact: Dr. Marion Wokeck, Dir.
E-mail: mwokeck@iupui.edu
Scope: Cultural environment in the United States.

33395 ■ Indiana University-Purdue University at Indianapolis–Center for the Study of Religion and American Culture
425 University Blvd., Rm. 341
Indianapolis, IN 46202-5140
Ph:(317)274-8409
Fax: (317)278-3354
Co. E-mail: pgoff@iupui.edu
URL: http://www.iupui.edu/~raac/
Contact: Dr. Philip K. Goff, Dir.
E-mail: pgoff@iupui.edu
Scope: Relationship between religion and aspects of American culture. **Publications:** Centers and Institutes Booklet (annually); News from the Center for the Study of Religion and American Culture (semiannually); Religion and American Culture: A Journal of Interpretation (semiannually). **Educational Activities:** Public lectures, conferences, and symposia; Young Scholars in American Religion Program. **Awards:** Awards and fellowships.

33396 ■ Indiana University-Purdue University at Indianapolis–CyberLab
719 Indiana Ave., Ste. 370
Indianapolis, IN 46202-5160
Ph:(317)278-2630
Fax: (317)610-8831
Co. E-mail: cyberlab@iupui.edu
URL: http://cyberlab.iupui.edu/
Contact: Ali Jafari PhD, Dir.
E-mail: cyberlab@iupui.edu
Scope: Worldwide web applications in teaching and learning, especially course management portals, campus portals, agent-based learning environment, and intelligent user interfaces.

33397 ■ Indiana University-Purdue University at Indianapolis–Nuclear Magnetic Resonance Laboratory
402 N Blackford St., Rm. 154
Indianapolis, IN 46202
Ph:(317)274-6901
Fax: (317)274-2393
Co. E-mail: brao@iupui.edu
Contact: Dr. B.D. Nageswara Rao, Dir.
E-mail: brao@iupui.edu
Scope: Structure-function relationships of biological macromolecules, using the techniques of nuclear magnetic resonance (NMR). The research is interdisciplinary, bringing together researchers from the School of Science and the School of Medicine. **Educational Activities:** Training, for scientists interested in learning or using NMR techniques.

33398 ■ Indiana University-Purdue University at Indianapolis–Peirce Edition Project
0010 Education/Social Work
902 W New York St.
Indianapolis, IN 46202-5157
Ph:(317)278-3374
Fax: (317)274-2170
Co. E-mail: cpeirce@iupui.edu
URL: http://www.iupui.edu/~peirce
Contact: Dr. Nathan Houser, Dir.
E-mail: cpeirce@iupui.edu
Scope: American philosophy and culture, focusing on the writings of scientist and philosopher Charles S. Peirce. **Publications:** Peirce Project Newsletter (periodically).

33399 ■ Institute for Forensic Imaging
383 S Arlington Ave., Ste. 111
Indianapolis, IN 46219
Ph:(317)356-0245
Fax: (317)356-0227
Co. E-mail: hblitzer@ifi-indy.org
URL: http://www.ifi-indy.org
Contact: Herbert Blitzer, Exec.Dir.
E-mail: hblitzer@ifi-indy.org
Scope: Forensic imaging in the investigation of crimes and legal questions. **Services:** Consulting; Research. **Educational Activities:** College courses, through the School of Informatics at IUPUI (Indiana University Purdue University Indianapolis); Student centered training; Training programs, certified by the Indiana Law Enforcement Academy.

33400 ■ Iowa Education Department–Financial and Information Services Division–Planning, Research and Evaluation Bureau
Grimes Bldg.
Des Moines, IA 50319-0146
Ph:(515)281-4837
Fax: (515)281-8777
Co. E-mail: shawn.snyder@iowa.gov
URL: http://www.state.ia.us/educate/
Contact: Shawn Snyder, Ch., Planning Res.
E-mail: shawn.snyder@iowa.gov
Scope: Educational policy.

33401 ■ Massachusetts Institute of Technology–Center for Technology, Policy and Industrial Development–International Motor Vehicle Program
Bldg. E40-207
1 Amherst St.
Cambridge, MA 02139-4307
Ph:(617)253-8973
Fax: (617)258-7140
Co. E-mail: Imvpmail@mit.edu
URL: http://imvp.mit.edu
Contact: John Paul MacDuffie, Co-Dir.
E-mail: Imvpmail@mit.edu
Scope: Product development, supply chain management, manufacturing, organization and human resources, distribution and marketing, environmental issues, and mobility in the motor vehicle industry. **Publications:** Working papers. **Educational Activities:** Workshops (periodically).

33402 ■ Massachusetts Institute of Technology–Japan Program
Bldg. E38, Rms 728/756
77 Massachusetts Ave.
Cambridge, MA 02139-4307
Ph:(617)253-2449
Fax: (617)258-7432
Co. E-mail: samuels@mit.edu
URL: http://web.mit.edu/mit-japan/
Contact: Dr. Richard J. Samuels, Dir.
E-mail: samuels@mit.edu
Scope: Japan and Asia, in particular Japanese foreign policy with regard to China, Asian energy and security, the changing role of Japan's technology at home and abroad. **Publications:** MIT Japan Science, Technology & Management Report; Newsletter (monthly); Sponsor Update (quarterly); Working Papers Series. **Educational Activities:** Japan Target Seminars, for technologically sophisticated professionals in business and government.

33403 ■ Massachusetts Institute of Technology–Program on the Pharmaceutical Industry
1 Broadway, 8th Fl, E 70
Cambridge, MA 02139-4307
Ph:(617)253-5194
Fax: (617)253-3033
Co. E-mail: popi-www@mit.edu
URL: http://web.mit.edu/popi/
Contact: Stan N. Finkelstein MD, Dir.
E-mail: popi-www@mit.edu
Scope: Competitiveness, performance, and productivity in the pharmaceutical field.

33404 ■ Nebraska Business Development Center
121 N Dewey, Ste. 208
North Platte, NE 69101
Ph:(308)534-5115
Fax: (308)534-5117
Co. E-mail: jtuller@mail.unomaha.edu
URL: http://www.nbdc.unomaha.edu/
Contact: Jason Tuller, Dir.
E-mail: jtuller@mail.unomaha.edu
Scope: Management education, market research, marketing plans, strategic planning, financial planning, cash flow budgeting, capital budgeting, loan packaging, and rural development. **Services:** Consulting. **Publications:** NBDC Business Calendar (annually). **Educational Activities:** Continuing education programs.

33405 ■ Pennsylvania State University–Center for the Study of Higher Education–NCTLA Project
400 Rackley Bldg.
University Park, PA 16802-3202
Ph:(814)865-6346
Fax: (814)865-3638
Co. E-mail: cshe@psu.edu
Contact: Carol L. Colbeck PhD, Dir.
E-mail: cshe@psu.edu
Scope: Postsecondary teaching and learning, minority student access and retention, higher education faculty, higher education organization and administration.

33406 ■ Rice University–Center for Education
6100 Main St.
Houston, TX 77005
Ph:(713)348-5145
Fax: (713)348-5459
Co. E-mail: Imcneil@rice.edu
URL: http://rice.edu/education/
Contact: Linda McNeil, Co-Dir.
E-mail: Imcneil@rice.edu
Scope: Teacher development, reorganization of schools, student evaluation methods, and educational policy and urban schools. **Publications:** CenterPiece.

33407 ■ Rice University–Center for the Study of Languages
MS 36
6100 Main St.
Houston, TX 77005
Ph:(713)348-5844
Fax: (713)348-5846
Co. E-mail: dnelson@rice.edu
URL: http://langcenter.rice.edu/
Contact: Dr. Deborah Nelson-Campbell, Dir.
E-mail: dnelson@rice.edu
Scope: Language teaching and learning. **Educational Activities:** Seminar, in language methodology; Workshops.

33408 ■ University of Connecticut–Institute for Teaching and Learning
Center for Undergraduate Education
348 Mansfield Rd., Unit 2142
Storrs, CT 06269
Ph:(860)486-2686
Fax: (860)486-5724
Co. E-mail: kb@uconn.edu
URL: http://www.itl.uconn.edu/
Contact: Dr. Keith Barker, Dir.
E-mail: kb@uconn.edu
Scope: Teaching and learning methods, pedagogy, media use and distance learning, and technology use in the classroom and online. **Services:** Consulting; Instructional design. **Publications:** The Journal of Graduate Teaching Assistant Development; TA Handbook. **Educational Activities:** Workshops.

33409 ■ University of Delaware–Delaware Education Research and Development Center
107 Pearson Hall
College of Human Services, Education & Public Policy
Newark, DE 19716
Ph:(302)831-4433
Fax: (302)831-4438
Co. E-mail: ajnoble@udel.edu
URL: http://www.rdc.udel.edu/index.asp
Contact: Audrey J. Noble PhD, Dir.
E-mail: ajnoble@udel.edu
Scope: Educational practice, policy reform, program evaluation.

33410 ■ University of Toronto–Ontario Institute for Studies in Education–Centre for Teacher Development
252 Bloor St., W.
Toronto, ON, Canada M5S 1V6
Ph:(416)923-6641
Fax: (416)926-4754
Co. E-mail: jmiller@oise.utoronto.ca
Contact: Dr. Jack Miller, Hd.
E-mail: jmiller@oise.utoronto.ca
Scope: Teacher education and development, including pre-service, induction, and in-service. **Educational Activities:** Presentation; Seminars; Teacher Development Conference.

33411 ■ University of Toronto–Ontario Institute for Studies in Education–International Centre for Educational Change
OISE/UT Bldg., 6th Fl. S
252 Bloor St. W.
Toronto, ON, Canada M5S 1V6
Ph:(416)923-6641
Fax: (416)926-4720
Co. E-mail: learl@oise.utoronto.ca
URL: http://fcis.oise.utoronto.ca/~icec/
Contact: Prof. Lorna Earl, Hd.
E-mail: learl@oise.utoronto.ca
Scope: Processes of educational change, including scheduling, teaching, curriculum, caring, assessment and decision-making; large-scale reform efforts, large-scale assessment, evaluation of programs and policies. **Services:** Practical field development, professional development activities, and consulting. **Educational Activities:** Study groups, presentations, discussions, and debates.

START-UP INFORMATION

33412 ■ *101 Internet Businesses You Can Start from Home: How to Choose and Build Your Own Successful E-Business*
Pub: Maximum Press
Ed: Susan Sweeney. **Released:** June 2006. **Price:** $29.95. **Description:** Guide for starting and growing an Internet business; information for developing a business plan, risk levels, and promotional techniques are included.

33413 ■ **"Automatic Riches"** in *Small Business Opportunities* (Vol. 13, No. 6, November 2001, pp. 66, 68)
Pub: Harris Publications, Inc.
Ed: Ken Mueller. **Description:** Profile of Toby McAdams, a former car salesman, who constructed a Web site to sell used vehicles. Mr. McAdams shares tips for targeting your niche on the Web.

33414 ■ **"Balancing the Books - by the Book"** in *Business Week Online* (February 4, 2002)
Pub: McGraw-Hill, Inc.
Description: Small business accounting practice and procedures for entrepreneurs are discussed, including the use of software such as QuickBooks and Peachtree.

33415 ■ *The Best Internet Businesses You Can Start*
Pub: Adams Media Corp.
Ed: Marian Betancourt. **Released:** 1999.

33416 ■ **"Booking the future"** in *Washington Business Journal* (Vol. 18, No. 44, March 3, 2000, pp. 30)
Pub: American City Business Journals, Inc.
Ed: Matthew Swibel. **Description:** Anyone can publish almost anything with Arlington-based eBranded-Books.com, a young company in the publishing industry. A company profile is included.

33417 ■ **"Bright Idea Takes Off"** in *Small Business Opportunities* (Vol. 16, No. 3, May 2004, pp. 70)
Pub: Harris Publications, Inc.
Ed: Chuck Green. **Description:** Profile of Philip Bonello, president and CEO of Top Bulb, an firm selling light bulbs online, with revenue of $8 million per year. Bonello says the company discouraged online sales, which now make up 40 percent of overall customer base.

33418 ■ **"Building on success"** in *Black Enterprise* (Vol. 32, No. 9, April 2002, pp. 70)
Pub: Earl Graves Publishing Co.
Ed: Carolyn M. Brown. **Description:** Profile of Freedie Lee and Yolanda Sherman and their business and Website, Illustrationsnetwork.com, that will showcase the artwork of minority artists and photographers to big corporations. Financial advice is offered to help the couple sustain their new business in the future and through their retirement by investing wisely.

33419 ■ **"Business Services"** in *PC Computing* (March 2000, pp. 159)
Pub: Ziff-Davis Inc.
Ed: Gordon Bass. **Description:** A profile of Smartonline.com, a virtual business center accessible from any browser. The site offers all the legal forms necessary to start and run a business, a complete reference suite, a business dictionary, exchange rates, driving directions, market research databases, and a calendar and contact manager.

33420 ■ **"Coaching Companies"** in *Black Enterprise* (Vol. 31, No. 2, September 2000, pp. 56)
Pub: Earl Graves Publishing Co.
Ed: Gerda Gallop-Goodman. **Description:** Suggestions for books, articles, and online assistance designed to coach small business owners and entrepreneurs on presenting their ideas and products to large retail companies.

33421 ■ **"Coffee mates"** in *Boston Business Journal* (Vol. 22, No. 3)
Pub: MCP, Inc.
Ed: Jill Lerner. **Description:** Profile of lonely man turned entrepreneur, who uses his aunt's advice to start his own online dating service.

33422 ■ *Complete Idiot's Guide to Starting an Ebay Business*
Pub: Penguin Books (USA) Incorporated
Ed: Barbara Weltman, Kara Gordon, Shirley Muse. **Released:** February 2005. **Price:** $19.95 (US), $29.00 (Canadian). **Description:** Guide for starting an eBay business includes information on products to sell, how to price merchandise, and details for working with services like PayPal, and how to organize fulfillment services.

33423 ■ *The Complete Small Business Start-up Guide*
Pub: John Wiley & Sons, Incorporated
Ed: Lisa Rogak. **Released:** November 2004. **Price:** $14.95. **Description:** Guide to starting a small company, focusing on development of a business plan, organizational structure, advertising, hiring, selection of suppliers, and using the Internet to market your firm.

33424 ■ **"Conversation with Randy Hinrichs"** in *Inc.* (November 15, 2000, pp. 83)
Pub: The Goldhirsh Group
Description: An intranet is no less than the foundation for a company's success. Advice to create powerful virtual spaces is offered by the author.

33425 ■ **"Culture Vultures Go Online"** in *Success* (Vol. 47, No. 2, June 2000, pp. 69)
Pub: Success Publishing, Inc.
Ed: Simeon Furman. **Description:** How a former cellist with no Internet experience is building an online ticketing market.

33426 ■ **"Daydream Believer"** in *My Business* (February/March 2003, pp. 52)
Pub: My Business Magazine
Ed: Jennifer Fuqua. **Description:** The online resource that assists entrepreneurs in their quest to

owning a business, USBX, is highlighted. USBX provides a forum to bring buyers and sellers of companies together.

33427 ■ **"Do This, Get Rich"** in *Business 2.0* (Vol. 6, May 2005, No. 4, pp. 78-86)
Pub: Time, Inc.
Ed: Michael V. Copeland, Om Malik, Erick Schonfeld. **Description:** Profiles of the eleven hottest business opportunities are presented, including computer upgrades, advertising on the Web, specialty baby furniture, professional medical employment services, interior design for hotels, Web-enabled subscription and service monitoring, search engines for podcasts, RFID tags to track drugs and supplies in hospitals, software to save energy in homes and businesses, software and hardware to monitor and control a boat's onboard systems.

33428 ■ **"Dot-Com Deathwatch"** in *Fortune* (Vol. 142, No. 3, July 24, 2000, pp. 48)
Pub: Time Inc.
Ed: Katrina Brooker. **Description:** Gloom was in the air at PC Expo in July 2000, because venture capitalists are not funding dot-com entrepreneurs as much as in the past.

33429 ■ **"Dot Com Fever Black-Oriented"** in *Black Enterprise* (Vol. 30, No. 8, March 2000, pp. 82)
Pub: Earl Graves Publishing Co.
Ed: Tariq K. Muhammad. **Description:** Websites are finally attracting capital. The key is in knowing how to get your share.

33430 ■ **"The downside of the upside of the downside: these days nothing succeeds like failure"** in *The New York Times Magazine* (Jan. 9, 2000)
Pub: The New York Times Company
Ed: Louis Menand. **Description:** Company failure in the Internet industry may be considered a badge of success because the downside of running a business has been experienced.

33431 ■ **"E-biz baffled"** in *Black Enterprise* (Vol. 32, No. 9, April 2002, pp. 48)
Pub: Earl Graves Publishing Co.
Ed: Alan Hughes. **Description:** Information is shared to successfully maintain an e-business, included is a listing of resources.

33432 ■ **"The e-changes are just beginning"** in *Hispanic Business* (Vol. 22, No. 6, June 2000, pp. 30)
Pub: Hispanic Business
Ed: Jorge Chapa. **Description:** Hispanic businesses are part of the Internet revolution, with most of them maintaining their own Web sites. Two areas where Hispanic entrepreneurs may have a competitive advantage are in the provision of services to the Hispanic population in the U.S. and connecting Hispanic Americans to their families and home countries.

33433 ■ **"E-Degree"** in *Entrepreneur* (Vol. 28, No. 1, January 2000, pp. 36)
Pub: Entrepreneur Media Inc.
Ed: Ellen Paris. **Description:** The world of e-commerce is exploding with opportunities, and universities are beginning to offer advanced degrees in cybercommerce.

33434 ■ **"eBay Fever"** in *Entrepreneur.com* (Vol. 34, February 2006, No. 2, pp. 114)
Pub: Entrepreneur Media Inc.
Ed: Janelle Elms. **Description:** About 724,000 individuals make a full-time or part-time living selling items on eBay. EBay items are selling at the rate of nearly $85,000 a minute. Entrepreneurs as well as established businesses are turning to the auction site to sell products.

33435 ■ **"Entrepreneurs"** in *Forbes* (February 28, 2000, pp. 74)
Pub: Forbes Magazine
Ed: Leigh Gallagher. **Description:** Web-based information services are targeting small business. By banding many small businesses together via the web, these portals offer services, prices and discounts that until recently were available only to much larger companies.

33436 ■ *Entrepreneurship with Online Learning Center Access Card*
Pub: McGraw-Hill Higher Education
Ed: Robert D. Hirich; Michael P. Peters; Dean A. Shepherd. **Released:** October 2006. **Price:** $103.25.
Description: Book instructs students on entrepreneurial processes that include starting a new business.

33437 ■ **"Fallen Idols"** in *Fortune* (Vol. 142, No. 10, October 30, 2000, pp. 108+)
Pub: Time Inc.
Ed: Melanie Warner. **Description:** Along the way people stopped seeing venture capitalists as just money guys. Once considered the gods of the new economy, venture capitalists heartily endorsed some of the most disastrous excesses of the dot-com age.

33438 ■ **"Find Your Partner"** in *Entrepreneur* (Vol. 28, No. 2, February 2000, pp. 72)
Pub: Entrepreneur Media Inc.
Ed: Robert McGarvey. **Description:** When industry giants and dot.coms come together, it's profits that fly round and round.

33439 ■ **"Flip Flipowski"** in *Internet World* (Vol. 6, No. 13, July 1, 2000, pp. 60)
Pub: Mecklermedia Corporation
Ed: Elizabeth Gardner. **Description:** A profile of Divine Interventures and CEO Andrew 'Flip' Flipowski, who aims to strengthen the reputation of Chicago in the Internet start-up world and move the Midwest into the New Economy. Flipowski, believing that traditional businesses have missed enormous opportunities on the Internet and emphasizing the business-to-business market, has already backed more than a dozen industry-specific online exchanges.

33440 ■ **"Get 'em while they're hot"** in *Entrepreneur* (Vol. 30, No. 12, December 2002, pp. 85)
Pub: Entrepreneur Media Inc.
Ed: Steve Cooper, Mark Henricks, Gisela M. Pedroza, April Y. Pennington, Chris Penttila, Chris Sandlund, Devlin Smith, Nichole L. Torres. **Description:** The hottest business opportunities for entrepreneurs in 2003 are listed, including online learning, outsourcing, home entertainment installation, health care technology, medi-spas, Instant Messaging-related services and products, sleep-related products, singles-related products and services, yoga studios, food supplements, online gaming, bankruptcy services, pet accessories, security, large-size clothing, online auction aftermarket services, scheduling software, and specialty ice cream shops.

33441 ■ **"Getrich.com: Join America's Newest Gold Rush"** in *Small Business Opportunities* (Vol. 12, No. 3, May 2000, pp. 22-24, 26, 28, 30, 32)
Pub: Harris Publications, Inc.
Description: An E-commerce crash course is offered. The fifteen steps needed to launch a global online venture are outlined.

33442 ■ **"Getting started on the Web"** in *Hispanic Business* (Vol. 22, No. 5, May 2000, pp. 98)
Pub: Hispanic Business
Ed: Roger Harris. **Description:** Small businesses wishing to establish a Web site must ensure that they find a site developer who really understands their requirements. It is also worth considering using pre-packaged site-builder software.

33443 ■ **"Going Digital"** in *Hispanic Business* (July-August 2000, pp. 76)
Pub: Hispanic Business
Ed: Nicole Lewis. **Description:** The successful use of electronic commerce by small companies is explored.

33444 ■ **"Going Places"** in *Success* (Vol. 47, No. 6, November 2000, pp. 38)
Pub: Success Publishing, Inc.
Ed: Debbie Selinsky. **Description:** Profile of Michael Thomas, the multilingual CEO and president of OneTravel.com who believes some of the best ideas are those that people won't see right away.

33445 ■ **"Homebased Moneymakers"** in *Small Business Opportunities* (Vol. 12, No. 5, September 2000, pp. 74, 76)
Pub: Harris Publications, Inc.
Description: Ten quick and easy businesses that can be started from home for less than $100, including an inventory service, apartment preparation service, summer snack shop, plant watering service, messenger/fast errand service, bartender for private parties, framing service, online auction business, gardening consultant, and making scrapbooks for clients.

33446 ■ **"Homeless entrepreneurs swap shopping carts"** in *Red Herring* (No. 76, March 2000, pp. 58)
Pub: Herring Communications, Inc.
Ed: Peter D. Henig. **Description:** The issue of homeless persons using the Internet at public libraries and shelters is discussed, including the success stories of homeless people successfully launching their own Web sites.

33447 ■ *How to Start a Home-Based Mail Order Business*
Pub: Globe Pequot Press
Ed: Georganne Fiumara. **Released:** January 2005.
Price: $17.95. **Description:** Step-by-step guide for starting and growing a home-based mail order business. Information about equipment, pricing, online marketing, are included along with worksheets and checklists for planning.

33448 ■ *How to Start a Home-Based Online Retail Business*
Pub: Globe Pequot Press
Ed: Jeremy Shepherd. **Released:** February 2007.
Price: $18.95. **Description:** Information for starting an online retail, home-based business is shared.

33449 ■ *How to Start an Internet Sales Business*
Pub: Lulu.com
Ed: Dan Davis. **Released:** August 2005. **Price:** $19.95. **Description:** Small business guide for launching an Internet sales company. Topics include business structure, licenses, and taxes.

33450 ■ **"Howdy, Partner"** in *Entrepreneur* (Vol. 32, October 2004, No. 10, pp. 104)
Pub: Entrepreneur Media Inc.
Ed: Nichole L. Torres. **Description:** When considering a virtual partnership with an entrepreneur met over the Internet, one must communicate, check references and histories, and establish set duties in writing.

33451 ■ **"I Bought It Through the Grapevine"** in *Success* (Vol. 47, No. 4, September 2000, pp. 4)
Pub: Success Publishing, Inc.
Ed: Carren Louise Bersch. **Description:** Uncorking a passion for wine leads to a world-class website.

33452 ■ **"If I Had an E-Hammer"** in *Success* (Vol. 47, No. 3, July 2000, pp. 24)
Pub: Success Publishing, Inc.
Description: A profile of Peter Hunt, president and COO of CornerHardware.com, an online hardware store based in San Francisco, California.

33453 ■ **"Info Overload"** in *Small Business Opportunities* (Vol. 13, No. 6, November 2001, pp. 82)
Pub: Harris Publications, Inc.
Description: Profile of the Internet-based customized news, information and alerting delivery service that is ready to launch a new wireless application.

33454 ■ **"Instantly International"** in *Inc.* (Volume 27, June 2005, No. 6, pp. 44)
Pub: Inc. Magazine
Ed: Darren Dahl. **Description:** Profile of John Buckman, owner of an email list-management company in Berkeley, California. Buckman also launched Magnatune.com, a global online music label. The entrepreneur started Magnatune.com after his wife, a composer of electronic music, had been dropped from her music label.

33455 ■ **"La Habra, Calif., Resident Builds Needlework Empire"** in *Orange County Register* (February 12, 2001)
Pub: Knight-Ridder/Tribune Business News
Ed: Jan Norman. **Description:** Profile of Candamar Designs, maker of art needlework, including cross-stitch, needlepoint and embroidery kits, both retail and through mail order catalogs and the Internet. Candi Martin began her business venture as a means to stay home with her three daughters.

33456 ■ **"The Leap: A Memoir of Love and Madness in the Internet Gold Rush"** in *Harvard Business Review* (Vol. 78, No. 4, July 2000, pp. 152)
Pub: Harvard Business School Publishing Corp.
Ed: John T. Landry. **Description:** Tom Ashbrook, a former foreign correspondent at the Boston Globe, discusses the history of Internet start-up companies. He focuses on the period before the onset of venture capital firms.

33457 ■ **"Making Ideas Fly"** in *Internet World* (Vol. 6, No. 12, June 15, 2000, pp. 31)
Pub: Mecklermedia Corporation
Ed: David Lipschultz. **Description:** Despite some setbacks, dot-com companies continue to pop up. Sometimes a start-up company would do well to go with a business incubator. These incubators can offer all manner of services from business to Web site development, but often take a large part of the company. Some start-ups work with venture capital companies who are eager to invest in Internet companies.

33458 ■ **"Making a Success of Failure"** in *Success* (Vol. 47, No. 4, September 2000, pp. 58)
Pub: Success Publishing, Inc.
Description: Nicholas Hall has had more comebacks than George Foreman. After his first three startups failed, the 30-year-old entrepreneur kept getting back into the ring. His latest creation, startupfailures.com, has been a cult hit.

33459 ■ **"Making waves"** in *San Francisco Business Times* (Vol. 16, No. 43)
Pub: San Francisco Business Times Inc.
Ed: Petra Pasternack. **Description:** Profile of Daniel Ko, founder of QIXO Inc., a travel search engine, the first such site to search all travel sites to find lowest fares.

33460 ■ "Master of your domain" in *WorkingWoman* (Vol. 25, No. 4, April 2000, pp. 54)
Pub: Lang Communications Inc.
Ed: Parry Aftab. Description: Legal advice for setting up a web site on the Internet and choosing and registering a domain name is explained.

33461 ■ "Mental health software company gets boost" in *Crain's Detroit Business* (Vol. 15, No. 49, December 6, 1999, pp. 45)
Pub: Crain Communications, Inc.
Ed: Matt Roush. Description: A year-old Ann Arbor, Michigan company that uses the Internet to deliver case-management software for mental health care received $5.1 million in venture capital financing.

33462 ■ "The Merchant of Bay Ridge" in *Forbes* (Vol. 174, December 27, 2004, No. 13, pp. 80)
Pub: Forbes Magazine Inc.
Ed: Phyllis Berman. Description: Profile of Joseph Cohen, the 17-year-old entrepreneur who developed a thriving online retail business called Bay Ridge.

33463 ■ "The Messenger" in *Black Enterprise* (Vol. 30, No. 12, July 2000, pp. 55)
Pub: Earl Graves Publishing Co.
Ed: Rebecca Rohan. Description: Build your customer base with an electric newsletter.

33464 ■ "My Short, Unhappy Life as an E-Tailer" in *Fortune* (Vol. 140, No. 11, December 6, 1999, pp. 313+)
Pub: Time Inc.
Ed: Jerry Useem. Description: A Fortune writer aims to become an Internet mogul, instead he ends up with $4.61 and a few pairs of tube socks.

33465 ■ "New Small Business Web Sites have Great Potential" in *Inc.* (April 2000, pp. 13)
Pub: The Goldhirsh Group
Description: Web sites designed to provide one-stop service for small business owners and managers offer three major benefits heretofore unavailable from any single source: Content on demand, Aggregation, Applications. The question is, how well do they deliver?

33466 ■ "The Nirve of These Guys" in *Success* (Vol. 47, No. 6, November 2000, pp. 20)
Pub: Success Publishing, Inc.
Ed: Simeon Furman. Description: Company profile of the Los Angeles-based startup Nirve, which produces and sells high-performance bikes, skateboards, snowboards, surfboards, and inline skates, along with cool clothing all under a single brand. Nirve is the only action sports company to distribute exclusively online, B2C and B2B.

33467 ■ "No Pain, All Gain" in *Success* (Vol. 47, No. 3, July 2000, pp. 24)
Pub: Success Publishing, Inc.
Description: It sounds ideal for Web commerce: a $15 billion small-business market that needs a variety of products from a variety of suppliers, but has limited time for ordering. Anesthesiologist, Dave Mayer, studying the market while working at Abbot Laboratories, came up with an idea to create an Amazon-style website that would make ordering medical supplies easy.

33468 ■ "No-Work Wonders" in *Small Business Opportunities* (Vol. 16, No. 2, March 2004, pp. 140)
Pub: Harris Publications, Inc.
Description: Online businesses that require only part time hours are listed, including online affiliation businesses. Review of Joseph T. Sinclair's book, eBay Business the Smart Way: Maximize Your Profits on the Web's No. 1 Auction Site. The book presents a comprehensive strategy and tips for selling on eBay as a full time enterprise.

33469 ■ "Nothing to Sneeze At" in *Success* (Vol. 47, No. 2, June 2000, pp. 58)
Pub: Success Publishing, Inc.

Ed: Simeon Furman, Michael S. Foley. Description: Profile of Soon-Chart Yu, founder and CEO of gazoontite.com, who carved his niche to capitalize on a $30 billion market.

33470 ■ "Office Search Engine" in *Success* (Vol. 47, No. 1, January 2000, pp. 23)
Pub: Success Publishing, Inc.
Ed: David Carnoy. Description: Offices2share.com finds corporate space for start-ups.

33471 ■ "On the Edge" in *Harvard Business Review* (Vol. 78, No. 3, May 2000, pp. 118)
Pub: Harvard Business School Publishing Corp.
Ed: Nicholas G. Carr. Description: An interview with Akamai's George Conrades, leader of the two year old Internet start-up with a multibillion dollar market.

33472 ■ "On the Internet Nobody Knows You're Not a VC" in *Red Herring* (No. 75, February 2000, pp. 148-150, 152, 154, 156, 158)
Pub: Herring Communications, Inc.
Ed: Dan Brekke. Description: Suddenly, the more desperate entrepreneurs are flocking to the new online venture capital firms. The article tells who these firms are, and who is behind their Web sites.

33473 ■ "One to Watch: Alpiri hopes to win the name game in e-commerce" in *Red Herring* (No. 105, October 1, 2001, pp. 26)
Pub: Herring Communications
Ed: Michael Fitzgerald. Description: Profile of Rob McCool and R.V. Guha, cofounders of Alpiri, a startup promising easier interaction among e-commerce programs based on Extensible Markup Language (XML), thus simplifying Web transactions.

33474 ■ "Online In A Flash" in *Small Business Opportunities* (Vol. 13, No. 5, September 2001, pp. 12, 130)
Pub: Harris Publications, Inc.
Ed: A. Michael Salim. Description: Five easy steps to start an online business are outlined.

33475 ■ "Online Moneymakers" in *Small Business Opportunities* (Vol. 16, No. 3, May 2004, pp. 102, 110, 120)
Pub: Harris Publications, Inc.
Description: Information to start an e-commerce business is shared, as well as 25 ideas for online businesses that can be started immediately.

33476 ■ "Our Kinda Town" in *Entrepreneur* (Vol. 28, No. 1, January 2000, pp. 26)
Pub: Entrepreneur Media Inc.
Ed: Robert McGarvey. Description: Information resources for entrepreneurs.

33477 ■ "Patent Chutzpah" in *Forbes* (November 13, 2000, pp. 58)
Pub: Forbes Magazine
Ed: Krysten A. Crawford. Description: An Example of the ways dubious patents for ideas, rather than a physical invention, are being deployed to extract ransom from companies.

33478 ■ "Pikesville-Based SafeDate and Dating Service Industry as a Whole Experiencing Growth" in *Daily Record* (July 18, 2003)
Pub: Dolan Media Newswires
Ed: Andrea Cecil. Description: Profiles of various dating services, including SafeDate and eHarmony.

33479 ■ "Podcast Startups Look Doomed from the Start" in *Venture Capital Journal* (October 1, 2005)
Pub: Thomason Financial Inc.
Description: Podcast service allows the user to get automatic updates of Website audio content and can listen to it on an iPod or other MP3 player. Problems being faced by Podcast startups are discussed.

33480 ■ "Read Smart, Grow Smart" in *Fast Company* (May 2001, pp. 202)
Pub: Fast Company
Ed: Christine Canabou. Description: Important information regarding data security and e-commerce to keep small business safe, is explored.

33481 ■ "Reality Check: Even the Best Execs Can Blow It When They Lose Tough" in *Entrepreneur* (Vol. 31, No. 8, August 2003, pp. 25)
Pub: Entrepreneur Media, Inc.
Ed: Mark Henricks. Description: Review of the book, "Why Smart Executives Fail", written by Sydney Finkelstein is presented. The author, a Dartmouth College professor, and his students studied over 50 commercial business failures and cite what went wrong to cause each company's demise.

33482 ■ "The Right Recipe: Successful E-Commerce Sites have Three Essential Ingredients in Common" in *Hispanic Business* (July-Aug.2000, pp.72)
Pub: Hispanic Business
Ed: Roger Harris. Description: The three essential ingredients for successfully launching a business online are integration, scalability, and flexibility. Tips on how to take advantage of the new technology are presented.

33483 ■ "Roberts' Internet venture to set up shop in Detroit" in *Crain's Detroit Business* (Vol. 16, No. 16, April 17, 2000, pp. 34)
Pub: Crain Communications, Inc.
Ed: Matt Roush. Description: Profile of Roy Roberts telling how he will move his new minority-vendor Internet trade exchange to downtown Detroit.

33484 ■ "Saga of an online pioneer" in *The New York Times* (March 3, 2000, pp. A25, A21)
Pub: The New York Times Company
Ed: Thomas L. Friedman. Description: Lessons learned from the demise of Positively-You.com, an e-business.

**33485 ■ *Scrapbooking for Profit: Cashing in on Retail, Home-Based and Internet Opportunities*
Pub: Allworth Press
Ed: Rebecca Pittman. Released: June 2005. Price: $19.95 (US), $22.95 (Canadian). Description: Eleven strategies for starting a scrapbooking business, including brick-and-mortar stores, home-based businesses, and online retail and wholesale outlets.

33486 ■ "Second Time Around" in *Entrepreneur* (Vol. 31, No. 7, July 2003, pp. 24)
Pub: Entrepreneur Media, Inc.
Ed: David Worrell. Description: Three Internet entrepreneurs are betting on Wireless startups and are bringing new ideas, perspectives and innovation to the industry.

33487 ■ "A secure net for agriculture" in *Hispanic Business* (Vol. 22, No. 10, October 2000, pp. 94)
Pub: Hispanic Business
Ed: A. Rojas. Description: The development of business-to-business markets within the agriculture industry is discussed. The successful launch of FoodTrader.com, which offers a global market place for food producers and buyers, is examined.

33488 ■ "Setting Up Shop" in *Black Enterprise* (Vol. 35, February 2005, No. 7, pp. 60)
Pub: Earl G. Graves Publishing Co. Inc.
Ed: James C. Johnson. Description: Advice for setting up a Website is offered to a business startup wishing to market and sell urban apparel via the Internet.

33489 ■ "Shoestring Start-Ups" in *Small Business Opportunities* (Vol. 16, November 2004, No. 6, pp. 22, 24, 26, 28, 30-32, 34, 36, 38, 40)
Pub: Harris Publications Inc.
Description: Fifty businesses that can be started for less than $500 are presented, including selling personalized products, event planning, flea markets, advertising, watches, Web site designer, home delivery service, mail order, lawn and landscape services, windshield repair, meal delivery, handmade bunk

beds, party lawn signs, computer repair, cruise travel, window washing, lingerie, online discount stores, pet sitting, ramps, security products, sunglasses, moving services, holiday decorating, birthday packages, errand service, online auctions, information broker, personal trainer, mortgage programs, and more.

33490 ■ "Sky Dayton" in *Internet World* **(Vol. 6, No. 7, April 1, 2000, pp. 94)**
Pub: Mecklermedia Corporation
Ed: Brian Caulfield. **Description:** EarthLink Network founder Sky Dayton plans to launch more new Web-based businesses, now that EarthLink has merged with rival MindSpring. Jake Winebaum's and Dayton's eCompanies, a business incubator for new Web companies, generates efficient Web start-ups within 180 days, including funding. Dayton looks for companies that blend commerce, community, and content.

33491 ■ "Small But Special" in *Entrepreneur* **(Vol. 28, No. 9, September 2000, pp. 170)**
Pub: Entrepreneur Media Inc.
Ed: Paul Edwards and Sarah Edwards. **Description:** The editors tell how a new company can compete in the online book market.

33492 ■ "Special Delivery" in *My Business* **(February/March 2003, pp. 54)**
Pub: My Business Magazine
Ed: Shannon Scully. **Description:** Profile of Dana Roy, who launched MaternitySolutions.com, an online catalog company specializing in upscale career and special occasion apparel for pregnant women.

33493 ■ *Start Your Own Business on eBay,* **2nd Edition**
Pub: Entrepreneur Press
Ed: Jacquelyn Lynn. **Released:** May 2007. **Price:** $19.95. **Description:** Tips for starring a new online business on eBay are shared.

33494 ■ *Starting a Yahoo! Business for Dummies*
Pub: John Wiley & Sons, Incorporated
Ed: Rob Snell. **Released:** June 2006. **Price:** $24.99. **Description:** Rob Snell offers advice for turning online browsers into buyers, increase online traffic, and build an online store from scratch.

33495 ■ "A Talk With the Net's Financiers" in *Internet World* **(Vol. 6, No. 6, March 15, 2000, pp. 60)**
Pub: Mecklermedia Corporation
Ed: David Lipschultz. **Description:** An interview with five leading venture capitalists to answer questions on the state of the Internet revolution. Questions are related to topics such as the types of businesses that venture capitalists are looking for and the possibility of emergence of another Yahoo or Cisco. The venture capitalists were also asked about the importance of the CEO in a company and predictions regarding when the Internet explosion was likely to end.

33496 ■ "Wanted" in *Black Enterprise* **(Vol. 32, No. 6, January 2002, pp. 3)**
Pub: Earl Graves Publishing Co.
Ed: Bridget McCrea. **Description:** Profile of David Vinson's company, Optate Inc, a Michigan-based online employee-relationship management firm. Vinson explains how his approach to staffing paid off when it came time to seek financing.

33497 ■ "Web-based publisher books investment from local sources" in *Kansas City Business Journal* **(Vol. 18, No. 22, February 4, 2000, pp. 6)**
Pub: American City Business Journals, Inc.
Ed: Suzanne King. **Description:** A profile of Kansas City-based BizSpace Inc., an Internet publishing company.

33498 ■ "Web Sites Help Small Companies Open Internet Stores" in *Wall Street Journal* **(April 25, 2000, pp. B2)**
Pub: Dow Jones & Co., Inc.
Ed: Jeffrey A. Tannenbaum. **Description:** E-business sites like Bigstep.com and BizLand.com, offering inexpensive e-business services, are profiled.

33499 ■ "Web.Preneuring" in *Small Business Opportunities* **(Vol. 13, No. 5, September 2001, pp. 46, 48)**
Pub: Harris Publications, Inc.
Description: Profile of Mike Moran, Chris Karl, and Ryan Moran, who launched their online business, Carepackages.com, which enables anyone to send creative gift packages with clever, customized themes.

33500 ■ "When It's Time to Market that Matters Most" in *Inc.* **(July 2000, pp. 92)**
Pub: The Goldhirsh Group
Ed: Thea Singer. **Description:** Business incubators for Internet start-ups are examined.

33501 ■ "Who let the blogs out? Blogging has become one of the hottest Web trends." in *Entrepreneur* **(Vol. 30, No. 10, October 2002, pp. 35)**
Pub: Entrepreneur Media Inc.
Ed: Amanda C. Kooser. **Description:** A blog is a frequently updated, timed and dated online journal with links involved. Blogs are a good resource for entrepreneurs to promote a business and to get other people to work with you on your business.

33502 ■ "Your Retail Riches" in *Small Business Opportunities* **(Winter 2005)**
Pub: Harris Publications Inc.
Description: Pricester.com offers affordable, easily implemented solutions for those wishing to start an online retail Website. Pricester acts as a complete online trading community and will facilitate barter transactions, auctions, and reverse auctions.

ASSOCIATIONS AND OTHER ORGANIZATIONS

33503 ■ Internet Alliance
1111 19th St. NW, Ste. 1100
Washington, DC 20035-5782
Ph:(202)861-2476
Co. E-mail: info@internetalliance.org
URL: http://www.internetalliance.org
Contact: Emily T. Hackett, Exec. Dir.
Membership: Companies offering Internet services.
Purpose: Seeks to "build the confidence and trust necessary for the Internet to become the global mass market medium of the 21st century". Represents members' commercial and regulatory interests; conducts promotional activities; facilitates communication and cooperation among members. **Publications:** *CyberBrief* (daily). **Telecommunication Services:** electronic mail, emilyh@internetalliance.org.

REFERENCE WORKS

33504 ■ "5 Tips to Make Your Web Site Work" in *My Business* **(December/January 2004, pp. 45)**
Pub: My Business Magazine
Ed: Lena Basha. **Description:** Tips to make a Web site more effective are listed. It is important to be able to find facts quickly and easily and to keep information current. Customers using dialup Internet services do not like to be slowed by unnecessary images on a Web site.

33505 ■ "6 Secrets of eBay Sales Success" in *My Business* **(December/January 2004, pp. 46)**
Pub: My Business Magazine
Ed: Kate Westbrook. **Description:** Small business owners are finding success selling products and services using eBay. Six tips to help a small business use eBay are provided.

33506 ■ *202 Things You Can Make and Sell for Big Profits*
Pub: Entrepreneur Press
Ed: James Stephenson. **Released:** September 2005. **Price:** $19.95. **Description:** Instructions for 202 products that can be made and sold over the Internet.

33507 ■ "A9.COM" in *Entrepreneur* **(Vol. 33, October 2005, No. 10, pp. 6)**
Pub: Entrepreneur Media Inc.
Ed: Steve Cooper. **Description:** Amazon.com's new subsidiary, A9.com, features Yellow Pages with click-to-call, customer reviews, recommendations and the ability to view images of a queried storefront. It also allows content providers the ability to publish search results for syndication as well as local, wikipedia, reference and book searches.

33508 ■ "About this index" in *Crain's Detroit Business* **(Vol. 18, No. 23, June 10, 2002, pp. E-14)**
Pub: Crain Communications Inc. - Detroit
Description: A directory of Web sites of companies, associations, nonprofits that provide assistance is presented.

33509 ■ "About Penny Stocks" in *Black Enterprise* **(Vol. 34, No. 4, November 2003, pp. 40)**
Pub: Earl Graves Publishing Co.
Ed: Matthew S. Scott. **Description:** Information about penny stocks, which are often small, early-stage, unknown companies trading at less than $1 per share, is presented. Websites offering investor information, market statistics, and company profiles are also included.

33510 ■ "Access Corporate Data on Your Wireless Phone" in *E-business Advisor* **(Vol. 18, No. 3, March 2000, pp. 16)**
Pub: Advisor Media, Inc.
Ed: Phillip Redman. **Description:** Decreasing costs, improved mobile devices and computer-telephone integration are spurring the use of wireless computing. Wireless networks are starting to offer data access as well as voice communications. High-speed wireless networks are expected to top 384-kbps performance by 2002-2004. Standards for operating systems and transmission protocols are needed for the development of tools and applications for both business and consumers. Wireless-enabled middleware will enable hardware and software to support mobile devices for e-mail, database and Internet access.

33511 ■ "Active.com Helps You Just Do It" in *Business Week Online* **(April 22, 2002)**
Pub: McGraw-Hill, Inc.
Description: Profile of Active.com Web site that offers sports and fitness event registration, fitness advice, nutritional and health advice, Web pages built by sports teams posting schedules, and sites for shopping for shoes and equipment.

33512 ■ "AcutionASAP: Another eBay But Without All the Hassles" in *Long Island Business News* **(April 2, 2004)**
Pub: Dolan Media Newswires
Ed: Adina Genn. **Description:** Profile of Jeff Nortman, who launched AuctionASAP, an eBay store in Plainview, New York. Nortman's customers drop goods off at his warehouse or Nortman picks the items up at the client's home or office, cleans the items up, packs and ships them. AuctionASAP sends the client a check as soon as the item is sold. Fees range 15-30 percent of final selling price.

33513 ■ "Ad Companies Probe Potential of Blog World" in *Chicago Tribune* **(February 22, 2005)**
Pub: Knight-Ridder/Tribune Business News
Ed: Mike Hughlett. **Description:** The blog world's potential as an avenue for advertising is investigated. Blogs can provide a resource to a targeted audience.

33514 ■ "Adapt or die: surviving the government's digital push" in *Black Enterprise* **(Vol. 33, No. 6, January 2003, pp. 42)**
Pub: Earl Graves Publishing Co.
Ed: Rebecca Rohan. **Description:** The economic survival of black-owned businesses depends on their knowledge of using technology. In the government's move towards a paperless operation, African American businesses must learn how to take advantage of the new opportunities that technology brings.

33515 ■ "Adcomparator" in *Entrepreneur. com* **(Vol. 34, January 2006, No. 1, pp. 6)**
Pub: Entrepreneur Media Inc.
Ed: Steve Cooper. **Description:** Free ad comparisons are offered by Adcomparator's Website, which allows users to test up to 15 aspects of advertising.

33516 ■ "Add An 'Inc' And Get Some Respect" in *Home Office Computing* **(Vol. 19, No. 1, January 2001, pp. 24)**
Pub: Scholastic Inc.
Ed: Jon Halpin. **Description:** The article discusses the fact that more small businesses are incorporating. Profiles of online incorporation services are provided.

33517 ■ "Advisor Answers" in *E-business Advisor* **(Vol. 18, No. 4, April 2000, pp. 42)**
Pub: Advisor Media, Inc.
Ed: Michael Cobb. **Description:** Information regarding denial-of-service (DOS) attacks, a major concern as much-publicized events are creating major headlines, is covered. These attacks involve overloading a Web site with bogus requests, making it impossible to process legitimate requests.

33518 ■ "Advisor Tips" in *E-business Advisor* **(Vol. 18, No. 12, December 2000, pp. 52)**
Pub: Advisor Media, Inc.
Description: Return on investment (ROI) is a major concern in the design of a Web business portal. The impact of the portal's touchpoints on customers, business partners, investors and employees should be evaluated. Business objectives should be identified and the site should be designed with the customers' needs as a primary objective.

33519 ■ "Adwatcher" in *Entrepreneur.com* **(Vol. 34, February 2006, No. 2, pp. 6)**
Pub: Entrepreneur Media Inc.
Description: AdWatcher tracks advertising campaigns across Websites, monitors search engines, banners and newsletters.

33520 ■ "Affordable branding 101" in *E-business Advisor* **(Vol. 18, No. 10, October 2000, pp. 12)**
Pub: Advisor Media, Inc.
Description: NetMediaVC helps startups and established business-to-consumer and business-to-business e-businesses plan and pay for traditional media campaigns (radio, magazines, television, etc.). Clients contribute 70 percent of the funds required and NetMedia kicks in the other 30 percent for an equity stake in the company.

33521 ■ "Against the Grain" in *Fast Company* **(May 2001, pp. 201)**
Pub: Fast Company
Ed: Cathy Olofson. **Description:** Taking a diversified company to the Web is no easy task, but Monica Morse, a managing director of Cargill's Eventures team, believes that the agribusiness company has what it takes to move B2B to a profit.

33522 ■ "Agreement on Internet taxes eludes deeply divided commission" in *The New York Times* **(March 21, 2000, pp. C1)**
Pub: The New York Times Company
Ed: David Cay Johnston. **Description:** The U.S. commission appointed to advise Congress on Internet taxes may have no recommendations to report after a political split between committee factions. Eleven of the 19 Committee members, representing the business and anti-tax factions have sided with Chairman James S. Gilmore III, favoring a moratorium on Internet taxation until at least 2006. The Internet Tax Freedom Act, which brought the commission into being, calls for a majority vote of two-thirds, or 13 of the commission members.

33523 ■ "Air Raid" in *Entrepreneur* **(Vol. 32, No. 4, April 2004, pp. 39)**
Pub: Entrepreneur Media, Inc.
Ed: Eric Bender. **Description:** Internet security is discussed, with a listing of steps to protect small businesses.

33524 ■ "The All-in-One Market" in *Harvard Business Review* **(Vol. 78, No. 3, May 2000, pp. 19)**
Pub: Harvard Business School Publishing Corp.
Ed: Paul Nunes, Diane Wilson, Ajit Kambil. **Description:** This article discusses all-in-one markets. The author describes how several companies use various online transaction mechanisms in order to gain more business from existing customers and bring in new buyers.

33525 ■ "All in One" in *Entrepreneur* **(Vol. 32, No. 2, February 2004, pp. 44)**
Pub: Entrepreneur Media, Inc.
Ed: Gisela M. Pedroza. **Description:** Profile of Samsung's new SPH-i700 Windows-powered Pocket PC. The device allows the user to manage work with desktop applications and to communicate through voice, email and photo images.

33526 ■ "All Systems Go" in *Entrepreneur* **(Vol. 32, December 2004, No. 12, pp. 52)**
Pub: Entrepreneur Media Inc.
Ed: Melissa Campanelli. **Description:** Importance for e-tailers to integrate accounting, inventory and customer management back-end systems is stressed. This setup will enable your Website to become a focal point of contact with customers from tracking packages, reviewing past orders, and viewing sales quotes, answering FAQs and logging support calls.

33527 ■ "All the Web's a Stage" in *Business Week* **(December 11, 2000, pp. 16)**
Pub: McGraw-Hill, Inc.
Description: London's Heritage Theater plans to bring some of it's finest theatre presentations to your desktop computer.

33528 ■ "The 'Always On' Economy" in *Inc.* **(Volume 27, June 2005, No. 6, pp. 59-60)**
Pub: Inc. Magazine
Ed: David H. Freedman. **Description:** New communications systems are able to keep companies in contact with employees and customers 24/7.

33529 ■ "Ambulance Chasing, Web-Style" in *Forbes* **(Vol. 174, December 27, 2004, No. 13, pp. 56)**
Pub: Forbes Magazine Inc.
Ed: David Whelan. **Description:** Law firms are paying large sums to place pay-per-click ads on Internet sites. The ads take the user to a law firm's Web site or a middleman, and a lawyer pays up to $160 to the Internet service provider.

33530 ■ "Amid Customer Backlash, eBay Reduces Some Fees" in *eWeek* **(February 7, 2005)**
Pub: Ziff Davis Media Inc.
Description: Online auction eBay has reduced some of its fees in response to customer complaints of price hikes imposed in January 2005.

33531 ■ "AMTDA members can self-update info online" in *Tooling & Production* **(Vol. 69, No. 1, January 2003, pp. 10)**
Pub: Nelson Publishing, Inc.
Description: The American Machine Tool Distributors' Association has selected Techspex to implement an Internet-based data entry platform for the collection and maintenance of the association's membership directory information, and publication of the annual directory.

33532 ■ "An Attractive Site" in *Black Enterprise* **(Vol. 36, November 2005, No. 4, pp. 74)**
Pub: Earl G. Graves Publishing Co. Inc.
Ed: James C. Johnson. **Description:** Tips to help a Website network with African American professionals and manage the costs associated with advertising on the site are listed.

33533 ■ "Analyze this: from "automation" to "effectiveness"" in *E-business Advisor* **(Vol. 18, No. 10, October 2000, pp. 10)**
Pub: Advisor Media, Inc.

Description: The market for analytics is rapidly expanding. The catch is that companies don't just need to identify who their customers are, they need to better figure out what customers do and why they do it.

33534 ■ "Analyze This" in *Entrepreneur.com* **(Vol. 34, February 2006, No. 2, pp. 42)**
Pub: Entrepreneur Media Inc.
Description: ClickTracks provides analysis of Web sites to be sure a company is getting the most from their Web traffic.

33535 ■ "The Anywhere Office" in *PC Computing* **(March 2000, pp. 146)**
Pub: Ziff-Davis Inc.
Ed: Jason Compton. **Description:** The article shows how to set up a virtual office.

33536 ■ "AOL woos small businesses with e-comm plan " in *Network World* **(September 18, 2000, pp. 12)**
Pub: Network World Inc.
Ed: Ellen Messmer. **Description:** A profile of AOL's new Netbusiness that helps small businesses start e-commerce sites.

33537 ■ "Application Integration for Real-Time B2B" in *E-business Advisor* **(Vol. 18, No. 9, September 2000, pp. 20)**
Pub: Advisor Media, Inc.
Ed: David S. Linthicum. **Description:** Business-to-business (B2B) application integration, an extension of enterprise application integration, is the unrestricted sharing of data and business processes among any connected applications and data sources, inside or outside the company. B2B application integration enables outside trading partners to access accurate information on demand.

33538 ■ "Application Service Providers on the Move" in *E-business Advisor* **(Vol. 17, No. 12, December 1999, pp. 18)**
Pub: Advisor Media, Inc.
Ed: Phillip Redman. **Description:** Application service providers (ASPs) are expanding services to mobile users, offering remote backup and data synchronization, as well as access to enterprise applications. In addition, ASPs are now offering unified messaging, with fax, e-mail and voice messaging on one number. ASPs must redesign their billing procedures, which typically charge by seats served, like standard software licenses.

33539 ■ "Apply Yourself" in *Entrepreneur* **(Vol. 32, October 2004, No. 10, pp. 98)**
Pub: Entrepreneur Media Inc.
Ed: Chris Penttila. **Description:** Three criteria used to define an online applicant for employers hiring via the Internet were set by the Department of Labor, the Equal Employment Opportunity Commission and other federal agencies. First, an employer must be filling a particular position, the online applicant must follow the employer's process when applying, and the online applicant must indicate interest in a specific position within the company.

33540 ■ "Are Portals Just Another Integration Problem?" in *E-business Advisor* **(Vol. 18, No. 7, July 2000, pp. 40)**
Pub: Advisor Media, Inc.
Ed: Rik Drummund. **Description:** While portals, or e-marketplaces, expand relationships with trading partners, no single integration standard has been defined. The standard that is being proposed is ebXML. With ebXML, implementing worldwide e-commerce can be done cost-effectively; with no standard, the amount of work is 500 times greater.

33541 ■ "Are the Tax-Free Net's Days Numbered?" in *Home Office Computing* **(Vol. 18, No. 7, July 2000, pp. 16)**
Pub: Scholastic Inc.
Ed: Jeffery D. Zbar. **Description:** With the three-year moratorium on Web taxes set to expire in October 2001, the federally appointed Advisory Commission on Electronic Commerce (ACEC) has submitted recommendations designed to kill or slow adoption of new taxes. That means dot-coms would be exempt from charging sales taxes, while traditional retailers would still be required to charge sales taxes.

33542 ■ "Arris trades road shows for online presentations" in *Atlanta Business Chronicle* (Vol. 25, No. 19, October 18, 2002, pp. 8B)
Pub: American City Business Publications, Inc.
Ed: Lee Hall. Description: Arris Group Inc., in Duluth, Georgia, has shifted most of its employee benefits education efforts onto the Internet, and away from putting its executives on the road. Initially intended to save the company money, the program also proved to be very effective and more popular with employees who found that they did not need to attend meetings. In addition, the program has encouraged employees to participate, due to the confidentiality afforded by the program.

33543 ■ "The art of Web selling: company finds a smart way to boost sales" in *Black Enterprise* (Vol. 33, No. 6, January 2003, pp. 41)
Pub: Earl Graves Publishing Co.
Ed: Rebecca Rohan. Description: Business owner, Glenn King, Exotica Art & Fashion, has found a unique way to sell imported art and artifacts using online auctions.

33544 ■ "As Web sites seek an attractive mix of content, a new type of business is providing the right stuff"in *The New York Times*(Sept25,2000)
Pub: The New York Times Company
Ed: Bob Tedeschi. Description: A discussion involving companies selling syndicated Web content to new sites.

33545 ■ "Assemble Your E-Business Team" in *E-business Advisor* (Vol. 17, No. 12, December 1999, pp. 30)
Pub: Advisor Media, Inc.
Ed: Zachary W. Esper. Description: Electronic business projects must be carefully staffed and managed. Traditional project structures work well, consisting of steering committee, project leader and supporting management team. Business-to-business projects can be led by operations or procurement managers. MIS managers, who traditionally maintain corporate Web sites, make good leaders for non-transactional Internet projects.

33546 ■ "At Deadline" in *Crain's New York Business* (Vol. 20, No. 12, March 22, 2004, pp. 1)
Pub: Crain Communications, Inc.
Description: Miscellaneous business briefs are cited, including information showing sixteen percent of New York City employers plan to hire more staff in the second quarter of 2004; Quickdrop International has been given state approval to begin selling franchises in New York for eBay drop-off centers.

33547 ■ "At Their Service" in *Entrepreneur* (Vol. 31, No. 7, July 2003, pp. 40)
Pub: Entrepreneur Media, Inc.
Ed: Melissa Campanelli. Description: Online retailers should never abandoned good customer services, even during a slower economy. Online shoppers have grown to expect excellent customer service from the Web sites in which they purchase.

33548 ■ "AT&T Sues eBay and PayPal" in *Cardline* (Vol. 3, No. 48, November 28, 2003, pp. 1)
Pub: Thomson Media
Description: AT&T Corporation has filed a patent infringement lawsuit against eBay and its subsidiary PayPal Inc over failure to reach a licensing agreement. EBAY PRODUCT/EBAY SERVICE

33549 ■ "Attention, Online Shoppers, Be Wary" in *Sacramento Bee* (November 28, 2005)
Pub: The Sacramento Bee
Ed: Clint Swett. Description: Internet safety for consumers is discussed. According to a survey conducted by the Business Software Alliance and Forrester Research, 61 percent of respondents are concerned about Internet security when making purchases. It is important to always use a secured Web page when entering personal information.

33550 ■ "Attract More Online Customers: Make Your Website Work Harder for You" in *Black Enterprise* (Vol. 37, November 2006, No. 4, pp. 66)
Pub: Earl G. Graves Publishing Co. Inc.
Ed: Description: Having an impressive presence on the Internet has become crucial. Detailed advice on making your website serve your business in the best way possible is included.

33551 ■ "Australian Computer Emergency Response Team: www.auscert.org.au" in *Entrepreneur* (Vol. 31, No. 10, October 2003, pp. 6)
Pub: Entrepreneur Media, Inc.
Ed: Steve Cooper. Description: The Australian Computer Emergency Response Team Website offers a free security threat alert service, giving American businesses nine to fifteen hours advance notice of issues.

33552 ■ "The Automated Agent" in *Rough Notes* (Vol. 146, No. 9, September 2003, pp. 92)
Pub: Rough Notes
Ed: Michael J. Weinberg. Description: An examination of newer technology making work easier and more efficient for insurance agents. Topics include laptops, cell phones, and email accounts.

33553 ■ "Automated advice sites turning up the heat on planners" in *The New York Times* (September 20, 2000, pp. D44, H44)
Pub: The New York Times Company
Ed: Patrick McGeehan. Description: Financial planning sites like www.financialengines.com, www.adviceamerica.com, www.directadvice.com, and others, are profiled. The article includes statistical data.

33554 ■ "Avoid the Supply Chain Squeeze" in *E-business Advisor* (Vol. 18, No. 7, July 2000, pp. 18)
Pub: Advisor Media, Inc.
Ed: Ben Chen, Lara Kass. Description: The next wave of e-commerce may result in significant disintermediation in select industry supply chains. It will be driven by the concurrent development of advanced computing technologies, such as high-definition text, with the implementation of new broadband Internet technologies that will redistribute the power within the supply chain to suppliers/manufacturers and consumers in certain industries. The article tells how these trends are transforming the book industry, home video industry and the music industry.

33555 ■ "B-to-b goes online: e-commerce among companies is rapidly changing the nature of procurement" in *Hispanic Business* (May 2000, pp. 50)
Pub: Hispanic Business
Ed: Jennifer Riley. Description: Online business deals by small- and medium-sized U.S. firms will reach a total of $1.3 trillion by 2003, according to Forrester Research. The Internet has become a key forum for firms seeking to purchase goods and services.

33556 ■ "B-to-B Takes Backseat to Infrastructure Deals" in *Venture Capital Journal* (Vol. 40, No. 10, October 2000, pp. 8, 10)
Pub: Venture Economics
Description: An overview of the B-to-B e-commerce and the fact that infrastructure investments could spark a rebirth to the industry.

33557 ■ "B2B Exchanges Survival Guide" in *Internet World* (Vol. 7, No. 1, January 15, 2001, pp. 48)
Pub: Mecklermedia Corporation
Ed: Ruhan Memishi. Description: It is estimated that the use and success of business-to-business exchanges will continue to grow and that by 2004 seven percent of the global economy could be fueled by these exchanges. An outline of the important steps a company needs to take in order to succeed in e-commerce.

33558 ■ "Back to Basics; Single Portal for Business" in *Crain's Detroit Business* (Vol. 19, No. 42, October 20, 2003, pp. 11)
Pub: Crain Communications Inc., Detroit
Ed: Amy Lane. Description: The State of Michigan intends to improve the state's telecommunications infrastructure, including a single state government Internet portal where businesses might handle all project-permit needs and new ways to expand high-speed Internet access to underserved areas.

33559 ■ "Back in the game. IT recruiters see selective improvement in local technology staffing markets" in *Business First Columbus* (Vol. 18)
Pub: Business First Columbus, Inc.
Ed: Craig Lovelace. Description: Central Ohio IT hiring is seeing improvements, yet the improvements are sporadic and not a major increase throughout the region. IT workers cannot expect the high salaries common before the turn around in the dot.com industry, these trends are indicative of the entire U.S.

33560 ■ "Back on the Tech Block" in *Black Enterprise* (Vol. 34, No. 7, February 2004, pp. 54)
Pub: Earl Graves Publishing Co.
Ed: Sonya A. Donaldson. Description: Profile of Brian Adams, former co-founder of Music Buddha Inc.; Adams has created AntiSpam Personal, an application that features a challenge and respond system that works with POP3 and SMTP compliant email services to fight spam.

33561 ■ "A bad rap: have you been slammed as a spammer? Here's how to fight back" in *Entrepreneur* (Vol. 31, No. 6, June 2003, pp. 83)
Pub: Entrepreneur Media Inc.
Ed: Catherine Seda. Description: Spamming is the act of sending email to individuals without their permission. SpamCop reports that it receives 9 million spam complaints monthly.

33562 ■ "Banks Try to Make Tele-Touch Satisfy Small Businesses" in *American Banker* (Vol. 171, November 27, 2006, No. 226, pp. 2)
Pub: SourceMedia, Inc.
Ed: Jim Cole. Description: Banks serving small businesses continue to offer personalized services, while incorporating call centers and online service models to small business strategies. Statistical data included.

33563 ■ "Banner Year" in *Entrepreneur* (Vol. 32, September 2004, No. 9, pp. 34)
Pub: Entrepreneur Media Inc.
Description: Online advertising has seen a dramatic increase in 2004. Statistical data included.

33564 ■ "The Battle of the Portals" in *The Economist* (Vol. 377, October 22-28, 2005, No. 8449, pp. 65-66)
Pub: The Economist Newspaper Ltd.
Description: Reasons Microsoft, Google and Yahoo! are fighting over AOL are discussed.

33565 ■ "Battle of the Wily Worms" in *Hispanic Business* (March 2004, pp. 42)
Pub: Hispanic Business
Ed: Judi Erickson. Description: On the front lines of the anti-virus war, companies such as Informatix struggle to say one step ahead of email viruses.

33566 ■ "BEA Ships Platform for Deploying Advanced Telecom Services" in *eWeek* (February 7, 2005)
Pub: Ziff Davis Media Inc.
Description: BEA Systems Inc. launched a suite of Java-based application development tools to make it easier for telecommunications companies to build advanced voice over Internet Protocol (VOIP), multimedia, and wireless services.

33567 ■ "BEA's Next Act" in *Barron's* (July 28, 2003, pp. T2)
Pub: Barron's
Ed: Mark Veverka. Description: Software firm, BEA Systems, is under competitive stress for market share

in applications servers sector, an arcane but highly lucrative back-end technology of great usefulness in e-commerce and Internet applications.

33568 ■ "Beat Those Bouncing Checks" in *Hispanic Business* **(December 2003, pp. 58)**
Pub: Hispanic Business
Ed: Roger Harris. **Description:** Profile of Justchex, the online service that can help a small business receive payment for about 80 percent of returned checks.

33569 ■ "Behind the Curve" in *Hispanic Business* **(Vol. 24, No. 5, May 2002, pp. 40-41)**
Pub: Hispanic Business Inc.
Ed: Teresa Talerico. **Description:** Hispanic small business owners are slow to accept technology. The importance of keeping up with technology for a small business is discussed.

33570 ■ "BellSouth drops hike in deposits" in *Atlanta Business Chronicle* **(Vol. 25, Jan. 10, 2003, No. 31, pp. 27A)**
Pub: American City Business Publications, Inc.
Ed: Mary Jane Credeur. **Description:** Citing potential financial burdens on young companies and a bias toward smaller companies, the Federal Communications Commission has denied pleas by the Baby Bells to hike security deposits for resellers of Bell services. BellSouth, Verizon Communications Inc., and SBC Communications Inc. were involved in the effort to sway FCC opinion.

33571 ■ "Best national Internet sites" in *Crain's Detroit Business* **(Vol. 18, No. 23, June 10, 2002, pp. E-15)**
Pub: Crain Communications Inc. - Detroit
Description: A listing of the best national Internet sites of various companies is presented. Illustrations are included.

33572 ■ "Best Travel Web Site: Hotwire.com" in *Entrepreneur* **(Vol. 32, No. 4, April 2004, pp. 47)**
Pub: Entrepreneur Media, Inc.
Description: Profile of Hotwire.com, which can save money for small business owners who are able to plan business travel on short notice.

33573 ■ "Best of the Web" in *Inc.* **(June 2000, pp. 137)**
Pub: The Goldhirsh Group
Ed: Ned Snell. **Description:** A panel of seasoned entrepreneurs share what they learned when they reviewed selected Web sites offering information and services to single-person businesses.

33574 ■ "Betting on the Net" in *Hispanic Business* **(Vol. 22, No. 6, June 2000, pp. 14)**
Pub: Hispanic Business
Ed: Jonathan Higuera. **Description:** Profile of Omar S. Rivero, founder and president of the new, Hispanic-run iMillenium Fund. Mr. Rivero says that the Internet will revolutionize the way that companies do business.

33575 ■ "Betty Crocker: can she cook in cyberspace?" in *The New York Times* **(December 13, 2000, pp. D13, H13)**
Pub: The New York Times Company
Ed: Stuart Elliott. **Description:** Consumer-products firms are using the Internet to market their goods.

33576 ■ "Beware of Love at First Byte" in *Success* **(Vol. 47, No. 6, November 2000, pp. 42)**
Pub: Success Publishing, Inc.
Ed: Suzy Girard. **Description:** Although the demand for Web developers has evolved into a thriving subindustry, there are only a handful of competent providers. Presented are six questions you may want to ask yourself when selecting a developer, one who will enable, not disable, your company's Web presence.

33577 ■ "Beyond the Banner Ad" in *Business Week* **(December 11, 2000, pp. 16)**
Pub: McGraw-Hill, Inc.
Description: An investigation of effective advertising on the Internet.

33578 ■ "Beyond dot.com" in *PC Computing* **(April 2000, pp. 112)**
Pub: Ziff-Davis Inc.
Ed: Jane Weaver. **Description:** It may seem like every Web address ends in .com, but there are plenty of options. Currently there are more than 35 top-level domains, and that number may soon grow. The article lists the best choices.

33579 ■ "Beyond the exchange: the future of B2B" in *Harvard Business Review* **(Vol. 78, No. 6, November-December 2000, pp. 86)**
Pub: Harvard Business School Publishing Corp.
Description: The evolution of business-to-business commerce on the Internet, and how it has been influenced by such revolutionary changes as an influx of specialists, a proliferation of creative business models, and new challenges for buyers and sellers. The article also forecasts the future of B2B on the Internet.

33580 ■ "Beyond Sales" in *My Business* **(June/July 2002, pp. 42)**
Pub: My Business Magazine
Ed: Mardy Fones. **Description:** Profile of owner Dan Santner, The Bakery in New Platz, New York, says that selling on his Web site helps keep him in touch with his customers.

33581 ■ "Biddeford, Maine, Partners Highlight Weirdest eBay 'Auctions on New Web Site" in *Portland Press Herald* **(July 8, 2005)**
Pub: Blethen Maine Newspapers, Inc.
Ed: Matt Wickenheiser. **Description:** Mark Greenlaw and partner Chaz Kraynak have created a new Website that collects the weirdest items from online auction house eBay.

33582 ■ "Bidding war" in *Entrepreneur* **(Vol. 30, No. 12, December 2002, pp. 32)**
Pub: Entrepreneur Media Inc.
Ed: Chris Sandlund. **Description:** EBay reports that nearly 12,000 businesses are posted for sale each month, up 35 percent from 2001. While eBay lists the businesses for sale, the Web site plays no role in working out details for the transaction.

33583 ■ "Big Box vs. Online" in *Hispanic Business* **(March 2003, pp. 25)**
Pub: Hispanic Business
Ed: Roger Harris. **Description:** Internet shoppers are finding very competitive pricing between purchasing online versus going to a brick and mortar store. An online shopping checklist is provided to assist consumers when making purchases online.

33584 ■ "Big Bucks" in *Entrepreneur* **(Vol. 28, No. 2, February 2000, pp. 28)**
Pub: Entrepreneur Media Inc.
Description: The business-to-business e-commerce marketplace is expected to reach $1.5 trillion in 2004, according to investment bankers Goldman, Sachs & Co.

33585 ■ "The Big Deals" in *PC Computing* **(April 2000, pp. 114)**
Pub: Ziff-Davis Inc.
Ed: Jane Weaver. **Description:** Some of the most notable domain name prices are listed, including Business.com, valued at $7.5 million.

33586 ■ "The Big Guns' Next Target: eBay" in *Business 2.0* **(Vol. 7, January/February 2006, No. 1, pp. 21-22)**
Pub: Time, Inc.
Ed: Michael V. Copeland. **Description:** eBay's lucrative auctions are being targeted by Google and Microsoft to move into classified advertising.

33587 ■ "Biggest and Best of the Internet? That's Diller's Goal" in *Barron's* **(August 25, 2003)**
Pub: Barron's
Ed: Jonathan R. Laing. **Description:** InterActiveCorporation, the newly minted e-commerce enterprise, formerly named USA Interactive, is headed by media tycoon Barry Diller of USA Networks. Diller discusses his strategy to dominate the growing e-commerce market, while conceding that the sector is threatening another bubble with overhauled stock values.

33588 ■ "The Bill's In the Mail"Bill Me Later" Payment Option" in *Entrepreneur.com* **(Vol. 34, February 2006, No. 2, pp. 36)**
Pub: Entrepreneur Media Inc.
Ed: Melissa Campanelli. **Description:** I4 Commerce's Bill Me Later Service provides payment options for Web customers, eliminating the need for clients to post their credit card numbers on the Internet.

33589 ■ "Bioigen Unchained" in *Harvard Business Review* **(Vol. 78, No. 3, May 2000, pp. 28)**
Pub: Harvard Business School Publishing Corp.
Ed: David Bovet, Joseph Martha. **Description:** When the biotech pioneer had to get a blockbuster drug to market fast, it joined with partners to become a virtual manufacturer.

33590 ■ "The Bite of the ASP" in *Forbes* **(November 27, 2000, pp. 296)**
Pub: Forbes Magazine
Ed: John C. Dvorak. **Description:** What happens when application service providers go bust? That question is answered, to help businesses protect themselves.

33591 ■ "Black Enterprise.com" in *Black Enterprise* **(Vol. 31, No. 5, December 2000, pp. 12)**
Pub: Earl Graves Publishing Co.
Description: Web features in the December 2000 virtual desktop for African Americans, including Black filmmakers, financial planning, and career choices, are reviewed.

33592 ■ "Black Ink brings dollars into the data-flow equation" in *Boston Business Journal* **(Vol. 22, No. 16, May 24, 2002, pp. 17)**
Pub: MCP, Inc.
Ed: Phil Sweeney. **Description:** Black Ink Systems is developing a product to assist telecommunications services firms to keep track of their financial information. This product will aid telecommunications services companies to make better decisions.

33593 ■ "Blackwell Inn using tech touch for high-end guests" in *Business First Columbus* **(Vol. 18, No. 38, May 10, 2002, pp. A6)**
Pub: Business First Columbus, Inc.
Ed: Jeff Bell. **Description:** The Roger D. Blackwell Inn, scheduled to open June 1, 2002, on the Ohio State University campus, will have its hotel rooms wired for computer and Internet use by guests. It is estimated that 60-80 percent of the hotel's guests will be transacting business or attending conferences at the University.

33594 ■ "Blog Me, Baby" in *Inc.* **(November 15, 2000, pp. 145)**
Pub: The Goldhirsh Group
Description: A concise list of services for Web logging, including Blogger, UserLand, and GrokSoup.

33595 ■ "A Blogger in Their Midst" in *Harvard Business Review* **(Vol. 81, No. 9, September 2003, pp. 30)**
Pub: Harvard Business School Press
Ed: Halley Suitt. **Description:** A hypothetical situation is presented where an indiscreet employee provides an online endorsement of a product that results in dramatically increased sales. Experts discuss how the CEO should deal with the matter.

33596 ■ "Blogger's Block: Sick of Blogging? Here's How to Deal with Business Blog Burnout" in *Entrepreneur* **(Vol. 32, December 2004, No. 12)**
Pub: Entrepreneur Media Inc.
Ed: Steve Cooper. **Description:** Debbie Well, a business blogging consultant founded WordBiz Report. Wells' publishing and consulting firm offers services in the area of e-newsletters and other Web content, including blogging.

33597 ■ **"Blogs Can Provide Testimonials"** in *Sales & Marketing Management* (Vol. 159, January-February 2007, No. 1, pp. 8)
Pub: VNU Business Media
Ed: Betsy Cummings. **Description:** Third party blogs are helping small companies market and promote products and services.

33598 ■ **"Bluetooth: Get Wired Without the Wires"** in *E-business Advisor* (Vol. 18, No. 10, October 2000, pp. 14)
Pub: Advisor Media, Inc.
Ed: Brent A. Miller, Chatschik Bisbikian. **Description:** Bluetooth is an emerging open specification that could revolutionize wireless communications in everything from desktop computers to telephone headsets. The basic idea is short-range communications that don't have to operate in licensed spectrum and a replacement for cables. This article takes a look at the uses of Bluetooth, and the origins and founders of the Bluetooth Special Users Group.

33599 ■ **"Book It! Using an Online Travel Site has its Advantages for Small Companies"** in *Entrepreneur* (Vol. 32, No. 1, January 2004, pp. 22)
Pub: Entrepreneur Media, Inc.
Description: Expedia, Orbitz, and Travelocity are the three top online travel services offering products to help small business save money on business travel. All three offer a small firm a private booking site ranging around $150 to startup and lower transaction costs.

33600 ■ **"Book Review: Summary judgment"** in *Red Herring* (No. 103, September 1, 2001, pp. 40)
Pub: Herring Communications
Ed: Mark Williams. **Description:** Book review of 'Inventing the Electronic Century', by Alfred D. Chandler. The author presents the story of the consumer electronics and computer industries.

33601 ■ **"Booting the Bear: E-Trade is Poised for the Bull's Return"** in *Barron's* (August 25, 2003, pp. MW17)
Pub: Barron's
Ed: Allison Krampf. **Description:** Online brokerage service E-Trade, victimized by the technology bubble collapse of 2000, has slowly and patiently retrenched, and now stands poised to exploit the return of the bull market that most analysts expect.

33602 ■ **"Booz Allen's Sweet Spot"** in *Forbes* (Vol. 170, No. 12, December 9, 2002, pp. 190)
Pub: Forbes Magazine
Ed: Andrew T. Gillies. **Description:** Booz Allen Hamilton, the McLean, Virginia consulting firm that is helping the Internal Revenue Service to modernize and create an effective Web site for users, is profiled.

33603 ■ **"BorderWare to ship e-commerce gateways for small business use"** in *Network World* (December 6, 1999, pp. NA)
Pub: Network World Inc.
Ed: Ellen Messmer. **Description:** A profile of BorderWare Technologies line of three firewall-based gateway products for use in small business e-commerce sites that require a minimum of technical expertise. The BorderWare Office Gateway is intended for use by organizations with ten or less employees.

33604 ■ **"Bosco Joins Clarity, Raising $1B Fund"** in *Venture Capital Journal* (Vol. 40, No. 10, November 2000, pp. 18)
Pub: Venture Economics
Description: Harry Bosco, former president of Lucent Technologies' Optical Networking Group, will join Clarity Partners on October 16, 2000. The firm will back early- to late-stage network infrastructure, wireless services and applications, e-commerce and broadband media companies.

33605 ■ **"BountyQuest Introduces New Service to Help Strengthen U.S. Patent System"** in *Information Today* (Vol. 17, No. 11, December 2000, pp. 6)
Pub: Information Today, Inc.
Ed: Nancy Lambert. **Description:** An overview of a new Web site launched by Boston based startup, BountyQuest Corporation. Via the site, interested companies offer a minimum $10,000 reward to the first "Bounty Hunter" who can provide the prior art (patents or published references) to invalidate specified new patent submissions.

33606 ■ **"BP Amoco wants to sell much more than gas at its new stations"** in *The New York Times* (July 25, 2000, pp. C6)
Pub: The New York Times Company
Ed: Kruti Trivedi. **Description:** BP Amoco is spending $7 billion to present a fresh brand image through BP Connect, a new round of service stations with cafilatte, solar panels, imaginatively-lit markets and e-commerce kiosks. Thus far, 20 percent of gas stations revenues come from the convenience markets. The bright green and yellow stations will be featured in ads, created by Ogilvy & Mather Worldwide promoting BP as a green company. The campaign will cost $100 million a year.

33607 ■ **"Bricks-and-Clicks World Needs Commercial Space"** in *The New York Times* (October 30, 2000, pp. C1)
Pub: The New York Times Company
Ed: Claudia H. Deutsch. **Description:** The need for warehouse distribution centers for online services is explored.

33608 ■ **"Bricks & Clicks"** in *Entrepreneur* (Vol. 33, October 2005, No. 10, pp. 64)
Pub: Entrepreneur Media Inc.
Ed: Gwen Moran. **Description:** Retailers are using eBay as a way to retail slow-moving merchandise from stores. Information for setting up a proper store on eBay is shared.

33609 ■ **"Briefing Book: E-Procurement"** in *Internet Week* (August 9, 2002)
Pub: CMP Media LLC
Ed: Tom Smith. **Description:** E-Procurement case studies and resources are presented.

33610 ■ **"Broadband Access"** in *Hispanic Business* (March 2005, pp. 14)
Pub: Hispanic Business
Description: According to a study by the Tomas Rivera Policy Institute, increasing broadband access to African Americans and Hispanics could equate to as much as $74 million in monthly revenue for technology providers.

33611 ■ **"Broadband Deluxe: High-Speed Firms Take the Stress Out of Networking"** in *Black Enterprise* (Vol. 35, November 2004, No. 4, pp. 68)
Pub: Earl G. Graves Publishing Co. Inc.
Ed: Rebecca Rohan. **Description:** Broadband provider, Comcast, will install and manage computer networks for customers.

33612 ■ **"Broadband Internet access"** in *Red Herring* (No. 105, October 1, 2001, pp. 34)
Pub: Herring Communications
Ed: Mark A. Mowrey. **Description:** According to a report by the Federal Communications Commission in August 2001, 96 percent of the U.S. population lives in the 75 percent of zip codes where at least one broadband provider offers service. Statistical data included.

33613 ■ **"Bronto Email Marketing Toolkit"** in *Entrepreneur.com* (Vol. 34, February 2006, No. 2, pp. 6)
Pub: Entrepreneur Media Inc.
Description: Free guide offered by Bronto software focuses on email marketing for small business.

33614 ■ **"Buck's Annual 401(k) Survey Shows Dramatic Growth In Web Administration"** in *Employee Benefit Plan Review* (Vol. 55, No. 7, Jan. 2001)
Pub: Charles D. Spencer & Associates, Inc.
Description: Buck Consultant's 11th annual survey reports a dramatic increase in the number of employers who make use of Web technology to administer 401(k) plans.

33615 ■ **"Bug Control"** in *Entrepreneur* (Vol. 32, No. 4, April 2004, pp. 34)
Pub: Entrepreneur Media, Inc.
Ed: Eric Bender. **Description:** Small companies have become a target for cyber attacks. Antivirus makers have started initiatives to respond more quickly and predictably to hackers by the use of antivirus software used along with a properly configured firewall.

33616 ■ **"Bugged out"** in *Entrepreneur* (Vol. 31, No. 5, May 2003, pp. 38)
Pub: Entrepreneur Media Inc.
Ed: Melissa Campanelli. **Description:** Information about Web bugs as a means to gather data on visitors to Web sites is presented. Most Web bugs are used through products and services from firms offering site analysis services or products.

33617 ■ **"Build Fault Reporting Into Your System"** in *E-business Advisor* (Vol. 18, No. 6, June 2000, pp. 41)
Pub: Advisor Media, Inc.
Ed: Amit Sharma. **Description:** Various ways of building fault reporting into a system to make optimal use of its system's fault tolerance is discussed. Fault reporting informs users what, when, and where things went wrong with their systems.

33618 ■ **"Build a Strong Customer-Brand Relationship"** in *E-business Advisor* (Vol. 18, No. 4, April 2000, pp. 34)
Pub: Advisor Media, Inc.
Ed: Doug Barton. **Description:** The article shows how the Internet is changing marketing practices as companies focus on developing customer loyalty instead of building brand images through advertising and traditional distribution channels. The two main factors driving sales are now customer loyalty and price.

33619 ■ **"Build a Successful Business Partner Network"** in *E-business Advisor* (Vol. 18, No. 5, May 2000, pp. 36)
Pub: Advisor Media, Inc.
Ed: Tim Claxton. **Description:** Business-to-business initiatives require online collaborative partnerships via a business partner network (BPN), also known as extranet. BPNs come with many benefits including speeding up joint projects, reducing costs and cycle times, supplies delivery on time and providing 24x7 customer service. Strategies for building an extranet, managing extranets and the future of BPNs are presented.

33620 ■ **"Build Your Business with eBay"** in *Home Business* (Vol. 13, January/February 2006, No. 1, pp. 58, 60)
Pub: Home Business Magazine
Description: According to the American Business Association, consumers are using online markets as a convenient way to buy products. Small companies should diversify into the online sector as a means to grow a business. Tips for opening an online shop are outlined.

33621 ■ **"Build Your Web Identity"** in *E-business Advisor* (Vol. 18, No. 5, May 2000, pp. 30)
Pub: Advisor Media, Inc.
Ed: Maria Szalay, James J. Datovech. **Description:** With about 800 million Web pages deployed over eight million Web sites, e-commerce companies have to follow certain fundamental design and marketing principles in their Web strategy. Key tips for such strategy are provided.

33622 ■ **"Building Downline...Online"** in *Success* (Vol. 47, No. 2, June 2000, pp. 80)
Pub: Success Publishing, Inc.

Ed: Greg Matusky, Mark Butler. **Description:** In the online world, brand is subordinate to the power of relationships. If relationships are the key to unlocking the wealth-building opportunities of multi-level marketing, then the Internet provides the electronic ways for creating the connections.

33623 ■ **"Building on the Web"** in *Pittsburgh Business Times* (Vol. 23, No. 7, September 5, 2003, pp. 19)
Pub: Pittsburgh Business Times
Ed: Christopher Davis. **Description:** Profile of the online management construction system, Facilities Information Technology System, developed by Valco Engineers, is presented.

33624 ■ **"Business Bookshelf"** in *Small Business Opportunities* (Vol. 13, No. 5, September 2001, pp. 118)
Pub: Harris Publications, Inc.
Description: Book reviews, including 'The E-Commerce Arsenal', which addresses 12 technologies needed to prevail in the digital arena; 'E-Business To Go', where the author believes now is the best time to start an e-business; and 'Lawn Care & Gardening', a down-to-earth guide to the lawn care business.

33625 ■ **"Business Challenge: Rex Bird Noticed Some Online Customers"** in *My Business* (October/November 2003, pp. 42)
Pub: My Business Magazine
Ed: Karen M. Kroll. **Description:** Profile of Rex Bird, owner of BodyTrends.com, a Web site selling fitness equipment. Bird recognized the patterns customers used while navigating his Website and offers solutions to help small business owners market successfully with Internet sites.

33626 ■ **"Business to E-Business"** in *Home Office Computing* (Vol. 18, No. 11, November 2000, pp. 52)
Pub: Scholastic Inc.
Ed: Amee Abel. **Description:** Guidelines are provided for setting up a Web site for a home-based business. The Web site should function as a kind of electronic brochure, providing potential customers with an attractive and inviting preview of the company's available products and services. The Web site should also provide links to related sites, and support associated marketing tasks.

33627 ■ **"Business Intelligence"** in *E-business Advisor* (Vol. 18, No. 8, August 2000, pp. 22)
Pub: Advisor Media, Inc.
Ed: Claudia Imhoff. **Description:** A description of the concept of Corporate Information Factory (CIF), which provides a high-level guide to developing an e-business plan.

33628 ■ **"Business and the Internet"** in *Ingram's* (Vol. 27, No. 4, April 2001, pp. 22)
Pub: Show Me Publishing, Inc.
Ed: Carol Rudder. **Description:** Online businesses have moved to online networks working together to provide solutions to complex business problems.

33629 ■ **"Business Services"** in *Entrepreneur* (Vol. 31, No. 5, May 2003, pp. 8)
Pub: Entrepreneur Media Inc.
Description: A directory of business services is presented, listing such services as franchise consultation, attorneys, entrepreneurial information radio shows, sales and marketing plans, business startup information, home-based businesses, raising business capital, e-businesses, B2B sales leads, and software.

33630 ■ **"Business Services"** in *PC Computing* (April 2000, pp. 180)
Pub: Ziff-Davis Inc.
Ed: Gordon Bass. **Description:** A listing of Internet Service Providers and their costs are provided.

33631 ■ **"Business-to-Consumer E-Commerce: What is(n't) the Problem?"** in *E-business Advisor* (Vol. 18, No. 8, August 2000, pp. 6)
Pub: Advisor Media, Inc.
Ed: Jane M. Falla. **Description:** Customers are grumbling, investors are threatening, and start-ups are sweating since the downturn of dot-coms. Despite the apparent dire straits, consumer online buying marches on and B2C e-commerce sights will need to outsource or find the correct packaged technology to keep pace with all of the changes occurring.

33632 ■ **"Business first Web site gets updated design, new URL"** in *Business First Columbus* (Vol. 18, No. 25, February 8, 2002, pp. A6)
Pub: Business First Columbus, Inc.
Description: Profile of Business First, periodical services, and the new Web site they designed.

33633 ■ **"The Business Week News You Need to Know"** in *Business Week* (January 23, 2006, No. 3968, pp. 30-31)
Pub: McGraw-Hill Companies
Ed: Harry Maurer. **Description:** News about the Detroit Auto Show, job growth, Home Depot's expansion plans, Internet search engines, new executive pay rules, the stock market, and more.

33634 ■ **"Business.com Pushes Portal Envelope"** in *Information Today* (Vol. 17, No. 11, December 2000, pp. 14)
Pub: Information Today, Inc.
Ed: Mick O'Leary. **Description:** Business.com is a giant directory of Web business sites. Its precise classification system permits easy identification of highly specific industry-sector information and news coverage.

33635 ■ **"Businesses work to offer wireless Internet access"** in *Crain's Detroit Business* (Vol. 18, No. 20, May 20, 2002, pp. 14)
Pub: Crain Communications Inc. - Detroit
Ed: Andrew Dietderich. **Description:** Profile of Wireless Fidelity, also called Wi-Fi, which is growing in popularity. Detroit currently has five access points.

33636 ■ **"Businesses Must Now Notify of Possible ID Theft"** in *Crain's Detroit Business* (Vol. 23, January 8, 2007, No. 2, pp. 6)
Pub: Crain Communications Inc. - Detroit
Ed: Amy Lane. **Description:** New bill requires businesses, state agencies, and local government to notify individuals of a security breech that is likely to cause individual loss, injury or identity theft.

33637 ■ **"Businesses Use Wireless Access to Draw Customers"** in *Crain's Detroit Business* (Vol. 19, No. 42, October 20, 2003, pp. 14)
Pub: Crain Communications Inc., Detroit
Ed: Andrew Dietderich. **Description:** Restaurants, book stores, office stores and hotels in Michigan are offering free wireless Internet access to draw businessmen and women to their shops.

33638 ■ **"Buying Online-Who Needs Contractors?"** in *Air Conditioning, Heating & Refrigeration News* (Vol. 219, No. 17, August 25, 2003, pp. 23)
Pub: Business News Publishing Co.
Ed: John Hall. **Description:** An overview of products and services available from eBay auctions, including information for air conditioning, heating and refrigeration contractors.

33639 ■ **"Buying Tunes Online"** in *Kiplinger's Personal Finance Magazine* (Vol. 54, No. 12, December 2000, pp. 28)
Pub: The Kiplinger Washington Editors, Inc.
Ed: Kathy Jones. **Description:** Digital-music subscriptions may be the answer for record companies for making music available through the Internet.

33640 ■ **"Buzzwords: Plog"** in *Inc.* (September 1, 2004)
Pub: Inc. Magazine
Ed: Ian Ybarra. **Description:** Plogs are Web-based tools where co-workers can create an archive of observations and data for projects. So far, companies using plogs have created the software in-house.

33641 ■ **"Cable cuts out slice of the broadband pie"** in *InfoWorld* (Vol. 23, No. 5, January 29, 2001, pp. 40)
Pub: InfoWorld
Ed: Jennifer Jones. **Description:** Cable modem service continues to hold a lead over DSL in the broadband sector. Industry leaders, such as AT&T and Media One, and America Online and Time Warner, are banking on that lead as part of their merger plans. These mergers are expected to bring high-speed Internet access to home users and focus on telecommuting.

33642 ■ **"Calculating clicks"** in *Entrepreneur* (Vol. 30, No. 2, February 2002, pp. 72)
Pub: Entrepreneur Media Inc.
Ed: Nichole L. Torres. **Description:** A review of the new guidelines recently released by the Interactive Advertising Bureau for selling ad space on a company's Web site.

33643 ■ **"California bill on Web sales tax"** in *The New York Times* (September 1, 2000, pp. C2)
Pub: The New York Times Company
Ed: Lawrence M. Fisher. **Description:** The California State Assembly passes a bill to collect state sales tax from Internet sales.

33644 ■ **"Can you keep a secret?"** in *Fast Company* (June 2001, pp. 186)
Pub: Fast Company
Ed: George Anders. **Description:** The push for online privacy threatens to kill the dream of super-sophisticated net-driven marketing, but there are simple ways that companies can have their data and also protect it.

33645 ■ **"Can you be a merchant vendor?"** in *Home Office Computing* (Vol. 18, No. 11, November 2000, pp. 20)
Pub: Scholastic Inc.
Ed: William Van Winkle. **Description:** A description of effective, online person-to-person (P2P) payment systems is provided.

33646 ■ **"Canada Rx offers access to Canadian pharmacies"** in *Atlanta Business Chronicle* (Vol. 25, January 10, 2003, No. 31, pp. 17A)
Pub: American City Business Publications, Inc.
Ed: Melissa Fowler. **Description:** Canada Rx Shop is described as an entity that supplies a Web-based ordering connection between clients in the U.S. and the pharmaceutical market in Canada. Tom Connell, owner of the company, stated that he and his wife became Rx affiliates to offer clients another way to manage their finances. Increasing prescription costs in the U.S. have sent many Americans, though primarily senior citizens, north of the border seeking cheaper drug prices. The article provides information on the service, the risks and the legal implications.

33647 ■ **"Canadian online pharmacy to open Springs storefront"** in *Colorado Springs Business Journal* (March 7, 2003)
Pub: Dolan Media Newswires
Ed: Marylou Doehrman. **Description:** Jeff Brooks, co-owner of Senior Co-Op, an online Canadian pharmacy will soon open a brick and mortar storefront in Colorado Springs, Colorado. The company has been providing prescription drugs to Americans at lower Canadian prices.

33648 ■ **"Card Tricks"** in *Entrepreneur* (Vol. 30, No. 2, February 2002, pp)
Pub: Entrepreneur Media Inc.
Ed: Amanda C. Kooser. **Description:** The biggest problem for online retailers comes with accepting

credit cards because of chargebacks when a customer disputes a charge on their bill, often due to unreceived merchandise or lack of quality in the product. The strict rules and dispute processes designed to protect consumers actually aids some people to use chargebacks as a vehicle for defrauding Internet businesses.

33649 ■ "Career Quarterly" in *Hispanic Business* **(April 2003, pp. 62, 64)**
Pub: Hispanic Business
Description: Profile of HireDiversity.com, the online service for diversity recruiting and career development is presented.

33650 ■ "CarsDirect.com Buys 2 Web Sites" in *American Banker* **(Vol. 170, February 4, 2005, No. 24, pp. 17)**
Pub: Thomson Financial Media Inc.
Ed: Erick Bergquist. **Description:** CarsDirect.com Inc. has bought a mortgage lead platform and two consumer Web sites, BestRate.com and LoanApp.com. The Los Angeles online car marketplace and lender says the move will help the company build on its business model of lead generation and mortgage brokering, along with adding the new component of subscription-based lender advertising.

33651 ■ "The Cash Flow Crunch" in *Home Office Computing* **(Vol. 19, No. 1, January 2001, pp. 88)**
Pub: Scholastic Inc.
Ed: Barbara Axelson. **Description:** Cash flow can become problematic when a small business is faced with an unexpected expense on top of normal monthly or yearly operating costs. Expert recommendations are offered for small businesses, including having cash reserves of up to three to six months available at all times.

33652 ■ "Catalog companies show the upstarts that they know a thing or two about Internet retailing" in *The New York Times* **(May 15,2000, pp.C16)**
Pub: The New York Times Company
Ed: Bob Tedeschi. **Description:** Well-established catalog firms see profits from e-commerce grow sharply, and have a high rate of success in converting online browsers into buyers.

33653 ■ "Cataloging the web" in *Incentive* **(Vol. 174, No. 10, October 2000, pp. 99)**
Pub: Bill Communications
Ed: Emily Hodnett. **Description:** Online award catalogs have a lot to offer, but before you follow this trend, don't forget the benefits of print copy.

33654 ■ "Caught In the Crossfire" in *Inc.* **(August 1, 2003)**
Pub: Gruner & Jahr USA Publishing
Ed: Ellen Neubone. **Description:** New spam filters are making it difficult for small companies relying on email for marketing strategies.

33655 ■ "Caught in the 'Net" in *Journal of Business Strategies* **(Vol. 21, No. 5, September 2000, pp. 4)**
Pub: Center for Business and Economic Research
Description: The Internet has become an obsession that's affecting the global economy, businesses of all sizes, and lifestyles. Statistical data included.

33656 ■ "Celecast Selling Sports Broadcasts" in *Atlanta Business Chronicle* **(Vol. 26, No. 11, August 22, 2003, pp. 5A)**
Pub: American City Business Publications, Inc.
Ed: Mary Jane Credeur. **Description:** Wireless broadcasts of college sports are available from Celecast Inc.

33657 ■ "Censorship" in *Business Week* **(January 23, 2006, No. 3968, pp. 32-34)**
Pub: McGraw-Hill Companies
Ed: Bruce Einhorn, Ben Elgin. **Description:** Security networks and compliant multinationals are keeping mainland China's Internet under government censorship.

33658 ■ "Center for Exhibition Industry Research (CEIR)" in *Entrepreneur* **(Vol. 32, No. 1, January 2004, pp. 10)**
Pub: Entrepreneur Media, Inc.
Ed: Steve Cooper. **Description:** Center for Exhibition Industry Research offer research and statistical information regarding trade show exhibitions and reports on topics of interest, many reports are industry-specific. Some reports cost a small fee, others are free.

33659 ■ "Chandler, Ariz., PostNet Among Chain's Stores that has eBay-Selling Service" in *The Tribune* **(November 25, 2003)**
Pub: Knight Ridder/Tribune Business News
Ed: Donna Hogan. **Description:** More than 850 shipping-service stores offer assistance to those individuals not familiar with using a computer to sell goods via eBay's auction site.

33660 ■ "Change of Address: There's a New Internet Protocol in Town. Is it Time to Upgrade?" in *Entrepreneur* **(Vol. 32, No. 1, January 2004)**
Pub: Entrepreneur Media, Inc.
Ed: Amanda C. Kooser. **Description:** Internet Protocol Version 6 (IPv6) will replace the previous Protocol Version.sub.4. Business hardware and software will eventually be required to work with the new version. IPv6 offers greater security, peer-to-peer possibilities and a nearly limitless supply of available addresses.

33661 ■ "Change, of Course" in *Entrepreneur.com* **(Vol. 34, February 2006, No. 2, pp. 79)**
Pub: Entrepreneur Media Inc.
Ed: David Worrell. **Description:** Profile of George Deeb, owner of iExplore Inc., a Chicago, Illinois-based adventure-travel firm with nearly $10 million in annual sales. Deeb offers his own tours and sells advertising on his Website.

33662 ■ "Change is Sweet" in *Fast Company* **(June 2001, pp. 169)**
Pub: Fast Company
Ed: Bill Breen. **Description:** When is a Net strategy more than just a Net strategy? When it enables a company to change an entire way of doing business. At Nestle USA, a bid to create the very best Web sites has become a vehicle for reinventing a staid, risk-averse culture.

33663 ■ "Changing hats" in *Black Enterprise* **(Vol. 31, No. 5, December 2000, pp. 71)**
Pub: Earl Graves Publishing Co.
Ed: Carolyn M. Brown. **Description:** Profile of Tim Cobb, founder of RelevantKnowledge, discussing his many business ventures.

33664 ■ "Charlotte, N.C., Jeweler Offers to Sell Stuff for You on eBay" in *Charlotte Observer* **(April 2, 2004)**
Pub: Knight-Ridder/Tribune Business News
Ed: Leigh Dyer. **Description:** Profile of Ernest Perry, owner of Perry's at SouthPark, a drop-off store where sellers can leave jewelry items to be sold on eBay. Drop-off stores appeal to those who lack Internet skills or have the time to maintain online auctions. Other drop-off operations include AuctionDrop, QuikDrop International, Snappy Auctions, iSold It and PictureIt-Sold.

33665 ■ "Check out our new book-What E-sourcing Means to You" in *Publishers Weekly* **(Vol. 249, No. 19, November 21, 2002, pp. 3)**
Pub: Reed Business Information
Description: This new book offers a comprehensive look at all possibilities, both good and bad, of the Internet, procurement strategies and purchases, and e-procurement. Case histories are included.

33666 ■ "Check 'Em Out" in *Entrepreneur* **(Vol. 28, No. 11, November 2000, pp. 40)**
Pub: Entrepreneur Media Inc.
Ed: Cynthia E. Griffin. **Description:** Guidelines to help evaluate online funding services are given.

33667 ■ "Checking Out" in *Harvard Business Review* **(Vol. 78, No. 2, March 2000, pp. 22)**
Pub: Harvard Business School Publishing Corp.
Description: Online shoppers routinely abandon their shopping carts without buying anything—and that's bad news for e-tailers.

33668 ■ "The Check's in the E-Mail" in *Entrepreneur* **(Vol. 32, October 2004, No. 10, pp. 66)**
Pub: Entrepreneur Media Inc.
Description: Banking law, Check 21, allows an electronic facsimile of a paper check to have the same legal standing of the original paper check it represents. This process will have a profound affect on the way businesses make and receive check payments.

33669 ■ "Choose the Right Application Server" in *E-business Advisor* **(Vol. 18, No. 1, January 2000, pp. 32)**
Pub: Advisor Media, Inc.
Ed: Guy Tal. **Description:** An application server can save time and money in an e-business environment, but choosing the wrong server can be costly. Essentially, an application server provides a way to reuse shared logic and data components. A Java application server is built on the Enterprise JavaBeans (EJB) component architecture. Choosing an application that relies on standard Java APIs is an effective way to build flexibility and scalability into a system.

33670 ■ "Cisco, SBA announce online learning program" in *Network World* **(July 24, 2000, pp. NA)**
Pub: Network World Inc.
Ed: Margaret Johnston. **Description:** The Small Business Administration and Cisco offer an online training partnership to help small businesses incorporate the Internet into their day-to-day business operations.

33671 ■ "A clarion call: the tech and telecom sectors are finally on the mend" in *Barron's* **(Vol. 82, No. 58, February 17, 2003, pp. 28)**
Pub: Barron's
Ed: Sandra Wood. **Description:** Tech and telecom research specialists, Scott Cleland and William Whyman, are optimistic about the end of the bear market in those sectors, including software, cable TV, and the Baby Bells.

33672 ■ "Class distinction" in *Entrepreneur* **(Vol. 30, No. 1, January 2)**
Pub: Entrepreneur Media Inc.
Ed: Amanda C. Kooser. **Description:** Web demographics studies show a fast rise in Internet use by blue-collar workers and seniors, and both groups are influencing e-business.

33673 ■ "A Click Away: Automotive Web Sites are Revved Up and Ready to Help You Buy" in *Entrepreneur* **(Vol. 31, No. 8, August 2003, pp. 22)**
Pub: Entrepreneur Media, Inc.
Ed: Jill Amadio. **Description:** Auto manufacturers have upgraded Websites offering the latest prices, reviews, surveys, advice, car care, links, and more to attract buyers. Websites offering automotive information are profiled.

33674 ■ "Click on a Fortune" in *Small Business Opportunities* **(Vol. 17, May 2005, No. 3, pp. 22-24, 26-28, 30, 32, 34, 36, 38, 40, 42, 44)**
Pub: Harris Publications Inc.
Description: Fifteen growing service franchises are highlighted. Profiles of the following franchise and independent startup opportunities include Island Ink-Jet, Wireless Toyz, homemade foods, Children's Orchard, carpet cleaning, concierge services, family books, Putt-Putt golf centers, glass replacement, online auction sales, mystery shoppers, Earl of Sandwich, Instant FX, senior care, and real estate investing.

33675 ■ "Clickalyzer www.clickalyzer.com" in *Entrepreneur* **(Vol. 32, No. 1, January 2004, pp. 10)**
Pub: Entrepreneur Media, Inc.
Ed: Steve Cooper. **Description:** Profile of the Website that tracks and monitors advertising, Web pages, sales letters and visitors.

33676 ■ "Clicking for Cash" in *Business Week* **(No. 3698, September 11, 2000, pp. F37)**
Pub: McGraw-Hill, Inc.
Description: Small businesses turn to online finance companies for loans and credit.

33677 ■ "Clicking online: mergers, consolidations predicted for Hispanic targeted Web sites in 2000" in *Hispanic Business* **(Dec. 1999, pp. 60)**
Pub: Hispanic Business
Ed: Vaughn Hagerty. **Description:** The emergence of Hispanic-targeted sites on the Internet is discussed. Developments of StarMedia Networks Inc. and quepasa.com are highlighted.

33678 ■ *Clicking Through: A Survival Guide for Bringing Your Company Online*
Pub: Bloomberg Press
Ed: Jonathan I. Ezor. **Released:** January 2000. **Price:** $19.95. **Description:** Summary of legal compliance issues faced by small companies doing business on the Internet, including copyright and patent laws.

33679 ■ "Clicks to Bricks" in *Entrepreneur* **(Vol. 33, August 2005, No. 8, pp. 44)**
Pub: Entrepreneur Media Inc.
Ed: Melissa Campanelli. **Description:** Following a current trend, more e-tailers are opening brick-and-mortar stores. This move will strengthen brand-name recognition, give local customers a place to shop or return merchandise, lower promotional fees, and expand a customer base.

33680 ■ "Clicks, not licks, as Green Stamps go digital" in *The New York Times* **(March 9, 2000, pp. D1, G1)**
Pub: The New York Times Company
Ed: Michelle Slatella. **Description:** S&H Green Stamps are back with green points, an online form of Green Stamps, given out as rewards for shopping online.

33681 ■ "Close to Home" in *Entrepreneur* **(Vol. 33, February 2005, No. 2, pp. 69)**
Pub: Entrepreneur Media Inc.
Ed: Catherine Seda. **Description:** Online advertising programs offering geographic-targeting plans can help a small business market to a specific audience. A listing of Websites offering online advertising programs is included.

33682 ■ "Closing the Book on Public Records" in *Kiplinger's Personal Finance Magazine* **(Vol. 55, No. 1, January, 2001, pp. 26)**
Pub: The Kiplinger Washington Editors, Inc.
Ed: Kathy Jones. **Description:** Thirty-one states have enacted, or are considering laws to keep personal information off the Internet, but these laws could end up limiting consumer access to important information.

33683 ■ "Club Planet Takes Off" in *Small Business Opportunities* **(Vol. 17, May 2005, No. 3, pp. 72)**
Pub: Harris Publications Inc.
Description: Profile of Andrew Fox who started Clubplanet.com from his New York City apartment. Later he and his sister founded Track Entertainment, a nightlife Website and entertainment marketing agency.

33684 ■ "Co-opting Customer Competence" in *Harvard Business Review* **(Vol. 78, No. 1, January 2000, pp. 79)**
Pub: Harvard Business School Publishing Corp.
Ed: C.K. Prahalad, Venkatram Ramaswamy. **Description:** In the new economy, companies must incorporate customer experience into their business models, in ways up until now were untapped. The challenges for doing that are addressed.

33685 ■ "Collectibles Cash-In" in *Small Business Opportunities* **(Vol. 17, November 2005, No. 6, pp. 100, 104)**
Pub: Harris Publications Inc.
Description: Profile of Vintage Stock, a leader in buying and selling new and pre-owned entertainment products. The company is the only retailer specializing in new and vintage merchandise.

33686 ■ "CollectiveGood and eBay Team Up to Recycle Cell Phones for Charity" in *PR Newswire* **(March 25, 2004)**
Pub: PR Newswire Association, Inc.
Description: Profile of CollectiveGood, the mobile phone recycler; the firm has partnered with eBay to collect and resell cellular/mobile phones, pagers and PDA devices from eBay to help charities.

33687 ■ "Come Fly With Me" in *Black Enterprise* **(Vol. 35, September 2004, No. 2, pp. 54)**
Pub: Earl G. Graves Publishing Co. Inc.
Ed: Tariq Muhammad. **Description:** Although online travel booking may offer great deals for domestic travel, for international travel, multiple destinations, or other special trips, a travel agent is recommended.

33688 ■ "Comic genius" in *Entrepreneur* **(Vol. 30, No. 2, February 2002, pp. 81)**
Pub: Entrepreneur Media Inc.
Ed: April Pennington. **Description:** Profile of Mark Silvestri, owner of Top Cow Productions Inc. in Los Angeles, who made $400,000 in four weeks by offering his hot new comic on the Web.

33689 ■ "Coming of age" in *Boston Business Journal* **(Vol. 22,)**
Pub: MCP, Inc.
Ed: Phil Sweeney. **Description:** Online retailers are learning ways to survive in a slowing economy.

33690 ■ "Commentary: 'About Us' Pages Spell Good Business, Consumer Confidence" in *Long Island Business News* **(February 27, 2004)**
Pub: Dolan Media Newswires
Ed: Adina Genn. **Description:** Small businesses are creating About Us pages on their Websites. These provide a site where a company can share information about its history, philosophies and mission. This information can be used as a marketing tool to attract new customers.

33691 ■ "Commentary: Testimonials-Let Your Customers Do the Talking" in *Long Island Business News* **(March 12, 2004)**
Pub: Dolan Media Newswires
Ed: Adina Genn. **Description:** Long Island businesses are cultivating customer testimonials on the Web, in brochures and on site. Tips for using customer praise to promote a business are included.

33692 ■ "Commentary: Testimonials-Let Your Customers Do the Talking" in *Long Island Business News* **(March 12, 2004)**
Pub: Dolan Media Newswires
Ed: Adina Genn. **Description:** Long Island businesses are cultivating customer testimonials on the Web, in brochures and on site. Tips for using customer praise to promote a business are included.

33693 ■ "Communicating - Building a community can be one of the biggest boosts to your site's stickiness" in *PC Magazine* **(Feb. 20, 2001, pp.13)**
Pub: Ziff-Davis Publishing Company
Ed: Troy Dreier. **Description:** Free message boards, chat rooms and e-mail can improve the usefulness of a Web site and attract repeat visitors. The message board Open Topic is reviewed.

33694 ■ "ComNet to showcase VOIP" in *InfoWorld* **(Vol. 23, No. 5, January 29, 2001, pp. 8)**
Pub: InfoWorld
Ed: Jennifer Jones, Heather Harreld. **Description:** WorldCom plans to migrate voice over IP (VoIP) tech-

nology at the ComNet 2001 trade show. Several other vendors, including hardware and network-management companies are expected to unveil new products at the show, but WorldCom is the first major carrier to pay serious attention to growing enterprise interest in VoIP.

33695 ■ "Compare Your Clicks: www. compareyourclicks.com" in *Entrepreneur* **(Vol. 32, November 2004, No. 11, pp. 6)**
Pub: Entrepreneur Media Inc.
Ed: Steve Cooper. **Description:** Profile of Compare Your Clicks, an online resource that lets marketers run live comparisons of keyword bid prices at multiple search engines.

33696 ■ "A Computer on Every Desk: Online Learning Takes Off" in *Long Island Business News* **(February 27, 2004)**
Pub: Dolan Media Newswires
Ed: Claude Solnik. **Description:** The Internet's impact on education at universities and colleges across the nation is discussed. Institutions have partnered with Blackboard.com, a company that offers a system for using and managing the Web in educational environments and allows instructors to control content and assignment management, online assessments, student tracking and virtual collaboration.

33697 ■ "Confessions of a Car Dot-Commer" in *Forbes* **(December 25, 2000, pp. 92)**
Pub: Forbes Magazine
Ed: Jerry Flint. **Description:** The reasons online car dealerships do not work.

33698 ■ "Consumer Finance" in *Business Week* **(January 16, 2006, No. 3967, pp. 38)**
Pub: McGraw-Hill Companies
Ed: Peter Burrows. **Description:** A new trend shows online brands offering shoppers Bill Me later payment options in order to spur sales growth and offer a billing method to consumers uneasy about using their credit cards on the Internet. So far 230 e-commerce sites offer this service.

33699 ■ "Consumer Research" in *Business 2.0* **(Vol. 6, September 2005, No. 8, pp. 36)**
Pub: Time Inc.
Ed: Bridget Finn. **Description:** Umbria Communications in Boulder, Colorado is turning the Internet into a marketing bonanza. The firm's software called Buzz Report searches 13 million blogs to uncover consumer's feelings about new products and trends.

33700 ■ "Contagious Commercials" in *Inc.* **(November 2006, pp. 31-32)**
Pub: Gruner & Jahr USA Publishing
Ed: Jennifer Gill. **Description:** Short videos on YouTube and MySpace can start a stream of information networks that can convey your business message. This process is known as viral video marketing and is rapidly growing on the web.

33701 ■ "Content sites find a way to keep e-tailer marketing booths on their page-without having lured their visitors away" in *The New York Times*
Pub: The New York Times Company
Ed: Bob Tedeschi. **Description:** Affiliate marketing between e-tailers and content Web sites is discussed.

33702 ■ "Contextual marketing" in *Harvard Business Review* **(Vol. 78, No. 6, November-December 2000, pp. 119)**
Pub: Harvard Business School Publishing Corp.
Description: Contextual marketing is examined and the ways new technologies will shift the focus of e-commerce from content to context, making many Web sites irrelevant.

33703 ■ "Control Your Content" in *E-business Advisor* **(Vol. 18, No. 10, October 2000, pp. 42)**
Pub: Advisor Media, Inc.
Ed: Andre McMillan. **Description:** As a business Web site grows, so does the need for managing the content of the site. This article explores content management

and how it differs from document management. The author strongly urges that before products are purchased, there be an advisory board for continuing management and operational committees that can help determine need.

33704 ■ "Convergence" in *Inc.* (November 15, 2000, pp. 88)
Pub: The Goldhirsh Group
Description: Technological innovations in the Internet sector are summarized.

33705 ■ "Cool New Software, Free of Charge" in *Inc.* (November 2006, pp. 42-43)
Pub: Gruner & Jahr USA Publishing
Ed: Michael Fitzgerald. Description: Free of charge software is available to help you run your business. From project management to managing email and customer relations, programs are available on line or free o charge to assist you. Six examples are highlighted in this article.

33706 ■ "Cool Tools" in *Inc.* (November 15, 2000, pp. 145)
Pub: The Goldhirsh Group
Description: If you are marketing to a special niche or need an online forum for new ideas, Web logs could be the answer. A Web log is a Web site, or a section of a Web site, whose overriding characteristic is its ever-changing list of links.

33707 ■ "Cool Tools" in *My Business* (February/March 2004, pp. 18-19)
Pub: My Business Magazine
Description: Profiles of new devices of interest to the small business owner, including Lingo Talking Translator, which translates nine languages aloud and/or onscreen, and includes a calculator, world clock, currency and metric converters, and an address book; the Auravision EluminX illuminated computer keyboard for working in dark or low-lit spaces; RedEnvelope's messaging pens; and Radio YourWay AM/FM Radio Recorder.

33708 ■ "Cost Transparency: The Net's Real Threat to Prices and Brands" in *Harvard Business Review* (Vol. 78, No. 2, March 2000, pp. 43)
Pub: Harvard Business School Publishing Corp.
Ed: Indrajit Sinha. Description: The vast sea of information about prices, competitors, and features that is readily available on the Internet helps buyers "see through" the costs of products and services. That's bad news for manufacturers and retailers, and there are ways to fight back.

33709 ■ "The costs of e-commerce" in *Hispanic Business* (Vol. 22, No. 4, April 2000, pp. 78)
Pub: Hispanic Business
Ed: Vaughn Hagerty. Description: The rapidly changing composition of businesses on the Internet makes it difficult for Internet-based companies to keep track of their competitors. The effects on business success of a lack of knowledge of competitors are discussed.

33710 ■ "The Counterfeit Catastrophe; Curbing Piracy Is As Urgent As Taking Down Trade Barriers" in *Business Week* (February 7, 2005, pp. 96)
Pub: McGraw-Hill Companies
Description: Issues involved with email spam, both nationally and internationally, are discussed, especially as it relates to international trade.

33711 ■ "Crafting a Web presence" in *Accounting Technology* (Vol. 19, No. 1, January-February 2003, pp. 16)
Pub: Thomson Financial Inc.
Ed: Richard McCausland. Description: Jim Schaefer, founder of Schaefer & Company, an 18-year old tax and accounting practice believes that a Web site keeps a business competitive.

33712 ■ "Crafts Americana Group to Expand Presence in Vancouver, Wash." in *The Columbian* (February 22, 2003)
Pub: Knight-Ridder/Tribune Business News
Ed: Gretchen Fehrenbacher. Description: Profile of Crafts American Group, the company specializing in catalog and Web sales of craft supplies, is planning to expand with 40,000 square foot of new space, which includes retail space. The new building will offer a larger area for crafts classes and products, including quilting, tole painting, and knitting.

33713 ■ "Craigslist Founder has a Hands-On Style" in *San Jose Mercury News* (March 4, 2005)
Pub: Knight-Ridder/Tribune Business News
Ed: Michael Bazeley. Description: Craig Newmark, founder of the classified ads Website, Craigslist, is profiled. Craigslist reports annual revenues from $7 million to $10 million. Employers pay a fee for listing job opportunities on the site, but there is no fee for individuals posting ads.

33714 ■ "Cranky consumer learns to knit" in *Wall Street Journal* (January 28, 2003, pp. D2)
Pub: Dow Jones & Co. Inc.
Ed: Elizabeth Schatz. Description: A comparison of learn-to-knit kits, obtained from five different mail-order or online sources, is presented.

33715 ■ "Crash and Burn" in *Entrepreneur* (Vol. 28, No. 4, April 2000, pp. 66)
Pub: Entrepreneur Media Inc.
Ed: Melissa Campanelli. Description: Your Web site will go down, but the right hosting company can keep disaster from being an everyday occurrence.

33716 ■ "A Crash Diet for Dot-Coms" in *Kiplinger's Personal Finance Magazine* (Vol. 54, No. 8, August 2000, pp. 21)
Pub: The Kiplinger Washington Editors, Inc.
Ed: Melynda Dovel Wilcox. Description: With Web downsizing, the Internet superhighway is no longer the road to riches. But, high-tech employees still have a ticket to ride.

33717 ■ "Create Compelling Web Content" in *E-business Advisor* (Vol. 18, No. 2, February 2000, pp. 24)
Pub: Advisor Media, Inc.
Ed: Laurie Windham. Description: Compelling content is an essential aspect of successful e-commerce Web sites. Updated and relevant content retains customer interest in the site and increases customer satisfaction. An infrastructure that supports the development of collaborative content publishing enables the Web master to focus on other issues, such as quality control. Good content, which personalizes, informs, supports, directs, sells and fulfills, is essential for solidifying customer relationships.

33718 ■ "Create Customer-Effective E-Services" in *E-business Advisor* (Vol. 18, No. 12, December 2000, pp. 26)
Pub: Advisor Media, Inc.
Ed: Jodie Dalgleish. Description: Effective customer services are essential for successful e-commerce operations. An e-commerce Web site must communicate clearly with the customers and make it easy for them to negotiate the site and make purchases. The site should make it simple to compare products within the site and across multiple sites, and be guided immediately to the more important parts of the site.

33719 ■ "A Crisis of Content: It's not just pop music." in *Time* (Vol. 156, No. 14, October 2, 2002, pp. 68)
Pub: Time Inc.
Description: Every industry that trades in intellectual property, from publishing to needlework patterns, could get Napsterized. Jim Hedgepath, president of Pegasus Originals, discusses problems encountered to protect his copyrighted cross-stitch needlework patterns.

33720 ■ *Crossing the Chasm: Marketing and Selling Disruptive Products to Mainstream Customers*
Pub: HarperInformation
Ed: Geoffrey A. Moore. Released: September 2002. Price: $17.95. Description: A guide for marketing in high-technology industries, focusing on the Internet.

33721 ■ "CueCat links printed ads to Web, but skeptics are wary" in *The New York Times* (September 28, 2000, pp. D8)
Pub: The New York Times Company
Ed: Katie Hafner. Description: A new device called CueCat, made by Digital Convergance and distributed for free at Radio Shack, makes it possible for computer users to scan printed ad barcodes which will direct them to relevant Web sites. Critics are worried that the data will be used in turn by e-tailers to gather information on Web shoppers using the devices in violation of the privacy rights.

33722 ■ "Culture Club: Many E-Tailers are Lining Up to Target the Growing Hispanic Market" in *Entrepreneur* (Vol. 31, No. 10, October 2003)
Pub: Entrepreneur Media, Inc.
Ed: Melissa Campanelli. Description: According to comScore Networks, nearly 12.5 million Hispanics are online, prompting online retailers to market to Hispanic consumers.

33723 ■ "Customer Driven" in *Success* (Vol. 47, No. 2, June 2000, pp. 60)
Pub: Success Publishing, Inc.
Ed: Mike Gorgan. Description: The Internet tunes up sales and satisfaction for car dealers and consumers.

33724 ■ "The Customer Loyalty Puzzle" in *E-business Advisor* (Vol. 17, No. 12, December 1999, pp. 10)
Pub: Advisor Media, Inc.
Ed: Laurie Windham. Description: E-business owners can offer excellent customer service on the Web by linking marketing, sales, delivery, and support into one rewarding experience. E-business owners should include fulfillment and support among customer services to build customer confidence and to reduce operating expenses. Developing trust is important to e-business relationships because the Web does not offer face-to-face contact.

33725 ■ "Customers Wary of Online Banking Security Breeches" in *Providence Business News* (Vol. 18, No. 13, July 14, 2003, pp. 3)
Pub: Providence Business News, Inc.
Ed: Patricia Resende. Description: Safety precautions undertaken by Rhode Island banks to protect online banking customers are discussed.

33726 ■ "Cut Travel Expenses" in *Inc.* (July 1, 2003)
Pub: Gruner & Jahr USA Publishing
Description: Big travel Websites are scrambling to help small companies cut business travel costs. Statistical data included.

33727 ■ "Cutbacks at another consultant" in *The New York Times* (December 8, 2000, pp. C3)
Pub: The New York Times Company
Ed: Matt Richtel. Description: E-commerce consultant Viant to layoff 125 employees.

33728 ■ "Cyber-battle for a piece of the pie" in *Hispanic Business* (Vol. 22, No. 11, November 2000, pp. 44)
Pub: Hispanic Business
Ed: Andrea Siedsma. Description: An overview of the influence of the Internet on the globalization of trade. The need for businesses to offer electronic commerce as a means of trading is discussed.

33729 ■ "Cyber contracting" in *Hispanic Business* (Vol. 22, No. 6, June 2000, pp. 122)
Pub: Hispanic Business
Ed: Janet Perez. Description: Two Internet sites are in the vanguard of the fast-growing area of online con-

tracting. Guru.com, begun in 1999, and MonsterTalent Market, an offshoot of Monster.com, both specialize in finding contract staff. They see their growth as a sign of the rapidly changing economy in the United States.

33730 ■ "Cyber-Sign" in *PC Magazine* **(February 6, 2001, pp. 26)**
Pub: Ziff-Davis Publishing Company
Ed: Sally Wiener Grotta. **Description:** Cyber-Sign Electronic Signature Verification Plug-In for Adobe Acrobat is able to verify that a signature is authentic and can establish intent, the two requirements for using e-signatures. The Cyber-Sign products are invaluable for online business communications, making an electronic signature more secure than a traditional paper signature.

33731 ■ "Cybercafe Cash-In" in *Small Business Opportunities* **(Vol. 12, No. 2, March 2000, pp. 108, 146)**
Pub: Harris Publications, Inc.
Ed: Marie Sherlock. **Description:** Cybercafes offer espresso and the Internet and can net six-figure incomes.

33732 ■ "Cybercare's Offices Empty Out Amid Tardy Filings" in *South Florida Business Journal* **(Vol. 24, No. 1, August 15, 2003, pp. 1)**
Pub: American City Business Journals
Ed: John T. Fakler. **Description:** Profile of Cyber-Care, the telehealth service provider, is presented.

33733 ■ "Cybersearch Specialist" in *Crain's New York Business* **(Vol. 23, January 29, 2007, No. 5 ,pp. F16)**
Pub: Crain Communications, Inc.
Ed: Amanda Fung. **Description:** Profile of Matthew Greitzer, director of search engine marketing for Avenue A/Razorfish. The firm has garnered more than twenty search marketing campaigns from clients such as Schering-Plough and Verizon and is the largest buyer of search advertising.

33734 ■ "Cybersecurity: Opportunities for Agents" in *Rough Notes* **(Vol. 145, No. 1, January 2003, pp. 110)**
Pub: Rough Notes
Ed: G. Edward Kalbaugh. **Description:** Any product or action to secure a wired or wireless work constitutes CyberSecurity, such as virus protection for computers, risk identification, insurance, risk assessment, and liability insurance. CyberSecurity promises to be one of the fastest growing businesses of the future, as more than $330 billion have been earmarked for the Department of Homeland Security.

33735 ■ "CyberStaking: Why Partnerships Matter" in *E-business Advisor* **(Vol. 18, No. 9, September 2000, pp. 10)**
Pub: Advisor Media, Inc.
Ed: Wendy Lea, Scott Creighton. **Description:** Partnerships, a start-up's key to success in the new economy, act to secure future markets, ease multi-channel strategies and lock out potential rivals. Electronic commerce partnerships often include the launching of joint ventures, formations of a third company, exclusivity agreements, and shared revenues and equity.

33736 ■ "The Daily Paper of Tomorrow" in *Business Week* **(January 9, 2006, No. 3966, pp. 20)**
Pub: McGraw-Hill Companies
Ed: Jon Fine. **Description:** A six-point list of things for the future of daily newspapers include using Google to advertise, offer a news-digest daily, put more information online, increase local coverage, redesign products for more appeal, and build communities and businesses around community-created content.

33737 ■ "Damm Dotcoms!" in *Entrepreneur* **(Vol. 28, No. 8, August 2000, pp. 78)**
Pub: Entrepreneur Media Inc.
Ed: Brian O'Connell. **Description:** Online companies present problems for traditional businesses, but the real winners in traditional business are positioning themselves to ride the e-coattails.

33738 ■ "Dare to Compare." in *Entrepreneur* **(Vol. 33, January 2005, No. 1, pp. 43)**
Pub: Entrepreneur Media Inc.
Ed: Melissa Campanelli. **Description:** Online merchants wishing to grow their business might consider placing products on comparison shopping Websites. These sites display product information in a simple format and lets buyers compare and choose the best product from a list of different retailers.

33739 ■ "Datatrac trucks in $3 million in venture capital funding" in *Atlanta Business Chronicle* **(Vol. 25, December 13, 2002, No. 27, pp. A3)**
Pub: American City Business Publications, Inc.
Ed: Mary Jane Credeur. **Description:** Datatrac Corporation has raised $3 in venture capital, led by Magunticook Management Inc., Boston, Massachusetts. The funds will allow Datatrac to further develop its eTrac online network providing real-time data for the transportation and logistics industries. Customers have expressed great interest in the eTrac product, and the funding will allow for increased capacity.

33740 ■ "David Wetherell" in *Internet World* **(Vol. 7, No. 2, January 15, 2001, pp. 30)**
Pub: Mecklermedia Corporation
Ed: Jason Black. **Description:** A profile of David Wetherell of the Internet holding company CMGI.

33741 ■ "Day of E-tonement" in *Forbes* **(December 25, 2000, pp. 262)**
Pub: Forbes Magazine
Ed: Elizabeth Corcoran. **Description:** A discussion involving Internet start-ups and the high failure rate seen in the industry.

33742 ■ "Dealflop: Good night, sweetheart" in *Red Herring* **(No. 103, September 1, 2001, pp. 33)**
Pub: Herring Communications
Ed: Julie Landry. **Description:** The demise of Tradia, a consumer-to-consumer e-commerce and swapping site, cost Accel Partners, Sequoia Capital, and angels Roger Sippl and Ron Conway $14 million.

33743 ■ "The Death and Life of Buy.com" in *Forbes* **(January 21, 2002, p. 86)**
Pub: Forbes Magazine
Ed: Quentin Hardy. **Description:** Profile of Scott Blum who hopes to rebuild the online retailer Buy.com. Blum founded the dot.com in 1997 and bought back control of the Internet retailer in November 2001.

33744 ■ "Delegating the dirty work of cleaning up" in *The New York Times* **(February 17, 2000, pp. D4, G4)**
Pub: The New York Times Company
Ed: Michelle Slatella. **Description:** Information to help hire contractors over the Internet is summarized.

33745 ■ "Dell and NetObjects make small business play" in *Network World* **(October 24, 2000, pp. NA)**
Pub: Network World Inc.
Ed: Ashlee Vance. **Description:** Dell plans to pre-install NetObject's software for building Web sites on some Dell desktops and notebooks. The software helps users build, publish and promote their own Web sites under the co-branded product title NetObjects Fusion Dell Edition.

33746 ■ "Dell to offer hosting of small business Web sites" in *Wall Street Journal* **(February 22, 2000, pp. B23)**
Pub: Dow Jones & Co., Inc.
Ed: Gary McWilliams. **Description:** As part of its E-Works initiative, Dell has launched a Web site hosting service for small business called Dellhost.com. The company will resell services of some of the ISPs that buy its servers. The site hosting market is expected to grow from $2 billion in 1999 to $17 billion 2003. Interliant Inc. will provide the Internet connection for Dell customers for $18 to $300 a month.

33747 ■ "Design Innovation Brings Communications Challenges" in *Employee Benefit Plan Review* **(Vol. 55, No. 7, January 2001, pp. 27)**
Pub: Charles D. Spencer & Associates, Inc.
Ed: Sue Burzawa. **Description:** The 401(k) plan design evolved rapidly in the late 1990s, and that trend is continuing. Recent innovations, including automatic enrollment and Web access for information and transactions of plans, are expected to soon be common practice.

33748 ■ Designing Websites for Every Audience
Pub: F & W Publications, Incorporated
Ed: Ilise Benun. **Released:** January 2003. **Price:** $34.99. **Description:** Twenty-five case studies targeting six difference audiences are used to help a business design, or make over, a Website.

33749 ■ "Despite the Growing Popularity of the WEB, 72 percent of small businesses don't sell goods & services online" in *Inc.* **(June2000, pp.80)**
Pub: The Goldhirsh Group
Description: With the new "almost free" e-commerce tools, it is easier for those companies to join the 28 percent already using the Web for their business.

33750 ■ "Detroit radio on the Web" in *Crain's Detroit Business* **(Vol. 16, No. 46, November 13, 2000, pp. 15)**
Pub: Crain Communications, Inc.
Description: The article includes a sampling of what some leading Detroit area commercial radio stations are offering on the Web.

33751 ■ "Develop a Solid E-Commerce Architecture" in *E-business Advisor* **(Vol. 18, No. 1, January 2000, pp. 22)**
Pub: Advisor Media, Inc.
Ed: Chris Koontz. **Description:** Building and maintaining effective e-commerce applications depends on working out clear definitions of business objectives. A six-step program is presented for helping IT professionals to react to today's changing conditions.

33752 ■ "Developing a brand" in *Black Enterprise* **(Vol. 32, No. 10, May 2002, pp. 47)**
Pub: Earl Graves Publishing Co.
Ed: Fabian Robinson, Rebecca Rohan. **Description:** A brand is the relationship between product and consumer. Advice is given to market a brand online and offline and ways to protect that brand online.

33753 ■ "Dialing Up a Degree" in *Crain's Detroit Business* **(Vol. 21, October 17, 2005, No. 43, pp. 11)**
Pub: Crain Communications Inc. - Detroit
Ed: Sherr Begin. **Description:** Online college and university courses are growing in popularity because of the convenience they offer.

33754 ■ "Different Stripes" in *Entrepreneur.com* **(Vol. 34, February 2006, No. 2, pp. 45)**
Pub: Entrepreneur Media Inc.
Ed: Karen Edwards. **Description:** Profile of Chris Lindland and partner Enrique Landa who produce horizontally striped corduroy pants and accessories available only online. The company expects revenues to reach $150,000 to $250,000 its first year.

33755 ■ "Digital Content Wars: Can't We All Just Get Along?" in *Red Herring* **(No. 87, December 18, 2000, pp. 19-20)**
Pub: Herring Communications, Inc.
Ed: Anthony B. Perkins. **Description:** The way the Internet has changed how we look at intellectual property is discussed, citing current court cases.

33756 ■ "Digital Defenses: A Business's Network Is its Castle" in *Red Herring* **(January 2003, pp. 52)**
Pub: Herring Communications Inc.
Ed: Lee Bruno. **Description:** The challenge for most small companies is to be able to keep the line of communication and commerce open, while securing and protecting critical business information.

33757 ■ "Digital Demographics" in *Red Herring* (No. 87, December 18, 2000, pp. 54-55)
Pub: Herring Communications, Inc.
Ed: Elizabeth Lamb. **Description:** An overview of digital demographics across the U.S. using graphs and charts projecting that by year 2005, there will be 20 million high-income households (making at least $75,000 annually) and 9 million low-income households (making less than $15,000) using the Internet.

33758 ■ "Digital Scammer" in *Entrepreneur* (Vol. 30, No. 2, February 2002, pp. 28)
Pub: Entrepreneur Media Inc.
Description: The ten most common online scams according to the National Consumer League are presented. Statistical data included.

33759 ■ "Digital Signatures vs. Electronic Signatures" in *E-business Advisor* (Vol. 18, No. 4, April 2000, pp. 48)
Pub: Advisor Media, Inc.
Ed: Tom Melling. **Description:** Confusion between the definitions of digital signatures and electronic signatures could result in poorly constructed legislation that may create barriers to e-commerce and make electronic contracts unenforceable.

33760 ■ "Digitally speaking, builders remain on the ground floor" in *The New York Times* (December 13, 2000, pp. D4, H4)
Pub: The New York Times Company
Ed: Charles V. Bagli. **Description:** Construction companies have yet to make full use of the Internet.

33761 ■ "The Dilemma of CNET's Success; It Gets Top Dollar For Online Ads, Most Tech-Oriented" in *Business Week Online* (February 9, 2005)
Pub: McGraw-Hill Companies
Ed: Sarah Lacy. **Description:** Technology-site ad rates rose 46 percent in 2004, but are mainstream marketers willing to pay for online ads? Statistical data included.

33762 ■ "Direct Hit: Can Direct Marketing Survive a Consumer Backlash?" in *Entrepreneur* (Vol. 31, No. 9, September 2003, pp. 23)
Pub: Entrepreneur Media, Inc.
Ed: Chris Penttila. **Description:** Congress, the states and large technology companies are taking action against telemarketing, junk mail and spam.

33763 ■ "The direct marketing industry hopes to get Internet retailers to see things in an old light" in *The New York Times* (Jul. 12, 2000, pp. C6)
Pub: The New York Times Company
Ed: Bernard Stamler. **Description:** Until recently, electronic commerce conducted their ad and marketing campaigns as if they were separate from the vagaries of those who learned to choose media carefully and control the cost of campaigns. Thus, online sellers spent lavishly, ignoring less expensive and often more effective direct marketing. Electronic retailers relied on branding alone, until the Internet boom went bust. Wall Street was more interested in profits than brand recognition. Now, many e-tailers are embracing direct marketing with a passion inspired by the potential of bankruptcy.

33764 ■ "Dirty laundry.com" in *Incentive* (Vol. 174, No. 9, September 2000, pp. 17)
Pub: Bill Communications
Ed: Don Mogelefsky. **Description:** Are Internet "gripe sites" beneficial for employees, or could employers benefit from them even more?

33765 ■ "Disappearing Ink" in *Kiplinger's Personal Finance Magazine* (Vol. 54, No. 10, October 2000, pp. 118)
Pub: The Kiplinger Washington Editors, Inc.
Ed: Ed Henry. **Description:** The Federal Electronic Signatures Law (E-Sign) that goes into effect October 1, 2000, will give e-signatures the same legal status as pen-and-ink signatures nationwide.

33766 ■ "Do it already!" in *Entrepreneur* (Vol. 30, No. 1, January 2002, pp. 43)
Pub: Entrepreneur Media Inc.
Ed: Amanda C. Kooser. **Description:** iBizResources.com encourages brick-and-mortar businesses to get online and use the new technologies available to small businesses. The site offers technical services, e-commerce tools, marketing, promotion and business products and services.

33767 ■ "Do-It-Yourself Due Diligence" in *Business Week* (January 16, 2006, No. 3967, pp. 93)
Pub: McGraw-Hill Companies
Ed: Anne Tergesen. **Description:** Ways to investigate hedge funds online before investing are offered.

33768 ■ "Do You Need E-Business Insurance" in *E-business Advisor* (Vol. 18, No. 9, September 2000, pp. 28)
Pub: Advisor Media, Inc.
Ed: Bernard P. Bell. **Description:** New types of insurance coverage are required to protect Internet businesses against new liabilities, such as system damage and intellectual property damage. For example, e-commerce is vulnerable to business interruptions caused by security breaches, natural disasters, internal systems problems, and failure of third parties.

33769 ■ "Do You Need Web Services?" in *E-business Advisor* (Vol. 18, No. 12, December 2000, pp. 16)
Pub: Advisor Media, Inc.
Ed: Jeri Dube, David Sink. **Description:** Business to business (B2B) transactions are complicated, but new Web-based services will provide new ways for companies to integrate their systems and applications over the Internet. The services will enable companies to leverage their strengths and respond to events in real time. Standards for the new services are still under development and not all applications are suitable for use on the Web. The Universal Description, Discovery and Integrations (UDDI) initiative has developed a specification that will enable businesses to discover each other and conduct business with each other over the Internet.

33770 ■ "Do Your Network: Curious About How Effective Wi-Fi Adapters Are? We've Got You Covered" in *Entrepreneur* (Vol. 31, No. 7, July 2003)
Pub: Entrepreneur Media, Inc.
Ed: Amanda C. Kooser. **Description:** Information regarding the new 802.11g and 54 Mbps speed wireless networking tools is discussed, and whether small companies should upgrade from their current 802.11b Wi-Fi standards.

33771 ■ "The Doctor Will E-Mail You Now" in *Black Enterprise* (Vol. 36, February 2006, No. 7, pp. 168)
Pub: Earl G. Graves Publishing Co. Inc.
Ed: Leslie E. Royal. **Description:** Many physicians across the nation are offering their patients online visits and several major insurance carriers are providing coverage for the service.

33772 ■ "Doing Away With the Old Resume" in *Success* (Vol. 47, No. 5, October 2000, pp. 18)
Pub: Success Publishing, Inc.
Ed: Debbie Selinsky. **Description:** Recruitsoft.com, e-recruiter, uses technology to match jobs to worker skills and shove that stack of resumes off employers' desks.

33773 ■ "Doing Business with Uncle Sam" in *My Business* (February/March 2003, pp. 14)
Pub: My Business Magazine
Description: The Small Business Administration will launch an online program designed to improve the procuring of government contracts, with an annual fee of $1,500 for using the e-commerce Web site.

33774 ■ "Domains of the Day: A New Domain Could Mean the Dawn of a New Mobile Age" in *Entrepreneur* (Vol. 32, August 2004, No. 8, pp. 31)
Pub: Entrepreneur Media Inc.
Ed: Amanda C. Kooser. **Description:** .mTLD, which stands for mobile Top Level Domain is a new domain suffix like .com, expressly for mobile use. Leaders like Hewlett-Packard, Microsoft, Nokia, Samsung Electronics, Sun Microsystems, T-Mobile International and Vodafone have partnered to set up a registry company to manage the new mTLD once the Internet Corporation for Assigned Names and Numbers grants approval.

33775 ■ "Don't call your doctor, send your symptoms over the Web" in *Crain's Detroit Business* (Vol. 16, No. 24, June 12, 2000, pp. 1)
Pub: Crain Communications, Inc.
Ed: Matt Roush. **Description:** Ann Arbor-based Cybernet Systems Inc. received a broad patent on transmitting medical information from patient monitoring devices over the Internet. Cybernet is also incorporating the patent into a launch of a centralized, national outpatient monitoring network for remote data capture, analysis, archive and display.

33776 ■ "Don't Get Scammed" in *Entrepreneur* (Vol. 28, No. 4, April 2000, pp. 42)
Pub: Entrepreneur Media Inc.
Ed: Robert McGarvey. **Description:** It is estimated that as many as one million small businesses have been a victim of fraud on the Internet.

33777 ■ "Don't throw out the old economy yet" in *Crain's Detroit Business* (Vol. 16, No. 17, April 24, 2000, pp. 8)
Pub: Crain Communications, Inc.
Ed: Keith Crain. **Description:** This may not be the new economy, but it sure has a lot to do with new Internet businesses.

33778 ■ "Dot-com Bust Fallout" in *Hispanic Business* (November 2002, pp. 14)
Pub: Hispanic Business
Description: Startups that received venture-backed funding in 1999 and 2000 are failing at a faster rate than startups initially funded between 1992 and 1998. Statistical data included.

33779 ■ "Dot-Com Distress" in *PC Magazine* (February 20, 2001, pp. 67)
Pub: Ziff-Davis Publishing Company
Ed: Sebastian Rupley. **Description:** A concise history of the dot-com industry is presented, including some optimism for the future of those e-tailers that survive.

33780 ■ "Dot-Com for Sale" in *E-business Advisor* (Vol. 18, No. 10, October 2000, pp. 48)
Pub: Advisor Media, Inc.
Ed: Ben Chen. **Description:** Gaining customers, skilled employees, knowledge, and strategic alliances are some of the reasons for the flurry of acquisitions and mergers in the dot.com world. This article examines reasons, and discusses the things to look for when contemplating a business move, including goal compatibility, cost for acquiring a new customer base, and whether the new company would have what the existing company does not have and needs.

33781 ■ "Dot-com Seeks Firm Footing" in *Boston Business Journal* (Vol. 22, No. 11, April 19, 2002, pp. 11)
Pub: MCP, Inc.
Ed: Scott Savitz. **Description:** Shoebuy.com Inc. has 10,000 products with 220 brands and increasing numbers of customers. By sticking to a disciplined marketing style, this dot.com online retailer has been able to grow steadily.

33782 ■ "Dotcom Damage" in *Entrepreneur* (Vol. 30, No. 1, January 200)
Pub: Entrepreneur Media Inc.
Ed: Aliza Pilar Sherman. **Description:** Gender issues following the dotcom crash are discussed. Despite what financiers may say, it seems women are still considered an investment risk.

33783 ■ "Double header" in *WorkingWoman* (Vol. 25, No. 5, May 2000, pp. 38)
Pub: Lang Communications Inc.
Ed: Eilene Zimmerman. **Description:** The Female Athlete company has 70 percent of its sales generated by catalogs and 30 percent from Web sites sales. Issues concerning marketing strategies to direct customers away from traditional catalog buying to purchasing on-line are presented.

33784 ■ "Double Play: Could Sending a Paper Catalog to Customers Boost Your E-Commerce Business?" in *Entrepreneur* (Vol. 32, September 2004)
Pub: Entrepreneur Media Inc.
Ed: Melissa Campanelli. **Description:** Many e-tailers are using catalogs to increase Internet sales. Statistical data included.

33785 ■ "Doyenne of Hip Proffers Hot Tips" in *Crain's New York Business* (Vol. 23, January 29, 2007, No. 5, pp. F9)
Pub: Crain Communications, Inc.
Ed: Elisabeth Butler. **Description:** Profile of Dany Levy and her trendy business, an e-newsletter, Daily Candy. Advertisers are flocking to this Internet publication which expects to generate revenues of $25 million this year.

33786 ■ "Dream of Zinfandel, delivered to the door" in *The New York Times* (September 27, 2000, pp. B14, F7)
Pub: The New York Times Company
Ed: Frank J. Prial. **Description:** Fewer wholesalers, more wineries, lead to legislative fights over online wine trade.

33787 ■ "DSL Users Brace for Bumpy Ride" in *Home Office Computing* (Vol. 18, No. 11, November 2000, pp. 19)
Pub: Scholastic Inc.
Ed: Bonny L. Georgia. **Description:** Tips for protecting yourself when dealing with DSL providers are given.

33788 ■ "E-Biz Buzz" in *E-business Advisor* (Vol. 18, No. 8, August 2000, pp. 58)
Pub: Advisor Media, Inc.
Ed: Buzz Hunter. **Description:** Web users are becoming less receptive to traditional forms of marketing. E-commerce providers will find a lucrative market in small businesses by offering solid support, quick answers to questions, and easy access to other services and products.

33789 ■ "E-Book vendors look to libraries for growth" in *Publishers Weekly* (Vol. 249, No. 40, October 7, 2002, pp. 12)
Pub: Reed Business Information
Ed: Calvin Reid. **Description:** E-publishing vendors, Fictionwise.com, netLibrary and Adobe have announced plans to offer libraries a variety of software and pricing options to encourage library patrons to check out digital reading materials. It is hoped this move will help increase sales.

33790 ■ "E-Brand Lessons" in *Small Business Opportunities* (Vol. 12, No. 5, September 2000, pp. 18)
Pub: Harris Publications, Inc.
Description: The results of a comprehensive study of Internet users' opinions and perceptions of 250 technology brands, ranking them on overall performance and key brand attributes are examined. These results can help small businesses improve their presence on the Web.

33791 ■ "E-Brands: Building an Internet Business at Breakneck Speed" in *Harvard Business Review* (Vol. 78, No. 4, July 2000, pp. 152)
Pub: Harvard Business School Publishing Corp.
Ed: John T. Landry. **Description:** Phil Carpenter, the founder of Point Cast, provides several case studies of Web consumer firms that have achieved success.

33792 ■ "E-bug exterminator: NetScreen nabs viruses and market share" in *Barron's* (Vol. 82, No. 58, February 17, 2003, pp. T8)
Pub: Barron's
Ed: Eric C. Fleming. **Description:** NetScreen Technologies' anti-virus hardware-software appliance is selling briskly, and its strong balance sheet fares well for its share price, currently near $20.

33793 ■ "E-Business Busters" in *Entrepreneur* (Vol. 28, No. 1, January 2000, pp. 46)
Pub: Entrepreneur Media Inc.
Ed: Melissa Campanelli. **Description:** What you read about the Internet is not always the real thing. Four e-commerce myths are debunked.

33794 ■ "E-Business Cards" in *Hispanic Business* (Vol. 23, No. 10, October, 2001, pp. 100)
Pub: Hispanic Business
Ed: Roger Harris. **Description:** Profile of the Web-based Scout service, a software system that automatically updates contact information in a user's computer address book. Scout is a service from Ants.com, a start-up backed by venture capital from such firms as Bertelsmann Venture Capital.

33795 ■ *e-Business, e-Government and Small and Medium-Size Enterprises: Opportunities and Challenges*
Pub: Idea Group Publishing
Ed: Brian J. Corbitt, Nabeel A.Y. Al-Qirim. **Released:** February 2004. **Price:** $79.95. **Description:** Electronic commerce and information technology research in small and medium-sized enterprises (SMEs). Policymakers, legislators, researchers and professionals address significant issues of importance to the small business sector.

33796 ■ "E-business firm spreads Influence to Ann Arbor" in *Crain's Detroit Business* (Vol. 16, No. 33, August 14, 2000, pp. 30)
Pub: Crain Communications, Inc.
Ed: Al Slavin. **Description:** St. Louis-based e-business firm Influence L.L.C., has joined Ann Arbor, Michigan's growing high-tech ranks, setting up a six-person shop. The company hopes to increase its workforce ten-fold over the next 16 months.

33797 ■ "E-Business for Tourism" in *Business Information Alert* (Vol. 14, No. 9, Oct. 2002, pp. 8)
Pub: Alert Publications
Ed: Ellen Shapley. **Description:** Review of the book, "World Tourism Organization", offering insightful look into e-tourism with online guides for Destination Management Systems and Web sites, extranet, and with tips for small and medium-sized tourism enterprises. The book is available in English, French and Spanish.

33798 ■ "E-commerce can pose legal risks for businesses" in *Crain's Detroit Business* (Vol. 16, No. 16, April 17, 2000, pp. 17)
Pub: Crain Communications, Inc.
Ed: Tim Moran. **Description:** The potential of legal risk when doing business on the Internet is examined.

33799 ■ "E-Commerce Complaints" in *Small Business Opportunities* (Vol. 14, No. 1, January 2002, pp. 16)
Pub: Harris Publications, Inc.
Description: Ten tips for dealing with customer complaints online offered by Karen Leland and Keith Bailey, authors of Online Customer Service For Dummies are investigated.

33800 ■ "E-Commerce Market Heats Up" in *Hispanic Business* (October 2003, pp. 98, 100)
Pub: Hispanic Business
Ed: Andrea Siedsma. **Description:** New studies indicate Hispanics are ready to buy online if merchants carry the right products, a strong brand, and financial security. A listing of the top sites for Hispanic online shoppers is included. Statistical data included.

33801 ■ "E-Commerce: Risky Business" in *Working Woman* (Vol. 25, No. 2, February 2000, pp. S20)
Pub: Lang Communications Inc.
Ed: Alice Sparberg Alexiou. **Description:** The risks of shopping online versus the convenience are discussed.

33802 ■ "E-commerce: Too Valuable to Tax" in *Success* (Vol. 47, No. 2, June 2000, pp. 22)
Pub: Success Publishing, Inc.
Ed: Fred A. Gray. **Description:** E-commerce may be the greatest tool small businesses can employ. All small-business people need is to learn the technology and then put it to work. Taxing the Internet could destroy the success of e-commerce.

33803 ■ "E-Commerce: When You Put Your 'John Hancock' on the Web Form!" in *Ingram's* (Vol. 27, No. 5, May 2001, pp. 33)
Pub: Show Me Publishing, Inc.
Ed: Arthur L. Smith. **Description:** Businesses are still finding ample opportunities from the electronic marketplace. Contracts made electronically are just as binding as the traditional paper contract.

33804 ■ "E-Government Catching On" in *Hispanic Business* (Vol. 23, No. 5, May 2001, pp. 22, 24)
Pub: Hispanic Business
Ed: Patricia Guadalupe. **Description:** The U.S. government is developing programs to access procurement, recruitment, and economic development. The FirstGov.gov links users to more than 20 million federal Web pages.

33805 ■ "E-Hubs: The New B2B Marketplaces" in *Harvard Business Review* (Vol. 78, No. 3, May 2000, pp. 97)
Pub: Harvard Business School Publishing Corp.
Ed: Steven Kaplan, Mohanbir Sawhney. **Description:** As business-to-business commerce shifts to the Internet, companies that control the online markets will exert enormous influence over the way transactions are carried out, relationships are formed, and profits flow. Understanding how these electronic hubs work is crucial to creating a successful e-business strategy.

33806 ■ "E-Learning Takes Off!" in *Small Business Opportunities* (Vol. 13, No. 6, November 2001, pp. 92, 94)
Pub: Harris Publications, Inc.
Description: Profile of Walden e-learning programs.

33807 ■ "E-Loyalty" in *Harvard Business Review* (Vol. 78, No. 4, July 2000, pp. 105)
Pub: Harvard Business School Publishing Corp.
Ed: Frederick F. Reichheld, Phil Schefter. **Description:** Bain and Company Inc. is studying the strategies and practices of top Internet companies. They have surveyed thousands of their customers to assess e-loyalty.

33808 ■ "E-Mail Alternative" in *Entrepreneur* (Vol. 32, No. 1, January 2004, pp. 47)
Pub: Entrepreneur Media, Inc.
Ed: Liane Cassavoy. **Description:** Eudora 6.0s new SpamWatch feature sends spam to a junk mail folder, making it an alternative to Outlook Express for email.

33809 ■ "E-Mail and Communications" in *PC Computing* (April, 2000, pp. 74)
Pub: Ziff-Davis Inc.
Ed: Marty Jerome. **Description:** Wireless products are becoming ubiquitous although cheap, dependable, one-stop communications, anytime, anywhere, are still three years away. The current crop of smart pagers, handheld PCs and smart phones, however, are providing users such functionality as e-mail, Internet access and basic PC features. Among the notable wireless products are, the Motorola PageWriter 2000X, the 3Com Palm VII, the Handspring Visor Deluxe, the Qualcomm pdQ 1900 Smartphone, the Samsung SCH-3500, and the Nokia 6185 phones.

33810 ■ "An E-Mail from the IRS? Don't Believe It" in *Long Island Business News* **(May 7, 2004)**
Pub: Dolan Media Newswires
Ed: David Reich-Hale. **Description:** The U.S. Internal Revenue Service has posted a warning to taxpayers about an email scam that tries to trick taxpayers into giving personal information. The email appears to be an official memo from the IRS.

33811 ■ "E-mail Marketer Looks for More Clout" in *Atlanta Business Chronicle* **(Vol. 25, December 13, 2002, No. 27, pp. A3)**
Pub: American City Business Publications, Inc.
Ed: Mary Jane Credeur. **Description:** Silverpop Systems Inc. has acquired Epigraphx LLC, Redwood, California. The acquisition took place in December 2002, as part of Silverpop's initiative to grow in the e-mail marketing industry. The deal will increase staff to 55 and will triple Silverpop's revenues, which remain undisclosed. The deal also expands Silverpop's client roster and increased profits are discussed by Silverpop CEO, Bill Nussey.

33812 ■ "E-Mail Marketing" in *Small Business Opportunities* **(Vol. 13, No. 5, September 2001, pp. 100, 102)**
Pub: Harris Publications, Inc.
Ed: Lin Grensing-Pophal. **Description:** The pros and cons to using e-mail as part of a marketing program are outlined. Spam, permission marketing, Internet services, are discussed. A list of online resources is included.

33813 ■ "E-mail Offers a Little Wit with Your News" in *Crain's Detroit Business* **(Vol. 19, No. 6, February 10, 2003, pp. 9)**
Pub: Crain Communications Inc., Detroit
Ed: Mary Kramer. **Description:** Crain's Detroit offers a free daily e-mail news service providing an online news summary by 3:30 p.m. daily. The service started in January and already has 16,000 people signed up.

33814 ■ "E-Mail Secrets Revealed" in *Home Office Computing* **(Vol. 18, No. 12, December 2000, pp. 48)**
Pub: Scholastic Inc.
Ed: Helen Bradley. **Description:** Tips for making effective use of E-mail software and services are presented.

33815 ■ "E-Mail the Way it Should Be" in *PC Computing* **(April 2000, pp. 117)**
Pub: Ziff-Davis Inc.
Ed: Bonny L. Georgia. **Description:** It is possible for a company to save a substantial amount of money if they outsource their e-mail. This article focuses in on some of the companies that offer these services and give brief evaluations.

33816 ■ "E-Marketplaces: Opportunity or Threat?" in *E-business Advisor* **(Vol. 18, No. 7, July 2000, pp. 32)**
Pub: Advisor Media, Inc.
Ed: Elizabeth Sara. **Description:** Businesses in the e-marketplace arena are obliged, not only to adapt their existing business processes to take advantage of the Web's inherent benefits, but also to keep their relatively new e-commerce solutions functionally current and flexible to keep in step with the market. Participating in private business-to-business (B2B) sales channels offer the advantage of enhanced contractual relationships with business partners. Price structures for products are included.

33817 ■ "E-Procurement Catching On" in *Hispanic Business* **(October 2002, pp. 88)**
Pub: Hispanic Business
Ed: Tim Dougherty. **Description:** An increasing number of small businesses are turning to the Internet to fulfill purchasing needs, and happy with the results.

33818 ■ "E-Procurement at Schlumberger" in *Harvard Business Review* **(Vol. 78, No. 3, May 2000, pp. 21)**
Pub: Harvard Business School Publishing Corp.
Description: Schlumberger, the world's largest oilfield services company, has introduced a Web-based procurement system. Now employees can act as their own purchasing agents by using the desktop system, thus speeding up the purchasing operation.

33819 ■ "E-retailers turn to the printed page to put their wares before consumers" in *The New York Times* **(July 10, 2000, pp. C12)**
Pub: The New York Times Company
Ed: Bob Tedeschi. **Description:** Online retailers have started using or developing programs that will mail catalogs to consumers.

33820 ■ "E-signing law seen as a boon to e-business" in *The New York Times* **(July 4, 2000, pp. C1)**
Pub: The New York Times Company
Ed: Barnaby J. Feder. **Description:** Analysts expect that the new law letting businesses and consumers sign legally binding accords with electronic signatures will increase the speed at which electronic businesses develop. The new process, called 'e-signing', will likely give rise to many personal identification technologies that can serve as alternatives to writing one's name on paper.

33821 ■ "E-Strategies" in *Inc.* **(November 15, 2000, pp. 98)**
Pub: The Goldhirsh Group
Description: A profile of Mrs. Beasley's bakery and how the owner has expanded into E-commerce, launching a Web site in 1999, which hit $2.1 million in sales during its first 60 days.

33822 ■ "E-Tail Therapy" in *Entrepreneur* **(Vol. 33, January 2005, No. 1, pp. 35)**
Pub: Entrepreneur Media Inc.
Ed: Heather Clancy. **Description:** Accessing marketing products via the Internet is growing in popularity.

33823 ■ "E-Tailers Pay a High Price for Free Shipping" in *Business Week Online* **(December 6, 2001)**
Pub: McGraw-Hill, Inc.
Description: The cost of offering free shipping by online retailers is discussed.

33824 ■ "E-Trade Financial Cuts Prices of Many Online Transactions" in *Kansas City Star* **(February 16, 2005)**
Pub: Knight-Ridder/Tribune Business News
Ed: Paul Wenske. **Description:** E-Trade Financial Corporation has announced a new commission schedule which will lower costs for some online stock and options trades on its Website. These changes will affect three customer groups. Customers will pay $9.99 commission when making five to 49 trades per month; power E-trades lowered to 75 cents to $1.25; and the serious investor fee is set at $11.99, down $1 from $12.99.

33825 ■ "E-Train" in *Sales and Marketing. com* **(Vol. 156, No. 3, March 2004, pp. 19)**
Pub: VNU eMedia, Inc.
Description: Profile of Ninth House Inc.'s Instant Advice E-Learning Solution. Using an online library of 500 business topics, users receive coaching from notable management gurus such as Tom Peters and Ken Blanchard.

33826 ■ "EAI Meets B2B" in *E-business Advisor* **(Vol. 18, No. 10, October 2000, pp. 34)**
Pub: Advisor Media, Inc.
Ed: David S. Linthicum. **Description:** Enterprise application integration (EAI) and business-to-business integration are coming together in the guise of middleware. Right now there are as many vendors as there are solutions. Vendors, however, generally divide their solutions into data (data federation and data integration), application, process, transaction and distributed object. It is up to the user to analyze their specific applications to determine their needs.

33827 ■ "Early warning" in *Black Enterprise* **(Vol. 32, No. 8, March 2002, pp.)**
Pub: Earl Graves Publishing Co.
Ed: Alan Hughes. **Description:** An interview with Ray Wilkins, president and CEO of SBC Pacific Bell, about last year's dotcom meltdown.

33828 ■ "EarthLink Inc. to purchase customers of Orlando ISP" in *Atlanta Business Chronicle* **(Vol. 25, No. 19, October 18, 2002, pp. 31A)**
Pub: American City Business Publications, Inc.
Ed: Chad Eric Watt. **Description:** Volaris Online, located in Orlando, Florida, will sell its base of dial-up Internet service customers to EarthLink Inc., Atlanta, Georgia. A total of 250,000 Volaris subscribers will be affected by the sale, and will likely result in Volaris trimming a large number of its 300-person staff. EarthLink has made a practice of building its subscriber base through the acquisition of smaller Internet service providers.

33829 ■ "Easy e-commerce" in *WorkingWoman* **(Vol. 25, No. 6, June 2000, pp. 107)**
Pub: Lang Communications Inc.
Ed: Nancy Henderson. **Description:** Intensive courses in the business use of the World Wide Web are described, with focus on choosing a course to fit your previous knowledge and your own requirements.

33830 ■ "Easy Read: Build Business Relationships with a Company Blog" in *Entrepreneur* **(Vol. 31, No. 12, December 2003, pp. 25)**
Pub: Entrepreneur Media Inc.
Ed: Laura Tiffany. **Description:** Before allowing customers, partners, investors, employees, or even competitors, to access company information via a blog, it is crucial to determine what you want your blog to accomplish.

33831 ■ "Ebank gains altitude after midflight change" in *Atlanta Business Chronicle* **(Vol. 24, No. 9, August 3, 2001, pp. 19A)**
Pub: American City Business Journals Inc.
Ed: Meredith Jordan. **Description:** Ebank.com Inc., based in Atlanta, Georgia, was headed for certain disaster as a dot-com bank. According to Jim Box, the new president and CEO, has turned the company around 100 percent, and the company is growing financially and considering acquisitions and still enjoys a presence on the Web.

33832 ■ "eBay Auction Integration Will Be a Major Player with Irun's Website Builder Tools" in *PR Newswire* **(December 2, 2003)**
Pub: PR Newswire Association, Inc.
Description: Irun Corporation announced that its Website builder now includes auction integration as part of its service. This service will allow businesses a single point for managing their e-commerce Website and eBay auctions.

33833 ■ "eBay" in *DSN Retail Fax* **(Vol. 10, No. 26, June 30, 2003)**
Pub: Lebhar-Friedman Inc.
Description: UPS and eBay have extended their partnership and introduced a new line of shipping tools for eBay customers.

33834 ■ "eBay Enters Electrical Market" in *Electrical Wholesaling* **(Vol. 84, No. 9, September 1, 2003)**
Pub: PRIMEDIA Business Magazines & Media Inc.
Ed: Jim Lucy. **Description:** eBay has added 110 new subcategories to its lineup, including categories for electrical distribution equipment, industrial automation and control, electrical tools and supplies, motors and lighting products.

33835 ■ "EBay Ex-Operating Chief Webb Joins LiveOps As Chief Executive" in *Wall Street Journal* **(Vol. 248, December 2006, No. 145, pp. B10)**
Pub: Dow Jones & Co. Inc.
Ed: Vauhini Vara **Description:** Profile of Maynard Webb, former EBay Inc. chief operating officer. Webb was largely responsible for upgrading Ebay's technology to keep up with rapid growth.

33836 ■ "eBay Phenomenon Embraced by Online Piano Company" in *PR Newswire* **(November 13, 2003)**
Pub: PR Newswire Association, Inc.

Description: Profile of PianoQuest.com, the company that has sold more than 200 pianos through eBay in two years, with a 98 percent positive feedback rating.

33837 ■ **"eBay Revs Up Its Industrial Sales: It's Now Easier for Engineers to Go Shopping Online"** in *Design News* (Vol.58, No.10, July 7, 2003)
Pub: Reed Business Information
Ed: Robert Spiegal. **Description:** eBay now has auctions posted across 18,000 categories, with 62 million registered users.

33838 ■ **"EBay Springs a Price Increase on eBay Store Owners"** in *Inc.* (April 1, 2005)
Pub: Inc. Magazine
Ed: Stephanie Clifford. **Description:** EBay's new price increases have many of the online's big sellers considering a move to selling on their own Websites.

33839 ■ **"EBay's Bid To Go Beyond Auctions Isn't Selling Well"** in *Wall Street Journal* (Vol. 248, December 2006, No. 145, pp. B1)
Pub: Dow Jones & Co. Inc.
Ed: Vauhine Vara **Description:** While trying to entice online shoppers with it's new eBay Express Website, the outlook seems bleak. Many of the early users report disappointment with the lack of increased exposure. In-Depth stock figures and projections included.

33840 ■ **"ebrary Snags Key Investors for Pay-Per-Use Service"** in *Information Today* (Vol. 17, No. 11, December 2000, pp. 41)
Pub: Information Today, Inc.
Ed: Paula J. Hane. **Description:** ebrary, an online research library, announced a joint investment by three leading publishing and information service companies: Random House, Inc., Pearson, and The McGraw-Hill Companies.

33841 ■ **"EBSCO Expands Book Services, Creates E-Journal Licensing Web Site"** in *Information Today* (Vol. 17, No. 10, November 2000, pp. 39)
Pub: Information Today, Inc.
Description: EBSCO Information Services is expanding its online book searching and ordering service to libraries and other organizations.

33842 ■ **"eC-T spins localized Web"** in *InfoWorld* (Vol. 22, No. 5, January 31, 2000, pp. 8)
Pub: InfoWorld
Ed: Geneva Sapp. **Description:** Defying the trend of faceless conglomerates, optimized supply chains, and the homogenization of the e-business marketplace, eC-T (e-Commerce Technology), a Web service company specializing in developing Internet-commerce strategies for local markets, plans to expand into the U.S. The company maintains that most shoppers, including small businesses, want to purchase from within their own communities.

33843 ■ **"The EDI revolution"** in *Hispanic Business* (Vol. 22, No. 4, April 2000, pp. 20)
Pub: Hispanic Business
Ed: Jennifer Riley. **Description:** The original vehicle for Governmental electronic procurement was the Electronic Data Interchange, but use of this system has been overtaken by the Internet due to its lower costs and ease of use. Small companies should take advantage of this change to ensure that they are able to respond to electronic procurement.

33844 ■ **"eFindOutTheTruth.com: www. efindoutthetruth.com"** in *Entrepreneur* (Vol. 32, November 2004, No. 11, pp. 6)
Pub: Entrepreneur Media Inc.
Ed: Steve Cooper. **Description:** Profile of the online service that provides background screening of prospective new hires.

33845 ■ **"8 Secrets of a Winning E-Mail Newsletter"** in *PC Magazine* (February 22, 2000, pp. 135)
Pub: Ziff-Davis Publishing Company
Ed: Brett Glass. **Description:** Eight tips are given to produce a successful newsletter to send to customers and clients via e-mail.

33846 ■ **"Eliminate Fulfillment Problems"** in *E-business Advisor* (Vol. 18, No. 3, March 2000, pp. 28)
Pub: Advisor Media, Inc.
Ed: Patrick Rigney. **Description:** The best ways to integrate an online system with an existing business is to establish a separate order fulfillment center, or to outsource order processing. Orders are then sent directly to the company's warehouse.

33847 ■ *Email Marketing by the Numbers: How to Use the World's Greatest Marketing Tool to Take Any Organization to the Next Level*
Pub: John Wiley and Sons Inc.
Ed: Chris Baggott. **Released:** April 2007. **Price:** $29.99 (CND). **Description:** Tips for using email to market small business products and services are provided.

33848 ■ **"Engler's tax web"** in *Wall Street Journal* (December 17, 2001, pp. A18)
Pub: Wall Street Journal
Description: An overview of Michigan's Governor John Engler's efforts to tax Internet Sales.

33849 ■ **"Enrolling online is No. 1 choice among workers, survey finds"** in *Crain's Detroit Business* (Vol. 18, No. 18, May 6, 2002, pp. 12)
Pub: Crain Communications Inc. - Detroit
Ed: Jerry Geisel. **Description:** The Internet has become the dominant way for workers to enroll into benefits programs offered by employers.

33850 ■ **"Enterprise Software: An industry finds order in the madness"** in *Red Herring* (No. 105, October 1, 2001, pp. 74-75)
Pub: Herring Communications
Ed: Justin Hibbard. **Description:** An overview of the enterprise software industry, which represents nearly 80 percent of the packaged application market, is presented. High market potential seems to exist with customer relationship management, supply chain management, and e-commerce software.

33851 ■ **"Enterprise Software Sector Analysis"** in *Red Herring* (No. 105, October 1, 2001, pp. 86-87)
Pub: Herring Communications
Description: Analysis of the enterprise software sector is presented in graphs and charts, including analytics, application servers, collaborative commerce, and Web services.

33852 ■ **"Entrepreneur Column"** in *Entrepreneur* (August 18, 2005)
Pub: Entrepreneur Media Inc.
Ed: Gail F. Goodman. **Description:** Electronic newsletters can be a great marketing tool if done properly. Email marketing solutions should include data that allows a firm to analyze and optimize any e-newsletter campaign.

33853 ■ **"Entrepreneur Seeks Riches In Pixels-Again"** in *Wall Street Journal* (Vol. 248, December 2006, No. 149, pp. B4)
Pub: Dow Jones & Co. Inc.
Ed: Gwendolyn Bounds **Description:** Profile of college student Alex Tew who sold $1 million in advertising by creating a new Internet advertising model.

33854 ■ **"Entrepreneurial Web Hub Debuts"** in *Hispanic Business* (September 2004, pp. 20)
Pub: Hispanic Business
Description: America Online Latino and Ford Motor Company have teamed to launch a Spanish-language Web hub that will assist Hispanics to start or grow small businesses.

33855 ■ **"The Eparty's Over"** in *Forbes* (December 11, 2000, pp. 144)
Pub: Forbes Magazine
Ed: Dorothy Pomerantz. **Description:** Of all the overhyped incubators launched during the heady days of 1999, Ecompanies and its two young founders seemed like a sure bet.

33856 ■ **"EPrize Touts Small Business"** in *Detroit Free Press* (January 17, 2007)
Pub: Knight-Ridder/Tribune Business News
Ed: Jewel Gopwani. **Description:** ePrize is targeting small businesses to advertise on its new Website, www.caffeinenow.com. The company designs promotions for larger companies but is offering space for small businesses to market their businesses by placing sweepstakes and rewards programs on the site.

33857 ■ **"Equal Time? Legal"** in *Entrepreneur* (Vol. 31, No. 9, September 2003, pp. 80)
Pub: Entrepreneur Media, Inc.
Ed: Jane Easter Bahls. **Description:** Labor unions may be able to use company email systems in order to communicate with members. A discussion regarding a recent decision by an administrative judge for the National Labor Relations Board involving Prudential Insurance's Office & Professional Employees International Union is cited.

33858 ■ **"The era of e-taxes"** in *Hispanic Business* (Vol. 22, No. 3, March 2000, pp. 62)
Pub: Hispanic Business
Ed: Milton Zall. **Description:** The Internal Revenue Service has implemented the electronic filing and payment of taxes in 2000. Issues concerning the effect of the new method of filing and payment on small businesses are discussed.

33859 ■ *The Essential Online Solution: The 5-Step Formula for Small Business Success*
Pub: John Wiley & Sons, Incorporated
Ed: Rick Segel; Barbara Callan-Bogia. **Released:** October 2006. **Price:** $22.95. **Description:** Strategies to help any small business increase its online presence and compete with big retail chains. Tips for success Web design are included.

33860 ■ *Essentials of Entrepreneurship and Small Business Management*
Pub: Prentice Hall PTR
Ed: Thomas W. Zimmerer; Norman M. Scarborough; Doug Wilson. **Released:** February 2007. **Price:** $106.67. **Description:** New venture creation and the knowledge required to start a new business are shared. The challenges of entrepreneurship, business plans, marketing, e-commerce, and financial considerations are explored.

33861 ■ **"Establish and Effective Privacy Policy"** in *E-business Advisor* (Vol. 18, No. 3, March 2000, pp. 34)
Pub: Advisor Media, Inc.
Ed: Joel B. Rothman. **Description:** The protection of a customer's personal information is a legal obligation that requires a comprehensive privacy policy. This policy should be clearly worded and linked to the home page through a distinctly labeled button.

33862 ■ **"Ethentica Ethenticator MS 3000 PC Card"** in *PC Magazine* (February 6, 2001, pp. 26)
Pub: Ziff-Davis Publishing Company
Ed: Sally Wiener Grotta. **Description:** Review of Ethentica Ethenticator MS 3000 PC Card, the fingerprint verification scanner used for mobile security. In addition to protecting the data on a laptop, the device replaces passwords on favorite Web sites and applications and even fills out personal information on user-selected Internet forms.

33863 ■ **"Even "E-Active" Organizations Have a Lot to Learn"** in *E-business Advisor* (Vol. 18, No. 3, March 2000, pp. 8)
Pub: Advisor Media, Inc.
Description: Most e-commerce companies understand the basic business concepts involved, such as Web portals, value chain and customer relations, but do not understand the issues of reintermediation, vortals and reverse markets. This article helps to bring meaning to these issues.

33864 ■ "Every Picture Tells a Story: New Web Displays Provide Market Data at a Glance" in *Barron's* (August 25, 2003, pp. T6)
Pub: Barron's
Ed: Theresa W. Carey. Description: Online securities trading services, such as those offered by Ameritrade and SmartMoney, are enhancing Web site displays of market activity with offerings such as QuoteScope and Map of the Market.

33865 ■ "Everything You Ever Wanted to Know About Email" in *Inc.* (October 2005, pp. 113-117, 119, 122)
Pub: Inc. Magazine
Ed: John Fried. Description: Guide to using email as an important business tool is presented. Tips to keep a system secure, efficient, and affordable are also included.

33866 ■ "The Evolution of E-Mail" in *Ingram's* (Vol. 28, No. 9, September 2002, pp. 62)
Pub: Show Me Publishing, Inc.
Ed: Tom Peterman. Description: E-mail is the most popular activity on the Internet and is being used in many ways, such as messaging, online teaching and learning, conferencing, and communication.

33867 ■ "The Evolution of XML Schemes" in *E-business Advisor* (Vol. 18, No. 5, May 2000, pp. 26)
Pub: Advisor Media, Inc.
Ed: James Tauber. Description: The idea behind the extensible markup language (XML) is to provide a standard way of attaching labels to unfamiliar objects, thus establishing a meaning for the objects. However, XML defines neither the meaning nor the set of familiar labels, which is a key part of its extensibility.

33868 ■ "Exbayer Online Trading Assistant Helps You Sell Items on eBay with New Store" in *PR Newswire* (March 15, 2004)
Pub: PR Newswire Association, Inc.
Description: Profile of Todd Quattlebaum, owner of Exbayer, the Houston, Texas store that offers easy and convenient services to people on fixed incomes, businesses with excess inventory, and attorneys legally bound to auction or probate goods to generate income. The store also provides UPS and Fed Ex shipping services.

33869 ■ "Exchange Overload" in *Red Herring* (No. 103, September 1, 2001, pp. 46-52)
Pub: Herring Communications
Ed: Christopher Locke, Michael V. Copeland. Description: Dominating North America's $400 billion gas and electricity market isn't enough for Enron. Now it wants to be the king of B2B trading. Can it work? A profile of Jeffrey Skilling, CEO and president, is included.

33870 ■ "Experienced players in the new economy" in *Hispanic Business* (Vol. 22, No. 7-8, July-August 2000, pp. 40)
Pub: Hispanic Business
Ed: Joel Russell. Description: A directory of the top 50 Hispanic American technology businesses is presented, ranked by revenue.

33871 ■ "Explaining XML" in *Harvard Business Review* (Vol. 78, No. 4, July 2000, pp. 18)
Pub: Harvard Business School Publishing Corp.
Ed: Eileen Roche. Description: J.P. Morgan and PricewaterhouseCoopers have proposed FpML, a dictionary that would standardize XML tags for foreign currency exchange and other financial transactions. This Internet technology development is based on XML, or extensible markup language.

33872 ■ "Exploding the Self-Service Myth" in *Harvard Business Review* (Vol. 78, No. 3, May 2000, pp. 26)
Pub: Harvard Business School Publishing Corp.
Ed: Youngme Moon, Frances X. Frei. Description: Instead of forcing customers to do all the work, the most successful e-commerce sites are taking over many aspects of the shopping process.

33873 ■ "Extra Special: Booking Sites Offer More Bang for Your Buck-And Then Some" in *Entrepreneur* (Vol. 32, November 2004, No. 11, pp. 22)
Pub: Entrepreneur Media Inc.
Ed: Chris McGinnis. Description: Low-fare airlines offer online booking sites for companies willing to book directly with them rather than using a travel agent. Airtran-A2B Corporate Travel, Jetblue-Companyblue, and Southwest-SWABIZ, are featured.

33874 ■ "Ezsupport Life" in *Entrepreneur.com* (Vol. 34, February 2006, No. 2, pp. 6)
Pub: Entrepreneur Media Inc.
Description: Profile of EzSupport Life, a free, automated online customer-support solution for small businesses.

33875 ■ "Face to face" in *Incentive* (Vol. 174, No. 9, September 2000, pp. 102)
Pub: Bill Communications
Ed: Andrea Nierenberg. Description: Tips for sales communication in the electronic age where less face-to-face meetings occur.

33876 ■ "Facing the Online Music" in *Inc.* (July 1, 2003)
Pub: Gruner & Jahr USA Publishing
Description: Entrepreneurs have a stake in the debate over downloading online music and are skeptical of the recording industry's attempts to rewrite intellectual property law.

33877 ■ "Failure is not an option" in *Fast Company* (June 2001, pp. 44)
Pub: Fast Company
Ed: Jennifer Reingold. Description: Unveiled in January 2001 by Plural Inc., the Wall Street Solutions Center (WSSC) was designed to help companies make big technology bets, without betting the future of the company in the process. Plural Inc. is an e-business consulting firm.

33878 ■ "Fake Microsoft Mail Is Sypware Phishing Attack" in *eWeek* (February 7, 2005)
Pub: Ziff Davis Media Inc.
Description: Microsoft plans to make its 'Windows Genuine Advantage' anti-piracy initiative mandatory in 2005. The plan will protect users from Internet scammers sending out emails that arrive with a subject line: Microsoft Windows Update.

33879 ■ "Falling in Gov" in *Entrepreneur* (Vol. 30, No. 3, March 200)
Pub: Entrepreneur Media Inc.
Ed: Amanda C. Kooser. Description: E-government is the next fertile, immense market space on which young entrepreneurs should set their focus. E-government is businesses that provide technical services to state agencies.

33880 ■ "Fantastic Forum" in *Entrepreneur* (Vol. 33, September 2005, No. 9, pp. 92)
Pub: Entrepreneur Media Inc.
Ed: Chris Penttila. Description: Video on Location Inc., a full-service video production firm located in Rockville, Maryland uses virtual collaboration software among its 16 employees to create commercials, Webcasts, instructional videos and more. The software allows workers to collaborate online from various locations.

33881 ■ "Farming IT Out" in *Home Office Computing* (Vol. 18, No. 10, October 2000, pp. 16)
Pub: Scholastic Inc.
Ed: Mark Kakkuri. Description: Information Technology (IT) outsourcing services are ready to help home office workers with everything from setting up a computer to building a broadband LAN.

33882 ■ "Fast Facts" in *Entrepreneur* (Vol. 28, No. 11, November 2000, pp. 30)
Pub: Entrepreneur Media Inc.
Ed: Robert McGarvey. Description: The latest information regarding electronic commerce. Statistical data is included.

33883 ■ "The Fast Track to CE Credits" in *Rough Notes* (Vol. 145, No. 2, February 2003, pp. 84)
Pub: Rough Notes
Ed: Barbara Morris. Description: Insurance agents can have their continuing education with online CE education, such as WEBCE.com or CEU.com with convenience, flexibility and speed.

33884 ■ "The Father of Spam: Half of All E-Mail Sent Today is Spam" in *Entrepreneur* (Vol. 31, No. 10, October 2003)
Pub: Entrepreneur Media Inc.
Ed: Geoff Williams. Description: Internet Spam costs companies $8 billion to $10 billion annually in the form of lost productivity as entrepreneurs and employees rid email boxes of unwanted email.

33885 ■ "Fear of Filing" in *Working Woman* (Vol. 25, No. 2, February 2000, pp. 84)
Pub: MacDonald Communications Corp.
Ed: Tamar Schreibman. Description: A professional e-organizer was hired to classify and manage the hundreds of documents on a company's PC to help the business run more smoothly.

33886 ■ "Fear of Filing" in *WorkingWoman* (Vol. 25, No. 2, February 2000, pp. 84)
Pub: Lang Communications Inc.
Ed: Tamar Schreibman. Description: An overview of a professional e-organizer who classifies and manages documents to help the business run more smoothly.

33887 ■ "FedEx to launch service that allows small companies to build online stores" in *Wall Street Journal* (June 12, 2000, pp. A6)
Pub: Dow Jones & Co., Inc.
Ed: Rick Brooks. Description: FedEx has launched a new program that assists small businesses in e-commerce.

33888 ■ "The Feds Are Following You" in *PC Computing* (March 2000, pp. 94)
Pub: Ziff-Davis Inc.
Description: The article addresses how easy it is to access personal information about anyone online, and suggests way to help protect yourself.

33889 ■ "Feed Me" in *Forbes* (Vol. 175, January 10, 2005, No. 1, pp. 38)
Pub: Forbes Magazine Inc.
Ed: Peter Kafka, David Whelan. Description: Profile of Flickr, a new photo Web site allowing users to post new photos to share with family and friends, using RSS technology. Experts are concerned that RSS could allow blogs to subvert media on the Internet.

33890 ■ "Feed the Need" in *Entrepreneur* (Vol. 32, July 2004, No. 7, pp. 47)
Pub: Entrepreneur Media Inc.
Ed: Amanda C. Kooser. Description: Web feeds bring news, updates and information to Internet users through XML-based RSS technology. These feeds could be a way for entrepreneurs to stay current on relevant news and updates affecting their industry.

33891 ■ "Feeding Frenzy" in *Entrepreneur.com* (Vol. 34, February 2006, No. 2, pp. 77)
Pub: Entrepreneur Media Inc.
Ed: Catherine Seda. Description: Creative marketers are using RSS feed in order to send successful marketing email. RSS is 100 percent opt-in. Users subscribe to a reader such as Bloglines, Newsgator, or Pluck and choose the feeds they wish to receive, no spam allowed. The number of RSS users is growing quickly making it an opportunity to market products and services for small companies.

33892 ■ "Fictionwise announces e-book lending solution for libraries" in *Information Today* (Vol. 19, No. 10, November 2002, pp. 44)
Pub: Information Today, Inc.
Description: Profile of Fictionwise, an e-book retailer that launched Libwise, a product that allows a library or group to loan e-books to their membership using a customized Web site branded by the library. Fictionwise provides complete hosting and customer technical support.

33893 ■ **"Find Anything on the Web"** in *Home Office Computing* (Vol. 18, No. 7, July 2000, pp. 48)
Pub: Scholastic Inc.
Ed: Susan Glinert. **Description:** Tips for using Web research tools effectively are presented. Government sites have some of the best information for anyone planning to start a home-based business, as do sites geared for particular industries.

33894 ■ **"Find Online Training That Pays Off"** in *Fortune* (Vol. 151, February 7, 2005, No. 3, pp. 34)
Pub: Time Inc.
Ed: Anne Fisher. **Description:** Online courses that help employees obtain needed knowledge are discussed. According to Pathlore Software, a firm that designs online curriculums for various companies, suggests a three-stage approach to online employee learning.

33895 ■ **"Find Out How To Reduce The Cost of Email"** in *Internet Wire* (October 30, 2001, pp. 100)
Pub: Internet Wire
Description: Profile of Oracle's eMail Center, a comprehensive email solution integrated with Oracle Interaction Center products, which can provide unified handling of email, telephony, and Web interactions.

33896 ■ **"Finding deals, small businesses buy more online"** in *The New York Times* (May 15, 2000, pp. C4)
Pub: The New York Times Company
Ed: Laurie J. Flynn. **Description:** The findings of a survey conducted by Access Markets International Partners regarding e-commerce.

33897 ■ **"Finding Prospects By Using The Internet"** in *Rough Notes* (Vol. 145, No. 9, September 2002, pp. 46)
Pub: Rough Notes
Ed: Steve Anderson. **Description:** Marketing for agencies has been helped by access to the Internet. There are business databases like Dun and Bradstreet and R.H. Donnelley from which lists of prospects are available.

33898 ■ **"Finding the Right Keyword"** in *Inc.* (October 1, 2003)
Pub: Gruner & Jahr USA Publishing
Ed: Ellen Neuborne. **Description:** Marketing via search engines like Yahoo and Google is difficult and costly, but it is still a good way to market products and services if done wisely.

33899 ■ **"Finding-Site search and geographic maps are an easy way to make a site more usable and useful to your visitors"** in *PC Magazine* (Feb.01)
Pub: Ziff-Davis Publishing Company
Ed: Troy Dreier. **Description:** Information about site search tools and geographic maps to make a Web site more useful are examined.

33900 ■ **"Finishing Touches - The Web is crowded and intensely competitive"** in *PC Magazine* (February 20, 2001, pp. 133)
Pub: Ziff-Davis Publishing Company
Ed: Neil Randall. **Description:** BeautyQ.com's Web site is designed to attract teen-age girls by offering health and style advice. The site enjoyed brisk traffic, but lacked repeat visitors until the organization added a bulletin board. The typical visitor now spends more than ten minutes on the site and many of them make repeat visits.

33901 ■ **"A Fire Wall for Unwanted E-Mail"** in *Kiplinger's Personal Finance Magazine* (Vol. 55, No. 1, January, 2001, pp. 97)
Pub: The Kiplinger Washington Editors, Inc.
Ed: Kristin Davis. **Description:** The software program SpamKiller, that detects spam, is described. Its publisher, Novasoft, has analyzed thousands of bulk commercial e-mails to come up with their 2,200 filters, which screen for addresses of known spammers and specific phrases used by spammers.

33902 ■ **"Firefox Is Hot; Thunderbird's Not"** in *St. Louis Post-Dispatch* (December 17, 2004)
Pub: Knight-Ridder/Tribune Business News
Ed: David Sheets. **Description:** Web browsers, Firefox and Thunderbird are profiled.

33903 ■ **"First Was Phishing, Next Is Pharming"** in *eWeek* (February 2, 2005)
Pub: Ziff Davis Media Inc.
Description: Security threats known as phishing and pharming are covered. Pharming is a new application of well-known security weaknesses, requiring banks and other institutions to upgrade their DNS systems and domain registrations in order to protect customers from attack when using their Websites.

33904 ■ **"Five Ideas to Watch"** in *Inc.* (January 1, 2005)
Pub: Inc. Magazine
Ed: Jess McCuan. **Description:** South Lake Tahoe, California's newest hotel caters specifically to snowboarders; products made from hemp seed and oil are the latest organic food trend; Ingenio has developed a Web advertising system to help small business; and a device that can shut off any television anywhere.

33905 ■ **"Five Questions"** in *Sales and Marketing.com* (Vol. 156, No. 3, March 2004, pp. 11)
Pub: VNU eMedia, Inc.
Description: Jay Fiore answers questions about his newest eBay campaign that targets small businesses.

33906 ■ **"Five Ways to Avoid Disaster"** in *Fast Company* (June 2001, pp. 46)
Pub: Fast Company
Description: Neil Isford, president and CEO of Plural, the e-business consulting firm, outlines five ways to avoid technology-enabled disasters.

33907 ■ **"Flexibility drove new revenue source"** in *Crain's Detroit Business* (Vol. 19, No. 13, March 31, 2003, pp. 14)
Pub: Crain Communications Inc., Detroit
Description: Founder, Mark Campbell of Stoneage. com, a Troy company, states that flexibility is the key to his successful online used-car database.

33908 ■ **"Florida Online Dating Service Tries to Find Love Link for Urban Professionals"** in *Miami Herald* (March 1, 2004)
Pub: Knight-Ridder/Tribune Business News
Description: Profile of Beatrice Louissaint and Yolanda Davis and their online dating service and event company, Soul Connections. The service targets urban professionals in search of love. The Website provides a place for users to post photos and information to meet other singles, while an event division organizes functions where singles can socialize.

33909 ■ **"Flying From the Computer"** in *The Economist* (Vol. 377, October 1-7, 2005, No. 8446, pp. 65-67)
Pub: The Economist Newspaper Ltd.
Description: The Internet has created intense competition among travel providers. Statistical data included.

33910 ■ **"Flying solo: pay more for a travel agent? Why not just go online?"** in *Entrepreneur* (Vol. 30, No. 9, September 2002, pp. 24)
Pub: Entrepreneur Media Inc.
Ed: Christopher Elliott. **Description:** According to the National Business Travel Association, more companies are using the Internet to book business travel in order to save booking fees for airline tickets.

33911 ■ **"Focus remained on primary customers"** in *Crain's Detroit Business* (Vol. 19, No. 13, March 31, 2003, pp. 14)
Pub: Crain Communications Inc., Detroit
Description: Profile of Troy, Michigan-based New World Systems Corporation, developer of software for public safety and public administration organizations.

33912 ■ **"Following the dollars online"** in *Hispanic Business* (Vol. 22, No. 5, May 2000, pp. 56)
Pub: Hispanic Business
Ed: Derek Reveron. **Description:** Hispanics are a key target market for many firms doing business via the Internet. Some 50 percent of Hispanic households could access the Internet in March 2000, from 46 percent of Anglo households.

33913 ■ **"For now, dealers win online battle for fleet buyers"** in *Hispanic Business* (Vol. 22, No. 6, June 2000, pp. 132)
Pub: Hispanic Business
Ed: Scott Williams. **Description:** U.S. consumers spent $360 billion on new cars in 1999, of which almost $6 billion was accounted for by Internet transactions. Auto industry research company J.D. Power forecasts that half of all new cars will be bought via the Internet by 2002. Most Internet sites focus on private customers, not fleet buyers.

33914 ■ **"For Offering Hope and Help to the Parents of Autistic Children"** in *Inc.* (April 1, 2005)
Pub: Inc. Magazine
Description: Profile of Julie Azuma, founder of Different Roads to Learning. After learning that her daughter Miranda was autistic, Azuma created an online retail business offering tools to help teach language and social skills to autistic children.

33915 ■ **"For Want of a Nail...The War Was Lost"** in *E-business Advisor* (Vol. 18, No. 12, December 2000, pp. 6)
Pub: Advisor Media, Inc.
Ed: John L. Hawkins. **Description:** Tips for e-commerce users include the use of the Sprint digital network for cell phone use when traveling. Sprint's voice mail and text messaging features are useless, taking days or even weeks for the notification of a message. IBM ThinkPad notebooks are good machines, but spare parts are in short supply. A battery replacement can take up to a year to receive. A Compaq desktop's automatic system for communicating with the company about updates occupies so much processing power, it slows the system's performance.

33916 ■ **"Forget About Bartering. For Start-Ups, It's All About the Freebies"** in *Inc.* (May 1, 2005)
Pub: Inc. Magazine
Ed: Stephanie Clifford. **Description:** Dave Morgan, founder of the Internet marketing firm Real Media shares ideas for starting a company with a minimal cash investment by offering employees benefits for working for him for free. Morgan recruited two recent college graduates to work unpaid for six months.

33917 ■ **"Former Information Warrior D'Amico Now Fighting Cyberwarfare"** in *Long Island Business News* (March 12, 2004)
Pub: Dolan Media Newswires
Ed: Ken Schachter. **Description:** Profile of Anita D'Amico, director of the 18-person company, Secure Decisions. The firm developed software used by the Navy Command and Control ship USS Blue Ridge for war games. A new initiative calls for the sale of the system to new markets, including epidemiology to track disease and outbreaks, and law enforcement to track crime patterns.

33918 ■ **"Forward: Thomas Middelhoff faces the music at Bertelsmann"** in *Red Herring* (No. 105, October 1, 2001, pp. 30-31)
Pub: Herring Communications
Ed: Robert LaFranco. **Description:** Despite the pronouncements given by Thomas Middelhoff, CEO of Bertelsmann, only one new-media investment he has spearheaded has paid off. In January 2000, Bertelsmann stated that his company wanted to be Number One in media e-commerce.

33919 ■ **"Found It! Building a Search-Engine Friendly Web Site"** in *My Business* (December/January 2004, pp. 44)
Pub: My Business Magazine
Ed: Lee Gimpel. **Description:** Ways to improve a Web site's ranking for a small business are examined,

including the use of search words and phrases and being listed in a directory of Web sites.

33920 ■ "A fourth frontier that technology has now crossed enables users to receive fat video files" in Inc. (November 15, 2000, pp. 88)
Pub: The Goldhirsh Group
Description: Companies are already using Internet video to communicate with customers and investors.

33921 ■ "Free-for-all on the name exchange" in The New York Times (March 27, 2000, pp. D3, H3)
Pub: The New York Times Company
Ed: Sue Cummings. **Description:** Internet domain names are discussed. Statistical data included.

33922 ■ "Free Online Bridal Registry Service Offers Total Flexibility to Add Any Gift..." in PR Newswire (Feb. 24, 2004)
Pub: PR Newswire Association, Inc.
Description: Prifle of FindGift.com, an Internet open gift registry. The gift registry is not tied to any particular store, but buyers can purchase registered gifts from any store they wish. The service is offered free to brides and grooms.

33923 ■ "Free Public Wireless Internet Access: Boom or Boondoggle?" in San Diego Business Journal (Vol. 28, January 1, 2007, No. 1, pp. 19)
Pub: San Diego Business Journal Associates
Ed: Andy Killion. **Description:** The pros and cons of offering free public wireless Internet access in San Diego County, California is discussed.

33924 ■ "Free Reign" in Home Office Computing (Vol. 18, No. 12, December 2000, pp. 45)
Pub: Scholastic Inc.
Ed: Douglas Gantenbein. **Description:** Many companies now offer free E-mail and Internet access service based on an advertiser-supported model. Home-based workers will find such free ISPs useful mainly as backups to a paid account.

33925 ■ "FriendFinder Online Dating Far Outranks the Competition; Multiple Awards Bestowed..." in PR Newswire (Jan. 5, 2004)
Pub: PR Newswire Association, Inc.
Description: Profile of FriendFinder online dating service. FriendFinder's strategy is to use a personalized approach that involves creating online communities with common interest areas, including categories based on key cultural, age, religious and sexual interests.

33926 ■ "Friends should never ask friends to spam-even if Big Blue says to do so" in InfoWorld (Vol. 22, No. 38, September 18, 2000 pp. 109)
Pub: InfoWorld
Ed: Ed Foster. **Description:** Internet marketers frequently use chain-letter methods to sell products and services, offering free items if a user agrees to spam friends. IBM has drawn several complaints from users by resorting to such tactics when marketing its Via-Voice speech-recognition product. Users received E-mail forms IBM titled 'How to Get ViaVoice Free' that offered a $169 copy of ViaVoice Millennium Pro at no charge if they persuaded five friends to sign up for the same small-business online newsletter. IBM asked users to forward a specific canned message to others offering an electronic Small Business Resource Guide as a bonus gift, but failed to mention that the person forwarding the message had received a bribe. Many people are appalled that IBM would stoop to spam methods.

33927 ■ "From big idea to big bust: the wild ride of Boo.com" in The New York Times (December 13 2000, pp. D3, H3)
Pub: The New York Times Company
Ed: Andrew Ross Sorkin. **Description:** How the dot.com used up $185 million in 18 months and went bankrupt.

33928 ■ "From Digital Image to Document" in Sales & Marketing Management (Vol. 158, November-December 2006, No. 11, pp. 62)
Pub: VNU Business Media
Ed: Tali Arbel. **Description:** Free Web-based application, scanR.com, allows users to convert camera phone snapshots into files that can be sent to email or faxed to other locations.

33929 ■ From Entrepreneur to Infopreneur: Make Money with Books, E-Books, and Other Information Products
Pub: John Wiley & Sons, Incorporated
Ed: Stephanie Chandler. **Released:** November 2006.
Price: $19.95. **Description:** Infopreneurs sell information online in the forms of books, e-books, special reports, audio and video products, seminars, and more.

33930 ■ "Fulfill the Promise of Electronic Billing" in E-business Advisor (Vol. 18, No. 7, July 2000, pp. 26)
Pub: Advisor Media, Inc.
Ed: Jim Flynn. **Description:** Electronic bill payment and presentment (EBPP) has not taken off as expected due to such problems as poor implementation of the technology for the consumer market and bill consolidation technology is still in the embryonic stage.

33931 ■ "Furniture.com stages revival, forges ties with non-com allies" in Boston Business Journal (Vol. 22, No. 11, April 19, 2002, pp. 1)
Pub: MCP, Inc.
Description: Furniture.com Inc., which went into bankruptcy, is making a comeback by partnering with brick-and-mortar retailers like Levitz Furniture Corporation and Seaman Furniture Company Inc.; Furniture.com is being backed by Resurgence Asset Management LLC.

33932 ■ "The Future of Commerce" in Harvard Business Review (Vol. 78, No. 1, January 2000, pp. 39)
Pub: Harvard Business School Publishing Corp.
Description: As we enter the twenty-first century, the business world is consumed by questions about e-commerce. To shed light on the changes we may see as the early years of our new century unfold, the article asks some close observers of electronic commerce to share their thoughts and speculations about the future.

33933 ■ "Ganging Up on the Web" in Business Week (June 12, 2000, pp. F4)
Pub: McGraw-Hill, Inc.
Description: Small business may group together for bargains in online purchases.

33934 ■ "Get the Best Domain Name" in E-business Advisor (Vol. 18, No. 6, June 2000, pp. 24)
Pub: Advisor Media, Inc.
Ed: Gene J. Riccoboni. **Description:** Companies who are unable to obtain a Web site domain name ending in '.com' should consider using Country Code Top Level Domain (CCTLD) names. Eighty-four countries do not require that name registrants be residents, and 70 countries have not even begun to register domain names. Register.com and Alldomains.com both provide registration services for CCTLD names.

33935 ■ "Get the Best Usability Expertise" in E-business Advisor (Vol. 18, No. 7, July 2000, pp. 36)
Pub: Advisor Media, Inc.
Ed: Kevin Scoresby. **Description:** Guidelines for choosing the appropriate usability services to enhance the value of a Web site's usability are discussed. Web site usability is becoming a hot issue partly because of the negative press and the 'un-user-friendliness' of some prominent Web sites.

33936 ■ "Get Bizzed" in Entrepreneur (Vol. 28, No. 4, April 2000, pp. 66)
Pub: Entrepreneur Media Inc.
Description: If you're looking for a one-stop portal for all your small business needs, try e-Citi, the e-commerce unit of Citigroup, formed to help entrepreneurs gain access to big-business resources easily and securely.

33937 ■ "Get Connected" in Business Week (No. 3761, December 10, 2001, pp. SB12)
Pub: McGraw-Hill Inc.
Description: Tips for bringing small business phone systems into the Internet age are offered, with focus on call centers.

33938 ■ "Get the Current View of Your Customers" in E-business Advisor (Vol. 18, No. 12, December 2000, pp. 42)
Pub: Advisor Media, Inc.
Ed: Claudia Imhoff. **Description:** Successful e-commerce businesses employ analytical and tactical customer relationship management (CRM) applications to offer personalized and current information to their customers. CRM applications are not easy to implement because they involve so many departments and require a significant change in business practices. The system must offer instant access to customer information from anywhere and quick analysis of the data.

33939 ■ "Get your fix: had enough of auctions?" in Entrepreneur (Vol. 31, No. 4, April 2003, pp. 75)
Pub: Entrepreneur Media Inc.
Ed: Mark Henricks. **Description:** An overview of the fixed-price marketplace is presented. The fixed-price marketplace is where pre-owned, overstocked and clearance items are listed and sold by prices set by the seller and make it easy to put large inventories of goods online for sale.

33940 ■ "Get a Piece of the Action" in PC Computing (April 2000, pp. 108)
Pub: Ziff-Davis Inc.
Ed: Jane Weaver. **Description:** Three ways to create a domain name for a Web site are listed, including a listing of name registry services.

33941 ■ "Get Ready for the Wireless Web" in E-business Advisor (Vol. 18, No. 9, September 2000, pp. 36)
Pub: Advisor Media, Inc.
Ed: Neerav Berry. **Description:** Businesses should create a separate Web site for wireless access due to the skyrocketing use of mobile phones. However, making over Web sites for wireless use is complex. Users will likely not tolerate push messaging or advertising because they are typically paying per minute for wireless Web access.

33942 ■ "Get the Right Mix of Bricks & Clicks" in Harvard Business Review (Vol. 78, No. 3, May 2000, pp. 107)
Pub: Harvard Business School Publishing Corp.
Ed: Ranjay Gulati, Jason Garino. **Description:** Many of the most innovative Internet players are integrating their virtual and physical company operations. The key to success lies in how you carry out the integration.

33943 ■ "Get There Faster" in PC Computing (April 2000, pp. 97)
Pub: Ziff-Davis Inc.
Ed: Jason Compton. **Description:** When flying into a city for a day of business meetings, the TravRoute Co-Pilot 2000, can plan the route and schedule appointments accordingly, and even redraw the route to accommodate any changes due to rescheduling.

33944 ■ "Get in tune: keep your site visitors dialed in and buying" in Entrepreneur (Vol. 31, No. 5, May 2003, pp. 79)
Pub: Entrepreneur Media Inc.
Ed: Catherine Seda. **Description:** Opt-in offers can provide a coupon, a free report, or a newsletter to customers.

33945 ■ "Get the Word Out" in Small Business Opportunities (Vol. 12, No. 5, September 2000, pp. 12)
Pub: Harris Publications, Inc.
Ed: Lin Grensing-Pophal. **Description:** Ways to let buyers know about a Web site and having them return are covered. Simple things such as putting the Web address on business cards, stationery, and printed materials, e-mail signature files and exchange links are explored.

33946 ■ "Get Your Digital Data Fix" in *Fast Company* (May 2001, pp. 196)
Pub: Fast Company
Ed: Daniel H. Pink. **Description:** Profile of Bob Drudge, father of cyberscribe Matt Drudge, and founder of the Refdesk Web site which contains links to hundreds of Web-based information tools.

33947 ■ "Getting Around" in *PC Magazine* (February 20, 2001, pp. 67)
Pub: Ziff-Davis Publishing Company
Ed: Walaika Haskins. **Description:** New Web services and software are attempting to make life easier for business travelers. Offerings from companies such as i-tinerary Travel Solutions and SideStep seek to provide hassle-free travel.

33948 ■ "Getting the Dish; Blogs Allow Everyone to be a Critic" in *Crain's New York Business* (Vol. 23, January 29, 2007, No. 5, pp. 48)
Pub: Crain Communications, Inc.
Description: Blogs are changing the landscape of the dining scene. Everyone can be a critic on such blogs as Chowmaster.com, Mouthfulsfood.com, or Thestrongbuzz.com among hosts of others.

33949 ■ "Getting in on the E-Signature Game" in *Inc.* (November 15, 2000, pp. 26)
Pub: The Goldhirsh Group
Description: The U.S. Congress has added "electronic sound, symbol, or process" to the list of legal signature types. Electronic signature is defined in the Electronic Signatures in Global and National Commerce Act, which went into effect on October 1, 2000.

33950 ■ "Getting a Leg up: Montemayor y Asociados Partners with Web-Hed Technologies" in *Hispanic Business* (Vol. 22, No. 5, May 2000, pp. 18)
Pub: Hispanic Business
Ed: Teresa Talerico. **Description:** Web development and hosting venture Web-Hed Technologies Inc. has formed a joint venture with advertising firm Montemayor y Asociados. Through this arrangement, Montemayor will be able to offer clients an extensive range of Web-Hed's interactive services.

33951 ■ "Getting Personal: Take a Closer Look at the Up-And-Coming Personalized Search Engine" in *Entrepreneur* (Vol. 33, February 2005, No. 2)
Pub: Entrepreneur Media Inc.
Ed: Steve Cooper. **Description:** Outline of search engines, including Google, WebSourced Inc., and SearchEngineLowdown.com.

33952 ■ "Getting Unwired" in *Internet World* (Vol. 7, No. 1, January 15, 2001, pp. 56)
Pub: Mecklermedia Corporation
Ed: Michael Cohn. **Description:** With the proliferation of wireless handheld services, there is a need to provide wireless Internet access and Web sites that will be able to deliver. This article takes a look at what the software and other industries are doing to enable Web sites to offer content to these devices and how they are doing it.

33953 ■ "Getting Your Head Around the Long Tail" in *Venture Capital Journal* (September 1, 2005)
Pub: Thomason Financial Inc.
Description: The Internet provides unlimited markets for consumers looking for mass-marketed products and services. Experts suggest that special businesses have yet to tap the potential that exists with e-commerce.

33954 ■ "GigaTrans hopes to get share of wireless market" in *Crain's Detroit Business* (Vol. 19, No. 16, April 21, 2003, pp. 12)
Pub: Crain Communications Inc., Detroit
Ed: Andrew Dietderich. **Description:** Profile of James Rose, CEO and his two-year-old firm GigaTrans, a wireless Internet service provider. The company hopes to serve small and medium-size business customers.

33955 ■ *Global E-Commerce: Impacts of National Environment and Policy*
Pub: Cambridge University Press
Ed: Kenneth L. Kraemer; Jason Dedrick; Nigel P. Melville; Kevin Zhu. **Released:** August 2006. **Price:** $75.00. **Description:** Global assessment of the impact of e-business on companies as well as countries.

33956 ■ *Global Electronic Business Research: Opportunities and Directions*
Pub: Idea Group Publishing
Ed: Nabeel A.Y. Al-Qirim. **Released:** October 2005. **Description:** Importance electronic commerce research plays in small to medium-sized enterprises in various countries.

33957 ■ "Go Live: They've Got Questions, You've Got Answers." in *Entrepreneur* (Vol. 33, March 2005, No. 3, pp. 90)
Pub: Entrepreneur Media Inc.
Ed: Catherine Seda. **Description:** When designing a Website, consider offering a live chat that helps customers with any frustrations navigating the site, while taking customer service to a higher level.

33958 ■ "Going digital for dollars" in *Black Enterprise* (Vol. 33, No. 3, October 2002, pp. 145)
Pub: Earl Graves Publishing Co.
Ed: Bernadette Williams. **Description:** The future of electronic commerce is discussed, including ways information technology can be used in the vision, creativity, and long-term planning for small business entrepreneurs. Security issues to protect small businesses, joint marketing between firms selling a similar product or service, and ways for African American small business owners can target their markets.

33959 ■ "Going Global" in *Home Office Computing* (Vol. 18, No. 10, October 2000, pp. 87)
Pub: Scholastic Inc.
Ed: David Harvey. **Description:** Small and home-based business are increasingly able to do business abroad by leveraging the power of the Internet and locating online tools and resources for tapping overseas markets. Steps to building an effective Web site are covered.

33960 ■ "Going, going, gone" in *Harvard Business Review* (Vol. 78, No. 6, November-December 2000, pp. 30)
Pub: Harvard Business School Publishing Corp.
Description: A discussion about companies using online reverse auctions to procure a variety of materials, services, and parts. Auctions force manufacturers to bid for contracts, and can produce great reductions in the cost of supplies, but they may also have risks.

33961 ■ "Going Green?" in *Crain's Detroit Business* (Vol. 22, November 20, 2006, No. 47, pp. 30)
Pub: Crain Communications Inc. - Detroit
Ed: Daniel Eizans. **Description:** Information and business links for green businesses are increasing online. Numerous sites are listed with job postings, event calendars, resource listings, and general news on the green industry are provided.

33962 ■ "Going Once, Going Twice..." in *Home Office Computing* (Vol. 18, No. 11, November 2000, pp. 90)
Pub: Scholastic Inc.
Ed: Mark Kakkuri. **Description:** Online auctions have become very popular recently. There are many reasons to sell online. It is a global market with many buyers, and instant feedback allows for a good sense of product value. Greater control over house, payment requirements, and buyer information is also an advantage. Sellers are encouraged to carefully read over terms and requirements because the work involved is substantial.

33963 ■ "Going Once, Going Twice: Online Auctions Offer Great Deals" in *Black Enterprise* (Vol. 34, No. 7, February 2004, pp. 140)
Pub: Earl Graves Publishing Co.

Ed: Raelyn C. Johnson. **Description:** Tips to use when shopping online auctions are presented.

33964 ■ "Gold Diggers" in *PC Magazine* (February 20, 2001, pp. 7a)
Pub: Ziff-Davis Publishing Company
Ed: Sarah L. Roberts-Witt. **Description:** The need for advanced E-business intelligence is driving the adoption of data warehousing and advanced analytical tools using such technologies as OLAP. Businesses who previously kept a tight hold on competitive information assets are now feeling compelled to share the information in order to retain market share. A few forward-thinking organizations now extend access to business-critical data to organizations outside their companies because they see information as an asset to be made widely available and tapped for profit.

33965 ■ "Gold Rush" in *Business Week* (January 9, 2006, No. 3966, pp. 68-72, 74, 76)
Pub: McGraw-Hill Companies
Ed: Brian Grow. **Description:** Online payment systems are facing security issues because online hackers are able to steal bank and credit card information. E-Gold is digital currency and customers using the service can enter false information in order to steal from an account.

33966 ■ "Good References, Easy to Find" in *Sales and Marketing.com* (Vol. 156, No. 3, March 2004, pp. 20)
Pub: VNU eMedia, Inc.
Ed: Daniel Tynan. **Description:** Profile of co-founders David Sroka and Darren Smith of Point of Reference, a Web site that manages customer testimonials. These testimonials can be used as a tool for closing sales.

33967 ■ "Goodwill Gets Back Into Retail Game" in *Crain's Detroit Business* (Vol. 21, January 17, 2005, No. 3, pp. 22)
Pub: Crain Communications Inc. - Detroit
Ed: Sherri Begin. **Description:** Goodwill Industries of Greater Detroit will launch a retail business using the Internet. Items donated will be sold on the Website at a fixed price rather auction format. Goodwill provides employee and training services to individuals with disabilities and other special needs.

33968 ■ "The Google Effect Kicks In" in *Venture Capital Journal* (December 1, 2004)
Pub: Thomason Financial Inc.
Ed: Lawrence Aragon. **Description:** The average price of venture capital-backed initial public offerings rose 32 percent in aftermarket, the biggest monthly gain in nine months. Statistical data included.

33969 ■ "Google Smackdown" in *Entrepreneur.com* (Vol. 34, January 2006, No. 1, pp. 6)
Pub: Entrepreneur Media Inc.
Ed: Steve Cooper. **Description:** Paul Bausch has developed Google Smackdown, a free site that allows users to input two words or phrases to help search for information on Google.

33970 ■ *The Google Story: Inside the Hottest Business, Media, and Technology Success of Our Time*
Pub: Random Housing Publishing Group
Ed: David A. Vise; Mark Malseed. **Price:** $26.00.

33971 ■ "Google Update Draws Criticism from Small Biz" in *Inc.* (January 1, 2004)
Pub: Gruner & Jahr USA Publishing
Ed: Rod Kurtz. **Description:** The recent upgrade at Google has small advertisers upset because ads will not longer be linked just to the specific keyword paid for. Google states the new system will help advertisers reach a wider audience, but some complain the system will also send irrelevant consumers to their sites.

33972 ■ "Google World: http://google. indicateur.com" in *Entrepreneur* (Vol. 31, No. 10, October 2003, pp. 6)
Pub: Entrepreneur Media, Inc.
Ed: Steve Cooper. **Description:** Ways the Google search engine can help a small business are discussed.

33973 ■ "Google's Banker" in *Fortune* (Vol. 149, No. 9, May 3, 2004, pp. 105)
Pub: Time, Inc.
Ed: Adam Lashinsky. Description: Venture capital information is discussed, including the impact of Google going public; Michael Moritz and his partners will likely reap hundreds of millions of dollars.

33974 ■ "Got Ideas? Book 'Em" in *Success* (Vol. 47, No. 6, November 2000, pp. 68)
Pub: Success Publishing, Inc.
Ed: Karen Fuller. Description: Profile of Firstuse. com, the world's central online registry for records, that could save your business millions.

33975 ■ "Government on Demand" in *Microsoft Executive Circle* (Vol. 1, No. 2, Q2 2001, pp. 38-40)
Pub: Putman Media
Ed: Marty Weil. Description: Constituents now have easier and faster access to government services and information via the Internet. Statistical data included.

33976 ■ "Government Hooks Man for Phishing" in *Cardline* (Vol. 4, No. 13, March 26, 2004, pp. 1)
Pub: Thomson Media Inc.
Description: An identity-theft scam has been shut down. Zachary Keith Hill used the logos of Internet service provider America Online (AOL) and the online payment service, PayPal to scam consumers into revealing credit card numbers and other confidential information.

33977 ■ "GoWholesale" in *Entrepreneur* (Vol. 33, October 2005, No. 10, pp. 6)
Pub: Entrepreneur Media Inc.
Ed: Steve Cooper. Description: Buyers and sellers of goods will love the new Go Wholesale portal offering paid and unpaid content, including pay-per-click advertising, wholesale online auctions, free classified, blogs and small business information.

33978 ■ "Graphiti: Eking out e-commerce" in *Red Herring* (No. 103, September 1, 2001, pp. 28)
Pub: Herring Communications
Ed: Elizabeth Lamb. Description: Online retail continues with steady growth; the number of online shoppers has risen by 50 percent worldwide, from 2000. Statistical data included.

33979 ■ "The Great Wall" in *Entrepreneur* (Vol. 32, No. 4, April 2004, pp. 38)
Pub: Entrepreneur Media, Inc.
Ed: Eric Bender. Description: For Internet security, it is essential for all small businesses to use a firewall to protect software and hardware. Information about Windows XP, Zone Labs' free ZoneAlarm and ZoneAlarm Pro is given.

33980 ■ "Groom Your Workforce" in *PC Computing* (March 2000, pp. 137)
Pub: Ziff-Davis Inc.
Ed: Leslie Ayers. Description: Internet training will teach employees the best way to do their jobs more effectively, with the convenience of learning on their own time and at their own pace.

33981 ■ "Grow Your Technology" in *Home Office Computing* (Vol. 18, No. 10, October 2000, pp. 52)
Pub: Scholastic Inc.
Ed: David Haskin. Description: Strategies for supporting a home business with best tech resources and support while staying within the budget are presented. The first step is to evaluate the existing tech set up, using a consultant, if necessary. Other tech strategies include developing a professional Web presence, providing adequate customer support and handling remote workers. Products and services for home office administration are listed.

33982 ■ "Growing apart: investment Websites keep advancing, even as the market retreats" in *Barron's* (Vol. 82, No. 59, Feb. 24, 2003, pp. T4)
Pub: Barron's
Ed: Kathy Yakal. Description: Evaluations of Web sites that provide financial information and portfolio management tips are given. The sites are Yahoo!Finance, Money.net from Nasdaq, WhisperNumber.com, Superstar Investor and MortgageSelect.com. Features of the sites are described to enable consumers to decide what sites might best fit personal needs.

33983 ■ "Guarding your turf: how the small guy can fend off big biz encroachment" in *Black Enterprise* (Vol. 33, No. 3, October 2002, pp. 56)
Pub: Earl Graves Publishing Co.
Ed: Bridget McCrea. Description: Strategies to help small business owners compete and successfully win contracts over larger firms are presented. Emphasis is given on the use of electronic commerce as a priority for doing business.

33984 ■ *Guerrilla Marketing for the New Millennium*
Pub: Morgan James Publishing, LLC
Ed: Jay Conrad Levinson. Released: September 2005. Price: $14.00. Description: Steps to successfully market a small business on the Internet.

33985 ■ *Guerrilla Marketing: Put Your Advertising on Steroids*
Pub: Morgan James Publishing, LLC
Ed: Jay Conrad Levinson. Released: October 2005. Price: $14.00. Description: Marketing concepts to successfully advertise any Internet business, featuring the ten most successful advertising campaigns of the 20th Century.

33986 ■ "Gulf Team With Corpedia on Ethics Course" in *Rough Notes* (Vol. 146, No. 9, September 2003, pp. 44)
Pub: Rough Notes
Ed: Dennis H. Pillsbury. Description: Profile of Gulf Insurance Group's underwriting division, including Internet marketing, importance of teamwork, and management of debt and business losses.

33987 ■ "Hack Attack:...And Other Threats From the Politically Offended" in *Entrepreneur* (Vol. 31, No. 10, October 2003, pp. 32)
Pub: Entrepreneur Media, Inc.
Ed: Julie Monahan. Description: Computer hackers can sabotage a small business directly by breaking through firewalls to steal and destroy data, or indirectly by using the company's network as a base from which to attack other targets.

33988 ■ "Hacked!" in *Entrepreneur* (Vol. 32, No. 4, April 2004, pp. 38)
Pub: Entrepreneur Media, Inc.
Ed: Eric Bender. Description: Standard security practices for small companies running an e-commerce business that is linked to other critical databases are discussed. Issues regarding the use of network security software versus hiring vendors are examined.

33989 ■ "The Hague: Laws without Borders" in *Red Herring* (No. 106, October 15, 2001, pp. 25-26)
Pub: Herring Communications
Ed: Julia Lawlor. Description: Important information regarding the Hague Convention on Jurisdiction and Foreign Judgments in Civil Matters is covered. The Hague treaty would deal with civil lawsuits and would require that laws regarding matters like libel, copyright, patents, and trademarks - which differ among countries - be enforced uniformly in the 53 nations participating in treaty talks.

33990 ■ "Hallmark, meet Hal" in *Crain's Detroit Business* (Vol. 16, No. 25, July 2000)
Pub: Crain Communications, Inc.
Ed: Matt Roush. Description: The way Mark Bennett saw it, if he could talk his family's Hallmark shop into using e-mail to build business, he could convince anybody.

33991 ■ "Handle Web Transactions with the BEA WebLogic Server" in *E-business Advisor* (Vol. 18, No. 2, February 2000, pp. 30)
Pub: Advisor Media, Inc.
Ed: Brian Benz. Description: A profile of BEA Systems' WebLogic Application Server, which offers excellent servlet development, deployment and management tools as well as outstanding class file selection and documentation.

33992 ■ "Hands On" in *Inc.* (September 2005, pp. 37-38)
Pub: Inc. Magazine
Ed: Alison Stein Wellner. Description: Email, Blackberrys, and text messaging are replacing face-to-face business communication. Facial expression and body language, voice inflection, and words can help derive meaning to business discussions.

33993 ■ "Happy Returns" in *Entrepreneur* (Vol. 32, No. 1, January 2004, pp. 39)
Pub: Entrepreneur Media, Inc.
Ed: Melissa Campanelli. Description: The importance of repeat business from customers, for both online retailers and brick-and-mortar businesses is discussed.

33994 ■ "Happy Returns" in *Entrepreneur. com* (Vol. 34, January 2006, No. 1, pp. 40)
Pub: Entrepreneur Media Inc.
Ed: Melissa Campanelli. Description: Online retailers should make the return process as easy as possible for customers by using a prepaid return label or box, give a longer time for returns, and to look at returns as an opportunity by providing good customer service.

33995 ■ "A Hard Sell" in *Entrepreneur* (Vol. 31, No. 8, August 2003, pp. 76)
Pub: Entrepreneur Media, Inc.
Ed: Jerry Fisher. Description: Ways advertising can convince tradition-bound prospects to switch to e-commerce are explored. Insure.com challenged parents to purchase insurance online, facing this issue head-on.

33996 ■ "Has the Divide Closed?" in *Hispanic Business* (July/August 2002, pp. 56-57)
Pub: Hispanic Business
Ed: Teresa Talerico. Description: Hispanics are rapidly embracing computer technology, but experts continue to debate the existence of a digital divide.

33997 ■ "Has Your Company Found Its Voice?" in *Fast Company* (August 2001, pp. 40)
Pub: Fast Company
Ed: Paul C. Judge. Description: Some brands really talk the talk, and sophisticated technology has the power to turn a customer's interaction with an automated call center into a virtual marketing conversation.

33998 ■ "Hatred of Spam Puts Crinkle in Faxing" in *Crain's Detroit Business* (Vol. 19, No. 45, November 10, 2003, pp. 9)
Pub: Crain Communications Inc., Detroit
Ed: Mary Kramer. Description: New rules adopted by the Federal Communications Commission require businesses to secure written approval from recipients before sending commercial faxes.

33999 ■ "Have Ricochet, Will Travel" in *PC Magazine* (February 20, 2001, pp. 35)
Pub: Ziff-Davis Publishing Company
Ed: Matthew D. Sarrel. Description: A profile of the recently launched Ricochet, a second-generation wireless data service now available in 22 major U.S. cities, including Atlanta, Baltimore, New York, San Diego and Washington, D.C., with plans to add 35 more cities this year.

34000 ■ "He knows if you've been naughty, but you can still send him e-mail" in *The New York Times* (December 13, 2000, pp. D10, H10)
Pub: The New York Times Company
Ed: James Barron. **Description:** Web sites having to do with Santa Claus see a huge rise in business.

34001 ■ "Heading for new domains" in *Entrepreneur* (Vol. 30, No. 3, March 2002, pp. 40)
Pub: Entrepreneur Media Inc.
Ed: Melissa Campanelli. **Description:** Seven new top-level domains (TLDs) are working their way onto the Internet, and business owners will have to decide if they want to register a new domain name. Along with the previous choices of business; .coop, for cooperatives; .info, for all uses; .museum, for museums; and accountants, will be available.

34002 ■ "Heard the News?" in *Entrepreneur* (Vol. 32, December 2004, No. 12, pp. 58)
Pub: Entrepreneur Media Inc.
Ed: Amanda C. Kooser. **Description:** Microsoft and Google have both rival services that gather news geared to the entrepreneur.

34003 ■ "Help! My brain's being eaten by a zillion dot-com ads!" in *The New York Times* (March 27, 2000, pp. D18, H18)
Pub: The New York Times Company
Description: A discussion about e-commerce between Sheri Baron, George Parker, David Wecal, Michael Zapolin, Roy Grace, Ellis Verdi, and Robert Bowman, moderated by Warren Berger.

34004 ■ "Helping You Realize Your Potential. ..on eBay" in *Journal Record (Oklahoma City, OK)* (October 2003)
Pub: Dolan Media Newswires
Ed: Matt Maile. **Description:** Profile of Door to Door Auctions, an auction firm that accurately represents the products it sells on eBay.

34005 ■ "The Hidden Value of Slow Sellers" in *Inc.* (October 2005, pp. 36)
Pub: Inc. Magazine
Description: According to a recent study that tracked sales at an online grocery store, a reduced choice of products led to a drop in sales, and fewer customers.

34006 ■ "High resolution" in *Entrepreneur* (Vol. 30, No. 2, February 2002, pp. 35)
Pub: Entrepreneur Media Inc.
Ed: Amanda C. Kooser. **Description:** Profile of Dispute Resolution Directory which offers online help in resolving business problems without using court action.

34007 ■ "High-Speed Web Access" in *Black Enterprise* (Vol. 35, February 2005, No. 7, pp. 162)
Pub: Earl G. Graves Publishing Co. Inc.
Ed: Leslie Guess Royal. **Description:** It is important for small businesses be equipped with high-speed Internet services to run a timely, efficient company. Statistical data, as well as pricing, is included.

34008 ■ "A high-tech domino effect: as dot-coms go, so go the e-commerce consultants" in *The New York Times* (December 16, 2000, pp. B1, C1)
Pub: The New York Times Company
Ed: Jonathan D. Glater. **Description:** All electronic-commerce consultant firms have suffered as a result of the weakness in the online sector. Firms like Scient Corporation and others that grew too rapidly are finding that demand for their services has evaporated, and are now having to lay off employees by the hundreds as they face a capital crunch.

34009 ■ "HighRankings.com: www.highrankings.com" in *Entrepreneur* (Vol. 31, No. 12, December 2003, pp. 8)
Pub: Entrepreneur Media Inc.
Ed: Steve Cooper. **Description:** Profile of a Web site offering tips for search engine optimization when designing a small business Internet site.

34010 ■ "Hired Guns: Is Enlisting Bloggers the Wave of the Future in Marketing?" in *Entrepreneur* (Vol. 31, No. 9, September 2003, pp. 30)
Pub: Entrepreneur Media, Inc.
Ed: Chris Penttila. **Description:** Blogs, Web logs or journals, are showing up all over the Internet and are being hired by companies to promote products.

34011 ■ "HispanicBusiness.com Expands" in *Hispanic Business* (Vol. 23, No. 5, May 2001, pp. 18)
Pub: Hispanic Business
Description: HispanicBusiness.com, the official Web site of Hispanic Business magazine, has launched a series of online and offline initiatives designed to reposition the site as a full-service resource center.

34012 ■ "Hispanics Flocking to the Web" in *Hispanic Business* (March 2002, pp. 12)
Pub: Hispanic Business
Description: According to a recent poll by Nielsen/Net Ratings, Hispanics are the fastest-growing ethnic group surfing the Web. Statistical data included.

34013 ■ "Hispanics Gravitating Toward the 'Net" in *Hispanic Business* (March 2003, pp. 24)
Pub: Hispanic Business
Description: According to a recent study called the America Online/Roper ASW U.S. Hispanic Cyberstudy, 48 percent of Hispanic Internet users have gone online in the last two years. Statistical data included.

34014 ■ "Hit the Mark" in *My Business* (August/September 2002, pp. 28-35)
Pub: My Business Magazine
Description: Seven small business trends that will position a company for success are profiled. These trends include mentoring programs, e-mail marketing, customer service, personalized products and services, employee stock ownership plans, targeting markets, and automation.

34015 ■ "Hitting the Links" in *Small Business Opportunities* (Vol. 13, No. 5, September 2001, pp. 84)
Pub: Harris Publications, Inc.
Ed: Marie Sherlock. **Description:** A primer to help small business owners maximize the use of links on their Web sites. The three essential types of links are outlined: outbound, inbound, and reciprocal.

34016 ■ "Holiday Bonus" in *Entrepreneur* (Vol. 33, September 2005, No. 9, pp. 48)
Pub: Entrepreneur Media Inc.
Ed: Melissa Campanelli. **Description:** According to a recent study, Websites offering a gift-idea center during the 2004 holidays were the most successful. Four ideas for adding special features to a Website for holiday 2005 are included.

34017 ■ "Hollywood, Silicon Valley at odds over digital piracy bills" in *Atlanta Business Chronicle* (Vol. 25, No. 21, Nov. 1, 2002, pp. 10B)
Pub: American City Business Publications, Inc.
Ed: Kent Hoover. **Description:** H.R. 5211, a bill introduced by California Democratic Representative Howard Berman, supports copyright owners in their efforts to stop unauthorized use of online music and movie materials. The bill permits copyright owners to use hacking as long as computer files are not damaged.

34018 ■ "Home Depot" in *Sales & Marketing Management* (Vol. 159, January-February 2007, No. 1, pp. 15)
Pub: VNU Business Media
Ed: Sarah Boehle. **Description:** Home Depot's Web-based training program is being used as a successful case study for other firms.

34019 ■ "Host With the Most" in *Small Business Opportunities* (Vol. 13, No. 5, September 2001, pp. 58)
Pub: Harris Publications, Inc.
Ed: Carla Vincent. **Description:** Seven-steps to guide small businesses in finding the right Web host, with the right size, a reasonable price, and competent technical support staff.

34020 ■ "Hot Disks" in *Entrepreneur* (Vol. 32, August 2004, No. 8, pp. 44)
Pub: Entrepreneur Media Inc.
Ed: Liane Cassavoy. **Description:** Profiles of small business tools include Avanquest's Design & Print Business Edition for creating marketing materials; Mozilla's Firefox 0.8 browser; Avidian Technologies' all-in-one Prophet 2004 that lets a business manage sales opportunities via email without switching applications; and Symantec's pcAnywhere, allows help-desk staff access the company's PCs without leaving the help desk.

34021 ■ "Hot Seat: Bruce Schneier" in *PC Computing* (April 2000, pp. 42)
Pub: Ziff-Davis Inc.
Ed: Thomas Claburn. **Description:** Bruce Schneier, founder and CTO of Counterpane Internet Security tells how to keep your company safe from Internet vandals. Mr. Schneier has also authored the book entitled, Secrets and Lies: Digital Security in the Networked World (John Wiley & Sons).

34022 ■ "Hot Stuff" in *Entrepreneur* (Vol. 32, No. 2, February 2004, pp. 43)
Pub: Entrepreneur Media, Inc.
Description: E-commerce analysts are researching the best online retail areas, predicting growth in food and beverage sales, used sporting goods, home products such as hardware, flowers and health and beauty products. Statistical data included.

34023 ■ "Hot on Their Trail: How to Use the Net to Track Offline Customers" in *Entrepreneur* (Vol. 32, December 2004, No. 12, pp. 94)
Pub: Entrepreneur Media Inc.
Ed: Catherine Seda. **Description:** Many small companies are using ad-tracking programs to monitor return on investment. When using the Internet to increase offline sales, be sure to offer a toll-free number, coupons, and printable order forms when designing the Website.

34024 ■ "How About a Little Browser Branding?" in *Sales & Marketing Management* (Vol. 159, January-February 2007, No. 1, pp. 45)
Pub: VNU Business Media
Description: Toolbars with built-in search engines can be customized to particular target markets.

34025 ■ "How to Acquire Customers on the Web" in *Harvard Business Review* (Vol. 78, No. 3, May 2000, pp. 179)
Pub: Harvard Business School Publishing Corp.
Ed: Donna L. Hoffman, Thomas P. Novak. **Description:** Customer acquisition is one of the biggest challenges facing online companies today. Success requires a fresh approach to managing the market mix.

34026 ■ "How ASPs Can Accelerate Your E-Business" in *E-business Advisor* (Vol. 18, No. 3, March 2000, pp. 20)
Pub: Advisor Media, Inc.
Ed: Lewis Ward. **Description:** E-commerce issues, including return policies, scalability and customer service are explored.

34027 ■ "How to Avoid Auction Scams" in *New York Times* (March 20, 2004, pp. C2)
Pub: New York Times Company
Ed: Katie Hafner. **Description:** Tips to avoid scams on eBay and other online auction sites. Issues covered include price, payment, the seller, photos and descriptions, location, off-site sales, private auctions and more.

34028 ■ "How to Be a Better Googler" in *My Business* (December/January 2004, pp. 24)
Pub: My Business Magazine
Description: Business research using the Internet is considered the second-most important use for small firms, after communication. Ways to use the Google search engine more effectively are listed.

34029 ■ "How Bluetooth Works" in *PC Computing* (April, 2000, pp. 87)
Pub: Ziff-Davis Inc.
Ed: Marty Jerome. **Description:** Named for the Danish King Harald Bluetooth, who unified Scandinavia, today's Bluetooth is a standard for unifying cordless voice and data communications among cell phones, PCs, LANs, entertainment systems, and other electronics.

34030 ■ "How to Create an E-Culture" in *E-business Advisor* (Vol. 18, No. 9, September 2000, pp. 16)
Pub: Advisor Media, Inc.
Ed: Shelly Wolf. **Description:** Companies can emulate an 'e-culture' model by adapting quickly to market changes, responding faster to customers and operating at the lowest possible cost. To accomplish this goal, companies' leadership teams must okay e-commerce projects and the company organization must be team-oriented.

34031 ■ "How Good Are Google's Extras?" in *Business Week* (January 16, 2006, No. 3967, pp. 88-90)
Pub: McGraw-Hill Companies
Ed: Description: An overview of Froogle, Maps, Gmail, and Picasa 2, Google's added services is presented. These extras offer shopping information, satellite and road maps, photo editing software, and email at no charge to users.

34032 ■ "How Good Is Your Online Nurse?" in *Business Week* (February 20, 2006, No. 3972, pp. 88)
Pub: McGraw-Hill Companies
Ed: Arlene Weintraub. **Description:** WellPoint, UnitedHealth Group, and Aetna offer patient Internet portals with tools to help manage health issues.

34033 ■ "How I Did It" in *Inc.* (Volume 27, December 2005, No. 12, pp. 118-120)
Pub: Inc. Magazine
Ed: Patrick J. Sauer. **Description:** In an interview, Reed Hastings, founder of Netflix an Internet-based subscription service.

34034 ■ "How Killer B-to-B's Slid to the Endangered List" in *The New York Times* (May 7, 2000, pp. BU1)
Pub: The New York Times Company
Ed: Bob Tedeschi. **Description:** Business-to-business Internet stocks plunge in value.

34035 ■ "How to Make Friends" in *Inc.* (October 1, 2003)
Pub: Gruner & Jahr USA Publishing
Ed: Bobbie Gossage, Matthew Fogel. **Description:** Want to build a professional network? Online Websites offering networking services are listed.

34036 ■ "How Much Am I Bid for This Imperfect Marketplace" in *The New York Times* (December 13, 2000, pp. D6, H6)
Pub: The New York Times Company
Ed: Tom Redburn. **Description:** Why e-business auctions have not caught on.

34037 ■ "How to Pick the Best Portal" in *E-business Advisor* (Vol. 18, No. 8, August 2000, pp. 30)
Pub: Advisor Media, Inc.
Ed: Tim Kounadis. **Description:** Information is provided about Enterprise information portals (EIP), or corporate portals, that employ a Web browser to provide a single point of access to critical business information. The portal, a fundamental aspect of any e-commerce strategy, is used by companies, their suppliers, partners, investors and customers.

34038 ■ "How a Virtual Supply Chain Can Help Your Business" in *E-business Advisor* (Vol. 18, No. 10, October 2000, pp. 22)
Pub: Advisor Media, Inc.
Ed: Bala Subramaniam, Romilla Subramaniam. **Description:** The Internet continues to change the way of doing business. Through an alliance of vendors, supply chains can now be managed using a virtual supply chain, meeting customers' needs almost instantly.

34039 ■ "Humanize Your Web Customer Service" in *E-business Advisor* (Vol. 18, No. 8, August 2000, pp. 12)
Pub: Advisor Media, Inc.
Ed: Kim M. Bayne. **Description:** The article tells how Lands' End chose WebLine Communications' applications to provide online customers with services similar to those of live sales clerks in a store.

34040 ■ "Hurricane Watch:Whether the Market's Boisterous or Becalmed, the Web's the Place to Vent and Pontificate" in *Barron's* (July 28, 2003)
Pub: Barron's
Ed: Kathy Yakal. **Description:** Traffic on Internet sites devoted to online trading and other financial services is measured based on market performance to evaluate trends in investor behavior.

34041 ■ "Hypermediation: Commerce as Clickstream" in *Harvard Business Review* (Vol. 78, No. 1, January 2000, pp. 46)
Pub: Harvard Business School Publishing Corp.
Ed: Nicholas G. Carr. **Description:** On the Web, profits will be made a penny at a time.

34042 ■ "IBM Corp." in *PC Magazine* (March 7, 2000, pp. 158)
Pub: Ziff-Davis Publishing Company
Ed: Bruce Brown, Cade Metz, Carol Venezia. **Description:** IBM's Netfinity 5000 server, priced at $3,960 with a 600MHz Pentium III CPU and dual 9GB hard disks, works well with its $2,259 PC 300PL desktop client and bundled software to create an excellent E-business solution. The company backs up its E-services solution with top-notch service and high-quality hardware. IBM offers customers the Home Page Creator and Small Business WebConnections products through its IBM Global Small Business organization. Both tools are very well designed; Home Page Creator is a Java tool that lets users build and publish a storefront from within the browser, while the higher-end WebConnections service package includes Internet access, E-mail and file sharing for five to 100 clients. IBM earns the Editors' Choice rating for the best E-business hardware, software and service solutions.

34043 ■ "IBM Has A Vision Too: Here's its answer to all those frustrated tech customers" in *Fortuneit* (Vol. 146, Nov. 25, 2002, pp. 158)
Pub: Time Inc.
Ed: David Kirkpatrick. **Description:** In an interview with Sam Palmisano, IBM CEO, on-demand computing is discussed. On demand-computing entails on-demand business, government, and health care provision.

34044 ■ "IBM, Microsoft, others plan alliance to help conduct business online" in *Wall Street Journal* (February 6, 2002, pp. B4)
Pub: Wall Street Journal
Description: The plans being made to form alliances for conducting business transactions online by such companies as IBM, Microsoft and others, are discussed.

34045 ■ "IBM Readies Linux Suite for Small Biz" in *Network World* (November 6, 2000, pp. NA)
Pub: Network World Inc.
Ed: Ed Scannell. **Description:** A profile of IBM's Linux suite for small businesses.

34046 ■ "Identifying and Developing Measures of Information Technology Ethical Work Climates" in *Journal of Business Ethics* (Sept. 15, 2003)
Pub: Kluwer Academic Publishers Group
Ed: Robert W. Stone, John W. Henry. **Description:** A model of information technology (IT) ethical work climates is presented using the ethical work climates and data collected from a national mail survey of the Association for Computing Machinery members.

34047 ■ "If BlackBerry Gets Smushed..." in *Business Week* (January 9, 2006, No. 3966, pp. 16)
Pub: McGraw-Hill Companies
Ed: Stephen H. Wildstrom. **Description:** Alternatives to using BlackBerry email services are discussed in the event of the service being shut down by patent infringement charges. GoodLink from Good Technology offers similar services as does Microsoft with its Exchange email system which is being upgraded.

34048 ■ "If Members Think Items are Overpriced, They'll Blame Barter Trust's Economy, says CEO Mike Edelhart" in *Inc.* (October 2000, pp. 58)
Pub: The Goldhirsh Group
Description: Although exchange customers display some ambivalence about barter, the latest generation of Web-enabled exchange operators is predictability bullish.

34049 ■ "If You Build It" in *Entrepreneur* (Vol. 31, No. 8, August 2003, pp. 30)
Pub: Entrepreneur Media, Inc.
Ed: Steve Cooper. **Description:** eBrain Market Research/Consumer Electronics Association present a survey asking consumers what features in a Web site make them more apt to purchase a product. Statistical data included.

34050 ■ "If You Market, They Will Come" in *Success* (Vol. 47, No. 1, January 2000, pp. 50)
Pub: Success Publishing, Inc.
Ed: Rivka Tadjer. **Description:** Three easy steps to draw customers to your online store.

34051 ■ "I'll Trade You" in *Black Enterprise* (Vol. 33, No. 6, January 2003, pp. 43)
Pub: Earl Graves Publishing Co.
Description: An overview of online bartering is presented, including tips for finding a legitimate site with an established reputation.

34052 ■ "I'll Trade You..." in *Home Office Computing* (Vol. 18, No. 9, September 2000, pp. 87)
Pub: Scholastic Inc.
Ed: Steven Van Yoder. **Description:** An overview of Internet sites such as BarterTrust.com, Big-Vine and Ubarter have brought back the ancient concept of barter by linking members with trading networks to create mini-economies.

34053 ■ "The Imagination Gap" in *Internet World* (Vol. 7, No. 1, January 15, 2001, pp. 8)
Pub: Mecklermedia Corporation
Ed: Tony Rizzo. **Description:** The so-called 'imagination gap', a concept noted by author Bob Crowley, is a growing issue as the technology and business strategy curves fail to keep pace with one another amid the growing importance of E-commerce. Internet and Web technology grew at a substantial rate between 1994 and 1999, but only a tiny percentage of traditional businesses took advantage of it effectively, and a few pure Internet businesses, such as Amazon.com, developed entirely new strategies. Companies often fail to adjust their business strategies to leverage new technology and fall behind as the economy moves to E-business.

34054 ■ "Imagining the Google Future" in *Business 2.0* (Vol. 7, January/February 2006, No. 1, pp. 78-80)
Pub: Time, Inc.
Ed: Chris Taylor. **Description:** Experts explore four scenarios that show where Google's leaders may be taking the company in the future.

34055 ■ "Imagining a Web Beyond the Browser: a new kind of dot" in *Fortune* (Vol. 141, No. 4, February 21, 2000, pp. 274+)
Pub: Time Inc.
Ed: Mark Gimein. **Description:** DoDots has developed a platform for producing Internet applications that could make the browser obsolete. Free applications called 'dots' would replace Web pages and be displayed on just part of a computer screen while other applications are running.

34056 ■ "In Brief: MBNA Issuing eBay Product in Canada" in *American Banker Newsletter* (Vol. 168, No. 208, October 29, 2003, pp. 9)
Pub: Thomson Media
Description: MBNA Corporation and eBay Inc. offers a Canadian version of the eBay Anything Points Master Card, a credit card product that allows individuals to earn points towards discounts when purchasing eBay auction items.

34057 ■ "In Demand" in *Entrepreneur* (Vol. 32, November 2004, No. 11, pp. 89)
Pub: Entrepreneur Media Inc.
Ed: Gwen Moran. **Description:** Brother filmmakers, Gregg and Evan Spiridellis, share ways to handle overnight success with a product. After producing an animated political film on their Website Jibjab, the entrepreneurs were not prepared for the number of phone calls, emails and national media appearances that followed. Hiring temp help and including an email contact on their Website could have helped.

34058 ■ "In Hot Water? Take a Closer Look at Your Marketing Materials, Or You May Get Burned" in *Entrepreneur* (Vol. 32, September 2004)
Pub: Entrepreneur Media Inc.
Ed: Catherine Seda. **Description:** Although not illegal, using another company's trademark or logo on a Website, banner ad, or newsletter could get a small company into legal trouble. Internet marketing law includes copyrights, privacy rights, trademark usage and order fulfillment and more aggressive legal action to protect brands is taking place.

34059 ■ "In My Humble Opinion: They gathered this past spring" in *Fast Company* (September 2001, pp. 92)
Pub: Fast Company
Ed: John Ellis. **Description:** Thanks to companies such as Recipio, PlanetFeedback.com, and InsightExpress, customers can vote on existing products and services.

34060 ■ "In Online Auctions of the Future, It'll Be Bot vs Bot vs. Bot." in *The New York Times* (August 17, 2000, pp. D8, G8)
Pub: The New York Times Company
Ed: Anne Eisenberg. **Description:** The world of e-commerce, with regard to the use of "intelligent" software Internet search programs or "bots" is about to change dramatically. A competition was held to determine how effective bots, or autonomous agents, were in finding and booking the best prices for round-trip airfare, hotel rooms and entertainment. Researchers say that consumers and businesses will have to be prepared for the changes bots will bring to the electronic marketplace.

34061 ■ "In Search of...Can Customers Search Your Website-And Actually Find What They Need?" in *Entrepreneur* (Vol. 32, November 2004, No. 11)
Pub: Entrepreneur Media Inc.
Ed: Melissa Campanelli. **Description:** Netpreneurs are improving search functions in order to compete with the success of Google. Options for upgrading Web sites are offered.

34062 ■ "In-Sync Web Authoring" in *PC Magazine* (February 20, 2001, pp. 38)
Pub: Ziff-Davis Publishing Company
Ed: Luisa Simone. **Description:** Macromedia has added to their hold on the Web authoring software market with recent releases of Dreamweaver and Fireworks. The three new products, Dreamweaver 4.0, Dreamweaver UltraDev 4.0, and Fireworks 4.0 have common interfaces and standardized keyboard shortcuts. New layouts and added features such as debugging, coding, and reference tools improve on the ease of use and capabilities of the products.

34063 ■ "Inbox 101: How to Manage the E-mail Avalanche" in *My Business* (December/January 2004, pp. 40)
Pub: My Business Magazine
Ed: Lena Basha. **Description:** Tips to improve email communication skills are presented, including ways to prevent spam.

34064 ■ "Industry News; Coinstar Expands Self-Service Kiosk Line" in *National Petroleum News* (Vol. 95, No. 13, December 2003, pp. 46)
Pub: Adams Business Media
Description: Coinstar Inc. has launched new self-service kiosks that deliver a variety of prepaid consumer products, including self-service bill payment, prepaid cash card, cell phone mobile content, online computer game time, prepaid wireless, prepaid long distance and prepaid Internet. These kiosks offer new revenue opportunities for convenience stores.

34065 ■ "Infectious Agents: A Growing Number of Uninvited Guests Are Pushing Their Way Onto Your PCs. Here Are the Latest Antidotes" in *Entrepreneur*
Pub: Entrepreneur Media Inc.
Ed: Mike Hogan. **Description:** The importance of a good firewall and anti-virus computer protection for small business is stressed. Experts estimate intruders have invaded 90 percent of all PCs and Dell identifies it as its top technical support problem.

34066 ■ *Information Technology for the Small Business: How to Make IT Work For Your Company*
Pub: TAB Computer Systems, Incorporated
Ed: T.J. Benoit. **Released:** June 2006. **Price:** $17.95. **Description:** Basics of information technology to help small companies maximize benefits are covered. Topics include pitfalls to avoid, email and Internet use, data backup, recovery and overall IT organization.

34067 ■ "Ingenta, Inc. Announces 19 New Publisher Portal Partnerships" in *Information Today* (Vol. 17, No. 11, December 2000, pp. 23)
Pub: Information Today, Inc.
Description: Ingenta, Inc. announces new partnerships to expand its research offerings.

34068 ■ "Inking the Deal" in *Kiplinger's Personal Finance Magazine* (Vol. 54, No. 12, December 2000, pp. 26)
Pub: The Kiplinger Washington Editors, Inc.
Ed: Catherine Siskos. **Description:** This holiday season, online retailers are publishing print catalogs to attract customers.

34069 ■ "Insurance Sites Aren't Closing the Sale" in *The New York Times* (December 13, 2000, pp. D8, H8)
Pub: The New York Times Company
Ed: Joseph B. Treaster. **Description:** Insurance is one area in which the Internet is not getting much use, due to consumer wariness.

34070 ■ "Integrate Enterprise Applications with XML" in *E-business Advisor* (Vol. 18, No. 5, May 2000, pp. 16)
Pub: Advisor Media, Inc.
Ed: David S. Linthicum. **Description:** The extensible markup language, or XML, can be used to develop enterprise application integration (EAI) software, as well as business-to-business (B2B) integration software. XML supports common metadata standards throughout the Internet to make B2B and internal enterprise application integration easier.

34071 ■ "Intern affairs: more and more companies are hiring virtual interns." in *Entrepreneur* (Vol. 31, No. 6, June 2003, pp. 74)
Pub: Entrepreneur Media Inc.
Ed: Chris Penttila. **Description:** The impact of hiring virtual interns performing tasks from information technology projects to customer service is investigated. A set of guidelines for hiring college students as virtual interns is presented.

34072 ■ "International E-Commerce: The Time is Now" in *E-business Advisor* (Vol. 18, No. 10, October 2000, pp. 28)
Pub: Advisor Media, Inc.
Ed: Donald DePalma. **Description:** Internet usage is not just limited to the United States. It is exploding worldwide, and therefore, offers the opportunity to gain international customers. It is important for Web sites to be designed to entice these international "visitors", while being aware of customs, laws and politics specific to the potential customer's country.

34073 ■ "Internet Auctions Rank High in U.S. Complaints about Online Fraud" in *Atlanta Journal-Constitution* (April 11, 2003)
Pub: Knight-Ridder/Tribune Business News
Ed: Tasgola Karla Bruner. **Description:** The number of complaints about online auction fraud tripled from 2001 to 2002, according to a report by the Internet Fraud Complaint Center. The dollar loss from cases reported in 2002 equaled $54 million.

34074 ■ "Internet Banking Can Improve Your Cash Management" in *Ingram's* (Vol. 28, No. 1, January 2002, pp. 42)
Pub: Show Me Publishing, Inc.
Ed: Gary Wilcutt. **Description:** The benefits of using Internet banking services for a small business are investigated.

34075 ■ "Internet Companies Learn How to Personalize Service" in *The New York Times* (August 28, 2000, pp. C8(L))
Pub: The New York Times Company
Ed: Susan Stellin. **Description:** Technologies for delivering customized, individually-oriented 'one to one marketing' or 'targeted merchandising' are still in the early stages of development, but are already in use by Amazon.com.

34076 ■ "Internet or Desktop" in *PC Magazine* (February 20, 2001, pp. 145)
Pub: Ziff-Davis Publishing Company
Ed: Wayne Kawamoto. **Description:** Reviews of accounting software packages that are available for the desktop or online.

34077 ■ "The Internet giveth, and it can also taketh away" in *Wall Street Journal* (May 23, 2000, pp. B2)
Pub: Dow Jones & Co., Inc.
Ed: Robert Johnson. **Description:** A survey of the economic impact of the Internet on small businesses.

34078 ■ "Internet Law Arena Marked by Issues About Spam, Pop-Up Ads, Domain Names, and File Sharing" in *Long Island Business News* (Feb.6, 2004)
Pub: Dolan Media Newswires
Ed: Rosmaria Mancini. **Description:** Microsoft and New York's State Attorney General have partnered and filed lawsuits against a spamming ring allegedly responsible for sending billions of deceptive and illegal emails. CAN-SPAM (Controlling the Assault of Non-Solicited Pornography and Marketing Act), is federal legislation that would require marketers to provide return addresses in emails so consumers can request being removed from mailing lists.

34079 ■ "Internet Marketing Focusing on Search Engines" in *Atlanta Business Chronicle* (Vol. 24, No. 14, September 7, 2001, pp. 4A)
Pub: American City Business Journals Inc.
Ed: Jim Lovel. **Description:** Companies such as Marketingcentral LLC and Socketware Inc. are using a new technology called search engine optimization, which moves their company to the top of the search engine list to market their Web sites. Stacy Williams, of Prominent Placement Inc. and Andrew Wetzler, of MoreVisibility.com had their companies work with Marketcentral and Socketware to remodel their Web sites. This is the latest technology in search engines, and as the demand increases, so do the companies providing these services.

34080 ■ "Internet Tax Won't Be Collected Anytime Soon" in *Crain's Detroit Business* (Vol. 17, No. 44, October 22, 2001, pp. 3)
Pub: Crain Communications, Inc.
Ed: Amy Lane, Brent Snavely. **Description:** The State of Michigan joins a multistate table to collect more taxes from Internet and mail-order companies, but it could be 2003 before collection begins.

34081 ■ "Internet Technologies-The constantly evolving Web is being driven by ever-growing human needs" in *PC Magazine* (Aug. 8, 2000, pp. 144)
Pub: Ziff-Davis Publishing Company
Ed: John Clyman. Description: Emerging technologies will dramatically change the Internet in the next few years. Networking will become all-pervasive with the popularity of handheld devices and even household appliances that can be Web-enabled, although there is still no universal standard for interoperability. Instant messaging will become standardized despite the well-publicized war between AOL and Microsoft, partly as a result of government scrutiny. Virtually every application will exploit connectivity tools. Digital certificates and biometric user ID systems will enhance security by providing two-stage authentication. Content delivery will become more intelligent. Crucial trends include software agents for coordinating devices, the Portable Network Graphics (PNG) format, and even Net connections from space probes on other planets.

34082 ■ "Internet To Go" in *Kiplinger's Personal Finance Magazine* (Vol. 54, No. 12, December 2000, pp. 150)
Pub: The Kiplinger Washington Editors, Inc.
Ed: Michael Martinez, Kathy Jones. Description: Most devices that link you wirelessly to the Web are often clunky and limited in their features.

34083 ■ "Internet Use by Manufacturers is Small for Business-to-Business Commerce" in *Wall Street Journal* (February 23, 2000, pp. B11C)
Pub: Dow Jones & Co., Inc.
Ed: John Connor. Description: A survey by the National Association of Manufacturers regarding Internet usage by manufacturers is examined.

34084 ■ "The Internet vs. the travel agent" in *Hispanic Business* (Vol. 22, No. 6, June 2000, pp. 146)
Pub: Hispanic Business
Ed: Barbara Beckley. Description: The World Wide Web offers many bargains for business travelers, but some businesspeople prefer a good travel agent. Around 3 percent of travel, valued at $4 billion, is booked via the Internet and this is set to rise to over $30 billion by 2004.

34085 ■ "Internet World Fall 2000 Conference" in *Information Today* (Vol. 17, No. 11, December 2000, pp. 28)
Pub: Information Today, Inc.
Ed: Jane Dysart, Stephen Abram, Pete Stair. Description: A review of the Fall 2000 Penton Media's Internet World show, held at New York's Jacob Javits Convention Center.

34086 ■ "Interview: Salesforce.com Adopts Amazon.com, eBay Model" in *InfoWorld.com* (November 17, 2003)
Pub: InfoWorld Media Group, Inc.
Ed: Mark Jones. Description: Salesforce.com has launched a new version of its hosted CRM application and developer platform. In an interview with chairman and CEO, Marc Benioff explains the company's vision.

34087 ■ "Intuit launches small business marketplace" in *Network World* (September 18, 2000, pp. NA)
Pub: Network World Inc.
Ed: Sam Costello. Description: A profile of Quick-Books Shopping Source, targeted at small businesses. The service will provide discounts on business supplies and services, ranging from computer to clothing, and even janitorial services.

34088 ■ "Intuit, Metiom build b-to-b marketplace" in *InfoWorld* (Vol. 22, No. 38, September 18, 2000, pp. 34)
Pub: InfoWorld
Description: Financial software maker Intuit last week joined with New York-based Metiom to create a business-to-business marketplace for its small business customers.

34089 ■ "Invasion of the Privacy Snatchers" in *Success* (Vol. 47, No. 4, September 2000, pp. 78)
Pub: Success Publishing, Inc.
Ed: Hollis Thomases. Description: Profiling. It's an ugly word, with lots of growing connotation surrounding it. It means that your purchasing habits are being recorded, cataloged, analyzed, and used for further direct-marketing efforts toward you.

34090 ■ "The IRS Wants You—Online" in *Home Office Computing* (Vol. 18, No. 12, December 2000, pp. 26)
Pub: Scholastic Inc.
Ed: Jeffery D. Zbar. Description: Information is given regarding the Internal Revenue Service's effort to get small businesses to file tax returns online.

34091 ■ "Is Excite@Home The AOL of Broadband?" in *Fortune* (Vol. , No. 11, December 6, 1999, pp. 156+)
Pub: Time Inc.
Ed: Eric Nee. Description: Excite@Home has become the leading supplier of broadband access to the Internet, with almost 1 million subscribers. It gained this position through the merger of @Home and Excite. Company strategy is to combine content and distribution.

34092 ■ "Is the Internet Second Nature" in *Fast Company* (July 2001, pp. 145)
Pub: Fast Company
Ed: Cheryl Dahle. Description: Ways to tap the real power of the Internet to transform small business are investigated.

34093 ■ "Is it theft, or is it freedom? 7 views of the Web's impact on culture clashes" in *The New York Times* (Sept. 20, 2000, pp. D40, H40)
Pub: The New York Times Company
Ed: Matthew Mirapaul. Description: Senator Orrin Hatch, Kevin Smith, Craig Newell, Hilary Rosen, Esther Dyson, David Boise, and Gene Kan discuss the impact of the Internet on culture clashes. Statistical data is included.

34094 ■ "Is Your Phone System Moving You Forward Or Chaining You Down?" in *Ingram's* (Vol. 29, No. 8, August 2003, pp. 15)
Pub: Show Me Publishing, Inc.
Ed: Kevin Tubbesing. Description: Benefits of Ethernet systems to companies looking to upgrade telephone systems are explored.

34095 ■ "ISPs Need To Keep Moving Against Spam" in *eWeek* (February 3, 2005)
Pub: Ziff Davis Media Inc.
Description: Internet service providers need to provide better security against spammers in order to protect customers on the Internet.

34096 ■ "It figures" in *Entrepreneur* (Vol. 31, No. 6, June 2003, pp. 36)
Pub: Entrepreneur Media Inc.
Ed: Steve Cooper. Description: A compilation of miscellaneous business statistics are presented, including women's wages, Web servers, and consumer confidence.

34097 ■ "It's 2006! Whatcha Gonna Do About It?" in *Inc.* (Volume 28, January 2006, No. 1, pp. 78-85, 113)
Pub: Inc. Magazine
Ed: Stephanie Clifford. Description: Various entrepreneurs give advice to help small businesses face new challenges in 2006. Topics include investments, the economy, small business trends, logistics, business communication such as blogs, energy issues, consumer products, real estate, interest rates and outsourcing.

34098 ■ "It's All About Results" in *Entrepreneur* (Vol. 32, October 2004, No. 10, pp. 92)
Pub: Entrepreneur Media Inc.
Ed: Catherine Seda. Description: Three steps to consider before engaging in a pay-for-performance marketing program are listed. Internet marketing agencies run performance-based advertising programs.

34099 ■ "It's the Law" in *Entrepreneur* (Vol. 30, No. 3, March 2002, pp. 42)
Pub: Entrepreneur Media Inc.
Ed: Amanda C. Kooser. Description: The Small Business Administration has created a Web site designed to help small business stay informed of laws and regulations.

34100 ■ "It's Never E-nough" in *Business Week* (No. 3689, July 10, 2000, pp. F14)
Pub: McGraw-Hill, Inc.
Description: Highlights of surveys of companies with 20-49 employees regarding the future of small business, including information about the Internet, Palmtops, networks, e-backlash, the bottom line, cost cutting, outsourcing, leasing, and Internet Telephony.

34101 ■ "It's a New Game: Killerspin Pushes Table Tennis to Extreme Heights" in *Black Enterprise* (Vol. 37, October 2006, No. 3, pp. 73)
Pub: Earl G. Graves Publishing Co. Inc.
Ed: Bridget McCrea. Description: Profile of Robert Blackwell and his company Killerspin L.L.C., which is popularizing the sport of table tennis. Killerspin has hit $1 million in revenues due to product sales primarily generated through the company's website, magazines, DVDs, and event ticket sales.

34102 ■ "It's That Time of Season" in *Entrepreneur* (Vol. 31, No. 8, August 2003, pp. 75)
Pub: Entrepreneur Media, Inc.
Ed: Catherine Seda. Description: Summer provides the perfect environment to increase online shopping for the holiday season by using perks such as free shipping, clearances, featured sale items, suggested items, and gift idea centers or personal shoppers.

34103 ■ "It's a Trap! Watch Your Step-Pharming Scams Are Lurking Around Every Corner" in *Entrepreneur* (Vol. 33, August 2005, No. 8, pp. 40)
Pub: Entrepreneur Media Inc.
Ed: Mike Hogan. Description: Netcraft, a network security company, identifies phishing emails that try to scam customers into giving up personal financial information. Ways to avoid these scams are listed.

34104 ■ "Jet Stream E-Mail" in *Inc.* (September 1, 2003)
Pub: Gruner & Jahr USA Publishing
Ed: Anton Piech. Description: Business travelers will now be able to access and send email while traveling on airplanes. No software downloading will be necessary to use this service.

34105 ■ "The job site evolution" in *Rough Notes* (Vol. 146, No. 3, March 2003, pp. 173)
Pub: Rough Notes
Ed: George Rusty Capulet. Description: Michael P. Tornesello, president of InsuranceJobChannel.com is an online career site available to the insurance industry. Nationwide Insurance is one of its customers.

34106 ■ "John Chambers after the deluge" in *Fast Company* (July 2001, pp. 100)
Pub: Fast Company
Ed: George Anders. Description: Interview with John Chambers, CEO of Cisco, where he explains how to slow down smart, why the Internet still matters, and what to do when customers stop buying.

34107 ■ "JP Morgan Rolls Out Tech-Heavy Branches" in *Houston Business Journal* (Vol. 34, No. 8, July 4, 2003, pp. 1)
Pub: American City Business Journals
Ed: Jim Greer. Description: JP Morgan Chase and Company has opened two new prototype banks in the Houston, Texas area equipped with Internet kiosks, video tellers, and plasma screens, all in order to bring in customers. Tim Olmstead, representative of the company states that the company is building the bank branch of the future.

34108 ■ "Judge, Jury, and Spam Executioner" in *Black Enterprise* (Vol. 34, No. 7, February 2004, pp. 53)
Pub: Earl Graves Publishing Co.
Ed: Anthony Calypso. Description: Profile of Paul Q. Judge, and his position as chief technology officer at Atlanta, Georgia-based CipherTrust Inc.; the firm offers solutions to the issues faced by small businesses when dealing with unwanted email spam.

34109 ■ "Judge, Jury, and Spam Executioner: Tech Exec Sets His Sights On Fighting E-Mail Menaces" in *Black Enterprise* (Vol. 34, No. 7)
Pub: Earl Graves Publishing Co.
Ed: Anthony Calypso. Description: Profile of Paul Q. Judge, and his position as chief technology officer at Atlanta, Georgia-based CipherTrust Inc.; the firm offers solutions to the issues faced by small businesses when dealing with unwanted email spam.

34110 ■ "Jury is still out: Is the bar ready for virtual law firms?" in *Boston Business Journal* (Vol. 22, No. 3, February 22, 2002, pp. 27)
Pub: MCP, Inc.
Ed: Sheri Qualters. Description: An investigation into the possibility of law firms using the Internet for legal services.

34111 ■ "Just Ask: Use e-mail to start a conversation with online buyers" in *My Business* (October/November 2002, pp. 17)
Pub: My Business Magazine
Description: Customer emails can be a good tool to target customers for online purchases.

34112 ■ "Just down the block" in *Entrepreneur* (Vol. 30, No. 1, January 2002, pp. 18)
Pub: Entrepreneur Media Inc.
Description: Adkey software has developed a program that denies access to users who used ad-filtering software that block a company's advertising.

34113 ■ "Just Browsing" in *Entrepreneur* (Vol. 32, November 2004, No. 11, pp. 66)
Pub: Entrepreneur Media Inc.
Ed: Amanda C. Kooser. Description: In June 2004, the U.S. Computer Emergency Readiness Team recommended using alternative Internet browsers instead of Internet Explorer for security reasons. Mozilla, Mozina's Firefox, and Netscape are offered free, and Opera costs $39.

34114 ■ "Just Can't Hack It" in *Entrepreneur* (Vol. 28, No. 11, November 2000, pp. 30)
Pub: Entrepreneur Media Inc.
Ed: Robert McGarvey. Description: The Web site www.sans.org/topten.html offers methods for small businesses to prevent hacking.

34115 ■ "Keen.com links experts to users via phone" in *InfoWorld* (Vol. 23, No. 5, January 29, 2001, pp. 44)
Pub: InfoWorld
Ed: Michael Vizard. Description: Keen.com CTO Mark Halstead is responsible for supporting a Web site that links users with experts through live telephone conversations. Halstead views his company as a liaison to the community, bringing together information with people who need it. The company's complex infrastructure enables people to obtain immediate answers to questions. The approach differs from most Internet companies because of the combination of the Web and telephony.

34116 ■ "Keep 'Em Clicking" in *Home Office Computing* (Vol. 19, No. 2, February 2001, pp. 73)
Pub: Scholastic Inc.
Ed: Mark Kakkuri. Description: Small business Web sites often lose out to competitors who can sell products for less. In order to achieve customer loyalty, a business must offer superior customer services and interaction. By personalizing customer services, a relationship will result that will bring customers back. One way to learn what customers want out of service is by conducting surveys and instant polls.

34117 ■ "Keep fit for free: personal training advice on the Web" in *Black Enterprise* (Vol. 33, No. 3, October 2002, pp. 179)
Pub: Earl Graves Publishing Co.
Description: Personalized diet and exercise plans are offered to anyone signing up for membership on www.freetrainers.com Web site. The service features chat rooms and message boards.

34118 ■ "Keeping Customers Clueless?" in *Home Office Computing* (Vol. 18, No. 8, August 2000, pp. 22)
Pub: Scholastic Inc.
Ed: Laura Turley. Description: A recent report by Jupiter Communications states that as e-commerce continues to grow, so does customer dissatisfaction. Results of the report are examined.

34119 ■ "KeepMedia Inc.: www.keepmedia. com" in *Entrepreneur* (Vol. 31, No. 12, December 2003, pp. 8)
Pub: Entrepreneur Media Inc.
Ed: Steve Cooper. Description: Profile of Keep-Media, an online database of more than 140 journals with ad-free magazine and newspaper articles.

34120 ■ "The Killer Ad Machine" in *Forbes* (December 11, 2000, pp. 168)
Pub: Forbes Magazine
Ed: Quentin Hardy. Description: Yahoo has the ability to provide ad feedback to its advertisers when the ad is online.

34121 ■ "Kleiner Perkins Adds Lane As New GP" in *Venture Capital Journal* (Vol. 40, No. 10, October 2000, pp. 34)
Pub: Venture Economics
Description: Raymond Lane, former chief operating officer at Oracle Corporation, has joined Kleiner, Perkins, Caufield & Byers. Lane will invest in all sectors, especially business-to-business, focusing on supply chain management.

34122 ■ "Know Your Customers" in *PC Computing* (April 2000, pp. 94)
Pub: Ziff-Davis Inc.
Ed: Jason Compton. Description: Software and online solutions for digital mapping are reviewed. MapInfo's MapInfo Professional 5.5 offers almost unlimited options for both generating maps and analyzing information. ESRI's BusinessMap Pro, is a collection of maps with solid graphing and charting features. The Corporate version adds extra business-to-business data. Microsoft's MapPoint 2000 is very easy to use, but has fewer features than BusinessMap Pro. DemographicsNow.com is a Web-based that includes interactive maps and helps users answer crucial questions about customers and works with the Autodesk Map Guide browser plug-in, which is easy to use.

34123 ■ "Knowledge On Demand" in *PC Computing* (March 2000, pp. 128)
Pub: Ziff-Davis Inc.
Ed: Leslie Ayers. Description: Companies are finding that it is easier to train employees via the Web, since it can be done from anywhere, anytime. This article focuses on companies that offer this service.

34124 ■ "Lancaster, Pa.-Area Restaurateur Markets Business with Internet-Based Kiosk" in *Lancaster New Era* (January 8, 2004)
Pub: Knight Ridder/Tribune Business News
Ed: Patricia A. Poist. Description: Terry Lee tells how he placed a kiosk at Park City Center to promote his restaurant. LiveWire International, a York County firm that designs and develops self-service, Internet-based kiosks, set up a kiosk for Lee at the mall to promote and sell gift certificates to his restaurant.

34125 ■ *Landscaping Business*
Pub: Globe Pequot Press
Ed: Owen E. Dell. Released: December 2005. Price: $18.95. Description: Guide to starting and running a successful home-based landscaping business, including tips for marketing on the Internet.

34126 ■ "Language Is a Virus" in *PC Computing* (March 2000, pp. 62)
Pub: Ziff-Davis Inc.
Ed: Wendy M. Grossman. Description: English is the cultural operating system of the Internet and the fragile common thread of global trade. But as trade barriers fall, cultural barriers are on the rise, and the Net is going to be multilingual.

34127 ■ "Law Firms Beef Up Extranets to Handle Complex Deals" in *Crain's Detroit Business* (Vol. 23, January 29, 2007, No. 5, pp. 26)
Pub: Crain Communications Inc. - Detroit
Ed: Robert Ankeny. Description: Virtual private computer networks eliminate multiple copies and shipping in complex legal and real estate deals. Documents can be displayed in War rooms with multiple parties exchanging information simultaneously. Huge savings in copying and shipping of paper copies are realized.

34128 ■ "Law firm creates privacy group" in *Atlanta Business Chronicle* (Vol. 24, No. 8, July 27, 2001, pp. 3A)
Pub: American City Business Journals Inc.
Ed: Mary Jane Credeur. Description: Concerned with Internet privacy, two partners with Morris, Manning, and Martin LLP formed a group within the firm that specializes in privacy issues. Concerns with Internet privacy and security have risen in the past regarding how online companies use offline and online personal information.

34129 ■ "Lawyers on War-Path Filing Wage and Hour Lawsuits" in *Kiplinger Letter* (Vol. 78, January 19, 2007, No. 2)
Pub: Kiplinger
Description: Attorneys are targeting clients with the use of Websites to looking for disgruntled employees. Major settlements are discussed.

34130 ■ "Lease Is More" in *Inc.* (August 1, 2003)
Pub: Gruner & Jahr USA Publishing
Ed: Bonnie Tsui. Description: Web sites offer information on renting apartment accommodations for holidays instead of staying at a hotel, which may save money.

34131 ■ "A Leg Up on Legal Fees" in *My Business* (October/November 2002, pp. 52)
Pub: My Business Magazine
Description: Web sites offering advice for writing simple legal documents, such as employment contracts and real estate leases, are listed.

34132 ■ "Legal Ease" in *My Business* (December/January 2004, pp. 53)
Pub: My Business Magazine
Ed: Lena Basha. Description: Profile of Legalzoom. com, an online legal document and resource center for small businesses.

34133 ■ "Legislation aims to tax Internet sales" in *Crain's Detroit Business* (Vol. 19, No. 1, January 6, 2003, pp. 20)
Pub: Crain Communications Inc., Detroit
Ed: Amy Lane. Description: The State of Michigan is considering imposing a multi-state agreement that would streamline processes for collecting sales tax on Internet purchases. The Michigan Department of Treasury estimates tax losses of $273 in the current fiscal year.

34134 ■ "Let Freedom Ring: The Internet is a Powerful Force for Telephone Deregulation" in *Barron's* (July 7, 2003, pp. 30)
Pub: Barron's
Ed: Christopher Whalen. Description: The advent of more sophisticated forms of Internet telephony will eventually force the government's hand in telecommunications deregulation.

34135 ■ "The Librarian's Internet Survival Guide" in *Information Today* (Vol. 20, No. 1, Jan. 2003, pp. 44)
Pub: Information Today, Inc.
Ed: Barbara Quint. Description: Review of a new guide for the Information Professional, particularly li-

brarians; the book features tips and advice for trouble-shooting, Web resources for answering reference questions, and strategies for information management.

34136 ■ "The Lid On Spam Is Still Loose" in *Business Week* (February 7, 2005, No. 3919, pp. 10)

Pub: McGraw-Hill Companies

Ed: Erin Chambers, Ira Sager. Description: Profile of the CAN-SPAM Act, passed by Congress in 2004. The Act sets restrictions on unsolicited email, but has done little to eliminate junk messages. According to MX Logic, 97 percent of unsolicited commercial email defies the law.

34137 ■ "Life after business" in *Women In Business* (Vol. 52, No. 2, March 2000, pp. 25)

Pub: The ABWA Co., Inc.

Ed: Rachel Warbington. Description: Memories can be preserved either in computerized form or in a traditional scrapbook. Photographs will not deteriorate if they are retained in digital format, but products are also available to preserve traditional scrapbooks.

34138 ■ "Linking Policies for Public Web Sites" in *Information Today* (Vol. 17, No. 10, November 2000, pp. 42)

Pub: Information Today, Inc.

Ed: Shirley Duglin Kennedy. Description: The article recommends information sites offering guidelines for setting up a Web site to avoid litigation.

34139 ■ "Listen and Judge" in *Black Enterprise* (Vol. 36, November 2005, No. 4, pp. 66)

Pub: Earl G. Graves Publishing Co. Inc.

Ed: Bridget McCrea. Description: American Idol Underground allows artists to upload their songs for $50 with a guarantee of at least 200 rotations. Music fans listen and rate songs.

34140 ■ "Listen Up! If You're Not Advertising on Internet Radio, You Could Be Missing Out" in *Entrepreneur* (Vol. 32, November 2004, No. 11)

Pub: Entrepreneur Media Inc.

Ed: Catherine Seda. Description: Internet radio has an estimated audience of nearly 19 million Americans, making it a great avenue for marketing. Tips based on audience demographics and behaviors are examined.

34141 ■ "Listen While You Work" in *Entrepreneur* (Vol. 31, No. 10, October 2003, pp. 120)

Pub: Entrepreneur Media, Inc.

Ed: Nichole L. Torres. Description: Profile of Joe Pezzillo of Music for Cubicles, an online music station for office workers.

34142 ■ "Listening for opportunity" in *Hispanic Business* (Vol. 22, No. 9, September 2000, pp. 16)

Pub: Hispanic Business

Ed: Peter Brennan. Description: Internet-based firm, Globe-1, assists minority companies to compete for government agency contracts by offering help in the procurement of contracts.

34143 ■ "Live Wire: Online Seminars Show 'Em What You've Got" in *Entrepreneur* (Vol. 31, No. 10, October 2003, pp. 91)

Pub: Entrepreneur Media, Inc.

Ed: Catherine Seda. Description: Ways to host interactive conferences via the Internet are presented.

34144 ■ "Living High on the Blog" in *Entrepreneur* (Vol. 33, February 2005, No. 2, pp. 65)

Pub: Entrepreneur Media Inc.

Ed: Gwen Moran. Description: Reach Communications Consulting founder, William Arruda, discovered an 800 percent hike in traffic on his firm's Website after being mentioned on an Internet blog; ways to add blogs to a public relations campaign are investigated.

34145 ■ "Living with Linux" in *PC Magazine* (February 6, 2001, pp. 63)

Pub: Ziff-Davis Publishing Company

Ed: Oliver Rist. Description: The initial furor over Linux is cooling and the open-source operating system is now assuming a role as a viable alternative to NT and Unix. Linux has established a reputation as a reliable server OS that will stand up under the most strenuous testing. It is a plug-and-forget OS that runs quickly over older hardware and will automatically scale to large numbers of users. Linux is a good choice for Web servers and Internet and E-mail gateways as well as file and print server chores. A new automated installation routine reflects the open-source community's efforts to improve ease of use.

34146 ■ "Local Business Changes Name" in *Bellingham Business Journal* (January 2007, pp. 3)

Pub: Sun News Inc.

Description: Profile of bridal self-help e-commerce website, TheSimplyOrganizedBride.com. The business name was changed from Weddings by Deborah to better reflect the nature of the business. Advertising opportunities for local wedding vendors, free tips and wedding articles, and a category for local bridal shows are now included in the content of the site.

34147 ■ "Lock it Away" in *Entrepreneur* (Vol. 31, No. 11, November 2003, pp. 62)

Pub: Entrepreneur Media, Inc.

Ed: Amanda C. Kooser. Description: California law S.B. 1386 requires public disclosure of any computer security breach that affects a California resident's private information, such as social security number or credit card numbers. The new privacy law will reduce identity theft, but also encourages data security to small companies.

34148 ■ "Log on for work" in *Black Enterprise* (Vol. 33, No. 3, October 2002, pp. 74)

Pub: Earl Graves Publishing Co.

Ed: Sonia Alleyne. Description: Advice is given for using the Internet to secure employment. Tips offered include using Web sites specializing in a particular field or company, to join industry organizations, and use caution when registering for a job listing.

34149 ■ "Looking for Leverage" in *Hispanic Business* (Vol. 23, No. 5, May 2001, pp. 32, 34, 36)

Pub: Hispanic Business

Ed: Scott Williams. Description: Companies looking to grow have a variety of high-tech options. Advice is given from Omni/Strat, a Miami-based consulting firm that helps companies leverage technology to improve customer relationships, business intelligence, and e-commerce. The Web Head Group, located in San Antonio, Texas, also offers technology advice to small businesses.

34150 ■ "Looks do matter" in *Black Enterprise* (Vol. 32, No. 9, April 2002, pp. 114)

Pub: Earl Graves Publishing Co.

Ed: Sonya A. Donaldson. Description: Tips for building a successful Web site that will attract new and repeat business are offered.

34151 ■ "Loud and Clear: CEO Hopes to Find International Audience For Multimedia Services" in *Black Enterprise* (Vol. 35, September 2004)

Pub: Earl G. Graves Publishing Co. Inc.

Ed: Anthony Calypso. Description: Ken Lipscomb is launching his virtual broadcasting network which will feature more than 100 Web channels of music, movies, sports and video content that can be enjoyed from computers, televisions, or stereo systems. DAVE Networks also offers in-house multimedia Web-casting production and post-production services to corporate as well as private individuals.

34152 ■ *Low-Budget Online Marketing for Small Business*

Pub: Self-Counsel Press, Incorporated

Ed: Holley Berkley. Released: July 2005. Price: $14.95, CD-Rom. Description: Low-cost, effective online marketing tips for small companies selling products or services over the Internet.

34153 ■ "Low-Cost Teleconferencing" in *My Business* (February/March 2004, pp. 17)

Pub: My Business Magazine

Description: Profile of Apple's new iSight, a cylindrical camera and microphone that connects to a Macintosh computer via high-speed firewire and Apple's proprietary multimedia Internet messaging software iCath-AV, providing always-on videoconferencing.

34154 ■ "Low-Income Residents First to Access Free Internet Services" in *San Diego Business Journal* (Vol. 28, January 8, 2007, No. 2, pp. 6)

Pub: San Diego Business Journal Associates

Ed: Andy Killion. Description: SoCalFreeNHet.org is offering free wireless Internet service to low income residents in Golden Hill apartments.

34155 ■ "M-commerce: does 'streaming media' give you the screaming meemies?" in *The New York Times Magazine* (March 19, 2000, pp. 32)

Pub: The New York Times Company

Ed: William Safire. Description: New language is being developed around m-commerce which is e-commerce done over mobile phones and hand-held devices.

34156 ■ "Mail Carriers Bring Home the Goods for Holiday Online Shoppers" in *Portland Press Herald* (December 22, 2005)

Pub: Blethen Maine Newspapers, Inc.

Ed: Elbert Aull. Description: U.S. Postal Service officials in Maine reported mail volume two to three times greater than normal on Wednesday, December 21, 2005, due in part to online holiday shopping.

34157 ■ "Main Street Moves Online" in *Business Week* (No. 3678, April 24, 2000, pp. F10)

Pub: McGraw-Hill, Inc.

Description: In a recent survey by the National Trust for Historic Preservation, 84 percent of small businesses located in historic downtown shopping districts said they had increased their Internet usage in 1999.

34158 ■ "Make 'Em an Offer: Entrepreneurs Can Save Big Bucks Bidding for Equipment on eBay. Learn Which Strategies Work Best" in *Entrepreneur*

Pub: Entrepreneur Media Inc.

Ed: Melissa Campanelli. Description: Small businesses are saving money purchasing equipment on eBay's online auction site. Some of eBay's loyal small business customers offer insight into this practice.

34159 ■ "Make It Usable" in *PC Magazine* (February 6, 2001, pp. 1a)

Pub: Ziff-Davis Publishing Company

Ed: Jakob Nielsen, Kara Pernice Coyne, Marie Tahir. Description: An overview of how to design Web sites that will make people want to stay on it and use it as well. The article stresses the importance of testing the site.

34160 ■ "Make Small Devices A Corporate Asset" in *E-business Advisor* (Vol. 18, No. 3, March 2000, pp. 10)

Pub: Advisor Media, Inc.

Ed: Eugene Tiller. Description: Small, wireless, computing devices are the next wave in intelligent systems. Smart phones, smart pagers and personal digital assistants (PDA) are typical of this genre. Over one billion mobile phones will be in use within five years and almost 56 million PDAs will be deployed by 2002. PCs will evolve to become hubs of a more flexible and mobile computing environment.

34161 ■ "Make Your Website Pop" in *Black Enterprise* (Vol. 36, November 2005, No. 4, pp. 70)

Pub: Earl G. Graves Publishing Co. Inc.

Ed: Bridget McCrea. Description: Search engine optimization is one way to maximize Website investment. Five tips for small business to distinguish itself online are offered.

34162 ■ "Making B2B Better" in *E-business Advisor* (Vol. 18, No. 5, May 2000, pp. 10)
Pub: Advisor Media, Inc.
Description: The next generation of business-to-business models is what Giga Research Fellow, Gig Graham, calls electronic partner networks (EPNs), where business partners share a common network, establish a trustworthy means of collaboration, and conduct business through the use of structured electronic contracts and agreements.

34163 ■ "Making E-Mail Work" in *Sales and Marketing.com* (Vol. 156, No. 3, March 2004, pp. 18)
Pub: VNU eMedia, Inc.
Ed: Ellen Neuborne. **Description:** Marketers are adjusting online newsletters sent to customers with the newly established spam laws. Four ways to send successful emails to customers that will help a small business grow are examined.

34164 ■ "Making Fast Food Faster" in *Altanta Journal-Constitution* (January 23, 2007)
Pub: Cox Newspapers, Inc.
Ed: Leon Stafford. **Description:** Fast food restaurants are working to reduce customer wait time at drive through restaurants through the use of the Internet to place and pay for orders.

34165 ■ "Making it" in *Wall Street Journal* (Dec. 9, 2002, pp. R5)
Pub: Dow Jones & Co. Inc.
Ed: Erin Schulte. **Description:** Home crafting has found its way to the Web, and that means small craft businesses are taking advantage of the Internet.

34166 ■ "Managing Your IT Managers" in *Ingram's* (Vol. 28, No. 5, May 2002, pp. 26)
Pub: Show Me Publishing, Inc.
Ed: Russ Johnson. **Description:** Guidelines for developing effective information technology leadership in a small company are presented.

34167 ■ "A Man's World?" in *Entrepreneur* (Vol. 31, No. 8, August 2003, pp. 26)
Pub: Entrepreneur Media, Inc.
Ed: Aliza Pilar Sherman. **Description:** Interview with three women entrepreneurs examining the challenges women entrepreneurs face in today's marketplace. The panel consisted of Cristi Cristich, CEO and founder of Cristek Interconnects Inc., maker of connectors and cabling for medical and military applications; Sheri L. Parrack, president and CEO of Texas Motor Transportation Consultants, a professional registration, tax and title service company; and Terrie Jones, owner of AGSI, a provider of information technology resource solutions.

34168 ■ "Manufacturers Group Wants End to Spam" in *Crain's Detroit Business* (Vol. 19, No. 10, March 10, 2003, pp. 6)
Pub: Crain Communications Inc., Detroit
Ed: Amy Lane. **Description:** The Michigan Manufacturers Association is fighting to stop spam on the Internet and is asking for the Michigan Legislature's help.

34169 ■ "Many analysts think the old-style expensive portal deals deserve more scrutiny from e-tailers" in *The New York Times* (May 1, 2000)
Pub: The New York Times Company
Ed: Bob Tedeschi. **Description:** Online retailers are re-evaluating how their advertising dollars are spent. Besides TV ads, the practice has been to buy ad space on Web portal pages. Portal companies, like Yahoo, MSN, or AOL, would create a category, then let e-tailers bid up the price for the top three slots. Often this led to $2-$3 million per year deals between the portal and e-tailer. Now online retailers are facing a cash squeeze as investors step back from Internet stocks. Also, the e-tail market is anticipating consolidation among different segments. If only 2 or 3 players remain in a given online retail category, bidding will fall off further, and portals will see a further erosion of revenue. At the same time, as portal sites gain traffic, advertisers will seek out the top 3 or 5 sites to place their ads.

34170 ■ "MAPICS Implements Web-based Self Service Tool to Enhance Customer Service For High Tech Manufacturers" in *PR Newswire* (Oct. 29, 2001)
Pub: PR Newswire Association, Inc.
Description: New solutions database offers on-demand support for MAPICS' ERP for extended systems customers. MAPICS is a leading provider of collaborative, extended enterprise applications for manufacturers.

34171 ■ "Maponics: www.maponics.com" in *Entrepreneur* (Vol. 32, November 2004, No. 11, pp. 6)
Pub: Entrepreneur Media Inc.
Ed: Steve Cooper. **Description:** A Website featuring custom mapping, geographic targeting and sales territory analysis is profiled.

34172 ■ "Maps on Tap" in *Entrepreneur.com* (Vol. 34, February 2006, No. 2, pp. 38)
Pub: Entrepreneur Media Inc.
Description: Profile of TomTom Navigator 5 Bluetooth GPS receiver that turns your PDA or smartphone into a GPS navigation system.

34173 ■ "Mark Hoffman" in *Internet World* (Vol. 7, No. 1, January 15, 2001, pp. 41)
Pub: Mecklermedia Corporation
Ed: Ruhan Memishi. **Description:** Mark Hoffman, chairman and CEO of Commerce One is interviewed about his views on business exchanges and his company. Hoffman believes there will be an increase in both business-to-business exchanges and growth in services for a competitive edge.

34174 ■ "Market Watch" in *Entrepreneur* (Vol. 28, No. 1, January 2000, pp. 46)
Pub: Entrepreneur Media Inc.
Ed: Melissa Campanelli. **Description:** The new Web-marketing service, eAnalytics from Adknowledge, is profiled.

34175 ■ "Marketers, a Lawyer, And a Techie—Cheap" in *FSB* (Vol. 10, No. 9, December 1, 2000, pp. 118)
Pub: Time Inc.
Ed: Maggie Overfelt. **Description:** A compilation of Web sites offering affordable advice for small businesses, with a brief description of each site.

34176 ■ *Marketing Without Money for Small and Midsize Businesses: 300 FREE and Cheap Ways to Increase Your Sales*
Pub: Halle House Publishing
Ed: Nicholas E. Bade. **Released:** July 2005. **Price:** $16.95. **Description:** Three hundred practical low-cost or no-cost strategies to increase sales, focusing on free advertising, free marketing assistance, and free referrals to the Internet.

34177 ■ *Marketing Your Product*
Pub: Self-Counsel Press, Incorporated
Ed: Donald Cyr, Douglas Gray. **Released:** September 2004. **Price:** $18.95. **Description:** Tips for marketing any product in today's competitive consumer environment. One chapter focuses on using the Internet as a marketing tool.

34178 ■ "Marketingfix: www.marketingfix. com" in *Entrepreneur* (Vol. 31, No. 10, October 2003, pp. 6)
Pub: Entrepreneur Media, Inc.
Ed: Steve Cooper. **Description:** E-marketing news from marketing consultant, Rick E. Bruner, is available from www.marketingfix.com.

34179 ■ "MarketingSherpa: www. marketingsherpa.com" in *Entrepreneur* (Vol. 33, February 2005, No. 2, pp. 8)
Pub: Entrepreneur Media Inc.
Description: MarketingSherpa provides marketers with statistics, case studies, and email marketing newsletters.

34180 ■ "A Match Made in Hormones" in *Business 2.0* (Vol. 7, January/February 2006, No. 1, pp. 24)
Pub: Time, Inc.
Ed: Susan Kuchinskas. **Description:** Profile of Match.com's new Chemistry.com, a spinoff that matches partners based on the levels of hormones in the brain.

34181 ■ *Maximum Marketing, Minimum Dollars: The Top 50 Ways to Grow Your Small Business*
Pub: Kaplan Books
Ed: Kim Gordon. **Released:** April 2006. **Price:** $24.00. **Description:** Marketing tips to increase sales are presented. Small business owners will learn to maximize marketing with 50 innovative and affordable methods, including online marketing.

34182 ■ "May I Help You?" in *Inc.* (Volume 28, January 2006, No. 1, pp. 31-32)
Pub: Inc. Magazine
Ed: Ellen Neuborne. **Description:** Life-chat software is helping online retailers attract buying customers. Life-chat vendors include LiveAdmins.com, LivePerson.com, and BoldChat.com.

34183 ■ "Mediation for Small Business: Cheaper and Faster Than The Courts" in *My Business* (February/March 2003, pp. 16)
Pub: My Business Magazine
Ed: Alvin M. Hattal. **Description:** Rather than using the court system, more small businesses are resolving disputes through mediation. Two online mediation services are also listed. Statistical data included.

34184 ■ "The Meet Market: Looking for New Business Leads? Networking Clubs on the Web Make it Easy" in *Entrepreneur* (Vol. 32, August 2004)
Pub: Entrepreneur Media Inc.
Ed: Catherine Seda. **Description:** Techniques that will help small business owners meet valuable contacts and secure new projects on the Internet are listed.

34185 ■ "Meet Your Customers' Needs Through Cultural Marketing" in *E-business Advisor* (Vol. 18, No. 8, August 2000, pp. 18)
Pub: Advisor Media, Inc.
Ed: Donald DePalma. **Description:** Few U.S. online businesses are focusing on the needs of culturally diverse groups of users. Cultural, or ethnic, marketing targets a specific national or linguistic group and includes such cross-border issues as currency conversion, shipping concerns, and export-import compliance. Statistical information is included.

34186 ■ "Meeting and Greeting" in *PC Magazine* (February 20, 2001, pp. 129)
Pub: Ziff-Davis Publishing Company
Ed: Walaika Haskins. **Description:** A profile of CoolE-mail.com, that offers traveling professionals wireless access to e-mail, faxes and voice mail at a central location.

34187 ■ "MeetingBridge" in *Entrepreneur* (Vol. 33, September 2005, No. 9, pp. 6)
Pub: Entrepreneur Media Inc.
Ed: Steve Cooper. **Description:** MeetingBridge offers teleconferencing, Web-conferencing and Webinar needs using a dial-in number and entry code. Web conferencing charges start at 12 cents per minute, teleconferencing at 15 center per minute (29 cents per minute with operation assistance), and Webinar tools and registration services are free.

34188 ■ "Meg Whitman" in *Fast Company* (May 2001, pp. 72)
Pub: Fast Company
Ed: Charles Fishman. **Description:** Profile of Meg Whitman, CEO of the e-commerce company eBay.

34189 ■ "Melville-Based DealerTrack Inc. Sue Rival Mich.-Based RouteOne" in *Long Island Business News* (February 6, 2004)
Pub: Dolan Media Newswires
Ed: Ken Schachter. **Description:** DealerTrack Inc. has filed a patent lawsuit against Michigan-based

RouteOne, a joint venture between DaimlerChrysler Service, Ford Motor Credit Company, General Motors Acceptance Corporation, and Toyota Financial Services. The lawsuit charges RouteOne of infringing on two patents related to a routing system, method and computer program for analyzing credit applications.

34190 ■ "Memo to Web shops" in *Crain's Detroit Business* **(Vol. 18,)**
Pub: Crain Communications Inc. - Detroit
Ed: Andrew Dietderich. **Description:** As companies look for ways to cut expenses, technology spending is coming under scrutiny.

34191 ■ "The Mentoring Advantage (Dearborn Trade) www.dearborn.com" in *Entrepreneur* **(Vol. 33, February 2005, No. 2, pp. 8)**
Pub: Entrepreneur Media Inc.
Description: Florence Stone addresses selecting mentors and implementing business mentoring programs.

34192 ■ "Mexican grocery gets wired" in *Hispanic Business* **(Vol. 22, No. 5, May 2000, pp. 14)**
Pub: Hispanic Business
Ed: Andrea Siedsma. **Description:** Mexgrocer.com, due to launch on May 5, 2000, will be the first online grocery to focus exclusively on Mexican food. It will target middle- to upper-income Hispanics, mainly Mexican Americans.

34193 ■ "Micron Technology Inc." in *PC Magazine* **(March 7, 2000, pp. 158)**
Pub: Ziff-Davis Publishing Company
Ed: Bruce Brown, Cade Metz, Carol Venezia. **Description:** Client and server machines from Micron Technology are reviewed as part of an E-services solution that includes software and services. The Net-Frame 3400 server is a 600MHz Pentium II machine with dual 9.1GB Wide Ultra3 SCSI hard drives and 256MB of RAM, while the ClientPro CS desktop PC has a similar CPU with an S3 graphics card, 40x CD-ROM, 13GB hard disk and 17-inch monitor. Micron does not offer its own small business portal and has fewer online applications than some competitors, but it does provide extensive Web-site development and hosting services as well as basic Internet access through its recently acquired HostPro ISP. Users can also obtain higher-speed access through Micron Internet Services (MIS) with a variety of access plans geared to different business types. The server is expensive but works well and has hot-swappable drives. The desktop PC is very expandable, but suffers from annoying design glitches.

34194 ■ "Microsoft Launches Small Business Web Services" in *Network World* **(September 25, 2000, pp. NA)**
Pub: Network World Inc.
Ed: George A. Chidi, Jr. **Description:** A profile of Microsoft's new program that brings small businesses into cyberspace. Microsoft's Business Web Services are designed for non-technical small business customers, providing domain registration, business e-mail, site creation and hosting, e-commerce and Web-based marketing services.

34195 ■ "Microsoft, Pfizer Target Fake Viagra Spammers" in *Boston Globe* **(February 11, 2005)**
Pub: New York Times Company
Ed: Christopher Rowland. **Description:** Pfizer Inc. and Microsoft Corporation have partnered to stop illegal Internet commerce, targeting email spammers peddling phony Viagra.

34196 ■ "MIMlist Draws Eclectic Crowd: Online Forums" in *Tradeshow Week* **(Vol. 34, November 29, 2004, No. 48, pp. 52)**
Pub: Reed Business Information
Ed: Rachelle Crum. **Description:** Exhibition industry associations provide a listserve or other online forum exclusively for its members. Profile of MIMlist, a forum of more than 4,000 members is profiled.

34197 ■ "Mind over Matter" in *Entrepreneur* **(Vol. 28, No. 9, September 2000, pp. 42)**
Pub: Entrepreneur Media Inc.
Ed: Robert McGarvey. **Description:** Web-based intellectual property exchanges are explored. The editor emphasizes the importance of doing a thorough investigation before sacrificing the control over your idea.

34198 ■ "MingleMatch Reaches Half-Million Member Milestone" in *PR Newswire* **(January 12, 2004)**
Pub: PR Newswire Association, Inc.
Description: Profile of MingleMatch, a fast growing online dating service offering more than 20 dating sites for specific audiences of various ethnic, religious persuasions, or geographic locations.

34199 ■ "Mining Online for the Bottom Line" in *Success* **(Vol. 47, No. 4, September 2000, pp. 82)**
Pub: Success Publishing, Inc.
Ed: Paul Gallagher. **Description:** Office services franchisors use the Internet to unearth more customers.

34200 ■ "The Missing Link?" in *Entrepreneur* **(Vol. 33, September 2005, No. 9, pp. 88)**
Pub: Entrepreneur Media Inc.
Ed: Catherine Seda. **Description:** The much-overlooked marketing strategy of getting links from other Websites to yours is examined. This tool will bring more visitors to a site while helping to achieve higher search engine rankings.

34201 ■ "Mohyr, Davidow Hires AOL Exec." in *Venture Capital Journal* **(Vol. 40, No. 10, November 2000, pp. 36)**
Pub: Venture Economics
Description: Mohr, Davidow Ventures hired Debby Meredith, former senior vice president and chief of quality officer at America Online Inc, in early September 2000. The firm backs and helps develop start-up companies, software services and infrastructure and business-to-business spaces. Ms. Meredith will focus on Internet companies, software services and infrastructure and business-to-business spaces.

34202 ■ "Molly Maid franchise owners have own site" in *Crain's Detroit Business* **(Vol. 16, No. 34, August 21, 2000, pp. E-6)**
Pub: Crain Communications, Inc.
Ed: Jewel Gopwani. **Description:** Molly Maid Inc., the Ann Arbor, Michigan-based cleaning company has developed two web sites, one for consumers and another to help the company communicate with franchise owners.

34203 ■ "MomandPop.com" in *PC Magazine* **(January 16, 2000, pp. 131)**
Pub: Ziff-Davis Publishing Company
Ed: Alan Cohen. **Description:** Scouring the Web for handy resources is a luxury small-business owners often don't have. A bevy of portals has simplified matters, bringing information, advice, and services to one place. Dozens of small-biz sites have popped up in the past year, but the best of the lot is AllBusiness. This site provides access to 250 business forms and agreements and how-to guides on everything from protecting trademarks to terminating an employee. Experts field questions in more than a dozen areas, including employment law; you can submit your own query or read through the site's archives.

34204 ■ "Monitor and Manage Your Web Server" in *E-business Advisor* **(Vol. 18, No. 1, January 2000, pp. 38)**
Pub: Advisor Media, Inc.
Ed: Terrance A. Crow. **Description:** A profile of Web-Manage Technologies Enterprise Reporter 5.0 network management software, which monitors Web traffic and online files at an affordable price.

34205 ■ "Monitor Your E-Business Systems' Health" in *E-business Advisor* **(Vol. 17, No. 12, December 1999, pp. 22)**
Pub: Advisor Media, Inc.
Ed: Bill Jaeger. **Description:** E-businesses should implement a program of ongoing systems monitoring, which tracks and reports key metrics on business-critical systems, as well as occasional performance testing. Ongoing systems monitoring makes it possible to warn users about slowdowns in advance, thus building customer loyalty. A directory of systems-monitoring software and services companies is included.

34206 ■ "Monkey Business" in *Entrepreneur* **(Vol. 28, No. 1, January 2000, pp. 26)**
Pub: Entrepreneur Media Inc.
Ed: Robert McGarvey. **Description:** If you're running an online store, or just thinking about it, Webmonkey's 'E-Business' page offers tips, links and information on e-business.

34207 ■ "The Moral Intensity of Privacy: An Empirical Study of Webmasters' Attitudes" in *Journal of Business Ethics* **(Vol. 46, Sept. 15, 2003)**
Pub: Kluwer Academic Publishers Group
Ed: Thomas R. Shaw. **Description:** Webmasters play an integral role as moral agent regarding the issue of Internet privacy.

34208 ■ "More Bang for Your Buck" in *Entrepreneur* **(Vol. 32)**
Pub: Entrepreneur Media Inc.
Ed: Nichole L. Torres. **Description:** Associated Surplus Dealers/Associated Merchandise Dealers (ASD/MD) Trade Show Las Vegas, produced by VNU Expositions, offers small business entrepreneurs and eBay resellers a cost-effective venue for selling products. The show includes 3,500 exhibitors with products ranging from dollar-store merchandise to general merchandise such as toys, gifts, electronics, health and beauty, and fashion accessories.

34209 ■ "More than friends" in *Entrepreneur* **(Vol. 30, No. 3, March 2002, pp. 66)**
Pub: Entrepreneur Media Inc.
Ed: Jennifer Pellet. **Description:** Profile of Circle Lending, an online service that enables would-be borrowers to create and administer business loans with family and friends.

34210 ■ "More steady growth: Hispanic ad expenditures increase 11 percent to reach nearly $1.9 billion" in *Hispanic Business* **(Dec. 1999, pp.56)**
Pub: Hispanic Business
Ed: Tim Dougherty. **Description:** Expansion in Hispanic advertising expenditures slowed to 11 percent in 1999, from 21 percent in 1998. However, the Top 50 Advertiser total rose 30 percent to $545.97 million. The impact of the Internet on Hispanic advertising is discussed.

34211 ■ "More, More, More" in *Entrepreneur* **(Vol. 33, September 2005, No. 9, pp. 52)**
Pub: Entrepreneur Media Inc.
Ed: Mike Hogan. **Description:** AOL's Callways offers voice calls, email, instant messaging, chat rooms and message boards with common inboxes, address books and buddy lists using one-click access.

34212 ■ "A More Profitable Harvest" in *Business 2.0* **(Vol. 6, May 2005, No. 4, pp. 66)**
Pub: Time, Inc.
Ed: Bridget Finn. **Description:** Blue Mountain Arts makes money by giving away free greeting cards online and selling flowers to go with the greetings. Pro-Flowers has grown to third-largest flower retailer in the nation.

34213 ■ "Mother, I'm the boss now: Internet executives hire their parents and traditions fall" in *The New York Times* **(July 4, 2000, pp. C1)**
Pub: The New York Times Company
Ed: Katie Hafner. **Description:** The ways reverse nepotism is opening a new dimension in child-parent relationships is discussed.

34214 ■ "Move Over, Internet Explorer; Why the Rush to Foxfire?" in *Business Week* **(February 7, 2005, No. 3919, pp. 89)**
Pub: McGraw-Hill Companies

Ed: Steve Hamm. **Description:** Profile of the new Web browser Firefox, which is becoming more popular than Microsoft's Internet Explorer because it is more secure.

34215 ■ "Moving from one product was their prize" in *Crain's Detroit Business* **(Vol. 19, No. 13, March 31, 2003, pp. 13)**
Pub: Crain Communications Inc., Detroit
Description: Profile of EPrize LLC, the company offers Web-based sweepstakes designed to draw Internet surfers with prizes and has expanded the enterprise in order to stay in business.

34216 ■ "MSCI-Red Herring Index" in *Red Herring* **(January 2003, pp. 72)**
Pub: Herring Communications Inc.
Description: An index comparison is presented, highlighting the following industries: communications equipment, Internet software & services, semiconductor equipment and products, wireless telecom services, electronic equipment and instruments, IT consulting and services, computers and peripherals, broadcasting and cable TV, software, diversified telecom services, and publishing.

34217 ■ "Municipal Wi-Fi: Let's Keep It Local" in *eWeek* **(February 3, 2005)**
Pub: Ziff Davis Media Inc.
Description: According to a report from the New Millennium Research Council, experts believe that the development of a municipally held Wi-Fi network would have a negative effect on city budgets and on competition.

34218 ■ "Music" in *Business Week* **(December 19, 2005, No. 3964, pp. 40)**
Pub: McGraw-Hill Companies
Ed: Peter Burrows. **Description:** Critics say iTunes-only downloads and inflexible pricing are hurting song sales.

34219 ■ "Music-Go-Round: Webcasters Reach Tentative Agreement with RIAA, DiMA" in *Black Enterprise* **(Vol. 34, No. 4, November 2003, pp. 52)**
Pub: Earl Graves Publishing Co.
Ed: Anthony Calypso. **Description:** A joint-royalty rate proposal between BlakeRadio.com, the Recording Industry Association of America, and the Digital Media Association has been submitted to the U.S. Copyright Office. The proposal would keep both sides from going through expensive and lengthy arbitration processes to determine appropriate royalty fees.

34220 ■ "Music Like Water" in *Forbes* **(Vol. 175, January 31, 2005, No. 2, pp. 42)**
Pub: Forbes Magazine Inc.
Ed: David Kusek. **Description:** Development of a music utility to distribute and market interactive digital music is discussed. The system would work like water, gas and utility systems.

34221 ■ "My Gadget" in *My Business* **(February/March 2004, pp. 17)**
Pub: My Business Magazine
Ed: Lena Basha. **Description:** Profile of AccuCard, a self-updating address book designed for use with Microsoft Outlook. The service will send personalized quarterly emails to every small business contact, requesting updated or confirmation of correct contact information and automatically updates information every three months.

34222 ■ *My Homemade Business*
Pub: Graphico Publishing Company
Ed: Victoria Ring. **Released:** January 2005. **Price:** $39.99. **Description:** Author shares insight into ways she marketed different businesses over a 16-year period. Free Web design software included.

34223 ■ "My Life as a Blogger: A Growing Number of VCs Are Opening Themselves Up in Online Diaries" in *Venture Capital Journal* **(Jan. 1, 2005)**
Pub: Thomason Financial Inc.
Ed: Tom Stein. **Description:** Information about the new blog-related technologies and startup companies emerging is shared. Currently there are about twelve venture-related blogs on the Internet.

34224 ■ "Myms, pings and vortals" in *The New York Times* **(March 27, 2000, pp. D4, H4)**
Pub: The New York Times Company
Ed: David Kirby, Henry Fountain. **Description:** The article covers computer jargon and how it is transferred to business conversation. Statistical data included.

34225 ■ "MyPayNet" in *Entrepreneur.com* **(Vol. 34, January 2006, No. 1, pp. 6)**
Pub: Entrepreneur Media Inc.
Ed: Steve Cooper. **Description:** MyPayNet is an electronic invoicing and payment service designed to help small companies send and receive payments electronically.

34226 ■ "MySpace for Business: Are You Connected?" in *Sales & Marketing Management* **(Vol. 158, November-December 2006, No. 11, pp. 20)**
Pub: VNU Business Media
Ed: Rebecca Aronauer. **Description:** Joining an online community can prove profitable to any salesperson.

34227 ■ "MyTechTool" in *My Business* **(June/July 2002, pp. 24)**
Pub: My Business Magazine
Description: Profile of Susan Soros, owner of Soap Goddess, a home-based business that makes and sells all-natural handmade soap online.

34228 ■ "The Name Game-Spending millions on a domain name?" in *PC Computing* **(April 2000, pp. 108)**
Pub: Ziff-Davis Inc.
Ed: Jane Weaver. **Description:** Businesses on the Internet rely on a good domain name and many are willing to pay millions of dollars for a name. This article describes some of the names and their prices.

34229 ■ "Name Grab-Cypersquaters, once a mere nuisance, now can go to prison for violating your trademark" in *PC Computing* **(April 2000, pp. 40)**
Pub: Ziff-Davis Inc.
Ed: Christopher Null. **Description:** The U.S. Anti-Cypersquatting Consumer Protection Act (ACPA), which was signed into law on November 29, 1999, has triggered a rash of lawsuits targeting cybersquatters. The most notable filing so far is the Coalition to Advance the Protection of Sports logos' (CAPS) case against FlairMail.com, which offers free e-mail addresses from sports domains like goavalanche.net and mightyducks1.com. Domain names have become very expensive commodities, as evidenced by the $7.5 million Business.com domain name.

34230 ■ "The Napsterization of B2B" in *Harvard Business Review* **(Vol. 78, No. 6, November-December 2000, pp. 18)**
Pub: Harvard Business School Publishing Corp.
Description: A business-to-business (B2B) report showing how companies are completing transactions among themselves through peer-to-peer networks, resulting in less need for centralized exchanges.

34231 ■ "Narrowing the divide" in *Black Enterprise* **(Vol. 32, No. 10, May 2002, pp. 26)**
Pub: Earl Graves Publishing Co.
Ed: Alan Hughes. **Description:** Internet use among African Americans has increased at an annual rate of 33 percent, rising to 18.5 million users, according to a study done by the National Telecommunications and Information Administration and the Economics and Statistics Administration.

34232 ■ "National trends in Webcast advertising" in *Crain's Detroit Business* **(Vol. 16, No. 46, November 13, 2000, pp. 15)**
Pub: Crain Communications, Inc.
Description: Market information and statistical data regarding online advertising, banner ads, sponsorship, e-mail, pop-ups, and buttons are discussed.

34233 ■ "Navigate the Application Framework Terrain" in *E-business Advisor* **(Vol. 18, No. 1, January 2000, pp. 16)**
Pub: Advisor Media, Inc.
Ed: Dan Sullivan. **Description:** Software vendors are bringing various, differing e-business tools, suites, and vertical applications to the marketplace, all classified as e-business application frameworks. Meanwhile, certain e-business developers' requirements are emerging as centrally important, including scalability, security and reduced time to market. Product overviews are included.

34234 ■ "Need Help? Don't Call Us" in *Inc.* **(August 2005, pp. 36)**
Pub: Inc. Magazine
Ed: Etelka Lehoczky. **Description:** Online forums are turning clients into a low-cost support staff. Nick Bradbury tells how he built a Web forum with 2,000 users.

34235 ■ "The Need for Speed in New Millennium Leadership Styles" in *Employment Relations Today* **(Vol. 27, No. 1, Spring 2000, pp. 61)**
Pub: John Wiley & Sons, Inc.
Ed: David Cottrell. **Description:** An overview of corporate management in an era of technological change, and the need for leadership styles that rely on quick decision-making and planning. Topics addressed include incorporating speed into company culture, streamlining processes, and implementing faster communication systems.

34236 ■ "Nervous About Bidding on eBay?" in *New York Times* **(November 17, 2003, pp. C7)**
Pub: The New York Times
Ed: Bob Tedeschi. **Description:** Hartford Financial Services Group and BuySafe have partnered to offer a buyer protection plan for eBay shoppers.

34237 ■ "'Net Attacks to Plague Small and Midsize Firms" in *Network World* **(October 16, 2000, pp. 108)**
Pub: Network World Inc.
Ed: David Legard. **Description:** Small and midsize companies are likely targets for Internet attacks, and many will suffer a successful attack between now and 2003, according to a report released by the market research firm Gartner Group.

34238 ■ "Net Company: Don't Shout, Listen" in *Fast Company* **(August 2001, pp. 129)**
Pub: Fast Company
Ed: Fara Warner. **Description:** The article shows how the Proctor & Gamble company has turned the Internet into a device for listening to customers, and also experiment with their brands.

34239 ■ "Net Crimes & Misdemeanors" in *Information Today* **(Vol. 20, No. 1, Jan. 2003, pp. 44)**
Pub: Information Today, Inc.
Description: A new book for Information Professionals is reviewed. The book helps individuals and business users of the Web to protect themselves, their children and their employees from online predators and cheats.

34240 ■ "Net Data Seller Can Be Sued in Stalking-Murder Case" in *Daily Business Review* **(Vol. 77, No. 190, March 12, 2003, pp. A7)**
Pub: American Lawyer Media LP
Ed: Peter Page. **Description:** The New Hampshire Supreme Court ruled that the family of a woman killed by a stalker can sue the Internet data broker hired by the stalker to locate his victim.

34241 ■ "Net Deposits" in *Entrepreneur* **(Vol. 33, October 2005, No. 10, pp. 54)**
Pub: Entrepreneur Media Inc.
Ed: C.J. Prince. **Description:** According to recent surveys, small business owners hesitate to move their business banking online.

34242 ■ "Net Gains" in *Incentive* (Vol. 174, No. 10, October 2000, pp. 9)
Pub: Bill Communications
Ed: Joan M. Steinauer. Description: The Internet has become the top source for planning trade show visits.

34243 ■ "Net Profits" in *Entrepreneur* (Vol. 27, No. 12, December 1999, pp. 48)
Pub: Entrepreneur Media Inc.
Ed: Melissa Campanelli. Description: If you sell on the Web, you know that fraud is part of the e-commerce game. Helpful hints to avoid online thieves.

34244 ■ "NetNose: www.netnose.com" in *Entrepreneur* (Vol. 31, No. 12, December 2003, pp. 8)
Pub: Entrepreneur Media Inc.
Ed: Steve Cooper. Description: Profile of the online search engine that allows users to vote on the relevancy of a Web site to its search terms.

34245 ■ "Netscape unveils Web site aimed at small firms" in *Wall Street Journal* (September 13, 2000, pp. B5)
Pub: Dow Jones & Co., Inc.
Ed: Julia Angwin. Description: A profile of the Netscape Netbusiness small business Web portal.

34246 ■ "Netting a bigger piece of the action" in *Hispanic Business* (Vol. 22, No. 5, May 2000, pp. 38)
Pub: Hispanic Business
Ed: Jonathan J. Higuera. Description: Ways in which Hispanic businesses can use the Internet are discussed. Tejas Office Products Inc., Burt Automotive Network and Gonzalez Plumbing are profiled.

34247 ■ "Net.Working" in *Small Business Opportunities* (Vol. 12, No. 2, March 2000, pp. 80)
Pub: Harris Publications, Inc.
Ed: Robert Spiegel. Description: One entrepreneur tells how net affiliations help him make an extra $250,000 a year by using them.

34248 ■ "New Deli Destination Coming to Town" in *Bellingham Business Journal* (December 2006, pp. A3)
Pub: Sun News Inc.
Description: Heidi Rosebush, a former Trader Joe's manager, will be opening Destination Deli, a sandwich cart serving sandwiches using local ingredients from bakeries and farms. Heidi will also develop a Web site that allows customers to place and pay for orders online.

34249 ■ "The new economy's currency is stock, stock, and stock" in *The New York Times* (March 27, 2000, pp. D12, H12)
Pub: The New York Times Company
Ed: Martha Baer. Description: An investigation into equity reimbursements for all Web business contractors.

34250 ■ "The New Edition" in *Internet World* (Vol. 7, No. 2, January 15, 2001, pp. 20)
Pub: Mecklermedia Corporation
Ed: Anastasia M. Ashman. Description: Electronic books currently represent a publishing segment so miniscule as to be virtually invisible, were it not receiving disproportionate media coverage. Market researchers, nevertheless, expect the market for E-books to reach $2.3 billion by 2005. E-publishing could dramatically transform the centuries-old industry and even revolutionize the way consumers use information, but the biggest obstacle may be publishers themselves, who have vast investments in the status quo.

34251 ■ "New Franchise Offers Customers Web Design Tech Without the Hassles" in *Small Business Opportunities* (March 2005)
Pub: Harris Publications Inc.
Description: Profile of the new franchise, InstantFX. The firm offers Website design, hosting services, email, e-commerce, and other Web-related services.

34252 ■ "The New Net CEO" in *Harvard Business Review* (Vol. 78, No. 3, May 2000, pp. S10)
Pub: Harvard Business School Publishing Corp.
Ed: Chuck Martin. Description: Executives in electronic commerce must understand the way in which the industry operates and must focus on the customer.

34253 ■ "New Online Dating Service Uses Psychoanalytic Approach; Dr. Freud: Log On!" in *PR Newswire* (March 8, 2004)
Pub: PR Newswire Association, Inc.
Description: Profile of Dr. Fred Levenson, New York psychoanalyst, and his new online dating service, TheraDate, that matches couples using psychoanalytic methods. Dr. Levenson has 30 years experience treating patients and his goal is to lower the current 50 percent divorce rate in America.

34254 ■ "The new pay paradigm" in *WorkingWoman* (Vol. 25, No. 7, August 2000, pp. 57)
Pub: Lang Communications Inc.
Ed: Elizabeth Wasserman. Description: Issues concerning the pay of women compared to men are discussed and the impact on wages of a large number of electronic commerce-based firms attracting highly paid women away from traditional market-place jobs. An annual review of women's salaries and interviews are included.

34255 ■ "New RCN Service Offers Net-Connected Surveillance" in *Boston Globe* (January 27, 2005)
Pub: New York Times Company
Ed: Peter J. Howe. Description: A new broadband service called WebWatch will allow parents and business owners to use Internet-connected cameras to secure their homes and companies. The fee for this service runs $10 per month.

34256 ■ "The New Spam" in *Entrepreneur* (Vol. 32, November 2004, No. 11, pp. 60)
Pub: Entrepreneur Media Inc.
Ed: Amanda C. Kooser. Description: Entrepreneurs need to educate their employees about the latest Internet security issue, Spim. Spim intrudes Internet connections through Instant Messaging systems.

34257 ■ "New Tacks for Tough Times" in *Business Week Online* (Oct. 17, 2002)
Pub: McGraw-Hill Inc.
Ed: Roger Franklin. Description: According to a small business survey, 75 percent of the 5,000 firms responding, have a positive attitude about the future, and predict bottom-line growth. One-third of the companies expect significant expansion.

34258 ■ "A New Vision for Network Marketing" in *Success* (Vol. 47, No. 3, July 2000, pp. 80)
Pub: Success Publishing, Inc.
Ed: Karin Fuller. Description: Profile of New Vision, a network-marketing company, whose co-founder shares some secrets of success.

34259 ■ "New Web Domains Bring Opportunity, Confusion" in *My Business* (November/December 2001, pp. 24)
Pub: My Business Magazine
Ed: Michael Grebb. Description: The registration of domain names can be expensive for small businesses, but the newly formed Internet Corporation for Assigned Names and Numbers (ICANN) has begun taking reservations for three new suffixes: offered.

34260 ■ "New Website for Women's Clothes" in *Marketing to Women* (Vol. 20, January 2007, No. 1, pp. 8)
Pub: EPM Communications, Inc.
Description: FrillyGirls.com is a new website catering to women between the ages of 21-45. The site is run by three stay-at-home mothers looking to reenter the workforce and specializes in designer clothing and accessories.

34261 ■ "News and Reviews" in *Home Business* (Vol. 13, January/February 2006, No. 1, pp. 98)
Pub: Home Business Magazine
Description: Information for closing business deals online, Web-based human resources small business software, noise canceling audio headphones, and tips for launching and marketing new products is given.

34262 ■ "Newsstand" in *Home Business* (Vol. 13, January/February 2006, No. 1, pp. 38-39)
Pub: Home Business Magazine
Description: Topics include marketing of office supplies and equipment, rising gas prices, toxic office environments, entrepreneurship, and online retailing.

34263 ■ "NEXIS Finally Goes Dot-Com" in *Information Today* (Vol. 17, No. 10, November 2000, pp. 32)
Pub: Information Today, Inc.
Ed: Mick O'Leary. Description: New nexis.com service blends old-style depth with new-style ease, with their news database and additional business and legislative data from LEXIS on the Web.

34264 ■ "The next best thing to being there?" in *E-business Advisor* (Vol. 18, No. 10, October 2000, pp. 11)
Pub: Advisor Media, Inc.
Description: A profile of PictureTel, who has developed the next generation of videoconferencing systems, called the Picture Tel900 Series. The systems are based on the iPower architecture, jointly developed by PictureTel and Intel Corporation.

34265 ■ "The next big e-thing" in *WorkingWoman* (Vol. 25, No. 5, May 2000, pp. 72)
Pub: Lang Communications Inc.
Ed: Calev Ben-David. Description: Isabel Maxwell is the president of Commtouch, the biggest provider of "branded e-mail", serving an enormous number of corporate web sites and individual e-mail accounts all over the world. Issues concerning her upbringing, career developments, and the success of Commtouch are presented.

34266 ■ "No Escape? Even the Internet May Not Be Able to Avoid Taxes" in *Entrepreneur* (Vol. 31, No. 4, April 2003, pp. 17)
Pub: Entrepreneur Media Inc.
Ed: Amanda C. Kooser. Description: The topic of taxation on the Internet is discussed.

34267 ■ "No More Free Rides: It's the End of the Free Lunch on the Web" in *Black Enterprise* (Vol. 32, No. 6, January 2002, pp. 39)
Pub: Earl Graves Publishing Co.
Ed: Rebecca Rohan. Description: Former free service providers know that their customer base is price-sensitive and charge less than fee-based competitors, but worry how their customers will cope with being charged after using free services for so long.

34268 ■ "No Pain, No Gain" in *Entrepreneur* (Vol. 28, No. 4, April 2000, pp. 42)
Pub: Entrepreneur Media Inc.
Ed: Robert McGarvey. Description: Small businesses with Web sites may benefit from Web marketplace sites.

34269 ■ "No Small Change" in *Black Enterprise* (Vol. 32, No. 8, March 2002, pp. 64)
Pub: Earl Graves Publishing Co.
Ed: Lee Anna Jackson. Description: Profile of Joyce Harris, Web page designer.

34270 ■ "Northeast Ohio Cottage Industry of eBay Drop-Off Stores Emerges" in *News-Herald, Willoughby* (April 3, 2004)
Pub: Knight-Ridder, Tribune Business News
Ed: Dave Truman. Description: Online eBay trading assistants, called Drop Off stores, not affiliated with eBay, work like consignment shops for customers. California has the most drop off stores, but the trend is spreading across the nation.

34271 ■ "Nothing but Net" in *Success* (Vol. 47, No. 4, September 2000, pp. 80)
Pub: Success Publishing, Inc.
Ed: Debbie Selinsky. **Description:** Quixtar combines the best in relationship sales and the Internet's unlimited potential.

34272 ■ "Now in 3-D" in *Entrepreneur* (Vol. 33, October 2005, No. 10, pp. 18)
Pub: Entrepreneur Media Inc.
Ed: Amanda C. Kooser. **Description:** 3-D Web graphics are being considered for use in electronic commerce applications.

34273 ■ "Now that they've come, what can we sell them?" in *The New York Times* (March 27, 2000, pp. D9, H9)
Pub: The New York Times Company
Ed: Bob Tedeschi. **Description:** How companies are converting free common interest sites to commercial ends is examined.

34274 ■ "Nurun Transforms Loews Hotels Website Into a More User-Friendly Experience" in *Canadian Corporate News* (February 7, 2007)
Pub: Comtex News Network, Inc.
Description: Loews Hotels has updated its Website to market its properties to online users.

34275 ■ "NY Bankruptcy Courts Shift to Online Filing" in *Long Island Business News* (February 6, 2004)
Pub: Dolan Media Newswires
Ed: Claude Solnik. **Description:** U.S. Bankruptcy Court for the Southern District of New York has begun accepting electronic Chapter 11 filing; the Eastern District has followed suit. Electronic filing for both non-bankruptcy and bankruptcy cases has also been accepted nationwide.

34276 ■ "OfficeMax launches e-book store" in *Publishers Weekly* (Vol. 249, No. 37, September 16, 2002, pp. 14)
Pub: Reed Business Information
Description: OfficeMax will offer e-books as a service to provide small businesses and mobile professionals with immediate access to best-selling authors, and technology guides and manuals from leading publishers.

34277 ■ "On the Agenda" in *Entrepreneur* (Vol. 30, No. 2, February 2002, pp. 39)
Pub: Entrepreneur Media Inc.
Ed: Amanda C. Kooser. **Description:** The Federal Trade Commission is taking a new approach to consumer privacy and electronic commerce.

34278 ■ "On-line Training Tips" in *Crain's Detroit Business* (Vol. 19, No. 17, April 28, 2003, pp. 12)
Pub: Crain Communications Inc., Detroit
Description: Issues to consider when making a decision to offer online training to employees are listed.

34279 ■ "On the Move?" in *Entrepreneur* (Vol. 31, No. 11, November 2003, pp. 65)
Pub: Entrepreneur Media Inc.
Ed: Jennifer Pellet. **Description:** E-Trade is offering a mortgage program that allows homeowners to move their current mortgages with the purchase of a new home.

34280 ■ "On the Radar" in *E-business Advisor* (Vol. 18, No. 4, April 2000, pp. 8)
Pub: Advisor Media, Inc.
Description: Several vendors have come up with products and services to help companies with e-business strategy. Bolero.net is aimed at helping multinational companies with international commerce. RadView Software's WebLoad Resource Manager and WebLoad Workstation electronic commerce software products are designed to test, analyze, and verify e-business applications. Other companies offering products and services are Primix Solutions, IBM and CyberTrust.

34281 ■ "On the Same Page" in *Crain's Detroit Business* ( )
Pub: Crain Communications Inc. - Detroit
Ed: Terry Kosdrosky. **Description:** Automakers, suppliers, and tooling companies are trying to standardize standard parts used by all facets of the industry, using a standard e-catalog, called e-tooling.

34282 ■ "On the Same Page: Small Booksellers Unite Online" in *Wall Street Journal* (June 29, 2000, pp. A1)
Pub: Dow Jones & Co., Inc.
Ed: Jeffrey A. Tannenbaum. **Description:** A profile of American Booksellers Association's BookSense.com, run by RH Associates & Co. Statistical data is included.

34283 ■ "On Top of the World" in *Home Business* (Vol. 13, January/February 2006, No. 1, pp. 92)
Pub: Home Business Magazine
Ed: Sandy Larson. **Description:** Profile of Jeff Dyrek who launched a company offering North Pole expeditions. Dyrek promotes the tours on his Website, www.YellowAirplane.com that offers information about military and aviation history and a hobby store with model airplanes, trains and ships.

34284 ■ "One Smart Customer" in *Fast Company* (September 2001, pp. 68)
Pub: Fast Company
Description: The CEO of NetSolve addresses the importance of customer service and ways to avoid problems.

34285 ■ "1,000 Crates of Sprinkles With That" in *The NewYork Times* (March 27, 2000, pp. D28, H28)
Pub: The New York Times Company
Ed: Stephen Mihm. **Description:** The structuring of business-to-business commerce online. Statistical data included.

34286 ■ "Online Appraisals Yield Ballpark Prices for Owners" in *Business First Columbus* (Vol. 18, No. 26, February 15, 2002, pp. 26)
Pub: Business First Columbus, Inc.
Ed: Scott Rawdon. **Description:** The impact of the Internet on the real estate industry is discussed.

34287 ■ "Online APPS and Quotes for E&O" in *Rough Notes* (Vol. 145, No. 9, September 2002, pp. 49)
Pub: Rough Notes
Ed: Len Strazewski. **Description:** Frederick J. Fisher, president of Executive Liability Managers Insurance Brokers Inc., discusses professional liability coverage.

34288 ■ "Online Banking is Evolution...Not Revolution" in *Ingram's* (Vol. 29, No. 1, January 2003, pp. 20)
Pub: Show Me Publishing, Inc.
Ed: Tom Mathis. **Description:** Online banking has grown to be a channel of choice for daily banking tasks and might be leading to a cashless and check-less society in the future.

34289 ■ "Online Banking - The Revolution That Really Is" in *Ingram's* (Vol. 29, No. 1, January 2003, pp. 65)
Pub: Show Me Publishing, Inc.
Ed: Jack Cashill. **Description:** Online banking has been growing at a tremendous rate while brick and mortar banks and ATM locations continue to build up around the country. The PEW Research Center survey estimates the rate of Americans who did their banking online increased 164 percent in two years, from March 2000 to October 2002.

34290 ■ "Online Content Reaches Bottom Line" in *Crain's New York Business* (Vol. 20, No. 12, March 22, 2004, pp. 4)
Pub: Crain Communications, Inc.
Ed: Anita Jain. **Description:** Online magazine publishers are seeing an increase in advertising sales as consumer confidence grows. Profiles of TheStreet.com, Nerve.com, and Slate are included, with each sharing the ways they are earning profits with online magazines.

34291 ■ "Online Employee Surveys Slow to Catch on" in *Atlanta Business Chronicle* (Vol. 25, No. 19, October 18, 2002, pp. 12C)
Pub: American City Business Publications, Inc.
Ed: Paige Bowers. **Description:** Online employee surveys are not being used by businesses for various reasons. It is considered that paper-based surveys are easier to use when dealing with cross-country truck drivers or assembly line workers, while the slowing economy has forced other businesses to set aside company Intranet projects.

34292 ■ "Online Insurance Exchanges Fail to Connect" in *Atlanta Business Chronicle* (Vol. 25, No. 19, October 18, 2002, pp. 6C)
Pub: American City Business Publications, Inc.
Ed: Lee Hall. **Description:** Online business-to-business insurance exchanges, once viewed as offering the insurance industry savings in time and money, have not gotten far beyond the conceptual stage, and may be as far as ten years away from completion.

34293 ■ "OnLine Job Sites, Take Two" in *Home Office Computing* (Vol. 18, No. 8, August 2000, pp. 24)
Pub: Scholastic Inc.
Ed: Todd Carter. **Description:** Odds are, posting your resume on an all-purpose job Web sites will not yield good results. According to a survey conducted by Cambridge, Massachusetts-based Forrester Research, online job seekers believe the quality of positions posted online is below average.

34294 ■ "The Online Lawyer" in *Hispanic Business* (October 2002, pp. 90)
Pub: Hispanic Business
Ed: Derek Reveron. **Description:** Caution is advised when seeking legal services online, however small businesses are finding reliable legal services online. A listing of Web site offering legal services is included.

34295 ■ "Online Markets for Private Equity Enter Second Season" in *Venture Capital Journal* (Vol. 40, No. 10, November 2000, pp. 50)
Pub: Venture Economics
Ed: George B. Moriarty. **Description:** Several new Web sites have been launched by private equity professionals who intend to take the relationship with the Internet beyond a profit experience.

34296 ■ "Online Office" in *Entrepreneur* (Vol. 32, No. 1, January 2004, pp. 47)
Pub: Entrepreneur Media, Inc.
Ed: Liane Cassovoy. **Description:** Profile of Microsoft's Web conferencing with Office Live Meeting, which includes tools for application viewing and sharing, attendance reposing and recording.

34297 ■ "Online Publisher Seeks Dismissal of Apple's Trade-Secret Lawsuit" in *San Jose Mercury News* (March 8, 2005)
Pub: Knight-Ridder/Tribune Business News
Ed: Dawn C. Chmielewski. **Description:** Website Think Secret has requested the court dismiss the computer company's trade-secret lawsuit with online publishers and Apple Computer. Apple sued Think Secret's creator of misappropriating trade secrets in his online posts about some of Apple's products.

34298 ■ "Online Retail Sales Jumper 13.1 Percent in Fourth Quarter" in *Wall Street Journal* (February 21, 2002, pp. B6)
Pub: Wall Street Journal
Description: Statistics showing a 13.1 increase in online retail sales is presented.

34299 ■ "Online Sales Booming; Retailers Rethink Web Biz as Sales Increase" in *Crain's Detroit Business* (Vol. 19, No. 1, Jan. 6, 2003, pp. 3)
Pub: Crain Communications Inc., Detroit
Ed: Brent Snavely. **Description:** Total consumer online sales were up 29 percent during the period November 1 and December 20, 2002. This increase has many retailers rethinking their online sales potential. Tips for developing successful Web sites are presented.

34300 ■ "Online Sales Continue To Climb at L.L. Bean, Other Retailers" in *Portland Press Herald* **(December 13, 2005)**
Pub: Blethen Maine Newspapers, Inc.
Ed: Edward D. Murphy. Description: L.L. Bean reports a 47 percent rise in sales over 2004. Other online retailers are also experiencing increased sales in 2004.

34301 ■ "Online Shoppers Begin Their Quest in Earnest" in *Sacramento Bee* **(November 28, 2005)**
Pub: The Sacramento Bee
Ed: Jim Wasserman. Description: Cyber Monday is the Monday after Thanksgiving. It is expected to be the largest online shopping day of the year, with spending reaching more than $400 million for the day.

34302 ■ "Online Sites are Registering with Couples" in *HFN* **(January 26, 2004, pp. 22)**
Pub: Fairchild Publications
Ed: Faye Musselman. Description: Only 16 percent of bridal couples register on Internet registries, the numbers are growing. A listing of Web sites offering bridal registries and their specialties is presented.

34303 ■ "Online Success: Go Fetch More Money!" in *My Business* **(June/July 2002, pp. 41)**
Pub: My Business Magazine
Ed: Shannon Scully. Description: Owners Larry and Charlene Woodward, discusses their e-commerce business www.dogwise.com. The Woodward's discuss the new challenges faced by selling on the Web.

34304 ■ "Online Trading Primer" in *Hispanic Business* **(October 2002, pp. 92)**
Pub: Hispanic Business
Ed: Derek Reveron. Description: The investment industry is going through a consolidation phase in order to attract big-asset accounts to trade online.

34305 ■ "Online Video Ads Get Ready to Grab You" in *Business 2.0* **(Vol. 6, May 2005, No. 4, pp. 25-26)**
Pub: Time, Inc.
Ed: Matthew Maier. Description: Spending for online video advertising is expected to grow from $100 million to $600 million in the next five years.

34306 ■ "Ontrackfitness.com Introduces the Fitness Accountability Trainer Service" in *PR Newswire* **(Nov. 25, 2003)**
Pub: PR Newswire Association, Inc.
Description: A new personalized telephone and email support service to help individuals stay on track with diet and/or exercise programs is being offered by Ontrackfitness.com. The company is committed to revolutionizing the way people approach fitness programs.

34307 ■ "Onvia Business Builder" in *Entrepreneur* **(Vol. 33, October 2005, No. 10, pp. 6)**
Pub: Entrepreneur Media Inc.
Ed: Steve Cooper. Description: Over 2 million procurement records across 55,500 government agencies are available through a subscription to Onvia's Business Builder.

34308 ■ "Onward, Christian Marketer" in *Inc.* **(July 1, 2004)**
Pub: Inc. Magazine
Ed: Nicole Gull. Description: The success of Mel Gibson's, The Passion of the Christ, proved to marketers that there is a demand for Christian-based movies, but also that Christians love the Internet.

34309 ■ "Open Source Solutions: Good Enough for E-Business?" in *E-business Advisor* **(Vol. 18, No. 6, June 2000, pp. 10)**
Pub: Advisor Media, Inc.
Ed: Dan Sullivan. Description: The most widely supported Open Source solutions, including Linux, Apache, and Perl, can be used to create a stable, reliable e-business architecture. Linux, while not as scalable or reliable as UNIX, works well for small- and mid-sized Web sites. Apache and Perl both have strong developer support in key areas, such as a database access and performance.

34310 ■ *Open Source Solutions for Small Business Problems*
Pub: Charles River Media
Ed: John Locke. Released: May 2004. Price: $39.95 (US), $55.95 (Canadian). Description: Open source software provides solutions to many small business problems such as tracking electronic documents, scheduling, accounting functions, managing contact lists, and reducing spam.

34311 ■ "Opt-In News" in *Entrepreneur* **(Vol. 31, No. 8, August 2003, pp. 6)**
Pub: Entrepreneur Media, Inc.
Ed: Steve Cooper. Description: A Website offering email marketing trends, players and news through daily updates is featured. The firm also offers a free newsletter and a resource directory with links to sources for email marketing consultants.

34312 ■ "Optimost" in *Entrepreneur* **(Vol. 33, August 2005, No. 8, pp. 4)**
Pub: Entrepreneur Media Inc.
Ed: Steve Cooper. Description: Optimost offers small companies feedback on a Website's content and whether the site is giving optimum results.

34313 ■ "Optimum Online Launches Online Arcade Service" in *Long Island Business News* **(February 13, 2004)**
Pub: Dolan Media Newswires
Description: Profile of Cablevision Systems Corporation's Optimum Online broadband service. The company has launched an Internet arcade service along with RealNetworks Inc. Customers can download more than 180 games, each allowing one hour of free play.

34314 ■ "Or you could call it schadenfreude.com" in *The New York Times* **(December 13, 2000, pp. D8, H8)**
Pub: The New York Times Company
Ed: Jane Fritsch. Description: Philip Kaplan's dotcom deathwatch Web site mockingly tracks business failures in the world of electronic commerce.

34315 ■ "Other Comments" in *Forbes* **(Vol. 170, No. 6, September 30, 2002, pp. 36)**
Pub: Forbes Magazine
Description: The depression in high technology and telecommunications, as well as telecommunications policies, and other business issues are analyzed.

34316 ■ "Out of Control" in *Inc.* **(September 1, 2003)**
Pub: Gruner & Jahr USA Publishing
Ed: Susan Hansen. Description: Profile of Travis Parsons, founder of Elogex, an Internet-based software application that would enable clients to coordinate shipping and delivery services across multiple warehouses and destinations. When Parsons sold the firm he also lost his decision-making power.

34317 ■ "Out of the box and onto the Web" in *Hispanic Business* **(Vol. 22, No. 6, June 2000, pp. 48)**
Pub: Hispanic Business
Ed: Vaughn Hagerty. Description: More than 70 percent of the largest Hispanic-owned businesses in the U.S. have an Internet presence in 2000, up from just 13.2 percent in 1996.

34318 ■ "Outsourced e-mail" in *PC Computing* **(April 2000, pp. 117)**
Pub: Ziff-Davis Inc.
Ed: Bonny L. Georgia. Description: Ferris Research predicts that within one year, e-mail traffic will increase three to five times, and storage requirements could more than double. The article shows how to outsource e-mail in order to increase business.

34319 ■ "Outsourcing" in *PC Computing* **(April 2000, pp. 185)**
Pub: Ziff-Davis Inc.
Ed: Christine Grech Wendin. Description: Small and medium-size companies are increasingly turning to the Web to get the business of running their businesses done. According to a recent Hambrecht and Quist study, the Internet business services market will grow to $6.6 billion in three years.

34320 ■ "Overcome E-Business Barriers" in *E-business Advisor* **(Vol. 18, No. 1, January 2000, pp. 10)**
Pub: Advisor Media, Inc.
Ed: Laurie Windham. Description: Today's e-business environment challenges managers to respond with effective online business strategies. Customers have already demonstrated their preference to do business over the Web, especially for routine tasks, and businesses that offer online services early are rewarded with customer loyalty and marketshare. Understanding how an e-business strategy influences time-to-market considerations is crucial to success.

34321 ■ "Overcome Your B2B Challenge" in *E-business Advisor* **(Vol. 18, No. 4, April 2000, pp. 22)**
Pub: Advisor Media, Inc.
Ed: Tom Hennings. Description: Developing a business-to-business (B2B) Web portal is more difficult than constructing a business-to-consumer (B2C0) e-commerce site. The article sites the differences and offers advice.

34322 ■ "OverDrive Inks Library, Yahoo! E-book Deals" in *Publishers Weekly* **(Vol. 250, No. 2, January 13, 2003, pp. 15)**
Pub: Reed Business Information
Ed: Calvin Reid. Description: OverDrive Inc. signs contracts with Cleveland Public Library and Yahoo. com to expand the availability of e-book titles to online consumers and library patrons.

34323 ■ "OverDrive Introduces Digital Kiosk" in *Information Today* **(Vol. 19, No. 5, May 2002, pp. 41)**
Pub: Information Today Inc.
Ed: Paula J. Hane. Description: Profile of Digital Kiosk, an all-in-one online vending machine for the sale of protected digital content, enabling publishers and retailers to protect and sell e-books, audiobooks, music, and digital media over the Web.

34324 ■ "Overview: The List" in *Inc.* **(October 17, 2000, pp. 115)**
Pub: The Goldhirsh Group
Ed: Edward O. Welles. Description: An overview of the Inc. 500 companies for the year.

34325 ■ "Panel on taxing Internet sales ends its meetings in disagreement" in *The New York Times* **(March 22, 2000, pp. D28, H28)**
Pub: The New York Times Company
Ed: David Cay Johnston. Description: The meeting of the 19 member Advisory Commission on Electronic Commerce agreed on every issue but one for extending sales taxes to Internet businesses. The panel couldn't agree on whether businesses that have sales personnel in a state and sell over the Internet should pay sales tax. The commission members seemed to fall into three groups: five against taxation, six business representatives, and eight from various government offices. The panel's report moves to Congress without a recommendation.

34326 ■ "Paper-Run Web Sites Prosper" in *Milwaukee Journal Sentinel* **(December 18, 2005)**
Pub: Journal Sentinel, Inc.
Ed: Paul Gores. Description: The trend towards Americans using online newspaper Websites is good news for the industry. Online newspaper sites saw an 11 percent increase in use over last year, prompting companies to develop new methods for delivery news in order to meet consumer demands.

34327 ■ "Parlez-vous e-Commerce? Here's How To Give Your Website International Appeal" in *Black Enterprise* **(Vol. 35, October 2004, No. 3)**
Pub: Earl G. Graves Publishing Co. Inc.
Ed: Carolyn M. Brown. Description: According to a recent study, more than $900 billion in Internet spending is expected to take place outside the U.S. It is advised for companies using the Internet to market a product or service to offer one or two foreign languages.

34328 ■ "Pathmark Adds Online Shopping Middletown, N.J., Store" in *The Record* (November 10, 2005)
Pub: New Jersey Media Group
Ed: Michael L. Diamond. **Description:** Pathmark Stores Inc. launched an online shopping site allowing customers to buy groceries without leaving their homes. Customers can choose from 35,000 items and pick the order up the next day.

34329 ■ "Patterns of Disruption in Retailing" in *Harvard Business Review* (Vol. 78, No. 1, January 2000, pp. 42)
Pub: Harvard Business School Publishing Corp.
Ed: Clayton M. Christensen, Richard S. Tedlow. **Description:** The past may not tell us everything about the future of electronic commerce, but it reveals more than we might expect.

34330 ■ "Paving the Cow Path" in *Rough Notes* (Vol. 146, No. 9, September 2003, pp. 40)
Pub: Rough Notes
Ed: John Ashenburst. **Description:** Overview of changes and future trends in the insurance industry. Topics covered include risk management services, Internet marketing of services, and insurance services offered through banks.

34331 ■ "Pay Per Sale" in *The Economist* (Vol. 377, October 1-7, 2005, No. 8446, pp. 62)
Pub: The Economist Newspaper Ltd.
Description: Microsoft launched its 'paid-search' or 'pay-per-click' advertising program which allows advertisers to bid in an online auction for the right to have their link displayed next to the results for specific search terms and pay only when a Web surfer actually links to the advertiser's site.

34332 ■ "Pay Up" in *PC Computing* (April 2000, pp. 37)
Pub: Ziff-Davis Inc.
Description: Electronic bill paying is the next e-commerce industry trend to be tapped. It is predicted that the Web could cut the cost of transactions in half and creditors would be paid more promptly, and checks would not bounce.

34333 ■ "Pay as You Click" in *Crain's New York Business* (Vol. 22, December 11, 2006, No. 50, pp. 19)
Pub: Crain Communications, Inc.
Description: Google Inc. started an online payment service, Google Checkout. It developed the service at its New York office. Google Checkout, which launched in June 2006, aims to compete with PayPal.

34334 ■ "Paying the piper for Internet access" in *Red Herring* (No. 105, October 1, 2001, pp. 38)
Pub: Herring Communications
Ed: Tim Jackson. **Description:** Issues regarding Internet taxing are explored.

34335 ■ "PayPal" in *Cardline* (Vol. 4, No. 13, March 26, 2004, pp. 1)
Pub: Thomson Media Inc.
Description: PayPal's payment service expansion into the online market provides opportunities into the international market. Statistical data included.

34336 ■ "PayPal Pushes For Business Use; A Hit With Consumers" in *Investor's Business Daily* (October 24, 2003, pp. A04)
Pub: Investor's Business Daily, Inc.
Ed: Pete Barlas. **Description:** Online payment firms are betting on Internet retail credit card sales to continue growth. Profile of the partnership created by PayPal and Cybersource Corporation is included.

34337 ■ "Penny-Wise, Site-Foolish" in *Inc.* (February 1, 2002)
Pub: Inc. Magazine
Ed: Jill Hecht Maxwell. **Description:** There are thousands of Web-hosting providers, information is provided to choose the right one, including a list of resources.

34338 ■ "PeopleProfileUSA" in *Entrepreneur* (Vol. 32, No. 1, January 2004, pp. 10)
Pub: Entrepreneur Media, Inc.
Ed: Steve Cooper. **Description:** PeopleProfileUSA searches consumer profiles gathered from phone directories, voter registrations and other sources to offer a projected profile and contact information, to be used as a marketing tool. The services are free.

34339 ■ "Perdue's home-work plan has failed past" in *Atlanta Business Chronicle* (Vol. 25, November 29, 2002, No. 25, pp. 1A)
Pub: American City Business Publications, Inc.
Ed: Sarah Rubenstein. **Description:** In an effort to reduce traffic congestion in Atlanta, Georgia, Governor-elect Sonny Perdue intends to persuade more companies to use telecommuting. Additionally, Perdue plans to identify 25,000 government employees who could telecommute at least part time.

34340 ■ "The Perfect Connection" in *Small Business Opportunities* (Vol. 16, No. 3, May 2004, pp. 72)
Pub: Harris Publications, Inc.
Ed: Chuck Green. **Description:** Profile of Jeff Liggett, ANET Internet Solutions, a bandwidth supplier. Liggett suggests it is important to expand gradually.

34341 ■ "The Perfect Niche" n *Hispanic Business* (Vol. 22, No. 7-8,July-August 2000, pp. 68)
Pub: Hispanic Business
Ed: Mario Hernandez. **Description:** Fernando Echeverria is founder of one of America's fastest-growing Internet-based educational sites, Toptutors. com. The company links students with a national network of tutors, and is backed by a $3 million investment from Idealab and Idealab Capital Partners.

34342 ■ "A perfect pair" in *Entrepreneur* (Vol. 30, No. 3, March 2002, pp. 37)
Pub: Entrepreneur Media Inc.
Ed: Mike Hogan. **Description:** An overview of the new wireless communications and wireless personal digital assistants. Resources for information as well as pricing about the Compaq Computer IPAQ PC Wireless Pack, Handspring Treo 180, Motient Mobile Modem for Palm VI, Motorola Accompit 009, Palm palm 1705, and Research in Motion BlackBerry 957, is included.

34343 ■ "Performing Triage" in *Entrepreneur* (Vol. 32, No. 4, April 2004, pp. 39)
Pub: Entrepreneur Media, Inc.
Ed: Heather Clancy. **Description:** Profile of Conqwest Inc., the Massachusetts firm specializing in fighting viruses and Internet spam for companies. Michelle Drolet, founder and CEO, uses a proactive approach to computer security. Conqwest started testing antispam technologies in 2002, long before these threats were as prevalent as today.

34344 ■ "Perquest Brings Payroll Industry Into 21st Century; PayPal Founder Seeds Silicon Valley Startups" in *PR Newswire* (Nov. 17, 2003)
Pub: PR Newswire Association, Inc.
Description: Online payroll services are now available online; profile of Perquest's payroll service is provided.

34345 ■ "Personal Decision" in *Entrepreneur* (Vol. 31, No. 8, August 2003, pp. 51)
Pub: Entrepreneur Media, Inc.
Ed: Frank Ohlhorst, Michael Gros. **Description:** Things to consider when purchasing a combination personal digital assistant (PDA) are discussed. The CRN Test Center evaluated five products that combine cell phone service, wireless email, instant messaging and Web accessibility.

34346 ■ "Personal issues" in *Entrepreneur* (Vol. 30, No. 2, February 2002, pp. 22)
Pub: Entrepreneur Media Inc.
Ed: Mark Henricks. **Description:** Review of the book entitled, "Making It Personal", by personalization and privacy expert Bruce Kasanoff. The books explores personalization and privacy issues, including technical complexity, ethical uncertainty and still-evolving legal oversight when customers share information.

34347 ■ "Pick A Topic" in *Entrepreneur* (Vol. 28, No. 3, March 2000, pp. 220)
Pub: Entrepreneur Media Inc.
Ed: Victoria Neal. **Description:** Analyst Melissa Shore discusses the opportunities in e-commerce.

34348 ■ "Pizza makers to add online orders" in *Crain's Detroit Business* (Vol. 16, No. 16, April 17, 2000, pp. 16)
Pub: Crain Communications, Inc.
Ed: Terry Kosdrosky. **Description:** Pizza chains will begin using the Internet for online ordering and a system to e-mail coupons to customers.

34349 ■ "Plan B from Cyberspace: A growing number of websites are going back to the future" in *Time Inc.* (Vol. 157, No. 1, Jan. 8, 2001, pp.57)
Pub: Time & Life Bldg., Rockefeller Center
Ed: Jeffrey Ressner. **Description:** Many dot.coms are publishing hard-copy magazines.

34350 ■ "Play Keyboard for Cash" in *Entrepreneur* (Vol. 28, No. 11, November 2000, pp. 38)
Pub: Entrepreneur Media Inc.
Ed: Cynthia E. Griffin. **Description:** How SalonsConnect.com found venture capital on the Internet.

34351 ■ "Playing the Business-to-Business Odds" in *Success* (Vol. 47, No. 1, January 2000, pp. 22)
Pub: Success Publishing, Inc.
Ed: Charles Pappas. **Description:** Purchase Pro is revolutionizing the way companies buy and sell to one another.

34352 ■ "Playing e-Detective" in *Entrepreneur* (Vol. 30, No.)
Pub: Entrepreneur Media Inc.
Ed: Chris Penttila. **Description:** The pros and cons of using the Internet for background checks on potential employees is discussed.

34353 ■ "Playing Favorites" in *Entrepreneur* (Vol. 31, Sept. 2003)
Pub: Entrepreneur Media, Inc.
Ed: Aliza Pilar Sherman. **Description:** Women entrepreneurs report favorite business Web sites they use to run their companies, with Google.com heading the list.

34354 ■ "Playing It Safe: What Can You Do to Protect Your E-Commerce Site From Fraud?" in *Entrepreneur* (Vol. 32, No. 4, April 2004, pp. 35)
Pub: Entrepreneur Media, Inc.
Ed: Amanda C. Kooser. **Description:** Entrepreneurs starting up an e-commerce business need to be sure the site is protected in order for customers to be able to use credit cards to make purchases. It is important when choosing a service that it is reputable and has secure credit card technologies.

34355 ■ "Plumbing Web Connection" in *Harvard Business Review* (Vol. 81, No. 9, September 2003, pp. 18)
Pub: Harvard Business School Press
Ed: Morse Gardiner. **Description:** Bob Sutor answers five questions about the future economic impact of the Internet on business, in particular Web service software.

34356 ■ "Plunkett's E-Commerce & Internet Business Almanac 2001-2002" in *Business Information Alert* (Vol. 14, No. 9, October 2002, pp. 9)
Pub: Alert Publications
Ed: Marther Jo Sani. **Description:** Profile of "Plunkett's E-Commerce & Internet Business Almanac 2001-2002" is presented. The publication serves as a general source of information that contributes to market research, strategic planning, and career building.

34357 ■ "Point, Click, File a Lawsuit" in *Sacramento Bee* (December 11, 2005)
Pub: The Sacramento Bee
Ed: Jim Wasserman. **Description:** LegalZoom.com will handle legal complaints online. The firm employs 120 workers to prepare legal complaints, send them to court, and even serve defendants.

34358 ■ "Point and Sniff" in *Kiplinger's Personal Finance Magazine* **(Vol. 55, No. 1, January, 2001, pp. 26)**
Pub: The Kiplinger Washington Editors, Inc.
Ed: Erin Burt. **Description:** With a new gizmo from DigiScents, you will be able to create, transmit and receive scents over the Web through a small device you hook up to your computer.

34359 ■ "Portals popping up again as links to customers" in *Atlanta Business Chronicle* **(Vol. 25, No. 21, November 1, 2002, pp. 5A)**
Pub: American City Business Publications, Inc.
Ed: Mary Jane Credeur. **Description:** Many companies are again putting considerable resources in to portals in attempts to save money. Delta Air Lines Inc., a portal user, obtains approximately 11 percent of its passenger sales via its Delta.com site that receives about 6 million visitors monthly. Other portal efforts are discussed.

34360 ■ "Post It and They Will Come" in *Home Office Computing* **(Vol. 18, No. 11, November 2000, pp. 40)**
Pub: Scholastic Inc.
Ed: Eileen Bien Calabro. **Description:** Ways to use message boards to expand your business are highlighted.

34361 ■ "Power to the Buyer With Group Buying Sites" in *E-business Advisor* **(Vol. 18, No. 2, February 2000, pp. 10)**
Pub: Advisor Media, Inc.
Ed: Erica Rugullies. **Description:** Group buying practices that enable customers to lower their acquisition costs and allow the vendor to reach new audiences, test new promotions and sell excess inventory are discussed.

34362 ■ "PR Exec: Agencies Share Blame for Crash" in *Atlanta Business Chronicle* **(Vol. 24, No. 13, August 31, 2001, pp. 3A)**
Pub: American City Business Journals Inc.
Ed: Jim Lovel. **Description:** Richard Edelman, CEO and president of Edelman Public Relations Worldwide, believes that public relations companies were largely involved in the crash of the dot-coms. Revenue for PR agencies rose 34 percent last year.

34363 ■ "PR Firms Tout the Value of 'Buzz' Marketing" in *Atlanta Business Chronicle* **(Vol. 25, November 15, 2002, No. 23 pp. S12)**
Pub: American City Business Publications, Inc.
Ed: Keith Reed. **Description:** Public relations companies are using 'guerrilla' and 'buzz' marketing as a more effective, less expensive method for taking messages directly to the audience. Virtual marketing is also being used, but often these emails are associated with spam and disregarded.

34364 ■ "Prepare for Y2K Litigation" in *E-business Advisor* **(Vol. 17, No. 12, December 1999, pp. 36)**
Pub: Advisor Media, Inc.
Ed: Sean P. Melvin. **Description:** Leaders of e-businesses should anticipate some lawsuits triggered by Y2K, so they should consider lawsuit defense strategies and start preventative maintenance measures.

34365 ■ "Priority" in *Inc.* **(Volume 27, March 2005, No. 3, pp. 23-26, 28, 30)**
Pub: Inc. Magazine
Description: Business information discussed includes information about the SEC looking into unlicensed investment brokers, the economy, freight co-ops to help shippers ease costs, hiring, Google, education, SBA assistance to women entrepreneurs, and new inventions.

34366 ■ "Priority Mail" in *Entrepreneur* **(Vol. 28, No. 1, January 2000, pp. 38)**
Pub: Entrepreneur Media Inc.
Ed: Gwen Moran. **Description:** If you think it's okay to wait a few days before returning e-mail inquiries, you could be committing customer service suicide.

34367 ■ "Privacy, the workplace and the Internet" in *Journal of Business Ethics* **(Vol. 28, No. 3, December 1, 2000, pp. 255)**
Pub: Kluwer Academic Publishers
Ed: Seumas Miller, John Weckert. **Description:** This paper examines surveillance and monitoring in the workplace, including Internet and e-mail privacy issues.

34368 ■ "Private Web hubs let companies build ties with their key buyers" in *Crain's Detroit Business* **(Vol. 16, No. 46, Nov. 13, 2000, pp. 19)**
Pub: Crain Communications, Inc.
Ed: Richard Karpinski. **Description:** Private marketplaces allow three things: they allow companies to control who has access to the marketplace, what kind of business gets carried out, and how everything is branded.

34369 ■ "Process Online Payments Quickly and Effectively" in *E-business Advisor* **(Vol. 18, No. 6, June 2000, pp. 34)**
Pub: Advisor Media, Inc.
Ed: Glenn T. Shesney. **Description:** Assessment Systems Inc. (ASI), a purveyor of electronically administered tests, has deployed Payment Plus' LiveProcessor electronic commerce software, greatly boosting the number of payments the company can transact per hour. LiveProcessor, a Linux-based system, can process hundreds of transactions per minute during periods of high volume, with per-transaction response time averaging less than three seconds.

34370 ■ "Profiting - Adding an affiliate program links site content to product sales" in *PC Magazine* **(February 20, 2001, pp. 133)**
Pub: Ziff-Davis Publishing Company
Ed: Neil Randall. **Description:** Banner ads are a way for Web site developers to make a profit. Placing a banner ad on the page directs interested site visitors to the advertiser's site. The affiliate network tracks the origin of the visit and pays the host of the originating site a percentage of all sales. Some pay a fee just for directing a visitor to a site. Commission Junction offers commissions from more than 1,600 companies in a wide variety of industries. LinkShare offers commissions from just over 500 companies, but they are major organizations.

34371 ■ "Profiting from Copyrighted Materials" in *Rough Notes* **(Vol. 146, No. 3, March 2003, pp. 104)**
Pub: Rough Notes
Ed: G. Edward Kalbaugh. **Description:** Owners of Internet sites with public access should understand copyright laws to protect information and themselves.

34372 ■ "Profiting from open source" in *Harvard Business Review* **(Vol. 78, No. 5, September-October 2000, pp. 22)**
Pub: Harvard Business School Publishing Corp.
Description: This article describes how Hewlett-Packard developed its e-speak software and plans to give it away. The company will relinquish all control of the code.

34373 ■ "A Progressive Sound" in *Washington Business Journal* **(Vol. 22, No. 15, August 15, 2003, pp. 16)**
Pub: Washington Business Journal
Ed: John Wilen. **Description:** Technology behind the success of Relatable's song-swapping technology is discussed. Topics include digital sound recording, downloading of MP3's, and company forecasts.

34374 ■ "Protect Customer's Web Privacy" in *E-business Advisor* **(Vol. 18, No. 4, April 2000, pp. 28)**
Pub: Advisor Media, Inc.
Ed: Dan Sullivan. **Description:** Protecting users' privacy is an increasingly important issue in the design of an e-commerce site. Users want to know what personal information is being collected by the site and how it will be used or disseminated. Trust is important in a business-customer relationship and a breach of privacy is considered a breach of trust. E-commerce

offers many opportunities to mine data for marketing purposes or the development of new products and services as well as to reduce costs by sharing information with other companies.

34375 ■ "Protecting Ideas" in *Black Enterprise* **(Vol. 35, February 2005, No. 7, pp. 54)**
Pub: Earl G. Graves Publishing Co. Inc.
Ed: James C. Johnson. **Description:** U.S. Patent and Trademark Office has a Website offering facts about patents, how to get one, and a list of registered patent attorneys and agents. It is best to use a nondisclosure agreement to protect an idea or invention.

34376 ■ "Proxity Electronic Commerce System" in *Entrepreneur* **(Vol. 33, August 2005, No. 8, pp. 4)**
Pub: Entrepreneur Media Inc.
Ed: Steve Cooper. **Description:** Proxity Inc. provides an online database of 12 million industrial parts, available from 150,000 sources, and includes government parts. State and local government requirements and contact information are also included in the database.

34377 ■ "The Public Library: Technology Lets You Browse the Stacks from Your Home Office" in *Black Enterprise* **(Vol. 34, No. 4, Nov. 2003)**
Pub: Earl Graves Publishing Co.
Ed: Jennifer L. Smith. **Description:** More than 3,000 libraries offer programs offering E-books, databases and online classes that can be accessed via computers for small and home businesses searching for materials on marketing and management topics.

34378 ■ "Publish or Perish" in *Forbes* **(November 13, 2000, pp. 252)**
Pub: Forbes Magazine
Ed: Brendan Coffey. **Description:** Struggling dotcoms are seeking more traditional forms of revenue from advertising and subscriptions. At least seven Weblets have created magazines in recent months, and more are considering the same.

34379 ■ "Publishing" in *Business Week* **(January 9, 2006, No. 3966, pp. 29-30)**
Pub: McGraw-Hill Companies
Ed: Louise Lee. **Description:** Web magazines are launching print versions of their publications in order to increase readership and advertising sales.

34380 ■ "Punching the Time Card" in *Incentive* **(Vol. 174, No. 8, August 2000, pp. 75)**
Pub: Bill Communications
Ed: Emily Hodnett. **Description:** Both busy consumers and hard-working employees like the time-saving nature of debit and stored value cards.

34381 ■ "Punta Gorda Interested in Wi-Fi Internet" in *Charlotte Observer* **(February 1, 2007)**
Pub: Knight-Ridder/Tribune Business News
Ed: Steve Reilly. **Description:** Punta Gorda officials are developing plans to provide free wireless Internet services to businesses and residents.

34382 ■ "Put Some Wow In Your Website" in *Inc.* **(September 2006, pp. 44-45)**
Pub: Gruner & Jahr USA Publishing
Ed: Michael Fitzgerald. **Description:** Websites get stale quickly and need constant changes to continue to attract attention to your message and products. New graphics, sounds, and more are provided as examples of techniques to accomplish this.

34383 ■ "Put Your Web Applications to the Test" in *E-business Advisor* **(Vol. 18, No. 7, July 2000, pp. 44)**
Pub: Advisor Media, Inc.
Ed: Guy Tal. **Description:** Testing Web applications has become more complex because the applications themselves have become increasingly sophisticated and interactive. The process of testing Web applications using Mercury Interactive's Astra Quick Test and Astra LoadTest is discussed.

34384 ■ **"Putting the 'E' in Your Business"** in *Hispanic Business* (Vol. 22, No. 5, May 2000, pp. 36)
Pub: Hispanic Business
Ed: Vaughn Hagerty. **Description:** It is important for Hispanic business enterprises to consider how electronic commerce will affect their business. It must be recognized that the Internet is now a permanent feature of the business environment.

34385 ■ **"Putting the Heat on Spam"** in *Entrepreneur* (Vol. 32, No. 4, April 2004, pp. 34)
Pub: Entrepreneur Media, Inc.
Ed: Amanda C. Kooser. **Description:** Internet spam costs small business in productivity time lost for employees. According to Ferris Research Inc., a market and technology research firm, American businesses lost more than $10 billion in 2003 from handling spam emails.

34386 ■ **"Putting their money where the future is"** in *The New York Times* (March 27, 2000, pp. D3, H3)
Pub: The New York Times Company
Ed: Jonathan Burton. **Description:** Venture capitalists and e-commerce is discussed. Statistical data included.

34387 ■ **"Putting the Screws to Google"** in *Business Week* (January 23, 2006, No. 3968, pp. 24)
Pub: McGraw-Hill Companies
Ed: Jon Fine. **Description:** How Old Media could take back market share of Google and Yahoo's! advertising market.

34388 ■ **"Q&A"** in *Home Office Computing* (Vol. 18, No. 11, November 2000, pp. 15)
Pub: Scholastic Inc.
Ed: Marilyn Zelinsky Syarto. **Description:** Are you drowning in e-mail? David Ferris, president of Ferris Research, a San Francisco-based consulting firm specializing in messaging and collaborative technology, discusses how to manage e-mail overload.

34389 ■ **"Q&A: Jack Bamberger"** in *Folio: the Magazine for Magazine Management* (Vol. 30, No. 1, January 2001, pp. 18)
Pub: Intertec Publishing Corp.
Ed: Caroline Jenkins. **Description:** An interview with Jack Bamberger addressing Folio's IdustryClick Web site, the company's ongoing integration with Intertec, and his view of the future of vertical online communities.

34390 ■ **"QEK's Intranet keeps life organized"** in *Crain's Detroit Business* (Vol. 16, No. 34, August 21, 2000, pp. E-8)
Pub: Crain Communications, Inc.
Ed: Jewel Gopwani. **Description:** QEK Global Solutions uses the Internet to keep up with its employees and keep track of its products.

34391 ■ **"Quest for the Next Great Search Company"** in *Venture Capital Journal* (December 1, 2004)
Pub: Thomason Financial Inc.
Ed: Katherine Heires. **Description:** Venture capital firms are investing in Internet search companies to the tune of $67 million in 15 companies for the first part of 2004. Google's initial public offering is fueling the trend to invest in Web search startups.

34392 ■ **"Quick Drop Franchise Opens in Virginia Beach, Va., for Storefront eBay Sales"** in *Virginian-Pilot* (March 16, 2004)
Pub: Knight-Ridder, Tribune Business News
Ed: Carolyn Shapiro. **Description:** Quik Drop has opened its seventh franchise. The new store is located in Virginia Beach, Virginia and is owned by Ned Griffith.

34393 ■ **"Quick fix: Help your IT staff save time and energy with PC Pinpoint"** in *Entrepreneur* (Vol. 30, No. 2, February 2002, pp. 34)
Pub: Entrepreneur Media Inc.

Ed: Liane Gouthro. **Description:** Profile of PC Pinpoint, a Web-based service from Distinctive Technologies, which automates PC repair by testing and evaluating each component of a computer, diagnosing and fixing both hardware and software problems.

34394 ■ **"QuickSeek"** in *Entrepreneur* (Vol. 33, September 2005, No. 9, pp. 6)
Pub: Entrepreneur Media Inc.
Ed: Steve Cooper. **Description:** Online directory, QuickSeek, lists more than 16 million businesses in a database. Information includes operating hours, business descriptions, email addresses, directions and links to corporate sites. Preferred listings, which include full-page design with graphics, photos and images, run $99 per year.

34395 ■ **"The quilted picker-upper: Celebrating the highs (and the lows) of dotcom culture with a needle and thread"** in *Entrepreneur* (Vol. 30)
Pub: Entrepreneur Media Inc.
Ed: Michelle Prather. **Description:** Amish quiltmakers have been recruited to stitch a quilt from 300 T-shirts, called the DotCom Quilt. The quilt will bear the logos from dotcom companies, both fallen icons and survivors, ranging from Midwestern start-ups to corporate spinoff dotcoms and international concerns, collected by friends and donated by the companies themselves.

34396 ■ **"Rapid Response"** in *Rough Notes* (Vol. 145, No. 9, September 2002, pp. 74)
Pub: Rough Notes
Description: Christina Nelson, President and CEO of SilverPlume, a broad-based online insurance company, agrees with the Insurance Services Office to distribute online insurance industry information services.

34397 ■ **"The Ratings Game"** in *Entrepreneur* (Vol. 31, No. 8, August 2003, pp. 45)
Pub: Entrepreneur Media, Inc.
Ed: Melissa Campanelli. **Description:** Many small business e-entrepreneurs are following the lead of Amazon.com and Drugstore.com by posting uncensored reviews and ratings of products sold on the firm's Website. The pros and cons of this practice are examined.

34398 ■ **"Reaching for less than the sky: as boldest fall, modest dreamers fly on"** in *The New York Times* (December 13, 2000, pp. D1, H1)
Pub: The New York Times Company
Ed: Saul Hansell. **Description:** Lessons on what works and what doesn't work for Internet-based businesses.

34399 ■ **"Reaching the Small Business Accounting Market"** in *Accounting Today* (Vol. 14, No. 12, July 10, 2000, pp. 41)
Pub: Faulkner & Gray, Inc.
Ed: Tracey Miller-Segarra. **Description:** There is a new crop of dot-coms seeking to stake their claims in the lucrative small business accounting software market by developing products designed exclusively for the Internet. A profile of three of these software products is presented.

34400 ■ **"ReachLocal"** in *Entrepreneur* (Vol. 33, August 2005, No. 8, pp. 4)
Pub: Entrepreneur Media Inc.
Ed: Steve Cooper. **Description:** ReachLocal is an online service that works in conjunction with Google, Overture, SuperPages.com and other sites that offer advertising channels. The service presents a business to online searchers looking for a product or service in their area. It tracks traffic, offers reports, and uses a performance-based payment system.

34401 ■ **"Ready to land"** in *Crain's Detroit Business* (Vol. 19, No. 16, April 21, 2003, pp. 11)
Pub: Crain Communications Inc., Detroit
Ed: Amy Lane. **Description:** Detroit Metropolitan Airport will offer wireless high-speed Internet access to

passengers waiting in the airport's terminals. Concourse Communications Group LLC, Springfield, Massachusetts, has an airport contract that includes providing the wireless access known as Wi-Fi in the new Midfield Terminal.

34402 ■ **"Ready? Set? Search! Rev Up Your Sales With Comparison-Shopping Engines"** in *Entrepreneur* (Vol. 31, No. 9, September 2003, pp. 87)
Pub: Entrepreneur Media, Inc.
Ed: Catherine Seda. **Description:** According to a survey conducted in January 2003, more than 50 percent of shoppers believe comparison-shopping search engines save time and money. The sites offer product descriptions, prices, and customer testimonials.

34403 ■ **"Refer madness"** in *Entrepreneur* (Vol. 30, No. 3, March 2002, pp. 87)
Pub: Entrepreneur Media Inc.
Ed: Nichole L. Torres. **Description:** The impact of word-of-mouth advertising by online customers is discussed.

34404 ■ **"Reinventing the wheel"** in *Hispanic Business* (Vol. 22, No. 4, April 2000, pp. 12)
Pub: Hispanic Business
Ed: Jonathan Higuera. **Description:** The expansion of the online advertising provider Adsmart NetFuerza is discussed. The company is achieving a 30 percent per month increase in the number of Internet sites, which it serves. It has a client base of 67 companies with Internet sites in 16 countries.

34405 ■ **"Relationship Advice"** in *Entrepreneur* (Vol. 32, No. 1, January 2004, pp. 47)
Pub: Entrepreneur Media, Inc.
Ed: Liane Cassavoy. **Description:** Profile of Salesnet's online Customer Relation Management application that includes tools for managing accounts and contacts.

34406 ■ **"Release the Hounds "** in *Entrepreneur*
Pub: Entrepreneur Media Inc.
Ed: Mike Hogan. **Description:** Competition in the Web search engine sector is fierce, providing advertising opportunities for small companies.

34407 ■ **"Rembrandts in the Attic"** in *Inc.* (October 2000, pp. 23)
Pub: The Goldhirsh Group
Description: Ian Peck, former gallery owner and art dealer founded an Internet-based company in 1999 that enables museums, galleries, family trusts and artists' estates to sell or lease their works of art to corporate clients.

34408 ■ **"Research methods"** in *Entrepreneur* (Vol. 31, No. 5, May 2003, pp. 40)
Pub: Entrepreneur Media Inc.
Ed: Amanda C. Kooser. **Description:** Forty-six of all Americans are more likely to shop at a physical store than purchase a product over the Internet.

34409 ■ **"Resources: Web Sites, Organizations, Events and More to Grow Your Business"** in *Entrepreneur* (Vol. 32, July 2004, No. 7, pp. 8)
Pub: Entrepreneur Media Inc.
Ed: Steve Cooper. **Description:** Online printing and mailing services are offered by Mailersclub; AuctionBytes is a free email newsletter that covers online auctions; Microsoft's Software Asset Management programs alerts companies when licenses are expiring and standardizes and centralizes the licensing process; U.S. Census Bureau's American Community Survey provides statistical data for small business marketing; Retailwire, provides news to retail professionals; Daypop is a specialized search engine; StumbleUpon is a free browser toolbar; and CoolSiteoftheDay spotlights good Web sites.

34410 ■ "Resources: Web Sites, Organizations, Events and More To Grow Your Business" in *Entrepreneur* (Vol. 32, September 2004, No. 9, pp. 8)
Pub: Entrepreneur Media Inc.
Ed: Steve Cooper. Description: Resources to help small business are featured including the Small Business Administration's effort to help teen entrepreneurs launch a business; KnockNow an online community of entrepreneurs, executives, venture capitalists, angel investors, service sector companies, and government; the SBA's business Website offering information on small business development, financial assistance, taxes, laws and regulations, international trade, workplace issues, buying and selling and federal forms.

34411 ■ "Retail Holdouts - But at What Price" in *Inc.* (March 2000, pp. 88)
Pub: The Goldhirsh Group
Description: According to the United States Small Business Administration, 70 percent of small businesses have no Web sales capabilities whatsoever. The article looks at small businesses with no Web sales.

34412 ■ "Return of the Agent" in *Entrepreneur.com* (Vol. 34, January 2006, No. 1, pp. 19)
Pub: Entrepreneur Media Inc.
Ed: Chris McGinnis. Description: Although 65 percent of all business travel is booked online, if a trip is complex, it is best to consult a travel expert.

34413 ■ "Reverse auctions online" in *Hispanic Business* (Vol. 22, No. 11, November 2000, pp. 94)
Pub: Hispanic Business
Ed: Roger Harris. Description: The popularity of reverse auctions which take place via the Internet are presented. The cost savings, which can be made from the use of reverse auctions by purchasing managers, is discussed.

34414 ■ "A rewarding experience" in *Incentive* (Vol. 174, No. 8, August 2000, pp. 12)
Pub: Bill Communications
Ed: Don Mogelefsky. Description: Inspiring a sales force, rewarding a customer, or recognizing an employee can all be done easily and efficiently online.

34415 ■ "Rewarding Rebates" in *Black Enterprise* (Vol. 36, November 2005, No. 4, pp. 166)
Pub: Earl G. Graves Publishing Co. Inc.
Ed: Stephanie Young. Description: The National Retail Federation reports that online rebate offers from stores provide ease in use while avoiding the hassle of finding serial numbers and product codes, filling out paperwork, and mailing in paperwork.

34416 ■ "Riding Out the Crash" in *Hispanic Business* (Vol. 23, No. 5, May 2001, pp. 42, 44-45)
Pub: Hispanic Business
Ed: Derek Reveron. Description: Hispanic-themed Web sites that focus on niche markets stand the best chance of long-term survival. An interview with Fernando Espuelas, CEO of StarMedia is presented.

34417 ■ "Riding the tech wave" in *Hispanic Business* (Vol. 22, No. 7-8, July-August 2000, pp. 30)
Pub: Hispanic Business
Ed: Jennifer Riley. Description: Ralph G. Moore, president of consulting firm RGMA believes that e-commerce and the Internet hold many opportunities for small, minority-owned businesses to take part in procurement.

34418 ■ "Right to the source" in *Entrepreneur* (Vol. 30, No. 1, January 2002, pp. 47)
Pub: Entrepreneur Media Inc.
Ed: Amanda C. Kooser. Description: Profile of some of the new e-sourcing services available for technical solutions to small businesses. E-sourcing can include various products and services, including Web hosting, data storage and network services.

34419 ■ "Rocket Science Retailing Is Almost Here Are You Ready?" in *Harvard Business Review* (Vol. 78, No. 4, July 2000, pp. 115)
Pub: Harvard Business School Publishing Corp.
Ed: Marshall L. Fisher, Ananth Raman, Anna Sheen McClelland. Description: Research shows that e-commerce firms are having problems delivering the products that customers order online while department stores increasingly rely on markdowns to attract customers.

34420 ■ "Room for Growth in the Big Apple" in *Black Enterprise* (Vol. 31, No. 5, December 2000, pp. 64)
Pub: Earl Graves Publishing Co.
Ed: Robyn D. Clarke. Description: The qualities that set Esystems Inc apart from the competition are discussed with owner Glenwood Elam Jr.

34421 ■ "RosettaNet: The Key to Supply Chain Efficiency?" in *E-business Advisor* (Vol. 17, No. 12, December 1999, pp. 16)
Pub: Advisor Media, Inc.
Ed: Rik Drummond. Description: The RosettaNet consortium, established in 1998 by Fadi Chehade, aims to create a single software standard throughout the IT supply chain, thus standardizing e-business operations. RosettaNet is presently defining open interfaces among supply chain manufacturers, distributors, resellers, and customers. RosettaNet's goal is to help computer makers and distributors defend their business against Dell and other Web-based made-to-order computer sellers.

34422 ■ "The Rules of E-etiquette" in *Incentive* (Vol. 174, No. 10, October 2000, pp. 140)
Pub: Bill Communications
Ed: Dana May Casperson. Description: Today more businesses are using E-mail communication to help turn prospects into clients. Some of the advantages to this are listed.

34423 ■ "Running Hot-and Cold-on the Web" in *Business Week Online* (Nov. 15, 2002)
Pub: McGraw-Hill Inc.
Ed: Karen E. Klein. Description: With the inception of annual search engine fees and a drop in Internet sales, a small retail business selling heating pads and ice packs online and wholesale to gift shops, is questioning the value of selling online.

34424 ■ "Sacramento Company Plans Public Stock Offering for Online Music Sales" in *Sacramento Bee* (October 1, 2005)
Pub: The Sacramento Bee
Ed: Clint Swett. Description: Digital Music Group Inc. plans a public stock offering to help finance its business selling music online at sites such as Apple's iTunes music store. Details of the move are included.

34425 ■ "A Safe Bet" in *Entrepreneur* (Vol. 31, No. 7, July 2003, pp. 42)
Pub: Entrepreneur Media, Inc.
Ed: Steve Cooper. Description: Profile of SonicWALL's TELE3 TZX combination firewall and VPN, allowing users to access office networks safely over a broadband connection while allowing Web browsing by other networked family members.

34426 ■ "Safety Measures" in *Washington Business Journal* (Vol. 22, No. 16, August 22, 2003, pp. 18)
Pub: Washington Business Journal
Ed: Tim Pappa. Description: Gary Noesner, from Control Risks Groups, points out the importance of travel information. Control Risks offers software and services to make data acquisition easier. Such information can result in saving the lives of employees of international businesses or government officials in the field.

34427 ■ "Sage unveils big plans for small business" in *Accounting Today* (Vol. 14, No. 13, July 24, 2000, pp. 29)
Pub: Faulkner & Gray, Inc.
Description: Accounting software development group Sage, announced plans to make several e-commerce innovations this year tied to its new accounting software product, BusinessWorks Gold. Sage said that the product, designed for companies of 50 or fewer employees, will be "the foundation for delivering e-commerce and e-management capabilities to the small business marketplace."

34428 ■ "Sagent Technology Unveils New Enterprise Information Portal" in *Information Today* (Vol. 17, No. 10, November 2000, pp. 44)
Pub: Information Today, Inc.
Description: Sagent Technology, Inc., a provider of real-time, e-business intelligence solutions, has released a second-generation information portal that integrates a broad range of content and applications, and serves many types of businesses.

34429 ■ "Salad Daze" in *Entrepreneur.com* (Vol. 34, January 2006, No. 1, pp. 32)
Pub: Entrepreneur Media Inc.
Ed: Sara Wilson. Description: Profile of Adam Cohen, Marc Meisel and Daren Herzberg, co-owners of New York City's healthy restaurant called Tossed. The eatery specializes in salads and offers an online salad bar that allows customers to create salads that are delivered to the homes or offices.

34430 ■ "" in *Sales & Marketing Management* (Vol. 158, October 2006, No. 10, pp. 11)
Pub: VNU Business Media
Description: Ideas for creating a business blog are presented. Blogs can feature ideas, criticisms, and insights.

34431 ■ "San Diego: Hielo Says Hello to Downtown" in *San Diego Business Journal* (Vol. 28, January 8, 2007, No. 2, pp. 27)
Pub: San Diego Business Journal Associates
Ed: Amy Yarnell. Description: Profile of Hielo LLC, a mobile service provider. The store offers patrons access to MySpace accounts and to try the newest games and music videos online.

34432 ■ "San Diego to Host Tech Summit" in *Hispanic Business* (Vol. 24, No. 5, May 2002, pp. 42)
Pub: Hispanic Business Inc.
Description: Technology and cross-border trade were among the issues of focus at the Hispanic Business Tech Summit held in November, 2001. Specific seminars included, B2B E-Commerce, E-Business Expansion, Strategic Online Alliances, Cross-Border Trends, and NAFTA.

34433 ■ "S&MM Pulse" in *Sales & Marketing Management* (Vol. 158, October 2006, No. 10, pp. 16)
Pub: VNU Business Media
Description: Information to help small companies embrace the Intered for IT and marketing is presented.

34434 ■ "S&MM Pulse" in *Sales and Marketing.com* (Vol. 156, No. 3, March 2004, pp. 10)
Pub: VNU eMedia, Inc.
Description: According to S&MM's Equation Research Survey of 529 executives, business-to-business marketers are predicting economic growth in 2004. Statistical data included.

34435 ■ "SBA Offers Free E-Commerce CD" in *Home Office Computing* (Vol. 19, No. 1, January 2001, pp. 22)
Pub: Scholastic Inc.
Ed: Lee Wertheimer. Description: The Small Business Administration (SBA) has teamed with a pair of small business Web sites to distribute a free CD-ROM with tools for creating an e-commerce site, plus advice on how to use it to make money. A profile of the disc, Build Your Own Business Web Site for Free, is included.

34436 ■ "SBC Can't Resist a Blast From Its Past" in *Fortune* (Vol. 151, February 21, 2005, No. 4, pp. 30)
Pub: Time Inc.
Ed: Stephanie N. Mehta. Description: SBC's plans to move into video services, aimed at transforming the phone company into a full-service media and communications leader is highlighted.

34437 ■ "Scammers Have Been Downloading Software From My Website Using Stolen PayPal Accounts. What Can I Do?" in *Inc.* (Vol. 27, July 2005)
Pub: Inc. Magazine
Description: PayPal accounts are being swiped with the identity-theft technique known as phishing. PayPal's seller-protection policy covers only physical goods, rendering dealers responsible for refunding any scammed customers.

34438 ■ "Scout New Business" in *PC Computing* (April 2000, pp. 90)
Pub: Ziff-Davis Inc.
Ed: Jason Compton. Description: A guide to digital-mapping resources for scouting new markets and studying demographics is presented. IAtlas Info Lens is a free service that gathers data on various industries sorted by region, state or metropolitan area and lets users target business-oriented products closely. Tetrad's PCensus has Profile and Target modes that output and input graphical/numerical data respectively. AnySite.com is a powerful Web-based service offering a wealth of demographic data from the U.S. Census and other sources. High-end GIS products include TTG Territory Mapper and ESRI ArcView.

34439 ■ "Screen Play" in *Hispanic Business* (December 2006, pp. 28-30, 32, 34)
Pub: Hispanic Business
Ed: Hildy Medina. Description: Advertisers and media companies are reaching the Hispanic marketing via the Internet. Statistical data included.

34440 ■ "SE Tools" in *Entrepreneur* (Vol. 33, October 2005, No. 10, pp. 6)
Pub: Entrepreneur Media Inc.
Ed: Steve Cooper. Description: SE Tools provides free tools to show the way search engines actually see a Website. The suite allows users to check keyword ranking, bloated pages, broken lines, and how a Flash site is indexed by major search engines.

34441 ■ "Search Engine Strategies" in *My Business* (October/November 2002, pp. 24)
Pub: My Business Magazine
Ed: Michael Grebb. Description: Web site advice for small businesses is covered, including research keywords for clients using search engines that will direct them to a particular site.

34442 ■ "Searching for Signs of Intelligent Life" in *Barron's* (August 11, 2003, pp. T1)
Pub: Barron's
Ed: Eric C. Fleming. Description: Internet search engine services, forecasted to profit from the growing use of the Web to find jobs, dates, information, and more are welcoming a stock bubble of sorts. LookSmart's 3.5 share price is four times its October 2002 low, while FindWhat has grown fivefold to more than 17. The competition for the paid search market, primarily between Overture and privately-held Google is detailed.

34443 ■ "Season's Ho! Ho! Turns No! No! No!" in *Atlanta Business Chronicle* (Vol. 25, January 3, 2003, No. 30, pp. 3B)
Pub: American City Business Publications, Inc.
Ed: Alf Nucifora. Description: Retailing over the holidays was not impressive. Internet sales were positive, posting double-digit, year-to-year, seasonal increases around 30-70 percent for various categories. Statistical data included.

34444 ■ "Seattle Book Co. offers e-book conversion" in *Publishers Weekly* (Vol. 249, No. 35, September 2, 2002, pp. 18)
Pub: Reed Business Information

Ed: Calvin Reid. Description: The Seattle Book Company is offering a Web-based, automated text-conversion service. The new c-publishing vendor will convert plain text files into any of seven e-book formats in a timely manner.

34445 ■ "Secret Shopper" in *Home Office Computing* (Vol. 18, No. 11, November 2000, pp. 12)
Pub: Scholastic Inc.
Description: Catalogs and Web sites can save time when purchasing, but getting help can prove much more challenging. Two resellers, pcconnection.com and CDW.com, were tested for customer service. While buying products was made easy, there was some difficulty in obtaining basic information about products from service representatives.

34446 ■ "Secrets of the Great White North-The world's hush-hush 3-commerce powerhouse is just a few miles away" in *PC Computing* (April 2000)
Pub: Ziff-Davis Inc.
Ed: Jim Conley. Description: Canadian retailers saw a banner year in 1999, with record sales both online and offline. Exchange rates, shipping costs, and support concerns have kept many U.S. companies from expanding to the Canadian market, but the article suggests the savvy retailer will realize the opportunity.

34447 ■ "Secure access; Carriersnet building Web-based system to track worldwide cargo" in *Crain's Detroit Business* (Jan. 13, 2003, pp. 3)
Pub: Crain Communications Inc., Detroit
Ed: Michael Strong. Description: Profile of Dearborn-based Carriersnet Group, Inc. The firm is working with the U.S. Customs service to develop an Internet-based system to ensure container security on cargo ships entering and departing the United States.

34448 ■ "Secure Your Database" in *E-business Advisor* (Vol. 18, No. 12, December 2000, pp. 34)
Pub: Advisor Media, Inc.
Ed: Bill Jaeger. Description: Database security is an essential aspect of a successful e-commerce operation. This article offers insight into using a security system for e-commerce sites.

34449 ■ "Security Lapse" in *Inc.* (August 2005, pp. 57-58)
Pub: Inc. Magazine
Ed: David H. Freedman. Description: Strategies to protect computer data systems from hackers are presented.

34450 ■ "Security Steps into the Spotlight" in *InfoWorld* (Vol. 23, No. 5, January 29, 2001, pp. 64)
Pub: InfoWorld
Ed: P.J. Connolly. Description: Security issues became more and more crucial in year 2000 as nearly every week brought news of another security lapse or breach at a major company. Firms that have lost sensitive, business-critical data to hackers find hope in several key improvements, although no technology can completely eradicate security problems. Digital certificates, which received federal legal authority in June 2000, will be important in future E-commerce initiatives.

34451 ■ "Seeing the Sites" in *Entrepreneur* (Vol. 33, September 2005, No. 9, pp. 120)
Pub: Entrepreneur Media Inc.
Ed: Sarah Pierce. Description: Profile of Heritage Web Solutions. The marketing company designs and hosts Websites for small companies for $1,000.

34452 ■ "Seeing Stars" in *Entrepreneur* (Vol. 33, August 2005, No. 8, pp. 18)
Pub: Entrepreneur Media Inc.
Ed: Chris McGinnis. Description: Tripadvisor.com, Hotelchatter.com, Hotelshark.com, travel.yahoo.com, and citysearch.com offer hotel reviews from real travelers.

34453 ■ "Self-Service" in *Inc.* (October 2005, pp. 124-125, 128)
Pub: Inc. Magazine
Description: When choosing software to manage email it is important to consider four basic questions: what you want the email to do, an access point, security, and costs. Comparisons of Microsoft Outlook 2003, IBM Lotus Notes 7.0, Qualcomm Eudora 6.2, and Mozilla Thunderbird 1.0 software are shown.

34454 ■ "Sell2All Launches DropShop Services for Selling on eBay" in *Comtex* (April 1, 2004)
Pub: Market Wire
Description: Profile of Sell2All, and the opening of its first location in Lincoln, Nebraska, as well as its DropShop services. The service will assist customers take their items into a DropShop location, utilize Sell2All's professional expertise and operations to place them on eBay and sell for the highest return possible.

34455 ■ "Selling Yourself" in *Kiplinger's Personal Finance Magazine* (Vol. 54, No. 12, December 2000, pp. 94)
Pub: The Kiplinger Washington Editors, Inc.
Ed: Kimberly Lankford, Justin Wiser. Description: The Internet opens up a world of opportunities for freelancers.

34456 ■ "Send E-Mail Securely" in *Home Office Computing* (Vol. 18, No. 11, November 2000, pp. 28)
Pub: Scholastic Inc.
Ed: Victoria Hall Smith. Description: E-mail is not a sure way to send anything sensitive or confidential. Messages hop from server to server as they traverse the Internet, sometimes becoming garbled or lost, and unauthorized copies are often left along the way. A profile of a proprietary message- and file-delivery software solution is presented.

34457 ■ "Set up shop" in *Entrepreneur* (Vol. 30, No. 3, March 2002, pp. 40)
Pub: Entrepreneur Media Inc.
Ed: Liane Gouthro. Description: Profile of Peachtree's WebsiteCreatorpro software that makes it easy to point and click your way to a new Web site.

34458 ■ "Set Up Shop in Europe" in *E-business Advisor* (Vol. 18, No. 2, February 2000, pp. 16)
Pub: Advisor Media, Inc.
Ed: Lars Hakan Sjoo. Description: The European e-commerce industry is estimated to be from one to four years behind the U.S., thus creating a myriad of opportunities for enterprising companies.

34459 ■ "Setting Up Shop" in *Home Office Computing* (Vol. 18, No. 10, October 2000, pp. 90)
Pub: Scholastic Inc.
Ed: William Van Winkle. Description: Online hosting companies have gone far beyond building Web storefronts and are evolving into E-business service providers (eBSPs) with wide assortments of front-end and back-end office tools. They often provide basics such as Web site setup and hosting free and generate revenue with premium value-added services such as marketing, site traffic monitoring, credit-card processing and inventory management. Tips for choosing a service provider are included.

34460 ■ "The Seven Laws of E-Commerce Strategy" in *Journal of Business Strategies* (Vol. 21, No. 5, September 2000, pp. 8)
Pub: Center for Business and Economic Research
Ed: Richard W. Oliver. Description: The author offers his seven tips for planners in order to thrive in the new Internet-driven economy.

34461 ■ "Sew What?" in *Black Enterprise* (Vol. 36, February 2006, No. 7, pp. 68)
Pub: Earl G. Graves Publishing Co. Inc.
Ed: James C. Johnson. Description: Entrepreneur seeks advice for starting an online sewing business.

34462 ■ **"SGS Automotive Services Offering Vehicle Inspections on eBay"** in *PR Newswire* (April 1, 2004)
Pub: PR Newswire Association, Inc.
Description: SGS Automotive Services will begin offering its comprehensive vehicle inspections services on eBay, providing the convenience of professional inspections done at individual's homes and offices. SGS is the nation's largest vehicle inspection firm.

34463 ■ **"Sharing the Wealth: Want to Get a Piece of the eBay Pie?"** in *Entrepreneur* (Vol. 33, February 2005, No. 2, pp. 40)
Pub: Entrepreneur Media Inc.
Ed: Melissa Campanelli. **Description:** Online affiliate programs offer banner advertising for companies in exchange for a percentage of any sales referred to the advertiser; one of the most lucrative programs is operated by online retailer, eBay.

34464 ■ **"Shawn Fanning's New Tune"** in *Business 2.0* (Vol. 6, May 2005, No. 4, pp. 38, 41)
Pub: Time, Inc.
Ed: John Heilemann. **Description:** Shawn Fanning, creator of Napster has developed a plan to help file-sharing networks legally make money for music labels.

34465 ■ **"She's only code and pixels, but she can help you shop"** in *The New York Times* (September 20, 2000, pp. D8, H8)
Pub: The New York Times Company
Ed: David J. Wallace. **Description:** A profile of the Emily program at ProFlowers, created by Kana Communications. Statistical data included.

34466 ■ **"Shipping out"** in *Entrepreneur* (Vol. 31, No. 6, June 2003, pp. 42)
Pub: Entrepreneur Media Inc.
Ed: Melissa Campanelli. **Description:** Many online retailers have followed Amazon.com and have begun offering free shipping with purchases. The advantages and downside to providing this service are discussed.

34467 ■ **"Shoe-String Your Site"** in *My Business* (June/July 2002, pp. 43)
Pub: My Business Magazine
Ed: Dan Rafter. **Description:** It is imperative that a Web site include essential information to avoid frustrating users.

34468 ■ **"Shoestring Marketing: Web Research: Is This Fantasy or Reality?"** in *Atlanta Business Chronicle* (Vol. 25, No. 21, Nov. 1, 2002)
Pub: American City Business Publications, Inc.
Ed: Alf Nucifora. **Description:** The advantages and disadvantages of online research are discussed. WebSurveyor, which has experienced online survey success, has received 2,000-plus customers globally via the hosting of 50,000 surveys in which 4 million responses were processed.

34469 ■ **"Shopping in palm of the hand is making its holiday debut"** in *The New York Times* (November 19, 2000, pp. A1)
Pub: The New York Times Company
Ed: Leslie Kaufman. **Description:** We are all used to making purchases online, particularly during the holiday season. But, this year, the new thing is wireless or mobile shopping. More people are making purchases over the Internet this year using their wireless digital assistants or their cellular telephones.

34470 ■ **"Shopping Pals"** in *Entrepreneur* (Vol. 27, No. 8, August 2000, pp. 20)
Pub: Entrepreneur Media Inc.
Ed: Robert McGarvey. **Description:** Earn a stellar ranking in e-tailing and watch customers come back for more.

34471 ■ **"Showcase Your Talent"** in *Black Enterprise* (Vol. 36, February 2006, No. 7, pp. 66)
Pub: Earl G. Graves Publishing Co. Inc.
Ed: Bridget McCrea. **Description:** Jonathon Alexander created Tap It FAME Inc., the firm that allows bands, singers, artists and designers to showcase their songs for $9.95 plus merchant service fees.

34472 ■ **"Sides Vie to Regulate Internet-Based Service; Michigan Wants to Play Role"** in *Crain's Detroit Business* (Vol. 21, January 24, 2005)
Pub: Crain Communications Inc. - Detroit
Ed: Amy Lane. **Description:** States across the nation, including Michigan, believe they should play a role in the regulation of Internet-based phone service, called Voice over Internet Protocol (VoIP).

34473 ■ **"Sign right here"** in *The New York Times* (October 8, 2000, pp. WK2)
Pub: The New York Times Company
Ed: John Schwartz. **Description:** An overview of electronic signatures in the Global Commerce Act.

34474 ■ **"Sign of the Times: Are You Missing Out on This Simple, Inexpensive Marketing Tool?"** in *Entrepreneur* (Vol. 33, January 2005, No. 1)
Pub: Entrepreneur Media Inc.
Ed: Catherine Seda. **Description:** Tactics to use email messages as an inexpensive marketing tool are given.

34475 ■ **"Sign of the Times"** in *Entrepreneur* (Vol. 28, No. 10, October 2000, pp. 29)
Pub: Entrepreneur Media Inc.
Ed: Amanda C. Kooser. **Description:** The Electronic Signatures in Global and National Commerce Act passed through Congress in June 2000. Popularly known as the Digital Signatures Bill, or E-SIGN Bill, will allow the use of electronic records and signatures the same legal weight as their paper counterparts.

34476 ■ **"Signing Internet Noncompetes And Working From Home"** in *Fortune* (Vol. 141, No. 5, March 6, 2000, pp. 430)
Pub: Time Inc.
Ed: Anne Fisher. **Description:** Questions answered by the editor concern signing noncompete contracts, working from home, and job interviews.

34477 ■ **"Signs of Life? You'll Need Plenty of Patience to Profit from M-Commerce"** in *Entrepreneur* (Vol. 31, No. 10, October 2003, pp. 28)
Pub: Entrepreneur Media, Inc.
Ed: Amanda C. Kooser. **Description:** M-Commerce, or mobile commerce, is discussed. The sector has seen disappointing early experiences, but many entrepreneurs are looking forward to a full-blown m-commerce future.

34478 ■ **"Simplify Web Development with Java Server Pages"** in *E-business Advisor* (Vol. 17, No. 12, December 1999, pp. 38)
Pub: Advisor Media, Inc.
Ed: Tom Valesky. **Description:** The Java Server Pages (JSP) standard is fast becoming the architecture of choice for active Web page development. JSP, vendor-neutral and highly portable, simplifies Web page creation by giving developers full access to Java APIs and third-party libraries. JSP, built on top of the Java Servlet API, permits developers to use all Java capabilities as a scripting language.

34479 ■ **"Sink or Swim"** in *My Business* (February/March 2004, pp. 20-25)
Pub: My Business Magazine
Ed: Shannon Scully. **Description:** The importance of e-commerce to small business marketing is discussed. The process of building a Website in order to improve a brick-and-mortar business is critical. A Website should be easy for a customer to surf; it is suggested to stay away from fancy Flash products.

34480 ■ **"The Sinking of the Dot-Com Fleet"** in *Information Today* (Vol. 17, No. 11, December 2000, pp. 42)
Pub: Information Today, Inc.
Ed: Robin Peek. **Description:** With the Web's golden era over, 2001 will be a saner year.

34481 ■ **"Site Seeing"** in *Business Week* (No. 3666, January 31, 2000, pp. F30)
Pub: McGraw-Hill, Inc.
Description: Useful Web sites for small businesses are discussed.

34482 ■ **"Site Watch for Home Workers"** in *Home Office Computing* (Vol. 18, No. 8, August 2000, pp. 20)
Pub: Scholastic Inc.
Ed: Cristina Gair, Sonya Donaldson. **Description:** Web sites offering services to home based workers, including financenter.com, midnightmac.com, fat-brain.com, and webentrepreneurs.com are profiled.

34483 ■ **"Six IT decisions your IT people shouldn't make"** in *Harvard Business Review* (Vol. 80, No. 11, November 2002, pp. 85)
Pub: Harvard Business School Press
Ed: Jeanne W. Peter, Ross Weill. **Description:** The need for senior managers to take leadership in making six key information technology decisions is investigated. These managers should decide how much to spend on IT, which business processes should receive IT funds, and which IT capabilities need to be company wide. Decisions must also be made regarding the quality of IT services, which privacy and security risks are acceptable and whom to blame if an IT initiative fails.

34484 ■ **"The Skinflint Goes Shopping"** in *Forbes* (December 24, 2001, p. 100)
Pub: Forbes Magazine
Ed: Stephen Manes. **Description:** The article explores shopping bargains online. Price-comparison Web sites are great places to gather information, but many often miss the best deals.

34485 ■ **"Skinnyguy.com Rekindles America's Love to Barter"** in *PR Newswire* (January 6, 2003)
Pub: PR Newswire Association, Inc.
Description: Profile of Skinnyguy.com, retailer of used and new DVC, CD, and VHS products via the Internet.

34486 ■ **"Slick Tricks"** in *Entrepreneur* (Vol. 31, No. 7, July 2003, pp. 73)
Pub: Entrepreneur Media, Inc.
Ed: Joanne Cleaver. **Description:** Telecommunications scams continue with newer attacks of hijacked phone accounts (slamming), unauthorized add-on charges (cramming). It is important for small business owners to warn employees of such scams to avoid problems.

34487 ■ **"Small Biz Tentative about Testing Web Waters"** in *Crain's Detroit Business* (Vol. 19, No. 9, March 3, 2003, pp. 29)
Pub: Crain Communications Inc., Detroit
Ed: Laura Bailey. **Description:** Small businesses continue to shy away from electronic commerce.

34488 ■ **"Small-Business Centers: E-Biz for Everyone"** in *PC Magazine* (July 1, 2000, pp. 189)
Pub: Ziff-Davis Publishing Company
Ed: Heath H. Herel. **Description:** Small businesses seeking to take advantage of the Web on a limited budget can turn to small-business portals for help. These centers bring what they consider best-of-breed services together into a single, convenient point of entry, often adding content of their own to round out the offerings. Bigstep.com, HyperMart Network, and Microsoft bCentral are three good choices for those just starting a Web presence. For those who want to improve their businesses, Office.com focuses on giving you information regarding e-business in general and preparing your company to move forward as technology continually improves.

34489 ■ **"Small-Business Centers"** in *PC Magazine* (June 6, 2000, pp. 141)
Pub: Ziff-Davis Publishing Company
Ed: Cade Metz. **Description:** The Internet's influence on small business continues to grow. An ever-increasing number of mom-and-pop operations are discovering the real earning potential that taking advantage of the Web opportunities can bring. Numerous small-business centers have risen to prominence online, each designed to facilitate or expand company operations. Many of these sites are maintained by

vendors that wish to attract new customers by pairing hardware products with business-centric online tools, but many act as standalone sites. A profile of the leading standalone centers intended for companies employing 1 to 100 employees is included.

34490 ■ *Small Business Clustering Technology: Applications in Marketing, Management, Finance, and IT*
Pub: Idea Group Publishing
Ed: Robert C. MacGregor; Ann Hodgkinson. Released: June 2006. Description: An overview of the development and role of small business clusters in disciplines that include economics, marketing, management and information systems.

34491 ■ "Small Business: Crunching numbers via the Internet" in *Crain's Detroit Business* (Vol. 16, May 29, 2000, pp. 54)
Pub: Crain Communications, Inc.
Ed: Joanne Cleaver. Description: With the growing acceptance of the Internet as a place to conduct business operations, Intuit Company's Quickbooks market position is being challenged.

34492 ■ *Small Business for Dummies*
Pub: John Wiley & Sons, Incorporated
Ed: Eric Tyson, Jim Schell. Released: November 2002. Price: $21.99. Description: Advice for launching and growing a small business; insights into using the Internet as business tool are included.

34493 ■ "Small-Business e-Loan" in *Hispanic Business* (March 2002, pp. 60)
Pub: Hispanic Business
Ed: Roger Harris. Description: The Small Business Administration has launched a new Web-hosted system that aids in the origination and management of SBA-backed and other traditional small-business loans.

34494 ■ *Small Business Management*
Pub: John Wiley & Sons, Incorporated
Ed: Margaret Burlingame. Released: March 2007. Price: $44.95. Description: Advice for starting and running a small business as well as information on the value and appeal of small businesses, is given. Topics include budgets, taxes, inventory, ethics, e-commerce, and current laws.

34495 ■ "Small-Business Services" in *PC Magazine* (February 8, 2000, pp. 156)
Pub: Ziff-Davis Publishing Company
Ed: Don Willmott. Description: A compilation of service sites geared to serve small businesses, including CenterBeam, eFax, myTalk, Stamps.com, and Zkey.com.

34496 ■ *Small Business Taxes Made Easy: How to Increase Your Deductions, Reduce What You Owe, and Boost Your Profits*
Pub: McGraw-Hill Companies
Ed: Eva Rosenberg. Released: December 2004. Price: $16.95 (US), $24.95 (Canadian). Description: Tax expert gives advice to small business owners regarding tax issues. TaxMamma.com, run by Eva Rosenberg, is one of the top seven tax advice Websites on the Internet.

34497 ■ "Small Businesses Don't Have to Spend Big for Web Sites" in *Crain's Detroit Business* (Vol. 18, No. 49, December 9, 2002, pp. 18)
Pub: Crain Communications Inc., Detroit
Ed: Laura Bailey. Description: Tips for building a successful Web site without spending lots of cash are presented for small businesses.

34498 ■ "Small Firms Slow to Board E-com Boat" in *Accounting Today* (Vol. 14, No. 14, August 7, 2000, pp. 27)
Pub: Faulkner & Gray, Inc.
Description: The National Federation of Independent Business found in its survey of 1,055 small business owners that the Internet is not perceived for its potential. Most small businesses use Web sites simply because it's the thing to do.

34499 ■ "Small Manufacturers Aren't Using the Internet" in *Wall Street Journal* (July 3, 2000, pp. B6)
Pub: Dow Jones & Co., Inc.
Description: The fact that small manufacturing companies have not jumped into Internet usage is explored.

34500 ■ "Smart Content Management" in *E-business Advisor* (Vol. 18, No. 6, June 2000, pp. 28)
Pub: Advisor Media, Inc.
Ed: Jon Radoff. Description: Managing content change on company Web sites must be done carefully or costs will skyrocket. Web site managers should ensure that their sites are scalable, meaning that per-unit costs decrease as usage increases. Web sites' content changes should be consistent with a strong brand identity, reflecting the company's unique, personalized views and content distribution methods.

34501 ■ "Smart customers, dumb companies" in *Harvard Business Review* (Vol. 78, No. 6, November-December 2000, pp. 187)
Pub: Harvard Business School Publishing Corp.
Description: An investigation into the ways in which the Internet is creating a variety of micromarkets, controlled by customers, not companies, and how marketers must realize this if they are going to make their companies successful.

34502 ■ *SMEs and New Technologies: Learning E-Business and Development*
Pub: Palgrave Macmillan
Ed: Banji Oyelaran-Oyeyinka; Kaushalesh Lal. Released: October 2006. Price: $85.00. Description: Adoption and learning of new information technologies in developing nations is covered. New technologies are opening opportunities for small companies in these countries.

34503 ■ "Smile: Your Company's Under Attack" in *PC Computing* (March 2000, pp. 42)
Pub: Ziff-Davis Inc.
Ed: Jamais Cascio. Description: Online consumer complaint sites, which are increasing in popularity, result in bad publicity for companies, and, the means by which the company chooses to handle the sites can be detrimental for company public relations. Companies have launched high-profile lawsuits and directly threatened the owner of the complaint domain. The reaction by the companies to the sites brings much more attention to the complaints than the original site. The best way to handle complaints is to respond to customers and work to resolve issues rather than ignoring them. Customer support sites are very easy to establish, and it is an easy way to keep in contact with customers.

34504 ■ "Smithtown-based LuminNet Helps Small Businesses Design and Market Their Own Web Sites" in *Long Island Business News* (Feb. 20, 2004)
Pub: Dolan Media Newswires
Ed: Adina Genn. Description: Profile of Annette Galarza, owner of LuminNet, a provider of Website development for small businesses. Galarza trains clients to understand ways to use a Website as a cost-effective business tool.

34505 ■ "Smooth Operator" in *Home Business* (Vol. 12, October 2005, No. 5, pp. 93)
Pub: Home Business Magazine
Ed: Sandy Larson. Description: Profile of Mark Williams, a California online retailer specializing in men's and women's grooming products.

34506 ■ "Snipers, Stalkers, and Nibblers: Online Auction Business Ethics" in *Journal of Business Ethics* (Vol. 46, No. 2, Aug. 15, 2003)
Pub: Kluwer Academic Publishers Group
Ed: Alexei M. Marcoux. Description: Spirited discussion exists among online auction participants over the ethics of sniping: delaying one's bid until the closing seconds of an online auction.

34507 ■ "Snowboarding Secrets" in *Forbes* (Vol. 175, February 14, 2005, No. 3, pp. 78)
Pub: Forbes Magazine Inc.
Ed: Melanie Wells. Description: Profile of Chris M. Bradley, founder of 2ndEdition, creator of $50 snowboards customized with vinyl graphics in camouflage, graffiti, etc. via the Web.

34508 ■ "Socialtext Update Knots Closer Enterprise Ties" in *eWeek* (February 7, 2005)
Pub: Ziff Davis Media Inc.
Description: Profile of Socialtext Workspace 1.5, which integrates the wiki service with enterprise directories based on lightweight directory access protocol and Microsoft Active Directory. Socialtext develops enterprise social software that allows people and companies to use the Web to communicate more effectively.

34509 ■ "Software that Asks Who Goes There?" in *Business Week Online* (February 26, 2002)
Pub: McGraw-Hill, Inc.
Description: The art and science of managing employee passwords is discussed, including the issues of tech support, legal requirements and the high costs involved for small business.

34510 ■ "Software for Rent" in *Hispanic Business* (Vol. 22, No. 6, June 2000, pp. 160)
Pub: Hispanic Business
Ed: Roger Harris. Description: The use of software leasing via the Internet is expected to show rapid growth as start-ups and small companies realize the cost-savings that can be achieved from a software vendor or an Application Service Provider.

34511 ■ "Sold for $20 Million" in *Black Enterprise* (Vol. 31, No. 5, December 2000, pp. 30)
Pub: Earl Graves Publishing Co.
Description: A profile of Charles "Chuck" H. James III, who sold his ProduceOnline.com, an online venture looking to streamline transactions between wholesale buyers and sellers of fresh produce.

34512 ■ "Soloella.com to launch" in *Hispanic Business* (Vol. 22, No. 4, April 2000, pp. 78)
Pub: Hispanic Business
Ed: Andrea Siedsma. Description: Soloella.com is to be launched on the Internet in April 2000, and is targeted at Hispanic women. Issues concerning the provision of Internet sites for Hispanics and for women are discussed.

34513 ■ "Somebody's Watching You" in *Inc.* (September 2005, pp. 75-76)
Pub: Inc. Magazine
Ed: David H. Freedman. Description: Search engines such as Google are having an impact on business in two ways. First, the ability to find information on the Web is critical to any business success; and companies are now freely examined by anyone, making it necessary to adapt a firm to public scrutiny.

34514 ■ "A Sore Site for Eyes" in *Entrepreneur* (Vol. 28, No. 10, October 2000, pp. 38)
Pub: Entrepreneur Media Inc.
Ed: Doug Hood and Marilea S. Hood. Description: If a sloppy Web site is your calling card, don't expect a call from lenders, a polished site will help attract funding.

34515 ■ "Spam Could Be a Scam: Internet Tricks Are Becoming High Crimes" in *Black Enterprise* (Vol. 35, August 2004, No. 1, pp. 30)
Pub: Earl G. Graves Publishing Co. Inc.
Ed: Siobhan Benet. Description: Internet crime, also called cybercrime, is the third priority after counterterrorism and counterintelligence for the Federal Bureau of Investigation.

34516 ■ "Spam Law Proposed in State House of Representatives" in *Journal Record* **(February 4, 2004)**
Pub: Dolan Media Company
Description: Oklahoma House Bill 2215 would require any unsolicited commercial email to include an automatic return mechanism enabling the recipient to send a reply without having to retype the sender's email address.

34517 ■ "A Spam Law That Slams Small Business" in *Business Week Online* **(November 5, 2003)**
Pub: McGraw-Hill Inc.
Ed: Christopher Kenton. **Description:** The impact of new California legislation that makes it a crime to send any unsolicited commercial email from or to any email account accessed from or billed to a California address is examined.

34518 ■ "Spam Stopper" in *Entrepreneur* **(Vol. 32, November 2004, No. 11, pp. 62)**
Pub: Entrepreneur Media Inc.
Ed: Liane Cassavoy. **Description:** Webroot Software offers an application that will keep unwanted emails away. The program is called Spam Shredder and works with all POP3 email clients.

34519 ■ "Spam Uncanned: Why the Recent Anti-Spam Legislation Isn't Protecting You" in *Entrepreneur* **(Vol. 32, July 2004, No. 7, pp. 72)**
Pub: Entrepreneur Media Inc.
Ed: Catherine Seda. **Description:** Can-Spam, the new legislation designed to protect Internet email users, does not prevent spam, it only attempts to regulate the way it is sent. Steps to help protect privacy while using a computer online are shared.

34520 ■ "Spam wars" in *Entrepreneur* **(Vol. 31, No. 4, April 2003, pp. 48)**
Pub: Entrepreneur Media Inc.
Ed: Amanda C. Kooser. **Description:** It is estimated that the amount of spam email received will more than double by the year 2007.

34521 ■ "SpamCheck http://spamcheck. sitesell.com" in *Entrepreneur* **(Vol. 32, No. 1, January 2004, pp. 10)**
Pub: Entrepreneur Media, Inc.
Ed: Steve Cooper. **Description:** SpamCheck will check a small businesses email and inform them with a spam score and recommend ways to decrease spam email.

34522 ■ "Speaking up" in *Entrepreneur* **(Vol. 31, No. 6, June 2003, pp. 46)**
Pub: Entrepreneur Media Inc.
Ed: Amanda C. Kooser. **Description:** According to a Yankee Group study, 25 percent of the 10-14 percent of small businesses that plan to upgrade or replace telephone systems in 2003, will move to Internet protocol telephony (IPT).

34523 ■ "Spider Simulator: http://tools. summitmedia.co.uk/spider" in *Entrepreneur* **(Vol. 33, February 2005, No. 2, pp. 8)**
Pub: Entrepreneur Media Inc.
Ed: Steve Cooper. **Description:** Search engine spiders grade the optimization of a Website based on page description, keywords, page size, image descriptions and more.

34524 ■ "The Spirit of Independence" in *Home Office Computing* **(Vol. 18, No. 7, July 2000, pp. 42)**
Pub: Scholastic Inc.
Ed: Dave Johnson. **Description:** An annotated list of 76 home-office Web site-based resources is presented. Categories include the following: Application Service Providers (ASP), finding clients, your business, your business plans, communications, education, finance/banking, finance/taxes, government, home networking, home office, Internet, legal, marketing, mobile, online storage, online support, reference library, shipping, shopping, telecommuting, tools, travel, and bookmarks.

34525 ■ "Sporting Goods Web Sites, Last Year's Costly Rage, Are Turned Over tothe Professionals" in *The New York Times* **(Sept. 4, 2000, pp. C5)**
Pub: The New York Times Company
Ed: Bob Tedeschi. **Description:** E-commerce Web sites formed by media companies are being handed over to outside companies with retail experience.

34526 ■ "Spread the Word" in *BlackEnterprise* **(Vol. 31, No. 10, May 2001, pp. 110)**
Pub: Earl Graves Publishing Co.
Ed: Holly Aguirre. **Description:** Successful ways to build a Web site for advertising a small business are shown, including search engines, links on other sites, and offline sources that include word-of-mouth and traditional advertising and marketing.

34527 ■ "Spreading Viruses Can be a Good Thing" in *Crain's Chicago Business* **(Vol. 30, January 2007, No. 3, pp. 18)**
Pub: Crain Communications, Inc.
Ed: Steve Hendershot. **Description:** Viral Marketing, spreading a company's message by email which directs consumers to the company's website, is another of the creative new marketing techniques finding success online. Downsides of this powerful tool are explored.

34528 ■ "Spring cleaning" in *Entrepreneur* **(Vol. 31, No. 4, April 2003, pp. 44)**
Pub: Entrepreneur Media Inc.
Ed: Melissa Campanelli. **Description:** There are a variety of software tools available to make sure a Web site is in good working order. Keynote NetMechanic spots and fixes common HTML code errors and generates a repaired file to upload to the Web host.

34529 ■ "Spy Games" in *Entrepreneur* **(Vol. 32, No. 4, April 2004, pp. 34)**
Pub: Entrepreneur Media, Inc.
Ed: Amanda C. Kooser. **Description:** Internet security and employee espionage are the topics covered. Protecting a small business from employee espionage requires a good policy written in both an employee handbook and employee contracts.

34530 ■ "Stake A Claim" in *Entrepreneur* **(Vol. 28, No. 1, January 2000, pp. 20)**
Pub: Entrepreneur Media Inc.
Ed: Laura Tiffany. **Description:** In the Internet gold rush, the United States Patent and Trademark Office is the lone barrier to technology infringement. Does it know what it's doing?

34531 ■ "Stamp It Out: A New Proposal Aims to Bring Spam Under Control" in *Entrepreneur* **(Vol. 32, July 2004, No. 7, pp. 28)**
Pub: Entrepreneur Media Inc.
Ed: Amanda C. Kooser. **Description:** Two proposals to help eliminated unwanted spam email are being considered. E-postage is an idea to attach a virtual stamp to email in order to reduce unwanted bulk email. Hashcash would require a sender's computer to solve a computational problem as proof of good faith. Good legislation will be required to alleviate the problem of spam.

34532 ■ "Starbucks Brews a New Strategy" in *Fast Company* **(August 2001, pp. 145)**
Pub: Fast Company
Ed: George Anders. **Description:** Starbucks is tying its online efforts closely to its central mission: building customer loyalty around cappuccinos, lattes, and other fancy beverages.

34533 ■ "Start Spreading the News" in *Business 2.0* **(Vol. 6, July 2005, No. 6, pp. 40, 42)**
Pub: Time, Inc.
Ed: John Heilemann. **Description:** Fred Wilson, venture capitalist and leader of the new firm, Union Square Adventures, is investing in New York. Wilson believes that as the Internet transforms the media, marketing, and finance new technologies will make investing in Internet startups profitable again.

34534 ■ "Start Your Blogs" in *Venture Capital Journal* **(January 1, 2005)**
Pub: Thomason Financial Inc.
Ed: Lawrence Aragon. **Description:** It is predicted that venture capital firms will use Internet blogs as a means for building business relationships. One by-product of blogs will be that brands will move away from venture firms to individual partners.

34535 ■ "Start Your Engines" in *My Business* **(June/July 2004, pp. 44)**
Pub: My Business Magazine
Ed: Paige Orr. **Description:** Ways to show up high on a search engine's list are shared.

34536 ■ "Starting From Zero: Entrepreneur Reaps Success During Rocky Tech Times" in *Black Enterprise* **(Vol. 34, July 2004, No. 12, pp. 53)**
Pub: Earl G. Graves Publishing Co. Inc.
Ed: Bridget McCrea. **Description:** Profile of Glenn Davis, owner of Virginia-based BranCore Technologies. Working from home, Davis borrowed $15,000 from his 401(k) to launch his minority-owned firm that provides project management and e-commerce consulting.

34537 ■ "Startup Hopes to Help Speed Payments to Vendors" in *Crain's Detroit Business* **(Vol. 19, No. 42, October 20, 2003, pp. 18)**
Pub: Crain Communications Inc., Detroit
Ed: Laura Bailey. **Description:** Profile of eFinNet Corporation, a startup financial services firm that speeds payments from large firms to small suppliers and eliminates direct banking, by linking the buyer, seller and lender through the Internet.

34538 ■ "State of the Banner" in *Forbes* **(December 25, 2000, pp. 273)**
Pub: Forbes Magazine
Ed: John C. Dvorak. **Description:** Banner advertising, now seen as ineffective and old-fashioned, may be on its last leg. Nobody likes banners, and the frequency of people clicking on them has fallen off drastically, to 0.5 percent, indicating that people simply ignore them.

34539 ■ "Steal This Customer" in *Internet World* **(Vol. 7, No. 1, January 15, 2001, pp. 32)**
Pub: Mecklermedia Corporation
Ed: Jason Black. **Description:** Acquiring and retaining customers is a major problem for online retailers, but need not be insurmountable. Many consumers use the Web for the online equivalent of window-shopping and price comparison; competing retailers have the opportunity to lure buyers with better offers, and Internet technology can greatly speed the process. Advertisements can be sent directly to the screen of a user browsing a competitor's site with the aid of Dash.com, Gator.com and other browser add-ons.

34540 ■ "Sticky Money" in *Entrepreneur* **(Vol. 28, No. 11, November 2000, pp. 38)**
Pub: Entrepreneur Media Inc.
Ed: Cynthia E. Griffin. **Description:** A growing number of Web sites connect business owners with financing resources ranging from banks and venture capitalists to private investors looking to purchase stock in direct public offerings.

34541 ■ "Stop, e-Thief!" in *Entrepreneur* **(Vol. 28, No. 11, November 2000, pp. 30)**
Pub: Entrepreneur Media Inc.
Ed: Robert McGarvey. **Description:** Web resources for stopping Internet fraud are investigated. Suggestions to protect your business are offered.

34542 ■ "Straight talking: to tell or not to tell?" in *Entrepreneur* **(Vol. 30, No. 10, October 2002, pp. 47)**
Pub: Entrepreneur Media Inc.
Ed: Melissa Campanelli. **Description:** A study conducted by the Consumer Web Watch shows that less than 30 percent of respondents trust information on Web sites that sell products and services.

34543 ■ **"Straight to video"** in *Entrepreneur* (Vol. 30, No. 2, February 2002, pp. 58)
Pub: Entrepreneur Media Inc.
Ed: Jennifer Pellet. **Description:** A free video player application debuted by www.bloomberg.com in November. The New York City-based financial news site video player not only provides streaming video access and archived news broadcasts, but also enables searches for specific content through the use of keywords.

34544 ■ **"Straight to Video"** in *Entrepreneur. com* (Vol. 34, January 2006, No. 1, pp. 22)
Pub: Entrepreneur Media Inc.
Ed: Amanda C. Kooser. **Description:** Microsoft's Small Business Center offers short clips to help small businesses market on the Internet. Businesses can test advertising, provide details on products and services, or show video tips to keep users returning to your site.

34545 ■ **"Strategic and Ethical Considerations in Managing Digital Privacy"** in *Journal of Business Ethics* (Vol. 46, No. 2, Aug. 15, 2003)
Pub: Kluwer Academic Publishers Group
Ed: Ravi Sarathy, Chrisopher J. Robertson. **Description:** Individualized customer information is at the heart of online commerce. Using increasing amounts of customer-specific data enhances the success and value of one-to-one online marketing, but the extensive gathering and use of data specific to individuals also causes alarm over the loss of digital privacy.

34546 ■ **"Strategize your e-mail newsletter to realize more grins than groans"** in *The Business Journal* (Vol. 18, No. 10, June 30, 2000, pp. 41)
Pub: Lee Enterprises, Inc.
Ed: Alf Nucifora. **Description:** An e-mail newsletter will help promote your business. Jupiter Communications Inc. predicts spending on commercial e-mail development and distribution will rise to $7.3 billion in 2005.

34547 ■ **"Strutting Your Cyber Stuff"** in *Folio: the Magazine for Magazine Management* (Vol. 30, No. 1, January 2001, pp. 15)
Pub: Intertec Publishing Corp.
Ed: Dale Buss. **Description:** From billboards to e-mail campaigns, magazine publishers are employing all sorts of multimedia marketing magic to promote their Internet properties.

34548 ■ **"Study shows businesses are slow to embrace e-commerce"** in *Black Enterprise* (Vol. 32)
Pub: Earl Graves Publishing Co.
Ed: Bevolyn Williams-Harold. **Description:** The Minority Business Development Agency is urging minority-owned businesses to use e-commerce to help grow their companies. Statistical data included.

34549 ■ **"Stumping in Cyberspace"** in *Hispanic Business* (June 2005, pp. 100, 102)
Pub: Hispanic Business
Ed: Scott Williams. **Description:** Ways the Internet is changing the political landscape are discussed using former Vermont Governor Howard Dean's run for office.

34550 ■ **"Sure, it would be easier on the Web - but let's haggle"** in *The New York Times* (December 13, 2000, pp. D13, H13)
Pub: The New York Times Company
Ed: Bernard Stamler. **Description:** Media buying is still done in an old-fashioned way, despite the availability of the Internet.

34551 ■ **"Surfing the Tongues"** in *Business Week* (December 11, 2000, pp. 18)
Pub: McGraw-Hill, Inc.
Description: The prevalence of foreign-language users of the Internet is increasing, and English has become the language of the World Wide Web.

34552 ■ **"Survey Says...Market Research on the Cheap is Just a Click Away"** in *Entrepreneur* (Vol. 32, September 2004, No. 9, pp. 73)
Pub: Entrepreneur Media Inc.
Ed: Nancy Michaels. **Description:** Tips for using on-line market surveys are presented.

34553 ■ **"Surviving the New Economy"** in *Inc.* (October 1, 2003)
Pub: Gruner & Jahr USA Publishing
Ed: Nadine Heintz. **Description:** Profile of Data Return and its management. Data Return is a Web-hosting firm sold by Sunny Vanderbeck, who is considering buying his company back.

34554 ■ **"Sweat rewards"** in *Entrepreneur* (Vol. 30, No. 3, Marc)
Pub: Entrepreneur Media Inc.
Ed: Amanda C. Kooser, Geoff Williams. **Description:** Predictions for hot business trends in 2002 are presented, including online learning, kiosks, online games, bartering, alternative health for pets, managing outsourcing, maternity clothing, life coaches, alternative energy, e-books, plus-size clothing, ethnic foods, personalization themes, boomer menopause, luxury products and services for middle income consumers, technology, marketing, money and management.

34555 ■ **"SwiftCD Taps PayPal as On-Demand Payment Engine"** in *DVD Report* (Vol. 8, No. 16, August 18, 2003)
Pub: PBI Media LLC
Description: SwiftCD signs a deal to have the PayPal e-commerce system handle transactions.

34556 ■ **"Swimgear Web Site Crosses Oceans"** in *My Business* (June/July 2002, pp. 46)
Pub: My Business Magazine
Ed: Shannon Scully. **Description:** Profile of Terry Gill Hammond, who began selling swimwear from her home. With five retail stores in the Atlanta area, Hammond decided to start selling her products online and discovered that Web customers require different service than in-store customers.

34557 ■ **"Switching Tracks"** in *Black Enterprise* (Vol. 34, July 2004, No. 12, pp. 124)
Pub: Earl G. Graves Publishing Co. Inc.
Ed: Sonya A. Donaldson. **Description:** Profile of BITco USA Inc., the Florida-based firm that installs equipment such as radios, surveillance cameras, and automatic fare boxes on buses and rail cars. The family owned business won the bid for a Website makeover that would help the build company's image.

34558 ■ **"Syndication: The Emerging Model for Business in the Internet Era"** in *Harvard Business Review* (Vol. 78, No. 3, May 2000, pp. 85)
Pub: Harvard Business School Publishing Corp.
Ed: Kevin Werbach. **Description:** Many of the new rules about competition and strategy can be found in the concept of syndication, a way of doing business that has its origins in the entertainment world, but is now expanding to define the structure of e-business.

34559 ■ **"Tackle Your International Logistics Obstacles"** in *E-business Advisor* (Vol. 18, No. 12, December 2004, pp. 22)
Pub: Advisor Media, Inc.
Ed: Beth Peterson. **Description:** International e-commerce offers excellent revenue opportunities and the Internet offers the needed business infrastructure, but shipping goods across international borders can be a problems. Logistics marketplaces are emerging to aid this process, but there are other challenges. The choice of the right Internet business infrastructure is critical for the success of global e-commerce.

34560 ■ **"Tag Sale"** in *Business 2.0* (Vol. 7, January/February 2006, No. 1, pp. 34, 37)
Pub: Time, Inc.
Ed: John Heilemann. **Description:** Profile of Joshua Schachter, founder of Del.icio.us, which offers a system for letting online users label Webpages with searchable keywords of their choice.

34561 ■ **"Take a virtual drive"** in *Hispanic Business* (Vol. 22, No. 3, March 2000, pp. 58)
Pub: Hispanic Business
Ed: Abel Magana. **Description:** Apple Computer's iMac was the first computer to be produced without a floppy drive. Following iMac's launch in 1998, several companies began offering digital information storage on the Internet. The services offered by such companies are discussed.

34562 ■ **"Taking Advantage of Technology"** in *Black Enterprise* (Vol. 31, No. 4, November 2000, pp. 57)
Pub: Earl Graves Publishing Co.
Ed: Paula McCoy-Pinderhughes. **Description:** Small business owners should "hire" the Internet to delegate and manage time-consuming activities such as accounting, marketing, office management, human resources, and administrative functions to cut operational costs and increase revenue.

34563 ■ **"Taking the Net by Storm"** in *Entrepreneur* (Vol. 28, No. 1, January 2000, pp. 50)
Pub: Entrepreneur Media Inc.
Ed: Melissa Campanelli. **Description:** According to a new study from high-tech market research firm, International Data Corporation, U.S. small businesses are accessing the Internet with a vengence.

34564 ■ **"The Talk of the Inc. 500"** in *Inc.* (October, 2000, pp. 13)
Pub: The Goldhirsh Group
Description: Attendees at the Inc. 500 conference contended that the biggest problems facing America's fastest growing companies in 2000 were related to financing business growth. Nearly 75 percent of attendees said they would consider a merger if the right offer came along and nearly two-thirds expressed difficulty implementing e-commerce solutions and many plan to spend more money on Internet marketing than on more traditional marketing media.

34565 ■ **"Talking Shop: Where Should You Focus Your Online Marketing? Try the Office"** in *Entrepreneur* (Vol. 31, No. 9, July 2003, pp. 83)
Pub: Entrepreneur Media, Inc.
Ed: Catherine Seda. **Description:** According to a study by ComScore Networks, about 60 percent of online shopping is being conducted at the workplace. Ways to market online products targeting workers are presented.

34566 ■ **"Talking tiger, hidden classroom"** in *Ingram's* (Vol. 28, No. 6, June 2002, pp. 53)
Pub: Show Me Publishing, Inc.
Description: A review of the forthcoming education systems and e-learning technologies that will be available to students in the future is presented. Product developments include synthespians, computer gaming, natural language interfaces, speech recognition, and bio-interfaces.

34567 ■ **"Tangled Web"** in *Hispanic Business* (December 2001, pp. 58)
Pub: Hispanic Business
Ed: Derek Reveron. **Description:** Estimated 2001 Internet revenues for Hispanic dot-coms are discussed, including StarMedia, one of the first Hispanic dot-coms. StarMedia is also facing an uncertain future.

34568 ■ **"Tap WAP for Enterprise Mobile Solutions?"** in *E-business Advisor* (Vol. 18, No. 5, May 2000, pp. 12)
Pub: Advisor Media, Inc.
Ed: Phillip Redman. **Description:** The Wireless Internet Protocol (WAP) will greatly expand the range of mobile capabilities, enabling mobile users to connect with e-mail, database, and scheduling servers and to receive text messages. However, because WAP technology is still immature, few devices are commercially available, and little compatibility exists among browsers and gateways.

34569 ■ "Tapping the Talent Pool of Hispanic Affluence" in *Hispanic Business* **(Vol. 24, No. 1/2, January/February 2002, pp. 6)**

Pub: Hispanic Business Inc.

Ed: Jesus Chavarria. **Description:** A brief overview of the growth of Hispanic affluence in America and the important role that plays for Hispanic entrepreneurs and marketers. Hispanic Business magazine plans to organize training and educational events with sessions on Latin American trade, B2B e-commerce strategies, Hispanic online consumers, and cross-border banking.

34570 ■ "Targeting a Tighter Audience" in *Hispanic Business* **(Vol. 22, No. 1/2, January/February, pp. 90)**

Pub: Hispanic Business

Ed: Vaughn Hagerty. **Description:** Money-focused Consejero.com represents a new breed of niche sites.

34571 ■ "Taxing News" in *Entrepreneur* **(Vol. 28, No. 2, February 2000, pp. 28)**

Pub: Entrepreneur Media Inc.

Description: Government officials say they're losing sales tax revenues because of the tax-free Internet.

34572 ■ "TCHI Consulting: www.tchiconsulting.com" in *Entrepreneur* **(Vol. 31, No. 12, December 2003, pp. 8)**

Pub: Entrepreneur Media Inc.

Ed: Steve Cooper. **Description:** Profile of a Web site offering tips and resources for setting up a business office.

34573 ■ "Team Players" in *Entrepreneur* **(Vol. 33, October 2005, No. 10, pp. 85)**

Pub: Entrepreneur Media Inc.

Ed: Catherine Seda. **Description:** Questions for planning an affiliate program for marketing a business are presented, focusing on hiring Internet marketers to promote your business with no up-front costs.

34574 ■ "Tech futures: Need a map for where business goes from here?" in *Entrepreneur* **(Vol. 30, No. 1, January 2002, pp. 27)**

Pub: Entrepreneur Media Inc.

Ed: Mark Henricks. **Description:** Book reviews of the title, "The Internet Galaxy", which suggests that the Internet's influence on commerce has just begun; and "The War for Talent", which offers five imperatives that can help hire the best people for a business.

34575 ■ "Technology" in *Crain's Detroit Business* **(Vol. 16, No. 46, November 13, 2000, pp. 20)**

Pub: Crain Communications, Inc.

Ed: Katie Merx. **Description:** CareerSite Corporation, an Ann Arbor, Michigan, company that runs a recruiting Web site is profiled.

34576 ■ "Technophobe Help Desk" in *Sales & Marketing Management* **(Vol. 158, October 2006, No. 10, pp. 22)**

Pub: VNU Business Media

Description: Traditional marketing channels are based on self-reported surveys, circulation audits and promotional code tracking, however, Web analytics provide actual site traffic, including page hits, number of visits, browser usage and visitors' regional origin.

34577 ■ "Technorati www.technorati.com" in *Entrepreneur* **(Vol. 32, No. 1, January 2004, pp. 10)**

Pub: Entrepreneur Media, Inc.

Ed: Steve Cooper. **Description:** Profile of Technorati, a blog research that tracks 1 million blogs, and also offers a tool called Watchlists that monitors changes in Google rankings.

34578 ■ "Tee Off Online" in *Black Enterprise* **(Vol. 37, January 2007, No. 6, pp. 52)**

Pub: Earl G. Graves Publishing Co. Inc.

Ed: James C. Johnson. **Description:** The E-Com Resource Center is one of many resources that are available for those interested in starting an e-commerce business. One of the first steps is to create a business plan, of which there are free samples available at BPlans.com.

34579 ■ "Telecom recession may have hit bottom" in *Atlanta Business Chronicle* **(Vol. 25, January 3, 2003, No. 30, pp. 3A)**

Pub: American City Business Publications, Inc.

Ed: Mary Jane Credeur. **Description:** In the year 2003, a slight recovery in the telecom recession could be in the making. Already BellSouth Corporation and other Baby Bells have experienced a rise in stock prices. In the fourth quarter 2002, BellSouth reported a shares' gain of 43.2 percent.

34580 ■ "Telecom Trickle-Up" in *Washington Business Journal* **(Vol. 22, No. 11, July 18, 2003, pp. 27)**

Pub: Washington Business Journal

Ed: Tania Anderson. **Description:** Jerry Cady, CEO of Herndon, Virginia-based PingTone Communications, reports that the company's phone service offers cost savings for small businesses. The phone service is integrated into a company's computer network.

34581 ■ "Telecom's transformation continues in Georgia" in *Atlanta Business Chronicle* **(Vol. 25, January 10, 2003, No. 31, pp. 17A)**

Pub: American City Business Publications, Inc.

Ed: Charles Davidson. **Description:** In the midst of a drastic recession, the communications industry is poised for recovery, even though full recovery may be a long way off. Trends in telecommunications like bundling - offering an array of communications services in one package with one price - are here to stay. Wireless device usage will continue to increase.

34582 ■ "Telephony Rising" in *Home Office Computing* **(Vol. 18, No. 10, October 2000, pp. 37)**

Pub: Scholastic Inc.

Ed: William Van Winkle. **Description:** Internet telephony is a booming industry, though a young technology. Frost & Sullivan predicts that revenues from Voice over IP services will reach over $102 billion in 2005, compared with $1.5 billion in 2000. The primary attraction of Internet telephony is the cost: no cost to PC to PC calls and low cost for PC to phone calls. Voice over IP issues including quality of service, broadband usage, use in e-commerce, availability of voice over IP phones, and government regulations are discussed.

34583 ■ "Tell-A-Friend Wizard" in *Entrepreneur* **(Vol. 33, September 2005, No. 9, pp. 6)**

Pub: Entrepreneur Media Inc.

Ed: Steve Cooper. **Description:** Tell-a-Friend Wizard helps to add customized buttons to any Website that allow visitors to recommend a product or service. The service starts at $5.95 per month.

34584 ■ "The 10 Least Wired Industries" in *PC Computing* **(April 2000, pp. 64)**

Pub: Ziff-Davis Inc.

Ed: Naomi Graychase. **Description:** As of August 1999, 158 Internet companies went public, raising more than $12.9 billion and have a total market cap of $278 billion. While it has become tougher to enter the online world, there are ten industries that are still up for grabs. These ten are dry cleaners, home and building supplies, funeral services, gas companies/stations, microbreweries, pawnbrokers, piano tuners/movers, plumbers, seamstresses/tailors, and taxis.

34585 ■ "That online religion with shopping, too" in *The New York Times* **(April 6, 2000, pp. D1)**

Pub: The New York Times Company

Ed: Lori Leibovich. **Description:** Beliefnet offers spiritual services as a for-profit company.

34586 ■ "The AdStop Inc.: www.theadstop.com" in *Entrepreneur* **(Vol. 31, No. 12, December 2003, pp. 8)**

Pub: Entrepreneur Media Inc.

Ed: Steve Cooper. **Description:** Profile of The AdStop Inc. Web site that offers resources for Internet advertising to help grow a business.

34587 ■ "There's More to E-Business Than Point and Click" in *Journal of Business Strategies* **(Vol. 21, No. 5, September 2000, pp. 11)**

Pub: Center for Business and Economic Research

Ed: Jerry Savin, Dave Silberg. **Description:** Companies that create an effective Web presence can streamline operations, shorten response time to customer requests, gather more market data, increase their geographic reach, and sell more goods.

34588 ■ "They clicked, they left: why aren't your web site visitors buying?" in *Entrepreneur* **(Vol. 31, No. 4, April 2003, pp. 85)**

Pub: Entrepreneur Media Inc.

Ed: Catherine Seda. **Description:** Business owners should evaluate the entry, or landing page of Web sites to see if their ad entices people to click for more information.

34589 ■ "Think Small" in *PC Magazine* **(November 21, 2000, pp. 5a)**

Pub: Ziff-Davis Publishing Company

Ed: Sarah L. Roberts-Witt. **Description:** E-commerce enablers are offering e-procurement and B2B e-commerce geared to small businesses.

34590 ■ "Thinking Outside the Box" in *E-business Advisor* **(Vol. 18, No. 10, October 2000, pp. 8)**

Pub: Advisor Media, Inc.

Ed: Jane Falla. **Description:** The only thing we can count on is change. The trick is to make the opportunities outweigh the obstacles. The challenge is to achieve the often delicate balance of risks and rewards.

34591 ■ "This Isn't Your Teenage Daughter's Diary: Web Logs Are a Big Hit With Everyone..." in *Black Enterprise* **(Vol. 34, December 2003)**

Pub: Earl Graves Publishing Co.

Ed: Rebecca Rohan. **Description:** Blogging, or Web logging, is journaling on the Web using special software that enables users to write directly in the blog, and is now being used by businesses.

34592 ■ "This Just In" in *Crain's Detroit Business* **(Vol. 19, No. 1, January 6, 2003, pp. 1)**

Pub: Crain Communications Inc., Detroit

Description: The possible acquisition of Rootlevel Inc. by Carriersnet Group Inc. is covered. Rootlevel is a Web application and database development company while Carriersnet, is an electronic-logistics company in international shipping. The deal was triggered by the need to develop a system that connects the shipping industry via the Internet.

34593 ■ "This Means War" in *Entrepreneur* **(Vol. 31, No. 11, November 2003, pp. 94)**

Pub: Entrepreneur Media, Inc.

Ed: Jane Easter Bahls. **Description:** Computer security for online retailers is crucial to being successful. Websites vulnerable to hackers can be held responsible in a lawsuit.

34594 ■ "This will keep you up at night" in *E-business Advisor* **(Vol. 18, No. 10, October 2000, pp. 10)**

Pub: Advisor Media, Inc.

Description: Business intelligence agency Cyveillance, who works with Global 2000 firms to understand Internet opportunities and risks, reports the five key risks that threaten revenue, decrease market share, and detract from customer and brand loyalty.

34595 ■ "This V-Day, Money Can Buy You Love" in *Fortune* **(Vol. 151, February 7, 2005, No. 3, pp. 32)**

Pub: Time Inc.

Ed: Thom Holden. **Description:** Profile of the Website offering singles a virtual girlfriend or boyfriend with no strings attached. The service allows users to choose someone they can communicate with via emails, handwritten letters, chat online, or even voicemail phone messages for a period of two months.

34596 ■ **"Threat Level"** in *Entrepreneur* **(Vol. 31, No. 8, August 2003, pp. 28)**
Pub: Entrepreneur Media, Inc.
Ed: Michael Miora, Geoff Williams. **Description:** Michael Miora, CEO and founder of ContingenZ Corporation in Playa del Rey, California, discusses the threat of cyberterrorism and business. Miora's incident management and planning firm offers expertise to the National Reconnaissance Office, the government agency that builds America's spy satellites.

34597 ■ **"Three Scary Words: Buy it Used"** in *Inc.* **(September 2006, pp. 29-31)**
Pub: Gruner & Jahr USA Publishing
Ed: Max Chafkin. **Description:** Secondhand items have become more attractive to consumers. Internet auctions like eBay or listings on Crain's list have given rise to tremendous growth of these items. Manufacturers are rethinking their product life strategies as the consequences could be serious.

34598 ■ **"Three Trends for 2005"** in *Forbes* **(Vol. 175, January 31, 2005, No. 2, pp. 39)**
Pub: Forbes Magazine Inc.
Ed: Rich Karlgaard. **Description:** Video Weblogs (V-blogs) and inexpensive technology are performing business chores and offer rewards for entrepreneurs who understand how to knit these trends together.

34599 ■ **"3G Wireless Networks: Worth the Wait?"** in *E-business Advisor* **(Vol. 18, No. 7, July 2000, pp. 12)**
Pub: Advisor Media, Inc.
Ed: Phillip Redman. **Description:** Third-generation wireless networks (3G) are about to be implemented in Asia and Europe, but North American users will have to wait a few years before the technology becomes available for them.

34600 ■ **"Through the grapevine: E-mail newsletter has owners tasting profits"** in *Entrepreneur* **(Vol. 31, No. 6, June 2003, pp. 81)**
Pub: Entrepreneur Media Inc.
Ed: April Y. Pennington. **Description:** Customer relations depend on communication and many companies are using email newsletters to stay in touch with customers.

34601 ■ **"Ticket Resellers Aim to Be Top Draws"** in *Business Week Online* **(February 3, 2005)**
Pub: McGraw-Hill Companies
Ed: Sarah Lacey. **Description:** Secondary-ticket companies are competing for customers. Profiles of industry leaders and companies are provided.

34602 ■ **"Time to Collect? Tacking Taxes Onto Internet Sales Could Soon Become Mandatory"** in *Entrepreneur.com* **(Vol. 34, February 2006, No. 2)**
Pub: Entrepreneur Media Inc.
Ed: Melissa Campanelli. **Description:** Online retailers can voluntarily add sales taxes to bills originating in the 19 states that have signed onto the Streamlined Sales and Use Tax Agreement, that makes it easier for retailers doing business in multiple states to calculate, collect and remit existing use taxes.

34603 ■ **"Time Saver"** in *My Business* **(June/July 2004, pp. 54)**
Pub: My Business Magazine
Ed: Lena Basha. **Description:** Basil Scaljon, owner of an antique Oriental rug business, is able to maintain a unique selection of rugs by using the Internet to locate auctions, exhibitions and antique road shows.

34604 ■ **"Tin Whiskers"** in *Fortune* **(Vol. 151, January 10, 2005, No. 1, pp. 27)**
Pub: Time Inc.
Ed: Ivan Amato. **Description:** The loss of the Galaxy 4 communications satellite short circuited and some 40 million pagers stopped working across the U.S. Tin whiskers in electronic and electrical systems, the process by which tin grows whiskers, is little-understood and can cause systems to short circuit. The cata-

strophic consequences to radar systems, pacemakers, fuse switches in air-to-air missiles, electronic relays in a nuclear power plant, and global positioning system receivers, as well as satellites have all fallen victim to tin whiskers, costing losses in billions of dollars.

34605 ■ **"Tip of the Month"** in *E-business Advisor* **(Vol. 17, No. 12, December 1999, pp. 44)**
Pub: Advisor Media, Inc.
Ed: Larry C. Whipple. **Description:** Tips for making banner advertisements eye-catching and effective are provided. Strategies include the correct choice of colors, keeping them simple, adding words such as 'free' and 'click here' and using small files. Programming tips are also provided for dealing with browser inconsistency in Web page creation and reducing Web graphic problems.

34606 ■ **"'Tis the Season"** in *Entrepreneur* **(Vol. 32, October 2004, No. 10, pp. 52)**
Pub: Entrepreneur Media Inc.
Ed: Melissa Campanelli. **Description:** It's never too early for online retailers to prepare for the holiday season. Fulfillment and inventory operations need to be assessed.

34607 ■ *Titanium EBay: A Tactical Guide to Becoming a Millionaire PowerSeller*
Pub: Penguin Group Incorporated
Ed: Skip McGrath. **Released:** June 2006. **Price:** $24.95. **Description:** Advice is given to help anyone selling items on eBay to become a Power Seller, an award presented based on monthly gross merchandise sales.

34608 ■ **"To e- or not to e-?"** in *Crain's Detroit Business* **(Vol. 16, No. 49, December 4, 2000, pp. 13)**
Pub: Crain Communications, Inc.
Ed: Kath Usitalo. **Description:** Online merchants are competing with traditional retailers and catalogs by trying to get shoppers to purchase from their sites.

34609 ■ **"To opt or not to opt"** in *Working Woman* **(Vol. 25, No. 6, June 2000, pp. 22)**
Pub: Lang Communications Inc.
Ed: Ananda Chaudhuri. **Description:** Internet retailers are adopting a new approach to selling goods and services to consumers, known as permission-based marketing, by asking electronic mail users to agree to opt to receive advertisements.

34610 ■ **"To serve and protect: want to avoid e-commerce nightmares?"** in *Black Enterprise* **(Vol. 33, No. 3, October 2002, pp. 63)**
Pub: Earl Graves Publishing Co.
Ed: Rebecca Rohan. **Description:** Encryption, authentication, firewalls, and certificates are all strategies used to secure information when doing business on the Internet.

34611 ■ **"To Serve and Protect: Want to Avoid E-commerce Nightmares?"** in *Black Enterprise* **(Vol. 33, No. 3, October 2002, pp. 63)**
Pub: Earl Graves Publishing Co.
Ed: Rebecca Rohan. **Description:** Encryption, authentication, firewalls, and certificates are all strategies used to secure information when doing business on the Internet.

34612 ■ **"To Tell the Truth"** in *Entrepreneur* **(Vol. 32, No. 4, April 2004, pp. 40)**
Pub: Entrepreneur Media, Inc.
Ed: Eric Bender. **Description:** Ways for small businesses to protect computers from email hoaxes. Employees should report suspicious email to appropriate authorities to keep company Internet use safe.

34613 ■ **"Tollhouses & cookies"** in *Entrepreneur* **(Vol. 30, No. 2,)**
Pub: Entrepreneur Media Inc.
Ed: Amanda C. Kooser. **Description:** The World Wide Web Consortium (W3C), the standards-making body for the Internet, has proposed allowing patent holders to charge fees for technologies that become part of the Web standards.

34614 ■ **"Top of the Heap"** in *Business 2.0* **(Vol. 6, May 2005, No. 4, pp. 54)**
Pub: Time, Inc.
Ed: Andrew Tilin. **Description:** Cutting-edge logistics and electronic commerce are the key ingredients to Copart's success in the salvage business. Copart processes about 40 percent of all cars salvaged in the U.S.

34615 ■ **"A Touch of Class"** in *Entrepreneur* **(Vol. 28, No. 10, October 2000, pp. 29)**
Pub: Entrepreneur Media Inc.
Ed: Amanda C. Kooser. **Description:** E-mail has evolved into a prime marketing tool for businesses. Jupiter Communications predicts the e-mail marketing industry will reach $7.3 billion by 2005.

34616 ■ **"Tower of label"** in *Entrepreneur* **(Vol. 30, No. 3, March 2002, pp. 47)**
Pub: Entrepreneur Media Inc.
Ed: Amanda C. Kooser. **Description:** The Internet Content Rating Association supports content-labeling systems for Web sites.

34617 ■ **"Toyota-eBay Deal Opens Floodgates"** in *Automotive News* **(Vol. 78, No. 6086, March 29, 2004, pp. 20B)**
Pub: Crain Communications, Inc.
Ed: Jason Stein. **Description:** Toyota Motor Sales USA has partnered with eBay to market its vehicles on an exclusive Web page linked to the auction site.

34618 ■ **"Trade Ya This"** in *PC Magazine* **(June 6, 2000, pp. 88)**
Pub: Ziff-Davis Publishing Company
Ed: Sebastian Rupley. **Description:** Proponents of the bartering model for online commerce are quick to point out that there is a big difference between a haggling model and a bartering model, because often bartering is a cashless transaction.

34619 ■ **"Traditional vs. On-Line Learning: It's Not an Either/or Proposition"** in *Employment Relations Today* **(Vol.27, No.1, Spring 2000, pp. 47)**
Pub: John Wiley & Sons, Inc.
Ed: James H.S. Davis. **Description:** Issues discussed concern the management of corporate training programs, focusing on the use of traditional and online education techniques. Topics addressed include how to most efficiently combine classroom and Internet-based training and methodologies to offer employees the opportunity to advance their skills.

34620 ■ **"Transform Your Business Into a B2B Portal"** in *E-business Advisor* **(Vol. 18, No. 4, April 2000, pp. 14)**
Pub: Advisor Media, Inc.
Ed: Nathaniel Palmer. **Description:** The concept of the corporate portal market evolved in less than a year to become one of the hottest sectors of the software industry as companies attempt to provide single access points for business transactions and the exchange of information.

34621 ■ **"Transforming online car buying"** in *Hispanic Business* **(Vol. 22, No. 5, May 2000, pp. 100)**
Pub: Hispanic Business
Ed: Vaughn Hagerty. **Description:** DriveOff.com is a business transformation model, according to Navidec President and CEO Ralph Armijo. He indicates that he is considering other online opportunities.

34622 ■ **"Transforming TV"** in *Hispanic Business* **(Vol. 22, No. 7-8, July-August 2000, pp. 14)**
Pub: Hispanic Business
Ed: Vivienne Heines. **Description:** Houston-based International eCommerce hopes that Hipanic families will use its new NetForAll interactive TV, Internet and e-mail service. The company expects to have up to 20,000 customers in Mexico, plus a further 15,000-plus in the U.S., by the end of the year 2000.

34623 ■ "Travel Agency Business All Over the Map" in *Pacific Business News* **(Vol. 41, No. 19, July 18, 2003, pp. 10)**
Pub: American City Business Journals
Ed: Eddy Conway. Description: Challenges facing the travel industry, highlighted by the difficulties facing Total Travel Inc., are examined. Topics include economic conditions, Internet use by customers, and business losses.

34624 ■ "Travel Web sites reaching out to business" in *Atlanta Business Chronicle* **(Vol. 25, January 3, 2003, No. 30, pp. 2A)**
Pub: American City Business Publications, Inc.
Ed: Robert Mullins. Description: Business travelers are being sought after more frequently by the online travel Web sites. New services and features are cropping up in order to cater to business travelers. One such new service is called SideStep, which began in July 2002.

34625 ■ "Treat me well when I visit" in *Crain's Detroit Business* **(Vol. 18, No. 23, June 10, 20)**
Pub: Crain Communications Inc. - Detroit
Ed: Joe Novak. Description: When creating a Web site, the developer has to walk a fine line to create something functional, while also being aesthetically pleasing.

34626 ■ "Trends" in *E-business Advisor* **(Vol. 17, No. 12, December 1999, pp. 8)**
Pub: Advisor Media, Inc.
Description: New business-to-business "e-market makers" are "reintermediaries" that enter supply chains and introduce new efficiencies and ways of buying and selling products and services. According to Dataquest, a unit of Gartner Group Inc., an e-market maker is an organization that develops a business-to-business, Internet Protocol (IP) network-based e-marketplace of buyers and sellers within a particular industry, geographic region, or affinity group.

34627 ■ "Trends Tips Ideas" in *Success* **(Vol. 47, No. 6, November 2000, pp. 12)**
Pub: Success Publishing, Inc.
Description: Inadequate customer service costs sales and goodwill. On the Internet, customer service can be particularly bad. A recent report estimated that more than $6 billion in online sales was lost last year due to inadequate customer service. The recent Web entry ServiceEngine allows e-commerce businesses to offer customer service over its platform, which automates the entire customer service process.

34628 ■ "Tricks of the Trade" in *Small Business Opportunities* **(Vol. 12, No. 5, September 2000, pp. 46, 48, 102-103)**
Pub: Harris Publications, Inc.
Ed: Richard Siedlecki. Description: Designing a Web site like a direct marketer instead of using conventional marketing techniques can generate more profitable sales and help grow an Internet business more successfully.

34629 ■ "Truly 'Small' Business" in *My Business* **(June/July 2002, pp. 45)**
Pub: My Business Magazine
Ed: Doug McPherson. Description: Profile of Evan and Elise Macmillan, age 16 and 13 respectively. Evan and Elise are co-founders of The Chocolate Farm that sells chocolate candies from a Web site, which employs 30-40 part-time workers.

34630 ■ "Tying a Lucrative Knot - WeddingNetwork.com sits on the brink of database-sharing bliss" in *PC Magazine* **(February 20, 2001, pp. 17a)**
Pub: Ziff-Davis Publishing Company
Ed: Judy DeYoung. Description: WeddingNetwork. com, a Web site that has sold wedding products and services since 1998, had to reinvent its business model when sales proved slow and developed extensive personalization capabilities.

34631 ■ "Tyrannosaurus Rep?" in *Incentive* **(Vol. 174, No. 10, October 2000, pp. 21)**
Pub: Bill Communications
Ed: Kenneth Hein. Description: E-commerce is transforming the process for buying and selling premiums. Does this mean ad specialty reps are headed for extinction?

34632 ■ "Ugly Salt and Pepper Shakers Spur Buffalo, N.Y., Woman's eBay Business" in *Buffalo News* **(March 29, 2004)**
Pub: Knight-Ridder/Tribune Business News
Ed: Lisa Haarlander. Description: Profile of Wendy Merkle, owner of an eBay drop-off center. Drop-off center work like consignment shops where customers drop off merchandise to be sold on eBay and the center collects a commission.

34633 ■ "The Ultimate Business Plan" in *Success* **(Vol. 47, No. 1, January 2000, pp. 44)**
Pub: Success Publishing, Inc.
Ed: C.J. Prince. Description: Miles Spencer, co-founder of MoneyHunt Properties in Norwalk, Connecticut, and a member of the venture fund Capital Express, advises no one write your business plan but you. Included are informative tips including: The Executive Summary, Management: Who's Running This Thing?, Marketing, Financials, and Your Tone.

34634 ■ *The Ultimate Guide to Electronic Marketing for Small Business: Low-Cost/ High Return Tools and Techniques That Really Work*
Pub: John Wiley & Sons, Incorporated
Ed: Tom Antion. Released: June 2005. Price: $19.95 (US), $25.99 (Canadian). Description: Online marketing techniques for small business to grow and increase sales.

34635 ■ "Uncle Same Eases Up on Barter" in *Business Week* **(March 27, 2000, pp. F6)**
Pub: McGraw-Hill, Inc.
Description: The IRS recently ruled that businesses are no longer required report barter transactions worth less than $1, which covers much of the free and low-cost banner-ad swaps popular among small companies.

34636 ■ "United Front" in *Entrepreneur* **(Vol. 33, January 2005, No. 1, pp. 47)**
Pub: Entrepreneur Media Inc.
Ed: Mike Hogan. Description: Unified messaging (UM) or unified communications (UC) will allow voice mail, email, and instant messaging to be delivered to the same inbox.

34637 ■ "Up in the Air: Dotcom Stocks Could be Poised for a Comeback" in *Entrepreneur* **(Vol. 31, No. 10, October 2003, pp. 38)**
Pub: Entrepreneur Media, Inc.
Ed: Julie Monahan. Description: Internet stocks seem to be climbing out of the dotcom doldrums; the first half 2003 showed the first real gains in three years.

34638 ■ "Up & Comers" in *Success* **(Vol. 47, No. 2, June 2000, pp. 20)**
Pub: Success Publishing, Inc.
Description: The owner of Medicalogic, Mark Leavitt, says that the privacy of medical records is history. Subscribing doctors can now keep patients' medical records online. Patients can go online to check their record, refill a prescription, make an appointment, or get an answer to a question regarding their medical condition.

34639 ■ "Up Front" in *Business Week* **(January 16, 2006, No. 3967, pp. 11-12, 14)**
Pub: McGraw-Hill Companies
Ed: Dan Beucke. Description: Information regarding construction wages in the U.S., Chrysler's new Baby Bentley sedan, teen trends, online sales taxes, and airline competition are among the topics discussed.

34640 ■ "Up to Speed? Wireless Could be Just What the Lagging Tech Market Needs to Get Moving Again" in *Entrepreneur* **(Vol. 31, August, 2003)**
Pub: Entrepreneur Media, Inc.
Ed: Amanda C. Kooser. Description: Despite a slowing economy and the Internet bust a few years ago, technology innovation and tech spending in the area of wireless technologies is playing a substantial role, especially phone technologies and Wi-Fi.

34641 ■ "Urban Media CTO pushes broadband envelope" in *InfoWorld* **(Vol. 22, No. 23, June 5, 2000, pp. 32)**
Pub: InfoWorld
Ed: Susan E. Fisher. Description: Paul Mockapetris, the CTO of Urban Media, is currently dedicating his time to the development of the technical means to deliver broadband to small and mid-sized businesses for free. Urban Media is taking the classic loss leader approach to business. The idea is that, once customers have whet their Internet appetite on the free 200Kbps access Urban Media serves to each desktop, they will be hungry for additional goodies from the on-site service provider. The Palo Alto, California company's menu of pay services includes local and long-distance voice, managed e-mail, videoconferencing, and VPNs.

34642 ■ "Use Webcasting to Grow Your Home Business" in *Home Business* **(Vol. 12, March/April 2005, No. 2, pp. 36, 38, 60-61)**
Pub: Home Business Magazine
Ed: Dr. Jeffrey Lant. Description: Online marketing is a good way for a home business to increase sales. Webcasting allows entrepreneurs to speak live to people through a computer.

34643 ■ "Use XML to Speed Application Development" in *E-business Advisor* **(Vol. 18, No. 9, September 2000, pp. 40)**
Pub: Advisor Media, Inc.
Ed: Chris Koontz, Dave DeBald. Description: Software developers can logically group the presentation, data, and transaction requirements for multiple categories of information into discrete units of work, describable as XML documents. Thus, XML can be used to create scalable, reliable Web-based applications, while greatly reducing development, testing, and maintenance time.

34644 ■ "UserLand Software Inc." in *Inc.* **(November 15, 2000, pp. 145)**
Pub: The Goldhirsh Group
Description: A profile of UserLand Software Inc., an eight-person software company in San Francisco.

34645 ■ "Users inch to security outsourcers" in *InfoWorld* **(Vol. 23, No. 5, January 29, 2001, pp. 10)**
Pub: InfoWorld
Ed: Brian Fonseca, Heather Harreld. Description: Distributed denial of service (DDoS) attacks by hackers on the Web sites of major U.S. companies are a continuing threat. Despite these attacks, many companies maintain a low-key attitude toward network security and are not allotting the necessary funds to stave off problems. Smaller companies may feel safe, but smaller to medium-size businesses are being used as launching sites for attacks on major organizations.

34646 ■ "Venture Capital: Arthritic corporations get a chance at a second childhood" in *Red Herring* **(No. 87, December 18, 2000, pp. 40)**
Pub: Herring Communications, Inc.
Ed: Guy Paisner. Description: Ways in which venture capital firms are competing to help dot.com corporations to develop new Internet strategies is discussed.

34647 ■ "Venturelab Launches $50M Targeted Fund" in *Venture Capital Journal* **(Vol. 40, No. 10, November 2000, pp. 22)**
Pub: Venture Economics
Description: Keystone Venture VI LP will back about 25-30 information technology companies, particularly in the wireless, tool, e-commerce and affinity marketing spaces. The firm will target early expansion-stage companies.

34648 ■ "Virtual Company Achieves Actual Savings" in *Home Business* (Vol. 12, March/April 2005, No. 2, pp. 48)
Pub: Home Business Magazine
Ed: Sandy Larson. Description: Profile of Karlin Sloan, who runs her executive coaching firm from her home using a telecommuting program.

34649 ■ "Virtual Money Chain: Company Changes the Rules of Wire Transfers Through the Internet" in *Black Enterprise* (Vol.34, No.4, Nov. 2003)
Pub: Earl Graves Publishing Co.
Ed: Tamara E. Holmes. Description: Profile of the technology firm, iKobo Inc., located in Atlanta, Georgia. The company offers electronic money transfer services and merchant payments, targeting foreign service sector workers and small- to medium-size businesses.

34650 ■ "A Virtual Wallet" in *PC Magazine* (December 14, 1999, pp. 12)
Pub: Ziff-Davis Publishing Company
Ed: Gary Gunnerson. Description: Micropayments technology, or 'electronic wallets', make it possible to purchase items over the Internet without using a credit card. Because online merchants have been slow to adopt e-wallet technologies, e-wallet products are beginning to support a standard way of filling out purchase forms, often via Electronic Commerce Markup Language (ECML) standardized tags.

34651 ■ "Voyeur-cams come to home furnishings: the idea is to check out the wares" in *The New York Times* (July 6, 2000, pp. G1)
Pub: The New York Times Company
Ed: Michelle Slatella. Description: Webcams, from Perceptual Robotics, let people view merchandise over the Internet.

34652 ■ "Wacky, fake Web sites grab attention, while only slyly referring to their sponsors" in *The New York Times* (August 14, 2000, pp. C8)
Pub: The New York Times Company
Ed: Allison Fass. Description: Companies, advertisers, and pranksters have found the fun of creating fake Web sites to enhance their image and be part of the giddy alternative to e-commerce. Sun Country Airlines, with BVK McDonald invented www.heybill.com which the company plays with for "relationship marketing" as opposed to its www.suncountry.com business site. Steve Fink and Steve Casino produced the fictional www.goblertoys.com merely for their own fancy. And Ted C. Fishman's parody site, www.FreeWhellz.com, eventually sold his domain name for his fake company for $25,000.

34653 ■ "Walled In" in *Entrepreneur* (Vol. 32, No. 4, April 2004, pp. 34)
Pub: Entrepreneur Media, Inc.
Ed: Amanda C. Kooser. Description: Profile of Firebox 700 from WatchGuard Technologies, offering security to a network with broadband Internet access.

34654 ■ "Wanted: A Few Good Hackers" in *Business Week* (December 11, 2000, pp. 14)
Pub: McGraw-Hill, Inc.
Description: These days there doesn't seem to be enough good hackers interested in honest work, and that has security types worried.

34655 ■ "Wanted: E-Business Professionals" in *E-business Advisor* (Vol. 17, No. 12, December 1999, pp. 6)
Pub: Advisor Media, Inc.
Ed: Jane Falla. Description: The article offers advice for attracting the top e-business talent to your business, including Director of E-Business, E-Commerce Consultant, Director of Business Development, E-Commerce, and E-Commerce Sales Executive.

34656 ■ "A wary welcome for the Net from Kentucky artisans" in *The New York Times* (June 7, 2000, pp. D34, H34)
Pub: The New York Times Company
Ed: Emily Yellin. Description: Statistical information about the Appalachian craft artisans in Berea, Kentucky and their feelings about the Internet.

34657 ■ "Way to Give!" in *Entrepreneur* (Vol. 31, No. 9, September 2003, pp. 53)
Pub: Entrepreneur Media, Inc.
Ed: Jennifer Pellet. Description: Because of high-profile cases of mismanagement by charitable programs, small businesses might consider online contribution systems for employees to contribute to worthy causes.

34658 ■ "We Have Liftoff" in *Entrepreneur* (Vol. 32, October 2004, No. 10, pp. 104)
Pub: Entrepreneur Media Inc.
Ed: Amanda C. Kooser. Description: Profile of Pursenickety's updated Website marketing handbags. Deborah Nail shares the work involved in creating the new site that won the Entrepreneur and Interland's Tech Makeover. The new site manages the company's inventory of purses and baby bags, offers separate wholesale pricing, and handles real-time credit card transactions.

34659 ■ "We Know Where You Live" in *Forbes* (November 13, 2000, pp. 332)
Pub: Forbes Magazine
Ed: Scott Woolley. Description: Established Web firms are developing ways to determine actual physical locations of Internet addresses, in order to sell the information to advertisers and Web sites.

34660 ■ "We Know Where You Live Work Shop Bank...And So Does Everyone Else!" in *PC Computing* (March 2000, pp. 80)
Pub: Ziff-Davis Inc.
Ed: Ed Bott. Description: Internet technology brings the world to PCs, but it also delivers our private information to the world. The e-commerce practice of profiling, or gathering information about customers, is a threat to personal privacy, even though most e-commerce vendors intend only to serve their customers better.

34661 ■ "We Know Who You Are" in *PC Computing* (March 2000, pp. 84)
Pub: Ziff-Davis Inc.
Ed: Robert Strohmeyer. Description: With just a few minutes and a few dollars, online snoops can track real-world activities of people, right down to a person's current location.

34662 ■ "Wearing Her Work on Her Sleeve" in *Home Business* (Vol. 13, January/February 2006, No. 1, pp. 80)
Pub: Home Business Magazine
Ed: Sandy Larson. Description: Profile of Eileen Parzek who sells work-at-home related merchandise including t-shirts, caps, mugs, mouse pads, and clocks.

34663 ■ "Web Attack" in *Harvard Business Review* (Vol. 78, No. 5, September-October 2000, pp. 20)
Pub: Harvard Business School Publishing Corp.
Description: Protest groups produce interesting and well-designed Web sites that attack corporate policies and practices. Any corporation could be attacked in this way at any time, and often attacks remain on the Web sites even after policies have been changed.

34664 ■ "Web Audio - You Can Take It With You" in *Fast Company* (May 2001, pp. 186)
Pub: Fast Company
Ed: Alison Overholt. Description: Profile of Vequette, the streaming-audio portal that's designed with business users in mind.

34665 ■ "Web-based Accounting" in *Home Office Computing* (Vol. 18, No. 11, November 2000, pp. 71)
Pub: Scholastic Inc.
Ed: Wayne Kawamoto. Description: A software buyer's guide featuring integrated accounting software packages and Web-based services of value to the home office user. Among the featured products are BAport Accounting from BAport, the eLedger 2.0 application from Application Service Provider (ASP) eLedger, Peachtree Software's ePeachtree 2.0, Intacct, an online service that offers general ledger, accounts payable, accounts receivable, and human resources functions, NetLedger 4.0, and Bizfinity.

34666 ■ "Web-based services provide easy access to no-cost employer-sponsored discount programs" in *Employee Benefit Plan Review* (Vol.55, No. 6)
Pub: Charles D. Spencer & Associates, Inc.
Ed: Miriam Basch Scott. Description: Internet companies exist which offer employee discount programs on products and services to businesses that wish to give their workers incentives outside of the workplace.

34667 ■ "Web Dating Service for 'Down-to-Earth' Singles Debuts in Bakersfield, Calif." in *Bakersfield Californian* (December 2003)
Pub: Knight Ridder/Tribune Business News
Ed: Erin Waldner. Description: A new Internet dating service marketed for down-to-earth singles is being test marketed in Bakersfield, California.

34668 ■ "Web Expertise in Novel Locales" in *Inc.* (June 2000, pp. 123)
Pub: The Goldhirsh Group
Description: For companies that cannot afford the high price for a business Web site, unconventional alternatives are explored.

34669 ■ "Web features" in *Black Enterprise* (Vol. 32, No. 6, January 2002, pp. 8)
Pub: Earl Graves Publishing Co.
Description: Websites featuring online employment services and the best cities for African Americans are highlighted.

34670 ■ "The Web: Land of Opportunists" in *Home Office Computing* (Vol. 18, No. 10, October 2000, pp. 11)
Pub: Scholastic Inc.
Ed: Lisa Roberts. Description: The Internet has become fertile ground for scams, many of them long in use before the new technology was available to spread ideas faster. E-mails and Web sites advertising fraudulent pyramid schemes abound. The FTC says online auctions account for 50 percent of all complaints about Internet scams; sellers routinely do not deliver what they promised. Offering a free Web site for 30 days is another scam.

34671 ■ "Web mortgage sites offer loans, plenty of advice" in *Business First Columbus* (Vol. 18, No. 26, February 15, 2002, pp. 26)
Pub: Business First Columbus, Inc.
Ed: Kim Komando. Description: Profile of online mortgage sites offering valuable advice along with offers for loans.

34672 ■ "Web Retailing: The prodigal e-commerce sites return" in *Red Herring* (No. 105, October 1, 2001, pp. 96-97)
Pub: Herring Communications
Ed: Dan Briody. Description: Both Wal-Mart and Kmart announced the buy-back of their independent Web sites, Walmart.com and BlueLight.com, and are reintegrating them back into their core businesses. Statistical data included.

34673 ■ "Web Services: Connection established" in *Red Herring* (No. 105, October 1, 2001, pp. 82)
Pub: Herring Communications
Ed: Christopher Locke. Description: Profile of Web services that help small businesses integrate their Internet services with software applications to improve business-to-business markets.

34674 ■ "Web Sets Sites on TV" in *Inc.* (October 1, 2003)
Pub: Gruner & Jahr USA Publishing
Ed: Nicole Gull. Description: Michael J. Smith, CEO of Classmates.com, and a former Web entrepreneur, has leveraged his brand on television.

34675 ■ "Web Site Guides Activists" in *Motor Age* (Vol. 122, No. 11, November 2003, pp. 86)
Pub: Advantstar Communications, Inc.
Description: A new resource for auto aftermarket firms to communicate with legislative officials has been developed by the Automotive Aftermarket Industry Association (AAIA). Located in the Government section of the association's Web site, users can click on an area of interest and write to legislators.

34676 ■ "Web Sites Can Make You Look Bigger, Better" in *Crain's Detroit Business* (Vol. 21, October 17, 2005, No. 43, pp. 20)
Pub: Crain Communications Inc. - Detroit
Ed: Sheena Harrison. Description: In order to compete, a small business must use its Website as a means of marketing products and services.

34677 ■ "Web Still Rules" in *Black Enterprise* (Vol. 34, No. 7, February 2004, pp. 56)
Pub: Earl Graves Publishing Co.
Ed: Sonya A. Donaldson. Description: Ways to present a small business on a Web site are discussed, including a review of the book, "Designing Websites".

34678 ■ "Web Surveys' Hidden Hazards" in *Harvard Business Review* (Vol. 81, No. 7, July 2003, pp. 16)
Pub: Harvard Business School Press
Ed: Palmer Morrel-Samuels. Description: The advantages and disadvantages of Web-based corporate surveys are compared.

34679 ■ "A Web Wake-Up; Posting of OU Student's Paper Turns Into Lesson That Helps Define Defamation in a New Medium" in *Crain's Detroit Business*
Pub: Crain Communications Inc. - Detroit
Ed: Andrew Dietderich. Description: Posting of student papers on the Internet can be a wake-up call for small businesses. An Oakland University professor posted an essay written by a student that contained statements about the student's former employer, who sued the school, student and professor when it discovered the paper through an Internet search.

34680 ■ "Web Wise" in *Harvard Business Review* (Vol. 78, No. 3, May 2000, pp. S4)
Pub: Harvard Business School Publishing Corp.
Ed: Patricia B. Seybold. Description: Electronic commerce can be successful through the careful management of the operation.

34681 ■ "Web Wise" in *Inc.* (November 15, 2000, pp. 130)
Pub: The Goldhirsh Group
Description: The four basic categories to address in order to make the Web work for businesses are addressed.

34682 ■ "Weblining" in *Business Week* (No. 3675, April 3, 2000, pp. EB22)
Pub: McGraw-Hill, Inc.
Description: Tracking personal information using Web technology is discussed.

34683 ■ "Web.Preneuring" in *Small Business Opportunities* (Vol. 17, November 2005, No. 6, pp. 90, 94)
Pub: Harris Publications Inc.
Ed: Chuck Green. Description: Profile of Scott Kolbe and Mike Stout, entrepreneurs who started Icon Digital Design in a basement. The partners base their success on being graphic designers with strong work ethics.

34684 ■ "Website redux" in *BlackEnterprise* (Vol. 32, No. 3, October 2001, pp. 64)
Pub: Earl Graves Publishing Co.
Ed: Sonya A. Donaldson. Description: Insight into putting a business on the Web is offered.

34685 ■ "Websites and Beyond" in *Entrepreneur* (Vol. 33, October 2005, No. 10, pp. 42)
Pub: Entrepreneur Media Inc.
Description: Five tips for choosing a Web solutions provider to help grow a business are listed.

34686 ■ "Websites" in *Black Enterprise* (Vol. 34, No. 5, December 2003, pp. S8)
Pub: Earl Graves Publishing Co.
Ed: Sonya Kimble-Ellis. Description: A listing of three Web sites offering startup advice to young entrepreneurs is presented.

34687 ■ "Webwise Service" in *Small Business Opportunities* (Vol. 13, No. 6, November 2001, pp. 10)
Pub: Harris Publications, Inc.
Ed: John Tschohl. Description: A study by Anderson Consulting found that 88 percent of online shopping carts were abandoned before checkout in 1998. Ten tips for successful online companies, including customer service are outlined.

34688 ■ "Welcome to the New Economy: Act III" in *Inc.* (November 15, 2000, pp. 139)
Pub: The Goldhirsh Group
Description: Extensive review of the books "From. com to .profit" and "How Digital Is Your Business?".

34689 ■ "Well Connected" in *My Business* (June/July 2004, pp. 36-40)
Pub: My Business Magazine
Ed: Shannon Scully. Description: The question whether new online networking sites will allow business deals to happen over the Internet as on the golf course is explored.

34690 ■ "What Conservatives, Liberals, Stores and States Share" in *The New York Times* (June 7, 2000, pp. D35, H35)
Pub: The New York Times Company
Ed: David Cay Johnston. Description: E-commerce tax policy is examined. Statistical data included.

34691 ■ "What is Del.icio.us and How Is It Used?" in *Sales & Marketing Management* (Vol. 159, January-February 2007, No. 1, pp. 17)
Pub: VNU Business Media
Description: Profile of the social book-marking Web service that allows users to see saved sites of other members of the service.

34692 ■ "What Do You Risk Using a Credit Card to Shop on the Net?" in *Wall Street Journal* (December 10, 2001, pp. B1)
Pub: Wall Street Journal
Ed: Thomas E. Weber. Description: The reasons why 94.5 percent of consumers are concerned about credit card security when purchasing online are outlined; safety tips for online shoppers are also listed.

34693 ■ "What Happened to the Paperless Society?" in *Automotive News* (Vol. 20, December 6, 2004, No. 49, pp. 8)
Pub: Crain Communications Inc.
Ed: Keith Crain. Description: Amid the growing use of the Internet, many companies are still sending catalogs to customers in order to sell products.

34694 ■ "What the Internet can do for the record labels" in *Red Herring* (March 2003, pp. 24)
Pub: Herring Communications Inc.
Ed: Lawrence Lessig. Description: Congress is contemplating acts to protect the recording industry and MP3 technology, issues of paid content and archived free content are discussed.

34695 ■ "What Office?" in *Entrepreneur* (Vol. 33, October 2005, No. 10, pp. 94)
Pub: Entrepreneur Media Inc.
Ed: Nichole L. Torres. Description: Building a virtual network of employees who communicate via phone, email and fax could be just the ticket to higher profits and business growth.

34696 ■ "What Works and What Doesn't - A Job Hunter's Primer to Looking for a Job on the Internet" in *Women in Business* (Vol.54, No.3 May-Jun.)
Pub: The ABWA Co Inc.
Ed: Kathleen Isaacson. Description: Job hunting and resume placement on the Internet are discussed.

34697 ■ "Whatcom E-View Moving to New Space" in *Bellingham Business Journal* (December 2006, pp. A3)
Pub: Sun News Inc.
Description: Eview.com, an Internet-based community which serves as a consumer ratings site and local search engine, recently moved its offices to a new five-acre property.

34698 ■ "What's in a Domain Name?" in *Home Office Computing* (Vol. 18, No. 8, August 2000, pp. 81)
Pub: Scholastic Inc.
Ed: William Van Winkle. Description: The task of selecting the right domain name is a critical one for a small business. The first step in the process is to settle on a name that is appropriate for the business, then searching the various domain registration sites to determine if the name is still available. Alternative strategies using Web services to select a domain name are also discussed.

34699 ■ "What's In a Name?" in *Entrepreneur* (Vol. 32)
Pub: Entrepreneur Media Inc.
Ed: Amanda C. Kooser. Description: The new .mail domain being considered could change the way businesses send out legitimate marketing emails, however the domain does not act as an anti-spam system.

34700 ■ "What's In Your Wallet? The Smartcard Is Emerging as a Major E-Commerce Tool" in *Black Enterprise* (Vol. 36, November 2005, No. 4)
Pub: Earl G. Graves Publishing Co. Inc.
Ed: Fiona Haley. Description: The trend towards the use of Smartcard technology could make cash transactions obsolete.

34701 ■ "What's Next: Data Disasters" in *Inc.* (November 1, 2003)
Pub: Gruner & Jahr USA Publishing
Ed: Robert X. Cringely. Description: Litigation may require a small business to produce every email employees have written.

34702 ■ "What's Next: Internet Phone Service is Here" in *Inc.* (October 1, 2003)
Pub: Gruner & Jahr USA Publishing
Ed: Robert X. Cringely. Description: Good, inexpensive Internet telephone services have arrived, and small businesses are eager to use it.

34703 ■ "What's Next for The Internet" in *Venture Capital Journal* (July 1, 2003)
Pub: Thomson Financial Inc.
Description: The future of the Internet is discussed. The value of the Philadelphia Internet Index has doubled since late 2002. One industry expert estimates that so far, the Internet revolution is less than 3 percent complete.

34704 ■ "What's the Secret to Successful CRM?" in *E-business Advisor* (Vol. 18, No. 8, August 2000, pp. 41)
Pub: Advisor Media, Inc.
Ed: Renee Sommer. Description: New technologies are offering effective customer relationship management (CRM), employing interactive, two-way communications that will provide new dimensions of customer satisfaction.

34705 ■ "When Bots Collide" in *Harvard Business Review* (Vol. 78, No. 4, July 2000, pp. 17)
Pub: Harvard Business School Publishing Corp.
Ed: Jeffrey O. Kephart, Amy R. Greenwald. Description: Online users are able to automatically search the Internet to locate the cheapest price for a product or service through companies like Buy.com, Evenbetter.com, and my Simon.com.

34706 ■ "When Commerce Moves Online, Competition Can Work in Strange Ways" in *The New York Times* (August 24, 2000, pp. C2)
Pub: The New York Times Company
Ed: Hal R. Varian. Description: An overview of electronic commerce.

34707 ■ "When You Really Lose Customers" in *Entrepreneur* (Vol. 30, No. 1)
Pub: Entrepreneur Media Inc.
Ed: Melissa Campanelli. Description: A recent study shows that less than one-third of consumers notify regularly visited Web sites, online newsletters and discussion lists with new email addresses. Statistical data included.

34708 ■ **"Where Ads Aimed at Kids Come to Life"** in *The New York Times* (December 13, 2000, pp. D14, H14)
Pub: The New York Times Company
Ed: Dulcie Leimbach. **Description:** Cereal and toy companies use their Web sites to market to children.

34709 ■ **"Where Are They Now? Working, but More Calmly"** in *Wall Street Journal* (April 8, 2002, pp. A17)
Pub: Wall Street Journal
Ed: Kara Swisher. **Description:** Current information about dot-com entrepreneurs and the industry is presented.

34710 ■ **"Where Do I E-Sign?"** in *Black Enterprise* (Vol. 31, No. 5, December 2000, pp. 61)
Pub: Earl Graves Publishing Co.
Ed: Craig Owen White. **Description:** The impact of electronic signatures on small business transactions is discussed.

34711 ■ **"Where's Big Brother? Orwell's Nightmare Won't Be Coming to the Internet Anytime Soon"** in *Entrepreneur* (Vol. 31, No. 7, July 2003)
Pub: Entrepreneur Media, Inc.
Ed: Mark Henricks. **Description:** Profile of Internet Corporation for Assigned Names and Numbers (ICANN), a private global Internet regulatory body, based in Marina Del Rey, California. The firm's only concern with the setting up and running of a domain-name system and has nothing to do with Internet security in the field of cyberterrorism.

34712 ■ **"Who Needs Publishers?"** in *Inc.* (November 15, 2000, pp. 139)
Pub: The Goldhirsh Group
Description: As more people learn about the opportunity of taking their message directly to the marketplace, the better the material is likely to be. The article shares information about the Internet sites Mighty Words and Soapbox.com.

34713 ■ **"Who pays to get it there? Net Profits"** in *Entrepreneur* (Vol. 3)
Pub: Entrepreneur Media Inc.
Ed: Melissa Campanelli. **Description:** The issue of shipping and handling charges is one of the most critical facing online merchants today.

34714 ■ **"Who Wants to be an Expert?"** in *Home Office Computing* (Vol. 18, No. 8, August 2000, pp. 22)
Pub: Scholastic Inc.
Ed: Sonya Donaldson. **Description:** An explanation of Web sites offering consulting services to small business is provided, with advice for choosing the right firm.

34715 ■ **"Wholesaler plans Web expansion"** in *Hispanic Business* (Vol. 22, No. 6, June 2000, pp. 114)
Pub: Hispanic Business
Ed: Christopher D. Lancette, Scott Williams, Joel Russell. **Description:** Hispanic-owned electronic wholesaler OneSource Distributors Inc. ranks 42nd in the Hispanic Business 500 table with 1999 revenues totaling $81.7 million. The company plans to grow through electronic commerce.

34716 ■ **"Who'll Be Left Standing?"** in *Folio: the Magazine for Magazine Management* (Vol. 30, No. 1, January 2001, pp. 5)
Pub: Intertec Publishing Corp.
Description: Due to the dot-com crash, many magazine publishers will face slow advertising growth in 2001, compared with last year's booming market.

34717 ■ **"Why 'Buy' Buttons Are Booming"** in *Business 2.0* (Vol. 6, July 2005, No. 6, pp. 36)
Pub: Time, Inc.
Ed: Elizabeth Esfahani. **Description:** Three technologies to help online e-tailers to close sales include customization, online catalogs, and dynamic imaging of products.

34718 ■ **"Why Clip When You Can Clip?"** in *Kiplinger's Personal Finance Magazine* (Vol. 54, No. 9, September 2000, pp. 24)
Pub: The Kiplinger Washington Editors, Inc.
Ed: Melynda Dovel Wilcox. **Description:** A new service links online discounts with off-line merchants, thus eliminating paper coupons.

34719 ■ **"Why I Read Business Blogs Every Day"** in *Inc.* (August 2005, pp. 104-106)
Pub: Inc. Magazine
Ed: Hillary Johnson. **Description:** Business blogs are being used to mentor entrepreneurs.

34720 ■ **"Why Online Exchanges Died"** in *Inc.* (August 1, 2003)
Pub: Gruner & Jahr USA Publishing
Ed: Cara Cannella. **Description:** According to a report by the Winter 2003 edition of the California Management Review, of the 1,500 business-to-business exchanges started, only 43 percent remain in operation, citing the fact that most buyers placed a premium on long-term relationships with vendors.

34721 ■ **"Why 'Real-Time' Business Takes Real Time"** in *Fast Company* (July 2001, pp. 158)
Pub: Fast Company
Ed: George Anders. **Description:** An overview of vendors that have developed Web-based software that promises to deliver up-to-the-minute access to essential enterprise data, known as the 'real-time Internet'.

34722 ■ **"Why the Small-Business Market is the Internet's new frontier"** in *Red Herring* (No. 76, pp. 185-186, 188, 192, 194, 198-200, 202, 204)
Pub: Herring Communications, Inc.
Description: Why venture capitalists, retail investors, and many Internet companies think they can make large profits by targeting the small business market. Extensive statistical data is included with charts and graphs.

34723 ■ **"Why There's No Escaping the Blog"** in *Fortune* (Vol. 151, January 10, 2005, No. 1, pp. 44)
Pub: Time Inc.
Ed: David Kirkpatrick, Daniel Roth, Oliver Ryan. **Description:** Microsoft has unveiled a plan to develop a new service called MSN Spaces, an online software that allows users to easily create and maintain blogs on the Internet. The power of blogs and bloggers to make or break a product or service is examined.

34724 ■ **"Why Wi-Fi?"** in *Hispanic Business* (November 2003, pp. 74)
Pub: Hispanic Business
Ed: Roger Harris. **Description:** According to one author, wireless Internet access has the potential to revolutionize operations at small companies.

34725 ■ **"Wi-Fi is a Must for New Office Space on Long Island"** in *Long Island Business News* (February 13, 2004)
Pub: Dolan Media Newswires
Ed: Nick Anastasi. **Description:** Small businesses are looking for office space offering high-speed wireless technology in the form of Wi-Fi connectivity.

34726 ■ **"Wi-Fi wherever"** in *Entrepreneur* (Vol. 31, No. 5, May 2003, pp. 35)
Pub: Entrepreneur Media Inc.
Ed: Eric Bender. **Description:** Gas stations, fast-food restaurants and convenience stores may be offering Internet services to customers.

34727 ■ **"Will E-Commerce Erode Liberty?"** in *Harvard Business Review* (Vol. 78, No. 3, May 2000, pp. 189)
Pub: Harvard Business School Publishing Corp.
Ed: Carl Shapiro. **Description:** Electronic commerce regulations should be established to ensure that individuals retain their privacy and companies obey their privacy policies.

34728 ■ **"Will Presentment Growth Enliven Online Bill Pay?"** in *American Banker* (Vol. 170, February 2, 2005, No. 22, pp. 17)
Pub: Thomson Financial Media Inc.
Ed: Steve Bills. **Description:** Banks are showing a growing interest in bill-pay technology vendors for presentment capabilities that will increase the amount of people choosing online bill payment.

34729 ■ **"Win Consumers with Better Usability"** in *E-business Advisor* (Vol. 18, No. 6, June 2000, pp. 16)
Pub: Advisor Media, Inc.
Ed: Kevin Scoresby. **Description:** Web sites' lack of usability is the main reason why 40 percent of experienced Web shoppers do not complete their purchases, according to market research firm Creative Good. Companies can make their Web sites more user-friendly by hiring professional Web site developers who understand human factors, such as catering to both novice vs. proficient users.

34730 ■ **"Wine Collectors' Service Getting Better with Age"** in *San Jose Mercury News* (February 21, 2005)
Pub: Knight-Ridder/Tribune Business News
Ed: John Boudreau. **Description:** Profile of Vinfolio. com, the Web-based wine service that offers collectors features to help manage wine inventories. Its database has photos of wine labels viewed online, wine reviews and notes on wine collectors. The firm also has a 16,000-square-foot climate controlled storage facility in San Francisco. Vinfolio will also manage sales and purchases for clients.

34731 ■ **"Winemakers Toast High Court Ruling"** in *Inc.* (Volume 27, July 2005, No. 7, pp. 23)
Pub: Inc. Magazine
Ed: John Anderson. **Description:** U.S. Supreme Court ruling, effective May 16, 2005, will allow the direct sale of wine across the nation. The new ruling is expected to impact sales via the Internet.

34732 ■ **"Winning with the big box retailers"** in *Harvard Business Review* (Vol. 78, No. 5, September-October 2000, pp. 26)
Pub: Harvard Business School Publishing Corp.
Ed: David Eric, Harding Schwalm. **Description:** The relationship of window maker Pella Corporation to the Wall-Mart chain is discussed. The manufacturer offered the big-box store a focused, branded product line.

34733 ■ **"Wired generation: polls indicate Hispanics are at home in the online market"** in *Hispanic Business* (Vol. 22, No. 5, May 2000, pp. 80)
Pub: Hispanic Business
Ed: Jeff D. Vitucci, Hillary Leon. **Description:** Online shopping has become a popular activity among Hispanic Americans. Research indicates that Hispanics are more likely to spend larger sums on the Internet than other groups.

34734 ■ **"Wireless Devices: The New Marketing Frontier"** in *E-business Advisor* (Vol. 18, No. 12, December 2000, pp. 10)
Pub: Advisor Media, Inc.
Ed: Kim M. Bayne. **Description:** The explosive popularity of mobile phones, personal digital assistants (PDAs) and two-way pagers will trigger a new wave of services development for wireless devices. The potential of mobile commerce, or m-commerce, is enormous. Roughly 31 percent of the U.S. population now uses cell phones, according to the Cellular Telecommunications Industry Association.

34735 ■ **"Wireless Metropolis"** in *Entrepreneur* (Vol. 32, October 2004, No. 10, pp. 24)
Pub: Entrepreneur Media Inc.
Ed: Eric Bender. **Description:** Plans for New York State's wireless backup system will be a boon for small and mid-size companies.

34736 ■ **"Wireless Web Boom" in** *Home Office Computing* **(Vol. 18, No. 11, November 2000, pp. 37)**
Pub: Scholastic Inc.
Ed: Dan Costa. Description: Thanks in part to the emergence of WAP, wireless Web services are poised to take off in the business world. WAP-based applications are expected to dramatically increase the efficiency of home-based workers, according to Joseph Fung, chief technology officer of Blueflame, a Hackensack, New Jersey-based wireless technology consulting firm. More than any other application, e-mail access is driving the wireless boom. WAP will also be used to bring Internet Protocol-based instant messaging to wireless devices.

34737 ■ **"The Wireless Web" in** *PC Computing* **(April 2000, pp. 78)**
Pub: Ziff-Davis Inc.
Ed: Marty Jerome. Description: Wireless networking services that enable users to access the Web from wherever they happen to be are starting to appear, and many more are being developed. Web phones and handheld PCs can access stock quotes, weather and news, and ABC, ESPN, USA Today, and The Wall Street Journal are among the organizations already transmitting information to wireless devices. MapQuest.com provides maps and directions, Fodor's yields information about restaurants, and MovieFone tells what is playing at theatres. Europe and Asia, where the cellular industry has standardized on GSM, are ahead in implementation of wireless technology, but analysts say the Wireless Application Protocol (WAP) will help America catch up.

34738 ■ **"Wiring the border" in** *Hispanic Business* **(Vol. 22, No. 7-8, July-August 2000, pp. 70)**
Pub: Hispanic Business
Ed: Scott Williams. Description: The U.S.-Mexico Chamber of Commerce is backing a program that will help 200 companies along the Mexican-U.S. border to be part of the Internet revolution. The public-private partnership, known as Wiring the Border, will provide hardware, software, training and Internet access, plus business-to-business connections with major companies.

34739 ■ **"Wish I'd Thought Of That! Aim small to make it big? You bet." in** *Fortune* **(Vol. 141, No. 10, May 15, 2000, pp. F372C+)**
Pub: Time Inc.
Ed: Arlyn Tobias Gajilan. Description: Small corners of the market ignored by others can be quite lucrative. Both online and off, small players need to burrow into ever narrower niches.

34740 ■ **"With dot-coms no longer soaring, financial backers get back to basics" in** *The New York Times* **(December 18, 2000, pp. C28)**
Pub: The New York Times Company
Ed: Jonathan Burton. Description: An interview with Venture Strategy founder Joanna Rees Gallanter.

34741 ■ **"With Rootlevel closed, Carriersnet to revise shipping-software project" in** *Crain's Detroit Business* **(Vol. 19, No. 16, Apr. 21, 2003)**
Pub: Crain Communications Inc., Detroit
Ed: Andrew Dietderich. Description: Carriersnet Group Inc., located in Dearborn, Michigan, plans to announce a new strategy for a $40 million Internet-based shipping software project.

34742 ■ **"With So Many Bed and Breakfast Values on the Internet, Why Stay Home for the Holidays?" in** *PR Newswire* **(November 11, 2003)**
Pub: PR Newswire Association, Inc.
Description: Bed and Breakfast Websites are featured to help with holiday or vacation planning.

34743 ■ **"Women of interest" in** *WorkingWoman* **(Vol. 25, No. 2, February 2000, pp. S10)**
Pub: Lang Communications Inc.
Ed: Dana Asher. Description: The prediction of death for brick and mortar banks has been made in this age of e-commerce. Bank presidents Kathleen Walsh Carr and Deborah C. Wright discuss the prediction.

34744 ■ **"Work At Home" in** *Black Enterprise* **(Vol. 34, July 2004, No. 12, pp. 145)**
Pub: Earl G. Graves Publishing Co. Inc.
Ed: Tanisha A. Sykes. Description: Work at home Websites are presented to help entrepreneurs seeking work-at-home opportunities, including the International Telework Association & Council, a non-profit that holds seminars in telecommuting; work-at-home. com, presents a listing of telecommuter-friendly companies; and IDC, an advisory firm offering information about information technology and telecommuting industries.

34745 ■ **"Work at Home-More bandwidth means better performance for an important business tool called a virtual private network" in** *PC Magazine*
Pub: Ziff-Davis Publishing Company
Ed: Frank J. Derfler, Jr. Description: Virtual private network (VPN) solutions are reviewed.

34746 ■ **"Work with me" in** *WorkingWoman* **(Vol. 25, No. 6, June 2000, pp. 40)**
Pub: Lang Communications Inc.
Ed: Eilene Zimmerman. Description: Georgina Curran and Petra Vester founded Lbdtogo.com in 1999 selling little black dresses. They wish to increase turnover by forming partnerships with other electronic retailers, and are seeking advice on the best way of doing this.

34747 ■ **"Workaholic Cooks Up Site" in** *Crain's New York Business* **(Vol. 23, January 29, 2007, No. 5, pp. F3)**
Pub: Crain Communications, Inc.
Ed: Lisa Fickenscher. Description: Profile of Jason R. Finger and his Internet company, SeamlessWeb. com, a service that allows consumers and corporate employees to order food from member restaurants. Food giant, Aramark bought the firm last year.

34748 ■ **"Working virtually works for her" in** *Black Enterprise* **(Vol. 32, No. 7, February 2002, pp. 51)**
Pub: Earl Graves Publishing Co.
Ed: Bridget McCrea. Description: Profile of Victoria Parham, owner and president of Virtual Support Services LLC. Parham's firm provides administrative support, such as email and database management, travel arrangements, scheduling, and customer-relationship management and support to a national client base, all done virtually.

34749 ■ **"Working Wonders on the Web" in** *Inc.* **(October 1, 2003)**
Pub: Gruner & Jahr USA Publishing
Ed: Leigh Buchanan. Description: The Internet isn't being used for decorative marketing sites only; small companies are using the Web to run some of their most strategic operations successfully.

34750 ■ **"Workplace 2005: Telecommuting, Virtual Offices, Dispersed Staff..." in** *Entrepreneur* **(Vol. 33, February 2005, No. 2, pp. 55)**
Pub: Entrepreneur Media Inc.
Ed: Amanda C. Kooser. Description: Overview of new trends and technologies to help a small business is presented. Several entrepreneurs offer insight into technologies that help them run their companies in an ever-changing business environment.

34751 ■ **"Wrestling for Web dominance" in** *Hispanic Business* **(Vol. 22, No. 7-8, July-August 2000, pp. 106)**
Pub: Hispanic Business
Ed: Vaughn Hagerty. Description: Global consolidation is taking place among the Internet's Hispanic-targeted Web sites. Among the companies set to gain a dominant position in the sector is Spanish telecom provider Terra Networks with its proposed $12.5 billion acquisition of Web service provider Lycos.

34752 ■ **"Writing her own e-ticket" in** *WorkingWoman* **(Vol. 25, No. 8, September 2000, pp. 20)**
Pub: Lang Communications Inc.
Ed: Susan Caminiti. Description: Priceline.com Chief Financial Officer (CFO) Heidi Miller talks about her plans for new role and of leaving Citigroup where she was also CFO.

34753 ■ **"Xign's Order-to-Pay Service Aims to Save Time, Money" in** *eWeek* **(February 2, 2005)**
Pub: Ziff Davis Media Inc.
Description: Profile of Xign Payment Services Network (XPSN), an electronic order delivery system that also processes invoices and payment services for business-to-business commerce.

34754 ■ **"XML for All" in** *Entrepreneur* **(Vol. 28, No. 11, November 2000, pp. 28)**
Pub: Entrepreneur Media Inc.
Ed: Amanda C. Kooser. Description: XML is the leading contender to replace HyperText Markup Language (HTML). Extensible Markup Language is more versatile than HTML, and allows for more advanced e-business applications on the Web.

34755 ■ **"XML offers flexibility, ebXML sorts it out" in** *Crain's Detroit Business* **(Vol. 16, No. 47, November 13, 2000, pp. 18)**
Pub: Crain Communications, Inc.
Ed: Jeffrey Kosseff. Description: Computer language that allows flexibility in communicating data is explored.

34756 ■ **"XML: The Only Chance for a Worldwide Standard" in** *E-business Advisor* **(Vol. 18, No. 4, April 2000, pp. 10)**
Pub: Advisor Media, Inc.
Ed: Rik Drummond. Description: The second meeting of the Electronic Business XML (ebXML) Initiative to produce a global standard for e-commerce was held in February 2000. There are eight project teams in ebXML. Activities of the project teams, are presented with special emphasis on the Transport/Routing and Packaging team, aimed at developing technical specifications for the e-commerce server intercommunications architecture are presented.

34757 ■ **"XML: What's Still Needed for B2B?" in** *E-business Advisor* **(Vol. 18, No. 5, May 2000, pp. 44)**
Pub: Advisor Media, Inc.
Ed: Rik Drummond. Description: Order fulfillment is an important component of B2B e-commerce and involved integration of many underlying applications. IT and business managers are finding XML to be a preferred means of integrating applications together into processes. The issues of security, semantics, and the choreography of how the applications interact with each other are discussed.

34758 ■ **"Y2K disasters? Never mind: Glitch fixers head for e-commerce opportunities" in** *Crain's Detroit Business* **(Vol. 16,No. 3, Jan. 17, 2000)**
Pub: Crain Communications, Inc.
Ed: Matt Roush. Description: The effects of the Y2K threat, and how computer companies that helped companies prepare for the new millennium are filling the gap with e-commerce.

34759 ■ **"Yahoo! Hooks Up with H&S to Promote Dating Service" in** *PR Week* **(August 18, 2003, pp. 3)**
Pub: Haymarket Business Publications Ltd.
Description: Online dating has proved to be very lucrative for Yahoo! The company reports that 70 percent of the company's subscription revenues come from four services, one of which is personal sites.

34760 ■ **"Yaknow?" in** *Entrepreneur* **(Vol. 28, No. 10, October 2000, pp. 15)**
Pub: Entrepreneur Media Inc.
Ed: Cynthia Harrington. Description: In the quickly evolving e-business world, one of the most important tasks facing netpreneurs is education. The latest changes in technology, marketing trends, evolving business models and financing deals are high priorities.

34761 ■ "You paid that bill with a single click. Or did you?" in *The New York Times* (July 2, 2000, pp. BU10)
Pub: The New York Times Company
Ed: Nancy Lloyd. Description: The problems with electronic bill paying are examined.

34762 ■ "You Data, Naked On the Net; What's Jeopardizing Your Privacy?" in *Business Week* (February 20, 2006, No. 3972)
Pub: McGraw-Hill Companies
Ed: Stephen H. Wildstrom. Description: Web sites are limited only by their privacy policies when obtaining information from users; the European Union Privacy Directive offers better protection to its residents than the U.S.

34763 ■ "Young Millionaires: Class of 2004" in *Entrepreneur* (Vol. 32, November 2004, No. 11, pp. 77)
Pub: Entrepreneur Media Inc.
Ed: Amanda C. Kooser, April Y. Pennington, Jonathan Riggs, Nichole L. Torres, Sara Wilson. Description: Profiles of successful entrepreneurs include Cristina Bartolucci and Laura Deluisa, manufacturers of specialty makeup and body creams; Ashton Palmer and Kristy Royce, founders of an Internet-based adventure travel company; Bernard Frei, who sells soccer and rugby apparel online; Christopher Faulkner, a Web-hosting and data center infrastructure provider; Marco and Sandra Johnson, who founded an accredited medical college; Shawn Nelson, owner of modular furniture stores; a media advertising company; James P. Funderburk Jr., owner of clothing stores, a private nightclub and real estate company; and a firm that manages online sites for clothing manufacturers.

34764 ■ "Your Boss is Watching" in *PC Computing* (March 2000, pp. 86)
Pub: Ziff-Davis Inc.
Description: Web monitoring software is used by 45 percent of all companies and 17 percent of Fortune 1000 companies to make sure employees are not misusing the Web while at work. The WinWhatWhere Investigator software can record every keystroke an employee enters on a PC, while Elron Software's CommandView has the Message Inspector module that filters, stores and blocks emails at the network server. The article recommends that employees should minimize non-business-related web browsing on the company's computer.

34765 ■ "Your Browser is Selling You Out" in *PC Computing* (March 2000, pp. 90)
Pub: Ziff-Davis Inc.
Description: The most dangerous threats to personal privacy while online are cookies, even though they hold only the personal information people volunteer and report to a single site. A report by the Electronic Privacy Information Center found that the top 1000 electronic commerce sites all collect personal information, and 86 use cookies, but only 21 of the sites appear to limit use of personal information to a specific transaction, and more than one-third use profile-based advertising without warning customers.

34766 ■ "Your Business needs to be E-Commerce - so what now?" in *Ingram's* (Vol. 27, No. 7, July 2001, pp. 19)
Pub: Show Me Publishing, Inc.
Description: Management techniques and theory are outlined for e-commerce management. Some techniques include treating online and offline sales the same way, organize and prioritize what the Website needs to accomplish, and consider market potential.

34767 ■ "Your Story Here" in *Black Enterprise* (Vol. 36, February 2006, No. 7, pp. 57)
Pub: Earl G. Graves Publishing Co. Inc.
Ed: Kenneth Meeks. Description: BlackNews.com will feature a press release on its Website, an email and fax to every African American newspaper, magazine, radio station and TV station for only $150. Diversity City Media Inc., the multicultural marketing and public relations firm not only runs the Website, but also Black PR.com a press release distribution service.

34768 ■ "Yourshop@Black Enterprise.com" in *Black Enterprise* (Vol. 31, No. 2, September 2000, pp. 215)
Pub: Earl Graves Publishing Co.
Ed: Dorett Smith. Description: Small business can join the e-commerce revolution. If you are considering a Web presence to sell your company's products online, you'll need to weigh a number of factors related to e-business planning, such as productivity and functionality, advertising, sales, and service.

34769 ■ "Zap It!" in *Entrepreneur* (Vol. 28, No. 2, February 2000, pp. 28)
Pub: Entrepreneur Media Inc.
Description: No more hassling with monstrous files, one click does the trick. To end the aggravation, try downloading Hermes.

34770 ■ "Zone of Defense" in *Entrepreneur* (Vol. 32, No. 4, April 2004, pp. 42)
Pub: Entrepreneur Media, Inc.
Ed: Amanda C. Kooser. Description: Profile of ZoneAlarm Pro, a firewall to protect computers from everything from worms to spyware, as well as ad-blockers and cookie controls.

34771 ■ "ZoomInfo" in *Entrepreneur* (Vol. 33, September 2005, No. 9, pp. 6)
Pub: Entrepreneur Media Inc.
Ed: Steve Cooper. Description: ZoomInfo offers a people-summarization search engine that provides personnel information such as employment history and contact information for free; a premium search engine will also narrow the search by geographic location, title and education level for $99 annually.

TRADE PERIODICALS

34772 ■ *Business 2.0*
Pub: eCompany Now
Contact: Amy Pietrasanta, Business Mgr
Released: Monthly. Price: $6.99; $10 two years; $9.65 Canada; $13.75 two years in Canada. Description: Trade magazine covering electronic commerce and business.

TRADE SHOWS AND CONVENTIONS

34773 ■ NetExpo Washington
Lindsay Communications Group, Inc.
2032 Virginia Ave.
McLean, VA 22101-4940
Ph:(703)536-2100
Fax: (703)536-2101
Released: Annual. Audience: Buyers of e-business services. Principal Exhibits: Companies offering e-business products and services for the B2B marketplace.

CONSULTANTS

34774 ■ Digital Deli Inc.
3145 Geary Blvd., Ste. 532
San Francisco, CA 94118
Ph:(415)992-8077
Free: 800-557-3354
Fax: (415)217-3636
Co. E-mail: sales@thedeli.com
URL: http://www.theDeli.com

E-mail: sales@thedeli.com
Scope: Specializes in interactive marketing development. Provides strategic and tactical planning for interactive media.

34775 ■ Digitas Inc.
33 Arch St.
Boston, MA 02199
Ph:(617)867-1000

Fax: (617)867-1111
Co. E-mail: contactus@digitas.com
URL: http://www.digitas.com

E-mail: contactus@digitas.com
Scope: Helps clients determine how to use the Internet and emerging technologies to create new business models and enterprise-wide customer value propositions to gain competitive advantages, improved market share, and enhanced profitability. Technology, Architecture, and Infrastructure Service Marketing and Creative Services are focused on enabling brands to connect with the right customer at the right time through the right channels in the most effective way possible. Performance Measurement provides the ultimate yardstick and continuous feedback mechanisms.

34776 ■ HyperClick Online Services
PO Box 235555
Honolulu, HI 96823-3509
Ph:(808)539-2545
Co. E-mail: hyperclick@hawaii.rr.com
URL: http://home.hawaii.rr.com/hyperclick

E-mail: hyperclick@hawaii.rr.com
Scope: An information management consulting firm that offers customized digital information products, services, and training. Specializes in building educational and business solutions for real-world end-users. Provides distance learning consultation and courseware; web publishing, web site analysis and evaluation reports; digitized collections; Internet training; online research and reference; information architecture, content development and interactivity; editing and copy-editing. Publications: "Pssst! Anybody Listening? Handheld Audio May Be the Next Big Thing," EContent, Jul, 2001; "It's a Small World After All: Content for Wireless & Mobile Appliances," EContent, May, 2001; "Click to Talk: Web Phones Spell OpportunIPy for Libraries," Online, Feb, 2001.

34777 ■ Inspired Arts Inc.
4225 Executive Sq., Ste. 1160
La Jolla, CA 92037
Ph:(619)623-3525
Free: 800-851-4394
Fax: (619)623-3534
Co. E-mail: info@inspiredarts.com

E-mail: info@inspiredarts.com
Scope: Provider of Internet business solutions and web design services. Specializes in Internet business plans, web site development, e-business and online marketing. Seminars: E-Commerce: Gone with the Net; The E-Business Buzz; Online Marketing: The Second Ten Commandments.

34778 ■ The Kelsey Group Inc.
600 Executive Dr.
Princeton, NJ 08540-1528
Ph:(609)921-7200
Fax: (609)921-2112
Co. E-mail: tkg@kelseygroup.com
URL: http://www.kelseygroup.com

E-mail: tkg@kelseygroup.com
Scope: A provider of research and fact-based analysis focusing on local advertising and electronic commerce.

34779 ■ Organic Inc.
555 Market St., 4th Fl.
San Francisco, CA 94105
Ph:(415)581-5300
Fax: (415)581-5400
Co. E-mail: newbiz@organic.com
URL: http://www.organic.com

E-mail: newbiz@organic.com
Scope: Strategic consulting, e-business, marketing solutions, e-commerce website creation, customer service and fulfillment.

34780 ■ Sapient Corp.
25 1st St.
Cambridge, MA 02141

Ph:(617)621-0200
Fax: (617)621-1300
Co. E-mail: info@sapient.com
URL: http://www.sapient.com

E-mail: info@sapient.com
Scope: An innovative e-services consultancy providing Internet strategy consulting and sophisticated Internet-based solutions to Global 1000 companies and start-up businesses.

34781 ■ Spherix Inc.
12051 Indian Creek Ct.
Beltsville, MD 20705
Ph:(301)419-3900
Fax: (301)210-4909
Co. E-mail: info@spherix.com
URL: http://www.biospherics.com

E-mail: info@spherix.com
Scope: Teleservices, ebusinesses, and IT solutions for the health and information industries.

34782 ■ Sterling Strategies Corp.
1821 Walden Office Sq.
Schaumburg, IL 60173
Ph:(847)431-0675
Fax: (847)517-6354
Co. E-mail: info@sterlingstrategies.com
URL: http://www.sterlingstrategies.com

E-mail: info@sterlingstrategies.com
Scope: A management consulting firm providing strategic planning services to the information technology industry.

34783 ■ Stratamar Inc.
5661 Seapine Rd.
Hilliard, OH 43026
Ph:(614)529-2945
Fax: (614)529-2945
Co. E-mail: info@stratamar.com
URL: http://www.stratamar.com

E-mail: info@stratamar.com
Scope: A full-spectrum strategic marketing consulting company. Areas of concentration include product development, product management, strategic planning,

development and implementation of tactical marketing plans, and internet marketing. The primary focus is upon maximizing the benefit/cost ratio of promotions through the use of direct marketing, low cost media, and the like. **Publications:** Newsletter:"Business Plans", February, 2006. **Special Services:** Includes web page designing and hosting services via an affiliate, Designing Web.

34784 ■ Xpedior Inc.
1 N Franklin St., Ste. 1500
Chicago, IL 60606
Ph:(312)251-2000
Free: 877-973-3467
Fax: (312)251-2999
URL: http://www.xpedior.com
Scope: Provides comprehensive eBusiness solutions to Global 2000 companies and emerging Internet businesses. eBusiness solutions integrate one or more of the following services, customized to fit a client's needs: digital business strategy, electronic commerce, digital branding and user experience design, ebusiness applications and integration, ebusiness technology management, ebusiness networks, ebusiness intelligence, and enterprise portals and knowledge management.

FRANCHISES AND BUSINESS OPPORTUNITIES

34785 ■ There it Was...Gone!
871 Victoria St. N, Unit 4
Kitchener, ON, Canada N2B 3S4
Ph:(519)745-4663
Free: 877-310-3229
Fax: (519)745-5229
Co. E-mail: franchise@thereitwasgone.com
URL: http://www.thereitwasgone.com
No. of Company-Owned Units: 1. **Founded:** 2005. **Franchised:** 2006. **Description:** Turns the worldwide untitled demand for eBay into serious profit. **Equity Capital Needed:** $75,000-$150,000. **Franchise Fee:** $25,000.

COMPUTERIZED DATABASES

34786 ■ *BtoB*
Crain Communications Inc.
1155 Gratiot Ave.
Detroit, MI 48207
Ph:(313)446-6000
Free: 800-678-2427
Fax: (313)446-0361
Co. E-mail: info@crain.com
URL: http://www.crain.com
Description: Contains news, articles, and features from the monthly print version of *BtoB*, as well as content exclusive to the online version. Contains daily news reports, analysis, and articles on business-to-business marketing and related issues. Includes coverage of e-commerce and current business events. Includes editorials and feature articles from the monthly magazine. **Availability:** Online: Crain Communications Inc. **Type:** Full text.

34787 ■ *Internet Law & Regulation*
Pike and Fischer Inc.
1010 Wayne Ave., Ste. 1400
Silver Spring, MD 20910
Ph:(301)562-1530
Free: 800-255-8131
Fax: (301)562-1521
Co. E-mail: customercare@pf.com
URL: http://www.pf.com
Description: Contains more than 500 laws, regulations, pleadings, and decisions related to Internet law and regulation. Focuses on United States statutes and regulations, European directives and conventions, and non-governmental policies affecting the Internet. Includes decisions from federal and state courts and administrative agencies, opinions from local and non-U.S. courts and agencies, and relevant briefs and motions. Includes the full text of cases, decisions, and other documents. Includes material on such areas as electronic commerce, freedom of speech, taxation, intellectual property, encryption, privacy, criminal liability, and other areas, all directly related to life and business on the Internet and World Wide Web. Includes full-text search capability. **Availability:** Online: Pike and Fischer Inc. **Type:** Full text; Bibliographic.

EDUCATIONAL PROGRAMS

34788 ■ AMA's Advanced Executive Leadership Program
American Management Association
1601 Broadway
New York, NY 10019
Ph:(212)586-8100
Free: 800-262-9699
Fax: (212)903-8168
Co. E-mail: customerservice@amanet.org
URL: http://www.amanet.org
Price: $2,195 for non-members; $1,995 for AMA members. **Description:** For managers who want effective leadership skills; covers motivational techniques, and practices to further corporate success. **Locations:** New York, NY; Chicago, IL; Atlanta, GA; Hilton Head Island, SC; and San Francisco, CA.

34789 ■ Developing Leaders at All Levels
American Management Association
1601 Broadway
New York, NY 10019
Ph:(212)586-8100
Free: 800-262-9699
Fax: (212)903-8168
Co. E-mail: customerservice@amanet.org
URL: http://www.amanet.org
Price: $1,795 for non-members; $1,595 for AMA members. **Description:** Covers the qualities needed at all levels of an organization, including self-motivation and confidence, accept and delegate responsibility, and accountability. **Locations:** New York, NY; Chicago, IL; Atlanta, GA; Washington, DC; and San Francisco, CA.

34790 ■ The Effective Facilitator: Maximizing Involvement and Results
American Management Association
1601 Broadway
New York, NY 10019
Ph:(212)586-8100
Free: 800-262-9699
Fax: (212)903-8168
Co. E-mail: customerservice@amanet.org
URL: http://www.amanet.org
Price: $1,795.00 for non-members; $1,595.00 for AMA members. **Description:** Covers achieving positive results in group settings such as meetings, project teams, and group work projects. **Locations:** Washington, DC; Atlanta, GA; and New York, NY.

34791 ■ The Effective Facilitator: Maximizing Involvement and Results (Canada)
Canadian Management Centre
150 York St., 5th Fl.
Toronto, ON, Canada M5H 3S5
Ph:(416)214-5678
Free: 800-262-9699
Fax: (416)313-4985
Co. E-mail: cmcinfo@cmctraining.org
URL: http://cmcamai.org
Price: $1,850.00 Canadian. **Description:** Covers achieving positive results in group settings such as meetings, project teams, and group work projects. **Locations:** Toronto, ON.

34792 ■ Effective Project Leadership: Building High Commitment Through Superior Communication (Canada)
Canadian Management Centre
150 York St., 5th Fl.
Toronto, ON, Canada M5H 3S5
Free: 877-CMC-2500
Fax: (416)313-4985
Co. E-mail: cmcinfo@cmctraining.org
URL: http://www.cma.org
Price: $1,895 Canadian. **Description:** Seminar that develops skills to build team commitment creating a predictable project environment that leads to completion of projects on time and within the budget. **Locations:** Toronto, ON.

34793 ■ The Essential Administrative Professional: The Skills and Know-How to Make You Invaluable
American Management Association
1601 Broadway
New York, NY 10019
Ph:(212)586-8100
Free: 800-262-9699
Fax: (212)903-8168
Co. E-mail: customerservice@amanet.org
URL: http://www.amanet.org
Price: $1,495.00 for non-members; $1,395.00 for AMA members. **Description:** Covers adapting to a changing role as the organization changes, confidence in performing new tasks, communication, and developing a positive attitude. **Locations:** Washington, DC.

34794 ■ Greater Productivity Through Improved Work Processes: A Guide for Administrative Professionals
American Management Association
1601 Broadway
New York, NY 10019
Ph:(212)586-8100
Free: 800-262-9699
Fax: (212)903-8168
Co. E-mail: customerservice@amanet.org
URL: http://www.amanet.org
Price: $1,345.00 for non-members; $1,245.00 for AMA members. **Description:** Two-day seminar for administrative professionals with three or more years of experience; covers increasing productivity and efficiency, dealing with change, improving your work, and assisting in improving various aspects of the organization. **Locations:** New York, NY.

34795 ■ How to Work Most Effectively with Your Boss
American Management Association
1601 Broadway
New York, NY 10019
Ph:(212)586-8100
Free: 800-262-9699
Fax: (212)903-8168
Co. E-mail: customerservice@amanet.org
URL: http://www.amanet.org
Price: $1,695 for non-members; $1,495 for AMA members. **Description:** Covers positive interaction with your boss to create a productive, and efficient work environment. **Locations:** New York, NY; San Francisco, CA; Chicago, IL; and Atlanta, GA.

34796 ■ Leadership and Team Development for Managerial Success (Canada)
Canadian Management Centre
150 York St., 5th Fl.
Toronto, ON, Canada M5H 3S5
Free: 877-CMC-2500
Fax: (416)313-4985
Co. E-mail: cmcinfo@cmctraining.org
URL: http://www.cma.org
Price: $1,695 Canadian. **Description:** Covers how to work in a horizontal mode of operation, including when to manage and when to lead your team, distinguishing the three team types, principles that make teams work, differentiating team content and process, and diagnosing work teams. **Locations:** Toronto, ON.

34797 ■ Motivating for Results: Bringing Out the Best in People
American Management Association
1601 Broadway
New York, NY 10019
Ph:(212)586-8100
Free: 800-262-9699
Fax: (212)903-8168
Co. E-mail: customerservice@amanet.org
URL: http://www.amanet.org
Price: $1,695.00 for non-members; $1,495.00 for AMA members. **Description:** Covers the benefits of high morale and a motivated team, overcoming motivational setbacks, increasing creativity, and motivational techniques. **Locations:** Chicago, IL.

34798 ■ Motivating for Results: Bringing Out the Best in People (Canada)
Canadian Management Centre
150 York St., 5th Fl.
Toronto, ON, Canada M5H 3S5
Ph:(416)214-5678
Free: 800-262-9699
Fax: (416)313-4985
Co. E-mail: cmcinfo@cmctraining.org
URL: http://cmcamai.org
Price: $1,695.00 Canadian. **Description:** Covers adapting a leadership style to effectively motivate others, solving motivation problems, key motivators, and setting and attaining goals. **Locations:** Toronto, ON.

34799 ■ Partnering with Your Boss: Strategic Skills for Administrative Professionals
American Management Association
1601 Broadway
New York, NY 10019
Ph:(212)586-8100
Free: 800-262-9699
Fax: (212)903-8168
Co. E-mail: customerservice@amanet.org
URL: http://www.amanet.org
Price: $1,345.00 for non-members; $1,245.00 for AMA members. **Description:** Covers skills for setting goals, prioritizing, making decisions, building relationships, and communicating in such a way as to repre-

sent your boss authoritatively and gain respect in the workplace. **Locations:** Anaheim, CA; San Francisco, CA; Washington, DC; Chicago, IL; Morristown, NJ; and New York, NY.

34800 ■ Power Thinking for powerful Results
American Management Association
1601 Broadway
New York, NY 10019
Ph:(212)586-8100
Free: 800-262-9699
Fax: (212)903-8168
Co. E-mail: customerservice@amanet.org
URL: http://www.amanet.org
Price: $1,795 for non-members; $1,595 for AMA members. **Description:** Covers problem solving, generating of innovative ideas, effective decision making skills, and learn how to understand the different thought patterns. **Locations:** New York, NY; Chicago, IL; Atlanta, GA; Orlando, FL; Washington, DC; and San Francisco, CA.

34801 ■ Projecting a Positive Professional Image
American Management Association
1601 Broadway
New York, NY 10019
Ph:(212)586-8100
Free: 800-262-9699
Fax: (212)903-8168
Co. E-mail: customerservice@amanet.org
URL: http://www.amanet.org
Price: $1,545.00 for non-members; $1,395.00 for AMA members. **Description:** Covers creating a self-image, including look, dress, and behavior, to project a positive image in your current position and to advance to new positions. **Locations:** Atlanta, GA; and New York, NY.

34802 ■ Situational Leadership II Workshop
American Management Association
1601 Broadway
New York, NY 10019
Ph:(212)586-8100
Free: 800-262-9699
Fax: (212)903-8168
Co. E-mail: customerservice@amanet.org
URL: http://www.amanet.org
Price: $1,895 for non-members; $1,695 for AMA members. **Description:** For individuals in leadership positions; that covers building relationships through delegating, supporting, coaching, and directing. **Locations:** New York, NY; Chicago, IL; Atlanta, GA; Washington, DC; and San Francisco, CA.

34803 ■ Strategic Planning (Canada)
Canadian Management Centre
150 York St., 5th Fl.
Toronto, ON, Canada M5H 3S5
Ph:(416)214-5678
Free: 800-262-9699
Fax: (416)313-4985
Co. E-mail: cmcinfo@cmctraining.org
URL: http://cmcamai.org
Price: $1,995.00 Canadian. **Description:** Covers the strategic planning process, identifying threats and opportunities for your company, and developing strategies and action plans. **Locations:** Toronto, ON.

REFERENCE WORKS

34804 ■ "The 100 Best Companies To Work For" in *Fortune* (Vol. 151, January 24, 2005, No. 2, pp. 72)
Pub: Time Inc.
Ed: Robert Levering, Milton Moskowitz, Ann Harrington, Nadira A. Hira, Christopher Tkaczyk. **Description:** Complete listing of the best 100 companies to work for in the U.S. is presented. Businesses are categorized by large company, 10,000-plus employees; midsize, 2,500 to 10,000 employees; and small, 1,000 to 2,500 employees. Republic Bancorp topped out as number one small company, followed by Xilinx and Griffin Hospital.

34805 ■ "The Activist Ingredient" in *Inc.* (July 1, 2003)
Pub: Gruner & Jahr USA Publishing
Ed: Bobbie Gossage. **Description:** Paul Osterman of the Sloan School of Management at MIT suggests that managers take lessons from grassroots political groups to avoid employee burnout while maintaining growth.

34806 ■ *The Adventures of a Self-Managing Team*
Pub: Pfeiffer & Co.
Ed: Mark Kelly. **Price:** $16.95 (paper). **Description:** A "novelette" that serves as a quick introduction to teaming and its benefits.

34807 ■ "All in a day's work" in *Harvard Business Review* (Vol. 79, No. 11, December 2001, pp. 54)
Pub: Harvard Business School Press
Description: A roundtable discussion with six experts from the corporate world, the nonprofit sector, and academia on tough questions about leadership is presented. Three common themes emerged: the need for a leader to formulate and communicate a vision for the organization, the need for the leader to add value to an enterprise and the organizational imperative for the leader to motivate followers.

34808 ■ *Alpha Dogs: How Your Small Business Can Become a Leader of the Pack*
Pub: HarperInformation
Ed: Donna Fenn. **Released:** December 2005. **Price:** $24.95. **Description:** Ways for an entrepreneur to outsmart competitors in the marketplace, to generate higher sales, and earn lasting customer and employee loyalty.

34809 ■ "Always Say Thank You" in *Incentive* (Vol. 175, No. 10, October 2001, pp. S14)
Pub: VNU Business Media
Description: According to an Accountemps survey, 1,400 corporate financial executives reported that they used financial rewards and/or regular communication with staff to motivate their workers.

34810 ■ "American Dreamers Nominations Due Thursday" in *Crain's Detroit Business* (Vol. 22, December 11, 2006, No. 50, pp. 9)
Pub: Crain Communications Inc. - Detroit
Description: Detroit was built on the hopes and dreams of many immigrants from other countries. Nominations of business successes of first-generation immigrants are ending soon and will be listed in March, 2007.

34811 ■ "Angling for workplace fun" in *Incentive* (Vol. 174, No. 10, October 2000, pp. 135)
Pub: Bill Communications
Ed: Phil Strand. **Description:** A motivational video shown to customer service employees, helped Sprint surpass employee retention goals and improve its customer service rating. The video was produced by ChartHouse Learning Video, and is called FISH! It was filmed at a Seattle world-famous fish market.

34812 ■ "Are American workers vacation deprived?" in *Incentive* (Vol. 174, No. 9, September 2000, pp. 7)
Pub: Bill Communications
Ed: Jeanie Casison. **Description:** Behind the booming economy lies the reality of over-worked and burned out employees working an average 50 hours per week. An initiative to make three week vacations mandatory is discussed, listing a website where readers can sign a petition.

34813 ■ "As virtual teaming arrives, discipline still an essential" in *Atlanta Business Chronicle* (Vol. 24, No. 13, August 31, 2001, pp. 42A)
Pub: American City Business Journals Inc.
Ed: Alf Nucifora. **Description:** Douglas Smith and Jon Katzenbach discuss their recent book, 'The Discipline of Teams', focusing on virtual teaming.

34814 ■ "Ask Inc. Profit Sharing" in *Inc.* (September 2006, pp. 53)
Pub: Gruner & Jahr USA Publishing
Description: Profit sharing plans can be changed without upsetting your employees. Numerous hints and strategies are provided to address this question

34815 ■ "Assemble Your E-Business Team" in *E-business Advisor* (Vol. 17, No. 12, December 1999, pp. 30)
Pub: Advisor Media, Inc.
Ed: Zachary W. Esper. **Description:** Electronic business projects must be carefully staffed and managed. Traditional project structures work well, consisting of steering committee, project leader and supporting management team. Business-to-business projects can be led by operations or procurement managers. MIS managers, who traditionally maintain corporate Web sites, make good leaders for non-transactional Internet projects.

34816 ■ *Assessing Your Team: 7 Measures of Team Success*
Pub: Pfeiffer & Co.
Ed: Dick Richards and Susan Smyth. **Price:** $24.95 (Leader's Package); $9.95 (each additional Team Member Manual). **Description:** Leader's Package includes one Team Leader's Manual and one Team Member Manual. Reveals your team's strengths and weaknesses, focusing on the team as opposed to individual performance.

34817 ■ "At-work weight watchers programs gain popularity" in *Business First Columbus* (Vol. 18, No. 26, February 15, 2002, pp. B5)
Pub: Business First Columbus, Inc.
Ed: Jon E. Hale. **Description:** Profile of the new Weight Watchers' At Work Program.

34818 ■ "Attract Stragglers" in *Sales & Marketing Management* (Vol. 159, January-February 2007, No. 1, pp. 14)
Pub: VNU Business Media
Ed: Leo Jakobson. **Description:** Employee sales incentive programs are profiled.

34819 ■ "Avoiding a Communication Breakdown: Keeping Employees Informed Benefits Business" in *Black Enterprise* (Vol. 34, September 2003)
Pub: Earl Graves Publishing Co.
Ed: John G. Clemons. **Description:** Profile of Ariel Capital Management Inc., an investment management company in the Chicago, Illinois area. The firm was rated Number One on Black Enterprise's Asset Managers list. The firm conducts a weekly Breakfast Club for employees to help them learn about the company's operations and services portfolio, honing presentation skills, and building professional skills. Ariel employs 67 people.

34820 ■ "Back to School" in *Inc.* (September 1, 2003)
Pub: Gruner & Jahr USA Publishing
Ed: Nicole Gull. **Description:** At Merkle Direct Marketing, education is not an option for its employees it is a requirement for working there.

34821 ■ "Balancing Act" in *Sales and Marketing.com* (Vol. 147, No. 2, February 2004, pp. 16)
Pub: VNU eMedia, Inc.
Ed: Julia Chang. **Description:** Many small businesses are learning that work/life balances, as well as financial rewards, for sales and marketing employees have become increasingly important.

34822 ■ *The Belbin Team-Roles Package*
Pub: Pfeiffer & Co.
Ed: Meredith Belbin. **Price:** $295.00. **Description:** Includes 5 user's guides; self-perception inventory and answer sheet; 25 looseleaf copies of the observer's assessment; one 3 inch IBM compatible diskette; 2 hardcover books: *Team Roles at Work* and *Management Teams: Why They Succeed or Fail*; and one VHS videocassette previewing two videos: *Building the Perfect Team* and *Selecting the Perfect Team*.

34823 ■ **"Benefits to Attract & Retain Key Employees"** in *Ingram's* (Vol. 27, No. 5, May 2001, pp. 35)
Pub: Show Me Publishing, Inc.
Ed: Mike Searcy. **Description:** Businesses need to attract and retain employees with good, competitive compensation packages, including flexible spending accounts and retirement packages.

34824 ■ **"The best-laid incentive plans"** in *Harvard Business Review* (Vol. 81, No. 1, January 2003, pp. 27)
Pub: Harvard Business School Press
Ed: Steve Kerr. **Description:** A case study is presented where a CFO and chief administrative officer of a consumer durables manufacturer has instituted a performance management system that seemed successful to him, but had negative results for employee morale and customer service. Four experts offer advice on ways the company should proceed.

34825 ■ **"A better way to deliver bad news"** in *Harvard Business Review* (Vol. 80, No. 9, Sept. 2002, pp. 114)
Pub: Harvard Business School Press
Ed: Jean-Francois Manzoni. **Description:** Managerial methods for the effective delivery of bad news to employees are examined.

34826 ■ **"The Big Comeback. How do you get a faltering team back on track?"** in *Harvard Business Review* (Vol. 80, No. 1, January 2002, pp. 20)
Pub: Harvard Business School Press
Ed: Roberta Fusaro. **Description:** Al Skinner, coach of the Boston College Basketball team, answered questions about how he turned around a losing team, which has implications for business.

34827 ■ **"Big Ideas for Small Biz"** in *Small Business Opportunities* (Vol. 16, No. 1, January 2004, pp. 92)
Pub: Harris Publications, Inc.
Ed: James Feldman. **Description:** Four ways to be innovative and creative with a small business include fostering a business climate, becoming number one with clients, creating a partnership with clients, and a partnership with employees.

34828 ■ **"Big Problem for Small Businesses: A Poor Work Ethic"** in *Wall Street Journal* (February 8, 2000, pp. A1)
Pub: Dow Jones & Co., Inc.
Ed: Albert R. Karr. **Description:** Poor work ethic among employees is a number one concern for small business owners. Statistical data is included.

34829 ■ **"Big Switch: Walk a Mile In Your Employees' Shoes-You Could Learn a Lot"** in *Entrepreneur* (Vol. 32, August 2004, No. 8, pp. 32)
Pub: Entrepreneur Media Inc.
Ed: April Y. Pennington. **Description:** Six corporate leaders switched places with employees in order to gain new perspectives, and respect for the people who work for them.

34830 ■ **"Black Hawk down at work"** in *Harvard Business Review* (Vol. 81, No. 1, January 2003, pp. 16)
Pub: Harvard Business School Press
Ed: Thomas W. Britt. **Description:** U.S. soldiers compare experiences in Somalia in 1992 with morale issues in business. In both situations ambiguity about work roles, inadequate resources and overwork lead to dissatisfaction and, in the business context, the defection of the best workers.

34831 ■ **"Bonus Round"** in *Entrepreneur* (Vol. 32, December 2004, No. 12, pp. 97)
Pub: Entrepreneur Media Inc.
Ed: Chris Penttila. **Description:** Alternatives to offer employees who reach the top of their pay scale include gift certificates, equity, tuition reimbursements, bonuses, job title enhancement, more benefits such as extra vacation days, or assigning high-profile projects to them.

34832 ■ **"Boosting moral"** in *Black Enterprise* (Vol. 32, No. 9, April 2002, pp. 43)
Pub: Earl Graves Publishing Co.
Ed: Bridget McCrea. **Description:** Suggestions are offered to managers to help boost company morale.

34833 ■ **"Boosting Morale with Work/Life Benefits"** in *Rough Notes* (Vol. 145, No. 12, December 2002, pp. 110)
Pub: Rough Notes
Ed: Len Strazewski. **Description:** Insurance agents can deepen business relations with clients by offering and explaining the issues that occupy them regarding health care benefits to employees.

34834 ■ **"Breaking Away"** in *Inc.* (October 1, 2004)
Pub: Inc. Magazine
Ed: Nadine Heintz. **Description:** Companies are offering employees paid sabbaticals as a new benefit for long-term workers.

34835 ■ *Building Community: The Human Side of Work*
Pub: South-Western Publishing Co.
Released: 1996. **Price:** $30.95.

34836 ■ *Building a Dynamic Team: Maximizing Team Performance*
Pub: Pfeiffer & Co.
Ed: Richard Y. Chang. **Price:** $12.95 (paper). **Description:** Part of the High Performance Team Series.

34837 ■ **"Building on History"** in *Philadelphia Inquirer* (October 16, 2006)
Pub: Philadelphia Newspapers LLC
Ed: Benjamin Y. Lowe. **Description:** Profile of Rick Skidmore, president and founder of Timberlane Inc. Skidmore, a former life insurance agent, discovered the need for custom made window shutters. The company allows employees to review the firm's financial performance on a quarterly basis.

34838 ■ *Building Team Power: How to Unleash the Collaborative Genius of Work Teams*
Pub: Irwin Professional Publishing
Ed: Thomas A. Kayser. **Released:** 1994. **Price:** $25.00.

34839 ■ **"Business, Employee Short-Term Focus Is on Survival"** in *Atlanta Business Chronicle* (Vol. 25, November 15, 2002, No. 23 pp. 2B)
Pub: American City Business Publications, Inc.
Ed: Emory Mulling. **Description:** As companies try to streamline, many are doing more work with fewer employees. Despite a tight market, employers should not assume that workers will tolerate miserable conditions. Maintaining spending on key areas and providing strong leadership remain vital to the health of a company.

34840 ■ **"Business and Pleasure"** in *Black Enterprise* (Vol. 35, September 2004, No. 2, pp. 46)
Pub: Earl G. Graves Publishing Co. Inc.
Ed: Bridget McCrea. **Description:** Profile of New York-based footwear designer, DETNY Footwear Inc. CEO Shawn Ward, who founded the firm with his twin brother, try to create a unique work environment in order to attract a young, energetic team. Ward believes employees are more productive when they are part of a team that not only works together, but has fun together.

34841 ■ *Business Upgrade: 21 Days to Reignite the Entrepreneurial Spirit in You and Your Team*
Pub: John Wiley & Sons, Incorporated
Ed: Richard P. Cordock. **Released:** January 2007. **Price:** $18.95. **Description:** Business consultant works to inspire and guide entrepreneurs to spark growth in their companies while motivating workers.

34842 ■ **"Buzzwords: Plog"** in *Inc.* (September 1, 2004)
Pub: Inc. Magazine
Ed: Ian Ybarra. **Description:** Plogs are Web-based tools where co-workers can create an archive of observations and data for projects. So far, companies using plogs have created the software in-house.

34843 ■ **"Can Loyalty Be Leased?"** in *Harvard Business Review* (Vol. 80, No. 9, Sept. 2002, pp. 24)
Pub: Harvard Business School Press
Ed: Elizabeth Craig, John Kimberly, Hamid Bouchikhi. **Description:** Research involving 400 mid-level executives from various companies throughout the world has shown that executive education that improve an executive's marketable talents, resulted in more executives staying with a company.

34844 ■ **"Can Spending A Day Stuck To A Velcro Wall Help Build A Team"** in *Wall Street Journal* (Vol. 248, December 2006, No. 149, pp. B1)
Pub: Dow Jones & Co. Inc.
Ed: Jared Sandberg **Description:** Profiles of several companies offering office and corporate team-building exercise outings and events. Alternative methods of company employee bonding are covered.

34845 ■ **"Can You Help Me?"** in *Black Enterprise* (Vol. 35, October 2004, No. 3, pp. 188)
Pub: Earl G. Graves Publishing Co. Inc.
Ed: Feona S. Huff. **Description:** Bonnie St. John, a motivational speaker, coach and author recommends asking for help as the surest way individuals, as well as entrepreneurs, can exceed limitations. Pointers to help with success are listed.

34846 ■ **"Can You 'Pass' on Passion?"** in *Women in Business* (Vol. 53, No. 5, September-October, 2001, pp. 12)
Pub: The ABWA Co. Inc.
Ed: Mary-Lane Kamberg. **Description:** Ways to ensure that the passion within an organization is pervasive throughout the company are to get employees involved, acknowledge employee contributions to the company, and reward top performing employees.

34847 ■ **"Can't Pay Like the Big Guys? Think Creatively."** in *Crain's Detroit Business* (Vol. 23, January 15, 2007, No. 3, pp. 18)
Pub: Crain Communications Inc. - Detroit
Ed: Sheena Harrison. **Description:** Smaller firms have an advantage in being flexible with non-monetary perks to attract high caliber recruits; this is sometimes necessary in order to compete against the larger companies offering higher salaries but are less flexible in their benefits and perks. Be creative, but within the law. Additional vacation, equity in the company, bonuses, and profit sharing are among the benefits suggested.

34848 ■ **"Casual rules"** in *Incentive* (Vol. 174, No. 9, September 2000, pp. 54)
Pub: Bill Communications
Ed: Joan M. Steinauer. **Description:** When motivating with business casual apparel, keep in mind the functionality of casual business attire for your employees.

34849 ■ **"Catch the Carrot"** in *Entrepreneur.com* (Vol. 34, February 2006, No. 2, pp. 74)
Pub: Entrepreneur Media Inc.
Ed: Barry Farber. **Description:** Being true to one's self, honesty and integrity, along with a bit of humor are the true secrets to successful salesmanship.

34850 ■ **"Celebrate Success. Embrace Innovation"** in *Black Enterprise* (Vol. 37, February 2007, No. 7, pp. 145)
Pub: Earl G. Graves Publishing Co. Inc.
Description: 2007 Women of Power Summit provides networking opportunities, empowerment sessions, and nightly entertainment. More than 500 executive women of color are expected to attend this inspiring summit in Phoenix, February 7-10.

34851 ■ "Central Perks" in *Entrepreneur*
(Vol. 33, September 2005, No. 9, pp. 34)
Pub: Entrepreneur Media Inc.
Ed: Aliza Pilar Sherman. **Description:** Most business women owners offer benefits that balances business needs with the needs of her employees.

34852 ■ "Collaboration is the Hottest Buzzword in Business Today. Too Bad it doesn't work." in *Inc.* **(September 2006, pp. 61-62)**
Pub: Gruner & Jahr USA Publishing
Ed: David H. Freedman. **Description:** Individual decision making, although frowned on in business circles today, is usually frowned upon when a consensus is bypassed in making that decision. Both strategies are important if properly used.

34853 ■ "Commuter Gains" in *Entrepreneur*
(Vol. 33, September 2005, No. 9, pp. 93)
Pub: Entrepreneur Media Inc.
Ed: Mark Henricks. **Description:** Bob Begle, owner of a design firm in Atlanta, Georgia, offers free monthly transit passes to his workers in order to attract and retain them.

34854 ■ "Companies encourage employees' artistic skill" in *Business First Columbus*
(Vol. 18, No. 38, May 10, 2002, pp. B1)
Pub: Business First Columbus, Inc.
Ed: Susan A. Pavilkey. **Description:** Retail Planning Associates LP and inChord Communications Inc., two creative companies in Columbus, have opened art galleries in their offices to showcase the artwork of their employees. The companies believe that displaying the artwork shows that they value the talent of their employees, and that employees have a sense of ownership in the business.

34855 ■ "A Confidence Boost" in *Sales & Marketing Management* **(Vol. 158, October 2006, No. 10, pp. 19)**
Pub: VNU Business Media
Ed: Bill Raymond. **Description:** Accountability is a key component of developing an effective sales staff.

34856 ■ "Consultant Outlines Steps For Measuring Effectiveness Of Communications Program" in *Employee Benefit Plan Review* **(Vol. 55, No. 12)**
Pub: Charles D. Spencer & Associates, Inc.
Description: Detroit, Michigan-based Aon Consulting Inc., a management consulting services firm, has developed an employee communication program that allows employers to measure the effectiveness of their program. The program, which is aimed at assessing employee job satisfaction, contains twelve key performance indicators.

34857 ■ "The cost center that paid its way" in *Harvard Business Review* **(Vol. 80, No. 4, April 2002, pp. 31)**
Pub: Harvard Business School Press
Ed: Julia Kirby. **Description:** A case study where four commentators review the workings of a fictional company's marketing communications department. Advice is offered on how its leader could have avoided the discontent within other departments.

34858 ■ "Crafting the most productive and efficient work force" in *Fairfield County Business Journal* **(Vol. 42, No. 3, Jan. 20, 2003, pp. 4)**
Pub: Westfair Communications, Inc.
Ed: Steven Drexel. **Description:** The importance of using both long-term and short-term recruitment strategies during slow economic times is discussed.

34859 ■ "Cultivating Teleworkers" in *Home Office Computing* **(Vol. 18, No. 12, December 2000, pp. 102)**
Pub: Scholastic Inc.
Ed: William Van Winkle. **Description:** Mutual fund company Putnam Investments used to be able to find qualified employees at job fairs. When that resource started to dry up they discovered that there is a ripe market for those workers that want to telecommute. This article takes a look at Putnam Investment's efforts and how well they have succeeded in their telecommuting program.

34860 ■ *Cute Little Store: Between the Entrepreneurial Dream and Business Reality*
Pub: Outskirts Press, Incorporated
Ed: Adeena Mignogna. **Released:** May 2006. **Price:** $11.95. **Description:** Challenges of starting and growing a retail business are profiled.

34861 ■ "Dealing With Bonus Backlash" in *Sales and Marketing.com* **(Vol. 147, No. 2, February 2004, pp. 7)**
Pub: VNU eMedia, Inc.
Ed: Melinda Ligos. **Description:** Three steps to help motivate a sales staff in a year of lower commissions and bonuses are listed, including short term rewards, holding a compensation seminar, and convincing the staff that management is committed to helping them increase their income.

34862 ■ "Departures Raise Questions About Loss of Women" in *Crain's Detroit Business* **(Vol. 22, November 27, 2006, No. 48, pp. 12)**
Pub: Crain Communications Inc. - Detroit
Ed: Brent Snaveley. **Description:** Female executives are leaving a void behind them in business and industry when they leave. Most of them leave the auto industry entirely and a few move to tier one and tier two suppliers. Strong message is sent to other women in the organization of the unrest.

34863 ■ *Design Your Own Effective Employee Handbook: How to Make the Most of Your Staff with Companion CD-ROM*
Pub: Atlantic Publishing Company
Ed: Michelle Devon. **Released:** June 2006. **Price:** $39.95. **Description:** An employee handbook should include clearly written policies covering the rights and responsibilities of workers.

34864 ■ *Designing Competence-Based Training*
Pub: Pfeiffer & Co.
Ed: Shirley Fletcher. **Price:** $19.95 (paper).

34865 ■ "Developing performers" in *Women in Business* **(Vol. 53, No. 3, May-June, 2001, pp. 8)**
Pub: The ABWA Co. Inc.
Ed: Rachel Warbington. **Description:** Small business owners need to find reliable staff whose skills can be developed to help ease some of the owner's workload. The business owner needs to recognize, develop and monitor their employees' potential.

34866 ■ "Developing a working relationship with your supervisor" in *Wome n in Business* **(Vol. 53, No. 1, January-February 2001, pp. 42)**
Pub: The ABWA Co. Inc.
Description: Ways to develop a working relationship with supervisors are discussed.

34867 ■ "The DHL EuroCup: Shots on Goal" in *Harvard Business Review* **(Vol. 81, No. 11, November 2003, pp. 43)**
Pub: Harvard Business School Press
Ed: Paul Hemp. **Description:** Increasing teamwork through competition in the business setting is shown in an examination of the DHL EuroCup soccer tournament.

34868 ■ "Dialing up devotion" in *Incentive* **(Vol. 174, No. 9, September 2000, pp. 72)**
Pub: Bill Communications
Ed: Libby Estell. **Description:** Telemarketing is a tough business, but computer seller Insight Enterprises calls upon incentives to boost both sales and spirits while putting turnover on hold. A brief overview of their program is discussed, including goals, strategies, and results.

34869 ■ "Dirty laundry.com" in *Incentive* **(Vol. 174, No. 9, September 2000, pp. 17)**
Pub: Bill Communications
Ed: Don Mogelefsky. **Description:** Are Internet "gripe sites" beneficial for employees, or could employers benefit from them even more?

34870 ■ *Discover the Limitless Power of Positive Team-Building Technology*
Pub: Continental Afrikan Publishers
Ed: Afrikan Culture Institute staff. **Released:** 1995.

34871 ■ "Disgruntled Workers Were Driving Vance Patterson Crazy" in *Inc.* **(Volume 27, July 2005, No. 7, pp. 42-43)**
Pub: Inc. Magazine
Ed: Stephanie Clifford. **Description:** Vance Patterson, CEO of Patterson Fan, discusses the way he handled disgruntled employees he felt were destroying his company.

34872 ■ "Do You Love What You Do?" in *Fast Company* **(March 2005, No. 92, pp. 88)**
Pub: Gruner & Jahr USA Publishing
Ed: Marshall Goldsmith. **Description:** Profile of Warren Bennis, founding chairman of the Leadership Institute at the University of Southern California. Bennis discusses job satisfaction.

34873 ■ "Does Your Team Need a Hug or a Prod?" in *Sales and Marketing.com* **(Vol. 147, No. 2, February 2004, pp. 14)**
Pub: VNU eMedia, Inc.
Ed: Michele Marchetti. **Description:** Finding the right style that works for managing a staff requires a quick lesson in behavioral science, according to Hellen Davis, president and CEO of a management counseling and training firm in Pennsylvania. Unless a manager uses the correct style, employees will not be motivated.

34874 ■ "Don't Get Mad, Get Practical" in *My Business* **(April/May 2004, pp. 39)**
Pub: My Business Magazine
Description: Ways to diffuse any difficult situation are listed in order to use conflict as a means for business growth.

34875 ■ "Don't subject those around you to cell hell" in *Atlanta Business Chronicle* **(Vol. 25, January 10, 2003, No. 31, pp. 3B)**
Pub: American City Business Publications, Inc.
Ed: Connie Glaser. **Description:** A relatively recent phenomenon is the explosion of cellular phone use, and on that also demands its own rules of etiquette, including the workplace. While cell phone use has increased rapidly, polite habits surrounding cell phone use has not. Cellular usage guidelines for the 21st century are discussed.

34876 ■ "The dynamics of team interaction" in *Women in Business* **(Vol. 53, No. 2, March-April, 2001, pp. 42)**
Pub: The ABWA Co. Inc.
Ed: Mary-Lane Kamberg. **Description:** Guidance on how to work effectively as a member of a team is presented. The effect of group dynamics, the management of conflict within a team and useful and counterproductive behavior within a team are explored.

34877 ■ "The Effect of Social Style on Peer Evaluation Ratings in Project Teams" in *Journal of Business Communications* **(Vol. 43, January 2006)**
Pub: Association for Business Communication
Ed: Gary L. May, Lisa E. Gueldenzoph. **Description:** A study of peer-to-peer performance appraisals in the team context is presented.

34878 ■ *Employee Incentive Contests: For Improved Marketing, Customer Service, and Morale*
Pub: Silverpoint Press
Ed: Dave Marley. **Released:** 1995. **Price:** $19.95.

34879 ■ *Employee Motivation: What to Do When What You Say Isn't Working*
Pub: SPC Press
Ed: Robert E. Wubbolding. **Released:** 1995. **Price:** $15.00.

34880 ■ "The employee strikes back" in *Wall Street Journal* **(April 16, 2002, pp. B1)**
Pub: Wall Street Journal
Ed: Kemba J. Dunham. **Description:** The trend towards employees holding positions at two different firms in order to hedge their bets is growing increasingly popular among workers. Related information included.

34881 ■ **"Employers Finding Low-Cost Ways to Motivate, Reward Staff"** in *San Diego Business Journal* (Vol. 22, No. 41, October 8, 2001, pp. 13)
Pub: San Diego Business Journal
Ed: Mandy Jackson. **Description:** Information is offered to help small businesses retain employees during economic downturns, with benefits playing a major role.

34882 ■ *Empowered Teams: Creating Self-Directed Work Teams That Improve Quality, Productivity, and Participation*
Pub: Pfeiffer & Co.
Ed: R. S. Wellins, W. C. Byham and J. M. Wilson. **Price:** $30.95.

34883 ■ *Empowering Employees*
Pub: Irwin Professional Publishing
Ed: L. Kristi Long. **Released:** 1995. **Price:** $10.00.

34884 ■ *Empowerment: A Practical Guide for Success*
Pub: Crisp Publications, Inc.
Ed: Dennis T. Jaffe and Cynthia Scott. **Price:** $10.95.
Description: Provides detailed plan to build an empowered workforce.

34885 ■ *Empowerment in Organizations: How to Spark Exceptional Performance*
Pub: Pfeiffer & Co.
Ed: Judith F. Vogt and Kenneth L. Murrell. **Price:** $34.95.

34886 ■ **"Encourage superior performance from people and teams through coaching"** in *Women In Business* (Vol. 52, No. 1, Jan.-Feb. 2000, pp. 38)
Pub: The ABWA Co., Inc.
Ed: Dennis C. Kinlaw. **Description:** Company, team, and individual performance can be greatly enhanced via coaching, which can include counseling, mentoring, tutoring, and confronting. Coaching technique is discussed.

34887 ■ *The Encyclopedia of Team-Building Activities*
Pub: Jossey-Bass
Ed: J. William Pfeiffer. **Price:** $89.95 (looseleaf).

34888 ■ *The Encyclopedia of Team-Development Activities*
Pub: Pfeiffer & Co.
Ed: J. William Pfeiffer. **Price:** $89.95 (looseleaf).

34889 ■ **"The enemies of trust"** in *Harvard Business Review* (Vol. 81, No. 2, February 2003, pp. 88)
Pub: Harvard Business School Press
Ed: Robert Galford, Ann Siebold Drapeau. **Description:** The relationship between a business and its client and a company's relationship with its employees is contrasted showing that the business/client relationship allows for trust to develop easier than that of the company/managers/employees relationships.

34890 ■ *Enlightened Leadership: Best Practice Guidelines and Timesaving Tools for Easily Implementing Learning Organizations*
Pub: Learning House Publishing, Incorporated
Ed: Alan G. Thomas; Ralph L. LoVuolo; Jeanne C. Hillson. **Released:** September 2006, printable 3 times/year. **Price:** $21.00. **Description:** Book provides the tools required to create a learning organization management model along with a step-by-step guide for team planning and learning. The strategy works as a manager's self-help guide as well as offering continuous learning and improvement for company-wide success.

34891 ■ **"Entrepreneur Column"** in *Entrepreneur.com* (January 12 2006)
Pub: Entrepreneur Media Inc.
Ed: David Javitch. **Description:** Ways to recognize and help prevent and rescue employees showing signs of being burnt-out on the job. Many factors in the workplace environment can cause employee burnout. Tardiness, absenteeism, apathy, moping, backstabbing, decreased quality, decreased productivity, increased errors, accidents or injuries are all signs of burnout.

34892 ■ **"ESOPs largely a positive tool, survey finds"** in *Employee Benefit Plan Review* (Vol. 56, No. 1, July 2001, pp. 42)
Pub: Charles D. Spencer & Associates, Inc.
Description: A survey of 500 companies which offer employee stock ownership plans found that 75 percent of those surveyed reported employee productivity and motivation increased as a result of having the stock ownership program. Statistical data included.

34893 ■ **"Establish strong team with game plan, feedback"** in *Minneapolis-St. Paul City Business* (Vol. 19, No. 15, September 14, 2001, pp. 12)
Pub: CityBusiness-Twin Cities, Inc.
Ed: Joan Lloyd. **Description:** Six tips to create a team environment in the workplace are spotlighted.

34894 ■ **"Evaluating promotion opportunities"** in *Women in Business* (Vol. 53, No. 2, March-April, 2001, pp. 36)
Pub: The ABWA Co. Inc.
Ed: Liz Hubler. **Description:** Advice on ways of assessing opportunities for promotion at work is presented. Guidance on how to weigh the opportunity costs of the promotion and the short- and long-term implications are explored.

34895 ■ *Fabled Service: Ordinary Acts, Extraordinary Outcomes*
Pub: Pfeiffer & Co.
Ed: Elizabeth A. Sanders. **Released:** 1995. **Price:** $19.95.

34896 ■ *Facilitation Skills for Team Leaders*
Pub: Crisp Publications, Inc.
Ed: Charles L. Martin and Donald Hackett. **Price:** $15.95.

34897 ■ **"Fair process: Managing in the knowledge economy"** in *Harvard Business Review* (Vol. 81, No. 1, January 2003)
Pub: Harvard Business School Press
Ed: W. Chan Kim, Renee Mauborgne. **Description:** A discussion of "fair process" is presented, pointing out that employees will commit to a management decision, even if they disagree, if they believe that the process used in arriving at the decision was fair.

34898 ■ **"Fantastic Forum"** in *Entrepreneur* (Vol. 33, September 2005, No. 9, pp. 92)
Pub: Entrepreneur Media Inc.
Ed: Chris Penttila. **Description:** Video on Location Inc., a full-service video production firm located in Rockville, Maryland uses virtual collaboration software among its 16 employees to create commercials, Webcasts, instructional videos and more. The software allows workers to collaborate online from various locations.

34899 ■ **"Fear of feedback"** in *Harvard Business Review* (Vol. 81, No. 4, April 2003, pp. 101)
Pub: Harvard Business School Press
Ed: Jay M. Jackman, Myra H. Strober. **Description:** The negative effects of the fear of feedback for workers and bosses are addressed. Ways to overcome that fear so employees can bring work into better alignment with organizational goals are discussed.

34900 ■ **"Fellowship of the rings"** in *Atlanta Business Chronicle* (Vol. 25, No. 19, October 18, 2002, pp. 1B)
Pub: American City Business Publications, Inc.
Ed: Lee Hall. **Description:** Innovative Service Technology Management Services Inc., located in Atlanta, Georgia, honors its 150 employees for a job well done with gifts of Godiva Chocolates, company rings, money and leather jackets emblazoned with the company logo, resulting in a more stable and efficient workforce.

34901 ■ **"Find Out How To Reduce The Cost of Email"** in *Internet Wire* (October 30, 2001, pp. 100)
Pub: Internet Wire
Description: Profile of Oracle's eMail Center, a comprehensive email solution integrated with Oracle Interaction Center products, which can provide unified handling of email, telephony, and Web interactions.

34902 ■ **"Firms Turn to Perks in Lieu of Bonus Checks"** in *Inc.* (December 1, 2004)
Pub: Inc. Magazine
Ed: Rod Kurtz. **Description:** According to a recent study, more employees are offering non-monetary awards rather than cash bonuses.

34903 ■ *The Five Dysfunctions of a Team: A Leadership Fable*
Pub: John Wiley & Sons, Incorporated
Ed: Patrick M. Lencioni. **Released:** April 2002. **Price:** $22.95. **Description:** Analysis of a hypothetical tale of the CEO of a struggling, high-profile firm with a dysfunctional executive team.

34904 ■ **"5 Honeymoon Hints"** in *My Business* (November/December 2001, pp. 46)
Pub: My Business Magazine
Description: The first few weeks in a new position are critical to small companies when hiring new employees. Five ways to assist new hires to adjust to working at a new company are listed.

34905 ■ **"Food for the soul"** in *Incentive* (Vol. 174, No. 7, July 2000, pp. 80)
Pub: Bill Communications
Ed: Jeanie Casison. **Description:** The employees at Morgan Stanley Dean Witter add a few artistic touches to a New York City intermediate school and boost their own morale in the process.

34906 ■ **"Found in Translation"** in *Inc.* (Oct, 2006, pp. 41-42)
Pub: Gruner & Jahr USA Publishing
Ed: Joshua Hyatt. **Description:** Two-thirds of the population growth by 2050 will comprise of immigrants. Adapting your business climate to the changing ethnicity has latent benefits in customer identification with your company.

34907 ■ **"From office catnaps to lunchtime jogs"** in *Wall Street Journal* (May 16, 2002, pp. D1)
Pub: Wall Street Journal
Ed: Sue Shellenbarger. **Description:** The art of balancing work and life is explored. Statistical data included.

34908 ■ *Frontline Teamwork: One Company's Story of Success*
Pub: Pfeiffer & Co.
Ed: Louis W. Joy and Jo A. Joy. **Price:** $24.95.

34909 ■ **"Generation Gap at the Office"** in *Hispanic Business* (November 2002, pp. 58, 60, 62)
Pub: Hispanic Business
Ed: Rosa Antonia Carrillo, Rachel Michelson. **Description:** Ways in which communication and a comprehensive transition plan can help family-owned businesses survive into the second generation and beyond.

34910 ■ **"Get the Mojo Working"** in *Small Business Opportunities* (Vol. 14, No. 1, January 2002, pp. 92, 124)
Pub: Harris Publications, Inc.
Ed: Roxanne Emmerich. **Description:** Ways to motivate employees during tough times, such as lending an empathetic ear, maintaining a positive attitude, maintaining focus, and showing appreciation are discussed.

34911 ■ **"Getting Their Slice: Save Money, and Keep Employees Happy With Stock Ownership Plans"** in *Entrepreneur* (Vol. 32, September 2004)
Pub: Entrepreneur Media Inc.
Ed: Joan Szabo. **Description:** Employee stock ownership plans and their tax-deferral benefits are examined.

34912 ■ **"Getting it together"** in *Incentive* (Vol. 174, No. 10, October 2000, pp. 138)
Pub: Bill Communications
Description: To enhance recruitment and retention efforts, employer work/life programs are examined.

34913 ■ **"A Gift is a Reward is an Incentive"** in *Incentive* (Vol. 174, No. 8, August 2000, pp. S8)
Pub: Bill Communications
Description: While many in the incentive industry tend to use the terms gift, reward and incentive interchangeably, management consultant and author, Alexander Hiam, who wrote the book Motivating & Rewarding Employees—New and Better Ways to Inspire Your People, claims these words should not be synonymous.

34914 ■ **"Give 'Em Space: A Well-Designed Work Space, that is"** in *Entrepreneur* (Vol. 32, No. 1, January 2004, pp. 77)
Pub: Entrepreneur Media, Inc.
Ed: Kimberly L. McCall. **Description:** By providing optimal work space to a sales team can improve their performance and increase sales.

34915 ■ **"Glass Ceiling Persists in the Board Room"** in *Marketing to Women* (Vol. 19, December 2006, No. 2, pp. 8)
Pub: EPM Communications, Inc.
Description: A study by search firm Heidrick & Struggles and Women Corporate Directors shows that executive inequality remains high despite the number of women who hold board seats. Although these women tend to mentor and recommend other women for candidates, only 54 percent say that at least one of the women recommended was actually elected to the board. Despite the meager statistics, 76 percent of women on boards surveyed stated that they oppose a legal quota that would mandate an increase of women occupying board seats.

34916 ■ **"Go major league"** in *Entrepreneur* (Vol. 31, No. 4, April 2003, pp. 81)
Pub: Entrepreneur Media Inc.
Ed: Kimberly L. McCall. **Description:** The benefits of team selling are good for the salesperson, team and the company overall. The team concept will help to close sales, maintain the client, create a happier customer environment, and provide unity within the firm.

34917 ■ **"Grist: Beyond the Vale of Smiles"** in *Inc.* (July 1, 2004)
Pub: Inc. Magazine
Ed: Adam Hanft. **Description:** Issues involved when encouraging employees to challenge their boss are addressed.

34918 ■ **"Groom Your Workforce"** in *PC Computing* (March 2000, pp. 137)
Pub: Ziff-Davis Inc.
Ed: Leslie Ayers. **Description:** Internet training will teach employees the best way to do their jobs more effectively, with the convenience of learning on their own time and at their own pace.

34919 ■ **"Grow Your Own Executive Team"** in *Journal of Accountancy* (Vol. 199, January 2005, No. 1, pp. 108)
Pub: American Institute of Certified Public Accountants
Ed: Stanley Zarowin. **Description:** Experts advise small business to establish a management incubator in order to promote present staff into key positions.

34920 ■ **"Guest Speaker. The Saltshaker Theory"** in *Inc.* (November 2006, pp. 69-70)
Pub: Gruner & Jahr USA Publishing
Ed: Danny Meyer. **Description:** Constant gentle pressure is invaluable in a growing company. Not so much to avoid problems, but to encourage participation and imaginative solutions to resolve those problems. Coaching and Communication are the two central keys to building consensus to resolve problems that arise.

34921 ■ **"Guide To Managing Employees: Forget Cash"** in *My Business* (November/December 2001, pp. 41)
Pub: My Business Magazine
Ed: Ivan Sylvester. **Description:** Because employees prefer recognition over money for a job well done, it is easier for a small company to retain good workers over a large corporation.

34922 ■ **"Gulf Team With Corpedia on Ethics Course"** in *Rough Notes* (Vol. 146, No. 9, September 2003, pp. 44)
Pub: Rough Notes
Ed: Dennis H. Pillsbury. **Description:** Profile of Gulf Insurance Group's underwriting division, including Internet marketing, importance of teamwork, and management of debt and business losses.

34923 ■ **"Handling conflict"** in *Black Enterprise* (Vol. 33, No. 7, February 2003, pp. 14)
Pub: Earl Graves Publishing Co.
Ed: Yvonne Abraham. **Description:** In response to an article about workplace conflict, a reader addresses the problems between her boss and project manager and provides a solution.

34924 ■ **"Handling people with tact and skill"** in *Women in Business* (Vol. 53, No. 5, September-October, 2001, pp. 5)
Pub: The ABWA Co. Inc.
Ed: Florence M. Stone. **Description:** Techniques for resolving work conflicts are presented. A six-step problem solving process and a conflict reduction process, are provided.

34925 ■ **"Harmony and bottom line: hm..."** in *The New York Times* (February 9, 2000, pp. G1)
Pub: The New York Times Company
Ed: Jobert E. Abueva. **Description:** Feng Shui in the workplace is explored.

34926 ■ **"Hate Performance Appraisals? Here's a better way to evaluate employees"** in *My Business* (November/December 2001, pp. 43)
Pub: My Business Magazine
Description: According to small business consultant, Mary Jenkins, traditional job performance appraisals do not work for small companies. The article further suggests that the key to evaluating employees effectively is to shift responsibility for feedback and coaching from the owner to the employee.

34927 ■ **"Have Kudos, Will Travel"** in *Hispanic Business* (July/August 2002, pp. 80)
Pub: Hispanic Business
Ed: Barbara Beckley. **Description:** The SITE Foundation released a report that states travel incentives to employees can increase work productivity by as much as 22 percent.

34928 ■ **"Healthy ways to handle rivalry in the workplace"** in *Atlanta Business Chronicle* (Vol. 25, December 20, 2002, No. 28, pp. 4B)
Pub: American City Business Publications, Inc.
Ed: Emory Mulling. **Description:** Managers need to know how to deal with workplace nemesis, someone who either gets in the way or is a challenge to deal with. These individuals can take a number of forms, such as those who are unknowingly annoying, to those who deliberately set out to obstruct. Whichever one the manager faces, each must be dealt with carefully. In addition, managers must be on the lookout for emerging problems, and must also understand the difference between negative friction and creative tension.

34929 ■ **"Here's a Late Resolution, But One to Be Taken Seriously"** in *St. Louis Post-Dispatch* (January 9, 2005)
Pub: Knight-Ridder/Tribune Business News
Ed: Repps Hudson. **Description:** A discussion involving politeness and consideration in the workplace is examined. Consideration of others in the work environment might improve business, boost morale and help with promotion opportunities.

34930 ■ **"The high cost of lost trust."** in *Harvard Business Review* (Vol. 80, No. 9, September 2002, pp. 18)
Pub: Harvard Business School Press
Ed: Tony Simons. **Description:** Advice is offered for managers to maintain trust by the company's employees.

34931 ■ **"Holding a Job, Having a Life: The Next Level in Work"** in *Employment Relations Today* (Vol. 27, No. 2, Summer 2000, pp. 29)
Pub: John Wiley & Sons, Inc.
Ed: Jill Casner-Lotto. **Description:** Many companies are employing new strategies that enhance business performance while helping employees experience a better balance between work and their personal lives. Research by the Work in America Institute is presented.

34932 ■ **"Housing Project"** in *Entrepreneur* (Vol. 31, No. 7, July 2003, pp. 50)
Pub: Entrepreneur Media, Inc.
Description: Many firms are offering employer-assisted housing programs to employees and newly hired employees to improve recruitment, retention and to boost employee morale.

34933 ■ **"How to Calm Workers' Fears"** in *Austin Business Journal* (Vol. 21, No. 25, September 7, 2001, pp. 17)
Pub: Austin Business Journal, Inc.
Description: Robert Half International offers tips on motivating employees during an economic slowdown.

34934 ■ **"How to Create an E-Culture"** in *E-business Advisor* (Vol. 18, No. 9, September 2000, pp. 16)
Pub: Advisor Media, Inc.
Ed: Shelly Wolf. **Description:** Companies can emulate an 'e-culture' model by adapting quickly to market changes, responding faster to customers and operating at the lowest possible cost. To accomplish this goal, companies' leadership teams must okay e-commerce projects and the company organization must be team-oriented.

34935 ■ **"How Departing Staff Can Still Help You"** in *My Business* (November/December 2001, pp. 46)
Pub: My Business Magazine
Ed: Drew Sullivan. **Description:** Advice for setting up exit interviews for small businesses is presented, including a listing of suggested topics to cover in the interview.

34936 ■ **"How to Fix Knowledge Management"** in *Harvard Business Review* (Vol. 81, No. 10, October 2003, pp. 16)
Pub: Harvard Business School Press
Ed: David Gilmour. **Description:** Businesses should stop trying to capture knowledge, and concentrate on improving employee connections.

34937 ■ *How to Lead Work Teams: Facilitation Skills*
Pub: Pfeiffer & Co.
Ed: Fran Rees. **Price:** $24.95 (paper).

34938 ■ *How to Meet, Think, and Work to Consensus*
Pub: Pfeiffer & Co.
Ed: Daniel Tagliere. **Price:** $14.95 (paper).

34939 ■ **"How to Motivate Your Problem People"** in *Harvard Business Review* (Vol. 81, No. 1, January 2003, pp. 57)
Pub: Harvard Business School Press
Description: Methods for motivating intractable employees are examined. A manager must pull solutions out of problem employees rather than pushing solutions on them. The article sites examples.

34940 ■ *How to Recognize & Reward Employees*
Pub: AMACOM
Ed: Donna Deeprose. **Released:** 1994. **Price:** $10.95 (paper).

34941 ■ *How to Recognize and Reward Employees: 150 Ways to Inspire Peak Performance*
Pub: American Management Association
Ed: Donna Deeprose. **Released:** 2006. **Price:** $13.95.

34942 ■ *How to Take a Training Audit*
Pub: Pfeiffer & Co.
Ed: Michael Applegarth. **Price:** $45.00 (paper).

34943 ■ "How To Be a Great Boss" in *Inc.*
(October 1, 2004)
Pub: Inc. Magazine
Ed: Rod Kurtz. **Description:** Management means directing workers, but a boss should also let employees know that you mean well when making decisions.

34944 ■ *How to Win at Work*
Pub: Inter-Graph Associates
Ed: Bill Hellstrom. **Released:** 1995. **Price:** $18.95.

34945 ■ *How to Write and Prepare Training Materials*
Pub: Pfeiffer & Co.
Ed: Nancy Stimson. **Price:** $19.95 (paper).

34946 ■ "Huddle Up" in *Entrepreneur* (Vol. 27, No. 12, December 1999, pp. 131)
Pub: Entrepreneur Media Inc.
Ed: Robert McGarvey. **Description:** Management techniques for motivating employees are explored.

34947 ■ "If you want honesty, break some rules" in *Harvard Business Review* (Vol. 80, No. 4, April 2002, pp. 42)
Pub: Harvard Business School Press
Ed: Ginger L. Graham. **Description:** Profile of CEO of Advanced Cardiovascular Systems, who worked to create a culture where people were not afraid to speak the truth. Two strategies were to assign non-executive coaches to senior managers to get grass roots feedback and to tell the whole truth to the rank and file.

34948 ■ "I'm Stuck. Can You Pass the Play-Doh?" in *Inc.* (August 2005, pp. 68)
Pub: Inc. Magazine
Ed: Lee Gimpel. **Description:** Meeting places designed to promote creativity are outlined. Contact information for six such sites is included.

34949 ■ *Improving Work Groups: A Practical Manual for Team Building*
Pub: Pfeiffer & Co.
Ed: Dave Francis and Don Young. **Released:** Revised edition. **Price:** $79.95 (paper).

34950 ■ "In High Spirits: How to Get Yourself and Your Business Fired up from the Inside out" in *Entrepreneur* (Vol. 31, No. 4, April 2003)
Pub: Entrepreneur Media Inc.
Ed: Barry Farber. **Description:** Four keys to help increase and maintain enthusiasm in a company include the following: learn something new everyday, revel in the smallest steps toward success, set goals and stick to them, and protect the environment around you.

34951 ■ *The In-House Trainer as Consultant*
Pub: Pfeiffer & Co.
Ed: Keith Holdaway and Mike Saunders. **Price:** $45.00 (paper).

34952 ■ "In the 'No': Pessimistic Employees May Not Be So Bad For Your Business After All" in *Entrepreneur* (Vol. 32, September 2004, No. 9)
Pub: Entrepreneur Media Inc.
Ed: Nichole L. Torres. **Description:** Pessimists tend to make safer choices with regard to gambling than optimistic counterparts, thus making them an asset to a small business.

34953 ■ "In Strictist Confidence" in *Entrepreneur* (Vol. 32, November 2004, No. 11, pp. 28)
Pub: Entrepreneur Media Inc.
Ed: Mark Henricks. **Description:** Review of Rosabeth Moss Kanter's book, Confidence. Kanter believes confidence rests on three pillars: accountability, collaboration and initiative.

34954 ■ "The ins and outs: Sales Force: Answering the eternal question" in *Entrepreneur* (Vol. 30, No. 3, March 2002, pp. 87)
Pub: Entrepreneur Media Inc.
Ed: Kimberly L. McCall. **Description:** Three myths regarding inside and outside sales teams are explored. In general, inside teams that do all their selling over the phone are generally less expensive to run and easier to manage, while outside teams working in the field establish the crucial personal link that allows a real glimpse into sales prospects.

34955 ■ *Inspiring Commitment: How to Win Employee Loyalty in Chaotic Times*
Pub: Irwin Professional Publishing
Released: 1995. **Price:** $19.95.

34956 ■ *ISO 9000: Motivating the People, Mastering the Process, Achieving Registration*
Pub: Irwin Professional Publishing
Ed: David Stevenson Huyink and Craig Westover. **Price:** $45.00. **Description:** Co-published with the National Center for Manufacturing Sciences. Shows how to successfully lead your organization through the ISO 9000 registration process. Provides examples of common conflicts and issues that aren't covered in most seminars and books.

34957 ■ "It's Cheaper to Keep 'Em" in *Black Enterprise* (Vol. 36, February 2006, No. 7, pp. 72)
Pub: Earl G. Graves Publishing Co. Inc.
Ed: Lee Anna Jackson. **Description:** According to a recent study, about 22 percent of all employees leave their job within the first year. The cost of replacing an employee varies, but can run an average of $13,000 per full-time worker, up 6.8 percent from 2002.

34958 ■ "It's an investment: Events require funds, planning" in *Atlanta Business Chronicle* (Vol. 24, No. 14, September 7, 2001, pp. S17)
Pub: American City Business Journals Inc.
Ed: Mary Kirkman. **Description:** Kristy Trenaman, Humana Inc.'s corporate communications manager, Eddie Kraft, Nanz & Kraft Florists part-owner, and Robin Hall, Dant Clayton Corporation's bid administrator, talk about budgeting for anniversary events planning. Anniversary celebrations are ways to gain employee loyalty and increase sales, having proven to be successful in these areas.

34959 ■ "It's a Scream" in *Incentive* (Vol. 174, No. 9, September 2000, pp. 92)
Pub: Bill Communications
Ed: Emily Hodnett. **Description:** Many businesses find that employees love company outings at local amusement parks.

34960 ■ "It's a Team Thing" in *Black Enterprise* (Vol. 35, December 2004, No. 5, pp. 67)
Pub: Earl G. Graves Publishing Co. Inc.
Ed: Bridget McCrea. **Description:** Larry Sheffield's ability to build and motivate teams in NEC's Solutions Platform Group is examined. Sheffield oversees the company's 200 employees in the firm's mobile solutions, software, server, advanced optical, customer and high-performance computing divisions.

34961 ■ "A Job Well Done" in *My Business* (June/July 2004, pp. 46)
Pub: My Business Magazine
Ed: Robyn A. Friedman. **Description:** Service Net Solutions offers employees not only a career path, but also allows workers to spend more time with their families.

34962 ■ "The Joy of Conflict" in *Inc.* (August 2005, pp. 112)
Pub: Inc. Magazine
Ed: Adam Hanft. **Description:** Workplace consensus versus workplace conflict is debated.

34963 ■ "Keeping to the fairway" in *Harvard Business Review* (Vol. 81, No. 4, April 2003, pp. 29)
Pub: Harvard Business School Press
Ed: Thomas J. Waite. **Description:** Four experts give opinions on the decision facing a fictional financial services company. Should the company continue to sponsor a golf tournament at a country club that has been attacked as sexist by a women's rights organization?

34964 ■ "Keeping It Positive" in *Small Business Opportunities* (Vol. 17, May 2005, No. 3, pp. 18, 20)
Pub: Harris Publications Inc.
Ed: Dave Anderson. **Description:** Small business owners can increase profits when boosting employee morale. Positive reinforcement should be given verbally or tangibly and should be as specific as possible.

34965 ■ "Keeping Mums" in *Entrepreneur* (Vol. 33, February 2005, No. 2, pp. 71)
Pub: Entrepreneur Media Inc.
Ed: Mark Henricks. **Description:** Owner of an advertising agency in San Antonio, Texas tells how he hired a pregnant woman in 1995. The two worked out a plan whereby she could telecommute two days a week in order for her to be with her new baby. She has since become a partner in the ad, marketing and public relations agency that reports $30 million in annual billings.

34966 ■ "Keys to Motivation" in *Small Business Opportunities* (Vol. 12, No. 2, March 2000, pp. 94, 96, 146)
Pub: Harris Publications, Inc.
Description: Fifteen ways to motivate employees in 15 days is presented by Alexander Hiam, trainer and consultant.

34967 ■ "Law Firm Recruiters Face Hurdles in Pay, Local Economy" in *Crain's Detroit Business* (Vol. 22, November 27, 2006, No. 48, pp. 18)
Pub: Crain Communications Inc. - Detroit
Ed: Robert Ankeny. **Description:** Recruitment and retention of new lawyers continues to be difficult for law firms in the Detroit area. Negative image of the area and the climate are major factors making recruitment from other areas difficult.

34968 ■ "Leadership Training" in *Black Enterprise* (Vol. 37, January 2007, No. 6, pp. 56)
Pub: Earl G. Graves Publishing Co. Inc.
Ed: Sonia Alleyne. **Description:** Profile of Theopolis Holman, Group Vice-President of Duke Energy, who discusses how he prepared for the merger between Duke Energy and Cinergy. Holman oversees a division of 9,000 service contractors and employees.

34969 ■ "Learning to lead" in *Incentive* (Vol. 174, No. 9, September 2000, pp. 32)
Pub: Bill Communications
Ed: Stephen Covey. **Description:** In strong organizations, leaders teach what they have learned to others so that knowledge is retained and recruits quickly learn to appreciate teamwork.

34970 ■ "Left Unsaid: How Ignoring Internal Conflict Can Kill Your Small Business" in *My Business* (April/May 2004, pp. 36-39)
Pub: My Business Magazine
Ed: Karen J. Bannan. **Description:** Conflict is necessary and important to a small business, it sparks creativity and keeps relationships from stagnating, however most small business owners do not understand that conflict really is an impetus for change.

34971 ■ "Let's celebrate! Use performance evaluations as a time to praise" in *Black Enterprise* (Vol. 32, No. 6, January 2002, pp. 45)
Pub: Earl Graves Publishing Co.
Ed: Monique R. Brown. **Description:** Strategies to transform year-end reviews and provide effective feedback on performance are outlined.

34972 ■ "Like It or Not...Culture Matters" in *Employment Relations Today* (Vol. 27, No. 2, Summer 2000, pp. 43)
Pub: John Wiley & Sons, Inc.
Ed: Caroline J. Fisher. Description: The true costs of an operational business culture that leaves employees feeling dispirited, disenfranchised and unmotivated are identified. Daniel Denison's model, which identifies the connection between a productive corporate culture and the bottom line, is discussed.

34973 ■ "Linking 'Em Up" in *Incentive* (Vol. 174, No. 10, October 2000, pp. 109)
Pub: Bill Communications
Ed: Joan M. Steinauer. Description: Golf professionals like Tiger Woods make the sport of golf a sought-after reward by employees, keeping the sport the top-requested award nationwide.

34974 ■ "Locker Room Tactics" in *Hispanic Business* (October 2002, pp. 76)
Pub: Hispanic Business
Ed: Teresa Talerico. Description: Professional coaching is used to help individuals and companies obtain results and reach goals. Corporate diversity training can work to combat workplace discrimination.

34975 ■ "Making a case for a four-day work week" in *Business First Columbus* (Vol. 18, No. 26, February 15, 2002, pp. A30)
Pub: Business First Columbus, Inc.
Ed: Michael Miller. Description: A discussion exploring the pros and cons of a four-day work week is presented.

34976 ■ "Making the Grade: Want to Create a Team of 'A' Players?" in *Sales and Marketing.com* (Vol. 156, No. 3, March 2004, pp. 24)
Pub: VNU eMedia, Inc.
Ed: Julia Chang. Description: During poor economic conditions, good managers focus on the "nearly there" team members, they are the players that show the potential to become good salespersons. Strategies for turning sales reps with potential into "A" players are outlined.

34977 ■ *Making Teams Work: A Guide to Creating and Managing Teams*
Pub: Pfeiffer & Co.
Ed: Organizational Dynamics, Inc. Price: $34.95 (spiralbound).

34978 ■ "Manage with care" in *Black Enterprise* (Vol. 32, No. 5, December 2001, pp. 61)
Pub: Earl Graves Publishing Co.
Ed: Monique R. Brown. Description: Suggestions are offered to ensure proper support to employees in times of crisis.

34979 ■ *Manage to the Individual, If You Want to Know How, Ask!: A Story about the Belief System of Motivation and Performance*
Pub: Belief System Institute
Ed: Thad Green. Released: 1995. Price: $14.95.

34980 ■ *Management Teams: Why They Succeed or Fail*
Pub: Pfeiffer & Co.
Ed: Meredith Belbin. Price: $34.95.

34981 ■ "Managerial Rudeness: Bad Attitudes Can Demoralize Your Staff" in *Black Enterprise* (Vol. 37, January 2007, No. 6, pp. 58)
Pub: Earl G. Graves Publishing Co. Inc.
Ed: Chauntelle Folds. Description: Positive leadership in the managerial realm leads to a more productive workplace. Managers who are negative, hostile, arrogant, rude or fail to accept any responsibility for their own mistakes find that employees will not give their all on the job.

34982 ■ *The Manager's Guide to Rewards: What You Need to Know to Get the Best of–and from–Your Employees*
Pub: American Management Association

Ed: Doug Jensen; Tom McMullen; Mel Stark. Released: 2006. Price: $24.95.

34983 ■ *Manager's Official Guide to Team Working*
Pub: Pfeiffer & Co.
Ed: Jerry Spiegel and Cresencio Torres. Price: $19.95.

34984 ■ *Managing Generation X: How to Bring Out the Best in Young Talent*
Pub: Merritt Co.
Ed: Bruce Tulgin. Released: 1995. Price: $19.95.

34985 ■ "Managing to Win" in *Small Business Opportunities* (Vol. 17, November 2005, No. 6, pp. 10, 20)
Pub: Harris Publications Inc.
Ed: Joe John Duran. Description: Business professional shares tips to help company leaders build championship teams. Tips to prevent identity theft are also listed.

34986 ■ "A Market-Driven Approach to Retaining Talent" in *Harvard Business Review* (Vol. 78, No. 1, January 2000, pp. 103)
Pub: Harvard Business School Publishing Corp.
Ed: Peter Cappelli. Description: Companies today are employing different strategies for retaining employees through incentive programs such as stock options and lucrative compensation packages. By designing and promoting longterm career employee development, the companies can win back the loyalty of their workforce.

34987 ■ "Maximizing Employee Performance: Grow Your Business by Empowering Your Workforce" in *Black Enterprise* (Vol. 35, February 2005, No. 7)
Pub: Earl G. Graves Publishing Co. Inc.
Ed: Arlene McKanic. Description: Guild Associates developed two entry-level management courses and the Leadership Development Program designed to develop and maximize leadership skills. The program features six steps that create a supportive culture that motivates and empowers a workforce.

34988 ■ *Measuring Team Performance: Tracking Team Success*
Pub: Pfeiffer & Co.
Ed: Richard Y. Chang, Audrey E. Bloom and Gloria E. Bader. Price: $12.95 (paper). Description: Part of the High Performance Team Series.

34989 ■ "Memo: Lift 1, Curl 2; Make No Excuses, Bassett & Bassett Employees Get Fit While They Work" in *Crain's Detroit Business* (Vol. 21)
Pub: Crain Communications Inc. - Detroit
Ed: Marti Benedetti. Description: Employees of Bassett & Bassett Inc. are able to discuss business ideas while using exercise equipment. The communications company installed a fully equipped fitness center above its offices in order to keep staff happy and healthy. CEO, Leland Bassett, believes this is a great way to motivate his team of workers.

34990 ■ "Millennial Madness" in *Entrepreneur* (Vol. 32, August 2004, No. 8, pp. 74)
Pub: Entrepreneur Media Inc.
Ed: Joanne Cleaver. Description: Millennials are the newest category of workers between the ages of 18 to 20s. Unlike Gen Xers, these employees are good team players and want to be included in a firm's growth strategies. Patrick Kulesa, global research director for a research and consulting firm reports that small businesses see an immediate difference when employing Millenials.

34991 ■ "Mind Over Matter" in *Entrepreneur* (Vol. 33, August 2005, No. 8, pp. 37)
Pub: Entrepreneur Media Inc.
Ed: Heather Clancy. Description: Infoblox founder Stuart Bailey offers Tae Kwon Do classes to employees on-site. Bailey feels the classes help foster a sense of community at his firm.

34992 ■ "Morale Boost Payoff" in *Small Business Opportunities* (Vol. 17, September 2005, No. 5, pp. 10, 20)
Pub: Harris Publications Inc.
Ed: Tess Marshall. Description: Happy employees are a key to small business success. Ten tips to help build a productive team are outlined.

34993 ■ "More bang" in *Entrepreneur* (Vol. 30, No. 2, February)
Pub: Entrepreneur Media Inc.
Ed: Chris Penttila. Description: Presentation of twenty-five tips for under $1,000 that will make a business better, from marketing to sales, and employees to equipment.

34994 ■ *Motivating People*
Pub: Crisp Publications, Inc.
Ed: Kurt Hanks. Price: $12.95.

34995 ■ *Motivating Today's Work Force: When the Carrot Can't Always Be Cash*
Pub: Self-Counsel Press, Inc.
Ed: Lin Grensing. Released: 1991. Price: $8.95.

34996 ■ *Motivating at Work: Empowering Employees to Give Their Best*
Pub: Crisp Publications, Inc.
Ed: Twyla Dell. Price: $9.95.

34997 ■ "Motivator Vehicles" in *Sacramento Bee* (October 31, 2005)
Pub: The Sacramento Bee
Ed: Rachel Osterman. Description: Experts recommend small companies reward hardworking employees with items used daily rather than a large company dinner or the like. Gift certificates to popular coffee houses or retailers motivate workers.

34998 ■ "Moving mountains" in *Harvard Business Review* (Vol. 81, No. 1, January 2003, pp. 41)
Pub: Harvard Business School Press
Description: Twelve business leaders, including Carly Fiorina of Hewlett-Packard and Robert Eckert of Mattel, discuss their approaches to motivating employees. Some managers stress a person's need for the rational and orderly while others speak of inspiring through example.

34999 ■ "Multiple Stakeholder Judgments of Employee Behaviors" in *Journal of Business Ethics* (Vol. 46, No. 3, September 2003, pp. 235)
Pub: Kluwer Academic Publishers Group
Ed: Elizabeth D. Scott, Karen A. Jehn. Description: Do moral judgments made by various stakeholders in determining whether an event, caused by an organizational employee, constitute dishonesty?

35000 ■ "Need to Boost Morale? Try Good Food, Fitness and Communication" in *Wall Street Journal* (May 28, 2002, pp. B1)
Pub: Wall Street Journal
Ed: Carol Hymowitz. Description: Suggestions are offered to help boost employee moral in the workplace.

35001 ■ "Negotiating Tips" in *Black Enterprise* (Vol. 37, December 2006, No. 5, pp. 70)
Pub: Earl G. Graves Publishing Co. Inc.
Description: Sekou Kaalund, head of strategy, mergers & acquisitions at Citigroup Securities & Fund Services, states that "Negotiation skills are paramount to success in a business environment because of client, employee, and shareholder relationships". He discusses how the book by George Kohlrieser, Hostage at the Table: How Leaders Can Overcome Conflict, Influence Others, and Raise Performance, has helped him negotiate more powerfully and enhance his skills at conflict-resolution.

35002 ■ "A New Game Plan for C Players" in *Harvard Business Review* (Vol. 80, No. 1, January 2002, pp. 81)
Pub: Harvard Business School Press

Ed: Beth Axelrod, Helen Handfield-Jones, Ed Michaels. **Description:** Corporate managers must find means to hire and retain quality managers, while finding an efficient means for dealing with managers that do not perform at needed levels; also important is improving the quality of existing managers.

35003 ■ **"A New Leaf" in** *Entrepreneur* **(Vol. 32, November 2004, No. 11, pp. 95)**
Pub: Entrepreneur Media Inc.
Ed: Mark Henricks. **Description:** Consulting firm, McKinsey & Company has designed a four-step process that assists entrepreneurs when making changes to a company. The first step involves convincing people, including employees, that a change is necessary for the firm.

35004 ■ **"Nonstop Innovation" in** *Inc.* **(Volume 27, July 2005, No. 7, pp. 34)**
Pub: Inc. Magazine
Ed: Larry Olmsted. **Description:** The firm Book 'em works to transform employees into entrepreneurs by having them develop ideas for innovative products and services.

35005 ■ **"Not Your Ordinary Perks" in** *My Business* **(April/May 2004, pp. 14)**
Pub: My Business Magazine
Description: The firm CoManage credits low employee turnover to perks such as flexible hours, free gourmet coffee, fresh-baked bread daily, and high-speed Internet connections to employee homes, as well as on-site pinball machines for de-stressing.

35006 ■ **"A Nursery Tale" in** *Inc.* **(June 2000, pp. 96)**
Pub: The Goldhirsh Group
Description: David Henry, CEO of Allegheny Child Care Academy, tells how his successful inner-city day care centers, serving welfare recipients, have a competitive edge in their non-traditional workforce: more than 25 percent of employees are themselves former welfare recipients.

35007 ■ **"October Recap" in** *Sales & Marketing Management* **(Vol. 159, January-February 2007, No. 1, pp. 48)**
Pub: VNU Business Media
Description: Problems among older and younger sales representatives are discussed.

35008 ■ **"On Boss Day, We Praise and Pan" in** *Sacramento Bee* **(October 17, 2005)**
Pub: The Sacramento Bee
Ed: Rachel Osterman. **Description:** October 16th has been held as National Boss Day since 1958. According to recent studies, many employees are unhappy with supervisors and would not want to be in charge; others feel the day is an opportunity for team building. Statistical data included.

35009 ■ **"On the Merge" in** *Entrepreneur* **(Vol. 33, October 2005, No. 10, pp. 87)**
Pub: Entrepreneur Media, Inc.
Ed: Sara Wilson. **Description:** Scott D'Entremont, co-founder of a conferencing services provider, shares insight into helping employees feel a sense of unity when merging two companies.

35010 ■ **101 Recognition Secrets: Tools for Motivating and Rewarding Today's Workers**
Pub: Performance Enhancement Group
Ed: Rosalind Jeffries. **Released:** 1996. **Price:** $6.95.

35011 ■ **"One More Time: How Do You Motivate Employees?" in** *Harvard Business Review* **(Vol. 81, No. 1, January 2003, pp. 87)**
Pub: Harvard Business School Press
Ed: Frederick Herzberg. **Description:** Employee motivation requires interesting work, challenge and increasing responsibility.

35012 ■ **"One Site Does Not Fit All" in** *Business 2.0* **(Vol. 6, July 2005, No. 6, pp. 110-111)**
Pub: Time, Inc.
Ed: Tom Price. **Description:** To get the most out of a business team's next retreat, the article recom-

mends sparing no expense and to tailor the destination to the manager's goal. Sites geared to team building, leadership retreats, brainstorming, and strategy sessions are highlighted.

35013 ■ **"Open Your Books To Grow Your Business" in** *My Business* **(November/December 2001, pp. 42)**
Pub: My Business Magazine
Ed: Shannon Scully. **Description:** Open book management (OBM), is described by its originator, Victor Ornelas owner of a Latino marketing firm in Dallas, Texas. Open book management is a company policy that requires the business owner to share the company's financial information with its employees.

35014 ■ **Overcoming the Five Dysfunctions of a Team: A Field Guide for Leaders, Manager, and Facilitators**
Pub: John Wiley & Sons, Incorporated
Ed: Patrick M. Lencioni. **Released:** March 2005. **Price:** $24.95. **Description:** Tools, exercises, assessment, and real-world examples for overcoming the five dysfunctions of a team.

35015 ■ **"The Pay-for-Performance Fallacy" in** *Business 2.0* **(Vol. 6, July 2005, No. 6, pp. 64)**
Pub: Time, Inc.
Ed: Jeffrey Pfeffer. **Description:** CEO pay and work performance are covered.

35016 ■ **"Paying off in the end" in** *BlackEnterprise* **(Vol. 31, No. 11, June 2001, pp. 71)**
Pub: Earl Graves Publishing Co.
Ed: Nancy Bearden Henderson. **Description:** Mentoring begins with a vision. The business owner who envisions his company to the next level while improving his performance and that of his employees is what the mentoring process is about. Recommendations for implementing a mentoring program for small companies, is included.

35017 ■ **"Paying your respects" in** *Entrepreneur* **(Vol. 31, No. 5, May 2003, pp. 70)**
Pub: Entrepreneur Media Inc.
Ed: Joanne Cleaver. **Description:** Managers who show respect for employees have a much higher rate of employee satisfaction, equating to employees staying on the job.

35018 ■ **"Peering In" in** *Entrepreneur* **(Vol. 33, January 2005, No. 1, pp. 70)**
Pub: Entrepreneur Media Inc.
Ed: Chris Penttila. **Description:** Peer-to-peer interviewing can help small companies; the applicant learns more about the company, employees help select future co-workers, and management can gain more insight into the applicant's personality.

35019 ■ **"Perk Avenue" in** *Entrepreneur* **(Vol. 31, No. 8, August 2003, pp. 71)**
Pub: Entrepreneur Media, Inc.
Ed: Kimberly L. McCall. **Description:** There are many ways to motivate sales reps to succeed while keeping within a budget by using perks. Lin Grensing-Pophal, author of "Motivating Today's Employees" feels that perks can help employees feel valued by the firm, which can lead to greater productivity, improved morale and loyalty. Tips are offered to motivate a sales staff.

35020 ■ **"Personal Relationships Key to Teamwork, Success" in** *San Diego Business Journal* **(Vol. 22, No. 41, October 8, 2001, pp. 14)**
Pub: San Diego Business Journal
Description: Things that motivate a work force are covered. A listing of seven principles to help demonstrate concern for a firm's workforce is included.

35021 ■ **"Perspective: Doing Well By Doing Nothing" in** *Inc.* **(July 1, 2004)**
Pub: Inc. Magazine
Ed: Jess McCuan. **Description:** Businesses are promoting meditation at work in order to keep employees healthy and happy.

35022 ■ **"Pet Projects: Cats and Dogs and Babies, Oh My!" in** *Entrepreneur* **(Vol. 32, November 2004, No. 11, pp. 30)**
Pub: Entrepreneur Media Inc.
Ed: Geoff Williams. **Description:** Small companies report on the success of allowing employees to bring pets to the office. Included are Hilary Kaye Associates, a public relations firm in California, with four adopted cats and allows employees to bring their cats to work with them. Small Dog Electronics, reseller of Macintosh computers, peripherals and software, believes dogs can be stress relievers in the workplace.

35023 ■ **"Planning is everything" in** *Ingram's* **(Vol. 27, No. 2, February 2001, pp. 28)**
Pub: Show Me Publishing, Inc.
Ed: Nancy Lauterbach. **Description:** The Small Business Advisor shows ways to use a company's annual meeting as a means of creating a sense of community among employees.

35024 ■ **"Power to the People" in** *Incentive* **(Vol. 174, No. 8, August 2000, pp. 18)**
Pub: Bill Communications
Ed: Don Mogelefsky. **Description:** To effectively recruit and retain employees in the tight job market, companies are treating workers with a lot more respect.

35025 ■ **The Power of Team Building: Using Ropes Techniques**
Pub: Pfeiffer & Co.
Ed: Harrison Snow. **Price:** $34.95. **Description:** Promotes teamwork through trust building.

35026 ■ **"Producer compensation linked to agency size" in** *Rough Notes* **(Vol. 146, No. 3, March 2003, pp. 16)**
Pub: Rough Notes
Ed: Phil Zinkewicz. **Description:** The Business Management Group has released its 2002 Owner, Executive and Producer Compensation Survey. The survey shows that the level of compensation for producers is related to agency size and individual production.

35027 ■ **"A Profile in Success" in** *Hispanic Business* **(Vol. 23, No. 5, May 2001, pp. 56)**
Pub: Hispanic Business
Ed: Vivienne Heines. **Description:** A beneficiary of early career encouragement, Frank Montano inspires others to realize their potential. Mr. Montano, president and CEO of Moto Photo Inc., uses goal-setting and planning in employee training sessions.

35028 ■ **"Program reawakens 'Spirit of Delta' in employees" in** *Atlanta Business Chronicle* **(Vol. 25, No. 19, October 18, 2002, pp. 7B)**
Pub: American City Business Publications, Inc.
Ed: Lee Hall. **Description:** Delta Air Lines Inc. has allocated $2 million to a voluntary employee education effort called the Business Literacy Initiative. The effort is designed to foster a sense of ownership among the airline's employees, as well as to inform them on the way business decisions are made.

35029 ■ **"Programs help keep troubled employees productive" in** *Atlanta Business Chronicle* **(Vol. 24, No. 13, August 24, 2001, pp. 4B)**
Pub: American City Business Journals Inc.
Ed: Eric Cravey. **Description:** Employee assistance programs (EAPs) are intended to help employees overcome personal problems so they can be productive in the workplace. EAPs can address problems ranging from alcoholism to family problems to personal finances to conflicts with managers. Statistics are presented indicating that every $1 spent on an EAP can save a company $3 in other costs such as absenteeism.

35030 ■ **"Promoting agency wellness" in** *Rough Notes* **(Vol. 146, No. 3, March 2003, pp. 171)**
Pub: Rough Notes
Ed: Wanda Shumaker. **Description:** Wellness programs for the staff contributes to the morale and mental health of the employees, creativity, production and reduced medical costs.

35031 ■ **"Protecting your company from high turnover"** in *Women in Busines s* (Vol. 53, No. 2, March-April, 2001, pp. 30)
Pub: The ABWA Co. Inc.
Ed: Melissa Will. **Description:** Strategies to attract and retain good caliber employees are addressed. Ways of reducing staff turnover through the use of flexible working hours, employee involvement and fair management practices are explored.

35032 ■ **"Pump 'em up at the office"** in *Incentive* (Vol. 174, No. 10, October 2000, pp. 149)
Pub: Bill Communications
Description: The principal cause of friction between independent sales representatives and their manufacturer is lack of understanding of each others' functions. Seven ways to motivate sales representatives and useful tips are discussed.

35033 ■ **"Pygmalion in management"** in *Harvard Business Review* (Vol. 81, No. 1, January 2003, pp. 97)
Pub: Harvard Business School Press
Ed: J. Sterling Livingston. **Description:** Ways some managers are able to inspire their subordinates to superior performance are listed. The high expectations these managers hold for themselves and their employees bring out the best in all.

35034 ■ **"Pyrotechnics fire up the crowd at meetings"** in *Atlanta Business Chronicle* (Vol. 24, No. 14, September 7, 2001, pp. S15)
Pub: American City Business Journals Inc.
Ed: Lucy Pritchett. **Description:** Pyrotechnics, the use of indoor lighting shows, has increased in popularity in recent years. Dawna VanHook, Axxis Inc.'s production manager discusses the use of pyrotechnics and how they appeal to company employees. This technology can be used for events such as product introductions, company peak sales announcements, and company mergers.

35035 ■ **"Quality Time: Not Getting What You Want Out of Your Sales Meeting? Here are 5 Tips to Point You in the Right Direction"** in *Entrepreneur*
Pub: Entrepreneur Media Inc.
Ed: Kimberly L. McCall. **Description:** Besides confidence building, information dissemination, and company strategies, sales meetings can also be used to inspire a sales team to produce. Steps to changing dull sales meetings into creative sales meetings are listed.

35036 ■ **"Raleigh, N.C.-Area Employers Decline to Offer Dating Service as Perk"** in *News & Observer* (February 1, 2004)
Pub: News & Observer
Ed: Karin Rives. **Description:** Owners of the William Ashley Agency, Lisa and Bill Horst, approached several Triangle North Carolina companies to offer their matchmaking service as a benefit to employees. The husband and wife team ran into issues such as employer concern about meddling in the personal life of employees, and the liability of matches that did not work out.

35037 ■ *Rapid Team Deployment*
Pub: Crisp Publications, Inc.
Ed: Sandy Pokras. **Price:** $9.95.

35038 ■ **"Reasons to celebrate"** in *Incentive* (Vol. 174, No. 9, September 2000, pp. 96)
Pub: Bill Communications
Ed: Glenn Parker, Jerry Adams, David Zielinski. **Description:** A description of the team-reward system that proved effective for the entire staff at a North Carolina-based Merck Pharmaceutical plant.

35039 ■ **"Rebuilding Shangri-la"** in *Inc.* (September 2005, pp. 154-159)
Pub: Inc. Magazine
Ed: Hillary Johnson. **Description:** When the Ojai Valley Inn was forced to close for renovations, it faced losing most of its workforce. Managers developed a job-retraining program to retain its employees. Details of the Inn and restaurant's renovation are included.

35040 ■ **"Rebuilding Your Business With Former and Current Customers"** in *Ingram's* (Vol. 27, No. 8, August 2001, pp. 19)
Pub: Show Me Publishing, Inc.
Ed: Tom Sight. **Description:** Advice for motivating employees and improving customer service within a small business is given.

35041 ■ **"Recharge Life and Business With a Vacation"** in *Crain's Detroit Business* (Vol. 22, December 18, 2006, No. 51, pp. 14)
Pub: Crain Communications Inc. - Detroit
Ed: Sheena Harrison. **Description:** Getting away from the office for a vacation offers a chance to balance home and business as well as the opportunity to explore new ideas from afar while refreshed. It's also an excellent chance to let employees develop new management skills and motivate them with the new challenges and responsibilities.

35042 ■ **"Recreation"** in *Inc.* (Volume 27, July 2005, No. 7, pp. 57-58)
Pub: Inc. Magazine
Ed: Patrick J. Sauer. **Description:** A well-planned company barbeque can be used as a business opportunity for recruitment, marketing, worker and customer loyalty, employee motivation, and finding new customers. Barbeque sauce recipe included.

35043 ■ **"Recruiting and Retaining Top Talent"** in *Success* (Vol. 47, No. 4, September 2000, pp. 84)
Pub: Success Publishing, Inc.
Ed: Jane Shealy. **Description:** In a recent poll of human resource executives, 80 percent characterized the labor shortage as bad, but manageable. Ten percent reported the situation so severe that they were turning business away.

35044 ■ **"Redefining Sick Days"** in *Sales & Marketing Management* (Vol. 157)
Pub: VNU Business Media
Ed: Kathryn Droullard. **Description:** Many companies are now offering flexible time-off policies whereby an employee can use sick time for reasons other than personal illness, such as family issues, personal needs, and stress. Allowing a workforce flexible time off not only motivates a staff, but can also lead to stronger management capabilities.

35045 ■ **"A Refreshing Way to Make a Living"** in *The Record* (November 6, 2005)
Pub: New Jersey Media Group
Ed: Teresa M. McAleavy. **Description:** Profile of Judson Kleinman, owner of Corporate Essentials, located in Fairfield, New Jersey. Kleinman sells coffee, tea and other refreshments to employers, who for less than a dollar a day per worker, give to their employees for free as an employee motivation benefit. He also provides clients with the equipment needed for making hot water and brewing gourmet coffee.

35046 ■ **"Remote Control"** in *Home Office Computing* (Vol. 18, No. 10, October 2000, pp. 46)
Pub: Scholastic Inc.
Ed: Jeffrey D. Zbar. **Description:** Organization strategies for telemanagers who work remotely, while the staff remains on-site at the corporate campus are outlined. Views of three telemanagers on such strategies, including keeping the office working seamlessly, tackling staff problems and maintaining morale are presented.

35047 ■ **"Retirement Benefits More Important to Workers"** in *Wall Street Journal* (January 14, 2003, pp. B5)
Pub: Dow Jones & Co. Inc.
Ed: Richard C. Breeden. **Description:** A new survey shows that employers are unaware of the fact that their employees prefer to have an employee-funded retirement.

35048 ■ *Reward Management: Employee Performance, Motivation and Pay*
Pub: Blackwell Publishers
Ed: David A. Hume. **Released:** 1995. **Price:** $36.95.

35049 ■ **"A rewarding experience"** in *Incentive* (Vol. 174, No. 8, August 2000, pp. 12)
Pub: Bill Communications
Ed: Don Mogelefsky. **Description:** Inspiring a sales force, rewarding a customer, or recognizing an employee can all be done easily and efficiently online.

35050 ■ *Rewarding & Recognizing Employees: Ideas for Individuals, Teams & Managers*
Pub: Irwin Professional Publishing
Ed: Joan P. Klubnik. **Released:** 1994. **Price:** $19.95.

35051 ■ **"The right carrot"** in *Entrepreneur* (Vol. 30, No. 2, February 20)
Pub: Entrepreneur Media Inc.
Ed: Kimberly L. McCall. **Description:** Ways to motivate and retain sales professionals are explored, including a discussion on the importance of a good compensation plan.

35052 ■ **"Right at Home with Telecommuting"** in *Business Week* (No. 3761, December 10, 2001, pp. SB4)
Pub: McGraw-Hill Inc.
Description: According to a survey of small business executives, conducted by Sales & Marketing Management, 86 percent believe that a sales staff can work as productively from home as in the office.

35053 ■ **"The right rewards"** in *WorkingWoman* (Vol. 25, No. 7, August 2000, pp. 40)
Pub: Lang Communications Inc.
Ed: Carol Leonetti Dannhauser. **Description:** Issues concerning the motivation and retention of employees through means and other pay raises are discussed.

35054 ■ **"Rookie Season"** in *Incentive* (Vol. 174, No. 10, October 2000, pp. 130)
Pub: Bill Communications
Ed: Caryn Meyers. **Description:** When is it time for a company to try its first incentive? When it's ready to do it correctly.

35055 ■ *Rules for Reaching Consensus: A Modern Approach to Decision Making*
Pub: Pfeiffer & Co.
Ed: James R. Lawson and Steven Saint. **Price:** $9.95 (paper).

35056 ■ **"Rural meeting settings draw groups from city"** in *Atlanta Business Chronicle* (Vol. 24, No. 14, September 7, 2001, pp. S8)
Pub: American City Business Journals Inc.
Ed: Judith Potwora. **Description:** Ann Godi, Benchmark Meetings & Incentives Inc. president and vice president of the Meeting Planners International Georgia chapter, states that rural settings are good places to have team-building and morale boosting retreats.

35057 ■ **"Saving your rookie managers from themselves"** in *Harvard Business Review* (Vol. 80, No. 4, April 2002, pp. 97)
Pub: Harvard Business School Press
Ed: Carol A. Walker. **Description:** Employees who are promoted to managerial positions based on technical competence often have difficulty translating that competence into good managerial performance. Strategies are presented to overcome the problem areas that rookie managers face: delegating, getting support from senior staffers, projecting confidence, thinking strategically and giving feedback.

35058 ■ **"School Is In for Entrepreneurs: Continuing Education Courses Abound."** in *Black Enterprise* (Vol. 35, October 2004, No. 3)
Pub: Earl G. Graves Publishing Co. Inc.
Ed: Bridget McCrea. **Description:** A growing number of small business owners are taking courses to help them better manage company growth, employees, financial operations, and other key issues.

35059 ■ "Screen Gems" in *Fast Company* (March 2005, No. 92, pp. 39)
Pub: Gruner & Jahr USA Publishing
Ed: Lucas Conley, Danielle Sacks. **Description:** Film industry leaders share insight into managing teams, coping with rejection and implementing the visions of others.

35060 ■ "Search Party" in *Entrepreneur* (Vol. 33, September 2005, No. 9, pp. 28)
Pub: Entrepreneur Media Inc.
Ed: Heather Clancy. **Description:** The latest trend in team building at small companies is to send employees on scavenger hunts. Two firms offering such events, Teambonding in Massachusetts and New York City's Paint the Town Red expect sales to reach $2 million in 2005, a 30 percent rise from 2004 to 2005 respectively.

35061 ■ *Secrets of Entrepreneurial Leadership: Building Top Performance Through Trust & Teamwork*
Pub: Dearborn Financial Publishing, Inc.
Ed: Ted Nicholas. **Released:** 1992. **Price:** $19.95.

35062 ■ "Security Blanket: Terrorists changed your employees" in *Entrepreneur* (Vol. 30, No. 3, March 2002, pp. 19)
Pub: Entrepreneur Media Inc.
Ed: Chris Penttila. **Description:** Since the terrorist attacks, employees want a sense of security combined with the opportunity to do good; work is no longer about making money. Employees also wish to find a better balance between work and home life. Advices is offered to management to help towards this trend.

35063 ■ "Seeing Is Believing: Creating a Vision To Guide Your Team To Success" in *Black Enterprise* (Vol. 35, September 2004, No. 2, pp. 181)
Pub: Earl G. Graves Publishing Co. Inc.
Ed: Kimberly J. Hamilton-Wright. **Description:** Small business success can be attributed to setting a vision of excellence for the entire team to follow.

35064 ■ "Seeking Up-and-Comers Under 30." in *Crain's Detroit Business* (Vol. 23, February 5, 2007, No. 6, pp. 26)
Pub: Crain Communications Inc. - Detroit
Description: Crain's is looking for the best twenty in their 20's feature. Unlike their forty in their 40's, which honors proven business successes, this feature emphasizes imaginative, out of the box, creative thinkers that are shaking things up.

35065 ■ *Self-Directed Work Teams: A Primer*
Pub: Pfeiffer & Co.
Ed: Cresencio Torres and Jerry Spiegel. **Price:** $19.95 (paper).

35066 ■ *Self-Directed Work Teams: The New American Challenge*
Pub: Pfeiffer & Co.
Ed: Jack D. Orsburn, Linda Moran, Ed Musselwhite and John H. Zenger. **Price:** $40.00.

35067 ■ *Self-Managing Teams*
Pub: Crisp Publications, Inc.
Ed: Robert Hicks and Diane Bone. **Price:** $9.95. **Description:** Explains what self-managing teams are, what makes them effective, and how to establish them.

35068 ■ *The Simple Art of Greatness: Building, Managing, & Motivating a Kick-Ass Work Force*
Pub: Viking Penguin, Inc.
Ed: James X. Mullen. **Released:** 1995. **Price:** $16.95.

35069 ■ "Singing the blues?" in *Entrepreneur* (Vol. 31, No. 4, April 2003, pp. 20)
Pub: Entrepreneur Media Inc.
Ed: Nichole L. Torres. **Description:** Profile of the band Face the Music. This blues band goes into companies to energize the workforce, increase teamwork, reduce stress, and improve communication.

35070 ■ "A site full of workers that isn't so sunny? Try this: give money" in *Wall Street Journal* (May 22, 2002, pp. B1)
Pub: Wall Street Journal
Ed: Suein L. Hwang. **Description:** Ideas for posters that encourage workers to relax to reduce stress in the workplace are presented.

35071 ■ "60 second strategist" in *Atlanta Business Chronicle* (Vol. 25, January 3, 2003, No. 30, pp. 6B)
Pub: American City Business Publications, Inc.
Ed: Jon Gordon. **Description:** Four tips for a post-holiday energy kick are presented to help get back into the work mode.

35072 ■ "Slack Off" in *Fast Company* (August 2001, pp. 27)
Pub: Fast Company
Ed: George Anders. **Description:** Who says being productive always means being busy? Not high-tech consultant Tom Demaro, who shares his reasons for being so up on downtime.

35073 ■ "Sleeping On the Job" in *Incentive* (Vol. 174, No. 10, October 2000, pp. 1S8)
Pub: Bill Communications
Ed: Rachel L. Fox. **Description:** In the book Power Sleep (Harper Collins, 1999), author Dr. James B. Maas explores ways that employees can enjoy the benefits of taking naps at work, suggesting improved performance may be just a snooze away!

35074 ■ "Small Biz Survivors" in *Small Business Opportunities* (Vol. 13, No. 6, November 2001, pp. 74-76, 80)
Pub: Harris Publications, Inc.
Description: Profile of Outward Bound, the adventure-based education organization, with more than 35 schools in 19 nations. Outward Bound Professional Development Programs benefit both small and large companies. A list of Outward Bound U.S. locations is provided.

35075 ■ "Sports Scenario: There's No Room for Ball Hogs on Your Team" in *Small Business Opportunities* (Vol. 16, No. 1, January 2004, pp. 54)
Pub: Harris Publications, Inc.
Ed: Pam Mitchell. **Description:** Teamwork is imperative in order for a small business to succeed. The four major issues that cause sub-optimal teamwork are investigated. Customer value programs can become strategic planning sessions.

35076 ■ "Standing Proud" in *Entrepreneur* (Vol. 31, No. 6, June 2003, pp. 28)
Pub: Entrepreneur Media Inc.
Ed: Mark Henricks. **Description:** Business consultant Jon R. Katzenbach contends that wages, salaries and benefits are just a starting point to keep and motivate employees, that encouraging pride and a sense of accomplishment can do more.

35077 ■ "Staying Ahead of the Curve" in *Fortune International* (Vol. 146, No. 4, March 3, 2003, pp. 41)
Pub: Time Inc.
Ed: Scott Spreier, Dawn Sherman. **Description:** According to a survey conducted by the magazine, the companies most admired are those focused on addressing critical strategic issues and maintaining the capability and commitment of their workforces. Statistical data included.

35078 ■ "Stiff upper lips: are your employees happy or just biding their time?" in *Black Enterprise* (Vol. 32, No. 9, April 2002, pp. 59)
Pub: Earl Graves Publishing Co.
Ed: Sonia Alleyne. **Description:** Low company morale in a downsized working environment is discussed. Suggestions to help lower stress levels in the workplace are offered by two experts.

35079 ■ "Stock option communications evolve; challenges remain" in *Employee Benefit Plan Review* (Vol. 56, No. 1, July 2001, pp. 36)
Pub: Charles D. Spencer & Associates, Inc.
Ed: Sue Burzawa. **Description:** Stock ownership plans should be discussed when the plan is introduced and when transactions take place. Employees should also be reminded that the program is in existence periodically. Supervisors and managers should receive more information so they can provide their employees with correct information about the program.

35080 ■ *Stop Managing, Start Coaching!: How Performance Coaching Can Enhance Commitment and Improve Performance*
Pub: Irwin Professional Publishing
Released: 1995. **Price:** $25.00.

35081 ■ *Streetwise Motivating and Rewarding Employees: New and Better Ways to Inspire Your People*
Pub: Adams Media Corporation
Ed: Alexander Hiam. **Released:** May 1999. **Price:** $19.95. **Description:** Ways for employers and business managers to motivate difficult employees.

35082 ■ "Stress Case? Is the Pressure to 'Get the Sale' Getting to You? Keep Your Cool With These Stress-Busters" in *Entrepreneur* (Vol. 32)
Pub: Entrepreneur Media Inc.
Ed: Barry Farber. **Description:** Effective remedies to alleviate stress for sales reps are presented, including the use of a 20-minute power nap.

35083 ■ *Succeeding as a Self-Managed Team: Operating as a Self-Managed Work Team*
Pub: Pfeiffer & Co.
Ed: Richard Y. Chang and Mark J. Curtin. **Price:** $12.95 (paper). **Description:** Part of the Quality Improvement Series.

35084 ■ "Surveys: Unhappiness growing in workforce" in *Austin Business Journal* (Vol. 21, No. 25, September 7, 2001, pp. 21)
Pub: Austin Business Journal, Inc.
Description: According to two recent surveys, the economic downturn is affecting workers' attitudes towards their employers; the surveys were conducted by CareerBuilder Inc., an online recruiting network, and Peter D. Hart Research.

35085 ■ "Taking Care of Baby?" in *Entrepreneur* (Vol. 32, July 2004, No. 7, pp. 78)
Pub: Entrepreneur Media Inc.
Ed: Joanne Cleaver. **Description:** According to the Society for Human Resource Management, fewer companies have parental leave policies than in the past. A good family leave policy can give a small business an advantage over big companies with confusing corporate policies, along with offering employees a benefit they want.

35086 ■ "Talent" in *Business Week* (January 9, 2006, No. 3966, pp. 26-28)
Pub: McGraw-Hill Companies
Ed: Jena McGregor. **Description:** Companies are questioning the value of rigid ranking systems that might hinder teamwork and innovation.

35087 ■ "Taming of the Crew: What Lion Tamers Teach Us About Team Management" in *Entrepreneur* (Vol. 33, January 2005, No. 1, pp. 26)
Pub: Entrepreneur Media Inc.
Ed: Geoff Williams. **Description:** In his book, Lion Taming: Working Successfully With Leaders, Bosses and Other Tough Customers, Steve Katz gathers insights from professional lion tamers to help entrepreneurs learn to tame suppliers, customers and competitors.

35088 ■ *The Tao of Teams: A Guide to Team Success*
Pub: Pfeiffer & Co.
Ed: Cresencio Torres. **Price:** $12.95. **Description:** Provides a spiritual approach to the practical issues of team leadership and participation.

35089 ■ *"Teacher in Chief"* in *Fast Company* (September 2001, pp. 66)
Pub: Fast Company
Ed: Jennifer Reingold. **Description:** Why would a CEO of a fast-growing company take time out every month to teach his new hires? He does this because he wants them to take customer service as seriously as he does.

35090 ■ *Team Building: A Practical Guide for Trainers*
Pub: The McGraw-Hill Companies
Ed: Neil Clark. **Released:** 1995. **Price:** $24.95 (paper). **Description:** Advice on the correct approach to use for training various teams according to their needs.

35091 ■ *Team Building: An Exercise in Leadership*
Pub: Crisp Publications, Inc.
Ed: Robert B. Maddox. **Released:** Revised edition. **Price:** $7.95.

35092 ■ *Team-Building for Diverse Work Groups: A Practical Guide to High-Performance and Diverse Teams*
Pub: Richard Chang Associates
Ed: Selma Myers. **Released:** 1995. **Price:** $12.95.

35093 ■ *Team Building for the Future: Beyond the Basics*
Pub: Pfeiffer & Co.
Ed: Robin Elledge. **Released:** 1994. **Price:** $99.95 (ringbound).

35094 ■ *"Team-Building Outings Heat Up"* in *Crain's Chicago Business* (Vol. 30, January 2007, No. 3, pp. 23)
Pub: Crain Communications, Inc.
Ed: Kevin Davis. **Description:** Team-building skills are often an important key to a successful business. Chicago-area cooking schools provide programs that bring corporate employees into the kitchen to prepare meals, working in teams.

35095 ■ *"Team-Building Remains Essential in Downturn"* in *Atlanta Business Chronicle* (Vol. 24, No. 14, September 7, 2001, pp. S11)
Pub: American City Business Journals Inc.
Ed: Judith Potwora. **Description:** Executives from team-building corporations discuss team-building and the services each company offers to small businesses.

35096 ■ *The Team-Building Source Book*
Pub: Pfeiffer & Co.
Ed: Steven L. Phillips and Robin L. Elledge. **Price:** $79.95 (looseleaf).

35097 ■ *Team Decision-Making Techniques: Successful Team Outcomes*
Pub: Pfeiffer & Co.
Ed: P. Keith Kelly. **Price:** $12.95 (paper). **Description:** Part of the High Performance Team Series.

35098 ■ *Team Games for Trainers*
Pub: The McGraw-Hill Companies
Ed: Carolyn Nilson. **Released:** 1995. **Price:** $24.95. **Description:** Provides over 100 ready-to-use games, exercises, and activities to aid in building and maintaining effective work teams.

35099 ■ *The Team Handbook: How to Use Teams to Improve Quality*
Pub: Pfeiffer & Co.
Ed: Peter R. Scholtes. **Price:** $39.00 (spiralbound).

35100 ■ *Team Problem Solving*
Pub: Crisp Publications, Inc.
Ed: Sandy Pokras. **Released:** 1995, revised edition. **Price:** $10.95.

35101 ■ *Team Roles at Work*
Pub: Pfeiffer & Co.
Ed: Meredith Belbin. **Price:** $34.95. **Description:** Guide to understanding each member's role within a team.

35102 ■ *The TeamNet Factor: Bringing the Power of Boundary Crossing into the Heart of Your Business*
Pub: Pfeiffer & Co.
Ed: Jessica Lipnack and Jeffrey Stamps. **Price:** $27.50.

35103 ■ *T.E.A.M.S.—Together Each Achieves More Success: How to Develop Peak Performance Teams for World-Class Results*
Pub: Dartnell Corp.
Ed: James L. Lundy. **Released:** 1994. **Price:** $14.95 (paper); $20.50 (Canada). **Description:** Step-by-step guide for team leaders, covering assessing company's needs and setting goals, improving leadership skills, performance and productivity tracking, feedback, and employee-management communication. Includes checklists and case studies.

35104 ■ *Teamwork*
Pub: Pfeiffer & Co.
Ed: Alban Associates, Inc. **Price:** $395.00 (game); $49.95 (set of 13 workbooks). **Description:** Game designed to foster teamwork and understanding. Includes one set of 13 Participant's Notebooks. Additional notebooks may be purchased.

35105 ■ *"Teamwork tips"* in *BlackEnterprise* (Vol. 32, No. 3, October 2001, pp. 68)
Pub: Earl Graves Publishing Co.
Ed: Quincy L. Lewis. **Description:** Book review of 'Team Troubleshooter: How To Find and Fix Team Problems', by Robert W. Barner. Team Troubleshooter presents a five-stage plan to strengthen teams by spotting and resolving problems, including identifying problems, exploring options, planning for action, gaining commitment for plans, and implementing and following up on the plans.

35106 ■ *Teamwork: What Must Go Right/What Can Go Wrong*
Pub: Sage Publications, Inc.
Ed: Carl E. Larson and Frank M. J. LaFasto. **Price:** $48.00. **Description:** Provides advice on maximizing team's working power while minimizing conflicts.

35107 ■ *"Tech Firm CEO's Solution: Unify Segments"* in *Crain's Chicago Business* (Vol. 30, January 2007, No. 5, pp. 6)
Pub: Crain Communications, Inc.
Description: Profile of Brandon Glenn, CEO of Technology Solutions Co., a Chicago-based information technology firm that is publicly traded. Although Glenn has never before served as a CEO, but feels he will be able to return Tech Solutions to the black by creating a unifying theme between the company's three business segments.

35108 ■ *"That'll never work!"* in *Entrepreneur* (Vol. 30, No. 2, February 2002, pp. 62)
Pub: Entrepreneur Media Inc.
Ed: Chris Sandlund. **Description:** Interview with author Robert Sutton on counterintuitive management techniques. In his book "Weird Ideas That Work: 11 1/2 Practices for Promoting, Managing and Sustaining Innovation", Sutton explores such counterintuitive techniques as getting happy people to fight and hiring people you don't need.

35109 ■ *"The A List"* in *Entrepreneur* (Vol. 31, No. 8, August 2003, pp. 65)
Pub: Entrepreneur Media, Inc.
Ed: Joanne Cleaver. **Description:** Kim Radeback, human resources manager for Spring Engineering and Manufacturing Corporation in Canton, Michigan, finds inexpensive ways to reward employees and bolster morale during a slumping economy. This practice won the company a spot on one of the Detroit, Michigan area's "101 Best and Brightest Companies to Work For" in the city's 2001 list.

35110 ■ *"The Champagne Group Launches 'Manager Makeover' Program"* in *Bellingham Business Journal* (January 2007, pp. 4)
Pub: Sun News Inc.
Description: Twelve-year-old business and leadership coaching company, The Champagne Group, is launching their new Manager Makeover Program. The five-step, customized program equips managers with techniques on becoming leaders who can resolve conflicts and increase performance.

35111 ■ *"The Solution's So Obvious, Yet So Hard to Follow Sometimes"* in *St. Louis Post-Dispatch* (February 27, 2005)
Pub: Knight-Ridder/Tribune Business News
Ed: Repps Hudson. **Description:** Some companies are providing employees with laptops and BlackBerry's in order to stay in touch with the office, even when home sick allowing them to work from home.

35112 ■ *"Their Life's Work"* in *Tampa Tribune* (November 25, 2005)
Pub: Media General, Inc.
Ed: Dave Simanoff. **Description:** Employees with long tenure become an integral part of any small business, creating a bond and trust between management and employee as well as customer satisfaction.

35113 ■ *"There's No Perk Like Home"* in *Inc.* (December 1, 2003)
Pub: Gruner & Jahr USA Publishing
Ed: Nadine Heintze. **Description:** Some small companies are offering assistance to home purchases to employees. ArchivesOne awards two low interest homes to employees annually.

35114 ■ *"They're not employees, they're people"* in *Harvard Business Review* (Vol. 80, No. 2, February 2002, pp. 70)
Pub: Harvard Business School Press
Ed: Peter F. Drucker. **Description:** Two fast-moving trends that are changing the way companies manage talent, the number of employees who are not longer traditional employees, and the growing number of companies that have outsourced employee relations is featured.

35115 ■ *"Throwing money away"* in *Incentive* (Vol. 174, No. 9, September 2000, pp. 8)
Pub: Bill Communications
Ed: Vincent Alonzo. **Description:** Two new surveys prove cash rewards, though popular, don't stick with employees.

35116 ■ *"The Time is Now"* in *My Business* (April/May 2004, pp. 14)
Pub: My Business Magazine
Ed: Lena Basha. **Description:** With a growing economy, it is important for small businesses to focus on employee retention; flexibility is an important incentive to employees.

35117 ■ *"Time on Their Side"* in *Entrepreneur* (Vol. 32, November 2004, No. 11, pp. 98)
Pub: Entrepreneur Media Inc.
Ed: Chris Penttila. **Description:** Giving employees an extra hour or two of flexible time or the option to telecommute occasionally, compressed workweeks, closing early on Fridays, are all ways to motivate employees.

35118 ■ *"Tips on managing older workers"* in *Crain's Detroit Business* (Vol. 17, No. 44, October 22, 2001, pp. 11)
Pub: Crain Communications, Inc.
Description: Tips for managing an older workforce are covered. Topics covered include compensation benefits, ergonomic equipment, stress management, flexible schedules, conflict resolution, and training.

35119 ■ *Tools for Team Excellence: A Practical Handbook for Making Teams Work: Building, Assessing, and Team Performance*
Pub: Davies-Black Publishing
Ed: Gregory E. Huszczo. **Released:** 1996. **Price:** $25.95.

35120 ■ "Top Executives Set the Tone for Treating Employees Well" in *St. Louis Post-Dispatch* **(January 16, 2005)**
Pub: Knight-Ridder/Tribune Business News
Ed: Repps Hudson. **Description:** Profile of Robert Levering, co-founder of Great Place to Work Institute. Levering scores U.S. companies on how they treat employees and what employees think about the companies in which they work.

35121 ■ "Tough choices" in *Entrepreneur* **(Vol. 31, No. 5, May 2003, pp. 70)**
Pub: Entrepreneur Media Inc.
Ed: Chris Penttila. **Description:** A big dilemma facing entrepreneurs these days is hiring fresh new talent. Ways to handle having to hire new employees at higher wages than existing employees are discussed.

35122 ■ "A tough review" in *Black Enterprise* **(Vol. 32, No. 10, May 2002, pp. 107)**
Pub: Earl Graves Publishing Co.
Ed: Alfred A. Edmond, Jr. **Description:** Advice is given on things to learn from an employee performance review which will help both an employee and manager.

35123 ■ "The tough work of turning around a team" in *Harvard Business Review* **(Vol. 78, No. 6, November-December 2000, pp. 179)**
Pub: Harvard Business School Publishing Corp.
Description: The article, written by Bill Parcells, director of football operations for the New York Jets, offers tips on company team building.

35124 ■ "The Tournament" in *Inc.* **(January 1, 2002)**
Pub: Inc. Magazine
Ed: Norm Brodsky. **Description:** The story of how a storage company in Brooklyn, whose employees witnessed the terrible events of September 11, organized a basketball tournament for their employees to help build morale. The tournament was so successful they are planning the second annual competition.

35125 ■ "Training as a Retention Tool" in *Internal Auditor* **(Vol. 58, No. 5, October 2001, pp. 47)**
Pub: Institute of Internal Auditors, Inc.
Ed: Diane Sears Campbell. **Description:** Many employers are introducing innovative ways to keep their internal auditors professionally challenged in order to retain them.

35126 ■ *Transforming the Mature Information Technology Organization: Reengineering and Motivating People*
Pub: Eagle Star Publishing
Ed: Robert A. Zawacki. **Released:** 1995. **Price:** $38.95.

35127 ■ *25 Activities for Teams*
Pub: Pfeiffer & Co.
Ed: Fran Rees. **Price:** $34.95 (paper).

35128 ■ "Under Attack? Think Another Woman is Out to Get You? Here's How to Watch Your Back" in *Entrepreneur* **(Vol. 32, August 2004, No. 8)**
Pub: Entrepreneur Media Inc.
Ed: Aliza Pilar Sherman. **Description:** Do women sabotage other women in business? According to a professional certified executive coach and behavioral analyst, both men and women commit sabotage, however women entrepreneurs understand the importance of a long-term relationship.

35129 ■ "Unselfish Teamwork Helps Gibson Insurance Agency Grow" in *Rough Notes* **(Vol. 146, No. 9, September 2003, pp. 18)**
Pub: Rough Notes
Ed: Dennis H. Pillsbury. **Description:** Profile of Gibson Insurance Agency; topics include teamwork, management styles, and market share.

35130 ■ *Validating Your Training*
Pub: Pfeiffer & Co.

Ed: Tony Newby. **Price:** $45.00 (paper). **Description:** Examines existing definitions of validation and gives reasons for using validation techniques in training. Includes guidelines for developing and implementing tests to validate training programs in interpersonal, technical/manual, business/office, and knowledge skills.

35131 ■ *Value Cards: Creating a Culture for Team Effectiveness*
Pub: Pfeiffer & Co.
Ed: Alan Barlow. **Price:** $99.95. **Description:** Workshop, with cards containing value statements that teams discuss, fostering a team environment. Includes 114 cards, 20 blank cards for creating your own value statements, 2 laminated placemats, and a trainer's manual.

35132 ■ "Virtual reality, chief whatiffer...this is EDS?" in *Crain's Detroit Business* **(Vol. 18, No. 22, June 3, 2002, pp. 22)**
Pub: Crain Communications Inc. - Detroit
Ed: Michelle Franzen Martin. **Description:** Moveable furniture, wireless laptops, picnic tables help describe the unusual workspace developed at Electronic Data Systems Corporation (EDS), located in Troy, MI.

35133 ■ *Vroom!: Turbo-Charged Team Building*
Pub: AMACOM
Ed: Michael Shandler. **Released:** 1996. **Price:** $14.95.

35134 ■ "Wanted: E-Business Professionals" in *E-business Advisor* **(Vol. 17, No. 12, December 1999, pp. 6)**
Pub: Advisor Media, Inc.
Ed: Jane Falla. **Description:** The article offers advice for attracting the top e-business talent to your business, including Director of E-Business, E-Commerce Consultant, Director of Business Development, E-Commerce, and E-Commerce Sales Executive.

35135 ■ "Web-based services provide easy access to no-cost employer-sponsored discount programs" in *Employee Benefit Plan Review* **(Vol.55, No. 6)**
Pub: Charles D. Spencer & Associates, Inc.
Ed: Miriam Basch Scott. **Description:** Internet companies exist which offer employee discount programs on products and services to businesses that wish to give their workers incentives outside of the workplace.

35136 ■ "The Wegman's Way" in *Fortune* **(Vol. 151, January 24, 2005, No. 2, pp. 62)**
Pub: Time Inc.
Ed: Matthew Boyle, Ellen Florian Kratz. **Description:** Profile of Wegmans, voted the best company to work for in America by its employees. The supermarket is also beating competitors in the tough grocery business.

35137 ■ "'Well dones' shouldn't be rare" in *BlackEnterprise* **(Vol. 32, No. 3, October 2001, pp. 67)**
Pub: Earl Graves Publishing Co.
Ed: Robyn D. Clarke. **Description:** In a survey conducted by Office Team, 60 percent of executives polled believed that companies do a somewhat effective job of acknowledging top performers, while 33 percent believed that staff recognition efforts are inadequate. Four employee incentives are listed by Liz Hubler, executive director of Office Team.

35138 ■ "What are you complaining about?" in *Fast Company* **(May 2001, pp. 66)**
Pub: Fast Company
Ed: Cheryl Dahle. **Description:** Many companies are stuck in the gripe mode, but Harvard researchers Robert Kegan and Lisa Laskow Lahey have a prescription to turn complaints into an agenda for change.

35139 ■ "What to Pay" in *My Business* **(November/December 2001, pp. 47)**
Pub: My Business Magazine
Ed: Description: Considerations to address when hiring and compensating employees are discussed, such as linking compensation of executives to performance and salary surveys for what other companies are paying in salaries.

35140 ■ "When Life Happens: A New Trend In Employee Benefits" in *Rough Notes* **(Vol. 145, No. 1, January 2003, pp. 46)**
Pub: Rough Notes
Ed: Elisabeth Boone. **Description:** Fortis Benefits Insurance Company and Work and Family Benefits, are the two companies dealing with broadened benefits packages that help employees balance their work and family responsibilities since 47 percent of them have a dependent care need.

35141 ■ "When the Love is Gone: How to Reignite Passion for the Job" in *Black Enterprise* **(Vol. 35, January 2005, No. 6, pp. 54)**
Pub: Earl G. Graves Publishing Co. Inc.
Ed: Lee Anna Jackson. **Description:** According to a study performed by the Conference Board, a nonprofit business leader resource, job satisfaction has been falling since 1995. Previous studies reported a direct connection between job satisfaction and top performing individuals and teams.

35142 ■ "When to Put the Brakes on Learning." in *Harvard Business Review* **(Vol. 81, No. 2, February 2003, pp. 20)**
Pub: Harvard Business School Press
Ed: J. Stuart Bunderson, Kathleen M. Sutcliffe. **Description:** Two fortune 100 companies' business units are compared to show that continued learning can reach a point of diminishing returns. Three suggestions are offered to help manage learning within a company.

35143 ■ "Where Everyone's a Winner: Sure, the Annual Trip to Hawaii Is a Great Reward For Your Top Performers" in *Sales & Marketing Management*
Pub: VNU Business Media
Ed: Julia Chang. **Description:** Motivational strategies that benefit an entire sales team, rather than rewarding only the top few salespeople, can provide greater success. In a recent survey, 68 percent of workers stated that more award opportunities would further motivate them in their jobs.

35144 ■ "Where is the new frontier of innovation?" in *Fast Company* **(September 2001, pp. 128)**
Pub: Fast Company
Ed: Fara Warner. **Description:** Fast-paced experimentation, distributed intelligence, total teamwork: the scientific formulation behind the new economy is still disrupting the status quo. In this case, 20,000 leagues under the sea; to appreciate the world-changing impact of digital technology, explore the world of the Monterey Bay Aquarium Research Institute.

35145 ■ "Where Jobs Are Plenty, Challenge is Finding Right People" in *Crain's Detroit Business* **(Vol. 22, November 27, 2006, No. 48, pp. 17)**
Pub: Crain Communications Inc. - Detroit
Ed: Anjali Fluker. **Description:** The environmental industry in Southeast Michigan has many job openings, but has difficulty finding educated and experienced workers. Part of the reason is most of the people working in that industry are content, and are not looking around.

35146 ■ "Whistle Blowers" in *Sales and Marketing.com* **(Vol. 156, No. 3, March 2004, pp. 30)**
Pub: VNU eMedia, Inc.
Ed: Julie Barker. **Description:** Profile of CIBA Vision's self-coaching model for sales executives is presented. Dow Jones Business News reported CIBA's fourth-quarter sales increased more than 20 percent after implementing the new program. In order for the program to be successful, sales reps must commit to their own learning, and must strategize and critique immediately before and after a sales call.

35147 ■ "Who Wants to Manage a Millionaire?" in *Harvard Business Review* **(Vol. 78, No. 4, July 2000, pp. 53)**
Pub: Harvard Business School Publishing Corp.
Ed: Suzy Wetlaufer. **Description:** Employees often become bored at Covad Communications and check out.

35148 ■ "Why Can't We Be Friends?" in *Inc.* **(January 1, 2004)**
Pub: Gruner & Jahr USA Publishing
Ed: Nadine Heintz. **Description:** Small companies may be informal but it is important for management to remain formal in relationships with employees.

35149 ■ "Why Employees Should Lead Themselves" in *Business 2.0* **(Vol. 7, January/February 2006, No. 1, pp. 76)**
Pub: Time, Inc.
Ed: Jeffrey Pfeffer. **Description:** Distributed management could help a small business become more innovative and productive.

35150 ■ "Why Good Employees Leave" in *Rough Notes* **(Vol. 145, No. 12, December 2002, pp. 121)**
Pub: Rough Notes
Ed: Emily Huling. **Description:** Good employees leave for various reasons that employers may not be aware. A listing of reasons is presented which includes employees feeling undervalued, used or exploited as well as frustration over office politics or favoritism.

35151 ■ "Why We Misread Motives" in *Harvard Business Review* **(Vol. 81, No. 1, January 2003)**
Pub: Harvard Business School Press
Description: Research by Stanford University professor, Chip Heath, suggests that managers tend to have an extrinsic incentives bias by assuming that others are more driven than they are by external rewards for work. Extrinsic rewards are such things as pay and job security, while intrinsic rewards are learning new skills and contributing to an organization.

35152 ■ *Why Work?: Motivating the New Workforce*
Pub: Miles River Press
Ed: Michael Maccoby. **Released:** 1995. **Price:** $24.95.

35153 ■ "Why You're Hiring All Wrong" in *Inc.* **(February 1, 2002)**
Pub: Inc. Magazine
Ed: Kate O'Sullivan. **Description:** Advice is offered for creating a long-range career plan for every employee hired, including the use of a consulting firm to review these plans annually.

35154 ■ "Winning the talent war for women: sometimes it takes a revolution" in *Harvard Business Review* **(Vol. 78, No. 6, Nov.- Dec. 2000)**
Pub: Harvard Business School Publishing Corp.
Description: The steps Deloitte and Touche is taking to retain women at its company.

35155 ■ "Winning at Work: What doesn't kill you will make you stronger" in *Atlanta Business Chronicle* **(Vol. 25, Nov. 8, 2002, No. 22 pp. 4B)**
Pub: American City Business Publications, Inc.
Ed: Connie Glaser. **Description:** Catch phrases concerning the resiliency of professional employees are presented. Suggestions for handling professional disappointments are discussed.

35156 ■ *The Wisdom of Teams*
Pub: NAPL
Ed: Jon R. Katzenbach and Douglas K. Smith. **Price:** $13.00 (non-member, paper); $10.50 (member, paper). **Description:** Provides guidance for creating a high-performance team, and for management to effectively use teams within the organization.

35157 ■ "The Wisdom of Thoughtfulness: In Tight Labor Market, Bosses Find Value in Being Nice" in *The New York Times* **(May 31, 2000, pp. C1)**
Pub: The New York Times Company
Ed: Amy Zipkin. **Description:** A new survey finds employees value a caring boss more than they value money or fringe benefits.

35158 ■ "With employee retention a headache, a small business builds entertainment into the work routine" in *Wall Street Journal* **(March 14, 2000)**
Pub: Dow Jones & Co., Inc.
Ed: Eleena De Lisser. **Description:** A profile of Mid-American Technologies.

35159 ■ "The Work-at-Home Hook" in *Home Office Computing* **(Vol. 18, No. 11, November 2000, pp. 92)**
Pub: Scholastic Inc.
Ed: Lisa Roberts. **Description:** Ways in which companies are using telework to recruit and retain employees is discussed.

35160 ■ *Work & Motivation*
Pub: Jossey-Bass, Inc.
Ed: Victor Vroom. **Released:** 1994. **Price:** $28.00 (paper).

35161 ■ "The work of leadership" in *Harvard Business Review* **(Vol. 79, No. 11, December 2001, pp. 131)**
Pub: Harvard Business School Press
Ed: Donald Laurie, Ronald A. Heifitz. **Description:** The authors argue that the most important task for leaders is to mobilize people in their organization to do adaptive work. Six principles for leading adaptive work are presented.

35162 ■ "Workforce Board Seeks To Improve Jobs" in *Bradenton Herald* **(January 28, 2005)**
Pub: Bradenton Herald
Ed: Matt Griswold. **Description:** The Suncoast Workforce Board is working to improve the Manatee-Sarasota business climate through education of employees. After a study of the region's economy, the area benefits from its desirable geography and is among the nation's top performing regions, but has issues with its workforce.

35163 ■ "Working It Out! How a Young Executive Overcomes Obstacles on the Job" in *Black Enterprise* **(Vol. 37, January 2007, No. 6, pp. 55)**
Pub: Earl G. Graves Publishing Co. Inc.
Ed: Laura Egodigwe. **Description:** Interview with Susan Chapman, Global Head of Operations for Citigroup Realty Services, in which she discusses issues such as the important skills necessary for overcoming obstacles in the workplace.

35164 ■ "Workplace" in *Business 2.0* **(Vol. 6, July 2005, No. 6, pp. 109)**
Pub: Time, Inc.
Ed: Michael V. Copeland. **Description:** Executives at Ventura, California's Patagonia hit the surf when the swell is good. The firm, an outdoor-gear maker, admits the outdoor recreation helps promote a dedicated staff.

35165 ■ "Workplace Column" in *Kansas City Star* **(January 20, 2005)**
Pub: Knight-Ridder/Tribune Business News
Ed: Diane Stafford. **Description:** Eddy Watkins ask his workers to help save the printing company, Watkins Lithographic, from bankruptcy. His employees worked hard to save the business and Watkins rewarded all 31 of them, plus a guest, to a 3-day, all-expense-paid vacation at a Florida resort.

35166 ■ "The workplace: learn to do more with less" in *Atlanta Business Chronicle* **(Vol. 25, No. 20, October 25, 2002, pp. 12B)**
Pub: American City Business Publications, Inc.
Ed: Emory Mulling. **Description:** Suggestions are given to improve workplace performance in these trying economic times. Training and matching the right person with the right skills for each job is important. Additionally, it is important to recognize that employees want to be developed and to increase their work skills base.

35167 ■ *Workplace Wars and How to End Them: Turning Personal Conflicts into Productive Teamwork*
Pub: Pfeiffer & Co.
Ed: Kenneth Kaye. **Price:** $19.95.

35168 ■ "Year-End Bonus Points" in *Inc.* **(November 1, 2003)**
Pub: Gruner & Jahr USA Publishing
Ed: Jess McCuan. **Description:** Employees prefer trips to cash as bonuses, with Mexico ranking the number one destination for incentive and Las Vegas as the first choice domestically.

35169 ■ "Your Employees" in *Small Business Opportunities* **(Vol. 14, No. 1, January 2002, pp. 76, 78)**
Pub: Harris Publications, Inc.
Ed: Lin Grensing-Pophal. **Description:** Twenty-five keys to creating positive employee relations are listed.

TRADE PERIODICALS

35170 ■ *The Journal for Quality and Participation*
Pub: American Society for Quality
Released: Quarterly, 4/yr. **Price:** $95 institutions international; $45 domestic, members; $70 international, members; $65 Canada, members; $75 domestic, non-members; $85 international, non-members; $85 Canada, non-members. **Description:** Journal covering total quality management and employee involvement processes.

35171 ■ *Teamwork*
Pub: The Dartnell Corp.
Released: Biweekly. **Price:** $286.70. **Description:** Focuses on successful teamwork in manufacturing and corporate businesses. Recurring features include columns titled What Would You Do?, Test Yourself and See, and Teamwork in Action.

VIDEOCASSETTES/ AUDIOCASSETTES

35172 ■ *Better Productivity Is Not By Chance—Dr. Robert Lorher*
Instructional Video
2219 C St.
Lincoln, NE 68502
Ph:(402)475-6570
Free: 800-228-0164
Fax: (402)475-6500
Co. E-mail: feedback@insvideo.com
URL: http://www.insvideo.com
Price: $169.00. **Description:** Dr. Robert Lorher offers five factors that will improve motivational skills and productivity, and support the importance of setting reachable goals. **Availability:** VHS.

35173 ■ *Building Blocks for Team Performance*
Instructional Video
2219 C St.
Lincoln, NE 68502
Ph:(402)475-6570
Free: 800-228-0164
Fax: (402)475-6500
Co. E-mail: feedback@insvideo.com
URL: http://www.insvideo.com
Price: $295.00. **Description:** Teaches the importance of teamwork and offers concepts to be used to build successful teams within your organization, including effective listening, developing top performers, and time management. Includes workbook. **Availability:** VHS.

35174 ■ *Building High Performing Teams*
Excellence in Training Corp.
1303 Marsh Ln.
Carrollton, TX 75006
Free: 800-747-6569

Released: 1991. Price: $995.00. Description: A presentation on the four steps of building an effective management team. Availability: VHS; 3/4U; Special order formats.

35175 ■ Coaching Skills: Developing a Better Employee
American Media, Inc.
4621 121st St.
Urbandale, IA 50323-2311
Ph:(515)224-0919
Free: 888-776-8268
Fax: (515)327-2555
Co. E-mail: custsvc@ammedia.com
URL: http://www.ammedia.com
Price: $495.00. Description: Focuses on ways to coach employees with training, motivation, and delegation to help employees grow in their positions. Two videos discuss coaching methods and show examples of good and bad coaching. A trainer's guide is included. Availability: VHS; 3/4U; 8mm.

35176 ■ Coaching for Top Performance
IVN Entertainment, Inc.
1390 Willow Pass Rd., Ste. 900
Concord, CA 94520
Ph:(925)688-0833
Free: 800-669-4486
Fax: (925)688-0848
Co. E-mail: ivn@ivn.com
URL: http://www.ivn.com
Released: 1992. Description: Get the best work possible out of your team by using these coaching strategies. Availability: VHS.

35177 ■ Colleagues As Customers: Internal Customer Service Begins with Teamwork
Government VideoSource, Inc.
461 Miller Dr.
Elgin, IL 60123-7232
Ph:(847)931-1955
Released: 1994. Price: $495.00. Description: Challenges employees to strive for optimal product quality and enhance their teamwork skills. Availability: VHS.

35178 ■ Dealing with Difficult People Volume Two
RMI Media
1365 N. Winchester
Olathe, KS 66061
Ph:(913)768-1696
Fax: (913)768-0184
Co. E-mail: actmedia@act.org
URL: http://www.rmimedia.com
Released: 1993. Price: $99.00. Description: Ed Greif explains how to handle very difficult problems with people. Availability: VHS.

35179 ■ Developing Strategies for Teamwork
Aspen Publishers
7201 McKinney Circ.
Frederick, MD 21704
Ph:(301)644-3599
Free: 800-638-8437
Fax: (301)644-3550
URL: http://www.aspenpublishers.com
Released: 1986. Price: $495.00. Description: Strategy tips to teach your supervisors how to get their employees working together and working harder are shown. Availability: VHS; 3/4U; Special order formats.

35180 ■ Discipline: A Matter of Judgment
Encyclopedia Britannica
331 N. LaSalle St.
Chicago, IL 60610
Ph:(312)347-7159
Free: 800-323-1229
Fax: (312)294-2104
URL: http://www.britannica.com
Released: 1989. Description: This video teaches that discipline must educate, not humiliate, and urges fair, prompt, and consistent disciplinary action. Availability: VHS; 3/4U.

35181 ■ Empowering Employees to Claim Their Autonomy
American Society for Training and Development (ASTD)
1640 King St.
Box 1443
Alexandria, VA 22313-2043
Ph:(703)683-8100
Free: 800-628-2783
Fax: (703)683-8103
URL: http://www.astd.org
Released: 1989. Description: Peter Block shows how to get past the passivity inherent in large organizations and help employees take charge of their individual needs, creating more creativity and energy in the workplace. Availability: VHS; 3/4U.

35182 ■ Empowerment: Communicating with Others
International Training Consultants, Inc.
1838 Park Oaks
Kemah, TX 77565
Free: 800-998-8764
Co. E-mail: itc@trainingitc.com
URL: http://www.trainingitc.com
Price: $495.00. Description: Part of the "Empowerment: The Employee Development Series." Provides instructional material for employees which helps them becoming better communicators. Covers both speaking and listening techniques. Availability: VHS.

35183 ■ Empowerment: Meeting Change Creatively
International Training Consultants, Inc.
1838 Park Oaks
Kemah, TX 77565
Free: 800-998-8764
Co. E-mail: itc@trainingitc.com
URL: http://www.trainingitc.com
Price: $495.00. Description: Part of the "Empowerment: The Employee Development Series." Helps employees learn to cope with change by showing them how to increase their tolerance to change and benefit from it. Availability: VHS.

35184 ■ Empowerment: Solving Problems Together
International Training Consultants, Inc.
1838 Park Oaks
Kemah, TX 77565
Free: 800-998-8764
Co. E-mail: itc@trainingitc.com
URL: http://www.trainingitc.com
Price: $495.00. Description: Part of the "Empowerment: The Employee Development Series." Illustrates skills which will help employees become better problem solvers. Availability: VHS.

35185 ■ Empowerment: Team Skills for Meeting Together
International Training Consultants, Inc.
1838 Park Oaks
Kemah, TX 77565
Free: 800-998-8764
Co. E-mail: itc@trainingitc.com
URL: http://www.trainingitc.com
Price: $495.00. Description: Part of the "Empowerment: The Employee Development Series." Teaches employees skills which help them become better meeting and team participants, including those of the group leader, recorder, facilitator, observer, and group member. Availability: VHS.

35186 ■ Empowerment: Working Effectively with Others
International Training Consultants, Inc.
1838 Park Oaks
Kemah, TX 77565
Free: 800-998-8764
Co. E-mail: itc@trainingitc.com
URL: http://www.trainingitc.com
Price: $495.00. Description: Part of the "Empowerment: The Employee Development Series." Examines methods which help employees work together more effectively. Covers two important areas which affect teamwork: individual behaviors and interaction. Availability: VHS.

35187 ■ Everything You Always Wanted to Know about Management
American Media, Inc.
4621 121st St.
Urbandale, IA 50323-2311
Ph:(515)224-0919
Free: 888-776-8268
Fax: (515)327-2555
Co. E-mail: custsvc@ammedia.com
URL: http://www.ammedia.com
Released: 1995. Price: $595. Description: Outlines the essentials of good management, including the six steps of delegation, employee empowerment, communication, feedback, and goal achievement. Includes course guide with participant exercises and case studies. Availability: VHS; CC.

35188 ■ Fostering Creativity and Innovation
J. Miller Associates
15669 Live Oak Springs Rd.
Santa Clarita, CA 91351-4712
Ph:(805)251-9310
Fax: (805)251-9192
Price: $99.00. Description: Part of the Management Speaks Series. Outlines how the success of a business is affected by its viewpoint on creativity and innovation. Availability: VHS.

35189 ■ How to Motivate Your People
1st Financial Training Services
1515 E. Woodfield Rd., Ste. 345
Schaumburg, IL 60173
Ph:(847)969-0900
Free: 800-442-8662
Fax: (847)969-0521
Co. E-mail: sales@1stfinancialtraining.com
URL: http://www.1stfinancialtraining.com
Released: 1987. Price: $250.00. Description: The program answers questions about how to motivate people and why some people are harder to motivate than others. Availability: VHS; 3/4U.

35190 ■ How to Supervise People
Nightingale-Conant Corp.
6245 W. Howard St.
Niles, IL 60714
Ph:(847)647-0300
Free: 800-560-6081
URL: http://www.nightingale.com
Price: $95.00. Description: Eileen Parkinson presents techniques for building a winning team by leading people, as opposed to managing them. Includes an audio cassette and book. Availability: VHS.

35191 ■ If at First: Overcoming the Fear of Failure
Government VideoSource, Inc.
461 Miller Dr.
Elgin, IL 60123-7232
Ph:(847)931-1955
Price: $895. Description: Offers tips on overcoming fear of failure. Availability: VHS.

35192 ■ Leading a Service Team
Government VideoSource, Inc.
461 Miller Dr.
Elgin, IL 60123-7232
Ph:(847)931-1955
Released: 1994. Price: $595.00. Description: Kathy Sweet, formerly a supervisor, becomes ingratiated in the role of Team Leader and learns how to empower herself and her team to enhance customer service. Availability: VHS.

35193 ■ Motivating/Directing/Leading—The Basics of Winning with People
RMI Media
1365 N. Winchester
Olathe, KS 66061
Ph:(913)768-1696
Fax: (913)768-0184
Co. E-mail: actmedia@act.org
URL: http://www.rmimedia.com
Released: 1989. Price: $129.00. Description: Find out how to get other people to do what you want them to do. Availability: VHS; 3/4U.

35194 ■ Motivating Others
American Management Association
9 Galen St.
PO Box 9119
Watertown, MA 02472
Ph:(617)926-4600
Free: 800-225-3215
Fax: (617)923-1875
URL: http://www.amanet.org
Released: 1993. **Price:** $215.00. **Description:** Provides tips on how to motivate employees to perform better. Contains information on proven, top-rated employee motivators and how to use them. **Availability:** VHS.

35195 ■ Motivating People Toward Peak Performance
Nightingale-Conant Corp.
6245 W. Howard St.
Niles, IL 60714
Ph:(847)647-0300
Free: 800-560-6081
URL: http://www.nightingale.com
Price: $95.00. **Description:** A look at motivational strategies for encouraging top-notch performance from ordinary people. Includes two audio cassettes and two workbooks. **Availability:** VHS.

35196 ■ Motivation & a Positive Attitude
University of Wisconsin-Madison Center on
    Education & Work
1025 W. Johnson St., Rm. 964
1025 W. Johnson St.
Madison, WI 53706-1796
Ph:(608)263-3696
Free: 800-446-0399
Co. E-mail: cewmail@education.wisc.edu
Released: 1997. **Price:** $79.00. **Description:** Looks at how to develop motivational behavior and a positive attitude. **Availability:** VHS.

35197 ■ Muppet Sales: Make-a-Buck
Video Arts, Inc.
c/o Aim Learning Group
8238-40 Lehigh
Morton Grove, IL 60053-2615
Free: 877-444-2230
Fax: (416)252-2155
Co. E-mail: service@aimlearninggroup.com
URL: http://www.aimlearninggroup.com
Price: $795.00. **Description:** Topic-specific selections from "The Muppets Show" provide motivation and humor to meetings and work related obligations. **Availability:** VHS.

35198 ■ Planning a Project and Building Your Project Team
Instrument Society of America
67 Alexander Dr.
Research Triangle Park, NC 27709
Ph:(919)549-8411
Co. E-mail: info@isa.org
URL: http://www.isa.org
Released: 199?. **Price:** $95.00. **Description:** An instrument technology training program on planning a project and building your project team. Includes a manual. **Availability:** VHS.

35199 ■ Team Building
Excellence in Training Corp.
1303 Marsh Ln.
Carrollton, TX 75006
Free: 800-747-6569
Released: 1991. **Price:** $495.00. **Description:** A detailed discussion of the ingredients of building an effective work team. A detailed leader's guide is included. **Availability:** VHS; 3/4U; Special order formats.

35200 ■ Team of Champions
Excellence in Training Corp.
1303 Marsh Ln.
Carrollton, TX 75006
Free: 800-747-6569
Released: 1991. **Price:** $595.00. **Description:** John Parker Stewart discusses how to combine empower-

ment, teamwork, and quality improvement to build a more effective working environment. A leader's guide is included. **Availability:** VHS; 3/4U; Special order formats.

35201 ■ Team Excellence
Home Vision Cinema
c/o Image Entertainment
20525 Nordhoff St., Ste. 200
Chatsworth, CA 91311
URL: http://www.homevision.com
Released: 1987. **Price:** $995.00. **Description:** Walter Cronkite emphasizes the importance of teamwork in the workplace. **Availability:** VHS; 3/4U.

35202 ■ Team Player
American Media, Inc.
4621 121st St.
Urbandale, IA 50323-2311
Ph:(515)224-0919
Free: 888-776-8268
Fax: (515)327-2555
Co. E-mail: custsvc@ammedia.com
URL: http://www.ammedia.com
Released: 1993. **Price:** $650.00. **Description:** Features a scene in which the main character develops a team approach to problem-solving in a very realistic way. **Availability:** VHS.

35203 ■ Together!
American Media, Inc.
4621 121st St.
Urbandale, IA 50323-2311
Ph:(515)224-0919
Free: 888-776-8268
Fax: (515)327-2555
Co. E-mail: custsvc@ammedia.com
URL: http://www.ammedia.com
Released: 1990. **Price:** $325.00. **Description:** Focuses on the importance of teamwork in business using a story about a group of boys and girls working together to perform a complicated task. **Availability:** VHS; 3/4U; 8mm.

35204 ■ Together We Can!
American Media, Inc.
4621 121st St.
Urbandale, IA 50323-2311
Ph:(515)224-0919
Free: 888-776-8268
Fax: (515)327-2555
Co. E-mail: custsvc@ammedia.com
URL: http://www.ammedia.com
Released: 1991. **Price:** $545.00. **Description:** Discusses actions individuals can take to ensure good teamwork. Includes a discussion guide. **Availability:** VHS; 3/4U; 8mm; CC.

35205 ■ Trust Your Team
Excellence in Training Corp.
1303 Marsh Ln.
Carrollton, TX 75006
Free: 800-747-6569
Released: 1987. **Price:** $595.00. **Description:** This video is designed to help managers open up their management styles, to allow all employees to function better, and take on more responsibility. **Availability:** VHS; 3/4U.

35206 ■ Where There's a Will...(Leadership and Motivation)
Video Arts, Inc.
c/o Aim Learning Group
8238-40 Lehigh
Morton Grove, IL 60053-2615
Free: 877-444-2230
Fax: (416)252-2155
Co. E-mail: service@aimlearninggroup.com
URL: http://www.aimlearninggroup.com
Released: 1988. **Price:** $790.00. **Description:** Find out how you can motivate your workers to a higher productivity level. **Availability:** VHS; 8mm; 3/4U; Special order formats.

35207 ■ Working Teams: Helping Your Team Succeed
American Management Association
9 Galen St.
PO Box 9119
Watertown, MA 02472

Ph:(617)926-4600
Free: 800-225-3215
Fax: (617)923-1875
URL: http://www.amanet.org
Price: $645.00. **Description:** Outlines the principles of being a contributing team member and not just a team player. **Availability:** VHS; CC.

35208 ■ Workplace Readiness: Teamwork
Agency for Instructional Technology (AIT)
1800 N. Stonelake Dr.
Box A
Bloomington, IN 47402-0120
Ph:(812)339-2203
Free: 800-457-4509
Fax: (812)333-4218
Co. E-mail: info@ait.net
URL: http://www.ait.net
Released: 1992. **Price:** $395.00. **Description:** Series of seven programs introducing students to the idea of teamwork in culturally diverse work forces. Programs deal with specific examples. Comes with guide. **Availability:** VHS; CC.

35209 ■ Workplace Teams
American Management Association
9 Galen St.
PO Box 9119
Watertown, MA 02472
Ph:(617)926-4600
Free: 800-225-3215
Fax: (617)923-1875
URL: http://www.amanet.org
Price: $975.00. **Description:** Contains information on the concept of building productive teams and the use of teamwork. **Availability:** VHS; CC.

35210 ■ Workteams and the Wizard of Oz
CRM Films
2215 Faraday Ave.
Carlsbad, CA 92008
Ph:(760)431-9800
Free: 800-421-0833
Fax: (760)931-5792
Co. E-mail: donna@crmfilms.com
URL: http://www.crmfilms.com
Released: 1996. **Price:** $595.00. **Description:** Gives an example, with "The Wizard of Oz" as a successful workteam with diverse characters. Includes a Leader's Guide and Workbook. **Availability:** VHS.

CONSULTANTS

35211 ■ Adventure Learning Associates Inc.
567 Hale Rd.
PO Box 6062
Brattleboro, VT 05302
Ph:(802)254-6160
Free: 800-551-3210
Fax: (802)254-3582
Co. E-mail: info@alrna.com
URL: http://www.alrna.com

E-mail: info@alrna.com
Scope: Provides consulting services and training in experiential training and development. Specifically provides teambuilding, communications skills, and empowerment skill sessions. Also focuses on needs analysis, strategic planning, and visioning for newly developing groups. Firm specializes in training trainers in experiential outdoor programming. Industries served: all including government and can work with intact groups at all levels from line staff to boards and executive committees. **Seminars:** Train the Adventure Trainer.

35212 ■ Advisory Management Services Inc.
9600 E 129th St., Ste. B
Kansas City, MO 64149-1025
Ph:(816)765-9611
Fax: (816)765-7447
Co. E-mail: amsi1@mindspring.com

E-mail: amsi1@mindspring.com
Scope: A management consulting and training firm specializing in employee relations, management and

staff training, organizational development, strategic planning, and continuous quality improvement.

35213 ■ Arete Ventures Administration L.L.C.
3 Bethesda Metro Ctr.
Bethesda, MD 20814-5330
Ph:(301)657-6268
Fax: (301)770-2877
Scope: Provides team-based management consulting services to organizations of all types. Provides a unique service in management consulting by bridging traditional strategic consulting that focuses on the numbers (and largely ignores the human side of organizations), and typical organization consulting that stresses team development (but avoids the pragmatic realities of running an organization). Focuses on strategic planning, organization design and effectiveness, managing human resources, and teambuilding/group dynamics.

35214 ■ The Axelrod Group Inc.
723 Laurel Ave.
Wilmette, IL 60091
Ph:(847)251-7361
Fax: (847)251-7370
Co. E-mail: info@axelrodgroup.com
URL: http://www.axelrodgroup.com

E-mail: info@axelrodgroup.com
Scope: Provides organizational development consulting services in the following areas: Conference Model® approach to redesign, strategic planning, organization assessment, self-directed work teams, cultural change and team development, and management. Clients include major corporations and nonprofit organizations. **Publications:** "You Don't Have to Do It Alone," Oct, 2004; "Terms of Engagement"; "The Conference Model"; "Harnessing Complexity"; "The Philosophy Behind Our Systems"; "Considerations Before You Build a Collaborative Process"; "Making Teams Work"; "Purpose is the Cornerstone"; "How to Build Relationships"; "How to Maximize Information Sharing"; "How to Promote Equity and Fairness"; "How to Create Freedom and Autonomy". **Seminars:** Conference Model® Professional Skills Seminar; Team Development; Creating Team Based Organizations; Conflict Management for Managers; Working Together; Communications Skills for Improving Productivity and Relationships; Designing for Engagement, Terms of Engagement.

35215 ■ Bloch Consulting Group
2033 Wild Cherry Ln.
Kalamazoo, MI 49009-9168
Ph:(616)375-6849
Fax: (616)375-6849
Scope: Managing creative processes to develop new ideas and products. Firm offers expertise in high performance work systems, teamwork, self-regulated teams, total quality management, employee involvement, and creativity session facilitation.

35216 ■ Business Development Group Inc.
220 E Huron, Ste. 250
Ann Arbor, MI 48104
Ph:(248)552-0821
Fax: (248)552-1924
Co. E-mail: info@busdevgroup.com
URL: http://www.busdevgroup.com

E-mail: info@busdevgroup.com
Scope: Consulting firm expertise in leadership development; strategic thinking; organizational transformation; team-based work systems; organizational learning; rapid change; knowledge management; competitive intelligence; crisis management; merger and acquisition integration; product integration and new product development. **Publications:** "Navigating in the Sea of Change," Competitive Intelligence Review Journal; "The Influence of Cultural Aspects of Strategic Information, Analysis, and Delivery"; "What Leadership Needs From Competitive Intelligence Professionals," Journal of Association for Global and Strategic Information. **Seminars:** Process of Self-Design for the Evolving Organization; Large System

Change Intervention; Self Assessment and the Transformational Process; The Knowledge Exchange - Shared Practices Workshop.

35217 ■ CFI Group USA L.L.C.
625 Avis Dr.
Ann Arbor, MI 48108
Ph:(734)930-9090
Fax: (734)930-0911
Co. E-mail: contactcfi@cfigroup.com
URL: http://www.cfigroup.com

E-mail: contactcfi@cfigroup.com
Scope: Management consulting firm that helps its clients worldwide to maximize shareholder value by optimizing customer and employee satisfaction. **Publications:** "Consumers Rate the Post-Boom Industry," Mortgage Banking, Jan, 2005"; "Interview with a Customer Satisfaction Guru," Rotman Magazine, 2005".

35218 ■ Charismedia
610 W End Ave.
New York, NY 10001
Ph:(212)362-6808
Fax: (212)362-6809
Co. E-mail: info@Charismedia.net
URL: http://www.charismedia.net

E-mail: info@Charismedia.net
Scope: Offers speech and image training as well as speech writing services for effective presentation skills. **Publications:** "The New Secrets of Charisma," McGraw-Hill. **Seminars:** Charisma Skills Training-The best investment for successful careers and relationships; Three-stage Anti-Stagefright Breathing.

35219 ■ Cole Financial Services Inc.
65 Cadillac Sq., Ste. 2850
Detroit, MI 48226
Ph:(313)962-7055
Free: 877-972-7055
Fax: 877-962-7815
Co. E-mail: colefinancial1@ameritech.net
URL: http://www.colefinancial1.net

E-mail: colefinancial1@ameritech.net
Scope: Offers services in business and human resource management and employee motivation. Industries served: engineering, construction, government, and other business entities. **Seminars:** How to Tap Your Potential and Discover Your Genius; What Every Woman Should Know before She Goes into Business; Four Phases of Business Ownership; Total Quality Management From the Bottom Up.

35220 ■ Competitive Edge Inc.
241 E Crestwood Rd.
PO Box 2418
Peachtree City, GA 30269
Ph:(770)487-6460
Fax: (770)487-2919
Co. E-mail: judy@competitiveedgeinc.com
URL: http://www.competitiveedgeinc.com

E-mail: judy@competitiveedgeinc.com
Scope: Human Resources consulting firm providing customized training and software solutions to assist clients in optimizing their human intellectual capital through effective selection, coaching, and training. Works with a network of consultants that are located throughout the United States, Canada, and Europe. **Publications:** "Energizing People: Unleashing The Power of DISC"; "The Ripple Effect: How the Global Model of Endorsement Opens Doors to Success"; "The Journey - Quotes to keep your boat afloat"; "The Universal Language DISC Reference Manual ". **Seminars:** How to Recruit and Retain High Performing Employees; The Importance of Values Matching For Sales Selection; How to Build a High Performance Team; Dynamic Communication Skills; Creating Nurturing Customer Relationships.

35221 ■ The Corlund Group L.L.C.
101 Federal St., Ste. 310
Boston, MA 02110
Ph:(617)423-9364

Fax: (617)423-9371
Co. E-mail: info@corlundgroup.com
URL: http://www.corlundgroup.com

E-mail: info@corlundgroup.com
Scope: Boutique firms offers services in the areas of leadership, governance, and change, with a particular focus on CEO and senior executive succession planning, including assessment, development, and orchestrating succession processes with management and Boards of Directors. Also Board governance effectiveness. **Publications:** "Leadership Due Diligence: The Neglected Governance Frontier," Directorship, Sep, 2001; "Leadership Due Diligence: Managing the Risks," The Corporate Board, Aug, 2001; "Succession: The need for detailed insight," Directors and Boards, 2001; "CEO Succession: Who's Doing Due Diligence?," 2001.

35222 ■ The Cradlerock Group
65 High Ridge Rd., Ste. 229
Stamford, CT 06905
Ph:(203)324-0088
Fax: (203)547-7778
Co. E-mail: info@cradlerock.com
URL: http://www.cradlerock.com

E-mail: info@cradlerock.com
Scope: Provides teambuilding and personal challenge programs for both corporate and nonprofit groups. Utilizing both team-challenge and personal initiative courses, along with a variety of other outdoor-based adventure activities, participants are encouraged to explore group dynamics and personal abilities. Cradlerock facilitators then help the participants to relate the outdoor experience to the business, education and social worlds. Industries served: large corporations, school districts, nonprofit organizations, and government agencies. **Seminars:** Team Start; Who Are We?; Whos On First?; Getting Past Stuck; Team Skills; Group Skills; Effective Team Leadership; Leading Global Teams; 360 Coaching; The Other Diversity; Harnessing Change; The Art of Sale.

35223 ■ Delta Systems
5621 Somerset Dr.
Brooklyn, MI 49230
Ph:(517)592-5463
Fax: (517)592-5463
Co. E-mail: renee@4deltasystems.com
URL: http://www.4deltasystems.com

E-mail: renee@4deltasystems.com
Scope: Organizational development consultant specializing in team-building training and keynote speeches. Industries served: manufacturing automotive suppliers, nuclear power plants. **Publications:** Checkered Flag Teams: Driving Your Workplace Into the Winners Circle; Success is a Team Effort; CAR-Styles™ - A Communication Style Model; The Life Challenge Inventory. **Seminars:** Team Leader Training; Fast Cycle Time: Change Leadership; Revitalizing Mature Teams; Fast Problem Solving; Pit Crew Challenge; Leadership Skills for Non-Supervisory People; Fast Start Teamwork.

35224 ■ Dimond Hospitality Consulting Group Inc.
5710 Stoneway Trl.
Nashville, TN 37209
Ph:(615)353-0033
Fax: (615)352-5290
Co. E-mail: dimond@dimondconsultinggroup.com
URL: http://www.dimondconsultinggroup.com

E-mail: dimond@dimondconsultinggroup.com
Scope: Specializes in strategic planning; start-up businesses; business process re-engineering; team building; competitive analysis; venture capital; competitive intelligence; and due diligence. Offers litigation support. Comprehensive hospitality consulting firm that serves as an adviser to leading hotel companies, independent hotels, lending institutions, trustees, law firms, investment companies and municipalities in the areas of:Asset management, Acquisition due diligence, Arbitration ,Disposition advisory services, Exit strategies, Financial review and analysis, Impact studies, Mediation.

35225 ■ Dropkin & Co.
390 George St.
New Brunswick, NJ 08901
Ph:(732)828-3211
Fax: (732)828-4118
Co. E-mail: murray@dropkin.com
URL: http://www.dropkin.com

E-mail: murray@dropkin.com
Scope: Firm specializes in feasibility studies; business management; business process re-engineering; and team building, healthcare and housing. **Publications:** "Guide to Auditing Nonprofit Organizations"; "The Cash Flow Management Book for Nonprofits"

35226 ■ The DuMond Group
5282 Princeton Ave.
Westminster, CA 92683-2753
Ph:(714)373-0610
Scope: Firm specializes in organizational development; small business management; employee surveys and communication; performance appraisals; and team building.

35227 ■ Dynamic Firm Management
4570 Campus Dr., Ste. 60
Newport Beach, CA 92660
Ph:(949)640-2220
Co. E-mail: info@dynamicfirm.com
URL: http://www.dynamicfirm.com

E-mail: info@dynamicfirm.com
Scope: Management consulting to law firms and other professional service providers. Emphasis on Partnership Relations, Compensation, Strategic Planning, Increasing Revenues, Profitable Firm Operations and Effective Management and Team building. Initial work includes the determination of your objectives; quantifying measurable accomplishments and outlining the consulting requirements. Industries served: Law Firms, attorneys, professional service. **Publications:** "Why Good Partnerships Go Bad", The Journal of Law Office Economics and Management, Feb, 2006; "Perfect Union", Daily Journal, Mar, 2004; "Future Perfect", Daily Journal, Dec, 2003. **Seminars:** Facilitates Partner retreats and management workshops. Topics covered include: Partner relations; compensations; management effectiveness; team building and strategic planning.

35228 ■ Eastern Point Consulting Group Inc.
75 Oak St.
Newton, MA 02464
Ph:(617)965-4141
Fax: (617)965-4172
Co. E-mail: info@eastpt.com
URL: http://www.eastpt.com

E-mail: info@eastpt.com
Scope: Specializes in bringing practical solutions to complex challenges. Provides consultation and training in managing diversity; comprehensive sexual-harassment policies and programs; organizational development; benchmarks 360 skills assessment; executive coaching; strategic human resource planning; team building; leadership development for women; mentoring programs; and gender issues in the workplace. **Seminars:** Leadership Development for Women.

35229 ■ Effective Resources Inc.
2803 Southfield Ct.
Holiday, FL 34691-2505
Ph:(727)944-2507
Free: 800-288-6044
Fax: (727)944-2607
Co. E-mail: customerservice@effectiveresources.com
URL: http://www.effectiveresources.com

E-mail: customerservice@effectiveresources.com
Scope: Concerned with technical aspects of human resource management. Specializes in compensation and incentive plans; performance appraisals; team building; and personnel policies and procedures; affirmative action plan preparation.

35230 ■ Employee Development Systems Inc.
7308 S Alton Way, Ste. 2J
Centennial, CO 80112
Ph:(303)221-0710
Free: 800-282-3374
Fax: (303)221-0704
Co. E-mail: info@edsiusa.com
URL: http://www.edsiusa.com

E-mail: info@edsiusa.com
Scope: Produces training systems that increase employee productivity by motivating employees to take responsibility for their own performance and by showing employees and managers how to improve communications and create productive team relationships. **Publications:** HR Manager. **Seminars:** Increasing Personal Effectiveness; Communicating to Manage Performance; ProAction: Responding to Change; and Just-in-Time Training: working successfully in a changing environment, challenging the status quo for continuous improvement, assertive communication, and reaching agreement. **Special Services:** eEducate, subsidiary, with over 3000 web-based training courses at www.eEducate.com.

35231 ■ Federer Resources Inc.
106 E 6th St.
Austin, TX 78701-3659
Ph:(512)476-8800
Scope: Firm specializes in feasibility studies; start-up businesses; small business management; mergers and acquisitions; joint ventures; divestitures; interim management; crisis management; turnarounds; production planning; team building; appraisals and valuations.

35232 ■ Goldore Consulting Inc.
120-5 St. NW
PO Box 590
Linden, AB, Canada T0M 1J0
Ph:(403)546-4208
Fax: (403)546-4208
Co. E-mail: goldore@leadershipessentials.com

E-mail: goldore@leadershipessentials.com
Scope: Provides consulting service in Leadership and management skills. Industries served: primarily charities, non-profits; some businesses. **Publications:** O Desafio de Lideranca; The Challenge Of Leadership; Le Challenge du Leadership; El Desafio de Liderazgo; Tantangan Kipeminpinan.

35233 ■ Grimmick Consulting Services
455 Donner Way
San Ramon, CA 94583
Ph:(925)735-9090
Fax: (925)735-1100
Co. E-mail: grimmick@pacbell.net

E-mail: grimmick@pacbell.net
Scope: Provides consulting services in the areas of strategic planning; organizational assessment; organizational development; leadership development and Baldrige Criteria.

35234 ■ Interpersonal Communication Programs Inc.
30772 Southview Dr., Ste. 200
Evergreen, CO 80439-7990
Ph:(303)674-2051
Free: 800-328-5099
Fax: (303)674-4283
Co. E-mail: icp@comskills.com
URL: http://www.couplecommunication.com

E-mail: icp@comskills.com
Scope: Provides team building and interpersonal communication training in small and large corporations. Serves private industries as well as government agencies. **Seminars:** Collaborative Team Skills for Intact Work Groups; Core Communication: Skills and Processes for Managers, Supervisors and Employees.

35235 ■ K & T Training
103 Greenville St.
Newnan, GA 30263-2630

Ph:(770)253-5870
Fax: (770)253-8866
Scope: Specializes in strategic planning; profit enhancement; organizational development; start-up businesses; interim management; crisis management; turnarounds; business process re-engineering; team building; cost controls.

35236 ■ The Ken Blanchard Cos.
125 State Pl.
Escondido, CA 92029
Ph:(760)839-8070
Free: 800-728-6000
Fax: (760)489-8407
Co. E-mail: info@kenblanchard.com
URL: http://www.kenblanchard.com

E-mail: info@kenblanchard.com
Scope: Full-service management development-training company known for development of the One-Minute Manager concept. Develops and sells quality products and services that enhance management and leadership skills. Offers seminars, workshops, in-house consulting, videos, audio tapes, slides, books, instruments and games. Areas of expertise include management training, team building, attitude and needs assessment, productivity improvement, motivation, and corporate development. Industries served: health, hospitality, financial, food service, telecommunications, retail, utilities, associations, aerospace, automotive, military, education, manufacturing, and government agencies. **Publications:** "Building High Performing Teams"; "Leadership Training for Supervisors"; "Legendary Service"; "The One Minute Manager". **Seminars:** Situational Leadership II; The One Minute Manager; Leadership and The One Minute Manager; Putting The One Minute Manager to Work; Ethical Management.

35237 ■ William E. Kuhn & Associates
234 Cook St.
Denver, CO 80206-5305
Ph:(303)322-8233
Fax: (303)322-9032
Co. E-mail: billkuhn1@cs.com

E-mail: billkuhn1@cs.com
Scope: Firm specializes in strategic planning; profit enhancement; small business management; mergers and acquisitions; joint ventures; divestitures; human resources management; performance appraisals; team building; sales management; appraisals and valuations.

35238 ■ LDG Associates
8094 Mission Vista Dr.
San Diego, CA 92120-1537
Ph:(619)583-0261
Fax: (619)583-4608
Co. E-mail: douggross@leadershipteam.com
URL: http://www.leadershipteam.com

E-mail: douggross@leadershipteam.com
Scope: Consultants in leadership training and development, coaching, 360 degree feedback, and team-building. Specialize in helping leaders build effective teams. Leaders learn specific skills to help them achieve individual and organizational objectives. Industries served: medical manufacturing, aerospace, electrical manufacturing, manufacturing, petroleum, and government agencies. **Seminars:** Leadership Styles and Strategies; Influencing Styles and Strategies; Organizing Yourself and Others; Team Building; 360 Degree Feedback; Executive Coaching; Stress Management.

35239 ■ May Toy Lukens
3226 NE 26th Ct.
Renton, WA 98056
Ph:(425)891-3226
Scope: Provide training to teach people to think of ways to improve their operations continuously by changing the way they think, and how they are motivated. Industries served: all, particularly financial. Operational analysis and training. **Seminars:** Seminars and workshops in maximizing resource utilization and staff potential.

35240 ■ Lupfer & Associates
92 Glen St.
South Natick, MA 01760
Ph:(508)655-3950
Fax: (508)655-7826
Co. E-mail: donlupfer@aol.com
URL: http://www.lupferassociates.com

E-mail: donlupfer@aol.com
Scope: Assists off shore hi-tech companies in entering United States markets and specializes in channel development for all sorts of products. Perform MARCOM support for hi-tech United States clients. **Publications:** "What's Next For Distribution-Feast or Famine?"; "The Changing Global Marketplace"; "Making Global Distribution Work". **Seminars:** How to do Business in the United States.

35241 ■ Management Advisory Associates Inc.
PO Box 703
Bowling Green, OH 43402
Ph:(419)352-7782
Fax: (419)354-8781
Co. E-mail: maa@wcnet.org
URL: http://www.maaconsulting.com

E-mail: maa@wcnet.org
Scope: Offers counsel in organizational diagnosis, development and change, as well as management development, manpower planning and forecasting, performance appraisal, management by objectives, team-building, related industrial and human relations areas, and a strong emphasis on self-directed work teams. Industries served: energy, health-care, auto parts manufacturers, chemical, financial, petroleum, and government agencies. **Publications:** The Discipline of Change Management, 2005; An Operational Definition of ODC, 2004. **Seminars:** Implementing Self-Directed Work Teams; SDWT Simulation; Managing Team Productivity; Navigating the Mine Fields of Change.

35242 ■ Mandalay Associates L.L.C.
3020 El Cerrito Plz.
PMB 226
El Cerrito, CA 94530-4002
Ph:(510)526-4651
Fax: (510)526-5774
Co. E-mail: contact@mandalayassociates.com
URL: http://www.mandalayassociates.com

E-mail: contact@mandalayassociates.com
Scope: Business management firm specializes in conflict resolution, employee relations, employment and placement, organizational analysis and development, human resources program development, program and project management, and staff development and training.

35243 ■ Miller, Hellwig Associates
150 W End Ave.
New York, NY 10023-5713
Ph:(212)799-0471
Fax: (212)877-0186
Co. E-mail: millerhelwig@earthlink.net

E-mail: millerhelwig@earthlink.net
Scope: Consulting services in the areas of start-up businesses; small business management; employee surveys and communication; performance appraisals; executive searches; team building; personnel policies and procedures; market research. Also involved in improving cross-cultural and multi-cultural relationships, particularly with Japanese clients. **Seminars:** Objectives and standards/recruiting for boards of directors.

35244 ■ Jane Moosbruker, Organization Development Consultant
72 Coventry Wood Rd.
Bolton, MA 01740
Ph:(978)779-5423
Fax: (978)779-6036
Co. E-mail: jamoos@ziplink.net

E-mail: jamoos@ziplink.net
Scope: Offers process-oriented consultation to organizations, in the areas of organizational change, team

building, management development, and conflict utilization. Industries served include biotechnology, information services, computer technology, aerospace, education, healthcare, and environmental. **Publications:** "Transitioning Work Groups into High Performing Teams," 1993; "Group Dynamics - History and Future," Vienna: WUV-Verlag, 1993; "Business Process Redesign and Organization Development-Applied Behavioral Science," 1998; "Forgotten Elements: Including Structure and Process in Recovery Efforts". **Seminars:** Managing Organizational Change; Facilitating and Managing Complex Systems Change; Team Leadership for Developing a High Productivity Team; Building a Team-based Organization; Conflict Utilization; Team Skills.

35245 ■ MW Corp.
2538 Crompond Rd.
Yorktown Heights, NY 10598-3713
Fax: (914)528-8889
Scope: Training firm provides training materials (books and videos) and conducts public workshops and custom-designed on-site training and development in the areas of management development, supervisor/technical leader training and development, team development, facilitator training, self-directed work teams, quality customer service workshops, and employee involvement programs. Serves all types of organizations. **Publications:** Leading a Service Team; A Team Leader's Day; The Changing Workplace; Self-Directed Work Teams; Supervisor in Transition. **Seminars:** Self-Directed Work Teams; The Management Workshop; First-line Supervisor/Technical Leader Workshop.

35246 ■ The Nelson Group Ltd.
5 Milk St., Ste. 4
Portland, ME 04101
Ph:(207)775-1199
Fax: (207)775-0141
URL: http://www.nelsonltd.com
Scope: Consulting services in the areas of strategic planning; organizational development; small business management; mergers and acquisitions; joint ventures; divestitures; interim management; crisis management; turnarounds; performance appraisals; executive searches; outplacement; and team building.

35247 ■ Organization Counselors Inc.
44 W Broadway, Ste. 1102
PO Box 987
Salt Lake City, UT 84101
Ph:(801)363-2900
Fax: (801)363-0861
Co. E-mail: jpanos@xmission.com

E-mail: jpanos@xmission.com
Scope: Firm specializes in organizational development; employee surveys and communication; outplacement; team building; total quality management (TQM) and continuous improvement. **Seminars:** Correcting Performance Problems; Total Quality Management; Employee Selection; Performance Management.

35248 ■ Organizational Futures
56 Pine St., Ste. 2b
Providence, RI 02903
Ph:(401)351-7110
Fax: (401)351-7158
Scope: Builder of agile human networks to champion innovation and mobilize change; to pursue business opportunities; to custom design agile organizations and communities, to foster civic engagement. **Seminars:** Facilitating for Results.

35249 ■ Organizational Transformations
PO Box 2553
Aptos, CA 95001-2553
Ph:(831)688-1344
Fax: (831)688-8091
Co. E-mail: postmaster@orgtrans.com
URL: http://www.orgtrans.com

E-mail: postmaster@orgtrans.com
Scope: A management and organizational consulting firm that provides customized strategies to help com-

panies increase productivity and profit. Specializes in organizational development, executive coaching, team building, conflict resolution and work comp reduction.

35250 ■ P2C2 Group Inc.
4101 Denfeld Ave.
Kensington, MD 20895-1514
Ph:(301)942-7985
Fax: (301)942-7986
Co. E-mail: info@p2c2group.com
URL: http://www.p2c2group.com

E-mail: info@p2c2group.com
Scope: Firm specializes in federal information technology management including capital investment management, strategic plans, policy, enterprise architecture, information security, documentation and knowledge management, OMB and NIST compliance, and IT program management. **Publications:** "How to Work with Proposal Consultants"; "Outside Reviewers for Proposals"; "The High Cost of Federal Information Technology".

35251 ■ Glenn M. Parker Associates Inc.
36 Otter Creek Rd.
Skillman, NJ 08558
Ph:(609)333-0203
Fax: (609)333-0203
Co. E-mail: glenn@glennparker.com
URL: http://www.glennparker.com

E-mail: glenn@glennparker.com
Scope: Provides the following services: team building without business teams, training workshops in team effectiveness, facilitation skills and meeting management, consulting to help organizations transition to a team-based operation, speaking at professional conferences and corporate meeting and diagnostic services to assess the effectiveness of teams and organizations. **Publications:** G. Parker, 50 Activities for Team Building, HRD Press (1992); Instruments: Parker Team Player Survey (1992)Team Development Survey,(1992) Consulting Psychologists Press; 50 Activities for Self-Directed Teams, HRD Press (1994); Cross-Functional Teams Tool Kit, Pfeiffer/Lossey Bass, 1997; Best Practices for Teams, Vol. 1 (1996), Vol. 2 (1998), HRD Press; 25 Instruments for Team Building, HRD Press (1998), Teamwork and Teamplay: Games and Activities for Building and Training Teams (with Sivasailam Thiagarajan), Jossey-Bass/Pfeiffer, 1999, Rewarding Teams: Lessons from the Trenches, Jossey-Bass/Wiley, 2000, Team Workout: A Trainer's Sourcebook of 50 Team Building Games and Activities, HRD Press, 2001, Team Depot: A Warehouse of 585 Tools to Reassess, Rehabilitate and Rejuvenate your Team, Jossey-Bass/Pfeiffer/Wiley, 2002, Cross-Functional Teams: Working with Allies, Enemies and Other Strangers, Completely Revised and Updates, JosseyBass/Wiley (2003); Video: Team Building II: What Makes a Good Team Player? CRM Learning, 1996. **Seminars:** How to Build Strong Teams and Develop Team Players (1 day); Effective Meetings (1 day). Building A Facilitators Tool Kit (1 day).

35252 ■ Parker Consultants Inc.
67 Mason St.
Greenwich, CT 06830
Ph:(203)869-9400
Scope: Firm specializes in strategic planning; organizational development; small business management; performance appraisals; executive searches; team building; and customer service audits.

35253 ■ Participative Dynamics Inc.
1327 Cottonwood Trl.
Sarasota, FL 34232
Ph:(941)377-3920
Free: 888-358-8848
Fax: (941)377-7328
Co. E-mail: ibens@ij.net
URL: http://www.participative-dynamics.com

E-mail: ibens@ij.net
Scope: OD consulting on change management initiatives. A consulting firm that specializes in helping or-

ganizations implement major culture change, team building, strategic planning lessons and group facilitation. **Publications:** "Advanced Facilitation Strategies contains," 2005; "Facilitating with Ease," 2000; "Facilitation at a Glance"; "Team Launch!". **Seminars:** Training workshops: Core Facilitation Skills & Advanced Facilitation Skills; Facilitating Better Meetings; Team Launch Preparation & Team Member Training; Internal Consulting Skills & Conflict Management.

35254 ■ Partnerwerks Inc.
PO Box 1046
Comfort, TX 78013
Ph:(830)995-4853
Fax: (830)995-4854
Co. E-mail: info@partnerwerks.com
URL: http://www.partnerwerks.com

E-mail: info@partnerwerks.com
Scope: Organizational development consultants specializing in development of leadership skills for managing relationships with a client company's customers, suppliers and employees through effective teamwork and new partnering practices. The firm currently has expertise in productive collaborations; teamwork, leadership and flat structures; power, influence, autonomy and empowerment; transformational learning, design, delivery, and evaluation; organizational culture diagnosis, analysis, and intervention; interactive broadcast education; interpersonal and organizational communication; technology transfer and risk-pooling; futures research, goals, motivation, and action planning; accident planning and response management; technical professional development; and post-modern organizing and management. Industries served: economic development, electric and gas utilities, electronics and computer production, healthcare systems and providers, insurance and financial services, manufacturing industrial goods, petroleum production and distribution, state government agencies, telecommunications services, broadcast journalism and education, and food development and packaging. **Publications:** "Teamwork Is An Individual Skill," Berrett-Kohler, 2001. **Seminars:** Project Team Leadership; Managing Teams; Team Planning.

35255 ■ Performance Consulting Associates Inc.
3700 Crestwood Pky., Ste. 100
Duluth, GA 30096
Ph:(770)717-2737
Fax: (770)717-7014
Co. E-mail: info@pcaconsulting.com
URL: http://www.pcaconsulting.com

E-mail: info@pcaconsulting.com
Scope: Maintenance consulting and engineering firm specializing in production planning, project management, team building, and re-engineering maintenance. **Publications:** "Asset Reliability Coordinator," Maintenance Technology; "Does Planning Pay," Plant Services; "Know What It Is You Have To Maintain," Maintenance Technology.

35256 ■ The Performance Engineering Group Inc.
765 Via Airosa, Ste. 220
Santa Barbara, CA 93110
Ph:(805)967-6568
Fax: (805)967-6533
Co. E-mail: inquiries@thepegroup.com
URL: http://www.thepegroup.com

E-mail: inquiries@thepegroup.com
Scope: A management consulting firm that provides organizational development, process re-engineering, team building, and other organizational change services. **Publications:** "Built to Learn"; "Software and Streaming Videos Let Companies Capture What's Unwritten". **Special Services:** QuickLearn™ a CBT tool that is produced at a fraction of the cost and time of traditional training solutions. It's an easy-to-use solution that lets employees learn at their own pace.

35257 ■ Performance Technologies Inc.
6756 Brantford Rd.
PO Box 13463
Dayton, OH 45414

Ph:(937)890-1243
Fax: (937)890-7853
Co. E-mail: info@performancetec.com
URL: http://www.performancetec.com

E-mail: info@performancetec.com
Scope: Services include: organizational transformation, creation of vision, values and operating philosophy, business analysis, impact analysis, innovation technology, succession planning, and process mapping. Training services include advanced sales strategies, sales coaching and management, training processes, management effectiveness, leadership development, performance management, measurement and assessment.

35258 ■ Pilot Consulting Corp.
126 Elk Ave.
PO Box 1249
Crested Butte, CO 81224
Ph:(970)349-1250
Fax: (970)349-1251
Co. E-mail: info@pilotconsulting.com
URL: http://www.pilotconsulting.com

E-mail: info@pilotconsulting.com
Scope: Firm specializes in the implementation of strategy, management of transition, and development of leadership.

35259 ■ Pioneering Management Possibilities
31000 Telegraph Rd., Ste. 260
Bingham Farms, MI 48025
Ph:(248)647-9290
Fax: (248)647-1537
URL: http://www.pioneeringmanagement.com
Scope: A team of management consultants and business coaches specializing in the application of management principles. Areas include team building, strategic planning, personal development, leadership development and management training. **Publications:** "Accountability - Compliance or Commitment"; "Leadership - The Missing Link"; "Succession Planning: An Imperative for Personal Growth"; "The Soft Stuff Yields Hard Results".

35260 ■ Positive Impact Consulting
9845 Horn Rd., Ste. 120
Sacramento, CA 95827
Ph:(916)366-3000
Free: 800-376-7484
Fax: (916)364-9860
Co. E-mail: info@positiveimpact.com
URL: http://www.positiveimpact.com

E-mail: info@positiveimpact.com
Scope: Management services in executive development, strategic planning, teambuilding, organization-wide surveys, customer surveys, systems and process redesigns, skills assessments, TQM overview training, TQM tools training, positive impact facilitator training, the coaching experience (TQM leadership training), customized course designing. **Seminars:** Cafe de la Facilitation, Jul, 2006; The Coaching Experience, Jul, 2006; Facilitator Boot Camp, Aug, 2006.

35261 ■ Profit Associates Inc.
26 Hunters Forest Dr.
PO Box 81018
Charleston, SC 29414
Ph:(843)763-5718
Free: 800-688-6304
Fax: (843)763-5719
Co. E-mail: bobrog@awod.com
URL: http://www.profit-associates.com

E-mail: bobrog@awod.com
Scope: A team of management and turnaround specialists providing consulting services. Focuses on the problems of small to mediumsized businesses in the manufacturing, distribution, construction, software, health care, and transportation industries. Specializes in employee productivity and incentives, management re-engineering, profit and expense controls, production planning, strategic business planning, marketing and public relations, or ISO 9000 support.

35262 ■ Renaissance Leadership
2500 Old King Cir.
Midlothian, VA 23113-9685
Ph:(804)423-4266
Fax: (804)423-4267
Co. E-mail: info@renlead.com
URL: http://www.renlead.com

E-mail: info@renlead.com
Scope: Specializes in the strategic building of high performance organizations and culture. Offer strategic consulting, executive coaching, team development and cultural transformation seminars which combine contemporary learning theory, leadership practice, and work-related outdoor adventures. Serves all industries in the United States, Europe, Central America and Asia. **Seminars:** Culture Change Leadership; Creating High Performance Learning Organizations; Life Planning; Thriving on Change; Team Building and Alignment; Creativity, Risk Taking, and Innovation; Creating a High Performance Culture; Servant Leadership; Capitalizing on Diversity; Coaching for Optimal Performance.

35263 ■ Soul Works
3809 County Rd. E
Swanton, OH 43558-9276
Ph:(419)825-2444
Scope: An organizational development consulting and training firm that specializes in leadership development and creating high performance work systems. Major focus is consulting to organizational system change and work redesign efforts. System change is also supported by a comprehensive and fully integrated curriculum of leadership development workshops. Workshops and consulting services develop: empowered entrepreneurial leadership, personal and organizational vision, teamwork and involvement, and a whole systems perspective when implementing change. Industries served: private industries including healthcare organizations, manufacturing, service, and nonprofit. **Seminars:** Mastering Leadership!; Organizational Control and Dependency; Aligned Teams.

35264 ■ Stier Associates
4 Dunellen
Cromwell, CT 06416-2702
Ph:(860)635-1590
Fax: (860)635-1591
Co. E-mail: s.stier@worldnet.att.net

E-mail: s.stier@worldnet.att.net
Scope: Personal development consulting. Subspecialty in Family-Owned businesses. Services include succession planning, executive coaching, strategic management, team building, board development. Consulting services for public companies include process consulting, team building, executive coaching, diversity management, and strategic management. Consulting to religious institutions.

35265 ■ Tamayo Consulting Inc.
169 Saxony Rd., Ste. 112
Encinitas, CA 92024-6779
Free: 800-580-9606
Fax: (760)479-1465
Co. E-mail: info@tamayoconsulting.com
URL: http://www.tamayoconsulting.com

E-mail: info@tamayoconsulting.com
Scope: Training and consulting firm specializing in: leadership and team development. Industries served: private, non-profit, government, educational.

35266 ■ Vision Management
149 Meadows Rd.
Lafayette, NJ 07848-3120
Ph:(973)702-1116
Fax: (201)702-8311
Scope: Firm specializes in profit enhancement; strategic planning; business process re-engineering; industrial engineering; facilities planning; team building; inventory management; and Total Quality Management (TQM).

35267 ■ Steve Wilson & Co.
1159 S Creekway Ct.
Columbus, OH 43230

Ph:(614)855-4733
Free: 800-669-5233
Fax: (614)855-4889
Co. E-mail: steve@stevewilson.com
URL: http://www.stevewilson.com

E-mail: steve@stevewilson.com
Scope: Specializing in teambuilding, staff development and personal growth, consultant presents the way humor works and awakens new ways of relating to ourselves and others. Consultant carries designation of Certified Speaking Professional (CSP) and is one of seven persons worldwide certified in I-Power program instruction. The topics that consultant specializes in are: health and humor, funny business, motivation and productivity, human relations, stress management, team building, communication, and creativity. Industries served: education, medical, telecommunications, service, allied medical, sales, training, real estate, associations, universities and colleges, temporary services, state and federal government, churches, and manufacturing worldwide. **Publications:** "The Steve Wilson Report"; "The Art of Mixing Work and Play," Sep, 1992; "Super Humor Power," Oct, 1992; "Remarried with Children," May, 1992; "Eat Dessert First," May, 1990. **Seminars:** Creating Positive Working Environments™; Putting Humor to Work at Work; Pulling Together Instead of Falling Apart; Winning over Customers from Hell; The Playshop Lab™; Humor For the Health of It; I-Power; Don't Postpone Joy™; Laughing Matters in the Classroom; The Art of Mixing Work and Play™; and Managing Stress Through Humor.

FRANCHISES AND BUSINESS OPPORTUNITIES

35268 ■ Turbo Leadership Systems Ltd.
36280 NE Wilsonville Rd.
Newberg, OR 97132
Ph:(503)625-1867
Fax: (503)625-2699
No. of Franchise Units: 1. **Founded:** 1985. **Franchised:** 1995. **Description:** Management training and team building training. **Equity Capital Needed:** $45,000. **Franchise Fee:** $29,000. **Financial Assistance:** No. **Training:** Yes.

COMPUTER SYSTEMS/ SOFTWARE

35269 ■ Facilitation Skills for Team Leaders–Crisp Learning–Thomson Learning (10650)
Chris Learning
10650 Toebben Dr.
Independence, KY 41051
Ph:800-442-7477
Free: 800-442-7477
Fax: (859)647-5963
URL: http://www.courseilt.com

Price: Description: Bring out the collaborative voices of your team members. Get started with this simple six-step plan. Increase participation and team efficiency. Develop feedback and clarification skills. Shortcut the path to team consensus.

35270 ■ Team Problem Solving–Crisp Learning
Chris Learning
PO Box 6900
Florence, KY 41022
Ph:800-442-7477
Free: 800-442-7477
Fax: (859)647-5963
Co. E-mail: courseiltcrisp@thomaslearning.com
URL: http://www.courseilt.com
Price: $99.00 (VCI CD-ROM). **Description:** Based on the *Team Problem-Solving and Decision-Making* video and book. Includes book and user's guide.

LIBRARIES

35271 ■ Employment Support Center–Library
1556 Wisconsin Ave., NW
Washington, DC 20001-3747
Ph:(202)628-2919
Fax: (703)790-1469
Co. E-mail: jobclubs@hotmail.com
URL: http://www.angelfire.com/biz/jobclubs
Scope: Employment networking, self-esteem, starting your own business, setting up job clubs, training facilitators, maintaining a large job bank, providing job-searching skills. **Services:** Library open to the public. **Holdings:** 150 articles; books; periodicals; videos on job search; interviews; reports; manuscripts. **Subscriptions:** 4 journals and other serials; 2 newspapers.

RESEARCH CENTERS

35272 ■ Loyola University Chicago–Center for Organization Development
820 N Michigan Ave.
Chicago, IL 60611
Ph:(312)915-6595
Fax: (312)915-6231
Contact: Dr. Homer H. Johnson, Dir.
Scope: Management of organizational change, including organizational design, total quality management, self-managed teams, employee empowerment, change management, facilitation skills, and high performance work systems. **Educational Activities:** Graduate courses and a master's degree in organizational development.

35273 ■ Riegel and Emory Human Resource Research Center
Darla-Moore School of Business
University of South Carolina at Columbia
1705 College St.
Columbia, SC 29208
Ph:(803)777-4901

Fax: (803)777-6876
Co. E-mail: klaasb@moore.sc.edu
URL: http://mooreschool.sc.edu/moore/riegelandemory
Contact: Brian S. Klaas, Dir.
E-mail: klaasb@moore.sc.edu
Scope: Improvement of understanding of how human resource practices can contribute to improved organizational performance, particularly employee values in the workplace, motivation and satisfaction of workers, and management skills. Aims to increase cooperation in the workplace and to preserve the values of the free market system. **Publications:** Values Research Project Reprint Series.

35274 ■ University of North Carolina at Chapel Hill–Frank Hawkins Kenan Institute of Private Enterprise
Kenan-Flagler Business School, CB 3440
Kenan Center
Chapel Hill, NC 27599-3440
Ph:(919)962-8201
Fax: (919)962-8202
Co. E-mail: john_kasarda@kenan-flagler.unc.edu
URL: http://www.kenan-flagler.unc.edu/KI
Contact: Dr. John D. Kasarda, Dir.
E-mail: john_kasarda@kenan-flagler.unc.edu
Scope: Free enterprise, including job creation, changing labor-force skill needs, factors affecting business competitiveness and employment growth, international trade and privatization, management in the financial services industry, policy issues relating to financial services, financial services markets, offshore sourcing in manufacturing, manufacturing quality, manufacturing forecasting, human resources supervision, team building, compensation, management development, and multidisciplinary research on global economic change and international marketing. **Educational Activities:** International Executive Series and MBA Enterprise Corps.

35275 ■ University of Southern California–Center for Effective Organizations
Marshall School of Business
3670 Trousdale Pky., BRI 204
Los Angeles, CA 90089-0806
Ph:(213)740-9814
Fax: (213)740-4354
Co. E-mail: ceo@usc.edu
URL: http://www.marshall.usc.edu/web/ceo.cfm?doc_id=11
Contact: Dr. Edward E. Lawler III, Dir.
E-mail: ceo@usc.edu
Scope: Action-research, conferences, workshops on issues of organizational effectiveness involving design and management of human systems, including organizational development and design, strategic planning and business policy, leadership, virtual teams, knowledge work teams and team performance management, performance appraisal, labor-management relations, career development, and job design. **Educational Activities:** Annual Human Resource Executive Seminar; Organization Design Workshop.

ASSOCIATIONS AND OTHER ORGANIZATIONS

35276 ■ International Association of Professional Security Consultants
525 SW 5th St., Ste. A
Des Moines, IA 50309-4501
Ph:(515)282-8192
Fax: (515)282-9117
Co. E-mail: iapsc@iapsc.org
URL: http://www.iapsc.org
Contact: Robert A. Schultheiss, Pres.
Description: Security management, technical, training, and forensic consultants. Promotes understanding and cooperation among members and industries or individuals requiring such services. Seeks to enhance members' knowledge through seminars, training programs, and educational materials. Works to foster public awareness of the security consulting industry; serves as a clearinghouse for consultants' requirements. Maintains code of conduct, ethics, and professional standards. Offers consultant referral service; operates speakers' bureau. **Publications:** *Consultants Directory* (annual); *Independent Consultant* (bimonthly). Also publishes registry. **Telecommunication Services:** phone referral service, Consultant Referral Service, (202)466-7212.

REFERENCE WORKS

**35277 ■ "Are Your Staffers Stealing" in *Inc.*
(November 2006, pp. 33-35)**
Pub: Gruner & Jahr USA Publishing
Ed: Scott Wescott. **Description:** Internal theft is a significant drain on resources and easier to prevent than amend. Selecting the right people, clear cut policies on theft, simplified accounting systems, all contribute to reducing this common problem in small companies.

35278 ■ "Crime and Small Business" in *Journal of Small Business Management* (Vol. 38, No. 3, July 2000, pp. 1)
Pub: West Virginia University
Ed: Donald F. Kuratko, Jeffrey S. Hornsby, Douglas W. Naffziger, Richard M. Hodgetts. **Description:** An examination of levels of crime and the methods of crime prevention in U.S. small business is presented.

35279 ■ *Employee Theft Control*
Pub: Prevention Press
Ed: Read Hayes. **Released:** 1993. **Price:** $14.99.

35280 ■ *Employee Theft: How to Spot It, How to Stop It!*
Pub: Business Owners Press
Ed: Ron Jennings. **Released:** 1994. **Price:** $12.95.

35281 ■ "Jonathan Hoffman Was Sure a Former Staffer Had Stolen His Company's Ideas" in *Inc.* (September 2005, pp. 55-56)
Pub: Inc. Magazine
Ed: Lora Kolodny. **Description:** Jonathan Hoffman, CEO of School Zone Publishing, maker of educational media; Hoffman discusses the way the family business handled litigation when a former employee stole his company's ideas.

35282 ■ "Mr. Clean" in *Crain's New York Business* (Vol. 23, January 8, 2007, No. 2, pp. 23)
Pub: Crain Communications, Inc.
Ed: Tom Fredrickson. **Description:** Profile of Joseph Spinelli, a former FBI agent who is the chief operating officer of Daylight Forensic & Advisory. Spinelli's specialty is discovering and preventing corruption in government agencies, schools, and corporations.

35283 ■ *Protect Your Business: Top Cops Help You Safeguard Against Shoplifting, Employee Theft and More*
Pub: Sourcebooks, Inc.
Ed: James Nelson. **Released:** 1993. **Price:** $8.95.

35284 ■ "Your Loss? Don't Risk Losing Your Laptop (or PDA or Phone) on Your Next Flight" in *Entrepreneur* (Vol. 31, No. 9, September 2003)
Pub: Entrepreneur Media, Inc.
Ed: Christopher McGinnis. **Description:** Thousands of laptops, mobile phones, PDAs and other devices are left behind at airports by business travelers; tips to help avoid loss, including labeling, are included.

TRADE PERIODICALS

35285 ■ *Corporate Security Newsletter*
Pub: Strafford Publications Inc.
Ed: Amanda Arnold, Editor, amanda_arnold@straffordpub.com. **Released:** Biweekly. **Price:** $330, individuals; $560, two years. **Description:** Focuses on all aspects of corporate security, including management issues, legal cases, new technologies, survey results, current events, trends, upcoming developments and new products. Articles regularly address workplace violence, employee theft, pre-employee screening, corporate liability, security policies, and information security.

35286 ■ *Private Security Case Law Reporter*
Pub: Strafford Publications Inc.
Contact: Jennifer F. Vaughan, Executive Editor
Released: 12/year. **Price:** $347, U.S.; $594, two years; $377, Canada; $402, elsewhere. **Description:** Contains judicial decisions on litigation involving private security operations.

35287 ■ *Security Letter*
Pub: Security Letter Inc.
Ed: Robert D. McCrie, Editor, rmccrie@mindspring.com. **Released:** 22/year. **Price:** $197, U.S. and Canada; $222, elsewhere. **Description:** Contains "solution-oriented information on security and protection of assets from loss," particularly for executives concerned about the following: internal checks and controls, personnel practices, management of change, fraud and embezzlement, business crime trends, security, and urban terrorism. Recurring features include news of research, a calendar of events, semiannual FBI crime data, quarterly financial news of major companies in the security industry, book reviews, security and safety pointers, and a question-and-answer feature.

VIDEOCASSETTES/ AUDIOCASSETTES

35288 ■ *Choices: How to Control Internal Shrink*
Excellence in Training Corp.
1303 Marsh Ln.
Carrollton, TX 75006
Free: 800-747-6569
Released: 1987. **Price:** $550.00. **Description:** Offers tips for retail stores to cut down employee theft through a look at two new employees: one conscientious, one not. **Availability:** VHS; 3/4U.

35289 ■ *Stop Business Crime: Shoplifting & Employee Theft*
Instructional Video
2219 C St.
Lincoln, NE 68502
Ph:(402)475-6570
Free: 800-228-0164
Fax: (402)475-6500
Co. E-mail: feedback@insvideo.com
URL: http://www.insvideo.com
Price: $79.95. **Description:** Offers solutions the problems of shoplifting and employee theft. Includes examples of how each is done followed by several alternatives that could be used to prevent them. **Availability:** VHS.

CONSULTANTS

35290 ■ AlixPartners L.L.C.
2000 Town Ctr., Ste. 2400
Southfield, MI 48075
Ph:(248)358-4420
Fax: (248)358-1969
URL: http://www.alixpartners.com
Scope: Corporate turnaround and crisis management consultants specialize in debt restructuring, Chapter 11 reorganizations, workout negotiations, refinancing, litigation support, forensic accounting, fraud investigations, valuation and expert testimony and information technology outsourcing management and realignment. **Seminars:** A Business Perspective on Bankruptcy and Insolvency; How to Avoid Corporate Bankruptcy; The Accountant's Role in Bankruptcy and Insolvency.

35291 ■ Assets Protection Inc.
421 Eastern Blvd.
Essex, MD 21221-6715
Ph:(410)780-0010
Fax: (410)327-3025

URL: http://www.sasi1968.com/api

Scope: Security consultants providing professional loss prevention assistance; development and maintenance of security programs for both small and large businesses (both retail and manufacturing). Loss prevention security surveys are conducted and from these, cost-effective strategies are designed to reduce and/or eliminate security hazards, risks and exposures. A confidential reward hot-line is operated for clients as well as security training and awareness seminars provided.

35292 ■ Assets Protection Systems Associates Inc.
11113 Bella Loma Dr.
Largo, FL 33774-4622
Ph:(727)596-9650
Fax: (813)596-8486
Co. E-mail: apsacorp@earthlink.net

E-mail: apsacorp@earthlink.net
Scope: Provides a broad range of loss control services, including development of policy and procedure manuals, expert witness testimony, loss control seminars, contingency planning/crisis management, loss control investigation, and competitive intelligence and counter-measures to the convenience store industry, other chain retailers and suppliers, high tech industrial firms, property management firms, parking lot management, and law firms worldwide. **Seminars:** Robbery Deterrence Measures; Internal Theft Deterrence; Management Controls for Loss Prevention; Crisis Management; Liability Aspects of Security.

35293 ■ Beall Investigation Bureau Inc.
318 Country Ln.
San Antonio, TX 78209-2319
Ph:(210)822-7197
Fax: (210)822-7197
Scope: Specializes in investigation and loss control/prevention. Assists with criminal, civil, domestic trial preparation. Assignments accepted on worldwide basis. Serves all industries including government. General practice and private investigation.

35294 ■ Frederick A. Bornhofen & Associates
1 Sunmere Ln.
Elverson, PA 19520
Ph:(610)942-9140
Fax: (610)942-9576
Co. E-mail: fborn@bellatlantic.net

E-mail: fborn@bellatlantic.net
Scope: Commercial and industrial security expert specializes in areas of robbery and violence prevention, business ethics, cargo security, commercial loss prevention techniques, and security management. Has developed a security quality review process now being used by several major clients which is to determine the overall effectiveness of their security programs. Also offers forensic services for the legal industry and conducts professional fraud investigations. Industries served: retail, convenience store, transportation, manufacturing, and energy. **Publications:** F.A. Bornhofen has authored numerous articles published nationally, and contributed to several books as well as It's a Matter of Judgement, ethics training tape; and I Shouldn't Be Telling You This, But, an information security training tape. **Seminars:** Business Ethics; Fraud in the Business World.

35295 ■ Dale System Inc.
1101 Stewart Ave.
Garden City, NY 11530
Ph:(516)794-2800
Free: 800-645-6366
Fax: (516)542-1063
Scope: Provides advice, guidance and services covering internal security to industrial firms, retail stores and theatre owners. Loss prevention services include undercover operations, shopping services, polygraph, and recreation/entertainment checking. Also surveys retail operations for price maintenance and product presentation. Additionally provides background investigations for business purposes. Serves private industries as well as government agencies.

35296 ■ Executive Management Services Inc.
416 7th Ave.
Pittsburgh, PA 15219
Ph:(412)471-8858
Fax: (412)221-5780
Scope: Security management loss prevention consulting and service company providing planning services and security awareness programs to its clients. Expertise focuses on providing solutions to internal theft issues, and loss prevention contingency planning.

35297 ■ Fidelity Polygraph & Investigation Consultants Inc.
2163 Pelham Pky., Ste. 218
Pelham, AL 35124-1160
Ph:(205)988-8644
Fax: (205)663-1489
Scope: Offers pre-employment screening as well as polygraph examinations and specific issue polygraph examinations; in-depth interviewing; loss prevention consulting; lectures on loss prevention; and shopping services interrogation, interviewing, and investigations. Serves retail businesses including clothing, hardware, auto, materials, and attorneys.

35298 ■ Greene Group
500 Market St.
Portsmouth, NH 03801
Ph:(603)433-8883
Fax: (603)433-8883
Scope: Firm specializes in business research and risk assessment; handles discreet, time-sensitive assignments, including site security systems and controls for clients in the United States, Latin America, and Southeast Asia.

35299 ■ Richard Haynes & Associates L.L.C.
1021 Temple St.
Charleston, WV 25312-2153
Ph:(304)346-6228
Fax: (304)346-9135
Co. E-mail: captrah@citynet.net

E-mail: captrah@citynet.net
Scope: Security management consultant. Offers the following services: security surveys and audits; security readiness for labor disputes; investigations; security training and awareness programs; special projects. Industries served: mining, petroleum, law enforcement, private security companies, and government agencies. **Publications:** Kanawha Valley Business Monthly - "Let's Talk Security," monthly series of articles on security topics. **Seminars:** Personal Protection Workshop: Workplace Violence.

35300 ■ Hub Kelsh Inc.
5312 Claridge Sq.
Atlanta, GA 30338
Ph:(770)457-2103
Fax: (770)457-2103
Co. E-mail: hubkelsh@dscga.com

E-mail: hubkelsh@dscga.com
Scope: Investigations, and loss prevention consulting for business (theft, harassment, drug activity, fraud, sabotage, hostile work environment & other inappropriate workplace conduct). Employee involvement programs for loss prevention and a drug-free workplace. Conducts physical security surveys. Inventory shrinkage a specialty. **Seminars:** Frequent speaker at conventions & business meetings. Theft By Employees & Outsiders; Substance Abuse in the Workplace; Sexual Harassment; Workplace Violence; Dealing with Diversity Issues. Seminars, keynote speaker on integrity, workplace substance abuse, and employee misconduct.

35301 ■ Kies Intelligence Agency
13630 Eldridge Ave.
PO Box 923572
Sylmar, CA 91392-3572
Ph:(818)367-8416
Fax: (818)367-4983
Co. E-mail: kies@intelligence.org
URL: http://www.intelligence.org

E-mail: kies@intelligence.org
Scope: Offers expertise in civil and criminal investigations, fingerprint analysis, missing persons and embezzlement investigations, employee background investigations and asset searches. Also specializes in messenger services, all kinds of investigative work and undercover assignments. Industries served: insurance companies, corporations and attorneys in the U.S. Branch office in Europe. **Special Services:** Offers numerous reports, such as Business Credit Report, Nationwide Social Security Number Trace and County Criminal Records Index Search. Contact firm for complete list. Skip Trace.

35302 ■ Navigator Research Group Inc.
4040 Desoto Farms Rd.
PO Box 14189
Tallahassee, FL 32309
Ph:(850)878-5437
Free: (866)620-4636
Fax: 800-814-7714
Co. E-mail: support@navigatorresearchgroup.com
URL: http://www.navigatorresearchgroup.com

E-mail: support@navigatorresearchgroup.com
Scope: Firm is a licensed private investigation agency specializing in locating missing persons and conducting background checks. Industries served: private investigators, insurance companies and adjustor's, law firms, and other corporations. The firm serves the state of Florida, but has a network of correspondents nationwide and access to various databases which provides coverage across the country.

35303 ■ Security & Loss Prevention Associates Inc.
4718 Sylvia Ln.
Manvel, TX 77578-3106
Ph:(281)489-1046
Fax: (281)489-8636
Scope: Security and loss control consultants in physical security, operating systems and procedures and personnel practices, investigations of internal and external fraud, and offers expert witness testimony in negligence litigation. Serve the convenience store industry, chain restaurants and health food industry.

RESEARCH CENTERS

35304 ■ University of Montreal–Université de Montréal–International Centre for Comparative Criminology
PO Box 6128, Downtown Station
Montreal, QC, Canada H3C 3J7
Ph:(514)343-7065
Fax: (514)343-2269
Co. E-mail: jean-paul.brodeur@umontreal.ca
URL: http://www.cicc.umontreal.ca
Contact: Jean-Paul Brodeur, Dir.
E-mail: jean-paul.brodeur@umontreal.ca
Scope: Criminal phenomenon as it exists in Quebec and Canada, including prevention of delinquency and protection of youth; delinquency that persists from adolescence to adulthood; female delinquency; victimology, white collar criminality (fraud, forgery, and counterfeiting and business crimes); crimes of violence (terrorism, group violence, and armed robbery); public reaction to various forms of deviance and criminality; functioning of the justice system, including functioning of the juvenile and adult courts; services for the execution of punishment (probation and pre-sentence reports); community participation in measures regarding criminals and delinquents; and clinical criminology and forensic psychiatry. **Publications:** Annales Internationales de Criminologie; Proceedings Collaborates in the publication of four specialized reviews: Criminologie (semiannually); Research Reports; Revue Canadienne de Criminologie; Revue Internationale de Criminologie et de Police technique et scientifique. **Educational Activities:** International congresses (semiannually); International courses, in cooperation with the International Society of Criminology; Research seminars.

35305 ■ Vera Institute of Justice, Inc. –Research Department
233 Broadway, 12th Fl.
New York, NY 10279
Ph:(212)334-1300

Fax: (212)941-9407
Co. E-mail: info@vera.org
URL: http://www.vera.org
Contact: Michael Jacobson, Exec.Dir.
E-mail: info@vera.org
Scope: Effects of community policing, alternatives to incarceration programs in New York City courts, the introduction of European dayfines into U.S. criminal courts, speed of felony case processing in New York City, alcohol and drug treatment strategies for parolees in New York City, mental health care in the justice system, policing, relationships between employment and crime, juveniles and the court system, immigration, violence against women, and indigent defense. **Publications:** Monographs; Reports.

START-UP INFORMATION

35306 ■ "The $50 Million Giveaway" in *Business 2.0* (Vol. 6, September 2005, No. 8, pp. 76)
Pub: Time, Inc.
Ed: Michael V. Copeland. **Description:** The visions of eleven venture capital firms are examined; each firm is looking for the right startup to fulfill these visions.

35307 ■ *The 100 Best Businesses to Start When You Don't Want to Work Hard Anymore*
Pub: Career Press
Ed: Lisa Rogak. **Price:** $14.99.

35308 ■ *101 Businesses You Can Satrt at with Less Thank One Thousand Dollars: For Retirees*
Pub: Atlantic Publishing Company
Ed: Christina Bultinck. **Released:** December 2006. **Price:** $21.95. **Description:** Business ideas to help retirees start a home-based business on a low budget.

35309 ■ *101 Businesses You Can Start at with Less Than One Thousand Dollars: For Stay-At-Home Moms and Dads*
Pub: Atlantic Publishing Company
Ed: Christina Bultinck. **Released:** December 2006. **Price:** $21.95. **Description:** Business ideas to help stay-at-home moms and dads start a home-based business on a low budget.

35310 ■ *101 Small Business Ideas for Under $5000*
Pub: John Wiley & Sons, Incorporated
Ed: Corey Sandler, Janice Keefe. **Released:** April 2005. **Price:** $19.95. **Description:** Entrepreneurial ideas for starting companies that can be run part-time or full-time, and some as an absentee owner.

35311 ■ "250 Unleash the Entrepreneur Within You!" in *Home Business* (Vol. 12, March/April 2005, No. 2, pp. 16, 20-23, 26-29, 100-101, 104-105)
Pub: Home Business Magazine
Ed: Sandy Larson. **Description:** Directory of 250 companies offering home-based businesses, franchises, and opportunities.

35312 ■ "2005: A Quiet, But Critical Year for Venture Capital" in *Venture Capital Journal* (January 1, 2005)
Pub: Thomason Financial Inc.
Description: Some industry experts are predicting a transformation in the venture capital industry for 2005, with a shift toward seed and early stage investing.

35313 ■ *The Accidental Entrepreneur: Practical Wisdom for People Who Never Expected to Work for Themselves*
Pub: Career Steps
Ed: Susan Urquhart-Brown. **Released:** August 2004. **Price:** $17.95. **Description:** Steps for launching, growing and running a successful small company.

35314 ■ "An agent for change" in *BlackEnterprise* (Vol. 31, No. 6, January 2001, pp. 99)
Pub: Earl Graves Publishing Co.
Ed: Robyn D. Clarke. **Description:** Profile of Sanyu Barnicoat, owner of the consulting firm, The Change Agents Group in West Orange, New Jersey. Ms. Barnicoat trains and coaches individuals, small groups, and major corporations on ways to make changes in an organization, and how to cope with those changes in the workplace.

35315 ■ "Airborne intelligence" in *Entrepreneur* (Vol. 30, No. 10, October 2002, pp. 114)
Pub: Entrepreneur Media Inc.
Ed: Devlin Smith. **Description:** The importance of signing up for the franchise advisory council when starting a new franchise is stressed.

35316 ■ "All new: be the first on the block with one of these 66 fresh opportunities" in *Entrepreneur* (Vol. 30, No. 12, Dec. 2002, pp. 118)
Pub: Entrepreneur Media Inc.
Description: A listing of franchises offered in 2001 and 2002, including contact information for researching each.

35317 ■ "Ambitious business women search for mentors during challenging times" in *San Francisco Business Times* (Vol. 16, No. 42, May 24, 2002)
Pub: San Francisco Business Times Inc.
Ed: Kristen Bole. **Description:** Mentoring Circles, a San Francisco nonprofit, connects women business owners with established women in business. Mentoring programs at San Francisco area companies are also discussed.

35318 ■ "American Megatrends vets start a new company" in *Atlanta Business Chronicle* (Vol. 24, No. 11, August 17, 2001, pp. 2A)
Pub: American City Business Journals Inc.
Ed: Mary Jane Credeur. **Description:** Two former engineers of American Megatrends Inc. have formed iVivity Inc., which has received over $11 million in venture capital backup. Sukha Ghosh and Sanjay Sehgal are now designing a data storage management storage product they hope will revolutionize the market. Their iDISX (Distributed Intelligent Storage exchange) product will operate, diagnose and repair data storage networks.

35319 ■ "Angel Investing Still Alive, Barely, in Chicago Area" in *Chicago Tribune* (November 10, 2002)
Pub: Knight Ridder/Tribune Business News
Ed: Rob Kaiser. **Description:** Profile of Bill Maulsby, founder of the Chicago-based BusBank charter bus service, tells how he was able to secure angel investments. The decline in angels to invest in startups is discussed.

35320 ■ "The art of making a plan and making it happen" in *The New York Times* (December 18, 2000, pp. C16)
Pub: The New York Times Company
Ed: Lisa Belkin. **Description:** Business plans for the self-employed are discussed.

35321 ■ *The Art of the Start: The Time-Tested, Battle-Hardened Guide for Anyone Starting Anything*
Pub: Penguin Books (USA) Incorporated
Ed: Guy Kawasaki. **Released:** September 2004. **Price:** $26.95. **Description:** Advice for someone starting a new business covering topics such as hiring employees, building a brand, business competition, and management.

35322 ■ "Ask Yourself What the Hell Really Works Here?" in *Fast Company* (May 2001, pp. 82)
Pub: Fast Company
Ed: Lee A. Iacocca. **Description:** Lee Iacocca, currently founder and chairman of EV Global Motors Inc., Los Angeles, California, offers advice to entrepreneurs, including the importance of customer service and standing behind products and service.

35323 ■ "Atlantis Group Plans to Back Start-ups" in *Venture Capital Journal* (Vol. 40, No. 10, November 2000, pp. 14)
Pub: Venture Economics
Description: Profile of Robbie Hardy, angel investor and entrepreneur, who founded The Atlantis Group LLC, to back seed-stage companies.

35324 ■ "Automatic Riches" in *Small Business Opportunities* (Vol. 13, No. 6, November 2001, pp. 66, 68)
Pub: Harris Publications, Inc.
Ed: Ken Mueller. **Description:** Profile of Toby McAdams, a former car salesman, who constructed a Web site to sell used vehicles. Mr. McAdams shares tips for targeting your niche on the Web.

35325 ■ "Barter's latest comeback" in *The Economist* (Vol. 357, No. 8, October 21, 2000, pp. 78)
Pub: Economist Newspaper Ltd.
Description: Most people know barter only from the playground, but a raft of American start-ups are trying to turn swapping into big business on the Internet.

35326 ■ "Be a Loan Shark" in *Success* (Vol. 47, No. 3, July 2000, pp. 59)
Pub: Success Publishing, Inc.
Ed: Michael A. Butler. **Description:** Small business has become huge in America. Each year, more and more entrepreneurs bypass the corporate ladder to take a shot at realizing a dream: owning their own businesses. Without proper preparation, the inspiration may not become reality because of the inability to obtain a small business loan.

35327 ■ *Be Your Own Boss*
Pub: Wet Feet, Incorporated
Ed: Marcia Passos. **Released:** November 2006. **Price:** $24.95. **Description:** Tips for starting a freelance business in any career or industry are covered.

35328 ■ **"Be Your Own Boss"** in *Small Business Opportunities* **(July 2005)**
Pub: Harris Publications Inc.
Description: Basic tips for starting your own business are outlined. Fifteen startups that can be launched for under $500 are listed, including sunglass sales, customized items, online auctions, children's music education, custom tea, vehicle ramps, waste management, pet businesses, sporting goods and sports merchandise, recipes, home improvement, wholesaling, personalized candy bars, promotional advertising products and more.

35329 ■ **"Beating the odds: remembering the basics of business can help"** in *Black Enterprise* **(Vol. 32, No. 6, January 2002, pp. 35)**
Pub: Earl Graves Publishing Co.
Ed: Glenn Townes. **Description:** The key to starting and sustaining a small business is to have a strong, basic understanding of business practices. Advice is given to manage small businesses.

35330 ■ **"Before he could set up a business, the founder of Portable Church Industries faced a more daunting task: inventing an industry"** in *Inc.*
Pub: The Goldhirsh Group
Description: A profile of Pete van der Harst and the industry he invented. Launching Portable Church Industries, based in Madison Heights, Michigan, involves the physical outfitting of nomadic congregations.

35331 ■ **"The Beginning of a Whole New Friendship"** in *Black Enterprise* **(Vol. 34, No. 5, December 2003, pp. S5)**
Pub: Earl Graves Publishing Co.
Ed: Jennifer L. Smith. **Description:** Financial Literacy for Teens group teaches young entrepreneurs how to start a new company, including tips for employing a startup.

35332 ■ **"Best of the best"** in *Entrepreneur* **(Vol. 31, No. 4, April 2003, pp. 88)**
Pub: Entrepreneur Media Inc.
Description: A directory of the top 116 franchise firms are ranked by best in category for 2003 to help would-be franchisees begin a search for the company that suits their interests.

35333 ■ **"Best of Times"** in *Entrepreneur* **(Vol. 31, No. 12, December 2003, pp. 14)**
Pub: Entrepreneur Media Inc.
Ed: Rieva Lesonsky. **Description:** The importance of timing as an essential ingredient to successful entrepreneurship is discussed. The fact that entrepreneurs have gained more respect during the recent recession is also examined.

35334 ■ **"Big Breaks"** in *Inc.* **(November 2000, pp. 90)**
Pub: The Goldhirsh Group
Description: Company profile of Wetzel's Pretzels, whose fans include famous celebrities.

35335 ■ **"Bigcat Systems leaves little to chance in Internet Marketing"** in *Crain's Detroit Business* **(Vol. , No. , pp.)**
Pub: Crain Communications, Inc.
Ed: Jeffrey Kosseff. **Description:** A profile of Bigcat Systems L.L.C. the 20-employee company located in Ann Arbor, Michigan, that specializes in interactive voice response systems.

35336 ■ **"Bird Biz Takes Off"** in *Small Business Opportunities* **(Vol. 12, No. 2, March 2000, pp. 64, 66)**
Pub: Harris Publications, Inc.
Ed: Marie Sherlock. **Description:** Shop owners, Brian and Janet Shelton, opened their bird biz emporium, Wild Bird Shop in 1993, and are now earning $500,000 a year.

35337 ■ **"Bizdom U. Set to Teach Next Gen of Startups"** in *Crain's Detroit Business* **(Vol. 22, November 13, 2006, No. 46, pp. 1)**
Pub: Crain Communications Inc. - Detroit

Ed: Sheena Harrison. **Description:** Local businessman invests $10M to form Bizdom U. that teaches entrepreneurs based on experience from other entrepreneurs' successes and failures. Focus will be on developing business plans for their own businesses on a two year program taught by actual local entrepreneurs.

35338 ■ **"BizWare"** in *Hispanic Business* **(Vol. 23, No. 11, November 2001, pp. 70)**
Pub: Hispanic Business Inc.
Ed: Roger Harris. **Description:** Hispanic programmers offer a software package for the mom-and-pop entrepreneur to develop a Web site for their business.

35339 ■ **"Blazing Profit"** in *Small Business Opportunities* **(Vol. 14, No. 1, January 2002, pp. 52-53)**
Pub: Harris Publications, Inc.
Ed: Annette Wood. **Description:** Profile of Fireplaces Plus, Inc., which sells traditional wood burning stoves, fireplaces and gas models, as well as accessories. After one year in business Fire Places Plus projects sales up to $320,000 and co-owner, Jerry Malcom, attributes customer service to the company's success.

35340 ■ **"Borrowing From Dad: Financing From Relatives and Friends Has Risks and Rewards"** in *Black Enterprise* **(Vol. 35, January 2005, No. 6)**
Pub: Earl G. Graves Publishing Co. Inc.
Ed: Carolyn M. Brown. **Description:** More than half of U.S. small businesses are started with money borrowed from family or friends. Banks do not like to make business loans in amounts less than $30,000. Borrowing from family and friends runs the risk of hurting relationships.

35341 ■ **"Bouncing back"** in *Entrepreneur* **(Vol. 30, No. 3, March 2002, pp. 134)**
Pub: Entrepreneur Media Inc.
Ed: Nichole L. Torres. **Description:** Valuable information for entrepreneurs starting a new business after losing a job is offered.

35342 ■ *Brewing Up a Business: Adventures in Entrepreneurship from the Founder of Dogfish Head Craft*
Pub: John Wiley & Sons, Incorporated
Ed: Sam Calagione. **Released:** October 2006. **Price:** $16.95. **Description:** Author shares nontraditional success secrets. Calgione began his business with a home brewing kit and grew it into Dogfish Head Craft Beer, the leading craft brewery in the U.S.

35343 ■ **"Bright Idea"** in *My Business* **(February/March 2004, pp. 48)**
Pub: My Business Magazine
Ed: Lena Basha. **Description:** Profile of IdeaCafe.com, offering resources on building a business plan to information on ways to de-stress.

35344 ■ **"Bringing home the dough"** in *BlackEnterprise* **(Vol. 32, No. 3, October 2001, pp. 68)**
Pub: Earl Graves Publishing Co.
Ed: Brandi Forte. **Description:** Profile of Paul Chisholm, personal chef, who consults with contracted clients to prepare fine cuisine to their specifications.

35345 ■ **"Buddy System"** in *Entrepreneur* **(Vol. 33, October 2005, No. 10, pp. 118)**
Pub: Entrepreneur Media Inc.
Ed: Nichole L. Torres. **Description:** Choosing a friend as a business partner is not always a good business decision, it is important to evaluate a person's knowledge and business skills before partnering a startup company.

35346 ■ **"Build Your Dream Home Business"** in *Home Business* **(Vol. 12, October 2005, No. 5, pp. 16, 18-22, 102, 104)**
Pub: Home Business Magazine
Ed: Sandy Larson. **Description:** Ten steps to starting a home-based business, starting from the initial planning phase to financing a venture as well as marketing strategies.

35347 ■ **"Building Business Leaders"** in *Hispanic Business* **(December 2002, pp. 64)**
Pub: Hispanic Business
Ed: Patricia Guadalupe. **Description:** Profile of the nonprofit organization, Young Americas Business Trust. The organization promotes entrepreneurism among young people.

35348 ■ **"Building on experience"** in *Black Enterprise* **(Vol. 33, No. 6, Jan. 2003, pp. 39)**
Pub: Earl Graves Publishing Co.
Ed: Bridget McCrea. **Description:** Profile of Angelo R. Perryman, who used his 22 years of experience in the construction industry to launch his own firm. Perryman used personal savings and loans from family members for his startup.

35349 ■ **"Building for the future"** in *Black Enterprise* **(Vol. 32, No. 7, February 2002, pp.)**
Pub: Earl Graves Publishing Co.
Ed: Glenn Townes. **Description:** Profile of Anthony Thompson's Kwame Building Group Inc., a St. Louis-based provider of construction management, contract-claims management, estimating, scheduling and engineering services.

35350 ■ **"Building vs. buying"** in *BlackEnterprise* **(Vol. 31, No. 6, January 2001, pp. 39)**
Pub: Earl Graves Publishing Co.
Ed: Glenn Townes. **Description:** Ideas are presented to would-be entrepreneurs on the advantages and disadvantages to buying an existing business or building one from scratch.

35351 ■ **"Burn, babay, Burn"** in *Entrepreneur* **(Vol. 28, No. 6, June 2000, pp. 76)**
Pub: Entrepreneur Media Inc.
Description: Presenting Entrepreneur and Dun & Bradstreet's Sixth Annual Hot 100 list of the fastest growing entrepreneurial businesses in America.

35352 ■ **"Business Incubator Has a Fish Wriggling Off of the Hook"** in *St. Louis Post-Dispatch* **(August 27, 2004)**
Pub: Knight-Ridder/Tribune Business News
Ed: David Nicklaus. **Description:** Marcia Mellitz, founder of Symbiontics Inc., is considering a move to Wisconsin because of lack of funding. The firm is developing treatments for genetic disorders known as lysosomal storage diseases. It was launched with $3.5 million.

35353 ■ **"Business plan pro"** in *Black Enterprise* **(Vol. 33, No. 6, January 2003, pp. 10)**
Pub: Earl Graves Publishing Co.
Description: The tools needed to write a successful business plan are provided at blackenterprise.com. The site helps entrepreneurs to write a plan, figure startup costs, find financing, along with tips on launching a Website for a new or existing small business.

35354 ■ **"Buying a Small Business? Beware!"** in *Business Week Online* **(December 4, 2002)**
Pub: McGraw-Hill Inc.
Description: An interview with attorney Mitchell Stern, explains pitfalls that entrepreneurs must avoid before purchasing a new business. Stern suggests that the perspective buyer also look at the historical analysis and financial records of a company and project their income when going forward with the firm.

35355 ■ *The Campus CEO: The Student Entrepreneur's Guide to Launching a Multi-Million Dollar Business*
Pub: Kaplan Books
Ed: Randal Pinkett. **Released:** February 2007. **Price:** $21.00 (CND). **Description:** Tips for generating income, while attending college is presented to students.

35356 ■ **"Can C.K. Prahalad Pass the Test?"** in *Fast Company* **(August 2001, pp. 108)**
Pub: Fast Company

Ed: Jennifer Reingold. **Description:** Profile of C.K. Prahalad, one of the business world's most influential professors and consultants, has left the University of Michigan and invested millions of dollars of his own money to put himself to the test. He wants to build a company around the ideas and principles he's been teaching others, and hopes to change the world in the process.

35357 ■ *Canadian Small Business Kit for Dummies*
Pub: CDG Books Canada, Incorporated
Ed: Margaret Kerr, JoAnn Kurtz. **Released:** August 2004. **Price:** $37.99 (Canadian). **Description:** Entrepreneurial guide to starting and running a small business in Canada.

35358 ■ "A Career, Not a Job" in *Forbes* (November 27, 2000, pp. 98)
Pub: Forbes Magazine
Ed: Eileen Glanton. **Description:** Profile of Twin Cities Rise job training program in Minneapolis, Minnesota. Steven Rothschild started the job training program in 1993 in order to help graduates launch substantial careers as computer technicians, accountants, and customer-service employees.

35359 ■ *Careers for Self-Starters and Other Entrepreneurial Types*
Pub: McGraw-Hill Companies
Ed: Blythe Camenson. **Released:** September 2004. **Price:** $13.95 (US), $19.95 (Canadian). **Description:** Advice to entrepreneurs wishing to start their own small company. Tips for turning hobbies into job skills are included.

35360 ■ "Cart Blanche: Think Retailing is Strictly Brick-and-Mortar Opportunity? Not So." in *Entrepreneur* (Vol. 31, No. 8, Aug. 2003, pp. 78)
Pub: Entrepreneur Media Inc.
Ed: Nichole L. Torres. **Description:** From hair products to cooking utensils to candy and cookies, entrepreneurs are making big money selling from kiosks in local malls. Examples of successful kiosks businesses are presented.

35361 ■ *Cash In On Cash Flow*
Pub: Simon & Schuster, Incorporated
Ed: Lawrence J. Pino. **Released:** July 2005. **Price:** $14.95. **Description:** Guide to assist entrepreneurs with starting a new business as a cash flow specialist.

35362 ■ "Change Of Face" in *Entrepreneur* (Vol. 28, No. 4, April 2000, pp. 125)
Pub: Entrepreneur Media Inc.
Ed: Mark Henricks. **Description:** Entrepreneurial shapeshifters may be in one business today and something entirely different tomorrow. The key is knowing when it's time to change focus.

35363 ■ "Choosing a Business Entity" in *Crain's Detroit Business* (Vol. 18, No. 49, December 9, 2002, pp. 15)
Pub: Crain Communications Inc., Detroit
Description: Questions for every aspiring entrepreneur to ask before starting a new venture are featured.

35364 ■ "Choosing an Incubator for your Business Baby" in *Ingram's* (Vol. 28, No. 6, June 2002, pp. 49)
Pub: Show Me Publishing, Inc.
Description: Small business management techniques are featured. An outline and review of some of the 900 business incubator programs offered by federal and state agencies to assist in the development of small businesses is presented.

35365 ■ "Cleaning Up" in *Small Business Opportunities* (Vol. 12, No. 3, May 2000, pp. 60)
Pub: Harris Publications, Inc.
Description: Natural and man-made disasters have created a boom for entrepreneurs who offer restoration and cleanup services. A profile of Servpro Industries, Inc., the nation's leading disaster restoration and cleaning franchise system, is included.

35366 ■ "Clients breathe easy thanks to outsourced tech support" in *Colorado Springs Business Journal* (March 7, 2003)
Pub: Dolan Media Newswires
Ed: Becky Huley. **Description:** Profile of Jeff Harrell, president and owner of Advanced Business Solutions, offering secure information technology services, Internet access filtered email and custom software services to companies.

35367 ■ "Close Up: Teen Sensations" in *Entrepreneur* (Vol. 28, No. 11, November 2000, pp. 24)
Pub: Entrepreneur Media Inc.
Ed: Devlin Smith. **Description:** Teen entrepreneurs give insights regarding teen consumers. A few of their suggestions include to know why a teenager buys a certain product, to set a good example, and to use humor. A listing of the top five magazines for teens is included.

35368 ■ "Coaching Companies" in *Black Enterprise* (Vol. 31, No. 2, September 2000, pp. 56)
Pub: Earl Graves Publishing Co.
Ed: Gerda Gallop-Goodman. **Description:** Suggestions for books, articles, and online assistance designed to coach small business owners and entrepreneurs on presenting their ideas and products to large retail companies.

35369 ■ "Coffee mates" in *Boston Business Journal* (Vol. 22, No. 3)
Pub: MCP, Inc.
Ed: Jill Lerner. **Description:** Profile of lonely man turned entrepreneur, who uses his aunt's advice to start his own online dating service.

35370 ■ "Cold Feet?" in *Entrepreneur* (Vol. 31, No. 11, November 2003, pp. 128)
Pub: Entrepreneur Media, Inc.
Ed: Todd D. Maddocks. **Description:** In a hypothetical scenario, a couple have signed a build-to-suit lease for the construction of a franchised oil-change operations. Details of the transaction are provided.

35371 ■ "Coming to America" in *Inc.* (November 1, 2004)
Pub: Inc. Magazine
Ed: David J. Dent. **Description:** Profile of StartSmart a program designed to help immigrants become entrepreneurs. The program is run by the not-for-profit economic development agency called Coastal Enterprises, and offers classes in entrepreneurship, one-on-one coaching, and start-up loans to immigrants and refugees. Five people helped by the program are highlighted.

35372 ■ "The Company You Keep" in *Success* (Vol. 47, No. 3, July 2000, pp. 58)
Pub: Success Publishing, Inc.
Ed: Debbie Phillips. **Description:** An entrepreneur discusses methods of success in self-employment, including building relationships with customers, vendors, family, or friends.

35373 ■ *The Complete Startup Guide for the Black Entrepreneur*
Pub: Career Press
Ed: Bill Bourdreaux. **Price:** $15.99.

35374 ■ "Computing Riches" in *Small Business Opportunities* (Vol. 12, No. 3, May 2000, pp. 108, 130)
Pub: Harris Publications, Inc.
Ed: Description: Despite his lack of business training, Barry P. Edwards, founded Creative Presentations, a company that offers computer presentation equipment products and services. His business now serves more than 3,000 clients and has become a $10 million dollar a year enterprise.

35375 ■ "Contest Challenges Teens to Consider Entrepreneurship" in *Kansas City Star* (March 8, 2005)
Pub: Knight-Ridder/Tribune Business News
Ed: Donna Vestal. **Description:** The National Association of Women Business Owners and Adams-

Gabbert & Associates Inc. in Kansas City have announced a contest for senior girls to enter. The competition is meant to promote entrepreneurship among young women.

35376 ■ "Crash Course" in *Entrepreneur* (Vol. 28, No. 1, January 2000, pp. 89)
Pub: Entrepreneur Media Inc.
Ed: Geoff Williams. **Description:** When your business is growing so fast it's out of control, here's how to pull the entrepreneurial equivalent of steering into the skid.

35377 ■ "Credit card financing: Tempting but risky for small businesses" in *Crain's Detroit Business* (Vol. 16, No. 33, August 14, 2000, pp. 13)
Pub: Crain Communications, Inc.
Ed: Brent Snavely. **Description:** Counselors from the Service Corps of Retired Executives believe that entrepreneurs should never use credit cards to finance a business. A variety of resources for advice and funding are investigated.

35378 ■ "Culture Vultures Go Online" in *Success* (Vol. 47, No. 2, June 2000, pp. 69)
Pub: Success Publishing, Inc.
Ed: Simeon Furman. **Description:** How a former cellist with no Internet experience is building an online ticketing market.

35379 ■ *Cute Little Store: Between the Entrepreneurial Dream and Business Reality*
Pub: Outskirts Press, Incorporated
Ed: Adeena Mignogna. **Released:** May 2006. **Price:** $11.95. **Description:** Challenges of starting and growing a retail business are profiled.

35380 ■ "A day of pondering leads to a life-altering change" in *Crain's Detroit Business* (Vol. 16, No. 50, December 11, 2000, pp. E-5)
Pub: Crain Communications, Inc.
Ed: Jeffrey Kosseff. **Description:** Tracy Lumley tells how she decided to begin her own printing company.

35381 ■ "Daydream Believer" in *My Business* (February/March 2003, pp. 52)
Pub: My Business Magazine
Ed: Jennifer Fuqua. **Description:** The online resource that assists entrepreneurs in their quest to owning a business, USBX, is highlighted. USBX provides a forum to bring buyers and sellers of companies together.

35382 ■ "Delivering a New (Business) Life" in *Ingram's* (Vol. 28, No. 5, May 2002, pp. 32)
Pub: Show Me Publishing, Inc.
Description: Profile of George Guile and Rob Waetzig, who have started a small delivery services firm named Plaza Couriers. Guile and Waetzig say their pricing and the fact that they are locals help to differentiate them from their competitors.

35383 ■ "The Design of an Ideal Business" in *Home Business* (Vol. 12, October 2005, No. 5, pp. 58, 60)
Pub: Home Business Magazine
Ed: Brad DeHaven. **Description:** Ten steps for starting a successful new business are outlined, including low start-up costs.

35384 ■ "Designing Women" in *Success* (Vol. 47, No. 3, July 2000, pp. 52)
Pub: Success Publishing, Inc.
Ed: Jane Shealy. **Description:** Two Texas sisters change the face of the cell phone industry by custom painting faceplates for Nokia phones.

35385 ■ "Designs on Success" in *Small Business Opportunities* (Vol. 13, No. 6, November 2001, pp. 48, 50, 122)
Pub: Harris Publications, Inc.
Description: Profile of Tamotsu, who launched his own design firm with a sewing machine in his New York City apartment, and grew his company into a $20-million-a-year successful small business. Tamotsu offers his insights into running a successful small company.

35386 ■ "Destined for success" in *Hispanic Business* (Vol. 22, No. 6, June 2000, pp. 20)
Pub: Hispanic Business
Ed: Vivienne Heines. **Description:** Profile of Mary Rodas, who began her business career when she was four years old. Ms. Rodas, now 24 years old, is president of Catalyst Toys. Daughter of Salvadoran immigrants, Ms. Rodas says the greatest obstacle to her success is her age, not her ethnicity.

35387 ■ "Detroit Free Press Small Business Column" in *Detroit Free Press* (September 12, 2005)
Pub: Knight-Ridder/Tribune Business News
Ed: Carol Cain. **Description:** Jeff Williams runs Biz-starters.com, a company that helps people over the age of 50 start new businesses. Williams offers a booklet that outlines ten tips to having fun while making money after age 50.

35388 ■ "Dialtone's Unlikely Arc" in *Hispanic Business* (Vol. 24, No. 5, May 2002, pp. 36, 38)
Pub: Hispanic Business Inc.
Ed: Jonathan J. Higuera. **Description:** Profile of Alvaro Albarracin and his successful Internet startup, Dialtone Internet Inc.

35389 ■ "A different kind of service" in *BlackEnterprise* (Vol. 32, No. 3, October 2001, pp. 54)
Pub: Earl Graves Publishing Co.
Ed: Quincy L. Lewis. **Description:** Profile of Reginald Ball, who served as a Secret Service agent for the U.S. Treasury Department. Ball has created RB Industries, a general-line industrial products distribution company based in Sterling Heights, Michigan.

35390 ■ "Digital Rules" in *Forbes* (February 19, 2001, pp. 51)
Pub: Forbes Magazine
Ed: Rich Karlgaard. **Description:** The article proves that, despite the New Economy, it still takes brains, salesmanship, guts and a whole lot of persistence to launch and run a startup.

35391 ■ "Direct Success" in *Small Business Opportunities* (Vol. 13, No. 6, November 2001, pp. 58, 60)
Pub: Harris Publications, Inc.
Ed: Patricia Gilbers. **Description:** Profile of Dennis Barnes, president of Marketing Direct, Inc. Mr. Barnes started his company with approximately $5,000 from his dining room, and grew it into a $5 million a year business.

35392 ■ "The Disruptive Startup" in *Inc.* (February 1, 2002)
Pub: Inc. Magazine
Ed: Nancy Lyons. **Description:** Interview with Harvard Business School professor and author, Clayton M. Christensen. Christensen helps identify strategies that allow new growth companies succeed.

35393 ■ "Does cutting costs sound like a good start-up idea?" in *Entrepreneur* (Vol. 30, No. 10, October 2002, pp. 134)
Pub: Entrepreneur Media Inc.
Description: Bob Meyer, publisher of BarterNews Magazine offers five tips for entrepreneurs to use the practice of bartering to reduce startup costs.

35394 ■ "Doing It for Themselves" in *Entrepreneur* (Vol. 28, No. 8, August 2000, pp. 40)
Pub: Entrepreneur Media Inc.
Ed: Cynthia E. Griffin. **Description:** Women investors are aiding women entrepreneurs.

35395 ■ "Doing Your Homework" in *Home Business* (Vol. 12, October 2005, No. 5, pp. 62)
Pub: Home Business Magazine
Ed: Kurt English, Esq. **Description:** Questions to ask before starting a home-based business are discussed. The importance of researching key issues is stressed.

35396 ■ "Don't get bogged down with futile procedures" in *Atlanta Business Chronicle* (Vol. 23, No. 46, April 20, 2001, pp. 66A)
Pub: American City Business Journals Inc.
Ed: Donna Chambers. **Description:** A small company should define its procedures from the start in order to provide for any circumstances that could arise, in both the short-term and the long-term for every department within the business.

35397 ■ "Dot-Com Deathwatch" in *Fortune* (Vol. 142, No. 3, July 24, 2000, pp. 48)
Pub: Time Inc.
Ed: Katrina Brooker. **Description:** Gloom was in the air at PC Expo in July 2000, because venture capitalists are not funding dot-com entrepreneurs as much as in the past.

35398 ■ "Down Economy Helps Incubate Small Businesses" in *Crain's Detroit Business* (Vol. 19, No. 45, November 10, 2003, pp. 11)
Pub: Crain Communications Inc., Detroit
Ed: Laura Bailey. **Description:** The State of Michigan reported 8,432 new business entities in 2003, and expects the trend to grow in 2004.

35399 ■ "Downhill and Dirty" in *Inc.* (February 1, 2002)
Pub: Inc. Magazine
Ed: Tahl Raz. **Description:** Profile of 30 year old entrepreneur, James Page. Page is putting another spin on Gen-X-style transport by inventing Crosskates, an all-terrain Hummer-like version of inline skates mounted on 10-inch mountain-bike tires.

35400 ■ "The downside of the upside of the downside: these days nothing succeeds like failure" in *The New York Times Magazine* (Jan. 9, 2000)
Pub: The New York Times Company
Ed: Louis Menand. **Description:** Company failure in the Internet industry may be considered a badge of success because the downside of running a business has been experienced.

35401 ■ "Dressed for Success" in *Small Business Opportunities* (Vol. 12, No. 3, May 2000, pp. 86, 130)
Pub: Harris Publications, Inc.
Ed: Annette Wood. **Description:** Owners share insight into their $20 million a year home-based men's pants business.

35402 ■ "DynamicDuo" in *Success* (Vol. 47, No. 3, July 2000, pp. 36)
Pub: Success Publishing, Inc.
Ed: Jane Shealy. **Description:** Twin brothers turn a backyard business into a corporate empire. A profile of William Howard West III and William Howard West IV, owners of Twin Tower Erection & Maintenance Inc., in Kernersville, North Carolina.

35403 ■ "E-mail Security Firm is Chaudry's Last Start-up" in *Atlanta Business Chronicle* (Vol. 24, No. 13, August 24, 2001, pp. 5A)
Pub: American City Business Journals Inc.
Ed: Mary Jane Credeur. **Description:** CipherTrust is a new company that offers IronMail, a security appliance that acts as a firewall to protect e-mail from hackers and viruses. Founder Jay Chaudry, who has started six companies, says that this will be his last start-up for the foreseeable future, since he wants to be able to focus, rather than spreading himself too thin.

35404 ■ "Eat Our Dust: Broadband infrastructure has made Redpoint the hottest VC firm you've never heard of" in *Fortune* (Oct. 9, 2000, pp. 200)
Pub: Time Inc.
Ed: Shawn Tully. **Description:** Entrepreneurial experience, cutting-edge technology, industry-transforming ideas - these are the things that have made the Redpoint partners among the hottest VC's in the land.

35405 ■ "Eco-Preneuring" in *Small Business Opportunities* (Vol. 12, No. 5, September 2000, pp. 94, 98)
Pub: Harris Publications, Inc.
Ed: Annette Wood. **Description:** A profile of Billy Darnell and Zoobee, the company he founded that makes exotic wildlife-themed watches.

35406 ■ "Electric Avenue" in *Small Business Opportunities* (Vol. 13, No. 6, November 2001, pp. 108)
Pub: Harris Publications, Inc.
Ed: Annette Wood. **Description:** Profile of R.S.C. Electronics, Inc., an electronics supply company that began in Wichita, Kansas.

35407 ■ "The Electronic Personal Touch" in *Fortune* (Vol. 141, No. 6, March 20, 2000, pp. 214)
Pub: Time Inc.
Ed: Erick Schonfeld. **Description:** Boston startup, Circles, is profiled. The new company offers virtual assistance to companies who, in turn, distribute as an employee benefit.

35408 ■ "Ellman: Building a VC Empire in the Empire State" in *Venture Capital Journal* (Vol. 40, No. 10, October 2000, pp. 48-49)
Pub: Venture Economics
Description: Profile of Stuart Ellman, 33, founder and general partner at RRE Ventures. Mr. Ellman tells how he and James Robinson IV, together with Robinson's father, created the New York-based venture capital firm.

35409 ■ "Empire Blossoms" in *Small Business Opportunities* (Vol. 12, No. 2, March 2000, pp. 86, 88)
Pub: Harris Publications, Inc.
Ed: Marie Sherlock. **Description:** Kari Moss was inspired by America's love of gardening when she started her business, Garden Rooms, one of a growing number of garden enterprises.

35410 ■ *Enterprise Planning and Development: Small Business and Enterprise Start-Up Survival and Growth*
Pub: Elsevier Science and Technology Books
Ed: David Butler. **Released:** August 2006. **Price:** $42.95. **Description:** Innovation, intellectual property, and exit strategies are among the issues discussed in this book involving current entrepreneurship.

35411 ■ "Entertainment Properties Trust" in *Ingram's* (Vol. 28, No. 5, May 2002, pp. 39)
Pub: Show Me Publishing, Inc.
Description: Profile of David Brain, who launched Entertainment Properties Trust, the real estate investment trust dedicated to the movie industry, by buying properties and leasing them back to theatres.

35412 ■ "Entrepreneur plans 31 strip malls for underserved areas" in *Crain's Detroit Business* (Vol. 16, No. 23, June 5, 2000, pp. 54)
Pub: Crain Communications, Inc.
Ed: Jennette Smith. **Description:** Djelosh "George" Juncaj plans to bring convenience retail to some of the most economically depressed areas of Detroit.

35413 ■ "Entrepreneur Column" in *Entrepreneur.com* (October 12, 2006)
Pub: Entrepreneur Media Inc.
Ed: Lisa Druxman. **Description:** Choice of a home-based business is critical to its success. Besides the many start up items such as permits, licenses, etc., make sure you have a passion for what you plan to do. Not all businesses can build upon past training and experience but there are those that lend themselves well to home based businesses like accounting, writing, editing, and others.

35414 ■ "Entrepreneur in Residence" in *Red Herring* (No. 87, December 18, 2000, pp. 212)
Pub: Herring Communications, Inc.
Ed: Desh Deshpande. **Description:** Desh Deshpande, cofounder and chairman of Sycamore Networks, offers advice to entrepreneurs on finding the right niche.

35415 ■ "Entrepreneur. Venturing Out" in *Boston Business Journal* (Vol. 23, No. 21, June 27, 2003, pp. 18)
Pub: American City Business Journals
Ed: Sean McFadden. Description: Matthew Roth and Sebastien Tran left jobs to found Veroxity Technology Partners (Boston, Massachusetts), a network infrastructure consulting and Internet services firm. The firm currently has 18 employees and offers services to both large and mid-size businesses.

35416 ■ "Entrepreneur of the Year: Bob Baron" in *Inc.* (January 1, 2005)
Pub: Inc. Magazine
Ed: Patrick J. Sauer. Description: Profile of Bob Baron, whose storm tracking technology helped the U.S. cope with a hyperactive Hurricane season in 2004. The firm's 3-D VIPIR system uses Doppler radar to pinpoint atmospheric disturbances a block away.

35417 ■ "Entrepreneur of the Year: Frank Altman" in *Inc.* (January 1, 2005)
Pub: Inc. Magazine
Ed: Jess McCuan. Description: Profile of Frank Alman, founder of Community Reinvestment Fund in Minneapolis, Minnesota. The company provides funding to small businesses in impoverished communities.

35418 ■ "Entrepreneur of the Year: Peter Provenzano" in *Inc.* (January 1, 2005)
Pub: Inc. Magazine
Ed: Allen Roberts. Description: Profile of Peter Provenzano, founder of the logistics company, SupplyCore, that delivers goods to American soldiers, even in Iraq's war zone. Provenzano was voted Entrepreneur of the Year.

35419 ■ "Entrepreneur of the Year: Shoba Purushothaman" in *Inc.* (January 1, 2005)
Pub: Inc. Magazine
Ed: Nadine Heintz. Description: Profile of Shoba Purushothaman, founder of NewsMarket, the firm that enables television broadcasters to transmit, watch and download video footage over the Internet. Purushothaman was voted Entrepreneur of the Year for 2004.

35420 ■ "Entrepreneur of the Year: The Ceja Family" in *Inc.* (January 1, 2005)
Pub: Inc. Magazine
Ed: Nicole Gull. Description: Profile of Pablo and Juanita Ceja, former migrant workers who now own their own vineyard producing 6,000 cases of wine annually. The couple left a small village in Mexico and became migrant workers picking grapes in Napa Valley, California.

35421 ■ "The Entrepreneurial Elite" in *Business Week* (No. 3658, December 6, 1999, pp. F46)
Pub: McGraw-Hill, Inc.
Description: A discussion with various business-affiliated people regarding small businesses, including how women entrepreneurs are changing the workplace and vice versa.

35422 ■ *Entrepreneurial Itch: What No One Tells You About Starting Your Own Business*
Pub: Self-Counsel Press Inc.
Ed: David Trahair. Released: December 2006. Price: $13.95. Description: Small business accountant shares a plan for starting a business.

35423 ■ *Entrepreneurial Itch: What No One Tells You about Starting Your Own Business*
Pub: Self-Counsel Press, Incorporated
Ed: David Trahair. Released: December 2006. Price: $13.95. Description: It is important for entrepreneurs to do research before starting a new business. Statistically, two out of three small businesses will fail within the first three years.

35424 ■ "Entrepreneurial Web Hub Debuts" in *Hispanic Business* (September 2004, pp. 20)
Pub: Hispanic Business

Description: America Online Latino and Ford Motor Company have teamed to launch a Spanish-language Web hub that will assist Hispanics to start or grow small businesses.

35425 ■ "Entrepreneurs" in *Forbes* (February 28, 2000, pp. 74)
Pub: Forbes Magazine
Ed: Leigh Gallagher. Description: Web-based information services are targeting small business. By banding many small businesses together via the web, these portals offer services, prices and discounts that until recently were available only to much larger companies.

35426 ■ "Entrepreneurs test start-ups-on the side" in *Wall Street Journal* (May 7, 2002, pp. B6)
Pub: Wall Street Journal
Ed: Jeff Bailey. Description: Many entrepreneurs are working fulltime jobs in order to finance their start-ups since venture capital and start-up funding has become more difficult to acquire.

35427 ■ "Entrepreneurs wanted" in *Boston Business Journal* (Vol. 22, No. 3, February 22, 2002, pp. 22)
Pub: MCP, Inc.
Description: Entrepreneurial opportunities are discussed.

35428 ■ *Entrepreneurship*
Pub: John Wiley and Sons Inc.
Ed: William D. Bygrave; Andrew Zacharakis. Released: March 2007. Price: $115.95. Description: Information for starting a new business is shared, focusing on marketing and financing a product or service.

35429 ■ *Entrepreneurship and the Financial Community Starting Up and Growing New Businesses*
Pub: Edward Elgar Publishing, Incorporated
Ed: Clarysse. Released: November 2006. Price: $75.00. Description: Understanding the role of private equity providers in the development and growth processes of small business.

35430 ■ *Entrepreneurship with Online Learning Center Access Card*
Pub: McGraw-Hill Higher Education
Ed: Robert D. Hirich; Michael P. Peters; Dean A. Shepherd. Released: October 2006. Price: $103.25. Description: Book instructs students on entrepreneurial processes that include starting a new business.

35431 ■ *Entrepreneurship Strategy: Changing Patterns in New Venture Creation, Growth, and Reinvention*
Pub: SAGE Publications, Incorporated
Ed: Lisa K. Gundry; Jill R. Kickul. Released: August 2006. Price: $69.95. Description: Entrepreneurial strategies that incorporate new venture emergence, early growth, and reinvention and innovation are examined.

35432 ■ *Entrepreneurship: Successfully Launching New Ventures*
Pub: Pearson Education Canada
Ed: Bruce Barringer; Duane Ireland. Released: January 2007. Price: $139.95 (CND). Description: Guide to help any entrepreneur successfully launch a new venture.

35433 ■ "Entrepreneurship, too, has its economic limits" in *Wall Street Journal* (October 1, 2002, pp. B4)
Pub: Dow Jones & Co. Inc.
Ed: Jeff Bailey. Description: Economic factors for entrepreneurs is presented. Statistical data included.

35434 ■ *Essentials of Entrepreneurship and Small Business Management*
Pub: Prentice Hall PTR
Ed: Thomas W. Zimmerer; Norman M. Scarborough; Doug Wilson. Released: February 2007. Price: $106.

67. Description: New venture creation and the knowledge required to start a new business are shared. The challenges of entrepreneurship, business plans, marketing, e-commerce, and financial considerations are explored.

35435 ■ "Eureka! I have an idea - how a business is born" in *Women in Business* (Vol. 54, No. 5, September-October 2002, pp. 30)
Pub: The ABWA Company, Inc.
Ed: Mia Katz. Description: The development of several businesses is discussed by the women who established them.

35436 ■ "Everyone's Doing It" in *Entrepreneur* (Vol. 28, No. 4, pp. 62)
Pub: Entrepreneur Media Inc.
Ed: Laura Tiffany. Description: Entrepreneurship is everywhere.

35437 ■ "Exercise your franchise" in *Ingram's* (Vol. 28, No. 3, March 2002, pp. 25)
Pub: Show Me Publishing, Inc.
Ed: Joe Bisogno. Description: It is important to investigate a franchising organization before making an investment. Some things to consider are: advertising and royalty fees, management personnel experience, and growth potential.

35438 ■ "Explosive Success" in *Small Business Opportunities* (Vol. 14, No. 1, January 2002, pp. 62-64)
Pub: Harris Publications, Inc.
Ed: Annette Wood. Description: Profile of Sandy Faust, who launched her circuit board company from her back porch, and has turned the business into a $1 million a year enterprise. Faust has won numerous business awards and plans to grow the business for her family then retire.

35439 ■ *Extraordinary Entrepreneurship: The Professional's Guide to Starting an Exceptional Enterprise*
Pub: John Wiley & Sons, Incorporated
Ed: Stephen C. Harper. Released: October 2006. Price: $45.00. Description: New rules to assist entrepreneurs in the 21st Century. The book focuses on thinking outside the box.

35440 ■ "Eye Candy: Life is Sweet for Two Visionaries Who Mix Sugary Treats with Style" in *Entrepreneur* (Vol. 32, No. 4, April 2004, pp. 168)
Pub: Entrepreneur Media, Inc.
Ed: April Y. Pennington. Description: Profile of Dylan Lauren and Jeff Rubin, co-founders of Dylan's Candy Bar. The New York City-based candy retailers project sales of more than $10 million for 2004.

35441 ■ "Faith, Determination, and a Little Marinara Sauce" in *Success* (Vol. 47, No. 1, January 2000, pp. 80)
Pub: Success Publishing, Inc.
Ed: Cynthia Kersey. Description: Domino's Pizza founder Tom Monaghan's hard-fought journey to success.

35442 ■ "Family Delivers on Father's Dream" in *Chicago Tribune* (March 9, 2005)
Pub: Knight-Ridder/Tribune Business News
Ed: Glenn Jeffers. Description: Profile of George Quinn who fell from a 30-foot ladder while painting a house, shattering a vertebra in his spine. Faced with years of rehabilitation, Quinn and his family fulfilled his dreams of owning his own pizzeria. His sons and wife work together to make the pizzas, work the cash register, and even deliver.

35443 ■ "The fast & the franchising" in *Entrepreneur* (Vol. 30, No. 3, March 2002, pp. 100)
Pub: Entrepreneur Media Inc.
Description: A listing of the 103 fastest growing franchises is presented. Franchises are ranked by growth in the number of franchises from 2000 to 2001.

35444 ■ *Fast-Track Business Start-Up Kit: California*
Pub: DP Group, Incorporated
Ed: Carolyn Usinger. **Released:** September 2006. **Price:** $29.00. **Description:** Step-by-step guide for starting and running a business in California, including information on sole proprietors, partnerships, limited liability companies, S and C corporations, as well as details concerning business entities, sales taxes, environmental issues, human resources, and more.

35445 ■ "Faster Tech Transfer" in *Inc.* (July 1, 2003)
Pub: Gruner & Jahr USA Publishing
Description: Technology transfer from colleges to private sector is discussed, using examples of universities tech transfer that fueled 450 business and 4,000 licenses in 2002. Transferring innovation from college laboratories to the private sector has startups and schools arguing over licensing and royalty deals.

35446 ■ "Fear factor: does the idea of starting your own business paralyze you?" in *Entrepreneur* (Vol. 31, No. 6, June 2003, pp. 92)
Pub: Entrepreneur Media Inc.
Ed: Romanus Wolter. **Description:** Doubt is probably the biggest fear faced by small business owners and new entrepreneurs. Ways to harness the energy of fear are examined.

35447 ■ "Feeling his oats" in *Entrepreneur* (Vol. 30, No. 2, February 2002, p)
Pub: Entrepreneur Media Inc.
Ed: April Pennington. **Description:** Profile of Lynn Rogers who started an oatmeal and oatmeal snacks company and donates a portion of profits to the athletic department at California State University, Fullerton.

35448 ■ "Feline Fortunes" in *Small Business Opportunities* (Vol. 12, No. 3, May 2000, pp. 62, 64)
Pub: Harris Publications, Inc.
Ed: Marie Sherlock. **Description:** Cat lover, Linda Wion, tells how she has turned her devotion to felines into a profitable business.

35449 ■ *Financial Times Guide to Business Start Up 2007*
Pub: Pearson Education, Limited
Ed: Sara Williams; Jonquil Lowe. **Released:** November 2006. **Price:** $52.50. **Description:** Guide for starting and running a new business is presented. Sections include ways to get started, direct marketing, customer relations, management and accounting.

35450 ■ "Find your working way" in *Black Enterprise* (Vol. 31, No. 5, December 2000, pp. 79)
Pub: Earl Graves Publishing Co.
Description: The question of loans to pay for career improvement is answered.

35451 ■ "Finding the Fault Line Where A New Business Can Grow" in *Fortune* (Vol. 142, No. 10, October 30, 2000, pp. 294+)
Pub: Time Inc.
Ed: Thomas A. Stewart. **Description:** The new company, 12 Entrepreneuring, an operating company whose mission is to reinvent business, is profiled.

35452 ■ "Finding financing" in *Black Enterprise* (Vol. 32, No. 6, January 2002, pp. 8)
Pub: Earl Graves Publishing Co.
Ed: Bevolyn Williams-Harold. **Description:** Minority entrepreneurs may need to look for more innovative capital resources, such as minority-focused venture capital funds or community-based securitization programs, to maintain cash flow.

35453 ■ "Finding Investors" in *Home Business* (Vol. 12, March/April 2005, No. 2, pp. 74)
Pub: Home Business Magazine
Ed: Nora Caley. **Description:** Home business startups need partners, rather than investors, to help with startup costs. And these partners expect to play a role in the business.

35454 ■ "A Fitting Memorial" in *Entrepreneur* (Vol. 32, No. 5, May 2004, pp. 130)
Pub: Entrepreneur Media, Inc.
Ed: Nichole L. Torres. **Description:** Profile of Mary Hickey and Bob Wheeler, founders of Renaissance Urn Company. The partners design and manufacturer decorative urn covers that allow families and friends to personalize funeral urns. Renaissance reported $100,000 in sales for 2003.

35455 ■ "Five Ways to Finance Your Business" in *Black Enterprise* (Vol. 31, No. 3, October 2000, pp. 43)
Pub: Earl Graves Publishing Co.
Ed: Glenn Townes. **Description:** The five best ways to find the cash to make your dream a reality are identified as: personal savings, trade credit, commercial banks, second mortgages, and angel investors.

35456 ■ "Flip the Switch" in *Entrepreneur. com* (Vol. 34, February 2006, No. 2, pp. 84)
Pub: Entrepreneur Media Inc.
Ed: Jennifer Alsever. **Description:** Experienced entrepreneurs share ideas to help start a successful business. Be sure to consider looking long term, get a prototype or test run, and be patient.

35457 ■ "Fly Solo: How to Build a Profitable Enterprise" in *Black Enterprise* (Vol. 30, No. 6, January 2000, pp. 72)
Pub: Earl Graves Publishing Co.
Ed: Millicent Lownes-Jackson and Gerda Gallop-Goodman. **Description:** Ways to assess your entrepreneurial sills are explored. Do you have the skills, abilities and knowledge required for the business you'd like to start? Do you have the ability to nurture and grow a business? Are you prepared to make sacrifices? Are you self-motivated? Do you like being in charge? Do you have the financial means to start a business? These questions must be answered truthfully before you move into self-employment.

35458 ■ "Flying Solo" in *Small Business Opportunities* (Vol. 12, No. 3, May 2000, pp. 20)
Pub: Harris Publications, Inc.
Ed: Lin Grensing-Pophal. **Description:** Going it alone when starting a new business requires some adjusting. The article addresses ways of coping.

35459 ■ "Food Frenzy" in *Small Business Opportunities* (Vol. 14, No. 1, January 2002, pp. 44)
Pub: Harris Publications, Inc.
Ed: Stan Roberts. **Description:** Selling fast food at a factory outlet created a $1.1 million business for Buddy Farr, an entrepreneur with no prior experience.

35460 ■ "Football Fever" in *Small Business Opportunities* (Vol. 13, No. 6, November 2001, pp. 54-55)
Pub: Harris Publications, Inc.
Ed: Stan Roberts. **Description:** Profile of Charlotte Begley, retailer who earns $500,000 a year selling licensed football products. Ms. Begley attends three trade shows a year to find the latest designs, colors and styles.

35461 ■ "For Love of the Game" in *Success* (Vol. 47, No. 6, November 2000, pp. 46)
Pub: Success Publishing, Inc.
Ed: Patrick Hoss. **Description:** Profile of Tim Walsh, a semi-professional baseball player in Mexico and exercise therapist, Walsh is also a board-game creator. As one of the creators of TriBond and the creator of Blurt, he shares the five things every entrepreneur should know in order to succeed.

35462 ■ "For the low, low price" in *Entrepreneur* (Vol. 30, No. 10, October 2002, pp. 100)
Pub: Entrepreneur Media Inc.
Description: A directory of franchises that can be started with investments of less than $25,000 is presented.

35463 ■ "Fore Profit Biz" in *Small Business Opportunities* (Vol. 13, No. 6, November 2001, pp. 72)
Pub: Harris Publications, Inc.
Description: Profile of Dale Bathum, who has built one of the golf shoe industry's most successful and fastest growing companies in the world of golf.

35464 ■ "Forget India, Outsource to Oregon!" in *Venture Capital Journal* (December 1, 2004)
Pub: Thomason Financial Inc.
Description: Reasons for venture capitals to target investments in Oregon and the Pacific Northwest rather than India or China are presented. Experienced angel investors and venture capitalists are taking the lead in building Oregon's high-tech entrepreneurial community.

35465 ■ "Fostering Urban Entrepreneurship" in *Black Enterprise* (Vol. 34, No. 4, November 2003, pp. 46)
Pub: Earl Graves Publishing Co.
Ed: Charlene Carter. **Description:** The winners of the third annual Miller Urban Entrepreneurs Business Grant Competition are highlighted. Each winner was awarded $20,000 to fund a business venture or expansion.

35466 ■ "The Four Questions" in *Home Business* (Vol. 12, March/April 2005, No. 2, pp. 64)
Pub: Home Business Magazine
Ed: Dr. Paul E. Adams. **Description:** Four questions to ask before applying to a bank for a new small business loan. It is important for entrepreneurs to understand their customer base.

35467 ■ "Franchise Finder" in *Black Enterprise* (Vol. 35, January 2005, No. 6, pp. 10)
Pub: Earl G. Graves Publishing Co. Inc.
Description: Black Enterprise offers a Website that helps aspiring entrepreneurs choose the franchise right for them.

35468 ■ "Franchise solutions" in *Black Enterprise* (Vol. 33, No. 7, February 2003, pp. 6)
Pub: Earl Graves Publishing Co.
Description: Blackenterprise.com can help entrepreneurs find the industry that suits their talents. The free Franchise Finder will locate business opportunities, information, and advice on running a business more efficiently, along with free consultation on financing and interviews with franchise CEOs.

35469 ■ "Franchising" in *Black Enterprise* (Vol. 32, No. 10, May 2002, pp. 101)
Pub: Earl Graves Publishing Co.
Ed: Carolyn M. Brown. **Description:** Franchising is one of the fastest growing segments of American business and is seen as an ideal partnership for an independent entrepreneur. More minorities are discovering franchising opportunities by increased recruiting by companies like Wendy's, Merry Maids, Jan Pro, Subway, Church's Chicken (TM), and Interim Healthcare. Profile of aforementioned franchise opportunities are included.

35470 ■ *Franchising for Dummies*
Pub: John Wiley & Sons, Incorporated
Ed: Dave Thomas, Michael Seid. **Released:** June 2000. **Price:** $19.99. **Description:** Advice to help entrepreneurs choose the right franchise, as well as financing, managing and expanding the business.

35471 ■ "Free Entrepreneurial Workshop" in *Minority Business Journal* (Vol. 17, No. 5, September/October 2001, pp. 2)
Pub: Minority Business Journal
Description: The Workshop in Business Opportunities (WIBO) has offered a free, 16-week intensive educational course for 35 years. The course, comparable to a short-course MBA curriculum, is taught by volunteer New York business owners and senior corporation executives. Alumni are entitled to free lifetime consulting services.

35472 ■ "From the Corner Office To Around the Corner" in *Fortune* (Vol. 141, No. 4, April 3, 2000, pp. 264J)
Pub: Time Inc.
Ed: Sam Hill. **Description:** In first person format, Sam Hill speaks about the loneliness of entrepreneurship.

35473 ■ "From the Firehouse to the Schoolhouse" in *Black Enterprise* (Vol. 33, No. 6, Jan. 2003, pp. 32)
Pub: Earl Graves Publishing Co.
Ed: Glenn Townes. **Description:** Profile of Marco Johnson, former firefighter, founded the Lancaster, California-based Antelope Valley Medical College where Johnson teaches individuals life-saving skills. Johnson outlines his road to entrepreneurship, from college, to football, to firehouse, to entrepreneur.

35474 ■ "From Vacation to Vocation" in *My Business* (September/October 2001, pp. 48)
Pub: My Business Magazine
Ed: Robyn and Tim Chilson. **Description:** Profile of Robyn and Tim Chilson, who turned their hobby of camping into the reality of owning the Brookdale Family Campground in Meadville, Pennsylvania.

35475 ■ "Full-time freelancers" in *Fast Company* (May 2001, pp. 62)
Pub: Fast Company
Ed: Christine Canabou. **Description:** A husband/wife team share their experiences that lead them to start their business, St. Aubyn, a company that emulates a freelance model, whereby staff members chose their work projects, manage their owns hours, and enjoy at least four weeks of paid vacation annually.

35476 ■ "Fun money" in *Entrepreneur* (Vol. 31, No. 4, April 2003, pp. 94)
Pub: Entrepreneur Media Inc.
Ed: Nichole L. Torres. **Description:** The benefits of starting a business based on a hobby gives the entrepreneur first-hand knowledge about the business, along with great passion for the work.

35477 ■ "Get 'em while they're hot" in *Entrepreneur* (Vol. 30, No. 12, December 2002, pp. 85)
Pub: Entrepreneur Media Inc.
Ed: Steve Cooper, Mark Henricks, Gisela M. Pedroza, April Y. Pennington, Chris Penttila, Chris Sandlund, Devlin Smith, Nichole L. Torres. **Description:** The hottest business opportunities for entrepreneurs in 2003 are listed, including online learning, outsourcing, home entertainment installation, health care technology, medi-spas, Instant Messaging-related services and products, sleep-related products, singles-related products and services, yoga studios, food supplements, online gaming, bankruptcy services, pet accessories, security, large-size clothing, online auction aftermarket services, scheduling software, and specialty ice cream shops.

35478 ■ "Get in the Game" in *Entrepreneur* (Vol. 33, January 2005, No. 1, pp. 106)
Pub: Entrepreneur Media Inc.
Ed: Andrew A. Caffey. **Description:** Five strategies to use in order to participate in a franchise program are listed.

35479 ■ "Getting off to the Right Start" in *Venture Capital Journal* (Vol. 40, No. 10, November 2000, pp. 40-41)
Pub: Venture Economics
Ed: Jay K. Hachigian. **Description:** Advice for entrepreneurs to avoid start-up problems, including ways to lay a proper foundation - setting up a common sense capital structure; ways to protect intellectual property; and good operating procedures.

35480 ■ "Getting Set for Success" in *Small Business Opportunities* (Vol. 16, No. 2, March 2004, pp. 162-163)
Pub: Harris Publications, Inc.
Ed: Stephen Kuslich. **Description:** According to the Small Business Administration's Office of Advocacy, over 600,000 new businesses are founded in the U.S. annually, and only two-thirds remain open at least two years, about half for four years, and only 40 percent remain at least six years. Eight keys for successful entrepreneurship are presented.

35481 ■ "Getting Set for Success with Your Own Small Business" in *Small Business Opportunities* (Vol. 12, No. 3, May 2000, pp. 110)
Pub: Harris Publications, Inc.
Description: Statistics regarding new business startups presented by the Small Business Administration (SBA) and Richard E. Irwin Research, Inc., along with advice for entrepreneurs, is provided.

35482 ■ "Goal for Entrepreneurs who have more equipment or employees than business demands" in *Business First Columbus* (Vol. 18, No. 25)
Pub: Business First Columbus, Inc.
Ed: Lisa Hooker. **Description:** Business plans for entrepreneurs with more equipment and employees than required to run their businesses.

35483 ■ "Going After Nike" in *Inc.* (October 1, 2004)
Pub: Inc. Magazine
Ed: Rob Walker. **Description:** Profile of Kalle Lasn, entrepreneur who intends to compete with Nike with his Blackspot sneaker.

35484 ■ "Going legit" in *BlackEnterprise* (Vol. 31, No. 12, July 2001, pp. 53)
Pub: Earl Graves Publishing Co.
Ed: Jason P. McKay. **Description:** Gregory D. Evans, the founder and CEO of the Cyber Group Network Corporation, has created E-Snitch, an electronic snitching device that uses wireless networks and satellites to locate missing or stolen computers anywhere in the world within a five-foot radius of the stolen PC.

35485 ■ "Going Places" in *Success* (Vol. 47, No. 6, November 2000, pp. 38)
Pub: Success Publishing, Inc.
Ed: Debbie Selinsky. **Description:** Profile of Michael Thomas, the multilingual CEO and president of OneTravel.com who believes some of the best ideas are those that people won't see right away.

35486 ■ "Goodbye B-School" in *Harvard Business Review* (Vol. 78, No. 2, March 2000, pp. 16)
Pub: Harvard Business School Publishing Corp.
Description: Two years ago, Jonathan Seelig left business school to co-found Akamai Technologies. In this interview he discusses how the company is now worth $20 billion.

35487 ■ "Got Fit?" in *Success* (Vol. 47, No. 6, November 2000, pp. 18)
Pub: Success Publishing, Inc.
Ed: Debbie Selinsky. **Description:** Jennifer Floren, a graduate of Dartmouth College, helps new college grads find their way into the work world. Three years into the business, experince.com has 100 employees across the country.

35488 ■ "Grandma's Recipe" in *Forbes* (December 25, 2000, pp. 242)
Pub: Forbes Magazine
Ed: Gail Buchalter. **Description:** Profile of Sorrells Pickard Gourmet Peanut Butter. In just two years since its launch, Sorrells Pickard Gourmet Peanut Butter expects sales of $3 million in 2000, and they predict $500,000 net on sales of $20 million in 2001.

35489 ■ "Grape Expectations: Are You Thinking About Getting Into the Wine Business?" in *Entrepreneur* (Vol. 31, No. 10, October 2003, pp. 106)
Pub: Entrepreneur Media, Inc.
Ed: Nichole L. Torres. **Description:** Winemaking has outpaced the economy in growth, even during recessions, and is expected to be a growth industry for the future.

35490 ■ "Grassroots Marketing" in *Home Business* (Vol. 12, March/April 2005, No. 2, pp. 58)
Pub: Home Business Magazine
Ed: Rich Sloan. **Description:** Finding unconventional ways to attract customers to a startup home-based business, called grassroots marketing, can cost much less than traditional advertising.

35491 ■ "Great Time to Go It Alone" in *Kiplinger's Personal Finance Magazine* (Vol. 58, No. 5, May 2004, pp. 20)
Pub: Kiplinger Washington Editors, Inc.
Ed: Melynda Dovel Wilcox. **Description:** Government statistics underestimate the number of jobs being created each month at small and startup companies, and the number of individuals becoming entrepreneurs.

35492 ■ "Growth Strategies" in *Inc.* (November 2000, pp. 78)
Pub: The Goldhirsh Group
Description: Chris Zane's bike shop was healthy and profitable, but he needed the skills of a CEO to make it grow.

35493 ■ "Guiding Light; Feeling a Little Lost at the Helm of Your Business?" in *Entrepreneur* (Vol. 31, No. 8, August 2003, pp. 84)
Pub: Entrepreneur Media, Inc.
Ed: Geoff Williams. **Description:** Profile of the Build Your Own Business (BYOB) 10-week program that helps entrepreneurs, targeting residents in underserved, urban neighborhoods. Entrepreneurs can receive ongoing free services upon completion of the classes, including financial counseling and tax preparation from BYOB's nonprofit organization, Smart Money Community Services in Cincinnati, Ohio.

35494 ■ "Hall of Mirrors" in *Small Business Opportunities* (Vol. 12, No. 3, May 2000, pp. 44)
Pub: Harris Publications, Inc.
Ed: Stan Roberts. **Description:** A profile of Tom Levine and how he worked part-time installing mirrors, before starting his own mirror business that now earns $300,000 annually.

35495 ■ "Halsey Minor's Virtual Train Station" in *Business Week Online* (February 9, 2005)
Pub: McGraw-Hill Companies
Description: Harry Minor, tech entrepreneur, talks about his latest venture, called Grand Central, that helps companies interconnect their software via the Internet. Minor has been working on Grand Central for five years.

35496 ■ "Handling Critics" in *Small Business Opportunities* (Vol. 12, No. 2, March 2000, pp. 58, 60)
Pub: Harris Publications, Inc.
Ed: Lin Grensing-Pophal. **Description:** Twelve tips to handle criticism effectively when starting a new business venture.

35497 ■ "Hands Off" in *Forbes* (December 25, 2000, pp. 270)
Pub: Forbes Magazine
Ed: Elizabeth Corcoran. **Description:** Profile of CenterBeam, a managed service provider, that loads computers with the latest software, networking features, and its own proprietary programming. That programming allows CenterBeam to manage the machines remotely. The company also becomes the client's Internet service provider.

35498 ■ "Hands On" in *Inc.* (September 2000, pp. 107)
Pub: The Goldhirsh Group
Ed: Mike Hoffman. **Description:** Small-fry entrepreneurs who can't afford top legal or Human Resource advice may be confused by arcane federal rules. A thorough rundown on regulations covering small companies is included.

35499 ■ "Hanging tough: Wilhelmina Bell-Taylor overcame cancer to launch a successful business" in *Black Enterprise* (Oct. 2002, pp. 55)
Pub: Earl Graves Publishing Co.
Ed: Phaedra Brotherton. **Description:** Profile of Wilhelmina Bell-Taylor, who was diagnosed with Hodgkin's disease when she was only 19 years old. At age 54, Bell-Taylor is the founder and president of BETAH Associates Inc., a management counseling, communications, information, and administrative services firm located in Bethesda, Maryland. The company started as a home-based operation, incorporated in 1994.

35500 ■ "Harnessing Rhino Power" in *Hispanic Business* **(July/August 2002, pp. 73)**
Pub: Hispanic Business
Description: Profile of Humberto Barrera, owner of Rhino Computer Systems. Barrera's computer consulting company is expected to gross more than $100,000 in its first fiscal year. The entrepreneur answers questions about his company, philosophy, employees, and marketing.

35501 ■ *The Harvard Entrepreneurs Club Guide to Starting Your Own Business*
Pub: John Wiley & Sons, Inc.
Ed: Sharma. **Released:** 1999. **Price:** $14.95.

35502 ■ "Health Crisis Inspires Medesto, Calif. Woman to Open Needlework Store" in *Modesto Bee* **(January 22, 2003)**
Pub: Knight-Ridder/Tribune Business News
Ed: Tim Moran. **Description:** Lois Mouriski Bear tells how she went from legal secretary to owner of the Elegant Stitch in Modesto, California. Mouriski Bear was diagnosed with breast cancer in 1997 and started her Internet business at home selling high-end needlework patterns and supplies.

35503 ■ "Here's the keys: looking for a new business idea?" in *Entrepreneur* **(Vol. 30, No. 10, October 2002, pp. 116)**
Pub: Entrepreneur Media Inc.
Ed: Gisela M. Pedroza. **Description:** Profile of Richard Weisman, Exotic Car Country Club, a club that provides high-end luxury cars to its members.

35504 ■ "High-Adventure Past, High-Speed Future" in *Success* **(Vol. 47, No. 4, September 2000, pp. 44)**
Pub: Success Publishing, Inc.
Ed: Paul Gallagher. **Description:** Chris Catranis, CEO of Skyway Partners, tells how he is maintaining a high-tech Internet business in a tiny village amid rural farmlands.

35505 ■ "Hold'Em" in *Entrepreneur* **(Vol. 28, No. 7, July 2000, pp. 78)**
Pub: Entrepreneur Media Inc.
Ed: Cynthia Harrington. **Description:** Takes a look at two entrepreneurs balancing the eternal choice between selling equity or borrowing.

35506 ■ "Hollister priorities: Loan, training programs" in *Crain's Detroit Business* **(Vol. 19, No. 3, January 20, 2003, pp. 24)**
Pub: Crain Communications Inc., Detroit
Ed: Amy Lane. **Description:** David Hollister was named by Jennifer Granholm, Michigan's new governor, to head the new Department of Labor, Economic Growth and Urban Development. The Department will provide low interest loans to entrepreneurs in targeted redevelopment areas of the state. The extension of the Michigan Economic Growth Authority is also discussed.

35507 ■ "Home Alone: Make an Effort to Fight Loneliness" in *My Business* **(October/November 2002, pp. 45)**
Pub: My Business Magazine
Ed: Doug McPherson. **Description:** Loneliness is a big factor to consider with deciding to start a home-based business; one such owner started a consultants group that meets monthly for breakfast, another takes time out for yoga classes and tennis.

35508 ■ "Home: Where the Money Is" in *Small Business Opportunities* **(Vol. 14, No. 1, January 2002, pp. 86)**
Pub: Harris Publications, Inc.
Description: Profile of Kalie Warren, Jr., an ex-homeless man who started a handyman service called Rent-A-Husband and now sells franchise opportunities in six states, Hong Kong, and Great Britain. Warren plans to expand the franchise operation to 1,000 by the year 2008.

35509 ■ "Homeless entrepreneurs swap shopping carts" in *Red Herring* **(No. 76, March 2000, pp. 58)**
Pub: Herring Communications, Inc.

Ed: Peter D. Henig. **Description:** The issue of homeless persons using the Internet at public libraries and shelters is discussed, including the success stories of homeless people successfully launching their own Web sites.

35510 ■ "Honey Rhymes with Money" in *Small Business Opportunities* **(Vol. 12, No. 2, March 2000, pp. 104)**
Pub: Harris Publications, Inc.
Ed: Stan Roberts. **Description:** A profile of Robin Bunting, owner of a honey-making company in Tangerine, Florida. Ms. Bunting tends her hives in her backyard on weekends and earns $30,000 or more annually.

35511 ■ "Honor Thy Self" in *Black Enterprise* **(Vol. 35, February 2005, No. 7, pp. 156)**
Pub: Earl G. Graves Publishing Co. Inc.
Ed: Tanisha A. Sykes. **Description:** Self-esteem, stress management, and dealing with difficult people are the issues discussed for an aspiring woman entrepreneur.

35512 ■ "Hot 100" in *Entrepreneur* **(Vol. 31, No. 6, June 2003, pp. 64)**
Pub: Entrepreneur Media Inc.
Ed: Amanda C. Kooser. **Description:** Twenty-five of the 100 companies hitting the year's hottest industry for 2003 come from the business services sector, nine providing logistics services (such as freight-handling, trucking and transportation) and six providing marketing and advertising services.

35513 ■ "How do Fast Companies Work Now?" in *Fast Company* **(September 2001, pp. 134)**
Pub: Fast Company
Ed: Keith H. Hammonds. **Description:** Imagine a company started by the best-connected investment bank in the world, by a leading management-consulting firm, and by one of the top venture capital firms - give it $300 million, and set it loose to reinvent big business - that is the formula guiding David Pecaut and his colleagues at Iformation.

35514 ■ "How to Get Started in Business" in *Crain's Detroit Business* **(Vol. 16, No. 50, December 11, 2000, pp. E-6)**
Pub: Crain Communications, Inc.
Description: The U.S. Small Business Administration provides the first steps an entrepreneur should take toward starting a business. Questions are provided to help create a focused, well-researched business plan that can serve as a blueprint for your business.

35515 ■ "How I Did It: Randy Slager" in *Inc.* **(January 1, 2005)**
Pub: Inc. Magazine
Ed: Patrick J. Sauer. **Description:** Profile of Randy Slager, founded Catapult Technology while battling a degenerative spinal injury incurred as an information systems officer in the Army. Slager has two goals: one is to continue expanding his $30 million dollar IT company, the other is to help disabled veterans achieve entrepreneurial success.

35516 ■ "How iWon Won the Web" in *Success* **(Vol. 47, No. 6, November 2000, pp. 28)**
Pub: Success Publishing, Inc.
Ed: Scott Smith, Paul Gallagher. **Description:** Profile of iWon.com, the Web portal that offers small business e-mail, news, services, and a chance to bag at least $10,000 a day. IWon.com's co-founders and co-CEO's, Bill Daugherty and Jonas Steinman, share some of the key ingredients that have helped them stay ahead of the curve.

35517 ■ "How to Stay on the Move...When the World is Slowing Down" in *Fast Company* **(July 2001, pp. 113)**
Pub: Fast Company
Ed: Scott Kirsner. **Description:** It is hard to remember a less-inviting time to have a great idea for a new company or to champion new ideas to change a big company. Leaders who think big aren't willing to downsize their ambitions they just work a little harder and smarter. Some battle-tested advice on how to stay fast in slow times is offered.

35518 ■ "How a Virtuoso Plays the Web: Eclectic, Inquisitive, and Academic, Yahoo's Jerry Yang Reinvents the Role of the Entrepreneur" in *Fortune*
Pub: Time Inc.
Ed: Brent Schlender. **Description:** Successful entrepreneurs are inventive people who conjure new technologies, contrive new business models, or figure out how to open new opportunities in the marketplace.

35519 ■ "Howdy, Partner" in *Entrepreneur* **(Vol. 32, October 2004, No. 10, pp. 104)**
Pub: Entrepreneur Media Inc.
Ed: Nichole L. Torres. **Description:** When considering a virtual partnership with an entrepreneur met over the Internet, one must communicate, check references and histories, and establish set duties in writing.

35520 ■ "I want to start my own business" in *Women in Business* **(Vol. 54, No. 5, September-October 2002, pp. 14)**
Pub: The ABWA Company, Inc.
Ed: Elizabeth Bradley. **Description:** The desire to start a business is discussed by several women business owners.

35521 ■ "I Did It My Way" in *Entrepreneur* **(Vol. 31, No. 8, August 2003, pp. 112)**
Pub: Entrepreneur Media, Inc.
Ed: Romanus Wolter. **Description:** The secret to entrepreneurial success is to discover what works for you by taking action according to your personality and instincts. A method to help create a business plan is presented.

35522 ■ "Identify All Possible Exits" in *Business Week Online* **(Dec. 6, 2002)**
Pub: McGraw-Hill Inc.
Ed: William J. Link. **Description:** Advice for entrepreneurs to keep exit strategies in mind when planning a start up company is given.

35523 ■ "If at First You Don't Succeed..." in *Black Enterprise* **(Vol. 34, No. 4, Nov. 2003, pp. 48)**
Pub: Earl Graves Publishing Co.
Ed: Zakiyyah El-Amin. **Description:** Profile of Linda A. Banks and Terri Michele, who, together, attempted various business ventures, but found their true calling when starting a childcare center in Pittsburgh, Pennsylvania.

35524 ■ "If I Had an E-Hammer" in *Success* **(Vol. 47, No. 3, July 2000, pp. 24)**
Pub: Success Publishing, Inc.
Description: A profile of Peter Hunt, president and COO of CornerHardware.com, an online hardware store based in San Francisco, California.

35525 ■ "I'm Game: What Hot, New Pastime is Inspiring Entrepreneurs to Launch Businesses?" in *Entrepreneur* **(Vol. 32, September 2004)**
Pub: Entrepreneur Media Inc.
Ed: Nichole L. Torres. **Description:** Cashflow 101 is the new business board game that teaches financial principles for accounting and investing. Profiles of entrepreneurs who launched a business after playing the game are included.

35526 ■ "Imperial forces" in *Entreprener* **(Vol. 30, No. 3, March 2002, pp. 109)**
Pub: Entrepreneur Media Inc.
Ed: Karen E. Klein. **Description:** Profile of various entrepreneurs and ways they started their empires.

35527 ■ "Import an Income" in *Small Business Opportunities* **(Vol. 12, No. 5, September 2000, pp. 100)**
Pub: Harris Publications, Inc.
Ed: Marie Sherlock. **Description:** Love to travel? Consider starting an import business that requires trips around the world.

35528 ■ "In for the Count" in *Entrepreneur* **(Vol. 28, No. 9, September 2000, pp. 60)**
Pub: Entrepreneur Media, Inc.
Ed: Cynthia E. Griffin. **Description:** Iris J. Burnett and Nell Merlino, developers of the innovative program called Count-Me-In had revolutionized business loans for women.

35529 ■ "In Jack he trusts; Ex-Decision Consultants owner starts new company" in *Crain's Detroit Business* **(Vol. 19, No. 1, Jan. 6, 2003, pp.3)**
Pub: Crain Communications Inc., Detroit
Ed: Andrew Dietderich. **Description:** Profile of Jack Krasula, past head of Decision Consultants Inc., a company providing information technology, application development, application outsourcing, and installation and support services. Having sold Decision Consultants Inc., Krasula has started a new company called Trustinus Inc. that will specialize in supply-chain-management services, or the middleman between Company A and the company it contracts for services.

35530 ■ "In a tough market, a tech executive chooses to gamble" in *Wall Street Journal* **(Jan. 24, 2003, pp. A1)**
Pub: Dow Jones & Co. Inc.
Ed: Pui-Wing Tam. **Description:** Profile of Barry Cottle, and his startup, Mobile Digital Media Inc. and the challenges he faces in the recession-struck Silicon Valley, California.

35531 ■ "The Inadvertent Entrepreneur" in *Success* **(Vol. 47, No. 6, November 2000, pp. 22)**
Pub: Success Publishing, Inc.
Ed: Richard E. Mueller. **Description:** Profile of Richard E. Mueller, founder and CEO of MTW Corporation. Mr. Mueller tells how, after 20 years as a CEO, he developed MTW, which began as a technical staffing company.

35532 ■ "Inc. Case Study" in *Inc.* **(November 2000, pp. 54)**
Pub: The Goldhirsh Group
Description: Marian Cihacek chronicles the business she founded, Great Harvest Bread Company, that practically runs itself.

35533 ■ "Inner-City Innovation" in *Entrepreneur* **(Vol. 28, No. 2, February 2000, pp. 136)**
Pub: Entrepreneur Media Inc.
Ed: Stephen Barlas. **Description:** President Clinton and Congress move toward increasing incentives for entrepreneurs ready to take on low-income communities.

35534 ■ "Inside the Customer-Focused Company" in *Harvard Business Review* **(Vol. 78, No. 3, May 2000, pp. S20)**
Pub: Harvard Business School Publishing Corp.
Ed: Cary Jehl Broussard. **Description:** The article shows how a change agent, or type of business consultant, and vocal consumers help structure an entire organization.

35535 ■ "Instant Phone Companies" in *Business 2.0* **(Vol. 6, July 2005, No. 6, pp. 28)**
Pub: Time, Inc.
Description: Michael Robertson has launched a beta version of Gizmo Project that will license technology to companies wishing to sell Voice over Internet Protocol (VoIP) services under their existing brand names.

35536 ■ "Is My Partnership Fair?" in *Inc.* **(July 1, 2004)**
Pub: Inc. Magazine
Description: A small business entrepreneur of a 50-50 partnership talks about protecting ideas and the pros and cons of leasing versus purchasing new technology.

35537 ■ "It's Not the First Time" in *Entrepreneur* **(Vol. 30, No. 2, February 2002, pp. 53)**
Pub: Entrepreneur Media Inc.
Ed: Jennifer Pellet. **Description:** Venture capitalists are looking for leadership experience when investing in startup companies.

35538 ■ "I've got an idea" in *Atlanta Business Chronicle* **(Vol. 25, January 3, 2003, No. 30, pp. 2B)**
Pub: American City Business Publications, Inc.

Ed: Tom Barry. **Description:** Profile of Jerry Eickhoff, founder and CEO of Enterpulse, the entrepreneur founding financial and Internet ventures. Enterpulse, an Internet technology firm, is currently on the brink of growth. Information is presented involving Eickhoff's other ventures.

35539 ■ "Just Desserts" in *Small Business Opportunities* **(Vol. 12, No. 3, May 2000, pp. 54)**
Pub: Harris Publications, Inc.
Ed: Jerilyn Kaufman. **Description:** Alicia Dargan, the mastermind behind AMK Specialty Gourmet, Inc., chronicles the family dessert shop from start-up to their current success, with earnings at $300,000 a year.

35540 ■ "Kick Back and Relax" in *Entrepreneur*
Pub: Entrepreneur Media Inc.
Ed: Romanus Wolter. **Description:** Relaxation time is essential to entrepreneurial success. Four tips to help avoid burnout are listed, focusing on making relaxation an essential part of a regular routine.

35541 ■ "Kid power! Adults need not apply" in *Black Enterprise* **(Vol. 32, No. 9, April 2002, pp. 135)**
Pub: Earl Graves Publishing Co.
Ed: Kenneth Meeks. **Description:** An overview of the Kidpreneurs Conference sponsored by Black Enterprise. The conference is designed to develop the entrepreneurial potential of young people.

35542 ■ "Lap of Luxury" in *Small Business Opportunities* **(Vol. 14, No. 1, January 2002, pp. 90)**
Pub: Harris Publications, Inc.
Ed: Stan Roberts. **Description:** Profile of Amy Evans, owner of Laptop Lane, the company that rents laptop computers to stranded travelers in airports. Laptop Lane averages 25,000 customers a month paying $20 per visit.

35543 ■ "The Last Frontier of Beer" in *Success* **(Vol. 47, No. 5, October 2000, pp. 32)**
Pub: Success Publishing, Inc.
Ed: Thomas Melville. **Description:** The article shows how Geoff and Marcy Larson used civic entrepreneurship to win over investors and raise $500,000 to begin their brewery in Juneau, Alaska.

35544 ■ "A launching point to the next step" in *Hispanic Business* **(Vol. 22, No. 6, June 2000, pp. 42)**
Pub: Hispanic Business
Ed: Derek Reveron. **Description:** Potomac Management Group Inc., founded as a part-time information technology and logistics consultancy by Dennis Garcia in 1992, has won a $22 million, 5-year contract from the U.S. Coast Guard. The company expects revenues to reach over $8 million in 2000.

35545 ■ "Laurel Touby" in *Entrepreneur* **(Vol. 30, No. 2, February 2002, pp. 18)**
Pub: Entrepreneur Media Inc.
Ed: Michelle Prather. **Description:** Profile of Laurel Touby, founder of Mediabistro.com in New York City. Mediabistro.com is an online and offline community for media and creative professionals.

35546 ■ "Lawn Ranger" in *My Business* **(September/October 2001, pp. 54)**
Pub: My Business Magazine
Ed: Ivan Sylvester. **Description:** Profile of Betty Jo Houck and her company called WeMailSmiles.com. The four-year-old company mails plastic lawn ornaments without wrapper, adorned with bows, for maximum attention.

35547 ■ "Learning Curves: How to Avoid 3 First-Time Mistakes" in *My Business* **(December/January 2004, pp. 48)**
Pub: My Business Magazine
Ed: Jamie Roberts. **Description:** Profile of Gary Heavin, founder and CEO of Curves International, the 30-minute strength and exercise club for women. It is estimated that a new Curves location opens every four hours.

35548 ■ "Learning the Game of Hard Knocks" in *Hispanic Business* **(October 2003, pp. 36, 38)**
Pub: Hispanic Business
Ed: Scott Williams. **Description:** A pair of aspiring marketers find out that unexpected problems are often part and parcel of starting new business ventures.

35549 ■ *Legal Guide for Starting and Running a Small Business*
Pub: NOLO
Ed: Fred S. Steingold. **Released:** August 2006. **Price:** $34.99. **Description:** Legal issues any small business owner needs to know for starting and running a successful business are outlined.

35550 ■ "Light Rider" in *Success* **(Vol. 47, No. 1, January 2000, pp. 13)**
Pub: Success Publishing, Inc.
Ed: Phoebe Chan. **Description:** Entrepreneur lights the way for neon's rebirth. Car repairman Jack Panzarella created special lighting to illuminate the road while a car is in motion.

35551 ■ "Lori & Ryan Pacchiano" in *Entrepreneur* **(Vol. 31, No. 7, July 2003, pp. 23)**
Pub: Entrepreneur Media, Inc.
Ed: April Y. Pennington. **Description:** Profile of, Lori and Ryan Pacchiano, co-founders of High Maintenance Bitch In Seattle. Lori has created a feather boa for dogs and cats which is sold by the brother and sister team at local pet stores. Ryan came up with the name, a synonym for the word dog, and is now trademarked.

35552 ■ "Love Story" in *Entrepreneur* **(Vol. 28, No. 8, August 2000, pp. 142)**
Pub: Entrepreneur Media Inc.
Ed: Paul Edwards and Sarah Edwards. **Description:** Help in finding a small business that fulfills personal passions.

35553 ■ "LSW Architects receives entrepreneurial spirit award in construction category" in *Vancouver, WA Business Journal* **(February 28, 2003)**
Pub: Dolan Media Newswires
Ed: Cami Joner. **Description:** LSW Architects was awarded the Entrepreneurial Spirit Award in the construction category for ongoing commitment to focused, quality work.

35554 ■ "Luck of the Draw: A Windfall Helps One Man's Small Business Dream Come True" in *Entrepreneur* **(Vol. 31, No. 10, October 2003)**
Pub: Entrepreneur Media, Inc.
Ed: Devlin Smith. **Description:** Profile of Timothy Tuttle, who won $1.9 million on a quarter slot machine in Las Vegas, Nevada, and started his own quick-service chain specializing in Orleans fare like gumbo and beignets.

35555 ■ "Maine Lawyer Launches Personal Chef and Catering Service" in *Portland Press Herald* **(August 9, 2002)**
Pub: Knight Ridder/Tribune Business News
Ed: Mark Shanahan. **Description:** Profile of Carrie Yardley, former attorney turned caterer. Yardley started Add More Thyme, a personal chef and catering service, from her home in Yarmouth, Maine.

35556 ■ "Making the grade" in *Entrepreneur* **(Vol. 31, No. 5, May 2003, pp. 96)**
Pub: Entrepreneur Media Inc.
Ed: Devlin Smith. **Description:** Profile of Angela F. Norman, owner of The Goddard School of Centerville, a childcare and education center in Ohio. Norman is a former district sales manager for a pharmaceutical company, and does not have a degree in education or early childhood development.

35557 ■ "Man for all Seasons" in *Small Business Opportunities* **(Vol. 12, No. 3, May 2000, pp. 102-103)**
Pub: Harris Publications, Inc.
Description: A profile of Michael Arnone, who can do it all from topiary and landscape design to pruning,

holiday decorating and incredible lawn displays. He tells how he completed several successful interior design projects, so he is adding decorating to his many talents.

35558 ■ "The Man Who Launched 4,000 Businesses" in *Fortune* **(Vol. 143, No. 3, February 5, 2001, pp. 180)**
Pub: Time Inc.
Ed: Carlye Adler. Description: Tony DeSio didn't set out to build the biggest non-food franchise ever. As with many entrepreneurial ventures, it just sort of happened that way.

35559 ■ "Master Builder" in *Success* **(Vol. 47, No. 5, October 2000, pp. 26)**
Pub: Success Publishing, Inc.
Ed: H. Lee Murphy. Description: Profile of Dan McLean, who built an empire from nothing, by knowing his market and taking risks. Now the world is at his feet. As chairman and CEO of MCL Cos., he expects to report revenues of %150 million this year.

35560 ■ "A matter of safety" in *Black Enterprise* **(Vol. 32, No. 9, April 2002)**
Pub: Earl Graves Publishing Co.
Ed: Alan Hughes. Description: Orlando Robinson tells how a tragic event in his life prompted him to launch his own company, D&D Innovations Inc. His first product is the Seatbelt Shifter Lock, which requires the seatbelt to be locked before the car can be taken out of the park position.

35561 ■ "Mavericks" in *Success* **(Vol. 47, No. 2, June 2000, pp. 18)**
Pub: Success Publishing, Inc.
Ed: Russell Wild. Description: A profile of Jack Barringer's Cactus Jack line of cleaning products.

35562 ■ "Max Polaner" in *Entrepreneur* **(Vol. 30, No. 3, March 2002, pp. 22)**
Pub: Entrepreneur Media Inc.
Ed: April Pennington. Description: Profile of Max Polaner, 35 year old founder and CEO of Impromptu Gourmet in Valley Cottage, New York. The startup earned $2 million in sales its first year.

35563 ■ "Mentor Wanted" in *Black Enterprise* **(Vol. 35, January 2005, No. 6, pp. 97)**
Pub: Earl G. Graves Publishing Co. Inc.
Ed: Tanisha A. Sykes. Description: Young African American man is looking for a mentor to help him start his own clothing business. The entrepreneur has placed some shirts in an area store, but is unsure of marketing and manufacturing of his clothing.

35564 ■ "The Merchant of Bay Ridge" in *Forbes* **(Vol. 174, December 27, 2004, No. 13, pp. 80)**
Pub: Forbes Magazine Inc.
Ed: Phyllis Berman. Description: Profile of Joseph Cohen, the 17-year-old entrepreneur who developed a thriving online retail business called Bay Ridge.

35565 ■ "Military Service Equips Future Business Owners" in *Home Business* **(Vol. 12, March/April 2005, No. 2, pp. 44)**
Pub: Home Business Magazine
Description: Twenty-two percent of American veterans are planning to purchase or start a small business, according to the Small Business Administration's Office of Advocacy.

35566 ■ "Milwaukee Mayor Says Federal Business Development Program Will Create Jobs" in *Milwaukee Journal Sentinel* **(December 8, 2005)**
Pub: Journal Sentinel, Inc.
Ed: Tom Daykin. Description: The Federal government is expanding its Renewal Community program in Milwaukee, Wisconsin. The program gives subsidies to new business development in poor neighborhoods.

35567 ■ "Minding Her Bees-Ness" in *Small Business Opportunities* **(Vol. 12, No. 5, September 2000, pp. 108)**
Pub: Harris Publications, Inc.

Description: A profile of Burt's Bees, famous for their earth-friendly, natural personal care products, and their commitment to giving back to nature by pledging $2 million to help preserve a remote forest in the state of Maine.

35568 ■ "Mining venture capital" in *Black Enterprise* **(Vol. 32, No. 7, February 2002,)**
Pub: Earl Graves Publishing Co.
Ed: Derek T. Dingle. Description: Strategies are given to entrepreneurs about finding capital to fund start-ups in today's economy. Statistical data included.

35569 ■ "Minneapolis" in *Entrepreneur* **(Vol. 28, No. 4, April 2000, pp. 162)**
Pub: Entrepreneur Media Inc.
Ed: Cynthia E. Griffin. Description: Use this incubator to hatch your business in 90 days or less. Entrenaut, a Minneapolis incubator is profiled.

35570 ■ "A model occupation: who says you can't turn business into play?" in *Entrepreneur* **(Vol. 31, No. 4, April 2003, pp. 102)**
Pub: Entrepreneur Media Inc.
Ed: Devlin Smith. Description: Profile of Gary Phillips who turned his knowledge of retailing and love of model railroads into becoming a franchisee for HobbyTown USA. Phillips and his wife are franchise partners. Information on three other franchising success stories is included.

35571 ■ "Money From Thin Air" in *Small Business Opportunities* **(Vol. 16, No. 1, January 2004, pp. 70)**
Pub: Harris Publications, Inc.
Ed: Annette Wood. Description: Profile of Michael Coup, who designs, manufactures and sells air moving products. Coup's Vornado Air Circulation Systems Inc., in Andover, Kansas, offers air fans, heaters, humidifiers, air cleaners and air circulators. The company's sales have grown to $29 million.

35572 ■ "Montana Champion Again, Joins F-of-F" in *Venture Capital Journal* **(Vol. 40, No. 10, November 2000, pp. 8, 9)**
Pub: Venture Economics
Description: Champion Ventures, the investment firm that invests in other venture capital funds, was founded in 1999 by San Francisco 49ers Ronnie Lott and Harris Barton. In mid-September 2000, Joe Montana joined the firm as a general partner.

35573 ■ "More than a green thumb" in *Black Enterprise* **(Vol. 32, No. 5, December 2001, pp. 46)**
Pub: Earl Graves Publishing Co.
Ed: Bridget McCrea. Description: Profile of Roderick Gay, founder and president of Preferred Landscape in College Park, Georgia.

35574 ■ "Moving Pictures" in *Hispanic Business* **(Vol. 23, No. 5, May 2001, pp. 66, 68)**
Pub: Hispanic Business
Ed: Andrea Siedsma. Description: Profile of Hispanic entrepreneurs Javier Jimenez and Matthew Cullen, co-founders of Motion Theory, a graphic design and production studio that combines motion graphics computer animation, Web-site design and programming, film and digital video shooting and, editing and post-production work.

35575 ■ "Mr. Koogle's Failed Return" in *Red Herring* **(January 2003, pp. 69)**
Pub: Herring Communications Inc.
Ed: Justin Hibbard. Description: Profile of Tim Koogle, former Yahoo CEO, who expected a return to the corporate stage, only to have his new venture close before it was able to open.

35576 ■ "Mr. Yoshida's Opus" in *Small Business Opportunities* **(Vol. 14, No. 1, January 2002, pp. 56)**
Pub: Harris Publications, Inc.
Description: Profile of Junki Yoshida, who launched a line of cooking sauces and markets them in such

unique ways as dressing like Elvis or a Roman gladiator in his advertisements. In addition to building a business that made more than $100 million in 2000, Yoshida finds the time to be a mentor and benefactor to many.

35577 ■ "Music to his Ears" in *Small Business Opportunities* **(Vol. 12, No. 5, September 2000, pp. 88, 90)**
Pub: Harris Publications, Inc.
Ed: Will Romano. Description: A profile of Bill Bennett, president of Off Wall Street Jam in Manhattan, and how he has built his recording studio business through word-of-mouth.

35578 ■ "The Name Game" in *Venture Capital Journal* **(Vol. 42, No. 10, October 2002, pp. 35-37)**
Pub: Thomas Venture Economics
Ed: Charles R. Fellers. Description: Young companies are changing names faster than they are changing their business plans. Strategies for naming a company are investigated.

35579 ■ "NASA Offers Free Rocket Scientists" in *Inc.* **(August 1, 2004)**
Pub: Inc. Magazine
Ed: Jess McCuan. Description: NASA has created a new outreach program that offers small businesses up to 40 hours of free high-tech and engineering advice under the Space Alliance Technology Outreach Program, which began as a state-run project in 1995 in the State of Florida and went national in 2001.

35580 ■ "National" in *Entrepreneur* **(Vol. 28, No. 10, October 2000, pp. 138)**
Pub: Entrepreneur Media Inc.
Ed: Cynthia E. Griffin. Description: As the number of entrepreneurial firms grow, corporate America is taking notice of the potential market that can also benefit small business. A roundup of some of the newest offerings is featured.

35581 ■ "Natural Instinct" in *Entrepreneur* **(Vol. 31, No. 8, August 2003, pp. 90)**
Pub: Entrepreneur Media, Inc.
Ed: Nichole L. Torres. Description: According to the Organic Trade Association, the organic market is growing 20 percent annually. All areas of the industry are experiencing this growth, especially spices, yogurt, coffee and meats.

35582 ■ "A New Century for Start-ups" in *Hispanic Business* **(Vol. 22, No. 3, March 2000, pp. 54)**
Pub: Hispanic Business
Ed: Christopher D. Lancette. Description: The importance of a comprehensive business plan to the successful winning of venture capital backing are explored. The calculation of required start-up capital is often underestimated and often results in business failure.

35583 ■ "New Economy" in *Inc.* **(November 2000, pp. 37)**
Pub: The Goldhirsh Group
Description: Profile of Dave Bell, a senior at Nashua High School, in Nashua, New Hampshire who is hard at work building his new company.

35584 ■ "New Group Creating Opportunities for Women" in *Atlanta Business Chronicle* **(Vol. 25, November 15, 2002, No. 23 pp. 10A)**
Pub: American City Business Publications, Inc.
Ed: Wendy Bowman-Littler. Description: Project Tsunami Inc., a nonprofit organization launched with a seed grant from the Ewing Marion Kaufmann Foundation in 2002, aims to provide women entrepreneurs with economic opportunities around the world.

35585 ■ "A New Hope" in *Entrepreneur* **(Vol. 30, No)**
Pub: Entrepreneur Media Inc.
Description: Some of the top franchise concepts for 2002 include space-age ice cream, weight loss, chicken wings and dating services. The top 50 new franchising concepts since 1997 are ranked. Contact information is provided for each franchise.

35586 ■ "New Me" in *Black Enterprise* (Vol. 35, November 2004, No. 4, pp. 188)
Pub: Earl G. Graves Publishing Co. Inc.
Ed: Tanisha A. Sykes. Description: Retired postal worker seeks advice for starting a business card/ brochure business.

35587 ■ "New Stratford, Conn., Needlework Quickly Gains Fans" in *Connecticut Post* (January 31, 2003)
Pub: Knight-Ridder/Tribune Business News
Ed: Stephania H. Davis. Description: Profile of Janet Kemp Fine Yarns and Needlework. Kemp tells how she and her husband obtained a second mortgage on their home in order to start her business. The store features high quality yarns, patterns, and accessories for the crafts of knitting, embroidering and needle-point.

35588 ■ "New Venture-Capital Group Wants to Keep Entrepreneurs in State" in *Crain's Detroit Business* (Vol. 18, No. 2, June 3, 2002, pp. 43)
Pub: Crain Communications Inc. - Detroit
Ed: Katie Merx. Description: Investors from across the state of Michigan hope that the Michigan Venture Capital Association will attract more venture capital-ists to the state and keep entrepreneurs from leaving.

35589 ■ "News from the Small Business Front" in *My Business* (August/September 2002, pp. 14)
Pub: My Business Magazine
Description: According to a survey by Dun & Brad-street, more small businesses provided health bene-fits to employees in 2002 than in the previous year; National Federation of Independent Business (NFIB) announced a new partnership with the International Fabricare Institute (ICPA); firms in America start smal-ler than new companies starting out in European countries.

35590 ■ "No Ticket to Easy Street" in *Black Enterprise* (Vol. 31, No. 4, November 2000, pp. 62)
Pub: Earl Graves Publishing Co.
Ed: Paula McCoy-Pinderhughes. Description: Is franchising your entrance into entrepreneurship? With approximately 320,000 franchised small businesses in the U.S., accounting for $1 trillion in annual retail sales, it is a proven way to achieve the American Dream.

35591 ■ *Nobody's Business but Your Own*
Pub: Hyperion
Ed: Carolyn M. Brown. Released: 1999. Price: $14.95.

35592 ■ "On the Internet Nobody Knows You're Not a VC" in *Red Herring* (No. 75, February 2000, pp. 148-150, 152, 154, 156, 158)
Pub: Herring Communications, Inc.
Ed: Dan Brekke. Description: Suddenly, the more desperate entrepreneurs are flocking to the new on-line venture capital firms. The article tells who these firms are, and who is behind their Web sites.

35593 ■ "On the Survival Prospects of Men's and Women's New Business Ventures" in *Journal of Business Venturing* (Vol. 15, July 2000, pp. 347)
Pub: Elsevier Science, Inc.
Ed: Richard J. Boden, Jr., Alfred R. Nucci. Descrip-tion: Issues are presented concerning the success of men and women entrepreneurs. Women were found to use less capital to start their businesses and the success of a business was found to relate directly to the amount of start-up capital employed.

35594 ■ "On the Waterfront" in *Inc.* (August 1, 2003)
Pub: Gruner & Jahr USA Publishing
Ed: David J. Dent. Description: Ways Portland, Maine encourages entrepreneurs to choose their city to start new companies are discussed.

35595 ■ "One to Watch: A Russian entrepreneur scores a wireless hit with teenagers" in *Red Herring* (No. 103, September 1, 2001, pp. 26)
Pub: Herring Communications
Ed: Eric Moskowitz. Description: Profile of David Yang, CEO of Cybiko, maker of a wireless personal digital assistant and gaming devices for teens.

35596 ■ "One to Watch: Alpiri hopes to win the name game in e-commerce" in *Red Herring* (No. 105, October 1, 2001, pp. 26)
Pub: Herring Communications
Ed: Michael Fitzgerald. Description: Profile of Rob McCool and R.V. Guha, cofounders of Alpiri, a startup promising easier interaction among e-commerce pro-grams based on Extensible Markup Language (XML), thus simplifying Web transactions.

35597 ■ "One to Watch: KnowNow tackles two-way computing" in *Red Herring* (No. 102, August 15, 2001, pp. 24)
Pub: Herring Communications
Ed: Om Malik. Description: Real-time computing is receiving renewed attention, prompting entrepreneurs to seek innovative ways of making corporations run more efficiently. Profile of KnowNow, the startup that has developed technology to network a company's in-formation technology (IT) infrastructure using the hy-pertext transfer protocol (HTTP) used to deliver Web pages one way, will allow users to send and receive information instantly through Web browsers, cell phones and email.

35598 ■ "Only a Few Sea Turtles Survive" in *Forbes* (February 21, 2000, pp. 96)
Pub: Forbes Magazine
Ed: James Champy. Description: Survival tactics for new technology companies are offered.

35599 ■ "Organizations" in *Black Enterprise* (Vol. 34, No. 5, December 2003, pp. S5)
Pub: Earl Graves Publishing Co.
Description: Profile of the Future Business Leaders of American (FBLA), a nonprofit for young entrepre-neurs and students preparing for careers in business.

35600 ■ "Our Kinda Town" in *Entrepreneur* (Vol. 28, No. 1, January 2000, pp. 26)
Pub: Entrepreneur Media Inc.
Ed: Robert McGarvey. Description: Information re-sources for entrepreneurs.

35601 ■ "Out of the blue into the black" in *Harvard Business Review* (Vol. 80, No. 4, April 2002, pp. 112)
Pub: Harvard Business School Press
Ed: Frank Batten. Description: A chronicle of the de-velopment of the Weather Channel, the brainchild of Frank Batten, chairman of Landmark Communica-tions. Batten's new concept in cable television, twenty years after its founding, is one of the world's most trusted media brands.

35602 ■ "Patent Chutzpah" in *Forbes* (November 13, 2000, pp. 58)
Pub: Forbes Magazine
Ed: Krysten A. Crawford. Description: An Example of the ways dubious patents for ideas, rather than a physical invention, are being deployed to extract ran-som from companies.

35603 ■ "Peachy Profits" in *Small Business Opportunities* (Vol. 12, No. 5, September 2000, pp. 114, 130)
Pub: Harris Publications, Inc.
Ed: Eileen Lockwood. Description: A profile of Fi-scher & Wieser Specialty Foods, Inc., in Fredericks-burg, Texas. Thirty years ago Mark Wieser's parents sold peaches and preserves from a roadside stand, today the company makes 75 kinds of jellies and con-diments and grosses more than $2.5 million a year.

35604 ■ "Pennsylvania" in *Entrepreneur* (Vol. 28, No. 6, June 2000, pp. 155)
Pub: Entrepreneur Media Inc.
Ed: Cynthia E. Griffin. Description: Pennsylvania has designed a program to encourage entrepreneurial business ventures.

35605 ■ "Perceived risks and choices in entrepreneurs' new venture decisions" in *Journal of Business Venturing* (Vol.15, No.4, Jul.2000, pp.305)
Pub: Elsevier Science, Inc.
Ed: David Forlani, John W. Mullins. Description: Is-sues are presented concerning the evaluation risk, the perception of risk and the willingness of entrepreneurs to make hazardous choices in the pursuit of potentially significant financial gains.

35606 ■ "The Perfect Niche" n *Hispanic Business* (Vol. 22, No. 7-8,July-August 2000, pp. 68)
Pub: Hispanic Business
Ed: Mario Hernandez. Description: Fernando Echeverria is founder of one of America's fastest-growing Internet-based educational sites, Toptutors.com. The company links students with a national net-work of tutors, and is backed by a $3 million invest-ment from Idealab and Idealab Capital Partners.

35607 ■ "Performing Triage" in *Entrepreneur* (Vol. 32, No. 4, April 2004, pp. 39)
Pub: Entrepreneur Media, Inc.
Ed: Heather Clancy. Description: Profile of Conq-west Inc., the Massachusetts firm specializing in fight-ing viruses and Internet spam for companies. Michelle Drolet, founder and CEO, uses a proactive approach to computer security. Conqwest started testing anti-spam technologies in 2002, long before these threats were as prevalent as today.

35608 ■ "Personality Test" in *Entrepreneur. com* (Vol. 34, February 2006, No. 2, pp. 122)
Pub: Entrepreneur Media Inc.
Ed: Romanus Wolter. Description: Business interac-tions must leave a positive impression as well as pro-vide exceptional results.

35609 ■ "Pikesville-Based SafeDate and Dating Service Industry as a Whole Experiencing Growth" in *Daily Record* (July 18, 2003)
Pub: Dolan Media Newswires
Ed: Andrea Cecil. Description: Profiles of various dating services, including SafeDate and eHarmony.

35610 ■ "Planning for Gold" in *Entrepreneur* (Vol. 32, November 2004, No. 11, pp. 112)
Pub: Entrepreneur Media Inc.
Ed: Nichole L. Torres. Description: Business plan competitions are growing in popularity. In order for en-trepreneurs to cash in and win cash, services or ven-ture capital they must understand the process. Many of the competitions are associated with university MBA programs, but there are also those produced by communities, which are open to anyone in the local area or a particular business sector.

35611 ■ "Playing favorites" in *Entrepreneur* (Vol. 31, No. 4, April 2003, pp. 22)
Pub: Entrepreneur Media Inc.
Ed: Julie Monahan. Description: Software compa-nies are finding venture capital funding easier be-cause they do not have a high inventory risk, along with the fact that needed changes can be implement-ed quickly.

35612 ■ "Primer for Profit" in *Small Business Opportunities* (Vol. 13, No. 6, November 2001, pp. 52, 56)
Pub: Harris Publications, Inc.
Description: Profile of Barry Penzel, owner of Certa ProPainters franchise in Minden, Nevada. Mr. Penzel, former army colonel, tells how he runs his successful company with military precision. Certa ProPainters franchise opportunities are listed.

35613 ■ "A private space race" in *Wall Street Journal* (Feb. 5, 2003, pp. B1)
Pub: Dow Jones & Co. Inc.
Ed: J. Lynn Lunsford. Description: Entrepreneur Peter Diamandis has founded and helped to fund the St. Louis, Missouri, based X Prize Foundation, which will award a $10 million prize to the first private venture

to fund, design and launch a manned space vehicle. Twenty-four entrepreneur-led teams are vying for the prize and the recent accident aboard the Space Shuttle Columbia has not deterred any in that quest. The foundation's rules for the spacecraft say only that it must be able to hold three passengers and must be able to fly 62 miles up and return safely two times in the course of two weeks.

35614 ■ *The Professional Chef: The Business of Doing Business As a Personal Chef*
Pub: John Wiley and Sons Inc.
Ed: Candy Wallace; Greg Forte. **Released:** February 2007. **Price:** $50.00. **Description:** Resources for starting a personal chef business are covered; CD-ROM included.

35615 ■ "Property Tax Woes Hit Indiana" in *Inc.* (October 1, 2004)
Pub: Inc. Magazine
Ed: Burt Helm. **Description:** Property tax hikes in Indiana have resulted in higher taxes for many entrepreneurs.

35616 ■ "Puncturing Myths" in *Kansas City Business Journal* (Vol. 18, No. 21, January 28, 2000, pp. 21)
Pub: American City Business Journals, Inc.
Ed: Anna Jaffe. **Description:** Christopher Powell, who started Missouri Acupuncture Services four years ago, is profiled.

35617 ■ "Rah-Rah rides" in *Entrepreneur* (Vol. 30, No. 2, February 2002, pp. 96)
Pub: Entrepreneur Media Inc.
Ed: Gisela M. Pedroza. **Description:** Profile of John D. Smith, president and CEO of Clever Covers. Smith designed a line of hubcaps emblazoned with logos of collegiate sports teams, which retail for $59.95 and are sold at team stores and through his company's Web site.

35618 ■ "Read Smart, Grow Smart" in *Fast Company* (May 2001, pp. 202)
Pub: Fast Company
Ed: Amy Wilson Sheldon. **Description:** Profile of Gil Elbaz, co-founder and CIO of Oingo, a search-technology firm based in Los Angeles, California. Elbaz shows how to create a company that's built to last when others are failing.

35619 ■ "Record setting: music industry veteran forms a label for Latin music performers who sing in English" in *Hispanic Business*(Jul-Aug2000)
Pub: Hispanic Business
Ed: Peter Brennan. **Description:** Bill Martin, a veteran of the music industry, has founded Demand Recordings, a label for Hispanics who sing in English. Martin, born in Ecuador, says he is close to signing a $5 million investment by a major label, which he refuses to name.

35620 ■ "Recovering Yuppie turns yoga hobby into a business" in *Sarasota Herald Tribune* (September 9, 2002, pp. 9)
Pub: Sarasota Herald Tribune
Ed: Alexander Coolidge. **Description:** Profile of Lynn Burgess, yuppie turned yoga instructor. Burgess started teaching friends out of her home, then on to offering classes at companies, country clubs and health clubs. The growing popularity of yoga has seen a large increase in health clubs offering yoga classes.

35621 ■ "Red-Tape Brainstorms" in *Inc.* (October 17, 2000, pp. 17)
Pub: The Goldhirsh Group
Description: Profile of Cherrill Fransworth, who has founded six companies since 1977.

35622 ■ "Reeling in the Big Ones" in *Entrepreneur* (Vol. 28, No. 1, January 2000, pp. 138)
Pub: Entrepreneur Media Inc.
Ed: Bill Kelley. **Description:** Most entrepreneurs would love to land large corporate accounts, but they often don't try for one simple reason: they're afraid.

35623 ■ "Remodeling Riches" in *Small Business Opportunities* (Vol. 12, No. 2, March 2000, pp. 126)
Pub: Harris Publications, Inc.
Ed: Annette Wood. **Description:** A profile of Cris Keeter, who started American Remodeling in 1992 from a backyard shed, and now earns $2.5 million yearly. Mr. Keeter tells how he has his business divided into three parts: remodeling, insurance restoration, and siding, windows and patio rooms.

35624 ■ "Rent-A-Mom" in *Forbes* (February 21, 2000, pp. 118)
Pub: Forbes Magazine
Ed: Brigid McMenamin. **Description:** A profile of Tammy Kumin and Joan Alfond who founded Concierge Services for Students Ltd., in 1992.

35625 ■ "Requiem for a Telecom" in *Forbes* (December 11, 2000, pp. 206)
Pub: Forbes Magazine
Ed: Brandon Copple. **Description:** James Kenefick started Nettel Communications four years ago with a few hundred thousand dollars and a lot of nerve. He planned to sell phone, data and Internet services to small businesses. October 23, 2000, Nettel filed for Chapter 7, after its largest backer pulled out.

35626 ■ "The right stuff" in *BlackEnterprise* (Vol. 32, No. 3, October 2001, pp. 51)
Pub: Earl Graves Publishing Co.
Ed: Paula McCoy-Pinderhughes. **Description:** Advice is offered to entrepreneurs wishing to bid on NASA contracts, including information on the Small and Disadvantaged Business Utilization at NASA headquarters in Washington DC, and the Training and Development for Small Businesses in Advanced Technologies (TADSBAT) program. Five African American-owned businesses are on NASA's FY 2000 Top 100 List of Prime Contractors.

35627 ■ "Rising money" in *Entrepreneur* (Vol. 30, No. 1, January 2002, pp. 36)
Pub: Entrepreneur Media Inc.
Ed: Steve Cooper. **Description:** A listing of financial sources used by entrepreneurs in 2001, information about customer trust, and other areas of interest to small business is presented. Statistical data included.

35628 ■ "Risk Is a Wonderful Thing" in *Success* (Vol. 47, No. 6, November 2000, pp. 24)
Pub: Success Publishing, Inc.
Ed: Peter Lowe. **Description:** Success demands that you push yourself outside of your comfort zone. Success requires risk, and risk requires guts. Success demands that you stretch your boundaries and challenge your limits. When you enter into a risky venture, there are specific steps you can use to minimize the possibility of failure. An acronym to help remember how to master RISK-taking is: Research, Invest, Strategize, Kiss off the critics.

35629 ■ "A Risky Business" in *Kiplinger's Personal Finance Magazine* (Vol. 54, No. 9, September 2000, pp. 94)
Pub: The Kiplinger Washington Editors, Inc.
Ed: Catherine Siskos, Matt Popowsky. **Description:** Some college students are quitting school to become Web entrepreneurs.

35630 ■ "The Root of the Business: Drawing on one's ethnicity leads to a passionate niche" in *My Business* (April/May 2002, pp. 36-39)
Pub: My Business Magazine
Ed: Kathleen Landis. **Description:** Ways in which creative entrepreneurs have taken their heritage and turned it into a profitable business are examined. Information to contact the Minority Business Development Agency, National Association of Asian American Professionals, Africa-American Business Link, AllSmallBiz.com, Shopping for Identity: The Marketing of Ethnicity, and Hispanic Business Magazine is provided.

35631 ■ "SBA's Office of Entrepreneurial Development: www.sba.gov/training" in *Entrepreneur* (Vol. 31, No. 10, October 2003, pp. 6)
Pub: Entrepreneur Media, Inc.
Ed: Steve Cooper. **Description:** Profile of the U.S. Small Business Administration's Website offering free online classes, workshops, and guides, as well as access to electronic counseling links.

35632 ■ "Seasonal Wonder" in *Small Business Opportunities* (Vol. 12, No. 2, March 2000, pp. 68)
Pub: Harris Publications, Inc.
Ed: Bill Watson. **Description:** The article shows how to make up to $500,000 a season with a snow removal business.

35633 ■ "Second Time Around" in *Entrepreneur* (Vol. 31, No. 7, July 2003, pp. 24)
Pub: Entrepreneur Media, Inc.
Ed: David Worrell. **Description:** Three Internet entrepreneurs are betting on Wireless startups and are bringing new ideas, perspectives and innovation to the industry.

35634 ■ "Secrets to Success: Yes, You Can Be a Successful Franchisee in 2003" in *Entrepreneur* (Vol. 31, No. 9, July 2003, pp. 86)
Pub: Entrepreneur Media, Inc.
Ed: Devlin Smith. **Description:** The major elements to start a new franchise are presented. Franchising insiders share secrets to being a successful franchisee.

35635 ■ *Seed-Stage Venture Investing: The Ins and Outs for Entrepreneurs, Start-Ups, and Investors on Successfully Starting a New Business*
Pub: Aspatore Books, Incorporated
Ed: William J. Robbins. **Released:** July 2006. **Price:** $199.95. **Description:** Ideas for starting, funding, and managing technology-based firms, also known as, venture capitalists, are featured.

35636 ■ "Selling Serenity" in *Small Business Opportunities* (Vol. 13, No. 5, September 2001, pp. 74, 130)
Pub: Harris Publications, Inc.
Ed: Marie Sherlock. **Description:** Profile of Judy Wallace, who runs a store called Serenity Shop, that sells inspirational products for those struggling with or recovering from addictions.

35637 ■ "Setting the Table: The Transforming Power of Hospitality in Business" in *New York Times* (January 14, 2007, pp. 15)
Pub: New York Times Company
Ed: Danny Meyer. **Description:** Profile of Danny Meyer, who offers advice to would-be restaurateurs that applies to anyone wishing to start a new business.

35638 ■ "Setting Up Shop" in *Black Enterprise* (Vol. 35, February 2005, No. 7, pp. 60)
Pub: Earl G. Graves Publishing Co. Inc.
Ed: James C. Johnson. **Description:** Advice for setting up a Website is offered to a business startup wishing to market and sell urban apparel via the Internet.

35639 ■ "Shape Up!" in *Entrepreneur* (Vol. 31, No. 10, October 2003, pp. 100)
Pub: Entrepreneur Media, Inc.
Ed: Chris Penttila. **Description:** Three entrepreneurial fitness tests are offered to entrepreneurs to see if they have what it takes to endure the startup phase.

35640 ■ "Shifting gears: Suit and tie gone, passion becomes his business" in *Crain's Detroit Business* (Vol. 18, No. 16, April 22, 2002, pp. 3)
Pub: Crain Communications Inc. - Detroit
Ed: Laura Bailey. **Description:** Profile of Eric Gorges, who launched his motorcycle business Voodoo Choppers LLC, three years ago.

35641 ■ "Shoestring Start-Ups" in *Small Business Opportunities* **(Vol. 13, No. 6, November 2001, pp. 22-24, 26, 28, 30, 32, 34, 36, 116)**
Pub: Harris Publications, Inc.
Description: The top 50 small business that can be started with little or no capital are previewed, some as little as $100 or less, including the ten steps to follow when starting a new business.

35642 ■ "Shop for Success" in *Small Business Opportunities* **(Vol. 12, No. 3, May 2000, pp. 46-48)**
Pub: Harris Publications, Inc.
Ed: Marie Sherlock. **Description:** To cash in on used sports equipment, this second-hand shop owner tells how he makes $500,000 a year selling used sporting goods.

35643 ■ "Silver Linings" in *My Business* **(June/July 2004, pp. 13)**
Pub: My Business Magazine
Description: Among the U.S. workforce, the number of self-employment among persons over the age of 50 is greater than any other age group.

35644 ■ "Six Degrees of Capitalization" in *Success* **(Vol. 47, No. 1, January 2000, pp. 16)**
Pub: Success Publishing, Inc.
Ed: Elaine Pofeldt. **Description:** Review of Neo Vision Hypersystems and the talk of a public offering for the company.

35645 ■ "Sky's the Limit: Think Your Product has Limited Appeal?" in *Entrepreneur* **(Vol. 32, No. 4, April 2004, pp. 132)**
Pub: Entrepreneur Media, Inc.
Ed: Don Debelak. **Description:** Profile of Dan Grace and Jeff Polke, two friends who invented The Everywhere Chair in 1996. The product is an outdoor chair with an adjustable back and seat and can be used on sloping surfaces. The startup cost the partners $10,000 for a patent and prototype, procured a $25,000 line of credit, and reported $2 million in sales in 2003, with projected sales close to $3 million in 2004.

35646 ■ *Small Business Entrepreneur: Launching a New Venture and Managing a Business on a Day-to-Day Basis*
Pub: Austin & Company, Incorporated
Ed: Rory Burke. **Released:** February 2006. **Price:** $19.95. **Description:** Comprehensive guide examining the management skills required to launch and run a small business.

35647 ■ *Small Business Management*
Pub: John Wiley & Sons, Incorporated
Ed: Margaret Burlingame. **Released:** March 2007. **Price:** $44.95. **Description:** Advice for starting and running a small business as well as information on the value and appeal of small businesses, is given. Topics include budgets, taxes, inventory, ethics, e-commerce, and current laws.

35648 ■ *The Small Business Start-Up Kit*
Pub: NOLO
Ed: Peri Pakroo. **Released:** April 2004. **Price:** $24.99. **Description:** Entrepreneurial advice for launching a new business. Topics include compliance with state regulations, sole proprietorships, partnerships, corporations, limited liability companies, as well as accounting and tax information.

35649 ■ *Small Business Start-Up Workbook: A Step-by-Step Guide to Starting the Business You've Dreamed Of*
Pub: How To Books
Ed: Cheryl D. Rickman. **Released:** February 2006. **Price:** $24.75. **Description:** Book provides practical exercises for starting a small business, including marketing and management strategies.

35650 ■ "Small-Business Wonder:SmartOnline.com provides the tools and experti se to take the trepidation out of launching a new business"in *PCMagazine*
Pub: Ziff-Davis Publishing Company
Ed: Greg Alwang. **Description:** SmartOnline.com provides Web-hosted business tools aimed at small businesses and entrepreneurs. SmartOnline.com assists with everything from starting, financing, and expanding a small business to corresponding with customers. More than just a resource for small-business owners, SmartOnline.com conveys the look and feel of a polished CD-based application in an up-to-date online form.

35651 ■ "Small Businesses Fuel Growth" in *Success* **(Vol. 47, No. 3, July 2000, pp. 16)**
Pub: Success Publishing, Inc.
Description: A study showing that small businesses are getting a boost from ever-cheaper information technology and easier access to financial assistance, and are helping to fuel the U.S. economy's record expansion. The study also predicts that this segment of the American economy will see a shift in management as well as the labor force over the next 15 years. Entrepreneurs will no longer be predominately young, white men. They will be older women, many of whom will also be Hispanic and African-American, reflecting the same shift in the U.S. population as a whole.

35652 ■ "Smart Business Tools" in *Black Enterprise* **(Vol. 32, No. 9, April 2002, pp. 54)**
Pub: Earl Graves Publishing Co.
Ed: Sonya A. Donaldson. **Description:** A profile of business plan authorship software called Plan Write Expert Edition for Business, produced by Business Resource Software.

35653 ■ "Solo Mission: Paul Stannard used to make software for other companies" in *Entrepreneur* **(Vol. 30, No. 3, March 2002, pp. 160)**
Pub: Entrepreneur Media Inc.
Ed: Michelle Prather. **Description:** Profile of Paul Stannard, founder and CEO of SmartDraw.com, located in San Diego, California. Stannard has been manufacturing diagramming software since 1994.

35654 ■ "Soul Progress" in *Fast Company* **(August 2001, pp. 22)**
Pub: Fast Company
Ed: Keith H. Hammonds. **Description:** Profile of the three co-founders of smartRay a Web editor for mobile communications devices: Troy Tyler, Andrew Playford, and David Kidder.

35655 ■ *Soul Proprietor: 101 Lessons from a Lifestyle Entrepreneur*
Pub: Crossing Press, Incorporated
Ed: Jane Pollak. **Released:** September 2004. **Price:** $14.95 (US), $21.95 (Canadian). **Description:** More than 100 tips and stores to inspire and guide any would-be entrepreneur to earn a living from a favorite hobby or passion.

35656 ■ "Sounds Like Success" in *Small Business Opportunities* **(Vol. 13, No. 5, September 2001, pp. 50, 103)**
Pub: Harris Publications, Inc.
Ed: Marie Sherlock. **Description:** Profile of Richard Stull, owner of a guitar shop called Guitar Crazy. Mr. Stull shares his experience of turning his hobby into a successful business.

35657 ■ "South Portland, Maine, College Develops Small-Business Incubator" in *Portland Press Herald* **(August 16, 2005)**
Pub: Blethen Maine Newspapers, Inc.
Ed: Ann S. Kim. **Description:** Southern Maine Community College in South Portland has developed a new small business incubator for area startups. Four students have enrolled in the incubator since January. They receive advice from faculty members on writing business plans and more.

35658 ■ "Sparkle Plenty" in *Success* **(Vol. 47, No. 4, September 2000, pp. 20)**
Pub: Success Publishing, Inc.
Ed: Debbie Selinsky. **Description:** Profile of Melody Kulp and how she developed a $40 million a year hair ornament business.

35659 ■ "Stake Your Claim: Contrary to Popular Belief, There's No Need to Ante Up a Fortune When You're Playing the Startup Game" in *Entrepreneur*
Pub: Entrepreneur Media Inc.
Ed: Karen E. Spaeder. **Description:** Three entrepreneurs share ways they started their high-cost businesses without large sums of money: Steve Bandovich, owner of Cloud 9 Specialty Car Rentals; Chi Conley, who started up with one hotel and now owns 31 hospitality businesses in Northern California; and Tom Hatten, who started Mountainside Fitness in 1991.

35660 ■ "Standing on Their Own: Couple Decides to Go It Alone With Their Own Woody's Hot Dogs Kiosk" in *Entrepreneur* **(Vol. 31, July 2003)**
Pub: Entrepreneur Media Inc.
Ed: Devlin Smith, Jodie Carter. **Description:** Profile of David and Chris Lycan, who operate a hot dog kiosk at the Lowe's Home Improvement Warehouse in Colorado, Springs, Colorado.

35661 ■ "The Starbucks Effect" in *Harvard Business Review* **(Vol. 78, No. 2, March 2000, pp. 17)**
Pub: Harvard Business School Publishing Corp.
Ed: Vijay Vishwanath, David Harding. **Description:** When a product suddenly becomes hip, the whole category can prosper.

35662 ■ "Start Achieving Your Goals" in *Success* **(Vol. 47, No. 5, October 2000, pp. 24)**
Pub: Success Publishing, Inc.
Ed: Peter Lowe. **Description:** Peter Lowe tells his story of success and shares his top five steps for setting and achieving your goals.

35663 ■ *Start Business in California, 3E*
Pub: Sourcebooks, Incorporated
Ed: John J. Talamo. **Released:** July 2006. **Price:** $24.95. **Description:** Information required for starting any business in California.

35664 ■ "Start with Nothing" in *Inc.* **(February 1, 2002)**
Pub: Inc. Magazine
Ed: Emily Barker. **Description:** Greg Gianforte, founder of the software company Brightwork Development Inc., shares his secrets for launching a successful new company, with a focus on sales.

35665 ■ "Start Up the Band" in *Inc.* **(January 1, 2002)**
Pub: Inc. Magazine
Ed: Andrew Raskin. **Description:** Profile of Andrew Raskin, cofounder and former CEO of Gazooba Corporation (now Qbiquity Corp.).

35666 ■ *Start-ups That Work: Surprise Research on What Makes or Breaks a New Company*
Pub: Penguin Group
Ed: Joel Kurtzman; Glenn Rifkin. **Released:** October 2005. **Price:** $25.95.

35667 ■ "Starting a business? Then get with the plan" in *Crain's Detroit Business* **(Vol. 18, No. 49, December 9, 2002, pp. 17)**
Pub: Crain Communications Inc., Detroit
Ed: Laura Bailey. **Description:** When starting a new company, it is imperative to have a good business plan.

35668 ■ "Starting in Style" in *Black Enterprise* **(Vol. 33, No. 6, January 2003, pp. 39)**
Pub: Earl Graves Publishing Co.
Ed: Alan Hughes. **Description:** Information is offered to an individual aspiring to start a fashion line firm. A Web site offering information on fashion careers and links to information and resources on the industry is included.

35669 ■ **"Starts Slow, Jobs Grow" in**
Business Week **(No. 3689, July 10, 2000, pp.
F8)**
Pub: McGraw-Hill, Inc.
Description: Many banks are tightening credit requirements for small business loans, venture capitalists are growing more demanding, and angel investors
may not be feeling so generous in an uncertain stock
market.

35670 ■ **"Staying within their niche yields
success for winners" in** *Atlanta Business
Chronicle* **(Vol. 23, No. 48, May 4, 2001, pp.
70A)**
Pub: American City Business Journals Inc.
Ed: Pamela Blackmon. **Description:** Sandy Morris
and Shaun Bradley of employee recruitment firm
Bradley-Morris Inc. have been awarded Georgia's
Small Business Persons of the Year award by the U.S.
Small Business Administration. They will compete
with other entrepreneurs from each state for the national Small Business of the Year award, which is selected based on increase in sales, innovative products
or services, staying power and employee growth.

35671 ■ **"A stealthier way to raise money" in**
Harvard Business Review **(Vol. 78, No. 5,
September-October 2000, pp. 18)**
Pub: Harvard Business School Publishing Corp.
Ed: David Champion. **Description:** Many entrepreneurs are seeking funding from private investors and
corporations rather than from venture capital companies. The dangers from venture capitalists are that
they demand control, and because of their networking,
they may inadvertently reveal company secrets.

35672 ■ *Steps to Small Business Start-Up*
Pub: Kaplan Books
Ed: Linda Pinson; Jerry Jinnett. **Released:** July 2006.
Price: $29.00. **Description:** Tips for starting and run-
ning a new company are presented.

35673 ■ **"Sterling Venture, Set to Close Fund
I" in** *Venture Capital Journal* **(Vol. 40, No. 10,
October 2000, pp. 24)**
Pub: Venture Economics
Description: Sterling Venture prefers to be the first to
back a company and work with entrepreneurs.

35674 ■ **"Storage titans would rather fight
than connect" in** *Red Herring* **(No. 105,
October 1, 2001, pp. 78, 80-81)**
Pub: Herring Communications
Ed: Scott Tyler Shafer. **Description:** Startup companies in the storage industry are focusing on two fields,
virtualization software and equipment standardized
for IP to eliminate the barriers between storage systems. A profile of Ziya Aral and George Teixeira, co-
founders of DataCore Software, a storage
virtualization company.

35675 ■ **"Street Smarts: Don't Sign Anything
Yet" in** *Inc.* **(January 1, 2005)**
Pub: Inc. Magazine
Ed: Norm Brodsky. **Description:** When starting a new
business, it is important for entrepreneurs to beware
of commitments made in the process.

35676 ■ **"Street Smarts" in** *Inc.* **(November
2000, pp. 35)**
Pub: The Goldhirsh Group
Ed: Norm Brodsky. **Description:** Sooner or later most
first-time entrepreneurs find themselves running out of
money and don't know where to turn for help.

35677 ■ **"Strike it Rich!" in** *Small Business
Opportunities* **(Vol. 16, No. 3, May 2004, pp.
22-24, 26, 28, 30, 32, 34, 36, 38, 40-42, 44, 98)**
Pub: Harris Publications, Inc.
Description: Profiles of fifteen service business to
consider, including electrical services, windshield repair, waste management, automotive repair, wedding
photography, dryer vent cleaning, home helpers, supermarket services, garage makeovers, window
blinds cleaning, concrete coating, carpet and upholstering cleaning, slip and fall prevention, and home
cleaning.

35678 ■ **"Strong Structure" in** *Black
Enterprise* **(Vol. 34, July 2004, No. 12, pp. 48)**
Pub: Earl G. Graves Publishing Co. Inc.
Ed: Alan Hughes. **Description:** Advice is given for
launching a small business. The entrepreneur needs
information for choosing the business structure that is
right for his new firm. Guidelines for choosing a sole
proprietorship, partnership, limited liability company,
C corporation, and S corporation are outlined.

35679 ■ **"Stump the slump" in** *Entrepreneur*
(Vol. 30, No. 2, February 2002, pp. 90)
Pub: Entrepreneur Media Inc.
Ed: Michele Marrinan. **Description:** Many entrepreneurs are taking advantage of the economic downturn
to start new businesses. Ways to work the economy
to find financing are discussed, including the importance of a solid business plan.

35680 ■ **"Success line" in** *Success* **(Vol. 47,
No. 3, July 2000, pp. 78)**
Pub: Success Publishing, Inc.
Description: Questions are answered on starting a
business, including loans and grants, patents, and
federal certification for minority- or woman-owned
business.

35681 ■ **"Success Rules!" in** *Success* **(Vol.
47, No. 4, September 2000, pp. 55)**
Pub: Success Publishing, Inc.
Ed: Thomas Melville. **Description:** Succeed with
these five rules from five entrepreneurs who have
made it.

35682 ■ **"Sweet success" in** *Black
Enterprise* **(Vol. 33, No. 3, October 2002, pp.
S6)**
Pub: Earl Graves Publishing Co.
Ed: Sonya Kimmble-Ellis. **Description:** Profile of Camilla Amber White, the 15 year old entrepreneur with
her own baking business. White offers a wide range
of pies, as well as cheesecakes, bread, and rice puddings.

35683 ■ *Swimming Against the Stream:
Launching Your Business and Making Your
Life*
Pub: Macmillan Publishers Limited
Ed: Tim Waterstone. **Released:** March 2007. **Price:**
$17.99. **Description:** Ten rules for launching a new
business are outlined using real-life experiences.

35684 ■ **"Take Our Outfit - Please! How do
you start a small business?" in** *Business
Week Online* **(December 23, 2002)**
Pub: McGraw-Hill Inc.
Ed: Gabor Garai. **Description:** Entrepreneurs are
finding that one way to start up a new company is to
purchase a division of a larger firm, thus allowing mid-
size companies to be rid of unprofitable divisions rather than shutting them down.

35685 ■ **"Take the Plunge! Teetering on the
Edge of Unemployment?" in** *Entrepreneur*
(Vol. 31, No. 11, November 2003, pp. 118)
Pub: Entrepreneur Media, Inc.
Ed: Nichole L. Torres. **Description:** Many individuals
faced with losing their jobs are starting their own busi-
nesses, a trend seen across the nation.

35686 ■ **"Taking care of business" in**
BlackEnterprise **(Vol. 31, No. 12, July 2001,
pp. 46)**
Pub: Earl Graves Publishing Co.
Ed: Bridget McCrea. **Description:** Brothers, Fred and
Richard Calloway, have founded a company that caters to a decidedly male customer base with its barber,
dry cleaning, and car wash services. In 1998, with approximately $30,000 of combined personal savings,
the brothers created Male Care.

35687 ■ **"Taking the 'dis' out of disability" in**
Black Enterprise **(Vol. 32, No. 9, March 2002,
pp. 102)**
Pub: Earl Graves Publishing Co.
Ed: Alan Hughes. **Description:** Profile of Carmen
Jones who triumphed over a crippling car accident
and built a marketing firm that serves disabled con-
sumers.

35688 ■ **"Talking the talk" in** *Black
Enterprise* **(Vol. 32, No. 9, April 2002, pp.
123)**
Pub: Earl Graves Publishing Co.
Ed: Alfred A. Edmond, Jr. **Description:** Tips are given
for starting a business as a motivational speaker. Resources are included.

35689 ■ **"TAMACC Launches Leadership
School" in** *Hispanic Business* **(July/August
2002, pp. 10)**
Pub: Hispanic Business
Description: A new initiative undertaken by the Texas
Association of Mexican American Chambers of Commerce, called Rules of Engagement: A Leadership Institute, will help Hispanic Texans to develop
businesses, reform education, and influence lawmakers.

35690 ■ **"Technology makes a comeback:
fizzling dotcoms were last year's news" in**
Black Enterprise **(Vol. 32, No. 8, March 2002,
pp. 87)**
Pub: Earl Graves Publishing Co.
Ed: Sonya A. Donaldson. **Description:** How African
Americans fit into the discussion of venture capitalists,
startups, and the technology industry is discussed. Interviews with various experts tell how African Americans can find the capital needed to fund a business
venture.

35691 ■ *Technology Ventures: From Idea to
Enterprise with Student DVD*
Pub: McGraw-Hill Higher Education
Ed: Richard C. Dorf; Thomas H. Byers. **Released:**
October 2006. **Price:** $100.68. **Description:** Text-
book examining technology entrepreneurship on a
global basis; technology management theories are
explored.

35692 ■ **"10 months, 10 minutes, $10
million" in** *The New York Times* **(June 7,
2000, pp. D3, H3)**
Pub: The New York Times Company
Ed: Courtney Barry. **Description:** The Texas Venture
Capitalist Conference was held in Austin; WebTag-
gers, one of 21 startups seeking funding is discussed.
Statistical data is included.

35693 ■ **"They Just Can't Stop Themselves"
in** *Inc.* **(Volume 27, March 2005, No. 3, pp. 98-
104)**
Pub: Inc. Magazine
Ed: Stephanie Clifford. **Description:** Entrepreneurs
share insight into starting more than one successful
company.

35694 ■ **"They'll Get Your Goat (Milk)" in** *My
Business* **(November/December 2001, pp. 13-
14)**
Pub: My Business Magazine
Ed: Jeff Louderback. **Description:** Profile of Patti and
Dennis Dean, who run a goat dairy in Ohio, and have
found their niche selling milk, cheese and fudge. The
couple uses tours to help change the perception people have regarding goat's milk products.

35695 ■ **"Third time's the charm" in**
BlackEnterprise **(Vol. 32, No. 2, September
2001, pp. 53)**
Pub: Earl Graves Publishing Co.
Ed: Bridget McCrea. **Description:** Profile of Reggie
P. Best of Netilla Networks Inc. Founded in 1999, the
30-employee networking service firm supplies secure
Web access to office applications, or simply put, it lets
small- to medium-size businesses use the Web as an
extension to the office network.

35696 ■ **"This Biz Is Smokin'" in** *Small
Business Opportunities* **(Vol. 13, No. 6,
November 2001, pp. 102, 122)**
Pub: Harris Publications, Inc.
Description: Profile of Bill Penny, founder of South-
ern Yankee Bar-B-Q. Mr. Penny came up with the idea
when he found himself out of work shortly before the
birth of his third child.

35697 ■ "Three Trends for 2005" in *Forbes* (Vol. 175, January 31, 2005, No. 2, pp. 39)
Pub: Forbes Magazine Inc.
Ed: Rich Karlgaard. **Description:** Video Weblogs (V-blogs) and inexpensive technology are performing business chores and offer rewards for entrepreneurs who understand how to knit these trends together.

35698 ■ "Throwing a Tea Party" in *Success* (Vol. 47, No. 4, September 2000, pp. 38)
Pub: Success Publishing, Inc.
Ed: Thomas Melville. **Description:** All-natural Honest is brewing up a national following.

35699 ■ "Time for a Change?" in *Entrepreneur* (Vol. 33, February 2005, No. 2, pp. 76)
Pub: Entrepreneur Media Inc.
Ed: Nichole L. Torres. **Description:** Things to ask would-be entrepreneurs in order to apply current skills to a new business.

35700 ■ "Tips for Entrepreneurial Leadership" in *Success* (Vol. 47, No. 3, July 2000, pp. 91)
Pub: Success Publishing, Inc.
Ed: Jerry Wilkerson. **Description:** Six tips for being a successful entrepreneur are offered.

35701 ■ "To get product on shelves, knock on a lot of doors" in *Crain's Detroit Business* (Dec. 16, 2002, pp. 18)
Pub: Crain Communications Inc., Detroit
Ed: Laura Bailey. **Description:** Various entrepreneurs share tips for successfully marketing new products.

35702 ■ "Told You So" in *Entrepreneur* (Vol. 28, No. 6, June 2000, pp. 90)
Pub: Entrepreneur Media Inc.
Ed: Laura Tiffany. **Description:** A directory of the Hot 100 businesses that proves there is life after recognition in Entrepreneur magazine. Statistical data is included.

35703 ■ "The Trading Post" in *Small Business Opportunities* (Vol. 12, No. 3, May 2000, pp. 94, 96, 98)
Pub: Harris Publications, Inc.
Ed: Marie Sherlock. **Description:** Sisters Paulette Wittwer and Tamara Patrick designed a business which specializes in folk art, clothing, and jewelry from around the world, while attempting to ensure that the sources for their merchandise are socially responsible.

35704 ■ "Trailblazing Entrepreneurs Prove that Hot Businesses Aren't Always Found in Industry Hotbeds" in *My Business* (February/March 2004)
Pub: My Business Magazine
Ed: Gwen Moran. **Description:** It is sometimes harder to create a new business concept when immersed in large cities like Los Angeles, California or New York City.

35705 ■ "Turning the Tables: You Worked for Them, and Now You Want Them to 'Work' for You" in *Entrepreneur* (Vol. 32, December 2004, No. 12)
Pub: Entrepreneur Media Inc.
Ed: Laura Koss-Feder. **Description:** The process for landing your former employer as your first client is outlined.

35706 ■ "20 Top Biz for 2002" in *Small Business Opportunities* (V. 14, No. 1, 1/2002, pp. 22-24, 26, 28, 30, 32, 34, 36, 38, 40, 130)
Pub: Harris Publications, Inc.
Description: Twenty recession-proof businesses for potential entrepreneurs to startup are profiled, including health food store, cleaning service, handyman service agency, cart vendors, window cleaning, dance studio, information broker, landscaping, sign shop, auto paint repair service, computer maintenance, closet/storage organizer, childproofing safety business, hair salon, specialty cake bakery, pet chauffer business, senior services, and delivery services.

35707 ■ *Ultimate Startup Directory: Expert Advice and 1,500 Great Startup Ideas*
Pub: Entrepreneur Press
Ed: James Stephenson. **Released:** February 2007. **Price:** $30.95 (CND). **Description:** Startup opportunities in over 30 industries are given, along with information on investment, earning potential, skills, legal requirements and more.

35708 ■ "Uncle Sam, Paralegal" in *Hispanic Business* (June 2002, pp. 22)
Pub: Hispanic Business
Ed: Teresa Talerico. **Description:** The Small Business Administration has launched a new Web site that assists entrepreneurs with legal questions. Since Hispanic entrepreneurs are eligible for a number of federal and state programs that are subject to changing regulations, the site will be very beneficial.

35709 ■ "Uncommon Enterprise: An inn that's down to earth" in *My Business* (November/December 2001, pp. 54)
Pub: My Business Magazine
Description: Brief profile of Sam and Virginia McCone, who rent their unusual bed and breakfast to pioneer wannabes, and call staying at their inn a true "Little House on the Prairie" adventure.

35710 ■ "Urban Legend: Do 90 Percent of Startups Really Fail to Make It Past Their First Year?" in *Entrepreneur* (Vol. 31, No. 8, Aug., 2003)
Pub: Entrepreneur Media, Inc.
Ed: Karen E. Spaeder. **Description:** According to an economist with the Small Business Administration's Office of Advocacy, a business closure does not necessarily mean failure; exit strategies for businesses are discussed.

35711 ■ "Useful Web sites for owners of small businesses" in *Crain's Detroit Business* (Vol. 16, No. 50, December 11, 2000, pp. E-6)
Pub: Crain Communications, Inc.
Description: A listing of places to find information on the Internet specifically for small business owners and would-be entrepreneurs.

35712 ■ "Venture investors start lending a hand" in *Red Herring* (January 2003, pp. 68)
Pub: Herring Communications Inc.
Ed: Julie Landry. **Description:** Entrepreneurs are finding it hard to procure seed money for new ventures. Venture Credit, a New York firm, is one of many venture lenders that went out of business in 2002.

35713 ■ "The Village Vanguard: Two new-economy entrepreneurs aim to jump-start businesses in college towns" in *Fortune* (July 10, 2000, pp.154)
Pub: Time Inc.
Ed: Andy Serwer. **Description:** Village Ventures wants to build businesses in places that are brainy and bucolic, and overlooked by venture capitalists.

35714 ■ "Vision and the Right Team Made This Dream Happen" in *Success* (Vol. 47, No. 2, June 2000, pp. 27)
Pub: Success Publishing, Inc.
Ed: Ian Widger. **Description:** Ian Widger, president and CEO, speaks to the success of AccessLine Communications, Inc., Seattle, Washington.

35715 ■ "A Walk in the Park" in *Small Business Opportunities* (Vol. 12, No. 3, May 2000, pp. 43)
Pub: Harris Publications, Inc.
Description: Making money is a Sunday stroll for a Vermont enterprise that packages walking tours.

35716 ■ "Wanda Wen" in *Entrepreneur* (Vol. 30, No. 10, October 2002, pp. 32)
Pub: Entrepreneur Media Inc.
Ed: April Y. Pennington. **Description:** Profile of Wanda Wen, 39-year-old designer and co-founder of Soolip Inc. located in West Hollywood, California. Soolip retails and wholesales fine papers and customized invitations.

35717 ■ "We Found It! The Venture Rebound" in *Fortune* (Vol. 149, No. 9, May 3, 2004, pp. 115)
Pub: Time, Inc.
Ed: Ellen Florian. **Description:** Using data from VentureOne, a research firm that tracks over 100 sectors, the article picked the five most funded sectors, proving that VC funding is good in a few key sectors.

35718 ■ "Wealth in Wanderlust" in *Small Business Opportunities* (Vol. 12, No. 2, March 2000, pp. 112, 114)
Pub: Harris Publications, Inc.
Ed: Marie Sherlock. **Description:** Cash in on the boom in travel with a fun tour business. Marie Lindt, former travel agent, and Carol Rivendell, former psychotherapist, started Wild Women Tour Company to provide fun tours for small groups of women who do not want to travel alone.

35719 ■ "Web.Preneuring" in *Small Business Opportunities* (Vol. 17, May 2005, No. 3, pp. 76, 110, 112)
Pub: Harris Publications Inc.
Description: Twenty-five step-by-step instructions are given for starting an electronic commerce business.

35720 ■ *Weekend Small Business Start*
Pub: Sourcebooks, Incorporated
Ed: Mark Warda. **Released:** June 2007. **Price:** $19.95. **Description:** Information for starting a new business is presented.

35721 ■ "We'll drink to that! " in *Entrepreneur* (Vol. 31, No. 4, April 2003, pp. 112)
Pub: Entrepreneur Media Inc.
Ed: Nichole L. Torres. **Description:** Profile of Christopher J. Miller, Craig Cook, Robert Pfeiffer, Heike Pfeiffer and Kerri Bryant, co-founders of Low Carb Living Inc. Inspired by the renewed popularity of the Atkins diet, the entrepreneurs produce low carbohydrate alternatives to traditional margarita mixes, including Baja Bob's Sugar Free and Low Garb Bar and Party Mixes.

35722 ■ *What No Ever Tells You About Starting Your Own Business: Real-Life Start-Up Advice from 101 Successful Entrepreneurs*
Pub: Kaplan Publishing
Ed: Jan Norman. **Released:** July 2004. **Price:** $18.95 (US), $28.95 (Canadian). **Description:** From planning to marketing, advice is given to entrepreneurs starting new companies. s.

35723 ■ *What No One Ever Tells You about Starting Your Own Business: Real Life Start-Up Advice from 101 Successful Entrepreneurs*
Pub: Upstart Publishing Co., Inc.
Ed: Jan Norman. **Released:** 1999. **Price:** $17.95.

35724 ■ "What Works: Start Last, Finish First" in *Business 2.0* (Vol. 7, January/February 2006, No. 1, pp. 41-43)
Pub: Time, Inc.
Ed: Michael V. Copeland. **Description:** Timing is right for entrepreneurial startups to successfully compete with industry leaders.

35725 ■ "What's For Dinner?" in *Entrepreneur* (Vol. 31, No. 8, August 2003, pp. 148)
Pub: Entrepreneur Media, Inc.
Ed: April Y. Pennington. **Description:** Profile of Dream Dinners Inc., a home meal-preparation service that has twelve customers, each paying $160, migrate around refrigerated stations, and preparing any 12 of the meals featured monthly. Tina Kuna and Stephanie Firchau, co-founders of Dream Dinners, have five locations in the Washington State area.

35726 ■ "What's your problem?" in *Entrepreneur* (Vol. 30, No. 12, Dec. 2002)
Pub: Entrepreneur Media Inc.
Ed: Paul Edwards, Sarah Edwards. **Description:** Advice for starting a new business for persons with bad credit history is offered.

35727 ■ "Who (Gonna) Dunnit" in *Forbes* (December 11, 2000, pp. 216)
Pub: Forbes Magazine
Ed: Michael Katz. **Description:** Profile of Annotated Digital Video for Intelligent Surveillance and Optimized Retrieval. The program, also known as the Advisor project, won't be ready for another three years. Once developed, cameras will add a brain to their roving eyes, allowing guards to not only monitor and track people, but to also predict what they will do.

35728 ■ "Who let the blogs out? Blogging has become one of the hottest Web trends." in *Entrepreneur* (Vol. 30, No. 10, October 2002, pp. 35)
Pub: Entrepreneur Media Inc.
Ed: Amanda C. Kooser. **Description:** A blog is a frequently updated, timed and dated online journal with links involved. Blogs are a good resource for entrepreneurs to promote a business and to get other people to work with you on your business.

35729 ■ "Winston-Salem, N.C. Area Attracts $567 Million in Venture Capital" in *Winston-Salem Journal* (April 11, 2003)
Pub: Knight-Ridder/Tribune Business News
Ed: Kristi E. Swartz. **Description:** Local investments in the Winston-Salem area helped place North Carolina in the ninth spot for venture capital investments nationally, according to a report by the Council for Entrepreneurial Development.

35730 ■ "Work It" in *Entrepreneur* (Vol. 33, October 2005, No. 10, pp. 34)
Pub: Entrepreneur Media Inc.
Ed: Mark Henricks. **Description:** The findings of a four-year study conducted by Joel Kurtzman and Glenn Riffkin are discussed. The authors of the study have identified nine key factors in successful startups that include market size, competitive position, business model and cash flow.

35731 ■ *Working for Yourself: An Entrepreneur's Guide to the Basics*
Pub: Kogan Page, Limited
Ed: Jonathan Reuvid. **Released:** September 2006. **Description:** Guide for starting a new business venture, focusing on raising financing, legal and tax issues, marketing, information technology, and site location.

35732 ■ "A World at their Feet" in *Kiplinger's Personal Finance Magazine* (Vol. 55, No. 1, January, 2001, pp. 128)
Pub: The Kiplinger Washington Editors, Inc.
Description: Lou-Ann and Randy Merrell, of Vernal, Utah, walked out on the corporate life to return to their roots by making hand-tooled western boots and teaching the craft to others.

35733 ■ "Yes, you can" in *Black Enterprise* (Vol. 31, No. 5, December 2000, pp. 64)
Pub: Earl Graves Publishing Co.
Ed: Feona Huff. **Description:** How to start, operate and grow a business while developing yourself and pursuing your personal goals.

35734 ■ "Yesterday & Today: How DFJ Went From Shrimp to Whale" in *Venture Capital Journal* (Vol. 42, No. 5, May 2002, pp. 12)
Pub: Thomas Venture Economics
Ed: Alistair Christopher. **Description:** Profile of Draper Fisher Jurvetson, an early-stage information technology firm that evolved from Draper & Associates. In ten years, Draper went from a $20 million fund to closing on a $640 million fund.

35735 ■ "You Don't Know Jackalope" in *Success* (Vol. 47, No. 4, September 2000, pp. 18)
Pub: Success Publishing, Inc.
Ed: Michael Barrier. **Description:** Darby McQuade, founder of a store called Jackalope in Santa Fe, New Mexico, has discovered a way to maintain a growing business while sharing his love for animals with his customers.

ASSOCIATIONS AND OTHER ORGANIZATIONS

35736 ■ Advancing Canadian Entrepreneurship
100 Adelaide St. W, Ste. 1302
Toronto, ON, Canada M5H 1S3
Ph:(416)304-1566
Free: 800-766-8169
Fax: (416)864-0514
Co. E-mail: amy@acecanada.ca
URL: http://www.acecanada.ca
Contact: Amy Harder, VP
Membership: Young people, business owners, or engaged in entrepreneurial activities. **Purpose:** Promotes growth and development of members' business interests. Provides support and services to businesses owned by young people; encourages communication and mutual support among collegiate entrepreneurs.

35737 ■ Canadian Association of Family Enterprise–Association Canadienne des Entreprises Familiales
1388 C Cornwall Rd.
Oakville, ON, Canada L6J 7W5
Ph:(416)538-9992
Free: (866)849-0099
Fax: (416)538-9556
Co. E-mail: office@cafenational.org
URL: http://www.cafemembers.org/cafenational
Contact: Lawrence Barns, Natl. CEO
Membership: Family-owned businesses. **Purpose:** Seeks to "encourage, educate, and inform members in disciplines unique to the family business." Fosters increased understanding of the importance of family-owned enterprises in the national economy among government agencies and the public. Gathers and disseminates information of interest to members. Conducts educational and lobbying activities. Provides technical support and advisory services to small businesses in areas including succession planning, taxation, family law, and arbitration and mediation. Maintains network of Family Councils, which serve as a forum for discussion of family and business matters. **Publications:** *Family Business Magazine* (quarterly); *Family Enterpriser* (quarterly); *International Magazine for Family Businesses* (bimonthly); Membership Directory (annual). **Telecommunication Services:** electronic mail, lbarns@cafenational.org.

35738 ■ Canadian Innovation Centre
Waterloo Research & Technology Park
Accelerator Centre
295 Hagey Blvd., Ste. 15
Waterloo, ON, Canada N2L 6R5
Ph:(519)885-5870
Fax: (519)513-2421
Co. E-mail: info@innovationcentre.ca
URL: http://www.innovationcentre.ca
Contact: Kathleen Barsoum, Mgr.
Membership: Investors, entrepreneurs, and innovative companies. **Purpose:** Promotes innovation in economic activity; seeks to ensure that developers of inventions or innovations receive full credit for their discoveries. Provides support and assistance to members. Conducts research and educational programs. **Publications:** *Eureka!* (quarterly).

35739 ■ Kauffman Center for Entrepreneurial Leadership
4801 Rockhill Rd.
Kansas City, MO 64110-2046
Ph:(816)932-1000
Co. E-mail: info@kauffman.org
Description: Works to accelerate entrepreneurship in America.

35740 ■ National Federation of Filipino American Associations
2607 24th St. NW, Ste. 4
Washington, DC 20008-2600
Ph:(202)986-1153
Fax: (202)478-5109
Co. E-mail: admin@naffaa.org

URL: http://www.naffaa.org
Contact: Jon Melegrito, Natl. Communications Dir.
Membership: Filipino American individuals and organizations. **Purpose:** Seeks to promote the interests and well-being of the 3 million Filipinos and Filipino Americans residing in the United States by getting them involved as leaders and participants in United States society. Major programs include citizenship and leadership development, voter education, entrepreneurial training, and community development.

35741 ■ National Foundation for Teaching Entrepreneurship
120 Wall St., 29th Fl.
New York, NY 10005
Ph:(212)232-3333
Free: 800-367-6383
Fax: (212)232-2244
Co. E-mail: nfte@nfte.com
URL: http://www.nfte.com
Contact: Steve Mariotti, Founder/Pres.
Description: Devoted to teaching entrepreneurship education to low-income young people, ages 11 through 18. **Publications:** *NFTE News* (quarterly).

35742 ■ United States Association for Small Business and Entrepreneurship
975 University Ave., No. 3260
Madison, WI 53706
Ph:(608)262-9982
Fax: (608)263-0818
Co. E-mail: jgillman@wisc.edu
URL: http://www.usasbe.org
Contact: Joan Gillman, Exec. Dir.
Description: Fosters business development through entrepreneurship education and research. Improves management knowledge, techniques and skills of small business owners and entrepreneurs. Develops an understanding of small businesses and entrepreneurship to promote a continuing exchange of expertise. **Publications:** *Liaison* (3/year).

REFERENCE WORKS

35743 ■ "19th Annual Entrepreneurial Woman's Conference" in *Entrepreneur* (Vol. 33, August 2005, No. 8, pp. 4)
Pub: Entrepreneur Media Inc.
Ed: Steve Cooper. **Description:** The Women's Business Development Center holds its annual Entrepreneurial Women's Conference for women business owners. The event presents a buyer's mart that allows the owners to market products and services to corporate and government buyers. There are also discussions and workshops addressing issues and trends affecting women-owned businesses.

35744 ■ "20 Keys to Leadership" in *Small Business Opportunities* (Vol. 16, No. 1, January 2004, pp. 12, 20)
Pub: Harris Publications, Inc.
Ed: Joanne G. Sujansky. **Description:** Joanne G. Sujansky, Certified Speaking Professional, shares twenty keys to help entrepreneurs and small business owners to become effective leaders.

35745 ■ "The '42 Formula' For Success" in *Inc.* (August 1, 2003)
Pub: Gruner & Jahr USA Publishing
Ed: Tahl Raz. **Description:** Author Nitin Nohria offers information and advice on why some small business owners succeed and others fail.

35746 ■ "60 Seconds On Doing the Impossible" in *Fast Company* (March 2005, No. 92, pp. 32)
Pub: Gruner & Jahr USA Publishing
Ed: Ryan Underwood. **Description:** Interview with Peter Diamandis, who created the competition that awarded the $10 million Ansari X Prize to SpaceShipOne for shuttling into suborbital space twice in two weeks. Diamandis is expanding his focus to include prizes for nanotechnology.

35747 ■ "The 75 Most Powerful African Americans in Corporate America" in *Black Enterprise* **(Vol. 35, February 2005, No. 7, pp. 104)**
Pub: Earl G. Graves Publishing Co. Inc.
Ed: Kenneth Meeks. **Description:** The 75 most powerful African American corporate leaders are highlighted, including 18 who hold CEO positions.

35748 ■ "75 Most Powerful Blacks on Wall Street" in *Black Enterprise* **(Vol. 37, October 2006, No. 3, pp. 136)**
Pub: Earl G. Graves Publishing Co. Inc.
Ed: Carolyn M. Brown. **Description:** Profiles of seventy-five African American top executives. The listing is a compilation of the brightest and best venture capitalists, asset managers, CEOs, traders, and investment bankers.

35749 ■ "75 Reasons to Be Glad You're an American Entrepreneur Right Now" in *Inc.* **(October 2005, pp. 88-95)**
Pub: Inc. Magazine
Ed: Michael S. Hopkins. **Description:** The diverse ways in which the culture, the economy, and entrepreneurship are making this the best time in history to build a business in America.

35750 ■ *201 Great Tips for Your Small Business: Increase Your Profit and Joy in Your Work*
Pub: Dundren Press Limited
Ed: Julie V. Watson. **Released:** April 2006. **Price:** $24.99. **Description:** Tips and hints for home-based, micro, and small businesses are presented.

35751 ■ *401 Questions Every Entrepreneur Should Ask*
Pub: Career Press, Incorporated
Ed: James L. Silvester. **Released:** October 2006. **Price:** $17.99. **Description:** Review of 25 functional areas of running a small business are covered along with questions entrepreneurs should ask in order to correct and avoid unwanted issues.

35752 ■ "2004 Corporate Elite Directory" in *Hispanic Business* **(January/February 2004, pp. 36, 38, 40, 42, 44, 46)**
Pub: Hispanic Business
Description: A listing of the Hispanic Business 2004 Corporate Elite Directory, with a brief profile of each winner.

35753 ■ "About His Life: Bob Dallmeyer" in *Tradeshow Week* **(Vol. 34, December 20, 2004, No. 51, pp. S4)**
Pub: Reed Business Information
Ed: Gary Tufel. **Description:** Profile of Bob Dallmeyer, exhibitor, show manager, author, teacher, lecturer, and mentor in the exhibition industry. Tradeshow Week named him one of the industry's 100 Most Influential People and one of its Top Five Industry Entrepreneurs in 2003.

35754 ■ "Add An 'Inc' And Get Some Respect" in *Home Office Computing* **(Vol. 19, No. 1, January 2001, pp. 24)**
Pub: Scholastic Inc.
Ed: Jon Halpin. **Description:** The article discusses the fact that more small businesses are incorporating. Profiles of online incorporation services are provided.

35755 ■ "Addicted to Success" in *Success* **(Vol. 47, No. 2, June 2000, pp. 50)**
Pub: Success Publishing, Inc.
Ed: Dina Ingber Stein. **Description:** Profile of Omni Computer Products and Gerald Chamales, President and CEO. Statistical data included.

35756 ■ "An African American in Paris: Ricki Stevenson's Entree to the City of Light" in *Black Enterprise* **(Vol. 35, January 2005, No. 6)**
Pub: Earl G. Graves Publishing Co. Inc.
Ed: Maureen Jenkins. **Description:** Profile of Paris as a city that attracts African Americans for business and pleasure. Many black entrepreneurs are enjoying Paris as a great place to grow their business.

35757 ■ "Agendas Cross in SHCC Boardroom" in *Hispanic Business* **(March 2002, pp. 56-58)**
Pub: Hispanic Business
Ed: Joel Russell. **Description:** Information regarding the U.S. Hispanic Chamber of Commerce's election of a new chairman is discussed, as well as economic issues.

35758 ■ "Agent of Change" in *Rough Notes* **(Vol. 145, No. 9, September 2002, pp. 38)**
Pub: Rough Notes
Ed: Elaine Tolen. **Description:** Dick Fournier, owner of Oregon Insurance Agency, attributes the independent insurance agency's success to former owner Martin K. Bowes, and his staff. He also favors updating the agency with technology and continuing education.

35759 ■ "Agent flips over high-flying sport" in *Atlanta Business Chronicle* **(Vol. 25, January 10, 2003, No. 31, pp. 28A)**
Pub: American City Business Publications, Inc.
Ed: Lisa R. Schoolcraft. **Description:** Heather Williams, a 28-year-old agent for Re/Max Realty Group, has an unusual hobby. Williams is a freestyle motocross jumper who has competed in the X-games XIII in Philadelphia, Pennsylvania.

35760 ■ "Ahead of Her Time" in *Success* **(Vol. 47, No. 3, July 2000, pp. 84)**
Pub: Success Publishing, Inc.
Ed: Jane R. Plitt. **Description:** The article uses Victorian entrepreneur Martha Matilda Harper as a teaching model for business education.

35761 ■ "Alchemist Among the Vines" in *Hispanic Business* **(Vol. 24, No. 4, April 2002, pp. 20-21)**
Pub: Hispanic Business Inc.
Ed: Scott Williams. **Description:** Profile of Reynaldo Robledo, a Mexican immigrant who rose to become owner of his own vineyard, winery, and vineyard management company.

35762 ■ "All About Me" in *My Business* **(February/March 2004, pp. 41)**
Pub: My Business Magazine
Ed: Melany Klinck. **Description:** The new 401(k), called the Solo 401(k) may be a tax-deferral tool for entrepreneurs, allowing them to defer more income.

35763 ■ "All Fired Up: With the Right Marketing Plan, Your Product Will Blaze Trails Across the Globe" in *Entrepreneur* **(Vol. 32, July 2004)**
Pub: Entrepreneur Media Inc.
Ed: Don Debelak. **Description:** Entrepreneurs share steps to successfully market products and services. Profile of Robustion Products Inc., maker of the Java-Log for fireplaces is included.

35764 ■ "Alone in Your Time Zone: Are You Plagued by Chronic Lateness?" in *Black Enterprise* **(Vol. 35, December 2004, No. 5, pp. 155)**
Pub: Earl G. Graves Publishing Co. Inc.
Ed: Alfred A. Edmond Jr. **Description:** Issues involved with chronic lateness are discussed with tips to better manage time.

35765 ■ *Alpha Dogs: How Your Small Business Can Become a Leader of the Pack*
Pub: HarperCollins Publishers, Inc.
Ed: Donna Fenn. **Released:** May 2007. **Price:** $14.95. **Description:** Profiles of eight successful entrepreneurs along with information for developing customer service, technology and competition.

35766 ■ "American Axle's Dauch rewarded handsomely for company success" in *Crain's Detroit Business* **(Vol. 19, No. 16, April 21, 2003, pp. 4)**
Pub: Crain Communications Inc., Detroit
Ed: David Sedgwick. **Description:** Two entrepreneurs who founded North America's largest auto supply firms may rank as the auto industry's top earners in 2002. Profiles of both Richard E. Dauch, founder of American Axle and Manufacturing Holdings Inc., and Frank Stronach, founder of Magna International Inc. are included.

35767 ■ "American Dreamers Nominations Due Thursday" in *Crain's Detroit Business* **(Vol. 22, December 11, 2006, No. 50, pp. 9)**
Pub: Crain Communications Inc. - Detroit
Description: Detroit was built on the hopes and dreams of many immigrants from other countries. Nominations of business successes of first-generation immigrants are ending soon and will be listed in March, 2007.

35768 ■ "America's Newest Entrepreneurial Patron" in *Inc.* **(October 1, 2003)**
Pub: Gruner & Jahr USA Publishing
Ed: Rod Kurtz. **Description:** Disney to sponsor the new U.S. Small Business Administration's National Entrepreneur Center in Orlando, Florida. The center will offer business courses, special software for creating business plans, and mentor programs.

35769 ■ "An Older Sibling In Your Corner Eases Entry Into The Real World" in *Wall Street Journal* **(Vol. 248, December 2006, No. 149, pp. B6)**
Pub: Dow Jones & Co. Inc.
Ed: Emily Meehan **Description:** Recent college grads often utilize the success, resources and connections of their older siblings while transitioning to life after college and establishing a foothold in their perspective careers.

35770 ■ "Andy Pearson Finds Love" in *Fast Company* **(August 2001, pp. 78)**
Pub: Fast Company
Ed: David Dorsey. **Description:** Profile of Andy Pearson, CEO of PepsiCo. Pearson shares his management skills and his new approach to leadership.

35771 ■ "Animal porter escapes economic dog days in shipshape" in *Houston Business Journal* **(Vol. 33, No. 48, April 11, 2003, pp. 2A)**
Pub: Houston Business Journal
Ed: Jenna Colley. **Description:** Biography of Tom Schooler and an explanation of his leadership style as owner of Animal Port Houston, an animal transit company, located in Houston, Texas.

35772 ■ *The Anonymous Entrepreneur, No. 1: 12 Steps to Build the Entrepreneurial Attitude*
Pub: The Corinth Press
Ed: Chad J. Simmons. **Released:** 1998. **Price:** $14.95.

35773 ■ "The Anti-FEMA" in *Inc.* **(Volume 27, December 2005, No. 12, pp. 100-102)**
Pub: Inc. Magazine
Ed: Patrick J. Sauer. **Description:** Profile of Richard Zuschlag, whose ambulance service rescued thousands of individuals from New Orleans after the devastation of Hurricane Katrina.

35774 ■ "Are We There Yet?" in *Entrepreneur* **(Vol. 28, No. 1, January 2000, pp. 328)**
Pub: Entrepreneur Media Inc.
Ed: Victoria Neal. **Description:** Souvenirs give small business a niche in the marketplace and America's love for regionally flavored items gives entrepreneurs the chance to counteract the homogeneity of huge corporate retail outlets.

35775 ■ "Are You Ready for Some Football Cliches?" in *Inc.* **(October 1, 2003)**
Pub: Gruner & Jahr USA Publishing
Ed: Patrick J. Sauer. **Description:** Ways the management of the New York Jets can benefit any small business are discussed.

35776 ■ "Armed for Profit-Taking" in *Small Business Opportunities* **(Vol. 16, November 2004, No. 6, pp. 90)**
Pub: Harris Publications Inc.
Description: Profile of Cactus Jack Barringer, inventor, entrepreneur, and marketer. Barringer's latest invention is The Enforcer, an arm wrestling machine.

35777 ■ "Art of Business" in *Entrepreneur. com* (Vol. 34, February 2006, No. 2, pp. 46)
Pub: Entrepreneur Media Inc.
Ed: Sara Wilson. **Description:** The MacDowell Colony serves not only as an inspiration to artists of all disciplines, but the Colony's methods for fostering creativity can be used to teach entrepreneurs the value of time and space in order to generate ideas.

35778 ■ "Art Lover Plays Fair Game" in *Crain's New York Business* (Vol. 23, January 29, 2007, No. 5, pp. F19)
Pub: Crain Communications, Inc.
Ed: Miriam Kreinin Souccar. **Description:** Profile of Helen Allen and her art fairs, including Pulse, a contemporary art fair in Miami which took in more than $10 million. Numerous dealers sold out their inventory on the first day of the fair. Her art fairs which in addition to Pulse include Ramsay and Art 212 are designed for a younger generation and feature more affordable pieces of work.

35779 ■ "The art of Web selling: company finds a smart way to boost sales" in *Black Enterprise* (Vol. 33, No. 6, January 2003, pp. 41)
Pub: Earl Graves Publishing Co.
Ed: Rebecca Rohan. **Description:** Business owner, Glenn King, Exotica Art & Fashion, has found a unique way to sell imported art and artifacts using online auctions.

35780 ■ "The Art of the Real" in *Inc.* (September 1, 2003)
Pub: Gruner & Jahr USA Publishing
Ed: Jess McCuan. **Description:** Profile of NBC's new reality show featuring Donald Trump. The show features contestants vying for an executive job with Trump that pays in the six figures. Street-smart entrepreneurs are expected to compete.

35781 ■ "The Art of the Woman Warrior" in *Inc.* (August 2005, pp. 26)
Pub: Inc. Magazine
Description: Two former Marines offer management training exclusively for businesswomen. The two sisters have created leadership workshops focusing on ten concepts they learned from the Marines.

35782 ■ "As seen on TV: Mark Burnett knows a little something about survival" in *Entrepreneur* (Vol. 30, No. 3, March 2002, pp.)
Pub: Entrepreneur Media Inc.
Ed: Geoff Williams. **Description:** In an interview with Mark Burnett, executive producer of CBS's Survivor and USA Network's Eco Challenge, he suggests that fear plays a major role in entrepreneur's failure to succeed.

35783 ■ "Ask Inc.: Do I Have to Go to School?" in *Inc.* (October 1, 2003)
Pub: Gruner & Jahr USA Publishing
Description: Advice is given to individuals considering entrepreneurship, focusing on sales strategies for individuals who hate to sell and the whether an entrepreneur needs a college degree.

35784 ■ "Ask Inc. Education" in *Inc.* (November 2006, pp. 51-52)
Pub: Gruner & Jahr USA Publishing
Ed: John Corsault **Description:** While there are many successful entrepreneurs who didn't attend or finish college, odds for successful businesses still favor those who complete their education seven to one.

35785 ■ "Ask yourself this" in *Entrepreneur* (Vol.)
Pub: Entrepreneur Media Inc.
Ed: Marc Diener. **Description:** Creative thinking can pay big dividends when making business deals. Many entrepreneurs often overlook creative ways to negotiate in business.

35786 ■ "Asking For It: You Can't Always Get What You Want, But Chances are Better If You Learn How To Ask" in *Entrepreneur* (August 2004)
Pub: Entrepreneur Media Inc.
Ed: Romanus Wolter. **Description:** Advice is offered to entrepreneurs when making requests in order to get the desired response.

35787 ■ "Asking Too Much? Not a Chance. Questions Are One of the Best Tools for Unlocking Creativity" in *Entrepreneur* (Vol. 31, October 2003)
Pub: Entrepreneur Media, Inc.
Ed: Juanita Weaver. **Description:** Ways to learn to be creative is answered using the "Seven Whys".

35788 ■ "Aspirations for '05" in *Inc.* (January 1, 2005)
Pub: Inc. Magazine
Ed: Darren Dahl, Lora Kolodny. **Description:** Various entrepreneurs of growing companies talk about what they hope to accomplish in 2005.

35789 ■ "At the Service of Charity" in *Business Week Online* (Oct. 23, 2002)
Pub: McGraw-Hill Inc.
Description: An interview with Mari Saso, founder of Aki Designs, explains how he is trying out a new strategy for making philanthropy a priority, despite hard times. Saso recently launched a competition on the firm's Web site that allows nonprofits to apply for pro bono design and branding work from Aki Designs.

35790 ■ "Atlanta ranked No. 1 in business owner diversity" in *Atlanta Business Chronicle* (Vol. 24, No. 10, August 10, 2001, pp. 45A)
Pub: American City Business Journals Inc.
Ed: G. Scott Thomas. **Description:** Compared to 180 other cities, Atlanta has the most diverse mix of entrepreneurs, according to a study by the Demographics Daily; Miami was second. The index has three components, which are divided along gender and racial lines: women in business, blacks in business, and Hispanics in business.

35791 ■ "Attacking Anxiety" in *Working Woman* (Vol. 25, No. 5, May 2000, pp. 40)
Pub: Lang Communications Inc.
Ed: Carol Leonetti Dannhauser. **Description:** Stress causes tension in workers, which in turn has an effect on productivity and efficiency, and often results in sickness and time off work. Companies such as HLB Communications and the Eliassen Group are finding methods to reduce stress levels in the workplace including massages, health club membership, play breaks and the use of communication consultants.

35792 ■ *Attracting Investors: A Marketing Approach to Finding Funds for Your Business*
Pub: John Wiley & Sons, Incorporated
Ed: Philip Kotler, Hermawan Kartajaya, S. David Young. **Released:** August 2004. **Price:** $29.95 (US), $42.99 (Canadian). **Description:** Marketing experts advise entrepreneurs in ways to find investors in order to raise capital for their companies.

35793 ■ "The Authority of Ideas" in *Harvard Business Review* (Vol. 81, No. 8, August 2003, pp. 144)
Pub: Harvard Business School Press
Ed: Lawrence Summers. **Description:** How good ideas are, and how fast a company can find/ implement will be a significant factor in the company's earnings. Business can gain insight into managing this asset by looking at research universities.

35794 ■ "Automotive Dealers Move Wheels" in *Hispanic Business* (Vol. 22, No. 6, June 2000, pp. 100)
Pub: Hispanic Business
Ed: Christopher D. Lancette, Scott Williams, Joel Russell. **Description:** Paul Young Auto Mall in Laredo, Texas, is one of the top ten Hispanic-owned auto dealerships in the United States, with revenues of $95. 97 million. Paul Young, Jr., owner of the company, says that the firm's growth is partially due to the town's population increase.

35795 ■ "Avoid litigation" in *Black Enterprise* (Vol. 32, No. 8, March 2002, pp. 49)
Pub: Earl Graves Publishing Co.
Ed: Bridget McCrea. **Description:** Entrepreneurs cannot afford the financial and emotional stress that comes with legal litigation. Key areas to help small business avoid lawsuits are examined.

35796 ■ "Back to Basics: Ex-Dotcommers Create New Beginnings through Low-Tech Businesses" in *Entrepreneur* (Vol. 31, No. 9, September 2003)
Pub: Entrepreneur Media, Inc.
Ed: Mark Henricks. **Description:** A growing number of ex-dotcommers are starting new businesses in low-technology fields associated with immigrant Americans.

35797 ■ "Back in bloom: Thrifty Florist owner buys back chain, plans to expand" in *Crain's Detroit Business* (Vol. 19, No. 7, Feb. 17, 2003)
Pub: Crain Communications Inc., Detroit
Ed: Brent Snavely. **Description:** Chris Rea sold Thrifty Florist to a national floral retail chain four years ago and has bought his company back and will build new stores.

35798 ■ "Back from the Brink" in *BlackEnterprise* (Vol. 31, No. 8, March 2001, pp. 47)
Pub: Earl Graves Publishing Co.
Ed: Glenn Townes. **Description:** Profiles of minority small business owners who were able to rebuild their businesses after facing major setbacks.

35799 ■ "Back from the Brink" in *Success* (Vol. 47, No. 3, July 2000, pp. 50)
Pub: Success Publishing, Inc.
Ed: Michael Barrier. **Description:** Profile of brothers Mike and Tim Hennessy, and Tim's wife, Sherry. The three chronicle the failure of their first company and how they became successful using their last $5 to buy another company.

35800 ■ "Back Talk with Chris Gardner" in *Black Enterprise* (Vol. 37, January 2007, No. 6, pp. 112)
Pub: Earl G. Graves Publishing Co. Inc.
Ed: Kenneth Meeks. **Description:** Profile of with Chris Gardner and his Chicago company, Gardner Rich L.L.C., a multimillion-dollar investment firm. During an interview, Gardner discusses his rise from homelessness. His story became a book, The Pursuit of Happyness and was recently released as a film starring Will Smith.

35801 ■ "Back Talk: With Billionaire & BET CEO Robert L. Johnson" in *Black Enterprise* (Vol. 35, January 2005, No. 6, pp. 112)
Pub: Earl G. Graves Publishing Co. Inc.
Ed: Kenneth Meeks. **Description:** In 1991, Robert L. Johnson became the first African American to take his company public on the New York Stock Exchange. Along with Black Entertainment Television, Johnson is also the first principle black owner of a major sports franchise, the NBA Charlotte Bobcats. Interview with Johnson explores his views on his accomplishments.

35802 ■ "Bad Apples: Business Owners Share their Hiring Horror Stories" in *Entrepreneur* (Vol. 32, No. 2, February 2004, pp. 26)
Pub: Entrepreneur Media, Inc.
Ed: Nichole L. Torres. **Description:** Three entrepreneurs share bad hiring experiences and offer advice for managers when hiring.

35803 ■ "Balance diet" in *Entrepreneur* (Vol. 30, No. 3, March 2002, p)
Pub: Entrepreneur Media Inc.
Ed: Aliza Pilar Sherman. **Description:** Despite the progress being made by women entrepreneurs, balancing work and family remains a major struggle for them.

35804 ■ *Balls!: 6 Rules for Winning Today's Business Game*
Pub: John Wiley & Sons, Incorporated
Ed: Alexi Venneri. **Released:** January 2005. **Price:** $19.95. **Description:** In order to be successful business leaders must be brave, authentic, loud, lovable, and spunky and they need to lead their competition.

35805 ■ "Banker Boosts Community" in *Crain's New York Business* (Vol. 23, January 29, 2007, No. 5, pp. F14)
Pub: Crain Communications, Inc.
Ed: Tom Fredrickson. **Description:** Profile of Maurice L. Coleman, New York Market Executive for Bank of America. Under his leadership, Bank of America is becoming a major player in community development in New York City, specifically targeting affordable housing and small businesses in low-income areas. Statistical data included.

35806 ■ "Banks: 'Atlanta's Quiet Ambassador of Good Will'" in *Atlanta Business Chronicle* (Vol. 25, No. 22, November 8, 2002, pp. 6C)
Pub: American City Business Publications, Inc.
Description: Walter Banks was recently inducted into the Atlanta Convention and Visitors Bureau Hospitality Hall of Fame following a lifetime of public service.

35807 ■ "Banks: Big vs. Small" in *Hispanic Business* (October 2002, pp. 36, 38)
Pub: Hispanic Business
Ed: Derek Reveron. **Description:** Entrepreneurs have traditionally had to choose between local lenders for customized service or larger institutions for more services, but statistics show that the margin difference between the two is narrowing.

35808 ■ "Barduous journey" in *Entrepreneur* (Vol. 30, No. 1, Januar)
Pub: Entrepreneur Media Inc.
Ed: Geoff Williams. **Description:** Richard Olivier, of Olivier Mythodrama Associates, son of the late Sir Laurence Olivier, uses Shakespeare to teach business executives and entrepreneurs about leadership. Olivier combines four elements to the seminars: theater skills, mythology, psychology and organizational development.

35809 ■ "The bargaining table: check your ego at the door." in *Atlanta Business Chronicle* (Vol. 25, Jan. 10, 2003, No. 31, pp. 1B)
Pub: American City Business Publications, Inc.
Ed: Tom Barry. **Description:** Negotiation skills are very valuable in today's business world; qualities of an effective negotiator, as well as how to negotiate effectively, are discussed.

35810 ■ "Bayla's Plea: Put Your Money Where Your Mouth Is" in *Fortune* (Vol. 142, No. 4, August 14, 2000, pp. 276+)
Pub: Time Inc.
Ed: Melanie Warner. **Description:** Meg Luttrell, CEO of Bayla Home, an online furniture retailer, shares her experiences searching for funding to save her company.

35811 ■ "B.E. Successpert Speaks" in *Black Enterprise* (Vol. 34, No. 5, December 2003, pp. 139)
Pub: Earl Graves Publishing Co.
Ed: Keisha Gaye-Anderson. **Description:** A lawyer and author offers advise to help others build their careers.

35812 ■ "Beating the Dream-Busters: Don't Let Loved Ones Keep You From Living Your Dream" in *Black Enterprise* (Vol. 34, No. 5, December 2003)
Pub: Earl Graves Publishing Co.
Description: Tips to help individuals avoid negativity and criticism from loved ones when trying to fulfill career/business visions and goals.

35813 ■ "Beating the Odds" in *Entrepreneur* (Vol. 27, No. 12, December 1999, pp. 154)
Pub: Entrepreneur Media Inc.

Ed: Geoff Williams. **Description:** Graham McFarland shares his plight to save his company, Express Digital.

35814 ■ "Beauty and the Bugs" in *Home Business* (Vol. 12, March/April 2005, No. 2, pp. 81)
Pub: Home Business Magazine
Ed: Sandy Larson. **Description:** Profile of Genma Stringer Holmes, founder of a home-based pest control company.

35815 ■ "Been there, done that: growing an entrepreneurial empire?" in *Entrepreneur* (Vol. 30, No. 9, September 2002, pp. 25)
Pub: Entrepreneur Media Inc.
Ed: Joshua Kurlantzick. **Description:** Many venture capital entrepreneurs are seeking businesses that have the same qualities that made their own companies successful.

35816 ■ "Behind the Veil" in *Entrepreneur* (Vol. 30, No. 2, Februa)
Pub: Entrepreneur Media Inc.
Ed: Nichole L. Torres. **Description:** Entrepreneurs are getting out of the traditional wedding-consultant role, and moving into the less traditional business of meeting needs not normally addressed, including Web sites for bridesmaids to wedding chapels.

35817 ■ "Being strong comes at high cost" in *Women In Business* (Vol. 52, No. 5, September-October 2000, pp. 18)
Pub: The ABWA Co., Inc.
Ed: Penny Shaffer. **Description:** Issues are presented concerning women's ability to cope with balancing careers, family life, and raising children. The increasing occurrence of burnout among women is covered.

35818 ■ "Belhaven College" in *Mississippi Business Journal* (Vol. 28, September 2006, No. 36, pp. 6)
Pub: Venture Publications, Inc.
Description: Profile of Belhaven College's three newest faculty members: Dr. Donnie Andrews, Dr. Brenda Redfern and Public Manager Randy Russ.

35819 ■ "" in *Bellingham Business Journal* (January 2007, pp.)
Pub: Sun News Inc.
Description: Profile of Christian bikers Mike and Pam Melland, owners of Biker's Oasis. The shop sells motorcycle parts and accessories, helmets, leather clothing, chrome accessories, intercom systems, and radio headsets.

35820 ■ *Ben Franklin: America's Original Entrepreneur, Franklin's Autobiography Adapted for Modern Times*
Pub: McGraw-Hill
Ed: Blaine McCormick; Benjamin Franklin. **Released:** September 2005.

35821 ■ "Best of 2005" in *Business Week* (December 19, 2005, No. 3964, pp. 58-64, 66, 68, 72)
Pub: McGraw-Hill Companies
Ed: Bruce Nussbaum. **Description:** Profiles of the best and most innovative business leaders in 2005.

35822 ■ "Best of the Best" in *Hispanic Business* (June 2002, pp. 32, 34, 36)
Pub: Hispanic Business
Ed: Holly Ocasio Rizzo. **Description:** The Hispanic Business 500 listing of the 500 largest Hispanic firms in the U.S. shows how managers have achieved success, despite the social barriers facing minority entrepreneurs.

35823 ■ "Best of Both Worlds" in *Entrepreneur* (Vol. 31, No. 9, July 2003, pp. 100)
Pub: Entrepreneur Media, Inc.
Ed: Nichole L. Torres. **Description:** Profile of Kevin D. Brewer, founder of Creative Visions Integrated Marketing Concepts, an agency producing commercials and promotional videos to TV pilots and product demonstrations.

35824 ■ "Best Business Books" in *Black Enterprise* (Vol. 36, February 2006, No. 7, pp. 165)
Pub: Earl G. Graves Publishing Co. Inc.
Ed: Tanisha A. Sykes. **Description:** A listing of the top eight business books geared towards black entrepreneurs and recommended by the journal are presented.

35825 ■ "The Best Jobs That Nobody Wants" in *Inc.* (September 2005, pp. 30, 32)
Pub: Inc. Magazine
Ed: Max Chafkin. **Description:** College entrepreneurship departments are having difficulty finding professors to teach classes.

35826 ■ "The best-laid incentive plans" in *Harvard Business Review* (Vol. 81, No. 1, January 2003, pp. 27)
Pub: Harvard Business School Press
Ed: Steve Kerr. **Description:** A case study is presented where a CFO and chief administrative officer of a consumer durables manufacturer has instituted a performance management system that seemed successful to him, but had negative results for employee morale and customer service. Four experts offer advice on ways the company should proceed.

35827 ■ *Best Practice in Business Advisory, Counseling and Information Services*
Pub: United Nations Publications
Ed: United Nations, Economic Commission for Europe Staff. **Released:** January 2005. **Price:** $20.00. **Description:** Second book in a series promoting entrepreneurship in small and medium-sized companies (SMEs) throughout United Nation's Economic Commission for Europe (UNECE) member states.

35828 ■ *Best Practice in Development of Entrepreneurship and SMEs in Countries in Transition: The Belarusian Experience*
Pub: United Nations Publications
Ed: United Nations, Economic Commission for Europe Staff. **Released:** January 2005. **Price:** $22.00. **Description:** Compilation of papers presented at the Forum on Best Practice in the Development of Entrepreneurship and Small and Medium-sized Enterprises (SMEs) in Countries in Transition: The Belarussian Experience, a forum organized by the United Nations Economic Commission for Europe. The book helps to assist Belarus with transitioning to a market economy.

35829 ■ "Best Practices" in *Entrepreneur* (Vol. 32, October 2004, No. 10, pp. 84)
Pub: Entrepreneur Media Inc.
Ed: Mark Henricks. **Description:** Doctors, lawyers and other professionals are taking the lead from entrepreneurs when running and building their businesses. Innovative solutions to grow a professional practice like an entrepreneur are shared.

35830 ■ "Best in Shoe" in *Entrepreneur* (Vol. 31, No. 9, September 2003, pp. 164)
Pub: Entrepreneur Media, Inc.
Ed: April Y. Pennington. **Description:** Profile of Udi Avshalom, president and CEO of Training Camp in New York, New York. Avshalom opened his first shoe store in 1996 and now has six locations with projected sales of about $15 million for 2003.

35831 ■ "Best of the Web" in *Inc.* (June 2000, pp. 137)
Pub: The Goldhirsh Group
Ed: Ned Snell. **Description:** Here's what a panel of seasoned entrepreneurs learned when they reviewed selected Web sites designed to help soloists excel.

35832 ■ "Beyond Big Macs" in *Hispanic Business* (December 2002, pp. 50-52)
Pub: Hispanic Business
Ed: Janet Perez. **Description:** Profile of John Lopez, who was named Entrepreneur of the Year by Hispanic Business Magazine. Lopez is president and CEO of Lopez Foods, a meat processing company that supplies products to McDonald's, Wal-Mart Supercenters, and Sam's Clubs.

35833 ■ "Beyond empowerment: Building a company of citizens" in *Harvard Business Review* **(Vol. 81, No. 1, January 2003, pp. 48)**
Pub: Harvard Business School Press
Ed: Brook Manville, Josiah Ober. **Description:** The ancient Greek city-state of Athens is used as a model for a democratic business organization suited to the knowledge economy of today. The Athenian model does not provide a simple set of prescriptions, but offers a window into how companies can create an atmosphere of dignity and trust without resorting to a stifling bureaucracy.

35834 ■ "Beyond Their Years: These Entrepreneurs Have It All" in *Entrepreneur* **(Vol. 31, No. 11, November 2003, pp. 74)**
Pub: Entrepreneur Media, Inc.
Ed: Amanda C. Kooser, April Y. Pennington, Karen E. Spaeder, Nichole L. Torres. **Description:** The best and brightest entrepreneurs offer advice to those considering starting their own business.

35835 ■ "Biddeford, Maine, Cord Business Weathers Trials of Domestic Textile Industry" in *Portland Press Herald* **(November 18, 2005)**
Pub: Blethen Maine Newspapers, Inc.
Ed: Seth Harkenss. **Description:** Bob Rice, entrepreneur and owner of Spurwink Cordage, discusses his success in an industry that is rapidly shrinking in the U.S. Spurwink Cordage reported nearly $1 million in annual sales, mostly to saddle manufacturers in western states.

35836 ■ "The Big Bang: How Franchising Became an Economic Powerhouse the World Over" in *Entrepreneur* **(Vol. 32, No. 1, January 2004, pp. 86)**
Pub: Entrepreneur Media, Inc.
Ed: David J. Kaufmann. **Description:** David J. Kaufmann offers a perspective on the ways franchising has change the economy and opportunity for entrepreneurs during the last 25 years.

35837 ■ "Big Biz on Campus: Class Is Now In Session For College Entrepreneurs." in *Entrepreneur* **(Vol. 32, December 2004, No. 12, pp. 130)**
Pub: Entrepreneur Media Inc.
Ed: Nichole L. Torres. **Description:** According to the Collegiate Entrepreneurs' Organization and the Institute for Entrepreneurial Studies at the University of Illinois, there has been an increased interest in entrepreneurship at colleges over the last five years, with more than 1,500 colleges and universities offering entrepreneurial training.

35838 ■ *The Big Book of Small Business: You Don't Have to Run Your Business by the Seat of Your Pants*
Pub: HarperCollins Publishers, Inc.
Ed: Tom Gegax; Phil Bolsta. **Released:** February 2007. **Price:** $29.95. **Description:** Entrepreneur shares his experiences starting and running his small business.

35839 ■ "The Big Cheese" in *Entrepreneur* **(Vol. 32, November 2004, No. 11, pp. 164)**
Pub: Entrepreneur Media Inc.
Ed: April Y. Pennington. **Description:** Profile of Kamhi World, maker of novelties and toys including the nine 'Spice Men' plush keychain characters.

35840 ■ "Big Ideas for Small Biz" in *Small Business Opportunities* **(Vol. 16, No. 1, January 2004, pp. 92)**
Pub: Harris Publications, Inc.
Ed: James Feldman. **Description:** Four ways to be innovative and creative with a small business include fostering a business climate, becoming number one with clients, creating a partnership with clients, and a partnership with employees.

35841 ■ "Big Plans" in *Entrepreneur* **(Vol. 30, No. 2, February 2002, p)**
Pub: Entrepreneur Media Inc.
Ed: Aliza Pilar Sherman. **Description:** A report released in late 2001 by the Center for Women's Business Research (formerly the National Foundation for Women Business Owners), states that women-owned firms formed in the last decade are more growth-oriented than their predecessors.

35842 ■ "Big Success Can Start With a Few Steps" in *Mississippi Business Journal* **(Vol. 29, January 2007, No. 4, pp. 5)**
Pub: Venture Publications, Inc.
Ed: Phil Hardwick **Description:** "ABC Volume One", published by the Boomtown Institute, is a new successful manual for many people in the world of economic and community development in small towns. Best used as a discussion guide in community development organizations, it is an offspring of Jack Schultz' "Boomtown USA- The 7-1/2 Keys to Big Success in Small Towns".

35843 ■ "Big Switch: Walk a Mile In Your Employees' Shoes-You Could Learn a Lot" in *Entrepreneur* **(Vol. 32, August 2004, No. 8, pp. 32)**
Pub: Entrepreneur Media Inc.
Ed: April Y. Pennington. **Description:** Six corporate leaders switched places with employees in order to gain new perspectives, and respect for the people who work for them.

35844 ■ "Bill Woodward: the Hollywood VC with staying power" in *Red Herring* **(No. 87, December 18, 2000, pp. 56, 58)**
Pub: Herring Communications, Inc.
Ed: Hildy Medina. **Description:** A profile of Bill Woodward, a Hollywood venture capitalist.

35845 ■ "A Billion in Baskets" in *Small Business Opportunities* **(Vol. 13, No. 6, November 2001, pp. 38, 40)**
Pub: Harris Publications, Inc.
Description: Profile of Longaberger Company, the largest handmade basket-making company in the United States. The company grew from a small family business to a billion-dollar empire, and is the 22nd largest woman-owned company in America.

35846 ■ "Billy Mitchell outstanding in industry and community" in *Atlanta Business Chronicle* **(Vol. 25, December 6, 2002, No. 26, pp. 3C)**
Pub: American City Business Publications, Inc.
Ed: Martin Sinderman. **Description:** Carter & Associates chairman, William A. "Billy" Mitchell has won The Carter/Mathis Award from the Georgia Chapter of the National Association of Industrial and Office Properties. The award recognizes a person or company that has made a lasting contribution to the real estate industry and the community.

35847 ■ "Biz Plan Competition" in *Black Enterprise* **(Vol. 34, No. 2, September 2003, pp. 12)**
Pub: Earl Graves Publishing Co.
Description: Blackenterprise.com is offering $1,000 or a copy of Business Plan Pro software to winners of its best business plan competition.

35848 ■ "Black Board Directors Form Network" in *Black Enterprise* **(Vol. 35, December 2004, No. 5, pp. 38)**
Pub: Earl G. Graves Publishing Co. Inc.
Ed: K. Terrell Reed. **Description:** According to the Investor Research Center, nearly 185 blacks sit on corporate boards, sharing 321 board seats out of 3,447. A recent gathering brought top black executives together to address a diversity agenda in board rooms.

35849 ■ "Black Hawk down at work" in *Harvard Business Review* **(Vol. 81, No. 1, January 2003, pp. 16)**
Pub: Harvard Business School Press
Ed: Thomas W. Britt. **Description:** U.S. soldiers compare experiences in Somalia in 1992 with morale issues in business. In both situations ambiguity about work roles, inadequate resources and overwork lead to dissatisfaction and, in the business context, the defection of the best workers.

35850 ■ "Blazing New Trails" in *Black Enterprise* **(Vol. 35, October 2004, No. 3, pp. 145)**
Pub: Earl G. Graves Publishing Co. Inc.
Ed: Nkechi I. Olisemeka. **Description:** Winners of the 2004 Black Enterprise Small Business Awards are profiled. These entrepreneurs help redefine small business excellence for black companies.

35851 ■ "The Bleeding-Heart Rationalist: William Morris b. 1911" in *New York Times* **(December 31, 2006, pp. 14)**
Pub: New York Times Company
Ed: Walter Kirn. **Description:** Profile of William Norris, founder of Control Data Corporation, now defunct, but at one time, one of the nation's largest computer manufacturing companies. Norris also founded an institute that promoted education and small business growth.

35852 ■ "Blind Ambition: Robert Jones Lost His Eyesight, But His Vision Is Crystal Clear" in *Black Enterprise* **(Vol. 34, No. 3, October 2003)**
Pub: Earl Graves Publishing Co.
Ed: Caroline V. Clark. **Description:** Profile of Robert Jones, who was blinded by a bullet at age 10. Jones did not let blindness keep him from performing songs in church and his developing talent and become a champion on Chicago's open mike circuit working as a songwriter and producer for Trakz Inkorporated Music Group, and graduating from Chicago's Columbia College. He is currently negotiating the launch of his own record label. Jones hopes to enter medical school next year to pursue a degree in psychiatry, in order to combine the knowledge of his passion for music and the inspiring perspective shaped by his life experiences to become a motivational speaker.

35853 ■ "Bloopers & Blunders" in *Small Business Opportunities* **(Vol. 16, November 2004, No. 6, pp. 72)**
Pub: Harris Publications Inc.
Ed: Joanne G. Sujansky. **Description:** Seven mistakes made by company leaders and ways to avoid them are explained: lack of trust, failure to shape and share vision, unclear expectations, insufficient modeling of desire behaviors, too little partnering, failure to retain top talent, and too little celebration of success.

35854 ■ "Blurred Vision" in *Entrepreneur* **(Vol. 28, No. 10, October 2000, pp. 118)**
Pub: Entrepreneur Media Inc.
Ed: Chris Penttila. **Description:** Don't expect your employees to be carbon copies of yourself. It takes an owner to have the dedication of an owner.

35855 ■ "Board certified" in *Black Enterprise* **(Vol. 33, No. 6, Jan. 2003, pp. 45)**
Pub: Earl Graves Publishing Co.
Ed: Phaedra Brotherton. **Description:** Landing a seat on a corporate board is an excellent opportunity to meet and network with high-level executives and industry leaders, as well as earning cash and stocks.

35856 ■ "Board gains" in *WorkingWoman* **(Vol. 25, No. 4, April 2000, pp. 42)**
Pub: Lang Communications Inc.
Ed: Carl Vogel. **Description:** Women executives working as volunteers on the boards of non-profit organizations share how this experience has also improved their business acumen.

35857 ■ "The board's missing link" in *Harvard Business Review* **(Vol. 81, No. 3, March 2003, pp. 86)**
Pub: Harvard Business School Press
Ed: Cynthia A. Montgomery, Rhonda Kaufman. **Description:** The relationship between boards of directors and shareholders is examined. Exchange of information is poor and shareholders fail to exert much influence over boards.

35858 ■ "The Bold and the Profitable?" in *Entrepreneur* **(Vol. 31, No. 10, October 2003)**
Pub: Entrepreneur Media, Inc.
Description: Profile of John Acres, founder of BiGHA Inc., an adventure bicycle manufacturer in Corvallis, Oregon.

35859 ■ *The Book of Entrepreneurs' Wisdom*
Pub: John Wiley and Sons Inc.
Ed: Peter Krass. **Price:** $26.95.

35860 ■ *The Book of Hard Choices: Making the Right Decisions at Work without Losing Your Self-Respect*
Pub: Broadway Books
Ed: Peter Roy; James A. Autry. **Released:** December 2006. **Price:** $23.95.

35861 ■ "**Boost Your Bottom Line By Taking the Guesswork Out of Pricing**" in *Inc.* (Volume 27, June 2005, No. 6, pp. 72-76, 78, 80, 82)
Pub: Inc. Magazine
Ed: Alison Stein Wellner. **Description:** Many business owners trust their instinct with pricing products and services. A better approach might be to ask what that product or service is really worth.

35862 ■ "**Bored Meeting**" in *Entrepreneur* (Vol. 31, No. 9, September 2003, pp. 78)
Pub: Entrepreneur Media, Inc.
Description: Business owners serving on commissions quickly find out it is not a way to gather intelligence about competitors, rather they should cultivate relationships with commercial real estate brokers and landlords.

35863 ■ "**Born Leaders? Learn to be the leader of your pack**" in *My Business* (April/May 2003, pp. 42)
Pub: My Business Magazine
Ed: Mardy Fones. **Description:** The success of any small business is directly related to its owner.

35864 ■ "**A Boss's Toughest Job; Grace was my first employee**" in *Business Week Online* (November 7, 2002)
Pub: McGraw-Hill Inc.
Ed: Gloria Washington. **Description:** An entrepreneur discusses the difficulties faced when having to fire an employee. Her experience was when her first employee hired, after many years of service, began alienating customers.

35865 ■ "**Bottom feeding for blockbuster businesses**" in *Harvard Business Review* (Vol. 81, No. 3, March 2003, pp. 52)
Pub: Harvard Business School Press
Ed: David Rosenblum, Doug Tomlinson, Larry Scott. **Description:** Research shows that companies can make profits from customers that are momentarily unprofitable and executives should ask themselves how they can make money from customers shunned by others, such as by serving small businesses that can't afford expensive services.

35866 ■ *Brag!: The Art of Tooting Your Own Horn Without Blowing It*
Pub: Warner Books, Incorporated
Ed: Peggy Klaus. **Released:** May 2004. **Price:** $13.95. **Description:** A plan to promote a small business by effectively selling one's self.

35867 ■ "**Brainstorming**" in *Small Business Opportunities* (Vol. 12, No. 2, March 2000, pp. 120)
Pub: Harris Publications, Inc.
Ed: Robert Spiegel. **Description:** Six ways to generate big ideas for small business are presented, including inviting friends, professionals, and relatives to brainstorm.

35868 ■ "**Brainy Is As Brainy Does**" in *BlackEnterprise* (Vol. 31, No. 7, February 2001, pp. 134)
Pub: Earl Graves Publishing Co.
Ed: Mary H. McCormack. **Description:** The article suggests that sometimes putting too much thought in a business plan can actually undermine the company. Tips to keep small business on track are presented.

35869 ■ "**A Brand New Day**" in *Entrepreneur* (Vol. 33, March 2005, No. 3, pp. 134)
Pub: Entrepreneur Media Inc.
Ed: Romanus Wolter. **Description:** Tips to help motivate entrepreneurs on a daily basis.

35870 ■ "**Break it up! Will Congress finally take a swing at contract bundling?**" in *Entrepreneur* (Vol. 30, No. 2, February 2002, pp. 23)
Pub: Entrepreneur Media Inc.
Ed: Stephen Barlas. **Description:** The topic of government contract bundling is addressed, including the Senate version of the fiscal 2002 Pentagon authorization bill, which would require a number of steps before contracts are combined in a package larger than $5 million.

35871 ■ "**Breaking Through Excuses**" in *Business 2.0* (Vol. 6, May 2005, No. 4, pp. 76)
Pub: Time, Inc.
Ed: Jeffrey Pfeffer. **Description:** Most managers are good at explaining why something can't be done; allowing excuses to inhibit change results in failure to improve.

35872 ■ "**Bridging the Gap: Networking Can Be Key to Creating Sales Opportunities.**" in *Entrepreneur* (Vol. 32, November 2004, No. 11, pp. 89)
Pub: Entrepreneur Media Inc.
Ed: Barry Farber. **Description:** Steps for successful business networking are listed to help entrepreneurs bridge the gap, a strategy that helps build a foundation of contacts that will provide sales opportunities.

35873 ■ "**Bright Ideas**" in *Entrepreneur* (Vol. 27, No. 12, December 1999, pp. 170)
Pub: Entrepreneur Media Inc.
Ed: Don Debelak. **Description:** The success story of Karen Alvarez and her invention of the Baby Comfort Strap, that safely secures a baby in a shopping cart.

35874 ■ "**Bringing the dead back to life**" in *BlackEnterprise* (Vol. 32, No. 3, October 2001, pp. 161)
Pub: Earl Graves Publishing Co.
Ed: Hasani Pettiford, Robyn D. Clarke. **Description:** Profile of Malachia Brantley, president of Newark, New Jersey-based Brantley Brothers Moving & Storage Company. Brantley purchased his first Dodge truck in 1967 for $1, and has expanded operations to include a company fleet of 25 trucks. Brantley has built a profitable company with a strong national and international presence.

35875 ■ "**Britt's Grit: Why He Left the Safety of JPMorgan in a Down Market**" in *Venture Capital Journal* (Vol. 42, No. 10, Oct. 2002, pp. 22)
Pub: Thomson Venture Economics
Ed: Dan Primack. **Description:** Profile of David Britts, partner in ComVentures. Britts left JPMorgan Partners to become a partner at ComVentures in Palo Alto, California.

35876 ■ "**Broadcast News: B.E. Breaks Ground With New TV Program**" in *Black Enterprise* (Vol. 34, No. 5, December 2003, pp. 159)
Pub: Earl Graves Publishing Co.
Description: Black Enterprise has teamed with Central City Productions Inc. to create a new program called, "The Black Enterprise Report", devoted to covering trends and accomplishments of minority business and professional executives.

35877 ■ "**Bruised but Unbowed**" in *Hispanic Business* (December 2001, pp. 66)
Pub: Hispanic Business
Ed: Barbara Beckley. **Description:** New York City is back in business while still recovering from the terrorist attacks of September 11, and hoping for a return of business and vacation travelers. Information for visiting New York City is provided.

35878 ■ *Building a Business the Buddhist Way*
Pub: Celestial Arts Publishing Company
Ed: Geri Larkin. **Released:** September 2004. **Price:** $18.95 (Canadian). **Description:** Principles of entrepreneurship for starting and growing a business while maintaining a balance between business goals and spiritual goals.

35879 ■ "**Building Character**" in *Black Enterprise* (Vol. 35, January 2005, No. 6, pp. 41)
Pub: Earl G. Graves Publishing Co. Inc.
Ed: Glenn Townes. **Description:** Mike Jones has launched, Discover Leadership Training, providing weekend training and development seminars designed to develop and improve leadership skills.

35880 ■ "**Building a Good Rep**" in *Black Enterprise* (Vol. 36, December 2005, No. 5, pp. 136)
Pub: Earl G. Graves Publishing Co. Inc.
Ed: Scott Westcott. **Description:** According to Jerome Henderson, former football star and manager of a team of mortgage bankers, reputation is the most important key to business success.

35881 ■ "**Building on History**" in *Philadelphia Inquirer* (October 16, 2006)
Pub: Philadelphia Newspapers LLC
Ed: Benjamin Y. Lowe. **Description:** Profile of Rick Skidmore, president and founder of Timberlane Inc. Skidmore, a former life insurance agent, discovered the need for custom made window shutters. The company allows employees to review the firm's financial performance on a quarterly basis.

35882 ■ "**Building the Perfect Tech CEO**" in *Hispanic Business* (Vol. 23, No. 5, May 2001, pp. 28, 30)
Pub: Hispanic Business
Ed: Jonathan J. Higuera. **Description:** Profile of Grey Reyes, president and CEO of the Silicon-based Brocade Communications Systems. Mr. Reyes has vowed to make the storage area network infrastructure provider an industry leader.

35883 ■ "**Building a Portfolio**" in *Crain's Detroit Business* (Vol. 21, October 3, 2005, No. 43)
Pub: Crain Communications Inc. - Detroit
Ed: Jennette Smith. **Description:** Profile of Fred Erb, who leased his Erb Lumber store locations to Carolina Holdings in 1993, however Erb did not sell the real estate. Erb has served the area as lumber baron, business mentor and philanthropist.

35884 ■ "**Built For Speed: Baba Garba Looks to Take His Broadband Business Abroad**" in *Black Enterprise* (Vol. 34, No. 5, December 2003, pp. 50)
Pub: Earl Graves Publishing Co.
Ed: Zakiyyah El-Amin. **Description:** Profile of Baba Garba, founder of Infonit LLC, launched in 2000 and located in Niles, Michigan. The firm provides broadband installation and information technology consulting.

35885 ■ *Built to Last: Successful Habits of Visionary Companies*
Pub: HarperCollins Publishers Inc.
Ed: James C. Collins; Jerry I. Porras. **Released:** January 2002. **Price:** $17.95 paperback.

35886 ■ "**The Bumpy Road to Success**" in *Home Business* (Vol. 12, October 2005, No. 5, pp. 56)
Pub: Home Business Magazine
Ed: Sandy Larson. **Description:** Jim Ziegler, author of the book, The Prosperity Equation, recounts his personal experiences from desolation to millionaire.

35887 ■ "**Bunny Money**" in *Entrepreneur* (Vol. 30, No. 3, March 2002)
Pub: Entrepreneur Media Inc.
Ed: Michelle Prather. **Description:** Gift basket retailers, as well as gift shops, are expecting higher profits on Easter sales this year.

35888 ■ "**Burned down to the wick**" in *Black Enterprise* (Vol. 31, No. 5, December 2000, pp. 165)
Pub: Earl Graves Publishing Co.
Ed: Robyn D. Clarke. **Description:** Identify your source of burnout and avoid future cases.

35889 ■ "Burrell CEO Steps Down" in *Black Enterprise* **(Vol. 35, August 2004, No. 1, pp. 23)**
Pub: Earl G. Graves Publishing Co. Inc.
Ed: Dahna M. Chandler. Description: Thomas J. Burrell, founder of a black-owned advertising firm, is stepping down as chairman and CEO of his Chicago, Illinois-based company. Burrell is credited with redefining the advertising industry.

35890 ■ "Business Bookshelf" in *Small Business Opportunities* **(Vol. 16, No. 1, January 2004, pp. 126)**
Pub: Harris Publications, Inc.
Description: Reviews of the books, "Beans: Four Principles For Running a Business In Good Times or Bad", by Leslie A. Yerkes and Charles Decker; and "Business Lessons with Sharkmaster, Jr.", by Randy Clay.

35891 ■ *Business Fairy Tales*
Pub: Thomson South-Western
Ed: Cecil W. Jackson. Released: July 2006. Price: $39.95. Description: The seven most-common business schemes are uncovered.

35892 ■ "Business Groups Look for Next Generation's Leaders" in *San Fernando Valley Business Journal* **(Vol. 12, January 2007, No. 2, pp. 1)**
Pub: San Fernando Valley Business Journal Associates
Ed: Mark R. Madler. Description: A number of business groups in the San Fernando Valley area are reaching out to embrace the younger generation by helping young business professionals make connections and learn leadership skills.

35893 ■ "Business Owners: Are You Getting Your Share of Investment Capital?" in *Women in Business* **(Vol. 54, No. 5, Sept.-Oct. 2002, pp. 28)**
Pub: The ABWA Company, Inc.
Ed: Mary-Lane Kamberg. Description: Sources of funding and techniques to obtain funding are discussed.

35894 ■ "Business Primer for Legislators" in *Hispanic Business* **(November 2002, pp. 32)**
Pub: Hispanic Business
Ed: Derek Reveron. Description: The National Commission on Entrepreneurship presented a guide to government officials stating small business concerns. The guide also provides CEOs a checklist of business-friendly government initiatives.

35895 ■ "Business Prophet" in *Business Week* **(January 23, 2006, No. 3968, pp. 68-73)**
Pub: McGraw-Hill Companies
Ed: Description: C.K. Prahalad shares lessons for executives in order to run their companies successfully. Prahalad's strategy suggests that the ingenuity used at work in poor nations, where success depends on brilliant deployment of minimal resources, has strong implications for executives worldwide.

35896 ■ "Business Services" in *Entrepreneur* **(Vol. 31, No. 5, May 2003, pp. 8)**
Pub: Entrepreneur Media Inc.
Description: A directory of business services is presented, listing such services as franchise consultation, attorneys, entrepreneurial information radio shows, sales and marketing plans, business startup information, home-based businesses, raising business capital, e-businesses, B2B sales leads, and software.

35897 ■ *The Business of Small Business: Succeeding and Prospering in Business for Reasonably Intelligent Entrepreneurs*
Pub: Allen-Reed Publishing Company
Released: August 2006. Price: $27.95. Description: Tips for running a successful company are presented to entrepreneurs.

35898 ■ *Business Unusual*
Pub: Thorsons
Ed: Anita Roddick. Price: $24.95.

35899 ■ *Business Upgrade: 21 Days to Reignite the Entrepreneurial Spirit in You and Your Team*
Pub: John Wiley & Sons, Incorporated
Ed: Richard P. Cordock. Released: January 2007. Price: $18.95. Description: Business consultant works to inspire and guide entrepreneurs to spark growth in their companies while motivating workers.

35900 ■ *Business Warrior: Strategy for Entrepreneurs*
Pub: Clearbridge Publishing
Ed: Sun Tzu. Released: September 2006. Price: $19.95. Description: Advice to help entrepreneurs understand competitive strategies in order to succeed, focusing on sales, marketing, and personnel management.

35901 ■ "The Business Year That Was" in *Inc.* **(December 1, 2003)**
Pub: Gruner & Jahr USA Publishing
Ed: Patrick J. Sauer. Description: A reflection on 2003 business issues is presented.

35902 ■ "The Buy-A-Wish Foundation Catalog" in *Fast Company* **(August 2001, pp. 148)**
Pub: Fast Company
Description: Humorous look at Dennis Tito, billionaire pension-fund manager, who, for a mere $20 million, enjoyed a week of orbital spaceflight aboard the Russian-manned International Space Station.

35903 ■ "By Gum!...It Is Possible to Beat Everyone-Even Big Companies-To Market..." in *Entrepreneur* **(Vol. 32, November 2004, No. 11, pp. 26)**
Pub: Entrepreneur Media Inc.
Ed: Geoff Williams. Description: Profile of Art Baer, who invested $20,000 of his own money to launch Impress Gum. Baer recognized the opportunity when Singapore lifted its ban on chewing gum, where residents chew gum for medicinal purposes.

35904 ■ "Calendar" in *San Fernando Valley Business Journal* **(Vol. 12, January 2007, No. 2, pp. 40)**
Pub: San Fernando Valley Business Journal Associates
Description: Listing of events, conferences, and other resources for small business owners and aspiring entrepreneurs.

35905 ■ "Can Entrepreneurship Be Taught? You Bet It Can" in *Entrepreneur* **(Vol. 31, No. 4, April 2003, pp. 62)**
Pub: Entrepreneur Media Inc.
Ed: David Newton, Mark Henricks. Description: The first Annual Top 100 Entrepreneurial Colleges and Universities lists the top schools teaching entrepreneurial skills in the United States.

35906 ■ "Can Gates Remember Being Small?" in *Fortune* **(Vol. 148, No. 12, December 8, 2003, pp. 204H)**
Pub: Time Inc.
Ed: David Lidsky, David Whitford. Description: In an interview with Bill Gates, he answers questions about his days of being a small businessman and the things that attributed to his success with Microsoft.

35907 ■ "Can a Nice Guy Finish First?" in *Washington Business Journal* **(Vol. 22, No. 3, May 23, 2003, pp. 28)**
Pub: Washington Business Journal
Ed: Suzanne White. Description: Profile of Daniel Bruce Karchem, president of Washington, DC area Karchem Properties. Topics include real estate development, management styles, and lifestyles.

35908 ■ "Can Spending A Day Stuck To A Velcro Wall Help Build A Team" in *Wall Street Journal* **(Vol. 248, December 2006, No. 149, pp. B1)**
Pub: Dow Jones & Co. Inc.
Ed: Jared Sandberg Description: Profiles of several companies offering office and corporate team-building exercise outings and events. Alternative methods of company employee bonding are covered.

35909 ■ "Can You Help Me?" in *Black Enterprise* **(Vol. 35, October 2004, No. 3, pp. 188)**
Pub: Earl G. Graves Publishing Co. Inc.
Ed: Feona S. Huff. Description: Bonnie St. John, a motivational speaker, coach and author recommends asking for help as the surest way individuals, as well as entrepreneurs, can exceed limitations. Pointers to help with success are listed.

35910 ■ "Can You Manage? Should the Office Hotshot Be Your Next Manager?" in *Entrepreneur* **(Vol. 31, No. 7, July 2003)**
Pub: Entrepreneur Media, Inc.
Ed: Chris Penttila. Description: Profile of Erika Mangrum, co-founder and president of Iatria Day Spa and Health Center in Raleigh, North Carolina. Mangrum realized she had promoted the wrong person to a management position, creating big problems as the company grew.

35911 ■ "Can You 'Pass' on Passion?" in *Women in Business* **(Vol. 53, No. 5, September-October, 2001, pp. 12)**
Pub: The ABWA Co. Inc.
Ed: Mary-Lane Kamberg. Description: Ways to ensure that the passion within an organization is pervasive throughout the company are to get employees involved, acknowledge employee contributions to the company, and reward top performing employees.

35912 ■ *Canadian Entrepreneurship and Small Business Management*
Pub: McGraw-Hill Ryerson, Limited
Ed: D. Wesley Balderson. Released: February 2005. Price: $79.95. Description: Successful entrepreneurship and small business management is shown through the use of individual Canadian small business experiences.

35913 ■ *Canadian Small Business Kit for Dummies*
Pub: John Wiley & Sons, Incorporated
Ed: Margaret Kerr; JoAnn Kurtz. Released: May 2006. Price: $28.99. Description: Resources include information on changes to laws and taxes for small businesses in Canada.

35914 ■ "Capital Access" in *Hispanic Business* **(July/August 2004, pp. 68, 70, 72, 74)**
Pub: Hispanic Business
Description: Top financial leaders discuss the challenges in mid-size company expansion. The growth of the U.S. Hispanic economy is paving the way for these businesses.

35915 ■ "Captains of Capital" in *Hispanic Business* **(March 2003, pp. 30-34, 36-38)**
Pub: Hispanic Business
Description: Ways in which the Hispanic Business 500 are finding growth capital are presented. Three Hispanic entrepreneurs are featured, showing how they met this investment challenge. Statistical data included.

35916 ■ "Cardenas' Star on the Rise" in *Hispanic Business* **(Vol. 23, No. 5, May 2001, pp. 12)**
Pub: Hispanic Business
Ed: Rick Laezman. Description: Profile of successful businessman, Tony Cardenas, and California Assemblyman (D-Sylmar, California), is the first Hispanic elected to represent the San Fernando Valley. Mr. Cardenas states that the number one issue for his district is healthcare.

35917 ■ "Career Patterns of the Self-Employed: Career Motivations and Career Outcomes" in *Journal of Small Business Management* **(Vol. 38, No. 3)**
Pub: West Virginia University
Ed: Daniel C. Feldman, Mark C. Bolino. Description: Little attention has been given to what motivates individuals to start small business enterprises and the extent to which self-employment fulfills important career needs. This study uses the "career Anchors" typology of Schein to determine which "constellations" of career goals, interests, and values attract individuals into, and keep them attached to, self-employment.

35918 ■ "Career smarts: Bouncing back from career setbacks" in *Women in Business* (Vol. 53, No. 1, January-February, 2001, pp. 26)
Pub: The ABWA Co. Inc.
Ed: Diane Domeyer. **Description:** Career setbacks, and ways to bounce back by taking stock, re-evaluating goals, and learning from mistakes are discussed.

35919 ■ "Career smarts" in *Women in Business* (Vol. 53, No. 4, July-August, 2001, pp. 38)
Pub: The ABWA Co. Inc.
Ed: Liz Hubler. **Description:** Issues concerning strategies for considering a career change are discussed. Particular attention is given to ways of assessing the need for a career change, including self-assessment techniques and ways of enhancing one's marketability.

35920 ■ *Careers for Homebodies and Other Independent Souls*
Pub: McGraw-Hill
Ed: Jan Goldberg. **Released:** March 2007. **Price:** $13.95. **Description:** The books offers insight into choosing the right career for individuals. Jobs range from office to outdoors, job markets, and levels of education requirements.

35921 ■ "Carrying Off the Gold" in *San Francisco Business Times* (Vol. 17, No. 48, July 4, 2003, pp. 3)
Pub: American City Business Journals
Ed: Steven E.F. Brown. **Description:** Profile of Brett Barron, owner of Capital Realty Group in Burlingame, California and U.S. Olympic coach of the U.S. Judo team.

35922 ■ "Case In Point" in *Entrepreneur* (Vol. 31, No. 8, August 2003, pp. 66)
Pub: Entrepreneur Media, Inc.
Ed: Joanne Cleaver. **Description:** Allowing a small firm to participate in a local business school's case study or class research project could help a small business become stronger. Faculty members in major metropolitan areas are always looking to do case studies on small companies in the area.

35923 ■ "Catering Company Expands Operations" in *Bellingham Business Journal* (December 2006, pp. A6)
Pub: Sun News Inc.
Description: Ciao Thyme, a catering company owned by Jessica and Mataio Gillis, will be moving to a larger space in March 2007. They plan to add an event space, a small private dining facility and will be offering cooking classes.

35924 ■ "Caviar Dreams" in *Black Enterprise* (Vol. 36, November 2005, No. 4, pp. 180)
Pub: Earl G. Graves Publishing Co. Inc.
Ed: Tennille M. Robinson. **Description:** Profile of David E. Mills, the 36-year-old owner of Emperor's Roe, the only black-owned caviar company in the U.S. Mills offers a breakdown of the four basic types of caviar, including Beluga, Oscetra, Sevruga, and American Sturgeon, along with tips for serving.

35925 ■ "Celeb-Savvy Publisher" in *Crain's New York Business* (Vol. 23, January 29, 2007, No. 5, pp. F24)
Pub: Crain Communications, Inc.
Ed: Matthew Flamm. **Description:** Profile of Jason Binn who is the founder and chief executive of Niche Media Holdings, a publisher of glossy magazines such as Gotham and Los Angeles Confidential. His innovative techniques led to a successful company which reports $40 million in annual revenues.

35926 ■ "Celebrate Success. Embrace Innovation" in *Black Enterprise* (Vol. 37, February 2007, No. 7, pp. 145)
Pub: Earl G. Graves Publishing Co. Inc.
Description: 2007 Women of Power Summit provides networking opportunities, empowerment sessions, and nightly entertainment. More than 500 executive women of color are expected to attend this inspiring summit in Phoenix, February 7-10.

35927 ■ "Celebrating Business Heroes" in *Hispanic Business* (December 2002, pp. 58-60)
Pub: Hispanic Business
Ed: Scott Williams. **Description:** Hispanic CEO's share their challenges while seeing a successful market niche, including an artist who designs pools, waterfalls, and water sculptures; founders of BLVD magazine, a doctor who treats varicose veins, and a magazine offering branding advice.

35928 ■ "CEO Incentives and Corporate Social Performance" in *Journal of Business Ethics* (Vol. 45, No. 4, July 15, 2003, pp. 341)
Pub: Kluwer Academic Publishers Group
Ed: Jean McGuire, Sandra Dow, Kamal Argheyd. **Description:** An examination of the relationship between CEO incentives and strong and weak corporate social performance is discussed.

35929 ■ "CEO Runs a Site with Bite" in *Crain's New York Business* (Vol. 23, January 29, 2007, No. 5, pp. F17)
Pub: Crain Communications, Inc.
Ed: Julie Satow. **Description:** Profile of chief executive, Ryan Slack of PropertyShark.com, a Brookly-based website that has a membership of over 200,000. The site offers users access to property information such as sales prices, code violations, appraisal values and previous owners.

35930 ■ "The CEO's Secret Handbook" in *Business 2.0* (Vol. 6, July 2005, No. 6, pp. 68-74)
Pub: Time, Inc.
Ed: Paul Kaihla. **Description:** Accidental guru, Bill Swanson, CEO at Raython shares a lifetime's worth of executive wisdom in his 760-page spiral-bound guidebook, Swanson's Unwritten Rules of Management.

35931 ■ "The Challenges of Equal Access" in *Atlanta Business Chronicle* (Vol. 23, No. 51, May 25, 2001, pp. 1B)
Pub: American City Business Journals Inc.
Ed: Edward Davis. **Description:** Edward Davis, dean of the School of Business at Clark Atlanta University, moderated a roundtable discussion with leaders of Atlanta's African-American business community. The group discussed capital issues, equal access as well as other key factors for entrepreneurship.

35932 ■ "Chamber Kicks Off Weekly Member-Appreciation Program" in *Bellingham Business Journal* (December 2006, pp. 4)
Pub: Sun News Inc.
Description: Bellingham Women Chamber of Commerce and Industry celebrates various businesses within its membership with a member appreciation program.

35933 ■ "A Chance at a Second Career" in *Home Business* (Vol. 13, January/February 2006, No. 1, pp. 81)
Pub: Home Business Magazine
Ed: Sandy Larson. **Description:** Profile of Dan Hicks Jr. and his wife Clara who run a tile and grout cleaning business in Texas.

35934 ■ "Change, of Course" in *Entrepreneur.com* (Vol. 34, February 2006, No. 2, pp. 79)
Pub: Entrepreneur Media Inc.
Ed: David Worrell. **Description:** Profile of George Deeb, owner of iExplore Inc., a Chicago, Illinois-based adventure-travel firm with nearly $10 million in annual sales. Deeb offers his own tours and sells advertising on his Website.

35935 ■ "The Change Makers" in *Harvard Business Review* (Vol. 81, No. 7, July 2003, pp. 20)
Pub: Harvard Business School Press
Ed: John T. Landry. **Description:** Review of the book featuring entrepreneurs who changed industries, including Bill Gates.

35936 ■ "Change the way you persuade" in *Harvard Business Review* (Vol. 80, No. 5, May 2002, pp. 65)
Pub: Harvard Business School Press
Ed: Robert B. Miller, Gary A. Williams. **Description:** Suggestions are offered for tailoring one's style of persuasion to the type of executive making the business decision. There are five types of decision makers: charismatics, thinkers, skeptics, followers and controllers.

35937 ■ "Changing gears: Gregory Blache pilots against the tide on the Mississippi River" in *Black Enterprise* (Vol. 33, No. 6, Jan. 2003)
Pub: Earl Graves Publishing Co.
Ed: Shani Smothers. **Description:** Profile of Gregory J. Blache, 33-year-old entrepreneur riverboat pilot, who guides over 95 percent of ship traffic on the Mississippi River.

35938 ■ "Changing hats" in *Black Enterprise* (Vol. 31, No. 5, December 2000, pp. 71)
Pub: Earl Graves Publishing Co.
Ed: Carolyn M. Brown. **Description:** Profile of Tim Cobb, founder of RelevantKnowledge, discussing his many business ventures.

35939 ■ "Charged Up" in *Entrepreneur* (Vol. 33, October 2005, No. 10, pp. 98)
Pub: Entrepreneur Media Inc.
Ed: Sara Wilson. **Description:** Profile of Russian-born Oleg Nikishin, who runs a successful Mr. Electric franchise in Pennsylvania. Nikishin offers advice to would-be entrepreneurs.

35940 ■ "Charmed, I'm Sure: Proper Business Etiquette Goes Beyond the Salad Fork" in *Black Enterprise* (Vol. 35, February 2005, No. 7, pp. 64)
Pub: Earl G. Graves Publishing Co. Inc.
Ed: Lee Anna Jackson. **Description:** Proper business etiquette is examined, offering a list of several things that develop effective business skills.

35941 ■ "Cheap Jet Update" in *Forbes* (Vol. 175, January 10, 2005, No. 1, pp. 31)
Pub: Forbes Magazine Inc.
Ed: Rich Karlgaard. **Description:** Profile of Bill Lear, creator of the Learjet, is presented. Lear is the last entrepreneur to build, certify and sell a business jet.

35942 ■ "Check It Out" in *Entrepreneur* (Vol. 32, November 2004, No. 11, pp. 14)
Pub: Entrepreneur Media Inc.
Description: Nancy Michaels latest offering, Perfecting Your Pitch: 10 Proven Strategies/or Winning the Clients Everyone Wants, shows how entrepreneurs can generate new clients or customers and close deals.

35943 ■ "Chief concern" in *Entrepreneur* (Vol. 31, No. 4, April 2003, pp. 51)
Pub: Entrepreneur Media Inc.
Ed: David Lipschultz. **Description:** The need for hiring a chief financial officer for companies is examined; one question to ask in making a determination is whether the bill from an accounting firm is higher than the salary of a seasoned financial manager.

35944 ■ "Chief Risk Officer No Solution" in *American Banker* (Vol. 170, February 4, 2005, No. 24, pp. 11)
Pub: Thomson Financial Media Inc.
Description: Separating business operations from risk management can lead to disjointed decision-making for a company. Ways to make risk management a business support function are critiqued.

35945 ■ *China's Rational Entrepreneurs: The Development of the New Private Business Sector*
Pub: Routledge
Ed: Barbara Krug. **Released:** March 2004. **Price:** $104.95 (US), $149.95 (Canadian). **Description:** Difficulties faced by entrepreneurs in China are discussed, including analysis for understanding their behavior and relations with local governments in order to secure long-term business success.

35946 ■ "A Class Act" in *Entrepreneur* (Vol. 32, December 2004, No. 12, pp. 61)
Pub: Entrepreneur Media Inc.
Ed: C.J. Prince. Description: Increasingly, entrepreneurs are taking courses designed to assist in running a business, including leadership, finance, accounting and economics.

35947 ■ "A Clean Slate" in *Entrepreneur* (Vol. 31, No. 11, November 2003, pp. 94)
Pub: Entrepreneur Media, Inc.
Ed: Juanita Weaver. Description: Entrepreneurial creativity can be hampered by those unwilling to make room for new ideas. Starting fresh can lead to new innovations.

35948 ■ "Cleantech Becomes Catalyst" in *Crain's Detroit Business* (Vol. 22, November 20, 2006, No. 47, pp. 13)
Pub: Crain Communications Inc. - Detroit
Ed: Tom Henderson. Description: Financial investment firm focuses in on green tech businesses for venture capital and funding. Brighton based firms now has three subsidiaries and holds trade shows in the U.S. and Europe to match investors with companies that market clean products and technology.

35949 ■ "The Clear Leader: Marcus Buckingham Has Spent a Lot of Time Watching Leadership At Its Best" in *Fast Company* (March 2005, No. 92)
Pub: Gruner & Jahr USA Publishing
Ed: Bill Breen. Description: Marcus Buckingham, researcher, discusses the heart of true leadership. Buckingham has authored a book that explains how strong, successful leaders are compelled by the future.

35950 ■ "Clear leadership" in *Women in Business* (Vol. 54, No. 5, September-October 2002, pp. 41)
Pub: The ABWA Company, Inc.
Ed: Andrew Harvey. Description: Leadership requires a vision of where an organization will be taken.

35951 ■ "Cloning Around" in *Entrepreneur* (Vol. 32, No. 1, January 2004, pp. 130)
Pub: Entrepreneur Media, Inc.
Ed: Andrew A. Caffey. Description: Things necessary to launch a successful franchise are examined.

35952 ■ "Colorado Man Helped Contribute to Overseas Tech Development" in *Colorado Springs Business Journal* (February 28, 2003)
Pub: Dolan Media Newswires
Ed: Marylou Doehrman. Description: Profile of Chet Sulewski, who retired from Johns Manville, after spending 35 years as senior vice president, promoting overseas technological development. Sulewski now owns a liquor store that is co-managed by his two sons.

35953 ■ "Coming of Age: Americans Are Hitting 50 and Finding They're Anything But Over the Hill" in *Entrepreneur*
Pub: Entrepreneur Media Inc.
Ed: Sara Wilson. Description: Several entrepreneurs over the age of 50 who purchased franchises are profiled.

35954 ■ "Commentary: Three Steps to Becoming a Business Leader in Your Field" in *Long Island Business News* (February 13, 2004)
Pub: Dolan Media Newswires
Description: Interview with Martha Ann Walther, one of the most impressive women in business today. Walther is vice president of operations for Triborough Bridge and Tunnel Authority and believes that being perceived as a leader can be a career-making factor for women in every industry at any stage of her career.

35955 ■ "Common Ground" in *Pittsburgh Business Times* (Vol. 23, No. 7, September 5, 2003, pp. 23)
Pub: Pittsburgh Business Times
Ed: Suzanne Elliott. Description: Profiles of six women-owned businesses on Penn Avenue in Pittsburgh, Pennsylvania are presented.

35956 ■ *Common Problems; Common Sense Solutions: Practical Advice for Small Business Owners*
Pub: iUniverse, Incorporated
Ed: Greg Hadley. Released: September 2004. Price: $14.95. Description: Common sense advice for entrepreneurs running a small business.

35957 ■ *Common Sense Business: Starting, Operating, and Growing Your Small Business-In Any Economy!*
Pub: HarperInformation
Ed: Steve Gottry. Released: August 2005. Price: $19.95 (US), $26.95 (Canadian). Description: Strategies for starting, operating and growing a small business in any economy. .

35958 ■ "Common Sense Still Rules in the Heartland" in *Ingram's* (Vol. 28, No. 5, May 2002, pp. 37)
Pub: Show Me Publishing, Inc.
Ed: Jack Cashill. Description: Profile of Pat McCown and Brett Gordon, who build McCown Gordon Construction LLC, a company based not on project but relationships. McCown Gordon is now one of the top 20 construction companies in Kansas City.

35959 ■ *The Commonsense Way to Build Wealth: One Entrepreneur Shares His Secrets*
Pub: Griffin Publishing Group
Ed: Jack Chou. Released: September 2004. Price: $19.95. Description: Entrepreneurial tips to accumulate wealth, select the proper business or franchise, choose and manage rental property, and how to negotiate a good lease.

35960 ■ "Community" in *Inc.* (September 2005, pp. 88)
Pub: Inc. Magazine
Ed: Darren Dahl. Description: Entrepreneurs, lawyers, MBAs and PhDs meet monthly in Newburyport, Massachusetts to discuss ways to apply business lessons learned from the book club's monthly selection.

35961 ■ "Company Crisis: CEO Under Fire" in *Hispanic Business* (March 2003, pp. 54-56)
Pub: Hispanic Business
Ed: Scott Williams. Description: Crisis management guidelines for CEOs and other top management executives are presented for times when a company is faced with an emergency.

35962 ■ *The Company We Keep: Reinventing Small Business for People, Community, and Place*
Pub: Chelsea Green Publishing
Ed: John Abrams. Released: May 2005. Price: $27.50 (US), $31.50 (Canadian). Description: The new business trend in social entrepreneurship as a business plan enables small business owners to meet the triple bottom line of profits for people (employees and owners), community, and the environment.

35963 ■ "Competing models of entrepreneurial intentions" in *Journal of Business Venturing* (Vol. 15, No. 5-6, September-November 2000, pp. 411)
Pub: Elsevier Science, Inc.
Ed: Norris F. Krueger, Jr., Michael D. Reilly, Alan L. Carsrud. Description: A new study compares the ability of two models designed to predict entrepreneurship.

35964 ■ *The Complete Idiot's Guide to Finance for Small Business*
Pub: Penguin Group Incorporated
Ed: Kenneth E. Little. Released: April 2006. Price: $19.95. Description: Financial experts helps small business owners through strategies for long-term financial success.

35965 ■ *The Complete Small Business Guide: A Sourcebook for New and Small Businesses*
Pub: John Wiley & Sons, Incorporated
Ed: Colin Barrow. Released: March 2006. Price: $27.95. Description: Sourcebook for creating new small companies and running established small businesses.

35966 ■ "Compliments to Piropos" in *Ingram's* (Vol. 28, No. 5, May 2002, pp. 52)
Pub: Show Me Publishing, Inc.
Description: Profile of Christina and Gary Worden, owners of Piropos, an upscale Argentinean restaurant located at Parkville, in Kansas City.

35967 ■ *Confessions of a Serial Entrepreneur: Why I Can't Stop Starting Over*
Pub: John Wiley and Sons Inc.
Ed: Stuart Skorman. Released: February 2007. Price: $27.99. Description: Profile of Stuart Skorman who was raised in a retail family; Skorman shares his business success.

35968 ■ "Connections for Business" in *Black Enterprise* (Vol. 35, November 2004, No. 4, pp. 81)
Pub: Earl G. Graves Publishing Co. Inc.
Ed: Matthew S. Scott. Description: Profile of Hamet Watt, former partner in a North Carolina venture capital firm called New Africa Opportunity Fund, that helps black and minority-owned companies secure funding. Four years later Watt joined NextMedium Inc., but is also committed to mentoring minority entrepreneurs.

35969 ■ "Consulting the Homeland" in *Crain's New York Business* (Vol. 23, January 29, 2007, No. 5, pp. F9)
Pub: Crain Communications, Inc.
Ed: Samantha Marshall. Description: Profile of Wendy Cai, director of Chinese Services Group, Deloitte & Touche USA, and one-time owner of e-commerce company Hagglers.com. She is one of the youngest directors in Deloitte's history and advises Fortune 500 companies on China investments ranging from $10 to $50 million.

35970 ■ "Contact sport: now that's how you play the networking game" in *Entrepreneur* (Vol. 31, No. 6, June 2003, pp. 28)
Pub: Entrepreneur Media Inc.
Ed: Joshua Kurlantzick. Description: The Ultimate Frisbee Game has become one of the fastest-growing participant sports, according to the Ultimate Players Association. The games popularity has attracted entrepreneurs, making it a great place for business networking.

35971 ■ "Convention Calendar" in *Black Enterprise* (Vol. 37, December 2006, No. 5, pp. 74)
Pub: Earl G. Graves Publishing Co. Inc.
Description: Listing of conferences and summits targeting African American business owners and executives.

35972 ■ "A Conversation With Robin Asher, Clark Hill, LLC" in *Crain's Detroit Business* (Vol. 23, February 5, 2007, No. 6, pp. 11)
Pub: Crain Communications Inc. - Detroit
Ed: Tom Henderson. Description: Patent attorney discusses new patent process rules expected to be in effect later this year that would streamline the patent process. Supreme Court decision could help define what makes an idea obvious and not rely on technicalities and fine print.

35973 ■ "A Cool $2 Billion" in *Hispanic Business* (June 2005, pp. 32, 34, 36, 38)
Pub: Hispanic Business
Ed: Joel Russell. Description: The Related Group of Florida is the first $2 billion company listed on the Hispanic Business 500. The firm builds upscale condominiums.

35974 ■ "Coping with change" in *Women In Business* (Vol. 52, No. 3, May 2000, pp. 22)
Pub: The ABWA Co., Inc.
Ed: Mary M. Witherspoon. Description: Four different personality types are identified and how each type manages change in their personal and/or professional lives.

35975 ■ *Corporate Crisis and Risk Management: Modeling, Strategies and SME Application*

Pub: Elsevier Science and Technology Books

Ed: M. Aba-Bulgu; S.M.N. Islam. **Released:** December 2006. **Price:** $115.00. **Description:** Methods and tools for handling corporate risk and crisis management are profiled for small to medium-sized businesses.

35976 ■ *Corporate Entrepreneurship & Innovation*

Pub: Thomson South-Western

Ed: Michael H. Morris; Donald F. Kuratko. **Released:** January 2007. **Price:** $104.95. **Description:** Innovation is the key to running a successful small business. The book helps entrepreneurs to develop the skills and business savvy to sustain a competitive edge.

35977 ■ *Corporate Entrepreneurship: Top Managers and New Business Creation*

Pub: Cambridge University Press

Ed: Vijay Sathe. **Released:** February 2007. **Price:** $35.00. **Description:** Studies covering entrepreneurship and business growth are examined.

35978 ■ **"Corporate Governance"** in *Atlanta Business Chronicle* (Vol. 25, Nov. 8, 2002, No. 22 pp. S1)

Pub: American City Business Publications, Inc.

Description: A panel discussion concerning corporate governance modifications resulting from the Sarbanes-Oxley Act of 2002 and various proposed regulations is presented. General counsels involved in the discussion came from Atlanta-based firms, including Acuity Brands Inc., ChoicePoint Inc., and Turner Broadcasting System Inc.

35979 ■ **"Corporate Ties"** in *Black Enterprise* (Vol. 34, July 2004, No. 12, pp. 41)

Pub: Earl G. Graves Publishing Co. Inc.

Ed: Nicole Lewis. **Description:** Profile of Alice Turner Byrd, owner of Turner Training USA. Byrd's firm provides corporate training to management and staff in CIGNA Corporation's customer service division.

35980 ■ *Country Studies in Entrepreneurship: A Historical Perspective*

Pub: Palgrave Macmillan

Ed: Ioanna Minoglou; Cassis Youssef. **Released:** July 2006. **Price:** $80.00. **Description:** Comparison of eight national entrepreneurial ventures, covering three continents, is discussed.

35981 ■ **"Cover Me: How to Spread the Risk of a Deal Around"** in *Entrepreneur* (Vol. 33, February 2005, No. 2, pp. 73)

Pub: Entrepreneur Media Inc.

Ed: Marc Diener. **Description:** Standards to be set by an attorney when a small business is making a large deal. These standards will help balance risks.

35982 ■ **"Cover Story: The mean streets"** in *Crain's Chicago Business* (Vol.23, September 11, 2000)

Pub: Crain Communications, Inc. Crain Communications, Inc.

Ed: Kevin Davis. **Description:** Patrick Macias has toughened it out in a neighborhood where many business owners have given up and fled. Not even an armed robbery ran him off.

35983 ■ **"Cracks in the Melting Pot"** in *Inc.* (Volume 27, December 2005, No. 12, pp. 27-29)

Pub: Inc. Magazine

Ed: Stephanie Clifford. **Description:** Because of stiff Visa restrictions, entrepreneurial immigrants are finding opportunities overseas. Statistical data included.

35984 ■ **"Craig Rosebraugh's War"** in *Inc.* (October 2005, pp. 136-139, 141-142)

Pub: Inc. Magazine

Ed: Bill Donahue. **Description:** Profile of Craig Rosebraugh, owner of an Oregon restaurant. Rosebraugh discusses his determination to make his business a success and is already working on his exit strategy.

35985 ■ **"Cream of the crop"** in *BlackEnterprise* (Vol. 31, No. 10, May 2001, pp. 47)

Pub: Earl Graves Publishing Co.

Ed: Paula McCoy-Pinderhughes, Roger Barnes. **Description:** The theme of the sixth annual Black Enterprise/Bank of America Entrepreneurs Conference is "Leading in a Changing Economy: Innovation, Transformation, Growth". The Black Enterprise Small Business Awards categories include Emerging Company of the Year, Business Innovator of the Year, the Rising Star Award, and the Kidpreneurs Award. Statistical data included.

35986 ■ **"Creating a Recipe for an Empire"** in *Crain's New York Business* (Vol. 23, January 29, 2007, No. 5, pp. F22)

Pub: Crain Communications, Inc.

Ed: **Description:** Profile of Kenny Lao, co-founder of Rickshaw Dumpling Bar, whose business plan for the casual Chelsea eatery won a contest at Stern and attracted the school's dean, Thomas Cooley, as an investor. Rickshaw's revenues in fiscal 2005 reached $1.3 million and are on track to rise another 12 percent in 2006. He intends to open six more Rickshaw bars within the next few years.

35987 ■ **"Creating Their Own Niche: 2001 Entrepreneurial Spirit Awards"** in *Hispanic Business* (December 2001, pp. 16-17)

Pub: Hispanic Business

Description: The winners of the 2001 Entrepreneurial Spirit Awards are profiled. New firms include Linx Bracelets Inc.; The Creative Partners, an advertising and graphic design firm; North American Latino Beer Industries, Inc., Saavedra Gehlhausen Architects, Zalia cosmetics, and the owners of a Gold's gym.

35988 ■ **"Creativity Regained"** in *Inc.* (September 1, 2003)

Pub: Gruner & Jahr USA Publishing

Ed: Stephen H. Zades. **Description:** Actor, Robert Redford, founded the Sundance Institute, and in the process changed an industry. His theories of innovation and creativity will inspire any entrepreneur to improve his or her business.

35989 ■ **"Crisis Mode: Economic Crises are Trickling Down to Entrepreneurs. How Are They Fighting Back?"** in *Entrepreneur* (Vol. 32, August 2004)

Pub: Entrepreneur Media Inc.

Ed: Chris Penttila. **Description:** Costs for running a small business are hurting entrepreneurs bottom line.

35990 ■ **"Crisis Mode"** in *Entrepreneur* (Vol. 32, December 2004, No. 12, pp. 32)

Pub: Entrepreneur Media Inc.

Ed: Geoff Williams. **Description:** When a personal crisis hits a small business owner, experts recommend giving full disclosure to employees.

35991 ■ **"Critical Mass"** in *Small Business Opportunities* (Summer 2005)

Pub: Harris Publications Inc.

Ed: Dave Anderson. **Description:** Five key issues to run a successful small business are outlined.

35992 ■ **"Crucibles of leadership"** in *Harvard Business Review* (Vol. 80, No. 9, September 2002, pp. 39)

Pub: Harvard Business School Press

Ed: Warren G. Bennis, Robert J. Thomas. **Description:** Various incidents recount the ways executives have successfully coped with adversity.

35993 ■ *Crunch Point: The Secret to Succeeding When it Matters Most*

Pub: American Management Association

Ed: Brian Tracy. **Released:** 2006. **Price:** $17.95.

35994 ■ **"Culture Shock"** in *Entrepreneur* (Vol. 31, No. 9, July 2003, pp. 77)

Pub: Entrepreneur Media, Inc.

Ed: Marc Diener. **Description:** With increasing numbers of international, multinational and transnational corporations, culture is playing a major role in negotiations.

35995 ■ **"Cup of Courtesy"** in *Entrepreneur* (Vol. 33, August 2005, No. 8, pp. 24)

Pub: Entrepreneur Media Inc.

Ed: Kelly Barron. **Description:** Entrepreneurs using a coffeehouse as an office should limit time at a table to one or two hours. Proper etiquette requires consideration of other patrons, especially when using cell phones.

35996 ■ **"Curtain Call?"** in *Entrepreneur* (Vol. 32, October 2004, No. 10, pp. 72)

Pub: Entrepreneur Media Inc.

Ed: David Worrell. **Description:** Profile of Chuck Hawkes, executive coach with DreamsFulfilled in Charlotte, North Carolina. Hawkes helps executives and entrepreneurs discover what they want to do after selling a business or retiring.

35997 ■ **"Cutting-Edge Accountant"** in *Crain's New York Business* (Vol. 23, January 29, 2007, No. 5, pp. F22)

Pub: Crain Communications, Inc.

Ed: Barbara Benson. **Description:** Profile of Vice President of Corporate Development for Health Insurance Plan of Greater New York, Steve Zeng. HIP plans to go public after a merger with Group Health Incorporated.

35998 ■ **"Cybersearch Specialist"** in *Crain's New York Business* (Vol. 23, January 29, 2007, No. 5 ,pp. F16)

Pub: Crain Communications, Inc.

Ed: Amanda Fung. **Description:** Profile of Matthew Greitzer, director of search engine marketing for Avenue A/Razorfish. The firm has garnered more than twenty search marketing campaigns from clients such as Schering-Plough and Verizon and is the largest buyer of search advertising.

35999 ■ **"Cycles teach you patience"** in *Fast Company* (May 2001, pp. 88)

Pub: Fast Company

Ed: Warren Bennis. **Description:** Leadership guru Warren Bennis, discusses economic cycles and how these cycles teach patience to business owners.

36000 ■ **"Dan Case's Next Great IPO"** in *Fast Company* (May 2001, pp. 175)

Pub: Fast Company

Ed: Paul C. Judge. **Description:** Profile of Dan Case, who is helping IPO-starved Silicon Valley adjust to the new realities of competition, finance, and innovation.

36001 ■ **"De la Torre Named to Hall of Fame"** in *Hispanic Business* (Vol. 23, No. 5, May 2001, pp. 20)

Pub: Hispanic Business

Description: Profile of Martha C. de la Torre, publisher of the Southern California Spanish language weekly El Clasificado. Ms. de la Torre was inducted into the National Association of Women Business Owners Hall of Fame in March 2001.

36002 ■ *Dead on Arrival: How the Anti-Business Backlash is Destroying Entrepreneurship in America and What We Can Still Do About It!*

Pub: HarperCollins Publishers, Inc.

Ed: Bernie Marcus; Steve Gottry. **Released:** November 2006. **Price:** $23.95. **Description:** Bernie Marcus, Home Depot leader, addresses regulations hurting small businesses in America.

36003 ■ **"Dealflop: Good night, sweetheart"** in *Red Herring* (No. 102, August 15, 2001, pp. 31)

Pub: Herring Communications

Ed: Om Malik. **Description:** Profile of Sabeer Bhatia, one of the two co-founders of the free Internet email service, Hotmail. Since selling Hotmail to Microsoft, Mr. Bhatia has failed to secure financing for his second startup, Arzoo.

36004 ■ **"Decisions, decisions: This book lets you be the judge"** in *Entrepreneur* (Vol. 30, No. 2, February 2002, pp. 22)

Pub: Entrepreneur Media Inc.

Ed: Mark Henricks. **Description:** Review of the book entitled, "Why Didn't I Think of That?", by Charles W.

McCoy Jr. The book is full of innovative-thinking exercises, checklists, anecdotes, challenges, puzzles and more.

36005 ■ *The Definitive Drucker: The Final Word from the Father of Modern Management*
Pub: McGraw-Hill
Ed: Elizabeth Haas Edersheim; A.G. Lafley. **Released:** December 2006. **Price:** $27.95.

36006 ■ **"Dell NFIB The Voice of Small Business"** in *My Business* (June/July 2004, pp. 26-27)
Pub: My Business Magazine
Description: Ten finalists chosen for the Small Business Excellence in Customer Experience Award are profiled. Winners were selected by members of the Herb Kelleher Center for Entrepreneurship at the University of Texas at Austin.

36007 ■ **"Demolition Man: This Entrepreneur Builds His Business by Tearing Things Down"** in *Black Enterprise* (Vol. 34, No. 5, December 2003)
Pub: Earl Graves Publishing Co.
Ed: Glenn Townes. **Description:** Profile of Jamie Potter and his small business, Cut Core Demolition Company. The Los Angeles, California-based firm specializes in demolition and site cleaning.

36008 ■ **"Designing Woman"** in *Hispanic Business* (January/February 2003, pp. 54-55)
Pub: Hispanic Business
Ed: Tim Dougherty. **Description:** Profile of Marisol Deluna, fashion designer, who donates proceeds from her fashions to fund-raising projects. Ms. Deluna says her designs are fashionable and stylish, but never trendy.

36009 ■ **"Desire-more than need-builds a business"** in *Wall Street Journal* (May 21, 2002, pp. B4)
Pub: Wall Street Journal
Ed: Jeff Bailey. **Description:** A survey conducted by Global Entrepreneurship Monitor showed that the most successful entrepreneurs started their business by choice, not necessity.

36010 ■ **"Detroit Free Press Small Business Column"** in *Detroit Free Press* (July 18, 2005)
Pub: Knight-Ridder/Tribune Business News
Ed: Carol Cain. **Description:** Profile of Philip Locke, entrepreneur with years of experience in starting and closing businesses; Locke describes his Cash Now company that advances cash to customers. His goal is to have ten master franchise agreements by December 2006.

36011 ■ **"Develop a Mission Statement for Your Business"** in *Home Business* (Vol. 13, January/February 2006, No. 1, pp. 64)
Pub: Home Business Magazine
Ed: Steven D. Strauss. **Description:** Mission statements help keep a business on track and the best time for an entrepreneur to reflect on a business is during the New Year period.

36012 ■ **"Developing performers"** in *Women in Business* (Vol. 53, No. 3, May-June, 2001, pp. 8)
Pub: The ABWA Co. Inc.
Ed: Rachel Warbington. **Description:** Small business owners need to find reliable staff whose skills can be developed to help ease some of the owner's workload. The business owner needs to recognize, develop and monitor their employees' potential.

36013 ■ **"Developing Your Leadership Pipeline"** in *Harvard Business Review* (Vol. 81, No. 12, December 2003, pp. 76)
Pub: Harvard Business School Press
Ed: Jay A conger, Robert M. Fulmer. **Description:** Key guidelines for effective leadership communication in succession management are examined, including identification of linchpin positions, making the transition process transparent, assessment of progress on a regular basis, and maintaining flexibility.

36014 ■ *Developmental Entrepreneurship: Adversity, Risk, and Isolation*
Pub: Elsevier Science and Technology Books
Ed: Craig Galbraith. **Released:** August 2006. **Price:** $99.95. **Description:** Volume five of the series, this book focuses on the fields of entrepreneurship, sociology, and economics. Fifteen articles related to entrepreneurship and small business development within a global environment are included.

36015 ■ **"Different Stripes"** in *Entrepreneur. com* (Vol. 34, February 2006, No. 2, pp. 45)
Pub: Entrepreneur Media Inc.
Ed: Karen Edwards. **Description:** Profile of Chris Lindland and partner Enrique Landa who produce horizontally striped corduroy pants and accessories available only online. The company expects revenues to reach $150,000 to $250,000 its first year.

36016 ■ **"Differentiating Legal Issues by Business Type"** in *Journal of Small Business Management* (Vol. 44, October 2006, No. 4, pp. 563)
Pub: Blackwell Publishing, Inc.
Ed: Sandra Malach; Peter Robinson; Tannis Radcliffe. **Description:** A fundamental issue when forming a business and its strategic operation is developing legal strategies to better protect the assets of the business and entrepreneur. An analysis of data indicated that certain legal issues are relevant to specific types of new ventures while certain legal issues are important to all new ventures. Depending on the category of business, the relevancy of individual legal issues will vary. Statistical data included.

36017 ■ **"Disabled Rise Up As Entrepreneurs"** in *Pacific Business News* (Vol. 41, No. 16, June 27, 2003, pp. 1)
Pub: American City Business Journals
Ed: Eddy Conway. **Description:** The Hawaiian government is sponsoring workshops designed to help disabled people start their own businesses, thus easing welfare roles.

36018 ■ **"Discovering a Spin-Off Business"** in *Home Business* (Vol. 12, March/April 2005, No. 2, pp. 40, 42-43)
Pub: Home Business Magazine
Ed: Priscilla Y. Huff. **Description:** Entrepreneurs share ways they used spin-off ventures to attract new customers and revitalize old ones.

36019 ■ *Divine Wisdom at Work: 10 Universal Principles for Enlightened Entrepreneurs*
Pub: Aha! House
Ed: Tricia Molloy. **Released:** July 2006. **Price:** $20.00. **Description:** Entrepreneurial advice for managing a small enterprise is given using inspiration, anecdotes and exercises.

36020 ■ **"DIY Renovator Gains Ground"** in *Crain's New York Business* (Vol. 23, January 29, 2007, No. 5, pp. F24)
Pub: Crain Communications, Inc.
Ed: Tom Fredrickson. **Description:** Profile of Sara Mirski, Managing Director of Development for Boymelgreen Developers, who leads a team of engineers, architects, and construction planners.

36021 ■ **"Do you have a well-designed organization?"** in *Harvard Business Review* (Vol. 80, No. 3, March 2002, pp. 117)
Pub: Harvard Business School Press
Ed: Michael Goold, Andrew Campbell. **Description:** An executive's job of creating a new organizational design and the nine tests of organization design, which can either evaluate an existing structure or create a new one are discussed.

36022 ■ **"Do You Work for Free?"** in *My Business* (February/March 2004, pp. 50)
Pub: My Business Magazine
Ed: Susan Palmquist. **Description:** When negotiating with potential clients, it is important to let a client have only a sampling of your expertise and to remain professional.

36023 ■ **"Don Coleman"** in *Crain's Detroit Business* (Vol. 19, No. 1, January 6, 2003, pp. 11)
Pub: Crain Communications Inc., Detroit
Ed: Jennette Smith. **Description:** Profile of Don Coleman, chairman and CEO of the GlobalHue advertising agency, a one-stop shop for all types of multicultural advertising.

36024 ■ **"Donny Deutsch"** in *Inc.* (Volume 27, June 2005, No. 6, pp. 104-109)
Pub: Inc. Magazine
Ed: Sasha Issenberg. **Description:** In an interview with Donny Deutsch, advertising executive and talk-show host, Deutsch discusses success.

36025 ■ **"Don't Be a Stranger"** in *Inc.* (January 1, 2005)
Pub: Inc. Magazine
Ed: Laura Rich. **Description:** Alumni programs can be a great way to network and increase business for small companies.

36026 ■ *Don't Bitch, Just Get Rich*
Pub: Simon and Schuster Incorporated
Ed: Toney Fitzgerald. **Released:** June 2006. **Price:** $16.00. **Description:** Advice is given to business leaders to help them shift from the position whereby money has power over you to taking responsibility for life choices in order to meet new challenges.

36027 ■ **"Don't Get Mad, Get Practical"** in *My Business* (April/May 2004, pp. 39)
Pub: My Business Magazine
Description: Ways to diffuse any difficult situation are listed in order to use conflict as a means for business growth.

36028 ■ **"A Dose of Change"** in *Fast Company* (August 2001, pp. 50)
Pub: Fast Company
Ed: Charles Fishman. **Description:** Profile of Kevin Sharer, CEO of Amgen, a biotech company that makes three leading drugs. Sharer discusses adaptability in the business world.

36029 ■ **"Down and Out: Surprise: Many Personal Bankruptcies are Really Business Failures in Disguise"** in *Entrepreneur* (Vol. 32, July 2004)
Pub: Entrepreneur Media Inc.
Ed: Joanne Cleaver. **Description:** Approximately 13 to 14 percent of all personal bankruptcies are really small business bankruptcies. In a recent study of 2,000 personal bankruptcies, it would take respondent small business owners 3.8 years to pay off money owed, and 2.9 years for non-business owners. Statistical data included.

36030 ■ **"Doyenne of Hip Proffers Hot Tips"** in *Crain's New York Business* (Vol. 23, January 29, 2007, No. 5, pp. F9)
Pub: Crain Communications, Inc.
Ed: Elisabeth Butler. **Description:** Profile of Dany Levy and her trendy business, an e-newsletter, Daily Candy. Advertisers are flocking to this Internet publication which expects to generate revenues of $25 million this year.

36031 ■ **"Drawing the Line: The Right Way To Do Business With Friends"** in *Sales & Marketing Management* (Vol. 157, February 2005, No. 2, pp. 18)
Pub: VNU Business Media
Ed: Sara Calabro. **Description:** The best way to handle business relationships with friends is to use the same client-customer principles of other deals, including putting everything in writing.

36032 ■ **"The Dream Achievers"** in *Women in Business* (Vol. 54, No. 2, March-April 2002, pp. 7)
Pub: The ABWA Co Inc.
Ed: Mia Katz. **Description:** Brenda L. Lawrence became the first African American and the first woman to be elected mayor of Southfield, Michigan. She is a member of the Millenium Chapter of the American Business Women's Association.

36033 ■ **"Dream Team or Nightmare Relationship"** in *My Business* (April/May 2003, pp. 34-37)
Pub: My Business Magazine
Ed: Nancy Mann Jackson. **Description:** The trials and tribulations of business partnerships are discussed by various business owners. Tips for making a partnership work successfully include communication, legal advice, and shared responsibilities.

36034 ■ **"Dream Your Way to Success: Think Visualization Is Easier Said than Done?"** in *Black Enterprise* (Vol. 33, No. 6, January 2003, pp. 84)
Pub: Earl Graves Publishing Co.
Ed: Caroline V. Clarke. **Description:** A technique for achieving success through creative visualization is presented.

36035 ■ *Dreams with a Deadline: How to Turn a Strategy for Tomorrow Into a Plan for Today*
Pub: Pearson Education, Limited
Ed: Jacques Horovitz; Anne-Valerie Ohlsson-Corboz. **Released:** November 2006. **Price:** $54.00. **Description:** Tips for successful entrepreneurship are covered.

36036 ■ *Drive a Modest Car: And 16 Other Keys to Small Business Success*
Pub: NOLO
Ed: Ralph E. Warner, Jake Warner. **Released:** September 2004. **Price:** $24.99. **Description:** Seventeen keys to successful entrepreneurship.

36037 ■ **"Duckworth Realty Inc."** in *Mississippi Business Journal* (Vol. 28, September 2006, No. 36, pp. 6)
Pub: Venture Publications, Inc.
Description: Profile of John Michael Holtmann of Duckworth Realty Inc. He serves as a commercial sales broker and focuses on leasing, sales, and tenant representation.

36038 ■ **"E-Brands: Building an Internet Business at Breakneck Speed"** in *Harvard Business Review* (Vol. 78, No. 4, July 2000, pp. 152)
Pub: Harvard Business School Publishing Corp.
Ed: John T. Landry. **Description:** Phil Carpenter, the founder of Point Cast, provides several case studies of Web consumer firms that have achieved success.

36039 ■ *E-Myth Mastery: The Seven Essential Disciplines for Building a World Class Company*
Pub: HarperCollins Publishers Inc.
Ed: Michael E. Gerber. **Released:** March 2007. **Price:** $16.95. **Description:** Leadership, marketing, money, management, lead conversion, lead generation, client fulfillment are the seven keys to successful entrepreneurship.

36040 ■ **"The Early Bird Gets the Worm"** in *Black Enterprise* (Vol. 37, January 2007, No. 6, pp. 111)
Pub: Earl G. Graves Publishing Co. Inc.
Ed: Tykisha N. Lundy. **Description:** General Motors hosts the Black Enterprise Conference And Expo: Where Deals Are Made at Walt Disney World's Swan and Dolphin Resort, May 9-12. The conference will offer great information to entrepreneurs.

36041 ■ **"East Meets West"** in *Entrepreneur* (Vol. 32, December 2004, No. 12, pp. 24)
Pub: Entrepreneur Media Inc.
Ed: Mark Henricks. **Description:** Review of The Art of Business. Author Raymond T. Yeh explores ways in which business leaders have created a new art of business that merges Eastern and Western concepts for success.

36042 ■ **"Easy Does It"** in *Entrepreneur* (Vol. 28, No. 6, June 2000, pp. 22)
Pub: Entrepreneur Media Inc.
Ed: Mark Henricks. **Description:** Michelle Paster's education business has no debt, more customers than it can handle, and a hands-on owner whose concern for quality requires her to do virtually everything herself.

36043 ■ **"Eat Your Heart Out"** in *Entrepreneur* (Vol. 33, February 2005, pp. 106)
Pub: Entrepreneur Media Inc.
Ed: Esther Nguonly. **Description:** Profile of Chuck DiRocco of Chuck D's LLC. DiRocco makes vanilla flavored cookies that are shaped into caricatures of famous celebrities. The startup was formed in 2003.

36044 ■ **"The Economic Ground War"** in *Hispanic Business* (March 2003, pp. 18)
Pub: Hispanic Business
Ed: Joel Russell. **Description:** Small business executives and economic experts are predicting a slowdown for the first half of 2003. It is hoped that spending will increase when global political threats are stabilized.

36045 ■ *The Economics of Entrepreneurship*
Pub: Edward Elgar Publishing, Incorporated
Ed: Parker. **Released:** April 2006. **Price:** $240.00. **Description:** Previously published articles influencing research into the economic structure of entrepreneurship are examined.

36046 ■ *The Economics of Self-Employment and Entrepreneurship*
Pub: Cambridge University Press
Ed: Simon C. Parker. **Released:** July 2006. **Price:** $50.00. **Description:** The importance of self-employment and entrepreneurship in a modern economy is explored.

36047 ■ **"Economy.sup.2"** in *Entrepreneur* (Vol. 30, No. 2, February 2002,)
Pub: Entrepreneur Media Inc.
Ed: Geoff Williams. **Description:** Profile of and interview with Nathan Myhrvold, CEO of Intellectual Ventures, a private entrepreneurial partnership in Bellevue, Washington.

36048 ■ **"Ed Otto, Director of Biotechnology at RCCC"** in *Charlotte Observer* (February 8, 2007)
Pub: Knight-Ridder/Tribune Business News
Ed: Gail Smith-Arrants. **Description:** Profile of Ed Otto, director of biotechnology at Rowan-Cabarrus Community College. Before taking the position at RCCC, Otto directed the Food and Drug Administration office responsible for regulating cellular, tissue and gene therapies products.

36049 ■ *Edgewalkers: People and Organizations That Take Risks, Build Bridges, and Break New Ground*
Pub: Greenwood Publishing Group, Inc.
Ed: Judi Neal. **Released:** October 2006. **Price:** $39.95. **Description:** Profiles of entrepreneurs who thrive on change and challenge in order to create successful companies in today's complex business climate.

36050 ■ *Effectuation*
Pub: Edward Elgar Publishing, Incorporated
Ed: Sarasvathy. **Released:** October 2006. **Price:** $85.00. **Description:** Effectuation is the idea that the future is unpredictable while being controllable. A study of 27 entrepreneurs shows effective effectuators.

36051 ■ **"The 80-20 Rule: It's Not Just a Glib Remark"** in *Barron's* (Vol. 82, No. 57, February, 10, 2003, pp. 39)
Pub: Barron's
Ed: Thomas G. Donlan. **Description:** Goldman Sachs CEO, Henry M. Paulson, Jr. was correct in citing the 80-20 rule, which is one of the most true management aphorisms ever invented. A small proportion of people almost always produce most of the work, innovation, and results in most organizations.

36052 ■ **"Elbows Off the Table"** in *My Business* (February/March 2004, pp. 14)
Pub: My Business Magazine
Ed: Julie Bawden Davis. **Description:** Rules of etiquette that still apply to be successful are listed. Manners are critical to business success.

36053 ■ **"Elite Company"** in *Hispanic Business* (December 2002, pp. 54)
Pub: Hispanic Business
Description: The four finalists in the Hispanic Business magazine's Entrepreneur of the Year award are profiled. The finalists hail from the aerospace, auto retailing, and telecommunications industries.

36054 ■ *The Emerging Digital Economy: Entrepreneurship, Clusters, and Policy*
Pub: Springer
Ed: Borje Johansson; Charlie Karlsson; Roger Stough. **Released:** August 2006. **Price:** $119.00. **Description:** The new economy, or digital economy, and its impact on the way industries and firms choose to locate and cluster geographically.

36055 ■ **"The empire strikes back; Counterrevolutionary strategies for industry leaders"** in *Harvard Business Review* (Vol. 80, Nov. 2002, pp. 66)
Pub: Harvard Business School Press
Ed: Richard D'Aveni. **Description:** Five ways that industry leaders can respond to revolutionary business models or disruptive technologies. The strategies are containment, shaping, absorption, neutralization and annulment.

36056 ■ *Employee Management for Small Business*
Pub: Self-Counsel Press, Incorporated
Ed: Lin Grensing-Pophal. **Released:** August 2005. **Price:** $17.95. **Description:** Management tools to help entrepreneurs maintain an effective human resources plan for a small company.

36057 ■ **"En Garde! Herby Raynaud's Fencing Fancy"** in *Black Enterprise* (Vol. 34, No. 3, October 2003, pp. 139)
Pub: Earl Graves Publishing Co.
Ed: Ashley Gibson. **Description:** Profile of Herby Raynaud, 32-year-old software developer for the Union Bank of Switzerland, located in Weehawken, New Jersey. Raynaud is an avid fencer and is currently training for the U.S. Olympic team.

36058 ■ *Encyclopedia of Small Business*
Pub: Thomson Gale
Ed: Arsen Darnay; Monique D. Magee; Kevin Hillstrom. **Released:** November 2006. **Description:** Concise encyclopedia of small business information.

36059 ■ **"The End of Entrepreneurship As We Know It"** in *Entrepreneur* (Vol. 28, No. 9, September 2000, pp. 18)
Pub: Entrepreneur Media Inc.
Ed: Brian O'Connell. **Description:** The fall in the NASDAQ exchange is hurting many entrepreneurs, but most are resisting the temptation to return to corporate life.

36060 ■ **"End of the Road? Success Isn't a Destination; It's Simply Undertaking the Journey"** in *Entrepreneur* (Vol. 31, No. 9, September 2003)
Pub: Entrepreneur Media, Inc.
Ed: Romanus Wolter. **Description:** Rules for entrepreneurs to follow when facing the challenges of an ever-changing business atmosphere are listed.

36061 ■ **"The enemies of trust"** in *Harvard Business Review* (Vol. 81, No. 2, February 2003, pp. 88)
Pub: Harvard Business School Press
Ed: Robert Galford, Ann Siebold Drapeau. **Description:** The relationship between a business and its client and a company's relationship with its employees is contrasted showing that the business/client relationship allows for trust to develop easier than that of the company/managers/employees relationships.

36062 ■ **"Engineer Turned Winemaker Became Toast of State Industry"** in *Milwaukee Journal Sentinel* (December 14, 2005)
Pub: Journal Sentinel, Inc.
Ed: Amy Rabideau Silvers. **Description:** Profile of Robert Wollersheim, former engineer, who bought an abandoned vineyard in 1972. After acquiring Cedar Creek Winery in 1990, he became one of the largest wine producers in the Midwest.

36063 ■ "Enlighten Me: One Entrepreneur Brings Business-and Spirituality-to New Heights" in *Entrepreneur* **(Vol. 33, March 2005, No. 3, pp. 93)**
Pub: Entrepreneur Media Inc.
Ed: Mark Henricks. **Description:** Profile of Marc Lesser, founder and former CEO of Brush Dance, a greeting card company, with 15 employees and $2.5 million in sales yearly.

36064 ■ *Enlightened Leadership: Best Practice Guidelines and Timesaving Tools for Easily Implementing Learning Organizations*
Pub: Learning House Publishing, Incorporated
Ed: Alan G. Thomas; Ralph L. LoVuolo; Jeanne C. Hillson. **Released:** September 2006, printable 3 times/year. **Price:** $21.00. **Description:** Book provides the tools required to create a learning organization management model along with a step-by-step guide for team planning and learning. The strategy works as a manager's self-help guide as well as offering continuous learning and improvement for company-wide success.

36065 ■ *Enterprise, Entrepreneurship and Innovation: Concepts, Context and Commercialization*
Pub: Elsevier Science and Technology Books
Ed: Robin Lowe, Sue Marriott. **Released:** June 2006. **Price:** $39.95. **Description:** Application of enterprise, innovation and entrepreneurship are discussed to help companies grow.

36066 ■ *Enterprise and Small Business: Principles, Practice and Policy*
Pub: Pearson Education, Limited
Ed: Sara Carter; Dylan Jones-Evans. **Released:** September 2006. **Price:** $79.50. **Description:** Introduction to small business, challenges of a changing environment, and the nature of entrepreneurship are among the issues covered.

36067 ■ "Entrepreneur Column" in *Entrepreneur Column* **(April 11, 2003)**
Pub: Knight-Ridder/Tribune Business News
Ed: David Meier. **Description:** Tax information when using a car for business purposes is provided.

36068 ■ "Entrepreneur Column" in *Entrepreneur.com* **(January 25, 2007)**
Pub: Entrepreneur Media Inc.
Ed: Kim T. Gordon. **Description:** Eight important considerations to help improve your marketing and advertising strategies by renown marketing expert.

36069 ■ "Entrepreneur Foundation Retools Its Teaching Model" in *Business First Columbus* **(Vol. 18, No. 40, March 24, 2002, pp. A11)**
Pub: Business First Columbus, Inc.
Ed: Laura Newpoff. **Description:** The non-profit Ohio Foundation for Entrepreneurial Education has decided to stop offering business development courses for small businesses, and will instead offer private label custom programs to small businesses.

36070 ■ *The Entrepreneur Next Door: Discover the Secrets to Financial Independence*
Pub: Entrepreneur Press
Ed: William F. Wagner. **Released:** May 2006. **Price:** $19.95. **Description:** Traits required to become a successful entrepreneur are highlighted.

36071 ■ *The Entrepreneur and Small Business Problem Solver*
Pub: John Wiley & Sons, Incorporated
Ed: William A. Cohen. **Released:** December 2005. **Price:** $24.95 (US), $31.99 (Canadian). **Description:** Revised edition of the resource for entrepreneurs and small business owners that covers everything from start-up financing and loans to new product promotion and more.

36072 ■ "Entrepreneur of the Year" in *Crain's Detroit Business* **(Vol. 16, No. 19, May 8, 2000, pp. 42)**
Pub: Crain Communications, Inc.
Description: Ernst & Young L.L.P. announced the 44 finalists for Michigan's 2000 Entrepreneur of the Year Awards. The awards honor successful entrepreneurs and business people who have encouraged entrepreneurs.

36073 ■ *The Entrepreneurial Culture Network Advantage Within Chinese and Irish Software Firms*
Pub: Edward Elgar Publishing, Incorporated
Ed: Tsang. **Released:** October 2006. **Price:** $95.00. **Description:** Ways national cultural heritage influences entrepreneurial ventures are discussed.

36074 ■ *Entrepreneurial Decision-Making Individuals, Tasks and Cognitions*
Pub: Edward Elgar Publishing, Incorporated
Ed: Gusfafsson. **Released:** December 2006. **Price:** $85.00. **Description:** Entrepreneurial decision-making is examined by comparing various individuals with differing levels of expertise and potential.

36075 ■ "Entrepreneurial Enthusiasm" in *Black Enterprise* **(Vol. 34, No. 7, February 2004, pp. 32)**
Pub: Earl Graves Publishing Co.
Ed: Carolyn M. Brown. **Description:** Approximately 41 percent of American youth feel that owning a business will provide more security than working for a company, and 81 percent believe there is more job satisfaction owning your own company rather working for someone else.

36076 ■ "Entrepreneurial Event at Automation Alley Jan. 12" in *Crain's Detroit Business* **(Vol. 22, January 2, 2006, No. 1, pp. 17)**
Pub: Crain Communications Inc. - Detroit
Ed: Joanne Scharich. **Description:** Three emerging technology companies, IMX, Check the Crib, and Secure Crossing, are scheduled to present business plans during the fourth Entrepreneurial Initiative of Southeast Michigan. Venture capitalists, bankers, and angel investors will provide feedback after the presentations.

36077 ■ *Entrepreneurial Finance*
Pub: Pearson Education, Limited
Ed: Philip J. Adelman; Alan M. Marks. **Released:** July 2006. **Price:** $87.35. **Description:** Financial aspects of running a small business are covered; topics include sole proprietorships, partnerships, limited liability companies, and private corporations.

36078 ■ *Entrepreneurial Finance: A Casebook*
Pub: John Wiley and Sons Inc.
Ed: Paul A. Gompers; William Sahlman. **Released:** September 2006. **Price:** $63.00. **Description:** Investment analysis, entrepreneurial financing, harvesting, and renewal in the entrepreneurial firm are among the topics discussed.

36079 ■ *The Entrepreneurial Imperative: How America's Economic Miracle Will Reshape the World (And Change Your Life)*
Pub: HarperCollins Publishers, Inc.
Ed: Carl J. Schramm. **Released:** October 2006. **Price:** $24.95. **Description:** Carl Schramm, president of Kauffman Foundation discusses the secret to America's economy.

36080 ■ *The Entrepreneurial PC*
Pub: Bell Springs Publishing
Ed: Bernard J. David. **Price:** $17.95. **Description:** Outlines a hundred businesses you can start using word processing, desktop publishing, online information research, database marketing, e-mail, computer graphics, and accounting, bookkeeping and payroll programs.

36081 ■ *Entrepreneurial Small Business Resources: Resource-Based Perspective*
Pub: Edgar Elgar Publishing, Incorporated
Ed: Dean A. Shepherd. **Released:** August 2005. **Price:** $110.00. **Description:** Analysis of entrepreneurial activities of small businesses focusing on why some businesses are successful, while others fail.

36082 ■ "Entrepreneurial Spirit Alive and Well in U.S." in *Hispanic Business* **(October 2006, pp. 18)**
Pub: Hispanic Business
Description: According to the seventh annual U.S. Global Entrepreneurship Monitor, business innovation is still on the rise.

36083 ■ "Entrepreneurial Spirit" in *Black Enterprise* **(Vol. 31, No. 4, November 2000, pp. 50)**
Pub: Earl Graves Publishing Co.
Ed: Chr150ine Albano. **Description:** Independent literary agent eyes financial freedom with aggressive investment and savings strategies.

36084 ■ *Entrepreneurial Strategies: New Technologies and Emerging Markets*
Pub: Blackwell Publishing Limited
Ed: Arnold Cooper; Sharon Alvarez; Alejandro Carrera; Luiz Mesquita; Robert Vassolo. **Released:** August 2006. **Price:** $69.95. **Description:** Ideas to help a small business expand into emerging market economies (EMEs) are discussed. Despite the high failure rate, this book helps a small firm develop a successful plan.

36085 ■ *Entrepreneurial Strategy Emerging Businesses in Declining Industries*
Pub: Edward Elgar Publishing, Incorporated
Ed: Cassia. **Released:** July 2006. **Price:** $110.00. **Description:** Role of entrepreneurship in context of older and declining industries is explored. The book offers insight into entrepreneurial dynamics behind emerging businesses in declining industries, especially the roles of resources processes and people.

36086 ■ *Entrepreneuring: The Ten Commandments for Building a Growth Company*
Pub: Addison Wesley Longman, Inc.
Ed: Steven C. Brandt. **Released:** 3rd ed. 1997. **Price:** $14.95.

36087 ■ "Entrepreneurs: Can Detroit Grow Them? :Part 2 of 2" in *Crain's Detroit Business* **(Vol. 22, November 27, 2006, No. 48, pp. 28)**
Pub: Crain Communications Inc. - Detroit
Description: Detroit lags behind other cities in developing entrepreneurs. Advice is provided in this column to address the things that hinder individual development and risk taking.

36088 ■ *The Entrepreneur's Edge: Finding Money, Making Money, Keeping Money*
Pub: Silver Lake Publishing
Ed: Daniel Hogan. **Released:** October 2006. **Price:** $24.95. **Description:** Advice for starting, running and growing a new business is given.

36089 ■ *Entrepreneur's Handbook*
Pub: SterlingHouse Publishers
Ed: Roberta E. Lonsdale and Lew Gaiter. **Released:** 1998. **Price:** $17.95.

36090 ■ "Entrepreneurs Have Accepted the Challenge" in *Hispanic Business* **(Vol. 23, No. 11, November 2001, pp. 30, 32)**
Pub: Hispanic Business Inc.
Description: Highlights from the Eleventh Annual Hispanic Business Magazine Entrepreneur of the Year Award ceremony are presented.

36091 ■ "Entrepreneurs Learn to Implement Ideas" in *San Fernando Valley Business Journal* **(Vol. 11, November 2006, No. 23, pp. 1)**
Pub: San Fernando Valley Business Journal Associates

Ed: Chris Coates. **Description:** Overview of the Dream and Discover 2006 Entrepreneurs Conference at College of the Canyons. The conference included four seminars ranging from small business practices, growth strategies and the various challenges of starting a business.

36092 ■ *The Entrepreneur's Strategy Guide: Ten Keys for Achieving Marketplace Leadership*
Pub: Greenwood Publishing Group, Incorporated
Ed: Tom Cannon. **Released:** September 2006. **Price:** $44.95. **Description:** Ten principles of marketplace leadership are explored. The book provides a plan for small businesses, including diagnostics, checklists, and other interactive exercises to study both external and internal principles.

36093 ■ *The Entrepreneur's Strategy Guide: Ten Keys for Achieving Marketplace Leadership and Operational Excellence*
Pub: Greenwood Publishing Group, Incorporated
Ed: Tom Cannon. **Released:** June 2006. **Price:** $38.45. **Description:** Business plan for entrepreneurs is offered from a fifty-year business veteran. The book is divided into tow parts: the marketplace and the internal environment.

36094 ■ *"Entrepreneurs Under Siege" in Hispanic Business* (Vol. 23, No. 11, November 2001, pp. 36-37)
Pub: Hispanic Business Inc.
Ed: Tim Dougherty. **Description:** The terrorist attacks in Washington and New York have cast a pall over small business community nationwide. Experts are divided on long-term forecasts and what the federal government's response should be to small business.

36095 ■ *Entrepreneurship*
Pub: Thomson South-Western
Ed: Donald F. Kuratko; Richard M. Hodgetts. **Released:** April 2006. **Price:** $125.95. **Description:** Understanding the process of entrepreneurship.

36096 ■ *Entrepreneurship: A Process Perspective*
Pub: Thomson South-Western
Ed: Robert A. Baron; Scott A. Shane. **Released:** February 2007. **Price:** $137.95. **Description:** Entrepreneurial process covering team building, finances, business plan, legal issues, marketing, growth and exit strategies.

36097 ■ *Entrepreneurship As Social Change: A Third New Movements in Entrepreneurship Book*
Pub: Edward Elgar Publishing, Incorporated
Ed: Steyaert. **Released:** February 2007. **Price:** $120.00. **Description:** Third book in a series, the edition examines entrepreneurship as a societal phenomenon.

36098 ■ *"Entrepreneurship Center Receives Gift" in Hispanic Business* (March 2005, pp. 14)
Pub: Hispanic Business
Description: Sergio Pino, chairman and CEO of Century Homebuilders, has given $2 million to Florida International University's Global Entrepreneurship Center.

36099 ■ *Entrepreneurship and Economic Growth*
Pub: Edward Elgar Publishing, Incorporated
Ed: Carree. **Released:** October 2006. **Price:** $195.00. **Description:** Historic and country-specific studies and articles regarding entrepreneurship and innovation, growth models, competition and productivity, and empirical evidence.

36100 ■ *Entrepreneurship and Economic Progress*
Pub: Routledge Inc.
Ed: Randall Holcombe. **Released:** October 2006. **Description:** Economic models of economic growth and the ways entrepreneurial progress are highlighted.

36101 ■ *"Entrepreneurship and Ethics: A Literature Review" in Journal of Business Ethics* (Vol. 46, No. 2, August 15, 2003, pp. 99)
Pub: Kluwer Academic Publishers Group
Ed: Francis T. Hannafey. **Description:** During the past twenty years, there has been an increase of new interest being shown in entrepreneurs and their activities; yet only recently has serious research attention been devoted to the ethical problems encountered by entrepreneurs and their organizations.

36102 ■ *Entrepreneurship: Frameworks and Empirical Investigations from Forthcoming Leaders of European Research*
Pub: Elsevier Science and Technology Books
Ed: Johan Wiklund; Dimo Dimov; Jerome A. Katz; Dean Shepherd. **Released:** July 2006. **Price:** $99.95. **Description:** Entrepreneurial research and theory cover the early growth of research-based startups and the role of learning in international entrepreneurship, focusing on Europe.

36103 ■ *Entrepreneurship: From Opportunity to Action*
Pub: Palgrave Macmillan
Ed: David Rae. **Released:** March 2007. **Price:** $63.95 (CND). **Description:** Learning enterprise theory is discussed, focusing on the individual as an entrepreneur and ways to create and take advantage of opportunities.

36104 ■ *Entrepreneurship, Geography, and American Economic Growth*
Pub: Cambridge University Press
Ed: Zoltan Acs; Catherine Armington. **Released:** June 2006. **Price:** $70.00. **Description:** Knowledge among college-educated workers was among the key reasons for economic growth throughout the U.S. in the 1990s.

36105 ■ *Entrepreneurship and the Growth of Firms*
Pub: Edward Elgar Publishing, Incorporated
Ed: Davidsson. **Released:** December 2006. **Price:** $100.00. **Description:** Relationships between entrepreneurial skills and business growth are explored.

36106 ■ *Entrepreneurship, Innovation and Economic Growth*
Pub: Edward Elgar Publishing, Incorporated
Ed: David B. Audretsch. **Released:** July 2006. **Price:** $145.00. **Description:** Links between entrepreneurship, innovation and economic growth are examined.

36107 ■ *Entrepreneurship, Innovation and the Growth Mechanism of the Free-Enterprise Economies*
Pub: Princeton University Press
Ed: Eytan Sheshinski; William J. Baumol. **Released:** January 2007. **Price:** $65.00. **Description:** Scholars address the free-enterprise Western economies.

36108 ■ *"The Entrepreneurship Institute: www.tei.net" in Entrepreneur* (Vol. 32, November 2004, No. 11, pp. 6)
Pub: Entrepreneur Media Inc.
Ed: Steve Cooper. **Description:** The Entrepreneurship Institute offers an online library of more than 100 presentations from 22 cities featuring entrepreneurs and business leaders.

36109 ■ *Entrepreneurship, Investment and Spatial Dynamics Lessons and Implications for an Enlarged EU*
Pub: Edward Elgar Publishing, Incorporated
Ed: Nijkamp. **Released:** September 2006. **Price:** $100.00. **Description:** Understanding the impact and interaction between investment, knowledge and entrepreneurship with an expanding European Union.

36110 ■ *"Entrepreneurship on the Rise" in Home Business* (Vol. 12, March/April 2005, No. 2, pp. 44)
Pub: Home Business Magazine
Description: According to a study by the Office of Advocacy of the U.S. Small Business Administration, entrepreneurship for women, blacks, and Latinos has risen from 1979 to 2003.

36111 ■ *Entrepreneurship and Small Business*
Pub: Palgrave Macmillan
Ed: Paul Burns. **Released:** January 2007. **Price:** $74.95. **Description:** Successful management practices are examined to encourage and develop entrepreneurial skills.

36112 ■ *Entrepreneurship & SME Research: On Its Way to the Next Millennium*
Pub: Ashgate Publishing Co.
Ed: Rik Donckels and Asko Miettinen. **Released:** 1998. **Price:** $63.95 (cloth).

36113 ■ *Entrepreneurship and SMEs in the Euro-Zone*
Pub: Imperial College Press
Ed: Dana. **Released:** May 2006. **Price:** $48.00. **Description:** Information regarding entrepreneurship and SMEs in Europe is presented.

36114 ■ *Entrepreneurship and Technology Policy*
Pub: Edward Elgar Publishing, Incorporated
Ed: Link. **Released:** August 2006. **Price:** $190.00. **Description:** Journal articles focusing how and the ways small businesses' technical contributions are affecting business. The book is divided into four parts: Government's Direct Support of R&D, Government's Leveraging of R&D, Government's Infrastructure Policies; and Knowledge Flows from Universities and Laboratories.

36115 ■ *Entrepreneurship: The Engine of Growth*
Pub: Greenwood Publishing Group, Incorporated
Ed: Maria Minniti; Andrew Zacharakis; Stephen Spinelli; Mark P. Rice; Timothy G. Habbershon. **Released:** November 2006. **Price:** $300.00. **Description:** Dynamics of entrepreneurship are examined.

36116 ■ *Entrepreneurship 2000*
Pub: Upstart Publishing Co., Inc.
Ed: Donald L. Sexton and Raymond W. Smilor. **Released:** 1996. **Price:** $63.95; $65.00.

36117 ■ *Entrepreneurship in the U.S.: The 2005 Assessment*
Pub: Springer
Ed: Paul Reynolds. **Released:** March 2007. **Price:** $79.95. **Description:** Entrepreneurship and its role in the U.S. economy is discussed, examining new business creation and its impact on job growth, productivity enhancements, innovation, and social mobility.

36118 ■ *"Entrepreneurship as a Utility Maximizing Response" in Journal of Business Venturing* (Vol. 15, No. 3, May 2000, pp. 231)
Pub: Elsevier Science, Inc.
Ed: Dean A. Shepherd. **Description:** Entrepreneurship is assessed as a utility maximizing response.

36119 ■ *"ERM to the rescue" in Rough Notes* (Vol. 146, No. 3, March 2003, pp. 116)
Pub: Rough Notes
Ed: Michael J. Moody. **Description:** After the recent passage of the Sarbanes-Oxley Act, regulations on corporate governance, as well as the PricewaterhouseCoopers study on risk management programs, management concerns are for renewed interest in enterprise risk management.

36120 ■ *"Ernst & Young Seeks Nominations for Southwest Area 2004 Entrepreneur of the Year" in Journal Record* (February 5, 2004)
Pub: Dolan Media Company
Description: Ernst & Young is looking for nominations for Southwest Area entrepreneurs for the 2004 Entrepreneur of the Year Awards, including those in Oklahoma, Arkansas and north Texas.

36121 ■ "Escondido: Sometimes, the Best Advice is Free" in *San Diego Business Journal* **(Vol. 28, January 8, 2007, No. 2, pp. 27)**
Pub: San Diego Business Journal Associates
Ed: Jessica Long. Description: Thursdays with Joe is a new program that offers free advice to small business owners in the Escondido, California area. Topics include marketing tips and financial planning advice.

36122 ■ *Essentials of Entrepreneurship & Small Business Management*
Pub: Prentice Hall
Ed: Thomas Zimmerer and Norman M. Scarborough. Released: 2nd ed. 1997. Price: $50.67 (paper).

36123 ■ "The ethical leader's decision tree." in *Harvard Business Review* **(Vol. 81, No. 2, February 2003, pp. 18)**
Pub: Harvard Business School Press
Ed: Constance E. Bagley. Description: The idea of a decision tree to help executives choose to continue an action is presented. The tree takes into consideration legal ramifications, shareholder value, and ethics.

36124 ■ "Ethical Problems, Conflicts and Beliefs of Small Business Professionals" in *Journal of Business Ethics* **(Vol. 28, No. 1, Nov. 1, 2000)**
Pub: Kluwer Academic Publishers
Ed: Scott J. Vitell, Erin Baca Dickerson, Troy A. Festervand. Description: This paper presents the results of a national study of the beliefs and perceptions of small business professionals concerning ethics within their company and business in general.

36125 ■ "Ethics of Justice and Care in Corporate Crisis Management" in *Journal of Business Ethics* **(Vol. 46, No. 4, Sept. 15, 2003, pp. 351)**
Pub: Kluwer Academic Publishers Group
Ed: Sheldene Simola. Description: The importance of ethics in corporate crisis management is discussed.

36126 ■ "Ex-BBDO Exec Forms New Agency" in *Crain's Detroit Business* **(Vol. 21, January 24, 2005, No. 4, pp. 18)**
Pub: Crain Communications Inc. - Detroit
Ed: Jean Halliday. Description: Profile of Mike Vogel, former CEO of Omnicom Group's BBDO Detroit has left that firm in order to form RTV Communications Group. Vogel's new firm will consist of RTV Consulting, Consolidated Purchasing Partners and Vineyard Group, all located in Auburn Hills, Michigan. RTV offers marketing, strategy, consulting, creative, public relations, advertising, media, events and printing services.

36127 ■ "The Excellence Group Helping Good Schools Become Great." in *Mississippi Business Journal* **(Vol. 28, September 2006, No. 37, pp. 30)**
Pub: Venture Publications, Inc.
Ed: Wally Northway Description: Profile of new educational consulting firm, The Excellence Group, LLC. The firm offers a unique blend of seasoned educators, administrators and an attorney who specializes in school law.

36128 ■ "Excellent leadership is all in the people leading" in *Atlanta Business Chronicle* **(Vol. 24, No. 14, September 7, 2001, pp. 9B)**
Pub: American City Business Journals Inc.
Ed: Michael H. Mescon, Timothy S. Mescon. Description: Dr. Timothy S. Mescon and Dr. Michael H. Mescon discuss leadership, and what makes good leaders. They use the business EBC Office Centers as an example of good leadership, with EBC employees and executives performing their jobs as professionals. Both doctors comment that a business is built from top to bottom, and from inside out.

36129 ■ "Exec has Firm Grip on Software Sales" in *Crain's New York Business* **(Vol. 23, January 29, 2007, No. 5, pp. F13)**
Pub: Crain Communications, Inc.

Ed: Amanda Fung. Description: Profile of Amanda Fung and her position as business and marketing officer for Microsoft Corp's New York/New Jersey district. Her precision helped bring in revenues of more than $492 million for her region in 2006 and her team expects this year's revenues to exceed $600 million.

36130 ■ "Executive Profile: Larry Hartwig" in *San Diego Business Journal* **(Vol. 28, January 8, 2007, No. 2, pp. 26)**
Pub: San Diego Business Journal Associates
Ed: Mike Allen. Description: Profile of Larry Hartwig, president and chief executive officer of California Community Bank. Hartwig shares his business philosophy of building relationships that matter and consistently delivering measurably superior service.

36131 ■ "Exit Strategy" in *Inc.* **(October 2005, pp. 80-81)**
Pub: Inc. Magazine
Ed: Allen P. Roberts Jr. Description: Mike Canney sold his defense company for $42.5 million. Canney now spends his time driving race cars.

36132 ■ "Expanding Your Network of Contacts" in *Black Enterprise* **(Vol. 35, January 2005, No. 6, pp. 111)**
Pub: Earl G. Graves Publishing Co. Inc.
Ed: Lisa Downer. Description: Invitation to business owners, entrepreneurs and corporate executives is extended for the 2005 Black Enterprise/General Motors Entrepreneurs Conference to be held in May 2005 in Dallas, Texas. The conference theme is, Seasons of Change, and explores the role that change management plays in gaining or retaining a competitive advantage.

36133 ■ "Extra scrutiny" in *Crain's Detroit Business* **(Vol. 19, No. 11, March 17, 2003, pp. 14)**
Pub: Crain Communications Inc., Detroit
Description: Robert Verdun presents his list of recovery methods for struggling companies.

36134 ■ "Eye to Eye" in *Entrepreneur* **(Vol. 32, October 2004, No. 10, pp. 89)**
Pub: Entrepreneur Media Inc.
Ed: Barry Farber. Description: Benefits to meeting business contact in person are listed. When looking into customers' eyes, an entrepreneur can communicate honesty and sincerity as well as confidence.

36135 ■ "Eyes Wide Shut? The Inspiration You Need Could Be Right Under Your Nose" in *Entrepreneur* **(Vol. 31, No. 9, July 2003, pp. 76)**
Pub: Entrepreneur Media, Inc.
Ed: Juanita Weaver. Description: Tips to broaden entrepreneurial perspective and to find inspiration are presented.

36136 ■ "Facing the Online Music" in *Inc.* **(July 1, 2003)**
Pub: Gruner & Jahr USA Publishing
Description: Entrepreneurs have a stake in the debate over downloading online music and are skeptical of the recording industry's attempts to rewrite intellectual property law.

36137 ■ "Failure of Genius" in *Inc.* **(August 1, 2003)**
Pub: Gruner & Jahr USA Publishing
Ed: Jess McCuan. Description: Profile of Future Beef. The founders of Future Beef were the smartest, most forward-thinking individuals in the beef business, yet the company did not succeed.

36138 ■ "Failure is Glorious" in *Fast Company* **(November 2001, pp. 35)**
Pub: Fast Company
Ed: Ian Wylie. Description: Alberto Alessi transformed his family's ho-hum housewares business into a trend setting design giant. His secret: walking the borderline between genius and failure.

36139 ■ "Fair process: Managing in the knowledge economy" in *Harvard Business Review* **(Vol. 81, No. 1, January 2003)**
Pub: Harvard Business School Press
Ed: W. Chan Kim, Renee Mauborgne. Description: A discussion of "fair process" is presented, pointing out that employees will commit to a management decision, even if they disagree, if they believe that the process used in arriving at the decision was fair.

36140 ■ "Falling Flat? How Flat is Too Flat When It Comes to Management?" in *Entrepreneur* **(Vol. 33, January 2005, No. 1, pp. 69)**
Pub: Entrepreneur Media Inc.
Ed: Mark Henricks. Description: The importance of a proper management hierarchy is highlighted.

36141 ■ "A family affair" in *Black Enterprise* **(Vol. 33, No. 3, October 2002, pp. 154)**
Pub: Earl Graves Publishing Co.
Ed: George Alexander. Description: The largest part of American wealth lies in the family-owned businesses that make up 80-90 percent of all business enterprises in North America. The importance of a succession plan for family-owned firms is discussed. A survey by the Family Firm Institute of 800 family-owned businesses showed that insufficient estate planning, failure to prepare for the inevitable transition, and lack of funds to pay estate taxes are the leading causes for most family-owned business failures.

36142 ■ *Fast Company's Greatest Hits: Ten Years of the Most Innovative Ideas in Business*
Pub: Penguin Group Incorporated
Ed: John Byrne; David Lidsky; Mark N. Vamos. Released: July 2006. Price: $24.95. Description: Offering of Fast Company's best articles covering business ideas and profiles of successful firms and their leaders.

36143 ■ "Fast Times" in *Entrepreneur* **(Vol. 32, November 2004, No. 11, pp. 28)**
Pub: Entrepreneur Media Inc.
Ed: Nichole L. Torres. Description: Three individuals share how working in fast food restaurants as teenagers actually helped prepare them to become successful entrepreneurs.

36144 ■ "Fast Track Business" in *Hispanic Business* **(March 2002, pp. 60-62)**
Pub: Hispanic Business
Ed: John H. Sullivan. Description: Profile of Hispanic businessman, Adrian Fernandez, who not only credits 150 race starts to his career, but is the only Championship Auto Racing Team (CART) driver who owns his own race team.

36145 ■ *Fast-Track Employer's Kit: California*
Pub: Kaplan Books
Ed: Carolyn Usinger. Released: May 2006. Price: $29.95. Description: Requirements for running a small business in California re outlined.

36146 ■ "Fear Factor" in *Entrepreneur.com* **(Vol. 34, February 2006, No. 2, pp. 144)**
Pub: Entrepreneur Media Inc.
Ed: Robert Kiyosaki. Description: Fear can keep an entrepreneur from growing a company to its full potential. It is important to have a clear, big vision for your business.

36147 ■ "Fear of feedback" in *Harvard Business Review* **(Vol. 81, No. 4, April 2003, pp. 101)**
Pub: Harvard Business School Press
Ed: Jay M. Jackman, Myra H. Strober. Description: The negative effects of the fear of feedback for workers and bosses are addressed. Ways to overcome that fear so employees can bring work into better alignment with organizational goals are discussed.

36148 ■ "Feast or Famine" in *Black Enterprise* **(Vol. 35, November 2004, No. 4, pp. 60)**
Pub: Earl G. Graves Publishing Co. Inc.

Ed: Alan Hughes. **Description:** Owner of a T-shirt business that uses heat transfers to create fashions is seeking marketing advice to balance workforce and cash flow with orders.

36149 ■ "The Fed Connection: 100 Most Influential Hispanics" in *Hispanic Business* (Vol. 23, No. 10, October, 2001)
Pub: Hispanic Business
Ed: Teresa Talerico. **Description:** This year's 'Influentials' list shows Hispanics making real headway within the Federal Government. A brief profile of each person on the list is included. Statistical data included.

36150 ■ "Fernandez: An Entrepreneur at Heart" in *Venture Capital Journal* (Vol. 40, No. 10, November 2000, pp. 52)
Pub: Venture Economics
Description: Profile of Manny Fernandez, a managing director at SI Ventures, a technology research firm. Despite working for SI Ventures for nearly ten years, Mr. Fernandez still considers himself an entrepreneur at heart.

36151 ■ "Filling big shoes at Adobe" in *Harvard Business Review* (Vol. 81, No. 3, March 2003, pp. 20)
Pub: Harvard Business School Press
Ed: Gardiner Morse. **Description:** Bruce Chizen, CEO of Adobe Systems, discusses how he took over leadership from the company's founders and used humility to win converts among the company's employees.

36152 ■ "Finding the potential in down and dirty jobs" in *Wall Street Journal* (April 23, 2002, pp. B5)
Pub: Wall Street Journal
Ed: Paulette Thomas. **Description:** Profile of a woman who runs a service that cleans up dog wastes for pet owners.

36153 ■ "Finishing Touches: the Fashion Statement is in the Detail" in *Black Enterprise* (Vol. 37, January 2007, No. 6, pp. 106)
Pub: Earl G. Graves Publishing Co. Inc.
Ed: Sonia Alleyne. **Description:** Men are discovering the importance of dressing for success. Paying attention to the details such as shoes, socks, cuffs, and collars are just as important as finding the right suit.

36154 ■ "Finning the Flames" in *Entrepreneur* (Vol. 31, No. 9, July 2003, pp. 126)
Pub: Entrepreneur Media, Inc.
Ed: Don Debelak. **Description:** Profile of Bob Evans, founder of Bob Evans Designs Inc. in Santa Barbara, California. Evans' company designed swimming fins designed to propel swimmers through water faster with less effort. Evans discusses how he stays ahead of a market where competitors sell lower-priced, more traditional products.

36155 ■ "Fire in the belly" in *WorkingWoman* (Vol. 25, No. 2, February 2000, pp. 48)
Pub: Lang Communications Inc.
Ed: Russell Wild. **Description:** Successful women give secrets for staying motivated, including patting oneself on the back and taking the long view.

36156 ■ *Fired Up: The Proven Principles of Successful Entrepreneurs*
Pub: Viking Penguin
Ed: Michael Gill. **Released:** 1999. **Price:** $8.95.

36157 ■ "Fisherman Joe's Reopens; Owner Hopes To Hook Customers With Late Hours" in *Bradenton Herald* (January 25, 2005)
Pub: Bradenton Herald
Ed: Kurt D. Schultheis. **Description:** Interview with Joe McDonald, owner of the newly expanded Fisherman Joe's restaurant. McDonald hopes to draw more customers with extended hours.

36158 ■ "Fit To Be Tied: New York Designer Directs Neckwear Fashions" in *Black Enterprise* (Vol. 35, September 2004, No. 2, pp. 194)
Pub: Earl G. Graves Publishing Co. Inc.
Ed: Laura Egodigwe. **Description:** Profile of Anthony T. Kirby, menswear designer and owner of Anthony T. New York Dress Furnishings. Kirby offers tips for choosing and preserving men's ties.

36159 ■ "The 5 Pitfalls Of CEO Succession" in *Fortuneit* (Vol. 146, No. 10, November 18, 2002, pp. 78)
Pub: Time Inc.
Ed: Ram Charan, Jerry Useem. **Description:** The five largest mistakes for grooming potential CEOs are listed. Succession planning is the key.

36160 ■ "Five Ways to Avoid Disaster" in *Fast Company* (June 2001, pp. 46)
Pub: Fast Company
Description: Neil Isford, president and CEO of Plural, the e-business consulting firm, outlines five ways to avoid technology-enabled disasters.

36161 ■ "Flaw and Order: Are You Apt to Make Mistakes? You're Not Alone" in *Entrepreneur* (Vol. 32)
Pub: Entrepreneur Media Inc.
Ed: Mark Henricks. **Description:** Eight strategy flaws identified by Charles Roxburgh, a director of consulting firm McKinsey & Company, are cited, with overconfidence being number one followed by mental accounting.

36162 ■ "Flight of Fancy? Launching a High-Tech Product Can be a Technical and Financial Challenge" in *Entrepreneur* (Vol. 32, August 2004)
Pub: Entrepreneur Media Inc.
Ed: Don Debelak. **Description:** Profile of William J. Boyer Jr. and partner and co-founder Ray Henson, who helped Boyer with the technical aspects of their digEplayer, a portable battery-operated in-flight entertainment system used on passenger tray tables. The company saw $1 millions in sales, first quarter 2004.

36163 ■ "Flip Taking Control of Online Auction House" in *Crain's Chicago Business*
Pub: Crain's Communications Inc. - Chicago
Ed: Lee H. Murphy. **Description:** Profile of Andrew J. Filipowski who acquired MastroNet Inc., an online sports memorabilia auction house.

36164 ■ "Florida Online Dating Service Tries to Find Love Link for Urban Professionals" in *Miami Herald* (March 1, 2004)
Pub: Knight-Ridder/Tribune Business News
Description: Profile of Beatrice Louissaint and Yolanda Davis and their online dating service and event company, Soul Connections. The service targets urban professionals in search of love. The Website provides a place for users to post photos and information to meet other singles, while an event division organizes functions where singles can socialize.

36165 ■ "Focus on Fundraising" in *Black Enterprise* (Vol. 35, September 2004, No. 2, pp. 63)
Pub: Earl G. Graves Publishing Co. Inc.
Ed: Sonia Alleyne. **Description:** Advice is given to a black woman pursuing a business management career organizing fundraising events.

36166 ■ "Follow the flight plan" in *Entrepreneur* (Vol. 30, No. 1,)
Pub: Entrepreneur Media Inc.
Ed: Geoff Williams. **Description:** The author suggests that learning to think like a fighter pilot will help entrepreneurs be successful. Many top managers from companies like Home Depot and FedEx have followed that trend.

36167 ■ "Follow Your Leader" in *Entrepreneur* (Vol. 32, No. 4, April 2004, pp. 124)
Pub: Entrepreneur Media, Inc.
Ed: Romanus Wolter. **Description:** Ways an entrepreneur can find someone to mentor them with business issues are listed. Mentors can help aspiring entrepreneurs to increase sales, create a business plan, as well as handling other challenges.

36168 ■ "Following your moral compass" in *Incentive* (Vol. 174, No. 10, October 2000, pp. 107)
Pub: Bill Communications
Ed: Stephen Covey. **Description:** The best leaders use an internal set of morals and principles to navigate the often treacherous waters of business and set a course for success.

36169 ■ "Following the Leader: Learn these Laws, and Employees Won't Be Far Behind You" in *Entrepreneur* (Vol. 32, July 2004, No. 7, pp. 34)
Pub: Entrepreneur Media Inc.
Description: Review of Michael Feiner's book, The Feiner Points of Leadership. The book offers insight into motivating employees and creating loyalty.

36170 ■ "Food for Thought: With a New Twist on Familiar Snack Foods" in *Entrepreneur* (Vol. 31, No. 9, July 2003, pp. 160)
Pub: Entrepreneur Media, Inc.
Ed: April T. Pennington. **Description:** Profile of James Lindsay, founder of Rap Snacks Inc. The Philadelphia, Pennsylvania company makes snack foods with 2003 sales projected at $4-5 million. Snacks include popcorn, chips and cheese curls featuring rap artists on the packaging.

36171 ■ "For Better Or. How Women Entrepreneurs Strike a Balance Between Business and Marriage" in *Entrepreneur* (Vol. 31, Oct. 2003)
Pub: Entrepreneur Media, Inc.
Ed: Aliza Pilar Sherman. **Description:** Two successful women entrepreneurs discuss marriage and business conflict and ways to deal with it.

36172 ■ "Forbes Keeps Track In It's Upscale Or Hot on the Lot" in *Sacramento Bee* (November 16, 2005)
Pub: The Sacramento Bee
Ed: Mark Glover. **Description:** Forbes magazine has launched a new website designed to attract successful business people. The Website, www.forbesautos.com is geared for the luxury automotive buyer. Tips for negotiating with automobile dealers, tests drives, financing and insurance are also included on the site.

36173 ■ "Ford Motor Company Is Sponsoring the Ford BEST Business Plan Contest..." in *Black Enterprise* (Vol. 34, No. 7, February 2004)
Pub: Earl Graves Publishing Co.
Ed: Carolyn M. Brown. **Description:** Ford Motor Company, in association with SCORE "Counselors to America's Small Business" and Diversity Inc., is sponsoring the BEST Business Plan contest. Prospective entrepreneurs submit a business plan to be reviewed by counselors at SCORE. The grand prize of $50,000 and two runner-up prizes of $25,000 each, will help the winners startup their businesses.

36174 ■ "Forget VC: Successful Entrepreneur Says Good Riddance" in *Venture Capital Journal* (October 1, 2004)
Pub: Thomason Financial Inc.
Description: In an interview, Harry Gruber, founder and CEO of Kintera Inc., a company providing software and services to help nonprofits conduct fundraising via the Internet. Gruber discusses the advantages, as well as the disadvantages of using venture capital to grow a business, particularly the control venture capitalists gain over a firm.

36175 ■ "Former Apprentice Candidate Launches Jewelry Line" in *Black Enterprise* (Vol. 37, October 2006, No. 3, pp. 36)
Pub: Earl G. Graves Publishing Co. Inc.
Ed: Philana Patterson. **Description:** Star of the second season of NBC's The Apprentice, Stacie J, has launched a line of jewelry and accessories which will be sold at Claire's stores nationwide.

36176 ■ **"Former Female Weightlifter Opens Yuba City, Calif., Women-Only Fitness Center" in** *Marysville Appeal-Democrat* **(January 26, 2003)**
Pub: Knight Ridder/Tribune Business News
Ed: Harold Kruger. **Description:** Profile of Sherry Gideons-Martin and her husband Gary, who own the Natural Woman Lifestyle Center, a women-only fitness business in Marysville, California. At age 37, Gideons-Martin is a former fitness model and power lifter, who has fought bulimia, drugs, homelessness and a near-fatal heart attack.

36177 ■ **"Former Wrestling Star Body Slams Private Equity" in** *Venture Capital Journal* **(Vol. 42, No. 9, September 2002, pp. 15-16)**
Pub: Thomas Venture Economics
Ed: Michael V. Copeland. **Description:** Profile of Ira Lubert, co-founder/principal of Lubert-Alder Management Inc. of Philadelphia, Pennsylvania; Lubert targets his market to mid- to late-stage companies that can't go public and don't want to be sold right away.

36178 ■ *Foundations of Small Business Enterprise*
Pub: Routledge Inc.
Ed: G. Reid. **Released:** December 2006. **Price:** $120.00. **Description:** Insight is given into the life cycle of entrepreneurial ventures; 150 new firms are tracked through early years.

36179 ■ **"Franchising" in** *Hispanic Business* **(Vol. 23, No. 5, May 2001, pp. 50)**
Pub: Hispanic Business
Description: The International Franchise Association reports the need to educate emerging entrepreneurs about the 75 various industries offering franchise opportunities to Hispanics.

36180 ■ **"Fred Smith" in** *Fast Company* **(June 2001, pp. 64)**
Pub: Fast Company
Ed: Charles Fishman. **Description:** An interview with Fred Smith, founder of Federal Express, the creator of overnight delivery.

36181 ■ **"Friends forever?" in** *Entrepreneur* **(Vol. 31, No. 6, June 2003, pp. 77)**
Pub: Entrepreneur Media Inc.
Ed: Marc Diener. **Description:** In the real world friendship is better for business than business in for friendship. When business deals get rocky, valued relationships often fall apart.

36182 ■ **"Friends in High Places" in** *Hispanic Business* **(Vol. 23, No. 7/8, July/August 2001, pp. 62, 64)**
Pub: Hispanic Business
Ed: Scott Williams. **Description:** Profile of the newly formed Hispanic Network of Entrepreneurs. The group hopes to ease the way for a new generation of Hispanic entrepreneurs in the high-tech industry, business development, venture capital financing, recruiting and exchange of ideas.

36183 ■ *From Entrepreneur to Infopreneur: Make Money with Books, E-Books, and Other Information Products*
Pub: John Wiley & Sons, Incorporated
Ed: Stephanie Chandler. **Released:** November 2006. **Price:** $19.95. **Description:** Infopreneurs sell information online in the forms of books, e-books, special reports, audio and video products, seminars, and more.

36184 ■ **"From Golf to Software" in** *Crain's Detroit Business* **(Vol. 19, No. 42, October 20, 2003, pp. 28)**
Pub: Crain Communications Inc., Detroit
Ed: Andrew Dietderich. **Description:** Profile of Thomas Itin, 69-year old entrepreneur who devotes his time between Ajay Sports Inc., CompuSonics Video Corporation, and Pro Golf of America Inc.

36185 ■ **"From Golf to Software; Entrepreneur Nixes Retirement to Build Businesses in Farmington Hills" in** *Crain's Detroit Business* **(Vol. 19)**
Pub: Crain Communications Inc., Detroit
Ed: Andrew Dietderich. **Description:** Profile of Thomas Itin, 69-year old entrepreneur who devotes his time between Ajay Sports Inc., CompuSonics Video Corporation, and Pro Golf of America Inc.

36186 ■ **"From Landscaper to Landowner" in** *Black Enterprise* **(Vol. 34, No. 5, December 2003, pp. S4)**
Pub: Earl Graves Publishing Co.
Ed: Sonya Kimble-Ellis. **Description:** Profile of young entrepreneur Airyque Ervin, who started a lawn service with his brother at age 14. Ervin found that owning land, selling it, and buying more was a more profitable venture.

36187 ■ **"From Mushing to Management" in** *Inc.* **(January 1, 2005)**
Pub: Inc. Magazine
Ed: Nicole Gull. **Description:** Lisa Wehl learned how to manage her 22 employees through a group of Alaskan husky dogs while competing in competitions such as the Knik 200 and the Klondike 300.

36188 ■ **"From Real Estate to Retirement Plan" in** *Black Enterprise* **(Vol. 34, No. 3, October 2003, pp. 29)**
Pub: Earl Graves Publishing Co.
Ed: Carmen Brown. **Description:** Profile of Bradley Simmons, the 40-year-old English teacher, who was encouraged by his brother, a real estate entrepreneur to switch careers and open Bestrow Realty in Harlem, New York. Simmons offers financial planning advice.

36189 ■ **"From Wish to Goal" in** *Black Enterprise* **(Vol. 35, January 2005, No. 6, pp. 97)**
Pub: Earl G. Graves Publishing Co. Inc.
Description: Gadsden's tips for setting and achieving goals are listed. These goals will help inspiring entrepreneurs follow their vision. Rev. Nathaniel Gadsden founded the Writers Wordshop, a not-for-profit agency that helps poets develop their writing skills.

36190 ■ **"From Zero to Hero: Even the Best Franchisor has to Start Somewhere" in** *Entrepreneur* **(Vol. 32, No. 1, January 2004, pp. 148)**
Pub: Entrepreneur Media, Inc.
Ed: Nichole L. Torres. **Description:** Profile of Fred DeLuca, founder of Subway restaurants. Subway expects to have 20,000 franchises in more than 70 countries in operation.

36191 ■ **"Frozen assets" in** *Entrepreneur* **(Vol. 31, No. 6, June 2003, pp. 114)**
Pub: Entrepreneur Media Inc.
Ed: Nichole L. Torres. **Description:** Profile of Mike Fanning and Bill Sammon of Hima Ice Towel Corporation, a manufacturer of ice-cold towels used in hot climates.

36192 ■ **"Full Esteem Ahead: Act Like an Executive-And Get the Respect You Deserve" in** *Entrepreneur* **(Vol. 31, No. 9, September 2003, pp. 104)**
Pub: Entrepreneur Media, Inc.
Description: Ways new entrepreneurs can learn to have the presence of a seasoned pro are listed, including the technique of talking slowly, standing with confidence, body language, and more.

36193 ■ **"A Full House" in** *Home Business* **(Vol. 12, October 2005, No. 5, pp. 40)**
Pub: Home Business Magazine
Ed: Sandy Larson. **Description:** Twin brothers, Shane and Shawn Ward, founders of DETNY Footwear, Inc., create shoes for fashion-conscious jetsetters. The young men run their business from their home with six employees.

36194 ■ **"Funny Business" in** *Black Enterprise* **(Vol. 36, December 2005, No. 5, pp. 71)**
Pub: Earl G. Graves Publishing Co. Inc.
Ed: Sean Drakes. **Description:** Profile of Ron Wilson, executive producer of the LAFFAPALOOZA! America's Urban International Comedy Arts Festival, a four-day comedy event held in Atlanta, Georgia. The festival attracts 250,000 attendees and 84 million viewers.

36195 ■ **"A Gambling Man: Career Transitions that Put a Vegas Hotshot on Top" in** *Black Enterprise* **(Vol. 37, October 2006, No. 3, pp. 89)**
Pub: Earl G. Graves Publishing Co. Inc.
Ed: Laura Egodigwe. **Description:** Interview with Lorenzo Creighton, president and chief operating officer of MGM Mirage's New York-New York Hotel and Casino. Creighton talks about his history and the challenges he faced since he didn't come from the casino industry.

36196 ■ **"Generation next" in** *San Francisco Business Times* **(Vol. 16, No. 42, May 24, 2002, pp. S4)**
Pub: San Francisco Business Times Inc.
Ed: Kristen Bole. **Description:** Changes in society which impact women executives and opportunities for women in business are discussed along with employee benefits. Women in the Bay Area are highlighted.

36197 ■ **"Georgia CEOs debate global leadership issues" in** *Atlanta Business Chronicle* **(Vol. 25, November 15, 2002, No. 23 pp. 10C)**
Pub: American City Business Publications, Inc.
Ed: Kelly Gay. **Description:** The Georgia Technology Forum of the Technology Association of Georgia provided Georgia's business leaders with the opportunity to participate in a round table discussion of the most pertinent business issues today. Overall, the panel showed optimism for the future.

36198 ■ **"Get Bizzed" in** *Entrepreneur* **(Vol. 28, No. 4, April 2000, pp. 66)**
Pub: Entrepreneur Media Inc.
Description: If you're looking for a one-stop portal for all your small business needs, try e-Citi, the e-commerce unit of Citigroup, formed to help entrepreneurs gain access to big-business resources easily and securely.

36199 ■ **"Get Inspired!" in** *My Business* **(April/May 2003, pp. 44)**
Pub: My Business Magazine
Ed: Mardy Fones. **Description:** Renewal strategies for small business leaders to keep creative and productive are presented.

36200 ■ **"Get Smart" in** *Entrepreneur* **(Vol. 32, July 2004, No. 7, pp. 34)**
Pub: Entrepreneur Media Inc.
Ed: Mark Henricks. **Description:** Review of the book, MBA In a Box, which offers practical ideas from top business leaders.

36201 ■ **"Get Your Digital Data Fix" in** *Fast Company* **(May 2001, pp. 196)**
Pub: Fast Company
Ed: Daniel H. Pink. **Description:** Profile of Bob Drudge, father of cyberscribe Matt Drudge, and founder of the Refdesk Web site which contains links to hundreds of Web-based information tools.

36202 ■ **"Getting Ahead" in** *Hispanic Business* **(June 2005, pp. 18)**
Pub: Hispanic Business
Description: According to a study from the Immigration Policy Center, immigrant women play an important role in the growth of women entrepreneurship in the U.S.

36203 ■ **"Getting Away and Meaning It" in** *Inc.* **(July 1, 2003)**
Pub: Gruner & Jahr USA Publishing
Description: Ways to make business a part of a vacation trip and avoid ruining please by keeping work distractions to a minimum.

36204 ■ "Getting on Board" in *Hispanic Business* **(March 2003, pp. 62)**
Pub: Hispanic Business
Description: Career development advice is given for Hispanic professionals wishing to increase their professional profile through board directorships.

36205 ■ "Getting No Respect?" in *Entrepreneur* **(Vol. 33, February 2005, pp. 110)**
Pub: Entrepreneur Media Inc.
Ed: Nichole L. Torres. **Description:** Young college entrepreneurs are offered advice to help them with credibility as business owners.

36206 ■ "Getting Props: Awards Can Boost Your Self-Esteem-And Your Business" in *Entrepreneur* **(Vol. 33, March 2005, No. 3, pp. 38)**
Pub: Entrepreneur Media Inc.
Ed: Aliza Pilar Sherman. **Description:** Awards focusing on female entrepreneurs can boost self-esteem and grow a business. Many national women's business awards are presented by organizations like the National Association of Women Business Owners and the National Association for Female Executives.

36207 ■ *Getting to Scale: Growing Your Business Without Selling Out*
Pub: Berrett-Koehler Publishers, Incorporated
Ed: Jill Bamburg. **Released:** July 2006. **Price:** $14.95. **Description:** Ways for entrepreneurs to preserve the value of their company while maintaining growth and competitiveness.

36208 ■ "Gilded Paper Route" in *Success* **(Vol. 47, No. 1, January 2000, pp. 20)**
Pub: Success Publishing, Inc.
Ed: Martha Visser. **Description:** Profile of Luke Pontifell, who turned his passion for printing into an international business, that manufactures fine writing paper for one of the world's leading luxury-goods corporations. Pontifell also produces premium leather-bound editions that are coveted by collectors, libraries, and even museums.

36209 ■ "Girl power" in *Entrepreneur* **(Vol. 31, No. 5, May 2003, pp. 28)**
Pub: Entrepreneur Media Inc.
Ed: Aliza Pilar Sherman. **Description:** Social entrepreneurship looks at the way a business fits into a community; an interview with business owners who did that and also found ways to help women and girls using their companies in included.

36210 ■ *The Girl's Guide to Being a Boss (Without Being a Bitch): Valuable Lessons, Smart Suggestions, and True Stories for Succeeding*
Pub: Random Housing Publishing Group
Ed: Caitlin Friedman; Kimberly Yorio. **Released:** April 2006.

36211 ■ "Give good presence" in *BlackEnterprise* **(Vol. 32, No. 2, September 2001, pp. 114)**
Pub: Earl Graves Publishing Co.
Ed: Phaedra Brotherton. **Description:** Appearance is often the thing people see first in the business world. Expert advice to help polish clothing and social skills in four critical areas are presented, including appearance, verbal presentation, networking, and business etiquette. A listing of books addressing these issues is included.

36212 ■ "Giving Back" in *Inc.* **(November 1, 2004)**
Pub: Inc. Magazine
Ed: Jess McCuan. **Description:** Profile of Cynthia McKay, owner of a gift-basket business in Castle Rock, Colorado, which is stacked high with dog food and cat litter to be donated as part of her employee charitable giving program. Giving programs like McKay's are on the rise in America because entrepreneurs feel the need to give back.

36213 ■ "Giving Where It Counts: Blackgiving.com Lets Consumers Choose Their Charities" in *Black Enterprise* **(Vol. 34, July 2004, No. 12)**
Pub: Earl G. Graves Publishing Co. Inc.
Ed: Anthony S. Calypso. **Description:** Profile of Blackgiving.com, developed by Vince Martin. The site is designed to reach African Americans and helps fund charitable causes that already exist.

36214 ■ "Glad that's over" in *Entrepreneur* **(Vol. 30, No. 12, December 2002, pp. 38)**
Pub: Entrepreneur Media Inc.
Ed: April Y. Pennington. **Description:** Profile of Kaleil D. Isaza Tuzman, co-creator of GovWorks.com, an Internet site that provided public access to government agencies. Currently Tuzman is president and managing partner of Recognition Group, which restructures companies on the brink of disaster.

36215 ■ "Global Entrepreneur" in *Inc.* **(September 2005, pp. 48, 50)**
Pub: Inc. Magazine
Ed: Lora Kolodny. **Description:** Chuck Foley, CEO of Tacit Networks, explains how he expanded his firm globally. Tacit makes software that enables instant file sharing between networks no matter the distance.

36216 ■ "Go For the Gold" in *Entrepreneur* **(Vol. 32, October 2004, No. 10, pp. 68)**
Pub: Entrepreneur Media Inc.
Ed: David Worrell. **Description:** Planning for the day an entrepreneur will sell their business is critical. Growth potential is key when determining a company's worth.

36217 ■ "Go West: Want a Few Business Pointers? Mosey on Over to Deadwood" in *Entrepreneur* **(Vol. 32, November 2004, No. 11, pp. 22)**
Pub: Entrepreneur Media Inc.
Ed: Steve Cooper. **Description:** HBO's new series Deadwood, based on a real-life town in South Dakota around 1876, offers insight into business leadership, contracts, property rights, marketing, managing and business expansion.

36218 ■ "Go With the Flow" in *Entrepreneur* **(Vol. 32, August 2004, No. 8, pp. 32)**
Pub: Entrepreneur Media Inc.
Ed: Mark Henricks. **Description:** Review of the book, Good Business: Leadership, Flow and the Making of Meaning, is presented. The author shows that setting clear goals, giving feedback and matching challenges to skills can make an entrepreneur successful.

36219 ■ "Goal Tending" in *Small Business Opportunities* **(Fall 2005)**
Pub: Harris Publications Inc.
Ed: Lonnie Pacelli. **Description:** Five tips to help a small business owner face challenges are outlined, including a good business plan.

36220 ■ "Going digital for dollars" in *Black Enterprise* **(Vol. 33, No. 3, October 2002, pp. 145)**
Pub: Earl Graves Publishing Co.
Ed: Bernadette Williams. **Description:** The future of electronic commerce is discussed, including ways information technology can be used in the vision, creativity, and long-term planning for small business entrepreneurs. Security issues to protect small businesses, joint marketing between firms selling a similar product or service, and ways for African American small business owners can target their markets.

36221 ■ "Going For a Whirl: Jamail Larkin Soars, Dips, and Shows Off a Few Stunts" in *Black Enterprise* **(Vol. 35, January 2005, No. 6, pp. 103)**
Pub: Earl G. Graves Publishing Co. Inc.
Ed: Jermine Benton. **Description:** Profile of Jamail Larkins, owner of an aviation marketing group. Larkins runs his business while attending Embry-Riddle Aeronautic University in Daytona, Florida. The entrepreneur decided to start a small business to pay for school, rather than work for minimum wage. The company is expected to show $200,000 in earnings for 2004.

36222 ■ *Golden Entrepreneuring*
Pub: Bell Springs Publishing
Ed: James B. Arkebauer. **Released: Price:** $169.95.
Description: Contains tips and ideas about how older entrepreneurs can use their years and experience to their advantage. Real hands-on help for those fed up with the corporate struggle or bored with retirement.

36223 ■ "Gone Fishing" in *Inc.* **(July 1, 2004)**
Pub: Inc. Magazine
Description: As a way to balance work and home life, one entrepreneur fills a goldfish bowl with ideas for day, weekend and weeklong vacations, then draws three ideas from the bowl and commits to making them a reality throughout the coming year.

36224 ■ "GOOD business and good BUSINESS" in *Harvard Business Review* **(Vol. 81, No. 3, March 2003, pp. 10)**
Pub: Harvard Business School Press
Ed: Thomas A. Stewart. **Description:** The editor of Harvard Business Review discusses stock options as too much of a good thing. Originally intended to link managers' interest with those of owners, they now create a means for executives to maximize their profit at the owners' expense.

36225 ■ "Good Deeds and Watchful Eyes" in *Business Week Online* **(March 8, 2002)**
Pub: McGraw-Hill, Inc.
Description: According to a survey of owners and managers of small businesses, conducted by Princeton Survey Research Associates on behalf of the Better Business Bureau's Wise Giving Alliance, most small firms actively support charities and local community groups so they can keep a close watch on how the money is being used.

36226 ■ "The Good Fight" in *Entrepreneur* **(Vol. 30, No. 3, March 2002, pp. 48)**
Pub: Entrepreneur Media Inc.
Ed: Janean Chun. **Description:** The author calls for entrepreneurs to change the corporate way of thinking in America, in other words a call to common sense.

36227 ■ *Good to Great*
Pub: Harper Business
Ed: Jim Collins. **Price:** $27.50.

36228 ■ "Good Libations?" in *Entrepreneur* **(Vol. 32, December 2004, No. 12, pp. 100)**
Pub: Entrepreneur Media Inc.
Ed: Jane Easter Bahls. **Description:** When planning a company party or event, it is essential to consider what could happen if alcohol was served and an employee drove home drunk.

36229 ■ "A Good Man(ager) is Hard to Find" in *My Business* **(August/September 2002, pp. 47)**
Pub: My Business Magazine
Ed: Shannon Scully. **Description:** The basics for understanding the franchising concept are listed, as well as a profile of James Rice, owner of 13 McDonald's franchises. Web sites offering franchising assistance are listed.

36230 ■ "Got Game?" in *Entrepreneur* **(Vol. 32, October 2004, No. 10, pp. 95)**
Pub: Entrepreneur Media Inc.
Ed: Chris Penttila. **Description:** Entrepreneurial introspection is a growing trend in small business. Strategic plans implemented inside a company help give employees and managers a realistic look at the business and its goals.

36231 ■ *Goventure: Live the Life of an Entrepreneur*
Pub: Houghton Mifflin College Division
Ed: Hatten. **Released:** May 2006. **Price:** $28.47. **Description:** Challenges of operating a small business are presented with more than 6,000 graphics, audio, and interactive video.

36232 ■ Great Big Book of Business Lists: All the Info You Need to Run a Small Business
Pub: Entrepreneur Press
Ed: Courtney Thurman; Ashlee Gardner. Released: April 2006. Price: $45.95. Description: Reference guide for small business that includes information for starting and running a small business; lists are organized for easy access and cover every aspect of small business.

36233 ■ "The Great Comeback" in My Business (April/May 2003, pp. 26-28, 30-32)
Pub: My Business Magazine
Ed: Shannon Scully. Description: Various business owners discuss their road from business failure and back again to running successful companies.

36234 ■ "The great unknown" in Entrepreneur (Vol. 31, No. 6, June 2003, pp. 19)
Pub: Entrepreneur Media Inc.
Ed: Chris Penttila. Description: The frustrations faced by entrepreneurs during a struggling economy are discussed.

36235 ■ "Green Machines" in Entrepreneur (Vol. 31, No. 7, July 2003, pp. 34)
Pub: Entrepreneur Media, Inc.
Ed: Geoff Williams. Description: Profile of Grant Goodman, CEO of Rockland Materials and five other companies, that make building materials such as ready-mix cement. Goodman runs his fleet of 120 truck on primarily biodiesel fuel made from soybeans. The fuel is biodegradable, nontoxic and free from sulfur.

36236 ■ "Grist: An Entrepreneurs Resolutions" in Inc. (January 1, 2005)
Pub: Inc. Magazine
Ed: Adam Hanft. Description: Small business New Year's resolutions are discussed, including recommendations to help grow a business.

36237 ■ "Grist: Micromanagers, Unite!" in Inc. (December 1, 2004)
Pub: Inc. Magazine
Ed: Adam Hanft. Description: Micromanagement is considered meddling, but small companies can benefit from micromanagers.

36238 ■ "Grist: The Inevitable Rise of the Entrepreneur" in Inc. (October 1, 2003)
Pub: Gruner & Jahr USA Publishing
Ed: Adam Henricks. Description: The natural life of the American economy always eventually favors the entrepreneur.

36239 ■ "Group Casts Another Line Into Seafood" in Crain's Chicago Business (Vol. 26, No. 50, December 15, 2003, pp. 22)
Pub: Crain Communications, Inc.
Ed: Anne Spiselman. Description: Profile of Roger Greenfield and Ted Kasemir's Restaurant Development Group. The owners of the 40-plus restaurant empire have a talent for recombining restaurant components to create new concepts. Stonefish Grill in Northbrook is their latest creation, specializing in seafood, but include chicken, steaks and burgers on the menu.

36240 ■ "Group dynamics" in Entrepreneur (Vol. 30, No. 12, December 2002, pp. 101)
Pub: Entrepreneur Media Inc.
Ed: Mark Henricks. Description: While large companies hire lobbyists to influence legislators and regulators, small firms join trade associations. There are more than 147,000 trade associations in the United States, most of which are state and local groups.

36241 ■ "Group Therapy" in Forbes (April 3, 2000, pp. 138)
Pub: Forbes Magazine
Ed: Leigh Gallagher. Description: The Young Entrepreneurs Association, the global association for small business operators under the age of 40, is profiled.

36242 ■ Groups in Context: Leadership and Participation in Small Groups
Pub: McGraw-Hill Companies
Ed: Gerald L. Wilson. Released: June 2004. Price: $70.00 (US), $105.95 (Canadian). Description: Small group communication skills for the workplace, in churches, social groups, or civic organizations.

36243 ■ "Grow Up: Teach Employees to Lead" in My Business (April/May 2003, pp. 44)
Pub: My Business Magazine
Ed: Melany Klink. Description: The importance of small business owners in hiring a team of leaders to run a company is stressed, using three key actions.

36244 ■ Growing Business Handbook: Inspirational Advice from Successful Entrepreneurs and Fast-Growing UK Companies
Pub: Kogan Page, Limited
Ed: Adam Jolly. Released: February 2007. Price: $49.95. Description: Tips for growing and running a successful business are covered, focusing on senior managers in middle market and SME companies.

36245 ■ "Growing a Business" in Small Business Opportunities (Vol. 16, No. 3, May 2004, pp. 80, 84)
Pub: Harris Publications, Inc.
Ed: Vicki Gerson. Description: Profile of Bill Meadows, who was born in a coal mining camp and now runs a chain of retail nurseries valued at $72 million. The nurseries focus exclusively on plants, shrubs, and trees.

36246 ■ Growing Local Value: How to Build Business Partnerships That Strengthen Your Community
Pub: Berrett-Koehler Publishers, Incorporated
Ed: Laury Hammel; Gun Denhart. Released: December 2006. Price: $15.00. Description: Advice and examples are provided for building socially responsible entrepreneurship.

36247 ■ Growing and Managing a Small Business: An Entrepreneurial Perspective
Pub: Houghton Mifflin College Division
Ed: Kathleen R. Allen. Released: July 2006. Price: $105.27. Description: Introduction to business ownership and management from startup through growth.

36248 ■ "Growing Pains" in Inc. (October 2000, pp. 20)
Pub: The Goldhirsh Group
Ed: Toby Toler. Description: The control of one's company and one's time are investigated, with comments from entrepreneurs about methods they have used in the past.

36249 ■ Growing Your Business
Pub: Routledge Inc.
Ed: Burke. Released: December 2006. Price: $150.00. Description: Growth strategies for small businesses are presented.

36250 ■ "Growth Guru: How to Turn Your Business Into a Hot Commodity" in Entrepreneur (Vol. 31, No. 7, July 2003, pp. 27)
Pub: Entrepreneur Media, Inc.
Ed: Mark Henricks. Description: Reviews of the books, "What I Learned Before I Sold to Warren Buffett", which deals with hiring, leading, communicating, decision-making and general management issues; and "What's The Big Idea", which deals with management ideas, are presented.

36251 ■ Growth Oriented Women Entrepreneurs and Their Businesses: A Global Research Perspective
Pub: Edward Elgar Publishing, Incorporated
Ed: Candida G. Brush. Released: June 2006. Price: $135.00. Description: Roles women play in entrepreneurship globally and their economic impact are examined.

36252 ■ "Growth Tales; Key Strategies Used by Young Firms" in Crain's New York Business (Vol. 22, December 11, 2006, No. 50, pp. 27)
Pub: Crain Communications, Inc.
Ed: Lisa Goff. Description: Profile of businesses who have used innovative marketing campaigns that cost little to no capital.

36253 ■ "Guide Advises Would-Be Entrepreneurs" in Marketing to Women (Vol. 20, January 2007, No. 1, pp. 8)
Pub: EPM Communications, Inc.
Description: Smart Women and Small Business: How to Make the Leap from Corporate Careers to the Right Small Enterprise, a new how-to guide book for women looking to leave their corporate careers and join the entrepreneurial workforce, offers tips on getting loans, starting a business, working with business partners, and finding and closing the right deals.

36254 ■ "Gurus in the garage" in Harvard Business Review (Vol. 78, No. 6, November-December 2000, pp. 71)
Pub: Harvard Business School Publishing Corp.
Description: Description of a special type of advisor who helps entrepreneurs with a variety of tasks, including recruiting staff and negotiating seed money.

36255 ■ "Guzman to Head CHCC" in Hispanic Business (December 2001, pp. 14)
Pub: Hispanic Business
Description: Profile of Melinda Guzman, the first woman elected president of the California Hispanic Chambers of Commerce. Ms. Guzman recently won the Luminary Award for business leadership from the National Association of Women Business Owners.

36256 ■ Habitual Entrepreneurs
Pub: Edward Elgar Publishing, Incorporated
Ed: Ucbasaran. Released: December 2006. Price: $100.00. Description: Habitual entrepreneurship is explored. Tools for developing a plan for successful leadership are offered.

36257 ■ Handbook of Quality Research in Entrepreneurship
Pub: Edward Elgar Publishing, Incorporated
Ed: Neergaard. Released: March 2007. Price: $215.00. Description: Advice for researchers to make informed choices and to design more stringent and sophisticated studies in the field of entrepreneurship.

36258 ■ "Handled Like a Pro" in Success (Vol. 47, No. 6, November 2000, pp. 34)
Pub: Success Publishing, Inc.
Ed: Melba Newsome. Description: After being widowed, Georgia Buchanan took her husband's construction company and rebuilt it from the ground up despite everyone's advice urging her to sell.

36259 ■ "Hangin' Tough: How to Beef Up Your Negotiating Game" in Entrepreneur (Vol. 32, August 2004, No. 8, pp. 72)
Pub: Entrepreneur Media Inc.
Ed: Marc Diener. Description: Negotiating skills out outlined, focusing on technique, not just game face. If you must give something, be sure to get something back in return.

36260 ■ Happy About Joint Venturing: The 8 Critical Factors of Success
Pub: Happy About
Ed: Valerie Orsoni-Vauthey. Released: June 2006. Price: $23.95. Description: An overview of joint venturing is presented.

36261 ■ "The Harder They Fall" in Harvard Business Review (Vol. 81, No. 10, October 2003, pp. 58)
Pub: Harvard Business School Press
Ed: Roderick M. Kramer. Description: Advice is given for executives, and by extension employees, wishing to avoid having careers come to an untimely end due to lapses of professional judgment.

36262 ■ **"Harrison, Maine, Homeland Security Consultant Telecommutes Around the Globe"** in *Portland Press Herald* (May 20, 2005)
Pub: Blethen Maine Newspapers, Inc.
Ed: Matt Wickenheiser. Description: Profile of Clifford A. Lewis, CEO of Strategy X, a new homeland security company. Lewis is committed to the idea of running a global business successfully from his hometown through the use of the Internet. Strategy X offers consulting services to assess and advise on security systems and processes of military bases, dams, power plants, and other facilities.

36263 ■ **"Have Faith, Not Fear"** in *Venture Capital Journal* (Vol. 42, No. 9, September 2002, pp. 31)
Pub: Thomas Venture Economics
Ed: Darryl E. Wash. Description: Darryl Wash, managing partner of Ascend Venture Group, a venture capital firm in New York City, feels the entrepreneurial spirit will keep the economy moving in the right direction.

36264 ■ **"Have Kid, Won't Travel"** in *Fast Company* (November 2001, pp. 48)
Pub: Fast Company
Ed: Christine Canabou. Description: Profile of David Peterson, cofounder, CEO and chairman of the Atlanta-based North Highland Company, the management and technology consulting firm. Mr. Peterson's work force is able to drive to their client's site, rather than having to spend much of their time away from their homes and families.

36265 ■ **"Hazlet, N.J., Firm Stays Ahead of Real Estate Trends"** in *The Record* (November 18, 2005)
Pub: New Jersey Media Group
Ed: William Conroy. Description: Profile of Warren Diamond, CEO of American Real Estate Management Associates. Diamond started a self-storage business in 1986 and explains the importance of getting in at the beginning of new trends when investing in real estate.

36266 ■ **"He Came. He Saw. He Took On the Whole Power-Tool Industry"** in *Inc.* (Volume 27, July 2005, No. 7, pp. 86-91)
Pub: Inc. Magazine
Ed: Melba Newsome. Description: Profile of Stephen Gass, inventor of the new SawStop, a power saw whose blade stops immediately when it comes into contact with the user's body.

36267 ■ **"He Has a Sky-High Outlook on His Business"** in *Charlotte Observer* (February 4, 2007)
Pub: Knight-Ridder/Tribune Business News
Ed: Stella M. Hopkins. Description: Profile of Chuck Boyle, former Army pilot; Boyle patrols over construction sites in the Charlotte, North Carolina area. The firm's team of engineers and geologists specialize in services such as: rock blasting, roads, testing concrete and other construction materials, and more.

36268 ■ **"Head of the class"** in *Black Enterprise* (Vol. 32, No. 10, May 2002)
Pub: Earl Graves Publishing Co.
Ed: Sonja D. Brown. Description: The editors have identified 12 companies that rank among the top guns of small business.

36269 ■ **"Health and Female Self-Employment"** in *Journal of Small Business Management* (Vol. 41, No. 3, July 2003, pp. 233)
Pub: International Council of Small Business
Ed: Arthur L. Dolinsky, Richard K. Caputo. Description: Data from the Mature Women's Cohort of the National Longitudinal Survey of Labor Market Experience was used to study self-employed, wage earning, and non-employed women showed that self-employment had no significant effect on health status in 1995.

36270 ■ **"Healthy Choice"** in *Entrepreneur* (Vol. 28, No. 11, November 2000, pp. 16)
Pub: Entrepreneur Media Inc.

Ed: Peter Kooiman. Description: How entrepreneurial lifestyle affects health is explored. Statistical data is included.

36271 ■ **"Healthy, Wealthy and Wise"** in *Home Business* (Vol. 13, January/February 2006, No. 1, pp. 40)
Pub: Home Business Magazine
Ed: Sandy Larson. Description: Brian Reinhardt, marketer of weight loss, fitness and personal development products shares his secret to staying physically and financially fit.

36272 ■ **"Heard the News?"** in *Entrepreneur* (Vol. 32, December 2004, No. 12, pp. 58)
Pub: Entrepreneur Media Inc.
Ed: Amanda C. Kooser. Description: Microsoft and Google have both rival services that gather news geared to the entrepreneur.

36273 ■ **"Heart of Gold: Nonprofits Are Reaping the Rewards of Starting For-Profit Ventures"** in *Entrepreneur* (Vol. 32, September 2004, No. 9)
Pub: Entrepreneur Media Inc.
Ed: Chris Penttila. Description: Nonprofit organizations are looking to for-profit ventures in order to diversify revenue streams.

36274 ■ **"Help me out, here"** in *Entrepreneur* (Vol. 30, No. 10, October 2002, pp. 40)
Pub: Entrepreneur Media Inc.
Ed: Aliza P. Sherman. Description: Successful women business owners discuss ways they are giving back through mentoring, sitting on corporate boards, and investing in their companies.

36275 ■ **"Henderson, Nev., Boot Camp Teaches How to Combat Hackers"** in *Las Vegas Review-Journal* (December 21, 2004)
Pub: Las Vegas Review-Journal
Ed: Emily Kumler. Description: Former computer hackers have formed a company that teaches information technology employees to run security tests on computer systems.

36276 ■ **"Here Comes the Sun"** in *Entrepreneur* (Vol. 32, December 2004, No. 12, pp. 16)
Pub: Entrepreneur Media Inc.
Ed: Gisela M. Pedroza. Description: Profile of the Luxury Atomic Solar G-Shock Watch, geared to the international business traveler. The watch features local time for 30 cities around the world.

36277 ■ **"Here's what I'm thinking: you'll get your best deal if prospects see things your way"** in *Entrepreneur* (Vol. 30, No. 10, Oct. 2002)
Pub: Entrepreneur Media Inc.
Ed: Marc Diener. Description: Preparation is the key to the power of persuasion when negotiating a business deal. Three important tips are offered by speaker and attorney, Marc Diener, author of the book, Deal Power.

36278 ■ **"Herman J. Russell"** in *Black Enterprise* (Vol. 36, December 2005, No. 5, pp. 28)
Pub: Earl G. Graves Publishing Co. Inc.
Ed: Alan Hughes. Description: Profile of Herman J. Russell, founder of H.J. Russell & Company; Russell helped create many Atlanta landmarks including the Georgia Dome and Coca-Cola headquarters.

36279 ■ **"Heroes Of Small Business"** in *Fortune* (Vol. 142, No. 11, November 13, 2000, pp. F348B+)
Pub: Time Inc.
Description: Fortune spotlights 15 people they consider to be heroes in the new Fortune Hall of Fame. From Apple's Steve Jobs to Kinko's founder Paul Orfalea to Earl Graves of Black Enterprise, meet some of the most influential entrepreneurs of the past two decades.

36280 ■ **"He's Still Standing"** in *Black Enterprise* (Vol. 34, No. 2, September 2003, pp. 43)
Pub: Earl Graves Publishing Co.
Ed: Nicole Lewis. Description: Profile of William Burton, owner of Professional Systems Inc., a firm that consults, implements, and customizes computer software and hardware for clients in the Chicago, Illinois area. Burton has been successful despite rejections for loans.

36281 ■ **"Hey, entrepreneurs! What's in your briefcase?"** in *Entrepreneur* (Vol. 30, No. 3, March 2002, pp. 22)
Pub: Entrepreneur Media Inc.
Ed: Mike Besack. Description: Entrepreneurs from various industries are asked the question: What do you carry in your briefcase?

36282 ■ **"Hey, Listen Up!"** in *Entrepreneur* (Vol. 31, No. 9, July 2003, pp. 124)
Pub: Entrepreneur Media, Inc.
Ed: Romanus Wolter. Description: Steps to help entrepreneurs grow a business and become open to ideas are listed.

36283 ■ **"High designs: the architect's career is taking flight"** in *Black Enterprise* (Vol. 33, No. 3, October 2002, pp. 74)
Pub: Earl Graves Publishing Co.
Ed: Christina Morgan. Description: Profile of Chauncey Tucker, architectural consultant in charge of the design, development and maintenance of new and existing plans for LaGuardia, Newark, and Teterboro airports for the Port Authority of New York and New Jersey.

36284 ■ **"A High-Flying Time: Ronald Mays Zips Through the Air with Jets of His Own"** in *Black Enterprise* (Vol. 34, No. 2, September 2003)
Pub: Earl Graves Publishing Co.
Ed: Raelyn C. Johnson. Description: Profile of Ronald Mays, owner of Montgomery Jet Center in Montgomery, Alabama. Mays was the 2002 winner of CLACK ENTERPRISE's Emerging Company of the Year. The center offers services ranging from chartering to pilot staffing.

36285 ■ *High-Tech Entrepreneurship: Managing Innovation in a World of Uncertainty*
Pub: Routledge Inc.
Ed: Michel Bernasconi; Simon Harris. Released: September 2006. Price: $42.95. Description: Profiles of successful high tech companies is included; high tech companies are driving innovation globally.

36286 ■ **"His Brother's Keeper: a Mentor Learns the True Meaning of Leadership"** in *Black Enterprise* (Vol. 37, December 2006, No. 5, pp. 69)
Pub: Earl G. Graves Publishing Co. Inc.
Ed: Laura Egodigwe. Description: Interview with Keith R. Wyche of Pitney Bowes Management Services which discusses the relationship between a mentor and mentee as well as sponsorship.

36287 ■ **"His stand on football: Reginald Rutledge creates a stadium rush"** in *Black Enterprise* (Vol. 33, No. 6, January 2003, pp. 89)
Pub: Earl Graves Publishing Co.
Ed: Sonia Alleyne. Description: Profile of Reginald Rutledge, telecommunications engineer in Texas. Rutledge has been building miniature football stadiums for years, and now sells his creations to clients that include the NFL Players Association, the NCAA, as well as private collectors.

36288 ■ **"His Word is Law"** in *Fast Company* (November 2001, pp. 66)
Pub: Fast Company
Ed: George Anders. Description: Interview with technology guru Gordon Moore, who won fame nearly 40 years ago as the creator of Moore's Law, a radical insight about computing.

36289 ■ "Hispanic Business 100 Influentials" in *Hispanic Business* (October 2003)
Pub: Hispanic Business
Description: Members of the Hispanic Business 100 Most Influential Hispanics for 2003 are profiled. As Hispanic leaders reach new levels of success and status, they dispel stereotypes and set the precedent for further progress.

36290 ■ "Hold On Tight" in *Entrepreneur* (Vol. 31, No. 8, August 2003, pp. 66)
Pub: Entrepreneur Media, Inc.
Ed: Chris Penttila. **Description:** During an economic downturn, it is recommended that company's begin maximizing loyalty in the workplace while it's still an employer's market. Look for ways to maintain a staff before they are enlisted by headhunters when the economy turns.

36291 ■ "Home Plate: Learning How to Let Go by Delegating" in *Crain's Detroit Business* (Vol. 19, No. 49, December 8, 2003, pp. 18)
Pub: Crain Communications Inc., Detroit
Ed: Joel Golden. **Description:** Delegating effectively can help a small business owner free up time, increase employee satisfaction and increase the company's bottom line.

36292 ■ "Home Sweet Equity" in *Hispanic Business* (October 2004, pp. 102, 104, 106)
Pub: Hispanic Business
Ed: John Cox. **Description:** Increasing homeownership rates are becoming a new source of capital for Hispanic entrepreneurs. Home equity loans in the Hispanic community have grown to 5.3 percent in 2001, up from 4 percent in 1993. Statistical data included.

36293 ■ "The Honored Few" in *Hispanic Business* (January/February 2004, pp. 48-50)
Pub: Hispanic Business
Description: Hispanics hold 69 board seats at Fortune 500 corporations, totaling about 1.6 percent of the available seats.

36294 ■ "Hospitality Hobnobber" in *Crain's New York Business* (Vol. 23, January 29, 2007, No. 5, pp. F10)
Pub: Crain Communications, Inc.
Ed: Julie Satow. **Description:** Profile of Mark Gordon, investment banker and managing director of Sonnenblick-Goldman. In the past twelve years he has completed $10 billion worth of transactions.

36295 ■ "The Hot List" in *Black Enterprise* (Vol. 34, No. 5, December 2003)
Pub: Earl Graves Publishing Co.
Ed: Tanisha A. Sykes, Robert Anthony, Siobhan Benet, Cliff Hocker, Tamara Holmes, Alan Hughes, Tykisha Lundy, Christina Morgan, Mayra R. Payne, Marcia Wade. **Description:** Highlights of 50 entrepreneurs and professionals under the age of 40 at the top of their field are presented.

36296 ■ "Hot Seat: Bruce Schneier" in *PC Computing* (April 2000, pp. 42)
Pub: Ziff-Davis Inc.
Ed: Thomas Claburn. **Description:** Bruce Schneier, founder and CTO of Counterpane Internet Security tells how to keep your company safe from Internet vandals. Mr. Schneier has also authored the book entitled, Secrets and Lies: Digital Security in the Networked World (John Wiley & Sons).

36297 ■ "Hotlist 05" in *Black Enterprise* (Vol. 36, December 2005, No. 5, pp. 102)
Pub: Earl G. Graves Publishing Co. Inc.
Description: Profiles of the top young powerful African Americans chosen by Black Enterprise to represent their Hotlist for 2005. These professionals and entrepreneurs are all under the age of 40 and have transformed American business using innovative products or practices.

36298 ■ *How to Be an Entrepreneur and Keep Your Sanity: The African-American Guide to Owning, Building and Maintaining Successfully Your Own Small Business*
Pub: Amber Books
Ed: Paula McCoy Pinderhughes. **Released:** May 2004. **Price:** $14.95. **Description:** Ten easy steps to becoming a successful African-American entrepreneur.

36299 ■ *How to Be an Entrepreneur: The Six Secrets of Self-Made Success*
Pub: Pearson Education, Limited
Ed: Steve Parks. **Released:** August 2006. **Price:** $37.50. **Description:** Entrepreneurial creativity is examined. Statistical data covering failure rates of small businesses is included.

36300 ■ "How to Be a Good Listener" in *Women in Business* (Vol. 54, No. 5, September-October 2002, pp. 17)
Pub: The ABWA Company, Inc.
Ed: Liz Hughes. **Description:** Good listening techniques for managers include paying attention and preventing interruptions.

36301 ■ "How David Steinberg Wins Friends, Influences People, and Moves a Whole Lot of Cell Phones" in *Inc.* (Volume 27, March 2005, No. 3)
Pub: Inc. Magazine
Ed: Ian Mount. **Description:** Profile of David Steinberg, CEO of InPhonic, maker of mobile phone handsets and Web services. Steinberg has grown his firm to nearly $200 million annual revenue in five years.

36302 ■ "How Do You Measure Up? They're Supposed to Follow, But Are You a Leader?" in *My Business* (April/May 2003, pp. 45)
Pub: My Business Magazine
Ed: Jackie Ross. **Description:** Characteristics shared by successful leaders are presented, including vision, dedication, charisma, communication, courage, intuition, and empathy.

36303 ■ "How EDS Got Its Groove Back" in *Fast Company* (November 2001, pp. 106)
Pub: Fast Company
Ed: Bill Breen. **Description:** Profile of Electronic Data Systems Corporation (EDS), and how Dick Brown turned the company around. Financial information included.

36304 ■ "How I Did It" in *Inc.* (Volume 27, March 2005, No. 3, pp. 88-90)
Pub: Inc. Magazine
Ed: John Fried. **Description:** Profile of R. Donahue Peebles, owner of the largest African American real estate development firm in America.

36305 ■ "How owners see themselves on the job" in *Wall Street Journal* (April 22, 2003, pp. A22)
Pub: Dow Jones & Co. Inc.
Ed: Richard C. Breeden. **Description:** Results of the Open Small Business Network Survey of small business owners reveals the way owners see themselves at work.

36306 ■ "How to Make Friends" in *Inc.* (October 1, 2003)
Pub: Gruner & Jahr USA Publishing
Ed: Bobbie Gossage, Matthew Fogel. **Description:** Want to build a professional network? Online Websites offering networking services are listed.

36307 ■ "How to Motivate Your Problem People" in *Harvard Business Review* (Vol. 81, No. 1, January 2003, pp. 57)
Pub: Harvard Business School Press
Description: Methods for motivating intractable employees are examined. A manager must pull solutions out of problem employees rather than pushing solutions on them. The article sites examples.

36308 ■ "How Networking Really Works" in *Black Enterprise* (Vol. 35, February 2005, No. 7, pp. 98)
Pub: Earl G. Graves Publishing Co. Inc.
Ed: Laura Egodigwe. **Description:** Networking is considered a two-way street by successful professionals and should benefit both parties.

36309 ■ "How Presidents Persuade" in *Harvard Business Review* (Vol. 81, No. 1, January 2003, pp. 20)
Pub: Harvard Business School Press
Ed: David R. Gergen. **Description:** An advisor to four presidents discusses how U.S. presidents establish trust and use their powers of oratory to persuade. He also points out the need for true humility and strict honesty with the American people.

36310 ■ *How to Run Your Business Like a Girl: Successful Strategies from Entrepreneurial Women Who Made It Happen*
Pub: Adams Media Corporation
Ed: Elizabeth Cogswell Baskin. **Released:** September 2005. **Price:** $14.95. **Description:** Tour of three women entrepreneurs and their successful companies.

36311 ■ *How to Succeed As a Lifestyle Entrepreneur*
Pub: Dearborn Trade Publishing Inc.
Ed: Gary Schine. **Price:** $18.95.

36312 ■ *How to Think Like an Entrepreneur*
Pub: Bret Publishing Limited Partnership
Ed: Michael B. Shane. **Released:** 1994. **Price:** $9.95.

36313 ■ "How To Assemble a Board of Directors" in *Inc.* (October 1, 2004)
Pub: Inc. Magazine
Ed: Nicole Gull. **Description:** Advice for putting together a Board of Directors that will best serve a small business is given.

36314 ■ "How To Be a Great Boss" in *Inc.* (October 1, 2004)
Pub: Inc. Magazine
Ed: Rod Kurtz. **Description:** Management means directing workers, but a boss should also let employees know that you mean well when making decisions.

36315 ■ "How To Conduct Due Diligence" in *Inc.* (October 1, 2004)
Pub: Inc. Magazine
Ed: Darren Dahl. **Description:** It is imperative to be sure there is nothing amiss when acquiring a new business. Things to keep in mind when conducting due diligence are listed.

36316 ■ "How To Create an Entrepreneurial Infrastructure" in *Venture Capital Journal* (January 1, 2005)
Pub: Thomason Financial Inc.
Ed: Tom Dickerson. **Description:** Development of a favorable entrepreneurial environment requires an increase in the quantity and quality of each of three critical elements: research and development, capital and entrepreneurs and each of these elements typically grow in relation to the others.

36317 ■ "How To Fire Decisively" in *Inc.* (October 1, 2004)
Pub: Inc. Magazine
Ed: Patrick J. Sauer. **Description:** Tips to assist managers in firing an employee are presented.

36318 ■ "How To Get the Kids On Your Side" in *Inc.* (October 1, 2004)
Pub: Inc. Magazine
Ed: Lora Kolodny. **Description:** Entrepreneurial parents need to articulate their values to their children, because business has to come first in certain family situations.

36319 ■ "How To Give Your Money Away" in *Inc.* (October 1, 2004)
Pub: Inc. Magazine
Ed: Jess McCuan. **Description:** Entrepreneurs have difficulty finding a satisfying way to give back. Possibilities besides giving to a nonprofit include starting a family foundation or sponsoring educational programs.

36320 ■ "How To Raise an Entrepreneur" in *Inc.* **(August 2005, pp. 80-85)**
Pub: Inc. Magazine
Ed: Jonathan Black. **Description:** The key to raising an entrepreneur was, for Michelle Rousseff Kemp, keeping her children away from the family business.

36321 ■ "How To Spot Trouble in Your Financials" in *Inc.* **(October 1, 2004)**
Pub: Inc. Magazine
Ed: Darren Dahl, Carol Hirsch. **Description:** One way to diagnose problems with your company is to look at the firm's financials.

36322 ■ "How To Stay on a Winning Streak" in *Inc.* **(October 1, 2004)**
Pub: Inc. Magazine
Ed: Nadine Heintz. **Description:** The four commandments created by Rosabeth Moss Kanater of the Harvard Business School are shared. Thou shalt not: panic, be rigid, deny change; thou shalt: celebrate success.

36323 ■ "How To Work (If You Must) With Your Spouse" in *Inc.* **(October 1, 2004)**
Pub: Inc. Magazine
Ed: Michael S. Hopkins. **Description:** The challenges of partnering with a spouse in a business venture are observed. Recommendations to overcome these challenges are offered.

36324 ■ "How To Work With a Partner (Year After Year After Year)" in *Inc.* **(October 1, 2004)**
Pub: Inc. Magazine
Ed: Patrick J. Sauer. **Description:** Ways to create a lasting business partnership are examined.

36325 ■ "How (Un)Ethical Are You?" in *Harvard Business Review* **(Vol. 81, No. 12, December 2003, pp. 56)**
Pub: Harvard Business School Press
Ed: Mahzaarin R. Banaji, Max H. Bazerman, Dolly Chugh. **Description:** Four sources of unintentional bias in management decision making are examined: conflict of interest, in-group favoritism, overclaiming credit, and implicit prejudice are shown. Methods for mitigating the sources of bias include shaping one's environment to reduce external cues, broadening the hypothetical influence of decision-making processes, and remaining vigilant.

36326 ■ "How to Win Big and Get Ahead Fast" in *Inc.* **(September 1, 2003)**
Pub: Gruner & Jahr USA Publishing
Description: College business-plan contests offer competitors the chance to win money to launch a startup.

36327 ■ "Howdy Partner!" in *Home Business* **(Vol. 12, March/April 2005, No. 2, pp. 44)**
Pub: Home Business Magazine
Description: Strategic alliances, agreements that establish exchange relationships between two cooperating companies, can help small businesses grow.

36328 ■ "Humanizing Leaders" in *Fast Company* **(March 2005, No. 92, pp. 82)**
Pub: Gruner & Jahr USA Publishing
Ed: Jennifer Vilaga. **Description:** Leadership courses are previewed, including a six-day course that allows business leaders to address the larger issues of leadership, innovation and creativity.

36329 ■ "I Consider Myself the Visionary Still" in *Business Week* **(December 19, 2005, No. 3964, pp. 54, 56)**
Pub: McGraw-Hill Companies
Description: Martha Stewart discusses her television shows, her return to work, and her time in jail.

36330 ■ "I was greedy, too" in *Harvard Business Review* **(Vol. 81, No. 2, February 2003, pp. 38)**
Pub: Harvard Business School Press
Ed: Diane L. Coutu. **Description:** Although greed has become an integral part of the U.S. psyche, the psy-chology of greed has not been studied well. Greed has ebbed and crested throughout this country's history, and most recently with the collapse of Internet companies, corporate malfeasance. However, business schools continue to graduate a high number of students.

36331 ■ "I Have One Life, and It Must Come Together" in *Inc.* **(October 1, 2003)**
Pub: Gruner & Jahr USA Publishing
Description: Five entrepreneurs define what the good life means to them.

36332 ■ "I Think I'll Pass: Do Women Have a Tougher Time Delegating Tasks?" in *Entrepreneur* **(Vol. 32, October 2004, No. 10, pp. 44)**
Pub: Entrepreneur Media Inc.
Ed: Aliza Pilar Sherman. **Description:** Although all entrepreneurs have trouble delegating tasks to employees, women business owners seem to have even more difficulty. Women also tend to be nurturing when delegating.

36333 ■ "Ideas on demand: you don't have to wait for inspiration" in *Entrepreneur* **(Vol. 31, No. 4, April 2003, pp. 78)**
Pub: Entrepreneur Media Inc.
Ed: Juanita Weaver. **Description:** The novel prompt creativity technique to promote innovation is examined. A novel prompt can be anything such as a word, a color, a fantasy, or an object that will launch thinking that will generate new ideas. Examples using the technique are given.

36334 ■ "The idol life" in *Entrepreneur* **(Vol. 30, No. 1, January 2002,)**
Pub: Entrepreneur Media Inc.
Ed: Aliza Pilar Sherman. **Description:** An interview with five of today's entrepreneurial icons and how they have changed from their early days in business through the current economic market, how they cope with ever-changing technology and ways they have endured their entrepreneurial spark.

36335 ■ "If At First You Don't Succeed" in *Inc.* **(July 1, 2003)**
Pub: Gruner & Jahr USA Publishing
Ed: Hillary Johnson. **Description:** Author describes how her father tried to reconcile his big ideas with a small-minded business world.

36336 ■ "If I knew then what I know now" in *WorkingWoman* **(Vol. 25, No. 7, August 2000, pp. 48)**
Pub: Lang Communications Inc.
Ed: Jeanne McDowell. **Description:** The views of seven successful American business women are shared, covering early working experience, combining family and work and competing in a male dominated sector.

36337 ■ "If Members Think Items are Overpriced, They'll Blame Barter Trust's Economy, says CEO Mike Edelhart" in *Inc.* **(October 2000, pp. 58)**
Pub: The Goldhirsh Group
Description: Although exchange customers display some ambivalence about barter, the latest generation of Web-enabled exchange operators is predictability bullish.

36338 ■ "The Impact of Immigrant Entrepreneurs" in *Business Week* **(February 7, 2007)**
Pub: McGraw-Hill Companies
Ed: Kerry Miller. **Description:** Overview of immigrant entrepreneur's impact on economic development and their status as a driving force for the U.S. economy.

36339 ■ "The Imposter Syndrome. Why Do So Many Successful Entrepreneurs Feel Like Fakes?" in *Inc.* **(September 2006, pp. 37-38)**
Pub: Gruner & Jahr USA Publishing
Ed: Leigh Buchanan. **Description:** Many successful entrepreneurs are embarrassed by their success and feel their success is due to timing and location than personal talent. This can be dangerous in the long range.

36340 ■ "In the Driver's Seat" in *Entrepreneur* **(Vol. 33, September 2005, No. 9, pp. 10)**
Pub: Entrepreneur Media Inc.
Ed: Rieva Lesonsky. **Description:** Small business owners have the same thing in common: they want to build something and be responsible for its success. Owning a business allows the entrepreneur to take ownership of his or her life.

36341 ■ "In His Element" in *Hispanic Business* **(Vol. 23, No. 7/8, July/August 2001, pp. 80, 82)**
Pub: Hispanic Business
Ed: Teresa Talerico. **Description:** Profile of Robert Rodriguez, the 33 year-old movie director.

36342 ■ "In Praise of the Paper Trail" in *Hispanic Business* **(June 2002, pp. 92)**
Pub: Hispanic Business
Description: The importance of documenting meetings, conversations, and agreements to protect a CEO when a deal goes array is stressed. Tips for documenting events is included.

36343 ■ "In Search of a Leader" in *Women in Business* **(Vol. 54, No. 2, March-April 2002, pp. 11)**
Pub: The ABWA Co Inc.
Ed: Linda S. Demorest, Deona Grady. **Description:** Specific personality traits are exhibited by leaders; some of these traits include charisma and motivational skills.

36344 ■ "In Strictest Confidence" in *Entrepreneur* **(Vol. 32, November 2004, No. 11, pp. 28)**
Pub: Entrepreneur Media Inc.
Ed: Mark Henricks. **Description:** Review of Rosabeth Moss Kanter's book, Confidence. Kanter believes confidence rests on three pillars: accountability, collaboration and initiative.

36345 ■ *Influence without Authority*
Pub: John Wiley and Sons Inc.
Ed: Allan R. Cohen; David L. Bradford. **Released:** March 2005. **Price:** $29.95.

36346 ■ *Innov and Entrepren in Biotech*
Pub: Edward Elgar Publishing, Incorporated
Ed: Hine. **Released:** April 2006. **Price:** $100.00. **Description:** Innovation processes underlying successful entrepreneurship in the biotechnology sector are explored.

36347 ■ *Innovation and Entrepreneurship*
Pub: HarperCollins Publishers, Inc.
Ed: Peter F. Drucker. **Released:** May 2006. **Price:** $16.95. **Description:** Presentation of entrepreneurship and innovation and a purposeful and systematic discipline and the challenges and opportunities of the American entrepreneurial economy.

36348 ■ *Innovation and Entrepreneurship: Practice and Principles*
Pub: Elsevier Science & Technology Books
Ed: Peter F. Drucker. **Released:** November 2004. **Description:** Profile of entrepreneurial innovation.

36349 ■ "The innovation toolkit" in *Entrepreneur* **(Vol. 31, No. 5, May 2003, pp. 52)**
Pub: Entrepreneur Media Inc.
Ed: Joshua Kurlantzick. **Description:** Innovation remains the most important component of small business success. A listing of 18 how-to's of innovation every entrepreneur should know are included.

36350 ■ "Inside Intel" in *Business Week* **(January 9, 2006, No. 3966, pp. 46-52, 54)**
Pub: McGraw-Hill Companies
Ed: Cliff Edwards. **Description:** Profile of Paul Otellini, CEO of Intel Corporation. Otellini is taking the computer chipmaker into sectors such as consumer electronics, wireless communications, and health care.

36351 ■ "Inspiring Black Investors" in *Black Enterprise* **(Vol. 35, January 2005, No. 6, pp. 58)**
Pub: Earl G. Graves Publishing Co. Inc.
Ed: Derek T. Dingle. Description: Profile of John W. Rogers Jr., owner of Airel Capital Management, one of the most powerful firms on Wall Street. In 1983, Rogers launched his first family of equity mutual funds managed by African Americans.

36352 ■ *Instant Income*
Pub: McGraw-Hill Inc.
Ed: Janet Switzer. Released: February 2007. Price: $30.95 (CND). Description: Book covers small business advertising techniques, marketing, joint ventures, and sales.

36353 ■ "Instantly International" in *Inc.* **(Volume 27, June 2005, No. 6, pp. 44)**
Pub: Inc. Magazine
Ed: Darren Dahl. Description: Profile of John Buckman, owner of an email list-management company in Berkeley, California. Buckman also launched Magnatune.com, a global online music label. The entrepreneur started Magnatune.com after his wife, a composer of electronic music, had been dropped from her music label.

36354 ■ *Instinct: Tapping Your Entrepreneurial DNA to Achieve Your Business Goals*
Pub: Warner Books, Incorporated
Ed: Mary H. Frakes; Thomas L. Harrison. Released: September 2006. Price: $15.99. Description: Research shows that entrepreneurs may attribute their success to genetics.

36355 ■ "Interiors By Design" in *Black Enterprise* **(Vol. 35, October 2004, No. 3, pp. 54)**
Pub: Earl G. Graves Publishing Co. Inc.
Ed: Virginia Myers Kelly. Description: Profile of Dennese Guadeloupe Rojas, a laid off direct mail worker, who earned a degree in interior design and is now the successful owner of Interiors By Design. Rojas offers interior and exterior design as well as home accessories to her clients. She started out working from home, but soon found she needed more space.

36356 ■ *International Entrepreneurship*
Pub: Edward Elgar Publishing, Incorporated
Ed: Oviatt. Released: March 2007. Price: $295.00. Description: Universities are focusing research efforts on international entrepreneurship. The book features critical articles on the topic.

36357 ■ *International Entrepreneurship Education Issues and Newness*
Pub: Edward Elgar Publishing, Incorporated
Ed: Fayolle. Released: August 2006. Price: $120.00. Description: Entrepreneurial education, focusing on economic, political and social needs of a changing world; ideas for reassessing, redeveloping, and renewing curricula and methods for teaching entrepreneurship are offered.

36358 ■ *International Entrepreneurship in Small and Medium Size Enterprises: Orientation, Environment and Strategy*
Pub: Edward Elgar Publishing, Incorporated
Ed: Hamid Etemad. Released: November 2004. Price: $110.00. Description: Issues involved in internationalizing small and medium sized (SME) businesses. Topics include an investigation into the emerging patterns of SME growth and international expansion in response to the changing competitive environment, dynamics of competitive behavior, entrepreneurial processes and a formulation of strategy.

36359 ■ *International Handbook of Women and Small Business Entrepreneurship*
Pub: Edward Elgar Publishing, Incorporated
Ed: Sandra L. Fielden. Released: June 2005. Price: $165.00. Description: The number of women entrepreneurs is growing at a faster rate than male counterparts worldwide. Insight into the phenomenon is targeted to scholars and students of women in management and entrepreneurship as well as policymakers and small business service providers.

36360 ■ "International corporate entrepreneurship and firm performance" in *Journal of Business Venturing* **(Vol. 15, No. 5-6, Sept.-Nov. 2000)**
Pub: Elsevier Science, Inc.
Ed: Shaker A. Zahra, Dennis M. Garvis. Description: A new study uses information for 98 U.S. companies to investigate their international corporate entrepreneurship activities.

36361 ■ "Is Anybody in Charge?" in *Fast Company* **(June 2001, pp. 52)**
Pub: Fast Company
Ed: Christine Canabou. Description: The changing face of management in the new technology-driven world is explored.

36362 ■ "Is There a Secret to Happiness in Retirement?" in *Women In Business* **(Vol. 52, No. 3, May 2000, pp. 9)**
Pub: The ABWA Co., Inc.
Ed: Kathie Dickenson. Description: Radford University Human Development Professor Janette Newhouse suggests good health, sufficient money and close relationships with family and friends will help people to have an enjoyable retirement.

36363 ■ "Is This Any Way to Run a Family" in *Inc.* **(Volume 27, December 2005, No. 12, pp. 122-131)**
Pub: Inc. Magazine
Ed: Robb Mandelbaum. Description: Profile of Tom Parsons who started a travel business with his 15-year-old son.

36364 ■ "Is Your Mate Ready For Your Success?" in *Black Enterprise* **(Vol. 34, July 2004, No. 12, pp. 139)**
Pub: Earl G. Graves Publishing Co. Inc.
Ed: Robyn D. Clarke. Description: Young entrepreneurs and business leaders need support from home in order to be comfortable with their successes.

36365 ■ "It figures" in *Entrepreneur* **(Vol. 31, No. 5, May 2003, pp. 32)**
Pub: Entrepreneur Media Inc.
Ed: Steve Cooper. Description: Statistical data is provided regarding various business issues, including entrepreneurial motivation, Internet Web sites and users, and germ warfare in the workplace.

36366 ■ "It's 2006! Whatcha Gonna Do About It?" in *Inc.* **(Volume 28, January 2006, No. 1, pp. 78-85, 113)**
Pub: Inc. Magazine
Ed: Stephanie Clifford. Description: Various entrepreneurs give advice to help small businesses face new challenges in 2006. Topics include investments, the economy, small business trends, logistics, business communication such as blogs, energy issues, consumer products, real estate, interest rates and outsourcing.

36367 ■ "It's All Relative" in *Entrepreneur* **(Vol. 33, March 2005, No. 3, pp. 74)**
Pub: Entrepreneur Media Inc.
Ed: Chris Penttila. Description: Three entrepreneurs offer insight into hiring a newcomer to help revitalize a family-run business.

36368 ■ "It's Business...and Personal" in *Black Enterprise* **(Vol. 34, July 2004, No. 12, pp. 38)**
Pub: Earl G. Graves Publishing Co. Inc.
Ed: Aissatou Sidime. Description: Anthony Harris, owner of Popular Demand clothing store and Popular Demand Unisex Salon in Cleveland, Ohio, reports how he has formed a retirement savings account by investing in mutual funds and government bonds through a financial advisor who also helped Harris find personal medical coverage and life insurance.

36369 ■ "It's Good to be King" in *Inc.* **(December 1, 2003)**
Pub: Gruner & Jahr USA Publishing
Ed: Jess McCuan. Description: In a study conducted by the Families and Work Institute, small business owners reported large personal satisfaction in entrepreneurship.

36370 ■ "It's a Good Time to Scare Up Business" in *St. Louis Post-Dispatch* **(October 11, 2004)**
Pub: Knight-Ridder/Tribune Business News
Ed: Mary Jo Feldstein. Description: Profile of Ray Sheetz, who co-manages Darkness, a haunted house in Soulard, Missouri. Sheetz's designs have earned the house one of the nation's best haunted houses award by Hauntworld.com, MSNBC, and Fangoria magazine.

36371 ■ "It's Important to Be Proactive about Risk Issues" in *Atlanta Business Chronicle* **(Vol. 24, No. 9, August 3, 2001, pp. 9B)**
Pub: American City Business Journals Inc.
Description: Major factors resulting in business failure include customer demand shortage, irregularities in accounting, issues concerning supply chain and competitive pressures. In protecting a business from risk of failure, in addition to purchasing insurance, a culture and organizational structure where risk management is seen as everyone's job, is essential.

36372 ■ "It's Never E-nough" in *Business Week* **(No. 3689, July 10, 2000, pp. F14)**
Pub: McGraw-Hill, Inc.
Description: Highlights of surveys of companies with 20-49 employees regarding the future of small business, including information about the Internet, Palmtops, networks, e-backlash, the bottom line, cost cutting, outsourcing, leasing, and Internet Telephony.

36373 ■ "It's a New Game: Killerspin Pushes Table Tennis to Extreme Heights" in *Black Enterprise* **(Vol. 37, October 2006, No. 3, pp. 73)**
Pub: Earl G. Graves Publishing Co. Inc.
Ed: Bridget McCrea. Description: Profile of Robert Blackwell and his company Killerspin L.L.C., which is popularizing the sport of table tennis. Killerspin has hit $1 million in revenues due to product sales primarily generated through the company's website, magazines, DVDs, and event ticket sales.

36374 ■ "It's Not Easy Being Green" in *Inc.* **(November 1, 2004)**
Pub: Inc. Magazine
Ed: Jess McCuan. Description: Jeffrey Hollender and Alan Newman disagreed about strategy, fought bitterly-and created two successful companies. They'd set out to change the world, but really changed each other in the end.

36375 ■ "It's Not about Money" in *Wall Street Journal* **(May 22, 2000, pp. R18)**
Pub: Dow Jones & Co., Inc.
Ed: Jeffrey A. Tannenbaum. Description: A profile of Vincent Pan.

36376 ■ "It's a Snap" in *Houston Business Journal* **(Vol. 34, No. 18, September 12, 2003, pp. 17)**
Pub: American City Business Journals
Ed: Allison Wollam. Description: Alvin Gee, owner of Alvin Gee Photography, has thrived during the economic downturn by leasing space to other businesses.

36377 ■ "It's the Sound Bite, Stupid" in *Inc.* **(Volume 27, June 2005, No. 6, pp. 128)**
Pub: Inc. Magazine
Ed: Adam Hanft. Description: Business leaders must understand the importance of good communications skills when conducting business.

36378 ■ "It's Swing Time" in *Inc.* **(September 1, 2004)**
Pub: Inc. Magazine
Ed: Adam Hanft. Description: Corporate America is suffering from bipolar management disorder.

36379 ■ "Ivan Allen Jr. helped build, and heal Atlanta" in *Atlanta Business Chronicle* **(Vol. 25, No. 22, November 8, 2002, pp. 4C)**
Pub: American City Business Publications, Inc.
Ed: Tom Barry. Description: A profile of Ivan Allen, Jr., one of the latest inductees of the Atlanta Convention and Visitors Bureau Hospitality Hall of Fame. Allen was noted for his support of civil rights while he was Mayor of Atlanta in the early 1960's.

36380 ■ "Jack of All Trades" in *Hispanic Business* (Vol. 23, No. 5, May 2001, pp. 70-71)
Pub: Hispanic Business
Ed: Teresa Talerico. Description: Profile of Charles Garcia, founder and CEO of Sterling Financial Investment Group. Under Mr. Garcia's leadership, Sterling Financial has seen a 3,800 percent growth rate over three years.

36381 ■ "Jack on Jack" in *Harvard Business Review* (Vol. 80, No. 2, February 2002, pp. 88)
Pub: Harvard Business School Press
Ed: Harris Collingwood, Diane L. Coutu. Description: An interview with Jack Welch, former CEO of General Electric, who stepped down from his position in September 2001. Welch's influence over future leaders is still unclear.

36382 ■ "James Bronce Henderson III" in *Crain's Detroit Business* (Vol. 19, No. 1, January 6, 2003, pp. 11)
Pub: Crain Communications Inc., Detroit
Ed: Michael Strong. Description: James Bronce Henderson III, owner of Utica Enterprises Inc. in Shelby Township, Michigan discusses his filing Chapter 11 bankruptcy and the impact it had on his employees.

36383 ■ "James L. McNeil" in *Entrepreneur* (Vol. 31, No. 10, October 2003, pp. 30)
Pub: Entrepreneur Media, Inc.
Ed: April Y. Pennington. Description: Profile of James L. McNeil, founder and CEO of McNeil Technologies Inc., in Springfield, Virginia. The firm offers language services, consulting services, information and securities services, and operates a subsidiary that publishes books, dictionaries and glossaries.

36384 ■ "Java Enabled" in *Entrepreneur* (Vol. 32, December 2004, No. 12, pp. 164)
Pub: Entrepreneur Media Inc.
Ed: April Y. Pennington. Description: Profile of Jeremy Gursey, founder of Mocha Kiss Coffee. Gursey runs catered coffee bars, retail stores on movie lots that serve hot and ice-blended coffee beverages, and sells gourmet coffee beans to wholesalers.

36385 ■ "J.C. Watts First Black John Deere Dealer" in *Black Enterprise* (Vol. 37, November 2006, No. 4, pp. 36)
Pub: Earl G. Graves Publishing Co. Inc.
Ed: Kiara Ashanti. Description: Profile of former Congressman J.C. Watts Jr., a man who grew up in rural America and is the first African American to own a John Deere Dealership.

36386 ■ *The Jewish Century*
Pub: Princeton University Press
Ed: Yuri Slezkins. Released: August 2006. Price: $18.95. Description: Success and vulnerability of individuals of Jewish descent is discussed, uncovering the 'Jewish Revolution' within the Russian Revolution.

36387 ■ "John Chambers after the deluge" in *Fast Company* (July 2001, pp. 100)
Pub: Fast Company
Ed: George Anders. Description: Interview with John Chambers, CEO of Cisco, where he explains how to slow down smart, why the Internet still matters, and what to do when customers stop buying.

36388 ■ "John Deere Named In Discrimination Suit" in *Black Enterprise* (Vol. 35, August 2004, No. 1, pp. 30)
Pub: Earl G. Graves Publishing Co. Inc.
Ed: Aisha Jefferson. Description: After working for John Deere for 30 years, Kenny Edwards wanted to become an entrepreneur by purchasing his own John Deere agricultural dealership. Edwards has sued the company for discrimination when it turned down his bid for ownership. Of the 1,400 John Deere agricultural dealerships in the U.S. non are African-American owned, and only 5 percent of owners include women, Hispanics, and Asians.

36389 ■ "The Joy Factory" in *WorkingWoman* (Vol. 25, No. 4, April 2000, pp. 48)
Pub: Lang Communications Inc.
Ed: Susan Caminiti. Description: Clincal psychologist, author, and television presenter, Dr. Joy Browne, talks about her move to television from radio broadcasting.

36390 ■ "The Juggling Act" in *My Business* (October/November 2003, pp. 36-39)
Pub: My Business Magazine
Ed: Nancy Mann Jackson. Description: Owning one business is not as difficult as it seems; tips to help entrepreneurs handle the operations of more than one business are given, including good organization skills.

36391 ■ "A Juice Guy Changes Lanes" in *Inc.* (December 1, 2003)
Pub: Gruner & Jahr USA Publishing
Ed: Nadine Heintz. Description: Profile of Tom First, cofounder of Nantucket Nectars. First and partner have sold the juice business to Ocean Spray, and is opening a gourmet grocery store in Concord, Massachusetts, called Concord Provisions.

36392 ■ "The Juice is Loose" in *My Business* (April/May 2004, pp. 16)
Pub: My Business Magazine
Ed: Gwen Moran. Description: Creative solutions can help a small business grow.

36393 ■ "Just 'To-Do' It: Having Trouble Getting Organized? Start by Getting a Grip on Your To-Do List" in *Entrepreneur* (August 2004)
Pub: Entrepreneur Media Inc.
Ed: Mark Hendricks. Description: Successful entrepreneurs create a weekly to-do list in order to stay focused and organized.

36394 ■ "Karaoke Nation" in *Entrepreneur* (Vol. 31, No. 8, August 2003, pp. 6)
Pub: Entrepreneur Media, Inc.
Ed: Steve Cooper. Description: Steve Fishman tells the story of his search for the American dream selling hip-hop karaoke.

36395 ■ "Kate and Andy Spade Are That Rare Thing: A Great Husband-and-Wife Business Team" in *Fast Company* (March 2005, No. 92, pp. 44)
Pub: Gruner & Jahr USA Publishing
Ed: Linda Tischler. Description: Profile of Kate and Andy Spade, husband and wife owners of the hip fashion company Kate Spade. It took only eleven years for the couple to build a $175 million business with a distinctive global brand.

36396 ■ "Kay Wagner" in *San Diego Business Journal* (Vol. 28, January 15, 2007, No. 3, pp. 34)
Pub: San Diego Business Journal Associates
Ed: Pat Broderick. Description: Profile of Kay Wagner, who has been executive director of the Children's Museum/Museo de Los Ninos since 1999. Wagner is responsible for the museum's new 50,000-square-foot complex.

36397 ■ "K.C. Hopps, Ltd." in *Ingram's* (Vol. 28, No. 5, May 2002, pp. 38)
Pub: Show Me Publishing, Inc.
Description: Profile of Ed Nelson and James Taylor who set up a brewpub in 1993, naming it the 75th Street Brewery. Ed Nelson bought Taylor out and is now president and CEO of the K.C. Hopps Ltd., which owns and manages several restaurants, brewpubs and eateries in Kansas and Missouri.

36398 ■ "Keeping America safe" in *Black Enterprise* (Vol. 32, No. 5, Decembe)
Pub: Earl Graves Publishing Co.
Ed: Michelle Buckley. Description: Profile of Reginald Daniel and his 1996 startup, Scientific & Engineering Solutions Information Technology consulting firm. Daniel was designated this year's Ernst & Young's IT Consulting Entrepreneur of the Year from Maryland, and National Black Chamber of Commerce name him Entrepreneur of the Year.

36399 ■ "Keeping the Balls Rolling" in *Entrepreneur* (Vol. 30, No. 10, October 2002, pp. 39)
Pub: Entrepreneur Media Inc.
Ed: Elizabeth J. Goodgold. Description: Profile of Jerry Swain, owner of Swain Creations and maker of Jer's IncrediBalls. Swain discovered that customers were more interested in the number of pieces of candy than weight when purchasing his chocolate confections.

36400 ■ "Keeping It All in the Family" in *Black Enterprise* (Vol. 31, No. 5, December 2000, pp. 66)
Pub: Earl Graves Publishing Co.
Ed: Glenn Townes. Description: Profile of James Olan Hutcheson, founder and president of ReGeneration Partners, offers advice in handling the future of family-owned businesses.

36401 ■ "Keeping It Positive" in *Small Business Opportunities* (Vol. 17, May 2005, No. 3, pp. 18, 20)
Pub: Harris Publications Inc.
Ed: Dave Anderson. Description: Small business owners can increase profits when boosting employee morale. Positive reinforcement should be given verbally or tangibly and should be as specific as possible.

36402 ■ "Ken Burn's Jeffersonian Pavilion" in *Inc.* (January 1, 2002)
Pub: Inc. Magazine
Ed: John Grossmann. Description: Filmmaker Ken Burns speaks to the importance of finding a space for one's self, in order to get away from daily business pressures.

36403 ■ "Keys to Communication" in *Small Business Opportunities* (Vol. 16, November 2004, No. 6, pp. 10)
Pub: Harris Publications Inc.
Ed: Lydia Ramsey. Description: Studies show that words account for only 7 percent of a message, 93 percent is non-verbal. In a business setting, body language must match your words in order to effectively communicate.

36404 ■ "Kid-Friendly Business Sources" in *Black Enterprise* (Vol. 37, January 2007, No. 6, pp. 40)
Pub: Earl G. Graves Publishing Co. Inc.
Ed: Carolyn M. Brown. Description: Financial or business camps are a great way to encourage a child who interested in starting his or her own business. A number of these camps are available each year including Kidpreneurs Conference and Bull and Bear Investment Camp. Other resources are available online. Resources included.

36405 ■ "Kid from the capital makes good" in *Hispanic Business* (Vol. 22, No. 11, November 2000, pp. 20)
Pub: Hispanic Business
Ed: Derek Reveron. Description: The lifestyle, political career and entrepreneurship of Raul Fernandez is profiled. His founding of the Internet based company Proxicom Inc. in 1991 is discussed.

36406 ■ "Kid stuff: want to light your child's entrepreneurial fire?" in *Entrepreneur* (Vol. 31, No. 5, May 2003, pp. 24)
Pub: Entrepreneur Media Inc.
Ed: Nichole L. Torres. Description: Information on camps focusing on hands-on training for young people to learn to be entrepreneurs is provided. Requirements and contact information for Camp Startup; Excellence in Youth Entrepreneurs; Wise Kid, Wealthy Kid Youth Entrepreneurship Camp, and Youth Entrepreneur Camp is also included.

36407 ■ "Killer Apps for Rent" in *Success* (Vol. 47, No. 3, July 2000, pp. 22)
Pub: Success Publishing, Inc.
Description: Bob Frankenberg has found a way to serve small businesses that want to connect to the Internet, through Encanto Networks, an Internet and applications service provider.

36408 ■ "KILO still rockin' after 25 years in the business" in *Colorado Springs Business Journal* **(February 28, 2003)**
Pub: Dolan Media Newswires
Ed: Lance Gurwell. **Description:** Profile of radio station KILO, 94.3 FM in Colorado Springs, Colorado. The station is celebrating its 25th anniversary.

36409 ■ *Kitchen Table Entrepreneurs: How Eleven Women Escaped Poverty and Became Their Own Bosses*
Pub: Westview Press
Ed: Martha Shirk, Anna S. Wadia. **Released:** February 2004. **Price:** $14.95. **Description:** Profile of eleven successful women entrepreneurs.

36410 ■ "Kitchen Table Entrepreneurs" in *Small Business Opportunities* **(Vol. 16, November 2004, No. 6, pp. 134)**
Pub: Harris Publications Inc.
Description: Book review of Kitchen Table Entrepreneurs, by Martha Shirk and Anna S. Wadia. The book shows how eleven women pulled themselves from poverty and became successful entrepreneurs.

36411 ■ *Know-Who Based Entrepreneurship from Knowledge Creation to Business Implementation*
Pub: Edward Elgar Publishing, Incorporated
Ed: Harryson. **Released:** August 2006. **Price:** $130.00. **Description:** Analysis of the knowledge and interconnected areas of entrepreneurship and networking across various levels is presented. Best practice companies are profiled.

36412 ■ "Knowing When It's Time" in *Black Enterprise* **(Vol. 35, December 2004, No. 5, pp. 65)**
Pub: Earl G. Graves Publishing Co. Inc.
Ed: Alan Hughes. **Description:** Ways to determine whether a part-time entrepreneur can afford to quit his fulltime job and devote full-time attention to his new company are discussed.

36413 ■ "La-Van Hawkins Linked to Philadelphia Corruption Probe" in *Black Enterprise* **(Vol. 35, September 2004, No. 2)**
Pub: Earl G. Graves Publishing Co. Inc.
Ed: Alan Hughes. **Description:** CEO of La-Van Hawkins Food & Entertainment Group LLC, La-Van Hawkins, has been connected to a Philadelphia corruption case where people have been charged for paying off former Philadelphia treasurer in a scandal in which 12 people have been indicted. Hawkins is charged with conspiring to commit honest services fraud, four counts of wire fraud, and four counts of perjuring himself before the Grand Jury investigating the case.

36414 ■ "Labor for Love" in *Entrepreneur* **(Vol. 33, February 2005, No. 2, pp. 68)**
Pub: Entrepreneur Media Inc.
Ed: Kirsten Osolind. **Description:** Three steps for entrepreneurs that help increase client base are listed, using love as the topic. Listening to customers, then initiating two-way dialogue is essential.

36415 ■ "A Labor of Love: Have You Lost That Lovin' Feeling For Your Business?" in *Entrepreneur* **(Vol. 32, November 2004, No. 11, pp. 130)**
Pub: Entrepreneur Media Inc.
Ed: Romanus Wolter. **Description:** Four ways to renew entrepreneurial passion are designed to bring happiness back into day-to-day business activities.

36416 ■ "Landing the big fish" in *Crain's Detroit Business* **(Vol. 19, No. 6, February 10, 2003, pp. 3)**
Pub: Crain Communications Inc., Detroit
Ed: Laura Bailey. **Description:** Networking and persistence are the two most important factors needed for small companies to win sales with major corporations.

36417 ■ "Language of the Middle Class" in *Hispanic Business* **(December 2003, pp. 28-30, 32)**
Pub: Hispanic Business
Description: English is the key, both for U.S. Hispanics who want to succeed in business, and the marketers wanting to appeal to them. Statistical data included.

36418 ■ "Laugh track" in *Entrepreneur* **(Vol. 30, No. 2, February 2002)**
Pub: Entrepreneur Media Inc.
Ed: April Pennington. **Description:** Profile of Sushil Bhatia, founder of the Laughing Clubs of America. The firm offers 30-45 minute sessions of laughter that encourage a more positive attitude, relaxation and a strengthened immune system.

36419 ■ "Leader of the Pack" in *Entrepreneur* **(Vol. 32, November 2004, No. 11, pp. 106)**
Pub: Entrepreneur Media Inc.
Ed: Jeri Yoshida. **Description:** Profile of Urmila Patel, the 46-year-old single mother who owns a PostalAnnex franchise. Patel had owned a clothing store in Belgium for 20 years before relocating to the U.S. She bought the franchise without knowing anything about postal, packaging and shipping services, but learned quickly, and now expects sales in 2004 to reach $500,000.

36420 ■ *Leadership 101: What Every Leader Needs to Know*
Pub: Nelson Business
Ed: John C. Maxwell. **Released:** September 2002. **Price:** $9.99. **Description:** Ways to enhance leadership skills focusing on following a vision and bringing others along.

36421 ■ "Leadership and followership" in *Physician Executive* **(Vol. 28, No. 1, January-February 2002, pp. 91)**
Pub: American College of Physician Executives
Ed: Mary Francis Lyons. **Description:** A discussion on leadership skills is presented. The traits highlighted include projecting a vision, being a team builder and leader, thinking strategically, understanding systems, and being able to read market forces.

36422 ■ "The leadership journey" in *Harvard Business Review* **(Vol. 80, No. 10, October 2002, pp. 42)**
Pub: Harvard Business School Press
Ed: Leonard D. Schaeffer. **Description:** Leonard D. Schaeffer, CEO of Blue Cross of California, discusses how he turned around losses at the organization. The company has changed its name to WellPoint Health Networks. Three management techniques are discussed, including the autocrat, the participative leader, and the reformer.

36423 ■ *The Leadership Secrets of Colin Powell*
Pub: McGraw-Hill Companies
Ed: Oren Harari. **Released:** January 2002. **Price:** $21.95. **Description:** Profile of Colin Powell, stressing his abilities as a world leader.

36424 ■ "Leadership Training" in *Black Enterprise* **(Vol. 37, January 2007, No. 6, pp. 56)**
Pub: Earl G. Graves Publishing Co. Inc.
Ed: Sonia Alleyne. **Description:** Profile of Theopolis Holman, Group Vice-President of Duke Energy, who discusses how he prepared for the merger between Duke Energy and Cinergy. Holman oversees a division of 9,000 service contractors and employees.

36425 ■ "Leading the Pack" in *Black Enterprise* **(Vol. 34, No. 4, November 2003, pp. 82)**
Pub: Earl Graves Publishing Co.
Ed: Marcia A. Wade. **Description:** The winners of the Black Enterprise Small Business Awards were announced at the 2003 Black Enterprise/Microsoft Entrepreneurs Conference in May. Among the winners were: John Sterling of Synch-Solutions Inc., Colleen Payne-Nabors of Mobile Cardiac Imaging LLC, Orlando Robinson of D&D Innovations Inc., and Kenya James of Blackgirl Magazine. Kenya is a 14-year-old entrepreneur publishing a magazine to improve the self-esteem of young women across the nation.

36426 ■ "Leading for value" in *Harvard Business Review* **(Vol. 81, No. 4, April 2003, pp. 41)**
Pub: Harvard Business School Press
Ed: Brian Pitman. **Description:** The former CEO of Lloyds Bank PLC describes how he and his team transformed the bank's corporate culture by focusing on increasing shareholder value and reaching decisions through debate, the key to agreement.

36427 ■ "Learn and Grow Rich" in *Black Enterprise* **(Vol. 32, No. 10, May 2002, pp. 106)**
Pub: Earl Graves Publishing Co.
Ed: Dennis P. Kimbro. **Description:** Tips to achieve success in life are presented by Dennis P. Kimbro, management consultant, educator, speaker, and author of the book 'What Makes the Great Great: Strategies for Extraordinary Achievement'.

36428 ■ "Learn the Importance of Being Perfect" in *Women In Business* **(Vol. 52, No. 2, March 2000, pp. 28)**
Pub: The ABWA Co., Inc.
Ed: Marci Bauman-Bork. **Description:** Women who seek perfection should realize that they would not be who they are if they were perfect, and should just do their best.

36429 ■ "Learning Curve" in *Entrepreneur* **(Vol. 33, September 2005, No. 9, pp. 126)**
Pub: Entrepreneur Media Inc.
Ed: Nichole L. Torres. **Description:** University of Washington in Seattle offers students the opportunity to consult for local businesses through its Business and Economic Development Program. The course offers real insight and experience into entrepreneurship.

36430 ■ "Leaving a legacy" in *Women In Business* **(Vol. 52, No. 4, July 2000, pp. 24)**
Pub: The ABWA Co., Inc.
Ed: Rachel Warbington. **Description:** The giving of personal time to charities that help people improve themselves can often be of more benefit than a legacy in a will. The satisfaction gained from helping others is reviewed.

36431 ■ "Leaving their Mark" in *Entrepreneur* **(Vol. 32, December 2004, No. 12, pp. 8)**
Pub: Entrepreneur Media Inc.
Ed: Rieva Lesonsky. **Description:** Baby boomers contributed more to entrepreneurial spirit than any other generation.

36432 ■ "Led poisoning" in *Entrepreneur* **(Vol. 30, No. 1, January 2002, pp. 18)**
Pub: Entrepreneur Media Inc.
Ed: Watts Wacker. **Description:** A brief discussion involving the qualities of leadership for the future of business.

36433 ■ "Left Unsaid: How Ignoring Internal Conflict Can Kill Your Small Business" in *My Business* **(April/May 2004, pp. 36-39)**
Pub: My Business Magazine
Ed: Karen J. Bannan. **Description:** Conflict is necessary and important to a small business, it sparks creativity and keeps relationships from stagnating, however most small business owners do not understand that conflict really is an impetus for change.

36434 ■ "Legendary Entrepreneur" in *Small Business Opportunities* **(Spring 2005)**
Pub: Harris Publications Inc.
Description: Profile of Jeno F. Paulucci, founder of Luigino's Inc. and creator of Michelina's brand. Paulucci was honored by Ernst & Young for his lifelong dedication to humanitarian efforts.

36435 ■ "Legends" in *Inc.* **(Volume 27, December 2005, No. 12, pp. 30, 32)**
Pub: Inc. Magazine
Ed: Darren Dahl. **Description:** Profiles of the well-known entrepreneurs who died in 2005 include Dr. Frederick H. Berenstein, John Delorean, Horace Hagedorn, John H. Johnson, Mortimer Levitt, James R. and Alice Lewis, Jerome Lippman, John J. McMullen, Gary Milgard, Robert Moog, Frank Perdue, Richard H. Sabot, John E. Struggles, Kenneth Taylor, Dale "The Hawk" Velzy, and Charles West.

36436 ■ "Lending a Helping Hand Even When Off Duty" in *Home Business* **(Vol. 12, March/April 2005, No. 2, pp. 62)**
Pub: Home Business Magazine
Ed: Sandy Larson. Description: Profile of Randy Gabel and Scott Mullins, licensed paramedics, who run a home-based company offering emergency training courses.

36437 ■ "Leo Rivera" in *Entrepreneur* **(Vol. 32, No. 4, April 2004, pp. 22)**
Pub: Entrepreneur Media, Inc.
Ed: Sara Wilson. Description: Profile of Leo Rivera, founder of Bishops Barbershop in Portland, Oregon. Bishop has designed his shops with rock 'n' roll themes, with startup costs in 2001 of $40,000 and now owns four shops, each catering to 90-130 customers daily. Projected sales for 2004 are $1.6 million for the four locations.

36438 ■ "A Lesson Learned" in *Black Enterprise* **(Vol. 34, No. 2, September 2003, pp. S2)**
Pub: Earl Graves Publishing Co.
Ed: Jennifer Smith. Description: Young entrepreneurs share the experiences as small business owners while, at the same time, attending school.

36439 ■ "Lessons From the Past: Entrepreneur Takes the Old World Approach to Business" in *Black Enterprise* **(Vol. 34, No. 3, October 2003)**
Pub: Earl Graves Publishing Co.
Ed: Marcia A. Wade. Description: Profile of George Banks, founder of Sentry Security International Inc. Banks used loans from friends and his own savings to start his security company in 1999. The firm generated $328,000 in revenue in 2002.

36440 ■ "Lessons from the Sandbox" in *Small Business Opportunities* **(Vol. 12, No. 5, September 2000, pp. 106)**
Pub: Harris Publications, Inc.
Description: Consulting guru and author, Alan S. Gregerman, tells how people should act more like kids in order to achieve lasting success. Mr. Gregerman believes the success of any business hinges on the ability to innovate quickly, and get the right new products, services and ideas to the right customers ahead of competitors.

36441 ■ "Lets get creative: creativity is what makes the world go round." in *Entrepreneur* **(Vol. 30, No. 10, Oct. 2002, pp. 42)**
Pub: Entrepreneur Media Inc.
Ed: Geoff Williams, Richard Florida. Description: Richard Florida, professor of regional economic development at the Heinz School of Public Policy and Management at Carnegie Mellon University in Pittsburgh, argues that entrepreneurs, artists and other innovators belong to a creative class of individuals. There are three dimensions to creativity: technological creativity, economic creativity or entrepreneurship and artistic/cultural creativity.

36442 ■ "Let's Do Lunch: Giving New Meaning to the Term 'Power Lunch'" in *Entrepreneur* **(Vol. 32, November 2004, No. 11, pp. 34)**
Pub: Entrepreneur Media Inc.
Ed: Nichole L. Torres. Description: In Good Company, founded by Nancy Michaels, accepts bids from entrepreneurs. The winners enjoy lunch with a powerful business owner or corporate CEO.

36443 ■ "A letter to the chief executive" in *Harvard Business Review* **(Vol. 80, No. 10, October 2002, pp. 94)**
Pub: Harvard Business School Press
Ed: Joseph Fuller. Description: This fictitious letter to the head of a company explores managerial faults within large companies that have recently been in the news, and that have challenged many long-held beliefs and misconceptions.

36444 ■ *The Life Cycle of Entrepreneurial Ventures*
Pub: Springer

36445 ■ "Life Is What You Make It" in *Entrepreneur.com* **(Vol. 34, February 2006, No. 2, pp. 28)**
Pub: Entrepreneur Media Inc.
Ed: Sara Wilson. Description: Profile of Dewayne McKinney who turned his life around and now owns 50 ATMs on the Big Island of Hawaii, Kauai, Maui and Oahu. McKinney's Island ATMs has become Hawaii's second largest ATM firm.

36446 ■ "The Life of a Landlord: Acquiring the Building is Just the Beginning." in *Black Enterprise* **(Vol. 35, August 2004, No. 1, pp. 94)**
Pub: Earl G. Graves Publishing Co. Inc.
Ed: Donald Jay Korn. Description: Harry Norton II, entrepreneur and real estate investor, offers boot camp seminars for landlords to be sure his properties are being maintained. Norton encourages tenants to inform him of any issues, especially before they become major problems. It is important for all real estate investors to have a strong system in place when buying and leasing property.

36447 ■ *Life's a Game So Fix the Odds: How to Be More Persuasive and Influential in Your Personal and Business*
Pub: John Wiley & Sons, Incorporated
Ed: Philip Hesketh. Released: September 2005. Price: $24.95 (US), $31.00 (Canadian). Description: Seven psychological reasons behind why and how people are persuaded and how to use these reasons to your advantage in both your personal and business life.

36448 ■ "Lightening the Workload: Entrepreneurs Should Know When It's Time to Delegate" in *Black Enterprise* **(Vol. 34, No. 2, September 2003)**
Pub: Earl Graves Publishing Co.
Ed: Bridget McCrea. Description: The importance of business owners realizing they need to delegate work to employees rather than continuing to adopt the theory, "if you want a job done right, you must do it yourself."

36449 ■ "A Little Equation that Creates Big Results" in *Home Business* **(Vol. 12, October 2005, No. 5, pp. 86)**
Pub: Home Business Magazine
Ed: Chris Widener. Description: Time management skills are essential to any successful business; entrepreneurs must learn to manage time properly.

36450 ■ "Living the Lifestyle of the Successful Businessperson" in *Hispanic Business* **(January/February 2005, pp. 63, 64)**
Pub: Hispanic Business
Ed: Leslie A. Westbrook. Description: Victor Lopez, senior vice president at Hyatt Hotels Corporation believes balance is the key to a successful executive lifestyle. Profile of X9 GPS that allows users to map a route and upload the information onto a watch is included.

36451 ■ "Local Businesses Discover There's No Place Like Home" in *Bradenton Herald* **(February 7, 2005)**
Pub: Bradenton Herald
Ed: Kurt D. Schultheis. Description: Profile of individuals who leave their hometowns, but return to raise their families and develop successful small businesses.

36452 ■ "Loehmann's New Owner Keeps the Faith" in *Fortune* **(Vol. 151, February 7, 2005, No. 3, pp. 26)**
Pub: Time Inc.
Ed: Barney Gimbel. Description: Profile of Bahrain's First Islamic Investment Bank, a Middle East-based investment firm located in the U.S. Through its American subsidiary, Crescent Capital Investment, the company has invested $2 billion into the U.S. market, particularly businesses that don't sell alcohol, charge interest, or allow gambling, produce tobacco, make unwholesome entertainment, or deal with pork.

36453 ■ "Longtime Pitchmen Started Chain" in *Tampa Tribune* **(November 17, 2005)**
Pub: Media General, Inc.
Ed: Michael Sasso. Description: Profile of Johnny Carrabba and his uncle Damian Mandola. In 1988, the two men teamed to start a chain of Carrabba's restaurants in Houston, Texas.

36454 ■ "Looking For Winning Small Businesses" in *Crain's Detroit Business* **(Vol. 23, February 5, 2007, No. 6, pp. 27)**
Pub: Crain Communications Inc. - Detroit
Description: Award recognizes small companies who are exceptionally innovative or who have grown through difficult problems to be stronger. It is open to all firms over three years old with one hundred fifty employees or less in Wayne, Oakland, Macomb, Livingston and Washtenaw counties.

36455 ■ "Looking Into the Sun" in *Inc.* **(Volume 27, July 2005, No. 7, pp. 76-79)**
Pub: Inc. Magazine
Ed: David H. Freedman. Description: Profile of David Slawson, who believes thermoelectric technology is twice as efficient as solar energy systems. He is committed to spreading his 38-foot emission-less dishes across the world.

36456 ■ "Low-Cost Teleconferencing" in *My Business* **(February/March 2004, pp. 17)**
Pub: My Business Magazine
Description: Profile of Apple's new iSight, a cylindrical camera and microphone that connects to a Macintosh computer via high-speed firewire and Apple's proprietary multimedia Internet messaging software iCath-AV, providing always-on videoconferencing.

36457 ■ "A Lucky journey" in *Crain's Detroit Business* **(Vol. 19, No. 10, March 10, 2003, pp. 34)**
Pub: Crain Communications Inc., Detroit
Ed: Andrew Dietderich. Description: Profile of Arthur Luck, founder of Luck's Music Library Inc., located in Madison Heights, Michigan. In the late 1940s Luck began selling and renting music to associates; the business is currently being run by one of Luck's son.

36458 ■ "Mad skills" in *Entrepreneur* **(Vol. 31, No. 4, April 2003, pp. 79)**
Pub: Entrepreneur Media Inc.
Ed: Marc Diener. Description: Anger can be used as another weapon in the negotiation process, but the proper use of anger is key.

36459 ■ "A Magazine on the Move" in *Tampa Tribune* **(December 22, 2005)**
Pub: Media General, Inc.
Ed: Will Rodgers. Description: Profile of the monthly magazine, Makes and Models, published by entrepreneur Samuel W. Ballinger. The magazine features high-end vehicles and flashy models. Ballinger discusses the challenges he faces as owner and publisher.

36460 ■ "Magic Carpet Ride" in *Small Business Opportunities* **(Vol. 17, May 2005, No. 3, pp. 46, 48)**
Pub: Harris Publications Inc.
Ed: Vicki Gerson. Description: Profile of Steven King, former financial advisor. King left his career and launched his own high-end carpet and area rug business. Tips on opening a rug business are provided.

36461 ■ "Maine Women's Fund Makes a Difference With Women Entrepreneurs" in *Portland Press Herald* **(April 26, 2005)**
Pub: Blethen Maine Newspapers, Inc.
Ed: Tux Turkel. Description: Maine Women's Fund helps fund startup businesses for women as well as supporting programs to stop domestic violence. The association works with 125 centers in the U.S. that support entrepreneurial development among women.

36462 ■ "Maintaining Momentum" in *Hispanic Business* **(October 2003, pp. 86)**
Pub: Hispanic Business
Description: Profile of Jamie Gutierrez Vela, president of Midwest Maintenance Company, reporting

sales that have more than tripled in the last five years. Ms. Gutierrez was named entrepreneur of the year by the University of Nebraska's Center for Entrepreneurship.

36463 ■ "Major Contributions to the Community" in *Home Business* (Vol. 12, March/April 2005, No. 2, pp. 44)
Pub: Home Business Magazine
Description: American small businesses donated nearly $40 billion to charities in 2004.

36464 ■ *Make It Big With Yuvi: How to Achieve Poolside Living by Growing Your Small Business*
Pub: AuthorHouse
Ed: Ron Peltier. **Released:** March 2006. **Price:** $17.00. **Description:** Successful entrepreneurship is profiled.

36465 ■ "Make a List, Check it Twice: Can You Check Off All the Items on Your List?" in *Entrepreneur* (Vol. 33, February 2005, pp. 92)
Pub: Entrepreneur Media Inc.
Ed: Guy Kawasaki. **Description:** Guy Kawasaki offers advice to entrepreneurs in developing business skills. His latest book, The Art of the Start: The Time-Tested, Battle-Hardened Guide for Anyone Starting Anything, offers his experience as an evangelist, entrepreneur, investment banker and venture capitalist.

36466 ■ "Make a List, Check it Twice: Ever Wonder What's on Other Entrepreneurs' To-Do Lists?" in *Entrepreneur* (Vol. 32, December 2004)
Pub: Entrepreneur Media Inc.
Ed: Sara Wilson. **Description:** A sampling of entrepreneurial to-do lists is presented.

36467 ■ "Make Up Your Mind" in *Black Enterprise* (Vol. 36, February 2006, No. 7, pp. 164)
Pub: Earl G. Graves Publishing Co. Inc.
Ed: Marcia A. Reed-Woodard. **Description:** Seven steps for making good decisions are outlined by Dr. Spencer Johnson, author of "Yes" or "No" The Guide To Better Decisions. Dr. Johnson believes a person's status is ruled by their choices.

36468 ■ *Make Your Business Survive and Thrive! 100+ Proven Marketing Methods to Help You Beat the Odds*
Pub: John Wiley & Sons, Incorporated
Ed: Priscilla Y. Huff. **Released:** December 2006. **Price:** $19.95. **Description:** Small business and entrepreneurial expert gives information to help small and home-based businesses grow.

36469 ■ "Make Your Company an Idea Factory" in *Fortune* (Vol. 141, No. 12, June 12, 2000, pp. 264N+)
Pub: Time Inc.
Description: Geoff Yang, venture capitalist, says there has never been a better time to back entrepreneurs who think their product or service is going to change the world.

36470 ■ "The Making of a Corporate Athlete" in *Harvard Business Review* (Vol. 79, No. 1, January 2001, pp. 120)
Pub: Harvard Business School Publishing Corp.
Ed: Jim Loehr, Tony Schwartz. **Description:** Quality work is produced by executives not only because of mental attributes, but also due to spiritual, emotional and physical characteristics.

36471 ■ "Making Entrepreneurship Job One" in *Black Enterprise* (Vol. 32, No. 10, May 2002, pp. 12)
Pub: Earl Graves Publishing Co.
Ed: Earl G. Graves Sr. **Description:** The state of minority-owned businesses is discussed. Statistical data included.

36472 ■ "Making the Most of Your Network" in *Women In Business* (Vol. 52, No. 4, July 2000, pp. 20)
Pub: The ABWA Co., Inc.
Ed: Donna Fisher. **Description:** The importance of networking and the measurement of the benefits of networking to a business are discussed. The positive benefits of involving all staff in networking are considered.

36473 ■ "Making Their 'Book' Mark" in *Boston Business Journal* (Vol. 22, No. 16, May 24, 2002, pp. 28)
Pub: MCP, Inc.
Ed: Jill Lerner. **Description:** Profile of owners of Barefoot Books, Nancy Traversy and Tessa Strickland. Barefoot Books, which started in 1993, publishes and sells children's books.

36474 ■ "The Malaria Fighter" in *Business 2.0* (Vol. 7, January/February 2006, No. 1, pp. 116-118, 120, 122, 124)
Pub: Time, Inc.
Ed: Michael Myser. **Description:** Profile of scientist, Stephen Hoffman, entrepreneur who's research is aimed at attacking global diseases.

36475 ■ "Malcolm Alexander" in *Entrepreneur* (Vol. 31, No. 5, May 2003, pp. 19)
Pub: Entrepreneur Media Inc.
Ed: April Y. Pennington. **Description:** Profile of Malcolm Alexander, founder of Alexander Global Promotions, located in Bellevue, Washington; Alexander created Bobble Dobbles bobbleheads to promote sports teams, as well as other promotional items. Sales are expected to reach $35 million in 2003.

36476 ■ "Man With the Golden Touch" in *Black Enterprise* (Vol. 35, October 2004, No. 3, pp. 53)
Pub: Earl G. Graves Publishing Co. Inc.
Ed: Demetria Lucas. **Description:** Profile of Darrick Lee Warfield, owner of the Atlanta-based Goldfinger C.S., with revenues of $300,000 reported in 2003. Warfield and his three employees design album covers, Websites, logos, and advertisements. While in high school, Warfield won a national design competition for the American Can Company.

36477 ■ "Man With a Plan" in *My Business* (December/January 2004, pp. 56)
Pub: My Business Magazine
Ed: N.C. Tognazzini. **Description:** Profile of a business owner who named his business plan Earl because he felt it was such an integral part of his success it deserved a name.

36478 ■ "Management by whose objectives?" in *Harvard Business Review* (Vol. 81, No. 1, January 2003, pp. 107)
Pub: Harvard Business School Press
Ed: Harry Levinson. **Description:** The argument that most performance appraisals fail because the do not take into account the aspirations of the employees is presented. Individual needs and organizational requirements must converge for self-motivation to occur.

36479 ■ *Managing for Results*
Pub: HarperCollins Publishers, Inc.
Ed: Peter F. Drucker. **Released:** October 2006. **Price:** $16.95. **Description:** Entrepreneurs running successful small companies focus on opportunity rather than problems.

36480 ■ *Managing a Small Business Made Easy*
Pub: Entrepreneur Press
Ed: Martin E. Davis. **Released:** September 2005. **Price:** $19.95 (US), $26.95 (Canadian). **Description:** Examination of the essential elements for an entrepreneur running a business, including advice on leadership, customer service, financials, and more.

36481 ■ "Managing for the next big thing" in *Harvard Business Review* (Vol. 79, No. 1, January 2001, pp. 131)
Pub: Harvard Business School Publishing Corp.
Ed: Paul Hemp. **Description:** Michael Ruettgers of data storage device manufacturer EMC discusses the company's success and how it has managed to stay ahead of the trends in the computer industry.

36482 ■ "Mane Attraction" in *Inc.* (August 1, 2003)
Pub: Gruner & Jahr USA Publishing
Ed: Heather Kenny. **Description:** Profile of Katrina Markoff, owner of a Chicago, Illinois chocolate boutique; Markoff unwinds by riding her horse, Euclide.

36483 ■ "A Man's World?" in *Entrepreneur* (Vol. 31, No. 8, August 2003, pp. 26)
Pub: Entrepreneur Media, Inc.
Ed: Aliza Pilar Sherman. **Description:** Interview with three women entrepreneurs examining the challenges women entrepreneurs face in today's marketplace. The panel consisted of Cristi Cristich, CEO and founder of Cristek Interconnects Inc., maker of connectors and cabling for medical and military applications; Sheri L. Parrack, president and CEO of Texas Motor Transportation Consultants, a professional registration, tax and title service company; and Terrie Jones, owner of AGSI, a provider of information technology resource solutions.

36484 ■ "Market Values: The virtue of unselfishness" in *Red Herring* (No. 106, October 15, 2001, pp. 42)
Pub: Herring Communications
Ed: Dinesh D'Souza. **Description:** Despite the perception by many that capitalists and entrepreneurs are greedy and selfish, entrepreneurs spend much of their time meeting the desires of others, thus entrepreneurial capitalism is not only efficient it is also moral.

36485 ■ "A marketing leader is made of life's experiences" in *Atlanta Business Chronicle* (Vol. 24, No. 9, August 3, 2001, pp. 2B)
Pub: American City Business Journals Inc.
Ed: Alf Nucifora. **Description:** The fundamentals of marketing and leadership are listed. Among the traits, marketing leaders should crave learning, learn to listen, seek wisdom, and speak well and write well.

36486 ■ *Marketing that Works: How Entrepreneurial Marketing Can Add Sustainable Value to Any Sized Company*
Pub: Wharton School Publishing
Ed: Leonard M. Lodish; Howard Morgan; Shellye Archambeau. **Released:** March 2007. **Price:** $36.99 (CND). **Description:** Entrepreneurial marketing techniques are shared in order to help a new company position and target products and services.

36487 ■ *The Martha Rules: 10 Essentials for Achieving Success as You Start, Build, or Manage a Business*
Pub: Rodale Press, Incorporated
Ed: Martha Stewart. **Released:** October 2005. **Price:** $24.95. **Description:** Martha Stewart offers insight into starting, building and managing a successful business.

36488 ■ *The Martha Rules: 10 Essentials for Achieving Success as You Start, Grow, or Manage a Business*
Pub: Rodale Press, Inc.
Ed: Martha Stewart. **Released:** October 2005.

36489 ■ "Mary Engelbreit: My Biggest Mistake" in *Inc.* (November 2000, pp. 97)
Pub: The Goldhirsh Group
Description: Profile of designer and founder of Mary Engelbreit Studios, a $100 million provider of greeting cards and gifts.

36490 ■ "Master of Disaster" in *Fast Company* (November 2001, pp. 46)
Pub: Fast Company
Ed: Annie F. Pyatak. **Description:** Profile of Gordon Ballinger, of MapInfo Corporation. Mr. Ballinger helps federal, state, and local authorities access the information they need to recover from disasters.

36491 ■ **"Master of Her Retail Space"** in *Crain's New York Business* **(Vol. 23, January 29, 2007, No. 5, pp. F11)**
Pub: Crain Communications, Inc.
Ed: Elisabeth Butler. **Description:** Profile of Amira Yunis and her position as executive vice president of Newmark Knight Frank Retail. Ms. Yunis won the Real Estate Board of New York's Retail Deal of the Year award for putting Trader Joe's into Union Square. She brokered $10 million in business last year as well.

36492 ■ **"Math Will Rock Your World"** in *Business Week* **(January 23, 2006, No. 3968, pp. 54-58, 60, 62)**
Pub: McGraw-Hill Companies
Ed: Stephen Baker. **Description:** Businesses are using math experts in ways that were unthinkable years ago. They are changing personal data, trends, and online content into math, crunching the numbers, and discovering new ways to market products and services.

36493 ■ **"Mattresses Beneath His Wings"** in *Sacramento Bee* **(October 10, 2005)**
Pub: The Sacramento Bee
Ed: Jon Ortiz. **Description:** Profile of Dale Carlsen and his mattress outlet stores. Carlsen's privately held company has made his Sleep Train marketing an advertising icon.

36494 ■ **"Maximizing Employee Performance: Grow Your Business by Empowering Your Workforce"** in *Black Enterprise* **(Vol. 35, February 2005, No. 7)**
Pub: Earl G. Graves Publishing Co. Inc.
Ed: Arlene McKanic. **Description:** Guild Associates developed two entry-level management courses and the Leadership Development Program designed to develop and maximize leadership skills. The program features six steps that create a supportive culture that motivates and empowers a workforce.

36495 ■ **"Mechanically inclined"** in *Entrepreneur* **(Vol. 31, No. 4, April 2003, pp. 168)**
Pub: Entrepreneur Media Inc.
Ed: April Y. Pennington. **Description:** Profile of Colin Angle, Helen Greiner, and Rod Brooks, co-founders of iRobot, a firm started with technology but no product.

36496 ■ *Medium Sized Firms and Economics Growth*
Pub: Nova Science Publishers, Incorporated
Ed: Janez Prasniker. **Released:** February 2005. **Price:** $79.00. **Description:** Medium sized companies should have a more definitive presence in modern microeconomic theory, the theory of entrepreneurship, and the theory of financial markets.

36497 ■ **"The Meet Market: Looking for New Business Leads? Networking Clubs on the Web Make it Easy"** in *Entrepreneur* **(Vol. 32, August 2004)**
Pub: Entrepreneur Media Inc.
Ed: Catherine Seda. **Description:** Techniques that will help small business owners meet valuable contacts and secure new projects on the Internet are listed.

36498 ■ **"Meet & Potatoes"** in *Entrepreneur* **(Vol. 30, No. 3, March 2002, pp. 89)**
Pub: Entrepreneur Media Inc.
Ed: Barry Farber. **Description:** Ideas to help entrepreneurs to network outside of a safe, familiar circle of contracts are presented.

36499 ■ **"Meetings & Clubs"** in *Bellingham Business Journal* **(January 2007, pp. C3)**
Pub: Sun News Inc.
Description: Calendar of clubs and meetings in the Bellingham area targeting business-minded individuals.

36500 ■ **"Membership Privileges: How To Benefit From Joining a Professional Organization"** in *Black Enterprise* **(Vol. 34, July 2004, No. 12)**
Pub: Earl G. Graves Publishing Co. Inc.

Ed: Lee Anna Jackson. **Description:** Belonging to an industry-related organization can help a small business owner or a company leader through the networking opportunities presented.

36501 ■ **"Memphis, Tenn., Entrepreneurs Urged to Stay Close to Customers"** in *Commercial Appeal* **(October 27, 2004)**
Pub: The Commercial Appeal
Ed: Maria Burnham. **Description:** Maria Fischer, owner of a virtual assistant business, found inspiration from L.D. Beard, founder of Biotechnology Inc. when he spoke to entrepreneurs about the importance of staying in close contact with customers.

36502 ■ *Millionaire Upgrade: Lessons in Success from Those Who Travel at the Sharp End of the Plane*
Pub: John Wiley & Sons, Incorporated
Ed: Richard Parkes Cordock. **Released:** September 2006. **Price:** $17.99. **Description:** Interviews with fifty successful millionaire entrepreneurs are used to help a frustrated employee understand the science and secrets behind their successful business ventures.

36503 ■ **"Mind Games: Jump-Start Your Problem-Solving Skills for a Better Business"** in *Entrepreneur* **(Vol. 31, No. 10, October 2003, pp. 34)**
Pub: Entrepreneur Media, Inc.
Ed: Mark Hendricks. **Description:** Review of the book, "Retrain Your Business Brain", by Donalee Markus, Lindsey Paige Markus and Pat Taylor; the book provides visual and verbal puzzles to small business owners to become better at solving business issues and spotting problems.

36504 ■ *Mind Your Own Business: Getting Started As an Entrepreneur*
Pub: JIST Works, Inc.
Ed: LaVerne Ludden. **Released:** 1994. **Price:** $9.95.

36505 ■ **"Mom and Pop Psychology"** in *Inc.* **(December 1, 2003)**
Pub: Gruner & Jahr USA Publishing
Ed: Bobbie Gossage. **Description:** Every small business has a personality all its own. Ways to help find that out are presented.

36506 ■ **"The Moment You Least Expect It"** in *Hispanic Business* **(December 2001, pp. FG1-FG2)**
Pub: Hispanic Business
Ed: Cathy Areu Jones. **Description:** After the terrorist attacks small businesses turned to the Federal Emergency Management Agency (FEMA) and local government for assistance. Luckily FEMA was prepared and on the scene within minutes. The things small businesses need to do to prepare for emergencies are investigated.

36507 ■ **"More bang"** in *Entrepreneur* **(Vol. 30, No. 2, February)**
Pub: Entrepreneur Media Inc.
Ed: Chris Penttila. **Description:** Presentation of twenty-five tips for under $1,000 that will make a business better, from marketing to sales, and employees to equipment.

36508 ■ **"More Tales of the Inner City"** in *Inc.* **(Volume 27, June 2005, No. 6, pp. 86-92, 94, 96-98, 100, 102-103)**
Pub: Inc. Magazine
Ed: Michael E. Porter. **Description:** Entrepreneurs across America are helping inner cities prosper economically and socially by growing their businesses in these areas. A listing of the top 100 street-smart companies is included.

36509 ■ **"Morning Glory"** in *Entrepreneur* **(Vol. 33, March 2005, No. 3, pp. 168)**
Pub: Entrepreneur Media Inc.
Ed: April Y. Pennington. **Description:** Profile of David Roth and Rick Bachers, partners in a quick-serve restaurants and cereal bars. The firm is expected to grow a dozen new stores nationwide in 2005.

36510 ■ **"Mother, I'm the boss now: Internet executives hire their parents and traditions fall"** in *The New York Times* **(July 4, 2000, pp. C1)**
Pub: The New York Times Company
Ed: Katie Hafner. **Description:** The ways reverse nepotism is opening a new dimension in child-parent relationships is discussed.

36511 ■ **"Moving mountains"** in *Harvard Business Review* **(Vol. 81, No. 1, January 2003, pp. 41)**
Pub: Harvard Business School Press
Description: Twelve business leaders, including Carly Fiorina of Hewlett-Packard and Robert Eckert of Mattel, discuss their approaches to motivating employees. Some managers stress a person's need for the rational and orderly while others speak of inspiring through example.

36512 ■ **"Moving On: Ex-Apprentices Find Life After 'The Donald' is All Business"** in *Entrepreneur* **(Vol. 32, October 2004, No. 10, pp. 28)**
Pub: Entrepreneur Media Inc.
Ed: April Y. Pennington. **Description:** Many of the runner-up contestants competing on The Apprentice television show are becoming entrepreneurs. Kwame Jackson and a friend started Legacy Communications Group, an entertainment financing company; Troy McClain co-Founded Solution Source Media, offering information and products related to credit and real estate; Sam Solovey founded an auctioneering business; Omarosa Manigault-Stallworth is working on a clothing line; Jessie Conners created an interactive real estate and investment resource firm; Katrina Campin, a residential and commercial full-service real estate brokerage company.

36513 ■ **"Mr. Clean"** in *Crain's New York Business* **(Vol. 23, January 8, 2007, No. 2, pp. 23)**
Pub: Crain Communications, Inc.
Ed: Tom Fredrickson. **Description:** Profile of Joseph Spinelli, a former FBI agent who is the chief operating officer of Daylight Forensic & Advisory. Spinelli's specialty is discovering and preventing corruption in government agencies, schools, and corporations.

36514 ■ **"Mrs., Mom, and CEO"** in *Black Enterprise* **(Vol. 32, No. 9, April 2)**
Pub: Earl Graves Publishing Co.
Ed: Monique R. Brown. **Description:** Profile of Vickie Clark, owner and founder of a family owned, home-based business that transports kids back and forth to various activities.

36515 ■ **"Multitasking"** in *Business First Columbus* **(Vol. 18, No. 26, February 15, 2002, pp. A17)**
Pub: Business First Columbus, Inc.
Ed: Susan Pavilkey. **Description:** The many challenges faced by owners of franchises, from doing their own accounting to cleaning floors, are covered. Statistical data included.

36516 ■ *My Big Idea: 30 Successful Entrepreneurs Reveal How They Found Inspiration*
Pub: Kogan Page, Limited
Ed: Rachel Bridge. **Released:** November 2006. **Price:** $29.95. **Description:** Thirty successful entrepreneurs share insight into starting and running a small business.

36517 ■ **"My Favorite Fiascos"** in *Fast Company* **(November 2001, pp. 38)**
Pub: Fast Company
Description: Alberto Alessi discusses his favorite business disasters, customer savvy, and customer loyalty.

36518 ■ **"My Focus Is My Children"** in *Inc.* **(October 1, 2003)**
Pub: Gruner & Jahr USA Publishing
Ed: Rita Cruz. **Description:** Profile of restaurateur, Monica Chitins and her husband who quit their New York careers and moved to Puerto Rico. It was there that Chitins opened her own restaurant, which allows her to spend time with her family.

36519 ■ "My Gadget" in *My Business* **(April/May 2002, pp. 18)**
Pub: My Business Magazine
Description: Profile of Jeremy Vos, owner of First Light Enterprises and Tri-County Water Conditioning, both located in Pella, Iowa.

36520 ■ "My 'Won't Do' List" in *My Business* **(February/March 2003, pp. 49)**
Pub: My Business Magazine
Ed: Terri Lonier. **Description:** Ways to streamline a small business owner's life are listed.

36521 ■ "Nathan's Reverses Loss, Posts Third Quarter Profit" in *Long Island Business News* **(February 13, 2004)**
Pub: Dolan Media Newswires
Description: Profile of the owner and operator of Nathan's Famous Inc. The company reported $237,000 in profits for third quarter 2003.

36522 ■ "National Treasure" in *Entrepreneur* **(Vol. 33, October 2005, No. 10, pp. 26)**
Pub: Entrepreneur Media Inc.
Ed: Sara Wilson. **Description:** Review of the book, "The Hypomanic Edge: The Link Between (A Little) Craziness and (A Lot of) Success in America." The book's author, John D. Gartner, suggests the theory that links hypomania, a medical condition resulting in elevated mood and increased activity, with our immigrant ancestors and the entrepreneurial successes of today.

36523 ■ "Neck and Neck" in *Entrepreneur* **(Vol. 32, No. 1, January 2004, pp. 134)**
Pub: Entrepreneur Media, Inc.
Ed: April Y. Pennington. **Description:** Entrepreneur magazine ranked Subway as its Number One franchise for the twelfth time, with 15,874 locations in the U.S. The firm's approach to capitalize on healthy dining has set it ahead of other fast food restaurants.

36524 ■ "Needful things?" in *Entrepreneur* **(Vol. 30, No. 12, December 2002, pp. 109)**
Pub: Entrepreneur Media Inc.
Ed: Nichole L. Torres. **Description:** Ways to sell non-essential items are examined.

36525 ■ "Negotiating without a net. A conversation with the NYPD's Dominick J. Misino" in *Harvard Business Review* **(Vol. 80, Oct. 2002, pp. 49)**
Pub: Harvard Business School Press
Ed: Diane L. Coutu. **Description:** Dominick J. Misino answers questions about management techniques used to run the New York City Police Department.

36526 ■ "The network of relationships between the economic environment and the entrepreneurial culture firms" in *Journal of Business Venturing*
Pub: Elsevier Science, Inc.
Ed: Antonio Minguzzi, Renato Passaro. **Description:** A new study theorizes that the entrepreneurial culture in small companies is influenced by their relationships with the economic environment.

36527 ■ "Networking is a Click Away" in *Black Enterprise* **(Vol. 34, No. 6, January 2004, pp. 101)**
Pub: Earl Graves Publishing Co.
Description: Information is given for the 2004 B.E. Entrepreneurs Conference to be held May 12-16, 2004 in Dallas, Texas. Nominations are also being accepted for BE Small Business Awards.

36528 ■ "Networking Provides Partnership's Funding" in *Wall Street Journal* **(October 14, 2003, pp. B4)**
Pub: Dow Jones & Co. Inc.
Ed: Paulette Thomas. **Description:** Case study of William G. Nelson showing ways to move from a career in finance to an entrepreneurial life on a shoe-string budget through networking.

36529 ■ "Net.Working" in *Small Business Opportunities* **(Vol. 12, No. 2, March 2000, pp. 80)**
Pub: Harris Publications, Inc.
Ed: Robert Spiegel. **Description:** One entrepreneur tells how net affiliations help him make an extra $250,000 a year by using them.

36530 ■ "Networking for Success: It Takes More Than Just Handling Out Business Cards" in *Black Enterprise* **(Vol. 34, No. 4, Nov. 2003, pp. 72)**
Pub: Earl Graves Publishing Co.
Ed: Wendy M. Harris. **Description:** Resources necessary to develop and maintain professional relationships for entrepreneurs are examined.

36531 ■ *Never Eat Alone: And Other Secrets to Success, One Relationship at a Time*
Pub: Doubleday Broadway Publishing Group
Ed: Keith Ferrazzi, Tahl Raz. **Released:** February 2005. **Price:** $24.95. **Description:** Business networking strategies are offered.

36532 ■ "New Beginnings for VIBE" in *Black Enterprise* **(Vol. 37, November 2006, No. 4, pp. 34)**
Pub: Earl G. Graves Publishing Co. Inc.
Ed: Mashaun D. Simon. **Description:** Danyel Smith replaced Mimi Valdes as editor-in-chief of VIBE magazine after the Wicks Group, private equity firm focused on selected segments of the media, communications, and information industries, purchased the magazine.

36533 ■ "New Biscotti Company Gets Cooking" in *Bellingham Business Journal* **(December 2006, pp. A5)**
Pub: Sun News Inc.
Description: Profile of Kyoung Croft, owner of Rainy Days Kitchen, a company that produces non-traditional biscotti.

36534 ■ "A New Breed of Entrepreneurs" in *Black Enterprise* **(Vol. 37, November 2006, No. 4, pp. 16)**
Pub: Earl G. Graves Publishing Co. Inc.
Description: Black entrepreneurs are an important part of the chain for providing economic opportunities within the community. Many black business owners are more likely to hire black employees and apply innovative strategies in building their businesses rather than taking the traditional route.

36535 ■ "New Business on Champion Street Uncorks a New Trend" in *Bellingham Business Journal* **(January 2007, pp. A4)**
Pub: Sun News Inc.
Description: Overview of Whatcom Winemakers which has developed a fresh new concept for the wine industry, do-it-yourself winemaking. The winemaking shop is slated to open in February.

36536 ■ "New Dynamic for Nonprofits" in *Hispanic Business* **(Vol. 23, No. 7/8, July/August 2001, pp. 104, 106)**
Pub: Hispanic Business
Ed: James E. Garcia. **Description:** A recent survey by Independent Sector, a national umbrella group of 700 non-profit agencies and foundations, found that Hispanic contributions have increased due to the growth of Hispanic middle class and wealthy entrepreneurs.

36537 ■ "New Entrepreneurs Arise from Bad Breaks" in *Altanta Journal-Constitution* **(January 20, 2007)**
Pub: Cox Newspapers, Inc.
Ed: Jill Young Miller. **Description:** Profile of Kimberly Morrison, owner of A Blue Lady, a floral shop in Georgia. Morrison discusses overcoming depression after her husband filed for divorce and starting her own business.

36538 ■ "New frontiers" in *Entrepreneur* **(Vol. 31, No. 6, June 2003, pp. 34)**
Pub: Entrepreneur Media Inc.
Ed: Geoff Williams. **Description:** In an interview, career consultant John Bradley offers insight into expanding a small business into Afghanistan.

36539 ■ "New Frontiers to Explore" in *Fast Company* **(September 2001, pp. 76)**
Pub: Fast Company
Ed: Chuck Salter. **Description:** Profile of John Fahey, president and CEO of a non-profit society, shares ways he is finding new sources of revenue, new corporate partnerships, and new identity for the 113-year-old institution.

36540 ■ "A New Game for Johnson: BET Founder Looking to Acquire Baseball Franchise" in *Black Enterprise* **(Vol. 33, No. 7, Feb. 2003, pp. 19)**
Pub: Earl Graves Publishing Co.
Ed: Cliff Hocker. **Description:** Profile of BET found and CEO Robert L. Johnson, the first African American majority owner of a Major League Baseball franchise.

36541 ■ "A New Leaf" in *Entrepreneur* **(Vol. 32, November 2004, No. 11, pp. 95)**
Pub: Entrepreneur Media Inc.
Ed: Mark Henricks. **Description:** Consulting firm, McKinsey & Company has designed a four-step process that assists entrepreneurs when making changes to a company. The first step involves convincing people, including employees, that a change is necessary for the firm.

36542 ■ "New Positions Emerging: How You Can Prepare for Them" in *Women In Business* **(Vol. 52, No. 2, March 2000, pp. 30)**
Pub: The ABWA Co., Inc.
Ed: Diane Domeyer. **Description:** Women should plan for the new roles anticipated in the workplace as a result of technological advances.

36543 ■ *The New Social Entrepreneurship What Awaits Social Entrepreneurship Ventures?*
Pub: Edward Elgar Publishing, Incorporated
Ed: Perrini. **Released:** October 2006. **Price:** $120.00. **Description:** Social entrepreneurship seeks to improve societal well-being within entrepreneurial organizations.

36544 ■ "New Space in an Old Place" in *Crain's Detroit Business* **(Vol. 21, February 7, 2005, No. 6, pp. 14)**
Pub: Crain Communications Inc. - Detroit
Ed: JoAnn Amicangelo. **Description:** Profile of Michael LaFontaine, the LaFontaine Automotive Group, which includes the Toyota, Kia, Scion, Suzuki, Hyundai, and Honda dealerships, all located in a Dearborn, Michigan location, as well as Pontiac, Cadillac, and GMC dealerships in Highland Township. The Group employs about 350 people and family members are involved in the management of different dealerships.

36545 ■ "A New Twist" in *Entrepreneur*
Pub: Entrepreneur Media Inc.
Ed: April Y. Pennington. **Description:** Profile of Kimberly and Scott Holstein, husband and wife co-founders of Kim & Scott's Gourmet Pretzels. Pretzels come in 20 flavors and the couple intends to open its first bakery cafe in 2005. The Chicago-based manufacturer expects to see $6 million in sales for 2004.

36546 ■ "A New Vision for Network Marketing" in *Success* **(Vol. 47, No. 3, July 2000, pp. 80)**
Pub: Success Publishing, Inc.
Ed: Karin Fuller. **Description:** Profile of New Vision, a network-marketing company, whose co-founder shares some secrets of success.

36547 ■ "New Year, New Laws" in *Inc.* **(Volume 28, January 2006, No. 1, pp. 24)**
Pub: Inc. Magazine
Description: An entrepreneur's guide to new state policies taking effect in 2006, along with their positive, negative, mixed and uncertain impacts.

36548 ■ "New Year's 2003: resolve to be a better boss" in *Atlanta Business Chronicle* **(Vol. 25, January 3, 2003, No. 30, pp. 2B)**
Pub: American City Business Publications, Inc.

Ed: Emory Mulling. **Description:** A list of ten resolutions for better business management are highlighted. These resolutions include learning to delegate, constructive criticism, information sharing, and to listen more.

36549 ■ "New York Stories" in *Venture Capital Journal* (Vol. 42, No. 9, September 2002, pp. 21, 22-23)
Pub: Thomas Venture Economics
Ed: Charles R. Fellers. **Description:** The impact of the terrorist attacks of September 11 is examined. Steve Brotman, managing director of Silicon Alley Venture Partners, feels New York enjoys the most entrepreneurial culture in the world.

36550 ■ "Newsstand" in *Home Business* (Vol. 13, January/February 2006, No. 1, pp. 38-39)
Pub: Home Business Magazine
Description: Topics include marketing of office supplies and equipment, rising gas prices, toxic office environments, entrepreneurship, and online retailing.

36551 ■ "The Next Management Revolution" in *Inc.* (July 1, 2004)
Pub: Inc. Magazine
Ed: Hillary Johnson. **Description:** Running a business like a household proved successful to the editor of a small newspaper.

36552 ■ "NFL Reaches Out" in *Crain's Detroit Business* (Vol. 21, January 3, 2005, No. 1, pp. 12)
Pub: Crain Communications Inc. - Detroit
Ed: Jennette Smith. **Description:** Super Bowl XL Host Committee and the National Football League have partnered to create an emerging-business program that encourages minority- and women-owned business to participate in the Super Bowl. The committee will also announce plans for a $2 million youth center to be located in Detroit.

36553 ■ "Nice meeting you!" in *Entrepreneur* (Vol. 30, No. 12, December 2002, pp. 111)
Pub: Entrepreneur Media Inc.
Ed: Nichole L. Torres. **Description:** Ideas for business networking to help grow a business are presented.

36554 ■ "Night of Stars" in *Hispanic Business* (January/February 2004, pp. 20, 22, 24)
Pub: Hispanic Business
Ed: Joel Russell. **Description:** CEO's put on the glitz for Hispanic Business magazine's Entrepreneur of the Year Awards. The ceremony was held at the Century Plaza Hotel, located on the Avenue of the Stars, Los Angeles, California. Headline sponsors of the event included Ford Motor Company and Office Depot.

36555 ■ "9/11 Call: When Crisis Hit, Business Owners Answered" in *Entrepeneur* (Vol. 30, No. 2, February 2002, pp. 46)
Pub: Entrepreneur Media Inc.
Ed: Geoff Williams. **Description:** Inspiring stories of entrepreneurs who responded to the 911 terrorist attacks are true examples of the meaning of the word 'hero'.

36556 ■ *Nirvana in a Cup: The Founding of Oregon Chai*
Pub: Moby Press
Ed: Tedde McMillen; Heather Hale. **Released:** July 2006. **Price:** $12.99. **Description:** Profile of a mother-daughter team who founded Oregon Chai, a tea company.

36557 ■ "No Small Plans" in *Inc.* (December 1, 2004)
Pub: Inc. Magazine
Ed: Patrick J. Sauer. **Description:** Profile of Harvey Robbins, small town entrepreneur, who sold his business and planned to retire with the $120 millions from the sale of his firm, National Floor Products. Robbins has made it his mission to revitalize his home town of Tuscumbia, Alabama.

36558 ■ "The Nonprofit Motive" in *Fortune* (Vol. 148, No. 8, October 13, 2003, pp. 214)
Pub: Time Inc.
Ed: David Whitford. **Description:** Profile of entrepreneur Art Mellor who co-founded three companies, including Midnight Networks, a computer network testing firm. Mellor was CTO of the computer network configuration management startup, Gold Wire Technology, when he was diagnosed with multiple sclerosis. Meller, with his neurologist, Dr. Tim Vartania, founded the Boston Cure Project.

36559 ■ "Nonstop Innovation" in *Inc.* (Volume 27, July 2005, No. 7, pp. 34)
Pub: Inc. Magazine
Ed: Larry Olmsted. **Description:** The firm Book 'em works to transform employees into entrepreneurs by having them develop ideas for innovative products and services.

36560 ■ "Northern Exposure: American Entrepreneurs are Finding Success by Heading for the Border" in *Entrepreneur* (Vol. 31, August 2003)
Pub: Entrepreneur Media, Inc.
Ed: Joshua Kurlantzick. **Description:** Canada is becoming more attractive to entrepreneurs because Canada has recorded the strongest economic growth of any industrialized nation in the past two years. Venture capitalists in Canada are usually more generous than those in the U.S.

36561 ■ "Northwest Mississippi Community College" in *Mississippi Business Journal* (Vol. 28, September 2006, No. 36, pp. 6)
Pub: Venture Publications, Inc.
Description: Profile of Dr. Chuck Strong, Northwest Mississippi Community College's vice president for educational affairs.

36562 ■ "Not so fast!: Studies show many of you aren't looking before you leap" in *Entrepreneur* (Vol. 31, No. 6, June 2003, pp. 30)
Pub: Entrepreneur Media Inc.
Ed: David Newton. **Description:** The topic of risk assessment for entrepreneurs is highlighted, stating that vision alone isn't enough to ensure success.

36563 ■ "Not Your Arena?" in *Entrepreneur* (Vol. 31, No. 8, August 2003, pp. 22)
Pub: Entrepreneur Media, Inc.
Ed: Mark Henricks. **Description:** Professional sports franchises and facilities do not provide opportunities for most local entrepreneurs. Nationally, more than $12 billion has gone into 80 different sports facilities in the last ten years, yet these stadiums generally yield few benefits locally.

36564 ■ "Note to Staff" in *My Business* (April/May 2004, pp. 44)
Pub: My Business Magazine
Ed: Lee Gimpel. **Description:** Small business owners should create a business manual for employees, allowing the owner time away from the company.

36565 ■ "Nothing is Unworkable" in *Home Office Computing* (Vol. 19, No. 1, January 2001, pp. 11)
Pub: Scholastic Inc.
Ed: Eric Grevstad. **Description:** The advantages to working at home are explored.

36566 ■ "A Nursery Tale" in *Inc.* (June 2000, pp. 96)
Pub: The Goldhirsh Group
Description: David Henry, CEO of Allegheny Child Care Academy, tells how his successful inner-city day care centers, serving welfare recipients, have a competitive edge in their non-traditional workforce: more than 25 percent of employees are themselves former welfare recipients.

36567 ■ "Off the Wall: Keith Collins' Larger-Than-Life Designs" in *Black Enterprise* (Vol. 37, February 2007, No. 7, pp. 138)
Pub: Earl G. Graves Publishing Co. Inc.
Description: Profile of Keith Collins, an entrepreneur who makes carpets for the likes of Jay Leno, Nicolas Cage, Arnold Schwartzenegger, Janet Jackson, and Will Smith. Collins is passionate about this ancient art form and saw a future in it despite the negative feedback from those around him.

36568 ■ "The Old Guard" in *Venture Capital Journal* (Vol. 42, No. 10, October 2002, pp. 24-30)
Pub: Thomas Venture Economics
Ed: Peter D. Henig. **Description:** Reid Dennis, Bill Draper, Pitch Johnson, Arthur Rock and Paul Wythes, better known as the "Old Guard" pioneered the venture capital business. The Old Guard offers advice on how to get the venture capital industry back on track.

36569 ■ "Older CEOs Plan to Work Past Age 65. They May Find That Harder Than They Expect" in *Inc.* (September 2005, pp. 27-29)
Pub: Inc. Magazine
Ed: Stephanie Clifford. **Description:** The entrepreneurial revolution was part of the baby boomer phenomenon. The trend toward older CEOs planning to work past the age of 65 is growing.

36570 ■ "Older is seen as better in small-business owners" in *Wall Street Journal* (August 20, 2002, pp. B4)
Pub: Dow Jones & Co. Inc.
Ed: Richard C. Breeden. **Description:** Global Entrepreneurship Monitor reports that age is an asset when it comes to owning a small business. Statistical data included.

36571 ■ "On Boss Day, We Praise and Pan" in *Sacramento Bee* (October 17, 2005)
Pub: The Sacramento Bee
Ed: Rachel Osterman. **Description:** October 16th has been held as National Boss Day since 1958. According to recent studies, many employees are unhappy with supervisors and would not want to be in charge; others feel the day is an opportunity for team building. Statistical data included.

36572 ■ "On the Business of Life" in *Forbes* (Vol. 175, January 31, 2005, No. 2, pp. 156)
Pub: Forbes Magazine Inc.
Description: It is proper business etiquette to call when people who accept business invitations to luncheons, dinners or other functions that involve planning of food, seating souvenirs, or other amenities cannot attend the event.

36573 ■ "On Her Best Behavior" in *Home Business* (Vol. 12, October 2005, No. 5, pp. 41)
Pub: Home Business Magazine
Ed: Sandy Larson. **Description:** Syndi Seid, founder of San-Francisco-based Advanced Etiquette, stresses the importance of using proper table manners while dining with clients.

36574 ■ "On the record" in *Entrepreneur* (Vol. 31, No. 4, April 2003, pp. 168)
Pub: Entrepreneur Media Inc.
Ed: April Y. Pennington. **Description:** Profile of Michael Koch, founder and CEO of Koch Entertainment, an independent music distribution and record company, with sales expected to reach more than $100 million in 2003.

36575 ■ "On a Roll! Why Small Business Is Like Duct Tape" in *My Business* (April/May 2003, pp. 51)
Pub: My Business Magazine
Ed: Harvey King. **Description:** The article compares the use of duct tape to American small business for its flexibility, creativity and ubiquity.

36576 ■ "On a Shoestring" in *Entrepreneur* (Vol. 32, September 2004, No. 9, pp. 107)
Pub: Entrepreneur Media Inc.
Description: Profile of Rick Kushel and Ed Vogelsong, who built their document storage company based on customer service. With $5,000 of startup money the two built a storage system that includes both hard copies and electronic copies, and currently consists of more than 400,000 square feet of storage space.

36577 ■ "On Top of the World" in *Home Business* (Vol. 13, January/February 2006, No. 1, pp. 92)
Pub: Home Business Magazine
Ed: Sandy Larson. **Description:** Profile of Jeff Dyrek who launched a company offering North Pole expeditions. Dyrek promotes the tours on his Website, www. YellowAirplane.com that offers information about military and aviation history and a hobby store with model airplanes, trains and ships.

36578 ■ "One Company Founder Learned the Hard Way" in *Wall Street Journal* (January 2, 2002, pp. A7)
Pub: Wall Street Journal
Ed: Hilary Stout. **Description:** Profile of Kristine Wilson, founder of Languages Unlimited; Wilson's advice is: don't try to do it all yourself.

36579 ■ "One Final Note: Why Your Last Impression Is As Important As Your First" in *Black Enterprise* (Vol. 35, November 2004, No. 4, pp. 76)
Pub: Earl G. Graves Publishing Co. Inc.
Ed: Erin Straker. **Description:** Final impressions in business are as important as first impressions. Show appreciation for time spent at a business meeting.

36580 ■ "The 100 most influential Hispanics" in *Hispanic Business* (Vol. 22, No. 10, October 2000, pp. 30)
Pub: Hispanic Business
Description: A list of the 100 most influential and innovative Hispanic citizens chosen by Hispanic Business magazine is presented. Their achievements, ideas and plans for their companies or sphere of influence are described.

36581 ■ "100 Most Influential Hispanics" in *Hispanic Business* (October 2002, pp. 40)
Pub: Hispanic Business
Description: The 100 most influential Hispanics chosen by Hispanic Business magazine for recent achievements having national impact are profiled. Forty-four winners are officials in federal agencies, with the rest working in state government, corporate America, nonprofits, and the entertainment or sports professions.

36582 ■ "One More For the Road" in *Sales & Marketing Management* (January 2005)
Pub: VNU Business Media
Ed: Denis Jensen. **Description:** Sales executives, as well as management, should avoid the pitfalls of drinking when entertaining business clients. One accident involving an employee under the influence will cause insurance rates to go up.

36583 ■ "One More Time: How Do You Motivate Employees?" in *Harvard Business Review* (Vol. 81, No. 1, January 2003, pp. 87)
Pub: Harvard Business School Press
Ed: Frederick Herzberg. **Description:** Employee motivation requires interesting work, challenge and increasing responsibility.

36584 ■ "One Tough Lesson Plan" in *Forbes* (Vol. 170, No. 9, October 28, 2002, pp. 238)
Pub: Forbes Magazine
Ed: Luisa Kroll. **Description:** Chosen as one of the 200 Best Companies by Forbes, co-founder and chief executive of Corinthian Colleges tells how he uses his past military career to oversee 4,800 faculty and staff and more than 34,000 students. Corinthian Colleges is one of the country's largest post-secondary education companies.

36585 ■ "Online Self-Publishing Services" in *Black Enterprise* (Vol. 37, November 2006, No. 4, pp. 90)
Pub: Earl G. Graves Publishing Co. Inc.
Description: Profiles of five online self-publishing services.

36586 ■ "Open Doors?" in *Entrepreneur* (Vol. 31, No. 9, September 2003, pp. 72)
Pub: Entrepreneur Media, Inc.
Ed: Joshua Kurlantzick. **Description:** Government deregulation in the real estate industry is discussed.

36587 ■ "Opening the Kimono" in *Inc.* (September 1, 2003)
Pub: Gruner & Jahr USA Publishing
Ed: Bobbie Gossage. **Description:** How much information should be revealed when negotiating with potential partners? Tips for successful negotiating are revealed.

36588 ■ "Opening Up the Baghdad Office" in *Inc.* (November 1, 2004)
Pub: Inc. Magazine
Ed: Nicole Gull. **Description:** Profile of Chris Exline, founder of Home Essentials, and one of the first entrepreneurs to set up a shop in Iraq after American troops swept the country in 2003. Exline, who speaks no Arabic, discusses the challenges and risks of working in Baghdad.

36589 ■ "Opportunities" in *Entrepreneur* (Vol. 30, No. 2, Fe)
Pub: Entrepreneur Media Inc.
Ed: Stephanie Soong. **Description:** Profile of Ray and Cyndi White who retired from their careers as rocket scientist and hearing specialist respectively to start their own business in a real estate franchise.

36590 ■ "Opportunity knocks at Kauffman" in *Ingram's* (Vol. 28, No. 3, March 2002, pp. 17)
Pub: Show Me Publishing, Inc.
Ed: Jack Cashill. **Description:** The Kauffman Foundation offers young people in the Kansas City area an opportunity to acquire real-world business skills.

36591 ■ "The Opportunity is Knocking" in *Black Enterprise* (Vol. 34, No. 7, February 2004)
Pub: Earl Graves Publishing Co.
Description: The 2004 "Black Enterprise/General Motors Entrepreneurs Conference" will be held in Dallas, Texas. This year's theme will be "Taking Business Beyond Boundaries", and will present industry experts, venture capitalists, and entrepreneurs. The event is geared to provide information and inspiration for African American executives, professionals, entrepreneurs, and wealth-accumulators.

36592 ■ "Opportunity Knocks" in *Rough Notes* (Vol. 145, No. 2, February 2003, pp. 36)
Pub: Rough Notes
Ed: Rick Dinger. **Description:** It is extremely helpful for youthful agents to involve themselves in industry events. Rick Dinger of Crescenta Valley Insurance, at the start of his career, joined Insurance Brokers and Agents of the West, and later the International Insurance Agents and Brokers of America.

36593 ■ "Organize Yourself" in *Fast Company* (September 2001, pp. 60)
Pub: Fast Company
Ed: Polly LaBarre. **Description:** Profile of Steven Johnson, cofounder of the Web zine Feed has written a book offering the secret history of decentralized thinking.

36594 ■ "OSDBU Directory" in *Hispanic Business* (December 2002, pp. FRG12-FRG14)
Pub: Hispanic Business
Description: Minority entrepreneurs use the Office of Small and Disadvantaged Business Utilization (OSDBU) as their first point of contact for selling products or services to the federal government. A directory of OSDBU agencies is presented. Statistical data included.

36595 ■ *Other Essentials of Business Ownership*
Pub: PublishAmerica, Incorporated
Ed: Charles Shaw. **Released:** May 2006. **Price:** $19.95. **Description:** Things a business owner, entrepreneur, or manager must be aware of in order to successfully manage a small business.

36596 ■ "Out of Control" in *Inc.* (September 1, 2003)
Pub: Gruner & Jahr USA Publishing

Ed: Susan Hansen. **Description:** Profile of Travis Parsons, founder of Elogex, an Internet-based software application that would enable clients to coordinate shipping and delivery services across multiple warehouses and destinations. When Parsons sold the firm he also lost his decision-making power.

36597 ■ "Out with the Old?" in *Entrepreneur* (Vol. 32, No. 1, January 2004, pp. 24)
Pub: Entrepreneur Media, Inc.
Ed: Chris Pentilla. **Description:** Young entrepreneurs are choosing not to join area Chambers of Commerce because they find them dull and uninteresting, some are focusing on networking groups instead.

36598 ■ "Owning Up" in *Entrepreneur* (Vol. 31, No. 8, August 2003, pp. 65)
Pub: Entrepreneur Media, Inc.
Ed: Mark Henricks. **Description:** Is a business better off renting or buying its location? This question is answered by looking at the benefits of purchasing property to build equity and control costs.

36599 ■ *The Oxford Handbook of Entrepreneurship*
Pub: Oxford University Press, Incorporated
Ed: Mark Casson; Bernard Young; Anuradha Basu. **Released:** October 2006. **Price:** $155.00. **Description:** Research covering entrepreneurship is presented by an international team of leading scholars.

36600 ■ "Paint Hustle: New Orleans Artist Went from the Streets to Mainstream" in *Black Enterprise* (Vol. 35, December 2004, No. 5, pp. 77)
Pub: Earl G. Graves Publishing Co. Inc.
Ed: Sean Drakes. **Description:** Profile of Lionel Milton, artist who went from painting graffiti on public sites in New Orleans, Louisiana, to creating sets for MTVs Real World and P.Diddy's show, Making the Band. Milton relates his path to finding a niche for his artwork as an African American artist.

36601 ■ "Paper Jam: Curtis Sherrod's Hip-Hop History Session" in *Black Enterprise* (Vol. 34, No. 5, December 2003, pp. 147)
Pub: Earl Graves Publishing Co.
Ed: Sonia Alleyne. **Description:** Profile of Curtis Sherrod, owner of a unique staffing service in New York City, called All Things Traffic Inc. Sherrod talks about his collection of party flyers.

36602 ■ "Parent Trap?" in *Entrepreneur* (Vol. 33, September 2005, No. 9, pp. 17)
Pub: Entrepreneur Media Inc.
Ed: Description: Entrepreneurial parents have positive things to offer their children; however there are obstacles to overcome in meeting the challenges of parenting while running a successful company.

36603 ■ "Parents for hire" in *Entrepreneur* (Vol. 31, No. 4, April 2003, pp. 76)
Pub: Entrepreneur Media Inc.
Ed: Patricia Schiff Estess. **Description:** Entrepreneurs often hire parents for their new companies because of their trust, savvy and availability, but it takes time to work out the role reversals in the new relationship.

36604 ■ "A Passion for the Work" in *Hispanic Business* (January/February 2004, pp. 30, 34)
Pub: Hispanic Business
Ed: Scott Williams. **Description:** Members of the Corporate Elite directory credit their cultural work ethic and enthusiasm for their success.

36605 ■ "Past Track to the Future" in *Fast Company* (May 2001, pp. 166)
Pub: Fast Company
Ed: Harriet Rubin. **Description:** Stephen E. Ambrose has written best-selling histories of great feats of leadership and human endeavor, from World Wars to the opening of the American West, to the building of the transcontinental railroad. His insights from the past have inspired Hollywood blockbusters such as 'Saving Private Ryan'. Ambrose thinks that the past is the way to navigate the future.

36606 ■ "Pat Croce's Bottom Line" in *Inc.* **(January 1, 2002)**
Pub: Inc. Magazine
Ed: Leslie Brokaw. **Description:** Former president of the Philadelphia 76ers discusses the benefits of fitness, and ways to fit exercise into a busy schedule.

36607 ■ "Pay Attention" in *Entrepreneur* **(Vol. 32, September 2004, No. 9, pp. 80)**
Pub: Entrepreneur Media Inc.
Description: Monitoring total pay earned by employees, broken down by gender and ethnicity will help a small business avoid inadvertent discrimination. Some studies indicate that women often receive 3 percent less than men performing similar jobs.

36608 ■ "Paying off in the end" in *BlackEnterprise* **(Vol. 31, No. 11, June 2001, pp. 71)**
Pub: Earl Graves Publishing Co.
Ed: Nancy Bearden Henderson. **Description:** Mentoring begins with a vision. The business owner who envisions his company to the next level while improving his performance and that of his employees is what the mentoring process is about. Recommendations for implementing a mentoring program for small companies, is included.

36609 ■ "Peace Maker" in *My Business* **(April/May 2003, pp. 43)**
Pub: My Business Magazine
Ed: Julie Bawden Davis. **Description:** Tips to consider when negotiating conflict among employees are outlined, the smaller a business, the more likely the conflict.

36610 ■ *The Peebles Principles: Insights from an Entrepreneur's Life of Business Success, Making Deals, and Creating a Fortune from Scratch*
Pub: John Wiley and Sons Inc.
Ed: R. Donahue Peebles. **Released:** April 2007. **Price:** $29.99. **Description:** Successful entrepreneur shares his business experience. Peebles went from CEO of the nation's largest Black-owned real estate development firm to founding his own firm.

36611 ■ "Peer group provides expertise firms lack" in *Wall Street Journal* **(December 17, 2002, pp. B7)**
Pub: Dow Jones & Co. Inc.
Ed: Jeff Bailey. **Description:** Profile of Young Entrepreneurs' Organization, a group that brings small business owners together in order to talk and exchange advice and insight into entrepreneurship.

36612 ■ "A Penchant for Profits" in *Entrepreneur* **(Vol. 33, August 2005, No. 8, pp. 53)**
Pub: Entrepreneur Media Inc.
Ed: David Worrell. **Description:** Profile of co-founder and CEO of Avidian Technologies, Bellevue, Washington is presented. James Wong's firm has grown 400 percent annually since 2003, with more than 7,000 registers users of its software.

36613 ■ "Penny wise, pound foolish" in *Black Enterprise* **(Vol. 32, No. 10, May 2002, pp. 44)**
Pub: Earl Graves Publishing Co.
Ed: Alan Hughes. **Description:** The importance of maintaining separate personal and business accounts is discussed.

36614 ■ "People" in *Ingram's* **(Vol. 28, No. 5, May 2002, pp. 49)**
Pub: Show Me Publishing, Inc.
Description: Profile of John McDonald, founder of Boulevard Brewing Company. McDonald was named the Small Business Philanthropist of the Year.

36615 ■ "A Perfect Brainstorm" in *Inc.* **(October 1, 2003)**
Pub: Gruner & Jahr USA Publishing
Ed: Alison Stein Wellner. **Description:** New scientific research suggests that brainstorming can help an entrepreneur attain business visions and goals.

36616 ■ "A Perfect Match?" in *Entrepreneur* **(Vol. 31, No. 10, October 2003, pp. 60)**
Pub: Entrepreneur Media, Inc.
Ed: Crystal Detamore-Rodman. **Description:** Profile of Ahmed and Reem Rahim, brother and sister entrepreneurs, and their first step in the half-million dollar expansion of their organic tea company.

36617 ■ "The Perfect Pitch" in *Hispanic Business* **(March 2005, pp. 38, 40)**
Pub: Hispanic Business
Ed: Scott Williams. **Description:** Tracy Lefteroff, global managing partner of VC arm of PriceWaterhouseCoopers believes it is a great time to be an entrepreneur. Pointers to help entrepreneurs win over private equity investors are shared. Statistical data included.

36618 ■ "Perfecting the Growth Spurt" in *Hispanic Business* **(Vol. 23, No. 11, November 2001, pp. 24-25, 28)**
Pub: Hispanic Business Inc.
Ed: James E. Garcia. **Description:** Profile of Juan Mencia, CEO of The Cube Corporation. The Cube Corporation provides facility management services to the federal government. Mencia was the winner of the Hispanic Business Entrepreneur of the Year 2001 Award. Brief profiles of runners up are included.

36619 ■ "The perils of starting a service firm" in *Wall Street Journal* **(May 28, 2002, pp. B5)**
Pub: Wall Street Journal
Ed: Jeff Bailey. **Description:** Must-know advice is offered for would-be entrepreneurs wishing to start a service firm, is presented. Statistical data included.

36620 ■ "Personal histories" in *Harvard Business Review* **(Vol. 79, No. 11, December 2001, pp.)**
Pub: Harvard Business School Press
Description: The responses of 17 leaders in business, academia and the arts respond to a request for stories of experiences that taught them about leadership at its best and worst. Among the respondents were Michael Eisner of Disney, Ben Bradlee, former Washington Post editor, and Xerox CEO, Anne Mulcahy.

36621 ■ "Personal Style" in *Hispanic Business* **(April 2005, pp. 62)**
Pub: Hispanic Business
Ed: Leslie A. Westbrook. **Description:** James Alvarez, successful executive and entrepreneur found himself unable to putt after an accident. Alvarez designed a putter with a longer grip and angled shaft that promotes a more open stance, allowing golfers to see the putting line with both eyes, optimizing accuracy.

36622 ■ "Personalize your management development" in *Harvard Business Review* **(Vol. 81, No. 3, March 2003, pp. 113)**
Pub: Harvard Business School Press
Ed: Natalie Shope Griffin. **Description:** The problems organizations have with leadership development are explored. An outline of specific training approaches for various types of prospective leaders, such as reluctant leaders, arrogant leaders, overlooked leaders, and workaholics is presented.

36623 ■ "Pet Sitters in St. Louis Area Will Sit With Fido When the Master is Out" in *Belleville News-Democrat* **(September 27, 2004)**
Pub: Belleville News-Democrat
Ed: Will Buss. **Description:** Profiles of entrepreneurs who own pet sitting businesses that offer customized pet sitting and other services to clients.

36624 ■ "Peter Falvey: Whiz Kid: Peter Falvey is Betting the Company on Tech Investment" in *Boston Business Journal* **(Vol. 23, July 11, 2003)**
Pub: American City Business Journals
Ed: Edward Mason. **Description:** Revolution Partners focuses on high technology investment; profile of the investment bank's co-founder Peter Falvey is included.

36625 ■ "Peters will help develop technology" in *Crain's Detroit Business* **(Vol. 16, No. 49, December 4, 2000, pp. 43)**
Pub: Crain Communications, Inc.
Ed: David Barkholz. **Description:** William Peters, M.D., is leaving the Barbara Ann Karmanos Cancer Center to run the Detroit Medical Center's new Institute of Strategic Analysis & Innovation and Karmanos' embryonic Center for Cancer Economics, Technology Assessment, Innovation and Development (CETAID).

36626 ■ *Petty Capitalists and Globalization: Flexibility, Entrepreneurship, and Economic Development*
Pub: State University of New York Press
Ed: Alan Smart, Josephine Smart. **Released:** March 2005. **Price:** $70.00. **Description:** Investigation into ways small businesses in Europe, Asia, and Latin America are required to operate and compete in the fast-growing transnational economy.

36627 ■ "Phone Home" in *My Business* **(April/May 2004, pp. 44)**
Pub: My Business Magazine
Ed: Marcia Layton Turner. **Description:** Ways a small business owner can get away from business and enjoy a vacation are discussed.

36628 ■ "Pick Your Battles" in *Entrepreneur* **(Vol. 31, No. 11, November 2003, pp. 95)**
Pub: Entrepreneur Media, Inc.
Ed: Marc Diener. **Description:** Ways to determine the difference between being outmaneuvered or outgunned during negotiations are presented.

36629 ■ "Planning Your Exit Strategy: Three Ways To Go" in *My Business* **(October/November 2003, pp. 30-35)**
Pub: My Business Magazine
Ed: Shannon Scully, Steve Becker. **Description:** Exit strategy plans help small businesses not only decide ways to get out of the company, but they also lay the groundwork for getting ahead. Profiles of small business owners and their exit strategies are investigated.

36630 ■ *The Platinum Rule for Small Business Success*
Pub: Morgan James Publishing, LLC
Ed: Scott Zimmerman; Tony Allesandra; Ron Finklestein. **Released:** August 2006. **Description:** Rules for running a successful and profitable small business are shared.

36631 ■ "Play Nice" in *Entrepreneur* **(Vol. 32, September 2004, No. 9, pp. 32)**
Pub: Entrepreneur Media Inc.
Ed: Mark Henricks. **Description:** Review of How Full Is Your Bucket? The book offers positive strategies for work and life management.

36632 ■ "Playbook" in *Business 2.0* **(Vol. 6, May 2005, No. 4, pp. 121-122, 126-127)**
Pub: Time, Inc.
Ed: Damon Darlin. **Description:** Leadership is the difference between enterprises that flourish and those that fail. Ways to turn a company into a thriving business are examined.

36633 ■ "Players-Accomplishments of the Area's Most Significant Producers" in *Ingram's* **(Vol. 29, No. 1, January 2003, pp. 10)**
Pub: Show Me Publishing, Inc.
Ed: Description: Profiles of Angela Bennett and Chuck Gatson, the most significant producers in the Kansas City, Missouri area, are highlighted.

36634 ■ "Playing Favorites" in *Entrepreneur* **(Vol. 31, Sept. 2003)**
Pub: Entrepreneur Media, Inc.
Ed: Aliza Pilar Sherman. **Description:** Women entrepreneurs report favorite business Web sites they use to run their companies, with Google.com heading the list.

36635 ■ "Positive Peer Pressure" in *My Business* **(December/January 2004, pp. 34-37)**
Pub: My Business Magazine
Ed: Karen J. Bannan. **Description:** A new trend seen for small companies, has owners relying on peer groups for dealing with the pressures of running a business. Networking options can offer advice, education and camaraderie.

36636 ■ "The Power of Ideas" in *Ingram's* **(Vol. 27, No. 8, August 2001, pp. 20)**
Pub: Show Me Publishing, Inc.
Ed: Ron Fredman. **Description:** The importance of inspiring ideas in small business marketing is discussed.

36637 ■ "Power Living: Teresa Kay-Aba Kennedy Says Executives Don't Get Enough S.E.X." in *Black Enterprise* **(Vol. 34, No. 6, January 2004)**
Pub: Earl Graves Publishing Co.
Ed: Sonia Alleyne. **Description:** Profile of Teresa Kay-Aba Kennedy, former vice president of business development operations at MTV Networks Interactive. Kennedy left her corporation position and founded a yoga center in Harlem, New York and is now president of Power Living Enterprises Inc., a lifestyle coaching company with programs that teach executives how to lead productive, healthy lives.

36638 ■ "Power is the great motivator" in *Harvard Business Review* **(Vol. 81, No. 1, January 2003, pp. 117)**
Pub: Harvard Business School Press
Ed: David C. McClelland, David H. Burnham. **Description:** Descriptions of three types of managers are discussed. Affiliative managers need to be liked more than they need to get things done, while personal power managers put their own achievement ahead of everything. The third group focuses on building power through influence, rather than promoting their own personal achievement, and are the most effective of the three groups.

36639 ■ "Power Shopping" in *Entrepreneur* **(Vol. 28, No. 4, April 2000, pp. 62)**
Pub: Entrepreneur Media Inc.
Ed: Cynthia E. Griffin. **Description:** When it comes to shopping for clothing, household items and cars, studies have shown women wield a tremendous amount of influence.

36640 ■ "Prepare for takeoff" in *Entrepreneur* **(Vol. 31, No. 6, June 2003, pp. 124)**
Pub: Entrepreneur Media Inc.
Ed: Romanus Wolter. **Description:** Advice is offered for would-be entrepreneurs to use when preparing a business plan.

36641 ■ "Preparing for evil" in *Harvard Business Review* **(Vol. 81, No. 4, April 2003, pp. 109)**
Pub: Harvard Business School Press
Ed: Ian I. Mitroff, Murat C. Alpaslan. **Description:** The lack of preparation for crises in organizations, including Fortune 500 companies, is discussed. Crisis-prepared companies use a systematic approach to focus efforts for planning for natural disasters and two types of manmade calamities, accidental and deliberate.

36642 ■ "Preparing for national leadership" in *Women in Business* **(Vol. 53, No. 4, July-August, 2001, pp. 20)**
Pub: The ABWA Co. Inc.
Ed: Mary-Lane Kamberg. **Description:** Issues concerning leadership development opportunities for women are discussed, with focus on women's opportunities to become national officers or to organize national conferences. Cases of women in leadership positions are examined.

36643 ■ "Preserving Tradition, Embracing Progress" in *Rough Notes* **(Vol. 145, No. 2, February 2003, pp. 26)**
Pub: Rough Notes

Ed: Elaine Tolen. **Description:** Profile of Trey Sherwood, a partner in Valdosta Insurance Services. The independent agency provides for the insurance needs of 98 percent of Lowndes County, Valdosta, Georgia.

36644 ■ "Primal Leadership: The hidden driver of great performance" in *Harvard Business Review* **(Vol. 79, No. 11, December 2001, pp. 42)**
Pub: Harvard Business School Press
Ed: Annie Richard, McKee Danile, Boyatzis Goleman. **Description:** Research into the effects of a leader's moods on the organization are presented. Leader's moods and behaviors are potent drivers of business success, since moods are literally contagious.

36645 ■ "Priority packets pay to fly first class" in *Red Herring* **(No. 87, December 18, 2000, pp. 44, 46)**
Pub: Herring Communications, Inc.
Ed: Scott Tyler Shafer. **Description:** A profile of Village Networks, the New Jersey high-tech start-up and its founder Kai Eng.

36646 ■ "Private Lives" in *Inc.* **(October 2005, pp. 84)**
Pub: Inc. Magazine
Ed: Lora Koldony. **Description:** Adam Seifer, CEO of Fotolog, the New York City-based photo company, places photos of every meal he's eaten in the last three years on his Internet blog. Seifer started the blog when he launched his business, which hosts millions of photoblogs for other companies.

36647 ■ "The Problem With Confidence" in *Inc.* **(September 2005, pp. 176)**
Pub: Inc. Magazine
Ed: Adam Hanft. **Description:** Entrepreneurs are eager to take risks, but when does self-confidence become a liability for the company.

36648 ■ "Productive Lessons from a Tech Meltdown" in *Hispanic Business* **(Vol. 23, No. 7/8, July/August 2001, pp. 6)**
Pub: Hispanic Business
Ed: Jesus Chavarria. **Description:** A brief look at the long-term effects of technology on the Hispanic economy, and the need to deal with Hispanics as consumers as well as entrepreneurial innovators.

36649 ■ "Professional athlete credits ABWA with the right 'assist'" in *Women in Business* **(Vol. 54, No. 5, September-October 2002, pp. 10)**
Pub: The ABWA Company, Inc.
Ed: Mia Katz. **Description:** American Business Women's Association member, Jeanette Simonsen, discusses her appreciation of the organization and its members. As a professional volleyball player, she enjoys the professional accomplishments of the other women in the association.

36650 ■ "Profile: Alan Patricof as entrepreneurial curmudgeon" in *Red Herring* **(No. 103, September 1, 2001, pp. 38, 40)**
Pub: Herring Communications
Ed: Julia Lawlor **Description:** Profile of venture capitalist, Alan Patricof, the chairman of Patricof & Co. Ventures.

36651 ■ "Profile: Don Green reigns as the don of optical networking" in *Red Herring* **(No. 105, October 1, 2001, pp. 44)**
Pub: Herring Communications
Ed: Om Malik. **Description:** Profile of Don Green, the chairman of Advanced Fibre Communications, a publicly traded company in Petaluma, California.

36652 ■ "A Profile in Success" in *Hispanic Business* **(Vol. 23, No. 5, May 2001, pp. 56)**
Pub: Hispanic Business
Ed: Vivienne Heines. **Description:** A beneficiary of early career encouragement, Frank Montano inspires others to realize their potential. Mr. Montano, president and CEO of Moto Photo Inc., uses goal-setting and planning in employee training sessions.

36653 ■ "Programs" in *Black Enterprise* **(Vol. 34, No. 5, December 2003, pp. S8)**
Pub: Earl Graves Publishing Co.
Description: Profile of Finding Leaders Among Minorities Everywhere (FLAME) program. The program is designed to build confidence and encourage professional growth.

36654 ■ "Promise-keeping has lost its importance as a core value" in *Atlanta Business Chronicle* **(Vol. 25, November 15, 2002, No. 23 pp. 27A)**
Pub: American City Business Publications, Inc.
Ed: Ellwood F. Oakley III. **Description:** Managers consider "promise keeping" to be a lower-level ethical priority in business activity. MindSpring Enterprises Inc. is a high-profile exception; the company lives up to its commitments. Senior management must practice promise-keeping in order for it to be reintroduced into a workplace.

36655 ■ "Protocol: Coming Soon: Ethernet as business model" in *Red Herring* **(No. 102, August 15, 2001, pp. 68-69)**
Pub: Herring Communications
Ed: Om Malik. **Description:** Profile of Bob Metcalfe, partner at Polaris Venture Partners, and inventor of the Ethernet.

36656 ■ "Prove Your Worth: Forget the Stock Market." in *Entrepreneur* **(Vol. 31, No. 7, July 2003, pp. 64)**
Pub: Entrepreneur Media, Inc.
Ed: Mark Henricks. **Description:** It is recommended that entrepreneurs invest in their own companies, rather than the stock market as a good investment.

36657 ■ *The Psychology of Entrepreneurship*
Pub: Lawrence/Erlbaum Associates
Ed: J. Robert Baum; Michael Frese. **Released:** July 2006. **Price:** $99.95. **Description:** Psychology as the basis for understanding successful entrepreneurship is used to discuss how these small firms impact international social and economic well-being and how they are the main source of job creation, market innovation, and economic growth in most societies.

36658 ■ "Publisher Evolves With Technology, Entrepreneurial Talent" in *Portland Press Herald* **(October 21, 2005)**
Pub: Blethen Maine Newspapers, Inc.
Ed: Edward D. Murphy. **Description:** Profile of Nancy Randolph, who started her business Just Write Books after spending years helping others get their books ready for publication. Randolph splits the profits with authors after a book is published.

36659 ■ "Pump it Up" in *Entrepreneur* **(Vol. 32, No. 2, February 2004, pp. 73)**
Pub: Entrepreneur Media, Inc.
Ed: Barry Farber. **Description:** Three things to build, maintain and project confidence when making a sale are explained.

36660 ■ *The Pursuit of Happyness*
Pub: HarperCollins Publishers Inc.
Ed: Chris Gardner. **Released:** May 2006. **Price:** $25.95. **Description:** Rags-to-riches saga of a homeless father who raised and cared for his son on the streets of San Francisco and worked to become a powerful leader on Wall Street.

36661 ■ "Pursuits" in *Inc.* **(Volume 27, March 2005, No. 3, pp. 62-63)**
Pub: Inc. Magazine
Ed: Jess McCuan. **Description:** Profile of Greg James, founder of Topics Entertainment, an educational software developer. After years of success, James is devoting time to environmental causes and is making changes in his personal life.

36662 ■ "Putting signage on shirts is a cinch for sign-a-Rama's founder" in *Entrepreneur* **(Vol. 30, No. 3, March 2002, pp. 106)**
Pub: Entrepreneur Media Inc.
Description: Profile of Ray Titus, founder of Sign-a-Rama and EmbraidMe. EmbraidMe began franchising in 2001 and has 20 locations.

36663 ■ "Puzzleman to the Rescue" in *My Business* **(December/January 2003, pp. 12-13)**
Pub: My Business Magazine
Ed: Melany Klinck. Description: Profile of Cypriana Porter, owner of the educational toy store called The Gingerbread House. Porter invented the superhero Puzzleman to increase sales.

36664 ■ "Pygmalion in management" in *Harvard Business Review* **(Vol. 81, No. 1, January 2003, pp. 97)**
Pub: Harvard Business School Press
Ed: J. Sterling Livingston. Description: Ways some managers are able to inspire their subordinates to superior performance are listed. The high expectations these managers hold for themselves and their employees bring out the best in all.

36665 ■ "Quick Fix: Do SBA Express Loans Really Shortchange Entrepreneurs?" in *Entrepreneur* **(Vol. 32, No. 4, April 2004, pp. 27)**
Pub: Entrepreneur Media, Inc.
Ed: Julie Monahan. Description: Profile of the U.S. Small Business Administration's Express program that guaranteed loans to thousands of entrepreneurs. Retailers with gross sales of $6 million or less, wholesalers with 100 employees or less, and manufacturers with 500 employees or less, are eligible for Express Loans.

36666 ■ "Radical Sabbaticals" in *Success* **(Vol. 47, No. 3, July 2000, pp. 68)**
Pub: Success Publishing, Inc.
Ed: Pamela Margoshes. Description: Can you afford to take time off? Can you afford not to?

36667 ■ "Raising the Bar Again" in *Hispanic Business* **(October 2002, pp. 72, 74)**
Pub: Hispanic Business
Ed: Tim Dougherty. Description: Profile of Michael Sanchez, co-founder of the nutrition bar Arriba, a health-oriented product line geared toward Hispanics. Arriba's former company is now a part of Kraft Foods.

36668 ■ "Raising children and working can be a challenge" in *Atlanta Business Chronicle* **(Vol. 24, No. 13, August 31, 2001, pp. 38A)**
Pub: American City Business Journals Inc.
Ed: Don Hutcheson, Bob D. McDonald. Description: Don Hutcheson and Bob D. McDonald discuss how to be a good parent and balance business life with family life. The article offers ways to raise children that will enhance and build relationships. Tips are offered for talking to children, playing with them, putting them to bed at night, and having meals together as a family.

36669 ■ "The Rat Pack" in *Forbes* **(Vol. 170, No. 9, October 28, 2002, pp. 228)**
Pub: Forbes Magazine
Ed: Nathan Vardi. Description: Profile of James Foster who breeds and maintains rodents for pharmaceutical and biotechnology companies researching genes and drugs, at the cost of $10 per animal per month.

36670 ■ "Rave Reviews" in *My Business* **(April/May 2003, pp. 42)**
Pub: My Business Magazine
Ed: Carolyn Denny. Description: Advice is given for setting up an employee review process.

36671 ■ "The Real Deal" in *Entrepreneur* **(Vol. 33, January 2005, No. 1, pp. 28)**
Pub: Entrepreneur Media Inc.
Ed: Mark Henricks. Description: Review of the book, Confronting Reality: The Discipline of Getting Things Right, by Larry Bossidy and Ram Charan. The book offers a program to help entrepreneurs understand if their businesses are positioned to make profits and how to set the right future direction.

36672 ■ "Real Estate Ambitions" in *Black Enterprise* **(Vol. 37, January 2007, No. 6, pp. 101)**
Pub: Earl G. Graves Publishing Co. Inc.
Ed: Description: National Real Estate Investors Association is a nonprofit trade association for both advanced as well as novice real estate investors that offers information on builders to contractors to banks. When looking to become a real estate investor utilize this organization, talk to various investors like the president of your local chapter, let people know your aspirations, and see if you can find a partner who has experience in the field. Resources included.

36673 ■ "Reality Checker" in *Forbes* **(February 19, 2001, pp. 95)**
Pub: Forbes Magazine
Ed: Jennifer Godwin. Description: A profile of Joseph W. Goodman, a retired electrical engineer, who has become a consultant for venture capital firms.

36674 ■ "Realizing the Spirit and Impact of Adam Smith's Capitalism through Entrepreneurship" in *Journal of Business Ethics* **(Vol.46, Sept.03)**
Pub: Kluwer Academic Publishers Group
Ed: Scott L. Newbert. Description: Adam Smith argued that in order to create an effective and productive capitalist system, individuals must pursue interests of both the self and society; despite this assertion, modern economic theory has become tightly focused on the pursuit of economic self-interests at the expense of other, higher order motives.

36675 ■ "A Reason for Ranting" in *Black Enterprise* **(Vol. 36, November 2005, No. 4, pp. 161)**
Pub: Earl G. Graves Publishing Co. Inc.
Ed: Robyn D. Clarke. Description: Three tips to vent constructively in order to resolve a problem or concern are listed.

36676 ■ "A Reason to Smile" in *Black Enterprise* **(Vol. 34, No. 2, September 2003, pp. 62)**
Pub: Earl Graves Publishing Co.
Ed: Ashley Gibson. Description: Of the 6,000 board certified oral surgeons in the U.S., about 100 are women. Profile of Dr. Ngozi Etufugh, who was born in Nigeria, operates two practices in New York. Etufugh tells how she empowered herself to become a top oral surgeon despite being black, being a woman, and being petite.

36677 ■ "Rebuilding and Revitalizing Lower Manhattan" in *Venture Capital Journal* **(Vol. 42, No. 9, September 2002, pp. 32)**
Pub: Thomas Venture Economics
Ed: Sheldon Silver. Description: Sheldon Silver, Speaker of the New York State Assembly, and represents the largest part of Silicon Alley, shares insight into the rebuilding and revitalizing of the Lower Manhattan area of New York after the terrorist attacks of September 11.

36678 ■ "Recession session" in *Entrepreneur* **(Vol. 30, No. 3, March 2002, pp.)**
Pub: Entrepreneur Media Inc.
Ed: Mark Henricks. Description: An interview with various experts and entrepreneurs to learn how and when they recommend aggressive or defensive positions in the areas of money management, people management, marketing, and technology.

36679 ■ "Recognizing Gifted Entrepreneurs" in *Black Enterprise* **(Vol. 34, No. 3, October 2003, pp. 150)**
Pub: Earl Graves Publishing Co.
Description: Black Enterprise is accepting nominations for the 2004 Black Enterprise Small Business Awards; the public is encouraged to nominate African-Americans from their communities.

36680 ■ "Reconnaissance" in *Inc.* **(August 2005, pp. 53-54)**
Pub: Inc. Magazine
Ed: Michael S. Hopkins. Description: Review of the book, Freakonomics. The book offers business lessons of interest to entrepreneurs.

36681 ■ "Recovering from Tragedy - How Alta Has Coped with Losses" in *Venture Capital Journal* **(Vol. 42, No. 9, September 2002, pp. 24-25)**
Pub: Thomas Venture Economics
Ed: Dan Primack. Description: Ways in which members of Alta Communications has coped in the aftermath of the terrorist attacks of 9/11 are discussed. Along with raising its new fund in a down market, each partner is very proud of their newly created foundation honoring two of their colleagues lost in the tragedy.

36682 ■ "Redefining my role" in *My Business* **(June/July 2002, pp. 48)**
Pub: My Business Magazine
Ed: Description: David Geller shares the challenge he faced as an entrepreneur and how he was able to help his firm reach the goals set out by he and his brother in 1996 when starting GV Financial Advisors, a financial planning firm in Atlanta, Georgia.

36683 ■ "Reel to Real" in *Success* **(Vol. 47, No. 2, June 2000, pp. 28)**
Pub: Success Publishing, Inc.
Ed: Scott Smith, Robert T. Wazeka. Description: Success Entrepreneurs of the Decade, Steven Spielberg and George Lucas, redefined an industry and changed the world along the way.

36684 ■ "Rembrandts in the Attic" in *Inc.* **(October 2000, pp. 23)**
Pub: The Goldhirsh Group
Description: Ian Peck, former gallery owner and art dealer founded an Internet-based company in 1999 that enables museums, galleries, family trusts and artists' estates to sell or lease their works of art to corporate clients.

36685 ■ "The Remote Control CEO" in *Inc.* **(October 2005, pp. 96-101, 144, 146)**
Pub: Inc. Magazine
Ed: Donna Fenn. Description: CEO, Stephen McConnell believes a major reason for his organic meat company's success is because he works from home four days a week. The success of his firm, Applegate Farms, reinforces this strategy.

36686 ■ "Remote Control" in *Entrepreneur* **(Vol. 33, February 2005, No. 2, pp. 56)**
Pub: Entrepreneur Media Inc.
Ed: Mark Henricks. Description: In 2003, 54 percent of companies internationally reported telecommuting programs for their staffs, that number rose to 80 percent in 2005. Skills for managing a telecommuting workforce are defined.

36687 ■ "Reporting for Boot Camp" in *Home Business* **(Vol. 13, January/February 2006, No. 1, pp. 56)**
Pub: Home Business Magazine
Ed: Sandy Larson. Description: Profile of Howard Dell, owner of a successful personal training firm in Newport Beach, California. Dell tells how he balances his business with an acting career.

36688 ■ "Required Reading" in *Entrepreneur* **(Vol. 31, No. 7, July 2003, pp. 32)**
Pub: Entrepreneur Media, Inc.
Ed: Aliza Pilar Sherman. Description: Reviews of books recommended for aspiring and current women entrepreneurs are shared. Many of these successful women are using the wisdom found in these books to improve business strategies.

36689 ■ "Required reading" in *Harvard Business Review* **(Vol. 79, No. 11, December 2001, pp. 15)**
Pub: Harvard Business School Press
Ed: Barbara Kellerman. Description: While there is no top ten list of books on leadership whose supremacy and currency are self-evident, leadership scholar Barbara Kellerman presents a list of works which she considers universal. The list includes Totalitarianism by Hannad Arendt; The Prince, by Machiavelli; Moses and Monotheism, by Freud; and Letter from Birmingham Jail, by Martin Luther King Jr.

36690 ■ "Resolving Owner Conflicts" in Rough Notes (Vol. 145, No. 9, September 2002, pp. 26)
Pub: Rough Notes
Ed: Paul J. DiStefano. Description: Lack of communications between owners of the insurance agency often results in disagreements. Unresolved conflict among owners can impede the future of an agency, whether the issue relates to money or operating philosophy.

36691 ■ "Resource line" in Black Enterprise (Vol. 33, No. 7, February 2003, pp. 6)
Pub: Earl Graves Publishing Co.
Ed: Latif Lewis. Description: Whatever your professional or entrepreneurial needs, blackenterprise.com's Interactive Media Editor Lewis' column provides useful resources for business owners, corporate executives, and investors.

36692 ■ "Restaurant Riches" in Small Business Opportunities (Vol. 17, November 2005, No. 6, pp. 76, 86)
Pub: Harris Publications Inc.
Ed: James Carlson. Description: Profile of Master Chef Michael Collins and partner, neon artist Tony Palumbo. The pair converted a church into a growing restaurant called Green Emporium in Colrain, Massachusetts.

36693 ■ "Retail Exec Stays in Style" in Crain's New York Business (Vol. 23, January 29, 2007, No. 5, pp. F3)
Pub: Crain Communications, Inc.
Ed: Elisabeth Butler. Description: Profile of Adrienne Lazarus and her position as President of Ann Taylor Stores Corp. The executive was brought in to revitalize the fashion chain.

36694 ■ "Retire Rich" in Entrepreneur (Vol. 33, September 2005, No. 9, pp. 68)
Pub: Entrepreneur Media Inc.
Ed: David Worrell. Description: Financial experts offer tips, strategies and secrets to help entrepreneurs accumulate wealth for retirement.

36695 ■ "Retired exec finds leisure time less than idle" in Atlanta Business Chronicle (Vol. 25, December 6, 2002, No. 26, pp. 26A)
Pub: American City Business Publications, Inc.
Ed: Meredith Jordan. Description: Roger Scovil, retired president of Lockwood Greene International, is presently chairman of the World Trade Center Atlanta's executive committee. Scovil has written a new book, "Get Ahead, Scovil's 7 Rules for Success in Management".

36696 ■ "The Return of the Black Entrepreneur" in Business Week Online (Oct. 8, 2002)
Pub: McGraw-Hill Inc.
Ed: Kimberly Weisul. Description: A recent study conducted by the Ewing Marion Kauffman Foundation shows that the number of African American entrepreneurs in the U.S. is on the rise. A second phase of the study will be published sometime in 2003.

36697 ■ "Revamping a Retirement Plan" in Black Enterprise (Vol. 35, October 2004, No. 3, pp. 43)
Pub: Earl G. Graves Publishing Co. Inc.
Ed: Carmen Brown. Description: Calvin and Jacqueline McGahee share investment strategies for a better retirement.

36698 ■ "Rich Man, Politician" in Inc. (September 1, 2003)
Pub: Gruner & Jahr USA Publishing
Ed: Patrick J. Sauer. Description: Will campaign finance reform put more entrepreneurs in political offices? The effects of the McCain-Feingold campaign finance reform law are discussed.

36699 ■ "Richard Rhodes" in Entrepreneur (Vol. 31, No. 8, August, 2003, pp. 19)
Pub: Entrepreneur Media, Inc.
Ed: April Y. Pennington. Description: Profile of Richard Rhodes, 42-year old founder and CEO of Rhodes Architectural Stone, located in Seattle, Washington. Rhodes started the firm in 1998 with $100,000 and projects sales at $10 million for 2003.

36700 ■ "Riding the Greenback" in Business Week (No. 3678, April 24, 2000, pp. F10)
Pub: McGraw-Hill, Inc.
Description: Small companies now comprise 97 percent of those selling overseas, according to the Small Business Administration. International finance for small business is covered.

36701 ■ "Rising to the Top" in Black Enterprise (Vol. 35, November 2004, No. 4, pp. 183)
Pub: Earl G. Graves Publishing Co. Inc.
Ed: Tanisha A. Sykes. Description: Profile of Donald Riley, host and producer of an Internet radio talk show. Riley suffers with a debilitating genetic birth defect that affects muscle development. Riley advocates Section 504 of the Rehabilitation Act of 1973 and the Americans With Disabilities Act, which prohibits discrimination against qualified individuals with disabilities.

36702 ■ Risk-Free Entrepreneur
Pub: Adams Media Corporation
Ed: Don Debelak. Released: June 2006. Price: $14.95. Description: Information is offered to help entrepreneurs to develop an idea for a product or service and have other companies provide the marketing, manufacturing and staff.

36703 ■ "Roamin' Holiday: Let a Vacation Put You On the Road to a Great Start-Up Idea" in Entrepreneur (Vol. 31, No. 9, September 2003)
Pub: Entrepreneur Media, Inc.
Ed: Nichole L. Torres. Description: Many entrepreneurs discover new business ideas while taking a relaxing vacation. Profile of Tie Wou, founder of Tote Le Monde, a handbag manufacturer in New York City is included.

36704 ■ "Robert L. Johnson" in Black Enterprise (Vol. 36, November 2005, No. 4, pp. 34)
Pub: Earl G. Graves Publishing Co. Inc.
Ed: Matthew S. Scott. Description: Profile of Robert L. Johnson, Black entrepreneur who founded the Black Entertainment Television network and sold it to build greater wealth.

36705 ■ "Roger Cass the Last Optimist" in Fast Company (July 2001, pp. 88)
Pub: Fast Company
Ed: Harriet Rubin. Description: Profile of Roger Cass, the man who invented the idea of the Long Boom, or, the notion that we're only seven years into a 27-year expansion.

36706 ■ "The Role of Integrity as a Mediator in Strategic Leadership" in Journal of Business Ethics (Vol. 46, No. 1, Aug. 2003, pp. 31)
Pub: Kluwer Academic Publishers Group
Ed: Skip Worden. Description: An examination of the role of integrity as a mediator within strategic leadership and its impact on credibility in reputational capital is discussed.

36707 ■ The Role of the Non-Executive Director in the Small to Medium-Sized Business
Pub: Palgrave Macmillan
Ed: John Smithson. Released: March 2004. Price: $75.00. Description: The role of the non-executive director in a small to medium-sized business is examined.

36708 ■ "Roll On: Davin Enjoys Just Spinning Your Wheels" in Black Enterprise (Vol. 34, No. 4, November 2003, pp. 180)
Pub: Earl Graves Publishing Co.
Ed: Linda S. Lawson. Description: Profile of Ian Hardman, CEO of Davin Wheels in Rhode Island. The company's patented chrome rims adorn the cars of executives and celebrities alike, ranging in price from $12,000-$14,000, with custom rims costing more.

36709 ■ "Round Table" in Atlanta Business Chronicle (Vol. 25, November 15, 2002, No. 23 pp. 7B)
Pub: American City Business Publications, Inc.
Description: Five Atlanta, Georgia-area executives respond to handling three potential dilemmas, which involve ethical issues. Responses are given by Arn Rubinoff of Powell, Goldstein, Frazer & Murphy LLC; John C. Knapp of The Southern Institute for Business and Professional Ethics; Dave Brookmire of Corporate Performance Strategies Inc.; Emmett Hawkins III of Leapfrog Services Inc.; and Larry Hart of The Executive Committee.

36710 ■ "Rule Book: Does Your Small Business Need an Employee Manual?" in My Business (June/July 2004, pp. 14)
Pub: My Business Magazine
Description: Review of the book, Create Your Own Employee Handbook: A Legal and Practical Guide, which teaches a company to express its culture and beliefs, ensure consistency for all employees, and clearly explain expectations of each employee in the form of an employee manual.

36711 ■ "Running on empty?" in Women in Business (Vol. 53, No. 2, March-April, 2001, pp. 32)
Pub: The ABWA Co. Inc.
Ed: Nancy Cloak. Description: Advice on methods of coping with stress is presented. Ways of changing behavior patterns from self-destructive habits to more positive soothing, adaptive, or reflective activities are suggested.

36712 ■ "Running Into Profits" in My Business (June/July 2004, pp. 16)
Pub: My Business Magazine
Description: Jogging sessions fit into tight schedules may actually improve a company's profits.

36713 ■ "Same Markets, New Marketplaces" in Black Enterprise (Vol. 35, September 2004, No. 2, pp. 34)
Pub: Earl G. Graves Publishing Co. Inc.
Ed: Malik Singleton. Description: According to a study performed by the Center for Women's Business Research, African American women entrepreneurs in nontraditional sectors rose between 1997 and 2002. Wisconsin, Delaware, and Oregon were among the top states experiencing the rise, with Wisconsin reporting 453 percent growth in the number of African American women-owned businesses. Statistical data included.

36714 ■ "San Diego: Stone Makes Rock-Solid Impression" in San Diego Business Journal (Vol. 28, January 15, 2007, No. 3, pp. 16)
Pub: San Diego Business Journal Associates
Ed: Amy Yarnall. Description: Profile of San Diego-based StoneImpressions and its Make-Mine-a-Million, a program that helps women entrepreneurs develop million dollar businesses.

36715 ■ "Saturday night event to celebrate Vancouver's entrepreneurial spirit" in Vancouver, WA Business Journal (February 28, 2003)
Pub: Dolan Media Newswires
Ed: Cami Joner. Description: The second annual Celebrating Entrepreneurial Spirit Awards event recognizes local successful businesses in the Vancouver area. The event will also award five scholarships to local high school DECA students.

36716 ■ "Save the Founder" in Inc. (October 2005, pp. 156)
Pub: Inc. Magazine
Ed: Adam Hanft. Description: No matter how large or successful a business becomes, it is necessary for its founder to remain its leader.

36717 ■ "Say Cheese, Fairhaven" in Bellingham Business Journal (December 2006, pp. A3)
Pub: Sun News Inc.
Description: Profile of Rachel Riggs, a lover of artisan cheeses, who opened a new shop in Fairhaven

named Quel Fromage. The store will supply restaurants and offers retail customers over 125 varieties of cheese and other specialty items not available locally to customers. It will also feature wine pairings, guest cheesemakers, and more.

36718 ■ **"SBA's Small Business Person of the Year Shares Her Story" in** *Portland Press Herald* **(May 6, 2005)**
Pub: Blethen Maine Newspapers, Inc.
Ed: Edward D. Murphy. **Description:** Profile of Marianne Sensale-Guerin, the Small Business Administration's new national Small Business Person of the Year. Sensale-Guerin tells how she started her business two months after her husband was killed in a work-related accident.

36719 ■ **"Scaling a Vertical Learning Curve" in** *Fortune* **(Vol. 141, No. 2, January 24, 2000, pp. 96+)**
Pub: Time Inc.
Ed: Eryn Brown. **Description:** Part two of a story following the paths of four graduates, three of which risked it all on a Net startup, to see how the lives of New Economy MBA's differ from those who follow a traditional path.

36720 ■ **"Scenic route" in** *Entrepreneur* **(Vol. 30, No. 3, March 2002, pp. 116)**
Pub: Entrepreneur Media Inc.
Description: Profile of Jenny Lefferts of MAD (Motor Adventure Destinations) Maps Inc. and John Codilis of PJ Squares LLC. Lefferts creates maps that chart scenic back roads, while Codilis produces individually wrapped peanut butter and jelly slices that can be eaten alone or with bread.

36721 ■ **"School Is In for Entrepreneurs: Continuing Education Courses Abound." in** *Black Enterprise* **(Vol. 35, October 2004, No. 3)**
Pub: Earl G. Graves Publishing Co. Inc.
Ed: Bridget McCrea. **Description:** A growing number of small business owners are taking courses to help them better manage company growth, employees, financial operations, and other key issues.

36722 ■ **"The science behind six degrees." in** *Harvard Business Review* **(Vol. 81, No. 2, Feb. 2003, pp. 16)**
Pub: Harvard Business School Press
Ed: Gardiner Morse. **Description:** Duncan Watts answers questions about his research into network science and how it can help explain why products sell, and how companies effectively manage themselves. Critical elements of this field of study are human behavior, group dynamics, and perception.

36723 ■ **"Scoring Big Goals" in** *Small Business Opportunities* **(Vol. 17, September 2005, No. 5, pp. 74)**
Pub: Harris Publications Inc.
Ed: Annette Wood. **Description:** Gary Proctor used his interest in soccer to build an empire selling high quality sporting goods at affordable prices. Proctor reported $6 million in equipment and sports supply sales.

36724 ■ **"Screen Gems" in** *Fast Company* **(March 2005, No. 92, pp. 39)**
Pub: Gruner & Jahr USA Publishing
Ed: Lucas Conley, Danielle Sacks. **Description:** Film industry leaders share insight into managing teams, coping with rejection and implementing the visions of others.

36725 ■ **"Sea Change" in** *Inc.* **(January 1, 2002)**
Pub: Inc. Magazine
Ed: John Grossmann. **Description:** Profile of Henry Lovejoy, wholesaler of ecologically acceptable fish and shellfish; Lovejoy shares ways he was able to brand his product.

36726 ■ *The Secret Language of Competitive Intelligence: How to See Through and Stay Ahead of Business Disruptions, Distortions, Rumors, and Smoke*
Pub: Crown Publishing Group
Ed: Leonard M. Fuld. **Released:** May 2006. **Price:** $24.95.

36727 ■ **"The Secret Life of a Tightwad" in** *My Business* **(April/May 2004, pp. 28-34)**
Pub: My Business Magazine
Ed: Shannon Scully. **Description:** Smart tips to help small business owners save on business expenses are shared.

36728 ■ *Secrets of Millionaire Moms*
Pub: McGraw-Hill
Ed: Tamara Monosoff. **Released:** March 2007. **Price:** $16.95. **Description:** Profiles of successful women/mother entrepreneurs are presented, including Julie Clark, Lane Nemeth, Lillian Vernon, Victoria Knight, Rachel Ashwell and other powerful businesswomen.

36729 ■ **"Secrets to Success" in** *Small Business Opportunities* **(Vol. 17, November 2005, No. 6, pp. 74, 86)**
Pub: Harris Publications Inc.
Ed: Mollie Neal. **Description:** Profile of Kelly Riddle, private investigator who offers services such as tracking down embezzlers and worker's compensation claims to finding missing persons and conducting bug sweeps and surveillance operations. Riddle employs 30 private investigators.

36730 ■ *Secrets of a Successful Entrepreneur: How to Start & Succeed at Running Your Own Business*
Pub: K & A Publications
Ed: Gene Dailey. **Released:** 1993. **Price:** $24.95.

36731 ■ **"Secure Fortune" in** *Small Business Opportunities* **(Vol. 16, No. 3, May 2004, pp. 54, 56)**
Pub: Harris Publications, Inc.
Ed: Vicki Gerson. **Description:** Profile of Dan Moceri and Greg Lernihan, who started their $43 million security systems and alarm enterprise with a laptop. The company closes one day a year to go into various communities to do work for the disadvantaged, working at food banks or other agencies.

36732 ■ **"Seeing Is Believing: Creating a Vision To Guide Your Team To Success" in** *Black Enterprise* **(Vol. 35, September 2004, No. 2, pp. 181)**
Pub: Earl G. Graves Publishing Co. Inc.
Ed: Kimberly J. Hamilton-Wright. **Description:** Small business success can be attributed to setting a vision of excellence for the entire team to follow.

36733 ■ **"Seeking Up-and-Comers Under 30." in** *Crain's Detroit Business* **(Vol. 23, February 5, 2007, No. 6, pp. 26)**
Pub: Crain Communications Inc. - Detroit
Description: Crain's is looking for the best twenty in their 20's feature. Unlike their forty in their 40's, which honors proven business successes, this feature emphasizes imaginative, out of the box, creative thinkers that are shaking things up.

36734 ■ *Sell Your Business Your Way: Getting Out, Getting Rich, and Getting on with Your Life*
Pub: American Management Association
Ed: Rick Rickertsen; Robert Gunther. **Released:** 2006. **Price:** $27.95.

36735 ■ **"Sense and reliability: A conversation with celebrated psychologist Karl E. Weick" in** *Harvard Business Review* **(Vol. 81, No. 4, Apr. 2003)**
Pub: Harvard Business School Press
Ed: Diane Coutu. **Description:** A noted psychologist examines the characteristics of high-reliability organizations, such as nuclear plants, firefighting units, and emergency rooms. Corporations can learn much from these organizations that cannot afford surprises in the workplace.

36736 ■ **"September 11, 2001. A CEO's story" in** *Harvard Business Review* **(Vol. 80, No. 10, October 2002, pp. 58)**
Pub: Harvard Business School Press
Ed: Jeffrey W. Greenberg. **Description:** Marsh & McLennan Companies' offices in the World Trade Center were destroyed on September 11, 2001. Jeffrey W. Greenberg, chairman of Marsh & McLennan Companies Inc., recounts his immediate response to the airplane attack, efforts to save lives, locate people, recapture company data, help with the healing, inspire confidence, and generally insure that the company and its employees were able to continue.

36737 ■ **"Service Providers" in** *Crain's Detroit Business* **(Vol. 16, No. 50, December 11, 2000, pp. E-13)**
Pub: Crain Communications, Inc.
Description: An extensive listing of services provided in Michigan that help startups and existing businesses get access to programs available to them.

36738 ■ **"Serving Up Success: There's Something to be Said for Doing Things Your Way" in** *Entrepreneur* **(Vol. 31, No. 11, November 2003, pp. 86)**
Pub: Entrepreneur Media, Inc.
Ed: Joshua Kurlantzick. **Description:** Profiles of Fred DeLuca, founder of Subway sandwich shops and Howard Schultz, founder of Starbucks coffee conglomerate. Each found success in his own way.

36739 ■ *Setting the Table*
Pub: HarperCollins Publishers Inc.
Ed: Danny Meyer. **Price:** $29.95. **Description:** Renowned restauranteur profiles his success in the hospitality business.

36740 ■ *Setting the Table: The Transforming Power of Hospitality in Business*
Pub: HarperCollins Publishers Inc.
Released: October 2006.

36741 ■ **"Shielding Your Home from Lawsuits" in** *Hispanic Business* **(October 2003, pp. 90)**
Pub: Hispanic Business
Ed: Glen M. Terrones, Christopher Jarvis, David Mandell. **Description:** Tools to help small business owners protect their homes from lawsuits are given, including the formation of limited liability companies and family limited partnerships.

36742 ■ **"Shout It Out" in** *Entrepreneur* **(Vol. 33, September 2005, No. 9, pp. 128)**
Pub: Entrepreneur Media Inc.
Ed: Romanus Wolter. **Description:** Four steps to help with entrepreneurial self-esteem are outlined: Be true to yourself; identify possibility in every conversation; be specific when answering questions; and trust instincts.

36743 ■ **"Show Me the Money!" in** *Success* **(Vol. 47, No. 6, November 2000, pp. 60)**
Pub: Success Publishing, Inc.
Ed: Phil Garfinkle. **Description:** Many companies are unable to secure financing, not because of a flaw in their business, but because of flaws in how they approach the capital formation process. A listing of some of the most common gaffes, and the steps entrepreneurs should take to avoid them.

36744 ■ **"Signs of Life? You'll Need Plenty of Patience to Profit from M-Commerce" in** *Entrepreneur* **(Vol. 31, No. 10, October 2003, pp. 28)**
Pub: Entrepreneur Media, Inc.
Ed: Amanda C. Kooser. **Description:** M-Commerce, or mobile commerce, is discussed. The sector has seen disappointing early experiences, but many entrepreneurs are looking forward to a full-blown m-commerce future.

36745 ■ **"Simplicity by Design" in** *Fast Company* **(September 2001, pp. 62)**
Pub: Fast Company
Ed: Christine Canabou. **Description:** Profile of Eileen Fisher, president and founder of Eileen Fisher Inc., based in Irvington, New York. The fashion designer shares the coping mechanisms she uses to help simplify her busy life.

36746 ■ "Six Degrees of Separation" in *Venture Capital Journal* **(October 1, 2005)**
Pub: Thomason Financial Inc.
Description: Isaac Applebaum has resigned from Lightspeed Venture Partners in order to form his own firm with two other partners.

36747 ■ "Sleep-state visualization in five easy steps" in *Black Enterprise* **(Vol. 33, No. 6, January 2003, pp. 84)**
Pub: Earl Graves Publishing Co.
Description: Five steps for creative visualization are presented, from formulating a question during the day to finding the answer while asleep; persistence is the key.

36748 ■ "Small Biz Barges into Cuba" in *Inc.* **(October 1, 2003)**
Pub: Gruner & Jahr USA Publishing
Ed: Anton Piach. **Description:** Profile of Maybank Shipping, the small South Carolina company that shipped goods to Cuba via chartered foreign vessels. Cuba licensed a large shipper called Crowley, in Oakland, California, to import goods on foreign vessels.

36749 ■ "Small-Biz Owners' Wild Mood Swings" in *Inc.* **(July 1, 2003)**
Pub: Gruner & Jahr USA Publishing
Description: The National Federation of Independent Businesses monthly index measuring small business optimism hit a 10-year low in March 2003.

36750 ■ "Small Biz Survivors" in *Small Business Opportunities* **(Vol. 13, No. 6, November 2001, pp. 74-76, 80)**
Pub: Harris Publications, Inc.
Description: Profile of Outward Bound, the adventure-based education organization, with more than 35 schools in 19 nations. Outward Bound Professional Development Programs benefit both small and large companies. A list of Outward Bound U.S. locations is provided.

36751 ■ "Small Business Advisor: Toy Story: Sharon P. John's Toy Company is Relaunching the Dawn Doll" in *Crain's Chicago Business* **(Vol. 23)**
Pub: Crain Communications, Inc. Crain Communications, Inc.
Ed: Barbara B. Buchholz. **Description:** A profile of Sharon P. John, Checkerboard Toys Inc., and her plans to relaunch the Dawn doll, first introduced in 1970.

36752 ■ *Small Business: An Entrepreneur*
Pub: Harcourt Brace College Publishers
Ed: Ryan. **Released:** 5th ed. 1998. **Price:** $39.00.

36753 ■ *Small Business: An Entrepreneur's Business Plan*
Pub: South-Western
Ed: J.D Ryan, Gail P. Hiduke. **Released:** June 2005. **Price:** $90.95. **Description:** Assistance in preparing a business plan that identifies opportunities and ways to target a customer market.

36754 ■ *Small Business: An Entrepreneur's Plan*
Pub: Nelson Thomson Learning
Ed: Ronald A. Knowles. **Released:** December 2006. **Description:** Entrepreneur's guide to planning a small business.

36755 ■ *Small Business, Big Life: Five Steps to Creating a Great Life with Your Own Small Business*
Pub: Rutledge Books Inc.
Ed: Louis Barajas. **Released:** May 2007. **Price:** $22.99. **Description:** Five steps for planning, starting and running a small business, while maintaining a good life, are presented.

36756 ■ "Small Business on the Big Screen" in *My Business* **(November/December 2001, pp. 36-39)**
Pub: My Business Magazine
Ed: Tom Ehrenfeld. **Description:** Entrepreneurs are rarely represented in a realistic manner in movies. A preview of the Top Ten small business movies and the messages they deliver on running a company, as well as several television sitcoms that focus on small businesses, are highlighted.

36757 ■ "Small Business: Houman Jewelry Design" in *San Diego Business Journal* **(Vol. 28, January 8, 2007, No. 2, pp. 26)**
Pub: San Diego Business Journal Associates
Ed: Jessica Long. **Description:** Profile of entrepreneur, Houman Omidifar, owner of Houman Jewelry Design in Coronado, California. Omidifar shares his secrets to success.

36758 ■ *Small Business Management*
Pub: John Wiley and Sons Inc.
Ed: Margaret Burlingame; Don Gulbrandsen; Richard M. Hodgetts; Donald F. Kuratko. **Released:** March 2007. **Price:** $44.95. **Description:** Tips for starting and running a successful small business are given, including advice on writing a business plan, financing, and the law.

36759 ■ *Small-Business Management Guide: Advice from the Brass-Tacks Entrepreneur*
Pub: Henry Holt & Company
Ed: Jim Schell. **Released:** October 1995. **Description:** Entrepreneurs offer advice for managing a small business.

36760 ■ "Small Business Spotlight" in *Small Business Opportunities* **(Vol. 17, November 2005, No. 6, pp. 112)**
Pub: Harris Publications Inc.
Description: Profiles of two successful entrepreneurs and the way they run their companies. Kevin Esteban owns Gotham Gardens, one of Manhattan's best known florists. Ollie Johnson sells Dr. Miracle's line of hair products designed to treat and condition African-American hair.

36761 ■ *Small Business Survival Guide: Starting, Protecting, and Securing Your Business for Long-Term Success*
Pub: Adams Media Corporation
Ed: Cliff Ennico. **Released:** October 2005. **Price:** $12.95 (US), $17.95 (Canadian). **Description:** Entrepreneurship in the new millennium. Topics include creditors, taxes, competition, business law, and accounting.

36762 ■ "Small Firms Emphasize Trade-Show Marketing" in *Crain's Detroit Business* **(Vol. 21, February 7, 2005, No. 6, pp. 24)**
Pub: Crain Communications Inc. - Detroit
Ed: DeAnna Belger. **Description:** According to a recent survey, more small companies in Michigan rely on trade shows than their larger competitors. Most respondents reported attending trade shows to generate sales leads, increase visibility, and to network.

36763 ■ *Small Firms: Entrepreneurship in the '90s*
Pub: Taylor & Francis, Inc.
Ed: David Deakins, Peter Jennings and Colin Mason. **Released:** 1997. **Price:** $85.00 (cloth).

36764 ■ "Smarter Than You" in *Inc.* **(September 2005, pp. 69, 72)**
Pub: Inc. Magazine
Ed: Michael S. Hopkins. **Description:** James Surowiecki's book, The Wisdom of Crowds, explains why so many entrepreneurial companies don't grow, or are unable to successfully produce a second product; the book also offers CEOs solutions to these challenges.

36765 ■ "Smith & Nephew's local spark" in *Boston Business Journal* **(Vol. 22, No. 15, May 17, 2002, p)**
Pub: MCP, Inc.
Ed: Allison Connolly. **Description:** Smith and Nephew Endoscopy president, Ron Sparks, kept his company in Massachusetts because of the talented potential labor pool. Sparks operates the company as an entrepreneurial enterprise.

36766 ■ "Snowboarding Secrets" in *Forbes* **(Vol. 175, February 14, 2005, No. 3, pp. 78)**
Pub: Forbes Magazine Inc.
Ed: Melanie Wells. **Description:** Profile of Chris M. Bradley, founder of 2ndEdition, creator of $50 snowboards customized with vinyl graphics in camouflage, graffiti, etc. via the Web.

36767 ■ "Soaring Salaries: It's Payback Time" in *Business Week* **(No. 3702, October 9, 2000, pp. F24)**
Pub: McGraw-Hill, Inc.
Description: Executive salaries are reaching record levels. Entrepreneurs are forced to offer as much as 40%-60% increases for new hires and better expand benefits for those already on the payroll. Statistical data included.

36768 ■ *Social Enterprise in Europe*
Pub: Routledge Inc.
Ed: Marthe Nyssens. **Released:** August 2006. **Price:** $145.00 hardcopy; $46.95 paperback. **Description:** Social enterprises in Europe are examined through three ideas: that they have a complex mixture of goals, that they mobilize various kinds of markets and non-market resources, and that they are embedded in the political context.

36769 ■ *Social Entrepreneurship*
Pub: Palgrave Macmillan
Ed: Johanna Mair; Jeffrey Robinson; Kai Hockerts. **Released:** June 2006. **Price:** $80.00. **Description:** Social entrepreneurship is the process involving innovative approaches to solving social problems while creating economic value.

36770 ■ "Soft Landing: James Garrett Took a Leap of Faith and Found Security" in *Black Enterprise* **(Vol. 34, No. 2, September 2003, pp. 51)**
Pub: Earl Graves Publishing Co.
Ed: Cristina Gair. **Description:** Profile of James Garrett, founder of Sentel Corporation, an engineering and software services company providing homeland security devices and other services. Garrett left a government position to become an entrepreneur and tried various businesses before finding his niche.

36771 ■ "Soldiers of fortune" in *Entrepreneur* **(Vol. 31, No. 5, May 2003, pp. 27)**
Pub: Entrepreneur Media Inc.
Ed: April Y. Pennington. **Description:** Profile of Advanced Internet Technologies in Fayetteville, North Carolina, a Web hosting firm founded by Clarence Briggs. Briggs uses the same sense of discipline and structure he learned while in the Army.

36772 ■ *Solo Success*
Pub: Crown Publishing Group, Inc.
Ed: David Perlstein. **Released:** 1998. **Price:** $13.00.

36773 ■ "Speak Easy" in *Fast Company* **(March 2005, No. 92, pp. 30)**
Pub: Gruner & Jahr USA Publishing
Ed: Ryan Underwood. **Description:** Five key steps to overcoming the fear of speaking in public are outlined.

36774 ■ "Speak Up: Hate to Negotiate? That's Still No Excuse to Avoid Learning This Skill" in *Entrepreneur* **(Vol. 32, September 2004)**
Pub: Entrepreneur Media Inc.
Ed: Marc Diener. **Description:** The art of negotiating is investigated. Tips are offered to entrepreneurs to improve their skills at the bargaining table.

36775 ■ "Special Opps" in *Entrepreneur* **(Vol. 32, October 2004, No. 10, pp. 38)**
Pub: Entrepreneur Media Inc.
Ed: Geoff Williams. **Description:** Profile of Mark Wilson, former Marine, who has restructured his company in order to tap into a new market in Iraq. Wilson is a franchisee of The Growth Coach, which works with self-employed and small business owners. He has created a Web site for entrepreneurs who are military reservists searching for strategies to keep their businesses operating while deployed in Iraq. Chris Exline, CEO of Home Essentials, generated $3.5 billion in revenue for 2003, by renting home essentials to individuals working in foreign countries.

36776 ■ "Specifically Speaking" in *Entrepreneur* (Vol. 28, No. 7, July 2000, pp. 150)
Pub: Entrepreneur Media Inc.
Ed: Paul Edwards and Sarah Edwards. **Description:** Finding the perfect niche for you business is discussed.

36777 ■ "Speed Reader" in *Crain's Chicago Business* (Vol. 30, February 2007, No. 6, pp. 58)
Pub: Crain Communications, Inc.
Ed: Laura Bianchi. **Description:** Interview with Paul Tamraz, president and CEO of Motor Werkes, which carries luxury vehicle lines like BMW, Porsche, and Mercedes-Benz. Tamraz discusses the importance of keeping up to speed with not only U.S. business but what is happening around the world.

36778 ■ "Spilling the Beans?" in *Entrepreneur* (Vol. 31, No. 11, November 2003, pp. 136)
Pub: Entrepreneur Media, Inc.
Ed: Romanus Wolter. **Description:** Secrets for entrepreneurs to share an idea while protecting their business is discussed. Tips for revealing only the most necessary details are listed.

36779 ■ "Spirit of business" in *Boston Business Journal* (Vol. 22, No. 11, April 19, 2002, pp. 27)
Pub: MCP, Inc.
Description: Richard Whiteley, who founded the Whiteley Group Inc., writes and speaks about management and the corporate world. His life's purpose is to bring spirit back to business.

36780 ■ *The Spirit of Entrepreneurship: Exploring the Essence of Entrepreneurship Through Personal Stories*
Pub: Springer
Ed: Sharda S. Nandram; Karel J. Samson. **Released:** October 2006. **Price:** $79.95. **Description:** Case studies involving 60 entrepreneurs and executives explores the fundamentals in starting a new business, techniques and mindsets.

36781 ■ "Spirited leadership: Carl Horton named President & CEO of Absolut" in *Black Enterprise* (Vol. 32, No. 9, April 2002, pp. 28)
Pub: Earl Graves Publishing Co.
Ed: Derek T. Dingle. **Description:** Profile of Carol Horton, new president and CEO of The Absolut Spirits Company. Horton has become the industry's top-ranking African American as well as one of the most powerful black executives in corporate America. Horton views his new role as a transition from corporate execute to an entrepreneur of a start-up.

36782 ■ "Spotlight Rick Chesley; Chairman Builds Law Office From Ground Up" in *Crain's Chicago Business* (Vol. 30, January 2007, No. 2, pp. 5)
Pub: Crain Communications, Inc.
Ed: Lorene Yue. **Description:** Profile of Rick Chesley, office chair for law firm, Paul Hastings Janofsky & Walker LLP's at the new Chicago location. Hastings' goal is to establish a strong Chicago presence for the firm.

36783 ■ "Standing Proud" in *Entrepreneur* (Vol. 31, No. 6, June 2003, pp. 28)
Pub: Entrepreneur Media Inc.
Ed: Mark Henricks. **Description:** Business consultant Jon R. Katzenbach contends that wages, salaries and benefits are just a starting point to keep and motivate employees, that encouraging pride and a sense of accomplishment can do more.

36784 ■ "Star quality" in *WorkingWoman* (Vol. 28, No. 5, May 2000, pp. 50)
Pub: Lang Communications, Inc.
Ed: Betsy Wiesendanger. **Description:** The stories of the winners in the second annual Entrepreneurial Excellence Awards include women who have exploited the technology boom, used innovative staffing solutions to beat labor problems, and offered free training to help women out of the welfare dependence scenario.

36785 ■ *The Starfish and the Spider*
Pub: Portfolio
Ed: Ori Brafman; Rod A. Beckstrom. **Released:** 2007.
Price: $24.95.

36786 ■ "Staring all over again" in *BlackEnterprise* (Vol. 31, No. 8, March 2001, pp. 50)
Pub: Earl Graves Publishing Co.
Ed: Bridget McCrea. **Description:** Profile of Gina and Raphael Bruce, co-founders of the former Millennium 2000 Computer Consulting Group, located in Georgia. The partners tell how they had to reinvent their business after helping companies prepare for Y2K.

36787 ■ "Start the Presses: Publishing a Magazine May Seem Like a Dream, But These Entrepreneurs Made It a Reality" in *Entrepreneur* (Vol. 32)
Pub: Entrepreneur Media Inc.
Ed: Nichole L. Torres. **Description:** Profiles of entrepreneurs sharing success in the magazine publishing industry are presented.

36788 ■ *Start, Run, and Grow a Successful Small Business, 2nd Edition*
Pub: CCH, Inc.
Ed: Susan M. Jacksack. **Price:** $24.95.

36789 ■ *Starting Over: How to Change Careers or Start Your Own Business*
Pub: Warner Books, Inc.
Ed: Stephen M. Pollan and Mark Levine. **Released:** 1997. **Price:** $10.00.

36790 ■ *Starting Up: An Interactive Adventure That Challenges Your Entrepreneurial Skills*
Pub: Prentice Hall
Ed: David E. Rye and Craig R. Hickman. **Released:** 1997. **Price:** $22.95 (cloth).

36791 ■ "Starting Up in High Gear" in *Harvard Business Review* (Vol. 78, No. 4, July 2000, pp. 93)
Pub: Harvard Business School Publishing Corp.
Ed: David Champion, Nicholas G. Carr. **Description:** Internet has opened unparalleled opportunities for entrepreneurs according to venture capitalists Vinod Khosla. He now works for Silicon Valley's Kleiner Perkins Caufield and Byers.

36792 ■ "Staying in the Loop: Continuing Education for Entrepreneurs" in *My Business* (December/January 2003, pp. 14)
Pub: My Business Magazine
Ed: Nancy Mann Jackson. **Description:** The importance for small business owners to continue learning is stressed. There are a number of venues for the entrepreneur to stay current, including networking, workshops, professional associations, and independent learning.

36793 ■ "Steve Richardson" in *Entrepreneur* (Vol. 30, No. 9, September 2002, pp. 25)
Pub: Entrepreneur Media Inc.
Ed: April Y. Pennington. **Description:** Profile of Steve Richardson, CEO of Stave Puzzles Inc., the maker of luxury wooden jigsaw puzzles; Bill and Melinda Gates, Barbara Bush and other high-profile families and celebrities are loyal customers of this company located in Norwich, Vermont.

36794 ■ "Stick-to-itiveness will always lead you to success" in *Atlanta Business Chronicle* (Vol. 24, No. 9, August 3, 2001, pp. 3B)
Pub: American City Business Journals Inc.
Ed: Jeffrey Gitomer. **Description:** The article outlines recommendations for the development of persistence, according to Napoleon Hill, author of 'Think and Grow Rich'. Four steps toward developing the habit of persistence are having a definite purpose, a definite plan, closing the mind to negative influences, and forming friendly alliances.

36795 ■ "Sticking to what she knows" in *BlackEnterprise* (Vol. 32, No. 2, September 2001, pp. 46)
Pub: Earl Graves Publishing Co.
Ed: Quincy Lewis. **Description:** Profile of Sheri Huguely, president of entertainment consulting firm Glue Inc. In 2000, the company had revenues of $252,000 with a goal of $350,000 for 2001.

36796 ■ *Stop Working: Start a Business, Globalize It, and Generate Enough Cash Flow to Get Out of the Rat Race*
Pub: Eye Contact Media
Ed: Rohan Hall. **Released:** November 2004. **Price:** $19.99. **Description:** Advice is given to small companies to compete in the global marketplace by entrepreneur using the same strategy for his own business.

36797 ■ "Stopping Office Snoops" in *Inc.* (November 1, 2003)
Pub: Gruner & Jahr USA Publishing
Ed: Patrick J. Sauer. **Description:** Review of the book, The Spy's Guide: Office Espionage? The book offers CIA-style tips for anyone running a small business.

36798 ■ "Storefront Column" in *Daily Press* (April 11, 2003)
Pub: Knight-Ridder/Tribune Business News
Ed: Audra Barlow. **Description:** Profile of John Robert Curtis, Jr., owner of a one-of-a-kind bookstore located in the heart of historic Williamsburg, Virginia. The Bookpress Ltd. prides itself on finding and selling rare books.

36799 ■ *Strategic Entrepreneurship*
Pub: Prentice Hall PTR
Ed: Philip A. Wickham. **Released:** September 2006. **Price:** $90.00. **Description:** Conceptual and practical ideas for managing a small business are explored.

36800 ■ *Strategic Partnerships: An Entrepreneur's Guide to Joint Ventures and Alliances*
Pub: Kaplan Publishing
Ed: Robert Wallace. **Released:** September 2004. **Price:** $22.00. **Description:** Ways to develop and execute joint venture relationships with larger business entities for small company owners.

36801 ■ "Strategies, Let's Be Friends" in *Inc.* (Volume 27, March 2005, No. 3, pp. 33-34)
Pub: Inc. Magazine
Ed: Allison Stein Wellner. **Description:** New research shows that CEOs who become friendly with competitors achieve more success than others.

36802 ■ "Strather Launches Hitsville Gaming-But Not in U.S." in *Crain's Detroit Business* (Vol. 22, December 18, 2006, No. 5, pp. 3)
Pub: Crain Communications Inc. - Detroit
Ed: Robert Ankeny **Description:** Innovative entrepreneur capitalizes on Motown heritage for his online casino. Only international wagers can be placed as internet gambling is illegal in the U.S. Hitsville name used due to copyright laws not permitting the use of Motown.

36803 ■ "Street Smarts. Are You Listening to Me?" in *Inc.* (November 2006, pp. 61-62)
Pub: Gruner & Jahr USA Publishing
Ed: Norm Brodsky. **Description:** As an entrepreneur, you ultimately need to make the final decisions. Sometimes too much advice from the wrong persons on the right things or the right person on the wrong things clouds the issue and can lead to a bad final decision you may have to live with.

36804 ■ "Street Smarts: Just Say Yes" in *Inc.* (November 1, 2004)
Pub: Inc. Magazine
Ed: Norm Brodsky. **Description:** One small business owner has found that a drug testing policy started at his company six years ago because of rumors about marijuana being used on the premises. The new policy not only decreased accidents and petty theft, but also helped employees.

36805 ■ "Street Smarts: Presumed Guilty" in _Inc._ (October 1, 2004)
Pub: Inc. Magazine
Ed: Norm Brodsky. **Description:** Experts recommend that small businesses let lawyers make legal decision, but to keep business decisions with company management.

36806 ■ _Street Smarts: Real Life Lessons from a Successful Entrepreneur_
Pub: Evanston Publishing, Inc.
Ed: John Fernandez. **Released:** 1994. **Price:** $14.95.

36807 ■ "Street Smarts: The King and I" in _Inc._ (July 1, 2003)
Pub: Gruner & Jahr USA Publishing
Ed: Norm Brodsky. **Description:** A visit with a king provides unexpected lessons for small business owners.

36808 ■ "Strike Up the Brand" in _Small Business Opportunities_ (Vol. 16, November 2004, No. 6, pp. 92, 94)
Pub: Harris Publications Inc.
Ed: Stan Roberts. **Description:** Profile of Michael Perlman, president of BrandsMartUSA. The retailer has earned awards and offers a Website of promotions ranging from art galleries for children to lunchtime specials. The discount house earns $580 million a year.

36809 ■ "Stuck in Mud?" in _My Business_ (October/November 2003, pp. 12)
Pub: My Business Magazine
Ed: Doug McPherson. **Description:** Ways to structure offices tasks should be structured in order for employees to become more proficient are addressed. Four tips for a more structured, smoother-running office are given.

36810 ■ "Students of Enterprise" in _Entrepreneur_ (Vol. 32, November 2004, No. 11, pp. 108)
Pub: Entrepreneur Media Inc.
Ed: April Y. Pennington, Devlin Smith. **Description:** Collegiate Entrepreneurs' Organization supports college students wanting to start their own businesses. The Chicago-based organization's membership has grown to 14,000 members nationwide. Profile of Fred DeLuca, who started a Subway sandwich shop when he was only seventeen, is included.

36811 ■ _Studies of Entrepreneurship, Business and Government in Hong Kong: The Economic Development of a Small Open Economy_
Pub: Edwin Mellen Press
Ed: Fu-Lai Tony Yu. **Released:** November 2006. **Price:** $109.95. **Description:** Institutional and Austrian theories are used to analyze the transformation taking place in Hong Kong's economy.

36812 ■ "Study: State 12th-best for small biz" in _Crain's Detroit Business_ (Vol. 17, No. 44, October 22, 2001, pp. 20)
Pub: Crain Communications, Inc.
Ed: Laura Bailey. **Description:** The state of Michigan was rated the 12th-most friendly state for entrepreneurs by a recent study conducted by the Small Business Survival Committee. The most business-friendly state is Nevada, followed by South Dakota and Washington; lowest were Maine, Hawaii, Rhode Island, and the District of Columbia.

36813 ■ "Study: Women Executives Want Corner Office, Too" in _Miami Herald_ (June 24, 2004)
Pub: Knight-Ridder/Tribune Business News
Ed: Gillian Wee. **Description:** According to a recent survey, female officials aspire to be chief executives at the same rate as male counterparts.

36814 ■ "Succeeding in adversity makes success all the sweeter" in _Fast Company_ (May 2001, pp. 84)
Pub: Fast Company
Ed: Sheila Wellington. **Description:** Profile of Sheila Wellington, author of the book 'Be Your Own Mentor:

Career Strategies for Women', published in February 2001 by Random House. Wellington suggests that during tough economic times, the strong become creative for survival.

36815 ■ "Success Products" in _Black Enterprise_ (Vol. 37, February 2007, No. 7, pp. 135)
Pub: Earl G. Graves Publishing Co. Inc.
Ed: Tanisha A. Sykes. **Description:** Using innovative resources that are already at your fingertips instead of trying to reach out to companies first is a great way to discover whether you have a viable idea or product. Be motivated to start an e-newsletter letting people know about your products and attend conferences like The Motivation Show, the world's largest exhibition of motivational products and services related to performance in business.

36816 ■ "Success: What's Your Definition?" in _My Business_ (December/January 2004, pp. 28-33, 52)
Pub: My Business Magazine
Ed: Rex Hammock, Shannon Scully. **Description:** Profiles of successful entrepreneurs with discussions on their definitions of success, including the ability to help others achieve their potential, balancing work and family, independence, loving your work, and the ability to earn money.

36817 ■ "Success Within Your Reach" in _Home Business_ (Vol. 13, January/February 2006, No. 1, pp. 36, 100)
Pub: Home Business Magazine
Ed: Sandy Larson. **Description:** Author, Jack Canfield, shares his secrets to building a successful publishing empire. Canfield is CEO of Chicken Soup for the Soul Enterprises.

36818 ■ _The Successful Entrepreneur's Guidebook: Where You Are Now, Where You Want to Be and How to Get There_
Pub: Kogan Page, Limited
Ed: Colin Barrow; Robert Brown. **Released:** January 2007. **Price:** $35.00. **Description:** Characteristics of successful entrepreneurship are examined. The book helps new business owners to develop and grow a business.

36819 ■ "Survival of the Fittest: As Your Business Grows, So Do the Challenges." in _Entrepreneur_ (Vol. 32, December 2004, No. 12)
Pub: Entrepreneur Media Inc.
Ed: Romanus Wolter. **Description:** Four steps to help entrepreneurs face new business challenges with confidence are featured.

36820 ■ "Survival of the Fittest: What Do Entrepreneurs Do to Stay Happy and Healthy?" in _Entrepreneur_ (Vol. 32, July 2004, No. 7, pp. 38)
Pub: Entrepreneur Media Inc.
Ed: April Y. Pennington. **Description:** Entrepreneurs share insight into their strategies for staying healthy and happy, while staying focused on their companies.

36821 ■ "Surviving Self-Employment" in _Black Enterprise_ (Vol. 35, October 2004, No. 3, pp. 84)
Pub: Earl G. Graves Publishing Co. Inc.
Ed: Carolyn M. Brown. **Description:** Profile of Ellen Hendrix tells how she is working as a video editor after being laid off from her job. She has invested in a rental property, but it is only making a small profit.

36822 ■ "The sweet smell of success" in _BlackEnterprise_ (Vol. 32, No. 3, October 2001, pp. 52)
Pub: Earl Graves Publishing Co.
Ed: Glenn Townes. **Description:** Profile of Bo-Dacious Baskets!!, the company that won the Minority Business Plan Competition in Philadelphia, Pennsylvania. Entrepreneur Cassandra Hayes is the owner of Bo-Dacious Baskets!!, the three year old, five-employee gift-service business.

36823 ■ "The Sweet Spot: A Sugar-Coated Pitch Paid Off Big Time" in _Black Enterprise_ (Vol. 37, November 2006, No. 4, pp. 71)
Pub: Earl G. Graves Publishing Co. Inc.
Ed: Laura Egodigwe. **Description:** In an interview with Debra Sandler, president of McNeil Nutritionals L. L.C., Sandler talks about the challenges of bringing a new product to the marketplace, how her personal experiences effect her business decisions, and the difficulties of re-entering the workforce.

36824 ■ _Swimming Against the Tide_
Pub: Macmillan Publishers Limited
Ed: Tim Waterstone. **Released:** October 2006. **Price:** $29.95. **Description:** Tim Waterstone shares ten rules for creating successful small businesses.

36825 ■ "Take It Or Leave It: The Only Guide to Negotiating You Will Ever Need" in _Inc._ (August 1, 2003)
Pub: Gruner & Jahr USA Publishing
Ed: Rob Walker. **Description:** In order to become a good negotiator it is important to change your mindset and your behavior. A guide to becoming a better negotiator is presented.

36826 ■ "Take it from me" in _Entrepreneur_ (Vol. 31, No. 4, April 2003, pp. 26)
Pub: Entrepreneur Media Inc.
Ed: Aliza Pilar Sherman. **Description:** An interview with two women business owners offering advice in management, business growth, and business downsizing.

36827 ■ "Take No For an Answer: Don't Dismiss Naysayers-Ask For Advice, and Turn It Into a Tool for Success" in _Entrepreneur_ (October 2004)
Pub: Entrepreneur Media Inc.
Ed: Romanus Wolter. **Description:** Entrepreneurs can ask the people who offer negative comments to also offer advice and not take comments personally.

36828 ■ "Taking the Emotions out of Business Decisions" in _Success from Failure_ (August 2000)
Pub: Vision Quest Publishing, Inc.
Ed: Charles K. Oppenheimer, Jr. **Description:** When you become emotionally involved in your business to the point it becomes a part of you, you are then unable to separate your emotional self from your logical and practical self. Without keeping your emotional self in check, you are unable to make the important decisions that are best for you, your company and your family.

36829 ■ "Taking Spiritual E-Path" in _Crain's New York Business_ (Vol. 23, November 20, 2006, No. 47, pp. 29)
Pub: Crain Communications, Inc.
Ed: Description: Profile of Cathy O'Brien and her position at Beliefnet, a website which combines blogs, news and videos, and a free e-mail newsletter on subjects of faith, spirituality and religion. O'Brien hopes to attract advertisers to the popular eight-year-old site.

36830 ■ "A tale of 25 Cities" in _Entrepreneur_ (Vol. 28, No. 10, October 2000, pp. 86)
Pub: Entrepreneur Media Inc.
Ed: Mark Henricks. **Description:** A listing of the cities in the top 10 large U.S. metropolitan areas in Entrepreneur and Dun & Bradstreet's Seventh Annual Ranking of the Best Cities in the Nation for Entrepreneurship.

36831 ■ "Uncommon Enterprise: A Tall Order" in _My Business_ (October/November 2003, pp. 58)
Pub: My Business Magazine
Ed: Shannon Scully. **Description:** Brief profile of Paul Hartmann, who launched Tall Paul's Tall Mall, a company that offers tall people longer beds, longer bed linens and shower arm extenders.

36832 ■ **"Taming of the Crew: What Lion Tamers Teach Us About Team Management"** in *Entrepreneur* (Vol. 33, January 2005, No. 1, pp. 26)
Pub: Entrepreneur Media Inc.
Ed: Geoff Williams. **Description:** In his book, Lion Taming: Working Successfully With Leaders, Bosses and Other Tough Customers, Steve Katz gathers insights from professional lion tamers to help entrepreneurs learn to tame suppliers, customers and competitors.

36833 ■ **"Tampa, Fla., Bike Shop Turns Off Its Engine"** in *Tampa Tribune* (November 5, 2005)
Pub: Media General, Inc.
Ed: Randy Diamond. **Description:** Profile of Patsy Ann Lovengreen, a feisty septuagenarian, who ran a motorcycle salvage and repair shop. Lovengreen is closing her store in order to spend more time caring for her collection of orchids and her husband, Bill.

36834 ■ *Target Success: How You Can Become a Successful Entrepreneur-Regardless of Your Background*
Pub: Adams Publishing
Ed: Don Dwyer. **Released:** 1993. **Price:** $5.95.

36835 ■ **"Targeting Options Threatens Innovation and Growth"** in *Venture Capital Journal* (Vol. 42, No. 5, May 2002, pp. 42)
Pub: Thomas Venture Economics
Ed: Craig A.T. Jones. **Description:** Stock options are critical in fostering innovation and entrepreneurship; the mandatory expensing of these options would make them too expensive to issue for most organizations.

36836 ■ **"Taxing Unfairly...Brand Mascots... Slotting Wars...The Genetic Jerk"** in *Fortune* (Vol. 141, No. 5, March 6, 2000, pp. 432L)
Pub: Time Inc.
Description: Dozens of Asian-American entrepreneurs in Los Angeles say the IRS has unfairly targeted them for audits and has selectively charged an "ozone tax".

36837 ■ **"Tech Firm CEO's Solution: Unify Segments"** in *Crain's Chicago Business* (Vol. 30, January 2007, No. 5, pp. 6)
Pub: Crain Communications, Inc.
Description: Profile of Brandon Glenn, CEO of Technology Solutions Co., a Chicago-based information technology firm that is publicly traded. Although Glenn has never before served as a CEO, but feels he will be able to return Tech Solutions to the black by creating a unifying theme between the company's three business segments.

36838 ■ *Technological Entrepreneurship*
Pub: Edward Elgar Publishing, Incorporated
Ed: Donald Siegel. **Released:** October 2006. **Price:** $230.00. **Description:** Technological entrepreneurship at universities is discussed. The book covers four related topics: university licensing and patenting; science parks and incubators; university-based startups; and the role of academic science in entrepreneurship.

36839 ■ **"Technology Can't Replace Your Best Asset: People"** in *My Business* (June/ July 2002, pp. 24)
Pub: My Business Magazine
Ed: Michael Grebb. **Description:** The pros and cons of replacing people with technology for small business are examined.

36840 ■ **"Tee for Two: Entrepreneurs Find a Swingingly Successful Venture in Arcade-Style Video Games"** in *Entrepreneur* (Vol. 31, October 2003)
Pub: Entrepreneur Media, Inc.
Ed: April Y. Pennington. **Description:** Profile of Elaine Hodgson and Richard Ditton, co-founders of Incredible Technologies Inc., manufacturer of coin-operated computer video games.

36841 ■ *The Ten Faces of Innovation*
Pub: Doubleday Broadway Publishing Group

Ed: Tom Kelley. **Price:** $29.95.

36842 ■ **"10 Rules for Bouncing Back"** in *My Business* (April/May 2003, pp. 32)
Pub: My Business Magazine
Description: A list of the top ten truths to motivate small business owners, compiled from motivational books, is presented.

36843 ■ **"Tennis Player Serves Mexican Meals"** in *Crain's New York Business* (Vol. 21, January 31, 2005, No. 5, pp. 25)
Pub: Crain Communications Inc.
Ed: Lisa Fickenscher. **Description:** Profile of Richard Sandoval, executive chef and owner of modern Mexican restaurants.

36844 ■ **"Texas' Big, Bold e-Experiment"** in *Success* (Vol. 47, No. 5, October 2000, pp. 50)
Pub: Success Publishing, Inc.
Ed: Tom Fetzer. **Description:** In a bold political/ entrepreneurial experiment, e-Texas' constituents will be provided with a single face of government that capitalizes on the power of the Internet.

36845 ■ **"That's My Baby: Who Says Running a Business and Motherhood Don't Mix?"** in *Entrepreneur* (Vol. 32, No. 2, February 2004, pp. 30)
Pub: Entrepreneur Media, Inc.
Ed: Aliza Pilar Sherman. **Description:** Profile of Alison Nelson, co-owner of a candy store called the Chocolate Bar; Caroline Caskey, president and CEO of a DNA identification service; and Adrienne Lumpkin, president of a converged communications firm specializing in business telecommunications tools. The three business women share their ideas and feelings about their pregnancies and ways they will handle being an entrepreneur along with motherhood.

36846 ■ **"The 100 Influentials"** in *Hispanic Business* (October 2004, pp. 38)
Pub: Hispanic Business
Description: Hispanic Business Directory of the 100 most influential Hispanics is presented. The list focuses on politics, the financial industry, and non-profit organizations, and the growing power and influence of these leaders. Profiles of these leaders are included.

36847 ■ **"The Inc. Life"** in *Inc.* (Volume 27, December 2005, No. 12, pp. 78-80)
Pub: Inc. Magazine
Description: Profile of Josh Reid, co-founder of Rome Snowboard Design Syndicate; Dominique Schurman, CEO of Schurman Fine Papers, selling greeting cards, gift bags, note cards, wrapping papers, etc.; and Fred Schwam, CEO of American Christmas Decorations, which creates holiday displays for New York City businesses.

36848 ■ **"The Zentrepreneur"** in *Inc.* (October 1, 2003)
Pub: Gruner & Jahr USA Publishing
Ed: Adam Hanft. **Description:** Profile of Phil Suarez, restaurateur of fine dining. Suarez has built his successful business intuitively.

36849 ■ **"There is no correlation at all between success and hours worked"** in *Fast Company* (June 2001, pp. 76)
Pub: Fast Company
Ed: Seth Godin. **Description:** The article makes the suggestion to take the time to look at the future, and think about how decisions made now will matter in years to come.

36850 ■ **"There's no place in business for these 4-letter words"** in *Success from Failure* (August 2000)
Pub: Vision Quest Publishing, Inc.
Ed: Harvey Mackay. **Description:** The four words that successful business owners never use: can't, bore, fear, and last. The author explains why these words can be harmful.

36851 ■ **"There's Something About Harry"** in *Venture Capital Journal* (Vol. 42, No. 5, May 2002, pp. 18-19)
Pub: Thomas Venture Economics
Ed: Charles R. Feller. **Description:** Profile of Harry Turner, Director of Park Street Capital. Turner believes he has an inside track on reviewing some of the really good partnerships that have established track records and are rather small.

36852 ■ **"They Almost Changed the World"** in *Forbes* (Vol. 170, No. 13, December 23, 2002, pp. 217)
Pub: Forbes Magazine
Ed: Michael Maiello. **Description:** Failed inventions and the entrepreneurial spirit to never give up are highlighted.

36853 ■ **"They Want You"** in *Inc.* (Volume 27, June 2005, No. 6, pp. 32)
Pub: Inc. Magazine
Ed: Michelle Leder. **Description:** To encourage growth, states are offering incentives to court entrepreneurs.

36854 ■ **"Things I Can't Live Without"** in *Inc.* (July 1, 2003)
Pub: Gruner & Jahr USA Publishing
Description: Profile of founder and CEO of Todd Parent, whose $5 million pizza chain offers toppings such as mandarin oranges, roasted walnuts, black beans and salsa, or hummus as alternatives to traditional pizzas.

36855 ■ **"Think Ahead"** in *Entrepreneur* (Vol. 32, October 2004, No. 10, pp. 40)
Pub: Entrepreneur Media Inc.
Ed: Mark Henricks. **Description:** Review of Seeing What's Next, written by Clayton M. Christensen, Scott D. Anthony, and Erik A. Roth. The book shows entrepreneurs ways to spot upcoming disruptive innovations that could threaten a company's success. A three-step process for predicting industry change is presented.

36856 ■ **"This Is Not About Charity"** in *Forbes* (August 21, 2000, pp. 70)
Pub: Forbes Magazine
Ed: Ann Marsh. **Description:** Academy of Business Leadership teaches teenagers to reach for their dreams.

36857 ■ **"This is War"** in *Entrepreneur* (Vol. 28, No. 2, February 2000, pp. 96)
Pub: Entrepreneur Media Inc.
Ed: Scott S. Smith. **Description:** According to author James Dunnigan, war and entrepreneurship are all the same to him.

36858 ■ **"Thoughts On the Business of Life"** in *Forbes* (Vol. 170, No. 13, December 23, 2002, pp. 396)
Pub: Forbes Magazine
Description: Thoughts gathered by several successful men from all walks of life, over some 85 years, are presented, from John D. Rockefeller, 1917 to Dennis Kozlowski, 2000.

36859 ■ **"3 Ways to improve your business by getting a life"** in *My Business* (June/July 2002, pp. 26-32)
Pub: My Business Magazine
Ed: Shannon Scully, Lisa Waddle. **Description:** Small business owners tell how they are able to make time for family, hobbies and relaxation, while running their successful firms. Although multitasking is essential for the small business owner, they must learn to delegate work, set limits, as well as separating personal identity from the company's identity.

36860 ■ **"Through Grieving"** in *Success from Failure* (August 2000)
Pub: Vision Quest Publishing, Inc.
Ed: Barbara Parton. **Description:** Barbara Parton, CEO of The Transpective Group, a business coaching and organization transformation firm, tells how she successfully led the family owned company "through grieving" after her husband died.

36861 ■ "The time for talk is over" in *Rough Notes* **(Vol. 146, No. 4, April 2003, pp. 16)**
Pub: Rough Notes
Ed: Michael J. Moody. **Description:** After Enron's collapse, enterprise risk management has become more important in corporate governance. Pricewaterhouse-Coopers Inc.'s research indicates that consumer trust can be regained by financial institutions through checks and balances in top managers.

36862 ■ "The Time Machine" in *Birmingham Business Journal* **(Vol. 20, No. 30, July 25, 2003, pp. 11)**
Pub: American City Business Journals, Inc.
Ed: Tom Bassing. **Description:** Profile of Emmett Godfrey, owner of The Baseball Card Shop, located in Hoover, Alabama.

36863 ■ "A Time to Shine: Awards Celebration Spotlights Today's Successful Entrepreneurs" in *Black Enterprise* **(Vol. 34, No. 4, November 2003)**
Pub: Earl Graves Publishing Co.
Description: Black Enterprise recognizes outstanding African American entrepreneurs, including small business owners and top-level executives who appear on the BE 100s lists.

36864 ■ "Timothy Askew: 54, Founder and CEO of Corporate Rain Inc (CRI)..." in *Entrepreneur* **(Vol. 32, No. 1, January 2004, pp. 23)**
Pub: Entrepreneur Media, Inc.
Ed: April Y. Pennington. **Description:** Profile of Timothy Askew, founder and CEO of Corporate Rain Inc., an executive sales outsourcing boutique. Askew invested $10,000 in his startup in 1996 and sales are estimated at $1.9 million for 2003. CRIs sales force is made up of entrepreneurs and former executives with PhDs or higher and use the peer-to-peer approach to selling.

36865 ■ "Tipping point leadership" in *Harvard Business Review* **(Vol. 81, No. 4, April 2003, pp. 60)**
Pub: Harvard Business School Press
Ed: W. Chan Kim, Renee Mauborgne. **Description:** Profile of the career of William Bratton in law enforcement administration, and the agencies that he has helped turn around, such as the New York City Police Department. Bratton's leadership style is referred to as tipping point leadership.

36866 ■ "Titan Up" in *Entrepreneur* **(Vol. 28, No. 11, November 2000, pp. 22)**
Pub: Entrepreneur Media Inc.
Ed: Amanda C. Kooser. **Description:** JA Titan Junior Achievement is helping shape young entrepreneurs through interactive business simulation.

36867 ■ "To Achieve It, Write It Down" in *Black Enterprise* **(Vol. 35, January 2005, No. 6, pp. 96)**
Pub: Earl G. Graves Publishing Co. Inc.
Ed: Marcia A. Wade. **Description:** The Small Business Administration recommends that entrepreneurs write down their visions and goals and offers a Website designed to give information for starting a new business. Rev. Nathaniel Gadsden, founder of the Writers Wordshop, suggests writing a business plan before embarking on a new career path.

36868 ■ "To the Future" in *Entrepreneur* **(Vol. 28, No. 11, November 2000, pp. 12)**
Pub: Entrepreneur Media Inc.
Description: This year's winner of the Junior Achievement JA Titan National Essay Contest, 17-year-old Mitch Wisniewski, describes how he would run Lycos.

36869 ■ "To Join Or Not To Join? Trade Groups Can Boost Business-If You Pick the Right One" in *Black Enterprise* **(Vol. 34, No. 3, October 2003)**
Pub: Earl Graves Publishing Co.
Ed: Bridget McCrea. **Description:** Issues to keep in mind before joining a trade group are presented, including the ways trade groups provide networking opportunities for entrepreneurs to help grow a small business.

36870 ■ "To L.L.C. or not to L.L.C.? That can be sticky question" in *Crain's Detroit Business* **(Vol. 18, No. 49, December 9, 2002, pp. 14)**
Pub: Crain Communications Inc., Detroit
Ed: Laura Bailey. **Description:** Important issues to be considered by all entrepreneurs regarding planning the structure of a new or existing small business are examined.

36871 ■ "To Thine Own Self" in *Entrepreneur* **(Vol. 33, August 2005, No. 8, pp. 34)**
Pub: Entrepreneur Media Inc.
Ed: Aliza Pilar Sherman. **Description:** Three tactics to boost a women entrepreneur's self-esteem are outlined by Jennifer Read Hawthorne, co-author of "Chicken Soup for the Woman's Soul".

36872 ■ "Tom McConnell: At Service to the Venture Community" in *Venture Capital Journal* **(Vol. 41, No. 8, August 2000, pp. 35-36)**
Pub: Venture Economics
Ed: Ken Ryan. **Description:** Profile of Tom McConnell, general partner with New Enterprise Associates, who also devotes his time to the National Venture Capital Association (NVCA) as its chairman.

36873 ■ "Too Much Information?" in *Black Enterprise* **(Vol. 37, December 2006, No. 5, pp. 59)**
Pub: Earl G. Graves Publishing Co. Inc.
Ed: James C. Johnson. **Description:** African American business owners often face the dilemma of whether or not to divulge their minority status when soliciting new customers and financial institutions. The quality of the products or services is always the key factor and race should never define one's business; however, is appropriate to market oneself as a minority or women-owned business, especially if the company is in an industry where those clients are offered top-tier contracts.

36874 ■ "Top 10 Business Schools for Hispanics" in *Hispanic Business* **(September 2004, pp. 78, 80, 82, 84)**
Pub: Hispanic Business
Description: The top ten business schools for Hispanics are profiled. Stanford University, Yale University, and New York University were listed as the top three, respectively.

36875 ■ "Top 10 Law Schools for Hispanics" in *Hispanic Business* **(September 2003, pp. 56, 58, 60, 62)**
Pub: Hispanic Business
Description: Top 10 law schools for Hispanic students to consider are listed, with University of Texas at Austin's School of Law rated number one, followed by University of Miami's School of Law.

36876 ■ "The Top 25" in *Entrepreneur* **(Vol. 31, No. 10, October 2003, pp. 22)**
Pub: Entrepreneur Media, Inc.
Description: The top 25 cities for entrepreneurs are ranked, with Las Vegas, Nevada leading the way for entrepreneurial activity and job growth.

36877 ■ "A top brand won't happen without top leadership" in *Atlanta Business Chronicle* **(Vol. 24, No. 10, August 10, 2001, pp. 43A)**
Pub: American City Business Journals Inc.
Ed: Michael H. Mescon, Timothy S. Mescon. **Description:** Leadership is key to building a brand. While goals, structure and people, are the basic elements in any organizational endeavor, the leader's vision and passion transforms an organization into an institution, an entity with a brand.

36878 ■ "Top-Heavy: Is it Time to Thin Out Your Management Pool" in *Entrepreneur* **(Vol. 32, No. 1, January 2004, pp. 30)**
Pub: Entrepreneur Media, Inc.
Ed: Nichole L. Torres. **Description:** Cynthia Shapiro, human resource consultant, recommends letting go unnecessary management. Tips for deciding which managers to pink slip are included.

36879 ■ "Total Tech LLC" in *San Diego Business Journal* **(Vol. 28, January 15, 2007, No. 3, pp. 34)**
Pub: San Diego Business Journal Associates
Ed: Jessica Long. **Description:** Profile of Kenneth Hamilton, president and chief executive officer of Total Tech LLC. Hamilton recalls his reasons for starting a business and shares his business weaknesses and strengths.

36880 ■ *Tough Choices: A Memoir*
Pub: Penguin Group
Ed: Carly Florina. **Released:** October 2006. **Price:** $24.95. **Description:** Former woman CEO at Hewlett-Packard is profiled.

36881 ■ "Tough choices" in *Entrepreneur* **(Vol. 31, No. 5, May 2003, pp. 70)**
Pub: Entrepreneur Media Inc.
Ed: Chris Penttila. **Description:** A big dilemma facing entrepreneurs these days is hiring fresh new talent. Ways to handle having to hire new employees at higher wages than existing employees are discussed.

36882 ■ "Tough Times build character" in *Fast Company* **(May 2001, pp. 86)**
Pub: Fast Company
Ed: Sir John Marks Templeton. **Description:** Profile of Sir John Marks Templeton who founded many investment funds, included the Templeton Growth Fund, which averaged 15.2 percent a year during its 45-year history, exceeding all other mutual funds during that time.

36883 ■ "A Trailblazer, Rediscovered" in *Inc.* **(September 1, 2003)**
Pub: Gruner & Jahr USA Publishing
Ed: Nadine Heintz. **Description:** Profile of Brownie Wise who built the multimillion-dollar Tupperware empire. A new documentary entitled, "In Tupperware!" will be seen on PBS in spring 2003. The film assesses Wise's marketing genius and her ouster in 1958.

36884 ■ "Transform Your Life" in *Black Enterprise* **(Vol. 37, January 2007, No. 6, pp. 14)**
Pub: Earl G. Graves Publishing Co. Inc.
Description: Through the magazine, television and radio programs, events, and the website, the various platforms of Black Enterprise will provide the tools necessary to achieve success in business ventures, career aspirations, and personal goals.

36885 ■ "Triple sport star: Steve Mills scores for the Knicks, Rangers, and the Liberty" in *Black Enterprise* **(Vol.33, No.3, Oct. 2002, pp. 72)**
Pub: Earl Graves Publishing Co.
Ed: Sonia Alleyne. **Description:** Profile of Steve Mills, president of sports team operations for Madison Square Garden in New York City. Mills manages business operations, finances, and marketing for the three teams, the Knicks, Rangers, and Liberty, housed at the Garden. Mills shares ways to successfully apply what is learned in sports to a business setting.

36886 ■ "Trouble on the horizon...isn't going away" in *Fast Company* **(May 2001, pp. 85)**
Pub: Fast Company
Ed: Peter C. Peterson. **Description:** Profile of Peter C. Peterson, a former U.S. Secretary of Commerce and former Chairman and CEO of Leisman Brothers, is chairman of the Council on Foreign Relations and of the Federal Reserve Bank of New York, among other organizations. He is also founding president of the Concord Coalition, an organization devoted to fiscal responsibility, and is a special limited-advisory partner to Millennium Technology Ventures LP.

36887 ■ "The Trouble With Lifestyle Entrepreneurs" in *Inc.* **(Volume 27, July 2005, No. 7, pp. 21-23)**
Pub: Inc. Magazine
Ed: Daniel McGinn. **Description:** New Zealand business owners are able to enjoy a work-life balance, but this trend is becoming a national crisis. American entrepreneurs can take note that growing a business in the U.S. requires a fast-paced, stressed lifestyle. The American economy is fueled by small business.

36888 ■ *True to Yourself: Leading a Values-Based Business*
Pub: Berrett-Koehler Publishers, Incorporated
Ed: Mark S. Albion. **Released:** June 2006. **Price:** $14.95. **Description:** Pressures faced by entrepreneurs running small companies are discussed. Advice is offered to help grow and maintain a profitable business.

36889 ■ *Trump University Entrepreneurship 101*
Pub: John Wiley & Sons, Incorporated
Ed: Mike Gordon. **Released:** January 2007. **Price:** $21.95. **Description:** Entrepreneurs, past, present or future, will find this book helpful. The book covers three objectives: to energize readers to be courageous when taking steps toward an entrepreneurial goal, works to demystify the entrepreneurial process, and to help individuals improve success.

36890 ■ "Trust is a must" in *Entrepreneur* (Vol. 30, No. 10, October 2002, pp. 70)
Pub: Entrepreneur Media Inc.
Ed: Chris Sandlund. **Description:** The importance of ethics in business is stressed. Trust underlies all business relationships, including employees, customers and suppliers.

36891 ■ "Try Again: Business Fell Flat? No Use Whining About It." in *Entrepreneur* (Vol. 32, December 2004, No. 12, pp. 102)
Pub: Entrepreneur Media Inc.
Ed: Nichole L. Torres. **Description:** Raymond T. Yeh and Stephanie H. Yeh, co-authors of The Art of Business: In the Footsteps of Giants, share histories of successful companies that experienced failure before becoming successful. Entrepreneurs can survive business failure by first taking a step back and taking stock of the issues.

36892 ■ "Tulsan Reflects on 35 Years of Polishing Shoes" in *Journal Record (Oklahoma City, OK)* (February 1, 2007)
Pub: Journal Record
Ed: Kirby Lee Davis. **Description:** Profile of William Herald Green, shoe repairman at Cherry Shoe Shine Parlor. Green started his career in 1928.

36893 ■ "Turning Designers Into Managers" in *Business Week* (No. 3761, December 10, 2001, pp. 60EU1)
Pub: McGraw-Hill Inc.
Description: Richard Koshalek tells how he is rebuilding Pasadena's Art Center College of Design curriculum to include courses on entrepreneurial leadership.

36894 ■ "The 2003 HBR List: Breakthrough Ideas for Tomorrow" in *Harvard Business Review* (Vol. 81, No. 4, 4/03, pp. 92)
Pub: Harvard Business School Press
Description: The editors consider strategy, organizations and leadership in the light of the events of the past year. They ponder the role of the leader, soft issues such as emotional intelligence and the unavoidable messiness of organizations.

36895 ■ "The Ultimate Employee Buy-In" in *Inc.* (Volume 27, December 2005, No. 12, pp. 107-111, 114-116)
Pub: Inc. Magazine
Ed: John Case. **Description:** Employee stock ownership plans, or ESOPs, are becoming a trend among small companies, an alternative to entrepreneurs rather than selling their firm.

36896 ■ *Ultimate Small Business Advisor*
Pub: Entrepreneur Press
Ed: Andi Axman. **Released:** May 2007. **Price:** $30.95. **Description:** Tip for starting and running a small business, including new tax rulings and laws affecting small business, are shared.

36897 ■ "Uncertainty and Information Search Activities" in *Journal of Small Business Management* (Vol. 41, No. 4, October 2003, pp. 385)
Pub: International Council of Small Business
Ed: Jeffrey E. McGee, Olukemi O. Sawyerr. **Description:** An examination of the relationship among perceived strategic uncertainty (PSU), environmental scanning, and the information sources used by owner-managers, using 153 small high-technology manufacturing firms.

36898 ■ "Uncharted Territory" in *Entrepreneur* (Vol. 32, No. 1, January 2004, pp. 27)
Pub: Entrepreneur Media, Inc.
Ed: Don Nichols. **Description:** Profile of Bill Davidson, author of Breakthrough: How Great Companies Set Outrageous Objectives-and Achieve Them. Davidson advises entrepreneurs to set outrageous objectives and to use creative thinking about customer care, cost reduction, and other issues to reach customers.

36899 ■ "Uncle Sam Wants YOU!" in *Business Week* (No. 3689, July 10, 2000, pp. F10)
Pub: McGraw-Hill, Inc.
Description: Information for procuring government contracts is covered, including a Web site that helps link small companies with federal contracts.

36900 ■ "Uncommon Enterprise: Chasing Business" in *My Business* (April/May 2003, pp. 54)
Pub: My Business Magazine
Description: Profile of David Marcks and his Border collies; Marcks has established two Geese Police Academies for Border collie training. Marcks, founder and president of New Jersey-based Geese Police, Inc. offers franchises in fives states to round up unwanted geese on corporate sites.

36901 ■ "Uncommon Enterprise: Rain Man" in *My Business* (December/January 2004, pp. 58)
Pub: My Business Magazine
Ed: Shannon Skully. **Description:** Profile of Richard Heinichen, bottler of rain water. Heinichen uses reverse osmosis to rid the rainwater of impurities making it safe for drinking; he also holds the first patent issued for bottling rainwater in the U.S.

36902 ■ *Understanding Small Business*
Pub: Tate Publishing and Enterprises, LLC
Ed: Edward McMahon. **Released:** May 2006. **Price:** $20.95. **Description:** Three step process to help an entrepreneur build a basic business plan and an effective cash flow statement to minimize risk.

36903 ■ "U.S. Soldier Returns from Iraq to Find How His Business Fared" in *Small Business Opportunities* (January 2006)
Pub: Harris Publications Inc.
Description: Joe Witte, vice-president and partner for CentricSource.com offers advice to soldiers leaving for overseas duties as well as issues when returning from active duty.

36904 ■ "Up Front: Stacking Up Sales Overseas" in *My Business* (December/January 2004, pp. 10-11)
Pub: My Business Magazine
Ed: Mike Doser. **Description:** U.S. entrepreneurs are finding success selling beverages overseas. Advice is given to research the market, utilize foreign links, and understand it takes more time to build a long-term relationship with an overseas firm.

36905 ■ "Up Front: Supersize It? No Thanks!" in *My Business* (October/November 2003, pp. 10-11)
Pub: My Business Magazine
Ed: Jackie Ross. **Description:** Profile of Sarah Cohen, owner of Route II Potato Chips, located in Middletown, Virginia; Cohen manufactures the snacks in retro packaging. The potato chips are fried in pure, monounsaturated sunflower and peanut oils and are hand-blended with salt and seasonings in order to produce an all natural product.

36906 ■ "Up To the Challenge" in *Entrepreneur.com* (Vol. 34, February 2006, No. 2, pp. 64)
Pub: Entrepreneur Media Inc.
Ed: Mark Henricks. **Description:** Three company founders discuss the obstacles that prevented them from reaching the next level of business. The companies represent three different industries at three different sales levels.

36907 ■ "Upfront: Be Flexible or Fold" in *My Business* (June/July 2002, pp. 13-14)
Pub: My Business Magazine
Ed: Karen E. Klein. **Description:** Sometimes a small firm needs to steer away from original business plans in order to grow. Martha C. de al Torre, Hispanic Business Woman of the Year 2000, tells how she learned to be flexible and creative with her business plan.

36908 ■ "Upfront: Saddle Up" in *My Business* (October/November 2002, pp. 13-14)
Pub: My Business Magazine
Ed: Alan Joch. **Description:** Profile of Robert Ferrand, owner of SaddleTech.com in Woodside, California. Ferrand sends his customers email greetings that are signed by his horse, Ace, and the customers love it. Tips for good customer relationship management are highlighted.

36909 ■ "Venetia Kontogouris: A Uniquely Different VC" in *Venture Capital Journal* (Vol. 41, No. 8, August 2000, pp. 34, 36)
Pub: Venture Economics
Ed: Ken Ryan. **Description:** Profile of Venetia Kontogouris, who works at Trident, the national VC firm that focuses on the information technology sector. Kontogouris says she uses her intuition regarding entrepreneurs.

36910 ■ "Venture Capitalism Inspires Hope in the Face of Tragedy" in *Venture Capital Journal* (Vol. 42, No. 9, September 2002, pp. 30)
Pub: Thomas Venture Economics
Ed: Mark G. Heesen. **Description:** Mark G. Heesen, president of the National Venture Capital Association, representing more than 400 venture capital and private equity firms, shares his views on the hope for the future that venture capital investments provide.

36911 ■ "A Venture Capitalist's View of 9-11" in *Venture Capital Journal* (Vol. 42, No. 9, September 2002, pp. 28-29)
Pub: Thomas Venture Economics
Ed: Alan Patricof. **Description:** Alan Patricof, vice chairman of Apax Partners Inc., an international private equity firm, shares his perspective of New York City after 9-11, including the economic impact of the attacks.

36912 ■ "Venture Philanthropist" in *Harvard Business Review* (Vol. 78, No. 4, July 2000, pp. 26)
Pub: Harvard Business School Publishing Corp.
Ed: Margaret Hanshaw. **Description:** Internet entrepreneur Martin Varsavsky is donating $11.2 million to help Argentina's Ministry of Education to provide Internet services to the country's 10 million grammar, high school, and university students.

36913 ■ "Verdi and Me" in *Inc.* (February 1, 2002)
Pub: Inc. Magazine
Ed: Donna Fenn. **Description:** Profile of high-tech entrepreneur Brent Habig speaks on singing opera, and how that makes him different from other entrepreneurs.

36914 ■ "Veteran CEO: Don't Fall for These Five Lines" in *Venture Capital Journal* (Vol. 42, No. 5, May 2002, pp. 38-39)
Pub: Thomas Venture Economics
Ed: Dean Goodermote. **Description:** An investigation into the five statements from small technology firms that should set off a red flag to venture capitalists, showing the misconception and the reality of the statement.

36915 ■ **"View Master"** in *Fast Company* (September 2001, pp. 72)
Pub: Fast Company
Ed: Paul C. Judge. **Description:** Profile of Adam Cohen, cofounder of Urban Data solutions. An architect by training, Cohen is able to master details from dozens of sources and apply them to the maps made by his company.

36916 ■ **"Viewer's Choice"** in *Entrepreneur* (Vol. 30, No. 3, March 2002, pp. 44)
Pub: Entrepreneur Media Inc.
Ed: Amanda C. Kooser. **Description:** Videoconferencing is offering entrepreneurs, as well as established small businesses, a safe, timesaving and economical choice to decrease the amount of business travel the would otherwise have to do. A resource guide for choosing the proper Web cam is included.

36917 ■ **"A Virtuous Cycle"** in *Forbes* (Vol. 170, No. 13, December 23, 2002, pp. 248)
Pub: Forbes Magazine
Ed: James Surowiecki. **Description:** The importance of trust and honesty in relation to capitalism is examined.

36918 ■ **"Voice of Experience"** in *Hispanic Business* (Vol. 23, No. 7/8, July/August 2001, pp. 32-33)
Pub: Hispanic Business
Ed: Janet Perez. **Description:** Federico Pena brings a lot to the table as the featured speaker at the 2001 Hispanic Business Entrepreneur of the Year Award gala. An interview with Mr. Pena is included, discussing his perspective on the challenges facing Hispanic entrepreneurs.

36919 ■ **"Voyage of a Lifetime"** in *Inc.* (September 1, 2004)
Pub: Inc. Magazine
Ed: Riza Cruz. **Description:** Profile of Kip Stone, owner of the T-shirt company called Artforms. Stone talks about his rethinking of his management strategy and hired managers with expertise in areas of production and inventory to accounting and sales who didn't need constant direction in order to allow him to continue to pursue his dreams of sailing.

36920 ■ **"Washington Insider: Small Business Overlooked?"** in *Hispanic Business* (March 2003, pp. 16)
Pub: Hispanic Business
Ed: Patricia Guadalupe. **Description:** Initiatives to address the current economic slowdown and its effect on minority entrepreneurs is addressed. Also discussed is the Small Business Administration's Internet site designed to assist small business owners with employees serving in the military reserves.

36921 ■ **"The Way he was"** in *Crain's Detroit Business* (Vol. 19, No. 2, January 13, 2003, pp. 11)
Pub: Crain Communications Inc., Detroit
Description: Profile of Ken Way, former CEO and chairman of Lear Seating Corporation.

36922 ■ **"We, the entrepreneurs"** in *Entrepreneur* (Vol. 30, No. 2, February 2002, pp. 8)
Pub: Entrepreneur Media Inc.
Ed: Rieva Lesonsky. **Description:** A discussion on the role entrepreneurs play in the United States economy.

36923 ■ *Wealth Without a Job: The Entrepreneur's Guide to Freedom and Security Beyond the 9 to 5 Lifestyle*
Pub: John Wiley & Sons, Incorporated
Ed: Phil Laut; Andy Fuehl. **Released:** May 2006. **Price:** $16.95. **Description:** Strategies for successful business ownership and job security are explored.

36924 ■ **"The Wealthiest Hispanics"** in *Hispanic Business* (March 2002, pp. 20, 22, 24, 26, 28, 30, 32, 34, 36)
Pub: Hispanic Business

Ed: Joel Russell. **Description:** A listing of the top 75 individuals and families on the 2002 Hispanic Business Rich List is presented. These individuals have a combined net worth totaling $11.4 billion, and have made their fortunes from automobiles to wire manufacturing, from big-budget movies to paper products.

36925 ■ **"Weathering the Storm; True, things have been better for the nation's entrepreneurs"** in *Business Week Online* (November 18, 2002)
Pub: McGraw-Hill Inc.
Ed: Alison Ogden. **Description:** According to a new survey conducted by the National Federation of Independent Businesses, small businesses are holding their own in the slow economy, and have defied the uncertain trends from the threats of terrorism and corporate scandals.

36926 ■ **"Web.Preneuring"** in *Small Business Opportunities* (Vol. 17, November 2005, No. 6, pp. 90, 94)
Pub: Harris Publications Inc.
Ed: Chuck Green. **Description:** Profile of Scott Kolbe and Mike Stout, entrepreneurs who started Icon Digital Design in a basement. The partners base their success on being graphic designers with strong work ethics.

36927 ■ **"Websites"** in *Black Enterprise* (Vol. 34, No. 5, December 2003, pp. S8)
Pub: Earl Graves Publishing Co.
Ed: Sonya Kimble-Ellis. **Description:** A listing of three Web sites offering startup advice to young entrepreneurs is presented.

36928 ■ **"Welcome aboard (but don't change a thing)"** in *Harvard Business Review* (Vol. 80, No. 10, October 2002, pp. 32)
Pub: Harvard Business School Press
Ed: Shannon McNulty. **Description:** The fictitious company, Lakeland Wonders, brought in a new CEO with fresh ideas, but the company balked at implementing them. Experts analyze the scenario.

36929 ■ **"Well Connected"** in *My Business* (June/July 2004, pp. 36-40)
Pub: My Business Magazine
Ed: Shannon Scully. **Description:** The question whether new online networking sites will allow business deals to happen over the Internet as on the golf course is explored.

36930 ■ **"Well-Suited Profits"** in *Small Business Opportunities* (Vol. 12, No. 2, March 2000, pp. 48-49)
Pub: Harris Publications, Inc.
Ed: Marie Sherlock. **Description:** Resale shop for men is dressed for success with sales of $300,000 a year. Profile of Gobor Vajda, owner of Suit Yourself.

36931 ■ **"Wells, Maine, Duo Start Custom Electronics Business"** in *Portland Press Herald* (August 26, 2005)
Pub: Blethen Maine Newspapers, Inc.
Ed: Edward D. Murphy. **Description:** Profile of Jeff Binette and Jason Robie, friends who started the company, SmartHome Solutions. The firm outfits homes with home theaters, whole-house audio systems, and multiple Internet and phone connections.

36932 ■ **"What Am I Worth? How to Increase Your Value to Your Company"** in *Black Enterprise* (Vol. 36, November 2005, No. 4, pp. 76)
Pub: Earl G. Graves Publishing Co. Inc.
Ed: Tennille M. Robinson. **Description:** As a business owner, setting your worth will help leverage monetary compensation as well as provide a better self-awareness of your role within your firm.

36933 ■ **"What Drives Inspiration?"** in *Entrepreneur* (Vol. 32, October 2004, No. 10, pp. 22)
Pub: Entrepreneur Media Inc.
Description: Tips to help entrepreneurs to be creative and successful are featured.

36934 ■ **"What Empowerment Requires"** in *Black Enterprise* (Vol. 33, No. 7, February 2003, pp. 9)
Pub: Earl Graves Publishing Co.
Ed: Earl G. Graves, Jr. **Description:** How the mid-term elections will affect African Americans as individuals and small business owners is discussed.

36935 ■ **"What Is Really Fueling This Economy, and Confounding the Grand Pooh-Bahs of the Old One"** in *Inc.* (November 2000, pp. 37)
Pub: The Goldhirsh Group
Description: Profile of entrepreneur Herb Kelleher, co-founder of Southwest Airlines.

36936 ■ **"What Leaders Really Do"** in *Harvard Business Review* (Vol. 79, No. 11, December 2001, pp. 85)
Pub: Harvard Business School Press
Ed: John P. Kotter. **Description:** Leadership is different from management. Leadership and management are two complementary systems. While management copes with complexity, leadership copes with change. Because the business world has become more competitive and demands more change, it also demands more leadership.

36937 ■ **"What Makes Owning a Business Fun? A Lesson Learned"** in *Black Enterprise* (Vol. 34, No. 5, December 2003, pp. S2)
Pub: Earl Graves Publishing Co.
Ed: Jennifer L. Smith. **Description:** Young entrepreneurs talk about their companies.

36938 ■ **"What Not To Do in a Press Release"** in *Inc.* (January 1, 2004)
Pub: Gruner & Jahr USA Publishing
Ed: Nicole Gull. **Description:** Entrepreneurs should double-check all information before allowing a press release to be printed.

36939 ■ *What Self-Made Millionaires Really Think, Know and Do: A Straight-Talking Guide to Business Success and Personal Riches*
Pub: John Wiley & Sons, Incorporated
Ed: Richard Dobbins; Barrie Pettman. **Released:** September 2006. **Price:** $24.95. **Description:** Guide for understanding the concepts of entrepreneurial success; the book offers insight into bringing an idea into reality, marketing, time management, leadership skills, and setting clear goals.

36940 ■ **"What about Small Business?"** in *Success* (Vol. 47, No. 1, January 2000, pp. 15)
Pub: Success Publishing, Inc.
Ed: Michael Caronna. **Description:** U.S. Governors are leery to address and encourage small business. During State of the State speeches, fewer than half said the words "small business" or "entrepreneur" in their addresses. Only a dozen made specific proposals that might encourage entrepreneurial growth.

36941 ■ **"What the Titans Can Teach Us"** in *Harvard Business Review* (Vol. 79, No. 11, December 2001, pp. 70)
Pub: Harvard Business School Press
Ed: Richard S. Tedlow. **Description:** Profile of legendary leaders of American business such as Andrew Carnegie, Henry Ford and Sam Walton of Wal-Mart. While some of their traits should not be emulated, the author argues that we can all learn from them. These people had the courage to bet on their vision of market potential, they shaped their vision into a mission for the company and they delivered more than they promised.

36942 ■ **"What's In a Name?"** in *Inc.* (July 1, 2004)
Pub: Inc. Magazine
Ed: Bobbie Gossage. **Description:** Choosing a company or brand name is critical to success. Ways to get the name your small company deserves are outlined.

36943 ■ *What's Stopping You?: Attitude Adjustment for the About-to-Be Entrepreneur*
Pub: Know How Now
Ed: William A. Remas. **Released:** 1995. **Price:** $5.00.

36944 ■ "What's Wrong with Executive Compensation" in *Harvard Business Review* (Vol. 81, No. 1, January 2003, pp. 69)
Pub: Harvard Business School Press
Ed: Charles Elson. **Description:** Harvard Business Review and the University of Delaware's Center for Corporate Governance convened a roundtable to discuss executive compensation. The twelve panelists discussed ways to align the interests of executives with long-term company interests and the broader questions of corporate governance and company values.

36945 ■ "What's Your Angle? Get Fresh Ideas When You Change Your Perspective" in *Entrepreneur* (Vol. 31, No. 9, September 2003, pp. 81)
Pub: Entrepreneur Media, Inc.
Ed: Juanita Weaver. **Description:** Reversing current ideas and beliefs can lead to new ways to develop a business, according to a creativity coach and business consultant.

36946 ■ "What's Your Problem? When to Tell Customers You Work From Your Home" in *Entrepreneur* (Vol. 32, December 2004, No. 12, pp. 104)
Pub: Entrepreneur Media Inc.
Description: Five factors to consider before telling a customer you work from a home-based business are explored.

36947 ■ "Wheels of Fortune" in *Entrepreneur* (Vol. 33, March 2005, No. 3, pp. 128)
Pub: Entrepreneur Media Inc.
Ed: Esther Nguonly. **Description:** Profile of Ross Evans and Kipchoge Spencer of Xtracycle in San Juan, California. Xtracycle offers a bicycle extension that can carry passengers and cargo; their primary product is the FreeRadical Kit, an extension for a traditional bicycle featuring modular racks and accessories that allow riders to carry up to 200 extra pounds.

36948 ■ "When in Doubt Grab a Mouse, or a Phone" in *Crain's Chicago Business* (Vol. 30, January 2007, No. 1, pp. 12)
Pub: Crain Communications, Inc.
Ed: Dee Gill. **Description:** Interview with Maria Meyers, network coordinator for U.S.SourceLink, a nonprofit designed to give entrepreneurs and small business owners easy access to resources. Meyers talks about the program, its history and impact on the community, the website itself, and the grass-roots marketing needed to inform consumers of the services available.

36949 ■ "When Everything Isn't Half Enough" in *Harvard Business Review* (Vol. 78, No. 2, March 2000, pp. 28)
Pub: Harvard Business School Publishing Corp.
Ed: Suzy Wetlaufer. **Description:** Entrepreneur Norman Spencer worked 22 years to make his company successful and his family wealthy. Now that they are, why does he feel so hollow?

36950 ■ "When Leadership Means Letting Go" in *Law Firm Inc.* (October 2004)
Pub: American Lawyer Media LP
Description: In law firms, it is important for the chief marketing officer to report to the firm's top leader in order for the position to be taken seriously. The chief marketing leader's expertise to handle marketing and sales efforts is critical.

36951 ■ "When the Love is Gone: How to Reignite Passion for the Job" in *Black Enterprise* (Vol. 35, January 2005, No. 6, pp. 54)
Pub: Earl G. Graves Publishing Co. Inc.
Ed: Lee Anna Jackson. **Description:** According to a study performed by the Conference Board, a nonprofit business leader resource, job satisfaction has been falling since 1995. Previous studies reported a direct connection between job satisfaction and top performing individuals and teams.

36952 ■ "Where Are They Now? Working, but More Calmly" in *Wall Street Journal* (April 8, 2002, pp. A17)
Pub: Wall Street Journal
Ed: Kara Swisher. **Description:** Current information about dot-com entrepreneurs and the industry is presented.

36953 ■ "Where Are You Going?" in *My Business* (April/May 2003, pp. 46)
Pub: My Business Magazine
Ed: Karen J. Bannan. **Description:** Business visions require identifying a target market, as well as the services and products a small business intends to supply.

36954 ■ "Where Are You Headed?" in *Women in Business* (Vol. 53, No. 7, January-February 2002, pp. 22)
Pub: The ABWA Co Inc.
Ed: Mary-Lane Kamberg. **Description:** It is important to establish goals and to develop a plan of action to achieve the goals. An individual must also be flexible because goals could change during their implementation.

36955 ■ "Where to Find Business Answers; Advice and Education" in *Crain's New York Business* (Vol. 22, November 13, 2006, No. 46, pp. 24)
Pub: Crain Communications, Inc.
Description: Listing of organizations and agencies that provide training, financial and managerial advice, and technical expertise to current or would-be business owners.

36956 ■ "Where It's a Woman's World" in *Inc.* (January 1, 2004)
Pub: Gruner & Jahr USA Publishing
Ed: Bobbie Gossage. **Description:** The U.S. ranked tenth with women entrepreneurs, among countries surveyed by researchers from Babson College, the London School of Economics and the Ewing M. Kauffman Foundation. Statistical data included.

36957 ■ "Where's the Beef? Has Your Business Lost Momentum?" in *Entrepreneur* (Vol. 31, No. 11, November 2003, pp. 92)
Pub: Entrepreneur Media, Inc.
Ed: Chris Penttila. **Description:** Many small businesses have the opportunity to beat larger companies because of the maneuverability of being small, but many times entrepreneurs 'sacred cows' prevent them from acting fast.

36958 ■ "Where's the Love?" in *Entrepreneur* (Vol. 31, No. 10, October 2003)
Pub: Entrepreneur Media, Inc.
Ed: Nichole L. Torres. **Description:** When entrepreneurs lose interest in their business, it is time for them to rediscover the passion they once had for their company.

36959 ■ "Who Are the Gurus' Gurus? One Thing is Clear: They're Not the Usual Suspects" in *Harvard Business Review* (Vol. 81, No. 12, Dec. 2003)
Pub: Harvard Business School Press
Ed: Lawrence Prusak, Thomas H. Davenport. **Description:** An examination of the various sources that dominate management literature and mass media; they reflect a wide range of intellectual specialties, including anthropology, history, psychology, and more. Implications of this diversity on management science and practice are briefly noted.

36960 ■ "Who Can You Trust?" in *Inc.* (October 1, 2004)
Pub: Inc. Magazine
Ed: Alison Stein Wellner. **Description:** One of the biggest problems faced by entrepreneurs is delegating responsibility to other employees.

36961 ■ "Who Needs Budgets?" in *Harvard Business Review* (Vol. 81, No. 2, February 2003, pp. 108)
Pub: Harvard Business School Press
Ed: Jeremy Hope, Robin Fraser. **Description:** The article advocates for the abolishment of budgeting within corporations using hypothetical scenarios and real situations to show that budgets can be detrimental to companies.

36962 ■ "Who Needs 'Em?" in *Entrepreneur* (Vol. 28, No. 7, July 2000, pp. 160)
Pub: Entrepreneur Media Inc.
Ed: Don Debelak. **Description:** Craig Winchell tells how he is marketing games through the Internet.

36963 ■ "Who Wants to be a Millionaire?" in *Entrepreneur* (Vol. 28, No. 11, November 2000, pp. 22)
Pub: Entrepreneur Media Inc.
Ed: Nichole L. Torres. **Description:** A survey finds that one-third of Americans do not want to be wealthy.

36964 ■ "Whoops! I won't let that happen again!" in *Women in Business* (Vol. 54, No. 5, September-October 2002, pp. 32)
Pub: The ABWA Company, Inc.
Ed: Elizabeth Bradley. **Description:** The mistakes made by several women business owners are recounted.

36965 ■ "Who's bringing you hot ideas, and how are you responding?" in *Harvard Business Review* (Vol. 81, No. 2, February 2003, pp. 58)
Pub: Harvard Business School Press
Ed: Thomas H. Davenport, Laurence Prusak, H. James Wilson. **Description:** Research into business management is presented, especially regarding management and executives who suggest meaningful ideas that benefit the company and calls these individuals idea practitioners.

36966 ■ "Why Bad Projects Are So Hard to Kill" in *Harvard Business Review* (Vol. 81, No. 2, February 2003, pp. 48)
Pub: Harvard Business School Press
Ed: Isabelle Royer. **Description:** Research into ways a company might continue to invest money in a technology that will never be marketable, and points out businesses don't often appreciate the need for those individuals who are willing to terminate a bad project.

36967 ■ "Why Bright Star Shines" in *Hispanic Business* (January/February 2004, pp. 14-16, 18)
Pub: Hispanic Business
Ed: Joel Russell. **Description:** Profile of Marcelo Claure, CEO of Brightstar and winner of the Hispanic Business Entrepreneur of the Year Award. Brightstar Corporation, a cellular phone distributor, reported double-digit growth for six years. Claure attributes the firm's success to smart use of technology and an aggressive approach to training.

36968 ■ "Why Democracy is America's Second Most Valuable Export" in *Inc.* (September 2005, pp. 23)
Pub: Inc. Magazine
Ed: Carl Schramm, Robert Litan. **Description:** If entrepreneurship is exported to China, democracy is sure to follow.

36969 ■ "Why Do So Many Salespeople Fail to Get It?" in *Home Business* (Vol. 12, March/April 2005, No. 2, pp. 54)
Pub: Home Business Magazine
Ed: Bill Brooks. **Description:** The importance for home-based business owners to understand the keys to successful selling is stressed.

36970 ■ "Why Hierarchies Thrive" in *Harvard Business Review* (Vol. 81, No. 3, March 2003, pp. 96)
Pub: Harvard Business School Press
Ed: Harold J. Leavit. **Description:** Despite the fact that hardly anyone likes them, hierarchies persist in business, because they fulfill the human need for order and security. However, they are always authoritarian.

36971 ■ "Why We Misread Motives" in *Harvard Business Review* (Vol. 81, No. 1, January 2003)
Pub: Harvard Business School Press
Description: Research by Stanford University professor, Chip Heath, suggests that managers tend to have

an extrinsic incentives bias by assuming that others are more driven than they are by external rewards for work. Extrinsic rewards are such things as pay and job security, while intrinsic rewards are learning new skills and contributing to an organization.

36972 ■ **"A Wild Ride: The Twists and Turns of Running Your Own Business Can Throw You for a Loop" in** *Entrepreneur* **(Vol. 31, October 2003)**
Pub: Entrepreneur Media, Inc.
Ed: Romanus Wolter. **Description:** Four tips to get a small business back on track are presented.

36973 ■ **"Will Power: What Would You Do If You Suddenly Inherited a Business?" in** *Entrepreneur* **(Vol. 32, September 2004, No. 9, pp. 28)**
Pub: Entrepreneur Media Inc.
Ed: Geoff Williams. **Description:** When his friend died, Dave Buck inherited his business. Buck explains how he had to rely on his instincts and to also make changes to the company in order to make it his own.

36974 ■ **"Wing Tips" in** *Inc.* **(February 1, 2002)**
Pub: Inc. Magazine
Ed: Mike Hofman. **Description:** Profile of James Murphy, owner of Afterburner Seminars Inc., the $3.1 million producer of management-training seminars, based in Atlanta.

36975 ■ **"And The Winner Is" in** *Inc.* **(October 1, 2003)**
Pub: Gruner & Jahr USA Publishing
Ed: Anton Piach. **Description:** Winning any one of the hundreds of small business competitions conducted across the nation can make all the difference for struggling entrepreneurs.

36976 ■ **"Winners' Circle: Lessons From Sports Superstars Help You Score Business Success" in** *Entrepreneur* **(Vol. 31, No. 10, October 2003)**
Pub: Entrepreneur Media, Inc.
Description: Profile of Brandon Steiner, founder of Steiner Sports, a sports marketing and sports collectibles company.

36977 ■ *Winning!*
Pub: HarperCollins Publishers Inc.
Ed: Jack and Suzy Welch. **Price:** $27.95.

36978 ■ **"Witness to history...and tragedy: a Wall Street veteran reflects on his 9/11 loss" in** *Barron's* **(Vol. 82, Sept. 9, 2002, pp. 26)**
Pub: Barron's
Ed: Erin E. Arvedlund. **Description:** Michael Pascuma, a 75-year veteran of the securities industry, is acknowledged as the oldest floor broker in the country. He built a small business with his only son, Michael Jr., who perished in the World Trade Center attacks. Pascuma reflects upon his life in the industry.

36979 ■ **"WKR-Small Business" in** *Entrepreneur* **(Vol. 28, No. 2, February 2000, pp. 38)**
Pub: Entrepreneur Media Inc.
Ed: Ellen Paris. **Description:** On the nation's radios, entrepreneurs are finally in the spotlight. Jim Blasingame hits the nation's airwaves and Intenet for three hours, five mornings a week, talking to and about small businesses.

36980 ■ **"Women" in** *Entrepreneur* **(Vol. 27, No. 12, December 1999, pp. 44)**
Pub: Entrepreneur Media Inc.
Ed: Cynthia E. Griffin. **Description:** A new study underscores the old adage that the most important thing in business is location, location, location. In the top 50 U.S. metropolitan areas, the number of women-owned firms has increased 33 to 59 percent in the past seven years, according to a 1999 report by the National Foundation for Women Business Owners (NFWBO).

36981 ■ *Women Entrepreneurs*
Pub: Edward Elgar Publishing, Incorporated

Ed: Andrea Smith-Hunter. **Released:** October 2006. **Price:** $120.00. **Description:** Focus is on women entrepreneurs; information includes human capital, network structures and financial capital, with comparative analysis across racial lines.

36982 ■ **"Women of Substance: Who Says It's a Man's World?" in** *Entrepreneur* **(Vol. 31, No. 11, November 2003, pp. 104)**
Pub: Entrepreneur Media, Inc.
Ed: Devlin Smith. **Description:** Women entrepreneurs share thoughts on ways franchising allows them to balance work and family lives.

36983 ■ **"Women mentoring women" in** *Women in Business* **(Vol. 53, No. 7, January-February 2002, pp. 28)**
Pub: The ABWA Co Inc.
Ed: Lisa Keating. **Description:** There are psychological and professional rewards for the mentor and the person who is mentored. Women mentors can assist new businesswomen to learn how to manage job stress and plan their careers or small business.

36984 ■ **"A Work of Art" in** *Entrepreneur* **(Vol. 32, December 2004, No. 12, pp. 24)**
Pub: Entrepreneur Media Inc.
Ed: Mark Henricks. **Description:** Business consultant, Frans Johansson has written a book called, The Medici Effect. Johansson gathered a team of individuals with various ideas, viewpoints and experiences to study successful idea-generators, or inventors, from business, science, the arts and elsewhere.

36985 ■ **"Work, Interrupted: Think Work Distractions Are a Pain? Top CEOs Tend to Disagree" in** *Entrepreneur* **(Vol. 32, September 2004, No. 9)**
Pub: Entrepreneur Media Inc.
Ed: Mark Henricks. **Description:** According to Stephanie Winston, an organization expert and author, top executives regard interruptions as a valuable tool for connecting with fellow workers.

36986 ■ **"Workaholic Cooks Up Site" in** *Crain's New York Business* **(Vol. 23, January 29, 2007, No. 5, pp. F3)**
Pub: Crain Communications, Inc.
Ed: Lisa Fickenscher. **Description:** Profile of Jason R. Finger and his Internet company, SeamlessWeb. com, a service that allows consumers and corporate employees to order food from member restaurants. Food giant, Aramark bought the firm last year.

36987 ■ **"Working It Out! How a Young Executive Overcomes Obstacles on the Job" in** *Black Enterprise* **(Vol. 37, January 2007, No. 6, pp. 55)**
Pub: Earl G. Graves Publishing Co. Inc.
Ed: Laura Egodigwe. **Description:** Interview with Susan Chapman, Global Head of Operations for Citigroup Realty Services, in which she discusses issues such as the important skills necessary for overcoming obstacles in the workplace.

36988 ■ *Working without a Net: The Realities of Going into Business for Yourself*
Pub: Vocational Video
Ed: Daniel J. Fardella. **Released:** 1995. **Price:** $7.95.

36989 ■ **"Working With Women" in** *My Business* **(April/May 2003, pp. 14)**
Pub: My Business Magazine
Ed: Mardy Fones. **Description:** Ways in which women business owners can grow a business by effectively managing female employees are addressed in a question/answer format.

36990 ■ *Working for Yourself: Law and Taxes for Independent Contractors, Freelancers and Consultants*
Pub: NOLO
Ed: Stephen Fishman. **Released:** October 2004. **Price:** $39.99. **Description:** Laws and tax rules governing independent contractors, freelancers and consultants.

36991 ■ **"The World According to Clark" in** *Business 2.0* **(Vol. 6, May 2005, No. 4, pp. 88)**
Pub: Time, Inc.
Description: Jim Clark, billionaire entrepreneur, offers insight into starting a new company.

36992 ■ **"A World of Difference" in** *Entrepreneur* **(Vol. 32, October 2004, No. 10, pp. 78)**
Pub: Entrepreneur Media Inc.
Ed: April Y. Pennington. **Description:** Entrepreneurs are committed to civic responsibility. They are actively working in communities for positive change through not only donations and in-house recycling programs, but also through a hands-on approach to social issues.

36993 ■ **"Would You Buy a Chinese Car From This Man?" in** *Inc.* **(Volume 27, July 2005, No. 7, pp. 68-72, 74)**
Pub: Inc. Magazine
Ed: Darren Dahl. **Description:** Profile of Malcolm Bricklin, CEO of Visionary Vehicles. Bricklin is on a quest to revolutionize the auto industry.

36994 ■ **"Write Stuff" in** *Crain's New York Business* **(Vol. 23, January 15, 2007, No. 3, pp. 47)**
Pub: Crain Communications, Inc.
Ed: Elisabeth Butler. **Description:** Profile of Karen Levy, a calligrapher, and her company Writer's Camp, a business that inscribes place cards, invitations and menus for individual clients as well as large companies including Saks Fifth Avenue and J.P. Morgan Chase.

36995 ■ **"The Write Stuff: Entrepreneurs Find Success with a New Take on a Familiar Product" in** *Entrepreneur* **(Vol. 32, November 2004, No. 11)**
Pub: Entrepreneur Media Inc.
Ed: Don Debelak. **Description:** Profile of Colin Roche and Bobby Ronsse, 33-year-old co-founders of Pacific Writing Instruments. The PenAgain is a writing tool shaped like a wishbone. The pair used about $15,000 to manufacture the first 5,000 units and predict sales to surpass $3 million in 2004.

36996 ■ **"Year In Review People" in** *Venture Capital Journal* **(February 1, 2006)**
Pub: Thomason Financial Inc.
Description: Leading venture capitalists in 2005 include Robert Alexander from Alta Partners, Stewart Alsop from Alsop Louie Partners, and Isaac Applebaum from Opus Capital.

36997 ■ **"Year to Success" in** *Small Business Opportunities* **(Vol. 17, May 2005, No. 3, pp. 126)**
Pub: Harris Publications Inc.
Description: Review of Year to Success, written by Bo Bennett. The book shares the wisdom and words of success stories and the insight of political leaders, CEOs, entrepreneurs, inventors and celebrities. The author highlights ways to handle mistakes, make a strong impression, make decisions, and create good situations from bad ones.

36998 ■ **"Yes, No, Maybe So" in** *Inc.* **(August 1, 2003)**
Pub: Gruner & Jahr USA Publishing
Ed: John Koten. **Description:** The silent treatment is one of the oldest tactics in journalism, but can also be used in business negotiations.

36999 ■ **"Yes, You Can!" in** *Entrepreneur* **(Vol. 32, No. 1, January 2004, pp. 32)**
Pub: Entrepreneur Media, Inc.
Ed: Aliza Pilar Sherman. **Description:** Entrepreneurs share visions and goals for their businesses.

37000 ■ **"You Can Count on Me: A Friend Can Make the Best Kind of Business Partner" in** *Entrepreneur* **(Vol. 32, November 2004, No. 11, pp. 36)**
Pub: Entrepreneur Media Inc.
Ed: Aliza Pilar Sherman. **Description:** Profiles of friends who ventured into businesses together. Lynn

Harris Medcalf and Susan Apgood teamed to launch News Generation, a public relations firm in Atlanta, Georgia. Sarah Eck and Brook Jay, partnered to create All Terrain Productions, an events-marketing firm in Chicago, Illinois.

37001 ■ "You Can Quote Him" in *Fast Company* **(July 2001, pp. 66)**
Pub: Fast Company
Ed: Charles Fishman. **Description:** Profile of Charles Schwab, who helped democratize the U.S. stock market when the government deregulated the fees that brokerage firms charged to trade stocks. While most brokerage firms raised their fees, Schwab did the opposite, and brought stock trading to ordinary individuals at the price of $50 per transaction.

37002 ■ "You First: An Opening Move May Make or Break a Deal-So Step Lightly" in *Entrepreneur* **(Vol. 33, March 2005, No. 3, pp. 96)**
Pub: Entrepreneur Media Inc.
Ed: Marc Diener. **Description:** Negotiation tips are offered to help close deals.

37003 ■ "You Should Be the Boss of Them" in *My Business* **(June/July 2004, pp. 51)**
Pub: My Business Magazine
Ed: Jackie Van Nice. **Description:** It is essential for small business owners to know and understand all employees and the jobs they perform.

37004 ■ "You Win! Poor You!" in *Entrepreneur* **(Vol. 28, No. 10, October 2000, pp. 82)**
Pub: Entrepreneur Media Inc.
Ed: Michelle Prather. **Description:** The article discusses some of the negative things entrepreneurs face after becoming successful.

37005 ■ "Young Entrepreneur of the Year Works Round the Clock" in *Portland Press Herald* **(March 24, 2005)**
Pub: Blethen Maine Newspapers, Inc.
Ed: Matt Wickenheiser. **Description:** Profile of Danny Bouzianis, co-owner of the Old Port Dunkin' Donuts. Bouzianis was named Maine's Young Entrepreneur of the Year by the U.S. Small Business Administration.

37006 ■ "Young Entrepreneurs Give the U.S. Mint Their Two Cents" in *Wall Street Journal* **(March 14, 2000, pp. B4)**
Pub: Dow Jones & Co., Inc.
Ed: Eleena De Lisser. **Description:** An overview of a program with the National Foundation for Teaching Entrepreneurship for marketing new coins.

37007 ■ "Young Millionaires: Class of 2004" in *Entrepreneur* **(Vol. 32, November 2004, No. 11, pp. 77)**
Pub: Entrepreneur Media Inc.
Ed: Amanda C. Kooser, April Y. Pennington, Jonathan Riggs, Nichole L. Torres, Sara Wilson. **Description:** Profiles of successful entrepreneurs include Cristina Bartolucci and Laura Deluisa, manufacturers of specialty makeup and body creams; Ashton Palmer and Kristy Royce, founders of an Internet-based adventure travel company; Bernard Frei, who sells soccer and rugby apparel online; Christopher Faulkner, a Web-hosting and data center infrastructure provider; Marco and Sandra Johnson, who founded an accredited medical college; Shawn Nelson, owner of modular furniture stores; a media advertising company; James P. Funderburk Jr., owner of clothing stores, a private nightclub and real estate company; and a firm that manages online sites for clothing manufacturers.

37008 ■ "Young Professional Share Ideas" in *San Fernando Valley Business Journal* **(Vol. 12, January 2007, No. 2, pp. 1)**
Pub: San Fernando Valley Business Journal Associates
Ed: Chris Coates. **Description:** Interview with four young business professionals from various fields who talk about gaining creditability in the workplace, image, and marketing.

37009 ■ "Younger But Wiser Than You Might Think" in *San Fernando Valley Business Journal* **(Vol. 12, January 2007, No. 2, pp. 51)**
Pub: San Fernando Valley Business Journal Associates
Ed: Jason Schaff. **Description:** Common traits are explored of successful business professionals under the age of forty.

37010 ■ "Your Annual Business Tune-Up" in *Business Week* **(December 28, 2006)**
Pub: McGraw-Hill Companies
Ed: Karen E. Klein. **Description:** Interview with entrepreneurial expert, Ty Freyvogel, founder of EntrpreneursLab.com. Freyvogel gives tips on how a thorough review of existing systems, vendors, customers, and employees could help keep an entrepreneur's business not only safe but highly successful in the upcoming year.

37011 ■ *Your Business, Your Future: How to Predict and Harness Growth*
Pub: Allen and Unwin Pty., Limited
Ed: Linda Hailey. **Released:** January 2007. **Price:** $16.95. **Description:** Four distinct phases every small companies faces during growth are profiled.

37012 ■ "Your Kind of News: Free Personalized Information for the Public" in *Black Enterprise* **(Vol. 34, No. 7, February 2004, pp. 140)**
Pub: Earl Graves Publishing Co.
Ed: Jennifer L. Smith. **Description:** Profile of a free Website offering articles and press releases from more than 70 major sources on topics relevant to business, including finance and computing.

37013 ■ "You're the Boss: There Are Some Things Beyond Your Control..." in *Entrepreneur* **(Vol. 31, No. 9, September 2003, pp. 90)**
Pub: Entrepreneur Media, Inc.
Ed: Devlin Smith. **Description:** Franchising may be the answer to an entrepreneur's dream of becoming a small business owner.

37014 ■ "You've Got Personality" in *Entrepreneur* **(Vol. 31, No. 8, August 2003, pp. 30)**
Pub: Entrepreneur Media, Inc.
Ed: Steve Cooper. **Description:** Statistics about the ways entrepreneurs see themselves in terms of personality are presented.

37015 ■ "You've got the power!" in *Black Enterprise* **(Vol. 31, No. 5, December 2000, pp. 166)**
Pub: Earl Graves Publishing Co.
Ed: Robyn D. Clarke. **Description:** The value of communicating with confidence and power through your body language is examined.

TRADE PERIODICALS

37016 ■ *Business Ideas & Shortcuts*
Pub: Editorial Board
Ed: Peter Joseph, Editor. **Released:** Monthly. **Price:** $99 year. **Description:** Contains special reports, practical ideas, tips, and guidelines on current business opportunities and shortcuts to profits. Covers specific topics, such as how to be a manufacturer without investing; how to get free national advertising; how to protect your business; and how to tap overlooked sources of financing. Recurring features include columns titled Business Shortcut of the Month and Unique Ideas for Entrepreneurs.

37017 ■ *Chief Executive Officer's Newsletter*
Pub: Chief Executive Officers Clubs
Ed: Joe Manuso, Editor. **Released:** Monthly. **Price:** Included in membership; $96, nonmembers. **Description:** "Designed to provide accurate and authoritative information relative to subjects of concern to entrepreneurial managers." Covers management, taxes, finance, marketing, information sources, and educational programs. Recurring features include news of seminars, book reviews, news of research and survey results, and columns titled Entrepreneurs's Hall of Fame, Mind Your Own Business, Resources, Accounting, Personal, Miscellaneous, and The Business Exchange.

37018 ■ *International Wealth Success*
Pub: IWS Inc.
Ed: Tyler Hicks, Editor. **Released:** Monthly. **Price:** $24, U.S.; $48 outside U.S.. **Description:** Covers methods of making money in a successful business, including sources of business capital, real estate income methods, mail order, import/export, franchising, and licensing of products. Recurring features include news of export/import opportunities and a column on capital sources.

37019 ■ *Journal of Entrepreneurial and Small Firm Finance*
Pub: University of California Press
Released: 3/yr. **Description:** Journal that focuses on small business and financial issues.

37020 ■ *The Small Business Advisor*
Pub: Small Business Advisors Inc.
Contact: Joseph Gelb, Publisher
Ed: Ann Liss, Editor. **Released:** Monthly. **Price:** $45, U.S.; $90, Canada. **Description:** Seeks to help emerging growth companies increase profits. Considers small business issues, including marketing sales, finance, taxes, organizing, competition, management, and human resources. Recurring features include letters to the editor, interviews, and columns titled Info Bank, In the Mail Box, Taxes, Human Resources, Marketing, Insurance, and Law. Remarks: Publication suspended in 1980; resumed publication Fall 1993.

VIDEOCASSETTES/ AUDIOCASSETTES

37021 ■ *The Achievement Challenge*
Beveridge Consulting Group
113 N. Grant St.
Barrington, IL 60010-3001
Ph:(847)381-7797
Free: 800-227-4332
Fax: (847)381-7301
Released: 1988. **Price:** $995.00. **Description:** A series of programs that explain things to be done and attitudes to be taken to do better in business. **Availability:** VHS.

37022 ■ *The American Entrepreneur Today*
GPN Educational Media
Box 80669
Lincoln, NE 68501-0669
Ph:(402)472-2007
Free: 800-228-4630
Fax: 800-306-2330
URL: http://gpn.unl.edu
Released: 1991. **Price:** $785.00. **Description:** A 14-part course focuses on the creativity and dedication needed to making a good idea work. Six successful entrepreneurs offer insight into their business success. Course text is "New Venture Creation: Entrepreneurship in the 1990s" by Jeffry A. Timmons. **Availability:** VHS.

37023 ■ *The Applied Management Series*
Thomson National Education Training Group (NETg)
14624 N. Scottsdale Rd., Ste. 300
Phoenix, AZ 85254
Ph:(480)315-4000
Free: 800-265-1900
Fax: (480)315-4001
Co. E-mail: info@netg.com
URL: http://www.netg.com
Released: 1984. **Description:** This series of four six hour programs will train people in current effective management techniques. **Availability:** 3/4U.

37024 ■ *Artful Negotiating*
Phoenix Learning Group
2349 Chaffee Dr.
St. Louis, MO 63146
Ph:(314)569-0211
Free: 800-221-1274
Fax: (314)569-2834
URL: http://www.phoenixlearninggroup.com
Released: 1989. **Price:** $650.00. **Description:** Herb Cohen demonstrates killer negotiating tactics. **Availability:** VHS; 3/4U.

37025 ■ *Business, Careers, and Lifestyle Series*
RMI Media
1365 N. Winchester
Olathe, KS 66061
Ph:(913)768-1696
Fax: (913)768-0184
Co. E-mail: actmedia@act.org
URL: http://www.rmimedia.com
Released: 1984. **Description:** In this series of 56 half-hour programs, host Dick Goldberg interviews top business leaders in various fields to find out what it takes to be successful in business. **Availability:** VHS; 3/4U.

37026 ■ *Change Your Mind: Inner Training for Women in Business*
American Bar Association
321 N. Clark St.
Chicago, IL 60610
Ph:(312)988-5000
Fax: (312)988-5528
Co. E-mail: abapubed@abanet.org
URL: http://www.abanet.org/publiced/
Released: 1988. **Price:** $495.00. **Description:** Dr. Kay Porter and Judy Foster give steps that will help women become better and more confident in the business world. **Availability:** VHS.

37027 ■ *Creativity in Business*
Kantola Productions, LLC
55 Sunnyside Ave.
Mill Valley, CA 94941-1935
Ph:(415)381-9363
Free: 800-989-8273
Fax: (415)381-9801
Co. E-mail: info@kantola.com
URL: http://kantola.com
Released: 1998. **Price:** $95.00. **Description:** Dr. Michael Ray demonstrates how to apply the principles of consciousness expansion, intuition and creativity to business ventures. **Availability:** VHS.

37028 ■ *Decision Analysis*
Massachusetts Institute of Technology (MIT)
Center for Advanced Educational Services
77 Massachusetts Ave., Rm. 9-234
Cambridge, MA 02139-4307
Ph:(617)253-7408
Fax: (617)253-8301
Co. E-mail: caes-courses@mit.edu
URL: http://www-caes.mit.edu
Released: 1988. **Price:** $8900.00. **Description:** Business managers are told how they can make the decisions that will be best for their company. **Availability:** VHS; 3/4U.

37029 ■ *Decision Making: How to Make Better, Faster, Smarter Decisions*
Instructional Video
2219 C St.
Lincoln, NE 68502
Ph:(402)475-6570
Free: 800-228-0164
Fax: (402)475-6500
Co. E-mail: feedback@insvideo.com
URL: http://www.insvideo.com
Price: $59.95. **Description:** Profiles effective decision-making techniques. Includes interactive guidebook. **Availability:** VHS.

37030 ■ *Empowerment: How to Receive Work Assignments*
International Training Consultants, Inc.
1838 Park Oaks
Kemah, TX 77565

Free: 800-998-8764
Co. E-mail: itc@trainingitc.com
URL: http://www.trainingitc.com
Price: $495.00. **Description:** Part of the "Empowerment: The Employee Development Series." Teaches employees proper procedures in receiving work assignments from their superiors. Includes instruction on how to obtain task objectives, ask for needed details, determine resources available, analyze contraints, ask for training, offer suggestions, and establish performance measures. Emphasis is placed on the employee's knowledge that it is their responsibility to finish the assignment correctly and on time. **Availability:** VHS.

37031 ■ *Empowerment: Moving from Criticism to Feedback*
International Training Consultants, Inc.
1838 Park Oaks
Kemah, TX 77565
Free: 800-998-8764
Co. E-mail: itc@trainingitc.com
URL: http://www.trainingitc.com
Price: $495.00. **Description:** Part of the "Empowerment: The Employee Development Series." Illustrates proper ways of giving and receiving criticism. Teaches a six-step method which helps turn criticism into constructive feedback. Also discusses methods which help an individual receive criticism without becoming defensive. Comes with leader's guide, self-study instructions, and five participant booklets. **Availability:** VHS.

37032 ■ *Empowerment: The Employee Development Series*
International Training Consultants, Inc.
1838 Park Oaks
Kemah, TX 77565
Free: 800-998-8764
Co. E-mail: itc@trainingitc.com
URL: http://www.trainingitc.com
Price: $10350.00. **Description:** Employee development series which prepares employees to meet the demands of today's workplace with skill and confidence. Covers such topics as time management, team work, communication, career advancement, working together, and problem solving. Comes with leader's guide, overhead transparencies, five participant booklets, and a complete participant's manual. **Availability:** VHS.

37033 ■ *Everything You Always Wanted to Know about Management*
American Media, Inc.
4621 121st St.
Urbandale, IA 50323-2311
Ph:(515)224-0919
Free: 888-776-8268
Fax: (515)327-2555
Co. E-mail: custsvc@ammedia.com
URL: http://www.ammedia.com
Released: 1995. **Price:** $595. **Description:** Outlines the essentials of good management, including the six steps of delegation, employee empowerment, communication, feedback, and goal achievement. Includes course guide with participant exercises and case studies. **Availability:** VHS; CC.

37034 ■ *The Good Business Basics Series: The Basics of Entrepreneuring*
Cambridge Educational
c/o Films Media Group
PO Box 2053
Princeton, NJ 08843-2053
Free: 800-257-5126
Fax: (609)671-0266
Co. E-mail: custserve@filmsmediagroup.com
URL: http://www.cambridgeol.com
Released: 1992. **Price:** $98.00. **Description:** So you think you have a good idea. How do you get started in business? This program overviews the basics of getting a business off the ground, from finding a niche in the marketplace, building a staff, learning from others' mistakes, and much more. **Availability:** VHS.

37035 ■ *Habits of Wealth, Volume 1: Achieving in the Futuristic Workplace*
Government VideoSource, Inc.
461 Miller Dr.
Elgin, IL 60123-7232
Ph:(847)931-1955
Released: 1994. **Price:** $89.95. **Description:** Addresses the entrepreneurial attitudes of a futuristic workplace which includes understanding the essentials of personal mission and defending core principals, understanding BALANCE and PEARL, and assimilating reality vs. expectations concept. **Availability:** VHS.

37036 ■ *Habits of Wealth, Volume 2: Conquering the Leadership Challenge*
Government VideoSource, Inc.
461 Miller Dr.
Elgin, IL 60123-7232
Ph:(847)931-1955
Released: 1994. **Price:** $89.95. **Description:** Discusses leader ethics, requirements of effective empowerment, establishing MUL, and assmilating futuristic leadership behavior. **Availability:** VHS.

37037 ■ *How You Can Start, Build, Manage, or Turn Around Any Business*
Nightingale-Conant Corp.
6245 W. Howard St.
Niles, IL 60714
Ph:(847)647-0300
Free: 800-560-6081
URL: http://www.nightingale.com
Price: $395.00. **Description:** Brian Tracy presents a mini-course in business management. **Availability:** VHS.

37038 ■ *I Can Do It! Ed Lewis*
Direct Cinema Ltd.
PO Box 10003
Santa Monica, CA 90410-1003
Ph:(310)636-8200
Free: 800-525-0000
Fax: (310)636-8228
Co. E-mail: orders@directcinemalimited.com
URL: http://www.directcinema.com
Released: 1984. **Description:** The creator of GMS explains the art, drive and knowledge necessary for successful entrepreneurism. **Availability:** VHS; 3/4U; Special order formats.

37039 ■ *If at First: Overcoming the Fear of Failure*
Government VideoSource, Inc.
461 Miller Dr.
Elgin, IL 60123-7232
Ph:(847)931-1955
Price: $895. **Description:** Offers tips on overcoming fear of failure. **Availability:** VHS.

37040 ■ *Leadership: Building Rainbows*
Eastern Kentucky University
Div. of Media Resources
521 Lancaster Ave.
Richmond, KY 40475-3102
Ph:(859)622-2474
Fax: (859)622-6276
URL: http://www.mediaresources.eku.edu
Released: 1984. **Description:** Professionals in leadership positions looking to gain personal and organizational goals are acquainted with effective persuasive communication skills. **Availability:** VHS.

37041 ■ *The Leadership Edge*
Salenger Films, Inc.
1635 12th St.
Santa Monica, CA 90404-9988
Ph:(310)450-1300
Free: 800-775-5025
Fax: (310)450-1010
Co. E-mail: salenger@aol.com
URL: http://salengerfilms.visualnet.com
Released: 1987. **Price:** $595.00. **Description:** Find out what it takes to be a good leader so you can become one yourself. **Availability:** VHS; 3/4U; Special order formats.

37042 ■ Love and Profit: The Art of Caring Leadership
Government VideoSource, Inc.
461 Miller Dr.
Elgin, IL 60123-7232
Ph:(847)931-1955
Released: 1994. **Price:** $695.00. **Description:** James Autry, Fortune 500 executive and business consultant, reviews four basic elements of progressive leadership: trust, honesty, special treatment, and courage. Includes leader's guide and a participant workbook. **Availability:** VHS.

37043 ■ Product Strategy: All the Right Moves
RMI Media
1365 N. Winchester
Olathe, KS 66061
Ph:(913)768-1696
Fax: (913)768-0184
Co. E-mail: actmedia@act.org
URL: http://www.rmimedia.com
Released: 1991. **Price:** $89.95. **Description:** Presents a case study of Carushka, a dance and exercise wear manufacturer, to demonstrate successful methods for increasing product use and customers; finding new uses for existing products; and broadening the product appeal to old and new markets. **Availability:** VHS.

37044 ■ Seven Habits of Highly Effective People
Format International
2421 E. Washington St.
Indianapolis, IN 46201-4123
Released: 1986. **Price:** $250.00. **Description:** Find out what has to be done in order for you to become a success in business. **Availability:** VHS; 3/4U.

37045 ■ Speaking of Success
RMI Media
1365 N. Winchester
Olathe, KS 66061
Ph:(913)768-1696
Fax: (913)768-0184
Co. E-mail: actmedia@act.org
URL: http://www.rmimedia.com
Released: 1988. **Price:** $69.95. **Description:** A series of business-oriented programs endeavoring to help the viewer improve his or her self, relations with others, and various manipulative techniques useful in business transactions. **Availability:** VHS; 3/4U.

37046 ■ Why Study Business?: Skills For the 21st Century
Cambridge Educational
c/o Films Media Group
PO Box 2053
Princeton, NJ 08843-2053
Free: 800-257-5126
Fax: (609)671-0266
Co. E-mail: custserve@filmsmediagroup.com
URL: http://www.cambridgeol.com
Released: 1990. **Price:** $98.00. **Description:** Introduces the various facets of the business world, and profiles careers in business which utilize several different skills. **Availability:** VHS.

CONSULTANTS

37047 ■ Association of Home-Based Women Entrepreneurs
11330 Olive Blvd., Ste. 106
Saint Louis, MO 63141-7161
Ph:(314)995-1455
Fax: (314)909-8179
Co. E-mail: aschaefer@advbizsol.com
URL: http://www.hbwe.org

E-mail: aschaefer@advbizsol.com
Scope: A non-profit womens organization who target the needs of women entrepreneurs/business owners working from home based offices. **Seminars:** Twenty Five Key Steps To Maintaining A Successful Home-Based Business, Nov, 2006; Pyro Marketing, Jan, 2007.

37048 ■ Beacon Management Group Inc.
1000 W McNab Rd.
Pompano Beach, FL 33069
Ph:(954)782-1119
Free: 800-771-8721
Fax: (954)969-2566
Co. E-mail: md@beaconmgmt.com
URL: http://www.beaconmgmt.com

E-mail: md@beaconmgmt.com
Scope: Provides entrepreneurial companies with managerial and financial expertise. Services include strategic and business planning; corporate finance; franchise development services; information management; turnaround management and consulting; and joint venture, strategic alliances and acquisition services, including due diligence, market intelligence, targeted searches, valuation, negotiation, and deal structure. Provides assistance for financially-troubled companies, not-for-profits and the public sector

37049 ■ Donna Cornell Enterprises Inc.
68 N Plank Rd., Ste. 204
Newburgh, NY 12550-2122
Ph:(845)565-0088
Fax: (845)565-0084
Co. E-mail: rc@cornellcareercenter.com
URL: http://www.dce.com

E-mail: rc@cornellcareercenter.com
Scope: Offers services in career consultant, professional search, job placement, and national professional search. **Publications:** "The Power of the Woman Within".

37050 ■ Entrepreneurial Strategies
107 S Yellowstone Ave., Ste. C
Bozeman, MT 59718
Ph:(406)587-5664
Fax: (406)586-0396
Scope: Academic consultants helping organizations become more entrepreneurial; helping communities become more entrepreneurial; market assessments for 'really new' products/technologies; strategic planning and marketing planning.

LIBRARIES

37051 ■ Canadian Federation of Independent Business–Research Library
4141 Yonge St.
Willowdale, ON, Canada M2P 2A6
Ph:(416)222-8022
Fax: (416)222-4337
Co. E-mail: infoctr@cfib-feei.ca
URL: http://www.cfib.ca/
Contact: Katalin Coorsh, Chf.Libn.
Scope: Small business, entrepreneurship, economic policy, politics and government. **Services:** Interlibrary loan; copying; Library open to the public by appointment. **Holdings:** 4000 volumes; 32 VF drawers of subject files; Annual reports. **Subscriptions:** 100 journals and other serials; 4 newspapers.

RESEARCH CENTERS

37052 ■ Baylor University–Center for Private Enterprise
PO Box 98003
Waco, TX 76798-8003
Ph:(254)710-2263
Fax: (254)710-1092
Co. E-mail: jim_truitt@baylor.edu
Contact: Dr. W. James Truitt, Dir.
E-mail: jim_truitt@baylor.edu
Scope: Entrepreneurship and private enterprise, including studies on characteristics of entrepreneurs, student and teacher attitudes toward the private enterprise system, business taxation, and women entrepreneurs. **Educational Activities:** Economic Forecast Conference; Leaderships programs, for high school seniors; Seminars, in-service workshops, and programs on teacher education and consumer economics.

37053 ■ Boston University–Entrepreneurial Management Institute
School of Management
595 Commonwealth Ave., Rm. 571
Boston, MA 02215
Ph:(617)353-9391
Fax: (617)353-5003
Co. E-mail: emi@bu.edu
URL: http://bu.edu/entrepreneurship
Contact: Prof. Peter Russo, Dir.
E-mail: emi@bu.edu
Scope: Entrepreneurship, women entrepreneurs, management policy, family-owned businesses, and marketing. **Educational Activities:** Annual Business Plan Competition; Business Plan Boot Camp.

37054 ■ Lehigh University–Small Business Development Center
Rauch Business Center
College of Business & Economics
621 Taylor St.
Bethlehem, PA 18015-3117
Ph:(610)758-3980
Fax: (610)758-5205
Co. E-mail: insbdc@lehigh.edu
URL: http://www.lehigh.edu/~insbdc/index2.htm
Contact: Sandra F. Holsonback, Exec.Dir.
E-mail: insbdc@lehigh.edu
Scope: Problems faced by small businesses, the impact of the general economy on the formation and operation of small business, and characteristics on entrepreneurs. **Services:** Administers various loan pools for lending to small businesses; Consulting and research in management assistance, international trade, government marketing, and financing assistance; Lehigh University Management Assistance Counseling (LUMAC) Program, a field studies course for senior students. **Publications:** Export Planning Guide; Financing Guide for Northampton; Financing Your Business; Lehigh and Berks County; Lehigh Valley Business Support Services; Market Planning Guide. **Educational Activities:** Seminars.

37055 ■ New York University–Berkley Center for Entrepreneurial Studies
NYU Stern School of Business
44 W 4th St., Ste 7-150, KMC
New York, NY 10012
Ph:(212)998-0070
Fax: (212)995-4211
Co. E-mail: baumolw@aol.com
URL: http://w4.stern.nyu.edu/berkley
Contact: William Baumol, Academic Dir.
E-mail: baumolw@aol.com
Scope: Factors that promote entrepreneurship and lead to the creation of new wealth and business revenues; business venturing within established firms. Topics include the major pitfalls and obstacles to start-ups, securing of venture capital, psychology and sociology of entrepreneurship, valuation and management of new ventures, technological innovation and new product development, emerging and creative industries, and cross-cultural environments that stimulate entrepreneurship. **Publications:** Case series; Working papers. **Educational Activities:** Business Plan Competition; Conferences; Entrepreneur in Residence Program; Forums and workshops. **Awards:** Harold Price Entrepreneurship Award; Rennert Entrepreneurial Prize.

37056 ■ Southern Methodist University–Caruth Institute of Entrepreneurship
Fincher Bldg., Rm. 143
Cox School of Business
PO Box 750333
Dallas, TX 75275-0333
Ph:(214)768-3689
Fax: (214)768-3604
Co. E-mail: jwhite@mail.cox.smu.edu
URL: http://www.cox.smu.edu/centers/caruthentrepreneurship
Contact: Prof. Jerry F. White, Dir.
E-mail: jwhite@mail.cox.smu.edu
Scope: Entrepreneurs as managers. **Publications:** Newsletter. **Educational Activities:** Southwest Venture Forum. **Awards:** Dallas 100 Award, recognizing the 100 fastest growing private companies in Dallas.

37057 ■ University of British Columbia–W. Maurice Young Entrepreneurship and Venture Capital Research Centre
2053 Main Mall
Vancouver, BC, Canada V6T 1Z2

Ph:(604)822-8483
Fax: (604)822-9362
Co. E-mail: ilan.vertinsk@sauder.ubc.ca

URL: http://www.sauder.ubc.ca/research/research_centres/evc.cfm
Contact: Dr. Ilan Vertinsky, Dir.
E-mail: ilan.vertinsk@sauder.ubc.ca
Scope: Entrepreneurship and venture capital.

START-UP INFORMATION

37058 ■ **"Automatic Riches"** in *Small Business Opportunities* (Vol. 13, No. 6, November 2001, pp. 66, 68)
Pub: Harris Publications, Inc.
Ed: Ken Mueller. **Description:** Profile of Toby McAdams, a former car salesman, who constructed a Web site to sell used vehicles. Mr. McAdams shares tips for targeting your niche on the Web.

37059 ■ *The Best Internet Businesses You Can Start*
Pub: Adams Media Corp.
Ed: Marian Betancourt. **Released:** 1999.

37060 ■ **"The e-changes are just beginning"** in *Hispanic Business* (Vol. 22, No. 6, June 2000, p. 30)
Pub: Hispanic Business
Ed: Jorge Chapa. **Description:** Hispanic businesses are part of the Internet revolution, with most of them maintaining their own Web sites. Two areas where Hispanic entrepreneurs may have a competitive advantage are in the provision of services to the Hispanic population in the U.S. and connecting Hispanic Americans to their families and home countries.

37061 ■ **"Going Digital"** in *Hispanic Business* (July-August 2000, pp. 76)
Pub: Hispanic Business
Ed: Nicole Lewis. **Description:** The successful use of electronic commerce by small companies is explored.

37062 ■ **"Howle turns to new tech start-up"** in *Atlanta Business Chronicle* (Vol. 24, No. 14, September 7, 2001, pp. 3A)
Pub: American City Business Journals Inc.
Ed: Mary Jane Credeur. **Description:** C. Tycho Howle, co-founder of Harbinger Corporation, recently formed a venture with a dozen other entrepreneurs called nuMethods LLC. The venture is currently in the process of developing a program that would allow businesses to electronically trade enormous amounts of information. Atlanta's Deloitte & Touche partner Joseph L. Morettini says the way the product is presented to potential buyers will determine if it will succeed.

37063 ■ **"I Bought It Through the Grapevine"** in *Success* (Vol. 47, No. 4, September 2000, pp. 4)
Pub: Success Publishing, Inc.
Ed: Carren Louise Bersch. **Description:** Uncorking a passion for wine leads to a world-class website.

37064 ■ **"Info Overload"** in *Small Business Opportunities* (Vol. 13, No. 6, November 2001, pp. 82)
Pub: Harris Publications, Inc.
Description: Profile of the Internet-based customized news, information and alerting delivery service that is ready to launch a new wireless application.

37065 ■ *Launching Onto the Web: A Small Business View*
Pub: Briarwood Publications
Ed: William J. Piniarski. **Released:** 1998. **Price:** $19.95.

37066 ■ **"Making a Success of Failure"** in *Success* (Vol. 47, No. 4, September 2000, pp. 58)
Pub: Success Publishing, Inc.
Description: Nicholas Hall has had more comebacks than George Foreman. After his first three startups failed, the 30-year-old entrepreneur kept getting back into the ring. His latest creation, startupfailures.com, has been a cult hit.

37067 ■ **"Master of your domain"** in *WorkingWoman* (Vol. 25, No. 4, April 2000, pp. 54)
Pub: Lang Communications Inc.
Ed: Parry Aftab. **Description:** Legal advice for setting up a web site on the Internet and choosing and registering a domain name is explained.

37068 ■ **"Moonlighting"** in *Forbes* (January 24, 2000, pp. 138)
Pub: Forbes Magazine
Ed: Tomas Kellner. **Description:** Online entrepreneurial startups are investigated.

37069 ■ **"Nothing to Sneeze At"** in *Success* (Vol. 47, No. 2, June 2000, pp. 58)
Pub: Success Publishing, Inc.
Ed: Simeon Furman, Michael S. Foley. **Description:** Profile of Soon-Chart Yu, founder and CEO of gazoontite.com, who carved his niche to capitalize on a $30 billion market.

37070 ■ **"On the Edge"** in *Harvard Business Review* (Vol. 78, No. 3, May 2000, pp. 118)
Pub: Harvard Business School Publishing Corp.
Ed: Nicholas G. Carr. **Description:** An interview with Akamai's George Conrades, leader of the two year old Internet start-up with a multibillion dollar market.

37071 ■ **"On the Edge"** in *Red Herring* (No. 106, October 15, 2001, pp. 62-64, 66)
Pub: Herring Communications
Ed: Michael Fitzgerald. **Description:** It could take a giant like Microsoft to get reluctant venture capitalists into funding the new software startups focusing on terminal nodes of networks where data transactions are executed from cellular phones and wireless-enabled handheld devices.

37072 ■ **"Online In A Flash"** in *Small Business Opportunities* (Vol. 13, No. 5, September 2001, pp. 12, 130)
Pub: Harris Publications, Inc.
Ed: A. Michael Salim. **Description:** Five easy steps to start an online business are outlined.

37073 ■ **"Prescription for Profit"** in *Small Business Opportunities* (Vol. 13, No. 6, November 2001, pp. 84, 86, 138)
Pub: Harris Publications, Inc.

Description: Electronic medical claims processing is the cutting edge of home-based businesses that can be grown as a home-based business, and offers a flexible schedule.

37074 ■ **"Rembrandts in the Attic"** in *Inc.* (October 2000, pp. 23)
Pub: The Goldhirsh Group
Description: Ian Peck, former gallery owner and art dealer founded an Internet-based company in 1999 that enables museums, galleries, family trusts and artists' estates to sell or lease their works of art to corporate clients.

37075 ■ **"The Right Recipe: Successful E-Commerce Sites have Three Essential Ingredients in Common"** in *Hispanic Business* (July-Aug.2000, pp.72)
Pub: Hispanic Business
Ed: Roger Harris. **Description:** The three essential ingredients for successfully launching a business online are integration, scalability, and flexibility. Tips on how to take advantage of the new technology are presented.

37076 ■ **"A Risky Business"** in *Kiplinger's Personal Finance Magazine* (Vol. 54, No. 9, September 2000, pp. 94)
Pub: The Kiplinger Washington Editors, Inc.
Ed: Catherine Siskos, Matt Popowsky. **Description:** Some college students are quitting school to become Web entrepreneurs.

37077 ■ **"Site-isfaction"** in *Entrepreneur* (Vol. 28, No. 10, October 2000, pp. 146)
Pub: Entrepreneur Media Inc.
Ed: Amanda C. Kooser. **Description:** The article suggests that, with the new "no-HTML-required" Web editors, small companies can design their own Web sites.

37078 ■ **"Sky Dayton"** in *Internet World* (Vol. 6, No. 7, April 1, 2000, pp. 94)
Pub: Mecklermedia Corporation
Ed: Brian Caulfield. **Description:** EarthLink Network founder Sky Dayton plans to launch more new Web-based businesses, now that EarthLink has merged with rival MindSpring. Jake Winebaum's and Dayton's eCompanies, a business incubator for new Web companies, generates efficient Web start-ups within 180 days, including funding. Dayton looks for companies that blend commerce, community, and content.

37079 ■ **"Small But Special"** in *Entrepreneur* (Vol. 28, No. 9, September 2000, pp. 170)
Pub: Entrepreneur Media Inc.
Ed: Paul Edwards and Sarah Edwards. **Description:** The editors tell how a new company can compete in the online book market.

37080 ■ **"A Talk With the Net's Financiers"** in *Internet World* (Vol. 6, No. 6, March 15, 2000, pp. 60)
Pub: Mecklermedia Corporation
Ed: David Lipschultz. **Description:** An interview with five leading venture capitalists to answer questions on

the state of the Internet revolution. Questions are related to topics such as the types of businesses that venture capitalists are looking for and the possibility of emergence of another Yahoo or Cisco. The venture capitalists were also asked about the importance of the CEO in a company and predictions regarding when the Internet explosion was likely to end.

37081 ■ "TechTalk: Big Bargain: 'Chipless' Semiconductor Startups" in *Venture Capital Journal* **(Vol. 42, No. 10, October 2002, pp. 38-39)**
Pub: Thomas Venture Economics
Ed: Ravi Chiruvolu. **Description:** The 'soft silicon' approach to manufacturing chips give customers absolute control over intellectual property, allowing for a faster time to market, and if there is an error in the chip, it can be corrected quickly and inexpensively.

37082 ■ "Third time's the charm" in *BlackEnterprise* **(Vol. 32, No. 2, September 2001, pp. 53)**
Pub: Earl Graves Publishing Co.
Ed: Bridget McCrea. **Description:** Profile of Reggie P. Best of Netilla Networks Inc. Founded in 1999, the 30-employee networking service firm supplies secure Web access to office applications, or simply put, it lets small- to medium-size businesses use the Web as an extension to the office network.

37083 ■ "Venture funding down sharply from June" in *Atlanta Business Chronicle* **(Vol. 24, No. 11, August 17, 2001, pp. 11B)**
Pub: American City Business Journals Inc.
Ed: Tony Heffernan. **Description:** Venture firms are remaining cautious about investing, with only three metro Atlanta-based high-tech startups raising $20.6 million in funding in July. This funding is discussed.

37084 ■ "Waning Risk Tolerance Haunts Tech IPOs" in *Venture Capital Journal* **(Vol. 42, No. 5, May 2002, pp. 6, 8, 10-11)**
Pub: Thomas Venture Economics
Ed: Colleen Marie O'Connor, Robyn Kurdek. **Description:** The level of risk the Initial Public Offering investors are willing to take continues to fall, causing problems for venture-backed technology startups.

37085 ■ "War Doesn't Pay" in *Venture Capital Journal* **(Vol. 42, No. 9, September 2002, pp. 18-23)**
Pub: Thomas Venture Economics
Ed: Michael V. Copeland. **Description:** Although technology to combat terrorism seemed like a good idea to profit from war, neither the government or venture capital firms proceeded with the idea. A listing of anti-terrorism startups funded after September 11 is presented.

37086 ■ "Web.Preneuring" in *Small Business Opportunities* **(Vol. 13, No. 5, September 2001, pp. 46, 48)**
Pub: Harris Publications, Inc.
Description: Profile of Mike Moran, Chris Karl, and Ryan Moran, who launched their online business, Carepackages.com, which enables anyone to send creative gift packages with clever, customized themes.

37087 ■ "What's Up Doc?" in *Entrepreneur* **(Vol. 28, No. 10, October 2000, pp. 132)**
Pub: Entrepreneur Media Inc.
Ed: Geoff Williams. **Description:** A profile of Health4her.com. The founders of this successful Internet-based business tell how they started with their own money.

37088 ■ "Yamacraw fund broadens its focus" in *Atlanta Business Chronicle* **(Vol. 24, No. 8, July 27, 2001, pp. 3A)**
Pub: American City Business Journals Inc.
Ed: Mary Jane Credeur. **Description:** Due to decreased demand for fiber-optics in the broadband industry, the Yamacraw Seed Capital Fund may invest in one or more of the following areas: antenna and wireless technology, data compression and decompression technology, and efficiency solutions for the cable industry. The $5 million fund was started in 1999 for the purpose of creating jobs in the traditionally high-paying technology sector.

37089 ■ "Yesterday & Today: How DFJ Went From Shrimp to Whale" in *Venture Capital Journal* **(Vol. 42, No. 5, May 2002, pp. 12)**
Pub: Thomas Venture Economics
Ed: Alistair Christopher. **Description:** Profile of Draper Fisher Jurvetson, an early-stage information technology firm that evolved from Draper & Associates. In ten years, Draper went from a $20 million fund to closing on a $640 million fund.

ASSOCIATIONS AND OTHER ORGANIZATIONS

37090 ■ Chief Executive Officers Club
47 West St., Ste. 5C
New York, NY 10006
Ph:(212)925-7911
Fax: (212)925-7463
Co. E-mail: main@ceoclubs.org
URL: http://ceoclubs.org
Contact: Joseph R. Mancuso, Pres.
Purpose: Serves as a management resource for entrepreneurial managers and their professional advisers. Selects and makes available publications on developing business plans, organizing an entrepreneurial team, attracting venture capital, and obtaining patents, trademarks, and copyrights. Develops, collects, and disseminates information on business trends, new laws and regulations, and tax guidance. Conducts intensive-study courses and seminars. Has identified stages of the entrepreneurial process and, through essays and audiocassettes, addresses problems pertinent to each stage. **Publications:** *Entrepreneurial Manager: The Entrepreneur's Source of Useful Information* (monthly).

37091 ■ The Entrepreneurship Institute
3592 Corporate Dr., Ste. 101
Columbus, OH 43231
Ph:(614)895-1153
Free: 800-736-3592
Fax: (614)895-1473
Co. E-mail: tei@tei.net
URL: http://www.tei.net
Contact: Dr. Jan W. Zupnick, Pres.
Description: Provides encouragement and assistance to entrepreneurs who operate companies with revenue in excess of $1 million. Unites financial, legal, and community resources to help foster the success of companies. Promotes sharing of information and interaction between members. Operates President's forums and projects which are designed to improve communication between businesses, develop one-to-one business relationships between small and midsize businesses and local resources, provide networking, and stimulate the growth of existing companies. **Publications:** *The President's Forum* (monthly).

EDUCATIONAL PROGRAMS

37092 ■ Hands-on Web Design
EEI Communications
66 Canal Center Plaza, Ste. 200
Alexandria, VA 22314
Ph:(703)683-0683
Fax: (703)683-4915
Co. E-mail: info@eeicommunications.com
URL: http://www.eeicommunications.com
Price: $1,595.00. **Description:** Covers planning and budgeting for a new site, using graphics, designing a site, and publishing the site online. **Locations:** Alexandria, VA.

37093 ■ Internet Marketing
EEI Communications
66 Canal Center Plaza, Ste. 200
Alexandria, VA 22314
Ph:(703)683-0683
Fax: (703)683-4915
Co. E-mail: info@eeicommunications.com
URL: http://www.eeicommunications.com
Price: $695.00. **Description:** Covers how businesses can use the Internet to market products, including increasing traffic to your site, and measuring results. **Locations:** Silver Spring, MD; and Alexandria, VA.

37094 ■ Web Design
EEI Communications
66 Canal Center Plaza, Ste. 200
Alexandria, VA 22314
Ph:(703)683-0683
Fax:(703)683-4915
Co. E-mail: info@eeicommunications.com
URL: http://www.eeicommunications.com
Price: $695.00. **Description:** Covers various aspects of graphic interface design for World Wide Web sites, including site conception; navigational and schematic design; processes from delivery of content to page layout for HTML; editorial, informational, and navigational graphics; and related topics. **Locations:** Silver Spring, MD; and Alexandria, VA.

37095 ■ Web Page Development I
EEI Communications
66 Canal Center Plaza, Ste. 200
Alexandria, VA 22314
Ph:(703)683-0683
Fax: (703)683-4915
Co. E-mail: info@eeicommunications.com
URL: http://www.eeicommunications.com
Price: $395.00. **Description:** Covers the fundamentals of Web page design, including formatting text, using graphics in a Web page, creating links, making simple tables in HTML, and avoiding common page design flaws. **Locations:** Silver Spring, MD; and Alexandria, VA.

37096 ■ Web Page Development II
EEI Communications
66 Canal Center Plaza, Ste. 200
Alexandria, VA 22314
Ph:(703)683-0683
Fax: (703)683-4915
Co. E-mail: info@eeicommunications.com
URL: http://www.eeicommunications.com
Price: $395.00. **Description:** Covers intermediate Web page design techniques, including creating forms, including radio buttons and check boxes, creating transparent and interlaced GIFs, using tables for page layout, and creating client-side image maps. **Locations:** Silver Spring, MD; and Alexandria, VA.

37097 ■ Web Page Development III
EEI Communications
66 Canal Center Plaza, Ste. 200
Alexandria, VA 22314
Ph:(703)683-0683
Fax: (703)683-4915
Co. E-mail: info@eeicommunications.com
URL: http://www.eeicommunications.com
Price: $395.00. **Description:** Covers advanced Web page development techniques, including using frames, animated GIFs, cascading style sheets, and javascript. **Locations:** Silver Spring, MD; and Alexandria, VA.

37098 ■ Writing for the Web
EEI Communications
66 Canal Center Plaza, Ste. 200
Alexandria, VA 22314
Ph:(703)683-0683
Fax: (703)683-4915
Co. E-mail: info@eeicommunications.com
URL: http://www.eeicommunications.com
Price: $6950.00. **Description:** Covers how to write and edit for sites on the World Wide Web, including understanding the Web's strengths and limitations, providing your audience the information it needs, organizing information with flowcharts and site maps, and using techniques of multimedia writing. **Locations:** Silver Spring, MD; and Alexandria, VA.

REFERENCE WORKS

37099 ■ "The Age of Disruption" in *Fast Company* **(September 2001, pp. 18)**
Pub: Fast Company
Description: The ways business and economics are changing are discussed by Harvard's Juan Enriquez, author of the book "As the Future Catches You: How Genomics and Other Forces Are Changing Your Life, Work, Health, and Wealth."

37100 ■ "Arthur Andersen announces YoungIT Entrepreneur Award" in *Crain's Detroit Business* (Vol. 26, No. 12, March 20, 2000, pp. 37)
Pub: Crain Communications, Inc.
Description: Arthur Andersen L.L.P. will sponsor the Young IT Entrepreneur Award at the second annual Michigan Information Technology Business Summit. The award will recognize entrepreneurs under 30 who have started Internet-based businesses.

37101 ■ "Atlanta to play host to cutting-edge tech thinkers" in *Atlanta Business Chronicle* (Vol. 24, No. 15, September 14, 2001, pp. 10A)
Pub: American City Business Journals Inc.
Ed: Mary Jane Credeur. **Description:** The wireless communication industry will meet in September 2001 to plan the industry's outlook and future uses of products such as hands free voice recognition. Industry executives portray how wireless communications can benefit other professions, such as doctors being able to retrieve patient information quickly and easily using quick communication devices.

37102 ■ "Atlanta's Top 10 Audiovisual Companies" in *Atlanta Business Chronicle* (Vol. 24, No. 14, September 7, 2001, pp. S37)
Pub: American City Business Journals Inc.
Description: The top ten audiovisual companies in Atlanta are ranked by the number of Atlanta employees. The top three are MCSi, with 170 employees, Hi-Tech Rentals Inc., with 286 employees, and Tech Rentals Inc., with 68 employees. Statistical data included.

37103 ■ "Attitude Adjustment" in *Fast Company* (November 2001, pp. 46)
Pub: Fast Company
Ed: Polly LaBarre. **Description:** Reviews of books written on attitude and attitude adjustments, focusing on Internet technology sectors.

37104 ■ "Auto News Digest" in *Automotive News* (Vol. 78, No. 6059, September 29, 2003, pp. 36)
Pub: Crain Communications, Inc.
Description: eBay Motors, the online auction service, offers access to Experian Automotive Autocheck in order to purchase vehicle history reports.

37105 ■ "Axion CEO heads in new, profitable direction" in *Atlanta Business Chronicle* (Vol. 24, No. 11, August 17, 2001, pp. 40A)
Pub: American City Business Journals Inc.
Ed: Mary Jane Credeur. **Description:** Axiom Solutions International is now focused on software integration, with the bulk of its business involving linking software via several satellite offices to a central network server for clients. The company became profitable in July and is expected to report revenue of $2.5 million by end-2001. The company and Hansjoerg Beha's management strategy are discussed.

37106 ■ "B2G Supplies Revenue Gains" in *Hispanic Business* (July/August 2002, pp. 32, 34)
Pub: Hispanic Business
Ed: Description: U. S. defense spending boosts revenues for the Hispanic Business High-Tech 50, the nation's largest Hispanic-owned high-tech businesses. A list of the 2002 High-Tech 50 is included, featuring ranking for 2002 and 2001, company/location, CEO, product/service, number of employees, and revenue for 2001.

37107 ■ "Betting on the Net" in *Hispanic Business* (Vol. 22, No. 6, June 2000, pp. 14)
Pub: Hispanic Business
Ed: Jonathan Higuera. **Description:** Profile of Omar S. Rivero, founder and president of the new, Hispanic-run iMillenium Fund. Mr. Rivero says that the Internet will revolutionize the way that companies do business.

37108 ■ "The Big Picture" in *Fast Company* (November 2001, pp. 134)
Pub: Fast Company
Ed: George Anders. **Description:** The five technologies that are gaining universal acceptance and massive impact are profiled.

37109 ■ "Biotech sector seeks advanced degrees" in *Atlanta Business Chronicle* (Vol. 24, No. 11, August 17, 2001, pp. 4B)
Pub: American City Business Journals Inc.
Ed: Erica Stephens. **Description:** Atlanta's biotechnology sector is hiring graduates with advanced degrees as fast as they graduate, but undergraduates are not having the same success. Educators and employers expect that to change as the young biotechnology companies continue to grow. Area research institutions are gearing up to offer undergraduate and high-level degrees in biotechnology and related fields.

37110 ■ "Broad's eye view" in *WorkingWoman* (Vol. 25, No. 8, September 2000, pp. 64)
Pub: Lang Communications Inc.
Description: 85Broads.com founder Janet Tiebout Hanson discussed her aims when starting up the online network aimed at women. The group has over 600 members who have worked for or are currently working for Goldman Sachs.

37111 ■ *Burn Rate: How I Survived the Gold Rush Years on the Internet*
Pub: Simon & Schuster Trade
Ed: Michael Wolff. **Released:** 1998. **Price:** $24.50; $25.00.

37112 ■ "Carry a Tune" in *Fast Company* (August 2001, pp. 38)
Pub: Fast Company
Ed: Alison Overholt. **Description:** Profile of the DUO-64 Digital E-Cassette from Digisette, that comes with software to access a library of more than 17,000 titles of audiobooks and periodicals.

37113 ■ "Cashflow: August 1-15, 2001" in *Red Herring* (No. 105, October 1, 2001, pp. 32)
Pub: Herring Communications
Ed: Mark A. Mowrey. **Description:** Although venture investment in the technology-related sectors remained low, activity in the biotechnology sector was increasing during the period of August 1-15, 2001. Statistical data included.

37114 ■ "Cashflow: August 15-31, 2001" in *Red Herring* (No. 105, October 1, 2001, pp. 36)
Pub: Herring Communications
Ed: Mark A. Mowrey. **Description:** Technology venture investing fell to its lowest level in the period of August 15-31, 2001, with only $353 million dollars being offered to young technology firms. Statistical data included.

37115 ■ "Chandler, Ariz., PostNet Among Chain's Stores that has eBay-Selling Service" in *The Tribune* (November 25, 2003)
Pub: Knight Ridder/Tribune Business News
Ed: Donna Hogan. **Description:** More than 850 shipping-service stores offer assistance to those individuals not familiar with using a computer to sell goods via eBay's auction site.

37116 ■ "Chasing the bottleneck" in *Red Herring* (No. 106, October 15, 2001, pp. 18)
Pub: Herring Communications
Ed: Rafe Needleman. **Description:** An overview of peer-to-peer content distribution networks, including Kontiki, OptiView Technologies, BlueKite.com, and Danger.

37117 ■ "Chip legend Carver Mead mixes analog and digital" in *Red Herring* (No. 106, October 15, 2001, pp. 26)
Pub: Herring Communications
Ed: Dean Takahashi. **Description:** Carver Mead, a pioneer of the chip industry, has started his 26th company with a former student. The Seattle-based communications chip start-up called Impinj, has patented a technique that uses a standard chip-manufacturing process to put analog components into digital chips, with a broad reach from cell phones to microprocessors.

37118 ■ "Choosy tenants are finding bargains, flexibility" in *Atlanta Business Chronicle* (Vol. 24, No. 9, August 3, 2001, pp. 4C)
Pub: American City Business Journals Inc.
Description: According to a worldwide survey, the high-technology company of today wants office space with Internet access, which ranks highest on the list of priorities. Additional options include flexible lease arrangements and closeness to public transportation.

37119 ■ "Climbing tech stocks can't match Nasdaq" in *Atlanta Business Chronicle* (Vol. 25, November 15, 2002, No. 23 pp. 7C)
Pub: American City Business Publications, Inc.
Ed: Tony Heffernan. **Description:** Georgia's high technology stocks grew 6 percent in November 2002, lower than the Nasdaq Composite Index and Dow Jones Industrial Average. A table ranks the most extreme stock increases and declines with details for various companies.

37120 ■ "Commerce: The bar code's high-tech sibling" in *Red Herring* (No. 105, October 1, 2001, pp. 27)
Pub: Herring Communications
Ed: Vinee Tong. **Description:** McDonalds restaurants in the Chicago area will be offering smart key chains to customers enabling them to pay for food in a wireless, cashless transaction. The devices, that use radio frequency identification (RFID), are the same as those being used by ExxonMobil gasoline stations.

37121 ■ "Companies struggle to define technology ROI" in *Atlanta Business Chronicle* (Vol. 25, November 15, 2002, No. 23 pp. 5C)
Pub: American City Business Publications, Inc.
Ed: Don Reichardt. **Description:** Defining the return on investment (ROI) for technology projects is difficult for most companies. Companies currently want to see a definite financial benefit before agreeing to additional investments. Projects are no longer justifiable by claiming they will permit better management.

37122 ■ "Dear Air Over America" in *Red Herring* (No. 105, October 1, 2001, pp. 42-46, 48)
Pub: Herring Communications
Ed: Dan Briody. **Description:** Without 3G spectrum, the U.S. wireless industry will fall further behind its international competitors. The article addresses the government's unwillingness to make the spectrum available in the U.S.

37123 ■ "Digital Rx" in *Fast Company* (May 2001, pp. 183)
Pub: Fast Company
Ed: Scott Kirsner. **Description:** Ways the Detroit Medical Center is using digital technology to repair its fiscal condition are presented.

37124 ■ *Doing Business on the Internet: How to Use the New Technology to Win a Competitive Edge*
Pub: Trans-Atlantic Publications, Inc.
Ed: Graham Jones. **Released:** 1997. **Price:** $19.95.

37125 ■ "A Dose of Change" in *Fast Company* (August 2001, pp. 50)
Pub: Fast Company
Ed: Charles Fishman. **Description:** Profile of Kevin Sharer, CEO of Amgen, a biotech company that makes three leading drugs. Sharer discusses adaptability in the business world.

37126 ■ "dot-com or dot-bomb?" in *Success* (Vol. 47, No. 5, October 2000, pp. 52)
Pub: Success Publishing, Inc.
Ed: Suzy Girard. **Description:** The Internet gold rush may have ended rather abruptly, but opportunities for huge success haven't ended for entrepreneurs who know how to build smart websites.

37127 ■ "E-Hubs: The New B2B Marketplaces" in *Harvard Business Review* (Vol. 78, No. 3, May 2000, pp. 97)
Pub: Harvard Business School Publishing Corp.
Ed: Steven Kaplan, Mohanbir Sawhney. Description: As business-to-business commerce shifts to the Internet, companies that control the online markets will exert enormous influence over the way transactions are carried out, relationships are formed, and profits flow. Understanding how these electronic hubs work is crucial to creating a successful e-business strategy.

37128 ■ "E-Scarcity" in *Entrepreneur* (Vol. 28, No. 8, August 2000, pp. 18)
Pub: Entrepreneur Media Inc.
Ed: Amanda C. Kooser. Description: The importance of choosing the right domain name for your new e-business is discussed.

37129 ■ "eBay" in *Travel Weekly* (Vol. 38, No. 13, December 2003, pp. 32)
Pub: NorthStar Travel Media, LLC
Description: eBay has launched new incentive gift certificates redeemable for merchandise.

37130 ■ "Electric Shoes and 'Breadcrumbs' for the Troops" in *Venture Capital Journal* (Vol. 42, No. 9, September 2002, pp. 26-27)
Pub: Thomas Venture Economics
Ed: Michael V. Copeland. Description: New defense technologies being developed to protect U.S. troops during wartime are presented.

37131 ■ "Entrepreneurs bring Michigan biz to Web" in *Crain's Detroit Business* (Vol. 16, No. 12, March 20, 2000, pp. 42)
Pub: Crain Communications, Inc.
Ed: Matt Roush. Description: The founder of Amazon.com Inc. has patented his system for "one-click" online ordering, leading to litigation among e-commerce providers.

37132 ■ "The fast track to fortitude - Helping harried tech pros confront adversity" in *eWeek* (April 2, 2001, pp. 49)
Pub: ZDNet
Ed: Lisa Kosan. Description: Employers can address adversity on the job by offering retreats or conflict resolution programs, or both, and by training managers to better listen to staff and pick up on stress-laden body language. Peak Learning Inc. offers adversity training to corporations. Its president and CEO, Paul Stoltz, has coined the term adversity quotient (AQ) to describe how people respond to adversity. Stoltz cites research studies that show people with a higher AQ make more money, have a higher level of innovation and are better problem solvers. Persons who score at the top take responsibility for fixing a problem, see problems as a result of circumstances (not their own personal flaws) and perceive problems as limited in scope.

37133 ■ "FC Shortlist" in *Fast Company* (October 2001, pp. 46)
Pub: Fast Company
Description: Review of the book "Gonzo Marketing: Winning Through Worst Practices" by Christopher Locke. The author describes micro-audiences and micro-markets as the new units of growth and competitive advantage. The book by Barbara Waugh, "The Soul in the Computer: The Story of a Corporate Revolutionary" is also reviewed. Ms. Waugh is the worldwide change manager at Hewlett-Packard and co-founder of HP's World e-Inclusion unit.

37134 ■ "Fear of Filing" in *WorkingWoman* (Vol. 25, No. 2, February 2000, pp. 84)
Pub: Lang Communications Inc.
Ed: Tamar Schreibman. Description: An overview of a professional e-organizer who classifies and manages documents to help the business run more smoothly.

37135 ■ "Firms shape students into future workers" in *Atlanta Business Chronicle* (Vol. 24, No. 11, August 17, 2001, pp. 3B)
Pub: American City Business Journals Inc.

Ed: Paige Boweres. Description: Companies, such as Zcorum Inc., are working with Atlanta-area colleges and universities through the Intellectual Capital Partnership Program, a statewide economic development initiative that teams universities with companies so that companies can meet their immediate information technology staff needs. The initiative and its impact are discussed.

37136 ■ "Five Ways to Avoid Disaster" in *Fast Company* (June 2001, pp. 46)
Pub: Fast Company
Description: Neil Isford, president and CEO of Plural, the e-business consulting firm, outlines five ways to avoid technology-enabled disasters.

37137 ■ "Flip the Competition" in *Fast Company* (August 2001, pp. 10)
Pub: Fast Company
Ed: Jennifer Reingold. Description: Review of the book, "The Art of Business Judo" is highlighted. The author, David B. Yoffie, is a master at decoding high-tech strategies.

37138 ■ "From big idea to big bust: the wild ride of Boo.com" in *The New York Times* (December 13 2000, pp. D3, H3)
Pub: The New York Times Company
Ed: Andrew Ross Sorkin. Description: How the dot.com used up $185 million in 18 months and went bankrupt.

37139 ■ "Gad Zeus!" in *Atlanta Business Chronicle* (Vol. 24, No. 10, August 10, 2001, pp. 1B)
Pub: American City Business Journals Inc.
Description: The Zeus Robotic Surgical System, a prototype robotic computer, is one of six undergoing a national trial of robotic surgery. Atlanta Medical Center is one of six undertaking the experiment of the systems, which are made by California-based Computer Motion.

37140 ■ "Georgia CEOs debate global leadership issues" in *Atlanta Business Chronicle* (Vol. 25, November 15, 2002, No. 23 pp. 10C)
Pub: American City Business Publications, Inc.
Ed: Kelly Gay. Description: The Georgia Technology Forum of the Technology Association of Georgia provided Georgia's business leaders with the opportunity to participate in a round table discussion of the most pertinent business issues today. Overall, the panel showed optimism for the future.

37141 ■ "Get the Right Mix of Bricks & Clicks" in *Harvard Business Review* (Vol. 78, No. 3, May 2000, pp. 107)
Pub: Harvard Business School Publishing Corp.
Ed: Ranjay Gulati, Jason Garino. Description: Many of the most innovative Internet players are integrating their virtual and physical company operations. The key to success lies in how you carry out the integration.

37142 ■ "Good night, sweetheart" in *Red Herring* (No. 106, October 15, 2001, pp. 35)
Pub: Herring Communications
Ed: Julie Landry. Description: The failure of Cerulic, the wireless-service provider, will open competition for MobileStart Network and Wayport.

37143 ■ "Greed Is Bad" in *Red Herring* (No. 106, October 15, 2001, pp. 92)
Pub: Herring Communications
Ed: Dan Briody. Description: The entire semiconductor has slumped over the past 12 months, but shares of Rambus have been hit particularly hard due to critical losses in patent litigation lawsuits. Rambus, a semiconductor designer, depends on the aggressive pursuit and defense of its patented intellectual property.

37144 ■ "The Hague: Laws without Borders" in *Red Herring* (No. 106, October 15, 2001, pp. 25-26)
Pub: Herring Communications

Ed: Julia Lawlor. Description: Important information regarding the Hague Convention on Jurisdiction and Foreign Judgments in Civil Matters is covered. The Hague treaty would deal with civil lawsuits and would require that laws regarding matters like libel, copyright, patents, and trademarks - which differ among countries - be enforced uniformly in the 53 nations participating in treaty talks.

37145 ■ "Has the Divide Closed?" in *Hispanic Business* (July/August 2002, pp. 56-57)
Pub: Hispanic Business
Ed: Teresa Talerico. Description: Hispanics are rapidly embracing computer technology, but experts continue to debate the existence of a digital divide.

37146 ■ "He's Giving It Away!" in *Entrepreneur* (Vol. 28, No. 9, September 2000, pp. 228)
Pub: Entrepreneur Media Inc.
Ed: Scott S. Smith. Description: A profile of Anthony D. Parks, Internet multimillionaire, and his commitment to share his success.

37147 ■ "His Word is Law" in *Fast Company* (November 2001, pp. 66)
Pub: Fast Company
Ed: George Anders. Description: Interview with technology guru Gordon Moore, who won fame nearly 40 years ago as the creator of Moore's Law, a radical insight about computing.

37148 ■ "How EDS Got Its Groove Back" in *Fast Company* (November 2001, pp. 106)
Pub: Fast Company
Ed: Bill Breen. Description: Profile of Electronic Data Systems Corporation (EDS), and how Dick Brown turned the company around. Financial information included.

37149 ■ "How To Pick Through the Optics Fire Sale" in *Venture Capital Journal* (Vol. 42, No. 9, September 2002, pp. 5-6)
Pub: Thomas Venture Economics
Ed: Danielle Fugazy, Lawrence Aragon. Description: In the first half of 2002, 63 optical networking companies secured nearly $950 million from more than 260 venture firms. A listing of the top ten deals are presented.

37150 ■ "IBM Has A Vision Too: Here's its answer to all those frustrated tech customers" in *Fortunet* (Vol. 146, Nov. 25, 2002, pp. 158)
Pub: Time Inc.
Ed: David Kirkpatrick. Description: In an interview with Sam Palmisano, IBM CEO, on-demand computing is discussed. On demand-computing entails on-demand business, government, and health care provision.

37151 ■ "Information Technology" in *Ingram's* (Vol. 27, No. 7, July 2001, pp. 76)
Pub: Show Me Publishing, Inc.
Description: Review of Kansas City's growing information technology industry is outlined. Local business professionals have put together a Technology Panel to address the needs of the growing industry.

37152 ■ "Innovation To Go" in *Fast Company* (July 2001, pp. 39)
Pub: Fast Company
Ed: Fara Warner. Description: Sometimes, it's the people who come late to a technology that push the industry. The article shares how firefighters and doctors learned to use their PDAs and became the apostles of the mobile economy.

37153 ■ "Investing in tomorrow" in *Success* (Vol. 47, No. 3, July 2000, pp. 32)
Pub: Success Publishing, Inc.
Ed: Eddy Goldberg. Description: Successful Internet entrepreneurs are changing the nature of giving.

37154 ■ "IPOs/Recent Issues" in *Venture Capital Journal* **(Vol. 41, No. 8, August 2000, pp. 42-45)**
Pub: Venture Economics
Description: Profile of seven venture-backed companies that went public during June 2001, including General Maritime Corporation, Monolithic System Technology Inc., MultiLink Technology Corporation, The Princeton Review, Torch Offshore Inc., Unilab Corporation, and United Surgical Partners International.

37155 ■ "IXL Enterprises to merge with Scient Corp." in *Atlanta Business Chronicle* **(Vol. 24, No. 9, August 3, 2001, pp. 12A)**
Pub: American City Business Journals Inc.
Description: Scient Corp, based in New York and iXL Enterprises Inc of Atlanta, Georgia have agreed to merge. The two companies will then become subsidiaries of the New York-based parent, called Scient Management, the new company will be headed by veteran leaders of both companies.

37156 ■ *Launching a Business on the Web*
Pub: Que
Ed: David Cook. **Released:** 3rd ed. 1997. **Price:** $39.99.

37157 ■ *Launching onto the Web: A Small Business View*
Pub: A K Peters, Ltd.
Ed: William J. Piniarski. **Released:** 1998. **Price:** $48.00.

37158 ■ "The Leap: A Memoir of Love and Madness in the Internet Gold Rush" in *Harvard Business Review* **(Vol. 78, No. 4, July 2000, pp. 152)**
Pub: Harvard Business School Publishing Corp.
Ed: John T. Landry. **Description:** Tom Ashbrook, a former foreign correspondent at the Boston Globe, discusses the history of Internet start-up companies. He focuses on the period before the onset of venture capital firms.

37159 ■ "Lear won't take a back seat" in *Fast Company* **(June 2001, pp. 179)**
Pub: Fast Company
Ed: Fara Warner. **Description:** For decades, Lear Corporation made car seats. Today, with the help of a virtual reality and other digital technologies, Lear makes a whole lot more, and makes it faster.

37160 ■ "Little Things Make a Big Difference at NanoOpto" in *Venture Capital Journal* **(Vol. 42, No. 10, October 2002, pp. 33-34)**
Pub: Thomas Venture Economics
Ed: Ken Ryan. **Description:** The growing field of nanotechnology is examined.

37161 ■ "Local tech firms mine for government gold" in *Atlanta Business Chronicle* **(Vol. 25, November 15, 2002, No. 23 pp. 6C)**
Pub: American City Business Publications, Inc.
Ed: Lee Hall. **Description:** The federal government's technology spending is expected to increase by 9.7 percent to $53.1 billion this year, and many companies are targeting this sector. About 1,100 Georgia firms interested in business with the federal government are currently working with the Georgia Tech Procurement Assistance Center. A ranking of Georgia's top civilian agency and defense department contractors is included.

37162 ■ "Long & Winding Road" in *Small Business Opportunities* **(Vol. 12, No. 5, September 2000, pp. 84)**
Pub: Harris Publications, Inc.
Ed: Marie Sherlock. **Description:** A profile of Andrea Dinard, who spent two decades as a used book shop owner in Portland, Oregon, and turned to the Internet to reduce overhead expenses, only to return to brick and mortar.

37163 ■ "LPs Carry Their Weight Beyond Venture Capital" in *Venture Capital Journal* **(Vol. 42, No. 9, September 2002, pp. 10-11)**
Pub: Thomas Venture Economics
Ed: Carolina Braunschweig. **Description:** A listing of the 10 venture capital firms making the most deals includes information on number of deals, investments and descriptions.

37164 ■ "MAPICS Implements Web-based Self Service Tool to Enhance Customer Service For High Tech Manufacturers" in *PR Newswire* **(Oct. 29, 2001)**
Pub: PR Newswire Association, Inc.
Description: New solutions database offers on-demand support for MAPICS' ERP for extended systems customers. MAPICS is a leading provider of collaborative, extended enterprise applications for manufacturers.

37165 ■ "Mark Hoffman" in *Internet World* **(Vol. 7, No. 1, January 15, 2001, pp. 41)**
Pub: Mecklermedia Corporation
Ed: Ruhan Memishi. **Description:** Mark Hoffman, chairman and CEO of Commerce One is interviewed about his views on business exchanges and his company. Hoffman believes there will be an increase in both business-to-business exchanges and growth in services for a competitive edge.

37166 ■ "Mechanical Minds" in *Red Herring* **(No. 105, October 1, 2001, pp. 64-69)**
Pub: Herring Communications
Ed: Thomas Maeder. **Description:** New surgical methods, devices, and research efforts could revolutionize the treatment of brain disorders. The article offers insight into current approaches, including brain salad surgery, shock therapy, neural networks, sound effects, eyes, and thought into action, which are all yielding new devices to improve quality of life for patients.

37167 ■ "Mediation Year 2051?" in *Dispute Resolution Journal* **(Vol. 56, No. 1, February-April 2001, pp. 24)**
Pub: American Arbitration Association
Ed: Luis Miguel Diaz. **Description:** Given the advances in high technology, the author imagines what might happen to mediators in the future if a software program is developed to replace the need for their services.

37168 ■ "Missing Part of the Equation" in *Hispanic Business* **(July/August 2002, pp. 50, 52, 54)**
Pub: Hispanic Business
Ed: Dora Elia, Gonzalez y Musielak. **Description:** Hispanic women continue to be underrepresented in the sciences and engineering fields. Statistical data included.

37169 ■ "The New Net CEO" in *Harvard Business Review* **(Vol. 78, No. 3, May 2000, pp. S10)**
Pub: Harvard Business School Publishing Corp.
Ed: Chuck Martin. **Description:** Executives in electronic commerce must understand the way in which the industry operates and must focus on the customer.

37170 ■ "A new venue for seeking capital" in *BlackEnterprise* **(Vol. 32, No. 3, October 2001, pp. 56)**
Pub: Earl Graves Publishing Co.
Ed: Paula McCoy-Pinderhughes. **Description:** The first-ever three-day conference aimed at helping African American and other minority technology-based businesses was held in Chantilly, Fairfax County, Virginia, from July 11-13, 2001. The Emerging Business Forum (EBF) will host its second conference next fall.

37171 ■ "No Respect: ONI Systems is the ugly stepchild of the networking market" in *Red Herring* **(No. 105, October 1, 2001, pp. 92)**
Pub: Herring Communications
Ed: Om Malik. **Description:** Profile of ONI Systems, which focuses on metropolitan area networks (MANs)

that connect businesses and other commercial enterprises to the optical fibers beneath city streets using metro dense wave division multiplexing (DWDM) equipment. Despite the fact that ONI has stronger fundamentals than many other networking companies, the firm's stock has fallen along with the telecom equipment sector.

37172 ■ "Nothing but Net" in *Fast Company* **(November 2001, pp. 36)**
Pub: Fast Company
Ed: Alison Overholt. **Description:** Profile of Wi-Fi networks, individual wireless network-access points and cards, which are growing in popularity.

37173 ■ *The Official Internet World Internet Mall*
Pub: Jupitermedia Corp.
Ed: Dave Taylor, Editor. **Price:** $24.99. **Covers:** More than 3,000 Internet sites selling products or services. **Entries Include:** Site name, URL, description of products/services sold.

37174 ■ "The Old Economy Meets the New Economy" in *Fast Company* **(November 2001, pp. 70)**
Pub: Fast Company
Description: Fast Company recently convened a session in Chicago with experts from the world's strongest and oldest brands with the objective of finding new insights on emerging best practices when it comes to customers, technology and business.

37175 ■ *101 Successful Businesses You Can Start on the Internet*
Pub: John Wiley & Sons, Inc.
Ed: Daniel S. Janal. **Released:** 2nd ed. 1997. **Price:** $29.95.

37176 ■ *121 Internet Businesses You Can Start from Your Home: A Guide to Starting a Business Online*
Pub: Actium Publishing, Inc.
Ed: Ron Gielgun. **Released:** 1997. **Price:** $19.95.

37177 ■ "Out of the box and onto the Web" in *Hispanic Business* **(Vol. 22, No. 6, June 2000, pp. 48)**
Pub: Hispanic Business
Ed: Vaughn Hagerty. **Description:** More than 70 percent of the largest Hispanic-owned businesses in the U.S. have an Internet presence in 2000, up from just 13.2 percent in 1996.

37178 ■ "Pay Up" in *PC Computing* **(April 2000, pp. 37)**
Pub: Ziff-Davis Inc.
Description: Electronic bill paying is the next e-commerce industry trend to be tapped. It is predicted that the Web could cut the cost of transactions in half and creditors would be paid more promptly, and checks would not bounce.

37179 ■ "Policy: The future of telecom lies at the steps of Capitol Hill" in *Red Herring* **(No. 106, October 15, 2001, pp. 24-25)**
Pub: Herring Communications
Ed: Dan Briody. **Description:** The impact of new regulations regarding the telecommunications industry will have a tremendous impact on consumers. Officials at Verizon Communications say that separating their retail and wholesale operations would cost nearly $1 billion per state.

37180 ■ "Profile: Don Green reigns as the don of optical networking" in *Red Herring* **(No. 105, October 1, 2001, pp. 44)**
Pub: Herring Communications
Ed: Om Malik. **Description:** Profile of Don Green, the chairman of Advanced Fibre Communications, a publicly traded company in Petaluma, California.

37181 ■ "Putting the 'E' in Your Business" in *Hispanic Business* **(Vol. 22, No. 5, May 2000, pp. 36)**
Pub: Hispanic Business
Ed: Vaughn Hagerty. **Description:** It is important for Hispanic business enterprises to consider how electronic commerce will affect their business. It must be recognized that the Internet is now a permanent feature of the business environment.

37182 ■ "Qwest's Napoleonic Ambitions" in *Red Herring* (No. 106, October 15, 2001, pp. 47-50, 52)
Pub: Herring Communications
Ed: Om Malik. **Description:** Qwest's CEO, Joe Nacchio, wants to redefine the way telecommunications companies operate by offering any service from anywhere in the world. Could Qwest become the world's first supercarrier?

37183 ■ "Rapid Motion" in *Fast Company* (August 2001, pp. 102)
Pub: Fast Company
Ed: Bell Breen. **Description:** Profile of the Canadian company, Research In Motion Ltd (RIM), which makes radio-based modems and wireless handheld communications devices. RIM launched the BlackBerry, a wireless device in January 1999.

37184 ■ "Reaching for less than the sky: as boldest fall, modest dreamers fly on" in *The New York Times* (December 13, 2000, pp. D1, H1)
Pub: The New York Times Company
Ed: Saul Hansell. **Description:** Lessons on what works and what doesn't work for Internet-based businesses.

37185 ■ "Reputations built now will outlast downturn" in *Atlanta Business Chronicle* (Vol. 24, No. 11, August 17, 2001, pp. 9B)
Pub: American City Business Journals Inc.
Ed: Chuck Johnson. **Description:** Measures that can be taken by those in the technology community to overcome the economic difficulties are discussed. These include coming to grips with the fact that times are tough and understanding that all industry sectors have been impacted, just not equally.

37186 ■ "Signing Internet Noncompetes And Working From Home" in *Fortune* (Vol. 141, No. 5, March 6, 2000, pp. 430)
Pub: Time Inc.
Ed: Anne Fisher. **Description:** Questions answered by the editor concern signing noncompete contracts, working from home, and job interviews.

37187 ■ "Slack Off" in *Fast Company* (August 2001, pp. 27)
Pub: Fast Company
Ed: George Anders. **Description:** Who says being productive always means being busy? Not high-tech consultant Tom Demaro, who shares his reasons for being so up on downtime.

37188 ■ *Small Business Internet Connections for Dummies*
Pub: I D G Books Worldwide
Ed: Greg Holden. **Released:** 1998. **Price:** $24.99.

37189 ■ *Small Business Internet Directory for Dummies*
Pub: I D G Books Worldwide
Ed: Esau Barchini. **Released:** 1998. **Price:** $24.99.

37190 ■ *Small Business Web Strategies for Dummies*
Pub: I D G Books Worldwide
Ed: Janine Warner. **Released:** 1998. **Price:** $24.99.

37191 ■ "Small Package" in *Fast Company* (August 2001, pp. 44)
Pub: Fast Company
Ed: Alison Overholt. **Description:** Profile of the Q.USB hard drive, by Agate Technologies Inc, plugs into any PC's port and operates like a standard external hard drive; the Pockey Portable Drive is also previewed.

37192 ■ "Sold for $20 Million" in *Black Enterprise* (Vol. 31, No. 5, December 2000, pp. 30)
Pub: Earl Graves Publishing Co.
Description: A profile of Charles "Chuck" H. James III, who sold his ProduceOnline.com, an online venture looking to streamline transactions between wholesale buyers and sellers of fresh produce.

37193 ■ "SWARM Online services seek small biz through CPAs" in *Accounting Today* (Vol. 14, No. 6, April 3, 2000, pp. 1)
Pub: Faulkner & Gray, Inc.
Ed: John M. Covaleski. **Description:** Internet entrepreneurs are seeking to leverage local tax and accounting firms to electronically deliver business products and services to small and mid-sized businesses.

37194 ■ "Tactics: Semiconductors will lead the tech recovery" in *Red Herring* (No. 105, October 1, 2001, pp. 102)
Pub: Herring Communications
Ed: Arnold Berman. **Description:** Economic indicators suggest that the technology sector is beginning to recover from the technology downturn, and the chip industry will remain at the leading edge of the recovery.

37195 ■ "Taking Stock" in *Fast Company* (May 2001, pp. 44)
Pub: Fast Company
Ed: Polly LaBarre. **Description:** The volatility of technology stocks is discussed, and information regarding the tech sector is covered.

37196 ■ "A Tale of Two Cities" in *Fast Company* (May 2001, pp. 143)
Pub: Fast Company
Ed: Scott Kirsner. **Description:** Seattle Mayor Paul Schell, says that his job is to turn the city into a 'platform for the creative experience', and the city is creating a place where telecommunications, biotech, software, and the Web are all coming together with music, architecture, and art.

37197 ■ "A Tale of Two Cities: Livin' La Vida Boca" in *Fast Company* (May 2001, pp. 155)
Pub: Fast Company
Ed: David Dorsey. **Description:** If you think of Boca Raton, Florida as a retirement village for New York snowbirds, you're wrong. It is the future of the Internet, and Boca-technos are convinced that they live at the epicenter of a new age in computing, a major global center for wireless technology, software development, and Internet traffic.

37198 ■ "Tech Detective: Lasers at PARC" in *Venture Capital Journal* (Vol. 42, No. 10, October 2002, pp. 31-32)
Pub: Thomas Venture Economics
Ed: Michael V. Copeland. **Description:** Profile of PARC laboratory located at the Palo Alto Research Center in California. PARC is an expert in laser technology.

37199 ■ "Tech firms uncertain about tech forecast" in *Atlanta Business Chronicle* (Vol. 25, November 15, 2002, No. 23 pp. 2C)
Pub: American City Business Publications, Inc.
Ed: Charles Davidson. **Description:** Many technology executives in Atlanta expect customers to buy more business products or services during the first or second quarter of 2003, and IDC expects the global information technology market to grow 9 percent to $1 trillion during 2003. Details on technology spending for various companies are included.

37200 ■ "TechTalk: How Maple Got Out of a Sticky Situation" in *Venture Capital Journal* (Vol. 42, No. 9, September 2002, pp. 38-39)
Pub: Thomas Venture Economics
Ed: Ravi Chiuvolu. **Description:** Problems faced by the firm funding Maple Optical, a company building technology for next-generation networks are investigated. Ravi Chiruvolu, general partner of Charter Venture Capital, advises venture capitalists to pay attention to the outside world when investing in companies.

37201 ■ "Telecom Services: Finding new life in a troubled industry" in *Red Herring* (No. 106, October 15, 2001, pp. 74-75)
Pub: Herring Communications
Ed: Lee Bruno. **Description:** A prospective of the telecommunications industry is highlighted offering information about how the industry is facing technical problems along with the slowing economy. Statistical data included.

37202 ■ "Telecommunications Sector Analysis" in *Red Herring* (No. 106, October 15, 2001, pp. 86-87)
Pub: Herring Communications
Description: Analysis of the telecommunications sector is presented in graphs and charts from 1999 through 2000, including fiber-optic service, local service, operational support systems, and voice over IP.

37203 ■ "Terrorism: After attacks, survivors use the Internet to say 'I'm OK'" in *Red Herring* (No. 106, October 15, 2001, pp. 28)
Pub: Herring Communications
Ed: Joanna Pearlstein. **Description:** It is the very technological contributions made by Daniel Lewin, the cofounder and chief technology officer of Akamai Technologies, that helped survivors of the September 11th attack on the World Trade Center to contact loved ones to let them know they were okay. Unfortunately, Mr. Lewin was among those killed when a Los Angeles-bound American Airlines jet crashed into one of the towers that day. The Internet proved a vital source for Americans, as well as those abroad, when telephone circuits became overloaded.

37204 ■ "A Touch of Class" in *Entrepreneur* (Vol. 28, No. 10, October 2000, pp. 29)
Pub: Entrepreneur Media Inc.
Ed: Amanda C. Kooser. **Description:** E-mail has evolved into a prime marketing tool for businesses. Jupiter Communications predicts the e-mail marketing industry will reach $7.3 billion by 2005.

37205 ■ "U.S. Needs Help from the Private Sector to Combat Terrorism" in *Venture Capital Journal* (Vol. 42, No. 9, September 2002, pp. 40)
Pub: Thomas Venture Economics
Ed: Leighton Read. **Description:** The private sector will play a major role in homeland security by developing and producing antiterrorism countermeasures.

37206 ■ "Venture Capital: First-round investments: now for the small and the brave" in *Red Herring* (No. 105, October 1, 2001, pp. 38-39)
Pub: Herring Communications
Ed: Lawrence Aragon, Julie Landry. **Description:** Venture capitalists are taking more time before investing in new investments and spending more time trying to raise follow-on rounds for their existing companies. Statistical data included.

37207 ■ *Web Commerce: Building a Digital Business*
Pub: John Wiley & Sons, Inc.
Ed: Kate Maddox and Dana Blankenhorn. **Released:** 1998. **Price:** $29.95 (cloth).

37208 ■ "Web Wise" in *Harvard Business Review* (Vol. 78, No. 3, May 2000, pp. S4)
Pub: Harvard Business School Publishing Corp.
Ed: Patricia B. Seybold. **Description:** Electronic commerce can be successful through the careful management of the operation.

37209 ■ "Web.Preneuring" in *Small Business Opportunities* (Vol. 14, No. 1, January 2002, pp. 88)
Pub: Harris Publications, Inc.
Ed: Marie Sherlock. **Description:** Ways to jumpstart an online business with a customer loyalty program are presented, including a reward system.

37210 ■ "Where is the new frontier of innovation?" in *Fast Company* (September 2001, pp. 128)
Pub: Fast Company
Ed: Fara Warner. **Description:** Fast-paced experimentation, distributed intelligence, total teamwork: the scientific formulation behind the new economy is still disrupting the status quo. In this case, 20,000 leagues under the sea; to appreciate the world-changing impact of digital technology, explore the world of the Monterey Bay Aquarium Research Institute.

37211 ■ **"Wireless security catches the eye of venture capitalists"** in *Red Herring* (No. 106, October 15, 2001, pp. 34-35)
Pub: Herring Communications
Ed: Scott Tyler Shafer. **Description:** The future of wireless is discussed. Several obstacles are addressed, including security and network management. Venture capitalists are backing startups creating the key technologies for the wireless industry.

37212 ■ **"Witness Systems adopts anti-takeover plan"** in *Atlanta Business Chronicle* (Vol. 25, November 15, 2002, No. 23 pp. 3A)
Pub: American City Business Publications, Inc.
Ed: Mary Jane Credeur. **Description:** Witness Systems Inc. has adopted a "shareholder rights" plan in 2002 to prevent hostile takeovers. The company believes its stock is currently undervalued. Other area technology companies have recently adopted similar plans.

37213 ■ **"Wrestling for Web dominance"** in *Hispanic Business* (Vol. 22, No. 7-8, July-August 2000, pp. 106)
Pub: Hispanic Business
Ed: Vaughn Hagerty. **Description:** Global consolidation is taking place among the Internet's Hispanic-targeted Web sites. Among the companies set to gain a dominant position in the sector is Spanish telecom provider Terra Networks with its proposed $12.5 billion acquisition of Web service provider Lycos.

37214 ■ **"Yaknow?"** in *Entrepreneur* (Vol. 28, No. 10, October 2000, pp. 15)
Pub: Entrepreneur Media Inc.
Ed: Cynthia Harrington. **Description:** In the quickly evolving e-business world, one of the most important tasks facing netpreneurs is education. The latest changes in technology, marketing trends, evolving business models and financing deals are high priorities.

CONSULTANTS

37215 ■ **Creative Computer Resources Inc.**
5001 Horizons Dr., Ste. 200
Columbus, OH 43220
Ph:(614)384-7557
Fax: (614)573-6331
Co. E-mail: team@Planet-CCR.com
URL: http://www.planet-ccr.com

E-mail: team@Planet-CCR.com
Scope: Offers information systems support, custom software development, web site design, development and implementation. Provides information technology support and management services to small and mid-size businesses.

RESEARCH CENTERS

37216 ■ **Center for the New West**
600 World Trade Center
1625 Broadway
Denver, CO 80202
Ph:(303)572-5400
Free: 800—795-9378
Fax: (303)572-5499
Contact: John Maddox, Pres.
Scope: Trade, technology, and education. Asian Pacific Rim region; human capital, including demographic trends and their impact on economic growth and productivity; and area and regional development, including infrastructure and innovative institutional arrangements. **Services:** Leadership development programs, including advisory services, training and technical assistance, and leadership forums and networks. **Publications:** Points West Publication Series: Advisories, Special Reports, and Newsletter (quarterly); Profile of the West Compendium. **Educational Activities:** Center Roundtable; Crossroads Seminars; National conferences.

37217 ■ **Corporation for Enterprise Development**
777 N Capitol St. NE, Ste. 800
Washington, DC 20002
Ph:(202)408-9788
Fax: (202)408-9793
Co. E-mail: andrea@cfed.org
URL: http://www.cfed.org
Contact: Andrea Levere, Pres.
E-mail: andrea@cfed.org
Scope: Entrepreneurial and asset-building policy initiatives at the local, state, and federal levels. Specific studies include economic climate of the states, job creation, globalization, seed capital assessment, international exchange, microenterprise, development finance, and state capital market analysis. Emphasizes economic empowerment of economically disadvantaged populations. **Publications:** Business Climate Tax Index; The Development Report Card for the States (annually); Investing In Technical Report

Series; State Enterprise Development Implementation Packets; State Strategy Memoranda. **Educational Activities:** National IDA Learning Conference (annually).

37218 ■ **University of California, Los Angeles–Harold and Paulina Price Center for Entrepreneurial Studies**
Anderson Graduate School of Management
110 Westwood Plz., Rm. C 305
PO Box 951481
Los Angeles, CA 90095-1481
Ph:(310)825-2985
Fax: (310)206-9102
Co. E-mail: esctr@anderson.ucla.edu
URL: http://www.anderson.ucla.edu/research/esc/
Contact: Alfred E. Osbome, Dir.
E-mail: esctr@anderson.ucla.edu
Scope: Entrepreneurship, venture initiation, family business, and interdisciplinary studies of business development, including finance, operations, information systems, organization, behavior, and oral histories of entrepreneurs. **Educational Activities:** Annual entrepreneurship conference for business people and students, in the spring; Research grants for selected faculty members for entrepreneurially related work; Roundtable sessions, entrepreneur-in-residence series, mentor programs, speaker series, venture proposal competitions, and student investment fund; Sponsors certificate programs in management development for entrepreneurs in various industries, including telecommunications and directors of early child care programs; Venture Fellows Program.

37219 ■ **University of South Florida–Small Business Development Center**
1101 Channelside Dr., Ste. 210
Tampa, FL 33602
Ph:(813)905-5800
Fax: (813)905-5801
Co. E-mail: sbdc@coba.usf.edu
URL: http://sbdc.usf.edu
Contact: Irene Hurst, Dir.
E-mail: sbdc@coba.usf.edu
Scope: Small business operations, entrepreneurship, and success and failure factors for small business development and management, including developing business plans, marketing strategy, and loan packages. **Services:** Counseling. **Publications:** Entrepreneurial Training Schedule (monthly); Minding Your Own Business (3/year). **Educational Activities:** Entrepreneurship seminars; Government contracting trade fair; Seminars on Small Business Management (monthly); Small Business Trade Conference; Training; Women Executive Forum.

Environmentally Responsible Business Practices

START-UP INFORMATION

37220 ■ "Do This, Get Rich" in *Business 2.0* (Vol. 6, May 2005, No. 4, pp. 78-86)
Pub: Time, Inc.
Ed: Michael V. Copeland, Om Malik, Erick Schonfeld.
Description: Profiles of the eleven hottest business opportunities are presented, including computer upgrades, advertising on the Web, specialty baby furniture, professional medical employment services, interior design for hotels, Web-enabled subscription and service monitoring, search engines for podcasts, RFID tags to track drugs and supplies in hospitals, software to save energy in homes and businesses, software and hardware to monitor and control a boat's onboard systems.

37221 ■ "Eco-Preneuring" in *Small Business Opportunities* (Vol. 13, No. 6, November 2001, pp. 42, 44)
Pub: Harris Publications, Inc.
Ed: John Marshall. **Description:** Profile of Eric Floyd, president and owner of EDF Associates, a Southern California-based environmental consulting firm.

ASSOCIATIONS AND OTHER ORGANIZATIONS

37222 ■ American Public Information on the Environment
PO Box 676
Northfield, MN 55057-0676
Free: 800-320-2743
Fax: (507)645-5724
Co. E-mail: info@americanpie.org
URL: http://www.AmericanPIE.org
Contact: Brad Easterson, Exec. Dir.
Membership: Individuals, organizations, and businesses. **Purpose:** Promotes "development of a land ethic and ecological consciousness essential to sustaining the environment". Gathers and disseminates information on "environmental quality, protection of natural resources and promotion of environmental health for all elements of the biotic community".

37223 ■ Association of Municipal Recycling Coordinators
127 Wyndham St. N, Ste. 100
Guelph, ON, Canada N1H 4E9
Ph:(519)823-1990
Fax: (519)823-0084
Co. E-mail: amrc@amrc.ca
URL: http://www.amrc.ca
Contact: Ben Bennett, Projects and
        Communications Mgr.
Membership: Municipal waste management professionals. **Purpose:** Promotes more effective and environmentally sustainable removal of solid wastes. Facilitates sharing of municipal waste management, reduction, recycling, and reuse information and facilities. Conducts continuing professional education

courses for members; operates job hotline; represents members' interests before government agencies and the public. Sponsors research; compiles statistics. **Publications:** *For R Information* (quarterly).

37224 ■ Canadian Association on Water Quality–Association canadienne sur la qualite de l'eau
PO Box 5050
Burlington, ON, Canada L7R 4A6
Ph:(905)336-6291
Fax: (905)336-4877
Co. E-mail: tyagi@inrs-eau.uquebec.ca
URL: http://www.cawq.ca
Contact: Dr. Yves Comeau, Pres.
Description: Corporations, learned societies, universities, organizations, and individuals. Promotes research on water quality and water pollution. Furthers the exchange of information and practical application of such research for public benefit. **Publications:** *Water Quality Research Journal of Canada* (quarterly). **Telecommunication Services:** electronic mail, yves.comeau@polymtl.ca.

37225 ■ Canadian Environmental Network–Reseau canadien de l'environnement
300-945 Wellington St.
Ottawa, ON, Canada K1Y 2X5
Ph:(613)728-9810
Fax: (613)728-2963
Co. E-mail: info@cen-rce.org
URL: http://www.cen-rce.org
Contact: Brigitte Gagne, Exec. Dir.
Membership: Environmental organizations. **Purpose:** Seeks to advance the projects and activities of members. Promotes ecologically sustainable development. Serves as a clearinghouse on environmental issues; provides support and assistance to members. **Publications:** *Canadian Environmental Network News* (annual).

37226 ■ Canadian Water Resources Association–Association Canadienne des Resources Hydriques
280 Albert St., Ste. 900
Ottawa, ON, Canada K1P 5G8
Ph:(613)237-9363
Fax: (613)594-5190
Co. E-mail: cwranat@aic.ca
URL: http://www.cwra.org
Contact: Russell Boals, Pres.
Description: Corporations, government agencies, public libraries, and individuals with an interest in water resources. Seeks to increase public awareness and understanding of water resources; serves as a forum for the exchange of information relating to their management and use. Encourages governments at all levels to recognize the importance of water as a resource and supports formulation of appropriate water use policies. Conducts educational programs. **Publications:** *Canadian Water Resources Journal* (quarterly); *ICID Bulletin* (quarterly); *Water News* (quarterly). **Telecommunication Services:** electronic mail, services@aic.ca.

37227 ■ Composting Council of Canada–Conseil canadien du Compostage
16, rue Northumberland St.
Toronto, ON, Canada M6H 1P7
Ph:(416)535-0240
Free: 877-571-GROW
Fax: (416)536-9892
Co. E-mail: ccc@compost.org
URL: http://www.compost.org
Contact: Susan Antler, Exec. Dir.
Purpose: Serves to advocate and advance composting and compost usage across Canada. Serves as the central resource and network for the composting industry in Canada. Contributes to the environmental sustainability of communities. Sponsors International Composting Awareness Week; "Plant a Row Grow a Row". Conducts seminars and educational programs. Compiles statistics, maintains speakers' bureau. **Publications:** *Communique*.

37228 ■ Ecology Action Centre
2705 Fern Ln.
Halifax, NS, Canada B3K 4L3
Ph:(902)429-2202
Fax: (902)405-3716
Co. E-mail: eac@ecologyaction.ca
URL: http://www.ecologyaction.ca
Contact: Carla Vanderberg, Office Mgr.
Description: Works to develop solutions to ecological problems. Fosters communication between members. **Publications:** *Between the Issues* (quarterly); Brochures (periodic); Reports (periodic).

37229 ■ Green Hotels Association
PO Box 420212
Houston, TX 77242-0212
Ph:(713)789-8889
Fax: (713)789-9786
Co. E-mail: info@greenhotels.com
URL: http://www.greenhotels.com
Contact: Patricia Griffin
Membership: Hotels, motels, inns, bed and breakfasts, and all other lodging establishments with an interest in protecting the environment. Encourages, promotes and supports ecological consciousness in the hospitality industry. **Publications:** *Greening Newsletter* (bimonthly); *Membership Conservation Guidelines and Ideas*. **Telecommunication Services:** electronic mail, green@greenhotels.com.

37230 ■ National Office Paper Recycling Project
1620 Eye St. NW
Washington, DC 20006
Ph:(202)293-7330
Fax: (202)293-2352
Co. E-mail: jwelfley@usmayors.org
URL: http://www.usmayors.org/uscm/uscm_
        projects_services/environment/national_paper_
        recycling_project.html
Contact: David Gatton
Membership: Corporations committed to increasing their recycling of office paper and use of recycled products. **Purpose:** Seeks to triple the amount of paper recycled by corporations. Disseminates infor-

mation. **Publications:** *Office Paper Recycling Guide*; *Recycling At Work* (quarterly); *Toner Cartridge Recycling*.

37231 ■ Pellet Fuels Institute
1901 N Moore St., Ste. 600
Arlington, VA 22209-1708
Ph:(703)522-6778
Fax: (703)522-0548
Co. E-mail: pfimail@pelletheat.org
URL: http://www.pelletheat.org
Contact: Don Kaiser, Exec. Dir.
Membership: Pellet and briquette manufacturers; processors of wood, and agricultural fuels; pellet burner manufacturers and distributors; combustion and handling equipment manufacturers and distributors; industry suppliers; and companies and organizations that use wood, agricultural residues, and paper as fuel. **Purpose:** Promotes the increased use of pellets, briquettes, chips, and other renewable fiber fuels. Supports lobbying efforts promoting fiber fuels. Acts as an information clearinghouse among members. **Publications:** *PFI Newsletter* (bimonthly).

37232 ■ Pembina Institute for Appropriate Development
Box 7558
Drayton Valley, AB, Canada T7A 1S7
Ph:(780)542-6272
Fax: (780)542-6464
Co. E-mail: info@pembina.org
URL: http://www.pembina.org
Contact: Marlo Raynolds, Exec. Dir.
Membership: Organizations and individuals with an interest in environmental protection and global development. **Purpose:** Promotes increased public awareness of environmental and development issues. Conducts environmental research and educational programs; provides corporate environmental strategic management services, sponsors charitable activities.

37233 ■ Planetary Association for Clean Energy–Societe Planetaire pour l'Assainissement de l'Energie
100 Bronson Ave., No. 1001
Ottawa, ON, Canada K1R 6G8
Ph:(613)236-6265
Fax: (613)235-5876
Co. E-mail: pacenet@canada.com
URL: http://pacenet.homestead.com
Contact: Dr. Andrew Michrowski, Pres.
Description: Researchers, individuals, corporations, and institutions worldwide seeking to facilitate research, development, demonstration, and evaluation of clean energy systems. Defines clean energy systems as those that utilize natural sources, and are inexpensive, non-polluting, and universally applicable. Concerns include the bioeffects of low-level electromagnetics, bioenergetics, new energy technology, decontamination of nuclear and toxic wastes, production of clean water from ambient air, and pesticide and fertilizer-free ultra-productive agricultural practices. Tests and recommends products that facilitate the implementation of clean energy systems. Serves as a consultant to governments and other agencies. Maintains speaker's bureau. **Publications:** Newsletter (periodic); Monograph (periodic); Proceedings (periodic).

37234 ■ Pollution Probe
625 Church St., Ste. 402
Toronto, ON, Canada M4Y 2G1
Ph:(416)926-1907
Fax: (416)926-1601
Co. E-mail: pprobe@pollutionprobe.org
URL: http://www.pollutionprobe.org
Contact: Ken Ogilvie, Exec. Dir.
Description: Works to define environmental problems through research; seeks to raise public awareness of environmental issues through education; lobbies for environmental protection and remediation before government agencies and industrial associations. Focuses on smog and climate change, reduction and elimination of mercury in water, child health and the environment, indoor air quality, and water quality. **Publications:** *ProbeAbilities* (3/year).

37235 ■ Recycling Council of Alberta
PO Box 23
Bluffton, AB, Canada T0C 0M0
Ph:(403)843-6563
Fax: (403)843-4156
Co. E-mail: info@recycle.ab.ca
URL: http://www.recycle.ab.ca
Contact: Al Tinholt, Pres.-Elect
Description: Promotes and facilitates waste reduction, recycling and resource conservation in the province of Alberta. **Publications:** *Connector* (quarterly); *Enviro Business Guide*.

37236 ■ Resource Efficient Agricultural Production - Canada
21, 111 Lakeshore Rd.
Box 125, Maison Glenaladale
Ste.-Anne-de-Bellevue, QC, Canada H9X 3V9
Ph:(514)398-7743
Fax: (514)398-7972
Co. E-mail: info@reap-canada.com
URL: http://www.reap-canada.com
Contact: Roger Samson, Exec. Dir.
Membership: Agricultural researchers and educators. **Purpose:** Promotes development and implementation of environmentally sustainable and economically viable agricultural techniques in Canada and internationally. Conducts research and disseminates results in areas including ecology, energy, agrifibre, and food production. Maintains on-farm research programs. **Publications:** Newsletter (annual).

37237 ■ Saskatchewan Environmental Society
Box 1372
Saskatoon, SK, Canada S7K 3N9
Ph:(306)665-1915
Fax: (306)665-2128
Co. E-mail: info@environmentalsociety.ca
URL: http://www.environmentalsociety.ca
Contact: Ann Coxworth
Description: Seeks to support and encourage the creation of a global community in which all needs are met in sustainable ways. **Publications:** *SES Newsletter* (bimonthly).

37238 ■ Society for Corporate Environmental and Social Responsibility
Dalhousie University
6100 University Ave.
Halifax, NS, Canada B3H3J5
Ph:(902)441-6756
Fax: (902)494-3728
Co. E-mail: cesr@dal.ca
URL: http://societyforcorporateenvironmentalandsocialresponsibility.ca
Contact: Kable Frank, Chair
Description: Promotes sustainable development, social justice, peace, corporate responsibility, ethics, democracy, good governance, and human rights.

37239 ■ Society Promoting Environmental Conservation
2150 Maple St.
Vancouver, BC, Canada V6J 3T3
Ph:(604)736-7732
Fax: (604)736-7115
Co. E-mail: info@spec.bc.ca
URL: http://www.spec.bc.ca
Contact: Gerry Thorne, Sec.
Description: Promotes environmental research, advocacy, and education. Operates the Vancouver Environmental Information Centre. **Publications:** *SPECTRUM* (quarterly). **Telecommunication Services:** electronic mail, gerrythorne@shaw.ca.

37240 ■ Women's Healthy Environments Network
24 Mercer St., Ste. 101
Toronto, ON, Canada M5V 1H3
Ph:(416)928-0880
Fax: (416)928-9640
Co. E-mail: when@web.ca
URL: http://www.whenvironments.ca
Contact: Kerri Brock, Co-Chair
Description: Women experts in environmental studies and issues. Works to implement community

development projects to improve the environment. Provides a forum for discussion, information exchange, and the conducting of research related to women in the fields of planning, health, workplace, design, economy, urban and rural sociology, and community development. Initiates and organizes community projects. Advocates environmental protection, anti-discriminatory zoning practices, and the development of affordable housing. **Publications:** *Whitewash*; *Women and Environments* (quarterly).

37241 ■ Yukon Conservation Society
302 Hawkins St.
Whitehorse, YT, Canada Y1A 1X6
Ph:(867)668-5678
Fax: (867)668-6637
Co. E-mail: ycs@ycs.yk.ca
URL: http://www.yukonconservation.org
Contact: Lisa Taylor
Description: Seeks to protect Canada's natural environment; particularly that of the Yukon region. Encourages the conservation of Yukon wilderness, wildlife and natural resources. **Publications:** *Walk Softly* (quarterly). **Telecommunication Services:** electronic mail, ycsoffice@ycs.yk.ca.

DIRECTORIES OF EDUCATIONAL PROGRAMS

37242 ■ *Recycling in America*
Pub: ABC-CLIO
Contact: Debra Kimball Strong, Author
Released: latest edition 2nd. **Price:** $25, individuals eBook. **Publication Includes:** Lists of private, state, and federal agencies and organizations, and online sources. Principal content of publication is a history of recycling; brief biographical section; facts on recycled materials; and laws and regulations.

REFERENCE WORKS

37243 ■ "Activists, pragmatists, technophiles, and tree-huggers?" in *Journal of Business Ethics* (Vol. 28, No. 3, December 1, 2000, pp. 211)
Pub: Kluwer Academic Publishers
Ed: Walter Wehrmeyer, Margaret McNeil. **Description:** The gender differences in employee's environmental attitudes is explored.

37244 ■ "Architects reframe strategy to suit slow year" in *Atlanta Business Chronicle* (Vol. 25, No. 21, November 1, 2002, pp. 20C)
Pub: American City Business Publications, Inc.
Ed: Tom Barry. **Description:** Atlanta, Georgia area architectural firms are not finding much work, but are procuring jobs in the public and institutional areas. Architectural firms have been focusing on the environmental friendliness of buildings. Heery International Inc. is currently involved in a $28.5 million project with Southeast Regional Archives that will be able to store 230,000 square feet of records.

37245 ■ "Are Green Funds True To Their Colors?" in *Fortune* (Vol. 151, February 7, 2005, No. 3, pp. 106)
Pub: Time Inc.
Ed: Marc Gunther. **Description:** Many social or environmental mutual funds do not own shares in any companies that promote alternative energy, organic farming, or other solutions to environmental problems. An example of such a practice is highlighted by the Sierra Club Stock Fund, that promises to 'invest for sustainable growth' but does not own shares in any environmental businesses.

37246 ■ *Audubon House: Building the Environmentally Responsible, Energy-Efficient Office*
Pub: John Wiley & Sons, Inc.
Ed: National Audubon Society staff. **Released:** 1994. **Price:** $24.95.

37247 ■ "Basis of Corporate Average Fuel Economy Could Change" in *Detroit Free Press* **(April 11, 2003)**
Pub: Knight-Ridder/Tribune Business News
Ed: Jocelyn Parker. Description: Environmentalists and safety groups are concerned that a new proposed change in government mandates for fuel economy could cause automakers to make larger, less fuel-efficient vehicles.

37248 ■ "The Best Sunset Provision Ever" in *Inc.* **(October 2005, pp. 34)**
Pub: Inc. Magazine
Ed: Lora Kolodny. Description: It is expected that all companies, regardless of size and industry, will benefit from the new Energy Act that extends daylight-savings time by four weeks, beginning March 2007. The Journal of Banking and Finance reports daylight-savings time will promote a healthier economy and higher stock market returns because exposure to full-spectrum light early in the day improves mood and concentration of employees.

37249 ■ "Building Design" in *Inc.* **(Volume 27, June 2005, No. 6, pp. 65-66)**
Pub: Inc. Magazine
Ed: Dimitra Kessenides. Description: Tax breaks, lower electric bills, and satisfied customers are a few of the benefits firms are experiencing after remodeling office space and buildings to conserve energy and protect the environment.

37250 ■ "Burst of Energy" in *Entrepreneur. com* **(Vol. 34, February 2006, No. 2, pp. 46)**
Pub: Entrepreneur Media Inc.
Ed: Kristin Ohlson. Description: Renewable, clean energy is a growing sector. Liquid Resources produces nearly 3 million gallons of ethanol annually, with water as its only waste product.

37251 ■ *Business & the Environment*
Pub: Island Press
Ed: Richard Welford. Released: 1995.

37252 ■ *The Business Environmental Handbook*
Pub: Oasis Press
Ed: Marty Westerman. Released: 1993. Price: $19. 95 (paper); $39.95 (ringbound paper). Description: Provides information on how businesses can profit by being environmentally aware, including recycling, precycling, conservation, and "green marketing" to customers.

37253 ■ *Business Guide to Waste Reduction and Recycling*
Pub: DIANE Publishing Co.
Released: 1993. Price: $60.00 (paper). Description: Covers how to develop and operate waste-reduction and recycling programs. Contains sample forms and schedules for administering conservation programs, cost-benefit worksheets, and sample contracts for vendors.

37254 ■ "California Regulator Seeks Cut in Lawn-Mower Emissions" in *Daily News* **(April 11, 2003)**
Pub: Knight-Ridder/Tribune Business News
Ed: Kerry Cavanaugh. Description: California State regulators are considering making major reductions in emissions from lawn mowers and are offering new electric lawn mowers for $150 along with the trade-in of old gas-powered mowers.

37255 ■ "Chicago Can Be Greener" in *Crain's Chicago Business* **(Vol. 30, January 2007, No. 1, pp. 15)**
Pub: Crain Communications, Inc.
Ed: Sarah A. Klein. Description: Overview of possible solutions to Chicago's problem of not putting enough resources into reducing carbon emissions and slowing global warming.

37256 ■ "Chrysler to Introduce Cleaner Diesel Engines" in *Altanta Journal-Constitution* **(January 24, 2007)**
Pub: Cox Newspapers, Inc.

Ed: Rob Douthit. Description: Chrysler will sell a heavy-duty diesel pickup truck meeting new emissions standards and a new diesel version of Jeep Grand Cherokee.

37257 ■ "Cleantech Becomes Catalyst" in *Crain's Detroit Business* **(Vol. 22, November 20, 2006, No. 47, pp. 13)**
Pub: Crain Communications Inc. - Detroit
Ed: Tom Henderson. Description: Financial investment firm focuses in on green tech businesses for venture capital and funding. Brighton based firms now has three subsidiaries and holds trade shows in the U.S. and Europe to match investors with companies that market clean products and technology.

37258 ■ "Common-Sense Approach to 'Safe' Building Materials" in *Business Journal-Milwaukee* **(Vol. 20, No. 43, July 11, 2003, pp. A13)**
Pub: American City Business Journals, Inc.
Ed: Kathy Bergstrom. Description: Safe Building Solutions owner, Andy Pace, will construct his home with the environmentally friendly building materials that he sells.

37259 ■ *The Company We Keep: Reinventing Small Business for People, Community, and Place*
Pub: Chelsea Green Publishing
Ed: John Abrams. Released: May 2005. Price: $27. 50 (US), $31.50 (Canadian). Description: The new business trend in social entrepreneurship as a business plan enables small business owners to meet the triple bottom line of profits for people (employees and owners), community, and the environment.

37260 ■ *Corporate Radar: Tracking the Forces That Are Shaping Your Business*
Pub: Amacom
Ed: Karl Albrecht. Released: October 1999. Price: $27.95. Description: Ways for a business to assess the forces operating in the external environment that can affect the business and solutions to protect from outside threats.

37261 ■ *Costing the Earth: The Challenge for Governments, the Opportunities for Business*
Pub: Harvard Business School Press
Ed: Frances Cairncross. Released: 1993. Price: $14. 95 (paper).

37262 ■ "Detroit, Inkster companies lead in removal of Rouge oil spill" in *Crain's Detroit Business* **(Vol. 18, No. 22, June 3, 2002, pp. 37)**
Pub: Crain Communications Inc. - Detroit
Ed: Joe Truini. Description: Investigators are focusing on those responsible for a mysterious oil spill in the Rouge River April 9. The cost of the cleanup has reached $3.5 million, and the culprit may have to pay as much as three times the cleanup costs plus fines of up to $27,500 per day.

37263 ■ "Diesel Gets Cleaner and Greener" in *Business Week* **(February 20, 2006, No. 3972, pp. 49)**
Pub: McGraw-Hill Companies
Ed: Gail Edmondson. Description: DaimlerChrysler has engineered a new emissions technology that promises to burn diesel fuels cleanly as gasoline. The automobile manufacturer has also unveiled its clean-diesel exhaust system in its Mercedes E-class sedans.

37264 ■ "Distributed Generation: Breaking the grid lock" in *Red Herring* **(No. 103, September 1, 2001, pp. 76-77)**
Pub: Herring Communications
Ed: Linda Rastelli. Description: In-depth article discussing legislation across the United States, that is working to restructure state electricity industries.

37265 ■ "Eco-Preneuring" in *Small Business Opportunities* **(Vol. 13, No. 5, September 2001, pp. 88, 90)**
Pub: Harris Publications, Inc.

Ed: Pat Gilbers. Description: Profile of Pedro (Peter) McMillan and Chuck Pass, founders of the retail store called Pedro's Planet. The young men started with $5,000 to open their business selling recycled and Earth-friendly products from toothpaste to computer paper.

37266 ■ "Eco-Products In Demand, But Labels Can Be Murky" in *Boston Globe* **(February 9, 2005)**
Pub: New York Times Company
Ed: Beth Daley. Description: Despite consumer demand for environmentally friendly products, labels can be misleading. A Website that helps consumers understand terminology on product labels is highlighted.

37267 ■ "Eco-Radicals Target Growth in Sierra Hills" in *San Jose Mercury News* **(March 9, 2005)**
Pub: Knight-Ridder/Tribune Business News
Ed: Dana Hull. Description: The Earth Liberation Front, an underground environmental network is attacking the foothill towns and fast-growing communities in the Bay Area of San Francisco, California.

37268 ■ *Ecopreneuring: The Complete Guide to Small Business Opportunities from the Environmental Revolution*
Pub: John Wiley & Sons, Inc.
Ed: Steven J. Bennett. Price: $60.00; $19.95 (paper). Description: Describes the opportunities available with environment-related products and services, including recycling, safe foods and packaging, and green products. Covers special equipment, marketing, overhead, and provides case studies.

37269 ■ "ECOWORKS Leeding The Way" in *Ingram's* **(Vol. 28, No. 1, January 2002, pp. 32)**
Pub: Show Me Publishing, Inc.
Ed: Chris Becicka. Description: An environmentally-friendly office building project, led by Hugh Zimmer, is highlighted.

37270 ■ "Energy: The changing balance of power" in *Red Herring* **(No. 103, September 1, 2001, pp. 66)**
Pub: Herring Communications
Ed: Lee Bruno. Description: A discussion regarding the need for standards to ensure that alternative power sources, such as micropower, can easily plug into the grid, which is critical for deregulated markets to move forward.

37271 ■ *Environmental Business Management*
Pub: International Labor Office
Ed: K. North. Released: 1992. Price: $31.50. Description: Covers the role of enterprise in the environment, including proposed and existing regulations and guidelines relating to environmental management.

37272 ■ *Environmental Guide to the Internet*
Pub: Government Institutes
Ed: Carol Briggs-Erickson, Editor. Released: latest edition 4th; published 1998. Price: $75 softcover. Covers: 1,200 resources covering the environment on the Internet, including organizations, products, and resources, including discussion groups, electronic journals, newsgroups, and discussion groups. Entries Include: Name, online address, description, e-mail address. Arrangement: Categories.

37273 ■ Ergonomics & Economics" in *Crain's Detroit Business* **(Vol. 21, November 7, 2005, No. 45, pp. 1)**
Pub: Crain Communications Inc. - Detroit
Ed: Amy Lane. Description: A Michigan advisory committee is meeting to devise rules to govern how employers must identify and address workplace conditions that put workers at risk for job-related injuries caused by repetitive motion, force and other factors. Business lobbyists charge the committee's work violates a provision of the Department of Labor and Economic Growth budget that prohibits the use of state funds to develop mandates stronger than federal voluntary ergonomics guidelines.

37274 ■ **"Ethanol Push Has Roots from Early 1990s, Support from Farmers"** in *Altanta Journal-Constitution* (February 4, 2007)
Pub: Cox Newspapers, Inc.
Ed: Jeff Nesmith. **Description:** National Farmers Union discusses renewable and alternative energy issues and the food vs. fuel debate.

37275 ■ *Fast-Track Business Start-Up Kit: California*
Pub: DP Group, Incorporated
Ed: Carolyn Usinger. **Released:** September 2006. **Price:** $29.00. **Description:** Step-by-step guide for starting and running a business in California, including information on sole proprietors, partnerships, limited liability companies, S and C corporations, as well as details concerning business entities, sales taxes, environmental issues, human resources, and more.

37276 ■ **"Finding Millions in the Trash"** in *Small Business Opportunities* (Vol. 13, No. 5, September 2001, pp. 52-54)
Pub: Harris Publications, Inc.
Description: Profile of Environmental Waste Solutions, the waste management consulting firm. Owners Darwyn Williams and Steve Ellis have developed an Affiliate Program to help small businesses start their own waste management consulting business.

37277 ■ **"Firms Paid $1.6 Million in Penalties, California Pesticide Regulators Report"** in *Sacramento Bee* (December 28, 2005)
Pub: The Sacramento Bee
Ed: Jim Wasserman. **Description:** Firms illegally selling pesticides in the State of California were fined a combined total of $1.6 million by the California Department of Pesticide Control. Most of the penalties incurred were due to chemical products that were not approved for sale in the state, while others were to firms not paying mandatory environmental fees.

37278 ■ **"Foundation Puts More Than $12M Behind Push For Design"** in *Crain's Detroit Business* (Vol. 22, November 20, 2006, No. 47, pp. 1)
Pub: Crain Communications Inc. - Detroit
Ed: Sherri Begin. **Description:** Kresge Foundation is encouraging non-profit businesses to incorporate sustainable design onto their capital projects. Grants to cover the usual extra costs to incorporate green as well as advice and referrals are available through Kresge on a national level.

37279 ■ **"Going for the green? Consultants can dig up all the dirt"** in *Boston Business Journal* (Vol. 22, No. 14, May 10, 2002, pp. 43)
Pub: MCP, Inc.
Ed: Philip Nannie. **Description:** Obtaining environmental consultation when planning, buying, constructing or selling a building would help avoid liability or environmental problems. Companies institute internal guidelines to prove compliance with regulations from the International Organization for Standardization.

37280 ■ **"Going Green?"** in *Crain's Detroit Business* (Vol. 22, November 20, 2006, No. 47, pp. 30)
Pub: Crain Communications Inc. - Detroit
Ed: Daniel Eizans. **Description:** Information and business links for green businesses are increasing online. Numerous sites are listed with job postings, event calendars, resource listings, and general news on the green industry are provided.

37281 ■ *Going Green: How to Communicate Your Company's Environmental Commitment*
Pub: Irwin Professional Publishing
Ed: E. Bruce Harrison. **Released:** 1993. **Price:** $32.50.

37282 ■ **"Governor Backs Solar-Panel Plan"** in *San Jose Mercury News* (March 2, 2005)
Pub: Knight-Ridder/Tribune Business News
Ed: Sue McAllister. **Description:** Governor Schwarzenegger announced support for legislation that would add 1 million energy-generating solar panels to rooftops statewide. The move would put California one step closer to self-sufficiency.

37283 ■ **"Grading confusion: Computer makers balk at report card's methods"** in *Waste News* (Vol. 7, No. 16, December 10, 2001, pp. 1)
Pub: Crain Communications Inc. - Akron
Ed: Joe Truini. **Description:** E-Waste is one of the fastest growing waste streams. The release of the Third Annual Computer Report Card that measures computer companies' effectiveness in clean production, protecting workers' health and making environmentally superior products was released. Results of the report are given.

37284 ■ **"The Great Rebate"** in *Entrepreneur* (Vol. 31, No. 9, September 2003, pp. 43)
Pub: Entrepreneur Media, Inc.
Description: Rebate opportunities are offered by computer companies to increase the sales of PCs.

37285 ■ **"Green Business Push Blooms"** in *Charlotte Observer* (February 7, 2007)
Pub: Knight-Ridder/Tribune Business News
Ed: Christopher D. Kirkpatrick. **Description:** Many energy companies are capitalizing on corporate guild about global warming. Companies offering environmental peace of mind are discussed.

37286 ■ **"Green Machines"** in *Entrepreneur* (Vol. 31, No. 7, July 2003, pp. 34)
Pub: Entrepreneur Media, Inc.
Ed: Geoff Williams. **Description:** Profile of Grant Goodman, CEO of Rockland Materials and five other companies, that make building materials such as ready-mix cement. Goodman runs his fleet of 120 truck on primarily biodiesel fuel made from soybeans. The fuel is biodegradable, nontoxic and free from sulfur.

37287 ■ **"Green Machines"** in *Entrepreneur. com* (Vol. 34, February 2006, No. 2, pp. 51)
Pub: Entrepreneur Media Inc.
Ed: Jennifer Pellet. **Description:** Under the Energy Tax Incentives Act of 2005, the government is offering tax incentives from $650 to $3,400 in tax credits for buying environmentally friendly vehicles.

37288 ■ *The Green PC: Making Choices That Make a Difference*
Pub: TAB Books, Inc.
Ed: Steven Anzovin. **Released:** 1993. **Price:** $9.95 (paper). **Description:** Provides 100 tips for reducing the environmental costs of computing.

37289 ■ **"Green Reporting"** in *Harvard Business Review* (Vol. 78, No. 1, January 2000, pp. 15)
Pub: Harvard Business School Publishing Corp.
Ed: Ans Kolk. **Description:** An investigation into the practice of publishing environmental performance reports. Thirty-five percent of the world's largest corporations now issue such reports.

37290 ■ **"Greenhouse Gas Limits are Called Affordable"** in *The Record* (November 21, 2005)
Pub: New Jersey Media Group
Ed: Alex Nussbaum. **Description:** Nine states are considering a new plan to cut greenhouse emissions over the next fifteen years. The plan would set limits on greenhouse gases allowed from power plants.

37291 ■ *The Greening of Business*
Pub: Ashgate Publishing Co., Inc.
Ed: Rhys A. David. **Released:** 1991. **Price:** $39.95. **Description:** Provides information for anyone concerned with determining environmental policy in industry, business, or the public sector.

37292 ■ **"A growing problem"** in *Electronic News* (Vol. 48, No. 11, March 11, 2002, pp)
Pub: Cahners Business Information
Ed: Jeff Chappell. **Description:** A recent investigation showed that much of the electronics turned over for recycling in the United States ends up in Asia, where it is either disposed of or recycled with little or no regard for environmental or worker health and safety.

37293 ■ **"Here's What You Can Do"** in *Crain's Chicago Business* (Vol. 30, January 2007, No. 1, pp. 15)
Pub: Crain Communications, Inc.
Ed: Sarah A. Klein. **Description:** Many developers want to be energy-efficient but good information is not available and most tips are put together by those not familiar with building science. Interview with John Porterfield, co-founder of Informed Energy Decisions LLC, a consulting firm that helps improve the energy performance of structures, talks about common defects in buildings which keep them from being efficient.

37294 ■ **"Higher Gas Prices Lead to More Hybrid Car Sales in Portland, Maine, Area"** in *Portland Press Herald* (September 13, 2005)
Pub: Blethen Maine Newspapers, Inc.
Ed: Ann S. Kim. **Description:** With the rising cost of gasoline, more people in the Portland, Maine area are purchasing new hybrid vehicles. Adam Lee, president of Lee Auto Malls, reports an increase in these sales due to car owners wanting to save money when filling up.

37295 ■ **"Hines blends architecture, environmental awareness"** in *Atlanta Business Chronicle* (Vol. 25, December 6, 2002, No. 26, pp. 5C)
Pub: American City Business Publications, Inc.
Ed: Sonny Lufrano. **Description:** Gerald D. Hines' real estate firm will receive the Development Firm of the Year Award from the Georgia Chapter of the National Association of Industrial Office Properties. The firm won the award for its dedication to innovate design, according to NAIOP Georgia president, Michael Pelt.

37296 ■ **"Hotels skip surcharges, focus on conservation"** in *Atlanta Business Chronicle* (Vol. 24, No. 14, September 7, 2001, pp. S6)
Pub: American City Business Journals Inc.
Ed: Erica Stephens. **Description:** Many hotels are eliminating surcharges, and instead focusing on ways to conserve energy. Matt Smith of the Ritz-Carlton Hotel Company has formed REACT, the Ritz-Carlton Energy Action and Conservation Teams. Hermann Gammeter has formed a committee to promote energy conservation. Due to the reactions from customers to surcharges, energy conservations are growing.

37297 ■ **"House Exempts Small Businesses From Superfund"** in *Atlanta Business Chronicle* (Vol. 23, No. 51, May 25, 2001, pp. 7A)
Pub: American City Business Journals Inc.
Ed: Kent Hoover. **Description:** The House Energy and Commerce Committee passed a bill that makes small business exempt from liability for cleanup costs at Superfund locations. The bill exempts those that dumped less than 110 gallons of nonhazardous liquids or less than 200 pounds of nonhazardous solid at a Superfund site, as well as businesses with less than 100 workers that dumped waste similar to that of household waste.

37298 ■ **"How microturbines generate megawatts"** in *Red Herring* (No. 103, September 1, 2001, pp. 72-73)
Pub: Herring Communications
Ed: Alan Zeichick. **Description:** An explanation of the technology that goes into microturbines, which allow for small, self-contained power generators that are quickly proving a viable means of supplying electricity.

37299 ■ **"In Tune With the Environment"** in *Fast Company* (February 2005, No. 91, pp. 26)
Pub: Gruner & Jahr USA Publishing
Ed: Ryan Underwood. **Description:** Gibson Guitar Corporation is committed to making its wood supply environmentally sustainable in order to ensure there is enough exotic wood, mostly mahogany, to continue making their guitars. The firm's electric-guitar division changed to a 100 percent fair-trade-certified wood in January 2005.

37300 ■ "Industrial Cleanser" in
Entrepreneur **(Vol. 28, No. 1, January 2000,**
pp. 132)
Pub: Entrepreneur Media Inc.
Ed: Stephen Barlas. Description: The EPA is targeting small business for pollution cleanup. The environmental laws governing small manufacturing businesses is explained.

37301 ■ "Keep Hand Injuries at Arm's
Length" in *San Jose Mercury News*
(February 28, 2005)
Pub: Knight-Ridder/Tribune Business News
Ed: Nicole C. Wong. Description: Facts to avoid carpal tunnel syndrome, trigger thumb, and Dequervain's tenosynovitis while using a keyboard are listed.

37302 ■ *Krupin's Toll-Free Environmental*
Directory
Pub: Direct Contact Publishing
Contact: Paul J. Krupin, Author
Price: $14.95, individuals. Covers: over 4,500 environmental organizations, companies, and government agencies that utilize toll-free phone numbers. Entries Include: Agency name, address, phone. Arrangement: Subject.

37303 ■ "Land use requires regional
cooperation" in *Crain's Detroit Business*
(Vol. 19, No. 14, April 7, 2003, pp. 9)
Pub: Crain Communications Inc., Detroit
Ed: Mary Kramer. Description: Agenda Ann Arbor held its annual meeting to discuss the city's public policy issues, such as regional land use planning.

37304 ■ "Learning to Walk; E-waste
stewardship takes first tentative steps" in
Waste News **(Vol. 8, No. 10, September 16,**
2002, pp. 10)
Pub: Crain Communications, Inc.
Ed: Joe Truini. Description: Profile of Houston-based Waste Management, Inc., the company that specializes in electronics recycling, offers the first electronics recycling environmental stewardship pledge. The intent of the pledge is to assure a high environmental standard when recycling electronic waste. A discussion into an industry-sponsored certification program is presented.

37305 ■ "Legislature considers energy tax
breaks" in *Crain's Detroit Business* **(Vol. 18,**
No. 16, April 22, 2002, pp. 23)
Pub: Crain Communications Inc. - Detroit
Ed: Amy Lane. Description: New corporate tax breaks for alternative energy technologies could head for Michigan's State Legislature soon.

37306 ■ "LI Banks $2 Million in State
Environmental Grants for Waterfront
Projects" in *Long Island Business News*
(March 12, 2004)
Pub: Dolan Media Newswires
Ed: Rosmaria Mancini. Description: New York State's Environmental Protection Fund program has awarded twelve Long Island municipalities more than $2 million in grants to improve waterfront districts. In Brookhaven, $400,000 will be used for the Port Jefferson Harborwalk project; Greenport will use $525,000 for continued implementation of the Mitchell Park and Marina project; Babylon Town will construct a fishing pier, hand-launch boat ramp and trail at Oak Beach with its $500,000; North Hempstead will implement sediment control devices to decrease pollution in Roslyn Pond and pollution reduction in Mill Pond.

37307 ■ "Local nonprofits benefit from
polluter-pay rulings" in *Crain's Detroit*
Business **(Vol. 19, No. 1, January 6, 2003, pp.**
19)
Pub: Crain Communications Inc., Detroit
Ed: Robert Ankeny. Description: Fines issued to U.S. Liquids of Detroit Inc. will benefit two Detroit areas charities. An increasing trend towards federal courts ordering companies convicted of polluting will also help offset environmental damage.

37308 ■ "Looking Into the Sun" in *Inc.*
(Volume 27, July 2005, No. 7, pp. 76-79)
Pub: Inc. Magazine
Ed: David H. Freedman. Description: Profile of David Slawson, who believes thermoelectric technology is twice as efficient as solar energy systems. He is committed to spreading his 38-foot emission-less dishes across the world.

37309 ■ "Maine Tribes Express Interest in
Naval Base Redevelopment Project" in
Portland Press Herald **(December 17, 2005)**
Pub: Blethen Maine Newspapers, Inc.
Ed: Kevin Wack. Description: The Penobscot Indian Nation and the Passamaquoddy Tribe are interested in redeveloping the Brunswick Naval Air Station. Plans include the manufacture of environmentally friendly wood-based products, aviation maintenance and manufacturing of airplane parts, and production of renewable energy.

37310 ■ "Microeconomics" in *Red Herring*
(No. 103, September 1, 2001, pp. 73)
Pub: Herring Communications
Ed: Ronald Recinto. Description: Although compatibility issues have slowed the adoption of microturbines in the United States, growth in the global markets looks promising.

37311 ■ "New Scooter Sales Store is Set to
Open on Iowa Street" in *Bellingham*
Business Journal **(December 2006, pp. A6)**
Pub: Sun News Inc.
Description: Profile of Urbano Moto, a new scooter store owned by Alan and Gretchen Taylor, will sell Roketa scooters, high-fuel-economy cars, including hybrids and those that run on diesel.

37312 ■ "Old Cell Phones" in *Black*
Enterprise **(Vol. 34, No. 5, December 2003,**
pp. 60)
Pub: Earl Graves Publishing Co.
Ed: Sonya A. Donaldson. Description: Ideas for small businesses to recycle old cell phones, by donating them to charitable organizations.

37313 ■ "Out With the Old" in *Entrepreneur*
(Vol. 31, No. 7, July 2003, pp. 46)
Pub: Entrepreneur Media, Inc.
Ed: Amanda C. Kooser. Description: Entrepreneurs can become environmentally responsible by donating or recycling old, unused computer equipment. Dell, Hewlett-Packard, Epson and IBM offer pickup or shipping services for a small fee. Dell either recycles the used computers or donates them to charities.

37314 ■ "PACE awards honor air-pollution
fighters" in *Atlanta Business Chronicle* **(Vol.**
25, No. 21, November 1, 2002, pp. 12C)
Pub: American City Business Publications, Inc.
Ed: Sonny Lufrano. Description: The 2002 PACE Awards, honoring anti-air pollution efforts in the Atlanta, Georgia area, were recently presented. Advantis Technologies Inc., Georgia Pacific Corporation, Turner Broadcasting System Inc., Solvay Pharmaceuticals Inc., and Worldspan LP were among the firms receiving awards.

37315 ■ "Pest-Control Companies
Increasingly Rely on Non-Chemical
Techniques" in *Portland Press Herald*
(September 2, 2005)
Pub: Blethen Maine Newspapers, Inc.
Description: Maine Board of Pesticides Control is hearing proposals to tighten indoor pesticide application in public and private buildings. Debates over the new proposal are outlined.

37316 ■ *Pollution Reduction and*
Contaminant Control
Pub: Gulf Publishing Co.
Ed: Paul N. Cheremisinoff. Released: 1993. Price: $155.00. Description: Volume 6 of *Encyclopedia of Environmental Control Technology*. Contains figures, tables, charts, and index.

37317 ■ "Potential Landfill Study Raises
Radiation Concerns" in *Bradenton Herald*
(January 27, 2005)
Pub: Bradenton Herald
Ed: Scott Radway. Description: Environmentalists are calling for a public hearing on a proposed study that would use phosphogypsum to extend the life of Florida landfills. Phosphogypsum is a low-level radioactive byproduct from fertilizer processing, and is expected to make decomposition occur twice as fast.

37318 ■ "The Power of Spin" in *The*
Economist **(Vol. 377, October 1-7, 2005, No.**
8446, pp. 76-77)
Pub: The Economist Newspaper Ltd.
Description: Canadian engineer, Louis Michaud, has developed a way to create artificial whirlwinds like a tornado, these whirlwinds can be controlled and harnessed in order to generate power. Michaud calls his invention the 'atmospheric vortex engine'.

37319 ■ "Pushing Green Building into
Mainstream" in *Crain's Detroit Business*
(Vol. 22, November 20, 2006, No. 47, pp. 16)
Pub: Crain Communications Inc. - Detroit
Ed: Jennette Smith. Description: Designing and building with the emphasis on green has grown in recent years. Michigan is a leader in the nation in green construction and is ranked fifth in the nation for its 34 projects certified by The U.S. Green Building Council.

37320 ■ "Recycled Fortune" in *Small*
Business Opportunities **(March 2005)**
Pub: Harris Publications Inc.
Description: Profile of Rapid Refill Ink; Dan P. White started his ink cartridge remanufacturing firm in 2002. The company uses state-of-the-art technology and equipment to refill 1,100 various inkjet cartridges and 200 models of laser toner cartridges.

37321 ■ "Recycling Adds Up to Big Savings
for Businesses, State, Says California
Agency" in *Sacramento Bee* **(December 13,**
2005)
Pub: The Sacramento Bee
Ed: Judy Lin. Description: The California Integrated Waste Management Board reported state businesses diverting nearly 1.8 million tons of materials from landfills to recycling. Seismic Computer Management of West Sacramento was recognized for its recycling as part of the 13th annual Waste Reduction Awards Program.

37322 ■ *Recycling and Waste Management*
Guide to the Internet
Pub: Government Institutes
Contact: Roger M. Guttentag, Author
Released: Latest edition 1997. Price: $65, individuals softcover. Covers: More than 350 web sites, discussion lists, and news groups on the internet covering waste management and recycling issues. Entries Include: Site name, address, subject, site summary, contact name and e-mail. Arrangement: Alphabetical. Indexes: Subject.

37323 ■ "Reporter's Notebook" in *Crain's*
Detroit Business **(Vol. 21, October 3, 2005,**
No. 43, pp. 33)
Pub: Crain Communications Inc. - Detroit
Ed: Jennette Smith. Description: According to Harrell Scarcello of Scarcello Associates Inc., interest is growing in green-building practices; rising energy prices are fueling the interest. State projects require LEED certification (Leadership in Energy and Environmental Design).

37324 ■ "Saving our energy" in *Red Herring*
(No. 103, September 1, 2001, pp. 67)
Pub: Herring Communications
Ed: Elizabeth Lamb. Description: According to the U.S. Energy Information Administration, commercial and residential energy consumption will decrease over the next 20 years due to slower population growth, fewer housing starts, increased energy efficiency, government efficiency programs, and innovations in technology.

37325 ■ "Small Business Spotlight" in *Small Business Opportunities* (Vol. 16, No. 2, March 2004, pp. 172)
Pub: Harris Publications, Inc.
Description: Profile of Jon Stocking who donates profits from his Endangered Species Chocolate Company to save threatened animals, an environmentally-friendly dry cleaner, and women and franchising.

37326 ■ "Social Grace" in *Entrepreneur* (Vol. 33, September 2005, No. 9, pp. 91)
Pub: Entrepreneur Media Inc.
Ed: Sara Wilson. **Description:** Profile of Jeffrey Hollender, president of Burlington, Vermont's Seventh Generation. Hollender manufactures environmentally safe household and personal-care products. The firm offers employee incentives for community involvement.

37327 ■ "State Coughs as Firms Seek Millions" in *Atlanta Business Chronicle* (Vol. 25, December 13, 2002, No. 27, pp. A3)
Pub: American City Business Publications, Inc.
Ed: Sara Rubenstein. **Description:** A group of some 130 Atlanta, Georgia area companies are suing the Georgia Environmental Protection Division and Department of Revenue in January 2003, seeking payment of over $9 million in fees for auto emissions tests that were allegedly collected illegally. The state contends that refunds would lead to cuts in the emissions inspection program, which is designed to help the metropolitan Atlanta region meet federal air quality standards. Georgia's Supreme Court ruled in 2001 that the fees were collected illegally.

37328 ■ "State Turns Up Heat on Green" in *Crain's Detroit Business* (Vol. 22, November 20, 2006, No. 47, pp. 11)
Pub: Crain Communications Inc. - Detroit
Ed: Amy Lane. **Description:** Governor Granholm has issued a directive that requires that all new construction and renovation for not only state agencies, but also that universities and colleges achieve the standards for green LEED (Leadership in Energy and Environmental Design) certification. It is hoped that this will spread into the private sector also.

37329 ■ "Stuck in a Storm of Controversy" in *Fortune* (Vol. 152, October 17, 2005, No. 8, pp. 41)
Pub: Time Inc.
Ed: Nicholas Varchaver. **Description:** An overview of the Shaw Group's contracts for reconstruction work in areas affected by Hurricane Katrina is presented.

37330 ■ "The Eco-Advantage. The Green 50" in *Inc.* (November 2006, pp. 79-103)
Pub: Gruner & Jahr USA Publishing
Ed: Larry Kanters **Description:** Fifty entrepreneurs are highlighted who have found a different way to do business that is more friendly to the environment. Some range from being directed at finding renewable sources of energy while others just wanted to find an eco-friendly business model.

37331 ■ "Toxic mold" in *Boston Business Journal* (Vol. 22, No. 3, February 22, 2002, pp. S4)
Pub: MCP, Inc.
Ed: Keith Regan. **Description:** Important information is given to property managers, but also applies to the general public, regarding issues of mold in buildings. The issues of mold cleanup, litigation and media attention are addressed.

37332 ■ "Unhelpful critique" in *Waste News* (Vol. 7, No. 16, December 10, 2001, pp. 8)
Pub: Crain Communications Inc. - Akron
Description: Problems associated with the computer report card recycling report are discussed.

37333 ■ "Watch That Bird's Rear" in *The Economist* (Vol. 376, July 16-22, 2005, No. 8435, pp. 30)
Pub: The Economist Newspaper Ltd.
Description: Oklahoma, home to some of the country's largest poultry businesses, has filed a lawsuit against 14 Arkansas poultry producers, claiming violations of federal and state environmental nuisance laws.

37334 ■ "What Every Executive Needs to Know About Global Warming" in *Harvard Business Review* (Vol. 78, No. 4, July 2000, pp. 129)
Pub: Harvard Business School Publishing Corp.
Ed: Kimberly O'Neill Packard, Forest Reinhardt. **Description:** The article covers the global warming issue and views and the problem from many points of view.

37335 ■ "When BlackBerry Use Causes Pain" in *San Jose Mercury News* (February 28, 2005)
Pub: Knight-Ridder/Tribune Business News
Ed: Nicole C. Wong. **Description:** Repetitive stress injuries are common among desktop and laptop computer users.

37336 ■ "Where Jobs Are Plenty, Challenge is Finding Right People" in *Crain's Detroit Business* (Vol. 22, November 27, 2006, No. 48, pp. 17)
Pub: Crain Communications Inc. - Detroit
Ed: Anjali Fluker. **Description:** The environmental industry in Southeast Michigan has many job openings, but has difficulty finding educated and experienced workers. Part of the reason is most of the people working in that industry are content, and are not looking around.

TRADE PERIODICALS

37337 ■ *Business and the Environment*
Pub: Cutter Information Corp.
Ed: Kate Victory, Editor. **Released:** Monthly. **Price:** $595. **Description:** Covers international trends in corporate environmental management and environmental regulation. Recurring features include a calendar of events and a monthly supplement on ISO 14,000.

37338 ■ *Clean Air News*
Pub: Progressive Business Publications
Ed: Fred Frazier, Editor, frazier@pbp.com. **Released:** Semimonthly. **Price:** $299. **Description:** Presents the inside story on the latest changes in the Clean Air Act rules. Recurring features include interviews, news of research, websites of interest, update on latest Federal & State regulation, and a column titled Sharpen Your Judgment.

37339 ■ *Composting News*
Pub: McEntee Media Corp.
Ed: Ken McEntee, Editor, ken@recycle.cc. **Released:** Monthly. **Price:** $83, individuals; $93, Canada and Mexico; $105, other countries. **Description:** Covers news and trends in the composting industry. Also reports on compost product prices. Recurring features include letters to the editor, interviews, news of research, a calendar of events, reports of meetings, and notices of publications available.

37340 ■ *The Davlin Report*
Pub: The Davlin Report Inc.
Ed: Andrew Davlin, Jr., Editor, aquaandy@aol.com. **Released:** Periodic. **Price:** $39.95, U.S. 4 issues; $59.95, U.S. 8 issues. **Description:** Reports on the aquaculture industry & companies, oil & gas companies & attractive common stocks.

37341 ■ *Defense Environment Alert*
Pub: Inside Washington Publishers
Contact: Suzanne Yohannan, Managing Editor
Released: Biweekly, every other Wednesday. **Price:** $615, U.S. and Canada; $665, elsewhere. **Description:** Reports on defense policies for cleanup, compliance, and pollution prevention.

37342 ■ *The Digest of Environmental Law*
Pub: Strafford Publications Inc.
Contact: Jennifer F. Vaughan, Exec. Ed.
E-mail: editors@straffordpub.com
Released: Monthly. **Price:** $547, U.S.; $994, two years. **Description:** Digest offers complete coverage of the expanding liability related to the full range of environmental issues. Recurring features include reports on cases of national significance.

37343 ■ *The Green Business Letter*
Pub: Tilden Press Inc.
Ed: Joel Makower, Editor. **Released:** Monthly. **Price:** $95 electronic edition; $45 for students and acdemics. **Description:** Helps companies integrate environmental considerations into their operations in a way that creates business value and environmental improvement. Recurring features include interviews, news of research, reports of meetings, book reviews, and notices of publications available.

37344 ■ *The GreenMoney Journal & Online Guide*
Pub: The Greenmoney Journal
Contact: Cliff Feigenbaum, Editor & Publisher
E-mail: cliff@greenmoney.com
Released: Bimonthly. **Price:** $50, individuals; $50, Canada plus $10 postage; $50, elsewhere plus $20 postage. **Description:** "Encourages and promotes the awareness of socially and environmentally responsible business, investing and consumer resources in publications and online. Our goal is to educate and empower individuals and businesses to make informed financial decisions through aligning their personal, corporate and financial principles." Recurring features include a calendar of events.

37345 ■ *GREENWIRE*
Pub: National Journal
Ed: Dale Curtis, Editor. **Released:** Daily, Monday-Friday. **Price:** $835, individuals and nonprofits; $1570, institutions. **Description:** Filters and digests over 200 sources on the environment. Recurring features include Interviews, news of research, environmental trend analysis, business opportunities, articles with a political focus, and a column titled P.S. Remarks: Available on the web, by e-mail, and by fax after 10:30 a.m. EST, Monday-Friday.

37346 ■ *Inside Cal/EPA*
Pub: Inside Washington Publishers
Contact: Rick Weber, Publisher
Released: Weekly (Fri.). **Price:** $585, U.S. and Canada; $635, elsewhere. **Description:** Reports on environmental legislation, regulation, and litigation.

37347 ■ *Journal of Vegetable Crop Production*
Pub: The Haworth Press Inc.
Contact: Bill Cohen Ph.D., Publisher
E-mail: vrusso-usda@lane-ag.org
Ed: Vincent M. Russo, PhD, Editor, vrusso-usda@lane-ag.org. **Released:** Biannual (2 issues per volume). **Description:** Journal of research about the production of vegetable crops.

37348 ■ *Recycling Canada*
Pub: Sydenham Publishing
Contact: Stella Coultas, Sr. Editor
Released: Monthly. **Price:** $110, Canada. **Description:** Spotlights waste management and recycling news. Recurring features include a calendar of events, reports of meetings, book reviews, and notices of publications available.

37349 ■ *Water Policy Report*
Pub: Inside Washington Publishers
Contact: Charlie Mitchell, Chief Editor
Released: Biweekly, every other Monday. **Price:** $650, U.S. and Canada; $700, elsewhere. **Description:** Reports on federal water quality programs and policies. Covers topics such as drinking water, toxics, enforcement, monitoring, and state/EPA relations.

37350 ■ *Wind Energy Weekly*
Pub: American Wind Energy Association
Ed: Thomas O. Gray, Editor, tom_gray@igc.org. **Released:** Weekly. **Price:** Included in membership; $595, nonmembers. **Description:** Provides wind energy trade news, plus covers energy and environmental policy. Recurring features include news of research, reports of meetings, job listings, and notices of publications available. Remarks: Available only via E-mail account.

VIDEOCASSETTES/ AUDIOCASSETTES

37351 ■ *Cleaning Up Toxics*
The Video Project
660 York St., Ste. 102
San Francisco, CA 94110
Free: 800-4-PLANET
Fax: (415)821-7204
Co. E-mail: video@videoproject.net
URL: http://www.videoproject.org
Released: 1990. **Price:** $59.95. **Description:** A series containing practical suggestions on reducing the amount of hazardous substances introduced into the environment from homes and businesses. **Availability:** VHS; 3/4U; Special order formats.

37352 ■ *Free Energy: The Race to Zero Point*
The Video Collection
PO Box 2284
South Burlington, VT 05407-2284
Released: 1998. **Price:** $29.95. **Description:** Documentary takes a look at the quest to find safe nonpolluting energy sources that are available to everyone. Features segments on Nikola Tesla's method of "broadcasting" free energy, electric cars, zero-point "space" energy and cold fusion. **Availability:** VHS.

37353 ■ *Greenbucks: The Challenge of Sustainable Development*
The Video Project
660 York St., Ste. 102
San Francisco, CA 94110
Free: 800-4-PLANET
Fax: (415)821-7204
Co. E-mail: video@videoproject.net
URL: http://www.videoproject.org
Released: 1992. **Price:** $195.00. **Description:** Major corporations change their attitudes and look for environmental solutions. Designed to inspire other businesses to higher ecological awareness. **Availability:** VHS.

37354 ■ *Grime Goes Green: Your Business & the Environment*
Video Arts, Inc.
c/o Aim Learning Group
8238-40 Lehigh
Morton Grove, IL 60053-2615
Free: 877-444-2230
Fax: (416)252-2155
Co. E-mail: service@aimlearninggroup.com
URL: http://www.aimlearninggroup.com
Released: 1991. **Price:** $435.00. **Description:** How to implement effective organizational enviromental policies. Shows how to avoid waste, use resources more efficiently, and institute re-cycling systems. **Availability:** VHS; 8mm; 3/4U; Special order formats.

37355 ■ *The Impact of Environmental Regulations on Business Transactions*
Practicing Law Institute
810 7th Ave.
New York, NY 10019
Ph:(212)824-5710
Free: 800-260-4PLI
Co. E-mail: info@pli.edu
URL: http://www.pli.edu
Released: 1988. **Price:** $245.00. **Description:** A look at how environmental standards affect business dealings. **Availability:** VHS.

37356 ■ *Nuclear Power: The Hot Debate*
Filmakers Library, Inc.
124 E. 40th St.
New York, NY 10016
Ph:(212)808-4980
Free: 800-555-9815
Fax: (212)808-4983
Co. E-mail: info@filmakers.com
URL: http://www.filmakers.com
Price: $395. **Description:** Looks at the pros and cons of nuclear power and at possible energy alternatives. **Availability:** VHS.

CONSULTANTS

37357 ■ Eco-Rating International Inc.
115 W California Blvd., Ste. 294
Pasadena, CA 91105
Ph:(818)792-3380
Fax: (818)792-7085
Co. E-mail: info@eco-rating.com

E-mail: info@eco-rating.com
Scope: A small consultancy, part of a nine company multinational, that scientifically evaluates and rates the environmental standing of companies, their products and projects.

37358 ■ Enviro MD Inc.
4400 E Broadway Blvd., Ste. 300
PO Box 66020
Tucson, AZ 85711-3553
Ph:(520)881-1000
Fax: (520)327-1572
Scope: Provides environmental consulting services to the private sector and governmental agencies.

37359 ■ Environmental Plus Inc.
PO Box 1348
Evergreen, CO 80437
Ph:(303)674-0803
Free: 800-368-7587
Fax: (303)674-1577
Co. E-mail: beldock@envplus.com
URL: http://www.envplus.com

E-mail: beldock@envplus.com
Scope: An environmental and energy company dedicated to developing and supporting clean and efficient energy technologies. Specialists in the areas of environmental and energy research, due diligence, project development, engineering, management, innovative project finance, and customer service.

37360 ■ Barbara Whyte Felicetti
606 Woodcrest Ave.
Ardmore, PA 19003-1920
Ph:(610)642-4939
Fax: (610)642-4939
Scope: Law library management consulting.

37361 ■ GE Energy
888 N Industrial Dr.
Elmhurst, IL 60126-1121
Ph:(630)530-6656
Free: (866)758-9042
Fax: (630)530-6630
Co. E-mail: daniel.grabowski@ge.com
URL: http://www.gepower.com

E-mail: daniel.grabowski@ge.com
Scope: Environmental compliance, permitting and site assessment services including compliance management systems environmental outsourcing, remediation design and management, asbestos project management, wetlands investigations, risk management planning, OSHA Compliance, and indoor air quality. **Publications:** "Energy consulting". **Special Services:** Positive Sequence Load Flow.

37362 ■ Occusafe Inc.
608 S Washington St., Ste. 9
Naperville, IL 60540
Ph:(630)851-3255
Free: 800-323-7597
Fax: (630)851-9339
Co. E-mail: info@occusafe-inc.com
URL: http://www.occusafe-inc.com

E-mail: info@occusafe-inc.com
Scope: Assist clients in resolving employee safety, health or environmental problems or concerns by providing practical and economical solutions.

37363 ■ Prindle Hinds Environmental Inc.
7208 Jefferson St. NE
Albuquerque, NM 87109
Ph:(505)345-8732
Fax: (505)345-0393

Scope: Provides environmental engineering/ consulting services needed by clients to prevent/solve regulatory compliance problems and/or reduce their potential liabilities. Services include: geology, hydrology, and engineering; hazardous waste management; non-hazardous waste management; permit preparation/delisting; site/risk assessments; and site characterization/remedial action planning and training. Additional specialized expertise includes underground storage tanks, regulatory negotiations, and expert witness testimony. **Seminars:** Firm has presented over a hundred specialized seminars/workshops, most pertaining to hazardous waste management.

37364 ■ Resource Applications Inc.
9291 Old Keene Mill Rd.
Burke, VA 22015-4202
Ph:(703)644-0401
Fax: (703)644-0404
Co. E-mail: psingh@rait.com

E-mail: psingh@rait.com
Scope: Provides engineering, planning, and research and development services. Extensive experience and expertise in hazardous waste management, including waste minimization, pollution prevention, and site remediation. Also offers seminars and workshops. Serves private industries as well as government agencies.

37365 ■ SENES Consultants Ltd.
121 Granton Ave., Ste. 12
Richmond Hill, ON, Canada L4B 3N4
Ph:(905)764-9380
Fax: (905)764-9386
Co. E-mail: info@senes.ca
URL: http://www.senes.ca

E-mail: info@senes.ca
Scope: Offers specialty services on many aspects of the environment including the aquatic ecosystem, atmospheric environment, terrestrial ecosystem, occupational health, radioactivity and hazardous and solid waste management. Typical projects involve provision of expert advice on specific environmental issues, preparation of environmental and risk assessments, environmental audits of existing facilities, site investigations, air quality assessment and air emission control, assessment of industrial and municipal water and waste treatment technologies, preparation of solid waste management master plans, development of waste management strategies, design and supervision of remedial action projects, data management and statistical analysis. Industries served: regulatory agencies from all levels of government, private sector companies, industrial associations, and public organizations. **Seminars:** Risk assessments; Environmental audits and other environmental matters.

37366 ■ Smyth Fivenson Co.
8513 Irvington Ave.
Bethesda, MD 20817-3815
Ph:(301)493-6600
Fax: (301)530-7557
URL: http://www.smythfivenson.com
Scope: A Human Resources consulting firm providing services to two business areas, both nationally. First, provides temporary human resource professionals to all industries. Second, Smyth Fivenson Co. performs recruiting and placement services for the environmental industry.

37367 ■ Versar Inc.
6850 Versar Ctr.
Springfield, VA 22151
Ph:(703)750-3000
Free: 800-283-7727
Fax: (703)642-6807
Co. E-mail: info@versar.com
URL: http://www.versar.com

E-mail: info@versar.com
Scope: Consultants offering environmental services; complete regulatory assistance to industry; applied research services to industry and government, emergency planning services; nuclear power plant

emergency plan development; engineering services; atmospheric and meteorological modeling; and recent experience in evaluation of off-site consequences of chemical accidents. Serves private industries as well as government agencies.

37368 ■ Vista Environmental Inc.
33324 Bergen Mtn. Rd., Ste. 110
Evergreen, CO 80439
Ph:(303)674-8420
Fax: (303)674-8161
Co. E-mail: ljvista@earthlink.net

E-mail: ljvista@earthlink.net
Scope: Firm designs innovative technical programs to enhance client image.

FRANCHISES AND BUSINESS OPPORTUNITIES

37369 ■ Biologix
BioLogix FMC
1561 Fairview Ave.
St. Louis, MO 63132
Ph:(314)423-1945
Free: 800-747-1885
No. of Franchise Units: 18. **No. of Company-Owned Units:** 3. **Founded:** 1989. **Franchised:** 1995. **Description:** Environmental waste disposal. **Equity Capital Needed:** $23,900-$43,600, including franchise fee. **Franchise Fee:** $15,000-$30,000. **Financial Assistance:** No. **Training:** Yes.

COMPUTERIZED DATABASES

37370 ■ *Business and the Environment*
Cutter Consortium
37 Broadway, Ste. 1
Arlington, MA 02474
Ph:(781)648-8700
Fax: (781)648-8707
Co. E-mail: info@cutter.com
URL: http://www.cutter.com
Description: Contains the complete text of *Business and the Environment*, a newsletter covering worldwide news and analyses of environmental regulatory and policy trends. Covers business opportunities, market developments, and company actions related to "green" innovations and regulatory actions. **Type:** Full text.

LIBRARIES

37371 ■ Environmental Bankers Association–Library
510 King St., Ste. 410
Alexandria, VA 22314

Ph:(703)549-0977
Fax: (703)548-5945
Co. E-mail: eba@envirobank.org
URL: http://www.envirobank.org
Scope: Environmental lender liability insurance, EPA and FDIC regulations, environment risk management. **Services:** Library not open to the public. **Holdings:** 50 books, periodicals, and clippings. **Subscriptions:** 125 journals and other serials.

37372 ■ Recycling Council of Ontario–Library
51 Wolseley, 2nd Fl.
Toronto, ON, Canada M5T 1A4
Ph:(416)960-1025
Fax: (416)960-8053
Co. E-mail: rco@rco.on.ca
URL: http://www.rco.on.ca
Contact: Sarah Mills
Scope: Waste management. **Services:** Library open to the public on a limited schedule. **Holdings:** 3550 books, reports, and documents. **Subscriptions:** 100 journals.

RESEARCH CENTERS

37373 ■ California State University, Hayward–California Urban Environmental Research and Education Center
25800 Carlos Bee Blvd., No. 109
Hayward, CA 94542
Ph:(510)885-3554
Fax: (510)885-4773
Co. E-mail: cuerec@greenstart.org
Contact: Prof. Samuel I. Doctors JD, Exec.Dir.
E-mail: cuerec@greenstart.org
Scope: Develops public policies that reduce environmental degradation and provides opportunities for sustainable economic development; assists environmental entrepreneurship and the development of public-private partnerships; and promotes the transfer and dissemination of ideas and appropriate technologies. **Services:** Provides services, to state and federal government concerning sustainable economic development. **Publications:** Government Reports.

37374 ■ Colorado State University–Industrial Assessment Center
Department of Mechanical Engineering
Fort Collins, CO 80523-1374
Ph:(970)491-7709
Fax: (970)491-3827
Co. E-mail: hittle@engr.colostate.edu
URL: http://www.engr.colostate.edu/IAC/
Contact: Prof. Douglas C. Hittle, Dir.
E-mail: hittle@engr.colostate.edu
Scope: Pollution prevention and energy conservation in manufacturing. **Services:** Pollution prevention, energy conservation & productivity improvement, to industry.

37375 ■ Tarleton State University–Texas Institute for Applied Environmental Research
Mail Stop T-0410
Stephenville, TX 76402

Ph:(254)968-9567
Fax: (254)968-9559
Co. E-mail: rjones@tiaer.tarleton.edu
URL: http://tiaer6.tarleton.edu
Contact: Ron Jones, Dir.
E-mail: rjones@tiaer.tarleton.edu
Scope: Environmental issues of state and national significance, focusing on the interface between the private sector and government as environmental policy is developed and implemented.

37376 ■ University of California, Davis–Information Center for the Environment
2120 Wickson Hall
Davis, CA 95616
Ph:(530)752-3026
Fax: (530)752-3350
Co. E-mail: jfquinn@ucdavis.edu
URL: http://ice.ucdavis.edu
Contact: Prof. James F. Quinn, Dir.
E-mail: jfquinn@ucdavis.edu
Scope: Environmental protection.

37377 ■ University of Florida–Powell Center for Construction and Environment
342 Rinker Hall
PO Box 115703
Gainesville, FL 32611-5703
Ph:(352)273-1172
Fax: (352)392-9606
Co. E-mail: ckibert@ufl.edu
URL: http://www.cce.ufl.edu
Contact: Dr. Charles J. Kibert, Dir.
E-mail: ckibert@ufl.edu
Scope: Environmental problems associated with planning and architecture activities, and the determination of the optimum materials and methods for use in minimizing environmental damage. **Publications:** Conference proceedings; Research reports. **Educational Activities:** Conferences; Continuing education courses; Workshops.

37378 ■ West Virginia University–Safety and Environmental Management Program
Industrial and Management Systems Engineering
PO Box 6107
Morgantown, WV 26506-6107
Ph:(304)293-4607
Fax: (304)293-4970
Co. E-mail: ralph.plummer@mail.wvu.edu
Contact: Dr. Ralph R. Plummer, Dir.
E-mail: ralph.plummer@mail.wvu.edu
Scope: Safety and environmental management; focusing on safety management; program development, highway safety, environmental management, behavioral based safety, ship dismantling, school violence and fire and emergency response. **Services:** Technical assistance and consulting, to industry and business organizations. **Publications:** The Lifesaver. **Educational Activities:** Annual conference and forums, on safety and environmental management; Off-campus education opportunities, on safety, health, and environment.

ASSOCIATIONS AND OTHER ORGANIZATIONS

37379 ■ Centre for Bioethics–Centre De Bioethique
Clinical Research Institute of Montreal
110 Pine Ave. W
Montreal, QC, Canada H2W 1R7
Ph:(514)987-5617
Fax: (514)987-5695
Co. E-mail: david.roy@ircm.qc.ca
URL: http://www.ircm.qc.ca/bioethique/index.html
Contact: Dr. David J. Roy, Dir.
Description: Works to identify and resolve ethical issues in medical practice and research. Monitors legal and policy issues such as "do not resuscitate" protocols and human experimentation. Facilitates exchange of information among physicians, medical scientists, and other health professionals. Conducts research and educational programs. **Publications:** *Bioethics in Canada*; *Journal of Palliative Care* (quarterly).

37380 ■ Council for Ethics in Economics
92 Jefferson Ave., Ste. 108
Columbus, OH 43215
Ph:(614)221-8661
Fax: (614)221-8707
Co. E-mail: cee@businessethics.org
URL: http://www.businessethics.org
Contact: Michael Distelhorst, Pres.
Membership: Leaders in business, education, and the professions. **Purpose:** Seeks to "strengthen the ethical fabric of business and economic life". Facilitates the development of international networks of businesspeople interested in economic ethics; sponsors educational programs and develops and distributes educational materials; advises and supports communities wishing to implement character educational programs; makes available consulting services.

37381 ■ National Council on Ethics in Human Research–Conseil national d'Ethique en recherche chez l'Humain
240 Catherine St., Ste. 208
Ottawa, ON, Canada K2P 2G8
Ph:(613)233-5445
Fax: (613)233-0658
Co. E-mail: office@ncehr-cnerh.org
URL: http://www.ncehr-cnerh.org
Contact: Dr. Glenn G. Griener, Pres.
Description: Encourages high ethical standards research involving human subjects. Consults with universities, government agencies and businesses engaged in human research; recommends standards for research projects using human subjects. Conducts educational programs. **Publications:** *Communique* (annual).

37382 ■ Society for Business Ethics
Department of Philosophy
College of St. Benedict, St. John's University
College Ave.
St. Joseph, MN 56374
Ph:(320)363-5915
Co. E-mail: jdesjardins@csbsju.edu
URL: http://www.societyforbusinessethics.org
Contact: Joe DesJardins, Exec. Dir.
Description: Philosophy and theology professors, business school professors, and business executives. Facilitates information exchange regarding research and activities in business ethics. **Publications:** *Business Ethics Quarterly* (quarterly); *Society for Business Ethics Newsletter* (quarterly).

REFERENCE WORKS

37383 ■ "About the Power Breakfast series" in *Crain's Detroit Business* (Vol. 19, No. 1, January 6, 2003, pp. 3)
Pub: Crain Communications Inc., Detroit
Description: Crain's Detroit Business is playing host to private roundtable discussions with executives and experts in the Detroit area. Key issues will focus on Southeast Michigan businesses, including suppliers, ethics, governance, and more.

37384 ■ "The Accounting Fraud Squads" in *Atlanta Business Chronicle* (Vol. 25, November 15, 2002, No. 23 pp. SS1)
Pub: American City Business Publications, Inc.
Ed: Lee Hall. **Description:** Following recent corporate scandals, more businesses are seeking fraud investigation and forensic accounting services. Businesses in the U.S. are expected to lose about $600 billion due to fraud in 2002, or $4,500 per employee. Details about the field of forensic accounting are included.

37385 ■ "Accounting Has Record of Trustworthiness" in *Crain's Detroit Business* (Vol. 18, No. 15, April 15, 2002, pp. 9)
Pub: Crain Communications Inc. - Detroit
Ed: Leslie Murphy. **Description:** The recent Enron scandal has obscured the accounting industry's reputation for dependability.

37386 ■ *Annual Editions: Business Ethics*
Pub: Dushkin Publishing Group, Inc.
Ed: John E. Richardson. **Released:** 1995. **Price:** $12.95.

37387 ■ "Are Race-Specific Drugs Unethical?" in *Black Enterprise* (Vol. 36, November 2005, No. 4, pp. 37)
Pub: Earl G. Graves Publishing Co. Inc.
Ed: Ron Chepesiuk, Joyce Jones. **Description:** BiDil, the first drug marketed for treatment of heart failure in African Americans was approved by the U.S. Food and Drug Administration in June 2005. Some in the African American community are questioning why the drug would work better for the Black population over other races.

37388 ■ "Atlanta businesswoman puts ethics over profit" in *Atlanta Business Chronicle* (Vol. 25, No. 22, November 8, 2002, pp. 9B)
Pub: American City Business Publications, Inc.
Ed: Lee Hall. **Description:** Professional Management Resources Inc., a healthcare consulting company, recently carried out its first mass layoffs in the ten years it existed. Although PMR has been experiencing problems, Laverne Poindexter, head, stopped the firm's relationship with an undisclosed customer that frequently failed to comply with government rules. PRM was victorious in getting a Georgia Business Ethics Award from the Society of Financial Service Professionals' Atlanta Chapter.

37389 ■ "Between Right And Right" in *Fortuneit* (Vol. 146, No. 9, November 11, 2002, pp. 66)
Pub: Time Inc.
Ed: Geoffrey Colvin. **Description:** Three specific corporate ethics issues are examined.

37390 ■ "Beware the Dotted Line" in *Hispanic Business* (December 2002, pp. 55)
Pub: Hispanic Business
Ed: Francisco Ramos, Jr. **Description:** The importance of reading the fine print before signing a contract is stressed. Ten traps to beware when signing a contract are outlined.

37391 ■ "Bird Dog" in *Barron's* (September 8, 2003, pp. 9)
Pub: Barron's
Ed: Alan Abelson. **Description:** New York State Attorney General, Eliot Spitzer's continuing crusade against corruption on Wall Street netted two more victims, a Canary Capital hedge fund, and mutual funds administered by such august firms as Bank of America, Bank One, Janus and others.

37392 ■ "A Blogger in Their Midst" in *Harvard Business Review* (Vol. 81, No. 9, September 2003, pp. 30)
Pub: Harvard Business School Press
Ed: Halley Suitt. **Description:** A hypothetical situation is presented where an indiscreet employee provides an online endorsement of a product that results in dramatically increased sales. Experts discuss how the CEO should deal with the matter.

37393 ■ "Boeing CEO Casualty of Company's Renewed Focus on Ethics" in *Atlanta Journal-Constitution* (March 8, 2005)
Pub: Knight-Ridder/Tribune Business News
Ed: Tammy Joyner. **Description:** U.S. companies are being pressured by stronger ethics laws and codes of conduct. The firing of Harry Stonecipher, chief executive at Boeing, is an example of poor judgment surrounding an alleged affair cost him his job.

37394 ■ "Business Bookshelf" in *Small Business Opportunities* (Vol. 17, September 2005, No. 5, pp. 134)
Pub: Harris Publications Inc.
Description: Reviews of three books of interest to small business owners and entrepreneurs are highlighted. Minding Her Own Business covers tax laws and financial matters to assist female business owners. Never Eat Alone covers networking and other business secrets to success. The Bottom Line On Integrity discusses business ethics and what it means to be honest.

37395 ■ "Business ethics issues cross all boundaries" in *Colorado Springs Business Journal* (March 7, 2003)
Pub: Dolan Media Newswires
Ed: Lance Gurwell. **Description:** Ethics issues of concern to chief executives of companies are discussed.

37396 ■ *Business Ethics*
Pub: The McGraw-Hill Companies

37397 ■ *Business Ethics: Concepts and Cases*
Pub: Prentice Hall
Ed: Manuel G. Velasquez. **Released:** Third edition, 1991. **Price:** $4.00 (paper).

37398 ■ *Business & Ethics: The Ethics of Economic Systems*
Pub: Eisenbrauns
Ed: Arthur Rich; introduction by Georges Enderle. **Released:** 1997. **Price:** $54.00.

37399 ■ *Business Fairy Tales*
Pub: Thomson South-Western
Ed: Cecil W. Jackson. **Released:** July 2006. **Price:** $39.95. **Description:** The seven most-common business schemes are uncovered.

37400 ■ "Can you trust your law firm?" in *Harvard Business Review* (Vol. 80, No. 11, November 2002, pp. 22)
Pub: Harvard Business School Press
Ed: Bronwyn Fryer. **Description:** A Boston University law professor and legal ethics expert advises managers to get legal advice in writing, record all oral communications, and seek second opinions.

37401 ■ "The case of the obsolete inventory" in *Red Herring* (March 2003, pp. 34)
Pub: Herring Communications Inc.
Ed: Justin Hibbard. **Description:** In February 2002, Solectron, an electronics manufacturer pressured an employee to write off outdated company inventory. The employee was fired seven months later, now his lawsuit could benefit honest employees throughout the U.S.

37402 ■ "The CEO's Secret Handbook" in *Business 2.0* (Vol. 6, July 2005, No. 6, pp. 68-74)
Pub: Time, Inc.
Ed: Paul Kaihla. **Description:** Accidental guru, Bill Swanson, CEO at Raython shares a lifetime's worth of executive wisdom in his 760-page spiral-bound guidebook, Swanson's Unwritten Rules of Management.

37403 ■ "Chapman Charged with Fraud" in *Black Enterprise* (Vol. 34, No. 2, September 2003, pp. 26)
Pub: Earl Graves Publishing Co.
Ed: Joyce Jones. **Description:** Nathan A. Chapman, Jr. was indicted by a federal grand jury on the charge of scheming to defraud the State Retirement & Pension System of Maryland, shareholders and his companies, and the public. The investment banker was charged on 39-counts with mail fraud, wire fraud, securities fraud and conspiracy.

37404 ■ "Community Theaters Mean More Than Just Entertainment" in *Mississippi Business Journal* (Vol. 28, January 2007, No. 36, pp. 29)
Pub: Venture Publications, Inc.
Ed: Lynn Lofton **Description:** With community theaters growing in Mississippi for several years, the Mississippi Theater Association has reached more than 500 members with many of those being community theaters. This represents a resurgence in the successful smaller independently run community theaters. Statistical data included.

37405 ■ "Compulsory ethics education and the cognitive moral development of salespeople" in *Journal of Business Ethics* (Vol. 28, No. 3)
Pub: Kluwer Academic Publishers
Ed: George Izzo. **Description:** The results of research conducted on the effect of compulsory ethics education on the moral development of real estate salespeople using comparative statistical measures of ethical reasoning ability.

37406 ■ "The Confidence Game" in *Forbes* (Vol. 170, No. 13, December 23, 2002, pp. 234)
Pub: Forbes Magazine
Ed: George Gilder. **Description:** The entire makeup of a successful company is based wholly on trust.

37407 ■ "Conflict of interest" in *Red Herring* (January 2003, pp. 23)
Pub: Herring Communications Inc.
Ed: Stacy Lawrence. **Description:** Most large U.S. firms still pay two-thirds of the money to auditors on non-audit services, however there is a shift toward spending their IT consulting budget elsewhere.

37408 ■ "Congress Scores One For Your Portfolio" in *Fortuneit* (Vol. 146, No. 4, September 2, 2002, pp. 184)
Pub: Time Inc.
Ed: Jeffrey H. Birnbaum. **Description:** Information about the Sarbanes-Oxley bill on corporate governance and accounting reform is presented.

37409 ■ "Consumers Ethics: The Role of Religiosity" in *Journal of Business Ethics* (Vol. 46, No. 2, August 15, 2003, pp. 151)
Pub: Kluwer Academic Publishers Group
Ed: Scott J. Vitell, Joseph G.P. Paolillo. **Description:** Results of a study investigating the role that religiosity plays in determining consumer attitudes/beliefs regarding various questionable consumer practice, along with other personal factors are offered.

37410 ■ *Contemporary Issues in Business Ethics*
Pub: Wadsworth Publishing Co.
Ed: Joseph R. DesJardins. **Released:** 4th ed. 1999. **Price:** $39.00 (mass market).

37411 ■ "Corporate Scandals Inspire Texas Fraud Bill" in *Houston Chronicle* (April 11, 2003)
Pub: Knight-Ridder/Tribune Business News
Ed: Janet Elliott. **Description:** In response to recent corporate scandals, the Senate unanimously approved a bill to crack down on business fraud. Senate Bill 1059 would create a corporate integrity unit in the Texas attorney general's office. Details of the bill are examined.

37412 ■ "Corporate Versus Individual Moral Responsibility" in *Journal of Business Ethics* (Vol. 46, No. 2, August 15, 2003, pp. 143)
Pub: Kluwer Academic Publishers Group
Ed: C. Soares. **Description:** There is a clear tendency in contemporary political/legal thought to limit agency to individual agents, thereby denying the existence and relevance of collective moral agency in general, and corporate agency in particular.

37413 ■ "A Corrupt Calculus: The Line Between 'Making the Numbers' and Making Them Up Remains Blurry" in *Barron's* (July 7, 2003, pp. 24)
Pub: Barron's
Ed: Michael Niemira, Bill Alpert, Jay Palmer. **Description:** Two books about corporate accounting and fraud are reviewed, "The Number" book, and "Born to Steal: When the Mafia Hit Wall Street".

37414 ■ "Courting Trouble" in *Inc.* (October 1, 2003)
Pub: Gruner & Jahr USA Publishing
Ed: Nadine Heintz. **Description:** Profile of an entrepreneur facing mail fraud charges engaged in a fraudulent scheme to obtain certification as a disadvantaged small business in 2000, in order to procure government road-construction contracts set aside for minorities and women.

37415 ■ "Crackdown on Mutual Fund Abuse" in *Black Enterprise* (Vol. 34, No. 5, December 2003, pp. 22)
Pub: Earl Graves Publishing Co.
Ed: Jeffrey McKinney. **Description:** The Securities and Exchange Commission is cracking down on U.S. firms improperly trading mutual funds. So far, 80 of the nation's largest mutual funds operations have received letters requesting information about ways they buy and sell mutual funds.

37416 ■ "Crossing the Gene Barrier" in *Business Week* (January 16, 2006, No. 3967, pp. 72-77, 80)
Pub: McGraw-Hill Companies
Ed: Arlene Weintraub. **Description:** Biotechnology scientists Harry M. Meade and Nils Lonberg are mixing the genetic materials of man and beats in new ways in order to develop treatments of life threatening diseases such as cancer and arthritis. Medical ethics of genetic research are also discussed.

37417 ■ "D&O: Hard and Getting Harder" in *Rough Notes* (Vol. 145, No. 9, September 2002, pp. 71)
Pub: Rough Notes
Ed: Phil Zinkewicz. **Description:** After Enron Corporation, Global Crossing, and WorldCom admitted to having overstated cash flow or profits, several insurance companies involved in potential directors and officers, liability policies are seeking protection against suits owing to alleged misrepresentations in the procurement of policies.

37418 ■ "D.C. Gets It Almost Right" in *Fortuneit* (Vol. 146, No. 4, September 2, 2002, pp. 38)
Pub: Time Inc.
Ed: Cait Murphy. **Description:** The Sarbanes-Oxley bill on corporate governance and accounting reform is profiled.

37419 ■ "Dean of Boston College Business School Wants to Emphasize Ethics and Values" in *Boston Globe* (March 8, 2005)
Pub: New York Times Company
Ed: Robert Weisman. **Description:** Boston College's School of Business is stressing ethics and values in its new curriculum.

37420 ■ "Delta Agrees to Settle Potential Allegations of Employee-Fund Misuse" in *Altanta Journal-Constitution* (February 7, 2007)
Pub: Cox Newspapers, Inc.
Ed: Russell Grantham. **Description:** Delta Airlines will pay $70 million into a fund for disabled employees and surviving relatives of retired employees in order to settle allegations that the airline used the fund after 9/11 for other expenses.

37421 ■ "Devil's advocate" in *Entrepreneur* (Vol. 31, No. 5, May 2003, pp. 75)
Pub: Entrepreneur Media Inc.
Ed: Kimberly L. McCall. **Description:** Ethics in sales is the topic covered. Good conscience sales make for good business sense.

37422 ■ "Do the Right Thing - Or Else" in *Inc.* (November 1, 2004)
Pub: Inc. Magazine
Ed: Darren Dahl. **Description:** New Federal ethics rules apply to all companies, regardless of size.

37423 ■ "Don Quixote In Court" in *Forbes* (Vol. 170, No. 8, October 14, 2002, pp. 97)
Pub: Forbes Magazine
Ed: Ashlea Ebeling. **Description:** Jeff Abraham won a $15 million verdict for blowing the whistle on his employer, South Korea's Hyundai Group. Abraham reflects on his experience and questions whether he would do the same thing again.

37424 ■ *E is for Ethics: Essentials for Entrepreneurs*
Pub: Lifelong Learning Options
Ed: Lorraine M. Zinn. **Released:** 1995. **Price:** $9.95.

37425 ■ "Entrepreneurship and Ethics: A Literature Review" in *Journal of Business Ethics* **(Vol. 46, No. 2, August 15, 2003, pp. 99)**
Pub: Kluwer Academic Publishers Group
Ed: Francis T. Hannafey. **Description:** During the past twenty years, there has been an increase of new interest being shown in entrepreneurs and their activities; yet only recently has serious research attention been devoted to the ethical problems encountered by entrepreneurs and their organizations.

37426 ■ *The Essence of Business Ethics*
Pub: Prentice Hall
Ed: Peter Pratley. **Released:** 1995. **Price:** $19.95.

37427 ■ *Essentials of Business Ethics*
Pub: NAL Dutton
Ed: Peter Madsen and Jay M. Shafritz, editors. **Released:** 1990. **Price:** $14.95. **Description:** Defines business ethics, and discusses ethical treatment of employees, management ethics, corporate ethics, corporate responsibility, business and environmental ethics, and multinational ethics.

37428 ■ "Ethical and fair work behavior" in *Journal of Business Ethics* **(Vol. 28, No. 3, December 1, 2000, pp. 187)**
Pub: Kluwer Academic Publishers
Ed: M.S. Singer. **Description:** The article explores three issues: the extent to which the normative criteria of ethics and justice prescribed by moral philosophers are indeed reflective in managers' subjective beliefs of ethic and just work behavior; the relationship between people's beliefs and their perceptions of actual ethical and just work behavior; and the relationship between the notions of ethics and justice.

37429 ■ *Ethical Conduct and the Professional's Dilemma: Choosing Between Service and Success*
Pub: Greenwood Publishing Group, Inc.
Ed: Banks McDowell. **Released:** 1991. **Price:** $49.95. **Description:** Examines choices faced by professionals regarding ethical behavior versus enhancing income.

37430 ■ *Ethical Issues in Business*
Pub: Harcourt Brace College Publishers
Ed: Michael Boylan. **Released:** 1995. **Price:** $46.25 (paper).

37431 ■ *Ethical Issues in Business: A Philosophical Approach*
Pub: Prentice Hall
Ed: Thomas Donaldson and Patricia H. Werhane, editors. **Released:** Fourth edition, 1992. **Price:** $41.00

37432 ■ "The ethical leader's decision tree." in *Harvard Business Review* **(Vol. 81, No. 2, February 2003, pp. 18)**
Pub: Harvard Business School Press
Ed: Constance E. Bagley. **Description:** The idea of a decision tree to help executives choose to continue an action is presented. The tree takes into consideration legal ramifications, shareholder value, and ethics.

37433 ■ "Ethical Problems, Conflicts and Beliefs of Small Business Professionals" in *Journal of Business Ethics* **(Vol. 28, No. 1, Nov. 1, 2000)**
Pub: Kluwer Academic Publishers
Ed: Scott J. Vitell, Erin Baca Dickerson, Troy A. Festervand. **Description:** This paper presents the results of a national study of the beliefs and perceptions of small business professionals concerning ethics within their company and business in general.

37434 ■ *Ethical Workplace*
Pub: Crisp Publications, Inc.
Ed: Steve Albrecht. **Released:** 1998. **Price:** $12.95.

37435 ■ *Ethics in the Business World*
Pub: Krieger Publishing Co., Inc.
Ed: Paul F. Hodapp. **Released:** 1994. **Price:** $19.95 (library binding).

37436 ■ "The Ethics of Consumer Sovereignty in an Age of High Tech" in *Journal of Business Ethics* **(Vol. 28, No. 1, November 1, 2000, pp. 1)**
Pub: Kluwer Academic Publishers
Ed: M. Joseph Sirgy, Chenting Su. **Description:** The world of high tech is increasingly responsible for changes in the opportunity, ability, and motivation of business firms to compete. Furthermore, it is also increasingly responsible for the same motivation of consumers to engage in rational decision-making.

37437 ■ "Ethics, Deception and Labor Negotiation" in *Journal of Business Ethics* **(Vol. 28, No. 2, November 15, 2000, pp. 145)**
Pub: Kluwer Academic Publishers
Ed: Chris Provis. **Description:** The importance of trust among all parties in the employment relationship, associated with a call for increased "integrative bargaining", is discussed.

37438 ■ "Ethics of Justice and Care in Corporate Crisis Management" in *Journal of Business Ethics* **(Vol. 46, No. 4, Sept. 15, 2003, pp. 351)**
Pub: Kluwer Academic Publishers Group
Ed: Sheldene Simola. **Description:** The importance of ethics in corporate crisis management is discussed.

37439 ■ *Ethics: The Enemy in the Workplace*
Pub: South-Western Publishing Co.
Ed: Laurence Barton. **Released:** 1995. **Price:** $38.95.

37440 ■ "Exaggeration Nation" in *Inc.* **(Volume 27, July 2005, No. 7, pp. 112)**
Pub: Inc. Magazine
Ed: Adam Hanft. **Description:** Few business owners tell the whole truth and inflate a company's revenue. Russell Simmons, hip-hop impresario was humiliated publicly for inflating the revenue of Phat Farm in 2003.

37441 ■ "Executive who was dismissed accuses firm of inflating profit" in *Wall Street Journal* **(February 3, 2003, pp. B6)**
Pub: Dow Jones & Co. Inc.
Description: A countersuit against Electronic Data Systems Corporation was filed by an employee fired by the firm. The employee was accused of stealing from the company.

37442 ■ "Federal suit alleges MVM overbilled" in *Washington Business Journal* **(Vol. 21, No. 50, April 11, 2003, pp. 1)**
Pub: Washington Business Journal
Ed: Sean Madigan. **Description:** A civil suit has been filed against MVM Inc. by the U.S. Department of Justice, alleging that MVM submitted 44 false invoices on a security services contract. MVM is alleged to have invoiced for 4 security guards in supervisory positions, before they were actually trained.

37443 ■ "Following your moral compass" in *Incentive* **(Vol. 174, No. 10, October 2000, pp. 107)**
Pub: Bill Communications
Ed: Stephen Covey. **Description:** The best leaders use an internal set of morals and principles to navigate the often treacherous waters of business and set a course for success.

37444 ■ "Folly and fortitude" in *Harvard Business Review* **(Vol. 80, No. 10, October 2002, pp. 10)**
Pub: Harvard Business School Press
Description: The exuberant spending by companies and consumers in the late 1990s has not produced high inflation; however, corporate corruption has increased, partly due to such spending and other factors.

37445 ■ "Former Couch Street Figure Heads to Prison" in *Business Journal-Portland* **(Vol. 20, No. 24, August 15, 2003, pp. 8)**
Pub: American City Business Journals, Inc.
Ed: Shelly Strom. **Description:** Cleburne Jr. Brigham has been sentenced to 37 years in prison for alleged falsification of a loan application, making false statements to the U.S. Small Business Administration, misuse of social security number, and using the Couch Street Fish House illegally.

37446 ■ "Four Steps to a Fundamental Ethical Vision through Meditation" in *Journal of Business Ethics* **(Vol. 28, No. 1, Nov. 1, 2000, pp. 25)**
Pub: Kluwer Academic Publishers
Ed: Paul G. LaForge. **Description:** The author suggests that modern business not only lacks ethics, but is also suffering form a loss of meaning, which prevents firms from maximizing their resources. Three types of meditation, as a source of recovery of meaning, are described.

37447 ■ "Friends should never ask friends to spam-even if Big Blue says to do so" in *InfoWorld* **(Vol. 22, No. 38, September 18, 2000 pp. 109)**
Pub: InfoWorld
Ed: Ed Foster. **Description:** Internet marketers frequently use chain-letter methods to sell products and services, offering free items if a user agrees to spam friends. IBM has drawn several complaints from users by resorting to such tactics when marketing its ViaVoice speech-recognition product. Users received E-mail forms IBM titled 'How to Get ViaVoice Free' that offered a $169 copy of ViaVoice Millennium Pro at no charge if they persuaded five friends to sign up for the same small-business online newsletter. IBM asked users to forward a specific canned message to others offering an electronic Small Business Resource Guide as a bonus gift, but failed to mention that the person forwarding the message had received a bribe. Many people are appalled that IBM would stoop to spam methods.

37448 ■ "Global accounting is coming" in *Harvard Business Review* **(Vol. 81, No. 4, April 2003, pp. 24)**
Pub: Harvard Business School Press
Ed: Richard G. Barker. **Description:** The recent accounting scandals have led to international influence on U.S. financial reporting. Under the emerging global standards, income statements will reveal more than has been the custom with U.S. firms.

37449 ■ "The Good Manager-A Moral Manager?" in *Journal of Business Ethics* **(Vol. 27, No. 3, October 1, 2000, pp. 247)**
Pub: Kluwer Academic Publishers
Ed: Per Sundman. **Description:** Two problems associated with the recently developed "practice or virtue approach" to business ethics are discussed. The first problem concerns an alleged harmony between common demands of morality and the internal goods of actual business practice. The second problem is related to the first and concerns the alleged relevance of a virtue perspective for business ethics.

37450 ■ "Good Vibes: Socially Responsible Investing is Gaining Fans...and Clout" in *Barron's* **(July 7, 2003, pp. L3)**
Pub: Barron's
Ed: Robin Goldwyn Blumenthal. **Description:** High profile corporate corruption scandals, such as Enron and WorldCom, have helped strengthen the position of socially responsible investing advocates, even in the Wall Street community, where they were most widely derided. A review of the increasing influence of socially responsible investing is provided.

37451 ■ "Green Machines" in *Entrepreneur* **(Vol. 31, No. 7, July 2003, pp. 34)**
Pub: Entrepreneur Media, Inc.
Ed: Geoff Williams. **Description:** Profile of Grant Goodman, CEO of Rockland Materials and five other companies, that make building materials such as ready-mix cement. Goodman runs his fleet of 120 truck on primarily biodiesel fuel made from soybeans. The fuel is biodegradable, nontoxic and free from sulfur.

37452 ■ "Gulf Team With Corpedia on Ethics Course" in *Rough Notes* **(Vol. 146, No. 9, September 2003, pp. 44)**
Pub: Rough Notes
Ed: Dennis H. Pillsbury. **Description:** Profile of Gulf Insurance Group's underwriting division, including Internet marketing, importance of teamwork, and management of debt and business losses.

37453 ■ **"HealthSouth Corp. Feels Fallout from Corporate Scandal"** in *Atlanta Journal-Constitution* **(April 11, 2003)**
Pub: Knight-Ridder/Tribune Business News
Ed: Patti Bond. **Description:** Despite the good care offered by professionals working for HealthSouth Corporation, fraud allegations against the HealthSouth headquarters, has made patients leery of having rehabilitation therapies performed there.

37454 ■ **"Hewlett-Packard Was Far From First To Try 'PreTexting'"** in *Wall Street Journal* **(Vol. 248, December 2006, No. 149, pp. A1)**
Pub: Dow Jones & Co. Inc.
Ed: John A. Emshwiller **Description:** Hewlett-Packard Co. as well as all the major lenders can no longer use 'Pretexting'- the practice of impersonating people in order to receive phone or financial records, as it is now being federally prohibited.

37455 ■ *Honest Business: A Superior Strategy for Starting & Maintaining Your Own Business*
Pub: Shambhala Publications, Inc.
Ed: Michael Phillips. **Released:** 1996.

37456 ■ *How Good People Make Tough Choices*
Pub: Simon & Schuster, Inc.
Released: 1996. **Price:** $11.00.

37457 ■ **"How Presidents Persuade"** in *Harvard Business Review* **(Vol. 81, No. 1, January 2003, pp. 20)**
Pub: Harvard Business School Press
Ed: David R. Gergen. **Description:** An advisor to four presidents discusses how U.S. presidents establish trust and use their powers of oratory to persuade. He also points out the need for true humility and strict honesty with the American people.

37458 ■ **"How (Un)Ethical Are You?"** in *Harvard Business Review* **(Vol. 81, No. 12, December 2003, pp. 56)**
Pub: Harvard Business School Press
Ed: Mahzaarin R. Banaji, Max H. Bazerman, Dolly Chugh. **Description:** Four sources of unintentional bias in management decision making are examined: conflict of interest, in-group favoritism, overclaiming credit, and implicit prejudice are shown. Methods for mitigating the sources of bias include shaping one's environment to reduce external cues, broadening the hypothetical influence of decision-making processes, and remaining vigilant.

37459 ■ **"The Hungry Wolf Syndrome"** in *Rough Notes* **(Vol. 145, No. 1, January 2003, pp. 92)**
Pub: Rough Notes
Ed: Donald S. Malecki. **Description:** Insurance agents sometimes add information on certificates or insurance, broaden contractual liability coverage, and misrepresent the truth to preserve a client whose demands are unreasonable.

37460 ■ **"I was greedy, too"** in *Harvard Business Review* **(Vol. 81, No. 2, February 2003, pp. 38)**
Pub: Harvard Business School Press
Ed: Diane L. Coutu. **Description:** Although greed has become an integral part of the U.S. psyche, the psychology of greed has not been studied well. Greed has ebbed and crested throughout this country's history, and most recently with the collapse of Internet companies, corporate malfeasance. However, business schools continue to graduate a high number of students.

37461 ■ **"Identifying and Developing Measures of Information Technology Ethical Work Climates"** in *Journal of Business Ethics* **(Sept. 15, 2003)**
Pub: Kluwer Academic Publishers Group
Ed: Robert W. Stone, John W. Henry. **Description:** A model of information technology (IT) ethical work climates is presented using the ethical work climates and data collected from a national mail survey of the Association for Computing Machinery members.

37462 ■ **"Impact of Personal and Situational Factors on Taxpayer Compliance"** in *Journal of Business Ethics* **(Vol. 47, No. 3, Oct. 15, 2003)**
Pub: Kluwer Academic Publishers Group
Ed: Viswanath Umashanker Trivedi, Mohamed Shehata, Bernadette Lynn. **Description:** A study using a laboratory experiment with monetary incentives to test the impact of three personal factors (moral reasoning, value orientation and risk preference), and three situational factors (the presence/absence of audits, tax inequity, and peer reporting behavior), while controlling for the impact of other demographic characteristics, on tax compliance is presented.

37463 ■ **"The Imposter Syndrome. Why Do So Many Successful Entrepreneurs Feel Like Fakes?"** in *Inc.* **(September 2006, pp. 37-38)**
Pub: Gruner & Jahr USA Publishing
Ed: Leigh Buchanan. **Description:** Many successful entrepreneurs are embarrassed by their success and feel their success is due to timing and location than personal talent. This can be dangerous in the long range.

37464 ■ **"In Corporate-Fraud Cases, Lawyer's Approval Can Let Client Avoid Charges"** in *Houston Chronicle* **(April 11, 2003)**
Pub: Knight-Ridder/Tribune Business News
Ed: Mary Flood. **Description:** The ramifications of an attorney's approval of a business deal are explored.

37465 ■ *Information & Responsibility: The Ethical Challenge*
Pub: Sage Publications, Inc.
Ed: Richard O. Mason. **Released:** 1995. **Price:** $48.00.

37466 ■ *Intentional Integrity*
Pub: Broadman & Holman Publishers
Ed: Millard N. MacAdam. **Released:** 1996. **Price:** $11.99.

37467 ■ **"It's a Trap! Watch Your Step-Pharming Scams Are Lurking Around Every Corner"** in *Entrepreneur* **(Vol. 33, August 2005, No. 8, pp. 40)**
Pub: Entrepreneur Media Inc.
Ed: Mike Hogan. **Description:** Netcraft, a network security company, identifies phishing emails that try to scam customers into giving up personal financial information. Ways to avoid these scams are listed.

37468 ■ **"Judge Rejects Effort to Keep Billing Records for Boston's Big Dig a Secret"** in *Boston Globe* **(April 11, 2003)**
Pub: Knight-Ridder/Tribune Business News
Ed: Sean P. Murphy. **Description:** Release of the records pertaining to Boston's Big Dig and the millions of dollars paid to private sector managers is discussed.

37469 ■ **"Keeping an Eye on Corporate America"** in *Fortuneit* **(Vol. 146, No. 11, November 25, 2002, pp. 44)**
Pub: Time Inc.
Ed: Alynda Wheat. **Description:** The gathering of the Ethics Officer Association's tenth anniversary is discussed. The meeting addressed many current compliance issues.

37470 ■ **"Kraft Not Alone"** in *Crain's Chicago Business* **(Vol. 30, February 2007, No. 6, pp. 8)**
Pub: Crain Communications, Inc.
Description: Consumer watchdog group, The Center for Science in the Public Interest, has been putting pressure on food companies to be more truthful on their product labels. Listing of companies who have had misleading claims on their products is included.

37471 ■ **"Liar, Liar: In the Race to Make Money, Some American Businesses Have Been Lying Their Pants Off"** in *Entrepreneur* **(Vol. 31, Oct. 2003)**
Pub: Entrepreneur Media, Inc.
Ed: Joshua Kurlantzick. **Description:** Despite the business scandals and legislation of 2002, lies and dishonesty are a more acceptable part of business in America.

37472 ■ **"Life After Enron"** in *Black Enterprise* **(Vol. 34, No. 4, November 2003)**
Pub: Earl Graves Publishing Co.
Ed: Sheryl Nance-Nash. **Description:** Profile of a human resources generalist working for Enron and had invested 60-70 percent of her retirement assets in Enron stock is presented. The family shares insight in ways they are coping.

37473 ■ **"Making ethical business decisions"** in *Women in Business* **(Vol. 53, No. 2, March-April, 2001, pp. 22)**
Pub: The ABWA Co. Inc.
Ed: Mary-Lane Kamberg. **Description:** Issues concerning the steps involved in ethical decision-making in business are discussed. The importance of establishing clear guidelines for staff on company policy regarding ethics, honesty, and behavior is stressed.

37474 ■ *Managing Business Ethics: Straight Talk about How to Do It Right*
Pub: John Wiley & Sons, Inc.
Ed: Linda K. Trevino and Katherine A. Nelson. **Released:** 2nd ed. 2000. **Price:** $35.95; $45.95.

37475 ■ **"Medieval or Modern? A Scholastic's View of Business Ethics, circa 1430"** in *Journal of Business Ethics* **(Vol. 28, No. 2, Nov. 15, 2000)**
Pub: Kluwer Academic Publishers
Ed: Daniel A. Wren. **Description:** There are varying opinions about whether or not the field of business ethics has a history or is a development of more modern times. This article looks at a book by a Dominican Friar, written ca. 1430, which provides a basis for a history of over 500 years.

37476 ■ **"The moonlighter"** in *Harvard Business Review* **(Vol. 80, No. 11, November 2002, pp. 33)**
Pub: Harvard Business School Press
Ed: Bronwyn Fryer. **Description:** In this fictional case study, an employee of one company is working on a project for another company in his free time in the first company's offices. Five experts discuss how the first company's managers should handle the situation.

37477 ■ **"The Moral Intensity of Privacy: An Empirical Study of Webmasters' Attitudes"** in *Journal of Business Ethics* **(Vol. 46, Sept. 15, 2003)**
Pub: Kluwer Academic Publishers Group
Ed: Thomas R. Shaw. **Description:** Webmasters play an integral role as moral agent regarding the issue of Internet privacy.

37478 ■ *Moral Issues in Business*
Pub: Wadsworth Publishing Co.
Ed: Shaw. **Released:** 8th ed. 2000. **Price:** $37.50.

37479 ■ *Moral Management: Integrating Ethics*
Pub: Irwin Professional Publishing
Ed: Andrew Sikula Sr. **Released:** 1995. **Price:** $20.005.

37480 ■ **"Multiple Stakeholder Judgments of Employee Behaviors"** in *Journal of Business Ethics* **(Vol. 46, No. 3, September 2003, pp. 235)**
Pub: Kluwer Academic Publishers Group
Ed: Elizabeth D. Scott, Karen A. Jehn. **Description:** Do moral judgments made by various stakeholders in determining whether an event, caused by an organizational employee, constitute dishonesty?

37481 ■ **"Net Crimes & Misdemeanors"** in *Information Today* **(Vol. 20, No. 1, Jan. 2003, pp. 44)**
Pub: Information Today, Inc.
Description: A new book for Information Professionals is reviewed. The book helps individuals and business users of the Web to protect themselves, their children and their employees from online predators and cheats.

37482 ■ **"New 'corporate sheriff' starts touch talk"** in *Atlanta Business Chronicle* (Vol. 25, No. 21, November 1, 2002, pp. 3A)
Pub: American City Business Publications, Inc.
Ed: Walter Woods. **Description:** U.S. Attorney General, William Duffey, vows to take action against corporate crooks. He is warning Atlanta, Georgia businesses their conduct will be eyed by his office.

37483 ■ **"New Ethics or No Ethics? Questionable behavior is Silicon Valley's next big thing"** in *Fortune* (Vol. 141, No. 6, Mar. 20, 2000, pp. 82)
Pub: Time Inc.
Ed: Jerry Useem. **Description:** Eventually our deeper values catch up to the new worlds we create. In the meantime, there will be a lot of shenanigans.

37484 ■ **"An old-fashioned fate: it takes the tax collector to really ruin somebody"** in *Barron's* (Vol. 82, No. 58, February 17, 2003, pp. 31)
Pub: Barron's
Ed: Thomas G. Donlan. **Description:** Former Sprint CEO, William T. Esprey, was doubly unethical in formulating the tax evasion scam that ruined him; he also leaned on the company auditors, Ernst & Young, to form an illicit tax shelter.

37485 ■ **"On the Internet, a Second Act"** in *Barron's* (July 28, 2003, pp. T1)
Pub: Barron's
Ed: Bill Alpert. **Description:** Michael Wachs, who conducts online interviews of executives for CEOcast, also spent nearly a year in federal prison for swindling Chase Manhattan Bank out of nearly $21 million. Questions are raised about the legality of his role with CEOcast on the provisions of his settlement with Chase.

37486 ■ **"Operation no safe haven: there's $400 billion in unregulated money stashed in offshore hedge accounts"** in *Red Herring* (Jan. 2003)
Pub: Herring Communications Inc.
Ed: Christopher Byron. **Description:** Offshore hedge funds provide an end run around the crackdown on U.S. companies. These accounts allow money to be moved anonymously in and out of the U.S. without going through a U.S. bank.

37487 ■ **"Oxymoron 101"** in *Forbes* (Vol. 170, No. 12, December 9, 2002, pp. 164)
Pub: Forbes Magazine
Ed: Dan Seligman. **Description:** Despite the increase in business ethics programs being increase at the nation's colleges and universities, there's no sign that the studies will prevent more business scandals such as Enron.

37488 ■ **"Pill Pusher: Drug Maker Biovail Sparks Controversy by Paying Doctors to Write Prescriptions"** in *Barron's* (July 21, 2003, pp. 17)
Pub: Barron's
Ed: Bill Alpert. **Description:** Biovail's offer of $1,000 to doctors who write 15 prescriptions for Cardizem LA blood-pressure treatment goes against medical ethics, according to many doctors and industry observers. Biovail developed the plan with the help of consulting firm, Quintiles Transnational.

37489 ■ **"The Postmodern Shift in Values and Jobs and the Implications for HR"** in *Employment Relations Today* (Vol. 26, No. 4, Winter 2000)
Pub: John Wiley & Sons, Inc.
Ed: Andy Himes. **Description:** A report concerning the impact of postmodern social values on corporate culture and human resource management. Topics addressed include industrial psychology, attracting and retaining postmodern workers, and the relationship between management and workers in a postmodern society.

37490 ■ *Practical Business Ethics*
Pub: Macmillan Publishing Co., Inc.
Ed: Warren A. French. **Released:** 1994. **Price:** $33.33.

37491 ■ *A Pragmatic Approach to Business Ethics*
Pub: Sage Publications, Inc.
Ed: Alex C. Michalos. **Released:** 1995. **Price:** $36.95; $21.95 (paper).

37492 ■ **"Pressure on appraisers creates risk for fraud"** in *Atlanta Business Chronicle* (Vol. 24, No. 13, August 31, 2001, pp. 4B)
Pub: American City Business Journals Inc.
Ed: Erica Stephens. **Description:** Real estate appraisers are at risk for fraud due to pressure that is put on them by real estate agents, lenders, and others in the industry, according to Jeff A. Lawson, Regions Bank's senior appraisal review officer. Lawson believes work by appraisers has become harder since the Financial Institutions Act Reform, Recovery and Enforcement Act was developed. Appraisers, said Lawson, should get in contact with clients who they can trust.

37493 ■ **"The Prevaricator"** in *Barron's* (July 28, 2003, pp. 7)
Pub: Barron's
Ed: Alan Abelson. **Description:** The tendency toward deception among financial services professionals is examined, which is engendered not only by inborn corruption, but by the drive to continue outperforming past results.

37494 ■ **"Private-to-Private Corruption"** in *Journal of Business Ethics* (Vol. 47, No. 3, October 15, 2003, pp. 253)
Pub: Kluwer Academic Publishers Group
Ed: Antonio Argandona. **Description:** Private-to-private corruption has been neglected and only recently receiving coverage by the media.

37495 ■ **"Promise-keeping has lost its importance as a core value"** in *Atlanta Business Chronicle* (Vol. 25, November 15, 2002, No. 23 pp. 27A)
Pub: American City Business Publications, Inc.
Ed: Ellwood F. Oakley III. **Description:** Managers consider "promise keeping" to be a lower-level ethical priority in business activity. MindSpring Enterprises Inc. is a high-profile exception; the company lives up to its commitments. Senior management must practice promise-keeping in order for it to be reintroduced into a workplace.

37496 ■ **"Reinforcing Ethical Decision Making Through Organizational Structure"** in *Journal of Business Ethics* (Vol. 28, No. 1, Nov. 1, 2000)
Pub: Kluwer Academic Publishers
Ed: Harvey S. James, Jr. **Description:** The article explores the way a firm's organizational structure will affect the ethical behavior of workers, including compensation practices, performance and evaluation systems, and decision-making assignments.

37497 ■ **"Right From Wrong"** in *Journal of Business Ethics* (Vol. 46, No. 1, Aug. 2003)
Pub: Kluwer Academic Publishers Group
Ed: Robert A. Giacalone, Carole L. Jurkiewicz. **Description:** A network sample of 162 employees across the U.S. was studied to assess the relationship between individual spirituality and perceptions of unethical business activities.

37498 ■ **"The Role of Integrity as a Mediator in Strategic Leadership"** in *Journal of Business Ethics* (Vol. 46, No. 1, Aug. 2003, pp. 31)
Pub: Kluwer Academic Publishers Group
Ed: Skip Worden. **Description:** An examination of the role of integrity as a mediator within strategic leadership and its impact on credibility in reputational capital is discussed.

37499 ■ **"Round Table"** in *Atlanta Business Chronicle* (Vol. 25, November 15, 2002, No. 23 pp. 7B)
Pub: American City Business Publications, Inc.
Description: Five Atlanta, Georgia-area executives respond to handling three potential dilemmas, which involve ethical issues. Responses are given by Arn Rubinoff of Powell, Goldstein, Frazer & Murphy LLC; John C. Knapp of The Southern Institute for Business and Professional Ethics; Dave Brookmire of Corporate Performance Strategies Inc.; Emmett Hawkins III of Leapfrog Services Inc.; and Larry Hart of The Executive Committee.

37500 ■ **"Scandal 101: Lessons From Ken Lay"** in *Fortuneit* (Vol. 146, No. 4, September 2, 2002, pp. 52)
Pub: Time Inc.
Ed: Julie Schlosser. **Description:** A listing of U.S. universities offering Ethics and Management Courses, starting fall 2002.

37501 ■ **"Shred of evidence: learn a lesson from Arthur Anderson"** in *Entrepreneur* (Vol. 30, No. 12, December 2002, pp. 106)
Pub: Entrepreneur Media Inc.
Ed: Steven C. Bahls, Jane Easter Bahls. **Description:** The importance of working with an attorney to ensure compliance with all laws on length of time to retain company documents is discussed.

37502 ■ **"Slick Tricks"** in *Entrepreneur* (Vol. 31, No. 7, July 2003, pp. 73)
Pub: Entrepreneur Media, Inc.
Ed: Joanne Cleaver. **Description:** Telecommunications scams continue with newer attacks of hijacked phone accounts (slamming), unauthorized add-on charges (cramming). It is important for small business owners to warn employees of such scams to avoid problems.

37503 ■ *Small Business Desk Reference*
Pub: Penguin Books (USA) Incorporated
Ed: Gene Marks. **Released:** December 2004. **Price:** $29.95 (US), $44.00 (Canadian). **Description:** Comprehensive guide for starting or running a successful small business, focusing on buying a business or franchise, writing a business plan, financial management, accounting, legal issues, human resources management, operations, marketing, sales, customer service, taxes, insurance, and ethics. Information for launching a restaurant, property management firm, retail outlet, consulting firm, and service business is included.

37504 ■ *Small Business Management*
Pub: John Wiley & Sons, Incorporated
Ed: Margaret Burlingame. **Released:** March 2007. **Price:** $44.95. **Description:** Advice for starting and running a small business as well as information on the value and appeal of small businesses, is given. Topics include budgets, taxes, inventory, ethics, e-commerce, and current laws.

37505 ■ **"Snipers, Stalkers, and Nibblers: Online Auction Business Ethics"** in *Journal of Business Ethics* (Vol. 46, No. 2, Aug. 15, 2003)
Pub: Kluwer Academic Publishers Group
Ed: Alexei M. Marcoux. **Description:** Spirited discussion exists among online auction participants over the ethics of sniping: delaying one's bid until the closing seconds of an online auction.

37506 ■ **"The Social Cost of Fraud and Bankruptcy"** in *Harvard Business Review* (Vol. 81, No. 12, December 2003, pp. 20)
Pub: Harvard Business School Press
Ed: Joseph Bower, Stuart Gilson. **Description:** The unfair advantage Chapter 11 bankruptcy law provides to companies that have operated outside the legally sanctioned business practices to which other firms have subscribed is addressed. Discussions focus on how firms obeying the laws are penalized, using the WorldCom Inc. case as an example.

37507 ■ *Social Responsibility in Marketing: A Proactive and Profitable Marketing Management Strategy*
Pub: Quorum Books
Ed: A. Coskum Samli. **Released:** 1992. **Price:** $49.95. **Description:** Covers socially responsible marketing strategies.

37508 ■ "A Spam Law That Slams Small Business" in *Business Week Online* (November 5, 2003)
Pub: McGraw-Hill Inc.
Ed: Christopher Kenton. **Description:** The impact of new California legislation that makes it a crime to send any unsolicited commercial email from or to any email account accessed from or billed to a California address is examined.

37509 ■ "Spies in the Boardroom?" in *Forbes* (Vol. 170, No. 5, September 16, 2002, pp. 45)
Pub: Forbes Magazine
Ed: Luisa Kroll. **Description:** CCBN.com's founder Jeffrey Parker filed a law suit against the Canadian information services corporation, Thomas Corporation in July 2002.

37510 ■ "Stopping Office Snoops" in *Inc.* (November 1, 2003)
Pub: Gruner & Jahr USA Publishing
Ed: Patrick J. Sauer. **Description:** Review of the book, The Spy's Guide: Office Espionage? The book offers CIA-style tips for anyone running a small business.

37511 ■ "Strategic and Ethical Considerations in Managing Digital Privacy" in *Journal of Business Ethics* (Vol. 46, No. 2, Aug. 15, 2003)
Pub: Kluwer Academic Publishers Group
Ed: Ravi Sarathy, Chrisopher J. Robertson. **Description:** Individualized customer information is at the heart of online commerce. Using increasing amounts of customer-specific data enhances the success and value of one-to-one online marketing, but the extensive gathering and use of data specific to individuals also causes alarm over the loss of digital privacy.

37512 ■ "Survey: Residents think scandal will shape up business behavior" in *Crain's Detroit Business* (Vol. 18, No. 22, June 3, 2002, pp. 1)
Pub: Crain Communications Inc. - Detroit
Ed: Brent Snavely. **Description:** Following the collapse of Enron Corporation, most Michigan residents think that the financial and accounting scandal will cause Michigan-based companies to act more responsibly and ethically than in the past.

37513 ■ "Sworn to secrecy" in *Women in Business* (Vol. 53, No. 4, July-August, 2001, pp. 22)
Pub: The ABWA Co. Inc.
Ed: Linda Helmig Braun, Mary Ann Clift. **Description:** Issues concerning ethical aspects of secrecy are discussed. Particular attention is given to reasons for keeping or disclosing a secret, emphasizing that according to the situation it could be more harmful to keep the secret rather than disclose it.

37514 ■ "Take a bow" in *Atlanta Business Chronicle* (Vol. 25, November 8, 2002, No. 22 pp. 1B)
Pub: American City Business Publications, Inc.
Ed: Lee Hall. **Description:** Party City of Atlanta, Inc. received recognition at the 2002 Georgia Business Ethics Awards given out by the Society of Financial Service Professionals' Atlanta chapter. The firm, a franchisee of Party City Corporation, runs 24 stores in the Atlanta area.

37515 ■ "Take a hard look, and do the right thing" in *Crain's Detroit Business* (Vol. 19, No. 5, February 3, 2003, pp. 9)
Pub: Crain Communications Inc., Detroit
Ed: Frank Hennessey. **Description:** The ethical aspects and regulation of business and accounting practices are investigated.

37516 ■ "Time Right To Let Sun Shine On AG, Outside Attorneys" in *Mississippi Business Journal* (Vol. 29, January 2007 , No. 29, pp. 4)
Pub: Venture Publications, Inc.
Ed: Joe D. Jones **Description:** Mississippi Open Lawyer Fees Act has been written and introduced to the Legislature to bring added openness, oversight and accountability to the Attorney General's Office when outside lawyers are hired to work on behalf of the state.

37517 ■ "Tougher rules likely to dry up boardroom candidates" in *Crain's Detroit Business* (Vol. 19, No. 6, February 10, 2003, pp. 14)
Pub: Crain Communications Inc., Detroit
Ed: Katie Merx. **Description:** The impact of the Sarbanes-Oxley Act are investigated, including the affect it will have on part-time directorships.

37518 ■ "Trust is a must" in *Entrepreneur* (Vol. 30, No. 10, October 2002, pp. 70)
Pub: Entrepreneur Media Inc.
Ed: Chris Sandlund. **Description:** The importance of ethics in business is stressed. Trust underlies all business relationships, including employees, customers and suppliers.

37519 ■ "The Truth Is Out There" in *Entrepreneur* (Vol. 33, August 2005, No. 8, pp. 8)
Pub: Entrepreneur Media Inc.
Ed: Rieva Lesonsky. **Description:** Entrepreneurs should be wary of using bad or misleading advertising in marketing campaigns.

37520 ■ "A Typology of Situational Factors" in *Journal of Business Ethics* (Vol. 46, No. 3, Sept. 2003, pp. 213)
Pub: Kluwer Academic Publishers Group
Ed: William T. Ross, Diana C. Robertson. **Description:** Two dimensions of situational factors expected to influence decision-making about ethical issues among sales representatives: universal vs. particular and direct vs. indirect, are explored.

37521 ■ "The virtue matrix" in *Harvard Business Review* (Vol. 80, No. 3, March 2002, pp. 69)
Pub: Harvard Business School Press
Ed: Roger L. Martin. **Description:** Corporate ethics issues are discussed at the Aspen Institute's Initiative for Social Innovation Through Business, and the virtue matrix, an analytical tool that helps executives think about corporate responsibility, designed after the Aspen Institute discussion.

37522 ■ "Virtue Theory as a Dynamic Theory of Business" in *Journal of Business Ethics* (Vol. 28, No. 2, November 15, 2000, pp. 159)
Pub: Kluwer Academic Publishers
Ed: Surendra Arjoon. **Description:** Virtue theory shows, firms that pursue ethically driven strategies can realize a greater profit potential than those firms who currently use profit-driven strategies.

37523 ■ "A Virtuous Cycle" in *Forbes* (Vol. 170, No. 13, December 23, 2002, pp. 248)
Pub: Forbes Magazine
Ed: James Surowiecki. **Description:** The importance of trust and honesty in relation to capitalism is examined.

37524 ■ *Wake Up Calls: Classic Cases in Business Ethics*
Pub: Wadsworth Publishing Co.
Ed: Lisa H. Newton. **Released:** 1996. **Price:** $26.95.

37525 ■ "Wall Street wooing wary investors with reforms" in *Atlanta Business Chronicle* (Vol. 25, No. 20, October 25, 2002, pp. 11C)
Pub: American City Business Publications, Inc.
Ed: Lee Hall. **Description:** The larger brokerage houses are revising the way they report on stocks. These houses are feeling the pressure from angry investors and threatened lawsuits and are going out of their way to polish their image.

37526 ■ "Wayne County chief creates post to watch ethics and efficiency" in *Crain's Detroit Business* (Vol. 19, No. 15, April 14, 2003)
Pub: Crain Communications Inc., Detroit
Ed: Robert Ankeny. **Description:** David Esper has been appointed by Wayne County Executive Robert Ficano to work as the county's ethics watchdog and efficiency expert. Esper feels the existing ethics ordinance in Wayne County, Michigan is limited in scope and may need to be expanded.

37527 ■ "We Need Reform To Curb Corporate Scandals, But Don't Get Excessive" in *Venture Capital Journal* (Vol. 42, No. 8, August 2002, pp. 40)
Pub: Thomas Venture Economics
Ed: Mark Heesen. **Description:** The Corporate and Auditing Accountability, Responsibility, and Transparency Act, which creates a new oversight body that will certify accountants and have the authority to punch, is profiled.

37528 ■ "Web.Preneuring" in *Small Business Opportunities* (Vol. 17, November 2005, No. 6, pp. 90, 94)
Pub: Harris Publications Inc.
Ed: Chuck Green. **Description:** Profile of Scott Kolbe and Mike Stout, entrepreneurs who started Icon Digital Design in a basement. The partners base their success on being graphic designers with strong work ethics.

37529 ■ *What's Ethical in Business?*
Pub: The McGraw-Hill Companies
Ed: Verne E. Henderson. **Released:** 1992. **Price:** $19.95; $12.95 (paper). **Description:** Provides a systematic method for managers and executives to approach ethical questions.

37530 ■ "What's Wrong with Computer-Generated Images of Perfection in Advertising?" in *Journal of Business Ethics* (Vol. 45, No. 3, July 2003)
Pub: Kluwer Academic Publishers Group
Ed: Earl W. Spurgin. **Description:** Advertisers often use computers to create fantastic images, however advertisers are ethically obligated to avoid certain aesthetic results that are produced by computer-generated images of perfection.

37531 ■ "When company values backfire" in *Harvard Business Review* (Vol. 80, No. 11, November 2002, pp. 18)
Pub: Harvard Business School Press
Ed: Amy C. Edmondson. **Description:** Ways the CEO of a company attempted to promote strong values but had his intentions misinterpreted by employees is described. The staff considered his decision to grow the company to be motivated by greed. The author advises leaders to work diligently to invite discussion and seek honest feedback.

37532 ■ "When Does Bending Rules Become Breaking Rules?" in *Atlanta Business Chronicle* (Vol. 24, No. 10, August 10, 2001, pp. 46A)
Pub: American City Business Journals Inc.
Ed: Emory Mulling. **Description:** Management needs to be consistent with the company's rules and core values. Company values need to be reiterated on a regular basis. In addition, people should not be expected to automatically absorb a corporate culture.

37533 ■ "Why business ethics is worthy of discussion" in *Atlanta Business Chronicle* (Vol. 25, November 15, 2002, No. 23 pp. 6B)
Pub: American City Business Publications, Inc.
Ed: John C. Knapp. **Description:** Business ethics is often associated with the aftermath of a scandal or fraud and is often thought of as negative. Businesses that embrace daily discussions tend to be the exception, but tremendous value can result from such discussions.

37534 ■ "Witness protection" in *Entrepreneur* (Vol. 31, No. 4, April 2003, pp. 78)
Pub: Entrepreneur Media Inc.
Ed: Steven C. Bahls, Jane Easter Bahls. **Description:** Profile of the Sarbanes-Oxley Act of 2002, which protects whistle-blowers reporting corporate wrong doing is presented, along with its impact on business.

TRADE PERIODICALS

37535 ■ Business Ethics
Pub: Business Ethics
Contact: Jean Madson, Advertising Department
E-mail: jean.madson@business-ethics.com
Ed: Marjorie Kelly, Editor, marjorie.kelly@business-ethics.com. Released: Quarterly. Description: Business newsletter.

37536 ■ Defense Environment Alert
Pub: Inside Washington Publishers
Contact: Suzanne Yohannan, Managing Editor
Released: Biweekly, every other Wednesday. Price: $615, U.S. and Canada; $665, elsewhere. Description: Reports on defense policies for cleanup, compliance, and pollution prevention.

37537 ■ Ethics & Policy
Pub: Center for Ethics and Social Policy
Ed: Chris Adams, Editor. Released: Quarterly. Price: Included in membership. Description: Voices the concerns of the Center, which "was founded to develop new modes of ethical analysis applicable to the major institutions of our society." Acts as a forum for various points of view on contemporary social problems. Recurring features include editorials from staff members; news of research in areas covering business ethics, economic policy, environmental ethics, religion and society, medical ethics, and book reviews.

37538 ■ Ethics Today
Pub: Ethics Resource Center Inc.
Ed: Lauren Larsen, Editor, lauren@ethics.org. Released: Monthly. Price: Free. Description: Presents discussions on issues in the field of organizational ethics and character education.

37539 ■ The GreenMoney Journal & Online Guide
Pub: The Greenmoney Journal
Contact: Cliff Feigenbaum, Editor & Publisher
E-mail: cliff@greenmoney.com
Released: Bimonthly. Price: $50, individuals; $50, Canada plus $10 postage; $50, elsewhere plus $20 postage. Description: "Encourages and promotes the awareness of socially and environmentally responsible business, investing and consumer resources in publications and online. Our goal is to educate and empower individuals and businesses to make informed financial decisions through aligning their personal, corporate and financial principles." Recurring features include a calendar of events.

37540 ■ Issues in Ethics
Pub: Markkula Center for Applied Ethics
Contact: Amy Gomersall, Designer
Ed: Miriam Schulman, Editor. Released: Semiannual. Price: $30. Description: Covers ethics in fields of education, business, biotech, healthcare, and technology. Recurring features include letters to the editor, interviews, news of research, and book reviews.

37541 ■ Poynter Center Newsletter
Pub: Poynter Center for the Study of Ethics and American Institutions
Ed: Judith A. Granbois, Editor, jgranboi@indiana.edu. Released: Semiannual. Price: Free. Description: Focuses on Center programs in American ethics and institutions, such as political institutions, research ethics and biomedical ethics.

VIDEOCASSETTES/ AUDIOCASSETTES

37542 ■ Concerns Quarterly with Footage from CBS News: General Business
Harcourt Brace College Publishers
301 Commerce, Ste. 3700
Fort Worth, TX 76102
Ph:(817)334-7500
Free: 800-237-2665
Fax: (817)334-0947

Co. E-mail: info@harcourt.com
URL: http://www.harcourt.com
Released: 1995. Price: $80.00. Description: Video newsletter containing footage from such CBS programs as CBS Evening News, 48 Hours, Street Stories, and CBS This Morning. Provides information on such topics as ethical responsibilities in business, people in business, competition, manufacturing, and marketing. Comes with instructor's guide. Available at an annual subscription rate of $300.00. Availability: VHS.

37543 ■ Ethics in American Business
Phoenix Learning Group
2349 Chaffee Dr.
St. Louis, MO 63146
Ph:(314)569-0211
Free: 800-221-1274
Fax: (314)569-2834
URL: http://www.phoenixlearninggroup.com
Released: 1988. Price: $475.00. Description: This video provides suggestions for formulating a legal code of business ethics. Availability: VHS; 3/4U.

37544 ■ Ethics: Is It Profitable in Business?
Salenger Films, Inc.
1635 12th St.
Santa Monica, CA 90404-9988
Ph:(310)450-1300
Free: 800-775-5025
Fax: (310)450-1010
Co. E-mail: salenger@aol.com
URL: http://salengerfilms.visualnet.com
Released: 1977. Description: A look at the roles ethics play in business decision-making, concluding that in the long run good ethics increases productivity. Availability: VHS; 3/4U.

37545 ■ Privacy in the Workplace: Unreasonable Intrusion or Legitimate Interest?
American Law Institute
American Bar Association Committee on Continuing Education
4025 Chestnut St.
Philadelphia, PA 19104
Ph:(215)243-1600
Free: 800-CLE-NEWS
Fax: (215)243-1664
Co. E-mail: PHunt@ali.org
URL: http://www.ali.org
Released: 1992. Price: $95. Description: Reviews issues of privacy in the workplace issues. Includes study guide. Availability: VHS.

CONSULTANTS

37546 ■ Frederick A. Bornhofen & Associates
1 Sunmere Ln.
Elverson, PA 19520
Ph:(610)942-9140
Fax: (610)942-9576
Co. E-mail: fborn@bellatlantic.net

E-mail: fborn@bellatlantic.net
Scope: Commercial and industrial security expert specializes in areas of robbery and violence prevention, business ethics, cargo security, commercial loss prevention techniques, and security management. Has developed a security quality review process now being used by several major clients which is to determine the overall effectiveness of their security programs. Also offers forensic services for the legal industry and conducts professional fraud investigations. Industries served: retail, convenience store, transportation, manufacturing, and energy. Publications: F.A. Bornhofen has authored numerous articles published nationally, and contributed to several books as well as It's a Matter of Judgement, ethics training tape; and I Shouldn't Be Telling You This, But, an information security training tape. Seminars: Business Ethics; Fraud in the Business World.

37547 ■ Siebrand-Wilton Associates Inc.
PO Box 337
Marlboro, NJ 07746-0337
Ph:(732)972-1456
Fax: (732)972-0214
Co. E-mail: clientsvcs@s-wa.com
URL: http://www.swausa.com

E-mail: clientsvcs@s-wa.com
Scope: Firm assesses, plans and implements human resources aspects of mergers/acquisitions. Offers human resources consulting in compensation and benefit plan design, mergers and acquisitions (HR aspects), business ethics assessment and development, editing, writing and association management services, and contract professionals and interim executives. Publications: "Should Government or Business Try to Save Medicare?," HR News; "Executive Temping," HR Horizons; "When is an Employee Truly an Employee?," HR Magazine; "Examining Your Insurance Carrier," HR Magazine.

LIBRARIES

37548 ■ Ethics Centre CA–Library
One Yonge St., Ste. 1801
Toronto, ON, Canada M5E 1W7
Ph:(416)368-7525
Fax: (416)368-0515
Co. E-mail: info@ethicscentre.ca
URL: http://www.ethicscentre.ca
Scope: Ethics, business, corporate policy. Services: Library open to the public for reference use only. Holdings: Books; periodicals; videocassettes.

37549 ■ University of South Florida, Saint Petersburg–Nelson Poynter Memorial Library–Special Collections (140 7)
140 7th Ave. S.
St. Petersburg, FL 33701-5016
Ph:(727)873-4094
Fax: (727)873-4196
Co. E-mail: schnur@nelson.usf.edu
URL: http://www.nelson.usf.edu/spccoll
Contact: Kathleen Arsenault, Dean of Lib.
Scope: Marine science and ichthyology, local and regional history, oral history, journalism and media studies, campus archives, ethics. Services: Copying; Library open to the public. Holdings: 4250 books; 200 bound periodical volumes; 100 reports; 500 lin.ft. of archival material; 1700 audio/visual materials.

RESEARCH CENTERS

37550 ■ Josephson Institute of Ethics
9841 Airport Blvd., Ste. 300
Los Angeles, CA 90045
Ph:(310)846-4800
Free: 800—711-2670
Fax: (310)846-4857
Co. E-mail: ji@jiethics.org
URL: http://www.josephsoninstitute.org
Contact: Michael S. Josephson, Pres.
E-mail: ji@jiethics.org
Scope: Ethical decision making and behavior, focusing on improving the ethical quality of personal, corporate, and governmental conduct by stimulating moral aspirations, reinforcing the motivation and abilities necessary to perceive the ethical dimensions of choices, and formulating optimal ethical responses. Services: Radio commentaries. Publications: Ethics in Action; Good Ideas Books—The Power of Character. Educational Activities: Aspen Summit Conference; Character Counts!, youth education project; Character Development Seminars; Ethics in the Workplace training; Pursuing Victory with Honor, sportsmanship campaign.

37551 ■ Loyola University Chicago–Center for Ethics and Social Justice
6525 N Sheridan Rd.
Chicago, IL 60626
Ph:(773)508-8349

Fax: (773)508-8879
Co. E-mail: ethics@luc.edu
URL: http://www.luc.edu/ethics
Contact: David T. Ozar, Dir.
E-mail: ethics@luc.edu
Scope: Ethics, particularly in the fields of business, health care, dental care, organizations, and journalism. **Services:** Consulting. **Educational Activities:** Ethics Breakfast Series; Integration Courses; Moral Reasoning Workshop; Nursing Ethics Workshops; Short courses, about health care ethics for ethics committees.

37552 ■ San Jose State University–Institute for Social Responsibility, Ethics, and Education
1 Washington Sq., FO 201
San Jose, CA 95192-0096
Ph:(408)924-1376
Fax: (408)924-4527
Co. E-mail: phadreas@earthlink.net
URL: http://www2.sjsu.edu/depts/social_resp/social_resp.html
Contact: Peter J. Hadreas, Dir.
E-mail: phadreas@earthlink.net
Scope: Social responsibility, including professional and business ethics. **Educational Activities:** Lecture

series, corporate roundtables, seminars, training session, and workshops.

37553 ■ Western Michigan University–Center for the Study of Ethics in Society
Kalamazoo, MI 49008-5201
Ph:(269)387-4397
Fax: (269)387-4390
Co. E-mail: michael.pritchard@wmich.edu
URL: http://www.wmich.edu/ethics
Contact: Dr. Michael S. Pritchard, Co.Dir.
E-mail: michael.pritchard@wmich.edu
Scope: Applied and professional ethics in all fields. **Services:** Consulting. **Publications:** Occasional papers (quarterly). **Educational Activities:** Colloquia; Public presentations, 20/academic year.

Family-Owned Business

START-UP INFORMATION

37554 ■ **"All in the Delivery"** in *Entrepreneur* (Vol. 31, No. 10, October 2003, pp. 112)
Pub: Entrepreneur Media, Inc.
Ed: Devlin Smith. Description: Profile of Randy and Melody Newman who started a dry cleaning delivery franchise after learning the company Randy worked for as a human resources director was being sold.

37555 ■ **"Bandy Resigns As President of TSEA: Six-Year Head To Start Association Management Firm With Wife in April"** in *Tradeshow Week* (Vol. 34)
Pub: Reed Business Information
Ed: Heidi Genoist. Description: Michael Bandy resigned as president of the Trade Show Exhibitors Association in order to launch an independent association management and consulting firm with his wife Dee Dee.

37556 ■ **"Bird Biz Takes Off"** in *Small Business Opportunities* (Vol. 12, No. 2, March 2000, pp. 64, 66)
Pub: Harris Publications, Inc.
Ed: Marie Sherlock. Description: Shop owners, Brian and Janet Shelton, opened their bird biz emporium, Wild Bird Shop in 1993, and are now earning $500,000 a year.

37557 ■ **"Building on success"** in *Black Enterprise* (Vol. 32, No. 9, April 2002, pp. 70)
Pub: Earl Graves Publishing Co.
Ed: Carolyn M. Brown. Description: Profile of Freedie Lee and Yolanda Sherman and their business and Website, Illustrationsnetwork.com, that will showcase the artwork of minority artists and photographers to big corporations. Financial advice is offered to help the couple sustain their new business in the future and through their retirement by investing wisely.

37558 ■ **"Class of their Own"** in *Entrepreneur* (Vol. 31, No. 11, November 2003, pp. 126)
Pub: Entrepreneur Media, Inc.
Ed: Olena Gerus. Description: Profile of Debra Tynan and Robert Tagliani who opened a child care center when they could not find one suitable for their daughter.

37559 ■ **"Documenting Profit"** in *Small Business Opportunities* (Vol. 16, No. 3, May 2004, pp. 58, 120)
Pub: Harris Publications, Inc.
Ed: Jan Fields. Description: Profile of Ira and Linda Distenfield, the couple behind We The People, a franchised legal document processing service. Currently there are 120 open or under construction franchises in 26 states. Total investment ranges between $139,500 to $151,500.

37560 ■ **"Dressed for Success"** in *Small Business Opportunities* (Vol. 12, No. 3, May 2000, pp. 86, 130)
Pub: Harris Publications, Inc.

Ed: Annette Wood. Description: Owners share insight into their $20 million a year home-based men's pants business.

37561 ■ **"Edgy Bistro Mixes Fancy and Casual"** in *Kansas City Star* (February 8, 2005)
Pub: Knight-Ridder/Tribune Business News
Ed: Joyce Smith. Description: Profile of Mike and Lisa McLaughlin who remodeled and upgraded a property for their bistro, Grace. Friends and relatives helped the couple in the process before opening their restaurant that serves breakfast, lunch and dinner, along with a $5.50 lunch special menu.

37562 ■ **"Entrepreneur of the Year: The Ceja Family"** in *Inc.* (January 1, 2005)
Pub: Inc. Magazine
Ed: Nicole Gull. Description: Profile of Pablo and Juanita Ceja, former migrant workers who now own their own vineyard producing 6,000 cases of wine annually. The couple left a small village in Mexico and became migrant workers picking grapes in Napa Valley, California.

37563 ■ **"Explosive Success"** in *Small Business Opportunities* (Vol. 14, No. 1, January 2002, pp. 62-64)
Pub: Harris Publications, Inc.
Ed: Annette Wood. Description: Profile of Sandy Faust, who launched her circuit board company from her back porch, and has turned the business into a $1 million a year enterprise. Faust has won numerous business awards and plans to grow the business for her family then retire.

37564 ■ **"Family Delivers on Father's Dream"** in *Chicago Tribune* (March 9, 2005)
Pub: Knight-Ridder/Tribune Business News
Ed: Glenn Jeffers. Description: Profile of George Quinn who fell from a 30-foot ladder while painting a house, shattering a vertebra in his spine. Faced with years of rehabilitation, Quinn and his family fulfilled his dreams of owning his own pizzeria. His sons and wife work together to make the pizzas, work the cash register, and even deliver.

37565 ■ **"Full-time freelancers"** in *Fast Company* (May 2001, pp. 62)
Pub: Fast Company
Ed: Christine Canabou. Description: A husband/wife team share their experiences that lead them to start their business, St. Aubyn, a company that emulates a freelance model, whereby staff members chose their work projects, manage their owns hours, and enjoy at least four weeks of paid vacation annually.

37566 ■ **"Graphically Speaking"** in *Small Business Opportunities* (Vol. 12, No. 2, March 2000, pp. 70, 72)
Pub: Harris Publications, Inc.
Ed: John Marshall. Description: Couple set to hit the $1 million mark with innovative graphics design firm.

37567 ■ **"How I Did It: Amber Chand"** in *Inc.* (September 1, 2004)
Pub: Inc. Magazine
Ed: Hillary Johnson. Description: Profile of Amber Chand, a businesswoman who went from running a museum gift shop to co-founding Eziba with her brother-in-law. Chand's mission to foster social change was the idea behind the artisan handicrafts retailer which provides a market for entrepreneurs worldwide, especially those in war-torn nations.

37568 ■ **"Investing in Communities"** in *Black Enterprise* (Vol. 35, January 2005, No. 6, pp. 42)
Pub: Earl G. Graves Publishing Co. Inc.
Ed: Zakiyyah El-Amin. Description: Profile of Kevin and Annie Byrd of Baltimore, Maryland. The couple took advantage of the city's housing revitalization market to become successful owners of the residential property and management firm, Signature Management. The company uses digital documentation and a customized property software management program, offering real estate investors services including leasing, management, maintenance, and construction.

37569 ■ **"Just Desserts"** in *Small Business Opportunities* (Vol. 12, No. 3, May 2000, pp. 54)
Pub: Harris Publications, Inc.
Ed: Jerilyn Kaufman. Description: Alicia Dargan, the mastermind behind AMK Specialty Gourmet, Inc., chronicles the family dessert shop from start-up to their current success, with earnings at $300,000 a year.

37570 ■ **"Lori & Ryan Pacchiano"** in *Entrepreneur* (Vol. 31, No. 7, July 2003, pp. 23)
Pub: Entrepreneur Media, Inc.
Ed: April Y. Pennington. Description: Profile of, Lori and Ryan Pacchiano, co-founders of High Maintenance Bitch In Seattle. Lori has created a feather boa for dogs and cats which is sold by the brother and sister team at local pet stores. Ryan came up with the name, a synonym for the word dog, and is now trademarked.

37571 ■ **"A model occupation: who says you can't turn business into play?"** in *Entrepreneur* (Vol. 31, No. 4, April 2003, pp. 102)
Pub: Entrepreneur Media Inc.
Ed: Devlin Smith. Description: Profile of Gary Phillips who turned his knowledge of retailing and love of model railroads into becoming a franchisee for HobbyTown USA. Phillips and his wife are franchise partners. Information on three other franchising success stories is included.

37572 ■ **"New mortgage company looks past the numbers"** in *Pueblo Business Journal* (February 28, 2003)
Pub: Dolan Media Newswires
Ed: William Dagendesh. Description: Profile of Southern Colorado Mortgages, and the family that started the firm that is designed to provide prime (good credit) and sub-prime (bad credit) services.

37573 ■ "Raising the Woof: Make No Bones About It-This Bakery Takes Dog Food to a Whole New Level" in *Entrepreneur* (Vol. 32, July 2004)

Pub: Entrepreneur Media Inc.

Ed: Jonathan Riggs. **Description:** Profile of Melanie Superack who founded Just Dogs! with her mother. The franchise, located in a shopping mall, offers gift ideas for dog lovers, including holiday cookies, dog lollipops and flavored barrel treats. Sales for the store are expected to reach nearly $170,000.

37574 ■ "Recipe for Riches" in *Small Business Opportunities* (Vol. 16, No. 1, January 2004, pp. 72)

Pub: Harris Publications, Inc.

Description: Profile of Cousins Subs franchises, founded by cousins James F. Sheppard and William F. Specht. The firm's goal is to open one store per week in 2005, concentrating in existing states that include Wisconsin, Minnesota, Michigan, Illinois, Indiana, North Dakota, Colorado, California, Texas, and Arizona. Total initial investment ranges from $159,300 to $291,600.

37575 ■ "Seeking Internet Interactivity" in *Crain's New York Business* (Vol. 23, January 22, 2007, No. 4, pp. 28)

Description: Profile of Santina Matwey and her husband's new Internet start-up Meetup.com. The website organizes events for couples such as game nights, dinners, and ice skating.

37576 ■ "The Trading Post" in *Small Business Opportunities* (Vol. 12, No. 3, May 2000, pp. 94, 96, 98)

Pub: Harris Publications, Inc.

Ed: Marie Sherlock. **Description:** Sisters Paulette Wittwer and Tamara Patrick designed a business which specializes in folk art, clothing, and jewelry from around the world, while attempting to ensure that the sources for their merchandise are socially responsible.

37577 ■ "What's Your Problem? A Mobile Photography Business Can Go a Long Way If You Know Where You're Going" in *Entrepreneur* (July 2004)

Pub: Entrepreneur Media Inc.

Ed: Nichole L. Torres. **Description:** Husband and wife team seek advice for starting a mobile photography business catering to dog and cat shows as well as motorcycle rallies.

ASSOCIATIONS AND OTHER ORGANIZATIONS

37578 ■ Canadian Association of Family Enterprise–Association Canadienne des Entreprises Familiales
1388 C Cornwall Rd.
Oakville, ON, Canada L6J 7W5
Ph:(416)538-9992
Free: (866)849-0099
Fax: (416)538-9556
Co. E-mail: office@cafenational.org
URL: http://www.cafemembers.org/cafenational
Contact: Lawrence Barns, Natl. CEO
Membership: Family-owned businesses. **Purpose:** Seeks to "encourage, educate, and inform members in disciplines unique to the family business." Fosters increased understanding of the importance of family-owned enterprises in the national economy among government agencies and the public. Gathers and disseminates information of interest to members. Conducts educational and lobbying activities. Provides technical support and advisory services to small businesses in areas including succession planning, taxation, family law, and arbitration and mediation. Maintains network of Family Councils, which serve as a forum for discussion of family and business matters. **Publications:** *Family Business Magazine* (quarterly); *Family Enterpriser* (quarterly); *International Magazine for Family Businesses* (bimonthly); Membership Directory (annual). **Telecommunication Services:** electronic mail, lbarns@cafenational.org.

37579 ■ Center for Family Business
PO Box 24219
Cleveland, OH 44124
Ph:(440)460-5409
Co. E-mail: grummi@aol.com
Contact: Dr. Leon A. Danco Ph.D., Chm.
Description: Presidents, owner/managers, founders, and inheritors of family-owned businesses and independent, private, or closely held companies. Develops educational programs for its members in the areas of business management, management succession, and business continuity. Provides consulting services. Conducts promotion, research, and public relations activities on behalf of its membership. **Publications:** *Beyond Survival*; *Inside the Family Business*; *Outside Directors in the Family Owned Business*; *Someday This Will All Be...Whose? The Lighter Side of Family Business*.

37580 ■ Focus on the Family
8605 Explorer Dr.
Colorado Springs, CO 80920
Ph:(719)531-3400
Free: 800-232-6459
Fax: (719)531-3424
Co. E-mail: paul.hetrick@fotf.org
URL: http://www.family.org
Contact: Jim Daly, Pres./CEO
Purpose: Promotes traditional Judeo-Christian values and strong family ties. Gathers and disseminates practical resource information on marriage, parenting, and other subjects related to family life. Produces fourteen different radio programs, aired in 96 countries. Conducts research and educational programs; sponsors charitable activities; makes available children's services; maintains speakers' bureau. Broadcasts and resources are also available in Hebrew, Hungarian, Indonesian, Italian, Japanese, Korean, Lithuanian, Norwegian, Polish, Portuguese, Romanian, Russian, Slovakian, Spanish, Swedish, Thai, Ukrainian and Zulu. **Publications:** *Boundless* (weekly); *Breakaway* (monthly); *Brio* (monthly); *Clubhouse* (monthly); *Clubhouse, Jr.* (monthly); *Focus on the Family Citizen* (monthly); *Focus on the Family Physician* (bimonthly); *LifeWise* (bimonthly); *Plugged In* (monthly); Magazine (monthly). Also produces films and videos.

37581 ■ National Family Business Council
1640 W Kennedy Rd.
Lake Forest, IL 60045
Ph:(847)295-1040
Fax: (847)295-1898
Co. E-mail: jmnfbc@msn.com
Contact: John E. Messervey, Pres.
Description: Serves as a consulting group and resource center on family-owned businesses. Offers consultation, speakers' bureau, and other communications with other family businesses; sponsors regional seminars on problems unique to family businesses. Conducts surveys. **Publications:** *Family Business Letter* (periodic); *Resource Guide to Family Business* (periodic).

EDUCATIONAL PROGRAMS

37582 ■ Kennesaw State University–Cox Family Enterprise Center
Family Business Academy
1000 Chastain Rd.
Kennesaw, GA 30144-5591
Ph:(770)423-6000
Fax: (770)423-6721
Co. E-mail: fec@coles2.kennesaw.edu
URL: http://www.kennesaw.edu
Released: Annual. **Price:** $1800.00 for first family member; $1500.00 for each additional family member. **Description:** Four-day course covering family business. Topics include: strategic and family business planning, leadership and management, conlict resolutions, total quality management (TQM), working with boards and other advisors, family and business values, and succession.

REFERENCE WORKS

37583 ■ "Accountability key factor in family business success" in *Business First Columbus* (Vol. 18, No. 25, February 8, 2002, pp. B3)

Pub: Business First Columbus, Inc.

Ed: Susan Pavilkey. **Description:** Management style, and the importance of personal accountability when running and working for a family business are discussed.

37584 ■ "Alchemist Among the Vines" in *Hispanic Business* (Vol. 24, No. 4, April 2002, pp. 20-21)

Pub: Hispanic Business Inc.

Ed: Scott Williams. **Description:** Profile of Reynaldo Robledo, a Mexican immigrant who rose to become owner of his own vineyard, winery, and vineyard management company.

37585 ■ "All work, All play" in *Entrepreneur* (Vol. 30, No. 3, March 2002, pp.)

Pub: Entrepreneur Media Inc.

Ed: Devlin Smith. **Description:** Profile of the family owned Woodplay franchise located in Tampa, Florida.

37586 ■ "Anjon's Sauces May Take the Lead" in *Portland Press Herald* (April 29, 2005)

Pub: Blethen Maine Newspapers, Inc.

Description: Profile of family business, Anjon's. The DiSanto family started jarring and selling its specialty pasta sauces in order to supplement their income from the family restaurant. The family is now considering selling the restaurant and focus on marketing the sauces.

37587 ■ "Answering the call" in *Crain's Detroit Business* (Vol. 19, No. 11, March 17, 2003, pp. 13)

Pub: Crain Communications Inc., Detroit

Description: Answering Service Inc., the telephone answering service located in Southfield, Michigan has revamped its infrastructure and wired its offices together, a move that should save the firm $150,000 annually.

37588 ■ "At Hallmark Cards, It's really all about family" in *Ingram's* (Vol. 27, No. 12, December 2001, pp. 42)

Pub: Show Me Publishing, Inc.

Description: Profile of Hallmark Cards Inc., focusing on the promotion of Donald J. Hall Jr. to president of the company.

37589 ■ "Avis Ford Owner Passes Reins of Dealerships to Sons" in *Crain's Detroit Business* (Vol. 21, January 24, 2005, No. 4, pp. 19)

Pub: Crain Communications Inc. - Detroit

Ed: Brent Snavely. **Description:** Walter Douglas Sr. has passed the day-to-day management over to his son Mark Douglas and is helping son Edmund Douglas to open a Jaguar-Land Rover dealership in Sylvania. Ohio. Walter Douglas will remain Avis' chairman.

37590 ■ "Bakery Wishes, Cake-Decorating Dreams" in *Bradenton Herald* (February 12, 2005)

Pub: Bradenton Herald

Ed: Tilde Herrera. **Description:** Profile of Deborah Naids and daughter, Jessica, co-owners of The Pour House. The shop offers four tables for those dining in, a counter across the back with 10 computer connections for laptops; the menu consists of baked goods, coffee, and a few breakfast and lunch-style sandwiches.

37591 ■ "Balancing Act" in *Black Enterprise* (Vol. 36, November 2005, No. 4, pp. 88)

Pub: Earl G. Graves Publishing Co. Inc.

Ed: Sakina P. Spruell. **Description:** Alexis James, 30-year-old purchasing manager tells how she is pursuing investments with the potential of high returns while also investing in her family's embroidery business by overseeing the computer-operated production of designs on t-shirts, hats, canvas bags, and more.

37592 ■ **"Bean Counter"** in *San Francisco Business Times* (Vol. 17, No. 53, August 8, 2003, pp. 27)
Pub: American City Business Journals
Ed: Steven E.F. Brown. Description: An overview and history of JBR Gourmet Foods, Inc., a family-owned company that has earnings of $25 million annually roasting and distributing its own blend of coffee beans.

37593 ■ **"Bean Enjoys Expanding Eat With Us Restaurants, Franchises"** in *Mississippi Business Journal* (Vol. 28, January 2007, No. 36, pp. 34)
Pub: Venture Publications, Inc.
Ed: Lynn Lofton Description: Profile of John Bean who started family business Eat With Us, a fast-growing Columbus-based company with several popular dining brands and several restaurants.

37594 ■ **""** in *Bellingham Business Journal* (January 2007, pp.)
Pub: Sun News Inc.
Description: Profile of Christian bikers Mike and Pam Melland, owners of Biker's Oasis. The shop sells motorcycle parts and accessories, helmets, leather clothing, chrome accessories, intercom systems, and radio headsets.

37595 ■ **"Beth Blake and Sophie Simmons: 34 and 32, Founders of Thread in New York City"** in *Entrepreneur* (Vol. 32, July 2004, No. 7, pp. 25)
Pub: Entrepreneur Media Inc.
Ed: Sara Wilson. Description: Profile of Beth Blake and Sophie Simmons, designers and manufacturers of bridesmaids' dresses. Word-of-mouth has helped the women grow their business.

37596 ■ **"Big Bucks in Boats"** in *Small Business Opportunities* (Vol. 17, September 2005, No. 5, pp. 126-127)
Pub: Harris Publications Inc.
Ed: Stan Roberts. Description: Profile of family-owned Regal Marine Industries, Inc. The firm produces luxury and performance boats and reported revenues of $108.4 million in 2003.

37597 ■ **"A Billion in Baskets"** in *Small Business Opportunities* (Vol. 13, No. 6, November 2001, pp. 38, 40)
Pub: Harris Publications, Inc.
Description: Profile of Longaberger Company, the largest handmade basket-making company in the United States. The company grew from a small family business to a billion-dollar empire, and is the 22nd largest woman-owned company in America.

37598 ■ **"Black Technology Pioneers Credit Family Support for Success"** in *San Jose Mercury News* (February 26, 2005)
Pub: Knight-Ridder/Tribune Business News
Ed: Jon Fortt. Description: IBM sponsored Black Family Technology Week at East Side Union High School; Mark Dean, one of the early inventors of the IBM PC, was a keynote speaker at the event.

37599 ■ **"Blood is Thicker than Ink"** in *Success* (Vol. 47, No. 4, September 2000, pp. 22)
Pub: Success Publishing, Inc.
Ed: Simeon Furman. Description: A family-run printing supply company finds its niche.

37600 ■ **"Book Reviews"** in *Crain's Chicago Business* (Vol. 23, October 23, 2000, pp. FB5)
Pub: Crain Communications, Inc. Crain Communications, Inc.
Ed: Barbara B. Buchholz. Description: A review of the five most useful family business books covering several significant issues.

37601 ■ **"Briefly"** in *Crain's Detroit Business* (Vol. 21, January 17, 2005, No. 3, pp. 29)
Pub: Crain Communications Inc. - Detroit
Description: Walsh College launched the Walsh Family Business Center, offering lunch and a discussion on running a family-owned business.

37602 ■ **"Broken plan"** in *Crain's Detroit Business* (Vol. 18, No. 19, May 13, 2002, pp. 1)
Pub: Crain Communications Inc. - Detroit
Ed: Terry Kosdrosky. Description: An interview with DCT owner, J. Bronce Henderson, whose family business filed for bankruptcy leaving workers without pay and medical bills.

37603 ■ **"Brothers Rev Up Roostertail"** in *Crain's Detroit Business* (Vol. 22, February 6, 2006, No. 6, pp. 22)
Pub: Crain Communications Inc. - Detroit
Ed: Brent Snavely. Description: Profile of Michael and John Schoenith, owners of Detroit's Roostertail banquet hall and catering business. The brothers have invested $1 - $2 million in renovations in the kitchen and Club Room.

37604 ■ **"Builders Land Rutenberg Deal"** in *Charlotte Observer* (February 2, 2007)
Pub: Knight-Ridder/Tribune Business News
Ed: Bob Fliss. Description: Jim and Larry Sanders purchased a franchise from builder, Arthur Rutenberg Homes. The brothers will build custom homes in the area.

37605 ■ **"Business After Divorce"** in *Entrepreneur* (Vol. 28, No. 4, April 2000, pp. 132)
Pub: Entrepreneur Media Inc.
Ed: Patricia Schiff Estess. Description: Promise to love, honor and cherish your business, even if you share it with your ex-spouse.

37606 ■ **"Business is business - when working with family"** in *Women In Business* (Vol. 52, No. 1, January-February 2000, pp. 34)
Pub: The ABWA Co., Inc.
Ed: Jane Thomas. Description: The difficulties associated with working with members of your own family are discussed. Parents often find it difficult to perceive their children as responsible adults.

37607 ■ **"Butler, Wis., Printing Plant Expands Operations"** in *Milwaukee Journal Sentinel* (December 17, 2005)
Pub: Journal Sentinel, Inc.
Ed: Joel Dresang. Description: Ries Graphics expanded its printing plant in Butler, Wisconsin by adding new equipment and employees in the hopes of increasing sales. The family-owned business is celebrating its 90th year with the $5 million expansion.

37608 ■ **"Catering Company Expands Operations"** in *Bellingham Business Journal* (December 2006, pp. A6)
Pub: Sun News Inc.
Description: Ciao Thyme, a catering company owned by Jessica and Mataio Gillis, will be moving to a larger space in March 2007. They plan to add an event space, a small private dining facility and will be offering cooking classes.

37609 ■ **"A Chance at a Second Career"** in *Home Business* (Vol. 13, January/February 2006, No. 1, pp. 81)
Pub: Home Business Magazine
Ed: Sandy Larson. Description: Profile of Dan Hicks Jr. and his wife Clara who run a tile and grout cleaning business in Texas.

37610 ■ **"Close-Knit"** in *Forbes* (December 25, 2000, pp. 134)
Pub: Forbes Magazine
Ed: Brigid McMenamin. Description: A look at two large, privately held firms that have come up with different solutions to keeping their family-owned, private companies family-owned and private. Cited are Milliken & Company, a big textile firm that remains in the hands of the family, and Hearst Corporation, a diversified media giant, that is still privately held.

37611 ■ **"Close Shave"** in *Portland Press Herald* (September 28, 2005)
Pub: Blethen Maine Newspapers, Inc.
Ed: Justin Ellis. Description: Lynden Pitt, owner of J & L Haircutters, is closing the shop he and his wife now run. Pitt's father opened the business nearly 60 years ago. Pitt plans to teach the art of barbering during his retirement.

37612 ■ **"Compliments to Piropos"** in *Ingram's* (Vol. 28, No. 5, May 2002, pp. 52)
Pub: Show Me Publishing, Inc.
Description: Profile of Christina and Gary Worden, owners of Piropos, an upscale Argentinean restaurant located at Parkville, in Kansas City.

37613 ■ **"Concrete Expansion; Doan Emerges as Major Player in Ready-Mix Business"** in *Crain's Detroit Business* (Vol. 19, October 27, 2003)
Pub: Crain Communications Inc., Detroit
Ed: Jennette Smith. Description: Profile of family-owned concrete company, Doan Company, based in Ypsilanti, Michigan. The firm has become one of the areas largest ready-mix concrete companies, with $10 million in acquisitions.

37614 ■ **"Connect the daughters: sons aren't the only offspring taking over family businesses"** in *Entrepreneur* (Vol. 30, No. 12, Dec. 2002)
Pub: Entrepreneur Media Inc.
Ed: Aliza Pilar Sherman. Description: According to Joseph H. Astrachan, director of the Cox Family Enterprise Center at Kennesaw State University in Georgia, it is often easier for daughters to take over a family business than for sons, because the daughters are not in competition with the father.

37615 ■ **"Construction Risk Management: Facing the Fire"** in *Rough Notes* (Vol. 145, No. 1, January 2003, pp. 98)
Pub: Rough Notes
Ed: Elisabeth Boone. Description: The International Risk Management Institute held its 22nd annual Construction Risk Management Conference in San Diego, California. The conference was attended by 1,240 contractors, owners, agents, and brokers, consultants, and insurers representatives, and Michael O'Neill, president of ACIG Insurance Agency Inc., was one of the key speakers at the event.

37616 ■ **"Contemporary Moon, Pa., Hotel to Become Bed-Breakfast-Ballroom"** in *Pittsburgh Post-Gazette* (March 24, 2004)
Pub: Knight-Ridder/Tribune Business News
Ed: Dan Gigler. Description: Profile of Tom and Valerie Sheehan, who are converting their contemporary Airport Plaza Hotel into a Colonial-style bed and breakfast and ballroom. The inn is scheduled to open in March 2005.

37617 ■ **"Convenience pushes pendulum back to PPO coverage"** in *Crain's Detroit Business* (Vol. 18, No. 16, April 22)
Pub: Crain Communications Inc. - Detroit
Ed: David Barkholz. Description: An interview with Kay Farnell, vice president of the family-owned Farnell Equipment Co. Farnell tells how her company's experiment with a health maintenance organization lasted only a year, only to return to a PPO.

37618 ■ **"Cooking Again"** in *Hispanic Business* (June 2005, pp. 78)
Pub: Hispanic Business
Ed: Luisa Beltran. Description: Profile of Goya Foods, the largest Hispanic-owned food company in the U.S. The firm produced $750 million in sales in 2003.

37619 ■ **"Couple First to Open Bed-and-Breakfast Under New Knoxville, Tenn. Rules"** in *Knoxville News-Sentinel* (November 30, 2003)
Pub: Knight-Ridder/Tribune Business News
Ed: Amy Nolan. Description: Profile of Tomica and David Miller, owners of a bed and breakfast at Tomica's Historic Old North Knoxville home. The Millers were the first to get a permit from the city to run a bed and breakfast operation. The Brimer House was set to open March 1, 2004.

37620 ■ "Crain's Family-Business Forum Set for Thursday" in *Crain's Detroit Business* (Vol. 21, October 3, 2005, No. 43, pp. 31)
Pub: Crain Communications Inc. - Detroit
Description: Stephen McClure of Gamily Business Consulting Group Inc. will speak at the first family-owned business forum sponsored by Crain's. Other sponsors include Derderian, Kann, Seyferth & Salucci PC; LaSalle Bank; Right Management Consultants; Michigan Business and Professional Association; and Andiamo Italia.

37621 ■ "Daddy Dearest" in *Forbes* (October 30, 2000, pp. 36)
Pub: Forbes Magazine
Ed: Katarzyna Moreno. **Description:** Profiles of four family-owned businesses and the ways they maintain a successful balance working together.

37622 ■ "The Daily Ground" in *Entrepreneur* (Vol. 28, No. 2, February 2000, pp. 147)
Pub: Entrepreneur Media Inc.
Ed: Michelle Prather. **Description:** In an industry of high-visibility brand names, they don't have one. So how does this family's coffee company stay in business?

37623 ■ "The Dairy News" in *Small Business Opportunities* (Spring 2005)
Pub: Harris Publications Inc.
Description: Profile of Oberweis Franchise Systems franchising Oberweis Ice Cream. Franchising information about the family-owned and operated dairy included.

37624 ■ "Dayton, Ohio, Inventor of Garden Tool Organizer Looks to Expand Business" in *Dayton Daily News* (July 29, 2004)
Pub: Dayton Daily News
Ed: LaToya Thompson. **Description:** Profile of Fred Utzinger III, founder and owner of Functional Fabrics Inc., which operates within his other business, Independent Awning and Canvas Co., a fourth-generation family business. Utzinger has invented a garden tool organizer.

37625 ■ "Despite Smaller Loans, SBA Breaks Records" in *Inc.* (November 1, 2004)
Pub: Inc. Magazine
Ed: Darren Dahl. **Description:** The U. S. Small Business Administration backed a record number of loans in 2004, providing $15 billion in loans to businesses. These loans have helped small and family-owned small business to create 1.5 million jobs.

37626 ■ "Detroit Free Press Macomb Small Business Column" in *Detroit Free Press* (June 16, 2005)
Pub: Knight-Ridder/Tribune Business News
Ed: Carol Cain. **Description:** Profile of three sisters who opened a restaurant named after their late parents.

37627 ■ "Detroit Free Press Oakland Small Business Column" in *Detroit Free Press* (July 28, 2005)
Pub: Knight-Ridder/Tribune Business News
Ed: Carol Cain. **Description:** Profile of brothers-in-law, Bill Rogers and Bob English who have grown their small company, Absolute Sales International, into four divisions offering closed-circuit television cameras to other small firms; audio and video products; security systems for boats, homes and businesses; as well as surveillance equipment for police and other organizations.

37628 ■ "Detroit Free Press Small Business Column" in *Detroit Free Press* (July 25, 2005)
Pub: Knight-Ridder/Tribune Business News
Ed: Carol Cain. **Description:** Profile of Stephen Pierce, high school dropout and founder of Impulsive Profits Inc., a firm offering investing advice over the Internet. Pierce and wife Alicia have branched out to include Innovation Marketers LLC, along with Thinkubator, which helps entrepreneurs and companies find creative solutions to company issues.

37629 ■ "Detroit Free Press Wayne Small Business Column" in *Detroit Free Press* (May 19, 2005)
Pub: Knight-Ridder/Tribune Business News
Ed: Carol Cain. **Description:** Walter and Mary Menard, owners of the Lotus Arts Gallery in Plymouth, Michigan began their career as marketers of fine art after looking for artwork to feature in high-end custom homes Walter used to build. Also included in the article is a profile of Jim Anderson, who started Urban Science Inc. in 1977. The firm creates computer-generated mapping solutions for automakers and dealers.

37630 ■ "Duly noted; Sheet-music company doesn't rest in copyright fight" in *Crain's Detroit Business* (Vol. 19, No. 10, March 10, 2003)
Pub: Crain Communications Inc., Detroit
Ed: Andrew Dietderich. **Description:** Profile of Arthur Luck, owner of the firm Luck's Music Library Inc.; the family business is the subject of two lawsuits filed by Luck's grandsons over copyrighted work becoming part of the public domain.

37631 ■ "Eminent Danger" in *Entrepreneur* (Vol. 33, January 2005, No. 1, pp. 19)
Pub: Entrepreneur Media Inc.
Ed: Joshua Kurlantzick. **Description:** Dino Paspalakis, owner of Joyland Amusement Center in Daytona Beach, Florida is concerned about losing his family business because of the city of Dayton Beach using the legal doctrine eminent domain to try to take his property from him. The city plans to give the land to developers to build high-rise condos and hotels.

37632 ■ "Engineering a Structure that's Lasted Generations" in *San Francisco Business Times* (Vol. 17, No. 48, July 4, 2003, pp. 18)
Pub: American City Business Journals
Ed: James Temple. **Description:** History of Bechtel and how it has managed to survive four generations, while many family-owned businesses fail after the third generation, is examined.

37633 ■ "Entrepreneur Column" in *Entrepreneur.com* (September 28, 2006)
Pub: Entrepreneur Media Inc.
Ed: David Javitch. **Description:** Working with family members has unique benefits, but also some possible pitfalls. There are ways to address the special relationships that will clarify the business needs and help build a more cohesive team.

37634 ■ *Entrepreneurship and Small Business*
Pub: Palgrave Macmillan
Ed: Paul Burns. **Released:** January 2007. **Price:** $74.95. **Description:** Entrepreneurial skills, focusing on good management practices are discussed. Topics include family businesses, corporate, international and social entrepreneurship.

37635 ■ "Estate of affairs" in *Entrepreneur* (Vol. 31, No. 4, April 2003, pp. 52)
Pub: Entrepreneur Media Inc.
Ed: Joshua Kurlantzick. **Description:** With the repealing of the federal estate tax in 2001, many entrepreneurs are taking advantage of the opportunity to inherit or pass on businesses without paying any tariff.

37636 ■ "The Exporting Advantage" in *Inc.* (August 2005, pp. 40, 42)
Pub: Inc. Magazine
Ed: Jeff Bailey. **Description:** Brothers Jon, Keith and Mark Pavlansky sell rubber dirt to Mexican growers. Their company, Hibco Plastics transformed their company while increasing sales by marketing their products in Mexico.

37637 ■ "Express to Success" in *Small Business Opportunities* (Vol. 17, November 2005, No. 6, pp. 126-128)
Pub: Harris Publications Inc.
Description: Robert A. Funk, CEO of Express Services, Inc., talks about the staffing firm he founded with his wife Nancy. The privately held company is rated sixth-largest in the nation and provides franchisor training at Express University in Oklahoma City.

37638 ■ "Failure is Glorious" in *Fast Company* (November 2001, pp. 35)
Pub: Fast Company
Ed: Ian Wylie. **Description:** Alberto Alessi transformed his family's ho-hum housewares business into a trend setting design giant. His secret: walking the borderline between genius and failure.

37639 ■ "Fairhaven Business Owners Open Pottery Production Facility" in *Bellingham Business Journal* (December 2006, pp. A6)
Pub: Sun News Inc.
Description: Fairhaven's Mud In Your Eye Pottery, owned by Cate Howell and husband Jeff McDougall, features dinnerware, mugs, serving and baking dishes, steins, and sushi trays. Due to demand from wholesalers they have opened Cascadia Stoneware USA, Inc., a pottery production facility which wholesales their wares to other businesses.

37640 ■ "Family keeps answering calls after 75 years" in *Crain's Detroit Business* (Vol. 19, No. 11, March 17, 2003, pp. 13)
Pub: Crain Communications Inc., Detroit
Ed: Laura Bailey. **Description:** Profile of Answering Service Inc., the 75-year-old telephone answering service based in Southfield, Michigan; the founder's grandson, James Robinson, credits innovation and generational transfer for the firm's success.

37641 ■ "A family affair" in *Black Enterprise* (Vol. 33, No. 3, October 2002, pp. 154)
Pub: Earl Graves Publishing Co.
Ed: George Alexander. **Description:** The largest part of American wealth lies in the family-owned businesses that make up 80-90 percent of all business enterprises in North America. The importance of a succession plan for family-owned firms is discussed. A survey by the Family Firm Institute of 800 family-owned businesses showed that insufficient estate planning, failure to prepare for the inevitable transition, and lack of funds to pay estate taxes are the leading causes for most family-owned business failures.

37642 ■ "A Family Affair" in *Pittsburgh Business Times* (Vol. 23, No. 9, September 19, 2003, pp. 25)
Pub: Pittsburgh Business Times
Ed: Tim Schooley. **Description:** Tom and Bill Northrop, co-publishers of the Washington Observer-Reporter are fifth generation executives of the family-owned newspaper. The paper has five family members on its executive board.

37643 ■ "Family-Biz Circle" in *Business Week Online* (February 17, 2006)
Pub: McGraw-Hill Companies
Description: Entrepreneurs must develop a business plan to pass the family-owned business to the next generation. Consultants at the Family Business Institute can help small business owners construct a plan designed for their small business.

37644 ■ *Family Business*
Pub: Ashgate Publishing Co., Inc.
Ed: Mary B. Rose. **Released:** 1995. **Price:** $250.00.

37645 ■ "Family-Business Psychology" in *Forbes* (December 25, 2000, pp. 134)
Pub: Forbes Magazine
Ed: Brigid McMenamin. **Description:** Over the past few years a large number of family-business experts, including lawyers, MBAs, accountants, and psychologists, have sprung up, all promising to help families prosper along with their businesses for generations to come.

37646 ■ *Family Business: Text, Readings, & Cases*
Pub: Kendall Hunt Publishing Co.
Ed: A. Bakr Ibrahim and Willard M. Ellis. **Released:** 1994. **Price:** $52.95.

37647 ■ "Family divisions threaten Jervis B. Webb" in *Crain's Detroit Business* (Vol. 19, No. 11, March 17, 2003, pp. 20)
Pub: Crain Communications Inc., Detroit

Ed: Michael Strong. **Description:** Farmington Hills, Michigan-based Jervis B. Webb Company, manufacturer of conveyor equipment, is involved in a struggle among family members that is now being heard in Oakland County Circuit Court.

37648 ■ "Family matters" in *Entrepreneur* **(Vol. 30, No. 12, December 2002, pp. 83)**
Pub: Entrepreneur Media Inc.
Ed: Jennifer Pellet. **Description:** Difficulties encountered by family-owned businesses when attempting to obtain venture capital backing are discussed.

37649 ■ "Family Partnerships Under Scrutiny" in *Inc.* **(Volume 27, July 2005, No. 7, pp. 26)**
Pub: Inc. Magazine
Ed: Allen P. Roberts Jr. **Description:** The Internal Revenue Service is taking steps to investigate the way business owners avoid paying estate taxes.

37650 ■ "Family Ties" in *Entrepreneur* **(Vol. 31, No. 7, July 2003, pp. 30)**
Pub: Entrepreneur Media, Inc.
Ed: Nichole L. Torres. **Description:** Revenues for family run businesses grew by 50 percent from 1997 to 2002, according to a study conducted by the Raymond Institute of Family Business and the Mass Mutual Financial Group. Sixty percent of family owned businesses felt optimistic about their company's future and 50 percent planned to hire new employees in the next year.

37651 ■ "Family Ties: Father and Sons Create Flooring Enterprise" in *Black Enterprise* **(Vol. 35, November 2004, No. 4, pp. 56)**
Pub: Earl G. Graves Publishing Co. Inc.
Ed: Zakiyyah El-Amin. **Description:** Franklin Shanklin Sr. and his two sons have partnered to create a family business. The Shanklins specialize in flooring, including carpets, hardwood, linoleum and vinyl tile for commercial and residential use.

37652 ■ "Father/Daughter Duo Finds Success in Classic Car Business" in *Macon Telegraph* **(January 31, 2005)**
Pub: Macon Telegraph
Ed: Mark Vanderhoek. **Description:** Profile of Bill Bonbrake and his daughter Traci, who turned their love for old things into an online auction for classic automobiles.

37653 ■ "Father Figure" in *Entrepreneur* **(Vol. 33, October 2005, No. 10, pp. 36)**
Pub: Entrepreneur Media Inc.
Ed: Aliza Pilar Sherman. **Description:** Issues faced by daughters who inherit their father's business are discussed.

37654 ■ "A 50-Year Legacy" in *Candy Industry* **(Vol. 167, April 2002, pp. 29)**
Pub: Stagnito Communications Inc.
Description: Profile of Anthony-Thomas Candy Company. The family owned business is celebrating its 50th anniversary.

37655 ■ "Food For Thought" in *Black Enterprise* **(Vol. 34, No. 3, October 2003, pp. 20)**
Pub: Earl Graves Publishing Co.
Ed: Latif Lewis. **Description:** Profile of Charles "Chuck" James III, owner of the 120-year-old family business, C.H. James & Company. James has partnered with Goldman Sachs Urban Investment Group to assess potential acquisitions in the food processing industry. James hopes to increase the presence of minority firms in the area of supplier diversity.

37656 ■ "For Better or Worse" in *Entrepreneur* **(Vol. 33, October 2005, No. 10, pp. 104)**
Pub: Entrepreneur Media Inc.
Ed: Nichole L. Torres. **Description:** Three couples share their experience of running their companies together.

37657 ■ "Franchisees of Huntington Station-based Relax the Back Find Success on Long Island" in *Long Island Business News* **(February 6, 2004)**
Pub: Dolan Media Newswires
Ed: Adina Genn. **Description:** Profile of Carey and CiCi Goldberg, husband and wife franchisees of Relax the Back, offering products to help find the right chair, mattress and pillow for customers in order to keep their spine aligned. The Goldbergs looked for a franchise that would allow them to target the baby boomers and senior citizens who drive the nation's economy.

37658 ■ *From the Other Side of the Bed: A Woman Looks at Life in the Family Business*
Pub: The Center for Family Business
Ed: Katharine L. Danco; introduction by Leon A. Danco. **Released:** 1997. **Price:** $19.95.

37659 ■ "From Vacation to Vocation" in *My Business* **(September/October 2001, pp. 48)**
Pub: My Business Magazine
Ed: Robyn and Tim Chilson. **Description:** Profile of Robyn and Tim Chilson, who turned their hobby of camping into the reality of owning the Brookdale Family Campground in Meadville, Pennsylvania.

37660 ■ "Full circle" in *Candy Industry* **(Vol. 167, No. 4, April 2002, pp. 24)**
Pub: Stagnito Communications Inc.
Ed: Carla Zanetos Cully. **Description:** Profile of ways the family-owned Anthony-Thomas Candy Company continues to reinvent itself in order to meet the demands of an ever-changing marketplace.

37661 ■ "A Full House" in *Home Business* **(Vol. 12, October 2005, No. 5, pp. 40)**
Pub: Home Business Magazine
Ed: Sandy Larson. **Description:** Twin brothers, Shane and Shawn Ward, founders of DETNY Footwear, Inc., create shoes for fashion-conscious jetsetters. The young men run their business from their home with six employees.

37662 ■ "Furniture Market Adapting Strategy to Combat Competition" in *Mississippi Business Journal* **(Vol. 29, January 2007, No. 2, pp. 17)**
Pub: Venture Publications, Inc.
Ed: C. Richard Cotton **Description:** Profile of family-owned Tupelo Furniture maker Spiller stores. The Spiller family has 17 stores.

37663 ■ "Gag Order" in *Entrepreneur* **(Vol. 28, No. 9, September 2000, pp. 132)**
Pub: Entrepreneur Media Inc.
Ed: Patricia Schiff Estess. **Description:** If the family business is seeping its way into every off-hours conversation, it's time to draw the line on shop talk.

37664 ■ "Gates Plans to Challenge Schnitzers" in *Business Journal-Portland* **(Vol. 20, No. 25, August 22, 2003, pp. 1)**
Pub: American City Business Journals, Inc.
Ed: Shelly Strom. **Description:** Bill Gates is attempting to reform the board of directors at Portland, Oregon-based Schnitzer Steel Industries. Gates, who has obtained support of shareholders for his proposal, is seeking to create a more independent board at the family-dominated company.

37665 ■ "Generation Gap at the Office" in *Hispanic Business* **(November 2002, pp. 58, 60, 62)**
Pub: Hispanic Business
Ed: Rosa Antonia Carrillo, Rachel Michelson. **Description:** Ways in which communication and a comprehensive transition plan can help family-owned businesses survive into the second generation and beyond.

37666 ■ *Getting Along in Family Business: The Relationship Intelligence Handbook*
Pub: Routledge
Ed: Edwin A. Hoover and Colette L. Hoover. **Released:** 1999. **Price:** $29.99.

37667 ■ "The Ghost in the Family Business" in *Harvard Business Review* **(Vol. 78, No. 3, May 2000, pp. 34)**
Pub: Harvard Business School Publishing Corp.
Ed: Warren D. Miller. **Description:** Ten years ago, the Monroe's oldest son died in a tragic accident. Now his memory hovers over Carolina Construction Supply. This article confronts what happens when a company is controlled by someone who isn't there.

37668 ■ "Going outside for expert help: Family businesses have options to get objective advice" in *Crain's Chicago Business* **(Vol.23,Nov.13,2000)**
Pub: Crain Communications, Inc. Crain Communications, Inc.
Ed: Barbara B. Buchholz. **Description:** How William Lane re-structured his family's 52-year-old manufacturing company around his family's needs.

37669 ■ "Good Sports" in *Entrepreneur* **(Vol. 32, September 2004, No. 9, pp. 104)**
Pub: Entrepreneur Media Inc.
Ed: Nichole Torres. **Description:** Profile of Deirdre and Phil Barrows and Faith and Rob Schroeder, partners in a business venture that sells penalty flags to sports fans. Deirdre came up with the idea while watching her husband throw things at the television when football officials made bad calls. The firm, Call Your Own! expects to gross around $40,000 in their first year.

37670 ■ "Got 20 Minutes? Gym Champions Quick, Occasional Workouts" in *Bradenton Herald* **(January 29, 2005)**
Pub: Bradenton Herald
Ed: Matt Griswold. **Description:** Al Roach, CEO of 20 Minutes to Fitness, offers a 20-minute workout for clients to be done once a week. Roach claims these workouts will build muscle faster and safer than traditional strength training, and will also burn fat in the process. Roach and his wife, Virginia Phillips, plan to sell franchise packages for the gyms.

37671 ■ "Hallmark, meet Hal" in *Crain's Detroit Business* **(Vol. 16, No. 25, July 2000)**
Pub: Crain Communications, Inc.
Ed: Matt Roush. **Description:** The way Mark Bennett saw it, if he could talk his family's Hallmark shop into using e-mail to build business, he could convince anybody.

37672 ■ "Hand Off" in *My Business* **(October/November 2002, pp. 26-31, 33)**
Pub: My Business Magazine
Ed: Shannon Scully. **Description:** Information for passing a family-owned business down to children is presented. According to the Small Business Administration, more than 70 percent of family businesses don't survive through a second generation, and only about 10 percent will survive a third.

37673 ■ "A Hand in Remarriage" in *Entrepreneur* **(Vol. 31, No. 9, September 2003, pp. 116)**
Pub: Entrepreneur Media, Inc.
Ed: Nichole L. Torres. **Description:** Profile of Bill and Cheryl Brown, owners of Twice is Nice Encore Bridal Creations LLC. The couple decided to start their own wedding planning service catering to second marriages after they had difficulty finding professionals to deliver their needs.

37674 ■ "Handing it over: businesses need a plan for passing the torch" in *Black Enterprise* **(Vol. 32, No. 8, March 2002, pp. 50)**
Pub: Earl Graves Publishing Co.
Ed: Alan Hughes. **Description:** A listing of things a sole proprietor should consider before having a succession plan drawn up for a business is presented. According to the U.S. Census Bureau, nearly 90 percent of the 823,500 African American-owned businesses in 1997, were sole proprietorships.

37675 ■ "Handle with care" in *Crain's Detroit Business* **(Vol. 18, N)**
Pub: Crain Communications Inc. - Detroit

Ed: Terry Kosdrosky. **Description:** Profile of Tom Abrams, who combined his love for classic cars with a business opportunity to transform a family owned business from a domestic mover into a national carrier of specialty cars.

37676 ■ **"Handled Like a Pro"** in *Success* **(Vol. 47, No. 6, November 2000, pp. 34)**
Pub: Success Publishing, Inc.
Ed: Melba Newsome. **Description:** After being widowed, Georgia Buchanan took her husband's construction company and rebuilt it from the ground up despite everyone's advice urging her to sell.

37677 ■ **"Healthy Transition"** in *Success* **(Vol. 47, No. 2, June 2000, pp. 52)**
Pub: Success Publishing, Inc.
Ed: Karen Fuller. **Description:** A profile of Molina Health Care showing how the lack of a succession plan could have cost the family their business. Instead, revenue is expected to reach $300 million this year.

37678 ■ **"Heir Raising"** in *Entrepreneur* **(Vol. 33, February 2005, No. 2, pp. 82)**
Pub: Entrepreneur Media Inc.
Ed: Sara Wilson. **Description:** Profile of Dave and Ellie Woodruff who purchased a Meineke Car Care Center franchise for their son, Michael. The couple has plans to open two more franchises for their two daughters. The family discusses their business plans intended to secure their children's future.

37679 ■ **"Her Line of Credit Was in Default. Her Partnership With Her Mom Was Faltering"** in *Inc.* **(Volume 27, December 2005, No. 12, pp. 59-60)**
Pub: Inc. Magazine
Ed: Nadine Heintz. **Description:** Heather Antonelli, CEO of Eminence Style, a furniture wholesaling business, tells why she decided to close her business and declare bankruptcy.

37680 ■ **"Herbal Remedies: Couple Looks to Make Bad Hair Days a Thing of the Past"** in *Black Enterprise* **(Vol. 34, No. 7, February 2004, pp. 48)**
Pub: Earl Graves Publishing Co.
Ed: Nicole Lewis. **Description:** Profile of Stephanie Suthers and her husband, who own Don-Vant Inc., manufacturer of herbal hair and scalp products. The firm's line of products include shampoos, conditioners, oils, and pomades.

37681 ■ **"Herman J. Russell Passes Torch"** in *Black Enterprise* **(Vol. 34, No. 6, January 2004, pp. 19)**
Pub: Earl Graves Publishing Co.
Ed: Tamara E. Holmes. **Description:** Herman J. Russell, founder and CEO of H.J. Russell & Company, one of the nation's largest black-owned firms, has stepped down. Russell's youngest son, Michael, will take over day-to-day operations while the elder Russell remains chairman.

37682 ■ **"High Profit in Play"** in *Small Business Opportunities* **(Vol. 16, No. 1, January 2004, pp. 62, 64)**
Pub: Harris Publications, Inc.
Ed: Stan Roberts. **Description:** Profile of Ron Kaplan who took over his family's toy distribution business, Action Products International in Orlando, Florida, in 1997. Kaplan decided to shift the focus of the company from supplying toys, books and souvenirs to museums, to concentrating on manufacturing educational toys. The company now reports sales of $6 million a year.

37683 ■ **"Historic Redevelopment Pushes Kirtland, Ohio Ice Cream Shop to Relocate"** in *Willoughby News-Herald* **(September 13, 2002)**
Pub: Knight-Ridder/Tribune Business News
Ed: Dave Truman. **Description:** Historic redevelopment has forced the owners of the family run Quirke's Carriage House ice cream shop to relocate. The historic development closed the street in front of the shop. Patty Quirke has run the business with her five children since the death of her husband Patrick in 1999.

37684 ■ **"History Bears Fruit for Maine Family's Apple Orchard"** in *Portland Press Herald* **(October 7, 2005)**
Pub: Blethen Maine Newspapers, Inc.
Ed: Matt Wickenheiser. **Description:** Family-owned Sweetser's Apple Barrel & Orchards of Cumberland, Maine, grows 37 varieties of apples. The company distributes its apples, cider and other products through a roadside stand.

37685 ■ **"History Lesson"** in *Entrepreneur* **(Vol. 33, September 2005, No. 9, pp. 19)**
Pub: Entrepreneur Media Inc.
Ed: Sara Wilson. **Description:** Melissa and Randy Rolston, founders of the Victorian Trading Company in Kansas, wholesale and retail Victorian-themed artifacts and antiques. The couple started with a $200 investment in 1986 and project 2005 sales to hit $15 million.

37686 ■ **"Hollinger VC Unit has Family Ties; Black's Nephew has Few Hits, Many Misses With Fund"** in *Crains Chicago Business* **(Vol. 26, No. 51)**
Pub: Crain Communications, Inc.
Ed: Jeremy Mullman. **Description:** Matthew Doullo is the nephew of Conrad Black, chairman of Hollinger International Inc. Doullo runs the venture investment unit of Hollinger International. A profile of Doullo is provided.

37687 ■ **"Hollinger VC Unit has Family Ties"** in *Crain's Chicago Business* **(Vol. 26, No. 51, December 22, 2003, pp. 3)**
Pub: Crain Communications, Inc.
Ed: Jeremy Mullman. **Description:** Matthew Doullo is the nephew of Conrad Black, chairman of Hollinger International Inc. Doullo runs the venture investment unit of Hollinger International. A profile of Doullo is provided.

37688 ■ **"Hollywood, Fla., Men's Shop is Tailor-Made for Success"** in *South Florida Sun-Sentinel* **(January 3, 2005)**
Pub: South Florida Sun-Sentinel
Ed: Karen-Janine Cohen. **Description:** Profile of Berlin, one of the oldest stores in Hollywood, Florida. The store is run by co-founder Lewis Cohen and his daughter Ronnie Cohen Coaches, who also serves as the stores personal shopper assisting customers in their purchases.

37689 ■ **"Hooked Up to Profit"** in *Small Business Opportunities* **(Vol. 17, May 2005, No. 3, pp. 92)**
Pub: Harris Publications Inc.
Ed: Stan Roberts. **Description:** Profile of Rob Wheeles, former salesman, who decided to start Mr. Hook-It-Up home theater solutions with his wife Donna. The firm now reports sales at $1.4 million annually.

37690 ■ **"Hot Fiscal Issues"** in *Small Business Opportunities* **(Vol. 16, November 2004, No. 6, pp. 70-71)**
Pub: Harris Publications Inc.
Ed: Gerry Murak. **Description:** Planning for compensation in a family business is critical. Seven signs to consider when planning a long-term compensation strategy are investigated.

37691 ■ **"How Don Zacharia Turned a Mom-and-Pop Liquor Store Into a Wine-Retailing Juggernaut"** in *Inc.* **(April 1, 2006)**
Pub: Inc. Magazine
Ed: John Anderson. **Description:** Profile of Don Zacharia who built the family's small liquor store in the suburbs of New York City into a giant wine retailer.

37692 ■ *How to Run a Family Business*
Pub: F & W Publishing, Inc.
Ed: Michael Friedman. **Released:** 1994. **Price:** $14.95 (paper).

37693 ■ **"How To Raise an Entrepreneur"** in *Inc.* **(August 2005, pp. 80-85)**
Pub: Inc. Magazine
Ed: Jonathan Black. **Description:** The key to raising an entrepreneur was, for Michelle Rousseff Kemp, keeping her children away from the family business.

37694 ■ **"How To Work (If You Must) With Your Spouse"** in *Inc.* **(October 1, 2004)**
Pub: Inc. Magazine
Ed: Michael S. Hopkins. **Description:** The challenges of partnering with a spouse in a business venture are observed. Recommendations to overcome these challenges are offered.

37695 ■ **"Humble Beginning"** in *Entrepreneur* **(Vol. 33, March 2005, No. 3, pp. 131)**
Pub: Entrepreneur Media Inc.
Ed: Esther Nguonly. **Description:** Profile of Crystal Belt and James Weathered of Apartment Personnel. The husband and wife team offer staffing services for the apartment industry.

37696 ■ **"I Fulfilled My Family Dream"** in *Success* **(Vol. 47, No. 5, October 2000, pp. 22)**
Pub: Success Publishing, Inc.
Ed: John O'Brien. **Description:** CEO and co-founder of the software company called iMarkup Solutions, describes the pleasures of running a family business.

37697 ■ **"Ice cream shop does its best to satisfy its customers' Cravings"** in *Sarasota Herald Tribune* **(November 21, 2002, pp. H12)**
Pub: Sarasota Herald Tribune
Ed: Nancy Konesko. **Description:** Profile of Carla Rolandi and her husband Victor Tirado, owners of Cravings Ice Cream and Coffee Shop. Rolandi discusses favorite flavors, as well as the gourmet coffee, nutritious Muscle Cruncher and Superman sundae served at the shop.

37698 ■ **"In the Black"** in *My Business* **(August/September 2002, pp. 45)**
Pub: My Business Magazine
Ed: Ivan Sylvester. **Description:** Profile of brothers, Andy and Doug Hoiland, who own a Jet-Black franchise that does driveway repair.

37699 ■ **"In critical decisions, often sole adviser is kin"** in *Wall Street Journal* **(September 24, 2002, pp. B6)**
Pub: Dow Jones & Co. Inc.
Ed: Richard C. Breeden. **Description:** Results of a survey of small business owners, conducted by Wells Fargo and National Federation of Independent Business, is presented. Statistical data included.

37700 ■ **"Industry standards set a base for family pay range"** in *Business First Columbus* **(Vol. 18, No. 25, February 8, 2002, pp. B9)**
Pub: Business First Columbus, Inc.
Ed: Betsy Butler. **Description:** Industry standards are presented for the management of a family-owned business.

37701 ■ **"Inheriting business as challenging as starting one"** in *Atlanta Business Chronicle* **(Vol. 24, No. 13, August 24, 2001, pp. 5B)**
Pub: American City Business Journals Inc.
Ed: Tara Milligan. **Description:** Taking over a business that is already operating has unique challenges. In the article is a case study of Carl Greenway's takeover of the Molly Maid franchise in Memphis five years ago, when it had six employees and eight dilapidated cars. It now has 24 employees, and competes against the national leader Merry Maids, which is also headquartered in Memphis.

37702 ■ **"Inn Vogue"** in *Black Enterprise* **(Vol. 35, November 2004, No. 4, pp. 124)**
Pub: Earl G. Graves Publishing Co. Inc.
Ed: James A. Anderson. **Description:** Profile of Monique Greenwood and husband Glenn Pogue, owners of three bed and breakfasts in New England. Greenwood describes a typical day that might start with cooking breakfast for ten guests. The three inns grossed $185,000 in revenues for 2003 with projected revenue of $370,000 for 2004.

37703 ■ "Is that Kosher? Here's a Food Niche You May Not Have Considered" in *Entrepreneur* **(Vol. 32, No. 2, February 2004, pp. 27)**
Pub: Entrepreneur Media, Inc.
Ed: Nichole L. Torres. **Description:** Profile of Erin Baker-Geschwill, owner of Baker's Breakfast Cookie Inc. in Bellingham, Washington. Baker provides a healthy, Kosher meal-replacement cookie. She got her kosher certification in June 2003; William Retin, owner of Lang's Premium Kosher Bakery, Deli and Foods in San Diego, California, a storefront bakery as well as Internet sales department. Retin manufactures and distributes Kosher breads, groceries, deli foods and meats; and Marc Michels and Martine Lacombe, co-owners of Kosher Pets Inc., husband and wife team who prepare Kosher pet food.

37704 ■ "Is This Any Way to Run a Family" in *Inc.* **(Volume 27, December 2005, No. 12, pp. 122-131)**
Pub: Inc. Magazine
Ed: Robb Mandelbaum. **Description:** Profile of Tom Parsons who started a travel business with his 15-year-old son.

37705 ■ "It's All in the Family for Craig Schnuck" in *St. Louis Post-Dispatch* **(November 5, 2004)**
Pub: Knight-Ridder/Tribune Business News
Ed: Linda Tucci. **Description:** Profile of Schnuck Markets Inc., the grocery company employing 17,000 people. In an interview, Craig Schnuck addresses the challenges and rewards of working in the family run business.

37706 ■ "It's All in the Family" in *Kansas City Star* **(March 8, 2005)**
Pub: Knight-Ridder/Tribune Business News
Ed: Joyce Smith. **Description:** Profile of the Tivol family jewelry company located in Kansas City, Missouri. Son, Tom, will begin offering appraisal services for jewelry and gemstones, including antique, estate and modern pieces. He plans to perform appraisals while customers wait in the shop.

37707 ■ "It's All Relative" in *Entrepreneur* **(Vol. 33, March 2005, No. 3, pp. 74)**
Pub: Entrepreneur Media Inc.
Ed: Chris Penttila. **Description:** Three entrepreneurs offer insight into hiring a newcomer to help revitalize a family-run business.

37708 ■ "Kate and Andy Spade Are That Rare Thing: A Great Husband-and-Wife Business Team" in *Fast Company* **(March 2005, No. 92, pp. 44)**
Pub: Gruner & Jahr USA Publishing
Ed: Linda Tischler. **Description:** Profile of Kate and Andy Spade, husband and wife owners of the hip fashion company Kate Spade. It took only eleven years for the couple to build a $175 million business with a distinctive global brand.

37709 ■ "Keeping Employees" in *Success* **(Vol. 47, No. 5, October 2000, pp. 12)**
Pub: Success Publishing, Inc.
Description: Equity compensation and employee stock ownership programs (ESOPs) as options for family-owned businesses to use as an exit strategy are discussed.

37710 ■ "Keeping it all in the family" in *BlackEnterprise* **(Vol. 31, No. 6, January 2001, pp. 40)**
Pub: Earl Graves Publishing Co.
Ed: Glenn Townes. **Description:** The importance of having a succession plan for a business is stressed and advice is given to develop such a plan.

37711 ■ "Keeping It All in the Family" in *Black Enterprise* **(Vol. 31, No. 5, December 2000, pp. 66)**
Pub: Earl Graves Publishing Co.
Ed: Glenn Townes. **Description:** Profile of James Olan Hutcheson, founder and president of ReGeneration Partners, offers advice in handling the future of family-owned businesses.

37712 ■ "The Lark" in *Crain's Detroit Business* **(Vol. 21, November 7, 2005, No. 45, pp. 16)**
Pub: Crain Communications Inc. - Detroit
Ed: Brent Snavely. **Description:** Profile of James and Mary Lark, husband and wife owners of West Bloomfield Michigan restaurant, The Lark. The Larks opened their European country inn twenty-five years ago and credit their long-term success to offering customers ambiance, service and quality.

37713 ■ "Lighting Their Way" in *Crain's Detroit Business* **(Vol. 21, October 3, 2005, No. 43, pp. 22)**
Pub: Crain Communications Inc. - Detroit
Ed: JoAnn Amicangelo. **Description:** Steve and Patty Gronow, owners of the automotive sales, service and parts company, Kensington Motors, found they had more fun and made a better living in the real estate development business. So they formed Chestnut LLC in Howell, in 1988.

37714 ■ "Long-Time Music Publisher Sings" in *San Fernando Valley Business Journal* **(Vol. 11, November 2006, No. 24, pp. 26)**
Pub: San Fernando Valley Business Journal Associates
Ed: Description: Profile of Alfred Publishing Co., a successful company that publishes music-related material and its acquisition of Daisy Rock Guitars, makers of acoustic and electrical guitars for women and girls.

37715 ■ "Longtime Pitchmen Started Chain" in *Tampa Tribune* **(November 17, 2005)**
Pub: Media General, Inc.
Ed: Michael Sasso. **Description:** Profile of Johnny Carrabba and his uncle Damian Mandola. In 1988, the two men teamed to start a chain of Carrabba's restaurants in Houston, Texas.

37716 ■ "Lou Fusz Cultivates Returns on Car-Selling Business" in *St. Louis Post-Dispatch* **(July 23, 2004)**
Pub: Knight-Ridder/Tribune Business News
Ed: Linda Tucci. **Description:** Louis F. Fusz Jr., owner of auto dealerships in the St. Louis area, discusses his sales philosophy. Fusz's five children are all interested in being a part of the business.

37717 ■ "A Lucky journey" in *Crain's Detroit Business* **(Vol. 19, No. 10, March 10, 2003, pp. 34)**
Pub: Crain Communications Inc., Detroit
Ed: Andrew Dietderich. **Description:** Profile of Arthur Luck, founder of Luck's Music Library Inc., located in Madison Heights, Michigan. In the late 1940s Luck began selling and renting music to associates; the business is currently being run by one of Luck's son.

37718 ■ "Maine Family Rolls Out 100 Flavors of Ice Cream" in *Portland Press Herald* **(July 15, 2005)**
Pub: Blethen Maine Newspapers, Inc.
Ed: Edward D. Murphy. **Description:** Profile of Beal's Old Fashioned Ice Cream, the family-owned firm run by Jim Malia. The company introduces two or three new flavors each year. Statistical data included.

37719 ■ "Make No Mistake" in *My Business* **(June/July 2002, pp. 34-35, 38-39)**
Pub: My Business Magazine
Ed: Alan Naditz. **Description:** The five mistakes that could sink a family business include poor communication, holding family to different standards, paying relatives to not work, failing to plan for Act II, and not preparing for life.

37720 ■ "Making Cents of It All" in *Home Business* **(Vol. 12, March/April 2005, No. 2, pp. 70)**
Pub: Home Business Magazine
Ed: Sandy Larson. **Description:** Profile of Trevor Ollivierre, the young entrepreneur helped his family create the new board game, All Around Spending.

37721 ■ "Making an Educated Decision" in *Business Week Online* **(February 16, 2006)**
Pub: McGraw-Hill Companies
Description: Business schools are helping entrepreneurs prepare to enter into family enterprises.

37722 ■ "Making New Memories at Little Cheese Shop" in *Business Journal-Milwaukee* **(Vol. 20, No. 45, July 25, 2003, pp. A15)**
Pub: American City Business Journals, Inc.
Ed: Becca Mader. **Description:** Profile of Linda Lutz and brother-in-law Howard Lutz, who reopened West Allis Cheese & Sausage Shop after it closed in 2001. They have rebranded the company, expanded the line of foods it makes, began marketing the foods to local shopping malls, as well as changing the labels to make the small company profitable.

37723 ■ "Making Waves: For the Brothers Who Made the Fish Taco a Million Dollar Industry, It's All Relative" in *Entrepreneur* **(Vol. 32)**
Pub: Entrepreneur Media Inc.
Ed: April Y. Pennington. **Description:** Profile of brothers, Mingo Lee, Wing Lam, and Ed Lee of Wahoo's Fish Taco, a casual Mexican restaurant, with hints of Chinese/Brazilian flavors.

37724 ■ "Malley's Chocolates opens first Summit County store" in *Crain's Cleveland Business* **(Vol. 22, No. 42, October 15, 2001, pp. 11)**
Pub: Crain Communications, Inc.
Description: The family-owned Malley's Chocolates of Cleveland will open its first Summit County store October 15, 2001, and plans to open two more stores at undisclosed locations in Northeast Ohio soon. Malley's currently has 12 stores in Cuyahoga, Lake and Lorain counties, in Ohio.

37725 ■ *Managing the Family Business*
Pub: Crisp Publications, Inc.
Ed: Marshall Northington. **Price:** $15.95. **Description:** Part of the Small Business & Entrepreneurship Series.

37726 ■ "Many Healthy Returns" in *Entrepreneur* **(Vol. 31, No. 9, September 2003, pp. 116)**
Pub: Entrepreneur Media, Inc.
Description: Profile of James and Geoff Murdock of Wolf Brothers Mobile Gourmet. The brothers own a food truck, providing nutritious and gourmet menu selections to customers.

37727 ■ *Married & Making a Living: Couples Who Own Small Franchise Businesses*
Pub: Garland Publishing, Inc.
Ed: Barbara Kranendonk. **Released:** 1997. **Price:** $48.00 (cloth).

37728 ■ "Married With Business" in *My Business* **(February/March 2003, pp. 28-32, 34)**
Pub: My Business Magazine
Ed: Shannon Scully. **Description:** Five tips for running a successful business with a spouse are listed, along with advice from couples running small businesses together.

37729 ■ "Mega Wal-Marts Crush Business Diversity" in *Bellingham Business Journal* **(January 2007, pp. C14)**
Pub: Sun News Inc.
Description: Small businesses are the backbone of the Bellingham economy. Wal-Mart threatens the economic diversity by flattening competition and erasing longtime family-owned businesses.

37730 ■ "Mexican Industries Goes Under" in *Hispanic Business* **(Vol. 23, No. 10, October, 2001, pp. 28, 30)**
Pub: Hispanic Business
Ed: Jonathan J. Higuera. **Description:** Profile of the Hispanic-owned automotive supplier Mexican Industries, which filed for bankruptcy in early 2001. The De-

troit-based company was founded by former Major Leaguer Hank Aguirre, and was being run by his three daughters and one son when it filed for Chapter 11. According to Yolanda Gomez-Stupka, president of the Michigan Hispanic Chamber of Commerce, portions of Mexican Industries may survive, but the company will not be the same.

37731 ■ "Mike and Wendy Sign, Seal and Deliver $450,000 a Year Sending Greeting Cards..." in *Small Business Opportunities* **(Vol. 17, May 2005)**
Pub: Harris Publications Inc.
Description: Profile of Mike and Wendy Zavilla who used customized software from Client Connection to create a greeting card mailing service. The couple shares insight into ways they are able to tap into each other's strengths.

37732 ■ *Mind Your Own Business and Keep It in the Family*
Pub: MasterMedia Ltd.
Ed: Marcy Syms. **Released:** 1993. **Price:** $18.95.

37733 ■ "Mom & Pop: Please Read" in *Inc.* **(September 1, 2003)**
Pub: Gruner & Jahr USA Publishing
Ed: Adam Hanft. **Description:** Perceptions and realities of family-owned businesses are investigated.

37734 ■ "Money-Preneuring" in *Small Business Opportunities* **(Vol. 17, September 2005, No. 5, pp. 68, 128)**
Pub: Harris Publications Inc.
Ed: Robert A. Adelson. **Description:** Three strategies to give non-family executives a share in the rewards of ownership without transferring any company stock are shared: offering a non-voting stock plan, a non-qualified deferred compensation plan, or a phantom stock plan.

37735 ■ "A More Perfect Business" in *Inc.* **(August 1, 2003)**
Pub: Gruner & Jahr USA Publishing
Ed: Matthew Fogel. **Description:** A family-business constitution could help direct a company through crisis and change. The constitution would consist of a statement of principles designed to guide issues of ownership, performance, accountability, and compensation, though would not be legally binding.

37736 ■ "Mother, I'm the boss now: Internet executives hire their parents and traditions fall" in *The New York Times* **(July 4, 2000, pp. C1)**
Pub: The New York Times Company
Ed: Katie Hafner. **Description:** The ways reverse nepotism is opening a new dimension in child-parent relationships is discussed.

37737 ■ "Mrs., Mom, and CEO" in *Black Enterprise* **(Vol. 32, No. 9, April 2)**
Pub: Earl Graves Publishing Co.
Ed: Monique R. Brown. **Description:** Profile of Vickie Clark, owner and founder of a family owned, home-based business that transports kids back and forth to various activities.

37738 ■ "Music To Your Ears" in *Entrepreneur.com* **(Vol. 34, February 2006, No. 2, pp. 113)**
Pub: Entrepreneur Media Inc.
Ed: James Park. **Description:** Profile of Mindy and Jerry Harvey, founders of Ultimate Ears, custom-made, high-end earpieces for professional musicians and music lovers.

37739 ■ "Never say die: how a family beat the odds (and the weather) to improve a franchise" in *Entrepreneur* **(Vol. 30, No. 12, Dec. 2002)**
Pub: Entrepreneur Media Inc.
Ed: Tracy Stapp. **Description:** Profile of Scott and Steven Prewitt and their brother-in-law Tony Mansoor; the three men were able to overcome the obstacles faced with their Back Yard Burgers restaurant, and revolutionized the franchise system along the way.

37740 ■ "New Scooter Sales Store is Set to Open on Iowa Street" in *Bellingham Business Journal* **(December 2006, pp. A6)**
Pub: Sun News Inc.
Description: Profile of Urbano Moto, a new scooter store owned by Alan and Gretchen Taylor, will sell Roketa scooters, high-fuel-economy cars, including hybrids and those that run on diesel.

37741 ■ "New Space in an Old Place" in *Crain's Detroit Business* **(Vol. 21, February 7, 2005, No. 6, pp. 14)**
Pub: Crain Communications Inc. - Detroit
Ed: JoAnn Amicangelo. **Description:** Profile of Michael LaFontaine, the LaFontaine Automotive Group, which includes the Toyota, Kia, Scion, Suzuki, Hyundai, and Honda dealerships, all located in a Dearborn, Michigan location, as well as Pontiac, Cadillac, and GMC dealerships in Highland Township. The Group employs about 350 people and family members are involved in the management of different dealerships.

37742 ■ "A New Twist" in *Entrepreneur*
Pub: Entrepreneur Media Inc.
Ed: April Y. Pennington. **Description:** Profile of Kimberly and Scott Holstein, husband and wife co-founders of Kim & Scott's Gourmet Pretzels. Pretzels come in 20 flavors and the couple intends to open its first bakery cafe in 2005. The Chicago-based manufacturer expects to see $6 million in sales for 2004.

37743 ■ "The Next Generation. Planning Ahead" in *San Francisco Business Times* **(Vol. 17, No. 48, July 4, 2003, pp. 15)**
Pub: American City Business Journals
Ed: Jessica Materna. **Description:** Sugarbowl Baker, owned and operated by Andrew Ly, is an example of a family-owned business that is trying to buck the trend of effectively passing on the company to the next generation. A recent study by the University of Connecticut's Family Business Program has found that only 30 percent of such companies can achieve this goal, and only 10 percent can survive a third generation change of ownership. Family rivalries are the given reason for such high failure rates.

37744 ■ *Nirvana in a Cup: The Founding of Oregon Chai*
Pub: Moby Press
Ed: Tedde McMillen; Heather Hale. **Released:** July 2006. **Price:** $12.99. **Description:** Profile of a mother-daughter team who founded Oregon Chai, a tea company.

37745 ■ "No Free Lunch" in *Entrepreneur* **(Vol. 32, October 2004, No. 10, pp. 107)**
Pub: Entrepreneur Media Inc.
Ed: Anna Buss. **Description:** Profile of Chris and Joan Lindner, who purchased a Togo franchise in California after Chris decided it was time for a career change. Since then, the couple has opened three more locations, including two co-branded Togo's and Baskin Robbins franchises as well as a stand-alone Togo's.

37746 ■ "No Place Like Home" in *Entrepreneur* **(Vol. 32, December 2004, No. 12, pp. 108)**
Pub: Entrepreneur Media Inc.
Ed: Rebecca Villaneda. **Description:** Husband and wife, Mike and Kerri Little, founders of Home Helpers, providing 24-hour-a-day home care to about 400 senior clients. Services include companionship, grocery shopping, personal care, transportation and laundry.

37747 ■ "Objectivity, Consensus Key For Survival of Family Biz" in *Crain's Detroit Business* **(Vol. 21, October 10, 2005, No. 43, pp. 23)**
Pub: Crain Communications Inc. - Detroit
Ed: Sheena Harrison. **Description:** Three keys to help family-owned companies survive into the fourth-generation and beyond are shared by Steve McClure of The Family Business Consulting Group Inc. The Marietta, Georgia-based consulting firm stresses objectivity, family organization and consensus on a business direction as key.

37748 ■ "On a Shoestring" in *Entrepreneur* **(Vol. 31, No. 9, September 2003, pp. 118)**
Pub: Entrepreneur Media, Inc.
Ed: April Y. Pennington. **Description:** Profile of Ellen and Jack Davies of Davies Gate, offering garden-inspired beauty and skincare products. Ellen Davies and her husband Jack spent $4,000 of their savings to buy paper wraps and labels to package their custom bars of soap.

37749 ■ "Opportunities" in *Entrepreneur* **(Vol. 30, No. 2, Fe)**
Pub: Entrepreneur Media Inc.
Ed: Stephanie Soong. **Description:** Profile of Ray and Cyndi White who retired from their careers as rocket scientist and hearing specialist respectively to start their own business in a real estate franchise.

37750 ■ "Oregon Food Producer Hitches Wagon to Big Brand-Name Star" in *Business Journal-Portland* **(Vol. 18, No. 33, October 12, 2001, pp. 16)**
Pub: American City Business Journals, Inc. (Portland)
Ed: Shelly Strom. **Description:** Family-owned YoCream has announced a partnership with Dannon Yogurt to produce frozen yogurt products.

37751 ■ "An outsider's perspective" in *Wall Street Journal* **(October 28, 2002, pp. R9)**
Pub: Dow Jones & Co. Inc.
Ed: Kemba J. Dunham. **Description:** Information is shared for managing a family-owned business.

37752 ■ *Partners at Work and at Home: How Couples Can Build a Successful Business Together without Killing Each Other*
Pub: Self-Counsel Press, Inc.
Ed: Annette O'Shea-Roche and Sieglinde Malmberg. **Released:** 1994, first edition. **Price:** $8.95 (paper).

37753 ■ "Passing the baton the importance of sequence, timing, technique and communication in executive succession" in *Journal of Business Venturing*
Pub: Elsevier Science, Inc.
Ed: Bruno Dyck, Michael Mauws, Frederick A. Starke, Gary A. Mischke. **Description:** Four factors said to influence the process of executive succession are discussed. These factors, sequence, timing, baton-passing techniques, and communication are examined within the analogy of a relay race, and plot the executive succession in a small manufacturing company, which is family owned.

37754 ■ *Passing the Torch: Succession, Retirement, and Estate Planning for Owners of Family Businesses*
Pub: The McGraw-Hill Companies
Ed: Mike Cohn. **Released:** Second edition, 1992. **Price:** $39.95; $17.95 (paper).

37755 ■ *Passing Your Family Business on to Your Family: Creating a Lifetime Succession Plan to Meet Your Changing Tax, Estate and Business Needs*
Pub: Probus Publishing Co., Inc.
Ed: Irving L. Blackman. **Released:** 1995. **Price:** $32.50.

37756 ■ "A Perfect Match?" in *Entrepreneur* **(Vol. 31, No. 10, October 2003, pp. 60)**
Pub: Entrepreneur Media, Inc.
Ed: Crystal Detamore-Rodman. **Description:** Profile of Ahmed and Reem Rahim, brother and sister entrepreneurs, and their first step in the half-million dollar expansion of their organic tea company.

37757 ■ "Plan to Avoid Confusion When Passing the Torch" in *Atlanta Business Chronicle* **(Vol. 23, No. 49, May 11, 2001, pp. 10B)**
Pub: American City Business Journals Inc.
Ed: James Lea. **Description:** Family-owned businesses must make careful plans for passing on of ownership and management, especially when divorce has complicated the family dynamics. Co-owners

must also be aware that they will not necessarily want to retire at the same time, and offspring may or may not want to continue in the family business. The economics of multiple ownership can also be complicated, especially if a business cannot support two or more families.

37758 ■ "Plan a legacy for your business and your family" in *Black Enterprise* (Vol. 33, No. 3, October 2002, pp. 104)
Pub: Earl Graves Publishing Co.
Description: Case studies for small, family-owned business planning are presented, including business planning, estate planning, and financial security.

37759 ■ "Planned transition" in *Business First Columbus* (Vol. 1)
Pub: Business First Columbus, Inc.
Ed: Drew Bracken. **Description:** Profile of family-owned business, Velvet Ice Cream, and how, together with a consultant, developed a flexible transition plan for the firm.

37760 ■ "Playing Cupid: These Matchmaking Sisters Aim to Give Busy Singles a Fast-and Fun-Way to Date" in *Entrepreneur* (September 2004)
Pub: Entrepreneur Media Inc.
Ed: Anna Buss. **Description:** Profile of Donna Heiser and Pat Maida, sisters, who operate the 4-Minute Date, a service geared to busy singles. The $35 service capitalizes on the speed-dating trend and allows couples to determine whether their 'date' is the perfect match...all in 4 minutes.

37761 ■ "Pottery studio offers a form of self-expression" in *Sarasota Herald Tribune* (December 19, 2002, pp. H1)
Pub: Sarasota Herald Tribune
Ed: Kelly Cramer. **Description:** Profile of Espresso Yourself, a paint-your-own-pottery studio located in Sarasota, Florida. Owners Andy and Kelly Minor, opened the shop in December 2002, which also houses a coffee shop.

37762 ■ *Preparing Your Family Business for Strategic Change*
Pub: Business Owner Resources
Ed: Craig E. Aronoff and John L. Ward. **Released:** 1997. **Price:** $14.95 (Vol. 9).

37763 ■ *Preserving the Legacy of a Small Business Family: Estate Planning & Business Succession*
Pub: Estate & Business Communications, Inc.
Ed: Tim Bachmeyer and William A. Snyder. **Released:** 1998. **Price:** $24.95.

37764 ■ "Proposed Apartments Meant For Those With Below-Median Income" in *Bradenton Herald* (January 26, 2005)
Pub: Bradenton Herald
Ed: Matt Griswold. **Description:** Brother and Sister, Andy and Beth Reasoner, are developing a $20 million apartment complex called the Royal Palm Terrace Apartments. The complex will house 220 affordable units targeted for families or individuals earning $35,000-$40,000 annually. Andy and Beth partnered with Venice estate-planning attorneys to take advantage of the county's land development code that allows them to build at a higher density in exchange for offering affordable rental property.

37765 ■ "Raleigh, N.C.-Area Employers Decline to Offer Dating Service as Perk" in *News & Observer* (February 1, 2004)
Pub: News & Observer
Ed: Karin Rives. **Description:** Owners of the William Ashley Agency, Lisa and Bill Horst, approached several Triangle North Carolina companies to offer their matchmaking service as a benefit to employees. The husband and wife team ran into issues such as employer concern about meddling in the personal life of employees, and the liability of matches that did not work out.

37766 ■ "Redefining my role" in *My Business* (June/July 2002, pp. 48)
Pub: My Business Magazine
Ed: Description: David Geller shares the challenge he faced as an entrepreneur and how he was able to help his firm reach the goals set out by he and his brother in 1996 when starting GV Financial Advisors, a financial planning firm in Atlanta, Georgia.

37767 ■ "Retired Couple Open Gift Shop, Bed-and-Breakfast in Jacksonville, Texas" in *Tyler Morning Telegraph* (February 10, 2004)
Pub: Knight-Ridder/Tribune Business News
Ed: Greg Junek. **Description:** Profile Susie and Ken Ripkowski, owners of the Love's Nest decor and gift shop, along with an upstairs bed-and-breakfast inn. The Ripkowski's moved to Jacksonville, Texas in order to spend their retirement time revitalizing a building and to run a business in the downtown district.

37768 ■ "Review with Care" in *Entrepreneur* (Vol. 28, No. 2, February 2000, pp. 125)
Pub: Entrepreneur Media Inc.
Description: Rating your sibling's performance means treading on delicate and potentially explosive ground.

37769 ■ "Ring Bearers: Some Would-Be Grooms Need a Little Direction in Finding the Perfect Diamond. Here Comes the Guides" in *Entrepreneur*
Pub: Entrepreneur Media Inc.
Ed: April Y. Pennington. **Description:** Profile of Skip and Steve Robbins, focusing exclusively on engagement rings. The brothers changed their family business, Robbins Brothers, and converted bank buildings into stores that feature Websites with ring combinations and a room with soda, coffee and ESPN.

37770 ■ "Robbins Bros. Executive to Manage Growth" in *San Fernando Valley Business Journal* (Vol. 11, December 2006, No. 25, pp. 16)
Pub: San Fernando Valley Business Journal Associates
Ed: Shelly Garcia. **Description:** Profile of Robbins Bros., the World's Biggest Engagement Ring Store, and the company's growth and vision for the future since hiring a new president after brother Skip Robbins moved on to pursue other ventures.

37771 ■ "A Rose by No Name" in *My Business* (June/July 2004, pp. 45)
Pub: My Business Magazine
Ed: Kathleen Landis. **Description:** Family owned Sparks Florist partnered with the U.S. Bank in nearby Reno, Nevada to create Good Neighbor Day. The event generated business for the flower shop.

37772 ■ "Rousches Celebrate 35 Years in Lawn Mower Business" in *Ledger* (March 2, 2005)
Pub: Knight-Ridder/Tribune Business News
Ed: Mike Grogan. **Description:** The Rousch family has been selling and servicing lawnmowers for 35 years. Dave Rousch talks about the many changes that have occurred in the past three decades.

37773 ■ "Safeguard your financial legacy" in *BlackEnterprise* (Vol. 32, No. 3, October 2001, pp. 75)
Pub: Earl Graves Publishing Co.
Ed: Carolyn M. Brown. **Description:** In small business, the transferring of wealth requires solid tax and estate planning. The article lists safeguards to secure a family legacy. Ten steps to financial empowerment are included.

37774 ■ "Second Time Around" in *Small Business Opportunities* (Vol. 12, No. 3, May 2000, pp. 18)
Pub: Harris Publications, Inc.
Ed: Sandy Weinberg. **Description:** Failing to properly plan for business succession can lead to a company's downfall. Three things that can help preserve a family business are examined.

37775 ■ "Selling guns: a tradition and a dilemma" in *The New York Times* (April 5, 2000, pp. B2(L))
Pub: The New York Times Company
Ed: Randy Kennedy. **Description:** An interview with New York City gun shop owner Anthony Imperato about his family-owned business.

37776 ■ "Sending Out an SOS: Our Franchisees Just Hit an Iceberg in Negotiating Their Land Deal" in *Entrepreneur* (Vol. 31, No. 9, July 2003)
Pub: Entrepreneur Media, Inc.
Ed: Todd D. Maddocks. **Description:** Issues a couple face when purchasing land to start their new franchise business are presented.

37777 ■ "Shock Value: A Belief in the Power of Batteries Charged This Couple Up for Franchise Ownership" in *Entrepreneur* (Vol. 32, Oct. 2004)
Pub: Entrepreneur Media Inc.
Ed: Sara Wilson. **Description:** Profile of Susan and Dan Manwaring, husband and wife team who purchased a Fast Batteries Plus franchise in Indiana. The couple has been in business for twelve years with six stores.

37778 ■ "Show me the money" in *Entrepreneur* (Vol. 31, No. 6, June 2003, pp. 108)
Pub: Entrepreneur Media Inc.
Ed: Todd D. Maddocks. **Description:** A couple have found the ideal property for their franchise business and need to secure financing for the deal.

37779 ■ "Sister Act" in *My Business* (February/March 2004, pp. 28-31)
Pub: My Business Magazine
Ed: Nancy Mann Jackson. **Description:** Profile of three sisters who started a coffee shop together; profile of a sister and brother who own an office furniture installation and facility management company together; another brother and sister team who run a successful mail sorting firm; and two brothers who own a telecommunications management company. Each team shares advice to others wishing to start a family business.

37780 ■ "Sisters in Fitness: Three Siblings Got Their Health Club Off the Ground" in *Black Enterprise* (Vol. 35, September 2004, No. 2, pp. 48)
Pub: Earl G. Graves Publishing Co. Inc.
Ed: Glenn Townes. **Description:** Three sisters from Milwaukee, Wisconsin opened a fitness center catering to African American women. SB Fitness Complex made nearly $250,000 in revenues for 2003.

37781 ■ "A Slice of Life" in *Entrepreneur* (Vol. 32, December 2004, No. 12, pp. 18)
Pub: Entrepreneur Media Inc.
Ed: Sara Wilson. **Description:** Profile of Michael and Meredith Wickliffe, founders of Wick's Pizza Parlor and Pub in Louisville, Kentucky. The restaurant offers pizzas, sandwiches and salads and features live entertainment.

37782 ■ "Smart Answers" in *Business Week* (No. 3694, August 14, 2000, pp. F14)
Pub: McGraw-Hill, Inc.
Description: The owner of a family-owned travel agency asks how to legally close the business.

37783 ■ "Split Personalities" in *Entrepreneur* (Vol. 32)
Pub: Entrepreneur Media Inc.
Ed: Nichole L. Torres. **Description:** Profile of Craig and Matt Steichen, father and son team who created custom sports jerseys combining two different teams or home/away uniforms.

37784 ■ "Stock of Ages" in *Entrepreneur* (Vol. 28, No. 8, August 2000, pp. 102)
Pub: Entrepreneur Media Inc.
Ed: Patricia Schiff Estess. **Description:** Every relative seems to want a piece of the family business pie, and the author offers insight in preventing your business from becoming a casualty of shareholding squabbles.

37785 ■ "Straub's Doesn't Fill its Baskets With a Lot of Gimmicks" in *St. Louis Post-Dispatch* **(October 29, 2004)**
Pub: Knight-Ridder/Tribune Business News
Ed: Linda Tucci. **Description:** Profile of Straub's Markets Inc., the 103 year-old-old family grocer. In an interview with Trip Straub, son of President Jack Straub, the fourth generation running the firm, he shares how he reinvented the stores through diversification of product line and remodeling shops. These steps have doubled total sales over an eight-year period.

37786 ■ "Street Smarts: Ya Gotta Love It" in *Inc.* **(November 1, 2003)**
Pub: Gruner & Jahr USA Publishing
Ed: Norm Brodsky. **Description:** Bobby and Helene Stone believe heartfelt enthusiasm can help create a successful business. The Stones run Data-Link Associates out of their basement, selling a range of computer supplies, from magnetic media to PC cleaning kits from their basement, and employ 6 people. The company reports $2.6 million in sales.

37787 ■ "Strictly Business" in *Entrepreneur* **(Vol. 28, No. 1, January 2000, pp. 118)**
Pub: Entrepreneur Media Inc.
Ed: Patricia Schiff Estess. **Description:** The topic of managing personnel issues in the family business is covered.

37788 ■ *The Successful Family Business*
Pub: Upstart Publishing Co., Inc.
Ed: Scott E. Friedman. **Released:** 1998. **Price:** $22.95.

37789 ■ "Succession-Planning Do's and Don'ts: Who Will Take Over When You're Ready to Retire?" in *Journal of Accountancy* **(February 2005)**
Pub: American Institute of Certified Public Accountants
Ed: Anita Dennis. **Description:** Few certified public accounting firms have set a succession plan into place for selling their firm or passing it down to the next generation.

37790 ■ "Super Success in Spas" in *Small Business Opportunities* **(Vol. 16, No. 2, March 2004, pp. 92, 95)**
Pub: Harris Publications, Inc.
Ed: Vicki Gerson. **Description:** Profile of Robert Hallam, founder of Dimension One Spas, designer and manufacturer of spas ranging in price from $4,000 to $30,000. Robert's wife handles the firm's customer service and is credited for its annual growth of 8-12 percent, reaching $48 million in 2002. Dimension Spas has partnered with Vision of Children Foundation by donating $100 for every spa sold to help end childhood blindness and vision disorders.

37791 ■ *Sustaining the Family Business: An Insider's Guide to Managing Across Generations*
Pub: Perseus Books
Ed: Marshall B. Paisner. **Released:** 1999. **Price:** $26.00.

37792 ■ "Sweet Scoop of Success" in *Small Business Opportunities* **(Vol. 16, No. 1, January 2004, pp. 50, 52)**
Pub: Harris Publications, Inc.
Ed: Justin Grensing. **Description:** Profile of Olson's Creamland Dairy, located in Chippewa Falls, Wisconsin. The family owned ice cream business is able to earn $450,000 annually in a town with a population of only 13,000 people.

37793 ■ "The sweet spot: a cathedral to candy brings together two very different worshipers" in *New York Times* **(October 27, 2002, pp. 81)**
Pub: The New York Times
Ed: Jonathan Reynolds. **Description:** Two candy stores in New York City are profiled. Dylan's Candy Bar is a stylish shop owned by Dylan Lauren, while Ruby et Violet is a family owned business. Recipes for candy and cookies are included.

37794 ■ "Switching Tracks" in *Black Enterprise* **(Vol. 34, July 2004, No. 12, pp. 124)**
Pub: Earl G. Graves Publishing Co. Inc.
Ed: Sonya A. Donaldson. **Description:** Profile of BITco USA Inc., the Florida-based firm that installs equipment such as radios, surveillance cameras, and automatic fare boxes on buses and rail cars. The family owned business won the bid for a Website makeover that would help the build company's image.

37795 ■ "Tax Bill Doesn't Repeal Estate Tax Uncertainty" in *Atlanta Business Chronicle* **(Vol. 24, No. 1, June 8, 2001, pp. 5A)**
Pub: American City Business Journals Inc.
Description: The federal estate law, which Congress repealed, can be reinstated in 2001 unless Congress passes a new law repealing it. Until then, the estate tax is phased out. The impact of estate tax on small business owners is discussed.

37796 ■ "A Tax Deal Too Good to Be True?" in *Business Week Online* **(July 25, 2003)**
Pub: McGraw-Hill Inc.
Ed: Anne Tergesen. **Description:** In May 2003, the U.S tax court declared tax breaks off-limits to a Texas partnership on the grounds that the donor had retained too much control over key decisions. The implications of this court order are discussed.

37797 ■ "Team Effort?" in *Entrepreneur* **(Vol. 28, No. 6, June 2000, pp. 125)**
Pub: Entrepreneur Media Inc.
Ed: Patricia Shiff Estess. **Description:** What happens when the founding partnership of a business was between two families? Will the future generations of each partner be as in tune with each other as their parents or grandparents were?

37798 ■ "Things I Can't Live Without..." in *Inc.* **(January 1, 2004)**
Pub: Gruner & Jahr USA Publishing
Ed: Riza Cruz. **Description:** Profile of Stephen Maharam, a principle in his family's textile company, Maharam with offices in New York City and Hauppauge, New York. Stephen and brother Michael report annual revenue of $100 million.

37799 ■ "Things I Can't Live Without: Marcy Zambelli" in *Inc.* **(July 1, 2004)**
Pub: Inc. Magazine
Ed: Ian Mount. **Description:** Interview with Marcy Zambelli, CEO of Zambelli Fireworks, a third generation family business. The firm was founded in 1893 and is worth $12 million.

37800 ■ "Through Grieving" in *Success from Failure* **(August 2000)**
Pub: Vision Quest Publishing, Inc.
Ed: Barbara Parton. **Description:** Barbara Parton, CEO of The Transpective Group, a business coaching and organization transformation firm, tells how she successfully led the family owned company "through grieving" after her husband died.

37801 ■ "Timing the Sale" in *Success* **(Vol. 47, No. 4, September 2000, pp. 74)**
Pub: Success Publishing, Inc.
Ed: Margaret Crane. **Description:** Selling a family business can be the right move. This article investigates the 10 reasons the owner of a family business made the sale.

37802 ■ "Tips for Tough Transitions" in *Business Week Online* **(February 16, 2006)**
Pub: McGraw-Hill Companies
Description: Options are offered to family members not interested in continuing a family business include selling the business or working with an investment firm.

37803 ■ "Tough Mama" in *Forbes* **(December 25, 2000, pp. 232)**
Pub: Forbes Magazine
Ed: Kelly Barron. **Description:** Profile of Gertrude Boyle, 76, and her son, who took their Portland, Oregon business, Columbia Sportswear public.

37804 ■ "The Trick is to Live" in *Journal of Political Economy* **(Vol. 111, No. 6, December 2003, pp. 18)**
Pub: University of Chicago Press
Ed: Wojciech Kopczuk. **Description:** Because estate tax liability usually depends on how long one lives, it implicitly provides annuity income. In the absence of annuity markets, lump-sum estate taxation may be used to achieve the first-best solution for individuals with a sufficiently strong bequest motive. Calculations of the annuity embedded in the U.S. estate tax show that people with $10 million of assets may be effectively receiving $100,000 a year financed at actuarially fair rates by their tax payments. The insurance effect might reduce the marginal cost of funds (MCF) for the estate tax by as much as 30 percent, and the resulting MCF is within the range of estimates for the MCF for the income tax.

37805 ■ "Truly 'Small' Business" in *My Business* **(June/July 2002, pp. 45)**
Pub: My Business Magazine
Ed: Doug McPherson. **Description:** Profile of Evan and Elise Macmillan, age 16 and 13 respectively. Evan and Elise are co-founders of The Chocolate Farm that sells chocolate candies from a Web site, which employs 30-40 part-time workers.

37806 ■ "Uncommon Enterprise: Breaking Up is Easy to Do" in *My Business* **(June/July 2004, pp. 56)**
Pub: My Business Magazine
Ed: Shannon Scully. **Description:** Happily married husband and wife team contact no-longer-beloveds for persons wishing to break off relationships. After a short interview, they construct a personalized letter to the person explaining the reasons for the breakup.

37807 ■ "Uncommon Enterprise: On the Map" in *My Business* **(June/July 2002, pp. 54)**
Pub: My Business Magazine
Description: Profile of husband and wife team, Helen and Larry Smith, owners of Professional Impressions, Inc. The company's signature product is the bandana-map, which features detailed topographical maps of the Grand Canyon, Yosemite National Park and surrounding area in Utah.

37808 ■ "Van Briggle Art Pottery" in *ColoradoBiz* **(Vol. 30, No. 1, January 2003, pp. 61)**
Pub: Wiesner Publishing, LLC
Ed: Eric Peterson. **Description:** Profile of Van Briggle Art Pottery, located in Colorado Springs. In 1970 Kenneth W. Stevenson bought the company, and his family continues to run the company today.

37809 ■ "Velvet Ice Cream Welcomes Return of Spring" in *PR Newswire* **(April 30, 2002, pp. CLTU00330042002)**
Pub: PR Newswire Association, Inc.
Description: Velvet Ice Cream Company and its Ye Old Mill celebrated its 88th anniversary. The company is a fourth generation, family owned business in Ohio.

37810 ■ "When Egos Collide" in *Entrepreneur* **(Vol. 28, No. 7, July 2000, pp. 113)**
Pub: Entrepreneur Media Inc.
Ed: Patricia Schiff Estess. **Description:** Don't let sparring egos tear the family business apart.

37811 ■ "When Taking Candy From Babies Makes Sense" in *Fortune* **(Vol. 141, No. 17, April 3, 2000, pp. 304)**
Pub: Time Inc.
Ed: Carolyn T. Geer. **Description:** Advice is given regarding partnership agreements, including information about the Uniform Transfers to Minors Act.

37812 ■ "When those at the Thanksgiving table are your team" in *Business First Columbus* **(Vol. 18, No. 25, February 8, 2002, pp. B6)**
Pub: Business First Columbus, Inc.
Ed: Carole W. Tomko. **Description:** Tips for running a family-owned business are presented, including issues presented when managing family members.

37813 ■ "Wholesale changes: Mom-and-Pop stores are so passe" in *Entrepreneur* (Vol. 30, No. 2, February 2002, pp. 19)
Pub: Entrepreneur Media Inc.
Ed: Nichole L. Torres. **Description:** Some retailers are revamping the layout of stores to give the look of a warehouse in order to attract more customers.

37814 ■ "Will Congress Act to Preserve Family Type Farming?" in *U.S. Farm News* (Vol. 25, No. 3, Autumn 2001, pp. 6-7)
Pub: U.S. Farmers Association
Ed: Lem Harris. **Description:** An overview of the new Farm Act being written by Congress is presented.

37815 ■ "The Winning Attitude" in *Small Business Opportunities* (Vol. 16, No. 2, March 2004, pp. 72, 74)
Pub: Harris Publications, Inc.
Ed: Chuck Green. **Description:** Profile of Taj Reneau and brother Darius, owners of Webley Systems, providing technology to companies such as telecommunications services providers. The firm is located in Deerfield, Illinois.

37816 ■ "Witness to history...and tragedy: a Wall Street veteran reflects on his 9/11 loss" in *Barron's* (Vol. 82, Sept. 9, 2002, pp. 26)
Pub: Barron's
Ed: Erin E. Arvedlund. **Description:** Michael Pascuma, a 75-year veteran of the securities industry, is acknowledged as the oldest floor broker in the country. He built a small business with his only son, Michael Jr., who perished in the World Trade Center attacks. Pascuma reflects upon his life in the industry.

37817 ■ *Work Smarter, Not Harder, the Service that Sells Workbook for Family Dining Operation*
Pub: Pencomm Inc.
Ed: Jim Sullivan. **Released:** 1995. **Price:** $9.95.

37818 ■ "Yessian Music hires Detroit producer, wins contract for ads" in *Crain's Detroit Business* (Vol. 18, No. 50, Dec. 16, 2002, pp. 16)
Pub: Crain Communications Inc., Detroit
Ed: Jennette Smith. **Description:** Yessian Music, located in Farmington Hills, Michigan hired producer, Gerard Smerek, and landed contracts for a number of high-profile commercials. Yessian Music is owned by Brian Yessian, along with his brother Michael, and his father Dan.

37819 ■ *Your Family Business—A Success Guide for Growth and Survival*
Pub: Dow Jones-Irwin
Ed: Benjamin Benson and Edwin T. Crego. **Released:** 1990. **Price:** $30.00.

TRADE PERIODICALS

37820 ■ *Estate Planners Alert*
Pub: Research Institute of America
Contact: Arthur Sabatini
Released: Monthly. **Price:** $200. **Description:** Spotlights critical developments in estate and financial planning.

37821 ■ *Family Business Advisor*
Pub: Family Enterprise Publishers
Ed: Craig E. Aronoff, Ph.D., Editor. **Released:** Monthly, 12/year. **Price:** $195, U.S.; $210, Canada; $225, elsewhere. **Description:** Covers business management, family relations, and asset protection. Addresses succession planning, estate planning, conflict management, compensation, family meetings, strategic planning, and board composition. Recurring features include news of research.

37822 ■ *Working Moms & Dads Magazine*
Pub: Corporate Marketing & Publishing
Ed: Patrick McGuire, Editor. **Released:** Monthly. **Description:** Contains national and local news on parenting, childcare, education, and work issues. For professional and working parents.

VIDEOCASSETTES/ AUDIOCASSETTES

37823 ■ *The Agony and the Ecstasy—The Special Problems of Running a Closely-Held or Family Business*
RMI Media
1365 N. Winchester
Olathe, KS 66061
Ph:(913)768-1696
Fax: (913)768-0184
Co. E-mail: actmedia@act.org
URL: http://www.rmimedia.com
Released: 1989. **Price:** $149.00. **Description:** About 90% of American businesses are family-owned. Find out their disadvantages and advantages and what makes them so special. **Availability:** VHS; 3/4U.

CONSULTANTS

37824 ■ **Calmas Associates**
62 Fairway Rd.
Chestnut Hill, MA 02467
Ph:(617)277-9244
Fax: (617)277-2021
Co. E-mail: wcalmas@calmasassociates.com
URL: http://www.calmasassociates.com

E-mail: wcalmas@calmasassociates.com
Scope: Offers sales productivity services, specializing in intra-corporate communications, employee relations, and motivation. Offers unique coaching program for increasing sales force productivity. Also serves in resolving family conflicts. Industries served: all, but primarily insurance and stock brokerage in New England. Executive coach. **Publications:** "How to Combat High Sales Force Turnover," Boston Business Journal. **Seminars:** Succession Issues for Family Owned Businesses; Role of Psychoanalysis in the Succession Process; The Sports Approach for Success in Sales.

37825 ■ **Center for Family Business**
PO Box 24219
Cleveland, OH 44124
Ph:(440)442-0800
Fax: (440)460-5407
Co. E-mail: grummi@aol.com

E-mail: grummi@aol.com
Scope: Family business specialists provide specialized seminars and consulting services devoted to the growth and successful continuity of family owned or closely held companies. Serves private industries worldwide. **Publications:** L. Danco, Beyond Survival, University Services Institute; Inside the Family Business, University Services Institute; Outside Directors in the Family Owned Business, University Services Institute; K. Danco, From the Other Side of the Bed, University Services Institute; purchasing information available from firm. **Seminars:** Seminar for Business Owners and Spouses; Managing Succession Without Conflict; Conferences for Heirs and Successors.

37826 ■ **Family Business Institute Inc.**
904 Steffi Ct.
Lawrenceville, GA 30044
Ph:(770)952-4085
Fax: (770)432-6660
Co. E-mail: asktheexpert@family-business-experts.com
URL: http://www.family-business-experts.com

E-mail: asktheexpert@family-business-experts.com
Scope: A multidisciplinary consulting team established to help families in business together achieve their personal, family, and organizational goals by meeting challenges that are unique to family-owned businesses. Provides coordinated and integrated assessments and solutions for family issues and needs; for company finance; and for human resource and operational requirements. **Publications:** "Professional

Intervention in the Family Owned Business"; "Building Consensus in a Family Business"; "Professionalizing Family Business Management"; "Recognizing generations - know them by their weekends"; "Succession planning tactics".

37827 ■ **Dean Fowler Associates Inc.**
17100 W North Ave., Ste. 202
Brookfield, WI 53005
Ph:(262)789-7367
Free: 800-203-3071
Fax: (262)789-5355
Co. E-mail: info@deanfowler.com
URL: http://www.deanfowler.com

E-mail: info@deanfowler.com
Scope: Offers management services in family dynamics in family- owned businesses. Services include: management development and peer interaction, maintaining family harmony and business success, and resolving personal and interpersonal issues. Industries served: family businesses, all industries. **Publications:** "Forums for Family Business," 2006; "The Family Forum," 2005; "The Bermuda Triangle," 2003; "Love, Power and Money: Family Business Between Generations," Glengrove Publishing, 2002.

37828 ■ **Frankel and Topche P.C.**
1700 Galloping Hill Rd.
Kenilworth, NJ 07033
Ph:(908)298-7700
Fax: (908)298-7701
Co. E-mail: info@frankelandtopche.com
URL: http://www.frankelandtopche.com

E-mail: info@frankelandtopche.com
Scope: Offers financial consulting for closely held businesses. Assists in mergers and acquisitions, tax planning, strategic business planning, family succession planning, accounting, auditing, and obtaining financing. The firm serves small businesses in the service, retail, wholesale, and manufacturing industries. Specializes in real estate, lumber and building materials, and service businesses.

37829 ■ **Management Growth Institute**
572 Washington St.
Wellesley, MA 02482
Ph:(781)235-1520
Fax: (781)235-8881
Co. E-mail: dtbarry@ziplink.net
URL: http://www.managementgrowth.com

E-mail: dtbarry@ziplink.net
Scope: Offers assistance in the specification, design, and implementation of management development programs. Clients include individuals, small businesses, national trade associations, and government agencies. **Seminars:** Profit Enhancement; Family-Owned Businesses; Strategic Planning; Survival and Growth in a Down Economy.

37830 ■ **Profit Planning Consultants**
617 Fields Dr.
Lafayette Hill, PA 19444
Ph:(610)828-1999
Fax: (610)828-5153
Co. E-mail: plf3plus5@aol.com

E-mail: plf3plus5@aol.com
Scope: Strengthening the Family Firm; Increasing the value of the business and preserving the heritage; Provides a full range of management services to independently-owned companies; Services cover such areas as operations analysis, planning and budgeting, marketing and sales, organizational development, succession planning, debt and equity financing, employee training and motivation as well as acquisitions, mergers and sales of business. Client's sales range from over $1 million to $50 million; Client base covers a broad range of family-owned businesses in all industries; Teaches the entrepreneur survival and growth techniques that become his own and develop with him/her the company's succession plan. **Seminars:** How to Enter International Markets; Time Management; Leadership, Professional Selling Skills; Manag-

ing a Family Owned Business; Profit Opportunities for Your Business; Family vs. Business; Doubling Your Net Profit; Transferring Management in a Family Owned Business (a series of interactive workshops under the heading of Managing a Family Owned Business).

37831 ■ ReGENERATION Partners
2 Turtle Creek Village, 3838 Oak Lawn, Ste. 999
Dallas, TX 75219
Ph:(214)559-3999
Free: 800-406-1112
Fax: (214)559-4299
Co. E-mail: info@regeneration-partners.com
URL: http://www.regeneration-partners.com

E-mail: info@regeneration-partners.com
Scope: Seeks to enable companies to find creative ways of confronting the crucial issues that can spell success or failure for family-owned businesses. Areas of specialization include business expertise growth strategies, competitive planning, crisis intervention, dispute resolution, interim management, bridge management, strategic planning, team selection, transitional management, employee assessment, business planning, management skills training, profit enhancement, family perspective, conflict management, communication barriers, family meetings, wealth preservation, succession planning, management mentoring, family values, family retreats. **Seminars:** The Essentials of Family Business.

37832 ■ Schneider Consulting Group Inc.
50 S Steele St., Ste. 390
Denver, CO 80209
Ph:(303)320-4413
Fax: (303)320-5795

Co. E-mail: info@scgfambus.com
URL: http://www.schneiderconsultinggroup.com

E-mail: info@scgfambus.com
Scope: Assists family-owned and privately-held business transition to the next generation and/or to a more professionally managed company, turnaround consulting for small and medium size companies.

37833 ■ Stier Associates
4 Dunellen
Cromwell, CT 06416-2702
Ph:(860)635-1590
Fax: (860)635-1591
Co. E-mail: s.stier@worldnet.att.net

E-mail: s.stier@worldnet.att.net
Scope: Personal development consulting. Subspecialty in Family-Owned businesses. Services include succession planning, executive coaching, strategic management, team building, board development. Consulting services for public companies include process consulting, team building, executive coaching, diversity management, and strategic management. Consulting to religious institutions.

37834 ■ The Titens Consulting Group
12612 Cedar St.
Leawood, KS 66209
Ph:(913)469-5279
Fax: (913)469-5192
Co. E-mail: knowthat@aol.com

E-mail: knowthat@aol.com
Scope: Provides market positioning, strategic planning and continuing education (design, standards,

certification) for trade associations, professional societies and professional service providers and family businesses. Industries served: banking, financial services, automotive, jewelry, healthcare, law, materials, joining, retail, environmental programs and distribution. **Publications:** "NFP"; "Applied Research at the Graduate Level," Parkway Press; "123 Secrets for Success in Your Family Business". **Seminars:** Making Family Business Work; Getting Started With Strategic Planning; Using the Internet as an Educational Tool. **Special Services:** Development of Public Domain Private Branded Websites; Development of Environmental Compliance Assistance Programs.

37835 ■ Turnaround Inc.
3415 A St. NW
Gig Harbor, WA 98335
Ph:(253)857-6730
Fax: (253)857-6344
Co. E-mail: info@turnround-inc.com
URL: http://www.turnaround-inc.com

E-mail: info@turnround-inc.com
Scope: Firm provides interim executive management assistance and management advisory to small, medium and family-owned businesses that are not meeting their goals. Services include acting as an interim executive or on-site manager. Extensive practices in arena of bankruptcy management. **Publications:** "How to Identify Problem and Promising Management"; "How to Tell if Your Company is a Bankruptcy Candidate"; "Signs that Your Company is in Trouble"; "The Turnaround Specialist: How to File a Petition Under 11 USC 11". **Seminars:** Competitive Intelligence Gathering.

START-UP INFORMATION

37836 ■ *Entrepreneurship and the Financial Community Starting Up and Growing New Businesses*
Pub: Edward Elgar Publishing, Incorporated
Ed: Clarysse. **Released:** November 2006. **Price:** $75.00. **Description:** Understanding the role of private equity providers in the development and growth processes of small business.

37837 ■ *"Hold'Em" in Entrepreneur* (Vol. 28, No. 7, July 2000, pp. 78)
Pub: Entrepreneur Media Inc.
Ed: Cynthia Harrington. **Description:** Takes a look at two entrepreneurs balancing the eternal choice between selling equity or borrowing.

37838 ■ *How to Get the Financing for Your New Small Business: Innovative Solutions from the Experts Who Do It Every Day*
Pub: Atlantic Publishing Company
Ed: Sharon L. Fullen. **Released:** August 2005. **Price:** $39.95, includes companion CD-Rom. **Description:** Ready capital is essential for starting and expanding a small business. Topics include traditional financing methods, financial statements, and a good business plan.

37839 ■ *How to Start a Bankruptcy Forms Processing Service*
Pub: Graphico Publishing Company
Ed: Victoria Ring. **Released:** September 2004. **Price:** $59.99. **Description:** Due to the increase in bankruptcy filings, attorneys are outsourcing related jobs in order to reduce overhead.

37840 ■ *"Money Master" in Entrepreneur* (Vol. 28, No. 9, September 2000, pp. 60)
Pub: Entrepreneur Media Inc.
Ed: Cynthia E. Griffin. **Description:** Finance is still an obstacle for businesswomen, and that is why expert Jennifer Openshaw has created a Web site to help women learn about personal finance.

37841 ■ *"Need Money?" in Inc.* (November 2006, pp.25-26)
Pub: Gruner & Jahr USA Publishing
Ed: Max Chafkin and Bobbie Gossage. **Description:** Private financial markets are difficult to navigate and dynamic. Various funding alternatives are discussed depending upon size of the venture. Trends are changing and reviewed in this article.

37842 ■ *Working for Yourself: An Entrepreneur's Guide to the Basics*
Pub: Kogan Page, Limited
Ed: Jonathan Reuvid. **Released:** September 2006. **Description:** Guide for starting a new business venture, focusing on raising financing, legal and tax issues, marketing, information technology, and site location.

EDUCATIONAL PROGRAMS

37843 ■ *Accessing the Financial Markets: Creating Strategies to Boost Corporate Profitability*
American Management Association
1601 Broadway
New York, NY 10019
Ph:(212)586-8100
Free: 800-262-9699
Fax: (212)903-8168
Co. E-mail: customerservice@amanet.org
URL: http://www.amanet.org
Price: $2,195.00 for non-members; $1,995.00 for AMA members. **Description:** Covers the changing financial markets and how to select investments, manage cash flow, and implement financial management systems. **Locations:** Washington, DC; and Chicago, IL.

37844 ■ *Advanced Strategies for Controllers (Canada)*
Canadian Management Centre
150 York St., 5th Fl.
Toronto, ON, Canada M5H 3S5
Ph:(416)214-5678
Free: 800-262-9699
Fax: (416)313-4985
Co. E-mail: cmcinfo@cmctraining.org
URL: http://cmcamai.org
Price: $1,695.00 Canadian. **Description:** Covers strategic planning; organizing, reporting, and managing financial information; creating a managerial information network; and budgeting and forecasting. **Locations:** Toronto, ON.

37845 ■ *AMA's Finance Workshop for Nonfinancial Executives*
American Management Association
1601 Broadway
New York, NY 10019
Ph:(212)586-8100
Free: 800-262-9699
Fax: (212)903-8168
Co. E-mail: customerservice@amanet.org
URL: http://www.amanet.org
Price: $1,195 for non-members; $1,995 for AMA members. **Description:** Covers the basic principles of finance; including making better business decisions from the financial perspective. **Locations:** San Francisco, CA; Washington, DC; New York, NY; Chicago, IL; Atlanta, GA.

37846 ■ *The Controller's Job in Today's Environment (Canada)*
Canadian Management Centre
150 York St., 5th Fl.
Toronto, ON, Canada M5H 3S5
Ph:(416)214-5678
Free: 800-262-9699
Fax: (416)313-4985
Co. E-mail: cmcinfo@cmctraining.org
URL: http://cmcamai.org
Price: $1,995.00 Canadian. **Description:** Covers the controller's role, working with corporate decision makers, accurate reporting, developing long-range plans, and cash forecasting. **Locations:** Toronto, ON.

37847 ■ *Corporate Performance Management: Optimizing Results Across the Organization*
American Management Association
1601 Broadway
New York, NY 10019
Ph:(212)586-8100
Free: 800-262-9699
Fax: (212)903-8168
Co. E-mail: customerservice@amanet.org
URL: http://www.amanet.org
Price: $1,995 for non-members; $1,795 for AMA members. **Description:** Covers understanding and implementing a corporate performance management system in the workplace, including its benefits, . **Locations:** San Francisco, CA; Chicago, IL; and New York, NY.

37848 ■ *Effective Internal Auditing*
American Management Association
1601 Broadway
New York, NY 10019
Ph:(212)586-8100
Free: 800-262-9699
Fax: (212)903-8168
Co. E-mail: customerservice@amanet.org
URL: http://www.amanet.org
Price: $1,895 for non-members; $1,695 for AMA members. **Description:** For anyone with less than two years of auditing experience and anyone responsible for The Sarbanes-Oxley Act of 2002. **Locations:** Newport Beach, CA; Chicago, IL; New York, NY; Washington, DC; and Atlanta, GA.

37849 ■ *The Essentials of Budgeting: From Creation Through Application*
American Management Association
1601 Broadway
New York, NY 10019
Ph:(212)586-8100
Free: 800-262-9699
Fax: (212)903-8168
Co. E-mail: customerservice@amanet.org
URL: http://www.amanet.org
Price: $1,995 for non-members; $1,795 for AMA members. **Description:** Covers budget plans as they relate to corporate objectives, including short and long-term, and be able to sell your budget to your superiors. **Locations:** Cities throughout the United States.

37850 ■ *The Essentials of Budgeting: From Creation Through Application (Canada)*
Canadian Management Centre
150 York St., 5th Fl.
Toronto, ON, Canada M5H 3S5
Free: 877-CMC-2500
Fax: (416)313-4985
Co. E-mail: cmcinfo@cmctraining.org
URL: http://www.cmcamai.org
Price: $1,795 Canadian. **Description:** Covers budget plans as they relate to corporate objectives, including short and long-term, and be able to sell your budget to your superiors. **Locations:** Toronto, ON.

37851 ■ Export/Import Procedures and Documentation
American Management Association
1601 Broadway
New York, NY 10019
Ph:(212)586-8100
Free: 800-262-9699
Fax: (212)903-8168
Co. E-mail: customerservice@amanet.org
URL: http://www.amanet.com
Price: $1,595.00 for non-members; $1,495.00 for AMA members. **Description:** Covers export and import guidelines and regulations, business documentation practices, using foreign trade zones, and financial aspects of importing and exporting. **Locations:** San Diego, CA; Atlanta, GA; and New York, NY.

37852 ■ Finance & Accounting for Non-Financial People
Fred Pryor Seminars
9757 Metcalf Ave.
Overland Park, KS 66212
Free: 800-944-8503
Fax: (913)967-8849
Co. E-mail: customerservice@pryor.com
URL: http://www.careertrack.com
Description: Covers basic accounting and financial management principals, terms, and tools. **Locations:** Cities throughout the United States.

37853 ■ Fundamentals of Finance and Accounting for Administrative Professionals (Canada)
Canadian Management Centre
150 York St., 5th Fl.
Toronto, ON, Canada M5H 3S5
Ph:(866)400-4941 ext. 2252
Free: 877-CMC-2500
Fax: (416)313-4985
Co. E-mail: cmcinfo@cmctraining.org
URL: http://www.cmcamai.org
Price: $1,550 Canadian. **Description:** Covers the financial concepts, including the understanding of financial statements, annual reports, and value of budgeting. **Locations:** Toronto, ON.

37854 ■ Fundamentals of Finance and Accounting for Non-Financial Executives (Canada)
Canadian Management Centre
150 York St., 5th Fl.
Toronto, ON, Canada M5H 3S5
Ph:(416)214-5678
Free: 800-262-9699
Fax: (416)313-4985
Co. E-mail: cmcinfo@cmctraining.org
URL: http://cmcamai.org
Price: $1,995.00 Canadian. **Description:** Seminar for nonfinancial professionals who need a basic understanding of financial data; covers financial concepts and statements, general accounting principles, and annual reports. **Locations:** Calgary, AB; Vancouver, BC; Mississauga, ON; and Toronto, ON.

37855 ■ Fundamentals of Finance and Accounting for Non-Financial Managers (Canada)
Canadian Management Centre
150 York St., 5th Fl.
Toronto, ON, Canada M5H 3S5
Ph:(866)400-4941 ext. 2252
Free: 877-CMC-2500
Fax: (416)313-4985
Co. E-mail: cmcinfo@cmctraining.org
URL: http://www.cmcamai.org
Price: $1,995 Canadian. **Description:** Covers the accounting, and financial processes as they relate to overall growth, and profit. **Locations:** Toronto, ON; Mississauga, ON; Calgary, Alberta.

37856 ■ Fundamentals of Finance and Accounting for Nonfinancial Managers
American Management Association
1601 Broadway
New York, NY 10019
Ph:(212)586-8100
Free: 800-262-9699

Fax: (212)903-8168
Co. E-mail: customerservice@amanet.org
URL: http://www.amanet.org
Price: $1,895 for non-members; $1,695 for AMA members. **Description:** Covers the basic accounting practices, including setting up financial statements and reports, how to analyze an annual report, and time planning as it pertains to budget. **Locations:** Cities throughout the United States.

37857 ■ Intermediate Finance and Accounting for Non-Financial Managers (Canada)
Canadian Management Centre
150 York St., 5th Fl.
Toronto, ON, Canada M5H 3S5
Ph:(416)214-5678
Free: 800-262-9699
Fax: (416)313-4985
Co. E-mail: cmcinfo@cmctraining.org
URL: http://cmcamai.org
Price: $1,695.00 Canadian. **Description:** Covers communicating with financial executives, reviewing financial statements, planning and budgeting, and financial analysis and forecasting. **Locations:** Toronto, ON.

37858 ■ Intermediate Fundamentals of Finance and Accounting for Non-Financial Managers (Canada)
Canadian Management Centre
150 York St., 5th Fl.
Toronto, ON, Canada M5H 3S5
Ph:(866)400-4941 ext. 2252
Free: 877-CMC-2500
Fax: (416)313-4985
Co. E-mail: cmcinfo@cmctraining.org
URL: http://www.cmcamai.org
Price: $1,695 Canadian. **Description:** Covers the analyzing of financial reports in order to make overall better business decisions, including balance sheets and income statements, apply activity-based and value-added breakdowns, and monitor your organization based on its past performance. **Locations:** Toronto, ON.

37859 ■ Managing Your Working Capital: How to Keep Your Assets Moving and Growing
American Management Association
1601 Broadway
New York, NY 10019
Ph:(212)586-8100
Free: 800-262-9699
Fax: (212)903-8168
Co. E-mail: customerservice@amanet.org
URL: http://www.amanet.org
Price: $1,995 for non-members; $1,795 for AMA members. **Description:** Covers the components of working capital management; including cash flow as it pertains to collection, disbursements, investing and borrowing, purchasing as it relates to accounts payable and cash management, increase short-term liquidity, and expand into the global market. **Locations:** Washington, DC; Atlanta, GA; New York, NY; San Francisco, CA.

37860 ■ Risk Management: Strategies and Tactics for Business
American Management Association
1601 Broadway
New York, NY 10019
Ph:(212)586-8100
Free: 800-262-9699
Fax: (212)903-8168
Co. E-mail: customerservice@amanet.org
URL: http://www.amanet.org
Price: $2,095 for non-members; $1,895 for AMA members. **Description:** For individuals that have the basic knowledge of finance and corporate strategy; covers the main corporate risks, and how they are integrated into the corporate environment. **Locations:** Washington, DC; Chicago, IL; New York, NY; Atlanta, GA.

REFERENCE WORKS

37861 ■ "The 5 Keys to Value Investing" in Black Enterprise (Vol. 36, December 2005, No. 5, pp. 52)
Pub: Earl G. Graves Publishing Co. Inc.
Ed: Matthew S. Scott. **Description:** The book, 5 Keys to Value Investing, teaches the fundamentals of value investing, how to assess the true value of a company, and understanding how events can work to move stock prices up or down. There is also a chapter showing how to build a portfolio of winning stocks.

37862 ■ "40-Year Plan" in Entrepreneur (Vol. 33, September 2005, No. 9, pp. 62)
Pub: Entrepreneur Media Inc.
Ed: Jennifer Pellet. **Description:** As mortgage rates climb, 40-year loans are becoming more attractive to home buyers. However, these longer-term mortgages will increase interest paid on the loan.

37863 ■ "The 2003 Teenpreneur Money Guide" in Black Enterprise (Vol. 34, No. 2, September 2003, pp. S10)
Pub: Earl Graves Publishing Co.
Ed: Tanisha A. Sykes. **Description:** Online resources for young entrepreneurs that will teach them how to be financially literate.

37864 ■ "About Penny Stocks" in Black Enterprise (Vol. 34, No. 4, November 2003, pp. 40)
Pub: Earl Graves Publishing Co.
Ed: Matthew S. Scott. **Description:** Information about penny stocks, which are often small, early-stage, unknown companies trading at less than $1 per share, is presented. Websites offering investor information, market statistics, and company profiles are also included.

37865 ■ Access to Finance
Pub: Brookings Institution Press
Ed: Barr. **Released:** December 2006. **Price:** $39.95. **Description:** Challenges to help make financial systems more inclusive to promote successful venture in new markets while utilizing new technologies and government policies to expand financial access to smaller companies.

37866 ■ "Account Balances Indicate That 401(k) Participants Have Heard The Long-Term Investor Message" in Employee Benefit Plan Review (Vol. 55)
Pub: Charles D. Spencer & Associates, Inc.
Ed: Sue Burzawa. **Description:** Lincolnshire, Illinois-based Hewitt Associates LLC, the health benefit plan consulting company, tracks pension fund activity through its 401(k) Index. Industry analysts said that institutional investors are remaining calm as the country suffers from a period of economic upheaval.

37867 ■ Account for Your Own Success: Everything You Need to Manage Your Own Business and Personal Finances
Pub: Management Communications Systems, Inc. (MCS)
Ed: Dan Meyer. **Released:** 1993. **Price:** $16.95 (paper). **Description:** Financial management guide for small businesses, covering accounting procedures for preparing budgets, cash flows, inventories, and tax returns. Includes examples, checklists, forms, tables, and worksheets.

37868 ■ Accounting and Finance for Your Small Business
Pub: John Wiley & Sons, Incorporated
Ed: Steven M. Bragg; E. James Burton. **Released:** April 2006. **Price:** $49.00. **Description:** Financial procedures and techniques for establishing and maintaining a profitable small company are outlined.

37869 ■ "Add fudge factor to cost to equal business success" in Crain's Detroit Business (Vol. 18, No. 49, December 9, 2002, pp. 12)
Pub: Crain Communications Inc., Detroit

Ed: Laura Bailey. **Description:** The issues of cost controls in managing a small business are discussed.

37870 ■ "Ahead of the Curve" in *Ingram's* **(Vol. 28, No. 9, September 2002, pp. 19)**
Pub: Show Me Publishing, Inc.
Ed: Stephanie Guerin. **Description:** A guide for taking tax advantages before changes take place, such as knowing tax laws, offsetting capital gains with capital losses, setting up foundations, etc.

37871 ■ "Aid package" in *Entrepreneur* **(Vol. 30, No. 12, December 2002, pp. 27)**
Pub: Entrepreneur Media Inc.
Ed: Julie Monahan. **Description:** Many business owners are assisting employees to get the most out of their 401(k)s and other retirement plans.

37872 ■ "All's Fair: In Love and Business, So You May Need a Prenup to Protect Your Company's Assets" in *Entrepreneur* **(Vol. 31, Sept. 2003)**
Pub: Entrepreneur Media, Inc.
Ed: Nichole L. Torres. **Description:** Pre-nuptial agreements can help to protect entrepreneurs in the event of a divorce.

37873 ■ "Ameribank Plans Branch in Palm Beach Gardens" in *South Florida Business Journal* **(Vol. 23, No. 47, June 27, 2003, pp. 2)**
Pub: American City Business Journals
Ed: Jim Freer. **Description:** Plans by Ameribank to open a branch office in Palm Beach, Florida are discussed.

37874 ■ *Analysis for Financial Management*
Pub: Richard D. Irwin, Inc.
Ed: Robert C. Higgins. **Released:** Fourth edition, 1994.

37875 ■ "Andrew Lo" in *Business Week* **(February 20, 2006, No. 3972, pp. 22)**
Pub: McGraw-Hill Companies
Ed: Christopher Farrell. **Description:** Andrew W. Lo, a finance professor at Massachusetts Institute of Technology, along with a group of economists are conducting research in the neurosciences and cognitive psychology to better understand how investors make financial decisions.

37876 ■ "Antigravity investing" in *Working Woman* **(Vol. 25, No. 2, February 2000, pp. 32)**
Pub: Lang Communications Inc.
Ed: James Pethokoukis. **Description:** Advice is given to select Internet stocks to avoid the roller-coaster effect.

37877 ■ "Are Some Stocks Too Cool: Wall Street Keeps Falling in Love With Growth Stocks. Why the Magic Fades" in *Barron's* **(August 18, 2003)**
Pub: Barron's
Ed: Michael Santoli. **Description:** Growth stock fads afflict Wall Street in every era, and are always disappointments. Investors bid up shares in the new trend beyond what is rationally supportable, competitors offer a good-enough alternative at a steep discount or reality intervenes in some other predictable way. An antidote to this way of thinking about stocks and investing is prescribed.

37878 ■ "Asia Rising" in *Black Enterprise* **(Vol. 35, October 2004, No. 3, pp. 46)**
Pub: Earl G. Graves Publishing Co. Inc.
Ed: Donald Jay Korn. **Description:** China and India are two emerging global economies making them attractive for investing. Manufacturing and high tech jobs are being outsourced to both countries. It is important to research before investing in China and India, as well as any international funds.

37879 ■ "Ask the Attorney" in *Red Herring* **(No. 99, June 15 & July 1, 2001, pp. 148)**
Pub: Herring Communications
Description: Legal questions are answered, including of employee termination, stock options, angel money, strategic finance, licensing, venture capital and financing, and copyrights.

37880 ■ "Ask Inc. Partnerships" in *Inc.* **(November 2006, pp. 57)**
Pub: Gruner & Jahr USA Publishing
Description: Buyouts of partners that leave the company require accurate assessment of the current value of the stock. That may require hiring a consultant to put a current value on the business to arrive at an amicable settlement.

37881 ■ "Asset managers become psychologists in recession" in *Atlanta Business Chronicle* **(Vol. 25, No. 20, October 25, 2002, pp. 4C)**
Pub: American City Business Publications, Inc.
Ed: Tom Barry. **Description:** In these difficult financial times, the role of the money manager is changing. In addition to advising investors, these managers are more skilled in communication, becoming part financial advisor, part psychologist.

37882 ■ "At Your Finger TIPS" in *Entrepreneur* **(Vol. 32, October 2004, No. 10, pp. 66)**
Pub: Entrepreneur Media Inc.
Ed: Scott Bernard Nelson. **Description:** Investors are looking at Treasury Inflation-Protected Securities, or TIPS, as a means of investing. TIPS are now available in five-year maturities, along with the standard 10- and 20-years investments. The interest rate is fixed from the time of purchase, but the principle changes with the Consumer Price Index.

37883 ■ "Atlanta's Top Stock Brokerage Firms" in *Atlanta Business Chronicle* **(Vol. 25, No. 20, October 25, 2002, pp. 12C)**
Pub: American City Business Publications, Inc.
Description: Table lists the top stock brokerage firms in Atlanta, Georgia. These firms are ranked by number of brokers and staff.

37884 ■ "Atlanta's Top 25 Financial Planning Firms" in *Atlanta Business Chronicle* **(Vol. 25, No. 20, October 25, 2002, pp. 8C)**
Pub: American City Business Publications, Inc.
Description: Table lists the top 25 financial planning firms in Atlanta, Georgia. The companies are ranked by total assets under management and other criteria.

37885 ■ "Automatic Turn-Off" in *My Business* **(April/May 2002, pp. 47)**
Pub: My Business Magazine
Description: According to Energize America Education, installing occupancy sensors can reduce office lighting energy use by 25-50 percent and up to 75 percent in warehouses and restrooms.

37886 ■ "Avoiding a Cash Flow Crunch: Accurate Projections Are Key To Your Business' Survival" in *Black Enterprise* **(Vol. 34, July 2004)**
Pub: Earl G. Graves Publishing Co. Inc.
Ed: Nicole Lewis. **Description:** According to small business financial experts, it is critical for businesses to pay attention to cash flow when engaging financial commitments that have a scheduled payback time.

37887 ■ "Avoiding Year-End Tax Traps" in *Black Enterprise* **(Vol. 34, No. 5, December 2003, pp. 85)**
Pub: Earl Graves Publishing Co.
Ed: Laura Washington. **Description:** Information regarding the Alternative Minimum Tax (AMT) and an end-of-the-year tax strategy is given.

37888 ■ "Back to the Future: Are Payouts Becoming a Top Priority Again?" in *Barron's* **(August 18, 2003, pp. 27)**
Pub: Barron's
Ed: Shirley A. Lazo. **Description:** Materials handling equipment maker NACCO announced its second dividend payout of 2003, nearly 50 percent higher from 25 to 38 cents per share. Electronics firm Maxim Integrated Products doubled its payout from two to four cents per share.

37889 ■ "Back to business with Staples: new chief works to reclaim the chain's roots" in *Barron's* **(Vol. 82, No. 59, Feb. 24, 2003, pp. T8)**
Pub: Barron's
Ed: Lawrence Strauss. **Description:** Profile of Ronald L. Sargent, newly appointed CEO of Staples. Sargent is refocusing the retailer on its original vision, the small business customer, and is committed to raising earnings as the best way to raising share prices.

37890 ■ "Back Talk with Chris Gardner" in *Black Enterprise* **(Vol. 37, January 2007, No. 6, pp. 112)**
Pub: Earl G. Graves Publishing Co. Inc.
Ed: Kenneth Meeks. **Description:** Profile of with Chris Gardner and his Chicago company, Gardner Rich L.L.C., a multimillion-dollar investment firm. During an interview, Gardner discusses his rise from homelessness. His story became a book, The Pursuit of Happyness and was recently released as a film starring Will Smith.

37891 ■ "Back to Technology" in *Black Enterprise* **(Vol. 34, No. 6, January 2004)**
Pub: Earl Graves Publishing Co.
Ed: Nicole Lewis. **Description:** Patrick Lyons, associate portfolio manager at NCM Capital Management Group in Durham, North Carolina is predicting a come back for the technology sector. He also expects a 4-5 percent growth in the economy over the next four quarters.

37892 ■ "Back to Technology: Patrick Lyons of NCM Capital Management Says a Tech Binge is Likely" in *Black Enterprise* **(Vol. 34, January 2004)**
Pub: Earl Graves Publishing Co.
Ed: Nicole Lewis. **Description:** Patrick Lyons, associate portfolio manager at NCM Capital Management Group in Durham, North Carolina is predicting a come back for the technology sector. He also expects a 4-5 percent growth in the economy over the next four quarters.

37893 ■ "Balancing Act" in *Black Enterprise* **(Vol. 36, November 2005, No. 4, pp. 88)**
Pub: Earl G. Graves Publishing Co. Inc.
Ed: Sakina P. Spruell. **Description:** Alexis James, 30-year-old purchasing manager tells how she is pursuing investments with the potential of high returns while also investing in her family's embroidery business by overseeing the computer-operated production of designs on t-shirts, hats, canvas bags, and more.

37894 ■ "A Bank, At Your Service" in *Inc.* **(Volume 28, January 2006, No. 1, pp. 21-23)**
Pub: Inc. Magazine
Ed: Dan Ackman. **Description:** In order to compete with larger banks, local bankers are focusing efforts on business owners.

37895 ■ "Bank CEO Aims to Compound Marketshare" in *Crain's Chicago Business* **(Vol. 30, January 2007, No. 3, pp. 6)**
Pub: Crain Communications, Inc.
Ed: Lorene Yue. **Description:** Profile of Bruce Taylor, CEO of Taylor Capital Group Inc., who aims to increase the bank's marketshare, expand the bank's financial management business and get more business from their existing customers.

37896 ■ "Bank branches go to battle for customers" in *Pittsburgh Business Times* **(Vol. 22, No. 42, May 2, 2003, pp. 3)**
Pub: Pittsburgh Business Times
Ed: Patty Tascarella. **Description:** Pittsburgh, Pennsylvania bank branches are offering free checking accounts and electronic bill payment services to obtain new small business and consumer customers.

37897 ■ "Bank deals draw fines" in *Business First of Buffalo* **(Vol. 18, No. 46, August 12, 2002, pp. 1)**
Pub: Knight-Ridder/Tribune Business News
Ed: Tom Hartley. **Description:** HSBC Bank USA, located in Buffalo, New York, has been fined more than

$71,000 for violating a law that prevents business dealings with nations on so-called U.S. enemies' lists, including dealings with the Taliban in Afghanistan, and Cuba, Kosovo, Iraq and Libya.

37898 ■ "Bank Stock Binge" in *Black Enterprise* **(Vol. 35, January 2005, No. 6, pp. 34)**
Pub: Earl G. Graves Publishing Co. Inc.
Ed: Nicole Lewis. **Description:** Bank analyst, Fred Cummings, discusses which banks are likely to survive the current economic conditions affecting the industry. Recent economic and business trends have created an environment for bank mergers and acquisitions in the Midwest, according to Cummings.

37899 ■ "Bank Wants Doubletree Novi Placed in Receivership" in *Crain's Detroit Business* **(Vol. 22, January 30, 2006, No. 5, pp. 41)**
Pub: Crain Communications Inc. - Detroit
Ed: Andrew Dietderich. **Description:** Doubletree Hotel Novi is facing receivership resulting from a legal battle over alleged mishandling of funds.

37900 ■ "Banker Boosts Community" in *Crain's New York Business* **(Vol. 23, January 29, 2007, No. 5, pp. F14)**
Pub: Crain Communications, Inc.
Ed: Tom Fredrickson. **Description:** Profile of Maurice L. Coleman, New York Market Executive for Bank of America. Under his leadership, Bank of America is becoming a major player in community development in New York City, specifically targeting affordable housing and small businesses in low-income areas. Statistical data included.

37901 ■ "Banker Right on the Money with Financial Powerhouse" in *Houston Business Journal* **(Vol. 34, No. 13, August 8, 2003, pp. 2)**
Pub: American City Business Journals
Ed: Jim Greer. **Description:** The growing success of Southwest Bank of Texas is presented. Topics include market development, strategic planning, and management styles.

37902 ■ "Bankers' Gaze Turns Northward" in *South Florida Business Journal* **(Vol. 23, No. 53, August 8, 2003, pp. 1A)**
Pub: American City Business Journals
Ed: Jim Freer. **Description:** The introduction of new bank branches in West Palm Beach, Florida, including an industry overview, is discussed.

37903 ■ "Banking on Culture" in *Boston Business Journal* **(Vol. 23, No. 31, September 5, 2003, pp. 3)**
Pub: American City Business Journals
Ed: Edward Mason. **Description:** Raymond K. Tung, president and CEO of Asian American Bank, reports the firm is targeting Asian Americans as a first phase of expansion strategy. Asian American, located in Boston, Massachusetts' Chinatown neighborhood, is celebrating its tenth anniversary.

37904 ■ "Bankruptcy Court Streamlines Rules - to Drum Up Business" in *Crain's Detroit Business* **(Vol. 21, January 3, 2005, No. 1, pp. 18)**
Pub: Crain Communications Inc. - Detroit
Ed: Brent Snavely. **Description:** Seventeen new rules designed to create new business for the U.S. Bankruptcy Court in Detroit, Michigan are discussed. The new rules will be evaluated over the next 18 months.

37905 ■ "Bankruptcy Law Would Mean Tougher Consequences for Consumers" in *Chicago Tribune* **(March 11, 2005)**
Pub: Knight-Ridder/Tribune Business News
Ed: Lorene Yue. **Description:** The newly created federal Bankruptcy Abuse Prevention and Consumer Protection Act of 2005 is outlined.

37906 ■ "Bankruptcy Reform Will Punish Debtors" in *Atlanta Business Chronicle* **(Vol. 25, No. 20, October 25, 2002, pp. 38A)**
Pub: American City Business Publications, Inc.
Ed: Mark Meltzer. **Description:** The lame-duck session of Congress will likely decide whether to reform the nation's bankruptcy laws. At issue is the reduction of the number of bankruptcies by making filing more difficult. Currently, Atlanta, Georgia is among the leading major metropolitan regions in bankruptcy filings.

37907 ■ "Banks, Groups Use Program to Improve Money Smarts" in *Memphis Business Journal* **(Vol. 25, No. 16, August 15, 2003, pp. 38)**
Pub: American City Business Journals
Ed: Leigh Ann Roman. **Description:** The Federal Deposit Insurance Corporation's new program called Money Smart has made an impact in Memphis. The program promotes financial assistance for low- and moderate-income neighborhoods.

37908 ■ "Banks Reaching Out to New Communities" in *San Francisco Business Times* **(Vol. 18, No. 6, September 19, 2003, pp. 22)**
Pub: American City Business Journals
Ed: Steven E.F. Brown. **Description:** Wells Fargo, Bank of America and other banks are trying to get Hispanic customers by signing them up at the Mexican consulate.

37909 ■ "The Barker Portfolio" in *Business Week* **(January 16, 2006, No. 3967, pp. 22)**
Pub: McGraw-Hill Companies
Ed: Robert Barker. **Description:** A look at past stock picks from the past include Chico's, Domino's Pizza, Goodyear Tire and Rubber, Krispy Kreme Doughnuts, Psychiatric Solutions, and Symantec.

37910 ■ "Barnes-Pettey Financial Advisors, LLC" in *Mississippi Business Journal* **(Vol. 29, January 2007, No. 4, pp. 6)**
Pub: Venture Publications, Inc.
Description: Profiles of Barnes-Pettey Financial Advisors, LLC financial advisors at the Clarksdale office of Raymond James Financial Services Inc. Statistical data included.

37911 ■ "Basket Case: A Lesson in Eggs, Baskets and Diversification" in *Entrepreneur* **(Vol. 33, January 2005, No. 1, pp. 49)**
Pub: Entrepreneur Media Inc.
Ed: Dian Vujovich. **Description:** Two levels of diversification need to be considered when constructing investment portfolios. The first is across the major asset classes: stocks, bonds and cash. The second level is within those classes.

37912 ■ "B.E. Wall St. All-Stars" in *Black Enterprise* **(Vol. 33, No. 3, October 2002, pp. 88)**
Pub: Earl Graves Publishing Co.
Ed: Matthew S. Scott, Alan Hughes, Laura Egodigwe, Sonia Alleyne, Sonya A. Donaldson, Latif Lewis, Sophia Rose, Reginald Hart, Daniel Brown. **Description:** The Top 50 African Americans on Wall Street are profiled. Black Enterprise chose these professionals and entrepreneurs as proven power hitters who consistently succeed despite market conditions.

37913 ■ "Best places to put your money now" in *Black Enterprise* **(Vol. 33, No. 6, Jan. 2003, pp. 72)**
Pub: Earl Graves Publishing Co.
Ed: Donald Jay Korn. **Description:** Diversification is the key to successful investment planning.

37914 ■ "Betting on Growth" in *Hispanic Business* **(June 2005, pp. 98)**
Pub: Hispanic Business
Ed: Joel Russell. **Description:** Top Hispanic finance companies are counting on strong demand and cash to grow their sector in 2005. Statistical data included.

37915 ■ "Beware of credit card offers ($s and sense)" in *Black Enterprise* **(Vol. 33, No. 3, October 2002, pp. S4)**
Pub: Earl Graves Publishing Co.
Ed: Carolyn M. Brown. **Description:** Advice is offered about the responsible use of credit and credit cards, especially for teens. Contact information is provided for the National Consumers League, and information for establishing and maintaining a clean credit report.

37916 ■ "Big Profits In Small Packages" in *Black Enterprise* **(Vol. 36, November 2005, No. 4, pp. 52)**
Pub: Earl G. Graves Publishing Co. Inc.
Ed: Dwight Oestricher. **Description:** Henry Jackson, chairman of Banneker Capital Management in Maryland offer a portfolio of small and mid-cap growth stocks that include Mueller Industries, Integra Life Sciences, and Global Payments.

37917 ■ "Big Returns in the Smallest Packages" in *Black Enterprise* **(Vol. 35, August 2004, No. 1, pp. 42)**
Pub: Earl G. Graves Publishing Co. Inc.
Ed: Donald Jay Korn. **Description:** Historically, small cap funds have performed better than large company stocks over the long-term. In the last few years, with a slowing economy, smaller companies were more likely to keep growing, and their stocks performed well.

37918 ■ "Big Taxes Top Lansing Agenda, Will Granholm Proposal Shift?" in *Crain's Detroit Business* **(Vol. 23, January 8, 2007, No. 2, pp. 1)**
Pub: Crain Communications Inc. - Detroit
Ed: Amy Lane. **Description:** Legislators still unsure how to budget in wake of large deficits. Tax shifts likely, but original proposal from the Governor's office may have to be revised with new figures to be announced.

37919 ■ "Big Winners Help State Stocks Top S&P; Housing, Finance Companies Boost Returns" in *Crain's Detroit Business* **(Vol. 21, Jan. 3, 2005)**
Pub: Crain Communications Inc. - Detroit
Ed: Katie Merx. **Description:** An overview of Michigan stocks, which performed better on average than the Standard & Poor's 500 Index for both fourth quarter and the entire year 2004. The S&P 500 Index was up 9.1 percent for the year, while Michigan stocks climbed 13.5 percent. Statistical data included.

37920 ■ "Biotech Balance: Mutual Fund Diversification Lets Investors Temper Biotech's Risk" in *Black Enterprise* **(Vol. 34, No. 4, Nov. 2003)**
Pub: Earl Graves Publishing Co.
Ed: James A. Anderson. **Description:** Information for investing in Biotechnology is examined.

37921 ■ "Biotech Believer" in *Fortune* **(Vol. 151, February 21, 2005, No. 4, pp. 128)**
Pub: Time Inc.
Ed: Stephanie N. Mehta. **Description:** Fund manager, Sam Isaly is predicting single-digit growth in the pharmacy industry, while expecting double-digit growth in the biotechnology sector for 2005.

37922 ■ "Bird Dog" in *Barron's* **(September 8, 2003, pp. 9)**
Pub: Barron's
Ed: Alan Abelson. **Description:** New York State Attorney General, Eliot Spitzer's continuing crusade against corruption on Wall Street netted two more victims, a Canary Capital hedge fund, and mutual funds administered by such august firms as Bank of America, Bank One, Janus and others.

37923 ■ "Black Gold: Oil is Key to the Success of this Russian Fund" in *Entrepreneur* **(Vol. 32, December 2004, No. 12, pp. 61)**
Pub: Entrepreneur Media Inc.
Ed: Dian Vujovich. **Description:** Investors looking to emerging markets, ING's Russia Fund has been a top performer. The fund's holdings consist of 35 holdings made up of oil and resource-type stocks.

37924 ■ "Black Investment Trends: Report Ranks What Buyers Care Most About" in *Black Enterprise* (Vol. 35, October 2004, No. 3, pp. 40)
Pub: Earl G. Graves Publishing Co. Inc.
Ed: Nkechi I. Olisemeka. Description: According to Carla A. Foster, vice president of Charles Schwab & Company, blacks consider the stock market more risky than other investments. However, blacks who actively trade in the market rose 68 percent in 2004.

37925 ■ "Bond Bonus" in *Black Enterprise* (Vol. 31, No. 5, December 2000, pp. 43)
Pub: Earl Graves Publishing Co.
Ed: Donald Jay Korn. Description: Will fixed-income vehicles continue to produce solid returns?

37926 ■ "Boomer Women Need Financial Advisors" in *Marketing to Women* (Vol. 19, October 2006, No. 10, pp. 8)
Pub: EPM Communications, Inc.
Description: Although most financially successful Boomer women don't have financial advisors, The Wall Street Journal reports, they need them. Financial services firms are eager to reach this market as they tend to give referrals.

37927 ■ "Breaking the bank" in *WorkingWoman* (Vol. 25, No. 2, February 2000, pp. S13)
Pub: Lang Communications Inc.
Ed: Dana Asher. Description: Ways to repair a shattered credit record are explored.

37928 ■ "Bridging the Gap" in *Black Enterprise* (Vol. 34, No. 5, December 2003, pp. 66)
Pub: Earl Graves Publishing Co.
Ed: Sonia Alleyne. Description: Profile of Careerbank, a Web site for individuals seeking jobs in the financial industry; the site provides job opportunities as well as current industry information.

37929 ■ "Bryson Buys Two Agencies" in *Mississippi Business Journal* (Vol. 29, January 2007, No. 2, pp. 8)
Pub: Venture Publications, Inc.
Ed: Wally Northway Description: Bryson Insurance acquires Banks Insurance and Shackleford Brothers & Fortenberry.

37930 ■ "Building on success" in *Black Enterprise* (Vol. 32, No. 9, April 2002, pp. 70)
Pub: Earl Graves Publishing Co.
Ed: Carolyn M. Brown. Description: Profile of Freedie Lee and Yolanda Sherman and their business and Website, Illustrationsnetwork.com, that will showcase the artwork of minority artists and photographers to big corporations. Financial advice is offered to help the couple sustain their new business in the future and through their retirement by investing wisely.

37931 ■ "The Bulls are Back" in *My Business* (June/July 2004, pp. 13)
Pub: My Business Magazine
Description: Privately held companies are predicting increased value and planning more mergers and acquisitions in the growing economy.

37932 ■ "The burden of borrowing" in *Entrepreneur* (Vol. 31, No. 4, April 2003, pp. 53)
Pub: Entrepreneur Media Inc.
Ed: Crystal Detamore-Rodman. Description: Many times the indirect costs of borrowing, such as collateral conditions, may have more impact on a growing business than the loan itself.

37933 ■ *Business Finance for the Numerically Challenged*
Pub: Career Press, Inc.
Ed: Career Press, Inc. Staff. Released: 1997. Price: $11.99.

37934 ■ "Business Plan Helps Set Goals, Draw Investors" in *Crain's Detroit Business* (Vol. 22, November 20, 2006, No. 47, pp. 18)
Pub: Crain Communications Inc. - Detroit

Ed: Sheena Harrison. Description: Financial investors always require a business plan before they will commit to investment in new or expanding ventures. Sound business planning and management also include a good business plan with time phased measurable goals to monitor progress and indicate need for adjustments of the plan.

37935 ■ "Buy, buy biotech?" in *Entrepreneur* (Vol. 30, No. 3, March 2002, pp. 72)
Pub: Entrepreneur Media Inc.
Ed: Jennifer Pellet. Description: Despite the warnings about bioterrorism, experts warn that biotech firms are difficult to evaluate before investing.

37936 ■ "Buying Stocks in a Slowing Economy" in *Black Enterprise* (Vol. 31, No. 5, December 2000, pp. 117)
Pub: Earl Graves Publishing Co.
Ed: Jeffery McKinney. Description: How to make smart moves in today's market.

37937 ■ "C & A Says Company Will Be Sold" in *Crain's Detroit Business* (Vol. 22, November 20, 2006, No. 47, pp. 4)
Pub: Crain Communications Inc. - Detroit
Ed: Brent Snaveley. Description: Southfield based interior supplier has decided to go out of business in wake of reduced sales volume and difficulty in emerging from bankruptcy. Entire company or individual assets are available for sale and will be consolidated and closed as the business winds down.

37938 ■ "Cable ready" in *WorkingWoman* (Vol. 25, No. 4, April 2000, pp. 38)
Pub: Lang Communications Inc.
Ed: Lisa Lee Freeman. Description: Cable News Network Financial Reporter, Willow Bay, talks about work on the television program 'Moneyline News Hour' and her life with husband, television executive Bob Iger.

37939 ■ "Calculating Profits" in *Black Enterprise* (Vol. 34, No. 6, January 2004, pp. 36)
Pub: Earl Graves Publishing Co.
Ed: Alan Hughes. Description: An explanation of profit margins and ways to calculate a profit margin are investigated.

37940 ■ "Calculating Savings Bonds Values" in *Black Enterprise* (Vol. 35, January 2005, No. 6, pp. 38)
Pub: Earl G. Graves Publishing Co. Inc.
Ed: Stephanie Young. Description: There are two types of Savings bonds, Series EE/E and Series I. A description of both to help investors choose which is best for their financial strategy is presented. The U.S. Treasury Department offers a Website to help individuals calculate a bond's worth.

37941 ■ "Can't Win For Losing: A Mutual Fund Tax Quirk Limits Your Capital Losses" in *Entrepreneur* (Vol. 31, No. 7, July 2003, pp. 52)
Pub: Entrepreneur Media, Inc.
Ed: Scott Bernard Nelson. Description: Investment losses stay within an investment fund even if the investment shows now gains.

37942 ■ "Capital Ideas" in *Hispanic Business* (March 2005, pp. 25-26, 28, 30, 34, 36)
Pub: Hispanic Business
Description: Top investment advisors Samuel A. Ramirez Jr., managing director of Samuel A. Ramirez and Company and Louis Baraja, certified financial planner and founder of Louis Barajas & Associates share their investment strategies for 2005. Statistical data included.

37943 ■ "Capstone Puts Skin in Game With First Project" in *Business Journal-Portland* (Vol. 20, No. 24, August 15, 2003, pp. 7)
Pub: American City Business Journals, Inc.
Ed: Heidi J. Stout. Description: Efforts of Capstone Partners, a new real estate development company, and the construction of its first building are discussed. The firm also provides financial services to consumers.

37944 ■ "Capturing the Potential: How CPA Firms are Building Successful Financial Services Practices" in *Journal of Accountancy* (Vol. 198)
Pub: American Institute of Certified Public Accountants
Ed: Patricia J. Abram, John J. Bowen Jr., Russ Alan Prince, Jeffrey A. Roush. Description: Certified public accounting firms are increasing profits by expanding into the financial services sector.

37945 ■ "Caribbean-type savings helps build businesses" in *Wall Street Journal* (October 27, 2000, pp. B1)
Pub: Dow Jones & Co., Inc.
Ed: Meera Louis. Description: A description of how friends and family members make weekly contributions into a "susu" or "partner" account to help build business.

37946 ■ "Cash in, cash out" in *Entrepreneur* (Vol. 31, No. 6, June 2003, pp. 53)
Pub: Entrepreneur Media Inc.
Ed: Crystal Detamore-Rodman. Description: The management of payables plays a critical role in cash-flow management. The article offers advise for small businesses to gain the best benefit from payment terms.

37947 ■ *Cash Traps: Small Business Secrets for Reducing Costs and Improving Cash Flow*
Pub: John Wiley & Sons, Inc.
Ed: Jeffrey P. Davidson and Charles W. Dean. Released: 1992. Price: $59.95; $14.95 (paper).

37948 ■ "Cashing In On Cash Flow" in *Business 2.0* (Vol. 6, September 2005, No. 8, pp. 119)
Pub: Time, Inc.
Ed: Carleen Hawn. Description: Seven strategies to help investors be successful are reviewed, including a list of three high-dividend stocks to buy and three to avoid. Tips are shared to help trade stock options like the pros.

37949 ■ "A Cautious Optimism" in *Forbes* (Vol. 175, February 14, 2005, No. 3, pp. 132)
Pub: Forbes Magazine Inc.
Ed: Laszlo Birinyi, Jr. Description: An overview of the stock market for 2004 is presented.

37950 ■ "CDs Unlocked" in *Business Week* (February 7, 2205, pp. 91)
Pub: McGraw-Hill Companies
Ed: Suzanne Woolley, Toddi Gutner. Description: Banks are promoting 'liquid' and 'bump up' certificates of deposit that offer penalty-free withdrawals or the ability to make use of a rise in rates.

37951 ■ "CEO Buyers's Guide: Financial" in *Hispanic Business* (November 2002, pp. BG12-13)
Pub: Hispanic Business
Description: A listing of fund managers for investments is provided, with a small profile of each investment firm.

37952 ■ "CFOs under pressure to disclose all transactions" in *Atlanta Business Chronicle* (Vol. 25, No. 20, October 25, 2002, pp. 14C)
Pub: American City Business Publications, Inc.
Ed: Alan Breznick. Description: In this climate of accounting scandals and corporate mistrust, disclosure has become the corporate buzzword. The landscape of financial accounting is changing and many chief financial officers are trying to adjust to the increased public scrutiny.

37953 ■ "Changing Course" in *Pittsburgh Business Times* (Vol. 23, No. 5, August 22, 2003, pp. 13)
Pub: Pittsburgh Business Times
Ed: Patty Tascarella. Description: Edwin Grinberg, president at Lionshead Financial Planning Company, will continue his role as counsel at Feldstein Grinberg Stein & McKee. Mr. Grinberg launched Lionshead to provide additional services to his law firm's clients.

37954 ■ "Changing times: tax relief for women business owners" in *Women in Business* (Vol. 54, No. 5, September-October 2002, pp. 12)
Pub: The ABWA Company, Inc.
Ed: Edward Jones. Description: Wise retirement plan changes that could be implemented by women business owners as a result of the passage of the Economic Growth and Tax Relief Reconciliation Act of 2001 are discussed.

37955 ■ "Chapman Charged with Fraud" in *Black Enterprise* (Vol. 34, No. 2, September 2003, pp. 26)
Pub: Earl Graves Publishing Co.
Ed: Joyce Jones. Description: Nathan A. Chapman, Jr. was indicted by a federal grand jury on the charge of scheming to defraud the State Retirement & Pension System of Maryland, shareholders and his companies, and the public. The investment banker was charged on 39-counts with mail fraud, wire fraud, securities fraud and conspiracy.

37956 ■ "Chapter 7 or Chapter 13? What Filing for Bankruptcy Really Means" in *Black Enterprise* (Vol. 35, February 2005, No. 7, pp. 159)
Pub: Earl G. Graves Publishing Co. Inc.
Ed: Tamara E. Holmes. Description: Information to consider before filing bankruptcy is provided, including a description of both Chapter 7 and Chapter 13 filings.

37957 ■ "Charm City" in *Forbes* (Vol. 174, December 27, 2004, No. 13, pp. 190)
Pub: Forbes Magazine Inc.
Ed: John W. Rogers, Jr. Description: Three Baltimore companies to consider investing in are profiled: McCormick & Company, Black & Decker, and T. Rowe Price Group.

37958 ■ "Charting a course" in *Black Enterprise* (Vol. 33, No. 6, Jan. 2003, pp. 30)
Pub: Earl Graves Publishing Co.
Ed: James A. Anderson. Description: Investment advice forecasts that the mild rally seen last fall will most likely be followed by another marked drop in share prices. Terry Bedford, money manager for Bedford & Associates Research Group, provides a listing of his private screening picks.

37959 ■ "Charts Show the Way" in *Black Enterprise* (Vol. 34, No. 6, January 2004, pp. 29)
Pub: Earl Graves Publishing Co.
Ed: Rhonda Reynolds. Description: Terry Bedford, CEO of Bedford and Associates Research Group Inc., explains the way he uses stock price charts and technical analysis to select stock investments. Statistical data included.

37960 ■ "Charts Show the Way: Money Manager Terry Bedford's Stock Selections Are Going in the Right Direction" in *Black Enterprise* (Vol. 34)
Pub: Earl Graves Publishing Co.
Ed: Rhonda Reynolds. Description: Terry Bedford, CEO of Bedford and Associates Research Group Inc., explains the way he uses stock price charts and technical analysis to select stock investments. Statistical data included.

37961 ■ "Checking with Interest" in *Business Week* (No. 3678, April 24, 2000, pp. F10)
Pub: McGraw-Hill, Inc.
Description: The House Banking Committee recently voted to lift a ban on interest for commercial checking accounts.

37962 ■ "Chemical Balance" in *Black Enterprise* (Vol. 34, No. 5, December 2003, pp. 38)
Pub: Earl Graves Publishing Co.
Ed: Sakina P. Spruell. Description: John Moten, former Deutsche Bank analyst, is recommending chemical stocks. Moten notes that chemical companies thrive when oil prices are down because they use oil for energy and production of raw materials.

37963 ■ "Chicago Tribune Market Report Column" in *Chicago Tribune* (April 11, 2003)
Pub: Knight-Ridder/Tribune Business News
Ed: Bill Barnhart. Description: Recent stock market information is presented. In February and March 2003, the economy lost 416,000 jobs. Statistical data included.

37964 ■ "Chief concern" in *Entrepreneur* (Vol. 31, No. 4, April 2003, pp. 51)
Pub: Entrepreneur Media Inc.
Ed: David Lipschultz. Description: The need for hiring a chief financial officer for companies is examined; one question to ask in making a determination is whether the bill from an accounting firm is higher than the salary of a seasoned financial manager.

37965 ■ "China Presents Opportunities, Risks for Investors" in *Sacramento Bee* (December 27, 2005)
Pub: The Sacramento Bee
Ed: Gilbert Chan. Description: China's capitalist economy ruled by a communist government makes investments risky. California's Public Employee's Retirement System is discussing plans on whether to invest in China, now one of the world's fastest growing economies.

37966 ■ "Chop, chop: Bush's plan changes all: tax planning" in *Barron's* (Vol. 82, No. 57, February 10, 2003, pp. 21)
Pub: Barron's
Ed: Karen Hube. Description: A detailed analysis of the President's proposed new dividend tax cut, lifetime savings account, retirement savings accounts, and employer retirement savings accounts is provided, with an emphasis on the impacts on individuals.

37967 ■ "Cineplex Galaxy Income Fund Reports Fourth Quarter and Year End Results" in *Canadian Corporate News* (February 7, 2007)
Pub: Comtex News Network, Inc.
Description: Financial results for fourth quarter 2006 were announced by Cineplex Galaxy Income Fund. The fund reported $195 million in revenue, up nearly $2 million for 2005. Statistical data included.

37968 ■ "Citibank announces credit card targeted to small businesses" in *Wall Street Journal* (May 22, 2000, pp. C24, C15)
Pub: Dow Jones & Co., Inc.
Description: Citibank offers credit to small businesses in the form of the CitiBusiness Platinum Select MasterCard.

37969 ■ "Citigroup Names President Of GDB" in *Wall Street Journal* (Vol. 248, December 2006, No. 145, pp. B10)
Pub: Dow Jones & Co. Inc.
Ed: Rick Carew Description: Profile of Michael Zink, new president of GDB of Citigroup. Zink played a top in the integration of South Korea's KorAm Bank, which Citigroup acquired in April 2004

37970 ■ "A clarion call: the tech and telecom sectors are finally on the mend" in *Barron's* (Vol. 82, No. 58, February 17, 2003, pp. 28)
Pub: Barron's
Ed: Sandra Wood. Description: Tech and telecom research specialists, Scott Cleland and William Whyman, are optimistic about the end of the bear market in those sectors, including software, cable TV, and the Baby Bells.

37971 ■ "Clicking for Cash" in *Business Week* (No. 3698, September 11, 2000, pp. F37)
Pub: McGraw-Hill, Inc.
Description: Small businesses turn to online finance companies for loans and credit.

37972 ■ *Code of Federal Regulations: Title 13: Business Credit and Assistance*
Pub: United States Government Printing Office
Ed: Department of Commerce Staff. Released: April 2005. Price: $55.00. Description: Title 13 covers regulations governing the activities of the Small Business Administration and the Department of Commerce. Book covers information on business credit, finance, and economic development.

37973 ■ "Columbia Credit Union branch targets 21st-century crowd" in *Vancouver, WA Business Journal* (February 28, 2003)
Pub: Dolan Media Newswires
Ed: Cami Joner. Description: The Columbia Credit Unions new branch is designed to appeal to Clark County's high tech community.

37974 ■ "Comeback Bank" in *Forbes* (Vol. 175, January 10, 2005, No. 1, pp. 142)
Pub: Forbes Magazine Inc.
Ed: Michael Maiello. Description: Profile of Raymond James Financial Inc., brokerage house, asset manager, and investment bank serving the mid- and small-cap markets. The firms reports profits of a record $127 million and revenue up 22 percent over 2003.

37975 ■ "A Comfortable Retirement" in *Black Enterprise* (Vol. 34, No. 4, Nov. 2003, pp. 65)
Pub: Earl Graves Publishing Co.
Ed: Lisa Armstrong. Description: Profile of Theresa and Johnny Knight, two retired teachers who were able to save for a comfortable retirement, while paying their mortgage off in ten years, paid private school and college tuition for their children's education, and now enjoy trips to Europe or a Caribbean cruise yearly.

37976 ■ "Coming Up Short" in *Entrepreneur* (Vol. 32, December 2004, No. 12, pp. 64)
Pub: Entrepreneur Media Inc.
Ed: Crystal Detamore-Rodman. Description: A major benefit of short-term financing is the flexibility it allows for a small business owner.

37977 ■ "Commerce in the Making" in *Washington Business Journal* (Vol. 22, No. 8, June 27, 2003, pp. 1)
Pub: Washington Business Journal
Ed: Tim Mazzucca. Description: Commerce Bank may open branches in the Washington, DC area. The bank has headquarters in Cherry Hill, New Jersey, and 240 branches operating in Pennsylvania, New Jersey, Delaware and New York.

37978 ■ "Common Cents" in *Success* (Vol. 47, No. 5, October 2000, pp. 46)
Pub: Success Publishing, Inc.
Ed: Paul Gallagher. Description: Five basic rules are presented as experts share tips with entrepreneurs on managing money and selecting advisors.

37979 ■ "Community Investing Online" in *Black Enterprise* (Vol. 31, No. 5, December 2000, pp. 52)
Pub: Earl Graves Publishing Co.
Ed: Carolyn M. Brown. Description: Web-based service helps investment clubs manage and track their accounts.

37980 ■ *The Complete Idiot's Guide to Finance for Small Business*
Pub: Penguin Group Incorporated
Ed: Kenneth E. Little. Released: April 2006. Price: $19.95. Description: Financial experts helps small business owners through strategies for long-term financial success.

37981 ■ "Con Fusion" in *Entrepreneur* (Vol. 33, February 2005, No. 2, pp. 53)
Pub: Entrepreneur Media Inc.
Ed: Jennifer Pellet. Description: Income depositary securities (IDSs) are hybrid securities that offer investors regular payment of a dividend-paying stock with some growth opportunity, as well as the interest payment of a fixed-income security. IDSs were approved by the U.S. Securities and Exchange Commission July 2004 and will be available in 2005.

37982 ■ *Controller's and Treasurer's Desk Reference*
Pub: The McGraw-Hill Companies
Ed: Christopher R. Malburg. Released: 1995. Price: $69.95. Description: Guide explaining 488 financial techniques and their uses in various business situations.

37983 ■ **"Corporate Coffers Full of Cash" in** *Kansas City Star* **(March 8, 2005)**
Pub: Knight-Ridder/Tribune Business News
Ed: Chris Lester. **Description:** Corporate finances are at their best, and what companies do with that money will determine economics on Wall Street and in general. If spent wisely, it could be positive for both financial markets and economic growth.

37984 ■ *Corporate Liquidity: A Guide to Managing Working Capital*
Pub: Professional Publishing
Ed: Kenneth L. Parkinson and Jarl G. Kallberg. **Released:** 1993. **Price:** $55.00. **Description:** Provides information on generating cash, including managing payables to locating suitable banks. Contains tables, charts, and checklists.

37985 ■ **"Court OKs Meridian Ch. 11 Plan" in** *Crain's Detroit Business* **(Vol. 22, December 11, 2006, No. 50, pp. 6)**
Pub: Crain Communications Inc. - Detroit
Ed: Bill Shea. **Description:** U.S. bankruptcy court approved reorganization plan to emerge from Chapter Eleven bankruptcy for local auto parts supplier. Management reorganization, reduced workforce, and price negotiations were part of plan filed last May.

37986 ■ **"Creating a strong foundation" in** *Black Enterprise* **(Vol. 33, No. 6, Jan. 2003, pp. 49)**
Pub: Earl Graves Publishing Co.
Ed: Curtis Simmons. **Description:** Members of the Theta Omega Chapter of Alpha Kappa Alpha Sorority Inc. are building assets in their community through grants, programs and scholarships. Tips for starting a foundation are included.

37987 ■ **"Credit Checkup" in** *Black Enterprise* **(Vol. 36, February 2006, No. 7, pp. 169)**
Pub: Earl G. Graves Publishing Co. Inc.
Ed: Tanisha A. Sykes. **Description:** TrueCredit lists five ways to maintain or improve a credit standing rating.

37988 ■ **"Credit Unions Share Branches to Compete with Bigger, National Banks" in** *Portland Press Herald* **(May 17, 2005)**
Pub: Blethen Maine Newspapers, Inc.
Ed: Edward D. Murphy. **Description:** A new trend shows credit unions sharing branches in order to compete with larger banking institutions which control about 80 percent of the market.

37989 ■ **"Cricket Still Clears the Bar For Leap" in** *Wall Street Journal* **(Vol. 248, December 2006, No. 149, pp. C1)**
Pub: Dow Jones & Co. Inc.
Ed: Amol Sharma **Description:** Profile of Leap Wireless International Inc., which has seen their shares sharply gaining traction. Leap's 'Cricket' brand service targets niche markets overlooked by larger carriers such as young, low-income and ethnic customers by offering flat-rate service and requiring no credit checks.

37990 ■ **"A Cruel, Cold January for Funds" in** *Business Week Online* **(February 9, 2005)**
Pub: McGraw-Hill Companies
Ed: Amey Stone. **Description:** The market did not rally in January 2005, higher interest rates hurt real estate funds, and the fear of slowing growth in the technology sector are blamed. Statistical data included.

37991 ■ **"Customers Wary of Online Banking Security Breeches" in** *Providence Business News* **(Vol. 18, No. 13, July 14, 2003, pp. 3)**
Pub: Providence Business News, Inc.
Ed: Patricia Resende. **Description:** Safety precautions undertaken by Rhode Island banks to protect online banking customers are discussed.

37992 ■ **"Cutting-Edge Accountant" in** *Crain's New York Business* **(Vol. 23, January 29, 2007, No. 5, pp. F22)**
Pub: Crain Communications, Inc.

Ed: Barbara Benson. **Description:** Profile of Vice President of Corporate Development for Health Insurance Plan of Greater New York, Steve Zeng. HIP plans to go public after a merger with Group Health Incorporated.

37993 ■ **"David Nicklaus Column" in** *St. Louis Post-Dispatch* **(September 24, 2004)**
Pub: Knight-Ridder/Tribune Business News
Ed: David Nicklaus. **Description:** Check 21, or the Check Clearing for the 21st Century Act, allows banks to convert a check into a digital image that can be transmitted electronically. The new process will draw money from an account within 24 hours from deposit and is expected to save the industry $2 billion annually.

37994 ■ **"The Deal of the Art" in** *Forbes* **(Vol. 174, December 27, 2004, No. 13, pp. 184)**
Pub: Forbes Magazine Inc.
Ed: Carrie Coolidge. **Description:** Profile of William Zachary, who invests in art. Zachary is among a pool of investors who back an art dealer specializing in 19th Century paintings.

37995 ■ **"Debit Cards Ease FSA Administration Burden" in** *Rough Notes* **(Vol. 145, No. 9, September 2002, pp. 34)**
Pub: Rough Notes
Ed: Len Strazewski. **Description:** Flexible spending accounts are not popular with employers nor employees owing to the heavy paperwork involved, but Congress may introduce legislation that will ease the administrative aspect so as to facilitate usage of the program.

37996 ■ **"Debit or Credit? Knowing the Benefits of Each Card Can Help You Manage Money Better" in** *Black Enterprise* **(Vol. 34, October 2003)**
Pub: Earl Graves Publishing Co.
Ed: Naeemah Khabir. **Description:** President and co-founder of www.Myvesta.org, recommends debit cards being used for day-to-day purchases, while credit cards should be used for bigger ticket purchases. Myvesta is a consumer education organization. Russell Simmons, founder of Rush Communications along with Unifund Corporation, has established the Rush Card, a prepaid Visa debit card.

37997 ■ **"Debt Collection" in** *Black Enterprise* **(Vol. 34, No. 3, October 2003, pp. 136)**
Pub: Earl Graves Publishing Co.
Ed: Tanisha A. Sykes. **Description:** According to a member activity report by the National Foundation for Credit Counseling, the average debt management client is 35 years of age, and 95 percent of his or her income is debt. The NCFF offers free and affordable financial advice to consumers. A plan for negotiating with a lender is presented.

37998 ■ **"Debt-defying acts: one woman's journey back from the brink of involvency" in** *WorkingWoman* **(Vol. 25, No. 2, February 2000, pp. 26)**
Pub: Lang Communications Inc.
Ed: Patricia Kitchen. **Description:** A woman reversed her negligent credit payment habits after realizing that she was not facing up to the self-limiting aspects of her deficit spending.

37999 ■ **"Debt End Ahead? Don't Let Debt Put Your Business in a Tight Spot-Learn How to Use Leverage to Your Advantage" in** *Entrepreneur* **(Vol.32)**
Pub: Entrepreneur Media Inc.
Ed: David Worrell. **Description:** Entrepreneurs must be wary of using family homes, credit cards and personal guarantees as leverage for solving financial business problems.

38000 ■ *Deduct It!: Lower Your Small Business Taxes*
Pub: NOLO
Ed: Stephen Fishman. **Released:** September 2005. **Price:** $34.99. **Description:** Ways to maximize business tax deductions for any type of small business owner (sole proprietor, partnership, LLC, corporation).

38001 ■ **"Delightful Dividends" in** *Black Enterprise* **(Vol. 35, November 2004, No. 4, pp. 46)**
Pub: Earl G. Graves Publishing Co. Inc.
Ed: James A. Anderson. **Description:** Historically, companies that pay dividends to shareholders tend to have stock shares that maintain better when interest rates rise.

38002 ■ **"Delphos Gets OK to Take $3.4B Cerberus-led offer" in** *Crain's Detroit Business* **(Vol. 23, January 15, 2007, No. 3, pp. 1)**
Pub: Crain Communications Inc. - Detroit
Ed: Brent Snaveley. **Description:** US Bankruptcy judge clears way for Delphos to proceed with Cerberus investment package. GM and UAW approval is still required to proceed.

38003 ■ **"Despite Loss, Lear Has Wall Street Impressed" in** *Crain's Detroit Business* **(Vol. 23, January 29, 2007, No. 5, pp. 4)**
Pub: Crain Communications Inc. - Detroit
Ed: Brent Snaveley. **Description:** Disposal of Interiors Division significantly improves restructuring plans at Lear, but accounts for large reported loss in 2006. Fourth quarter results were much stronger than forecast. Shift in Asia supply from domestic Big 3 attributed to positive outcome.

38004 ■ **"Detroit Free Press Oakland Small Business Column" in** *Detroit Free Press* **(May 19, 2005)**
Pub: Knight-Ridder/Tribune Business News
Ed: Carol Cain. **Description:** National City, Rochester Downtown Development Authority, and the City of Rochester, Michigan have joined forces to offer downtown Rochester firms free business consulting services. Brad and Valerie Huyck are also profiled in the article. The Huyck's opened Karma Tea and Tonics in 2001, a California Asian-style tearoom on West Nine Mile Road in Ferndale.

38005 ■ **"Detroit Free Press Small Business Column" in** *Detroit Free Press* **(July 18, 2005)**
Pub: Knight-Ridder/Tribune Business News
Ed: Carol Cain. **Description:** Profile of Philip Locke, entrepreneur with years of experience in starting and closing businesses; Locke describes his Cash Now company that advances cash to customers. His goal is to have ten master franchise agreements by December 2006.

38006 ■ *The Dhandho Investor: The Low Risk Value Method to High Returns*
Pub: John Wiley and Sons Inc.
Ed: Mohnish Pabrai. **Released:** April 2007. **Price:** $27.95. **Description:** Value investing is described using the Dhandho capital allocation framework for successfully investing in the stock market.

38007 ■ **"The Dirty Dozen" in** *Forbes* **(Vol. 175, January 31, 2005, No. 2, pp. 108)**
Pub: Forbes Magazine Inc.
Description: A listing of the twelve most expensive investment funds are listed, with Dreyfus Founders Passport Fund leading the pack.

38008 ■ **"The Dirty Little Secret About Buybacks" in** *Business Week* **(January 23, 2006, No. 3968, pp. 74-75)**
Pub: McGraw-Hill Companies
Ed: David Henry. **Description:** Stock repurchases made by companies do little good for its shareholders because they are not reducing the number of shares outstanding.

38009 ■ **"Discount Days for Closed-End Funds" in** *Business Week* **(January 16, 2006, No. 3967, pp. 94)**
Pub: McGraw-Hill Companies
Ed: Aaron Pressman. **Description:** Closed-end funds look like mutual funds but are bought and sold like stocks. Depending on market conditions, they trade at prices different from the value of their holdings, many times at discounted prices.

38010 ■ "Dividends Gushing from Tax Cut" in *Houston Business Journal* (Vol. 34, No. 13, August 8, 2003, pp. 1)
Pub: American City Business Journals
Ed: Jim Greer. Description: Changes in the federal tax laws have resulted in substantial profits for investors of Kinder Morgan Inc. Topics include value of company shares, tax laws, and dividend payments.

38011 ■ "Do-It-Yourself Due Diligence" in *Business Week* (January 16, 2006, No. 3967, pp. 93)
Pub: McGraw-Hill Companies
Ed: Anne Tergesen. Description: Ways to investigate hedge funds online before investing are offered.

38012 ■ "Do the REIT Thing? When It Comes to Returns on Real Estate, Think Long-Term Investment" in *Entrepreneur* (Vol. 31, September 2003)
Pub: Entrepreneur Media, Inc.
Ed: Scott Bernard Nelson. Description: Real Estate Investment Trusts (REITs) are discussed. REITs gained an average of 3.6 percent in 2002, making them less desirable to investors.

38013 ■ "Do You Rate?" in *Entrepreneur* (Vol. 31, No. 10, October 2003, pp. 59)
Pub: Entrepreneur Media, Inc.
Ed: Joshua Kurlantzick. Description: Many small companies are struggling to maintain good credit ratings because of the continued weak economy.

38014 ■ "Does New Watchdog Have Teeth?" in *Business Journal-Portland* (Vol. 20, No. 23, August 8, 2003, pp. 1)
Pub: American City Business Journals, Inc.
Ed: Aliza Earnshaw. Description: The passage of the federal Sarbanes-Oxley Act of 2002 resulted in the formation of the Public Companies Accounting Oversight Board (PCAOB). The PCAOB will attempt to restore investor confidence in corporations by monitoring financial reports.

38015 ■ "Don't chicken out in 2003" in *Red Herring* (March 2003, pp. 70)
Pub: Herring Communications Inc.
Ed: Arnie Berman. Description: The basic fundamentals for investing in high tech stocks are presented.

38016 ■ "Don't Believe the Hype; Many of the Tax Benefits of Variable Annuities No Longer Exist" in *Business Week* (February 7, 2005, No. 3919)
Pub: McGraw-Hill Companies
Ed: Ellen Hoffman. Description: Some 7,000 complaints by angry buyers of variable annuities have been made to the National Association of Securities Dealers. Statistical information is presented regarding variable annuities.

38017 ■ "Don't Go Long: For Fixed-Income Investors, Low Interest Rates Make Short-Term CDs the Best Choice" in *Entrepreneur* (Vol. 32)
Pub: Entrepreneur Media Inc.
Ed: Scott Bernard Nelson. Description: Currently, short-term CDs may be the wisest choice for fixed-income investors because of low interest rates.

38018 ■ "Don't Watch This Curve Too Closely" in *Business Week* (January 9, 2006, No. 3966, pp. 22)
Pub: McGraw-Hill Companies
Description: A description of the inverted yield curve is presented. The yield curve is a graph of interest rate levels across all the various maturities, from the overnight federal funds rate to the 10-year Treasury note. The current curve inverted yield curve, which occurs when short rates are higher than long rates, no longer appears ominous to economists.

38019 ■ "Down and Out: Surprise: Many Personal Bankruptcies are Really Business Failures in Disguise" in *Entrepreneur* (Vol. 32, July 2004)
Pub: Entrepreneur Media Inc.

Ed: Joanne Cleaver. Description: Approximately 13 to 14 percent of all personal bankruptcies are really small business bankruptcies. In a recent study of 2,000 personal bankruptcies, it would take respondent small business owners 3.8 years to pay off money owed, and 2.9 years for non-business owners. Statistical data included.

38020 ■ "Down to a Science" in *Entrepreneur* (Vol. 31, No. 8, August 2003, pp. 54)
Pub: Entrepreneur Media, Inc.
Ed: Dian Vujovich. Description: Profile of the Eaton Vance Worldwide Health Sciences Fund (ETHSX), which has a five-year average total return of 12.67 percent. The fund invests in health, sciences and biotechnology firms worldwide.

38021 ■ "Drugmaker Ups Dosage; Acquisition Expected to Double Revenue" in *Crain's New York Business* (Vol. 23, January 22, 2007, No. 4, pp. 4)
Pub: Crain Communications, Inc.
Description: Barr Pharmaceuticals Inc. won a bidding war to acquire Pliva for $2.5 billion. The acquisition is expected to double Barr's revenue which had been falling over the last two years.

38022 ■ "Dueling North Carolina Bills Would Revive Payday Lending" in *Charlotte Observer* (April 11, 2003)
Pub: Knight-Ridder/Tribune Business News
Ed: Rick Rothacker. Description: The debate over payday lending continues for North Carolina's General Assembly. There are two controversial bills for making short-term, high-interest loans introduced in April, consumer advocates support one, lenders the other.

38023 ■ "E-bug exterminator: NetScreen nabs viruses and market share" in *Barron's* (Vol. 82, No. 58, February 17, 2003, pp. T8)
Pub: Barron's
Ed: Eric C. Fleming. Description: NetScreen Technologies' anti-virus hardware-software appliance is selling briskly, and its strong balance sheet fares well for its share price, currently near $20.

38024 ■ "E-Trade Financial Cuts Prices of Many Online Transactions" in *Kansas City Star* (February 16, 2005)
Pub: Knight-Ridder/Tribune Business News
Ed: Paul Wenske. Description: E-Trade Financial Corporation has announced a new commission schedule which will lower costs for some online stock and options trades on its Website. These changes will affect three customer groups. Customers will pay $9.99 commission when making five to 49 trades per month; power E-trades lowered to 75 cents to $1.25; and the serious investor fee is set at $11.99, down $1 from $12.99.

38025 ■ "Earnings Gain, Wealth Loss" in *Black Enterprise* (Vol. 35, January 2005, No. 6, pp. 30)
Pub: Earl G. Graves Publishing Co. Inc.
Ed: Nadirah Sabir. Description: Family income rose in the late 1990s in both black and white families, and at their highest in 2000 for both. Employment rates also rose during the same time period. Statistical data included.

38026 ■ "The Easy Way to Find the Best" in *Business Week* (January 23, 2006, No. 3968, pp. 78-82)
Pub: McGraw-Hill Companies
Ed: Lauren Young. Description: A Mutual Fund Scoreboard is presented for investors, featuring the top stocks in their class, and ways to compare stock picks.

38027 ■ "Eight Moves for Your Money" in *Black Enterprise* (Vol. 35, October 2004, No. 3, pp. 98)
Pub: Earl G. Graves Publishing Co. Inc.
Ed: Matthew S. Scott. Description: Eight ways to implement a sound financial strategy in today's market are listed.

38028 ■ "11th Hour" in *Entrepreneur* (Vol. 27, No. 12, December 1999, pp. 20)
Pub: Entrepreneur Media Inc.
Ed: Cynthia E. Griffin. Description: A bill in Congress could fundamentally change the way small business bankruptcies are handled. Information about the Bankruptcy Reform Act of 1998 is covered.

38029 ■ "An Embarrassment of riches" in *WorkingWoman* (Vol. 25, No. 5, May 2000, pp. 66)
Pub: Lang Communications Inc.
Ed: Marlys Harris. Description: Issues concerning the plethora of books written on financial guides for women are presented, including details on a selection of seven of the more "inspirational" books.

38030 ■ "Enjoy your income today while saving for your future" in *Black Enterprise* (Vol. 33, No. 3, October 2002, pp. 102)
Pub: Earl Graves Publishing Co.
Description: Case study is presented for a young account executive to meet family obligations, while investing in a retirement account.

38031 ■ "Enjoy It While It Lasts: Charts Suggest the Market Will Resume a Long-Term Decline at Summer's End" in *Barron's* (July 7, 2003)
Pub: Barron's
Ed: Michael Kahn. Description: Technical analysis of the purported recovery in the stock market that attended success in the Iraq war indicates a longer-lasting downturn.

38032 ■ *Entrepreneurial Finance*
Pub: Pearson Education, Limited
Ed: Philip J. Adelman; Alan M. Marks. Released: July 2006. Price: $87.35. Description: Financial aspects of running a small business are covered; topics include sole proprietorships, partnerships, limited liability companies, and private corporations.

38033 ■ *Entrepreneurial Finance: A Casebook*
Pub: John Wiley and Sons Inc.
Ed: Paul A. Gompers; William Sahlman. Released: September 2006. Price: $63.00. Description: Investment analysis, entrepreneurial financing, harvesting, and renewal in the entrepreneurial firm are among the topics discussed.

38034 ■ "Entrepreneurial Spirit" in *Black Enterprise* (Vol. 31, No. 4, November 2000, pp. 50)
Pub: Earl Graves Publishing Co.
Ed: Chirstine Albano. Description: Independent literary agent eyes financial freedom with aggressive investment and savings strategies.

38035 ■ *The Entrepreneur's Edge: Finding Money, Making Money, Keeping Money*
Pub: Silver Lake Publishing
Ed: Daniel Hogan. Released: October 2006. Price: $24.95. Description: Advice for starting, running and growing a new business is given.

38036 ■ "Equality through equities: African Americans turning to stocks to build wealth" in *Black Enterprise* (Vol.33, No.3, Oct. 2002, pp. 40)
Pub: Earl Graves Publishing Co.
Ed: Daniel R. Brown. Description: The 2002 Ariel-Schwab Black Investor Survey compared 500 blacks with household incomes of at least $50,000 with the same number of Caucasians. The survey showed that 74 percent of high-income blacks own stock and funds today, 30 percent higher than in 1998. Statistical data included.

38037 ■ "Equity Strategies: Small caps could be the best bet for big gains" in *Red Herring* (No. 103, September 1, 2001, pp. 90-92)
Pub: Herring Communications
Ed: Beverly Goodman. Description: Small-cap stock indices have outperformed technology stocks and the overall market during the last two years.

38038 ■ **"Escondido: Sometimes, the Best Advice is Free"** in *San Diego Business Journal* (Vol. 28, January 8, 2007, No. 2, pp. 27)
Pub: San Diego Business Journal Associates
Ed: Jessica Long. **Description:** Thursdays with Joe is a new program that offers free advice to small business owners in the Escondido, California area. Topics include marketing tips and financial planning advice.

38039 ■ *Essentials of Entrepreneurship and Small Business Management*
Pub: Prentice Hall PTR
Ed: Thomas W. Zimmerer; Norman M. Scarborough; Doug Wilson. **Released:** February 2007. **Price:** $106.67. **Description:** New venture creation and the knowledge required to start a new business are shared. The challenges of entrepreneurship, business plans, marketing, e-commerce, and financial considerations are explored.

38040 ■ **"Every Picture Tells a Story: New Web Displays Provide Market Data at a Glance"** in *Barron's* (August 25, 2003, pp. T6)
Pub: Barron's
Ed: Theresa W. Carey. **Description:** Online securities trading services, such as those offered by Ameritrade and SmartMoney, are enhancing Web site displays of market activity with offerings such as QuoteScope and Map of the Market.

38041 ■ **"Exchange Rate: Here's the Skinny on Exchange-Traded Funds"** in *Entrepreneur* (Vol. 32, August 2004, No. 8, pp. 47)
Pub: Entrepreneur Media Inc.
Ed: Dian Vujovich. **Description:** Exchange-traded funds (ETFs) may be an alternative to mutual funds. ETFs are like an index fund and closed end fund combination, each representing various indices, and trade like stocks.

38042 ■ **"Expensing stock options in not inevitable"** in *Red Herring* (January 2003, pp. 14)
Pub: Herring Communications Inc.
Ed: John Doerr. **Description:** The expensing of employee stock options is discussed.

38043 ■ **"Expensing Stock Options: A Fair-Value Approach"** in *Harvard Business Review* (Vol. 81, No. 12, December 2003, pp. 105)
Pub: Harvard Business School Press
Ed: Robert S. Kaplan, Krishna G. Palepu. **Description:** An examination of methods for fair-value expensing employee stock options, thus eliminating measurement and forecasting errors over time. Estimated option prices, amortized expenses, adjustment to paid-in capital, and total end-of-year reported expenses are calculated in two theoretical scenarios over a four-year period.

38044 ■ **"Factor Hurt by Funding Investments"** in *South Florida Business Journal* (Vol. 24, No. 7, September 26, 2003, pp. 1)
Pub: American City Business Journals
Ed: Jim Freer. **Description:** In changing from a factoring company to an investing company, E.S. Bankest has become bankrupt.

38045 ■ *Factoring Small Receivables: How to Make Money in Little Deals the Big Guys Brush Off*
Pub: Coastline Financial Group, LLC
Ed: Jeff Callender. **Released:** 4th ed. 1998. **Price:** $59.95 (ringbound).

38046 ■ **"Fair Game"** in *Entrepreneur* (Vol. 32, September 2004, No. 9, pp. 55)
Pub: Entrepreneur Media Inc.
Description: Profile of the Standard & Poor's Neural Fair Value 20 portfolio is presented. This portfolio uses computer models to select stocks with good returns.

38047 ■ **"Fallen and Can't Get Up: Even Greenspan Can't Hold Off the Bond Bears"** in *Barron's* (July 21, 2003, pp. MW11)
Pub: Barron's
Ed: Jennifer Ablan. **Description:** Bond markets continued to unravel, despite mollifying statements from Federal Reserve Chairman Alan Greenspan. Analysts were disheartened by the Federal government's plan to buy long-term treasury securities to keep rates under control, a program similar to Japan's price-keeping operations (PKO) of the early 1990s.

38048 ■ **"FAM Matters: This is Not Your Father's Equity-Income Fund"** in *Entrepreneur* (Vol. 33, February 2005, No. 2, pp. 49)
Pub: Entrepreneur Media Inc.
Ed: Dian Vujovich. **Description:** FAM Equity-Income Fund (FAMEX) is a concentrated fund that currently holds 31 stocks in its portfolio and all companies must pay a dividend each quarter. The fund is ranked No. 2 in its category for threeand five-year performance records.

38049 ■ **"Fed Model is Pointing to Some Upside for Stocks"** in *Barron's* (August 18, 2003, pp. 15)
Pub: Barron's
Ed: Robin Goldwyn Blumenthal. **Description:** The forward-earnings yield, an inverse indicator of the price-earnings ration, augers a favorable future for stocks, despite a short-term downturn forecasted for the S and P 500, according to Puglisi and Company analysts.

38050 ■ **"Federal-Mogul Reaches Ch. 11 Deal"** in *Crain's Detroit Business* (Vol. 19, No. 45, November 10, 2003, pp. 4)
Pub: Crain Communications Inc., Detroit
Ed: Brent Snavely. **Description:** Federal-Mogul Corporation, the Michigan-based automotive supplier, has reached an agreement on a proposed Chapter 11 reorganization plan with unsecured creditors, asbestos claimants, and banks.

38051 ■ **"Filing for Bankruptcy"** in *Black Enterprise* (Vol. 34, No. 7, February 2004, pp. 12)
Pub: Earl Graves Publishing Co.
Description: Personal bankruptcy filings have increased in 2003, however business bankruptcy filings decreased in the same year.

38052 ■ *Finance & Accounting: How to Keep Your Books and Manage Your Finances with an MBA, a CPA, or a Ph.D*
Pub: Adams Media Corporation
Ed: Suzanne Caplan. **Price:** $19.95.

38053 ■ **"Financial bootstrapping in small businesses"** in *Journal of Business Venturing* (Vol. 16, No. 3, May 2001, pp. 235)
Pub: Elsevier Science, Inc.
Ed: Joakim Winborg, Hans Landstrom. **Description:** Research into the financial bootstrapping methods used by managers of small businesses to acquire resources is presented.

38054 ■ *Financial Essentials for Small Business Success: Accounting, Planning & Recordkeeping Techniques for a Healthy Bottom Line*
Pub: Upstart Publishing Co., Inc.
Ed: Joe Tabet. **Released:** 1994. **Price:** $19.95 (paper).

38055 ■ **"Financial Industry Expects Growth Amid Radical Changes"** in *Crain's Detroit Business* (Vol. 19, No. 45, November 10, 2003, pp. 24)
Pub: Crain Communications Inc., Detroit
Ed: Katie Merx. **Description:** Southeast Michigan banks are expecting increases across the board in commercial lines of business, credit unions are expected to expand, and mortgage companies and brokers are offering new services to keep business brisk when interest rates rise. Venture capital and mergers-and-acquisition are also projected to do well.

38056 ■ *Financial Management*
Pub: South-Western Publishing Co.
Released: 1997. **Price:** $64.95.

38057 ■ *Financial Management 101: Get a Grip on Your Business Numbers*
Pub: Self-Counsel Press, Incorporated
Ed: Angie Mohr. **Released:** September 2004. **Price:** $14.95. **Description:** An overview of business planning, financial statements, budgeting and advertising for small businesses. s.

38058 ■ *Financial Management: How to Make a Go of Your Business*
Pub: Gordon Press Publishers
Released: 1997. **Price:** $251.95 (library binding).

38059 ■ *Financial Management for the Small Business*
Pub: Kogan Page, Limited
Ed: Colin Barrow. **Released:** April 2006. **Description:** Keys to successful financial management are presented to help small business owners to address the principles and problems associated with financial planning.

38060 ■ *Financial Management Techniques for Small Business*
Pub: Oasis Press
Ed: Art R. De Thomas. **Price:** $39.95 (looseleaf binder); $19.95 (paper). **Description:** Provides information on financial management for small businesses, covering monitoring trends in financial activities and changing cash behavior. Software available for IBM-PC and compatible computers.

38061 ■ **"Financial services firms foresee mixed results"** in *Atlanta Business Chronicle* (Vol. 25, January 10, 2003, No. 31, pp. 18A)
Pub: American City Business Publications, Inc.
Ed: Tony Heffernan. **Description:** The University of Georgia's Georgia Economic Outlook 2003 indicates that financial services companies will have mixed performances this coming year. One performance issue is that community banks will do better than bigger banks because they are not dependent on venture capital lending.

38062 ■ **"Financial Services: Institutions Bank on Information Technology"** in *Microsoft Executive Circle* (Vol. 1, No. 2, Q2 2001, pp. 50)
Pub: Putman Media
Ed: Craig A. Shutt. **Description:** Chase Manhattan Bank recently introduced a retail Internet Banking platform to provide a responsive system that customers can use 24 hours a day, slashing transaction time from 3 months to 10 days. Statistical data included.

38063 ■ **"Financial Services Market Changing"** in *Rough Notes* (Vol. 146, No. 3, March 2003, pp. 68)
Pub: Rough Notes
Ed: Phil Zinkewicz. **Description:** The feared consequences of the Financial Services Modernization Act of 1999 were of ensuing mergers and acquisitions among banks and insurers, never occurred. What followed was more competition and business among insurers and banks and more choices for consumers.

38064 ■ *Financial Troubleshooting: An Action Plan for Money Management in the Small Business*
Pub: Inc. Publishing
Ed: David H. Bangs, Jr. and Michael Pellecchia. **Released:** 1998. **Price:** $15.95.

38065 ■ **"Financially Sound"** in *Black Enterprise* (Vol. 35, October 2004, No. 3, pp. 44)
Pub: Earl G. Graves Publishing Co. Inc.
Ed: Rhonda Reynolds. **Description:** Robert McMillan, analyst at Standard & Poor's, offers stock market updates.

38066 ■ *Financing Your Business*
Pub: Prentice Hall

Ed: Iris Lorenz-Fife. **Released:** 1997. **Price:** $13.95. **Description:**

38067 ■ *Financing Your Business Dreams with Other People's Money: How & Where to Find Money for Start-Up & Growing Businesses*
Pub: Rhodes & Easton
Ed: Harold R. Lacy. **Released:** 1998. **Price:** $15.95.

38068 ■ "Finding the Middle Ground" in *Black Enterprise* (Vol. 34, No. 6, January 2004)
Pub: Earl Graves Publishing Co.
Ed: James A. Anderson. **Description:** According to market experts, mid-sized companies offer opportunity in most market conditions and are recommended in 2004. Statistical data included.

38069 ■ "Finding More Funds for Retirement" in *Black Enterprise* (Vol. 31, No. 5, December 2000, pp. 56)
Pub: Earl Graves Publishing Co.
Ed: Derek T. Dingle. **Description:** Ways to improve retirement benefits are explored.

38070 ■ "First-Time Investor: Where Should You Put Your Money Straight Out of College?" in *Black Enterprise* (Vol. 35, November 2004, No. 4)
Pub: Earl G. Graves Publishing Co. Inc.
Ed: Erin Straker. **Description:** Advice is offered to young adults for first-time investing. Dale Bryant, portfolio manager of the Bryant Group and Angela Bledsoe, a financial consultant with AXA Advisors offer insight into investing right out of college.

38071 ■ "Fit to Commit: This Small-Cap Fund Wants Investors for the Long Haul" in *Entrepreneur* (Vol. 31, No. 7, July 2003, pp. 50)
Pub: Entrepreneur Media, Inc.
Ed: Dian Vujovich. **Description:** To understand how an investment fund is managed, it is suggested to look into the fund's portfolio manager. A profile of Royce Special Equity Fund (RYSEX), which began in 1998, is presented.

38072 ■ "Fit and Trim" in *Entrepreneur* (Vol. 31, No. 7, July 2003, pp. 74)
Pub: Entrepreneur Media, Inc.
Ed: Joanne Cleaver. **Description:** It is necessary for small business owners to examine where overhead is out of control in order to trim expenses.

38073 ■ "Five Checking Account Mistakes to Avoid" in *Black Enterprise* (Vol. 34, No. 5, December 2003, pp. S11)
Pub: Earl Graves Publishing Co.
Ed: Tamekia Reece. **Description:** Five tips to help small businesses avoid accounting mistakes with the firm's checking account.

38074 ■ "The Five Don'ts" in *Forbes* (Vol. 175, February 14, 2005, No. 3, pp. 110)
Pub: Forbes Magazine Inc.
Ed: David Dreman. **Description:** Five ideas to avoid when suggested by your broker are presented.

38075 ■ "The Flaw of averages" in *Harvard Business Review* (Vol. 80, No. 11, November 2002, pp. 20)
Pub: Harvard Business School Press
Ed: Sam Savage. **Description:** The use of an average figure to represent an uncertain quantity can lead to a wrong answer in accounting, investment and sales. Software exists that can fix this flaw.

38076 ■ "Follow the Corporate Insiders" in *Black Enterprise* (Vol. 36, November 2005, No. 4, pp. 50)
Pub: Earl G. Graves Publishing Co. Inc.
Ed: Nicole Lewis. **Description:** Ty Burroughs, president of Burroughs Financial Group in Atlanta, Georgia predicts the infusion of new capital into the equities market sending the Dow and S&P 500 over 11,000 and 1,300 respectively.

38077 ■ "Food for thought" in *Black Enterprise* (Vol. 32, No. 9, Ma rch 2002, pp. 102)
Pub: Earl Graves Publishing Co.
Ed: James A. Anderson. **Description:** Five funds concentrating on the food industry and consumer staples are highlighted. Statistical data included.

38078 ■ "For Small Businesses, Future of Biz Taxes Will be Crucial" in *Crain's Detroit Business* (Vol. 22, November 27, 2006, No. 48, pp. 15)
Pub: Crain Communications Inc. - Detroit
Ed: Sheena Harrison. **Description:** With the cancellation of the Single Business Tax, small businesses will be central in the talks and discussions on changes necessary to replace revenue losses. Also of concern is the difficulty of hiring qualified employees with affordable wages and benefits.

38079 ■ "Former Collection Attorney Needs Consultants to Offer Bulletproof Asset Protection" in *Success* (Vol. 47, No. 2, June 2000, pp. 88)
Pub: Success Publishing, Inc.
Description: Bill Reed, former collection attorney and author, tells how he changed his career to start a consultant agency to help people protect their assets. Mr. Reed trains Asset Protection Consultants nationwide to work with clients in their own areas.

38080 ■ "Foundation Puts More Than $12M Behind Push For Design" in *Crain's Detroit Business* (Vol. 22, November 20, 2006, No. 47, pp. 1)
Pub: Crain Communications Inc. - Detroit
Ed: Sherri Begin. **Description:** Kresge Foundation is encouraging non-profit businesses to incorporate sustainable design onto their capital projects. Grants to cover the usual extra costs to incorporate green as well as advice and referrals are available through Kresge on a national level.

38081 ■ "401 Ok?" in *Entrepreneur* (Vol. 30, N pp. 81)
Pub: Entrepreneur Media Inc.
Ed: Jennifer Pellet. **Description:** The growing dissatisfaction with 401(k) investment plans is explored.

38082 ■ "From Football to Financial Plan" in *Black Enterprise* (Vol. 36, November 2005, No. 4, pp. 85)
Pub: Earl G. Graves Publishing Co. Inc.
Ed: Carmen Brown. **Description:** Three years after signing a contract with the Cincinnati Bengals, defensive back Forey Duckett was sidelined by an injury in which he never fully recovered. Duckett shares his investment strategy, which has turned $130,000 in 2002 to $265,000 in 2005.

38083 ■ "Fund Sharks" in *Entrepreneur* (Vol. 31, No. 8, August 2003, pp. 54)
Pub: Entrepreneur Media, Inc.
Ed: Jennifer Pellet. **Description:** Congress is looking into allegations of mutual fund companies fleecing investors with high fees which decreased returns on investment.

38084 ■ "The future of financial services and the information professional" in *Business Information Alert* (Vol. 15, No. 1, Jan. 2003, pp. 1)
Pub: Alert Publications
Ed: Sylvia James. **Description:** In the past 20 years there has been a large increase in the number of information professionals working directly or indirectly for the financial services sector. Suggestions are offered for future opportunities in the financial services sector for business information professionals.

38085 ■ "Gearing Up for the Golden Years" in *Black Enterprise* (Vol. 34, No. 3, October 2003)
Pub: Earl Graves Publishing Co.
Ed: Alan Hughes. **Description:** More African Americans are planning for retirement, according to the Minority Retirement Confidence Survey (MRCS),

although confidence tends to be lower and preparations further behind other Americans. The reason for this disparity is examined by William Spriggs, director of Research and Public Policy for the National Urban League and a member of the Black Enterprise Board of economists.

38086 ■ "Georgia's a Peach for Profits" in *Black Enterprise* (Vol. 34, No. 7, February 2004, pp. 38)
Pub: Earl Graves Publishing Co.
Ed: Nicole Lewis. **Description:** The Malachi Group (TMG) is focusing on Georgia-based companies as good selections for investors; TMG's criteria for selecting stocks is explained.

38087 ■ "Get fiscally fit" in *BlackEnterprise* (Vol. 31, No. 6, January 2001, pp. 102)
Pub: Earl Graves Publishing Co.
Ed: Monique R. Brown. **Description:** The first chapter in a series of exercises designed to teach effective money management and consumer empowerment is presented.

38088 ■ "Getting Back on the Bull" in *Black Enterprise* (Vol. 34, No. 4, November 2003, pp. 91)
Pub: Earl Graves Publishing Co.
Ed: James A. Anderson. **Description:** New strategies for a successful portfolio in 2004 are addressed.

38089 ■ "Getting More Bang for Your Buck" in *Black Enterprise* (Vol. 34, No. 6, January 2004)
Pub: Earl Graves Publishing Co.
Ed: Sheryl Nance-Nash. **Description:** Profile of a Sicklerville, New Jersey couple who have invested wisely for their retirement. The couple ranks among the top 6 percent of African American households with an income of $120,000.

38090 ■ "Getting Out of an IRS Mess" in *Black Enterprise* (Vol. 37, December 2006, No. 5, pp. 53)
Pub: Earl G. Graves Publishing Co. Inc.
Ed: Carolyn M. Brown. **Description:** Owing back taxes to the IRS can lead to huge penalties and interest. Here are some tips on how to handle paying the IRS what you owe them.

38091 ■ "Getting on the Road Toward Financial Freedom" in *Black Enterprise* (Vol. 35, October 2004, No. 3, pp. 125)
Pub: Earl G. Graves Publishing Co. Inc.
Ed: Lynnette Khalfani. **Description:** Three strategies to economically empower individuals are examined. Eliminating debt, setting up a financial record-keeping system, and tossing old records are a few suggestions offered.

38092 ■ "Getting your bucks in a row" in *WorkingWoman* (Vol. 25, No. 5, May 2000, pp. 34)
Pub: Lang Communications Inc.
Ed: James Pethokoukis. **Description:** There is a danger of losing money and investment opportunity if one's finances are not properly organized. A plan to reorganize suggests seven stages: assess, check, let go, consolidate, transfer, make a list, and fine-tuning. Information on useful web sites is included.

38093 ■ "Give Me a Tax Break" in *Black Enterprise* (Vol. 36, February 2006, No. 7, pp. 40)
Pub: Earl G. Graves Publishing Co. Inc.
Ed: Joyce Jones. **Description:** If passed, the Mortgage Insurance Fairness Act would allow homeowners with a combined income under $100,000 to deduct the total amount of mortgage insurance payments on federal tax returns.

38094 ■ "Go For the Big Ones" in *Forbes* (Vol. 175, January 31, 2005, No. 2, pp. 146)
Pub: Forbes Magazine Inc.
Ed: John W. Rogers, Jr. **Description:** Investment industry experts are advising investors to buy big company stocks.

38095 ■ **"Go Where the Money Is"** in *Black Enterprise* (Vol. 36, November 2005, No. 4, pp. 54)
Pub: Earl G. Graves Publishing Co. Inc.
Ed: Donald Jay Korn. **Description:** Financial services mutual funds are listed as a good investment. These funds hold stocks in banks, brokerage firms, insurers, and other financial companies.

38096 ■ **"Go With the Flow"** in *Small Business Opportunities* (Vol. 13, No. 6, November 2001, pp. 114)
Pub: Harris Publications, Inc.
Ed: Jim Schabarum II, Michael Strahan. **Description:** Proper cash flow management can help a small business generate income and also plan for slower times.

38097 ■ **"Going for Brokers: Recent Enthusiasm for Shares of Street Firms Appears Premature"** in *Barron's* (August 18, 2003, pp. 17)
Pub: Barron's
Ed: Leslie P. Norton. **Description:** Securities brokerages such as Merrill Lynch, Bear Stearns, and Lehman Brothers are witnessing a recovery in share valuations, to an 18-month high of twice book, compared to a bear-market low of less than 1.5. Some analysts, however, fear that the recovery is not warranted, and detail their reasoning.

38098 ■ **"Gold Rush"** in *Business Week* (January 9, 2006, No. 3966, pp. 68-72, 74, 76)
Pub: McGraw-Hill Companies
Ed: Brian Grow. **Description:** Online payment systems are facing security issues because online hackers are able to steal bank and credit card information. E-Gold is digital currency and customers using the service can enter false information in order to steal from an account.

38099 ■ **"Good Calls: Gains, Losses and Straddles"** in *Barron's* (July 7, 2003, pp. 19)
Pub: Barron's
Ed: Joseph F. Gelband. **Description:** Techniques for negotiating the tax consequences of straddle investments, or plays both for and against a stock at the same time, are detailed. The Economic Recovery Tax Act of 1981 has made this process more difficult.

38100 ■ **"Good Vibes: Socially Responsible Investing is Gaining Fans...and Clout"** in *Barron's* (July 7, 2003, pp. L3)
Pub: Barron's
Ed: Robin Goldwyn Blumenthal. **Description:** High profile corporate corruption scandals, such as Enron and WorldCom, have helped strengthen the position of socially responsible investing advocates, even in the Wall Street community, where they were most widely derided. A review of the increasing influence of socially responsible investing is provided.

38101 ■ **"Goodbye, Retainers"** in *Inc.* (November 2006, pp. 35,38)
Pub: Gruner & Jahr USA Publishing
Ed: Stefanie Clifford. **Description:** Pay-as-you-go, results based public relations are replaced the traditional retainer system. Significant costs are realized on a timely basis.

38102 ■ **"Granholm to Propose New Revenue-Sharing Plan"** in *Crain's Detroit Business* (Vol. 23, January 29, 2007, No. 5, pp. 32)
Pub: Crain Communications Inc. - Detroit
Ed: Amy Lane. **Description:** Revenue sharing to be a major part of Governor's fiscal 2008 budget proposal. This adds to the list of other legislative issues such as increased gas tax, replacing the single-business tax revenues, and changes to the broader tax structure.

38103 ■ **"Grassley Offers Discussion Draft on COLI Policies"** in *Tax Notes* (Vol. 102, No. 3, January 19, 2004, pp. 323-325)
Pub: Tax Notes International
Ed: Patti Mohr, Christine Harris. **Description:** Discussion with Senate Finance Committee Chair, Charles E. Grassley, regarding corporate-owned life insurance.

38104 ■ **"Greektown Casino Seeks Financial Extension"** in *Crain's Detroit Business* (Vol. 22, December 11, 2006, No. 50, pp. 25)
Pub: Crain Communications Inc. - Detroit
Ed: Robert Ankeny. **Description:** Greektown Casino seeks second extension from Michigan Gaming Control Board in 30 days. Revenue shortages are blamed on parking and traffic problems associated with the demolition of the Foster-Winter parking garage.

38105 ■ **"Greener Pastures: Exodus from Fidelity Continues as Another Hot Manager Heads to a Hedge Fund"** in *Barron's* (July 21, 2003, pp. F2)
Pub: Barron's
Ed: Erin E. Arvedlund. **Description:** David Glancy is one of a growing number of fund managers leaving Fidelity to start their own funds. Some analysts are encouraging investors to follow their fund managers, posing a graver threat to Fidelity. Investigations by state attorneys general and an investor lawsuit are among the plagues afflicting Morgan Stanley.

38106 ■ **"Growing apart: investment Websites keep advancing, even as the market retreats"** in *Barron's* (Vol. 82, No. 59, Feb. 24, 2003, pp. T4)
Pub: Barron's
Ed: Kathy Yakal. **Description:** Evaluations of Web sites that provide financial information and portfolio management tips are given. The sites are Yahoo!Finance, Money.net from Nasdaq, WhisperNumber.com, Superstar Investor and MortgageSelect.com. Features of the sites are described to enable consumers to decide what sites might best fit personal needs.

38107 ■ **"The Growing Opportunity in Server Consolidation"** in *Venture Capital Journal* (Vol. 42, No. 9, September 2002, pp. 36-37)
Pub: Thomas Venture Economics
Ed: Roger Lee. **Description:** Reducing the number of servers to a manageable number allows corporations to save money on real estate, power consumption, security, and IT administration.

38108 ■ *The Guide to Understanding Financial Statements*
Pub: The McGraw-Hill Companies
Ed: S.B. Costales and Geza Szurovy. **Released:** Second edition, 1995. **Price:** $12.95. **Description:** Provides explanations on balance sheets, profit and loss statements, and other financial statements.

38109 ■ *The Handbook of Financing Growth: Strategies and Capital Structure*
Pub: John Wiley & Sons, Incorporated
Ed: Kenneth H. Marks, John P. Funkhouser, Larry E. Robbins. **Released:** March 2005. **Price:** $79.95 (US), $123.95 (Canadian). **Description:** Using empirical data and actual case studies, strategies are presented to illustrate capital structures and fund raising techniques for emerging growth and middle-market companies.

38110 ■ **"A Happy Return on Equities"** in *Black Enterprise* (Vol. 34, No. 7, February 2004, pp. 40)
Pub: Earl Graves Publishing Co.
Ed: Rhonda Reynolds. **Description:** In an interview with Derek Batts, portfolio manager for Union Heritage Capital Management in Detroit, Michigan, Batts discussed the portfolio he put together last year that earned 29.96 percent.

38111 ■ **"Hazards of 401(k) debt"** in *Hispanic Business* (Vol. 22, No. 11, November 2000, pp. 92)
Pub: Hispanic Business
Ed: Milton Zall. **Description:** Issues are presented concerning the dangers of borrowing from retirement plans. The loss of interest until loans are repaid and loss of taxation benefits on the repayments of loans are discussed.

38112 ■ **"HB Diversity Stock Index"** in *Hispanic Business* (December 2006, pp. 10)
Pub: Hispanic Business

Description: Listing of top 45 Hispanic businesses shows stock symbol and values from January 3 to November 6, 2006, along with percent of change.

38113 ■ **"Hedging Its Bets"** in *Hispanic Business* (October 2003, pp. 44, 46, 48)
Pub: Hispanic Business
Ed: Derek Reveron. **Description:** Global Partners Group (GPG) launches an innovated program to create the next generation of hedge fund managers. GPG is based in Fort Lauderdale, Florida and is Hispanic-owned.

38114 ■ **"Her Line of Credit Was in Default. Her Partnership With Her Mom Was Faltering"** in *Inc.* (Volume 27, December 2005, No. 12, pp. 59-60)
Pub: Inc. Magazine
Ed: Nadine Heintz. **Description:** Heather Antonelli, CEO of Eminence Style, a furniture wholesaling business, tells why she decided to close her business and declare bankruptcy.

38115 ■ **"Here's to 5 Years of DOFE"** in *Black Enterprise* (Vol. 35, January 2005, No. 6, pp. 61)
Pub: Earl G. Graves Publishing Co. Inc.
Ed: Sakina P. Spruell. **Description:** Profile of the Wealth Building Kit offered by Black Enterprise. The program helps readers take control of their finances.

38116 ■ **"Hidden Expenses"** in *Forbes* (Vol. 175, January 31, 2005, No. 2, pp. 108)
Pub: Forbes Magazine Inc.
Ed: James M. Clash, Michale Maiello. **Description:** Mutual fund expense ratios are discussed to help investors choose a fund.

38117 ■ **"High Hopes: Ralph Mitchell's Picks Have Growth Potential"** in *Black Enterprise* (Vol. 37, February 2007, No. 7, pp. 42)
Pub: Earl G. Graves Publishing Co. Inc.
Ed: Carolyn M. Brown. **Description:** Ralph Mitchell, president and senior financial advisor of Braintree-Carthage Financial Group, offers three recommendations: Toll Brothers, Home Depot, and Lowe's.

38118 ■ **"High On Energy, Wary of Inflation"** in *Business Week Online* (February 8, 2005)
Pub: McGraw-Hill Companies
Description: In an interview with Stephen Leeb of Leeb Capital Management, he shares advice for investing in the stock market. Leeb addresses two major factors affecting the market: oil prices and inflation.

38119 ■ **"Home-building firms post double-digit profits, but Wall Street remains unimpressed"** in *Daily Business Review* (Vol. 77, Jan. 7, 2003)
Pub: American Lawyer Media LP
Description: Fourth quarter 2002, showed double-digit earnings for homebuilders, but the industry's stocks continue to under-perform.

38120 ■ **"A Home is the Foundation for Wealth"** in *Black Enterprise* (Vol. 34, No. 6, January 2004)
Pub: Earl Graves Publishing Co.
Ed: Lisa Armstrong. **Description:** Daphne and Gary Dixon use rental income to pay mortgages on their properties, building equity to be used for future acquisitions.

38121 ■ **"The Home Stretch"** in *Entrepreneur* (Vol. 33, January 2005, No. 1, pp. 52)
Pub: Entrepreneur Media Inc.
Ed: Scott Bernard Nelson. **Description:** If a down payment is the only thing keeping you from a home mortgage, borrowing from an Individual Retirement Account (IRA) is allowable for first time home buyers ($10,000 each or $20,000 for a couple).

38122 ■ **"Hospitality Hobnobber"** in *Crain's New York Business* (Vol. 23, January 29, 2007, No. 5, pp. F10)
Pub: Crain Communications, Inc.
Ed: Julie Satow. **Description:** Profile of Mark Gordon, investment banker and managing director of Sonnenblick-Goldman. In the past twelve years he has completed $10 billion worth of transactions.

38123 ■ **"How to Boost Your Portfolio's Performance"** in *Black Enterprise* **(Vol. 34, No. 4, November 2003)**
Pub: Earl Graves Publishing Co.
Ed: Lynnette Khalfani. **Description:** Information to make the most of stock market investments is provided.

38124 ■ *How to Finance a Growing Business: An Insider's Guide to Negotiating the Capital Markets*
Pub: Merritt Publishing
Ed: Royce Diener. **Released:** 5th ed. 1997. **Price:** $24.95.

38125 ■ **"How Much Cash Does Your Company Need?"** in *Harvard Business Review* **(Vol. 81, No. 11, November 2003, pp. 119)**
Pub: Harvard Business School Press
Ed: Richard Passov. **Description:** The economic benefits of wise knowledge management are discussed.

38126 ■ *How to Protect and Manage Your 401K: Shield, Save, and Grow Your Money, Guard Against Corporate Corruption, Do What It Takes to Protect Your Future*
Pub: Career Press, Incorporated
Ed: Elizabeth Opalka. **Released:** May 2003. **Price:** $15.99. **Description:** Ways to protect and manage 401(K) investments.

38127 ■ **"How the Quest for Efficiency Corroded the Market"** in *Harvard Business Review* **(Vol. 81, No. 7, July 2003, pp. 76)**
Pub: Harvard Business School Press
Ed: Paul M. Healy, Krishna G. Palepu. **Description:** Analysis of the U.S. financial system is provided.

38128 ■ *How to Start & Finance a Business That Works for You*
Pub: International Wealth Success, Inc.
Ed: Tyler G. Hicks; edited by S. David Hicks. **Released:** 1999. **Price:** $24.75.

38129 ■ **"How To Choose an Annuity"** in *Black Enterprise* **(Vol. 34, July 2004, No. 12, pp. 104)**
Pub: Earl G. Graves Publishing Co. Inc.
Ed: Aissatou Sidime, Jeffrey McKinney. **Description:** Variable annuities address multiple financial goals. Investors contributed $223.1 billion into annuities in 2002. Annuities tend to be more practical for individuals over the age of 50 and closer to retirement than for younger people.

38130 ■ **"How To Spot Trouble in Your Financials"** in *Inc.* **(October 1, 2004)**
Pub: Inc. Magazine
Ed: Darren Dahl, Carol Hirsch. **Description:** One way to diagnose problems with your company is to look at the firm's financials.

38131 ■ **"How To Talk to an Investment Bank"** in *Inc.* **(October 1, 2004)**
Pub: Inc. Magazine
Ed: Darren Dahl. **Description:** Investment banks are supposed to advise you on big deals, therefore it is important to know that your advisor is looking out for your interests.

38132 ■ *How to Write a Great Business Plan for Your Small Business in 60 Minutes or Less*
Pub: Atlantic Publishing
Ed: Sharon L. Fullen. **Released:** September 2005. **Price:** $39.95 includes CD-Rom. **Description:** A good business plan outlines goals and works as a company's resume to obtain funding, credit from suppliers, management of the operations and finances, promotion and marketing, and more.

38133 ■ **"Hurricane Watch:Whether the Market's Boisterous or Becalmed, the Web's the Place to Vent and Pontificate"** in *Barron's* **(July 28, 2003)**
Pub: Barron's

Ed: Kathy Yakal. **Description:** Traffic on Internet sites devoted to online trading and other financial services is measured based on market performance to evaluate trends in investor behavior.

38134 ■ **"In the Balance: A Good Blend Scales Down This Fund's Risk"** in *Entrepreneur* **(Vol. 32, October 2004, No. 10, pp. 59)**
Pub: Entrepreneur Media Inc.
Ed: Dian Vujovich. **Description:** It is wise for investors to include both stock and bond funds in their portfolio. Oakmark Equity and Income Fund (OAKBX) is an all-in-one fund boasting top three- and five-year performance rankings, with 57 percent of assets invested in value-oriented stocks.

38135 ■ **"In the Balance: Learn the Factors Banks Really Weight When Setting Loan Terms"** in *Entrepreneur* **(Vol. 31, No. 7, July 2003, pp. 30)**
Pub: Entrepreneur Media, Inc.
Ed: David Newton. **Description:** The size of a small company is not the most important issue banks look at when setting loan terms. When a small firm is seeking a bank loan, it should focus on the development and maintenance of good banking relationships, working with more than one bank.

38136 ■ **"In the Black"** in *Hispanic Business* **(May 2005, pp. 18)**
Pub: Hispanic Business
Ed: Joel Russell. **Description:** Projected surpluses brighten the future outlook for the U.S. Hispanic Chamber of Commerce. Statistical data included.

38137 ■ **"In Defense of the CEO Chair"** in *Harvard Business Review* **(Vol. 81, No. 9, September 2003, pp. 24)**
Pub: Harvard Business School Press
Ed: William T. Allen, William R. Berkeley. **Description:** The disadvantages to a company and its shareholders if the company separates the roles of CEO and chairman are examined.

38138 ■ **"Income for life: Dawn Greene needs a plan to help her live beyond her injuries"** in *Black Enterprise* **(Vol. 33, No. 6, Jan. 2003)**
Pub: Earl Graves Publishing Co.
Ed: Carmen Brown. **Description:** When former magazine editor Dawn Greene was disabled by a botched surgery, she contacted Merrill Lynch Financial advisor, William Betts in New York City, to take steps to regain solid financial footing. Betts is advising Greene on an investment philosophy emphasizing asset allocation, wealth preservation, and retirement/estate planning.

38139 ■ **"Independents' Day: Would Giving More Power to Outside Directors Boost Funds' Performance?"** in *Barron's* **(July 7, 2003, pp. L12)**
Pub: Barron's
Ed: Loren Fox. **Description:** Congress is moving against lax governance by the boards of mutual fund companies in the wake of corporate corruption scandals involving the likes of Enron and WorldCom. Mutual funds have largely been savaged, not only by exposure to scandal-ridden companies, but by the fallout from the tech-bubble collapse, and it is hoped outside influence on directors will boost accountability.

38140 ■ **"Inflation Woes: Secure Your Portfolio Against Rising Prices"** in *Black Enterprise* **(Vol. 37, January 2007, No. 6, pp. 40)**
Pub: Earl G. Graves Publishing Co. Inc.
Ed: Donald Jay Korn. **Description:** Inflation has a huge impact on investing and it is important to take the steady increase on cost into account when looking at your financial goals and investing in your future. Statistical data included.

38141 ■ **"Inspiring Black Investors"** in *Black Enterprise* **(Vol. 35, January 2005, No. 6, pp. 58)**
Pub: Earl G. Graves Publishing Co. Inc.

Ed: Derek T. Dingle. **Description:** Profile of John W. Rogers Jr., owner of Airel Capital Management, one of the most powerful firms on Wall Street. In 1983, Rogers launched his first family of equity mutual funds managed by African Americans.

38142 ■ *Instant Cashflow: Hundreds of Proven Strategies to Win Customers, Boost Margins and Take More Money Home*
Pub: McGraw-Hill Companies
Ed: Bradley J. Sugars. **Released:** December 2005. **Price:** $16.95 (US), $22.95 (Canadian). **Description:** Nearly 300 proven marketing and sales strategies are shared by the author, a self-made millionaire. Advice on creating the proper mindset, generating new leads, boosting the conversion rate of leads to sales, maximizing the value of the average sale, and measuring results is included.

38143 ■ *Instant Profit: Successful Strategies to Boost Your Margin and Increase the Profitability of Your Business*
Pub: McGraw-Hill Companies
Ed: Bradley J. Sugars. **Released:** December 2005. **Price:** $16.95 (US), $22.95 (Canadian). **Description:** Advice on management, money, marketing, and merchandising a successful small business is offered.

38144 ■ **"Institute for Financial Literacy Thrives Teaching Adults to Manage Money"** in *Portland Press Herald* **(December 2, 2005)**
Pub: Blethen Maine Newspapers, Inc.
Ed: Tux Turkel. **Description:** Institute for Financial Literacy helps adults learn to manage personal finances. The new federal bankruptcy laws will require the firm to add another 150 workers in late 2006.

38145 ■ **"Interest Alone May Not Be Enough"** in *Hispanic Business* **(November 2003, pp. 79)**
Pub: Hispanic Business
Ed: Glenn M. Terrones, Christopher Jarvis. **Description:** Living off the interest alone during retirement is not as simple as it sounds. Statistical data is included.

38146 ■ **"Introducing the art of second-derivative investing"** in *Red Herring* **(No. 99, June 15 & July 1, 2001, pp. 140)**
Pub: Herring Communications
Ed: Pip Coburn. **Description:** Three examples of second-derivative investing is highlighted. Second-derivative investing means playing the cyclical-growth game, buying when a stock goes low, and hopefully, riding the investment back up.

38147 ■ *Introduction to Financial Management*
Pub: Richard D. Irwin, Inc.
Ed: C. P. Jones. **Released:** 1991. **Price:** $62.95.

38148 ■ **"Intuitively clear: the king of personal-finance software sets sights on small business"** in *Barron's* **(Vol. 82, Feb. 24, 2003, pp.17)**
Pub: Barron's
Ed: Jay Palmer. **Description:** Demand for software products by Intuit Inc. is likely to continue to increase, thereby positively affecting the company's stock price. One analyst predicts that the new company's earnings growth will exceed 50 percent in 2003, as more small businesses buy the new software packages.

38149 ■ **"Invest in the Basics"** in *Women In Business* **(Vol. 52, No. 5, September-October 2000, pp. 44)**
Pub: The ABWA Co., Inc.
Ed: Edward Jones. **Description:** Issues are presented concerning the investment decisions that need to be taken regularly by business owners. The provision of good employee facilities as a means of retaining quality employees is covered.

38150 ■ **"Investing To Fight Disease; It May Be Better For Your Soul Than For Your Bottom Line"** in *Business Week* **(February 7, 2005, No. 3919)**
Pub: McGraw-Hill Companies
Ed: Carol Marie Cropper. **Description:** Investment trusts that target diseases such as Alzheimer's, breast

and ovarian cancer, diabetes, prostate cancer and rheumatoid arthritis are discussed. Developed by WellSpring BioCapital Partners in 2004, VIOLTs, short for Vertical Investments of Life Sciences Trusts, hold shares of companies developing or marketing treatments for these diseases.

38151 ■ "Investment Camps" in *Black Enterprise* (Vol. 34, No. 5, December 2003, pp. S11)
Pub: Earl Graves Publishing Co.
Ed: Siobhan Benet. **Description:** Profile of Money Camp for Kids, which teaches middle school and high school students the importance of financial independence.

38152 ■ "Investment Chat Rooms Can Be Hazardous" in *Women in Business* (Vol. 53, No. 2, March-April, 2001, pp. 26)
Pub: The ABWA Co. Inc.
Ed: Edward Jones. **Description:** Issues concerning the use of Internet chat rooms are discussed. The potential risks involved in following unsound investment tips or falling for scams are explored and the need to conduct independent advice, is stressed.

38153 ■ "Investment Clubs Offer Education and Fun" in *Women In Business* (Vol. 52, No. 1, January-February 2000, pp. 36)
Pub: The ABWA Co., Inc.
Description: The identification of potential members is essential for the formation of a successful investment club. A structured, but flexible agenda is also recommended, along with member involvement.

38154 ■ "Investment Intelligence" in *Hispanic Business* (January/February 2003, pp. 58)
Pub: Hispanic Business
Ed: Joel Russell. **Description:** A brief overview of leading financial newsletters is presented, including a list of top newsletters for the bear market.

38155 ■ "An Investment TIP For Unsure Times" in *My Business* (November/December 2001, pp. 16)
Pub: My Business Magazine
Ed: William J. Lynott. **Description:** Information is offered about treasury inflation-protected securities, or TIPS, as a good investment tactic during unsure economic times.

38156 ■ "Investor: Boarding School" in *Red Herring* (No. 99, June 15 & July 1, 2001, pp. 130, 132)
Pub: Herring Communications
Ed: Beverly Goodman. **Description:** An overview of the new audit committee rules adopted by the stock exchanges is presented. The volatility of today's market is discussed.

38157 ■ "Investor, Know Thyself" in *Black Enterprise* (Vol. 33, No. 3, October 2002, pp. 128)
Pub: Earl Graves Publishing Co.
Ed: Donald Jay Korn. **Description:** Ways to match investments with an individual's personality are discussed in order to receive positive returns in today's unstable stock market. A money personality profile is offered to place persons into one of nine investment categories.

38158 ■ "Investor, know thyself" in *Black Enterprise* (Vol. 33, No. 3, October 2002, pp. 128)
Pub: Earl Graves Publishing Co.
Ed: Donald Jay Korn. **Description:** Ways to match investments with an individual's personality are discussed in order to receive positive returns in today's unstable stock market. A money personality profile is offered to place persons into one of nine investment categories.

38159 ■ "Investors Apathetic about Re-entering Stock Market" in *Atlanta Business Chronicle* (Vol. 25, No. 20, October 25, 2002, pp. 6C)
Pub: American City Business Publications, Inc.

Ed: Leslie Williams Johnson. **Description:** Current events, such as threats of terrorism and accounting scandals taint the appeal of the stock market for many investors. According to a poll by the Associated Press, when the stock market declined to its lowest level in years, nearly two-thirds of Americans felt it was unwise to make a large investment.

38160 ■ "The Investors Next Door: Trying to Figure out the Best Moves in Today's Market?" in *Black Enterprise* (Vol. 33, Oct. 2002, pp. 134)
Pub: Earl Graves Publishing Co.
Ed: Matthew S. Scott. **Description:** Strategies for investing are offered by some of the nation's leading investment clubs. Topics include investing in tough markets and maintaining a financial commitment to investing; changing strategies and philosophies; stocks to avoid; goals; the differences in individual portfolios versus club portfolios; and information for future investments. Statistical data included.

38161 ■ "The investors next door: trying to figure out the best moves in today's market?" in *Black Enterprise* (Vol. 33, Oct. 2002, pp. 134)
Pub: Earl Graves Publishing Co.
Ed: Matthew S. Scott. **Description:** Strategies for investing are offered by some of the nation's leading investment clubs. Topics include investing in tough markets and maintaining a financial commitment to investing; changing strategies and philosophies; stocks to avoid; goals; the differences in individual portfolios versus club portfolios; and information for future investments. Statistical data included.

38162 ■ "Investors Retrench with Bond in Shaky Market" in *Atlanta Business Chronicle* (Vol. 25, No. 20, October 25, 2002, pp. 3C)
Pub: American City Business Publications, Inc.
Ed: Tony Heffernan. **Description:** Investors are seeing safety amid a volatile stock market and an uncertain economy. For investors, safety translates to bonds, especially U.S. Treasury securities, rather than corporate securities.

38163 ■ "Investors Wary of IPOs as New Charges Emerge" in *Atlanta Business Chronicle* (Vol. 25, No. 20, October 25, 2002, pp. 7C)
Pub: American City Business Publications, Inc.
Ed: Paige Bowers. **Description:** Allegations of insider favoritism is tainting the IPO market. Some financial underwriters, such as Salomon Smith Barney, are being questioned about preferential treatment of clients such as Global Crossing and Enron.

38164 ■ "IPOs: Things of the Past" in *Crain's New York Business* (Vol. 23, January 1, 2007, No. 1, pp. 14)
Pub: Crain Communications, Inc.
Description: Relegence Corp., a Manhattan-based company that gathers business information from around the globe and allows people to personalize the news delivered to their desktops, was acquired by AOL. The new trend in the business realm is to slowly grow then be acquired by a larger company instead of going public.

38165 ■ "Is it time to consolidate IRAs?" in *Women in Business* (Vol. 53, No. 5, September-October, 2001, pp. 46)
Pub: The ABWA Co. Inc.
Ed: Edward Jones. **Description:** The importance of consolidating individual retirement accounts is discussed. Paperwork, fee and distribution calculations can be kept to a minimum if all accounts are kept in one financial institution.

38166 ■ "It's 2006! Whatcha Gonna Do About It?" in *Inc.* (Volume 28, January 2006, No. 1, pp. 78-85, 113)
Pub: Inc. Magazine
Ed: Stephanie Clifford. **Description:** Various entrepreneurs give advice to help small businesses face new challenges in 2006. Topics include investments, the economy, small business trends, logistics, business communication such as blogs, energy issues, consumer products, real estate, interest rates and outsourcing.

38167 ■ "It's Optional: What Do You Really Need, and What Can You Live Without?" in *Entrepreneur* (Vol. 31, No. 7, July 2003, pp. 26)
Pub: Entrepreneur Media, Inc.
Ed: Jill Amadio. **Description:** Today's vehicles can come equipped with the latest technology. It is important to understand options that are not necessary when leasing or purchasing company vehicles.

38168 ■ "It's all about the profits (you're the boss)" in *Black Enterprise* (Vol. 33, No. 3, October 2002, pp. S3)
Pub: Earl Graves Publishing Co.
Ed: Carolyn M. Brown. **Description:** Financial management advice is given for student-owned businesses. A formula is provided for pricing services or products.

38169 ■ "Ja-Da must make its plan more palatable" in *Crain's Detroit Business* (Vol. 16, No. 49, December 4, 2000, pp. 41)
Pub: Crain Communications, Inc.
Ed: Terry Kosdrosky. **Description:** Downtown Detroit barbecue restaurant shares its financial woes in this article.

38170 ■ "Jackson CEO: company growing from within" in *Atlanta Business Chronicle* (Vol. 25, No. 20, October 25, 2002, pp. 26A)
Pub: American City Business Publications, Inc.
Ed: Meredith Jordan. **Description:** Profile of Jackson Securities Inc. Reuben McDaniel III, president and CEO of Jackson Securities, an investment banking concern and is owned by former Atlanta, Georgia mayor, Maynard Jackson, is the only company that covers all publicly traded minority companies.

38171 ■ "Just a Little Bit Public" in *Inc.* (August 2005, pp. 32, 34)
Pub: Inc. Magazine
Ed: Jennifer Gill. **Description:** Private placements are on the rise as the stock market falters. Private placement expert, Mike Haider, CEO of BioE has raised $22.5 million from investors.

38172 ■ "Keep Large and Small in the Mix" in *Black Enterprise* (Vol. 34, No. 2, September 2003, pp. 36)
Pub: Earl Graves Publishing Co.
Ed: James A. Anderson. **Description:** Portfolio manager, Dawn Alston Page, at Piedmont Investment Advisors in North Carolina, predicts a better than expected corporate growth in 2004. Paige advises investors to split money between stocks with good earnings growth prospects and stocks that are trading at a discount, making sure they include both large and small companies.

38173 ■ "Keep it Simple" in *Entrepreneur.com* (Vol. 34, February 2006, No. 2, pp. 60)
Pub: Entrepreneur Media Inc.
Ed: Chris Penttila. **Description:** Twenty-five tips for fine tuning a small business are outlined, focusing on technology, money, banking, taxes, credit and collection, accounting systems, mergers, management, and marketing ideas.

38174 ■ "Keeping Their Options Open" in *Boston Business Journal* (Vol. 23, No. 26, August 1, 2003, pp. 3)
Pub: American City Business Journals
Description: Profile of Boston, Massachusetts-based Progressive Software Inc., including an examination of Boston-area technology companies as highlighted by the plight of Progressive Software Inc. Topics include economic conditions, competition, and financial management.

38175 ■ "Knowing When It's Time" in *Black Enterprise* (Vol. 35, December 2004, No. 5, pp. 65)
Pub: Earl G. Graves Publishing Co. Inc.
Ed: Alan Hughes. **Description:** Ways to determine whether a part-time entrepreneur can afford to quit his fulltime job and devote full-time attention to his new company are discussed.

38176 ■ "L.A. County Econowatch" in *San Fernando Valley Business Journal* (Vol. 12, January 2007, No. 1, pp. 23)
Pub: San Fernando Valley Business Journal Associates
Description: Statistical data included for factors affecting the L.A. County's economy, including numbers of bankruptcies, electricity accounts, tourism activity, real estate figures and others

38177 ■ "Lack o' tax: the return from these funds all yours" in *Entrepreneur* (Vol. 30, No. 3, March 2002, pp. 66)
Pub: Entrepreneur Media Inc.
Ed: Dian Vujovich. **Description:** Profile of the Thomburg Limited Term Municipal National Bond Fund, a tax free municipal bond fund.

38178 ■ "Land Bank South Distributes $3 Million" in *Mississippi Business Journal* (Vol. 29, January 2007, No. 2, pp. 8)
Pub: Venture Publications, Inc.
Ed: Wally Northway **Description:** Land Bank South, FLCA, and it's board of directors and management has paid a cash patronage distribution of $3 million to its members based on the association's financial performance over the past year.

38179 ■ "Large Potential in Small Companies" in *Forbes* (Vol. 172, No. 13, December 22, 2003, pp. 220)
Pub: Forbes Magazine
Ed: Fei Mei Chan. **Description:** The potential of small company growth funds is discussed.

38180 ■ "Last Year Was Good to Investors in the American Century Value Fund" in *Kansas City Star* (January 23, 2005)
Pub: Knight-Ridder/Tribune Business News
Ed: Mark Davis. **Description:** Fees can determine how much an individual will actually earn when investing in a mutual fund. Despite the 14.6 percent return on American Century Value Fund, some investors gained 9.5 percent, others 7.5 percent or 13.4 percent depending on fees incurred by each.

38181 ■ "Laughing All the Way to the Bank" in *Harvard Business Review* (Vol. 81, No. 9, September 2003, pp. 16)
Pub: Harvard Business School Press
Ed: Fabio Sala. **Description:** Studies conducted of executives to determine humor in management, found that those using humor intended to build bridges rather than interfere with the flow of conversation or otherwise be undermining, tended to receive more money.

38182 ■ "Law Away" in *Entrepreneur* (Vol. 31, No. 8, August 2003, pp. 53)
Pub: Entrepreneur Media, Inc.
Ed: Jennifer Pellet. **Description:** Financial planners recommend that small companies establish an emergency fund that would last six months in case of business decline or a low stock market. Low risk and liquidity are the key investment criteria such as CD or money market accounts or short-term bond funds.

38183 ■ "Law of the Land" in *Entrepreneur* (Vol. 33, October 2005, No. 10, pp. 89)
Pub: Entrepreneur Media Inc.
Ed: Marc Diener. **Description:** Six rules to make the most of a company's money are listed.

38184 ■ *Law for the Small and Growing Business*
Pub: Jordans Publishing Limited
Ed: P. Bohm. **Released:** February 2007. **Price:** $59.98. **Description:** Legal and regulatory issues facing small businesses, including employment law, health and safety, commercial property, company law and finance are covered.

38185 ■ "Lawsuit, Tax Lien Plague Post-Bankruptcy Orbcomm" in *Washington Business Journal* (Vol. 22, No. 9, July 4, 2003, pp. 5)
Pub: Washington Business Journal
Ed: Roger Hughlett. **Description:** Orbcomm's post-bankruptcy battles to survive in light of the recent lawsuits and tax liens are discussed.

38186 ■ "Lending Tree earns first profit, branches out" in *Atlanta Business Chronicle* (Vol. 25, No. 22, November 8, 2002, pp. 8A)
Pub: American City Business Publications, Inc.
Ed: Jen Zoghby. **Description:** Lending Tree Inc. anticipates generating a profit in fourth quarter 2002 and all of 2003 when revenue is expected to total $131 million. Lending Tree has been increasing business from realty services offerings and is considering various ideas for 2003 to aid its growth efforts. The firm will continue its free membership program that offers discounts on various services.

38187 ■ "Lentek Lands in Chapter 11" in *Orlando Business Journal* (Vol. 20, No. 5, July 18, 2003, pp. 1)
Pub: American City Business Journals, Inc.
Ed: Chad Eric Watt. **Description:** Reasons behind Lentek International's filing for Chapter 11 bankruptcy protection are listed. Topics include business losses, economic conditions, and business management.

38188 ■ "A Less Taxing Way to Invest" in *Black Enterprise* (Vol. 35, December 2004, No. 5, pp. 48)
Pub: Earl G. Graves Publishing Co. Inc.
Ed: Donald Jay Korn. **Description:** Long-term municipal bond funds are an attractive means for investors looking to increase their portfolio's yield. If these bonds are held in a taxable account rather than a tax-deferred retirement plan, taxes must be paid.

38189 ■ "Let It Roll: Reginald Bowser Bends Over Backward to Create Convenient 401(k) Transfers" in *Black Enterprise* (Vol. 34, December 2003)
Pub: Earl Graves Publishing Co.
Ed: Marcia A. Wade. **Description:** Profile of Rollover-Systems Inc., provides job changers a free and easy service to reallocate 401(k) investments to a tax-deferred IRA in less than 25 minutes.

38190 ■ "Levitt on the street" in *Harvard Business Review* (Vol. 81, No. 4, April 2003, pp. 22)
Pub: Harvard Business School Press
Ed: Ben Gerson. **Description:** The former chairman of the Securities and Exchange Commission discusses the eroded state of investor confidence and what business and the SEC need to do about this issue.

38191 ■ "Life After Enron" in *Black Enterprise* (Vol. 34, No. 4, November 2003)
Pub: Earl Graves Publishing Co.
Ed: Sheryl Nance-Nash. **Description:** Profile of a human resources generalist working for Enron and had invested 60-70 percent of her retirement assets in Enron stock is presented. The family shares insight in ways they are coping.

38192 ■ "Living on the Hedge" in *Entrepreneur* (Vol. 31, No. 7, July 2003, pp. 49)
Pub: Entrepreneur Media, Inc.
Ed: Jennifer Pellet. **Description:** Hedge fund products tend to do well in down markets, but are risky investments. These funds hedge against risk by holding opposite-directions, instruments or futures.

38193 ■ "Local Hero: Ken Enright of MFS Bets on Underdogs-and Usually Wins" in *Barron's* (September 8, 2003)
Pub: Barron's
Description: Ken Enright has steered the MFS Strategic Value Fund to nearly 15 percent growth rate in the five years since its 1998 inception. Enright lays out his strategy of isolating well-managed companies with strong fundamentals that have fallen from grace.

38194 ■ "Lockport, N.Y.-Based First Niagara Financial to Open More Branches, Buy Bank" in *The Buffalo News* (April 11, 2203)
Pub: Knight-Ridder/Tribune Business News
Ed: Chet Bridger. **Description:** First Niagara Financial Groups intends to open new branches in Buffalo, Rochester and Syracuse, New York markets and is looking for a bank acquisition in Pennsylvania.

38195 ■ "Long Live the New King of Bonds" in *Business Week* (January 16, 2006, No. 3967, pp. 68, 70)
Pub: McGraw-Hill Companies
Ed: Christopher Palmeri. **Description:** Profile of Ken Leech, chief investment officer at Western Asset Management Company (Wamco). Wamco manages about $5.5 billion in 11 mutual funds. Experts believe the key to Wamco's success has been it consistent focus on large institutional bond clients.

38196 ■ "Long-term bunker: Louis A. Holland thinks more turbulence is ahead" in *Black Enterprise* (Vol. 33, No. 3, Oct. 2002, pp. 48)
Pub: Earl Graves Publishing Co.
Ed: James A. Anderson. **Description:** Louis A. Holland, money manager, speaks about the state of the stock market in the U.S. Holland makes predictions and stock picks and provides statistical data.

38197 ■ "Long-Term Bunker: Louis A. Holland Thinks More Turbulence Is Ahead" in *Black Enterprise* (Vol. 33, No. 3, Oct. 2002, pp. 48)
Pub: Earl Graves Publishing Co.
Ed: James A. Anderson. **Description:** Louis A. Holland, money manager, speaks about the state of the stock market in the U.S. Holland makes predictions and stock picks and provides statistical data.

38198 ■ "Long-term dare" in *WorkingWoman* (Vol. 25, No. 7, August 2000, pp. 36)
Pub: Lang Communications Inc.
Ed: Lisa Holton. **Description:** Issues and advice are given concerning the planning for and selection of long term care financial plans.

38199 ■ "Long-Term Technology" in *Black Enterprise* (Vol. 34, No. 4, November 2003, pp. 34)
Pub: Earl Graves Publishing Co.
Ed: Nicole Lewis. **Description:** Financial managers for the Philadelphia Public Employee Retirement System has used a long-term approach to investing and maintains the fund's allocation in technology without changes.

38200 ■ "Looking for a bull market" in *BlackEnterprise* (Vol. 32, No. 3, October 2001, pp. 38)
Pub: Earl Graves Publishing Co.
Ed: Nicole Halsey. **Description:** African American mutual funds are growing as the slow market recovery continues. A brief overview of the Ariel Appreciation (CAAPX) and Ariel (ARGFX) Funds, Brown Capital Management Small Co. Fund (BCSIX), as well as the DEM Equity Investor Fund (DEMEX) is presented. The DEM fund invests in companies owned or controlled by women, African, Hispanic, Asian, and Native Americans, and is managed by Nathan A. Chapman Jr., president of Chapman Capital Management in Baltimore, Maryland.

38201 ■ "Looking for a club that's more than just for fun?" in *Women in Business* (Vol. 53, No. 1, January-February, 2001, pp. 41)
Pub: The ABWA Co. Inc.
Ed: Edward Jones. **Description:** Investment clubs and their significance in the investment education process are discussed.

38202 ■ "Lop Legal Costs" in *My Business* (April/May 2002, pp. 16)
Pub: My Business Magazine
Ed: Deborah L. Jacobs. **Description:** Ten ways to reduce legal fees are listed.

38203 ■ "Losing Stream: Smart Moves: Is Your Business Leaking Profits?" in *Entrepreneur* (Vol. 31, No. 9, September 2003, pp. 77)
Pub: Entrepreneur Media, Inc.
Ed: Mark Henricks. **Description:** Ways to get more sales revenue back into a small company are discussed.

38204 ■ "Lower Fees, Higher Returns" in
Black Enterprise **(Vol. 34, No. 3, October**
2003, pp. 82)
Pub: Earl Graves Publishing Co.
Ed: Donald Jay Korn. **Description:** During the past
five years, financial markets have been divided so that
when either stocks or bonds went up, the other went
down. The second quarter of 2003 was a winner for
both stocks and bonds. Highlights of the fist half of the
2003 stock market is presented.

38205 ■ "LP's Loans to Executives Raises
Issues" in *Business Journal-Portland* **(Vol.**
20, No. 27, September 5, 2003, pp. 1)
Pub: American City Business Journals, Inc.
Ed: Shelly Strom. **Description:** In a policy that runs
counter to efforts to reduce a $1 billion debt, Louisiana
Pacific Corporation, a timber products company, continues to increase benefits to its top executives, critics
point to the company's loan program for these executives.

38206 ■ "Macro Money Maker" in *Forbes*
(Vol. 174, December 27, 2004, No. 13, pp.
121)
Pub: Forbes Magazine Inc.
Ed: Dyan Machan. **Description:** Profile of Louis
Bacon, the 48 year old hedge fund trader and founder
of Moore Capital Management. Bacon is a global
macro trader and new member of The Forbes 400.

38207 ■ "Made in America?" in *Entrepreneur*
(Vol. 31, No. 10, October 2003, pp. 72)
Pub: Entrepreneur Media, Inc.
Ed: Joshua Kurlantzick. **Description:** The consequences of U.S. businesses using overseas labor to
produce products and reduce costs to small U.S. manufacturers are examined.

38208 ■ "Maine Thing: Camden Tries New
Approach" in *American Banker* **(Vol. 172,**
January 18, 2007, No. 12, pp. 1)
Pub: SourceMedia, Inc.
Ed: Bonnie McGeer. **Description:** Camden National
Bank, located in Maine, is offering small business fi-
nancial centers in order to expand business. The cen-
ters target small and medium-sized firms, relying on
referrals from accountants and attorneys. Statistical
data included.

38209 ■ "Make the Change Today" in *Black*
Enterprise **(Vol. 34, No. 6, January 2004, pp.**
53)
Pub: Earl Graves Publishing Co.
Description: The ten wealth-building principles creat-
ed by Black Enterprise in 2000 anchor the Declaration
of Financial Empowerment and are helping African
Americans achieve financial goals.

38210 ■ "Making Sense of Stocks" in *Black*
Enterprise **(Vol. 31, No. 5, December 2000,**
pp. 147)
Pub: Earl Graves Publishing Co.
Ed: James A. Anderson. **Description:** All the information needed to build wealth by owning shares in the
market is covered.

38211 ■ *Management Accounts: How to Use*
Them To Control Your Business
Pub: Ashgate Publishing Co., Inc.
Ed: Tony Skone. **Released:** 1995. **Price:** $49.95

38212 ■ "Management Makes a Difference:
Bill Thomason Managed His Way to
Outstanding Gains" in *Black Enterprise* **(Vol.**
34, November 2003)
Pub: Earl Graves Publishing Co.
Ed: Sakina P. Spruell. **Description:** Interview with
hedge fund manager, Bill Thomason, CEO of Thomason Capital Management in Oakland, California; Thomason's theory to emphasize the effect of
management on a company's bottom line proved correct in 2003.

38213 ■ *Managing Business Growth: Get a*
Grip on the Numbers That Count
Pub: Self-Counsel Press, Incorporated
Ed: Angie Mohr. **Released:** September 2004. **Price:**
$14.95. **Description:** Fourth book in the Numbers 101

for Small Business Series, teaches how small company owners can expand their businesses using sound
financial planning.

38214 ■ *Managing by the Numbers: Financial*
Essentials for the Growing Business
Pub: Upstart Publishing Co., Inc.
Ed: David H. Bangs, Jr. **Released:** 1992. **Price:** $19.
95 (paper). **Description:** Discusses accounting help,
balance sheets and P&L statements, cash flow and
outflow, and financial projections.

38215 ■ *Managing a Small Business Made*
Easy
Pub: Entrepreneur Press
Ed: Martin E. Davis. **Released:** September 2005.
Price: $19.95 (US), $26.95 (Canadian). **Description:**
Examination of the essential elements for an entrepre-
neur running a business, including advice on leader-
ship, customer service, financials, and more.

38216 ■ "Market Guru Does a Reality Check
on Forecasting" in *St. Louis Post-Dispatch*
(January 14, 2005)
Pub: Knight-Ridder/Tribune Business News
Ed: David Nicklaus. **Description:** Market expert,
Larry Swedroe, recommends that individuals ignore
new-year investment predictions. He sites the negative outlook for 2003, yet the market rose 25 percent,
the best showing in decades.

38217 ■ "Market Upswing" in *Black*
Enterprise **(Vol. 34, No. 5, December 2003)**
Pub: Earl Graves Publishing Co.
Ed: Nicole Lewis. **Description:** Portfolio manager,
Ted Parrish, predicts a robust economy in the next 18
months. Parrish is the principal and director of invest-
ments for G.W. Henssler & Associates Ltd., located in
Marietta, Georgia.

38218 ■ *The McGraw-Hill Thirty-Six Hour*
Course in Finance for Nonfinancial Managers
Pub: The McGraw-Hill Companies
Ed: Robert A. Cooke. **Released:** 1995. **Price:** $40.00;
$19.95 (paper). **Description:** Provides information on
finance for managers, including figuring cost of sales,
budgeting for expenses, constructing a balance sheet,
and analyzing assets.

38219 ■ "Measuring Progress: A Look at the
Economic Strides of African Americans in
Recent Decades" in *Black Enterprise*
(December 2003)
Pub: Earl Graves Publishing Co.
Ed: Latif Lewis. **Description:** Homeownership among
African Americans rose in the 1990s to 42.7 percent.
Statistical data included.

38220 ■ *Microfinance*
Pub: Palgrave Macmillan
Ed: Mario La Torre; Gianfranco A. Vento; Philip
Molyneux. **Released:** October 2006. **Price:** $80.00.
Description: Microfinance involves the analysis of
operational, managerial and financial aspects of a
small business.

38221 ■ "Middle of the Road" in *Black*
Enterprise **(Vol. 31, No. 5, December 2000,**
pp. 44)
Pub: Earl Graves Publishing Co.
Ed: Donald J. Korn. **Description:** Midcap growth
funds continue their drive for top performance.

38222 ■ *Millionaire Republican*
Pub: Penguin Group Incorporated
Ed: Wayne Allyn Root. **Released:** September 2006.
Price: $12.95. **Description:** Eighteen steps to create
personal wealth in a Republican-dominated era.

38223 ■ "Minding the Money" in *Hispanic*
Business **(May 2005, pp. 16)**
Pub: Hispanic Business
Description: Results of a study conducted by Roper
Public Affairs showed that 74 percent of Hispanics
aged 45 to 64 with household incomes of at least
$45,000 feel they are financially successful. Fifty-eight
percent of Hispanics find life insurance policies con-
fusing.

38224 ■ "Minimum Credit Payments Will
Rise" in *Sacramento Bee* **(October 16, 2005)**
Pub: The Sacramento Bee
Ed: Jon Ortiz. **Description:** Along with the new bankruptcy rules making it more difficult to file for bankruptcy credit card companies will require larger minimum
monthly payments on outstanding credit accounts.

38225 ■ "Minority Banks are Thriving:
Deposits Jumped 213 percent in Five Years"
in *Atlanta Business Chronicle* **(Vol. 25, Jan.**
10, 2003, pp.1A)
Pub: American City Business Publications, Inc.
Ed: Meredith Jordan. **Description:** According to the
Federal Reserve Bank, Georgia's minority-owned
banks have experienced robust growth in the past five
years, outpacing even state and national banks. For
example, Capitol City Bank and Trust deposits have
grown 218 percent since 1997.

38226 ■ "Mix it Up" in *Entrepreneur* **(Vol. 32,**
No. 2, February 2004, pp. 47)
Pub: Entrepreneur Media, Inc.
Ed: Jennifer Pellet. **Description:** According to Ross
Levin, president of financial planning at Accredited In-
vestors Inc., a combination of a slower market along
with a new tax law that lowers the tax rate on divi-
dends is changing the way individuals are investing.
The new law taxes most dividends at 15 percent, as
low as 5 percent for low income earners.

38227 ■ "A Mixed Blessing" in *Entrepreneur*
(Vol. 31, No. 7, July 2003, pp. 68)
Pub: Entrepreneur Media, Inc.
Ed: Mark Henricks. **Description:** If not invested wisely, a windfall for a small business, could turn into a
negative. When a small firm receives unexpected
money, it should use that money to help expand production, pay off debts, fund new marketing, and/or to
motivate employees.

38228 ■ "Mixed Grill: A Quarter's Menu:
Good-and Some Bad—News" in *Barron's*
(July 7, 2003, pp. 22)
Pub: Barron's
Ed: Shirley A. Lazo. **Description:** Nearly one hundred
companies reported dividend increases in June 2003,
up 10 percent from 2002, reflecting the influence of reduced taxes on certain corporate dividends. A corresponding and irregular increase in cutback is the
negative counter to this trend.

38229 ■ "Money to Burn? Before You Go On
a Spending Spree With Your Surplus Cash,
Get Your Priorities Straight" in *Entrepreneur*
(July 2004)
Pub: Entrepreneur Media Inc.
Ed: C.J. Prince. **Description:** Small business owners
should meet with their CFO and accountant to plan
projections before spending or investing.

38230 ■ "Money Corner" in *Home Business*
(Vol. 13, January/February 2006, No. 1, pp.
78)
Pub: Home Business Magazine
Description: Small Business Administration loans,
retirement information, small business taxes, and Valentine's Day gift-buying tips are included.

38231 ■ "Money-Counting for Growth" in
Hispanic Business **(June 2002, pp. 70)**
Pub: Hispanic Business
Ed: Scott Williams. **Description:** Financial manage-
ment is critical to running a small business, yet corpo-
rate executives often fail to make it a high priority.

38232 ■ "Money-Preneuring" in *Small*
Business Opportunities **(Vol. 16, No. 2,**
March 2004, pp. 96, 166)
Pub: Harris Publications, Inc.
Ed: Fred Siegel. **Description:** The need for a sound
investment strategy is critical in today's changing economic climate. The chicken stock strategy, which refers to creating a portfolio that's appropriate for
individuals leery of investing in the stock market is outlined.

38233 ■ *Money Smart Secrets for the Self-Employed*
Pub: Random House, Inc.
Ed: Linda Stern. **Released:** 1997. **Price:** $20.00.

38234 ■ "Mortgage Delinquencies in 2007" in *Kiplinger Letter* (Vol. 78, January 19, 2007, No. 2)
Pub: Kiplinger
Description: Late mortgage payments are expected to reach 5 percent by mid-2007, the highest rate in five years. Adjustable rate mortgages and higher home equity payments are to blame.

38235 ■ "Most small businesses say credit access is good" in *Wall Street Journal* (October 16, 2000, pp. A4)
Pub: Dow Jones & Co., Inc.
Ed: Rodney Ho. **Description:** National Federation of Independent Business report regarding business credit. Statistical data included.

38236 ■ "Mutual Attraction: Despite the Headlines, Mutual Funds are Still a Good Thing" in *Entrepreneur* (Vol. 32, July 2004, No. 7, pp. 32)
Pub: Entrepreneur Media Inc.
Ed: Dian Vujovich. **Description:** Mutual funds continue to post good returns, making them a wise investment.

38237 ■ "Natural Hedge" in *The Economist* (Vol. 377, October 1-7, 2005, No. 8446, pp. 72)
Pub: The Economist Newspaper Ltd.
Description: Interest increases in financial tools that offset the economic damage caused by Hurricanes Katrina and Rita. Weather-risk management contracts and natural-catastrophe bonds are two such tools.

38238 ■ "Nearly Three Years Into an Economic Recovery" in *St. Louis Post-Dispatch* (October 15, 2004)
Pub: Knight-Ridder/Tribune Business News
Ed: David Nicklaus. **Description:** Despite the economic recovery of the last three years, small businesses are using profits for savings or to repay debt, rather than upgrades or expansion of the company.

38239 ■ "Net Deposits" in *Entrepreneur* (Vol. 33, October 2005, No. 10, pp. 54)
Pub: Entrepreneur Media Inc.
Ed: C.J. Prince. **Description:** According to recent surveys, small business owners hesitate to move their business banking online.

38240 ■ *Never Bet the Farm*
Pub: Jossey-Bass Publishers
Ed: Anthony L. Iaquinto; Stephen Spinelli, Jr. **Price:** R19.95 paperback.

38241 ■ "New Frontiers" in *Entrepreneur* (Vol. 33, October 2005, No. 10, pp. 54)
Pub: Entrepreneur Media Inc.
Ed: Dian Vujovich. **Description:** Exchange-traded funds offer an opportunity to invest in markets not otherwise accessible to individual investors.

38242 ■ "New Issues: There's a Side Door into the Public Markets" in *Red Herring* (No. 99, June 15 & July 1, 2001, pp. 138)
Pub: Herring Communications
Ed: Stephen Lacey. **Description:** The alternative to an Initial Public Offering (IPO), is coming back into style: Divestiture. Divestiture is when a company simply distributes shares of a subsidiary to its own stockholders, in a one-step spin-off.

38243 ■ "The New Roth 401(k)" in *Black Enterprise* (Vol. 36, December 2005, No. 5, pp. 50)
Pub: Earl G. Graves Publishing Co. Inc.
Ed: Rene Brinkley. **Description:** Both Roth IRA and the Roth 401(k) plans will allow workers to save money for retirement after taxes have been paid and pay no taxes on the money invested when withdrawn from the account in retirement. Suggestions are made for determining the use of a 401(k) versus a Roth 401(k).

38244 ■ "A new terminal at National?" in *Washington Business Journal* (Vol. 22, No. 3, May 23, 2003, pp. 1)
Pub: Washington Business Journal
Ed: John Wilen. **Description:** U.S. Airways plans construction of a new airport terminal at Washington's Reagan National Airport. Data covering U.S. Airways growth, design and construction and financial management is included.

38245 ■ "New Year's Resolutions" in *Black Enterprise* (Vol. 34, No. 6, January 2004, pp. 10)
Pub: Earl Graves Publishing Co.
Description: Black Enterprise offers a Web site to help keep finances in line.

38246 ■ "The Next Big Things: Nothing is more profitable than an investment idea whose time has come" in *Fortune* (Vol. 140, December 20, 1999)
Pub: Time Inc.
Description: From bricks and mortar to biotech, seven themes for the next century and ten stocks to profit from are outlined.

38247 ■ "No Fast Cash Class" in *Black Enterprise* (Vol. 37, December 2006, No. 5, pp. 72)
Pub: Earl G. Graves Publishing Co. Inc.
Ed: **Description:** There are no shortcuts to a obtaining a career as a financial planner. Certified Financial Planner Board of Standards has specific requirements for certification which include having a bachelor's degree from an accredited U.S. school before candidates are even eligible for taking the certification exam. Other criteria and requirements are discussed.

38248 ■ "No Guts, Some Glory" in *Entrepreneur* (Vol. 31, No. 10, October 2003, pp. 60)
Pub: Entrepreneur Media, Inc.
Ed: Dian Vujovich. **Description:** Treasury securities provide safety and security for investors because they are backed by full faith and credit of the U.S. Government and are rated triple A.

38249 ■ "No More Debt" in *Black Enterprise* (Vol. 37, November 2006, No. 4, pp. 159)
Pub: Earl G. Graves Publishing Co. Inc.
Ed: Tanisha A. Sykes. **Description:** Eliminating debt is not necessarily easy and can be overwhelming. Here are some tips for reducing and eventually getting out of debt.

38250 ■ "Nonprofit Consolidation to Increase" in *Crain's Detroit Business* (Vol. 22, November 27, 2006, No. 48, pp. 20)
Pub: Crain Communications Inc. - Detroit
Ed: Sherri Begin. **Description:** Reduced funding from foundations and pension shortfalls have resulted in consolidation of the nonprofit industry in Michigan. Efficiencies are to be gained by eliminating duplication of services.

38251 ■ "Nonprofits Eye New Revenue Ideas as Gifts, Grants Dwindle" in *Boston Business Journal* (Vol. 23, No. 31, September 5, 2003, pp. 1)
Pub: American City Business Journals
Ed: Jill Lerner. **Description:** Nonprofit organizations in the Boston, Massachusetts-area are facing a sharp decline in revenues as the national economy continues to drop. Nonprofits, such as the Freedom Trail Foundation, are depending on major annual fundraising events and innovative financing to survive.

38252 ■ "Not just for a rainy day" in *Black Enterprise* (Vol. 33, No. 6, Jan. 2003, pp. 87)
Pub: Earl Graves Publishing Co.
Ed: Lee Anna Jackson. **Description:** BET.com has joined with Consumer Federation of America to establish a Black America Saves Club, part of BET.com's Building Black Wealth Initiative.

38253 ■ "OKC-based Advanced Financial Solutions Releases New Check Image Exchange System" in *Journal Record* (February 4,2004)
Pub: Dolan Media Company
Description: Profile of Advanced Financial Solutions' new AFS xVision solution that enables the nation's larger financial institutions to exchange check images with other financial institutions, regardless of any system or platform processing differences.

38254 ■ "OKC-based Devon Energy's Fourth-Quarter Profits Dip 40 Percent" in *Journal Record (Oklahoma City, OK)* (February 8, 2007)
Pub: Journal Record
Ed: Jerry Shottenkirk. **Description:** Devon Energy reported a 40-percent drop in profits for fourth quarter 2006. Statistical details included.

38255 ■ "On a Bank Roll" in *Black Enterprise* (Vol. 33, No. 6, Jan. 2003, pp. 31)
Pub: Earl Graves Publishing Co.
Ed: Matthew S. Scott. **Description:** Raymond C. Steward, CEO of Briarcliff Manor, New York-based RASARA Strategies, presents his private screening performance on bank stocks.

38256 ■ "On Edge" in *Entrepreneur* (Vol. 33, October 2005, No. 10, pp. 62)
Pub: Entrepreneur Media Inc.
Ed: Scott Bernard Nelson. **Description:** Problems associated with investing in hedge funds are examined. It is recommended to include only a small portion of hedge funds into any investment portfolio.

38257 ■ "On the road to financial fitness" in *Black Enterprise* (Vol. 33, No. 3, Oct. 2002, pp. 79)
Pub: Earl Graves Publishing Co.
Ed: Carolyn M. Brown. **Description:** According to the 2002 Ariel/Schwab Black Investor Survey, the percentage of high-income African Americans earning more than $50,000 per year and investing in the stock market has risen by 30 percent, and the number investing in mutual funds or brokerage accounts is up 21 percent. The Black Enterprise January winners are profiled.

38258 ■ "On Good Terms" in *Entrepreneur. com* (Vol. 34, February 2006, No. 2, pp. 51)
Pub: Entrepreneur Media Inc.
Ed: Crystal Detamore-Rodman. **Description:** Interest rates have been rising steadily since 2004. Now might be the time for small business owners to consider refinancing loans.

38259 ■ "On the Rise: What Will Expected Interest-Rate Hikes Mean To You?" in *Entrepreneur* (Vol. 32, September 2004, No. 9, pp. 30)
Pub: Entrepreneur Media Inc.
Ed: Julie Monahan. **Description:** Interest rates are rising and small business must plan strategies for the changing economy.

38260 ■ "On the Road to Financial Fitness" in *Black Enterprise* (Vol. 33, No. 3, Oct. 2002, pp. 79)
Pub: Earl Graves Publishing Co.
Ed: Carolyn M. Brown. **Description:** According to the 2002 Ariel/Schwab Black Investor Survey, the percentage of high-income African Americans earning more than $50,000 per year and investing in the stock market has risen by 30 percent, and the number investing in mutual funds or brokerage accounts is up 21 percent. The Black Enterprise January winners are profiled.

38261 ■ "On the Road" in *Sales and Marketing.com* (Vol. 156, No. 3, March 2004, pp. 48)
Pub: VNU eMedia, Inc.
Ed: Betsy Cummings. **Description:** Six tips for sales managers to follow when purchasing vehicles for a sales fleet are offered by fleet experts. These strategies will help save money while making sales reps more productive.

38262 ■ *100% Deductible: Retirement Plans for Small Business*
Pub: International Legal Publishing
Ed: D. Kirk Buchanan; edited by Lon L. Davis. **Released:** 1997. **Price:** $14.95.

38263 ■ "One-stop shop? Brokerage firms make a play for your bank business, too" in *Entrepreneur* (Vol. 31, No. 5, May 2003, pp. 48)
Pub: Entrepreneur Media Inc.
Ed: Scott Bernard Nelson. **Description:** Stock brokerages are getting into the banking business. Merrill Lynch launched a new program called Beyond Banking in 2003.

38264 ■ "Online Banking is Evolution...Not Revolution" in *Ingram's* (Vol. 29, No. 1, January 2003, pp. 20)
Pub: Show Me Publishing, Inc.
Ed: Tom Mathis. **Description:** Online banking has grown to be a channel of choice for daily banking tasks and might be leading to a cashless and check-less society in the future.

38265 ■ "Online Trading Primer" in *Hispanic Business* (October 2002, pp. 92)
Pub: Hispanic Business
Ed: Derek Reveron. **Description:** The investment industry is going through a consolidation phase in order to attract big-asset accounts to trade online.

38266 ■ "Open Bar for Health Costs" in *Forbes* (Vol. 174, December 27, 2004, No. 13, pp. 192)
Pub: Forbes Magazine Inc.
Ed: A. Gary Shilling. **Description:** Despite rising healthcare costs, health care investments are still a good risk. Statistical data included.

38267 ■ "Options vigilantes" in *Forbes* (Vol. 170, No. 13, December 23, 2002, pp. 88)
Pub: Forbes Magazine
Ed: Robert Lenzner. **Description:** Ways in which portfolio managers believe stock options should be reported by companies are discussed. Statistical data included.

38268 ■ "Other People's Money: A Pension Fund Learns About Soft Dollars-the Hard Way" in *Barron's* (July 7, 2003, pp. L7)
Pub: Barron's
Ed: Erin E. Arvedlund. **Description:** The increasing influence wielded over pension funds by Wall Street, including which portfolio managers they hire and what companies they invest in, is a troubling trend, as evidenced in the case of the Nashville Municipal fund and consultant, William Keith Phillips.

38269 ■ "Out of control? Has individualized investing come and gone?" in *Entrepreneur* (Vol. 30, No. 2, February 2002, pp. 22)
Pub: Entrepreneur Media Inc.
Ed: Karen Epper Hoffman. **Description:** Information about individualized investing is discussed, including community stock funds, where online members help pick stocks within a fund; and folios, or stock baskets, where each investor can choose a customized list of stocks or removed unwanted companies from a preselected list.

38270 ■ "Over the Limit" in *Entrepreneur* (Vol. 33, October 2005, No. 10, pp. 56)
Pub: Entrepreneur Media Inc.
Ed: Crystal Detamore-Rodman. **Description:** Many banks offer small companies overdraft lines of credit to eliminate overdraft fees.

38271 ■ "Over the Wall" in *Entrepreneur. com* (Vol. 34, February 2006, No. 2, pp. 58)
Pub: Entrepreneur Media Inc.
Ed: Scott Bernard Nelson. **Description:** Smart ways to invest in China's growing economy are presented. Mutual funds or exchange-traded funds with exposure to China are considered the best strategy.

38272 ■ "Overreaching for the Roof" in *Black Enterprise* (Vol. 36, December 2005, No. 5, pp. 38)
Pub: Earl G. Graves Publishing Co. Inc.
Ed: Cliff Hocker. **Description:** According to a report by the Joint Center for Housing Studies at Harvard University, home price increases outpaced income increased by nearly five times from 2003 and 2004. Buyers are taking desperate measures in order to own a home.

38273 ■ "Own or Rent? Revisiting the Pros and Cons of Leasing vs. Purchasing" in *Black Enterprise* (Vol. 34, No. 6, January 2004, pp. 44)
Pub: Earl Graves Publishing Co.
Ed: Rebecca Rohan. **Description:** Information for small-to-medium-sized companies to consider regarding the purchase or rental of PCs, printers, fax machines, and copiers for their offices is examined.

38274 ■ "Passing the bucks" in *WorkingWoman* (Vol. 25, No. 4, April 2000, pp. 28)
Pub: Lang Communications Inc.
Ed: Lisa Holton. **Description:** Advice on making a will and estate planning are covered.

38275 ■ "Paulson Changes Name of Business" in *Bellingham Business Journal* (January 2007, pp. A19)
Pub: Sun News Inc.
Description: Judith Paulson, certified financial planner, changed the name of her business from Financial Counseling Services to Paulson Financial Services. With the change of the name also comes a new focus in which she plans to provide insurance and tax planning, financial education, and retirement planning.

38276 ■ "Pay Dirt! Finally Making a Profit? Put It Where It Belongs-Back in Your Business" in *Entrepreneur* (Vol. 31, No. 11, November 2003)
Pub: Entrepreneur Media, Inc.
Ed: Geoff Williams. **Description:** Small businesses should invest profits back into the company.

38277 ■ "Payback Time: Mutual Funds are Paying the Price, But Will You Get Your Fair Share?" in *Entrepreneur* (Vol. 32, August 2004, No. 8)
Pub: Entrepreneur Media Inc.
Ed: Julie Monahan. **Description:** Settlement money from the Security Exchange Commission's investigation into mutual fund malfeasance will most likely go to the funds themselves rather than investors.

38278 ■ "A Penny Not Saved" in *Entrepreneur* (Vol. 31, No. 8, August 2003, pp. 30)
Pub: Entrepreneur Media, Inc.
Ed: Steve Cooper. **Description:** According to a survey sponsored by the Employee Benefit Research Institute, the American Savings Education Council and Mathew Greenwald & Associates, more employees are planning to work more years before deciding to retire. Statistical data included.

38279 ■ "Personal Business" in *Business Week* (January 9, 2006, No. 3966, pp.)
Pub: McGraw-Hill Companies
Description: Stock and mutual fund figures for the week of January 1-8, 2005, as well as interest rates and forecasts for the week ahead.

38280 ■ "The Peterman Principle" in *Business Week* (January 9, 2006, No. 3966, pp. 62-63)
Pub: McGraw-Hill Companies
Ed: Roben Farzad. **Description:** John O'Hurley has turned his acting career on the television show Seinfeld into a profitable investing career.

38281 ■ "Pick of the Pack" in *Black Enterprise* (Vol. 34, No. 3, October 2003, pp. 30)
Pub: Earl Graves Publishing Co.
Ed: James A. Anderson. **Description:** According to Robert McMillan, financial advisor, a slow economic

stretch for an industry does not ruin every company within that industry. McMillan oversees brokerage companies and consumer credit firms.

38282 ■ "Picking apart company reports" in *Hispanic Business* (Vol. 22, No. 3, March 2000, pp. 60)
Pub: Hispanic Business
Ed: Jennifer Riley. **Description:** The importance of comparing performance ratios, such as price-to-cash flow, and price-to-net asset value, before investing in companies is presented. The value of information from ratios for Internet stock investments is discussed.

38283 ■ "Plan for a comfortable retirement while you save for your children's education" in *Black Enterprise* (Vol.33, No.3, Oct. 2002, pp.103)
Pub: Earl Graves Publishing Co.
Description: Ways to plan for retirement, while also investing for children's college education are discussed.

38284 ■ "Planning Ahead: Steven Taylor Mulls a Second Career After Retirement" in *Black Enterprise* (Vol. 37, November 2006, No. 4, pp. 82)
Pub: Earl G. Graves Publishing Co. Inc.
Ed: Sheryl Nance Nash. **Description:** Many workers are unprepared for retirement. Profile of Steven Taylor, a soon to retire dietary correctional officer who looked to Walt Clark, president of Clark Capital Financial in Maryland, to assess his retirement goals. Detailed advice and statistical data included.

38285 ■ "Playing the Money Game" in *Washington Business Journal* (Vol. 22, No. 8, June 27, 2003, pp. 26)
Pub: Washington Business Journal
Ed: Tim Mazzucca. **Description:** Profile of Ron Rubin, founder of the investment advisory firm, Bridgewater Financial Management.

38286 ■ *PPC's Guide to Audits of Small Businesses*
Pub: Practitioners Publishing Co.
Ed: Douglas R. Carmichael, Howard P. McMurrian, Jerry Anderson, L. Scott Spradline, D. Keith Wilson, David R. Frazier, Judith H. O'Dell, Glenn J. Vice, Cherie W. Shipp and Todd S. Lundy. **Released:** 1997. **Price:** $156.00 (ringbound) 4 vols.

38287 ■ "The Price Makes the Stock" in *Forbes* (Vol. 175, February 14, 2005, No. 3, pp. 138)
Pub: Forbes Magazine Inc.
Ed: Vahan Janjigian. **Description:** Investors need to distinguish between a company and its stock when deciding where to invest money.

38288 ■ "The Price is Right" in *Black Enterprise* (Vol. 31, No. 5, December 2000, pp. 56)
Pub: Earl Graves Publishing Co.
Ed: Donald J. Korn. **Description:** Can you stomach the highs and lows of index options? More adventurous investors use stock index options to protect their portfolios against stock market corrections.

38289 ■ "The Price is Right" in *Inc.* (July 1, 2003)
Pub: Gruner & Jahr USA Publishing
Description: Profiles of profit-analyzing software to help small businesses set pricing for products and services are investigated.

38290 ■ "Priority" in *Inc.* (Volume 27, March 2005, No. 3, pp. 23-26, 28, 30)
Pub: Inc. Magazine
Description: Business information discussed includes information about the SEC looking into unlicensed investment brokers, the economy, freight co-ops to help shippers ease costs, hiring, Google, education, SBA assistance to women entrepreneurs, and new inventions.

38291 ■ "Private investors manage for the long haul" in *Crain's Detroit Business* (Vol. 19, No. 15, April 14, 2003, pp. 9)
Pub: Crain Communications Inc., Detroit
Ed: Daniel Ajamian. **Description:** Are stock market investments made because of some kind of connection to a particular industry, or are they made to make a financial gain?

38292 ■ "The Problem: Getting Stung by a B" in *St. Louis Post-Dispatch* (January 16, 2005)
Pub: Knight-Ridder/Tribune Business News
Ed: Jack Naudi. **Description:** Ways to determine if B share stocks are a good investment is shared.

38293 ■ "Proceed With Caution" in *Black Enterprise* (Vol. 35, December 2004, No. 5, pp. 44)
Pub: Earl G. Graves Publishing Co. Inc.
Ed: Nicole Lewis. **Description:** Alfred Jackson, partner at Davis Hamilton Jackson & Associates LP, believes the nation has realized its highest levels of growth and is investing with caution. Ideas for lowering investment risk are presented.

38294 ■ "The Producers: Fixed Payouts Mimic Hit Yield. But Will the Hit Keep Playing?" in *Barron's* (August 25, 2003, pp. F2)
Pub: Barron's
Ed: Erin E. Arvedlund. **Description:** New tax rules that punish investors in mutual funds with fixed payout schemes are prompting managers such as Martin E. Zweig to consider pulling out of the closed-end sector.

38295 ■ "Production Co. Enters Familiar Chapter: 11" in *Washington Business Journal* (Vol. 22, No. 17, August 29, 2003, pp. 1)
Pub: Washington Business Journal
Ed: Greg A. Lohr. **Description:** Reasons behind Roland House's filing for Chapter 11 bankruptcy protection is examined. Topics include economic conditions, debt management, and long term planning.

38296 ■ "Profit or Paycheck?" in *Hispanic Business* (June 2002, pp. 96)
Pub: Hispanic Business
Ed: Milton Zall. **Description:** There are two factors to consider when determining the salary of an owner-employee. The first is whether the corporation can accumulate earnings without a tax penalty and the second whether the IRS will disallow deductions on an owner's salary increase. A table showing owner taxes vs. corporate taxes is presented.

38297 ■ "Protecting the Dream" in *Ingram's* (Vol. 28, No. 5, May 2002, pp. 28)
Pub: Show Me Publishing, Inc.
Ed: Cynthia Grimes. **Description:** Legal advice is given to protect small businesses from bankruptcy, lawyers, accounting, cash flow planning, employee benefits and estate planning.

38298 ■ "Putting Pension Funds to Work" in *Hispanic Business* (November 2003, pp. 38, 40)
Pub: Hispanic Business
Ed: Holly Ocasio Rizzo. **Description:** New America Alliance has launched an initiative to channel state pension fund money into Hispanic investment firms.

38299 ■ "Rabbi trusts give execs a false sense of security" in *Atlanta Business Chronicle* (Vol. 25, No. 20, October 25, 2002, pp. 2C)
Pub: American City Business Publications, Inc.
Ed: Tom Barry. **Description:** The rabbi trust is a nonqualified retirement plan that provides deferred compensation for middle and high level executives. In 1981, a synagogue in Brooklyn, New York wanted to reward a rabbi and established the first trust of its kind. The pros and cons of this type of trust are presented.

38300 ■ *Raising Money to Start of Expand Your Business Through a SCOR*
Pub: Infoware
Ed: Eileen Savid. **Released:** 1997. **Price:** $34.00 (spiral).

38301 ■ "A Rally Deferred" in *Black Enterprise* (Vol. 34, No. 2, September 2003, pp. 38)
Pub: Earl Graves Publishing Co.
Ed: Jeffrey McKinney. **Description:** William Young, president of Buford, Dickson, Harper & Sparrow Inc., discusses how the economy, the war in Iraq and low consumer spending foiled his strategic approach to investing.

38302 ■ "Ranks of Banker-Brokers Growing at Local Banks" in *Business Journal-Portland* (Vol. 20, No. 22, August 1, 2003, pp. 3)
Pub: American City Business Journals, Inc.
Ed: Robert Goldfield. **Description:** Profile of the growing diversification of financial products offered by local Portland, Oregon-area banks.

38303 ■ "Reaching For Financial Success" in *Black Enterprise* (Vol. 34, No. 5, December 2003, pp. 71)
Pub: Earl Graves Publishing Co.
Ed: Sheryl Nance-Nash. **Description:** Using advice from financial planners, the 2002 Financial Fitness Contest winners made changes to their financial lives and adopted the 10 principles of the Declaration of Financial Empowerment (DOFE).

38304 ■ "Reaching For Financial Success: Our 2002 Financial Fitness Contest Winners Are Achieving Their Goals" in *Black Enterprise* (Vol. 34)
Pub: Earl Graves Publishing Co.
Ed: Sheryl Nance-Nash. **Description:** Using advice from financial planners, the 2002 Financial Fitness Contest winners made changes to their financial lives and adopted the 10 principles of the Declaration of Financial Empowerment (DOFE).

38305 ■ "Reap What You Grow" in *Entrepreneur.com* (Vol. 34, February 2006, No. 2, pp. 52)
Pub: Entrepreneur Media Inc.
Ed: Jennifer Pellet. **Description:** Total return stocks are those that pay dividends with an annualized compound five-year total return of 20 percent or more, which combines yields with growth potential. It is recommended to diversify across industries.

38306 ■ "Rebound or Release?" in *Black Enterprise* (Vol. 34, No. 3, October 2003, pp. 69)
Pub: Earl Graves Publishing Co.
Ed: Matthew S. Scott. **Description:** Four high-powered money managers evaluate the current economic conditions and predict the fourth quarter of 2003 and beyond. Members of the discussion include Mary Pugh, CEO of Pugh Capital Management; Isaac Green, president and chief investment office of Piedmont Investment Advisors; Randall Eley, president of The Edgar Lomax Company; and Raymond Stewart, president and chief investment officer of Rasara Strategies.

38307 ■ "Rebuilding Interest; Bank One Brings in New Credit Chief to Ease Lending Rules, Win Back Middle-Market Business" in *Crain's Detroit Business*
Pub: Crain Communications Inc., Detroit
Ed: Katie Merx. **Description:** Bank One's new chief credit officer, is charged with bringing middle-market business to the firm.

38308 ■ "Rebuilding Interest" in *Crain's Detroit Business* (Vol. 19, No. 45, November 10, 2003, pp. 1)
Pub: Crain Communications Inc., Detroit
Ed: Katie Merx. **Description:** Bank One's new chief credit officer, is charged with bringing middle-market business to the firm.

38309 ■ "Recession session" in *Entrepreneur* (Vol. 30, No. 3, March 2002, pp.)
Pub: Entrepreneur Media Inc.
Ed: Mark Henricks. **Description:** An interview with various experts and entrepreneurs to learn how and when they recommend aggressive or defensive positions in the areas of money management, people management, marketing, and technology.

38310 ■ "Recovery for Some; Chicago's Economy Will Lag the State and Nation Next Year" in *Crain's Chicago Business* (December 22, 2003)
Pub: Crain Communications, Inc.
Ed: Sandra Jones. **Description:** Chicago's economy is expected to see a 2.96 percent rise in 2004, with the warehousing and distribution, financial services, and hospitality sectors feeling strongest growth with an increase in business travel to the area. However, Chicago's economy is expected to grow at a slower pace than the state or the nation.

38311 ■ "Reduce your tax bill" in *Women In Business* (Vol. 52, No. 2, March 2000, pp. 37)
Pub: The ABWA Co., Inc.
Description: To reduce tax on investments it is advised to invest in products that earn a tax-free income. U.S. tax-free investments include various mutual funds, unit investment trusts, and municipal bonds.

38312 ■ "Reforming pro forma" in *Entrepreneur* (Vol. 31, No. 5, May 2003, pp. 50)
Pub: Entrepreneur Media Inc.
Ed: Jennifer Pellet. **Description:** The issue of pro forma financial reports used by small businesses in the past is discussed. The SEC is working to bring pro forma reporting under control.

38313 ■ "Reliant's refinancing package could be a model for industry" in *Houston Business Journal* (Vol. 33, No. 48, April 11, 2003, pp. 10A)
Pub: Houston Business Journal
Ed: Monica Perin. **Description:** Reliant Resources Inc. received a $6.2 billion refinancing deal from Barclays Bank PLC, BankAmerica Corporation, and Deutsche Bank AG. The banks agreed to lower interest rates, offer a longer term, and payment deadline extensions.

38314 ■ "Relief Valve? Done Right, a Private Investment in Public Equity, Or Pipe, Could Bring Your Business Much-Needed Cash" in *Entrepreneur*
Pub: Entrepreneur Media Inc.
Ed: C.J. Prince. **Description:** Private Investment in Public Equity (PIPE) allow public companies to do a limited distribution of securities in common stocks or convertible debt to accredited or institutional investors, working like a hybrid of private and public capital.

38315 ■ "Renewed Biotech Interest Boosts BioCryst" in *Birmingham Business Journal* (Vol. 20, No. 35, August 29, 2003, pp. 1)
Pub: American City Business Journals, Inc.
Ed: Tom Bassing. **Description:** Difficult financial times facing BioCryst Pharmaceuticals Inc. are discussed, especially falling stock prices, cash flow problems, and financial management.

38316 ■ "Report Reveals Best Lenders for Black Business" in *Black Enterprise* (Vol. 36, November 2005, No. 4, pp. 38)
Pub: Earl G. Graves Publishing Co. Inc.
Ed: Glenn Townes. **Description:** The Greenlining Institute, a public policy research and advocacy group, ranks U.S. financial institutions for the Small Business Administration according to loans to minorities. Bank of America and JPMorgan Chase were at the top of the list. Statistical data included.

38317 ■ "Retail Rut: Sears Holders Might Get a $10 Payout. But Don't Expect Much More from the Stock" in *Barron's* (July 21, 2003, pp. 15)
Pub: Barron's
Ed: Robin Goldwyn Blumenthal. **Description:** Sears Roebuck's credit-loan subsidiary went to Citigroup for $6 billion, considerably less than the expected $7 billion, but was still enough to give $10/share in cash to stockholders.

38318 ■ "Rethinking Refinancing" in *Black Enterprise* (Vol. 34, No. 5, December 2003, pp. 33)
Pub: Earl Graves Publishing Co.

Ed: Carl Unegbu. **Description:** Mortgage rates are better than two years ago, despite the recent rise in rates. Experts agree that low interest rates are the reason behind most refinancing decisions.

38319 ■ "Rethinking Refinancing: With Mortgage Rates on the Rise, Does It Still Make Sense to Refinance?" in *Black Enterprise* **(Vol. 34)**
Pub: Earl Graves Publishing Co.
Ed: Carl Unegbu. **Description:** Mortgage rates are better than two years ago, despite the recent rise in rates. Experts agree that low interest rates are the reason behind most refinancing decisions.

38320 ■ "Retire Rich" in *Entrepreneur* **(Vol. 33, September 2005, No. 9, pp. 68)**
Pub: Entrepreneur Media Inc.
Ed: David Worrell. **Description:** Financial experts offer tips, strategies and secrets to help entrepreneurs accumulate wealth for retirement.

38321 ■ "Retirement Plan Shopping" in *Hispanic Business* **(Vol. 23, No. 5, May 2001, pp. 76)**
Pub: Hispanic Business
Ed: Javier R. Jimenez. **Description:** Information for sound financial planning is presented. Retirement plans for self-employed and small businesses are discussed, including a SEP (Simplified Employee Pension), a simplified IRA, 401(k) plans, and profit-sharing and money purchase pension plans.

38322 ■ "Retirement Plans for Small Business" in *Ingram's* **(Vol. 28, No. 5, May 2002, pp. 31)**
Pub: Show Me Publishing, Inc.
Ed: Michael Searcy. **Description:** Retirement plans for small business owners are presented, including Individual Retirement Arrangement, Simplified Employee Pension IRA and 401(k)Profit Sharing.

38323 ■ "Revamping a Retirement Plan" in *Black Enterprise* **(Vol. 35, October 2004, No. 3, pp. 43)**
Pub: Earl G. Graves Publishing Co. Inc.
Ed: Carmen Brown. **Description:** Calvin and Jacqueline McGahee share investment strategies for a better retirement.

38324 ■ "Revamping Roth" in *Entrepreneur* **(Vol. 33, October 2005, No. 10, pp. 60)**
Pub: Entrepreneur Media Inc.
Ed: Jennifer Pellet. **Description:** The Economic Growth and Tax Relief Reconciliation Act of 2001 allows employers to offer employees a retirement-savings vehicle, similar to a Roth IRA, within their 401(k) plans starting in 2006.

38325 ■ "A Rich New Niche" in *Hispanic Business* **(June 2005, pp. 80, 82)**
Pub: Hispanic Business
Ed: Judi Erickson. **Description:** Private equity funds provide a powerful investment opportunity.

38326 ■ "Risky Business: Hedge fund chic is both undeserved - and dangerous" in *Red Herring* **(No. 103, September 1, 2001, pp. 84-85)**
Pub: Herring Communications
Ed: Eric Moskowitz. **Description:** An overview of the popular hedge funds. Hedge funds allow managers to not only buy stocks, but to short them (a bet that a stock will go down) or to employ more exotic financial instruments, like derivative securities.

38327 ■ "Robert Wagner Hosts The Litigation Explosion" in *Entrepreneur* **(Vol. 33, January 2005, No. 1, pp. 104)**
Pub: Entrepreneur Media Inc.
Description: The rewards of high income and owning your own business as a consultant providing asset protection, financial privacy and tax reduction are highlighted.

38328 ■ "Rolling the Dice on Hedge Funds" in *Business 2.0* **(Vol. 6, May 2005, No. 4, pp. 34)**
Pub: Time, Inc.
Ed: Jonathan Weber. **Description:** Investing in hedge funds is the latest trend in investing. Tips to help make money investing in these funds are discussed.

38329 ■ "Rough Ride to Recovery: Black-Owned Mutual Funds Brace for a Bumpy Bull Ride" in *Black Enterprise* **(Vol. 34, No. 5, December 2003)**
Pub: Earl Graves Publishing Co.
Ed: Tanisha A. Sykes. **Description:** Profile of black-owned mutual funds and the problems faced by these funds in a weak economy.

38330 ■ "Running Dry" in *Entrepreneur* **(Vol. 33, August 2005, No. 8, pp. 20)**
Pub: Entrepreneur Media Inc.
Ed: Crystal Detamore-Rodman. **Description:** The U.S. government's Small Business Investment Company (SBIC) provides equity capital to entrepreneurs. Currently the SBIC Participating Securities Program provides as much as $2 for every $1 of capital raised by venture funds licensed by the SBA; this program is in jeopardy of being discontinued.

38331 ■ "Safeguard your financial legacy" in *BlackEnterprise* **(Vol. 32, No. 3, October 2001, pp. 75)**
Pub: Earl Graves Publishing Co.
Ed: Carolyn M. Brown. **Description:** In small business, the transferring of wealth requires solid tax and estate planning. The article lists safeguards to secure a family legacy. Ten steps to financial empowerment are included.

38332 ■ "San Diego Public Stocks" in *San Diego Business Journal* **(Vol. 28, January 8, 2007, No. 2, pp. 23)**
Pub: San Diego Business Journal Associates
Description: Statistical table showing San Diego public stocks from December 26, 2006 to January 2, 2007, including net change and percent of change.

38333 ■ "Save It For Later" in *Entrepreneur* **(Vol. 32, December 2004, No. 12, pp. 68)**
Pub: Entrepreneur Media Inc.
Description: Studies indicate that more than one-third of the eligible work force does not participate in 401(k) retirement plans. Employers might automatically enroll employees into a plan with the option of their opting out.

38334 ■ "Save Some Green" in *My Business* **(August/September 2002, pp. 13-14)**
Pub: My Business Magazine
Ed: Janet Cass. **Description:** One way for small business to save money on lawn maintenance is to plant a "xeriscape" containing native plants. Native plants are adapted to a region's soil and climate, thus watering and mowing bills can save a small firm up to 80 percent in lawn care.

38335 ■ "Saving money, saving lives" in *Harvard Business Review* **(Vol. 78, No. 6, November-December 2000, pp. 57)**
Pub: Harvard Business School Publishing Corp.
Description: Jon Meliones, the chief medical director at Duke Children's Hospital (DCH) improved the quality of care at the hospital by focusing less like a nonprofit that loses money, and more like a profitable corporation.

38336 ■ *Saving Your Business: How to Survive Chapter 11 Bankruptcy and Successfully Reorganize Your Company*
Pub: Prentice Hall
Ed: Suzanne Caplan. **Released:** 1992. **Price:** $17.95 (paper).

38337 ■ *Schaum's Outline Financial Management, Third Edition*
Pub: McGraw-Hill
Ed: Jae K. Shim; Joel G. Siegel. **Released:** May 2007. **Price:** $22.95 (CND). **Description:** Rules and regulations governing corporate finance, including the Sarbanes-Oxley Act are discussed.

38338 ■ "School Is In for Entrepreneurs: Continuing Education Courses Abound." in *Black Enterprise* **(Vol. 35, October 2004, No. 3)**
Pub: Earl G. Graves Publishing Co. Inc.
Ed: Bridget McCrea. **Description:** A growing number of small business owners are taking courses to help them better manage company growth, employees, financial operations, and other key issues.

38339 ■ "Score Savvy: Business Credit Scores are on the Horizon" in *Entrepreneur* **(Vol. 31, Oct. 2003)**
Pub: Entrepreneur Media, Inc.
Ed: Joanne Cleaver. **Description:** Lenders will begin using credit scores, similar to those assigned to most consumers, by summer 2004, making the loan process difficult for businesses with complicated credit histories.

38340 ■ "SEC Acts to Curb Cash Flow Shenanigans" in *Inc.* **(Volume 27, June 2005, No. 6, pp. 26)**
Pub: Inc. Magazine
Description: According to a new study by Georgia Tech's business school cash flow statements need to be scrutinized. Companies regularly wrongly categorize money due from venders, such as members of their distribution network.

38341 ■ "Second Act" in *Entrepreneur* **(Vol. 32, December 2004, No. 12, pp. 42)**
Pub: Entrepreneur Media Inc.
Ed: Jill Amadio. **Description:** Certified Pre-Owned vehicles can save small businesses money. Most of these vehicles carry a warranty.

38342 ■ "SEC's Harness Might Help Hedge Funds More Than it Hurts" in *St. Louis Post-Dispatch* **(October 31, 2004)**
Pub: Knight-Ridder/Tribune Business News
Ed: David Nicklaus. **Description:** According to some experts, the competition among hedge funds has decreased their profitability.

38343 ■ "Seeing Green" in *Entrepreneur* **(Vol. 33, September 2005, No. 9, pp. 56)**
Pub: Entrepreneur Media Inc.
Ed: Dian Vujovich. **Description:** Sixty-eight percent of the Forward/Emerald Banking and Finance Fund (HSSAX) is invested in community banks.

38344 ■ "Severed Ties" in *Entrepreneur* **(Vol. 33, October 2005, No. 10, pp. 30)**
Pub: Entrepreneur Media Inc.
Ed: Crystal Detamore-Rodman. **Description:** New laws aimed at reforming the bankruptcy system will slow the growth of new companies as well expansion of existing companies.

38345 ■ "ShareBuilder by Netstock" in *Black Enterprise* **(Vol. 33, No. 7, February 2003, pp. 6)**
Pub: Earl Graves Publishing Co.
Description: ShareBuilder and blackenterprise.com offer investors ways to invest for the long-term. Through this site individuals can set up an account, build a portfolio, choose desired stocks, investment schedule, all with no account or investment minimums.

38346 ■ "Shifting Fortunes" in *Black Enterprise* **(Vol. 35, October 2004, No. 3, pp. 114)**
Pub: Earl G. Graves Publishing Co. Inc.
Ed: Donald Jay Korn. **Description:** Ninety mutual funds to consider are presented; domestic equity funds were up about 1.4 percent on average, taxable bond funds lost more principle than they paid out in interest, and only a few subcategories of funds lost.

38347 ■ "Shopping for Investment Advice" in *Ingram's* **(Vol. 29, No. 7, July 2003, pp. 42)**
Pub: Show Me Publishing, Inc.
Description: Adam Bold began The Mutual Fund Store offering fee-based investment advice to small investors with a minimum of $50,000.

38348 ■ "Shopping for Value" in *Forbes* (Vol. 175, January 31, 2005, No. 2, pp. 110)
Pub: Forbes Magazine Inc.
Ed: Fei Mei Chan. **Description:** The Investment Company Institute reports the costs of owning stock funds have steadily decreased over the last 20 years. Average overhead expenses for ten domestic funds have fallen from 89 cents per $100 in assets to 83 cents.

38349 ■ *Six SIGMA for Small Business*
Pub: Entrepreneur Press
Ed: Greg Brue. **Released:** October 2005. **Price:** $19.95 (US), $26.95 (Canadian). **Description:** Jack Welch's Six SIGMA approach to business covers accounting, finance, sales and marketing, buying a business, human resource development, and new product development.

38350 ■ *The Small Business Bible: Everything You Need to Know to Succeed in Your Small Business*
Pub: John Wiley & Sons, Incorporated
Ed: Steven D. Strauss. **Released:** December 2004. **Price:** $19.95 (US), $28.99 (Canadian). **Description:** Comprehensive guide to starting and running a successful small business. Topics include bookkeeping and financial management, marketing, publicity, and advertising.

38351 ■ *Small Business Cash Flow: Strategies for Making Your Business a Financial Success*
Pub: John Wiley & Sons, Incorporated
Ed: Denise O'Berry. **Released:** October 2006. **Price:** $19.95. **Description:** Tips to help small businesses manage money are given.

38352 ■ *Small Business Clustering Technology: Applications in Marketing, Management, Finance, and IT*
Pub: Idea Group Publishing
Ed: Robert C. MacGregor; Ann Hodgkinson. **Released:** June 2006. **Description:** An overview of the development and role of small business clusters in disciplines that include economics, marketing, management and information systems.

38353 ■ *Small Business Desk Reference*
Pub: Penguin Books (USA) Incorporated
Ed: Gene Marks. **Released:** December 2004. **Price:** $29.95 (US), $44.00 (Canadian). **Description:** Comprehensive guide for starting or running a successful small business, focusing on buying a business or franchise, writing a business plan, financial management, accounting, legal issues, human resources management, operations, marketing, sales, customer service, taxes, insurance, and ethics. Information for launching a restaurant, property management firm, retail outlet, consulting firm, and service business is included.

38354 ■ *Small Business Finance*
Pub: Prentice Hall
Ed: Phillip J. Adelman and Alan M. Marks. **Released:** 1997. **Price:** $36.00; $27.00; $37.60.

38355 ■ *Small Business Financing: How & Where to Get It*
Pub: CCH Inc.
Ed: Alice H. Magos, SmallOffice Home Office Editorial Group Staff; illustrated by Tim Kaage, introduction by Martin Bush. **Released:** 1998. **Price:** $17.95.

38356 ■ *Small Business Insiders Guide to Bankers*
Pub: PSI Research
Ed: Suzanne Caplan and Thomas M. Nunnally. **Released:** 1997. **Price:** $18.95.

38357 ■ *The Small Business Money Guide: How to Get It, Use It, Keep It*
Pub: John Wiley & Sons, Inc.
Ed: Terri Lonier and Lisa M. Aldisert. **Released:** 1998. **Price:** $16.95.

38358 ■ *The Small Business Savings Plan: 101 Tactics for Controlling Costs and Boosting the Bottom Line*
Pub: Kaplan Books
Ed: Timothy R. Gase. **Released:** May 2007. **Price:** $28.00. **Description:** Strategies for small business owners to develop a savings plan and increase profits are outlined.

38359 ■ *The Small Business Valuation Book*
Pub: Adams Media Corp.
Ed: Lawrence W. Tuller. **Released:** 1998. **Price:** $9.95.

38360 ■ "Small Caps, Big Value" in *Black Enterprise* (Vol. 35, November 2004, No. 4, pp. 40)
Pub: Earl G. Graves Publishing Co. Inc.
Ed: James A. Anderson. **Description:** Profile of Henry O. Jackson, minority owner of Banneker Capital Management. The firm invests in small and mid-cap growth companies with a stock market value between $100 million and $4 billion.

38361 ■ "Small Caps Gain Affection" in *Black Enterprise* (Vol. 31, No. 5, December 2000, pp. 48)
Pub: Earl Graves Publishing Co.
Ed: Tanisha Ann Sykes. **Description:** In this topsy-turvy stock market, investors are warming up to small-cap plays and that's a cozy proposition for fund managers who specialize in such sectors.

38362 ■ *Small Firm Finance: An Entrepreneurial Analysis*
Pub: Dryden Press
Ed: Jerome S. Osteryoung, Derek L. Newman and Leslie G. Davies. **Released:** 1997. **Price:** $61.50; $40.50.

38363 ■ "So What's Your Story?" in *Forbes* (October 30, 2000, pp. 274)
Pub: Forbes Magazine
Ed: Brett Nelson. **Description:** How coverage or lack of coverage by investment banks and analysts affects a company's finances is explored.

38364 ■ "The Social Cost of Fraud and Bankruptcy" in *Harvard Business Review* (Vol. 81, No. 12, December 2003, pp. 20)
Pub: Harvard Business School Press
Ed: Joseph Bower, Stuart Gilson. **Description:** The unfair advantage Chapter 11 bankruptcy law provides to companies that have operated outside the legally sanctioned business practices to which other firms have subscribed is addressed. Discussions focus on how firms obeying the laws are penalized, using the WorldCom Inc. case as an example.

38365 ■ "Soft Landing Strategy" in *Forbes* (December 25, 2000, pp. 300)
Pub: Forbes Magazine
Ed: Robert S. Salomon. **Description:** This is clearly a better time to invest than was the case a year ago. A plan for investing in an economic slow down is discussed.

38366 ■ "Speaking volumes on the dollar" in *WorkingWoman* (Vol. 25, No. 2, February 2000, pp. S19)
Pub: Lang Communications Inc.
Ed: Dana Asher. **Description:** Book reviews of various financial books of interest to women in business.

38367 ■ "The Spirit of Independence" in *Home Office Computing* (Vol. 18, No. 7, July 2000, pp. 42)
Pub: Scholastic Inc.
Ed: Dave Johnson. **Description:** An annotated list of 76 home-office Web site-based resources is presented. Categories include the following: Application Service Providers (ASP), finding clients, your business, your business plans, communications, education, finance/banking, finance/taxes, government, home networking, home office, Internet, legal, marketing, mobile, online storage, online support, reference library, shipping, shopping, telecommuting, tools, travel, and bookmarks.

38368 ■ "Spitzer's Stand" in *Entrepreneur* (Vol. 33, September 2005, No. 9, pp. 64)
Pub: Entrepreneur Media Inc.
Ed: Jacquelyn Lynn. **Description:** Eliot Spitzer, New York state attorney general, recommends employers in all states to scrutinize 401(k) plan providers to ensure employees are not being overcharged for benefits, otherwise they may face legal action.

38369 ■ "Spotlight On" in *Crain's Detroit Business* (Vol. 21, October 24, 2005, No. 43, pp. 16)
Pub: Crain Communications Inc. - Detroit
Description: A listing of Munder Capital Management's assets from 1995 through 2004 is presented.

38370 ■ *Start up Financing: An Entrepreneur's Guide to Financing a New or Growing Business*
Pub: Career Press, Inc.
Ed: William J. Stolze. **Released:** 1997. **Price:** $16.99.

38371 ■ "State Budget Panel's Report Due this Week" in *Crain's Detroit Business* (Vol. 23, January 29, 2007, No. 5, pp. 6)
Pub: Crain Communications Inc. - Detroit
Ed: Amy Lane. **Description:** Advisory panel to issue recommendations to Governor for a way forward plan to address the chronic budget shortfalls and gloomy outlook; two ex-Michigan governors lead the panel.

38372 ■ "Stay Out of Foreclosure: Here's What to Do If You Miss a Mortgage Payment" in *Black Enterprise* (Vol. 35, February 2005, No. 7)
Pub: Earl G. Graves Publishing Co. Inc.
Ed: Naeemah Khabir. **Description:** Tips to help homeowners avoid foreclosure on a home mortgage are outlined, stressing the importance of savings.

38373 ■ "Staying Afloat" in *Black Enterprise* (Vol. 30, No. 10, May 2000, pp. 50)
Pub: Earl Graves Publishing Co.
Ed: Lori Rohlk Pfeiffer. **Description:** Strategies for surviving a cash flow crisis.

38374 ■ *Step-by-Step Bookkeeping: The Complete Handbook for the Small Business*
Pub: Sterling Publishing Co., Inc.
Ed: Robert C. Ragan. **Released:** Revised edition, 1992. **Price:** $7.95 (paper). **Description:** Guide to financial management for small businesses. Provides information on keeping accounts-receivable and -payable records, producing and analyzing profit-and-loss statements, and preparing monthly financial statements.

38375 ■ "Stewart & Stevenson Treads Through Tough Times" in *Houston Business Journal* (Vol. 34, No. 19, September 19, 2003, pp. 2A)
Pub: American City Business Journals
Ed: Jim Greer. **Description:** Stewart & Stevenson Services Inc., has announced the resignation of its president and CEO Michael Grimes; the truck maker has been plagued by financial problems.

38376 ■ "Stick with the Trends" in *Black Enterprise* (Vol. 36, February 2006, No. 7, pp. 48)
Pub: Earl G. Graves Publishing Co. Inc.
Ed: Nicole Lewis. **Description:** Ralph Mitchell, portfolio manager for Carthage Financial Group, recommends investing in companies that will most likely benefit from recent world events.

38377 ■ "Stock Options" in *Business Week* (December 19, 2005, No. 3964, pp. 34, 36)
Pub: McGraw-Hill Companies
Ed: Jane Sasseen. **Description:** Companies are finding new ways to lower options costs, despite stricter rules. Statistical data included.

38378 ■ "Stock uncertainty treats state better than nation as a whole" in *Crain's Detroit Business* (Vol. 19, No. 1, January 6, 2003, pp. 4)
Pub: Crain Communications Inc., Detroit

Ed: Katie Merx. **Description:** The four key reasons why Michigan stocks fared better than the Standard & Poors 500 are listed. Experts project that the state will finish 2003 flat or slightly up.

38379 ■ "A storm offshore" in *Crain's Detroit Business* (Vol. 19, No. 5, Feb. 3, 2003, pp. 11)
Pub: Crain Communications Inc., Detroit
Ed: Katie Merx. **Description:** The Internal Revenue Service will be scrutinizing offshore investments made by small businesses.

38380 ■ "Strategic Mission" in *Black Enterprise* (Vol. 31, No. 5, December 2000, pp. 54)
Pub: Earl Graves Publishing Co.
Ed: Christine Albano. **Description:** Military veteran navigates a financially sound retirement game plan.

38381 ■ "Strategy for a Weak Market" in *Forbes* (Vol. 175, January 31, 2005, No. 2, pp. 144)
Pub: Forbes Magazine Inc.
Ed: David Dreman. **Description:** Higher inflation rates are likely to slow the market in 2005. Experts predict only a 5 percent gain for the year. Stock picks are highlighted.

38382 ■ *Streetwise Finance and Accounting for Entrepreneurs: Set Budgets, Manage Costs, Keep Your Business Profitable*
Pub: Adams Media Corporation
Ed: Suzanne Caplan. **Released:** November 2006. **Price:** $25.95. **Description:** Book offers a basic understanding of accounting and finance for small businesses, including financial statements, credits and debits, as well as establishing a budget. Strategies for small companies in financial distress are included.

38383 ■ "Strike a Balance" in *Entrepreneur.com* (Vol. 34, February 2006, No. 2, pp. 50)
Pub: Entrepreneur Media Inc.
Ed: Dian Vujovich. **Description:** Fidelity's Balanced Fund has ranked eighth out of 629 balanced funds in 2005 and earned a five-star overall rating from Morningstar based on its three-, five- and 10-year performance records.

38384 ■ "Student Teachers" in *Inc.* (November 2006, pp. 44,46)
Pub: Gruner & Jahr USA Publishing
Ed: Max Chafkin. **Description:** Hiring college undergraduates give fresh eyes approach at low investment. Many universities have programs that work with smaller local businesses as part of their hands on education programs. Large savings can accumulate without the cost of expensive consultant fees.

38385 ■ "Study" in *Portland Press Herald* (May 18, 2005)
Pub: Blethen Maine Newspapers, Inc.
Ed: Edward D. Murphy. **Description:** According to a recent study performed by CFED, a non-profit economic research organization, citizens of the state of Maine are more financially secure than those in other states. The state ranked in the top 10 of 21 and of 31 measures that included household net worth and savings, home ownership, business ownership, education, and healthcare coverage.

38386 ■ "Success Off the Shelf" in *Hispanic Business* (October 2003, pp. 88)
Pub: Hispanic Business
Ed: Joel Russell. **Description:** Two Hispanic authors share expertise on branding and on managing money.

38387 ■ "Survey finds optimism up at businesses" in *Pittsburgh Business Times* (Vol. 22, No. 46, May 30, 2003, pp. 3)
Pub: Pittsburgh Business Times
Ed: Kent Bernhard, Jr. **Description:** The results of a business survey of small businesses in the Pittsburgh, Pennsylvania area is presented, including economic conditions, capital investment planning, and economic forecasts.

38388 ■ "Survey Finds Workers Confident of Living Comfortable Retirement" in *Baltimore Sun* (April 11, 2003)
Pub: Knight-Ridder/Tribune Business News
Ed: Eileen Ambrose. **Description:** The majority of employees feel optimistic about retirement, according to the 13th Annual Retirement Confidence Survey, conducted in January 2003, for the Employee Benefit Research Institute and its affiliate, the American Savings Education Council.

38389 ■ "Switch Gears: Flexibility is Key Feature of Convertible Funds" in *Entrepreneur* (Vol. 32, November 2004, No. 11, pp. 69)
Pub: Entrepreneur Media Inc.
Ed: Dian Vujovich. **Description:** Convertible securities are bonds or preferred stocks in which the holder has the option to convert either form into the underlying common stock. Convertibles are a conservative way for an investor to play the market.

38390 ■ "The Switch from a SEP-IRA" in *Business Week Online* (Dec. 24, 2002)
Pub: McGraw-Hill Inc.
Ed: Karen E. Klein. **Description:** Information is offered regarding the Economic Growth & Tax Relief Reconciliation Act of 2001, the tax relief bill signed by President Bush that makes changes in the estate-tax rates and amended pension-plan rules. The Act allows a rollover of a subchapter S company's SEP-IRA funds into a 401(k) and also allows for borrowing against the account.

38391 ■ "Synthetic funds draw scrutiny from regulators" in *Crain's Detroit Business* (Vol. 16, No. 46, November 13, 2000, pp. 22)
Pub: Crain Communications, Inc.
Ed: David Hoffman. **Description:** An Ann Arbor, Michigan-based mutual fund Web site has developed a twist on a novel investment that critics claim skirts federal regulations.

38392 ■ "The T. Rowe Small-Cap Gauge" in *Forbes* (Vol. 175, January 31, 2005, No. 2, pp. 102)
Pub: Forbes Magazine Inc.
Ed: Ira Carnahan. **Description:** The relative multiple of small to large cap companies is plotted on an inverted scale to help investors decide when to purchase certain stocks.

38393 ■ "Take It to the Bank" in *Washington Business Journal* (Vol. 22, No. 15, August 15, 2003, pp. 3)
Pub: Washington Business Journal
Ed: Tim Mazzucca. **Description:** Profile of Washington's newest bank, Congressional Bank, examining management goals and plans, including long term planning, market development, and management styles.

38394 ■ "Take Me To Your Leaders: A New Research Tool Helps You Find Leading Mutual Funds" in *Entrepreneur* (Vol. 31, No. 9, September 2003)
Pub: Entrepreneur Media, Inc.
Ed: Dian Vujovich. **Description:** Morningstar's Mutual Fund Reports and Lipper Leaders are two research tools to help find mutual funds for investing.

38395 ■ "Take a vacation" in *Women in Business* (Vol. 54, No. 2, March-April 2002, pp. 20)
Pub: The ABWA Co Inc.
Description: Personal investments should be planned; appropriate changes in an investment plan can be developed with the assistance of an investment counselor.

38396 ■ "Taking the mystery out of investor behavior" in *Harvard Business Review* (Vol. 80, No. 9, September 2002, pp. 68)
Pub: Harvard Business School Press
Ed: Kevin P. Coyne, Jonathan W. Witter. **Description:** Advice is offered to companies for understanding the investors most important to a firm.

38397 ■ "Taking Care of Business: Downloadable Programs For Your Enterprise" in *Black Enterprise* (Vol. 34, July 2004, No. 12, pp. 145)
Pub: Earl G. Graves Publishing Co. Inc.
Ed: Jennifer L. Smith. **Description:** Websites offering free, downloadable small business software are presented. Everything from accounting, computer security, as well as investment programs is available from these sites.

38398 ■ *Taking Money Out of Your Corporation: Perfectly Legal Methods to Maximize Your Income*
Pub: John Wiley & Sons, Inc.
Ed: M. John Storey. **Released:** 1993. **Price:** $75.00 cloth; $17.95 (paper). **Description:** Describes how to achieve more net compensation.

38399 ■ "Taking Stock" in *Fast Company* (May 2001, pp. 44)
Pub: Fast Company
Ed: Polly LaBarre. **Description:** The volatility of technology stocks is discussed, and information regarding the tech sector is covered.

38400 ■ "Taking stock" in *Harvard Business Review* (Vol. 81, No. 1, January 2003, pp. 19)
Pub: Harvard Business School Press
Ed: Roger L. Martin. **Description:** The Dean of Rotman School of Management at the University of Toronto disputes the theory that managers should be compensated with company stock or options; he suggests bonuses based on real earnings growth.

38401 ■ "Tastes great? Less taxing?" in *Barron's* (Vol. 82, No. 57, February 10, 2003, pp. T4)
Pub: Barron's
Ed: Randall W. Forsyth, Theresa W. Carey, Kathy Yakal. **Description:** Reviews of tax preparation software, including Intuit Turbo Tax Premier, TaxCut Platinum, and TaxACT Online.

38402 ■ "Tax relief leads boomers to planned giving" in *Crain's Detroit Business* (Vol. 16, No. 48, November 27, 2000, pp. 13)
Pub: Crain Communications, Inc.
Ed: Jeffrey Kosseff. **Description:** As baby boomers retire and investors reap the rewards of the strong stock market, estate planning has become more important than ever. Estate planning and tax breaks are covered.

38403 ■ "Taxes on Roth IRAs" in *Black Enterprise* (Vol. 34, No. 7, February 2004, pp. 42)
Pub: Earl Graves Publishing Co.
Ed: Matthew S. Scott. **Description:** Things to consider before converting a traditional IRA to a Roth IRA are discussed.

38404 ■ "Technology still troubles investors" in *BlackEnterprise* (Vol. 32, No. 2, September 2001, pp. 36)
Pub: Earl Graves Publishing Co.
Ed: Marie Evan. **Description:** An overview of investment recommendations made by Stephen Coleman, portfolio manager and chief investment officer for St. Louis-based Daedalus Capital.

38405 ■ "Technology Stocks Show Some Life" in *Black Enterprise* (Vol. 35, January 2005, No. 6, pp. 36)
Pub: Earl G. Graves Publishing Co. Inc.
Ed: Nicole Lewis. **Description:** An overview of technology stocks is given. The technology sector was expected to show strong growth in 2004, but so far it has shown small returns.

38406 ■ "10 ways to improve small business cash flow" in *Journal of Accountancy* (Vol. 189, No. 3, March 2000, pp. 14)
Pub: Harborside Financial Center
Description: Cash flow is the lifeblood of any small business. A healthy stream is essential if a business is to succeed. In general, the key is to accelerate the flow of money coming in and delay what goes out. Ten tips a business can use to improve cash flow are given.

38407 ■ *Ten Keys to Sales & Financial Success for Small Business*
Pub: Wave Communications, Inc.
Ed: Ron Torrence. **Released:** 1994.

38408 ■ "This Is a Test" in *Entrepreneur* (Vol. 32, December 2004, No. 12, pp. 97)
Pub: Entrepreneur Media Inc.
Ed: Mark Henricks. **Description:** According to the Small Business Administration, return on investment (ROI) is the single most important measure of a company's financial status. ROI reveals overall profitability, and is calculated by dividing net profit by total assets, and can be easily misinterpreted.

38409 ■ *Thomson Bank Directory*
Pub: Accuity
Contact: Marideth Johnson
E-mail: marideth.johnson@tfp.com
Released: Semiannual, June and December. **Covers:** in three volumes, about 11,000 banks and 50,000 branches of United States banks, and 60,000 foreign banks and branches engaged in foreign banking; Federal Reserve system and other United States government and state government banking agencies; 500 largest North American and International commercial banks; paper and automated clearinghouses. Volumes 1 and 2 contain North American listings; volumes 3 and 4, international listings (also cited as 'M Thomson International Bank Directory'); volume 5, Worldwide Correspondents Guide containing key correspondent data to facilitate funds transfer. **Entries Include:** For domestic banks—Bank name, address, phone, telex, cable, date established, routing number, charter type, bank holding company affiliation, memberships in Federal Reserve System and other banking organizations, principal officers by function performed, principal correspondent banks, and key financial data (deposits, etc.). For international banks—Bank name, address, phone, fax, telex, cable, SWIFT address, transit or sort codes within home country, ownership, financial data, names and titles of key personnel, branch locations. For branches—Bank name, address, phone, charter type, ownership and other details comparable to domestic bank listings. **Arrangement:** Geographical. **Indexes:** Alphabetical, geographical.

38410 ■ *Thomson North American Financial Institutions Directory*
Pub: Accuity
Contact: Marideth Johnson
E-mail: marideth.johnson@tfp.com
Released: Semiannual, January and July. **Price:** $495, individuals. **Covers:** 15,000 banks and their branches; over 2,000 head offices, and 15,500 branches of savings and loan associations; over 5,500 credit unions with assets over $5 million; Federal Reserve System and other U.S. government and state government banking agencies; bank holding, commercial finance, and leasing companies; ocverage includes the United States, Canada, Mexico, and Central America. **Entries Include:** Bank name, address, phone, fax, telex, principal officers and directors, date established, financial data, association memberships, attorney or counsel, correspondent banks, out-of-town branch, holding company affiliation, ABA transit number and routing symbol, MICR number with check digit, credit card(s) issued, trust powers, current par value and dividend of common stock, kind of charter. **Arrangement:** Geographical. **Indexes:** Alphabetical.

38411 ■ "A thousand bottles of beer on the wall" in *Washington Business Journal* (Vol. 22, No. 3, May 23, 2003, pp. 31)
Pub: Washington Business Journal
Ed: Sean Madigan. **Description:** Profile of the management of a Washington, DC area tavern called the Brickskeller. Topics include management styles, product lines, and financial management.

38412 ■ "Three Cheers for Bankruptcy" in *Fortune* (Vol. 152, October 17, 2005, No. 8, pp. 33)
Pub: Time Inc.
Ed: Justin Fox, Kate Bonamici. **Description:** New bankruptcy laws taking effect October 17, 2005 will make it harder for individuals and corporations to file Chapter 11.

38413 ■ "Time For a Checkup" in *Sales and Marketing.com* (Vol. 156, No. 3, March 2004, pp. 68)
Pub: VNU eMedia, Inc.
Ed: Marc S. Daner. **Description:** Executives should have a financial plan prepared every three years, and every other year within ten years of retirement. A financial planner can assist in planning long and short-term goals.

38414 ■ "A Time to Sell?" in *Black Enterprise* (Vol. 35, September 2004, No. 2, pp. 95)
Pub: Earl G. Graves Publishing Co. Inc.
Ed: Sakina P. Spruell. **Description:** Two reasons for selling a stock include the move to achieve desired asset allocation or because of deterioration of a company's fundamentals. Strategies for successful investing are examined.

38415 ■ "Tips for cutting costs" in *Crain's Detroit Business* (Vol. 18, No. 32, August 12, 2002, pp. 12)
Pub: Crain Communications Inc., Detroit
Description: The Small Business Administration offers advice to small businesses for cutting business expenses, including inventory, payments, overhead, management compensation, equipment costs, expansion, joint ventures, risk management, and the use of buying groups.

38416 ■ "Todd Brown" in *Black Enterprise* (Vol. 34, No. 5, December 2003, pp. 68)
Pub: Earl Graves Publishing Co.
Description: Profile of Todd Brown, vice chairman of ShoreBank Corporation and chairman of the board of directors for the company's banking operations in Chicago, Illinois and Detroit, Michigan.

38417 ■ "Too Much Information?" in *Black Enterprise* (Vol. 37, December 2006, No. 5, pp. 59)
Pub: Earl G. Graves Publishing Co. Inc.
Ed: James C. Johnson. **Description:** African American business owners often face the dilemma of whether or not to divulge their minority status when soliciting new customers and financial institutions. The quality of the products or services is always the key factor and race should never define one's business; however, it is appropriate to market oneself as a minority or women-owned business, especially if the company is in an industry where those clients are offered top-tier contracts.

38418 ■ "Top Area Stock Brokerage Firms" in *Ingram's* (Vol. 29, No. 1, January 2003, pp. 27)
Pub: Show Me Publishing, Inc.
Description: Edward Jones and Company, UBS Paine Webber Inc., and A.G. Edwards and Sons Inc., are among the Kansas City, Missouri area's top registered stock brokerage firms.

38419 ■ "Top Cop" in *Forbes* (Vol. 175, January 10, 2005, No. 1, pp. 154)
Pub: Forbes Magazine Inc.
Ed: Victoria Murphy. **Description:** Profile of security software and services provided by Symantec and Thompson. Symantec's stock is up fivefold in the past five years, making it a good investment. Thompson buys new technology to keep pace with computer hackers.

38420 ■ "Top-drawer advice: new software tells you how much your charitable contributions are worth" in *Barron's* (Vol.82, Feb.17, 2003, pp.T7)
Pub: Barron's
Ed: Randall W. Forsyth, Theresa W. Carey. **Description:** Two programs that help value donations of used clothing and other goods and work well, include H & R Block Deduction Pro and Income Dynamics ItsDeductible tax preparation software.

38421 ■ "Top Drawer" in *Forbes* (Vol. 174, December 27, 2004, No. 13, pp. 156)
Pub: Forbes Magazine Inc.
Ed: Christopher Helman. **Description:** Profile of Jim Halperin, a leading rare coin dealer in the U.S. Halperin is the co-owner of Heritage Galleries & Auctioneer in Dallas, a rare coin auction house in Dallas, Texas.

38422 ■ "Tougher Test for Bankruptcy" in *Black Enterprise* (Vol. 36, November 2005, No. 4, pp. 56)
Pub: Earl G. Graves Publishing Co. Inc.
Ed: Melissa S. Monroe. **Description:** The new Bankruptcy Abuse Prevention and Consumer Protection Act of 2005 was made law October 17, 2005. The Act forces many who intended to file for Chapter 7 bankruptcy to file for Chapter 13 bankruptcy instead, and commit to a payment plan.

38423 ■ "Towns, Counties Grow With Interest" in *The Record* (November 5, 2005)
Pub: New Jersey Media Group
Ed: Scott Fallon. **Description:** Consumers are enjoying higher earnings on investments ranging from traditional savings accounts to high-end money market investments with the Federal Reserve's recent hikes in interest rates.

38424 ■ "Trading Takes a Breather" in *Red Herring* (No. 105, October 1, 2001, pp. 30)
Pub: Herring Communications
Ed: Elizabeth Lamb. **Description:** The volume of daily stock trading executed online during the second and third quarters has fallen, with about 5 percent of the 1.2 billion shares traded on the New York Stock Exchange (NYSE) being transacted through its wireless trading system. Statistical data included.

38425 ■ "Traditional VS. Roth IRA" in *Black Enterprise* (Vol. 37, October 2006, No. 3, pp. 58)
Pub: Earl G. Graves Publishing Co. Inc.
Ed: K. Parker; Carolyn M. Brown. **Description:** Government taxes the traditional IRAs different than it taxes Roth IRAs.

38426 ■ "Transitions" in *Inc.* (Volume 28, January 2006, No. 1, pp. 27)
Pub: Inc. Magazine
Description: Three key institutions, the Federal Reserve Board, the National Federation of Independent Business, and the Congressional Budget Office are changing leaders in 2006.

38427 ■ "Turning Market Pain Into Prosperity" in *Black Enterprise* (Vol. 34, No. 3, October 2003, pp. 32)
Pub: Earl Graves Publishing Co.
Ed: Matthew S. Scott. **Description:** Louis A. Holland, managing partner and CIO of Holland Capital Management LP, believes that markets tend to experience three phases: love, hate, and indifference. He predicts the market has passed the hate stage and could have a little more volatility to go through.

38428 ■ *203 Home-Based Businesses That Will Make You Rich*
Pub: Prima Publishing
Ed: Tyler G. Hicks. **Released:** 1998. **Price:** $14.95.

38429 ■ *Understanding Business Valuation: A Practical Guide to Valuing Small to Medium-Sized Businesses*
Pub: American Institute of Certified Public Accountants
Ed: Gary R. Trugman. **Released:** 1998. **Price:** $99.00.

38430 ■ *Understanding Financial Statements*
Pub: Crisp Publications, Inc.
Ed: James O. Gill. **Price:** $12.95.

38431 ■ *Understanding and Managing Financial Information: The Non-financial Manager's Guide*
Pub: Self-Counsel Press, Inc.

Ed: Michael M. Coltman. **Released:** 1993. **Price:** $9.95 (paper).

38432 ■ "The Unlevel Playing Field: At Some Mutual Funds, Big Investors Got Big Breaks" in *Barron's* (September 8, 2003, pp. F2)
Pub: Barron's
Ed: Erin E. Arvedlund. **Description:** An investigation by New York State attorney general Eliot Spitzer has revealed that, for a long time, mutual funds have rewarded larger investors disproportionately at the expense of smaller ones. The long-term effects on the sector from investor backlash are considered.

38433 ■ "Use the index: The scoop on fully tradable ETFs" in *Entrepreneur* (Vol. 30, No. 2, February 2002, pp. 54)
Pub: Entrepreneur Media Inc.
Ed: Dian Vujovich. **Description:** Profile of exchange traded funds (ETFs), a combination of both index mutual funds and individual stocks, is presented.

38434 ■ "Valley Econowatch" in *San Fernando Valley Business Journal* (Vol. 11, December 2006, No. 25, pp. 25)
Pub: San Fernando Valley Business Journal Associates
Description: Statistical data included for factors affecting the San Fernando Valley's economy, including numbers of bankruptcies, electricity accounts, tourism activity, real estate figures and others.

38435 ■ "Valuable Goods" in *Black Enterprise* (Vol. 31, No. 5, December 2000, pp. 46)
Pub: Earl Graves Publishing Co.
Ed: Tanisha Ann Sykes. **Description:** Union Heritages' Derek Batts picks stocks that offer value with growth.

38436 ■ *Valuing the Closely Held Firm*
Pub: Oxford University Press
Ed: Michael S. Long; Thomas A. Bryant. **Released:** March 2007. **Price:** $65.00. **Description:** The differences between a large and small firm and their ability to generate future cash flow are discussed.

38437 ■ "VC Company to Double One Fund, Add $40M Fund." in *Crain's Detroit Business* (Vol. 23, January 15,2007, No. 3, pp. 26)
Pub: Crain Communications Inc. - Detroit
Ed: Tom Henderson. **Description:** Local Venture Capital firm adds personnel and expands funds to increase business. First fund is doubled to $20M and began raising money for a second fund of $40M.

38438 ■ "Vendors tweak strategies to help clients buy" in *Atlanta Business Chronicle* (Vol. 25, November 15, 2002, No. 23 pp. 3C)
Pub: American City Business Publications, Inc.
Ed: Don Reichardt. **Description:** As companies need to re-engineer costly legacy system, some are seeking less expensive alternatives. Leasing and outsourcing are becoming more popular alternatives. Details on alternatives being offered by vendors are included.

38439 ■ "Venerable Financial Firms to Join" in *Altanta Journal-Constitution* (February 7, 2007)
Pub: Cox Newspapers, Inc.
Ed: Tom Walker. **Description:** Atlanta Life Financial Group acquired Jackson Securities LLC, merging the two largest black-owned enterprises in Atlanta, Georgia.

38440 ■ "Venture Michigan Makes First Investment Commitments" in *Crain's Detroit Business* (Vol. 23, January 29, 2007, No. 5, pp. 17)
Pub: Crain Communications Inc. - Detroit
Ed: Amy Lane. **Description:** First investment commitments to smaller venture capital fund providers is made by state venture group. Investments are in capital funds that support start-up firms with a Michigan presence that engage in new product development, research, and technology in non-manufacturing sectors.

38441 ■ "Virtual Money Chain: Company Changes the Rules of Wire Transfers Through the Internet" in *Black Enterprise* (Vol.34, No.4, Nov. 2003)
Pub: Earl Graves Publishing Co.
Ed: Tamara E. Holmes. **Description:** Profile of the technology firm, iKobo Inc., located in Atlanta, Georgia. The company offers electronic money transfer services and merchant payments, targeting foreign service sector workers and small- to medium-size businesses.

38442 ■ "Vive les funds" in *WorkingWoman* (Vol. 25, No. 8, September 2000, pp. 24)
Pub: Lang Communications Inc.
Ed: Virginia Munger Kahn. **Description:** Advice for investors on opportunities for investing in international stocks is presented. Four suitable funds are described.

38443 ■ "Waive Goodbye" in *Entrepreneur* (Vol. 32, October 2004, No. 10, pp. 60)
Pub: Entrepreneur Media Inc.
Ed: Description: Various mutual fund families are being investigated for questionable practices. Included are Invesco, Janus, Merrill Lynch, and Putnam Investments. Experts advise to check a fund's net asset value (NAV) transfer before purchasing.

38444 ■ "Wall Street wooing wary investors with reforms" in *Atlanta Business Chronicle* (Vol. 25, No. 20, October 25, 2002, pp. 11C)
Pub: American City Business Publications, Inc.
Ed: Lee Hall. **Description:** The larger brokerage houses are revising the way they report on stocks. These houses are feeling the pressure from angry investors and threatened lawsuits and are going out of their way to polish their image.

38445 ■ "WaMu Whiplash: Fast Expansion Yields Problems" in *Wall Street Journal* (Vol. 248, December 2006, No. 142, pp. B1)
Pub: Dow Jones & Co. Inc.
Ed: Ann Carrns **Description:** Despite rapid growth from 2000-2003, Washington Mutual Bank has closed 80 branches and halted entering new markets.

38446 ■ "War Earnings" in *Forbes* (Vol. 175, January 10, 2005, No. 1, pp. 140)
Pub: Forbes Magazine Inc.
Ed: David Serchuk. **Description:** Profile of Perini Corporation, the company rebuilding power stations in Iraq and installing new military bases in Afghanistan. The firm has seen revenues grow 71.2 percent in the last year and average three-year earnings-per-share is up 63.7 percent.

38447 ■ "Watch Out!" in *Entrepreneur* (Vol. 28, No. 11, November 2000, pp. 40)
Pub: Entrepreneur Media Inc.
Ed: Dian Vujovich. **Description:** The complicated and expensive aspect of owning mutual funds is discussed.

38448 ■ "Way to Grow: A Computer Model Picks This Fund's Winners" in *Entrepreneur* (Vol. 32, September 2004, No. 9, pp. 49)
Pub: Entrepreneur Media Inc.
Ed: Dian Vujovich. **Description:** Quantitative funds use computer-driven models to sort through equity funds and create large-cap growth funds, such as the Touchstone Large Cap Growth Fund.

38449 ■ "Wealth on the Go" in *Black Enterprise* (Vol. 34, No. 3, October 2003, pp. 61)
Pub: Earl Graves Publishing Co.
Ed: Nicole Lewis. **Description:** Profile of Chris Galloway, a radiation therapist and real estate investor in Washington, DC; Galloway keeps up to date by using the latest in radiation treatment technology to treat patients with cancer and other diseases.

38450 ■ "West L.A. CPA Firm Opening Valley Office" in *San Fernando Valley Business Journal* (Vol. 11, December 2006, No. 25, pp. 1)
Pub: San Fernando Valley Business Journal Associates

Ed: Shelly Garcia. **Description:** Singer Lewak Greenbaum & Goldstein LLP will open a Warner Center office in hopes of keeping workers in what has become a fiercely competitive employment market and capturing larger ground in the growing financial services market.

38451 ■ "What Eliot Spitzer's Investigations Mean For You" in *Inc.* (May 1, 2005)
Pub: Inc. Magazine
Ed: Stephanie Clifford. **Description:** If a 401(k) provider or insurance company overcharges employees, a small business owner may be held liable. It is recommended that employers check fees, commission structures, and overrides with health care providers carefully.

38452 ■ "What a Long Strange Trip It's Been...Where We Have Been" in *Ingram's* (Vol. 29, No. 1, January 2003, pp. 24)
Pub: Show Me Publishing, Inc.
Ed: John Hanahan. **Description:** The history of the bull market at the start of the 1990s through the early 2000s when it turned into a bull market is explored. One expert suggests that the current market is an opportunity to buy stocks.

38453 ■ "What Rate Hike?" in *Business Week* (No. 3658, December 6, 1999, pp. F9)
Pub: McGraw-Hill, Inc.
Description: How the interest rate affects small business.

38454 ■ "What to do when bad news hits your stocks" in *Women in Business* (Vol. 53, No. 3, May-June, 2001, pp. 20)
Pub: The ABWA Co. Inc.
Description: Investors must not panic when a stock price is affected by bad news. Any decline may be temporary, so investors must try to assess the long-term outlook for the stock. A diversified portfolio also helps minimize risk.

38455 ■ "What To Do When Your Client Declares Bankruptcy" in *Home Business* (Vol. 13, January/February 2006, No. 1, pp. 76)
Pub: Home Business Magazine
Ed: Kurt English, Esq. **Description:** In a slow economy, small and home-based businesses should collect money in advance from clients whenever possible. Legal steps to take when accounts become delinquent are discussed.

38456 ■ "What's New" in *Entrepreneur.com* (Vol. 34, February 2006, No. 2, pp. 104)
Pub: Entrepreneur Media Inc.
Description: The Online Trading Academy helps individuals to buy and sell stocks. The company plans to expand its franchise opportunities to about 100 major cities worldwide.

38457 ■ "What's Your Company Worth Now?" in *Inc.* (July 1, 2003)
Pub: Gruner & Jahr USA Publishing
Description: Information for calculating a small company's value is offered.

38458 ■ "When the Going Gets Tough...many turn to financial counselors" in *Business Week Online* (November 15, 2002)
Pub: McGraw-Hill Inc.
Ed: Sandra Block. **Description:** Small business owners often turn to financial counselors for advice on careers, family and security. Nearly 60 percent of all people will consult a financial adviser after a major catastrophe or change in their lives. Since the terrorist attacks of 911, many professionals are seeking ways to leave the corporate life behind, while others are facing changes due to the recession.

38459 ■ "When to Roll Over" in *Black Enterprise* (Vol. 37, November 2006, No. 4, pp. 50)
Pub: Earl G. Graves Publishing Co. Inc.
Ed: Carolyn M. Brown. **Description:** Being proactive and rolling over your funds if you own stock of your former employee will give you more control over your money, especially if the company merges or is sold.

38460 ■ "Where Are the 529 Plans?" in *Black Enterprise* (Vol. 34, No. 5, December 2003, pp. 40)
Pub: Earl Graves Publishing Co.
Ed: Matthew S. Scott. **Description:** Information about the 529 state-sponsored college savings plan, giving individuals the ability to invest money in a pre-selected portfolio of stocks and bonds for future education expenses.

38461 ■ "Where Do You Go From Here" in *Black Enterprise* (Vol. 31, No. 5, December 2000, pp. 87)
Pub: Earl Graves Publishing Co.
Ed: Carolyn M. Brown. **Description:** The Black Wealth Initiative is used to review financial goals and adjust strategy to ensure a brighter future.

38462 ■ *Where to Get the Money & Management Help for New Business Start-Ups & Small Business Growth: East-North Central Region, IL, IN, MI, OH, WI*
Pub: Special Reports, Inc.
Ed: Richard S. Guyer and Frank J. Domeracki. **Released:** 1998. **Price:** $197.00.

38463 ■ *Where to Get the Money & Management Help for New Business Start-Ups & Small Business Growth: Mountain Region, AZ, CO, ID, MT, NV, NM, UT, WY*
Pub: Special Reports, Inc.
Ed: Richard S. Guyer and Frank J. Domeracki. **Released:** 1998. **Price:** $197.00.

38464 ■ *Where to Get the Money & Management Help for New Business Start-Ups & Small Business Growth: Pacific Region, AK, CA, HI, OR, WA*
Pub: Richard S. Guyer and Frank J. Domeracki
Ed: Richard S. Guyer and Frank J. Domeracki. **Released:** 1998. **Price:** $197.00.

38465 ■ *Where to Get the Money & Management Help for New Business Start-Ups & Small Business Growth: South Atlantic Region, DE, DC, FL, GA, MD, NC, SC, VA, WV*
Pub: Special Reports, Inc.
Ed: Richard S. Guyer and Frank J. Domeracki. **Released:** 1997. **Price:** $197.00.

38466 ■ *Where to Get the Money & Management Help for New Business Start-Ups & Small Business Growth: West-North Central Region, IA, KS, MN, MO, NE, ND, SD*
Pub: Special Reports, Inc.
Ed: Richard S. Guyer and Frank J. Domeracki. **Released:** 1998. **Price:** $197.00.

38467 ■ *Where to Get the Money & Management Help for New Business Start-Ups & Small Growth: West-South Central Region, AR, LA, OK, TX*
Pub: Special Reports, Inc.
Ed: Richard S. Guyer and Frank J. Domeracki. **Released:** 1998. **Price:** $197.00.

38468 ■ "'A Whole New Era' for Once-Ignored Stockholders" in *Daily Business Review* (Vol. 77, No. 198, March 24, 2003, pp. A5)
Pub: American Lawyer Media LP
Description: With the public outcry over the way shareholders' fates were dealt with behind closed doors, shareholders may be having some say at the negotiation table.

38469 ■ "Why S&P Is Standing Pat on HP" in *Business Week* (February 10, 2005)
Pub: McGraw-Hill Companies
Description: Megan Graham-Hackett, a computer-hardware analyst covering Hewlett-Packard Company for Standard & Poor's Equity Research, talked about Carly Fiorina's resignation and what it means to the company's strategy. Graham-Hackett has listed HP stock as a hold, or 3-STARS.

38470 ■ "Will Power: Build Flexibility Into Your Estate Plan so Heirs Can Avoid the Pitfalls of Changing Tax Laws" in *Entrepreneur* (Vol. 32)
Pub: Entrepreneur Media Inc.
Ed: Scott Bernard Nelson. **Description:** Information about the ever-changing death tax law is cited. Currently the federal government allows heirs to inherit $1.5 million of an estate, the amount rises to $2 million in 2006 and $3-5 million in 2009, then disappears entirely for 2010, but reappears in 2011 with a $1 million exemption.

38471 ■ "Wisconsin is Among States With Best Savers" in *Milwaukee Journal Sentinel* (December 13, 2005)
Pub: Journal Sentinel, Inc.
Ed: Avrum D. Lank. **Description:** According to the Nest Egg Index compiled by A.G. Edwards, Wisconsin ranked as the ninth highest state of best savers in the U.S.; Milwaukee came in at 64 out of 200 metropolitan areas.

38472 ■ "Women Business Owners Seek Financing" in *Marketing to Women* (Vol. 19, December 2006, No. 2, pp. 8)
Pub: EPM Communications, Inc.
Description: A study by the Center for Women's Business Research shows that women business owners have become more savvy when seeking financial support for their business ventures. Statistical data included.

38473 ■ "Worth the Drive? Your Company Cars Could Be Gulping More than Just Gas if You Don't Know What Your Ownership Costs Are" in *Entrepreneur*
Pub: Entrepreneur Media Inc.
Ed: Jill Amadio. **Description:** Four major fixed cost factors are involved when determining the cost of owning a company car: depreciation, state fees, financing and insurance.

38474 ■ "Wrestling with the bear" in *Black Enterprise* (Vol. 33, No. 3, Oct. 2002, pp. 46)
Pub: Earl Graves Publishing Co.
Ed: Nicole Halsey. **Description:** An overview of black-owned mutual fund companies is presented, including Ariel, Brown Cap, DEM Equity, Edgar Lomax, Kenwood Growth, Lou Holland Growth, MDL Broad Market, and Profit Value. Statistical data included.

38475 ■ "The Year of the Convertible" in *Forbes* (Vol. 175, February 14, 2005, No. 3, pp. 134)
Pub: Forbes Magazine Inc.
Ed: Richard Lehmann. **Description:** Experts are advising people to invest in convertible preferred stocks in 2005. Convertibles are considered a safe alternative for achieving above-average returns in a growing economy.

38476 ■ "You Can Take It with You: Clubs that Let the Stocks Travel with Individual Owners" in *Black Enterprise* (Vol. 33, Oct. 2002, pp. 43)
Pub: Earl Graves Publishing Co.
Ed: Carolyn M. Brown. **Description:** An overview of traveling investment clubs. These investment clubs allow the members to invest on their own, while enjoying the benefits of being a member of the club. Statistical data included.

38477 ■ "You Must Be Crazy" in *Entrepreneur.com* (Vol. 34, February 2006, No. 2, pp. 18)
Pub: Entrepreneur Media Inc.
Ed: Jennifer Pellet. **Description:** According to researchers from Stanford Graduate School of Business, Carnegie Mellon University, and the University of Iowa, functional psychopaths make better investment decisions.

38478 ■ "You can take it with you: clubs that let the stocks travel with individual owners" in *Black Enterprise* (Vol. 33, Oct. 2002, pp. 43)
Pub: Earl Graves Publishing Co.

Ed: Carolyn M. Brown. **Description:** An overview of traveling investment clubs. These investment clubs allow the members to invest on their own, while enjoying the benefits of being a member of the club. Statistical data included.

38479 ■ "Your Father's Bank" in *Inc.* (September 1, 2004)
Pub: Inc. Magazine
Ed: Ed Welles. **Description:** Citigroup is feeling competition from smaller, traditional community banks such as Burke & Herbert.

38480 ■ "Your Kind of News: Free Personalized Information for the Public" in *Black Enterprise* (Vol. 34, No. 7, February 2004, pp. 140)
Pub: Earl Graves Publishing Co.
Ed: Jennifer L. Smith. **Description:** Profile of a free Website offering articles and press releases from more than 70 major sources on topics relevant to business, including finance and computing.

38481 ■ "Your money: be sure you have access to your cash" in *Atlanta Business Chronicle* (Vol. 25, No. 20, October 25, 2002, pp. 6B)
Pub: American City Business Publications, Inc.
Ed: Dan Kolber. **Description:** Dan Kolber dispenses financial advise for the next twelve months.

TRADE PERIODICALS

38482 ■ *CFO & Controller Alert*
Pub: Progressive Business Publications
Contact: John Hiatt
Ed: John Hiatt, Editor, hiatt@pbp.com. **Released:** Semimonthly. **Price:** $299, individuals. **Description:** Assists busy financial executives to boost cash flow, control expenses, manage resources, and comply with changing regulations. Recurring features include case studies, success stories, financial and tax developments, cost-saving ideas and columns titled Management and Sharpen Your Judgment.

38483 ■ *The COINfidential Report*
Pub: Bale Publications
Ed: Don Bale, Jr., Editor. **Released:** Bimonthly, except July and August. **Price:** $19.95, individuals; $99 lifetime subscription. **Description:** Features coin, stock and bullion market forecasts and analyses, plus inside information and best coin and stock bets. Recurring features include interviews, book reviews, and notices of publications available.

38484 ■ *Deposit Growth Strategies*
Pub: Siefer Consultants Inc.
Ed: Joe Sheller, Editor. **Released:** Monthly. **Price:** $329, U.S.; $259 charter rate. **Description:** Cover methods to increase deposits at financial institutions, as well as marketing strategies for deposit growth. Both personal accounts and commercial accounts are covered.

38485 ■ *Directorship*
Pub: Directorship Search Group Inc.
Released: 11/year. **Price:** $495, U.S.. **Description:** Covers corporate governance issues of interest to directors and CEOs, including legal matters, compensation, shareholders, and board committees and director responsibilities.

38486 ■ *Eternal Value Review: World Report and Market Monitor*
Pub: Mulberry Press Inc.
Contact: Joyce Hahn
Ed: Wilfred J. Hahn, Editor. **Released:** 6/year. **Price:** Free. **Description:** Provides information on the economy and investment markets worldwide with a Christian perspective. Includes topics such as social security and pensions, market trends, and population/age statistics. Recurring features include columns titled World Market Update, Facts/Stats and Ends/Trends, and Editor's Notes.

38487 ■ Executive's Tax and Management Report
Pub: Aspen Publishers Inc.
Ed: Sara Vine, Editor, sara.vine@aspenpublishers. com. **Released:** 2/month. **Price:** $255. **Description:** Supplies information on how to obtain more tax-free cash from a company or business, cut a company's tax bill, increase personal deductions, and deal with new tax crackdowns.

38488 ■ Financial Services Review
Pub: Cadmus Journal Services
Ed: Conrad S. Ciccotello, Editor, cciccotello@gsu. edu. **Released:** Quarterly. **Price:** $75; $100 institutions; $150 institutions, other countries. **Description:** Journal that covers personal finance.

38489 ■ Financial Studies of the Small Business
Pub: Financial Research Associates Inc.
Released: Annual. **Description:** Trade magazine covering financial standards for small businesses.

38490 ■ Journal of Entrepreneurial and Small Firm Finance
Pub: University of California Press
Released: 3/yr. **Description:** Journal that focuses on small business and financial issues.

38491 ■ Journal of Management
Pub: University of California Press
Ed: Daniel Feldman, Editor. **Released:** Bimonthly. **Price:** $165; $441 institutions. **Description:** Scholarly journal.

38492 ■ NACOMEX Insider
Pub: NACOMEX USA Inc.
Contact: Robert Zises
Ed: Robert Zises, Editor, zises@nacomex.com. **Released:** Quarterly. **Price:** $199, U.S.. **Description:** Provides information on historical values, current tactics, and residual value forecasting for ad valorem tax, bankruptcy, loss compensation, and related purposes. Recurring features include news of research and a column titled Industry Round-up.

38493 ■ North American Journal of Economics and Finance
Pub: Elsevier Science B.V.
Contact: Sven W. Arndt, Managing Editor
E-mail: sven.arndt@claremontmckenna.edu
Released: 3/year. **Price:** $99; $427 institutions. **Description:** Scholarly journal sponsored by the North American Economics and Finance Association.

38494 ■ Quarterly Journal of Business & Economics
Pub: University of Nebraska
Contact: Margo Young, Managing Editor
E-mail: myoung1@unl.edu
Ed: George M. McCabe, Editor, gmccabe1@unl.edu. **Released:** Quarterly. **Price:** $24; $45 institutions; $37 out of country; $55 institutions out of country. **Description:** Journal reporting on finance and economics.

VIDEOCASSETTES/
AUDIOCASSETTES

38495 ■ Accounting and Finance for Non-Financial Managers
Center for Video Education
56 Lafayette Ave.
North White Plains, NY 10603
Ph:(914)428-9620
Free: 800-621-0043
Fax: (914)428-0180
Released: 1986. **Description:** This tape shows non-financial executives how to handle and process business finances. **Availability:** VHS; 3/4U.

38496 ■ American Institute of Small Business: Your Personal Financial Guide to Success, Power & Security
American Institute of Small Business (AISB)
7515 Wayzata Blvd., Ste. 126
Minneapolis, MN 55426
Ph:(612)545-7001
Free: 800-328-2906
Fax: (612)545-7020
Co. E-mail: AISBOFMN@AOL.COM
URL: http://www.accessil.com/aisb
Released: 199?. **Price:** $69.95. **Description:** Covers money management, financial planning, budgeting, record keeping, and spending and savings plans. **Availability:** VHS.

38497 ■ Corporate Financial Management: Emerging Trends and Recent Developments
Bisk Education
9417 Princess Palm Ave.
Tampa, FL 33619
Free: 800-874-7877
Co. E-mail: info@bisk.com
URL: http://www.bisk.com
Price: $179.00. **Description:** Discusses financial management techniques and recent developments in corporate finance. Furnishes information on Activity-Based Cost Management (ABC), Total Quality Management (TQM), and Internal Controls and Management Accounting. Includes workbook and quizzer. **Availability:** VHS.

38498 ■ Financial Success Strategies for the 1990s
Cambridge Educational
c/o Films Media Group
PO Box 2053
Princeton, NJ 08843-2053
Free: 800-257-5126
Fax: (609)671-0266
Co. E-mail: custserve@filmsmediagroup.com
URL: http://www.cambridgeol.com
Released: 1992. **Price:** $99.00. **Description:** Best-selling financial author Charles J. Givens gives advice that could save or earn viewers thousands of dollars. **Availability:** VHS.

38499 ■ Money in America
Ambrose Video Publishing, Inc.
145 W. 45th St., Ste. 1115
New York, NY 10036
Ph:(212)768-7373
Free: 800-526-4663
Fax: (212)768-9292
Co. E-mail: customerservice@ambrosevideo.com
URL: http://www.ambrosevideo.com
Released: 1989. **Price:** $795.00. **Description:** A video series which explains everything about banks and banking. **Availability:** VHS.

38500 ■ Reading Financial Reports: The Income Statement
Phoenix Learning Group
2349 Chaffee Dr.
St. Louis, MO 63146
Ph:(314)569-0211
Free: 800-221-1274
Fax: (314)569-2834
URL: http://www.phoenixlearninggroup.com
Released: 1985. **Description:** An explanation of the income statement-how to read it and use it. **Availability:** VHS; 3/4U; Special order formats.

38501 ■ Return on Investment
Video Arts, Inc.
c/o Aim Learning Group
8238-40 Lehigh
Morton Grove, IL 60053-2615
Free: 877-444-2230
Fax: (416)252-2155
Co. E-mail: service@aimlearninggroup.com
URL: http://www.aimlearninggroup.com
Released: 1986. **Price:** $790.00. **Description:** For the business owner, a look at assessing and justifying capital expenditures. **Availability:** VHS; 8mm; 3/4U; Special order formats.

TRADE SHOWS AND
CONVENTIONS

38502 ■ ABA/BMA National Conference for Community Bankers
American Bankers Association
1120 Connecticut Ave. NW
Washington, DC 20036
Free: 800-BAN-KERS
Co. E-mail: custserv@aba.com
URL: http://www.aba.com
Released: Annual. **Audience:** Chairmen and presidents, mainly of banks with less than $500 million in assets, community bank CEOs, bank directors, and other community bank executives. **Principal Exhibits:** Products and services related to investment management, customer service improvements, advertising, asset/liability management, bank management, electronic data interchange, employee recruitment/training, insurance, strategic planning models, including preparation for the 21st century, new revenue sources, cost control techniques, mainframe computers, market research, MCIF technology, minicomputers in community banking applications, software: platform, optical disk, and loan pricing, sweep accounts, and relationship banking for community bankers. **Dates and Locations:** 2007 Feb 18-21.

38503 ■ ABA Sales Management Workshop
American Bankers Association
1120 Connecticut Ave. NW
Washington, DC 20036
Free: 800-BAN-KERS
Co. E-mail: custserv@aba.com
URL: http://www.aba.com
Released: Annual. **Audience:** Senior community bank executives, marketing directors, mid-level bank retail managers, sales managers. **Principal Exhibits:** Services related to creating and maintaining customers.

38504 ■ BMA Annual Marketing Forum
American Bankers Association
1120 Connecticut Ave. NW
Washington, DC 20036
Free: 800-BAN-KERS
Co. E-mail: custserv@aba.com
URL: http://www.aba.com
Released: Annual. **Audience:** Bankers including community bank CEO's, marketing directors, sales managers, advertising directors, public relations managers. **Principal Exhibits:** Financial services marketing offering banking solutions in advertising services, bank equipment/systems, computer software, database marketing, direct marketing/sales, incentive/premium programs, insurance services, investment services, marketing consulting, merchandising, publishing, research, retail delivery, sales training, service quality, signage, and telemarketing.

38505 ■ BMA Private Wealth Sales Management Workshop, an ABA Program
American Bankers Association
1120 Connecticut Ave. NW
Washington, DC 20036
Free: 800-BAN-KERS
Co. E-mail: custserv@aba.com
URL: http://www.aba.com
Released: Annual. **Audience:** Trust, private banking and asset management officers, bank brokerage managers, sales managers, business development managers, and regional department managers. **Principal Exhibits:** Provides marketing education and information, professional growth and networking resources to marketing professionals in the financial services industry.

38506 ■ Financial Managers Society Annual Conference
Financial Managers Society
100 W. Monroe St., Ste. 810
Chicago, IL 60603-1959
Ph:(312)578-1300
Free: 800-ASK-4FMS
Fax: (312)578-1308

URL: http://www.fmsinc.org
Released: Annual. **Audience:** CEO's, CFO's, treasurers, controllers, investment officers, internal auditors of banks, thrift and credit unions. **Principal Exhibits:** Companies offering products/services to CEO's, CFO's, treasurers, controllers, investment officers, and internal auditors of banks, thrifts, and credit unions. **Dates and Locations:** 2007 Jun 24-26; 2008 Jun 08-10, Orlando, FL.

38507 ■ National Agricultural Bankers Conference
American Bankers Association
1120 Connecticut Ave. NW
Washington, DC 20036
Free: 800-BAN-KERS
Co. E-mail: custserv@aba.com
URL: http://www.aba.com
Released: Annual. **Audience:** Bank CEOs, mainly from community banks in rural areas, executive vice presidents, senior vice presidents, economists, analysts. **Principal Exhibits:** The latest developments in the agricultural lending business, as well as strategies for better market share, profitability and customer service.

CONSULTANTS

38508 ■ 2010 Fund 5
24351 Spartan St., Ste. 120
Mission Viejo, CA 92691
Ph:(949)583-1992
Scope: Funds in formation that will invest in technologies licensed from 30 universities. **Seminars:** Chair, Corporate Investment and Strategic Alliance Conferences.

38509 ■ ADG Group
4261 Northside Dr., Ste. 200
Atlanta, GA 30327
Ph:(404)264-9301
Fax: (404)261-3439
Scope: Corporate finance advisory firm specializing in arranging venture capital financing for emerging companies. Assists with mergers, acquisitions, and divestitures. Offers balance sheet restructuring services for bankrupt and financially troubled companies. Also offers independent due diligence investigations.

38510 ■ Aurora Management Partners Inc.
4485 Tench Rd., Ste. 340A
Suwanee, GA 30024
Ph:(770)904-5207
Co. E-mail: rturcotte@auroramp.com
URL: http://www.auroramp.com

E-mail: rturcotte@auroramp.com
Scope: Firm specializes in turnaround management and reorganization consulting. **Publications:** Back From The Brink - Bland Farms; New Breed of Turnaround Managers; Key Performance Drivers - Bland Farms; The Missing Element in Corporate Governance Ratings.

38511 ■ Automated Accounting
13800 Heacock St.
Moreno Valley, CA 92553
Ph:(951)653-5053
Co. E-mail: autoacc@earthlink.net

E-mail: autoacc@earthlink.net
Scope: A business management consulting firm that caters to small businesses. Services include part-time chief, financial officer services. Also offers software installation services, tax preparation services and business plan advisory services.

38512 ■ Beacon Management Group Inc.
1000 W McNab Rd.
Pompano Beach, FL 33069
Ph:(954)782-1119
Free: 800-771-8721
Fax: (954)969-2566
Co. E-mail: md@beaconmgmt.com
URL: http://www.beaconmgmt.com

E-mail: md@beaconmgmt.com
Scope: Provides entrepreneurial companies with managerial and financial expertise. Services include strategic and business planning; corporate finance; franchise development services; information management; turnaround management and consulting; and joint venture, strategic alliances and acquisition services, including due diligence, market intelligence, targeted searches, valuation, negotiation, and deal structure. Provides assistance for financially-troubled companies, not-for-profits and the public sector

38513 ■ Benchmark Consulting Group Inc.
110 Broad St.
Boston, MA 02110-3030
Ph:(617)482-7661
Fax: (617)423-2158
Scope: Provides financial and management services to companies. Helps companies grow through debt and equity sourcing and restructuring, business valuation, acquisition/divestiture, computer information systems, and improved operation profitability.

38514 ■ Samuel E. Bodily
100 Darden Blvd.
Charlottesville, VA 22903
Ph:(434)924-4813
Fax: (434)243-7677
Co. E-mail: bodilys@virginia.edu

E-mail: bodilys@virginia.edu
Scope: Consultant specializes in financial analysis, capital investment, business/product/market planners, financial risk analysis, and decision sciences. **Publications:** "I Can't Get No Satisfaction: How Bundling and Multi-Part Pricing Can Satisfy Consumers and Suppliers," Feb, 2006; "Organizational Use of Decision Analysis," Oct, 2004; "Real Options," Oct, 2004.

38515 ■ The Business Guide Inc.
Torbay Rd.
PO Box 29077
Saint John's, NL, Canada A1A 5B8
Ph:(709)754-8433
Free: 877-754-8433
Fax: (709)754-8434
Co. E-mail: info@businessguide.net
URL: http://www.businessguide.net

E-mail: info@businessguide.net
Scope: Assists private sector firms in acquiring financial assistance to start or expand a business.

38516 ■ CBIZ Inc.
6050 Oak Tree, Blvd. S, Ste. 500
Cleveland, OH 44131
Ph:(216)447-9000
Fax: (216)447-9007
Co. E-mail: info@cbiz.com
URL: http://www.cbiz.com

E-mail: info@cbiz.com
Scope: A business consulting and tax services firm providing financial, consulting, tax and business services through seven groups: financial management, tax advisory, construction and real estate, healthcare, litigation support, capital resource, and CEO outsource.

38517 ■ Chartered Management Co.
125 S Wacker Dr., Ste. 300
Chicago, IL 60606-4402
Ph:(312)214-2575
Scope: Operations improvement consultants. Specializes in strategic planning; feasibility studies; management audits and reports; profit enhancement; start-up businesses; mergers and acquisitions; joint ventures; divestitures; interim management; crisis management; turnarounds; business process re-engineering; venture capital; and due diligence.

38518 ■ Clayton/Curtis/Cottrell
1722 Madison Ct.
Louisville, CO 80027
Ph:(303)665-2005

Fax: (303)665-2276
Scope: Firm specializes packaged goods, telecommunications, direct marketing & printing, & packaging industries. Services include strategic planning; profit enhancement; start-up businesses; mergers and acquisitions; joint ventures; divestitures; interim management; crisis management; turnarounds; market size, segmentation and rates of growth; competitor intelligence; image & reputation, & competitive analysis.

38519 ■ John Alan Cohan
415 N Camden Dr., Ste. 100
Beverly Hills, CA 90210
Ph:(310)557-9900
Free: 800-255-1529
Fax: (310)859-8656
Co. E-mail: johnalancohan@aol.com

E-mail: johnalancohan@aol.com
Scope: Development of business plans for startups in the fields of livestock, horses, farming, or aviation. Tax consultations and tax opinion letters to support deductions.

38520 ■ C.C. Comfort Consulting
3370 N Hayden Rd.
Scottsdale, AZ 85251
Ph:(602)483-8364
Co. E-mail: cccomfortcfe@martindalemail.com

E-mail: cccomfortcfe@martindalemail.com
Scope: Evaluates, develops and implements financial, operational and compliance management systems' strategies, programs and practices. Professional recognition as Certified Public Accountant, Internal Auditor, Cost Analyst and Fraud Examiner plus investigatory, law enforcement, and court experience ensure confidential handling of sensitive and legal matters. Works with management, audit, legal, security and outside personnel to evaluate and improve compliance, efficiency and effectiveness.

38521 ■ Comprehensive Planning Services
3201 Lucas Cir.
Lafayette, CA 94549
Ph:(925)283-8272
Fax: (925)283-8272
Scope: Business/financial consultants with related experience in marketing, finance, organization, business planning, and profit development. Industries served include construction, manufacturing, and wholesale.

38522 ■ Comprehensive Professional Management Inc.
222 E Dundee Rd.
Wheeling, IL 60090-3009
Ph:(847)520-0101
Fax: (847)520-0372
Co. E-mail: bob@cpmincfs.com

E-mail: bob@cpmincfs.com
Scope: Services include accounting, financial planning, litigation support, pension profit sharing administration, practice surveys, professional corporation issues, retirement and estate planning, and tax advice.

38523 ■ Controlled Resources
1021 E 1st Ave., Apt. 822
Broomfield, CO 80020
Ph:(303)798-2978
Fax: (303)798-2979
Scope: Strategic planning, with focus on human performance and financial issues. Also offers institutional ergonomics.

38524 ■ Corporate Consulting Inc.
3333 Belcaro Dr.
Denver, CO 80209
Ph:(303)698-9292
Fax: (303)698-9292
Co. E-mail: corpcons@compuserve.com

E-mail: corpcons@compuserve.com
Scope: Specializes in feasibility studies; organizational development; small business management; merg-

ers and acquisitions; joint ventures; divestitures; interim management; crisis management; turnarounds; financing; appraisals and valuations; and due diligence studies.

38525 ■ Crystal Clear Communications Inc.
8989 N Port Washington Rd., Ste. 210
Milwaukee, WI 53217-1667
Ph:(414)228-8799
Scope: Specializes in strategic planning; organizational development; small business management; mergers and acquisitions; joint ventures; divestitures; strategy implementation; executive coaching.

38526 ■ Dubuc Lucke & Co.
414 Walnut St., Ste607
Cincinnati, OH 45202
Ph:(513)579-8330
Fax: (513)241-6669
Scope: Consulting services in the areas of profit enhancement; small business management; mergers and acquisitions; joint ventures; divestitures; interim management; crisis management; turnarounds; appraisals; valuations; due diligence; and international trade.

38527 ■ Effective Compensation Inc.
3609 S Wadsworth Blvd., Ste. 260
Lakewood, CO 80235
Ph:(303)854-1000
Free: 877-746-4324
Fax: (303)854-1030
Co. E-mail: eci@effectivecompensation.com
URL: http://www.effectivecompensation.com

E-mail: eci@effectivecompensation.com
Scope: Helps organizations determine how to competitively pay their employees. Provides quality, culture sensitive, compensation consulting assistance to all types of employers. **Publications:** Industry Compensation Surveys.

38528 ■ Everett & Co.
3126 S Franklin St.
Englewood, CO 80113
Ph:(303)761-7999
Fax: (303)781-8296
Co. E-mail: everettco@qwest.net
URL: http://www.everettco.com

E-mail: everettco@qwest.net
Scope: Management and financial consultants provide business planning, start-up assistance as well as in-depth financial and project analysis. Helps plan for increased cash flow and working capital reduction. Industries served: manufacturing, wholesaling, service and technological. Corporate United States subsidiary creation and maintenance services for international firms.

38529 ■ Federer Resources Inc.
106 E 6th St.
Austin, TX 78701-3659
Ph:(512)476-8800
Scope: Firm specializes in feasibility studies; start-up businesses; small business management; mergers and acquisitions; joint ventures; divestitures; interim management; crisis management; turnarounds; production planning; team building; appraisals and valuations.

38530 ■ Steven S. Feinberg
412 Beacon St.
Boston, MA 02115
Ph:(617)247-2881
Fax: (617)247-2881
Scope: Offers small business consulting with emphasis on budgeting and financial management needs of small manufacturing firms. Also offers plant layout and work simplification services. Serves private industries.

38531 ■ Financial Management Solutions Inc.
1720 Windward Concourse, Ste. 200
Alpharetta, GA 30005
Ph:(770)619-3443
Free: 877-887-3022
Fax: (770)619-3095

Co. E-mail: info@fmsi.com
URL: http://www.fmsi.com

E-mail: info@fmsi.com
Scope: Firm provides staff models, industry comparative and benchmark data, measurement and monitoring systems. Also offers data processing evaluations, process improvements, and operational reviews. They have also developed resource management and sales management systems. Industries served: communications, banking, insurance, retail. **Publications:** "Teller Management System and Empowered Process Improvement". **Seminars:** Staff Productivity: Effective Use of Databases to Improve Performance and Statistical Models - the New Wave of Management; Micro-Analysis process to Profitability in the Financial Services Industry. **Special Services:** The Teller Management System™; The Resource Management System™; The Sales Management System™.

38532 ■ Focus Financial Consulting Inc.
201 E Washington St.
Middleburg, VA 20117
Ph:(540)687-3369
Scope: Provides management with financial expertise in planning goal achievement, evaluating historical results, and analyzing variances from plan. Performs the functions of a Financial Officer whose primary responsibility is the efficient management of scarce financial resources. Administers loan funds and develops custom software applications. **Publications:** Ecker and Altman, Building a Microloan Program, Community Reinvestment Fund, Inc. (April 1993). **Special Services:** Markets LoanServ, a loan servicing system developed by firm to meet the needs of development lenders. Develops custom business applications for small businesses (including nonprofit ones) and professional associations.

38533 ■ The Foster Group Inc.
330 N Wabash Ave., Ste. 3500
Chicago, IL 60611
Ph:(312)609-1009
Fax: (312)609-1109
Co. E-mail: info@thefostergroup.com
URL: http://www.thefostergroup.com

E-mail: info@thefostergroup.com
Scope: Offers information systems and data security, financial accounting services, and management consulting.

38534 ■ Frankel and Topche P.C.
1700 Galloping Hill Rd.
Kenilworth, NJ 07033
Ph:(908)298-7700
Fax: (908)298-7701
Co. E-mail: info@frankelandtopche.com
URL: http://www.frankelandtopche.com

E-mail: info@frankelandtopche.com
Scope: Offers financial consulting for closely held businesses. Assists in mergers and acquisitions, tax planning, strategic business planning, family succession planning, accounting, auditing, and obtaining financing. The firm serves small businesses in the service, retail, wholesale, and manufacturing industries. Specializes in real estate, lumber and building materials, and service businesses.

38535 ■ Glass & Associates Inc.
623 5th Ave., Fl. 15
New York, NY 10022
Ph:(212)223-2002
Free: (866)452-7716
Fax: (212)223-5477
Co. E-mail: jmansell@glass-consulting.com
URL: http://www.glass-consulting.com

E-mail: jmansell@glass-consulting.com
Scope: Works with troubled companies, functioning as agents of change to help organizations deal with extraordinary needs in situations ranging from the early stages of financial decline to "life-or-death" crisis conditions. Provides in-depth analysis and strategic planning, backed up by leadership and decisive action

to help under-performing companies change the way they operate and survive crisis situations. Assists management, creditors, lenders and other "parties in interest" involved with financially troubled companies; crisis management services include on-site interim crisis management, including direction of the Chapter 11 process, for insolvent companies; human resources services include personnel for temporary senior-level management and professional staff assignments; executive search, selection and placement; specialized advisory services in human resource areas such as worker's compensation and health benefits.

38536 ■ Global Technology Transfer
1500 Dixie Hwy.
Covington, KY 41011
Ph:(859)431-1262
Fax: (859)431-5148
Co. E-mail: arzembrodt@worldnet.att.net

E-mail: arzembrodt@worldnet.att.net
Scope: Firm specializes in product development; quality assurance; new product development; and total quality management focusing on household chemical specialties, especially air fresheners. Utilizes latest technology from global resources. Specializes in enhancement products for home and automobile.

38537 ■ Joseph Goldsten & Associates
401 Jackson Ave.
Lexington, VA 24450
Ph:(540)463-4593
Fax: (540)463-5921
Scope: Offers counsel to financial institutions, corporations and individuals on planning, financial management, new ventures, small business development, investment counseling, real estate and banking. Active in mergers, acquisitions and valuations. Clients primarily financial institutions and manufacturers.

38538 ■ Gordian Concepts & Solutions
16 Blueberry Ln.
Lincoln, MA 01773
Ph:(617)259-8341
Co. E-mail: gordian@usa1.com

E-mail: gordian@usa1.com
Scope: An engineering and management consultancy, the firm offers a broad range of general, financial, and valuation services, civil and tax litigation support, helps clients to enter new businesses, to plan new products and services, to evaluate feasibility, and assists with their due diligence efforts. Targets industrial concerns engaged in manufacturing, assembly, warehousing, energy production, process systems and biotechnology, steel, paper, and electronics. Also services businesses such as retailing, financial services, health-care, satellite broadcasting and cable television, outdoor advertising, and professional practices.

38539 ■ The Greystone Group Inc.
678 Front St., Ste. 159
Grand Rapids, MI 49504
Ph:(616)451-8880
Fax: (616)451-9180
Co. E-mail: consult@greystonegp.com
URL: http://www.greystonegp.com

E-mail: consult@greystonegp.com
Scope: Firm specializes in strategic planning and communications; organizational development; startup businesses; business management; mergers and acquisitions; joint ventures; divestitures; business process re-engineering.

38540 ■ Herpers Gowling L.L.P.
4 Hughson St., Ste. 300
Hamilton, ON, Canada L8N 3Z1
Ph:(905)529-3328
Free: 888-735-9909
Fax: (905)529-3980
Co. E-mail: dgowling@herpersgowling.com
URL: http://www.herpersgowling.com

E-mail: dgowling@herpersgowling.com
Scope: Provides services to small and medium size businesses in the areas of financial management, strategic planning, mergers and acquisitions and re-engineering/restructuring.

38541 ■ Hewitt Development Enterprises
1717 N Bayshore Dr., Ste. 2154
Miami, FL 33132
Ph:(305)372-0941
Free: 800-631-3098
Fax: (305)372-0941
Co. E-mail: info@hewittdevelopment.com
URL: http://www.hewittdevelopment.com

E-mail: info@hewittdevelopment.com
Scope: A manufacturing management consulting firm. Specializes in strategic planning; profit enhancement; start-up businesses; interim management; crisis management; turnarounds; production planning; Just-in-Time inventory management; and project management.

38542 ■ Hickey & Hill Inc.
1009 Oak Hill Rd., Ste. 201
Lafayette, CA 94549
Ph:(925)283-7802
Fax: (925)283-4259
Scope: Firm provides management consulting services to companies in financial distress. Expertise area: corporate restructuring and turnaround.

38543 ■ Guy C. Hill, G H Associates
8677 Highwood Dr.
San Diego, CA 92119-1410
Fax: (619)464-6573
Co. E-mail: ciconsd@worldnet.att.net

E-mail: ciconsd@worldnet.att.net

38544 ■ C. W. Hines and Associates Inc.
344 Churchill Cir., Sanctuary Bay
White Stone, VA 22578
Ph:(804)435-8844
Fax: (804)435-8855
Co. E-mail: turtlecwh@aol.com
URL: http://www.cwhinesassociates.org

E-mail: turtlecwh@aol.com
Scope: Management consultants with expertise in the following categories: advertising and public relations, health and human resources, management sciences, organizational development, computer sciences, financial management, behavioral sciences, environmental design, technology transfer, project management, facility management, program evaluation, and business therapy. Also included are complementary areas such as sampling procedures, job training, managerial effectiveness, corporate seminars, gender harassment, training for trainers, and leadership and management skills development. **Publications:** Money Muscle, 120 Exercises To Build Spiritual And Financial Strength, 2004; Inside Track: Executives Coaching Executives. **Seminars:** Career Development; Coaching and Counseling for Work Success; Communicating More Effectively in a Diverse Work Environment; Communications 600: Advanced Skills for Relationship Building; Customer Service: Building a Caring Culture.

38545 ■ Hollingsworth & Associates
1200 Commissioners Rd. E, Ste. 2
London, ON, Canada N5Z 4R3
Ph:(519)649-2001
Fax: (519)649-7880
Co. E-mail: jack@hollingsworth.net

E-mail: jack@hollingsworth.net
Scope: Acts as management accountants, tax and management consultants, and offsite controllers. Consulting services include software selection, and financial information systems. Accounting and tax preparation.

38546 ■ Holt Capital
1100 Dexter Ave. N
Seattle, WA 98109

Ph:(206)676-3822
Fax: (206)789-8034
Co. E-mail: info@holtcapital.com
URL: http://www.holtcapital.com

E-mail: info@holtcapital.com
Scope: Connects companies with capital. Mergers and acquisitions, finance through debt and leasing, private equity and venture capital. Is a registered Investment Advisor. **Publications:** "Is Your First Paragraph a Turn-off?"; "Bubble Rubble: Bridging the Price Gapfor an Early-Stage Business"; "Are You Ready For The New New Economy?"; "Could I Get Money or Jail Time With That? The Sarbanes-Oxley Act Of 2002 gives early-stage companies More Risks". **Seminars:** Attracting Private Investors; Five Proven Ways to Finance Your Company.

38547 ■ Human Capital Research Corp.
1735 N Paulina St., Ste. 401
Chicago, IL 60622
Ph:(773)342-0440
Fax: (773)342-0498
Co. E-mail: humancap@humancapital.com

E-mail: humancap@humancapital.com
Scope: Economic research including financial aid analysis, curriculum development and market demand studies, strategic peer analysis, alumni follow-up, institutional research, and executive information.

38548 ■ Idi-Supply Inc.
3866 N Fratney St.
PO Box 12050
Milwaukee, WI 53212
Ph:(414)961-2365
Fax: (414)961-1582
Scope: Firm specializes in start-up businesses; small business management; mergers and acquisitions; joint ventures; divestitures; venture capital; appraisals; valuations; and international trade.

38549 ■ InfoSource Management Services Inc.
PO Box 590
Sicamous, BC, Canada V0E 2V0
Ph:(250)804-6113
Free: 888-804-4700
Fax: (250)836-3667
Scope: Provides customized financial reports that highlight the areas where change will improve the bottom line. **Seminars:** Provides a series of seminars on cash flow management issues.

38550 ■ Integrated Financial Consultants
3625 Dufferin St., Ste. 340
Toronto, ON, Canada M3K 1Z2
Ph:(416)630-4000
Fax: (416)642-1458
Co. E-mail: info@ifc-inc.ca
URL: http://www.ifc-inc.ca

E-mail: info@ifc-inc.ca
Scope: Designs and implements a financial plan for the shareholders/partners of small businesses. Services include investment management, tax planning, risk management in the form of structuring and funding shareholder's agreements, estate planning and creditor protection.

38551 ■ Johnston Co.
1646 Massachusetts Ave., Ste. 22
Lexington, MA 02420
Ph:(781)862-7595
Fax: (781)862-9066
Co. E-mail: info@johnstoncompany.com
URL: http://www.johnstoncompany.com

E-mail: info@johnstoncompany.com
Scope: Firm specializes in management audits and reports; start-up businesses; small business management; mergers and acquisitions; joint ventures; divestitures; interim management; crisis management; turnarounds; cost controls; financing; venture capital.

38552 ■ Keiei Senryaku Corp.
19191 S Vermont Ave., Ste. 530
Torrance, CA 90502

Ph:(310)366-3331
Free: 800-951-8780
Fax: (310)366-3330
Co. E-mail: takenakaes@earthlink.net

E-mail: takenakaes@earthlink.net
Scope: Consulting services in the areas of strategic planning; feasibility studies; profit enhancement; organizational development; start-up businesses; mergers and acquisitions; joint ventures; divestitures; executive searches; sales management; competitive analysis. Entering Japanese market.

38553 ■ Key Communications Group Inc.
5617 Warwick Pl.
Chevy Chase, MD 20815-5503
Ph:(301)656-0450
Free: 800-705-5353
Fax: (301)656-4554
Co. E-mail: mr.dm@verizon.net

E-mail: mr.dm@verizon.net
Scope: Direct marketing and publishing consultants specializing in subscriber and member acquisition for newsletters and other niche B2B publications, organizations and associations. Specialties: small and start-up businesses; mergers and acquisitions; joint ventures; divestitures; product development; employee surveys and communication; market research; customer service audits; new product development; direct marketing; and competitive intelligence.

38554 ■ Charles A. Krueger
1908 Innsbrooke Dr.
Sun Prairie, WI 53590
Ph:(608)837-5247
Fax: (608)825-7538
Co. E-mail: ckrueger@bus.wisc.edu

E-mail: ckrueger@bus.wisc.edu
Scope: Financial management consultant specializing in professional education programs for managers and executives. Programs include: finance and accounting for nonfinancial executives, financial management for executives, and developing and using financial information for decision making. Major industries served include manufacturing, service, healthcare and insurance. **Publications:** "Monitoring Financial Results, chapter in Corporate Controllers Manual", Warren Gorham and Lamont **Seminars:** Finance and Accounting for Nonfinancial Executives; Financial Management for Health Care Executives; Financial Management for Insurance Executives; Direct Costing; Flexible Budgeting; Contribution Reporting; Building Value and Driving Profits - A Business Simulation.

38555 ■ William E. Kuhn & Associates
234 Cook St.
Denver, CO 80206-5305
Ph:(303)322-8233
Fax: (303)322-9032
Co. E-mail: billkuhn1@cs.com

E-mail: billkuhn1@cs.com
Scope: Firm specializes in strategic planning; profit enhancement; small business management; mergers and acquisitions; joint ventures; divestitures; human resources management; performance appraisals; team building; sales management; appraisals and valuations.

38556 ■ Lacloche Manitoulin Business Assistance Corp.
30 Meredith St.
PO Box 130
Gore Bay, ON, Canada P0P 1H0
Ph:(705)282-3215
Free: 800-461-5131
Fax: (705)282-2989
Co. E-mail: info@lambac.org
URL: http://www.lambac.org

E-mail: info@lambac.org
Scope: Encourages a strong, vibrant, sustainable, environmentally-friendly, business community

through financial investment and support services. **Publications:** Packed Panniers on Manitoulin, Sept., 2005; One Wind Farm Gains License, Another Proposes 60 Windmills, Jul, 2005.

38557 ■ Management Resource Partners
181 2nd Ave., Ste. 542
San Mateo, CA 94401-3813
Ph:(650)401-5850
Fax: (650)401-5850
Scope: Firm specializes in strategic planning; small business management; mergers and acquisitions; joint ventures; divestitures; interim management; crisis management; turnarounds; venture capital; appraisals and valuations.

38558 ■ McShane Group Inc.
2345 York Rd.
Timonium, MD 21093
Ph:(410)560-0077
Fax: (410)560-2718
Co. E-mail: tmcshane@mcshanegroup.com
URL: http://www.mcshanegroup.com

E-mail: tmcshane@mcshanegroup.com
Scope: Management consulting firm specializing in helping financially troubled companies. All senior level business executives with strong operations backgrounds. Focuses on turnarounds, interim management, crisis management, debt restructuring, organizational restructuring, operating business and asset sales.

38559 ■ Mefford, Knutson & Associates Inc.
6437 Lyndale Ave. S
Richfield, MN 55423-1465
Ph:(612)869-8011
Free: 800-831-0228
Fax: (612)893-1806
Co. E-mail: don@mkaonline.net
URL: http://www.mkaonline.net

E-mail: don@mkaonline.net
Scope: Firm specializes in start-up businesses; strategic planning; mergers and acquisitions; joint ventures; divestitures; business process re-engineering; personnel policies and procedures; market research; new product development and cost controls.

38560 ■ Colmen Menard Company Inc.
The Woods, 994 Old Eagle School Rd., Ste. 1000
Wayne, PA 19087
Ph:(484)367-0300
Fax: (484)367-0305
Co. E-mail: cmci@colmenmenard.com
URL: http://www.colmenmenard.com

E-mail: cmci@colmenmenard.com
Scope: Merger and acquisition corporate finance and business advisory services for public and private companies located in North America.

38561 ■ Merrimac Associates Inc.
1236 Brace Rd., Ste. F
Cherry Hill, NJ 08034-2634
Ph:(856)428-4350
Free: 888-777-5215
Fax: (856)428-4333
Co. E-mail: mo@merrimac.com
URL: http://www.merrimac.com

E-mail: mo@merrimac.com
Scope: Offers financial management consulting to help with financial problems of small or medium sized businesses of any type on a long or short term basis. Assists with a wide variety of management problems. **Special Services:** XtremePM™.

38562 ■ Metro Accounting Services Inc.
167 Oxmoor Blvd.
Birmingham, AL 35209-5955
Ph:(205)916-0900
Fax: (205)945-1784
Scope: Consults on tax planning, retirement planning, investment analysis and personal financial planning on a fee basis for individuals and small businesses;

and on real estate partnerships. Also specializes in employee benefit analysis, pension investment analysis and investment management for small businesses. **Seminars:** How to Win the Money Game; Using Mutual Funds for Financial Independence; IRA's, Keogh and Other Retirement Plans; How to Quit Paying Income Taxes. **Special Services:** IRS problem solving. Quick Books® installation and training.

38563 ■ Miller/Cook & Associates Inc.
1316 2nd St.
Roanoke, VA 24016
Ph:(540)345-4393
Free: 800-591-1141
Fax: (239)394-2652
Co. E-mail: ccook2412@aol.com
URL: http://www.millercook.com

E-mail: ccook2412@aol.com
Scope: Enrollment management, specializing in revenue-based enrollment: helping admissions and financial aid with the important business of balancing head count, net revenue, and quality, communications strategies. **Publications:** "Capital Gains: Surviving in an Increasingly For-Profit World"; "Making Steps to a Brighter Future".

38564 ■ Mitchell & Titus L.L.P.
1 Battery Park Plz., 27th Fl.
New York, NY 10004
Ph:(212)709-4500
Fax: (212)709-4680
Co. E-mail: newyork.office@mitchelltitus.com
URL: http://www.mitchelltitus.com

E-mail: newyork.office@mitchelltitus.com
Scope: Minority-controlled certified public accounting and management consulting firm audit and accounting services tax planning and preparation services management and business advisory services.

38565 ■ The Nelson Group Ltd.
5 Milk St., Ste. 4
Portland, ME 04101
Ph:(207)775-1199
Fax: (207)775-0141
URL: http://www.nelsonltd.com
Scope: Consulting services in the areas of strategic planning; organizational development; small business management; mergers and acquisitions; joint ventures; divestitures; interim management; crisis management; turnarounds; performance appraisals; executive searches; outplacement; and team building.

38566 ■ Partners for Market Leadership Inc.
400 Galleria Pky., Ste. 1500
Atlanta, GA 30339
Ph:(770)850-1409
Free: 800-984-1110
Co. E-mail: dcarpenter@market-leadership.com
URL: http://www.market-leadership.com

E-mail: dcarpenter@market-leadership.com
Scope: Change management firm. Provides consulting services in the areas of strategic planning, start-up businesses, mergers and acquisitions, joint ventures, divestitures, interim management, crisis management, turnarounds, new product development, sales management and competitive analysis.

38567 ■ Penny & Associates Inc.
16100 Old Simcoe Rd.
Port Perry, ON, Canada L9L 1P3
Ph:(905)985-0712
Free: 800-699-6190
Fax: (905)985-9461
Co. E-mail: mail@pennyinc.com
URL: http://www.pennyinc.com

E-mail: mail@pennyinc.com
Scope: Develops financial reports by providing outsourced accounting and management support services.

38568 ■ Kevin L. Pohle
5820 Main St., Ste. 316-317
Buffalo, NY 14221

Ph:(716)565-0565
Scope: Firm specializes in business strategic planning services, compensation and benefits consulting, special projects management, cost and productivity analysis, and business crisis management. Industries served: manufacturing, retail, healthcare facilities, educational institutions, and local government and municipalities.

38569 ■ Queens Business Consulting
Queens School of Business, Goodes Hall, 143 Union St.
Kingston, ON, Canada K7L 3N6
Ph:(613)533-2309
Fax: (613)533-2370
Co. E-mail: qbc@business.queensu.ca
URL: http://www.business.queensu.ca/qbc

E-mail: qbc@business.queensu.ca
Scope: Provides business plans, feasibility studies, financial planning, competitor analysis, market research, marketing strategies, production planning, and systems implementation.

38570 ■ Rainwater-Gish & Associates
317 3rd St., Ste. 3
Eureka, CA 95501
Ph:(707)443-0030
Fax: (707)443-5683
Scope: Offers financial management for small business: includes asset management (controlling cash, inventory, A/R), cashflow control, credit policies, and securing/structuring financing for growth. Also offers assistance in business planning, preparing proforma statements and other loan documents to secure financing. Majority of financial loan packages have been SBA loans. Firm provides SBA marketing and portfolio management services to banks. **Seminars:** Consultant frequently lectures on financial management for small business owners.

38571 ■ Scannell & Kurz Inc.
40B Grove St.
Pittsford, NY 14534
Ph:(585)381-1120
Fax: (585)381-2383
Co. E-mail: info@scannellkurz.com
URL: http://www.scannellkurz.com

E-mail: info@scannellkurz.com
Scope: Provides pricing and financial aid strategies, admissions market analysis, enrollment management, and retention strategies. **Publications:** "Enrollment Management Grows Up," May, 2006; "Just One Stop, But Many Potential Pitfalls," Mar, 2006; "Bond Rating: Beyond the Balance," Jan, 2006; "Strategy and Operations in Financial Aid," Nov, 2005.

38572 ■ Harvey C. Skoog
3737 N Robert Rd., No. A
Prescott Valley, AZ 86314
Ph:(928)772-1448
Scope: Firm has expertise in taxes, payroll, financial planning, budgeting, buy/sell planning, business start-up, fraud detection, troubled business consulting, acquisition, and marketing. Serves the manufacturing, construction, and retailing industries in Arizona.

38573 ■ The Stillwater Group
920 E Shore Dr.
PO Box 168
Stillwater, NJ 07875
Ph:(973)579-7080
Fax: (973)579-7970
Co. E-mail: education@stillwater.com
URL: http://www.stillwater.com

E-mail: education@stillwater.com
Scope: Provides strategic planning, budget and financial management, process improvement, organizational design and assessment, and college student services operations.

38574 ■ Strategic MindShare Consulting
1401 Brickell Ave., Ste. 640
Miami, FL 33131
Ph:(305)377-2220

Fax: (305)377-2280
Co. E-mail: dee@strategicmindshare.com
URL: http://www.strategicmindshare.com

E-mail: dee@strategicmindshare.com
Scope: Firm specializes in strategic planning; feasibility studies; profit enhancement; organizational development; start-up businesses; mergers and acquisitions; joint ventures; divestitures; interim management; crisis management; turnarounds; new product development and competitive analysis. **Publications:** "Top Ten CEO Burning Issues for 2005"; "Top Ten Consumer Behavioral Trends for 2005"; "The Influence Factors".

38575 ■ Swigert and Associates Inc.
505 Chicago Ave.
Evanston, IL 60202
Ph:(847)864-4690
Scope: Offers assistance to businesses and individuals on matters related to finance, investment decisions, taxes and general management concerns.

38576 ■ Syed Hussayn TMCI
95 October Ln.
Aurora, ON, Canada L4G 7A1
Ph:(905)949-4555
Fax: (905)949-9116
Co. E-mail: syedn.hussain@sympatico.ca

E-mail: syedn.hussain@sympatico.ca
Scope: Business process re-engineering, change management, financial restructuring & insolvency, consumer & corporate bankruptcy, financial/debt management, investments & insurance advisory services, management/executive development, marketing management, organizational development, needs assessment, financial counselling, succession planning, performance management/measurement, program evaluation, project management, strategic planning and import/export advisory. **Publications:** "Innovative Management"; "Team Building and Leadership"; "Financial Planning"; "Estate Planning"; "Risk Management"; "Export/Import Trade Finance Mechanics"; "Marketing and Sales Management"; "What Your Banker Needs to Know"; "Building A Successful Financial Plan". **Seminars:** Workplace Solutions Seminars; Export Development; Executive Education & Leadership Development; Financial Planning; Estate Planning; Succession Planning; Wealth Accumulation and Management; Strategic Planning/Competitive Positioning.

38577 ■ Value Creation Group Inc.
7820 Scotia Dr., Ste. 2000
Dallas, TX 75248-3115
Ph:(972)980-7407
Fax: (972)980-4619
Co. E-mail: john.antos@valuecreationgroup.com
URL: http://www.valuecreationgroup.com

E-mail: john.antos@valuecreationgroup.com
Scope: General business experts offering predictive strategic planning, Activity-Based Costing (ABC), Activity-Based Management (ABM), mergers and acquisitions, outsourcing, re-engineering, process management, web-enabling technology, bench marking, installation of financial systems, executive search, training, teams, activity based budgeting, operational auditing, feature costing. Industries served: financial services, food, health-care, insurance, manufacturing, electronics, real estate, consumer products, nonprofit, telecommunication, oil, service, data processing, hotel and resort and government agencies. **Publications:** Handbook of process management based (predictive accounting), ALCPA 2002; Activity Based Management for Service Environments, Government Entities, & Nonprofit Organizations; Driving Value Using Activity Based Budgeting; Process Based Accounting leveraging Processes to Predict Results; Handbook of Supply Chain Management; Economic Value Management Applications and Techniques; The Change Handbook: Group Methods for Creating the Future. **Seminars:** Predictive Accounting; Performance measures; ABM for Manufacturing; ABM for Service Organizations; Finance and Accounting for

Non-Financial Executives; Return on Investment/Capital Expenditure Evaluation; Planning and Cost Control; The Next Step Intermediate Finance and Accounting for Non-financial Managers; Activity-Based Budgeting; Friendly Finance for Fund Raisers; Strategic Outsourcing.

38578 ■ ValueNomics Value Specialists
10 Almaden Blvd., Ste. 1450
San Jose, CA 95113-2226
Ph:(408)257-8521
Fax: (408)257-1146
Co. E-mail: value@valuenomics.com
URL: http://www.valuenomics.com

E-mail: value@valuenomics.com
Scope: Specializes in valuations; appraisals; strategic planning; feasibility studies; mergers and acquisitions; joint ventures; divestitures; competitive intelligence; and due diligence. Acts as an expert witness. Offers litigation support. **Publications:** "The Business of Business Valuation and the CPA as an expert witness". **Special Services:** ValueNomics®.

38579 ■ Mark Vanderstelt
9831 Gulfstream Ct.
Fishers, IN 46038
Ph:(317)576-9328
Fax: (317)576-9328
Scope: Consulting services include financial planning and analysis, inventory control, cash management, return on investment, budgeting, pricing, system design and analysis, mergers and acquisitions, feasibility studies, data processing, cost systems and controls, and performance measurement. Also performs operational and financial reviews.

38580 ■ VelociTel Inc.
18071 Fitch Ave.
Irvine, CA 92614
Ph:(949)809-4999
Fax: (949)553-3919
Co. E-mail: corporateinfo@velocitel.net
URL: http://www.velocitel.com

E-mail: corporateinfo@velocitel.net
Scope: Provides expertise in developing wireless networks. Services include project management; site acquisition; land use planning; architecture and engineering; construction and construction management. **Special Services:** VELOCITEL®.

38581 ■ VenturEdge Corp.
4711 Yonge St., Ste. 1105
Toronto, ON, Canada M2N 6K8
Ph:(416)224-2000
Fax: (416)224-2376
Co. E-mail: info@venturedge.com
URL: http://www.venturedge.com

E-mail: info@venturedge.com
Scope: Services include strategy formulation; performance improvement; business coaching; competitive intelligence; business planning; acquiring capital; financial management; and succession planning in mergers and acquisitions.

38582 ■ Verbit & Co.
19 Bala Ave.
Bala Cynwyd, PA 19004
Ph:(610)668-9840
Scope: The management consulting services of Verbit & Company apply to practically every facet of a business, from operations and administration to financial and information systems management. These services include: general management - to assist executives and managers fulfill their mission and to assure that adequate planning of day-to-day operations occurs; that controls are sufficient to safeguard valuable resources; and that results of decisions are reviewed in sufficient time to effect continuing action. Financial planning and control - to develop accounting, budgeting, forecasting, and other information systems for the management of resources and evaluation of strategies. Information systems and electronic data processing - to promote efficient and effective use of

computers in company operations; operations planning and control - to design systems to promote effective management of production facilities; cost accounting and management - to design systems to record and report costs of operations; and human resources - to review organizational structures, personnel planning and compensation programs. Other services include: evaluation of desk-top computer systems for small firms; CAD/CAM implementation plan and orderly introduction of CAD/CAM to client company; and public sector services to assist with evaluation and implementation of governmental accounting systems and law enforcement information systems. Industries served: manufacturing, distribution, metals casting, equipment and components, professional services, healthcare, retail, nonprofit, and government. **Seminars:** Presents seminars on Integrating Manufacturing Management Systems with Business Systems; Negotiating Information Systems Agreements with Suppliers. **Special Services:** Low volume document/image scanning; low volume document scanning -OCR editing.

38583 ■ Vision Management
149 Meadows Rd.
Lafayette, NJ 07848-3120
Ph:(973)702-1116
Fax: (201)702-8311
Scope: Firm specializes in profit enhancement; strategic planning; business process re-engineering; industrial engineering; facilities planning; team building; inventory management; and Total Quality Management (TQM).

38584 ■ WestCap Partners Inc.
750 Lexington Ave., 24th Fl.
New York, NY 10022
Ph:(212)949-1825
Fax: (212)223-7363
Scope: Business and financial consultants provide corporate finance (debt, equity, private placements) and advisory services to emerging and medium-sized companies; investment and merchant banking; trade assistance, planning, strategy and financing; and financial consulting. Also temporarily assist growing companies in operational roles. Offer troubled company assistance through work-outs and turnarounds. Industries served: all including environmental, manufacturing, information technology (hardware, software, systems integration and implementation), direct marketing, sales service/wholesaling/distribution, construction materials and services, advertising, financial services, and emerging technologies. **Seminars:** Financial Negotiations for Mergers, Acquisitions and Projects. **Special Services:** Maintains a database of individuals, groups and firms interested in investing/participating in growing companies, turnarounds, or technologies in a variety of industries and service areas; and a database of international business contacts by country, area of expertise, past experiences and industry.

38585 ■ Western Capital Holdings Inc.
10050 E Applwood Dr.
Parker, CO 80138
Ph:(303)841-1022
Fax: (303)770-1945
Scope: Specialists in all phases of financial and management consulting. Provide strong emphasis in strategic planning and corporate development, financial analysis, acquisitions, investment banking and corporate finance. Projects range in size and duration to fit clients needs. Services can be applied to many diverse financial projects that may include the following: business plan development, budgeting and forecasting, strategic planning, cash flow analysis, cash flow management, corporate development, banking relations, asset management, and financial analysis. Industries served: food industry, manufacturing, distribution, retailing, computer services, agribusiness, financial services, insurance, and government agencies. **Seminars:** Buy Low, Sell High, Collect Early and Pay Late; Preparing Your Company for Sale; Venture Capital - Finding an Angel.

38586 ■ Wetmore Associates
625 North Ct., Ste. 150
Palatine, IL 60067-8174

Ph:(847)705-1585
Fax: (847)705-1598
Co. E-mail: wetmoreassoc@wetmoreassoc.com

E-mail: wetmoreassoc@wetmoreassoc.com
Scope: Financial specialists offer consulting services in the following areas: financial statement preparation, tax planning and preparation, pension/profit sharing plan audits, computerized accounting systems, start-up companies, and international taxation. Industries served: manufacturing, service, distribution, and international trade.

38587 ■ Donald C. Wright
3906 Lawndale Ln. N
Minneapolis, MN 55446-2940
Ph:(763)478-5595
Co. E-mail: donaldwright@compuserve.com

E-mail: donaldwright@compuserve.com
Scope: Consultant offers expertise in accounting and taxes, personal financial planning, strategic planning, pension/profit sharing planning and administration, professional practice management and surveys. Surveys and consultations performed worldwide. **Seminars:** Qualified pension plans and employee welfare benefit plans.

FRANCHISES AND BUSINESS OPPORTUNITIES

38588 ■ Brooke Insurance & Financial Services
Brooke Corp.
10895 Grandview Dr., Bldg. 24, Ste. 250
Overland Park, KS 66210
Free: 800-642-1872
Fax: 888-292-4196
No. of Franchise Units: 150. **Founded:** 1986. **Franchised:** 1988. **Description:** Sale of insurance and financial services. **Equity Capital Needed:** $1,900-$22,100. **Franchise Fee:** $1,000. **Financial Assistance:** Yes. **Training:** Yes.

COMPUTERIZED DATABASES

38589 ■ e-JEP
American Economic Association
2014 Broadway, Ste. 305
Nashville, TN 37203
Ph:(615)322-2595
Fax: (615)343-7590
Co. E-mail: aeainfo@vanderbilt.edu
URL: http://www.vanderbilt.edu/AEA
Description: Contains the full text of the *Journal of Economic Perspectives*. Includes articles, reports, and other material for economists and economics professionals. Features analysis and critiques of recent research findings and developments in public policy. Includes coverage of global economics issues and developments. Features articles on education in economics, employment issues for economists, and other issues of concern to professional economists. **Availability:** Online: American Economic Association, Thomson West; CD-ROM: American Economic Association. **Type:** Full text.

38590 ■ *InvestmentNews*
Crain Communications Inc.
1155 Gratiot Ave.
Detroit, MI 48207
Ph:(313)446-6000
Free: 800-678-2427
Fax: (313)446-0361
Co. E-mail: info@crain.com

URL: http://www.crain.com
Description: Contains investment news, articles, and features from the print version of *InvestmentNews*. Includes material for investors, financial planners, investment advisors, and other players in the stock market. Includes interviews, company profiles, investment analysis, calendars of upcoming events, and more. Includes classified advertisements for jobs, services, products, and other resources. Includes news archives, company reports, and a financial services stock index. **Availability:** Online: Crain Communications Inc. **Type:** Full text; Numeric.

38591 ■ *Offshore Funds*
iMoneyNet Inc.
1 Research Dr.
Westborough, MA 01581-5193
Ph:(508)616-6600
Fax: (508)616-5511
Co. E-mail: info@imoneynet.com
URL: http://www.imoneynet.com
Description: Tracks money market mutual fund performance for funds domiciled in International financial centers, including Dublin, Cayman Islands, Bermuda, The Bahamas, and Luxembourg. Each issue provides assets, yields, portfolio composition, returns, ratings and more. For benchmarking purposes, averages for U.S. dollar, the Euro, and Pound Sterling currencies are also included. **Availability:** Online: iMoneyNet Inc. **Type:** Full text; Numeric.

38592 ■ *Vickers Weekly Insider Report*
Argus Research Group
61 Broadway St., Ste. 1700
New York, NY 10006
Ph:(212)425-7500
Free: 800-405-9723
Fax: (212)809-2975
Co. E-mail: clientservices@vickers-stock.com
URL: http://www.vickers-stock.com
Description: Contains details on insider activity on Wall Street as it happens each week. Offers market commentary, sample stock portfolios, and a list of the most and least popular stocks as determined by their insider transactions. Available for online browsing or download in Adobe PDF format. **Availability:** Online: Argus Research Group. **Type:** Full text; Numeric.

LIBRARIES

38593 ■ Business Development Bank of Canada–Research & Information Centre
5 Place Ville Marie, Ste. 300
Montreal, QC, Canada H3B 5E7
Ph:(514)283-7632
Fax: (514)283-0439
Co. E-mail: odette.lavoie@bdc.ca
Contact: Odette Lavoie, Sr.Info.Spec.
Scope: Small business, management, Canadian business and industry, banking and finance, development banking. **Services:** Interlibrary loan; Library not open to the public. **Holdings:** 5000 books; CD-ROMs. **Subscriptions:** 100 journals and other serials; 7 newspapers.

38594 ■ Carnegie Library of Pittsburgh–Library Center
Business Dept.
612 Smithfield St.
Pittsburgh, PA 15222
Ph:(412)281-7141
Fax: (412)471-1724
Co. E-mail: wernerr@carnegielibrary.org
URL: http://www.clpgh.org/locations/business/
Contact: Roye Werner, Dept.Hd.
Scope: Investments, small business, entrepreneurship, management, marketing, insurance, advertising, personal finance, accounting, real estate, job and ca-

reer, international business. **Services:** Interlibrary loan; Library open to the public. **Holdings:** 14,000 business volumes; VF materials; microfilm; looseleaf services; AV cassettes. **Subscriptions:** 350 business journals, serials, and newspapers.

38595 ■ Nichols College–Conant Library
Center Rd.
Dudley, MA 01571
Ph:(508)213-2222
Free: 877-266-2681
Co. E-mail: reference@nichols.edu
URL: http://www.nichols.edu/library/
Contact: Jim Douglas, Lib.Dir.
Scope: Management, advertising, finance and accounting, small business, marketing, taxation, economics, International trade, humanities. **Services:** Interlibrary loan; copying; information service to groups; document delivery; Library open to Dudley and Webster residents. **Holdings:** 48,000 volumes; 1677 audio/visual titles; 3804 reels of microfilm. **Subscriptions:** 278 journals and electronic subscriptions.

38596 ■ Strategic Account Management Association–Library
150 N. Wacker Dr., Ste. 2222
Chicago, IL 60606
Ph:(312)251-3131
Fax: (312)251-3132
Co. E-mail: sama@strategicaccounts.org
URL: http://www.strategicaccounts.org
Contact: Elisabeth Cornell, Dir. of Educ.
Scope: National and global account management programs, account managers, strategic account management, strategic partnering and alliances, cross-functional teams, channel conflict, supply chain management, internal selling, customer viewpoint, value-added selling, account planning, account segmentation, compensation. **Services:** Library not open to the public (numerous sample documents available to non-members, and most can be purchased). **Holdings:** 1500 documents, periodicals, audiocassettes, case studies, white papers, research studies, books, reports, archives, PDFs, and presentation materials. **Subscriptions:** 1 journal; 3 newsletters.

38597 ■ University of Kentucky–Business & Economics Information Center
B&E Info. Ctr., Rm. 116
100 W. Gatton College of Business
Lexington, KY 40406-0093
Ph:(859)257-5868
Fax: (859)323-9496
Co. E-mail: mrazeeq@pop.uk.edu
URL: http://www.uky.edu/~BEIC
Contact: Michael A. Razeeq, Bus.Ref.Libn.
Scope: Business, economics, business management, marketing, finance, accounting. **Services:** Library open to the public for reference use only.

RESEARCH CENTERS

38598 ■ University of Oklahoma–Center for Financial Studies
Adams Hall, Rm. 205A
Finance Division
Michael F. Price College of Business
307 W Brooks, Adams Hall
Norman, OK 73019-0450
Ph:(405)325-5591
Fax: (405)325-7688
Co. E-mail: cfernando@ou.edu
URL: http://price.ou.edu/finance/cfs.html
Contact: C.S. Fernando, Dir.
E-mail: cfernando@ou.edu
Scope: Finance. **Educational Activities:** Executive Education Courses; Seminar (annually).

START-UP INFORMATION

38599 ■ **"250 Unleash the Entrepreneur Within You!" in** *Home Business* **(Vol. 12, March/April 2005, No. 2, pp. 16, 20-23, 26-29, 100-101, 104-105)**
Pub: Home Business Magazine
Ed: Sandy Larson. Description: Directory of 250 companies offering home-based businesses, franchises, and opportunities.

38600 ■ **"Actioncoaching.com" in** *Entrepreneur.com* **(Vol. 34, January 2006, No. 1, pp. 6)**
Pub: Entrepreneur Media Inc.
Ed: Steve Cooper. Description: The Business Coaching Franchise has launched its new Action-Coaching.com, a franchise offering small business owners topics for growing a business, marketing, and selling products and services.

38601 ■ **"Airborne intelligence" in** *Entrepreneur* **(Vol. 30, No. 10, October 2002, pp. 114)**
Pub: Entrepreneur Media Inc.
Ed: Devlin Smith. Description: The importance of signing up for the franchise advisory council when starting a new franchise is stressed.

38602 ■ **"All in the Delivery" in** *Entrepreneur* **(Vol. 31, No. 10, October 2003, pp. 112)**
Pub: Entrepreneur Media, Inc.
Ed: Devlin Smith. Description: Profile of Randy and Melody Newman who started a dry cleaning delivery franchise after learning the company Randy worked for as a human resources director was being sold.

38603 ■ **"All new: be the first on the block with one of these 66 fresh opportunities" in** *Entrepreneur* **(Vol. 30, No. 12, Dec. 2002, pp. 118)**
Pub: Entrepreneur Media Inc.
Description: A listing of franchises offered in 2001 and 2002, including contact information for researching each.

38604 ■ **"All the Rage: Wondering What Everyone Will Be Crazy About in the Coming Year?" in** *Entrepreneur* **(Vol. 33, January 2005, No. 1, pp. 84)**
Pub: Entrepreneur Media Inc.
Ed: Sara Wilson. Description: Fitness and weight-loss, technical consulting, eBay drop-off stores, child tutoring/enrichment programs and senior care are among the top franchises for 2005.

38605 ■ **"At Your Service" in** *Small Business Opportunities* **(Vol. 12, No. 3, May 2000, pp. 70, 72, 74, 76, 78, 80-82, 84)**
Pub: Harris Publications, Inc.
Description: Service businesses sell the commodities of time and convenience. The article presents the 15 best businesses to start and run from the home, including landscape/gardening, computer/internet tutor,

e-commerce specialist, elder care, window washing, reunion planner, bookkeeper, children's party planner, personalized products, errand service, food delivery service, children's taxi service, personal chef, and repair/restoration services.

38606 ■ **"Be a Savvy Franchise Sleuth" in** *My Business* **(December/January 2004, pp. 49)**
Pub: My Business Magazine
Description: Matthew Shay, executive vice president of the International Franchise Association, offers information to prospective franchise entrepreneurs.

38607 ■ **"Best of the best" in** *Entrepreneur* **(Vol. 31, No. 4, April 2003, pp. 88)**
Pub: Entrepreneur Media Inc.
Description: A directory of the top 116 franchise firms are ranked by best in category for 2003 to help would-be franchisees begin a search for the company that suits their interests.

38608 ■ **"Big Breaks" in** *Inc.* **(November 2000, pp. 90)**
Pub: The Goldhirsh Group
Description: Company profile of Wetzel's Pretzels, whose fans include famous celebrities.

38609 ■ **"Big Bucks in Bojangles" in** *Small Business Opportunities* **(Vol. 16, No. 2, March 2004, pp. 76-79)**
Pub: Harris Publications, Inc.
Description: Profile of Bojangles' Famous Chicken 'n Biscuits. The firm's strategic approach to growth and development focuses on four principles. Franchise startup costs range from $264,100 to $460,000.

38610 ■ **"Big Bucks in Little Gym" in** *Small Business Opportunities* **(Winter 2005)**
Pub: Harris Publications Inc.
Description: Profile of the multi-unit franchise The Little Gym with 160 units in 14 countries. The gyms are designed to help children develop motor skills.

38611 ■ **"Biz Paved With Gold" in** *Small Business Opportunities* **(Vol. 14, No. 1, January 2002, pp. 50-51, 54)**
Pub: Harris Publications, Inc.
Description: Profile of Systems Paving, the franchise that markets, sells and installs interlocking paving stones for outdoor paving areas, such as driveways, pool decks, and patios.

38612 ■ **"Breaking Into the Chains" in** *Hispanic Business* **(October 2004, pp. 108, 110, 112)**
Pub: Hispanic Business
Ed: Julie Bennett. Description: Several Hispanic leaders are among the owners of franchises across the nation. Information regarding general franchising opportunities is included.

38613 ■ **"Building Permitted" in** *Entrepreneur.com* **(Vol. 34, February 2006, No. 2, pp. 104)**
Pub: Entrepreneur Media Inc.

Description: Profile of Tom Pfister who purchased a franchise from a condominium builder in Pickerington, Ohio. Pfister has no previous experience in construction or real estate and received assistance from his franchisor, Epcon Communities, on market opportunity, sales materials and employee training.

38614 ■ *The Canadian Small Business Survival Guide: How to Start and Operate Your Own Successful Business*
Pub: Dundurn Group
Ed: Benjamin Gallander. FRQ September 2004. Price: $18.99. Description: Ideas for starting and running a successful small business. Topics include selecting a business, financing, government assistance, locations, franchises, and marketing ideas.

38615 ■ **"Cash From Trash: 1-800-Got-Junk?" in** *Fortune* **(Vol. 148, No. 9, October 27, 2003, pp. 196)**
Pub: Time Inc.
Ed: Justin Martin. Description: Profile of Brian Scudamore's startup franchise called Got-Junk. The firm is one of the fastest growing franchises in North America with $12.6 million in revenue in 2003.

38616 ■ **"Cash In At Home" in** *Small Business Opportunities* **(Vol. 16, No. 2, March 2004, pp. 22)**
Pub: Harris Publications, Inc.
Description: Seventy-five businesses that can be started and run from a home-based business are profiled, along with the top ten things anyone considering a home-based business should do before starting. Important questions are answered before pursuing a particular opportunity, as well as a listing of free resources and loan programs available from the U.S. Small Business Administration. Strategies for organizing paperwork for entrepreneurs are also presented.

38617 ■ **"Catch 'Em If You Can" in** *Entrepreneur.com* **(Vol. 34, February 2006, No. 2, pp. 90)**
Pub: Entrepreneur Media Inc.
Description: Rankings of the fastest growing 100 U.S. and Canadian franchise opportunities are presented along with contact information.

38618 ■ **"Chem-dry, a Franchise Rated No. 1 in its Category for 15 Years Straight..." in** *Entrepreneur* **(Vol. 32, No. 5, May 2004, pp. 131)**
Pub: Entrepreneur Media, Inc.
Description: Profile of the 27-year-old carpet and upholstery cleaning franchise, Chem-Dry. The firm is the leading carpet and upholstery cleaning business worldwide, with nearly 4,000 franchises around the world. The franchise credits their services as well as support and training to franchisees as keys to their success. New franchises can be started with less than $25,000, with financing offered and monthly payments equal to a car payment.

38619 ■ "Cleaning Up" in *Small Business Opportunities* **(Vol. 12, No. 3, May 2000, pp. 60)**
Pub: Harris Publications, Inc.
Description: Natural and man-made disasters have created a boom for entrepreneurs who offer restoration and cleanup services. A profile of Servpro Industries, Inc., the nation's leading disaster restoration and cleaning franchise system, is included.

38620 ■ "Click on a Fortune" in *Small Business Opportunities* **(May 2005)**
Pub: Harris Publications Inc.
Description: Franchise expo, Future Business Owners Spring Into Action, sponsored by the International Franchise Association, offers information to individuals interested in starting their own franchise business. Fifteen franchise opportunities are profiled in the article.

38621 ■ "Cold Feet?" in *Entrepreneur* **(Vol. 31, No. 11, November 2003, pp. 128)**
Pub: Entrepreneur Media, Inc.
Ed: Todd D. Maddocks. Description: In a hypothetical scenario, a couple have signed a build-to-suit lease for the construction of a franchised oil-change operations. Details of the transaction are provided.

38622 ■ "Cracking the Code" in *My Business* **(October/November 2003, pp. 49)**
Pub: My Business Magazine
Description: The top ten franchising industries are listed in the following order: fast food, retail, service, automotive, restaurants, maintenance, building and construction, retail-food, business services, and lodging. It is advised to seek legal advice before purchasing a franchise business.

38623 ■ "Cream of the Crop" in *Entrepreneur.com* **(Vol. 34, January 2006, No. 1, pp. 25)**
Pub: Entrepreneur Media Inc.
Ed: April Y. Pennington. Description: Profile of Cold Stone Creamery's founder, Doug Ducey, who discusses the firm's emphasis on customer service. The company is offering franchising opportunities throughout the country.

38624 ■ "The Dairy News" in *Small Business Opportunities* **(Spring 2005)**
Pub: Harris Publications Inc.
Description: Profile of Oberweis Franchise Systems franchising Oberwies Ice Cream. Franchising information about the family-owned and operated dairy included.

38625 ■ "Decorating Dollars" in *Small Business Opportunities* **(Vol. 16, No. 2, March 2004, pp. 110, 112)**
Pub: Harris Publications, Inc.
Description: Profile of Karen Price and Josie Cicerale, founders of Decor & You, a home-based decorating franchise. Professionally trained interior decorators go to client's homes and change the looks of rooms using wall and window coverings, furnishings, carpets and other elements. Currently 24 franchises are operating.

38626 ■ "Detroit Free Press Small Business Column" in *Detroit Free Press* **(July 18, 2005)**
Pub: Knight-Ridder/Tribune Business News
Ed: Carol Cain. Description: Profile of Philip Locke, entrepreneur with years of experience in starting and closing businesses; Locke describes his Cash Now company that advances cash to customers. His goal is to have ten master franchise agreements by December 2006.

38627 ■ "Documenting Profit" in *Small Business Opportunities* **(Vol. 16, No. 3, May 2004, pp. 58, 120)**
Pub: Harris Publications, Inc.
Ed: Jan Fields. Description: Profile of Ira and Linda Distenfield, the couple behind We The People, a franchised legal document processing service. Currently there are 120 open or under construction franchises in 26 states. Total investment ranges between $139,500 to $151,500.

38628 ■ "Dramatic Success" in *Small Business Opportunities* **(Vol. 17, November 2005, No. 6, pp. 52, 54)**
Pub: Harris Publications Inc.
Description: Profile of Drama Kids, the $10.5 million a year children's after-school drama program. The program offers original lessons with a focus on advancing language, speech and acting skills.

38629 ■ "Drawing Attention" in *Small Business Opportunities* **(Vol. 16, No. 3, May 2004, pp. 92, 130)**
Pub: Harris Publications, Inc.
Description: Profile of Young Rembrandts, a franchised home-based business that teaches a drawing program to preschool and elementary children. The program offers parents an alternative before and after school educational program for children interested in art.

38630 ■ "Exercise your franchise" in *Ingram's* **(Vol. 28, No. 3, March 2002, pp. 25)**
Pub: Show Me Publishing, Inc.
Ed: Joe Bisogno. Description: It is important to investigate a franchising organization before making an investment. Some things to consider are: advertising and royalty fees, management personnel experience, and growth potential.

38631 ■ "Expanding an Empire" in *Small Business Opportunities* **(Vol. 16, November 2004, No. 6, pp. 62, 64, 138)**
Pub: Harris Publications Inc.
Description: Profile of franchisor, Martinizing Dry Cleaning, headquartered in Loveland, Ohio. The upscale dry cleaning franchisor targets white collar customers with incomes more than $60,000 and are between the ages of 25 and 59. The company was launched in 1949. Growth strategies and predictions are included.

38632 ■ "Express to Success" in *Small Business Opportunities* **(Vol. 17, November 2005, No. 6, pp. 126-128)**
Pub: Harris Publications Inc.
Description: Robert A. Funk, CEO of Express Services, Inc., talks about the staffing firm he founded with his wife Nancy. The privately held company is rated sixth-largest in the nation and provides franchisor training at Express University in Oklahoma City.

38633 ■ "Find the Perfect Biz" in *Small Business Opportunities* **(Vol. 13, No. 5, September 2001, pp. 20)**
Pub: Harris Publications, Inc.
Description: Profile of FranChoice, a network of independent consultants who provide franchises with pre-screened, high quality leads to selected franchisors across the U.S. A list of the top ten franchise industries is provided.

38634 ■ "Flower Power: A Nearly Overlooked Opportunity is Blooming Into an Ideal Business" in *Entrepreneur* **(Vol. 32, July 2004, No. 7, pp. 87)**
Pub: Entrepreneur Media Inc.
Ed: Sarah Pierce. Description: Profiles of Kim Lohnes, who started a KaBloom franchise after being laid off from her technology job and Mary C. Rogers who established the successful Computertots franchise and is now embarking on another franchise, Abrakadoodle, she hopes will inspire the artist in every child.

38635 ■ "For the low, low price" in *Entrepreneur* **(Vol. 30, No. 10, October 2002, pp. 100)**
Pub: Entrepreneur Media Inc.
Description: A directory of franchises that can be started with investments of less than $25,000 is presented.

38636 ■ "Former Execs Go Franchising" in *Boston Business Journal* **(Vol. 23, No. 24, July 18, 2003, pp. 1)**
Pub: American City Business Journals
Ed: Jill Lerner. Description: Several executives from the Boston, Massachusetts area that have been laid off by their firms, are starting their own franchises.

38637 ■ "Franchise Fever" in *Home Business* **(Vol. 13, January/February 2006, No. 1, pp. 24, 26-27, 54-55)**
Pub: Home Business Magazine
Description: Excerpts from the Federal Trade Commission's Consumer Guide to Buying a Franchise by the International Franchise Association help entrepreneurs wishing to purchase a franchise. Statistical data included.

38638 ■ "Franchise Finder" in *Black Enterprise* **(Vol. 35, January 2005, No. 6, pp. 10)**
Pub: Earl G. Graves Publishing Co. Inc.
Description: Black Enterprise offers a Website that helps aspiring entrepreneurs choose the franchise right for them.

38639 ■ "Franchise Finds" in *Small Business Opportunities* **(Vol. 16, No. 2, March 2004, pp. 146)**
Pub: Harris Publications, Inc.
Description: Profile of three franchises, including Window Butler, offering residential and commercial window cleaning; More Space Place, a specialty retail company featuring Murphy Beds, space saving furniture, custom closets, garage and home products; and Wild Noodles, a quick-serve restaurant offer ethnic noodle dishes.

38640 ■ "A Franchise of Her Own" in *Entrepreneur* **(Vol. 28, No. 6, June 2000, pp. 163)**
Pub: Entrepreneur Media Inc.
Ed: Ellen Paris. Description: Meet a few exceptions to the rule that women don't do franchising, and why don't they anyway?

38641 ■ "Franchise solutions" in *Black Enterprise* **(Vol. 33, No. 7, February 2003, pp. 6)**
Pub: Earl Graves Publishing Co.
Description: Blackenterprise.com can help entrepreneurs find the industry that suits their talents. The free Franchise Finder will locate business opportunities, information, and advice on running a business more efficiently, along with free consultation on financing and interviews with franchise CEOs.

38642 ■ "Franchising" in *Black Enterprise* **(Vol. 32, No. 10, May 2002, pp. 101)**
Pub: Earl Graves Publishing Co.
Ed: Carolyn M. Brown. Description: Franchising is one of the fastest growing segments of American business and is seen as an ideal partnership for an independent entrepreneur. More minorities are discovering franchising opportunities by increased recruiting by companies like Wendy's, Merry Maids, Jan Pro, Subway, Church's Chicken (TM), and Interim Healthcare. Profile of aforementioned franchise opportunities are included.

38643 ■ *Franchising for Dummies*
Pub: John Wiley & Sons, Incorporated
Ed: Dave Thomas, Michael Seid. Released: June 2000. Price: $19.99. Description: Advice to help entrepreneurs choose the right franchise, as well as financing, managing and expanding the business.

38644 ■ "Franchising, Franchising" in *Inc.* **(Volume 27, June 2005, No. 6, pp. 24, 26)**
Pub: Inc. Magazine
Description: A group of entrepreneurs have launched Franchising Ventures Group, with $10 million to invest. The VC is looking for profitable companies that show franchise potential.

38645 ■ "Franchising" in *Hispanic Business* **(Vol. 23, No. 5, May 2001, pp. 50)**
Pub: Hispanic Business
Description: The International Franchise Association reports the need to educate emerging entrepreneurs about the 75 various industries offering franchise opportunities to Hispanics.

38646 ■ **"Franchisor Contacts"** in *Hispanic Business* (October 2004, pp. 114)
Pub: Hispanic Business
Ed: Description: Contact information for franchising opportunities of interest to Hispanic entrepreneurs is presented. Opportunities in the following sectors is presented: automotive, business aids and services, education and training, cleaning and sanitation, employment services, grocery and specialty stores, tutoring and learning aids, packaging and mailing, rentals, restaurants, carry-outs and drive-ins.

38647 ■ **"Fresh-Tossed Profits"** in *Small Business Opportunities* (Vol. 17, November 2005, No. 6, pp. 48, 50)
Pub: Harris Publications Inc.
Description: Fast growing Saladworks franchise is profiled. The firm plans to open more than 350 locations by 2010. The Saladworks menu includes more than 12 salads, made to order in front of customers and complemented by 12 dressings prepared on-site; fresh sandwiches and pasta dishes are also served.

38648 ■ **"Funding a Franchise Startup"** in *Hispanic Business* (Vol. 23, No. 5, May 2001, pp. 52, 54)
Pub: Hispanic Business
Ed: Barbara Beckley. **Description:** Funding sources available for franchise start-ups are presented. The Certified Development Company, a private, non-profit organization licensed by the SBA; the Small Business Investment Companies (SBICs), which provide equity capital and long-term debt financing; and the Community Development Corporations (CDCs) are among the resources profiled.

38649 ■ **"Get in the Game"** in *Entrepreneur* (Vol. 33, January 2005, No. 1, pp. 106)
Pub: Entrepreneur Media Inc.
Ed: Andrew A. Caffey. **Description:** Five strategies to use in order to participate in a franchise program are listed.

38650 ■ **"Get Rich in 2004"** in *Small Business Opportunities* (Vol. 16, No. 1, January 2004, pp. 22)
Pub: Harris Publications, Inc.
Description: Profiles of the best twenty franchise businesses to startup in 2004 are listed, including profiles and contact information for each. The companies features are Contours Express, Blind Butler, Best Personalized Books, Bark Busters, Home Helpers, Blind Brokers Network, Hometeam Inspections Service Inc., Lazylawn, Handyman Service, Lantis Fireworks, retail shops from Liberty Opportunities (Dollar Store), advanced window tinting systems, Green Concepts, Christmas Concepts, window washing, Badge-A-Minit, LeGourmet Gift Basket, Homeowner Referral Network, and Ding King.

38651 ■ **"Graduating with Wings"** in *Small Business Opportunities* (Vol. 16, No. 3, May 2004, pp. 76, 130)
Pub: Harris Publications, Inc.
Description: Profile of Wing Zone's franchise opportunities. The restaurants menu features 25 unique flavors of fresh, cooked-to-order chicken wings, and also offers salads, grilled sandwiches, and appetizers.

38652 ■ **"Home: Where the Money Is"** in *Small Business Opportunities* (Vol. 14, No. 1, January 2002, pp. 86)
Pub: Harris Publications, Inc.
Description: Profile of Kalie Warren, Jr., an ex-homeless man who started a handyman service called Rent-A-Husband and now sells franchise opportunities in six states, Hong Kong, and Great Britain. Warren plans to expand the franchise operation to 1,000 by the year 2008.

38653 ■ **"Imperial forces"** in *Entrepener* (Vol. 30, No. 3, March 2002, pp. 109)
Pub: Entrepreneur Media Inc.
Ed: Karen E. Klein. **Description:** Profile of various entrepreneurs and ways they started their empires.

38654 ■ **"Inc. Case Study"** in *Inc.* (November 2000, pp. 54)
Pub: The Goldhirsh Group
Description: Marian Cihacek chronicles the business she founded, Great Harvest Bread Company, that practically runs itself.

38655 ■ **"The Inside Scoop: What's It Really Like to Buy a Franchise?"** in *Entrepreneur* (Vol. 33, January 2005, No. 1, pp. 96)
Pub: Entrepreneur Media Inc.
Ed: Nichole L. Torres. **Description:** Profile of a woman who purchased a Cold Stone Creamery franchise.

38656 ■ **"Learning the Ropes"** in *Entrepreneur* (Vol. 33, October 2005, No. 10, pp. 99)
Pub: Entrepreneur Media Inc.
Description: A.D. Banker & Company helps individuals wishing to buy a franchise obtain licenses in the insurance, security, legal and accounting industries through classroom, online and self-study courses.

38657 ■ **"Less Is More"** in *Entrepreneur* (Vol. 33, October 2005, No. 10, pp. 100)
Pub: Entrepreneur Media Inc.
Description: A listing of 107 franchises that cost less than $25,000 to start up are listed, including phone numbers and Websites.

38658 ■ **"Love's Rewards"** in *Success* (Vol. 47, No. 1, January 2000, pp. 63)
Pub: Success Publishing, Inc.
Ed: Martha Visser. **Description:** By bringing together good research and a devoted support staff, Paul Falzone forged a successful dating-service franchise.

38659 ■ **"Luck of the Draw: A Windfall Helps One Man's Small Business Dream Come True"** in *Entrepreneur* (Vol. 31, No. 10, October 2003)
Pub: Entrepreneur Media, Inc.
Ed: Devlin Smith. **Description:** Profile of Timothy Tuttle, who won $1.9 million on a quarter slot machine in Las Vegas, Nevada, and started his own quick-service chain specializing in Orleans fare like gumbo and beignets.

38660 ■ **"The Man Who Launched 4,000 Businesses"** in *Fortune* (Vol. 143, No. 3, February 5, 2001, pp. 180)
Pub: Time Inc.
Ed: Carlye Adler. **Description:** Tony DeSio didn't set out to build the biggest non-food franchise ever. As with many entrepreneurial ventures, it just sort of happened that way.

38661 ■ **"McDonald's goes to church"** in *BlackEnterprise* (Vol. 32, No. 2, September 2001, pp. 24)
Pub: Earl Graves Publishing Co.
Ed: Lloyd Gite. **Description:** Brentwood Baptist Church in Houston is the first church in the nation to have a McDonald's hamburger franchise on its grounds. The Rev. Joe Ratliff, Brentwood's 51-year-old pastor, came up with the idea for the McDonald's at the church.

38662 ■ **"A model occupation: who says you can't turn business into play?"** in *Entrepreneur* (Vol. 31, No. 4, April 2003, pp. 102)
Pub: Entrepreneur Media Inc.
Ed: Devlin Smith. **Description:** Profile of Gary Phillips who turned his knowledge of retailing and love of model railroads into becoming a franchisee for Hobby-Town USA. Phillips and his wife are franchise partners. Information on three other franchising success stories is included.

38663 ■ **"A New Career for You Might Start at Franchise U"** in *Success* (Vol. 47, No. 3, July 2000, pp. 82)
Pub: Success Publishing, Inc.
Ed: Richard Landesberg. **Description:** Franchises are discussed as a way to become self-employed.

38664 ■ **"New Curves franchise serves up fast fitness"** in *Sarasota Herald Tribune* (August 12, 2002, pp. 8)
Pub: Sarasota Herald Tribune
Description: Short profiles of new businesses opening in the Sarasota area in August 2002, including Curves for Women, fitness and weight loss franchise; an Acupuncture and Alternative Medicine Center; a psychiatric practice; The Oasis Café; and the Floor Doctor and The Wood Floor Store.

38665 ■ **"A New Hope"** in *Entrepreneur* (Vol. 30, No)
Pub: Entrepreneur Media Inc.
Description: Some of the top franchise concepts for 2002 include space-age ice cream, weight loss, chicken wings and dating services. The top 50 new franchising concepts since 1997 are ranked. Contact information is provided for each franchise.

38666 ■ **"No Ticket to Easy Street"** in *Black Enterprise* (Vol. 31, No. 4, November 2000, pp. 62)
Pub: Earl Graves Publishing Co.
Ed: Paula McCoy-Pinderhughes. **Description:** Is franchising your entrance into entrepreneurship? With approximately 320,000 franchised small businesses in the U.S., accounting for $1 trillion in annual retail sales, it is a proven way to achieve the American Dream.

38667 ■ **"Out with the Old"** in *Entrepreneur* (Vol. 32, December 2004, No. 12, pp. 110)
Pub: Entrepreneur Media Inc.
Description: A listing of 102 companies that started offering franchising opportunities in 2003 or 2004 is presented.

38668 ■ **"Perk Up Profits"** in *Small Business Opportunities* (Vol. 12, No. 5, September 2000, pp. 82)
Pub: Harris Publications, Inc.
Description: Information to start a drive-through coffee kiosk enterprise is offered. A profile of two sisters-in-law who operate 17 Mountain Mudd locations in Montana is included.

38669 ■ **"Personalized Profits"** in *Small Business Opportunities* (Vol. 13, No. 5, September 2001, pp. 82)
Pub: Harris Publications, Inc.
Description: Profile of franchise embroidery shops, EmbroidMe, the newest franchise venture from SIGN*A*RAMA, and owner and president Ray Titus. EmbroidMe has partnered with Brother, the leading manufacturer of embroidery equipment and accessories, in order to provide lettering on everything from baby blankets to corporate logos. Facts and figures for investing are included.

38670 ■ **"Primer for Profit"** in *Small Business Opportunities* (Vol. 13, No. 6, November 2001, pp. 52, 56)
Pub: Harris Publications, Inc.
Description: Profile of Barry Penzel, owner of Certa ProPainters franchise in Minden, Nevada. Mr. Penzel, former army colonel, tells how he runs his successful company with military precision. Certa ProPainters franchise opportunities are listed.

38671 ■ **"Purchasing Power"** in *Small Business Opportunities* (Spring 2005)
Pub: Harris Publications Inc.
Description: Profile of Save It Now!, the franchised group purchasing organization. The firm negotiated for Fortune 500 volume discounted prices for up to 40 percent and service guarantees with national vendors. Currently the service boasts membership of 4,000 small to medium-sized businesses.

38672 ■ **"Raising the Woof: Make No Bones About It-This Bakery Takes Dog Food to a Whole New Level"** in *Entrepreneur* (Vol. 32, July 2004)
Pub: Entrepreneur Media Inc.
Ed: Jonathan Riggs. **Description:** Profile of Melanie Superack who founded Just Dogs! with her mother. The franchise, located in a shopping mall, offers gift ideas for dog lovers, including holiday cookies, dog lollipops and flavored barrel treats. Sales for the store are expected to reach nearly $170,000.

38673 ■ "Real Estate" in *Sarasota Herald Tribune* (January 20, 2003, pp. 5)
Pub: Sarasota Herald Tribune
Description: Announcement of the opening of a new Curves For Women, 30 Minute Fitness and Weight Loss Center in Sarasota, Florida, by Maureen Barnett and Christine Cassanelli.

38674 ■ "Recipe for Riches" in *Small Business Opportunities* (Vol. 16, No. 1, January 2004, pp. 72)
Pub: Harris Publications, Inc.
Description: Profile of Cousins Subs franchises, founded by cousins James F. Sheppard and William F. Specht. The firm's goal is to open one store per week in 2005, concentrating in existing states that include Wisconsin, Minnesota, Michigan, Illinois, Indiana, North Dakota, Colorado, California, Texas, and Arizona. Total initial investment ranges from $159,300 to $291,600.

38675 ■ "Secrets to Success: Yes, You Can Be a Successful Franchisee in 2003" in *Entrepreneur* (Vol. 31, No. 9, July 2003, pp. 86)
Pub: Entrepreneur Media, Inc.
Ed: Devlin Smith. **Description:** The major elements to start a new franchise are presented. Franchising insiders share secrets to being a successful franchisee.

38676 ■ "Service Franchises Hold Advantages Over Retail Operations" in *Long Island Business News* (May 7, 2004)
Pub: Dolan Media Newswires
Ed: Adina Genn. **Description:** The advantages service franchises have over owning a retail franchise are discussed. Discussions with various franchise owners are included.

38677 ■ "Show Me the Money" in *Entrepreneur* (Vol. 33, September 2005, No. 9, pp. 102)
Pub: Entrepreneur Media Inc.
Ed: April Y. Pennington. **Description:** Franchise ownership is not as costly as perceived. Stan Harris tells how he secured a loan from a bank to fund his wrap-sandwich restaurant, while a Hawaiian couple secured two loans, one from franchisee and one from a bank, to start their smoothie franchise that promotes healthy eating and living.

38678 ■ "A Sizzling Fortune" in *Small Business Opportunities* (Vol. 17, September 2005, No. 5, pp. 48, 50)
Pub: Harris Publications Inc.
Ed: Stan Roberts. **Description:** Profile of Brian Wheeler and Camp Fitch, owners of the Tijuana Flats franchise. Initial investment costs run from $133,000 to $236,000 with at least two years of restaurant experience required to startup.

38679 ■ "Sizzling Sales" in *Small Business Opportunities* (Winter 2005)
Pub: Harris Publications Inc.
Description: Profile of franchise, El Pollo Loco, the country's leading quick-service restaurant chain. The restaurant serves citrus-marinated, flame grilled chicken and is aggressively seeking franchisees.

38680 ■ "A Slice of Happiness" in *Small Business Opportunities* (Vol. 17, September 2005, No. 5, pp. 72, 138)
Pub: Harris Publications, Inc.
Description: Profile of Figaro's Italian Pizzas, Inc., headquartered in Salem, Oregon. Startup costs run $200,000 to $300,000 and include training in every aspect of starting and running a Figaro pizza restaurant.

38681 ■ "Small Business Spotlight" in *Small Business Opportunities* (Vol. 14, No. 1, January 2002, pp. 110)
Pub: Harris Publications, Inc.
Description: Profiles of three franchise startups, including a Sign-A-Rama that opened in a Puerto Rican neighborhood in Chicago's north side through the Latino Economic Development Assistance Corporation (LEDAC); Hi Frequency Marketing, a Carrboro, North Carolina-based company focusing on the youth marked; and Buffalo Lube Associates, operator of 15 Valvoline Instant Oil Change centers in New York.

38682 ■ "Smoothie Operators" in *Small Business Opportunities* (Vol. 16, No. 2, March 2004, pp. 82)
Pub: Harris Publications, Inc.
Description: Profile of Maui Wowi, the franchisor of Hawaiian Blend gourmet, all natural refreshments sold at kiosks. The franchise is also adding FIJI Water to its line of products. Founders Jeff and Jill Summerhays are also profiled.

38683 ■ "Stress Relief" in *Entrepreneur.com* (Vol. 34, February 2006, No. 2, pp. 104)
Pub: Entrepreneur Media Inc.
Ed: Sara Wilson. **Description:** Profile of Jeni Garrett who mastered three businesses by age 27. Garrett sold clothing and jewelry line, raised and sold cattle, and created a new spa brand in 2001. Garrett founded The Woodhouse Day Spa in Victoria, Texas and offers franchising opportunities.

38684 ■ "Stretch Your Limits" in *Entrepreneur* (Vol. 32, December 2004, No. 12, pp. 108)
Pub: Entrepreneur Media Inc.
Ed: Natalia Olenicoff. **Description:** IM=X Pilates franchises are now available. Pilates is one of the fastest growing fitness trends in the U.S.

38685 ■ "Strike it Rich!" in *Small Business Opportunities* (Vol. 16, No. 3, May 2004, pp. 22-24, 26, 28, 30, 32, 34, 36, 38, 40-42, 44, 98)
Pub: Harris Publications, Inc.
Description: Profiles of fifteen service business to consider, including electrical services, windshield repair, waste management, automotive repair, wedding photography, dryer vent cleaning, home helpers, supermarket services, garage makeovers, window blinds cleaning, concrete coating, carpet and upholstering cleaning, slip and fall prevention, and home cleaning.

38686 ■ "Strike While the Iron's Red Hot!" in *Success* (Vol. 47, No. 2, June 2000, pp. 92)
Pub: Success Publishing, Inc.
Ed: Jerry Wilkerson. **Description:** Across most industries, the business of franchise development is projecting a decisive 12 percent increase in the year 2000.

38687 ■ "Strong Future Brewing" in *Small Business Opportunities* (Spring 2005)
Pub: Harris Publications Inc.
Description: Profile of The Coffee Beanery, Ltd. The franchise supports upscale cafes, retail stores, carts and kiosks specializing in Arabica coffee. Franchise facts included.

38688 ■ "Super Success in Spas" in *Small Business Opportunities* (Vol. 16, No. 2, March 2004, pp. 92, 95)
Pub: Harris Publications, Inc.
Ed: Vicki Gerson. **Description:** Profile of Robert Hallam, founder of Dimension One Spas, designer and manufacturer of spas ranging in price from $4,000 to $30,000. Robert's wife handles the firm's customer service and is credited for its annual growth of 8-12 percent, reaching $48 million in 2002. Dimension Spas has partnered with Vision of Children Foundation by donating $100 for every spa sold to help end childhood blindness and vision disorders.

38689 ■ "Supply Side Economics" in *Small Business Opportunities* (Vol. 16, No. 2, March 2004, pp. 64, 68)
Pub: Harris Publications, Inc.
Description: Profile of Shane's Office Supply, franchise business in Downers Grove, Illinois. The office supply company earns $8 million annually selling office products such as pens, pads and toner cartridges to businesses of all sizes. Total startup costs run between $76,000 and $137,000.

38690 ■ "Tips & Trends" in *Small Business Opportunities* (Vol. 13, No. 5, September 2001, pp. 14)
Pub: Harris Publications, Inc.
Description: The latest tips and trends for small business are presented, including the Fastsigns Interna-

tional, Inc. franchisor; VeriPack.com shipping company; Seaga Manufacturing, supplier of compact vending machines and refrigerated venders; the wireless handheld device LinkPoint 9000; and the Motorola Spirit GT walkie-talkie.

38691 ■ "20 Top Biz for 2002" in *Small Business Opportunities* (V. 14, No. 1, 1/2002, pp. 22-24, 26, 28, 30, 32, 34, 36, 38, 40, 130)
Pub: Harris Publications, Inc.
Description: Twenty recession-proof businesses for potential entrepreneurs to startup are profiled, including health food store, cleaning service, handyman service agency, cart vendors, window cleaning, dance studio, information broker, landscaping, sign shop, auto paint repair service, computer maintenance, closet/storage organizer, childproofing safety business, hair salon, specialty cake bakery, pet chauffer business, senior services, and delivery services.

38692 ■ "Web.Preneuring" in *Small Business Opportunities* (Vol. 17, September 2005, No. 5, pp. 90, 94)
Pub: Harris Publications, Inc.
Description: Profile of Jeremiah Hutchins, who launched his Safe Kids Card, Inc. venture in 2002 and started offering franchise opportunities in March 2003. The card acts as an all-in-one identification card for children and holds photographs, a biometric fingerprint, and personal and medical information. Franchising information included.

38693 ■ "What's New" in *Entrepreneur.com* (Vol. 34, February 2006, No. 2, pp. 104)
Pub: Entrepreneur Media Inc.
Description: The Online Trading Academy helps individuals to buy and sell stocks. The company plans to expand its franchise opportunities to about 100 major cities worldwide.

38694 ■ "Winning Recipe-Superhot & Sizzling" in *Small Business Opportunities* (January 2006)
Pub: Harris Publications Inc.
Description: Profile of FiltaFry franchise that cleans deep fryers and recycles oil for restaurants.

38695 ■ "Word to the Wise" in *Entrepreneur* (Vol. 32, July 2004, No. 7, pp. 82)
Pub: Entrepreneur Media Inc.
Ed: April Y. Pennington. **Description:** Several key factors to consider when choosing a franchise opportunity are listed.

ASSOCIATIONS AND OTHER ORGANIZATIONS

38696 ■ American Association of Franchisees and Dealers
3500 5th Ave., Ste. 103
PO Box 81887
San Diego, CA 92138-1887
Ph:(619)209-3775
Free: 800-733-9858
Fax:(619)209-3777
Co. E-mail: benefits@aafd.org
URL: http://www.aafd.org
Contact: Robert L. Purvin Jr., Chm./CEO
Membership: Franchise business owners. **Purpose:** Represents the interests of franchise business owners. Seeks to bring fairness to franchising. Maintains legal and financial referral services, speakers' bureau, and suppliers network; conducts research and educational programs; compiles statistics. **Publications:** *Franchisee Voice* (quarterly).

38697 ■ American Franchisee Association
53 W Jackson Blvd., Ste. 1157
Chicago, IL 60604
Ph:(312)431-0545
Fax: (312)431-1469
Co. E-mail: info@franchisee.org
URL: http://www.franchisee.org
Contact: Susan P. Kezios, Pres.
Description: Works to promote and enhance the economic interests of small business franchisees; pro-

mote the growth and development of members' enterprises; assist in the formation of independent franchisee associations; offer support, assistance, and legal referral services to members. **Publications:** *E-news* (monthly); *Forming an Independent Franchisee Association - A Turn-Key Approach*; *How to Form an Association?*.

38698 ■ Canadian Alliance of Franchise Operators

1201 Bayfield St. N
Midhurst, ON, Canada L0L 1X1
Ph:(705)737-4635
Fax: (705)737-4950
Co. E-mail: mail@cafo.net
URL: http://www.cafo.net
Contact: Les Stewart MBA, Founder/Pres.
Description: Offers advisory services on issues facing franchisees.

38699 ■ Canadian Franchise Association–Association Canadienne de la Franchise

5399 Eglinton Ave. W, Ste. 116
Toronto, ON, Canada M9C 5K6
Ph:(416)695-2896
Free: 800-665-4232
Fax: (416)695-1950
Co. E-mail: info@cfa.ca
URL: http://www.cfa.ca
Contact: Monika Dickson, Office Mgr.
Membership: Franchise businesses. **Purpose:** Represents the shared interests of businesses and professionals active in the Canadian franchise sector. Provides information and guidance to aspiring franchisees. **Publications:** *Franchise Canada* (bimonthly); Directory (annual).

38700 ■ International Franchise Association

1501 K St. NW, Ste. 350
Washington, DC 20005
Ph:(202)628-8000
Fax: (202)628-0812
Co. E-mail: ifa@franchise.org
URL: http://www.franchise.org
Contact: Cecelia Bond, Exec.Asst.
Description: Firms in 100 countries utilizing the franchise method of distribution for goods and services in all industries. **Publications:** *Franchise Opportunities Guide* (semiannual); *Franchising World Magazine* (bimonthly).

38701 ■ Women in Franchising

53 W Jackson Blvd., Ste. 1157
Chicago, IL 60604
Ph:(312)431-1467
Fax: (312)431-1469
Co. E-mail: info@womeninfranchising.com
URL: http://www.womeninfranchising.com
Contact: Susan P. Kezios, Pres.
Description: Assists women interested in all aspects of franchise business development including those buying a franchised business and those expanding their businesses via franchising. Provides franchise technical assistance in both of these areas. Surveys the industry on the status of women. **Publications:** *Buying a Franchise: How to Make the Right Choice*; *Growing Your Business: The Franchise Option*.

DIRECTORIES OF EDUCATIONAL PROGRAMS

38702 ■ *Bond's Franchise Guide 2007*

Pub: Source Book Publications.
Ed: Robert E. Bond. **Released:** December 2006. **Price:** $34.95. **Description:** Directory of 1,000 franchise opportunities, includes supplemental profiles on franchise attorneys and consultants. The companies are divided into 45 business categories with comparisons.

REFERENCE WORKS

38703 ■ "View from the Top: Subway Takes the Title of the 1 Franchise for the 13th Time." in *Entrepreneur* (Vol. 33, January 2005, No. 1)

Pub: Entrepreneur Media Inc.
Ed: Nichole L. Torres. **Description:** Subway reports 21,444 franchises worldwide in 2004, making it the number one franchise in Entrepreneur's Franchise 500 for the 13th time. Fred Deluca, owner of Subway, talks about the good feeling he has knowing he has helped thousands of entrepreneurs to start their own business.

38704 ■ "10 Hottest Deals in Franchising" in *Black Enterprise* (Vol. 35, September 2004, No. 2, pp. 77)

Pub: Earl G. Graves Publishing Co. Inc.
Ed: Wendy Harris. **Description:** According to industry experts, a new franchise business opens in the U.S. every eight minutes. A listing of the best ten franchising opportunities for African Americans is presented.

38705 ■ "A North Carolina Entrepreneur Sets His Sights On Creating the H&R Block of Public Relations" in *Inc.* (May 1, 2005)

Pub: Inc. Magazine
Ed: Stephanie Clifford. **Description:** Mike Butler has launched his new public relations firm, PR Store, focusing on small businesses. Butler has franchises in Charlotte, North Carolina; Detroit and Grand Rapids, Michigan; and plans to expand nationwide.

38706 ■ "Affordable Franchises" in *BlackEnterprise* (Vol. 32, No. 2, September 2001, pp. 88)

Pub: Earl Graves Publishing Co.
Ed: Bridget McCrea. **Description:** A list of 15 franchises that offer opportunities for African American business owners, based on a national survey franchisors that are members of the of the International Franchise Association (IFA), the existing number of African American franchise units, and companies that have franchises within three price ranges: $10,000-$50,000, $50,000-$150,000, and $150,000-$350,000 (inclusive of total start-up costs and franchise fee). Franchises listed include Coverall Cleaning Concepts, Molly Maid Inc., Liberty Tax Service, Kumon North America, ECW Corp., Crown Trophy, SIGN-A-RAMA, Ace Cash Express Inc., MGW Group Inc., Express Personnel Services, Meineke Discount Muffler Shops Inc., Cinnabon Inc., Jiffy Lube International Inc., Denny's Inc., Church's Chicken.

38707 ■ "All work, All play" in *Entrepreneur* (Vol. 30, No. 3, March 2002, pp.)

Pub: Entrepreneur Media Inc.
Ed: Devlin Smith. **Description:** Profile of the family owned Woodplay franchise located in Tampa, Florida.

38708 ■ "An American Icon" in *Entrepreneur* (Vol. 33, January 2005, No. 1, pp. 76)

Pub: Entrepreneur Media Inc.
Ed: April Y. Pennington. **Description:** There are more than 387,000 franchises, listed are the five ways in which franchising has affected the U.S.

38709 ■ "Amortization of Certain Intangible Assets" in *Journal of Accountacncy*

Pub: American Institute of Certified Public Accountants
Ed: Jennifer M. Mueller. **Description:** Intangible assets that are the result of contractual or legal rights are explained, including patents, licenses, trademarks, franchise and servicing rights.

38710 ■ "Applebee Int'l Sets Up Loans for Remodeling by Franchises" in *Long Island Business News* (March 12, 2004)

Pub: Dolan Media Newswires
Description: Applebee's International has instituted a new loan program for its franchisees in order to remodel stores. The Overland Park, Kansas-based Applebee's will allow franchisees to draw on a credit line up to $75 million. Statistical data included.

38711 ■ "At Deadline" in *Crain's New York Business* (Vol. 20, No. 12, March 22, 2004, pp. 1)

Pub: Crain Communications, Inc.
Description: Miscellaneous business briefs are cited, including information showing sixteen percent of New York City employers plan to hire more staff in the second quarter of 2004; Quickdrop International has been given state approval to begin selling franchises in New York for eBay drop-off centers.

38712 ■ "AT & T Heads Into TV Fray With Passage of Video Bill" in *Crain's Detroit Business* (Vol. 22, December 18, 2006, No. 51, pp. 5)

Pub: Crain Communications Inc. - Detroit
Ed: Amy Lane. **Description:** AT&T is making a large investment in Michigan as a result of the new bill passed last week to open competition amongst high tech cable suppliers; franchising process is revised opening the doors to a new video battle amongst Comcast and AT&T.

38713 ■ "The Attention Getter" in *My Business* (June/July 2004, pp. 48)

Pub: My Business Magazine
Ed: Jamie Roberts. **Description:** Profile of Greg Grimaud, owner of nine Precision Tune Auto Care franchises. Grimaud shares secrets to his marketing success. He advertises in both English and Spanish and promotes his stores by driving Hummer automobiles with the company logos.

38714 ■ *Best Home-Based Franchises*

Pub: Doubleday & Co., Inc.
Ed: Compiled by Philip Lief Group, Inc., staff. **Released:** 1992. **Price:** $15.00 (paper).

38715 ■ *The Best Nonfranchise Business Opportunities: The Smart Entrepreneur's Guide to Dealerships, License Agreements, Distributors, and More*

Pub: Henry Holt & Co., Inc.
Ed: Andrew J. Sherman and Donna T. Cavanagh. **Released:** 1993. **Price:** $19.95 (paper). **Description:** Provides information on business opportunities, such as license agreements, distributorships, and dealerships. Covers 75 opportunities and offers advice on evaluating a nonfranchise opportunity.

38716 ■ "Beyond Burgers" in *My Business* (December/January 2004, pp. 49)

Pub: My Business Magazine
Ed: Lena Basha. **Description:** Top ten hottest franchises are ranked: McDonald's Corporation, 7-Eleven Inc., Subway Sandwiches & Salads, Pizza Hut Inc., Burger King Corporation, Jani-King International Inc., RadioShack, Cendant Corporation, International Dairy Queen Inc., and KFC Corporation. Brief profiles of Three Dog Bakery, My Gym, and American Pool-players Association are also presented.

38717 ■ "The Big Bang: How Franchising Became an Economic Powerhouse the World Over" in *Entrepreneur* (Vol. 32, No. 1, January 2004, pp. 86)

Pub: Entrepreneur Media, Inc.
Ed: David J. Kaufmann. **Description:** David J. Kaufmann offers a perspective on the ways franchising has change the economy and opportunity for entrepreneurs during the last 25 years.

38718 ■ "Big Boy Plans Big Growth in Franchises; Deals Signed for 23 Diners, One for 60 in Works" in *Crain's Detroit Business* (Vol. 21)

Pub: Crain Communications Inc. - Detroit
Ed: Brent Snavely. **Description:** Big Boy Restaurants International LLC will expand its operations with about 23 new restaurants over the next six years. The company is also close to closing a deal for 60 restaurants in southern California. Brief history of the company is included.

38719 ■ "Boise fitness centers brace for challenge from Gold's Gym" in *Vancouver Business Journal* (December 2, 2002)

Pub: Dolan Media Newswires

Ed: Steve Martin. **Description:** Profile of Gold's Gyms, and its expansion, particularly in the Boise, Idaho area. Gold's Gyms are working to stay current with workout trends, including not only free-weights and workout machines, but martial arts, tanning and massage, child-care, Pilates, yoga, even specific exercise regimens for golfers, etc.

38720 ■ Bond's Franchise Guide
Pub: Source Book Publications
Ed: Bond staff. **Released:** 1996. **Price:** $29.95.

38721 ■ Bond's Franchise Guide 2007
Pub: Source Book Publications
Ed: Robert E. Bond. **Released:** December 2006. **Price:** $34.95. **Description:** Comprehensive directory of franchise opportunities, divided into 45 categories.

38722 ■ "Bottle Perfection" in Entrepreneur (Vol. 33, February 2005, No. 2, pp. 83)
Pub: Entrepreneur Media Inc.
Description: Profile of franchise, Let's Make Wine, in Boca Raton, Florida. Customers can select a wine, and then personalize the bottle, cork, and label after fermentation.

38723 ■ "Breaking the Chain: A Declaration of Independents Against Chain Restaurants" in Entrepreneur (Vol. 32, July 2004, No. 7, pp. 30)
Pub: Entrepreneur Media Inc.
Ed: Judith Potwara. **Description:** Independent restaurant owners are partnering in order to compete with chain restaurants as they continue to expand. According to the Council of Independent Restaurants in America (CIRA), 8,000 to 10,000 new restaurants open every year in the U.S.

38724 ■ "Briefly" in Crain's Detroit Business (Vol. 21, January 24, 2005, No. 4, pp. 10)
Pub: Crain Communications Inc. - Detroit
Ed: Jennette Smith, Brent Snavely, Amy Lane. **Description:** Pro Golf, headquartered in Farmington Hills, Michigan plans to open eight new franchises with locations in Florida, Indiana, Georgia, Massachusetts, New York, and Nevada.

38725 ■ "Builders Land Rutenberg Deal" in Charlotte Observer (February 2, 2007)
Pub: Knight-Ridder/Tribune Business News
Ed: Bob Fliss. **Description:** Jim and Larry Sanders purchased a franchise from builder, Arthur Rutenberg Homes. The brothers will build custom homes in the area.

38726 ■ "Building Your Business" in Small Business Opportunities (Vol. 17, May 2005, No. 3, pp. 12)
Pub: Harris Publications Inc.
Ed: Carla Longley Vincent. **Description:** Seven ways for a small business to tap into customers and increase profits include the development of alliances, franchising, adding wholesale clients, sell to the government, work with nonprofits, market yourself, and create new goods or services.

38727 ■ "Burger King Corp" in Black Enterprise (Vol. 34, No. 6, January 2004, pp. 51)
Pub: Earl Graves Publishing Co.
Description: Clyde Rucker, senior vice president of diversity for Burger King Corporation, will co-chair the firm's Diversity Advisory Council along with CEO Brad Blum. The council will oversee development of minority franchises and suppliers.

38728 ■ "Burger King Franchisees, Parent Squabble Over Firm's Declining Fortunes" in Portland Press Herald (November 8, 2005)
Pub: Blethen Maine Newspapers, Inc.
Ed: Edward D. Murphy. **Description:** Burger King franchisees contend that the company's corporate headquarters' bad management has left them with declining profits. Continual turnover in leadership, quick changes in promotional strategies, and the change of the company's logo have all cost franchisees large sums of money, especially changing signs and restaurant supplies to reflect the new logo.

38729 ■ "The Business of Fitness" in Birmingham Business Journal (Vol. 20, No. 31, August 1, 2003, pp. 11)
Pub: American City Business Journals, Inc.
Ed: Lauren Bishop. **Description:** Fitness Together, a personal training company, is expanding its franchise in Alabama and North Carolina under the leadership of Forrest Walden and Aaron Crocker. Fitness Together is owned by Castlerock, the Colorado-based Fitness for Life Franchise Corporation.

38730 ■ "Business Near You: Beverly Hills Franchise Offers Directors for Smaller Firms" in Detroit Free Press (January 21, 2007)
Pub: Knight-Ridder/Tribune Business News
Ed: Carol Cain. **Description:** Profile of Carl Ammaccapane, president of The Alternative Board in Beverly Hills. The firm assists small to mid-sized businesses organize an outside board of directors consisting of owners of companies of similar size.

38731 ■ "Business Services" in Entrepreneur (Vol. 32, No. 1, January 2004, pp. 168)
Pub: Entrepreneur Media, Inc.
Description: Listing of various business service franchises opportunities is presented.

38732 ■ Buying Your First Franchise
Pub: Crisp Publications, Inc.
Ed: Rebecca Luhn. **Released:** 1994. **Price:** $15.95. **Description:** Part of the Small Business & Entrepreneurship Series.

38733 ■ "California based Robeks Fruit Smoothies Sets Expansion in NY Metro..." in Long Island Business News (Feb.27,2004)
Pub: Dolan Media Newswires
Ed: Nick Anastasi. **Description:** Profile of Robeks Fruit Smoothies & Healthy Treats, a franchise eatery based in Manhattan Beach, California. Founded in 1995, the franchise currently has 45 stores in three states and expects to expand into 26 metropolitan areas in the U.S.

38734 ■ "Card Shark" in Entrepreneur (Vol. 33, October 2005, No. 10, pp. 99)
Pub: Entrepreneur Media Inc.
Description: Profile of CardSmart franchise, featuring half-price cards, soy candles, and silk plants.

38735 ■ "CEO of Fort Lauderdale, Fla., Women's Fitness Chain Creates Smaller Outlets" in Miami Herald (November 11, 2002)
Pub: Knight Ridder/Tribune Business News
Description: Profile of Roger Wittenberns, the man behind Lady of America fitness centers for women. Wittenberns opened his first women-only fitness center in Houston in 1984, and has expanded to 290 franchise locations to date.

38736 ■ "Chain Lightening" in Hispanic Business (May 2005, pp. 72, 74)
Pub: Hispanic Business
Ed: Dale Buss. **Description:** Hispanics are fueling the growth in franchise ownership. Franchising tips are shared by Detroit's Ruben Acosta, franchising expert and lawyer, and founder of Pizza Patron.

38737 ■ "Change is Good" in Success (Vol. 47, No. 5, October 2000, pp. 6)
Pub: Success Publishing, Inc.
Ed: Ripley Hotch. **Description:** The annual Franchise Gold survey and ranking of the top franchisors in the country is presented.

38738 ■ "Changing Lanes; Retirements Spur Wave of Sales of Ford Dealerships" in Crain's Detroit Business (Vol. 20, December 20, 2004, No. 51)
Pub: Crain Communications Inc. - Detroit
Ed: Brent Snavely. **Description:** Retirement is changing ownership of Ford new car dealerships throughout Michigan. Details on the sales of Ray Whitfield Ford, Alan Ford, and Jorgenson Ford are presented.

38739 ■ "Charged Up" in Entrepreneur (Vol. 33, October 2005, No. 10, pp. 98)
Pub: Entrepreneur Media Inc.
Ed: Sara Wilson. **Description:** Profile of Russian-born Oleg Nikishin, who runs a successful Mr. Electric franchise in Pennsylvania. Nikishin offers advice to would-be entrepreneurs.

38740 ■ "Children's Products and Services" in Entrepreneur (Vol. 32, No. 1, January 2004, pp. 178)
Pub: Entrepreneur Media, Inc.
Description: Franchise opportunities in available for retail children's products and children's services industries.

38741 ■ "Chili Shack Draws Interest" in Kansas City Star (February 15, 2005)
Pub: Knight-Ridder/Tribune Business News
Ed: Joyce Smith. **Description:** Profile of John David DiCapo's new Chili Shack restaurant. DiCapo promotes his food products through his restaurants and hopes to open 10 franchise or license operations by 2006. He is also offering a line of hot sauces.

38742 ■ "Chocolate Factory is a sweet deal" in (Vol. 16, No. 2, February, 2002, pp. B6)
Pub: The Wenatchee Business Journal Inc.
Ed: Rebecca Dudley. **Description:** Profile of the Rocky Mountain Chocolate Factory, a franchise headquartered in Durango, Colorado. The international franchiser and confectionery manufacturer has eight company-owned and 213 franchised stores.

38743 ■ "Click on a Fortune" in Small Business Opportunities (Vol. 17, May 2005, No. 3, pp. 22-24, 26-28, 30, 32, 34, 36, 38, 40, 42, 44)
Pub: Harris Publications Inc.
Description: Fifteen growing service franchises are highlighted. Profiles of the following franchise and independent startup opportunities include Island Ink-Jet, Wireless Toyz, homemade foods, Children's Orchard, carpet cleaning, concierge services, family books, Putt-Putt golf centers, glass replacement, online auction sales, mystery shoppers, Earl of Sandwich, Instant FX, senior care, and real estate investing.

38744 ■ "Cloning Around" in Entrepreneur (Vol. 32, No. 1, January 2004, pp. 130)
Pub: Entrepreneur Media, Inc.
Ed: Andrew A. Caffey. **Description:** Things necessary to launch a successful franchise are examined.

38745 ■ "Coming of Age: Americans Are Hitting 50 and Finding They're Anything But Over the Hill" in Entrepreneur
Pub: Entrepreneur Media Inc.
Ed: Sara Wilson. **Description:** Several entrepreneurs over the age of 50 who purchased franchises are profiled.

38746 ■ The Commonsense Way to Build Wealth: One Entrepreneur Shares His Secrets
Pub: Griffin Publishing Group
Ed: Jack Chou. **Released:** September 2004. **Price:** $19.95. **Description:** Entrepreneurial tips to accumulate wealth, select the proper business or franchise, choose and manage rental property, and how to negotiate a good lease.

38747 ■ "Couldn't hurt" in Entrepreneur (Vol. 30, No. 3, March 2002, pp. 28)
Pub: Entrepreneur Media Inc.
Description: Will 'healthy fast food' chains be successful in America?

38748 ■ "Creaming up the competition" in Atlanta Business Chronicle (Vol. 24, No. 13, August 31, 2001, pp. 3A)
Pub: American City Business Journals Inc.
Ed: Jarred Schenke. **Description:** Cold Stone Creamer, a Scottsdale, Arizona-based ice cream parlor, is planning to open 30 stores in Atlanta during the

next three to four years, according to Stone's co-owner of the region franchise rights, Brad Spratte. Ice cream with the normal levels of butter fat, which Stone sells, has increases in sales by 6 percent from 2000. Although Cold Stone is doing well, Baskin-Robbins, the largest chain of ice cream parlors, has been successful in the Atlanta area.

38749 ■ "Creating a Recipe for an Empire" in *Crain's New York Business* (Vol. 23, January 29, 2007, No. 5, pp. F22)
Pub: Crain Communications, Inc.
Ed: Description: Profile of Kenny Lao, co-founder of Rickshaw Dumpling Bar, whose business plan for the casual Chelsea eatery won a contest at Stern and attracted the school's dean, Thomas Cooley, as an investor. Rickshaw's revenues in fiscal 2005 reached $1.3 million and are on track to rise another 12 percent in 2006. He intends to open six more Rickshaw bars within the next few years.

38750 ■ "Dairy Queen phasing out frozen yogurt" in (Vol. 14, No. 9, August 29, 2001, pp. 1)
Pub: Howard Waxman
Description: Due to waning sales, Dairy Queen International will no longer sell frozen yogurt at its shops. Dairy Queen has hired Dimension Data/Proxicom to develop an extranet for the company's franchises in the hopes that better communications and information sharing will increase efficiency.

38751 ■ "Delivering At Domino's Pizza" in *Fortune* (Vol. 151, February 7, 2005, No. 3, pp. 28)
Pub: Time Inc.
Ed: Julia Boorstin. **Description:** Domino's Pizza has seen its stock climb 26 percent since going public in July 2004. In an interview with Domino's CEO, David Brandon, he tells how he helped overhaul the company's training program and dropped the employee turnover rate by 60 percent. The franchiser has also opened 1,200 new stores in the past five years, two-thirds of them overseas.

38752 ■ "Despite Flaws, Franchise System is Solid" in *Automotive News* (Vol. 79, January 31, 2005, No. 6132, pp. 12)
Pub: Crain Communications Inc.
Ed: Keith Crain. **Description:** Franchising is still the best method for selling and distributing vehicles in the U.S.

38753 ■ "Detroit Free Press Wayne Small Business Column" in *Detroit Free Press* (July 21, 2005)
Pub: Knight-Ridder/Tribune Business News
Ed: Carol Cain. **Description:** Mark Slagle, owner of Mr. Handyman of Southeastern Wayne County franchise, discusses growing a small business in a tough economy. Mr. Handyman offers full-service repair and maintenance for homeowners.

38754 ■ "Dishin' Up Profits" in *My Business* (April/May 2004, pp. 46-47)
Pub: My Business Magazine
Ed: Jamie Roberts. **Description:** Profile Yaron Goldman, owner of seven McAlister's Deli franchises in the Charlotte, North Carolina area. Goldman offers three rules that helped him become a successful franchise owner.

38755 ■ "Dixie Queen Plans to Grow by 200 Units" in *Memphis Business Journal* (Vol. 25, No. 17, August 22, 2003, pp. 1)
Pub: American City Business Journals
Ed: Michael Sheffield. **Description:** Dixie Queen plans to franchise its fast food restaurants outside the Memphis, Tennessee area. Owner, David Raffanty, has hired UrbanArch Associates PC to remodel the company's existing buildings.

38756 ■ "Does the Franchisor Provide Value to Franchisees?" in *Journal of Small Business Management* (Vol. 41, No. 4, October 2003, pp. 366)
Pub: International Council of Small Business
Ed: Marko Grunhagen, Michael J. Dorsch. **Description:** The degree to which a franchise system penetrates a target market over time is often influenced by the rate its individual franchisees expand.

38757 ■ "Domino's says new system saves dough" in *Crain's Detroit Business* (Vol. 19, No. 8, February 24, 2003, pp. 13)
Pub: Crain Communications Inc., Detroit
Ed: Michael Strong. **Description:** Domino's Pizza LLC has begun a new computerized system, called Pulse that will save the company and franchisees both time and money.

38758 ■ "The Doughnut Industry can make room for one more" in *Entrepreneur* (Vol. 30, No. 2, February 2002, pp. 88)
Pub: Entrepreneur Media Inc.
Description: Profile of Tim Matthews, who used his mother's doughnut recipe to grow a franchise.

38759 ■ "Dressed for Success" in *Small Business Opportunities* (Vol. 17, September 2005, No. 5, pp. 112)
Pub: Harris Publications Inc.
Ed: Stan Roberts. **Description:** Profile of Brian and Jamey Elrod who started their uniform clothing store from their garage; sales reached $1.3 million in 2004. Educational Outfitters offers franchising opportunities starting from $82,000 to $198,000 which includes franchise fee, initial rent, inventory, furniture, equipment, insurance and marketing.

38760 ■ "Dry Cleaning Dons a Corporate Veneer" in *Tampa Tribune* (December 9, 2005)
Pub: Media General, Inc.
Ed: Mary Shedden. **Description:** Independently run dry cleaning stores are facing stiff competition from national franchise chains. Dryclean USA is expanding into the Florida market and boasts nearly 400 shops in the U.S., Caribbean, Mexico, and Brazil.

38761 ■ "Dunkin' Donuts" in *Hispanic Business* (March 2002, pp. 66)
Pub: Hispanic Business
Description: Profile of Joe Boveda, and his experience as the owner of a combination Dunkin' Donuts/Togo's location. Contact information is provided for those interested in franchising opportunities.

38762 ■ "Early-Bird Special" in *Success* (Vol. 47, No. 1, January 2000, pp. 58)
Pub: Success Publishing, Inc.
Ed: Azriela Jaffe. **Description:** When buying in to a new system, you may get in on the ground floor of the next McDonald's. Often, new franchisees who get in on the start of a hot new trend, usually become successful before the concept peaks.

38763 ■ "Eight Black Physicians Partnered to Open an International House of Pancakes in Harlem..." in *Black Enterprise* (Vol. 35, Dec. 2004)
Pub: Earl G. Graves Publishing Co. Inc.
Ed: Nkechi Olisemeka. **Description:** In its first month of operation, a restaurant opened by eight African American doctors is ranked 14th in sales among the International House of Pancakes franchises. The franchise has 1,167 franchises located throughout 48 states and Canada.

38764 ■ "El Pollo Loco" in *Hispanic Business* (March 2002, pp. 64)
Pub: Hispanic Business
Description: Information for obtaining an El Pollo Loco restaurant franchise is presented.

38765 ■ "Entrepreneur Column" in *Entrepreneur.com* (November 30, 2006)
Pub: Entrepreneur Media Inc.
Ed: Jeff Elgin. **Description:** Three types of technical franchises are explored: Educational, Creative, and Troubleshooting. All three require the importance of being a businessman first and a tech expert second.

38766 ■ *Entrepreneur Magazine—Franchise 500 Survey Issue*
Pub: Entrepreneur Media Inc.
Contact: Maria Anton, Exec. Ed.
E-mail: manton@entrepreneur.com
Ed: Rieva Lesonsky, Editor. **Released:** Annual, January. **Publication Includes:** Listing and ranking of top

500 franchises in the United States and Canada. **Entries Include:** Company name, address, and, in tabular form, key statistics. **Arrangement:** Classified by industry and ranking.

38767 ■ *Entrepreneur's Be Your Own Boss*
Pub: Entrepreneur Media Inc.
Ed: Maria Anton, Editor, manton@entrepreneur.com.
Released: 3x/yr.; Feb., May., Sept. **Covers:** over 1,100 franchise and business opportunities; coverage includes Canada; Feb: low-investment franchises; May issue: directory of homebased franchises and business opportunites; Sept issue: completed directory of franchise and business opportunities. **Entries include:** Company name, address, phone, description of opportunity, geographical areas available, costs. **Arrangement:** Classified by line of business.

38768 ■ "Ex-burger king teams with Hawkins; Group may be pursuing KFC deal" in *Crain's Detroit Business* (Vol. 18, No.51, Dec. 23, 2002, pp. 1)
Pub: Crain Communications Inc., Detroit
Ed: Michael Strong. **Description:** Profile of La-Van Hawkins, owner of 117 Pizza Hut restaurants in Michigan. Hawkins has hired Robert Lowes, a former CEO of Burger King Inc., and is hoping to acquire KFC Inc., the chicken fast food chain.

38769 ■ "Expanding Its Menu and Changing Its Business Strategy Have Helped IHOP" in *The Record* (November 4, 2005)
Pub: New Jersey Media Group
Ed: Michael L. Diamond. **Description:** Clifford and Mitzy Moore successfully reached out to the community in order to run their IHOP franchise restaurant as a neighborhood restaurant rather than a national chain.

38770 ■ "Extreme Pizza eying Atlanta for expansion" in *Atlanta Business Chronicle* (Vol. 25, No. 19, October 18, 2002, pp. 21A)
Pub: American City Business Publications, Inc.
Ed: Mark Chediak. **Description:** Extreme Pizza, headquartered in San Francisco, California, is looking to expand into almost 12 metropolitan areas in 2003, and may include Atlanta, Georgia. Emboldened by revenue growth of 50 percent in 2002, the pizza parlor chain is hoping to more than double the number of its outlets. The highest level of interest include Arizona, Colorado, and Oregon.

38771 ■ "Fantastic Sams To Open Manatee County, Fla. Hair Salon" in *Bradenton Herald* (January 5, 2005)
Pub: Bradenton Herald
Ed: Kurt D. Schultheis. **Description:** Lee Kline, owner of the new Fantastic Sams hair salon explains reasons for his site selection in the Cortez Commons Plaza in Manatee County, Florida.

38772 ■ "The fast & the franchising" in *Entrepreneur* (Vol. 30, No. 3, March 2002, pp. 100)
Pub: Entrepreneur Media Inc.
Description: A listing of the 103 fastest growing franchises is presented. Franchises are ranked by growth in the number of franchises from 2000 to 2001.

38773 ■ *The Fifty Best Low-Investment, High-Profit Franchises*
Pub: Prentice Hall
Ed: Robert L. Perry. **Released:** 1994. **Price:** $14.95.
Description: Provides information on fifty available franchises with investments as low as $2500, including start-up costs, expected training, and potential profits.

38774 ■ "Fight Brews in Senate Over Bill to Change TV Franchises" in *Crain's Detroit Business* (Vol. 22, November 20, 2006, No. 47, pp. 25)
Pub: Crain Communications Inc. - Detroit
Ed: Amy Lane. **Description:** State issuing guideline template to communities to permit more competition in the video provider market. Currently awarding franchises is a city by city function without any clear guidelines for standardization from one community to another. AT and T is making a major investment in Michigan and challenging existing cable franchises in local communities.

38775 ■ *Financing Your Franchise*
Pub: The McGraw-Hill Companies
Ed: Andrew J. Sherman, Ripley Hotch, and Meg Whittemore. **Released:** 1993. **Price:** $32.95; $16.95 (paper).

38776 ■ "FIOS TV" in *Crain's New York Business* (Vol. 22, November 27, 2006, No. 48, pp. 33)
Pub: Crain Communications, Inc.
Description: FiOs TV is a television service offered by Verizon and is currently available in small cities and suburban areas in seven states. The company won a statewide TV franchise in New Jersey and is doing business in forty Long Island communities.

38777 ■ "First Finishes" in *Entrepreneur* (Vol. 32, No. 1, January 2004, pp. 84)
Pub: Entrepreneur Media, Inc.
Description: A listing of the Number One winners of Entrepreneur's Franchise 500 from 1980-2004, with Subway scoring first twelve times, McDonald's eight times.

38778 ■ "Fitness Chain Curves Makes Boston Push" in *Boston Business Journal* (Vol. 23, No. 30, August 29, 2003, pp. 3)
Pub: American City Business Journals
Ed: Jill Lerner. **Description:** The growing success of Curves for Women locations in the Boston, Massachusetts area is explored. Topics include the franchise company's marketing plans, strategic planning, and market development.

38779 ■ "Flower Power" in *My Business* (February/March 2004, pp. 45-46)
Pub: My Business Magazine
Ed: Jamie Roberts. **Description:** Profile of John Halaris, who owns three floral KaBloom retail chains in Rhode Island. KaBloom is presently the fastest growing floral retail chain in the U.S.

38780 ■ "Food/Full-Service Restaurants" in *Entrepreneur* (Vol. 32, No. 1, January 2004, pp. 202)
Pub: Entrepreneur Media, Inc.
Description: Franchise opportunities in the food/full service restaurant sector.

38781 ■ "Food Industry Veteran Has It His Way" in *Black Enterprise* (Vol. 35, February 2005, No. 7, pp. 36)
Pub: Earl G. Graves Publishing Co. Inc.
Ed: Latif Lewis. **Description:** Charles H. James III became Burger King's largest African American franchise. James now owns 37 stores in the Chicago area. Profile of James is included.

38782 ■ "Food/Quick Service" in *Entrepreneur* (Vol. 32, No. 1, January 2004, pp. 184)
Pub: Entrepreneur Media, Inc.
Description: Franchise opportunities in the food/ quick service restaurant sector.

38783 ■ "Food/Retail Sales" in *Entrepreneur* (Vol. 32, No. 1, January 2004, pp. 206)
Pub: Entrepreneur Media, Inc.
Description: Profiles of food and retail franchises available to entrepreneurs, including candy shops.

38784 ■ *Franchise Bible: How to Buy a Franchise or Franchise Your Own Business*
Pub: Oasis Press
Ed: Erwin J. Keup. **Released:** 1994. **Price:** $39.95; $19.95 (paper). **Description:** Provides information for franchisees and franchisors. Includes sample franchise documents, a list of state statutes relating to franchising, and a directory of state franchise law offices.

38785 ■ "Franchise country" in *Entrepreneur* (Vol. 31, No. 6, June 2003, pp. 86)
Pub: Entrepreneur Media Inc.
Ed: Todd D. Maddocks. **Description:** An overview of the franchise industry is presented.

38786 ■ "Franchise Financing" in *Black Enterprise* (Vol. 35, September 2004, No. 2, pp. 50)
Pub: Earl G. Graves Publishing Co. Inc.
Ed: Alan Hughes. **Description:** Many times franchisors offer financing for new franchisees, or help them find an independent firm that provides loans.

38787 ■ "Franchise to go: despite a recession some of these businesses are hot" in *Black Enterprise* (Vol. 32, No. 9, April 2002, pp. 46)
Pub: Earl Graves Publishing Co.
Ed: Alan Hughes. **Description:** The advantages of buying a franchise business are examined. Recommendations for choosing a franchise are also discussed.

38788 ■ "Franchise Gold 200" in *Success* (Vol. 47, No. 5, October 2000, pp. 58)
Pub: Success Publishing, Inc.
Ed: Jane Shealy. **Description:** Surveys such as Success Magazine's annual Franchise Gold 200 provide a good source for prospective franchisees and consumers wanting to evaluate and compare different systems. A list of ranking is included along with information about franchises such as Sylvan Learning Centers, who ranked number one, Mail Boxes, Inc., and Dunkin Donuts.

38789 ■ *Franchise Handbook*
Pub: Enterprise Magazines Inc.
Contact: Poulsen Marsha
E-mail: marsha@franchisehandbook.com
Ed: Michael J. McDermott, Editor. **Released:** Quarterly. **Covers:** Firms offering franchises. **Entries Include:** Franchisor name, headquarters address, phone, president or other contact, description of operation, number of franchises, year founded, equity capital needed, financial assistance available, training provided, managerial assistance available. **Arrangement:** Classified by line of business, alphabetical. **Indexes:** Franchising company name.

38790 ■ *Franchise Kit: A Nuts & Bolts Guide to Owning & Running a Franchise Business*
Pub: The McGraw-Hill Companies
Released: 1995. **Price:** $14.95.

38791 ■ *Franchise Opportunities*
Pub: Sterling Publishing Co., Inc.
Released: 1995. **Price:** $14.95.

38792 ■ *Franchise Opportunities Handbook*
Pub: Superintendent of Documents
Released: 1991. **Price:** $21.00. **Description:** Lists equal opportunity franchisors, providing terms, requirements, and conditions under which the franchises are available. Includes government and private organizations that can assist minority group entrepreneurs, and checklists.

38793 ■ *Franchise Riches Success Kit*
Pub: International Wealth Success, Inc.
Ed: Tyler G. Hicks. **Released:** 1996. **Price:** $99.50.

38794 ■ *The Franchise Survival Guide: Real-World Solutions for Turning Your Investment into a Money-Making Business*
Pub: Probus Publishing Co., Inc.
Ed: Carol B. Green. **Released:** 1993. **Price:** $21.95 (paper). **Description:** Guide to selecting and operating a franchise, covering marketing and management. Includes case examples.

38795 ■ "Franchisee Satisfaction Critical to Success" in *Success* (Vol. 47, No. 3, July 2000, pp. 90)
Pub: Success Publishing, Inc.
Description: The most important factors for a successful franchise is overall satisfaction and the franchisee/franchisor relationship, according to a recent franchise partner survey conducted by AFC Enterprises.

38796 ■ "Franchisees of Huntington Station-based Relax the Back Find Success on Long Island" in *Long Island Business News* (February 6, 2004)
Pub: Dolan Media Newswires
Ed: Adina Genn. **Description:** Profile of Carey and CiCi Goldberg, husband and wife franchisees of Relax the Back, offering products to help find the right chair, mattress and pillow for customers in order to keep their spine aligned. The Goldbergs looked for a franchise that would allow them to target the baby boomers and senior citizens who drive the nation's economy.

38797 ■ *Franchises: Dollars & Sense—A Guide for Evaluating Franchises and Projecting Franchise Earnings*
Pub: Kendall/Hunt Publishing Co.
Ed: Warren L. Lewis. **Released:** 1993. **Price:** $49.95.
Description: Provides franchise sales and profit data from hundreds of franchise companies.

38798 ■ *Franchising 101: The Complete Guide to Evaluating, Buying & Growing Your Franchised Business*
Pub: Upstart Publishing Co., Inc.
Ed: Ann Dugan. **Released:** 1998. **Price:** $22.95.

38799 ■ *Franchising: A Case-Study Approach*
Pub: Ashgate Publishing Co., Inc.
Ed: Antony Dnes. **Released:** 1992. **Price:** $76.95 (trade cloth).

38800 ■ *Franchising in America: The Development of a Business Method, 1840-1980*
Pub: University of North Carolina Press
Ed: Thomas S. Dicke. **Released:** 1992. **Price:** $32.50; $13.95 (paper).

38801 ■ *Franchising in Canada: Pros & Cons*
Pub: Self-Counsel Press, Inc.
Ed: Michael M. Coltman. **Released:** 1995. **Price:** $8.95.

38802 ■ "Franchising Contacts" in *Hispanic Business* (Vol. 23, No. 5, May 2001, pp. 60)
Pub: Hispanic Business
Description: A listing of contact information for franchises, including the automotive sector, business aids and services, cleaning and sanitation, clothing and shoes, employment services, grocery and specialty stores, home care, home inspections, learning aids, lodging, printing, rentals, restaurants, food, retail, tools and hardware.

38803 ■ *Franchising: Contemporary Issues & Research*
Pub: The Haworth Press, Inc.
Ed: Patrick J. Kaufmann. **Released:** 1995. **Price:** $39.95.

38804 ■ "The Franchising Formula" in *Hispanic Business* (Vol. 22, No. 5, May 2000, pp. 60)
Pub: Hispanic Business
Ed: Vivienne Heins, Scott Williams. **Description:** It has become increasingly common for Hispanic Americans to become involved in franchising ventures. Successful franchise operations are profiled, including Kentucky Fried Chicken, Minuteman Press, and U-Save Auto Rental.

38805 ■ "Franchising" in *Hispanic Business* (Vol. 24, No. 5, May 2002, pp. 44, 46)
Pub: Hispanic Business Inc.
Description: Profile of various franchising opportunities including hotels, cleaning and sanitation, art supplies, business aids and services, grocery and specialty stores, printing, and restaurants, drive-ins and carry-outs.

38806 ■ "The franchising industry continues to heighten" in *Atlanta Business Chronicle* (Vol. 24, No. 11, August 17, 2001, pp. 48A)
Pub: American City Business Journals Inc.

Ed: Alf Nucifora. **Description:** Franchising generates an estimated $1 trillion annually in the U.S., with the top franchise industries including fast food, retail, service, automotive, restaurants, maintenance, building and construction, retail-food, business services, and lodging. The service sector is creating the news.

38807 ■ *Franchising and Licensing: Two Ways to Build Your Business*
Pub: AMACOM
Ed: Andrew J. Sherman. **Released:** 1991. **Price:** $27.95 ($25.15 for AMA members). **Description:** Covers the management, legal, and operational issues when creating a franchise program.

38808 ■ **"Franchising: Model of Success"** in *Hispanic Business* (September 2004, pp. 90)
Pub: Hispanic Business
Ed: Monica Valencia. **Description:** Hispanics are a growing force for the franchise industry. Many Hispanics choose franchising because of the business model already provided.

38809 ■ **"Franchising Opportunities"** in *Hispanic Business* (March 2002, pp. 66)
Pub: Hispanic Business
Description: A listing of franchising opportunities is presented, featuring art supply stores, business aids and services, cleaning and sanitation, grocery and specialty stores, hotels, and printing services.

38810 ■ *Franchising: The Business Strategy That Changed the World*
Pub: Prentice Hall
Ed: Carrie Shook and Robert L. Shook. **Released:** 1993. **Price:** $19.95.

38811 ■ **"From Zero to Hero: Even the Best Franchisor has to Start Somewhere"** in *Entrepreneur* (Vol. 32, No. 1, January 2004, pp. 148)
Pub: Entrepreneur Media, Inc.
Ed: Nichole L. Torres. **Description:** Profile of Fred DeLuca, founder of Subway restaurants. Subway expects to have 20,000 franchises in more than 70 countries in operation.

38812 ■ *The Fundamentals of Franchising*
Pub: American Bar Association
Ed: Rupert M. Barkoff and Andrew C. Selden. **Released:** 1997. **Price:** $89.95.

38813 ■ **"The Future of Franchising: Taking Advantage of the Changing Complexion of the American Economy"** in *Black Enterprise* (Vol. 32, No. 2)
Pub: Earl Graves Publishing Co.
Ed: C. Everett Wallace. **Description:** Franchising remains one of the fastest growing segments of the American business economy. The article addresses the potential business franchise opportunity in minority communities with information for the following franchises: Jan-Pro Cleaning Systems, AAMCO Transmissions, SIGN-A-RAMA, Chick-fil-A, Sunoco Inc., Kumon Math and Reading Centers, Choice Hotels, Liberty Tax Service, Dunhill Staffing Systems Inc., The Athlete's Foot, KFC, Meineke, Denny's, Subway, Coverall Cleaning Concepts, Church's Chicken, and Wendy's.

38814 ■ **"Getting Noticed"** in *Entrepreneur* (Vol. 31, No. 10, October 2003, pp. 114)
Pub: Entrepreneur Media, Inc.
Ed: Todd D. Maddocks. **Description:** The question of leasing or owning a new oil-change location is discussed.

38815 ■ **"Girl Franchising Power"** in *Black Enterprise* (Vol. 36, February 2006, No. 7, pp. 155)
Pub: Earl G. Graves Publishing Co. Inc.
Ed: Bridget McCrea. **Description:** The Women's Franchise Committee (WFC) was created in 1996 by the International Franchise Association. The 18-member committee helps women become leaders in the field through mentoring, education, and training programs.

38816 ■ **"Global Fitness, Weight-Loss Franchise Opens Sites in Willoughby, Ohio Area"** in *Willoughby News-Herald* (December 17, 2002)
Pub: Knight-Ridder/Tribune Business News
Ed: Cathleen S. Murphy. **Description:** Information is given about the new Curves For Women locations in Lyndhurst and Painesville Township, Ohio. Unlike traditional health spas, Curves favors the four no's: no men, no classes, no lines, and no weights to stack, and uses a 30-minute quickfit circuit workout anytime during opening hours.

38817 ■ **"Good as Gold"** in *Entrepreneur* (Vol. 32, No. 1, January 2004, pp. 106)
Pub: Entrepreneur Media, Inc.
Ed: Devlin Smith. **Description:** The hottest franchising trends for 2004 include senior care, child products and services, technology, home improvement, fitness, income tax preparation, business consulting, specialty ice cream and coffee.

38818 ■ **"A Good Man(ager) is Hard to Find"** in *My Business* (August/September 2002, pp. 47)
Pub: My Business Magazine
Ed: Shannon Scully. **Description:** The basics for understanding the franchising concept are listed, as well as a profile of James Rice, owner of 13 McDonald's franchises. Web sites offering franchising assistance are listed.

38819 ■ **"Goodwill Hunting?"** in *Entrepreneur* (Vol. 31, No. 9, September 2003, pp. 108)
Pub: Entrepreneur Media, Inc.
Ed: Devlin Smith. **Description:** Many new franchises are supporting charity and community causes as a primary mission, rather than the tradition side project of the organization.

38820 ■ **"Got 20 Minutes? Gym Champions Quick, Occasional Workouts"** in *Bradenton Herald* (January 29, 2005)
Pub: Bradenton Herald
Ed: Matt Griswold. **Description:** Al Roach, CEO of 20 Minutes to Fitness, offers a 20-minute workout for clients to be done once a week. Roach claims these workouts will build muscle faster and safer than traditional strength training, and will also burn fat in the process. Roach and his wife, Virginia Phillips, plan to sell franchise packages for the gyms.

38821 ■ **"Groom to Grow: Animal Grooming is More Than a Pet Project for a Former HR Executive"** in *Entrepreneur* (Vol. 32, December 2004, No. 12)
Pub: Entrepreneur Media Inc.
Ed: Jeri Yoshida. **Description:** Profile of Kerri Evans who left her corporate job to run her Aussie Pet Mobile. The franchise provides pet-grooming services.

38822 ■ **"Hawkins wins support in his suit against Burger King"** in *Crain's Detroit Business* (Vol. 16, No. 46, November 13, 2000, pp. 3)
Pub: Crain Communications, Inc.
Ed: Terry Kosdrosky. **Description:** Some details regarding the Detroit franchisee La-Van Hawkins and his law suit against Burger King Corporation.

38823 ■ **"Health Businesses"** in *Entrepreneur* (Vol. 32, No. 1, January 2004, pp. 208)
Pub: Entrepreneur Media, Inc.
Description: Profiles of health care franchise opportunities, including vision care and dental services.

38824 ■ **"Heir Raising"** in *Entrepreneur* (Vol. 33, February 2005, No. 2, pp. 82)
Pub: Entrepreneur Media Inc.
Ed: Sara Wilson. **Description:** Profile of Dave and Ellie Woodruff who purchased a Meineke Car Care Center franchise for their son, Michael. The couple has plans to open two more franchises for their two daughters. The family discusses their business plans intended to secure their children's future.

38825 ■ **"Heller Family Pays $4.1M for Warehouse"** in *Journal Record (Oklahoma City, OK)* (February 6, 2007)
Pub: Journal Record
Ed: Kirby Lee Davis. **Description:** Heller Family Investments LLC purchased the Airpark Distribution Center industrial building, the 19th property in the family portfolio. The family is expected to purchase two more properties in 2007.

38826 ■ **"Here's the Scoop: Five Sweet Advantages to Owning a Franchise"** in *My Business* (October/November 2003, pp. 48)
Pub: My Business Magazine
Ed: Jamie Roberts. **Description:** Profile of Paul Sumrall, owner of two Marble Slab Creameries in two different states. The homemade ice cream company is a good example of successful franchising. Tips for running a successful franchise are given.

38827 ■ **"Hey, Get a Clue!"** in *Entrepreneur* (Vol. 32, No. 1, January 2004, pp. 112)
Pub: Entrepreneur Media, Inc.
Ed: Andrew A. Caffey. **Description:** Profile of the Uniform Franchise Offering Circular (UFOC), a document designed to make a franchise investment a fully informed decision. The federal franchise law has required franchisors to deliver this document to prospective franchisees a couple weeks before closing.

38828 ■ **"Home Improvements"** in *Entrepreneur* (Vol. 32, No. 1, January 2004, pp. 210)
Pub: Entrepreneur Media, Inc.
Description: Complete listing of franchise opportunities in the home improvement sector, including building services, decorating services, handyman services, home organization systems, remodeling, windows and floors, restoration, and more.

38829 ■ **"Home Instead Senior Care"** in *Small Business Opportunities* (Vol. 16, November 2004, No. 6, pp. 112)
Pub: Harris Publications Inc.
Description: Profile of Home Instead Senior Care. The franchisor provides opportunity in non-medical eldercare in 46 states, as an affordable alternative to nursing home care.

38830 ■ **"Hot Scoop"** in *Small Business Opportunities* (March 2005)
Pub: Harris Publications Inc.
Description: Profile of Cold Stone Creamery, the country's fastest growing premium ice cream franchise. Currently there are stores in 44 states including Hawaii, Alaska and the Caribbean.

38831 ■ *How to Buy and Manage a Franchise*
Pub: Simon & Schuster, Inc.
Ed: Joseph R. Mancuso and Donald Boroian. **Released:** 1993. **Price:** $11.00 (paper) **Description:** Provides information on buying and running a franchise. Covers choosing the right product/service, working with a franchisor, royalties, ongoing costs, and legal issues.

38832 ■ *How to Open a Franchise Business*
Pub: Avon Books
Ed: Michael Powers. **Released:** 1995. **Price:** $12.50.

38833 ■ **"Howell Twp. May Get Import Motor Mall"** in *Crain's Detroit Business* (Vol. 21, January 31, 2005, No. 5, pp. 40)
Pub: Crain Communications Inc. - Detroit
Ed: Sheena Harrison. **Description:** Chestnut Development LLC, residential and commercial builder in Howell, Michigan, plans to build a motor mall featuring four Japanese imports.

38834 ■ **"Hungry Howie's Plans 50 Stores"** in *Crain's Detroit Business* (Vol. 19, No. 49, December 8, 2003, pp. 3)
Pub: Crain Communications Inc., Detroit
Ed: Michael Strong. **Description:** Hungry Howie's Pizza and Subs Inc. will add 50 additional stores nationally in 2004 by opening up new territories and franchises.

38835 ■ "Hungry for More: With Four Food Franchises on His Plate, This Owner Reveals His Recipe for Success" in *Entrepreneur* **(August 2004)**
Pub: Entrepreneur Media Inc.
Ed: Sara Wilson. **Description:** Profile of Stan Given, who shares his entrepreneurial successes as owner of four franchises: location, commitment and homework before purchasing.

38836 ■ "In the Black" in *My Business* **(August/September 2002, pp. 45)**
Pub: My Business Magazine
Ed: Ivan Sylvester. **Description:** Profile of brothers, Andy and Doug Hoiland, who own a Jet-Black franchise that does driveway repair.

38837 ■ "Inheriting business as challenging as starting one" in *Atlanta Business Chronicle* **(Vol. 24, No. 13, August 24, 2001, pp. 5B)**
Pub: American City Business Journals Inc.
Ed: Tara Milligan. **Description:** Taking over a business that is already operating has unique challenges. In the article is a case study of Carl Greenway's takeover of the Molly Maid franchise in Memphis five years ago, when it had six employees and eight dilapidated cars. It now has 24 employees, and competes against the national leader Merry Maids, which is also headquartered in Memphis.

38838 ■ *International Franchise Association—Franchise Opportunities Guide*
Pub: International Franchise Association
Contact: Jack Burris, Director
E-mail: jack@frachise.org
Ed: Diego Cardona, Editor, diego@franchise.org. **Released:** Semiannual, October and April. **Price:** $17 plus $8.00 shipping; $15 for Web Visitors. **Covers:** over 5,000 companies offering franchises. **Entries Include:** Company name, address, phone, type of business, contact, number of franchised and company-owned outlets, years in business, qualifications expected of prospective franchisees, investment required, training & support provided. **Arrangement:** Classified.

38839 ■ *International Franchising Law*
Pub: Matthew Bender & Co., Inc.
Ed: Dennis Campbell, editor. **Released:** 1993.

38840 ■ "It's a Chic Thing: Boutique Hotel Chains Are Going Strong With Cheap, Stylish Offerings" in *Entrepreneur* **(Vol. 32, September 2004)**
Pub: Entrepreneur Media Inc.
Ed: Chris McGinnis. **Description:** Reasonably priced all-suite hotels are growing in popularity. Profiles of Affinia Hospitality, the Kimpton Group, and Joie de Vivre Hospitality are included.

38841 ■ "It's a 'go' in Detroit" in *BlackEnterprise* **(Vol. 32, No. 2, September 2001, pp. 50)**
Pub: Earl Graves Publishing Co.
Ed: Roger Barnes. **Description:** Blimpie will open restaurants in Empowerment Zones throughout the country, including one in Detroit, Michigan. Empowerment Zones are neighborhoods in urban and rural areas throughout the United States designated by the federal government for revitalization.

38842 ■ "Keys to Successful Multiple-Unit Franchising" in *Black Enterprise* **(Vol. 34, No. 4, November 2003, pp. 157)**
Pub: Earl Graves Publishing Co.
Description: Multi-unit franchising has increased over the last few years. According to FRANdata, a franchise firm located in Washington, reports 27,000 franchisees own and operate two or more franchises in the U.S. Statistical data included.

38843 ■ "Labor of Love" in *Entrepreneur* **(Vol. 31, No. 9, September 2003, pp. 110)**
Pub: Entrepreneur Media, Inc.
Ed: Todd D. Maddocks. **Description:** Profile of a hypothetical couple starting a fast change oil center franchise, including financing and site location. Typically, a franchise license is really no more than a cash-flow machine unless the franchisee owns the real estate.

38844 ■ "Larry Nelson" in *Black Enterprise* **(Vol. 34, No. 5, December 2003, pp. 68)**
Pub: Earl Graves Publishing Co.
Description: Profile of Larry Nelson, recently named senior vice president and associate general counsel, development for Wendy's International. Nelson will oversee legal matters for the corporation, including franchising and real estate.

38845 ■ "Leader of the Pack" in *Entrepreneur* **(Vol. 32, November 2004, No. 11, pp. 106)**
Pub: Entrepreneur Media Inc.
Ed: Jeri Yoshida. **Description:** Profile of Urmila Patel, the 46-year-old single mother who owns a PostalAnnex franchise. Patel had owned a clothing store in Belgium for 20 years before relocating to the U.S. She bought the franchise without knowing anything about postal, packaging and shipping services, but learned quickly, and now expects sales in 2004 to reach $500,000.

38846 ■ "Lessons Learned: The franchising road can be hard, expensive" in *My Business* **(August/September 2002, pp. 46)**
Pub: My Business Magazine
Ed: Melany Klinck. **Description:** Kelly Fleming, owner of Pickles and Ice Cream maternity fashion franchises discusses her journey to selling franchises of her company. Fleming offers advice to those planning to franchise.

38847 ■ "Lighthouse starts sign biz to boost revenue, people" in *Crain's Detroit Business* **(Vol. 18, No. 20, May 20, 2002, pp. 18)**
Pub: Crain Communications Inc. - Detroit
Ed: Katie Merx. **Description:** Profile of Lighthouse of Oakland County Inc. The emergency-services provider hopes that the launch of a sign franchise will help move more unemployed people from crisis to independence while providing some financial stability for the agency itself.

38848 ■ "Longtime Pitchmen Started Chain" in *Tampa Tribune* **(November 17, 2005)**
Pub: Media General, Inc.
Ed: Michael Sasso. **Description:** Profile of Johnny Carrabba and his uncle Damian Mandola. In 1988, the two men teamed to start a chain of Carrabba's restaurants in Houston, Texas.

38849 ■ "Low-Volume Chevy Dealers Criticize Incentive Program" in *Automotive News* **(Vol. 79, February 7, 2005, No. 6133, pp. 42)**
Pub: Crain Communications Inc.
Ed: K.C. Crain. **Description:** Many low-volume Chevy dealers have expressed dissatisfaction with the Chevrolet Standards of Excellence program, which has been in effect for six months. The sign-up fee is $30,000 regardless of franchise size.

38850 ■ "Maintenance" in *Entrepreneur* **(Vol. 32, No. 1, January 2004, pp. 218)**
Pub: Entrepreneur Media, Inc.
Description: Profiles of franchise opportunities, including Jan Pro and Jani-King.

38851 ■ "Making Fast Food Faster" in *Atlanta Journal-Constitution* **(January 23, 2007)**
Pub: Cox Newspapers, Inc.
Ed: Leon Stafford. **Description:** Fast food restaurants are working to reduce customer wait time at drive through restaurants through the use of the Internet to place and pay for orders.

38852 ■ "Mark to sell 9 Weight Watchers franchises" in *Crain's Detroit Business* **(Vol. 19, No. 10, March 10, 2003, pp. 1)**
Pub: Crain Communications Inc., Detroit
Ed: Brent Snavely. **Description:** Florine Mark announced plans to sell nine franchises to Weight Watchers International Inc. Mark plans to concentrate her efforts on four Michigan and two Canadian franchises.

38853 ■ "Maui Wowi Fresh Hawaiian Blends" in *Small Business Opportunities* **(Vol. 16, November 2004, No. 6, pp. 112)**
Pub: Harris Publications Inc.
Description: Profile of Maui Wowi Fresh Hawaiian Blends, offering gourmet, all-natural Hawaiian beverages sold at malls, universities, stadiums, and other events.

38854 ■ "MHV Opens 100th SONIC" in *Mississippi Business Journal* **(Vol. 28, September 2006, No. 36, pp. 8)**
Pub: Venture Publications, Inc.
Description: Profile of McClain, Harvey, Vaughn (MHV), SONICS's third largest franchise group. The group has just opened its 100th SONIC drive in. Statistical data included.

38855 ■ "Michigan Firm Buys Signs Now" in *Bradenton Herald* **(February 11, 2005)**
Pub: Bradenton Herald
Ed: Matt Griswold. **Description:** Allegra Network LLC, a Michigan-based sign company has purchased Signs Now Corporation's assets and franchise agreements. The sale will have little impact on local stores. Allegra is the franchisor for six various printing brands in the U.S., Canada and Japan; leading brands include Allegra Print & Imaging, American Speedy Printing Centers, and Insty-Prints.

38856 ■ "Mining Online for the Bottom Line" in *Success* **(Vol. 47, No. 4, September 2000, pp. 82)**
Pub: Success Publishing, Inc.
Ed: Paul Gallagher. **Description:** Office services franchisors use the Internet to unearth more customers.

38857 ■ "Molly Maid franchise owners have own site" in *Crain's Detroit Business* **(Vol. 16, No. 34, August 21, 2000, pp. E-6)**
Pub: Crain Communications, Inc.
Ed: Jewel Gopwani. **Description:** Molly Maid Inc., the Ann Arbor, Michigan-based cleaning company has developed two web sites, one for consumers and another to help the company communicate with franchise owners.

38858 ■ "More than Fare" in *Success* **(Vol. 47, No. 1, January 2000, pp. 67)**
Pub: Success Publishing, Inc.
Description: An investigation into the top fifteen food-related franchises in America.

38859 ■ "Mr. Pita legal woes haven't put a wrap on expansion" in *Crain's Detroit Business* **(Vol. 18, No. 24, June 17, 2002, pp. 22)**
Pub: Crain Communications Inc. - Detroit
Ed: Michael Strong. **Description:** Shelby Township-based Mr. Pita, plans to open eight more locations, despite internal legal problems that could hinder the company's expansion.

38860 ■ "Mr. Pita Wagons Rolling Along" in *Crain's Detroit Business* **(Vol. 22, February 6, 2006, No. 6, pp. 21)**
Pub: Crain Communications Inc. - Detroit
Ed: Brent Snavely. **Description:** Mr. Pita Franchise Corporation is using three lunch wagons to deliver both hot and cold lunches to workers at various locations. Mr. Pita has 37 franchised locations in Michigan with plans to expand in Florida, Tennessee, Ohio and Illinois.

38861 ■ "Multitasking" in *Business First Columbus* **(Vol. 18, No. 26, February 15, 2002, pp. A17)**
Pub: Business First Columbus, Inc.
Ed: Susan Pavilkey. **Description:** The many challenges faced by owners of franchises, from doing their own accounting to cleaning floors, are covered. Statistical data included.

38862 ■ "Neck and Neck" in *Entrepreneur* **(Vol. 32, No. 1, January 2004, pp. 134)**
Pub: Entrepreneur Media, Inc.
Ed: April Y. Pennington. **Description:** Entrepreneur magazine ranked Subway as its Number One fran-

chise for the twelfth time, with 15,874 locations in the U.S. The firm's approach to capitalize on healthy dining has set it ahead of other fast food restaurants.

38863 ■ "Never say die: how a family beat the odds (and the weather) to improve a franchise" in *Entrepreneur* **(Vol. 30, No. 12, Dec. 2002)**
Pub: Entrepreneur Media Inc.
Ed: Tracy Stapp. **Description:** Profile of Scott and Steven Prewitt and their brother-in-law Tony Mansoor; the three men were able to overcome the obstacles faced with their Back Yard Burgers restaurant, and revolutionized the franchise system along the way.

38864 ■ "New Franchise Offers Customers Web Design Tech Without the Hassles" in *Small Business Opportunities* **(March 2005)**
Pub: Harris Publications Inc.
Description: Profile of the new franchise, InstantFX. The firm offers Website design, hosting services, email, e-commerce, and other Web-related services.

38865 ■ "New Lease on Life" in *Small Business Opportunities* **(Vol. 16, No. 1, January 2004, pp. 102-103)**
Pub: Harris Publications, Inc.
Description: Profile of Charles Loudermilk, founder of Aaron's Sales Lease Ownership and Aaron's Rents Inc., providing rental, sales and lease ownership and the specialty retailing of residential and office furniture, consumer electronics, and home appliances. Aaron's operates 468 corporate stores and 232 franchises in 43 states and Puerto Rico.

38866 ■ "No Free Lunch" in *Entrepreneur* **(Vol. 32, October 2004, No. 10, pp. 107)**
Pub: Entrepreneur Media Inc.
Ed: Anna Buss. **Description:** Profile of Chris and Joan Lindner, who purchased a Togo franchise in California after Chris decided it was time for a career change. Since then, the couple has opened three more locations, including two co-branded Togo's and Baskin Robbins franchises as well as a stand-alone Togo's.

38867 ■ *No Money down Financing for Franchising*
Pub: PSI Research
Ed: Roger C. Rule. **Released:** 1998. **Price:** $19.95.

38868 ■ "Oh So Good" in *My Business* **(August/September 2002, pp. 44)**
Pub: My Business Magazine
Ed: Doug McPherson. **Description:** Four keys to franchising, along with advice from top franchises are offered. Information about Krispy Kreme, Merry Maids and Mail Boxes Etc. franchises is also presented.

38869 ■ "One World Seeking to Expand Beyond Its Local Universe" in *San Diego Business Journal* **(Vol. 28, January 15, 2007, No. 3, pp. 12)**
Pub: San Diego Business Journal Associates
Ed: Jessica Long. **Description:** Profile of One World Fine Foods, San Diego Retailer, is offering franchise opportunities. The company hopes to expand to 25 franchises. .

38870 ■ "Opportunities" in *Entrepreneur* **(Vol. 30, No. 2, Fe)**
Pub: Entrepreneur Media Inc.
Ed: Stephanie Soong. **Description:** Profile of Ray and Cyndi White who retired from their careers as rocket scientist and hearing specialist respectively to start their own business in a real estate franchise.

38871 ■ *Opportunities in Franchising Careers*
Pub: N T C Contemporary Publishing Co.
Ed: Kent B. Banning. **Released:** 1995. **Price:** $10.95.

38872 ■ *Owning Your Own Franchise*
Pub: Prentice Hall
Ed: Herbert Rust. **Released:** 1991. **Price:** $24.95; $14.95 (paper). **Description:** Covers profiting from the franchising boom.

38873 ■ "Package Deal" in *Entrepreneur* **(Vol. 28, No. 8, August 2000, pp. 138)**
Pub: Entrepreneur Media Inc.
Ed: Zaheera Wahid. **Description:** Today's postal franchises are making sure they beat the "snail mail" rap by providing unmatched service alongside access to the latest technologies. By not only changing the way we communicate, but the way we do business, modern technology has been a springboard from which the postal industry has taken off.

38874 ■ "Painting by numbers" in *Hispanic Business* **(Vol. 22, No. 9, September 2000, pp. 82)**
Pub: Hispanic Business
Ed: Scott Williams. **Description:** Standards in workmanship and encouraging the use of business management skills are just two of the aims of franchise operation Certa ProPainters.

38875 ■ "Paying to lose" in *Sarasota Herald Tribune* **(Nov. 11, 2002, pp. 10)**
Pub: Sarasota Herald Tribune
Description: Franchises in Southwest Florida offering weight loss solutions are profiled, including Shapes Family Fitness, Gold's Gyms, Curves for Women, Weight Watchers, Jenny Craig, and LA Weight Loss. Health and medical statistics included.

38876 ■ "Personal Care" in *Entrepreneur* **(Vol. 32, No. 1, January 2004, pp. 228)**
Pub: Entrepreneur Media, Inc.
Description: Profiles of franchise opportunities that offer restoration and cleaning services and elderly care.

38877 ■ "Pets" in *Entrepreneur* **(Vol. 32, No. 1, January 2004, pp. 232)**
Pub: Entrepreneur Media, Inc.
Description: Profiles of franchises that provide pet supplies, pets, animal day care and boarding services, and dog grooming.

38878 ■ "Pigtails & Crewcuts" in *Small Business Opportunities* **(Vol. 16, November 2004, No. 6, pp. 112)**
Pub: Harris Publications Inc.
Description: Profile of Pigtails & Crewcuts franchise opportunities. The franchises offer hair styling for children done while sitting in an airplane, flower mobile, a fire engine or police car.

38879 ■ "Piling It On" in *Crain's Detroit Business* **(Vol. 19, No. 45, November 10, 2003, pp. 3)**
Pub: Crain Communications Inc., Detroit
Ed: Michael Strong. **Description:** Smaller, local sandwich chains are struggling to keep up with national restaurants moving into the area.

38880 ■ "Piling It On; Local Sandwich Chains Face Onslaught of Competition from National Companies" in *Crain's Detroit Business* **(Vol. 19)**
Pub: Crain Communications Inc., Detroit
Ed: Michael Strong. **Description:** Smaller, local sandwich chains are struggling to keep up with national restaurants moving into the area.

38881 ■ "Pizza Hut" in *Hispanic Business* **(March 2002, pp. 64)**
Pub: Hispanic Business
Description: Profile of Gene Camarena, the first Hispanic Pizza Hut franchisee. Contact information is provided for owning a Pizza Hut franchise.

38882 ■ "Plato's Closet, a Retail Outlet, Sells Teenagers Brand-Name Labels for Less" in *Long Island Business News* **(March 5, 2004)**
Pub: Dolan Media Newswires
Ed: Adina Genn. **Description:** Profile of Plato's Closet, a retail outlet offering used, current teen fashions with designer labels from Abercrombie & Fitch, Bebe, South Pole and Tommy Hilfiger, with an average price of $10. Plato's Closet offers franchise opportunities.

38883 ■ "Playing Cupid: These Matchmaking Sisters Aim to Give Busy Singles a Fast-and Fun-Way to Date" in *Entrepreneur* **(September 2004)**
Pub: Entrepreneur Media Inc.
Ed: Anna Buss. **Description:** Profile of Donna Heiser and Pat Maida, sisters, who operate the 4-Minute Date, a service geared to busy singles. The $35 service capitalizes on the speed-dating trend and allows couples to determine whether their 'date' is the perfect match...all in 4 minutes.

38884 ■ "Portland, Maine-Based Amato's Sandwich Shops Spread Across New England" in *Portland Press Herald* **(September 16, 2005)**
Pub: Blethen Maine Newspapers, Inc.
Ed: Edward D. Murphy. **Description:** Amato's sandwich shops have grown into one of the biggest franchise chains based in Maine. The stores offer Italian sandwiches, pizza, pasta, calzones and salads. Profile of owner, Dominic Reali is included.

38885 ■ "Portland, Maine, Woman Builds Successful Child-Care Business" in *Portland Press Herald* **(June 10, 2005)**
Pub: Blethen Maine Newspapers, Inc.
Ed: Edward D. Murphy. **Description:** Profile of Cheryl Carrier and her booming child care business, Toddle Inn, in the Portland, Maine area. Carrier also plans a franchise in Brewer, Maine, and also runs an early-stage furniture business.

38886 ■ "Prewitt With Prudential" in *Mississippi Business Journal* **(Vol. 29, January 2007, No.4, pp. 9)**
Pub: Venture Publications, Inc.
Ed: Wally Northway **Description:** Prudential Real Estate Affiliates Inc., awarded its' newest franchise to Ann Prewitt & Associates. Aligning with Prudential Real Estate Network will enable Prudential Ann Prewitt Realty to enhance the quality of their service.

38887 ■ "Price is Right: 114 Franchises You Can Buy for Less than $25,000" in *Entrepreneur* **(Vol. 31, No. 10, October 2003, pp. 94)**
Pub: Entrepreneur Media, Inc.
Description: An alphabetical listing of 114 franchise opportunities for under $25,000 is given, along with contact phone numbers and Web addresses.

38888 ■ "Putting signage on shirts is a cinch for sign-a-Rama's founder" in *Entrepreneur* **(Vol. 30, No. 3, March 2002, pp. 106)**
Pub: Entrepreneur Media Inc.
Description: Profile of Ray Titus, founder of Sign-a-Rama and EmbraidMe. EmbraidMe began franchising in 2001 and has 20 locations.

38889 ■ "Quick Drop Franchise Opens in Virginia Beach, Va., for Storefront eBay Sales" in *Virginian-Pilot* **(March 16, 2004)**
Pub: Knight-Ridder, Tribune Business News
Ed: Carolyn Shapiro. **Description:** Quik Drop has opened its seventh franchise. The new store is located in Virginia Beach, Virginia and is owned by Ned Griffith.

38890 ■ "QuikDrop Authorized by State of Illinois and State of MI to Offer eBay Drop-Off Store Franchises" in *PR Newswire* **(Mar. 29, 2004)**
Pub: PR Newswire Association, Inc.
Description: QuikDrop International has obtained the rights by both Michigan and Illinois to franchise eBay drop-off stores, and approval is pending in Maryland and Virginia. QuickDrop is now approved in 41 states.

38891 ■ "Ramps to Riches" in *Small Business Opportunities* **(Vol. 17, May 2005, No. 3, pp. 66)**
Pub: Harris Publications Inc.
Description: Gator Ramps are compact ramps that are installed on pick-up trucks. The franchise provides a good home-based opportunity.

38892 ■ *Rating Guide to Franchises*
Pub: Facts on File, Inc.
Ed: Dennis L. Foster. **Released:** Revised edition, 1991. **Price:** $40.00. **Description:** Contains listings for more than 400 franchises. Includes a discussion of recent trends, franchising and the law, and the outlook for franchising in the 1990s. Also offers a ranking of the 500 leading franchisors, and a ranking of franchisors within specific categories.

38893 ■ "Raw Deal" in *Forbes* (December 25, 2000, pp. 238)
Pub: Forbes Magazine
Ed: Dorothy Pomerantz. **Description:** Profile of Papa Murphy's pizza, the nation's seventh-largest pizza chain, and how the franchise has cornered the take-and-bake niche.

38894 ■ "Recipe for Profit" in *Small Business Opportunities* (Fall 2005)
Pub: Harris Publications Inc.
Description: Profile of Breadsmith Franchising, Inc., offering a six-week training program covering all aspects of store operation for up to two individuals. Franchise costs start at $30,000.

38895 ■ "Recreation" in *Entrepreneur* (Vol. 32, No. 1, January 2004, pp. 234)
Pub: Entrepreneur Media, Inc.
Description: Profiles of franchise opportunities that include Batteries Plus; Country Clutter, offering country gifts, collectibles and home decor; Verlo Mattress Factory Stores, selling sleep products; Play It Again Sports, offering new and used sports and fitness equipment; and Pressed4Time, the first drycleaning/shoe repair franchise offering pick up and delivery services.

38896 ■ "The Restaurant Business" in *The Economist* (Vol. 376, July 16-22, 2005, No. 8435, pp. 60)
Pub: The Economist Newspaper Ltd.
Description: American restaurants, including franchise fast-food stores, are facing a decline in sales due to the slow economy.

38897 ■ "Restaurant chains look for bite of local market" in *Crain's Detroit Business* (Vol. 18, No. 19, May 13, 2002, pp. 1)
Pub: Crain Communications Inc. - Detroit
Ed: Michael Strong. **Description:** National restaurant chains are looking to metro Detroit for new markets because of the area's rise in new housing and retail developments, strong franchise owners and lack of restaurant diversity.

38898 ■ "Restaurateur Inks Subway Deal for Eastern Wayne County" in *Crain's Detroit Business* (Vol. 19, No. 45, November 10, 2003, pp. 44)
Pub: Crain Communications Inc., Detroit
Ed: Michael Strong. **Description:** Nikolaos Moschouris signed a $1.5 million deal with Subway to build at least 30 Subway franchise restaurants in Detroit, Highland Park and Hamtramck, Michigan over the next two years.

38899 ■ "Retail" in *Entrepreneur* (Vol. 32, No. 1, January 2004, pp. 238)
Pub: Entrepreneur Media, Inc.
Description: Profiles of an art and custom framing franchise and franchise opportunities for owning a UPS Store.

38900 ■ "Rolling dough: do you go with original butter and salt or almond crunch?" in *Entrepreneur* (Vol. 31, No. 6, June 2003, pp. 106)
Pub: Entrepreneur Media Inc.
Ed: Jodie Carter. **Description:** Profile of Mike Jacobs who opened a Wetzel's Pretzels franchise in Stone Ridge Mall in Pleasanton, California in 2000; and Beth and Mike Bulpit and their House Medic franchise located in Springfield, Illinois.

38901 ■ "Scouting a Perfect Site" in *My Business* (October/November 2003, pp. 49)
Pub: My Business Magazine
Description: The art and science of selecting a site to start a franchise is discussed, including the use of costly global positioning systems.

38902 ■ "Sending Out an SOS: Our Franchisees Just Hit an Iceberg in Negotiating Their Land Deal" in *Entrepreneur* (Vol. 31, No. 9, July 2003)
Pub: Entrepreneur Media, Inc.
Ed: Todd D. Maddocks. **Description:** Issues a couple face when purchasing land to start their new franchise business are presented.

38903 ■ "Senior In-Home Care a Burgeoning Business" in *Colorado Springs Business Journal* (July 23, 2004)
Pub: Dolan Media Newswires
Ed: Marylou Doehrman. **Description:** Profile of the Home Instead Senior Care franchise, providing respite care to families and support services to the elderly or disabled who wish to remain in their own home. Profile of Kathryn Curry, who opened a Home Instead franchise with exclusive rights for Teller and El Paso County, Colorado, is included.

38904 ■ "Services" in *Entrepreneur* (Vol. 32, No. 1, January 2004, pp. 242)
Pub: Entrepreneur Media, Inc.
Description: Profiles of service industry franchises available, including FiltaFry, a mobile cooking oil filtration management service; Music Go Round, a used musical instrument dealer; AmeriSpec, home inspection service.

38905 ■ "Shaping Up" in *Entrepreneur* (Vol. 33, September 2005, No. 9, pp. 100)
Pub: Entrepreneur Media Inc.
Ed: Sara Wilson. **Description:** Profile of Mitch and Heather Naro, teachers turned entrepreneurs. The couple used Heather's background as a physical education teacher to start their Cuts Fitness for Men franchise.

38906 ■ "Shattered Magazine: A Monthly for the Global Businesswoman" in *Marketing to Women* (Vol. 19, December 2006, No. 2, pp. 6)
Pub: EPM Communications, Inc.
Ed: Julie Ros. **Description:** Shattered is a glossy magazine distributed monthly and run by veteran financial journalist, Julie Ros. Shattered concentrates its focus on the business world and puts special emphasis on the global impact women are having in the leadership roles of the business community.

38907 ■ "She's not afraid to flex her sales muscles" in *Selling* (October 2002, pp. 15)
Pub: Institutional Investor, Inc.
Ed: Jenny McCune. **Description:** Profile of Ann Power, National Franchise Sales Director of Lady of America, a women-only fitness chain with 500 locations worldwide; Power started her career selling for a weight-loss company, and became successful in sales.

38908 ■ "Shock Value: A Belief in the Power of Batteries Charged This Couple Up for Franchise Ownership" in *Entrepreneur* (Vol. 32, Oct. 2004)
Pub: Entrepreneur Media Inc.
Ed: Sara Wilson. **Description:** Profile of Susan and Dan Manwaring, husband and wife team who purchased a Fast Batteries Plus franchise in Indiana. The couple has been in business for twelve years with six stores.

38909 ■ "Show me the money" in *Entrepreneur* (Vol. 31, No. 6, June 2003, pp. 108)
Pub: Entrepreneur Media, Inc.
Ed: Todd D. Maddocks. **Description:** A couple have found the ideal property for their franchise business and need to secure financing for the deal.

38910 ■ *Small Business Desk Reference*
Pub: Penguin Books (USA) Incorporated
Ed: Gene Marks. **Released:** December 2004. **Price:** $29.95 (US), $44.00 (Canadian). **Description:** Comprehensive guide for starting or running a successful small business, focusing on buying a business or franchise, writing a business plan, financial management, accounting, legal issues, human resources management, operations, marketing, sales, customer service, taxes, insurance, and ethics. Information for launching a restaurant, property management firm, retail outlet, consulting firm, and service business is included.

38911 ■ "Small Business Spotlight" in *Small Business Opportunities* (Vol. 16, No. 2, March 2004, pp. 172)
Pub: Harris Publications, Inc.
Description: Profile of Jon Stocking who donates profits from his Endangered Species Chocolate Company to save threatened animals, an environmentally-friendly dry cleaner, and women and franchising.

38912 ■ "Something's fishy: More Captain D's coming" in *Atlanta Business Chronicle* (Vol. 25, No. 21, November 1, 2002, pp. 8A)
Pub: American City Business Publications, Inc.
Ed: Walter Woods. **Description:** Captain D's Seafood Inc., a fast food seafood restaurant chain, intends to start up 36 new outlets in the Atlanta, Georgia area in the next five years. The chain has 562 existing outlets, and would like the majority to be franchised.

38913 ■ "Sonic Profits, Sales Up for Quarter" in *Journal Record* (June 24, 2003)
Pub: Dolan Media Company
Description: Profile of Sonic Corporation, the drive-in restaurant firm reporting increased franchising income fueled by drive-in openings. Third quarter net income increased 9 percent to $16.2 million over previous year.

38914 ■ "South Carolina Duo Cashes in By Buying Ugly Houses as Fixer-Uppers" in *Sun News* (January 9, 2005)
Pub: Knight-Ridder/Tribune News
Ed: Jenny Burns. **Description:** Profile of Bennie Marshall and Jack Rockey, who bought a franchise that buys homes in need of work, renovates them, and sells them for a profit. The franchise uses billboards advertising, We Buy Ugly Houses.

38915 ■ "State Franchise Laws and the Small Business Franchise Act of 1999" in (Vol. 55, No. 4, August 2000, pp. 1699)
Pub: American Bar Association
Ed: Thomas J. Collin. **Description:** Unless a business sells to customers directly or through factory branches, they will need to take a close account of state franchise laws as they make decisions about distribution changes, and they may find that these laws raise significant barriers to change.

38916 ■ "Students of Enterprise" in *Entrepreneur* (Vol. 32, November 2004, No. 11, pp. 108)
Pub: Entrepreneur Media Inc.
Ed: April Y. Pennington, Devlin Smith. **Description:** Collegiate Entrepreneurs' Organization supports college students wanting to start their own businesses. The Chicago-based organization's membership has grown to 14,000 members nationwide. Profile of Fred DeLuca, who started a Subway sandwich shop when he was only seventeen, is included.

38917 ■ "Sub chains target Detroit: Quizno's, Panera want bite of market" in *Crain's Detroit Business* (Vol. 16, No. 6, February 7, 2000, pp. 3)
Pub: Crain Communications, Inc.
Ed: Terry Kosdrosky. **Description:** Panera Bread Company of Webster Groves, Missouri and Quizno's Corporation of Denver, Colorado hope to corner part of Michigan's submarine sandwich market.

38918 ■ "Super Bowl Sundae" in *Entrepreneur* (Vol. 32, October 2004, No. 10, pp. 107)
Pub: Entrepreneur Media Inc.

Ed: Sara Wilson. **Description:** Little Scoops franchises offer an alternative to traditional birthday parties. Children's parties come complete with pizza, dancing and games, all in a 1950s ice cream parlor setting.

38919 ■ "Taco Treasure" in *Small Business Opportunities* **(Vol. 16, November 2004, No. 6, pp. 84, 86)**
Pub: Harris Publications Inc.
Description: Profile of Craig Slavin, former franchise consultant, turned franchise owner. El Taco Tote offers real Mexican food prepared in view of guests. The franchisor provides initial and ongoing training programs with franchisees beginning training in a company-owned restaurant.

38920 ■ "Take a bow" in *Atlanta Business Chronicle* **(Vol. 25, November 8, 2002, No. 22 pp. 1B)**
Pub: American City Business Publications, Inc.
Ed: Lee Hall. **Description:** Party City of Atlanta, Inc. received recognition at the 2002 Georgia Business Ethics Awards given out by the Society of Financial Service Professionals' Atlanta chapter. The firm, a franchisee of Party City Corporation, runs 24 stores in the Atlanta area.

38921 ■ "Taking It Outside: Outsourcing Can Be a Great Time Saver-But Mind the Costs" in *Black Enterprise* **(Vol. 34, No. 5, December 2003)**
Pub: Earl Graves Publishing Co.
Ed: Bridget McCrea. **Description:** Profile of C. Michael Greer, owner of The Little Coupon Book, and ways he is marketing his franchise venture in the Atlanta, Georgia area.

38922 ■ "Taking It Outside: Outsourcing Can Be a Great Time Saver-But Mind the Costs" in *Black Enterprise* **(Vol. 34, No. 5, December 2003)**
Pub: Earl Graves Publishing Co.
Ed: Bridget McCrea. **Description:** Profile of C. Michael Greer, owner of The Little Coupon Book, and ways he is marketing his franchise venture in the Atlanta, Georgia area.

38923 ■ "Team players" in *Crain's Detroit Business* **(Vol. 18, No. 17, April 29,)**
Pub: Crain Communications Inc. - Detroit
Ed: Michael Strong. **Description:** Profile of Hawkins Food Group LLC, whose co-owners, Van Hawkins and Conrad Mallet, hope to prepare for an initial public offering.

38924 ■ "Tech" in *Entrepreneur* **(Vol. 32, No. 1, January 2004, pp. 252)**
Pub: Entrepreneur Media, Inc.
Description: Profiles of three technical franchise opportunities, including Friendly Computers; Geeks On Call, providing computer repair, networks, and one-on-one training; Expetec, provides mobile, on-site, high-level technology services to business and consumer customers; Concerto Networks Inc., offers nationwide information technology computer and network services; and ACE America's Cash Express, gives customers financial services that include check cashing, short-term loans, money orders, wire transfers, bill payments, pre-paid telecommunications and more.

38925 ■ "The Ten Hottest New Franchises" in *Success* **(Vol. 47, No. 2, June 2000, pp. 82)**
Pub: Success Publishing, Inc.
Ed: Jane Shealy. **Description:** A comprehensive listing of the top ten franchises, including a brief profile of each.

38926 ■ "TGIFridays to Open Restaurant at Islip MacArthur Airport" in *Long Island Business News* **(February 6, 2004)**
Pub: Dolan Media Newswires
Description: TGIFridays will open a new restaurant in the food court at Islip MacArthur Airport, part of the airports expansion.

38927 ■ "Think fast" in *Entrepreneur* **(Vol. 31, No. 5, May 2003, pp. 82)**
Pub: Entrepreneur Media Inc.
Description: The top 100 fastest-growing franchises in the United States are listed alphabetically, based on growth in the number of franchises from 2001 to 2002.

38928 ■ "This Biz is Growing by Leaps and Bounds" in *Small Business Opportunities* **(Vol. 16, November 2004, No. 6, pp. 90)**
Pub: Harris Publications Inc.
Description: Firehouse Subs has announced a new program, American Dream, that will convert its 30 corporate stores where managers can become equity partners or owners. The program provides financing.

38929 ■ "Those China Franchises are Risky" in *Automotive News* **(Vol. 78, July 5, 2004, No. 6101, pp. 12)**
Pub: Crain Communications Inc.
Ed: Keith Crain. **Description:** Entrepreneurs are warned about vehicle franchises being offered to sell cars manufactured in China.

38930 ■ "Tips & Trends" in *Small Business Opportunities* **(Vol. 17, September 2005, No. 5, pp. 14)**
Pub: Harris Publications Inc.
Description: Tips and trends important to small business include the addition of a coffeemaker that also makes soup, tea or cocoa; paper shredders; headsets; a sales resource guide for retailers; information for the Federal Citizen Information Center; and Creative Colors, the franchise offering mobile equipment to home-based businesses.

38931 ■ "To the Rescue" in *Entrepreneur* **(Vol. 31, No. 8, August 2003, pp. 98)**
Pub: Entrepreneur Media, Inc.
Ed: Todd D. Maddocks. **Description:** When Jack's potential real estate developer pulled out of the deal, Jacks franchisee met with his bank to gain re-approval of the deal.

38932 ■ "A Toast to Innovation" in *Small Business Opportunities* **(Vol. 16, November 2004, No. 6, pp. 48, 50)**
Pub: Harris Publications Inc.
Description: Profile of Bill and Ann Rosenberg who have founded Let's Make Wine franchise. Customers can select a wine and personally bottle it and also request a special label to celebrate events.

38933 ■ "Toasting High Profits" in *Small Business Opportunities* **(July 2005)**
Pub: Harris Publications Inc.
Description: Vino 100 plans to open more than 50 franchise locations by the end of the year with projected sales equaling $50 million in 2006. Each store offers more than 100 varieties of wines, champagnes and cognacs with prices under $25.

38934 ■ "Too Much Too Soon?" in *Inc.* **(November 1, 2003)**
Pub: Gruner & Jahr USA Publishing
Description: Perils of franchising are investigated.

38935 ■ "Tulsa-based Dollar Thrifty Automotive Group Buys Franchise" in *Journal Record (Oklahoma City, OK)* **(February 5, 2007)**
Pub: Journal Record
Description: Details of Dollar Thrifty Automotive Groups purchase of Thrifty Car Rental franchise are presented.

38936 ■ "Tulsa-based Dollar Thrifty Buys Franchises" in *Journal Record* **(February 4, 2004)**
Pub: Dolan Media Company
Description: Growth strategy to acquire Dollar and Thrifty franchisees in key U.S. and Canadian operations by Dollar Thrifty Automotive Group is discussed.

38937 ■ "Two Franchisees Buy Buffalo's Wings Chain" in *Atlanta Journal-Constitution* **(January 18, 2007)**
Pub: Cox Newspapers, Inc.

Ed: Leon Stafford. **Description:** Buffalo's Franchise Concepts sold two of its franchises; the Marietta, Georgia firm has 38 restaurants in ten states, Puerto Rico and Kuwait with thirty-four stores franchised.

38938 ■ *The Two Hundred Twenty Best Franchises to Buy*
Pub: Bantam Books, Inc.
Ed: Compiled by Philip Lief Group, Inc. staff. **Released:** Revised edition, 1993. **Price:** $13.95.

38939 ■ *Ultimate Guide to Buying or Selling Your Business*
Pub: Entrepreneur Press
Ed: Ira N. Nottonson. **Released:** September 2004. **Price:** $24.95 (US), $35.95 (Canadian). **Description:** Proven strategies to evaluate, negotiate, and buy or sell a small business. Franchise and family business succession planning is included.

38940 ■ "Uncommon Enterprise: Chasing Business" in *My Business* **(April/May 2003, pp. 54)**
Pub: My Business Magazine
Description: Profile of David Marcks and his Border collies; Marcks has established two Geese Police Academies for Border collie training. Marcks, founder and president of New Jersey-based Geese Police, Inc. offers franchises in fives states to round up unwanted geese on corporate sites.

38941 ■ "Under the Big Top" in *Hispanic Business* **(Vol. 23, No. 5, May 2001, pp. 58)**
Pub: Hispanic Business
Ed: Vivienne Heines. **Description:** An overview of the 2001 International Franchise Expo held May 18-20, at the Washington Convention Center in Washington, DC.

38942 ■ "UnitedAuto Sells Properties" in *Crain's Detroit Business* **(January 26, 2004, pp. 20)**
Pub: Crain Communications Inc., Detroit
Ed: Brent Snavely. **Description:** UnitedAuto Group Inc. sold property and buildings to Capital Automotive REIT, based in McLean, Virginia. UnitedAuto's strategy is to acquire and upgrade clusters of automotive dealerships, and presently operates 134 automotive franchises in the U.S., as well as 83 internationally.

38943 ■ "Vista: Dave's Seeks Fame, Fortune in North County" in *San Diego Business Journal* **(Vol. 28, January 15, 2007, No. 3, pp. 17)**
Pub: San Diego Business Journal Associates
Ed: Connie Lewis. **Description:** Famous Dave's barbeque restaurant chain is opening a franchise store in Minneapolis.

38944 ■ "What One Man Can Do" in *Inc.* **(September 2005, pp. 144-153)**
Pub: Inc. Magazine
Ed: John Brant. **Description:** Profile of Bill Strickland who is in the business of changing lives. He is committed to ending poverty and uses beauty to help individuals compete in the marketplace. Strickland is looking to franchise his brand of hope.

38945 ■ "What's Cookin'?" in *Entrepreneur* **(Vol. 32, December 2004, No. 12, pp. 30)**
Pub: Entrepreneur Media Inc.
Ed: Stephen Barlas. **Description:** The Federal Trade Commission's amendments to its Franchise Rule may ban post-sale encroachment on franchisees, market territory and restrictions on suppliers.

38946 ■ "With the Big Dogs" in *Crain's Detroit Business* **(Vol. 21, December 19, 2005, No. 51, pp. 3)**
Pub: Crain Communications Inc. - Detroit
Ed: Brent Snavely. **Description:** Profile of Pet Supplies 'Plus' franchises. The pet food retailer's expansion makes it the third-largest pet food retailers in the nation. Statistical data included.

38947 ■ "A Woman's Job" in *My Business* (June/July 2004, pp. 50)
Pub: My Business Magazine
Ed: Lena Basha. **Description:** Women franchisees are moving into a traditionally male-dominated market.

38948 ■ "Women of Substance: Who Says It's a Man's World?" in *Entrepreneur* (Vol. 31, No. 11, November 2003, pp. 104)
Pub: Entrepreneur Media, Inc.
Ed: Devlin Smith. **Description:** Women entrepreneurs share thoughts on ways franchising allows them to balance work and family lives.

38949 ■ "Worth His Weight" in *Entrepreneur* (Vol. 31, No. 8, August 2003, pp. 96)
Pub: Entrepreneur Media, Inc.
Ed: Devlin Smith. **Description:** Profile of Neal Smith and the LA Weight Loss Centers franchise system. These centers provide clients with nutritional advice and weight-loss support. Before purchasing his first two franchises, Smith worked with another weight-loss system and owned discounts stores.

38950 ▣ "Would You Like a Franchise With That?" in *Entrepreneur* (Vol. 33, January 2005, No. 1, pp. 120)
Pub: Entrepreneur Media Inc.
Ed: April Y. Pennington. **Description:** Things to consider when considering a franchise are discussed.

38951 ■ "You're the Boss: There Are Some Things Beyond Your Control..." in *Entrepreneur* (Vol. 31, No. 9, September 2003, pp. 90)
Pub: Entrepreneur Media, Inc.
Ed: Devlin Smith. **Description:** Franchising may be the answer to an entrepreneur's dream of becoming a small business owner.

TRADE PERIODICALS

38952 ■ *Business Opportunities Journal(online)*
Pub: Business Service Corp.
Contact: Carl Rawlins, Advertising Mgr
E-mail: carlrawlins@cox.net
Released: Monthly. **Description:** Newspaper covering businesses for sale.

38953 ■ *Canadian Pizza Magazine*
Pub: Annex Publishing & Printing Inc.
Contact: Diane Geerlinks, Publisher
E-mail: dgeerlinks@annexweb.com
Ed: Cameron Wood, Editor, cwood@annexweb.com.
Released: 8/yr. **Price:** $19.26 Canada; $50 in U.S.; $60 other countries. **Description:** Trade magazine for the pizza industry.

38954 ■ *Franchise News*
Pub: Franchise News
Ed: C. Richey, Editor. **Released:** Quarterly. **Price:** Included in membership. **Description:** Provides information about franchising. Recurring features include letters to the editor, interviews, news of research, a calendar of events, news of educational opportunities, reports of meetings, notices of publications available, and legal and global franchising news.

38955 ■ *Franchise Times*
Pub: Sparks Publishing & Reporting Corp.
Ed: Nancy Weingartner, Editor. **Released:** Biweekly, plus four special reports. **Price:** $195, U.S.; $225, elsewhere. **Description:** Provides analysis and information on franchising, including trends and legal and financial aspects. Recurring features include domestic and international franchising news, questions and answers, and an editorial column.

38956 ■ *Franchising Business and Law Alert*
Pub: Law Journal Newsletter
Contact: Erik B. Wulff, Editor-in-Chief
Released: Monthly. **Price:** $299, individuals for print version per year; $329, individuals for electronic version per year; $379, individuals for print and electronic version per year. **Description:** Provides articles on franchising business and law. Topics include tips on selecting a good franchise; the multi-branded concept; the FTC rule and national and international transactions; securitizing franchisor receivables; franchise expansions; litigation and arbitrations.

38957 ■ *Franchising World*
Pub: International Franchise Association
Released: Monthly, 8/year. **Price:** $50. **Description:** Trade magazine covering topics of interest to franchise company executives and the business world.

38958 ■ *Info Franchise Newsletter*
Pub: Info Press Inc.
Contact: Jo-Anne Rittenhouse, Asst. Editor
Ed: Edward L. Dixon, Jr., Editor. **Released:** Monthly. **Price:** $96. **Description:** Covers business format franchising in the U.S., Canada, and overseas; reports on trends, legislation and litigation, and on developments in the franchising business scene. Recurring features include lists of new franchisors, including descriptions, contact addresses and telephone numbers for each; and address changes of franchisor headquarters. Spotlights upcoming seminars, conferences and business opportunity shows.

38959 ■ *International Journal of Franchising and Distribution Law*
Pub: Kluwer Academic/Plenum Publishing Corp.
Ed: Martin Mendelsohn, Editor. **Released:** Quarterly. **Description:** Journal covering franchise law worldwide.

VIDEOCASSETTES/ AUDIOCASSETTES

38960 ■ *The Franchising Explosion*
GPN Educational Media
Box 80669
Lincoln, NE 68501-0669
Ph:(402)472-2007
Free: 800-228-4630
Fax: 800-306-2330
URL: http://gpn.unl.edu
Released: 1989. **Price:** $29.95. **Description:** The business phenomenon of franchising is explained by the experts at the University of Nebraska-Lincoln. **Availability:** VHS; 3/4U.

38961 ■ *How to Buy a Franchise*
Chesney Communications
2302 Martin St., Ste. 125
Irvine, CA 92612
Ph:(949)263-5500
Free: 800-223-8878
Fax: (949)263-5506
Released: 1987. **Price:** $39.95. **Description:** Find out how to become a francisee. **Availability:** VHS; 3/4U.

TRADE SHOWS AND CONVENTIONS

38962 ■ Franchising Conference & Expo
E.J. Krause & Associates, Inc.
6550 Rock Spring Dr., Ste. 500
Bethesda, MD 20817
Ph:(301)493-5500
Fax: (301)493-5705
Co. E-mail: ejkinfo@ejkrause.com
URL: http://www.ejkrause.com
Released: Annual. **Principal Exhibits:** Franchise systems and conference about purchasing a franchise.

CONSULTANTS

38963 ■ Damas & Associates
6810 S Cedar St., Ste. 2B
Lansing, MI 48911-6961
Ph:(517)694-0910
Fax: (517)694-1377
Scope: Franchise developers and consultants for franchisors in such areas as structuring the franchise, drafting agreements and disclosures statements, registering the franchise offerings where necessary, advising on matters pertaining to anti-trust trade name and trademark protection and rights, and corporate matters, developing marketing materials and operating manuals, and marketing franchises.

38964 ■ Follow-Up News
185 Pine St., Ste. 818
Manchester, CT 06040-5882
Ph:(860)647-0696
Free: 800-708-0696
Fax: (860)646-6544
Co. E-mail: followupnews@aol.com

E-mail: followupnews@aol.com
Scope: Offers low cost, low volume, "Target Marketing" solutions, to small and medium size businesses that never thought before, they had the time or money to advertise, and implement "Loyalty", "Referral", "Frequency", "Retention", "Reference", "Name Recognition", and "New Customer Prospecting" programs. **Special Services:** Database management.

38965 ■ Franchise Architects
2275 Half Day Rd., Ste. 350
Bannockburn, IL 60015
Ph:(847)465-3400
Free: 888-237-2624
Fax: (847)821-2610
Co. E-mail: info@franchisearchitects.com
URL: http://www.franchisearchitects.com

E-mail: info@franchisearchitects.com
Scope: Firm will create and/or manage indirect channels of distribution, which includes franchising, licensing, dealerships and distributorships. Development/consulting services include strategic planning, positioning, naming, creation or refinement of training programs, operational manuals, marketing strategies and collateral brochures; organizational surveys and development; and human resource assessment. Industries served: retail, transportation, food service, technology, service and communications. **Seminars:** Making the Transition from Entrepreneurial to a Professionally Managed Company; Franchising - Is It for You?; The Franchise Success System. **Special Services:** Franchise Navigator, an "interactive" assessment and educational program.

38966 ■ Franchise Brokers Network
3617-A Silverside Rd.
Wilmington, DE 19810-5117
Ph:(302)478-0200
Fax: (302)478-9217
Scope: Serves companies that are interested in expanding their business by way of franchising: provides all services including feasibility studies, contracts, disclosure statement, brochure, marketing plan, advertising program and a sales organization to bring the franchise to market. Active with manufacturing, sales, service, retail and food and beverage companies. Services individuals who are interested into going into their own business.

38967 ■ Franchise Developments Inc.
4730 Centre Ave.
Pittsburgh, PA 15213
Ph:(412)687-8484
Free: 800-576-5115
Fax: (412)687-0541
Co. E-mail: fdi@sgi.net
URL: http://www.franchise-dev.com

E-mail: fdi@sgi.net
Scope: Offers clients full development services for the purpose of designing and implementing a total fran-

chise program. **Publications:** Franchising Your Business. **Seminars:** Has presented franchising seminars under auspices of American Management Association, Management Center Europe and International Franchise Association. Recent programs include Expanding Your Business by Franchising; Writing Effective Franchise Operations Manuals. Also has franchise seminar on Prodigy. **Special Services:** Prepares operations manuals, training programs, feasibility studies, franchise agreements, disclosure documents, brochures/ads and videos.

38968 ■ Franchise Masters Inc.
8301 Golden Valley Rd., Ste. 230
Golden Valley, MN 55427
Ph:(763)541-1385
Free: 800-328-4158
Fax: (763)542-2246
Co. E-mail: johnca@franchisemasters.com
URL: http://www.franchisemasters.com

E-mail: johnca@franchisemasters.com
Scope: Provides franchise development and consulting services that include franchise legal services, advertising brochures and media advertising, manual preparation, video presentation, training programs, franchisor/franchisee relations, franchise sales and marketing, venture capital funding, business planning and human resource evaluation and planning. **Seminars:** How to Choose a Business or a Franchise.

38969 ■ Francorp Inc.
20200 Governors Dr.
Olympia Fields, IL 60461
Ph:(708)481-2900
Free: 800-372-6244
Fax: (708)481-5885
Co. E-mail: info@francorp.com
URL: http://www.francorp.com

E-mail: info@francorp.com
Scope: A management consulting firm specializing in franchise development. Provides full development programs, including feasibility studies, business plans, legal documents, operations manuals and marketing materials. Also provides post-development services for established franchisers including lead generation programs, franchise brochures, videotapes, international brokerage, public relations and expert witness services. **Seminars:** Franchise Your Business, Sep, 2006. **Special Services:** Francorp®.

38970 ■ General Business Services Corp.
1020 N University Parks Dr.
PO Box 3146
Waco, TX 76707
Ph:(817)745-2525
Free: 800-583-6181
Fax: (817)745-2544
Scope: Firm provides financial management, business counseling, and tax-related products and services to business owners and professionals. Additional services include proper record-keeping systems, accurate tax return preparation, computer software services, and financial planning services. Initial and continuous training is available to franchisees in all areas: business and tax counseling, client acquisition and business operations. Training provided at headquarters in Waco, Texas and in the field. Ongoing managerial and technical support from field support managers and national office. Manuals, sales aids, advertising materials, tax services, product development and media relations training are also included. **Publications:** 1993 Tax Tips for the Small Business Owner and Professional. **Seminars:** National Office conducts local seminars across the nation and annual conventions for franchisees. Franchisees may conduct seminars for business owners and professionals.

38971 ■ David Goodwin, PhD
23 Barnsley Cres.
Mount Sinai, NY 11766
Ph:(631)474-3290
Fax: (631)234-2649
Scope: Specializes in franchise and organizational development, sales and operation support, and business and marketing plans.

38972 ■ ISO Healthcare Consulting
641 6th Ave.
New York, NY 10011
Ph:(917)408-6900
Free: 888-715-1500
Fax: (917)408-6990
Co. E-mail: info@isohc.com
URL: http://www.isohc.com

E-mail: info@isohc.com
Scope: Provides strategic management consulting services to major pharmaceutical, medical device and biotech companies worldwide. ISO helps its clients create and implement strategies that drive top-line growth, performance and competitiveness. The company provides customized services that enhance commercial and R&D performance and alignment. The firm's areas of focus include corporate, functional and brand strategy; marketing and sales effectiveness; R&D portfolio management; R&D productivity; life cycle management; franchise planning; and organizational effectiveness design. **Publications:** List of publications available from firm upon request. **Seminars:** Strategy workshops are customized to specific client needs.

38973 ■ JC Ventures Inc.
4 Arnold St.
Old Greenwich, CT 06870-1203
Ph:(203)698-1990
Free: 800-698-1997
Fax: (203)698-2638
Scope: Specialize in business strategy consulting services to the middle market and provide venture management services. Venture management services include development of business plans, franchise advisory services, and assistance in attaining financing. Industries served: financial services and high-technology. **Publications:** Authored "The Commandants of Franchising." **Seminars:** Provide seminars for individuals looking for franchise opportunities.

38974 ■ Harold L. Kestenbaum P.C.
EAB Plz., 14th Fl.
W Twr.
Uniondale, NY 11556
Ph:(516)745-0099
Fax: (516)745-0293
Co. E-mail: hkestenbaum@farrellfritz.com
URL: http://www.franchiseatty.com

E-mail: hkestenbaum@farrellfritz.com
Scope: Provides consulting services for start-up and existing franchisors. Practices franchise law and provides marketing services as well. Serves all industries. **Publications:** Principal has published many articles related to franchising.

38975 ■ Koach Enterprises
5529 N 18th St.
Arlington, VA 22205
Ph:(703)241-8361
Fax: (703)241-8623
Scope: Business consultants specializing in franchise development, distribution and small business start-ups. Services include business development plans, preparation of operations manuals, marketing programs and training programs. Serves private industries as well as government agencies. **Publications:** "How to Franchise Your Business and How to Buy a Franchise". **Seminars:** Taking the Mystique Out of Franchising; Franchising in the 1990's; Franchising Internationally; How to Avoid Bankruptcy; International Franchising.

38976 ■ Kushell Associates Inc.
235 Greystone
Pittsboro, NC 27312
Ph:(919)542-3500
Fax: (919)542-1156
Co. E-mail: info@kushellassociates.com
URL: http://www.kushellassociates.com

E-mail: info@kushellassociates.com
Scope: Offers services in the areas of developing franchise programs for multinational entrepreneur to

minority companies domestically and internationally. Franchisee or franchisor development and franchise investments and acquisitions. Serves as an expert witness on all matters involving franchising. **Seminars:** Growth and Development of a Franchise System; Buying or Selling of a Franchise Company; Franchise Relationship.

38977 ■ Lupfer & Associates
92 Glen St.
South Natick, MA 01760
Ph:(508)655-3950
Fax: (508)655-7826
Co. E-mail: donlupfer@aol.com
URL: http://www.lupferassociates.com

E-mail: donlupfer@aol.com
Scope: Assists off shore hi-tech companies in entering United States markets and specializes in channel development for all sorts of products. Perform MARCOM support for hi-tech United States clients. **Publications:** "What's Next For Distribution-Feast or Famine?"; "The Changing Global Marketplace"; "Making Global Distribution Work". **Seminars:** How to do Business in the United States.

38978 ■ Management Action Programs Inc.
4725 Hazeltine Ave.
Sherman Oaks, CA 91423
Ph:(818)380-1177
Free: 888-834-3040
Co. E-mail: info@mapconsulting.com
URL: http://www.mapconsulting.com

E-mail: info@mapconsulting.com
Scope: Counsels distributors of products and services in improving productivity and profitability through the MAP management system. Also specializes in dealer/distributor systems, franchised companies, strategic planning, and business planning to use investment capital. **Seminars:** How to Finance a Growing Business; Venture Capital for Growing Business; Franchise Relations for the Large Accounting Firm; Should You Franchise Your Business; The Pitfalls of TQM; Productivity in the Manufacturing Sector and Re-engineering to Get Results.

38979 ■ Marketing Resources Group Franchise Consulting
7158 Austin St.
Forest Hills, NY 11375
Ph:(718)261-8882
Scope: Franchise sales, development and consulting.

38980 ■ National Cooperative Bank, Corporate Banking Div.
1725 I St. NW, Ste. 600
Washington, DC 20006
Ph:(202)336-7700
Free: 800-955-9622
Fax: (202)336-7800
URL: http://www.ncb.com
Scope: In addition to offering various banking services to franchise cooperatives, this Division consults on the establishment of employee stock ownership plans within the franchising system.

38981 ■ National Franchise Associates Inc.
240 Lake View Ct.
Lavonia, GA 30553-2018
Ph:(770)945-0660
Fax: (770)338-1603
Co. E-mail: nfa@nationalfranchise.com
URL: http://www.nationalfranchise.com

E-mail: nfa@nationalfranchise.com
Scope: An international franchise consulting firm providing full-service program to franchise companies. Services include: feasibility studies, franchise plans, venture capital, franchise agreement, FTC disclosure document, state registration applications, operations manuals, training materials, advertising and public relations, computer software programs and sales and marketing of franchises. **Seminars:** Offers franchise seminars throughout the southeastern United States.

38982 ■ National Franchise Sales
1601 Dove St., Ste. 150
Newport Beach, CA 92660
Ph:(949)428-0480
Free: 888-982-4446
Fax: (949)428-0490
Co. E-mail: mi@nationalfranchisesales.com
URL: http://www.nationalfranchisesales.com

E-mail: mi@nationalfranchisesales.com
Scope: A business brokerage firm specializing in the resale of franchise businesses and small chains. Assists in the asset recovery of non-performing franchise businesses in bankruptcy, foreclosure, or default, by re-franchising the businesses. **Seminars:** Franchising - How to Start a Franchise; Franchising - How to Market Your Franchise.

38983 ■ Nationwide Franchise Marketing Services
18715 Gibbons Dr.
Dallas, TX 75287-4045
Ph:(972)733-9942
Fax: (972)335-6581
Co. E-mail: fmmigdol@comcast.net

E-mail: fmmigdol@comcast.net
Scope: Founded primarily to aid franchisors in such areas as food services, automotive products and services, apparel, education, personnel, health and beauty aids, maintenance, entertainment and service businesses. Serves individuals who are contemplating the purchase of a franchise or distributorship with all aspects of franchise establishment. **Publications:** The following publications are available from the firm: Starting a Business, Winning in the 90s, How to Get Organized in 30 Days, 25 Tips for Producing an Effective Direct Mail Brochure; How to Land That Job, How to Keep a Job, How to Buy the Right Franchise, Fundraising for Business, Fund-raising for Non-profit Organizations, Public Relations: A Growing Management Function for Today; How to Prevent Legal problems in Hiring, Comics as a Public Relations Tool in Communications, and Greater Virility. **Seminars:** Sponsors numerous seminars, workshops and conferences, particularly in the areas of training, motivation, entrepreneurship, business start-ups and finance.

38984 ■ Sommers Consultants Inc.
301 N Main St.
New City, NY 10956-4021
Ph:(845)638-4111
Free: 800-332-2229
Fax: (845)638-3878
Scope: Provides the full scope of services necessary for planning, designing and implementing franchise programs. Industries presently served include: juvenile furniture, uniforms and maternity, fashion and footwear, instant shoe repair, and specialty baking and foods. Other services provided include: business forms and systems, marketing programs and services, real estate site selection and lease negotiations, and small business development.

38985 ■ Tarbutton Associates Inc.
1072 Laskin Rd., Ste. 202
Virginia Beach, VA 23451
Ph:(757)422-2020
Fax: (757)425-2959
Co. E-mail: ltarbutton@aol.com

E-mail: ltarbutton@aol.com
Scope: A consulting firm specializing in franchise consulting worldwide for expert witness court and legislative testimony as well as the sale or acquisition of franchising parent companies. **Publications:** Dr. Lloyd T. Tarbutton, Franchising: The How-To Book, Prentice-Hall Inc., available from firm. **Seminars:** 21st Century Management Techniques; Developing Your Business for Franchising; Developing People Into Producers; The Franchising Possiblities.

38986 ■ Venture Marketing Association, Business Development Services
800 Palisade Ave., Ste. 907
Fort Lee, NJ 07024
Ph:(201)924-7435

Fax: (201)224-8757
Co. E-mail: venturemkt@aol.com
URL: http://www.myventure.biz

E-mail: venturemkt@aol.com
Scope: Specializes in franchise program development and small businesses. Provides hands-on assistance in planning and implementing strategic marketing/management plans. Clients include franchisors, small business owners and individuals. Cost-effective fees for those in transition, facing unemployment, researching a franchise or starting a business. Industries served: service, retail, and distribution. **Seminars:** Franchise Your Business; How to Research a Franchise Services.

FRANCHISES AND BUSINESS OPPORTUNITIES

38987 ■ Brightscape Investment Centers, Inc.
9130 S Dadeland Blvd., Ste. 1602
Miami, FL 33156
Ph:(305)670-4880
Fax: (305)670-4332
No. of Franchise Units: 1. **Founded:** 1999. **Franchised:** 2003. **Description:** High margin financial services franchise. **Equity Capital Needed:** $5,000-$15,000, depending upon build out of franchise. **Franchise Fee:** $5,000. **Financial Assistance:** No. **Training:** Yes.

38988 ■ Business Alliance Inc.
130 Fifth Ave., 10th Fl.
New York, NY 10011-4399
Ph:(212)242-4399
Description: Home-based business franchise consultant, helping others find the ideal business. No previous business ownership experience is necessary. **Equity Capital Needed:** $20,000-$24,999 cash required. **Managerial Assistance:** Offers consultants a private website with all the forms and information, multiple conference calls each week, where consultants can learn more about the franchise concepts in their portfolio, plus the home office of the Business Alliance does all the negotiating with franchisors, so consultants can focus on matching prospective with franchisees. **Training:** Provides training and ongoing support.

38989 ■ Distinction Service Plus Inc.
7750 Garry East
Anjou, QC, Canada H1J 2M3
Ph:(514)351-7744
Fax: (514)351-5793
Co. E-mail: cmercier@distinction.ca
No. of Franchise Units: 80. **No. of Company-Owned Units:** 1. **Founded:** 1998. **Franchised:** 1998. **Description:** The Distinction Plus Franchise Network is built on and around a solid core of independent entrepreneurs that have chosen work for themselves and control their own destiny. It offers above all the possibility to start one's own janitorial service enterprise, while being able to count on the reputation, support and viability of a strong network. **Equity Capital Needed:** $2,000. **Training:** Technical and administrative support.

38990 ■ Franchise Development International, LLC
370 SE 15 Ave.
Pompano Beach, FL 33060
Ph:(954)942-9424
Fax: (954)783-5177
Founded: 1991. **Description:** Franchise development and marketing.

38991 ■ Franchise Developments, Inc.
4730 Centre Ave.
Pittsburgh, PA 15213
Ph:(412)521-4988
Fax: (412)687-0541
Founded: 1970. **Description:** Develop, implement and launch franchise programs.

38992 ■ Franchise Foundations
4157 23rd St.
San Francisco, CA 94114
Free: 800-942-4402
Founded: 1980. **Description:** Franchise consulting.

38993 ■ Franchise Masters International
8301 Golden Valley Rd., Ste. 230
Minneapolis, MN 55427
Ph:(763)541-0832
Free: 800-541-1385
Fax: (763)542-2246
Founded: 1980. **Description:** Planning, legal, manuals, advertising and marketing.

38994 ■ Franchise Officer
Franchise Officer, Inc.
3300 Don Mills Rd., Ste. 2101
Toronto, ON, Canada M2J 4X7
Ph:(905)668-1102
Free: (866)449-5558
Fax: (905)668-6758
Founded: 2003. **Franchised: Description:** Franchise due-diligence services and consulting.

38995 ■ Franchise Recruiters Ltd.
3500 Innsbruck
Lincolnshire Country Club
Village of Crete, IL 60417
Ph:(708)757-5595
Free: 800-334-6257
Fax: (708)758-8222
Founded: 1977. **Description:** Placement of franchise management professionals.

38996 ■ Franchise Sales
1315 S Villa Ave.
Villa Park, IL 60181
Ph:(630)571-1504
Fax: (630)827-0174
Founded: 1991. **Description:** Self franchisees in business now.

38997 ■ Franchise Search, Inc.
Kushell Associates Inc.
48 Burd St., Ste. 101
Nyack, NY 10960
Ph:(845)727-4103
Founded: 1982. **Description:** International executive search firm for franchisors.

38998 ■ Franchise Specialists, Inc.
1234 Maple St. Ext.
Moon Twp, PA 15108
Free: 800-261-5055
Founded: 1978. **Description:** Professional franchise development and sales.

38999 ■ FranchiseBuyersAgent
Franchise One, Inc.
9463 Hwy 377 S, Ste.111
Fort Worth, TX 76126
Ph:(817)249-2126
Free: 800-505-7380
Fax: (817)249-7524
Co. E-mail: info@franchise-one.com
URL: http://www.franchisebuyersagent.com
Founded: 1992. **Description:** Representing franchise buyers exclusively.

39000 ■ Franchisee Financialine
American Association of Franchisees and Dealers
PO Box 81887
San Diego, CA 92138-1887
Ph:(619)209-3775
Free: 800-733-9858
Fax: (619)209-3777
Founded: 1992. **Description:** Accounting services for franchisees.

39001 ■ Franchoice, Inc.
7500 Flying Cloud Dr., Ste. 600
Eden Prairie, MN 55344
Ph:(952)942-5561
Fax: (952)942-5793
Co. E-mail: info@franchoice.com
URL: http://www.franchoice.com

Founded: 2000. **Description:** Provides consumers with free guidance and advice to help them select a franchise that matches their individual interests and financial qualifications. **Financial Assistance:** Must have a minimum $100,000 net worth; $20,000 available capital.

39002 ■ Francorp, Inc.
20200 Governors Dr.
Olympia Fields, IL 60461
Ph:(708)481-2900
Free: 800-372-6244
Co. E-mail: info@francorp.com
URL: http://www.francorp.com
Founded: 1976. **Description:** Offers consultancy on franchising business. Consultants have provided full development programs, including feasibility studies, business plans, legal documents, operations manuals, and marketing materials for clients since 1976. **Training:** Provides post-development services for establishing franchisors, including lead generation programs, brochures, videotapes, international brokerage, PR, and expert witness service.

39003 ■ Franquest
Douglas Matheson & Co., Inc.
PO Box 2038
Pismo Beach, CA 93448
Ph:(805)773-5377
Free: 800-794-0117
Fax: (805)773-5687
Founded: 1978. **Description:** Offers consultancy on franchising issues.

39004 ■ Fransearch, Inc.
450 E 1000 N, Ste. 101
North Salt Lake, UT 84054-1925
Ph:(801)397-3726
Description: Franchise executive recruiting.

39005 ■ Franstaff, Inc.
73 S Palm Ave., Ste. 219
Sarasota, FL 34236
Ph:(941)952-9555
Description: Provides consultancy on franchising matters.

39006 ■ iFranchise Group
905 W 175th St., Ste. 2-N
Homewood, IL 60430
Ph:(708)957-2300
Fax: (708)957-2395
Co. E-mail: info@ifranchise.net
URL: http://www.ifranchise.com
Description: Offers services on strategic planning, franchise law, operations documentation, marketing and sales, and executive recruiting for franchisors.

39007 ■ Inc Plan (USA)
26C Trolley Sq.
Wilmington, DE 19806
Ph:(302)428-1200
Free: 800-462-4633
Fax: (302)428-1274
Description: Forms corporations in 50 states.

39008 ■ Information Services Inc.
2811 NE 46th St.
Lighthouse Pt., FL 33064
Ph:(954)942-0242

Fax: (954)783-2570
Founded: 1982. **Description:** Sell franchise and business opportunities.

39009 ■ Intel Marketing Associates, Inc.
227 Bellevue Way NE, Ste. 178
Bellevue, WA 98004
Ph:(206)781-1047
Description: Franchise marketing and consulting firm.

39010 ■ International Center for Entrepreneurial Development, Inc.
12715 Telge Rd.
Cypress, TX 77429
Free: 888-280-2053
Fax: (281)256-4178
Description: Entrepreneurial and franchising development.

39011 ■ International Franchise Dev./Frannet Div. LLC
29125 Chargrin Blvd., No. 200
Cleveland, OH 44122
Ph:(216)831-2610
Fax: (216)765-7118
Founded: 1990. **Description:** Franchise selection advice and development.

39012 ■ Kanouse & Walker, P.A.
2255 Glades Rd.
Boca Raton, FL 33431
Ph:(561)451-8090
Fax: (561)451-8089
Founded: 1974. **Description:** Represents franchisees in buying a franchise.

39013 ■ L. Michael Schwartz, P.A.
10561 Barkley Pl., Ste. 510
Overland Park, KS 66212-1860
Ph:(913)341-1919
Fax: (913)341-0007
Description: Franchise consulting and full legal services.

39014 ■ Leon Gottlieb USA/Int'l Franchise/ Restaurant Consultants
Leon Gottlieb & Associates
4601 Sendero Pl.
Tarzana, CA 91356-4821
Ph:(818)757-1131
Fax: (818)757-1816
Founded: 1960. **Description:** Consultant, expert witness, arbitrator.

39015 ■ Mark W. Carnes & Associates Inc.
5770 Hopkins Rd.
Richmond, VA 23234
Ph:(804)271-7522
Founded: 1988. **Description:** Franchise insurance and benefit programs.

39016 ■ Marketing Resources Group
71-58 Austin St.
Forest Hills, NY 11375
Ph:(718)261-8882
Description: Franchise development, marketing, and sales.

39017 ■ National Franchise Associates Inc.
240 Lake View Ct.
Lavonia, GA 30553
Ph:(770)945-0660
Fax: (770)338-1603
Co. E-mail: nfa@nationalfranchise.com
URL: http://www.nationalfranchise.com
Founded: 1981. **Description:** Full service consulting and developmental firm with expertise in feasibility studies, Franchise agreements and UFOC's, advertising and public relations campaigns, operations and training manuals, franchise sales programs, and ongoing franchise consulting.

LIBRARIES

39018 ■ Alberta Securities Commission–Resource Centre
300-5th Ave. SW, 4th Fl.
Calgary, AB, Canada T2P 3C4
Ph:(403)297-6454
Fax: (403)297-6156
Co. E-mail: yanming.fei@seccom.ab.ca
URL: http://www.albertasecurities.com
Contact: Yanming Fei, Libn.
Scope: Securities legislation, corporate law. **Services:** Library open to the public by appointment. **Holdings:** Figures not available.

39019 ■ Franchise Consultants International Association–Library
5147 S. Angela Rd.
Memphis, TN 38117
Ph:(901)368-3361
Fax: (901)368-1144
Co. E-mail: Franmark@msn.com
URL: http://www.FranchiseStores.com
Contact: R. Richey
Scope: Franchise law, demographics, statistics, logistics, suppliers, technology, advertising, management, legal consulting. **Services:** Members only participants for reference use. **Holdings:** 2800 books, periodicals, clippings, audio/visuals, and audio recordings; reports; manuscripts; archives; patents. **Subscriptions:** 143 magazines.

RESEARCH CENTERS

39020 ■ The Nature Conservancy–New Jersey Chapter Office
200 Pottersville Rd.
Chester, NJ 07930
Ph:(908)879-7262
Fax: (908)879-2172
Co. E-mail: newjersey@tnc.org
URL: http://nature.org/wherewework/northamerica/ states/newjersey
Contact: Barbara Brummer PhD, Exec.Dir.
E-mail: newjersey@tnc.org
Scope: Identifies rare plants and animals and the lands where they live; protects land through acquisition by gift or purchase and managing it using staff and volunteer land stewards. Also uses innovative strategies involving community and corporate partnerships. **Publications:** Brochures and fact sheets; Nature Conservancy Magazine; The Oak Leaf. **Educational Activities:** Field trips and special events throughout the state.

START-UP INFORMATION

39021 ■ *The 100 Best Businesses to Start When You Don't Want to Work Hard Anymore*
Pub: Career Press
Ed: Lisa Rogak. **Price:** $14.99.

39022 ■ *101 Businesses You Can Satrt at with Less Thank One Thousand Dollars: For Retirees*
Pub: Atlantic Publishing Company
Ed: Christina Bultinck. **Released:** December 2006. **Price:** $21.95. **Description:** Business ideas to help retirees start a home-based business on a low budget.

39023 ■ *101 Businesses You Can Start at with Less Than One Thousand Dollars: For Stay-At-Home Moms and Dads*
Pub: Atlantic Publishing Company
Ed: Christina Bultinck. **Released:** December 2006. **Price:** $21.95. **Description:** Business ideas to help stay-at-home moms and dads start a home-based business on a low budget.

39024 ■ *101 Small Business Ideas for Under $5000*
Pub: John Wiley & Sons, Incorporated
Ed: Corey Sandler, Janice Keefe. **Released:** April 2005. **Price:** $19.95. **Description:** Entrepreneurial ideas for starting companies that can be run part-time or full-time, and some as an absentee owner.

39025 ■ *The Accidental Entrepreneur: Practical Wisdom for People Who Never Expected to Work for Themselves*
Pub: Career Steps
Ed: Susan Urquhart-Brown. **Released:** August 2004. **Price:** $17.95. **Description:** Steps for launching, growing and running a successful small company.

39026 ■ *The Art of the Start: The Time-Tested, Battle-Hardened Guide for Anyone Starting Anything*
Pub: Penguin Books (USA) Incorporated
Ed: Guy Kawasaki **Released:** September 2004. **Price:** $26.95. **Description:** Advice for someone starting a new business covering topics such as hiring employees, building a brand, business competition, and management.

39027 ■ *Be Your Own Boss*
Pub: Wet Feet, Incorporated
Ed: Marcia Passos. **Released:** November 2006. **Price:** $24.95. **Description:** Tips for starting a free-lance business in any career or industry are covered.

39028 ■ *"Be Your Own Boss" in Small Business Opportunities* (July 2005)
Pub: Harris Publications Inc.
Description: Basic tips for starting your own business are outlined. Fifteen startups that can be launched for under $500 are listed, including sunglass sales, customized items, online auctions, children's music edu-cation, custom tea, vehicle ramps, waste management, pet businesses, sporting goods and sports merchandise, recipes, home improvement, wholesaling, personalized candy bars, promotional advertising products and more.

39029 ■ *Brewing Up a Business: Adventures in Entrepreneurship from the Founder of Dogfish Head Craft*
Pub: John Wiley & Sons, Incorporated
Ed: Sam Calagione. **Released:** October 2006. **Price:** $16.95. **Description:** Author shares nontraditional success secrets. Calgione began his business with a home brewing kit and grew it into Dogfish Head Craft Beer, the leading craft brewery in the U.S.

39030 ■ *"Build Your Dream Home Business" in Home Business* (Vol. 12, October 2005, No. 5, pp. 16, 18-22, 102, 104)
Pub: Home Business Magazine
Ed: Sandy Larson. **Description:** Ten steps to starting a home-based business, starting from the initial plan-ning phase to financing a venture as well as marketing strategies.

39031 ■ *"Business information centers" in BlackEnterprise* (Vol. 31, No. 12, July 2001, pp. 48)
Pub: Earl Graves Publishing Co.
Ed: Roger Barnes. **Description:** Profile of the Small Business Administration's (SBA) Business Informa-tion Center (BIC), the government-funded business resource with more than 65 BIC offices in more than 35 states. BICs provide a one-stop location for infor-mation, education, workshops, and training designed to address a broad variety of business start-up and development issues.

39032 ■ *A Business of My Own? 21 Steps to Successfully Starting and Running a Small Business*
Pub: Enfield Publishing
Ed: Marjorie Cleveland Fisher. **Released:** January 2005. **Price:** $24.95. **Description:** New ideas to start or grow a small business, including ideas for writing business plans with examples, adopting a business structure, and setting goals and objectives.

39033 ■ *"Business plan pro" in Black Enterprise* (Vol. 33, No. 6, January 2003, pp. 10)
Pub: Earl Graves Publishing Co.
Description: The tools needed to write a successful business plan are provided at blackenterprise.com. The site helps entrepreneurs to write a plan, figure startup costs, find financing, along with tips on launch-ing a Website for a new or existing small business.

39034 ■ *Canadian Small Business Kit for Dummies*
Pub: CDG Books Canada, Incorporated
Ed: Margaret Kerr, JoAnn Kurtz. **Released:** August 2004. **Price:** $37.99 (Canadian). **Description:** Entre-preneurial guide to starting and running a small busi-ness in Canada.

39035 ■ *The Canadian Small Business Survival Guide: How to Start and Operate Your Own Successful Business*
Pub: Dundurn Group
Ed: Benjamin Gallander. FRQ September 2004. **Price:** $18.99. **Description:** Ideas for starting and running a successful small business. Topics include selecting a business, financing, government assis-tance, locations, franchises, and marketing ideas.

39036 ■ *Careers for Self-Starters and Other Entrepreneurial Types*
Pub: McGraw-Hill Companies
Ed: Blythe Camenson. **Released:** September 2004. **Price:** $13.95 (US), $19.95 (Canadian). **Description:** Advice to entrepreneurs wishing to start their own small company. Tips for turning hobbies into job skills are included.

39037 ■ *Cash In On Cash Flow*
Pub: Simon & Schuster, Incorporated
Ed: Lawrence J. Pino. **Released:** July 2005. **Price:** $14.95. **Description:** Guide to assist entrepreneurs with starting a new business as a cash flow specialist.

39038 ■ *"Choosing a Business Entity" in Crain's Detroit Business* (Vol. 18, No. 49, December 9, 2002, pp. 15)
Pub: Crain Communications Inc., Detroit
Description: Questions for every aspiring entrepre-neur to ask before starting a new venture are featured.

39039 ■ *"Click on a Fortune" in Small Business Opportunities* (May 2005)
Pub: Harris Publications Inc.
Description: Franchise expo, Future Business Own-ers Spring Into Action, sponsored by the International Franchise Association, offers information to individu-als interested in starting their own franchise business. Fifteen franchise opportunities are profiled in the arti-cle.

39040 ■ *Coin Laundries - Road to Financial Independence: A Complete Guide to Starting and Operating Profitable Self-Service Laundries*
Pub: Mountain Publishing Company
Ed: Emerson G. Higdon. **Released:** June 2001. **Price:** $44.95. **Description:** Guide to starting and op-erating a self-service laundry.

39041 ■ *Common Sense Business: Starting, Operating, and Growing Your Small Business-In Any Economy!*
Pub: HarperInformation
Ed: Steve Gottry. **Released:** August 2005. **Price:** $19.95 (US), $26.95 (Canadian). **Description:** Strate-gies for starting, operating and growing a small busi-ness in any economy. .

39042 ■ *Complete Idiot's Guide to Starting an Ebay Business*
Pub: Penguin Books (USA) Incorporated
Ed: Barbara Weltman, Kara Gordon, Shirley Muse. **Released:** February 2005. **Price:** $19.95 (US), $29.

00 (Canadian). **Description:** Guide for starting an eBay business includes information on products to sell, how to price merchandise, and details for working with services like PayPal, and how to organize fulfillment services.

39043 ■ *The Complete Small Business Start-up Guide*
Pub: John Wiley & Sons, Incorporated
Ed: Lisa Rogak. **Released:** November 2004. **Price:** $14.95. **Description:** Guide to starting a small company, focusing on development of a business plan, organizational structure, advertising, hiring, selection of suppliers, and using the Internet to market your firm.

39044 ■ *The Complete Startup Guide for the Black Entrepreneur*
Pub: Career Press
Ed: Bill Bourdreaux. **Price:** $15.99.

39045 ■ *Corporation: Small Business Start-Up Kit*
Pub: Nova Publishing Company
Ed: Daniel Sitarz. **Released:** February 2005. **Price:** $29.95. **Description:** Guidebook to help entrepreneurs start up and run a small business corporation. Book includes state and federal forms with instructions.

39046 ■ *"The Design of an Ideal Business"* in *Home Business* (Vol. 12, October 2005, No. 5, pp. 58, 60)
Pub: Home Business Magazine
Ed: Brad DeHaven. **Description:** Ten steps for starting a successful new business are outlined, including low start-up costs.

39047 ■ *"Doing Your Homework"* in *Home Business* (Vol. 12, October 2005, No. 5, pp. 62)
Pub: Home Business Magazine
Ed: Kurt English, Esq. **Description:** Questions to ask before starting a home-based business are discussed. The importance of researching key issues is stressed.

39048 ■ *The Elements of Small Business*
Pub: Silver Lake Publishing
Ed: John Thaler. **Released:** October 2004. **Price:** $24.95. **Description:** Concepts, markets, worksheets, letters, business plans, and sample legal forms for starting and running a small business are included.

39049 ■ *Enterprise Planning and Development: Small Business and Enterprise Start-Up Survival and Growth*
Pub: Elsevier Science and Technology Books
Ed: David Butler. **Released:** August 2006. **Price:** $42.95. **Description:** Innovation, intellectual property, and exit strategies are among the issues discussed in this book involving current entrepreneurship.

39050 ■ *Entrepreneurial Itch: What No One Tells You About Starting Your Own Business*
Pub: Self-Counsel Press Inc.
Ed: David Trahair. **Released:** December 2006. **Price:** $13.95. **Description:** Small business accountant shares a plan for starting a business.

39051 ■ *Entrepreneurial Itch: What No One Tells You about Starting Your Own Business*
Pub: Self-Counsel Press, Incorporated
Ed: David Trahair. **Released:** December 2006. **Price:** $13.95. **Description:** It is important for entrepreneurs to do research before starting a new business. Statistically, two out of three small businesses will fail within the first three years.

39052 ■ *The Entrepreneur's Edge: Finding Money, Making Money, Keeping Money*
Pub: Silver Lake Publishing
Ed: Daniel Hogan. **Released:** October 2006. **Price:** $24.95. **Description:** Advice for starting, running and growing a new business is given.

39053 ■ *Entrepreneurship: Successfully Launching New Ventures*
Pub: Pearson Education Canada
Ed: Bruce Barringer; Duane Ireland. **Released:** January 2007. **Price:** $139.95 (CND). **Description:** Guide to help any entrepreneur successfully launch a new venture.

39054 ■ *Extraordinary Entrepreneurship: The Professional's Guide to Starting an Exceptional Enterprise*
Pub: John Wiley & Sons, Incorporated
Ed: Stephen C. Harper. **Released:** October 2006. **Price:** $45.00. **Description:** New rules to assist entrepreneurs in the 21st Century. The book focuses on thinking outside the box.

39055 ■ *Fast-Track Business Start-Up Kit: California*
Pub: DP Group, Incorporated
Ed: Carolyn Usinger. **Released:** September 2006. **Price:** $29.00. **Description:** Step-by-step guide for starting and running a business in California, including information on sole proprietors, partnerships, limited liability companies, S and C corporations, as well as details concerning business entities, sales taxes, environmental issues, human resources, and more.

39056 ■ *Financial Times Guide to Business Start Up 2007*
Pub: Pearson Education, Limited
Ed: Sara Williams; Jonquil Lowe. **Released:** November 2006. **Price:** $52.50. **Description:** Guide for starting and running a new business is presented. Sections include ways to get started, direct marketing, customer relations, management and accounting.

39057 ■ *"Flip the Switch"* in *Entrepreneur.com* (Vol. 34, February 2006, No. 2, pp. 84)
Pub: Entrepreneur Media Inc.
Ed: Jennifer Alsever. **Description:** Experienced entrepreneurs share ideas to help start a successful business. Be sure to consider looking long term, get a prototype or test run, and be patient.

39058 ■ *Franchising for Dummies*
Pub: John Wiley & Sons, Incorporated
Ed: Dave Thomas, Michael Seid. **Released:** June 2000. **Price:** $19.99. **Description:** Advice to help entrepreneurs choose the right franchise, as well as financing, managing and expanding the business.

39059 ■ *"Get 'em while they're hot"* in *Entrepreneur* (Vol. 30, No. 12, December 2002, pp. 85)
Pub: Entrepreneur Media Inc.
Ed: Steve Cooper, Mark Henricks, Gisela M. Pedroza, April Y. Pennington, Chris Penttila, Chris Sandlund, Devlin Smith, Nichole L. Torres. **Description:** The hottest business opportunities for entrepreneurs in 2003 are listed, including online learning, outsourcing, home entertainment installation, health care technology, medi-spas, Instant Messaging-related services and products, sleep-related products, singles-related products and services, yoga studios, food supplements, online gaming, bankruptcy services, pet accessories, security, large-size clothing, online auction aftermarket services, scheduling software, and specialty ice cream shops.

39060 ■ *"Getting Set for Success"* in *Small Business Opportunities* (Vol. 16, No. 2, March 2004, pp. 162-163)
Pub: Harris Publications, Inc.
Ed: Stephen Kuslich. **Description:** According to the Small Business Administration's Office of Advocacy, over 600,000 new businesses are founded in the U.S. annually, and only two-thirds remain open at least two years, about half for four years, and only 40 percent remain at least six years. Eight keys for successful entrepreneurship are presented.

39061 ■ *How to Form Your Own California Corporation*
Pub: NOLO
Ed: Anthony Mancuso. **Released:** March 2005. **Price:** $59.99. **Description:** Instructions and forms required to incorporate any business in the State of California.

39062 ■ *How to Get the Financing for Your New Small Business: Innovative Solutions from the Experts Who Do It Every Day*
Pub: Atlantic Publishing Company
Ed: Sharon L. Fullen. **Released:** August 2005. **Price:** $39.95, includes companion CD-Rom. **Description:** Ready capital is essential for starting and expanding a small business. Topics include traditional financing methods, financial statements, and a good business plan.

39063 ■ *How to Start a Home-Based Mail Order Business*
Pub: Globe Pequot Press
Ed: Georganne Fiumara. **Released:** January 2005. **Price:** $17.95. **Description:** Step-by-step guide for starting and growing a home-based mail order business. Information about equipment, pricing, online marketing, are included along with worksheets and checklists for planning.

39064 ■ *How to Start an Internet Sales Business*
Pub: Lulu.com
Ed: Dan Davis. **Released:** August 2005. **Price:** $19.95. **Description:** Small business guide for launching an Internet sales company. Topics include business structure, licenses, and taxes.

39065 ■ *How to Start, Operate and Market a Freelance Notary Signing Agent Business*
Pub: Gom Publishing, LLC
Ed: Victoria Ring. **Released:** September 2004. **Price:** $19.99. **Description:** Due to the changes in the 2001 Uniform Commercial Code allowing notary public agents to serve as a witness to mortgage loan closings (eliminating the 2-witness requirement under the old code), notaries are working directly for mortgage, title and signing companies as mobile notaries.

39066 ■ *"It's in the card"* in *BlackEnterprise* (Vol. 31, No. 12, July 2001, pp. 50)
Pub: Earl Graves Publishing Co.
Ed: Paula McCoy-Pinderhughes. **Description:** American Express launches the Community Business Card, a new source of funding for entrepreneurs and small business owners who want to start and grow their companies. The program, called AmEx Community Business Credit Card, is designed for microenterprises with less than five employees and a capital need of less than $35,000 a year. Each time the business owner uses the card, AmEx will contribute one percent of that purchase to one of three select Microenterprise Development Organizations (MDO), which in turn provide loans and technical assistance to the microenterprise requesting the capital.

39067 ■ *Kick Start Your Dream Business: Getting it Started and Keeping You Going*
Pub: Ten Speed Press
Ed: Romanus Wolter. **Released:** March 2004. **Price:** $26.95 (Canadian). **Description:** Comprehensive guide covering the start-up process for any new company.

39068 ■ *Legal Guide for Starting and Running a Small Business*
Pub: NOLO
Ed: Fred Steingold, Lisa Guerin. **Released:** March 2005. **Price:** $34.99. **Description:** Information for starting a new business focusing on choosing a business structure, taxes, employees and independent contractors, trademark and service marks, licensing and permits, leasing and improvement of commercial space, buying and selling a business, and more.

39069 ■ *"The Name Game"* in *Venture Capital Journal* (Vol. 42, No. 10, October 2002, pp. 35-37)
Pub: Thomas Venture Economics
Ed: Charles R. Fellers. **Description:** Young companies are changing names faster than they are changing their business plans. Strategies for naming a company are investigated.

39070 ■ *The Owners Manual for Small Business*
Pub: Planning Shop
Ed: Rhonda Abrams. **Released:** December 2005. **Price:** $19.95. **Description:** Reference book offering tips for starting a small business, low-cost marketing, and communicating effectively.

39071 ■ *Partnership: Small Business Start-Up Kit*
Pub: Nova Publishing Company
Ed: Daniel Sitarz. **Released:** November 2005. **Price:** $29.95. **Description:** Guidebook detailing partnership law by state covering the formation and use of partnerships as a business form. Information on filing requirements, property laws, legal liability, standards, and the new Revised Uniform Partnership Act is covered.

39072 ■ *"Personality Test" in Entrepreneur.com* (Vol. 34, February 2006, No. 2, pp. 122)
Pub: Entrepreneur Media Inc.
Ed: Romanus Wolter. **Description:** Business interactions must leave a positive impression as well as provide exceptional results.

39073 ■ *"Pick Your Startup Tool" in Black Enterprise* (Vol. 36, November 2005, No. 4, pp. 74)
Pub: Earl G. Graves Publishing Co. Inc.
Ed: Sonya Donaldson. **Description:** Besides being a good business plan, financial management tools are an asset for planning a marketing strategy. Business Plan Pro Standard, QuickBooks, Peachtree, and Business Resource Software can help startups write business plans that include pricing strategy, advertising, and budgeting.

39074 ■ *"Shoestring Start-Ups" in Small Business Opportunities* (Vol. 17, November 2005, No. 6)
Pub: Harris Publications Inc.
Description: Fifty low-cost businesses to start on a part-time basis and grow into a full-time entrepreneurial venture are profiled.

39075 ■ *Small Business for Dummies*
Pub: John Wiley & Sons, Incorporated
Ed: Eric Tyson, Jim Schell. **Released:** November 2002. **Price:** $21.99. **Description:** Advice for launching and growing a small business; insights into using the Internet as business tool are included.

39076 ■ *Small Business Entrepreneur: Launching a New Venture and Managing a Business on a Day-to-Day Basis*
Pub: Austin & Company, Incorporated
Ed: Rory Burke. **Released:** February 2006. **Price:** $19.95. **Description:** Comprehensive guide examining the management skills required to launch and run a small business.

39077 ■ *Small Business Legal Tool Kit*
Pub: Entrepreneur Press
Ed: Ira Nottonson; Theresa A. Pickner. **Released:** May 2007. **Price:** $36.95. **Description:** Legal expertise is provided by two leading entrepreneurial attorneys. Issues covered include forming and operating a business: taxes, contracts, leases, bylaws, trademarks, small claims court, etc.

39078 ■ *Small Business Management: Launching and Managing New Ventures*
Pub: Nelson Thomson Learning
Ed: Justin G. Longenecker. **Released:** March 2006. **Price:** $78.95. **Description:** Tips for starting and running a successful new company are provided.

39079 ■ *The Small Business Owner's Manual: Everything You Need to Know to Start Up and Run Your Business*
Pub: Career Press, Incorporated
Ed: Joe Kennedy. **Released:** June 2005. **Price:** $19.99 (US), $26.95 (Canadian). **Description:** Comprehensive guide for starting a small business, focusing on twelve ways to obtain financing, business plans, selling and advertising products and services, hiring and firing employees, setting up a Web site, business law, accounting issues, insurance, equipment, computers, banks, financing, customer credit and collection, leasing, and more.

39080 ■ *"Small Business Spotlight" in Small Business Opportunities* (Vol. 16, No. 1, January 2004, pp. 112)
Pub: Harris Publications, Inc.
Description: National Aeronautics and Space Administration (NASA) funds the Space Alliance Technology Outreach Program (SATOP). The program provides small businesses with free technical assistance through the use of the U.S. Space Program, as well as aerospace contractors, NASA field centers, universities and colleges. Profiles of two companies that improved and developed their designs through the SATOP program are presented.

39081 ■ *The Small Business Start-Up Kit*
Pub: NOLO
Ed: Peri Pakroo. **Released:** April 2004. **Price:** $24.99. **Description:** Entrepreneurial advice for launching a new business. Topics include compliance with state regulations, sole proprietorships, partnerships, corporations, limited liability companies, as well as accounting and tax information.

39082 ■ *The Small Business Start-Up Kit for California*
Pub: NOLO
Ed: Peri Pakroo. **Released:** April 2004. **Price:** $24.99. **Description:** Handbook covering all aspects of starting a business in California, including information about necessary fees, forms, and taxes.

39083 ■ *Small Business Start-Up Workbook: A Step-by-Step Guide to Starting the Business You've Dreamed Of*
Pub: How To Books
Ed: Cheryl D. Rickman. **Released:** February 2006. **Price:** $24.75. **Description:** Book provides practical exercises for starting a small business, including marketing and management strategies.

39084 ■ *"Small business package passes Congress" in BlackEnterprise* (Vol. 31, No. 10, May 2001, pp. 22)
Pub: Earl Graves Publishing Co.
Ed: Joyce Jones. **Description:** Information regarding the package of small business legislation passed by the 106th Congress will keep some programs intact and secure the future of others. SBA budget agreement appropriations, including venture capital assistance are presented. Statistical data included.

39085 ■ *Small Time Operator: How to Start Your Own Business, Keep Your Books, Pay Your Taxes, and Stay Out of Trouble*
Pub: Bell Springs Publishing
Ed: Bernard B. Kamoroff. **Released:** February 2005. **Price:** $17.95. **Description:** Comprehensive guide for starting any kind of business.

39086 ■ *Solo Private Practice: A Step by Step Guide to Opening Your Private Practice*
Pub: Empowerment Publications
Ed: B.J. Patchett. **Released:** August 2004. **Price:** $12.95. **Description:** Launching a medical facility offering clinical services, while adhering to the highest professional standards, requires an efficiently run office.

39087 ■ *Soul Proprietor: 101 Lessons from a Lifestyle Entrepreneur*
Pub: Crossing Press, Incorporated
Ed: Jane Pollak. **Released:** September 2004. **Price:** $14.95 (US), $21.95 (Canadian). **Description:** More than 100 tips and stores to inspire and guide any would-be entrepreneur to earn a living from a favorite hobby or passion.

39088 ■ *"South Portland, Maine, College Develops Small-Business Incubator" in Portland Press Herald* (August 16, 2005)
Pub: Blethen Maine Newspapers, Inc.
Ed: Ann S. Kim. **Description:** Southern Maine Community College in South Portland has developed a new small business incubator for area startups. Four students have enrolled in the incubator since January. They receive advice from faculty members on writing business plans and more.

39089 ■ *The Spirit of Entrepreneurship: Exploring the Essence of Entrepreneurship Through Personal Stories*
Pub: Springer
Ed: Sharda S. Nandram; Karel J. Samson. **Released:** October 2006. **Price:** $79.95. **Description:** Case studies involving 60 entrepreneurs and executives explores the fundamentals in starting a new business, techniques and mindsets.

39090 ■ *Start Business in California, 3E*
Pub: Sourcebooks, Incorporated
Ed: John J. Talamo. **Released:** July 2006. **Price:** $24.95. **Description:** Information required for starting any business in California.

39091 ■ *Start and Run a Bookkeeping Business*
Pub: Self-Counsel, Incorporated
Ed: Angie Mohr. **Released:** October 2005. **Price:** $17.95 (US), $22.95 (Canadian). **Description:** Advice for starting and running a bookkeeping service business. Includes MS Word and PDF formats for use in Windows-based PC.

39092 ■ *Start, Run, and Grow a Successful Small Business, 2nd Edition*
Pub: CCH, Inc.
Ed: Susan M. Jacksack. **Price:** $24.95.

39093 ■ *Start-ups That Work: Surprise Research on What Makes or Breaks a New Company*
Pub: Penguin Group
Ed: Joel Kurtzman; Glenn Rifkin. **Released:** October 2005. **Price:** $25.95.

39094 ■ *Start Your Own Lawn Care Business: Your Step-by-Step Guide to Success*
Pub: Entrepreneur Press
Ed: Eileen Figure Sandlin. **Released:** December 2003. **Price:** $14.95. **Description:** Steps for starting and running a lawn care service.

39095 ■ *Start Your Own Wedding Consultant Business*
Pub: Entrepreneur Press
Ed: Eileen Figure Sandlin. **Released:** December 2003. **Price:** $14.95. **Description:** Advice for starting and running a wedding consulting business.

39096 ■ *"Staying within their niche yields success for winners" in Atlanta Business Chronicle* (Vol. 23, No. 48, May 4, 2001, pp. 70A)
Pub: American City Business Journals Inc.
Ed: Pamela Blackmon. **Description:** Sandy Morris and Shaun Bradley of employee recruitment firm Bradley-Morris Inc. have been awarded Georgia's Small Business Persons of the Year award by the U.S. Small Business Administration. They will compete with other entrepreneurs from each state for the national Small Business of the Year award, which is selected based on increase in sales, innovative products or services, staying power and employee growth.

39097 ■ *Steps to Small Business Start-Up*
Pub: Kaplan Books
Ed: Linda Pinson; Jerry Jinnett. **Released:** July 2006. **Price:** $29.00. **Description:** Tips for starting and running a new company are presented.

39098 ■ *Stop Working: Start a Business, Globalize It, and Generate Enough Cash Flow to Get Out of the Rat Race*
Pub: Eye Contact Media
Ed: Rohan Hall. **Released:** November 2004. **Price:** $19.99. **Description:** Advice is given to small companies to compete in the global marketplace by entrepreneur using the same strategy for his own business.

39099 ■ *Straight Talk About Small Business Success in New Jersey: How to Maximize the Growth, Cash Flow and Profitability of Your Small Business*
Pub: Business Success Systems, Incorporated

Ed: Salim Omar. **Released:** April 2004. **Price:** $18.95. **Description:** Small business information geared to new and existing small businesses in New Jersey.

39100 ■ *Swimming Against the Stream: Launching Your Business and Making Your Life*
Pub: Macmillan Publishers Limited
Ed: Tim Waterstone. **Released:** March 2007. **Price:** $17.99. **Description:** Ten rules for launching a new business are outlined using real-life experiences.

39101 ■ *"They Just Can't Stop Themselves"* in *Inc.* (Volume 27, March 2005, No. 3, pp. 98-104)
Pub: Inc. Magazine
Ed: Stephanie Clifford. **Description:** Entrepreneurs share insight into starting more than one successful company.

39102 ■ *"20 Top Biz for 2002"* in *Small Business Opportunities* (V. 14, No. 1, 1/2002, pp. 22-24, 26, 28, 30, 32, 34, 36, 38, 40, 130)
Pub: Harris Publications, Inc.
Description: Twenty recession-proof businesses for potential entrepreneurs to startup are profiled, including health food store, cleaning service, handyman service agency, cart vendors, window cleaning, dance studio, information broker, landscaping, sign shop, auto paint repair service, computer maintenance, closet/storage organizer, childproofing safety business, hair salon, specialty cake bakery, pet chauffer business, senior services, and delivery services.

39103 ■ *Ultimate Startup Directory: Expert Advice and 1,500 Great Startup Ideas*
Pub: Entrepreneur Press
Ed: James Stephenson. **Released:** February 2007. **Price:** $30.95 (CND). **Description:** Startup opportunities in over 30 industries are given, along with information on investment, earning potential, skills, legal requirements and more.

39104 ■ *The Unofficial Guide to Starting a Small Business*
Pub: John Wiley & Sons, Incorporated
Ed: Marcia Layton Turner. **Released:** October 2004. **Price:** $16.99. **Description:** Information and tools for starting a small business, covering the start-up process, from market research, to business plans, to marketing programs.

39105 ■ *Up and Running: Opening a Chiropractic Office*
Pub: PageFree Publishing, Incorporated
Ed: John L. Reizer. **Released:** March 2004. **Price:** $30.00. **Description:** Tips for starting a chiropractic business.

39106 ■ *Weekend Small Business Start*
Pub: Sourcebooks, Incorporated
Ed: Mark Warda. **Released:** June 2007. **Price:** $19.95. **Description:** Information for starting a new business is presented.

39107 ■ *What No Ever Tells You About Starting Your Own Business: Real-Life Start-Up Advice from 101 Successful Entrepreneurs*
Pub: Kaplan Publishing
Ed: Jan Norman. **Released:** July 2004. **Price:** $18.95 (US), $28.95 (Canadian). **Description:** From planning to marketing, advice is given to entrepreneurs starting new companies. s.

39108 ■ *"What Works: Start Last, Finish First"* in *Business 2.0* (Vol. 7, January/February 2006, No. 1, pp. 41-43)
Pub: Time, Inc.
Ed: Michael V. Copeland. **Description:** Timing is right for entrepreneurial startups to successfully compete with industry leaders.

39109 ■ *"Work It"* in *Entrepreneur* (Vol. 33, October 2005, No. 10, pp. 34)
Pub: Entrepreneur Media Inc.
Ed: Mark Henricks. **Description:** The findings of a four-year study conducted by Joel Kurtzman and Glenn Riffkin are discussed. The authors of the study have identified nine key factors in successful startups that include market size, competitive position, business model and cash flow.

39110 ■ *Working for Yourself: An Entrepreneur's Guide to the Basics*
Pub: Kogan Page, Limited
Ed: Jonathan Reuvid. **Released:** September 2006. **Description:** Guide for starting a new business venture, focusing on raising financing, legal and tax issues, marketing, information technology, and site location.

39111 ■ *Your First Business Plan: A Simple Question-and-Answer Format Designed to Help You Write Your Own Plan*
Pub: Sourcebooks, Incorporated
Ed: Joseph A. Covello. **Released:** May 2005. **Price:** $14.95. **Description:** Writing a good first business plan outlines successful business growth.

ASSOCIATIONS AND OTHER ORGANIZATIONS

39112 ■ Association for Enterprise Integration
2111 Wilson Blvd., Ste. 400
Arlington, VA 22201
Ph:(703)247-9474
Fax: (703)522-3192
Co. E-mail: info@afei.org
URL: http://www.afei.org
Contact: Dave Chesebrough, Pres.
Description: Strives to advance enterprise integration and electronic business practices for industries and governments.

39113 ■ Association for International Business
725 G St.
Salida, CO 81201
Ph:(719)539-0500
Free: 800-359-5166
Fax: (719)539-6925
Co. E-mail: director@aibcenter.com
URL: http://www.creditman.co.uk/internat/aiblink.html
Contact: Ray Gabriel, Managing Dir.
Description: Global business community whose members are in all areas of International business. Provides a network for the international business community where members can provide and share information, resources, and help with problem solving. Hosts in 70 countries to assist visitors. Conducts a mentorship program. **Publications:** *International Business Discussion Group* (daily).

39114 ■ BC Innovation Council
1188 W Georgia St., 9th Fl.
Vancouver, BC, Canada V6E 4A2
Ph:(604)438-2752
Free: 800-665-7222
Fax: (604)438-6564
Co. E-mail: info@bcinnovationcouncil.com
URL: http://www.bcinnovationcouncil.com
Contact: David Dolphin, CEO

39115 ■ Canadian Federation of Independent Business–Federation Canadienne de l'Entreprise Independante
4141 Yonge St., Ste. 401
Willowdale, ON, Canada M2P 2A6
Ph:(416)222-8022
Fax: (416)222-7593
Co. E-mail: cfib@cfib.ca
URL: http://www.cfib.ca
Contact: Catherine Swift, Pres./CEO
Membership: Independent businesses. **Purpose:** Promotes economic well-being of members and seeks to maintain a healthy domestic business climate. Represents members' interests before government agencies, labor and industrial organizations, and the public.

39116 ■ International Association for Business Organizations
3 Woodthorn Ct., Ste. 12
Owings Mills, MD 21117
Ph:(410)581-1373
Co. E-mail: nahbb@msn.com

Contact: Rudolph Lewis, Exec. Officer
Description: Business organizations that develop and support small businesses that have the capability to provide their products or services on an international level. Establishes international business training institutions; promotes a business code of ethics for members. Conducts market studies; supplies member organizations with management assistance. Encourages joint marketing services and international trade assistance among members. Certifies international traders. **Publications:** Newsletter (periodic).

39117 ■ International Council for Small Business
The George Washington University
Scholarship of Business
2201 G St. NW, Funger 315
Washington, DC 20052
Ph:(202)994-0704
Fax: (202)994-4930
Co. E-mail: icsb@gwu.edu
URL: http://www.icsb.org
Contact: Rob Van der Horst, Pres.
Membership: Management educators, researchers, government officials, and professionals in 80 countries. **Purpose:** Fosters discussion of topics pertaining to the development and improvement of small business management. **Publications:** *ICSB Bulletin* (quarterly); *Journal of Small Business Management* (quarterly); Membership Directory (annual); Proceedings (annual).

39118 ■ National Association for Business Organizations
3 Woodthorne Ct., No. 12
Owings Mills, MD 21117
Ph:(410)363-3698
Co. E-mail: nahbb@msn.com
Contact: Rudolph Lewis, Pres.
Purpose: Business organizations that develop and support small businesses that have the capability to provide their products or services on a national level. Promotes small business in a free market system; represents the interests of small businesses to government and community organizations on small business affairs; monitors and reviews laws that affect small businesses; promotes a business code of ethics. Supplies members with marketing and management assistance; encourages joint marketing services between members. Operates a Home Based Business Television Network that provides an affordable audio/visual media for small and home based businesses. **Publications:** Newsletter (periodic).

39119 ■ National Association of Entrepreneurial Parents
PO Box 320722
Fairfield, CT 06825
Ph:(203)371-6212
Fax: (203)371-6212
Co. E-mail: members@en-parent.com
URL: http://www.en-parent.com/NAEP.htm
Contact: Lisa Roberts, Dir.
Membership: Parents with home-based business careers. **Purpose:** Seeks to assist "parents who are looking to balance work and family on their own terms." Facilitates networking among entrepreneurial parents; provides ad opportunities for members; organizes support groups for members; makes available discount programs and services to members. Conducts home career counseling sessions. **Publications:** *The Entrepreneurial Parent; EPnews* (quarterly); *How to Raise a Family and a Career Under One Roof;* Membership Directory (annual).

39120 ■ National Association of Small Business Investment Companies
666 11th St. NW, Ste. 750
Washington, DC 20001
Ph:(202)628-5055
Fax: (202)628-5080
Co. E-mail: nasbic@nasbic.org
URL: http://www.nasbic.org
Contact: Lee W. Mercer, Pres.
Membership: Firms licensed as Small Business Investment Companies (SBICs) under the Small Busi-

ness Investment Act of 1958. **Publications:** *Layman's Guide to the Legal Aspects of Venture Investments; NASBIC Membership Directory* (annual); *NASBIC News* (quarterly); *Today's SBICs: Investing in America's Future.*

39121 ■ National Small Business Association
1156 15th St. NW, Ste. 1100
Washington, DC 20005
Ph:(202)293-8830
Free: 800-345-6728
Fax: (202)872-8543
Co. E-mail: press@nsba.biz
URL: http://www.nsba.biz
Contact: Paul Hense, Chm.
Membership: Small businesses including manufacturing, wholesale, retail, service, and other firms. **Purpose:** Works to advocate at the federal level on behalf of smaller businesses. **Publications:** *Advocate* (bimonthly).

39122 ■ SCORE
409 3rd St. SW, 6th Fl.
Washington, DC 20024
Ph:(202)205-6762
Free: 800-634-0245
Fax: (202)205-7636
Co. E-mail: media@score.org
URL: http://www.score.org
Contact: W. Kenneth Yancey Jr., CEO
Description: Serves as volunteer program sponsored by U.S. Small Business Administration in which working and retired business management professionals provide free business counseling to men and women who are considering starting a small business, encountering problems with their business, or expanding their business. Offers free one-on-one counseling, online counseling and low cost workshops on a variety of business topics. **Publications:** *SCORE eNews* (monthly) ; *SCORE Expert Answers* (monthly); *SCORE Today* (monthly) ; Annual Report (annual).

EDUCATIONAL PROGRAMS

39123 ■ AMA's 5-day "MBA" Workshop
American Management Association
1601 Broadway
New York, NY 10019
Ph:(212)586-8100
Free: 800-262-9699
Fax: (212)903-8168
Co. E-mail: customerservice@amanet.org
URL: http://www.amanet.org
Price: $2,995 for non-members; $2,695 for AMA members. **Description:** Covers accounting, finance, strategy, marketing, and management to provide an integrated overview of the business world. **Locations:** Cities throughout the United States.

DIRECTORIES OF EDUCATIONAL PROGRAMS

39124 ■ *Entrepreneurs Directory*
Pub: infoUSA Inc.
Price: $1,100 annual subscription print, CD, DVD or internet. **Covers:** 4.5 million small business owners and 671,000 entrepreneurs in the U.S. **Entries Include:** Owner's name, gender and title; company name, address, phone, fax; type of business, number of employees, sales volume, franchise and brand information.

REFERENCE WORKS

39125 ■ "3-D Negotiation: Playing the Whole Game" in *Harvard Business Review* (Vol. 81, No. 11, November 2003, pp. 64)
Pub: Harvard Business School Press
Ed: David A. Lax, James K. Sebenius. **Description:** Business negotiations require thorough planning and development in order to be successful.

39126 ■ *The 7 Irrefutable Rules of Small Business Growth*
Pub: John Wiley & Sons, Incorporated
Ed: Steven S. Little. **Released:** February 2005. **Price:** $18.95. **Description:** Proven strategies to maintain small business growth are outlined, covering topics such as technology, business plans, hiring, and more.

39127 ■ "75 Reasons to Be Glad You're an American Entrepreneur Right Now" in *Inc.* (October 2005, pp. 88-95)
Pub: Inc. Magazine
Ed: Michael S. Hopkins. **Description:** The diverse ways in which the culture, the economy, and entrepreneurship are making this the best time in history to build a business in America.

39128 ■ "101 Dumbest Moments in Business" in *Business 2.0* (Vol. 7, January/February 2006, No. 1, pp. 98-102, 104-106, 108, 110, 136)
Pub: Time, Inc.
Ed: Adam Horowitz; David Jacobson; Mark Lasswell; and Owen Thomas. **Description:** Lessons to be learned by mistakes made by other businesses.

39129 ■ *201 Great Tips for Your Small Business: Increase Your Profit and Joy in Your Work*
Pub: Dundren Press Limited
Ed: Julie V. Watson. **Released:** April 2006. **Price:** $24.99. **Description:** Tips and hints for home-based, micro, and small businesses are presented.

39130 ■ *401 Questions Every Entrepreneur Should Ask*
Pub: Career Press, Incorporated
Ed: James L. Silvester. **Released:** October 2006. **Price:** $17.99. **Description:** Review of 25 functional areas of running a small business are covered along with questions entrepreneurs should ask in order to correct and avoid unwanted issues.

39131 ■ "The 2003 Tax Relief Act: What Does It Mean for You?" in *My Business* (October/November 2003, pp. 26)
Pub: My Business Magazine
Description: Three provisions of the 2003 Tax Relief Act are especially beneficial for small businesses, including the increase in spending, accelerated reduction in income-tax rates, and accelerating the reduction in the top marginal rate. Tax information is also provided for small businesses using trucks or SUVs, and the 50 percent bonus depreciation deduction.

39132 ■ "2007 Conference Calendar" in *Journal of Business Communication* (Vol. 44, January 2007, No. 1, pp. 103)
Pub: Association for Business Communication
Description: Overview of 2007 Conference Calendar.

39133 ■ "About the Power Breakfast series" in *Crain's Detroit Business* (Vol. 19, No. 1, January 6, 2003, pp. 3)
Pub: Crain Communications Inc., Detroit
Description: Crain's Detroit Business is playing host to private roundtable discussions with executives and experts in the Detroit area. Key issues will focus on Southeast Michigan businesses, including suppliers, ethics, governance, and more.

39134 ■ "Add fudge factor to cost to equal business success" in *Crain's Detroit Business* (Vol. 18, No. 49, December 9, 2002, pp. 12)
Pub: Crain Communications Inc., Detroit
Ed: Laura Bailey. **Description:** The issues of cost controls in managing a small business are discussed.

39135 ■ "Affirmative Action on Trial" in *Hispanic Business* (September 2003, pp. 40-42, 44)
Pub: Hispanic Business
Ed: Holly Ocasio Rizzo. **Description:** The nation's law and business schools are struggling to raise minority enrollment, and the new U.S. Supreme Court ruling struck down a plan giving Hispanics and other minorities extra points toward undergraduate admission.

39136 ■ "Agency with a Small Focus" in *Hispanic Business* (September 2003, pp. 24, 26, 28)
Pub: Hispanic Business
Ed: Patricia Guadalupe. **Description:** Hector Barreto, Small Business Administration's Administrator, addresses the 20 million businesses the SBA has assisted in its fifty years of existence. Statistical data included.

39137 ■ "Agenda Items" in *Fast Company* (June 2001, pp. 147)
Pub: Fast Company
Description: A collection of the best-of-the-best innovations and technologies that set the business agenda are listed, including the bar code scanning device, the Honda Insight, the lab mouse, the catalytic converter, Perl programming language, and the Hertz Number One Gold Program.

39138 ■ "All's Fair: In Love and Business, So You May Need a Prenup to Protect Your Company's Assets" in *Entrepreneur* (Vol. 31, Sept. 2003)
Pub: Entrepreneur Media, Inc.
Ed: Nichole L. Torres. **Description:** Pre-nuptial agreements can help to protect entrepreneurs in the event of a divorce.

39139 ■ *Alpha Dogs: How Your Small Business Can Become a Leader of the Pack*
Pub: HarperCollins Publishers, Inc.
Ed: Donna Fenn. **Released:** May 2007. **Price:** $14.95. **Description:** Profiles of eight successful entrepreneurs along with information for developing customer service, technology and competition.

39140 ■ "The American Cancer Society's Next Crusade" in *Fast Company* (November 2001, pp. 58)
Pub: Fast Company
Ed: Bill Breen. **Description:** For nearly 90 years, the American Cancer Society has led the war against cancer, now the society faces another do-or-die challenge: to identify the next generation of leaders who will continue the battle.

39141 ■ "An American Icon" in *Entrepreneur* (Vol. 33, January 2005, No. 1, pp. 76)
Pub: Entrepreneur Media Inc.
Ed: April Y. Pennington. **Description:** There are more than 387,000 franchises, listed are the five ways in which franchising has affected the U.S.

39142 ■ *America's Corporate Families*
Pub: Dun & Bradstreet Corp.
Released: Annual. **Covers:** Approximately 12,700 U.S. corporations . Ultimate companies must meet all of the following criteria for inclusion: two or more business locations, 250 or more employees at that location or in excess of $25 million in sales volume or a tangible net worth greater than $500,000, and controlling interest in one or more subsidiary company. **Entries Include:** D&B D-U-N-S number, company name, address, phone, state of incorporation, line of business, primary/secondary SIC codes, sales volume, net worth, number of employees, current ownership date, year started, number of sites, key executives' names/titles, directors and than officers, primary bank and accounting firm, import/export designation, stock exchange symbol and indicator for publicly owned companies, parent company and location. **Arrangement:** Alphabetical, geographical, industry classication. **Indexes:** Geographical, SIC code (both with address and SIC code).

39143 ■ "America's Labor Federation" in *The Economist* (Vol. 376, July 30-August 5, 2005, No. 8437, pp. 25-26)
Pub: The Economist Newspaper Ltd.
Description: Will the split in the AFL-CIO help or hurt organized labor in the U.S.? Union membership has been on a decline since for the last forty years.

39144 ■ "America's Newest Entrepreneurial Patron" in *Inc.* (October 1, 2003)
Pub: Gruner & Jahr USA Publishing

Ed: Rod Kurtz. **Description:** Disney to sponsor the new U.S. Small Business Administration's National Entrepreneur Center in Orlando, Florida. The center will offer business courses, special software for creating business plans, and mentor programs.

39145 ■ "An Older Sibling In Your Corner Eases Entry Into The Real World" in *Wall Street Journal* (Vol. 248, December 2006, No. 149, pp. B6)
Pub: Dow Jones & Co. Inc.
Ed: Emily Meehan **Description:** Recent college grads often utilize the success, resources and connections of their older siblings while transitioning to life after college and establishing a foothold in their perspective careers.

39146 ■ "Annual meetings an extension of nonprofit mission" in *Atlanta Business Chronicle* (Vol. 24, No. 14, September 7, 2001, pp. S12)
Pub: American City Business Journals Inc.
Ed: Anya Martin. **Description:** Various executives from non-profit organizations talk about annual meetings and key factors to consider.

39147 ■ "Anti-Recession Strategies" in *Small Business Opportunities* (Vol. 14, No. 1, January 2002, pp. 10)
Pub: Harris Publications, Inc.
Ed: Jerry Buchs. **Description:** Recession-proof business strategies to help small businesses cope during an economic downturn are presented.

39148 ■ *Are Government Purchasing Policies Failing Small Business?: Congressional Hearing*
Pub: DIANE Publishing Company
Ed: John F. Kerry. **Released:** November 2004. **Price:** $35.00. **Description:** Covers Congressional hearing: Steven App, Treasury Department; Fred Armendariz and Major Clark, Small Business Administration; Susan Allen, Pan Asian American Chamber of Commerce; Stephen Denlinger, Latin American Management Association; Charles Henry, National Veteran's Business Development Corporation; Morris Hudson, MO Procurement Technology Assistance Centers; Bar Kasoff, Women Impact, Public Policy; Pam Mazza, Piliero, Massa and Pargament; Ron Newlan, HubZone Contract National Council; Pat Parker, Native American Management Service; Joann Payne, Women First National Legislative Commission; Mike Robinson, MA Small Business Development Centers; Ramon Rodriguez, Hispanic Chamber of Commerce; Angela Styles, Office of Management and Budget; Ralph Thomas, NASA; John Turner, MN Business Enterprise Legal Defense Fund; James Turpin, American Subcontractor's Association, Inc.; and Henry Wilfong, National Association of Small Disadvantaged Business.

39149 ■ "Arlington the Site of HD Career Expo" in *Hispanic Business* (Vol. 23, No. 10, October, 2001, pp. 104)
Pub: Hispanic Business
Description: The diversity recruitment division of Hispanic Business, HireDiversity.com, will host a national Diversity Career Expo November 13, 2001, at the Hyatt Regency Crystal City in Arlington, Virginia.

39150 ■ "Art of Business" in *Entrepreneur. com* (Vol. 34, February 2006, No. 2, pp. 46)
Pub: Entrepreneur Media Inc.
Ed: Sara Wilson. **Description:** The MacDowell Colony serves not only as an inspiration to artists of all disciplines, but the Colony's methods for fostering creativity can be used to teach entrepreneurs the value of time and space in order to generate ideas.

39151 ■ "The Art of the Perfect Business Gift" in *Crain's Detroit Business* (Vol. 21, October 3, 2005, No. 43, pp. 14)
Pub: Crain Communications Inc. - Detroit
Ed: Constance Crump. **Description:** Etiquette regarding business gift giving, broken down by various sectors, is presented. Food gifts are always a good option.

39152 ■ "The Art and Science of Networking" in *Sales and Marketing.com* (Vol. 153, No. 3, March 2004, pp. 49)
Pub: VNU eMedia, Inc.
Ed: Mark Haering. **Description:** Networking is a key to finding new employment. Guidelines for participating in an organized network setting are presented.

39153 ■ "Arts Group Adopts New Name, Look, Enhanced Agenda" in *Mississippi Business Journal* (Vol. 28, September 2006, No. 36, pp. 28)
Pub: Venture Publications, Inc.
Ed: Wally Northway **Description:** Profile of the Greater Jackson Arts Council. With a new look, name, and logo to add to their enhanced agenda, the Greater Jackson Arts Council boasts a higher degree of professionalism in the portrayal of the arts in the Jackson community. Statistical data included.

39154 ■ "Assist.com www.assist.com/assist. htm" in *Entrepreneur* (Vol. 32, No. 1, January 2004, pp. 10)
Pub: Entrepreneur Media, Inc.
Ed: Steve Cooper. **Description:** When a small business is searching for a white paper or any research, Assist.com's search engine indexes PDF files that are downloadable free.

39155 ■ "Attention Readers!" in *Fast Company* (July 2001, pp. 50)
Pub: Fast Company
Ed: Polly LaBarre. **Description:** Review of the book titled, 'The Attention Economy: Understanding the New Currency of Business'. The book explores human attention factors and offers ways of capturing and holding the attention of customers, employees, and shareholders.

39156 ■ "Author, Expert to Discuss Socially Responsible Business Methods" in *Portland Press Herald* (April 20, 2005)
Pub: Blethen Maine Newspapers, Inc.
Ed: Victoria Gannon. **Description:** Hunter Lovins, co-author of the book, Natural Capitalism-Creating the Next Industrial Revolution, spoke to a group of business owners regarding the three main tenets of natural capitalism.

39157 ■ "Back from the Brink" in *BlackEnterprise* (Vol. 31, No. 8, March 2001, pp. 47)
Pub: Earl Graves Publishing Co.
Ed: Glenn Townes. **Description:** Profiles of minority small business owners who were able to rebuild their businesses after facing major setbacks.

39158 ■ "Baker, Donelson, Bearman, Caldwell & Berkowitz, PC" in *Mississippi Business Journal* (Vol. 29, January 2007, No. 4, pp. 6)
Pub: Venture Publications, Inc.
Description: Profile of William S. Painter of law firm Baker, Donelson, Bearman, Caldwell & Berkowitz, PC, who concentrates his practice in the areas of corporate, tax and healthcare restructuring.

39159 ■ "Balancing act" in *Entrepreneur* (Vol. 31, No. 5, May 2003, pp. 19)
Pub: Entrepreneur Media Inc.
Ed: Chris Penttila. **Description:** The proposed new pension rules by President Bush will make it easier for employers to implement cash-balance pension plans, a type of defined-benefit plan that looks like a 401(k), but accumulate at the same rate regardless of how long an employee stays with the company.

39160 ■ *Balls!: 6 Rules for Winning Today's Business Game*
Pub: John Wiley & Sons, Incorporated
Ed: Alexi Venneri. **Released:** January 2005. **Price:** $19.95. **Description:** In order to be successful business leaders must be brave, authentic, loud, lovable, and spunky and they need to lead their competition.

39161 ■ "Banks Try to Make Tele-Touch Satisfy Small Businesses" in *American Banker* (Vol. 171, November 27, 2006, No. 226, pp. 2)
Pub: SourceMedia, Inc.
Ed: Jim Cole. **Description:** Banks serving small businesses continue to offer personalized services, while incorporating call centers and online service models to small business strategies. Statistical data included.

39162 ■ "Bargaining a good-bye" in *BlackEnterprise* (Vol. 32, No. 2, September 2001, pp. 61)
Pub: Earl Graves Publishing Co.
Ed: Robyn D. Clarke. **Description:** Strategies to negotiate a job departure deal are examined.

39163 ■ "Barnes-Pettey Financial Advisors, LLC" in *Mississippi Business Journal* (Vol. 29, January 2007, No. 4, pp. 6)
Pub: Venture Publications, Inc.
Description: Profiles of Barnes-Pettey Financial Advisors, LLC financial advisors at the Clarksdale office of Raymond James Financial Services Inc. Statistical data included.

39164 ■ "Be Prepared" in *Inc.* (Volume 28, January 2006, No. 1, pp. 53-54)
Pub: Inc. Magazine
Ed: Norm Brodsky. **Description:** The greatest competitive edge a company can have, is to know more than your competitor knows when a longtime client's contract is due to expire.

39165 ■ *Beans: Four Principles for Running a Business in Good Times or Bad*
Pub: John Wiley & Sons, Incorporated
Ed: Leslie Yerkes, Charles Decker, Bob Nelson **Released:** June 2003. **Price:** $19.95. **Description:** Profile of Monorail Espresso, the popular Seattle coffee company that has become prosperous by intentionally staying small and building a strong customer service program.

39166 ■ *Being Self-Employed: How to Run a Business Out of Your Home, Claim Travel and Depreciation and Earn a Good Income Well into Your 70s or 80s*
Pub: Allyear Tax Guides
Ed: Holmes F. Crouch, Irma Jean Crouch, Barbara J. MacRae. **Released:** September 2004. **Price:** $24.95 (US), $37.95 (Canadian). **Description:** Guide for small business to keep accurate tax records.

39167 ■ *Ben Franklin: America's Original Entrepreneur, Franklin's Autobiography Adapted for Modern Times*
Pub: McGraw-Hill
Ed: Blaine McCormick; Benjamin Franklin. **Released:** September 2005.

39168 ■ "Best of 2005" in *Business Week* (December 19, 2005, No. 3964, pp. 58-64, 66, 68, 72)
Pub: McGraw-Hill Companies
Ed: Bruce Nussbaum. **Description:** Profiles of the best and most innovative business leaders in 2005.

39169 ■ "Best Business Books" in *Black Enterprise* (Vol. 36, February 2006, No. 7, pp. 165)
Pub: Earl G. Graves Publishing Co. Inc.
Ed: Tanisha A. Sykes. **Description:** A listing of the top eight business books geared towards black entrepreneurs and recommended by the journal are presented.

39170 ■ "The Best" in *Forbes* (May 13, 2002, p. 104)
Pub: Forbes Magazine
Description: A listing of the best chief executive officers, executive salaries and shareholder returns is featured.

39171 ■ "Best Ideas" in *Business Week* (December 19, 2005, No. 3964, pp. 74-78, 80-82)
Pub: McGraw-Hill Companies

Ed: Diane Brady. **Description:** Concepts that came to the forefront in 2005 may have a great impact on the future.

39172 ■ Best Practice in Business Advisory, Counseling and Information Services
Pub: United Nations Publications
Ed: United Nations, Economic Commission for Europe Staff. **Released:** January 2005. **Price:** $20.00. **Description:** Second book in a series promoting entrepreneurship in small and medium-sized companies (SMEs) throughout United Nation's Economic Commission for Europe (UNECE) member states.

39173 ■ "Best Products" Business Week (December 19, 2005, No. 3964, pp. 84-88, 90-92)
Pub: McGraw-Hill Companies
Ed: Larry Armstrong. **Description:** Best products introduced in 2005 are highlighted, from the cellular phones, kitchen, Internet, even medicine.

39174 ■ "Beyond empowerment: Building a company of citizens" in Harvard Business Review (Vol. 81, No. 1, January 2003, pp. 48)
Pub: Harvard Business School Press
Ed: Brook Manville, Josiah Ober. **Description:** The ancient Greek city-state of Athens is used as a model for a democratic business organization suited to the knowledge economy of today. The Athenian model does not provide a simple set of prescriptions, but offers a window into how companies can create an atmosphere of dignity and trust without resorting to a stifling bureaucracy.

39175 ■ The Big Book of Small Business: You Don't Have to Run Your Business by the Seat of Your Pants
Pub: HarperCollins Publishers, Inc.
Ed: Tom Gegax; Phil Bolsta. **Released:** February 2007. **Price:** $29.95. **Description:** Entrepreneur shares his experiences starting and running his small business.

39176 ■ "Big Boxes of the Road" in Hispanic Business (March 2002, pp. 5052)
Pub: Hispanic Business
Ed: Ralph Gray. **Description:** Profile of commercial vans used for business fleets is presented.

39177 ■ "Big Ideas for Small Biz" in Small Business Opportunities (Vol. 16, No. 1, January 2004, pp. 92)
Pub: Harris Publications, Inc.
Ed: James Feldman. **Description:** Four ways to be innovative and creative with a small business include fostering a business climate, becoming number one with clients, creating a partnership with clients, and a partnership with employees.

39178 ■ "Big Success Can Start With a Few Steps" in Mississippi Business Journal (Vol. 29, January 2007, No. 4, pp. 5)
Pub: Venture Publications, Inc.
Ed: Phil Hardwick **Description:** "ABC Volume One", published by the Boomtown Institute, is a new successful manual for many people in the world of economic and community development in small towns. Best used as a discussion guide in community development organizations, it is an offspring of Jack Schultz' "Boomtown USA- The 7-1/2 Keys to Big Success in Small Towns".

39179 ■ Bigger Isn't Always Better
Pub: AMACOM
Ed: Robert M. Tomasko. **Price:** $24.95.

39180 ■ "Bills would allow government land banks" in Crain's Detroit Business (Vol. 18, No. 21, May 27, 2002, pp. 6)
Pub: Crain Communications Inc. - Detroit
Description: Land banks that could help Detroit and other urban areas redevelop and sell thousands of acres of vacant land would be a boon for the city.

39181 ■ "The Bleeding-Heart Rationalist: William Morris b. 1911" in New York Times (December 31, 2006, pp. 14)
Pub: New York Times Company
Ed: Walter Kirn. **Description:** Profile of William Norris, founder of Control Data Corporation, now defunct, but at one time, one of the nation's largest computer manufacturing companies. Norris also founded an institute that promoted education and small business growth.

39182 ■ The Book of Entrepreneurs' Wisdom
Pub: John Wiley and Sons Inc.
Ed: Peter Krass. **Price:** $26.95.

39183 ■ Brag!: The Art of Tooting Your Own Horn Without Blowing It
Pub: Warner Books, Incorporated
Ed: Peggy Klaus. **Released:** May 2004. **Price:** $13.95. **Description:** A plan to promote a small business by effectively selling one's self.

39184 ■ "Bruised but Unbowed" in Hispanic Business (December 2001, pp. 66)
Pub: Hispanic Business
Ed: Barbara Beckley. **Description:** New York City is back in business while still recovering from the terrorist attacks of September 11, and hoping for a return of business and vacation travelers. Information for visiting New York City is provided.

39185 ■ "Budget hole brings tax-hike whispers" in Crain's Detroit Business (Vol. 19, No. 4, January 27, 2003, pp. 6)
Pub: Crain Communications Inc., Detroit
Ed: Amy Lane. **Description:** The Michigan Chamber of Commerce is vehemently opposed to proposed state tax hikes, suggesting the state should cut spending before raising taxes.

39186 ■ Building a Business the Buddhist Way
Pub: Celestial Arts Publishing Company
Ed: Geri Larkin. **Released:** September 2004. **Price:** $18.95 (Canadian). **Description:** Principles of entrepreneurship for starting and growing a business while maintaining a balance between business goals and spiritual goals.

39187 ■ "Building a Professional Pipeline" in Hispanic Business (March 2004, pp. 44-45)
Pub: Hispanic Business
Ed: Janet Perez. **Description:** A new report finds schools need to do more to prepare Hispanics for business careers.

39188 ■ Built to Last: Successful Habits of Visionary Companies
Pub: HarperCollins Publishers Inc.
Ed: James C. Collins; Jerry I. Porras. **Released:** January 2002. **Price:** $17.95 paperback.

39189 ■ "The Business of Base Closures" in Inc. (September 2005, pp. 34)
Pub: Inc. Magazine
Description: Economic impact of the Pentagon's announcement to close as many as 150 military bases across the country is examined.

39190 ■ "Business gurus talk about practicing basics" in Atlanta Business Chronicle (Vol. 25, January 10, 2003, No. 31, pp. 4B)
Pub: American City Business Publications, Inc.
Ed: Timothy S. Mescon, Michael H. Mescon. **Description:** In today's business environment, fad philosophies have been replaced by a new appreciation for the corny, basic, time-tested sage advice. Nine nuggets of corny business wisdom from a recent business event are discussed.

39191 ■ "Business Bookshelf" in Small Business Opportunities (Vol. 16, No. 1, January 2004, pp. 126)
Pub: Harris Publications, Inc.
Description: Reviews of the books, "Beans: Four Principles For Running a Business In Good Times or Bad", by Leslie A. Yerkes and Charles Decker; and "Business Lessons with Sharkmaster, Jr.", by Randy Clay.

39192 ■ Business Buying Basics
Pub: Robert Erdmann Publishing
Ed: Martin Bloom. **Released:** 1992. **Price:** $12.95 (paper).

39193 ■ Business Fairy Tales
Pub: Thomson South-Western
Ed: Cecil W. Jackson. **Released:** July 2006. **Price:** $39.95. **Description:** The seven most-common business schemes are uncovered.

39194 ■ Business Know-How: An Operational Guide for Home-Based and Micro-Sized Businesses with Limited Budgets
Pub: Adams Media Corporation
Ed: Janet Attard. **Price:** $17.95.

39195 ■ Business Organizations, Agencies, and Publications Directory
Pub: Thomson Gale
Ed: Amy Darga, Editor. **Released:** Annual, latest edition 19th, published March 2006. **Price:** $585, individuals. **Covers:** more than 40,000 organizations and publications of all kinds that are helpful in business, including trade, business, commercial, and labor associations; government agencies and advisory organizations; commodity and stock exchanges; United States and foreign diplomatic offices; regional planning and development agencies; convention, fair, and trade organizations; franchise companies; information centers; computerized information services; research centers; graduate schools of business; special libraries; periodicals, directories; national, state and local chambers of commerce. **Entries Include:** Name, address, phone, fax, contact person; some entries include annotations. Contents are based in part on information selected from other Gale publications. **Arrangement:** Classified by type of organization, publication, or service. **Indexes:** Name and keyword.

39196 ■ "Business schools vying for professors with Ph.D.s" in Atlanta Business Chronicle (Vol. 24, No. 13, August 31, 2001, pp. 2C)
Pub: American City Business Journals Inc.
Ed: Anya Martin. **Description:** Business schools are aggressively seeking to hire professors with PhDs for their Business Administration programs. Candidates are able to demand high salaries and many benefits. The shortage is said to be less critical in the Atlanta area than in other regions of the country.

39197 ■ Business Plans Kit for Dummies, 2nd Edition
Pub: John Wiley and Sons Inc.
Released: September 2005.

39198 ■ Business Plans That Work: A Guide for Small Business
Pub: McGraw-Hill Companies
Ed: Jeffry A. Timmons, Stephen Spinelli, Andrew Zacharakis. **Released:** May 2004. **Price:** $16.95 (US), $24.95 (Canadian). **Description:** Guide for preparing a small business plan along with an analysis of potential business opportunities.

39199 ■ "Business Primer for Legislators" in Hispanic Business (November 2002, pp. 32)
Pub: Hispanic Business
Ed: Derek Reveron. **Description:** The National Commission on Entrepreneurship presented a guide to government officials stating small business concerns. The guide also provides CEOs a checklist of business-friendly government initiatives.

39200 ■ "Business Products" in Ingram's (Vol. 29, No. 8, August 2003, pp. 43)
Pub: Show Me Publishing, Inc.
Description: Businesses in Kansas City, Missouri offering a wide range of consumer products, including cars, books, flowers, gourmet food, jewelry, and more are listed.

39201 ■ **"A Business Real Estate Appraisal Problem"** in *American Banker* (Vol. 170, February 4, 2005, No. 24, pp. 10)
Pub: Thomson Financial Media Inc.
Ed: Kathleen W. Collins, Zonnie Breckinridge. Description: Federal banking agencies are considering a move toward establishing a formal position on real estate appraisals. The Federal Reserve Board and Office of the Comptroller of the Currency had confirmed a position that could affect the value of real estate used in business, including hotels, gas stations, convenience stores, bowling alleys, restaurants and nursing homes.

39202 ■ *The Business of Small Business: Succeeding and Prospering in Business for Reasonably Intelligent Entrepreneurs*
Pub: Allen-Reed Publishing Company
Released: August 2006. Price: $27.95. Description: Tips for running a successful company are presented to entrepreneurs.

39203 ■ *Business Unusual*
Pub: Thorsons
Ed: Anita Roddick. Price: $24.95.

39204 ■ *Business Warrior: Strategy for Entrepreneurs*
Pub: Clearbridge Publishing
Ed: Sun Tzu. Released: September 2006. Price: $19.95. Description: Advice to help entrepreneurs understand competitive strategies in order to succeed, focusing on sales, marketing, and personnel management.

39205 ■ *Business Week—1,000 Issue*
Pub: McGraw-Hill Inc.
Released: Annual, March. Publication Includes: List of 1,000 U.S. Corporations by market value in all business, industrial, and financial categories, with financial results for preceding year and extensive analytical text. Entries Include: Company name, several types of sales and earnings data in dollars, line of business. Arrangement: Ranked by market value.

39206 ■ **"The Business Week"** in *Business Week* (December 19, 2005, No. 3964, pp. 28-29)
Pub: McGraw-Hill Companies
Ed: Harry Maurer. Description: Stocks, tax reform, a weak Japanese economy, wages, international investment, and airplane orders are among issues discussed.

39207 ■ *Business Week—Corporate Scoreboard Issue*
Pub: McGraw-Hill Inc.
Contact: Frederick F. Jespersen, Bureau Reports
Released: Quarterly, March, May, August, November. Publication Includes: List of sales and profits for 900 major U.S. Companies in all business, industrial, and financial categories, with extensive analytical text. Entries Include: Company name, several types of sales and earnings data. Arrangement: Alphabetical within line of business categories.

39208 ■ **"The Business Week News You Need to Know"** in *Business Week* (January 23, 2006, No. 3968, pp. 30-31)
Pub: McGraw-Hill Companies
Ed: Harry Maurer. Description: News about the Detroit Auto Show, job growth, Home Depot's expansion plans, Internet search engines, new executive pay rules, the stock market, and more.

39209 ■ **"The Business Week News You Need To Know"** in *Business Week* (January 9, 2006, No. 3966, pp. 24-25)
Pub: McGraw-Hill Companies
Ed: Harry Maurer. Description: Information of 2005 holiday sales, interest rates, a medical device lawsuit, television cable news programming, the retailer Wal-Mart, Albertson's grocery stores, Alaska drilling, Microsoft's European business, and other issues is offered.

39210 ■ **"The Business Year That Was"** in *Inc.* (December 1, 2003)
Pub: Gruner & Jahr USA Publishing
Ed: Patrick J. Sauer. Description: A reflection on 2003 business issues is presented.

39211 ■ **"Businesses' Cost From Flu Are Nothing To Sneeze At"** in *Tampa Tribune* (November 3, 2005)
Pub: Media General, Inc.
Ed: Dave Simanoff. Description: Experts predict this year's flu season will cost about $8 billion in paid sick leave for businesses, equating to 70 million missed work days.

39212 ■ **"Businesses hope comments don't mean a tense border"** in *Crain's Detroit Business* (Vol. 19, No. 14, April 7, 2003, pp. 39)
Pub: Crain Communications Inc., Detroit
Ed: Michael Strong. Description: U.S. companies bordering Canada fear that Canada's lack of support for the U.S.-led war on Iraq will affect business relations.

39213 ■ **"Businesses Get Creative in Wake of Storm"** in *Memphis Business Journal* (Vol. 25, No. 14, August 1, 2003, pp. 3)
Pub: American City Business Journals
Ed: Scott Shepard. Description: Businesses in the Memphis, Tennessee area describe the ways they coped with the loss of electricity and damaged buildings experienced in the worst weather-related disaster in nine years, which occurred July 22, 2003.

39214 ■ **"The Buy-A-Wish Foundation Catalog"** in *Fast Company* (August 2001, pp. 148)
Pub: Fast Company
Description: Humorous look at Dennis Tito, billionaire pension-fund manager, who, for a mere $20 million, enjoyed a week of orbital spaceflight aboard the Russian-manned International Space Station.

39215 ■ **"Cadence Bank"** in *Mississippi Business Journal* (Vol. 29, January 2007, No. 3, pp. A6)
Pub: Venture Publications, Inc.
Description: Profile of Jim McAlexander, president of Cadence Bank's Columbus Banking Center. McAlexander has been with Cadence Bank since 1973.

39216 ■ **"California Teaming"** in *Fast Company* (November 2001, pp. 30)
Pub: Fast Company
Ed: Heath Row. Description: Profile of Company of Friends, the organization whose mission is to bring southern California's multiple business communities closer and help other teams and organizations worldwide with collaboration.

39217 ■ **"Callon Adds Inventory"** in *Mississippi Business Journal* (Vol. 28, September 2006, No. 36, pp. 24)
Pub: Venture Publications, Inc.
Description: Callon Petroleum Co. has acquired 12 offshore oil drilling tracts at the Outer Continental Shelf.

39218 ■ **"Can This Off-Site Be Saved?"** in *Fast Company* (November 2001, pp. 119)
Pub: Fast Company
Ed: Cheryl Dahle. Description: A seven-point guide to planning and managing off-site business events is offered.

39219 ■ *Canadian Small Business Kit for Dummies*
Pub: John Wiley & Sons, Incorporated
Ed: Margaret Kerr; JoAnn Kurtz. Released: May 2006. Price: $28.99. Description: Resources include information on changes to laws and taxes for small businesses in Canada.

39220 ■ **"Capital City Beverage To Distribute Energy Drink"** in *Mississippi Business Journal* (Vol. 29, January 2007, No. 2, pp. 30)
Pub: Venture Publications, Inc.

Description: Capital City Beverage Company has created a distribution deal with Who's Your Daddy Inc. CCBC will distribute the entire line of Who's Your Daddy "King of Energy" drinks in 18 counties of Central Mississippi.

39221 ■ **"Capitol Coverage: A Report on Politics and Policy from NFIB"** in *My Business* (October/November 2003, pp. 16-17)
Pub: My Business Magazine
Description: The National Federation of Independent Business (NFIB) addresses current issues of importance to small businesses in the U.S., including economic impact of policies, white collar overtime, health insurance, and the 2004 NFIB Summit, to be held in Washington, DC in June 2004.

39222 ■ **"Career Guide"** in *Black Enterprise* (Vol. 33, No. 7, February 2003, pp. 6)
Pub: Earl Graves Publishing Co.
Description: Black Enterprise magazine offers a Web site that provides information to guide individuals through various stages of their career, tools to help assist career advancement with links to job search engines, interviewing tips, and a resume guide. Additional topics include management, COBRA, plus the top ten cities for African Americans to live, work and play.

39223 ■ **"Career smarts: Bouncing back from career setbacks"** in *Women in Business* (Vol. 53, No. 1, January-February, 2001, pp. 26)
Pub: The ABWA Co. Inc.
Ed: Diane Domeyer. Description: Career setbacks, and ways to bounce back by taking stock, re-evaluating goals, and learning from mistakes are discussed.

39224 ■ **"Career smarts"** in *Women in Business* (Vol. 53, No. 4, July-August, 2001, pp. 38)
Pub: The ABWA Co. Inc.
Ed: Liz Hubler. Description: Issues concerning strategies for considering a career change are discussed. Particular attention is given to ways of assessing the need for a career change, including self-assessment techniques and ways of enhancing one's marketability.

39225 ■ **"Cashing in Before You Join: Negotiating a Signing Bonus"** in *Black Enterprise* (Vol. 37, October 2006, No. 3, pp. 90)
Pub: Earl G. Graves Publishing Co. Inc.
Ed: Chauntelle Folds. Description: Information on how to research and negotiate a signing deal, including how to avoid a tax hit.

39226 ■ **"Causes and Effects"** in *Harvard Business Review* (Vol. 81, No. 7, July 2003, pp. 95)
Pub: Harvard Business School Press
Ed: Carol L. Cone, Mark A. Feldman, Alison T. DaSilva. Description: Companies must select the social causes they wish to become involved in and identified with carefully.

39227 ■ *CCH Toolkit Tax Guide 2007*
Pub: CCH, Inc.
Ed: Paul Gada. Released: January 2007. Price: $17.95. Description: Guide for filing 2007 tax forms for both personal and small businesses with expert line-by-line explanations.

39228 ■ **"Chamber Kicks Off Weekly Member-Appreciation Program"** in *Bellingham Business Journal* (December 2006, pp. 4)
Pub: Sun News Inc.
Description: Bellingham Women Chamber of Commerce and Industry celebrates various businesses within its membership with a member appreciation program.

39229 ■ "Chamber Puts Spotlight on Small-Business Issues" in *Crain's Detroit Business* **(Vol. 19, No. 42, October 20, 2003, pp. 31)**
Pub: Crain Communications Inc., Detroit
Ed: Laura Bailey. Description: The Detroit Regional Chamber is offering several new programs for companies with less than 50 employees, about 96 percent of the Chamber's 20,000-plus membership, including the Small Business Central program.

39230 ■ "The Change Makers" in *Harvard Business Review* **(Vol. 81, No. 7, July 2003, pp. 20)**
Pub: Harvard Business School Press
Ed: John T. Landry. Description: Review of the book featuring entrepreneurs who changed industries, including Bill Gates.

39231 ■ "Charmed, I'm Sure: Proper Business Etiquette Goes Beyond the Salad Fork" in *Black Enterprise* **(Vol. 35, February 2005, No. 7, pp. 64)**
Pub: Earl G. Graves Publishing Co. Inc.
Ed: Lee Anna Jackson. Description: Proper business etiquette is examined, offering a list of several things that develop effective business skills.

39232 ■ "Chart-Toppers; Largest M&A Deals in U.S. History" in *Crain's Chicago Business* **(Vol. 30, January 2007, No. 4, pp.30)**
Pub: Crain Communications, Inc.
Ed: Michelle Evans; Christina Galoozis. Description: Profiles of the largest mergers and acquisitions of 2006, which rose to $1.6 trillion. This is close to the record year of 2000 during the peak of the dot-com boom.

39233 ■ *China's Rational Entrepreneurs: The Development of the New Private Business Sector*
Pub: Routledge
Ed: Barbara Krug. Released: March 2004. Price: $104.95 (US), $149.95 (Canadian). Description: Difficulties faced by entrepreneurs in China are discussed, including analysis for understanding their behavior and relations with local governments in order to secure long-term business success.

39234 ■ "The clumsy multinational" in *Harvard Business Review* **(Vol. 80, No. 9, September 2002, pp. 128)**
Pub: Harvard Business School Press
Ed: John Kenneth Galbraith. Description: Reprints of material from "The defense of the multinational company", printed in Harvard Business Review, April 1978, in which the author criticizes many existing business attitudes.

39235 ■ *Code of Federal Regulations: Title 13: Business Credit and Assistance*
Pub: United States Government Printing Office
Ed: Department of Commerce Staff. Released: April 2005. Price: $55.00. Description: Title 13 covers regulations governing the activities of the Small Business Administration and the Department of Commerce. Book covers information on business credit, finance, and economic development.

39236 ■ "Coming Up Short on Nonfinancial Performance Measurement" in *Harvard Business Review* **(Vol. 81, No. 11, November 2003, pp. 88)**
Pub: Harvard Business School Press
Ed: Christopher D. Ittner, David F. Larcker. Description: The influence of non-financial performance criteria, such as customer loyalty and corporate profits is examined.

39237 ■ *Common Problems; Common Sense Solutions: Practical Advice for Small Business Owners*
Pub: iUniverse, Incorporated
Ed: Greg Hadley. Released: September 2004. Price: $14.95. Description: Common sense advice for entrepreneurs running a small business.

39238 ■ *The Commonsense Way to Build Wealth: One Entrepreneur Shares His Secrets*
Pub: Griffin Publishing Group
Ed: Jack Chou. Released: September 2004. Price: $19.95. Description: Entrepreneurial tips to accumulate wealth, select the proper business or franchise, choose and manage rental property, and how to negotiate a good lease.

39239 ■ "Community Colleges Near Capacity for Retraining Workers" in *Crain's Detroit Business* **(Vol. 21, October 17, 2005, No. 43, pp. 15)**
Pub: Crain Communications Inc. - Detroit
Ed: Sherri Begin. Description: Displaced workers are filling area community colleges for retraining in the areas of nursing, health care services, automotive service technology, digital media, culinary and hospitality programs.

39240 ■ "Community Theaters Mean More Than Just Entertainment" in *Mississippi Business Journal* **(Vol. 28, January 2007, No. 36, pp. 29)**
Pub: Venture Publications, Inc.
Ed: Lynn Lofton Description: With community theaters growing in Mississippi for several years, the Mississippi Theater Association has reached more than 500 members with many of those being community theaters. This represents a resurgence in the successful smaller independently run community theaters. Statistical data included.

39241 ■ "Companies Still Evaluating Blackout Toll" in *Pittsburgh Business Times* **(Vol. 23, No. 5, August 22, 2003, pp. 1)**
Pub: Pittsburgh Business Times
Ed: Christopher Davis. Description: The recent power failure on the East Coast had a significant impact on many businesses in the greater Pittsburgh, Pennsylvania area. But companies, such as financial services and legal service firms did not suffer as great a hardship.

39242 ■ *The Company We Keep: Reinventing Small Business for People, Community, and Place*
Pub: Chelsea Green Publishing
Ed: John Abrams. Released: May 2005. Price: $27.50 (US), $31.50 (Canadian). Description: The new business trend in social entrepreneurship as a business plan enables small business owners to meet the triple bottom line of profits for people (employees and owners), community, and the environment.

39243 ■ "The Competitiveness of Small and Medium Enterprises" in *Journal of Business Venturing* **(Vol. 17, No. 2, March 2002, pp. 123)**
Pub: Elsevier Science, Inc.
Ed: Thomas W.Y. Man, Theresa Lau, K.F. Chan. Description: The development of a conceptual model, patterned after the notion of competitiveness and the competency approach, is discussed. This conceptual model was developed to connect the performance of the traits small and medium-sized enterprises (SME), owner-managers and their companies have in common.

39244 ■ *The Complete Idiot's Guide to Finance for Small Business*
Pub: Penguin Group Incorporated
Ed: Kenneth E. Little. Released: April 2006. Price: $19.95. Description: Financial experts helps small business owners through strategies for long-term financial success.

39245 ■ *The Complete Small Business Guide: A Sourcebook for New and Small Businesses*
Pub: John Wiley & Sons, Incorporated
Ed: Colin Barrow. Released: March 2006. Price: $27.95. Description: Sourcebook for creating new small companies and running established small businesses.

39246 ■ "Consorting with Competitors" in *Harvard Business Review* **(Vol. 80, No. 1, January 2002, pp. 21)**
Pub: Harvard Business School Press
Ed: Christopher Kurt. Description: Personal insight is given in forming industry consortia, using specifications called Universal Description, Discover, and Integration (UDDI). UDDI allows for integrations of ideas electronically via a directory, and keeps the consortia on track.

39247 ■ "Consumer Joe: Harassing Corporate America, One Letter at a Time" in *Entrepreneur* **(Vol. 31, No. 8, August 2003, pp. 6)**
Pub: Entrepreneur Media, Inc.
Ed: Steve Cooper. Description: Profile of Broadway Books, the Website that tries to bring information about all books to the public.

39248 ■ "Consumers Ethics: The Role of Religiosity" in *Journal of Business Ethics* **(Vol. 46, No. 2, August 15, 2003, pp. 151)**
Pub: Kluwer Academic Publishers Group
Ed: Scott J. Vitell, Joseph G.P. Paolillo. Description: Results of a study investigating the role that religiosity plays in determining consumer attitudes/beliefs regarding various questionable consumer practice, along with other personal factors are offered.

39249 ■ "Contact sport: now that's how you play the networking game" in *Entrepreneur* **(Vol. 31, No. 6, June 2003, pp. 28)**
Pub: Entrepreneur Media Inc.
Ed: Joshua Kurlantzick. Description: The Ultimate Frisbee Game has become one of the fastest-growing participant sports, according to the Ultimate Players Association. The games popularity has attracted entrepreneurs, making it a great place for business networking.

39250 ■ "Contents; Book of Lists 2005 Edition" in *Crain's Detroit Business* **(Vol. 20, December 27, 2004, No. 52, pp. 1)**
Pub: Crain Communications Inc. - Detroit
Description: A listing of business information compiled from surveys Crain's sends to businesses and other organizations in Southeast Michigan is provided.

39251 ■ "Contents; Book of Lists - 2006 Edition" in *Crain's Detroit Business* **(Vol. 21, December 26, 2005, No. 52, pp. 1)**
Pub: Crain Communications Inc. - Detroit
Description: Crain's Book of Lists, 2006 edition is highlighted. This is used as a reference and business tool and is a culmination of the previous year's data on businesses in Southeast Michigan.

39252 ■ "Controlling the Outcome" in *Ingram's* **(Vol. 29, No. 1, January 2003, pp. 40)**
Pub: Show Me Publishing, Inc.
Ed: Joe Sweeney. Description: Joe Sweeney, editor of Ingram's, has introduced Corporate Kansas City, as a supplement to the magazine. This publication will allow businesses to publish corporate profiles.

39253 ■ "Convention Calendar" in *Black Enterprise* **(Vol. 37, February 2007, No. 7, pp. 68)**
Pub: Earl G. Graves Publishing Co. Inc.
Description: Listing of conventions and trade show of interest to minority and women business leaders.

39254 ■ "Conventions" in *Crain's Chicago Business* **(Vol. 30, January 2007, No. 5, pp. 15)**
Pub: Crain Communications, Inc.
Description: Listings of business oriented conferences and conventions through the month of March.

39255 ■ *Corporate Affiliations Library*
Pub: LexisNexis Group
Contact: Tanya Hurst
Released: Annual, latest edition 2004. Description: a 8-volume set listing public and private companies

worldwide. Comprises the following: Master Index (volumes 1 and 2); U.S. Public Companies (volume 3 & 4), listing 6,200 parent companies and 52,000 subsidiaries, affiliates, and divisions worldwide; U.S. Private Companies (volume 5), listing 20,000 privately held companies and 24,000 U.S. and international subsidiaries; and International Public and Private Companies (volume 7 & 8), listing 4,800 parent companies and 69,000 subsidiaries worldwide. **Entries Include:** Parent company name, address, phone, fax, telex, e-mail addresses, names and titles of key personnel, financial data, fiscal period, type and line of business, SIC codes; names and locations of subsidiaries, divisions, and affiliates, outside service firms (accountants, legal counsel, etc.). **Arrangement:** Alphabetical within each volume. **Indexes:** Each volume includes company name index; separate Master Index volumes list all company names in the set in one alphabetic sequence in five indexes including private, public, international, alphabetical, geographical, brand name, SIC, and corporate responsibilities.

39256 ■ *Corporate Crisis and Risk Management: Modeling, Strategies and SME Application*
Pub: Elsevier Science and Technology Books
Ed: M. Aba-Bulgu; S.M.N. Islam. **Released:** December 2006. **Price:** $115.00. **Description:** Methods and tools for handling corporate risk and crisis management are profiled for small to medium-sized businesses.

39257 ■ **"Corporate Diversity"** in *Hispanic Business* (January/February 2005, pp. 50, 52, 54)
Pub: Hispanic Business
Description: In response to the ever-changing consumer and workforce demographics, corporate diversity means creating programs that integrate with core company values and accountability measures. Ways to measure the return on investment for these practices are presented.

39258 ■ *Corporate Entrepreneurship & Innovation*
Pub: Thomson South-Western
Ed: Michael H. Morris; Donald F. Kuratko. **Released:** January 2007. **Price:** $104.95. **Description:** Innovation is the key to running a successful small business. The book helps entrepreneurs to develop the skills and business savvy to sustain a competitive edge.

39259 ■ *Corporate Radar: Tracking the Forces That Are Shaping Your Business*
Pub: Amacom
Ed: Karl Albrecht. **Released:** October 1999. **Price:** $27.95. **Description:** Ways for a business to assess the forces operating in the external environment that can affect the business and solutions to protect from outside threats.

39260 ■ **"A Corporate Science Project"** in *Business Week* (December 19, 2005, No. 3964, pp. 108)
Pub: McGraw-Hill Companies
Ed: Craig R. Barrett. **Description:** U.S. businesses need to help turn out more mat and science graduates in order to stay competitive in a global economy.

39261 ■ **"Court Sides With Biz on Disability"** in *Inc.* (August 1, 2003)
Pub: Gruner & Jahr USA Publishing
Description: The Supreme Court ruled that businesses can reject employee disability benefits when the employer's doctor disagrees with the treating physician. A case involving a Black & Decker employee is cited.

39262 ■ **"Cream of the crop"** in *BlackEnterprise* (Vol. 31, No. 10, May 2001, pp. 47)
Pub: Earl Graves Publishing Co.
Ed: Paula McCoy-Pinderhughes, Roger Barnes. **Description:** The theme of the sixth annual Black Enterprise/Bank of America Entrepreneurs Conference is "Leading in a Changing Economy: Innovation, Transformation, Growth". The Black Enterprise Small Busi-

ness Awards categories include Emerging Company of the Year, Business Innovator of the Year, the Rising Star Award, and the Kidpreneurs Award. Statistical data included.

39263 ■ **"Credit crunch unlikely for most small businesses"** in *Atlanta Business Chronicle* (Vol. 23, No. 51, May 25, 2001, pp. 8A)
Pub: American City Business Journals Inc.
Ed: Kent Hoover. **Description:** According to a survey by the National Federation of Independent Business and the Federal Reserve Board, small businesses should not have problems obtaining financing despite the tightening of standards by banks. Only 5 percent of small businesses that responded to the survey reported that obtaining loans was more difficult. Only 3 percent of NFIB members reported credit as their top problem.

39264 ■ **"A Crisis Waiting to Happen?"** in *My Business* (August/September 2002, pp. 16)
Pub: My Business Magazine
Ed: Ivan Sylvester. **Description:** The top 15 crises that can happen in a business are listed, along with seven steps to prepare for and manage any small business crisis.

39265 ■ **"Critical Mass"** in *Small Business Opportunities* (Summer 2005)
Pub: Harris Publications Inc.
Ed: Dave Anderson. **Description:** Five key issues to run a successful small business are outlined.

39266 ■ *Crunch Point: The Secret to Succeeding When it Matters Most*
Pub: American Management Association
Ed: Brian Tracy. **Released:** 2006. **Price:** $17.95.

39267 ■ **"CSA Acquires Political Science Abstracts"** in *Information Today* (Vol. 17, No. 11, December 2000, pp. 8)
Pub: Information Today, Inc.
Description: Cambridge Scientific Abstracts, a leading publisher of bibliographic databases and print journals, acquired the publishing rights to the Political Science Abstracts database. Political Science Abstracts provides references and abstracts from multiple sources devoted to politics and political analysis.

39268 ■ **"Cup of Courtesy"** in *Entrepreneur* (Vol. 33, August 2005, No. 8, pp. 24)
Pub: Entrepreneur Media Inc.
Ed: Kelly Barron. **Description:** Entrepreneurs using a coffeehouse as an office should limit time at a table to one or two hours. Proper etiquette requires consideration of other patrons, especially when using cell phones.

39269 ■ **"Current Events"** in *Forbes* (January 21, 2002, p. 29)
Pub: Forbes Magazine
Ed: Paul Johnson. **Description:** Information is presented regarding the antitrust case against Microsoft; legal information is discussed about the equality for businesses, regardless of size, under the law.

39270 ■ **"Cymfony: www.cymfony.com"** in *Entrepreneur* (Vol. 33, February 2005, No. 2, pp. 8)
Pub: Entrepreneur Media Inc.
Description: Cymfony is an online application that monitors business trends by scanning all online and offline media, broadcast mentions, message-board postings, blogs and more, capturing what journalists and consumers think about a company.

39271 ■ **"D&PL Reports Loss"** in *Mississippi Business Journal* (Vol. 29, January 2007, No. 2, pp. 8)
Pub: Venture Publications, Inc.
Ed: Wally Northway **Description:** Delta and Pine Land Company reported a net loss during the first quarter ended November 2006. Due to the seasonal nature of the seed business, D&PL typically incurs sizeable losses during the first and fourth fiscal quarters. Statistical data included.

39272 ■ **"Data Disposal Questions"** in *Hispanic Business* (Vol. 23, No. 7/8, July/August 2001, pp. 112, 114)
Pub: Hispanic Business
Ed: Roger Harris. **Description:** The legal, technical, and financial issues involved in disposing office equipment are discussed.

39273 ■ *Dead on Arrival: How the Anti-Business Backlash is Destroying Entrepreneurship in America and What We Can Still Do About It!*
Pub: HarperCollins Publishers, Inc.
Ed: Bernie Marcus; Steve Gottry. **Released:** November 2006. **Price:** $23.95. **Description:** Bernie Marcus, Home Depot leader, addresses regulations hurting small businesses in America.

39274 ■ **"Dean of Boston College Business School Wants to Emphasize Ethics and Values"** in *Boston Globe* (March 8, 2005)
Pub: New York Times Company
Ed: Robert Weisman. **Description:** Boston College's School of Business is stressing ethics and values in its new curriculum.

39275 ■ **"Defusing disasters"** in *Atlanta Business Chronicle* (Vol. 24, No. 8, July 27, 2001, pp. 1B)
Pub: American City Business Journals Inc.
Ed: Chaundra Frierson. **Description:** Workplace violence has become an important issue facing small businesses. The article offers ways to address workplace violence.

39276 ■ **"A delicate balance"** in *Red Herring* (March 2003, pp. 44)
Pub: Herring Communications Inc.
Ed: John Micklethwait, Adrian Wooldridge. **Description:** A review of the book, "The Company: A Short History of a Revolutionary Idea", by John Micklethwait and Adrian Wooldridge.

39277 ■ *Delivering Knock Your Socks Off Service, 4th Edition*
Pub: American Management Association
Ed: Performance Research Associates. **Released:** 2006.

39278 ■ **"Dell NFIB The Voice of Small Business"** in *My Business* (June/July 2004, pp. 26-27)
Pub: My Business Magazine
Description: Ten finalists chosen for the Small Business Excellence in Customer Experience Award are profiled. Winners were selected by members of the Herb Kelleher Center for Entrepreneurship at the University of Texas at Austin.

39279 ■ **"Delta Industries Inc"** in *Mississippi Business Journal* (Vol. 29, January 2007, No. 4, pp. 6)
Pub: Venture Publications, Inc.
Description: Profile of Les Howell Jr., vice president of Delta Industries Inc. Howell has been chief engineer of Delta for seven years.

39280 ■ **"Disastrous effects"** in *Entrepreneur* (Vol. 30, No. 1, Ja)
Pub: Entrepreneur Media Inc.
Ed: Mark Henricks. **Description:** Various businesses affected by the 911 terrorist attacks tell ways they are surviving by using their survivor mentality to salvage what they can while seeking ways to rebound and generate more opportunity than before the attacks.

39281 ■ *Divine Wisdom at Work: 10 Universal Principles for Enlightened Entrepreneurs*
Pub: Aha! House
Ed: Tricia Molloy. **Released:** July 2006. **Price:** $20.00. **Description:** Entrepreneurial advice for managing a small enterprise is given using inspiration, anecdotes and exercises.

39282 ■ "DMC, city dispute hospital control" in *Crain's Detroit Business* (Vol. 19, No. 16, April 21, 2003, pp. 3)
Pub: Crain Communications Inc., Detroit
Ed: Katie Merx. **Description:** Regional and state leaders in Michigan are considering the creation of a health and hospital authority to assist the region's safety-net hospitals to provide indigent care. The move would keep Detroit Receiving Hospital open.

39283 ■ "Doing business in a dangerous world" in *Harvard Business Review* (Vol. 80, No. 4, April 2002, pp. 22)
Pub: Harvard Business School Press
Ed: Gardiner Morse. **Description:** A discussion with former chairman of the National Commission on Terrorism, L. Paul Bremer, about the risks to American businesses from terrorism and the resentment in developing economies toward the dominant position of the U.S. in the world.

39284 ■ "Dollars for Scholars" in *Hispanic Business* (September 2003, pp. 64, 66, 68)
Pub: Hispanic Business
Description: A select guide to scholarships for the study of business or law is presented.

39285 ■ "The domino effect: ripples from September 11 spread FAR and WIDE" in *Black Enterprise* (Vol. 32, No. 6, January 2002, pp. 53)
Pub: Earl Graves Publishing Co.
Ed: Sonya A. Donaldson, Alan Hughes, Terrell Reed. **Description:** The impacts on business after the September 11 terrorist attacks, including consumer reaction, are discussed with an optimistic outlook for the future.

39286 ■ "Don't Tell It To The Judge" in *Entrepreneur* (Vol. 28, No. 6, June 2000, pp. 127)
Pub: Entrepreneur Media Inc.
Ed: Steven C. Bahls and Jane Aster Bahls. **Description:** It's good to fire bad employees. It's not so good to talk about how bad they were at unemployment hearings.

39287 ■ "The Dress Code: How Business Style is Communicated" in *Black Enterprise* (Vol. 34, No. 2, September 2003, pp. 60)
Pub: Earl Graves Publishing Co.
Ed: Laura Egodigwe. **Description:** Women business leaders tend to set standards by their business style. The basis of any executive's wardrobe is a great suit and wearing the best affordable quality.

39288 ■ *Drive a Modest Car: And 16 Other Keys to Small Business Success*
Pub: NOLO
Ed: Ralph E. Warner, Jake Warner. **Released:** September 2004. **Price:** $24.99. **Description:** Seventeen keys to successful entrepreneurship.

39289 ■ "The Dubious Dole" in *Entrepreneur* (Vol. 28, No. 10, October 2000, pp. 123)
Pub: Entrepreneur Media Inc.
Ed: Jacquelyn Lynn. **Description:** Unemployment compensation is an insurance program designed to provide income to people who are out of work. Don't treat claims for unemployment compensation by former employees lightly, and the reasons why are covered.

39290 ■ *The Dynamic Small Business Manager*
Pub: Lulu.com
Ed: Frank Vickers. **Released:** March 2006. **Price:** $39.99. **Description:** Practical advice is given to help small business owners successfully manage their company.

39291 ■ *e-Business, e-Government and Small and Medium-Size Enterprises: Opportunities and Challenges*
Pub: Idea Group Publishing
Ed: Brian J. Corbitt, Nabeel A.Y. Al-Qirim. **Released:** February 2004. **Price:** $79.95. **Description:** Electron-

ic commerce and information technology research in small and medium-sized enterprises (SMEs). Policymakers, legislators, researchers and professionals address significant issues of importance to the small business sector.

39292 ■ *The E-Myth Revisited: Why Most Small Businesses Don't Work and What to Do About It*
Pub: HarperInformation
Ed: Michael E. Gerber. **Released:** April 1995. **Price:** $16.00. **Description:** Keys for developing a prosperous small business is presented in an updated version of the author's best-seller published in the nineties.

39293 ■ "East Meets West" in *Entrepreneur* (Vol. 32, December 2004, No. 12, pp. 24)
Pub: Entrepreneur Media Inc.
Ed: Mark Henricks. **Description:** Review of The Art of Business. Author Raymond T. Yeh explores ways in which business leaders have created a new art of business that merges Eastern and Western concepts for success.

39294 ■ "Easy Read: Build Business Relationships with a Company Blog" in *Entrepreneur* (Vol. 31, No. 12, December 2003, pp. 25)
Pub: Entrepreneur Media Inc.
Ed: Laura Tiffany. **Description:** Before allowing customers, partners, investors, employees, or even competitors, to access company information via a blog, it is crucial to determine what you want your blog to accomplish.

39295 ■ "Economics Focus" in *The Economist* (Vol. 376, July 30-August 5, 2005, No. 8437, pp. 70)
Pub: The Economist Newspaper Ltd.
Description: The strength of the American labor market is examined, focusing on 5.1 million workers missing from the reported unemployment figures.

39296 ■ *The Economics of Small Firms*
Pub: Routledge Inc.
Ed: Johnson. **Released:** December 2006. **Price:** $41.95. **Description:** Introduction to the economics of small business, covering both theoretical and empirical issues.

39297 ■ *Edgewalkers: People and Organizations That Take Risks, Build Bridges, and Break New Ground*
Pub: Greenwood Publishing Group, Inc.
Ed: Judi Neal. **Released:** October 2006. **Price:** $39.95. **Description:** Profiles of entrepreneurs who thrive on change and challenge in order to create successful companies in today's complex business climate.

39298 ■ *Effectuation*
Pub: Edward Elgar Publishing, Incorporated
Ed: Sarasvathy. **Released:** October 2006. **Price:** $85.00. **Description:** Effectuation is the idea that the future is unpredictable while being controllable. A study of 27 entrepreneurs shows effective effectuators.

39299 ■ "Elbows Off the Table" in *My Business* (February/March 2004, pp. 14)
Pub: My Business Magazine
Ed: Julie Bawden Davis. **Description:** Rules of etiquette that still apply to be successful are listed. Manners are critical to business success.

39300 ■ "The empire strikes back; Counterrevolutionary strategies for industry leaders" in *Harvard Business Review* (Vol. 80, Nov. 2002, pp. 66)
Pub: Harvard Business School Press
Ed: Richard D'Aveni. **Description:** Five ways that industry leaders can respond to revolutionary business models or disruptive technologies. The strategies are containment, shaping, absorption, neutralization and annulment.

39301 ■ *Encyclopedia of Small Business*
Pub: Thomson Gale
Ed: Arsen Darnay; Monique D. Magee; Kevin Hillstrom. **Released:** November 2006. **Description:** Concise encyclopedia of small business information.

39302 ■ "The energy roller coaster" in *Red Herring* (No. 103, September 1, 2001, pp. 42-43)
Pub: Herring Communications
Ed: Peter Schwartz. **Description:** Advice is given to aid in understanding the future of energy markets, what drives them and how they work, is discussed.

39303 ■ "Engler and business" in *Crain's Detroit Business* (Vol. 18, No. 50, December 16, 2002, pp. 21)
Pub: Crain Communications Inc., Detroit
Description: A list of the key business accomplishments made by Michigan's outgoing Governor, John Engler is presented.

39304 ■ *Enterprise, Entrepreneurship and Innovation: Concepts, Context and Commercialization*
Pub: Elsevier Science and Technology Books
Ed: Robin Lowe, Sue Marriott. **Released:** June 2006. **Price:** $39.95. **Description:** Application of enterprise, innovation and entrepreneurship are discussed to help companies grow.

39305 ■ *Enterprise and Small Business: Principles, Practice and Policy*
Pub: Pearson Education, Limited
Ed: Sara Carter; Dylan Jones-Evans. **Released:** September 2006. **Price:** $79.50. **Description:** Introduction to small business, challenges of a changing environment, and the nature of entrepreneurship are among the issues covered.

39306 ■ "Entrepreneur Column" in *Entrepreneur* (August 11, 2005)
Pub: Entrepreneur Media Inc.
Ed: Tim Berry. **Description:** Effective business plans include at least three vital pro forma statements based on three main accounting statements. These statements are outlined in detail.

39307 ■ *The Entrepreneur Next Door: Discover the Secrets to Financial Independence*
Pub: Entrepreneur Press
Ed: William F. Wagner. **Released:** May 2006. **Price:** $19.95. **Description:** Traits required to become a successful entrepreneur are highlighted.

39308 ■ *The Entrepreneur and Small Business Problem Solver*
Pub: John Wiley & Sons, Incorporated
Ed: William A. Cohen. **Released:** December 2005. **Price:** $24.95 (US), $31.99 (Canadian). **Description:** Revised edition of the resource for entrepreneurs and small business owners that covers everything from start-up financing and loans to new product promotion and more.

39309 ■ *Entrepreneurial Small Business Resources: Resource-Based Perspective*
Pub: Edgar Elgar Publishing, Incorporated
Ed: Dean A. Shepherd. **Released:** August 2005. **Price:** $110.00. **Description:** Analysis of entrepreneurial activities of small businesses focusing on why some businesses are successful, while others fail.

39310 ■ *The Entrepreneur's Strategy Guide: Ten Keys for Achieving Marketplace Leadership and Operational Excellence*
Pub: Greenwood Publishing Group, Incorporated
Ed: Tom Cannon. **Released:** June 2006. **Price:** $38.45. **Description:** Business plan for entrepreneurs is offered from a fifty-year business veteran. The book is divided into tow parts: the marketplace and the internal environment.

39311 ■ *Entrepreneurship*
Pub: Thomson South-Western
Ed: Donald F. Kuratko; Richard M. Hodgetts. **Released:** April 2006. **Price:** $125.95. **Description:** Understanding the process of entrepreneurship.

39312 ■ *Entrepreneurship: A Process Perspective*
Pub: Thomson South-Western

Ed: Robert A. Baron; Scott A. Shane. **Released:** February 2007. **Price:** $137.95. **Description:** Entrepreneurial process covering team building, finances, business plan, legal issues, marketing, growth and exit strategies.

39313 ■ *Entrepreneurship: From Opportunity to Action*
Pub: Palgrave Macmillan
Ed: David Rae. **Released:** March 2007. **Price:** $63.95 (CND). **Description:** Learning enterprise theory is discussed, focusing on the individual as an entrepreneur and ways to create and take advantage of opportunities.

39314 ■ *Entrepreneurship and Small Business*
Pub: Palgrave Macmillan
Ed: Paul Burns. **Released:** January 2007. **Price:** $74.95. **Description:** Successful management practices are examined to encourage and develop entrepreneurial skills.

39315 ■ *ERC Directory of Real Estate Appraisers and Brokers*
Pub: Employee Relocation Council (ERC)
Released: Annual, March. **Covers:** about 9,000 member brokers and appraisers worldwide, equipped to handle the relocation of employees. **Entries Include:** For brokers—Firm name, address, phone, e-mail, number of offices, median price, code indicating services offered, list of corporations served, code indicating means of working with other brokers. For appraisers—Name, firm affiliation (if any), address, phone, e-mail, code indicating professional designations, names of corporations served. **Arrangement:** Appraisers and brokers are geographical.

39316 ■ *"Escondido: Sometimes, the Best Advice is Free" in San Diego Business Journal* (Vol. 28, January 8, 2007, No. 2, pp. 27)
Pub: San Diego Business Journal Associates
Ed: Jessica Long. **Description:** Thursdays with Joe is a new program that offers free advice to small business owners in the Escondido, California area. Topics include marketing tips and financial planning advice.

39317 ■ *"Evaluating promotion opportunities" in Women in Business* (Vol. 53, No. 2, March-April, 2001, pp. 36)
Pub: The ABWA Co. Inc.
Ed: Liz Hubler. **Description:** Advice on ways of assessing opportunities for promotion at work is presented. Guidance on how to weigh the opportunity costs of the promotion and the short- and long-term implications are explored.

39318 ■ *"Evenhandedly Political: VCs Back Candidates in Both Camps" in Venture Capital Journal* (Vol. 40, No. 10, October 2000, pp. 5)
Pub: Venture Economics
Description: An overview of campaign contributions made by the venture capital community is presented.

39319 ■ *"Everything I know about business I learned from Monopoly" in Harvard Business Review* (Vol. 80, No. 3, March 2002, pp. 51)
Pub: Harvard Business School Press
Ed: Phil Orbanes. **Description:** Profile of Phil Orbanes, one of the world's prominent game designers and an executive at Winning Moves Games. Orbanes reflects on competition and winning.

39320 ■ *"Ex-Im Bank cuts effect on small business unclear" in Atlanta Business Chronicle* (Vol. 24, No. 3, June 22, 2001, pp. 54A)
Pub: American City Business Journals Inc.
Ed: Kent Hoover. **Description:** The Export-Import Bank has been targeted by the Bush Administration for a budget cut from $863 million to $633 million, resulting in a total of $11.4 billion available for export credit authorizations. Although the Small Business Administration says small businesses will be protected from budget cuts, many small business owners are not convinced. The Export-Import Bank is considering lowering coverage on export transactions and raising fees in order to stabilize its resources.

39321 ■ *"Exchange may improve small-business lending" in Atlanta Business Chronicle* (Vol. 23, No. 36, February 9, 2001, pp. 52A)
Pub: American City Business Journals Inc.
Ed: Jean Capriotti. **Description:** Equifax Inc. and 19 lenders have started a database to help evaluate small business loan applications. The database will help protect lenders from extending loans to businesses that may already be overextended on other loans, and will help small businesses by taking some of the guesswork out of the loan process, thus increasing the amount of money available in some cases. The service will be tested beginning in March, and will be available in June 2001.

39322 ■ *"Executive who was dismissed accuses firm of inflating profit" in Wall Street Journal* (February 3, 2003, pp. B6)
Pub: Dow Jones & Co. Inc.
Description: A countersuit against Electronic Data Systems Corporation was filed by an employee fired by the firm. The employee was accused of stealing from the company.

39323 ■ *"Experts Advise Office Workers on the Fine Art of Holiday Gift-Giving" in Portland Press Herald* (December 16, 2005)
Pub: Blethen Maine Newspapers, Inc.
Ed: Matt Wickenheiser. **Description:** Pitfalls to avoid for company gift giving should include the avoidance of gag gifts and personal items; and it is essential to follow a company's gift-giving policy.

39324 ■ *"Extra scrutiny" in Crain's Detroit Business* (Vol. 19, No. 11, March 17, 2003, pp. 14)
Pub: Crain Communications Inc., Detroit
Description: Robert Verdun presents his list of recovery methods for struggling companies.

39325 ■ *"Family matters" in Entrepreneur* (Vol. 31, No. 5, May 2003, pp. 30)
Pub: Entrepreneur Media Inc.
Ed: Geoff Williams. **Description:** In an interview with Marie C. Wilson, president of the Ms. Foundation for Women, Wilson stresses the benefits of providing paid family leave to employees. Entrepreneurs are wondering how they will afford the benefit.

39326 ■ *Fast Company's Greatest Hits: Ten Years of the Most Innovative Ideas in Business*
Pub: Penguin Group Incorporated
Ed: John Byrne; David Lidsky; Mark N. Vamos. **Released:** July 2006. **Price:** $24.95. **Description:** Offering of Fast Company's best articles covering business ideas and profiles of successful firms and their leaders.

39327 ■ *Fast-Track Employer's Kit: California*
Pub: Kaplan Books
Ed: Carolyn Usinger. **Released:** May 2006. **Price:** $29.95. **Description:** Requirements for running a small business in California re outlined.

39328 ■ *"Fastest Growth by Revenue Category" in San Fernando Valley Business Journal* (Vol. 11, November 2006, No. 24, pp. 21)
Pub: San Fernando Valley Business Journal Associates
Description: Listing of statistical data on fifty of the San Fernando Valley area's fastest growing private companies based on revenue.

39329 ■ *"The Fed Connection: 100 Most Influential Hispanics" in Hispanic Business* (Vol. 23, No. 10, October, 2001)
Pub: Hispanic Business
Ed: Teresa Talerico. **Description:** This year's 'Influentials' list shows Hispanics making real headway within the Federal Government. A brief profile of each person on the list is included. Statistical data included.

39330 ■ *Financial Management 101: Get a Grip on Your Business Numbers*
Pub: Self-Counsel Press, Incorporated

Ed: Angie Mohr. **Released:** September 2004. **Price:** $14.95. **Description:** An overview of business planning, financial statements, budgeting and advertising for small businesses. s.

39331 ■ *Financing Your Business: Get a Grip on Finding the Money*
Pub: Self-Counsel Press, Incorporated
Ed: Angie Mohr. **Released:** September 2004. **Price:** $14.95 (US), $19.95 (Canadian). **Description:** Recommendations to help raise capital for a new or expanding small company.

39332 ■ *"Finding Ideas" in Harvard Business Review* (Vol. 81, No. 11, November 2003, pp. 18)
Pub: Harvard Business School Press
Ed: Bronwyn Fryer. **Description:** A diverse workforce with many different ideas can introduce organizational change and enhance business creativity.

39333 ■ *"Finishing Touches: the Fashion Statement is in the Detail" in Black Enterprise* (Vol. 37, January 2007, No. 6, pp. 106)
Pub: Earl G. Graves Publishing Co. Inc.
Ed: Sonia Alleyne. **Description:** Men are discovering the importance of dressing for success. Paying attention to the details such as shoes, socks, cuffs, and collars are just as important as finding the right suit.

39334 ■ *"Firms rate terrorist attack as No. 1 concern" in Wall Street Journal* (December 17, 2002, pp. B7)
Pub: Dow Jones & Co. Inc.
Ed: Richard C. Breeden. **Description:** A poll of small business executives, taken by TEC International Inc., shows that firms rate terrorist attacks as their number one concern.

39335 ■ *First, Break All the Rules: What the World's Greatest Managers Do Differently*
Pub: Simon & Schuster, Incorporated
Ed: Marcus Buckingham, Curt Coffman. **Released:** May 1999. **Price:** $27.00. **Description:** Great managers break virtually every rule revered by conventional wisdom.

39336 ■ *"First Impressions" in Black Enterprise* (Vol. 36, December 2005, No. 5, pp. 62)
Pub: Earl G. Graves Publishing Co. Inc.
Description: Sonya Lowerey, author of The Secret Language of Business Cards, discusses the eight common business card mistakes made by small companies.

39337 ■ *"The 5 Pitfalls Of CEO Succession" in Fortuneit* (Vol. 146, No. 10, November 18, 2002, pp. 78)
Pub: Time Inc.
Ed: Ram Charan, Jerry Useem. **Description:** The five largest mistakes for grooming potential CEOs are listed. Succession planning is the key.

39338 ■ *"5 Ways to Get Rid of Clutter: Spring Cleaning" in My Business* (April/May 2003, pp. 12)
Pub: My Business Magazine
Ed: Julie Bawden Davis. **Description:** Experts offer five tips for eliminating clutter in work areas, thus increasing productivity.

39339 ■ *"FMLA Needs to be Fixed to Stop Abuse" in Crain's Detroit Business* (Vol. 21, January 10, 2005, No. 2, pp. 9)
Pub: Crain Communications Inc. - Detroit
Ed: Nancy McKeague. **Description:** Sixty-eight federal lawsuits have been filed challenging the validity of the Family and Medical Leave Act. Managers and business owners struggle to provide these benefits because federal rules make it difficult to administer them.

39340 ■ *"For some companies, it pays to be private" in Red Herring* (March 2003, pp. 66)
Pub: Herring Communications Inc.
Ed: Michael V. Copeland. **Description:** Currently, an increasing number of private companies are being valued at a higher multiple than public counterparts.

39341 ■ *Forbes—Platinum 400-America's Best Big Companies*
Pub: Forbes Magazine
Ed: William Baldwin, Editor, wbaidwin@forbes.com. **Released:** Annual, December. **Publication Includes:** List of 400 leading publicly owned corporations. **Entries Include:** Company name, sales and net income growth rates, return on capital, debt/capital, net profit margin, and operating margin. **Arrangement:** Classified alphabetically by industry. **Indexes:** Alphabetical.

39342 ■ *Forbes—Up-and-Comers 200*
Pub: Forbes Magazine
Contact: Michael K. Ozanian
Ed: Steve Kichen, Editor. **Released:** Weekly. **Publication Includes:** List of 200 small companies judged to be high quality and fast-growing on the basis of 5-year return on equity and other qualitative measurements. Also includes a list of the 100 best small companies outside the U.S. Note: Issue does not carry address or CEO information for the foreign companies. **Entries Include:** Company name, shareholdings data on chief executive officer; financial data. **Arrangement:** Alphabetical. **Indexes:** Ranking.

39343 ■ *Foundations of Small Business Enterprise*
Pub: Routledge Inc.
Ed: G. Reid. **Released:** December 2006. **Price:** $120.00. **Description:** Insight is given into the life cycle of entrepreneurial ventures; 150 new firms are tracked through early years.

39344 ■ "Free Art! Gallery Loans Visual Art to the Public" in *Black Enterprise* (Vol. 34, No. 3, October 2003, pp. 136)
Pub: Earl Graves Publishing Co.
Ed: Jennifer Smith. **Description:** The National Gallery of Art in Washington, D.C. offers free art collections to the public, as well as videocassettes, CD-Roms, and slides.

39345 ■ "Friend or Faux? Why Big Businesses Want to Look Like You" in *My Business* (February/March 2003, pp. 51)
Pub: My Business Magazine
Ed: Harvey King. **Description:** To move away from the tarnished images of corporate executives, more big companies are spending money trying to appear small to the consumer.

39346 ■ "Friendly firing" in *WorkingWoman* (Vol. 25, No. 4, April 2000, pp. 36)
Pub: Lang Communications Inc.
Ed: Carol Leonetti Dannhauser. **Description:** Expert advice is given on dismissing an employee without incurring a legal action.

39347 ■ "The future of professional organizations" in *Women in Business* (Vol. 53, No. 3, May-June, 2001, pp. 18)
Pub: The ABWA Co. Inc.
Ed: Rachel Warbington. **Description:** Professional organizations have changed significantly in the last few decades, but their future is still bright. One problem they must tackle is cutting their attrition rates, and this requires good communication.

39348 ■ "Ga. Chamber seeking 'civil justice' reform" in *Atlanta Business Chronicle* (Vol. 25, November 29, 2002, No. 25 pp. 28A)
Pub: American City Business Publications, Inc.
Ed: David Allison. **Description:** The main objective of the Georgia Chamber of Commerce in the next session of state legislature is to amend civil justice in Georgia. Chamber leaders have outlined nine reforms they hope to introduce into law.

39349 ■ *Gen X*
Pub: Entrepreneur Press
Ed: Brian O'Connell. **Price:** $17.95.

39350 ■ "Gender Inequity at Top" in *Crain's Detroit Business* (Vol. 19, No. 42, October 20, 2003, pp. 8)
Pub: Crain Communications Inc., Detroit

Description: Fewer than 10 percent of the top positions and board seats in the Michigan Index 100, are held by women. The index is a collaboration of the Center for the Education of Women at University of Michigan and the Women's Leadership Forum, a nonprofit affiliated with the Women's Economic Club in Detroit and supported financially by Ford Motor Company, General Motors Corporation and the forum.

39351 ■ *Gendered Processes: Korean Small Business Ownership*
Pub: LFB Scholarly Publishing LLC
Ed: Eunju Lee. **Released:** November 2005. **Price:** $60.00. **Description:** Examination of the gender processes among Korean immigrants becoming small business owners in the New York City metropolitan area.

39352 ■ *The Geography of Small Firm Innovation*
Pub: Springer
Ed: Grant Black. **Released:** January 2005. **Price:** $39.95. **Description:** Concentration of high-tech innovation across metropolitan areas in the U.S. during the 1990s and the role geography plays in innovation.

39353 ■ "Get carded" in *Entrepreneur* (Vol. 30, No. 2, February 2002, pp. 61)
Pub: Entrepreneur Media Inc.
Ed: Chris Sandlund. **Description:** Creative ways to boost profits for small businesses are explored.

39354 ■ "Getting Noticed at Work" in *Women in Business* (Vol. 53, No. 1, January-February, 2001, pp. 22)
Pub: The ABWA Co. Inc.
Ed: Mary-Lane Kamberg. **Description:** Ways of getting noticed at work, such as communicating, remaining flexible, dressing appropriately, taking pride in work and keeping a positive attitude are discussed.

39355 ■ "Getting the truth into workplace surveys" in *Harvard Business Review* (Vol. 80, No. 1, January 2002, pp. 111)
Pub: Harvard Business School Press
Ed: Palmer Morrel-Samuels. **Description:** Workplace surveys and the differences between good ones and bad ones, which seems to be informed design, are discussed.

39356 ■ *Getting Things Done: The Art of Stress-Free Productivity*
Pub: Penguin Books (USA) Incorporated
Ed: David Allen. **Released:** December 2002. **Price:** $15.00. **Description:** Coach and management consultant recommends methods for stress-free performance under the premise that productivity is directly related to our ability to relax.

39357 ■ "Give good presence" in *BlackEnterprise* (Vol. 32, No. 2, September 2001, pp. 114)
Pub: Earl Graves Publishing Co.
Ed: Phaedra Brotherton. **Description:** Appearance is often the thing people see first in the business world. Expert advice to help polish clothing and social skills in four critical areas are presented, including appearance, verbal presentation, networking, and business etiquette. A listing of books addressing these issues is included.

39358 ■ "Glass Ceiling Persists in the Board Room" in *Marketing to Women* (Vol. 19, December 2006, No. 2, pp. 8)
Pub: EPM Communications, Inc.
Description: A study by search firm Heidrick & Struggles and Women Corporate Directors shows that executive inequality remains high despite the number of women who hold board seats. Although these women tend to mentor and recommend other women for candidates, only 54 percent say that at least one of the women recommended was actually elected to the board. Despite the meager statistics, 76 percent of women on boards surveyed stated that they oppose a legal quota that would mandate an increase of women occupying board seats.

39359 ■ "Goal Tending" in *Small Business Opportunities* (Fall 2005)
Pub: Harris Publications Inc.
Ed: Lonnie Pacelli. **Description:** Five tips to help a small business owner face challenges are outlined, including a good business plan.

39360 ■ "Godwin Group" in *Mississippi Business Journal* (Vol. 29, January 2007, No. 3, pp. A6)
Pub: Venture Publications, Inc.
Description: Profile of Joey Lee, vice president, coastal region of Godwin Group. Lee has previously served as Godwin Group's account manager, strategic communications.

39361 ■ "Golden opportunities: Older workers bring experience and special needs" in *Crain's Detroit Business* (Vol. 17, No. 44, Oct. 22, 2001)
Pub: Crain Communications, Inc.
Ed: Mike Scott. **Description:** According to a survey conducted by AARP, 12.8 percent of seniors work full or part-time, and that men over 65 were more likely to work than women, with 17.5 percent of those interviewed in the workforce in 2000. The differences between senior workers and baby boomer workers are compared.

39362 ■ "Gone Fishin'" in *Entrepreneur* (Vol. 31, No. 10, October 2003, pp. 82)
Pub: Entrepreneur Media, Inc.
Ed: Joanne Cleaver. **Description:** Advice for small firms that close the last week of the year, citing the fact that some companies actually profit from the shutdown.

39363 ■ "Gonzales and Lizarraga Speak Out" in *Hispanic Business* (January/February 2003, pp. 20, 22)
Pub: Hispanic Business
Ed: Joel Russell. **Description:** A new coalition of 130 local chambers have created the Coalition of Hispanic Chambers of Commerce for Fairness and Inclusion, in the hopes of changing the U.S. Hispanic Chamber of Commerce.

39364 ■ "Good Deeds and Watchful Eyes" in *Business Week Online* (March 8, 2002)
Pub: McGraw-Hill, Inc.
Description: According to a survey of owners and managers of small businesses, conducted by Princeton Survey Research Associates on behalf of the Better Business Bureau's Wise Giving Alliance, most small firms actively support charities and local community groups so they can keep a close watch on how the money is being used.

39365 ■ "The Good Fire" in *Entrepreneur* (Vol. 28, No. 3, March 2000, pp. 127)
Pub: Entrepreneur Media Inc.
Ed: Jacquelyn Lynn. **Description:** Try a kinder, gentler termination to help avoid workplace violence.

39366 ■ *Good to Great*
Pub: Harper Business
Ed: Jim Collins. **Price:** $27.50.

39367 ■ *Good to Great: Why Some Companies Make the Leap...and Others Don't*
Pub: HarperInformation
Ed: Jim Collins. **Released:** October 2001. **Price:** $27.50. **Description:** Management styles for growing a modern business.

39368 ■ "Goodwill for Your Ex" in *Inc.* (September 1, 2003)
Pub: Gruner & Jahr USA Publishing
Ed: Mike Hofman. **Description:** Should 'goodwill' be considered divisible property for small business owners in divorce cases?

39369 ■ *Goventure: Live the Life of an Entrepreneur*
Pub: Houghton Mifflin College Division
Ed: Hatten. **Released:** May 2006. **Price:** $28.47. **Description:** Challenges of operating a small business are presented with more than 6,000 graphics, audio, and interactive video.

39370 ■ "GoWholesale" in *Entrepreneur* **(Vol. 33, October 2005, No. 10, pp. 6)**
Pub: Entrepreneur Media Inc.
Ed: Steve Cooper. **Description:** Buyers and sellers of goods will love the new Go Wholesale portal offering paid and unpaid content, including pay-per-click advertising, wholesale online auctions, free classified, blogs and small business information.

39371 ■ *Great Big Book of Business Lists: All the Info You Need to Run a Small Business*
Pub: Entrepreneur Press
Ed: Courtney Thurman; Ashlee Gardner. **Released:** April 2006. **Price:** $45.95. **Description:** Reference guide for small business that includes information for starting and running a small business; lists are organized for easy access and cover every aspect of small business.

39372 ■ "Group dynamics" in *Entrepreneur* **(Vol. 30, No. 12, December 2002, pp. 101)**
Pub: Entrepreneur Media Inc.
Ed: Mark Henricks. **Description:** While large companies hire lobbyists to influence legislators and regulators, small firms join trade associations. There are more than 147,000 trade associations in the United States, most of which are state and local groups.

39373 ■ "Growing Influence" in *Hispanic Business* **(January/February 2005, pp. 18, 20)**
Pub: Hispanic Business
Ed: Craig Mauro. **Description:** Increasing political clout and attention will help Hispanic small business and lead to immigration reform.

39374 ■ *Growing Local Value: How to Build Business Partnerships That Strengthen Your Community*
Pub: Berrett-Koehler Publishers, Incorporated
Ed: Laury Hammel; Gun Denhart. **Released:** December 2006. **Price:** $15.00. **Description:** Advice and examples are provided for building socially responsible entrepreneurship.

39375 ■ *Growing and Managing a Small Business: An Entrepreneurial Perspective*
Pub: Houghton Mifflin College Division
Ed: Kathleen R. Allen. **Released:** July 2006. **Price:** $105.27. **Description:** Introduction to business ownership and management from startup through growth.

39376 ■ "Guardian of the Past" in *Crain's Detroit Business* **(Vol. 21, January 3, 2005, No. 1, pp. 19)**
Pub: Crain Communications Inc. - Detroit
Ed: Jennette Smith. **Description:** The Guardian Building is experiencing an increase in tenants after being purchased by the Sterling Group, led by Gary Torgow. Since $1 million in renovations, the building's occupancy rate rose from 6 percent in 2003 to 43 percent in 2004.

39377 ■ "Guarding gizmos" in *Atlanta Business Chronicle* **(Vol. 24, No. 8, July 27, 2001, pp. 1C)**
Pub: American City Business Journals Inc.
Ed: Mary Jane Credeur. **Description:** Since more and more business persons rely on digital datebooks, laptops, and cellular phones, there is an increased risk of losing important information by theft or loss. According to the National Business Travelers Association, nearly 400,000 laptops were taken from their owners in 2000. Disastrous scenarios involving lost planners and laptops and ways to reduce the risk of losing important devices are discussed.

39378 ■ "Hands off small business!" in *My Business* **(September/October 2001, pp. 23)**
Pub: My Business Magazine
Description: The results of a recent survey by NFIB to its members is displayed. The survey included such issues as taxes, compensatory time off, pay disparities, ergonomics, competition with prisons, federal contract bundling, and Internet taxes.

39379 ■ *Happy About Joint Venturing: The 8 Critical Factors of Success*
Pub: Happy About
Ed: Valerie Orsoni-Vauthey. **Released:** June 2006. **Price:** $23.95. **Description:** An overview of joint venturing is presented.

39380 ■ "Help! I Need a Job" in *Crain's New York Business* **(Vol. 23, January 8, 2007, No. 2, pp. 23)**
Pub: Crain Communications, Inc.
Description: January is the best time to search for a new job. Companies bring in new management, have gotten their budgets and know the amount of staff that is required to meet their goals.

39381 ■ "Here's a Late Resolution, But One to Be Taken Seriously" in *St. Louis Post-Dispatch* **(January 9, 2005)**
Pub: Knight-Ridder/Tribune Business News
Ed: Repps Hudson. **Description:** A discussion involving politeness and consideration in the workplace is examined. Consideration of others in the work environment might improve business, boost morale and help with promotion opportunities.

39382 ■ "HFMA identifies financial implications of workforce shortages" in *Healthcare Financial Management* **(Vol. 56, Sept. 2002, pp. 26)**
Pub: Healthcare Financial Management Association
Description: An overview of the report, "Investing in Your Workforce: Overcoming the Financial Impact of Labor Shortage", the study sponsored by Kronos, Inc. is presented.

39383 ■ "Hispanic Business Top 50 Companies for Diversity" in *Hispanic Business* **(September 2006, pp. 32-34)**
Pub: Hispanic Business
Ed: Jenn Holmes. **Description:** Hispanic influence on the American corporate world is explored. Statistical data included.

39384 ■ *A History of Small Business in America*
Pub: University of North Carolina Press
Ed: Mansel G. Blackford. **Released:** January 2003. **Price:** $18.95. **Description:** History of American small business from the colonial era to present, showing how it has played a role in the nation's economic, political, and cultural development across manufacturing, sales, services and farming.

39385 ■ "Hollywood Opens Ahead Of Schedule" in *Mississippi Business Journal* **(Vol. 28, September 2006, No. 36, pp. 20)**
Pub: Venture Publications, Inc.
Description: Former Bay St. Louis Casino, Casino Magic reopened early despite severe storm damage. Now called Hollywood Casino, the casino has more than 75 percent of the original employees and many upgrades.

39386 ■ "Hometown Heroes: Doing Good by Doing Well" in *My Business* **(November/December 2001, pp. 26-30, 33-35)**
Pub: My Business Magazine
Ed: Shannon Scully, Lisa Waddle. **Description:** Small business owners have long been in the forefront of giving back to their communities. The article takes a look at dozens of Main Street businesses that are making a difference since the terrorist attacks on 9-11.

39387 ■ "Hot or Not?" in *Inc.* **(Volume 28, January 2006, No. 1, pp. 102-105)**
Pub: Inc. Magazine
Description: The most and least valuable industries in today's marketplace are discussed. Investors are putting more capital into entrepreneurial firms, but it is important to understand the hottest sectors. Statistical data included.

39388 ■ "Hot Shots: 200 Up And Coming Companies" in *Forbes* **(Vol. 172, No. 9, October 27, 2003, pp. 139)**
Pub: Forbes Magazine
Ed: Cecily J. Fluke, Lesley Kump. **Description:** Share prices of 200 entrepreneurial firms are up an average of 58 percent over the last years, earnings per share increased 19 percent and return on equity rose 15 percent. Statistical data showing the companies recent performance is included.

39389 ■ "Hot Shots: U.S. Top 15" in *Forbes* **(Vol. 6, No. 20, October 27, 2003, pp. 53)**
Pub: Forbes Magazine
Description: A ranking of America's top small companies (under $500 million in revenues, but otherwise according to criteria similar to those ranked under $1 billion).

39390 ■ *How to Make Big Money in Your Own Small Business: Unexpected Rules Every Small Business Owner Needs to Know*
Pub: Hyperion Press
Ed: Jeffrey J. Fox. **Released:** May 2004. **Price:** $16.95. **Description:** Former sales and marketing pro offers advice on growing a small business.

39391 ■ "How to Make Friends" in *Inc.* **(October 1, 2003)**
Pub: Gruner & Jahr USA Publishing
Ed: Bobbie Gossage, Matthew Fogel. **Description:** Want to build a professional network? Online Websites offering networking services are listed.

39392 ■ "How to beat the Monday blues" in *Women in Business* **(Vol. 53, No. 3, May-June, 2001, pp. 16)**
Pub: The ABWA Co. Inc.
Ed: Liz Hubler. **Description:** Many people experience the 'Monday blues' feeling sometimes with regard to their work, but it can be overcome. Tips include suggestions for changing routines, asking for help, taking regular breaks and controlling time schedules.

39393 ■ *How to Raise Capital: Techniques and Strategies for Financing and Valuing Your Small Business*
Pub: McGraw-Hill Companies
Ed: Jeffrey A. Timmons, Stephen Spinelli, Andrew Zacharakis. **Released:** September 2004. **Price:** $16.95 (US), $24.95 (Canadian). **Description:** Small business financing process is examined. Tips for identifying the financial life cycle of new ventures, developing a framework for financial strategies, and understanding an investor's prospective.

39394 ■ *How to Run Your Business Like a Girl: Successful Strategies from Entrepreneurial Women Who Made It Happen*
Pub: Adams Media Corporation
Ed: Elizabeth Cogswell Baskin. **Released:** September 2005. **Price:** $14.95. **Description:** Tour of three women entrepreneurs and their successful companies.

39395 ■ *How to Succeed As a Lifestyle Entrepreneur*
Pub: Dearborn Trade Publishing Inc.
Ed: Gary Schine. **Price:** $18.95.

39396 ■ *How Walmart is Destroying America (And the World): And What You Can Do About It*
Pub: Ten Speed Press
Ed: Bill Quinn. **Released:** April 2005. **Price:** $10.95. **Description:** Wal-Mart employs 1.5 million employees and operates more than 3,500 stores, making it the largest private employer globally. Wal-Mart's impact on mom-and-pop business is discussed.

39397 ■ *How to Write a Business Plan*
Pub: NOLO
Ed: Mike McKeever. **Released:** January 2007. **Price:** $34.99. **Description:** Author, teacher and financial manager shows how to write an effective business plan. Examples and worksheets are included.

39398 ■ *How to Write a Great Business Plan for Your Small Business in 60 Minutes or Less*
Pub: Atlantic Publishing
Ed: Sharon L. Fullen. **Released:** September 2005. **Price:** $39.95 includes CD-Rom. **Description:** A good business plan outlines goals and works as a company's resume to obtain funding, credit from suppliers, management of the operations and finances, promotion and marketing, and more.

39399 ■ *HRD in Small Organizations: Research and Practice*
Pub: Routledge
Ed: Jim Steward, Graham Beaver. **Released:** February 2004. **Price:** $124.95 (US), $165.00 (Canadian). **Description:** Approaches to human resource development in small organizations are evaluated.

39400 ■ *Human Resources for Small Business Made Easy*
Pub: Skilled Learning Incorporated
Ed: Ruth Zimmerman. **Released:** November 2006. **Description:** Guide for human resource development for small businesses.

39401 ■ "Hyper business or just... hyperbusy?" in *Women in Business* (Vol. 53, No. 3, May-June, 2001, pp. 12)
Pub: The ABWA Co. Inc.
Ed: Sheryl Dawson. **Description:** The apparent trend for Americans to be working longer hours is due to factors including personnel cuts and an aging workforce. The rising cost of living and growing consumer demand for material goods also keeps Americans working longer hours.

39402 ■ "I-5 Corridor: Nurturing Its Economic Potential" in *San Fernando Valley Business Journal* (Vol. 11, December 2006, No. 25, pp. 35)
Pub: San Fernando Valley Business Journal Associates
Ed: Jason Schaff. **Description:** North Valley area sticks out when compared to the remade cities of Burbank and Gendale due to its lack of industrial diversity and cohesiveness that would make it a larger contributor to the economy of the region. Statistical data included.

39403 ■ "I Have One Life, and It Must Come Together" in *Inc.* (October 1, 2003)
Pub: Gruner & Jahr USA Publishing
Description: Five entrepreneurs define what the good life means to them.

39404 ■ "IBM Has A Vision Too: Here's its answer to all those frustrated tech customers" in *Fortuneit* (Vol. 146, Nov. 25, 2002, pp. 158)
Pub: Time Inc.
Ed: David Kirkpatrick. **Description:** In an interview with Sam Palmisano, IBM CEO, on-demand computing is discussed. On demand-computing entails on-demand business, government, and health care provision.

39405 ■ *ICTs and SMEs Antecedents and Consequences of Technology Adoption*
Pub: Edward Elgar Publishing, Incorporated
Ed: Ordanini. **Released:** November 2006. **Price:** $85.00. **Description:** Issues involving information communication technology adoption among small and medium-sized firms are discussed.

39406 ■ "Identity crisis" in *Entrepreneur* (Vol. 31, No. 4, April 2003, pp. 24)
Pub: Entrepreneur Media Inc.
Ed: Nichole L. Torres. **Description:** An estimated 52,400 businesses were affected by identity theft as of June 2002. Tips to avoid identity theft, as well as two Web sites offering more advice is included.

39407 ■ "In critical decisions, often sole adviser is kin" in *Wall Street Journal* (September 24, 2002, pp. B6)
Pub: Dow Jones & Co. Inc.
Ed: Richard C. Breeden. **Description:** Results of a survey of small business owners, conducted by Wells Fargo and National Federation of Independent Business, is presented. Statistical data included.

39408 ■ "In office of the future, we'll all be scanned like a can of beans" in *Wall Street Journal* (April 10, 2002, pp. B1)
Pub: Wall Street Journal
Ed: Suein L. Hwang. **Description:** It is predicted that barcodes on employees and cubicles will be used in the future in order to save space and money.

39409 ■ "In Praise of Boundaries: A Conversation with Miss Manners" in *Harvard Business Review* (Vol. 81, No. 12, December 2003, pp. 41)
Pub: Harvard Business School Press
Ed: Diane L. Coutu. **Description:** Judith Martin, known as the syndicated columnist Miss Manners, argues in favor of establishing formal limits to govern behavior in the office, as the personalization of business relations interferes with efficiency and in some cases, can have legal repercussions, such as sexual harassment.

39410 ■ *Inc.—The Inc. 500 Issue*
Pub: Gruner & Jahr USA Publishing
Contact: John Koten, EDC
Released: Annual, October. **Publication Includes:** List of 500 fastest-growing privately held companies based on percentage increase in sales over the five year period prior to compilation of current year's list. **Entries Include:** Company name, headquarters city, description of business, year founded, number of employees, sales five years earlier and currently, profitability range, and growth statistics. **Arrangement:** Ranked by sales growth.

39411 ■ "Indiana Electric Utility for Sale" in *Crain's Chicago Business* (Vol. 30, January 2007, No. 5, pp. 12)
Pub: Crain Communications, Inc.
Description: Northern Indiana's electric utility is for sale and is expected to fetch between $3.4 and $4 billion.

39412 ■ "Influence-Peddling" in *Business Week* (January 16, 2006, No. 3967, pp. 32)
Pub: McGraw-Hill Companies
Ed: Description: A guilty plea by Jack Abramoff could mean tighter rules for corporate lobbyists. Abramoff plead guilty to charges of conspiracy, mail fraud and tax evasion. Senator John McCain has proposed a bill that would require lobbyists to disclose all fees, report who's giving to charities, and make gifts to lawmakers illegal.

39413 ■ "Inner-City Light" in *Hispanic Business* (September 2006, pp. 28, 30)
Pub: Hispanic Business
Ed: Yolanda Perdomo Bindert. **Description:** Detroit Hispanic Development Corporation and local Detroit employers are helping young adults with educational and career opportunities.

39414 ■ "The Innovation Conversation" in *Fast Company* (July 2001, pp. 70)
Pub: Fast Company
Description: Fast Company gathered ten business leaders for a 90-minute roundtable discussion in San Francisco, California. The following questions were addressed: What is the state of innovation? How are leaders competing on innovation?

39415 ■ *Innovation Methodologies in Enterprise Research*
Pub: Edward Elgar Publishing, Incorporated
Ed: Hine. **Released:** December 2006. **Price:** $75.00. **Description:** The importance of qualitative, interpretist research in the field of enterprise research is discussed. The book stresses how enterprise research is a new method and permits a wide scope for new and innovative research studies.

39416 ■ "Intel is putting its chips on the Net" in *Fast Company* (July 2001, pp. 152)
Pub: Fast Company
Ed: Cheryl Dahle. **Description:** Profile of Craig Barrett, Intel CEO. Barrett discusses his experiences running the Intel, after replacing former CEO Andy Grove.

39417 ■ "The IRS Goes Fishin'" in *Inc.* (July 1, 2003)
Pub: Gruner & Jahr USA Publishing
Ed: Rod Kurtz. **Description:** Regulations governing small company's annual outings or party for employees are discussed.

39418 ■ "It figures" in *Entrepreneur* (Vol. 31, No. 5, May 2003, pp. 32)
Pub: Entrepreneur Media Inc.
Ed: Steve Cooper. **Description:** Statistical data is provided regarding various business issues, including entrepreneurial motivation, Internet Web sites and users, and germ warfare in the workplace.

39419 ■ "It's 2006! Whatcha Gonna Do About It?" in *Inc.* (Volume 28, January 2006, No. 1, pp. 78-85, 113)
Pub: Inc. Magazine
Ed: Stephanie Clifford. **Description:** Various entrepreneurs give advice to help small businesses face new challenges in 2006. Topics include investments, the economy, small business trends, logistics, business communication such as blogs, energy issues, consumer products, real estate, interest rates and outsourcing.

39420 ■ "It's Good to be King" in *Inc.* (December 1, 2003)
Pub: Gruner & Jahr USA Publishing
Ed: Jess McCuan. **Description:** In a study conducted by the Families and Work Institute, small business owners reported large personal satisfaction in entrepreneurship.

39421 ■ "It's Settled: A New Law Makes it Easier to Reach Settlements" in *Entrepreneur* (Vol. 33, February 2005, No. 2, pp. 74)
Pub: Entrepreneur Media Inc.
Ed: Jane Easter Bahls. **Description:** American Jobs Creation Act of 2004, Section 703, the Civil Rights Tax Relief Acts overturns a tax rule that no longer requires the winner of wrongful termination or workplace discrimination to pay taxes on any money awarded in the lawsuit.

39422 ■ "Job Titles of the Future: Chief Academic Officer" in *Fast Company* (September 2001, pp. 60)
Pub: Fast Company
Ed: Erika Germer. **Description:** Profile of Jack Leonard, formerly assistant headmaster for curriculum at Dorchester High School near Boston, Massachusetts, has been assigned the new title of chief academic officer.

39423 ■ "The Juggling Act" in *My Business* (October/November 2003, pp. 36-39)
Pub: My Business Magazine
Ed: Nancy Mann Jackson. **Description:** Owning one business is not as difficult as it seems; tips to help entrepreneurs handle the operations of more than one business are given, including good organization skills.

39424 ■ "Just Zip It: A Confidentiality Agreement Can Give You the Upper Hand" in *Entrepreneur* (Vol. 32, November 2004, No. 11, pp. 96)
Pub: Entrepreneur Media Inc.
Ed: Marc Diener. **Description:** When planning a confidentiality agreement it is essential to determine what information is confidential, to whom information can be disclosed, and how long it is to remain confidential. Always make the confidentiality agreement a separate document from other contracts.

39425 ■ "Keep it Simple" in *Entrepreneur.com* (Vol. 34, February 2006, No. 2, pp. 60)
Pub: Entrepreneur Media Inc.
Ed: Chris Penttila. **Description:** Twenty-five tips for fine tuning a small business are outlined, focusing on technology, money, banking, taxes, credit and collection, accounting systems, mergers, management, and marketing ideas.

39426 ■ "Keeping an Eye on Corporate America" in *Fortuneit* (Vol. 146, No. 11, November 25, 2002, pp. 44)
Pub: Time Inc.
Ed: Alynda Wheat. **Description:** The gathering of the Ethics Officer Association's tenth anniversary is discussed. The meeting addressed many current compliance issues.

39427 ■ "Know Thy Worth" in *Entrepreneur.com* **(Vol. 34, February 2006, No. 2, pp. 50)**
Pub: Entrepreneur Media Inc.
Ed: C.J. Prince. **Description:** A business valuation can help an owner put a precise number on the company's present and future value. It will help when choosing to sell the business, gifting the business to heirs, recruiting new investors, or bringing employees into ownership.

39428 ■ "Land of the Free" in *Fast Company* **(May 2001, pp. 125)**
Pub: Fast Company
Ed: Daniel H. Pink. **Description:** During an economic downturn, the rules of supply and demand, profit and loss, and the art of value creation remain the same.

39429 ■ *Law (in Plain English) for Small Business*
Pub: Sourcebooks, Incorporated
Ed: Leonard D. DuBoff. **Released:** November 2006.
Description: Small business law is described in easy to read format.

39430 ■ "Lead Softly, but Carry a Big Baton" in *Fast Company* **(July 2001, pp. 46)**
Pub: Fast Company
Ed: Jill Rosenfeld. **Description:** Symphony conductor, Roger Nierenberg, knows a thing or two about creative management. How else do you get the piccolos and the percussion to stay on the same page?

39431 ■ "Leaders for the Long Haul" in *Fast Company* **(July 2001, pp. 56)**
Pub: Fast Company
Ed: Keith H. Hammonds. **Description:** When workers and executives from Roadway Express came together to strategize about the company's future, they made a startling discovery: everyone wanted the same things.

39432 ■ "Leadership Training in Uniform" in *Hispanic Business* **(Vol. 23, No. 7/8, July/August 2001, pp. 20)**
Pub: Hispanic Business
Ed: Vivienne Heines. **Description:** Profile of Command Sergeant Major Daniel Chavez, highlighting his leadership skills, which he compares to that of a small business manager.

39433 ■ "Leading Indicators; Slow (But Steady) Growth" in *My Business* **(December/January 2003, pp. 48)**
Pub: My Business Magazine
Ed: Bill Dunkelberg. **Description:** Small business optimism, small business hiring plans, and inventory plans are among the items discussed. Growth in real gross domestic product averaged 3 percent in the 12 months following the September 11 tragedy, down only by one-half percent of the average trend.

39434 ■ "Leading in Times of Trauma" in *Harvard Business Review* **(Vol. 80, No. 1, January 2002, pp. 55)**
Pub: Harvard Business School Press
Ed: Jane E. Dutton. **Description:** Using three years of research conducted at the Compassion Lab (jointly operated by the University of Michigan Business School and the University of British Columbia), recommendations are offered for dealing with trauma, disaster, and grief within a business environment.

39435 ■ *Lean Six Sigmas That Works: A Powerful Action Plan for Dramatically Improving Quality, Increasing Speed, and Reducing Waste*
Pub: American Management Association
Ed: Bill Carreira; Bill Trudell. **Released:** 2006. **Price:** $21.95.

39436 ■ "Leave small business alone!" in *My Business* **(April/May 2002, pp. 51)**
Pub: My Business Magazine
Description: According to a National Federation of Independent Business Member Ballot, small business owners want fewer government regulations and mandates in order to run their firms. Statistical data included.

39437 ■ "Leaving their Mark" in *Entrepreneur* **(Vol. 32, December 2004, No. 12, pp. 8)**
Pub: Entrepreneur Media Inc.
Ed: Rieva Lesonsky. **Description:** Baby boomers contributed more to entrepreneurial spirit than any other generation.

39438 ■ "Legal Aid: Sample Legal Documents can Lower Your Attorney Fees" in *Black Enterprise* **(Vol. 37, October 2006, No. 3, pp. 210)**
Pub: Earl G. Graves Publishing Co. Inc.
Ed: Tamara E. Holmes. **Description:** FreeLegalForms.net provides thousands of free legal forms. These forms are not a substitute for consultation with an attorney but the sample documents can help save you time and money.

39439 ■ "Legends" in *Inc.* **(Volume 27, December 2005, No. 12, pp. 30, 32)**
Pub: Inc. Magazine
Ed: Darren Dahl. **Description:** Profiles of the well-known entrepreneurs who died in 2005 include Dr. Frederick H. Berenstein, John Delorean, Horace Hagedorn, John H. Johnson, Mortimer Levitt, James R. and Alice Lewis, Jerome Lippman, John J. McMullen, Gary Milgard, Robert Moog, Frank Perdue, Richard H. Sabot, John E. Struggles, Kenneth Taylor, Dale "The Hawk" Velzy, and Charles West.

39440 ■ *Lessons in Service From Charlie Trotter*
Pub: Ten Speed Press
Ed: Edmund Lawler. **Released:** $19.95 (US), $29.95 (Canadian). **Price:** $19.95 (US), $29.95 (Canadian).
Description: Chef Charlie Trotter, owner of a restaurant, shares insight into managing any business successfully.

39441 ■ "Let's Do Launch" in *Entrepreneur* **(Vol. 32, No. 4, April 2004, pp. 26)**
Pub: Entrepreneur Media, Inc.
Ed: Jill Amadio. **Description:** Ford and Mercury have announced their new 2005 models, with the Futura, Mariner, and Montego targeted to the business market.

39442 ■ "Let's Do Lunch: Giving New Meaning to the Term 'Power Lunch'" in *Entrepreneur* **(Vol. 32, November 2004, No. 11, pp. 34)**
Pub: Entrepreneur Media Inc.
Ed: Nichole L. Torres. **Description:** In Good Company, founded by Nancy Michaels, accepts bids from entrepreneurs. The winners enjoy lunch with a powerful business owner or corporate CEO.

39443 ■ *The Life Cycle of Entrepreneurial Ventures*
Pub: Springer
Ed: Simon Parker. **Released:** October 2006. **Price:** $199.00. **Description:** Issues involved in creating a new business are explored, including venture creation, development and performance.

39444 ■ "Loans can be more than just the numbers" in *Atlanta Business Chronicle* **(Vol. 23, No. 52, June 1, 2001, pp. 52A)**
Pub: American City Business Journals Inc.
Ed: Linda Kercher. **Description:** Nationwide, the top small business lenders use Fair Issac's credit-scoring models, but in Atlanta, Georgia, lenders do not use the automated process, opting for a one-on-one relationship between the banker and borrower.

39445 ■ "The Magic Number" in *Inc.* **(September 1, 2003)**
Pub: Gruner & Jahr USA Publishing
Ed: Norm Brodsky. **Description:** Small businesses all have key numbers to track on a daily or weekly basis. These numbers are an essential part of running a successful enterprise. Key numbers give financial information needed to take timely action. Tips to help small companies forecast critical issues are shared.

39446 ■ "Magna Carta for the Virtual Age" in *Home Office Computing* **(Vol. 18, No. 12, December 2000, pp. 21)**
Pub: Scholastic Inc.
Ed: Jeffrey D. Zbar. **Description:** Jennifer Johnson outlines 10 key practices a company needs in order to maintain "professionalism in the virtual workplace".

39447 ■ "Maine Faces Slow Population Growth, Aging Workforce" in *Portland Press Herald* **(May 6, 2005)**
Pub: Blethen Maine Newspapers, Inc.
Ed: Tux Turkel. **Description:** Maine is experiencing slow population growth coupled with an aging workforce, making the state's ability to expand its economy over the next ten years a challenge.

39448 ■ "Make Corporate America Work for You" in *Inc.* **(July 1, 2003)**
Pub: Gruner & Jahr USA Publishing
Ed: Alison Stein Wellner. **Description:** Corporate America wants your business, but whom can you trust? Information is provided to sort out responsible vendors.

39449 ■ *Make It Big With Yuvi: How to Achieve Poolside Living by Growing Your Small Business*
Pub: AuthorHouse
Ed: Ron Peltier. **Released:** March 2006. **Price:** $17.00. **Description:** Successful entrepreneurship is profiled.

39450 ■ "Make a List, Check it Twice: Can You Check Off All the Items on Your List?" in *Entrepreneur* **(Vol. 33, February 2005, pp. 92)**
Pub: Entrepreneur Media Inc.
Ed: Guy Kawasaki. **Description:** Guy Kawasaki offers advice to entrepreneurs in developing business skills. His latest book, The Art of the Start: The Time-Tested, Battle-Hardened Guide for Anyone Starting Anything, offers his experience as an evangelist, entrepreneur, investment banker and venture capitalist.

39451 ■ "Make a List, Check it Twice: Ever Wonder What's on Other Entrepreneurs' To-Do Lists?" in *Entrepreneur* **(Vol. 32, December 2004)**
Pub: Entrepreneur Media Inc.
Ed: Sara Wilson. **Description:** A sampling of entrepreneurial to-do lists is presented.

39452 ■ *Make Your Business Survive and Thrive! 100+ Proven Marketing Methods to Help You Beat the Odds*
Pub: John Wiley & Sons, Incorporated
Ed: Priscilla Y. Huff. **Released:** December 2006. **Price:** $19.95. **Description:** Small business and entrepreneurial expert gives information to help small and home-based businesses grow.

39453 ■ "Making a case for a four-day work week" in *Business First Columbus* **(Vol. 18, No. 26, February 15, 2002, pp. A30)**
Pub: Business First Columbus, Inc.
Ed: Michael Miller. **Description:** A discussion exploring the pros and cons of a four-day work week is presented.

39454 ■ "Male and female in organizational behavior" in *Journal of Organizational Behavior* **(Vol. 23, No. 2, March 2002, pp. 149)**
Pub: John Wiley & Sons Inc.
Ed: Lloyd E. Sandelands. **Description:** The influence of a person's sex on the operation of an organization is discussed. The lack of published information on this topic is also discussed.

39455 ■ "The Man Who Started It All" in *Hispanic Business* **(January/February 2003, pp. 24, 26)**
Pub: Hispanic Business
Description: In an interview, David Lizarraga, answers questions about his role as new leader of the Coalition of Hispanic Chambers for Fairness and Inclusion.

39456 ■ "Managing emotional fallout" in *Harvard Business Review* **(Vol. 80, No. 2, February 2002, pp. 55)**
Pub: Harvard Business School Press
Ed: Steven E. Hyman. **Description:** The opinions of Dr. Steven E. Hyman, the former director of the National Institute of Mental Health, regarding stress and depression in the workplace, especially in the aftermath of the terrorist attacks of September 11, 2001, are presented.

39457 ■ *Managing Labour in Small Firms*
Pub: Routledge
Ed: Susan Marlow, Dean Patton, Monder Ram. **Released:** December 2004. **Price:** $105.00 (US), $147.00 (Canadian). **Description:** Essays addressing conditions of workers in small business.

39458 ■ *Managing a Small Business Made Easy*
Pub: Entrepreneur Press
Ed: Martin E. Davis. **Released:** September 2005. **Price:** $19.95 (US), $26.95 (Canadian). **Description:** Examination of the essential elements for an entrepreneur running a business, including advice on leadership, customer service, financials, and more.

39459 ■ "Many things matter, and here's what matters most" in *Fast Company* **(June 2001, pp. 70)**
Pub: Fast Company
Ed: John Ellis. **Description:** Understanding the many things that matter in the modern economy are addressed, including money, strategy, leadership, values, IT networks, peer-to-peer computing, reengineering, and profits.

39460 ■ "Marketing Spreads Hawaiian Message" in *Pacific Business News* **(Vol. 41, No. 22, August 8, 2003, pp. 1)**
Pub: American City Business Journals
Ed: Nina Wu. **Description:** Marketing campaign that supports federal self-determination legislation for Native Hawaiians and the impact of the legislation on Hawaiian businesses are discussed

39461 ■ *The Martha Rules: 10 Essentials for Achieving Success as You Start, Build, or Manage a Business*
Pub: Rodale Press, Incorporated
Ed: Martha Stewart. **Released:** October 2005. **Price:** $24.95. **Description:** Martha Stewart offers insight into starting, building and managing a successful business.

39462 ■ *The Martha Rules: 10 Essentials for Achieving Success as You Start, Grow, or Manage a Business*
Pub: Rodale Press, Inc.
Ed: Martha Stewart. **Released:** October 2005.

39463 ■ *Mastering Business Growth and Change Made Easy*
Pub: Entrepreneur Press
Ed: Jeffrey A. Hansen. **Released:** October 2005. **Price:** $19.95 (US), $26.95 (Canadian). **Description:** Tips for growing a small business, regardless of state or environment.

39464 ■ "A Mediation on Risk" in *Fortune* **(Vol. 152, October 3, 2005, No. 7, pp. 50)**
Pub: Time Inc.
Ed: Justin Fox. **Description:** Home Depot's effective disaster planning had them among the first company's to reopen its stores after Hurricane Katrina hit the Gulf Coast.

39465 ■ *Medium Sized Firms and Economics Growth*
Pub: Nova Science Publishers, Incorporated
Ed: Janez Prasniker. **Released:** February 2005. **Price:** $79.00. **Description:** Medium sized companies should have a more definitive presence in modern microeconomic theory, the theory of entrepreneurship, and the theory of financial markets.

39466 ■ "Memo to Rex Tillerson" in *Business Week* **(January 9, 2006, No. 3966, pp. 36)**
Pub: McGraw-Hill Companies
Description: Advice given to Mobil Corporation's future CEO, Rex Tillerson, who will be stepping into Lee F. Raymonds position when he retires from the company.

39467 ■ "Mending Fences" in *Entrepreneur* **(Vol. 33, October 2005, No. 10, pp. 90)**
Pub: Entrepreneur Media Inc.
Ed: Jane Easter Bahls. **Description:** Processes to help settle a conflict with a neighboring business are discussed. To avoid a legal battle, mediation may help find a mutually agreeable solution.

39468 ■ "Metro firms maintain pay for called-up reservists" in *Crain's Detroit Business* **(Vol. 19, No. 14, April 7, 2003, pp. 1)**
Pub: Crain Communications Inc., Detroit
Ed: Robert Sherefkin, Robert Ankeny. **Description:** Major Detroit area firms, including auto suppliers and DTE Energy are paying salary differences for employees called up for active military duty. Many are also maintaining medical, dental and life insurance for several months, and some for years.

39469 ■ "Michigan Department of Consumer and Industry Services: What it does" in *Crain's Detroit Business* **(Vol. 18, Dec. 9, 2002, pp. 14)**
Pub: Crain Communications Inc., Detroit
Description: An overview of the Michigan Department of Consumer and Industry Services, and the services the department provides to small businesses in the state.

39470 ■ "Middays of Thunder" in *Inc.* **(January 1, 2002)**
Pub: Inc. Magazine
Ed: Rebecca Dorr. **Description:** Robert River, founder of Spectrum Communications Cabling Services Inc., tells how he took his top customers and some employees to a race track to race cars, rather than dinner or a ball game.

39471 ■ "Mind Games: Jump-Start Your Problem-Solving Skills for a Better Business" in *Entrepreneur* **(Vol. 31, No. 10, October 2003, pp. 34)**
Pub: Entrepreneur Media, Inc.
Ed: Mark Hendricks. **Description:** Review of the book, "Retrain Your Business Brain", by Donalee Markus, Lindsey Paige Markus and Pat Taylor; the book provides visual and verbal puzzles to small business owners to become better at solving business issues and spotting problems.

39472 ■ "Mind over manners" in *Entrepreneur* **(Vol. 31, No. 5, May 2003, pp. 118)**
Pub: Entrepreneur Media Inc.
Ed: Nichole L. Torres. **Description:** Proper business etiquette is discussed to help make a good impression at a dinner business meeting.

39473 ■ "Mind Your P's and Q's" in *Entrepreneur* **(Vol. 32, September 2004, No. 9, pp. 77)**
Pub: Entrepreneur Media Inc.
Ed: Joanne Cleaver. **Description:** Misspelled words can destroy a small business' credibility, not to mention the costs involved in misspelling in an advertisement or business contract.

39474 ■ "Mind Your P's and Q's" in *Rough Notes* **(Vol. 145, No. 2, February 2003, pp. 43)**
Pub: Rough Notes
Ed: Emily Huling. **Description:** Business etiquette is important to observe whether in or out of the office, and when meeting people. The article provides a few do's and don'ts.

39475 ■ "Mingling at Business Holiday Parties Made Easier for Some" in *Sacramento Bee* **(November 29, 2005)**
Pub: The Sacramento Bee

Ed: Gilbert Chan. **Description:** Tips to ease anxiety over attending holiday business parties are shared, including the use of networking for career building.

39476 ■ "Mississippi Children's Home Services" in *Mississippi Business Journal* **(Vol. 29, January 2007, No. 4, pp. 6)**
Pub: Venture Publications, Inc.
Description: Profile of Kelly Shannon, Development Coordinator of Mississippi Children's Home Services. She was previously Special Projects Officer of the Mississippi Department of Health's Communications Office.

39477 ■ "A Mixed Blessing" in *Entrepreneur* **(Vol. 31, No. 7, July 2003, pp. 68)**
Pub: Entrepreneur Media, Inc.
Ed: Mark Henricks. **Description:** If not invested wisely, a windfall for a small business, could turn into a negative. When a small firm receives unexpected money, it should use that money to help expand production, pay off debts, fund new marketing, and/or to motivate employees.

39478 ■ "Mom and Pop Psychology" in *Inc.* **(December 1, 2003)**
Pub: Gruner & Jahr USA Publishing
Ed: Bobbie Gossage. **Description:** Every small business has a personality all its own. Ways to help find that out are presented.

39479 ■ "Money & Manners" in *Small Business Opportunities* **(Vol. 17, September 2005, No. 5, pp. 12)**
Pub: Harris Publications Inc.
Ed: Lydia Ramsey. **Description:** Rudeness can cost a small business sales and revenue. A true/false quiz is offered to judge a company's business etiquette.

39480 ■ "More bang" in *Entrepreneur* **(Vol. 30, No. 2, February)**
Pub: Entrepreneur Media Inc.
Ed: Chris Penttila. **Description:** Presentation of twenty-five tips for under $1,000 that will make a business better, from marketing to sales, and employees to equipment.

39481 ■ "More Checks in the Mail" in *Hispanic Business* **(Vol. 23, No. 7/8, July/August 2001, pp. 30)**
Pub: Hispanic Business
Ed: Vivienne Heines. **Description:** According to Tirso Del Junco, member of the Board of Governors of the U.S Postal Service, in order to meet rising labor costs, the postal system will be forced to raise rates again.

39482 ■ "Motorola to Cut 3,500 Jobs" in *Crain's Chicago Business* **(Vol. 30, January 2007, No. 4, pp. 12)**
Pub: Crain Communications, Inc.
Description: Ed Zander, CEO of Motorola, said the cell phone maker will cut 5 percent of its workforce as it tries to improve operating costs after a disappointing fourth quarter.

39483 ■ "My Bad! Playing the Blame Game is Out." in *Entrepreneur* **(Vol. 33, March 2005, No. 3, pp. 94)**
Pub: Entrepreneur Media Inc.
Ed: Chris Penttila. **Description:** A growing number of CEOs are concerned with credibility, and are offering apologies for mistakes.

39484 ■ "My 'Won't Do' List" in *My Business* **(February/March 2003, pp. 49)**
Pub: My Business Magazine
Ed: Terri Lonier. **Description:** Ways to streamline a small business owner's life are listed.

39485 ■ "National Association for the Exchange of Industrial Resources" in *Entrepreneur* **(Vol. 33, August 2005, No. 8, pp. 4)**
Pub: Entrepreneur Media Inc.
Ed: Steve Cooper. **Description:** The National Association for the Exchange of Industrial Resources assists U.S. businesses in the donation of excess inventory to the ill, needy or minors. These donations earn federal income tax deductions.

39486 ■ "National Treasure" in *Entrepreneur* (Vol. 33, October 2005, No. 10, pp. 26)
Pub: Entrepreneur Media Inc.
Ed: Sara Wilson. **Description:** Review of the book, "The Hypomanic Edge: The Link Between (A Little) Craziness and (A Lot of) Success in America." The book's author, John D. Gartner, suggests the theory that links hypomania, a medical condition resulting in elevated mood and increased activity, with our immigrant ancestors and the entrepreneurial successes of today.

39487 ■ "Natural Gas Prices Pinch Businesses" in *Tampa Tribune* (October 28, 2005)
Pub: Media General, Inc.
Ed: Will Rodgers. **Description:** Natural gas prices are driving the cost of running a small business; the price of natural gas for commercial use rose nearly 41 percent between 2000 and 2004.

39488 ■ *Never Bet the Farm*
Pub: Jossey-Bass Publishers
Ed: Anthony L. Iaquinto; Stephen Spinelli, Jr. **Price:** R19.95 paperback.

39489 ■ "The New Chairman" in *Hispanic Business* (January/February 2003, pp. 22, 24)
Pub: Hispanic Business
Description: J.R. Gonzales will assume leadership of the U.S. Hispanic Chamber of Commerce. In an interview Gonzales answers questions regarding his platform as new chairman.

39490 ■ "New Frontiers to Explore" in *Fast Company* (September 2001, pp. 76)
Pub: Fast Company
Ed: Chuck Salter. **Description:** Profile of John Fahey, president and CEO of a non-profit society, shares ways he is finding new sources of revenue, new corporate partnerships, and new identity for the 113-year-old institution.

39491 ■ "New Growth in the Garden State" in *Fast Company* (August 2001, pp. 36)
Pub: Fast Company
Ed: Heath Row. **Description:** In March 2001, two longtime members of the Fast Company community launched a CoF cell in Morristown, New Jersey, with more than 75 people joining within two months. Cell members have established a set of design principles for their organization, principles that any networking group, team or company should take seriously.

39492 ■ "New Lessons to Learn" in *Fortune* (Vol. 152, October 3, 2005, No. 7, pp. 87)
Pub: Time Inc.
Ed: Howard Schultz. **Description:** Eight Fortune 500 CEOs discuss how Hurricane Katrina changed the way they think about crisis management. Focus is on caring for employees, keeping communication lines open, and preparation for the next disaster.

39493 ■ "New York Stories" in *Venture Capital Journal* (Vol. 42, No. 9, September 2002, pp. 21, 22-23)
Pub: Thomas Venture Economics
Ed: Charles R. Fellers. **Description:** The impact of the terrorist attacks of September 11 is examined. Steve Brotman, managing director of Silicon Alley Venture Partners, feels New York enjoys the most entrepreneurial culture in the world.

39494 ■ "Next Round on Adarand" in *Hispanic Business* (Vol. 23, No. 7/8, July/August 2001, pp. 26)
Pub: Hispanic Business
Ed: Jonathan J. Higuera. **Description:** The Justice Department brief is expected to articulate the Bush administration's take on government contracting.

39495 ■ "NFIB Lays Groundwork for 108th Congress" in *My Business* (February/March 2003, pp. 18)
Pub: My Business Magazine
Description: New members of Congress were indoctrinated into the workings of the National Federation of Independent Business advocacy group during the past few weeks.

39496 ■ "NFIB Report From The State Capitols" in *My Business* (December/January 2003, pp. 20-23)
Pub: My Business Magazine
Description: A look at small business issues particular to each of the fifty states.

39497 ■ "NFIB Report from the State Capitals" in *My Business* (June/July 2002, pp. 20-22)
Pub: My Business Magazine
Description: Current issues confronting small businesses are listed by state.

39498 ■ "NFIB Report from the State Capitols" in *My Business* (April/May 2003, pp. 20-23)
Pub: My Business Magazine
Description: Small businesses issues are listed by state.

39499 ■ "Nice meeting you!" in *Entrepreneur* (Vol. 30, No. 12, December 2002, pp. 111)
Pub: Entrepreneur Media Inc.
Ed: Nichole L. Torres. **Description:** Ideas for business networking to help grow a business are presented.

39500 ■ "9/11 Call: When Crisis Hit, Business Owners Answered" in *Entrepeneur* (Vol. 30, No. 2, February 2002, pp. 46)
Pub: Entrepreneur Media Inc.
Ed: Geoff Williams. **Description:** Inspiring stories of entrepreneurs who responded to the 911 terrorist attacks are true examples of the meaning of the word 'hero'.

39501 ■ "NMSDC Confab" in *Hispanic Business* (Vol. 23, No. 10, October, 2001, pp. 22)
Pub: Hispanic Business
Description: The 2001 National Minority Supplier Development Council Conference and Business Opportunity Fair was held October 28-31 at the Georgia World Congress Center in Atlanta.

39502 ■ "Not so fast!: Studies show many of you aren't looking before you leap" in *Entrepreneur* (Vol. 31, No. 6, June 2003, pp. 30)
Pub: Entrepreneur Media Inc.
Ed: David Newton. **Description:** The topic of risk assessment for entrepreneurs is highlighted, stating that vision alone isn't enough to ensure success.

39503 ■ "Nothing Personal" in *Entrepreneur* (Vol. 31, No. 10, October 2003, pp. 85)
Pub: Entrepreneur Media, Inc.
Ed: Marc Diener. **Description:** The art of negotiation to make better business deals is discussed.

39504 ■ "The Number Cruncher Versus the Vision Guy" in *Inc.* (Volume 28, January 2006, No. 1, pp. 90-93, 96, 99)
Pub: Inc. Magazine
Ed: Alison Stein Wellner. **Description:** Two business assessors value the worth of three companies. Five ways to boost the final value of a company are listed.

39505 ■ "Numbers Game" in *Entrepreneur* (Vol. 32, December 2004, No. 12, pp. 46)
Pub: Entrepreneur Media Inc.
Ed: Jill Amadio. **Description:** An individual or company is required to purchase at least five or more vehicles from major automakers in order to qualify as a fleet member.

39506 ■ "Obesity costing billions" in *Atlanta Business Chronicle* (Vol. 24, No. 14, September 7, 2001, pp. 1A)
Pub: American City Business Journals Inc.
Ed: Julie Bryant. **Description:** According to Innovus Research, employee obesity is costing U.S. employers nearly $70 billion annually. Primary health problems leading to increased costs include heart disease, gastrointestinal tract disease, cancer, type 2 diabetes, and high blood pressure. Roche Laboratories Inc. and Verizon Wireless are two companies that offer their employees a free pilot weight loss program.

39507 ■ "Oceanside: Chamber Gets in Networking Fast Lane" in *San Diego Business Journal* (Vol. 28, January 15, 2007, No. 3, pp. 16)
Pub: San Diego Business Journal Associates
Ed: Pat Broderick. **Description:** The Oceanside Chamber of Commerce is offering five-minute networking sessions to members.

39508 ■ "Oklahoma Business Roundtable Elects Officers" in *Journal Record* (June 24, 2003)
Pub: Dolan Media Company
Description: The Oklahoma Business Roundtable has elected new officers, with William Talley, The Rams Company, elected as chairman. The Roundtable has 107 member companies.

39509 ■ "The Old Economy Meets the New Economy" in *Fast Company* (November 2001, pp. 70)
Pub: Fast Company
Description: Fast Company recently convened a session in Chicago with experts from the world's strongest and oldest brands with the objective of finding new insights on emerging best practices when it comes to customers, technology and business.

39510 ■ "Older is seen as better in small-business owners" in *Wall Street Journal* (August 20, 2002, pp. B4)
Pub: Dow Jones & Co. Inc.
Ed: Richard C. Breeden. **Description:** Global Entrepreneurship Monitor reports that age is an asset when it comes to owning a small business. Statistical data included.

39511 ■ "Omniplex on the Case" in *Black Enterprise* (Vol. 37, December 2006, No. 5, pp. 38)
Pub: Earl G. Graves Publishing Co. Inc.
Ed: Glenn Townes. **Description:** Office of Personnel Management in Washington D.C. recently awarded a service contract to Omniplex World Services Corp. Virginia-based, The Chantilly, will perform security investigations and background checks on current and prospective federal employees and military personnel and contractors.

39512 ■ "On Her Best Behavior" in *Home Business* (Vol. 12, October 2005, No. 5, pp. 41)
Pub: Home Business Magazine
Ed: Sandy Larson. **Description:** Syndi Seid, founder of San-Francisco-based Advanced Etiquette, stresses the importance of using proper table manners while dining with clients.

39513 ■ "On a Roll! Why Small Business Is Like Duct Tape" in *My Business* (April/May 2003, pp. 51)
Pub: My Business Magazine
Ed: Harvey King. **Description:** The article compares the use of duct tape to American small business for its flexibility, creativity and ubiquity.

39514 ■ "On Your Mind" in *Forbes* (February 19, 2001, pp. 34)
Pub: Forbes Magazine
Ed: Katarzyna Moreno. **Description:** The pros and cons of using a personal name as the name of a business are investigated.

39515 ■ "Out with the Old?" in *Entrepreneur* (Vol. 32, No. 1, January 2004, pp. 24)
Pub: Entrepreneur Media, Inc.
Ed: Chris Pentilla. **Description:** Young entrepreneurs are choosing not to join area Chambers of Commerce because they find them dull and uninteresting, some are focusing on networking groups instead.

39516 ■ *Outfoxing the Small Business Owner*
Pub: Adams Media Corporation
Ed: Gene Marks. **Released:** January 2005. **Price:** $12.95 (US), $18.95 (Canadian). **Description:** Special skill sets are required to sell, service or deal with small business customers.

39517 ■ *The Oxford Handbook of Entrepreneurship*
Pub: Oxford University Press, Incorporated
Ed: Mark Casson; Bernard Young; Anuradha Basu.
Released: October 2006. **Price:** $155.00. **Description:** Research covering entrepreneurship is presented by an international team of leading scholars.

39518 ■ "Package deal" in *Entrepreneur* (Vol. 31, No. 4, April 2003, pp. 22)
Pub: Entrepreneur Media Inc.
Ed: Stephen Barlas. **Description:** The new economic stimulus package proposed by President George W. Bush would increase the annual allowance for expensing of capital investments from $25,000 to $75,000 for small businesses, and tie the ceiling in the future to inflation.

39519 ■ "Peace Maker" in *My Business* (April/May 2003, pp. 43)
Pub: My Business Magazine
Ed: Julie Bawden Davis. **Description:** Tips to consider when negotiating conflict among employees are outlined, the smaller a business, the more likely the conflict.

39520 ■ "Peer group provides expertise firms lack" in *Wall Street Journal* (December 17, 2002, pp. B7)
Pub: Dow Jones & Co. Inc.
Ed: Jeff Bailey. **Description:** Profile of Young Entrepreneurs' Organization, a group that brings small business owners together in order to talk and exchange advice and insight into entrepreneurship.

39521 ■ "Personal Business" in *Business Week* (January 9, 2006, No. 3966, pp. 94)
Pub: McGraw-Hill Companies
Ed: Mara der Hovanesian. **Description:** Topics include a takeover of auto lender Americredit, overseas shipping, and retail shopping in China.

39522 ■ "Peter Drucker, still essential" in *Red Herring* (No. 102, August 15, 2001, pp. 35)
Pub: Herring Communications
Ed: Mark Williams. **Description:** A review of the book, The Essential Drucker, issued in three volumes, one on management, one on the individual in organizations, and one on society in general.

39523 ■ *Petty Capitalists and Globalization: Flexibility, Entrepreneurship, and Economic Development*
Pub: State University of New York Press
Ed: Alan Smart, Josephine Smart. **Released:** March 2005. **Price:** $70.00. **Description:** Investigation into ways small businesses in Europe, Asia, and Latin America are required to operate and compete in the fast-growing transnational economy.

39524 ■ "Pharmed Wins for Innovation" in *Hispanic Business* (Vol. 23, No. 7/8, July/August 2001, pp. 6)
Pub: Hispanic Business
Description: The Pharmed Group, ranked 24th on the Hispanic Business 500, won the 2001 Cutting Edge Award from the Greater Miami Chamber of Commerce, for exceptional innovative business techniques.

39525 ■ *A Piece of the Pie*
Pub: Outskirts Press, Incorporated
Ed: Shelton P. Rhodes, Peter Fretty. **Released:** July 2005. **Price:** $34.95. **Description:** Examination of the U.S. Small Business Administration's program 8(a), designed to help disadvantaged individuals grow their small businesses.

39526 ■ "Pinstriped Populist" in *New York Times* (November 12, 2006, pp. 15)
Pub: New York Times Company
Ed: David Sirota. **Description:** Profile of Lou Dobbs, author of How the Government, Big Business, and Special Interest Groups Are Waging War on the American Dream and How to Fight Back. Dobbs, a financial journalist, examines wages, corruption, trade, outsourcing, immigration and health care.

39527 ■ "Planners say the best defense is preparation" in *Atlanta Business Chronicle* (Vol. 24, No. 14, September 7, 2001, pp. S7)
Pub: American City Business Journals Inc.
Ed: Anya Martin. **Description:** Jackson Planners president, Melanie Jackson, talks about pre-planning for meetings.

39528 ■ *The Platinum Rule for Small Business Success*
Pub: Morgan James Publishing, LLC
Ed: Scott Zimmerman; Tony Allesandra; Ron Finklestein. **Released:** August 2006. **Description:** Rules for running a successful and profitable small business are shared.

39529 ■ "Playing Favorites" in *Entrepreneur* (Vol. 31, Sept. 2003)
Pub: Entrepreneur Media, Inc.
Ed: Aliza Pilar Sherman. **Description:** Women entrepreneurs report favorite business Web sites they use to run their companies, with Google.com heading the list.

39530 ■ "Plugging In: Networking Skills That Promise Success" in *Black Enterprise* (Vol. 34, No. 7, February 2004, pp. 61)
Pub: Earl Graves Publishing Co.
Ed: Lee Anna Jackson. **Description:** Reviews are presented of two books that teach business networking skills.

39531 ■ "Power Up!" in *Entrepreneur* (Vol. 31, No. 9, September 2003, pp. 20)
Pub: Entrepreneur Media, Inc.
Description: Steps to take a company to the next level are examined.

39532 ■ *PPC's Guide to Compensation Planning for Small Business*
Pub: Practitioners Publishing Company
Released: September 2004. **Price:** $104.00. **Description:** Technical guide for developing a compensation system for small business. Forms and letters included.

39533 ■ *Principles of Private Firm Valuation*
Pub: John Wiley & Sons, Incorporated
Ed: Stanley J. Feldman. **Released:** April 2005. **Price:** $79.95 (US); $115.99 (Canadian). **Description:** Tools and techniques to correctly perform private firm valuation, including value and how to measure it, valuing control, determining the size of the marketability discount, creating transparency and the implications for value, the value of tax pass-through entities versus a C corporation, etc.

39534 ■ *Print Solutions—Buyers' Guide Issue*
Pub: Document Management Industries Association
Contact: Brad Holt, Mng. Ed.
Released: Annual, October. **Publication Includes:** List of about 600 suppliers of business forms and other business printing, such as ad specialties, barcoded forms & labels, commercial printing calendars, tags, cards, labels, and printed stationery. **Entries Include:** name, address, phone, fax, capabilities, product/service. **Arrangement:** Alphabetical. **Indexes:** Product/service.

39535 ■ "Priority" in *Inc.* (Volume 27, March 2005, No. 3, pp. 23-26, 28, 30)
Pub: Inc. Magazine
Description: Business information discussed includes information about the SEC looking into unlicensed investment brokers, the economy, freight co-ops to help shippers ease costs, hiring, Google, education, SBA assistance to women entrepreneurs, and new inventions.

39536 ■ "The Problem With Confidence" in *Inc.* (September 2005, pp. 176)
Pub: Inc. Magazine
Ed: Adam Hanft. **Description:** Entrepreneurs are eager to take risks, but when does self-confidence become a liability for the company.

39537 ■ "Profits In Penalty Box as NHL Lockout Takes Toll on Businesses" in *Crain's Detroit Business* (Vol. 21, January 31, 2005, No. 5, pp. 43)
Pub: Crain Communications Inc. - Detroit
Ed: Anjali Fluker. **Description:** Restaurants, bars, taxi and shuttles services and parking vendors are suffering without Red Wing Hockey Games this season. Most owners report 20 to 40 percent losses over last year.

39538 ■ *Project Management for Small Business Made Easy*
Pub: Entrepreneur Press
Ed: Sid Kemp. **Released:** April 2006. **Price:** $26.95. **Description:** Strategies for implementing project management for small business are offered.

39539 ■ "The promise of solidarity" in *BlackEnterprise* (Vol. 32, No. 2, September 2001, pp. 14)
Pub: Earl Graves Publishing Co.
Ed: Earl G. Graves, Sr. **Description:** An overview of the political activism of minority-owned businesses in the U.S.

39540 ■ "Promotion Creativity Through the Logic of Contradiction" in *Journal of Organizational Behavior* (Vol. 23, No. 3, May 2002, pp. 321)
Pub: John Wiley & Sons Inc.
Ed: Linda Parrack Livinstone, Leslie E. Palicyh, Gary R. Carini. **Description:** The logic of contradiction which embraces paradox and contradiction as vehicles through which positive change and growth in the organization occur, is proposed and Intel Corporation of the microprocessor industry is used as an illustration. Intel crated new powerful microprocessor chips which were not yet in use so it invested in firms that promised to create need for their increased computing power.

39541 ■ "Protecting the Dream" in *Ingram's* (Vol. 28, No. 5, May 2002, pp. 28)
Pub: Show Me Publishing, Inc.
Ed: Cynthia Grimes. **Description:** Legal advice is given to protect small businesses from bankruptcy, lawyers, accounting, cash flow planning, employee benefits and estate planning.

39542 ■ "Pull the Plug on Stress" in *Harvard Business Review* (Vol. 81, No. 7, July 2003, pp. 102)
Pub: Harvard Business School Press
Ed: Bruce Cryer, Rollin McCraty, Doc Childre. **Description:** The benefits of stress management are discussed.

39543 ■ *The Pursuit of Happyness*
Pub: HarperCollins Publishers Inc.
Ed: Chris Gardner. **Released:** May 2006. **Price:** $25.95. **Description:** Rags-to-riches saga of a homeless father who raised and cared for his son on the streets of San Francisco and worked to become a powerful leader on Wall Street.

39544 ■ "Put It In Drive" in *Entrepreneur.com* (Vol. 34, February 2006, No. 2, pp. 34)
Pub: Entrepreneur Media Inc.
Ed: Mike Hogan. **Description:** According to a study conducted by The Dieringer Research Group, 21 million Americans work in their automobiles; mobile workers are taking care of business in planes, trains and automobiles. Requirements to equip your automobile for teleworking are outlined.

39545 ■ "Raising children and working can be a challenge" in *Atlanta Business Chronicle* (Vol. 24, No. 13, August 31, 2001, pp. 38A)
Pub: American City Business Journals Inc.
Ed: Don Hutcheson, Bob D. McDonald. **Description:** Don Hutcheson and Bob D. McDonald discuss how to be a good parent and balance business life with family life. The article offers ways to raise children that will enhance and build relationships. Tips are offered for talking to children, playing with them, putting them to bed at night, and having meals together as a family.

39546 ■ **"Raising Response Rates In Mail Surveys of Small Business Owners"** in *Journal of Small Business Management* (Vol. 41, No. 3, July 2003)

Pub: International Council of Small Business

Ed: William J. Dennis, Jr. Description: The article covers survey treatments that enhance mail survey response among small business owners.

39547 ■ **"Rating reasonable risks"** in *Women in Business* (Vol. 53, No. 4, July-August, 2001, pp. 18)

Pub: The ABWA Co. Inc.

Ed: Melissa Will. Description: Issues concerning strategies of identifying, setting, managing and analyzing the effects of risks in everyday life are discussed. Particular attention is given to techniques of coping with risks, including considering in advance the ways in which they may affect the risk taker.

39548 ■ **"Reading for retention"** in *Women in Business* (Vol. 53, No. 4, July-August, 2001, pp. 26)

Pub: The ABWA Co. Inc.

Ed: Ron Fry. Description: An excerpt from the book 'Improve Your Memory' is presented, with focus on techniques of memorization, including evaluating the reading material, identifying the essential facts, taking notes, and outlining the text's headlines and keywords.

39549 ■ **"Reading, writing, and protection"** in *Black Enterprise* (Vol. 32, No. 5,)

Pub: Earl Graves Publishing Co.

Ed: Roger Barnes. Description: Three commonly overlooked provisions when a small business enters a contract, ways to construct a contract, and finding legal help are highlighted.

39550 ■ **"Ready, Set Strategize"** in *Inc.* (October 2005, pp. 41-42, 44, 46)

Pub: Inc. Magazine

Ed: Darren Dahl. Description: Strategic planning can be time-consuming and labor-intensive. Advice for developing a new strategic business plan in 48 hours is outlined.

39551 ■ **"Reality Check"** in *InfoWorld* (Vol. 27, May 16, 2005, No. 20, pp. 22)

Pub: InfoWorld Media Group, Inc.

Ed: Ephraim Schwartz. Description: Ways to create a data recovery plan after a natural disaster or an attack on the U.S. telecommunications infrastructure are discussed.

39552 ■ **"Realizing the Spirit and Impact of Adam Smith's Capitalism through Entrepreneurship"** in *Journal of Business Ethics* (Vol.46, Sept.03)

Pub: Kluwer Academic Publishers Group

Ed: Scott L. Newbert. Description: Adam Smith argued that in order to create an effective and productive capitalist system, individuals must pursue interests of both the self and society; despite this assertion, modern economic theory has become tightly focused on the pursuit of economic self-interests at the expense of other, higher order motives.

39553 ■ **"Reawakening your passion for work"** in *Harvard Business Review* (Vol. 80, No. 4, April 2002, pp. 86)

Pub: Harvard Business School Press

Ed: Daniel Richard, Annie Richard, Goleman Richard, McKee Boyatzis. Description: Signals that alert a person that it is time to reevaluate work and career choices and strategies to take stock of one's life are examined.

39554 ■ **"Reconnaissance"** in *Inc.* (August 2005, pp. 53-54)

Pub: Inc. Magazine

Ed: Michael S. Hopkins. Description: Review of the book, Freakonomics. The book offers business lessons of interest to entrepreneurs.

39555 ■ **"Recruitment Contacts"** in *Hispanic Business* (Vol. 23, No. 10, October, 2001, pp. 94)

Pub: Hispanic Business

Description: A listing of corporations seeking multicultural and bilingual candidates for various positions is listed, along with information for submitting resumes.

39556 ■ **"Recruitment: Federal File"** in *Hispanic Business* (December 2002, pp. FRG4)

Pub: Hispanic Business

Description: Information on future U.S. postal service, head start programs, the federal government's General Schedule that determines salaries, and personnel security is offered.

39557 ■ **"Regional Leaders Search for Solutions to Water Problems"** in *Orlando Business Journal* (Vol. 20, No. 13, September 12, 2003, pp. 32)

Pub: American City Business Journals, Inc.

Ed: Noelle Haner-Dorr. Description: The future of the water supply of Central Florida has brought together a coalition of political and business leaders. The rapid growth in the area, in which the population has grown to 1.75 million people, has focused public attention on water resources.

39558 ■ **"Reproduction Right"** in *Fast Company* (July 2001, pp. 52)

Pub: Fast Company

Ed: Alison Overholt. Description: Profile of the SiPix Pocket Printer A6, from SiPix Inc. The SiPix Pocket Printer A6 is a handheld peripheral that is as light as a Discman and is small enough to slip into a briefcase.

39559 ■ **"Requisite Relief"** in *Entrepreneur. com* (Vol. 34, January 2006, No. 1, pp. 26)

Pub: Entrepreneur Media Inc.

Ed: Joshua Kurlantzick. Description: Programs that would benefit small businesses hurt by the hurricanes of 2005 are discussed by various entrepreneurs.

39560 ■ **"Resource Directory"** in *Entrepreneur* (Vol. 32, August 2004, No. 8, pp. 53)

Pub: Entrepreneur Media Inc.

Description: A listing of resources of interest to small businesses is presented, along with contact information and brief descriptions.

39561 ■ **"Retirement-Plan Administer To Be Bought For $115 Million"** in *Wall Street Journal* (Vol. 248, December 2006, No. 149, pp. C5)

Pub: Dow Jones & Co. Inc.

Ed: Wall Street Journal News Description: Charles Schwab Corp. acquires 401(K) Co. for $115 million. 401(K) overseas $22 billion in retirement assets.

39562 ■ *The RFA at 25: Needed Improvements for Small Business Regulatory Relief*

Pub: United States Government Printing Office

Released: February 2006. Price: $62.00. Description: Information regarding the hearing on needed improvements for small business regulatory relief before the Committee on Small Business, House of Representatives, One Hundred Ninth Congress, First Session, Washington, DC, March 16, 2005 is provided.

39563 ■ **"Right From Wrong"** in *Journal of Business Ethics* (Vol. 46, No. 1, Aug. 2003)

Pub: Kluwer Academic Publishers Group

Ed: Robert A. Giacalone, Carole L. Jurkiewicz. Description: A network sample of 162 employees across the U.S. was studied to assess the relationship between individual spirituality and perceptions of unethical business activities.

39564 ■ **"Roger Cass the Last Optimist"** in *Fast Company* (July 2001, pp. 88)

Pub: Fast Company

Ed: Harriet Rubin. Description: Profile of Roger Cass, the man who invented the idea of the Long Boom, or, the notion that we're only seven years into a 27-year expansion.

39565 ■ **"Room for More"** in *Business First Columbus* (Vol. 18, No. 38, May)

Pub: Business First Columbus, Inc.

Ed: Lisa Hooker. Description: Owners of small businesses find that donating services can benefit charities. Greater Relocation Group, a Columbus, Ohio moving and storage company volunteers by storing items for the Komen Columbus Race for the Cure, which contributes funds for breast cancer treatment, services and education.

39566 ■ **"SEC Offers Small Banks Internal Controls Leeway"** in *American Banker* (Vol. 171, December 14, 2006, No. 239, pp. 3)

Pub: SourceMedia, Inc.

Ed: Ben Jackson. Description: American Bankers Association is supporting the Securities and Exchanges Commission's move to give small companies, including most community banks, more flexibility within the Sarbanes-Oxley Act of 2002. The proposal would ease the compliance burden for small banks.

39567 ■ *The Secret of Exiting Your Business Under Your Terms!*

Pub: Outskirts Press, Incorporated

Ed: Gene H. Irwin. Released: August 2005. Price: $29.95. Description: Topics include how to sell a business for the highest value, tax laws governing the sale of a business, finding the right buyer, mergers and acquisitions, negotiating the sale, and using a limited auction to increase future value of a business.

39568 ■ **"Seeing the Light"** in *Entrepreneur* (Vol. 33, September 2005, No. 9, pp. 92)

Pub: Entrepreneur Media Inc.

Ed: Chris Penttila. Description: It is predicted that a move to extend daylight savings time would be an economic boom to small businesses. Consumers would spend the extra daylight time shopping, dining at restaurants, working out at fitness centers, etc.

39569 ■ **"Self-Employed Boost the Economic Recovery"** in *Wall Street Journal* (December 1, 2003, pp. A2)

Pub: Dow Jones & Co. Inc.

Ed: Jon E. Hilsenrath. Description: Small businesses are aiding in the economic recovery.

39570 ■ **"Sense and reliability: A conversation with celebrated psychologist Karl E. Weick"** in *Harvard Business Review* (Vol. 81, No. 4, Apr. 2003)

Pub: Harvard Business School Press

Ed: Diane Coutu. Description: A noted psychologist examines the characteristics of high-reliability organizations, such as nuclear plants, firefighting units, and emergency rooms. Corporations can learn much from these organizations that cannot afford surprises in the workplace.

39571 ■ **"September 11, 2001. A CEO's story"** in *Harvard Business Review* (Vol. 80, No. 10, October 2002, pp. 58)

Pub: Harvard Business School Press

Ed: Jeffrey W. Greenberg. Description: Marsh & McLennan Companies' offices in the World Trade Center were destroyed on September 11, 2001. Jeffrey W. Greenberg, chairman of Marsh & McLennan Companies Inc., recounts his immediate response to the airplane attack, efforts to save lives, locate people, recapture company data, help with the healing, inspire confidence, and generally insure that the company and its employees were able to continue.

39572 ■ *Serves You Right!*

Pub: Serves You Right!, Incorporated

Ed: Susan Brooks. Released: May 2004. Price: $15. 95. Description: Profile of excellence in customer service.

39573 ■ **"Service with a smile"** in *Entrepreneur* (Vol. 30, No. 2, February 2002, pp. 66)

Pub: Entrepreneur Media Inc.

Ed: Steven C. Bahls, Jane Easter Bahls. Description: The legal aspects for managing employees who are signed up with the armed forces reserves are discussed.

39574 ■ Setting the Table: The Transforming Power of Hospitality in Business
Pub: HarperCollins Publishers Inc.
Released: October 2006.

39575 ■ "Severe Storm Watch" in Inc. (August 1, 2003)
Pub: Gruner & Jahr USA Publishing
Ed: Rod Kurtz. Description: Small business owners must understand the need to protect companies from potential storm damage if they are in an area prone to hurricanes. The U.S. Small Business Administration paid out 5,458 business recovery loans for more than $257 million from small business losses due to Hurricane Andrew.

39576 ■ Simplified Incorporation Kit
Pub: Nova Publishing Company
Ed: Daniel Sitarz. Released: March 2007. Price: $19.95. Description: Kit includes all the forms, instructions, and information necessary for incorporating any small business in any state (CD-ROM included).

39577 ■ Six SIGMA for Small Business
Pub: Entrepreneur Press
Ed: Greg Brue. Released: October 2005. Price: $19.95 (US), $26.95 (Canadian). Description: Jack Welch's Six SIGMA approach to business covers accounting, finance, sales and marketing, buying a business, human resource development, and new product development.

39578 ■ Small Business: An Entrepreneur's Business Plan
Pub: South-Western
Ed: J.D Ryan, Gail P. Hiduke. Released: June 2005. Price: $90.95. Description: Assistance in preparing a business plan that identifies opportunities and ways to target a customer market.

39579 ■ Small Business: An Entrepreneur's Plan
Pub: Nelson Thomson Learning
Ed: Ronald A. Knowles. Released: December 2006. Description: Entrepreneur's guide to planning a small business.

39580 ■ The Small Business Bible: Everything You Need to Know to Succeed in Your Small Business
Pub: John Wiley & Sons, Incorporated
Ed: Steven D. Strauss. Released: December 2004. Price: $19.95 (US), $28.99 (Canadian). Description: Comprehensive guide to starting and running a successful small business. Topics include bookkeeping and financial management, marketing, publicity, and advertising.

39581 ■ Small Business, Big Life: Five Steps to Creating a Great Life with Your Own Small Business
Pub: Rutledge Books Inc.
Ed: Louis Barajas. Released: May 2007. Price: $22.99. Description: Five steps for planning, starting and running a small business, while maintaining a good life, are presented.

39582 ■ "Small Business on the Big Screen" in My Business (November/December 2001, pp. 36-39)
Pub: My Business Magazine
Ed: Tom Ehrenfeld. Description: Entrepreneurs are rarely represented in a realistic manner in movies. A preview of the Top Ten small business movies and the messages they deliver on running a company, as well as several television sitcoms that focus on small businesses, are highlighted.

39583 ■ Small Business Desk Reference
Pub: Penguin Books (USA) Incorporated
Ed: Gene Marks. Released: December 2004. Price: $29.95 (US), $44.00 (Canadian). Description: Comprehensive guide for starting or running a successful small business, focusing on buying a business or franchise, writing a business plan, financial management, accounting, legal issues, human resources management, operations, marketing, sales, customer service, taxes, insurance, and ethics. Information for launching a restaurant, property management firm, retail outlet, consulting firm, and service business is included.

39584 ■ "Small Business Growth: Intention, Ability, and Opportunity" in Journal of Small Business Management (Vol. 41, No. 4, October 2003)
Pub: International Council of Small Business
Ed: Alison Morrison, John Breen, Shameem Ali. Description: Small businesses are recognized as vital contributors to economic development, job creation, and general health and welfare of economies, representing a significant proportion of the world economy.

39585 ■ A Small Business Handbook
Pub: Key Porter Books
Ed: Susan Kennedy-Loewen. Released: April 2002. Price: $16.95. Description: Guidebook for small business owners.

39586 ■ Small Business Legal Strategies
Pub: Aspatore Books, Incorporated
Released: July 2004. Price: $37.95. Description: Corporate Chairs and Partners from top firms in the U.S. offering insight into selecting, engaging, employing, and benefiting from external corporate counsel for the small business owner or executive.

39587 ■ Small Business Sourcebook
Pub: Gale Group
Released: July 2005. Price: $430.00. Description: Two-volume guide to more than 27,300 listings of live and print sources for small business startups as well as small business growth and development. Over 30,500 topics are included.

39588 ■ Small Business Survival Guide
Pub: Adams Media Corporation
Ed: Cliff Ennico. Price: $12.95.

39589 ■ Small Business Survival Guide: Starting, Protecting, and Securing Your Business for Long-Term Success
Pub: Adams Media Corporation
Ed: Cliff Ennico. Released: October 2005. Price: $12.95 (US), $17.95 (Canadian). Description: Entrepreneurship in the new millennium. Topics include creditors, taxes, competition, business law, and accounting.

39590 ■ Small Business Taxes 2006: Your Complete Guide to a Better Bottom Line
Pub: John Wiley & Sons, Incorporated
Ed: Barbara Weltman. Released: November 2005. Price: $16.95 (US), $21.99 (Canadian). Description: Detailed information on new tax laws and IRS rules for small businesses.

39591 ■ Small Business Taxes Made Easy: How to Increase Your Deductions, Reduce What You Owe, and Boost Your Profits
Pub: McGraw-Hill Companies
Ed: Eva Rosenberg. Released: December 2004. Price: $16.95 (US), $24.95 (Canadian). Description: Tax expert gives advice to small business owners regarding tax issues. TaxMamma.com, run by Eva Rosenberg, is one of the top seven tax advice Websites on the Internet.

39592 ■ Small Business Turnaround
Pub: Adams Media Corporation
Ed: Marc Kramer. Price: $17.95 paperback.

39593 ■ "Small Businesses Are Engine to American Economy" in Atlanta Business Chronicle (Vol. 24, No. 9, August 3, 2001, pp. 10B)
Pub: American City Business Journals Inc.
Ed: Paige Bowers. Description: Senator Max Cleland discusses what he has done in support of small business in America. The Senator's support includes reducing taxes on small businesses, broadening health care options and boosting the opportunities for minority and women-owned enterprises.

39594 ■ Small Businesses and Workplace Fatality Risk: An Exploratory Analysis
Pub: RAND Corporation
Ed: John F. Mendeloff; Christopher Nelson; Kilkon Ko. Released: June 2006. Price: $20.00. Description: According to previous research, small business worksites report higher rates of deaths or serious injuries than larger corporations. Statistical data included.

39595 ■ A Small Enterprise
Pub: Lulu.com
Ed: Tsvi Reiss. Released: October 2005. Price: $16.36. Description: Eleven issues involved in the process of completion for Small Enterprise Management.

39596 ■ Small Giants: Companies that Choose to Be Great Instead of Big
Pub: Penguin Group
Ed: Bo Burllingham. Price: $19.96.

39597 ■ Small and Medium-Sized Enterprises in Countries in Transition
Pub: United Nations Publications
Released: January 2005. Price: $18.00. Description: Characteristics of small and medium enterprise (SME) sector in transition countries and emerging market economies.

39598 ■ "Small businesses dissatisfied with SBA" in Black Enterprise (Vol. 31, No. 5, December 2000, pp. 29)
Pub: Earl Graves Publishing Co.
Ed: Joyce Jones. Description: A report issued by the General Accounting Office (GAO) shows that the Small Business Administration is not effective in securing contracts for 8(a) program participants.

39599 ■ "Smart Businesses See Value, and Profit, in Promoting Women" in Crain's Chicago Business (Vol. 30, February 2007, No. 6, pp. 30)
Pub: Crain Communications, Inc.
Ed: Marc J. Lane. Description: Despite U.S. corporations making little progress in advancing women to leadership positions over the past ten years, enlightened corporate decision makers understand that gender diversity is good business as the highest percentages of women officers yielded, on average, a 34 percent higher total return to shareholders and a 35.1 percent higher return on equity than those firms with the lowest percentages of women officers, according to a 2004 Catalyst study of Fortune 500 companies.

39600 ■ "Smart growth advocates push for change" in Atlanta Business Chronicle (Vol. 24, No. 14, September 7, 2001, pp. 10C)
Pub: American City Business Journals Inc.
Description: Several participants from various organizations took part in a discussion by Atlanta Business Chronicle focusing on Smart Growth. Those present were Steve Macauley, Dough Spohn, Dan Reuter, Billy Mitchell, Jim Durrett, Kevin Green, Egbert Perry, Sam Williams, Larry Frank, M. von Nkosi, Hattie Dorsey, Gregg T. Logan, and Ron Terwilliger.

39601 ■ SME Cluster Development: A Dynamic View on Survival Clusters in Developing Countries
Pub: Palgrave Macmillan
Ed: Mario Davide Parrilli. Released: April 2007. Price: $90.00. Description: Survival clustering in developing countries is discussed in order to increase effectiveness of policy-making and development operations in local contexts.

39602 ■ "The Social Security Conundrum" in Hispanic Business (Vol. 23, No. 10, October, 2001, pp. 36, 38)
Pub: Hispanic Business
Ed: Patricia Guadalupe. Description: As debate over proposals to privatize portions of Social Security, one thing is beyond dispute, the status quo is not an option. Social Security rates of return for average-income Hispanic Americans are discussed. Statistical data included.

39603 ■ "Solving the regional puzzle" in Crain's Detroit Business (Vol. 19, No. 17, April 28, 2003, pp. 1)
Pub: Crain Communications Inc., Detroit
Description: An introduction to a survey conducted by Crain's Detroit Business regarding regional issues affecting business and the economy in the Detroit area.

39604 ■ *The Starfish and the Spider*
Pub: Portfolio
Ed: Ori Brafman; Rod A. Beckstrom. **Released:** 2007.
Price: $24.95.

39605 ■ *Start Small, Finish Big*
Pub: Warner Business Books
Ed: Fred DeLuca. **Price:** $14.95.

39606 ■ "Staying power" in *Black Enterprise*
(Vol. 32, No. 9, April 2002, pp. 108)
Pub: Earl Graves Publishing Co.
Ed: Sonia Alleyne. **Description:** Five critical factors
in acquiring and maintaining a vice presidential posi-
tion in a company are outlined.

39607 ■ "Stopping Office Snoops" in *Inc.*
(November 1, 2003)
Pub: Gruner & Jahr USA Publishing
Ed: Patrick J. Sauer. **Description:** Review of the
book, The Spy's Guide: Office Espionage? The book
offers CIA-style tips for anyone running a small business.

39608 ■ *Strategic Entrepreneurship*
Pub: Prentice Hall PTR
Ed: Philip A. Wickham. **Released:** September 2006.
Price: $90.00. **Description:** Conceptual and practical
ideas for managing a small business are explored.

39609 ■ *Strategizing, Disequilibrium, and
Profit*
Pub: Stanford University Press
Ed: John A. Mathews. **Released:** June 2006. **Price:**
$24.95. **Description:** Author proposes the use of a
conceptual framework that is consistent with real
economies instead of equilibrium-based foundations
when creating a business strategy.

39610 ■ "Street Smarts: The King and I" in
Inc. (July 1, 2003)
Pub: Gruner & Jahr USA Publishing
Ed: Norm Brodsky. **Description:** A visit with a king
provides unexpected lessons for small business own-
ers.

39611 ■ *Streetwise Small Business Book of
Lists: Hundreds of Lists to Help You Reduce
Costs, Increase Revenues, and Boost Your
Profits!*
Pub: Adams Media Corporation
Ed: Gene Marks. **Released:** September 2006. **Price:**
$25.95. **Description:** Strategies to help small busi-
ness owners locate services, increase sales, and
lower expenses.

39612 ■ "Student teachers" in *Entrepreneur*
(Vol. 30, No. 10, October 2002, pp. 93)
Pub: Entrepreneur Media Inc.
Ed: Nichole L. Torres. **Description:** Information about
small business participation in Emory University's
business school competition is provided.

39613 ■ "Study" in *Crain's Detroit Business*
(Vol. 18, No. 18, May 6, 2002, pp. 6)
Pub: Crain Communications Inc. - Detroit
Ed: Amy Lane. **Description:** Michigan ranks well
against competitor states on many business factors,
but remains bogged down by high business costs, according to a study performed by SRI International, formerly known as the Stanford Research Institute. The
study compared Michigan with 17 other states.

39614 ■ "Study: State 12th-best for small
biz" in *Crain's Detroit Business* (Vol. 17, No.
44, October 22, 2001, pp. 20)
Pub: Crain Communications, Inc.
Ed: Laura Bailey. **Description:** The state of Michigan
was rated the 12th-most friendly state for entrepreneurs by a recent study conducted by the Small Business Survival Committee. The most business-friendly
state is Nevada, followed by South Dakota and Washington; lowest were Maine, Hawaii, Rhode Island, and
the District of Columbia.

39615 ■ "Study: Women Executives Want
Corner Office, Too" in *Miami Herald* (June
24, 2004)
Pub: Knight-Ridder/Tribune Business News
Ed: Gillian Wee. **Description:** According to a recent
survey, female officials aspire to be chief executives
at the same rate as male counterparts.

39616 ■ *Succeeding in Small Business: The
101 Toughest Problems and How to Solve
Them*
Pub: NAL Dutton
Ed: Jane Applegate. **Released:** 1992. **Price:** $13.95
(paper).

39617 ■ "Success: What's Your Definition?"
in *My Business* (December/January 2004, pp.
28-33, 52)
Pub: My Business Magazine
Ed: Rex Hammock, Shannon Scully. **Description:**
Profiles of successful entrepreneurs with discussions
on their definitions of success, including the ability to
help others achieve their potential, balancing work
and family, independence, loving your work, and the
ability to earn money.

39618 ■ *The Successful Entrepreneur's
Guidebook: Where You Are Now, Where You
Want to Be and How to Get There*
Pub: Kogan Page, Limited
Ed: Colin Barrow; Robert Brown. **Released:** January
2007. **Price:** $35.00. **Description:** Characteristics of
successful entrepreneurship are examined. The book
helps new business owners to develop and grow a
business.

39619 ■ *Successful Proposal Strategies for
Small Business: Using Knowledge
Management to Win Government, Private-
Sector, and International Contracts, Fourth E*
Pub: Artech House, Incorporated
Ed: Robert S. Frey. **Released:** February 2005. **Price:**
$99.00. **Description:** Front-end proposal planning
and storyboarding, focusing on the customer mission
in proposals, along with the development of grant pro-
posals.

39620 ■ "Support for Rapid-Growth Firms" in
Journal of Small Business Management
(Vol. 41, No. 4, October 2003, pp. 346)
Pub: International Council of Small Business
Ed: Eileen Fischer, A. Rebecca Reuber. **Description:**
Perspectives of small business owners, government
policymakers, and external resource providers on
ways rapid-growth firms should be supported.

39621 ■ "Survey: Small-biz owners seeing
better economic outlook ahead" in *Business
First Columbus* (Vol. 18, No. 25, February 8,
2002, pp. A3)
Pub: Business First Columbus, Inc.
Ed: Kathy Showalter. **Description:** According to a recent small business survey, owners feel optimistic
about the economy.

39622 ■ "Susan McMillan Appointed
Executive Director of the Long Island Better
Business Bureau" in *Long Island Business
News* (Feb. 6, 2004)
Pub: Dolan Media Newswires
Ed: Ryan McCormick. **Description:** Profile of Susan
McMillan, newly appointed executive director of the
Long Island Better Business Bureau. McMillan also
serves on the Consumer Affairs Committee of the Bar
Association of the City of New York and is an active
member of the Small Business Advisory Committee.

39623 ■ *Swimming Against the Tide*
Pub: Macmillan Publishers Limited
Ed: Tim Waterstone. **Released:** October 2006. **Price:**
$29.95. **Description:** Tim Waterstone shares ten
rules for creating successful small businesses.

39624 ■ "Sworn to secrecy" in *Women in
Business* (Vol. 53, No. 4, July-August, 2001,
pp. 22)
Pub: The ABWA Co. Inc.
Ed: Linda Helmig Braun, Mary Ann Clift. **Description:**
Issues concerning ethical aspects of secrecy are dis-

cussed. Particular attention is given to reasons for
keeping or disclosing a secret, emphasizing that according to the situation it could be more harmful to
keep the secret rather than disclose it.

39625 ■ "Take a Peek: What Does Congress
Have in Mind for 2005?" in *Entrepreneur*
(Vol. 33, January 2005, No. 1, pp. 27)
Pub: Entrepreneur Media Inc.
Ed: Stephen Barlas. **Description:** Agenda set by
Congress for 2005, and how it relates to business, is
examined.

39626 ■ "Telemarketers Plan to Do-Not-Call"
in *Providence Business News* (Vol. 18, No.
20, September 1, 2003, pp. 1)
Pub: Providence Business News, Inc.
Ed: Mike Colias. **Description:** The possible effect of
the Do-Not-Call list will have on the direct marketing
industry is examined. Topics include business closures, layoffs, and economic hardship.

39627 ■ *The Ten Faces of Innovation*
Pub: Doubleday Broadway Publishing Group
Ed: Tom Kelley. **Price:** $29.95.

39628 ■ "This just in" in *Crain's Detroit
Business* (Vol. 19, No. 17, April 28, 2003, pp.
1)
Pub: Crain Communications Inc., Detroit
Ed: Brett Snavely, Laura Bailey, Robert Ankeny. **De-
scription:** AlixPartners LLC, based in Southfield,
Michigan has landed the high-profile bankrupt Flem-
ing Cos. Inc., Dallas, Texas. Quadrants Inc. of Wixom,
Michigan plans to develop a $55 million, 68-acre in-
dustrial park in Green Oak Township, Michigan.

39629 ■ *This Is Not Your Parents'
Retirement: A Revolutionary Guide for a
Revolutionary Generation*
Pub: Entrepreneur Press
Ed: Patrick P. Astre. **Released:** July 2005. **Price:**
$19.95 (US), $26.95 (Canadian). **Description:** Mutual
funds, stocks, bonds, insurance products, and tax
strategies for retirement planning.

39630 ■ "Tips for collecting performance
numbers" in *Crain's Detroit Business* (Vol.
19, No. 3, January 20, 2003, pp. 14)
Pub: Crain Communications Inc., Detroit
Description: Key indicators for checking small business performance are listed. It is advised that the indicators be reported regularly, and the use of software
programs, called dashboard products, can help track
performance numbers.

39631 ■ "Tips & Trends" in *Small Business
Opportunities* (Vol. 13, No. 5, September
2001, pp. 14)
Pub: Harris Publications, Inc.
Description: The latest tips and trends for small business are presented, including the Fastsigns International, Inc. franchisor; VeriPack.com shipping
company; Seaga Manufacturing, supplier of compact
vending machines and refrigerated venders; the wireless handheld device LinkPoint 9000; and the Motorola Spirit GT walkie-talkie.

39632 ■ "To Join Or Not To Join? Trade
Groups Can Boost Business-If You Pick the
Right One" in *Black Enterprise* (Vol. 34, No.
3, October 2003)
Pub: Earl Graves Publishing Co.
Ed: Bridget McCrea. **Description:** Issues to keep in
mind before joining a trade group are presented, including the ways trade groups provide networking opportunities for entrepreneurs to help grow a small
business.

39633 ■ "Top 10 Business Schools for
Hispanics" in *Hispanic Business* (September
2004, pp. 78, 80, 82, 84)
Pub: Hispanic Business
Description: The top ten business schools for Hispanics are profiled. Stanford University, Yale University, and New York University were listed as the top
three, respectively.

39634 ■ "Tough Sell" in *Black Enterprise* (Vol. 37, October 2006, No. 3, pp. 92)
Pub: Earl G. Graves Publishing Co. Inc.
Ed: Sonia Alleyne. **Description:** Career coaches can evaluate your talents and skills. In an era where more companies are downsizing a coach can help you decide if you are suited for your industry or should try switching careers.

39635 ■ "Tough Times build character" in *Fast Company* (May 2001, pp. 86)
Pub: Fast Company
Ed: Sir John Marks Templeton. **Description:** Profile of Sir John Marks Templeton who founded many investment funds, included the Templeton Growth Fund, which averaged 15.2 percent a year during its 45-year history, exceeding all other mutual funds during that time.

39636 ■ *Trading Places: SMEs in the Global Economy, A Critical Research Handbook*
Pub: Edward Elgar Publishing, Incorporated
Ed: Lloyd-Reason. **Released:** September 2006. **Price:** $110.00. **Description:** An overview of international research for small and medium-sized companies wishing to expand in the global economy.

39637 ■ "Traffic Turn Says Downriver Site, Public Money Best for Border" in *Crain's Detroit Business* (Vol. 21, January 31, 2005, No. 5, pp. 42)
Pub: Crain Communications Inc. - Detroit
Ed: Michelle Martinez. **Description:** Details of a study recommending a bridge location for a second border crossing between Windsor, Ontario, Canada, and Detroit, Michigan are reported.

39638 ■ "Tragic taste" in *Entrepreneur* (Vol. 30, No. 1, January 2002, p)
Pub: Entrepreneur Media Inc.
Ed: Michelle Prather. **Description:** Since the September terrorist attacks, Atlanta-based Zyman Marketing Group suggests that the political climate cannot be separated from the marketing climate and as Americans strive to return to normal, marketing tactics cannot.

39639 ■ "Trailblazing Entrepreneurs Prove that Hot Businesses Aren't Always Found in Industry Hotbeds" in *My Business* (February/March 2004)
Pub: My Business Magazine
Ed: Gwen Moran. **Description:** It is sometimes harder to create a new business concept when immersed in large cities like Los Angeles, California or New York City.

39640 ■ "Transitions" in *Inc.* (Volume 28, January 2006, No. 1, pp. 27)
Pub: Inc. Magazine
Description: Three key institutions, the Federal Reserve Board, the National Federation of Independent Business, and the Congressional Budget Office are changing leaders in 2006.

39641 ■ "The trouble I've seen" in *Harvard Business Review* (Vol. 80, No. 3, March 2002, pp. 42)
Pub: Harvard Business School Press
Ed: David N. James. **Description:** The experiences of crisis manager, David N. James, are profiled. James has 30 years of experience and offers advice about rescuing companies about to go under.

39642 ■ "Trust toppers" in *Realtor Magazine* (Vol. 35, No. 9, September 2002, pp. 22)
Pub: Real Estate University
Description: A USA Today/CNN Gallup Poll finds that Americans place high trust in small business owners. Raj Nisankarao of the National Business Association says this is because of the one-on-one relationship small business owners are able to develop with customers.

39643 ■ "Turn Public Problems into Private Account" in *Harvard Business Review* (Vol. 81, No. 8, August 2003, pp. 129)
Pub: Harvard Business School Press
Ed: Rodman C. Rockefeller. **Description:** Four criteria are offered to guide companies looking to balance philanthropy and corporate earnings.

39644 ■ "$25M to Aid Slow Border Crossings on Fast Track" in *Crain's Detroit Business* (V. 17, No. 44, 10/22/2001)
Pub: Crain Communications, Inc.
Ed: Terry Kosdrosky. **Description:** Forty percent of all trade between Canada and the U.S. occurs at the Detroit-Windsor border. A new proposal would give the U.S. Customs Service an additional $25 million for more officers in order to ease delays at the border crossings since the 9-11 terrorist attack.

39645 ■ "200 Best Small Companies" in *Forbes* (Vol. 170,No. 9, October 28, 2002, pp. 227)
Pub: Forbes Magazine
Ed: Katrina Keller, Cecily J. Fluke. **Description:** Over the past 12 months, sales growth has increased some 17 percent for the 200 best small companies listed by Forbes; earnings rose 23 percent.

39646 ■ "2003 Black Enterprise Convention Calendar" in *Black Enterprise* (Vol. 33, No. 6, January 2003)
Pub: Earl Graves Publishing Co.
Description: The 2003 Black Enterprise convention calendar is presented.

39647 ■ "The 2003 HBR List: Breakthrough Ideas for Tomorrow" in *Harvard Business Review* (Vol. 81, No. 4, 4/03, pp. 92)
Pub: Harvard Business School Press
Description: The editors consider strategy, organizations and leadership in the light of the events of the past year. They ponder the role of the leader, soft issues such as emotional intelligence and the unavoidable messiness of organizations.

39648 ■ *The Ugly Truth About Small Business: 50 Things That Can Go Wrong... and What You Can Do About It*
Pub: Sourcebooks, Incorporated
Ed: Ruth King. **Released:** November 2005. **Price:** $14.95. **Description:** More than 50 percent of small businesses fail within their first year and 95 percent fail within the first five years.

39649 ■ *Ultimate Guide to Project Management*
Pub: Entrepreneurial Press
Ed: Sid Kemp. **Released:** October 2005. **Price:** $29.95 (US), $39.95 (Canadian). **Description:** Project management strategies including writing a business plan and developing a good advertising campaign.

39650 ■ *Ultimate Small Business Advisor*
Pub: Entrepreneur Press
Ed: Andi Axman. **Released:** May 2007. **Price:** $30.95. **Description:** Tip for starting and running a small business, including new tax rulings and laws affecting small business, are shared.

39651 ■ "Unemployment changes are 'mixed bag' for business, labor" in *Crain's Detroit Business* (Vol. 18, No. 15, 2002, pp. 6)
Pub: Crain Communications Inc. - Detroit
Ed: Amy Lane. **Description:** An explanation of the recent changes to Michigan's unemployment benefits. Statistical data included.

39652 ■ "Union Station Has the Blues Over Loss of Hockey, Low Sales" in *St. Louis Post-Dispatch* (January 13, 2005)
Pub: Knight-Ridder/Tribune Business News
Ed: Martin Van Der Werf. **Description:** The loss of St. Louis hockey games has owners of kiosks at Union Station reporting slow to no sales, along with restaurants and gift shops in the station.

39653 ■ "U.S. Soldier Returns from Iraq to Find How His Business Fared" in *Small Business Opportunities* (January 2006)
Pub: Harris Publications Inc.
Description: Joe Witte, vice-president and partner for CentricSource.com offers advice to soldiers leaving for overseas duties as well as issues when returning from active duty.

39654 ■ "Vector Marketing" in *Mississippi Business Journal* (Vol. 29, January 2007, No. 2, pp. 6)
Pub: Venture Publications, Inc.
Description: Profile of Rebecca Huckeby, of Vector Marketing. Huckeby placed in the Top 25 sales reps from more than 40,000 sales representatives nationwide.

39655 ■ "Voice of America" in *Fortune* (Vol. 151, June 27, 2005, No. 13 pp. F184)
Pub: Time Inc.
Ed: David Whitford. **Description:** The National Federation of Independent Business (NFIB) believes small business directly impacts the economy of the U.S.

39656 ■ "WaMu Whiplash: Fast Expansion Yields Problems" in *Wall Street Journal* (Vol. 248, December 2006, No. 142, pp. B1)
Pub: Dow Jones & Co. Inc.
Ed: Ann Carrns **Description:** Despite rapid growth from 2000-2003, Washington Mutual Bank has closed 80 branches and halted entering new markets.

39657 ■ "Wanted: stimulus: report says GOP is not doing all it can for small business" in *Black Enterprise* (Vol. 33, No. 7, Feb. 2003)
Pub: Earl Graves Publishing Co.
Ed: Joyce Jones. **Description:** Federal funding and legislation important to small business is discussed.

39658 ■ *Ward's Business Directory of U.S. Private and Public Companies*
Pub: Thomson Gale
Ed: Deborah J. Baker, Editor. **Released:** Annual, latest edition 47; September, 2004; volumes 1 to 8 and supplement. **Covers:** approximately 114,500 companies, 90% of which are privately owned, representing all industries. **Entries Include:** Company name, address, phone, fax, toll-free, e-mail, URL, names and titles of up to five officers, up to four Standard Industrial Classification (SIC) codes, NAICS code, revenue figure, number of employees, year founded, ticker symbol, stock exchange, immediate parent, fiscal year end, import/export, type of company (public, private, subsidiary, etc.). In Vol. 4, lists of top 1,000 privately held companies ranked by sales vol., top 1,000 publicly held companies ranked by sales volume, and top 1,000 employers ranked by number of employees; analyses of public and private companies by state, revenue per employee for top 1,000 companies, public and private companies by SIC code and NAICS code. In volume 5, national Standard Industrial Classification (SIC) code rankings are listed, while volumes 6 and 7 lists Standard Industrial Classification (SIC) code rankings by state. In all volumes, guide to abbreviations, codes, and symbols; explanation of classification system; numerical and alphabetical listings of SIC and NAICS codes. In volume 8, NAICS rankings. In the supplement, 10,000 new listings not contained in the main edition are included. **Arrangement:** Volumes 1, 2, and 3, alphabetical; volume 4 is geographical by state, then ascending zip; volume 5 is classified by 4-digit SIC code, then ranked by sales; volumes 6 and 7 are classified by Standard Industrial Classification (SIC) code within state; volume 8 classified by NAICS, then ranked; supplement arranged alphabetical and Standard Industrial Classification (SIC) code. **Indexes:** Company name index in volumes 5, 7, and 8.

39659 ■ "Washington Insider: Small Business Overlooked?" in *Hispanic Business* (March 2003, pp. 16)
Pub: Hispanic Business
Ed: Patricia Guadalupe. **Description:** Initiatives to address the current economic slowdown and its effect

on minority entrepreneurs is addressed. Also discussed is the Small Business Administration's Internet site designed to assist small business owners with employees serving in the military reserves.

39660 ■ "Weathering the Storm; True, things have been better for the nation's entrepreneurs" in *Business Week Online* (November 18, 2002)
Pub: McGraw-Hill Inc.
Ed: Alison Ogden. **Description:** According to a new survey conducted by the National Federation of Independent Businesses, small businesses are holding their own in the slow economy, and have defied the uncertain trends from the threats of terrorism and corporate scandals.

39661 ■ "A Web Wake-Up; Posting of OU Student's Paper Turns Into Lesson That Helps Define Defamation in a New Medium" in *Crain's Detroit Business*
Pub: Crain Communications Inc. - Detroit
Ed: Andrew Dietderich. **Description:** Posting of student papers on the Internet can be a wake-up call for small businesses. An Oakland University professor posted an essay written by a student that contained statements about the student's former employer, who sued the school, student and professor when it discovered the paper through an Internet search.

39662 ■ "Webvan, Microsoft, and the second-mover advantage" in *Red Herring* (No. 102, August 15, 2001, pp. 100)
Pub: Herring Communications
Ed: Jason Pontin. **Description:** Discussion regarding the second-mover advantage. The rule of the second-mover advantage states that, market dominance rarely goes to the pluck startup that first releases a product, but to the second company, sometimes an established business, that most effectively markets and sells the products, and which then gives the best customer service.

39663 ■ "What are you complaining about?" in *Fast Company* (May 2001, pp. 66)
Pub: Fast Company
Ed: Cheryl Dahle. **Description:** Many companies are stuck in the gripe mode, but Harvard researchers Robert Kegan and Lisa Laskow Lahey have a prescription to turn complaints into an agenda for change.

39664 ■ "What Am I Worth? How to Increase Your Value to Your Company" in *Black Enterprise* (Vol. 36, November 2005, No. 4, pp. 76)
Pub: Earl G. Graves Publishing Co. Inc.
Ed: Tennille M. Robinson. **Description:** As a business owner, setting your worth will help leverage monetary compensation as well as provide a better self-awareness of your role within your firm.

39665 ■ "What Empowerment Requires" in *Black Enterprise* (Vol. 33, No. 7, February 2003, pp. 9)
Pub: Earl Graves Publishing Co.
Ed: Earl G. Graves, Jr. **Description:** How the midterm elections will affect African Americans as individuals and small business owners is discussed.

39666 ■ "What Goes Up: Now There's a New Way to Track Small Business's Ups and Downs" in *Entrepreneur* (Vol. 32, No. 1, January 2004, pp. 30)
Pub: Entrepreneur Media, Inc.
Description: The Small Business Index (SBI) will help entrepreneurs track 19 economic indicators affecting small businesses. The indicators are grouped in four categories: costs factors, credit conditions, industry metrics, and trade competitiveness.

39667 ■ "Whatever it takes" in *BlackEnterprise* (Vol. 32, No. 3, October 2001, pp. 54)
Pub: Earl Graves Publishing Co.
Ed: Mark Richard Moss. **Description:** Review of the publication, 'Off-the-Wall Marketing Ideas.' The book offers advice on such diverse topics as business card design, generating publicity and "Pro Bono: Civic Marketing."

39668 ■ "What's the Biggest Problem in American Business? An Excess of Loyalty" in *Inc.* (May 1, 2005)
Pub: Inc. Magazine
Ed: Adam Hanft. **Description:** The difference between loyalty and trust in the world of business are discussed.

39669 ■ "What's your real cost of capital?" in *Harvard Business Review* (Vol. 80, No. 10, October 2002, pp. 114)
Pub: Harvard Business School Press
Ed: James J. McNulty. **Description:** The article suggests that corporate capital asset pricing models are flawed and provides a new analysis technique.

39670 ■ "What's the Deal?" in *Entrepreneur* (Vol. 31, No. 10, October 2003, pp. 34)
Pub: Entrepreneur Media, Inc.
Ed: Mark Hendricks. **Description:** Book review of, "The Only Negotiating Guide You'll Ever Need", written by Peter B. Stark and Jane Flaherty. Stark and Flaherty, both business consultants, stress that negotiators must always consider the other side's needs in order to win repeat customers and develop strong vendor relationships.

39671 ■ "What's the Plan? How President Bush's Second-Term Agenda Will Affect You" in *Entrepreneur* (Vol. 33, January 2005, No. 1, pp. 24)
Pub: Entrepreneur Media Inc.
Ed: Crystal Detamore-Rodman. **Description:** President Bush is expected to carryover his first term agenda of making his income tax cuts permanent, a permanent repeal of estate tax, and an expansion of health savings accounts.

39672 ■ "What's on Your Agenda?" in *Fast Company* (June 2001, pp. 85)
Pub: Fast Company
Description: Fast Company asked ten senior executives and thinkers to explain the most crucial item on their particular leadership agenda.

39673 ■ "What's Your Company Worth Now?" in *Inc.* (July 1, 2003)
Pub: Gruner & Jahr USA Publishing
Description: Information for calculating a small company's value is offered.

39674 ■ "When a partner doesn't work out" in *My Business* (November/December 2001, pp. 48)
Pub: My Business Magazine
Ed: Denise O'Berry. **Description:** Issues to consider before starting a business with a partner are examined.

39675 ■ "When Duty Calls" in *Entrepreneur* (Vol. 28, No. 3, March 2000, pp. 127)
Pub: Entrepreneur Media Inc.
Ed: Jacquelyn Lynn. **Description:** Know your responsibilities when it comes to employees on military leave.

39676 ■ "When You Speak, Lawmakers Listen" in *My Business* (June/July 2004, pp. 41)
Pub: My Business Magazine
Description: Lawmakers are interested in small business. The National Federation of Independent Business (NFIB) advocates for small business through its Member Ballot, the largest opinion-gathering effort of its type. Results are given to lawmakers. Currently issues revolved around employer retirement savings accounts, postal rates, debit cards, project labor agreements, and OSHA regulations.

39677 ■ "Where can you improve? Get the numbers" in *Crain's Detroit Business* (Vol. 19, No. 3, January 20, 2003, pp. 14)
Pub: Crain Communications Inc., Detroit
Ed: Laura Bailey. **Description:** First article to appear under Crain's Detroit Business's Small Business Solutions column. The column will offer advice from local small businesses for solving specific problems. This column address issues involved with time management.

39678 ■ "Which School is Right?" in *Hispanic Business* (September 2003, pp. 46)
Pub: Hispanic Business
Ed: Joel Russell. **Description:** For Hispanic students, selecting an MBA or a law school program involves academic, social, personal, and financial considerations.

39679 ■ "Who Gets Disaster Aid? Who Doesn't?" in *Business Week Online* (January 22, 2002)
Pub: McGraw-Hill, Inc.
Description: A decision by President Bush has made all small businesses across the nation affected by the terror attacks of September 11, 2001 eligible for government assistance. Statistical data included.

39680 ■ "Who has the next big idea?" in *Fast Company* (September 2001, pp. 108)
Pub: Fast Company
Ed: Daniel H. Pink. **Description:** Michael Hammer, consultant, author, evangelical business revolutionary, unleashed re-engineering on an unsuspecting public in the early 1990s, now he's back with a new book, a new agenda, and a bunch of new ideas.

39681 ■ "A Whole New Chamber" in *Hispanic Business* (November 2003, pp. 32, 34)
Pub: Hispanic Business
Ed: Joel Russell. **Description:** Leadership plots a new course for the U.S. Hispanic Chamber of Commerce. A listing of the newly elected U.S. Hispanic Chamber of Commerce Board is presented.

39682 ■ "Who's Next? Smart Moves" in *Entrepreneur* (Vol. 30, No. 3, March 2002, pp. 77)
Pub: Entrepreneur Media Inc.
Ed: Mark Hendricks. **Description:** The importance of having a plan for succession is stressed for all businesses.

39683 ■ "Why Hierarchies Thrive" in *Harvard Business Review* (Vol. 81, No. 3, March 2003, pp. 96)
Pub: Harvard Business School Press
Ed: Harold J. Leavit. **Description:** Despite the fact that hardly anyone likes them, hierarchies persist in business, because they fulfill the human need for order and security. However, they are always authoritarian.

39684 ■ "Why I Read Business Blogs Every Day" in *Inc.* (August 2005, pp. 104-106)
Pub: Inc. Magazine
Ed: Hillary Johnson. **Description:** Business blogs are being used to mentor entrepreneurs.

39685 ■ "Why Image Matters" in *My Business* (December/January 2003, pp. 28-31)
Pub: My Business Magazine
Ed: Shannon Scully. **Description:** Solutions for building a small business' image are explored, using various companies as examples, including a home remodeling company, garage door/window sales company, retail bicycle shop, candy and snack food manufacturer and retailer, and a public relations firm.

39686 ■ *Wikinomics: How Mass Collaboration Changes Everything*
Pub: Penguin Group
Ed: Don Tapscott. **Released:** November 2006. **Price:** $25.95. **Description:** Guide to collaborate plans change beliefs about business hierarchies.

39687 ■ "Will Power: What Would You Do If You Suddenly Inherited a Business?" in *Entrepreneur* (Vol. 32, September 2004, No. 9, pp. 28)
Pub: Entrepreneur Media Inc.
Ed: Geoff Williams. **Description:** When his friend died, Dave Buck inherited his business. Buck explains how he had to rely on his instincts and to also make changes to the company in order to make it his own.

39688 ■ *Winning!*
Pub: HarperCollins Publishers Inc.
Ed: Jack and Suzy Welch. Price: $27.95.

39689 ■ *The Wisdom of Crowds: Why the Many Are Smarter Than the Few and How Collective Wisdom Shapes Business, Economies, Societies and Nations*
Pub: Doubleday Canada, Limited
Ed: James Surrowiecki. Released: May 2004. Price: $24.95. Description: The premise that the many are smarter than the few and its impact on business, economics, societies and nations is discussed.

39690 ■ "Women Business Owners Seek Financing" in *Marketing to Women* (Vol. 19, December 2006, No. 2, pp. 8)
Pub: EPM Communications, Inc.
Description: A study by the Center for Women's Business Research shows that women business owners have become more savvy when seeking financial support for their business ventures. Statistical data included.

39691 ■ "Women Find 'Grass Ceiling' of Men-Only Clubs Impediment to Business" in *Chicago Tribune* (February 3, 2003)
Pub: Knight Ridder/Tribune Business News
Ed: Greg Burns. Description: Executive women speak out on the difficulties encountered when golf courses exclude them from grillrooms, member-guest tournaments and Saturday morning tee times. Maureen Grzelakowski decided to solve her problem by purchasing her own nine-hole golf course in the southwest suburbs of Chicago.

39692 ■ "Work and Play" in *Fast Company* (November 2001, pp. 48)
Pub: Fast Company
Ed: Alison Overholt. Description: Profile of the Shark MX personal digital assistant, which allows the user to move from game playing to sending and receiving email, schedule appointments, or to use the calculator and address book.

39693 ■ "Working It Out! How a Young Executive Overcomes Obstacles on the Job" in *Black Enterprise* (Vol. 37, January 2007, No. 6, pp. 55)
Pub: Earl G. Graves Publishing Co. Inc.
Ed: Laura Egodigwe. Description: Interview with Susan Chapman, Global Head of Operations for Citigroup Realty Services, in which she discusses issues such as the important skills necessary for overcoming obstacles in the workplace.

39694 ■ *The World Is Flat: A Brief History of the Twenty-First Century*
Pub: Picador USA
Ed: Thomas L. Friedman. Released: July 2006. Price: $16.00. Description: Globalization's impact on business.

39695 ■ "Worried on Woodward; Police Caucus on Robbers of Oakland Businesses" in *Crain's Detroit Business* (Vol. 21, January 31, 2005, No. 5)
Pub: Crain Communications Inc. - Detroit
Ed: Sheena Harrison, Anjali Fluker. Description: Royal Oak, Birmingham and Farmington Hills, Michigan police departments are joining forces in an attempt to share strategies and information to find suspects who are committing armed robbery against area businesses. One robbery resulted in the shooting of two employees.

39696 ■ "Worst-case scenario" in *Entrepreneur* (Vol. 30, No. 2, February 2)
Pub: Entrepreneur Media Inc.
Ed: Chris Penttila. Description: Tips that may save employees lives in a crisis are examined.

39697 ■ "Year In Review Fund-Raising" in *Venture Capital Journal* (February 1, 2006)
Pub: Thomason Financial Inc.
Description: A total of 182 U.S.-based venture funds raised $25.2 billion in 2005, lower in number than in 2005 but a 46 percent surge in dollar amount. Statistical data included.

39698 ■ "A Year Into The Job, He's Making Progress Slowly But Surely" in *Fortuneit* (Vol. 146, No. 12, December 9, 2002, pp. 217)
Pub: Time Inc.
Ed: Jeffrey H. Birnbaum. Description: Profile of the new president of the Small Business Administration, Hector Barreto, Jr. Barreto's goal is to transform the SBA from an old-time Beltway bureaucracy into a relevant resource for small business. Four specific issues to be addressed under the new administration are listed.

39699 ■ "Yes to English, No to Espanol?" in *Hispanic Business* (Vol. 23, No. 10, October, 2001, pp. 26)
Pub: Hispanic Business
Ed: Domenico Maceri. Description: According to the article, lower income and a lack of language skills conspire against Hispanic and other immigrant children. These challenges require compensatory education to enable these children to become employable.

39700 ■ "You can't lead without making sacrifices" in *Fast Company* (June 2001, pp. 106)
Pub: Fast Company
Ed: Randy Hopper. Description: Profile of the U.S. Military Academy, recognized for its Grassroots Leadership Home Base, located in West Point, New York.

39701 ■ "Younger But Wiser Than You Might Think" in *San Fernando Valley Business Journal* (Vol. 12, January 2007, No. 2, pp. 51)
Pub: San Fernando Valley Business Journal Associates
Ed: Jason Schaff. Description: Common traits are explored of successful business professionals under the age of forty.

39702 ■ "Your Employees" in *Small Business Opportunities* (Vol. 14, No. 1, January 2002, pp. 76, 78)
Pub: Harris Publications, Inc.
Ed: Lin Grensing-Pophal. Description: Twenty-five keys to creating positive employee relations are listed.

39703 ■ *Your Lawyer: An Owner's Manual*
Pub: Agate Publishing, Incorporated
Ed: Henry C. Krasnow. Released: November 2005. Price: $14.00. Description: Small business guide that assists owners and managers to find, work with, and inspire attorneys. Includes an overview of the legal processes involved in running a small company.

39704 ■ "Your own time" in *BlackEnterprise* (Vol. 32, No. 3, October 2001, pp. 162)
Pub: Earl Graves Publishing Co.
Description: Ways to relax away from business stress are explored.

39705 ■ "Your Vote Really Does Count: Changing Political Dynamics of an Evenly Divided Congress" in *Venture Capital Journal* (Vol. 40, No. 10)
Pub: Venture Economics
Description: The article points out the importance for business owners to vote during elections.

39706 ■ "You've Got Personality" in *Entrepreneur* (Vol. 31, No. 8, August 2003, pp. 30)
Pub: Entrepreneur Media, Inc.
Ed: Steve Cooper. Description: Statistics about the ways entrepreneurs see themselves in terms of personality are presented.

TRADE PERIODICALS

39707 ■ *Business Asia*
Pub: Economist Intelligence Unit
Released: Biweekly. Price: $985. Description: Provides news on political, economic, and legal developments throughout the region, including business and e-business news; regulatory changes; distribution, human resources, market-entry strategies and regulatory development issues; economic and political risk analysis; company case studies; business intelligence.

39708 ■ *Business China*
Pub: Economist Intelligence Unit
Released: Biweekly. Price: $985. Description: Provides news on political, economic, and legal developments throughout the region, including business and e-business news; regulatory changes; distribution, human resources, market-entry strategies and regulatory development issues; company case studies; business intelligence.

39709 ■ *Business Eastern Europe*
Pub: Economist Intelligence Unit
Released: Weekly. Price: $1455, individuals for print version; $1530, individuals for online version per year; $85, single issue; $85 for most recent online issue. Description: Provides news on political, economic, and legal developments throughout the region, including business and e-business news; regulatory changes; distribution, human resources, market-entry strategies and regulatory development issues; economic and political risk analysis; company case studies; business intelligence.

39710 ■ *Business India Intelligence*
Pub: Economist Intelligence Unit
Released: Monthly. Price: $845, individuals for print version; $895 for online version per year; $105 for most recent print issue; $105 for most recent online issue. Description: Provides news on political, economic, and legal developments throughout the region, including business and e-business news; regulatory changes; distribution, human resources, market-entry strategies and regulatory development issues; economic and political risk analysis; company case studies; business intelligence.

39711 ■ *Business Middle East*
Pub: Economist Intelligence Unit
Released: Biweekly. Price: $1055, individuals for print version; $1095 for online version per year; $85 for most recent print issue; $85 for most recent online issue. Description: Provides news on political, economic, and legal developments throughout the region, including business and e-business news; regulatory changes; distribution, human resources, market-entry strategies and regulatory development issues; economic and political risk analysis; company case studies; business intelligence.

39712 ■ *Business Periodicals Index*
Pub: The H.W. Wilson Co.
Ed: Hiyol Yang, Editor. Released: Monthly. Description: Index of business periodicals.

39713 ■ *Business Russia*
Pub: Economist Intelligence Unit
Released: Monthly. Price: $955 for online version per year; $90 for most recent online issue. Description: Provides news on political, economic, and legal developments throughout the region, including business and e-business news; regulatory changes; distribution, human resources, market-entry strategies and regulatory development issues; political and economic risk analysis; company case studies; business intelligence.

39714 ■ *Business Week*
Pub: McGraw-Hill Inc.
Contact: Stephen B. Shepard, Editor-in-Chief
Released: Weekly, 51/year. Price: $45.97 for 51 issues plus free premium online access. Description: Magazine providing business news and intelligence for executives.

39715 ■ *Catalog Success Magazine*
Pub: North American Publishing Co.
Contact: Matt Griffin, Assoc. Ed.
Released: Monthly. Description: Professional journal covering information for executives involved in the business-to-business and consumer catalog industry.

39716 ■ *Cincy Business Magazine*
Pub: Great Lakes Publishing Co.
Contact: Eric Harmon, Publisher
E-mail: eharmon@cincybusinessmag.com
Ed: Felix Winternitz, Editor, editorial@cincybusinessmag.com. Description: Magazine featuring information of interest to Cincinnati, Ohio-area businesspersons.

39717 ■ *Forbes*
Pub: Forbes Magazine
Contact: Malcolm S. Forbes Jr., Editor-in-Chief
Released: Biweekly, 26/year. **Price:** $29.99 Per year; $1.15 single issue. **Description:** Magazine reporting on industry, business and finance management.

39718 ■ *Fortune*
Pub: Time Inc.
Contact: Michael Federle, Group Publisher
Released: 28/year. **Price:** $19.99. **Description:** Business and industry magazine printed in regional and demographic editions.

39719 ■ *Inc.*
Pub: Gruner & Jahr USA
Contact: John Koten, Editor-in-Chief
Ed: George Gendron, Editor. **Released:** 13/year. **Price:** $14; $31 Canada; $50 out of country. **Description:** Business and finance magazine for business owners and managers.

39720 ■ *Independent Operations*
Pub: American Financial Services Association (AFSA)
Ed: Thomas L. Thomas, Editor. **Released:** Quarterly. **Price:** Included in membership; $15, nonmembers. **Description:** Furnishes members with news of the financial services industry, small business, and other areas of concern to the members of the Association's Section on Independent Operations. Provides news of current legislation, regulations, and individual/company profiles. Recurring features include letters to the editor, interviews, reports of meetings, news of Association events and conferences, and notices of publications available. Also contains columns titled Chairman's Report, Profile, Marketplace, Want Ads, For Your Information, and Question and Answer.

39721 ■ *Interface Tech News*
Pub: InterfaceMediaGroup
Contact: Morten Asbjornsen, MESDA Board of Dir.
Ed: John Farrell, Editor, johnf@interfacenow.com. **Released:** Monthly. **Price:** Free to qualified subscribers; $34 out of area; $50 Canada. **Description:** Newspaper covering local technology and business.

39722 ■ *The Journal of Business Valuation*
Pub: Carswell
Released: Annual. **Price:** $80 Canada; $73.39 U.S. **Description:** Journal including papers presented at the Business Valuation Conference in Canada.

39723 ■ *Journal of Industry, Competition and Trade*
Pub: Kluwer Academic/Plenum Publishing Corp.
Contact: Karl Aiginger, Editor-in-Chief
Released: 4/year. **Price:** $267 institutions print or online ed., add 20% for both together; $66 print ed. **Description:** Journal covering research on industry, competition and trade.

39724 ■ *Marple's Pacific Northwest Letter*
Pub: Newsletter Publishing Corp.
Ed: Michael J. Parks, Editor. **Released:** Biweekly. **Price:** $125; $225 2 years. **Description:** Reports business and economic conditions in the Pacific Northwest (Washington, Oregon, Idaho, Montana), with some coverage of Alaska. Includes coverage of publicly-held companies of the region, with emphasis on basic industry such as forest products. Includes an analysis of long-term regional economic trends.

39725 ■ *Ohio Business*
Pub: Great Lakes Publishing Co.
Contact: Julie Perlmuter, Advertising Coord.
E-mail: perlmuter@Inside-Business.com
Released: 3/yr. **Description:** Magazine providing information relevant to businesspersons in the state of Ohio.

39726 ■ *Ohio Entrepreneur*
Pub: Great Lakes Publishing Co.
Released: Monthly. **Description:** Magazine covering entrepreneurs in the state of Ohio.

39727 ■ *Print Solutions*
Pub: Document Management Industries Association
Released: Monthly. **Description:** Trade magazine on business forms and other printed products, document management, electronic data interchange, and electronic forms.

39728 ■ *Review of Business Information Systems*
Pub: The Clute Institute for Academic Research
Contact: Ronald C. Clute, Managing Editor
E-mail: cluter@CluteInstitute.org
Released: Quarterly. **Price:** $275 institutions. **Description:** Accounting Information Systems magazine.

VIDEOCASSETTES/ AUDIOCASSETTES

39729 ■ *The Business File*
PBS Home Video
Catalog Fulfillment Center
PO Box 751089
Charlotte, NC 28275-1089
Ph:800-531-4727
Free: 800-645-4PBS
Co. E-mail: info@pbs.org
URL: http://www.pbs.org
Released: 1985. **Price:** $130.00. **Description:** An extensive course for college students, introducing them to the basic concepts of business. **Availability:** VHS; 3/4U.

39730 ■ *Career Insights*
RMI Media
1365 N. Winchester
Olathe, KS 66061
Ph:(913)768-1696
Fax: (913)768-0184
Co. E-mail: actmedia@act.org
URL: http://www.rmimedia.com
Released: 1987. **Description:** Describes 50 occupations, including skill requirements and interviews with people employed in these fields. **Availability:** VHS; 3/4U.

39731 ■ *Great Leaders in Business and Administration*
Video Collectibles
PO Box 385
Lewiston, NY 14092-0385
Free: 800-268-3891
Fax: 800-269-8877
Co. E-mail: info@collectablesdirect.com
URL: http://www.collectablesdirect.com
Released: 1988. **Price:** $140.00. **Description:** A ongoing series of interviews with important figures in business and management, who discuss with students their current thoughts and forecasts of future developments. Viewer's guide included with each tape. **Availability:** VHS; EJ; 3/4U.

39732 ■ *Managing the Emerging Company*
Leslie T. McClure
PO Box 1223
Pebble Beach, CA 93953
Ph:(831)647-0680
Fax: (831)647-0682
Released: 1997. **Price:** $990.00. **Description:** Ten-volume set deals with the functions of developing and running a business. **Availability:** VHS.

39733 ■ *Take It from the Top: The Business of Business Success*
Video Arts, Inc.
c/o Aim Learning Group
8238-40 Lehigh
Morton Grove, IL 60053-2615
Free: 877-444-2230
Fax: (416)252-2155
Co. E-mail: service@aimlearninggroup.com
URL: http://www.aimlearninggroup.com
Released: 1991. **Price:** $295.00. **Description:** David Frost interviews three of England's most successful businessmen, who share their secrets of success. In the first tape, Lord Hanson talks about organization and change. In the second, Sir John Harvey-Jones tells the difference between leadership and management. In the third, Sir James Goldsmith shares his business philosophy. **Availability:** VHS; 8mm; 3/4U; Special order formats.

39734 ■ *What They Don't Teach You at Harvard Business School*
Bullfrog Films, Inc.
PO Box 149
Oley, PA 19547
Ph:(610)779-8226
Free: 800-543-3764
Fax: (610)370-1978
Co. E-mail: video@bullfrogfilms.com
URL: http://bullfrogfilms.com
Released: 1985. **Price:** $995.00. **Description:** A business theory program by Mark McCormack, packed with methods and hints not traditionally used in the mainstream. **Availability:** VHS; 3/4U.

TRADE SHOWS AND CONVENTIONS

39735 ■ *Age Small Business Show*
Business Connect
PO Box 576
Crows Nest, New South Wales 1585, Australia
Ph:61 2 9437 9333
Principal Exhibits: Small Business equipment, supplies, and services.

39736 ■ *Sydney Morning Herald Small Business Show*
Business Connect
PO Box 576
Crows Nest, New South Wales 1585, Australia
Ph:61 2 9437 9333
Released: Annual. **Principal Exhibits:** Small Business equipment, supplies, and services.

CONSULTANTS

39737 ■ *Shriner-Midland Co.*
7347 Stuart Cir.
Warrenton, VA 20187
Ph:(540)349-8193
Fax: (540)349-8799
Co. E-mail: shrinermidland@aol.com

E-mail: shrinermidland@aol.com
Scope: Business and economic analysis for corporations, investors, associations, and law firms. Services include development of management strategies, financial management and analysis, financial due diligence, turnaround, and work-out support. Also provides analysis and expert testimony for legislative, regulatory, and trial proceedings. Specializes in high-tech, services, and nonprofit organizations. **Publications:** "Economic Impact Estimates of the Clinton Health Plan"; "Modeling Product Liability Costs in Large Class Action Cases"; "Minimum Wage Research Review"; cost analysis for nonprofit organizations.

39738 ■ *Value Creation Group Inc.*
7820 Scotia Dr., Ste. 2000
Dallas, TX 75248-3115
Ph:(972)980-7407
Fax: (972)980-4619
Co. E-mail: john.antos@valuecreationgroup.com
URL: http://www.valuecreationgroup.com

E-mail: john.antos@valuecreationgroup.com
Scope: General business experts offering predictive strategic planning, Activity-Based Costing (ABC), Activity-Based Management (ABM), mergers and acquisitions, outsourcing, re-engineering, process management, web-enabling technology, bench marking, installation of financial systems, executive search,

training, teams, activity based budgeting, operational auditing, feature costing. Industries served: financial services, food, health-care, insurance, manufacturing, electronics, real estate, consumer products, nonprofit, telecommunication, oil, service, data processing, hotel and resort and government agencies. **Publications:** Handbook of process management based (predictive accounting), ALCPA 2002; Activity Based Management for Service Environments, Government Entities, & Nonprofit Organizations; Driving Value Using Activity Based Budgeting; Process Based Accounting leveraging Processes to Predict Results; Handbook of Supply Chain Management; Economic Value Management Applications and Techniques; The Change Handbook: Group Methods for Creating the Future. **Seminars:** Predictive Accounting; Performance measures; ABM for Manufacturing; ABM for Service Organizations; Finance and Accounting for Non-Financial Executives; Return on Investment/Capital Expenditure Evaluation; Planning and Cost Control; The Next Step Intermediate Finance and Accounting for Non-financial Managers; Activity-Based Budgeting; Friendly Finance for Fund Raisers; Strategic Outsourcing.

COMPUTERIZED DATABASES

39739 ■ *BtoB*
Crain Communications Inc.
1155 Gratiot Ave.
Detroit, MI 48207
Ph:(313)446-6000
Free: 800-678-2427
Fax: (313)446-0361
Co. E-mail: info@crain.com
URL: http://www.crain.com
Description: Contains news, articles, and features from the monthly print version of *BtoB*, as well as content exclusive to the online version. Contains daily news reports, analysis, and articles on business-to-business marketing and related issues. Includes coverage of e-commerce and current business events. Includes editorials and feature articles from the monthly magazine. **Availability:** Online: Crain Communications Inc. **Type:** Full text.

39740 ■ *Business Periodicals Index*
H.W. Wilson Co.
950 University Ave.
Bronx, NY 10452
Ph:(718)588-8400
Free: 800-367-6770
Fax: 800-590-1617
Co. E-mail: custserv@hwwilson.com
URL: http://www.hwwilson.com
Description: Contains citations to articles and book reviews in more than 600 general business periodicals and trade journals, covering 25 business specialties. Includes feature articles, interviews, biographical sketches of business leaders, book reviews, research developments, new product reviews, and reports of associations, societies, and conferences. Features indexing of publications from 1982 to date. Covers such general topics as accounting, advertising, economics, finance, management, marketing, and occupational health and safety, as well as such specific industries as banking, computers, and real estate. Corresponds to *Business Periodicals Index*. **Availability:** Online: H.W. Wilson Co., Ovid Technologies Inc., Ovid Technologies Inc; CD-ROM: H.W. Wilson Co., Ovid Technologies Inc. **Type:** Bibliographic.

39741 ■ *Business Week*
McGraw-Hill Companies Inc.
1221 Avenue of the Americas
New York, NY 10020-1095
Ph:(212)512-2000
Free: (866)436-8502
Fax: (212)512-3840
Co. E-mail: customer.service@mcgraw-hill.com
URL: http://www.mcgraw-hill.com
Description: Contains the complete text (including images) of *Business Week*, a business and industry

news magazine. Covers finance, labor and production, corporate news and investment policies, and the effects of legislative and regulatory developments on commerce. Includes analyses of the economic outlook. Provides daily business briefings, market news, investing coverage, and other business information. Provides information on global business, technology, small business, investing, and electronic commerce. Offers reviews of hundreds of business books, including sample chapters. Provides data on the best business schools and provides coverage of work and career issues. Allows users to search back issues of the magazine. **Availability:** Online: LexisNexis, Financial Times, Dow Jones & Co. Inc., Thomson Dialog, ProQuest, GENIOS Wirtschaftsdatenbanken; Handheld: Financial Times. **Type:** Full text.

39742 ■ *The CorpTech Directory of Technology Companies*
Corporate Technology Information Services, Inc. (CorpTech)
5711 S 86th Cir.
Ohmaha, NE 68127
Ph:(866)313-6367
Co. E-mail: webmaster@corptech.com
URL: http://www.corptech.com
Description: Contains directory information on more than 90,000 technology companies and developers in 18 major high-technology industries throughout the United States. Includes more than 230,000 executive contacts. Provides company address, telephone, web and e-mail contact information, industry type, estimated sales, and brief description. Provides more detailed profiles and descriptions on a fee basis. Includes additional information such as stock quotes, SEC filing details, top 20 lists, detailed analysis, and more. Offers particular focus on web-related technologies such as the Internet, ISDN, multimedia, web infrastructure and security, and web searching. Includes indexes of manufacturers, products and technologies, and non-U.S. parent companies. Provides search capability on company name, stock symbol, or CorpTech URI. **Availability:** Online: Executive Grapevine International Ltd., Corporate Technology Information Services, Inc. (CorpTech); CD-ROM: Corporate Technology Information Services, Inc. (CorpTech). **Type:** Full text; Directory.

39743 ■ *NewsEdge Live*
Thomson Dialog
11000 Regency Pky., Ste. 10
Cary, NC 27511
Ph:(919)462-8600
Free: 800-334-2564
Fax: (919)468-9890
Co. E-mail: contact@dialog.com
URL: http://www.dialog.com
Description: Provides real-time news delivery from more than 1000 comprehensive global business news sources. Provides scrolling news 24 hours a day, 7 days a week. Subscribers can set up alerts to notify them of breaking news through auditory and visual cues. Subscribers can also define customized profiles to bring in the news they're most interested in. Provides quick, real-time access to equity prices, stock quotes, market trends, and breaking news headlines. Includes a browser-based interface to make this database easy to use and easy to distribute throughout an intranet or business organization. Offers a free trial of the service at NewsEdge's web site. **Availability:** Online: Thomson Dialog. **Type:** Full text; Numeric; Statistical.

39744 ■ *U.S. Business Directory File*
Acxiom Corp.
1 Information Way
Little Rock, AR 72202
Ph:(501)342-1000
Free: 888-3-ACXIOM
Fax: (501)342-3913
Co. E-mail: info@acxiom.com
URL: http://www.acxiom.com
Description: Contains approximately 18 million records of white pages telephone listings for businesses throughout the United States. Includes information compiled from current white pages and associated

telephone directories in the U.S. Includes such data as business name, address, phone number, and Standard Industrial Classification (SIC) code. **Availability:** Online: Online Computer Library Center Inc. (OCLC). **Type:** Directory.

LIBRARIES

39745 ■ **College of William and Mary–Mason School of Business–Professional Resource Center (PO Bo)**
PO Box 8795
Tyler Hall, Rm. 107
Williamsburg, VA 23187-8795
Ph:(757)221-2916
Fax: (757)221-2937
Co. E-mail: charlotte.brown@business.wm.edu
URL: http://mason.wm.edu/Mason/
Contact: Charlotte Brown, Dir.
Scope: Business. **Holdings:** Reference materials; corporation records; video cassettes; periodicals.

39746 ■ **New Hampshire Technical Institute, Concord–Library**
31 College Dr.
Concord, NH 03301-7412
Ph:(603)271-7186
Co. E-mail: nhtilibrary@nhctc.edu
URL: http://www.nhti.edu/library/
Scope: Business, computers, education, engineering, health, justice/legal studies, architecture, autism. **Services:** Library open to the public. **Holdings:** 30,000 books; 50,000 microfilms, videotapes, recordings, CDs, and other media. **Subscriptions:** 800 journals and other serials.

39747 ■ **Southern Methodist University–Cox School of Business–Business Information Center (6212)**
6212 Bishop Blvd,
PO Box 0333
Dallas, TX 75275-0333
Ph:(214)768-4107
Fax: (214)768-1884
URL: http://bic.cox.smu.edu/index.html
Contact: Paulette Hasier, Dir.
Scope: Business. **Holdings:** Reference materials; faculty papers. **Subscriptions:** 50 journals and other serials.

39748 ■ **Touro College–Bensonhurst Library**
1870 Stillwell Ave., No. 86
Brooklyn, NY 11223
Ph:(718)265-6534, x1006
Fax: (718)265-0616
Co. E-mail: miriamm@touro.edu
URL: http://www.touro.edu/library/directories/Directory.asp
Contact: Miriam Magill
Scope: Business, computer science, human services, ESL. **Holdings:** Books; diskettes; audio and video tapes; CD-ROMs; DVDs; microfiche.

39749 ■ **Touro College–Boro Park (53rd Street) Library**
1273 53rd St.
Brooklyn, NY 11219
Ph:(718)871-6187, x-17
Fax: (718)686-7071
Co. E-mail: leibk@touro.edu
URL: http://www.touro.edu/library/directories/Directory.asp
Contact: Leib Klein, Libn.
Scope: Business, computer science, human services, ESL. **Holdings:** Books; diskettes; audio and video tapes; CD-ROMs; DVDs; microfiche.

39750 ■ **Touro College–Brighton Beach Library**
532 Neptune Ave.
Brooklyn, NY 11224
Ph:(718)449-6160, x-118
Fax: (718)265-6341
Co. E-mail: bellar@touro.edu
URL: http://www.touro.edu/library/directories/Directory.asp

Contact: Bella Reytblat
Scope: Business, computer science, human services, ESL. **Holdings:** Books; diskettes; audio and video tapes; CD-ROMs; DVDs; microfiche.

39751 ■ Touro College–Flushing Library
133-35 Roosevelt Ave.
Flushing, NY 11354
Ph:(718)353-6400, x-112
Fax: (718)353-8952
Co. E-mail: xuanwenh@touro.edu
URL: http://www.touro.edu/library/directories/
     Directory.asp
Contact: Xuan Wen Huang
Scope: Business, computer science, human services, ESL. **Holdings:** Books; diskettes; audio and video tapes; CD-ROMs; DVDs; microfiche.

39752 ■ Touro College–Forest Hills Library
71-02 113th St.
Forest Hills, NY 11375
Ph:(718)261-4719
Fax: (718)793-3610
Co. E-mail: shulmanr@touro.edu
URL: http://www.touro.edu/library/directories/
     Directory.asp
Contact: Rachel Shulman
Scope: Business, computer science, human services, ESL. **Holdings:** Books; diskettes; audio and video tapes; CD-ROMs; DVDs; microfiche.

39753 ■ Touro College–Lander College for Men Library
75-31 150th St.
Kew Gardens Hills, NY 11367
Ph:(718)820-4894
Fax: (718)820-4825
Co. E-mail: zhannama@touro.edu
URL: http://www.touro.edu/library/directories/
     Directory.asp
Contact: Zhanna S. Marina, Libn.
Scope: Biology, business, computer science, management information science, political science, psychology, social sciences, Judaica. **Holdings:** Books; diskettes; audio and video tapes; CD-ROMs; DVDs; microfiche.

39754 ■ Touro College–Midtown Library
43 W. 23rd St.
New York, NY 10010
Ph:(212)463-0400
Fax: (212)627-9144
Co. E-mail: marinaz@touro.edu
URL: http://www.touro.edu/library/directories/
     Directory.asp
Contact: Marina Zilberman, MLIS, Chf.Libn.
Scope: Business, education, ethnic studies, psychology, pre-clinical and clinical medicine, occupational and physical therapy, physician assistant, Oriental medicine. **Holdings:** Books; diskettes; audio and video tapes; CD-ROMs; DVDs; microfiche.

39755 ■ Touro College–Midwood (Flatbush) Library
1602 Ave. J
Brooklyn, NY 11230
Ph:(718)252-7800
Fax: (718)338-7732
Co. E-mail: simonb@touro.edu
URL: http://www.touro.edu/library/directories/
     Directory.asp
Contact: Bashe Simon, Dp.Dir. of Libs.
Scope: Business, computer science, education, human services, neuroscience, political science, psychology, speech pathology, Judaica. **Holdings:** Books; diskettes; audio and video tapes; CD-ROMs; DVDs; microfiche.

39756 ■ Touro College–Starrett City Library
1390 Pennsylvania Ave.
Brooklyn, NY 11239
Ph:(718)642-6562, x-104
Fax: (718)642-6807
Co. E-mail: ritah@touro.edu
URL: http://www.touro.edu/library/directories/
     Directory.asp
Contact: Rita Hilu
Scope: Business, computer science, human services, ESL. **Holdings:** Books; diskettes; audio and video tapes; CD-ROMs; DVDs; microfiche.

39757 ■ Touro College–Sunset Park Library
475 53rd St.
Brooklyn, NY 11220

Ph:(718)748-2776, x-4
Fax: (718)492-9031
Co. E-mail: fainak@touro.edu
URL: http://www.touro.edu/library/directories/
     Directory.asp
Contact: Faina G. Katsnelson
Scope: Business, computer science, human services, ESL. **Holdings:** Books; diskettes; audio and video tapes; CD-ROMs; DVDs; microfiche.

39758 ■ University of Nevada, Reno–University Library–Business and Government Information Center (1664)
1664 N. Virginia St.
Mail Stop 322
Reno, NV 89557-0001
Ph:(775)784-6500, x-309
Fax: (775)784-4398
Co. E-mail: ragains@unr.edu
URL: http://www.library.unr.edu/depts/bgic/
Contact: Patrick Ragains, Lib./Dept.Hd.
Scope: Business, government. **Holdings:** Presidential papers; Indian agency correspondence; documents on terrorism; census materials.

RESEARCH CENTERS

39759 ■ Appalachian State University–Appalachian Regional Development Institute
231 Appalachian State University Hall
Boone, NC 28608
Ph:(828)262-2907
Fax: (828)262-6553
Co. E-mail: combsjp@appstate.edu
URL: http://www.ardi.appstate.edu
Contact: J. Paul Combs, Dir.
E-mail: combsjp@appstate.edu
Scope: Business and economic development in northwestern North Carolina, international trade. **Educational Activities:** Leadership Summit.

START-UP INFORMATION

39760 ■ **"Alameda high-tech incubator is expanding"** in *Kiplinger California Letter* (Vol. 38, No. 17, September 4, 2002) Pub: Kiplinger Washington Editors, Inc. **Description:** Profile of Advancing California's Emerging Technologies high-tech incubator. The high-tech incubator will construct a 40,000 square foot laboratory and offices with $6.5 million in federal money.

39761 ■ **"Business information centers"** in *BlackEnterprise* (Vol. 31, No. 12, July 2001, pp. 48) Pub: Earl Graves Publishing Co. **Ed:** Roger Barnes. **Description:** Profile of the Small Business Administration's (SBA) Business Information Center (BIC), the government-funded business resource with more than 65 BIC offices in more than 35 states. BICs provide a one-stop location for information, education, workshops, and training designed to address a broad variety of business start-up and development issues.

39762 ■ *The Canadian Small Business Survival Guide: How to Start and Operate Your Own Successful Business* Pub: Dundurn Group **Ed:** Benjamin Gallander. FRQ September 2004. **Price:** $18.99. **Description:** Ideas for starting and running a successful small business. Topics include selecting a business, financing, government assistance, locations, franchises, and marketing ideas.

39763 ■ **"Choosing an Incubator for your Business Baby"** in *Ingram's* (Vol. 28, No. 6, June 2002, pp. 49) Pub: Show Me Publishing, Inc. **Description:** Small business management techniques are featured. An outline and review of some of the 900 business incubator programs offered by federal and state agencies to assist in the development of small businesses is presented.

39764 ■ **"Credit card financing: Tempting but risky for small businesses"** in *Crain's Detroit Business* (Vol. 16, No. 33, August 14, 2000, pp. 13) Pub: Crain Communications, Inc. **Ed:** Brent Snavely. **Description:** Counselors from the Service Corps of Retired Executives believe that entrepreneurs should never use credit cards to finance a business. A variety of resources for advice and funding are investigated.

39765 ■ **"EISC partners start-up with unique technology"** in *Toledo Business Journal* (Vol. 19, No. 2, February 2003, pp. 23) Pub: Telex Communications, Inc. **Ed:** Susan Ford. **Description:** Profile of Energystics Technologies, Ltd. and Tom Sheperak, president and CEO, who is working on three applications for his unique Energy Beam(TM) technology that has the capability to move electricity through the air without a

wire to heat, melt, or vaporize materials. EISC, the Small Business Development Center for technology and manufacturing, has established an on-site lab where Sheperak is developing and testing prototypes.

39766 ■ **"Federal funds may spur Legislature to re-enact transit bill"** in *Crain's Detroit Business* (Vol. 19, No. 1, January 6, 2003, pp. 5)** Pub: Crain Communications Inc., Detroit **Ed:** Amy Lane. **Description:** Legislation regarding the Federal startup funds that may be available in the metro Detroit area for regional transportation is discussed. Two lawmakers plan to introduce new bills for the Detroit Area Regional Transportation Authority.

39767 ■ **"Finding financing"** in *Black Enterprise* (Vol. 32, No. 6, January 2002, pp. 8) Pub: Earl Graves Publishing Co. **Ed:** Bevolyn Williams-Harold. **Description:** Minority entrepreneurs may need to look for more innovative capital resources, such as minority-focused venture capital funds or community-based securitization programs, to maintain cash flow.

39768 ■ **"Finding Funding"** in *Black Enterprise* (Vol. 34, No. 7, February 2004, pp. 48) Pub: Earl Graves Publishing Co. **Ed:** Alan Hughes. **Description:** An overview of government grants offered to minority startup businesses is presented, along with information about the U.S. Small Business Association's resources.

39769 ■ **"Hollister priorities: Loan, training programs"** in *Crain's Detroit Business* (Vol. 19, No. 3, January 20, 2003, pp. 24) Pub: Crain Communications Inc., Detroit **Ed:** Amy Lane. **Description:** David Hollister was named by Jennifer Granholm, Michigan's new governor, to head the new Department of Labor, Economic Growth and Urban Development. The Department will provide low interest loans to entrepreneurs in targeted redevelopment areas of the state. The extension of the Michigan Economic Growth Authority is also discussed.

39770 ■ **"Inner-City Innovation"** in *Entrepreneur* (Vol. 28, No. 2, February 2000, pp. 136) Pub: Entrepreneur Media Inc. **Ed:** Stephen Barlas. **Description:** President Clinton and Congress move toward increasing incentives for entrepreneurs ready to take on low-income communities.

39771 ■ **"Keep them flying"** in *BlackEnterprise* (Vol. 31, No. 11, June 2001, pp. 74) Pub: Earl Graves Publishing Co. **Ed:** Paula McCoy-Pinderhughes. **Description:** Advice is given to an airplane mechanic who is interested in becoming a minority business supplier of aircraft components and parts. Sources such as the Small

Business Development Council, under the auspices of the SBA; the Boeing Company's Supplier Diversity Program; the National Minority Supplier Development Council; and the National Black Chamber of Commerce are all profiled.

39772 ■ **"Market Planning 101"** in *Home Business* (Vol. 12, October 2005, No. 5, pp. 42, 44-45) Pub: Home Business Magazine **Ed:** Christopher J. Bachler. **Description:** A quick marketing plan for any small business is presented and includes all the basic information required to attract loans, partners, business services and even Small Business Administration assistance.

39773 ■ **"Milwaukee Mayor Says Federal Business Development Program Will Create Jobs"** in *Milwaukee Journal Sentinel* (December 8, 2005) Pub: Journal Sentinel, Inc. **Ed:** Tom Daykin. **Description:** The Federal government is expanding its Renewal Community program in Milwaukee, Wisconsin. The program gives subsidies to new business development in poor neighborhoods.

39774 ■ **"Pennsylvania"** in *Entrepreneur* (Vol. 28, No. 6, June 2000, pp. 155) Pub: Entrepreneur Media Inc. **Ed:** Cynthia E. Griffin. **Description:** Pennsylvania has designed a program to encourage entrepreneurial business ventures.

39775 ■ **"SBA's Office of Entrepreneurial Development: www.sba.gov/training"** in *Entrepreneur* (Vol. 31, No. 10, October 2003, pp. 6) Pub: Entrepreneur Media, Inc. **Ed:** Steve Cooper. **Description:** Profile of the U.S. Small Business Administration's Website offering free online classes, workshops, and guides, as well as access to electronic counseling links.

39776 ■ **"Show Me the Money"** in *Black Enterprise* (Vol. 34, No. 3, October 2003, pp. 40) Pub: Earl Graves Publishing Co. **Ed:** Alan Hughes. **Description:** The U.S. Small Business Administration (SBA) offers the 7(a) Loan Guaranty Program to small startup companies. Private lenders make loans to a business, up to $150,000 and the SBA will guarantee up to 85 percent, or 75 percent on loans for more than $150,000. For loans under $150,000, the SBALowDoc (low documentation) loans are available, or the SBA Microloan Program for loans $35,000 or less.

39777 ■ **"Small Business Spotlight"** in *Small Business Opportunities* (Vol. 16, No. 1, January 2004, pp. 112) Pub: Harris Publications, Inc. **Description:** National Aeronautics and Space Administration (NASA) funds the Space Alliance Technology Outreach Program (SATOP). The program provides small businesses with free technical assistance through the use of the U.S. Space Program, as well as aerospace contractors, NASA field centers, universities and colleges. Profiles of two companies that improved and developed their designs through the SATOP program are presented.

39778 ■ "Small business package passes Congress" in *BlackEnterprise* (Vol. 31, No. 10, May 2001, pp. 22)
Pub: Earl Graves Publishing Co.
Ed: Joyce Jones. Description: Information regarding the package of small business legislation passed by the 106th Congress will keep some programs intact and secure the future of others. SBA budget agreement appropriations, including venture capital assistance are presented. Statistical data included.

39779 ■ "States' aid for tech start-ups: more talk than action" in *Wall Street Journal* (January 4, 2000, pp. B2)
Pub: Dow Jones & Co., Inc.
Ed: Ellena De Lisser. Description: A compilation of entrepreneurial news, including information about state aid for high-tech start-ups.

39780 ■ "Success line" in *Success* (Vol. 47, No. 3, July 2000, pp. 78)
Pub: Success Publishing, Inc.
Description: Questions are answered on starting a business, including loans and grants, patents, and federal certification for minority- or woman-owned business.

39781 ■ "Uncle Sam, Paralegal" in *Hispanic Business* (June 2002, pp. 22)
Pub: Hispanic Business
Ed: Teresa Talerico. Description: The Small Business Administration has launched a new Web site that assists entrepreneurs with legal questions. Since Hispanic entrepreneurs are eligible for a number of federal and state programs that are subject to changing regulations, the site will be very beneficial.

39782 ■ "You better shop around" in *Atlanta Business Chronicle* (Vol. 23, No. 46, April 20, 2001, pp. 65A)
Pub: American City Business Journals Inc.
Ed: Jean Capriotti. Description: The founders of Front Page News restaurant in the Atlanta area offer an example of the work needed to find a bank willing to work with risky new enterprises. They finally went to a bank in New Orleans for their loan. Capitol City Bank of Atlanta does specialize in small business loans, and is willing to lend up to 80 percent of the money needed by a start-up company. Charles Anderson of the Small Business Administration says that his agency can help entrepreneurs obtain loans and can provide assistance on how to run a business.

ASSOCIATIONS AND OTHER ORGANIZATIONS

39783 ■ National Association of Government Guaranteed Lenders
424 S Squires St., Ste. 130
Stillwater, OK 74074
Ph:(405)377-4022
Fax: (405)377-3931
Co. E-mail: info@naggl.com
URL: http://www.naggl.org
Contact: Anthony R. Wilkinson, Pres./CEO
Description: Aims to serve the needs and represents the interests of the small business lending community who utilize the Small Business Administrations and other government guaranteed loan programs.

REFERENCE WORKS

39784 ■ "7(a) Program Restored" in *Black Enterprise* (Vol. 35, October 2004, No. 3, pp. 36)
Pub: Earl G. Graves Publishing Co. Inc.
Ed: Joyce Jones. Description: Funding for the Small Business Administration's 7(a) program has been restored, with $79.1 million reallocated to the program after it ran out of money in January 2004.

39785 ■ "Adviser: Temporary tax act makes planning tough" in *Crain's Cleveland Business* (Vol. 22, No. 43, October 22, 2001, pp. 11)
Pub: Crain Communications, Inc.
Ed: Scott Snow. Description: The Economic Growth and Tax Relief Act of 2001 provides the largest tax cut in more than 20 years. The new law will benefit small business owners and individuals rather and corporations.

39786 ■ "Agency with a Small Focus" in *Hispanic Business* (September 2003, pp. 24, 26, 28)
Pub: Hispanic Business
Ed: Patricia Guadalupe. Description: Hector Barreto, Small Business Administration's Administrator, addresses the 20 million businesses the SBA has assisted in its fifty years of existence. Statistical data included.

39787 ■ "Are sec. 529 plans a better choice than education IRAs?" in *The Tax Adviser* (Vol. 32, No. 10, October 2001, pp. 668)
Pub: Harborside Financial Center
Ed: Philip E. Moore. Description: A comparison is made between Education IRAs and qualified tuition programs (Sec. 529 plans), to help parents identify the best way to save for their children's education.

39788 ■ "Around ground zero, an effort to rescue mom-and-pop shops" in *Wall Street Journal* (February 8, 2002, pp. A1)
Pub: Wall Street Journal
Ed: Lucette Lagnado. Description: The article asks the question: Is the microlender's program merely delaying layoffs by small businesses near the former World Trade Center after 9-11?

39789 ■ "Arrested Development?" in *Entrepreneur* (Vol. 32, November 2004, No. 11, pp. 75)
Pub: Entrepreneur Media Inc.
Description: Small businesses backed by venture capital may soon be eligible for the Small Business Administration's Small Business Innovation Research Program.

39790 ■ "Bill Would Boost Small Businesses" in *Bradenton Herald* (February 13, 2007)
Pub: Bradenton Herald
Ed: Brian Neill. Description: U.S. Representative Vern Buchanan has introduced a bill in Congress that includes a provision that would enable small businesses to offer health insurance more readily through the formation of associations. The bill would also benefit small business owners by allowing them to deduct a larger portion of taxes for labor and capital expenditures.

39791 ■ "Biomedical, Marine Research Funds Could Grow If Voters Approve Seed Money" in *Portland Press Herald* (November 2, 2005)
Pub: Blethen Maine Newspapers, Inc.
Ed: Edward D. Murphy. Description: Maine's Department of Economic and Community Development says the $20 million on the state's election ballot would not be enough to fund projects designed to help biomedical and marine research programs.

39792 ■ "Broadband agency makes its first loan" in *Crain's Detroit Business* (Vol. 19, No. 12, March 24, 2003, pp. 6)
Pub: Crain Communications Inc., Detroit
Ed: Amy Lane. Description: The Michigan Broadband Development Authority has approved its first loan to the mid-Michigan wireless provider ISP Wireless Group Inc., located in Alma. The company intends to install wireless broadband antennae and equipment in small towns from Clare to Ithaca.

39793 ■ "Bush may trim SBA budget" in *BlackEnterprise* (Vol. 32, No. 1, August 2001, pp. 28)
Pub: Earl Graves Publishing Co.
Ed: Joyce Jones. Description: The proposed reduction of funding to the Small Business Administration (SBA), is discussed.

39794 ■ "Businesses Assessing Granholm's Plans for SBT Overhaul" in *Crain's Detroit Business* (Vol. 21, January 31, 2005, No. 5, pp. 6)
Pub: Crain Communications Inc. - Detroit
Ed: Amy Lane. Description: Under a business-tax proposal, Michigan's single-business tax will not expire at the end of 2009. The pros and cons of this move are discussed with business experts from the state.

39795 ■ "Can't Save the Farm" in *Black Enterprise* (Vol. 31, No. 5, December 2000, pp. 34)
Pub: Earl Graves Publishing Co.
Ed: Hamil R. Harris. Description: Legal relief arrives too late to harvest benefits for black farmers.

39796 ■ "Capital infusion" in *Entrepreneur* (Vol. 30, No. 10, October 2002, pp. 60)
Pub: Entrepreneur Media Inc.
Ed: Jennifer Pellet. Description: Senator Kit Bond (R-MO) has introduced a bill that would direct investment capital into Small Business Investment Company Capital Access Act Bond.

39797 ■ "Caps off to you!" in *Entrepreneur* (Vol. 31, No. 6, June 2003, pp. 51)
Pub: Entrepreneur Media Inc.
Ed: C.J. Prince. Description: The U.S. Small Business Administration has restored the maximum loan amount of its 7(a) small business loan program to $2 million.

39798 ■ "Cisco, SBA announce online learning program" in *Network World* (July 24, 2000, pp. NA)
Pub: Network World Inc.
Ed: Margaret Johnston. Description: The Small Business Administration and Cisco offer an online training partnership to help small businesses incorporate the Internet into their day-to-day business operations.

39799 ■ *Code of Federal Regulations: Title 13: Business Credit and Assistance*
Pub: United States Government Printing Office
Ed: Department of Commerce Staff. Released: April 2005. Price: $55.00. Description: Title 13 covers regulations governing the activities of the Small Business Administration and the Department of Commerce. Book covers information on business credit, finance, and economic development.

39800 ■ "Companies in low-income neighborhoods seize opportunity" in *Wall Street Journal* (April 4, 2000, pp. B2)
Pub: Dow Jones & Co., Inc.
Ed: Joshua Harris Prager. Description: An overview of the HUBZone program.

39801 ■ "Company Looks to Link Rural Firms with City Buyers" in *St. Louis Post-Dispatch* (February 17, 2005)
Pub: Knight-Ridder/Tribune Business News
Ed: Martin Van Der Werf. Description: Profile of Rural Business Consultants, led by Robert Fowler. The firm links interested buyers with rural companies, mostly manufacturers. Many of the buyers will be able to take advantage of a federal program that guarantees loans for businesses in rural areas.

39802 ■ "Congress rejects plan to raise SBA loan fees" in *Atlanta Business Chronicle* (Vol. 24, No. 7, July 20, 2001, pp. 5A)
Pub: American City Business Journals Inc.
Ed: Ken Hoover. Description: The U.S. House Appropriations Committee has approved a $728 million budget for the Small Business Administration, adding 40 percent to the $539 million budget proposed by the Bush Administration, but still $130 million less than the 2001 budget. The increase means the agency does not need to raise fees for its flagship 7(a) loans and charge for consultation services at its Small Business Development Centers.

39803 ■ "Connecting Firms with Needed Funds; Financial Assistance" in Crain's New York Business (Vol. 22, November 13, 2006, No. 46, pp. 32)
Pub: Crain Communications, Inc.
Description: Listing of organizations that provide incentives or financial assistance to firms that are based in New York or are relocating to the area.

39804 ■ "A Contracting Conundrum" in Hispanic Business (October 2003, pp. 32, 34)
Pub: Hispanic Business
Ed: Ron Utt, Grace Napolitano. Description: Two opinions are expressed regarding government contracts, one insisting bundling results in cost savings and improved service, while the other believes bundling succeeds only in excluding small businesses from the federal procurement marketplace.

39805 ■ "CRS reports on the so-call 'tax rebate'" in Tax Notes (Vol. 92, No. 4, July 23, 2001, pp. 567-570)
Pub: Tax Notes International
Ed: Gregg Esenwein, Steve Maguire. Description: Issues concerning the so-called tax rebate created by the Economic Growth and Tax Relief Reconciliation Act of 2001 are examined. Topics include a report by the Congressional Research Service that states the payment is not technically a tax rebate but is, instead, an advance on reduced tax liability for 2001 income, and that more than a quarter of all taxpayers, including low-income taxpayers, will not receive a payment.

39806 ■ "Despite Smaller Loans, SBA Breaks Records" in Inc. (November 1, 2004)
Pub: Inc. Magazine
Ed: Darren Dahl. Description: The U. S. Small Business Administration backed a record number of loans in 2004, providing $15 billion in loans to businesses. These loans have helped small and family-owned small business to create 1.5 million jobs.

39807 ■ "Disabled Rise Up As Entrepreneurs" in Pacific Business News (Vol. 41, No. 16, June 27, 2003, pp. 1)
Pub: American City Business Journals
Ed: Eddy Conway. Description: The Hawaiian government is sponsoring workshops designed to help disabled people start their own businesses, thus easing welfare roles.

39808 ■ "Doing Business with Uncle Sam" in My Business (February/March 2003, pp. 14)
Pub: My Business Magazine
Description: The Small Business Administration will launch an online program designed to improve the procuring of government contracts, with an annual fee of $1,500 for using the e-commerce Web site.

39809 ■ "E-Government Catching On" in Hispanic Business (Vol. 23, No. 5, May 2001, pp. 22, 24)
Pub: Hispanic Business
Ed: Patricia Guadalupe. Description: The U.S. government is developing programs to access procurement, recruitment, and economic development. The FirstGov.gov links users to more than 20 million federal Web pages.

39810 ■ "The earned income tax credit and the child tax credit under the Tax Act of 2001" in Tax Notes (Vol. 92, No. 4, July 23, 2001)
Pub: Tax Notes International
Ed: Laurence S. Seidman, Saul D. Hoffman. Description: Issues concerning the interaction of the earned income tax credit (EITC), the child tax credit, the reduction of EITC marriage penalties, and the resulting structure of marginal tax rates, as they occur within the Economic Growth and Tax Relief Act of 2001, are examined. Topics include the introduction of a new 10 percent tax bracket, and the need for further marriage penalty tax reform and future marginal tax rate reduction. Statistical data included.

39811 ■ "Easy Target? Budget-Cutters in Congress Have Set Their Sights on the SBA" in Entrepreneur.com (Vol. 34, January 2006, No. 1, pp. 18)
Pub: Entrepreneur Media Inc.
Ed: Chris Penttila. Description: Congress is considering cutting billions of dollars in federal programs, creating fear for small companies that rely on the Small Business Administration for assistance.

39812 ■ "EBay Shippers Receive Special Service at Virginia Beach, Va., Post Office" in Virginian-Pilot (September 9, 2004)
Pub: Virginian-Pilot
Ed: Benita D. Newton. Description: Profile of Quick Ship Unit at the Witchduck postal station, a free service designed to help get small business owners and eBay sellers with many parcels out of lobby lines. Virginia Beach postmaster, Gerald A. Roane, states that the service is available for anyone with multiple packages.

39813 ■ Economic Development Assistance Programs in State Government
Pub: DIANE Publishing Co.
Ed: Wendy Umino. Released: 1994. Price: $35.00 (paper).

39814 ■ "EGTRRA lowers rates and expands credits, education benefits" in The Tax Adviser (Vol. 32, No. 10, October 2001, pp. 677)
Pub: Harborside Financial Center
Ed: Ronald B. Hegt. Description: A summary of the Economic Growth and Tax Relief Reconciliation Act of 2001 is presented, including information on individual rate reductions, personal exemption phaseout repeal, itemized deduction phaseout repeal, AMT changes, child credit, adoption credit, dependent care credit, employer-provided childcare facilities, marriage penalty relief, education IRAs, student loan interest, QHEE deduction, and employer-provided education assistance.

39815 ■ "Employers Can Use State Programs to Help Employees Save for College Education" in Employee Benefit Plan Review (Vol. 55, No. 6)
Pub: Charles D. Spencer & Associates, Inc.
Ed: Sue Burzawa. Description: Most states offer either prepaid tuition programs or college savings plans, which allow workers to set aside tax deferred income to pay for college.

39816 ■ "Employers' extra credit" in Hispanic Business (Vol. 22, No. 6, June 2000, pp. 156)
Pub: Hispanic Business
Ed: Milton Zall. Description: A small business can earn between $1,500 and $8,500 per employee by hiring members of targeted group and qualifying for Work Opportunity Tax Credit and the Welfare to Work Tax Credit.

39817 ■ "Ex-Im Bank cuts effect on small business unclear" in Atlanta Business Chronicle (Vol. 24, No. 3, June 22, 2001, pp. 54A)
Pub: American City Business Journals Inc.
Ed: Kent Hoover. Description: The Export-Import Bank has been targeted by the Bush Administration for a budget cut from $863 million to $633 million, resulting in a total of $11.4 billion available for export credit authorizations. Although the Small Business Administration says small businesses will be protected from budget cuts, many small business owners are not convinced. The Export-Import Bank is considering lowering coverage on export transactions and raising fees in order to stabilize its resources.

39818 ■ "Expert Help" in Entrepreneur (Vol. 28, No. 8, August 2000, pp. 135)
Pub: Entrepreneur Media Inc.
Ed: Cynthia E. Griffin. Description: The President's Resource Organization helps small businesses form boards of advisors.

39819 ■ Exporter's Guide to Federal Resources for Small Business
Pub: Gordon Press Publishers
Released: 1995. Price: $255.99.

39820 ■ "Fattah's Plan for Small Business" in Philadelphia Inquirer (February 6, 2007)
Pub: Philadelphia Newspapers LLC
Ed: Michael Currie Schaffer. Description: Philadelphia Mayoral candidate, Chaka Fattah, plans to create an emergency loan fund for small business in the city, if elected. The micro-loans would be available for small and home-based businesses.

39821 ■ "Federal Resource Guide 2002-2003" in Hispanic Business (December 2002, pp. FRG1-FRG2)
Pub: Hispanic Business
Description: Minority suppliers made up 5.7 percent of total federal procurement for the year 2000, with 1,585 Hispanic companies participating in the Minority Business Development program, making up 24.8 percent of all firms participating. Statistical data included.

39822 ■ "Firm Wins Grant for Robotic Vehicle" in Pittsburgh Business Times (Vol. 23, No. 4, August 15, 2003, pp. 3)
Pub: Pittsburgh Business Times
Ed: Maria Guzzo. Description: A U.S. Army research grant will be used at Applied Perception Inc. to develop a robotic vehicle; topics include military research, robotic vehicles, and battlefield applications of the vehicle.

39823 ■ "Follow the Leader" in Crain's Detroit Business (Vol. 18, No. 20, May 2)
Pub: Crain Communications Inc. - Detroit
Ed: Amy Lane. Description: A new state agency will offer low-interest loans to spur the development of statewide high-speed Internet access.

39824 ■ "Foreclosures: Troubled Owners Offered Free Help" in Altanta Journal-Constitution (February 1, 2007)
Pub: Cox Newspapers, Inc.
Ed: Julie B. Hairston. Description: Georgia Department of Labor and Federal Reserve Bank have partnered to offer assistance to homeowners facing mortgage foreclosure, information can be ascertained by calling 1-888-995-HOPE.

39825 ■ "Foreign currency" in Entrepreneur (Vol. 30, No. 10, October 2002, pp. 58)
Pub: Entrepreneur Media Inc.
Ed: Crystal Detamore-Rodman. Description: Profile of Steve Lamond, who launched International Turbine Systems Inc. in 1992; Lamond tells how he was able to borrow capital through government-guaranteed loans to start his firm.

39826 ■ Foundation for a New Century: A Report to the President & Congress: The White House Conference on Small Business Commission
Pub: DIANE Publishing Co.
Ed: Alan J. Patricof. Released: 1997. Price: $35.00. Description: Contains the 1995 conference delegates' action agenda for small business-60 public-policy recommendations that will further shape small business' role as the nation's job creators, innovators & risk takers. The agenda included: perennial challenges for small businesses; new challenges for small businesses; small businesses' policy priorities; entrepreneurship & self-employment; human capital; international trade; & reinventing & strengthening SBA. Also, prospects for small business & entrepreneurship in the 21st century.

39827 ■ "Free rein" in Entrepreneur (Vol. 31, No. 5, May 2003, pp. 23)
Pub: Entrepreneur Media Inc.
Ed: Stephen Barlas. Description: President Bush's proposed Fiscal 2004 Budget, while tightening the SBA's 7(a) loan program, would provide more in the way of the 504 Certified Development Loan Program.

39828 ■ "Funding from the Feds: Local interest in Small Business Investment Corporations is growing" in *Crain's Detroit Business* **(Vol.16, No.33)**
Pub: Crain Communications, Inc.
Ed: Matt Roush. **Description:** A venture capital program instituted during the Eisenhower administration is growing in Southeast Michigan. Several local groups are studying the creation of Small Business Investment Corporations, or SBICs, that are venture capital-like investment companies chartered by the federal SBA, and matches organizers' money up to $2-for-$1.

39829 ■ "Get that SBA Loan" in *My Business* **(September/October 2001, pp. 40)**
Pub: My Business Magazine
Ed: Juan Hovey. **Description:** The essential elements needed to procure a small business loan are profiled.

39830 ■ "Government on Demand" in *Microsoft Executive Circle* **(Vol. 1, No. 2, Q2 2001, pp. 38-40)**
Pub: Putman Media
Ed: Marty Weil. **Description:** Constituents now have easier and faster access to government services and information via the Internet. Statistical data included.

39831 ■ *Government Loans & Assistance Small Business Directory*
Pub: National Information Corp.
Ed: Chris D. Shemwell; Nicole S. Bruck. **Released:** 1997. **Price:** $44.99.

39832 ■ "Grants for Rural Biz" in *Inc.* **(September 1, 2003)**
Pub: Gruner & Jahr USA Publishing
Ed: Amy Gunderson. **Description:** States with a number of farms and fields are making more grants available to small businesses. The program, EPSCor, is funded mostly by the National Science Foundation and fosters scientific research in rural areas.

39833 ■ "Groups Push Forward on Mass Transit Proposals" in *Crain's Detroit Business* **(Vol. 23, February 5, 2007, No. 6, pp. 1)**
Pub: Crain Communications Inc. - Detroit
Ed: Andrew Dietderich. **Description:** Fast transit study proposals from Ann Arbor to Detroit are being backed by Amtrak and state and local governments. Three year trial to be undertaken patterned after other successful systems in other cities.

39834 ■ "Guardian Angel" in *Entrepreneur* **(Vol. 33, March 2005, No. 3, pp. 58)**
Pub: Entrepreneur Media Inc.
Ed: David Worrell. **Description:** Profile of the ACE-Net, the Angel Capital Electronic Network, which helps entrepreneurs with angel capital. Since it began in 1995, ACE-Net has helped entrepreneurs raise over $100 million.

39835 ■ "Healthy prospects" in *Black Enterprise* **(Vol. 32, No. 9, April 2002, pp.)**
Pub: Earl Graves Publishing Co.
Ed: Wendy Pelle-Beer. **Description:** Profile of Juanita Simmons, owner of an exercise studio, who worked through the StoreWorks program to purchase a new building for her studio. StoreWorks is a collaborative partnership between the Neighborhood Housing Services Community Development Corp., the City of New York's Department of Housing Preservation and Development, the Department of Housing and Urban Development, and participating private lenders; available only in New York City.

39836 ■ "Helping the Economy, One Snip at a Time" in *New York Times* **(November 2, 2003, pp. 1)**
Pub: The New York Times
Ed: Joseph P. Fried. **Description:** Profile of a hair salon owner who has grown her business by borrowing from people close to her, as well as loans from the Small Business Administration and the Women's Venture Fund, a nonprofit group.

39837 ■ "Helping Hands Overseas" in *Hispanic Business* **(November 2003, pp. 52, 54)**
Pub: Hispanic Business
Ed: Scott Williams. **Description:** Companies on the Hispanic Business Top 50 Exporters directory look to federal programs to help in foreign markets. Statistical data included.

39838 ■ "Hire Education" in *Hispanic Business* **(May 2005, pp. 56)**
Pub: Hispanic Business
Ed: Joel Russell. **Description:** A new job training program SER National helps Hispanic seniors, ages 55 and over, train for jobs. SER National was awarded a $26 million grant from the U.S. Labor Department.

39839 ■ "Home-Based Resources" in *Small Business Opportunities* **(Vol. 16, No. 2, March 2004, pp. 184)**
Pub: Harris Publications, Inc.
Description: Twenty resources to help run a home-based business, including information about the U.S. Small Business Administration small business programs.

39840 ■ "Housing Pilot Plan Updated" in *Mississippi Business Journal* **(Vol. 29, January 2007, No. 4, pp. 8)**
Pub: Venture Publications, Inc.
Ed: Wally Northway **Description:** Mississippi has been granted more than $280 million in funding from FEMA for the Alternative Housing Pilot Program. Under this plan some FEMA trailers would be replaced with more sustainable alternative housing. Plan aims to demonstrate that safer, more livable emergency housing can be produced for victims of major natural disasters.

39841 ■ "How Can I Find the Right Business Contacts in China?" in *Inc.* **(Volume 27, June 2005, No. 6, pp. 48)**
Pub: Inc. Magazine
Description: Information for starting an export-import business with Chinese businesses is offered. The U.S. Department of Commerce arranges meetings between American companies and foreign agents through its Gold Key Matching Service.

39842 ■ "In Brief: SBA Assesses Role Of Scores in Lending" in *American Banker* **(Vol. 171, November 17, 2006, No. 222, pp. 8)**
Pub: SourceMedia, Inc.
Ed: Alan Kline. **Description:** Small Business Administration's Office of Advocacy reported 47 percent of banks responding to a survey say they use credit scoring to aid in small business lending decisions. Statistical data included.

39843 ■ "In business with the U.S." in *Black Enterprise* **(Vol. 33, No. 3, October 2002, pp. 60)**
Pub: Earl Graves Publishing Co.
Ed: Alan Hughes. **Description:** Information for becoming designated as an 8(a) company with the federal government is given. The Small Business Administration runs the 8(a) Business Development program that provides business development and technical assistance to assist socially and economically disadvantaged small business growth. Contact information is provided.

39844 ■ "It's a 'go' in Detroit" in *BlackEnterprise* **(Vol. 32, No. 2, September 2001, pp. 50)**
Pub: Earl Graves Publishing Co.
Ed: Roger Barnes. **Description:** Blimpie will open restaurants in Empowerment Zones throughout the country, including one in Detroit, Michigan. Empowerment Zones are neighborhoods in urban and rural areas throughout the United States designated by the federal government for revitalization.

39845 ■ "Jadi's Journey; Move to OU Incubator Could Lead to Funding" in *Crain's Detroit Business* **(Vol. 22, January 9, 2006, No. 2, pp. 3)**
Pub: Crain Communications Inc. - Detroit

Ed: Sheena Harrison. **Description:** Jadi Inc. should receive $3 million in grants and federal funding for its new navigation systems for military robots. The firm has moved into the SmartZone Business Incubator at Oakland University in Michigan.

39846 ■ "Jeep Adds to Legacy of Federal Program Gone Well" in *San Diego Business Journal* **(Vol. 28, January 8, 2007, No. 2, pp. 12)**
Pub: San Diego Business Journal Associates
Ed: Cordell Koland. **Description:** Profile of the Jeep Wrangler and its beginnings as a military light reconnaissance vehicle in the 1940s.

39847 ■ "JSU Receives Record Funding" in *Mississippi Business Journal* **(Vol. 28, September 2006, No. 36, pp. 23)**
Pub: Venture Publications, Inc.
Description: Jackson State University has been granted a record $56 million in research and other sponsored programs awards for the external funding of 175 projects from federal and state agencies.

39848 ■ "Just a Mirage? Proposed Legislation May Expand SBIC Financing-Someday" in *Entrepreneur* **(Vol. 31, No. 8, August 2003, pp. 24)**
Pub: Entrepreneur Media, Inc.
Ed: Stephen Barlas. **Description:** Profile of the Small Business Investment Company (SBIC) loan enhancement bill proposed by Senator Olympia Snowe (R-Maine) is presented. The bill would increase the stream of capital into Debenture SBICs. Money from these loans could be used by small companies to finance inventories, accounts receivable and more, the only exception would be real estate.

39849 ■ "Lack of Lease Could Cost US Airways" in *Pittsburgh Business Times* **(Vol. 23, No. 5, August 22, 2003, pp. 3)**
Pub: Pittsburgh Business Times
Ed: Christopher Davis. **Description:** US Airway's future at Pittsburgh International Airport is in jeopardy following the airline's decision to reject its leases. The airline, led by CEO David Siegel, has been offered a $264 million financial incentive package by the City of Pittsburgh.

39850 ■ "Lawmakers take aim at living-wage laws" in *Crain's Detroit Business* **(Vol. 19, No. 8, February 24, 2003, pp. 7)**
Pub: Crain Communications Inc., Detroit
Ed: Amy Lane. **Description:** Republican lawmakers are working on ordinances that would allow local governments to require higher minimum wage from businesses that are vendors or receive other forms of local government assistance; Governor Granholm opposes the bill.

39851 ■ *Leadership Library on CD-ROM*
Pub: Leadership Directories Inc.
Released: Quarterly, Published 1997. **Price:** $3,420, individuals annual subscription; $3,249, individuals automatic renewal subscriptions. **Database Covers:** Integrated database of all 14 Yellow Books, searchable and exportable.

39852 ■ "Lenders rebuke SBA plan to address 7(a) shortfall" in *Business First Columbus* **(Vol. 18, No. 18, March 1, 2002, pp. A14)**
Pub: Business First Columbus, Inc.
Ed: Kent Hoover. **Description:** Small Business Administration lenders dispute the loan program cuts. Statistical data included.

39853 ■ "Lenders wary of plan to make up SBA program shortfall" in *Wall Street Journal* **(March 19, 2002, pp. B2)**
Pub: Wall Street Journal
Ed: Jeff Bailey. **Description:** The requirements of the SBA's new loan program are complicating the use of funding authority from another loan category. Statistical data included.

39854 ■ "LI Banks $2 Million in State Environmental Grants for Waterfront Projects" in *Long Island Business News* **(March 12, 2004)**
Pub: Dolan Media Newswires
Ed: Rosmaria Mancini. **Description:** New York State's Environmental Protection Fund program has awarded twelve Long Island municipalities more than $2 million in grants to improve waterfront districts. In Brookhaven, $400,000 will be used for the Port Jefferson Harborwalk project; Greenport will use $525,000 for continued implementation of the Mitchell Park and Marina project; Babylon Town will construct a fishing pier, hand-launch boat ramp and trail at Oak Beach with its $500,000; North Hempstead will implement sediment control devices to decrease pollution in Roslyn Pond and pollution reduction in Mill Pond.

39855 ■ "Loan Stars" in *Hispanic Business* **(March 2004, pp. 38, 40)**
Pub: Hispanic Business
Ed: Johanna Knapschaefer. **Description:** From micro-loans to Small Business Administration (SBA) programs, banks are slowly waking up to the possibilities of the Hispanic market.

39856 ■ "Loans, grants, and more" in *BlackEnterprise* **(Vol. 32, No. 2, September 2001, pp. 46)**
Pub: Earl Graves Publishing Co.
Ed: Paul McCoy-Pinderhughes. **Description:** A list of government-sponsored programs, small business loans, and grants for small business are highlighted, including the Commerce Business Daily lists of government-awarded contracts; the Federal Procurement Data System; the U.S. Department of Housing and Urban Development; the 7(a) loan program; and the Small Business Innovation Research program.

39857 ■ "Loanworthy Women" in *Business Week* **(June 12, 2000, pp. F8)**
Pub: McGraw-Hill, Inc.
Description: The conditions are favorable for loans for small women-owned companies.

39858 ■ "Long Island Development Corp. Steps Up Loan Programs in 2003" in *Long Island Business News* **(March 5, 2004)**
Pub: Dolan Media Newswires
Ed: Nick Anastasi. **Description:** The Long Island Development Company has provided 86 loans in the amount of $36.8 million from October 1, 2002 to September 30, 2003. The firm also assisted companies obtain $302 million in government and big business contracts through its Procurement Technical Assistance Program. Statistical data included.

39859 ■ "Long-Term Care Insurance is Growing Option Among Munster, Ind.-Area Families" in *The Times* **(July 4, 2004)**
Pub: The Times
Ed: Dan Rafter. **Description:** The State of Indiana has partnered with private insurance companies to offer residents long-term care policies to help them protect their assets and life savings should they ever require long-term care.

39860 ■ "Love of Country" in *Entrepreneur* **(Vol. 33, March 2005, No. 3, pp. 62)**
Pub: Entrepreneur Media Inc.
Ed: Jennifer Pellet. **Description:** The Rural Business Investment Program (RBIP), a joint effort of the Department of Agriculture and the Small Business Administration are working to make $60 million available to rural entrepreneurs for equity investing and $3 million in grant-funded technical assistance for businesses.

39861 ■ "Maine Office of Innovation Releases Plan for Research Development" in *Portland Press Herald* **(November 4, 2005)**
Pub: Blethen Maine Newspapers, Inc.
Ed: Matt Wickenheiser. **Description:** Maine's Office of Innovation is proposing a plan that would double the amount of money spent on research and development statewide. The plan proposes $1 billion in annual spending for 2010, with increases from both private and public organizations.

39862 ■ "Maine Program Helps Businesses Apply for Federal Grants" in *Portland Press Herald* **(September 23, 2005)**
Pub: Blethen Maine Newspapers, Inc.
Ed: Matt Wickenheiser. **Description:** Maine's Technology Institute program helps small businesses with the grant application process.

39863 ■ "Maine Program Merges On-The-Job Trainings with College Education" in *Portland Press Herald* **(August 30, 2005)**
Pub: Blethen Maine Newspapers, Inc.
Ed: Matt Wickenheiser. **Description:** Maine residents can enroll in apprenticeship programs in the child care, marine trades, construction and other industries. Funding for the program was set at $600,000 for fiscal year 2005.

39864 ■ "Make Over Magic" in *Entrepreneur* **(Vol. 31, No. 7, July 2003, pp. 49)**
Pub: Entrepreneur Media, Inc.
Ed: C.J. Prince. **Description:** The U.S. Small Business Administration's 504 Certified Development Company Program offers below-market, fixed-rate loans to small businesses for real estate and heavy equipment purchases, yet few small firms use the program.

39865 ■ "Massachusetts Jobless Insurance Trust Fund May Need Federal Help" in *Boston Globe* **(April 11, 2003)**
Pub: Knight-Ridder/Tribune Business News
Ed: Matthew Brelis. **Description:** The State of Massachusetts' unemployment insurance trust fund is facing insolvency after two years of rising unemployment rates and will require federal loans to pay benefits in 2003.

39866 ■ "Michigan Department of Consumer and Industry Services: What it does" in *Crain's Detroit Business* **(Vol. 18, Dec. 9, 2002, pp. 14)**
Pub: Crain Communications Inc., Detroit
Description: An overview of the Michigan Department of Consumer and Industry Services, and the services the department provides to small businesses in the state.

39867 ■ "The microbe warrior. (Bioterrorism)" in *Red Herring* **(January 2003, pp. 58)**
Pub: Herring Communications Inc.
Ed: Suzanne McGee. **Description:** Profile AgION Technologies, the company developing products financed from the Homeland Security Fund. The firm's products show great promise in the areas of national security, intelligence, or military applications.

39868 ■ "Microlending - Arizona Style" in *Hispanic Business* **(March 2002, pp. 16)**
Pub: Hispanic Business
Ed: Jonathan J. Higuera. **Description:** Profile of Frank Ballesteros, who borrows from the U.S. Small Business Administration and other financial institutions and lends to the working poor.

39869 ■ "Microloans Face Budgetary Ax" in *Black Enterprise* **(Vol. 35, November 2004, No. 4, pp. 60)**
Pub: Earl G. Graves Publishing Co. Inc.
Ed: Tamara E. Holmes. **Description:** Profile of the Small Business Association's Microloan Program, designed to loan startup businesses loans under $35,000.

39870 ■ "Money Corner" in *Home Business* **(Vol. 13, January/February 2006, No. 1, pp. 78)**
Pub: Home Business Magazine
Description: Small Business Administration loans, retirement information, small business taxes, and Valentine's Day gift-buying tips are included.

39871 ■ "Money Matters" in *Small Business Opportunities* **(Vol. 13, No. 5, September 2001, pp. 10)**
Pub: Harris Publications, Inc.
Ed: Carla Vincent. **Description:** Ways for small businesses to generate venture capital are explored, including a list of government agencies that provide small business funding.

39872 ■ "New DOE contracts: small business is the focus of several new agency initiatives" in *Hispanic Business* **(Vol.22,No. 7-8, July-Aug. 2000)**
Pub: Hispanic Business
Ed: Patricia Guadalupe. **Description:** The U.S. Department of Energy is presenting small businesses with over 250 contract opportunities in fields including energy resources, national security and environmental quality.

39873 ■ "New Face at the SBA" in *Hispanic Business* **(Vol. 23, No. 10, October, 2001, pp. 32, 34)**
Pub: Hispanic Business
Ed: Scott Williams. **Description:** Profile of Hector V. Barreto, the new administrator of the U.S. Small Business Administration (SBA), hopes to make the agency more responsive to the small-business community. Statistical data included.

39874 ■ "New Law Offers Tax Relief for Individuals - But Only Temporarily" in *Practical Tax Strategies* **(Vol. 67, No. 1, July 2001, pp. 30)**
Pub: Warren, Gorham and Lamont
Ed: Robert E. Ward. **Description:** The author examines the Economic Growth and Tax Relief Reconciliation Act of 2001 and the tax benefits it offers individuals.

39875 ■ "New Law Significantly Alters Retirement Plan Landscape" in *Warren, Gorham and Lamont* **(Vol. 67, No. 1, July 2001, pp. 36)**
Pub: Warren, Gorham and Lamont
Ed: Barry Salkin. **Description:** The author examines the retirement planning effects, especially in regards to employee benefits and pension funds, of the Economic Growth and Tax Relief Reconciliation Act of 2001.

39876 ■ "New Way to 7(a)" in *Entrepreneur* **(Vol. 33, February 2005, No. 2, pp. 49)**
Pub: Entrepreneur Media Inc.
Ed: C.J. Prince. **Description:** Information regarding the bill that will eliminate the $79 million federal subsidy for the Small Business Administration's loan guarantee program is presented. The bill is supposed to make the program self-sustaining.

39877 ■ "New to You?" in *Entrepreneur* **(Vol. 28, No. 9, September 2000, pp. 50)**
Pub: Entrepreneur Media Inc.
Ed: Doug Hood and Marilea S. Hood. **Description:** The Small Business Administration 504 Certified Development Companies program, a new government-guaranteed loan program with a fixed rate-separate from the SBA, is outlined in question/answer format.

39878 ■ "No Slowdown Likely for Rising Health Costs" in *Crain's Detroit Business* **(Vol. 22, November 27, 2006, No. 48, pp. 21)**
Pub: Crain Communications Inc. - Detroit
Ed: Andrew Dietderich. **Description:** Double digit increases in health care are forecast for 2007. Health carriers say too many people who can afford to pay for medical treatment are leaving Michigan. This leaves a more indigent population behind. Governor is proposing assistance for access to universal health care.

39879 ■ "A not-so-taxing CHANGE" in *Pittsburgh Business Times* **(Vol. 20, No. 53, July 20, 2001, pp. 25)**
Pub: Pittsburgh Business Times
Ed: Tracy Carbasho. **Description:** The Reconciliation Act features changes in four areas: updated 401(k) contribution schedule, increased employer contribution limits, shortened vesting schedule, and added 401(k) options.

39880 ■ "The Occupational Safety & Health Administration (OSHA)" in *Entrepreneur* **(Vol. 32, No. 1, January 2004, pp. 10)**
Pub: Entrepreneur Media, Inc.
Ed: Steve Cooper. **Description:** Occupational Safety & Health Administration (OSHA) has added informa-

tion for small businesses regarding workplace emergency preparedness, covering issues of preparing for chemical and biological attacks, personal protective equipment, bioterrorism, training and education, and safety equipment.

39881 ■ "Orchestrating Assistance; Chambers of Commerce" in *Crain's New York Business* **(Vol. 22, November 13, 2006, No. 46, pp. 38)**
Pub: Crain Communications, Inc.
Description: Listing of local chapters of New York's chambers of commerce. These organizations serve as sources of information and representation for local business interest provide a number of services and a wide variety of programs for small businesses.

39882 ■ "OSDBU Directory" in *Hispanic Business* **(December 2001, pp. FG18, FG20)**
Pub: Hispanic Business
Description: A listing of the Office of Small and Disadvantaged Business Utilization agencies is presented. The OSDBU is the first point of contact for minority entrepreneurs wishing to sell goods or services to the federal government.

39883 ■ "Panel Chief Set To Reopen SBA Budget Debate" in *American Banker* **(Vol. 171, November 30, 2006, No. 229, pp. 1)**
Pub: SourceMedia, Inc.
Ed: Ben Jackson. Description: New York Democrat, Nydia Velazquez, is committed to changing the Small Business Administration's loan programs. Her plan would lower user fees for borrowers as well as lenders.

39884 ■ "Partnership: Cisco, SBA team on online learning" in *InfoWorld* **(Vol. 22, No. 30, July 24, 2000, pp. 20)**
Pub: InfoWorld
Ed: Carolyn A. April. Description: The U.S. Small Business Administration (SBA) and Cisco Systems last week announced an online training partnership to help small businesses incorporate the Internet into their day-to-day business operations.

39885 ■ "Pension Reform Enhances Sponsored Retirement Plans" in *San Diego Business Journal* **(Vol. 22, No. 41, October 8, 2001, pp. 16)**
Pub: San Diego Business Journal
Ed: Laura Just. Description: A listing of the new pension revisions effective in 2002 by the Economic Growth and Tax Relief Reconciliation Act of 2001 are presented.

39886 ■ *A Piece of the Pie*
Pub: Outskirts Press, Incorporated
Ed: Shelton P. Rhodes, Peter Fretty. Released: July 2005. Price: $34.95. Description: Examination of the U.S. Small Business Administration's program 8(a), designed to help disadvantaged individuals grow their small businesses.

39887 ■ "Plan Would Share Wealth From $1B Fund" in *Crain's Detroit Business* **(Vol. 21, October 24, 2005, No. 43, pp. 26)**
Pub: Crain Communications Inc. - Detroit
Ed: Amy Lane. Description: Life-sciences, technology, tourism, manufacturing, agriculture, film-production, and defense companies will all benefit from $101 million in government funds to support growing or technology-oriented businesses.

39888 ■ "Port of Pittsburgh to Start Weekday Water Taxi Service" in *Pittsburgh Business Times* **(Vol. 23, No. 8, September 12, 2003, pp. 1)**
Pub: Pittsburgh Business Times
Ed: Christopher Davis. Description: The Port of Pittsburgh Commission has launched a new weekday water taxi service with $3 million federal financing. The taxi service will link the Pittsburgh downtown area to Homestead, Pennsylvania.

39889 ■ "President signs tax cut bill with pension reform" in *Employee Benefit Plan Review* **(Vol. 56, No. 1, July 2001, pp. 10)**
Pub: Charles D. Spencer & Associates, Inc.
Description: President George W. Bush signed the Economic Growth and Tax Relief Reconciliation Act of 2001. Changes in the pension law were made in vesting provisions and compensation limits.

39890 ■ "Priority" in *Inc.* **(Volume 27, March 2005, No. 3, pp. 23-26, 28, 30)**
Pub: Inc. Magazine
Description: Business information discussed includes information about the SEC looking into unlicensed investment brokers, the economy, freight co-ops to help shippers ease costs, hiring, Google, education, SBA assistance to women entrepreneurs, and new inventions.

39891 ■ "Qualified state tuition programs: EGTRRA update" in *The Tax Adviser* **(Vol. 32, No. 10, October 2001, pp. 672)**
Pub: Harborside Financial Center
Ed: Philip E. Moore. Description: The impact that the Economic Growth and Tax Relief Reconciliation Act (EGTRRA) will have on qualified state tuition programs (Sec. 529 plans) is discussed. The new law, will most likely, make Sec. 29 plans more popular.

39892 ■ "Quick Fix: Do SBA Express Loans Really Shortchange Entrepreneurs?" in *Entrepreneur* **(Vol. 32, No. 4, April 2004, pp. 27)**
Pub: Entrepreneur Media, Inc.
Ed: Julie Monahan. Description: Profile of the U.S. Small Business Administration's Express program that guaranteed loans to thousands of entrepreneurs. Retailers with gross sales of $6 million or less, wholesalers with 100 employees or less, and manufacturers with 500 employees or less, are eligible for Express Loans.

39893 ■ "Rating the Governors" in *Inc.* **(November 2006, pp. 95-98, 100, 102, 104, 106)**
Pub: Gruner & Jahr USA Publishing
Ed: Mike Hofman. Description: Best governors for business are the least partisan. Governors of various states are discussed and rated on several criteria: tax and fiscal policy, health care, education, regulation, and work force and economic development.

39894 ■ "Recruitment: Federal File" in *Hispanic Business* **(December 2002, pp. FRG4)**
Pub: Hispanic Business
Description: Information on future U.S. postal service, head start programs, the federal government's General Schedule that determines salaries, and personnel security is offered.

39895 ■ "Recruitment: Hispanic Employment Program Managers" in *Hispanic Business* **(December 2002, pp. FRG6-FRG8)**
Pub: Hispanic Business
Description: Contact information is provided from the Hispanic Employment Program Manager's Directory (HEPM); these managers are responsible with improving the representation of Hispanics in the work force.

39896 ■ "Regulatory Rescue" in *Entrepreneur* **(Vol. 31, No. 8, August 2003, pp. 24)**
Pub: Entrepreneur Media, Inc.
Ed: Stephen Barlas. Description: The bill authorizing 20 Small Business Development Centers across the U.S. is expected to be passed by Congress. The Small Business Regulatory Assistance Act (H.R. 205) was approved by the House in April 2003.

39897 ■ "Requisite Relief" in *Entrepreneur.com* **(Vol. 34, January 2006, No. 1, pp. 26)**
Pub: Entrepreneur Media Inc.
Ed: Joshua Kurlantzick. Description: Programs that would benefit small businesses hurt by the hurricanes of 2005 are discussed by various entrepreneurs.

39898 ■ "Rescue Plan" in *Entrepreneur* **(Vol. 33, October 2005, No. 10, pp. 53)**
Pub: Entrepreneur Media Inc.
Ed: David Worrell. Description: The Federal Emergency Management Agency's emergency loan of $300,000 helped save Colleen Molter's information technology staffing firm, QED National. Molter's company has grown about 33 percent annually since the attack on the World Trade Center that could have put her out of business.

39899 ■ "Resources: Web Sites, Organizations, Events and More To Grow Your Business" in *Entrepreneur* **(Vol. 32, September 2004, No. 9, pp. 8)**
Pub: Entrepreneur Media Inc.
Ed: Steve Cooper. Description: Resources to help small business are featured including the Small Business Administration's effort to help teen entrepreneurs launch a business; KnockNow an online community of entrepreneurs, executives, venture capitalists, angel investors, service sector companies, and government; the SBA's business Website offering information on small business development, financial assistance, taxes, laws and regulations, international trade, workplace issues, buying and selling and federal forms.

39900 ■ "Richmond Times-Dispatch, Va., Business Briefs Column" in *Knight-Ridder/Tribune Business News* **(October 23, 2001, pp. ITEM01296031)**
Pub: Knight-Ridder/Tribune Business News
Description: The Richmond Economic Development Corporation in Virginia, has been awarded $450,000 by the U.S. Treasury Department to create a loan source for small businesses lacking access to traditional financing.

39901 ■ "Ripple Effects" in *Hispanic Business* **(May 2005, pp. 68, 70)**
Pub: Hispanic Business
Ed: Holly Ocasio Rizzo. Description: Congress is considering a move to restore small business equity funding; the program was stopped when the technology and telecom bubble burst.

39902 ■ "Romney Set To Unveil Jobs Program" in *Boston Globe* **(February 3, 2005)**
Pub: New York Times Company
Ed: Sasha Talcott. Description: Massachusetts State has partnered with Citizens Financial Group to create jobs. The new program is funded by Citizens and will be administered by the State's Department of Business and Technology.

39903 ■ "Running Dry" in *Entrepreneur* **(Vol. 33, August 2005, No. 8, pp. 20)**
Pub: Entrepreneur Media Inc.
Ed: Crystal Detamore-Rodman. Description: The U.S. government's Small Business Investment Company (SBIC) provides equity capital to entrepreneurs. Currently the SBIC Participating Securities Program provides as much as $2 for every $1 of capital raised by venture funds licensed by the SBA; this program is in jeopardy of being discontinued.

39904 ■ "The SBA All-Stars" in *Inc.* **(August 2005, pp. 22)**
Pub: Inc. Magazine
Ed: Mina Azodi. Description: Listing of the top ten Small Business Administration's field offices is presented, with San Diego, California making the number one spot, followed by Utah.

39905 ■ "SBA Bad Loans on the Rise" in *Hispanic Business* **(January/February 2003, pp. 12)**
Pub: Hispanic Business
Description: The number of bad loans the Small Business Administration has been required to cover have nearly doubled from 1995 to 2002.

39906 ■ "SBA can be a boon, but it doesn't make loans" in *Crain's Detroit Business* **(Vol. 18, No. 49, December 9, 2002, pp. 16)**
Pub: Crain Communications Inc., Detroit

Ed: Laura Bailey. **Description:** The misconceptions about the U.S. Small Business Administration regarding grants and loans are discussed.

39907 ■ "SBA Chief: Storm Relief Advances" in *American Banker* (Vol. 172, February 2, 2007, No. 23, pp. 3)
Pub: SourceMedia, Inc.
Ed: Derek Klobucher. **Description:** The Small Business Administration has disbursed more than $5 billion in disaster relief loans to individuals and small business owners affected by the 2005 Gulf Coast hurricanes. The SBA also reports an additional $2 billion in funding available.

39908 ■ "SBA Creates Contracting Opportunities for Disabled Veterans" in *St. Charles Business Record* (May 7, 2004)
Pub: Dolan Media Company
Description: A new procurement program created by the U.S. Small Business Administration will help service-disabled veteran-owned small businesses procure federal contracts.

39909 ■ "SBA Finds Another Billion for Loans" in *Inc.* (August 1, 2003)
Pub: Gruner & Jahr USA Publishing
Ed: Bobbie Gossage. **Description:** The U.S. Small Business Administration has created an additional $1.4 billion lending authority for its primary 7(a) loan program for fiscal 2003, increasing total lending authority to more than $11 billion.

39910 ■ "SBA Head Opposes Relaxing 'Minority' Terms" in *Wall Street Journal* (December 13, 1999, pp. A2)
Pub: Dow Jones & Co., Inc.
Ed: Paulette Thomas. **Description:** An interview with the Small Business Administration head, Aida Alvarez.

39911 ■ "SBA Hearing Scheduled" in *Journal Record (Oklahoma City, OK)* (February 5, 2007)
Pub: Journal Record
Description: Small business owners, community organization and trade association representatives, and community and business leaders will attend the U.S. Small Business Administration's Federal Regulatory Fairness Hearing to be held February 23, 2007 in the Oklahoma State Capital building.

39912 ■ "SBA info" in *Crain's Detroit Business* (Vol. 18, No. 49, December 9, 2002, pp. 16)
Pub: Crain Communications Inc., Detroit
Description: Profile of important information for small businesses regarding the Small Business Administration. Contact information included.

39913 ■ "SBA urged to tighten oversight of lenders" in *Atlanta Business Chronicle* (Vol. 25, January 10, 2003, No. 31, pp. 4B)
Pub: American City Business Publications, Inc.
Ed: Kent Hoover. **Description:** A report from the General Accounting Office claims that the Small Business Administration needs tighter oversight with respect to private-sector lenders who make government-guaranteed loans. Existing reviews of private-sector lenders have been criticized for their cursory nature.

39914 ■ "SBA Loan Lenders Ranked by Value of 7(a) Loans" in *American Banker* (Vol. 170, February 1, 2005, No. 270, pp. 6)
Pub: Thomson Financial Media Inc.
Description: Listing of Small Business Administration's loan lenders, ranked by value of 7(a) loans.

39915 ■ "SBA Preferred Lenders" in *Crain's Detroit Business* (Vol. 19, No. 42, October 20, 2003, pp. 18)
Pub: Crain Communications Inc., Detroit
Description: A listing of the U.S. Small Business Administration's preferred lenders is presented. These banks are SBA approved to review and process loans with contacts in Southeast Michigan.

39916 ■ "SBA Program Falls Short on Helping Firms Win Jobs" in *Wall Street Journal* (August 1, 2000, pp. B2)
Pub: Dow Jones & Co., Inc.
Ed: Eleena De Lisser. **Description:** According to a report published by the General Accounting Office, the Small Business Administration (SBA) has not helped small business procure government contracts.

39917 ■ "SBA limits program's loan amounts to $500,000" in *Crain's Detroit Business* (Vol. 18, No. 40, October 7, 2002, pp. 43)
Pub: Crain Communications Inc., Detroit
Ed: Laura Bailey. **Description:** The U.S. Small Business Administration has lowered the amount of loans falling under the 7(a) program from $2 million to $500,000. This move could cost the State of Michigan 4,663 jobs over a year's time.

39918 ■ "SBA Raises Size Standards for Small-Business Eligibility" in *Business First Columbus* (Vol. 18, No. 25, February 8, 2002, pp. A17)
Pub: Business First Columbus, Inc.
Ed: Ken Hoover. **Description:** Recent changes in the Small Business Administration's size standards for small business eligibility is explained.

39919 ■ "SBA Spared Budget Blues" in *Hispanic Business* (Vol. 22, No. 1/2, January/February, pp. 16)
Pub: Hispanic Business
Ed: Patricia Guadalupe. **Description:** Congress gives the agency a boost in its fiscal 2000 budget. Various programs of the SBA are highlighted, including The New Market Venture Capital Program, an initiative aimed at increasing the number of minority businesses.

39920 ■ "SBA Suspends VC Program, Future in Doubt" in *Venture Capital Journal* (January 1, 2005)
Pub: Thomason Financial Inc.
Description: Faced with nearly $2 billion in losses, the Small Business Administration's Small Business Investment Companies (SBIC) program will stop licensing new SBIC firms until October 1, 2005. The program provides about one-fifth of U.S. venture funds.

39921 ■ "SBA's main loan program faces deep cut for fiscal 2003" in *Wall Street Journal* (March 12, 2002, pp. B2)
Pub: Wall Street Journal
Ed: Jeff Bailey. **Description:** Information is presented regarding the impending cuts in the SBA's main loan program for fiscal year 2003.

39922 ■ "SBA's future up to whoever controls Congress" in *Atlanta Business Chronicle* (Vol. 25, No. 20, October 25, 2002, pp. 4A)
Pub: American City Business Publications, Inc.
Ed: Kent Hoover. **Description:** The winner of control of Congress in 2003 will play a pivotal role in mapping out the future of the Small Business Administration. The majority of the SBA's programs are set for reauthorization in 2003.

39923 ■ "Seminars focus on bio-research" in *Hispanic Business* (Vol. 22, No. 6, June 2000, pp. 28)
Pub: Hispanic Business
Description: The U.S. Government will provide $495 million funding for research into nanotechnology in 2001. Small businesses wishing to participate in the new technological revolution are being helped by the National Institutes of Health, which is sponsoring a symposium on nanotechnology.

39924 ■ "Service Providers" in *Crain's Detroit Business* (Vol. 16, No. 50, December 11, 2000, pp. E-13)
Pub: Crain Communications, Inc.
Description: An extensive listing of services provided in Michigan that help startups and existing businesses get access to programs available to them.

39925 ■ "Small-Business e-Loan" in *Hispanic Business* (March 2002, pp. 60)
Pub: Hispanic Business
Ed: Roger Harris. **Description:** The Small Business Administration has launched a new Web-hosted system that aids in the origination and management of SBA-backed and other traditional small-business loans.

39926 ■ *The Small Business Guide to HSAs*
Pub: Brick Tower Press
Ed: JoAnn Mills Laing. **Released:** September 2004. **Price:** $14.95. **Description:** Government-assisted Health Savings Accounts (HSAs) offer employees a tax-free way to accumulate savings to be used for qualified medical expenses, they can be rolled over without penalty for future spending, or invested to accumulate savings to pay for health needs after retirement. Employers offering HSAs can save up to two-thirds of business expenses on health insurance costs.

39927 ■ *Small Business Loan Program Kit*
Pub: International Wealth Success, Incorporated
Ed: Tyler G. Hicks. **Released:** 2006. **Price:** $100.00. **Description:** Guide to the Small Business Loan Program that offers loans to small and minority-owned companies doing work for government agencies, large corporations, hospitals, universities, and similar organizations.

39928 ■ "Small Business Protests Loan Program Shift" in *Long Island Business News* (March 12, 2004)
Pub: Dolan Media Newswires
Ed: Adina Genn. **Description:** The U.S. Small Business Administration did not request funding for the Centereach-based Community Development Corporation of Long Island for 2005. Advocates of microloans say the cut in funding would hurt small businesses and slow job creation.

39929 ■ "Small Business Resource Guide: Service Providers: Part 1 of 2" in *Crain's Detroit Business* (Vol. 15, No. 50, Dec. 13, 1999, pp. E-11)
Pub: Crain Communications, Inc.
Description: The Michigan Economic Development Corporation is the State of Michigan's one-stop resource for businesses seeking growth in the state. Includes a listing of the SBA's programs and contact information.

39930 ■ "Small Business Resource Guide: Service Providers: Part 2 of 2" in *Crain's Detroit Business* (Vol. 15, No. 50, Dec. 13, 1999, pp. E-13)
Pub: Crain Communications, Inc.
Description: More contact information for small and start-up business in the State of Michigan, including information about Michigan State University Extension Service, the public library systems, organizations, IRS publications, regulators, Michigan Unemployment Agency, and the Michigan Department of Environmental Quality.

39931 ■ "Small Businesses Now Can Afford Big Benefits" in *National Underwriter Life & Health-Financial Services Edition* (Vol. 105, No. 42)
Pub: The National Underwriter Co.
Ed: Peter A. Welsh. **Description:** A review of the Economic Growth & Tax Relief Reconciliation Act of 2001 (EGTRBA) is presented, focusing on the impact this new law will have on small businesses. Statistical data included.

39932 ■ "Small Firms Seeking Government Contracts Will Get More Help" in *Kiplinger Letter* (Vol. 78, January 19, 2007, No. 2)
Pub: Kiplinger
Description: Business Matchmaking program run by the Small Business Administration, along with new rules to do away with unfair competition for government contracts, will help small companies compete for government work. The Small Business Administration will also lower fees for new loans to small companies.

39933 ■ "Small businesses dissatisfied with SBA" in *Black Enterprise* **(Vol. 31, No. 5, December 2000, pp. 29)**
Pub: Earl Graves Publishing Co..
Ed: Joyce Jones. **Description:** A report issued by the General Accounting Office (GAO) shows that the Small Business Administration is not effective in securing contracts for 8(a) program participants.

39934 ■ "State, Utilities to Debate How to Meet Power Needs" in *Crain's Detroit Business* **(Vol. 22, November 27, 2006, No. 48, pp. 14)**
Pub: Crain Communications Inc. - Detroit
Ed: Amy Lane. **Description:** Michigan Public Service Commission will chair discussions with state power companies on meeting the energy needs for 2007. New policies are on the agenda from building new power plants to purchasing required amounts of energy from renewable sources.

39935 ■ "Take It For Granted" in *Entrepreneur* **(Vol. 33, January 2005, No. 1, pp. 50)**
Pub: Entrepreneur Media Inc.
Ed: David Worrell. **Description:** U.S. Small Business Innovative Research grants and contracts provide funding for small companies to develop high tech products. The programs are divided into two phases: one is to study the feasibility of a new technology or idea, the second to encourage commercialization of a particular technology.

39936 ■ "Task Force Recommends Strategies to Improve Maine's Forest Products Industry" in *Portland Press Herald* **(April 6, 2005)**
Pub: Blethen Maine Newspapers, Inc.
Ed: Tux Turkel. **Description:** Maine's Governor John Baldacci created a task force to address the state's forest products industry. The report outlines eight specific initiatives for the Governor to consider for improving the industry.

39937 ■ "The Tax Act of 2001" in *Hawaii Business* **(Vol. 47, No. 2, August 2001, pp. 208)**
Pub: Hawaii Business Publishing Co.
Ed: Scott Butera. **Description:** A review of the Economic Growth and Tax Relief Reconciliation Act of 2001 is presented. The law provides both tax-saving and financial-planning opportunities, the four areas of focus include personal taxation, education funding, retirement planning and estate planning.

39938 ■ "Tax Cut Bill Includes Pension Reform, Other Provisions Affecting Employee Benefits" in *Employee Benefit Plan Review* **(Vol. 55, No. 12)**
Pub: Charles D. Spencer & Associates, Inc.
Description: The Economic Growth and Tax Relief Reconciliation Act of 2001 represents a major advance in pension reform. The new law, which President George W. Bush expects to sign, includes an increase of the annual dollar limit for defined benefit plans.

39939 ■ "Tax 'Rebate' Notices Continue to Rankle Democrats" in *Tax Notes* **(Vol. 92, No. 1, July 2, 2001, pp. 25-27)**
Pub: Tax Notes International
Ed: Amy Hamilton. **Description:** Issues concerning the political ramifications of an IRS notice sent to U.S. taxpayers announcing tax relief under the Economic Growth and Tax Relief Reconciliation Act of 2001 are examined, focusing on the political benefits Republicans and President George W. Bush may gain from the wording of the notice.

39940 ■ "Terrorism Insurance" in *The Economist* **(Vol. 376, July 16-22, 2005, No. 8435, pp. 71)**
Pub: The Economist Newspaper Ltd.
Description: In the aftermath of the terrorist bombings in London, England, American insurers are looking at the Congressional scheme called TRIA, which offers a back-stop to private insurers in the event of a terrorist incident in the nation.

39941 ■ "The U.S. Commercial Service: www.export.gov/comm_svc" in *Entrepreneur* **(Vol. 32, November 2004, No. 11, pp. 6)**
Pub: Entrepreneur Media Inc.
Ed: Steve Cooper. **Description:** U.S. Commercial Service offers global business solutions in the areas of market research, trade events to promote businesses and services, introductions between buyers and distributors, and export counseling.

39942 ■ "Thumbs Up" in *Hispanic Business* **(July/August 2002, pp. 16)**
Pub: Hispanic Business
Ed: Patricia Guadalupe. **Description:** Hector Barreto wins praise for his stewardship of the Small Business Administration, but the Bush administration receives criticism.

39943 ■ "Tight-Lipped Banks" in *Entrepreneur* **(Vol. 28, No. 7, July 2000, pp. 40)**
Pub: Entrepreneur Media Inc.
Ed: Doug Hood and Marilea Hood. **Description:** Information about SBA loans is shared.

39944 ■ "Tips & Trends" in *Small Business Opportunities* **(Vol. 17, September 2005, No. 5, pp. 14)**
Pub: Harris Publications Inc.
Description: Tips and trends important to small business include the addition of a coffeemaker that also makes soup, tea or cocoa; paper shredders; headsets; a sales resource guide for retailers; information for the Federal Citizen Information Center; and Creative Colors, the franchise offering mobile equipment to home-based businesses.

39945 ■ "To lend or not to lend" in *Atlanta Business Chronicle* **(Vol. 24, No. 13, August 31, 2001, pp. 1B)**
Pub: American City Business Journals Inc.
Ed: Linda Kercher. **Description:** Small business loan activity may be slowing, either due to tightening loan standards or reduced demand from small business owners, as both groups deal with an uncertain future. Lower interest rates have helped buoy demand for loans, and Small Business Administration loan guarantees help ensure that lenders will be interested in making loans. The article provides opinions from several lenders and from the National Federation of Independent Business.

39946 ■ "Trading For Success" in *Business First Buffalo* **(Vol. 19, No. 46, August 8, 2003, pp. 17)**
Pub: American City Business Journals, Inc.
Ed: Joe Iannarelli. **Description:** Integrated Thermal Solutions, led by president Richard Perez, faces an array of new regulations for pallets and other shipping products. The Buffalo, New York region is a hub for international trade, prompting local companies to seek assistance to boost their operations.

39947 ■ "Two Detroit Riverfront Projects Win Tax Breaks" in *Crain's Detroit Business* **(Vol. 22, November 27, 2006, No. 48, pp. 25)**
Pub: Crain Communications Inc. - Detroit
Ed: Amy Lane. **Description:** Tax credits and other assistance were approved by the Michigan Economic Growth Authority for two brownfield-redevelopment projects. Townhomes and retail space to be built just East of the Renaissance Center.

39948 ■ *The Ultimate Insider's Guide to SBA and Other Loans*
Pub: Entrepreneur Press
Ed: Dan M. Koehler. **Released:** July 2004. **Price:** $23.95. **Description:** Guide to understanding Small Business Administration government small business loans.

39949 ■ "Unfinished business: the disappearing Tax Act of 2001" in *Tax Notes* **(Vol. 91, No. 11, June 4, 2001, pp. 1652-1653)**
Pub: Tax Notes International
Ed: Martin A. Sullivan. **Description:** The political implications of a sunset provision that would cause the

entire Economic Growth and Tax Relief Reconciliation Act of 2001 to expire December 31, 2001, are examined, focusing on how the provision acts as a political defeat for Republicans who have supported President George W. Bush's tax cut proposals.

39950 ■ *The United States Government Manual*
Pub: Superintendent of Documents
Released: Annual. **Price:** $36.00. **Description:** Includes complete information on all agencies, boards, commissions, and committees in the federal government. Entries include a list of principal officers, descriptions of programs and services, and contact information.

39951 ■ "An Unsure Thing: Can't Pay Your Federal Tax Bill?" in *Entrepreneur* **(Vol. 31, No. 7, July 2003, pp. 55)**
Pub: Entrepreneur Media, Inc.
Ed: Joan Szabo. **Description:** The U.S. Internal Revenue Service's Offer-In-Compromise (OIC) program, which allows taxpayers to settle tax bills for a lower amount than owed, needs a complete overhaul, according to the IRS Oversight Board.

39952 ■ "Utilities Boost Companies; Utility Services" in *Crain's New York Business* **(Vol. 22, November 13, 2006, No. 46, pp. 36)**
Pub: Crain Communications, Inc.
Description: Listing of companies that provide utility programs, incentives and benefits to small businesses looking to relocate within the five boroughs of New York City or expand their businesses in the area.

39953 ■ "Wanted: stimulus: report says GOP is not doing all it can for small business" in *Black Enterprise* **(Vol. 33, No. 7, Feb. 2003)**
Pub: Earl Graves Publishing Co.
Ed: Joyce Jones. **Description:** Federal funding and legislation important to small business is discussed.

39954 ■ "What Gives?" in *Entrepreneur* **(Vol. 28, No. 9, September 2000, pp. 20)**
Pub: Entrepreneur Media Inc.
Ed: Julie Monahan. **Description:** An audit finds problems with the Small Disadvantaged Business Certification program.

39955 ■ "When in Doubt Grab a Mouse, or a Phone" in *Crain's Chicago Business* **(Vol. 30, January 2007, No. 1, pp. 12)**
Pub: Crain Communications, Inc.
Ed: Dee Gill. **Description:** Interview with Maria Meyers, network coordinator for U.S.SourceLink, a nonprofit designed to give entrepreneurs and small business owners easy access to resources. Meyers talks about the program, its history and impact on the community, the website itself, and the grass-roots marketing needed to inform consumers of the services available.

39956 ■ "Who Gets Disaster Aid? Who Doesn't?" in *Business Week Online* **(January 22, 2002)**
Pub: McGraw-Hill, Inc.
Description: A decision by President Bush has made all small businesses across the nation affected by the terror attacks of September 11, 2001 eligible for government assistance. Statistical data included.

39957 ■ "Who's small enough to get SBA aid? Some ceilings are raised" in *Wall Street Journal* **(July 18, 2000, pp. B2)**
Pub: Dow Jones & Co., Inc.
Ed: Jeffrey A. Tannenbaum. **Description:** An update on the new requirements for obtaining SBA loans.

39958 ■ *Winning Government Grants and Contracts for Your Small Business*
Pub: The McGraw-Hill Companies
Ed: Mark Rowh. **Released:** 1992. **Price:** $16.95 (paper). **Description:** Provides information on obtaining money through government agencies, including developing proposals and creating budgets. Also contains sample proposals and glossary.

39959 ■ "Wiring the border" in *Hispanic Business* **(Vol. 22, No. 7-8, July-August 2000, pp. 70)**
Pub: Hispanic Business
Ed: Scott Williams. **Description:** The U.S.-Mexico Chamber of Commerce is backing a program that will help 200 companies along the Mexican-U.S. border to be part of the Internet revolution. The public-private partnership, known as Wiring the Border, will provide hardware, software, training and Internet access, plus business-to-business connections with major companies.

39960 ■ "Wisconsin Biotech Aims to Create Artificial Heart Tissue" in *Milwaukee Journal Sentinel* **(December 8, 2005)**
Pub: Journal Sentinel, Inc.
Ed: Kathleen Gallagher. **Description:** InvivoSciences LLC plans to make artificial heart tissue. The firm has chosen Wisconsin for its location because of the Medical College of Wisconsin's support for entrepreneurs along with several state programs that support young companies.

39961 ■ "Wisconsin Grants Economic Assistance to Four Companies, One Technical College" in *Milwaukee Journal Sentinel* **(December 1, 2005)**
Pub: Journal Sentinel, Inc.
Ed: Rick Barrett. **Description:** MCL Industries, Moraine Park Technical College, Burns Best Company, ABC Computers, and SMT Engineering will receive nearly $2 million in state assistance for employee training and expansion projects.

39962 ■ "Women" in *Entrepreneur* **(Vol. 27, No. 12, December 1999, pp. 44)**
Pub: Entrepreneur Media Inc.
Ed: Cynthia E. Griffin. **Description:** A new study underscores the old adage that the most important thing in business is location, location, location. In the top 50 U.S. metropolitan areas, the number of women-owned firms has increased 33 to 59 percent in the past seven years, according to a 1999 report by the National Foundation for Women Business Owners (NFWBO).

39963 ■ "Women Entrepreneurship in the 21st Century" in *Entrepreneur* **(Vol. 31, No. 8, August 2003, pp. 6)**
Pub: Entrepreneur Media, Inc.
Ed: Steve Cooper. **Description:** A Website created by the U.S. Department of Labor and the U.S. Small Business Administration is featured. The site assists women business owners in finding federal resources and business in general.

39964 ■ "Women's Business Centers Fight for Funding" in *Inc.* **(August 1, 2004)**
Pub: Inc. Magazine
Ed: Bobbie Gossage. **Description:** U.S. Small Business Administration announced the opening of 11 new Women's Business Centers.

39965 ■ "The Women's Business Centers: the help women business owners need?" in *WorkingWoman* **(Vol. 25, No. 2, February 2000, pp. S32)**
Pub: Lang Communications Inc.
Ed: Joanne Symons. **Description:** Questions regarding the Women's Business Centers Bill are answered.

39966 ■ "A Year Into The Job, He's Making Progress Slowly But Surely" in *Fortuneit* **(Vol. 146, No. 12, December 9, 2002, pp. 217)**
Pub: Time Inc.
Ed: Jeffrey H. Birnbaum. **Description:** Profile of the new president of the Small Business Administration, Hector Barreto, Jr. Barreto's goal is to transform the SBA from an old-time Beltway bureaucracy into a relevant resource for small business. Four specific issues to be addressed under the new administration are listed.

COMPUTERIZED DATABASES

39967 ■ *Small Business Innovative Research Current Solicitations*
Wheeling Jesuit University
316 Washington Ave.
Wheeling, WV 26003

Ph:(304)243-4341
Free: 800-678-6882
Fax: (304)243-4388
Co. E-mail: technology@nttc.edu
URL: http://www.nttc.edu
Description: Contains solicitations for the Small Business Innovation Research (SBIR) Program and the Small Business Technology Transfer (STTR) Pilot Program. Programs seek to stimulate U.S. technological innovation by funding small business research projects. The database assists users in exploring topics for which funding is available. **Type:** Full text.

RESEARCH CENTERS

39968 ■ Center for International Private Enterprise
1155 15th St. NW, Ste. 700
Washington, DC 20005
Ph:(202)721-9200
Fax: (202)721-9250
Co. E-mail: cipe@cipe.org
URL: http://www.cipe.org/
Contact: John D. Sullivan, Exec.Dir.
E-mail: cipe@cipe.org
Scope: Worldwide democracy through the promotion of private enterprise, market-oriented reform, and legal, regulatory and business institutions, including supporting strategies and techniques that address market-based democratic development and working with indigenous organizations in emerging democracies. Provides matching funds to a variety of developing country institutions for political and economic development. **Publications:** Economic Reform Feature Service. **Educational Activities:** Training program for Business Association Management.

START-UP INFORMATION

39969 ■ **"Business On Her Own Terms"** in *Black Enterprise* (Vol. 35, August 2004, No. 1, pp. 57)
Pub: Earl G. Graves Publishing Co. Inc.
Ed: Bridget McCrea. **Description:** Profile of Fay Coleman, president and CEO of her Silver Spring, Maryland firm, Westover Consultants Inc. Coleman started her business in the basement of her home and began developing educational training programs, planning events, creating public outreach programs, and conducting surveys for government agencies. Today, the firm comprises three divisions: Health and Behavior Sciences, Management Support Services, and Information Technology Services.

39970 ■ **"A launching point to the next step"** in *Hispanic Business* (Vol. 22, No. 6, June 2000, pp. 42)
Pub: Hispanic Business
Ed: Derek Reveron. **Description:** Potomac Management Group Inc., founded as a part-time information technology and logistics consultancy by Dennis Garcia in 1992, has won a $22 million, 5-year contract from the U.S. Coast Guard. The company expects revenues to reach over $8 million in 2000.

39971 ■ **"Opportunity of the Fly"** in *Entrepreneur* (Vol. 28, No. 8, August 2000, pp. 40)
Pub: Entrepreneur Media Inc.
Ed: Cynthia E. Griffin. **Description:** The Air Force has launched an outreach campaign in order to contract with more women business owners.

ASSOCIATIONS AND OTHER ORGANIZATIONS

39972 ■ **Coalition for Government Procurement**
1990 M St. NW, Ste. 400
Washington, DC 20036
Ph:(202)331-0975
Fax: (202)822-9788
Co. E-mail: info@thecgp.org
URL: http://www.thecgp.org
Contact: Paul Caggiano, Pres.
Description: Represents large and small businesses interested in commercial product procurement issues. Works to help protect the interests of federal government commercial product suppliers; to monitor commercial product legislation, policies, regulations, and procurement trends of federal agencies. Provides members with current information, changes, and developments in procurement policies and their impact. Conducts phone consultations. **Publications:** *Friday Flash* (weekly); *Off the Shelf* (monthly); *Official Coalition for Government Procurement Yearbook* (annual).

39973 ■ **Coalition for Prompt Pay**
11242 Waples Mill Rd., Ste. 200
Fairfax, VA 22030
Ph:(703)273-7200
Free: 800-659-7469
Fax: (703)278-8082
Co. E-mail: membership@infocomm.org
URL: http://www.icia.org
Contact: Walter G. Blackwell, Exec.Dir.
Description: National trade associations representing companies that sell services and products or do construction work under federal government contracts. Lobbies Congress for improvements in the Prompt Pay Act of 1982 (amended in 1988); encourages strict enforcement of the act by the Executive Branch. **Publications:** *Quick Reference Guide and Side-By-Side Explanation of Federal Prompt Pay Regulations*; Newsletter (periodic).

39974 ■ **Contract Services Association of America**
1000 Wilson Blvd., Ste. 1800
Arlington, VA 22209
Ph:(703)243-2020
Fax: (703)243-3601
Co. E-mail: info@csa-dc.org
URL: http://www.csa-dc.org
Contact: Chris Jahn, Pres.
Membership: Companies that provide, by contract, technical and support services to the federal government, particularly in defense and space programs, and to state, local and other public and international agencies. **Purpose:** Supports reliance on the free enterprise system and improvement in the work environment for the private sector. Disseminates information on the "economies, efficiencies, and flexibility" afforded by government on use of private corporations in providing technical and support services. Corporations have contracted such services to the government as the space shuttle, the DEW Line, and National Aeronautics and Space Administration's tracking and data network. Maintains speakers' bureau. Compiles statistics. **Publications:** *Linkage* (quarterly); *Service Scope* (monthly). **Telecommunication Services:** electronic mail, chris@csa-dc.org.

39975 ■ **National Contract Management Association**
8260 Greensboro Dr., Ste. 200
McLean, VA 22102
Ph:(571)382-0082
Free: 800-344-8096
Fax: (703)448-0939
Co. E-mail: couture@ncmahq.org
URL: http://www.ncmahq.org
Contact: Neal J. Couture CPCM, Exec.Dir.
Description: Professional individuals concerned with administration, procurement, acquisition, negotiation and management of contracts and subcontracts. Works for the education, improvement and professional development of members and nonmembers through national and chapter programs, symposia and educational materials. Offers certification in Contract Management (CPCM, CFCM, and CCCM) designations as well as a credential program. Operates speakers' bureau. **Publications:** *Contract Management* (monthly); *Journal of Contract Management* (annual).

REFERENCE WORKS

39976 ■ **"$1 Million Grant Program Aims to Boost Renewable Energy"** in *Milwaukee Journal Sentinel* (December 13, 2005)
Pub: Journal Sentinel, Inc.
Ed: Thomas Content. **Description:** Wisconsin's Governor Jim Doyle has proposed a $1 million grant to invest in renewable energy technologies for the state, including ethanol, biodiesel and waste-to-energy power.

39977 ■ **"19th Annual Entrepreneurial Woman's Conference"** in *Entrepreneur* (Vol. 33, August 2005, No. 8, pp. 4)
Pub: Entrepreneur Media Inc.
Ed: Steve Cooper. **Description:** The Women's Business Development Center holds its annual Entrepreneurial Women's Conference for women business owners. The event presents a buyer's mart that allows the owners to market products and services to corporate and government buyers. There are also discussions and workshops addressing issues and trends affecting women-owned businesses.

39978 ■ **"Action Yet in Need of Affirming"** in *Hispanic Business* (Vol. 23, No. 7/8, July/August 2001, pp. 29)
Pub: Hispanic Business
Ed: Harry P. Pachon. **Description:** An overview of data that supports the continued use of affirmative action programs.

39979 ■ **"Aegis of Success"** in *Hispanic Business* (June 2002, pp. 16)
Pub: Hispanic Business
Ed: Rick Laezman. **Description:** New York manufacturer, Aegis Electronic Systems, has procured federal contracts for aerospace and military programs.

39980 ■ **"Anti-bundling plan may give small firms contracts"** in *Atlanta Business Chronicle* (Vol. 25, No. 22, November 8, 2002, pp. 7B)
Pub: American City Business Publications, Inc.
Ed: Kent Hoover. **Description:** The Bush administration would like to curtail contract bundling in order to allow small businesses an opportunity to procure more government contracts. Small firms have been hurt by bundling, the method in which contracts were placed into large packages that favored large businesses.

39981 ■ ***Are Government Purchasing Policies Failing Small Business?: Congressional Hearing***
Pub: DIANE Publishing Company
Ed: John F. Kerry. **Released:** November 2004. **Price:** $35.00. **Description:** Covers Congressional hearing: Steven App, Treasury Department; Fred Armendariz and Major Clark, Small Business Administration; Susan Allen, Pan Asian American Chamber of Commerce; Stephen Denlinger, Latin American Management Association; Charles Henry, National Veteran's

Business Development Corporation; Morris Hudson, MO Procurement Technology Assistance Centers; Bar Kasoff, Women Impact, Public Policy; Pam Mazza, Piliero, Massa and Pargament; Ron Newlan, HubZone Contract National Council; Pat Parker, Native American Management Service; Joann Payne, Women First National Legislative Commission; Mike Robinson, MA Small Business Development Centers; Ramon Rodriguez, Hispanic Chamber of Commerce; Angela Styles, Office of Management and Budget; Ralph Thomas, NASA; John Turner, MN Business Enterprise Legal Defense Fund; James Turpin, American Subcontractor's Association, Inc.; and Henry Wilfong, National Association of Small Disadvantaged Business.

39982 ■ "Area Arab-Americans can help rebuild Iraq" in *Crain's Detroit Business* **(Vol. 19, No. 15, April 14, 2003, pp. 8)**
Pub: Crain Communications Inc., Detroit
Description: Arab-American professionals and companies owned by Arab-Americans can act as a bridge to rebuilding not only Iraq, but also the American image in the Middle East.

39983 ■ "Army Extends Contract With Maine Company to Improve Armor On Humvees" in *Portland Press Herald* **(December 3, 2005)**
Pub: Blethen Maine Newspapers, Inc.
Ed: Bart Jansen. **Description:** Maine Readiness Sustainment Center's Maine Military Authority was awarded a temporary contract with the U.S. Army to improve the armor on its Humvees. The contract will save 250 local jobs for workers.

39984 ■ "Army's Tech Needs Boost General Dynamics' Role" in *Crain's Detroit Business* **(Vol. 21, January 17, 2005, No. 3, pp. 14)**
Pub: Crain Communications Inc. - Detroit
Ed: Brent Snavely. **Description:** General Dynamics Land Systems is being asked to deliver high tech equipment to the U.S. Army ahead of schedule. The company moved to a 52,000 square foot center on 14 Mile Road to facilitate the design of a new set of vehicles for a demonstration scheduled for 2014.

39985 ■ "B2G Supplies Revenue Gains" in *Hispanic Business* **(July/August 2002, pp. 32, 34)**
Pub: Hispanic Business
Ed: **Description:** U. S. defense spending boosts revenues for the Hispanic Business High-Tech 50, the nation's largest Hispanic-owned high-tech businesses. A list of the 2002 High-Tech 50 is included, featuring ranking for 2002 and 2001, company/location, CEO, product/service, number of employees, and revenue for 2001.

39986 ■ "Back to Basics; Single Portal for Business" in *Crain's Detroit Business* **(Vol. 19, No. 42, October 20, 2003, pp. 11)**
Pub: Crain Communications Inc., Detroit
Ed: Amy Lane. **Description:** The State of Michigan intends to improve the state's telecommunications infrastructure, including a single state government Internet portal where businesses might handle all project-permit needs and new ways to expand high-speed Internet access to underserved areas.

39987 ■ "Bath Iron Works Wins Contract for Tri-Hulled Navy Warship" in *Portland Press Herald* **(October 15, 2005)**
Pub: Blethen Maine Newspapers, Inc.
Ed: Matt Wickenheiser. **Description:** Bath Iron Works secured a $223 million contract with the U.S. Navy to build its first tri-hulled warship that would operate in coastal waters. The Navy expects delivery of the ship in October 2007.

39988 ■ "Big Goals, Small Steps" in *Hispanic Business* **(January/February 2003, pp. 46, 48)**
Pub: Hispanic Business
Ed: Frank McCoy. **Description:** Since the Minority Business Development Agency (MBDA) no longer documents contracts awarded to minority-owned companies, minority business owners feel they are not getting their share of contracts.

39989 ■ "Black Firm Sues SBA, Alleges Funding Bias" in *Boston Business Journal* **(Vol. 23, No. 30, August 29, 2003, pp. 18)**
Pub: American City Business Journals
Ed: Kent Hoover. **Description:** The racial discrimination lawsuit filed by minority-owned Small Business Investment Corporation against the U.S. Small Business Administration is addressed. Topics include management teams, funding of minority business, and business start-up loans.

39990 ■ "Break it up! Will Congress finally take a swing at contract bundling?" in *Entrepreneur* **(Vol. 30, No. 2, February 2002, pp. 23)**
Pub: Entrepreneur Media Inc.
Ed: Stephen Barlas. **Description:** The topic of government contract bundling is addressed, including the Senate version of the fiscal 2002 Pentagon authorization bill, which would require a number of steps before contracts are combined in a package larger than $5 million.

39991 ■ "BresaGen moves slowly to grow stem cell work" in *Atlanta Business Chronicle* **(Vol. 25, November 8, 2002, No. 22 pp. 1A)**
Pub: American City Business Publications, Inc.
Ed: Julie Bryant. **Description:** BresaGen Inc., located in Athens, Georgia, is working with stem cells to find treatments for various human conditions. BresaGen has received $1.6 million in U.S. government grants and has entered into various licensing and distribution accords with the National Institutes of Health.

39992 ■ "Briefly" in *Crain's Detroit Business* **(Vol. 19, No. 2, January 13, 2003, pp. 10)**
Pub: Crain Communications Inc., Detroit
Description: The U.S. Small Business Administration and the U.S. Department of Defense have integrated the Procurement Marketing and Access Network and the Central Contractor Registration databases. This move will let vendors to enter information through a single registration, allowing small businesses to market products or services. Contact information is included.

39993 ■ "Bush Backs Contracting Program" in *Hispanic Business* **(Vol. 23, No. 10, October, 2001, pp. 22)**
Pub: Hispanic Business
Ed: Patricia Guadalupe. **Description:** The Bush Administration will defend before the U.S. Supreme Court a federal program that uses race as a factor in determining contract awards. The Republican Party, in conjunction with the Republican National Hispanic Assembly, is offering training sessions for Spanish-speaking political activists and would-be GOP candidates. Ida Castro has been named director of the DNC's Women's Vote Center.

39994 ■ "Business Briefs" in *Salt Lake Tribune* **(February 24, 2005)**
Pub: Knight-Ridder/Tribune Business News
Description: Business information involving Extra Space Storage, a real estate investment trust that owns and operates self-storage properties; Cirtran Corp. a contract manufacturer; Maxwell Publishing; Trio Restaurant Group; Raser Technologies, who received a contract to develop mobile power generation technology for the government; and Cyprus Credit Union's fundraiser for Primary Children's Medical Center, is spotlighted.

39995 ■ "California Auto Dealers Attack Government Vehicle Plan" in *Sacramento Bee* **(November 19, 2005)**
Pub: The Sacramento Bee
Ed: Andrew McIntosh. **Description:** California auto dealers met with the Department of General Services to discuss its procurement process along with its secrecy. Dealers complained that contracts will now be awarded to dealers earning high scores on a rating system, rather than lowest bidders.

39996 ■ "Cartel Creativo wins army contract" in *Hispanic Business* **(Vol. 22, No. 10, October 2000, pp. 24)**
Pub: Hispanic Business
Ed: Teresa Talerico. **Description:** An advertising contract aimed at recruiting more Hispanics into the U.S. Army has been won by Hispanic-owned Cartel Creativo. The Army plans to recruit 80,000 new soldiers in 2000 and to increase the proportion from ethnic minorities.

39997 ■ "Case Study" in *Inc.* **(October 1, 2004)**
Pub: Inc. Magazine
Ed: Rod Kurtz. **Description:** Government contractor, DefenseWeb is considering a move to the private sector.

39998 ■ *Constructing the Team - Final Report of Government-Industry Review of Procurement*
Pub: UNIPUB
Ed: HMSO staff. **Released:** 1994. **Price:** $45.00 (paper).

39999 ■ "Contacts for Contracts" in *Hispanic Business* **(Vol. 23, No. 7/8, July/August 2001, pp. 98)**
Pub: Hispanic Business
Description: As the energy sector heats up, opportunities for minority vendors should also increase. Contacts for minority vendors seeking contracts are listed, including Web sites for the Small Business Administration (SBA) and the National Minority Supplier Development Council are included.

40000 ■ "A Contracting Conundrum" in *Hispanic Business* **(October 2003, pp. 32, 34)**
Pub: Hispanic Business
Ed: Ron Utt, Grace Napolitano. **Description:** Two opinions are expressed regarding government contracts, one insisting bundling results in cost savings and improved service, while the other believes bundling succeeds only in excluding small businesses from the federal procurement marketplace.

40001 ■ *Contractor's Directory*
Pub: Government Data Publications Inc.
Contact: S. Lobel
Released: Annual, February. **Price:** $49.50 Diskette edition; $15; $49.95 CD-ROM. **Covers:** contractors who have received government contract under Public Law 95-507, which requires preferential treatment of small business for subcontracts. **Entries Include:** Contractor name and address. Supplementary to 'Small Business Preferential Subcontracts Opportunities Monthly,' which lists companies with government contracts over $500,000 ($1,000,000 for construction). **Arrangement:** Same information given alphabetically and by ZIP code.

40002 ■ "Convicts Stealing Small Business Jobs" in *My Business* **(September/October 2001, pp. 19)**
Pub: My Business Magazine
Description: Awarding federal contracts to Federal Prison Industries (FPI) is costing small businesses millions of dollars annually.

40003 ■ "Courting Trouble" in *Inc.* **(October 1, 2003)**
Pub: Gruner & Jahr USA Publishing
Ed: Nadine Heintz. **Description:** Profile of an entrepreneur facing mail fraud charges engaged in a fraudulent scheme to obtain certification as a disadvantaged small business in 2000, in order to procure government road-construction contracts set aside for minorities and women.

40004 ■ "Dealt a double blow" in *Hispanic Business* **(Vol. 22, No. 10, October 2000, pp. 20)**
Pub: Hispanic Business
Ed: Patricia Guadalupe. **Description:** The alleged misuse of the Small Business Administration's (SBA) funds and the lack of contracts awarded to minority firms are examined. An audit of the SBA criticizes its spending of $22 million on certification of only 3,000 firms.

40005 ■ "Detroiters eye Iraq contracts" in *Crain's Detroit Business* (Vol. 19, No. 15, April 14, 2003, pp. 1)
Pub: Crain Communications Inc., Detroit
Ed: Jennette Smith, Brent Snavely. Description: Many metropolitan Detroit companies are hoping to win contracts to help rebuild Iraq. U.S. Representative John Dingell is calling for the General Accounting Office to investigate the process of contracting awards.

40006 ■ "Discrimination's new name" in *Hispanic Business* (Vol. 22, No. 9, September 2000, pp. 12)
Pub: Hispanic Business
Ed: Christopher Lancette. Description: Issues concerning the exclusion of Hispanic contractors from the minority-contracting program of the Memphis School Board, Tennessee, is discussed.

40007 ■ "The Diversity Game" in *Forbes* (Vol. 170, No. 12, December 9, 2002, pp. 140)
Pub: Forbes Magazine
Ed: Tomas Kellner. Description: Information about the Small Business Administration's Section 8(a) program and its reform are examined. The program was created by President Nixon to foster black capitalism and sets aside up to $6 billion a year worth of government contracts for small companies owned by minorities or women.

40008 ■ *DOD FAR Supplement*
Pub: Superintendent of Documents
Released: Annual. Price: $37.50. Description: Contains instructions for implementing the Federal Acquisition Regulations (FAR) within the Department of Defense (DOD). Includes directives on what provisions, clauses, and procedures are authorized for DOD contracts. Also includes information on additional procedures necessary for awarding and administering DOD contracts.

40009 ■ *Doing Business with the Government Using EDI: A Guide for Small Businesses*
Pub: John Wiley & Sons, Inc.
Ed: Jan Zimmerman. Released: 1997. Price: $30.95.

40010 ■ "Doing Business with Uncle Sam" in *My Business* (February/March 2003, pp. 14)
Pub: My Business Magazine
Description: The Small Business Administration will launch an online program designed to improve the procuring of government contracts, with an annual fee of $1,500 for using the e-commerce Web site.

40011 ■ *e-Business, e-Government and Small and Medium-Size Enterprises: Opportunities and Challenges*
Pub: Idea Group Publishing
Ed: Brian J. Corbitt, Nabeel A.Y. Al-Qirim. Released: February 2004. Price: $79.95. Description: Electronic commerce and information technology research in small and medium-sized enterprises (SMEs). Policymakers, legislators, researchers and professionals address significant issues of importance to the small business sector.

40012 ■ "E-Government Catching On" in *Hispanic Business* (Vol. 23, No. 5, May 2001, pp. 22, 24)
Pub: Hispanic Business
Ed: Patricia Guadalupe. Description: The U.S. government is developing programs to access procurement, recruitment, and economic development. The FirstGov.gov links users to more than 20 million federal Web pages.

40013 ■ "The EDI revolution" in *Hispanic Business* (Vol. 22, No. 4, April 2000, pp. 20)
Pub: Hispanic Business
Ed: Jennifer Riley. Description: The original vehicle for Governmental electronic procurement was the Electronic Data Interchange, but use of this system has been overtaken by the Internet due to its lower costs and ease of use. Small companies should take advantage of this change to ensure that they are able to respond to electronic procurement.

40014 ■ "8(a) Advantage or Disadvantage?" in *Hispanic Business* (March 2003, pp. 60)
Pub: Hispanic Business
Description: The advantages and disadvantages of participating in the Small Business Administration's program are discussed by a few Hispanic small business owners currently contracting with the U.S. government.

40015 ■ "Electric Shoes and 'Breadcrumbs' for the Troops" in *Venture Capital Journal* (Vol. 42, No. 9, September 2002, pp. 26-27)
Pub: Thomas Venture Economics
Ed: Michael V. Copeland. Description: New defense technologies being developed to protect U.S. troops during wartime are presented.

40016 ■ "Eyes on Iraq; 'I'd rather go with a Michigan company'" in *Crain's Detroit Business* (Vol. 19, No. 16, April 21, 2003, pp. 3)
Pub: Crain Communications Inc., Detroit
Ed: Michael Strong. Description: An Iraqi-born scientist living in the metropolitan Detroit area, and owner of an environmental consulting business, feels American companies should be a part of rebuilding the country of Iraq.

40017 ■ "FedBizOpps Opens for Biz" in *Hispanic Business* (Vol. 23, No. 10, October, 2001, pp. 24)
Pub: Hispanic Business
Ed: Derek Reveron. Description: The Federal Acquisition Regulation Council (FARC), has set up a Web site providing information on all government contracts worth $25,000 or more. The FARC oversees government procurement. As of October 1, 2001, all government agencies will post procurement notices on the site, and several links to other helpful sites are included.

40018 ■ *Federal Acquisition Regulation*
Pub: Global Engineering Documents
Released: 1993. Price: $195.00. Description: Includes basic manual and supplementary material. Primary source of procurement regulations used by Federal agencies in the acquisition of supplies and services with appropriated funds. Details all provisions and clauses used in government contracting.

40019 ■ "Federal Contracts Draw New Scrutiny" in *Inc.* (August 2005, pp. 24)
Pub: Inc. Magazine
Ed: Darren Dahl. Description: The Small Business Administration reported ways that large companies are erroneously categorized in order to procure federal government contracts.

40020 ■ "Federal File: News & Developments in the Business of Government" in *Hispanic Business* (December 2001, pp. FG4, FG6, FG14, FG16)
Pub: Hispanic Business
Description: The Department of Agriculture has an Outreach Office that helps socially disadvantaged farmers and farm workers gain access to federal programs. Federal government employment opportunities for minorities are presented with a listing of internship opportunities. Hispanic entrepreneurs owning 8(a) firms secured 14.4 percent of federal contracts for fiscal year 2000.

40021 ■ "Federal Resource Guide 2002-2003" in *Hispanic Business* (December 2002, pp. FRG1-FRG2)
Pub: Hispanic Business
Description: Minority suppliers made up 5.7 percent of total federal procurement for the year 2000, with 1,585 Hispanic companies participating in the Minority Business Development program, making up 24.8 percent of all firms participating. Statistical data included.

40022 ■ "Focused Fundraising" in *Entrepreneur.com* (Vol. 34, February 2006, No. 2, pp. 49)
Pub: Entrepreneur Media Inc.
Ed: David Worrell. Description: Phil Libin discusses his experiences when seeking venture capital for his national security technology firm; Libin also secured million-dollar contracts with the Department of Defense.

40023 ■ "For the People" in *Entrepreneur. com* (Vol. 34, February 2006, No. 2, pp. 68)
Pub: Entrepreneur Media Inc.
Ed: Joshua Kurlantzick. Description: The U.S. government's contract budget has grown to $300 billion and is growing due to more outsourcing to contractors. Entrepreneurs share secrets to procuring government contracts.

40024 ■ "Frank Otto Named EDO's COO" in *Long Island Business News* (February 27, 2004)
Pub: Dolan Media Newswires
Description: Profile of Frank Otto, newly appointed COO of defense contractor, Long Island Forum for Technology.

40025 ■ "Frontier Online" in *Business Week* (No. 3694, August 14, 2000, pp. F8)
Pub: McGraw-Hill, Inc.
Description: The number of federal contracts awarded to small businesses dropped by 23 percent from 1997 to 1999, from 6.4 million to 4.9 million, with minority- and women-owned companies hardest hit.

40026 ■ "GAO: Small Firms are Losing Out on Federal Contracts" in *Hispanic Business* (March 2003, pp. 20)
Pub: Hispanic Business
Description: According to a report published by the Los Angeles Times, small companies are losing out to larger corporations in procuring government contracts. The General Accounting Office began an investigation in 2002 after a California small business group filed a complaint.

40027 ■ "General Dynamics will build 2,131 vehicles for Army" in *Crain's Detroit Business* (Vol. 16, No. 49, December 4, 2000, pp. 2)
Pub: Crain Communications, Inc.
Ed: Brent Snavely. Description: Having a light-combat vehicle already in production, helped Sterling Heights, Michigan-based General Dynamics Land Systems win a contract to build armored vehicles. This contract is the largest of its kind in the U.S. in years.

40028 ■ "Getting Out of an IRS Mess" in *Black Enterprise* (Vol. 37, December 2006, No. 5, pp. 53)
Pub: Earl G. Graves Publishing Co. Inc.
Ed: Carolyn M. Brown. Description: Owing back taxes to the IRS can lead to huge penalties and interest. Here are some tips on how to handle paying the IRS what you owe them.

40029 ■ "Getting Paid Faster" in *Black Enterprise* (Vol. 36, February 2006, No. 7, pp. 58)
Pub: Earl G. Graves Publishing Co. Inc.
Ed: Bridget McCrea. Description: Large corporations and the government are using credit-card-like accounts through Visa and MasterCard for purchasing products and services. Visa has launched a program to introduce to small businesses in order to setup accounts to accept the purchasing cards in order to grow their businesses.

40030 ■ "Getting a Piece of the Federal Pie" in *Hispanic Business* (Vol. 23, No. 7/8, July/August 2001, pp. 38)
Pub: Hispanic Business
Ed: Joel Russell. Description: The number of large Hispanic high-tech firms that sell to the federal government has dropped by half in the last five years.

40031 ■ *Getting Started in Federal Contracting*
Pub: Panoptic Enterprises
Released: Irregular, previous edition September 1995; latest edition 1996. Publication Includes: Lists of 26 offices of small and disadvantaged business utilization; 10 Department of Labor regional offices, 11 General Services Administration business service centers, and 11 Small Business Administration regional offices, plus 14 Government resource offices; 35 commercial resources; training; books; newslet-

ters; and associations. These agencies are of use to those privately-owned businesses wishing to sell their products and services to the federal government. Plus 26 Federal Acquisition Computer Network (FACNET) Certified Value Added Networks (VANS). **Entries Include:** Agency name, address, phone, geographical territory covered. Principal content is discussion of current procurement regulations and information on how to submit proposals. **Arrangement:** Classified by agency represented; type of resource. **Indexes:** Organization name.

40032 ■ *Government Contract Negotiations: A Practical Guide for Small Business*
Pub: John Wiley & Sons, Inc.
Ed: David C. Moore. **Released:** 1996. **Price:** $70.00.

40033 ■ *Government Contracts & Subcontract Leads Directory*
Pub: Government Data Publications Inc.
Released: Annual, March. **Price:** $89.50, individuals print; $89.50, individuals CD-ROM; $89.50, individuals disk. **Covers:** firms which received prime contracts for production of goods or services from federal government agencies during the preceding twelve months. **Entries Include:** Name and address of recipient, awarding agency, product, quantity, contract number, and dollar amount. Cumulates listings in 'Government Primecontracts Monthly.' **Arrangement:** Classified by product.

40034 ■ *Government Prime Contractors Directory*
Pub: Government Data Publications Inc.
Released: Annual, July. **Price:** $15, individuals; $49.95, individuals diskettes; $49.95, individuals CD-ROM. **Covers:** organizations that received government prime contracts during the previous two years. **Entries Include:** Contractor name and address, product/service; contractors with contracts of more than $500,000 are marked. **Arrangement:** In two parts; Part 1 is alphabetical by company name and Part 2 is classified by zip code.

40035 ■ "Growth in a streamling sector" in *Hispanic Business* (Vol. 22, No. 4, April 2000, pp. 24)
Pub: Hispanic Business
Ed: Jonathan J. Higuera, Joel Russell. **Description:** Engineering services company, L&M Technologies, has improved personnel management, technical services and knowledge specialization in order to maintain its competitiveness in the federal contract market. The teaming of companies to improve expertise is discussed.

40036 ■ *A Guide to Doing Business with the Department of State*
Pub: U.S. Government Printing Office
Price: $3.25. **Description:** Guide for small, minority, and women-owned businesses interested in doing business with the State Department. Includes list of subcontracting opportunities and contacts for trade- and investment-related issues.

40037 ■ "Hands off small business!" in *My Business* (September/October 2001, pp. 23)
Pub: My Business Magazine
Description: The results of a recent survey by NFIB to its members is displayed. The survey included such issues as taxes, compensatory time off, pay disparities, ergonomics, competition with prisons, federal contract bundling, and Internet taxes.

40038 ■ "Health care guide gets the Army's OK" in *Crain's Detroit Business* (Vol. 19, No. 15, April 14, 2003, pp. 12)
Pub: Crain Communications Inc., Detroit
Ed: Ian McClure. **Description:** The American Institute for Preventive Medicine has published a medical guide approved for distribution to U.S. Army soldiers.

40039 ■ "Health care, federal contracts high on Bush's small business agenda" in *Crain's Detroit Business* (Vol. 18, No. 22, June 3, 2002, pp.50)
Pub: Crain Communications Inc. - Detroit
Ed: Laura Bailey. **Description:** Under President Bush's small business agenda, companies can expect more affordable health insurance and fairer competition for government contracts.

40040 ■ "High and Dry? A New Federal Contract Program May Not Be an Oasis After All" in *Entrepreneur* (Vol. 32, No. 4, April 2004, pp. 20)
Pub: Entrepreneur Media, Inc.
Ed: Stephen Barlas. **Description:** Other than defense and Homeland Security, federal contracts have been down. Procurement rules for Homeland Security contracts are being questioned by the U.S. Small Business Administration.

40041 ■ "Hispanic Outreach Takes Off" in *Hispanic Business* (March 2003, pp. 62, 64)
Pub: Hispanic Business
Ed: Janet Perez. **Description:** The Federal Aviation Administration is among the government agencies promoting Hispanic recruitment and retention.

40042 ■ "In business with the U.S." in *Black Enterprise* (Vol. 33, No. 3, October 2002, pp. 60)
Pub: Earl Graves Publishing Co.
Ed: Alan Hughes. **Description:** Information for becoming designated as an 8(a) company with the federal government is given. The Small Business Administration runs the 8(a) Business Development program that provides business development and technical assistance to assist socially and economically disadvantaged small business growth. Contact information is provided.

40043 ■ "InDyne's $440M Launch Pad" in *Washington Business Journal* (Vol. 22, No. 12, July 25, 2003, pp. 1)
Pub: Washington Business Journal
Ed: Roger Hughlett. **Description:** The USAF has awarded a $440 million contract to McLean, Virginia, InDyne for a missile defense systems program. The Small Business Administration reports that the contract is the largest federal contract issued for small business.

40044 ■ "Jadi's Journey; Move to OU Incubator Could Lead to Funding" in *Crain's Detroit Business* (Vol. 22, January 9, 2006, No. 2, pp. 3)
Pub: Crain Communications Inc. - Detroit
Ed: Sheena Harrison. **Description:** Jadi Inc. should receive $3 million in grants and federal funding for its new navigation systems for military robots. The firm has moved into the SmartZone Business Incubator at Oakland University in Michigan.

40045 ■ "Jeff Jonas" in *Entrepreneur* (Vol. 32, September 2004, No. 9, pp. 24)
Pub: Entrepreneur Media Inc.
Ed: Sara Wilson. **Description:** Profile of Jeff Jonas, founder of SRD, a company specializing in the large-scale identification of individuals and their relationships with others. SRD focuses on the production of patent-pending technologies and software products, particularly with the government to address issues of national concern while protecting individual's privacy.

40046 ■ "Laser Business Fails to Shine" in *Orlando Business Journal* (Vol. 20, No. 5, July 18, 2003, pp. 1)
Pub: American City Business Journals, Inc.
Ed: Chad Eric Watt. **Description:** Information about Orlando, Florida-based Electro Optics' failure to land a military contract for development and production of military lasers.

40047 ■ "Lessons from the 8(A) Leaders" in *Hispanic Business* (March 2005, pp. 54, 56)
Pub: Hispanic Business
Ed: Jonathan J. Higuera. **Description:** Hispanic contractors are finding more opportunity in the U.S. government's 8(a) minority business development program. Top Hispanic 8(a) companies are listed.

40048 ■ "Letters count at keypadding design firm Digit Wireless" in *Boston Business Journal* (Vol. 22, No. 14, May 10, 2002, pp. 19)
Pub: MCP, Inc.
Ed: Phil Sweeney. **Description:** Founder David Levy and CEO, John Facella of Digit Wireless LLC, are promoting the use of their patented keyboard that has letters alongside numbers on mobile phones.

40049 ■ "Level Playing Field" in *Entrepreneur* (Vol. 32, No. 2, February 2004, pp. 28)
Pub: Entrepreneur Media, Inc.
Ed: Stephen Barlas. **Description:** U.S. Small Business Administration has created new rules that will prohibit the bundling of small contracts, thus enabling more small businesses to compete with larger firms.

40050 ■ "Listening for opportunity" in *Hispanic Business* (Vol. 22, No. 9, September 2000, pp. 16)
Pub: Hispanic Business
Ed: Peter Brennan. **Description:** Internet-based firm, Globe-1, assists minority companies to compete for government agency contracts by offering help in the procurement of contracts.

40051 ■ "Loans, grants, and more" in *BlackEnterprise* (Vol. 32, No. 2, September 2001, pp. 46)
Pub: Earl Graves Publishing Co.
Ed: Paul McCoy-Pinderhughes. **Description:** A list of government-sponsored programs, small business loans, and grants for small business are highlighted, including the Commerce Business Daily lists of government-awarded contracts; the Federal Procurement Data System; the U.S. Department of Housing and Urban Development; the 7(a) loan program; and the Small Business Innovation Research program.

40052 ■ "Local tech firms mine for government gold" in *Atlanta Business Chronicle* (Vol. 25, November 15, 2002, No. 23 pp. 6C)
Pub: American City Business Publications, Inc.
Ed: Lee Hall. **Description:** The federal government's technology spending is expected to increase by 9.7 percent to $53.1 billion this year, and many companies are targeting this sector. About 1,100 Georgia firms interested in business with the federal government are currently working with the Georgia Tech Procurement Assistance Center. A ranking of Georgia's top civilian agency and defense department contractors is included.

40053 ■ "Long Island's Patent Production Falls Nearly 20 Percent Since 1988" in *Long Island Business News* (March 5, 2004)
Pub: Dolan Media Newswires
Ed: Ken Schachter. **Description:** Long Island's future economic health is tied to industries such as life sciences, software development and defense-industry prototyping and design rather than large-scale manufacturing. Patent growth is used to gauge the economic progress of the area.

40054 ■ "Looming Large: Are Small-Business Contracts Really Going to the Big Guys?" in *Entrepreneur* (Vol. 31, No. 9, September 2003, pp. 22)
Pub: Entrepreneur Media, Inc.
Ed: Stephen Barlas. **Description:** According to a report by the Microcomputer Industry Suppliers Association, too many big businesses are listed as small in the federal government's vendor database.

40055 ■ "Maine Tribes Express Interest in Naval Base Redevelopment Project" in *Portland Press Herald* (December 17, 2005)
Pub: Blethen Maine Newspapers, Inc.
Ed: Kevin Wack. **Description:** The Penobscot Indian Nation and the Passamaquoddy Tribe are interested in redeveloping the Brunswick Naval Air Station. Plans include the manufacture of environmentally friendly wood-based products, aviation maintenance and manufacturing of airplane parts, and production of renewable energy.

40056 ■ "Many federal contractors ignore subcontracting goals" in *Atlanta Business Chronicle* (Vol. 25, No. 22, November 8, 2002, pp. 5B)
Pub: American City Business Publications, Inc.
Ed: Kent Hoover. **Description:** The U.S. government does not appear to be concerned about the large number of contractors that do not submit plans. Although

the Small Business Administration examines subcontracting compliance, a General Accounting Office report expresses concerns that the effectiveness of that monitoring.

40057 ■ **"Marine One, Sikorsky Zero"** in *Business Week* (February 14, 2005, No. 3920, pp. 40)
Pub: McGraw-Hill Companies
Ed: Diane Brady. **Description:** United Technologies Corporation's chairman and CEO, George David, talks about losing the contract for providing the presidential Sikorsky helicopter. The U.S. Navy awarded the contract to Lockheed Martin Corporation.

40058 ■ **"Military Now One of the Big Guns in Tech Financing"** in *Washington Business Journal* (Vol. 22, No. 16, August 22, 2003, pp. 30)
Pub: Washington Business Journal
Ed: Roger Hughlett. **Description:** Sentel, Alexandria, Virginia, is one of a growing number of small high-tech companies foregoing traditional efforts at raising funds by, instead, contacting the U.S. Military and other U.S. government agencies.

40059 ■ **"More tech firms feed off federal defense, IT spending growth"** in *Boston Business Journal* (Vol. 22, No. 14, May 10, 2002, pp. 1)
Pub: MCP, Inc.
Description: Defense contractors are relying on increased spending by the government on defense, information technology and homeland security.

40060 ■ **"MSU Enlists Biz Help On $1B Isotope Project Bid"** in *Crain's Detroit Business* (Vol. 21, January 24, 2005, No. 4, pp. 1)
Pub: Crain Communications Inc. - Detroit
Ed: Sherri Begin. **Description:** Michigan State University is calling in help from the Michigan Business Group to bring the Rare Isotope Accelerator to its campus. The project is a $1 billion project of the U.S. Department of Energy.

40061 ■ **"The Myth of Benign 'Resistance'"** in *Hispanic Business* (Vol. 23, No. 7/8, July/August 2001, pp. 28)
Pub: Hispanic Business
Ed: Todd Gaziano. **Description:** Government contract procurement preferences are inherently discriminatory. The U.S. government must follow the same laws that apply to everyone else. The article suggests, that programs to help the disadvantaged without regard to ethnicity are fine; those that use racial or ethnic stereotypes are not.

40062 ■ **"NASA Logs on for Team Encounter in Space"** in *Houston Business Journal* (Vol. 34, No. 18, September 12, 2003, pp. 1)
Pub: American City Business Journals
Ed: Jenna Colley. **Description:** Team Encounter LLC, Houston, Texas, a private space vehicles company, is preparing to send a spacecraft into orbit in 2005. Team Encounter has obtained a contract from NASA to send the Inertial Stellar Compass into orbit aboard its spacecraft.

40063 ■ **"Navy assesses small-biz impact of intranet deal"** in *Network World* (April 3, 2000, pp. NA)
Pub: Network World Inc.
Ed: Dan Verton. **Description:** The Small Business Administration has urged the Navy to disclose the number of small businesses that could be cut off from future Navy business once the service awards its $16 billion Intranet contract.

40064 ■ **"New DOE contracts: small business is the focus of several new agency initiatives"** in *Hispanic Business* (Vol.22,No. 7-8, July-Aug. 2000)
Pub: Hispanic Business
Ed: Patricia Guadalupe. **Description:** The U.S. Department of Energy is presenting small businesses with over 250 contract opportunities in fields including energy resources, national security and environmental quality.

40065 ■ **"New Face at the SBA"** in *Hispanic Business* (Vol. 23, No. 10, October, 2001, pp. 32, 34)
Pub: Hispanic Business
Ed: Scott Williams. **Description:** Profile of Hector V. Barreto, the new administrator of the U.S. Small Business Administration (SBA), hopes to make the agency more responsive to the small-business community. Statistical data included.

40066 ■ **"New Law Reduced Liability for Architects, Engineers"** in *Crain's Detroit Business* (Vol. 21, January 10, 2005, No. 2, pp. 22)
Pub: Crain Communications Inc. - Detroit
Ed: Amy Lane. **Description:** Michigan Governor Jennifer Granholm signed into law a small bill that will reduce the liability architects and engineers face on state construction projects.

40067 ■ **"Next Round on Adarand"** in *Hispanic Business* (Vol. 23, No. 7/8, July/August 2001, pp. 26)
Pub: Hispanic Business
Ed: Jonathan J. Higuera. **Description:** The Justice Department brief is expected to articulate the Bush administration's take on government contracting.

40068 ■ **"NY State Senator Introduces Bill to Obtain Federal Funding for Genetic Research"** in *Long Island Business News* (February 13, 2004)
Pub: Dolan Media Newswires
Ed: Rosmaria Mancini. **Description:** A bill introduced by Senator Ken LaValle, R-New York, would create an 'institute' that would work to obtain federal grant money for genetics research at institutions throughout New York State.

40069 ■ **"OKC-based The Benham Cos. Lands Military Housing Contract"** in *Journal Record (Oklahoma City, OK)* (February 8, 2007)
Pub: Journal Record
Ed: Kelley Chambers. **Description:** Details of The Benham Companies contract to construct and maintain military housing on four bases is discussed.

40070 ■ **"On the March: War and Peace Aid General Dynamics"** in *Barron's* (July 7, 2003, pp. 22)
Pub: Barron's
Ed: Dimitra Defotis. **Description:** Defense contractor, General Dynamics, has yet to profit from the flurry of defense spending as a result of the Iraq war and the Pentagon's restructuring efforts. The firm's $75 share price is 30 percent lower than its 52-week high, but a strengthening economy and diversification of defense offerings stand to profit the firm.

40071 ■ **"Onvia Business Builder"** in *Entrepreneur* (Vol. 33, October 2005, No. 10, pp. 6)
Pub: Entrepreneur Media Inc.
Ed: Steve Cooper. **Description:** Over 2 million procurement records across 55,500 government agencies are available through a subscription to Onvia's Business Builder.

40072 ■ **"Orbit International Corp. Expects $1M in UPS Orders"** in *Long Island Business News* (February 6, 2004)
Pub: Dolan Media Newswires
Description: Orbit International Corporation expects more than $1 million in orders for its MK 119 gun-control power-supply system to the U.S. Navy's Aegis Destroyers.

40073 ■ **"OSDBU Directory"** in *Hispanic Business* (December 2001, pp. FG18, FG20)
Pub: Hispanic Business
Description: A listing of the Office of Small and Disadvantaged Business Utilization agencies is presented. The OSDBU is the first point of contact for minority entrepreneurs wishing to sell goods or services to the federal government.

40074 ■ **"Panel to Monitor Minority Contracts"** in *Hispanic Business* (March 2004, pp. 12)
Pub: Hispanic Business
Ed: Patricia Guadalupe. **Description:** The National Minority Compliance Board in Washington DC will monitor corporate and governmental minority purchasing activities.

40075 ■ **"Powerhouse Tech Companies Merge"** in *Black Enterprise* (Vol. 35, November 2004, No. 4, pp. 28)
Pub: Earl G. Graves Publishing Co. Inc.
Ed: Cliff Hocker. **Description:** Two high-tech firms in Alexandria, Virginia have merged to better compete for homeland defense contracts.

40076 ■ **"Procurement: Federal File"** in *Hispanic Business* (December 2002, pp. FRG10)
Pub: Hispanic Business
Description: An overview of the Small Business Administration new PRO-Net Contractor Registration Merge program. This program will streamline contracting by helping create a single, user-friendly acquisition system.

40077 ■ **"Profile: Local Web Developer Plays a Starring Role in NASA's Mission to Mars"** in *Crain's Chicago Business* (December 22, 2003)
Pub: Crain Communications, Inc.
Ed: Paul Merrion. **Description:** Profile of Web site developer Critical Mass Inc., the firm that designed a Web site for the National Aeronautics and Space Administration, one of the highest traffic Web sites in history. Critical Mass partnered with eTouch Systems Corporation, whose software updates the NASA site continuously. Web site visitors can access information on humans in space or exploration of the universe with links to specialized sites for children, students, educators and journalists.

40078 ■ **"Proving That You Have the Right Stuff"** in *Inc.* (Volume 27, July 2005, No. 7, pp. 28)
Pub: Inc. Magazine
Ed: Alison Stein Wellner. **Description:** QuVIS, located in Topeka, Kansas landed a federal contract for technology it developed that quickly transmits digital pictures without blurred images. QuVIS technology will be used when the space shuttle Discovery takes off in July 2005.

40079 ■ **"Proxity Electronic Commerce System"** in *Entrepreneur* (Vol. 33, August 2005, No. 8, pp. 4)
Pub: Entrepreneur Media Inc.
Ed: Steve Cooper. **Description:** Proxity Inc. provides an online database of 12 million industrial parts, available from 150,000 sources, and includes government parts. State and local government requirements and contact information are also included in the database.

40080 ■ **"Qcorps Scores Military Coup"** in *Houston Business Journal* (Vol. 34, No. 17, September 5, 2003, pp. 1)
Pub: American City Business Journals
Ed: Jennifer Dawson. **Description:** Examination of the U.S. Army contract awarded to Houston, Texas-based Qcorps Residential Inc. Topics include other defense contracts held by the company, limiting competition, and managing moving services for military personnel.

40081 ■ **"Raytheon, SRM Awarded U.S. Navy Contracts"** in *Providence Business News* (Vol. 18, No. 15, July 28, 2003, pp. 3)
Pub: Providence Business News, Inc.
Description: An examination of the specifics of contracts awarded by the U.S. Navy to Raytheon and Systems Resource Management for work on the Navy's Littoral Combat Ship Program.

40082 ■ "Resources: Web Sites, Organizations, Events and More to Grow Your Business" in *Entrepreneur* **(Vol. 32, No. 2, February 2004, pp. 8)**
Pub: Entrepreneur Media, Inc.
Ed: Steve Cooper. Description: Profiles of Websites to help grow a small business include Zagat Survey covering 2003 restaurants and hotels offering Wi-Fi to customers; NewIdeaTrade, an online forum for buying and selling inventions, patents, copyrights and other intellectual property; Yahoo's small business Merchant Solutions, with shopping carts, coupons and 24-hour toll-free phone support; WordBiz Report, an e-newsletter focusing on online copywriting and content; Plan-Alyzer, evaluates outcomes of marketing plans; Bob Ely, an independent copywriter and consultant; Meeting & Event Planning for Dummies; and Business Matchmaking, a service to help small business procure government contracts.

40083 ■ "The right stuff" in *BlackEnterprise* **(Vol. 32, No. 3, October 2001, pp. 51)**
Pub: Earl Graves Publishing Co.
Ed: Paula McCoy-Pinderhughes. Description: Advice is offered to entrepreneurs wishing to bid on NASA contracts, including information on the Small and Disadvantaged Business Utilization at NASA headquarters in Washington DC, and the Training and Development for Small Businesses in Advanced Technologies (TADSBAT) program. Five African American-owned businesses are on NASA's FY 2000 Top 100 List of Prime Contractors.

40084 ■ "Sacramento, Calif., Light-Rail Plant Gets $84 Million Deal" in *Sacramento Bee* **(October 21, 2005)**
Pub: The Sacramento Bee
Ed: Dale Kasler. Description: Siemens Transportation Systems Inc. in Sacramento, California has secured a contract with the city of Edmonton, Alberta, Canada to produce 26 light-rail cars for the city's transit system. The company plans to add 75 new jobs in order to assemble the outer shells of the rail cars.

40085 ■ "SBA Creates Contracting Opportunities for Disabled Veterans" in *St. Charles Business Record* **(May 7, 2004)**
Pub: Dolan Media Company
Description: A new procurement program created by the U.S. Small Business Administration will help service-disabled veteran-owned small businesses procure federal contracts.

40086 ■ "SBA Government Procurement Office Directory" in *Hispanic Business* **(December 2002, pp. FRG16)**
Pub: Hispanic Business
Description: A listing of the Small Business Administration's Government Procurement Offices is presented. These offices assist small businesses obtain federal contracts.

40087 ■ "SBA Increases Bond Maximum" in *Hispanic Business* **(Vol. 23, No. 5, May 2001, pp. 24)**
Pub: Hispanic Business
Description: The U.S. Small Business Administration (SBA) has increased the size of surety bonds to increase contracting opportunities for small, minority, and women contractors. In fiscal year 2000, the Surety Bond Guarantee Program backed more than 1,795 final bonds on contracts valued at nearly $328.9 million.

40088 ■ "SBA Moves to Protect Small Firms from Bundling" in *Hispanic Business* **(Vol. 22, No. 1/2, January/February, pp. 84)**
Pub: Hispanic Business
Description: The Small Business Administration (SBA) regulations limiting bundling of federal procurement contracts are explained. Bundling is considered detrimental to small businesses.

40089 ■ "Scorecard & Blueprint" in *Hispanic Business* **(Vol. 24, No. 5, May 2002, pp. 48)**
Pub: Hispanic Business Inc.
Ed: Joel Russell. Description: The 2003 Federal budget rates agencies on five different management criteria. Under the plan, nearly one-quarter of all federal workers will have their jobs outsourced.

40090 ■ *Selling to the Military*
Pub: Superintendent of Documents
6 Released: 1992. Price: $30.00. Description: Provides information for small businesses interested in contracting with agencies of the U.S. Department of Defense. Contains general information on contracting, including lists of products and services, list of buying offices and service centers, and samples of standard forms.

40091 ■ *Selling To Uncle Sam*
Pub: Bell Springs Publishing
Ed: C. L. Crownover and M. Henricks. Price: $15.95. Description: The Federal government is now required to give more of their contracts to small businesses. Each year, Find out how you can join the many businesses successfully selling to the government, how to get your company on the government's select bid list, how to maneuver through the rules and red tape.

40092 ■ "Senator Urges 'Measurable Standard' for Awarding Farm Subsidies" in *Chicago Tribune* **(February 16, 2005)**
Pub: Knight-Ridder/Tribune Business News
Ed: Andrew Martin. Description: Although an individual must be actively engaged in a farm in order to received federal farm subsidies, the U.S. Department of Agriculture has paid out millions of dollars to dead farmers and wealthy businessmen who did nothing more than participate in conference calls.

40093 ■ "Shift to Military Contracts Could Help Excel Stay Afloat" in *Crain's Detroit Business* **(Vol. 21, October 10, 2005, No. 43, pp. 36)**
Pub: Crain Communications Inc. - Detroit
Ed: Sheena Harrison. Description: Excel Pattern Works Inc. is looking to reinvent itself by moving its focus away from the automotive industry to military contracts. The Dearborn, Michigan plastics molder reports 75 percent of its present business coming from tier-one and tier-two automotive suppliers.

40094 ■ "Sizing Things Up" in *Entrepreneur* **(Vol. 33, October 2005, No. 10, pp. 17)**
Pub: Entrepreneur Media Inc.
Ed: Christopher Moraff. Description: An overview of the American Small Business League's investigation into the way the U.S. Small Business Administration's awards contracts to private companies is presented.

40095 ■ "Small Firms Seeking Government Contracts Will Get More Help" in *Kiplinger Letter* **(Vol. 78, January 19, 2007, No. 2)**
Pub: Kiplinger
Description: Business Matchmaking program run by the Small Business Administration, along with new rules to do away with unfair competition for government contracts, will help small companies compete for government work. The Small Business Administration will also lower fees for new loans to small companies.

40096 ■ "Small businesses dissatisfied with SBA" in *Black Enterprise* **(Vol. 31, No. 5, December 2000, pp. 29)**
Pub: Earl Graves Publishing Co.
Ed: Joyce Jones. Description: A report issued by the General Accounting Office (GAO) shows that the Small Business Administration is not effective in securing contracts for 8(a) program participants.

40097 ■ "Software Pacts Handed Off" in *Sacramento Bee* **(November 3, 2005)**
Pub: The Sacramento Bee
Ed: Andrew McIntosh. Description: California's Department of Technology Services awarded a $31.1 million contract to Computer Associates International Inc. for computer software maintenance. The company will help negotiate and consolidate the state's existing mainframe computer software maintenance contracts for security, data storage, and systems management software.

40098 ■ "A Soldier's Story" in *Black Enterprise* **(Vol. 34, No. 6, January 2004, pp. 91)**
Pub: Earl Graves Publishing Co.
Ed: Alfred E. Edmond, Jr. Description: An African American woman, soon to retire from a military procurement job, and wishes to become an author is offered advice for both careers.

40099 ■ "Some prison program deals not using inmates" in *Atlanta Business Chronicle* **(Vol. 25, No. 21, November 1, 2002, pp. 11B)**
Pub: American City Business Publications, Inc.
Ed: Kent Hoover. Description: Michigan Republican Representative Peter Hoekstra offered a bill whereby prison inmate labor projects would have to compete with businesses concerning contract bids. Federal Prison Industries, which employs 22,560 inmates, generated sales of $583 million in 2001, versus $546 in 2000.

40100 ■ "Squeezed out? Is there any room left for small businesses in federal contracting?" in *Entrepreneur* **(Vol. 31, No. 4, April 2003)**
Pub: Entrepreneur Media Inc.
Ed: Chris Penttila. Description: In 2001, contract bundling cost small businesses an estimated $13 billion. Technology, engineering and outsourcing companies are expected to benefit from new Homeland Security projects, but the question is, will that include small companies.

40101 ■ "State eyes contracts in quest to get lean" in *Crain's Detroit Business* **(Vol. 19, No. 6, Feb. 10, 2003, pp. 1)**
Pub: Crain Communications Inc., Detroit
Ed: Amy Lane. Description: In an effort to cut spending, Governor Jennifer Granholm will scrutinize all major purchases made by the State of Michigan.

40102 ■ *Successful Proposal Strategies for Small Businesses: Winning Government, Private Sector, & International Contracts*
Pub: Artech House, Inc.
Ed: Robert S. Frey. Released: 1997. Price: $59.95 (cloth).

40103 ■ "Texas considers outsourcing real estate needs" in *Atlanta Business Chronicle* **(Vol. 25, December 6, 2002, No. 26, pp. 30C)**
Pub: American City Business Publications, Inc.
Ed: Matt Hudgins. Description: The Texas Building and Procurement Commission is considering outsourcing the administration of over 1,100 state-government leases. The outsourcing deal could be worth $4-$6 million per year in landlord commissions. The article discusses competing firms for the contract.

40104 ■ "Trouble in Tennessee" in *Hispanic Business* **(October 2002, pp. 18)**
Pub: Hispanic Business
Ed: Jonathan J. Higuera. Description: Hispanic small business owners charge they are being blocked from local government contract work, officials deny the charge.

40105 ■ "Uncle Sam Wants YOU!" in *Business Week* **(No. 3689, July 10, 2000, pp. F10)**
Pub: McGraw-Hill, Inc.
Description: Information for procuring government contracts is covered, including a Web site that helps link small companies with federal contracts.

40106 ■ "War Earnings" in *Forbes* **(Vol. 175, January 10, 2005, No. 1, pp. 140)**
Pub: Forbes Magazine Inc.
Ed: David Serchuk. Description: Profile of Perini Corporation, the company rebuilding power stations in Iraq and installing new military bases in Afghanistan. The firm has seen revenues grow 71.2 percent in the last year and average three-year earnings-per-share is up 63.7 percent.

40107 ■ "What Your Country Can Do For You" in *Inc.* (July 1, 2003)
Pub: Gruner & Jahr USA Publishing
Description: Ways to assist small companies to procure government contracts are highlighted.

40108 ■ "Why Small Firms Can't Do Their Part" in *Hispanic Business* (Vol. 23, No. 11, November 2001, pp. 22)
Pub: Hispanic Business Inc.
Ed: Patricia Guadalupe. **Description:** As the government begins a buildup, a new report questions how much small business contractors will benefit. Statistics showing contracts to small disadvantaged businesses made by the SBA from 1997 to 2000 are presented.

40109 ■ *Win Government Contracts for Your Small Business*
Pub: CCH, Inc.
Ed: John DiGiacomo. **Released:** June 2007. **Price:** $24.95. **Description:** Techniques to help small companies negotiate and win government contracts.

40110 ■ *Winning Government Grants and Contracts for Your Small Business*
Pub: The McGraw-Hill Companies
Ed: Mark Rowh. **Released:** 1992. **Price:** $16.95 (paper). **Description:** Provides information on obtaining money through government agencies, including developing proposals and creating budgets. Also contains sample proposals and glossary.

TRADE PERIODICALS

40111 ■ *Defense Information and Electronics Report*
Pub: Inside Washington Publishers
Contact: Richard Lardner, Gen Mgr
Released: Weekly (Fri.). **Price:** $300, members to insidedefense.com at http://insidedefense.com/. **Description:** Publishes defense information and electronic warfare programs, procurement and policymaking.

40112 ■ *Government Market Report*
Pub: Amtower & Co.
Ed: Mark Amtower, Editor. **Released:** Quarterly. **Price:** Free to qualified subscribers. **Description:** Offers resources for companies selling to goods and services to the federal government. Recurring features include news of research, a calendar of events, book reviews, notices of publications available, and a column titled Marketing and Selling to Government. Remarks: Also available via e-mail.

40113 ■ *Inside Missile Defense*
Pub: Inside Washington Publishers
Ed: Thomas Duffy, Editor. **Released:** Biweekly, every other Wednesday. **Price:** $645, U.S. and Canada; $695, elsewhere. **Description:** Reports on U.S. missile defense programs, procurement, and policymaking.

40114 ■ *Mark Amtower's B-to-Government Report*
Pub: Amtower & Co.
Ed: Mark Amtower, Editor, amtower@erols.com. **Released:** Bimonthly. **Price:** $195, Free via e-mail; Free. **Description:** Provides information pertaining to direct marketing of products and services to the $200 billion/yr. U.S. Federal government marketplace. Recurring features include letters to the editor, interviews, a calendar of events, reports of meetings, notices of publications available, and Federal department and agency mail (incoming) regulations. Remarks: Also available via e-mail.

40115 ■ *The Nash & Cibinic Report*
Pub: West Group
Ed: Ralph Nash, Editor. **Released:** Monthly. **Price:** $1,300. **Description:** Discusses government contracts analysis and reporting. Topics include procurement management, contractor claims, and competition and awards.

TRADE SHOWS AND CONVENTIONS

40116 ■ Alliance Texas
Showorks Inc.
1325 W. 1st Ave., Ste. 312
Spokane, WA 99201
Ph:(509)838-8755
Fax: (509)838-2838
Co. E-mail: showorks@showorksinc.com
URL: http://www.showorksinc.com
Audience: Buyers and contracting officers from military bases. **Principal Exhibits:** Small business procurement opportunities.

CONSULTANTS

40117 ■ Margiloff & Associates
621 Royalview St.
Duarte, CA 91010-1346
Ph:(626)303-1266
Fax: (626)303-0127
Co. E-mail: margiloff@compuserve.com

E-mail: margiloff@compuserve.com
Scope: Energy and water conservation studies, analysis of research and development, licensing, economics and project management. Projects involve development, training, utility review, cost analysis, manufacturing system improvement, process modeling and expert witness services. Clients are in the food, chemical, fermentation, energy, financial and legal services, government and general manufacturing fields.

40118 ■ Moorhead Associates Inc.
2571 Vernon Dr. NE
Palm Bay, FL 32905-2501
Ph:(321)723-2031
Scope: Marketing, business development, public relations, video production, and writing.

COMPUTERIZED DATABASES

40119 ■ *Commerce Business Daily Online*
UCG
11300 Rockville Pke., Ste. 1100
Rockville, MD 20852-3030
Ph:(301)287-2700
Free: 800-824-1195
Fax: (301)816-8945
Co. E-mail: webmaster@ucg.com
URL: http://www.ucg.com
Description: Contains the complete text of the *Commerce Business Daily*, covering business news; contract awards of $25,000 or more by civil agencies and $100,000 or more by military agencies; proposed U.S. government procurements for services, supplies, equipment, and material of $25,000 or more for civilian and military agencies; research and development sources sought; special notices, including some international information, e.g., foreign government standards; and surplus property sales. Includes requests for proposals and quotations, invitations for bids, and solicitations. Also contains "Bluetops" announcements of contract awards of $3 million or more by the U.S. Department of Defense. Provides descriptions of non-U.S. government standards which may affect U.S. exports. Includes notifications of the government's interest in specific research and development fields and programs. NOTE: On DIALOG, the Commerce Business Daily database is available in three files: 194 (October 1992-start of File 195); 195 (most recent 60-90 days); CBDMENU (menu version). **Type:** Full text; Directory.

40120 ■ *Federal Contracts Report*
The Bureau of National Affairs Inc.
1231 25th St. NW
Washington, DC 20037
Ph:(202)452-4200
Free: 800-372-1033
Fax: (202)452-4226
Co. E-mail: customercare@bna.com
URL: http://www.bna.com
Description: Contains the complete text of *Federal Contracts Report*, covering significant developments and controversies in procurement policies and regulations at the government and individual agency level. Covers government agencies, including the U.S. Department of Defense, General Accounting Office, executive agencies, courts, and the Congress. Topics covered include minority contracting and subcontracting, grant programs, competitive and "sole source" contracting, research and development procedures, privatizing, and congressional budget actions. Includes coverage of ongoing fraud and enforcement activities, significant litigation, appeals, and more. **Availability:** Online: Thomson West, The Bureau of National Affairs Inc. **Type:** Full text.

40121 ■ *Federal Prime Contracts Data Base*
Eagle Eye Publishers Inc.
10560 Main St., PH-18
Fairfax, VA 22030-7182
Ph:(703)359-8980
Free: 800-875-4201
Fax: (703)359-8981
Co. E-mail: info@eagleeyeinc.com
URL: http://www.eagleeyeinc.com
Ed: Paul Murphy, Editor, pmurphy@eagleeyeinc.com. **Released:** Quarterly. **Price:** $3,495 annual subsciption; $7,495 5-year disc. **Covers:** More than 400,000 prime contracts awarded by U.S. government departments a nd agencies to more than 30,000 companies. **Entries Include:** Recipient company name, address, phone, name and title of contact; issuing agency and purchase office; parent company affiliations; 5-year contract payment history; 3-year company contract revenue history; links to CBD Award Announcements; product/service code, SIC code; place of performance city, country; SMSA; Congressional District, state, country; weapon system; solicitation terms; small business socioeconomic data.

LIBRARIES

40122 ■ Georgia State University–Small Business Development Center
PO Box 3986
10 Park Pl. S., Ste. 450
Atlanta, GA 30302
Ph:(404)651-3550
Fax: (404)651-1035
Co. E-mail: sbdrec@langate.gsu.edu
URL: http://www.gsu.edu/sbdc
Contact: Bernie Meineke, Res.Dir.
Scope: Small business, marketing, finance, international business, government procurement. **Services:** Counseling; center open to the public for reference use only. **Holdings:** Business directories; government publications and journals, periodicals, training manuals and videotapes. **Subscriptions:** 11 journals and other serials.

40123 ■ National Institute of Governmental Purchasing, Inc.–Specifications/Searchable Forms/Documents
151 Spring St., Ste. 200
Herndon, VA 20170
Ph:(703)736-8900
Fax: (703)736-9639
Co. E-mail: fabutaleb@nigp.org
URL: http://www.nigp.org
Scope: Governmental purchasing. **Services:** Library open to NIGP members. **Holdings:** Files of specifications, government procurement (13,000), searchable forms and documents (350).

Government Regulations

START-UP INFORMATION

40124 ■ "Inner-City Innovation" in *Entrepreneur* **(Vol. 28, No. 2, February 2000, pp. 136)**
Pub: Entrepreneur Media Inc.
Ed: Stephen Barlas. **Description:** President Clinton and Congress move toward increasing incentives for entrepreneurs ready to take on low-income communities.

40125 ■ "Pennsylvania" in *Entrepreneur* **(Vol. 28, No. 6, June 2000, pp. 155)**
Pub: Entrepreneur Media Inc.
Ed: Cynthia E. Griffin. **Description:** Pennsylvania has designed a program to encourage entrepreneurial business ventures.

40126 ■ *The Small Business Start-Up Kit*
Pub: NOLO
Ed: Peri Pakroo. **Released:** April 2004. **Price:** $24.99. **Description:** Entrepreneurial advice for launching a new business. Topics include compliance with state regulations, sole proprietorships, partnerships, corporations, limited liability companies, as well as accounting and tax information.

40127 ■ "Small business package passes Congress" in *BlackEnterprise* **(Vol. 31, No. 10, May 2001, pp. 22)**
Pub: Earl Graves Publishing Co.
Ed: Joyce Jones. **Description:** Information regarding the package of small business legislation passed by the 106th Congress will keep some programs intact and secure the future of others. SBA budget agreement appropriations, including venture capital assistance are presented. Statistical data included.

40128 ■ "Small or Not, It's the Law" in *Inc.* **(September 2000, pp. 107)**
Pub: The Goldhirsh Group
Ed: Ilan Mochari. **Description:** Frequent legal consultations add up, but many small business owners believe the cost is worth it for peace of mind and avoided litigation.

40129 ■ "Uncle Sam, Paralegal" in *Hispanic Business* **(June 2002, pp. 22)**
Pub: Hispanic Business
Ed: Teresa Talerico. **Description:** The Small Business Administration has launched a new Web site that assists entrepreneurs with legal questions. Since Hispanic entrepreneurs are eligible for a number of federal and state programs that are subject to changing regulations, the site will be very beneficial.

ASSOCIATIONS AND OTHER ORGANIZATIONS

40130 ■ American Small Businesses Association
206 E College St., Ste. 201
Grapevine, TX 76051
Free: 800-942-2722
Fax: (817)251-8578
Co. E-mail: rsawyer@utaic.com
URL: http://www.asbaonline.org
Contact: James C. Musser
Description: Represents small business owners. Supports legislation favorable to the small business enterprise; organizes members to collectively oppose unfavorable legislation. Informs members of proposed legislation affecting small businesses; conducts business education programs. Operates scholarship program. **Publications:** *ASBA Benefits Guide* (annual); *ASBA Today* (bimonthly).

40131 ■ National Federation of Independent Business
53 Century Blvd., Ste. 250
Nashville, TN 37214
Ph:(615)872-5800
Free: 800-NFI-BNOW
Fax: (615)232-4035
Contact: Todd Stottlemyer, Pres./CEO
Membership: Independent business and professional people. **Purpose:** Presents opinions of small and independent business to state and national legislative bodies. Conducts surveys at the state level with area directors and government affairs representatives working with state legislatures. Maintains 50 person legislative, research, and public affairs office in Washington, DC. Compiles statistics. **Publications:** *Independent Business* (bimonthly); *NFIB Mandate* (bimonthly). Also prepares and disseminates weekly press releases to daily papers, trade associations, and chambers of commerce nationwide, and monthly materials to high schools, colleges, and universities throughout the U.S.

40132 ■ Small Business Council of America
PO Box 2283
Wilmington, DE 19899
Ph:(302)691-7222
Free: 877-404-1329
Co. E-mail: calimafd@paleyrothman.com
URL: http://www.sbca.net
Contact: Paula Calimafde, Chair
Description: Small business and professional organizations. Goals are to keep federal tax and employee benefit legislation from becoming burdensome, and to support legislation creating economic incentives for small businesses. Lobbies Congress on behalf of members; alerts members to proposed legislation so that opposition or support can be mustered before a bill becomes law; operates ad hoc committees on specific legislation. Maintains speakers' bureau; compiles statistics. **Publications:** *News Flashes* (periodic); *SBCA Member and Congressional Directory* (annual); *Tax Report* (monthly).

40133 ■ Small Business Legislative Council
1100 H St. NW, Ste. 540
Washington, DC 20005
Ph:(202)639-8500
Fax: (202)296-5333
Co. E-mail: email@sblc.org
URL: http://www.sblc.org
Contact: John Satagaj, Pres./Gen. Counsel
Description: Serves as an independent coalition of trade and professional associations that share a common commitment to the future of small business. Represents the interests of small businesses in such diverse economic sectors as manufacturing, retailing, distribution, professional and technical services, construction, transportation, and agriculture. **Publications:** Newsletter (monthly).

EDUCATIONAL PROGRAMS

40134 ■ Adobe Acrobat Section 508 Accessibility
EEI Communications
66 Canal Ctr. Plz., Ste. 200
Alexandria, VA 22314-5507
Ph:(703)683-7453
Free: 888-253-2762
Fax: (703)683-7310
Co. E-mail: train@eeicommunications.com
URL: http://www.eeicommunications.com/training
Price: $395. **Description:** Covers the regulations by the Federal Government's Section 508 accessibility and the features of Adobe Acrobat software designed to meet the regulations, including definition of accessibility, authoring for accessibility, working with existing PDF files, forms, and scanned documents, using the accessibility checker, and tags palette, and testing your PDF files for accessibility. **Locations:** Alexandria, VA; Silver Spring, MD; and Washington, DC.

DIRECTORIES OF EDUCATIONAL PROGRAMS

40135 ■ *Neal-Schuman Guide to Finding Legal and Regulatory Information on the Internet*
Pub: Neal-Schuman Publishers Inc.
Ed: Yvonne J. Chandler, Editor. **Released:** new edition expected 2005. **Price:** $135, individuals. **Covers:** 947 Internet sites offering local, state, and federal legal and government information. **Entries Include:** Title, publishing agency, URL, brief description of the site.

REFERENCE WORKS

40136 ■ "2 Lawsuits Challenge State's Canker Policy" in *Tampa Tribune* **(December 22, 2005)**
Pub: Media General, Inc.
Ed: Cheryl N. Schmidt. **Description:** Two lawsuits filed by Florida citrus growers challenge the legality of Florida's citrus canker eradication program, mainly due to the recent hurricanes making it impossible to eradicate the canker. Canker does not harm humans but can cause fruit trees to loose nearly half their yields.

40137 ■ "The "A" team" in *WorkingWoman* **(Vol. 25, No. 5, May 2000, pp. 24)**
Pub: Lang Communications Inc.
Ed: Adele M. Stan. Description: The work of the President's Interagency Council on Women covers both international and domestic issues, including universal equality for females in education, health care and economic opportunity. It also provides a forum for career-minded women to be publicly noticed.

40138 ■ "Aastrom Gets \$22M Financing Boost; Stem-Cell Trials Pique Wall Street's Interest" in *Crain's Detroit Business* **(January 17, 2005)**
Pub: Crain Communications Inc. - Detroit
Ed: Andrew Dietderich. Description: Aastrom Biosciences Inc. is committed to obtaining approval by the U.S. Food and Drug Administration for approval of stem-cell-based products for general medical use. The firm has secured \$22 million capital to conduct clinical stem-cell trial tests at William Beaumont Hospital.

40139 ■ "About the Power Breakfast series" in *Crain's Detroit Business* **(Vol. 19, No. 1, January 6, 2003, pp. 3)**
Pub: Crain Communications Inc., Detroit
Description: Crain's Detroit Business is playing host to private roundtable discussions with executives and experts in the Detroit area. Key issues will focus on Southeast Michigan businesses, including suppliers, ethics, governance, and more.

40140 ■ "The ABSc of ESOPs" in *My Business* **(February/March 2003, pp. 36-38)**
Pub: My Business Magazine
Ed: Nancy Mann Jackson. Description: Employee Stock Ownership Programs (ESOPs), established by Congress in 1974, are examined. Five myths regarding ESOPs are also listed.

40141 ■ "Abuse-awareness initiative lets employers help parents" in *Business First Columbus* **(Vol. 18, No. 26, February 15, 2002, pp. B7)**
Pub: Business First Columbus, Inc.
Ed: Betsy Butler. Description: A new government initiative is allowing employers to assist employees in abuse cases.

40142 ■ *Access to Finance*
Pub: Brookings Institution Press
Ed: Barr. Released: December 2006. Price: \$39.95. Description: Challenges to help make financial systems more inclusive to promote successful venture in new markets while utilizing new technologies and government policies to expand financial access to smaller companies.

40143 ■ "Accounting for intangible assets" in *Rough Notes* **(Vol. 146, No. 3, March 2003, pp. 128)**
Pub: Rough Notes
Ed: Wayne A. Walkotten. Description: The Financial Accounting Standards Board issued statements on acquisitions and intangible assets. These statements have resulted in changes in accounting procedures that now affect agency acquisitions.

40144 ■ "Action Sacked" in *Entrepreneur* **(Vol. 33, August 2005, No. 8, pp. 18)**
Pub: Entrepreneur Media Inc.
Ed: Jane Easter Bahls. Description: President Bush signed the Class Action Fairness Act of 2005 in February. The new law is expected to protect small businesses from class-action lawsuits.

40145 ■ "Action Yet in Need of Affirming" in *Hispanic Business* **(Vol. 23, No. 7/8, July/August 2001, pp. 29)**
Pub: Hispanic Business
Ed: Harry P. Pachon. Description: An overview of data that supports the continued use of affirmative action programs.

40146 ■ "Addressing the Inhibitors" in *Washington Business Journal* **(Vol. 21, No. 50, April 11, 2003, pp. 28)**
Pub: Washington Business Journal
Ed: Chris Silva. Description: Drugs designed to bolster viral fusion inhibitors are being developed by Panacos Pharmaceuticals Inc. An anti-HIV drug was approved by the U.S. Food and Drug Administration in March, which offers opportunities for a new type of drug.

40147 ■ "Affirmative Action Front and Center" in *Hispanic Business* **(March 2003, pp. 20, 22, 24)**
Pub: Hispanic Business
Ed: Tim Dougherty. Description: The Supreme Court will consider two related cases with implications for college-bound Hispanic students.

40148 ■ "Affirmative Action on Trial" in *Hispanic Business* **(September 2003, pp. 40-42, 44)**
Pub: Hispanic Business
Ed: Holly Ocasio Rizzo. Description: The nation's law and business schools are struggling to raise minority enrollment, and the new U.S. Supreme Court ruling struck down a plan giving Hispanics and other minorities extra points toward undergraduate admission.

40149 ■ "Age On Your Side" in *Black Enterprise* **(Vol. 36, February 2006, No. 7, pp. 74)**
Pub: Earl G. Graves Publishing Co. Inc.
Ed: L. Taylor. Description: The Age Discrimination Act of 1967 is examined.

40150 ■ "Age Rage: Younger Employees are Crying Age Discrimination" in *Entrepreneur* **(Vol. 32, No. 4, April 2004, pp. 24)**
Pub: Entrepreneur Media, Inc.
Ed: Chris Penttila. Description: Employees in the forty-something age bracket are filing discrimination suits against employers charging they are being excluded from particular retirement health benefits older employees receive.

40151 ■ "Ahead of the Law" in *Adweek* **(Vol. 46, January 17, 2005, No. 3, pp. 16)**
Pub: VNU Business Media
Ed: Wendy Melillo. Description: Laws and regulations involving television advertising are examined.

40152 ■ "Alarcon Backs McCain Bill" in *Hispanic Business* **(March 2003, pp. 18)**
Pub: Hispanic Business
Description: The president and CEO of Spanish Broadcasting System, Raul Alercon, is in favor of the Telecommunications Ownership Diversification Act of 2003, introduced by Senator John McCain (R-AZ). The bill would provide a tax deferral for companies that sell broadcast properties to minority-owned broadcasters and new entrants into the industry.

40153 ■ "Amendment to Thwart Scavengers Could Hurt Scrap Dealers" in *Crain's Detroit Business* **(Vol. 22, December 4, 2006, No. 49, pp. 27)**
Pub: Crain Communications Inc. - Detroit
Ed: Anjali Fluker. Description: New city ordinance may drive legitimate scrap dealers out of the city limits. Intent was to prevent theft and stripping of copper from residences and businesses.

40154 ■ "Analog TV" in *Business Week* **(January 23, 2006, No. 3968, pp. 22)**
Pub: McGraw-Hill Companies
Ed: Stephen H. Wildstrom. Description: Congress has decreed that television broadcasters must end analog transmissions by February 17, 2009 and switch to digital technology.

40155 ■ "Anti-bundling plan may give small firms contracts" in *Atlanta Business Chronicle* **(Vol. 25, No. 22, November 8, 2002, pp. 7B)**
Pub: American City Business Publications, Inc.
Ed: Kent Hoover. Description: The Bush administration would like to curtail contract bundling in order to allow small businesses an opportunity to procure more government contracts. Small firms have been hurt by bundling, the method in which contracts were placed into large packages that favored large businesses.

40156 ■ "The Anti-FEMA" in *Inc.* **(Volume 27, December 2005, No. 12, pp. 100-102)**
Pub: Inc. Magazine
Ed: Patrick J. Sauer. Description: Profile of Richard Zuschlag, whose ambulance service rescued thousands of individuals from New Orleans after the devastation of Hurricane Katrina.

40157 ■ "Apple Squares Off Against Resellers" in *Inc.* **(September 1, 2004)**
Pub: Inc. Magazine
Ed: Cara Cannella. Description: The legal battle between Apple and its resellers that began four years ago is examined. The battle started when resellers concluded that Apple was mistreating them by opening outlets near their businesses.

40158 ■ "Apply Yourself" in *Entrepreneur* **(Vol. 32, October 2004, No. 10, pp. 98)**
Pub: Entrepreneur Media Inc.
Ed: Chris Penttila. Description: Three criteria used to define an online applicant for employers hiring via the Internet were set by the Department of Labor, the Equal Employment Opportunity Commission and other federal agencies. First, an employer must be filling a particular position, the online applicant must follow the employer's process when applying, and the online applicant must indicate interest in a specific position within the company.

40159 ■ *Are Government Purchasing Policies Failing Small Business?: Congressional Hearing*
Pub: DIANE Publishing Company
Ed: John F. Kerry. Released: November 2004. Price: \$35.00. Description: Covers Congressional hearing: Steven App, Treasury Department; Fred Armendariz and Major Clark, Small Business Administration; Susan Allen, Pan Asian American Chamber of Commerce; Stephen Denlinger, Latin American Management Association; Charles Henry, National Veteran's Business Development Corporation; Morris Hudson, MO Procurement Technology Assistance Centers; Bar Kasoff, Women Impact, Public Policy; Pam Mazza, Piliero, Massa and Pargament; Ron Newlan, HubZone Contract National Council; Pat Parker, Native American Management Service; Joann Payne, Women First National Legislative Commission; Mike Robinson, MA Small Business Development Centers; Ramon Rodriguez, Hispanic Chamber of Commerce; Angela Styles, Office of Management and Budget; Ralph Thomas, NASA; John Turner, MN Business Enterprise Legal Defense Fund; James Turpin, American Subcontractor's Association, Inc.; and Henry Wilfong, National Association of Small Disadvantaged Business.

40160 ■ "Are the Tax-Free Net's Days Numbered?" in *Home Office Computing* **(Vol. 18, No. 7, July 2000, pp. 16)**
Pub: Scholastic Inc.
Ed: Jeffery D. Zbar. Description: With the three-year moratorium on Web taxes set to expire in October 2001, the federally appointed Advisory Commission on Electronic Commerce (ACEC) has submitted recommendations designed to kill or slow adoption of new taxes. That means dot-coms would be exempt from charging sales taxes, while traditional retailers would still be required to charge sales taxes.

40161 ■ "Arm yourself for the coming battle over social security" in *Harvard Business Review* **(Vol. 80, No. 11, November 2002, pp. 52)**
Pub: Harvard Business School Press
Description: A visiting professor at Harvard Law School and a former member of the President's Committee to Strengthen Social Security describes the problems ahead for the Social Security system. He outlines three alternatives to reforming the system, including increasing contributions, decreasing growth of benefits for the affluent, and increasing returns on Social Security assets.

40162 ■ **"Ask the attorney"** in *Red Herring* (March 2003, pp. 73)
Pub: Herring Communications Inc.
Description: Legal issues are addressed that include the following topics, pharmaceutical patents, government support for research and development, global commerce, intellectual property rights, the transfer of customer lists from European subsidiary to its U.S. parent company, trademark dilution, venture financing, selling a business, stock options, corporate tax deductions, small business patent methods, and employee use of Instant Messaging with clients.

40163 ■ **"Ask Inc, Marketing"** in *Inc.* (November 2006, pp. 53)
Pub: Gruner & Jahr USA Publishing
Ed: Doug Houte **Description:** Federal "Do Not Call" registry injured much of the telemarketing business to consumer marketers, but did not affect business to business as deeply. The key is to discover who needs what you have to sell, rather than mass canvassing. Help is available online or with companies that specialize in this.

40164 ■ **"ASPA President Shares Regulatory Outlook, Plans New Association Initiatives"** in *Employee Benefit Plan Review* (Vol. 55, No. 7, Jan.2001)
Pub: Charles D. Spencer & Associates, Inc.
Ed: Seymour LaRock. **Description:** George Taylor, president of the American Society of Pension Actuaries, is critical of President Bush's Social Security proposals. He feels the Social Security system must provide all Americans with a floor retirement benefit in conjunction with a healthy private retirement system.

40165 ■ **"Attorney General to offer olive branch to Silicon Valley"** in *The New York Times* (April 5, 2000, pp. C2)
Pub: The New York Times Company
Ed: John Markoff. **Description:** Janet Reno to fight computer crime and strengthen network security.

40166 ■ **"Bad credit and employment"** in *Black Enterprise* (Vol. 31, No. 5, December 2000, pp. 172)
Pub: Earl Graves Publishing Co.
Ed: Bevolyn Williams-Harold. **Description:** The issue of screening job applicants based on credit history is discussed.

40167 ■ **"Bank deals draw fines"** in *Business First of Buffalo* (Vol. 18, No. 46, August 12, 2002, pp. 1)
Pub: Knight-Ridder/Tribune Business News
Ed: Tom Hartley. **Description:** HSBC Bank USA, located in Buffalo, New York, has been fined more than $71,000 for violating a law that prevents business dealings with nations on so-called U.S. enemies' lists, including dealings with the Taliban in Afghanistan, and Cuba, Kosovo, Iraq and Libya.

40168 ■ **"Bank Reform: Should You Be Celebrating?"** in *Business Week* (No. 3658, December 6, 1999, pp. F8)
Pub: McGraw-Hill, Inc.
Description: Lists ways in which financial services deregulation will affect small business.

40169 ■ **"Bankruptcy Court Streamlines Rules - to Drum Up Business"** in *Crain's Detroit Business* (Vol. 21, January 3, 2005, No. 1, pp. 18)
Pub: Crain Communications Inc. - Detroit
Ed: Brent Snavely. **Description:** Seventeen new rules designed to create new business for the U.S. Bankruptcy Court in Detroit, Michigan are discussed. The new rules will be evaluated over the next 18 months.

40170 ■ **"Bankruptcy Reform Trying to Scale Final Hurdle"** in *Atlanta Business Chronicle* (Vol. 24, No. 8, July 27, 2001, pp. 4A)
Pub: American City Business Journals Inc.
Ed: Kent Hoover. **Description:** A bill crafted by creditors and designed to change the laws regarding bankruptcy may be signed into law before Labor Day.

Because wealthy debtors may abuse the current system by shielding their assets in states such as Florida that keep homes from the reach of creditors, the new law will allow debtors to only protect $125,000 of home equity. Analysts predict that if the bill becomes law, bankruptcies will increase dramatically in the months before it goes into effect.

40171 ■ **"Bankruptcy Reform Will Punish Debtors"** in *Atlanta Business Chronicle* (Vol. 25, No. 20, October 25, 2002, pp. 38A)
Pub: American City Business Publications, Inc.
Ed: Mark Meltzer. **Description:** The lame-duck session of Congress will likely decide whether to reform the nation's bankruptcy laws. At issue is the reduction of the number of bankruptcies by making filing more difficult. Currently, Atlanta, Georgia is among the leading major metropolitan regions in bankruptcy filings.

40172 ■ **"Bar None"** in *Entrepreneur* (Vol. 32, December 2004, No. 12, pp. 24)
Pub: Entrepreneur Media Inc.
Ed: Amanda C. Kooser. **Description:** New bar code regulations affecting retailers and suppliers, called Sunrise 2005, go into effect January 1, 2005. This process allows businesses to scan different types of codes used worldwide, and ultimately, the 14-digit Global Trade Item Number.

40173 ■ **"Bar None"** in *My Business* (December/January 2004, pp. 11)
Pub: My Business Magazine
Ed: Tamara E. Holmes. **Description:** The 2005 Sunrise mandate, instituted by the Uniform Code Council Inc., will require all retailers to have systems able to read 13-digit bar codes in addition to the 12-digit bar code numbers already standard in the U.S. The change is required EAN International, the global body that issues product codes overseas, currently uses an 8-digit and 13-digit system.

40174 ■ **"Battle over restaurant smoking still smolders in state Capitol"** in *Crain's Detroit Business* (Vol. 18, No. 22, June 3, 2002, pp. 41)
Pub: Crain Communications Inc. - Detroit
Ed: Michael Strong. **Description:** The legal battle in the war over banning smoking in restaurants is building, and Detroit area restaurants are caught in the middle.

40175 ■ **"Battle brews against tort reform"** in *Atlanta Business Chronicle* (Vol. 25, Dec. 13, 2002, No. 27, pp. A1)
Pub: American City Business Publications, Inc.
Ed: Julie Bryant. **Description:** As political move towards tort reform in Georgia gathers strength with the election of Sonny Perdue, trial attorneys and the victims they represent are presenting data indicating that such reforms do not halt medical malpractice insurance premium hikes. Caps on jury awards are, however, sought by physicians as they face mounting insurance premiums.

40176 ■ **"Beating the Odds"** in *Success* (Vol. 47, No. 3, July 2000, pp. 28)
Pub: Success Publishing, Inc.
Ed: Joan Szabo. **Description:** Alan Greenspan has achieved an important distinction in his 13-year tenure as chairman of the Federal Reserve Board. Under his leadership, the United States has enjoyed the longest economic expansion in its history.

40177 ■ **"Before You Sign on the Dotted Line..."** in *Black Enterprise* (Vol. 35, October 2004, No. 3, pp. 200)
Pub: Earl G. Graves Publishing Co. Inc.
Ed: Tamara Holmes. **Description:** Before hiring any company, it is imperative to check with the Better Business Bureau and your state attorney general's office. Web sites are also featured for checking a company before signing a contract.

40178 ■ **"BellSouth drops hike in deposits"** in *Atlanta Business Chronicle* (Vol. 25, Jan. 10, 2003, No. 31, pp. 27A)
Pub: American City Business Publications, Inc.
Ed: Mary Jane Credeur. **Description:** Citing potential financial burdens on young companies and a bias toward smaller companies, the Federal Communications Commission has denied pleas by the Baby Bells to hike security deposits for resellers of Bell services. BellSouth, Verizon Communications Inc., and SBC Communications Inc. were involved in the effort to sway FCC opinion.

40179 ■ **"Belmont Annexation Approved"** in *Charlotte Observer* (February 7, 2007)
Pub: Knight-Ridder/Tribune Business News
Ed: Jefferson George. **Description:** Belmont, North Carolina City Council approved annexation of nearly 64 acres. The land will be used to develop a residential community.

40180 ■ **"Beluga Import Ban Benefits Two Area Companies"** in *Sacramento Bee* (November 7, 2005)
Pub: The Sacramento Bee
Ed: Jon Ortiz. **Description:** The U.S. federal government has imposed a ban on beluga sturgeon products from the Caspian and Black Seas. The move will help two Sacramento area businesses.

40181 ■ **"Bennett Pursues Public Input On Growth Issues"** in *Bradenton Herald* (February 2, 2005)
Pub: Bradenton Herald
Ed: Stephen Majors. **Description:** Florida Senator Mike Bennett will not make a decision on the state's impending state-growth-management legislation until more planning experts and the public have had input. Senator Bennett will hold workshops throughout the state to explore better ways to plan business growth.

40182 ■ **"The Best Sunset Provision Ever"** in *Inc.* (October 2005, pp. 34)
Pub: Inc. Magazine
Ed: Lora Kolodny. **Description:** It is expected that all companies, regardless of size and industry, will benefit from the new Energy Act that extends daylight-savings time by four weeks, beginning March 2007. The Journal of Banking and Finance reports daylight-savings time will promote a healthier economy and higher stock market returns because exposure to full-spectrum light early in the day improves mood and concentration of employees.

40183 ■ **"Beware the Venture Catalyst"** in *Inc.* (August 2000, pp. 127)
Pub: The Goldhirsh Group
Description: Newfangled venture catalysts may have great connections to angel investors and venture capitalists, but they may also be breaking the law. A warning from a former counsel for the National Association of Securities Dealers.

40184 ■ **"Big Bonus"** in *Entrepreneur* (Vol. 30, No. 3, March 2002, pp. 77)
Pub: Entrepreneur Media Inc.
Ed: Chris Sandlund. **Description:** Complying with government regulations costs small businesses with fewer than 20 employees 56 percent more per employee than those with 500 or more employees.

40185 ■ **"The Big Issues for Small Concerns: Listen up, candidates"** in *Time Inc.* (Vol. 156, No. 3, July 17, 2000, pp. B7)
Pub: Time & Life Bldg., Rockefeller Center
Description: Small-business owners hate excessive regulations, taxes, red tape, and healthcare costs.

40186 ■ **"Big Taxes Top Lansing Agenda, Will Granholm Proposal Shift?"** in *Crain's Detroit Business* (Vol. 23, January 8, 2007, No. 2, pp. 1)
Pub: Crain Communications Inc. - Detroit
Ed: Amy Lane. **Description:** Legislators still unsure how to budget in wake of large deficits. Tax shifts likely, but original proposal from the Governor's office may have to be revised with new figures to be announced.

40187 ■ **"Bill Requiring State Copy of Tax Form on Way to Granholm"** in *Crain's Detroit Business* (Vol. 19, No. 45, November 10, 2003, pp. 6)
Pub: Crain Communications Inc., Detroit

Ed: Amy Lane. **Description:** Information on Michigan's Senate Bill 770, which requires employers to file with the state a copy of the federal form that lists income paid to non-employees such as independent contractors, is provided. The bill is designed to help track income earned by independent contractors and the taxes owed to the State.

40188 ■ "Bill Will Allow Consumers to Order Wine Shipped Directly from Maker" in *Atlanta Journal-Constitution* **(February 2, 2007)**
Pub: Cox Newspapers, Inc.
Ed: James Salzer. **Description:** Lawmakers are backing legislation that would allow Georgia citizens to purchase wine directly from wineries in other states.

40189 ■ "Bill Would Ease Rules on Store Price Tags" in *Crain's Detroit Business* **(Vol. 22, December 4, 2006, No. 49, pp. 6)**
Pub: Crain Communications Inc. - Detroit
Ed: Amy Lane. **Description:** New bill will aid attraction of new members of the retailing industry to come to Michigan. Video scanning is now permissible to replace individual pricing tags or labels if certain conditions are met.

40190 ■ "Bill Would Let Biz Keep Unclaimed $100 Paychecks" in *Crain's Detroit Business* **(Vol. 18, No. 18, May 6, 2002, pp. 24)**
Pub: Crain Communications Inc. - Detroit
Ed: Amy Lane. **Description:** Many businesses may not know that they are supposed to give the state any unclaimed employee payroll checks, but a bill, if passed, would allow the employer the ability to keep unclaimed checks of $100 or less.

40191 ■ "Billion-Dollar Plan in Limbo" in *Pacific Business News* **(Vol. 41, No. 20, July 25, 2003, pp. 1)**
Pub: American City Business Journals
Ed: Terrence Sing. **Description:** A law suit has been filed in the 3rd Circuit Court trying to prevent 1250 Oceanside Partners from developing a track of agricultural land into a $1 billion residential complex.

40192 ■ "Bills would allow government land banks" in *Crain's Detroit Business* **(Vol. 18, No. 21, May 27, 2002, pp. 6)**
Pub: Crain Communications Inc. - Detroit
Description: Land banks that could help Detroit and other urban areas redevelop and sell thousands of acres of vacant land would be a boon for the city.

40193 ■ "Biloxi, Miss., Bed, Breakfast Law Upheld" in *Sun Herald* **(January 7, 2004)**
Pub: Knight-Ridder/Tribune Business News
Ed: Tom Wilemon. **Description:** Supreme Court Justice Oliver Diaz Jr. and former wife Jennifer, founders of Green Oaks LLC, dispute the city of Biloxi's law that would prohibit weddings at bed-and-breakfast inns in residential areas. The Diazes were indicted in July 2003 on federal fraud and bribery charges along with lawyer Paul Minor, who was also charged with racketeering.

40194 ■ "Bird Dog" in *Barron's* **(September 8, 2003, pp. 9)**
Pub: Barron's
Ed: Alan Abelson. **Description:** New York State Attorney General, Eliot Spitzer's continuing crusade against corruption on Wall Street netted two more victims, a Canary Capital hedge fund, and mutual funds administered by such august firms as Bank of America, Bank One, Janus and others.

40195 ■ "Biz has an interest in keeping Prop A" in *Crain's Detroit Business* **(Vol. 18, No. 18, May 6, 2002, pp. 8)**
Pub: Crain Communications Inc. - Detroit
Description: An examination of Michigan's Proposal A, that slashed taxes from an average of 34 mills to 6 mills for education.

40196 ■ "Biz Travelers Adapting To Ever-Changing Security Measures" in *Mississippi Business Journal* **(Vol. 28, September 2006, No. 36, pp. 12)**
Pub: Venture Publications, Inc.
Ed: Lynne Jeter **Description:** Since escalating airplane terrorist suspects have been arrested worldwide, airports have ramped-up their security measures. Business people and others who constantly travel the skies have had no choice but to exercise extreme tolerance and patience concerning the new security measures. But despite these changes, airline traveler numbers have been relatively unaffected. Statistical data included.

40197 ■ "Black Firm Sues SBA, Alleges Funding Bias" in *Boston Business Journal* **(Vol. 23, No. 30, August 29, 2003, pp. 18)**
Pub: American City Business Journals
Ed: Kent Hoover. **Description:** The racial discrimination lawsuit filed by minority-owned Small Business Investment Corporation against the U.S. Small Business Administration is addressed. Topics include management teams, funding of minority business, and business start-up loans.

40198 ■ "Blue Bag Site Faces Scrutiny" in *Chicago Tribune* **(February 17, 2005)**
Pub: Knight-Ridder/Tribune Business News
Description: Authorities are investigating an Indiana farmer who allegedly accepted more than six times the amount of waste from blue bag recycling centers than he reported spreading on his fields. Officials are trying to determine whether the farm's operator is dumping more material than allowed on his fields.

40199 ■ "Boeing CEO Casualty of Company's Renewed Focus on Ethics" in *Atlanta Journal-Constitution* **(March 8, 2005)**
Pub: Knight-Ridder/Tribune Business News
Ed: Tammy Joyner. **Description:** U.S. companies are being pressured by stronger ethics laws and codes of conduct. The firing of Harry Stonecipher, chief executive at Boeing, is an example of poor judgment surrounding an alleged affair cost him his job.

40200 ■ "Booz Allen's Sweet Spot" in *Forbes* **(Vol. 170, No. 12, December 9, 2002, pp. 190)**
Pub: Forbes Magazine
Ed: Andrew T. Gillies. **Description:** Booz Allen Hamilton, the McLean, Virginia consulting firm that is helping the Internal Revenue Service to modernize and create an effective Web site for users, is profiled.

40201 ■ "Border Patrol" in *Entrepreneur* **(Vol. 33, September 2005, No. 9, pp. 22)**
Pub: Entrepreneur Media Inc.
Ed: Stephen Barlas. **Description:** Members of Congress are trying to reverse a decision handed down by the Sixth U.S. Circuit Court of Appeals, covering the states of Kentucky, Michigan, Ohio and Tennessee. The ruling states it is unconstitutional for the state of Ohio to offer tax incentives to existing Ohio companies to expand within the state.

40202 ■ "Bradenton Central CRA To Launch New Business Development Center" in *Bradenton Herald* **(January 29, 2005)**
Pub: Bradenton Herald
Ed: Tim W. McCann. **Description:** The Bradenton Central Community Redevelopment Agency is working to grow the economy of the area. The Agency will create a small business center with a professional counselor to assist small business owners in applying for a business loan, advertising, marketing and legal issues.

40203 ■ "Brasfield & Gorrie captures award" in *Atlanta Business Chronicle* **(Vol. 25, December 6, 2002, No. 26, pp. 8C)**
Pub: American City Business Publications, Inc.
Ed: Anya Martin. **Description:** Brasfield & Gorrie LLC, Birmingham, Alabama, has won the Associate Firm of the Year Award from the National Association of Industrial and Office Properties' Georgia Chapter. The company was chosen from 10 companies.

40204 ■ "Briefly" in *Crain's Detroit Business* **(Vol. 19, No. 2, January 13, 2003, pp. 10)**
Pub: Crain Communications Inc., Detroit
Description: The U.S. Small Business Administration and the U.S. Department of Defense have integrated the Procurement Marketing and Access Network and the Central Contractor Registration databases. This move will let vendors to enter information through a single registration, allowing small businesses to market products or services. Contact information is included.

40205 ■ "Broader Wheelchair Access Rules Proposed" in *Inc.* **(September 2005, pp. 32)**
Pub: Inc. Magazine
Ed: Allen P. Roberts Jr. **Description:** The Justice Department is considering changing the Americans With Disabilities Act to require companies to make all entryways wheelchair accessible, a move that would impact all small companies.

40206 ■ "Brookhaven Revising Commercial Development Codes After Developer Backlash" in *Long Island Business News* **(March 12, 2004)**
Pub: Dolan Media Newswires
Ed: Nick Anastasi. **Description:** Developers are fighting the changes made to the commercial development code in Brookhaven, New York. Opponents say the code would reduce the amount of developable space, leading to higher costs and overall reduction in property value.

40207 ■ "Broward Commission moves to take control of redevelopment" in *Daily Business Review* **(Vol. 77, No. 146, January 7, 2003, pp. A1)**
Pub: American Lawyer Media LP
Ed: Terry Sheridan. **Description:** The Broward County Commission will be exerting more control over land-use issues and redevelopment than in the past. The new policy will consider "densities, intensity, contiguous properties and transportation".

40208 ■ "Budget cuts target cities with living-wage laws" in *Crain's Detroit Business* **(Vol. 18, No. 24,)**
Pub: Crain Communications Inc. - Detroit
Ed: Amy Lane. **Description:** Detroit and other communities in Southeast Michigan with living-wage ordinances have become targets of state budget cuts, endangering millions in revenue-sharing payments.

40209 ■ "Building vital region requires teamwork" in *Crain's Detroit Business* **(Vol. 19, No. 17, April 28, 2003, pp. 9)**
Pub: Crain Communications Inc., Detroit
Ed: Richard Rassel. **Description:** The necessary upgrades needed to establish the Detroit region as a competitive economic region are discussed, including the importance for lawmakers to work together for a common goal.

40210 ■ "Building Your Business" in *Small Business Opportunities* **(Vol. 17, May 2005, No. 3, pp. 12)**
Pub: Harris Publications Inc.
Ed: Carla Longley Vincent. **Description:** Seven ways for a small business to tap into customers and increase profits include the development of alliances, franchising, adding wholesale clients, sell to the government, work with nonprofits, market yourself, and create new goods or services.

40211 ■ "Bush Backs Contracting Program" in *Hispanic Business* **(Vol. 23, No. 10, October, 2001, pp. 22)**
Pub: Hispanic Business
Ed: Patricia Guadalupe. **Description:** The Bush Administration will defend before the U.S. Supreme Court a federal program that uses race as a factor in determining contract awards. The Republican Party, in conjunction with the Republican National Hispanic Assembly, is offering training sessions for Spanish-speaking political activists and would-be GOP candidates. Ida Castro has been named director of the DNC's Women's Vote Center.

40212 ■ "Bush may trim SBA budget" in *BlackEnterprise* **(Vol. 32, No. 1, August 2001, pp. 28)**
Pub: Earl Graves Publishing Co.
Ed: Joyce Jones. Description: The proposed reduction of funding to the Small Business Administration (SBA), is discussed.

40213 ■ "Business dodges budget ax; But fee hikes, tax moves raise concerns" in *Crain's Detroit Business* **(Vol. 19, No. 10, March 10, 2003)**
Pub: Crain Communications Inc., Detroit
Ed: Amy Lane. Description: Michigan Governor Jennifer Granholm spared small business on some issues and programs in her proposed 2004 budget.

40214 ■ "Business by the Book" in *Home Office Computing* **(Vol. 18, No. 12, December 2000, pp. 99)**
Pub: Scholastic Inc.
Description: An explanation of licenses and permits needed to get a small business up and running.

40215 ■ "Business groups urge caution on pension law changes" in *Business First Columbus* **(Vol. 18, No. 25, February 8, 2002, pp. A5)**
Pub: Business First Columbus, Inc.
Description: Brief review of potential changes to pension laws, including the concerns expressed by business groups.

40216 ■ "Business Groups Divided Over Cuts to MEDC Funding" in *Crain's Detroit Business* **(Vol. 19, No. 17, April 28, 2003, pp. 6)**
Pub: Crain Communications Inc., Detroit
Description: The Michigan Manufacturers Association, the Detroit Regional Chamber and eight other local chambers have formed a new coalition to urge lawmakers to not go beyond Governor Granholm's recommended reductions in the budget of the Michigan Economic Development Corporation because it would damage the state's ability to compete for business investments and jobs.

40217 ■ "Business Primer for Legislators" in *Hispanic Business* **(November 2002, pp. 32)**
Pub: Hispanic Business
Ed: Derek Reveron. Description: The National Commission on Entrepreneurship presented a guide to government officials stating small business concerns. The guide also provides CEOs a checklist of business-friendly government initiatives.

40218 ■ "A Business Real Estate Appraisal Problem" in *American Banker* **(Vol. 170, February 4, 2005, No. 24, pp. 10)**
Pub: Thomson Financial Media Inc.
Ed: Kathleen W. Collins, Zonnie Breckinridge. Description: Federal banking agencies are considering a move toward establishing a formal position on real estate appraisals. The Federal Reserve Board and Office of the Comptroller of the Currency had confirmed a position that could affect the value of real estate used in business, including hotels, gas stations, convenience stores, bowling alleys, restaurants and nursing homes.

40219 ■ "The Business Week" in *Business Week* **(January 16, 2006, No. 3967, pp. 26-27)**
Pub: McGraw-Hill Companies
Ed: Harry Maurer. Description: Topics include Federal Reserve rate hikes, management at BASF, Hilton Hotels, China's economy, issues facing the airline industry, and more.

40220 ■ "The Business Week News You Need To Know" in *Business Week* **(January 9, 2006, No. 3966, pp. 24-25)**
Pub: McGraw-Hill Companies
Ed: Harry Maurer. Description: Information of 2005 holiday sales, interest rates, a medical device lawsuit, television cable news programming, the retailer Wal-Mart, Albertson's grocery stores, Alaska drilling, Microsoft's European business, and other issues is offered.

40221 ■ "Businesses Hope to Limit Lawsuits, Expand Health-Care Access" in *Atlanta Business Chronicle* **(Vol. 24, No. 7, July 20, 2001, pp. 3A)**
Pub: American City Business Journals Inc.
Ed: Kent Hoover. Description: A managed-care reform bill sponsored by Rep. Ernest Fletcher would allow patients to file lawsuits over medical coverage decisions, but only after they go through an administrative review. The bill would require most of the lawsuits to be filed in federal court and would cap punitive damages at $500,000. By comparison, the Patients' Bill of Rights, would cap the damages at $5 million.

40222 ■ "Businesses Must Now Notify of Possible ID Theft" in *Crain's Detroit Business* **(Vol. 23, January 8, 2007, No. 2, pp. 6)**
Pub: Crain Communications Inc. - Detroit
Ed: Amy Lane. Description: New bill requires businesses, state agencies, and local government to notify individuals of a security breech that is likely to cause individual loss, injury or identity theft.

40223 ■ "Businesses Oppose Family Leave Change" in *Crain's Detroit Business* **(Vol. 16, No. 4, January 24, 2000, pp. 4)**
Pub: Crain Communications, Inc.
Ed: Amy Lane. Description: Michigan's small business community is concerned about the impending federal rule that would allow workers to receive unemployment benefits if they take time off to care for newly born or adopted children.

40224 ■ "Businesses Warn State: Don't Hurt Economy to Fix Budget" in *Crain's Detroit Business* **(Vol. 19, No. 42, October 20, 2003, pp. 29)**
Pub: Crain Communications Inc., Detroit
Ed: Amy Lane. Description: Business officials are warning Michigan's governor that any new or increased taxes or fees could increase job losses in the state.

40225 ■ "Buy, Sell & Rent" in *Black Enterprise* **(Vol. 34, July 2004, No. 12, pp. 116)**
Pub: Earl G. Graves Publishing Co. Inc.
Ed: Donald Jay Korn. Description: Real estate investors must be aware of and understand the housing laws and regulations when buying, selling and renting properties.

40226 ■ "Buying Tunes Online" in *Kiplinger's Personal Finance Magazine* **(Vol. 54, No. 12, December 2000, pp. 28)**
Pub: The Kiplinger Washington Editors, Inc.
Ed: Kathy Jones. Description: Digital-music subscriptions may be the answer for record companies for making music available through the Internet.

40227 ■ "By Land, Air, and Sea: New Passport Rules in Effect" in *Black Enterprise* **(Vol. 37, January 2007, No. 6., pp. 101)**
Pub: Earl G. Graves Publishing Co. Inc.
Ed: Stephanie Young. Description: As part of a new security measure by the Western Hemisphere Travel Initiative, a passport will now be required for U.S. citizens traveling by air between Mexico, Canada, South and Central America, and the Caribbean. This initiative, designed to easily identify travelers and enforce border security, will most likely extend to land or sea travel no later than January 1, 2008.

40228 ■ "CAFTA Action" in *Hispanic Business* **(September 2006, pp. 14)**
Pub: Hispanic Business
Ed: Patricia Guadalupe. Description: Guatemala has implemented the Central America Free Trade Agreement (CAFTA-DR) joining several Central American countries and the United States. The agreement removes barriers to trade while expanding U.S. export opportunities.

40229 ■ "California Commissioner Proposes Overhaul to Auto Insurance Premiums" in *Sacramento Bee* **(December 23, 2005)**
Pub: The Sacramento Bee

Ed: Gilbert Chan. Description: California insurance commissioner, John Garamendi, is proposing new rules that would require auto insurance carriers to base their premiums primarily on a driver's safety record instead of the insured's residence. The move would close a major loophole to the state's Proposition 103 that allows insurers to rely heavily on zip codes when determining rates.

40230 ■ "California Offers Paid Leave for All Workers" in *Inc.* **(October 1, 2004)**
Pub: Inc. Magazine
Ed: Burt Helm. Description: Information is presented regarding California's new paid family leave benefit and its affect on the state's economy.

40231 ■ "California Regulator Seeks Cut in Lawn-Mower Emissions" in *Daily News* **(April 11, 2003)**
Pub: Knight-Ridder/Tribune Business News
Ed: Kerry Cavanaugh. Description: California State regulators are considering making major reductions in emissions from lawn mowers and are offering new electric lawn mowers for $150 along with the trade-in of old gas-powered mowers.

40232 ■ "California bill on Web sales tax" in *The New York Times* **(September 1, 2000, pp. C2)**
Pub: The New York Times Company
Ed: Lawrence M. Fisher. Description: The California State Assembly passes a bill to collect state sales tax from Internet sales.

40233 ■ "Call of the Wi-Fi: Digital Edge" in *Entrepreneur* **(Vol. 31, No. 9, September 2003, pp. 39)**
Pub: Entrepreneur Media, Inc.
Ed: Mike Hogan. Description: Today, the federal government protects businesses selling narrowband communications to people, allowing anyone to set up a combined phone service.

40234 ■ "Can the Fed Keep Things Cooking At a Low Boil?" in *Business Week* **(January 9, 2006, No. 3966, pp. 21)**
Pub: McGraw-Hill Companies
Ed: James C. Cooper. Description: The Federal Reserve is committed to lifting interest rates to a neutral level that will not stimulate or restrict economic growth, while keeping inflation under control.

40235 ■ "Can Firms Ban Weapons?" in *St. Louis Post-Dispatch* **(December 6, 2004)**
Pub: Knight-Ridder/Tribune Business News
Ed: Repps Hudson. Description: Potential for workforce violence and the fight over whether employees should have the right to carry firearms at work is examined.

40236 ■ "Can't Save the Farm" in *Black Enterprise* **(Vol. 31, No. 5, December 2000, pp. 34)**
Pub: Earl Graves Publishing Co.
Ed: Hamil R. Harris. Description: Legal relief arrives too late to harvest benefits for black farmers.

40237 ■ "Capital Coverage" in *My Business* **(October/November 2002, pp. 18-19)**
Pub: My Business Magazine
Description: NFIB presents small business legislation, health care cost information, tax administration.

40238 ■ "Capital Crunch" in *Hispanic Business* **(March 2002, pp. 44, 46, 48, 50, 52)**
Pub: Hispanic Business
Ed: Joel Russell. Description: After September 11, federal funds have been shifted from community development to emergency response. A listing of Hispanic nonprofit organizations, located in all 50 states and the District of Columbia, is presented.

40239 ■ "Capital infusion" in *Entrepreneur* **(Vol. 30, No. 10, October 2002, pp. 60)**
Pub: Entrepreneur Media Inc.
Ed: Jennifer Pellet. Description: Senator Kit Bond (R-MO) has introduced a bill that would direct investment capital into Small Business Investment Company Capital Access Act Bond.

40240 ■ "Capitol Briefings" in *Crain's Detroit Business* (Vol. 16, No. 49, December 4, 2000, pp. 7)

Pub: Crain Communications, Inc.

Ed: Amy Lane. **Description:** Two bills that offer an alternative to mandated diabetes coverage are reviewed, as well as information about the Michigan Department of Consumer and Industry Services' new Web site, which assists architects and engineers.

40241 ■ "Capitol Coverage: A Report on Politics and Policy from NFIB" in *My Business* (October/November 2003, pp. 16-17)

Pub: My Business Magazine

Description: The National Federation of Independent Business (NFIB) addresses current issues of importance to small businesses in the U.S., including economic impact of policies, white collar overtime, health insurance, and the 2004 NFIB Summit, to be held in Washington, DC in June 2004.

40242 ■ "Capitol Coverage" in *My Business* (December/January 2004, pp. 16-17)

Pub: My Business Magazine

Ed: Description: The National Federation of Independent Business (NFIB) addresses current issues of importance to small businesses in the U.S., including unemployment insurance benefits, unfair trade regulation, health insurance, and taxes.

40243 ■ "Capitol hits brakes on tax plan" in *Crain's Detroit Business* (Vol. 19, No. 15, April 14, 2003, pp. 3)

Pub: Crain Communications Inc., Detroit

Ed: Amy Lane. **Description:** Michigan governor, Jennifer Granholm is seeking new business- and income-tax changes totaling nearly $100 million.

40244 ■ "The Case of A Lifetime" in *Hispanic Business* (April 2005, pp. 22, 24-25)

Pub: Hispanic Business

Ed: Joel Russell. **Description:** Profile of Brigida Benitez whose affirmative action suit put her in the winning circle. She was voted 2005 Woman of the Year by Hispanic Magazine. Benitz' well-publicized case involving three white college applicants who filed discrimination suits because race was considered in the application processes is discussed.

40245 ■ "Cash in: Tax talk: Cash accounting is about to get more use" in *Entrepreneur* (Vol. 30, No. 3, March 2002, pp. 74)

Pub: Entrepreneur Media Inc.

Ed: Joan Szabo. **Description:** A recently issued Internal Revenue Service procedure allows certain businesses with gross receipts of up to $10 million to use the cash method of accounting for income and expenses, rather than using the accrual method, making income taxable when received and expenses deductible when paid.

40246 ■ "Casino Case Hits Legal Jackpot" in *Inc.* (August 1, 2003)

Pub: Gruner & Jahr USA Publishing

Ed: Bobbie Gossage. **Description:** A new ruling against Caesars Palace in Las Vegas, Nevada, will affect all companies when firing employees. The Supreme Court affirmed that circumstantial evidence in the casino's firing of an employee would suffice for a female warehouse worker fired for brawling with a co-worker.

40247 ■ "Cell Tower Potential" in *Black Enterprise* (Vol. 37, October 2006, No. 3, pp. 86)

Pub: Earl G. Graves Publishing Co. Inc.

Ed: James C. Johnson. **Description:** Due to local zoning that does not allow new cell towers to be too close to existing ones along with other issues only certain properties are eligible as leasing cites to wireless carriers.

40248 ■ "Chamber prepares for fight over tax changes" in *Crain's Detroit Business* (Vol. 19, No. 13, March 31, 2003, pp. 5)

Pub: Crain Communications Inc., Detroit

Ed: Amy Lane. **Description:** The Michigan Chamber of Commerce is opposed to the new budget measures planned by Governor Jennifer Granholm, saying they are disguised tax increases.

40249 ■ "The Chamber Steps Up Its War On the SEC" in *Business Week* (February 14, 2005, No. 3920, pp. 45)

Pub: McGraw-Hill Companies

Ed: Richard S. Dunham. **Description:** The U.S. Chamber of Commerce is continuing its battle with the Securities & Exchange Commission by filing a brief in support of Siebel Systems, which the SEC has charged with violating a 2000 rule that bars businesses from selectively disclosing material information.

40250 ■ "Changes at issue" in *Crain's Detroit Business* (Vol. 19, No. 15, April 14, 2003, pp. 33)

Pub: Crain Communications Inc., Detroit

Description: Changes in Michigan tax laws opposed by the Michigan Chamber of Commerce are detailed. Statistical data included.

40251 ■ "Changing Economic Factors Put Nursing Homes at Risk" in *Crain's Detroit Business* (Vol. 16, No. 49, December 4, 2000, pp. 28)

Pub: Crain Communications, Inc.

Ed: Mike Scott. **Description:** Detroit area nursing homes are experiencing a high number of closings due to such issues as high costs, stiff federal regulations, staff turnover and increasing competition.

40252 ■ "Changing of the Guard" in *Hispanic Business* (Vol. 24, No. 1/2, January/February 2002, pp. 57)

Pub: Hispanic Business Inc.

Description: The 2002 Hispanic Business Federal Elite Directory, listing 20 members of Congress, 51 judges, 13 military leaders, and 93 government executives, including officers in all three branches of government.

40253 ■ "Changing times: tax relief for women business owners" in *Women in Business* (Vol. 54, No. 5, September-October 2002, pp. 12)

Pub: The ABWA Company, Inc.

Ed: Edward Jones. **Description:** Wise retirement plan changes that could be implemented by women business owners as a result of the passage of the Economic Growth and Tax Relief Reconciliation Act of 2001 are discussed.

40254 ■ "Checking with Interest" in *Business Week* (No. 3678, April 24, 2000, pp. F10)

Pub: McGraw-Hill, Inc.

Description: The House Banking Committee recently voted to lift a ban on interest for commercial checking accounts.

40255 ■ "Chicago Can Be Greener" in *Crain's Chicago Business* (Vol. 30, January 2007, No. 1, pp. 15)

Pub: Crain Communications, Inc.

Ed: Sarah A. Klein. **Description:** Overview of possible solutions to Chicago's problem of not putting enough resources into reducing carbon emissions and slowing global warming.

40256 ■ "Chicago Observer: Owners Hope to Keep Plumbing Problems from Leaking" in *Crain's Chicago Business* (Vol. 26, December 15, 2003)

Pub: Crain Communications, Inc.

Ed: Steven R. Strahler. **Description:** Builders Plumbing & Heating Supply Company has filed bankruptcy and has the firm's owners concerned about Kitchen Distributors of America, another company they control, facing the same fate. KDA has $1.7 million in customer deposits for kitchen work to be done.

40257 ■ "ChoicePoint's Actions Could be Damaging, Experts Say" in *Atlanta Journal-Constitution* (March 5, 2005)

Pub: Knight-Ridder/Tribune Business News

Ed: Matt Kempner. **Description:** State and federal investigators are looking into ChoicePoint's steps since the discovery of its selling at least 145,000 Americans' personal information to a bogus company. This data is normally sold to insurance companies, law enforcement agencies, companies screening potential employees and landlords considering renters.

40258 ■ "Church Case May Impact Land Use" in *Crain's Detroit Business* (Vol. 23, January 8, 2007, No. 2, pp. 18)

Pub: Crain Communications Inc. - Detroit

Ed: Jennette Smith. **Description:** Southfield legal battle to be precedent setting for the issue of conversion of business property to church and other nonprofit use. Loss of tax revenue is the central issue. This is a universal problem nationally and may end up at the U.S. Supreme Court.

40259 ■ "Cities Talk Taxes; Mt. Clemens, Ann Arbor Look at Adding Income Levels to Help Fix Budgets" in *Crain's Detroit Business* (Vol. 21)

Pub: Crain Communications Inc. - Detroit

Ed: Anjali Fluker, Sheena Harrison. **Description:** Mt. Clemons and Ann Arbor, Michigan are both considering an increase in city taxes. There are 22 cities in Michigan that levy an income tax, including Detroit, Pontiac, Hamtramck, Highland Park, Flint, Saginaw, and Grand Rapids.

40260 ■ "City Policy Slows Efforts to Rehab Homes" in *Crain's Detroit Business* (Vol. 19, No. 10, March 10, 2003, pp. 9)

Pub: Crain Communications Inc., Detroit

Ed: Mary Kramer. **Description:** Issues confronting the Boston Edison Development Inc., a group of homeowners committed to rehabilitating the residential area, are presented. The city of Detroit requires the group to pay $20,000-$30,000 for abandoned houses, making it difficult for the group to continue.

40261 ■ "City building department slow, costly, audit says" in *Crain's Detroit Business* (Vol. 16, No. 49, December 4, 2000, pp. 1)

Pub: Crain Communications, Inc.

Ed: Robert Ankeny. **Description:** Detroit's Buildings and Safety Engineering Department has improved its operations in recent years, but it still has a way to go according to a recently released performance audit.

40262 ■ "CIWMB wants e-waste law signed, looks at zero waste, landfills" in *Solid Waste Report* (Vol. 34, No. 1, January 10, 2003)

Pub: Business Publishers, Inc.

Description: The California Integrated Waste Management Board will focus on three things in 2003, creating electronic waste legislation, the 2001 Strategic Plan, and landfills.

40263 ■ "Clearer Regs on Wellness Programs in the Workplace" in *Kiplinger Letter* (Vol. 78, January 19, 2007, No. 2)

Pub: Kiplinger

Description: Employers are creating employee incentives through wellness programs in order cut healthcare costs. Such programs can give employees rewards in the form of a discount or rebate in premiums; a waiver of deductibles, copays or coinsurance; or perhaps a gym membership.

40264 ■ "Clocking In: For Low-Wage Workers, Overtime May Get More Lucrative" in *Entrepreneur* (Vol. 31, No. 7, July 2003, pp. 22)

Pub: Entrepreneur Media, Inc.

Ed: Stephen Barlas. **Description:** The U.S. Labor Department has proposed changes to the law dictating overtime pay. The changes to the "white collar exemptions" of the Fair Labor Standards Act would entitle more hourly employees to time and half and further clarifies provisions that have allowed salaried employees to sue employers for overtime.

40265 ■ "Clybourn Ave.'s PMD Corridor Leads Nowhere" in *Crain's Chicago Business* (Vol. 30, January 2007, No. 1, pp. 8)

Pub: Crain Communications, Inc.

Description: In an effort to stem the loss of manufacturing jobs the city created planned manufacturing districts. A. Finkl & Sons Co. is moving its manufacturing plant to a new location and real estate developers are clamoring to turn the site into one of Chicago's hottest neighborhoods but are not able to make the purchase since the plant sits in a PMD.

40266 ■ *Code of Federal Regulations: Title 13: Business Credit and Assistance*
Pub: United States Government Printing Office
Ed: Department of Commerce Staff. **Released:** April 2005. **Price:** $55.00. **Description:** Title 13 covers regulations governing the activities of the Small Business Administration and the Department of Commerce. Book covers information on business credit, finance, and economic development.

40267 ■ "Cold Remedy Control has Pharmacies on Hot Seat" in *Milwaukee Journal Sentinel* (December 6, 2005)
Pub: Journal Sentinel, Inc.
Ed: Doris Hajewski. **Description:** A new Wisconsin law classifies cold remedies with pseudoephedrine a controlled substance. A controlled substance can be sold only by a licensed pharmacist in the state. Grocers, convenience stores and other retail outlets can no longer sell any cold remedies containing pseudoephedrine.

40268 ■ "Commentary: Real Estate Binders: Are They Enforceable?" in *Long Island Business News* (February 20, 2004)
Pub: Dolan Media Newswires
Description: The rights and obligations to parties involved in a residential real estate binder are explained.

40269 ■ "Companies Have Spent a Lot of Money To Comply with ISO's Popular Management Standards" in *Inc.* (May 1, 2006)
Pub: Inc. Magazine
Ed: Stephanie Clifford. **Description:** By 2003, more than 600,000 companies had been certified to ISO management standards worldwide. Certification is costly and time-consuming making it difficult for entrepreneurs.

40270 ■ "Competitors, biz groups worry bills would help Blues too much" in *Crain's Detroit Business* (Vol. 19, No. 11, March 17, 2003, pp. 23)
Pub: Crain Communications Inc., Detroit
Ed: Katie Merx. **Description:** House Bills 4278 through 4282 are examined. The newly introduced legislation would help Blue Cross Blue Shield of Michigan add more healthy residents to its insurance rolls, a move that has BCBS of Michigan competitors upset.

40271 ■ "Computer Recycling Bill Sent to California Governor" in *San Jose Mercury News* (September 1, 2002)
Pub: Knight-Ridder/Tribune Business News
Ed: Noam Levey. **Description:** California is leading the nation with a movement to recycle electronics, which will place a fee on new computer monitors and televisions. Technical manufacturers are set to fight the plan.

40272 ■ "Condo Builder Doubles Down" in *Crain's Chicago Business* (Vol. 26, No. 51, December 22, 2003, pp. 1)
Pub: Crain Communications, Inc.
Ed: Alby Gallun. **Description:** Harris Smith intends to build a 28-story condominium complex, despite the City of Chicago's attempts to stop the project. The city claims that a zoning change to permit the condos is illegal, while Smith contends the project would be legal under existing zoning.

40273 ■ "Congress considers legislation on 401(k)s after Enron scandal" in *Crain's Detroit Business* (Vol. 18, No. 18, May 6, 2002, pp. 13)
Pub: Crain Communications Inc. - Detroit
Ed: Laura Bailey. **Description:** There is pending federal legislation to regulate everything from 401(k) plans to accounting practices as a result of the collapse of Enron Corp. in 2001.

40274 ■ "Congress debates cable, DSL regulation" in *Crain's Detroit Business* (Vol. 18, No. 20, May 20, 2002, pp. 12)
Pub: Crain Communications Inc. - Detroit
Ed: Amy Lane. **Description:** An overview of the continuing debate in Washington over cable and DSL regulations.

40275 ■ "Congress Debates Fate of U.S. Agriculture" in *U.S. Farm News* (Vol. 25, No. 3, Autumn 2001, pp. 7)
Pub: U.S. Farmers Association
Ed: Lem Harris. **Description:** Both Houses of Congress and both major parties are conducting hearings and holding grassroots sessions in farm regions in order to prepare the new Farm Act due in 2002.

40276 ■ "Congress Looking at Proposed Tax Deferral Program" in *Atlanta Business Chronicle* (Vol. 24, No. 10, August 10, 2001, pp. 40A)
Pub: American City Business Journals Inc.
Ed: Andisheh Nouraee. **Description:** Tatum CFO Partners LLP is proposing the Bridge Act, a tax deferral program that will allow growing businesses (those with a growth rate of 10 percent during the previous two years, but under $10 million in gross annual revenue) to defer $250,000 in federal tax liability over two years. A coalition of small business groups and the House of Representatives Small Business Committee member Rep. Jim DeMint support Tatum.

40277 ■ "Congress Moves to Repeal Business Sale Lump-Sum Rule" in *Accounting Today* (Vol. 14, No. 8, May 1, 2000, pp. 3)
Pub: Faulkner & Gray, Inc.
Ed: David Cho. **Description:** Heeding the calls of the American Institute of CPAs and small business advocacy groups, the House of Representatives has fast-tracked a repeal of the law enacted last year that forces small business owners who are selling their businesses to immediately pay all taxes resulting from the sale in one lump sum.

40278 ■ "Congress Scores One For Your Portfolio" in *Fortuneit* (Vol. 146, No. 4, September 2, 2002, pp. 184)
Pub: Time Inc.
Ed: Jeffrey H. Birnbaum. **Description:** Information about the Sarbanes-Oxley bill on corporate governance and accounting reform is presented.

40279 ■ "Congress Waking Up to Stock Options" in *Venture Capital Journal* (Vol. 40, No. 10, November 2000, pp. 42)
Pub: Venture Economics
Ed: Howard Cox. **Description:** The importance of stock options to companies is addressed by Howard Cox, General Partner of Greylock in Boston, Massachusetts.

40280 ■ "Construction Defect Bill Is Progressing in Nevada, Lobbyist Says" in *Las Vegas Review-Journal* (April 11, 2003)
Pub: Knight-Ridder/Tribune Business News
Ed: Hubble Smith. **Description:** According to a lobbyist for the construction industry in Nevada, legislation aimed at reforming construction defect laws could help lower liability insurance rates.

40281 ■ "Consumer Bankers Assn. Files Petition With FCC Seeking Clarification About Do Not Call" in *Long Island Business News* (Feb. 13, 2004)
Pub: Dolan Media Newswires
Ed: Claude Solnik. **Description:** Consumers Bankers Association has filed a petition asking clarification of and relief from the Federal Communications Commission for its Do Not Call registry. Banks are claiming technological difficulties with Caller ID issues.

40282 ■ "The Content Crunch" in *Venture Capital Journal* (July 1, 2003)
Pub: Thomson Financial Inc.
Description: The new changes in FCC rules are examined, focusing on how these changes will impact the private equity business.

40283 ■ "A Conversation With Robin Asher, Clark Hill, LLC" in *Crain's Detroit Business* (Vol. 23, February 5, 2007, No. 6, pp. 11)
Pub: Crain Communications Inc. - Detroit
Ed: Tom Henderson. **Description:** Patent attorney discusses new patent process rules expected to be in effect later this year that would streamline the patent process. Supreme Court decision could help define what makes an idea obvious and not rely on technicalities and fine print.

40284 ■ "Corporate Scandals Inspire Texas Fraud Bill" in *Houston Chronicle* (April 11, 2003)
Pub: Knight-Ridder/Tribune Business News
Ed: Janet Elliott. **Description:** In response to recent corporate scandals, the Senate unanimously approved a bill to crack down on business fraud. Senate Bill 1059 would create a corporate integrity unit in the Texas attorney general's office. Details of the bill are examined.

40285 ■ *Counterattack: The New Government Attack on Small Business & How to Fight Back*
Pub: Regnery Publishing, Inc., an Eagle Publishing Co.
Ed: Jack Faris. **Released:** 1998. **Price:** $24.95.

40286 ■ "Court Sides With Biz on Disability" in *Inc.* (August 1, 2003)
Pub: Gruner & Jahr USA Publishing
Description: The Supreme Court ruled that businesses can reject employee disability benefits when the employer's doctor disagrees with the treating physician. A case involving a Black & Decker employee is cited.

40287 ■ "Courting the future" in *Crain's Detroit Business* (Vol. 19, No. 14, April 7, 2003, pp. 1)
Pub: Crain Communications Inc., Detroit
Ed: Robert Ankeny. **Description:** Profile of Reginald Turner, president of the State Bar of Michigan is presented. Turner's successful career includes partnerships at two prestigious Detroit law firms, presidencies of two major Michigan bar associations and significant roles in city, county and state affairs and in the Democratic Party.

40288 ■ "Courting Trouble" in *Inc.* (October 1, 2003)
Pub: Gruner & Jahr USA Publishing
Ed: Nadine Heintz. **Description:** Profile of an entrepreneur facing mail fraud charges engaged in a fraudulent scheme to obtain certification as a disadvantaged small business in 2000, in order to procure government road-construction contracts set aside for minorities and women.

40289 ■ "Crackdown on Mutual Fund Abuse" in *Black Enterprise* (Vol. 34, No. 5, December 2003, pp. 22)
Pub: Earl Graves Publishing Co.
Ed: Jeffrey McKinney. **Description:** The Securities and Exchange Commission is cracking down on U.S. firms improperly trading mutual funds. So far, 80 of the nation's largest mutual funds operations have received letters requesting information about ways they buy and sell mutual funds.

40290 ■ "Cracks in the Melting Pot" in *Inc.* (Volume 27, December 2005, No. 12, pp. 27-29)
Pub: Inc. Magazine
Ed: Stephanie Clifford. **Description:** Because of stiff Visa restrictions, entrepreneurial immigrants are finding opportunities overseas. Statistical data included.

40291 ■ "Credit Unions Win A Door-Opener For PassMark?" in *American Banker* (Vol. 170, February 4, 2005, No. 24, pp. 12)
Pub: Thomson Financial Media Inc.
Ed: Daniel Wolfe. **Description:** A new anti-phishing system from PassMark Security LLC, allows customers to select a personal image, such as a photo of a pet or relative, that is displayed when logging into their bank's Website. This system should help users recognize their bank's Website, making them less vulnerable to being fooled by an imposter site by phishers.

40292 ■ "Criminal records" in *Entrepreneur* (Vol. 31, No. 5, May 2003, pp. 72)
Pub: Entrepreneur Media Inc.
Ed: Steven C. Bahls, Jane Easter Bahls. **Description:** Under the Sarbanes-Oxley Act it is a federal crime for businesses to intentionally destroy documents that might be evidence in a federal investigation.

40293 ■ "Crooks and Books" in *The Economist* **(Vol. 376, July 30-August 5, 2005, No. 8437, pp. 14)**
Pub: The Economist Newspaper Ltd.
Description: Account reform is creating as many problems as it is solving.

40294 ■ "Crossing the finish line at full speed" in *Hispanic Business* **(Vol. 22, No. 6, June 2000, pp. 52)**
Pub: Hispanic Business
Ed: Joel Russell. **Description:** The 2000 directory of the largest Hispanic-owned businesses in the U.S. shows that their total revenues have risen 7.6 percent to $18.78 billion. Among them, MasTec Inc. and Burt Automotive each have revenues of over $1 billion.

40295 ■ "Customs dictates" in *Entrepreneur* **(Vol. 30, No. 3, March 2)**
Pub: Entrepreneur Media Inc.
Ed: Michelle Prather. **Description:** Since September 11, 2001, importers and exporters can expect to experience greater unpredictability and harsher penalties for violating import/export regulations.

40296 ■ "Customs Expansion Would Hurt Riverfront" in *Crain's Detroit Business* **(Vol. 21, October 24, 2005, No. 43, pp. 8)**
Pub: Crain Communications Inc. - Detroit
Ed: Description: Plans for a new customs inspection area in Detroit would improve international crossings for both freight and vehicle traffic. The plan might also include major retail shops. Some experts fear the plan, which calls for a new road in the middle of downtown, would hurt the new pedestrian-friendly promenade which is bringing visitors to the area.

40297 ■ "Cyber-Sign" in *PC Magazine* **(February 6, 2001, pp. 26)**
Pub: Ziff-Davis Publishing Company
Ed: Sally Wiener Grotta. **Description:** Cyber-Sign Electronic Signature Verification Plug-In for Adobe Acrobat is able to verify that a signature is authentic and can establish intent, the two requirements for using e-signatures. The Cyber-Sign products are invaluable for online business communications, making an electronic signature more secure than a traditional paper signature.

40298 ■ "The Dangers of a Lack of Accountability" in *Automotive News* **(Vol. 20, October 4, 2004, No. 40, pp. 8)**
Pub: Crain Communications Inc.
Ed: Keith Crain. **Description:** Plans for developing a downtown district, called African Town, in Detroit that would fund money to black-owned businesses is discussed. Many individuals claim the plan is both discriminatory and illegal.

40299 ■ "David Nicklaus Column" in *St. Louis Post-Dispatch* **(September 24, 2004)**
Pub: Knight-Ridder/Tribune Business News
Ed: David Nicklaus. **Description:** Check 21, or the Check Clearing for the 21st Century Act, allows banks to convert a check into a digital image that can be transmitted electronically. The new process will draw money from an account within 24 hours from deposit and is expected to save the industry $2 billion annually.

40300 ■ "D.C. Gets It Almost Right" in *Fortuneit* **(Vol. 146, No. 4, September 2, 2002, pp. 38)**
Pub: Time Inc.
Ed: Cait Murphy. **Description:** The Sarbanes-Oxley bill on corporate governance and accounting reform is profiled.

40301 ■ *Dead on Arrival: How the Anti-Business Backlash is Destroying Entrepreneurship in America and What We Can Still Do About It!*
Pub: HarperCollins Publishers, Inc.
Ed: Bernie Marcus; Steve Gottry. **Released:** November 2006. **Price:** $23.95. **Description:** Bernie Marcus, Home Depot leader, addresses regulations hurting small businesses in America.

40302 ■ "Debate Over State-Mandated Costs Threatens Georgia Health Insurance Measures" in *Atlanta Journal-Constitution* **(March 2, 2005)**
Pub: Knight-Ridder/Tribune Business News
Ed: Andy Miller. **Description:** Georgia legislation that aims to bring health insurance to the uninsured by removing some or all benefits required by the state is examined. Meanwhile, Senate Bill 174 offers business owners the choice of offering employees a policy with all coverages or one with fewer benefits.

40303 ■ "Debit Cards Ease FSA Administration Burden" in *Rough Notes* **(Vol. 145, No. 9, September 2002, pp. 34)**
Pub: Rough Notes
Ed: Len Strazewski. **Description:** Flexible spending accounts are not popular with employers nor employees owing to the heavy paperwork involved, but Congress may introduce legislation that will ease the administrative aspect so as to facilitate usage of the program.

40304 ■ "A Decade of NAFTA" in *Hispanic Business* **(July/August 2004, pp. 42, 44)**
Pub: Hispanic Business
Ed: Debra Beachy. **Description:** Successes and frustrations that have created the new platform for future growth are discussed. Trade investments have increased but there is still controversy over NAFTA's impact.

40305 ■ *Democratization Without Representation: The Politics of Small Industry in Mexico*
Pub: Pennsylvania State University Press
Ed: Kenneth C. Shalden. **Released:** July 2005. **Price:** $27.00. **Description:** Opportunities for individuals to participate in Mexico's democracy and how it is affecting the way industries do business.

40306 ■ "Democrats fall short: McCall, Kirk lose major elections" in *Black Enterprise* **(Vol. 33, No. 6, January 2003, pp. 23)**
Pub: Earl Graves Publishing Co.
Ed: K. Terrell Reed. **Description:** The impact of the November 2002 election on African Americans and minority small businesses is discussed.

40307 ■ *The Department of Labor's Overtime Regulations Effect on Small Business: Congressional Hearing*
Pub: DIANE Publishing Company
Ed: W. Todd Akin. **Released:** April 2006. **Price:** $20.00. **Description:** An overview of the Congressional hearing regarding the Department of Labor's regulations governing overtime and how they impact small business.

40308 ■ "Determination of a profit motive" in *Journal of Accountancy* **(Vol. 190, No. 3, September 2000, pp. 94)**
Pub: Harborside Financial Center
Ed: Cynthia Bolt Lee. **Description:** Information about the IRC section 183, "Activities Not Engaged in For Profit", which contains nine factors a taxpayer can use to determine whether an activity has a profit motive or is a hobby.

40309 ■ "Detroit, Inkster companies lead in removal of Rouge oil spill" in *Crain's Detroit Business* **(Vol. 18, No. 22, June 3, 2002, pp. 37)**
Pub: Crain Communications Inc. - Detroit
Ed: Joe Truini. **Description:** Investigators are focusing on those responsible for a mysterious oil spill in the Rouge River April 9. The cost of the cleanup has reached $3.5 million, and the culprit may have to pay as much as three times the cleanup costs plus fines of up to $27,500 per day.

40310 ■ "Developers pleased with changes in brownfield laws" in *Crain's Detroit Business* **(Vol. 19, No. 2, January 13, 2003, pp. 19)**
Pub: Crain Communications Inc., Detroit
Ed: Jennette Smith. **Description:** Changes to state and federal brownfield laws will encourage more development of contaminated sites in Michigan. The law will extend until the end of 2007.

40311 ■ "Developers See Trouble in Petitions" in *South Florida Business Journal* **(Vol. 23, No. 53, August 8, 2003, pp. 1A)**
Pub: American City Business Journals
Ed: Stephen Van Drake. **Description:** Real estate developers are concerned about potential legislation that would place land use decisions with voters rather than elected officials.

40312 ■ "Digital Signatures vs. Electronic Signatures" in *E-business Advisor* **(Vol. 18, No. 4, April 2000, pp. 48)**
Pub: Advisor Media, Inc.
Ed: Tom Melling. **Description:** Confusion between the definitions of digital signatures and electronic signatures could result in poorly constructed legislation that may create barriers to e-commerce and make electronic contracts unenforceable.

40313 ■ "Direct Hit: Can Direct Marketing Survive a Consumer Backlash?" in *Entrepreneur* **(Vol. 31, No. 9, September 2003, pp. 23)**
Pub: Entrepreneur Media, Inc.
Ed: Chris Penttila. **Description:** Congress, the states and large technology companies are taking action against telemarketing, junk mail and spam.

40314 ■ "Disappearing Ink" in *Kiplinger's Personal Finance Magazine* **(Vol. 54, No. 10, October 2000, pp. 118)**
Pub: The Kiplinger Washington Editors, Inc.
Ed: Ed Henry. **Description:** The Federal Electronic Signatures Law (E-Sign) that goes into effect October 1, 2000, will give e-signatures the same legal status as pen-and-ink signatures nationwide.

40315 ■ "Diversity in the Workplace" in *My Business* **(February/March 2004, pp. 15)**
Pub: My Business Magazine
Ed: Dennis McCafferty. **Description:** Legal experts offer advice on workplace practices involving ethnic diversity.

40316 ■ "DMC, city dispute hospital control" in *Crain's Detroit Business* **(Vol. 19, No. 16, April 21, 2003, pp. 3)**
Pub: Crain Communications Inc., Detroit
Ed: Katie Merx. **Description:** Regional and state leaders in Michigan are considering the creation of a health and hospital authority to assist the region's safety-net hospitals to provide indigent care. The move would keep Detroit Receiving Hospital open.

40317 ■ "Do the Right Thing - Or Else" in *Inc.* **(November 1, 2004)**
Pub: Inc. Magazine
Ed: Darren Dahl. **Description:** New Federal ethics rules apply to all companies, regardless of size.

40318 ■ "Do We Have Lift-Off? VoIP is a Bottle Rocket, but Red Tape Could Ground It" in *Entrepreneur* **(Vol. 32, No. 4, April 2004, pp. 27)**
Pub: Entrepreneur Media, Inc.
Ed: Mike Hogan. **Description:** Issues facing Voice over Internet Protocol (VoIP) are discussed, including the security and law enforcement protections of the technology. VoIP diverts the nation's phone calls from the Public Switched Telephone Network (PSTN), costing millions in tax dollars.

40319 ■ "Docs Face Big Financial Hit" in *Pittsburgh Business Times* **(Vol. 23, No. 9, September 19, 2003, pp. 1)**
Pub: Pittsburgh Business Times
Ed: Lynne Glover. **Description:** Diane Koken, the Pennsylvania insurance commissioner, ordered insurance companies to follow new billing procedures when issuing medical malpractice insurance. The new billing procedures are mandated under the 2003 Medical Care Availability and Reduction of Error Fund (MCARE).

40320 ■ "Does New Watchdog Have Teeth?" in *Business Journal-Portland* **(Vol. 20, No. 23, August 8, 2003, pp. 1)**
Pub: American City Business Journals, Inc.

Ed: Aliza Earnshaw. **Description:** The passage of the federal Sarbanes-Oxley Act of 2002 resulted in the formation of the Public Companies Accounting Oversight Board (PCAOB). The PCAOB will attempt to restore investor confidence in corporations by monitoring financial reports.

40321 ■ "Don't Bet Your Life On It" in *Inc.* **(August 2005, pp. 24-25)**
Pub: Inc. Magazine
Description: The Internal Revenue Service is cracking down on split-dollar insurance, a common benefit given to company executives.

40322 ■ "Double taxation is double wrong" in *Atlanta Business Chronicle* **(Vol. 25, January 10, 2003, No. 31, pp. 33A)**
Pub: American City Business Publications, Inc.
Ed: Jeff Dickerson. **Description:** George W. Bush's plan to eliminate the tax on dividends is far from an attempt to help the rich, for nearly half of all tax-filers in 2000 who claimed dividend income earned less than $50,000. Bush's stimulus plan will help everyday Americans, and the class warfare crowd will have a difficult time finding fault with the plan.

40323 ■ "Down the chute" in *Daily Business Review* **(Vol. 77, No. 198, March 24, 2003, pp. A8)**
Pub: American Lawyer Media LP
Ed: Laurie Cunningham. **Description:** The Florida Supreme Court has ruled that out-of-state lawyers could not represent clients in securities arbitration.

40324 ■ "Drug Importation and the Capital Markets" in *Venture Capital Journal* **(November 1, 2004)**
Pub: Thomason Financial Inc.
Description: Issues involving the importation of prescription drugs are covered. An examination of the economics behind cross-border shipment of drugs is essential in order to understand the affects of importation. Canadian and European governments are able to name the price they will pay for a particular drug and the Canadian government pays only the cost of manufacturing with a small markup, while American consumers not only pay manufacturing costs, but also research and development, administrative along with a markup.

40325 ■ "The Dubious Dole" in *Entrepreneur* **(Vol. 28, No. 10, October 2000, pp. 123)**
Pub: Entrepreneur Media Inc.
Ed: Jacquelyn Lynn. **Description:** Unemployment compensation is an insurance program designed to provide income to people who are out of work. Don't treat claims for unemployment compensation by former employees lightly, and the reasons why are covered.

40326 ■ "Dueling North Carolina Bills Would Revive Payday Lending" in *Charlotte Observer* **(April 11, 2003)**
Pub: Knight-Ridder/Tribune Business News
Ed: Rick Rothacker. **Description:** The debate over payday lending continues for North Carolina's General Assembly. There are two controversial bills for making short-term, high-interest loans introduced in April, consumer advocates support one, lenders the other.

40327 ■ "Duty on Canadian lumber may raise home prices" in *Atlanta Business Chronicle* **(Vol. 24, No. 13, August 31, 2001, pp. 9B)**
Pub: American City Business Journals Inc.
Ed: Martin Sinderman. **Description:** Following a ruling by the U.S. government for new tariffs on softwood lumber from Canada, the marketplace is feeling the pressure of price increases.

40328 ■ "E-commerce can pose legal risks for businesses" in *Crain's Detroit Business* **(Vol. 16, No. 16, April 17, 2000, pp. 17)**
Pub: Crain Communications, Inc.
Ed: Tim Moran. **Description:** The potential of legal risk when doing business on the Internet is examined.

40329 ■ "E-Commerce: When You Put Your 'John Hancock' on the Web Form!" in *Ingram's* **(Vol. 27, No. 5, May 2001, pp. 33)**
Pub: Show Me Publishing, Inc.
Ed: Arthur L. Smith. **Description:** Businesses are still finding ample opportunities from the electronic marketplace. Contracts made electronically are just as binding as the traditional paper contract.

40330 ■ "E-waste Bill in Oregon" in *Solid Waste Report* **(Vol. 33, No. 39, December 27, 2002)**
Pub: Business Publishers, Inc.
Description: A new representative in Oregon is proposing a bill to prohibit computer monitors and televisions from being disposed of in Oregon landfills.

40331 ■ "E-waste Management Muddled as Agencies Grope for Solutions" in *Solid Waste Report* **(Vol. 33, No. 32, September 20, 2002)**
Pub: Business Publishers, Inc.
Description: Problems associated with electronic products waste is examined, including the nation's efforts to solve these issues. The article suggests various types of remedies that should be considered, including recycling grants, hazardous waste exemptions, the banning of waste export, and regulation.

40332 ■ "Ease up on us, one industry that finances small firms asks the U.S." in *Wall Street Journal* **(July 18, 2000, pp. B2)**
Pub: Dow Jones & Co., Inc.
Ed: Jeffrey A. Tannenbaum. **Description:** Investment firms request an easing of regulations on financing small business.

40333 ■ "Easy Target? Budget-Cutters in Congress Have Set Their Sights on the SBA" in *Entrepreneur.com* **(Vol. 34, January 2006, No. 1, pp. 18)**
Pub: Entrepreneur Media Inc.
Ed: Chris Penttila. **Description:** Congress is considering cutting billions of dollars in federal programs, creating fear for small companies that rely on the Small Business Administration for assistance.

40334 ■ "Eateries Fend Off Nutrition Labels" in *Tampa Tribune* **(November 8, 2005)**
Pub: Media General, Inc.
Ed: Michael Sasso. **Description:** Legislators in at least 12 states want to require restaurants and fast food eateries to list fat and calorie content on their menus.

40335 ■ "Eateries Shut In Raids Over Labor Laws" in *Sacramento Bee* **(November 15, 2005)**
Pub: The Sacramento Bee
Ed: Rachel Osterman. **Description:** State officials temporarily closed more than a dozen restaurants in the Sacramento, California area. Of 20 establishments inspected, 16 were in violation of labor laws, including workers' compensation, overtime, meal breaks, and minimum wage rules.

40336 ■ "Eco-Products In Demand, But Labels Can Be Murky" in *Boston Globe* **(February 9, 2005)**
Pub: New York Times Company
Ed: Beth Daley. **Description:** Despite consumer demand for environmentally friendly products, labels can be misleading. A Website that helps consumers understand terminology on product labels is highlighted.

40337 ■ "The economics of ergonomics" in *Atlanta Business Chronicle* **(Vol. 23, No. 35, February 2, 2001, pp. 51A)**
Pub: American City Business Journals Inc.
Ed: Chaundra Frierson. **Description:** A new ergonomics regulation has been enacted recently which requires businesses to set up programs to reduce the amount of work-related injuries that take place. Small businesses oppose the regulation because it will increase costs dramatically. An accompanying sidebar includes an ergonomics timeline, while another provides statistics about who will be covered by this new regulation and its costs.

40338 ■ *Effect of the Overvalued Dollar on Small Exporters: Congressional Hearing*
Pub: DIANE Publishing Company
Ed: Donald Manzullo. **Released:** October 2004. **Price:** $30.00. **Description:** Congressional hearing: Witnesses: Dr. Lawrence Chimerine, Economist; Tony Raimondo, President and CEO, Behlen Manufacturing Company; Robert J. Weskamp, President, Wes-Tech, Inc.; Wayne Dollar, President, Georgia Farm Bureau; and Vargese George, President and CEO, Westex International, Inc. Appendix includes correspondence sent to committee on the overvalued dollar.

40339 ■ "Electricity, natural gas facing uncertain future" in *Atlanta Business Chronicle* **(Vol. 25, January 10, 2003, No. 31, pp. 24A)**
Pub: American City Business Publications, Inc.
Ed: Don Reichardt. **Description:** According to the Georgia Economic Outlook 2003 survey, electric utilities are positioned for growth while natural gas utilities will have to deal with the effects of deregulation and volatile prices.

40340 ■ "11th Hour" in *Entrepreneur* **(Vol. 27, No. 12, December 1999, pp. 20)**
Pub: Entrepreneur Media Inc.
Ed: Cynthia E. Griffin. **Description:** A bill in Congress could fundamentally change the way small business bankruptcies are handled. Information about the Bankruptcy Reform Act of 1998 is covered.

40341 ■ "Emergency care for Detroit's health system" in *Crain's Detroit Business* **(Vol. 19, No. 15, April 14, 2003, pp. 11)**
Pub: Crain Communications Inc., Detroit
Ed: Katie Merx. **Description:** Issues involving Detroit's health care system are discussed, including the crises in rising benefit rates for businesses, drug costs, the growing number of working persons without healthcare insurance, and the level of federal and state reimbursement for Medicaid patients.

40342 ■ "Eminent Danger" in *Entrepreneur* **(Vol. 33, January 2005, No. 1, pp. 19)**
Pub: Entrepreneur Media Inc.
Ed: Joshua Kurlantzick. **Description:** Dino Paspalakis, owner of Joyland Amusement Center in Daytona Beach, Florida is concerned about losing his family business because of the city of Dayton Beach using the legal doctrine eminent domain to try to take his property from him. The city plans to give the land to developers to build high-rise condos and hotels.

40343 ■ "Employment Law at the Dawn of the New Millennium" in *Employment Relations Today* **(Vol. 26, No. 4, Winter 2000, pp. 109)**
Pub: John Wiley & Sons, Inc.
Ed: William C. Martucci and Jeffrey M. Place. **Description:** The interpretation and construction of employment law at the turn of the 21st century are described. Topics addressed include protection for employees under anti-discrimination laws, employee privacy rights, and flexible working environments.

40344 ■ *Enabling Environments for Jobs and Entrepreneurship: The Role of Policy and Law in Small Enterprise Employment*
Pub: International Labour Office
Ed: Gerhard Reinecke, Simon White. **Released:** February 2004. **Price:** $22.95. **Description:** National policies, laws and regulations governing workplace safety.

40345 ■ "End of the Road" in *Entrepreneur* **(Vol. 31, No. 8, August 2003, pp. 24)**
Pub: Entrepreneur Media, Inc.
Ed: Joshua Kurlantzick. **Description:** Two Department of Commerce programs, the Advanced Technology Program (ATP) and the Manufacturing Extension Partnership (MEP) may be discontinued as part of the 2004 federal budget. The ATP program assists small firms by supporting research and development, while the MEP aids manufacturers in upgrading technology and human resources.

40346 ■ "End of Some Tariffs a Boon to Suppliers" in *Crain's Detroit Business* **(Vol. 22, December 18, 2006, No. 51, pp. 6)**
Pub: Crain Communications Inc. - Detroit
Ed: Brent Snavely. **Description:** Relaxation of tariffs on corrosion resistant steels will reduce supply costs for automotive suppliers. Tariffs were removed for imports from France, Canada, Australia, and Japan but remain in effect for Korea and Germany.

40347 ■ "Engler and business" in *Crain's Detroit Business* **(Vol. 18, No. 50, December 16, 2002, pp. 21)**
Pub: Crain Communications Inc., Detroit
Description: A list of the key business accomplishments made by Michigan's outgoing Governor, John Engler is presented.

40348 ■ "Entrepreneur Column" in *Entrepreneur* **(August 29, 2005)**
Pub: Entrepreneur Media Inc.
Ed: Gail F. Goodman. **Description:** The U.S. government's CAN-SPAM Act of 2004 and the E-Mail Service Provider Coalition (ESPC) are working to end unwanted spam email. Steps to ensure small businesses do not delete important email are listed, along with four basic rules for commercial email compliance.

40349 ■ *Entrepreneurship and Technology Policy*
Pub: Edward Elgar Publishing, Incorporated
Ed: Link. **Released:** August 2006. **Price:** $190.00. **Description:** Journal articles focusing how and the ways small businesses' technical contributions are affecting business. The book is divided into four parts: Government's Direct Support of R&D, Government's Leveraging of R&D, Government's Infrastructure Policies; and Knowledge Flows from Universities and Laboratories.

40350 ■ "Equal Time? Legal" in *Entrepreneur* **(Vol. 31, No. 9, September 2003, pp. 80)**
Pub: Entrepreneur Media, Inc.
Ed: Jane Easter Bahls. **Description:** Labor unions may be able to use company email systems in order to communicate with members. A discussion regarding a recent decision by an administrative judge for the National Labor Relations Board involving Prudential Insurance's Office & Professional Employees International Union is cited.

40351 ■ "Ergonomics & Economics" in *Crain's Detroit Business* **(Vol. 21, November 7, 2005, No. 45, pp. 1)**
Pub: Crain Communications Inc. - Detroit
Ed: Amy Lane. **Description:** A Michigan advisory committee is meeting to devise rules to govern how employers must identify and address workplace conditions that put workers at risk for job-related injuries caused by repetitive motion, force and other factors. Business lobbyists charge the committee's work violates a provision of the Department of Labor and Economic Growth budget that prohibits the use of state funds to develop mandates stronger than federal voluntary ergonomics guidelines.

40352 ■ "Estate of affairs" in *Entrepreneur* **(Vol. 31, No. 4, April 2003, pp. 52)**
Pub: Entrepreneur Media Inc.
Ed: Joshua Kurlantzick. **Description:** With the repealing of the federal estate tax in 2001, many entrepreneurs are taking advantage of the opportunity to inherit or pass on businesses without paying any tariff.

40353 ■ "Estate tax foes awaiting more shots at a repeal" in *Business First Columbus* **(Vol. 18, No. 26, February 15, 2002, pp. A16)**
Pub: Business First Columbus, Inc.
Ed: Kent Hoover. **Description:** A discussion regarding the issues facing estate tax reform is presented.

40354 ■ "An Evening with the Brain Trust" in *Hispanic Business* **(October 2003, pp. 40)**
Pub: Hispanic Business
Description: Academics, diplomats, investors, and CEOs come together to discuss public policy at the U.S. Hispanic Economic Summit, hosted at the Organization of American States in the Hall of the Americas.

40355 ■ "Ex-Im Bank cuts effect on small business unclear" in *Atlanta Business Chronicle* **(Vol. 24, No. 3, June 22, 2001, pp. 54A)**
Pub: American City Business Journals Inc.
Ed: Kent Hoover. **Description:** The Export-Import Bank has been targeted by the Bush Administration for a budget cut from $863 million to $633 million, resulting in a total of $11.4 billion available for export credit authorizations. Although the Small Business Administration says small businesses will be protected from budget cuts, many small business owners are not convinced. The Export-Import Bank is considering lowering coverage on export transactions and raising fees in order to stabilize its resources.

40356 ■ "Excluded Taxi Groups Aren't Hailing Rival's Airport Deal" in *Sacramento Bee* **(November 16, 2005)**
Pub: The Sacramento Bee
Ed: Judy Lin. **Description:** Sacramento County officials approved a three-year pact with the Sacramento Independent Taxi Owners Association for exclusive pickup privileges at the Sacramento International Airport. The three other taxi groups competed for the contract charge the County is imposing a monopoly of services, thus hurting the taxi industry and denying airport passengers cheaper fares.

40357 ■ "Execs getting more political: Efforts to influence policy growing" in *Crain's Chicago Business* **(Vol. 23, October 9, 2000, pp. SB2)**
Pub: Crain Communications, Inc. Crain Communications, Inc.
Ed: Mary Ellen Podmolik. **Description:** As small business has grown an economic force, so too, has its collective voice in local, state and national politics, but many small business owners often are too busy running successful companies during a bull market.

40358 ■ "The Explosion of Chinese Imports Has Changed U.S. Manufacturers In Many Ways" in *Inc.* **(May 1, 2005)**
Pub: Inc. Magazine
Ed: Darren Dahl. **Description:** The need for a policy that does not allow the U.S. to be abused by liberalized trade is discussed, focusing on Chinese competitors.

40359 ■ "The Explosion of Chinese Imports Has Changed US Manufacturers In Many Ways-Including How They Lobby in Washington" in *Inc.* **(May1,2005)**
Pub: Inc. Magazine
Ed: Darren Dahl. **Description:** The need for a policy that does not allow the U.S. to be abused by liberalized trade is discussed, focusing on Chinese competitors.

40360 ■ "Export Advice" in *Entrepreneur* **(Vol. 33, January 2005, No. 1, pp. 72)**
Pub: Entrepreneur Media Inc.
Ed: Joshua Kurlantzick. **Description:** Small business exporters are among the fastest-growing sectors of American entrepreneurs in the U.S. The Department of Commerce has developed a new Website geared to assist smaller American export companies.

40361 ■ "Extra Credit" in *Entrepreneur* **(Vol. 31, No. 5, May 2003, pp. 69)**
Pub: Entrepreneur Media Inc.
Ed: Joanne Cleaver. **Description:** Information about the state income tax child-care credits offered by 25 states is given. Specifics of this credit vary from state to state, and most companies don't understand the specifics of the credit.

40362 ■ "Exxon Damages for Valdez Spill Are Cut In Half" in *Wall Street Journal* **(Vol. 248, December 2006, No. 149, pp. A2)**
Pub: Dow Jones & Co. Inc.
Ed: Associated Press **Description:** A federal appeals court cut in half a $5 billion jury award for punitive damages against Exxon Mobil Corp. for the 1989 Valdez oil spill in Alaska.

40363 ■ "Facing the Online Music" in *Inc.* **(July 1, 2003)**
Pub: Gruner & Jahr USA Publishing
Description: Entrepreneurs have a stake in the debate over downloading online music and are skeptical of the recording industry's attempts to rewrite intellectual property law.

40364 ■ "Families and Work: Some Future Probabilities" in *Employment Relations Today* **(Vol. 26, No. 4, Winter 2000, pp. 17)**
Pub: John Wiley & Sons, Inc.
Ed: David Macarov. **Description:** Issues discussed concern the relationship between family and work within the context of society, economics, and public policy. Topics addressed include the definition of family, government regulations regarding family rights and responsibilities, and the impact of stress and poverty on families.

40365 ■ "Farmers' Livelihood Dried Up by Federal Regs" in *My Business* **(September/ October 2001, pp. 19)**
Pub: My Business Magazine
Description: Brief discussion involving the EPA's move to protect suckerfish by shutting the headgates of the Upper Klamath Lake Dam in Oregon, cutting water off to 1,500 farms. The owner of a fertilizer company testified before Congress that his business is in jeopardy.

40366 ■ *Fast-Track Business Start-Up Kit: California*
Pub: DP Group, Incorporated
Ed: Carolyn Usinger. **Released:** September 2006. **Price:** $29.00. **Description:** Step-by-step guide for starting and running a business in California, including information on sole proprietors, partnerships, limited liability companies, S and C corporations, as well as details concerning business entities, sales taxes, environmental issues, human resources, and more.

40367 ■ "Fax Regs Rethought" in *Inc.* **(December 1, 2004)**
Pub: Inc. Magazine
Ed: Darren Dahl. **Description:** Federal regulations regarding mass faxes could hurt small businesses. The new law would allow businesses to fax any customer they have done businesses with in the last seven years.

40368 ■ "Fed Model is Pointing to Some Upside for Stocks" in *Barron's* **(August 18, 2003, pp. 15)**
Pub: Barron's
Ed: Robin Goldwyn Blumenthal. **Description:** The forward-earnings yield, an inverse indicator of the price-earnings ration, augers a favorable future for stocks, despite a short-term downturn forecasted for the S and P 500, according to Puglisi and Company analysts.

40369 ■ "Federal Contracts Draw New Scrutiny" in *Inc.* **(August 2005, pp. 24)**
Pub: Inc. Magazine
Ed: Darren Dahl. **Description:** The Small Business Administration reported ways that large companies are erroneously categorized in order to procure federal government contracts.

40370 ■ "Federal agencies generate most e-waste" in *Waste News* **(Vol. 8, No. 10, September 16, 2002, pp. 12)**
Pub: Crain Communications, Inc.
Ed: Joe Truini. **Description:** The U.S. Federal government is developing procurement and disposition guidelines for electronics. The Federal government is the nation's largest consumer of electronics, and the recycling industry may not be prepared for the amount of materials the government needs recycled. Information about the Federal Electronics Stewardship Work Group is provided.

40371 ■ "Federal File: News & Developments in the Business of Government" in *Hispanic Business* **(December 2001, pp. FG4, FG6, FG14, FG16)**
Pub: Hispanic Business
Description: The Department of Agriculture has an Outreach Office that helps socially disadvantaged farmers and farm workers gain access to federal programs. Federal government employment opportunities for minorities are presented with a listing of internship opportunities. Hispanic entrepreneurs owning 8(a) firms secured 14.4 percent of federal contracts for fiscal year 2000.

40372 ■ "Federal Legislation Lays Groundwork for Electronic Check Exchange" in *Long Island Business News* **(February 13, 2004)**
Pub: Dolan Media Newswires
Ed: Claude Solnik. **Description:** Federal legislation will allow banks to process checks using electronic transfers of scanned checks, making deposits almost immediate. The new system will cut costs for financial institutions.

40373 ■ "Federal funds may spur Legislature to re-enact transit bill" in *Crain's Detroit Business* **(Vol. 19, No. 1, January 6, 2003, pp. 5)**
Pub: Crain Communications Inc., Detroit
Ed: Amy Lane. **Description:** Legislation regarding the Federal startup funds that may be available in the metro Detroit area for regional transportation is discussed. Two lawmakers plan to introduce new bills for the Detroit Area Regional Transportation Authority.

40374 ■ "Federal stimulus can ensure recovery" in *Atlanta Business Chronicle* **(Vol. 25, January 10, 2003, No. 31, pp. 32A)**
Pub: American City Business Publications, Inc.
Ed: Jim Molis. **Description:** A stimulus package from the Federal Government will go a long way in helping the economy on its way to recovery. However, war with Iraq or North Korea would most certainly bring the economy back down.

40375 ■ "Federal Reserve Raises Key Interest Rate by Quarter Point" in *Boston Globe* **(February 3, 2005)**
Pub: New York Times Company
Ed: Robert Gavin. **Description:** The Federal Reserve raised key interest rates which will lead to higher charges on credit cards, home equity lines of credit, and other short-term loans. Savings and money market accounts are not expected to see a rise in interest rates.

40376 ■ "Feel the Burn" in *Entrepreneur* **(Vol. 33, August 2005, No. 8, pp. 28)**
Pub: Entrepreneur Media Inc.
Ed: Stephen Barlas. **Description:** The Workforce Health Improvement Program Act would allow small companies to deduct the costs for reimbursing employees' health club fees.

40377 ■ "The 51 percent rule fallout" in *Hispanic Business* **(Vol. 22, No. 3, March 2000, pp. 40)**
Pub: Hispanic Business
Ed: Derek Reveron. **Description:** The decision of the National Minority Supplier Development Council to alter the minority status of businesses is examined. Minority status will now be given to companies with 30 percent of their non-voting stock owned by minorities compared with 51 percent previously.

40378 ■ "The 51 Percent Solution" in *Hispanic Business* **(Vol. 21, No. 12, December 1999, pp. 74)**
Pub: Hispanic Business
Ed: Joel Russell. **Description:** The National Minority Supplier Development Council board has postponed a vote on whether to alter the definition of a minority-owned firm. This change has been opposed by the U.S. Hispanic Chamber of Commerce and other groups.

40379 ■ "Fifty States, a Thousand New Tax Laws" in *Inc.* **(Volume 27, June 2005, No. 6, pp. 21-23)**
Pub: Inc. Magazine
Ed: Amy Feldman. **Description:** States are decoupling tax codes from the federal government's tax code. Two key areas of divergence between state and federal tax codes are depreciation and estate taxes.

40380 ■ "Fight Brews in Senate Over Bill to Change TV Franchises" in *Crain's Detroit Business* **(Vol. 22, November 20, 2006, No. 47, pp. 25)**
Pub: Crain Communications Inc. - Detroit
Ed: Amy Lane. **Description:** State issuing guideline template to communities to permit more competition in the video provider market. Currently awarding franchises is a city by city function without any clear guidelines for standardization from one community to another. AT and T is making a major investment in Michigan and challenging existing cable franchises in local communities.

40381 ■ "Filling the Gap" in *My Business* **(April/May 2003, pp. 10)**
Pub: My Business Magazine
Ed: Tamara E. Holmes. **Description:** Information regarding the Uniformed Services Employment and Re-employment Rights Act is covered. The Act requires businesses to give employees leaves of absence for active duty, training, drills or other military operations.

40382 ■ "Firm Suiting Up for New Space Flights" in *San Fernando Valley Business Journal* **(Vol. 12, January 2007, No. 1, pp. 12)**
Pub: San Fernando Valley Business Journal Associates
Ed: Mark R. Madler. **Description:** Profile on Orbital Outfitters, a company that wants to revolutionize the space industry by designing the next generation of space suits targeting crew and passengers for space travel through commercial and privately funded space flight. The firm also has an administrative office in Washington, D.C. to better deal with the regulations which oversee the New Space industry.

40383 ■ "Firms Paid $1.6 Million in Penalties, California Pesticide Regulators Report" in *Sacramento Bee* **(December 28, 2005)**
Pub: The Sacramento Bee
Ed: Jim Wasserman. **Description:** Firms illegally selling pesticides in the State of California were fined a combined total of $1.6 million by the California Department of Pesticide Control. Most of the penalties incurred were due to chemical products that were not approved for sale in the state, while others were to firms not paying mandatory environmental fees.

40384 ■ "Fishermen's Days Numbered; New Regs Would Cut Time at Sea" in *Providence Business News* **(Vol. 18, No. 23, September 22, 2003, pp. 1)**
Pub: Providence Business News, Inc.
Ed: Laura Ricketson. **Description:** New government regulations that take effect May 2004, will reduce the number of fishing days, thus reducing fishermen's catch by 65 percent; the regulations will affect both Canadian and New England fisheries.

40385 ■ "Flea-market bill would ban sales of certain items" in *Crain's Detroit Business* **(Vol. 16, No. 49, December 4, 2000, pp. 44)**
Pub: Crain Communications, Inc.
Ed: Amy Lane. **Description:** At the urging of Michigan retailers, legislators have introduced a bill that targets products that retailers claim thieves are prone to steal from stores then turn over to flea markets, swap meets and other "unused property markets".

40386 ■ "FMLA Needs to be Fixed to Stop Abuse" in *Crain's Detroit Business* **(Vol. 21, January 10, 2005, No. 2, pp. 9)**
Pub: Crain Communications Inc. - Detroit
Ed: Nancy McKeague. **Description:** Sixty-eight federal lawsuits have been filed challenging the validity of the Family and Medical Leave Act. Managers and business owners struggle to provide these benefits because federal rules make it difficult to administer them.

40387 ■ "Focus on Finances" in *Entrepreneur.com* **(Vol. 34, January 2006, No. 1, pp. 24)**
Pub: Entrepreneur Media Inc.
Ed: Crystal Detamore-Rodman. **Description:** The Internal Revenue Service is starting to examine 5,000 random S corporation tax returns from the 2003 and 2004 tax years. The IRS is concerned that some S corporation owners are skimping on salaries in favor of a larger dividend distribution, which isn't subject to self-employment taxes.

40388 ■ "Focus on Prohibitive Health-Care Costs: Government help may be on the way" in *Time Inc.* **(Vol. 156, No. 3, July 17, 2000, pp. B13)**
Pub: Time & Life Bldg., Rockefeller Center
Ed: Daniel Kadlec. **Description:** Some 44 million Americans are without health insurance and 60 percent of them work in businesses employing fewer than 500 people or are family members of those who do.

40389 ■ "Focused Vision" in *Hispanic Business* **(April 2005, pp. 34, 36)**
Pub: Hispanic Business
Ed: Janet Perez. **Description:** Profile of Janet Murguia, president and CEO of the National Council of La Raza (NCLR). Murguia works to advance the organization's presence and advocacy among policymakers and constituents. NCLR is committed to improving the lives of Hispanics.

40390 ■ "Follow that bill; E-waste and landfill policies just some of new changes" in *Waste News* **(Vol. 8, No. 8, August 19, 2002, pp. 1)**
Pub: Crain Communications, Inc.
Ed: Bruce Geiselman. **Description:** Compliance issues being faced by waste haulers and recycling firms handling electronic and other recycling issues, are examined.

40391 ■ "Following the Leader: Learn these Laws, and Employees Won't Be Far Behind You" in *Entrepreneur* **(Vol. 32, July 2004, No. 7, pp. 34)**
Pub: Entrepreneur Media Inc.
Description: Review of Michael Feiner's book, The Feiner Points of Leadership. The book offers insight into motivating employees and creating loyalty.

40392 ■ "Food may become next public enemy" in *Atlanta Business Chronicle* **(Vol. 24, No. 14, September 7, 2001, pp. 1A)**
Pub: American City Business Journals Inc.
Ed: Julie Bryant. **Description:** The U.S. Surgeon General will issue a report on the fast food industry, linking it to the growing obesity problem in America.

40393 ■ "Food Fight! How Should Restaurateurs Deal With the Weighty Problem of Customer's Obesity?" in *Entrepreneur* **(Vol. 31, July 2003)**
Pub: Entrepreneur Media, Inc.
Ed: Julie Monahan. **Description:** Should restaurants be held liable for customer's weight problems? Industry associations are developing consumer education campaigns emphasizing a balanced diet and exercise to lose or maintain weight and stay healthy.

40394 ■ "For Small Businesses, Future of Biz Taxes Will be Crucial" in *Crain's Detroit Business* **(Vol. 22, November 27, 2006, No. 48, pp. 15)**
Pub: Crain Communications Inc. - Detroit
Ed: Sheena Harrison. **Description:** With the cancellation of the Single Business Tax, small businesses will be central in the talks and discussions on changes necessary to replace revenue losses. Also of concern is the difficulty of hiring qualified employees with affordable wages and benefits.

40395 ■ "For Some, ITC's Steel Stance a Lose-Lose Deal" in *Pittsburgh Business Times* **(Vol. 23, No. 8, September 12, 2003, pp. 1)**
Pub: Pittsburgh Business Times
Ed: Christopher Davis. **Description:** Monaca, Pennsylvania-based Beaver Valley Alloy Foundry Compa-

ny, a small steel producer, may be affected by any changes in U.S. steel tariffs. The tariffs are under review by the U.S. International Trade Commission.

40396 ■ "Former B.E. 100s CEO Convicted" in Black Enterprise (Vol. 35, October 2004, No. 3, pp. 33)
Pub: Earl G. Graves Publishing Co. Inc.
Ed: K. Terrell Reed. Description: Nathan A. Chapman, former investment banker, has been convicted of fraud. Chapman was convicted of 15 counts of wire fraud, two counts of mail fraud, three counts of investment advisory fraud, one count of making false statements to Securities and Exchange Commission, and two counts of making false statements on tax returns.

40397 ■ "Former Computer Associates Executive Pleads Guilty in U.S. District Court in Brooklyn" in Long Island Business News (Jan. 30, 2004)
Pub: Dolan Media Newswires
Description: Former senior vice president, Lloyd Silverstein, of Computer Associates International, pleaded guilty to charges of obstruction of justice in the federal investigation of the software maker's accounting practices. The company has also received notice that it will be the target of civil charges by the Securities and Exchange Commission.

40398 ■ "Former Couch Street Figure Heads to Prison" in Business Journal-Portland (Vol. 20, No. 24, August 15, 2003, pp. 8)
Pub: American City Business Journals, Inc.
Ed: Shelly Strom. Description: Cleburne Jr. Brigham has been sentenced to 37 years in prison for alleged falsification of a loan application, making false statements to the U.S. Small Business Administration, misuse of social security number, and using the Couch Street Fish House illegally.

40399 ■ "Fund Sharks" in Entrepreneur (Vol. 31, No. 8, August 2003, pp. 54)
Pub: Entrepreneur Media, Inc.
Ed: Jennifer Pellet. Description: Congress is looking into allegations of mutual fund companies fleecing investors with high fees which decreased returns on investment.

40400 ■ "Funds Face Unexpected Antitrust Problem" in Venture Capital Journal (January 1, 2005)
Pub: Thomason Financial Inc.
Description: Profile of the Clayton Act Section 8 of federal antitrust law is examined. The Act, which prohibits an end-run around the Sherman Act's ban on monopolization and agreements in restraint of trade by prohibiting the same person from serving on boards of competitive companies, has rarely been enforced by either private litigants or by the federal government.

40401 ■ "Ga. Chamber seeking 'civil justice' reform" in Atlanta Business Chronicle (Vol. 25, November 29, 2002, No. 25 pp. 28A)
Pub: American City Business Publications, Inc.
Ed: David Allison. Description: The main objective of the Georgia Chamber of Commerce in the next session of state legislature is to amend civil justice in Georgia. Chamber leaders have outlined nine reforms they hope to introduce into law.

40402 ■ "GAO blames IRS, Congress for small business tax woes" in Accounting Today (Vol. 14, No. 16, September 4, 2000, pp. 3)
Pub: Faulkner & Gray, Inc.
Ed: Ken Rankin. Description: The General Accounting Office found, in a study done for the Senate Small Business Committee, that Congress itself, creates problems by the complexity of the tax code and the IRS adds to them when it focuses attention on enforcement activities rather than efforts to prevent small business taxpayers from falling out of compliance in the first place.

40403 ■ "Gas Station Owners May Be Pumping Red Ink" in Business Week (No. 3699, September 18, 2000, pp. 156)
Pub: McGraw-Hill, Inc.
Description: Owners of service stations face upgrades of diesel tanks to accommodate law changes, but the pace of this change causes concerns.

40404 ■ "A Generally Beneficial Law" in Hispanic Business (Vol. 23, No. 10, October, 2001, pp. 98)
Pub: Hispanic Business
Ed: Milton Zall. Description: The effects of President Bush's tax cut package on individual small business owners may vary significantly. Small businesses operated as sole proprietorships, partnerships, or S corporations will directly benefit from the lowered tax rates.

40405 ■ "Georgia Senate Panel Approves Right to Buy, Sell Water Permits" in Atlanta Journal-Constitution (April 11, 2003)
Pub: Knight-Ridder/Tribune Business News
Ed: Stacy Shelton. Description: A committee voted in April 2003, allowing industries, cities, and farmers the right to buy and sell water permits they obtained free. The practice is called "permit trading" and is opposed by various environmental groups, while economists say it will help mold state water policy.

40406 ■ "Get in the Zone: Checking Local Zoning Ordinances First Stops Problems Later" in My Business (October/November 2002, pp. 4)
Pub: My Business Magazine
Ed: Joan E. Lisante. Description: It is advised to check with the local municipality for zoning laws regarding home-based businesses before setting up shop.

40407 ■ "Getting Clocked" in Entrepreneur (Vol. 33, October 2005, No. 10, pp. 88)
Pub: Entrepreneur Media Inc.
Ed: Chris Penttila. Description: The U.S. Department of Labor is investigating off-the-clock work. Employers should set rules for on-the-clock and off-the-clock working. It is important to record all time worked and to allot a small window for tasks that may need to be done off the clock.

40408 ■ "Getting in on the E-Signature Game" in Inc. (November 15, 2000, pp. 26)
Pub: The Goldhirsh Group
Description: The U.S. Congress has added "electronic sound, symbol, or process" to the list of legal signature types. Electronic signature is defined in the Electronic Signatures in Global and National Commerce Act, which went into effect on October 1, 2000.

40409 ■ "Getting Out of an IRS Mess" in Black Enterprise (Vol. 37, December 2006, No. 5, pp. 53)
Pub: Earl G. Graves Publishing Co. Inc.
Ed: Carolyn M. Brown. Description: Owing back taxes to the IRS can lead to huge penalties and interest. Here are some tips on how to handle paying the IRS what you owe them.

40410 ■ "Give Me a Tax Break" in Black Enterprise (Vol. 36, February 2006, No. 7, pp. 40)
Pub: Earl G. Graves Publishing Co. Inc.
Ed: Joyce Jones. Description: If passed, the Mortgage Insurance Fairness Act would allow homeowners with a combined income under $100,000 to deduct the total amount of mortgage insurance payments on federal tax returns.

40411 ■ "Global accounting is coming" in Harvard Business Review (Vol. 81, No. 4, April 2003, pp. 24)
Pub: Harvard Business School Press
Ed: Richard G. Barker. Description: The recent accounting scandals have led to international influence on U.S. financial reporting. Under the emerging global standards, income statements will reveal more than has been the custom with U.S. firms.

40412 ■ "Global Trader" in Hispanic Business (April 2005, pp. 40, 42)
Pub: Hispanic Business
Ed: Luisa Beltran. Description: Profile of Carmen Suro-Bredie, Assistant U.S. Trade Representative for Policy Coordination. Suro-Bredie believes women are natural negotiators with a commitment to the peace process that ensures a more Democratic trade agreement.

40413 ■ "Good intentions, bad policy" in Crain's Detroit Business (Vol. 16, No. 49, December 4, 2000, pp. 8)
Pub: Crain Communications, Inc.
Description: Mandating the coverage of diabetes will boost the cost of providing insurance to Michigan workers, thus setting a precedent for future mandates for other diseases.

40414 ■ "GOP tells business owners that effort to finance fights against OSHA is lost" in Wall Street Journal (February 16, 2000, pp. A6)
Pub: Dow Jones & Co., Inc.
Ed: Jim VandeHei. Description: The efforts to fund fights against OSHA was lost to union opposition. Statistical data is included.

40415 ■ "Government Hooks Man for Phishing" in Cardline (Vol. 4, No. 13, March 26, 2004, pp. 1)
Pub: Thomson Media Inc.
Description: An identity-theft scam has been shut down. Zachary Keith Hill used the logos of Internet service provider America Online (AOL) and the online payment service, PayPal to scam consumers into revealing credit card numbers and other confidential information.

40416 ■ "Governor Backs Solar-Panel Plan" in San Jose Mercury News (March 2, 2005)
Pub: Knight-Ridder/Tribune Business News
Ed: Sue McAllister. Description: Governor Schwarzenegger announced support for legislation that would add 1 million energy-generating solar panels to rooftops statewide. The move would put California one step closer to self-sufficiency.

40417 ■ "Granholm Criticized for HMO Bill Inaction" in Crain's Detroit Business (Vol. 21, January 3, 2005, No. 1, pp. 20)
Pub: Crain Communications Inc. - Detroit
Ed: Amy Lane. Description: Governor Jennifer Granholm killed a bill that would give health maintenance organizations greater pricing flexibility because of concerns the ruling would increase the health care costs of patients.

40418 ■ "Granholm to Propose New Revenue-Sharing Plan" in Crain's Detroit Business (Vol. 23, January 29, 2007, No. 5, pp. 32)
Pub: Crain Communications Inc. - Detroit
Ed: Amy Lane. Description: Revenue sharing to be a major part of Governor's fiscal 2008 budget proposal. This adds to the list of other legislative issues such as increased gas tax, replacing the single-business tax revenues, and changes to the broader tax structure.

40419 ■ "Granholm wants to scrap workers' comp appeal board" in Crain's Detroit Business (Vol. 19, No. 11, March 17, 2003, pp. 6)
Pub: Crain Communications Inc., Detroit
Ed: Amy Lane. Description: Michigan Governor Jennifer Granholm wants to eliminate the Workers' Compensation Appellate Commission; manufacturers feel they would lose an important place to adjudicate claims for disability benefits outside of court.

40420 ■ "Grassley Offers Discussion Draft on COLI Policies" in Tax Notes (Vol. 102, No. 3, January 19, 2004, pp. 323-325)
Pub: Tax Notes International
Ed: Patti Mohr, Christine Harris. Description: Discussion with Senate Finance Committee Chair, Charles E. Grassley, regarding corporate-owned life insurance.

40421 ■ "Greektown Casino Seeks Financial Extension" in *Crain's Detroit Business* (Vol. 22, December 11, 2006, No. 50, pp. 25)
Pub: Crain Communications Inc. - Detroit
Ed: Robert Ankeny. Description: Greektown Casino seeks second extension from Michigan Gaming Control Board in 30 days. Revenue shortages are blamed on parking and traffic problems associated with the demolition of the Foster-Winter parking garage.

40422 ■ "Greener Pastures: Exodus from Fidelity Continues as Another Hot Manager Heads to a Hedge Fund" in *Barron's* (July 21, 2003, pp. F2)
Pub: Barron's
Ed: Erin E. Arvedlund. Description: David Glancy is one of a growing number of fund managers leaving Fidelity to start their own funds. Some analysts are encouraging investors to follow their fund managers, posing a graver threat to Fidelity. Investigations by state attorneys general and an investor lawsuit are among the plagues afflicting Morgan Stanley.

40423 ■ "Greenhouse Gas Limits are Called Affordable" in *The Record* (November 21, 2005)
Pub: New Jersey Media Group
Ed: Alex Nussbaum. Description: Nine states are considering a new plan to cut greenhouse emissions over the next fifteen years. The plan would set limits on greenhouse gases allowed from power plants.

40424 ■ "The Greens Bite Back" in *The Economist* (Vol. 377, October 22-28, 2005, No. 8449, pp. 35)
Pub: The Economist Newspaper Ltd.
Description: Oregon's strict land-use laws protect the area's rural character, but in November 2004 a new initiative was placed on the ballot, Measure 37, which gave landowners previously banned from turning rural land into houses the right to develop.

40425 ■ "Greenspan Floats Sales Tax" in *Chicago Tribune* (March 4, 2005)
Pub: Knight-Ridder/Tribune Business News
Ed: William Neikirk. Description: Alan Greenspan, chairman of the U.S. Federal Reserve, is recommending consideration of a national sales tax as part of the restructuring of the federal tax system.

40426 ■ "Gridlock Alert; Who is Driving" in *Crain's New York Business* (Vol. 22, December 11, 2006, No. 50, pp. 14)
Pub: Crain Communications, Inc.
Description: Traffic jams in Manhattan impose enormous costs on the economy, argued The Partnership for New York City. The Business Advocacy Group called for greater study of the issue before establishing congestion pricing fees for cars that enter the most crowded sections of Manhattan.

40427 ■ "Growing Influence" in *Hispanic Business* (January/February 2005, pp. 18, 20)
Pub: Hispanic Business
Ed: Craig Mauro. Description: Increasing political clout and attention will help Hispanic small business and lead to immigration reform.

40428 ■ "Guest Article" in *Venture Capital Journal* (February 1, 2006)
Pub: Thomason Financial Inc.
Description: Section 409A of the Internal Revenue Code for non-qualified deferred compensation plans is outlined. The new rule could hurt venture capital-backed companies.

40429 ■ "A Guide through the Garnishment Jungle" in *Employment Relations Today* (Vol. 27, No. 1, Spring 2000, pp. 117)
Pub: John Wiley & Sons, Inc.
Ed: Marilyn E. Culp, Deanna R. Lindquist, Chaton Turner Williams, Tamila V. Lee, and Charles M. Rice. Description: Accounting of federal and state garnishment laws that impact the ability of employers to withhold an employees pay because of financial obligations of the employee to his or her creditor. Federal limits on garnishment laws due to the Consumer Credit Protection Act are addressed. Statistical data included.

40430 ■ "The Hague: Laws without Borders" in *Red Herring* (No. 106, October 15, 2001, pp. 25-26)
Pub: Herring Communications
Ed: Julia Lawlor. Description: Important information regarding the Hague Convention on Jurisdiction and Foreign Judgments in Civil Matters is covered. The Hague treaty would deal with civil lawsuits and would require that laws regarding matters like libel, copyright, patents, and trademarks - which differ among countries - be enforced uniformly in the 53 nations participating in treaty talks.

40431 ■ "Harris Teeter sued by black employees" in *Atlanta Business Chronicle* (Vol. 24, No. 14, September 7, 2001, pp. 1A)
Pub: American City Business Journals Inc.
Ed: Matt Gove. Description: Harris Teeter Inc. and Ruddick Corporation, its parent, are both being sued by nine African-Americans for racial discrimination. Gordon, Silberman, Wiggins, & Childs, the law firm handling the case, sought class-action status following the original suit.

40432 ■ "Hatred of Spam Puts Crinkle in Faxing" in *Crain's Detroit Business* (Vol. 19, No. 45, November 10, 2003, pp. 9)
Pub: Crain Communications Inc., Detroit
Ed: Mary Kramer. Description: New rules adopted by the Federal Communications Commission require businesses to secure written approval from recipients before sending commercial faxes.

40433 ■ "Health care, federal contracts high on Bush's small business agenda" in *Crain's Detroit Business* (Vol. 18, No. 22, June 3, 2002, pp.50)
Pub: Crain Communications Inc. - Detroit
Ed: Laura Bailey. Description: Under President Bush's small business agenda, companies can expect more affordable health insurance and fairer competition for government contracts.

40434 ■ "Health Care Coverage Reform Introduced in Congress" in *My Business* (April/May 2003, pp. 18)
Pub: My Business Magazine
Description: Legislation that could help small businesses with health care costs using association health plans (AHPs) is presented.

40435 ■ "Healthcare Insurance" in *Black Enterprise* (Vol. 34, No. 2, September 2003, pp. 48)
Pub: Earl Graves Publishing Co.
Ed: Alan Hughes. Description: Healthcare insurance is becoming increasingly more difficult for small business owners to provide to employees, especially for a small home-based business wishing to expand. The House Small Business Committee introduced the Self-Employed Health Care Affordability Act of 2003 (H.R. 1873) in April 2003, this bill allows self-employed business owners to deduct health insurance costs when calculating payroll taxes, thus effectively reducing those costs by more than 15 percent.

40436 ■ "Hewlett-Packard Was Far From First To Try 'PreTexting'" in *Wall Street Journal* (Vol. 248, December 2006, No. 149, pp. A1)
Pub: Dow Jones & Co. Inc.
Ed: John A. Emshwiller Description: Hewlett-Packard Co. as well as all the major lenders can no longer use 'Pretexting'- the practice of impersonating people in order to receive phone or financial records, as it is now being federally prohibited.

40437 ■ "HHS lawsuit allowed" in *Healthcare Purchasing News* (Vol. 24, No. 8, August 2000, pp. 13)
Pub: Medical Economics Co.
Description: The American Chiropractic Association may sue the Department of Health and Human Services over guidelines that allegedly all but exclude chiropractic services from the MedicareChoice program.

40438 ■ "Higher Revenue Boosts Call for Tax Cut" in *Boston Globe* (February 2, 2005)
Pub: New York Times Company
Ed: Scott S. Greenberger. Description: Massachusetts Governor Mitt Romney is proposing an income tax cut that would cost the state $225 million in fiscal 2006. The state's tax total for January 2005 was 11.9 percent higher than January 2004, predicting projected revenue of $16.5 billion for fiscal 2005.

40439 ■ "HIPAA hysteria" in *Atlanta Business Chronicle* (Vol. 25, November 29, 2002, No. 25, pp. 1C)
Pub: American City Business Publications, Inc.
Ed: Julie Bryant. Description: The Health Insurance Portability and Accountability Act has caused disorder and confusion in health care and insurance industries. The new privacy and security regulations were added to protect electronic patient information.

40440 ■ "Home Builder Falls Under SEC Scrutiny" in *Orlando Business Journal* (Vol. 20, No. 10, August 22, 2003, pp. 1)
Pub: American City Business Journals, Inc.
Ed: Jill Krueger. Description: The merger with a Colorado petroleum company gave Whitemark Homes Inc. an entry to the stock exchange. Whitemark also purchased a consulting firm, which collapsed and was brought under investigation.

40441 ■ "Home Rules" in *Business Week* (No. 3667, February 7, 2000, pp. 53)
Pub: McGraw-Hill, Inc.
Description: Representative Thomas M. Davis (R-Va.) supports the law to keep government from regulating home offices.

40442 ■ "House Exempts Small Businesses From Superfund" in *Atlanta Business Chronicle* (Vol. 23, No. 51, May 25, 2001, pp. 7A)
Pub: American City Business Journals Inc.
Ed: Kent Hoover. Description: The House Energy and Commerce Committee passed a bill that makes small business exempt from liability for cleanup costs at Superfund locations. The bill exempts those that dumped less than 110 gallons of nonhazardous liquids or less than 200 pounds of nonhazardous solid at a Superfund site, as well as businesses with less than 100 workers that dumped waste similar to that of household waste.

40443 ■ "House Rules: Before You Let Your People Work at Home, Find Out What You're Liable For-And Cover Your Bases" in *Entrepreneur* (Vol. 32)
Pub: Entrepreneur Media Inc.
Ed: Jane Easter Bahls. Description: Safety and liability issues involved in allowing employees to work from home are examined. It is critical for a small business owner to have a policy that addresses office arrangements, hours, responsibilities and who pays for what, as well as safety, security of company property and proprietary information, workers' compensation and insurance.

40444 ■ "How well is Appeals doing?" in *Tax Notes* (Vol. 96, No. 12, September 16, 2002, pp. 1564-1567)
Pub: Tax Notes International
Ed: George Guttman. Description: The effectiveness of the IRS Appeals Division is analyzed by measuring employee and taxpayer satisfaction and the length of time it takes the Appeals Division to process cases.

40445 ■ "How to Improve Georgia's Economy" in *Atlanta Business Chronicle* (Vol. 25, December 6, 2002, No. 26, pp. 35A)
Pub: American City Business Publications, Inc.
Ed: Georgia Description: Governor-elect, Sonny Perdue, should back the Metro Atlanta Chamber of Commerce's attempts to attract the secretariat of the Free Trade Area of the Americas to the city. He should also consider opening field offices of the Georgia Department of Industry, Trade and Tourism in Latin American cities.

40446 ■ "How Well is Appeals Doing?" in *Tax Notes* **(Vol. 96, No. 12, September 16, 2002, pp. 1564-1567)**
Pub: Tax Notes International
Ed: Warren Rojas. Description: Republicans in the U.S. House are developing a tax plan that would include provisions on unemployment benefits, corporate inversions, executive compensation and tax relief for small businesses. However, they may not have time to put it on the legislative calendar.

40447 ■ "Hunting Season: Feds Try to Protect the Little Guy From Payroll Tax Predators" in *Entrepreneur* **(Vol. 32, September 2004, No. 9)**
Pub: Entrepreneur Media Inc.
Ed: Stephen Barlas. Description: The Tax Administration Good Government Act gives the Internal Revenue Service tools to go after payroll/accounting firms that steal a client's employment tax payments, while protecting small businesses that hire the services.

40448 ■ "If I had had more experience, if I was more careful, if I was more competent" in *Fast Company* **(June 2001, pp. 161)**
Pub: Fast Company
Ed: Michael Saylor. Description: Profile of Micro-Strategy Inc., and the ongoing investigation of the company, by the U.S. Securities and Exchange Commission.

40449 ■ "Illicit Affairs?" in *Entrepreneur* **(Vol. 32)**
Pub: Entrepreneur Media Inc.
Ed: Jane Easter Bahls. Description: The Foreign Corrupt Practice Act (FCPA), enacted by Congress in 1977, prohibits the use of bribery of officials in other countries in order to do business overseas. It is illegal to make payments, promises, or offers of anything of value to foreign officials to obtain or retain business, or to make payments to a third party.

40450 ■ "Illinois Businesses Anxious about Governor's Plans on Fees, Taxes" in *Chicago Tribune* **(April 11, 2003)**
Pub: Knight-Ridder/Tribune Business News
Ed: John Schmeltzer. Description: Governor Rod Blagojevich plans to boost fees and taxes on Illinois businesses by as much as $600 million annually.

40451 ■ "Illinois Gov. Pushes More Pension Reform" in *Venture Capital Journal* **(October 1, 2005)**
Pub: Thomason Financial Inc.
Description: Illinois Governor Rod Blagojevich has announced new rules to eliminate contingency fees paid to placement agents and require board of trustee members to disclose more financial information in order to reform pension systems within the state.

40452 ■ "Illinois Regulators Investigate Possible Title Insurance Kickbacks" in *Chicago Tribune* **(February 23, 2005)**
Pub: Knight-Ridder/Tribune Business News
Description: State regulators across the nation are investigating a kickback scheme whereby housing developers and lenders direct title insurance business to particular companies, causing higher closing costs for homeowners.

40453 ■ "Immigration Reform" in *Hispanic Business* **(March 2004, pp. 14)**
Pub: Hispanic Business
Description: Issues regarding U.S. immigration policies are examined.

40454 ■ "Immigration Reform, Latin American Trade Issues Piled on Congress's Plate" in *Hispanic Business* **(November 2006, pp. 24)**
Pub: Hispanic Business
Ed: Patricia Guadalupe. Description: Immigration and trade issues with Latin American countries and Mexico are discussed.

40455 ■ "In Brief: Firms Eager to Avoid Illegal Workers" in *American Banker* **(Vol. 171, November 2, 2006, No. 211, pp. 17)**
Pub: SourceMedia, Inc.
Ed: H. Michael Jalili. Description: According to a survey conducted by Discover Financial Services, most small businesses and their customers are willing to pay more for services and goods if such costs would help curb illegal immigration.

40456 ■ "In Brief: Grassley Offers a Bankruptcy Bill" in *American Banker* **(Vol. 170, February 4, 2005, No. 24, pp. 3)**
Pub: Thomson Financial Media Inc.
Ed: Hannah Bergman. Description: Finance Committee Chairman, Senator Charles Grassley, has introduced a bill that would revamp bankruptcy laws. The bill would require credit card companies to disclose the risks of minimum payment, ban deceptive advertising of low introductory rates, and require the companies to establish a toll-free number for consumers. It would also make permanent the Chapter 12 protections to help farmers from going bankrupt.

40457 ■ "In Corporate-Fraud Cases, Lawyer's Approval Can Let Client Avoid Charges" in *Houston Chronicle* **(April 11, 2003)**
Pub: Knight-Ridder/Tribune Business News
Ed: Mary Flood. Description: The ramifications of an attorney's approval of a business deal are explored.

40458 ■ "In Hot Water? Take a Closer Look at Your Marketing Materials, Or You May Get Burned" in *Entrepreneur* **(Vol. 32, September 2004)**
Pub: Entrepreneur Media Inc.
Ed: Catherine Seda. Description: Although not illegal, using another company's trademark or logo on a Website, banner ad, or newsletter could get a small company into legal trouble. Internet marketing law includes copyrights, privacy rights, trademark usage and order fulfillment and more aggressive legal action to protect brands is taking place.

40459 ■ "In a Policy Shift, Hewlett-Packard Backs Computer Recycling in California" in *San Jose Mercury News* **(December 3, 2002)**
Pub: Knight-Ridder/Tribune Business News
Ed: Karl Schoenberger. Description: Hewlett-Packard will support California state legislation that will require PC manufacturers to bear the cost of disposing of discarded computers.

40460 ■ *Incorporate Your Business: A 50 State Legal Guide to Forming a Corporation*
Pub: Nolo
Ed: Anthony Mancuso. Released: August 2001. Price: $50.00. Description: Legal guide to incorporating a business in the U.S., covering all 50 states.

40461 ■ "Independent Testing" in *Inc.* **(November 2000, pp. 97)**
Pub: The Goldhirsh Group
Description: Rules vary from state to state, so it is recommended to talk to a Human Resources expert in order to comply with state and federal regulations when hiring contractors.

40462 ■ "Independents' Day: Would Giving More Power to Outside Directors Boost Funds' Performance?" in *Barron's* **(July 7, 2003, pp. L12)**
Pub: Barron's
Ed: Loren Fox. Description: Congress is moving against lax governance by the boards of mutual fund companies in the wake of corporate corruption scandals involving the likes of Enron and WorldCom. Mutual funds have largely been savaged, not only by exposure to scandal-ridden companies, but by the fallout from the tech-bubble collapse, and it is hoped outside influence on directors will boost accountability.

40463 ■ "Indiana Bill Would Multiply U.S. Development Tax Credit" in *American Banker* **(Vol. 170, February 4, 2005, No. 24, pp. 4)**
Pub: Thomson Financial Media Inc.
Ed: Ben Jackson. Description: Legislation is being considered for a bill that would give state tax breaks to small banks for investing in local development in Indiana. The bill is modeled after the Treasury Department's New Markets Tax Credit program. Indiana banks and thrifts whose investments qualify for the federal credit would also get state credit.

40464 ■ "Industry Fights Law on Violent Video Games" in *Crain's Detroit Business* **(Vol. 21, October 24, 2005, No. 43, pp. 1)**
Pub: Crain Communications Inc. - Detroit
Ed: Andrew Dietderich. Description: If passed, a new law would limit the sale or rental of certain violent video games to individuals under the age of 17. Retailers could be fined up to $5,000 for each offense.

40465 ■ "Influence-Peddling" in *Business Week* **(January 16, 2006, No. 3967, pp. 32)**
Pub: McGraw-Hill Companies
Ed: Description: A guilty plea by Jack Abramoff could mean tighter rules for corporate lobbyists. Abramoff plead guilty to charges of conspiracy, mail fraud and tax evasion. Senator John McCain has proposed a bill that would require lobbyists to disclose all fees, report who's giving to charities, and make gifts to lawmakers illegal.

40466 ■ "Insiders' Tax Break" in *Forbes* **(August 7, 2000, pp. 134)**
Pub: Forbes Magazine
Ed: Ashlea Ebeling. Description: Reducing or eliminating capital gains taxes from stock investments using the three-year-old Section 1045 of the tax code is described.

40467 ■ "Inspection Indigestion; Chicago Restaurant Owners Deal with a Dizzying Array of Bureaucrats and Licensing Fees" in *Crains Chicago Business*
Pub: Crain Communications, Inc.
Ed: Greg Hinz. Description: The City of Chicago, Illinois is considering changing regulations to make it easier for the city's restaurants to do business, while still protecting the public.

40468 ■ "Inspection Indigestion" in *Crain's Chicago Business* **(Vol. 26, No. 51, December 22, 2003, pp. 3)**
Pub: Crain Communications, Inc.
Ed: Greg Hinz. Description: The City of Chicago, Illinois is considering changing regulations to make it easier for the city's restaurants to do business, while still protecting the public.

40469 ■ "Intellectual property rights are cyberspace issue" in *Crain's Detroit Business* **(Vol. 16, No. 12, March 20, 2000, pp. 23)**
Pub: Crain Communications, Inc.
Ed: Joseph Serwach. Description: When it comes to intellectual property cases, even a hyphen can make a big difference. The Internet explosion is accelerating the concern about maximizing the value of knowledge assets.

40470 ■ "Interest in Commercial Brownfield Properties High, but Action Still on Hold" in *Long Island Business News* **(March 12, 2004)**
Pub: Dolan Media Newswires
Ed: Nick Anastasi. Description: New York's Brownfield's Law is expected to jump-start the redevelopment of about 7,000 commercial brownfield properties. The Law has set out provisions for cleanup, groundwater protection and remediation, and funding.

40471 ■ "International E-Commerce: The Time is Now" in *E-business Advisor* **(Vol. 18, No. 10, October 2000, pp. 28)**
Pub: Advisor Media, Inc.
Ed: Donald DePalma. Description: Internet usage is not just limited to the United States. It is exploding worldwide, and therefore, offers the opportunity to gain international customers. It is important for Web sites to be designed to entice these international "visitors", while being aware of customs, laws and politics specific to the potential customer's country.

40472 ■ *International Handbook of Women and Small Business Entrepreneurship*
Pub: Edward Elgar Publishing, Incorporated
Ed: Sandra L. Fielden. **Released:** June 2005. **Price:** $165.00. **Description:** The number of women entrepreneurs is growing at a faster rate than male counterparts worldwide. Insight into the phenomenon is targeted to scholars and students of women in management and entrepreneurship as well as policymakers and small business service providers.

40473 ■ "Internet Law Arena Marked by Issues About Spam, Pop-Up Ads, Domain Names, and File Sharing" in *Long Island Business News* (Feb.6, 2004)
Pub: Dolan Media Newswires
Ed: Rosmaria Mancini. **Description:** Microsoft and New York's State Attorney General have partnered and filed lawsuits against a spamming ring allegedly responsible for sending billions of deceptive and illegal emails. CAN-SPAM (Controlling the Assault of Non-Solicited Pornography and Marketing Act), is federal legislation that would require marketers to provide return addresses in emails so consumers can request being removed from mailing lists.

40474 ■ "Investing" in *Business Week* (January 23, 2006, No. 3968, pp. 36)
Pub: McGraw-Hill Companies
Ed: Amy Borrus. **Description:** Chris Cox, new chairman at the Securities & Exchange Commission, wants all CEO pay revealed, stiff enforcement, and post-Enron reforms.

40475 ■ "IPO Scandal Means Venture Capitalists Need To Be More Vigilant" in *Venture Capital Journal* (Vol. 42, No. 10, October 2002, pp. 50)
Pub: Thomas Venture Economics
Ed: Thomas C. McConnell. **Description:** Initial Public Offering practices are the latest business practices to come under regulatory, Congressional and media scrutiny.

40476 ■ "IRS changes and finalizes 2000 cafeteria plan rules" in *Employee Benefit Plan Review* (Vol. 55, No. 8, February 2001, pp. 13)
Pub: Charles D. Spencer & Associates, Inc.
Description: The changes made by the Internal Revenue Service regarding the status change, cost and coverage rules for cafeteria plans, and published in March 2000, are covered. These changes will be effective for cafeteria plan years beginning on or after January 1, 2001.

40477 ■ "IRS Boosts Enforcement Collections" in *The Record* (November 4, 2005)
Pub: New Jersey Media Group
Ed: Kathleen Lynn. **Description:** The Internal Revenue Service has collected a record $47.3 billion in the last year in payments, penalties and interest payments through enforcement activities.

40478 ■ "IRS to aid businesses, but tax code is a problem" in *Birmingham Business Journal* (Vol. 17, No. 22, June 2, 2000, pp. 10)
Pub: American City Business Journals, Inc.
Ed: Ken Hoover. **Description:** The Internal Revenue Service has developed a new small business/self-employed division this year, but for many small business owners the problem is not within the agency, but within the tax code itself.

40479 ■ "Is It Time for the Fed to Take a Good, Long Vacation?" in *Barron's* (August 18, 2003, pp. 14)
Pub: Barron's
Ed: Robin Goldwyn Blumenthal. **Description:** The Federal Open Market Committee's wavering positions on inflation and deflation having ruffled bond markets sufficiently, the Fed moved to mollify traders.

40480 ■ "IT Risk Assessment: Who Needs It?" in *Ingram's* (Vol. 29, No. 7, July 2003, pp. 23)
Pub: Show Me Publishing, Inc.

Ed: Scott Brouillette. **Description:** Businesses that fail to embrace technology put themselves at a disadvantage. However, companies that fail to plan for implementing information technology and related government regulations could suffer financially.

40481 ■ "It's the Law" in *Entrepreneur* (Vol. 30, No. 3, March 2002, pp. 42)
Pub: Entrepreneur Media Inc.
Ed: Amanda C. Kooser. **Description:** The Small Business Administration has created a Web site designed to help small business stay informed of laws and regulations.

40482 ■ "It's Not Personal" in *Entrepreneur* (Vol. 33, September 2005, No. 9, pp. 94)
Pub: Entrepreneur Media Inc.
Ed: Jane Easter Bahls. **Description:** Most state and federal laws entitle employees to review personnel files and also make copies of them. Documents that should be kept in a personnel file are listed.

40483 ■ "It's Son of NAFTA" in *Inc.* (Volume 27, July 2005, No. 7, pp. 26-27)
Pub: Inc. Magazine
Ed: Darren Dahl. **Description:** Will the new Central America Free Trade Agreement (CAFTA), which eliminates duties on trade between the U.S. and six Central American countries, help American businesses stay competitive?

40484 ■ "Jobless benefits on family leave? Not here" in *Crain's Detroit Business* (Vol. 16, No. 32, August 7, 2000, pp. 7)
Pub: Crain Communications, Inc.
Ed: Amy Lane. **Description:** Workers throughout the country could become eligible for unemployment benefits if they take time off to care for newly born or adopted children.

40485 ■ "Jolting Joe" in *Washington Business Journal* (Vol. 22, No. 12, July 25, 2003, pp. 23)
Pub: Washington Business Journal
Ed: Eleni Kretikos. **Description:** Dwayne Walker, operational chief of M.E. Swing Coffee Roasters, has been working at the 87-year-old coffee company since 1989. The coffee company's retail operations expanded after new city regulations forced it to halt wholesaling roasting.

40486 ■ "Judge Rejects Effort to Keep Billing Records for Boston's Big Dig a Secret" in *Boston Globe* (April 11, 2003)
Pub: Knight-Ridder/Tribune Business News
Ed: Sean P. Murphy. **Description:** Release of the records pertaining to Boston's Big Dig and the millions of dollars paid to private sector managers is discussed.

40487 ■ "Judge Stays Implementation of Massachusetts Governor's Auto Insurance Plan" in *Boston Globe* (February 2, 2005)
Pub: New York Times Company
Ed: Bruce Mohl. **Description:** Judge Raymond J. Brassard stayed the initial implementation of Governor Mitt Romney's proposed changes to the way high-risk drivers are apportioned among the state's insurance companies.

40488 ■ "Jump-starting broadband" in *Barron's* (Vol. 82, No. 54, January 20, 2003, pp. T1)
Pub: Barron's
Ed: Bill Alpert. **Description:** Federal Communications Commissioners disagreed with FCC Chairman Michael K. Powell's planned broadband deregulation of local Bell lines in Congressional testimony. However, the future of competition in broadband is likely to be 802.11/Wi-Fi networks.

40489 ■ "Just Call Him George W. Reagan" in *Business Week Online* (Jan. 8, 2003)
Pub: McGraw-Hill Inc.
Ed: Joseph Weber. **Description:** President George W. Bush's new economic stimulus program is examined, focusing on the program's gains for small businesses.

40490 ■ "Just a Mirage? Proposed Legislation May Expand SBIC Financing Someday" in *Entrepreneur* (Vol. 31, No. 8, August 2003, pp. 24)
Pub: Entrepreneur Media, Inc.
Ed: Stephen Barlas. **Description:** Profile of the Small Business Investment Company (SBIC) loan enhancement bill proposed by Senator Olympia Snowe (R-Maine) is presented. The bill would increase the stream of capital into Debenture SBICs. Money from these loans could be used by small companies to finance inventories, accounts receivable and more, the only exception would be real estate.

40491 ■ "Justice's warning" in *Black Enterprise* (Vol. 33, No. 198, March 24, 2003, pp. A3)
Pub: Earl Graves Publishing Co.
Ed: Laurie Cunningham. **Description:** Florida Supreme Court Justice Raoul Cantero III, warns of inadequate funding for the justice system in his state.

40492 ■ "Katrina Relief Bill May Produce Windfall For a Few Nonprofits" in *Crain's Detroit Business* (Vol. 21, November 7, 2005, No. 45)
Pub: Crain Communications Inc. - Detroit
Ed: Sherri Begin. **Description:** The Katrina relief bill allows individuals to deduct charitable gifts up to 100 percent of their gross adjusted income in 2005. The new law lifts the cap on corporate charitable deductions form 10 percent of taxable income as long as the gift is for hurricane relief and is made between August 28, 2005 and the end of the year.

40493 ■ "Keep it coming" in *Entrepreneur* (Vol. 30, No. 3, March)
Pub: Entrepreneur Media Inc.
Ed: Michelle Prather. **Description:** The SBA has received a special grant of funds to meet the additional needs of the disaster loan program.

40494 ■ "Keeping It Legal" in *Small Business Opportunities* (Vol. 12, No. 2, March 2000, pp. 76)
Pub: Harris Publications, Inc.
Ed: Lin Grensing-Pophal. **Description:** Guidelines for creating advertising to stay on the right side of the law are presented.

40495 ■ "Kiss Privacy Goodbye" in *Fortune* (Vol. 151, January 10, 2005, No. 1, pp. 55)
Pub: Time Inc.
Ed: Peter H. Lewis. **Description:** Surveillance devices aimed at humans are being developed at historical rates. These devices can be anything ranging from lasers that monitor members of a crowd for abnormal vital signs, to biometric scanners that find individual travelers from a distance and link them to commercial or governmental databases. The Biometric Group, a consulting company, predicts worldwide sales and licensing of fingerprinting, facial recognition, and other biometic devices to increase to more than $1.8 billion in 2005 and $4.8 billion by 2008.

40496 ■ "Know your limits" in *Entrepreneur* (Vol. 31, No. 6, June 2003, pp. 73)
Pub: Entrepreneur Media Inc.
Ed: Joanne Cleaver. **Description:** The U.S. Circuit Court of Appeals in California ruled that failure to fulfill a contract is just that and no more, fueling an emerging national precedent.

40497 ■ "Know the Rules" in *Black Enterprise* (Vol. 35, December 2004, No. 5, pp. 56)
Pub: Earl G. Graves Publishing Co. Inc.
Ed: Arlene McKanic. **Description:** Rules and regulations governing home-based businesses have become more complex, especially tax laws. The Internal Revenue Service is unfair to home-based companies when it comes to deductions, while zoning codes create other barriers.

40498 ■ "La-Van Hawkins Linked to Philadelphia Corruption Probe" in *Black Enterprise* (Vol. 35, September 2004, No. 2)
Pub: Earl G. Graves Publishing Co. Inc.

Ed: Alan Hughes. **Description:** CEO of La-Van Hawkins Food & Entertainment Group LLC, La-Van Hawkins, has been connected to a Philadelphia corruption case where people have been charged for paying off former Philadelphia treasurer in a scandal in which 12 people have been indicted. Hawkins is charged with conspiring to commit honest services fraud, four counts of wire fraud, and four counts of perjuring himself before the Grand Jury investigating the case.

40499 ■ "Labor Department Seeks Repeal of Regulation Threatening UI Reserves" in *My Business* **(February/March 2003, pp. 19)**
Pub: My Business Magazine
Description: Many states have been using state unemployment compensation reserves to fund Baby UI for employees following the birth or adoption of a child under the Birth and Adoption Unemployment Compensation Rule. Now small businesses fear that larger taxes will be needed to increase UI funds.

40500 ■ "Labor pains: if immigration laws tighten, all entrepreneurs could feel the squeeze" in *Entrepreneur* **(Vol. 31, No. 5, May 2003)**
Pub: Entrepreneur Media Inc.
Ed: Mark Henricks. **Description:** According to an analysis of Census data by the Center for Labor Market Studies, the American economic boom of the 1990s was fueled from laborers coming from foreign countries. With immigration laws being tightened in the wake of 9/11, many entrepreneurs are concerned about a reduced flow of immigrant workers.

40501 ■ "Lafayette 148 Had High Hopes For Its New Chinese Factory" in *Inc.* **(Volume 27, December 2005, No. 12, pp. 62, 66)**
Pub: Inc. Magazine
Ed: Catherine Curan. **Description:** Profile of Deirdre Quinn and her fashion business, Lafayette 148. Quinn discusses how she and partner, Shun Yen Siu were able to get her warehouse full of fine women's apparel from China to the U.S.

40502 ■ "Lawmakers to tackle e-waste issue" in *Waste News* **(Vol. 8, No. 20, January 6, 2002, pp. 15)**
Pub: Crain Communications, Inc.
Ed: Bruce Geiselman. **Description:** Legislation regarding the recycling of electronics, including computers and monitors, is discussed. One plan would establish a nationwide computer recycling program to divert personal computers from landfills.

40503 ■ "Lawmakers take aim at living-wage laws" in *Crain's Detroit Business* **(Vol. 19, No. 8, February 24, 2003, pp. 7)**
Pub: Crain Communications Inc., Detroit
Ed: Amy Lane. **Description:** Republican lawmakers are working on ordinances that would allow local governments to require higher minimum wage from businesses that are vendors or receive other forms of local government assistance; Governor Granholm opposes the bill.

40504 ■ "Lawmakers Working on Insurance Issues" in *Miami Herald* **(March 10, 2005)**
Pub: Knight-Ridder/Tribune Business News
Ed: Beatrice E. Garcia. **Description:** The Senate Banking and Insurance Committee approved a bill that will require insurers to offer multiple deductibles for policies covering commercial properties, including condominium associations.

40505 ■ "Laws Mandating Paid Sick Leave Will Pass in Several States" in *Kiplinger Letter* **(Vol. 78, January 19, 2007, No. 2)**
Pub: Kiplinger
Description: Massachusetts, Wisconsin, Washington, Main, Montana, Vermont, and Maryland are among the states considering a law to mandate paid sick leave to employees.

40506 ■ "Lawsuit: EPA ignored impact of lead regulation" in *Atlanta Business Chronicle* **(Vol. 23, No. 46, April 20, 2001, pp. 11A)**
Pub: American City Business Journals Inc.

Ed: Kent Hoover. **Description:** The Small Business Regulatory Enforcement Fairness Act will be sued to challenge a recent Environmental Protection Agency regulation that requires reports from any company that makes or uses at least 100 pounds of lead per year. A lawsuit filed by a coalition of 36 trade associations says that the EPA did not consider the effect of the regulation on small businesses. The National Federation of Independent Business will also file suit.

40507 ■ "Lease reviews can help avoid extra expenses" in *Business First Columbus* **(Vol. 18, No. 28, March 1, 2002, pp. B13)**
Pub: Business First Columbus, Inc.
Ed: Dan Lacey. **Description:** Information is offered for using a lease compliance strategy to avoid added expenses.

40508 ■ "Lease on Life?" in *Entrepreneur* **(Vol. 32, November 2004, No. 11, pp. 98)**
Pub: Entrepreneur Media Inc.
Ed: Jane Easter Bahls. **Description:** According to the National Association of Professional Employer Organizations, 2 to 3 million Americans are co-employed in professional employer organizations (PEO) arrangements. The employer and the PEO are both legally responsible for payment of payroll taxes and workers' compensation, and compliance with government regulations.

40509 ■ "Leave small business alone!" in *My Business* **(April/May 2002, pp. 51)**
Pub: My Business Magazine
Description: According to a National Federation of Independent Business Member Ballot, small business owners want fewer government regulations and mandates in order to run their firms. Statistical data included.

40510 ■ "Legal Eagle?" in *Entrepreneur* **(Vol. 32, October 2004, No. 10, pp. 89)**
Pub: Entrepreneur Media Inc.
Ed: Gwen Moran. **Description:** Important updates on marketing law are shared, including an amendment to telemarketing sales rules, Internet spam, and security software.

40511 ■ "Legislation aims to tax Internet sales" in *Crain's Detroit Business* **(Vol. 19, No. 1, January 6, 2003, pp. 20)**
Pub: Crain Communications Inc., Detroit
Ed: Amy Lane. **Description:** The State of Michigan is considering imposing a multi-state agreement that would streamline processes for collecting sales tax on Internet purchases. The Michigan Department of Treasury estimates tax losses of $273 in the current fiscal year.

40512 ■ "Legislature considers energy tax breaks" in *Crain's Detroit Business* **(Vol. 18, No. 16, April 22, 2002, pp. 23)**
Pub: Crain Communications Inc. - Detroit
Ed: Amy Lane. **Description:** New corporate tax breaks for alternative energy technologies could head for Michigan's State Legislature soon.

40513 ■ "Let Freedom Ring: The Internet is a Powerful Force for Telephone Deregulation" in *Barron's* **(July 7, 2003, pp. 30)**
Pub: Barron's
Ed: Christopher Whalen. **Description:** The advent of more sophisticated forms of Internet telephony will eventually force the government's hand in telecommunications deregulation.

40514 ■ "Let the (Political) Games Begin" in *Inc.* **(Volume 27, June 2005, No. 6, pp. 51-52, 54, 56)**
Pub: Inc. Magazine
Ed: Description: Information to assist companies who are faced with the government wanting to take their land.

40515 ■ "Little urgency seen over HIPAA" in *Crain's Detroit Business* **(Vol. 18, No.)**
Pub: Crain Communications Inc. - Detroit
Ed: David Barkholz, Andrew Dietderich. **Description:** Profile of the Health Insurance Portability and Accountability Act, which is intended to standardize and simplify security and privacy in health care.

40516 ■ "Living wage lands on death row; Legislature nears ban on ordinances" in *Crain's Detroit Business* **(Vol. 16, No. 49, Dec. 4, 2000)**
Pub: Crain Communications, Inc.
Ed: Amy Lane. **Description:** The legislature is poised to kill the living wage bill (House Bill 4766, sponsored by Rep. Andrew Richner, R-Grosse Pointe Park) that would prohibit local governments from enacting, enforcing or maintaining minimum-wage requirements higher than Michigan's rate of $5.15 per hour.

40517 ■ "LMSB Deputy Commissioner stresses fairness for taxpayers" in *Journal of Accountancy* **(Vol. 190, No. 4, October 2000, pp. 113)**
Pub: Harborside Financial Center
Description: An interview with Deborah M. Nolan, IRS Deputy Commissioner of the Large and Mid-Size Business (LMSB) division. Ms. Nolan spoke of the service's strategic goals that would make filing tax returns easier and increase fairness of compliance enforcement.

40518 ■ "LoanGiant.com Files for Chapter 11" in *Crain's Detroit Business* **(Vol. 21, October 10, 2005, No. 43, pp. 3)**
Pub: Crain Communications Inc. - Detroit
Ed: Description: LoanGiant, based in Southfield, Michigan, has filed for Chapter 11 bankruptcy protection. The firm has been accused of fraudulent mortgage loan and documentation practices.

40519 ■ "Local nonprofits benefit from polluter-pay rulings" in *Crain's Detroit Business* **(Vol. 19, No. 1, January 6, 2003, pp. 19)**
Pub: Crain Communications Inc., Detroit
Ed: Robert Ankeny. **Description:** Fines issued to U.S. Liquids of Detroit Inc. will benefit two Detroit areas charities. An increasing trend towards federal courts ordering companies convicted of polluting will also help offset environmental damage.

40520 ■ "Localizing the Brand" in *Inc.* **(October 2005, pp. 54-56)**
Pub: Inc. Magazine
Ed: Allen P. Roberts Jr. **Description:** Henry Estate shares insight into marketing and exporting and selling his wine in China. The global entrepreneur may also look into expanding not only to China, but also Guatemala, Honduras, Dominican Republic, El Salvador, Costa Rica, and Nicaragua with the Central American Free Trade Agreement in place.

40521 ■ "Long Island Financial Briefs: March 5, 2004" in *Long Island Business News* **(March 5, 2004)**
Pub: Dolan Media Newswires
Description: The Long Island Housing Partnership, along with Freddie Mac, are commencing an anti-predatory campaign against advertising and outreach efforts targeted against deceptive refinance mortgage schemes that can lead to foreclosures.

40522 ■ "The Long Road to Free Trade" in *Hispanic Business* **(July/August 2004, pp. 46)**
Pub: Hispanic Business
Ed: Debra Beachy. **Description:** An overview of the Central American Free Trade Agreement and the Free Trade Area of the Americas pact is presented.

40523 ■ "Losing the race: is the Patent Office's slowness putting U.S. innovation at risk?" in *Entrepreneur* **(Vol. 31, No. 5, May 2003)**
Pub: Entrepreneur Media Inc.
Ed: Joshua Kurlantzick. **Description:** The U.S. Patent and Trademark Office is no longer able to keep pace with the number of patent applications it receives.

40524 ■ "Loss-Limit Repeal May be Tied to Tax Boost" in *Kansas City Star* **(March 8, 2005)**
Pub: Knight-Ridder/Tribune Business News
Ed: Rick Alm. **Description:** The repeal of Missouri's $500 loss limit for casino gamblers is debated.

40525 ■ "Maine Debate Imposing Stricter Standards for Auto Emissions" in *Portland Press Herald* (October 7, 2005)
Pub: Blethen Maine Newspapers, Inc.
Ed: John Richardson. **Description:** Maine's Board of Environmental Protection is considering a proposal that would require new cars and trucks sold in Maine to release 30 percent less greenhouse gases by 2016.

40526 ■ "Making Family Leave Family-Friendly; California is considering subsidizing parental leave" in *Business Week Online* (Sept. 20, 2002)
Pub: McGraw-Hill Inc.
Ed: Aaron Bernstein, Ronald Grover, Cliff Edwards. **Description:** Small business owners share growing concern over the California legislation calling for a paid-family-leave law that would be too costly for small firms to handle. Massachusetts is also considering similar legislation.

40527 ■ "Manufacturers Group Wants End to Spam" in *Crain's Detroit Business* (Vol. 19, No. 10, March 10, 2003, pp. 6)
Pub: Crain Communications Inc., Detroit
Ed: Amy Lane. **Description:** The Michigan Manufacturers Association is fighting to stop spam on the Internet and is asking for the Michigan Legislature's help.

40528 ■ "Many federal contractors ignore subcontracting goals" in *Atlanta Business Chronicle* (Vol. 25, No. 22, November 8, 2002, pp. 5B)
Pub: American City Business Publications, Inc.
Ed: Kent Hoover. **Description:** The U.S. government does not appear to be concerned about the large number of contractors that do not submit plans. Although the Small Business Administration examines subcontracting compliance, a General Accounting Office report expresses concerns that the effectiveness of that monitoring.

40529 ■ "Marketing Spreads Hawaiian Message" in *Pacific Business News* (Vol. 41, No. 22, August 8, 2003, pp. 1)
Pub: American City Business Journals
Ed: Nina Wu. **Description:** Marketing campaign that supports federal self-determination legislation for Native Hawaiians and the impact of the legislation on Hawaiian businesses are discussed.

40530 ■ "M.D.s, business group seek to shape patients' bill" in *Atlanta Business Chronicle* (Vol. 24, No. 8, July 27, 2001, pp. 8A)
Pub: American City Business Journals Inc.
Ed: Julie Bryant. **Description:** Doctors are supporting patient protection laws, like the Patients' Bill of Rights now before the House of Representatives, because such laws provide protection from managed care organizations.

40531 ■ "A Mediation on Risk" in *Fortune* (Vol. 152, October 3, 2005, No. 7, pp. 50)
Pub: Time Inc.
Ed: Justin Fox. **Description:** Home Depot's effective disaster planning had them among the first company's to reopen its stores after Hurricane Katrina hit the Gulf Coast.

40532 ■ *Meltdown on Main Street: How Government is Obstructing Small Business in America*
Pub: NAL Dutton
Ed: Richard Lesher; foreword by Newt Gingrich. **Released:** 1997. **Price:** $11.95.

40533 ■ "The Merry Go-Round" in *The Economist* (Vol. 377, October 1-7, 2005, No. 8446, pp. 60)
Pub: The Economist Newspaper Ltd.
Description: In the global drug industry, no regulation is more important than that of the U.S. Food and Drug Administration. The industry boasts $550 billion in annual sales.

40534 ■ "MGM Taking Bids for Two Casinos in Detroit" in *Crain's Detroit Business* (Vol. 21, February 7, 2005, No. 6, pp. 3)
Pub: Crain Communications Inc. - Detroit
Ed: Robert Ankeny. **Description:** MGM Mirage Inc. announced plans for a buyout in spring 2004, but under Michigan law, no casino owner can have more than 10 percent interest in more than one casino.

40535 ■ "Military leave" in *Ingram's* (Vol. 27, No. 12, December 2001, pp. 24)
Pub: Show Me Publishing, Inc.
Description: The obligations to both the employer and employee regarding military leave are discussed. The Uniformed Employment and Re-employment Act of 1994 is explained in detail.

40536 ■ "The Mini-K Advantage" in *Rough Notes* (Vol. 144, No. 12, December 2001, pp. 80)
Pub: Rough Notes
Description: Information about the new tax laws that benefit small business 401(k) retirement plans is given. Under the new tax laws, an individual making $100,000 per year can contribute $28,000 to a 401(k) plan.

40537 ■ "Minimum Wage Hikes Eyed Nationwide" in *Inc.* (October 1, 2004)
Pub: Inc. Magazine
Ed: Jess McCuan. **Description:** New York may become the 13th state to raise its minimum wage above the federal level now set at $5.15 per hour.

40538 ■ "A Model Chamber Tackles Complex Issues" in *Hispanic Business* (July/August 2002, pp. 64-66)
Pub: Hispanic Business
Ed: Joel Russell. **Description:** The Mexican American Network of Odessa (MANO), Texas shows how local leadership can make a difference for constituent businesses. Profile of Iris Correa, executive director of the model Hispanic chamber is also highlighted.

40539 ■ "Modular Home Center Opens in Arcadia" in *Charlotte Observer* (February 1, 2007)
Pub: Knight-Ridder/Tribune Business News
Ed: John Lawhorne. **Description:** Arcadia Home Center features modular homes constructed on a steel frame; regulations regarding the manufacture and moving of these homes are included.

40540 ■ "Money-Preneuring" in *Small Business Opportunities* (Vol. 17, September 2005, No. 5, pp. 68, 128)
Pub: Harris Publications Inc.
Ed: Robert A. Adelson. **Description:** Three strategies to give non-family executives a share in the rewards of ownership without transferring any company stock are shared: offering a non-voting stock plan, a non-qualified deferred compensation plan, or a phantom stock plan.

40541 ■ "More protection means less worry over suits" in *Wall Street Journal* (October 8, 2002, pp. B4)
Pub: Dow Jones & Co. Inc.
Ed: Richard Breeden. **Description:** An examination of tort reform for small business is presented.

40542 ■ "Nanotech Steve Jurvetson" in *Venture Capital Journal* (January 1, 2005)
Pub: Thomason Financial Inc.
Description: Steve Jurvetson's firm Draper Fisher Jurvetson, has invested in more than 20 nanotech, MEMS and novel materials startups. Jurvetson suggests the best thing to happen to the nanotechnology sector in 2005 would be a major restructuring of immigration and education policy to prioritize science and engineering, the worst, more federal restrictions on immigration or freedom of scientific research like stem cell policy.

40543 ■ "Nassau Democrats Propose Reforms to Prevent Mismanagement" in *Long Island Business News* (March 12, 2004)
Pub: Dolan Media Newswires

Ed: Rosmaria Mancini. **Description:** Nassau County Legislatures have proposed procedural reforms to protect the county from mismanagement scandals in its Department of Economic Development. The Legislature cites serious issues in the personnel management, and purchasing and procurement practices and voice a need for new rules, regulations and policies.

40544 ■ "The Need for Tort Reform" in *My Business* (October/November 2002, pp. 49)
Pub: My Business Magazine
Ed: Hilda Bankston. **Description:** The former owner of a Fayette, Mississippi family-owned drug store tells how her and her pharmacist husband were named in a class action lawsuit over the prescription drug Fen-Phen. The lawsuit has devastated the family as well as the community and its small businesses.

40545 ■ "A New Abacus for Pensions" in *Business Week* (January 9, 2006, No. 3966, pp. 91)
Pub: McGraw-Hill Companies
Description: New Financial Accounting Standards Board rules on post-retirement accounting will change how companies account for pensions and other employee benefits, especially retiree health insurance.

40546 ■ "New Adult-Home Reforms Announced" in *Westchester County Business Journal* (Vol. 43, July 5, 2004, No. 27, pp. 16)
Pub: Westfair Communications Inc.
Description: New York State's Governor George E. Pataki has announced a new package of reforms to better protect adult-home residents in the state. An examination of the proposal is presented.

40547 ■ "New Burdens on Home Builders Hurt Local Government" in *Atlanta Business Chronicle* (Vol. 25, December 6, 2002, No. 26, pp. 38A)
Pub: American City Business Publications, Inc.
Ed: Mark Fitzgerald. **Description:** Delays in permits for housing projects in Atlanta, Georgia, might add a substantial amount to the cost of a home; the problem also results in the delay of tax dollars being collected.

40548 ■ "New Congress may give business some gains" in *Atlanta Business Chronicle* (Vol. 25, November 15, 2002, No. 23 pp. 7A)
Pub: American City Business Publications, Inc.
Ed: Kent Hoover. **Description:** Various issues are being considered by Congress, including tax cuts and health care reform.

40549 ■ "New EEOC and OFCCP Issues for the Year 2000 and Beyond" in *Employment Relations Today* (Vol. 26, No. 4, Winter 2000, pp. 99)
Pub: John Wiley & Sons, Inc.
Ed: Morgan D. Hodgson, Ronald S. Cooper, and Lloyd C. Loomis. **Description:** Reviews federal regulations regarding employment discrimination, focusing on the policies enacted by the US Equal Opportunity Commission and the Office of Federal Contract Compliance Programs. Topics addressed include the interpretation of the Americans with Disabilities Act of 1990, immigration and work policies, and enforcing discrimination law compliance within government organizations.

40550 ■ "New Jersey Acting Governor Seeks Deal to Ban Smoking in Bars, Eateries" in *The Record* (November 18, 2005)
Pub: New Jersey Media Group
Description: New Jersey's Acting Governor Codey is considering a plan that would ban smoking in the state's bars, restaurants and other indoor locations; establishment owners strongly oppose the plan.

40551 ■ "New Land-Use Council Set to Tackle Urban Sprawl" in *Crain's Detroit Business* (Vol. 19, No. 9, March 3, 2003, pp. 7)
Pub: Crain Communications Inc., Detroit
Ed: Amy Lane. **Description:** The Land Use Leadership Council will submit ideas to Michigan Governor Jennifer Granholm; the council will study urban sprawl and recommend ways to minimize the effects of current land-use trends.

40552 ■ "New Law Likely to Save Businesses Money on Terrorism Insurance" in *Crain's Detroit Business* (Vol. 19, No. 1, Jan. 6, 2003, pp. 16)

Pub: Crain Communications Inc., Detroit

Ed: Katie Merx. **Description:** Investigation into terrorism risk insurance coverage for small businesses is presented. Passage of the Terrorism Risk Insurance Act should help save businesses money because the government will assume most of the risk for coverage.

40553 ■ "New Law Reduced Liability for Architects, Engineers" in *Crain's Detroit Business* (Vol. 21, January 10, 2005, No. 2, pp. 22)

Pub: Crain Communications Inc. - Detroit

Ed: Amy Lane. **Description:** Michigan Governor Jennifer Granholm signed into law a small bill that will reduce the liability architects and engineers face on state construction projects.

40554 ■ "New Laws Take On Delaware Subsidiaries" in *Inc.* (January 1, 2005)

Pub: Inc. Magazine

Ed: Lora Kolodny. **Description:** New York Tax Courts have imposed taxes on revenue derived from intellectual property.

40555 ■ "New OSHA Rules to Reduce Injuries" in *Home Office Computing* (Vol. 18, No. 8, August 2000, pp. 15)

Pub: Scholastic Inc.

Ed: William Van Winkle. **Description:** Being ergonomically correct is about to become the law of the land; The Occupational Safety & Health Administration (OSHA) is set to implement new ergonomic rules that could send businesses, both large and small, hurrying for compliance, including companies with teleworkers in home offices.

40556 ■ "A New Pain in the Neck-OSHA lays down ergonomic standards for businesses great and small" in *PC Computing* (April 2000, pp. 44)

Pub: Ziff-Davis Inc.

Ed: Jennifer Powell. **Description:** The Occupational Safety and Health Administration's (OSHA) move to protect knowledge workers from workplace injuries caused by musculoskeletal disorders (MSD) is facing stiff opposition from businesses and some members of Congress. OSHA estimates that more than 600,000 people suffer from lost-workday MSDs each year and that MSDs account for more than one-third of all occupational injuries. Opponents of the regulations argue that there is not enough scientific data to know what causes injuries due to MSD or what workplace changes will stop them.

40557 ■ "New Political Players on the Scene" in *Hispanic Business* (January/February 2005, pp. 14)

Pub: Hispanic Business

Ed: Patricia Guadalupe. **Description:** Henry Cuellar, John Salazar and Luis Fortuno are the new Hispanic member of the U.S. Senate. Issues involving the Central American Free Trade Agreement (CAFTA) and visa concerns are addressed.

40558 ■ "New Rules for Corporate Counsel" in *Inc.* (September 1, 2003)

Pub: Gruner & Jahr USA Publishing

Ed: Anton Piech. **Description:** Specific steps attorneys should take to become more independent of a client company's executive team are outlined.

40559 ■ "New Rules Cut Health Risks from Lead in Children's Jewelry" in *Kansas City Star* (February 9, 2005)

Pub: Knight-Ridder/Tribune Business News

Ed: Paul Wenske. **Description:** In a move to reduce health risks for children, the U.S. Consumer Product Safety Commission has established guidelines for children's metal jewelry. New procedures for manufacturers, importers and retailers for testing lead in the jewelry have also been developed.

40560 ■ "New Rules Lift Cost of Grease" in *Atlanta Business Chronicle* (Vol. 24, No. 14, September 7, 2001, pp. 3A)

Pub: American City Business Journals Inc.

Ed: Walter Woods. **Description:** Due to the overwhelming amount of grease that builds up in Atlanta's restaurants, an astounding amount that reaches 25 gallons, the city government has passed a law that requires restaurants to get rid of their grease once every 90 days. Although this solves the grease problem, it is also requiring restaurants to pay excessive disposal costs.

40561 ■ "New Rules Stall Foreign Vessels" in *Pacific Business News* (Vol. 41, No. 23, August 15, 2003, pp. 1)

Pub: American City Business Journals

Ed: Prabha Natarajan. **Description:** The U.S. Department of Homeland Security has issued new immigration regulations that may harm Hawaii's maritime and tourism industries.

40562 ■ "New SEC Rule Means Business" in *Business Journal-Milwaukee* (Vol. 20, No. 47, August 8, 2003, pp. A13)

Pub: American City Business Journals, Inc.

Ed: Michael Muckian. **Description:** An examination of how Vista 360 Inc. regulatory compliance services for investment advisors is booming following new reporting rules by the U.S. Securities and Exchange Commission.

40563 ■ "New SEC Rules Regarding Selective Disclosure and Insider Trading Increase Risks" in *Venture Capital Journal* (Vol.40, No.10, Oct. 2000)

Pub: Venture Economics

Description: In depth report examining the Regulation Fair Disclosure (FD), issued by the Securities and Exchange Commission, and two new insider trading rules.

40564 ■ "A new standard" in *Entrepreneur* (Vol. 30, No. 10, October 2002, pp. 83)

Pub: Entrepreneur Media Inc.

Ed: Mark Henricks. **Description:** Profile of the International Organization for Standardization is presented. Currently more than 1,500 U.S. firms are certified under the ISO 14001 banner.

40565 ■ *New Technology-Based Firms in the New Millennium, Volume 3*

Pub: Elsevier Science & Technology Books

Ed: Ray Oakey, Wim During, Seleema Kauser. **Released:** June 2004. **Price:** $110.00. **Description:** Collection of papers from the Annual International High Technology Firms (HTSFs) Conference covering issues of importance to governments as they develop technological program. Papers are grouped into three sections: strategy, spin-off firms, clusters, networking, and global issues.

40566 ■ *New Technology-Based Firms in the New Millennium, Volume 4*

Pub: Elsevier Science & Technology Books

Ed: Ray Oakey, Wim During, Seleema Kauser. **Released:** December 2005. **Price:** $135.00. **Description:** Collection of papers from the Annual International High Technology Firms (HTSFs) Conference cover issues of importance to governments as they develop technological program. Papers are grouped into three sections: theory, strategy and clustering, and spin-off firms.

40567 ■ "New War Means New Contracts" in *Hispanic Business* (March 2002, pp. 58)

Pub: Hispanic Business

Ed: Patricia Guadalupe, Frank McCoy. **Description:** Outsourcing and a security buildup will impact procurement for minority firms in the U.S. Statistics for the Department of Defense, the Department of Transportation, and the Department of Justice, all concerned with terrorist threats, are presented.

40568 ■ "New World Border" in *Hispanic Business* (Vol. 23, No. 7/8, July/August 2001, pp. 14)

Pub: Hispanic Business

Ed: Scott Williams. **Description:** A group of business representatives from California, Arizona, New Mexico, and Texas have formed the non-profit Southwest Hispanic Economic Alliance (SHEA) to address Mexico/U.S. border and other issues of concern to the region's large Hispanic population.

40569 ■ "A New Wrinkle On Age Bias" in *Inc.* (Volume 27, July 2005, No. 7, pp. 36)

Pub: Inc. Magazine

Ed: Darren Dahl. **Description:** The Supreme Court made it easier to file age discrimination claims in federal court. There were 8,000 age discrimination cases filed in the U.S. in 2004 against companies with less than 500 employees.

40570 ■ "New York State Officials May Allow Wine Sales in Supermarkets" in *Buffalo News* (April 11, 2003)

Pub: Knight-Ridder/Tribune Business News

Ed: Matt Glynn. **Description:** New York officials are considering a move to allow the sale of wine in food stores and Sunday business hours for liquor stores in an attempt to ease the state's fiscal woes.

40571 ■ "New to You?" in *Entrepreneur* (Vol. 28, No. 9, September 2000, pp. 50)

Pub: Entrepreneur Media Inc.

Ed: Doug Hood and Marilea S. Hood. **Description:** The Small Business Administration 504 Certified Development Companies program, a new government-guaranteed loan program with a fixed rate-separate from the SBA, is outlined in question/answer format.

40572 ■ "News from the Small Business Front" in *My Business* (August/September 2002, pp. 14)

Pub: My Business Magazine

Description: According to a survey by Dun & Bradstreet, more small businesses provided health benefits to employees in 2002 than in the previous year; National Federation of Independent Business (NFIB) announced a new partnership with the International Fabricare Institute (ICPA); firms in America start smaller than new companies starting out in European countries.

40573 ■ "NextEnergy gets $2M from feds" in *Crain's Detroit Business* (Vol. 19, No. 10, March 10, 2003, pp. 29)

Pub: Crain Communications Inc., Detroit

Ed: Laura Bailey. **Description:** The state of Michigan's alternative-fuel research center, NextEnergy, received $2 million from an appropriations bill signed by President George W. Bush.

40574 ■ "NFIB Lays Groundwork for 108th Congress" in *My Business* (February/March 2003, pp. 18)

Pub: My Business Magazine

Description: New members of Congress were indoctrinated into the workings of the National Federation of Independent Business advocacy group during the past few weeks.

40575 ■ "NFIB Report From The State Capitals" in *My Business* (August/September 2002, pp. 20-22)

Pub: My Business Magazine

Description: Issues important to small businesses are listed by state.

40576 ■ "NFIB Report From The State Capitols" in *My Business* (December/January 2003, pp. 20-23)

Pub: My Business Magazine

Description: A look at small business issues particular to each of the fifty states.

40577 ■ "NFIB Report from the State Capitals" in *My Business* (April/May 2002, pp. 22-25)

Pub: My Business Magazine

Description: Current small business issues are presented in a listing by state.

40578 ■ "NFIB Report from the State Capitols" in *My Business* (April/May 2003, pp. 20-23)
Pub: My Business Magazine
Description: Small businesses issues are listed by state.

40579 ■ "No Bankruptcy Break for Hurricane Victims" in *Credit Union Journal* (Vol. 9, October 3, 2005, No. 39, pp. 12)
Pub: SourceMedia, Inc.
Description: An overview of the new consumer bankruptcy law is presented. The new law takes effect October 17, 2005.

40580 ■ "Not for sale" in *BlackEnterprise* (Vol. 32, No. 3, October 2001, pp. 165)
Pub: Earl Graves Publishing Co.
Ed: Leslie E. Royal. **Description:** Profile of the GrammLeach-Bliley Financial Services Modernization Act signed into law by President Clinton in 1999. The bill requires all financial institutions to inform their current and former customers how their personal and financial information is to be disclosed, shared, and sold to its affiliates and other companies.

40581 ■ "Number-Portability Change to Increase Wireless Competition" in *Crain's Detroit Business* (Vol. 19, No. 45, November 10, 2003, pp. 28)
Pub: Crain Communications Inc., Detroit
Ed: Amy Lane. **Description:** New Federal Communications Commission rules allow wireless customers in the Detroit and Ann Arbor, Michigan regions, as well as other large areas of the country, to switch wireless carrier while maintaining current phone numbers.

40582 ■ "Numbers Game" in *Entrepreneur* (Vol. 32, No. 1, January 2004, pp. 30)
Pub: Entrepreneur Media, Inc.
Ed: Stephen Barlas. **Description:** High technology firms relying on the H-1B Visa to fill engineering and technical jobs with foreign workers face a drop in the number of visas available in 2004.

40583 ■ "NY Bankruptcy Courts Shift to Online Filing" in *Long Island Business News* (February 6, 2004)
Pub: Dolan Media Newswires
Ed: Claude Solnik. **Description:** U.S. Bankruptcy Court for the Southern District of New York has begun accepting electronic Chapter 11 filing; the Eastern District has followed suit. Electronic filing for both non-bankruptcy and bankruptcy cases has also been accepted nationwide.

40584 ■ "NY State Senator Introduces Bill to Obtain Federal Funding for Genetic Research" in *Long Island Business News* (February 13, 2004)
Pub: Dolan Media Newswires
Ed: Rosmaria Mancini. **Description:** A bill introduced by Senator Ken LaValle, R-New York, would create an 'institute' that would work to obtain federal grant money for genetics research at institutions throughout New York State.

40585 ■ "OFCCP Contractor Survey; New Worker Economic Opportunity Law" in *Employment Relations Today* (Vol. 27, No. 2, Summer 2000, pp. 81)
Pub: John Wiley & Sons, Inc.
Ed: Morgan D. Hodgson and Ronald S. Cooper. **Description:** The Labor Department's office of Federal Contract Compliance's proposed rule to revise its affirmative action regulations contains a survey requesting detailed information concerning the employee pay policies of federal contractors. The Equal Employment Opportunity Commission's manual offers guidelines for pursuing charges of discrimination in the workplace.

40586 ■ "Officials discuss deferred comp, guidance and legislation for EOs" in *Tax Notes* (Vol. 96, No. 13, September 23, 2002, pp. 1693-1697)
Pub: Tax Notes International
Ed: Fred Stokeld, J. Christine Harris. **Description:** At an SBA conference, government officials discussed tax issues relating to employee benefits of nonprofit organizations and government entities.

40587 ■ "Oil changers may face oversight" in *Crain's Detroit Business* (Vol. 18, No. 17, April 29, 2002, pp. 6)
Pub: Crain Communications Inc. - Detroit
Description: Michigan considers new auto-related regulations that would affect oil-change shops.

40588 ■ "Oil Slicks" in *Inc.* (October 1, 2003)
Pub: Gruner & Jahr USA Publishing
Ed: Tahl Raz. **Description:** Tim Marquez and Rod Eson were on their way to revolutionizing the oil industry until they ran into legal issues that tore them apart.

40589 ■ "Oklahoma Insurance Commissioner Orders Tribal Companies Out of State" in *Journal Record* (February 5, 2004)
Pub: Dolan Media Company
Description: Carroll Fisher, Oklahoma Insurance Commissioner, ordered a group of companies claiming tribal sovereignty to stop doing business in the state. Fisher alleges the companies are required to be licensed by the Oklahoma Insurance Department, while the companies claim tribal sovereignty since they are affiliated with the Ponca Tribe of Nebraska.

40590 ■ "Omniplex on the Case" in *Black Enterprise* (Vol. 37, December 2006, No. 5, pp. 38)
Pub: Earl G. Graves Publishing Co. Inc.
Ed: Glenn Townes. **Description:** Office of Personnel Management in Washington D.C. recently awarded a service contract to Omniplex World Services Corp. Virginia-based, The Chantilly, will perform security investigations and background checks on current and prospective federal employees and military personnel and contractors.

40591 ■ "On the Agenda" in *Entrepreneur* (Vol. 30, No. 2, February 2002, pp. 39)
Pub: Entrepreneur Media Inc.
Ed: Amanda C. Kooser. **Description:** The Federal Trade Commission is taking a new approach to consumer privacy and electronic commerce.

40592 ■ "On the Internet, a Second Act" in *Barron's* (July 28, 2003, pp. T1)
Pub: Barron's
Ed: Bill Alpert. **Description:** Michael Wachs, who conducts online interviews of executives for CEOcast, also spent nearly a year in federal prison for swindling Chase Manhattan Bank out of nearly $21 million. Questions are raised about the legality of his role with CEOcast on the provisions of his settlement with Chase.

40593 ■ "One More For the Road" in *Sales & Marketing Management* (January 2005)
Pub: VNU Business Media
Ed: Denis Jensen. **Description:** Sales executives, as well as management, should avoid the pitfalls of drinking when entertaining business clients. One accident involving an employee under the influence will cause insurance rates to go up.

40594 ■ "The Online Lawyer" in *Hispanic Business* (October 2002, pp. 90)
Pub: Hispanic Business
Ed: Derek Reveron. **Description:** Caution is advised when seeking legal services online, however small businesses are finding reliable legal services online. A listing of Web site offering legal services is included.

40595 ■ "Open Doors?" in *Entrepreneur* (Vol. 31, No. 9, September 2003, pp. 72)
Pub: Entrepreneur Media, Inc.
Ed: Joshua Kurlantzick. **Description:** Government deregulation in the real estate industry is discussed.

40596 ■ "Opus Seen In Talks To Buy Rare Westlake Property" in *San Fernando Valley Business Journal* (Vol. 12, January 2007, No. 2, pp. 33)
Pub: San Fernando Valley Business Journal Associates
Ed: Shelly Garcia. **Description:** Industry sources say that Opus is close to a deal to acquire property currently owned by Lowe's. The Russell Ranch Road parcel had been at the center of a re-zoning effort in Westlake Village.

40597 ■ "Orchestrating Assistance; Chambers of Commerce" in *Crain's New York Business* (Vol. 22, November 13, 2006, No. 46, pp. 38)
Pub: Crain Communications, Inc.
Description: Listing of local chapters of New York's chambers of commerce. These organizations serve as sources of information and representation for local business interest provide a number of services and a wide variety of programs for small businesses.

40598 ■ "Organizer's Laud Bigger Javits" in *Tradeshow Week* (Vol. 34)
Pub: Reed Business Information
Ed: Margo McCall. **Description:** New York State legislators approved the expansion of the Jacob K. Javits Convention Center. The move is expected to increase the number of shows drawn to the area.

40599 ■ "OSHA's Proposed Ergonomic Standard and Clarification on Home Work Policy" in *Employment Relations Today* (Vol. 27, No. 1, Spring 2000)
Pub: John Wiley & Sons, Inc.
Ed: John J. Gallagher and Gregory R. Watchman. **Description:** Several federal regulations that impacted US workers in 1999 are discussed, focusing on home work, foreign worker, and overtime policies. Topics addressed include the US Occupational Safety and Health Administration's ergonomic standards, protection for illegal aliens, and the calculation of overtime under the Fair Labor Standards Act.

40600 ■ "Out of the Zone" in *Home Office Computing* (Vol. 18, No. 12, December 2000, pp. 97)
Pub: Scholastic Inc.
Ed: Steven Van Yoder. **Description:** This article takes a look at home-based business and zoning laws. The author contends that many home business workers are violating zoning laws with or without knowing it. Advice is given to avoid this problem.

40601 ■ "Overtime Reform Overdoses on Politics" in *Inc.* (July 1, 2004)
Pub: Inc. Magazine
Ed: Jess McCuan. **Description:** New rules governing overtime will be part of the overhauling of the Fair Labor Standards Act in 2004, but politics are leaving rules unclear.

40602 ■ "Package deal" in *Entrepreneur* (Vol. 31, No. 4, April 2003, pp. 22)
Pub: Entrepreneur Media Inc.
Ed: Stephen Barlas. **Description:** The new economic stimulus package proposed by President George W. Bush would increase the annual allowance for expensing of capital investments from $25,000 to $75,000 for small businesses, and tie the ceiling in the future to inflation.

40603 ■ "Paid family leave better if voluntary" in *Crain's Detroit Business* (Vol. 16, No. 5, January 31, 2000, pp. 8)
Pub: Crain Communications, Inc.
Description: Information regarding a proposed federal rule to allow employees on unpaid family leave to apply for jobless benefits while taking care of newborns or newly adopted children.

40604 ■ "Panel Seeks to Put Organic Loophole Out to Pasture" in *Chicago Tribune* (March 3, 2005)
Pub: Knight-Ridder/Tribune Business News
Ed: Andrew Martin. **Description:** An advisory board has recommended that the U.S. Department of Agriculture strengthen existing rules requiring organic livestock to be raised and fed on open pasture rather than confined pens. The move would most directly affect the dairy business.

40605 ■ "Passing Marks?" in *Entrepreneur* (Vol. 31, No. 11, November 2003, pp. 70)
Pub: Entrepreneur Media, Inc.
Ed: Joan Szabo. **Description:** Information on the Regulatory Flexibility Act (RFA) is presented. The RFA is a law designed to make sure federal agencies address the needs of small business when issuing rules and regulations.

40606 ■ "The Patent Epidemic" in *Business Week* (January 9, 2006, No. 3966, pp. 60-62)
Pub: McGraw-Hill Companies
Ed: Michael Orey. **Description:** Defeating suspicious patents can take years, cost millions, and slow innovation, however, the Supreme Court may reshape patent law.

40607 ■ *Patent Reexamination and Small Business Innovation: Congressional Hearing*
Pub: DIANE Publishing Company
Ed: Howard Coble. **Released:** February 2004. **Price:** $25.00. **Description:** Congressional hearing: Witness: Peter Theis, President, Theis Research, Inc.; Paul Heckel, Independent Inventor; Nancy Linck, Senior Vice President, General Counsel and Secretary, Guilford Pharmaceuticals, Inc.; and Mark H. Webbink, Senior Vice President and General Counsel, Red Hat, Inc.

40608 ■ "Payback Time: Mutual Funds are Paying the Price, But Will You Get Your Fair Share?" in *Entrepreneur* (Vol. 32, August 2004, No. 8)
Pub: Entrepreneur Media Inc.
Ed: Julie Monahan. **Description:** Settlement money from the Security Exchange Commission's investigation into mutual fund malfeasance will most likely go to the funds themselves rather than investors.

40609 ■ "Paying for Your Mistakes: Are You Overlooking Allowable Deductions in Your Business?" in *My Business* (February/March 2003, pp. 43)
Pub: My Business Magazine
Ed: Nancy Mann Jackson. **Description:** Most small business owners end up paying more in taxes because they overlook allowable deductions.

40610 ■ "The PCAOB and the Future of Oversight" in *Journal Of Accountancy*
Pub: American Institute of Certified Public Accountants
Ed: Patrick J. McDonnell. **Description:** Review of the Sarbanes-Oxley Act of 2002 created by the Public Company Accounting Oversight Board (PCAOB) is presented. The role of the PCAOB is discussed.

40611 ■ "Pension Pain" in *Forbes* (Vol. 170, No. 4, September 2, 2002, pp. 144)
Pub: Forbes Magazine
Ed: A. Gary Shilling. **Description:** Companies will no longer be allowed to boost earnings by including pension plans.

40612 ■ "A Phony Cure; Shifting Class Actions to Federal Courts Is No Reform" in *Business Week* (February 7, 2005, No. 3919, pp. 33)
Pub: McGraw-Hill Companies
Ed: Lorraine Woellert. **Description:** New legislation would require class action lawsuits to be filed in Federal Courts rather than in rural areas that have strong consumer-protection laws, anti-business jurors, and judges who help the local plaintiffs' bar.

40613 ■ "Pill Pusher: Drug Maker Biovail Sparks Controversy by Paying Doctors to Write Prescriptions" in *Barron's* (July 21, 2003, pp. 17)
Pub: Barron's
Ed: Bill Alpert. **Description:** Biovail's offer of $1,000 to doctors who write 15 prescriptions for Cardizem LA blood-pressure treatment goes against medical ethics, according to many doctors and industry observers. Biovail developed the plan with the help of consulting firm, Quintiles Transnational.

40614 ■ "A Place for More Hispanics?" in *Hispanic Business* (March 2002, pp. 56)
Pub: Hispanic Business
Ed: Patricia Guadalupe. **Description:** Currently there is a push to get more Hispanics on the federal payroll, to help diversity government agencies.

40615 ■ "Plan would gut MEDC to fund scholarships" in *Crain's Detroit Business* (Vol. 19, No. 14, April 7, 2003, pp. 1)
Pub: Crain Communications Inc., Detroit
Ed: Robert Ankeny. **Description:** The Michigan Economic Development Corporation could lose operating money if the House Republican proposal to cut $59 million from the business-attraction agency passes; the funds would be shifted to fully restore merit-scholarship funding in the 2004 state budget.

40616 ■ "Policy: The future of telecom lies at the steps of Capitol Hill" in *Red Herring* (No. 106, October 15, 2001, pp. 24-25)
Pub: Herring Communications
Ed: Dan Briody. **Description:** The impact of new regulations regarding the telecommunications industry will have a tremendous impact on consumers. Officials at Verizon Communications say that separating their retail and wholesale operations would cost nearly $1 billion per state.

40617 ■ "Politics of Design" in *San Francisco Business Times* (Vol. 18, No. 1, August 15, 2003, pp. 15)
Pub: American City Business Journals
Ed: Ryan Tate. **Description:** Heller-Manus Architects, led by principals Jeffrey Heller and Clark Manus, has designed several proposed residential towers in San Francisco, California. Heller-Manus must face an array of government regulations to get its construction projects approved.

40618 ■ "Pollution Rules to Cost Illinois Firms" in *Chicago Tribune* (March 11, 2005)
Pub: Knight-Ridder/Tribune Business News
Ed: Robert Manor. **Description:** The federal government has issued firmer limits on air pollution for most of the country. This move will cost billions of dollars for Illinois power generators. The state is among the top polluters of the nation.

40619 ■ "Postal Rate Hikes" in *Kiplinger Letter* (Vol. 78, January 5, 2007, No. 1)
Pub: Kiplinger
Description: Postal rates are expected to rise from 39 cents to 42 cents for first-class stamps. Business mailers will increase by 9 percent for invoices and ad mailings.

40620 ■ "Power Broker Gets 7 1/2 Years in Prison" in *Black Enterprise* (Vol. 35, January 2005, No. 6, pp. 28)
Pub: Earl G. Graves Publishing Co. Inc.
Ed: Carolyn M. Brown. **Description:** Nathan Chapman Jr. has been sentenced to 7-1/2 years in prison and fined for defrauding Maryland's retirement system and stealing from his own firm.

40621 ■ "Power and Influence on the Hill" in *Hispanic Business* (March 2005, pp. 12)
Pub: Hispanic Business
Ed: Patricia Guadalupe. **Description:** Lobby groups are helping Hispanics to enjoy greater representation in Washington, D.C.

40622 ■ "Power PACs" in *Hispanic Business* (March 2005, pp. 16, 18)
Pub: Hispanic Business
Ed: Joel Russell. **Description:** Hispanic political action committees almost tripled campaign contributions to political parties during the 2003-2004 election cycle. Statistical data included.

40623 ■ "Predatory Towing" in *San Fernando Valley Business Journal* (Vol. 12, January 2007, No. 2, pp. 37)
Pub: San Fernando Valley Business Journal Associates
Ed: Vanessa Herman. **Description:** State Towing Inc. and the company's owner, Reza Nowrooz, was found guilty of two counts of unlawfully taking vehicles and one count of attempted extortion.

40624 ■ "Prepare for Y2K Litigation" in *E-business Advisor* (Vol. 17, No. 12, December 1999, pp. 36)
Pub: Advisor Media, Inc.
Ed: Sean P. Melvin. **Description:** Leaders of e-businesses should anticipate some lawsuits triggered by Y2K, so they should consider lawsuit defense strategies and start preventative maintenance measures.

40625 ■ "Pressure mounting for terrorism insurance relief" in *Atlanta Business Chronicle* (Vol. 25, No. 21, November 1, 2002, pp. 5C)
Pub: American City Business Publications, Inc.
Ed: Jan R. Costello. **Description:** The U.S. House of Representatives and the U.S. Senate are both working on terrorism insurance reform legislation. Terrorism coverage costs have risen tremendously and a majority of policies launched after the September 11, 2001 terrorist attacks do not cover terrorism.

40626 ■ "Private Matters: Retail Alert: Keep an Eye on New RFID Privacy Legislation" in *Entrepreneur* (Vol. 32, October 2004, No. 10, pp. 38)
Pub: Entrepreneur Media Inc.
Ed: Amanda C. Kooser. **Description:** Wireless capabilities that track products as they move through the supply chain, known as radio frequency identification (RFID) are growing in popularity with retailers. Several states are considering privacy legislation to regulate RFID so companies could not collect and use data collected regarding customers.

40627 ■ "The Privatization Question" in *Hispanic Business* (October 2002, pp. 22, 24)
Pub: Hispanic Business
Ed: Loretta Sanchez, L. Jacobo Rodriguez. **Description:** Both sides of the issues involving privatizing social security are presented, with commentary by Representative Loretta Sanchez, Democrat from California, and L. Jacob Rodriguez, an analyst from the Cato Institute.

40628 ■ "Q&A" in *Home Office Computing* (Vol. 18, No. 7, July 2000, pp. 13)
Pub: Scholastic Inc.
Ed: Cristina Gair. **Description:** Jay Westermeier, attorney at Piper, Maybury, Rudnick & Wolfe, in Washington, D.C., discusses ways to avoid legal problems when selling goods and services online.

40629 ■ "Raines Stays Cool Under Fire" in *Black Enterprise* (Vol. 35, December 2004, No. 5, pp. 34)
Pub: Earl G. Graves Publishing Co. Inc.
Ed: Hamil Harris. **Description:** Overview of the case against Franklin Raines, CEO of Fannie Mae, the nation's largest source of financing for home mortgages. Franklin has been charged with engaging in accounting violations.

40630 ■ "Ray-gulation" in *Inc.* (July 1, 2003)
Pub: Gruner & Jahr USA Publishing
Ed: Nadine Heintz. **Description:** Proposed safety regulations regarding the tanning industry are examined. According to some experts, tighter rules are needed because ultraviolet exposure during childhood can lead to skin cancer later; currently some states enforce a tanning age limit, while some require parental consent.

40631 ■ "Read the fine print" in *Black Enterprise* (Vol. 33, No. 7, February 2003, pp. 6)
Pub: Earl Graves Publishing Co.
Ed: Alan Hughes. **Description:** Information regarding the black business community and the progress of the BE 100s, as well as insight into issues affecting African Americans on Capitol Hill is provided by Alan Hughes at blackenterprise.com.

40632 ■ "Ready for Progress" in *Hispanic Business* (January/February 2005, pp. 44, 46, 48)
Pub: Hispanic Business
Description: With corporate board diversity in a holding pattern, new regulations may work as a vehicle for change. Hispanics hold 95 seats on boards of directors at Fortune 500 companies, down by one from 2004.

40633 ■ "Recent State Legislative Developments Concerning Employment Discrimination..." in *Employment Relations Today* **(Summer 2000, pp. 89)**
Pub: John Wiley & Sons, Inc.
Ed: William C. Martucci and Eric W. Smith. **Description:** A summary of recent state legislative activity regarding employment discrimination and whistle-blower protections is presented. The legislation is of importance to multi-state employees who must ensure their operations comply with state laws and regulations.

40634 ■ "Reforming pro forma" in *Entrepreneur* **(Vol. 31, No. 5, May 2003, pp. 50)**
Pub: Entrepreneur Media Inc.
Ed: Jennifer Pellet. **Description:** The issue of pro forma financial reports used by small businesses in the past is discussed. The SEC is working to bring pro forma reporting under control.

40635 ■ "Regulation Nation" in *Entrepreneur* **(Vol. 32, October 2004, No. 10, pp. 32)**
Pub: Entrepreneur Media Inc.
Ed: Joshua Kurlantzick. **Description:** Federal regulations are limiting the growth of small business in America. The Small Business Administration's Office of Advocacy estimates small firms with less than 20 employees pay nearly $7,000 per employee in regulatory costs.

40636 ■ "Regulatory Rescue" in *Entrepreneur* **(Vol. 31, No. 8, August 2003, pp. 24)**
Pub: Entrepreneur Media, Inc.
Ed: Stephen Barlas. **Description:** The bill authorizing 20 Small Business Development Centers across the U.S. is expected to be passed by Congress. The Small Business Regulatory Assistance Act (H.R. 205) was approved by the House in April 2003.

40637 ■ "Remember The Nanny Tax? Now It's the Granny Tax" in *Fortune* **(Vol. 141, No. 1, January 10, 2000, pp. 218)**
Pub: Time Inc.
Ed: Carolyn T. Geer. **Description:** Determining when taxes are due for people who provide elder care are investigated. The tax that shook up the nanny world threatens those who employ home health-care workers.

40638 ■ "Renewed Effort for Reintroduced Rural Credit Bill" in *American Banker* **(Vol. 170, February 2, 2005, No. 22, pp. 5)**
Pub: Thomson Financial Media Inc.
Ed: Ben Jackson. **Description:** Rural Economic Invest Act was reintroduced at the end of January 2005. The bill gives banks and thrifts tax breaks for lending in rural areas.

40639 ■ "Report proposes update of copyright act: panel seeks liability for violations by Internet access services" in *The New York Times*
Pub: The New York Times Company
Ed: Jeri Clausing. **Description:** The Progressive Policy Institute is releasing a report discussing the need for privacy on the Internet, specifically in the area of copyright infringement. The report states the sites like Napster should not be allowed to offer Internet users free trade of music and MP3 files. A House Small Business Committee meeting is scheduled to discuss the problems of copyright in the Internet music industry.

40640 ■ "Reporters' Notebook; Weighing Fed's Tough-guy Tactics" in *Crain's Detroit Business* **(Vol. 22, December 11, 2006, No. 50, pp. 11)**
Pub: Crain Communications Inc. - Detroit
Ed: Robert Ankeny. **Description:** U.S. Justice Department Thompson Memorandum demands that corporations under investigation waive the attorney-client privilege and also pressures those companies to stop paying attorney fees for employees facing charges.

40641 ■ "Representation for hire" in *Black Enterprise* **(Vol. 32, No. 10, May 2002, pp. 24)**
Pub: Earl Graves Publishing Co.
Ed: Joyce Jones. **Description:** Ways in which small businesses can lobby politicians are presented.

40642 ■ "Republican Leaders Push More SBT Cuts" in *Crain's Detroit Business* **(Vol. 21, December 19, 2005, No. 51, pp. 6)**
Pub: Crain Communications Inc. - Detroit
Ed: Amy Lane. **Description:** Lawmakers are pushing for small business tax relief and a single-business tax rate cut.

40643 ■ "Research's reward" in *Crain's Detroit Business* **(Vol. 18, No. 51, Dec. 23, 2002, pp. 1)**
Pub: Crain Communications Inc., Detroit
Ed: Laura Bailey. **Description:** Since starting their firm in 1991, James Downward and Judith Erb, have developed six patents and have 6 patents pending. Their company IA Inc, and its subsidiary Threefold Sensors, has developed the Endotect biosensor for widespread detection of compounds that mimic estrogen and appear to cause birth defects.

40644 ■ "Resources: Web Sites, Organizations, Events and More to Grow Your Business" in *Entrepreneur* **(Vol. 32, August 2004, No. 8, pp. 8)**
Pub: Entrepreneur Media Inc.
Ed: Steve Cooper. **Description:** Showcase of information to help small business include: Global Advisor offers services from United Parcel Service to help companies learn ways to conduct business overseas, including trade tools and terminology, a global time clock and HAP, supply chain management, and a guide to international shipping; a CAN-SPAM Act of 2003 summary; RE:INVENTION INC is a daily blog dedicated to women entrepreneurs; and a directory of venture capital and private equity firms.

40645 ■ "Resources: Web Sites, Organizations, Events and More To Grow Your Business" in *Entrepreneur* **(Vol. 32, September 2004, No. 9, pp. 8)**
Pub: Entrepreneur Media Inc.
Ed: Steve Cooper. **Description:** Resources to help small business are featured including the Small Business Administration's effort to help teen entrepreneurs launch a business; KnockNow an online community of entrepreneurs, executives, venture capitalists, angel investors, service sector companies, and government; the SBA's business Website offering information on small business development, financial assistance, taxes, laws and regulations, international trade, workplace issues, buying and selling and federal forms.

40646 ■ "Restaurants Watch Helplessly As Wait Staff Applications Dry Up" in *Bradenton Herald* **(January 31, 2005)**
Pub: Bradenton Herald
Ed: Tilde Herrera. **Description:** Restaurant owners in the Bradenton area are having difficulty hiring professional wait staff. Sean Murphy, owner of Beach Bistro and Mangrove Grill, believes waiting tables has become less attractive because of the tip reporting system used by the Internal Revenue Service.

40647 ■ "Revamped Retiring Plans" in *My Business* **(April/May 2002, pp. 15)**
Pub: My Business Magazine
Ed: Milt Zall. **Description:** Tax legislation signed into law by President Bush in 2001 made significant changes to retirement plans, including loans allowed, limit on annual additions raised, employer's tax deduction increase, increased limit for defined benefit plans, increased compensation limits, and small business tax credits.

40648 ■ "Rewarding Bad Behavior" in *Rough Notes* **(Vol. 145, No. 12, December 2002, pp. 118)**
Pub: Rough Notes
Description: The National Conference of State Legislatures, using the National Association of Insurance

Commissioners, has much influence in contributing to state revenues; they are now involved in preserving state regulations and dealing with federal government pressures.

40649 ■ *The RFA at 25: Needed Improvements for Small Business Regulatory Relief*
Pub: United States Government Printing Office
Released: February 2006. **Price:** $62.00. **Description:** Information regarding the hearing on needed improvements for small business regulatory relief before the Committee on Small Business, House of Representatives, One Hundred Ninth Congress, First Session, Washington, DC, March 16, 2005 is provided.

40650 ■ "Rich Man, Politician" in *Inc.* **(September 1, 2003)**
Pub: Gruner & Jahr USA Publishing
Ed: Patrick J. Sauer. **Description:** Will campaign finance reform put more entrepreneurs in political offices? The effects of the McCain-Feingold campaign finance reform law are discussed.

40651 ■ "Richard Whitmer" in *Crain's Detroit Business* **(Vol. 19, No. 1, January 6, 2003, pp. 12)**
Pub: Crain Communications Inc., Detroit
Ed: Katie Merx. **Description:** Profile of Richard Whitmer, who works to prevent changes to laws regarding health insurance and Blue Cross and Blue Shield of Michigan.

40652 ■ "The Right to Regulate Off-Duty Conduct" in *Employment Relations Today* **(Vol. 27, No. 2, Summer 2000, pp. 101)**
Pub: John Wiley & Sons, Inc.
Ed: Arthur F. Silbergeld and Stephanie T. Sasaki. **Description:** Many employers are attempting to exert control over off-duty conduct of employees that could be detrimental to profitability. The laws have not been well developed in most jurisdictions, but many companies have implemented policies restricting employees dating other employees and setting up or participating in competing businesses.

40653 ■ "Ripple Effects" in *Hispanic Business* **(May 2005, pp. 68, 70)**
Pub: Hispanic Business
Ed: Holly Ocasio Rizzo. **Description:** Congress is considering a move to restore small business equity funding; the program was stopped when the technology and telecom bubble burst.

40654 ■ "Rising to the Top" in *Black Enterprise* **(Vol. 35, November 2004, No. 4, pp. 183)**
Pub: Earl G. Graves Publishing Co. Inc.
Ed: Tanisha A. Sykes. **Description:** Profile of Donald Riley, host and producer of an Internet radio talk show. Riley suffers with a debilitating genetic birth defect that affects muscle development. Riley advocates Section 504 of the Rehabilitation Act of 1973 and the Americans With Disabilities Act, which prohibits discrimination against qualified individuals with disabilities.

40655 ■ "Road Weary No More" in *Hispanic Business* **(Vol. 24, No. 1/2, January/February 2002, pp. 10)**
Pub: Hispanic Business Inc.
Ed: Tim Dougherty. **Description:** Two constitutional amendments approved by Texas voters will benefit cross-border trade and the state's Hispanic population. Proposition 2 will improve local roads along the Mexican border, while Proposition 15 provides for the creation of the Texas Mobility Fund to finance state highway and other transportation projects.

40656 ■ "Romney, Businesses Wrangle On 'Loopholes'" in *Boston Globe* **(January 31, 2005)**
Pub: New York Times Company
Description: Governor Mitt Romney is working to create business-friendly policies to create jobs in Massachusetts. So far, an estimated $210 million has been collected by closing corporate tax loopholes.

40657 ■ **"Romney Set To Unveil Jobs Program"** in *Boston Globe* **(February 3, 2005)**
Pub: New York Times Company
Ed: Sasha Talcott. **Description:** Massachusetts State has partnered with Citizens Financial Group to create jobs. The new program is funded by Citizens and will be administered by the State's Department of Business and Technology.

40658 ■ **"Ruling on Tax Incentives May Head to High Court"** in *Crain's Detroit Business* **(Vol. 21, January 31, 2005, No. 5, pp. 33)**
Pub: Crain Communications Inc. - Detroit
Ed: Amy Lane. **Description:** A legal dispute in Ohio could have an impact of Michigan's main business-tax incentive, the Michigan Economic Growth Authority program whereby Michigan grants single-business-tax credits for incentives for corporate investment.

40659 ■ **"Rumblings"** in *Crain's Detroit Business* **(Vol. 16, No. 50, December 11, 2000, pp. 26)**
Pub: Crain Communications, Inc.
Description: For anyone caught short of change at a Detroit parking meter, the city's Municipal Parking Department is issuing meter cards. The debit cards are usable at four business areas: downtown, the Detroit Medical Center, Wayne State University/Culture Center, and the New Center area.

40660 ■ **"Safe Seats Don't Make Sound Politics"** in *Hispanic Business* **(Vol. 24, No. 5, May 2002, pp. 26, 28)**
Pub: Hispanic Business Inc.
Ed: Joel Russell. **Description:** Hispanic representation in Congress is increasing, but not at the same rate as the population increases in the United States.

40661 ■ **"St. Catherine of Siena Medical Center Seeks to Block LIRR"** in *Long Island Business News* **(March 12, 2004)**
Pub: Dolan Media Newswires
Ed: Claude Solnik. **Description:** The Long Island Rail Road is being asked by St. Catherine of Siena Medical Center to remove a site adjacent to the hospital from its list of potential locations for a new rail yard. The Medical Center is citing potential health risks as their reason to halt the rail road's plans.

40662 ■ **"Sales"** in *Inc.* **(Volume 27, March 2005, No. 3, pp. 38)**
Pub: Inc. Magazine
Ed: Mike Brewster. **Description:** Large corporations require a request for proposal when purchasing products or services in order to comply with corporate governance standards.

40663 ■ **"San Francisco Job Applicants Do Not Have to Admit to Former Convictions"** in *Sacramento Bee* **(October 26, 2005)**
Pub: The Sacramento Bee
Ed: Rachel Osterman. **Description:** The city of San Francisco has adopted a ruling that allows applicants with criminal records to apply for jobs without disclosing that information. The move was made in order to help erase the stigma faced by felons applying for public sector positions.

40664 ■ **"Say What? Decipher Common Contract Legalese"** in *Entrepreneur* **(Vol. 32, December 2004, No. 12, pp. 98)**
Pub: Entrepreneur Media Inc.
Ed: Marc Diener. **Description:** Common clauses to beware of when entering into legal contracts are examined.

40665 ■ **"SBA can be a boon, but it doesn't make loans"** in *Crain's Detroit Business* **(Vol. 18, No. 49, December 9, 2002, pp. 16)**
Pub: Crain Communications Inc., Detroit
Ed: Laura Bailey. **Description:** The misconceptions about the U.S. Small Business Administration regarding grants and loans are discussed.

40666 ■ **"SBA Hearing Scheduled"** in *Journal Record (Oklahoma City, OK)* **(February 5, 2007)**
Pub: Journal Record

Description: Small business owners, community organization and trade association representatives, and community and business leaders will attend the U.S. Small Business Administration's Federal Regulatory Fairness Hearing to be held February 23, 2007 in the Oklahoma State Capital building.

40667 ■ **"SBA adjusts revenue standards for inflation"** in *Boston Business Journal* **(Vol. 22, No. 3, February 22, 2002, pp. 22)**
Pub: MCP, Inc.
Description: The Small Business Administration adjusted revenue standards for inflation.

40668 ■ **"SBA info"** in *Crain's Detroit Business* **(Vol. 18, No. 49, December 9, 2002, pp. 16)**
Pub: Crain Communications Inc., Detroit
Description: Profile of important information for small businesses regarding the Small Business Administration. Contact information included.

40669 ■ **"SBA Moves to Protect Small Firms from Bundling"** in *Hispanic Business* **(Vol. 22, No. 1/2, January/February, pp. 84)**
Pub: Hispanic Business
Description: The Small Business Administration (SBA) regulations limiting bundling of federal procurement contracts are explained. Bundling is considered detrimental to small businesses.

40670 ■ **"SBA Offers Free E-Commerce CD"** in *Home Office Computing* **(Vol. 19, No. 1, January 2001, pp. 22)**
Pub: Scholastic Inc.
Ed: Lee Wertheimer. **Description:** The Small Business Administration (SBA) has teamed with a pair of small business Web sites to distribute a free CD-ROM with tools for creating an e-commerce site, plus advice on how to use it to make money. A profile of the disc, Build Your Own Business Web Site for Free, is included.

40671 ■ **"SBA Program Falls Short on Helping Firms Win Jobs"** in *Wall Street Journal* **(August 1, 2000, pp. B2)**
Pub: Dow Jones & Co., Inc.
Ed: Eleena De Lisser. **Description:** According to a report published by the General Accounting Office, the Small Business Administration (SBA) has not helped small business procure government contracts.

40672 ■ **"SBA Suspends VC Program, Future in Doubt"** in *Venture Capital Journal* **(January 1, 2005)**
Pub: Thomason Financial Inc.
Description: Faced with nearly $2 billion in losses, the Small Business Administration's Small Business Investment Companies (SBIC) program will stop licensing new SBIC firms until October 1, 2005. The program provides about one-fifth of U.S. venture funds.

40673 ■ **"SBA's future up to whoever controls Congress"** in *Atlanta Business Chronicle* **(Vol. 25, No. 20, October 25, 2002, pp. 4A)**
Pub: American City Business Publications, Inc.
Ed: Kent Hoover. **Description:** The winner of control of Congress in 2003 will play a pivotal role in mapping out the future of the Small Business Administration. The majority of the SBA's programs are set for reauthorization in 2003.

40674 ■ **"SBC, Other Providers Spar on Phone Rules"** in *Crain's Detroit Business* **(Vol. 21, October 3, 2005, No. 43, pp. 6)**
Pub: Crain Communications Inc. - Detroit
Ed: Amy Lane. **Description:** Competitive land-line systems in Michigan are important for small businesses. The Michigan Alliance for Competitive Telecommunications wants to see provisions that ensure competition at the basic calling level.

40675 ■ **"SBS Suit Thrown Out"** in *Hispanic Business* **(March 2003, pp. 18)**
Pub: Hispanic Business
Description: The antitrust lawsuit filed by Spanish Broadcasting System against Clear Channel Communications and Hispanic Broadcasting Corporation has been dismissed from federal court.

40676 ■ **"Scorecard & Blueprint"** in *Hispanic Business* **(Vol. 24, No. 5, May 2002, pp. 48)**
Pub: Hispanic Business Inc.
Ed: Joel Russell. **Description:** The 2003 Federal budget rates agencies on five different management criteria. Under the plan, nearly one-quarter of all federal workers will have their jobs outsourced.

40677 ■ **"SEC Comes Down Hard On Unregistered Stock Giveaways"** in *Venture Capital Journal* **(Vol. 40, No. 10, November 2000, pp. 5)**
Pub: Venture Economics
Description: In recent months the Securities Exchange Commission has begun cracking down on Web site operators caught giving away free shares of unregistered stock to online visitors.

40678 ■ **"SEC Offers Small Banks Internal Controls Leeway"** in *American Banker* **(Vol. 171, December 14, 2006, No. 239, pp. 3)**
Pub: SourceMedia, Inc.
Ed: Ben Jackson. **Description:** American Bankers Association is supporting the Securities and Exchanges Commission's move to give small companies, including most community banks, more flexibility within the Sarbanes-Oxley Act of 2002. The proposal would ease the compliance burden for small banks.

40679 ■ **"Second Chance"** in *Entrepreneur* **(Vol. 33, September 2005, No. 9, pp. 58)**
Pub: Entrepreneur Media Inc.
Ed: Joan Szabo. **Description:** The Streamlined Sales Tax Project (SSTP), if passed, would simplify and modernize sales and use tax collection and administration. An outline of the program is included.

40680 ■ **"Security Steps into the Spotlight"** in *InfoWorld* **(Vol. 23, No. 5, January 29, 2001, pp. 64)**
Pub: InfoWorld
Ed: P.J. Connolly. **Description:** Security issues became more and more crucial in the year 2000 as nearly every week brought news of another security lapse or breach at a major company. Firms that have lost sensitive, business-critical data to hackers find hope in several key improvements, although no technology can completely eradicate security problems. Digital certificates, which received federal legal authority in June 2000, will be important in future E-commerce initiatives.

40681 ■ **"Seeing the Light"** in *Entrepreneur* **(Vol. 33, September 2005, No. 9, pp. 92)**
Pub: Entrepreneur Media Inc.
Ed: Chris Penttila. **Description:** It is predicted that a move to extend daylight savings time would be an economic boom to small businesses. Consumers would spend the extra daylight time shopping, dining at restaurants, working out at fitness centers, etc.

40682 ■ **"Seeing Red Over Big Blue's China Deal"** in *Business Week* **(February 14, 2005, No. 3920, pp. 45)**
Pub: McGraw-Hill Companies
Ed: Stan Crock, Richard S. Dunham. **Description:** U.S. Homeland Security Department and the FBI are concerned over the sale of IBM's PC business that could help China's military. Issues involved include the possible transfer of encryption technology and the higher-end IBM operations in Research Triangle Park, North Carolina, which could make industrial espionage easier. China has an estimated $400 billion in dollar reserves, which could start a strategic buying spree by China.

40683 ■ **"Selling to Audit Committees"** in *Journal of Accountancy*
Pub: American Institute of Certified Public Accountants
Ed: Gale Crosley. **Description:** Suggestions to help certified public accounting firms approach and obtain committee boards in each of the three target markets for auditing services: publicly held companies, large private and public-interest entities, and smaller private and public-interest entities.

40684 ■ "Senate Debates Bill That Shields Gunmakers From Some Lawsuits" in *Portland Press Herald* **(July 27, 2005)**
Pub: Blethen Maine Newspapers, Inc.
Ed: Bart Jansen. Description: Debate over lawsuits filed by customers against gun manufacturers over misuse of weapons is covered.

40685 ■ "Senate votes to ease effect of high SBT bills" in *Crain's Detroit Business* **(Vol. 18, No. 49, December 9, 2002, pp. 6)**
Pub: Crain Communications Inc., Detroit
Ed: Amy Lane. Description: Information about the new single-business tax and certificate-of-need legislation is presented

40686 ■ "Senate Targets Payroll Tax Scam" in *Inc.* **(August 1, 2004)**
Pub: Inc. Magazine
Ed: Nadine Heintz. Description: Roger Cyr, owner of Lily Moon Cafe in Saco, Maine alleges that his payroll tax accountant stole tax payments from dozens of companies, including his own.

40687 ■ "Senator Urges 'Measurable Standard' for Awarding Farm Subsidies" in *Chicago Tribune* **(February 16, 2005)**
Pub: Knight-Ridder/Tribune Business News
Ed: Andrew Martin. Description: Although an individual must be actively engaged in a farm in order to received federal farm subsidies, the U.S. Department of Agriculture has paid out millions of dollars to dead farmers and wealthy businessmen who did nothing more than participate in conference calls.

40688 ■ "Sensing the System Is Being Abused, Congress Passed a Bill in March to Help Creditors Recover More Debt From Businesses That Have Filed Bankruptcy" i
Pub: Inc. Magazine
Ed: Mike Hoffman. Description: Congress passed a bill in March 2005 that will help creditors recover more debt from businesses filing bankruptcy.

40689 ■ "Service with a smile" in *Entrepreneur* **(Vol. 30, No. 2, February 2002, pp. 66)**
Pub: Entrepreneur Media Inc.
Ed: Steven C. Bahls, Jane Easter Bahls. Description: The legal aspects for managing employees who are signed up with the armed forces reserves are discussed.

40690 ■ "Shell Shock?" in *Entrepreneur* **(Vol. 32, December 2004, No. 12, pp. 15)**
Pub: Entrepreneur Media Inc.
Ed: David Worrell. Description: Lawmakers and regulators are working to implement tougher rules for public companies, which will impact future initial public offerings and mergers.

40691 ■ "Side Lines" in *Forbes* **(Vol. 170, No. 3, August 12, 2002, pp. 22)**
Pub: Forbes Magazine
Ed: William Baldwin. Description: The consequences of government regulations are examined, including the ways new regulations can have unintended consequences.

40692 ■ "Sides Vie to Regulate Internet-Based Service; Michigan Wants to Play Role" in *Crain's Detroit Business* **(Vol. 21, January 24, 2005)**
Pub: Crain Communications Inc. - Detroit
Ed: Amy Lane. Description: States across the nation, including Michigan, believe they should play a role in the regulation of Internet-based phone service, called Voice over Internet Protocol (VoIP).

40693 ■ "Sign of the Times" in *Entrepreneur* **(Vol. 28, No. 10, October 2000, pp. 29)**
Pub: Entrepreneur Media Inc.
Ed: Amanda C. Kooser. Description: The Electronic Signatures in Global and National Commerce Act passed through Congress in June 2000. Popularly known as the Digital Signatures Bill, or E-SIGN Bill, will allow the use of electronic records and signatures the same legal weight as their paper counterparts.

40694 ■ "Simplify CRA? Not So Fast: Citi, GE Say Keep As Is; JPM Offers Alternative" in *American Banker* **(Vol. 170, Feb. 4, 2005, No. 24)**
Pub: Thomson Financial Media Inc.
Ed: Hannah Bergman. Description: Currently, 50 percent of a large thrift's Community Reinvestment Act's rating is based on its lending record, 25 percent on service and 25 percent on investments. A new proposal would allow large thrifts decide if any of their rating would be based on community service or investments.

40695 ■ "Slick Tricks" in *Entrepreneur* **(Vol. 31, No. 7, July 2003, pp. 73)**
Pub: Entrepreneur Media, Inc.
Ed: Joanne Cleaver. Description: Telecommunications scams continue with newer attacks of hijacked phone accounts (slamming), unauthorized add-on charges (cramming). It is important for small business owners to warn employees of such scams to avoid problems.

40696 ■ "Small-Biz Leaders Mixed on Retirement Proposal" in *Crain's Detroit Business* **(Vol. 22, January 30, 2006, No. 5, pp. 6)**
Pub: Crain Communications Inc. - Detroit
Ed: Amy Lane. Description: Michigan's Governor Jennifer Granholm seeks to create a new retirement-savings program for small business employee working for firms not offering pension coverage. Details of the plan are included.

40697 ■ *Small Business Access to Health Care: Congressional Hearing*
Pub: DIANE Publishing Company
Ed: Donald A. Manzullo. Released: August 2004. Price: $25.00. Description: Congressional hearing held at Crystal Lake, Illinois. Witnesses: Mary Blankenbaker, Co-Owner, Benjamin's Restaurant; Ryan Brauns, Senior Vice President, Rockford Consulting and Brokerage; Scott Shalek, RHU, Shalek Financial Services; Brad Close, National Federation of Independent Businesses; Ken Koehler, Flowerwood, Inc.; Brad Buxton, Vice President of Networks and Medical Management, Blue Cross and Blue Shield of Illinois; Isabella Wilson, Chief Financial Office, Illinois Blower, Inc.; and James Milam, Illinois State Medical Society.

40698 ■ *Small Business Handbook: Laws, Regulations & Technical Assistance Services - U.S. Department of Labor*
Pub: DIANE Publishing Co.
Ed: Mario DiStasio. Released: 1994. Price: $25.00 (paper).

40699 ■ "Small Business Owners Want Tax Cuts, Less Regulation" in *St. Louis Business Journal* **(Vol. 20, No. 40, June 12, 2000, pp. 23)**
Pub: American City Business Journals, Inc.
Ed: Kent Hoover. Description: Small business owners surveyed by the National Federation of Independent Business list lower taxes as the main issue they want their state and federal elected officials to address.

40700 ■ "Small Business Protests Loan Program Shift" in *Long Island Business News* **(March 12, 2004)**
Pub: Dolan Media Newswires
Ed: Adina Genn. Description: The U.S. Small Business Administration did not request funding for the Centereach-based Community Development Corporation of Long Island for 2005. Advocates of microloans say the cut in funding would hurt small businesses and slow job creation.

40701 ■ "Small Businesses Driving for 'Fast Track' on Trade" in *Atlanta Business Chronicle* **(Vol. 24, No. 9, August 3, 2001, pp. 11B)**
Pub: American City Business Journals Inc.
Ed: Kent Hoover. Description: Small businesses in the U.S. want Congress to grant President Bush trade promotion authority, which is the ability to negotiate trade agreements with countries outside of the U.S. These agreements would be brought back to Congress for a vote of 'yes' or 'no', with no amendments.

40702 ■ "Small Firms, Consumers Have PWBA Health Care Benefit Tools" in *Employee Benefit Plan Review* **(Vol. 55, No. 8, February 2001, pp. 40)**
Pub: Charles D. Spencer & Associates, Inc.
Description: A discussion regarding online and paper publications of the Pension and Welfare Benefits Administration of the Department of Labor. These tools for helping individuals and small businesses in making decisions about health care benefits have resulted from the Health Benefits Education Campaign.

40703 ■ "Small-Group Reform, Blue Changes on Hold" in *Crain's Detroit Business* **(Vol. 18, No. 50, December 16, 2002, pp. 6)**
Pub: Crain Communications Inc., Detroit
Ed: Amy Lane. Description: Small-group insurance reform and Michigan's item-pricing law, and how businesses must deal with unclaimed property, as well as the single-business-tax credit for redeveloping blighted or contaminated property are examined.

40704 ■ "Small-group insurance reforms are in works" in *Crain's Detroit Business* **(Vol. 19, No. 16, April 21, 2003, pp. 7)**
Pub: Crain Communications Inc., Detroit
Ed: Amy Lane. Description: Blue Cross Blue Shield of Michigan is seeking the 75 percent rule, whereby carriers have the option of denying coverage to employers who don't enroll 75 percent of their employees with the insurer.

40705 ■ "The Social Security Conundrum" in *Hispanic Business* **(Vol. 23, No. 10, October, 2001, pp. 36, 38)**
Pub: Hispanic Business
Ed: Patricia Guadalupe. Description: As debate over proposals to privatize portions of Social Security, one thing is beyond dispute, the status quo is not an option. Social Security rates of return for average-income Hispanic Americans are discussed. Statistical data included.

40706 ■ "Some prison program deals not using inmates" in *Atlanta Business Chronicle* **(Vol. 25, No. 21, November 1, 2002, pp. 11B)**
Pub: American City Business Publications, Inc.
Ed: Kent Hoover. Description: Michigan Republican Representative Peter Hoekstra offered a bill whereby prison inmate labor projects would have to compete with businesses concerning contract bids. Federal Prison Industries, which employs 22,560 inmates, generated sales of $583 million in 2001, versus $546 in 2000.

40707 ■ "Sonoma County, Calif., Voters Set to Decide Whether to Ban Biotech Crops" in *Sacramento Bee* **(November 2, 2005)**
Pub: The Sacramento Bee
Ed: Jim Wasserman. Description: Sonoma County voters will decide whether to ban biotech crops. If passed, the county will be included among Mendocino, Marin and Trinity counties banning these crops that are used to repel insects and chemical weed killers. In 2004 growers in the county produced $526 million from wine grapes, dairy cows and poultry.

40708 ■ "South Florida Braces From New Overtime Law" in *South Florida Business Journal* **(Vol. 23, No. 47, June 27, 2003, pp. 1)**
Pub: American City Business Journals
Ed: John T. Fakler. Description: New federal laws effecting the rates of payment to employees working overtime are examined.

40709 ■ "Spam Could Be a Scam: Internet Tricks Are Becoming High Crimes" in *Black Enterprise* **(Vol. 35, August 2004, No. 1, pp. 30)**
Pub: Earl G. Graves Publishing Co. Inc.
Ed: Siobhan Benet. Description: Internet crime, also called cybercrime, is the third priority after counterterrorism and counterintelligence for the Federal Bureau of Investigation.

40710 ■ "Spam Law Proposed in State House of Representatives" in *Journal Record* **(February 4, 2004)**
Pub: Dolan Media Company
Description: Oklahoma House Bill 2215 would require any unsolicited commercial email to include an automatic return mechanism enabling the recipient to send a reply without having to retype the sender's email address.

40711 ■ "Spam Uncanned: Why the Recent Anti-Spam Legislation Isn't Protecting You" in *Entrepreneur* **(Vol. 32, July 2004, No. 7, pp. 72)**
Pub: Entrepreneur Media Inc.
Ed: Catherine Seda. **Description:** Can-Spam, the new legislation designed to protect Internet email users, does not prevent spam, it only attempts to regulate the way it is sent. Steps to help protect privacy while using a computer online are shared.

40712 ■ "Spitzer's Stand" in *Entrepreneur* **(Vol. 33, September 2005, No. 9, pp. 64)**
Pub: Entrepreneur Media Inc.
Ed: Jacquelyn Lynn. **Description:** Eliot Spitzer, New York state attorney general, recommends employers in all states to scrutinize 401(k) plan providers to ensure employees are not being overcharged for benefits, otherwise they may face legal action.

40713 ■ "Sports Authority Faces Fourth Down" in *Houston Business Journal* **(Vol. 34, No. 19, September 19, 2003, pp. 1A)**
Pub: American City Business Journals
Ed: Jennifer Dawson. **Description:** Oliver Luck, CEO of the Harris County-Houston Sports Authority, has developed three major sports venues, but the future of the Harris County-Houston Sports Authority is being debated by local and state officials.

40714 ■ "Spot-condemnation law better for neighborhoods, leaders say" in *Crain's Detroit Business* **(Vol. 18, No. 21, May 27, 2002, pp. 40)**
Pub: Crain Communications Inc. - Detroit
Ed: Robert Ankeny. **Description:** A new anti-blight law aimed at redeveloping deteriorating property will probably be more useful in Detroit's neighborhoods than downtown, according to many city and business leaders.

40715 ■ "Squeezed out? Is there any room left for small businesses in federal contracting?" in *Entrepreneur* **(Vol. 31, No. 4, April 2003)**
Pub: Entrepreneur Media Inc.
Ed: Chris Penttila. **Description:** In 2001, contract bundling cost small businesses an estimated $13 billion. Technology, engineering and outsourcing companies are expected to benefit from new Homeland Security projects, but the question is, will that include small companies.

40716 ■ "Stamp It Out: A New Proposal Aims to Bring Spam Under Control" in *Entrepreneur* **(Vol. 32, July 2004, No. 7, pp. 28)**
Pub: Entrepreneur Media Inc.
Ed: Amanda C. Kooser. **Description:** Two proposals to help eliminated unwanted spam email are being considered. E-postage is an idea to attach a virtual stamp to email in order to reduce unwanted bulk email. Hashcash would require a sender's computer to solve a computational problem as proof of good faith. Good legislation will be required to alleviate the problem of spam.

40717 ■ "State Begins Hitting Biz for 'SUTA Dumping'" in *Crain's Detroit Business* **(Vol. 21, February 7, 2005, No. 6, pp. 1)**
Pub: Crain Communications Inc. - Detroit
Ed: Amy Lane. **Description:** According to the state of Michigan, employers try to lower their unemployment insurance tax rate by shifting payrolls to a new corporation or buying a firm with a lower tax rate, costing the state about $100 million in cumulative tax losses.

40718 ■ "State Budget Panel's Report Due this Week" in *Crain's Detroit Business* **(Vol. 23, January 29, 2007, No. 5, pp. 6)**
Pub: Crain Communications Inc. - Detroit
Ed: Amy Lane. **Description:** Advisory panel to issue recommendations to Governor for a way forward plan to address the chronic budget shortfalls and gloomy outlook; two ex-Michigan governors lead the panel.

40719 ■ "State Coughs as Firms Seek Millions" in *Atlanta Business Chronicle* **(Vol. 25, December 13, 2002, No. 27, pp. A3)**
Pub: American City Business Publications, Inc.
Ed: Sara Rubenstein. **Description:** A group of some 130 Atlanta, Georgia area companies are suing the Georgia Environmental Protection Division and Department of Revenue in January 2003, seeking payment of over $9 million in fees for auto emissions tests that were allegedly collected illegally. The state contends that refunds would lead to cuts in the emissions inspection program, which is designed to help the metropolitan Atlanta region meet federal air quality standards. Georgia's Supreme Court ruled in 2001 that the fees were collected illegally.

40720 ■ "State, local bodies work to police e-waste" in *Waste News* **(Vol. 8, No. 10, September 16, 2002, pp. 11)**
Pub: Crain Communications, Inc.
Ed: Joe Truini. **Description:** State and local legislators are taking steps to regulate produce stewardship for scrap electronics, proposing measures such as banning electronic devices from landfills and incinerators, and to also hold the electronics industry accountable for its products.

40721 ■ "State Franchise Laws and the Small Business Franchise Act of 1999" in (Vol. 55, No. 4, August 2000, pp. 1699)
Pub: American Bar Association
Ed: Thomas J. Collin. **Description:** Unless a business sells to customers directly or through factory branches, they will need to take a close account of state franchise laws as they make decisions about distribution changes, and they may find that these laws raise significant barriers to change.

40722 ■ "State Investigates 'Tribal Coverage" in *San Francisco Business Times* **(Vol. 18, No. 6, September 19, 2003, pp. 1)**
Pub: American City Business Journals
Ed: Daniel S. Levine. **Description:** Native Americans are being hired and leased back to avoid workers compensation costs to employers, which may be against California law.

40723 ■ "State Joins War on Use of Trans Fats" in *Crain's Detroit Business* **(Vol. 23, January 29, 2007, No. 5, pp. 1)**
Pub: Crain Communications Inc. - Detroit
Ed: Amy Lane. **Description:** Michigan joins 16 other states in requiring restaurants to inform public on the use of trans fats and could lead to a ban on their use. Trans fats increase the risk of heart disease by raising cholesterol.

40724 ■ "State Manufacturers Ready to Raise Voices" in *Crain's Detroit Business* **(Vol. 19, No. 49, December 8, 2003, pp. 1)**
Pub: Crain Communications Inc., Detroit
Ed: Michael Strong. **Description:** More worker training and streamlined regulatory procedures are among the issues small and mid-sized manufacturers want, according to a survey of more than 1,000 manufacturers in the State of Michigan.

40725 ■ "State OKs Minimum Wage Boost" in *Atlanta Journal-Constitution* **(February 2, 2007)**
Pub: Cox Newspapers, Inc.
Ed: Marilyn Geewax. **Description:** Senate voted in favor of raising the minimum wage from $5.15 to $7.25 an hour over two years, but the deal is not completed. Complex negotiations will take place between the House and Senate.

40726 ■ "State Senate Passes Bill To Cut $1B from SBT" in *Crain's Detroit Business* **(Vol. 21, October 31, 2005, No. 44, pp. 28)**
Pub: Crain Communications Inc. - Detroit
Ed: Amy Lane. **Description:** A new plan to cut Michigan's single-business tax by $1 billion over six years would start by instituting a $100 million single-business tax cut in 2006.

40727 ■ "State Tells Poker Rooms to Fold 'Em" in *Tampa Tribune* **(November 11, 2005)**
Pub: Media General, Inc.
Ed: Steven Isbitts. **Description:** Florida officials have shut down poker tournaments because they determined the games pose a threat to public health, safety and welfare of its citizens.

40728 ■ "State Turns Up Heat on Green" in *Crain's Detroit Business* **(Vol. 22, November 20, 2006, No. 47, pp. 11)**
Pub: Crain Communications Inc. - Detroit
Ed: Amy Lane. **Description:** Governor Granholm has issued a directive that requires that all new construction and renovation for not only state agencies, but also that universities and colleges achieve the standards for green LEED (Leadership in Energy and Environmental Design) certification. It is hoped that this will spread into the private sector also.

40729 ■ "State, Utilities to Debate How to Meet Power Needs" in *Crain's Detroit Business* **(Vol. 22, November 27, 2006, No. 48, pp. 14)**
Pub: Crain Communications Inc. - Detroit
Ed: Amy Lane. **Description:** Michigan Public Service Commission will chair discussions with state power companies on meeting the energy needs for 2007. New policies are on the agenda from building new power plants to purchasing required amounts of energy from renewable sources.

40730 ■ "States Target Outsourcing" in *Inc.* **(July 1, 2004)**
Pub: Inc. Magazine
Ed: Darren Dahl. **Description:** Several states hope legislation efforts will help curb the trend toward outsourcing to companies overseas.

40731 ■ "Status Woe: Contractors' Illegal Workers Could Put You in a Legal Pickle" in *Entrepreneur* **(Vol. 32, No. 4, April 2004, pp. 23)**
Pub: Entrepreneur Media, Inc.
Ed: Chris Penttila. **Description:** Small businesses can face lawsuits and fines up to $10,000 per illegal alien employee for every day worked on-site. It is important for small firms, when outsourcing, to review contracts with vendors supplying contract workers.

40732 ■ "Staying Out of Court" in *Business Week* **(No. 3702, October 9, 2000, pp. F16)**
Pub: McGraw-Hill, Inc.
Description: Alternatives to a courtroom battle are covered, including mediation, where a neutral party helps negotiate a settlement, and arbitration, where the neutral's decision is binding.

40733 ■ "Stepping On It: Will New Measures Really Rev Up U.S. Manufacturers' Engines?" in *Entrepreneur* **(Vol. 32, July 2004, No. 7, pp. 35)**
Pub: Entrepreneur Media Inc.
Ed: Stephen Barlas. **Description:** Under Executive Order by President Bush, federal agencies are to emphasize manufacturing in the Small Business Innovation Research (SBIR) and Small Business Technology Transfer (STTR) programs.

40734 ■ "Stimulus plan offers some firms tax windfall" in *Wall Street Journal* **(April 9, 2002, pp. B6)**
Pub: Wall Street Journal
Ed: Jeff Bailey. **Description:** An overview of the Job Creation and Worker Assistance Act of 2002.

40735 ■ "Stock answers: Workers need 401(K) advice? Too bad! You can't give it!" in *Entrepreneur* (Vol. 30, No. 3, March 2002, pp. 28)
Pub: Entrepreneur Media Inc.
Ed: Stephen Barlas. **Description:** An overview of the proposed Retirement Security Advice Act, which is opposed by labor and some Democrats, is presented.

40736 ■ "Straining Under Sarbanes-Oxley" in *Business Journal-Milwaukee* (Vol. 20, No. 48, August 15, 2003, pp. A1)
Pub: American City Business Journals, Inc.
Ed: Michael Muckian. **Description:** Small businesses that are publicly traded may suffer under the new Sarbanes-Oxley Act of 2002. The new law was passed in an effort to protect public shareholders from corporate scandals.

40737 ■ "Stressed Out" in *PC Computing* (April 2000, pp. 44)
Pub: Ziff-Davis Inc.
Ed: Jennifer Powell. **Description:** The seriousness of musculoskeletal disorders and their impact is covered. Musculoskeletal disorders (MSDs), also known as repetitive strain injuries (RSIs), can begin whenever a part of the body is used in the same way repeatedly, especially when twisting or lifting.

40738 ■ "Striving for 'Critical Mass'" in *Hispanic Business* (Vol. 23, No. 10, October, 2001, pp. 16)
Pub: Hispanic Business
Ed: Rick Laezman. **Description:** The LaRaza Lawyers Association of California is working to strengthen Hispanic legal influence. Despite the fact that Hispanics account for more than 30 percent of California's population, only 4 percent are attorneys.

40739 ■ "Stuck in a Storm of Controversy" in *Fortune* (Vol. 152, October 17, 2005, No. 8, pp. 41)
Pub: Time Inc.
Ed: Nicholas Varchaver. **Description:** An overview of the Shaw Group's contracts for reconstruction work in areas affected by Hurricane Katrina is presented.

40740 ■ *Studies of Entrepreneurship, Business and Government in Hong Kong: The Economic Development of a Small Open Economy*
Pub: Edwin Mellen Press
Ed: Fu-Lai Tony Yu. **Released:** November 2006. **Price:** $109.95. **Description:** Institutional and Austrian theories are used to analyze the transformation taking place in Hong Kong's economy.

40741 ■ "Suit May Force SBC Refunds" in *Atlanta Journal-Constitution* (February 17, 2004)
Pub: Knight-Ridder/Tribune Business News
Ed: Purva Patel. **Description:** SBC business customers have filed a class-action suit against the phone company for overcharging them.

40742 ■ "Suits Mount Against Salons" in *San Jose Mercury News* (March 5, 2005)
Pub: Knight-Ridder/Tribune Business News
Ed: Esther Landhuis. **Description:** Santa Clara County is investigating reported infections caused from pedicures. There have been at least 20 lawsuits filed by customers from the Nails National. The spa is cited for negligence in sanitation procedures that have cultivated the disease-causing mycobacteria at the foot spas.

40743 ■ "Summerford, Dixon Odom Cite Sarbanes in Breakup" in *Birmingham Business Journal* (Vol. 20, No. 31, August 1, 2003, pp. 1)
Pub: American City Business Journals, Inc.
Ed: Leslie Zganjar. **Description:** A forensic accountant unit of Dixon Odom has declared independence from its parent firm. Ralph Summerford, the top executive at the new accounting company, attributed the breakup of the company to the new Sarbanes-Oxley Act.

40744 ■ "Support for Rapid-Growth Firms" in *Journal of Small Business Management* (Vol. 41, No. 4, October 2003, pp. 346)
Pub: International Council of Small Business
Ed: Eileen Fischer, A. Rebecca Reuber. **Description:** Perspectives of small business owners, government policymakers, and external resource providers on ways rapid-growth firms should be supported.

40745 ■ "Supreme Court Rules Regal Entertainment's Style is Unfair to Disabled Customers" in *Miami Herald* (June 29, 2004)
Pub: Knight-Ridder/Tribune Business News
Ed: Gillian Wee. **Description:** U.S. Supreme Court has ruled Regal Entertainment Group's theaters discriminate against disabled customers. The stadium-style seating in the theater requires handicapped guests to sit in seats located at the front of the show, and they claim these seats are uncomfortable.

40746 ■ "...Survey Shows Employees Using Work Computers for Romantic/Sexual Activity" in *Long Island Business News* (Feb. 27, 2004)
Pub: Dolan Media Newswires
Ed: Rosamaria Mancini. **Description:** Statistics involving computer use for personal activity in the workplace are presented, with nearly 25 percent of Americans saying they or their coworkers use office computers to participate in sexually explicit online activity.

40747 ■ "Symbolism with a Bottom Line" in *Hispanic Business* (Vol. 23, No. 7/8, July/August 2001, pp. 16)
Pub: Hispanic Business
Ed: Leigh Miller. **Description:** In April 2001, Georgia Governor Roy Barnes signed a state law designating Hispanics as an official minority group. Hispanic businesses will now qualify as minority-owned firms.

40748 ■ "Synthetic funds draw scrutiny from regulators" in *Crain's Detroit Business* (Vol. 16, No. 46, November 13, 2000, pp. 22)
Pub: Crain Communications, Inc.
Ed: David Hoffman. **Description:** An Ann Arbor, Michigan-based mutual fund Web site has developed a twist on a novel investment that critics claim skirts federal regulations.

40749 ■ "Take a hard look, and do the right thing" in *Crain's Detroit Business* (Vol. 19, No. 5, February 3, 2003, pp. 9)
Pub: Crain Communications Inc., Detroit
Ed: Frank Hennessey. **Description:** The ethical aspects and regulation of business and accounting practices are investigated.

40750 ■ "Take a Peek: What Does Congress Have in Mind for 2005?" in *Entrepreneur* (Vol. 33, January 2005, No. 1, pp. 27)
Pub: Entrepreneur Media Inc.
Ed: Stephen Barlas. **Description:** Agenda set by Congress for 2005, and how it relates to business, is examined.

40751 ■ "Taking a Dive: A Federally Chartered Insurer of Pensions has Fallen on Hard Times. Taxpayers, Beware" in *Barron's* (July 21, 2003)
Pub: Barron's
Ed: Jim McTague. **Description:** The government-run Pension Benefit Guaranty Corporation, which insures more than 30,000 defined-benefit plan payments comprising more than 40 million workers, could be bankrupt in ten years, according to Congress. A bailout would tax citizens in the tens of billions.

40752 ■ "A Tax Act" in *Entrepreneur* (Vol. 31, No. 8, August 2003, pp. 55)
Pub: Entrepreneur Media, Inc.
Ed: Scott Bernard Nelson. **Description:** Latest tax cuts approved by Congress are investigated, citing investors and married couples with children being the winners of the new legislation.

40753 ■ "Tax-Free College Savings" in *My Business* (August/September 2002, pp. 15)
Pub: My Business Magazine
Ed: Phillip L. Pennartz. **Description:** An overview of the 529 Plan that allows individuals to invest in mutual funds for a child's or grandchild's education with tax-free earnings.

40754 ■ "Tax Lien Sales: Money and Politics" in *Atlanta Business Chronicle* (Vol. 25, January 10, 2003, No. 31, pp. 33A)
Pub: American City Business Publications, Inc.
Ed: Arthur E. Ferdinand. **Description:** Last year tax lien sales were a hot political topic, and were a way to raise tax revenue in the past. The politics surrounding tax lien sales in Atlanta, Georgia are discussed in detail.

40755 ■ "Tax Rule Crimps Small Business Deals; Firms Get Creative in Seeking Remedy" in *Wall Street Journal* (January 26, 2000, pp. C1)
Pub: Dow Jones & Co., Inc.
Ed: Karen Hube. **Description:** Innovative ways small businesses are using to avoid taxes when making deals are investigated.

40756 ■ "Tech firms like Granholm's economic plan" in *Crain's Detroit Business* (Vol. 18, No. 22, June 3, 2002, pp. 53)
Pub: Crain Communications Inc. - Detroit
Ed: Andrew Dietderich. **Description:** The Michigan State Attorney General has called for the creation of the Michigan Technology Tri-Corridor, which would expand the state's $40 million Life Sciences Corridor and promote automotive technology and homeland security research and development programs.

40757 ■ "Telecom Rewrite Has New Rules for Wireless" in *Crain's Detroit Business* (Vol. 21, October 17, 2005, No. 43, pp. 7)
Pub: Crain Communications Inc. - Detroit
Ed: Amy Lane. **Description:** A Michigan telecommunications law rewrite was passed by the Senate in October 2005. The law places new regulations on wireless and carriers and required business-call offerings.

40758 ■ "Telecommuter Denied Jobless Benefits" in *Inc.* (October 1, 2003)
Pub: Gruner & Jahr USA Publishing
Ed: Patrick J. Sauer. **Description:** An unemployed Florida telecommuter was denied unemployment benefits from the New York company she worked for.

40759 ■ "Telephony Rising" in *Home Office Computing* (Vol. 18, No. 10, October 2000, pp. 37)
Pub: Scholastic Inc.
Ed: William Van Winkle. **Description:** Internet telephony is a booming industry, though a young technology. Frost & Sullivan predicts that revenues from Voice over IP services will reach over $102 billion in 2005, compared with $1.5 billion in 2000. The primary attraction of Internet telephony is the cost: no cost to PC to PC calls and low cost for PC to phone calls. Voice over IP issues including quality of service, broadband usage, use in e-commerce, availability of voice over IP phones, and government regulations are discussed.

40760 ■ "Terrorism Backup Legislation Raises Many Questions" in *Rough Notes* (Vol. 145, No. 2, February 2003, pp. 34)
Pub: Rough Notes
Ed: Phil Zinkewicz. **Description:** Terrorism insurance, its back up legislation, and obligations of agents and insurance companies in regard to disclosure requirements has turned out to be so complex it raises serious questions on compliance.

40761 ■ "Texas Doctors Take Pains to Follow Privacy Rules" in *Houston Chronicle* (April 11, 2003)
Pub: Knight-Ridder/Tribune Business News
Description: Measures to protect patient's privacy are being taken by doctors at medical facilities in the Houston, Texas area. These rules will comply with the new federal privacy standards.

40762 ■ "That Bites" in *Entrepreneur* (Vol. 33, January 2005, No. 1, pp. 69)
Pub: Entrepreneur Media Inc.
Ed: Joshua Kurlantzick. **Description:** Ninety percent of small companies are not compliant with new COBRA regulations. Employers with more than 20 employees must now give written notice explaining COBRA. Brokers can assist small business owners with COBRA compliance.

40763 ■ "The Supreme Court" in *Business Week* (December 19, 2005, No. 3964, pp. 42)
Pub: McGraw-Hill Companies
Description: Stock holdings of justices can keep corporate cases off the docket.

40764 ■ "There are no magic words to alter tax law" in *Crain's Detroit Business* (Vol. 19, No. 11, March 17, 2003, pp. 9)
Pub: Crain Communications Inc., Detroit
Ed: James Jenkins. **Description:** The double taxation of corporate profits is destructive to the American economy, according to Alan Greenspan, Federal Reserve Chairman, as well as leading academics.

40765 ■ "There's More Than One Way to Bust a Trust" in *Inc.* (Volume 27, December 2005, No. 12, pp. 24)
Pub: Inc. Magazine
Ed: Robert Litan. **Description:** The Federal Government failed to break Microsoft's monopoly; details of Microsoft's case are investigated.

40766 ■ "This Week: McD's Tests Trans-Free Oil in 1,200 Locations" in *Crain's Chicago Business* (Vol. 29, December 2006, No. 50, pp. 1)
Pub: Crain Communications, Inc.
Ed: Julie Jargon. **Description:** Just under ten percent of McDonald's U.S. outlets are performing initial tests with trans fat-free oil in their foods. Pressure is high as rival fast food restaurants have already introduced these trans fat-free foods and New York passed the ban which takes place in July.

40767 ■ "Three Cheers for Bankruptcy" in *Fortune* (Vol. 152, October 17, 2005, No. 8, pp. 33)
Pub: Time Inc.
Ed: Justin Fox, Kate Bonamici. **Description:** New bankruptcy laws taking effect October 17, 2005 will make it harder for individuals and corporations to file Chapter 11.

40768 ■ "Tight-Lipped Banks" in *Entrepreneur* (Vol. 28, No. 7, July 2000, pp. 40)
Pub: Entrepreneur Media Inc.
Ed: Doug Hood and Marilea Hood. **Description:** Information about SBA loans is shared.

40769 ■ "Time to Collect? Tacking Taxes Onto Internet Sales Could Soon Become Mandatory" in *Entrepreneur.com* (Vol. 34, February 2006, No. 2)
Pub: Entrepreneur Media Inc.
Ed: Melissa Campanelli. **Description:** Online retailers can voluntarily add sales taxes to bills originating in the 19 states that have signed onto the Streamlined Sales and Use Tax Agreement, that makes it easier for retailers doing business in multiple states to calculate, collect and remit existing use taxes.

40770 ■ "Time Right To Let Sun Shine On AG, Outside Attorneys" in *Mississippi Business Journal* (Vol. 29, January 2007 , No. 29, pp. 4)
Pub: Venture Publications, Inc.
Ed: Joe D. Jones **Description:** Mississippi Open Lawyer Fees Act has been written and introduced to the Legislature to bring added openness, oversight and accountability to the Attorney General's Office when outside lawyers are hired to work on behalf of the state.

40771 ■ "Time's Up: New Laws Tell You Who Gets Overtime-And Who Doesn't" in *Entrepreneur* (Vol. 32, October 2004, No. 10, pp. 40)
Pub: Entrepreneur Media Inc.
Ed: Chris Penttila. **Description:** New U.S. Department of Labor rules state that employees earning over $100,000 annually in executive, administrative and professional positions are no longer eligible for overtime, workers earning less than $23,660 annually are.

40772 ■ "To be competitive, press 1" in *Crain's Detroit Business* (Vol. 19, No. 7, February 17, 2003, pp. 11)
Pub: Crain Communications Inc., Detroit
Ed: Amy Lane. **Description:** Beginning in February 2003, SBC Communications customers will see lower line charges on their phone bills. State lawmakers are concerned about the legitimacy of common-line charges.

40773 ■ "To Fax or Not to Fax?" in *My Business* (October/November 2003, pp. 11)
Pub: My Business Magazine
Description: Information regarding the new rules for advertising and telemarketing via fax machines is addressed, including information about the do-not-call rules, whereby companies violating the law can be fined up to $2,000 per violation.

40774 ■ "Tollhouses & cookies" in *Entrepreneur* (Vol. 30, No. 2,)
Pub: Entrepreneur Media Inc.
Ed: Amanda C. Kooser. **Description:** The World Wide Web Consortium (W3C), the standards-making body for the Internet, has proposed allowing patent holders to charge fees for technologies that become part of the Web standards.

40775 ■ "Too Sensible to Survive" in *The Economist* (Vol. 377, October 22-28, 2005, No. 8449, pp. 33-34)
Pub: The Economist Newspaper Ltd.
Description: The tax reform panel has some good ideas, but they are not expected to be adopted because revenue-neutral tax reform will create both winners and losers.

40776 ■ "A Tough Row to Hoe" in *Hispanic Business* (October 2002, pp. 26, 28)
Pub: Hispanic Business
Ed: Lou Gallegos. **Description:** An increasing number of Hispanics in the U.S. are taking up farming. Lou Gallegos, a U.S. Department of Agriculture official, discusses current trends and offers policy recommendations to promote Hispanic farming owner and prosperity.

40777 ■ "Tougher Test for Bankruptcy" in *Black Enterprise* (Vol. 36, November 2005, No. 4, pp. 56)
Pub: Earl G. Graves Publishing Co. Inc.
Ed: Melissa S. Monroe. **Description:** The new Bankruptcy Abuse Prevention and Consumer Protection Act of 2005 was made law October 17, 2005. The Act forces many who intended to file for Chapter 7 bankruptcy to file for Chapter 13 bankruptcy instead, and commit to a payment plan.

40778 ■ "Towns, Counties Grow With Interest" in *The Record* (November 5, 2005)
Pub: New Jersey Media Group
Ed: Scott Fallon. **Description:** Consumers are enjoying higher earnings on investments ranging from traditional savings accounts to high-end money market investments with the Federal Reserve's recent hikes in interest rates.

40779 ■ "Trade Policy" in *The Economist* (Vol. 376, July 30-August 5, 2005, No. 8437, pp. 66)
Pub: The Economist Newspaper Ltd.
Description: Details of the Central American Free Trade Agreement (CAFTA), passed July 28, 2005, are presented.

40780 ■ "Trading For Success" in *Business First Buffalo* (Vol. 19, No. 46, August 8, 2003, pp. 17)
Pub: American City Business Journals, Inc.
Ed: Joe Iannarelli. **Description:** Integrated Thermal Solutions, led by president Richard Perez, faces an array of new regulations for pallets and other shipping products. The Buffalo, New York region is a hub for international trade, prompting local companies to seek assistance to boost their operations.

40781 ■ "Trainers of Racing Horses Face New Drug Fine" in *Chicago Tribune* (February 18, 2005)
Pub: Knight-Ridder/Tribune Business News
Ed: Michael Higgins. **Description:** Racing Board officials in Illinois voted to fine trainers whose horses test positive for drugs, but are letting them keep prize money for wins. The board voted to impose a $250 fine for the first offense, $500 for the second, and $1,000 for all subsequent offenses.

40782 ■ "Treasury Officials Discuss Role of the OPR, Circular 230" in *Tax Notes* (Vol. 102, No. 3, January 19, 2004, pp. 320-323)
Pub: Tax Notes International
Ed: Kenneth A. Gary. **Description:** Information is presented about the IRS Office of Professional Responsibility and Circular 230, regarding tax shelters.

40783 ■ "Trouble in Little Cuba" in *Hispanic Business* (Vol. 23, No. 10, October, 2001, pp. 20)
Pub: Hispanic Business
Ed: Scott Williams. **Description:** An overview of the problems facing the Cuban American National Foundation (CANF) under its current leadership. The CANF was formed to oppose the revolutionary government of Cuban dictator Fidel Castro.

40784 ■ "Trustbuster" in *Forbes* (Vol. 175, February 14, 2005, No. 3, pp. 86)
Pub: Forbes Magazine Inc.
Ed: Scott Woolley. **Description:** Tobacco companies are being fined for hiding evidence of the health risks from smoking cigarettes.

40785 ■ "Trying to Play their Cards Right" in *Crain's New York Business* (Vol. 20, No. 12, March 22, 2004, pp. 20)
Pub: Crain Communications, Inc.
Description: Pharmacists can decline participation in the new Medicare discount card program when filling prescriptions for contracts that have unfavorable terms. However, they risk losing customers.

40786 ■ "Tuning In?" in *Entrepreneur* (Vol. 32, No. 4, April 2004, pp. 26)
Pub: Entrepreneur Media, Inc.
Ed: Steve Cooper. **Description:** Legal issues facing the used-digital-music market are discussed. The industry is seeing accelerated sales in 2004.

40787 ■ "Two Identity-Theft Bills Filed In Oklahoma House of Representatives" in *Journal Record* (February 5, 2004)
Pub: Dolan Media Company
Description: Two bills filed in the Oklahoma House of Representatives would tighten state laws against identity theft.

40788 ■ "Udder Irony" in *Forbes* (Vol. 174, December 27, 2004, No. 13, pp. 54)
Pub: Forbes Magazine Inc.
Ed: Bernard Condon. **Description:** The U.S. Department of Justice has launched an investigation into the Dairy Farmers of America (DFA) cooperative. The government is looking into whether the DFA has used processing plants it controls to force farmers into joining the cooperative and to pay below-market prices for milk. The State of Florida has also begun its own investigation.

40789 ■ "Uncle Same Eases Up on Barter" in *Business Week* (March 27, 2000, pp. F6)
Pub: McGraw-Hill, Inc.
Description: The IRS recently ruled that businesses are no longer required report barter transactions worth less than $1, which covers much of the free and low-cost banner-ad swaps popular among small companies.

40790 ■ "Unemployment changes are 'mixed bag' for business, labor" in *Crain's Detroit Business* (Vol. 18, No. 15, 2002, pp. 6)
Pub: Crain Communications Inc. - Detroit
Ed: Amy Lane. **Description:** An explanation of the recent changes to Michigan's unemployment benefits. Statistical data included.

40791 ■ "Unemployment, workers' comp may split again" in *Crain's Detroit Business* (Vol. 19, No. 5, February 3, 2003, pp. 7)
Pub: Crain Communications Inc., Detroit
Ed: Amy Lane. **Description:** In 2002, then Michigan Governor John Engler merged the state's workers' compensation and unemployment programs; in 2003 new Governor Jennifer Granholm is considering splitting them apart again.

40792 ■ "Union's Job is to Protect Due Process, Not Bad Teachers" in *Crain's Chicago Business* (Vol. 29, December 2006, No. 51, pp.)
Pub: Crain Communications, Inc.
Ed: Marilyn Stewart. **Description:** Unions do not want to protect professionals who do not perform well. Overview of union member's rights and the reason they can be an important functional institution for employees.

40793 ■ "Unions shouldn't labor in financial secrecy" in *Crain's Detroit Business* (Vol. 18, No. 16, April 22, 2002, pp. 8)
Pub: Crain Communications Inc. - Detroit
DES It is suggested that unions should be required to make financial disclosure statements.

40794 ■ "U.S. District Court of Appeals Sides with Baby Bells Over 1996 Telecommunications Act" in *Long Island Business News* (March 12, 2004)
Pub: Dolan Media Newswires
Ed: Claude Solnik. **Description:** Small local telecommunications carriers worry about the new court ruling that they feel will undo the Telecommunications Act of 1996. The small firms worry the new ruling will take away ability to lease infrastructure at a wholesale rate from Baby Bells, thus inhibiting them from remaining competitive in the industry.

40795 ■ "U.S. Fails to Deal with Threat of Cyberattack, Experts Says" in *San Jose Mercury News* (February 17, 2005)
Pub: Knight-Ridder/Tribune Business News
Ed: Dan Lee. **Description:** Government experts are predicting a large-scale electronic attack against the nation's computer systems.

40796 ■ "Updates on sugar, peanut reform" in *Candy Industry* (Vol. 167, No. 2, February 2002, pp. 18)
Pub: Stagnito Communications Inc.
Ed: Stephen Lodge. **Description:** New sugar legislation and peanut reform issues being considered for the Senate version of the Farm Bill (S. 1731) are discussed.

40797 ■ "Upping the Minimum Wage: Small Business Bust or Low-Income Boost?" in *Black Enterprise* (Vol. 35, October 2004, No. 3, pp. 60)
Pub: Earl G. Graves Publishing Co. Inc.
Ed: Cliff Hocker. **Description:** Legislation sponsored by Senator Edward M. Kennedy could raise the federal minimum wage from $5.15 per hour to $5.85 within 60 days of the bill's passage. Hikes in the minimum wage could hurt small businesses.

40798 ■ "UPS Drives Changes to Postal Service" in *Atlanta Business Chronicle* (Vol. 26, No. 12, August 29, 2003, pp. 1)
Pub: American City Business Publications, Inc.
Ed: Sarah Rubenstein. **Description:** United Parcel Service Inc. has been active in providing input into a Presidential commission looking into the Postal Services' business practice. UPS is the leader in U.S. delivery of packages.

40799 ■ "U.S." in *Business Week* (February 20, 2006, No. 3972, pp. 29)
Pub: McGraw-Hill Companies
Ed: James C. Cooper. **Description:** The question is asked: When should U.S. lawmakers and investors start to worry about the inflation implications of tight labor markets? Statistical data included.

40800 ■ "US Supreme Court Rules on Punitive Damages in Title VII Discrimination Cases" in *Employment Relations Today* (Vol. 27, No.1, Spring2000)
Pub: John Wiley & Sons, Inc.
Ed: Arthur F. Silbergeld and Tracy L. Turner. **Description:** A study of punitive damages under Title VII of the Civil Rights Act of 1964, focusing on employer liability in the US Supreme Court case of Kolstad v. American Dental Association. Topics addressed include employer liability for discrimination, and the influence of the Kolstad case on the amount of punitive damages awarded.

40801 ■ "USDA Plans to Charge Farm Commodity Groups a Fee for Research" in *Kiplinger Letter* (Vol. 78, January 5, 2007, No. 1)
Pub: Kiplinger
Description: Farm commodity groups can expect to pay fees for research. The Agricultural Department's research services already charges 10 percent for companies and other agencies while farm commodity groups and other nonprofits were exempt.

40802 ■ "Used Car Dealers' Business Held Up by NY Department of Motor Vehicles" in *Long Island Business News* (February 13, 2004)
Pub: Dolan Media Newswires
Ed: Rosmaria Mancini. **Description:** Because of the increase in salvage- and junk-vehicle applications in the New York Department of Motor Vehicles, used car dealers are suffering because this increase has resulted in a 10-week backlog to process applications.

40803 ■ "VCs Buoyed by $3B for Stem Cell Research" in *Venture Capital Journal* (December 1, 2004)
Pub: Thomason Financial Inc.
Description: Proposal 71 in California approves a stem cell research initiative in California, a big win for the venture capital industry.

40804 ■ "Verizon Told to Widen Service" in *The Record* (November 17, 2005)
Pub: New Jersey Media Group
Ed: Martha McKay. **Description:** New Jersey legislation required Verizon to build its new high-speed fiber network in all 526 towns where the company currently offers phone service.

40805 ■ "Viewpoint: Rule on Race, Gender Data Has Outlived Its Intent" in *American Banker* (Vol. 171, December 15, 2006, No. 240, pp. 11)
Pub: SourceMedia, Inc.
Ed: David Lizarraga; Fred Jordan. **Description:** Information regarding the Federaladopted Regulation B is presented. The regulation bars regulated financial institutions from targeting minorities in marketing or advertising campaigns or tracking or recording lending data by race, ethnicity, or gender.

40806 ■ "Voice of America" in *Fortune* (Vol. 151, June 27, 2005, No. 13 pp. F184)
Pub: Time Inc.
Ed: David Whitford. **Description:** The National Federation of Independent Business (NFIB) believes small business directly impacts the economy of the U.S.

40807 ■ "Voters May Rule on Export Tax for Maine's Drinking Water" in *Portland Press Herald* (September 24, 2005)
Pub: Blethen Maine Newspapers, Inc.
Ed: Seth Harkness. **Description:** Voters in Maine are voting on a measure that would tax nearly 20 cents of each gallon of bottled water taken from Maine wells. Supports believe the move is necessary to ensure bottled water companies do not extract too much water from the state's aquifiers.

40808 ■ "Wall Street Rogues: Fast Cars, Women, and Cash. These Financial Whizzes Had It All" in *Black Enterprise* (Vol. 35, August 2004, No. 1)
Pub: Earl G. Graves Publishing Co. Inc.
Ed: Alan Hughes. **Description:** Alan Brian Bond, one time Wall Street all-star, conspired with a broker to inflate client fees from 1993 to 1998. Bonds clients, mostly African Americans, lost nearly $57 million.

40809 ■ "Walz wants to extend NAIOP's reach" in *Atlanta Business Chronicle* (Vol. 25, December 6, 2002, No. 26, pp. 9C)
Pub: American City Business Publications, Inc.
Ed: Tom Barry. **Description:** The Georgia Chapter of the National Association of Industrial and Office Properties has a new president, Gregory J. Walz, who aims to bolster the body's voice in matters of government.

40810 ■ "Wanted: stimulus: report says GOP is not doing all it can for small business" in *Black Enterprise* (Vol. 33, No. 7, Feb. 2003)
Pub: Earl Graves Publishing Co.
Ed: Joyce Jones. **Description:** Federal funding and legislation important to small business is discussed.

40811 ■ "Washington gridlock worries small business groups" in *Wall Street Journal* (November 1, 2000, pp. A1)
Pub: Dow Jones & Co., Inc.
Ed: Tom Herman. **Description:** Groups want repeal of 1999 law that says businesses that sell operations at a profit must pay a lump-sum capital gains tax.

40812 ■ "Washington Insider: Hispanics Crash House Small-Biz Groups" in *Hispanic Business* (March 2003, pp. 12)
Pub: Hispanic Business
Ed: Patricia Guadalupe. **Description:** Profiles of Hispanic government officials and the offering of bonds in Mexico are highlighted.

40813 ■ "Washington Insider: Issues Count More Than Affiliation" in *Hispanic Business* (July/August 2004, pp. 12)
Pub: Hispanic Business
Ed: Patricial Guadalupe. **Description:** Political issues affecting Hispanic business are examined.

40814 ■ "Washington Insider: Small Business Overlooked?" in *Hispanic Business* (March 2003, pp. 16)
Pub: Hispanic Business
Ed: Patricia Guadalupe. **Description:** Initiatives to address the current economic slowdown and its effect on minority entrepreneurs is addressed. Also discussed is the Small Business Administration's Internet site designed to assist small business owners with employees serving in the military reserves.

40815 ■ "Washington State Apple Commission Shuts Down Soon after Ruling on Fees" in *News Tribune* (April 11, 2003)
Pub: Knight-Ridder/Tribune Business News
Ed: C.R. Roberts. **Description:** The Washington State Apple Commission closed its doors after a federal court decided the commission's collection of mandatory fees from growers was unconstitutional. The Commission was in charge of promoting the state's apple industry.

40816 ■ "Watchdog groups say evidence shows Canada continues to export e-waste" in *Solid Waste Report* (Vol. 33, No. 36, November 15, 2002)
Pub: Business Publishers, Inc.
Description: An overview of e-waste recycling in Canada is presented. Some Canadian provinces, such as Manitoba, are looking into progressive systems of end-of-life electronics management, as is the United States with its National Electronic Product Stewardship Initiative.

40817 ■ "We Must Discuss Regional Government" in *Crain's Detroit Business* (Vol. 21, January 10, 2005, No. 2, pp. 8)
Pub: Crain Communications Inc. - Detroit
Ed: Keith Crain. **Description:** The impact of Detroit's dwindling population is discussed. The city's popula-

tion is expected to be below 1 million, while suburbs continue growing at a rapid pace. Regional government must address how this impacts the city's economy.

40818 ■ "We Need Reform To Curb Corporate Scandals, But Don't Get Excessive" in *Venture Capital Journal* **(Vol. 42, No. 8, August 2002, pp. 40)**
Pub: Thomas Venture Economics
Ed: Mark Heesen. **Description:** The Corporate and Auditing Accountability, Responsibility, and Transparency Act, which creates a new oversight body that will certify accountants and have the authority to punch, is profiled.

40819 ■ "A Web Wake-Up; Posting of OU Student's Paper Turns Into Lesson That Helps Define Defamation in a New Medium" in *Crain's Detroit Business*
Pub: Crain Communications Inc. - Detroit
Ed: Andrew Dietderich. **Description:** Posting of student papers on the Internet can be a wake-up call for small businesses. An Oakland University professor posted an essay written by a student that contained statements about the student's former employer, who sued the school, student and professor when it discovered the paper through an Internet search.

40820 ■ "What Comes Next" in *Business Week* **(No. 3658, December 6, 1999, pp. F30)**
Pub: McGraw-Hill, Inc.
Description: According to experts, small businesses will face similar problems over the next decade: low unemployment rates will continue, which means workers will be choosier; increasing health care costs; regulations; and work-family balancing. But the good news is that the trend seems to show these workers will still prefer working for small companies over large ones. Data from the U.S. Department of Labor is included.

40821 ■ "What Eliot Spitzer's Investigations Mean For You" in *Inc.* **(May 1, 2005)**
Pub: Inc. Magazine
Ed: Stephanie Clifford. **Description:** If a 401(k) provider or insurance company overcharges employees, a small business owner may be held liable. It is recommended that employers check fees, commission structures, and overrides with health care providers carefully.

40822 ■ "What Gives?" in *Entrepreneur* **(Vol. 28, No. 9, September 2000, pp. 20)**
Pub: Entrepreneur Media Inc.
Ed: Julie Monahan. **Description:** An audit finds problems with the Small Disadvantaged Business Certification program.

40823 ■ "What a Governance Referee Thinks" in *Journal of Accountancy* **(Vol. 199, February 2005, No. 2, pp. 43)**
Pub: American Institute of Certified Public Accountants
Ed: Michael Hayes. **Description:** Rules for obtaining a certified public accounting firm are changing as the Sarbanes-Oxley Act is implemented. Experts believe the Sarbanes-Oxley Act is requiring accounting firms to do the things they should have been doing all along.

40824 ■ "What the One Hand Giveth" in *Ingram's* **(Vol. 28, No. 9, September 2002, pp. 15)**
Pub: Show Me Publishing, Inc.
Ed: Jack Cashill. **Description:** While being stimulated by local governments, rural economies are being stifled by too many regulations and programs from the federal government, the most oppressive of which is the Hazard Analysis and Critical Control Point, issued by the Food and Drug Administration.

40825 ■ "What about Small Business?" in *Success* **(Vol. 47, No. 1, January 2000, pp. 15)**
Pub: Success Publishing, Inc.
Ed: Michael Caronna. **Description:** U.S. Governors are leery to address and encourage small business. During State of the State speeches, fewer than half said the words "small business" or "entrepreneur" in their addresses. Only a dozen made specific proposals that might encourage entrepreneurial growth.

40826 ■ "What will Wall Street do on a red alert?" in *Wall Street Journal* **(February 27, 2003, pp. C1)**
Pub: Dow Jones & Co. Inc.
Ed: Susanne Craig, Paul Beckett. **Description:** Companies have only vague guidelines from the U.S. government regarding steps to take in the event of the terrorism warning moving to red alert status.

40827 ■ "What Will Remain of PGE" in *Business Journal-Portland* **(Vol. 20, No. 29, September 19, 2003, pp. 1)**
Pub: American City Business Journals, Inc.
Ed: Robert Goldfield. **Description:** Portland General Electric's assets may be sold by financially-troubled Enron Corporation. The breakup of PGE is feared among community activist groups who believe the sale of PGE's assets will allow owners to bypass state energy regulations.

40828 ■ "What's Cookin'?" in *Entrepreneur* **(Vol. 32, December 2004, No. 12, pp. 30)**
Pub: Entrepreneur Media Inc.
Ed: Stephen Barlas. **Description:** The Federal Trade Commission's amendments to its Franchise Rule may ban post-sale encroachment on franchisees, market territory and restrictions on suppliers.

40829 ■ "What's New for 2002 Returns?" in *My Business* **(February/March 2003, pp. 42)**
Pub: My Business Magazine
Ed: Barbara Weltman. **Description:** The changes for filing 2002 small business tax returns are presented.

40830 ■ "What's the Plan? How President Bush's Second-Term Agenda Will Affect You" in *Entrepreneur* **(Vol. 33, January 2005, No. 1, pp. 24)**
Pub: Entrepreneur Media Inc.
Ed: Crystal Detamore-Rodman. **Description:** President Bush is expected to carryover his first term agenda of making his income tax cuts permanent, a permanent repeal of estate tax, and an expansion of health savings accounts.

40831 ■ "What's Your Fiscal Year" in *My Business* **(February/March 2003, pp. 44)**
Pub: My Business Magazine
Ed: John Rubino. **Description:** Advice if given to small business owners for setting up a fiscal year, along with regulations for compliance.

40832 ■ "What's Your Problem?" in *Entrepreneur* **(Vol. 31, No. 9, September 2003, pp. 106)**
Pub: Entrepreneur Media, Inc.
Description: Registering a business name varies from state to state. It is recommended to log onto the state's Web site to find the requirements.

40833 ■ "When Duty Calls" in *Entrepreneur* **(Vol. 28, No. 3, March 2000, pp. 127)**
Pub: Entrepreneur Media Inc.
Ed: Jacquelyn Lynn. **Description:** Know your responsibilities when it comes to employees on military leave.

40834 ■ "When You Speak, Lawmakers Listen" in *My Business* **(June/July 2004, pp. 41)**
Pub: My Business Magazine
Description: Lawmakers are interested in small business. The National Federation of Independent Business (NFIB) advocates for small business through its Member Ballot, the largest opinion-gathering effort of its type. Results are given to lawmakers. Currently issues revolved around employer retirement savings accounts, postal rates, debit cards, project labor agreements, and OSHA regulations.

40835 ■ "When You're no Longer Home Alone" in *Inc.* **(December 1999, pp. 92)**
Pub: The Goldhirsh Group
Description: An overview of the legal issues regarding hiring employees for home-based business.

40836 ■ "Where Small Business Stands: Your Voice Sends A Clear Message to Lawmakers" in *My Business* **(December/January 2003, pp. 47)**
Pub: My Business Magazine
Description: Results of the National Federation of Independent Business (NFIB) Member Ballot are presented. This information is then relayed to government lawmakers to help them understand the issues important to small business in the U.S. Statistical data included on alternative minimum tax, English proficiency, generic drugs, medical malpractice, strict liability and health care tax credits.

40837 ■ "Where There's Smoke...One Entrepreneur Feels the Heat of Anti-Smoking Laws" in *Entrepreneur* **(Vol. 32, No. 2, February 2004, pp. 32)**
Pub: Entrepreneur Media, Inc.
Ed: Geoff Williams. **Description:** Nick Sanders, owner of a restaurant and cigar bar in Ohio and Kentucky. Sanders does not believe it would be right to prohibit smoking in a bar that has been specifically designated a cigar bar, but if the law is upheld, he will follow and enforce it in his bar.

40838 ■ "Who Needs The Aggravation?" in *Forbes* **(Vol. 170, No. 8, October 14, 2002, pp. 56)**
Pub: Forbes Magazine
Ed: Carrie Coolidge. **Description:** With the new tough accounting rules, some small companies are deciding that it is better to not be a publicly traded firm.

40839 ■ "Who's small enough to get SBA aid? Some ceilings are raised" in *Wall Street Journal* **(July 18, 2000, pp. B2)**
Pub: Dow Jones & Co., Inc.
Ed: Jeffrey A. Tannenbaum. **Description:** An update on the new requirements for obtaining SBA loans.

40840 ■ "Who's Working in Our Interest" in *Crain's Detroit Business* **(Vol. 23, January 15, 2007, No. 3, pp. 8)**
Pub: Crain Communications Inc. - Detroit
Ed: Christopher Crain. **Description:** Northwest loses bid for direct flight to Shanghai; $200M business potential lost. Decision may have adverse affect on expansion and growth in the Chinese market for local businesses.

40841 ■ "Whose drug is it, anyway?" in *Washington Business Journal* **(Vol. 21, No. 44, Feb. 28, 2003, pp. 2,6)**
Pub: Washington Business Journal
Ed: Jennifer Taylor. **Description:** Alleged legal loopholes abound keeping generic drug companies from getting their products to market faster. President Bush has proposed new rules that might fix one of those loopholes. Large companies with costly employee benefit plans are getting involved also. Drug companies with blockbuster drugs try to keep patents in effect as long as possible, claiming that research and development costs are astronomical.

40842 ■ "Why Businesses Should Have Judge Dread" in *Inc.* **(Volume 27, June 2005, No. 6, pp. 24)**
Pub: Inc. Magazine
Ed: Allen P. Roberts Jr. **Description:** Because of increasing business-related cases moving from state to federal district courts on issues of interstate commerce, as well as employment law and intellectual property disputes, it is important for federal judge nominees to be scrutinized on business law.

40843 ■ "Why Must China Die?" in *Minority Business Journal* **(Vol. 17, No. 5, September/October 2001, pp. 4)**
Pub: Minority Business Journal
Description: Foreign investment in China and China's hardline business arrangements are discussed.

40844 ■ "Why Small Firms Can't Do Their Part" in *Hispanic Business* **(Vol. 23, No. 11, November 2001, pp. 22)**
Pub: Hispanic Business Inc.

Ed: Patricia Guadalupe. **Description:** As the government begins a buildup, a new report questions how much small business contractors will benefit. Statistics showing contracts to small disadvantaged businesses made by the SBA from 1997 to 2000 are presented.

40845 ■ "Widespread Ignorance of Regulation and Labeling of Vitamins, Minerals and Food Supplements" in *PR Newswire* **(December 23, 2002)**
Pub: PR Newswire Association, Inc.
Description: According to a National Harris Interactive Survey, large majorities of the public are very skeptical of anti-aging medicine, but do believe that a healthy lifestyle and good nutrition can help slow the aging process. The survey was based on 1,010 telephone interviews with a national cross-section of adults. Statistical data included.

40846 ■ "Will Congress Act to Preserve Family Type Farming?" in *U.S. Farm News* **(Vol. 25, No. 3, Autumn 2001, pp. 6-7)**
Pub: U.S. Farmers Association
Ed: Lem Harris. **Description:** An overview of the new Farm Act being written by Congress is presented.

40847 ■ "Will E-Commerce Erode Liberty?" in *Harvard Business Review* **(Vol. 78, No. 3, May 2000, pp. 189)**
Pub: Harvard Business School Publishing Corp.
Ed: Carl Shapiro. **Description:** Electronic commerce regulations should be established to ensure that individuals retain their privacy and companies obey their privacy policies.

40848 ■ "Wine Battle May Be Aging Toward Compromise" in *Crain's Detroit Business* **(Vol. 21, October 10, 2005, No. 43, pp. 42)**
Pub: Crain Communications Inc. - Detroit
Ed: Amy Lane. **Description:** Progress is being made in an attempt to settle a House-passed bill that would allow limited wine shipments by Michigan and out-of-state wineries to individual Michigan consumers, but bans shipping directly to retailers and restaurants.

40849 ■ "Winemakers Toast High Court Ruling" in *Inc.* **(Volume 27, July 2005, No. 7, pp. 23)**
Pub: Inc. Magazine
Ed: John Anderson. **Description:** U.S. Supreme Court ruling, effective May 16, 2005, will allow the direct sale of wine across the nation. The new ruling is expected to impact sales via the Internet.

40850 ■ "Witness protection" in *Entrepreneur* **(Vol. 31, No. 4, April 2003, pp. 78)**
Pub: Entrepreneur Media Inc.
Ed: Steven C. Bahls, Jane Easter Bahls. **Description:** Profile of the Sarbanes-Oxley Act of 2002, which protects whistle-blowers reporting corporate wrong doing is presented, along with its impact on business.

40851 ■ "Women" in *Entrepreneur* **(Vol. 27, No. 12, December 1999, pp. 44)**
Pub: Entrepreneur Media Inc.
Ed: Cynthia E. Griffin. **Description:** A new study underscores the old adage that the most important thing in business is location, location, location. In the top 50 U.S. metropolitan areas, the number of women-owned firms has increased 33 to 59 percent in the past seven years, according to a 1999 report by the National Foundation for Women Business Owners (NFWBO).

40852 ■ "The Women's Business Centers: the help women business owners need?" in *WorkingWoman* **(Vol. 25, No. 2, February 2000, pp. S32)**
Pub: Lang Communications Inc.
Ed: Joanne Symons. **Description:** Questions regarding the Women's Business Centers Bill are answered.

40853 ■ "Workers' Comp Claims Filed Have Decreased in Okla., Statistics Show" in *Journal Record (Oklahoma City, OK)* **(February 8, 2007)**
Pub: Journal Record
Ed: Marie Price. **Description:** Workers' compensation reform has reduced the number of claims filed in Oklahoma. Statistical data included.

40854 ■ "Workers' Con" in *Forbes* **(Vol. 175, February 28, 2005, No. 4, pp. 34)**
Pub: Forbes Magazine Inc.
Ed: Nathan Vardi. **Description:** American businesses are cheating on workers' compensation, costing billions in added premiums and leaving employees at risk.

40855 ■ "You Know My Name (Don't Call My Number)" in *Inc.* **(July 1, 2003)**
Pub: Gruner & Jahr USA Publishing
Description: The legal status of the no-call list for telemarketers is presented.

40856 ■ "Your Man On The Hill" in *Fortune* **(Vol. 142, No. 9, October 16, 2000, pp. 312B)**
Pub: Time Inc.
Ed: Julie Rose. **Description:** Senator Kit Bond, who runs the Committee on Small Business, has become an unrelenting advocate for small business interests, and agencies like the SBA and OSHA pay attention.

STATISTICAL SOURCES

40857 ■ *Regulatory Spending Soars: An Analysis of the US Budget for 2003*
Pub: Weidenbum Center
Price: Free. **Description:** Provides information on government regulation, covering 2004 overall cost, barriers to economic growth, and benefits of deregulation, Includes graphs, charts, and statistics.

TRADE PERIODICALS

40858 ■ *China Telecom*
Pub: Information Gatekeepers Inc.
Contact: Hui Pan
Ed: Hui Pan, Editor, editor@igigroup.com. **Released:** Monthly. **Price:** $695, U.S. and Canada; $745, elsewhere; $695 email, one user. **Description:** Reports on current events in telecommunications developments occuring in China. Recurring features include a calendar of events.

40859 ■ *Compliance Action*
Pub: Compliance Action
Contact: George B. Milner Jr., Publisher
Ed: Lucy Griffin, Editor. **Released:** 16/year. **Price:** $299. **Description:** Covers issues pertaining to regulatory compliance in financial institutions.

40860 ■ *Defense Environment Alert*
Pub: Inside Washington Publishers
Contact: Suzanne Yohannan, Managing Editor
Released: Biweekly, every other Wednesday. **Price:** $615, U.S. and Canada; $665, elsewhere. **Description:** Reports on defense policies for cleanup, compliance, and pollution prevention.

40861 ■ *Dickinson's FDA Review*
Pub: Ferdic Inc.
Ed: James G. Dickinson, Editor. **Released:** Monthly. **Price:** $735, U.S. and Canada. **Description:** Recurring features include interviews, news of research, a calendar of events, reports of meetings, and notices of publications available.

40862 ■ *Document Center—Update*
Pub: Document Center
Contact: Claudia Bach, President
Description: Informs of the Center's specifications and standards services available to customers.

40863 ■ *FDA News*
Pub: Technomic Publishing Company Inc.
Contact: Dr. Y.H. Hui, Editor-in-Chief
Released: Monthly. **Price:** $245, U.S.. **Description:** Reports on major FDA announcements, as well as recalls and field corrections for drugs, cosmetics, devices, and biologics.

40864 ■ *FDA Week*
Pub: Inside Washington Publishers
Ed: Donna Haseley, Editor. **Released:** Weekly (Fri.). **Price:** $595, U.S. and Canada; $645, elsewhere. **Description:** Reports on Food and Drug Administration policy, regulation, and enforcement.

40865 ■ *HYDRO ■ WIRE*
Pub: HCI Publications
Contact: Leslie Eden, Publisher
Ed: John Braden, Editor. **Released:** Biweekly. **Price:** $425, U.S.; $720, two years; $20, single issue. **Description:** Publishes on the hydroelectric industry, including national and regional news. Also includes Federal Energy Regulatory Commission notices. Recurring features include a calendar of events.

40866 ■ *Internet Regulation Alert*
Pub: Inside Washington Publishers
Contact: Joe Burey, Publisher
Released: Weekly. **Price:** $745, U.S. and Canada; $795, elsewhere. **Description:** "The Inside Washington look at federal telecommunications policymaking." Covers phone, video, cable and satellite companies.

40867 ■ *Legislative Watch*
Pub: American Tort Reform Association
Ed: Lissa Astilla, Editor, lastilla@atra.org. **Released:** Weekly. **Price:** Included in membership. **Description:** Membership newsletter of the American Tort Reform Association.

40868 ■ *The Nash & Cibinic Report*
Pub: West Group
Ed: Ralph Nash, Editor. **Released:** Monthly. **Price:** $1,300. **Description:** Discusses government contracts analysis and reporting. Topics include procurement management, contractor claims, and competition and awards.

40869 ■ *Ottawa Letter*
Pub: CCH Canadian Ltd.
Contact: Anna Wong
E-mail: awong@cch.ca
Released: Biweekly. **Price:** $650. **Description:** Reports on current events and topics of Canada, such as free trade, human rights, employment, and defense. Also provides statistics, lending, and foreign exchange rates.

40870 ■ *PCS Direct Marketing Newsletter*
Pub: PCS Mailing List Company
Contact: Ed Nasser, Associate Editor
E-mail: ednasser@pcslist.com
Ed: Ann Guyer, Editor, aguyer@pcslist.com. **Released:** Bimonthly. **Price:** Free. **Description:** Offers research tools, publications, and other advice on legal, medical, financial & consumer, direct marketing. Also covers mailing lists, databases, and software to assist with direct mailings. Reports on news and conferences in this field as well. Recurring features include notices of publications available and book reviews.

40871 ■ *Russian Telecom Newsletter*
Pub: Information Gatekeepers Inc.
Contact: Jeremy Awori, Publisher
Ed: Prof. Sergei L. Galkin, Editor. **Released:** Monthly. **Price:** $695, U.S. and Canada; $745, elsewhere; $695 PDF email version. **Description:** Covers the telecommunications industry in Russia, including competition, government regulations, international business and ventures, cellular, satellites, and market intelligence. Also features new products and conference reports.

40872 ■ *The Small Business Advocate*
Pub: Office of Advocacy
Contact: Kathryn Tobias, Senior Editor

Ed: Rebecca Kraft, Editor. **Released:** Bimonthly, Monthly or Bi-monthly. **Price:** Free. **Description:** Provides updates on activities and issues of the Office of Advocacy, which examines the impact of legislative proposals and other public policy issues on small businesses.

40873 ■ *The Tan Sheet*
Pub: F-D-C Reports Inc.
Contact: Ramsey Baghdadi, Managing Editor
Ed: Christopher Walker, Editor. **Released:** Weekly, 51/year. **Price:** $1,285, U.S. print and web. **Description:** Provides "in-depth coverage of nonprescription pharmaceuticals and dietary supplement/nutritionals." Topics include congressional hearings and legislation, business and marketing news, FDA recalls and seizures, regular listing of product trademarks, and activities of FTC, CPSC, and FDA.

40874 ■ *Utilities Telecommunications News*
Pub: Information Gatekeepers Inc.
Contact: Paul Polishuk, Managing Editor
Released: Monthly. **Price:** $695, U.S. and Canada; $745, elsewhere; $695 PDF email version. **Description:** Focuses on the role of utilities in telecommunications. Topics include government and regulations, business, and the Internet. Also features new products and conferences.

40875 ■ *Water Policy Report*
Pub: Inside Washington Publishers
Contact: Charlie Mitchell, Chief Editor
Released: Biweekly, every other Monday. **Price:** $650, U.S. and Canada; $700, elsewhere. **Description:** Reports on federal water quality programs and policies. Covers topics such as drinking water, toxics, enforcement, monitoring, and state/EPA relations.

40876 ■ *Windstar Wildlife Garden Weekly*
Pub: WindStar Wildlife Institute
Contact: Thomas D. Patrick, Editor & Publisher
Released: Weekly. **Price:** Included in membership; $25, nonmembers. **Description:** Communicates how to attract wildlife to one's property and improve wildlife habitat at the same time, including personal experiences. Includes profiles of wildlife and plants, and what to plant and feed. Recurring features include interviews, news of research, reports of meetings, news of educational opportunities, book reviews, and notices of publications available. Also includes a column titled From the President.

CONSULTANTS

40877 ■ ARDITO Information & Research Inc.
1019 Sedwick Dr., Ste. G
Wilmington, DE 19803
Ph:(302)479-5373
Free: 800-836-9068
Fax: (302)479-5375
Co. E-mail: sardito@ardito.com
URL: http://www.ardito.com

E-mail: sardito@ardito.com
Scope: A full-service information and research firm. Provides information in area of financial data, published research, demographic data, industry-specific publications, competitor data, marketing and sales trends, new product developments, government relations, bibliographies. Industries served are pharmaceutical, health, publishing, and environment, and business.

40878 ■ Blasland, Bouck & Lee Inc.
6723 Towpath Rd.
PO Box 66
Syracuse, NY 13214-0066
Ph:(315)446-9120
Fax: (315)449-0017
Co. E-mail: info@bbl-inc.com
URL: http://www.bbl-inc.com

E-mail: info@bbl-inc.com
Scope: Firm offers expertise in hazardous waste remediation, environmental compliance and programs,

life sciences, air quality engineering, solid waste management, and water and waste-water engineering. **Publications:** "Chemical contamination of aquatic organisms from an urbanized estuarine river," 2004; "Phragmites and environmental management: A question of values," Estuaries, 2003; "The Passaic River creel/angler survey: Expert panel review, findings, and recommendations," 2003; "A Common Tragedy: History of An Urban Waterway," Amherst Scientific Publishers, 2002; "Potential long-term ecological impacts caused by disturbance of contaminated sediments: A case study," Environ Manage, 2002.

40879 ■ Daniel Bloom and Associates Inc.
11517 128th Ave. N
PO Box 1233
Largo, FL 33779-1233
Ph:(727)581-6216
Co. E-mail: dan@dbalconsulting.com
URL: http://www.dbaiconsulting.com

E-mail: dan@dbalconsulting.com
Scope: Human resources management consultant with a specialization in corporate relocation. Offers clients a turn key service aimed at meeting the unique relocation needs of their employees. Develops and implements training programs within the relocation industry. **Publications:** "Recoup Your Hiring Investment," Brainbuzz.com, Aug, 2000.

40880 ■ Capitol City Services Inc.
1865 Lamplight Dr.
PO Box 25038
Woodbury, MN 55125-0038
Ph:(651)702-2533
Fax: (651)204-1668
Co. E-mail: lwatkins2@comcast.net

E-mail: lwatkins2@comcast.net
Scope: An information gathering, document retrieval, monitoring, research and reporting service.

40881 ■ Compliance Consultants
1151 Hope St.
Stamford, CT 06907
Ph:(203)329-2700
Fax: (203)329-2345
Co. E-mail: rkeen@fda-complianceconsultants.com
URL: http://www.fda-complianceconsultants.com

E-mail: rkeen@fda-complianceconsultants.com
Scope: A consultancy with expertise in regulatory engineering, product development, and medical devices. Firm advises manufacturers of regulatory requirements and submits detailed engineering facts and marketing reports to obtain market approval from Federal Drug Administration. Serves domestic and foreign clients who wish to market products in the United States.

40882 ■ Envar Services Inc.
505 Milltown Rd.
North Brunswick, NJ 08902-3326
Ph:(732)296-9601
Fax: (732)296-9602
Co. E-mail: mail@envarservices.com
URL: http://www.envarservices.com

E-mail: mail@envarservices.com
Scope: Firm advises in the following areas: engineering design and construction; environmental compliance; plant and process appraisals and upgrades; environmental audits and impact statements; air/oil pollution control and test analyses; feasibility studies; spill prevention; underground storage tank upgrades, removals, and remediation; waste-water treatment studies; and groundwater remediation. Industries served include chemical, petrochemical, pharmaceutical, and manufacturing. Serves eastern United States and Texas. **Publications:** "Method of Detoxification and Stabilization of Soils Contaminated with Chromium Ore Waste".

40883 ■ Environmental Affairs Management Inc.
455 Dan St.
PO Box 13255
Akron, OH 44310-3906

Ph:(330)384-9150
Free: 888-878-3664
Fax: (330)384-9169
Co. E-mail: envafsmgt@aol.com

E-mail: envafsmgt@aol.com
Scope: Company provides facilities support services and Phase I and Phase II site assessment, regulatory compliance management, and training programs, including OSHA HAZ-COM training, remedial operations, and maintenance of underground storage tanks throughout the United States, Eastern seaboard, and southern states. Also facility decontamination and demolition services. **Seminars:** Hazard communication.

40884 ■ Environmental Assessment Services Inc.
124 S Main St.
Middletown, OH 45044-4023
Ph:(513)424-3400
Fax: (513)424-2020
Co. E-mail: easdave@aol.com

E-mail: easdave@aol.com
Scope: Offers environmental and health and safety services in compliance auditing, program management and implementation, field services (monitoring/testing), and real estate assessment.

40885 ■ Environmental Design Group Inc.
450 Grant St., Ste. 201
Akron, OH 44311-1183
Ph:(330)375-1390
Fax: (330)375-9485
Scope: Manages environmental affairs such as assessments, compliance reviews, audits, remedial investigations and feasibility studies, asbestos inspection and abatement management, pollution prevention and spill plans, hazardous and solid waste management, modeling, environmental risk assessments, remediation, and underground storage tank management.

40886 ■ Environmental Management Consultants Inc.
427 Main St.
Evansville, IN 47708-1501
Ph:(812)424-7768
Fax: (812)424-7797
Co. E-mail: emc@emcevv.com
URL: http://www.emcevv.com

E-mail: emc@emcevv.com
Scope: Offers environmental consulting in the following areas: air and water quality monitoring; environmental site assessments; training; underground and above-ground storage tanks; industrial regulatory compliance; and hazardous materials cleanups. Serves all industries in Indiana, Kentucky, and Illinois areas.

40887 ■ Environmental Monitoring Inc.
5730 Industrial Park Rd.
PO Box 1190
Norton, VA 24273
Ph:(276)679-6544
Free: 888-236-4522
Fax: (276)679-6549
Co. E-mail: info@emilab.com
URL: http://www.emilab.com

E-mail: info@emilab.com
Scope: Offers environmental inspections for permit compliance, geotechnical drilling and split spoon soil sampling, underground storage tank investigations and remediation, hazardous materials handling, and Phase I, II, and III environmental assessments. Also offers groundwater monitoring, industrial waste characterization, visible emissions evaluations, indoor air quality monitoring, municipal and industrial waste sampling and analysis, and hazardous and non-hazardous waste disposal management. Provides environmental impact studies, landfill monitoring, leachate characterization, bench tests and studies, baseline data surveys and evaluation, expert testimony, laboratory costs and operations evaluations, labo-

ratory quality control programs, consultation on testing problems, and water quality investigations and remediation. Industries served: commercial, state and federal agencies, and coal.

40888 ■ Environmental Solutions Inc.
1023 Business Park Dr.
PO Box 2127
Traverse City, MI 49686-8372
Ph:(231)941-2025
Free: 800-968-0400
Fax: (231)941-8752
Co. E-mail: dianel@esi-tc.com

E-mail: dianel@esi-tc.com
Scope: Full service environmental consulting firm providing environmental management systems, auditing, hydro-geological, regulatory, Title V of the CAA, waste minimization, site redevelopment, and remediation services. It serves all industries.

40889 ■ Environmental Support Network Inc.
5376 Fulton Dr. NW
Canton, OH 44718-1808
Ph:(330)494-0905
Fax: (330)494-1650
Co. E-mail: esn@sssnet.com

E-mail: esn@sssnet.com
Scope: Provides environmental, health, and safety consulting and project management services. These include compliance auditing and remediation specifications concerning air, groundwater, and soil quality. Also offers health and safety reviews, asbestos and lead-based paint handling, noise sampling, industrial permitting, and UST management. Industries served: education, finance, industry, and government. **Seminars:** Environmental Health and Safety Management in Ohio; Managing Compliance in Ohio; Environmental Site Remediation in Ohio and Surrounding States; Conducting ESAs by ASTM Standards; Health and Safety Management in the Medical Setting; Exposure Monitoring in Schools and Public Buildings.

40890 ■ G. Ferrell & Associates
251 Mulholland St.
Ann Arbor, MI 48103
Ph:(734)663-1230
Fax: (734)663-1230
Co. E-mail: gferrell@umich.edu

E-mail: gferrell@umich.edu
Scope: Firm provides a full range of services to assist businesses with meeting their regulatory and compliance obligations under Affirmative Action and Equal Employment Opportunity (EEO) requirements. These services include: Affirmative Action Plan (AAP) development for government contractors, preparation and management of government compliance audits; personnel and EEO data tracking systems; statistical discrimination analysis; technical compliance assessment for affirmative action and non-discrimination requirements; risk management strategies; EEO census data research; public policy and economic research; Americans with Disabilities Act (ADA) compliance assistance; I-9 audit preparation and management. Serves all industries except construction. Firm also provides training and instructional services in computer software applications. **Publications:** *Affirmative Action Planning for Individuals with Disabilities* (training manual); *Excel Exercises: Spreadsheet Applications Workbook; EEO Checklist for Employers.* **Seminars:** How to Prepare an Affirmative Action Plan; Affirmative Action Planning for Individuals with Disabilities; I-9 Compliance Training; ADA Compliance Training; Sexual Orientation in the Workplace. **Special Services:** Computerized applications for the preparation of Affirmative Action Plans and meeting other EEO compliance requirements (such as EEO-1s and Impact Ratio Analyses); training classes in the use of PC application software, such as Word and Excel; web page design and consulting services.

40891 ■ Safety Management Services
4012 Santa Nella Pl.
San Diego, CA 92130-2291

Ph:(858)259-0591
Fax: (858)792-2350
Scope: Offers safety consulting services: evaluates safety policies and procedures to determine degree of effectiveness; advises on compliance with OSHA standards; and provides safety programs for managers, supervisors, and workers. Industries served: general contractors in new construction, renovation, and demolition; and tenant improvement companies which hire general contractors to perform construction activities on their premises. Also assists litigation as construction safety expert witness. Safety training programs customized to meet clients needs. **Publications:** "What Can Go Wrong?," *International Cranes* magazine, Apr 1994; and "Construction Safety - A Study in Failure," *EXCEL Newletter*, West Virginia University, 1994. **Seminars:** Federal OSHA Construction Safety and Health Course for Trainers, University of California, San Diego; OSHA 10-Hour Construction Safety Course; 90-Hour Construction Safety Management Certificate Course - 1991 to 1993; Fall Protection; Confined Space Standards; Cranes and Rigging; Scaffold or Trenching and Excavation; and Safe Construction Work Practices.

40892 ■ Verk Consultants Inc.
1190 Olive St.
PO Box 11277
Eugene, OR 97440-3477
Ph:(541)687-9170
Fax: (541)687-9758
Co. E-mail: larry@verk.com
URL: http://www.verk.com

E-mail: larry@verk.com
Scope: Specializes in vocational rehabilitation, worksite evaluations for managing workers'compensation and the Americans with Disabilities Act, Title I. **Seminars:** ADA Title I, Workers Compensation, Disability Management.

COMPUTERIZED DATABASES

40893 ■ American Journey: The Constitution and Supreme Court
Thomson Gale
27500 Drake Rd.
Farmington Hills, MI 48331-3535
Ph:(248)699-4253
Free: 800-877-GALE
Fax: (248)699-8069
Co. E-mail: gale.galeord@thomson.com
URL: http://www.gale.com
Description: Contains Supreme Court decisions that interpreted it and the enduring issues that contribute to the public debate in America. Major themes include: the Constitutional Convention and James Madison's detailed debate notes, the role of the Supreme Court, including complete decisions and dissenting opinions on a wide range of constitutional questions, state's rights, original intent, separation of powers, and republican government and a hyperlinked version of the Constitution. **Availability:** Online: Thomson Gale; CD-ROM: Thomson Gale. **Type:** Full text; Audio; Image.

40894 ■ CCH PROTOS
CCH Inc.
2700 Lake Cook Rd.
Riverwoods, IL 60015
Ph:(847)267-7000
Free: 800-525-3335
Fax: (773)866-3095
URL: http://www.cch.com
Description: Contains information on taxes in Canada. Includes interpretation bulletins, circulars, rulings, Department of Finance releases, Revenue Canada releases, court cases, Internal Revenue Canada documents, draft legislation and explanatory notes, CCH Tax newsletters, and more. **Type:** Bulletin board.

40895 ■ EZ-DOCS : Government Documents for the People
Auto-Graphics Inc.
3201 Temple Ave.
Pomona, CA 91768-3279
Ph:(909)595-7004
Free: 800-776-6939
Fax: (909)595-3506
Co. E-mail: info@auto-graphics.com
URL: http://www.auto-graphics.com
Description: Contains citations to 400,000 publications distributed and cataloged by the U.S. Government Printing office since 1976. Publications indexed cover consumer education, environmental issues, finance, business, demographics, education, career planning, agriculture, health, nutrition, medicine, congressional hearings, presidential reports, census information, and more. Each record identifies local depository libraries where the item may be found. Also includes complete directory information for each depository library, including name, address, phone number, and designation date. Includes onscreen function key map, User Guide, Depository Library Directory, and toll-free support. Enables the user to browse by author, title, subject, or combination of all three; search by number in Sudoc, Report, Item, Stock, Monthly Catalog Entry, Shipping Lists, and OCLC Control Number fields (Boolean search is available at Research level). **Type:** Bibliographic; Directory.

40896 ■ KeyCite
Thomson West
610 Opperman Dr.
Eagan, MN 55123
Ph:(651)687-7000
Free: 800-344-5008
Fax: (651)687-5827
Co. E-mail: west.customer.service@thomson.com
URL: http://www.westlaw.com
Description: Contains citing references, including case law and secondary law. Provides direct history, negative indirect history, and related references to the history of a case. **Availability:** Online: Thomson West. **Type:** Bibliographic; Full text.

40897 ■ Product Safety & Liability Reporter
The Bureau of National Affairs Inc.
1231 25th St. NW
Washington, DC 20037
Ph:(202)452-4200
Free: 800-372-1033
Fax: (202)452-4226
Co. E-mail: customercare@bna.com
URL: http://www.bna.com
Description: Contains product liability cases, legislation and federal regulatory developments. Also includes text of laws and regulations administered by the CPSC and NHTSA. Subjects include asbestos, building and construction equipment, consumer product safety commission, drugs and medical devices, electrical equipment, enforcement actions, expert testimony, farm equipment, industrial machinery, motor vehicles, national highway traffic safety administration, pending litigation, product recalls, sports equipment, toxic products, and tobacco. Sections include Highlights, Topical Summary, Product Liability, Product Safety, Table of Cases, Journal, Analysis & Perspective, and Indexes. **Availability:** Online: The Bureau of National Affairs Inc. **Type:** Full text.

40898 ■ Tax Directory
Tax Analysts
510 N Washington St., Ste. 400
Falls Church, VA 22046
Ph:(703)533-4400
Free: 800-955-2444
Co. E-mail: cservice@tax.org
URL: http://www.taxanalysts.com
Description: Contains information on more than 20,00 tax professionals. Vol. One Government Officials Worldwide including state and federal officials, including taxwriting committees U.S. Department of Treasury and IRS, Tax Court Judges, International Financial Specialists, Tax and Business Journalists, Professional Associations, and Tax Groups and Coalitions. Vol. Two Corporate Tax Managers including

names and contact information for tax managers in largest U.S corporations. Entries including industry description derived from the Securities and Exchange Commission's four-digit Standard Industry Classification code used by the listed companies for filing purposes. **Availability:** Online: LexisNexis; CD-ROM: Tax Analysts. **Type:** Directory.

40899 ■ *TOMES Plus System*
Thomson Microdex
6200 S Syracuse Way, Ste. 300
Greenwood Village, CO 80111-4740
Ph:(303)486-6400
Free: 800-525-9083
Fax: (303)486-6464
Co. E-mail: mdx.info@thomson.com
URL: http://www.micromedex.com
Description: Contains chemical, medical, and toxicological information for the industrial and occupational medicine markets. Covers clinical effects, range of toxicity, workplace standards, kinetics, and physiochemical standards. Comprises 16 files:; MEDITEXT Medical Managements—contains protocols on the evaluation, medical response, and treatment of individuals acutely exposed to industrial chemicals. Includes Occupational Safety and Health Administration (OSHA) occupational exposure standards.; HAZARDTEXT Hazard Managements—contains initial response protocols to incidents involving hazardous materials (e.g., fires, spills, leaks). Includes Occupational Safety and Health Administration (OSHA) occupational exposure standards.; Hazardous Substances Data Bank (HSDB)—contains data on more than 4200 chemical substances that are of known or potential toxicity and to which substantial populations are exposed.; OHM/TADS (Oil and Hazardous Materials/ Technical Assistance Data System)—contains data gathered from published literature on 1402 materials that have been designated oil or hazardous materials. Provides technical support for dealing with potential or actual dangers resulting from the discharge of oil or hazardous substances. Up to 126 data fields, some textual and some numeric, may be present for each record (i.e., one material). A record includes identification of the substance (CAS Registry Number, common and trade names, and chemical formula), physical properties, uses, toxicity, handling procedures, and suggested methods for disposing of spilled materials. Produced by the U.S. Environmental Protection Agency (EPA). Corresponds to the OHM-TADS online database.; Chemical Hazards Response Information System (CHRIS)—contains information on approximately 1200 chemical substances for use in spill situations. Includes chemical names and synonyms, molecular formula, biological and fire hazard potential, and chemical and physical properties. Also includes information on water pollution and toxicity of chemicals to aquatic life. Produced by the U.S. Coast Guard. Corresponds to the Chemical Hazards Response Information System (CHRIS) online database.; IRIS (Integrated Risk Information System)—contains information on the health risk assessment of more than 450 hazardous substances. Covers toxicity, carcinogenicity, chemical and physical properties, and applicable regulations. Includes reference doses (i.e., concentrations of substances below which adverse health effects are not expected to occur), and carcinogenic risk assessment of varying concentrations of substances in air and drinking water. Also includes summaries of EPA regulatory actions. Produced by the U.S. Environmental Protection Agency (EPA). Corresponds to the IRIS online database.; INFOTEXT Documents—provides general health and safety data on nonchemical-specific topics such as ergonomics and human health risk assessments.; Registry of Toxic Effects of Chemical Substances (RTECS)—offers toxicity data on more than 135,000 substances, extracted from scientific literature worldwide, includes specifics on mutagenicity, carcinogenicity, reproductive hazards, and acute and chronic toxicity of hazardous substances.; 1996 North American Emergency Response Guidebook (NAERG).; NIOSH (National Institute for Occupational Safety and Health) Pocket Guide—contains critical industrial hygiene data for approximately 675 chemicals with information on exposure limits, U.S. IDLH concentrations,

incompatibilities and reactivities, personal protection, and recommendations for respirator selection.; New Jersey Fact Sheets from the N.J. Department of Health—offers employee-oriented exposure risk information useful when addressing worker right-to-know issues and developing training programs. Includes generic, non-technical worker safety and training information, frequently asked questions & answers, and a glossary of terms for more than 700 hazardous substances. **Availability:** Online: Thomson Microdex. **Type:** Bibliographic; Full text; Numeric.

40900 ■ *U.S. Government Management Policy*
U.S. General Services Administration
1800 F St. NW
Washington, DC 20405
Ph:(202)501-1021
Fax: (202)401-8233
Co. E-mail: public.affairs@gsa.gov
URL: http://www.cfda.gov
Description: Includes: Federal Information Resources Management Regulation & Bulletins Federal Acquisition Regulation & Circulars, Defense Logistics Acquisition Regulation, Federal Property Management Regulation Chapters E,G,H, Federal Travel Regulations Preface & Chapters 301-304 as well as other publications. **Type:** Full text.

LIBRARIES

40901 ■ Bryan Cave LLP–Law Library
700 13th St. NW, Ste. 600
Washington, DC 20005-3960
Ph:(202)508-6000
Fax: (202)508-6200
Co. E-mail: laura.green@bryancave.com
Contact: Laurie Green, Mgr., Lib. & Res.Svcs.
Scope: Government and politics; law - commercial, corporate, environmental, intellectual property, taxation. **Services:** Interlibrary loan; copying; faxing; Library open to the public with restrictions. **Holdings:** 11,000 volumes. **Subscriptions:** 200 journals and other serials.

RESEARCH CENTERS

40902 ■ American Enterprise Institute
1150 17th St. NW
Washington, DC 20036
Ph:(202)862-5800
Fax: (202)862-7177
Co. E-mail: cdemuth@aei.org
URL: http://www.aei.org
Contact: Christopher DeMuth, Pres.
E-mail: cdemuth@aei.org
Scope: Economic policy, including domestic taxing, spending, and regulatory programs, and international trade and competitiveness; foreign and defense policy, including the spread of democracy and free enterprise, and the development of stable international security arrangements; social and political studies, including U.S. politics and public opinion, the Constitution and legal policy, and social welfare, educational and cultural issues. **Publications:** AEI Newsletter (monthly); The American Enterprise (bimonthly). **Educational Activities:** Debates and meetings, featuring discussions among experts on major public policy issues.

40903 ■ New Jersey Attorney General's Office–Law and Public Safety Department–Research Services
Justice Complex
PO Box 115
Trenton, NJ 08625
Ph:(609)292-4958
Fax: (609)633-6555
Co. E-mail: maria.baratta@lps.state.nj.us
Contact: Maria Baratta, Ch.
E-mail: maria.baratta@lps.state.nj.us
Scope: Law and public safety.

START-UP INFORMATION

40904 ■ "Do This, Get Rich" in *Business 2.0* **(Vol. 6, May 2005, No. 4, pp. 78-86)**
Pub: Time, Inc.
Ed: Michael V. Copeland, Om Malik, Erick Schonfeld.
Description: Profiles of the eleven hottest business opportunities are presented, including computer upgrades, advertising on the Web, specialty baby furniture, professional medical employment services, interior design for hotels, Web-enabled subscription and service monitoring, search engines for podcasts, RFID tags to track drugs and supplies in hospitals, software to save energy in homes and businesses, software and hardware to monitor and control a boat's onboard systems.

40905 ■ "Obesity Whets VC Appetites" in *Inc.* **(Volume 27, June 2005, No. 6, pp. 26)**
Pub: Inc. Magazine
Ed: Michelle Leder. **Description:** Venture capitalists have invested millions in six anti-obesity companies in the past year.

40906 ■ *Solo Private Practice: A Step by Step Guide to Opening Your Private Practice*
Pub: Empowerment Publications
Ed: B.J. Patchett. **Released:** August 2004. **Price:** $12.95. **Description:** Launching a medical facility offering clinical services, while adhering to the highest professional standards, requires an efficiently run office.

40907 ■ *Up and Running: Opening a Chiropractic Office*
Pub: PageFree Publishing, Incorporated
Ed: John L. Reizer. **Released:** March 2004. **Price:** $30.00. **Description:** Tips for starting a chiropractic business.

ASSOCIATIONS AND OTHER ORGANIZATIONS

40908 ■ AcademyHealth
1801 K St. NW, No. 701-L
Washington, DC 20006
Ph:(202)292-6700
Fax: (202)292-6800
Co. E-mail: info@academyhealth.org
URL: http://www.academyhealth.org
Contact: W. David Helms PhD, Pres./CEO
Description: Promotes interaction across the health research and policy arenas by bringing together a broad spectrum of players to share their perspectives, learn from each other and strengthen their working relationships. Convenes national scientific and health policy conferences; helps public and private policymakers transform research and policy into workable programs; educates policymakers, researchers, government officials, and business leaders; disseminates vital information through research syntheses, special report findings, newsletters and website; and conducts major programs that serve the research community, health policy leaders, and business and government decision-makers. **Publications:** *AcademyHealth Reports* (quarterly); *Health Affairs* (bimonthly); Annual Report (annual).

40909 ■ American Health Care Association
1201 L St. NW
Washington, DC 20005
Ph:(202)842-4444
Fax: (202)842-3860
Co. E-mail: update@ahca.org
URL: http://www.ahca.org
Contact: Dr. Hal Daub, Pres./CEO
Description: Federation of state associations of long-term health care facilities. Promotes standards for professionals in long-term health care delivery and quality care for patients and residents in a safe environment. Focuses on issues of availability, quality, affordability, and fair payment. Operates as liaison with governmental agencies, Congress, and professional associations. Compiles statistics. **Publications:** *AHCA Notes* (monthly); *Provider: For Long Term Care Professionals* (monthly). Also produces audiovisual aids.

40910 ■ American Managed Behavioral Healthcare Association
1101 Pennsylvania Ave. NW, 6th Fl.
Washington, DC 20004
Ph:(202)756-7726
Fax: (202)756-7308
Co. E-mail: mike_strand@excite.com
URL: http://www.ambha.org
Contact: Pamela Greenberg MPP, Exec.Dir.
Membership: Managed behavioral healthcare organizations. **Purpose:** Works to advance the value of managed behavioral healthcare and promotes the inclusion of mental illnesses and addiction disorders in benefit coverage. **Publications:** *Catalog of Special Reports*.

40911 ■ Associated Medical Services
162 Cumberland St., Ste. 228
Toronto, ON, Canada M5R 3N5
Ph:(416)924-3368
Fax: (416)323-3338
Co. E-mail: seidelman@ams-inc.on.ca
URL: http://www.ams-inc.on.ca
Contact: William E. Seidelman MD, Pres./CEO
Membership: Health services. **Purpose:** Promotes increased availability of quality health care. Facilitates communication and cooperation among members; represents members' interests before government agencies, professional medical organizations, and the public. **Publications:** *Corporate Report* (biennial); Newsletter (3/year).

40912 ■ Canadian Academy of Periodontology–Academie Canadienne de Parodontologie
1815 Alta Vista Dr., No. 105
Ottawa, ON, Canada K1G 3Y6
Ph:(613)523-9800
Fax: (613)523-1968
Co. E-mail: central-office@cap-acp.ca
URL: http://www.cap-acp.ca
Membership: Periodontologists, educators, and students. **Purpose:** Promotes advancement in the practice and teaching of periodontology. Conducts continuing professional education courses for members. Maintains speakers' bureau. **Publications:** *CAPsule* (3/year); Directory (annual).

40913 ■ Canadian Association of Gerontology–Association canadienne de gerontologie
329 March Rd., Ste. 232
Box 11
Ottawa, ON, Canada K2K 2E1
Ph:(613)271-1083
Fax: (613)599-7027
Co. E-mail: cagacg@igs.net
URL: http://www.cagacg.ca
Contact: Sandra P. Hirst, Pres.
Description: Focuses on the problems and process of aging. **Publications:** *CAG Newsletter* (quarterly); *Canadian Journal on Aging* (quarterly).

40914 ■ Canadian Association for School Health
2835 Country Woods Dr.
Surrey, BC, Canada V4P 9P9
Ph:(604)535-7664
Fax: (604)531-6454
Co. E-mail: dmccall@netcom.ca
URL: http://www.schoolfile.com/cash/acknowledgements.htm
Contact: Doug S. McCall, Exec. Dir.
Membership: School health services. **Purpose:** Promotes increased availability and quality of school health programs. Serves as a clearinghouse on school health services; facilitates communication and cooperation among members.

40915 ■ Canadian Cancer Society–Societe Canadienne du Cancer
1639 Yonge St.
Toronto, ON, Canada M4T 2W6
Ph:(416)488-5400
Free: 800-268-8874
Fax: (416)488-2872
Co. E-mail: info@cis.cancer.ca
URL: http://www.cancer.ca
Contact: Peter Vaudry, Pres.
Membership: Community-based volunteers. **Purpose:** Promotes research into the causes, detection, and cure of cancer; seeks to improve the quality of life of people with cancer. Conducts fundraising activities benefiting cancer research; sponsors volunteer training programs; makes available educational courses. **Publications:** *Daffodil* (annual); *Progress Against Cancer* (3/year).

40916 ■ Canadian Cardiovascular Society–Societe Canadienne de Cardiologie
222 Queen St., Ste. 1403
Ottawa, ON, Canada K1P 5V9
Ph:(613)569-3407
Free: 877-569-3407
Fax: (613)569-6574
Co. E-mail: info@ccs.ca

URL: http://www.ccs.ca
Contact: Anne Ferguson, Exec. Dir./CEO
Description: Physicians, surgeons, and scientists practicing or conducting research in cardiology and related fields. Works to advance the cardiovascular health and care of Canadians through leadership on professional development, advocacy, and the promotion, dissemination of research. **Publications:** *Canadian Journal of Cardiology*; *CCS News* (biweekly).

40917 ■ Canadian College of Health Service Executives–College canadien des directeurs de services de sante
292 Somerset St. W
Ottawa, ON, Canada K2P 0J6
Ph:(613)235-7218
Free: 800-363-9056
Fax: (613)235-5451
Co. E-mail: cchse@cchse.org
URL: http://www.cchse.org
Contact: Dr. John Hylton, Pres./CEO
Description: Serves health service executives in Canada. Offers a forum for the exchange of ideas and information, a career network, and professional development opportunities. **Publications:** *Healthcare Management Forum* (quarterly). **Telecommunication Services:** electronic mail, jhylton@cchse.org.

40918 ■ Canadian Council on Health Services Accreditation–Conseil canadien d'agrement des services de sante
1730 St. Laurent Blvd., Ste. 100
Ottawa, ON, Canada K1G 5L1
Ph:(613)738-3800
Free: 800-814-7769
Fax: (613)738-7755
Co. E-mail: nowl@cchsa.ca
URL: http://www.cchsa.ca
Contact: Wendy Nicklin, Exec. Dir.
Membership: Agencies and organizations accrediting health care services including mental health care, cancer treatment centers, home health care, and community health. **Purpose:** Seeks to ensure high standards of ethics, practice, and equipment and facilities among Canadian health services. Formulates and enforces standards; conducts research and educational programs. **Publications:** *The Accreditation Standard* (quarterly); *Standards*; Annual Report (annual).

40919 ■ Canadian Dermatology Association–Association Canadienne de Dermatologie
1385 Bank St., Ste. 425
Ottawa, ON, Canada K1H 8N4
Ph:(613)738-1748
Free: 800-267-3376
Fax: (613)738-4695
Co. E-mail: contact.cda@dermatology.ca
URL: http://www.dermatology.ca
Contact: Ms. Michelle Albagli, Exec. Dir.
Description: Certified dermatologists and related professionals interested in the professional advancement of dermatology. Promotes continuing education programs in dermatology. Provides public education program on skin cancer prevention. Holds an annual National Sun Awareness Week. Recognizes sun protection products. **Publications:** *Journal of Cutaneous Medicine and Surgery* (quarterly); *Membership and Corporate Directory* (annual); Bulletin (3/year).

40920 ■ Canadian Health Coalition–Coalition Canadienne de la Sante
2841 Riverside Dr.
Ottawa, ON, Canada K1V 8X7
Ph:(613)521-3400
Fax: (613)521-9638
Co. E-mail: info@healthcoalition.ca
URL: http://www.healthcoalition.ca
Contact: Kathleen Connors, Chair
Membership: Individuals and organizations with an interest in health care. **Purpose:** Promotes increased availability and quality of health services. Monitors the performance of health care facilities and services and makes recommendations for their improvement.

40921 ■ Canadian Healthcare Association–Association canadienne des soins de sante
17 York St.
Ottawa, ON, Canada K1N 9J6
Ph:(613)241-8005
Fax: (613)241-5055
Co. E-mail: info@cha.ca
URL: http://www.cha.ca
Contact: Sharon Sholzberg-Gray, Pres./CEO
Description: Promotes a humane, effective, and efficient health system of the highest quality. **Publications:** *Canada's Health Care System: Its Funding and Organization*; *Guide to Canadian Healthcare Facilities* (annual); Annual Report (annual). **Telecommunication Services:** electronic mail, chapresident@cha.ca.

40922 ■ Canadian Medical Association
1867 Alta Vista Dr.
Ottawa, ON, Canada K1G 3Y6
Free: 800-457-4205
Fax: (613)236-8864
Co. E-mail: cmamsc@cma.ca
URL: http://www.cma.ca
Contact: Dr. Louise M.C. Cloutier, Chair
Description: Seeks to improve medical care for persons living in Canada. Works to maintain high standards of hospital care and health related services. Encourages constant improvement in the medical profession.

40923 ■ Canadian Medical Protective Association–Association Canadienne de Protection Medicale
PO Box 8225, Sta. T
Ottawa, ON, Canada K1G 3H7
Ph:(613)725-2000
Free: 800-267-6522
Fax: (613)725-1300
URL: http://www.cmpa-acpm.ca
Contact: Dr. John E. Gray, Exec.Dir./CEO
Description: Defense organization for physicians practicing in Canada. **Publications:** *Risk Identification*.

40924 ■ Canadian Mental Health Association–Association Canadienne pour la Sante Mentale
8 King St. E, Ste. 810
Toronto, ON, Canada M5C 1B5
Ph:(416)484-7750
Fax: (416)484-4617
Co. E-mail: info@cmha.ca
URL: http://www.cmha.ca
Contact: Penelope Marrett, CEO
Description: Mental health professionals and other individuals with an interest in community mental health. Works to enable individuals, groups and communities to increase control over and enhance their mental health. Serves as a social advocate to encourage public action to strengthen community mental health services; conducts lobbying activities. Promotes mental health research; organizes and operates grass roots programs to help people whose mental health is at risk make use of the services available to them. Sponsors educational programs. **Publications:** *Mental Health Promotion-Train the Trainer*; Newsletter (quarterly); Annual Report (annual).

40925 ■ Canadian Paediatric Society–Societe Canadienne de Pediatrie
2305 St. Laurent Blvd.
Ottawa, ON, Canada K1G 4J8
Ph:(613)526-9397
Fax: (613)526-3332
Co. E-mail: info@cps.ca
URL: http://www.cps.ca
Contact: Elizabeth Moreau, Dir. of Communications
Membership: Professional organization of pediatricians serving on committees and sections focusing on adolescent medicine, bioethics, drug therapy, hazardous substances, fetus and newborns, Indian and Inuit health, infectious disease and immunization, injury prevention, pediatric practice, nutrition, and psychological pediatrics. **Purpose:** Provides services to Canadian children and to its membership. Serves as an

advocate on issues relating to child health and welfare. Provides continuing education for the maintenance of competence of its members. Establishes Canadian standards/guidelines for pediatric care and practice, and promotes the interest of pediatricians. **Publications:** *Clinical Practice Guidelines* (periodic); *CPS News* (5/year); *Pediatrics & Child Health* (10/year).

40926 ■ Canadian Pain Society–La Societe Canadienne De La Douleur
701 Rossland Rd. E, Ste. 373
Whitby, ON, Canada L1N 9K3
Ph:(905)668-9545
Fax: (905)668-3728
Co. E-mail: ellen@canadianpainsociety.ca
URL: http://www.canadianpainsociety.ca
Contact: Ellen Maracle-Benton, Office Mgr.
Membership: Health care professionals and medical and pharmaceutical researchers with an interest in pain and its alleviation. **Purpose:** Fosters research on the causes of pain; seeks improved methods of pain management. Facilitates communication and cooperation among pain researchers and clinicians; sponsors educational and research programs. **Publications:** *CPS Newsletter* (quarterly); *Pain Research and Management* (quarterly); Membership Directory (annual).

40927 ■ Canadian Psychiatric Association–Association des Psychiatres du Canada
141 Laurier Ave. W, Ste. 701
Ottawa, ON, Canada K1P 5J3
Ph:(613)234-2815
Fax: (613)234-9857
Co. E-mail: cpa@cpa-apc.org
URL: http://www.cpa-apc.org
Contact: Alex Saunders, CEO/Dir. Gen.
Description: Works to improve mental health and psychiatric care delivery systems in Canada. Fosters high standards among Canadian psychiatrists; promotes continuing education of members; encourages and participates in educational programs for patient care providers; promotes research into psychiatric disorders; advocates for mental health system reforms and on related issues affecting the practice of psychiatry. **Publications:** *Canadian Journal of Psychiatry* (monthly); Bulletin (bimonthly).

40928 ■ Canadian Public Health Association–Association Canadienne De Sante Publique
400-1565 Carling Ave.
Ottawa, ON, Canada K1Z 8R1
Ph:(613)725-3769
Fax: (613)725-9826
Co. E-mail: info@cpha.ca
URL: http://www.cpha.ca
Contact: Elinor E. Wilson RN, CEO
Description: Works to mobilize national charitable and volunteer resources to address public health concerns worldwide. Conducts immunization, maternal and child health, and HIV/AIDS programs in at-risk areas.

40929 ■ Canadian Society for Clinical Investigation–Societe canadienne de recherches cliniques
774 Echo Dr.
Ottawa, ON, Canada K1S 5N8
Ph:(613)730-6240
Fax: (613)730-1116
Co. E-mail: csci@rcpsc.edu
URL: http://www.csci-scrc.org
Contact: Dr. Jody Ginsberg, Pres.
Description: Canadian clinical investigators working in the field of human health. Represents members' interests. **Publications:** *Clinical and Investigative Medicine* (periodic).

40930 ■ Canadian Society for International Health–La Societe Canadienne de Sante Internationale
1 Nicholas St., Ste. 1105
Ottawa, ON, Canada K1N 7B7
Ph:(613)241-5785
Fax: (613)241-3845

Co. E-mail: csih@csih.org
URL: http://www.csih.org
Contact: Ms. Janet Hatcher Roberts, Exec. Dir.
Membership: Health care services and individuals and organizations with an interest in global public health. **Purpose:** Promotes increased availability and quality of health services in previously underserved areas worldwide. Advocates for health policy and programming that contributes to global objectives of health for all; equity, and social justice through partnership building with Canadian and other institutions and organizations. **Publications:** *Online Synergy* (weekly); *PAHO News* (weekly).

40931 ■ Catholic Health Association of Canada–Association catholique canadienne de la sante
1247 Kilborn Pl.
Ottawa, ON, Canada K1H 6K9
Ph:(613)731-7148
Fax: (613)731-7797
Co. E-mail: info@chac.ca
URL: http://www.chac.ca
Contact: Mr. Gerard Lewis, Pres./CEO
Description: Represents the interests of Catholic Hospitals and nursing homes in Canada. Works to administer Christian principles within the Canadian healthcare system. Fosters competent and efficient health care services.

40932 ■ College of Family Physicians of Canada - Ontario Chapter–College des Medecins de Famille du Canada
2630 Skymark Ave.
Mississauga, ON, Canada L4W 5A4
Ph:(905)629-0900
Free: 800-387-6197
Fax: (905)629-0893
Co. E-mail: ocfp@cfpc.ca
URL: http://www.cfpc.ca
Contact: Dr. Calvin Gutkin, Exec. Dir./CEO
Description: National medical association of family physicians and general practitioners. Members must maintain a minimum of 50 hours of continuing medical education credits annually. Works to maintain standards of family medicine training in the 16 Canadian medical schools through support of the Departments of Family Medicine and the accreditation of family practice residency programs. Administers certification examinations in emergency medicine and family medicine. Runs practice assessment program. Offers public education programs on family medicine topics. **Publications:** *Canadian Family Physician* (monthly); *CFPC-Liaison Newsletter* (quarterly); *Self-Evaluation* (bimonthly).

40933 ■ Community Health Nurses Association of Canada–Association canadienne des infirmieres et infirmiers en sante communantaire
1185 Eglinton Ave. E, Ste. 104
Toronto, ON, Canada M3C 3C6
Ph:(416)426-7029
Fax: (416)426-7280
Co. E-mail: info@chnac.ca
URL: http://www.communityhealthnursescanada.org
Contact: Rosemarie Goodyear, Pres.
Membership: Community health nurses and provincial organizations. **Purpose:** Seeks to advance the practice of community health nursing and enhance members' professional status. Represents members' interests before government agencies and medical associations; provides support, services, and assistance to members. **Publications:** *National Headlines* (3/year); Annual Report (annual).

40934 ■ Community and Hospital Infection Control Association - Canada–Association Pour La Prevention Des Infections A l'hopital et dans La Communaute
PO Box 46125
Winnipeg, MB, Canada R3R 3S3
Ph:(204)897-5990
Free: (866)999-7111
Fax: (204)895-9595
Co. E-mail: chicacanada@mts.net
URL: http://www.chica.org
Contact: Gerry Hansen, Admin./Conference Planner

Membership: Health care professionals engaged in the prevention and control of infections. **Purpose:** Seeks to improve the health of Canadians by promoting excellence in the practice of infection prevention and control. Serves as a clearinghouse on infection control standards and practices; facilitates communication and exchange of information among members; conducts continuing professional education programs for members. Collaborates with government agencies responsible for public health in the formulation and enforcement of certification standards and in the development of public policies. Provides advice and assistance to organizations and agencies concerned with specific diseases, including AIDS. Maintains speakers' bureau. **Publications:** *Canadian Journal of Infection Control* (quarterly).

40935 ■ Epilepsy Canada–Epilepsie Canada
2255B Queen St. E, Ste. 336
Toronto, ON, Canada M4E 1G3
Free: 877-734-0873
Fax: (905)764-1231
Co. E-mail: epilepsy@epilepsy.ca
URL: http://www.epilepsy.ca
Contact: Denise Crepin, Natl. Exec. Dir.
Membership: People with epilepsy and their families; health care professionals with an interest in epilepsy and related disorders. **Purpose:** Seeks to improve the quality of life of people affected by epilepsy through promotion and support of research. Offers education and awareness initiatives that build understanding and acceptance of epilepsy. **Publications:** *Lumina* (semiannual); Brochure (semiannual).

40936 ■ Foundation for Health
337 East Ave.
Watertown, NY 13601-3829
Ph:(315)782-6664
Free: 800-724-7460
Fax: (315)782-6664
Co. E-mail: geobonadio@westelcom.com
Contact: George Bonadio, Exec. Dir.
Description: Gathers and disseminates information regarding health; seeks to publicize "natural" laws of health in an effort to make excellent health and long, useful lives common throughout the world. Proclaims the simplicity and inexpensiveness of maintaining one's health in contrast to the complexity and expense of disease. Researches and develops nutrition and health related projects and programs. Convention/Meeting: none. **Publications:** *Ask the Nutritionist* (weekly) ; *Seven Disciplines of Health*. Also contributes weekly health column to newspapers; plans to publish book.

40937 ■ Health Information Resource Center
1850 W Winchester Rd., Ste. 213
Libertyville, IL 60048
Ph:(847)816-8660
Free: 800-828-8225
Fax: (847)816-8662
Co. E-mail: info@fitnessday.com
URL: http://www.healthawards.com
Contact: Patricia Henze, Exec. Dir.
Purpose: Provides information and referral services to many organizations that use or produce consumer health information materials. Conducts market research. Convention/Meeting: none. **Publications:** *Consumer Health Information Online* (annual); *Consumer Health Information: The Professional Guide to the Nations' Best Consumer Health Information Programs and Materials* (annual) ; *Health and Medical Media '99* (annual); *The Health Events Calendar* (annual). **Telecommunication Services:** electronic mail, healthprograms@aol.com.

40938 ■ International Institute of Concern for Public Health
PO Box 80523
Toronto, ON, Canada M1P 4Z5
Ph:(416)755-3685
Co. E-mail: info@iicph.org
URL: http://www.iicph.org
Contact: Dr. Marion Odell, VP/Coor.
Purpose: Promotes dissemination of information on public health and related topics including environmen-

tal and occupational health and human rights. Serves as a clearinghouse on international public health and related issues; assists in the development of model health-related human rights legislation. Conducts research and educational programs; compiles statistics; maintains speakers' bureau. Provides support and assistance to communities wishing to maintain their own public health databases. **Publications:** *International Perspectives in Public Health* (annual); Newsletter (bimonthly).

40939 ■ Let's Face It USA
University of Michigan
School of Dentistry
Dentistry Library
Ann Arbor, MI 48109-1078
Co. E-mail: faceit@umich.edu
URL: http://www.dent.umich.edu/faceit
Contact: Betsy Wilson, Founder/Dir.
Purpose: Provides information and support for people who have or who care for those with facial disfigurement. Website and annual publication with over 150 resources for professionals and families. Links to all related networks for specific conditions i.e. Genetic Disorders, Burns, Cancer, etc. **Publications:** *Resources for People with Facial Difference* (semiannual).

40940 ■ National Coalition for Cancer Research
2300 N St. NW
Washington, DC 20004
Ph:(202)544-1880
Fax: (202)543-2565
Co. E-mail: md@capitolassociates.com
URL: http://www.cancercoalition.org
Contact: Carolyn R. Aldige, Pres./Founder
Membership: Lay and professional organizations committed to the eradication of cancer. **Purpose:** Dedicated to strengthening the National Cancer Program through public education and communication about the value of cancer research, treatment, and prevention.

40941 ■ National Council Against Health Fraud
119 Foster St., Bldg. R, 2nd Fl.
Peabody, MA 01960
Ph:(978)532-9383
Fax: (978)532-9450
Co. E-mail: ncahf.office@verizon.net
URL: http://www.ncahf.org
Contact: Dr. Robert S. Baratz MD, Pres.
Description: Health professionals, researchers, legal professionals, and other interested individuals. Seeks to educate the public on fraud and quackery in health care. Offers advice to consumers. Provides witnesses for health fraud trials. Assists law enforcement officials with health fraud cases. Sponsors speaker's bureau and research programs. Offers aid to victims in the form of free legal screening. **Publications:** *Consumer Health Digest* (weekly). Also publishes position statement on various topics.

40942 ■ National Health Policy Forum
2131 K St. NW, Ste. 500
Washington, DC 20037
Ph:(202)872-1390
Fax: (202)862-9837
Co. E-mail: nhpf@gwu.edu
URL: http://www.nhpf.org
Contact: Judith Miller Jones, Dir.
Description: Nonpartisan education program serving primarily senior federal legislative and executive branch health staff but also addressing the interests of state officials and their Washington representatives. Seeks to foster more informed government decision-making. Helps decision makers forge the personal acquaintances and understanding necessary for cooperation among government agencies and between government and the private sector. **Publications:** *Background Papers*; *Basics* (periodic); *Issue Briefs*; *Site Visit Reports* (periodic).

40943 ■ Occupational and Environmental Medical Association of Canada–Association canadienne de la medecine du travail et de l'environnement

344 Lakeshore Rd. E, Ste. B
Oakville, ON, Canada L6J 1J6
Free: (866)513-9925
Fax: (905)849-8606
Co. E-mail: oemac@oemac.org
URL: http://www.oemac.org
Contact: Dr. Jeremy Beach, Pres.
Membership: Health care professionals with an active interest in occupational and environmental medicine. **Purpose:** Promotes improved standards of education and practice in the field. Serves as a unified voice for Canadian occupational and environmental medicine; acts as a forum for exchange of scientific and professional information. Conducts continuing professional education programs. **Publications:** *Liaison* (quarterly); *Occupational Medicine*; Directory (annual).

40944 ■ Operation Eyesight Universal

4 Parkdale Crescent NW
Calgary, AB, Canada T2N 3T8
Ph:(403)283-6323
Free: 800-585-8265
Fax: (403)270-1899
Co. E-mail: info@operationeyesight.ca
URL: http://www.operationeyesight.ca
Contact: Mrs. Pat Ferguson, Pres./CEO
Description: Individuals, firms, churches, schools, service clubs, and other organizations united to promote sight restoration and blindness prevention through programs in developing countries. Provides medical and educational assistance to needy individuals. Assists in the establishment of: special programs to combat blindness due to malnutrition; eye care hospitals; eye care departments in health care institutions; rural mobile eye programs. Works with local blindness prevention societies. Operates training programs. **Publications:** *Sightlines* (triennial); Annual Report (annual).

40945 ■ Osteoporosis Canada–Osteoporose Canada

1090 Don Mills Rd., Ste. 301
Toronto, ON, Canada M3C 3R6
Ph:(416)696-2663
Free: 800-463-6842
Fax: (416)696-2673
Co. E-mail: osc@osteoporosis.ca
URL: http://www.osteoporosis.ca
Contact: Karen Ormerod MM, Pres./CEO/Board Sec.
Description: Individuals and organizations interested in the prevention, diagnosis, and treatment of osteoporosis. Supports research programs that seek to improve the quality of life for women with osteoporosis. Promotes education about osteoporosis among professional health practitioners. Disseminates informational materials to individuals with osteoporosis, physicians, and the public. Offers audio visual programs; participates in public forums. **Publications:** *Osteoblast* (quarterly); *Osteoporosis Update* (quarterly).

40946 ■ People's Medical Society

PO Box 868
Allentown, PA 18105-0868
Ph:(610)770-1670
Free: 800-624-8773
Fax: (610)770-0607
Co. E-mail: cbi@peoplesmed.org
URL: http://www.peoplesmed.org
Contact: Pamela Maraldo PhD, Chair
Description: Promotes citizen involvement in the cost, quality, and management of the American health care system. Seeks to: train and encourage individuals to study local health care systems, practitioners, and institutions and promote preventive health care and medical cost control by these groups; address major policy issues and control health costs; encourage more preventive practice and research; promote self-care and alternative health care procedures; launch an information campaign to assist individuals in maintaining personal health and to prepare them for appointments with medical professionals. Convention/Meeting: none. **Publications:** *Allergies: Questions You Have...Answers You Need*; *Alzheimer's and Dementia: Questions You Have...Answers You Need*; *Arthritis: Questions You Have, Answers You Need*; *Asthma: Questions You Have, Answers You Need*; *Breathe Better, Feel Better*; *The Consumer's Medical Desk Reference*; *Depression: Questions You Have, Answers You Need*; *Headaches: 47 Ways to Stop the Pain*; *Hearing Loss: Questions, You Have, Answers You Need*; *Long-Term Care and Alternatives*; *Medicare Made Easy*; *Medicine on Trial*; *Misdiagnosis: Woman as a Disease*; *Natural Recipes for the Good Life*; *150 Ways to Be a Savvy Medical Consumer*; *People's Medical Society Newsletter* (bimonthly); *Prostate: Questions You Have...Answers You Need*; *77 Ways to Beat Colds and Flu*; *Take This Book to the Gynecologist With You*; *Take This Book to the Hospital With You*.

40947 ■ Physicians Committee for Responsible Medicine

5100 Wisconsin Ave. NW, Ste. 400
Washington, DC 20016
Ph:(202)686-2210
Fax: (202)686-2216
Co. E-mail: pcrm@pcrm.org
URL: http://www.pcrm.org
Contact: Neal D. Barnard MD, Pres.
Description: Physicians, scientists, healthcare professionals, and interested others. Increases public awareness about the importance of preventive medicine and nutrition, and raises scientific and ethical questions pertaining to the use of humans and animals in medical research. Supports research into U.S. agricultural and public health policies. Promotes the New Four Food Groups, a no-cholesterol, low-fat alternative to U.S.D.A. dietary recommendations. Maintains the Gold Plan program, which includes information on low-fat, cholesterol-free entrees and nutrition for institutional food services. Offers fact sheets on nutrition, preventive medicine, and non-animal research topics. Maintains speakers' bureau. **Publications:** *Alternatives in Medical Education*; *Best in the World (Cookbook)*; *Eat Right, Live Longer*; *Food for Life*; *Foods That Fight Pain*; *Good Medicine* (quarterly); *PCRM Online* (monthly); *The Power of Your Plate*. Also publishes fact sheets.

40948 ■ SMARTRISK

790 Bay St., Ste. 401
Toronto, ON, Canada M5G 1N8
Ph:(416)977-7350
Fax: (416)596-2700
Co. E-mail: info@smartrisk.ca
URL: http://www.smartrisk.ca
Contact: Dr. Robert Conn, CEO
Description: Works to reduce the number of injuries in Canada. Sponsors campaigns to raise public awareness of preventable causes of injury in all aspects of daily life. **Publications:** *Heads Up* (monthly); *Will It Float*.

40949 ■ Society for the Psychological Study of Social Issues

208 I St. NE
Washington, DC 20002-4340
Ph:(202)675-6956
Fax: (202)675-6902
Co. E-mail: spssi@spssi.org
URL: http://www.spssi.org
Contact: Shari Miles PhD, Exec. Dir.
Description: Psychologists, sociologists, anthropologists, psychiatrists, political scientists, and social workers. Works to: obtain and disseminate to the public scientific knowledge about social change and other social processes; promote psychological research on significant theoretical and practical questions of social issues; encourage application of findings to problems of society. **Publications:** *Analyses of Social Issues and Public Policy (ASAP)* (quarterly); *Journal of Social Issues* (quarterly); *Social Psychological Applications to Social Issues* (3/year); *SPSSI Newsletter* (3/year).

40950 ■ Society for the Study of Social Problems

901 McClung Tower
University of Tennessee
Knoxville, TN 37996-0490
Ph:(865)689-1531
Fax: (865)689-1534
Co. E-mail: tomhood@utk.edu
URL: http://www.sssp1.org
Contact: Thomas C. Hood, Exec. Officer
Description: An interdisciplinary community of scholars, activists, practitioners, and students endeavoring to create greater social justice through social research. Members are often social scientists working in colleges and universities, in non-profit organizations and in other applied and policy settings. **Publications:** *Anthologies of Articles from Social Problems* (periodic); *Social Problems* (quarterly); Membership Directory (monthly); Newsletter (3/year).

40951 ■ Society for Women's Health Research

1025 Connecticut Ave. NW, Ste. 701
Washington, DC 20036
Ph:(202)223-8224
Fax: (202)833-3472
Co. E-mail: info@womenshealthresearch.org
URL: http://www.womenshealthresearch.org
Contact: Phyllis Greenberger MSW, Pres./CEO
Purpose: Seeks to improve the health of women by promoting equity in research. Advocates policies which promotes the inclusion of women in clinical trials; informs government agencies and private industry of issues affecting women's health and sex-based biology; educates women consumers on conditions that affect women; promotes funding for women's health research. **Publications:** *Journal of Women's Health* (10/year); *Sexx Matters* (quarterly).

40952 ■ United Methodist Association of Health and Welfare Ministries

407 Corporate Center Dr., Ste. B
Vandalia, OH 45377
Ph:(937)415-3624
Free: 800-411-9901
Fax: (937)222-7364
Co. E-mail: info@umassociation.org
URL: http://www.umassociation.org
Contact: Rev. Dr. Mearle L. Griffith, CEO/Pres.
Description: Offers communications and church relations guidance. Provides leadership development training for health and human service professionals in United Methodist related organizations and agencies. Develops ethical and theological statements on institutional care. Operates Educational Assessment Guidelines Leading Toward Excellence (EAGLE), a self-assessment and peer review accreditation program. Operates a Field Consultation Program; members may access skilled professionals to assist with governance questions. Offers audiovisual services to members. Administers the Order of Good Shepherds program designed to recognize ministry in the workplace by employees at member organizations. Maintains speakers' bureau; compiles statistics. **Publications:** *Children, Youth, and Family Services Section Salary and Benefit Study*; *National Directory of all United Methodist Related Health and Welfare Ministries* (annual); *Older Adult Ministries Section Salary and Benefit Study*.

REFERENCE WORKS

40953 ■ "Account Balances Indicate That 401(k) Participants Have Heard The Long-Term Investor Message" in *Employee Benefit Plan Review* (Vol. 55)

Pub: Charles D. Spencer & Associates, Inc.
Ed: Sue Burzawa. **Description:** Lincolnshire, Illinois-based Hewitt Associates LLC, the health benefit plan consulting company, tracks pension fund activity through its 401(k) Index. Industry analysts said that institutional investors are remaining calm as the country suffers from a period of economic upheaval.

40954 ■ *Adoption Resource Book*
Pub: HarperCollins
Contact: Lois Gilman, Author
Released: Irregular, latest edition 4. Price: $16.95, individuals paper. Publication Includes: List of public and private adoption agencies, support groups, and services. Entries Include: Agency name, address, phone, special requirements. Principal content of the publication is a discussion of adoption procedures and requirements, including adoption of foreign children and open adoption. Arrangement: Geographical.

40955 ■ "Aetna to Expand to Pompano Beach" in *Miami Herald* (March 10, 2005)
Pub: Knight-Ridder/Tribune Business News
Ed: Patrick Danner. Description: Aetna healthcare will open a new prescription mail order facility in Pompano Beach, Florida. The new facility will employ about 800 people. Another facility in Kansas City, Missouri, owned by Aetna, fills nearly 6 million prescriptions annually.

40956 ■ "Age Rage: Younger Employees are Crying Age Discrimination" in *Entrepreneur* (Vol. 32, No. 4, April 2004, pp. 24)
Pub: Entrepreneur Media, Inc.
Ed: Chris Penttila. Description: Employees in the forty-something age bracket are filing discrimination suits against employers charging they are being excluded from particular retirement health benefits older employees receive.

40957 ■ "Ailing Wellness Plan considers job cuts" in *Crain's Detroit Business* (Vol. 19, No. 9, March 3, 2003, pp. 3)
Pub: Crain Communications Inc., Detroit
Ed: Katie Merx. Description: The State of Michigan's largest Medicaid health maintenance organization is considering laying off workers in an attempt to save money.

40958 ■ "Ambulance Chasing, Web-Style" in *Forbes* (Vol. 174, December 27, 2004, No. 13, pp. 56)
Pub: Forbes Magazine Inc.
Ed: David Whelan. Description: Law firms are paying large sums to place pay-per-click ads on Internet sites. The ads take the user to a law firm's Web site or a middleman, and a lawyer pays up to $160 to the Internet service provider.

40959 ■ "American Trends Column" in *Richmond Times-Dispatch* (February 7, 2005)
Pub: Richmond Times-Dispatch
Ed: Gary Robertson. Description: A new trend in medicine is the hiring of a personal physician. There are currently about 250 concierge physicians in the U.S., but the numbers are growing because many affluent baby-boomers are willing to pay a premium price for a doctor's time.

40960 ■ "Answer the phone and have a good time" in *Rough Notes* (Vol. 146, No. 4, April 2003, pp. 18)
Pub: Rough Notes
Ed: Dennis Pillsbury. Description: Mike Heffernan is the CEO of Heffernan Group, which includes Heffernan Insurance Brokers, an insurance retail agency and Presidio and Advanced Risk Technologists. Nearly 50 percent of business is derived from niche practices and programs such as nonprofits, healthcare, property owners, construction and technology.

40961 ■ "Appetite for Destruction" in *Washington Business Journal* (Vol. 22, No. 14, August 8, 2003, pp. 29)
Pub: Washington Business Journal
Ed: Tim Pappa. Description: Brad Schofield, president of Safeguard Shredding, said that the mobile document shredding company is planning a major expansion program. The firm's business is increasing since medical companies are required to destroy patient records under the 2003 Health Insurance Portability Accountability Act.

40962 ■ "Are Race-Specific Drugs Unethical?" in *Black Enterprise* (Vol. 36, November 2005, No. 4, pp. 37)
Pub: Earl G. Graves Publishing Co. Inc.
Ed: Ron Chepesiuk, Joyce Jones. Description: BiDil, the first drug marketed for treatment of heart failure in African Americans was approved by the U.S. Food and Drug Administration in June 2005. Some in the African American community are questioning why the drug would work better for the Black population over other races.

40963 ■ "Ask Inc." in *Inc.* (August 1, 2004)
Pub: Inc. Magazine
Description: Examples to jump-start sales are offered for a managed-care consulting firm and a small skin care business.

40964 ■ "Attention to Nonmedical Factors Can Facilitate Return-To-Work For Workers' Comp Claimants" in *Employee Benefit Plan Review* (Vol. 55)
Pub: Charles D. Spencer & Associates, Inc.
Ed: Jay E. Betz. Description: Workers' compensation insurance is the focus of an interview with Jay E. Betz, an executive at Milwaukee, Wisconsin-based CareNetwork Inc. The goal of workers' compensation services is to return the injured employee to work in a safe and timely manner.

40965 ■ "Baker, Donelson, Bearman, Caldwell & Berkowitz, PC" in *Mississippi Business Journal* (Vol. 29, January 2007, No. 4, pp. 6)
Pub: Venture Publications, Inc.
Description: Profile of William S. Painter of law firm Baker, Donelson, Bearman, Caldwell & Berkowitz, PC, who concentrates his practice in the areas of corporate, tax and healthcare restructuring.

40966 ■ "Belt-Tightening at Pfizer?" in *Business Week Online* (February 9, 2005)
Pub: McGraw-Hill Companies
Ed: Amy Barrett. Description: Pfizer is expected to announce a major restructuring of the company in order to cut costs, but its sales force is believed to be safe from cuts.

40967 ■ "Benefits Costs Averaged 36.8 Percent Of Payroll In 1999" in *Employee Benefit Plan Review* (Vol. 55, No. 10, April 2001 pp. 14)
Pub: Charles D. Spencer & Associates, Inc.
Description: The U.S. Chamber of Commerce annual survey, "The 2000 Employee Benefits Study", shows the most costly company benefit in 1999 was still paid time off at 30 percent. The second most expensive was medical benefits, which accounted for 26 percent of the benefit dollar.

40968 ■ "Best Practices" in *Entrepreneur* (Vol. 32, October 2004, No. 10, pp. 84)
Pub: Entrepreneur Media, Inc.
Ed: Mark Henricks. Description: Doctors, lawyers and other professionals are taking the lead from entrepreneurs when running and building their businesses. Innovative solutions to grow a professional practice like an entrepreneur are shared.

40969 ■ "Big Pharm's Favorite Gadfly" in *Business Week* (December 19, 2005, No. 3964, pp. 50-51)
Pub: McGraw-Hill Companies
Ed: Amy Barrett. Description: Dr. Steven E. Nissen, leader of clinical trials, works to ascertain drug safety.

40970 ■ "Bill Would Boost Small Businesses" in *Bradenton Herald* (February 13, 2007)
Pub: Bradenton Herald
Ed: Brian Neill. Description: U.S. Representative Vern Buchanan has introduced a bill in Congress that includes a provision that would enable small businesses to offer health insurance more readily through the formation of associations. The bill would also benefit small business owners by allowing them to deduct a larger portion of taxes for labor and capital expenditures.

40971 ■ "Blues losses decline for small-group business coverage" in *Crain's Detroit Business* (Vol. 18, No. 17, April 29, 2002, pp. 22)
Pub: Crain Communications Inc. - Detroit
Ed: David Barkholz. Description: Blue Cross and Blue Shield of Michigan has cut underwriting losses in its troubled small-group business at a time when legislation is aimed at changing Blues governance and health insurance in Michigan.

40972 ■ "Borders of Life" in *Crain's Detroit Business* (Vol.22, December 18, 2006, No. 51, pp. 1)
Pub: Crain Communications Inc. - Detroit
Ed: Andrew Dieterich. Description: Southeast Michigan offers faster serious health care options to Canadian residents in nearby Windsor and southwest Ontario. Statistics on available facilities are included in this article.

40973 ■ "Broader Wheelchair Access Rules Proposed" in *Inc.* (September 2005, pp. 32)
Pub: Inc. Magazine
Ed: Allen P. Roberts Jr. Description: The Justice Department is considering changing the Americans With Disabilities Act to require companies to make all entryways wheelchair accessible, a move that would impact all small companies.

40974 ■ "Bush Signs HSAs Into Law" in *Tax Notes* (Vol. 101, No. 11, December 15, 2003, pp. 1250-1251)
Pub: Tax Notes International
Ed: Patti Mohr. Description: An overview of the health savings accounts President Bush signed into law.

40975 ■ "Business On Her Own Terms" in *Black Enterprise* (Vol. 35, August 2004, No. 1, pp. 57)
Pub: Earl G. Graves Publishing Co. Inc.
Ed: Bridget McCrea. Description: Profile of Fay Coleman, president and CEO of her Silver Spring, Maryland firm, Westover Consultants Inc. Coleman started her business in the basement of her home and began developing educational training programs, planning events, creating public outreach programs, and conducting surveys for government agencies. Today, the firm comprises three divisions: Health and Behavior Sciences, Management Support Services, and Information Technology Services.

40976 ■ "Businesses' Cost From Flu Are Nothing To Sneeze At" in *Tampa Tribune* (November 3, 2005)
Pub: Media General, Inc.
Ed: Dave Simanoff. Description: Experts predict this year's flu season will cost about $8 billion in paid sick leave for businesses, equating to 70 million missed work days.

40977 ■ "CAN Forms In Capital City" in *Mississippi Business Journal* (Vol. 29, January 2007, No. 3, pp. A10)
Pub: Venture Publications, Inc.
Description: New non-profit company The Certified Nursing Assistant Programs Training Center Inc., has formed with the mission of remedying the shortage of nurses in Mississippi. They are located in the Jackson Medical Mall Thad Cochran Center.

40978 ■ "Candidates' Take on Premiums" in *Inc.* (October 1, 2003)
Pub: Gruner & Jahr USA Publishing
Ed: Alison Stein Wellner. Description: A guide to Democratic presidential candidates' proposals, particularly regarding health insurance.

40979 ■ *CARES Directory*
Pub: United Way of New York City
Contact: Raquel Dasilva
Released: Biennial. Covers: over 2,469 nonprofit social service agencies in the greater New York area. Entries Include: Name, address, phone, names and titles of key personnel, agency mission, programs of-

fered, eligibility requirements, fees, application procedure, geographic area served, other locations, site director name and title, accessibility to the handicapped, hours open, languages spoken, transportation facilities. **Arrangement:** Alphabetical by agency name. **Indexes:** Program, Keyword/Target Group.

40980 ■ *Case Management Resource Guide*
Pub: Dorland Healthcare Information
Contact: V. Kelly
E-mail: vkelly@dorlandhealth.com
Released: Annual, latest edition 2005-2006. **Price:** $60, individuals for additional copy, per volume. **Entries Include:** Facility name, address, phone names and titles of key personnel; number of employees, geographical area served, type of service or programs provided branch office or parent organization name and phone, and credentials. **Database Covers:** in four regional volumes, lists 110,000 health care facilities and support services, including homecare, rehabilitation, psychiatric, and addiction treatment program; hospices, adult day care, and burn and cancer centers. **Arrangement:** Classified by service provided and location. **Indexes:** Company name, advertiser.

40981 ■ "Changes in Care" in *Pittsburgh Business Times* (Vol. 23, No. 1, July 25, 2003, pp. 1s)
Pub: Pittsburgh Business Times
Ed: Lynne Glover. **Description:** Lutheran Affiliated Services, led by CEO Greg Hughes, operates a chain of nursing homes and is the ninth-largest elder care firm in the Pittsburgh, Pennsylvania area. Hughes creates a more homelike atmosphere at the facilities.

40982 ■ "Charging an Arm and a Leg?" in *Orlando Business Journal* (Vol. 20, No. 2, June 27, 2003, pp. 1)
Pub: American City Business Journals, Inc.
Ed: Susan Lundine. **Description:** An examination of the results of a survey of Florida hospitals, including medical care prices and rates, hospital prices and rates, and medical care surveys.

40983 ■ "Chicago Tribune Inside Health Care" in *Chicago Tribune* (March 3, 2005)
Pub: Knight-Ridder/Tribune Business News
Ed: Bruce Japsen. **Description:** The Leapfrog Group is helping employers in the Chicago area to determine if hospitals are providing quality care to their employees. The measures will recommend that hospitals adopt three primary safety practices.

40984 ■ "Citigroup Names President Of GDB" in *Wall Street Journal* (Vol. 248, December 2006, No. 145, pp. B10)
Pub: Dow Jones & Co. Inc.
Ed: Rick Carew **Description:** Profile of Michael Zink, new president of GDB of Citigroup. Zink played a top in the integration of South Korea's KorAm Bank, which Citigroup acquired in April 2004

40985 ■ "Cleaning Up in Health Care" in *Boston Business Journal* (Vol. 23, No. 27, August 8, 2003, pp. 16)
Pub: American City Business Journals
Ed: Mark Micheli. **Description:** Profile of Equipment Systems Inc. located in Weston, Massachusetts, which does business as SonicScrub, is presented.

40986 ■ "Club Meds: Could Drug-Buying Clubs Cure High Prescription Costs?" in *Entrepreneur* (Vol. 32, November 2004, No. 11, pp. 24)
Pub: Entrepreneur Media Inc.
Ed: Julie Monahan. **Description:** Fifty employers from the Fortune 500 are teaming to negotiate better prices with pharmaceutical companies to help ease the burden of high costs of prescription drugs for employees.

40987 ■ "Combined Health Agencies" in *San Diego Business Journal* (Vol. 28, January 15, 2007, No. 3, pp. 33)
Pub: San Diego Business Journal Associates
Ed: Stacey Bengtson. **Description:** Listing of combined health agencies includes agency leader, contact information, and the organization's mission.

40988 ■ "Consumers Hit Harder by Medicine Copayments" in *Boston Globe* (February 8, 2005)
Pub: New York Times Company
Ed: Christopher Rowland. **Description:** Consumers reported the biggest change in health insurance for 2004 was the increase in co-payments for prescription drugs. Statistical data included.

40989 ■ *Council for Health and Human Service Ministries—Directory of Services*
Pub: Council for Health and Human Service Ministries
Released: Annual, latest edition 2002-2003. **Covers:** about 300 social welfare agencies, retirement homes, children's residential homes, hospitals, and other health and human service facilities affiliated with the United Church of Christ. **Entries Include:** Agency name, type of institution and summary of services offered, certifications and memberships, name of chief administrator, mailing address, phone, and conference assignment. **Arrangement:** Alphabetical. **Indexes:** Service.

40990 ■ "Creative Control" in *Washington Business Journal* (Vol. 22, No. 9, July 4, 2003, pp. 16)
Pub: Washington Business Journal
Ed: Chris Silva. **Description:** Management style, marketing and strategic planning of Washington, DC-based Healthcare Ventures LLC is discussed.

40991 ■ "Crossing the Gene Barrier" in *Business Week* (January 16, 2006, No. 3967, pp. 72-77, 80)
Pub: McGraw-Hill Companies
Ed: Arlene Weintraub. **Description:** Biotechnology scientists Harry M. Meade and Nils Lonberg are mixing the genetic materials of man and beats in new ways in order to develop treatments of life threatening diseases such as cancer and arthritis. Medical ethics of genetic research are also discussed.

40992 ■ "A Cure for Health Concerns" in *Black Enterprise* (Vol. 35, November 2004, No. 4, pp. 141)
Pub: Earl G. Graves Publishing Co. Inc.
Ed: James A. Anderson. **Description:** Without long-term care insurance, families will have trouble providing health care later in life.

40993 ■ "Cybercare's Offices Empty Out Amid Tardy Filings" in *South Florida Business Journal* (Vol. 24, No. 1, August 15, 2003, pp. 1)
Pub: American City Business Journals
Ed: John T. Fakler. **Description:** Profile of Cyber-Care, the telehealth service provider, is presented.

40994 ■ "Deducting the Cost of Laser Eye Surgery" in *Journal of Accountancy* (Vol. 198, December 2004, No. 6, pp. 92)
Pub: American Institute of Certified Public Accountants
Ed: W. Terry Dancer. **Description:** The Internal Revenue Service has issued a letter ruling that addresses whether surgical procedures to correct nearsightedness, farsightedness and astigmatism can be used as a tax deduction.

40995 ■ "Dental, vision plan vendors use the Web to administer, communicate, market benefits" in *Employee Benefit Plan Review* (Vol. 55, No. 6)
Pub: Charles D. Spencer & Associates, Inc.
Ed: Robert Pruter. **Description:** Dental and vision insurance plan providers are redesigning their Web sites to offer better services to employers and to better market themselves to small businesses.

40996 ■ *Dial 800 for Health*
Pub: People's Medical Society
Contact: Karla Morales
Released: Irregular. **Covers:** health related organizations providing toll-free numbers. **Entries Include:** Organization name, location, toll-free phone number, geographical area served, description of service and e-mail address when available; hours of operation; hearing/visually impaired access. **Arrangement:** Classified by subject. **Indexes:** Subject.

40997 ■ *Directory of Catholic Charities USA Directories*
Pub: Catholic Charities USA
Ed: Mary Reed, Editor. **Released:** Annual. **Price:** $25, individuals. **Covers:** nearly 1,200 Catholic community and social service agencies. Listings include diocesan agencies, state Catholic conferences. **Entries Include:** Organization name, address, name and title of director, phone, fax. **Arrangement:** Geographical by state, then classified by diocese.

40998 ■ *Directory of Community Care Facilities*
Pub: California Department of Social Services
Contact: Tanya De La Cruz
Ed: Tanya De La Cruz, Editor. **Released:** Quarterly. **Price:** $75. **Covers:** adoption and home finding agencies, residential care facilities for adults and children, preschool care centers, and day care centers located in California and licensed by the California Department of Social Services. Health facilities are not listed. **Entries Include:** Facility name, address, phone; name of director or administrator; capacity; license limitations (age, sex, hours of care, etc.) **Arrangement:** Geographical.

40999 ■ *Directory of Human Services and Self Help Support Groups-Maricopa County*
Pub: Community Information & Referral Inc.
Contact: Roberto Armijo, Exec. Dir.
Released: Annual, January. **Covers:** More than 2,300 governmental and private non-profit human service organizations in Maricopa County, Arizona. **Entries Include:** Organization name, address, phone, fax, e-mail, URL, name and title of contact, affiliations, location, geographical area served, eligibility requirements, description of services, days and hours of operation, complete program and service descriptions. **Arrangement:** Alphabetical. **Indexes:** Subject, alphabetical.

41000 ■ "Do I Have a Choice?" in *Inc.* (September 2005, pp. 40)
Pub: Inc. Magazine
Ed: Stephanie Clifford. **Description:** Greg Roderick's firm offers three health plans to his employees, which encourages competition among providers. Statistical data included.

41001 ■ "The Doctor Will E-Mail You Now" in *Black Enterprise* (Vol. 36, February 2006, No. 7, pp. 168)
Pub: Earl G. Graves Publishing Co. Inc.
Ed: Leslie E. Royal. **Description:** Many physicians across the nation are offering their patients online visits and several major insurance carriers are providing coverage for the service.

41002 ■ *Dorland's Medical Directory*
Pub: Dorland Healthcare Information
Contact: Virginia Kelly
E-mail: vkelly@dorlandhealth.com
Released: Annual, latest edition 2004. **Price:** $71.95, individuals plus $3.95 shipping. **Covers:** nearly 15,000 physicians in Eastern Pennsylvania and Southern New Jersey, Northern Delaware. Also includes group practices, hospitals, healthcare facilities, and medical organizations. **Entries Include:** For physicians—Name, office and home addresses and phone, fax numbers, email addresses, medical school attended and year graduated, medical specialties, certifications, hospital affiliations. For hospitals—Name, address, names and specialties of staff members. **Arrangement:** Geographical, subject. **Indexes:** Speciality.

41003 ■ "Drug Importation and the Capital Markets" in *Venture Capital Journal* (November 1, 2004)
Pub: Thomason Financial Inc.
Description: Issues involving the importation of prescription drugs are covered. An examination of the economics behind cross-border shipment of drugs is essential in order to understand the affects of importation. Canadian and European governments are able to name the price they will pay for a particular drug and

the Canadian government pays only the cost of manufacturing with a small markup, while American consumers not only pay manufacturing costs, but also research and development, administrative along with a markup.

41004 ■ "Emageon Vies With Big Guns" in Birmingham Business Journal (Vol. 20, No. 39, September 26, 2003, pp. 1)
Pub: American City Business Journals, Inc.
Ed: Tom Bassing. Description: Profile of Emageon Inc., maker of inter-connectable software for hospital diagnostic equipment.

41005 ■ "Employee Health Costs Rose 6.1 Percent" in Tampa Tribune (November 22, 2005)
Pub: Media General, Inc.
Ed: Dave Simanoff. Description: According to a survey conducted by Mercer Health & Benefits LLC, annual health care costs rose to $7,089 for American employees, up 6.1 percent over 2004.

41006 ■ Episcopal Church Annual
Pub: Morehouse Publishing
Contact: Ken Quigley
Ed: Kenneth H. Quigley, Editor. Released: Annual, February. Covers: the churches and clergy of the Episcopal Church; seminaries, training schools, retreat centers, and social service agencies; dioceses, and provinces of Anglican Communion. Entries Include: Name, address, phone of churches; name and address of clergy members; staff size, membership; the organizations, officers, and other information for the Episcopal Church in the United States of America with contacts, addresses, and phone numbers. Arrangement: Clergy list is alphabetical; diocesan list is alphabetical. Indexes: Alphabetical by categories; Classified Buyers' Guide classified by subject; alphabetical by advertisers.

41007 ■ "Feel the Burn" in Entrepreneur (Vol. 33, August 2005, No. 8, pp. 28)
Pub: Entrepreneur Media Inc.
Ed: Stephen Barlas. Description: The Workforce Health Improvement Program Act would allow small companies to deduct the costs for reimbursing employees' health club fees.

41008 ■ "Fighting alcohol abuse can benefit insurers" in Rough Notes (Vol. 146, No. 3, March 2003, pp. 114)
Pub: Rough Notes
Ed: Phil Zinkewicz. Description: Alcoholism is a disease and teenage drinking results in incalculable loss of human lives and suffering, insurance claims for death, health, medical treatment and property damage; Van Wagner, owner of the Van Wagner Group, wants the insurance agency to tackle alcohol abuse head on.

41009 ■ "Fill-In Physicians" in Birmingham Business Journal (Vol. 20, No. 20, July 4, 2003, pp. 15)
Pub: American City Business Journals, Inc.
Ed: Tom Bassing. Description: Birmingham, Alabama-based Preferred MedSearch Consultants Inc. provides a professional recruitment service for the health care industry. Preferred MedSearch, led by president, Stephen Cannon, provides temporary health care staffing services.

41010 ■ "Five Ideas to Watch" in Inc. (August 1, 2004)
Pub: Inc. Magazine
Ed: Nicole Gull. Description: Five new ideas for products are presented, including a new window-mounted device that can detect brush fires; a new dog tag for the armed forces containing a wireless chip that carries medical and other key information for medics; pumps and motors that respond to electrical impulses; shopping carts that double as exercise equipment; and Steak n Shake's eight new milk shake flavors.

41011 ■ "Fly By Night? Don't Fall for a Scam-Use These Tips Before You Buy Health Insurance" in Entrepreneur (Vol. 31, No. 10, October 2003)
Pub: Entrepreneur Media, Inc.
Ed: Jacquelyn Lynn. Description: Health insurance scams targeting small businesses and their employees often collect millions of dollars before vanishing when claims start coming in. Tips to avoid fraudulent insurance companies are listed.

41012 ■ "For Offering Hope and Help to the Parents of Autistic Children" in Inc. (April 1, 2005)
Pub: Inc. Magazine
Description: Profile of Julie Azuma, founder of Different Roads to Learning. After learning that her daughter Miranda was autistic, Azuma created an online retail business offering tools to help teach language and social skills to autistic children.

41013 ■ "Genetic Medicine's Next Big Step" in Fortune (Vol. 151, January 10, 2005, No. 1, pp. 54)
Pub: Time Inc.
Ed: John Simons. Description: RNA interference (RNAi) is a process that is able to block threatening genetic signals in diseased cells, such as those that can proliferate a virus. This process could lead to the breakthrough needed for the struggling drug industry. Profile of Alnylam Pharmaceutical in Cambridge, Massachusetts is included.

41014 ■ "Get Used to the Pain" in Business Week (No. 3854, October 20, 2003, pp. 42)
Pub: McGraw-Hill Inc.
Ed: William C. Symonds, Brian Grow, Carol Marie Cropper, Diane Brady. Description: Health insurance costs for employers are expected to rise by 16 percent in 2004.

41015 ■ Global Health Directory
Pub: Global Health Council
Ed: Annmarie Christensen, Editor, achristensen@globalhealth.org. Released: Irregular, latest edition 2003-2004. Price: $50, nonmembers payment must accompany order; $25, members payment must accompany order plus $5.95 shipping and handling. Covers: over 450 private voluntary organizations, universities, civic groups, professional associations, and other groups involved with global health. Entries Include: Organization name, address, e-mail, website, contact name, number of employees, mission, services, regions served, publications, internships available, and volunteer information. Arrangement: Classified by title of organization.

41016 ■ "Good for Business: Houston is a Hot Spot for Economic Growth" in Black Enterprise (Vol. 37, October 2006, No. 3, pp. 216)
Pub: Earl G. Graves Publishing Co. Inc.
Ed: Jeanette Valentine. Description: Fast-growing sectors in the biotechnology and healthcare industries are among the driving forces of Houston's economic growth. More than 76,000 small businesses in the area employ about one in four area workers, according to the Small Business Administration. Housing and business costs are 26 and 11 percent below the national average, respectively, garnering the attention of corporate giants.

41017 ■ "HAP boosts employee-pay plans" in Crain's Detroit Business (Vol. 19, No. 6, Feb. 10, 2003, pp. 3)
Pub: Crain Communications Inc., Detroit
Ed: Katie Merx. Description: Henry Ford Health System's insurance sector is promoting its product line that will help cut the increasing costs of health care to employers.

41018 ■ "Health Businesses" in Entrepreneur (Vol. 32, No. 1, January 2004, pp. 208)
Pub: Entrepreneur Media, Inc.
Description: Profiles of health care franchise opportunities, including vision care and dental services.

41019 ■ "Health Care Battle Heats Up" in San Francisco Business Times (Vol. 17, No. 50, July 18, 2003, pp. 1)
Pub: American City Business Journals
Ed: Meg Walker. Description: Growing competition between Sutter Health and Kaiser Permanente in Marin, California is examined. Topics include marketing strategy, membership prices and rates, and market share.

41020 ■ "Health care, federal contracts high on Bush's small business agenda" in Crain's Detroit Business (Vol. 18, No. 22, June 3, 2002, pp.50)
Pub: Crain Communications Inc. - Detroit
Ed: Laura Bailey. Description: Under President Bush's small business agenda, companies can expect more affordable health insurance and fairer competition for government contracts.

41021 ■ "Health Care: California's Next Freakout?" in Business Week Online (September 5, 2003)
Pub: McGraw-Hill Inc.
Ed: Arlene Weintraub. Description: Universal health care is at the top of California legislator's agenda. The impact of universal health care on small business and the state is examined.

41022 ■ Health Groups in Washington
Pub: National Health Council Inc.
Contact: Myrl Weinberg, Pres.
E-mail: weinberg@nhcouncil.org
Released: Biennial, August of odd years. Price: $40, members; $50, nonmembers. Covers: over 800 professional, voluntary, consumer, insurance, union, business, and academic organizations with some impact on the development of federal health policies. Entries Include: Name of organization, address, phone, e-mail address, website address, names of Washington representatives. Arrangement: Alphabetical. Indexes: Subject index; personnel index.

41023 ■ "Health Insurance Rates Still Rising as Hospitals Struggle" in Crain's Detroit Business (Vol. 19, No. 45, November 10, 2003, pp. 25)
Pub: Crain Communications Inc., Detroit
Ed: Katie Merx. Description: Health insurance rate increases have slowed but continue to rise at double-digit rates and the number of working people without insurance is expected to grow, according to the Small Business Association of Michigan.

41024 ■ "Health Savings Accounts Not Getting Much Attention from Garden City-Area Employers" in Long Island Business News (January 30, 2004)
Pub: Dolan Media Newswires
Ed: Ben Abelson. Description: Health savings accounts could impact the health insurance industry in the U.S. These accounts allow employees with high health-insurance deductibles to set aside pre-tax income to cover the balance of deductibles.

41025 ■ "Healthcare Insurance" in Black Enterprise (Vol. 34, No. 2, September 2003, pp. 48)
Pub: Earl Graves Publishing Co.
Ed: Alan Hughes. Description: Healthcare insurance is becoming increasingly more difficult for small business owners to provide to employees, especially for a small home-based business wishing to expand. The House Small Business Committee introduced the Self-Employed Health Care Affordability Act of 2003 (H.R. 1873) in April 2003, this bill allows self-employed business owners to deduct health insurance costs when calculating payroll taxes, thus effectively reducing those costs by more than 15 percent.

41026 ■ "Heart of the Matter" in Hispanic Business (March 2005, pp. 58, 60)
Pub: Hispanic Business
Ed: Luisa Beltran. Description: Jose Nino, CEO of El Nino Group, discusses cardiovascular disease, the number one cause of death. Nino shares healthy choices to decrease risk factors for busy executives.

41027 ■ **"Helping Doctors Go Digital"** in *Business 2.0* **(Vol. 6, July 2005, No. 6, pp. 54-55)**
Pub: Time, Inc.
Ed: Erick Schonfeld. Description: Epocrates Essentials grew its subscriber base by offering important medical information to doctors, and in the process is able to profit from advertisers targeting the medical industry. Subscriptions to the service start at $60 annually.

41028 ■ **"Henry Schein Expands Office Space in Melville"** in *Long Island Business News* **(February 27, 2004)**
Pub: Dolan Media Newswires
Ed: Nick Anastasi. Description: Henry Schein Inc. is relocating to a 150,000-square foot building. The distributor of health care products will also hold the right to expand 80 Bayliss. Schein is the largest distributor of healthcare products and services to office-based healthcare practitioners in the combined North American and European markets and has operations in Australia and New Zealand.

41029 ■ **"He's Boss of the Blues; Phillip Pope Stays a Fiscally Prudent Course"** in *Birmingham Business Journal* **(Vol. 20, October 3, 2003)**
Pub: American City Business Journals, Inc.
Ed: Tom Bassing. Description: Profile of Phillip Pope, who was promoted from within the ranks of Blue Cross and Blue Shield of Alabama. The company is successful at membership retention, investments and growth and is planning strategies to offer services to aging baby boomers.

41030 ■ **"Hospitals Across Long Island Shift to Digital Imaging Technology"** in *Long Island Business News* **(February 20, 2004)**
Pub: Dolan Media Newswires
Ed: Claude Solnik. Description: In order to speed up and improve service, Long Island hospitals are changing over to digital imaging technology that allows doctors to view x-rays from home and confirm diagnoses with radiologists at the hospital.

41031 ■ **"Hospitals Turn to Ads as the Rx for Blahs"** in *San Francisco Business Times* **(Vol. 17, No. 51, July 25, 2003, pp. 20)**
Pub: American City Business Journals
Ed: Meg Walker. Description: Advertising campaigns of San Francisco, California hospitals are discussed.

41032 ■ **"How Good Is Your Online Nurse?"** in *Business Week* **(February 20, 2006, No. 3972, pp. 88)**
Pub: McGraw-Hill Companies
Ed: Arlene Weintraub. Description: WellPoint, UnitedHealth Group, and Aetna offer patient Internet portals with tools to help manage health issues.

41033 ■ **"How to Win a Marquee Account"** in *Sales and Marketing.com* **(Vol. 156, No. 3, March 2004, pp. 72)**
Pub: VNU eMedia, Inc.
Ed: John Zimmer. Description: Profile of Toshiba America Medical Systems, which sells medical imaging products for the diagnosis and treatment of heart disease, cancer and stroke. Toshiba's marketing strategy has helped them achieve double-digit growth in an otherwise sluggish market.

41034 ■ **"Inside Intel"** in *Business Week* **(January 9, 2006, No. 3966, pp. 46-52, 54)**
Pub: McGraw-Hill Companies
Ed: Cliff Edwards. Description: Profile of Paul Otellini, CEO of Intel Corporation. Otellini is taking the computer chipmaker into sectors such as consumer electronics, wireless communications, and health care.

41035 ■ **"Internet Facilities Defined Contribution Model For Employer-Sponsored Health Benefits"** in *Employee Benefit Plan Review* **(Vol. 55, No.12)**
Pub: Charles D. Spencer & Associates, Inc.
Ed: Miriam Basch Scott. Description: Defined contribution health benefits plans have been transformed

through the advent of the Internet. Regence Blue Cross Blue Shield of Oregon, working with Portland, Oregon-based Myhealthbank Inc., offers self-directed health benefit services.

41036 ■ **"IPO an Inner City 100 First"** in *Inc.* **(October 1, 2003)**
Pub: Gruner & Jahr USA Publishing
Ed: Jess McCuan. Description: Molina Healthcare becomes the first Inc. Inner City company to go public.

41037 ■ **"IRS changes and finalizes 2000 cafeteria plan rules"** in *Employee Benefit Plan Review* **(Vol. 55, No. 8, February 2001, pp. 13)**
Pub: Charles D. Spencer & Associates, Inc.
Description: The changes made by the Internal Revenue Service regarding the status change, cost and coverage rules for cafeteria plans, and published in March 2000, are covered. These changes will be effective for cafeteria plan years beginning on or after January 1, 2001.

41038 ■ **"IRS Will Remove Tax Trap for One-Person S Corporations"** in *Kiplinger Letter* **(Vol. 82, January 12, 2007, No. 1)**
Pub: Kiplinger
Description: Internal Revenue Service is developing a new system that will clarify S corporation owners in states that are not allowed to deduct one-participant group health insurance plans, however, to get the deduction, the S firm must pay the medical premium.

41039 ■ **"It's OK If You Shop Til You Drop"** in *Tampa Tribune* **(November 19, 2005)**
Pub: Media General, Inc.
Ed: Ted Jackovics. Description: Quick Quality Care is opening mini-clinics in retail stores offering non-emergency medical treatment to shoppers. Shoppers check in and are given a beeper to carry enabling them to shop until they can be seen by a medical professional.

41040 ■ *It's Your Life!*
Pub: Blue Dolphin Publishing Inc.
Contact: James A. Schaller, Author
Released: published 1997. Price: $16.95, individuals Retail price. Publication Includes: Resources covering health care for women. Entries Include: Publication name, address. Principal content of publication is articles and suggestions on health care and social and emotional issues for women.

41041 ■ **"Job Market Thaw"** in *Sales and Marketing.com* **(Vol. 156, No. 3, March 2004, pp. 24)**
Pub: VNU eMedia, Inc.
Description: Future job market trends for ten different industries are examined. The ten featured industries include construction, energy, financial services, healthcare/pharmaceutical, hospitality/travel, real estate, services, technology, telecommunications, and transportation.

41042 ■ **"Kaiser Getting a Transplant"** in *San Francisco Business Times* **(Vol. 18, No. 1, August 15, 2003, pp. 1)**
Pub: American City Business Journals
Ed: Meg Walker. Description: Dr. Sharon Inokuchi is leading a team that is launching a new kidney transplant program at San Francisco's Kaiser Permanent. The new transplant program may help the health maintenance organization build a reputation as a leading medical research facility.

41043 ■ **"Less than Half of Small Firms Offer Health Plans"** in *Wall Street Journal* **(November 4, 2003, pp. B9)**
Pub: Dow Jones & Co. Inc.
Ed: Richard C. Breeden. Description: It is estimated that less than half of all small businesses are able to offer health care plans to employees.

41044 ■ **"Lifestyle, research drugs cloud benefit decisions"** in *Business First Columbus* **(Vol. 18, No. 40, May 24, 2002, pp. B8)**
Pub: Business First Columbus, Inc.

Ed: Michael Nikunen, Timothy Dickman. Description: Companies will continue to find challenges with offering medical coverage to their employees.

41045 ■ **"Lights, Camera, Trauma!"** in *Crain's Chicago Business* **(Vol. 26, No. 50, December 15, 2003, pp. 1)**
Pub: Crain Communications, Inc.
Ed: Sarah A. Klein. Description: Chicago-area hospitals are enjoying the publicity they are gaining through reality television shows featuring births, women's specials, and documentaries about children's hospitals. Despite the costs incurred to accommodate camera crews, the hospitals are seeing a rise in donations.

41046 ■ **"Little urgency seen over HIPAA"** in *Crain's Detroit Business* **(Vol. 18, No.)**
Pub: Crain Communications Inc. - Detroit
Ed: David Barkholz, Andrew Dietderich. Description: Profile of the Health Insurance Portability and Accountability Act, which is intended to standardize and simplify security and privacy in health care.

41047 ■ **"LiveWell Center Opens"** in *Mississippi Business Journal* **(Vol. 29, January 2007, No. 2, pp. 10)**
Pub: Venture Publications, Inc.
Ed: Wally Northway Description: Forrest General Hospital has opened a new health center. The new LiveWell Center, located in the Cloverleaf Medical Plaza, seeks to empower individuals to take action in their own health.

41048 ■ **"Local Labs are Working to Perfect DNA Probes"** in *Kansas City Star* **(March 8, 2005)**
Pub: Knight-Ridder/Tribune Business News
Ed: Julius A. Karash. Description: Children's Mercy Hospital and Phylogenetix Laboratories Inc. have partnered to complete the development of patented DNA probes for detecting diseases; when completed the probes will be brought to market.

41049 ■ **"Lose Weight, Get a Toaster"** in *Inc.* **(January 1, 2005)**
Pub: Inc. Magazine
Ed: Bobbie Gossage. Description: Destiny Health offers consumer-driven health plans for small businesses. The insurer offers the Vitality program that awards points to participants who take care of themselves. The points can be converted into frequent-flier miles on three airlines.

41050 ■ **"MacroChem Advances Relaunch of Viagra Rival"** in *Boston Business Journal* **(Vol. 23, No. 31, September 5, 2003, pp. 1)**
Pub: American City Business Journals
Ed: Mark Hollmer. Description: Lexington, Massachusetts-based MacroChem Corporation, led by president and CEO Bob DeLuccia, is expanding Phase II clinical trials for a new topical hormone drug that will rival Viagra.

41051 ■ *Managing Health Benefits in Small and Mid-Sized Organizations*
Pub: Amacom
Ed: Patricia Halo. Released: July 1999. Price: $35.00. Description: Comprehensive guide for developing health care plans for companies employing between 50 and 5,000 employees in order to provide employees with better health care at lower prices.

41052 ■ *Maternal and Child Health*
Pub: Springer-Verlag New York Inc.
Contact: Donna J. Petersen, Co-editor
Released: Published 2004. Publication Includes: International health programs and trends, research and evaluation, U.S. Programs for mothers and children. Entries Include: Organization name, programs name, address, phone number. Principal content of publication is articles on maternal and child health.

41053 ■ **"Med Tech Carl Goldfischer"** in *Venture Capital Journal* **(January 1, 2005)**
Pub: Thomason Financial Inc.
Description: According to Carl Goldfischer, managing director at Bay City Capital, the best thing that could happen to the medical device market in 2005 is that large and small companies continue creating new products that improve disease management.

41054 ■ "Medfone Expanding Its Wantagh Headquarters" in *Long Island Business News* **(March 5, 2004)**
Pub: Dolan Media Newswires
Ed: Nick Anastasi. **Description:** Medfone National Inc. is expanding and renovating its corporate headquarters in New York. The firm acts as a call center serving all fields of the health industry, specializing in outsourced calling and Web-based solutions for the electronic retailing, direct marketing, pharmaceuticals, hospital, medical practice and managed care segments.

41055 ■ *Medical Directory of the Dakotas & Montana*
Pub: Jola Publications
Contact: Dennis Schapiro
Released: Biennial, latest edition 1st. **Price:** $18. **Covers:** Approximately 5,000 doctors, hospitals, clinics, nursing homes, and other selected health care providers in North Dakota, South Dakota, and Montana. **Entries Include:** Doctor or facility name, address, phone. **Arrangement:** Classified by type of facility or care provided. **Indexes:** Name, product/service, subject.

41056 ■ "Medical Emergency" in *Hispanic Business* **(May 2005, pp. 76, 78)**
Pub: Hispanic Business
Ed: Susan Kreimer. **Description:** The U. S. healthcare industry is struggling to meet the needs of hiring enough qualified Hispanic professionals including nurses, doctors, administrative staff, executives, and emergency personnel. Statistical data included.

41057 ■ *Medical and Health Information Directory*
Pub: Thomson Gale
Released: Annual, latest edition 18th, Published October 2005. **Price:** $285, individuals 15th volume; $805, individuals 18th edition. **Covers:** in Volume 1, more than 26,500 medical and health oriented associations, organizations, institutions, and government agencies, including health maintenance organizations (HMOs), preferred provider organizations (PPOs), insurance companies, pharmaceutical companies, research centers, and medical and allied health schools. In Volume 2, over 12,000 medical book publishers; medical periodicals, directories, audiovisual producers and services, medical libraries and information centers, electronic resources, and health-related internet search engines. In Volume 3, more than 35,500 clinics, treatment centers, care programs, and counseling/diagnostic services for 34 subject areas. **Entries Include:** Institution, service, or firm name, address, phone, fax, email and URL; many include names of key personnel and, when pertinent, descriptive annotation. Volume 3 was formerly listed separately as Health Services Directory. **Arrangement:** Classified by organization activity, service, etc. **Indexes:** Each volume has a complete alphabetical name and keyword index.

41058 ■ *Medicare & You Handbook*
Pub: Health Care Financing Administration
Released: Irregular, latest edition 2003. **Price:** Free. **Publication Includes:** Lists of medicare carriers in individual states. Principal content includes discussion of what Medicare is, what its various options are, and what new benefits have been added recently. ·

41059 ■ "Medicine Man" in *Forbes* **(June 10, 2002, p. 146)**
Pub: Forbes Magazine
Ed: Matthew Swibel. **Description:** Profile of Michael Caradimitropoulo of health discount-card seller Pinnacle Choice; Caradimitropoulo discusses ways selling discount health care cards to the uninsured can work.

41060 ■ "Medstat Acquisition May Bring More Jobs" in *Crain's Detroit Business* **(Vol. 22, September 25-October 1, 2006, No. 39, pp. 1, 38-39)**
Pub: Crain Communications Inc. - Detroit
Ed: Michelle Martinez. **Description:** Health care cost data and analysis company purchases competitor for expansion in local market. Consolidation in Ann Arbor may bring more jobs to this area.

41061 ■ "The Merry Go-Round" in *The Economist* **(Vol. 377, October 1-7, 2005, No. 8446, pp. 60)**
Pub: The Economist Newspaper Ltd.
Description: In the global drug industry, no regulation is more important than that of the U.S. Food and Drug Administration. The industry boasts $550 billion in annual sales.

41062 ■ *Minority Health Resources Directory*
Pub: ANROW Publishing
Contact: Marian Williams
Ed: Patricia President, Editor. **Released:** Published 1991. **Price:** $50 plus $6.95 shipping. **Covers:** 360 federal government programs and agencies, organizations, and foundations offering health services and products to minority group members. **Entries Include:** Name, address, phone, description, activities for minorities, publications and other communications, meetings and conferences. **Arrangement:** Classified by type of organization. **Indexes:** Organization name, subject, minority group served.

41063 ■ "MSA Withdrawals: Rules on Tax Exclusion" in *Employee Benefit Plan Review* **(Vol. 55, No. 12, June 2001, pp. 8)**
Pub: Charles D. Spencer & Associates, Inc.
Description: Questions and answers focus on Cobra rules and tax rules for employee health plans. Employees are advised that they may pay medical bills by using an employer's medical savings account, which are known as Archer MSAs.

41064 ■ *National Directory of Private Social Agencies*
Pub: Croner Publications Inc.
Contact: Rosa Padilla, Subscription Mgr.
E-mail: repadilla@ucdavis.edu
Ed: Ruth Jordan, Editor. **Released:** Base edition supplied upon order; monthly updates. **Price:** $109.95, individuals base and supplements; plus $9.95 shipping. **Entries Include:** Agency name, address, phone, name and title of contact, description of services. **Arrangement:** Geographical. **Indexes:** Service, agency type.

41065 ■ *National Wellness Institute-Member Directory*
Pub: National Wellness Institute
Contact: Anne Helmke
Ed: Linda R. Chapin, DDS, Editor. **Released:** updated daily. **Covers:** more than 1,600 health and wellness promotion professionals in corporations, hospitals, colleges, government agencies, universities, community organizations, schools (K-12), and consulting firms, and managed care. **Entries Include:** Member name, address, and phone, fax, email. **Arrangement:** Same information given in alphabetical, and geographical and work setting arrangements.

41066 ■ "Needed on the Frontline" in *Pittsburgh Business Times* **(Vol. 23, No. 8, September 12, 2003, pp. 19)**
Pub: Pittsburgh Business Times
Ed: Lynne Glover. **Description:** Profile of Frontline Healthcare LLC, founded by three local women, provides healthcare products designed by nurses. The firm, founded in 2002, introduced its new Personal Products Caddy Pack for hospital patients.

41067 ■ "A New Abacus for Pensions" in *Business Week* **(January 9, 2006, No. 3966, pp. 91)**
Pub: McGraw-Hill Companies
Description: New Financial Accounting Standards Board rules on post-retirement accounting will change how companies account for pensions and other employee benefits, especially retiree health insurance.

41068 ■ "New disease has businesses cautious, but few effects seen" in *Crain's Detroit Business* **(Vol. 19, No. 14, April 7, 2003, pp. 46)**
Pub: Crain Communications Inc., Detroit
Ed: Michael Strong. **Description:** Businesses in the metropolitan Detroit, Michigan area are keeping an eye on the progression of severe acute respiratory syndrome and keeping travel to China for business-critical issues only.

41069 ■ "No Slowdown Likely for Rising Health Costs" in *Crain's Detroit Business* **(Vol. 22, November 27, 2006, No. 48, pp. 21)**
Pub: Crain Communications Inc. - Detroit
Ed: Andrew Dietderich. **Description:** Double digit increases in health care are forecast for 2007. Health carriers say too many people who can afford to pay for medical treatment are leaving Michigan. This leaves a more indigent population behind. Governor is proposing assistance for access to universal health care.

41070 ■ "Nobody's Fool? Health Insurance Scams Target Entrepreneurs" in *Entrepreneur* **(Vol. 32, August 2004, No. 8, pp. 21)**
Pub: Entrepreneur Media Inc.
Ed: Joan Szabo. **Description:** Phony health insurance plan promoters are preying on entrepreneurs promising coverage at premiums below charges by licensed insurers. These fraudulent plans escape state regulators with false claims of federally regulated plans under the Employee Retirement Income Security Act (ERISA), a law that pre-empts states from regulating ERISA-covered employee benefit plans sponsored by private employers.

41071 ■ "Obesity costing billions" in *Atlanta Business Chronicle* **(Vol. 24, No. 14, September 7, 2001, pp. 1A)**
Pub: American City Business Journals Inc.
Ed: Julie Bryant. **Description:** According to Innovus Research, employee obesity is costing U.S. employers nearly $70 billion annually. Primary health problems leading to increased costs include heart disease, gastrointestinal tract disease, cancer, type 2 diabetes, and high blood pressure. Roche Laboratories Inc. and Verizon Wireless are two companies that offer their employees a free pilot weight loss program.

41072 ■ "On The Board" in *Inc.* **(October 1, 2004)**
Pub: Inc. Magazine
Ed: Patrick J. Sauer. **Description:** Profile of Benecard Services, the New Jersey company that processes and administers prescription drug and vision programs for health plans. The firm sponsors a New Jersey State Prison chess tournament by donating boards, pieces, clocks, and books.

41073 ■ "One of Portland, Maine's Fastest Growing Tech Companies is Sold" in *Portland Press Herald* **(December 20, 2005)**
Pub: Blethen Maine Newspapers, Inc.
Ed: Matt Wickenheiser. **Description:** IntelliCare Inc., one of Portland, Maine's largest technology companies was recently acquired by PolyMedica Corporation. The firm is a telemedicine company offering telephone-based nursing services and technology.

41074 ■ "Open Bar for Health Costs" in *Forbes* **(Vol. 174, December 27, 2004, No. 13, pp. 192)**
Pub: Forbes Magazine Inc.
Ed: A. Gary Shilling. **Description:** Despite rising healthcare costs, health care investments are still a good risk. Statistical data included.

41075 ■ "Pall Corp. Plans to Sell New Bacteria-Detection System to Blood Banks" in *Long Island Business News* **(February 20, 2004)**
Pub: Dolan Media Newswires
Description: The U.S. Food and Drug Administration (FDA) has approved Pall Corporation's system for detecting bacteria in blood platelets. The new system will cut testing time by about 20 percent, increasing the supply of blood available for transfusion.

41076 ■ "PartnerMD Finds Customers Willing to Pay More for Individualized Health Care" in *Richmond Times-Dispatch* **(February 7, 2005)**
Pub: Richmond Times-Dispatch
Ed: Delanie Mayhew. **Description:** Profile of PartnerMD, the concierge medical group where members are provided with 24-hour access to their primary physicians and reduced waiting room times.

41077 ■ **"People Growers Deals With Personal Growing Pains"** in *Business Journal-Portland* (Vol. 20, No. 22, August 1, 2003, pp. 3)
Pub: American City Business Journals, Inc.
Ed: Robin J. Moody. **Description:** Profile of Windy Baty, owner of People Growers. The home-based firm helps companies organize on-site health fairs and promotes wellness among employees.

41078 ■ **"The Perfect Storm? Employers Need Navigation Tools For The Newest Set of Health Cost Waves"** in *Employee Benefit Plan Review* (Vol. 55)
Pub: Charles D. Spencer & Associates, Inc.
Ed: Stephen A. Huth. **Description:** Reports from the Department of Labor show that, for the year ended September 30, 2000, benefits costs for private industry workers rose to 6 percent. The largest portion was for health care, and employers will try many strategies to reduce costs, including passing some on to their employees.

41079 ■ **"Perfect Storm Strikes CEOs"** in *Hispanic Business* (Vol. 24, No. 4, April 2002, pp. 16, 18)
Pub: Hispanic Business Inc.
Ed: Derek Reveron. **Description:** A new study shows that insurance premiums will rise during the next few years, squeezing profits and swelling the ranks of the uninsured, and small Hispanic-owned businesses and their employees are said to be among those hardest hit.

41080 ■ **"Pinstriped Populist"** in *New York Times* (November 12, 2006, pp. 15)
Pub: New York Times Company
Ed: David Sirota. **Description:** Profile of Lou Dobbs, author of How the Government, Big Business, and Special Interest Groups Are Waging War on the American Dream and How to Fight Back. Dobbs, a financial journalist, examines wages, corruption, trade, outsourcing, immigration and health care.

41081 ■ **"Premium pain"** in *Boston Business Journal* (Vol. 22, No. 16, Ma)
Pub: MCP, Inc.
Ed: Allison Connolly, Jill Lerner. **Description:** Small business in the Boston, MA area have had their health insurance premiums increased dramatically. Health insurance premiums increased by 12-15 percent in Massachusetts in 2002.

41082 ■ **"Programs help keep troubled employees productive"** in *Atlanta Business Chronicle* (Vol. 24, No. 13, August 24, 2001, pp. 4B)
Pub: American City Business Journals Inc.
Ed: Eric Cravey. **Description:** Employee assistance programs (EAPs) are intended to help employees overcome personal problems so they can be productive in the workplace. EAPs can address problems ranging from alcoholism to family problems to personal finances to conflicts with managers. Statistics are presented indicating that every $1 spent on an EAP can save a company $3 in other costs such as absenteeism.

41083 ■ **"Promoting agency wellness"** in *Rough Notes* (Vol. 146, No. 3, March 2003, pp. 171)
Pub: Rough Notes
Ed: Wanda Shumaker. **Description:** Wellness programs for the staff contributes to the morale and mental health of the employees, creativity, production and reduced medical costs.

41084 ■ *Public Human Services Directory*
Pub: American Public Human Services Association
Contact: Amy J. Plotnick, Publications Mgr.
Ed: Sybil Walker Barnes, Editor, aplotnick@aphsa. org. **Released:** Annual, September. **Price:** $99 for members; $115, nonmembers. **Covers:** federal, state, territorial, county, and major municipal public human service agencies. **Entries Include:** Agency name, address, phone, fax, e-mail address, web site address, names of key personnel, program area. **Arrangement:** Geographical.

41085 ■ **"A Reason to Smile"** in *Black Enterprise* (Vol. 34, No. 2, September 2003, pp. 62)
Pub: Earl Graves Publishing Co.
Ed: Ashley Gibson. **Description:** Of the 6,000 board certified oral surgeons in the U.S., about 100 are women. Profile of Dr. Ngozi Etufugh, who was born in Nigeria, operates two practices in New York. Etufugh tells how she empowered herself to become a top oral surgeon despite being black, being a woman, and being petite.

41086 ■ **"Reed Jumps Onto the Medical Bandwagon "** in *Tradeshow Week* (Vol. 3)
Pub: Reed Business Information
Ed: Rachelle Crum. **Description:** Reed Exhibitions has launched a new show division along with its sister company, publisher Elsevier Health Sciences. The new division will focus on continuing medical education. Reed Medical Education is committed to improving health care delivery.

41087 ■ **"A Remedy for Malpractice Malaise"** in *Business Week* (February 7, 2005, No. 3919, pp. 38)
Pub: McGraw-Hill Companies
Ed: Arlene Weintraub. **Description:** In order to retain physicians, hospitals are offering malpractice insurance through not-for-profit entities known as captives. Statistical data included.

41088 ■ **"RenaLab Acquired"** in *Mississippi Business Journal* (Vol. 29, January 2007, No. 3, pp. A10)
Pub: Venture Publications, Inc.
Description: Renal Advantage Inc. has completed it's previously announced acquisition of RenaLab from Fresenius Medical Care North America.

41089 ■ **"Retail Stores Taking Health Care Debit Cards Must Upgrade Systems"** in *Kiplinger Letter* (Vol. 82, January 12, 2007, No. 1)
Pub: Kiplinger
Description: Internal Revenue Services is requiring retailers accepting health care debit cards to install electronic systems that restrict debit card purchases to qualified medical expenses. The system upgrades must be in place by 2009.

41090 ■ *Rhode Island Directory of Human Service Agencies & Government Agencies*
Pub: Travelers Aid Society of Rhode Island
Released: Biennial. **Covers:** about 1,200 public and private nonprofit human service agencies and organizations in Rhode Island. **Entries Include:** Agency name, address, phone, name of contact or director; description of services; hours open; eligibility requirements; ages and geographic area served; fee for service; funding. **Arrangement:** Alphabetical. **Indexes:** Service, alphabetical, government agency name.

41091 ■ **"Ritz-Carlton Offers Henry Ford Patients a Place to Recuperate"** in *Crain's Detroit Business* (Vol. 21, October 10, 2005, No. 43)
Pub: Crain Communications Inc. - Detroit
Ed: Michelle Martinez. **Description:** The Ritz-Carlton hotel in Dearborn, Michigan is offering discounted luxury recuperation packages to cancer patients undergoing surgery at Henry Ford Hospital.

41092 ■ *RurAL CAP's Directory of Rural Alaskan Organizations*
Pub: Rural Alaska Community Action Program Inc.
Contact: David Hardenbergh, Exec. Dir.
Released: Biennial, January of even years. **Covers:** about 550 social services agencies, community service organizations; village councils and officials in rural Alaska. **Entries Include:** Agency, organization, or council name, address, phone, names and titles of key personnel. **Arrangement:** Agencies and organizations are alphabetical; village councils are alphabetical. **Indexes:** Agency/organization name.

41093 ■ **"SciTech Developments to Watch"** in *Business Week* (January 16, 2006, No. 3967, pp. 87)
Pub: McGraw-Hill Companies
Description: Scientific and technological developments discussed include a pain-free alternative to pricking fingers for blood sugar readings for diabetics through the use of infrared light bounced off the white of an individual's eye; carbon nanotubes for electronic components; and information about tree farms.

41094 ■ **"Seeing Face Value: Cosmetic Medical Spa Captures Ethnic Skin Care Market"** in *Black Enterprise* (Vol. 35, February 2005, No. 7, pp. 51)
Pub: Earl G. Graves Publishing Co. Inc.
Ed: Bridget McCrea. **Description:** When owners opened their cosmetic medical spa, they chose to avoid advertising for reputation, media exposure and physician referrals to grow their business. Drs. Eliot F. Battle and Monte O. Harris, noted academic physicians and researchers, have developed a customized approach to ethnic skin care.

41095 ■ **"Seeking outside help"** in *Crain's Detroit Business* (Vol. 19, No. 8, February 24, 2003, pp. 11)
Pub: Crain Communications Inc., Detroit
Ed: Katie Merx. **Description:** Area hospitals have begun outsourcing essential medical services as well as the traditionally outsourced non-medical services.

41096 ■ **"Shake 'Em Up"** in *Forbes* (Vol. 175, February 14, 2005, No. 3, pp. 58)
Pub: Forbes Magazine Inc.
Ed: Andy Stone. **Description:** Profile of Kevin Goodwin, founder of SonoSite and creator of a handheld ultrasound device, a laptop-size machine that scans patients immediately.

41097 ■ **"Share the Health: When Encouraging Healthy Living, You've Got to Walk the Walk"** in *Entrepreneur* (Vol. 33, January 2005, No. 1)
Pub: Entrepreneur Media Inc.
Ed: Kimberly Olson. **Description:** Small companies are promoting healthy lifestyles by offering lunchtime walks, nutrition seminars, and subscriptions to health information Websites. They could also offer prizes for participation.

41098 ■ **"Shopping For Good Health: Perception Strategies Adds 'Mystery' to Medicine"** in *Indianapolis Business Journal* (September 27, 2004)
Pub: Indianapolis Business Journal Corp.
Ed: Shelley Swift. **Description:** Mystery shoppers are helping to shape the standard for patient satisfaction at health care facilities nationwide. Kevin Billingsley, founder of Perception Strategies Inc., applies the mystery shopping technique to the field of health care.

41099 ■ **"Should Doctors Own Hospitals?"** in *Business Week* (February 20, 2006, No. 3972, pp. 63)
Pub: McGraw-Hill Companies
Ed: Arlene Weintraub. **Description:** Controversy over the practice of doctors owning and running hospitals is discussed.

41100 ■ *Small Business Access and Alternatives to Health Care: Congressional Hearing*
Pub: DIANE Publishing Company
Ed: Donald A. Manzullo. **Released:** July 2006. **Price:** $35.00. **Description:** Congressional hearings regarding the health care crisis facing America's small businesses is discussed.

41101 ■ *Small Business Access to Health Care: Congressional Hearing*
Pub: DIANE Publishing Company
Ed: Donald A. Manzullo. **Released:** August 2004. **Price:** $25.00. **Description:** Congressional hearing held at Crystal Lake, Illinois. Witnesses: Mary Blankenbaker, Co-Owner, Benjamin's Restaurant; Ryan Brauns, Senior Vice President, Rockford Con-

sulting and Brokerage; Scott Shalek, RHU, Shalek Financial Services; Brad Close, National Federation of Independent Businesses; Ken Koehler, Flowerwood, Inc.; Brad Buxton, Vice President of Networks and Medical Management, Blue Cross and Blue Shield of Illinois; Isabella Wilson, Chief Financial Office, Illinois Blower, Inc.; and James Milam, Illinois State Medical Society.

41102 ■ *The Small Business Guide to HSAs*
Pub: Brick Tower Press
Ed: JoAnn Mills Laing. **Released:** September 2004. **Price:** $14.95. **Description:** Government-assisted Health Savings Accounts (HSAs) offer employees a tax-free way to accumulate savings to be used for qualified medical expenses, they can be rolled over without penalty for future spending, or invested to accumulate savings to pay for health needs after retirement. Employers offering HSAs can save up to two-thirds of business expenses on health insurance costs.

41103 ■ "Small Business Strains to Provide Health Care" in *Bradenton Herald* (December 6, 2006)
Pub: Bradenton Herald
Ed: Robin Roger. **Description:** Florida's small businesses want to provide their employees health insurance but find that the expense is too prohibitive. According to a survey conducted by the National Federation of Independent Business, the number of small businesses in Florida that offer health insurance has declined.

41104 ■ "Small Firms, Consumers Have PWBA Health Care Benefit Tools" in *Employee Benefit Plan Review* (Vol. 55, No. 8, February 2001, pp. 40)
Pub: Charles D. Spencer & Associates, Inc.
Description: A discussion regarding online and paper publications of the Pension and Welfare Benefits Administration of the Department of Labor. These tools for helping individuals and small businesses in making decisions about health care benefits have resulted from the Health Benefits Education Campaign.

41105 ■ "Some D.C. Health enters Quietly Filling Urgent Needs" in *Washington Business Journal* (Vol. 22, No. 8, June 27, 2003, pp. 34)
Pub: Washington Business Journal
Ed: Chris Silva. **Description:** Services at various Washington, DC health facilities are discussed.

41106 ■ "Spreading the Word On Translation" in *Business Week Online* (February 16, 2006)
Pub: McGraw-Hill Companies
Description: Language skills alone may not be enough to become a health-care interpreter.

41107 ■ "State Joins War on Use of Trans Fats" in *Crain's Detroit Business* (Vol. 23, January 29, 2007, No. 5, pp. 1)
Pub: Crain Communications Inc. - Detroit
Ed: Amy Lane. **Description:** Michigan joins 16 other states in requiring restaurants to inform public on the use of trans fats and could lead to a ban on their use. Trans fats increase the risk of heart disease by raising cholesterol.

41108 ■ "Studies push for analysis of quality in health care" in *Business First Columbus* (Vol. 18, No. 40, May 24, 2002, pp. B7)
Pub: Business First Columbus, Inc.
Ed: Andrea Tortora. **Description:** Two major studies of Cincinnati's health care delivery system addressed issues of choosing a physician and low pay to doctors, both issues being endemic throughout the U.S.

41109 ■ "Study Looks at Benefits of Nonprofits Teaming Up to Buy Health Insurance" in *Pittsburgh Business Times* (Vol. 23, August 8, 2003)
Pub: Pittsburgh Business Times
Ed: Lynne Glover. **Description:** The increasing price of health insurance may force nonprofit organizations to join together in a group buying plan. Dewey and Kaye, a management consulting firm, will conduct a feasibility study of the option.

41110 ■ "Suits Mount Against Salons" in *San Jose Mercury News* (March 5, 2005)
Pub: Knight-Ridder/Tribune Business News
Ed: Esther Landhuis. **Description:** Santa Clara County is investigating reported infections caused from pedicures. There have been at least 20 lawsuits filed by customers from the Nails National. The spa is cited for negligence in sanitation procedures that have cultivated the disease-causing mycobacteria at the foot spas.

41111 ■ "Superior Consultant Holdings sees demand for health care IT" in *Crain's Detroit Business* (Vol. 19, No. 13, March 31, 2003, pp. 4)
Pub: Crain Communications Inc., Detroit
Ed: Andrew Dietderich. **Description:** Compliance with the Health Insurance Portability and Accountability Act, quality mandates and physician connectivity are fueling demand for hardware and software and Southfield-based Superior Consultant Holdings Corporation is planning a new $5 million data-processing center.

41112 ■ "Take your pick" in *Entrepreneur* (Vol. 31, No. 5, May 2003, pp. 69)
Pub: Entrepreneur Media Inc.
Ed: Mark Henricks. **Description:** Cafeteria health insurance plans let employees preset an amount to pay for selections from various insurances and other benefit providers. Employers prefer cafeteria-style packages because they shift some of the healthcare costs onto employees.

41113 ■ "Taking it to the Street" in *Hispanic Business* (March 2004, pp. 30, 32, 34)
Pub: Hispanic Business
Ed: Scott Williams. **Description:** An IPO provided the fuel to help propel Molina Healthcare from a midsize care provider to a major company. Profile of CEO, J. Mario Molina is included.

41114 ■ "Tampa, Fla.-Area Project Gets Grant to Put Medical Data Online" in *Tampa Tribune* (December 22, 2005)
Pub: Media General, Inc.
Ed: Carol Gentry. **Description:** The state of Florida is launching its first Internet-based medical records system in the Tampa Bay region. The area was awarded $467,000 in state grants for planning and starting a medical data-sharing system.

41115 ■ "Tax-Free Bill of Health: Health-Care Accounts with Tax Benefits" in *Entrepreneur* (Vol. 33, January 2005, No. 1, pp. 50)
Pub: Entrepreneur Media Inc.
Ed: Joan Szabo. **Description:** Health Savings Accounts (HSAs), Health Reimbursement Arrangements (HRAs), Flexible Spending Accounts (FSAs), and Medical Savings Accounts (MSAs) are health-care spending accounts designed to help employees pay for health costs, while saving on taxes.

41116 ■ "Tiered pricing plans have benefits and disadvantages" in *Business First Columbus* (Vol. 18, No. 40, May 24, 2002, pp. B11)
Pub: Business First Columbus, Inc.
Ed: David Miller. **Description:** Tiered pricing is a new idea within the health insurance industry that allows customers to pay a fixed price for services regardless of the actual cost of the service.

41117 ■ "Tips to Keep Your Medical Renewal Cost Under Control" in *Ingram's* (Vol. 29, No. 9, September 2003, pp. 52)
Pub: Show Me Publishing, Inc.
Ed: Matt Krull. **Description:** Ways to reduce insurance costs for small businesses in the Greater Kansas City, Missouri area are covered. Topics include employment practices liability insurance, employee medical coverage, and long-term planning.

41118 ■ "To your health: an old health insurance bill gets a second chance at life" in *Entrepreneur* (Vol. 31, No. 6, June 2003, pp. 26)
Pub: Entrepreneur Media Inc.

Ed: Stephen Barlas. **Description:** The Small Business Health Fairness Act (H.R. 660) would allow trade associations to create federally regulated national health insurance plans for small businesses, but Congressional Democrats are strongly opposed to the bill.

41119 ■ "Top Ten Schools for Hispanics: Medical" in *Hispanic Business* (September 2006, pp. 82, 84, 86)
Pub: Hispanic Business
Description: Top ten universities offering medical degrees geared towards Hispanic students include, Stanford University, University of Texas Health Science Center, University of Texas Medical Branch, University of New Mexico, University of Miami, University of Texas Southwestern Medical Center at Dallas, University of Illinois, University of Texas at Houston, University of Arizona, and Texas A&M.

41120 ■ "TPA business for self-funded plans balanced in 2000" in *Employee Benefit Plan Review* (Vol. 56, No. 1, July 2001, pp. 18)
Pub: Charles D. Spencer & Associates, Inc.
Description: The use of third party administrators for self-funded health insurance programs is discussed, including such topics as fees paid and programs provided.

41121 ■ "Trickle Up: Small Companies Slowly Build Momentum in the Job Market" in *Wall Street Journal* (December 4, 2003, pp. A1)
Pub: Dow Jones & Co. Inc.
Ed: Clare Ansberry. **Description:** As the economy improves, more small companies are hiring new employees, health care and construction sectors are improving.

41122 ■ "Trying to Play their Cards Right" in *Crain's New York Business* (Vol. 20, No. 12, March 22, 2004, pp. 20)
Pub: Crain Communications, Inc.
Description: Pharmacists can decline participation in the new Medicare discount card program when filling prescriptions for contracts that have unfavorable terms. However, they risk losing customers.

41123 ■ "2001 Brought Steep Increase in Uninsured" in *Business First Columbus* (Vol. 18, No. 26, Feb. 15, 2002, pp. A16)
Pub: Business First Columbus, Inc.
Ed: Kent Hoover. **Description:** Nearly two million Americans lost their health care insurance in 2001.

41124 ■ "UDM Hopes Move Will Help Renew Detroit Neighborhood" in *Crain's Detroit Business* (Vol. 22, December 11, 2006, No.50, pp. 3)
Pub: Crain Communications Inc. - Detroit
Ed: Sheena Harrison **Description:** University of Detroit plans to move its dental school to Detroit's Core City neighborhood in January, 2008. Developers hope it has the effect of attracting other small businesses around and further aid in the restructuring of that area.

41125 ■ "UM Licenses System to Cigna" in *Crain's Detroit Business* (Vol. 22, December 18, 2006, No. 51, pp. 18)
Pub: Crain Communications Inc. - Detroit
Ed: Andrew Dietderich. **Description:** University of Michigan and Cigna HealthCare have entered an agreement to license a system to identify and address health risks for individuals. Health Risks and wellness programs at the worksite are also available to employers.

41126 ■ "Unhealthy Costs" in *Hispanic Business* (November 2006, pp. 58, 60, 62)
Pub: Hispanic Business
Ed: Jenn Holmes. **Description:** Small business owners are having difficulty paying high insurance premiums for their employees.

41127 ■ "Union, Nursing Home Owners in Tense Negotiations" in *Chicago Tribune* (March 2, 2005)
Pub: Knight-Ridder/Tribune Business News
Ed: Barbara Rose. **Description:** Contract negotiations between local nursing union and nursing home

owners in the Chicago area are examined. Nursing home owners deny union accusations they collect millions in fees yet deny their lowest paid employees adequate raises.

41128 ■ "Up and away to better health" in *BlackEnterprise* **(Vol. 32, No. 3, October 2001, pp. 168)**
Pub: Earl Graves Publishing Co.
Ed: Ann Brown. Description: According to Diana Fairechild, a former flight attendant who logged more than 10 million miles before authoring Jet Smarter: The Air Traveler's Rx, 90 percent of airline passengers get sick after flying. Tips for frequent flyers to avoid problems are cited.

41129 ■ "Use It or Lose It: Is Your Business Usable-or Disposable? Figure It Out Before Your Competitors Gain an Edge" in *Entrepreneur* **(Vol.32)**
Pub: Entrepreneur Media Inc.
Ed: Mark Henricks. Description: Geoffrey Hart explains his concerns of usability when setting out to develop a medical device for soothing and entertaining children during the process of anesthetizing them for medial or dental procedures.

41130 ■ "VCs See Jumbo Opportunity in Fighting Obesity" in *Venture Capital Journal* **(January 1, 2005)**
Pub: Thomason Financial Inc.
Description: Obesity-fighting companies saw $234 million invested from January through November 2004. Obesity is a growing problem, with estimates that one-third of all American adults are obese. Statistical data included.

41131 ■ "VitalMed Absorbs Doctors' Paperwork" in *Birmingham Business Journal* **(Vol. 20, No. 20, July 4, 2003, pp. 1)**
Pub: American City Business Journals, Inc.
Ed: Tom Bassing. Description: Profile of Birmingham, Alabama-based VitalMed Inc., led by Clete Walker. The firm offers administrative services for physicians' practices.

41132 ■ "Waiting in the Wings" in *Entrepreneur* **(Vol. 32, No. 1, January 2004, pp. 21)**
Pub: Entrepreneur Media, Inc.
Ed: David Worrell. Description: Market experts are predicting a rise in the number of Initial Public Offerings (IPOs) in 2004, although there is still strength in biotech and pharmaceutical companies, other sectors such as real estate, business services, healthcare and manufacturing are growing.

41133 ■ "Wealth on the Go" in *Black Enterprise* **(Vol. 34, No. 3, October 2003, pp. 61)**
Pub: Earl Graves Publishing Co.
Ed: Nicole Lewis. Description: Profile of Chris Galloway, a radiation therapist and real estate investor in Washington, DC; Galloway keeps up to date by using the latest in radiation treatment technology to treat patients with cancer and other diseases.

41134 ■ "Wellness programs" in *Rough Notes* **(Vol. 146, No. 3, March 2003, pp. 134)**
Pub: Rough Notes
Ed: Len Strazewski. Description: The benefits of providing physical fitness programs to employees are seen in increased productivity as well as savings to the employer.

41135 ■ "While I'm Gone: Transitioning Into- and Back From-Family and Medical Leave" in *Black Enterprise* **(Vol. 35, September 2004, No. 2)**
Pub: Earl G. Graves Publishing Co. Inc.
Ed: Carla Thompson. Description: According to the 2000 Family and Medical Leave Act (FMLA) survey, conducted by the U.S. Department of Labor, 75 percent of workers took some form of family leave in 1999.

41136 ■ "Winter has Me Down. What Can I Do at Work" in *Crain's New York Business* **(Vol. 23, January 29, 2007, No. 5, pp. 47)**
Pub: Crain Communications, Inc.
Description: Getting enough sunlight is important to a person's health. If you are not getting enough sunlight due to long days at the office, a good remedy is light therapy, products can be purchased as inexpensive as $89.

41137 ■ Wisconsin Medical Directory
Pub: Jola Publications
Contact: Dennis Schapiro
Released: Annual, latest edition 2nd 2005. Price: $24, individuals Orderpoint tentative price. Covers: Approximately 15,000 doctors, hospitals, clinics, nursing homes, and other selected health care providers in Wisconsin. Entries Include: Doctor or facility name, address, phone, fax, doctors' UPINS. Arrangement: Classified by type of facility or care provided. Indexes: Name, product/service, subject.

41138 ■ Women's Health Concerns Sourcebook
Pub: Omnigraphics Inc.
Ed: Amy L. Sutton, Editor. Released: Irregular, latest edition 2nd; Published 2004. Price: $78, individuals. Publication Includes: Resources on women's health issues. Entries Include: Publication name, address. Principal content of publication is articles on specific health issues, definitions, symptoms, risks, treatment, and answers to frequently asked questions. Arrangement: Topic. Indexes: subject index/alpha.

41139 ■ "Words Fail Them" in *Hispanic Business* **(May 2005, pp. 58)**
Pub: Hispanic Business
Ed: Joel Russell. Description: The lack of qualified bilingual counselors is making it difficult to manage the growing demand for Latino behavioral health programs.

41140 ■ "Workplace Wellness" in *Small Business Opportunities* **(March 2005)**
Pub: Harris Publications Inc.
Description: Ergonomics is the applied science of design, particularly in the workplace. Ten steps to assure a better and healthier workplace that is ergonomically sound are listed.

SOURCES OF SUPPLY

41141 ■ Community Service Directory
Pub: United Way of Greater St. Louis Inc.
Contact: Kay Archer
Released: Biennial, even years. Covers: over 900 not-for-profit and tax-supported health, social welfare, recreation, education, and related agencies in the metropolitan St. Louis area. Entries Include: Organization or program name, address, phone, names and titles of key personnel; branch or satellite office address, phone, and director; description of activities or services provided. Custom reports, mailing labels, and supplemental directories available. Arrangement: First section contains agency profiles; agencies by programs are listed in an index. Indexes: Alphabetical, program.

41142 ■ Directory of Community Resources
Pub: Hotline
Released: Annual, January of odd years. Covers: about 200 nonprofit health and social service agencies in Cass County, North Dakota and Clay County, Minnesota. Entries Include: Organization name, address, phone, toll-free phone, contact name, hours and days of operation, services, purpose, eligibility requirements, fees, source of funding, whether accessible to the handicapped. Arrangement: Alphabetical. Indexes: Subject and alphabetical.

41143 ■ Directory of Human Services
Pub: United Way of the Columbia-Willamette
Price: $20 per edition; payment must accompany order. Covers: human service agencies and organizations in the Portland, Oregon area; separate editions for Multnomah, Clackamas, and Washington counties. Entries Include: Provider name, address, phone, days and hours of operation, fees, restrictions, wheelchair access, geographical.

41144 ■ Directory of Human Services for Delaware
Pub: Division of State Service Centers
Released: Biennial, previous edition March 2001, latest edition February 2004. Covers: about 567 social service agencies and volunteer organizations providing a variety of health care, social welfare, counseling, and other human services in Delaware. Entries Include: Organization name, address, phone, hours of operation, branch locations and phone numbers, eligibility requirements, geographic area served, name and title of contact, description of services, fees. Arrangement: Geographical; statewide services are listed separately. Indexes: Organization name, subject.

TRADE PERIODICALS

41145 ■ The AARP Pharmacy Service Enjoying Good Health Newsletter
Pub: Retired Persons Services Inc.
Contact: Joan M. Zimmermann
Ed: Joan M. Zimmermann, Editor, jzimmermann@rpsrx.com. Released: Bimonthly. Description: Offers health information and medical tips on topics relevant for the elderly. Recurring features include notices of publications available.

41146 ■ Abbeyfield Houses Society of Canada Newsletter
Pub: Abbeyfield Houses Society of Canada
Ed: Robert McMullan, Editor. Released: Quarterly. Description: Reports on news of Abbeyfield Houses Society of Canada, a provider of care and companionship for the elderly. Also features articles related to aging, housing, and lifestyle in Canada and internationally. Recurring features include letters to the editor, and columns titled News of Local Societies and Bits 'n Bites.

41147 ■ a.b.c. Reports
Pub: League for the Hard of Hearing
Contact: Arlene Romoff, Editor-in-Chief
E-mail: aromoff@aol.com
Released: Semiannual. Price: Included in membership. Description: Advocates better communication for the hearing impaired. Reports on the latest advances in technology, computers, broadcasting, travel, healthcare, the arts, and other services that assist deaf and hard of hearing people.

41148 ■ Academic Emergency Medicine
Pub: Hanley & Belfus Inc.
Contact: Michelle H. Biros MD, Editor-in-Chief
Released: Monthly. Price: $145 domestic; $239 institutions international; $226 institutions domestic; $155 other countries; $74 students domestic; $80 students international. Description: Journal of emergency medicine.

41149 ■ Advances
Pub: The Robert Wood Johnson Foundation (RWJF 2003)
Ed: Larry Blumenthal, Editor, lblumen@rwjf.org. Released: Quarterly. Price: Included in membership. Description: "The National Newsletter of The Robert Wood Johnson Foundation." Reports on issues related to the Foundations grantmaking. Recurring features include interviews, news of research, and columns titled Profile, Abridge, Grants, and People.

41150 ■ Advances in Pharmacy
Pub: Facts & Comparisons
Released: Quarterly. Description: Journal devoted to the management of hospital pharmacy services.

41151 ■ Aesthetic Surgery Journal
Pub: Mosby
Contact: Kathleen Gaffney, Publisher

Released: Bimonthly. **Price:** $165 outside U.S.; $235 institutions outside U.S.; $82 other countries students and residents; $206 institutions; $138; $69 students. **Description:** Official journal of the American Society for Aesthetic Plastic Surgery. Covers information on procedures, medications, and surgical supplies.

41152 ■ AHA News
Pub: Health Forum L.L.C.
Contact: Mary Grayson, Publisher
E-mail: mgrayson@healthforum.com
Released: Biweekly. **Description:** Tabloid for healthcare industry professionals covering related business issues, legislative policies, and hospital management issues.

41153 ■ AIDS Reference Guide
Pub: Atlantic Information Services Inc.
Contact: J. Schnuer
Ed: Steve Goodwin, Editor. **Released:** Monthly. **Price:** $392, U.S. **Description:** Acts as an information clearinghouse for planning services and managing the epidemic in workplaces, hospitals, clinics, classrooms and communities.

41154 ■ Air Medical Journal
Pub: Mosby Inc.
Contact: Michael Targowski, Advertising Sales
E-mail: m.targowski@elsevier.com
Ed: David J. Dries, MD, Editor, david.j.dries@healthpartners.com. **Released:** Bimonthly. **Price:** $88 U.S.; $116 Canada; $116 Mexico; $116 international; $44 students U.S.; $58 students Canada; $58 students Mexico; $58 students international. **Description:** Journal for air medical transport professionals.

41155 ■ AJIC (American Journal of Infection Control)
Pub: Mosby Inc.
Contact: Elaine Larson Ph.D., Editor-in-Chief
E-mail: ajic@columbia.edu
Released: 10/year. **Price:** $124; $358 institutions; $62 students; $149 other countries; $386 institutions, other countries; $74 students other countries. **Description:** Journal for infection control practitioners. Includes peer-reviewed articles in the field of infection control, and case studies and reports of innovations in control of infections.

41156 ■ Alcohol, Health and Research World
Pub: U.S. Government Printing Office and
    Superintendent of Documents
Released: Quarterly. **Price:** $25; $35 other countries; $12 single issue; $16.80 single issue in other countries. **Description:** Magazine presenting results of alcohol research.

41157 ■ Alive
Pub: Alive Publishing Group Inc.
Released: Monthly, 12/year. **Price:** $37 1 year; $69 2 years; $94 3 years. **Description:** Magazine promoting healthy living, alternative health, and nutrition.

41158 ■ American Journal of Electroneurodiagnostic Technology
Pub: American Society of Electroneurodiagnostic
    Technologists Inc.
Ed: Janet Ghigo, Editor. **Released:** Quarterly. **Price:** $50 U.S.; $60 outside the U.S.; $90 U.S. institutions/libraries; $100 out of country institutions/libraries. **Description:** Professional Journal.

41159 ■ American Journal of Hospice and Palliative Care
Pub: Prime National Publishing Corp.
Contact: Richard A. DeVito, President
Ed: Donna Vallaincorte, Editor. **Released:** Bimonthly. **Price:** $158 qualified individuals only; $225 institutions and library; $262 institutions Canadian Library; $185 Canada qualified individuals only; $354 institutions, other countries; $232 out of country qualified individuals only; $40 single issue; $45 single issue, Canada; $60 other countries. **Description:** Professional journal of hospice practitioners. Provides information to physicians, nurses, clergy, social workers, and volunteers providing care to the terminally ill.

41160 ■ American Journal on Mental Retardation
Pub: American Association on Mental Retardation
Ed: William E. MacLean, Jr, Editor. **Released:** Bimonthly, 6/yr. **Price:** $246 institutions with online tier 1; $286 institutions, other countries with online; $221 institutions only online; $283 institutions with online tier 2; $323 institutions, other countries with online; $255 institutions only online; $325 with online tier 3; $365 institutions, other countries with online; $293 institutions only online; $384 institutions with online tier 4. **Description:** Journal concerning research about mental retardation.

41161 ■ Anesthesia Malpractice Prevention
Pub: Lippincott Williams & Wilkins
Contact: K.R. Orourke
Ed: Nora Macready, Editor, medrite@aol.com. **Released:** Monthly. **Price:** $305. **Description:** Presents case lessons and their verdicts concerning anesthesiology. Recurring features include letters to the editor, interviews, news of research, reports of meetings, and a column titled Reader Question.

41162 ■ The Arc News
Pub: The Arc of Carroll County Inc.
Price: Included in membership. **Description:** Spotlights issues concerning the mentally and physically disabled. Discusses rehabilitation, safety, housing, and centers.

41163 ■ Archives of Environmental Health
Pub: Heldref Publications
Released: Monthly. **Price:** $382 add $21 for postage outside the U.S. **Description:** Journal providing objective documentation of the effects of environmental agents on human health. Official publication of the Society for Occupational and Environmental Health.

41164 ■ BETA (Bulletin of Experimental Treatments for AIDS)
Pub: San Francisco AIDS Foundation
Ed: Reilly O'Neal, Editor. **Released:** Biennial. **Description:** Magazine reporting medical information about treatment for HIV infection.

41165 ■ Body Positive
Pub: Body Positive
Released: Monthly. **Description:** Magazine for people who are HIV-infected/affected.

41166 ■ Briefings on Assisted Living (BAL)
Pub: HCPro Inc.
Contact: Suzanne Perney, Publisher
Released: Monthly. **Price:** Free. **Description:** Covers topics of interest to developers and managers of assisted living facilities. Recurring features include interviews and news of research.

41167 ■ Business & Health Institute
Pub: Advanstar Communications
Ed: Wayne N. Burton, M.D., Editor. **Released:** 10/year. **Description:** Magazine covering health care costs, quality and access issues, and health care policy at the federal, state, and local levels.

41168 ■ Business Insurance
Pub: Crain Communications Inc.
Contact: Martin J. Ross, Publisher
E-mail: mross@crain.com
Ed: Regis J. Coccia, Editor. **Released:** Weekly. **Price:** $97. **Description:** International newsweekly reporting on corporate risk and employee benefit management news.

41169 ■ Cambridge Quarterly of Healthcare Ethics
Pub: Cambridge University Press
Contact: Dr. Doris Thomasma, Managing Editor
E-mail: dathomasma@comcast.net
Ed: Steve Heilig, Editor, heilig@sfms.org. **Released:** Quarterly. **Price:** $256 institutions online & print; $214 institutions online; $85 print; $153 institutions online & print; $132 institutions online; $51 print. **Description:** Journal focusing on ethics as applied to medicine.

41170 ■ Canadian Journal of Dietetic Practice and Research
Pub: Dietitians of Canada
Released: Quarterly. **Price:** $25 Canada single copies; $85 Canada in Canada; $85 other countries and the U.S.; $25 U.S. and overseas cost. **Description:** Professional journal for dietitians and nutritionists in Canada (English and French).

41171 ■ Canadian Journal of Public Health
Pub: Canadian Public Health Association
Contact: Jeanette Ward, Interim Sci. Ed.
Released: Bimonthly. **Price:** $103.79 Canada regular rate; $111.55 Canada regular rate; $125 U.S. regular rate; $161 other countries regular rate; $21.40 Canada single issue rate; $23 Canada single issue rate; $26 U.S. single issue rate; $31 other countries single issue rate. **Description:** Journal featuring peer-reviewed scientific articles on all aspects of public health, including health promotion, disease prevention, and healthy public policy.

41172 ■ Canadian Journal of Respiratory Therapy
Pub: Canadian Society of Respiratory Therapists
Contact: Rita Hansen, Editor-in-Chief
E-mail: rhansen@csat.com
Released: 5/yr. **Description:** Journal covering respiratory therapy.

41173 ■ Canadian Journal of Rural Medicine–Journal canadien de la medecine rurale
Pub: Canadian Medical Association
Contact: Suzanne Kingsmill, Managing Editor
E-mail: advertising@cma.ca
Released: Quarterly. **Price:** $65 postage extra; $33 student/resident; postage extra; $105 institutions postage extra; $30 single issue; $71 out of country; $105 institutions, other countries; $30 single issue foreign. **Description:** Peer-reviewed journal focusing on rural medicine. A publication of the Canadian Medical Association for the Society of Rural Physicians of Canada.

41174 ■ Canadian Respiratory Journal
Pub: Pulsus Group Inc.
Contact: N.R. Anthonisen, Editor-in-Chief
Released: 8/year. **Price:** $240 USA and Canada; $380 other countries. **Description:** Journal featuring articles, investigations, and clinical reports dealing with respiratory therapy, pulmonary medicine, and cardiocirculatory conditions.

41175 ■ Care Management Journals
Pub: Springer Publishing Co.
Contact: Matt Felton, Production Mgr.
E-mail: springer@springerpub.com
Ed: Joan Quinn, MD, Editor. **Released:** Quarterly. **Price:** $70; $120 two years; $160 institutions; $260 two years institution. **Description:** Journal presenting research, analysis of current issues, and reports on programs in case management and current programs and policies in the long term home health care field.

41176 ■ Caring People
Pub: National Association for Home Care
Contact: Val Halamandaris, Publisher
Ed: Heather Dittbrenner, Editor. **Released:** Monthly. **Price:** $7.50 single issue. **Description:** Magazine spotlighting individuals who care and service others.

41177 ■ The Case Manager
Pub: Mosby Inc.
Ed: Catherine M. Mullahy, RN, Editor. **Released:** Bimonthly, 6 /yr. **Price:** $124 institutions other countries; $89 other countries; $89 students other countries; $94 institutions; $66; $66 students. **Description:** Targeted to medical case managers and other related professionals who coordinate and manage patient care in hospital, home, long-term care, rehabilitation, mental health, and managed care settings.

41178 ■ Child and Youth Services
Pub: The Haworth Press Inc.
Contact: Jerome Beker, Ed. Emeritus
Released: Semiannual, 2/yr. **Price:** $60 U.S.; $81 Canada; $87 other countries; $135 institutions U.S.;

$182 institutions, Canada; $196 institutions, other countries; $400 libraries agencies, U.S.; $540 libraries agencies, Canada; $580 libraries agencies, other countries. **Description:** Journal on youth services.

41179 ■ *Children's Voice*
Pub: Child Welfare League of America Inc.
Contact: Karen Dunn, Editor-in-Chief
E-mail: sboehm@cwla.org
Released: Bimonthly, 6/year. **Price:** $25 U.S. individual; $40 international. **Description:** Magazine providing information on child welfare programs and policy developments.

41180 ■ *Clinical Laboratory News*
Pub: American Association for Clinical Chemistry
Contact: Richard G. Flaherty
Ed: Nancy Sasavage, PhD, Editor, nsasavage@aacc.org. **Released:** Monthly. **Description:** Scholarly magazine providing current news in the field of clinical laboratory science.

41181 ■ *Clinical Leadership and Management Review*
Pub: Clinical Laboratory Management Association
Contact: Scott Kober, Publications, Communications Mgr.
Released: Bimonthly. **Description:** Business magazine for clinical laboratory managers.

41182 ■ *CMA News*
Pub: Canadian Medical Association
Contact: Josephine Sciortino, Managing Editor
Ed: John Hoey, Editor. **Released:** Biweekly, January to December - 25 issues. **Price:** $199 postage extra; $35 single issue student/resident; postage extra; $295 institutions postage extra; $20 single issue; $268 out of country; $316 institutions, other countries; $20 single issue foreign. **Description:** Provides coverage of events affecting the medical profession and health care delivery in Canada.

41183 ■ *The CMA Today*
Pub: American Association of Medical Assistants
Ed: Jean M. Lynch, Editor. **Released:** Bimonthly. **Price:** $30 nonmembers. **Description:** Professional health journal.

41184 ■ *Contemporary Long Term Care*
Pub: Leisure Publications Inc.
Contact: Karen Cavallo, Publisher
E-mail: karen@cltcmag.com
Ed: Pervin Lakdawalla, Editor, pervin@cltcmag.com. **Released:** 11/year. **Price:** $79.95; $94.95 Canada and Mexico; $130 two years; $129 other countries. **Description:** Magazine covering the long term healthcare trade.

41185 ■ *The Counselor*
Pub: The Counselor
Ed: Steve Erickson, Editor. **Released:** 6/year. **Description:** Reports on membership news and other public relations topics.

41186 ■ *Dentaletter*
Pub: MPL Communications Inc.
Contact: John Hobez, Managing Editor
Ed: Dr. Brian Waters, Editor. **Released:** 11/year. **Price:** $119. **Description:** Publishes news of dental research. Also covers related web sites.

41187 ■ *Dietary Manager Magazine*
Pub: Dietary Managers Association (DMA)
Ed: Diane Everett, Editor. **Released:** Monthly. **Price:** $40 one year (10 issues). **Description:** Professional magazine focusing on nutrition and management issues encountered by dietary managers in non-commerical food service.

41188 ■ *Emergency*
Pub: Bobit Business Media
Ed: Doug Fiske, Editor. **Released:** Monthly. **Price:** $23.95. **Description:** Trade journal covering prehospital medical and rescue techniques for paramedics, firefighters, EMTS, RN's, EMS physicians and other emergency services.

41189 ■ *Encounters*
Pub: Venice Family Clinic
Contact: Rachel Taylor, Dev.Assoc.
Released: Biennial. **Price:** Free. **Description:** Reports on news, events, programs, and activities of the Venice Family Clinic in Los Angeles, California whose mission is "to provide comprehensive primary health care that is affordable, accessible and compassionable for people with no other access to such care."

41190 ■ *Epilepsy Wellness Newsletter*
Pub: Epilepsy Wellness Newsletter
Contact: Patricia Murphy, Editor & Publisher
Released: Quarterly. **Price:** $12, individuals; $4.50, single issue; $18, institutions; out of country. **Description:** Covers scientific and anecdotal research regarding alternative treatments for seizure disorders, particularly nutrition, and also covers lifestyle issues important to people with epilepsy. Recurring features include book reviews and interviews with health professionals.

41191 ■ *Equilibrium*
Pub: The Mood Disorders Association of Ontario
Ed: Eric Jonasson, Editor. **Released:** Quarterly. **Price:** $25. **Description:** Reports on news, events, and updates of The Mood Disorders Association of Metropolitan Toronto, as well as related topics.

41192 ■ *European Clinical Laboratory*
Pub: International Scientific Communications Inc.
Contact: Brian Howard, Publisher/Editor in Chief
Released: Bimonthly. **Price:** $210; $226 foreign. **Description:** Magazine for clinical laboratory scientists.

41193 ■ *Evaluation & the Health Professions*
Pub: Sage Publications Inc.
Contact: Carolyn F. Waltz, Fouding Editor
Ed: R. Barker Bausell, Editor, bbausell@compmed.umm.edu. **Released:** Quarterly. **Price:** $105 Print only; $441.75 institutions E-access; $446.40 institutions Print only; $465 institutions Combined (Print & E-access); $34 single issue Print only; $123 single issue Institutions, Print only. **Description:** Journal providing information relating to research and practice in health settings.

41194 ■ *FDA Week*
Pub: Inside Washington Publishers
Ed: Donna Haseley, Editor. **Released:** Weekly (Fri.). **Price:** $595, U.S. and Canada; $645, elsewhere. **Description:** Reports on Food and Drug Administration policy, regulation, and enforcement.

41195 ■ *Fertility Weekly*
Pub: Keith Key
Contact: Keith Key, Publisher
E-mail: keithkey@mindspring.com
Released: Weekly. **Price:** $759, U.S. and Canada; $859, elsewhere; $1,289, U.S. and Canada two years; $1,460, elsewhere two years. **Description:** Discusses information pertaining to fertility. Recurring features include news of research, a calendar of events, reports of meetings, and a column titled Periodical Review.

41196 ■ *Fitness Management Magazine*
Pub: Leisure Publications Inc.
Contact: Chris Ballard, Publisher
E-mail: chris@fitnessmgmt.com
Released: 12/year. **Price:** Free to qualified subscribers. **Description:** Fitness, preventive health care, and management magazine for owners, managers, and program directors of physical fitness facilities.

41197 ■ *Focus on Autism and Other Developmental Disabilities*
Pub: PRO-ED Inc.
Contact: Donald D. Hammill, Publisher
Ed: John Kregel, Editor, rsimpson@kumc.edu. **Released:** Quarterly. **Price:** $45; $120 institutions in North America; $74 other countries; $151 institutions, other countries. **Description:** Journal provides practical management, treatment, and planning strategies for professionals working with people with autism and developmental disabilities.

41198 ■ *Forensic Drug Abuse Advisor*
Pub: Forensic Drug Abuse Advisor Inc.
Ed: Steven B. Karch, M.D., Editor. **Released:** 10/year. **Price:** $197, individuals. **Description:** Acts as a drug information source. Emphasizes the latest scientific discoveries in drug abuse, workplace drug testing, federal drug law, and forensic pathology. "An absolute necessity in drug related litigation." Recurring features include letters to the editor, news of research, a calendar of events, reports of meetings, news of educational opportunities, book reviews, and notices of publications available. Continuing medical education available.

41199 ■ *Frontiers of Health Services Management*
Pub: Health Administration Press
Ed: Audrey Kaufman, Editor. **Released:** Quarterly. **Price:** $85; $23 single issue. **Description:** Journal presenting commissioned articles by leaders in health services administration on the future of the field, policy, and management issues.

41200 ■ *Georgia Tech Sports and Performance Newsletter*
Pub: Georgia Tech University
Ed: H.G. Knuttgen, Ph.D., Editor. **Released:** Monthly. **Price:** $34, U.S.; $42, Canada; $48, elsewhere. **Description:** Discusses sports training, nutrition, injury prevention, and sports medicine research and news. Recurring features include letters to the editor, interviews, and news of research.

41201 ■ *Good Health Bulletin*
Pub: Harvey W. Watt & Company Inc.
Ed: Bill Maness, Editor. **Released:** Monthly. **Price:** $19.95, U.S. and Canada. **Description:** Contains up-to-date helpful medical and related information concerning health, fitness, and longevity. Recurring features include news of research.

41202 ■ *Government Recreation and Fitness*
Pub: Executive Business Media Inc.
Released: Bimonthly, 7/yr. **Description:** Government administration magazine concentrating on fitness centers, recreation concepts, and facilities.

41203 ■ *Health Affairs*
Pub: Project HOPE
Contact: Meredith S. Zimmerman, Production Mgr
E-mail: mzimmerman@projecthope.org
Ed: John K. Iglehart, Editor, jiglehart@projecthope.org. **Released:** Bimonthly, 6/year. **Price:** $122 U.S. and Canada; $162 internationa; $208 U.S. and Canada; print & online; $248 internationa; $293 U.S. and Canada; print & online; $333 internationane; $78 students other countries; print & online; $118 students internationa; $295 institutions U.S. & Canada print online; $335 institutions other countries. **Description:** Number one cited health policy and health services research journal.

41204 ■ *Health Care Analysis*
Pub: Springer Netherlands
Ed: A.R. Edgar, Editor. **Released:** Quarterly, 4/yr. **Price:** $528.32 institutions. **Description:** Journal seeking to analyze health care from multiple perspectives: public policy and health-related education, health services organisation and decision-making health care professional practice.

41205 ■ *Health Care Management REVIEW (HCMR)*
Pub: Aspen Publishers Inc.
Released: Quarterly. **Price:** $97.91; $272.96 institutions; $52.49 other countries; $167.49; $340.94 institutions. **Description:** Journal devoted to management issues in health care and administration.

41206 ■ *The Health Care Manager (HCM)*
Pub: Aspen Publishers Inc.
Contact: Kevin Entricken, CFO
Released: Quarterly. **Price:** $92.49; $256.49 institutions; $150.49 international; $309.49 institutions international. **Description:** Journal providing cost-effective solutions and guidance for health care supervisors.

41207 ■ Health Care for Women International
Pub: Taylor & Francis
Ed: Eleanor Krassen Covan, Ph.D., Editor, covane@uncw.edu. **Released:** 10/year. **Price:** $662 institutions; $182. **Description:** Interdisciplinary journal on women's health care. Covers cultural differences, psychological challenges, alternative lifestyles, aging, wife abuse, childbearing and ethical issues.

41208 ■ Health Progress
Pub: Catholic Health Association of the United States
Contact: Rev. Michael Place, Publisher
Released: Bimonthly. **Price:** Free to qualified subscribers; $50; $60 out of country; $10 single issue to non-members. **Description:** Magazine for administrative-level and other managerial personnel in Catholic healthcare and related organizations. Featured are articles on management concepts, legislative and regulatory trends, and theological, sociological, ethical, legal, and technical issues.

41209 ■ Health and Safety Science Abstracts
Pub: Cambridge Scientific Abstracts
Released: Monthly. **Price:** $850 web edition. **Description:** Journal covering health and safety research.

41210 ■ Health Science
Pub: National Health Association
Released: Quarterly. **Price:** $35 U.S. and Canada; $55 other countries. **Description:** Health and natural hygiene magazine, for members of ANHS.

41211 ■ Healthcare Advertising Review
Pub: The Business Word
Contact: Tom Rees, Associate Editor
E-mail: tom.rees@businessword.com
Released: Bimonthly. **Price:** $294 print or online. **Description:** Magazine for healthcare providers and advertising agencies reviewing print, direct mail, outdoor and television advertising done by healthcare institutions.

41212 ■ Healthcare Corporate Finance News
Pub: Irving Levin Associates Inc.
Contact: Stephen M. Monroe, Managing Editor
Ed: Gretchen S. Swanson, Editor. **Released:** Monthly. **Price:** $495. **Description:** Reports on the growth strategies of managed care providers, hospitals, drug companies, medical device manufacturers, and other healthcare organizations. Also reports on the latest deals in the healthcare sector, and how healthcare companies are doing on Wall Street.

41213 ■ Healthcare Executive
Pub: American College of Healthcare Executives
Released: Bimonthly. **Price:** $65; $75 other countries; $15 single issue. **Description:** Health care management magazine examining trends, issues, and innovations.

41214 ■ Healthcare Fraud and Abuse
Pub: Law Journal Newsletter
Contact: Michael E. Clark, Editor-in-Chief
Price: $2255. **Description:** Covers healthcare fraud and abuse cases, administrative decisions, new legislation and regulations, developments in investigative techniques and discovery, defense strategies, and more. Also provides analysis.

41215 ■ Healthcare Purchasing News
Pub: Nelson Publishing Inc.
Ed: James M. Berklan, Editor, jberklan@nelsonpub.com. **Released:** Monthly. **Price:** $44.95 U.S.; $54.95 Canada; $59.95 foreign; $5 single issue; $9 single issue back issue. **Description:** Magazine for healthcare material management, central services, operating room and infection control professionals, and others involved in supply chain issues with hospitals and outpatient settings.

41216 ■ Heart and Lung
Pub: Mosby
Released: Bimonthly, Jan, Mar, May, July, Sept, Nov. **Price:** $71; $253 institutions; $34 students; $99 other countries; $50 students, other countries; $289 institutions, other countries. **Description:** Journal offering articles prepared by nurse and physician members of the critical care team, recognizing the nurse's role in the care and management of major organ-system conditions in critically ill patients.

41217 ■ Hemophilia Ontario News
Pub: Hemophilia Ontario
Released: Quarterly, 3-4/yr. **Price:** $15, individuals in Canada; $20, institutions in Canada. **Description:** "Hemophilia Ontario is commited to improve the quality of life of people affected by hemophilia and related blood conditions, and to work towards a cure." Publishes on current events, new treatments, volunteer update, and advocacy news. Recurring features include news of research, a calendar of events, and job listings.

41218 ■ Home Health Care Management and Practice
Pub: Sage Publications Inc.
Ed: Barbara Stover Gingerich, Editor, Bgingerich1@suscom.net. **Released:** Bimonthly. **Price:** $380 institutions print and e-access; $361 institutions e-access only; $365 institutions print only; $132 print only. **Description:** Journal covering issues and practical concerns in home health care.

41219 ■ Home Health Care Services Quarterly
Pub: The Haworth Press Inc.
Contact: David Cherin PhD, Assoc. Ed.
E-mail: dcherin@picf.org
Ed: Lynn Goforth, PhD, Editor, jsimmons@picf.org. **Released:** Quarterly. **Price:** $75 U.S.; $101 Canada; $109 other countries; $160 institutions U.S.; $216 institutions, Canada; $232 institutions, other countries; $580 libraries agencies, U.S.; $783 libraries agencies, Canada; $841 libraries agencies, other countries. **Description:** Professional journal.

41220 ■ Homecare Administrative HORIZONS
Pub: Beacon Health Corp.
Contact: Diane J. Omdahl RN, MS, Editor-in-Chief
Released: Monthly. **Price:** $249, individuals. **Description:** Provides homecare agency management information on all kinds of business and personnel topics. Incorporates comprehensive how-to information, current regulatory requirements, and documentation strategies. Runs a series of articles, including how to move into managed care, how to manage and measure outcomes, how to survive scrutiny by medicare's fraud squad, strengthening agency/physician relationships, and personnel issues. Recurring features include columns titled Peaks & Valleys, Fine-tuning the Fundamentals, Clearing the Fog, and Higher Ground.

41221 ■ Hospital News Canada
Pub: Trader Media Corp.
Contact: Connie Michalsky, Gen Mgr
Ed: Julie Abelsohn, Editor. **Released:** Monthly. **Price:** $29.40 single issue in U.S.; $77 in U.S.; $104.50 in U.S.; $187 in U.S.; $330 in U.S.; $374 in U.S. **Description:** Publication focusing on the health industry for healthcare professionals, including adminstrative and medical staff.

41222 ■ Hospital Topics
Pub: Heldref Publications
Contact: Chante Douglas, Advertising Mgr
E-mail: advertise@heldref.org
Released: Quarterly. **Price:** $52 plus postage charges for outside U.S.; $105 institutions plus postage charges for outside U.S. **Description:** Journal for upper and middle management in the changing hospital and health care industry.

41223 ■ Industrial Hygiene News
Pub: Rimbach Publishing Inc.
Contact: Norberta Rimbach, Publisher
Ed: David Lavender, Editor. **Released:** Bimonthly. **Price:** Free to qualified subscribers. **Description:** Magazine covering industrial hygiene, occupational health, and safety.

41224 ■ The Informer
Pub: The Simon Foundation for Continence
Contact: Cheryle B. Gartley, President
Released: Quarterly. **Price:** $15, U.S.. **Description:** Discusses topics concerned with bladder or bowel incontinence.

41225 ■ Inside MS
Pub: National Multiple Sclerosis Society
Contact: Rochell Ratner, Assoc. Ed.
E-mail: rochelle.ratner@nmiss.com
Released: Bimonthly, 6/year. **Price:** $25 members. **Description:** Magazine for people with multiple sclerosis, their families, attending professionals, and interested donors. Provides information on coping, research, legislation, medical advances and disability rights advocacy.

41226 ■ International Journal of Health Planning and Management
Pub: John Wiley & Sons Inc.
Contact: Prof. Bie Nio Ong, Joint Ed.
Released: Quarterly, 4/yr. **Price:** $1,235 worldwide, in Canada, add 7% GST; $1,645 institutions worldwide, in Canada, add 7% GST; $1,810 institutions worldwide, in Canada, add 7% GST, print & online. **Description:** Journal discussing major issues in health planning and management systems and practices.

41227 ■ International Journal of Health Services
Pub: Baywood Publishing Company Inc.
Contact: Linda Strange, Copy Ed.
Ed: Debabar Banerji, Editor. **Released:** Quarterly, 4/yr. **Price:** $300 institutions; $75. **Description:** International health services journal covering social policy, political economy, sociology, history, philosophy, ethics, and law.

41228 ■ International Journal of Technology Assessment in Health Care
Pub: Cambridge University Press
Ed: Prof. Egon Jonsson, Editor, ejonsson@ihe.ca. **Released:** Quarterly, 4/yr. **Price:** $202 institutions online & print; $175 institutions online; $183 print; $335 institutions online & print; $285 institutions online; $305 print. **Description:** Journal covering advancements in health care technology.

41229 ■ International Quarterly of Community Health Education
Pub: Baywood Publishing Company Inc.
Ed: George P. Cernada, Editor. **Released:** Quarterly, 4/yr. **Price:** $75; $300 institutions. **Description:** Publication on the relationship between community health education and social change.

41230 ■ The Joint Commission Journal on Quality Improvement
Pub: The Joint Commission Journal on Quality Improvement
Ed: Steven Berman, Editor, sberman@jcaho.org. **Released:** Monthly. **Description:** Magazine directed to health care providers and administrators quality assurance/improvement managers and researchers concerned with the quality of health care; specifically quality improvement, CQI/TQM, and risk management.

41231 ■ Journal of Agromedicine
Pub: The Haworth Press Inc.
Ed: William M. Simpson, Editor. **Released:** Quarterly, 4 issues/volume. **Price:** $75 U.S.; $101 Canada; $109 other countries; $125 institutions U.S.; $169 institutions, Canada; $181 institutions, other countries; $185 libraries agencies, U.S.; $250 libraries agencies, Canada; $268 libraries agencies, other countries. **Description:** Journal on the health effects of agricultural operations on workers and their families, consumers, and the environment.

41232 ■ Journal of AHIMA
Pub: American Health Information Management Association (AHIMA)
Contact: Kevin Heubusch, Managing Editor
E-mail: kevin.heubusch@ahima.org

Released: Monthly, 10/yr. **Price:** $100. **Description:** A professional development tool for health information managers. Disseminates new knowledge, best practices, and industry news.

41233 ■ *Journal of the American Board of Family Medicine*
Pub: American Board of Family Medicine
Contact: James C. Puffer MD, Exec. Ed.
Released: Bimonthly. **Price:** $130 institutions print; $65 print; $30 print; $160 print international; $95 print international; $40 print, international. **Description:** Medical journal.

41234 ■ *Journal of American College Health*
Pub: Heldref Publications
Contact: Alison Mayhew, Advertising Mgr
E-mail: advertise@heldref.org
Released: Bimonthly. **Price:** $76 plus postage charges for outside U.S.; $140 institutions plus postage charges for outside U.S. **Description:** Journal covering developments and research in the college healthcare field.

41235 ■ *Journal of the American Dietetic Association*
Pub: American Dietetic Association
Ed: Elaine R. Monsen, Editor. **Released:** Monthly. **Description:** Journal reporting original research on nutrition, diet therapy, education and administration.

41236 ■ *Journal of the Association of Nurses in AIDS Care*
Pub: Sage Publications Inc.
Contact: Elizabeth Haigh, Publisher
Released: Bimonthly. **Price:** $85 U.S.D; $354 institutions U.S.D. **Description:** Professional magazine focusing on quality care for people with HIV/AIDS.

41237 ■ *Journal of Behavioral Health Services & Research*
Pub: Springer-Verlag New York Inc.
Contact: Dr. Bruce L. Levin, Editor-in-Chief
E-mail: levin@fmhi.usf.edu
Released: Quarterly. **Price:** $71.95; $201.95 institutions; $49 single issue institutions. **Description:** Journal on the organization, financing, delivery, and outcome of behavioral health services.

41238 ■ *Journal of Cutaneous Medicine & Surgery*
Pub: Springer-Verlag New York Inc.
Contact: Aditya Gupta, Assoc. Ed.
Released: Bimonthly. **Description:** Journal containing article summaries on dermatology.

41239 ■ *Journal of Developmental and Learning Disorders*
Pub: International Universities Press Inc.
Ed: Stanley Greenspan, MD, Editor. **Released:** Semiannual. **Price:** $42; $70. **Description:** Journal concerned with the identification, prevention, and treatment of disorders that interfere with adaptive developmental and learning processes.

41240 ■ *Journal of Ethnic & Cultural Diversity in Social Work*
Pub: The Haworth Press Inc.
Contact: Bill Cohen Ph.D., Publisher
E-mail: ddeanda@ucla.edu
Ed: Diane de Anda, PhD, Editor. **Released:** Quarterly. **Price:** $75 U.S.; $101 Canada; $109 other countries; $150 institutions U.S.; $203 institutions, Canada; $218 institutions, other countries; $340 libraries agencies, U.S.; $459 libraries agencies, Canada; $493 libraries agencies, other countries. **Description:** Journal examines multicultural social issues related to social work policy, research, theory, and practice.

41241 ■ *Journal of Health Care Chaplaincy*
Pub: The Haworth Press Inc.
Contact: Bill Cohen, Publisher
Ed: Larry VandeCreek, DMin, Editor, lvandecreek2001@yahoo.com. **Released:** Biannual (2 issues per volume). **Price:** $50 U.S.; $68 Canada; $73

other countries; $95 institutions U.S.; $128 institutions, Canada; $138 institutions, other countries; $225 libraries agencies, U.S.; $304 libraries agencies, Canada; $326 libraries agencies, other countries. **Description:** Journal on chaplaincy in health care institutions.

41242 ■ *Journal of Health Care Finance*
Pub: Aspen Publishers Inc.
Contact: Richard H. Kravitz
Released: Quarterly. **Description:** Journal offering advice, effective management strategies, and information on new financing alternatives for competing in today's health care financial environment.

41243 ■ *Journal of Health Care for the Poor and Underserved*
Pub: The Johns Hopkins University Press
Ed: Kimyona Roberts, Editor, kroberts@mmc.edu. **Released:** Quarterly, (February, May, August, and November). **Price:** $60 print; $25 students print; $285 institutions print; $285 institutions online; $399 institutions print and online. **Description:** Journal covering the health problems of the poor, elderly, rural and inner-city residents.

41244 ■ *Journal of Health & Social Behavior*
Pub: American Sociological Association
Released: Quarterly. **Description:** Sociology journal on problems of health and illness. Features analyses of health-related institutions, occupations, programs, and behaviors.

41245 ■ *Journal of Health and Social Policy*
Pub: The Haworth Press Inc.
Ed: Stanley F. Battle, PhD, Editor, sbattle@coppin.edu. **Released:** Quarterly. **Price:** $75 U.S.; $150 institutions U.S.; $450 libraries agencies, U.S.; $101 Canada; $203 institutions, Canada; $608 libraries agencies, Canada; $109 other countries; $218 institutions, other countries; $653 libraries agencies, other countries. **Description:** Journal for people interested in health and social policy issues.

41246 ■ *Journal for Healthcare Quality*
Pub: National Association for Healthcare Quality
Contact: Robert Rosati, Quality Network Ed.
Released: Bimonthly. **Price:** $105 nonmembers per year; $150 institutions per year; $175 out of country per year. **Description:** Professional publication that explores safe, cost-effective, quality healthcare.

41247 ■ *Journal of Intensive Care Medicine*
Pub: Sage Publications Inc.
Ed: James M. Rippe, M.D., Editor, bporcaro@rippelifestyle.com. **Released:** Bimonthly. **Price:** $546 institutions print & e-access; $518.70 institutions e-access only; $524.16 institutions print only; $218 print only; $96 single issue institutions; $47 single issue. **Description:** Medical journal for specialists working in intensive care units.

41248 ■ *Journal of Nuclear Cardiology*
Pub: Mosby
Contact: Jane Grochowski MD, Publisher
Ed: Barry L. Zaret, MD, Editor. **Released:** Bimonthly. **Price:** $186; $259 institutions; $227; $304 institutions, other countries. **Description:** Official journal of the American Society of Nuclear Cardiology (ASNC). Covers all aspects of nuclear cardiology including interpretation, diagnosis, radiopharmaceuticals, and imaging equipment.

41249 ■ *Journal of Nutraceuticals, Functional & Medical Foods*
Pub: The Haworth Press Inc.
Contact: Nancy M. Childs PhD, Journal Co-Editor
E-mail: nchilds@sju.edu
Released: Quarterly, (4 issues per volume). **Price:** $32 U.S.; $43.20 Canada taxes; $60 institutions U.S.; $86.67 institutions, Canada can taxes taxes; $130 libraries U.S.; $187.78 libraries agencies, Canada 35%(7% on whole amount); $188.50 libraries agencies, other countries. **Description:** Journal focusing on 'superfoods, food products with potentially strong health preventative or therapeutic properties.' Con-

tains research and review articles, book and report reviews, and announcements of upcoming seminars. Chiefly directed toward professionals involved in or concerned with superfoods, such as nutritionists, physicians, dieticians, and pharmaceutical scientists.

41250 ■ *Journal of School Health*
Pub: American School Health Association
Ed: Morgan R. Pigg, Jr., Editor. **Released:** Monthly, (not published in June and July). **Description:** Journal on health promotion in school settings.

41251 ■ *Journal of Social Service Research*
Pub: The Haworth Press Inc.
Contact: Bill Cohen Ph.D., Publisher
E-mail: cmcmille@wustl.edu
Released: Quarterly. **Price:** $40 U.S.; $54; $58 other countries; $150 institutions U.S.; $203 institutions, Canada; $218 institutions, other countries; $520 libraries agencies, U.S.; $702 libraries agencies, Canada; $754 libraries agencies, other countries. **Description:** Journal addressing issues of design, delivery, and management of social services.

41252 ■ *Journal of the Society of Pediatric Nurses*
Pub: Nursecom Inc.
Contact: Margo Neal RN, Publisher
E-mail: margoneal@cs.com
Ed: Roxie L. Foster, R.N., Editor, margocneal@cs.com. **Released:** Quarterly. **Price:** $68 print and online, U.S.; $139 institutions print and standard online, U.S.; $120 institutions premium online, U.S.; $71 Europe, print and online; $88 institutions Europe, print and standard online; $97 institutions, other countries premium online; $47 other countries print and online; $97 institutions print and premium online, U.S.; $88 institutions, other countries print and premium online. **Description:** Journal for pediatric nurses promoting infant, child, and adolescent health.

41253 ■ *The League Letter*
Pub: League for the Hard of Hearing
Price: Included in membership. **Description:** Reports on news and events of the The League for the Hard of Hearing. Recurring features include a calendar of events. **Remarks:** TTY available at (917)305-7999.

41254 ■ *Leaven*
Pub: La Leche League International Inc.
Contact: Judy Torgus, Exec. Editor
E-mail: jtorgus@llli.org
Released: Bimonthly. **Description:** Magazine for volunteer lactation specialists who help mothers breastfeed their infants.

41255 ■ *Managed Care Quarterly*
Pub: Aspen Publishers Inc.
Contact: Wolters Kluwer
Ed: Allan Fine, Editor. **Released:** Quarterly. **Description:** Journal providing current information to health care executives who require in-depth material on specific managed care issues.

41256 ■ *Managed Care Week*
Pub: Atlantic Information Services Inc.
Contact: Jill Brown
Released: 45/year. **Price:** $622, individuals include e-mail issues, e-mail news alerts. **Description:** Provides the news on innovative managed care arrangements and the business affairs and compliance strategies of HMOs, PPOs, and POS plans. Recurring features include inserts.

41257 ■ *Managed Healthcare Executive*
Pub: Advanstar Communications
Contact: Daniel J. Corcoran, Publisher
Released: Monthly. **Price:** Free to qualified subscribers; $64 U.S.; $12 single issue U.S.; $114 two years U.S.; $84 Canada and Mexico; $134 two years Canada and Mexico; $14 single issue Canada and Mexico; $124 other countries; $229 two years other countries; $14 single issue other countries. **Description:** Professional magazine reporting news and information pertinent to healthcare purchasing decisions made in the managed care industry. Topics include quality assurance, technology, disease management, and trends in integrated health systems.

41258 ■ Marketing Health Services
Pub: American Marketing Association
Contact: Jack Hollfelder, Publisher
E-mail: jhollfelder@ama.org
Released: Quarterly. **Price:** $55 AMA member; $80 nonmembers tax extra for Canadian residents; $110 institutions tax extra for Canadian residents; $120 other countries; $135 institutions other countries. **Description:** Periodical that provides practitioners and academics with the latest research on techniques and applications.

41259 ■ Massage Therapy Journal
Pub: American Massage Therapy Association
Contact: Christina Rompon, Media Sales & Svcs.
Ed: Michael Schwanz, Editor. **Released:** Annual. **Price:** $25 U.S. and Canada per year; $45 two years 2 years; $70 elsewhere per year; $120 elsewhere 2 years. **Description:** Magazine focusing on professional massage therapy benefits, techniques, research, news, and practitioners.

41260 ■ Materials Management in Health Care
Pub: Health Forum L.L.C.
Contact: John Sukenik, COO
E-mail: jsukenik@healthforum.com
Ed: Erin Burke, Editor. **Released:** Monthly. **Description:** Trade magazine for purchasers, managers, and manufacturers of health care equipment and supplies.

41261 ■ McKnight's Long-Term Care News
Pub: McKnight's Long-Term Care News
Contact: Jim Berklan
E-mail: jim.berklan@mltcn.com
Released: 16/year. **Price:** Free to qualified subscribers; $5 single issue; $9 single issue back issue; $54.95 Canada; $59.95 foreign. **Description:** Professional magazine.

41262 ■ Mealey's Managed Care Liability Report
Pub: Mealey Publications
Contact: A. Spencer
Ed: Beth Caputo, Editor, bcaputo@mealeys.com. **Released:** Semimonthly. **Price:** $675, U.S.; $795, elsewhere. **Description:** "Details legal battles arising from the sweeping and controversial changes in the U.S. health care system. Topics include HMO vicarious liability for medical malpractice, ERISA preemption, antitrust, trade practices, contractual disputes, coverage denials, negligent credentialing, Medicare/Medicaid fraud and abuse."

41263 ■ Medical Care
Pub: Lippincott Williams & Wilkins
Ed: Catarina Kiefe, PhD, Editor. **Released:** Monthly. **Price:** $373; $475 international; $813 institutions; $869 institutions, other countries. **Description:** Journal publishing original papers on developments in the medical care field. Also covers findings of investigations into health services research, planning, organization, financing, and evaluation.

41264 ■ Medical Environment Update Newsletter
Pub: Medical Environment Inc.
Contact: George W. Hunt, Editor & Publisher
E-mail: george@medicalenvironment.com
Released: Monthly. **Price:** $165, individuals; $300, two years. **Description:** Provides news and items of interest to medical facilities. Covers government mandated policies and standards, as well as training materials designed to make work easier for the facility's safety officer. Recurring features include letters to the editor and news of research.

41265 ■ Medicine on the Net
Pub: COR Healthcare Resources
Contact: Joyce Flory
Ed: Bridget Meaney, Editor. **Released:** Monthly. **Price:** $147, U.S. and Canada; $159, elsewhere. **Description:** Spotlights developing issues in the use of the Internet by medical professionals. Recurring features include letters to the editor, interviews, news of research, and book reviews.

41266 ■ Michigan Health and Hospitals
Pub: Michigan Hospital Association
Contact: Gretchen Christensen, Advertising Mgr
E-mail: gretchenchris@villagepress.com
Ed: Patty Dextrom, Editor, pdextrom@lans.mha.org. **Released:** Bimonthly. **Description:** Trade magazine for Michigan hospital leaders and healthcare policy makers.

41267 ■ Modern Healthcare
Pub: Crain Communications Inc.
Contact: Neil McLaughlin, Managing Editor
E-mail: nmclaughlin@crain.com
Ed: David Burda, Editor, dburda@crain.com. **Released:** Weekly. **Price:** $145; $236 Canada; $199 other countries. **Description:** Weekly Business news magazine for Healthcare Management

41268 ■ Morbidity and Mortality Weekly Report
Pub: Centers for Disease Control and Prevention
Ed: Mary Lou Lindegren, MD, Editor. **Released:** Weekly (Fri.). **Description:** Magazine focusing on public health problems and diseases.

41269 ■ The Nation's Health
Pub: American Public Health Association
Contact: Melanie Padgett, Asst. Ed./Reporter
E-mail: melanie.padgett@apha.org
Ed: Michele Late, Editor, michele.late@apha.org. **Released:** 10/year. **Price:** $50 U.S. and Canada; $63 other countries by airmail; $5 single issue; $10 single issue other countries. **Description:** Public health policy, research and legislation news.

41270 ■ NCPD National Update
Pub: National Catholic Office for Persons with Disabilities
Contact: Mary Jane Owen, Executive Director
Released: Quarterly. **Price:** Free. **Description:** Focuses on disabled persons with a Catholic slant.

41271 ■ New Beginnings
Pub: La Leche League International Inc.
Contact: Judy Torgus, Exec. Editor
E-mail: jtorgus@llli.org
Released: Bimonthly. **Price:** $20; $25 Canada; $26 other countries. **Description:** Magazine offering education, information, and support to women who wish to breastfeed their infants.

41272 ■ New Horizons
Pub: San Fernando Valley Association for the Retarded
Ed: Nancy Banks, Editor. **Released:** 3/year. **Price:** Included in membership. **Description:** Reports on membership news of the San Fernando Valley Association for the Retarded. Spotlights volunteers, activities, and events. Recurring features include columns titled Legislative Corner and President's Corner.

41273 ■ Nursing Education Perspectives
Pub: National League for Nursing
Contact: Leslie Block, Managing Editor
E-mail: lblock@nln.org
Ed: Joyce Fitzpatrick, Editor, jfitz@nln.org. **Released:** Bimonthly, January, March, May, July, September, and November. **Price:** $40 members one year; $70 nonmembers; $125 institutions libraries and institutions; $90 nonmembers Canada; $98 nonmembers other countries; $145 institutions, Canada; $153 institutions, other countries. **Description:** Professional journal for nurses. Includes articles on health policy, social and economic issues affecting health care, and nursing education and practice.

41274 ■ Nutrition & Mental Health
Pub: International Schizophrenia Foundation
Contact: Steven Carter, Managing Editor
Released: Quarterly. **Price:** $30, U.S. and Canada; $35, other countries. **Description:** Acquaints readers with the effects of nutrition on mental health, with on emphasis on schizophrenia.

41275 ■ Nutrition Today
Pub: Lippincott Williams & Wilkins
Ed: Johanna Dwyer, Editor. **Released:** Bimonthly, 6/yr. **Price:** $82.91 U.S.; $228.96 institutions U.S.; $42.49 U.S. in-training; $114.94 international:; $319.94 institutions international. **Description:** Health science journal.

41276 ■ Occupational Hazards
Pub: Penton Media Inc.
Contact: John DiPaola, Vice President
E-mail: jdipaola@penton.com
Ed: Sandy Smith, Editor, ssmith@penton.com. **Released:** Monthly. **Price:** $72 Canada; $126 two years; $50 Canada digital version; $99 international; $162 international; $80 international digital version. **Description:** Monthly publication for safety professionals featuring information to meet OSHA and EPA compliance requirements,improve management of safety, industrial hygiene and environmental programs and find products and services to protect employees and property.

41277 ■ Occupational Therapy in Health Care
Pub: The Haworth Press Inc.
Contact: Bill Cohen, Publisher
Ed: Anne Elizabeth Dickerson, PhD, Editor, dickersona@mail.ecu.edu. **Released:** Quarterly. **Price:** $75 U.S.; $101 Canada; $109 other countries; $150 institutions U.S.; $203 institutions, Canada; $218 institutions, other countries; $315 libraries agencies, U.S.; $425 libraries agencies, Canada; $457 libraries agencies, other countries. **Description:** Journal for occupational therapists.

41278 ■ Operative Techniques in Sports Medicine
Pub: Elsevier
Ed: J.C. DeLee, Jr., Editor. **Released:** 4/yr. **Price:** $409 institutions outside U.S.; $343 institutions U.S.; $286 outside U.S.; $208 U.S.; $105 students U.S.; $142 students outside U.S.; $52 single issue U.S. (individuals); $71.50 single issue outside U.S. (individuals); $85.75 single issue U.S. (institutions); $102.25 single issue outside U.S. (institutions). **Description:** Journal covering the field of orthopedics in sports medicine.

41279 ■ Osteoporosis International
Pub: Springer-Verlag New York Inc.
Contact: R. Lindsay, Editor-in-Chief
E-mail: ralbano@springer-ny.com
Released: Monthly, 12/yr. **Price:** $145.30 single issues. **Description:** Journal featuring papers, articles, and reports regarding osteoporosis.

41280 ■ Outpatient Care Technology
Pub: Reilly Communications Group
Contact: Sean P. Reilly, President
E-mail: sean.r@ix.netcom.com
Ed: Maureen Leahy, Editor, mleahy@flash.net. **Released:** Bimonthly. **Description:** Trade magazine (tabloid) serving physician specialists, chief medical officers, administrators, business managers, and others concerned with product evaluation and procurement in freestanding ambulatory, diagnostic and surgical centers, group practices, HMOs, and PPOs.

41281 ■ Peritoneal Dialysis International
Pub: Multimed Inc.
Contact: Lorne Cooper, Vice President
Released: Bimonthly. **Description:** Magazine for health professionals.

41282 ■ Physical and Occupational Therapy in Pediatrics
Pub: The Haworth Press Inc.
Contact: Bill Cohen, Publisher
Ed: Robert J. Palisano, PT, Editor, robert.j.palisano@drexel.edu. **Released:** Quarterly. **Price:** $75 U.S.; $101 Canada; $109 other countries; $150 institutions U.S.; $203 institutions, Canada; $218 institutions, other countries; $545 libraries agencies, U.S.; $736 libraries agencies, Canada; $790 libraries agencies, other countries. **Description:** Journal for therapists involved in developmental and physical rehabilitation of infants and children.

41283 ■ Physician Executive
Pub: American College of Physician Executives
Ed: Susan Sasenick, Editor. **Released:** Bimonthly. **Price:** Free to qualified subscribers; $72 institutions; $10 single issue; $84 other countries. **Description:** Journal focusing on health care management and medical management for physician executives.

41284 ■ Physician Magazine
Pub: Focus on the Family
Contact: Jim Daly, President
Ed: Scott Denicola, Editor. **Released:** Bimonthly. **Description:** Magazine for medical professionals addressing personal and family growth, public policy and community involvement, patient care and research.

41285 ■ The Prevention Researcher
Pub: Integrated Research Services Inc.
Ed: Steven Ungerleider, Ph.D., Editor, suinteg@attglobal.net. **Released:** Quarterly, 4/year. **Price:** $36, individuals; $48 libraries. **Description:** Specializes in prevention topics for at-risk youth.

41286 ■ Provider
Pub: American Health Care Association
Released: Monthly. **Price:** $48 U.S.; Free to qualified subscribers; $61 Canada and Mexico; $85 other countries foreign. **Description:** Provider Magazine.

41287 ■ Psychoanalytic Social Work
Pub: The Haworth Press Inc.
Contact: Jerrold Brandell PhD, Journal Editor
E-mail: JBRANDS451@aol.com
Released: Biannual. **Price:** $60 USA; $81 Canada; $87 other countries; $125 institutions USA; $169 institutions, Canada; $181 institutions, other countries; $325 libraries Agencies, USA; $439 libraries Agencies, Canada; $471 libraries Agencies, other countries. **Description:** Journal devoted to relationship of clinical social work to psychoanalysis.

41288 ■ PT, Magazine of Physical Therapy
Pub: American Physical Therapy Association
Contact: Maryann DiGiacomo, News Editor
E-mail: maryanndigiacomo@apta.org
Ed: Donald Tepper, Editor, donaldtepper@apta.org. **Released:** Monthly. **Price:** $70; $70 members; $90 other countries by surface mail; $90 members out of USA; $150 out of country by Airmail; $95 institutions; $120 institutions, other countries by surface mail; $180 institutions, other countries by airmail; $15 single issue. **Description:** Magazine for physical therapy professionals.

41289 ■ Qualitative Health Research
Pub: Sage Publications Inc.
Ed: Janice M. Morse, PhD, Editor. **Released:** Monthly, 10/yr. **Price:** $850 institutions print and e-access; $808 institutions e-access only; $816 institutions print only; $176 print only; $90 single issue institutions; $23 single issue institutions. **Description:** Journal featuring research, theoretical, and methodological articles on qualitative health issues.

41290 ■ Quality Management in Health Care (QMHC)
Pub: Aspen Publishers Inc.
Released: Quarterly. **Description:** Journal providing a forum to explore and assist in the theoretical, technical, and strategic elements of quality management in health care.

41291 ■ Respiratory Care Manager
Pub: HCPro Inc.
Contact: Paul Nash, Assoc. Editor
Ed: Cathy Rossi, Editor. **Released:** Monthly. **Price:** $229, individuals print; $412, two years print. **Description:** Covers topics related to cardiopulmonary and respiratory care management. Recurring features include interviews and news of research.

41292 ■ Revista Panamericana de Salud Publica
Pub: Pan American Health Organization
Ed: Celia Maria de Almeida, Editor. **Released:** Monthly. **Price:** $44 electronic; $72 institutions electronic; $81 two years electronic; $133 institutions two years, electronic. **Description:** Multilingual public health journal providing information on medical and health progress in America.

41293 ■ Roswellness
Pub: Roswell Park Cancer Institute
Contact: Colleen Karuza, Managing Editor
E-mail: Colleen.Karuza@roswellpark.org

Released: 3/year. **Price:** Free. **Description:** Focuses on health and wellness with a special emphasis on cancer prevention, research, and patient care. Features include patient testimonials and special events.

41294 ■ Seizure
Pub: Elsevier
Contact: P. Boon, Editor-in-Chief
Released: 8/yr. **Price:** $628 institutions European countries; $587 institutions for all countries except Europe and Japan; $71.40 institutions Japan. **Description:** Journal including topics related to epilepsy and seizure disorders.

41295 ■ Share
Pub: SHARE
Released: Semiannual. **Description:** Acts as a forum for information, meetings, resources, and support groups for women with breast or ovarian cancer.

41296 ■ SIECUS Report
Pub: Sexuality Information and Education Council of the United States
Released: Quarterly. **Price:** $49; $9.20 single issue. **Description:** Journal providing information and education on all aspects of human sexuality.

41297 ■ Sleep
Pub: American Academy of Sleep Medicine
Ed: Christian Guilleminault, MD, Editor. **Released:** Monthly, 1 issue comprised of the abstracts presented at the APSS Annual. **Price:** $195 U.S.; $290 institutions U.S.; $260 other countries; $360 institutions other countries. **Description:** Journal covering findings on sleep and circadian rhythms.

41298 ■ Social Work with Groups
Pub: The Haworth Press Inc.
Contact: Andrew Malekoff ACSW, Publisher
E-mail: Anjru@aol.com
Released: Quarterly. **Price:** $75 U.S.; $175 institutions U.S.; $500 libraries agencies, U.S.; $101 Canada; $236 institutions, Canada; $675 libraries agencies, Canada; $109 other countries; $254 institutions, other countries; $725 libraries agencies, other countries. **Description:** Journal for social workers focusing on groups and groupwork in psychiatric, rehabilitative, and multipurpose social work.

41299 ■ Social Work in Health Care
Pub: The Haworth Press Inc.
Contact: Toba Schwaber Kerson PhD, Publisher
Released: Quarterly, (4 issues per vol. / 2 vols. per year). **Price:** $75 U.S.; $101 Canada; $109 other countries; $150 institutions U.S.; $203 institutions, Canada; $218 institutions, other countries; $350 libraries agencies, U.S.; $473 libraries agencies, Canada; $508 libraries agencies, other countries. **Description:** Quality articles in Research Clinical Practice Education in Health Care.

41300 ■ Sports Medicine Alert
Pub: Mountainview Publishing L.L.C.
Contact: Rob Johnson MD, Editor-in-Chief
Released: Monthly. **Price:** $187, U.S.; $207, Canada. **Description:** Provides the latest multidisciplinary research for active patents in the field of primary care sports medicine. Also features clinical reviews, briefs, abstracts, and commentary. Recurring features include letters to the editor, interviews, news of research, and notices of publications available.

41301 ■ Therapeutic Recreation Journal
Pub: National Recreation and Park Association
Ed: Colleen Deyell Hood, Editor, hoodc@okstate.edu. **Released:** Quarterly. **Price:** $28 members; $66 non-members; $34 out of country member; $72 out of country nonmember; $60 libraries. **Description:** Journal providing forum for research and discussion of therapeutic recreation for persons with disabilities.

41302 ■ Topics in Clinical Nutrition (TICN)
Pub: Aspen Publishers Inc.
Ed: Judith A. Gilbride, PhD, Editor. **Released:** Quarterly. **Price:** $88.49; $252.49 institutions; $150.49 other countries; $309.49 institutions, other countries. **Description:** Journal addressing the challenges and problems of dietitians and others involved in dietary care in a health care setting.

41303 ■ Trustee
Pub: Health Forum L.L.C.
Contact: Mary Grayson, Publisher
E-mail: mgrayson@healthforum.com
Ed: Karen Gardner, Editor, kgardner@healthforum.com. **Released:** 10/year. **Price:** $40. **Description:** Magazine for hospital and health care system governing board members containing information about events and issues affecting the health care industry.

41304 ■ Women and Health
Pub: The Haworth Press Inc.
Contact: Bill Cohen, Publisher
Ed: Ellen B. Gold, Ph.D., Editor. **Released:** 4 issues per vol. / 2 vols. per year. **Price:** $75 USA; $101 Canada; $109 other countries; $200 institutions USA; $270 institutions, Canada; $290 institutions, other countries; $480 libraries Agencies, USA; $648 libraries Agencies, Canada; $696 libraries Agencies, other countries. **Description:** Multidisciplinary journal on health for women.

41305 ■ Worksight
Pub: Rehabilitation Research and Training Center on Blindness and Low Vision
Ed: Kelly S. Schaefer, Editor, schaefer@ra.msstate.edu. **Released:** Annual. **Price:** Free. **Description:** Discusses news, activities, research, and training programs of the Rehabilitation Research and Training Center on Blindness and Low Vision. Remarks: TDD available at (662)325-8693.

VIDEOCASSETTES/ AUDIOCASSETTES

41306 ■ Confidentiality: Ethical and Legal Considerations
Channing Bete Company
One Community Pl.
South Deerfield, MA 01373-0200
Ph:(413)665-7611
Free: 800-477-4776
Fax: 800-499-6464
Co. E-mail: custsvcs@channing-bete.com
URL: http://www.channing-bete.com
Released: 1994. **Price:** $295.00. **Description:** Discusses privacy issues, defamation, instances when information must be shared, patient and family access to information, and the impact of computers on confidentiality. Program approved for 1 hour of CEU credits. **Availability:** VHS.

41307 ■ Continuous Quality Improvement in Health Care
Channing Bete Company
One Community Pl.
South Deerfield, MA 01373-0200
Ph:(413)665-7611
Free: 800-477-4776
Fax: 800-499-6464
Co. E-mail: custsvcs@channing-bete.com
URL: http://www.channing-bete.com
Released: 1993. **Price:** $199.00. **Description:** Discusses leadership, training, empowerment, data collection, and tools for interpreting data. Program approved for 3 hours of CEU credits. **Availability:** VHS.

41308 ■ Continuous Quality Improvement in Long-Term Care
Channing Bete Company
One Community Pl.
South Deerfield, MA 01373-0200
Ph:(413)665-7611
Free: 800-477-4776
Fax: 800-499-6464
Co. E-mail: custsvcs@channing-bete.com
URL: http://www.channing-bete.com
Released: 1993. **Price:** $99.00. **Description:** Discusses leadership, training, empowerment, data collection, and tools for interpreting data. Program approved for 2 hours of CEU credits. **Availability:** VHS.

41309 ■ *Controlling Violence in Health Care*
Channing Bete Company
One Community Pl.
South Deerfield, MA 01373-0200
Ph:(413)665-7611
Free: 800-477-4776
Fax: 800-499-6464
Co. E-mail: custsvcs@channing-bete.com
URL: http://www.channing-bete.com
Released: 1994. **Price:** $199.00. **Description:** Covers verbal de-escalation, limit setting, pharmacological intervention, and physical containment. Program approved for 1 hour of CEU credit. **Availability:** VHS.

41310 ■ *Coronary Artery Disease*
Concept Media
PO Box 19542
Irvine, CA 92623-9542
Ph:(949)660-0727
Free: 800-233-7078
Fax: (949)660-0206
Co. E-mail: info@conceptmedia.com
URL: http://www.conceptmedia.com
Released: 1997. **Description:** Four-volume series discusses nursing assessment, diagnosis, intervention and evaluation of patients with this condition. **Availability:** VHS.

41311 ■ *Exercise Echocardiography*
Futura Publishing Co., Inc.
c/o Blackwell Publishing
350 Main St.
Malden, MA 02148
Ph:(781)388-8200
URL: http://www.blackwellpublishing.com
Released: 1997. **Price:** $95.00. **Description:** Demonstrates how to perform exercise stress echocardiography and interpret studies. Also discusses how stress-provoked changes effect coronary angiography. **Availability:** VHS.

41312 ■ *Health Care for the Homeless*
National Film Board of Canada
1123 Broadway, Ste 307
New York, NY 10010
Ph:(212)629-8890
Free: 800-542-2164
Fax: (866)299-9928
URL: http://www.nfb.ca
Released: 1989. **Price:** $295.00. **Description:** This program examines the nexus of poverty and ill health in its extremes, and asks questions about the responsibility of physicians to treat any and all ill people that come to them. **Availability:** VHS; 3/4U.

41313 ■ *Issues in Homecare Nursing*
Concept Media
PO Box 19542
Irvine, CA 92623-9542
Ph:(949)660-0727
Free: 800-233-7078
Fax: (949)660-0206
Co. E-mail: info@conceptmedia.com
URL: http://www.conceptmedia.com
Released: 1997. **Description:** Four-volume series that helps healthcare professionals, experienced practitioners and students address aspects of care in the home. **Availability:** VHS.

41314 ■ *Patient Rights: The Art of Caring*
Channing Bete Company
One Community Pl.
South Deerfield, MA 01373-0200
Ph:(413)665-7611
Free: 800-477-4776
Fax: 800-499-6464
Co. E-mail: custsvcs@channing-bete.com
URL: http://www.channing-bete.com
Released: 1990. **Price:** $199.00. **Description:** Explains patients rights to information, self-determination, communication, privacy, personal property, and freedom from abuse and restraint. Program approved for 2 hours of CEU credits. **Availability:** VHS.

41315 ■ *S.O.S. Kids: Infant/Child Emergency Life Saving Video*
Tapeworm Video Distributors
27833 Hopkins Ave., Unit 6
Valencia, CA 91355
Ph:(661)257-4904
Fax: (661)257-4820
Co. E-mail: sales@tapeworm.com
URL: http://www.tapeworm.com
Released: 1997. **Price:** $19.95. **Description:** EMT Paramedic Richard Hardman describes and demonstrates what to do in various medical emergencies. **Availability:** VHS.

41316 ■ *What Tadoo*
Tapeworm Video Distributors
27833 Hopkins Ave., Unit 6
Valencia, CA 91355
Ph:(661)257-4904
Fax: (661)257-4820
Co. E-mail: sales@tapeworm.com
URL: http://www.tapeworm.com
Released: 1997. **Price:** $14.95. **Description:** Puppet frogs, What and Tadoo help children deal with issues of child abuse and prevention. **Availability:** VHS.

TRADE SHOWS AND CONVENTIONS

41317 ■ American Public Health Association Public Health Expo
American Public Health Association
800 I St. NW
Washington, DC 20001
Ph:(202)777-2742
Fax: (202)777-2534
Co. E-mail: comments@apha.org
URL: http://www.apha.org/
Released: Annual. **Audience:** Public health professionals, physicians, nurses, and health administrators. **Principal Exhibits:** Medical, products-related and pharmaceutical, health services, publishers, computer/software, educational, government, schools of public health. **Dates and Locations:** 2007 Nov 03-07, Washington, DC; 2008 Oct 25-29, San Diego, CA; 2009 Nov 07-11, Philadelphia, PA.

41318 ■ American School Health Association National School Health Conference
American School Health Association
7263 State Rte. 43
PO Box 708
Kent, OH 44240
Ph:(330)678-1601
Free: 800-445-2742
Fax: (330)678-4526
Co. E-mail: asha@ashaweb.org
URL: http://www.ashaweb.org
Released: Annual. **Audience:** School nurses, health educators, physicians, teachers, school administrators, dentists, school counselors, physical educators, and school health coordinators. **Principal Exhibits:** Publications, pharmaceuticals, clinical and medical equipment and supplies, information on health organizations, and health education methods and materials. **Dates and Locations:** 2007 Jul 09-13, Honolulu, HI.

41319 ■ American Society for Healthcare Risk Management Convention
American Society for Healthcare Risk Management
1 N Franklin
Chicago, IL 60606
Ph:(312)422-3980
Fax: (312)422-4580
Co. E-mail: ashrm@aha.org
URL: http://www.ashrm.org
Released: Annual. **Principal Exhibits:** Healthcare industry risk management equipment, supplies, and services.

41320 ■ Association for Research on Nonprofit Organizations and Voluntary Action Conference (ACNOVA)
Association for Research on Nonprofit Organizations and Voluntary Action
550 W N St., Ste. 301
Indianapolis, IN 46202
Ph:(317)684-2120
Fax: (317)684-2128
Co. E-mail: aplotin@indyvax.iupui.edu
URL: http://www.arnova.org
Released: Annual. **Audience:** Scholars and nonprofit organization professionals. **Principal Exhibits:** Exhibits for citizen participation and voluntary action, including social movements, interest groups, consumer groups, political participation, community development, and religious organizations.

41321 ■ Health and Fitness Expo
Jerry Hanson & Associates
PO Box 200201
303 N. Roberts
Billings, MT 59104-0392
Ph:(406)245-0404
Fax: (406)245-3897
Released: Annual. **Audience:** Health professionals and general public. **Principal Exhibits:** Lawn and garden products, home improvements/repair products, spas, computers, interior decorating, nurseries, entertainment and health related services and products.

41322 ■ Virginia Health Care Association Annual Convention and Trade Show
Virginia Health Care Association
2112 W. Laburnum Ave., Ste. 206
Richmond, VA 23227
Ph:(804)353-9101
Fax: (804)353-3098
Co. E-mail: kathy.robertson@vhca.org
URL: http://www.vhca.org
Released: Annual. **Audience:** Nursing homeowners, administrators, purchasing agents, and nurses; dietary, housekeeping, social services, and activities departments heads. **Principal Exhibits:** Equipment, supplies, and services for nursing home operations, including food, medical supplies, furniture, computer systems, linen, medical equipment, insurance, pharmaceuticals, optometrists, psychologists, and transportation.

CONSULTANTS

41323 ■ Alternative Services Inc.
32625 7 Mile Rd., Ste. 10
Livonia, MI 48152-4269
Ph:(248)471-4880
Fax: (248)471-5230
Scope: Provides social services management support to group homes for the mentally disabled. Also offers marketing, training, and financial services to businesses and nonprofit organizations.

41324 ■ BioSciCon Inc.
14905 Forest Landing Cir.
Rockville, MD 20850
Ph:(301)610-9130
Fax: (301)610-7662
Co. E-mail: info@BioSciCon.com
URL: http://www.bioscicon.com

E-mail: info@BioSciCon.com
Scope: Sponsoring development of the technology of the Pap test accuracy via introduction of a new biomarker that enhances visibility of abnormal cells on Pap smears or monolayers of cervical cells obtained in solution. Conducts clinical trials for assessment of the test efficacy and safety, manufactures research tools for conduct of trials, and markets IP to license manufacturing, marketing, sales and distribution rights of the new technology line of products. **Publications:** "Cervical acid phosphatase: A biomarker of cervical dysplasia and potential surrogate endpoint for colposcopy," 2004; "Journal of Clinical Oncology," 2004. **Special Services:** MarkPap®.

41325 ■ Center for Lifestyle Enhancement - Columbia Medical Center of Plano
Medical Center of Plano, 3901 W 15th St.
Plano, TX 75075
Ph:(972)596-6800
Fax: (972)519-1299

Co. E-mail: mcp.cle@hcahealthcare.com
URL: http://www.medicalcenterofplano.com

E-mail: mcp.cle@hcahealthcare.com
Scope: Provides professional health counseling in the areas of general nutrition for weight management, eating disorders, diabetic education, cholesterol reduction, and adolescent weight management. Offers work site health promotion and preventive services. Also coordinates speaker's bureau, cooking classes, and physician referrals. Industries served: education, insurance, healthcare, retail/wholesale, data processing, and manufacturing in Dallas, Ft. Worth, and Collin County, Texas. **Seminars:** Rx Diet and Exercise; Smoking Cessation; Stress Management; Health Fairs; Fitness Screenings; Body Composition; Nutrition Analysis; Exercise Classes; Prenatal Nutrition; SHAPEDOWN; Successfully Managing Diabetes.

41326 ■ The Children's Psychological Trauma Center
31 Clara Ave.
South San Francisco, CA 94080
Ph:(650)589-7989
Fax: (650)589-7989
Co. E-mail: gil.kliman@cphc-sf.org
URL: http://www.expertchildpsychiatry.org

E-mail: gil.kliman@cphc-sf.org
Scope: Treats those with psychological trauma claimed from stressors including institutional negligence, vehicular and aviation accidents, wrongful death in the family, rape, molestation, fire, explosion, flood, earthquake, loss of parents, terrorism, kidnapping, disfiguring events, emotional damage from social work, medical malpractice or defective products. Provides evaluation and reports to referring professionals. Experienced in forensic consultation and testimony. **Publications:** "The practice of behavioural treatment in the acute rehabilitation setting"

41327 ■ Continuing Education Consulting
PO Box 600
Bomoseen, VT 05732
Ph:(802)468-3200
Fax: (802)468-8989
Co. E-mail: sunshinebirdie@aol.com

E-mail: sunshinebirdie@aol.com
Scope: Consultant for healthcare systems. Services include analysis, planning and management services for health clinics, ambulance services, hospitals, and nursing homes. **Seminars:** ACLS and Emergency Nursing Courses; Stress Management.

41328 ■ Diversified Health Resources Inc.
875 N Michigan Ave., Ste. 3250
Chicago, IL 60611-1901
Ph:(312)266-0466
Fax: (312)266-0715
URL: http://www.diversifiedhealth.net
Scope: Offers healthcare consulting for hospitals, nursing homes (including homes for the aged), and other health-related facilities and companies. Specializes in planning and marketing. Also conducts executive searches for top level healthcare administrative positions. Serves private industries as well as government agencies.

41329 ■ Environmental Health Science Inc.
418 Wall St.
Princeton, NJ 08540
Ph:(609)924-7616
Free: 800-841-8923
Fax: (609)924-0793
Co. E-mail: info@speechgeneratingdevices.com
URL: http://www.speechgeneratingdevices.com

E-mail: info@speechgeneratingdevices.com
Scope: Specialists in rehabilitation technology for speech disorder and physically disabled persons. Offers demonstrations, evaluations and sales of the following types of equipment: augmentative speech communication systems, adaptive switches and specialty controls, and computer access devices. Industries served: hospitals and rehabilitation centers,

schools, and special service organizations such as United Cerebral Palsy Association, Department of Human Services, etc. **Seminars:** Augmentative Communication and Assistive Devices.

41330 ■ Family Resource Center on Disabilities
20 E Jackson Blvd., Rm. 300
Chicago, IL 60604
Ph:(312)939-3513
Free: 800-952-4199
Fax: (312)939-7297
Co. E-mail: contact@frcd.org
URL: http://www.frcd.org

E-mail: contact@frcd.org
Scope: Provides consulting services to advocacy groups and individuals seeking support for children with disabilities. **Publications:** "How to Get Services by Being Assertive"; "How to Organize an Effective Parent/Advocacy Group and Move Bureaucracies"; "MAINROADS Travel to Tomorrow - a Road Map for the Future". **Seminars:** How to Support Parents as Effective Advocates; How to Get Services by Being Assertive; How to Develop an Awareness Program for Nondisabled Children; How to Organize a Parent Support Group; How to Move Bureaucratic Mountains; How to Raise Money Painlessly through Publishing; How to Use Humor in Public Presentations.

41331 ■ Grief Counseling & Support Services
8600 W Chester Pke., Ste. 304
Upper Darby, PA 19082
Ph:(610)789-7707
Fax: (610)949-9499
Scope: Specializing in consulting and training services for organizations dealing with loss, trauma and grief issues. These services may include management consultations, crisis intervention, educational programming, policy development, program design, group process work, individual counseling or other support services. Training and support services also provided for loss issues for mental retardation service providers. Serves private industries as well as government agencies. **Seminars:** Seminars on grief, mourning, Drug, alcohol, sex addiction, loss designed to meet individual situations. All seminars tailor-made to specific organizational needs.

41332 ■ Health Information Referral System
RR1 Box 850
Woodstock, VT 05091
Ph:(802)457-3455

41333 ■ Jest for the Health of It Services
PO Box 8484
Santa Cruz, CA 95061-8484
Ph:(831)425-8436
Fax: (831)425-8437
Co. E-mail: pwooten@jesthealth.com
URL: http://www.jesthealth.com

E-mail: pwooten@jesthealth.com
Scope: Develops and presents seminars, keynotes, and skill shops about the power of humor. Provides consulting services for development of humor rooms and comedy carts in hospitals. Conducts training for clowns to make visits in hospitals and nursing homes. Industries served: health professionals and businesses wishing to educate staff about healthy lifestyle choices. **Publications:** "Heart Humor and Healing and Compassionate Laughter:Jest for your Health"; "The Hospital Clown: A Closer Look". **Seminars:** Professional Survival-You Can Laugh or Cry: Stress Control; Choosing the Amusing-Humor Techniques for Work and Home; What's So Funny-What Humor Is, Isn't and Should Be; You've Got To Be Kidding Learning to Laugh at Life's Upsets and Setbacks; Tickle While You Teach-Learning with Laughter.

41334 ■ Occupational & Environmental Health Consulting Services
635 Harding Rd.
Hinsdale, IL 60521-4814
Ph:(630)325-2083
Fax: (630)325-2098

URL: http://www.safety-epa.com
Scope: Provides consulting to industry on safety program development and implementation, industrial hygiene monitoring programs, occupational health nursing, wellness programs, medical monitoring, accident trending and statistics, emergency response planning, multilingual training, right-to-know compliance and training, hazardous waste management, radon monitoring and mitigation, asbestos school inspection, and project management. Also offers indoor air quality, expert witnessing service. **Publications:** "Global Occupational Exposure Limits for over 5,000 Specific Chemicals"; "Post-Remediation Verification and Clearance Testing for Mold and Bacteria Risk Based Levels of Cleanliness". **Seminars:** Right-To-Know Compliance; Setting Internal Exposure Standards; Hospital Right-to-Know and Contingency Response; Ethylene Oxide Control; Industrial Hygiene Training; Asbestos Worker Training; Biosafety; Asbestos Operations and Maintenance. **Special Services:** Firm offers Safety Software Program.

41335 ■ Pathways To Wellness
13845 Flintlock Dr.
Corpus Christi, TX 78418
Ph:(361)949-4790
Fax: (361)949-4627
Co. E-mail: path2wellness@earthlink.net
URL: http://www.path2wellness.com

E-mail: path2wellness@earthlink.net
Scope: Offer natural holistic health counseling, yoga classes and teachers training programs for individuals and companies. R.Y.T.500 and R.Y.Training Center through the Yoga Alliance. Hatha Yoga style is traditional and includes all aspects of yoga from jnana, bhakti, karma, and hatha for all levels of student. Health counseling includes nutritional guidance, kinesiology, iridology, reflexology, energy healing, massage therapy and reflexology, herbal and supplemental direction, creative visualization and meditation. Teachers training program will qualify students for registry with the Yoga Alliance. **Publications:** Is It You Holding You Back?; Is Yoga For Everyone?; The Balancing Act for Staying Healthy; Spring Housecleaning for your Body; Who Needs Nutritional Support...What are the Indicators?; Get Quality work from Healthy Employees!; Creating a Healthy Work Environment. **Seminars:** Is It You Holding You Back?; Introduction to Natural Health and Healthy Living; Introduction to Yoga and Meditation; Creative Visualization for Creating a Healthy Life; Mind/Body Connections for a Wealth of Health; The Eyes Are the Windows to the Soul: Explanations of non-invasive ways to get and stay healthy through Iris interpretations.

41336 ■ Professional Counseling Centers of Indiana
543 Coventry Way
Noblesville, IN 46060-9024
Ph:(317)846-7999
Fax: (317)574-5063
Scope: Business counselors offer expertise in the following areas: employee assistance, managed care, alcohol and drug treatment, labor and union consultation, and industrial mental health.

FRANCHISES AND BUSINESS OPPORTUNITIES

41337 ■ Boston Bartenders School of America
Boston Bartenders School Associates, Inc.
PO Box 176
Wilbraham, MA 01095
Free: 800-357-3210
Fax: (413)596-4630
No. of Franchise Units: 10. **No. of Company-Owned Units:** 3. **Founded:** 1968. **Franchised:** 1994. **Description:** Program in mixology and alcohol awareness. **Equity Capital Needed:** $25,000. **Franchise Fee:** $6,999. **Financial Assistance:** Yes. **Training:** Yes.

41338 ■ ComForcare Senior Services

ComForcare Healthcare Holdings Inc.
2510 Telegraph Rd.
Bloomfield Hills, MI 48302
Ph:(248)745-9700
Free: 800-886-4044
Fax: (248)745-9763
URL: http://www.ComForcare.com
No. of Franchise Units: 70. **No. of Company-Owned Units:** 1. **Founded:** 1996. **Franchised:** 2001. **Description:** Franchise provides home health care for seniors. **Equity Capital Needed:** $48,000-$68,000 total operating capital for one year. **Franchise Fee:** $19,500. **Financial Assistance:** No. **Training:** 1 week on-site training program, and ongoing support available.

41339 ■ The Corporate Body Franchise, L. L.C.

370 SE 15 Ave.
Pompano Beach, FL 33060
Ph:(954)942-9424
Free: 800-790-6930
Fax: (954)783-5177
No. of Company-Owned Units: 1. **Founded:** 1995. **Franchised:** 2001. **Description:** Alternative medicine franchise. **Equity Capital Needed:** $88,000-$178,999. **Franchise Fee:** $15,000. **Financial Assistance:** No. **Training:** Yes.

41340 ■ CPR Services

CPR Services, Inc.
22 Stoneybrook Dr.
Ashland, MA 01721
Ph:(508)881-5107
Free: 800-547-5107
Fax: (508)881-4718
No. of Franchise Units: 1. **No. of Company-Owned Units:** 1. **Founded:** 1985. **Franchised:** 1998. **Description:** CPR and First Aid Training. **Equity Capital Needed:** $13,500-$16,500. **Franchise Fee:** $7,500. **Financial Assistance:** No. **Training:** Yes.

41341 ■ The Dentist Choice, Inc.

34700 Coast Hwy., Ste. 307
Capistrano Beach, CA 92624
Ph:(949)443-2070
Free: 800-757-1333
Fax: (949)443-2074
No. of Franchise Units: 99 **Founded:** 1994. **Franchised:** 1994. **Description:** Dental health services. **Equity Capital Needed:** $25,200-$28,600. **Franchise Fee:** $15,000. **Financial Assistance:** Yes. **Training:** Yes.

41342 ■ ELDirect Homecare

716 W Sycamore
Fayetteville, AR 72703
Ph:(479)443-7173
Fax: (479)443-0183
Co. E-mail: eldirecthomecare@yahoo.com
URL: http://www.eldirecthomecare.com
No. of Company-Owned Units: 2. **Founded:** 1996. **Franchised:** 2002. **Description:** Homecare for elderly and senior people. **Equity Capital Needed:** $21,900-$29,700. **Franchise Fee:** $15,000. **Royalty Fee:** 5%. **Financial Assistance:** No. **Training:** Provides up to 5 days at headquarters, and up to 5 days onsite.

41343 ■ Interim Health Care

1601 Sawgrass Corporate Pky.
Sunrise, FL 33323
Free: 800-338-7786
Fax: (954)858-2720
No. of Franchise Units: 267. **No. of Company-Owned Units:** 20. **Founded:** 1966. **Franchised:** 1966. **Description:** Franchises nursing and home health care personnel services. **Equity Capital Needed:** Medical staffing $100,000-$125,000; home health care $250,000-$400,000. **Franchise Fee:** $20,000-$30,000. **Financial Assistance:** No. **Training:** Yes.

41344 ■ Superior Senior Care

Superior Senior Care Franchises, L.L.C.
PO Box 505
Hot Springs, AR 71902

Ph:(479)783-1206
Fax: (479)783-1232
Co. E-mail: Franchise@SuperiorSeniorCare.com
URL: http://www.SuperiorSeniorCare.com
No. of Franchise Units: 7. **No. of Company-Owned Units:** 7. **Founded:** 1985. **Franchised:** 2000. **Description:** Provider of light housekeeping and home management, meal preparation, shopping, transportation and companionship. **Equity Capital Needed:** $18,771. **Franchise Fee:** $15,000. **Financial Assistance:** No. **Training:** Yes.

COMPUTERIZED DATABASES

41345 ■ *ESPICOM Country Health Care Reports*

Espicom Business Intelligence
Lincoln House
City Fields Business Park
City Fields Way
Chichester PO20 2FS, United Kingdom
Ph:44 1243 533322
Fax: 44 1243 533418
Co. E-mail: sales_desk@espicom.com
URL: http://www.espicom.com
Description: Contains information from *Medistat: World Medical Market Analysis*. Includes reports which are profiles for 70 countries worldwide. Includes countries located in Eastern and Western Europe, the Middle East, Africa, Asia, the Pacific Rim and the Americas. Provides information on the medical device, equipment and supplies markets. Allows users to plan strategy and business decisions for the international markets. Includes contact directories and comparative data. **Availability:** Online: Thomson Dialog. **Type:** Full text; Directory.

41346 ■ *ESPICOM Pharmaceutical & Medical Device News*

Espicom Business Intelligence
Lincoln House
City Fields Business Park
City Fields Way
Chichester PO20 2FS, United Kingdom
Ph:44 1243 533322
Fax: 44 1243 533418
Co. E-mail: sales_desk@espicom.com
URL: http://www.espicom.com
Description: Provides news articles from three newsletters covering the field of pharmaceutical and medical devices: *Medistat News*-contains information on health care markets worldwide, including regulation, health structure, expenditure, health provision, market size, and trade. Covers January 1995 to date.; *MDCA News*-provides news intelligence on the global medical device industry, including company performance, products, mergers, acquisitions, and alliances. Covers January 1996 to date.; *PCA News*-reports on pharmaceutical company developments worldwide, including company results, performance, products, mergers and acquisitions, and agreements. Covers January 1996 to date. **Availability:** Online: Thomson Dialog, Thomson Dialog. **Type:** Full text.

41347 ■ *GrantSelect*

Greenwood Publishing Group Inc.
88 Post Rd. W
Westport, CT 06881
Ph:(203)226-3571
Co. E-mail: webmaster@greenwood.com
URL: http://www.greenwood.com
Description: Contains descriptions of over 10,000 funding opportunities provided by more than 4000 sponsoring organizations including nonprofit organizations; U.S. federal, state, and local governments; commercial organizations; professional associations; private and community foundations; and private organizations. Includes approximately 500 Canadian grants from private and government organizations. Provides information on grants in areas such as arts and humanities; children and youth; health care and biomedical; K-12 schools and adult basic education; community development, and more. Also includes in-

formation on international programs and operating grants. Information for each grant includes name, grant program description, requirements, restrictions, contact person and address information, funding amounts, deadline and renewal information, and samples of previously awarded grants. Corresponds to the annual *Directory of Research Grants*, *Directory of Biomedical and Health Care Grants*, *Directory of Grants in the Humanities*, *Directory of Funding Sources for Community Development*, and *Funding Sources for K-12 Schools and Adult Basic Education*. **Availability:** Online: Thomson Dialog, Online Computer Library Center Inc. (OCLC), UTEK Corp., Greenwood Publishing Group Inc., Thomson Dialog; CD-ROM: Thomson Dialog, Greenwood Publishing Group Inc;Magnetic Tape: Greenwood Publishing Group Inc. **Type:** Directory; Numeric.

41348 ■ *Health Care Daily Report*

The Bureau of National Affairs Inc.
1231 25th St. NW
Washington, DC 20037
Ph:(202)452-4200
Free: 800-372-1033
Fax: (202)452-4226
Co. E-mail: customercare@bna.com
URL: http://www.bna.com
Description: Contains information on all aspects of health care, including state and federal court decisions, tax-related legislation and regulation, insurance issues, national policy-making, union concerns, collective bargaining, and Medicare. Provides up-to-date information on policy proposals, debates, and outcomes in federal, state, and private sector areas. Provides coverage of background issues and emerging trends as well as major court cases and legal developments. Covers such subjects as abortion, AIDS, malpractice, medical devices, managed care, ERISA and employee benefits, access to health care, bioethics, pharmaceuticals, patient dumping, health care reform, and much more. **Availability:** Online: Thomson West, The Bureau of National Affairs Inc. **Type:** Full text.

41349 ■ *Health Care Policy Report*

The Bureau of National Affairs Inc.
1231 25th St. NW
Washington, DC 20037
Ph:(202)452-4200
Free: 800-372-1033
Fax: (202)452-4226
Co. E-mail: customercare@bna.com
URL: http://www.bna.com
Description: Contains concise reporting and information on federal, state, and private sector efforts to reform and manage the U.S. health care system. Covers federal and state regulatory and legislative developments. Provides detailed information on the activities of businesses, health care providers, insurance companies, consumers, special interest groups, and private sector coalitions. Contains important documents, early notification on key personnel moves, and advance notice of agency policy proposals. Provides analysis and reporting on key health care issues. Covers such topics as managed care, cost containment, medical savings accounts, ERISA and employee benefits policy, hospital and physician reimbursement, insurance regulation, malpractice, and much more. **Availability:** Online: Thomson West, The Bureau of National Affairs Inc. **Type:** Full text.

41350 ■ *Health Reference Center*

Thomson Gale
27500 Drake Rd.
Farmington Hills, MI 48331-3535
Ph:(248)699-4253
Free: 800-877-GALE
Fax: (248)699-8069
Co. E-mail: gale.galeord@thomson.com
URL: http://www.gale.com
Description: Contains information for health and wellness research, drawing from medical and consumer periodicals, health newsletters, reference books, topical overviews, and pamphlets. Provides information in clearly understandable terms. Includes: indexing of approximately 195 medical periodicals, eight reference books, over 700 pamphlets, more than

1800 overviews from *Clinical Reference Systems*, selective indexing for articles in approximately 1500 additional general interest titles, full text for more than 185 periodicals, all reference books, overviews, and pamphlets. Reference books include: *Mosby's Medical, Nursing, and Allied Health Dictionary*; *USP-DI Volume II: Advice for the Patient*; *The Consumer Health Information Source Book*; *The Gale Encyclopedia of Medicine*; *The Complete Directory for People with Chronic Illness*; and *PDR Family Guide to Nutrition and Health*. **Availability:** Online: Thomson Gale; CD-ROM: Thomson Gale. **Type:** Full text; Directory.

41351 ■ *Health & Wellness InSite*
Thomson Dialog
11000 Regency Pky., Ste. 10
Cary, NC 27511
Ph:(919)462-8600
Free: 800-3-DIALOG
Fax: (919)468-9890
Co. E-mail: intelligence.data@tfn.com
URL: http://www.dialog.com/sources/intelligence_data
Description: Contains complete information about health, medicine, fitness, and nutrition. Provides access to 170 of the world's leading professional and consumer health publications, including *The Lancet* and *Nutrition Today*; 550 health and medical pamphlets; 200,000 health-related articles from more than 3000 other publications; and 1800 overviews of different diseases and medical conditions published by Clinical Reference Systems, Ltd. Includes six medical reference books: *Columbia University College of Physicians & Surgeons Complete Home Medical Guide*; *Mosby's Medical, Nursing, and Allied Health Dictionary*; *Consumer Health Information Source Book*; *The People's Book of Medical Tests*; *USP DI-Vol. II Advice for the Patient*; *Drug Information in Lay Language*; and *The Complete Directory for People With Chronic Illness*.. Allows searches by article title, article type, author, company name, person discussed in the article, publication name, publication date range, publication type, target audience, ticker symbol, words in the title, and words that appear anywhere in the article. **Availability:** Online: Thomson Dialog. **Type:** Full text.

41352 ■ *Healthfinder*
U.S. Department of Health and Human Services
200 Independence Ave. SW
Washington, DC 20201
Ph:(202)619-0257
Free: 877-696-6775
Fax: (202)453-8282
Co. E-mail: healthfinder@nhic.org
URL: http://www.healthfinder.gov/
Ed: David Baker, Editor. **Released:** April. **Price:** Free. **Entries Include:** Site name, description, link to site. **Database Covers:** Online health publications, clearinghouses, web sites, self-help groups, government agencies, academic centers, and nonprofit agencies.

LIBRARIES

41353 ■ Association of Gospel Rescue Missions–Library
1045 Swift
North Kansas City, MO 64116
Ph:(816)471-8020
Fax: (816)471-3718
Co. E-mail: agrm@agrm.org
URL: http://www.agrm.org
Scope: Homelessness, urban ministry, alcohol and drug assistance, history of Christian efforts to inner city poor. **Services:** Library open to the public for reference use only. **Holdings:** 2118 periodicals, books, clippings, audio/visuals, and archival material.

41354 ■ National Families in Action–Library
2957 Clairmont Rd. NE, Ste. 150
Atlanta, GA 30329
Ph:(404)248-9676
Fax: (404)248-1312
Co. E-mail: nfia@nationalfamilies.org
URL: http://www.nationalfamilies.org
Scope: Drug use, drug legalization, drug usage prevention. **Services:** Library open to the public for refer-

ence use only. **Holdings:** 1 million books, periodicals, clippings, audio/visuals, monographs, and archival material.

41355 ■ Wisconsin HIV/STD/Hepatitis Information & Referral Center
820 N. Plankinton Ave.
PO Box 510498
Milwaukee, WI 53203
Ph:(414)225-1539
Free: 800-334-2437
Fax: (414)273-2357
Co. E-mail: irc-wisconsin@arcw.org
URL: http://www.irc-wisconsin.org/
Contact: Angie Clark
Scope: AIDS, HIV, STDs, hepatitis. **Services:** Library open to the public.

RESEARCH CENTERS

41356 ■ African Medical and Research Foundation, U.S.A.
19 W 44th St., Rm. 710
New York, NY 10036
Ph:(212)768-2440
Fax: (212)768-4230
Co. E-mail: amrefusa@amrefusa.org
URL: http://www.amref.org/
Contact: Lisa Meadowcraft, Exec.Dir.
E-mail: amrefusa@amrefusa.org
Scope: The spread and prevention of AIDS, malaria, and hydatid disease. Also creates health care and training models used by developing countries worldwide. **Educational Activities:** Health education courses.

41357 ■ American College of Apothecaries–Research and Education Resource Center
PO Box 341266
Memphis, TN 38184
Ph:(901)383-8119
Free: 800—828-5933
Fax: (901)383-8882
Co. E-mail: dana@acainfo.org
URL: http://www.acainfo.org
Contact: Dana D. Easton, Dir. of Finance
E-mail: dana@acainfo.org
Scope: Three-fold objective of the Foundation is to promote public welfare through development of services in institutions providing health care, encourage and conduct research to improve health care and education, and encourage health care practitioners to improve the quality and availability of their services. **Educational Activities:** Community pharmacy residency program; Community education program; Conferences; Speakers bureau.

41358 ■ American Council on Consumer Awareness, Inc.
7669 W Copper Crest Pl.
Tucson, AZ 85743-5302
Co. E-mail: accaus@aol.com
Contact: Kenneth J. Benner, Pres.
E-mail: accaus@aol.com
Scope: Conducts survey research on consumer issues, including credit card interest rates, credit file access abuse, banks, medical billing abuse, bait and switch advertising, funeral home charges, and electrical and telephone rates. **Services:** Narrated video programs (annually), for consumer and community groups; Public service radio announcements (annually), Facility provides spot radio production. **Publications:** The OC3PF Project.

41359 ■ Baylor College of Medicine–Center for Medical Ethics and Health Policy
1 Baylor Plz.
Houston, TX 77030
Ph:(713)798-6290
Fax: (713)798-5678
Co. E-mail: bbrody@bcm.tmc.edu
Contact: Dr. Baruch Brody, Dir.
E-mail: bbrody@bcm.tmc.edu
Scope: Priorities for health care services, methods of funding health care services, and social controls on

health care service, including studies on ethics in clinical decision making and value issues in controlling the cost of medicine. **Services:** Consultation Services. **Publications:** News Bulletin (semimonthly). **Educational Activities:** Clinical Instruction; Continuing Education Programs; Education Courses, in medical ethics; Lectures, visiting scholars.

41360 ■ Benaroya Research Institute at Virginia Mason
1201 9th Ave.
Seattle, WA 98101-2795
Ph:(206)583-6525
Fax: (206)223-7543
Co. E-mail: info@benaroyaresearch.org
URL: http://benaroyaresearch.org
Contact: Dr. Gerald T. Nepom, Dir.
E-mail: info@benaroyaresearch.org
Scope: Immunology, diabetes and clinical research. **Publications:** Bulletin of the Virginia Mason Clinic. **Educational Activities:** Educational opportunities through high school programs and postdoctoral training.

41361 ■ Blanton-Peal Institute
3 W 29th St., 5th Fl.
New York, NY 10001
Ph:(212)725-7850
Fax: (212)689-3212
Co. E-mail: info@blantonpeale.org
URL: http://www.blantonpeale.org
Contact: Kathryn Madden PhD, Pres./CEO
E-mail: info@blantonpeale.org
Scope: Policy studies related to psychoanalysis, marriage and family therapy, pastoral care, and the dialogue between theology and psychology. **Publications:** Journal of Religion and Health (quarterly); Labyrinth Newsletter (semiannually). **Educational Activities:** Lectures; Marriage and Family Therapy Residency; Pastoral Care Studies Program; Psychoanalytic Residency.

41362 ■ Brandeis University–Schneider Institute for Health Policy
Heller School for Social Policy & Management, MS 035
415 South St.
Waltham, MA 02454-9110
Ph:(781)736-3900
Fax: (781)736-3905
Co. E-mail: wallack@brandeis.edu
URL: http://sihp.brandeis.edu
Contact: Stanley S. Wallack PhD, Exec.Dir.
E-mail: wallack@brandeis.edu
Scope: Health services research and policy analysis, focusing on the design, development, implementation, and evaluation of innovative financing and delivery systems. Specific areas of research include establishing and implementing national health care expenditure limits, all-payer payment systems, an Alcohol and Drug Services Survey, the changing trends of substance abuse, financing and reimbursement of drug abuse treatment programs, and long-term care for the elderly, including home care services for the disabled elderly and cost effective models and standards for assisted living. Operates the Center for Substance Abuse Services Research, Center for Drug Abuse Policy Analysis, Center on Vulnerable Populations, and the National Resource Center. **Publications:** Annual Report; Background Reports; Major Issue Papers; Newsletter (semimonthly); Program Analyses; Publication Catalogue. **Educational Activities:** Brandeis Pew Scholars Program; Scholars in Health Policy Program; Social Health Maintenance Organization Demonstration Project; Two-Year Doctoral Program, in health policy.

41363 ■ Brown University–Watson Institute for International Studies
111 Thayer St.
PO Box 1970
Providence, RI 02912-1970
Ph:(401)863-2809
Fax: (401)863-1270
Co. E-mail: Watson_institute@brown.edu
URL: http://www.watsoninstitute.org
Contact: Thomas J. Biersteker, Dir.

E-mail: Watson_institute@brown.edu
Scope: Contemporary global problems and challenges in security, economy, ecology, identity and culture. **Services:** Extensive outreach activities, for community and policy makers. **Publications:** Annual Report; Blogs; Conference Reports; Documentaries; Newsletters; Streaming video; Studies in Comparative International Development (Journal). **Educational Activities:** Choices for the 21st Century Education program; Development studies undergraduate major; Faculty and student foreign exchange programs; International relations undergraduate major; Lectures; Seminars.

41364 ■ California State University, Los Angeles–Edmund G. "Pat" Brown Institute of Public Affairs
5151 State University Dr.
Los Angeles, CA 90032-8261
Ph:(323)343-3770
Fax: (323)343-3774
Co. E-mail: jregala@calstatela.edu
URL: http://www.patbrowninstitute.org/
Contact: Jaime A. Regalado PhD, Exec.Dir.
E-mail: jregala@calstatela.edu
Scope: Applied research and analysis of public policy issues of California and greater Los Angeles area, including ethnic community participation in politics, futures planning, the environment, mental health, law and justice, water, the homeless, history, infrastructure, the judicial system, health care, education, transportation, and emergency disaster management. **Services:** Technical assistance and consulting, on policy issues.

41365 ■ Center for the Study of Social Policy
1575 Eye St. NW, Ste. 500
Washington, DC 20005
Ph:(202)371-1565
Fax: (202)371-1472
URL: http://www.cssp.org
Contact: Frank Farrow, Dir.
Scope: Social policy, including studies on children and youth, income support, long-term care, health, disability, and minorities. Focus on children and family services and policy.

41366 ■ Dalhousie University–Population Health Research Unit
5790 of Community Health & Epidemiology
Faculty of Medicine
5790 University Ave.
Halifax, NS, Canada B3H 1V7
Ph:(902)494-1785
Fax: (902)494-1597
Co. E-mail: mark.smithhart@dal.ca
URL: http://www.phru.dal.ca/
Contact: George Kephart, Dir.
E-mail: mark.smithhart@dal.ca
Scope: Health and social sciences, particularly population health, health services utilization and their interrelationships.

41367 ■ Dartmouth College–Center for Evaluative Clinical Sciences
Dartmouth Medical School
7251 Strasenburgh
Hanover, NH 03755-3863
Ph:(603)650-1684
Fax: (603)650-1225
Co. E-mail: cecsweb@dartmouth.edu
URL: http://www.dartmouth.edu/~cecs/
Contact: John E. Wennberg MD, Dir.
E-mail: cecsweb@dartmouth.edu
Scope: Evaluative clinical science and health care delivery, including medical care epidemiology, health policy, health behavior, efficacy of medical procedures, quality of medical and surgical care, distribution of health care resources, medical interventions and consequences for patients, care at the end of life, distribution of health care resources across hospital market areas, geriatric health, and sociology of medical organizations. **Publications:** The Dartmouth Atlas of Health Care. **Educational Activities:** Fellowships to physicians, administrators, and health policy makers; Graduate programs in evaluative clinical science.

41368 ■ Economic and Social Research Institute
2100 M St., N W, Ste. 605
Washington, DC 20037
Ph:(202)833-8877
Fax: (202)833-8932
Co. E-mail: announcements@esresearch.org
URL: http://www.esresearch.org
Contact: Jack A. Meyer PhD, Pres./CEO
E-mail: announcements@esresearch.org
Scope: Health care and social services reforms, focusing on enhancing the effectiveness of social programs, improving the organization and delivery of health care services, and making quality health care accessible and affordable, assessing the impact of proposed health policy reforms, and designing early childhood reforms.

41369 ■ Evergreen Freedom Foundation
PO Box 552
Olympia, WA 98507
Ph:(360)956-3482
Fax: (360)352-1874
Co. E-mail: effwa@effwa.org
URL: http://www.effwa.org
Contact: Bob Williams, Pres.
E-mail: effwa@effwa.org
Scope: Health care, budget, taxes, education, welfare reform, citizenship and governance issues, with emphasis on limited, accountable, representative government, and working partnerships between governing bodies and the private sector. **Services:** Briefings,, during legislative session when requested. **Publications:** In-Briefs; Newsletter (monthly); Policy Highlighters. **Educational Activities:** Speaking engagements, at service clubs and community organizations.

41370 ■ Forum for State Health Policy Leadership
National Conference of State Legislatures
444 N Capital St. NW, Ste. 515
Washington, DC 20001
Ph:(202)624-5400
Fax: (202)737-1069
Co. E-mail: donna.folkemer@ncsl.org
URL: http://www.ncsl.org/programs/health/forum
Contact: Donna Folkemer, Dir.
E-mail: donna.folkemer@ncsl.org
Scope: Health laws and programs of the states, including research in such areas as alternatives to institutional care, state health care reform, managing and funding health care programs, preventive health services for children, state Medicaid programs, state comprehensive and catastrophic health insurance programs, Medicaid cost containment, state health promotion and disease prevention initiatives, AIDS, and private health insurance benefits for alcoholism, drug abuse, and mental illness. **Services:** Assistance, on particular issues and research projects; Legislative and state clearinghouses; Maintains a network of health policy correspondents, in each of the 50 states who keep the project abreast of significant developments in the states; State legislative tracking service. **Publications:** Primary Care News; Reports on long-term care, primary care, and children's health; State Health Notes (semimonthly). **Educational Activities:** Health Policy Conference (annually).

41371 ■ Georgia State University–Center for Risk Management and Insurance Research
PO Box 4036
Atlanta, GA 30302-4036
Ph:(404)651-4250
Fax: (404)651-1897
Co. E-mail: rwklein@gsu.edu
URL: http://rmictr.gsu.edu
Contact: Robert Klein, Dir.
E-mail: rwklein@gsu.edu
Scope: Insurance, finance, and economics. Provides technical materials and policy research in the areas of health care financing, international issues, law and regulation, corporate finance, retirement financing, risk, risk management, insurance, finance, economics. Research focuses on risk management and insurance including insurance markets, catastrophe risk, financial instruments, social insurance, health care financing, retirement, law, public policy, and regulation. **Services:** Consultation; Develops technical and professional materials; Issues working papers; Responds to proposal requests. **Publications:** Reprint series; Research report series; Working paper series. **Educational Activities:** Seminars and workshops, on risk management and insurance industry financial, actuarial and regulatory topics.

41372 ■ Health Research and Educational Trust
1 N Franklin
Chicago, IL 60606-3421
Ph:(312)422-2600
Fax: (312)422-4568
Co. E-mail: mpittman@aha.org
URL: http://www.hret.org
Contact: Dr. Mary Pittman, Pres.
E-mail: mpittman@aha.org
Scope: Improvement in the delivery of hospital and health care. **Publications:** Health Services Research (bimonthly). **Educational Activities:** Conference (annually).

41373 ■ Health Research and Educational Trust of New Jersey
760 Alexander Rd.
PO Box 1
Princeton, NJ 08543-0001
Ph:(609)275-4000
Fax: (609)275-4271
Co. E-mail: gcarter@njha.com
URL: http://www.njha.com/hret/
Contact: Gary S. Carter, Pres./CEO
E-mail: gcarter@njha.com
Scope: Health services in New Jersey. Topics explored include access to primary healthcare, parenting education, breast cancer, newborn screening. **Publications:** Shaping Healthier Tomorrows. **Educational Activities:** Continuing education courses; HRET Annual Meeting; Specialized training workshops. **Awards:** Community outreach awards.

41374 ■ Heartland Institute
19 S LaSalle St., Ste. 903
Chicago, IL 60603
Ph:(312)377-4000
Fax: (312)377-5000
Co. E-mail: think@heartland.org
URL: http://www.heartland.org
Contact: Joseph L. Bast, Pres./CEO
E-mail: think@heartland.org
Scope: Privatization, deregulation, tax reform, education reform, health care policy, environmental policy, and telecommunications. Seeks alternatives to government-provided services at the national, state and local levels. Also examines state business climates and their impact on economic growth. **Publications:** Budget & Tax News (monthly); Environment and Climate News (monthly); Health Care News (monthly); IT&T News (monthly); Policy Studies; School Reform News (monthly). **Educational Activities:** Book tours (occasionally); Mealtime conferences and seminars (periodically), open to the public. **Awards:** Heartland Liberty Prize.

41375 ■ Indiana University-Purdue University at Indianapolis–Center for Law and Health
Inlow Hall, Rm. 136
School of Law
530 W New York St.
Indianapolis, IN 46202-3225
Ph:(317)274-1912
Fax: (317)274-0455
Co. E-mail: maawelsh@iupui.edu
URL: http://indylaw.indiana.edu/centers/clh/
Contact: Margie A. Welsh, Coord.
E-mail: maawelsh@iupui.edu
Scope: All issues related to law and the legal environment. **Educational Activities:** Information resource, on law issues.

41376 ■ Indiana University-Purdue University at Indianapolis–Indiana AIDS Clinical Trials Unit
550 N University Blvd., Rm. 5510
Indianapolis, IN 46202

Ph:(317)274-8456
Free: 800—421-3316
Fax: (317)274-1876
Co. E-mail: actg.indiana@fstrf.org
Contact: Mitchell Goldman, Prin. Investigator
E-mail: actg.indiana@fstrf.org
Scope: AIDS treatment, including an antiretroviral approach; treatment and prevention of AIDS complications, including pneumocystis, pneumonia, cryptococcal meningitis, histoplasmosis, cytomegalovirus infection, Kaposi's sarcoma, and dementia.

41377 ■ Institute for SocioEconomic Studies
10 New King St.
White Plains, NY 10604
Ph:(914)686-7112
Fax: (914)686-0581
Co. E-mail: mail@socioeconomic.org
URL: http://www.socioeconomic.org
Contact: Leonard M. Greene, Pres.
E-mail: mail@socioeconomic.org
Scope: Quality of life, economic development, social motivation, poverty, urban regeneration, problems of the elderly, health care and other related socioeconomic issues. **Publications:** Socioeconomic Bulletin (bimonthly).

41378 ■ Institute for Women's Policy Research
1707 L St. NW, Ste. 750
Washington, DC 20036
Ph:(202)785-5100
Fax: (202)833-4362
Co. E-mail: hartmann@iwpr.org
URL: http://www.iwpr.org
Contact: Heidi I. Hartmann PhD, Pres./CEO
E-mail: hartmann@iwpr.org
Scope: Causes and consequences of women's poverty, particularly of minority women; costs and benefits of family and work policies; pay equity; wages and employment opportunities; impact of tax policy on women and families; and access to and costs of health care. Specific issues include the impact of the Pregnancy Discrimination Act, the costs and benefits of family and medical leave, pay equity in 20 state civil service systems, the wage gap between women of color and white women, low-wage work, welfare reform, microenterprise, women and labor unions (labor law reform), and women's economic agendas. **Services:** First Friday Forums, a discussion series. **Educational Activities:** Conferences; Workshops.

41379 ■ International Development Research Centre–Centre de recherches pour le développment international
250 Albert St.
PO Box 8500
Ottawa, ON, Canada K1G 3H9
Ph:(613)236-6163
Fax: (613)238-7230
Co. E-mail: info@idrc.ca
URL: http://www.idrc.ca
Contact: Maureen O'Neil, Pres.
E-mail: info@idrc.ca
Scope: Supports scientific and technical research projects identified and carried out by research institutions in developing countries. IDRC maintains the following program initiative areas: strategies and policies for healthy societies; sustainable employment; equity in natural resources management; biodiversity conservation; food security; information and communication; peace building and reconstruction. Research activities focus on integrating environmental, social, and economic policies; technology and the environment; information and communication for development; health and the environment; and biodiversity. Supports research that is essential to sustainable and equitable development through three areas of enquiry: social and economic equity; environmental and natural resource management; and information and communication technologies for development. Research activities focus areas include water resource management; ecosystem management; biodiversity control, governance, delivery of public services (health, education, social security), small enterprise and livelihoods, information access, information ca-

pacity-building, macroeconomic policy, regional integration, and global threats to health (social instability, AIDS, malnutrition, tobacco use). **Publications:** Annual Report; IDRC Reports (quarterly); Searching Series. **Awards:** Young Canadian Researchers Award.

41380 ■ Jacobs Institute of Women's Health
409 12th St. SW
Washington, DC 20024-2188
Ph:(202)863-4990
Fax: (202)488-4229
Co. E-mail: djames@jiwh.org
URL: http://www.jiwh.org
Contact: Diane James, Exec.Dir.
E-mail: djames@jiwh.org
Scope: Women's health care issues, focusing on the interaction of medical and social systems. **Publications:** InTouch (quarterly); Women's Health Issues (bimonthly). **Educational Activities:** Seminars; Symposia. **Awards:** Charles E. Gibbs MD Leadership Prize.

41381 ■ Johns Hopkins University–Center for Hospital Finance and Management
624 N Broadway, Rm. 304
Baltimore, MD 21205
Ph:(410)955-3241
Fax: (410)955-2301
Co. E-mail: ganderso@jhsph.edu
Contact: Gerard Anderson PhD, Dir.
E-mail: ganderso@jhsph.edu
Scope: Hospital finance and management, technology assessment, reform of cost containment and payment, policies, clinical education, managed care, and medical effectiveness. **Services:** Offers Congressional testimony. **Educational Activities:** Training to pre- and postdoctoral fellows.

41382 ■ Johns Hopkins University–Health Services Research and Development Center
624 N Broadway, Rm. 650
Baltimore, MD 21205-1996
Ph:(410)955-6562
Fax: (410)955-0470
Co. E-mail: dsteinwa@jhsph.edu
Contact: Dr. Donald M. Steinwachs, Dir.
E-mail: dsteinwa@jhsph.edu
Scope: Health services, including determinants of health outcomes; the impacts of alternative health care systems on cost and quality; effective strategies for health promotion and disease prevention; and methods of meeting the needs of high risk populations such as the poor, elderly, mentally ill, disabled, and children. **Services:** Technical assistance, for local and national groups. **Educational Activities:** Presentations, at national meetings.

41383 ■ Kaiser Permanente Center for Health Research
3800 N Interstate Ave.
Portland, OR 97227-1098
Ph:(503)335-2400
Fax: (503)335-2424
Co. E-mail: mary.durham@kpchr.org
URL: http://www.kpchr.org/
Contact: Mary L. Durham PhD, Dir.
E-mail: mary.durham@kpchr.org
Scope: Organization, financing, costs and quality of medical care in an HMO; mental health; medical informatics; patient safety; health behavior interventions; epidemiology; effectiveness of alternative therapies and services; nutrition; genetics; dental research; and biometry and research methods. **Educational Activities:** Residence program, in public health; Saward Lecture (annually).

41384 ■ Kaiser Permanente Medical Care Program–Division of Research
3505 Broadway
Oakland, CA 94611
Ph:(510)891-3400
Fax: (510)450-2073
Co. E-mail: jvs@dor.kaiser.org
URL: http://www.dor.kaiser.org/
Contact: Dr. Joseph V. Selby, Dir.
E-mail: jvs@dor.kaiser.org
Scope: Epidemiology, biometrics and biostatistics, technology assessment, health services research,

and health education research and evaluation. Supports clinical research in medical centers. **Services:** Staff teaches at local universities and performs editorial and review services for scientific and medical journals. **Educational Activities:** In-house seminars and conferences.

41385 ■ La Rabida Children's Hospital and Research Center
E 65th St. at Lake Michigan
Chicago, IL 60649
Ph:(773)363-6700
Fax: (773)363-7160
Co. E-mail: info@larabida.org
URL: http://www.larabida.org
Contact: Raoul Wolf MD, Dir.
E-mail: info@larabida.org
Scope: Economic, educational, cultural, and medical effects of childhood chronic illness and disability on families and society. Areas of research include patterns of health care financing, medically complex children, community-based service systems, and the nature of family constellations, including the tracking of child development in family contexts, and intervention studies. **Services:** Technical assistance and consulting for the community. **Educational Activities:** Informal mentoring program; Professional symposium, at pediatricians, therapists, social workers, psychologists and other health care professionals; Seminars and workshops (periodically).

41386 ■ Marshall University Research Corp.
401 11th St., Ste. 1400
Huntington, WV 25701
Ph:(304)696-6598
Fax: (304)697-3789
Co. E-mail: schellin@marshall.edu
URL: http://www.marshall.edu/murc/
Contact: Ron Schelling, Exec.Dir.
E-mail: schellin@marshall.edu
Scope: Provides technical and research assistance to West Virginia businesses and governments, focusing on business and industry, including business and job development, marketing research, and feasibility studies; community and government, including housing, zoning, recreation, criminology, traffic safety, transportation, personnel administration, and finance; education, including basic teaching skills, educational financing, and extended training for primary and secondary instructors; arts and culture, including developing, coordinating, and promoting cultural activities, and assisting local arts and cultural organizations in obtaining funding; health, including basic and applied research, and mechanisms for continuing growth of health care services and education; family and consumer, including problems of families in transition, support of displaced workers, housing norms, retirement preparation and adjustment, and consumer issues. **Services:** Counseling and referral services; Technical and research assistance. **Educational Activities:** Educational seminars, workshops, and lectures; Graduate cooperative education programs.

41387 ■ Medical Technology and Practice Patterns Institute, Inc.
4733 Bethesda Ave., Ste. 510
Bethesda, MD 20814
Ph:(301)652-4005
Fax: (301)652-8335
Co. E-mail: info@mtppi.org
URL: http://www.mtppi.org
Contact: Dennis J. Cotter, Pres./Founder
E-mail: info@mtppi.org
Scope: New and emerging health-care technologies and their implications for local, national, and international policy. Research efforts fall into three broad areas: Health Services Research, encompassing patient outcomes, pharmacoeconomics, quality-of-life assessments, and cost-effectiveness analyses; International Activities, including conducting surveys of health technology assessment activities worldwide technology assessment modeling, and sponsorship of workshops and seminars on health policy issues; and Special Programs, encompassing health-facility planning, vaccine research and development, and educational outreach. Technologies studied include

magnetic resonance imaging, extracorporeal shock-wave lithotripsy, endocardial electrical stimulation, implantable cardiac defibrillators, percutaneous transluminal coronary angioplasty, percutaneous lithotripsy, heart transplantation, ambulatory blood pressure monitoring, total parenteral nutrition, liver transplantation, bone marrow transplantation, and dialysis treatment for end-stage renal disease. **Services:** Consulting for public and private organizations. **Publications:** Diagnostic Imaging and Child Abuse; Direct and Indirect Costs of Diabetes; Implications of NAFTA for Trade in Health Care Technology; Rational Use of Health Technologies; Reports on various health technologies. **Educational Activities:** Senior Resident Scholar Program.

41388 ■ Methodist Research Institute
1701 N Senate Blvd.
PO Box 1367
Indianapolis, IN 46206
Ph:(317)962-3554
Fax: (317)962-5954
Co. E-mail: gzaloga@clarian.org
URL: http://mri.clarian.com
Contact: Gary P. Zaloga MD, Med.Dir.
E-mail: gzaloga@clarian.org
Scope: Pharmaceutical and device clinical trials, experimental cell research, cell signalling, ion channel physiology, immunology, nutrition angiogenesis, cancer, shock. Other research involves heart, kidney, lung, pancreas, and liver transplants; biliary and renal extracorporeal shock wave lithotripsy; and clot lysis programs. **Services:** Statistical analysis, abstract and manuscript preparation, and grant proposal writing. **Educational Activities:** Educational seminars on research topics; Seminars; Staff physician training in surgical techniques; Summer Student Research Program.

41389 ■ Michigan Family Forum
PO Box 15216
Lansing, MI 48901-5216
Ph:(517)374-1171
Free: 800—644-9111
Fax: (517)374-6112
Co. E-mail: info@michiganfamily.org
URL: http://www.michiganfamily.org
Contact: Brad Snavely, Exec.Dir.
E-mail: info@michiganfamily.org
Scope: Public policy issues and responsible citizenship, focusing on strengthening families. Areas of study include education, sex education, educational choice, educational curriculum, divorce, adoption, euthanasia, marriage and marriage protection, welfare reform, and health care. **Publications:** The Forum (quarterly); Forum Online (weekly); Voter Guides.

41390 ■ Mount Sinai School of Medicine of City University of New York–International Longevity Center
60 E 86th St.
New York, NY 10028
Ph:(212)288-1468
Fax: (212)288-3132
Co. E-mail: robertb@ilcusa.org
URL: http://www.ilcusa.org
Contact: Robert N. Butler MD, Pres./CEO
E-mail: robertb@ilcusa.org
Scope: Health, long-term care, and productive aging, emphasizing policy implications for future generations and institutions. **Services:** Consulting services, for policymakers, the general public, and the media. **Publications:** Annual Report (annually); Productive Aging News. **Educational Activities:** Exchange program, for scholars and students.

41391 ■ New Jersey Health and Senior Services Department–Health Planning and Regulation–Health Care Systems Analysis–Research and Development
225 E State St., 8th Fl.
PO Box 360
Trenton, NJ 08625-0360
Ph:(609)292-9354
Fax: (609)292-6523
Co. E-mail: emmanuel.noggoh@doh.state.nj.us
Contact: Emmanuel Noggoh, Dir.

E-mail: emmanuel.noggoh@doh.state.nj.us
Scope: Health care.

41392 ■ New Mexico Clinical Research and Osteoporosis Center
300 Oak NE
Albuquerque, NM 87106
Ph:(505)855-5525
Fax: (505)884-4006
Co. E-mail: nmbonecare@aol.com
URL: http://www.nmbonecare.com
Contact: Lance Rudolph MD, Dir.
E-mail: nmbonecare@aol.com
Scope: Health care quality, health promotion, clinical research, and continuing medical education. **Publications:** Newsletter (quarterly).

41393 ■ The New School–Center for New York City Affairs
72 5th Ave., 6th Fl.
New York, NY 10011
Ph:(212)229-5400
Fax: (212)229-5335
Co. E-mail: whitea@newschool.edu
URL: http://www.milano.newschool.edu/nycaffairs
Contact: Andrew White, Dir.
E-mail: whitea@newschool.edu
Scope: Applied research and journalism on public policy in urban centers, including children and families, immigrant communities, poverty and politics. **Publications:** Child Welfare Watch (semiannually); Monographs. **Educational Activities:** Debates, conferences, short courses, and seminars.

41394 ■ Northwestern University–Institute for Health Services Research and Policy Studies
717 Wieboldt Hall
339 E Chicago Ave.
Chicago, IL 60611
Ph:(312)503-2937
Fax: (847)491-2202
Co. E-mail: k-weiss@northwestern.edu
URL: http://www.northwestern.edu/ihsrps
Contact: Dr. Kevin B. Weiss, Dir.
E-mail: k-weiss@northwestern.edu
Scope: Health services research and policy analysis focusing on the relationship between health care delivery systems and health outcomes, health economics, organization behavior in health, competition in the delivery of health services, physician and institutional incentives. **Publications:** Working paper series. **Educational Activities:** Annual Health Services Research Symposium, in collaboration with other Chicago-area research centers; Executive education opportunities and student research; Seminar series.

41395 ■ Oklahoma Family Policy Council
3908 N Peniel Ave., Ste. 100
Bethany, OK 73008-3458
Ph:(405)787-7744
Free: 888—381-0044
Fax: (405)787-3900
Co. E-mail: info@okfamilypc.org
URL: http://www.okfamilypc.org
Contact: Michael L. Jestes, Exec.Dir.
E-mail: info@okfamilypc.org
Scope: Public policy analysis, including health care, education, taxes, family policy, welfare reform, and institutional reform. **Publications:** Community Impact Bulletin; Fact Sheet; Oklahoma Citizen (quarterly); Viewpoint on Public Issues. **Educational Activities:** Title V abstinence-only education program, in Oklahoma City; Training courses, on citizenship and policy issues.

41396 ■ Pacific Health Research Institute
846 S Hotel St., Ste. 301
Honolulu, HI 96813
Ph:(808)524-4411
Fax: (808)524-5559
Co. E-mail: info@phrihawaii.org
URL: http://www.phrihawaii.org
Contact: J. David Curb MD, Pres./CEO/Medical Dir.
E-mail: info@phrihawaii.org
Scope: Health services and clinical research, including breast cancer, hypertension, osteoporosis, diabe-

tes, heart attacks, drug studies, effects of chemical exposure, and cost-effectiveness analysis. Specific studies focus on risk factors associated with breast cancer, methods of delaying or preventing postmenopausal osteoporosis, isolated systolic hypertension among the elderly, outcomes research, leprosy, interactive videodiscs, geriatrics, and prostate, lung, colorectal, and ovarian cancer screening. Participates in a statewide consortium of hospitals to address quality and cost of care. Hawaii MEDTEP (Medical Treatment Effectiveness Program) Research Center, outcomes research with a focus on minority populations.

41397 ■ Pacific Research Institute for Public Policy
755 Sansome St., No. 450
San Francisco, CA 94111
Ph:(415)989-0833
Co. E-mail: info@pacificresearch.org
URL: http://www.pacificresearch.org
Contact: Sally C. Pipes, Pres./CEO
E-mail: info@pacificresearch.org
Scope: Public policy issues. Administers a publishing program focusing on health care, environment, education, technology, and privatization, with an outreach program of breakfasts, luncheons, conferences, briefings, and opinion editorials. **Publications:** Capital Ideas; The Contrarian; Impact; Newsletter (quarterly); Pacific Clips; Policy Briefings; Studies. **Educational Activities:** Breakfasts (monthly); Conferences (quarterly); Luncheon Lecture Series; National Privatization Dinner (annually).

41398 ■ Pennsylvania State University–Network for Policy Research
603 Oswald Tower
University Park, PA 16802
Ph:(814)865-6909
Fax: (814)865-8342
Co. E-mail: dpb4@psu.edu
Contact: Mark D. Hayward PhD, Dir.
E-mail: dpb4@psu.edu
Scope: Principal fields of research are organized into four centers: Center for Health Policy Research, which seeks to advance the study of health policy and the delivery of services; Center for Public Policy Research, which conducts studies on the impacts of research and development on economic growth, the economic aspects of environmental pollution, the effects of government regulation, the diffusion of technology in the public sector, and the relationship between government and science; Center for Prevention Evaluation and Research, which utilizes best-practice evaluation and research methods in examining substance abuse policies and programs and assessing prevention programs in community agencies, business and industry, and schools; and Center for Regional Research and Industry Studies, which conducts regional economic analyses, industry studies, and policy evaluations using qualitative and quantitative research methods. **Educational Activities:** Conferences; Seminars.

41399 ■ Portland VA Research Foundation, Inc.
PO Box 69539
Portland, OR 97201-0539
Ph:(503)273-5228
Fax: (503)402-2866
Co. E-mail: david.hickam@med.va.gov
Contact: David Hickam MD, Pres.
E-mail: david.hickam@med.va.gov
Scope: Medicine and medical research.

41400 ■ Public Citizen–Health Research Group
1600 20th St. NW
Washington, DC 20009
Ph:(202)588-1000
Fax: (202)588-7796
URL: http://www.citizen.org/hrg
Contact: Sidney M. Wolfe MD, Dir.
Scope: Health care delivery, workplace safety and health, drug regulation, food additives, medical device safety, and environmental influences on health. Conducts consumer advocacy and lobbying on health

matters and monitors the enforcement of health and safety legislation. **Publications:** Health Letter (monthly); Health Research Group List of Publications (annually); Worst Pills, Best Bills; Worst Pills Best Pills News (monthly).

41401 ■ Regenstrief Institute, Inc.
1050 Wishard Blvd., RG 6
Indianapolis, IN 46202-2872
Ph:(317)630-7604
Co. E-mail: mgray@regenstrief.org
URL: http://www.regenstrief.org
Contact: Mary Gray
E-mail: mgray@regenstrief.org
Scope: Health care, including use of computers in health care delivery, and use of engineering and computer techniques to improve medical diagnosis and therapy.

41402 ■ Rockburn Institute
6581 Belmont Woods Rd.
Elkridge, MD 21075
Ph:(410)796-4554
Fax: (410)796-3173
Contact: Dale N. Schumacher MD, Pres.
Scope: Health care services and effective and efficient management of health care institutions. **Services:** Promotes development and dissemination of health information to community; Technical assistance for health care organizations.

41403 ■ RTI International
3040 Cornwallis Rd.
PO Box 12194
Research Triangle Park, NC 27709-2194
Ph:(919)485-2666
Fax: (919)541-5985
Co. E-mail: listen@rti.org
URL: http://www.rti.org
Contact: Victoria F. Haynes PhD, Pres./CEO
E-mail: listen@rti.org
Scope: Public health, medicine, environmental protection, electronic technology, and public policy. **Publications:** Annual report; Hypotenuse (8/year).

41404 ■ Rush University–Center for Health Management Studies
Rush-Presbyterian-St. Luke's Medical Center
1700 W Van Burren St., Rm. 126-B
Chicago, IL 60612
Ph:(312)942-5402
Fax: (312)942-3833
Co. E-mail: rush_hsm@rush.edu
Contact: Dr. Denise M. Oleske, Dir.
E-mail: rush_hsm@rush.edu
Scope: Health care organizations, including studies in organization and administration, organizational behavior, research design and statistics, cost containment, health economics, health care financial management, quantitative methods and epidemiology, long-term care, and information systems. **Services:** Methodological and statistical assistance to health care clinicians, managers, and students for developing research projects. **Publications:** Annual Report; Working Paper Series (semiannually). **Educational Activities:** Annual Symposium of Health Affairs, current topics in healthcare management research and policy; Faculty Development Program; Journal Club; Symposia, seminars, and continuing education/executive development programs, and other special programs.

41405 ■ Rush University–Office of Research Affairs
Rush University Medical Center
1653 W Congress Pky.
Chicago, IL 60612
Ph:(312)942-3351
Fax: (312)942-8119
Co. E-mail: hblack@rush.edu
Contact: Dr. Henry Black, Assoc.VP,Res.
E-mail: hblack@rush.edu
Scope: Medical sciences including, surgical sciences, nursing, and health sciences. **Publications:** Finance report; Research activities report. **Educational Activities:** OPRR Regional Conference.

41406 ■ Rutgers University–Institute for Health, Health Care Policy, and Aging Research
30 College Ave.
New Brunswick, NJ 08901-1293
Ph:(732)932-8413
Fax: (732)932-6872
Co. E-mail: caboyer@rci.rutgers.edu
URL: http://www-ihhcpar.rutgers.edu/
Contact: Dr. David Mechanic, Dir.
E-mail: caboyer@rci.rutgers.edu
Scope: Research divisions include and focus on the following activities: the Division of Health studies the impact of stress on emotional states and health and risk behaviors and how these latter factors influence the immune system and morbidity and mortality, and studies how stress and emotional states affect symptom appraisal and the decision to use health care; the Division of Health Care Policy analyzes the health and cost outcomes of the current allocation of health resources, with emphasis on preventive care and chronic illnesses; analyzes the evolution of managed care and its impact on patient outcomes, medical professions and utilization of services; examines trust relationships among consumers and physicians and managed care organizations; the Division on Aging measures income inequality, investigates the role of instrumental and social support as buffers against stress and chronic illness, and identifies predictors of poor self-assessments of health among the elderly; the AIDS Policy Research Group measures health care utilization and cost among patients with HIV illness; the Mental Health Services and Criminal Justice Research Division conducts research on improving care and treatment of persons with mental illness in the criminal justice systems; the Center for the Study of Health Beliefs and Behavior targets the relationships among cognitions, emotions, personality, social relationships and health and health behavior. Investigators are developing models to improve communications among practitioners, clients and families to facilitate quality health outcomes; the Center for Obesity Research and Intervention investigates the treatment of obesity; the Center for Health Services Research on Pharmacotherapy, Chronic Disease Management and Outcomes fosters collaborative research on pharmacotherapy for persons with chronic illness, including more effective use of drugs, the impact of policy changes and sociocultural influences on utilization; the Center for State Health Policy analyzes and researches state health policy; the Center for Education and Research in Therapeutics studies the use of antidepressant and antipsychotic medications among children and adolescents, psychotropic drug use among adults and the frail elderly, and the outcomes of pharmaceutical care. **Publications:** Peer-reviewed articles. **Educational Activities:** Brown Bag luncheon seminars (semimonthly), on health, mental health and health policy; Research training, for undergraduates from minority backgrounds; Seminars (weekly), open to the public.

41407 ■ Rutgers University–Institute for Health, Health Care Policy, and Aging Research–Division on Aging–AIDS Policy Research Group
30 College Ave.
New Brunswick, NJ 08901-1293
Ph:(732)932-8579
Fax: (732)932-6872
Co. E-mail: scrystal@rci.rutgers.edu
URL: http://www.ihhcpar.rutgers.edu
Contact: Stephen Crystal PhD, Dir.
E-mail: scrystal@rci.rutgers.edu
Scope: AIDS, and gerontology, focusing on policy issues and applying social science methodology to the planning and evaluation of programs and policies designed to meet public health objectives. Specific areas of research include HIV health services, long-term care, social networks, mental health programs, the social context of health-related behavior in Hispanic and black subcultures, health cognition and health belief systems, legal aspects of serving endangered and high-risk populations, and cost of care and services utilization studies. Special areas of emphasis include quality of life and long-term care for the elderly, inter-

vention-focused behavioral science research, increasing patient-provider communication, furthering methods of research in the health services field, adherence and access to prescription drugs and medical care, social and behavioral AIDS research, and mental health issues in relation to previous areas listed. **Educational Activities:** Training programs for graduate and postdoctoral students.

41408 ■ Seton Hall University–Center for Public Service
Kozlowski Hall, 5th Fl.
400 S Orange Ave.
South Orange, NJ 07079
Ph:(973)761-9510
Fax: (973)275-2463
Co. E-mail: wishnaom@shu.edu
URL: http://artsci.shu.edu/cps
Contact: Dr. Naomi Wish, Dir.
E-mail: wishnaom@shu.edu
Scope: Nonprofit management education; health policy issues, finance, and management; nonprofit information technology; service learning; strategic planning; etc. **Services:** Technical assistance and training. **Educational Activities:** Distinguished Lecture Series in Philanthropy; Graduate certificates, in Health Care Administration and Nonprofit Organization Management; Master's program, in public and healthcare administration.

41409 ■ Southern Illinois University at Carbondale–Center for Rural Health and Social Service Development
Office of Economic & Regional Development, MC 6892
Carbondale, IL 62901-6892
Ph:(618)453-1262
Fax: (618)453-5040
Co. E-mail: tessh@siu.edu
URL: http://www.siu.edu/~crhssd/
Contact: Tess D. Ford, Dir.
E-mail: tessh@siu.edu
Scope: Health care and social service issues that impact the lives and productivity of the citizens in Illinois and the nation, including alternative service delivery systems and policy alternatives. Studies include rural health care, rural safety, mental health and substance use, violence prevention, tobacco initiatives, and obesity. **Services:** Community needs assessments; Program evaluations; Project development and management. **Publications:** Staff publications. **Educational Activities:** Training, curriculum development.

41410 ■ Texas A&M University–Institute for Science, Technology and Public Policy
George Bush School of Government & Public Services
113A Allen Bldg., 4350 TAMU
College Station, TX 77843-4350
Ph:(979)862-1521
Fax: (979)862-8856
Co. E-mail: avedlitz@bushschool.tamu.edu
URL: http://bush.tamu.edu/Research/ISTPP/
Contact: Dr. Arnold Vedlitz, Dir.
E-mail: avedlitz@bushschool.tamu.edu
Scope: Impact of policy formation and implementation in Texas and the U.S. Specific research areas include health and health policy, environment and natural resources policy, infrastructure and the built environment, information technology and biotechnology. **Educational Activities:** Conferences, workshops.

41411 ■ Texas Tech University–Center for Health Care Leadership and Strategy
College of Business Administration
15th & Flint St.
Lubbock, TX 79409-2102
Ph:(806)742-0432
Fax: (806)742-2308
Co. E-mail: tnix@ba.ttu.edu
URL: http://chcs.ba.ttu.edu
Contact: Tim Nix PhD, Dir.
E-mail: tnix@ba.ttu.edu
Scope: Information that builds bridges between strategic Management theory and practice in healthcare

Organization. Develops strategic Management theory. **Publications:** Advances in Health Care Management (annually). **Educational Activities:** Graduate programs, on health organization management; John A. Buesseler Lecture Series; Management education and development series; Professional development programming, related to healthcare organizations.

41412 ■ Texas Tech University–Institute for Leadership Research
Box 42101
Rawls College of Business, BA Rm. 1013
15th St. & Flint Ave.
Lubbock, TX 79409-2101
Ph:(806)742-2111
Fax: (806)742-2308
Co. E-mail: ilr@ttu.edu
URL: http://ilr.ba.ttu.edu
Contact: William L. Gardner, Dir.
E-mail: ilr@ttu.edu
Scope: Develops and tests state of the art leadership theory. Applies theory to leaders at all organizational levels. Incorporates effective existing and emerging leadership practice into the development of new theory for managerial leaders. **Publications:** Journal of Management Inquiry (quarterly); Monographs. **Educational Activities:** Distinguished lecturer and panel discussions; Forums for chief executive officers.

41413 ■ Thomas Jefferson University–Center for Research in Medical Education and Health Care
Jefferson Medical College
1025 Walnut St., Rm. 119
Philadelphia, PA 19107-5083
Ph:(215)955-5492
Fax: (215)923-6939
Co. E-mail: joseph.gonnella@jefferson.edu
URL: http://www.tju.edu/jmc/crmehc
Contact: Joseph S. Gonnella MD, Dir.
E-mail: joseph.gonnella@jefferson.edu
Scope: Medical education process and factors affecting the quality of cost of health care. Medical education research focuses on the following areas: measurement of physician competence; long-term follow-up study of graduates; program evaluation; specialty choice; and refinement of evaluation methods. Health services research focuses on the concept and system of disease staging for classification of severity of illness, cost, and quality of care. **Services:** Consultation and technical services. **ABSTRACTS:** Longitudinal Study of Medical Students and Graduates; Annual report. **Educational Activities:** Provides abstracts of graduating students' performance to graduate program coordinators; Seminars.

41414 ■ Tufts-New England Medical Center–Division of Clinical Care Research
750 Washington St., Box 63
Boston, MA 02111
Ph:(617)636-5009
Fax: (617)636-8023
Co. E-mail: hselker@tufts-nemc.org
URL: http://www.nemc.org/dccr
Contact: Dr. Harry P. Selker, Ch.
E-mail: hselker@tufts-nemc.org
Scope: Ongoing research programs in clinical trials in emergency room based cardiovascular health services research, mathematical modeling and statistics, meta-analysis and other evidence-based research methodologies. **Services:** Statistical and study design consulting and contract research. **Educational Activities:** Affiliated MPH Program with Tufts University School of Medicine; Clinical Epidemiology and Biostatistics instruction; Postdoctoral training in Health Services/Clinical Care Research.

41415 ■ University of Alabama at Birmingham–Lister Hill Center for Health Policy
330 Ryals Public Health Bldg.
1665 University Blvd.
Birmingham, AL 35294-0022
Ph:(205)975-8966
Fax: (205)934-3347
Co. E-mail: morrisey@uab.edu
URL: http://www.healthpolicy.uab.edu

Contact: Michael A. Morrisey PhD, Dir.
E-mail: morrisey@uab.edu
Scope: Health policy research, focusing on health care markets and managed care, maternal and child health, management in public health organizations, aging policy, and outcomes research. **Publications:** Health Policy Abstract (monthly). **Educational Activities:** Methods workshops (semiannually); Research seminars (monthly). **Awards:** Intramural Grant Program (annually).

41416 ■ University of Arizona–Native American Research and Training Center
1642 E Helen
Tucson, AZ 85719
Ph:(520)621-5075
Fax: (520)621-9802
Co. E-mail: jrjoe@email.arizona.edu
URL: http://www.fcm.arizona.edu/research/nartc/
Contact: Jennie R. Joe PhD, Dir.
E-mail: jrjoe@email.arizona.edu
Scope: Health and rehabilitation of disabled and chronically ill Native Americans. Core areas include the following: needs assessment, service delivery, and evaluation as determined by or in cooperation with the tribal community and empowerment that is sensitive to Indian values and needs. Also studies the impact of government policy on the delivery of health care. Promotes self determination and parity among Native Americans in health and rehabilitation. Serves as a national resource for all North American tribes and Alaska natives. **Publications:** Books; Dual track videotapes; Reports. **Educational Activities:** Conferences and workshops; Training programs for indigenous trainers and direct-service providers.

41417 ■ University of California at Berkeley–Center for Labor Research and Education
2521 Channing Way, No. 5555
Berkeley, CA 94720-5555
Ph:(510)642-7213
Fax: (510)642-6432
Co. E-mail: laborcenter@berkeley.edu
URL: http://laborcenter.berkeley.edu
Contact: Carol Zabin, Ch.
E-mail: laborcenter@berkeley.edu
Scope: Labor standards: job quality, living wages, health care. Organizing models: human services, immigrant workers, young workers, Black workers, workers in the global economy. **Publications:** California Workers Rights, and various pamphlets; Eyes on the Fries; Falling Apart: Declining Job-Based Health Coverage for Working Families in California and the United States; Hidden Costs of Wal-Mart Jobs; Hidden Public Costs of Low Wage Work; Kids at Risk: Declining Employer-Based Health Coverage in California and the U.S.; Organize to Improve the Quality of Jobs in the Black Community; The State of Labor Education in the U.S.; Trade Secrets; The Weingarten Decision and the Right to Representation on the Job; Winning at Work. **Educational Activities:** California Lead Organizers Institute; California Union Leadership School; China labor rights curriculum; C.L. Dellums African American Leadership School; Export processing zone workers organizing curriculum; Financial Skills Workshop; Labor summer internships, in unions and community organizations; Latino American Leadership School; Latino American Leadership School; Media Skills Workshop; Strategic Campaigns Workshop; Strategic Research Workshop.

41418 ■ University of California, San Francisco–Institute for Health Policy Studies
3333 California St., Ste. 265
San Francisco, CA 94118
Ph:(415)476-4921
Fax: (415)476-0705
Co. E-mail: ihpsweb@itsa.ucsf.edu
URL: http://ihps.ucsf.edu
Contact: Harold S. Luft, Dir.
E-mail: ihpsweb@itsa.ucsf.edu
Scope: Health policy and health services research.

41419 ■ University of Colorado—Denver–Center for Health Services Research
1355 S Colorado Blvd., Ste. 306
Denver, CO 80222

Ph:(303)756-8350
Fax: (303)759-8196
Co. E-mail: pete.shaughnessy@uchsc.edu
Contact: Peter W. Shaughnessy PhD, Dir.
E-mail: pete.shaughnessy@uchsc.edu
Scope: Health services research and health policy research for federal and state governments, foundations, and related organizations, emphasizing general health policy topics and issues in long-term care quality, access, cost and cost effectiveness. Studies emphasize Medicare and Medicaid quality assurance and reimbursement for long-term care providers, including home health agencies, subacute care facilities, swing-bed hospitals, and traditional nursing homes. Studies focus on the collection and analysis of extensive primary and secondary cross-sectional and longitudinal data at the patient and facility levels. Contributes to federal and state policy deliberations on regulatory and reimbursement issues in long-term care, and to clinical practice and decision making (especially in quality assurance.).

41420 ■ University of Colorado—Denver–Center for Human Investment Policy
1445 Market St., Ste. 350
Denver, CO 80202
Ph:(303)820-5631
Fax: (303)820-5656
Contact: Donna Garnett, Exec.Dir.
Scope: Ethical and policy issues in health care, including health care for the medically indigent, cost of care, rural health care, medical malpractice costs, prenatal care, public health, euthanasia, and the role of public opinion in policy formation. **Services:** Consultation research and policy analysis, for public and private sectors; Policy formulation assistance. **Publications:** FrontLines. **Educational Activities:** Educates students, health care providers, business leaders, and policy makers on health policy and ethics; Serves on boards and committees in public and private sectors; Workshops.

41421 ■ University of Connecticut–Center for International Community Health Studies
Department of Community Medicine & Health Care
School of Medicine, MC 6325
263 Farmington Ave.
Farmington, CT 06030-6325
Ph:(860)679-1570
Fax: (860)679-5464
Co. E-mail: schensul@nso2.uchc.edu
URL: http://www.commed.uchc.edu/cichs/default.htm
Contact: Stephen L. Schensul PhD, Dir.
E-mail: schensul@nso2.uchc.edu
Scope: The health of underprivileged people in the U.S. and abroad, emphasizing international primary health care and community health, including international health policy, urban health in developing and developed countries, maternal and child health, health programs and problems in Peru, Sri Lanka, Kenya, Mauritius, and Connecticut, effects of economic development on health, and the role of the hospital in the developing world. Facilitates international health research for faculty and graduate students through consultation on grant proposals, networking with international contacts, advocating for researchers within international agencies, and establishing foreign research and educational placements. **Publications:** Annual Training Program Catalogue; CICHS Connections Newsletter. **Educational Activities:** Develops curricula in the medical, dental, and other health professional schools; Language training programs, short-term research, evaluation, curriculum design, and management training programs, for health professionals from Africa, Asia, the Middle East, Latin America, and The New Independent States (NIS).

41422 ■ University of Illinois–Health Systems Research
College of Medicine
1601 Parkview Ave.
Rockford, IL 61107
Ph:(815)395-5639
Fax: (815)395-5602
Co. E-mail: joelc@uic.edu
URL: http://www.uirockford.com/research/health_whatis.asp

Contact: Joel B. Cowen, Asst. Dean
E-mail: joelc@uic.edu
Scope: Community health, primary care, public health, geriatrics, substance abuse, evaluation of delivery of health services, mental health services, demographic studies, health care planning, program evaluation. **Publications:** Information Service Letter (quarterly).

41423 ■ University of Illinois at Chicago–Institute for Health Research and Policy–Center for Health Services Research
Westside Research Office Bldg., MC 275
1747 W Roosevelt Rd.
Chicago, IL 60608
Ph:(312)996-1062
Fax: (312)996-2703
Co. E-mail: jzwanzig@uic.edu
URL: http://www.uic.edu/depts/ovcr/hrpc/centers/ hsr_content.html
Contact: Jack Zwanziger PhD, Dir.
E-mail: jzwanzig@uic.edu
Scope: New health care technologies, medical informatics, health manpower, observation unit medicine in the hospital emergency room, and performance of preventive through tertiary healthcare delivery at the systems, program, and specific intervention levels. Studies focus on access, appropriateness, acceptability, cost, safety, availability, effectiveness, benefits, and overall quality of healthcare. Specific topics include clinical decision-making, health information management, psychological and social sciences, and public health policy analysis. **Educational Activities:** Internships and independent studies.

41424 ■ University of Manitoba–Manitoba Nursing Research Institute
Helen Glass Centre, Rm. 213
Winnipeg, MB, Canada R3T 2N2
Ph:(204)474-9080
Fax: (204)474-7683
Co. E-mail: nursing_research@umanitoba.ca
URL: http://www.umanitoba.ca/nursing/research/mnri
Contact: Dr. Maureen Heaman
E-mail: nursing_research@umanitoba.ca
Scope: Surveys of nursing graduates, program evaluation and health outcomes. **Services:** Consultation, for faculty, graduate students and community nurses; Research support, for research grant applications and knowledge translation activities. **Educational Activities:** Research seminars, workshops and training. **Awards:** Manitoba Nursing Research Institute research grants, for outcomes research.

41425 ■ University of Maryland–Center on Aging
2367 HHP Bldg.
College Park, MD 20742-2611
Ph:(301)405-2469
Fax: (301)405-2542
Co. E-mail: lwilson@umd.edu
URL: http://www.hhp.umd.edu/AGING
Contact: Dr. Laura B. Wilson, Dir.
E-mail: lwilson@umd.edu
Scope: Gerontology, including senior service and volunteerism, long-term care financing, service credit banking, informal caregiving, aging and disabilities, productive aging, lifelong learning and engagement, health care delivery systems and cost containment. Conducts health assessment and longitudinal data base projects on aging, lifelong learning and civil engagement. **Services:** Curriculum development. **Publications:** Community Gerontology. **Educational Activities:** Graduate Gerontology Certificate Program; Legacy College, for age 50 and over; Legacy Leadership Institutes.

41426 ■ University of Memphis–Center for Health Services Research
119 Mccord Hall
Division of Health Administration
Memphis, TN 38152
Ph:(901)678-2794
Fax: (901)678-2981
Co. E-mail: peftzgrl@memphis.edu
Contact: Dr. Paul Fitzgerald, Dir.
E-mail: peftzgrl@memphis.edu

Scope: Health services research, including health administration, health utilization and access, health finance, health policy and law, guardianship, medical malpractice, mental health policy and law, health ethics, research methodology in health services research, and health decision making. **Services:** Consulting to government officials and the local community on health care and mental health policy; Provides legal testimony on health and mental health policy. **Educational Activities:** Internships and master's degrees in health and public administration.

41427 ■ University of Michigan–Health Management Research Center
1027 E Huron St.
Ann Arbor, MI 48104-1688
Ph:(734)763-2462
Co. E-mail: dwe@umich.edu
URL: http://www.umich.edu/~hmrc
Contact: Dr. D.W. Edington, Dir.
E-mail: dwe@umich.edu
Scope: Examines the relationships between lifestyle behaviors, quality of life, organizational productivity, and health care costs. **Services:** Consultation on wellness programs. **Publications:** Cost Benefit Analysis (annually). **Educational Activities:** Wellness in the Workplace Seminar.

41428 ■ University of Minnesota–Division of Health Policy and Management
Mayo Mail Code 729
School of Public Health
420 Delaware St. SE
Minneapolis, MN 55455-0392
Ph:(612)624-6151
Fax: (612)624-2196
Co. E-mail: ogbon001@umn.edu
URL: http://www.hsr.umn.edu
Contact: Geroge C. Ogbonna Sr.
E-mail: ogbon001@umn.edu
Scope: Long-term care, health insurance, managed health care, patient care outcomes, rural health services, and health policy analysis. **Publications:** Institute News (3/year); Research brief (monthly). **Educational Activities:** Minnesota Health Services Research Conference (annually); Postdoctoral training program.

41429 ■ University of Pennsylvania–Leonard Davis Institute of Health Economics
Colonial Penn Ctr.
3641 Locust Walk
Philadelphia, PA 19104-6218
Ph:(215)898-5611
Fax: (215)898-0229
Co. E-mail: levyj@wharton.upenn.edu
URL: http://www.upenn.edu/ldi/
Contact: David A. Asch MD, Exec.Dir.
E-mail: levyj@wharton.upenn.edu
Scope: Health economics; health care financing; systems design, organization, and management; evaluation of medical practices; and related policy issues that address the efficient allocation of health resources, the appropriate use of health services, the development of innovative health care delivery systems, and changing patient and provider behavior. Areas of concern include evaluation and optimization of clinical care and new technologies; access to health care; payment/reimbursement mechanisms and insurance; and institutional structure, management, and governance. **Publications:** Brochures; Issue briefs (occasionally). **Educational Activities:** Advanced management education programs, to senior health care executives and other health care professionals; Health Policy Seminar Series; Research conference (semimonthly); Research Seminar Series; Summer Undergraduate Minority Research Program.

41430 ■ University of South Florida–Center for HIV Education and Research
13301 Bruce B. Downs Blvd.
Tampa, FL 33612
Ph:(813)974-4430
Fax: (813)974-8451
Co. E-mail: knox@fmhi.usf.edu
URL: http://www.usfcenter.org
Contact: Dr. Michael D. Knox, Dir.

E-mail: knox@fmhi.usf.edu
Scope: Treatment of persons infected with HIV, study of HIV risk factors, and AIDS prevention. Provides current AIDS and HIV treatment information to physicians, psychologists, dentists, nurses, and other health care providers. **Services:** Responds to requests for education by medical professionals, hospitals, clinics, public health centers, community health centers, and substance abuse centers. **Publications:** HIV/AIDS Primary Care Guide. **Educational Activities:** Annual Florida/Caribbean HIV Conference; Clinical tutorial, for mental health professionals; Clinical mini-residencies, to primary care physicians; Educational events and workshops, on HIV and AIDS for physicians and other primary care clinicians; Florida/Caribbean AIDS education and training center; Perinatal transmission prevention program; Workshops, on clinical management for public health and correctional medical personnel.

41431 ■ University of Tennessee, Knoxville–Society for the Study of Social Problems, Inc.
Department of Sociology
901 McClung Tower
Knoxville, TN 37996-0490
Ph:(865)689-1531
Fax: (865)689-1534
Co. E-mail: sssp@utk.edu
URL: http://www.sssp1.org
Contact: Dr. Thomas C. Hood, Exec.Off.
E-mail: sssp@utk.edu
Scope: Community research and development; crime and juvenile delinquency; drinking and drugs; racial and ethnic minorities; conflict, social action, and change; the family; poverty, class, and inequality; social problems theory; mental health; teaching social problems; sociology and social welfare; youth, aging, and the life course; educational problems; environment and technology; labor studies; sexual behavior, politics and communities; law and society; health, health policy and health services; and institutional ethnography. **Publications:** Newsletters (3/year); Social Problems (quarterly). **Educational Activities:** Panels; Symposia; Training workshops. **Awards:** C. Wright Mills Award; Edwin O. Smigel Award; Lee Scholar-Activist Support Fund; Lee Student Support Fund; Lee-Founders Award; Social Action Award.

41432 ■ University of Texas at Dallas–Bruton Center for Development Studies
School of Social Sciences
PO Box 830688
Richardson, TX 75083-0688
Ph:(972)883-2992
Fax: (972)883-2735
Co. E-mail: jargo@utdallas.edu
URL: http://www.bruton.utdallas.edu
Contact: Prof. Paul A. Jargowsky, Dir.
E-mail: jargo@utdallas.edu
Scope: Real estate, transportation, and urban/regional analysis, with an emphasis on geospatial analysis. **Publications:** Working papers.

41433 ■ University of Wisconsin—Madison–Center for Health System Research and Analysis
WARF Bldg., 11th Fl.
610 Walnut St.
Madison, WI 53726-2397
Ph:(608)263-5722
Fax: (608)263-4523
Co. E-mail: david_zimmerman@chsra.wisc.edu
URL: http://www.chsra.wisc.edu
Contact: David R. Zimmerman PhD, Dir.
E-mail: david_zimmerman@chsra.wisc.edu
Scope: Five major research areas: quality assessment and improvement, long term care, public health policy and program evaluation, consumer decision making, and patient education and support.

41434 ■ Vanderbilt University–Center for Health Policy
1207 18th Ave S
Nashville, TN 37212
Ph:(615)322-0045
Fax: (615)322-8081

URL: http://www.vanderbilt.edu/VIPPS/HPC/
 HPChome.html
Contact: James F. Blumstein, Dir.
Scope: Health care reform, hospital competition, effects of medicaid policy on long term care decisions, hospital investment behavior, and choice of physicians.

41435 ■ Vanderbilt University–Institute for Public Policy Studies
2201 W End Ave.
Nashville, TN 37212
Ph:(615)322-7311
Fax: (615)322-8081
Co. E-mail: daniel.b.cornfield@vanderbilt.edu
URL: http://www.vanderbilt.edu/VIPPS/
Contact: Dr. Daniel B. Corfield, Actg.Dir.
E-mail: daniel.b.cornfield@vanderbilt.edu
Scope: Strives to provide a bridge between academic research on child and family policy options and the worlds of state and local policy makers. Fosters collaboration among faculty members at the University by operating the following research centers: the Center for Evaluation Research and Methodology works on both technical and substantive questions, the former including developing methods for cross-site evaluations of substance abuse treatment programs and improving metaanalytic tools, and the latter including identifying risk and protective factors for drug use and delinquency; the Center for Psychotherapy Research and Policy studies a variety of community mental health program issues, such as adaptation of mental health treatments for Southeast Asian refugee children; the Center for Health Policy studies health care reform and related issues; the Center for Mental

Health Policy specializes in the evaluation of programs for innovative mental health care for children; the Vanderbilt Center for Environmental Management Studies works on building environmental management considerations into corporate decision making; the Center for State and Local Policy provides research and analysis to government agencies and regional nonprofits; and the Center for U.S.-Japan Studies and Cooperation analyzes issues of international security involving the U.S. and Japan and compares the two nations' approaches to domestic policy problems such as education and the environment. **Publications:** Annual Report; Semiannual Newsletter. **Educational Activities:** Conferences; Faculty discussion groups; Freshman Tennessee Legislator Issue Workshop (biennially); Orientation and budget workshops; Technical and general interest seminars.

41436 ■ Veterans Affairs Medical Center
1 Veterans Dr.
Minneapolis, MN 55417-2300
Ph:(612)725-2033
Fax: (612)725-2093
Co. E-mail: michael.levitt@med.va.gov
Contact: Dr. Michael D. Levitt
E-mail: michael.levitt@med.va.gov
Scope: Health services, including cooperative clinical trials, psychiatry, prostate cancer, and kidney disease.

41437 ■ Walther Cancer Institute, Inc.–Mary Margaret Walther Program for Cancer Care Research
School of Nursing
1111 Middle Dr., Rm. 340
Indianapolis, IN 46202
Ph:(317)274-7563

Fax: (317)278-2021
Co. E-mail: vchampio@iupui.edu
Contact: Dr. Victoria L. Champion, Dir.
E-mail: vchampio@iupui.edu
Scope: Cancer prevention/control, survivorship, and cancer care delivery, focusing on developing an interdisciplinary effort to conduct behavioral research improving the quality of life for cancer patients and their families. Research addresses the psychological, economic, sociological and spiritual needs of those going through the cancer experience; increasing early detection of cancer and decreasing the occurrence of cancer through individual, family, and community behaviors; and improving the delivery of cost-effective cancer care by health professionals to cancer patients and their families. **Publications:** Brochures (annually).

41438 ■ Welfare Research, Inc.
112 State St.
Albany, NY 12207
Ph:(518)432-2563
Fax: (518)432-2564
Co. E-mail: administration@welfareresearch.org
URL: http://www.welfareresearch.org
Contact: Virginia Hayes Sibbison, Exec.Dir.
E-mail: administration@welfareresearch.org
Scope: Child welfare, AIDS, human services, health services, mental hygiene, nutrition assistance, public housing, employment and training, and nonprofit organization management. **Services:** Management assistance; Program evaluation projects, health and human services and public administration. **Publications:** Annual Report. **Educational Activities:** Communication and public information programs.

START-UP INFORMATION

41439 ■ **"7 Mesh Networking Startups Snag Funding"** in *Venture Capital Journal* (September 1, 2005)
Pub: Thomason Financial Inc.
Description: Venture capital firms are investing in mesh network companies who will build or expand wireless technology for the home and workplace. Kiyon Inc. and PacketHop Inc are the two most recent recipients of startup funding.

41440 ■ **"Alameda high-tech incubator is expanding"** in *Kiplinger California Letter* (Vol. 38, No. 17, September 4, 2002)
Pub: Kiplinger Washington Editors, Inc.
Description: Profile of Advancing California's Emerging Technologies high-tech incubator. The high-tech incubator will construct a 40,000 square foot laboratory and offices with $6.5 million in federal money.

41441 ■ **"The Amazing, Real-Life Adventures of Microfly"** in *Venture Capital Journal* (Vol. 42, No. 8, August 2002, pp. 30-31)
Pub: Thomas Venture Economics
Ed: Michael V. Copeland. **Description:** Profile of a robotic fly that weighs less than a paper clip and its promising technological value is discussed.

41442 ■ **"Anatomy of a Startup"** in *Black Enterprise* (Vol. 35, November 2004, No. 4, pp. 112)
Pub: Earl G. Graves Publishing Co. Inc.
Ed: Sonya A. Donaldson. **Description:** Profile of Ken Coleman, founder of the technology startup ITM Software in Silicon Valley, California. Coleman started his new firm after retiring from Silicon Graphics Inc.

41443 ■ **"Beacon Telco Aims To Jumpstart Optics"** in *Venture Capital Journal* (Vol. 40, No. 10, November 2000, pp. 6, 8)
Pub: Venture Economics
Description: Beacon Telco, a venture capital development company, was launched in mid-September 2000, to focus on optical networking and broadband communications. The venture capital firm will provide its portfolio companies with $1 million to $3 million in funding, noting that companies which choose to participate in the incubation program will also need to pay a program cost for incubator services.

41444 ■ **"Business Incubator Has a Fish Wriggling Off of the Hook"** in *St. Louis Post-Dispatch* (August 27, 2004)
Pub: Knight-Ridder/Tribune Business News
Ed: David Nicklaus. **Description:** Marcia Mellitz, founder of Symbiontics Inc., is considering a move to Wisconsin because of lack of funding. The firm is developing treatments for genetic disorders known as lysosomal storage diseases. It was launched with $3.5 million.

41445 ■ **"Business On Her Own Terms"** in *Black Enterprise* (Vol. 35, August 2004, No. 1, pp. 57)
Pub: Earl G. Graves Publishing Co. Inc.
Ed: Bridget McCrea. **Description:** Profile of Fay Coleman, president and CEO of her Silver Spring, Maryland firm, Westover Consultants Inc. Coleman started her business in the basement of her home and began developing educational training programs, planning events, creating public outreach programs, and conducting surveys for government agencies. Today, the firm comprises three divisions: Health and Behavior Sciences, Management Support Services, and Information Technology Services.

41446 ■ **"Designing Women"** in *Success* (Vol. 47, No. 3, July 2000, pp. 52)
Pub: Success Publishing, Inc.
Ed: Jane Shealy. **Description:** Two Texas sisters change the face of the cell phone industry by custom painting faceplates for Nokia phones.

41447 ■ **"Detroit Free Press Small Business Column"** in *Detroit Free Press* (May 23, 2005)
Pub: Knight-Ridder/Tribune Business News
Ed: Carol Cain. **Description:** Profile of Detroit-based Mobius Microsystems Inc., a firm that designs and sells patented intellectual property to microchip makers. Co-owners are looking to raise $5.5 million in venture capital to grow the firm.

41448 ■ **"Digital Rules"** in *Forbes* (August 21, 2000, pp. 51)
Pub: Forbes Magazine
Ed: Rich Karlgaard. **Description:** The importance of having a relaxed attitude in being a technology entrepreneur is discussed.

41449 ■ **"Do This, Get Rich"** in *Business 2.0* (Vol. 6, May 2005, No. 4, pp. 78-86)
Pub: Time, Inc.
Ed: Michael V. Copeland, Om Malik, Erick Schonfeld. **Description:** Profiles of the eleven hottest business opportunities are presented, including computer upgrades, advertising on the Web, specialty baby furniture, professional medical employment services, interior design for hotels, Web-enabled subscription and service monitoring, search engines for podcasts, RFID tags to track drugs and supplies in hospitals, software to save energy in homes and businesses, software and hardware to monitor and control a boat's onboard systems.

41450 ■ **"EISC partners start-up with unique technology"** in *Toledo Business Journal* (Vol. 19, No. 2, February 2003, pp. 23)
Pub: Telex Communications, Inc.
Ed: Susan Ford. **Description:** Profile of Energystics Technologies, Ltd. and Tom Sheperak, president and CEO, who is working on three applications for his unique Energy Beam(TM) technology that has the capability to move electricity through the air without a wire to heat, melt, or vaporize materials. EISC, the Small Business Development Center for technology and manufacturing, has established an on-site lab where Sheperak is developing and testing prototypes.

41451 ■ **"Engineering a Culture"** in *Crain's Detroit Business* (Vol. 19, No. 45, November 10, 2003, pp. 41)
Pub: Crain Communications Inc., Detroit
Ed: Andrew Dietderich. **Description:** Profile of Troy, Michigan-based Altair Engineering Inc. The firm was started in 1985 by three ex-General Motors Corporation employees and now employs 700 employees in 11 countries, with revenue expected to reach $75 in 2003.

41452 ■ **"Entrepreneur of the Year: Bob Baron"** in *Inc.* (January 1, 2005)
Pub: Inc. Magazine
Ed: Patrick J. Sauer. **Description:** Profile of Bob Baron, whose storm tracking technology helped the U.S. cope with a hyperactive Hurricane season in 2004. The firm's 3-D VIPIR system uses Doppler radar to pinpoint atmospheric disturbances a block away.

41453 ■ **"Forget India, Outsource to Oregon!"** in *Venture Capital Journal* (December 1, 2004)
Pub: Thomason Financial Inc.
Description: Reasons for venture capitals to target investments in Oregon and the Pacific Northwest rather than India or China are presented. Experienced angel investors and venture capitalists are taking the lead in building Oregon's high-tech entrepreneurial community.

41454 ■ **"Forward: Startups: Network-chip makers may be in danger of extinction"** in *Red Herring* (No. 102, August 15, 2001, pp. 22-23)
Pub: Herring Communications
Ed: Dean Takahaski. **Description:** Theoretically, network-processor startups could be saved by large company acquisitions, but several large firms have already purchased their favorites.

41455 ■ **"From the Ground Floor: The business paths to nanotech"** in *Red Herring* (No. 99, June 15 & July 1, 2001, pp. 42, 44)
Pub: Herring Communications
Ed: Steve Jurvetson. **Description:** A discussion involving nanotechnology and the startup opportunities, which paths will receive U.S. government grants, and which are market-driven businesses that attract venture capital.

41456 ■ **"Getting off to the Right Start"** in *Venture Capital Journal* (Vol. 40, No. 10, November 2000, pp. 40-41)
Pub: Venture Economics
Ed: Jay K. Hachigian. **Description:** Advice for entrepreneurs to avoid start-up problems, including ways to lay a proper foundation - setting up a common sense capital structure; ways to protect intellectual property; and good operating procedures.

41457 ■ **"GigaTrans hopes to get share of wireless market"** in *Crain's Detroit Business* (Vol. 19, No. 16, April 21, 2003, pp. 12)
Pub: Crain Communications Inc., Detroit

Ed: Andrew Dietderich. **Description:** Profile of James Rose, CEO and his two-year-old firm GigaTrans, a wireless Internet service provider. The company hopes to serve small and medium-size business customers.

41458 ■ "Going legit" in *BlackEnterprise* (Vol. 31, No. 12, July 2001, pp. 53)
Pub: Earl Graves Publishing Co.
Ed: Jason P. McKay. **Description:** Gregory D. Evans, the founder and CEO of the Cyber Group Network Corporation, has created E-Snitch, an electronic snitching device that uses wireless networks and satellites to locate missing or stolen computers anywhere in the world within a five-foot radius of the stolen PC.

41459 ■ "Goodbye B-School" in *Harvard Business Review* (Vol. 78, No. 2, March 2000, pp. 16)
Pub: Harvard Business School Publishing Corp.
Description: Two years ago, Jonathan Seelig left business school to co-found Akamai Technologies. In this interview he discusses how the company is now worth $20 billion.

41460 ■ "Halsey Minor's Virtual Train Station" in *Business Week Online* (February 9, 2005)
Pub: McGraw-Hill Companies
Description: Harry Minor, tech entrepreneur, talks about his latest venture, called Grand Central, that helps companies interconnect their software via the Internet. Minor has been working on Grand Central for five years.

41461 ■ "High Tech, High Sales" in *Small Business Opportunities* (Vol. 13, No. 5, September 2001, pp. 76, 78)
Pub: Harris Publications, Inc.
Ed: Lin Grensing-Pophal. **Description:** An overview of the use of CD-Rom's as marketing tools, including a profile of Jim O'Reilly and his software company, DCA Holdings, Inc. of Minneapolis, Minnesota.

41462 ■ *High Tech Start Up*
Pub: Free Press
Ed: John L. Nesheim. **Price:** $50.00.

41463 ■ "How I Did It: Randy Slager" in *Inc.* (January 1, 2005)
Pub: Inc. Magazine
Ed: Patrick J. Sauer. **Description:** Profile of Randy Slager, founded Catapult Technology while battling a degenerative spinal injury incurred as an information systems officer in the Army. Slager has two goals: one is to continue expanding his $30 million dollar IT company, the other is to help disabled veterans achieve entrepreneurial success.

41464 ■ "Image is Everything" in *Red Herring* (No. 99, June 15 & July 1, 2001, pp. 114, 116)
Pub: Herring Communications
Ed: Dean Takahashi. **Description:** Profile of Bob Weinschenk, CEO of Pixim, producer of image-sensor chips for digital cameras and other imaging devices. Statistical data included.

41465 ■ "In a tough market, a tech executive chooses to gamble" in *Wall Street Journal* (Jan. 24, 2003, pp. A1)
Pub: Dow Jones & Co. Inc.
Ed: Pui-Wing Tam. **Description:** Profile of Barry Cottle, and his startup, Mobile Digital Media Inc. and the challenges he faces in the recession-struck Silicon Valley, California.

41466 ■ "Learning business was key" in *Crain's Detroit Business* (Vol. 19, No. 13, March 31, 2003, pp. 13)
Pub: Crain Communications Inc., Detroit
Description: Profile of David Fry, president and CEO of Fry Inc. Fry, a former Harvard University professor, started his firm with financing from family members. The company tripled in size in a short period of time, and Fry shares his experiences of learning about his business as it grew.

41467 ■ "Merit Networks offshoot draws $5M in venture capital funding" in *Crain's Detroit Business* (Vol. 16, No. 37, Sept. 11, 2000, pp. 55)
Pub: Crain Communications, Inc.
Ed: Matt Roush. **Description:** Profile of Merit Networks Inc. and its spin-off company, Interlinks Networks Inc.

41468 ■ "Miami Upstart Goes National" in *Hispanic Business* (October 2002, pp. 86)
Pub: Hispanic Business
Ed: Roger Harris. **Description:** Profile of Nextrox, an Internet service provider based in Miami, Florida, has grown into a national information technology company in less than seven years.

41469 ■ "Montreal: A Fertile Ground For VC Exploration" in *Venture Capital Journal* (Vol. 42, No. 5, May 2002, pp. 54)
Pub: Thomas Venture Economics
Description: Montreal, Quebec is becoming the hot spot for technological development, and is supported by a strong investment community and world-class local venture capital environment.

41470 ■ "Mr. Koogle's Failed Return" in *Red Herring* (January 2003, pp. 69)
Pub: Herring Communications Inc.
Ed: Justin Hibbard. **Description:** Profile of Tim Koogle, former Yahoo CEO, who expected a return to the corporate stage, only to have his new venture close before it was able to open.

41471 ■ "NASA Offers Free Rocket Scientists" in *Inc.* (August 1, 2004)
Pub: Inc. Magazine
Ed: Jess McCuan. **Description:** NASA has created a new outreach program that offers small businesses up to 40 hours of free high-tech and engineering advice under the Space Alliance Technology Outreach Program, which began as a state-run project in 1995 in the State of Florida and went national in 2001.

41472 ■ "One to Watch: A Russian entrepreneur scores a wireless hit with teenagers" in *Red Herring* (No. 103, September 1, 2001, pp. 26)
Pub: Herring Communications
Ed: Eric Moskowitz. **Description:** Profile of David Yang, CEO of Cybiko, maker of a wireless personal digital assistant and gaming devices for teens.

41473 ■ "One to Watch: KnowNow tackles two-way computing" in *Red Herring* (No. 102, August 15, 2001, pp. 24)
Pub: Herring Communications
Ed: Om Malik. **Description:** Real-time computing is receiving renewed attention, prompting entrepreneurs to seek innovative ways of making corporations run more efficiently. Profile of KnowNow, the startup that has developed technology to network a company's information technology (IT) infrastructure using the hypertext transfer protocol (HTTP) used to deliver Web pages one way, will allow users to send and receive information instantly through Web browsers, cell phones and email.

41474 ■ "Only a Few Sea Turtles Survive" in *Forbes* (February 21, 2000, pp. 96)
Pub: Forbes Magazine
Ed: James Champy. **Description:** Survival tactics for new technology companies are offered.

41475 ■ "Podcast Startups Look Doomed from the Start" in *Venture Capital Journal* (October 1, 2005)
Pub: Thomason Financial Inc.
Description: Podcast service allows the user to get automatic updates of Website audio content and can listen to it on an iPod or other MP3 player. Problems being faced by Podcast startups are discussed.

41476 ■ "Powerful forces" in *Black Enterprise* (Vol. 32, No. 6, January 2002, pp. 69)
Pub: Earl Graves Publishing Co.
Ed: Bridget McCrea. **Description:** Profile of three women entrepreneurs who took on the high tech industry and succeeded with their startup companies. The articles discusses the fact that African American women are forging ahead in this male-dominated field.

41477 ■ "Priority packets pay to fly first class" in *Red Herring* (No. 87, December 18, 2000, pp. 44, 46)
Pub: Herring Communications, Inc.
Ed: Scott Tyler Shafer. **Description:** A profile of Village Networks, the New Jersey high-tech start-up and its founder Kai Eng.

41478 ■ "A private space race" in *Wall Street Journal* (Feb. 5, 2003, pp. B1)
Pub: Dow Jones & Co. Inc.
Ed: J. Lynn Lunsford. **Description:** Entrepreneur Peter Diamandis has founded and helped to fund the St. Louis, Missouri, based X Prize Foundation, which will award a $10 million prize to the first private venture to fund, design and launch a manned space vehicle. Twenty-four entrepreneur-led teams are vying for the prize and the recent accident aboard the Space Shuttle Columbia has not deterred any in that quest. The foundation's rules for the spacecraft say only that it must be able to hold three passengers and must be able to fly 62 miles up and return safely two times in the course of two weeks.

41479 ■ "The Quebec Story: Low Cost, Low Risk, Tremendous Opportunity" in *Venture Capital Journal* (Vol. 42, No. 5, May 2002, pp. 48, 50)
Pub: Thomas Venture Economics
Ed: Peter Diekmeyer. **Description:** Canada's venture capital center has become a hotbed of technology startups because of the unique incentives, including tax incentives, low business costs, Montreal's close ties to Europe, and an educated workforce focused on technology.

41480 ■ "Second Time Around" in *Entrepreneur* (Vol. 31, No. 7, July 2003, pp. 24)
Pub: Entrepreneur Media, Inc.
Ed: David Worrell. **Description:** Three Internet entrepreneurs are betting on Wireless startups and are bringing new ideas, perspectives and innovation to the industry.

41481 ■ *Seed-Stage Venture Investing: The Ins and Outs for Entrepreneurs, Start-Ups, and Investors on Successfully Starting a New Business*
Pub: Aspatore Books, Incorporated
Ed: William J. Robbins. **Released:** July 2006. **Price:** $199.95. **Description:** Ideas for starting, funding, and managing technology-based firms, also known as, venture capitalists, are featured.

41482 ■ "Silicon Peninsula?" in *Crain's Detroit Business*
Pub: Crain Communications, Inc.
Ed: Matt Roush. **Description:** There's still a lack of venture capital in Michigan to back tech spin-offs.

41483 ■ "States' aid for tech start-ups: more talk than action" in *Wall Street Journal* (January 4, 2000, pp. B2)
Pub: Dow Jones & Co., Inc.
Ed: Ellena De Lisser. **Description:** A compilation of entrepreneurial news, including information about state aid for high-tech start-ups.

41484 ■ "Street Talk" in *Barron's* (July 21, 2003, pp. 7)
Pub: Barron's
Ed: Alan Abelson. **Description:** The term burn rate, used to describe the profligate spending of Internet startups and biotechnology firms, has been latched on to by Donald Rumsfeld to describe the cost of the Iraq war.

41485 ■ *Strengthening Technology Incubation System for Creating High Technology-Based Enterprises in Asia and the Pacific*
Pub: United Nations Publications
Released: January 2005. **Price:** $75.00. **Description:** Report reviewing policy guidelines and practices

to establish technology incubators that will help entrepreneurs develop small technology-based enterprises in different national economies.

41486 ■ "Technology makes a comeback: fizzling dotcoms were last year's news" in *Black Enterprise* **(Vol. 32, No. 8, March 2002, pp. 87)**
Pub: Earl Graves Publishing Co.
Ed: Sonya A. Donaldson. **Description:** How African Americans fit into the discussion of venture capitalists, startups, and the technology industry is discussed. Interviews with various experts tell how African Americans can find the capital needed to fund a business venture.

41487 ■ *Technology Ventures: From Idea to Enterprise with Student DVD*
Pub: McGraw-Hill Higher Education
Ed: Richard C. Dorf; Thomas H. Byers. **Released:** October 2006. **Price:** $100.68. **Description:** Textbook examining technology entrepreneurship on a global basis; technology management theories are explored.

41488 ■ "This VC Firm's Motto: Make Money, Not War" in *Fortune* **(Vol. 142, No. 3, July 24, 2000, pp. 54)**
Pub: Time Inc.
Ed: Jane M. Folpe. **Description:** Military Commercial Technologies, an Orlando venture capital firm and high-tech incubator, has a winning formula for bringing defense technology to the public sector.

ASSOCIATIONS AND OTHER ORGANIZATIONS

41489 ■ Organization of Pakistani Entrepreneurs of North America
4 Maxwell Cir.
Hudson, MA 01749
Ph:(781)266-2141
Fax: (781)266-2141
Co. E-mail: info@open-us.org
URL: http://www.open-us.org
Description: Provides networking opportunities for Pakistani entrepreneurs and professionals in hightech industries in the Nascent Community of Massachusetts. **Telecommunication Services:** electronic mail, rsvp@open-us.org.

EDUCATIONAL PROGRAMS

41490 ■ Business Systems Analysis and Design
American Management Association
1601 Broadway
New York, NY 10019
Ph:(212)586-8100
Free: 800-262-9699
Fax: (212)903-8168
Co. E-mail: customerservice@amanet.org
URL: http://www.amanet.org
Price: $1,895 for non-members; $1,695 for AMA members. **Description:** Covers knowledge of information technology to enhance productivity, including recognizing matters that need attention, monitoring throughout the process, and implementation. **Locations:** New York, NY; and Chicago, IL.

41491 ■ Information Technology for the Non-IT Manager
American Management Association
1601 Broadway
New York, NY 10019
Ph:(212)586-8100
Free: 800-262-9699
Fax: (212)903-8168
Co. E-mail: customerservice@amanet.org
URL: http://www.amanet.org
Price: $1,695 for non-members; $1,495 for AMA members. **Description:** Covers the core components of information technology, and how it can enhance corporate productivity. **Locations:** New York, NY; Chicago, IL; Atlanta, GA; Washington, DC; and San Francisco, CA.

REFERENCE WORKS

41492 ■ "$1 Million Grant Program Aims to Boost Renewable Energy" in *Milwaukee Journal Sentinel* **(December 13, 2005)**
Pub: Journal Sentinel, Inc.
Ed: Thomas Content. **Description:** Wisconsin's Governor Jim Doyle has proposed a $1 million grant to invest in renewable energy technologies for the state, including ethanol, biodiesel and waste-to-energy power.

41493 ■ *The 7 Irrefutable Rules of Small Business Growth*
Pub: John Wiley & Sons, Incorporated
Ed: Steven S. Little. **Released:** February 2005. **Price:** $18.95. **Description:** Proven strategies to maintain small business growth are outlined, covering topics such as technology, business plans, hiring, and more.

41494 ■ "60 Seconds On Doing the Impossible" in *Fast Company* **(March 2005, No. 92, pp. 32)**
Pub: Gruner & Jahr USA Publishing
Ed: Ryan Underwood. **Description:** Interview with Peter Diamandis, who created the competition that awarded the $10 million Ansari X Prize to SpaceShipOne for shuttling into suborbital space twice in two weeks. Diamandis is expanding his focus to include prizes for nanotechnology.

41495 ■ "12.1 Inch SVGA Modules From Toshiba..." in *PR Newswire* **(Dec. 9, 2003)**
Pub: PR Newswire Association, Inc.
Description: Toshiba's new electronic components, offering high luminance and wide viewing angle displays are suitable for a wide range of industrial, terminal, kiosk, medical, and EPOS applications. Statistical data included.

41496 ■ "A Market for Ideas" in *The Economist* **(Vol. 377, October 22-28, 2005, No. 8449, pp. 3-6, 8-10, 12-18)**
Pub: The Economist Newspaper Ltd.
Description: The magazine presents information collected from a survey conducted on issues of patents and technology. Protection of intellectual property can be good for both the technology industry and its customers. The patent system, companies preparing for intellectual-property battles, a new intellectual-property business model, sharing intellectual property, Indian and Chinese competition in innovation, and new markets for intellectual property are among issues investigated.

41497 ■ "Acquisitions helped increase offerings" in *Crain's Detroit Business* **(Vol. 19, No. 13, March 31, 2003, pp. 12)**
Pub: Crain Communications Inc., Detroit
Description: Special report on Integration Projects Inc., now called Dewpoint Inc. after acquisition the company modified service offerings in order to cope with the market.

41498 ■ *Advanced Manufacturing Technology*
Pub: John Wiley & Sons Inc. Scientific/Technical/Medical Publishing
Ed: Leo O'Connor, Editor. **Released:** Monthly. **Publication Includes:** List of companies involved in developing advanced manufacturing technologies such as robotics, artificial intelligence in computers, ultrasonics, lasers, and waterjet cutters; also lists sources of information and education on high-technology. **Entries Include:** Company or organization name, address, phone, name of contact; description of process, product, or service. Principal content is articles and analysis of advanced manufacturing technology. **Arrangement:** Classified by subject.

41499 ■ "Advertisers Want to Leave Their Message on Your Cell Phone" in *Crain's Detroit Business* **(Vol. 23, January 15, 2007, No. 3, pp. 13)**
Pub: Crain Communications Inc. - Detroit
Ed: Bill Shea. **Description:** Mobile phones are becoming more interactive with the Internet for online local information. Triggered by a voluntary request of the user, things like Google search can be used as either audio or text message advertising specifically targeted at the requestor.

41500 ■ "Aether Systems Unveils $125M Venture Arm" in *Venture Capital Journal* **(Vol. 40, No. 10, October 2000, pp. 6)**
Pub: Venture Economics
Description: In order to expand its markets, Aether Systems Inc., provider of wireless data products and services, launched Aether Capital as its venture capital arm.

41501 ■ "Aftermarket Hits Its Stride" in *Venture Capital Journal* **(November 1, 2004)**
Pub: Thomason Financial Inc.
Ed: Lawrence Aragon. **Description:** Of the six venture-backed companies listed in September 2004, most posted strong aftermarket performances. Thereavance Inc., a drug company in San Francisco; IntraLase Corporation, maker of software for lasers used in eye surgery; and PlanetOut Inc., which operates gay and lesbian-themed Websites, went public as of October 15, 2004.

41502 ■ "Air Campaign: Think Wireless Devices and Air Travel Don't Mix?" in *Entrepreneur* **(Vol. 32, November 2004, No. 11, pp. 60)**
Pub: Entrepreneur Media Inc.
Ed: Amanda C. Kooser. **Description:** Entrepreneurs and other business travelers prefer taking care of business in-flight and American Airlines and Qualcomm have teamed to offer an in-cabin cellular station to send and receive calls and text messages.

41503 ■ "Albany's High-Tech Park Already Creating Jobs" in *Tampa Tribune* **(November 28, 2005)**
Pub: Media General, Inc.
Ed: Gary Haber. **Description:** Albany NanoTech, located 150 miles north of New York City, is a $3 billion research and development complex for researchers from industry, as well as professors and students from the University at Albany who are working on next-generation miniature computer chips.

41504 ■ "Alcatel Draws Contract" in *San Fernando Valley Business Journal* **(Vol. 11, December 2006, No. 25, pp. 28)**
Pub: San Fernando Valley Business Journal Associates
Description: Alcatel, a company that provides innovative products that allow for seamless communication by integrating data and voice networks, signed a $300 million deal to provide an integrated phone system for over 400 medical facilities in Pennsylvania.

41505 ■ *Alpha Dogs: How Your Small Business Can Become a Leader of the Pack*
Pub: HarperCollins Publishers, Inc.
Ed: Donna Fenn. **Released:** May 2007. **Price:** $14.95. **Description:** Profiles of eight successful entrepreneurs along with information for developing customer service, technology and competition.

41506 ■ "Alternative Energy Companies" in *Crain's Detroit Business* **(Vol. 22, February 6, 2006, No. 6, pp. 14)**
Pub: Crain Communications Inc. - Detroit
Description: A directory of Southeast Michigan's alternative energy companies is presented.

41507 ■ "Alternative Energy Powers Up In Michigan - Part 1 of 2" in *Crain's Detroit Business* **(Vol. 22, February 6, 2006, No. 6, pp. 10)**
Pub: Crain Communications Inc. - Detroit
Ed: Amy Lane. **Description:** McKenzie Bay International Ltd. Located in Farmington Hills, Michigan is launching a commercial wind-energy system that generates and distributes electricity at customer locations, and supplements power from a conventional utility.

41508 ■ "Alternative Energy Powers Up In Michigan - Part 2 of 2" in *Crain's Detroit Business* **(Vol. 22, February 6, 2006, No. 6, pp. 10)**
Pub: Crain Communications Inc. - Detroit
Ed: Amy Lane. **Description:** Michigan is pushing to become the nations' epicenter for research and development into new technology for biodiesel fuels made from renewable resources such as vegetable oil recycled from restaurants or produced from sunflowers, soybeans and canola plants.

41509 ■ "The 'Always On' Economy" in *Inc.* **(Volume 27, June 2005, No. 6, pp. 59-60)**
Pub: Inc. Magazine
Ed: David H. Freedman. **Description:** New communications systems are able to keep companies in contact with employees and customers 24/7.

41510 ■ "Americans Have Grown Very Attached to Their Gadgets, Survey Finds" in *Portland Press Herald* **(December 23, 2005)**
Pub: Blethen Maine Newspapers, Inc.
Ed: Kelley Bouchard. **Description:** Americans are attached to high tech gadgets such as laptop computers, cellular phones, think pads, iPods, digital media receivers, etc. Demographics include every age group except seniors with annual incomes over $50,000.

41511 ■ "Analog TV" in *Business Week* **(January 23, 2006, No. 3968, pp. 22)**
Pub: McGraw-Hill Companies
Ed: Stephen H. Wildstrom. **Description:** Congress has decreed that television broadcasters must end analog transmissions by February 17, 2009 and switch to digital technology.

41512 ■ "Analyze This" in *Black Enterprise* **(Vol. 34, No. 6, January 2004, pp. 41)**
Pub: Earl Graves Publishing Co.
Ed: Ashley Gibson. **Description:** Profile of Charles Phillips, technology expert and rated America's best software analyst, has been appointed new executive vice president of Oracle Corporation.

41513 ■ "Analyze This: Charles Phillips Makes Bold Career Move to Oracle as Executive Vice President" in *Black Enterprise* **(Vol. 34, No. 6)**
Pub: Earl Graves Publishing Co.
Ed: Ashley Gibson. **Description:** Profile of Charles Phillips, technology expert and rated America's best software analyst, has been appointed new executive vice president of Oracle Corporation.

41514 ■ "Andrews & Kurth goes high-tech with ex-Brobeck attorneys" in *Houston Business Journal* **(Vol. 33, No. 49, April 18, 2003, pp. 2A)**
Pub: Houston Business Journal
Ed: Jim Greer. **Description:** The law firm of Andrews & Kurth has hired three attorneys specializing in securities law.

41515 ■ "'Angels' Seek to Expand Territory; Investors Begin to Target Waukesha County" in *Milwaukee Journal Sentinel* **(December 12, 2005)**
Pub: Journal Sentinel, Inc.
Ed: Kathleen Gallagher. **Description:** IQ Corridor Angel Network is targeting Waukesha County to help develop a series of high-tech companies from Chicago through Milwaukee and Madison onto Minneapolis. The firm is seeking ideas related to manufacturing equipment needed by biotech and other high-tech companies, especially those in Madison, Wisconsin.

41516 ■ "The Angler: With more opportunities comes more isolation" in *Red Herring* **(No. 103, September 1, 2001, pp. 16)**
Pub: Herring Communications
Ed: Anthony B. Perkins. **Description:** Results of a study by the Stanford Institute for the Quantitative Study of Society (SIQSS) are presented. The study was conducted to determine whether the sociopolitical changes brought about by the Internet will be liberating or harmful, or both.

41517 ■ "Answer the phone and have a good time" in *Rough Notes* **(Vol. 146, No. 4, April 2003, pp. 18)**
Pub: Rough Notes
Ed: Dennis Pillsbury. **Description:** Mike Heffernan is the CEO of Heffernan Group, which includes Heffernan Insurance Brokers, an insurance retail agency and Presidio and Advanced Risk Technologists. Nearly 50 percent of business is derived from niche practices and programs such as nonprofits, healthcare, property owners, construction and technology.

41518 ■ "Anything but Boring; CBS Boring Draws Big Attention with New Robotic System" in *Crain's Detroit Business* **(Vol. 19, No. 40)**
Pub: Crain Communications Inc., Detroit
Ed: Terry Kosdrosky. **Description:** Profile of the robotic cell-based production system created by CBS Boring & Machine Company. The new technology enabled CBS Boring to meet low prices demanded by automakers.

41519 ■ "Anything but Boring" in *Crain's Detroit Business* **(Vol. 19, No. 40, October 13, 2003, pp. 3)**
Pub: Crain Communications Inc., Detroit
Ed: Terry Kosdrosky. **Description:** Profile of the robotic cell-based production system created by CBS Boring & Machine Company. The new technology enabled CBS Boring to meet low prices demanded by automakers.

41520 ■ "Apex Venture Partners Preps for Fifth Vehicle" in *Venture Capital Journal* **(Vol. 40, No. 10, November 2000, pp. 16)**
Pub: Venture Economics
Description: Apex Venture Partners began raising its fifth fund in January 2001. The new fund will invest in about 25-35 companies with initial investments in the $2 million range. Apex mainly backs telecommunications, software, information technology, and consumer-related companies in the U.S.

41521 ■ "Apple Wanted Cornice To Supply Tiny Hard Drives for a New Device, the iPod Mini" in *Inc.* **(October 2005, pp. 59-60)**
Pub: Inc. Magazine
Ed: Michael Fitzgerald. **Description:** Carmillo Martino, CEO of Cornice, maker of tiny hard drives with one-inch planters for storing music or digital files, offers insight into his decision to turn down Apple's offer to supply these hard drives for the iPod Mini.

41522 ■ "Arlington, Texas, High-Tech Incubator Gets $2.85 Million Boost" in *Dallas Morning News* **(October 27, 2002)**
Pub: Knight Ridder/Tribune Business News
Ed: Jenni Smith. **Description:** The Arlington Technology Incubator, a joint venture of the University of Texas at Arlington and the Arlington Chamber of Commerce, received a $150,000 technical assistance grant from the U.S. Economic Development Administration and will get another $2.7 million from the research portion of the defense bill signed by President Bush in October.

41523 ■ "Army's Tech Needs Boost General Dynamics' Role" in *Crain's Detroit Business* **(Vol. 21, January 17, 2005, No. 3, pp. 14)**
Pub: Crain Communications Inc. - Detroit
Ed: Brent Snavely. **Description:** General Dynamics Land Systems is being asked to deliver high tech equipment to the U.S. Army ahead of schedule. The company moved to a 52,000 square foot center on 14 Mile Road to facilitate the design of a new set of vehicles for a demonstration scheduled for 2014.

41524 ■ "AT & T Heads Into TV Fray With Passage of Video Bill" in *Crain's Detroit Business* **(Vol. 22, December 18, 2006, No. 51, pp. 5)**
Pub: Crain Communications Inc. - Detroit
Ed: Amy Lane. **Description:** AT&T is making a large investment in Michigan as a result of the new bill passed last week to open competition amongst high tech cable suppliers; franchising process is revised opening the doors to a new video battle amongst Comcast and AT&T.

41525 ■ "ATI's Moment of Glory" in *Barron's* **(August 18, 2003, pp. T1)**
Pub: Barron's
Ed: Bill Alpert. **Description:** ATI Technologies, with NVIDIA one of the two major players in the computer graphics chip market, welcomed a 12 percent surge in share price as the market responded to its deal to supply the graphics engine for Microsoft's next generation X-Box.

41526 ■ "Automation Alley Awards" in *Crain's Detroit Business* **(Vol. 22, September 25-October 1, 2006, No. 39, pp. E1-E7)**
Pub: Crain Communications Inc. - Detroit
Description: Top technology leaders and organizations with significant contributions through Southeast Michigan are honored. Automation Alley is a consortium of businesses that promote Southeast Michigan as a good place to do business.

41527 ■ "Aven Hopes Portable Microscope Drives Growth" in *Crain's Detroit Business* **(Vol. 22, December 18, 2006, No. pp. 16)**
Pub: Crain Communications Inc. - Detroit
Ed: Tom Henderson. **Description:** New portable microscope and digital camera to be marketed by Ann Arbor firm. This product combines a high resolution camera, with a series of in-house developed lenses. Target markets are crime scene investigations and quality control in manufacturing.

41528 ■ "Avienda: A New Avenue for Communications" in *Venture Capital Journal* **(Vol. 40, No. 10, November 2000, pp. 38)**
Pub: Venture Economics
Description: Profile of Avienda, the Internet technology company co-founded by former Columbia University Business School classmates, Aaron Shapiro and David Bloom. The company is a global point-to-point delivery network, that is, it provides a content delivery and storage solution for personalized data and perishable information.

41529 ■ "Back to Basics: Ex-Dotcommers Create New Beginnings through Low-Tech Businesses" in *Entrepreneur* **(Vol. 31, No. 9, September 2003)**
Pub: Entrepreneur Media, Inc.
Ed: Mark Henricks. **Description:** A growing number of ex-dotcommers are starting new businesses in low-technology fields associated with immigrant Americans.

41530 ■ "Back to Basics; Single Portal for Business" in *Crain's Detroit Business* **(Vol. 19, No. 42, October 20, 2003, pp. 11)**
Pub: Crain Communications Inc., Detroit
Ed: Amy Lane. **Description:** The State of Michigan intends to improve the state's telecommunications infrastructure, including a single state government Internet portal where businesses might handle all project-permit needs and new ways to expand high-speed Internet access to underserved areas.

41531 ■ "Back in the game. IT recruiters see selective improvement in local technology staffing markets" in *Business First Columbus* **(Vol. 18)**
Pub: Business First Columbus, Inc.
Ed: Craig Lovelace. **Description:** Central Ohio IT hiring is seeing improvements, yet the improvements are sporadic and not a major increase throughout the region. IT workers cannot expect the high salaries common before the turn around in the dot.com industry, these trends are indicative of the entire U.S.

41532 ■ "Back to Technology" in *Black Enterprise* **(Vol. 34, No. 6, January 2004)**
Pub: Earl Graves Publishing Co.
Ed: Nicole Lewis. **Description:** Patrick Lyons, associate portfolio manager at NCM Capital Management Group in Durham, North Carolina is predicting a come back for the technology sector. He also expects a 4-5 percent growth in the economy over the next four quarters.

41533 ■ "Back to Technology: Patrick Lyons of NCM Capital Management Says a Tech Binge is Likely" in *Black Enterprise* (Vol. 34, January 2004)

Pub: Earl Graves Publishing Co.

Ed: Nicole Lewis. **Description:** Patrick Lyons, associate portfolio manager at NCM Capital Management Group in Durham, North Carolina is predicting a come back for the technology sector. He also expects a 4-5 percent growth in the economy over the next four quarters.

41534 ■ "Bandleader" in *Entrepreneur* (Vol. 30, No. 2, February 2002, pp. 31)

Pub: Entrepreneur Media Inc.

Ed: Mike Hogan. **Description:** Profile of the new network wireless technology that can achieve speeds of up to 108Mbps.

41535 ■ "Banks Try to Make Tele-Touch Satisfy Small Businesses" in *American Banker* (Vol. 171, November 27, 2006, No. 226, pp. 2)

Pub: SourceMedia, Inc.

Ed: Jim Cole. **Description:** Banks serving small businesses continue to offer personalized services, while incorporating call centers and online service models to small business strategies. Statistical data included.

41536 ■ "Battenberg is riding along with Segway" in *Crain's Detroit Business* (Vol. 18, No. 24, June 17, 2002, pp. 8)

Pub: Crain Communications Inc. - Detroit

Ed: Mary Kramer. **Description:** Profile of the Segway Human Transporter, a two-wheel scooter designed to help overweight Americans.

41537 ■ "Beaming in on safety business" in *Atlanta Business Chronicle* (Vol. 25, December 20, 2002, No. 28, pp. 3A)

Pub: American City Business Publications, Inc.

Ed: Mary Jane Credeur. **Description:** ScanTech Sciences Inc.'s electron beam technology can be used to scan through large steel shipping containers as a way of detecting nuclear material that may be smuggled into U.S. ports as well as irradiating potentially contaminated meat or produce.

41538 ■ "Before You Do That 'Amazing' Biotech Deal, Read This Story" in *Venture Capital Journal* (Vol. 42, No. 8, August 2002, pp. 36-37)

Pub: Thomas Venture Economics

Ed: Ravi Chiruvolu. **Description:** Biotechnology startups always require a longer incubation period. The author shares his experiences with biotechnology deals.

41539 ■ "Behind the Curve" in *Hispanic Business* (Vol. 24, No. 5, May 2002, pp. 40-41)

Pub: Hispanic Business Inc.

Ed: Teresa Talerico. **Description:** Hispanic small business owners are slow to accept technology. The importance of keeping up with technology for a small business is discussed.

41540 ■ "Behind the looking glass" in *Red Herring* (March 2003, pp. 58)

Pub: Herring Communications Inc.

Ed: Celeste Biever. **Description:** A listing of everyday products manufactured through nanotechnology is presented, including antibacterial products, self-cleaning glass, sunscreens, tennis balls and more.

41541 ■ "Berridge Confident of Evolving Work Force" in *Ledger* (March 6, 2005)

Pub: Knight-Ridder/Tribune Business News

Ed: Kyle Kennedy. **Description:** Florida High Tech Corridor Council's president, Randy Berridge is committed to bringing more high tech business and jobs to Central Florida.

41542 ■ "Betting the Farm" in *Business 2.0* (Vol. 6, September 2005, No. 8, pp. 108)

Pub: Time, Inc.

Ed: Erick Schonfeld. **Description:** The continual advancement of genetically modified crops is paying off for Monsanto after the company took the big risk on biotechnology.

41543 ■ "Big Communications Deals Keep On Coming" in *Venture Capital Journal* (Vol. 40, No. 10, October 2000, pp. 10, 12)

Pub: Venture Economics

Description: Venture capital firms are financing communications businesses, with optical switching technology being strongest.

41544 ■ "The Big Disconnect" in *Barron's* (Vol. 82, No. 59, February 24, 2003, pp. T1)

Pub: Barron's

Ed: Eric J. Savitz. **Description:** The technology industry is fundamentally weak, and a recent rally is not likely to provide long-term relief to the industry. Several inventions introduced at a February 2003 Demo conference are described.

41545 ■ "Big Projects Give Some Life to Sluggish Real Estate Sector" in *Crain's Detroit Business* (Vol. 19, No. 45, November 10, 2003, pp. 15)

Pub: Crain Communications Inc., Detroit

Ed: Jennette Smith. **Description:** Upcoming high-technology automotive projects by Hyundai Motor American, BorgWarner Inc., and Visteon Corporation will help the stalled real estate sector.

41546 ■ "Bio-Layoffs Cool Once-Booking Job Market" in *Boston Business Journal* (Vol. 23, No. 21, June 27, 2003, pp. 1)

Pub: American City Business Journals

Ed: Allison Connolly. **Description:** Massachusetts' biotechnology industry has suffered 1,000 job losses in the past six months. Though expectations are that the industry will play a significant role in improving the state's economy, experts predict that in the short-term, the industry will continue to decline.

41547 ■ "Biocentric Security" in *PC Magazine* (February 6, 2001, pp. 26)

Pub: Ziff-Davis Publishing Company

Ed: Sally Wiener Grotta. **Description:** Biometrics, the use of physical characteristics to confirm identity, are explained.

41548 ■ "Biomedical, Marine Research Funds Could Grow If Voters Approve Seed Money" in *Portland Press Herald* (November 2, 2005)

Pub: Blethen Maine Newspapers, Inc.

Ed: Edward D. Murphy. **Description:** Maine's Department of Economic and Community Development says the $20 million on the state's election ballot would not be enough to fund projects designed to help biomedical and marine research programs.

41549 ■ "Biometric conversion" in *Red Herring* (January 2003, pp. 63)

Pub: Herring Communications Inc.

Ed: Andrew P. Madden. **Description:** Biometrics is the use of technology to verify a person's identity based on physical or behavioral characteristics, such as fingerprints and facial recognition. Profile of Identix, the market leader in the use of biometrics is included.

41550 ■ "Biotech Balance: Mutual Fund Diversification Lets Investors Temper Biotech's Risk" in *Black Enterprise* (Vol. 34, No. 4, Nov. 2003)

Pub: Earl Graves Publishing Co.

Ed: James A. Anderson. **Description:** Information for investing in Biotechnology is examined.

41551 ■ "Biotech Believer" in *Fortune* (Vol. 151, February 21, 2005, No. 4, pp. 128)

Pub: Time Inc.

Ed: Stephanie N. Mehta. **Description:** Fund manager, Sam Isaly is predicting single-digit growth in the pharmacy industry, while expecting double-digit growth in the biotechnology sector for 2005.

41552 ■ "Biotech Hotbeds: Where Are They, and How Do You Get One?" in *Venture Capital Journal* (October 1, 2004)

Pub: Thomason Financial Inc.

Ed: Dan Primack. **Description:** Boston, San Diego, San Francisco, and Research Triangle Park are earn-

ing the reputation in the life sciences sector as biotech hotbeds, clusters or hubs. These centers rely on four things: there is at least one large, nonprofit research institution strong in the field of biomedicine, close proximity to venture capital firms investing in biotech companies, local government officials have an interest in enhancing business environment for biotech companies, and there are a few publicly-traded biotech companies in the area.

41553 ■ "Biotech II Alan Frazier" in *Venture Capital Journal* (January 1, 2005)

Pub: Thomason Financial Inc.

Description: In an interview with Alan Frazier, founder of Frazier Healthcare Ventures in Seattle, Washington, he discusses the best and worst things that could happen in biotechnology in 2005. Frazier sites a continued IPO market that prices good companies appropriately along with mergers and acquisitions would be positive for the sector.

41554 ■ "Biotech Takes Heart in Potential New Drug" in *Pacific Business News* (Vol. 41, No. 23, August 15, 2003, pp. 1)

Pub: American City Business Journals

Ed: Terrance Sing. **Description:** Hawaii-based Hawaii Biotech Inc. has developed a new drug that is expected to reduce heart tissue damage. The new drug, called Cardax, has achieved positive results in clinical tests at the Medical College of Wisconsin.

41555 ■ "Black Board Directors Form Network" in *Black Enterprise* (Vol. 35, December 2004, No. 5, pp. 38)

Pub: Earl G. Graves Publishing Co. Inc.

Ed: K. Terrell Reed. **Description:** According to the Investor Research Center, nearly 185 blacks sit on corporate boards, sharing 321 board seats out of 3,447. A recent gathering brought top black executives together to address a diversity agenda in board rooms.

41556 ■ "Blade server firm sharpens up with funding" in *Houston Business Journal* (Vol. 33, No. 51, May 2, 2003, pp. 2A)

Pub: Houston Business Journal

Ed: Jennifer Dawson. **Description:** Doug Erwin has moved from PentaSafe Security Technologies Inc CEO and president to CEO and Chairman of RLX Technologies Inc. Investors offered more than $16 million in new funds after Erwin's move.

41557 ■ "Bluetooth babble: not all wireless gadgets speak the same language" in *Entrepreneur* (Vol. 31, No. 5, May 2003, pp. 36)

Pub: Entrepreneur Media Inc.

Ed: Daniel Tynan. **Description:** Gartner Inc. predicts that it will cost businesses approximately $70 per employee to workout the handshake and security settings of Bluetooth devices.

41558 ■ "BM enmeshed in grid computing " in *Red Herring* (No. 103, September 1, 2001, pp. 27)

Pub: Herring Communications

Ed: Om Malik. **Description:** Discussion involving distributed, or grid, computing is presented. Grid computing uses groups of computers to perform very complex processing tasks.

41559 ■ "BofA Cutting 70 Charlotte Tech Jobs" in *Charlotte Observer* (January 31, 2007)

Pub: Knight-Ridder/Tribune Business News

Ed: Rick Rothacker. **Description:** Bank of America announced the elimination of 70 technology positions at their Charlotte, North Carolina facility. The move is part of the company's effort to increase efficiency.

41560 ■ "Book Review: Summary judgment" in *Red Herring* (No. 103, September 1, 2001, pp. 40)

Pub: Herring Communications

Ed: Mark Williams. **Description:** Book review of 'Inventing the Electronic Century', by Alfred D. Chandler. The author presents the story of the consumer electronics and computer industries.

41561 ■ "Booting the Bear: E-Trade is Poised for the Bull's Return" in *Barron's* **(August 25, 2003, pp. MW17)**
Pub: Barron's
Ed: Allison Krampf. **Description:** Online brokerage service E-Trade, victimized by the technology bubble collapse of 2000, has slowly and patiently retrenched, and now stands poised to exploit the return of the bull market that most analysts expect.

41562 ■ "Born in an infertility clinic, nursed in a dish" in *Atlanta Business Chronicle* **(Vol. 25, No. 22, November 8, 2002, pp. 20A)**
Pub: American City Business Publications, Inc.
Ed: Julie Bryant. **Description:** BresaGen Inc. has four stem cell lines for use in research on finding new treatments for various debilitating illnesses. The firm has not revealed the name of the Atlanta, Georgia infertility clinic from which it received the needed human embryos to obtain the stem cell lines. The stem cell process is examined.

41563 ■ "Bosco Joins Clarity, Raising $1B Fund" in *Venture Capital Journal* **(Vol. 40, No. 10, November 2000, pp. 18)**
Pub: Venture Economics
Description: Harry Bosco, former president of Lucent Technologies' Optical Networking Group, will join Clarity Partners on October 16, 2000. The firm will back early- to late-stage network infrastructure, wireless services and applications, e-commerce and broadband media companies.

41564 ■ "Bowling for drug research: families take entrepreneurial tack in signing up biotech firms" in *Wall Street Journal* **(Feb. 27, 2003)**
Pub: Dow Jones & Co. Inc.
Ed: Vanessa Fuhrmans. **Description:** Families of Spinal Muscular Atrophy signed a contract with Decode Genetics Inc. to fund their research programs.

41565 ■ "Brave New Tech World" in *Black Enterprise* **(Vol. 34, July 2004, No. 12, pp. 58)**
Pub: Earl G. Graves Publishing Co. Inc.
Ed: Sonya A. Donaldson. **Description:** Advice if offered to help choose a personal computer.

41566 ■ "Breaking out" in *Barron's* **(Vol. 82, No. 58, February 17, 2003, pp. 23)**
Pub: Barron's
Ed: Rhonda Brammer. **Description:** Lifetime Hoan's household wares is enjoying steady sales growth and improving margins, making its share of $5 a good value. The only stock sector to enjoy a positive mark in January 2003 was high tech.

41567 ■ "Briefing: Semiconductors" in *Red Herring* **(No. 99, June 15 & July 1, 2001, pp. 100-101)**
Pub: Herring Communications
Ed: Dean Takahashi. **Description:** An overview of the downturn in the high tech sector.

41568 ■ "Bright Lights" in *Red Herring* **(No. 99, June 15 & July 1, 2001, pp. 55-56, 58)**
Pub: Herring Communications
Ed: Lee Bruno. **Description:** With nanotechnology lighting the way, a new class of optical switches are vying to usher in more efficient communications networks.

41569 ■ "Broadband Access" in *Hispanic Business* **(March 2005, pp. 14)**
Pub: Hispanic Business
Description: According to a study by the Tomas Rivera Policy Institute, increasing broadband access to African Americans and Hispanics could equate to as much as $74 million in monthly revenue for technology providers.

41570 ■ "Broadband Deluxe: High-Speed Firms Take the Stress Out of Networking" in *Black Enterprise* **(Vol. 35, November 2004, No. 4, pp. 68)**
Pub: Earl G. Graves Publishing Co. Inc.
Ed: Rebecca Rohan. **Description:** Broadband provider, Comcast, will install and manage computer networks for customers.

41571 ■ "Broadband agency makes its first loan" in *Crain's Detroit Business* **(Vol. 19, No. 12, March 24, 2003, pp. 6)**
Pub: Crain Communications Inc., Detroit
Ed: Amy Lane. **Description:** The Michigan Broadband Development Authority has approved its first loan to the mid-Michigan wireless provider ISP Wireless Group Inc., located in Alma. The company intends to install wireless broadband antennae and equipment in small towns from Clare to Ithaca.

41572 ■ "Broadband Wagon: Greater Connectivity is Coming to a Neighborhood Near You." in *Entrepreneur* **(Vol. 32, November 2004, No. 11, pp. 59)**
Pub: Entrepreneur Media Inc.
Ed: Mike Hogan. **Description:** Fiber to the Premises (FTTP) is a new blend of fiber optic and Ethernet cable and is available for homes and businesses, promising unlimited bandwidth.

41573 ■ "Build a Better Business" in *Black Enterprise* **(Vol. 35, October 2004, No. 3, pp. 136)**
Pub: Earl G. Graves Publishing Co. Inc.
Ed: Robert Anthony, Sonya A. Donaldson. **Description:** Emerging new technologies can help small businesses seem larger than they really are. Co-founder of Krazy Kickz, Sam Robinson, tells how upgrading the company's phone system led to a better customer service system.

41574 ■ "Building the Minority High-Tech Work Force" in *Hispanic Business* **(Vol. 23, No. 7/8, July/August 2001, pp. 116)**
Pub: Hispanic Business
Description: The Council on Competitiveness has received a $23 million grant to establish a non-profit organization to address the critical shortage of women and minorities in the high-tech industries sector in the U.S.

41575 ■ "Building the Perfect Tech CEO" in *Hispanic Business* **(Vol. 23, No. 5, May 2001, pp. 28, 30)**
Pub: Hispanic Business
Ed: Jonathan J. Higuera. **Description:** Profile of Grey Reyes, president and CEO of the Silicon-based Brocade Communications Systems. Mr. Reyes has vowed to make the storage area network infrastructure provider an industry leader.

41576 ■ "Built For Speed: Baba Garba Looks to Take His Broadband Business Abroad" in *Black Enterprise* **(Vol. 34, No. 5, December 2003, pp. 50)**
Pub: Earl Graves Publishing Co.
Ed: Zakiyyah El-Amin. **Description:** Profile of Baba Garba, founder of Infonit LLC, launched in 2000 and located in Niles, Michigan. The firm provides broadband installation and information technology consulting.

41577 ■ "Business Briefs" in *Salt Lake Tribune* **(February 24, 2005)**
Pub: Knight-Ridder/Tribune Business News
Description: Business information involving Extra Space Storage, a real estate investment trust that owns and operates self-storage properties; Cirtran Corp. a contract manufacturer; Maxwell Publishing; Trio Restaurant Group; Raser Technologies, who received a contract to develop mobile power generation technology for the government; and Cyprus Credit Union's fundraiser for Primary Children's Medical Center, is spotlighted.

41578 ■ "Business Integrator Entrepreneur Marries Technology and Advertising to Grow Business" in *Black Enterprise* **(Vol. 35, Jan. 2005, No. 6)**
Pub: Earl G. Graves Publishing Co. Inc.
Ed: Nichole Lewis. **Description:** Interactive marketing strategies have helped POWERi to grow in the travel and tourism industry despite a slowdown since the terrorist attacks of 9-11. The firm operates three lines of business: technology within an advertising agency that could also provide marketing strategy and graphic design services. The firm reported revenues of $1 million in 2003.

41579 ■ "The Business of Nanotech" in *Business Week* **(February 14, 2005, No. 3920, pp. 64)**
Pub: McGraw-Hill Companies
Ed: Stephen Baker, Adam Aston. **Description:** Soon cars, chips and even golf balls will be produced using new materials engineered down to the level of individual atoms. Some 1,200 nano startups have emerged globally.

41580 ■ "Businesses Use Wireless Access to Draw Customers" in *Crain's Detroit Business* **(Vol. 19, No. 42, October 20, 2003, pp. 14)**
Pub: Crain Communications Inc., Detroit
Ed: Andrew Dietderich. **Description:** Restaurants, book stores, office stores and hotels in Michigan are offering free wireless Internet access to draw businessmen and women to their shops.

41581 ■ "Buy, buy biotech?" in *Entrepreneur* **(Vol. 30, No. 3, March 2002, pp. 72)**
Pub: Entrepreneur Media Inc.
Ed: Jennifer Pellet. **Description:** Despite the warnings about bioterrorism, experts warn that biotech firms are difficult to evaluate before investing.

41582 ■ "The Buzz About HD Radio" in *Black Enterprise* **(Vol. 37, February 2007, No. 7, pp. 58)**
Pub: Earl G. Graves Publishing Co. Inc.
Ed: James C. Johnson. **Description:** HD radio broadcasting will send CD quality sound and extra information to more radio stations using the same amount of bandwidth.

41583 ■ "C2G-Network" in *Entrepreneur.com* **(Vol. 34, January 2006, No. 1, pp. 6)**
Pub: Entrepreneur Media Inc.
Ed: Steve Cooper. **Description:** College students can be certified and placed on C2G-Network that puts them in contact with fast-growing small businesses. Students have backgrounds in technology, engineering, marketing and sales, human resources, finance, communications and more.

41584 ■ "California Regulators Approve SBC, AT&T Merger" in *Sacramento Bee* **(November 19, 2005)**
Pub: The Sacramento Bee
Description: Details of the $16 billion merger of telephone companies SBC Communications Inc. and AT&T Corporation are discussed. The merger will create the largest telecommunications company in the U.S.

41585 ■ "Calling All VoIP Adopters: Tech Shows" in *Tradeshow Week* **(Vol. 34, November 29, 2004, No. 48, pp. 54)**
Pub: Reed Business Information
Ed: Margo McCall. **Description:** Ways Voice over Internet protocol can improve small business are discussed, including information about established companies and startups providing the service.

41586 ■ "Calling security" in *Entrepreneur* **(Vol. 30, No. 9, September 2002, pp. 23)**
Pub: Entrepreneur Media Inc.
Ed: Melissa Campanelli. **Description:** Both large and small businesses are implementing security-related technologies, including mailing services like PaperlessPOBox located in San Francisco, California.

41587 ■ "Can I get into IT?" in *Black Enterprise* **(Vol. 31, No. 3, October 2000, pp. 59)**
Pub: Earl Graves Publishing Co.
Description: The article tells what high-tech entrepreneurs look for when hiring non-IT degreed employees.

41588 ■ "Canadian companies ponder best options for e-waste" in *Computing Canada* **(Vol. 28, No. 21, October 25, 2002, pp. 1)**
Pub: Plesman Publications
Ed: Liam Lahey. **Description:** More than 42,000 tons of electronic waste, or e-waste, will be generated by Canadian homes and businesses in the year 2005. Obsolete computers and peripherals are increasing at alarming rates across North America.

41589 ■ "Cancer Drug May Hold Key to Company's Survival" in *Crain's Detroit Business* (Vol. 18, No. 21, May 27, 2002, pp. 3)
Pub: Crain Communications Inc. - Detroit
Ed: Andrew Dietderich. Description: Profile of Biotherapies, Inc., located in Ann Arbor, Michigan. The 7-year-old privately held firm has developed a patented drug to treat breast cancer, and has pending patents in the treatment of ovarian, colon, prostate and lung cancers.

41590 ■ "Cancer Scans a Lifesaver for Crystal Maker" in *Orlando Business Journal* (Vol. 20, No. 8, August 8, 2003, pp. 2)
Pub: American City Business Journals, Inc.
Ed: Chad Eric Watt. Description: Profile of Crystal Photonics, founded by physicist Bruce Chai to produce artificial crystals. The firm has become one of the top crystal makers in the world.

41591 ■ "Capitol Connections" in *Pittsburgh Business Times* (Vol. 23, No. 1, July 25, 2003, pp. 1)
Pub: Pittsburgh Business Times
Ed: Patty Tascarella. Description: GSP Consulting Corporation offers lobbying services for the biotechnology and technology sectors and is expected to earn over $1 million in revenues in 2003.

41592 ■ "Caritas Seeking Cambridge Lab Space" in *Boston Globe* (February 4, 2005)
Pub: New York Times Company
Ed: Jeffrey Krasner. Description: Caritas Christi Health Care is planning to lease 100,000 square feet of laboratory space in Cambridge to increase its healthcare and biotechnology research. The move is expected to give the firm a higher profile and better access to scientists and local companies.

41593 ■ "A case for clinical informatics" in *Ingram's* (Vol. 28, No. 6, June 2002, pp. 61)
Pub: Show Me Publishing, Inc.
Description: Ideas and forecasting of future genetic and clinical trends in the health care industry are examined. Analysts believe genomics and medical informatics will combine to form clinical informatics, which will be a hybrid of laboratory testing and genetic analysis.

41594 ■ "Cashflow: July 1-15, 2001" in *Red Herring* (No. 102, August 15, 2001, pp. 28)
Pub: Herring Communications
Ed: Elizabeth Lamb. Description: Presentation using graphs and charts showing the seven companies that went public during the first two weeks of July 2001. Only one of the firms was a technology company.

41595 ■ "Cell Tower Potential" in *Black Enterprise* (Vol. 37, October 2006, No. 3, pp. 86)
Pub: Earl G. Graves Publishing Co. Inc.
Ed: James C. Johnson. Description: Due to local zoning that does not allow new cell towers to be too close to existing ones along with other issues only certain properties are eligible as leasing cites to wireless carriers.

41596 ■ "Centerpoint is sidelined" in *Red Herring* (March 2003, pp. 67)
Pub: Herring Communications Inc.
Ed: Om Malik. Description: The demise of Centerpoint Broadband Technologies, a high-profile startup, developing wireless technologies and a new optical-transport mechanism, is chronicled.

41597 ■ "Central Indiana's High-Tech Incubator Lands First Tenant" in *Indianapolis Star* (September 24, 2002)
Pub: Knight Ridder/Tribune Business News
Ed: Jack Naudi. Description: Profile of central Indiana's newest high-tech incubator, the Haelan Group, a small company with a big high-tech vision to improve health care. The startup firm is geared toward life sciences, and will be run by Indiana University's Advanced Research and Technology Institute.

41598 ■ "CEO sells IT company to help it grow" in *Crain's Detroit Business* (Vol. 18, No.)
Pub: Crain Communications Inc. - Detroit
Ed: Andrew Dietderich. Description: Ciber Inc. has purchased Southfield, Michigan's Decision Consultants Inc., an information technology services company.

41599 ■ "The changing face of technology" in *Hispanic Business* (Vol. 22, No. 10, October 2000, pp. 26)
Pub: Hispanic Business
Ed: Scott Williams. Description: The representation of Hispanic professionals in U.S. business is discussed. Barriers to Hispanics achieving their full potential at school or university and the growing number of Hispanics graduating in math, science and engineering are analyzed.

41600 ■ "China Syndrome" in *Boston Business Journal* (V)
Pub: MCP, Inc.
Ed: Tom Witkowski. Description: Massachusetts-based semiconductor device firms are establishing operations in China.

41601 ■ "Chip Demand Worldwide Drives Up 1Q Earnings for Intel" in *San Jose Mercury News* (March 11, 2005)
Pub: Knight-Ridder/Tribune Business News
Ed: Dean Takahashi. Description: International sales will drive first quarter earnings for Intel higher than projected. Statistical data included.

41602 ■ "Chip Shot. Teradyne's New President is Crafting a Comeback after an Industry Slump" in *Boston Business Journal* (Vol. 23, Jul. 4, 03)
Pub: American City Business Journals
Ed: Tom Witkowski. Description: Biography of Michael A. Bradley, the new president of Teradyne Inc. is presented. Teradyne Inc. manufactures automatic test equipment and interconnection systems to semiconductor, electronics and network systems companies.

41603 ■ "City Guide for Moms Launched" in *Marketing to Women* (Vol. 20, January 2007, No. 1, pp. 3)
Pub: EPM Communications, Inc.
Description: ModernMom.com has launched a series of city guides on the Internet designed to highlight local businesses that offer goods and services a mother may need. Los Angeles, San Francisco, Chicago, New York City, Seattle, Austin Minneapolis, Atlanta, San Diego, Boston, Philadelphia and Washington D.C. are cities included so far in Modern Mom City Guides.

41604 ■ "A clarion call: the tech and telecom sectors are finally on the mend" in *Barron's* (Vol. 82, No. 58, February 17, 2003, pp. 28)
Pub: Barron's
Ed: Sandra Wood. Description: Tech and telecom research specialists, Scott Cleland and William Whyman, are optimistic about the end of the bear market in those sectors, including software, cable TV, and the Baby Bells.

41605 ■ "Clearwater Man Puts Technology To Work" in *Tampa Tribune* (November 27, 2005)
Pub: Media General, Inc.
Ed: Will Rodgers. Description: Denny Klein of Airport Business Center has developed a gas that speeds welding and fusing times and also improves automobile fuel efficiency by at least 30 percent.

41606 ■ "A CLEC Clicks" in *Boston Business Journal* (Vol. 23, No. 27, August 8, 2003, pp. 19)
Pub: American City Business Journals
Ed: Mark Hollmer. Description: Profile of the local exchange carrier, Conversent Communications is presented.

41607 ■ "Click on a Fortune" in *Small Business Opportunities* (Vol. 17, May 2005, No. 3, pp. 22-24, 26-28, 30, 32, 34, 36, 38, 40, 42, 44)
Pub: Harris Publications Inc.
Description: Fifteen growing service franchises are highlighted. Profiles of the following franchise and independent startup opportunities include Island Ink-Jet, Wireless Toyz, homemade foods, Children's Orchard, carpet cleaning, concierge services, family books, Putt-Putt golf centers, glass replacement, online auction sales, mystery shoppers, Earl of Sandwich, Instant FX, senior care, and real estate investing.

41608 ■ "Clicking against the Current" in *Crain's Detroit Business* (Vol. 19, No. 9, March 3, 2003, pp. 3)
Pub: Crain Communications Inc., Detroit
Ed: Andrew Dietderich. Description: Despite reports that technology spending is down and won't increase until 2004, local area technology firms are growing.

41609 ■ "Cloning: Venture capitalists decline a visit to the animal farm" in *Red Herring* (No. 103, September 1, 2001, pp. 34)
Pub: Herring Communications
Ed: Lawrence Aragon. Description: Profile of Lou Hawthorne, CEO of GS&C, based in Mill Valley, California. Mr. Hawthorne is considering making his gene bank, and eventually pet cloning services, available free of charge.

41610 ■ "Close to Finding RedZone's Niche" in *Pittsburgh Business Times* (Vol. 4, August 15, 2003, pp. 14)
Pub: Pittsburgh Business Times
Ed: Maria Guzzo. Description: Profile of Pittsburgh, Pennsylvania-based RedZone Robotics Inc.; topics include market development, management styles, and management of small business.

41611 ■ "Cobasys Powers Up for Possible IPO; New Deal, HQ Spur Optimism" in *Crain's Detroit Business* (Vol. 20, December 20, 2004, No. 51)
Pub: Crain Communications Inc. - Detroit
Ed: Andrew Dietderich. Description: Cobasys LLC is planning an initial public offering in 2006 or 2007. Meanwhile, the firm plans to consolidate its executive, engineering and product development under one roof in Orion Township, Michigan.

41612 ■ "Colorado Man Helped Contribute to Overseas Tech Development" in *Colorado Springs Business Journal* (February 28, 2003)
Pub: Dolan Media Newswires
Ed: Marylou Doehrman. Description: Profile of Chet Sulewski, who retired from Johns Manville, after spending 35 years as senior vice president, promoting overseas technological development. Sulewski now owns a liquor store that is co-managed by his two sons.

41613 ■ "Come Together" in *Entrepreneur* (Vol. 32)
Pub: Entrepreneur Media Inc.
Ed: Mike Hogan. Description: Information of importance to small business regarding wireless LANs and Voice over Internet Protocol (VoIP) is presented.

41614 ■ "Communications Jonathan Silver" in *Venture Capital Journal* (January 1, 2005)
Pub: Thomason Financial Inc.
Description: Jonathan Silver, managing director of Core Capital Partners in Washington DC, offers predictions in the communications market for 2005. Silver believes the best thing is that venture capitalists are regaining interest in communications.

41615 ■ "Companies Bid for Wireless Washtenaw" in *Crain's Detroit Business* (Vol. 21, December 19, 2005, No. 51, pp. 20)
Pub: Crain Communications Inc. - Detroit
Ed: Andrew Dietderich. Description: Twenty-three companies are expected to bid on developing and maintaining a wireless Internet network for the 720 square mile county in Michigan.

41616 ■ "Compuware to Buy Back up to 34 Million Shares" in *Crain's Detroit Business* (Vol. 22, December 18, 2006, No. 51 pp. 4)
Pub: Crain Communications Inc. - Detroit
Ed: Tom Henderson. Description: Stock buyback approved by board for 34 million shares of company stock. This will start immediately and continue through June 30.Also approved was the purchase of $200M in additional stock at management's discretion with no timing specified.

41617 ■ "Consumer Tech II Oren Zeev" in *Venture Capital Journal* (January 1, 2005)
Pub: Thomason Financial Inc.
Description: In an interview with Oren Zeev, consumer technology investments are discussed. Ultra wide band-wireless technology, primarily used for the home, will have a large impact in 2005. Zeev discusses trends in consumer technology and where he is putting his money.

41618 ■ "Copy Cop Fights Back, Takes the Digital Plunge" in *Boston Business Journal* (Vol. 23, No. 30, August 29, 2003, pp. 4)
Pub: American City Business Journals
Ed: Jill Lerner. Description: Efforts by Boston, Massachusetts-based Copy Cop to recapture lost market share is examined. Topics include making capital investments in the company, developing new markets, and taking on competition.

41619 ■ "Corporate Image-Maker Sees Hope for Symbol, Pain for Computer Associates" in *Long Island Business News* (March 5, 2004)
Pub: Dolan Media Newswires
Ed: Ken Schachter. Description: Ann Stephenson, chief executive of Stephenson Group, a corporate image-maker specializing in technology companies, discusses ways she would rehabilitate the images of Symbol Technologies and Computer Associates. Both firms are facing government investigations into accounting procedures and the sudden departure of high-ranking executives.

41620 ■ "Court Battles" in *Business Week* (December 19, 2005, No. 3964, pp. 33-34)
Pub: McGraw-Hill Companies
Ed: Catherine Yang. Description: A settlement of the patent fight could net $1 billion for the late Tom Campana's NTP.

41621 ■ "Creation of tech corridor to spur Midtown's growth" in *Atlanta Business Chronicle* (Vol. 25, No. 20, October 25, 2002, pp. 6)
Pub: American City Business Publications, Inc.
Ed: Tony Heffernan. Description: Technology Square is Georgia Tech's $180 million project that is currently underway. According to Wayne Clough, president of the university, he and a main developer envision the project to stretch from the campus to 14th Street.

41622 ■ "Cricket Still Clears the Bar For Leap" in *Wall Street Journal* (Vol. 248, December 2006, No. 149, pp. C1)
Pub: Dow Jones & Co. Inc.
Ed: Amol Sharma Description: Profile of Leap Wireless International Inc., which has seen their shares sharply gaining traction. Leap's 'Cricket' brand service targets niche markets overlooked by larger carriers such as young, low-income and ethnic customers by offering flat-rate service and requiring no credit checks.

41623 ■ *Crossing the Chasm: Marketing and Selling Disruptive Products to Mainstream Customers*
Pub: HarperInformation
Ed: Geoffrey A. Moore. Released: September 2002. Price: $17.95. Description: A guide for marketing in high-technology industries, focusing on the Internet.

41624 ■ "A Cruel, Cold January for Funds" in *Business Week Online* (February 9, 2005)
Pub: McGraw-Hill Companies
Ed: Amey Stone. Description: The market did not rally in January 2005, higher interest rates hurt real estate funds, and the fear of slowing growth in the technology sector are blamed. Statistical data included.

41625 ■ "Cutting the Cord: Investing in Wireless" in *Venture Capital Journal* (February 1, 2005)
Pub: Thomason Financial Inc.
Description: The growth of the wireless industry has created opportunity for private equity investors to expand their portfolios. Current issues facing private equity investment in the wireless sector are discussed.

41626 ■ "The cycle turns for technology in 2003" in *Red Herring* (January 2003, pp. 70)
Pub: Herring Communications Inc.
Ed: Arnie Berman. Description: The economic future for the technology industry is examined.

41627 ■ "Dealflop: Good night, sweetheart" in *Red Herring* (No. 102, August 15, 2001, pp. 31)
Pub: Herring Communications
Ed: Om Malik. Description: Profile of Sabeer Bhatia, one of the two co-founders of the free Internet email service, Hotmail. Since selling Hotmail to Microsoft, Mr. Bhatia has failed to secure financing for his second startup, Arzoo.

41628 ■ "Dealing with Reality" in *Pittsburgh Business Times* (Vol. 23, No. 6, August 29, 2003, pp. 15)
Pub: Pittsburgh Business Times
Ed: Christopher Davis. Description: Robotics Foundry president, William Thomasmeyer, hopes to develop robotics research into viable business opportunities in the Pittsburgh, Pennsylvania area.

41629 ■ "Death to Cool" in *Inc.* (July 1, 2003)
Pub: Gruner & Jahr USA Publishing
Description: Profile of iRobot, a boutique high-tech firm reinvented itself as an appliance company and now sells new products on the Home Shopping Network.

41630 ■ "Delagardelle Joins Sprout Group" in *Venture Capital Journal* (Vol. 40, No. 10, November 2000, pp. 36)
Pub: Venture Economics
Description: The Sprout Group hired Jeani Delagardelle, former general partner at Weiss, Peck & Greer Venture Partners. Ms. Delagardelle came to Sprout because of their dedication to investments in healthcare technologies.

41631 ■ "Demo 2002 Cuts the Fluff" in *Business Week Online* (Februa)
Pub: McGraw-Hill, Inc.
Description: An overview of the annual Demo conference held in Phoenix during February is presented.

41632 ■ "Detection Redirection" in *Washington Business Journal* (Vol. 22, No. 9, July 4, 2003, pp. 13)
Pub: Washington Business Journal
Ed: Chris Silva. Description: Marketing of cancer detection technology by Washington, DC-based biotechnology firm Protiveris Inc. is examined.

41633 ■ "Detroit Public Schools Pick IT Firms" in *Crain's Detroit Business* (Vol. 22, December 18, 2006, No. 51, pp. 18)
Pub: Crain Communications Inc. - Detroit
Ed: Tom Henderson. Description: Vision IT was retained by the City of Detroit for a five year contract at $9.8M per year. Vision IT was one of five minority owned firms picked to share five year, $58M contracts previously held by Comcast and Strategic Staffing. Three of the contracts were rescinded after a protest over the bidding process and results was filed by the previous contractors.

41634 ■ "Dialogue Picks Up on St. Louis' Status in IT and Biotech" in *St. Louis Post-Dispatch* (November 3, 2004)
Pub: Knight-Ridder/Tribune Business News
Ed: David Nicklaus. Description: St. Louis reports dozens of startup biotechnology companies and venture capital funds to back them. According to a study conducted by the Battelle Institute, St. Louis has become competitive in both life sciences and information technology sectors.

41635 ■ "Digital Detroit gathering helps build new economy in Motown" in *Crain's Detroit Business* (Vol. 16, No. 49, December 4, 2000, pp. 42)
Pub: Crain Communications, Inc.
Ed: Katie Merx. Description: The Digital Detroit L.L.C. conference provided the much-needed jumpstart for Detroit's high tech industry. Internet startup gurus, tech-side workers from traditional businesses, lawyers and economic development officials were in attendance.

41636 ■ "The Digital Disruptors" in *Red Herring* (No. 102, August 15, 2001, pp. 58-59)
Pub: Herring Communications
Ed: Jon Maples. Description: Profile of the ten companies, and the sector they represent, that stand to upend the entertainment markets, including Anonymous Content, advertising; News Corporation, television; Clear Channel, radio; Realnetworks, streaming media; Microsoft, gaming; Adobe Systems, publishing; NTT Docomo, wireless; Nothing Real, film; Loudeye, digital-rights management; and Audiogalaxy, music.

41637 ■ "The Digital Schusser" in *Business Week* (January 16, 2006, No. 3967, pp. 92-93)
Pub: McGraw-Hill Companies
Ed: Jay Greene. Description: The latest high-tech gear designed with the snow skier in mind include headphones in hats and cellular phones in sunglasses.

41638 ■ "DigitalLife Tries New Approach: Reaching Consumers" in *Tradeshow Week* (Vol. 34, November 29, 2004, No. 48, pp. 56)
Pub: Reed Business Information
Ed: Margo McCall. Description: Profile of DigitalLife, a consumer tradeshow held in New York, October 2004. The show featured cell phones, digital cameras, music players, and handheld computers and the benefits they serve to small business.

41639 ■ "Directors of High-Tech Incubator in Tampa, Fla., Vote to Shut Down" in *Tampa Tribune* (October 4, 2002)
Pub: Knight Ridder/Tribune Business News
Ed: Frank Witsil. Description: Profile of TechVillage Tampa Bay, a one year old high-tech incubator, announced its closing in October 2002. The incubator had a budget of $120,000, but after nine months encountered financial problems.

41640 ■ "Distributed Generation: Breaking the grid lock" in *Red Herring* (No. 103, September 1, 2001, pp. 76-77)
Pub: Herring Communications
Ed: Linda Rastelli. Description: In-depth article discussing legislation across the United States, that is working to restructure state electricity industries.

41641 ■ "Diversification, Efficiency Boosts Firm" in *San Fernando Valley Business Journal* (Vol. 11, November 2006, No. 24, pp. 23)
Pub: San Fernando Valley Business Journal Associates
Ed: Chris Coates. Description: Profile of Systech Solutions, a professional services firm that specializes in the Internet. The company's client list includes Wal-Mart.com, Disney, IHOP Corp., American Express Co., and a host of other Fortune 500 and 1000 companies.

41642 ■ "Do Your Network: Curious About How Effective Wi-Fi Adapters Are? We've Got You Covered" in *Entrepreneur* (Vol. 31, No. 7, July 2003)
Pub: Entrepreneur Media, Inc.
Ed: Amanda C. Kooser. Description: Information regarding the new 802.11g and 54 Mbps speed wireless networking tools is discussed, and whether small companies should upgrade from their current 802.11b Wi-Fi standards.

41643 ■ "Doctor's Little Helpers" in *Red Herring* **(No. 99, June 15 & July 1, 2001, pp. 50-52, 54)**
Pub: Herring Communications
Ed: Stephan Herrera. Description: Nanotechnology doesn't look so far out and flimsy for medical applications anymore. Quantum Dot, in Hayward, California and C Sixty, in Toronto, Canada are profiled.

41644 ■ "Domains of the Day: A New Domain Could Mean the Dawn of a New Mobile Age" in *Entrepreneur* **(Vol. 32, August 2004, No. 8, pp. 31)**
Pub: Entrepreneur Media Inc.
Ed: Amanda C. Kooser. Description: .mTLD, which stands for mobile Top Level Domain is a new domain suffix like .com, expressly for mobile use. Leaders like Hewlett-Packard, Microsoft, Nokia, Samsung Electronics, Sun Microsystems, T-Mobile International and Vodafone have partnered to set up a registry company to manage the new mTLD once the Internet Corporation for Assigned Names and Numbers grants approval.

41645 ■ "Don Quixote In Court" in *Forbes* **(Vol. 170, No. 8, October 14, 2002, pp. 97)**
Pub: Forbes Magazine
Ed: Ashlea Ebeling. Description: Jeff Abraham won a $15 million verdict for blowing the whistle on his employer, South Korea's Hyundai Group. Abraham reflects on his experience and questions whether he would do the same thing again.

41646 ■ "Don't chicken out in 2003" in *Red Herring* **(March 2003, pp. 70)**
Pub: Herring Communications Inc.
Ed: Arnie Berman. Description: The basic fundamentals for investing in high tech stocks are presented.

41647 ■ "Down, not out" in *Black Enterprise* **(Vol. 32, No. 7, February 2002, pp. 184)**
Pub: Earl Graves Publishing Co.
Description: Technology is hoping to make a comeback.

41648 ■ "Drives Provide New Electronics Avenue" in *Inc.* **(September 1, 2003)**
Pub: Gruner & Jahr USA Publishing
Ed: Bobbie Gossage. Description: Profile of Cornice Inc., the electronics company that uses inexpensive materials and found ways to cut assembly costs in order to design circuitry that can fit 1.5 gigabytes of storage onto a one-inch square, and sells for about $70. Their drives hold 15,000 MP3 songs.

41649 ■ "Dumars company diversifies with deal for Troy tech firm" in *Crain's Detroit Business* **(Vol. 19, No. 4, January 27, 2003, pp. 26)**
Pub: Crain Communications Inc., Detroit
Ed: Terry Kosdrosky. Description: Profile of Joe Dumars who heads up companies in the automotive supply industry and telecommunications, has just acquired the Troy-based Technical Solutions Inc., giving Detroit Technologies Inc. the capability to install telecommunications and computer software, hardware and infrastructure.

41650 ■ "Dynamic capabilities and new product development in high technology ventures" in *Journal of Business Venturing* **(Vol.15, No.3, May2000)**
Pub: Elsevier Science, Inc.
Ed: David L. Deeds, Dona DeCarolis, Joseph Coombs. Description: A new product development model was tested on a sample of pharmaceutical biotechnology companies.

41651 ■ "E-business firm spreads Influence to Ann Arbor" in *Crain's Detroit Business* **(Vol. 16, No. 33, August 14, 2000, pp. 30)**
Pub: Crain Communications, Inc.
Ed: Al Slavin. Description: St. Louis-based e-business firm Influence L.L.C., has joined Ann Arbor, Michigan's growing high-tech ranks, setting up a six-person shop. The company hopes to increase its workforce ten-fold over the next 16 months.

41652 ■ "Early Adopters' Paradise: What Else Is Popping In Tech? Plenty" in *Fortune* **(Vol. 151, January 10, 2005, No. 1, pp. 52)**
Pub: Time Inc.
Ed: Adam Lashinsky. Description: Profile of Roku HD 1000 digital medial player that allows users to display digitized photos and art on a screen, which is part of the new digital home. These new devices connect televisions, stereos, computers, and game machines throughout a household and allows for images, music and files to be swapped from machine to machine.

41653 ■ "Early Stage Deals Could Come Back" in *Venture Capital Journal* **(October 1, 2204)**
Pub: Thomason Financial Inc.
Ed: Tom York. Description: Life sciences sector is expected to see a surge in investment opportunities in 2005, which will result in turning promising technologies into new companies.

41654 ■ "Easy Router" in *Entrepreneur* **(Vol. 32, No. 2, February 2004, pp. 45)**
Pub: Entrepreneur Media, Inc.
Ed: Steve Cooper. Description: Profile of the new wireless gear by Netgear; its new WGT624 108Mbps Wireless Firewall Router offers twice the data throughput of 54Mbps 802.11 wireless routers and is as much as 10 times faster than 802.11b devices, yet maintains backward compatibility with both.

41655 ■ "EBay Ex-Operating Chief Webb Joins LiveOps As Chief Executive" in *Wall Street Journal* **(Vol. 248, December 2006, No. 145, pp. B10)**
Pub: Dow Jones & Co. Inc.
Ed: Vauhini Vara Description: Profile of Maynard Webb, former EBay Inc. chief operating officer. Webb was largely responsible for upgrading Ebay's technology to keep up with rapid growth.

41656 ■ "Economy: So much for technology's third-quarter save" in *Red Herring* **(No. 103, September 1, 2001, pp. 24)**
Pub: Herring Communications
Ed: Dan Briody. Description: A bleak forecast for the third quarter 2001 in the technology sector is discussed.

41657 ■ "Electric Avenue" in *Entrepreneur* **(Vol. 32, December 2004, No. 12, pp. 46)**
Pub: Entrepreneur Media Inc.
Ed: Jill Amadio. Description: Many high-tech features seen only in cars, are making their way into trucks as either standard features or options.

41658 ■ "Electronic Arts to Convert Some of Its Salaried Employees to Hourly Pay" in *San Jose Mercury News* **(March 10, 2005)**
Pub: Knight-Ridder/Tribune Business News
Description: Electronic Arts has transitioned some of its salaried workers to hourly wage earners. The employees will be allowed to collect overtime pay, but will no longer be eligible for company stock options or bonuses. The video game firm's move is one example of the changing nature of the tech economy since the dot-com collapse.

41659 ■ "Electronics recycling firm looks to power up $8M plant in Oakland County" in *Crain's Detroit Business* **(Vol. 19, Feb. 10, 2003)**
Pub: Crain Communications Inc., Detroit
Ed: Andrew Dietderich. Description: Construction of a new electronic-waste recycling plant in Oakland County is expected to begin soon. The plant is estimated to cost up to $8M.

41660 ■ "Elephants on a chip" in *Barron's* **(Vol. 82, No. 58, February 17, 2003, pp. T1)**
Pub: Barron's
Ed: Bill Alpert. Description: Smaller 'point solution' semiconductor firms may be pushed aside in the Texas Instruments vs. Intel battle for market share, including Broadcom, Marvell, and Intersill.

41661 ■ "End of the Road" in *Entrepreneur* **(Vol. 31, No. 8, August 2003, pp. 24)**
Pub: Entrepreneur Media, Inc.
Ed: Joshua Kurlantzick. Description: Two Department of Commerce programs, the Advanced Technology Program (ATP) and the Manufacturing Extension Partnership (MEP) may be discontinued as part of the 2004 federal budget. The ATP program assists small firms by supporting research and development, while the MEP aids manufacturers in upgrading technology and human resources.

41662 ■ "Energy Conference in Novi March 23" in *Crain's Detroit Business* **(Vol. 22, February 6, 2006, No. 6, pp. 13)**
Pub: Crain Communications Inc. - Detroit
Ed: Laura Bommarito. Description: The 2006 DTE Energy Conference and Exhibition in Partnership with The Engineering Society of Detroit will hold its one-day event on alternative energy sources and energy efficiency in Novi, Michigan at the Rock Financial Showplace March 23, 2006.

41663 ■ "Energy Firm Surges with High-Tech Utility Meters" in *Atlanta Business Chronicle* **(Vol. 26, No. 14, September 12, 2003, pp. 4A)**
Pub: American City Business Publications, Inc.
Ed: Mary Jane Credeur. Description: USI Energy Inc., Atlanta, Georgia, has reported $20 million in annual revenues from sales of its high tech utility meters; the firm, founded in 1996, is headed by Michael Anderson.

41664 ■ "Energy: The changing balance of power" in *Red Herring* **(No. 103, September 1, 2001, pp. 66)**
Pub: Herring Communications
Ed: Lee Bruno. Description: A discussion regarding the need for standards to ensure that alternative power sources, such as micropower, can easily plug into the grid, which is critical for deregulated markets to move forward.

41665 ■ "Entering a Hot Zone" in *Black Enterprise* **(Vol. 35, February 2005, No. 7, pp. 58)**
Pub: Earl G. Graves Publishing Co. Inc.
Ed: Anthony S. Calypso. Description: Philadelphia Mayor, John Street, is committed to making his city the first urban community to offer wireless, low-cost Internet access to its residents.

41666 ■ "Entrepreneur Column" in *Entrepreneur.com* **(November 20, 2006)**
Pub: Entrepreneur Media Inc.
Ed: John Williams. Description: Branding requires utilizing the proper medium to reach the target market. Use high tech approaches to brand high tech products.

41667 ■ "Entrepreneurial Event at Automation Alley Jan. 12" in *Crain's Detroit Business* **(Vol. 22, January 2, 2006, No. 1, pp. 17)**
Pub: Crain Communications Inc. - Detroit
Ed: Joanne Scharich. Description: Three emerging technology companies, IMX, Check the Crib, and Secure Crossing, are scheduled to present business plans during the fourth Entrepreneurial Initiative of Southeast Michigan. Venture capitalists, bankers, and angel investors will provide feedback after the presentations.

41668 ■ *Entrepreneurial Finance: A Casebook*
Pub: John Wiley and Sons Inc.
Ed: Paul A. Gompers; William Sahlman. Released: September 2006. Price: $63.00. Description: Investment analysis, entrepreneurial financing, harvesting, and renewal in the entrepreneurial firm are among the topics discussed.

41669 ■ *Entrepreneurial Strategies: New Technologies and Emerging Markets*
Pub: Blackwell Publishing Limited
Ed: Arnold Cooper; Sharon Alvarez; Alejandro Carrera; Luiz Mesquita; Robert Vassolo. Released: Au-

gust 2006. **Price:** $69.95. **Description:** Ideas to help a small business expand into emerging market economies (EMEs) are discussed. Despite the high failure rate, this book helps a small firm develop a successful plan.

41670 ■ *Entrepreneurship and Technology Policy*
Pub: Edward Elgar Publishing, Incorporated
Ed: Link. **Released:** August 2006. **Price:** $190.00. **Description:** Journal articles focusing how and the ways small businesses' technical contributions are affecting business. The book is divided into four parts: Government's Direct Support of R&D, Government's Leveraging of R&D, Government's Infrastructure Policies; and Knowledge Flows from Universities and Laboratories.

41671 ■ "Equity Strategies: Small caps could be the best bet for big gains" in *Red Herring* (No. 103, September 1, 2001, pp. 90-92)
Pub: Herring Communications
Ed: Beverly Goodman. **Description:** Small-cap stock indices have outperformed technology stocks and the overall market during the last two years.

41672 ■ "The Essential Tech Toolbox" in *Hispanic Business* (Vol. 23, No. 5, May 2001, pp. 38, 40)
Pub: Hispanic Business
Ed: Gina Binole. **Description:** A list of tech must-haves for the competitive business owner, including profiles of the Palm Pilot, cellular phones, Application Service Providers (ASP), firewall protection, anti-virus software, wireless local area network, wireless broadband, Web services, and P3P (privacy enhancing technology).

41673 ■ "The Ethics of Consumer Sovereignty in an Age of High Tech" in *Journal of Business Ethics* (Vol. 28, No. 1, November 1, 2000, pp. 1)
Pub: Kluwer Academic Publishers
Ed: M. Joseph Sirgy, Chenting Su. **Description:** The world of high tech is increasingly responsible for changes in the opportunity, ability, and motivation of business firms to compete. Furthermore, it is also increasingly responsible for the same motivation of consumers to engage in rational decision-making.

41674 ■ "ety8 Bluetooth Earphones: Music to Your Ears" in *Sales & Marketing Management* (Vol. 159, January-February 2007, No. 1, pp. 40)
Pub: VNU Business Media
Ed: Julia Chang. **Description:** Profile of Etymotic Research's new Bluetooth earphones with an iPod adapter, starting at $199.

41675 ■ "Executives see trouble spreading" in *The New York Times* (December 4, 2000, pp. C1)
Pub: The New York Times Company
Ed: Andrew Ross Sorkin. **Description:** The high technology industry, particularly the online, software, computer equipment, and semiconductor segments are bracing for a continued slowdown. Telecom and consulting firms are also watching for signs of retrenchment. Some executives said that recent investor-sell off had driven stock prices too low. Others said any problems were limited to particular companies, not whole industries. The computer peripherals area was held up as a bright spot. Presently there are stock bargains out there for investors willing to wait for renewed growth, and the stomach for near term uncertainty. Statistical data included.

41676 ■ "Experienced players in the new economy" in *Hispanic Business* (Vol. 22, No. 7-8, July-August 2000, pp. 40)
Pub: Hispanic Business
Ed: Joel Russell. **Description:** A directory of the top 50 Hispanic American technology businesses is presented, ranked by revenue.

41677 ■ "Extreme hunter scores big with tiny funds" in *Red Herring* (March 2003, pp. 52)
Pub: Herring Communications Inc.
Ed: Niall McKay. **Description:** Profile of Jonathan Trent, an astrobiologist at NASA. Trent discovered a breakthrough in 1991 that may revolutionize a segment of nanotechnology known as molecular manufacturing.

41678 ■ "The fabric of consumer reality" in *Red Herring* (March 2003, pp. 54)
Pub: Herring Communications Inc.
Ed: Alan Zeichick. **Description:** The economics of nanotechnology are discussed. In order for a particular consumer good to be priced competitively, the nano-scale components required must be manufactured in bulk, using techniques similar to those used in making larger-scale products.

41679 ■ "Fabricating Photons" in *Red Herring* (No. 99, June 15 & July 1, 2001, pp. 110, 112-113)
Pub: Herring Communications
Ed: Om Malik. **Description:** Optical chips will revolutionize computer networks, but it will remain on the fringe of networks until many obstacles to its commercialization are overcome.

41680 ■ "Faster Tech Transfer" in *Inc.* (July 1, 2003)
Pub: Gruner & Jahr USA Publishing
Description: Technology transfer from colleges to private sector is discussed, using examples of universities tech transfer that fueled 450 business and 4,000 licenses in 2002. Transferring innovation from college laboratories to the private sector has startups and schools arguing over licensing and royalty deals.

41681 ■ "Feel the Burn" in *Entrepreneur* (Vol. 32, August 2004, No. 8, pp. 40)
Pub: Entrepreneur Media Inc.
Ed: Amanda C. Kooser. **Description:** DVD-burner technology has become popular for small business with double-layer (DL) DVD technology being the best in terms of storage space for companies looking for a new data backup method.

41682 ■ "FEI's Strategy for Reaching Big Leagues" in *Business Journal-Portland* (Vol. 20, No. 24, August 15, 2003, pp. 1)
Pub: American City Business Journals, Inc.
Ed: Aliza Earnshaw. **Description:** Profile of FEI Company, manufacturer of three-dimensional inspection technology used in semiconductor manufacturing. The firm's goal is to have $1 billion in revenue.

41683 ■ "Finding Your Way: Navigation Systems Move Beyond High-End Cars" in *Black Enterprise* (Vol. 35, January 2005, No. 6, pp. 48)
Pub: Earl G. Graves Publishing Co. Inc.
Ed: Anthony Calypso. **Description:** Positioning system-based navigation systems are being used in commercial, mass transit, and public safety applications. Companies are offering mounted or handheld personal navigation systems for cars, laptop computers, and even PDAs.

41684 ■ "Firm is Managing Increase in Data" in *San Fernando Valley Business Journal* (Vol. 11, November 2006, No. 24, pp. 37)
Pub: San Fernando Valley Business Journal Associates
Ed: Mark R. Madler. **Description:** Profile of NovaStor Corp., a company whose demand rose almost overnight due to the need of companies needing to store larger amounts of data on servers and personal electronics gear such as the iPod.

41685 ■ "Firm Suiting Up for New Space Flights" in *San Fernando Valley Business Journal* (Vol. 12, January 2007, No. 1, pp. 12)
Pub: San Fernando Valley Business Journal Associates
Ed: Mark R. Madler. **Description:** Profile on Orbital Outfitters, a company that wants to revolutionize the

space industry by designing the next generation of space suits targeting crew and passengers for space travel through commercial and privately funded space flight. The firm also has an administrative office in Washington, D.C. to better deal with the regulations which oversee the New Space industry.

41686 ■ "Firm Wins Grant for Robotic Vehicle" in *Pittsburgh Business Times* (Vol. 23, No. 4, August 15, 2003, pp. 3)
Pub: Pittsburgh Business Times
Ed: Maria Guzzo. **Description:** A U.S. Army research grant will be used at Applied Perception Inc. to develop a robotic vehicle; topics include military research, robotic vehicles, and battlefield applications of the vehicle.

41687 ■ "Firm's New President to Push Digital Experience" in *San Fernando Valley Business Journal* (Vol. 11, November 2006, No. 24, pp. 48)
Pub: San Fernando Valley Business Journal Associates
Ed: Mark R. Madler. **Description:** Profile of Rob Hummel, entertainment industry veteran who is the new president of Dalsa Digital Cinema. Hummel's responsibility is to get the Dalsa Origin, a new digital camera, into the reluctant Hollywood market.

41688 ■ "Firms Will Spend Less on Buildings and Equipment This Year" in *Kiplinger Letter* (Vol. 78, January 19, 2007, No. 2)
Pub: Kiplinger
Description: Small business will spend about 2 percent less in building and equipment purchases in 2007. Industrial equipment, telecommunications and diesel engines will be the hardest hit.

41689 ■ "First Data: New Terminal POS Lift for Small Outfits" in *American Banker* (Vol. 172, January 17, 2006, No. 11, pp. 17)
Pub: SourceMedia, Inc.
Ed: David Breitkopf. **Description:** First Data Corporation has partnered with Microsoft Corporation and Hewlett Packard Company to devise a more complete point of sale terminal for small retailers. The terminal will accept most transactions and will track account information, track inventory, and work with customer relationship software.

41690 ■ "Flexibility drove new revenue source" in *Crain's Detroit Business* (Vol. 19, No. 13, March 31, 2003, pp. 14)
Pub: Crain Communications Inc., Detroit
Description: Founder, Mark Campbell of Stoneage. com, a Troy company, states that flexibility is the key to his successful online used-car database.

41691 ■ "Flight of Fancy? Launching a High-Tech Product Can be a Technical and Financial Challenge" in *Entrepreneur* (Vol. 32, August 2004)
Pub: Entrepreneur Media Inc.
Ed: Don Debelak. **Description:** Profile of William J. Boyer Jr. and partner and co-founder Ray Henson, who helped Boyer with the technical aspects of their digEplayer, a portable battery-operated in-flight entertainment system used on passenger tray tables. The company saw $1 millions in sales, first quarter 2004.

41692 ■ "FNC, HomeSafe Team Up" in *Mississippi Business Journal* (Vol. 29, January 2007, No. 2, pp. 19)
Pub: Venture Publications, Inc.
Description: Mississippi technology companies FNC Inc., and HomeSafe Inspection Inc. are teaming up to help provide lenders with easy access to advanced home inspection technologies.

41693 ■ "Focus remained on primary customers" in *Crain's Detroit Business* (Vol. 19, No. 13, March 31, 2003, pp. 14)
Pub: Crain Communications Inc., Detroit
Description: Profile of Troy, Michigan-based New World Systems Corporation, developer of software for public safety and public administration organizations.

41694 ■ **"For U.S. Small Biz, Fertile Soil in Europe"** in *Business Week Online* (April 3, 2002)
Pub: McGraw-Hill, Inc.
Description: This year 2002 is turning out to be a great year for many small and midsize American companies selling to or operating in Europe, especially high-tech companies.

41695 ■ **"Former B.E. 100s Clerk Faces Prison Time"** in *Black Enterprise* (Vol. 35, September 2004, No. 2, pp. 30)
Pub: Earl G. Graves Publishing Co. Inc.
Ed: Tamara E. Holmes. Description: Joanna L. Cook, former accounts payable clerk for TeleCommunication Systems Inc., pleaded guilty to one count of bank fraud for stealing more than $1 million from the company between 2000 and 2003. An assistant controller and accounting supervisor discovered her fraudulent activity.

41696 ■ **"Former Nortel VP Joins Enterprise"** in *Venture Capital Journal* (Vol. 40, No. 10, October 2000, pp. 36)
Pub: Venture Economics
Description: Enterprise Partners Venture Capital recently hired Naser Partovi as a general partner. Partovi will focus on telecommunications, specifically the optical and wireless spaces.

41697 ■ **"Forward: Patents"** in *Red Herring* (No. 99, June 15 & July 1, 2001, pp. 34-35)
Pub: Herring Communications
Ed: Stephan Herrera. Description: Overview of the biotech legal case, Festo, a recent patent-infringement decision that has fundamentally changed the balance of power that has long favored patent holders over those who deliberately or incidentally design products based on similar science.

41698 ■ **"Frank Otto Named EDO's COO"** in *Long Island Business News* (February 27, 2004)
Pub: Dolan Media Newswires
Description: Profile of Frank Otto, newly appointed COO of defense contractor, Long Island Forum for Technology.

41699 ■ **"Free Public Wireless Internet Access: Boom or Boondoggle?"** in *San Diego Business Journal* (Vol. 28, January 1, 2007, No. 1, pp. 19)
Pub: San Diego Business Journal Associates
Ed: Andy Killion. Description: The pros and cons of offering free public wireless Internet access in San Diego County, California is discussed.

41700 ■ **"Free! (With Purchase)"** in *Business 2.0* (Vol. 7, January/February 2006, No. 1, pp. 113-115)
Pub: Time, Inc.
Ed: John Battelle. Description: Profile of Scott McNealy, CEO of Sun Microsystems. McNealy is giving away software in order to sell the company's hardware.

41701 ■ **"Friends in High Places"** in *Hispanic Business* (Vol. 23, No. 7/8, July/August 2001, pp. 62, 64)
Pub: Hispanic Business
Ed: Scott Williams. Description: Profile of the newly formed Hispanic Network of Entrepreneurs. The group hopes to ease the way for a new generation of Hispanic entrepreneurs in the high-tech industry, business development, venture capital financing, recruiting and exchange of ideas.

41702 ■ **"From Cow Pies to Clean Power"** in *Business 2.0* (Vol. 7, January/February 2006, No. 1, pp. 24)
Pub: Time, Inc.
Ed: Elizabeth Esfahani. Description: Panda Energy is developing a method that converts cow dung into bio-gas fuel which would in turn power the production of ethanol.

41703 ■ **"Full-Figured Women are Avid Online Shoppers"** in *Marketing to Women* (Vol. 19, November 2006, No. 11, pp. 11)
Pub: EPM Communications, Inc.
Description: According to a study by Anderson Analytics, commissioned by lingerie retailer, GiGi's Closet, a wider range of items are purchased online by full-figured women than by women weighing less. Statistical data included.

41704 ■ **"Gadget: Why I Wi-Fi"** in *Red Herring* (No. 103, September 1, 2001, pp. 18)
Pub: Herring Communications
Ed: Rafe Needleman. Description: Useful information for setting up a wireless network is presented.

41705 ■ **"Genetic Medicine's Next Big Step"** in *Fortune* (Vol. 151, January 10, 2005, No. 1, pp. 54)
Pub: Time Inc.
Ed: John Simons. Description: RNA interference (RNAi) is a process that is able to block threatening genetic signals in diseased cells, such as those that can proliferate a virus. This process could lead to the breakthrough needed for the struggling drug industry. Profile of Alnylam Pharmaceutical in Cambridge, Massachusetts is included.

41706 ■ **"Genzyme Battles An Old Adversary"** in *Boston Globe* (January 25, 2005)
Pub: New York Times Company
Ed: Jeffrey Krasner. Description: A new battle over intellectual property has erupted between Genzyme Corporation and Transkaryotic Therapies Inc. (TKT) of Cambridge, Massachusetts. Genzyme has sued TKT claiming that the firm's method of purifying a treatment for a particular disease infringed on Genzyme's proprietary technology.

41707 ■ *The Geography of Small Firm Innovation*
Pub: Springer
Ed: Grant Black. Released: January 2005. Price: $39.95. Description: Concentration of high-tech innovation across metropolitan areas in the U.S. during the 1990s and the role geography plays in innovation.

41708 ■ **"Georgia medical device business growing"** in *Atlanta Business Chronicle* (Vol. 25, No. 19, October 18, 2002, pp. 3A)
Pub: American City Business Publications, Inc.
Ed: Julie Bryant. Description: The number of medical device companies operating in the state of Georgia currently totals more than 225, with growth centered in the small- to medium-size category. However, industry leaders in the state contend that the medical device industry has yet to take-off in the state. Many of these firms are divisions of much larger companies.

41709 ■ **"Get Lost! While You Still Can, That Is."** in *Entrepreneur* (Vol. 32, October 2004, No. 10, pp. 49)
Pub: Entrepreneur Media Inc.
Ed: Mike Hogan. Description: Global positioning system navigation displays are being offered in new cars, boats, and handheld devices. Equipment sales have doubled since 2000 to $15 billion in 2004 and are expected to reach $22 billion by 2008. Global Tracking Communications in California helps growing businesses track outbound employees and vehicles.

41710 ■ **"Get the Message? SMS Technology Could Bring Mobile Commerce Within Your Reach"** in *Entrepreneur* (Vol. 32, October 2004, No. 10)
Pub: Entrepreneur Media Inc.
Ed: Amanda C. Kooser. Description: The international popularity of mobile-commerce is spreading to the U.S. Short Message Service (SMS) enables users to send queries as text messages over a mobile phone or device and receive answers to questions without links or web pages.

41711 ■ **"Getting a Piece of the Federal Pie"** in *Hispanic Business* (Vol. 23, No. 7/8, July/August 2001, pp. 38)
Pub: Hispanic Business

Ed: Joel Russell. Description: The number of large Hispanic high-tech firms that sell to the federal government has dropped by half in the last five years.

41712 ■ **"Glam Media Launches Fashion Week Site"** in *Marketing to Women* (Vol. 19, October 2006, No. 10, pp. 5)
Pub: EPM Communications, Inc.
Description: GlamCentral.com, a website being launched by Glam Media, offers blog hosting for fashion fans and highlights fashion-related articles. The site is designed to help fashion editorial get wider exposure and focuses on coverage of New York Fashion Week.

41713 ■ **"GM Set To Unleash $3B In IT Deals"** in *Crain's Detroit Business* (Vol. 21, December 19, 2005, No. 51, pp. 1)
Pub: Crain Communications Inc. - Detroit
Ed: Andrew Dietderich. Description: General Motors Corporation announced plans for $3 Billion worth of information technology contracts to be awarded to more than 40 technology contractors and subcontracts from the Detroit area.

41714 ■ **"GM's Way Or the Highway"** in *Business Week* (December 19, 2005, No. 3964, pp. 48-49)
Pub: McGraw-Hill Companies
Ed: Steve Hamm. Description: With $15 billion in deals to discourse, General Motors is changing technology outsourcing business.

41715 ■ **"Going Medium-Tech"** in *Inc.* (Volume 27, December 2005, No. 12, pp. 77-78)
Pub: Inc. Magazine
Ed: David H. Freedman. Description: Most successful companies place themselves somewhere in the middle of technology.

41716 ■ **"Going Nuclear"** in *Business 2.0* (Vol. 6, May 2005, No. 4, pp. 90-95)
Pub: Time, Inc.
Ed: G. Pascal Zachary. Description: Randy Edington, troubleshooter for sick nuclear plants, explains how Entergy is making aging atomic power plants successful, fueling the industry's doubtful resurgence.

41717 ■ *The Google Story: Inside the Hottest Business, Media, and Technology Success of Our Time*
Pub: Random Housing Publishing Group
Ed: David A. Vise; Mark Malseed. Price: $26.00.

41718 ■ **"A Graphic Shoot-Em Up"** in *Barron's* (July 7, 2003, pp. T1)
Pub: Barron's
Ed: Bill Alpert. Description: Canada-based ATI Technologies is beating rival NVIDIA of Silicon Valley, California, in the battle for the computer graphics market, but the latter still boasts a share price more than 50 times projected earning, perplexing analysts.

41719 ■ **"Great Expectations: Think Your Business Technology Is All That and a Bag of Microchips? Well, It's Not"** in *Entrepreneur*
Pub: Entrepreneur Media Inc.
Ed: Amanda C. Kooser. Description: Upgrading technologies like radio frequency identification (RFID), computers to tablet PCs, ultrawideband (UWB), VoIP and Wi-Fi are new technologies designed to have an impact of the way business is conducted.

41720 ■ **"A grim adventure: Amphion Capital's venture fund loses all"** in *Barron's* (Vol. 82, No. 58, February 17, 2003, pp. T8)
Pub: Barron's
Ed: Eric J. Savitz. Description: Amphion's portfolio of tech stocks all collapsed in the past two years, as the fund's assets under management dropped from $91.8 million January 30, 2000 to below zero at the end of 2002. Major losses were Axcess and Biocentric Solutions.

41721 ■ "Ground Control" in *Entrepreneur* (Vol. 32, August 2004, No. 8, pp. 34)
Pub: Entrepreneur Media Inc.
Ed: Gisela M. Pedroza. **Description:** One-Touch NAP 2500 is a mobile satellite system that is mounted to the top of a vehicle. The wireless device can launch a high-speed network for up to five local computers, making it perfect for construction or field-service businesses whose employees are always changing job sites but need to be connected to the company network, Internet or IP phone service.

41722 ■ "Group Sees Window of Opportunity" in *Pittsburgh Business Times* (Vol. 23, No. 3, August 8, 2003, pp. 1)
Pub: Pittsburgh Business Times
Ed: Christopher Davis. **Description:** A new company, jointly owned by GE Plastics and Bayer Polymers, will sell a new polycarbonate glazing technology; the new company, called Exatec, will be led by CEO Clemens Kaiser.

41723 ■ "Groups Pick Up Push for Women in Tech World" in *Crain's Detroit Business* (Vol. 22, December 4, 2006, No. 49, pp. 13)
Pub: Crain Communications Inc. - Detroit
Ed: Sheena Harrison. **Description:** Local groups, such as Ann Arbor Women in Computing, assist in providing opportunities for women in the local technology industry through networking, training, scholarships, job fairs and other means.

41724 ■ "Growth Spurt: Thanks to the Spread of Bluetooth, Now Your Business Can Be As Wireless As You Want It To Be" in *Entrepreneur* (Vol. 32)
Pub: Entrepreneur Media Inc.
Ed: Amanda C. Kooser. **Description:** Bluetooth technology is being used for cell phones, computers, and digital cameras. Profiles of the Concord Eye-Q Go Wireless digital camera with built-in Bluetooth, Plantronics M2500 Bluetooth headset, Cardo Systems' always Bluetooth headset, and Logitech's MX900 Bluetooth Optical Mouse are included.

41725 ■ "The 'Guerrilla' Approach" in *Hispanic Business* (July/August 2004, pp. 28)
Pub: Hispanic Business
Ed: Anthony Limon. **Description:** Profile of Jorge Granados, owner of the Miami-based telecommunications provider Latin Node Inc. The firm listed revenue growth of 107,993 percent from 1999 to 2003.

41726 ■ "gWHIZ!: swimming through the alphabet soup of today's wireless standards" in *Entrepreneur* (Vol. 31, No. 6, June 2003, pp. 39)
Pub: Entrepreneur Media Inc.
Ed: Daniel Tynan. **Description:** By the end of 2003, products supporting combinations of wireless devices will be available. The Institute of Electrical and Electronics Engineers will finalize specification this summer enabling the Wi-Fi Alliance to begin testing and certifying the interoperability of various "g" devices.

41727 ■ "Half Pints: Wireless Routers Have the Size Advantage" in *Entrepreneur* (Vol. 33, January 2005, No. 1, pp. 42)
Pub: Entrepreneur Media Inc.
Ed: Amanda C. Kooser. **Description:** Business travelers can now access the Internet in hotel rooms via a wireless travel router. These devices are manufactured by D-Link, Netgear, SMC and 3Com.

41728 ■ "Hands-On Experience: Tech Exec Rolls Up Sleeves to Tackle Homeland Security" in *Black Enterprise* (Vol. 35, November 2004, No. 4)
Pub: Earl G. Graves Publishing Co. Inc.
Ed: Bridget McCrea. **Description:** Profile of Darryl B. Moody, creator of BearingPoint's Homeland Security Program Management Office, a project that serves as a conduit between the Department of Homeland Security and small companies offering technology solutions.

41729 ■ "Hauppauge-based Spellman High Voltage Electronics Doubles the Size of Its Bohemia Facility" in *Long Island Business News* (Jan.30,2004)
Pub: Dolan Media Newswires
Ed: Nick Anastasi. **Description:** The nation's largest independent manufacturer of high-voltage power conversion products, Spellman High Voltage Electronics Corporation, has doubled the size of its Bohemia facility. The expansion will include metal fabrication and machining divisions.

41730 ■ "Have Kid, Won't Travel" in *Fast Company* (November 2001, pp. 48)
Pub: Fast Company
Ed: Christine Canabou. **Description:** Profile of David Peterson, cofounder, CEO and chairman of the Atlanta-based North Highland Company, the management and technology consulting firm. Mr. Peterson's work force is able to drive to their client's site, rather than having to spend much of their time away from their homes and families.

41731 ■ "Health of a Nation" in *Entrepreneur* (Vol. 33, March 2005, No. 3, pp. 70)
Pub: Entrepreneur Media Inc.
Ed: Joshua Kurlantzick. **Description:** Insurance premium costs have risen 10 to 15 percent annually over the past six years for high tech firms employing young employees who are getting married and starting families.

41732 ■ "Healthcare: Information Systems Help Patients and Providers Breathe Easier" in *Microsoft Executive Circle* (Vol. 1, No. 2, Q2 2001)
Pub: Putman Media
Ed: Craig A. Shutt. **Description:** New technology is trimming costs while improving patient-physician interaction in the healthcare industry.

41733 ■ "Helping Doctors Go Digital" in *Business 2.0* (Vol. 6, July 2005, No. 6, pp. 54-55)
Pub: Time, Inc.
Ed: Erick Schonfeld. **Description:** Epocrates Essentials grew its subscriber base by offering important medical information to doctors, and in the process is able to profit from advertisers targeting the medical industry. Subscriptions to the service start at $60 annually.

41734 ■ "Hewlett-Packard leading the assault on e-waste" in *Computing Canada* (September 13, 2002, pp. 22)
Pub: Plesman Publications
Ed: Shane Schick. **Description:** Hewlett-Packard has launched a take-back equipment program in Canada that puts the company in the role of high-tech garbage collector to businesses and consumers.

41735 ■ "A Hidden Gem? Quebec Looks To Flex Muscle" in *Venture Capital Journal* (Vol. 42, No. 5, May 2002, pp. 44-45)
Pub: Thomas Venture Economics
Ed: Danielle Fugazy. **Description:** American venture capitalists have not invested much in Quebec's industry in the past, but the continuous growth Quebec is seeing in the fields of engineering, transportation, telecommunications, aeronautics and aerospace technology, medical research, computer science and biotechnology, has American VCs taking a second look.

41736 ■ "A high-tech domino effect: as dotcoms go, so go the e-commerce consultants" in *The New York Times* (December 16, 2000, pp. B1, C1)
Pub: The New York Times Company
Ed: Jonathan D. Glater. **Description:** All electronic-commerce consultant firms have suffered as a result of the weakness in the online sector. Firms like Scient Corporation and others that grew too rapidly are finding that demand for their services has evaporated, and are now having to lay off employees by the hundreds as they face a capital crunch.

41737 ■ *High-Tech Entrepreneurship: Managing Innovation in a World of Uncertainty*
Pub: Routledge Inc.
Ed: Michel Bernasconi; Simon Harris. **Released:** September 2006. **Price:** $42.95. **Description:** Profiles of successful high tech companies is included; high tech companies are driving innovation globally.

41738 ■ *High Tech, High Hope: Turning Your vision of Technology into Business Success*
Pub: John Wiley & Sons, Inc.
Ed: Paul Franson. **Released:** 1998. **Price:** $27.95 (cloth).

41739 ■ "High-tech, low-tech methods can help cut costs for training" in *Crain's Detroit Business* (Vol. 19, No. 17, April 28, 2003, pp. 12)
Pub: Crain Communications Inc., Detroit
Ed: Ian McClure. **Description:** Employee training can range from using the intranet for in-house training and testing materials, as well as tuition reimbursement for employees to attend classes. Various approaches to effectively and efficiently train employees for different types of companies are discussed.

41740 ■ "High-Tech Trade Shows" in *Sales and Marketing.com* (Vol. 147, No. 2, February 2004, pp. 12)
Pub: VNU eMedia, Inc.
Ed: Megan Sweas. **Description:** A marketing strategy by Biovail Pharmaceuticals Inc. at trade shows, is to use an interactive video game called, Race Under Pressure. The game helped to generate 900 leads at the 2003 American College of Cardiology Show, up from only 250 leads in 2002.

41741 ■ *High Technology Market Place Directory*
Pub: Princeton Hightech Group Inc.
Ed: Susan Jacob, Editor. **Released:** Annual, Latest edition November 2003. **Price:** $225, individuals. **Covers:** over 2,000 advanced technology companies in such fields as consumer electronics, robotics, telecommunication, CAD/CAM, and others. **Entries Include:** Company name, address, phone, year established, description of products and services, sales revenue and breakdown, number of employees, names of key personnel; amount of current assets and liabilities, and long-term debt, stock market membership and symbol. **Arrangement:** Classified by industry. **Indexes:** Geographical, alphabetical, product/service, ranking by revenue.

41742 ■ "High Tech's Unwavering Champion" in *Hispanic Business* (March 2002, pp. 24-26)
Pub: Hispanic Business
Ed: Derek Reveron. **Description:** Amerindo's Alberto Vilar predicts that, despite recent setbacks, the world is on the verge of another technology revolution.

41743 ■ "High-Wired Competition" in *Inc.* (November 15, 2000, pp. 26)
Pub: The Goldhirsh Group
Description: The articles tells how high-tech competitors are setting up shop in a 400,000 square-foot renovated building in New York City.

41744 ■ "Holding pattern: It's not time to go 3G quite yet" in *Entrepreneur* (Vol. 30, No. 2, February 2002, pp. 31)
Pub: Entrepreneur Media Inc.
Ed: Mike Hogan. **Description:** Plans for a 30-enabling bandwidth auction can be expected sometime in 2004 and network rollouts in 2006 when applications will be compelling enough to get customers to buy.

41745 ■ "Hollywood, Silicon Valley at odds over digital piracy bills" in *Atlanta Business Chronicle* (Vol. 25, No. 21, Nov. 1, 2002, pp. 10B)
Pub: American City Business Publications, Inc.
Ed: Kent Hoover. **Description:** H.R. 5211, a bill introduced by California Democratic Representative Howard Berman, supports copyright owners in their efforts to stop unauthorized use of online music and movie materials. The bill permits copyright owners to use hacking as long as computer files are not damaged.

41746 ■ "The Holy Wafer" in *Red Herring* **(No. 99, June 15 & July 1, 2001, pp. 106-107)**
Pub: Herring Communications
Ed: Alan Zeichick. **Description:** Alan Zeichick, principal technology analysts with Camden Associates, explains how a single silicon water is transformed into the hundreds of microchips that make up an integrated circuit, including step-by-step illustrations.

41747 ■ "Hook up" in *Entrepreneur* **(Vol. 30, No. 1, January 2002, pp. 43)**
Pub: Entrepreneur Media Inc.
Ed: Mike Hogan. **Description:** Profile of the Belkin USB 10/100 Ethernet Adapter that provides instant network access for any desktop or laptop with a USB port.

41748 ■ "Hospitals Across Long Island Shift to Digital Imaging Technology" in *Long Island Business News* **(February 20, 2004)**
Pub: Dolan Media Newswires
Ed: Claude Solnik. **Description:** In order to speed up and improve service, Long Island hospitals are changing over to digital imaging technology that allows doctors to view x-rays from home and confirm diagnoses with radiologists at the hospital.

41749 ■ "The Hot List" in *Black Enterprise* **(Vol. 34, No. 5, December 2003)**
Pub: Earl Graves Publishing Co.
Ed: Tanisha A. Sykes, Robert Anthony, Siobhan Benet, Cliff Hocker, Tamara Holmes, Alan Hughes, Tykisha Lundy, Christina Morgan, Mayra R. Payne, Marcia Wade. **Description:** Highlights of 50 entrepreneurs and professionals under the age of 40 at the top of their field are presented.

41750 ■ "House Wants Bigger Business-Tax Cut" in *Crain's Detroit Business* **(Vol. 21, October 31, 2005, No. 44, pp. 6)**
Pub: Crain Communications Inc. - Detroit
Ed: Amy Lane. **Description:** A new plan that would heighten and accelerate business tax-cuts was passed by the Senate in October 2005. The plan would use $700 million to support growth and technology-oriented businesses while $300 million would go to programs that support life-sciences, emerging technology and related sectors.

41751 ■ "Houston-Based ChaseCom L.P." in *Black Enterprise* **(Vol. 35, December 2004, No. 5, pp. 38)**
Pub: Earl G. Graves Publishing Co. Inc.
Ed: Malik Singleton. **Description:** ChaseCom LP in Houston, Texas has opened a new call center in Fort Smith, Arkansas creating 140 jobs paying $8 to $12 per hour. The firm provides telecom services and customer support.

41752 ■ "Houston Leads Research in Superconducting Wire" in *Houston Business Journal* **(Vol. 34, No. 7, June 27, 2003, pp. 27A)**
Pub: American City Business Journals
Ed: Andrew P. Coleman. **Description:** The University of Houston has brought in $300 million in 15 years in grants for technology research.

41753 ■ "How microturbines generate megawatts" in *Red Herring* **(No. 103, September 1, 2001, pp. 72-73)**
Pub: Herring Communications
Ed: Alan Zeichick. **Description:** An explanation of the technology that goes into microturbines, which allow for small, self-contained power generators that are quickly proving a viable means of supplying electricity.

41754 ■ "How do you narrow your product options?" in *Wall Street Journal* **(March 17, 2003, pp. R3)**
Pub: Dow Jones & Co. Inc.
Ed: Carl Bialik. **Description:** Profile of DNA-testing device developers Kalyan Handique and Sundaresh Brahmasandra and the founders of HandyLab Inc.

41755 ■ "How to Ride the Fifth Wave" in *Business 2.0* **(Vol. 6, July 2005, No. 6, pp. 78-83, 85)**
Pub: Time, Inc.
Ed: Michael V. Copeland, Om Malik. **Description:** Affordable computing, infinite bandwidth, and open standards are driving an epic technological transformation expected to create new tech opportunities, as well as problems for those who are not able to adapt to the changes.

41756 ■ "How to identify your enemies before they destroy you" in *Harvard Business Review* **(Vol. 80, No. 10, October 2002, pp. 115)**
Pub: Harvard Business School Press
Ed: Paul J. Farshad. **Description:** Genuine threats to an established business are discussed, including the tools necessary to determine what emerging technologies constitute disruptive innovations and must be addressed and which technologies can be ignored.

41757 ■ "I Tune, You Tune" in *Forbes* **(Vol. 175, January 31, 2005, No. 2, pp. 60)**
Pub: Forbes Magazine Inc.
Ed: Chana R. Schoenberger. **Description:** Profile of Jonathan Axelrod and Robert Khedouri, who hope to launch MusicGremlin in 2005. The firm will offer the first mobile music subscription service.

41758 ■ "I Want My Cell TV" in *Entrepreneur.com* **(Vol. 34, February 2006, No. 2, pp. 42)**
Pub: Entrepreneur Media Inc.
Ed: Mike Hogan. **Description:** Vodcasts can be made with any videocam or even some cellular phones. Open Media Network offers free distribution and MPEG Nation charges $5 to host a video for six months. FilmLoop and Pic2Vid allow users to build a video using digital pictures and a voice-over.

41759 ■ *IBM on Demand Technology for the Growing Business: How to Optimize Your Computing Environment for Today and Tomorrow*
Pub: Maximum Press
Ed: Jim Hoskins. **Released:** June 2005. **Price:** $29.95. **Description:** IBM is offering computer solutions to small companies entering the On Demand trend in business.

41760 ■ "IBM Unveils Intel-Based Servers to Improve Business Security and Efficiency" in *Internet Wire* **(February 14, 2005)**
Pub: COMTEX News Network Inc.
Description: IBM has introduced five servers based on Intel's 64-bit Xeon DP processor. These new systems offer clients more control over their processing power and help them manage their options for and secure their systems against the threat of intrusion and instability.

41761 ■ *ICTs and SMEs Antecedents and Consequences of Technology Adoption*
Pub: Edward Elgar Publishing, Incorporated
Ed: Ordanini. **Released:** November 2006. **Price:** $85.00. **Description:** Issues involving information communication technology adoption among small and medium-sized firms are discussed.

41762 ■ "If BlackBerry Gets Smushed..." in *Business Week* **(January 9, 2006, No. 3966, pp. 16)**
Pub: McGraw-Hill Companies
Ed: Stephen H. Wildstrom. **Description:** Alternatives to using BlackBerry email services are discussed in the event of the service being shut down by patent infringement charges. GoodLink from Good Technology offers similar services as does Microsoft with its Exchange email system which is being upgraded.

41763 ■ "The Importance of Well-Crafted Terms" in *Law Firm Inc.* **(August 2004)**
Pub: American Lawyer Media LP
Ed: Mark Hanchet, Edward Hansen. **Description:** Agreements involving complex technology relationships should be negotiated and drafted with the idea of avoiding future litigation because of the long-term partnerships they create. These contracts cover such issues as outsourcing and enterprise resources planning (ERP) licensing and implementation agreements; risk avoidance, scope of services, service levels and cost need to be agreed upon before the contract is signed.

41764 ■ "In Hub, biotech discoveries outpace demand" in *Boston Business Journal* **(Vol. 22, No. 15, May 17, 2002, pp. 1)**
Pub: MCP, Inc.
Ed: Allison Connolly. **Description:** Many technologies in Boston and Cambridge, including medical laboratories are awaiting commercial development and the supply of potential new products much greater than the demand creating cautious venture capital investors.

41765 ■ "Increased Spending, Shakeout Seen in IT Industry" in *Crain's Detroit Business* **(Vol. 21, January 31, 2005, No. 5, pp. 22)**
Pub: Crain Communications Inc. - Detroit
Ed: Andrew Dietderich. **Description:** Increased tech spending in Michigan has spurred dozens of mergers and acquisitions in the technology sector. Market research firms estimate an increase in tech spending for 2005 between 6 and 9 percent.

41766 ■ *Information Technology for the Small Business: How to Make IT Work For Your Company*
Pub: TAB Computer Systems, Incorporated
Ed: T.J. Benoit. **Released:** June 2006. **Price:** $17.95. **Description:** Basics of information technology to help small companies maximize benefits are covered. Topics include pitfalls to avoid, email and Internet use, data backup, recovery and overall IT organization.

41767 ■ "Injector Gadget" in *Inc.* **(February 1, 2002)**
Pub: Inc. Magazine
Ed: Mike Hofman. **Description:** Profile of new category of medical devices designed to take the pain out of administering medications and vaccines by replacing speed for sharpness is presented.

41768 ■ "Inking Up: Now Coming to a Printer Near You-Files From a Cell Phone or PDA" in *Entrepreneur* **(Vol. 31, No. 7, July 2003, pp. 37)**
Pub: Entrepreneur Media, Inc.
Ed: Mike Hogan. **Description:** Nokia and other cell phone and handset makers are equipping models to read email, contact lists and photos to network printers or to infrared- or Bluetooth-enabled printers.

41769 ■ "Innotrac tries to get back on track after telecom woes" in *Atlanta Business Chronicle* **(Vol. 25, November 29, 2002, No. 25, pp. 3A)**
Pub: American City Business Publications, Inc.
Ed: Mary Jane Credeur. **Description:** Innotrac Corporation has suffered financially as telecommunications firms cut costs to make up for reduced demand in services. The company posted a 36 percent decline in revenue for the first nine months of 2002 compared to the same period in 2001.

41770 ■ *Innov and Entrepren in Biotech*
Pub: Edward Elgar Publishing, Incorporated
Ed: Hine. **Released:** April 2006. **Price:** $100.00. **Description:** Innovation processes underlying successful entrepreneurship in the biotechnology sector are explored.

41771 ■ "Inside Intel" in *Business Week* **(January 9, 2006, No. 3966, pp. 46-52, 54)**
Pub: McGraw-Hill Companies
Ed: Cliff Edwards. **Description:** Profile of Paul Otellini, CEO of Intel Corporation. Otellini is taking the computer chipmaker into sectors such as consumer electronics, wireless communications, and health care.

41772 ■ "Intel Inside: The Chips Get Hot" in *Barron's* **(August 25, 2003, pp. T1)**
Pub: Barron's
Ed: Bill Alpert. **Description:** Growing demand for Intel's market-leading Pentium microprocessors has moved the company to project an 11-percent increase for third quarter sales. Investors welcomed the news by bidding Intel's share price up a dollar, or nearly 4 percent, to more than $27/share.

41773 ■ "Internet To Go" in *Kiplinger's Personal Finance Magazine* **(Vol. 54, No. 12, December 2000, pp. 150)**
Pub: The Kiplinger Washington Editors, Inc.
Ed: Michael Martinez, Kathy Jones. **Description:** Most devices that link you wirelessly to the Web are often clunky and limited in their features.

41774 ■ "InterWest Fund VIII Nears $750M Mark" in *Venture Capital Journal* **(Vol. 40, No. 10, October 2000, pp. 16)**
Pub: Venture Economics
Description: InterWest Partners is aiming for a post-Labor Day final close on $750 million for the firm's latest vehicle, InterWest Partners VIII. The fund will back companies in the telecommunications/ communications infrastructure space, medical technology and the Internet economy.

41775 ■ "Invention: Scientist puts circuits on paper" in *Red Herring* **(No. 102, August 15, 2001, pp. 25)**
Pub: Herring Communications
Ed: Avi Machlis. **Description:** Profile of Andrew Shipway, the scientist who invented the patent-pending process which allows electrical circuits to be created using a standard laser printer.

41776 ■ "Investor: Earnings projections for technology are still too lofty" in *Red Herring* **(No. 103, September 1, 2001, pp. 82-83)**
Pub: Herring Communications
Ed: J.P. Vicente. **Description:** Predictions that technology earnings will not return to the high levels seen in 2000 until 2004, at the earliest.

41777 ■ "Irby Buys Two Companies" in *Mississippi Business Journal* **(Vol. 29, January 2007, No. 4, pp. 8)**
Pub: Venture Publications, Inc.
Ed: Wally Northway **Description:** Stuart C. Irby Co., a subsidiary of Sonepar USA acquires Burmeister Electric Co. and High Voltage Testing Laboratories. Profiles of both acquired companies included.

41778 ■ "The Iridian Authenticam" in *PC Magazine* **(February 6, 2001, pp. 26)**
Pub: Ziff-Davis Publishing Company
Ed: Sally Wiener Grotta. **Description:** Iridian Technologies holds key patents on iris recognition technology. The Authenticam is a computer-tethered camera that takes a picture of a person's iris from a distance of 18-20 inches. The image is then analyzed and compared to a database to determine an individual's authorization level.

41779 ■ "The I's Have It: A More Secure Wireless Standard Is On Its Way" in *Entrepreneur* **(Vol. 32, November 2004, No. 11, pp. 59)**
Pub: Entrepreneur Media Inc.
Ed: Amanda C. Kooser. **Description:** The new standard 802.11i protects data with one of the strongest types of encryption to date.

41780 ■ "It Even Makes Calls!" in *Fortune* **(Vol. 151, January 10, 2005, No. 1, pp. 55)**
Pub: Time Inc.
Ed: Stephanie N. Mehta. **Description:** Advances in technology have brought about cellular phones that can take pictures, browse the Internet, send email messages, play MP3 music files, record short videos, as well as making telephone calls.

41781 ■ "IT Risk Assessment: Who Needs It?" in *Ingram's* **(Vol. 29, No. 7, July 2003, pp. 23)**
Pub: Show Me Publishing, Inc.

Ed: Scott Brouillette. **Description:** Businesses that fail to embrace technology put themselves at a disadvantage. However, companies that fail to plan for implementing information technology and related government regulations could suffer financially.

41782 ■ "It's Alive! New Software You Play Dr. Frankenstein" in *Black Enterprise* **(Vol. 35, November 2004, No. 4, pp. 64)**
Pub: Earl G. Graves Publishing Co. Inc.
Ed: Schuyler K. Esprit. **Description:** Review of Peter Plantec's book, Virtual Humans: Creating the Illusion Personality. The book is a resource for graphic designers, scientific researchers, students, technophobes and is accompanied by a CD-ROM that allows the user to build a virtual character.

41783 ■ "It's a Team Thing" in *Black Enterprise* **(Vol. 35, December 2004, No. 5, pp. 67)**
Pub: Earl G. Graves Publishing Co. Inc.
Ed: Bridget McCrea. **Description:** Larry Sheffield's ability to build and motivate teams in NEC's Solutions Platform Group is examined. Sheffield oversees the company's 200 employees in the firm's mobile solutions, software, server, advanced optical, customer and high-performance computing divisions.

41784 ■ "Jadi's Journey; Move to OU Incubator Could Lead to Funding" in *Crain's Detroit Business* **(Vol. 22, January 9, 2006, No. 2, pp. 3)**
Pub: Crain Communications Inc. - Detroit
Ed: Sheena Harrison. **Description:** Jadi Inc. should receive $3 million in grants and federal funding for its new navigation systems for military robots. The firm has moved into the SmartZone Business Incubator at Oakland University in Michigan.

41785 ■ "Jazzin' Up the Chips" in *Red Herring* **(No. 99, June 15 & July 1, 2001, pp. 118)**
Pub: Herring Communications
Ed: Scott Tyler Shafer. **Description:** Profile of Jazio, developer of technology that allows faster chip-to-chip communications.

41786 ■ "JCJC, SMG Partner" in *Mississippi Business Journal* **(Vol. 29, January 2007, No. 4, pp. 9)**
Pub: Venture Publications, Inc.
Ed: Wally Northway **Description:** Jones County Junior College began a unique partnership with local area high-tech business Service Management Group, Inc. SMG will train sophomore computer information systems technology students at JCJC and transition them to full-time SMG employees after graduation from JCJC.

41787 ■ "Job Market Thaw" in *Sales and Marketing.com* **(Vol. 156, No. 3, March 2004, pp. 24)**
Pub: VNU eMedia, Inc.
Description: Future job market trends for ten different industries are examined. The ten featured industries include construction, energy, financial services, healthcare/pharmaceutical, hospitality/travel, real estate, services, technology, telecommunications, and transportation.

41788 ■ "John Ladaga" in *Hispanic Business* **(January/February 2005, pp. 56)**
Pub: Hispanic Business
Description: Profile of John Ladaga, vice president and general manager service delivery for EDS America discusses his company's diversity program in detail.

41789 ■ "JP Morgan Rolls Out Tech-Heavy Branches" in *Houston Business Journal* **(Vol. 34, No. 8, July 4, 2003, pp. 1)**
Pub: American City Business Journals
Ed: Jim Greer. **Description:** JP Morgan Chase and Company has opened two new prototype banks in the Houston, Texas area equipped with Internet kiosks, video tellers, and plasma screens, all in order to bring in customers. Tim Olmstead, representative of the company states that the company is building the bank branch of the future.

41790 ■ "Just a Little Bit Public" in *Inc.* **(August 2005, pp. 32, 34)**
Pub: Inc. Magazine
Ed: Jennifer Gill. **Description:** Private placements are on the rise as the stock market falters. Private placement expert, Mike Haider, CEO of BioE has raised $22.5 million from investors.

41791 ■ "Just the Tiqit" in *Red Herring* **(January 2003, pp. 26)**
Pub: Herring Communications Inc.
Ed: Dean Takahashi. **Description:** Profile of Tiqit Computers, a Silicon Valley startup, developing a PC into a device that could fit into a pants pocket.

41792 ■ "Ka-Boom! Looks Like the Economy is Finally Growing-And Guess What's Leading the Way?" in *Entrepreneur* **(Vol. 32, August 2004)**
Pub: Entrepreneur Media Inc.
Ed: Mike Hogan. **Description:** Technology is being credited as the catalyst for the growing economy in the U.S., which averaged 5.5 percent growth over the last two years. The U.S. Bureau of Labor Statistics expects continued growth in the economy at the rate of about 4 percent or more in 2005.

41793 ■ "Keep it Simple" in *Entrepreneur. com* **(Vol. 34, February 2006, No. 2, pp. 60)**
Pub: Entrepreneur Media Inc.
Ed: Chris Penttila. **Description:** Twenty-five tips for fine tuning a small business are outlined, focusing on technology, money, banking, taxes, credit and collection, accounting systems, mergers, management, and marketing ideas.

41794 ■ "Keeping America safe" in *Black Enterprise* **(Vol. 32, No. 5, Decembe)**
Pub: Earl Graves Publishing Co.
Ed: Michelle Buckley. **Description:** Profile of Reginald Daniel and his 1996 startup, Scientific & Engineering Solutions Information Technology consulting firm. Daniel was designated this year's Ernst & Young's IT Consulting Entrepreneur of the Year from Maryland, and National Black Chamber of Commerce name him Entrepreneur of the Year.

41795 ■ "Keeping It Together: Maryland Family's Home is a Hub of Tech Activity" in *Black Enterprise* **(Vol. 35, November 2004, No. 4, pp. 66)**
Pub: Earl G. Graves Publishing Co. Inc.
Ed: Rebecca Rohan. **Description:** Profile of Hollins Riley, owner of a managed care consulting firm and his wife Diana who started her own travel center. The couple uses a wireless network through a broadband provider.

41796 ■ "Keeping Their Options Open" in *Boston Business Journal* **(Vol. 23, No. 26, August 1, 2003, pp. 3)**
Pub: American City Business Journals
Description: Profile of Boston, Massachusetts-based Progressive Software Inc., including an examination of Boston-area technology companies as highlighted by the plight of Progressive Software Inc. Topics include economic conditions, competition, and financial management.

41797 ■ "KFC Forms Moms' Advisory Board" in *Marketing to Women* **(Vol. 19, October 2006, No. 10, pp. 3)**
Pub: EPM Communications, Inc.
Description: Kentucky Fried Chicken has formed an advisory board, KFC Moms Matter, to consul the company on how it can best meet mother's needs. The board consists of employees who are mothers as well as moms recruited from across the country.

41798 ■ "Kiss Privacy Goodbye" in *Fortune* **(Vol. 151, January 10, 2005, No. 1, pp. 55)**
Pub: Time Inc.
Ed: Peter H. Lewis. **Description:** Surveillance devices aimed at humans are being developed at historical rates. These devices can be anything ranging from lasers that monitor members of a crowd for abnormal

vital signs, to biometric scanners that find individual travelers from a distance and link them to commercial or governmental databases. The Biometric Group, a consulting company, predicts worldwide sales and licensing of fingerprinting, facial recognition, and other biometic devices to increase to more than $1.8 billion in 2005 and $4.8 billion by 2008.

41799 ■ "Landlords keep on plugging" in *San Francisco Business Times* **(Vol. 16, No. 42, May 24, 2002, pp. 3)**
Pub: San Francisco Business Times Inc.
Ed: Steve Ginsberg. **Description:** Bay Area commercial real estate landlords are offering incentives such as free furniture to gain tenants. Carr America Realty Corporation's efforts, high technology industry sublessor's needs, and other aspects of the market are discussed.

41800 ■ "Laser 'Breakthrough': Changing the Silicon Game" in *San Jose Mercury News* **(March 7, 2005)**
Pub: Knight-Ridder/Tribune Business News
Ed: Dean Takahashi. **Description:** Mario Paniccia discusses the continuous wave silicon laser being developed by him and his team of researchers at Intel. The laser could launch a new stage in electronics.

41801 ■ "Laser Business Fails to Shine" in *Orlando Business Journal* **(Vol. 20, No. 5, July 18, 2003, pp. 1)**
Pub: American City Business Journals, Inc.
Ed: Chad Eric Watt. **Description:** Information about Orlando, Florida-based Electro Optics' failure to land a military contract for development and production of military lasers.

41802 ■ "Law Firms Beef Up Extranets to Handle Complex Deals" in *Crain's Detroit Business* **(Vol. 23, January 29, 2007, No. 5, pp. 26)**
Pub: Crain Communications Inc. - Detroit
Ed: Robert Ankeny. **Description:** Virtual private computer networks eliminate multiple copies and shipping in complex legal and real estate deals. Documents can be displayed in War rooms with multiple parties exchanging information simultaneously. Huge savings in copying and shipping of paper copies are realized.

41803 ■ "Leading the Pack" in *Black Enterprise* **(Vol. 34, No. 4, November 2003, pp. 82)**
Pub: Earl Graves Publishing Co.
Ed: Marcia A. Wade. **Description:** The winners of the Black Enterprise Small Business Awards were announced at the 2003 Black Enterprise/Microsoft Entrepreneurs Conference in May. Among the winners were: John Sterling of Synch-Solutions Inc., Colleen Payne-Nabors of Mobile Cardiac Imaging LLC, Orlando Robinson of D&D Innovations Inc., and Kenya James of Blackgirl Magazine. Kenya is a 14-year-old entrepreneur publishing a magazine to improve the self-esteem of young women across the nation.

41804 ■ "Leading the Way" in *Black Enterprise* **(Vol. 35, February 2005, No. 7, pp. 57)**
Pub: Earl G. Graves Publishing Co. Inc.
Ed: Bridget McCrea. **Description:** Profile of Lisa Williams, one of a few African American women leaders in the high-tech logistics and supply management field. Williams' firm conducts original research and offers technology services to help clients move information, goods, and capital within and between organizations.

41805 ■ "Legislature considers energy tax breaks" in *Crain's Detroit Business* **(Vol. 18, No. 16, April 22, 2002, pp. 23)**
Pub: Crain Communications Inc. - Detroit
Ed: Amy Lane. **Description:** New corporate tax breaks for alternative energy technologies could head for Michigan's State Legislature soon.

41806 ■ "Let Your Fingers Do the Locking: Forgotten That Password?" in *Fortune* **(Vol. 151, January 24, 2005, No. 2, pp. 42)**
Pub: Time Inc.

Ed: Peter Lewis. **Description:** Profile of the new technology that allows users to access computers with fingerprint-reading devices. American Power Conversion, Sony, IBM, and other firms have developed password-management devices that can act as a lock and key for encrypting specific files and folders on a computer.

41807 ■ "Life Sciences Industry Outlook" in *Ingram's* **(Vol. 28, No. 6, June 2002, pp. 65)**
Pub: Show Me Publishing, Inc.
Description: The life sciences industry in Kansas City, Missouri is profiled. Topics covered include media aspects, industry funding, workforce issues, collaboration, and commercialization.

41808 ■ "Lightning Speed" in *Entrepreneur* **(Vol. 28, No. 3, March 2000, pp. 26)**
Pub: Entrepreneur Media Inc.
Ed: Gene Koprowski. **Description:** DSL's are quickly growing in popularity among cost-conscious businesses, according to a report by Cahners h-Stat Group, a leading industry research firm.

41809 ■ "Listen Up! Get the Scoop on Bluetooth Headsets With This Guide" in *Entrepreneur.com* **(Vol. 34, February 2006, No. 2, pp. 34)**
Pub: Entrepreneur Media Inc.
Ed: Amanda C. Kooser. **Description:** Profile of the new Bluetooth m9obile phone headset. The Essentials Network features a guide that helps individuals choose the headset suited to them.

41810 ■ "Local Investors Eye Chip Plant" in *Orlando Business Journal* **(Vol. 20, No. 11, August 29, 2003, pp. 1)**
Pub: American City Business Journals, Inc.
Ed: Chad Eric Watt. **Description:** Profile of Bill Cochrane, a former research and development vice president at Agere Systems Inc., has joined with others in an effort to buy and reopen Agere Systems Inc, a microchip factory in Orlando, Florida.

41811 ■ "Local ISPs NAS, Open Access Join Forces" in *Bellingham Business Journal* **(January 2007, pp. A6)**
Pub: Sun News Inc.
Description: Local Internet service providers, OpenAccess ad Network Access Services, Inc., have recently joined forces.

41812 ■ "Long Island Banks Upgrade IT to Improve Service, Sales" in *Long Island Business News* **(February 13, 2004)**
Pub: Dolan Media Newswires
Ed: Claude Solnik. **Description:** Many banks, including Astoria, have redesigned computer hardware and software to create a single system whereby tellers and customer services representatives can obtain a customer's complete profile. The new system will improve a company's ability to cross-sell products and make follow-up calls.

41813 ■ "Long-Term Technology" in *Black Enterprise* **(Vol. 34, No. 4, November 2003, pp. 34)**
Pub: Earl Graves Publishing Co.
Ed: Nicole Lewis. **Description:** Financial managers for the Philadelphia Public Employee Retirement System has used a long-term approach to investing and maintains the fund's allocation in technology without changes.

41814 ■ "Long in the Tooth" in *Red Herring* **(January 2003, pp. 72)**
Pub: Herring Communications Inc.
Ed: Duff McDonald. **Description:** Statistical information regarding the November 2001 rally, especially in the tech sector, is presented.

41815 ■ "Look to the Future" in *Atlanta Business Chronicle* **(Vol. 25, No. 20, October 25, 2002, pp. 1)**
Pub: American City Business Publications, Inc.
Ed: Tonya Layman. **Description:** Phase 1 of the High Museum of Art expansion in Atlanta, Georgia's Midtown corridor will be completed in 2005. This expansion will join Georgia Tech's new Technology Square, along with the new Centergy office development, slated to be completed in August 2003.

41816 ■ "Look for a Sign" in *Entrepreneur* **(Vol. 31, No. 8, August 2003, pp. 44)**
Pub: Entrepreneur Media, Inc.
Ed: Mike Hogan. **Description:** Information on Wi-Fi hot spots is discussed. Storefronts offering the service will feature the Wi-Fi ZONE logo, which means a firm has agreed to meet certain standards of service and security set by the Wi-Fi Alliance, an independent association located in Mountain View, California. The alliance certifies 802.11 product interoperability.

41817 ■ "Looking for Leverage" in *Hispanic Business* **(Vol. 23, No. 5, May 2001, pp. 32, 34, 36)**
Pub: Hispanic Business
Ed: Scott Williams. **Description:** Companies looking to grow have a variety of high-tech options. Advice is given from Omni/Strat, a Miami-based consulting firm that helps companies leverage technology to improve customer relationships, business intelligence, and e-commerce. The Web Head Group, located in San Antonio, Texas, also offers technology advice to small businesses.

41818 ■ "The Lookout: It's time to play some war games" in *Red Herring* **(No. 103, September 1, 2001, pp. 94)**
Pub: Herring Communications
Ed: Paul R. LaMonica. **Description:** Profile of CACI International, an information technology company whose number one customer was the U.S. Department of Defense. The article discusses the firm's successful initiatives to diversify.

41819 ■ "LPs Give Redpoint $1.25B Green Light" in *Venture Capital Journal* **(Vol. 40, No. 10, October 2000, pp. 16, 17)**
Pub: Venture Economics
Description: Redpoint Ventures announced in August that it held a $1.25 billion final close on its second investment vehicle. The fund will focus on the type of Internet infrastructure plays that make up approximately 60 percent of Redpoint's current investments.

41820 ■ "The Lure of Bay State Technology" in *Boston Globe* **(February 7, 2005)**
Pub: New York Times Company
Ed: Robert Weisman. **Description:** Overseas investors are seeking acquisitions in Massachusetts, focusing on the state's high-technology and life sciences start-ups. Two deals are presented.

41821 ■ "M/C Venture Partners Close on $550M" in *Venture Capital Journal* **(Vol. 40, No. 10, November 2000, pp. 24, 26)**
Pub: Venture Economics
Description: M/C Venture Partners will us its latest vehicle, M/C Venture Partners V LP, to back nearly 30 companies with average initial investments between $15-$20 million. The firm will target early-stage communications services and information technology services companies, splitting capital evenly between the two sectors.

41822 ■ "M-protection" in *Entrepreneur* **(Vol. 30, No. 1, January 2002, pp. 40)**
Pub: Entrepreneur Media Inc.
Ed: Mike Hogan. **Description:** Most wireless devices lack the power to accommodate traditional desktop security algorithms, many companies are developing new, lighter data encryption algorithms suited to these devices.

41823 ■ "A Macro View at Microsoft" in *Hispanic Business* **(January/February 2005, pp. 24, 26, 28)**
Pub: Hispanic Business
Ed: Judi Erickson. **Description:** Orlando Ayala is targeting small and mid-size companies around the world to increase the global reach of technology firm Microsoft. Orlando discusses marketing strategies for selling Microsoft Business Solutions worldwide.

41824 ■ "Madler: Local Venues Replace Exotic Locales" in *San Fernando Valley Business Journal* **(Vol. 12, January 2007, No. 2, pp. 43)**
Pub: San Fernando Valley Business Journal Associates

Ed: Mark R. Madler. **Description:** Highlights of the Consumer Electronics Show in Las Vegas include high definition products such as broadband cell phones that allow downloading of video, ultra mobile PC's, and new equipment such as monitors that are capable of showing imagery in 3D without the need for special glasses.

41825 ■ "Making it" in *Wall Street Journal* **(Dec. 9, 2002, pp. R5)**
Pub: Dow Jones & Co. Inc.
Ed: Erin Schulte. **Description:** Home crafting has found its way to the Web, and that means small craft businesses are taking advantage of the Internet.

41826 ■ "A Man's World?" in *Entrepreneur* **(Vol. 31, No. 8, August 2003, pp. 26)**
Pub: Entrepreneur Media, Inc.
Ed: Aliza Pilar Sherman. **Description:** Interview with three women entrepreneurs examining the challenges women entrepreneurs face in today's marketplace. The panel consisted of Cristi Cristich, CEO and founder of Cristek Interconnects Inc., maker of connectors and cabling for medical and military applications; Sheri L. Parrack, president and CEO of Texas Motor Transportation Consultants, a professional registration, tax and title service company; and Terrie Jones, owner of AGSI, a provider of information technology resource solutions.

41827 ■ "Manufacturing: Industrial Strength Integration" in *Microsoft Executive Circle* **(Vol. 1, No. 2, Q2 2001, pp. 56-58)**
Pub: Putman Media
Ed: Marty Weil. **Description:** The Internet has forced manufacturers to rethink business in order to stay competitive. One global chemical maker handles 4.5 million transactions every month with a 2-3 second response time using the Internet to transact business.

41828 ■ "Market Drifts While Tech Stocks Wilt" in *Barron's* **(August 11, 2003, pp. MW3)**
Pub: Barron's
Ed: Vito J. Racanelli. **Description:** Stock markets, which seemed willing to rally on the thinnest of premises in the second quarter, now appear resolved to stagnate despite genuinely positive indicators. Factory orders increased nearly 2 percent in June, while labor productivity gained almost 6 percent.

41829 ■ "Marriage of Expedience" in *Red Herring* **(No. 99, June 15 & July 1, 2001, pp. 108)**
Pub: Herring Communications
Ed: Bridget Eklund. **Description:** University of California Berkeley Professor Dave Patterson, is developing a chip called intelligent random access memory (IRAM), which will connect a microprocessor and a memory chip to improve speed and efficiency.

41830 ■ "Mechanically inclined" in *Entrepreneur* **(Vol. 31, No. 4, April 2003, pp. 168)**
Pub: Entrepreneur Media Inc.
Ed: April Y. Pennington. **Description:** Profile of Colin Angle, Helen Greiner, and Rod Brooks, co-founders of iRobot, a firm started with technology but no product.

41831 ■ "Med Tech Carl Goldfischer" in *Venture Capital Journal* **(January 1, 2005)**
Pub: Thomason Financial Inc.
Description: According to Carl Goldfischer, managing director at Bay City Capital, the best thing that could happen to the medical device market in 2005 is that large and small companies continue creating new products that improve disease management.

41832 ■ "The microbe warrior. (Bioterrorism)" in *Red Herring* **(January 2003, pp. 58)**
Pub: Herring Communications Inc.
Ed: Suzanne McGee. **Description:** Profile AgION Technologies, the company developing products financed from the Homeland Security Fund. The firm's products show great promise in the areas of national security, intelligence, or military applications.

41833 ■ "Microchip Delays Start in Gresham" in *Business Journal-Portland* **(Vol. 20, No. 22, August 1, 2003, pp. 1)**
Pub: American City Business Journals, Inc.
Ed: Aliza Earnshaw. **Description:** Profile of Microchip Technology Inc. and production delays being encountered, as well as competition, production management, and market conditions.

41834 ■ "Microeconomics" in *Red Herring* **(No. 103, September 1, 2001, pp. 73)**
Pub: Herring Communications
Ed: Ronald Recinto. **Description:** Although compatibility issues have slowed the adoption of microturbines in the United States, growth in the global markets looks promising.

41835 ■ "Military Now One of the Big Guns in Tech Financing" in *Washington Business Journal* **(Vol. 22, No. 16, August 22, 2003, pp. 30)**
Pub: Washington Business Journal
Ed: Roger Hughlett. **Description:** Sentel, Alexandria, Virginia, is one of a growing number of small high-tech companies foregoing traditional efforts at raising funds by, instead, contacting the U.S. Military and other U.S. government agencies.

41836 ■ "Milwaukee, Wis., to Host Biotech Finance Gathering in 2007" in *Milwaukee Journal Sentinel* **(December 14, 2005)**
Pub: Journal Sentinel, Inc.
Ed: Kathleen Gallagher. **Description:** Venture capitalists representing more than $7 billion and biotechnology and medical device startups will meet in Milwaukee in September 2007 for the largest industry event in the Midwest. The BIO Med-America Venture-Forum expects 75 to 100 VCs to attend.

41837 ■ "MIMlist Draws Eclectic Crowd: Online Forums" in *Tradeshow Week* **(Vol. 34, November 29, 2004, No. 48, pp. 52)**
Pub: Reed Business Information
Ed: Rachelle Crum. **Description:** Exhibition industry associations provide a listserve or other online forum exclusively for its members. Profile of MIMlist, a forum of more than 4,000 members is profiled.

41838 ■ "Mining Mars" in *CMA Management* **(Vol. 76, No. 6, Sept. 2002, pp. 38)**
Pub: Society of Management Accountants of Canada
Ed: John Cooper. **Description:** Information regarding high-tech incubators in Ontario, Canada is presented, examining the possibilities for space firms.

41839 ■ "Mirra, Mirra" in *Entrepreneur* **(Vol. 32, No. 1, January 2004, pp. 38)**
Pub: Entrepreneur Media, Inc.
Ed: Mike Hogan. **Description:** A recent study conducted by the University of California, Berkeley, found that nearly 800MB of new information is generated by each person per year. Much is in multimedia files, such as digital photos, music, movies, and Microsoft Office output.

41840 ■ "Mobile Situation UT Starcom Soars" in *Barron's* **(July 21, 2003, pp. 16)**
Pub: Barron's
Ed: Leslie P. Norton. **Description:** Alameda, California-based UT Starcom is welcoming a 75 percent increase in second-quarter revenue, to more than $400 million, based on increased demand from China for its wireless local-loop equipment.

41841 ■ "Mohyr, Davidow Hires AOL Exec." in *Venture Capital Journal* **(Vol. 40, No. 10, November 2000, pp. 36)**
Pub: Venture Economics
Description: Mohr, Davidow Ventures hired Debby Meredith, former senior vice president and chief of quality officer at America Online Inc, in early September 2000. The firm backs and helps develop start-up companies. Ms. Meredith will focus on Internet companies, software services and infrastructure and business-to-business spaces.

41842 ■ "Money talks" in *Black Enterprise* **(Vol. 32, No. 9, April 2002, pp. 52)**
Pub: Earl Graves Publishing Co.
Ed: Holly Aguirre. **Description:** An introduction to the new talking automated teller machines, designed for the visually impaired.

41843 ■ "More tech firms feed off federal defense, IT spending growth" in *Boston Business Journal* **(Vol. 22, No. 14, May 10, 2002, pp. 1)**
Pub: MCP, Inc.
Description: Defense contractors are relying on increased spending by the government on defense, information technology and homeland security.

41844 ■ "More than luck was required to remake San Diego's economy" in *Wall Street Journal* **(June 13, 2000, pp. B4)**
Pub: Dow Jones & Co., Inc.
Ed: Jeffrey Tannenbaum. **Description:** A report showing that the San Diego area became an incubator for high-tech firms thanks to superb cooperation between government, entrepreneurs and academics.

41845 ■ "Most Likely to Succeed" in *Inc.* **(Volume 28, January 2006, No. 1, pp. 26)**
Pub: Inc. Magazine
Ed: Jim Melloan. **Description:** Innovative technology companies are launching new products in 2006.

41846 ■ "Motherhood Maternity Debuts Canadian Site" in *Marketing to Women* **(Vol. 19, November 2006, No. 11, pp. 5)**
Pub: EPM Communications, Inc.
Description: Motherhoodcanada.ca, a Website serving residents of Canadian provinces, with the exception of Quebec, was launched by Motherhood Maternity.

41847 ■ "Motorola to Cut 3,500 Jobs" in *Crain's Chicago Business* **(Vol. 30, January 2007, No. 4, pp. 12)**
Pub: Crain Communications, Inc.
Description: Ed Zander, CEO of Motorola, said the cell phone maker will cut 5 percent of its workforce as it tries to improve operating costs after a disappointing fourth quarter.

41848 ■ "Moving from one product was their prize" in *Crain's Detroit Business* **(Vol. 19, No. 13, March 31, 2003, pp. 13)**
Pub: Crain Communications Inc., Detroit
Description: Profile of EPrize LLC, the company offers Web-based sweepstakes designed to draw Internet surfers with prizes and has expanded the enterprise in order to stay in business.

41849 ■ "MRI and the national defense" in *Ingram's* **(Vol. 28, No. 6, June 2002, pp. 73)**
Pub: Show Me Publishing, Inc.
Description: A review of the increased role in biological terrorism research given to the Midwest Research Institute is offered. The organization receives 75 percent of its funding from the national government, and has seen an increased need for biological terrorism research after the terrorist mailings of anthrax.

41850 ■ "MSCI-Red Herring Index" in *Red Herring* **(January 2003, pp. 72)**
Pub: Herring Communications Inc.
Description: An index comparison is presented, highlighting the following industries: communications equipment, Internet software & services, semiconductor equipment and products, wireless telecom services, electronic equipment and instruments, IT consulting and services, computers and peripherals, broadcasting and cable TV, software, diversified telecom services, and publishing.

41851 ■ "Municipal Wi-Fi: Let's Keep It Local" in *eWeek* **(February 3, 2005)**
Pub: Ziff Davis Media Inc.
Description: According to a report from the New Millennium Research Council, experts believe that the development of a municipally held Wi-Fi network would have a negative effect on city budgets and on competition.

41852 ■ "Naked at Work: Psst! The Boss is Watching" in *Black Enterprise* (Vol. 34, No. 5, December 2003, pp. 55)
Pub: Earl Graves Publishing Co.
Ed: Sonja D. Brown. Description: Review of the book, "The Naked Employee: How Technology is Compromising Workplace Privacy". The book argues that technology is robbing employees their right to privacy at work.

41853 ■ "Nanomaterials: The Road to Lilliput" in *Red Herring* (No. 99, June 15 & July 1, 2001, pp. 48-50)
Pub: Herring Communications
Ed: Philip E. Ross. Description: A pot of gold awaits those who can manufacture materials atom by atom, if they can actually pull it off. Statistical data included.

41854 ■ "Nanotech Grows" in *Red Herring* (No. 99, June 15 & July 1, 2001, pp. 46-47)
Pub: Herring Communications
Description: A brief chronology of nanotechnology. Nanotechnology is the science of the extremely small, nano meaning one-billionth.

41855 ■ "Nanotech Steve Jurvetson" in *Venture Capital Journal* (January 1, 2005)
Pub: Thomason Financial Inc.
Description: Steve Jurvetson's firm Draper Fisher Jurvetson, has invested in more than 20 nanotech, MEMS and novel materials startups. Jurvetson suggests the best thing to happen to the nanotechnology sector in 2005 would be a major restructuring of immigration and education policy to prioritize science and engineering, the worst, more federal restrictions on immigration or freedom of scientific research like stem cell policy.

41856 ■ "NASA Logs on for Team Encounter in Space" in *Houston Business Journal* (Vol. 34, No. 18, September 12, 2003, pp. 1)
Pub: American City Business Journals
Ed: Jenna Colley. Description: Team Encounter LLC, Houston, Texas, a private space vehicles company, is preparing to send a spacecraft into orbit in 2005. Team Encounter has obtained a contract from NASA to send the Inertial Stellar Compass into orbit aboard its spacecraft.

41857 ■ "Navigation-Technology Startup Seeks Investors" in *Portland Press Herald* (August 5, 2005)
Pub: Blethen Maine Newspapers, Inc.
Ed: Matt Wickenheiser. Description: Profile of Zachariah Conover, founder of CrossRate Technology LLC. Conover returned to his hometown after earning his MBA at Drexel University in Pennsylvania. He hired two childhood friends and is seeking investors for his backup device for a global positioning system.

41858 ■ "NEA Fund 10 $2B Hard Cap" in *Venture Capital Journal* (Vol. 40, No. 10, October 2000, pp. 18, 20, 22)
Pub: Venture Economics
Description: NEA will continue targeting start-up companies in the information technology, communications, software, B-to-B e-commerce and semiconductor sectors, as well as medical, biotech and life sciences companies.

41859 ■ "New CEO: So What is Moto, Anyway?" in *Crain's Chicago Business* (Vol. 26, No. 51, December 22, 2003, pp. 20)
Pub: Crain Communications, Inc.
Ed: Julie Johnsson. Description: Newly appointed CEO of Motorola, Edward Zander, wants to fashion a distinctive corporate image for the electronics giant. The firm reports $27 billion in revenues and Zander feels the firm needs to better define itself.

41860 ■ "The New Kid: Another Wireless Technology is Moving into the Neighborhood" in *Entrepreneur* (Vol. 32, July 2004, No. 7, pp. 25)
Pub: Entrepreneur Media Inc.
Ed: Steve Cooper. Description: Ultra Wide Band (UWB) wireless communication technology transmits

data in short, low-powered pulses over a wide range of frequency spectrums. The new technology could help entrepreneurs to use UWB as wireless backup drives, transferring data from a scanner or connecting with a camera for videoconferencing wirelessly.

41861 ■ "New Products Hit Showfloor: Expo! Expo!" in *Tradeshow Week* (Vol. 34, November 29, 2004, No. 48, pp. 47)
Pub: Reed Business Information
Ed: Margo McCall. Description: New technology products and services were unveiled at the Expo! Expo! Show. The show's highlights include Accumanage, a new software program that provides an exhibitor management system that can be used by show management or exhibitors to complete company profiles for a directory listing.

41862 ■ "The New School" in *Entrepreneur.com* (Vol. 34, February 2006, No. 2, pp. 28)
Pub: Entrepreneur Media Inc.
Ed: Mark Henricks. Description: The School of the Future, backed by Microsoft Corporation, will give each pupil a PC and teachers will present lessons on interactive whiteboards that are connected to the Internet and equipped with speakers and capable of playing DVDs. Graduates will have digital literacy skills to meet employer demands.

41863 ■ *New Technology-Based Firms in the New Millennium, Volume 3*
Pub: Elsevier Science & Technology Books
Ed: Ray Oakey, Wim During, Seleema Kauser. Released: June 2004. Price: $110.00. Description: Collection of papers from the Annual International High Technology Firms (HTSFs) Conference covering issues of importance to governments as they develop technological program. Papers are grouped into three sections: strategy, spin-off firms, clusters, networking, and global issues.

41864 ■ *New Technology-Based Firms in the New Millennium, Volume 4*
Pub: Elsevier Science & Technology Books
Ed: Ray Oakey, Wim During, Seleema Kauser. Released: December 2005. Price: $135.00. Description: Collection of papers from the Annual International High Technology Firms (HTSFs) Conference cover issues of importance to governments as they develop technological program. Papers are grouped into three sections: theory, strategy and clustering, and spin-off firms.

41865 ■ *New Technology-Based Firms in the New Millennium, Volume 5*
Pub: Elsevier Science and Technology Books
Ed: Ray Oakey; Saleema Kauser; Aard Groen; Peter van der Sijde. Released: November 2006. Price: $145.00. Description: Papers from the Annual High Technology Smal Firms conference are presented. Experts address strategic growth for these small firms.

41866 ■ "A New Tone" in *Hispanic Business* (September 2004, pp. 86, 88)
Pub: Hispanic Business
Ed: Sam Diaz. Description: Profiles of the new wireless phones are presented, including the Motorola MPX, Handspring Treo 600, Nokia 6820, Samsung VM-A680, Nokia N0Gage, and Mobitv.

41867 ■ "New Wireless Service to Debut in 2006" in *Crain's Detroit Business* (Vol. 21, October 10, 2005, No. 43, pp. 1)
Pub: Crain Communications Inc. - Detroit
Ed: Andrew Dietderich. Description: As part of a $739 million investment in MetroPCS Inc., two buyout and private-equity firms are backing the startup of a new wireless service planned for the Detroit area; the plan also includes opening as many as 12 company-owned stores in metropolitan Detroit, Michigan.

41868 ■ "News Blog Highlights Women's Careers" in *Marketing to Women* (Vol. 19, November 2006, No. 11, pp. 5)
Pub: EPM Communications, Inc.
Description: NewsonWomen.com, a news blog for businesswomen and their career achievements, has added executive job postings to its content.

41869 ■ "Next step: Bricks and mortar" in *Crain's Detroit Business* (Vol. 19, No. 10, March 10, 2003, pp. 11)
Pub: Crain Communications Inc., Detroit
Ed: Laura Bailey. Description: Howard Bell, the newly appointed head of Wayne State University's Research and Technology Park is working towards a 10-20 year project that will result in a mix of emerging companies with satellite offices of Wayne State's largest industry partners.

41870 ■ "NextEnergy gets $2M from feds" in *Crain's Detroit Business* (Vol. 19, No. 10, March 10, 2003, pp. 29)
Pub: Crain Communications Inc., Detroit
Ed: Laura Bailey. Description: The state of Michigan's alternative-fuel research center, NextEnergy, received $2 million from an appropriations bill signed by President George W. Bush.

41871 ■ "NextEnergy May Get HQ" in *Crain's Detroit Business* (Vol. 22, February 6, 2006, No. 6, pp. 11)
Pub: Crain Communications Inc. - Detroit
Ed: Amy Lane. Description: Nextek Power Systems Inc. is considering a move to the Detroit area in order to be a major player in the state's NextEnergy Center. NextEnergy is a nonprofit corporation charged with advancing Michigan's alternative-energy industry.

41872 ■ "NextWave to Buy Go Networks, Lists on Nasdaq" in *San Diego Business Journal* (Vol. 28, January 8, 2007, No. 2, pp. 5)
Pub: San Diego Business Journal Associates
Ed: Brad Graves. Description: NextWave Wireless Inc. will pay $13.3 million and assume $7.46 million in debt purchasing Go Networks Inc. Details of the agreement are shared.

41873 ■ "9/11 Calls: Wireless Devices in the Post-Attacks Era"in *Entrepeneur* (Vol. 30, No. 1, January 2002, pp. 39)
Pub: Entrepreneur Media Inc.
Ed: Mike Hogan. Description: After 9/11, Americans learned that wireless communications will be important in future emergencies.

41874 ■ "North Highland creates transportation service" in *Atlanta Business Chronicle* (Vol. 25, No. 21, November 1, 2002, pp. 10A)
Pub: American City Business Publications, Inc.
Ed: Mary Jane Credeur. Description: North Highland Company, a technology consulting and management company, has launched TranSCORE, a new consulting service that enables firms to find transportation and scheduling flaws.

41875 ■ "Northfield Hits Blood-Test Hurdle" in *Wall Street Journal* (Vol. 248, December 2006, No. 145, pp. A10)
Pub: Dow Jones & Co. Inc.
Ed: Thomas M Burton Description: Northfield Laboratories Inc., is expected to be first to market with a blood-substitute. Stock plummets after reports of numerous deaths hint to FDA approval setback.

41876 ■ "Northrop Grumman in Bethpage Celebrates National Engineers Week..." in *Long Island Business News* (March 5, 2004)
Pub: Dolan Media Newswires
Description: Northrop Grumman holds an annual paper airplane contest in Bethpage, as well as the company's three other sites in St. Augustine, Florida, Hollywood, Maryland, and Niceville, Florida. Categories include distance, accuracy, and longest flight time.

41877 ■ "Northrop Grumman in Bethpage Celebrates National Engineers Week with Paper Airplane Contest" in *Long Island Business News* (Mar. 5, 04)
Pub: Dolan Media Newswires
Description: Northrop Grumman holds an annual paper airplane contest in Bethpage, as well as the company's three other sites in St. Augustine, Florida, Hollywood, Maryland, and Niceville, Florida. Categories include distance, accuracy, and longest flight time.

41878 ■ "Novel microarray applications" in *Small Business Economic Trends* (February 2002, pp. 1)

Pub: National Federation of Independent Business Foundation

Ed: Neil McKenna. Description: Companies are exploring new applications and protocols in the areas of data-analysis software that is linked to microarrays obtained from gene expression and protein-drug interactions.

41879 ■ "Nth Power Energizes New $120M Fund" in *Venture Capital Journal* (Vol. 40, No. 10, November 2000, pp. 26, 28)

Pub: Venture Economics

Description: With its new close, Nth Power Technologies Inc., intends to maintain its investment focus on distributed energy and storage, energy-related communications, power quality and transmission, and distribution automation.

41880 ■ "Nuance Gains Voice in Noisy Speech Market" in *San Francisco Business Times* (Vol. 18, No. 2, August 22, 2003, pp. 3)

Pub: American City Business Journals

Ed: Lizette Wilson. Description: Examination of ScanSoft's acquisition of rival SpeechWorks International Inc., maker of speech recognition products. Topics include market development plans, market share, and strategic planning.

41881 ■ "Numbers Game" in *Entrepreneur* (Vol. 32, No. 1, January 2004, pp. 30)

Pub: Entrepreneur Media, Inc.

Ed: Stephen Barlas. Description: High technology firms relying on the H-1B Visa to fill engineering and technical jobs with foreign workers face a drop in the number of visas available in 2004.

41882 ■ "Offshoring Could Boost Your Career" in *Fortune* (Vol. 151, January 24, 2005, No. 2, pp. 36)

Pub: Time Inc.

Ed: Anne Fisher. Description: According to a study conducted by Duke University's Fuqua School of Business and Archstone Consulting, American businesses with offshore operations will ship 81 percent more research jobs, 55 percent more engineering, and 75 percent more human resources overseas (69 percent of which are already in India). American managers will be needed to oversee these operations.

41883 ■ "Old Media's Mobile Future" in *Business Week* (January 16, 2006, No. 3967, pp. 20)

Pub: McGraw-Hill Companies

Ed: Jon Fine. Description: America is rated sixteen among the world's county's using broadband technology, as well as for mobile phone use. Jeffrey Cole, director of the University of Southern California's Center for the Digital Future oversees the World Internet Project that tracks the Internet's impact in 20 industrialized countries.

41884 ■ "On the Fast Track: How Technology Is Speeding Incentive Delivery" in *Sales & Marketing Management* (Vol. 157, February 2005)

Pub: VNU Business Media

Ed: Alan Horowitz. Description: Profile of the software company Synygy Inc. and its enterprise incentive management product. The software and services help to manage incentive compensation for sales staff, or any employee of a company, which promotes sales growth and employee motivation.

41885 ■ "On the Road? Then Don't Forget to Pack These Tech Essentials" in *Entrepreneur* (Vol. 32, November 2004, No. 11, pp. 39)

Pub: Entrepreneur Media Inc.

Ed: Heather Clancy. Description: Profiles of the latest mobile devices important to small companies are presented.

41886 ■ "One of Portland, Maine's Fastest Growing Tech Companies is Sold" in *Portland Press Herald* (December 20, 2005)

Pub: Blethen Maine Newspapers, Inc.

Ed: Matt Wickenheiser. Description: IntelliCare Inc., one of Portland, Maine's largest technology companies was recently acquired by PolyMedica Corporation. The firm is a telemedicine company offering telephone-based nursing services and technology.

41887 ■ "Online Education: Global Questions, Local Answers" in *Journal of Business Communication* (Vol. 44, January 2007, No. 1, pp. 96)

Pub: Association for Business Communication

Ed: Christopher Lam. Description: A collection of essays entitled, Online Education: Global Questions, Local Answers looks at professional communication and the effect of online education. Although the focus is mainly on technical communication, business communication scholars and practitioners will also find this collection a valuable read.

41888 ■ "The operators" in *Red Herring* (March 2003, pp. 28)

Pub: Herring Communications Inc.

Ed: Om Halik. Description: After the grim economy of the high tech industry, many companies are either trying to unload assets or reduce business plans; many new firms are seeing this as an opportunity.

41889 ■ "Opportunities emerge in a new age of miracle materials. (Nanotechnology)" in *Red Herring* (March 2003, pp. 50)

Pub: Herring Communications Inc.

Ed: Lee Bruno. Description: An overview of nanotechnology, the study of materials smaller than 100 nanometers, or approximately 1/100th the width of a human hair. Nanotechnology involves two main areas of research.

41890 ■ "Optics' Second Wave: Test-and-measurement stocks burn brightly" in *Red Herring* (No. 102, August 15, 2001, pp. 86)

Pub: Herring Communications

Ed: Stephen Lucey. Description: Profiles of three optical equipment and testing companies that have solid growth prospects, including Acterna, Digital Lightwave, and EXFO, are presented.

41891 ■ "Oracle chief puts CEOs to the test" in *San Francisco Business Times* (Vol. 16, No. 43, May 31, 2002, pp. 1)

Pub: San Francisco Business Times Inc.

Ed: Lizette Wilson. Description: Former Oracle employees who have gone on to success outside the company, such as Craig Conway of PeopleSoft and Tim Siebel of Siebel Systems, are discussed along with Oracle CEO Larry Ellison's management style. More than half of all top technical firms have Oracle workers in their top ranks.

41892 ■ "Other Comments" in *Forbes* (Vol. 170, No. 6, September 30, 2002, pp. 36)

Pub: Forbes Magazine

Description: The depression in high technology and telecommunications, as well as telecommunications policies, and other business issues are analyzed.

41893 ■ "Out in the Cold? If Wi-Fi 'Cold Spots' Are Leaving You in the Lurch, Try These Solutions" in *Entrepreneur* (Vol. 32, August 2004)

Pub: Entrepreneur Media Inc.

Ed: Amanda C. Kooser. Description: Wi-Fi signals might not reach every area of an office building, called cold spots, where Wi-Fi fades or drops off. Antennas, wireless repeaters and bridges will help to expand any wireless network.

41894 ■ "Pall Corp. Plans to Sell New Bacteria-Detection System to Blood Banks" in *Long Island Business News* (February 20, 2004)

Pub: Dolan Media Newswires

Description: The U.S. Food and Drug Administration (FDA) has approved Pall Corporation's system for detecting bacteria in blood platelets. The new system will cut testing time by about 20 percent, increasing the supply of blood available for transfusion.

41895 ■ "Papermaster in startup mode" in *Austin Business Journal* (Vol. 22, No. 28, September 27, 2002, pp. 1)

Pub: Austin Business Journal Inc.

Ed: Spacey Higginbotham. Description: Steve Papermaster's software company Agillion Inc. was sold at auction when dot-com companies crashed. He is back now as chairman of a high tech business company formed through incubator Powershift Ventures LLP, and co-investor with Azure Capital Partners LP, called CooperaTech Inc., which develops risk and opportunity management software.

41896 ■ "Patient Capital: How Life Sciences Investments Touch Us All" in *Venture Capital Journal* (December 1, 2004)

Pub: Thomason Financial Inc.

Description: National Venture Capital Association's report explains the role venture capital plays in the expansion and enhancement of health and medical systems. The venture capital industry has invested almost $41 billion in more than 6,600 biotechnology and medical device companies in the last 20 years. Statistical data included.

41897 ■ "Paying Your Dues" in *Entrepreneur* (Vol. 32)

Pub: Entrepreneur Media Inc.

Ed: David Worrell. Description: Stephen Forte, founder and president of Ascendent, a telecommunication technology company that connects wireless phones to traditional phone systems. Forte addresses the issue of due-diligence, an investor's process of fact-finding.

41898 ■ "Peer Pressure" in *Red Herring* (No. 103, September 1, 2001, pp. 62-65)

Pub: Herring Communications

Ed: Justin Hibbard. Description: An overview of the new content-delivery business, including profiles of startup companies. Forecasts for content-delivery revenue is optimistic, despite the lows in this sector seen on Wall Street.

41899 ■ "Personal Business" in *Business Week* (December 19, 2005, No. 3964, pp. 95)

Pub: McGraw-Hill Companies

Ed: Gene G. Marcial. Description: Profile of Expeditors International of Seattle, Washington, a freight forwarder and customs broker; licensing and patents for intellectual property; and biotech firm Sonus Pharaceuticals.

41900 ■ "Peter Falvey: Whiz Kid: Peter Falvey is Betting the Company on Tech Investment" in *Boston Business Journal* (Vol. 23, July 11, 2003)

Pub: American City Business Journals

Ed: Edward Mason. Description: Revolution Partners focuses on high technology investment; profile of the investment bank's co-founder Peter Falvey is included.

41901 ■ "Peters will help develop technology" in *Crain's Detroit Business* (Vol. 16, No. 49, December 4, 2000, pp. 43)

Pub: Crain Communications, Inc.

Ed: David Barkholz. Description: William Peters, M.D., is leaving the Barbara Ann Karmanos Cancer Center to run the Detroit Medical Center's new Institute of Strategic Analysis & Innovation and Karmanos' embryonic Center for Cancer Economics, Technology Assessment, Innovation and Development (CETAID).

41902 ■ "Pick a niche and fill it" in *Hispanic Business* (Vol. 22, No. 7-8, July-August 2000, pp. 44)

Pub: Hispanic Business

Description: An analysis is presented showing how Hispanic American chief executive officers have achieved fast-growing companies in slow growing industries.

41903 ■ "Picking Up the Pace of the Space Tourism Race" in *Business Week* (February 7, 2005, No. 3919, pp. 81)

Pub: McGraw-Hill Companies

Ed: Otis Port. Description: Richard Branson, chief of Virgin Atlantic Airways, is planning to launch a suborbital space tourism business in 2008. Branson plans to have five spaceliners; 13,500 people have requested reservations for space flights.

41904 ■ "Picking Up the Pieces" in *Black Enterprise* **(Vol. 32, No. 9, April 2002, pp. 44)**
Pub: Earl Graves Publishing Co.
Ed: Bridget McCrea. **Description:** Patrick Duroseau, founder and president of Marnic Technologies, tell how he and his firm and employees are carrying on after the terrorist attacks of September 11, 2001.

41905 ■ "Plan Would Share Wealth From $1B Fund" in *Crain's Detroit Business* **(Vol. 21, October 24, 2005, No. 43, pp. 26)**
Pub: Crain Communications Inc. - Detroit
Ed: Amy Lane. **Description:** Life-sciences, technology, technology, manufacturing, agriculture, film-production, and defense companies will all benefit from $101 million in government funds to support growing or technology-oriented businesses.

41906 ■ "Planned obsolescence, the tech way" in *Recycling Today* **(Vol. 40, No. 19, September 2002, pp. 4)**
Pub: G.I.E. Media, Inc.
Ed: Brian Taylor. **Description:** An overview of the computer industry and waste management, including information about Gold Circuit Inc. of Chandler, Arizona. Information from the 2002 Paper Recycling Conference are included.

41907 ■ "Plastics recovery technology developer tackles post-consumer electronics scrap" in *Modern Plastics* **(Vol. 79, Dec. 2002, pp. 65)**
Pub: Chemical Week Associates
Ed: Mark Rosenzweig. **Description:** Profile of Recovery Plastics International (RPI), Salt Lake City, Utah; RPI is developing the technology for a commercial process for retrieving plastics from post-consumer computer and television scrap.

41908 ■ "Podcast Network Focuses on Wedding Plans" in *Marketing to Women* **(Vol. 19, October 2006, No. 10, pp. 5)**
Pub: EPM Communications, Inc.
Description: The newly launched Wedding Podcast Network provides couples with programming dedicated to planning their wedding. Shows include a diversity of topics ranging from getting in shape for the big day to tips from expert wedding planners to popular wedding destinations.

41909 ■ "Pond Venture Partners Closes $78M Fund II" in *Venture Capital Journal* **(Vol. 40, No. 10, October 2000, pp. 24, 26)**
Pub: Venture Economics
Description: Pond Venture Partners Ltd. will focus its investments into early-stage communications companies, including firms in Western Europe.

41910 ■ "Portland Seeks Biotech Park to Stimulate New Business" in *Portland Press Herald* **(December 13, 2005)**
Pub: Blethen Maine Newspapers, Inc.
Ed: Kelley Bouchard. **Description:** Portland, Maine officials are proposing the development of a biotechnology park in order to compete for tenants seeking similar locations in the Boston, Massachusetts area.

41911 ■ "Positive defense for networks" in *Red Herring* **(January 2003, pp. 60)**
Pub: Herring Communications Inc.
Ed: Sarah Fallon. **Description:** An overview of intrusion detection systems is presented.

41912 ■ "Power House" in *Entrepreneur* **(Vol. 32, No. 1, January 2004, pp. 37)**
Pub: Entrepreneur Media, Inc.
Ed: Mike Hogan. **Description:** Computer networking, connectivity and large files are among the devices that are no longer used exclusively in offices, but are being used in homes for mobile workers.

41913 ■ *Power Up Your Small-Medium Business: A Guide to Enabling Network Technologies*
Pub: Cisco Press
Ed: Robyn Aber. **Released:** March 2004. **Price:** $39.95 (US), $57.95 (Canadian). **Description:** Network technologies geared to small and medium-size business, focusing on access, IP telephony, wireless technologies, security, and computer network management.

41914 ■ "Powerhouse Tech Companies Merge" in *Black Enterprise* **(Vol. 35, November 2004, No. 4, pp. 28)**
Pub: Earl G. Graves Publishing Co. Inc.
Ed: Cliff Hocker. **Description:** Two high-tech firms in Alexandria, Virginia have merged to better compete for homeland defense contracts.

41915 ■ "Powering the imagination" in *Red Herring* **(No. 103, September 1, 2001, pp. 74)**
Pub: Herring Communications
Ed: Bridget Eklund. **Description:** Information explaining the way fuels cells produce electricity is presented using illustrations.

41916 ■ "Primus Fund V Eyes $250M Close" in *Venture Capital Journal* **(Vol. 40, No. 10, October 2000, pp. 22, 24)**
Pub: Venture Economics
Description: The Primus Fund V will focus on four industry sectors: telecommunications, Internet/e-commerce, out-sourced business services, and health care.

41917 ■ "Private Company Profiles" in *Red Herring* **(No. 103, September 1, 2001, pp. 80)**
Pub: Herring Communications
Ed: Stasia Bochnowski. **Description:** A cross section of five privately held companies in the energy market, including Metallic Power, NxtPhase, RealEnergy, Serveron, and USPowerSolutions.

41918 ■ "Private Matters: Retail Alert: Keep an Eye on New RFID Privacy Legislation" in *Entrepreneur* **(Vol. 32, October 2004, No. 10, pp. 38)**
Pub: Entrepreneur Media Inc.
Ed: Amanda C. Kooser. **Description:** Wireless capabilities that track products as they move through the supply chain, known as radio frequency identification (RFID) are growing in popularity with retailers. Several states are considering privacy legislation to regulate RFID so companies could not collect and use data collected regarding customers.

41919 ■ "Program Off To A Great Start Providing Capital for Gazelles" in *Mississippi Business Journal* **(Vol. 29, January 2007, No. 2, pp. 21)**
Pub: Venture Publications, Inc.
Ed: Becky Gillette **Description:** High-performance emerging technology companies known as gazelles are getting seed and growth capitol from the newly established Mississippi Angel Network.

41920 ■ "A Progressive Sound" in *Washington Business Journal* **(Vol. 22, No. 15, August 15, 2003, pp. 16)**
Pub: Washington Business Journal
Ed: John Wilen. **Description:** Technology behind the success of Relatable's song-swapping technology is discussed. Topics include digital sound recording, downloading of MP3's, and company forecasts.

41921 ■ "Promised Land" in *Entrepreneur* **(Vol. 33, August 2005, No. 8, pp. 26)**
Pub: Entrepreneur Media Inc.
Ed: Mark Henricks. **Description:** As the Israeli-Palestinian conflict abates American entrepreneurs, particularly in technology areas, are looking to Israel as a new business opportunity.

41922 ■ "Proving That You Have the Right Stuff" in *Inc.* **(Volume 27, July 2005, No. 7, pp. 28)**
Pub: Inc. Magazine
Ed: Alison Stein Wellner. **Description:** QuVIS, located in Topeka, Kansas landed a federal contract for

technology it developed that quickly transmits digital pictures without blurred images. QuVIS technology will be used when the space shuttle Discovery takes off in July 2005.

41923 ■ "Public Company Profiles" in *Red Herring* **(No. 103, September 1, 2001, pp. 81)**
Pub: Herring Communications
Ed: Mark Chediak. **Description:** A cross section of four publicly held companies in the energy market, including Capstone Turbine, Catalytica Energy Systems, FuelCell Energy, and Vestas Wind Systems.

41924 ■ "The Pulse" in *Sales & Marketing Management* **(Vol. 159, January-February 2007, No. 1, pp. 9)**
Pub: VNU Business Media
Description: According to a survey conducted by Extraprise, 63 percent of all business-to-business companies will implement marketing automation technology in 2007.

41925 ■ "Punta Gorda Interested in Wi-Fi Internet" in *Charlotte Observer* **(February 1, 2007)**
Pub: Knight-Ridder/Tribune Business News
Ed: Steve Reilly. **Description:** Punta Gorda officials are developing plans to provide free wireless Internet services to businesses and residents.

41926 ■ "Pushing the Right Buttons" in *Crain's Detroit Business* **(Vol. 23, January 15,2007, No. 3, pp. 11)**
Pub: Crain Communications Inc. - Detroit
Ed: Amy Lane. **Description:** Speed, flexibility, and time compression advantages are driving wireless companies to expand networks and facilities in Southeastern Michigan to further serve small business needs. Significant cost savings can be realized when converting from land-based fax and phone lines.

41927 ■ "Put Some Wow In Your Website" in *Inc.* **(September 2006, pp. 44-45)**
Pub: Gruner & Jahr USA Publishing
Ed: Michael Fitzgerald. **Description:** Websites get stale quickly and need constant changes to continue to attract attention to your message and products. New graphics, sounds, and more are provided as examples of techniques to accomplish this.

41928 ■ "A quantum leap" in *Red Herring* **(January 2003, pp. 54)**
Pub: Herring Communications Inc.
Ed: Martin LaMonica. **Description:** An overview of quantum cryptography, the technique that secures data transmission by putting quantum theory into practice.

41929 ■ "QuikTrip Policy Points to Dismissal" in *Kansas City Star* **(February 24, 2005)**
Pub: Knight-Ridder/Tribune Business News
Ed: Diane Stafford. **Description:** Biometric systems are being used as an employee tracking system at many companies now. This system replaced traditional time clocks and records employee fingerprints rather than punching a card or filling out a time sheet.

41930 ■ "R and D Spending Jumps as Firms Foresee Recovery" in *Atlanta Business Chronicle* **(Vol. 26, No. 10, August 15, 2003, pp. 1)**
Pub: American City Business Publications, Inc.
Ed: Mary Jane Credeur. **Description:** The first signs of economic recovery for the greater Atlanta, Georgia area are in the form of higher research and development spending by local technology firms.

41931 ■ "Radio Frequency Identification" in *Journal of Accountancy*
Pub: American Institute of Certified Public Accountants
Ed: Harold E. Davis, Michael S. Luehlfing. **Description:** Radio frequency identification (RFID) consists of tags, transceivers and a computer system that share the characteristics, location, arrival/shipment time and other information about inventories. RFID is expected to reduce costs and improve efficiency for managing and accounting inventory.

41932 ■ "Rapiscan Opens Plant" in *Mississippi Business Journal* (Vol. 28, September 2006, No. 36, pp. 22)
Pub: Venture Publications, Inc.
Description: Profile of Rapiscan Systems, a division of OSI Systems Inc., Rapiscan has opened a new factory in Ocean Springs to manufacture Rapiscan Gamma Radiographic Detection Systems for deployment around the world. Statistical data included.

41933 ■ "Reaching Out to Low-Wage Countries" in *Washington Business Journal* (Vol. 22, September 26, 2003)
Pub: Washington Business Journal
Ed: Tania Anderson. **Description:** Outsourcing of work overseas by engineering and computer firms has increased during the economic recession.

41934 ■ "Ready to land" in *Crain's Detroit Business* (Vol. 19, No. 16, April 21, 2003, pp. 11)
Pub: Crain Communications Inc., Detroit
Ed: Amy Lane. **Description:** Detroit Metropolitan Airport will offer wireless high-speed Internet access to passengers waiting in the airport's terminals. Concourse Communications Group LLC, Springfield, Massachusetts, has an airport contract that includes providing the wireless access known as Wi-Fi in the new Midfield Terminal.

41935 ■ "Reality TV for Business" in *Hispanic Business* (September 2003, pp. 74)
Pub: Hispanic Business
Ed: Roger Harris. **Description:** Profile of the new lower priced and higher quality videoconferencing devices affordable for all small companies.

41936 ■ "Recession session" in *Entrepreneur* (Vol. 30, No. 3, March 2002, pp.)
Pub: Entrepreneur Media Inc.
Ed: Mark Henricks. **Description:** An interview with various experts and entrepreneurs to learn how and when they recommend aggressive or defensive positions in the areas of money management, people management, marketing, and technology.

41937 ■ "The Red Herring Portfolio: Going nowhere fast" in *Red Herring* (No. 103, September 1, 2001, pp. 96)
Pub: Herring Communications
Description: Presentation of the Red Herring Portfolio, including stock profiles of AOL Time Warner, Atmel, Cisco Systems, Comcast, Electronic Data Systems, EMC, Immunex, Integrated Circuit Systems, IntraNet Solutions, Nokia, Oracle, and Peregrine Systems.

41938 ■ "The Red Herring Portfolio: Stuck inside a sideways pattern with the market" in *Red Herring* (No. 102, August 15, 2001, pp. 96)
Pub: Herring Communications
Description: Presentation of the Red Herring Portfolio, including stock profiles of AOL Time Warner, Atmel, Cisco Systems, Comcast, Electronic Data Systems, EMC, Immunex, Integrated Circuit Systems, IntraNet Solutions, Nokia, Oracle, and Peregrine Systems.

41939 ■ "Redleaf, UPenn Launch PenNetWorks" in *Venture Capital Journal* (Vol. 40, No. 10, October 2000, pp. 6, 8)
Pub: Venture Economics
Description: The technology operating company, Redleaf Group Inc., partnered with the University of Pennsylvania in August to form PenNetWorks, an on-campus Internet accelerator. The accelerator is owned by the University and managed by Redleaf.

41940 ■ "Reed Acquires Manufacturing Shows" in *Tradeshow Week* (Vol. 34, December 13, 2004, No. 50, pp. 3)
Pub: Reed Business Information
Description: Reed Exhibitions has acquired a series of regional manufacturing tradeshows with the purchase of Advanced Manufacturing and Productivity Exposition series from the Technical Exhibitions and Conferences. The shows focus on automated manufacturing, assembly systems and information technology.

41941 ■ "Remote Control" in *My Business* (February/March 2004, pp. 14)
Pub: My Business Magazine
Ed: Lee Gimpel. **Description:** Five questions to ask a mobile solution vendor before hiring their services are listed.

41942 ■ "Renewed Biotech Interest Boosts BioCryst" in *Birmingham Business Journal* (Vol. 20, No. 35, August 29, 2003, pp. 1)
Pub: American City Business Journals, Inc.
Ed: Tom Bassing. **Description:** Difficult financial times facing BioCryst Pharmaceuticals Inc. are discussed, especially falling stock prices, cash flow problems, and financial management.

41943 ■ "Researchers Test Bioterrorism Sensors in Greenwich Village and on Long Island" in *Long Island Business News* (March 5, 2004)
Pub: Dolan Media Newswires
Ed: Ken Schachter. **Description:** Researchers are testing bioterrorism sensors for the Long Island Partnership for Homeland Security. The project includes area defense contractors, technology companies and research institutions.

41944 ■ "Resource Line" in *Black Enterprise* (Vol. 35, January 2005, No. 6, pp. 10)
Pub: Earl G. Graves Publishing Co. Inc.
Description: Black Enterprise offers a Website offering advice to small business owners, executives and investors.

41945 ■ "Resources: Web Sites, Organizations, Events and More to Grow Your Business" in *Entrepreneur* (Vol. 32, No. 2, February 2004, pp. 8)
Pub: Entrepreneur Media, Inc.
Ed: Steve Cooper. **Description:** Profiles of Websites to help grow a small business include Zagat Survey covering 2003 restaurants and hotels offering Wi-Fi to customers; NewIdeaTrade, an online forum for buying and selling inventions, patents, copyrights and other intellectual property; Yahoo's small business Merchant Solutions, with shopping carts, coupons and 24-hour toll-free phone support; WordBiz Report, an e-newsletter focusing on online copywriting and content; Plan-Alyzer, evaluates outcomes of marketing plans; Bob Ely, an independent copywriter and consultant; Meeting & Event Planning for Dummies; and Business Matchmaking, a service to help small business procure government contracts.

41946 ■ "Resources: Web Sites, Organizations, Events and More To Grow Your Business" in *Entrepreneur* (Vol. 32, September 2004, No. 9, pp. 8)
Pub: Entrepreneur Media Inc.
Ed: Steve Cooper. **Description:** Resources to help small business are featured including the Small Business Administration's effort to help teen entrepreneurs launch a business; KnockNow an online community of entrepreneurs, executives, venture capitalists, angel investors, service sector companies, and government; the SBA's business Website offering information on small business development, financial assistance, taxes, laws and regulations, international trade, workplace issues, buying and selling and federal forms.

41947 ■ "Restart: Network Engines Finds Profits After the Tech Bubble Burst" in *Boston Business Journal* (Vol. 23, No. 27, August 8, 2003)
Pub: American City Business Journals
Ed: Tom Witkowski. **Description:** The operations and growth of Canton, Massachusetts-based Network Engines are discussed.

41948 ■ "Retail/Hospitality" in *Microsoft Executive Circle* (Vol. 1, No. 2, Q2 2001, pp. 34-37)
Pub: Putman Media
Ed: Craig A. Shutt. **Description:** New technology is providing consumers faster, more personalized service at restaurants, while cutting costs for restaurant owners.

41949 ■ "RFID Due Diligence: RFID Technologies Hold Great Promise for VCs" in *Venture Capital Journal* (January 1, 2005)
Pub: Thomason Financial Inc.
Description: Radio frequency identification (RFID) investing requires an understanding of the markets the technology serves. RFID technology is composed of three components: tags that can store data about anything as well as transmit and receive that data over low or high frequencies; an infrastructure platform that creates a wireless network whereby data can be transmitted and received; and a software solutions component that can then manipulate and analyze that data, store it and share it with existing software systems.

41950 ■ "RFID: Plenty of Mixed Signals" in *Business Week Online* (January 31, 2005)
Pub: McGraw-Hill Companies
Ed: Sarah Lacy. **Description:** Suppliers remain skeptical of radio-frequency identification technology to manage inventories.

41951 ■ "Riding the Telecom-Computer Convergence" in *Hispanic Business* (Vol. 23, No. 7/8, July/August 2001, pp. 60)
Pub: Hispanic Business
Ed: Joel Russell. **Description:** An overview of the fast-growth, high-tech Hispanic firms specializing in networking and system integration. Statistical data included.

41952 ■ "Riding the tech wave" in *Hispanic Business* (Vol. 22, No. 7-8, July-August 2000, pp. 30)
Pub: Hispanic Business
Ed: Jennifer Riley. **Description:** Ralph G. Moore, president of consulting firm RGMA believes that e-commerce and the Internet hold many opportunities for small, minority-owned businesses to take part in procurement.

41953 ■ "Ring It Up. Way Systems Helps Convert Cell Phones into Portable Cash Registers" in *Boston Business Journal* (Vol. 23, Aug. 22, 2003)
Pub: American City Business Journals
Ed: Mark Hollmer. **Description:** Way Systems Inc., Medford, Massachusetts, expects to manufacture a device that can be attached to a cell phone and would convert it into a portable point of sale terminal.

41954 ■ "Riparian Unveils Village Ventures' R.I. Fund" in *Venture Capital Journal* (Vol. 40, No. 10, November 2000, pp. 20)
Pub: Venture Economics
Description: The investment banking firm, Riparian Partners, will back technology-related companies in high-growth industries, including telecommunications, Internet plays, some medical technology companies, and marine-related technologies.

41955 ■ "Rivaling a Giant" in *Boston Business Journal* (Vol. 23, No. 30, August 29, 2003, pp. 3)
Pub: American City Business Journals
Ed: Tom Witkowski. **Description:** Profile of Enterasys Networks efforts to capture market share away from rival giant Cisco Systems Inc. Topics include market development, product development, and competition.

41956 ■ "Running a Biotech Operation Here is Reasonably Cheap, Study Finds" in *Pittsburgh Business Times* (Vol. 23, No. 2, August 1, 2003)
Pub: Pittsburgh Business Times
Ed: Maria Guzzo. **Description:** Industry analysts report that the Pittsburgh, Pennsylvania region offers a wide range of benefits to biotechnology firms. A new report from Boyd Company has found that the region offers economic advantages for biomedical research firms.

41957 ■ "Safe and Secure" in *Business First Columbus* (Vol. 18, No. 26, February 15, 2002, pp. A21)
Pub: Business First Columbus, Inc.
Ed: Drew Bracken. **Description:** Columbus, Ohio scientist develops a method for password security by typing bar-code.

41958 ■ "Safety Measures" in *Washington Business Journal* (Vol. 22, No. 16, August 22, 2003, pp. 18)
Pub: Washington Business Journal
Ed: Tim Pappa. Description: Gary Noesner, from Control Risks Groups, points out the importance of travel information. Control Risks offers software and services to make data acquisition easier. Such information can result in saving the lives of employees of international businesses or government officials in the field.

41959 ■ "San Diego to Host Tech Summit" in *Hispanic Business* (Vol. 24, No. 5, May 2002, pp. 42)
Pub: Hispanic Business Inc.
Description: Technology and cross-border trade were among the issues of focus at the Hispanic Business Tech Summit held in November, 2001. Specific seminars included, B2B E-Commerce, E-Business Expansion, Strategic Online Alliances, Cross-Border Trends, and NAFTA.

41960 ■ "S&P Top 10: Covance In, Amgen Out" in *Business Week Online* (January 31, 2005)
Pub: McGraw-Hill Companies
Ed: Kenneth Shea, Robert Gold, Steve Biggar. Description: A listing of the Standard & Poor's Top Ten Portfolio is presented. A drug development services firm has replaced Amgen for Top Investment Ranking. Statistical data included.

41961 ■ "Telecommunications: 'Press ' for Satisfied Users" in *Microsoft Executive Circle* (Vol. 1, No. 2, Q2 2001, pp. 42-44)
Pub: Putman Media
Ed: Marty Weil. Description: New telecommunication programs could generate 30 percent of revenue for companies within five years and improve customer satisfaction and loyalty.

41962 ■ "Saving our energy" in *Red Herring* (No. 103, September 1, 2001, pp. 67)
Pub: Herring Communications
Ed: Elizabeth Lamb. Description: According to the U.S. Energy Information Administration, commercial and residential energy consumption will decrease over the next 20 years due to slower population growth, fewer housing starts, increased energy efficiency, government efficiency programs, and innovations in technology.

41963 ■ "SBV Venture Partners Eyes $75M First Fund" in *Venture Capital Journal* (Vol. 40, No. 10, November 2000, pp. 24)
Pub: Venture Economics
Description: SBV Venture Partners aimed for a late fall or early 2001 second close for its inaugural fund and the fund's companion vehicle. The two funds Sigefi Burnette & Vallee I and Sigefi, Burnette & Vallee IA, considered one vehicle by the firm, will focus primarily on network infrastructure companies and companies arising from the convergence between communications and computing.

41964 ■ "Scanning For Dollars" in *Fortune* (Vol. 151, January 10, 2005, No. 1, pp. 60)
Pub: Time Inc.
Ed: Julie Schlosser. Description: New technology is being used by marketers to study consumer emotions and motivations. Functional magnetic resonance imaging (fMRI) detects the flow of blood to the brain's centers of pleasure, thought or memory. Researchers suggest that blood flow increases in areas of the prefrontal cortex when an individual likes what he or she is seeing.

41965 ■ "SciTech Developments to Watch" in *Business Week* (January 16, 2006, No. 3967, pp. 87)
Pub: McGraw-Hill Companies
Description: Scientific and technological developments discussed include a pain-free alternative to pricking fingers for blood sugar readings for diabetics through the use of infrared light bounced off the white of an individual's eye; carbon nanotubes for electronic components; and information about tree farms.

41966 ■ "Secret Weapon: Synopsys is Thriving Behind the Scenes in the Semiconductor Business" in *Barron's* (August 11, 2003, pp. 16)
Pub: Barron's
Ed: Mark Veverka. Description: CEO, Art de Geus's Synopsys, headquartered in Silicon Valley, California, is quietly making its case as a leading electronic-design automation firm, creating the software that semiconductor firms like Intel and AMD use to design microchips.

41967 ■ "Security Companies Expect War to Increase Business" in *Crain's Detroit Business* (Vol. 19, No. 12, March 24, 2003, pp. 24)
Pub: Crain Communications Inc., Detroit
Ed: Andrew Dietderich. Description: Raj Patel, manager of Plante & Moran LLP, the Southfield, Michigan-based security consulting firm, expects a rise in business due to the war in Iraq.

41968 ■ "The Security-Industrial Complex" in *Forbes* (Vol. 174, November 29, 2004, No. 11, pp. 44)
Pub: Forbes Magazine Inc.
Ed: Mark P. Mills. Description: Security is a growing technology business in the U.S. The money flowing into the military and homeland infrastructure will revolutionize technologies and materials. Terror-sensing tools will expand to applications in medicine, industry, transportation, telecommunications and entertainment driving a tech boom.

41969 ■ "Security's New Face: 3-D Face-Recognition Technology" in *San Jose Mercury News* (March 7, 2005)
Pub: Knight-Ridder/Tribune Business News
Ed: Dan Lee. Description: Grant Evans, chief executive of A4Vision discusses 3-D face recognition technology. Face scanning is becoming the first choice for biometric identification of humans.

41970 ■ "Seeing the future in real time" in *Red Herring* (No. 99, June 15 & July 1, 2001, pp. 21-22)
Pub: Herring Communications
Ed: Anthony B. Perkins. Description: Discussion highlighting a speech made by Vinod Khosla at the recent Venture 2001 conference in reference to the information technology industry. Mr. Khosla, called the most successful venture capitalist on the planet by Red Herring, discussed the impact the Internet is having on the entire model of computing.

41971 ■ "Seizing the Sun" in *Boston Business Journal* (Vol. 23, No. 25, July 25, 2003, pp. 20)
Pub: American City Business Journals
Ed: Mark Micheli. Description: Konarka Technologies, led by CEO and president, William M. Bechenbaugh, produces solar cell material that is light and flexible; the firm states that the new product is more cost-effective than traditional hard solar cells.

41972 ■ "The semi swing" in *Red Herring* (No. 99, June 15 & July 1, 2001, pp. 142, 144)
Pub: Herring Communications
Ed: J.P. Vicente. Description: The prediction that semiconductor stocks will rise during the summer months is highlighted.

41973 ■ "Semiconductor Industry's Growth Will Slow" in *Kiplinger Letter* (Vol. 78, January 19, 2007, No. 2)
Pub: Kiplinger
Description: Semiconductor manufacturers are expecting a 3 percent drop in sales worldwide in 2007.

41974 ■ "Semiconductors Pierre Lamond" in *Venture Capital Journal* (January 1, 2005)
Pub: Thomason Financial Inc.
Description: Pierre Lamond shares insight into the best and worst that could happen to the semiconductor industry for 2005. Lamond believes continued growth in the global economy is essential.

41975 ■ "Seminars focus on bio-research" in *Hispanic Business* (Vol. 22, No. 6, June 2000, pp. 28)
Pub: Hispanic Business
Description: The U.S. Government will provide $495 million funding for research into nanotechnology in 2001. Small businesses wishing to participate in the new technological revolution are being helped by the National Institutes of Health, which is sponsoring a symposium on nanotechnology.

41976 ■ "Send In the Robots!" in *Fortune* (Vol. 151, January 24, 2005, No. 2, pp. 140)
Pub: Time Inc.
Ed: Stuart F. Brown. Description: New generation industrial robots can strip paint, inspect buried gas mains, traverse desserts, and even cut grass for golf courses. Computer and navigational technology costs have fallen making these robots affordable to most small businesses.

41977 ■ "Server it Right" in *Entrepreneur* (Vol. 31, No. 11, November 2003, pp. 57)
Pub: Entrepreneur Media, Inc.
Ed: Steve Cooper. Description: Profile of D-Link's DP-311P Wireless Print Server that allows users to use printers wirelessly.

41978 ■ "Service With a Smile" in *Inc.* (October 2005, pp. 75-76)
Pub: Inc. Magazine
Ed: David H. Freedman. Description: The article exams the ways in which technology has harmed customer service and ways three startup companies plan to rescue it. According to one study, 37 percent of callers who reach an automated voice system press zero in the hopes of speaking to an actual person.

41979 ■ "Setting aside a reliance on set-asides" in *Washington Business Journal* (Vol. 22, No. 3, May 23, 2003, pp. 35)
Pub: Washington Business Journal
Ed: Tania Anderson. Description: An examination of the management and development of Native Technologies, an American Indian-owned company is presented.

41980 ■ "Shady Business" in *Entrepreneur* (Vol. 30, No. 2, February 2002, pp. 22)
Pub: Entrepreneur Media Inc.
Ed: Gisela M. Pedroza. Description: Profile of eShades, made by Inviso Inc., are glasses that project an image the size of a desktop monitor at a comfortable distance.

41981 ■ "Shopping List" in *Entrepreneur* (Vol. 32, August 2004, No. 8, pp. 43)
Pub: Entrepreneur Media Inc.
Description: Versions of Bluetooth technology are highlighted, including manufacturer, contact information, and features.

41982 ■ "Sides Vie to Regulate Internet-Based Service; Michigan Wants to Play Role" in *Crain's Detroit Business* (Vol. 21, January 24, 2005)
Pub: Crain Communications Inc. - Detroit
Ed: Amy Lane. Description: States across the nation, including Michigan, believe they should play a role in the regulation of Internet-based phone service, called Voice over Internet Protocol (VoIP).

41983 ■ "Signs of Life? You'll Need Plenty of Patience to Profit from M-Commerce" in *Entrepreneur* (Vol. 31, No. 10, October 2003, pp. 28)
Pub: Entrepreneur Media, Inc.
Ed: Amanda C. Kooser. Description: M-Commerce, or mobile commerce, is discussed. The sector has seen disappointing early experiences, but many entrepreneurs are looking forward to a full-blown m-commerce future.

41984 ■ *Silicon Gold Rush: The Next Generation of High-Tech Stars Rewrite the Rules of Business*
Pub: John Wiley & Sons, Inc.
Ed: Karen Southwick. Released: 1999. Price: $24.95.

41985 ■ "The Silicon Killer" in *Red Herring* (No. 99, June 15 & July 1, 2001, pp. 102, 104-105)
Pub: Herring Communications
Ed: Glenn Zorpette. Description: The discovery of gallium nitride (GaN) could lead researchers to a supertransistor; if the transistors could be fabricated economically, GaN could be the cornerstone of several communication technologies.

41986 ■ "Silicon Still Matters" in *Forbes* (March 25, 2002, p. 60)
Pub: Forbes Magazine
Ed: Edward Clendaniel. Description: The ups and downs of the high tech industry are highlighted showing how the leaders are able to cope during the down times.

41987 ■ "Silverado's Clean Coal Technology Coming To Choctaw County" in *Mississippi Business Journal* (Vol. 29, January 2007, No. 2, pp. 22)
Pub: Venture Publications, Inc.
Ed: Lynn Lofton Description: Silverado Green Fuel Inc. will build a new $26 million clean coal technology project in Choctaw County which promises to help decrease the country's dependence on foreign oil and make Mississippi the center of alternative fuel production.

41988 ■ "Similac Launches Online Moms' Community" in *Marketing to Women* (Vol. 19, November 2006, No. 11, pp. 3)
Pub: EPM Communications, Inc.
Description: Similacmomsalliance.com, a Website by Abbott Laboratories who manufacture Similac baby formulas, launched the site to provide a community forum for mothers. Panel members include Itsy Bitsy Yoga founder Helen Garabedian, Pediatrician Julie Segal and Olympic swimmer and mom Summer Sanders.

41989 ■ "Sister Act" in *My Business* (February/March 2004, pp. 28-31)
Pub: My Business Magazine
Ed: Nancy Mann Jackson. Description: Profile of three sisters who started a coffee shop together; profile of a sister and brother who own an office furniture installation and facility management company together; another brother and sister team who run a successful mail sorting firm; and two brothers who own a telecommunications management company. Each team shares advice to others wishing to start a family business.

41990 ■ "Sleepy Little Towns Turn High Tech" in *Home Office Computing* (Vol. 19, No. 1, January 2001, pp. 17)
Pub: Scholastic Inc.
Ed: Lisa Roberts. Description: The agricultural town of Petaluma, California suddenly found itself a high-tech center when local firm Ceret Corp was acquired by networking giant Cisco Systems and 40 other telecom firms established facilities in the area. Petaluma has become a model for many other rural areas whose economies are disappearing. Tazwell County, Virginia has adopted a similar strategy in an effort to attract high-technology companies to an area where population has been declining.

41991 ■ *Small Business Clustering Technology: Applications in Marketing, Management, Finance, and IT*
Pub: Idea Group Publishing
Ed: Robert C. MacGregor; Ann Hodgkinson. Released: June 2006. Description: An overview of the development and role of small business clusters in disciplines that include economics, marketing, management and information systems.

41992 ■ "Smart Set" in *Inc.* (November 1, 2003)
Pub: Gruner & Jahr USA Publishing
Ed: Bobbie Gossage. Description: Hiring incentives and tax abatements are attracting new business to the Lawrence, Kansas area, especially in the area of biotechnology.

41993 ■ "Smarter highways to revolutionize the way we drive" in *Ingram's* (Vol. 28, No. 2, February 2002, pp. 53)
Pub: Show Me Publishing, Inc.
Description: Information regarding the implementation of smart highways is discussed. By utilizing global positioning systems in automobiles and highway systems, drivers will be advised immediately on changes in driving conditions, thus allowing for less traffic congestion and accidents.

41994 ■ *SMEs and New Technologies: Learning E-Business and Development*
Pub: Palgrave Macmillan
Ed: Banji Oyelaran-Oyeyinka; Kaushalesh Lal. Released: October 2006. Price: $85.00. Description: Adoption and learning of new information technologies in developing nations is covered. New technologies are opening opportunities for small companies in these countries.

41995 ■ "Software/Hardware Sector Seconds August VC Spending" in *Venture Capital Journal* (Vol. 40, No. 10, October 2000, pp. 14)
Pub: Venture Economics
Description: Venture capitalists invested in 74 computer software and hardware companies during August, for a total of nearly $1 billion, compared with $500 million for 53 firms in July.

41996 ■ "Solar Cells: The New Light Fantastic" in *Business Week Online* (January 31, 2005)
Pub: McGraw-Hill Companies
Ed: Olga Kharif. Description: Solar cell prices have fallen 5 to 6 percent a year, but that trend is expected to change since they will be manufactured through complex processes similar to those used for making computer processors and memory cards.

41997 ■ "Soldiers of fortune" in *Entrepreneur* (Vol. 31, No. 5, May 2003, pp. 27)
Pub: Entrepreneur Media Inc.
Ed: April Y. Pennington. Description: Profile of Advanced Internet Technologies in Fayetteville, North Carolina, a Web hosting firm founded by Clarence Briggs. Briggs uses the same sense of discipline and structure he learned while in the Army.

41998 ■ "Some Relief Over End of Pixelworks Merger" in *Business Journal-Portland* (Vol. 20, No. 23, August 8, 2003, pp. 8)
Pub: American City Business Journals, Inc.
Ed: Aliza Earnshaw. Description: The proposed merger between Pixelworks Inc. and Genesis Microchip Inc. has been scrapped. Genesis Microchip, led by CEO Eric Erdman, reported lower than expected revenues for the second quarter 2003.

41999 ■ "Sonoma County, Calif., Voters Set to Decide Whether to Ban Biotech Crops" in *Sacramento Bee* (November 2, 2005)
Pub: The Sacramento Bee
Ed: Jim Wasserman. Description: Sonoma County voters will decide whether to ban biotech crops. If passed, the county will be included among Mendocino, Marin and Trinity counties banning these crops that are used to repel insects and chemical weed killers. In 2004 growers in the county produced $526 million from wine grapes, dairy cows and poultry.

42000 ■ "Space and Technology" in *The Economist* (Vol. 376, July 16-22, 2005, No. 8435, pp. 75-76)
Pub: The Economist Newspaper Ltd.
Description: NASA's new administrator, Dr. Mike Griffin, wants to capitalize on existing technical and workforce assets as a cost-effective and efficient means for building a new space vehicle; good news for Texas and Florida where many workers live.

42001 ■ "Special Report" in *The Economist* (Vol. 376, July 16-22, 2005, No. 8435, pp. 65-67)
Pub: The Economist Newspaper Ltd.

Description: New, faster computer chips are impacting the business-software industry.

42002 ■ "Spinoff Doctors" in *Entrepreneur* (Vol. 32, November 2004, No. 11, pp. 18)
Pub: Entrepreneur Media Inc.
Ed: David Worrel. Description: Trends in the venture capital industry are spotlighted.

42003 ■ "Spy tech" in *Crain's Detroit Business* (Vol. 19, No. 11, March 17, 2003, pp. 11)
Pub: Crain Communications Inc., Detroit
Ed: Jennette Smith. Description: Ann Arbor-based research and development firm, Veridian, is a specialist in national security work. The firm reported 2002 revenue of nearly $79 million, and has increased sales by 10 percent a year for the past few years.

42004 ■ "Squeezed out? Is there any room left for small businesses in federal contracting?" in *Entrepreneur* (Vol. 31, No. 4, April 2003)
Pub: Entrepreneur Media Inc.
Ed: Chris Penttila. Description: In 2001, contract bundling cost small businesses an estimated $13 billion. Technology, engineering and outsourcing companies are expected to benefit from new Homeland Security projects, but the question is, will that include small companies.

42005 ■ "Stacking the Digital Deck" in *Hispanic Business* (May 2005, pp. 32, 34, 36, 38)
Pub: Hispanic Business
Ed: Kevin Savetz. Description: The newest technology systems and business software can help small companies target new markets, increase productivity, and lower costs.

42006 ■ "Stand by NASA research" in *Red Herring* (March 2003, pp. 17)
Pub: Herring Communications Inc.
Description: NASA research and development has resulted in growth in technology sectors such as communications, energy and the robotics industry.

42007 ■ "Starting From Zero: Entrepreneur Reaps Success During Rocky Tech Times" in *Black Enterprise* (Vol. 34, July 2004, No. 12, pp. 53)
Pub: Earl G. Graves Publishing Co. Inc.
Ed: Bridget McCrea. Description: Profile of Glenn Davis, owner of Virginia-based BranCore Technologies. Working from home, Davis borrowed $15,000 from his 401(k) to launch his minority-owned firm that provides project management and e-commerce consulting.

42008 ■ "State broadband authority begins funding programs" in *Crain's Detroit Business* (Vol. 19, No. 7, February 17, 2003, pp. 12)
Pub: Crain Communications Inc., Detroit
Ed: Amy Lane. Description: The Michigan Broadband Development Authority is close to finalizing on $100 million loans in 2003, its first full year in business.

42009 ■ "State to seek VC to ease biotech cuts" in *Crain's Detroit Business* (Vol. 19, No. 8, February 24, 2003, pp. 1)
Pub: Crain Communications Inc., Detroit
Ed: Amy Lane. Description: Governor Jennifer Granholm, in an attempt to cut the state's budget, has cut $12.5 million from Michigan life sciences funding and is seeking venture capitalists to pick up the slack.

42010 ■ "Sterling Venture, Set to Close Fund I" in *Venture Capital Journal* (Vol. 40, No. 10, October 2000, pp. 24)
Pub: Venture Economics
Description: Sterling Venture prefers to be the first to back a company and work with entrepreneurs.

42011 ■ **"Stockholders in Cyberspace: Weick's Sensemaking Online"** in *Journal of Business Communication* (Vol. 44, January 2007, No. 1, pp. 13)
Pub: Association for Business Communication
Ed: Andrew F. Herrmann. **Description:** Stockholders are using the Internet's discussion boards to make sense of their financial holdings.

42012 ■ **"Stocks Go Up, Stocks Go Down, But Innovators Keep Innovating"** in *San Jose Mercury News* (March 8, 2005)
Pub: Knight-Ridder/Tribune Business News
Ed: Chris O'Brien. **Description:** Profile of software developer, Paul Mercer. Mercer's self-financed start-tup, Iventor of Palo Alto, is creating a new generation of software for mobile devices.

42013 ■ **"Strather Launches Hitsville Gaming-But Not in U.S."** in *Crain's Detroit Business* (Vol. 22, December 18, 2006, No. 5, pp. 3)
Pub: Crain Communications Inc. - Detroit
Ed: Robert Ankeny **Description:** Innovative entrepreneur capitalizes on Motown heritage for his online casino. Only international wagers can be placed as internet gambling is illegal in the U.S. Hitsville name used due to copyright laws not permitting the use of Motown.

42014 ■ **"Strength in numbers"** in *Washington Business Journal* (Vol. 22, No. 3, May 23, 2003, pp. 3)
Pub: Washington Business Journal
Ed: John Wilen. **Description:** The economic outlook for the Washington, DC area is discussed, including employment levels, layoffs, and growth within the computer industry.

42015 ■ **"Study shows businesses are slow to embrace e-commerce"** in *Black Enterprise* (Vol. 32)
Pub: Earl Graves Publishing Co.
Ed: Bevolyn Williams-Harold. **Description:** The Minority Business Development Agency is urging minority-owned businesses to use e-commerce to help grow their companies. Statistical data included.

42016 ■ **"Sun Microsystems Remakes Its Sales Force"** in *Wall Street Journal* (Vol. 248, December 2006, No. 149, pp. B3)
Pub: Dow Jones & Co. Inc.
Ed: Christopher Lawton **Description:** Sun Microsystems makes a dramatic change in the retraining of its' sales force to focus on customers' needs in growing their businesses.

42017 ■ **"Super Cell"** in *Forbes* (Vol. 175, February 14, 2005, No. 3, pp. 46)
Pub: Forbes Magazine Inc.
Ed: Benjamin Fulford, David Whelan. **Description:** Profile of the new chip called Cell. Cell is a powerful microprocessor produced by a consortium of Sony, Toshiba and IBM and will be the brains behind the next-generation Sony PlayStation 3, due on the market in 2006.

42018 ■ **"Superior Consultant Holdings sees demand for health care IT"** in *Crain's Detroit Business* (Vol. 19, No. 13, March 31, 2003, pp. 4)
Pub: Crain Communications Inc., Detroit
Ed: Andrew Dietderich. **Description:** Compliance with the Health Insurance Portability and Accountability Act, quality mandates and physician connectivity are fueling demand for hardware and software and Southfield-based Superior Consultant Holdings Corporation is planning a new $5 million data-processing center.

42019 ■ **"Supplier Innovation Key to Industry Future, Exec Says"** in *Crain's Detroit Business* (Vol. 21, January 24, 2005, No. 4, pp. 5)
Pub: Crain Communications Inc. - Detroit
Ed: Terry Kosdrosky. **Description:** According to Paul Wilbur, president of ASC Inc., suppliers need to bring the latest and best technology to automakers in order to survive, despite added costs.

42020 ■ **"Surfing the Virtual Wave"** in *Business 2.0* (Vol. 6, May 2005, No. 4, pp. 116-118)
Pub: Time, Inc.
Ed: John Battelle. **Description:** Sky Dayton, founder of EarthLink is developing a plan to put Korea's version of wireless broadband on U.S. cellular phones.

42021 ■ **"Survey: Tech Spending Likely to Stabilize, but Not Show Big Increase This Year"** in *Daily Business Review* (Vol. 77, March 12, 2003)
Pub: American Lawyer Media LP
Description: Goldman Sachs polled technology buyers in February 2003 and found that many executives expect information technology spending to increase in 2003. Further results of the survey are discussed.

42022 ■ **"Suspended Animation: New Technology Lets You Take Your PC Anywhere—Virtually"** in *Black Enterprise* (Vol. 35, November 2004, No. 4)
Pub: Earl G. Graves Publishing Co. Inc.
Ed: Rebecca Rohan. **Description:** New technology allows individuals to leave a computer at home or the workplace and return to exactly where the users left off at another computer in another location, via the Internet.

42023 ■ **"Symbol Technologies Appoints Steinberg as CTO and VP of Its Mobility Solutions Group"** in *Long Island Business News* (February 6, 2004)
Pub: Dolan Media Newswires
Ed: Ryan McCormick. **Description:** Profile of Lou Steinberg, newly appointed CTO and vice president of Symbol Technologies; Steinberg will be responsible for coordinating the firm's global sales, and development of end-to-end product requirements. He will also create marketing communications around the company's mobile solutions.

42024 ■ **"Symbol Technologies Inc. Hires Former IBM Executive"** in *Long Island Business News* (March 5, 2004)
Pub: Dolan Media Newswires
Description: Profiles of Verlin P. Youd, vice president of retail systems for Symbol Technologies Inc., and Anthony Bartolo, vice president and general manager of wireless infrastructure division.

42025 ■ **"Tactics: Technology's earnings riddle"** in *Red Herring* (No. 103, September 1, 2001, pp. 88)
Pub: Herring Communications
Ed: Pip Coburn. **Description:** For the last four years, the technology sector experienced either the largest or second-largest gains in earnings. However, for 2001, it's on track to come in dead last.

42026 ■ **"Tactics: Will better be good enough?"** in *Red Herring* (No. 102, August 15, 2001, pp. 94)
Pub: Herring Communications
Ed: Arnold Berman. **Description:** In 2002, the questions about technology stocks will have more to do with valuation, rather than the broad spending environment.

42027 ■ **"Take It For Granted"** in *Entrepreneur* (Vol. 33, January 2005, No. 1, pp. 50)
Pub: Entrepreneur Media Inc.
Ed: David Worrell. **Description:** U.S. Small Business Innovative Research grants and contracts provide funding for small companies to develop high tech products. The programs are divided into two phases: one is to study the feasibility of a new technology or idea, the second to encourage commercialization of a particular technology.

42028 ■ **"Take a peek at tech site"** in *Crain's Detroit Business* (Vol. 16, No. 49, December 4, 2000, pp. 9)
Pub: Crain Communications, Inc.
Description: Information regarding the Crain Web site, including its newly expanded technology section.

42029 ■ **"Taking Technology Curbside and Beyond"** in *Black Enterprise* (Vol. 35, October 2004, No. 3, pp. 63)
Pub: Earl G. Graves Publishing Co. Inc.
Ed: Bridget McCrea. **Description:** Wyndham International Inc. is offering smooth check-ins for visitors with the use of handheld wireless devices used by employees to check guests in right at curbside. Lyndon A. Brown, who developed the new system, was nominated for USBE & Information Technology magazine's 2003 Black Engineer of the Year award.

42030 ■ **"Talented work force credited for right ideas"** in *Crain's Detroit Business* (Vol. 19, No. 13, March 31, 2003, pp. 14)
Pub: Crain Communications Inc., Detroit
Description: Profile of Menlo Institute LLC, the software development services company. Rick Sheridan, co-founder and instructor believes the success of the firm lies in having the right product at the right time developed by the right people.

42031 ■ **"A Team Sport"** in *Entrepreneur* (Vol. 31, No. 9, September 2003, pp. 27)
Pub: Entrepreneur Media, Inc.
Ed: Mark Henricks. **Description:** Review of the book, "How Breakthroughs Happen", describing technology brokering, the processes that occurs when inventors borrow existing ideas from one or more fields and gather the people, funding and other assets needed to assemble and apply those ideas elsewhere.

42032 ■ **"Tech Biz. Tough Crowd"** in *Boston Business Journal* (Vol. 23, No. 21, June 27, 2003, pp. 16)
Pub: American City Business Journals
Description: Silicon Dimensions Inc. (Marlborough, Massachusetts) acquired $3 million in investment from Globespan Capital Partners and Kodiak Venture Partners. Michael Naum, one of the three founders of the company, had to learn how to successfully give effective presentations in order to gain venture capital.

42033 ■ **"Tech and the City: What Cities Are Rising Fast on the High-Tech Horizon?"** in *Entrepreneur* (Vol. 32, October 2004, No. 10, pp. 36)
Pub: Entrepreneur Media Inc.
Ed: Melissa Campanelli. **Description:** U.S. cities offering opportunity for high-tech companies include Camden, New Jersey where the New Jersey Economic Development Authority is developing the Camden Waterfront Technology Center; Madison, Wisconsin's economic development initiative, Technology Zone Program; Tucson, Arizona, with area companies working with the SBA SBIR and SBTT federal grant programs to attract high tech companies; and South Lafayette, Louisiana's Acadiana Technology Immersion Center.

42034 ■ **"Tech"** in *Entrepreneur* (Vol. 32, No. 1, January 2004, pp. 252)
Pub: Entrepreneur Media, Inc.
Description: Profiles of three technical franchise opportunities, including Friendly Computers; Geeks On Call, providing computer repair, networks, and one-on-one training; Expetec, provides mobile, on-site, high-level technology services to business and consumer customers; Concerto Networks Inc., offers nationwide information technology computer and network services; and ACE America's Cash Express, gives customers financial services that include check cashing, short-term loans, money orders, wire transfers, bill payments, pre-paid telecommunications and more.

42035 ■ **"Tech Firm CEO's Solution: Unify Segments"** in *Crain's Chicago Business* (Vol. 30, January 2007, No. 5, pp. 6)
Pub: Crain Communications, Inc.
Description: Profile of Brandon Glenn, CEO of Technology Solutions Co., a Chicago-based information technology firm that is publicly traded. Although Glenn has never before served as a CEO, but feels he will be able to return Tech Solutions to the black by creating a unifying theme between the company's three business segments.

42036 ■ "Tech Firms Prepare as Upgrade Cycle Set to Drive Growth" in *Crain's Detroit Business* **(Vol. 19, No. 45, November 10, 2003, pp. 20)**
Pub: Crain Communications Inc., Detroit
Ed: Andrew Dietderich. Description: Computer networks and security will be the area small companies will need to upgrade during 2004, and Troy-based Data Management Inc. hopes to cash in on the trend.

42037 ■ "Tech firms' juicy new prospect" in *Wall Street Journal* **(April 22, 2002, pp. B1)**
Pub: Wall Street Journal
Ed: Lee Gomes. Description: An overview of customer relationship management, including terrorism-tracking programs are presented.

42038 ■ "Tech futures: Need a map for where business goes from here?" in *Entrepreneur* **(Vol. 30, No. 1, January 2002, pp. 27)**
Pub: Entrepreneur Media Inc.
Ed: Mark Henricks. Description: Book reviews of the title, "The Internet Galaxy", which suggests that the Internet's influence on commerce has just begun; and "The War for Talent", which offers five imperatives that can help hire the best people for a business.

42039 ■ "Tech firms like Granholm's economic plan" in *Crain's Detroit Business* **(Vol. 18, No. 22, June 3, 2002, pp. 53)**
Pub: Crain Communications Inc. - Detroit
Ed: Andrew Dietderich. Description: The Michigan State Attorney General has called for the creation of the Michigan Technology Tri-Corridor, which would expand the state's $40 million Life Sciences Corridor and promote automotive technology and homeland security research and development programs.

42040 ■ "Tech the Halls" in *Black Enterprise* **(Vol. 34, No. 5, December 2003)**
Pub: Earl Graves Publishing Co.
Ed: Sonya A. Donaldson. Description: Profile of new technology devices available for the holidays, including Pentax Optio S4 camera, Siemens SL56 cellular phone, Apple Power Mac G5 computer, Sony Personal Entertainment Communicator, Palm Tungsten T3 wireless handheld device, Canon Optura 20 camera, Archos A120 MP4 video player, Panasonic SV-AV100sd video camera, Iomega Super DVD-RW, Canon i900D digital camera, RIM Blackberry 7210 device, Fuji Film Finepix S5000 digital camera, a Tablet PC by Acer, and KDS Rad-7xp color computer monitor.

42041 ■ "Tech, Please: 'Next-Generation CIOs' Offer More Than Just Tech Advice" in *Entrepreneur* **(Vol. 33, January 2005, No. 1, pp. 22)**
Pub: Entrepreneur Media Inc.
Ed: Mark Henricks. Description: Successful chief information officers understand the business in which they work. They should continually examine new technologies and competitors' IT practices, and bring in new products, services and process improvements.

42042 ■ "Tech Stock Knockout" in *Black Enterprise* **(Vol. 35, November 2004, No. 4, pp. 42)**
Pub: Earl G. Graves Publishing Co. Inc.
Ed: Rhonda Reynolds. Description: Anthony K. Johnson, CIO for the Philadelphia Public Employee Retirement System, believes in the technology stocks in the system's portfolio.

42043 ■ *Tech Support Yellow Pages*
Pub: CyberMedia
Price: $19.95, individuals. Covers: 2,000 computer companies and 500 personal computer user groups. Entries Include: Company name, address, phone, web addresses, user group web addresses.

42044 ■ "Tech Talk" in *St. Louis Post-Dispatch* **(December 31, 2004)**
Pub: Knight-Ridder/Tribune Business News
Ed: David Sheets. Description: Joseph E. Walsh Jr., patent attorney, explains how he nearly fell prey to

techno-fraud in the form of an email that appeared to be from his bank. Phishing, carding or spoofing are techniques that try to extract important information from individuals using fake emails that appear to be authentic.

42045 ■ "Tech towns: which U.S. cities are today's hotbeds of technology?" in *Entrepreneur* **(Vol. 31, No. 6, June 2003, pp. 24)**
Pub: Entrepreneur Media Inc.
Ed: Amanda C. Kooser. Description: Atlanta, Georgia; Austin, Texas, and Boise, Idaho are becoming the largest growing cities for the technology industries.

42046 ■ "Tech Toy" in *Entrepreneur* **(Vol. 31, No. 10, October 2003, pp. 26)**
Pub: Entrepreneur Media, Inc.
Ed: Gisela M. Pedroza. Description: Profile of Sony's robot dog called AIBO Cyber-Blue, when connected with AIBO EYES software, the robot dog connects to Internet-enabled PC or mobile devices and can take digital snapshots and email them to another location.

42047 ■ "The Tech Track" in *Hispanic Business* **(January/February 2005, pp. 56, 58)**
Pub: Hispanic Business
Ed: Anthony Limon. Description: The Information Technology Association of America reports a 2 percent increase in employment for first quarter periods of 2003 and 2004. The technology sector is slowly re-absorbing displaced workers, however banking, finance, manufacturing, food service and transportation accounted for 89 percent of new IT jobs. Statistical data included.

42048 ■ "Tech-wreck survivors" in *Crain's Detroit Business* **(Vol. 19, No. 13, March 31, 2003, pp. 11)**
Pub: Crain Communications Inc., Detroit
Ed: Andrew Dietderich. Description: Information on seven metro Detroit area high tech companies that have prospered while others have gone out of business is discussed. The CEOs of Clarity LLC, Dewpoint Inc., ePrize LLC, Fry Inc., The Menlo Institute LLC, New World Systems, and Stoneage.com are interviewed.

42049 ■ *Technological Entrepreneurship*
Pub: Edward Elgar Publishing, Incorporated
Ed: Donald Siegel. Released: October 2006. Price: $230.00. Description: Technological entrepreneurship at universities is discussed. The book covers four related topics: university licensing and patenting; science parks and incubators; university-based startups; and the role of academic science in entrepreneurship.

42050 ■ "Technology" in *Crain's Detroit Business* **(Vol. 19, No. 45, November 10, 2003, pp. 20)**
Pub: Crain Communications Inc., Detroit
Description: Aging wire and cable networks, as well as other issues will face small businesses in 2004. High speed, secure wireless networks is just one of the issues listed.

42051 ■ "Technology Evolving At Beall's" in *Bradenton Herald* **(February 14, 2005)**
Pub: Bradenton Herald
Ed: Dana Sanchez. Description: Profile of Don Keller, production manager of one of Beall's Inc.'s two large distribution centers. Keller is phasing in voice recognition technology in its warehouses to increase efficiency in handling inventories.

42052 ■ "Technology and Human Vulnerability" in *Harvard Business Review* **(Vol. 81, No. 9, September 2003, pp. 43)**
Pub: Harvard Business School Press
Description: Researchers at MIT and Caltech are investigating the benefits and drawbacks of computer technology in our society.

42053 ■ "Technology Stocks Show Some Life" in *Black Enterprise* **(Vol. 35, January 2005, No. 6, pp. 36)**
Pub: Earl G. Graves Publishing Co. Inc.
Ed: Nicole Lewis. Description: An overview of technology stocks is given. The technology sector was expected to show strong growth in 2004, but so far it has shown small returns.

42054 ■ "The technology trade-off" in *Red Herring* **(No. 102, August 15, 2001, pp. 33)**
Pub: Herring Communications
Ed: Tim Jackson. Description: The impact of technologies such as the Internet and mobile-commuting is making people step back and appreciate the more traditional, non-technical parts of life.

42055 ■ "Technology's Growth Champs" in *Forbes* **(Vol. 175, February 14, 2005, No. 3, pp. 100)**
Pub: Forbes Magazine Inc.
Ed: Jody Yen. Description: Profiles of the 25 fastest growing technology companies in the U.S. are presented. AtRoad of Fremont, California is number one in five-year sales growth.

42056 ■ "Technophobe Help Desk" in *Sales & Marketing Management* **(Vol. 158, November-December 2006, No. 11, pp. 20)**
Pub: VNU Business Media
Description: Keylogging is a form of Internet theft, whereby keylogging programs copy the keystrokes of computer users then sends the data to thieves.

42057 ■ "Telecom recession may have hit bottom" in *Atlanta Business Chronicle* **(Vol. 25, January 3, 2003, No. 30, pp. 3A)**
Pub: American City Business Publications, Inc.
Ed: Mary Jane Credeur. Description: In the year 2003, a slight recovery in the telecom recession could be in the making. Already BellSouth Corporation and other Baby Bells have experienced a rise in stock prices. In the fourth quarter 2002, BellSouth reported a shares' gain of 43.2 percent.

42058 ■ "Telecom Rewrite Has New Rules for Wireless" in *Crain's Detroit Business* **(Vol. 21, October 17, 2005, No. 43, pp. 7)**
Pub: Crain Communications Inc. - Detroit
Ed: Amy Lane. Description: A Michigan telecommunications law rewrite was passed by the Senate in October 2005. The law places new regulations on wireless and carriers and required business-call offerings.

42059 ■ "Telecom's transformation continues in Georgia" in *Atlanta Business Chronicle* **(Vol. 25, January 10, 2003, No. 31, pp. 17A)**
Pub: American City Business Publications, Inc.
Ed: Charles Davidson. Description: In the midst of a drastic recession, the communications industry is poised for recovery, even though full recovery may be a long way off. Trends in telecommunications like bundling - offering an array of communications services in one package with one price - are here to stay. Wireless device usage will continue to increase.

42060 ■ "Tenet Healthcare Ends Fight over Heart Program at Stuart, Fla. Medical Center" in *Palm Beach Post* **(April 11, 2003)**
Pub: Knight-Ridder/Tribune Business News
Ed: Phil Galewitz. Description: Tenet Healthcare Corporation has dropped its long-standing opposition to a new open-heart surgery program at Martin Memorial Medical Center, located in Stuart, Florida. There are four hospitals in the area now performing open-heart surgery and are among the most profitable hospitals in the region.

42061 ■ "That's the Spot" in *Entrepreneur. com* **(Vol. 34, February 2006, No. 2, pp. 35)**
Pub: Entrepreneur Media Inc.
Description: JiWire and Wi Finder help locate hot spots for Internet access before you hit the roads. The software can be downloaded at no charge and includes a directory of more than 70,000 hot spots in 103 countries.

42062 ■ "The 'IT' Factor" in *Hispanic Business* **(November 2006, pp. 26, 28, 30)**
Pub: Hispanic Business
Ed: Keith Rosenblum. Description: Profile of Abba Tech, the New Mexico information technology firm that is competing with large companies through service and knowledge.

42063 ■ "There's No There There" in *Red Herring* (No. 99, June 15 & July 1, 2001, pp. 134)
Pub: Herring Communications
Ed: David Lipschultz. **Description:** Distressed investors are those who assign value to companies that other investors avoid. Distressed investors do not believe there is hidden value in the recent bankrupt technology firms.

42064 ■ "Think Tech; Automation Alley" in *Crain's Detroit Business* (Vol. 21, October 3, 2005, No. 43, pp. 1)
Pub: Crain Communications Inc. - Detroit
Ed: Andrew Dietderich, Sheena Harrison. **Description:** Two technology companies are working to keep and attract technology companies and jobs to Southeastern Michigan. The state lost 17,600 tech jobs between 2002 and 2003. Automation Alley of Troy and Sparks of Ann Arbor hope to double the number of tech companies and triple the number of tech workers by 2010.

42065 ■ "Threat Level" in *Entrepreneur* (Vol. 31, No. 8, August 2003, pp. 28)
Pub: Entrepreneur Media, Inc.
Ed: Michael Miora, Geoff Williams. **Description:** Michael Miora, CEO and founder of ContingenZ Corporation in Playa del Rey, California, discusses the threat of cyberterrorism and business. Miora's incident management and planning firm offers expertise to the National Reconnaissance Office, the government agency that builds America's spy satellites.

42066 ■ *301 Great Ideas for Using Technology to Grow Your Business*
Pub: Inc. Publishing
Ed: Phaedra Hise. **Released:** 1998. **Price:** $14.95.

42067 ■ "Through a Wall, Clearly" in *Business 2.0* (Vol. 7, January/February 2006, No. 1, pp. 28)
Pub: Time, Inc.
Ed: Rebecca Jarvis. **Description:** Radar imaging technology could assist police and firefighters in saving lives.

42068 ■ "Ticker Takes: Jmar Technologies" in *San Diego Business Journal* (Vol. 28, January 15, 2007, No. 3, pp. 10)
Pub: San Diego Business Journal Associates
Ed: Mike Allen. **Description:** Jmar Technologies was delisted form the Nasdaq exchange based on the firm's inability to meet the $1 minimum price per share.

42069 ■ "Tin Whiskers" in *Fortune* (Vol. 151, January 10, 2005, No. 1, pp. 27)
Pub: Time Inc.
Ed: Ivan Amato. **Description:** The loss of the Galaxy 4 communications satellite short circuited and some 40 million pagers stopped working across the U.S. Tin whiskers in electronic and electrical systems, the process by which tin grows whiskers, is little-understood and can cause systems to short circuit. The catastrophic consequences to radar systems, pacemakers, fuse switches in air-to-air missiles, electronic relays in a nuclear power plant, and global positioning system receivers, as well as satellites have all fallen victim to tin whiskers, costing losses in billions of dollars.

42070 ■ "Titans Tune In" in *Hispanic Business* (May 2005, pp. 46, 48)
Pub: Hispanic Business
Ed: Kevin Brass. **Description:** The ever-expanding Hispanic technology market is increasing sales for computers and helping to equip the small to mid-size Hispanic firms who spent $14.8 billion on IT in 2004. Statistical data included.

42071 ■ "TodaysMama.com Relaunches Website" in *Marketing to Women* (Vol. 20, January 2007, No. 1, pp. 3)
Pub: EPM Communications, Inc.
Description: TodaysMama.com, an online resource for mothers, debuted its enhanced Website. They have partnered with Kiva, a charitable organization, to fund microloans to entrepreneurs in developing nations.

42072 ■ "TomTom GO910: On the Road Again" in *Black Enterprise* (Vol. 37, January 2007, No. 6, pp. 52)
Pub: Earl G. Graves Publishing Co. Inc.
Ed: Stephanie Young. **Description:** TomTom GO 910 is a GPS navigator that offers detailed maps of the U.S., Canada, and Europe. Consumers view their routes by a customizable LCD screen showing everything from the quickest to the shortest routes available or how to avoid toll roads. Business travelers may find this product invaluable as it also functions as a cell phone and connects to a variety of other multi-media devices.

42073 ■ "Total Tech LLC" in *San Diego Business Journal* (Vol. 28, January 15, 2007, No. 3, pp. 34)
Pub: San Diego Business Journal Associates
Ed: Jessica Long. **Description:** Profile of Kenneth Hamilton, president and chief executive officer of Total Tech LLC. Hamilton recalls his reasons for starting a business and shares his business weaknesses and strengths.

42074 ■ "Treo" in *Business Week* (January 16, 2006, No. 3967, pp. 18)
Pub: McGraw-Hill Companies
Ed: Stephen H. Wildstrom. **Description:** Profile of the new Treo 700w which runs on Microsoft software. The new device is the first Pocket PC that offers home screen features such as speed-dial buttons and two boxes for entering text.

42075 ■ "Trouble In PDA Paradise" in *Entrepreneur* (Vol. 31, No. 7, July 2003, pp. 44)
Pub: Entrepreneur Media, Inc.
Ed: Amanda C. Kooser. **Description:** An overview of information for entrepreneurs when choosing personal digital assistant devices is provided. Many entrepreneurs will find built-in Wi-Fi or Bluetooth, flash memory and wireless communication capabilities attractive.

42076 ■ "The true believer" in *Red Herring* (March 2003, pp. 56)
Pub: Herring Communications Inc.
Ed: Lee Bruno. **Description:** Scientific developments that are transforming nanotechnology from science fiction to reality are explored, including challenges facing the nanotechnology industry and the talents and skills needed for newcomers to the industry.

42077 ■ "Truly Personal Entertainment" in *Sales & Marketing Management* (Vol. 158, October 2006, No. 10, pp. 52)
Pub: VNU Business Media
Ed: Tali Arbel. **Description:** DVD/VCD players or a video iPod can help business travelers pass time on airlines or buses.

42078 ■ "Truth or Consequences" in *Red Herring* (No. 99, June 15 & July 1, 2001, pp. 120)
Pub: Herring Communications
Ed: Dean Takahashi **Description:** The worldwide market for chip-verification software is expected to grow nearly 16 percent annually.

42079 ■ "Turing the Page" in *Business 2.0* (Vol. 6, July 2005, No. 6, pp. 98-100)
Pub: Time, Inc.
Ed: John Battelle. **Description:** Xerox CEO Anne Mulcahy is digitizing the company she helped save. In an interview, Mulcahy discusses the humility that comes from turning a business around.

42080 ■ "Turning South; Sterling Heights Pushes Redevelopment of Older Areas as Vacant Land Dries Up" in *Crain's Detroit Business* (Vol. 21)
Pub: Crain Communications Inc. - Detroit
Ed: Anjali Fluker. **Description:** Many areas in the city of Sterling Heights, Michigan are zoned for mixed-use projects. The city is seeking developers to renovate vacant sites to bring a lifestyle center that combines retail, commercial and residential space.

42081 ■ "TV to Go" in *Entrepreneur* (Vol. 32, October 2004, No. 10, pp. 24)
Pub: Entrepreneur Media Inc.
Ed: Gisela M. Pedroza. **Description:** Profile of the Location-Free LF-X1 television from Sony. The set is a wireless portable set with a broadband connection to the Internet.

42082 ■ "The 2001 Hispanic Business High-Tech 50 Directory" in *Hispanic Business* (Vol. 23, No. 7/8, July/Aug. 2001, pp. 40)
Pub: Hispanic Business
Description: Presentation of the top 50 high-tech Hispanic businesses in the U.S. for 2001. The directory includes each company's location, CEO, product or service, number of employees, and year 2000 revenue.

42083 ■ "Uncertainty and Information Search Activities" in *Journal of Small Business Management* (Vol. 41, No. 4, October 2003, pp. 385)
Pub: International Council of Small Business
Ed: Jeffrey E. McGee, Olukemi O. Sawyerr. **Description:** An examination of the relationship among perceived strategic uncertainty (PSU), environmental scanning, and the information sources used by owner-managers, using 153 small high-technology manufacturing firms.

42084 ■ "Universal connectivity" in *Entrepreneur* (Vol. 30, No. 1, January 2002, pp. 43)
Pub: Entrepreneur Media Inc.
Ed: Mike Hogan. **Description:** Profile of the Toshiba Portege 4000 portable computer, that adds Wi-Fi and Bluetooth wireless technologies to its motherboard, along with an Ethernet adapter and a 56Kbps modem.

42085 ■ "Unleash the Wireless Future" in *Microsoft Executive Circle* (Vol. 1, No. 2, Q2 2001, pp. 28-29, 31)
Pub: Putman Media
Ed: Rex Davenport. **Description:** The benefits for using wireless networks in business are highlighted, including the listing of benefits from the Wireless LAN Association; a wireless checklist according to the Meta Group's Peter Firstbrook; and a listing of terms used when communicating about wireless networks.

42086 ■ "Up to Speed? Wireless Could be Just What the Lagging Tech Market Needs to Get Moving Again" in *Entrepreneur* (Vol. 31, August, 2003)
Pub: Entrepreneur Media, Inc.
Ed: Amanda C. Kooser. **Description:** Despite a slowing economy and the Internet bust a few years ago, technology innovation and tech spending in the area of wireless technologies is playing a substantial role, especially phone technologies and Wi-Fi.

42087 ■ "An Uptick In the Local Tech Index" in *Sacramento Bee* (November 25, 2005)
Pub: The Sacramento Bee
Ed: Clint Swett. **Description:** The Sacramento Area Regional Technology Alliance Technology Index rose 2.7 percent in third quarter 2005; the rise is fueled by higher stock prices and a small rise in hiring among private companies.

42088 ■ "Vacaville, Calif.-Based Biotech Firm Ends Operations" in *Sacramento Bee* (December 23, 2005)
Pub: The Sacramento Bee
Ed: Jim Wasserman. **Description:** Large Scale Biology Corporation, manufacturer of proteins and vaccines for tobacco plants closed its operations in Vacaville, California as well as its site in Kentucky, due to lack of funds. The firm went public five years ago.

42089 ■ "Valley Record Label Goes Back to Future" in *San Fernando Valley Business Journal* (Vol. 11, November 2006, No. 24, pp. 1)
Pub: San Fernando Valley Business Journal Associates
Ed: Mark R. Madler. **Description:** Profile of independent record label, Your Music America.

42090 ■ "Vanguard Adds Eilers, Wraps on Fund Seven" in *Venture Capital Journal* (Vol. 40, No. 10, November 2000, pp. 34)
Pub: Venture Economics
Description: Vanguard Venture Partners hired Daniel Eilers as the firm's fourth general partner. The firm backs early-stage communications equipment, Internet infrastructure and life sciences companies.

42091 ■ "VC infusions flagged: Tech firms hope year better than tough '01" in *Business First Columbus* (Vol. 18, No. 25, Feb. 8, 2002, pp. A3)
Pub: Business First Columbus, Inc.
Ed: Laura Newpoff. **Description:** Tech firms in Ohio are hoping that venture capitalists will provide more funding in 2002 than the previous year.

42092 ■ "VC Whispers: Glowing optimism" in *Red Herring* (No. 103, September 1, 2001, pp. 78)
Pub: Herring Communications
Ed: Lawrence Aragon. **Description:** Despite the fact that venture deals in energy-related companies have slowed, venture capitalists predict a bright future for the sector. Statistical data included.

42093 ■ "VC Whispers: Optical components shine brightly in a dreary market" in *Red Herring* (No. 102, August 15, 2001, pp. 76)
Pub: Herring Communications
Ed: Julie Landry. **Description:** Communications investors continue to put money into companies building optical components for carrier networks, because carriers continue to move forward with network upgrades to integrate smaller, cheaper, and more advanced components.

42094 ■ "VCs raid biotechs, nab talent" in *San Francisco Business Times* (Vol. 16, No. 42, May 24, 2002, pp. 1)
Pub: San Francisco Business Times Inc.
Ed: Brendan Doherty. **Description:** Venture capital companies are hiring scientists and other experts from the biotechnology industry, making it harder for research firms to get good talent.

42095 ■ "VCs Buoyed by $3B for Stem Cell Research" in *Venture Capital Journal* (December 1, 2004)
Pub: Thomason Financial Inc.
Description: Proposal 71 in California approves a stem cell research initiative in California, a big win for the venture capital industry.

42096 ■ "Venturelab Launches $50M Targeted Fund" in *Venture Capital Journal* (Vol. 40, No. 10, November 2000, pp. 22)
Pub: Venture Economics
Description: Keystone Venture VI LP will back about 25-30 information technology companies, particularly in the wireless, tool, e-commerce and affinity marketing spaces. The firm will target early expansion-stage companies.

42097 ■ "Verdi and Me" in *Inc.* (February 1, 2002)
Pub: Inc. Magazine
Ed: Donna Fenn. **Description:** Profile of high-tech entrepreneur Brent Habig speaks on singing opera, and how that makes him different from other entrepreneurs.

42098 ■ "Verizon Taps Strigl To Become President, Chief Operating Officer" in *Wall Street Journal* (Vol. 248, December 2006, No. 145, pp. B10)
Pub: Dow Jones & Co. Inc.
Ed: Wallstreet Journal News **Description:** Profile of Denny Strigl, newly appointed president and chief operating officer of Verizon Wireless. Strigl helped propel Verizon Wireless into a leadership position in the cellphone market.

42099 ■ "Veteran GPs Launch Maven" *Venture Capital Journal* (February 1, 2006)
Pub: Thomason Financial Inc.
Ed: Constance Loizos. **Description:** In January 2006, Jennifer Gill Roberts and Marc Friend were set to

launch fund-raising efforts for $150 million for an inaugural fund. The firm will focus on smart mobile services.

42100 ■ "Vonage V-Phone: Use Your Laptop to Make Calls Via the Internet" in *Black Enterprise* (Vol. 37, January 2007, No. 6, pp. 52)
Pub: Earl G. Graves Publishing Co. Inc.
Ed: James C. Johnson. **Description:** Overview of the Vonage V-Phone, which is small flash drive device that lets you make phone calls through a high-speed Internet connection and plugs into any computer's USB port. Business travels may find this product to be a wonderful solution as it includes 250MB of memory and can store files, digital photos, MP3s, and more.

42101 ■ "Voom Direct-Broadcast Satellite Service Offers High Definition News" in *Long Island Business News* (February 13, 2004)
Pub: Dolan Media Newswires
Ed: Ken Schachter. **Description:** Cablevision Systems' News 12 Long Island made television history with the country's first nationwide news broadcasts in high definition.

42102 ■ "Waiting in the Wings" in *Entrepreneur* (Vol. 32, No. 1, January 2004, pp. 21)
Pub: Entrepreneur Media, Inc.
Ed: David Worrell. **Description:** Market experts are predicting a rise in the number of Initial Public Offerings (IPOs) in 2004, although there is still strength in biotech and pharmaceutical companies, other sectors such as real estate, business services, healthcare and manufacturing are growing.

42103 ■ "Wall-To-Wall: Wireless Jacks are the 'In' Thing for Networking" in *Entrepreneur* (Vol. 33, January 2005, No. 1, pp. 41)
Pub: Entrepreneur Media Inc.
Ed: Amanda C. Kooser. **Description:** Wi-Fi jacks are the newest hardware offering to make Wi-Fi easier and less expensive for small businesses.

42104 ■ "Wealth on the Go" in *Black Enterprise* (Vol. 34, No. 3, October 2003, pp. 61)
Pub: Earl Graves Publishing Co.
Ed: Nicole Lewis. **Description:** Profile of Chris Galloway, a radiation therapist and real estate investor in Washington, DC; Galloway keeps up to date by using the latest in radiation treatment technology to treat patients with cancer and other diseases.

42105 ■ *Western Hi-Tech Companies Database*
Pub: Harris InfoSource
Ed: Fran Carlsen, Editor. **Released:** latest edition 2003. **Price:** $1,295. **Entries Include:** Company name, address, phone, fax, toll-free, names and titles of key personnel, number of employees, geographical area served, financial data, descriptions of product/service, Standard Industrial Classification (SIC) code, year established, annual revenues, plant size, legal structure, export/import information. **Database Covers:** Over 14,900 technology-based manufacturers, software developers, and other high tech companies in Alaska, Arizona, California, Colorado, Hawaii, Idaho, Kansas, Missouri, North Dakota, Nebraska, Oklahoma, South Dakota, Texas, Montana, New Mexico, Nevada, Oregon, Utah, Washington, Wyoming; names of owners, CEOs, and key executives.

42106 ■ "WFI Lays Out Restructuring Plan" in *San Diego Business Journal* (Vol. 28, January 8, 2007, No. 2, pp. 4)
Pub: San Diego Business Journal Associates
Ed: Andy Killion. **Description:** WFI, communications infrastructure designer and provider, shares its plans to reduce operating expenses, increase profits, and free cash flow by divesting or exiting portions of business that show no profitability.

42107 ■ "What Drives Inspiration?" in *Entrepreneur* (Vol. 32, December 2004, No. 12, pp. 20)
Pub: Entrepreneur Media Inc.
Description: Four tips for entrepreneurs to remain flexible in managing their business include: being realistic, updating technology, customer satisfaction, and being a good boss.

42108 ■ "What I Think of Pink" in *Marketing to Women* (Vol. 20, January 2007, No. 1, pp. 2)
Pub: EPM Communications, Inc.
Ed: Ellen Neuborne. **Description:** Marketers have embraced women by using the color pink to entice them into buying their products.

42109 ■ "What Works" in *Business 2.0* (Vol. 6, May 2005, No. 4, pp. 49-51)
Pub: Time, Inc.
Ed: G. Pascal Zachary. **Description:** Technology pioneer Seagate is reporting new growth due in part to its plan to team innovation with automation and standardization.

42110 ■ "What's Next" in *Business 2.0* (Vol. 6, July 2005, No. 6, pp. 27-28)
Pub: Time, Inc.
Description: Cell phone providers Nokia and Qualcomm introduce plans to bring television to cell phones using UHF band technology.

42111 ■ "What's Next? Hardware that Can Straddle Wireless LANs and Cellular Networks" in *Entrepreneur* (Vol. 32, December 2004, No. 12, pp. 49)
Pub: Entrepreneur Media Inc.
Ed: Amanda C. Kooser. **Description:** Integration of services like voice over Internet Protocol (VoIP) can create more flexible work environments between cellular phones, software and computers.

42112 ■ "What's Next" in *Inc.* (Volume 27, March 2005, No. 3, pp. 59-60)
Pub: Inc. Magazine
Ed: David H. Freedman. **Description:** High tech companies expand in pieces and turn fast-growth units into stand-alone entities. Tips to develop a successful fractural approach to business growth are shared.

42113 ■ "When the Chips are Down" in *Red Herring* (No. 99, June 15 & July 1, 2001, pp. 122)
Pub: Herring Communications
Ed: Tom Stein. **Description:** As the semiconductor sector cools off, venture capitalists seek companies with staying power.

42114 ■ "When Technology Runs Amok" in *Inc.* (Volume 27, July 2005, No. 7, pp. 53-54)
Pub: Inc. Magazine
Ed: David H. Freedman. **Description:** Small companies need to use caution when developing computer systems for their business.

42115 ■ "White Joins Pequot, Heads West Coast Ops." in *Venture Capital Journal* (Vol. 40, No. 10, November 2000, pp. 34, 36)
Pub: Venture Economics
Description: Pequot Capital Management Inc. hired Karen White, former senior vice president of worldwide business development at Oracle Corporation, as a general partner in the firm's private equity group. Pequot's private equity group backs early- to expansion-stage technology, telecommunications and healthcare companies.

42116 ■ "Why the Old Rules Don't Apply" in *Business Week* (February 14, 2005, No. 3920, pp. 68)
Pub: McGraw-Hill Companies
Ed: Stephen Baker, Adam Aston. **Description:** An overview of nanotechnology. Venture capital firm Draper Fisher Jurvetson has invested $95 million in eleven nanotechnology startup companies.

42117 ■ "Why the Street Isn't Hip to Electronic Arts' Game" in *Fortune* **(Vol. 151, February 21, 2005, No. 4, pp. 53)**
Pub: Time Inc.
Ed: Andy Serwer. **Description:** Electronic Arts stock has tripled in the last five years. As the world's largest video game publisher for computers and handheld devices, the company has produced Madden football, the Sims, and Need for Speed, with market share of 57.5 percent in North America.

42118 ■ "Wi-Fi is a Must for New Office Space on Long Island" in *Long Island Business News* **(February 13, 2004)**
Pub: Dolan Media Newswires
Ed: Nick Anastasi. **Description:** Small businesses are looking for office space offering high-speed wireless technology in the form of Wi-Fi connectivity.

42119 ■ "Wi-Fi Reloaded: Maybe All Your 802.11B Network Needs is a Boost" in *Entrepreneur* **(Vol. 31, No. 7, July 2003, pp. 38)**
Pub: Entrepreneur Media, Inc.
Ed: Mike Hogan. **Description:** Various ways to boost existing 802.11b networks are examined, including the use of software and adaptors.

42120 ■ "Wi-Fi, Where Are You? Where to Find the Nearest Free Hot Spot" in *Entrepreneur.com* **(Vol. 34, February 2006, No. 2, pp. 19)**
Pub: Entrepreneur Media Inc.
Ed: Chris McGinnis. **Description:** Business travelers are increasingly depending on fast and easy wireless Internet connections when on the road. Hotel chains often offer free Wi-Fi.

42121 ■ "Wi-Fi wherever" in *Entrepreneur* **(Vol. 31, No. 5, May 2003, pp. 35)**
Pub: Entrepreneur Media Inc.
Ed: Eric Bender. **Description:** Gas stations, fast-food restaurants and convenience stores may be offering Internet services to customers.

42122 ■ "The Winning Attitude" in *Small Business Opportunities* **(Vol. 16, No. 2, March 2004, pp. 72, 74)**
Pub: Harris Publications, Inc.
Ed: Chuck Green. **Description:** Profile of Taj Reneau and brother Darius, owners of Webley Systems, providing technology to companies such as telecommunications services providers. The firm is located in Deerfield, Illinois.

42123 ■ "A Wireless Decision" in *Hispanic Business* **(Vol. 23, No. 5, May 2001, pp. 78)**
Pub: Hispanic Business
Ed: Roger Harris. **Description:** Wireless networking equipment and services are examined for small business.

42124 ■ "Wireless Metropolis" in *Entrepreneur* **(Vol. 32, October 2004, No. 10, pp. 24)**
Pub: Entrepreneur Media Inc.
Ed: Eric Bender. **Description:** Plans for New York State's wireless backup system will be a boon for small and mid-size companies.

42125 ■ "Wireless Poised to Explode, but Problems Remain, Panel Says" in *Daily Camera* **(April 11, 2003)**
Pub: Knight-Ridder/Tribune Business News
Ed: Erika Stutzman. **Description:** The future of wireless technology is discussed.

42126 ■ "Wireless Wealth: The Wi-Fi Revolution is Coming" in *Entrepreneur* **(Vol. 31, No. 9, July 2003, pp. 92)**
Pub: Entrepreneur Media, Inc.
Ed: Sky Dayton, David Worrell. **Description:** Wi-Fi is becoming the industry standard for wireless networking, being used by both business and homes. Wi-Fi provides consumers and business travelers, as well as home workers, with wireless Internet access at broadband speeds.

42127 ■ "Wisconsin Biotech Aims to Create Artificial Heart Tissue" in *Milwaukee Journal Sentinel* **(December 8, 2005)**
Pub: Journal Sentinel, Inc.
Ed: Kathleen Gallagher. **Description:** InvivoSciences LLC plans to make artificial heart tissue. The firm has chosen Wisconsin for its location because of the Medical College of Wisconsin's support for entrepreneurs along with several state programs that support young companies.

42128 ■ "Workplace 2005: Telecommuting, Virtual Offices, Dispersed Staff..." in *Entrepreneur* **(Vol. 33, February 2005, No. 2, pp. 55)**
Pub: Entrepreneur Media Inc.
Ed: Amanda C. Kooser. **Description:** Overview of new trends and technologies to help a small business is presented. Several entrepreneurs offer insight into technologies that help them run their companies in an ever-changing business environment.

42129 ■ "World Wide Technology Expands" in *Black Enterprise* **(Vol. 37, December 2006, No. 5, pp. 34)**
Pub: Earl G. Graves Publishing Co. Inc.
Ed: Marcia A. Wade. **Description:** World Wide Technology Inc. opened a streamlined, higher capacity 12,000-square-foot Integration Technology Center near its corporate headquarters in St. Louis. The new venture will transfer lower costs to customers.

42130 ■ "WTC mission is 'call to service' for Ann Arbor biotech firm" in *Crain's Detroit Business* **(Vol. 18, No. 18, May 6, 2002, pp. 1)**
Pub: Crain Communications Inc. - Detroit
Ed: Laura Bailey. **Description:** Software developed by the Ann Arbor biotech firm, Gene Codes Corporation, helped investigators in identifying victims from the attacks on the World Trade Center.

42131 ■ "Year In Review IPO Market" in *Venture Capital Journal* **(February 1, 2006)**
Pub: Thomason Financial Inc.
Description: Initial public offerings for 2005 was the highest since 2000 with biotechnology and medical technology, semiconductors and computer chips leading the way.

42132 ■ "You Can Run" in *Entrepreneur* **(Vol. 31, No. 6, June 2003, pp. 39)**
Pub: Entrepreneur Media Inc.
Ed: Mike Hogan. **Description:** The importance of wireless technology and its impact for small businesses and workers is discussed.

42133 ■ "Zander's Chip Shot; New CEO Faces Tough Call on Semiconductor Unit" in *Crain's Chicago Business* **(Vol. 26, No. 51, December 22, 2003)**
Pub: Crain Communications, Inc.
Ed: Julie Johnsson. **Description:** Edward Zander, new CEO of Motorola Inc., is faced with the dilemma to sell or spin off the company's struggling semiconductor unit. The company is making plans for an initial public offering of its chip business, which saw $5 billion in revenue, but is also considering interest from rivals and private-equity firms.

SOURCES OF SUPPLY

42134 ■ *High-Tech Materials Alert*
Pub: John Wiley & Sons Inc. Scientific/Technical/ Medical Publishing
Released: Monthly. **Publication Includes:** List of manufacturers and suppliers of high performance alloys, metals, ceramics, plastics, graphite, and other materials. **Entries Include:** Company name, address, phone. Principal content is articles and analyses of new materials for industrial processes.

TRADE PERIODICALS

42135 ■ *AIA Today!*
Pub: Automated Imaging Association (AIA)
Ed: Kirsten L. Erickson, Editor. **Released:** Quarterly. **Price:** Included in membership. **Description:** Provides information on machine vision and scientific imaging market trends, events, standards, publications, shows, and conferences. Recurring features include a calendar of events and notices of publications available.

42136 ■ *Optics & Photonics News*
Pub: Optical Society of America
Contact: John Childs, Publisher
Released: Monthly. **Price:** Free. **Description:** Concerned with optical research, instruction, applications, manufacturing, and equipment. Supplies information on developments in all branches of optics, such as space optics, medical optics, fiber optics, lasers, color optics, and optical communications. Recurring features include reports on Society activities, news of members, and a calendar of events.

42137 ■ *Robot Times*
Pub: Robotic Industries Association
Ed: Jeffrey A. Burnstein, Editor. **Released:** Quarterly. **Price:** Included in membership; Free. **Description:** Promotes "the use and acceptance of robotic technology through the exchange of technical and trade-related information." Provides news of the Association and its affiliate organization, the Automated Imaging Association.

42138 ■ *Sales Automation Success*
Pub: Denali Group Inc.
Ed: Steve Pokin, Editor. **Released:** 10/year. **Description:** Reviews sales automation software. Offers advice for applying technology to sales and marketing problems, and how to sell more now through effective use of high technology. Recurring features include interviews, news of research, and book reviews.

42139 ■ *Sensor Technology*
Pub: Technical Insights/M John Wiley & Sons Inc.
Ed: Leo O'Connor, Editor. **Released:** Monthly. **Price:** $650, U.S. and Canada year; $710, elsewhere year. **Description:** Informs readers of the latest scientific and technological developments in the field of sensors. Focuses on process and machine control, including robotics; also covers environmental and medical uses. Recurring features include a calendar of events, news of research, book reviews, and columns titled Key Patents and Keep an Eye On.

CONSULTANTS

42140 ■ I.H.R. Solutions
3333 E Bayaud Ave., Ste. 219
Denver, CO 80209
Ph:(303)588-4243
Fax: (303)978-0473
Co. E-mail: dhollands@ihrsolutions.com
URL: http://www.ihrsolutions.com

E-mail: dhollands@ihrsolutions.com
Scope: Provides joint-venture and start-up human resource consulting services as well as advice on organization development for international human capital. Industries Served: high-tech and telecommunications.

42141 ■ ProActive English
1001 Pine St., Ste. 1004
San Francisco, CA 94109
Ph:(415)752-2270
Co. E-mail: infopae@proactive-english.com
URL: http://www.proactive-english.com

E-mail: infopae@proactive-english.com
Scope: Offers on-site individual and small group language and communication training. Sets up learning plans tailored to the needs and schedules of managers and executives who are non-native English speakers. Serves all industries. **Seminars:** Communicating in Business Situations; Presentations and Pronunciation.

FRANCHISES AND BUSINESS OPPORTUNITIES

42142 ■ Medspa Boutique
Walpert Healthcare Corp.
1563 Solano Ave., No. 405
Berkeley, CA 94707
Ph:(415)205-5123
Fax: (510)614-2791
No. of Franchise Units: 6. **Founded:** 2002. **Franchised:** 2003. **Description:** Laser hair removal and skin care. **Equity Capital Needed:** $200,000. **Franchise Fee:** $95,000. **Financial Assistance:** Yes. **Training:** Yes.

COMPUTERIZED DATABASES

42143 ■ TechKnow
Global Environment & Technology Foundation
2900 S Quincy St., Ste. 410
Arlington, VA 22003
Ph:(703)379-2713
Fax: (703)820-6168
Co. E-mail: gnet@getf.org
URL: http://www.gnet.org
Description: Provides environmental technology information. Includes profiles of user-owned technology; summaries and full descriptions of technologies; related information from DOE and other sources; demonstration, intellectual property, and licensing status; technology needs, limitations, applications, and costs; and technology developer contact information.
Type: Directory; Full text.

RESEARCH CENTERS

42144 ■ Georgia Institute of Technology–Advanced Technology Development Center
75 5th St., NW Ste. 100
Atlanta, GA 30308
Ph:(404)894-3575
Fax: (404)894-4545
Co. E-mail: wayne.hodges@edi.gatech.edu
URL: http://www.atdc.org
Contact: H. Wayne Hodges, Dir.
E-mail: wayne.hodges@edi.gatech.edu
Scope: Promotes the development of advanced technology-based companies throughout Georgia. including firms involved in advanced structural materials, electronic equipment, biotechnology, health and medical products, artificial intelligence, environmental sciences, telecommunications, aerospace systems,

instrumentation and test equipment, robotics, and related technolgies. **Services:** Business assistance, to start-up technology companies; General management consulting; Technical and business management services, to entrepreneurs. **Publications:** Technology Partners (quarterly).

42145 ■ National Center for Technology Planning
PO Box 2393
Tupelo, MS 38803-2393
Ph:(662)844-9630
Fax: (662)844-9630
Co. E-mail: larry@nctp.com
URL: http://www.nctp.com
Contact: Larry S. Anderson EdD, Dir.
E-mail: larry@nctp.com
Scope: Technology planning, with dissemination looking to guide those developing technology plans, working on unfinished technology plans, implementing new technology plans, or evaluating current plans. **Services:** Consulting. **Educational Activities:** Speeches and presentations; Workshops.

42146 ■ Progress Corporate Park
13709 Progress Blvd.
PO Box 10
Alachua, FL 32615
Ph:(386)462-4040
Free: 877—457-6489
Fax: (386)462-3932
Co. E-mail: sandy@progresscorporatepark.com
URL: http://progresscorporatepark.com
Contact: Sandra Burgess, Mgr.
E-mail: sandy@progresscorporatepark.com
Scope: 200-acre research and technology park open to both public and private research and manufacturing organizations emphasizing high-technology development, including electronics, biotechnology, advanced materials, pharmacology, and agriculture. Center provides a link between University researchers and industry and transfers new technologies from the laboratory to the marketplace. **Services:** Assistance, in entrepreneurial development, commercialization of scientific and technological innovations, and international marketing.

42147 ■ University of California at Berkeley–Berkeley Roundtable on International Economy
2234 Piedmont Ave.
Berkeley, CA 94720-2322
Ph:(510)642-3067
Fax: (510)643-6617
Co. E-mail: brie@socrates.berkeley.edu
URL: http://brie.berkeley.edu/~briewww
Contact: Prof. Stephen S. Cohen, Co-Dir.
E-mail: brie@socrates.berkeley.edu
Scope: Policy studies of the interaction of high technology development and the international economy.
Publications: BRIE Working Paper Series.

42148 ■ University of Connecticut–University Center for Instructional Media and Technology
CUE Bldg. Rm. 403, Unit 2001
368 Fairfield Rd.
Storrs, CT 06269-2001
Ph:(860)486-2530
Fax: (860)486-1766
Co. E-mail: steven.mcdermott@uconn.edu
URL: http://www.ucimt.uconn.edu
Contact: Steven McDermott, Dir.
E-mail: steven.mcdermott@uconn.edu
Scope: Instructional media, communications, telecommunications, radio, television, multi-image systems, interactive video, video disc systems, high technology, and instructional development. **Educational Activities:** Seminars for University and state personnel (monthly).

42149 ■ University of Illinois at Urbana-Champaign–Technology Commercialization Laboratory
2004 S Wright St.
Urbana, IL 61802
Ph:(217)244-7742
Fax: (217)333-4050
Co. E-mail: kybrown@uiuc.edu
URL: http://www.tech.com
Contact: Karolee Brown, Prog.Admin.Asst.
E-mail: kybrown@uiuc.edu
Scope: Assists new and growing business by providing affordable space, shared services, and access to University of Illinois expertise, entrepreneurs, start-up firms, and satellite units of established companies. **Services:** Assistance in identifying specialists in the areas of accounting, business start-up, planning and budgeting, and financial management; Provides specialists in industrial relations, manufacturing operations, organizational development, and strategic planning; Provides specialists in management of marketing and sales, human resources, and personnel areas.

42150 ■ Washington Technology Center
300 Fluke Hall, Box 352140
Seattle, WA 98195-2140
Ph:(206)685-1920
Fax: (206)543-3059
Co. E-mail: info@watechcenter.org
URL: http://www.watechcenter.org
Contact: R. Lee Cheatham, Exec.Dir.
E-mail: info@watechcenter.org
Scope: Commercially viable technologies, particularly advanced materials and manufacturing systems technology, biotechnology/biomedical devices, microelectronics technology, and computer systems and software technology. **Services:** Statewide Technology Assistance Program. **Publications:** At-A-Glance Newsletter (quarterly); Index of Innovation (annually); WTC Annual Report. **Educational Activities:** SBIR training; Workshops and seminars, on future research projects.

START-UP INFORMATION

42151 ■ *The Art of the Start: The Time-Tested, Battle-Hardened Guide for Anyone Starting Anything*
Pub: Penguin Books (USA) Incorporated
Ed: Guy Kawasaki **Released:** September 2004. **Price:** $26.95. **Description:** Advice for someone starting a new business covering topics such as hiring employees, building a brand, business competition, and management.

42152 ■ *"Blending In Family" in Ingram's* (Vol. 28, No. 5, May 2002, pp. 35)
Pub: Show Me Publishing, Inc.
Ed: Chuck Vogt, Sr. **Description:** One of the challenges facing the owner of a startup small business is recruiting the right employees. Four objectives are listed to help a firm be successful.

42153 ■ *The Complete Small Business Start-up Guide*
Pub: John Wiley & Sons, Incorporated
Ed: Lisa Rogak. **Released:** November 2004. **Price:** $14.95. **Description:** Guide to starting a small company, focusing on development of a business plan, organizational structure, advertising, hiring, selection of suppliers, and using the Internet to market your firm.

42154 ■ *"Desperate Times" in Entrepreneur* (Vol. 28, No. 4, April 2000, pp. 56)
Pub: Entrepreneur Media Inc.
Ed: Ellen Paris. **Description:** America's tight job market has caused some entrepreneurs to relax their hiring policies and lower their standards. It is recommended to choose employees wisely, and not lower standards.

42155 ■ *"Inside or Out?" in Black Enterprise* (Vol. 35, October 2004, No. 3, pp. 60)
Pub: Earl G. Graves Publishing Co. Inc.
Ed: Alan Hughes. **Description:** The pros and cons of outsourcing for a newly formed company are addressed.

42156 ■ *Legal Guide for Starting and Running a Small Business*
Pub: NOLO
Ed: Fred Steingold, Lisa Guerin. **Released:** March 2005. **Price:** $34.99. **Description:** Information for starting a new business focusing on choosing a business structure, taxes, employees and independent contractors, trademark and service marks, licensing and permits, leasing and improvement of commercial space, buying and selling a business, and more.

42157 ■ *"Wanted" in Black Enterprise* (Vol. 32, No. 6, January 2002, pp. 3)
Pub: Earl Graves Publishing Co.
Ed: Bridget McCrea. **Description:** Profile of David Vinson's company, Optate Inc, a Michigan-based online employee-relationship management firm. Vinson explains how his approach to staffing paid off when it came time to seek financing.

42158 ■ *"Web.Preneuring" in Small Business Opportunities* (Vol. 16, November 2004, No. 6, pp. 66, 68)
Pub: Harris Publications Inc.
Ed: Lin Grensing-Pophal. **Description:** Online recruiting is a $7 billion industry. Information is offered to help entrepreneurs plan an online recruiting business.

ASSOCIATIONS AND OTHER ORGANIZATIONS

42159 ■ **International Association of Corporate and Professional Recruitment**
327 N Palm Dr., Ste. 201
Beverly Hills, CA 90210
Ph:(310)550-0304
Fax: (213)413-1914
Co. E-mail: office@iacpr.org
URL: http://www.iacpr.org
Contact: Kay Kennedy, Exec. Dir.
Description: Human resources executives and executive search professionals who are leaders in executive recruitment and retention. Serves as a communications network for sharing information and solving problems within the corporate recruiting industry. **Publications:** *Impact* (semiannual); *Quick Takes* (bimonthly).

42160 ■ **National Association of Executive Recruiters**
1901 N Roselle Rd., Ste. 920
Schaumburg, IL 60195
Ph:(847)885-1453
Fax: (847)885-8393
Co. E-mail: naerinfo@naer.org
URL: http://www.naer.org
Contact: Bob Zahra, Chm.
Description: Executive recruitment and search specialist firms providing counsel and assistance in identifying and hiring candidates for middle- and senior-level management positions. Promotes and enhances the public image, awareness, and understanding of the executive search profession. Serves as a forum for exchange of ideas among members; conducts educational programs and owners' roundtable. Maintains code of ethics and professional practice guidelines. **Publications:** Membership Directory (annual).

EDUCATIONAL PROGRAMS

42161 ■ **Effective Recruiting, Selecting and Behavioral Interviewing: A Practical Techniques Workshop (Canada)**
Canadian Management Centre
150 York St., 5th Fl.
Toronto, ON, Canada M5H 3S5
Ph:(866)400-4941 ext. 2252
Free: 877-CMC-2500
Fax: (416)313-4985
Co. E-mail: cmcinfo@cmctraining.org
URL: http://www.cmcamai.org
Price: $1,595 Canadian. **Description:** Covers effective recruiting skills to locate the right person for the job, to eliminate turnover and cost. **Locations:** Toronto, ON.

REFERENCE WORKS

42162 ■ *The 7 Irrefutable Rules of Small Business Growth*
Pub: John Wiley & Sons, Incorporated
Ed: Steven S. Little. **Released:** February 2005. **Price:** $18.95. **Description:** Proven strategies to maintain small business growth are outlined, covering topics such as technology, business plans, hiring, and more.

42163 ■ *"2006 Hispanic Business Diversity Report: Employment" in Hispanic Business* (September 2006, pp. 40, 42, 44, 48, 50)
Pub: Hispanic Business
Description: Fifty businesses promoting business with the Hispanic community are profiled.

42164 ■ *"Accentuating the accent" in The New York Times* (September 3, 2000, pp. BU10)
Pub: The New York Times Company
Ed: Mickey Meece. **Description:** Research by Dianne Markley and Patricia Cukor-Avila shows that employers base hiring decisions on the way they judge a candidate's regional accent.

42165 ■ *"Age On Your Side" in Black Enterprise* (Vol. 36, February 2006, No. 7, pp. 74)
Pub: Earl G. Graves Publishing Co. Inc.
Ed: L. Taylor. **Description:** The Age Discrimination Act of 1967 is examined.

42166 ■ *The Agile Manager's Guide to Hiring Excellence*
Pub: Velocity Business Publishing, Inc.
Ed: Hardy Caldwell. **Released:** 1998. **Price:** $9.95.

42167 ■ *"Apply Yourself" in Entrepreneur* (Vol. 32, October 2004, No. 10, pp. 98)
Pub: Entrepreneur Media Inc.
Ed: Chris Penttila. **Description:** Three criteria used to define an online applicant for employers hiring via the Internet were set by the Department of Labor, the Equal Employment Opportunity Commission and other federal agencies. First, an employer must be filling a particular position, the online applicant must follow the employer's process when applying, and the online applicant must indicate interest in a specific position within the company.

42168 ■ *"Are you picking the right leaders?" in Harvard Business Review* (Vol. 80, No. 2, February 2002, pp. 58)
Pub: Harvard Business School Press
Ed: Melvin Sorcher, James Brant. **Description:** Advice is given to help executives choose the right leaders for their firms. Executives often overvalue certain traits and skills while overlooking more leadership-related ones.

42169 ■ "Arlington the Site of HD Career Expo" in *Hispanic Business* (Vol. 23, No. 10, October, 2001, pp. 104)
Pub: Hispanic Business
Description: The diversity recruitment division of Hispanic Business, HireDiversity.com, will host a national Diversity Career Expo November 13, 2001, at the Hyatt Regency Crystal City in Arlington, Virginia.

42170 ■ "The Art and Science of Networking" in *Sales and Marketing.com* (Vol. 153, No. 3, March 2004, pp. 49)
Pub: VNU eMedia, Inc.
Ed: Mark Haering. **Description:** Networking is a key to finding new employment. Guidelines for participating in an organized network setting are presented.

42171 ■ "Ask the Attorney" in *Red Herring* (No. 99, June 15 & July 1, 2001, pp. 148)
Pub: Herring Communications
Description: Legal questions are answered, including issues of employee termination, stock options, angel money, strategic finance, licensing, venture capital and financing, and copyrights.

42172 ■ "Ask Inc." in *Inc.* (January 1, 2005)
Pub: Inc. Magazine
Description: A firm asks if international expansion is right for the company; many small companies hire senior executives through recruitment agencies.

42173 ■ "Attracting the talent you need now" in *Incentive* (Vol. 174, No. 9, September 2000, pp. 98)
Pub: Bill Communications
Ed: Bruce Tulgan. **Description:** Advice for developing a compelling recruiting message and eight factors workers of the future look for in employment offers.

42174 ■ "Back in the game. IT recruiters see selective improvement in local technology staffing markets" in *Business First Columbus* (Vol. 18)
Pub: Business First Columbus, Inc.
Ed: Craig Lovelace. **Description:** Central Ohio IT hiring is seeing improvements, yet the improvements are sporadic and not a major increase throughout the region. IT workers cannot expect the high salaries common before the turn around in the dot.com industry, these trends are indicative of the entire U.S.

42175 ■ "Bad Apples: Business Owners Share their Hiring Horror Stories" in *Entrepreneur* (Vol. 32, No. 2, February 2004, pp. 26)
Pub: Entrepreneur Media, Inc.
Ed: Nichole L. Torres. **Description:** Three entrepreneurs share bad hiring experiences and offer advice for managers when hiring.

42176 ■ "Bad credit and employment" in *Black Enterprise* (Vol. 31, No. 5, December 2000, pp. 172)
Pub: Earl Graves Publishing Co.
Ed: Bevolyn Williams-Harold. **Description:** The issue of screening job applicants based on credit history is discussed.

42177 ■ "Banking on Diversity" in *Hispanic Business* (November 2006, pp. 74, 76)
Pub: Hispanic Business
Ed: Leanndra Martinez. **Description:** Analysis and advice for recruiting and hiring a multicultural workforce is presented.

42178 ■ "Benefits to Attract & Retain Key Employees" in *Ingram's* (Vol. 27, No. 5, May 2001, pp. 35)
Pub: Show Me Publishing, Inc.
Ed: Mike Searcy. **Description:** Businesses need to attract and retain employees with good, competitive compensation packages, including flexible spending accounts and retirement packages.

42179 ■ "Beyond the resume" in *Women In Business* (Vol. 52, No. 4, July 2000, pp. 36)
Pub: The ABWA Co., Inc.
Ed: Diane Domeyer. **Description:** Issues regarding the recruitment of personnel are presented. The importance of interpersonal skills, knowledge technology, enthusiasm, and adaptability are discussed.

42180 ■ "Bio-Layoffs Cool Once-Booking Job Market" in *Boston Business Journal* (Vol. 23, No. 21, June 27, 2003, pp. 1)
Pub: American City Business Journals
Ed: Allison Connolly. **Description:** Massachusetts' biotechnology industry has suffered 1,000 job losses in the past six months. Though expectations are that the industry will play a significant role in improving the state's economy, experts predict that in the short-term, the industry will continue to decline.

42181 ■ "Blurred Vision" in *Entrepreneur* (Vol. 28, No. 10, October 2000, pp. 118)
Pub: Entrepreneur Media Inc.
Ed: Chris Penttila. **Description:** Don't expect your employees to be carbon copies of yourself. It takes an owner to have the dedication of an owner.

42182 ■ "Boosting Corporate Diversity" in *Hispanic Business* (April 2005, pp. 14)
Pub: Hispanic Business
Description: Many corporate managers believe that diversity programs provide a competitive edge because they improve a company's performance and leadership. The University of Texas, Austin started a program to expand the number of diverse students for their MBA program.

42183 ■ "Bridging the Gap" in *Black Enterprise* (Vol. 34, No. 5, December 2003, pp. 66)
Pub: Earl Graves Publishing Co.
Ed: Sonia Alleyne. **Description:** Profile of Careerbank, a Web site for individuals seeking jobs in the financial industry; the site provides job opportunities as well as current industry information.

42184 ■ "Builder Bandits" in *Tampa Tribune* (December 12, 2005)
Pub: Media General, Inc.
Ed: Shannon Behnken. **Description:** Florida's booming economy and hurricane damage has forced building trade subcontractors to compete over workers by raising hourly wages by $3-$5.

42185 ■ "Building the Minority High-Tech Work Force" in *Hispanic Business* (Vol. 23, No. 7/8, July/August 2001, pp. 116)
Pub: Hispanic Business
Description: The Council on Competitiveness has received a $23 million grant to establish a non-profit organization to address the critical shortage of women and minorities in the high-tech industries sector in the U.S.

42186 ■ "Buyer's Mentality" in *Sales & Marketing Management* (Vol. 159, January-February 2007, No. 1, pp. 45)
Pub: VNU Business Media
Ed: John Boe. **Description:** Sales managers should approach hiring interviews with the same logic as a buyer's mentality.

42187 ■ "Bystrom Providing In-Room Massages at Lakeway Inn & Convention Center" in *Bellingham Business Journal* (January 2007, pp. A17)
Pub: Sun News Inc.
Description: Profile of Charisma Bystrom who has been selected as the exclusive massage practitioner for the guests of Bellingham's Lakeway Inn & Convention Center. Bystrom collaborates with her husband, Scott MacGregor, on tandem massages.

42188 ■ "C2G-Network" in *Entrepreneur.com* (Vol. 34, January 2006, No. 1, pp. 6)
Pub: Entrepreneur Media Inc.
Ed: Steve Cooper. **Description:** College students can be certified and placed on C2G-Network that puts them in contact with fast-growing small businesses. Students have backgrounds in technology, engineering, marketing and sales, human resources, finance, communications and more.

42189 ■ "Cable TV Firm Announces Hundreds of Job Openings in Atlanta" in *Atlanta Journal-Constitution* (January 18, 2007)
Pub: Cox Newspapers, Inc.
Ed: Peralte C. Paul. **Description:** Comcast is set to hire about 600 new employees in the metro Atlanta, Georgia area. The firm currently employs 2,100 workers in the area.

42190 ■ "California Lost Jobs in September" in *Sacramento Bee* (October 22, 2005)
Pub: The Sacramento Bee
Ed: Dale Kasler. **Description:** Californians saw the first job decline for 2005 in September with unemployment rates falling to 5.1 percent, only a tenth of a point. Economists believe the drop was due mainly from some schools opening earlier than usual.

42191 ■ "Can I get into IT?" in *Black Enterprise* (Vol. 31, No. 3, October 2000, pp. 59)
Pub: Earl Graves Publishing Co.
Description: The article tells what high-tech entrepreneurs look for when hiring non-IT degreed employees.

42192 ■ "Career Quarterly" in *Hispanic Business* (April 2003, pp. 62, 64)
Pub: Hispanic Business
Description: Profile of HireDiversity.com, the online service for diversity recruiting and career development is presented.

42193 ■ "Career smarts: Negotiate salary from a strength position" in *Women In Business* (Vol. 52, No. 1, January-February 2000, pp. 23)
Pub: The ABWA Co., Inc.
Ed: Diane Domeyer. **Description:** Prospective employees are advised to be aware of their market skills when negotiating their salary. Salary negotiations should present themselves in a professional manner and be aware of good timing.

42194 ■ "Careful planning can ease stress of layoffs" in *Atlanta Business Chronicle* (Vol. 25, No. 19, October 18, 2002, pp. 4B)
Pub: American City Business Publications, Inc.
Ed: Emory Mulling. **Description:** Slow economies bring with them the prospect of employee layoffs. A stressful situation, companies can take steps to mitigate the impact on all concerned by implementing a well thought out plan that takes into account those who will and will not be affected.

42195 ■ "Case Study" in *Inc.* (January 1, 2005)
Pub: Inc. Magazine
Ed: Patrick J. Sauer. **Description:** Magnetech Industrial Services is considering the implementation of an apprenticeship program in order to triple its work force in a slowing industry.

42196 ■ "Cashing in Before You Join: Negotiating a Signing Bonus" in *Black Enterprise* (Vol. 37, October 2006, No. 3, pp. 90)
Pub: Earl G. Graves Publishing Co. Inc.
Ed: Chauntelle Folds. **Description:** Information on how to research and negotiate a signing deal, including how to avoid a tax hit.

42197 ■ "Casino Case Hits Legal Jackpot" in *Inc.* (August 1, 2003)
Pub: Gruner & Jahr USA Publishing
Ed: Bobbie Gossage. **Description:** A new ruling against Caesars Palace in Las Vegas, Nevada, will affect all companies when firing employees. The Supreme Court affirmed that circumstantial evidence in the casino's firing of an employee would suffice for a female warehouse worker fired for brawling with a co-worker.

42198 ■ "Cautious Hiring in January Report" in *Charlotte Observer* (February 3, 2007)
Pub: Knight-Ridder/Tribune Business News
Ed: Kerry Hall. **Description:** U.S. Labor Department released a report that shows 111,000 new positions in January 2007, compared to 206,000 in December 2006. Employers remain cautious about hiring.

42199 ■ **"CFO's Exit Returns CPI Aerostructures Inc. to Recruiting Market"** in *Long Island Business News* **(February 6, 2004)**
Pub: Dolan Media Newswires
Ed: Ken Schachter. **Description:** Profile of CPI Aerostructures Inc., the defense contractor; CPI is looking for a new chief financial officer, and Edward Fred, CPI's president and chief executive said he will resume duties as the CFO until a new manager is hired.

42200 ■ **"Changing Times Require Changes in Recruiting Styles"** in *Rough Notes* **(Vol. 145, No. 2, February 2003, pp. 65)**
Pub: Rough Notes
Ed: Troy Korsgaden. **Description:** The insurance and financial services industry must create deliberate recruitment processes to maintain seamless and expert service to customers.

42201 ■ **"Chicago Tribune Business Agenda"** in *Chicago Tribune* **(February 28, 2005)**
Pub: Knight-Ridder/Tribune Business News
Description: Economic predictions, unemployment rates, and manufacturing are issues discussed.

42202 ■ **"Class Reunion: Corporate Alumni Groups Keep Business Connections Going"** in *Sales & Marketing Management* **(Vol. 157, January 2005)**
Pub: VNU Business Media
Ed: Julia Chang. **Description:** Alumni organizations are becoming a new source for hiring and business networking.

42203 ■ **"Closer Call"** in *Entrepreneur* **(Vol. 33, October 2005, No. 10, pp. 85)**
Pub: Entrepreneur Media Inc.
Ed: Kimberly L. McCall. **Description:** Five traits to look for when hiring a sales staff are investigated.

42204 ■ **"Cochran Firm Wins Record $1.62 Billion Insurance Fraud Case"** in *Black Enterprise* **(Vol. 34, July 2004, No. 12, pp. 21)**
Pub: Earl G. Graves Publishing Co. Inc.
Ed: Carolyn M. Brown. **Description:** The Cochran Firm's record winning insurance fraud case could help bring about reform in the insurance industry. The verdict has impacted the way insurance agents are being hired and trained.

42205 ■ **"Commentary: Research is Key To Getting Hired in 'Jobless Recovery'"** in *Long Island Business News* **(January 30, 2004)**
Pub: Dolan Media Newswires
Description: In a slow job market, basic job search networking may not be enough to land a new position. Job seekers should focus on providing value and demonstration of skills and talents when contacting hiring managers, as well as doing research in finding good jobs that are available. Tips for doing this type of research are given.

42206 ■ **"Companies Increasingly Turn to Perks to Retain, Lure Quality Employees"** in *Atlanta Journal-Constitution* **(February 3, 2007)**
Pub: Cox Newspapers, Inc.
Ed: Tammy Joyner. **Description:** Various perks provided by different companies are shared; Chick-fil-A offers free lunch to its employees.

42207 ■ *Complying with the ADA: A Small Business Guide to Hiring and Employing the Disabled*
Pub: John Wiley & Sons, Inc.
Ed: Jeffrey G. Allen. **Released:** 1993. **Price:** $55.00; $17.95 (paper). **Description:** Guide to the American with Disabilities Act (ADA), covering hiring and employing the disabled, construction requirements, and economic implications of the ADA.

42208 ■ **"Corporate social performance and attractiveness as an employer to different job seeking populations"** in *Journal of Business Ethics*
Pub: Kluwer Academic Publishers
Ed: Heather Schmidt Albinger, Sarah J. Freeman. **Description:** This study investigates the hypothesis that the advantage corporate social performance (CSP) yields in attracting employees depends on the degree of job choice possessed by the people seeking employment.

42209 ■ **"Crafting the most productive and efficient work force"** in *Fairfield County Business Journal* **(Vol. 42, No. 3, Jan. 20, 2003, pp. 4)**
Pub: Westfair Communications, Inc.
Ed: Steven Drexel. **Description:** The importance of using both long-term and short-term recruitment strategies during slow economic times is discussed.

42210 ■ **"Craigslist Founder has a Hands-On Style"** in *San Jose Mercury News* **(March 4, 2005)**
Pub: Knight-Ridder/Tribune Business News
Ed: Michael Bazeley. **Description:** Craig Newmark, founder of the classified ads Website, Craigslist, is profiled. Craigslist reports annual revenues from $7 million to $10 million. Employers pay a fee for listing job opportunities on the site, but there is no fee for individuals posting ads.

42211 ■ **"Creative Recruiting"** in *Small Business Opportunities* **(Vol. 13, No. 6, November 2001, pp. 90, 138)**
Pub: Harris Publications, Inc.
Ed: Lin Grensing-Pophal. **Description:** Fifteen tips for creative recruiting that will benefit small businesses are outlined.

42212 ■ **"Cultivating Teleworkers"** in *Home Office Computing* **(Vol. 18, No. 12, December 2000, pp. 102)**
Pub: Scholastic Inc.
Ed: William Van Winkle. **Description:** Mutual fund company Putnam Investments used to be able to find qualified employees at job fairs. When that resource started to dry up they discovered that there is a ripe market for those workers that want to telecommute. This article takes a look at Putnam Investment's efforts and how well they have succeeded in their telecommuting program.

42213 ■ **"The Curse of the superstar CEO"** in *Harvard Business Review* **(Vol. 80, No. 9, September 2002, pp. 60)**
Pub: Harvard Business School Press
Ed: Rakesh Khurana. **Description:** Recent examples are used to show how destructive the process for recruiting for a CEO can be, especially if the CEO is charismatic, yet prone to crucial errors.

42214 ■ **"Cuts in Retail, Manufacturing Hurt Northern New Jersey's Job Growth"** in *The Record* **(November 9, 2005)**
Pub: New Jersey Media Group
Ed: Kathleen Lynn. **Description:** According to the federal Bureau of Labor Statistics, northern New Jersey firms are not hiring new employees. Statistical data included.

42215 ■ **"Delegating the dirty work of cleaning up"** in *The New York Times* **(February 17, 2000, pp. D4, G4)**
Pub: The New York Times Company
Ed: Michelle Slatella. **Description:** Information to help hire contractors over the Internet is summarized.

42216 ■ **"Desperate Measures"** in *Entrepreneur* **(Vol. 31, No. 8, August 2003, pp. 25)**
Pub: Entrepreneur Media, Inc.
Ed: Karen Axelton. **Description:** The Creative Group, an employment service located in Menlo Park, California, conducted a survey that asked executives to describe the most unusual maneuver they had seen job candidates use to get their attention. The results of that survey are presented.

42217 ■ **"Desperately Seeking Sales Stars"** in *Sales & Marketing Management* **(Vol. 158, October 2006, No. 10, pp. 44)**
Pub: VNU Business Media
Ed: Julia Chang. **Description:** Competition to hire sales personnel is growing; companies strategic plans for recruiting successful sales teams are presented.

42218 ■ **"Devalued by Diversity"** in *Black Enterprise* **(Vol. 35, January 2005, No. 6, pp. 53)**
Pub: Earl G. Graves Publishing Co. Inc.
Description: Key factors to determine whether diversity is managed effectively in a company are presented.

42219 ■ **"Developing the Workforce"** in *Ingram's* **(Vol. 28, No. 9, September 2002, pp. 61)**
Pub: Show Me Publishing, Inc.
Ed: Rick Beasley. **Description:** Industries complain about a lack of skilled workers therefore educators, business leaders, and policy makers should work together to provide education and training towards a highly skilled workforce.

42220 ■ **"Diversity in the Big City"** in *Hispanic Business* **(June 2002, pp. 80)**
Pub: Hispanic Business
Ed: Vivienne Heines. **Description:** The New York Times conducted a study that reveals that both hiring managers and job seekers in the New York metropolitan area equate diversity with equal opportunity and fairness, thus seeing diversity as a contribution to a good work environment. Statistical data included.

42221 ■ **"Diversity Defined"** in *Hispanic Business* **(January/February 2003, pp. 64, 66)**
Pub: Hispanic Business
Description: Results of the Hispanic Business Corporate Diversity Survey show that diversity is defined in different terms from company to company. In a recent online poll, IBM was named the country's number one company for providing opportunity to minority-owned firms. A listing of corporations seeking multicultural and bilingual workers is included.

42222 ■ **"Driving Force"** in *Hispanic Business* **(April 2005, pp. 56, 58)**
Pub: Hispanic Business
Ed: Anthony Limon. **Description:** Analysis and advice relating to recruitment and career development in the auto industry is given. Due to the high volume of car sales in 2005, new sales and service professionals will be recruited by dealerships.

42223 ■ **"Economy Expands Modestly, but Unemployment Rate Rises"** in *Atlanta Journal-Constitution* **(February 3, 2007)**
Pub: Cox Newspapers, Inc.
Ed: Michael E. Kanell. **Description:** Despite a modest jump in the economy, unemployment numbers rose, according to the U.S. Department of Labor Statistics.

42224 ■ *Effective Hiring & ADA Compliance*
Pub: AMACOM
Ed: Arlene Vernon-Oehmke. **Released:** 1994. **Price:** $49.95.

42225 ■ **"eFindOutTheTruth.com: www.efindoutthetruth.com"** in *Entrepreneur* **(Vol. 32, November 2004, No. 11, pp. 6)**
Pub: Entrepreneur Media Inc.
Ed: Steve Cooper. **Description:** Profile of the online service that provides background screening of prospective new hires.

42226 ■ *Employee Matters: A Legal Guide to Hiring, Firing & Setting Employee Policies*
Pub: Probus Publishing Co., Inc.
Ed: E. Kenneth Snyder. **Released:** 1991. **Price:** $24.95 (paper).

42227 ■ **"Employee Matters"** in *Home Business* **(Vol. 12, March/April 2005, No. 2, pp. 90)**
Pub: Home Business Magazine

Ed: Kurt English. **Description:** Home-based businesses face unique challenges when hiring additional employees.

42228 ■ "The employee strikes back" in *Wall Street Journal* **(April 16, 2002, pp. B1)**
Pub: Wall Street Journal
Ed: Kemba J. Dunham. **Description:** The trend towards employees holding positions at two different firms in order to hedge their bets is growing increasingly popular among workers. Related information included.

42229 ■ "Employment Will Be Stable, Survey Says" in *Milwaukee Journal Sentinel* **(December 13, 2005)**
Pub: Journal Sentinel, Inc.
Ed: Joel Dresang. **Description:** According to the Manpower Employment Outlook Survey, 23 percent of 16,000 employers will add employees in first quarter 2006, while 10 percent report plans to downsize.

42230 ■ "Equal Work, Unequal Pay?" in *Hispanic Business* **(October 2004, pp. 26)**
Pub: Hispanic Business
Description: According to a Hudson survey, race is a dominant factor when determining wages, more significant than gender. Overall, more than half of working men and women believe they are being paid on par with others, but only 37 percent of Hispanics and 33 percent of African Americans feel the same.

42231 ■ "Exit interviews can reveal wealth of information" in *Crain's Detroit Business* **(Vol. 18, No. 49, December 9, 2002, pp. 13)**
Pub: Crain Communications Inc., Detroit
Ed: Laura Bailey. **Description:** The pros and cons of hiring outside a company are explored.

42232 ■ *Fair, Square, & Legal: Safe Hiring, Managing & Firing Practices to Keep You & Your Company Out of Court*
Pub: AMACOM
Ed: Donald H. Weiss. **Released:** Second edition, 1995. **Price:** $24.95.

42233 ■ "Find a Job" in *Black Enterprise* **(Vol. 34, No. 6, January 2004, pp. 10)**
Pub: Earl Graves Publishing Co.
Description: Black Enterprise offers an online Career Center to help those seeking employment to match skills using a job search function, and figures worth in the job market using salary estimates.

42234 ■ *Finding, Hiring, and Keeping the Right People*
Pub: Self-Counsel Press, Inc.
Ed: Lin Grensing. **Price:** $31.95 (business package); $16.95 (audiocassettes only). **Description:** Business package includes two books, *A Small Business Guide to Employee Selection* and *Motivating Today's Work Force*, and two audiocassettes.

42235 ■ *Finding, Hiring, Training, Motivating & Keeping Employees Honest*
Pub: Success Publishing Co.
Ed: Allan Smith. **Released:** 1991. **Price:** $7.00 (paper).

42236 ■ "Finding Ideas" in *Harvard Business Review* **(Vol. 81, No. 11, November 2003, pp. 18)**
Pub: Harvard Business School Press
Ed: Bronwyn Fryer. **Description:** A diverse workforce with many different ideas can introduce organizational change and enhance business creativity.

42237 ■ "Finding and Keeping Good Employees" in *Ingram's* **(Vol. 28, No. 1, January 2002, pp. 69)**
Pub: Show Me Publishing, Inc.
Description: Strategies for retaining valued employees are presented.

42238 ■ "Finding Permanence in Temporary Assignments" in *Home Office Computing* **(Vol. 18, No. 10, October 2000, pp. 20)**
Pub: Scholastic Inc.
Ed: Jeffery D. Zbar. **Description:** Many workers are choosing temping as a career choice and employers are catching on, finding loyal workers for short or long term assignments.

42239 ■ "Fire fight" in *Entrepreneur* **(Vol. 30, No. 2, February)**
Pub: Entrepreneur Media Inc.
Ed: Michelle Prather. **Description:** Employers of H-1B workers are coming under fire, facing accusations that they are laying off American workers in order to hire applicants from other countries who are willing to work for lower wages.

42240 ■ "5 Honeymoon Hints" in *My Business* **(November/December 2001, pp. 46)**
Pub: My Business Magazine
Description: The first few weeks in a new position are critical to small companies when hiring new employees. Five ways to assist new hires to adjust to working at a new company are listed.

42241 ■ "401(k) Becomes Benefit of Choice to Woo Employees" *Crain's Detroit Business* **(Vol.16, No.13, Mar. 27, 2000)**
Pub: Crain Communications, Inc.
Ed: Jennie Phipps. **Description:** One of the first things many managers talk about when interviewing a prospective new employee is the company's 401(k) plan.

42242 ■ "From Barracks to Boardroom" in *Hispanic Business* **(Vol. 24, No. 1/2, January/February 2002, pp. 59-60)**
Pub: Hispanic Business Inc.
Ed: Vivienne Heines. **Description:** Because of the technical training and education received during military service, many recruits are developing a work ethic proven to improve employment prospects.

42243 ■ *From Hiring to Firing: The Legal Survival Guide for Employers in the 90's*
Pub: Legal Strategies, Inc.
Ed: Steven M. Sack. **Released:** 1994. **Price:** $34.95.

42244 ■ "From the Recruiter: Enliven Your Resume" in *Sales & Marketing Management* **(Vol. 157, January 2005, No. 1, pp. 51)**
Pub: VNU Business Media
Ed: Dan Martin. **Description:** Because employers do not have the time to read through every resume, it is imperative to design a resume with something that captures attention quickly.

42245 ■ "Get Hired Now! A 28-Day Program for Landing the Job You Want" in *Black Enterprise* **(Vol. 37, October 2006, No. 3, pp. 119)**
Pub: Earl G. Graves Publishing Co. Inc.
Ed: C.J. Hayden; Frank Traditi. **Description:** Finding a job can be a challenge. Surveys estimate that 74 to 85 percent of those available are never advertised. Tips for searching out employment opportunities and landing the job you desire are explored.

42246 ■ "Getting it together" in *Incentive* **(Vol. 174, No. 10, October 2000, pp. 138)**
Pub: Bill Communications
Description: To enhance recruitment and retention efforts, employer work/life programs are examined.

42247 ■ "Golden opportunities: Older workers bring experience and special needs" in *Crain's Detroit Business* **(Vol. 17, No. 44, Oct. 22, 2001)**
Pub: Crain Communications, Inc.
Ed: Mike Scott. **Description:** According to a survey conducted by AARP, 12.8 percent of seniors work full or part-time, and that men over 65 were more likely to work than women, with 17.5 percent of those interviewed in the workforce in 2000. The differences between senior workers and baby boomer workers are compared.

42248 ■ "Goldmining for Internships" in *Black Enterprise* **(Vol. 34, No. 5, December 2003, pp. S6)**
Pub: Earl Graves Publishing Co.
Ed: Raelyn C. Johnson. **Description:** Information is provided for individuals wishing to intern at a company in order to get hands-on experience.

42249 ■ "Gone Fishin'" in *Entrepreneur* **(Vol. 28, No. 3, March 2000, pp. 86)**
Pub: Entrepreneur Media Inc.
Ed: Brian O'Connell. **Description:** Using the right bait while recruiting top executives for your business.

42250 ■ "Good-bye Doesn't Mean Forever" in *Inc.* **(January 1, 2002)**
Pub: Inc. Magazine
Ed: Emily Barker. **Description:** Profile of SelectMinds maintains a database of former employees for employers.

42251 ■ "Got anything smaller?" in *Entrepreneur* **(Vol. 30, No. 10, October 2002, pp. 83)**
Pub: Entrepreneur Media Inc.
Ed: Chris Sandlund. **Description:** A new trend shows that two out of three corporate executives prefer to work for smaller firms.

42252 ■ "Great Expectation" in *Entrepreneur* **(Vol. 33, February 2005, No. 2, pp. 72)**
Pub: Entrepreneur Media Inc.
Ed: Chris Penttila. **Description:** According to a recent study conducted by the Corporate Leadership Council, 40 percent of newly hired employees will be fired within their first year and half with a company.

42253 ■ "Growing Pains" in *Home Business* **(Vol. 13, January/February 2006, No. 1, pp. 88, 90-91)**
Pub: Home Business Magazine
Ed: Jodi Helmer. **Description:** Home-based business owners can hire employees to help grow a company. Tips to discover if your home-based firm is ready to hire an employee are included.

42254 ■ "Gurus in the garage" in *Harvard Business Review* **(Vol. 78, No. 6, November-December 2000, pp. 71)**
Pub: Harvard Business School Publishing Corp.
Description: Description of a special type of advisor who helps entrepreneurs with a variety of tasks, including recruiting staff and negotiating seed money.

42255 ■ "Hack away" in *Entrepreneur* **(Vol. 30, No. 3, March)**
Pub: Entrepreneur Media Inc.
Ed: Amanda C. Kooser. **Description:** With cyberterrorism becoming a greater threat, more small businesses are hiring computer hackers as computer consultants.

42256 ■ "Help! I Need a Job" in *Crain's New York Business* **(Vol. 23, January 8, 2007, No. 2, pp. 23)**
Pub: Crain Communications, Inc.
Description: January is the best time to search for a new job. Companies bring in new management, have gotten their budgets and know the amount of staff that is required to meet their goals.

42257 ■ "Help Wanted" in *Entrepreneur.com* **(Vol. 34, February 2006, No. 2, pp. 80)**
Pub: Entrepreneur Media Inc.
Ed: Chris Penttila. **Description:** Globalization, outsourcing and competition for capital are putting pressure on small companies to operate more like large businesses. Ideas for hiring CEOs for a small firm are included.

42258 ■ "Here to Stay: When You're Looking for New Hires, Temps May Not be as Temporary as You Might Think" in *Entrepreneur* **(Vol. 32, July 2004)**
Pub: Entrepreneur Media Inc.
Ed: Chris Penttila. **Description:** Temporary staffing agencies have filled at least 162,200 new temporary positions from April to July 2004, according to the U.S. Bureau of Labor Statistics. Companies are wary of hiring new full-time employees and are opting for temporary workers.

42259 ■ **"HFMA identifies financial implications of workforce shortages" in** *Healthcare Financial Management* **(Vol. 56, Sept. 2002, pp. 26)**
Pub: Healthcare Financial Management Association
Description: An overview of the report, "Investing in Your Workforce: Overcoming the Financial Impact of Labor Shortage", the study sponsored by Kronos, Inc. is presented.

42260 ■ **"Hickory Unemployment Stays Steady" in** *Charlotte Observer* **(February 2, 2007)**
Pub: Knight-Ridder/Tribune Business News
Ed: Jen Aronoff. **Description:** Unemployment rates remained unchanged in Hickory, North Carolina area; the region reported 6.1 percent unemployment.

42261 ■ *High Performance Hiring*
Pub: Crisp Publications, Inc.
Ed: Robert Wendover. **Price:** $9.95.

42262 ■ **"Hire for Attitude, Train for Skills" in** *Rough Notes* **(Vol. 145, No. 9, September 2002, pp. 106)**
Pub: Rough Notes
Ed: Nancy Doucette. **Description:** Managing employees starts with hiring them for attitude and then training them for skills. Thus, hiring is pure expense initially.

42263 ■ **"Hire Diversity: Diversity Leaders" in** *Hispanic Business* **(October 2004, pp. 130)**
Pub: Hispanic Business
Description: A listing of top corporations dedicated to workplace diversity and seeking multicultural and bilingual employees is presented.

42264 ■ **"Hire Education" in** *Hispanic Business* **(May 2005, pp. 56)**
Pub: Hispanic Business
Ed: Joel Russell. **Description:** A new job training program SER National helps Hispanic seniors, ages 55 and over, train for jobs. SER National was awarded a $26 million grant from the U.S. Labor Department.

42265 ■ **"Hire Ground" in** *Entrepreneur* **(Vol. 33, March 2005, No. 3, pp. 28)**
Pub: Entrepreneur Media Inc.
Ed: Mark Henricks. **Description:** According to the Small Business Scoreboard, compiled by SurePayroll, a payroll services company, hiring was up, but wages were down in 2004.

42266 ■ **"Hire Learning" in** *Entrepreneur* **(Vol. 32, November 2004, No. 11, pp. 100)**
Pub: Entrepreneur Media Inc.
Ed: Nichole L. Torres. **Description:** According to Kathleen Miller, founder of Miller Consultants Inc., entrepreneurs who take the time to teach newly hired employees find they become more productive.

42267 ■ **"Hire Power" in** *Entrepreneur* **(Vol. 33, March 2005, No. 3, pp. 128)**
Pub: Entrepreneur Media Inc.
Ed: Jessica Hong. **Description:** Profile of Shawn Boyer, co-founder and CEO of SnagAJob.com Inc. The Website matches prospective employees to hourly positions in specific sectors.

42268 ■ **"Hire purpose" in** *Entrepreneur* **(Vol. 31, No. 4, April 2003, pp. 56)**
Pub: Entrepreneur Media Inc.
Ed: Joan Szabo. **Description:** Tax credits from the Job Creation and Worker Assistance Act of 2002 have been extended through 2003, and could provide savings and help defray costs of maintaining employees on the payroll of small businesses.

42269 ■ **"HireDiversity.com Named a Top Site" in** *Hispanic Business* **(Vol. 24, No. 1/2, January/February 2002, pp. 60)**
Pub: Hispanic Business Inc.
Description: HireDiversity.com, the recruitment arm of Hispanic Business Inc., was named a top Web site for the 2002 edition of CareerXroads, a directory of leading online job, resume, and career management information providers.

42270 ■ **"Hiring an Accountant" in** *Crain's Detroit Business* **(Vol. 19, No. 49, December 8, 2003, pp. 14)**
Pub: Crain Communications Inc., Detroit
Description: Questions an employer should ask when hiring an accountant are listed.

42271 ■ *Hiring the Best*
Pub: Irwin Professional Publishing
Ed: Ann M. McGill. **Released:** 1993. **Price:** $10.00 (paper).

42272 ■ **"Hiring Employees With Disabilities" in** *Inc.* **(October 2005, pp. 29-32)**
Pub: Inc. Magazine
Ed: Darren Dahl. **Description:** Habitat International, a carpet, turf and contract manufacturing firm in Chattanooga, Tennessee hires employees with disabilities. Three in four firms in the U.S. have no disabled workers employed. Statistical data included.

42273 ■ *The Hiring, Firing and Everything in Between Personnel Forms Book*
Pub: Round Lake Publishing Co.
Ed: James M. Jenks. **Released:** 1992. **Price:** $19.95 (paper).

42274 ■ *Hiring Handbook Special Report: Avoiding Employee Lawsuits*
Pub: Aspen Publishers, Inc.
Released: 1994. **Price:** $45.00.

42275 ■ **"Hiring, Hollywood Style" in** *Inc.* **(January 1, 2004)**
Pub: Gruner & Jahr USA Publishing
Ed: Bobbie Gossage. **Description:** Typecasting is used in business according to a study conducted by Ezra Zuckerman, a Massachusetts Institute of Technology professor. Zuckerman's research found that employers are more likely to hire an individual who is easily typecast into a particular role, especially early in careers. However, typecasting could be a bad policy.

42276 ■ *Hiring: More Than a Gut Feeling*
Pub: Career Press, Inc.
Ed: Richard Deems. **Released:** 1995. **Price:** $12.99 (paper).

42277 ■ *Hiring Right: A Practical Guide*
Pub: Sage Publications, Inc.
Ed: Susan J. Herman. **Released:** 1993. **Price:** $46.00. **Description:** Provides guidelines for writing job descriptions, interviewing, testing, reference-checking, negotiating contracts, and other aspects of the hiring process. Includes exercises and worksheets.

42278 ■ **"Hiring the Right People to Rep Your Products" in** *Black Enterprise* **(Vol. 35, November 2004, No. 4, pp. 54)**
Pub: Earl G. Graves Publishing Co. Inc.
Ed: Robert Janis. **Description:** Tips for finding the right salesperson for a new product are presented.

42279 ■ **"Hiring is Slow Despite Optimism About Economy" in** *Wall Street Journal* **(August 12, 2003, pp. B9)**
Pub: Dow Jones & Co. Inc.
Ed: Richard C. Breeden. **Description:** According to the National Federation of Independent Business survey, companies are slow to hire new employees, despite good news on the economy.

42280 ■ *Hiring Strategies for Long-Term Success: How to Hire the Best People & Keep Them!*
Pub: Global Insights Publications
Ed: Edward E. Hubbard. **Released:** 1992. **Price:** $24.95 (paper).

42281 ■ **"Hiring True Believers" in** *Sacramento Bee* **(November 14, 2005)**
Pub: The Sacramento Bee
Ed: Rachel Osterman. **Description:** Many retailers hire loyal customers during the holiday season because they understand that shoppers who know and love their store can be the best possible sales staff.

42282 ■ *Hiring Winners*
Pub: Human Resource Development Press
Ed: Phillip Faris. **Released:** 1993. **Price:** $99.95 (ringbound).

42283 ■ **"Hispanic Employment Program Managers Directory" in** *Hispanic Business* **(December 2001, pp. FG8, FG10 FG12)**
Pub: Hispanic Business
Description: The Hispanic Employment Program Manager program assists in increasing the number of Hispanics employed in the U.S. workforce. A list of participating agencies is included.

42284 ■ **"Hispanic Outreach Takes Off" in** *Hispanic Business* **(March 2003, pp. 62, 64)**
Pub: Hispanic Business
Ed: Janet Perez. **Description:** The Federal Aviation Administration is among the government agencies promoting Hispanic recruitment and retention.

42285 ■ **"Hispantelligence Report" in** *Hispanic Business* **(January/February 2004, pp. 8)**
Pub: Hispanic Business
Description: Stock market indexes compared to Hispanic companies, changes in Hispanic occupations and Hispanic employment by the numbers is presented. Statistical data included.

42286 ■ **"Hold Your Tongue" in** *Black Enterprise* **(Vol. 34, No. 3, October 2003, pp. 54)**
Pub: Earl Graves Publishing Co.
Ed: Sonia Alleyne. **Description:** Advice is given to the unemployed when going on a job interview, including the resources: 101 Great Answers to the Toughest Interview Questions and 101 Greatest Questions to Ask on Your Interview.

42287 ■ **"Holding Pattern" in** *Entrepreneur* **(Vol. 33, September 2005, No. 9, pp. 26)**
Pub: Entrepreneur Media Inc.
Ed: Mark Henricks. **Description:** Small business hiring has been at a standstill in 2005 and small business salaries fell 2.2 percent from January to June. Statistical data included.

42288 ■ **"Holiday Headache" in** *The Record* **(November 14, 2005)**
Pub: New Jersey Media Group
Ed: David P. Willis. **Description:** As workers plan vacations around the holiday season from Thanksgiving through New Years, employers scramble to hire replacements.

42289 ■ **"Home Depot Swings into Spring Hiring Season" in** *Altanta Journal-Constitution* **(January 30, 2007)**
Pub: Cox Newspapers, Inc.
Ed: Matt Kempner. **Description:** Home Depot shares its plan to create 15,000 new jobs nationwide. The retailer added the same number in 2006.

42290 ■ **"Hot commodities" in** *WorkingWoman* **(Vol. 25, No. 2, February 2000, pp. 40)**
Pub: Lang Communications Inc.
Ed: Joanne Cleaver, Carrie Patton, and Lisa Holton. **Description:** Corporate recruiters from Time Warner and Yahoo, along with top job applicants, offer job-search secrets.

42291 ■ **"Hot Tips" in** *Inc.* **(May 2000, pp. 161)**
Pub: The Goldhirsh Group
Description: Tips regarding hiring an executive recruiter and information regarding the Family and Medical Leave Act (FMLA) are covered.

42292 ■ **"Housing Project" in** *Entrepreneur* **(Vol. 31, No. 7, July 2003, pp. 50)**
Pub: Entrepreneur Media, Inc.
Description: Many firms are offering employer-assisted housing programs to employees and newly hired employees to improve recruitment, retention and to boost employee morale.

42293 ■ "How High Can Low Go Without Adverse Effects on Economy?" in *St. Louis Post-Dispatch* (March 9, 2005)
Pub: Knight-Ridder/Tribune Business News
Ed: David Nicklaus. **Description:** Minimum wage laws are discussed. The Senate rejected two proposals to raise the minimum wage from $5.15 an hour in March.

42294 ■ "How to Hire A Workers" in *Success* (Vol. 47, No. 1, January 2000, pp. 25)
Pub: Success Publishing, Inc.
Ed: Sarah Duran. **Description:** An overview for hiring young and inexperienced workers.

42295 ■ *How to Hire, Train, and Keep the Best Employees for Your Small Business*
Pub: Atlantic Publishing Company
Ed: Dianna Podmoroff. **Released:** June 2004. **Price:** $29.95. **Description:** Costs of hiring, training, and lost productivity costs related to losing employees.

42296 ■ *How to Make Money While You Look for a Job*
Pub: Booklocker.com, Incorporated
Ed: Donna Boyette. **Released:** March 2005. **Price:** $11.95. **Description:** Six steps to make money while searching for employment are outlined, from setting up a home-based office to selling a service.

42297 ■ "How to Net Vets" in *Entrepreneur* (Vol. 28, No. 10, October 2000, pp. 44)
Pub: Entrepreneur Media Inc.
Ed: Ellen Paris. **Description:** The U.S. Department of Labor has launched a new program called UMET (Use your Military Experience and Training), a web site designed to link employers with soon-to-be civilians.

42298 ■ *How to Recruit, Interview, & Hire the Right Person: A Step by Step System for Selecting the Best Person for Every Job*
Pub: Pryor Resources, Inc.
Released: 1997. **Price:** $199.95 (VHS; 3 cassettes).
Description: Successful hiring is not a matter of luck. Knowledge & well tuned skills are required to recruit, interview, & hire the right person. In this program, you'll get the knowledge & skills you need. You'll learn to accurately identify job requirements & how to find qualified applicants. You'll learn how to protect yourself & your organization by using proper interviewing techniques. Find out how to properly test candidates before interviewing. You'll learn how to ensure success through effective orientation of new employees.

42299 ■ "How To Hire Wisely" in *Inc.* (October 1, 2004)
Pub: Inc. Magazine
Ed: Patrick J. Sauer. **Description:** Tips to help hire quality employees without using gimmicky tests and interview books.

42300 ■ "How You Can Hire Gray Hairs" in *FSB* (Vol. 10, No. 9, December 1, 2000, pp. 79)
Pub: Time Inc.
Ed: Lee Smith. **Description:** Tips for hiring seasoned executives are outlined. Highest in demand are marketing directors, business development directors, CFOs, and CEOs according to recruiters across the country.

42301 ■ "HR Battles to Conquer" in *Hispanic Business* (June 2002, pp. 72)
Pub: Hispanic Business
Ed: Derek Reveron. **Description:** Human resource managers are facing several issues since the terrorist attacks against the U.S. Despite these issues, Hispanic Business 500 firms grew at a 4.9 percent rate last year.

42302 ■ *The HR Book: Human Resources Management for Small Business*
Pub: Self-Counsel Press, Incorporated
Ed: Lin Grensing-Pophal. **Released:** September 2004. **Price:** $22.95. **Description:** Keys to hiring and maintaining productive workforce are outlined.

42303 ■ "I Can't Seem to Hire the Right Bookkeeper. Should I Try Using a Personality Test?" in *Inc.* (October 2005, pp. 62)
Pub: Inc. Magazine
Description: Personality tests that screen job applicants for traits like reliability and dishonesty have become commonplace in most industries.

42304 ■ "If You Have Rules, You Have To Be Prepared to Stick With Them-Even When It's Hard" in *Inc.* (May 1, 2005)
Pub: Inc. Magazine
Ed: Norm Brodsky. **Description:** Problems encountered when hiring an employee who has falsified his/her applications are examined.

42305 ■ "In search of hire principles" in *Incentive* (Vol. 174, No. 7, July 2000, pp. 16)
Pub: Bill Communications
Ed: Stephen Covey. **Description:** Finding a body as quickly as possible should not be a manager's top priority when trying to fill a position. Strategic recruiting and selection are vital to success.

42306 ■ "In a World of Pay" in *Harvard Business Review* (Vol. 81, No. 11, November 2003, pp. 31)
Pub: Harvard Business School Press
Ed: Bronwyn Fryer. **Description:** Compensation for expatriate staff and executives is analyzed.

42307 ■ "Intern affairs: more and more companies are hiring virtual interns." in *Entrepreneur* (Vol. 31, No. 6, June 2003, pp. 74)
Pub: Entrepreneur Media Inc.
Ed: Chris Penttila. **Description:** The impact of hiring virtual interns performing tasks from information technology projects to customer service is investigated. A set of guidelines for hiring college students as virtual interns is presented.

42308 ■ "Intern Burn: Hired the Ultimate Intern from Hell?" in *Entrepreneur* (Vol. 32, November 2004, No. 11, pp. 96)
Pub: Entrepreneur Media Inc.
Ed: Chris Penttila. **Description:** Intership programs offer an inexpensive labor source, as well as a good recruiting tool. Advice for hiring interns is discussed.

42309 ■ "The Internship Edge" in *Hispanic Business* (Vol. 23, No. 10, October, 2001, pp. 90, 92)
Pub: Hispanic Business
Ed: Janet Perez. **Description:** For young Hispanics entering the work force, internships can provide an advantage. A profile of Belinda Stubblefield, vice president of global diversity at Delta Airlines, has developed initiatives that enable Delta to attract and leverage a highly skilled, diverse work force.

42310 ■ *Interviewing, Hiring & Firing*
Pub: SkillPath Publications
Ed: Keith Shannon; read by Keith Shannon. **Released:** 1998. **Price:** $29.95 (analog audio cassette); includes workbook. **Description:** Compilation of the must-have tools required by today's changing, challenging workplace.

42311 ■ "The Ire Next Time" in *Business Week* (March 27, 2000, pp. F28)
Pub: McGraw-Hill, Inc.
Description: Ticket to Work and Work Incentives Improvement Act of 1999 are discussed.

42312 ■ "Jetblue Outlines Massive Logan Expansion" in *Boston Globe* (February 3, 2005)
Pub: New York Times Company
Ed: Keith Reed. **Description:** JetBlue's plans for expansion at Logan International Airport in Boston are outlined. The expansion could make JetBlue one of the largest airlines operating out of Logan and calls for the hiring of about 500 new employees.

42313 ■ "Job Board for NAIA Looks Like a Winner" in *Kansas City Star* (February 8, 2005)
Pub: Knight-Ridder/Tribune Business News
Ed: Diane Stafford. **Description:** HCap Search and the National Association of Intercollegiate Athletics have partnered to form an online job listing. The board will assist college graduates from small liberal arts colleges and employers to connect. Statistical data on employment issues is also included.

42314 ■ "Job Flight: Is it Real: Evidence is Scant, but a Shift Would be Welcome" in *Barron's* (August 11, 2003, pp. 26)
Pub: Barron's
Ed: Gene Epstein. **Description:** Forecasts of a mass migration overseas of U.S. white collar jobs, representing nearly $150 billion in wages, may be fresh meat for a media frenzy, but are not supported by the data.

42315 ■ "Job Market for 2004 Show Improvement, but Not Higher Starting Salaries" in *Hispanic Business* (January/February 2004, pp. 57)
Pub: Hispanic Business
Description: Results of a survey conducted by the National Association of Colleges and Employers (NACE) showed that although the job market will improve, starting wages will not.

42316 ■ "Job Market May Be Turning Around" in *Hispanic Business* (October 2003, pp. 111)
Pub: Hispanic Business
Description: According to a career services Internet company, the job market in North America is stabilizing. Statistical data included.

42317 ■ "Job Market Thaw" in *Sales and Marketing.com* (Vol. 156, No. 3, March 2004, pp. 24)
Pub: VNU eMedia, Inc.
Description: Future job market trends for ten different industries are examined. The ten featured industries include construction, energy, financial services, healthcare/pharmaceutical, hospitality/travel, real estate, services, technology, telecommunications, and transportation.

42318 ■ "Job Outlook Stays Bright in Florida" in *Tampa Tribune* (December 16, 2005)
Pub: Media General, Inc.
Ed: Dave Simanoff. **Description:** Tampa, Florida is seeing an increase in job growth, leading the nation by adding 255,100 jobs in the last year.

42319 ■ "The job site evolution" in *Rough Notes* (Vol. 146, No. 3, March 2003, pp. 173)
Pub: Rough Notes
Ed: George Rusty Capulet. **Description:** Michael P. Tornesello, president of InsuranceJobChannel.com is an online career site available to the insurance industry. Nationwide Insurance is one of its customers.

42320 ■ "Jobs Are Back; Too Bad Wages Aren't" in *Fortune* (Vol. 149, No. 9, May 3, 2004, pp. 40)
Pub: Time, Inc.
Ed: Anna Bernasek. **Description:** Despite the number of newly created jobs, wages are remaining the same. One factor accounting for this is the benefits workers receive, which increase costs for employers. Insurance premiums have risen 32 percent over the past five years.

42321 ■ "Jobs Increase in Milwaukee Area" in *Milwaukee Journal Sentinel* (December 22, 2005)
Pub: Journal Sentinel, Inc.
Ed: Joel Dresang. **Description:** According to the Wisconsin Department of Workforce Development, Milwaukee showed an increase in jobs over the last year, including the manufacturing sector. From November 2004 to November 2005, 1,300 new factory jobs were created paying an average of $17.37 an hour.

42322 ■ "Joining the Ranks" in *Entrepreneur* (Vol. 33, October 2005, No. 10, pp. 89)
Pub: Entrepreneur Media Inc.
Ed: Mark Henricks. **Description:** American entrepreneurs are finding returning military personnel to be attractive employees for their small companies due to their work experience combined with an eagerness to prove themselves.

42323 ■ "Keeping Employees" in *Success* (Vol. 47, No. 5, October 2000, pp. 12)
Pub: Success Publishing, Inc.
Description: Equity compensation and employee stock ownership programs (ESOPs) as options for family-owned businesses to use as an exit strategy are discussed.

42324 ■ "Labor pains: if immigration laws tighten, all entrepreneurs could feel the squeeze" in *Entrepreneur* (Vol. 31, No. 5, May 2003)
Pub: Entrepreneur Media Inc.
Ed: Mark Henricks. **Description:** According to an analysis of Census data by the Center for Labor Market Studies, the American economic boom of the 1990s was fueled from laborers coming from foreign countries. With immigration laws being tightened in the wake of 9/11, many entrepreneurs are concerned about a reduced flow of immigrant workers.

42325 ■ "Law Firm Recruiters Face Hurdles in Pay, Local Economy" in *Crain's Detroit Business* (Vol. 22, November 27, 2006, No. 48, pp. 18)
Pub: Crain Communications Inc. - Detroit
Ed: Robert Ankeny. **Description:** Recruitment and retention of new lawyers continues to be difficult for law firms in the Detroit area. Negative image of the area and the climate are major factors making recruitment from other areas difficult.

42326 ■ "Lawyering Up" in *Boston Business Journal* (Vol. 23, No. 30, August 29, 2003, pp. 1)
Pub: American City Business Journals
Ed: Sheri Qualters. **Description:** Forecasts by officers of Boston, Massachusetts-based Legal Staffing Solutions regarding the state of employment in the legal services market. Topics include levels of employee recruitment, economic conditions, and effects of past layoffs.

42327 ■ "Litigation's price boosts arbitration's appeal" in *Atlanta Business Chronicle* (Vol. 25, November 15, 2002, No. 23 pp. SS15)
Pub: American City Business Publications, Inc.
Ed: Linda Goodspeed. **Description:** The number of arbitration cases has increased to 218,032 in 2001, from 60,808 in 1990, as litigation costs continue to rise. Arbitration is used to settle a variety of disputes. Employment contracts represent a newer and more controversial use for arbitration, and some pros and cons are discussed.

42328 ■ "The Little Guys Spy a Slowdown" in *Business Week* (No. 3691, July 24, 2000, pp. 26)
Pub: McGraw-Hill, Inc.
Description: Recent reports of sluggish hiring gains, flat vehicle sales and weak consumer spending confirm the findings from the National Federation of Independent Business' month survey of members, that small business optimism fell to 97.9 in June, its lowest level since the fall of 1993.

42329 ■ "Log on for work" in *Black Enterprise* (Vol. 33, No. 3, October 2002, pp. 74)
Pub: Earl Graves Publishing Co.
Ed: Sonia Alleyne. **Description:** Advice is given for using the Internet to secure employment. Tips offered include using Web sites specializing in a particular field or company, to join industry organizations, and use caution when registering for a job listing.

42330 ■ "The Low Down" in *My Business* (June/July 2004, pp. 46)
Pub: My Business Magazine
Ed: Karen J. Bannan. **Description:** Pre-hire tests can give employers more insight into job candidates than a resume alone.

42331 ■ "Lowest bid is not always best for hiring contractor" in *Business First Columbus* (Vol. 18, No. 25, February 8, 2002, pp.)
Pub: Business First Columbus, Inc.
Ed: Susanna Barton. **Description:** Tips for choosing the correct contractor for the job are offered.

42332 ■ "Making a Comeback" in *Entrepreneur* (Vol. 32, August 2004, No. 8, pp. 71)
Pub: Entrepreneur Media Inc.
Ed: Joanne Cleaver. **Description:** Advantages as well as disadvantages to rehiring an employee to serve as a consultant are explored.

42333 ■ "Making Strides in Building Jobs" in *Milwaukee Journal Sentinel* (December 3, 2005)
Pub: Journal Sentinel, Inc.
Ed: Joel Dresang. **Description:** Big Step, also known as the Building Industry Group Skilled Trades Employment Program, shares its plans to train Milwaukee, Wisconsin residents for skilled trades in the construction industry. Statistical and detailed plans are included.

42334 ■ "Manatee Boat Makers Are Hiring, But Workers Aren't Plentiful" in *Bradenton Herald* (February 4, 2005)
Pub: Bradenton Herald
Ed: Tilde Herrera. **Description:** Growth of the boating industry has increased significantly, with Chris-Craft reporting above 15 percent increase in sales for 2004. However, companies are having difficulty finding skilled labor to produce the growing demand.

42335 ■ "Manufacturing History: Tales of Turning Points in Factory Jobs are Just That" in *Barron's* (July 28, 2003, pp. 30)
Pub: Barron's
Ed: Gene Epstein. **Description:** The continuing erosion of manufacturing jobs in the U.S. may have produced a nearly 40-year low, with less than 15 million factory-related jobs; and its percentage of total private employment, at less than 15 percent, may be nearly 20 percent less than the previous low; but that still does not indicate anything structurally wrong, or any harmful effect of foreign manufacturing.

42336 ■ "Manufacturing: Industrial Strength Integration" in *Microsoft Executive Circle* (Vol. 1, No. 2, Q2 2001, pp. 56-58)
Pub: Putman Media
Ed: Marty Weil. **Description:** The Internet has forced manufacturers to rethink business in order to stay competitive. One global chemical maker handles 4.5 million transactions every month with a 2-3 second response time using the Internet to transact business.

42337 ■ "Manufacturing Job Losses Hit Other Sectors" in *Crain's Detroit Business* (Vol. 22, November 20, 2006,No. 47, pp. 3)
Pub: Crain Communications Inc. - Detroit
Ed: Amy Lane. **Description:** Detroit area service industry job market is flat as a result of the decline in manufacturing job. Service sector jobs are still growing in the rest of the state, however.

42338 ■ "Match Made in Heaven" in *Hispanic Business* (June 2002, pp. 82)
Pub: Hispanic Business
Description: The Web site HireDiversity.com links professionals with corporations seeking multicultural and bilingual job candidates from entry- to senior-management-level positions. A listing of 24 such companies and contacts are included.

42339 ■ "Matchmaker" in *Forbes* (Vol. 175, February 28, 2005, No. 4, pp. 48)
Pub: Forbes Magazine Inc.

Ed: Joanne Gordon. **Description:** Profile of Debra Feldman, a job coach who helps individuals find employment.

42340 ■ "Meet the Gatekeepers" in *Crain's Chicago Business* (Vol. 30, February 2007, No. 6, pp. 40)
Pub: Crain Communications, Inc.
Ed: Kate Ryan. **Description:** Recruiters at big investment banking firms agree that the way to get your foot in the door requires common sense issues such as not answering your phone in the middle of an interview, proofreading your cover letter, and research. Interviews with three top executives give more insight and advice.

42341 ■ "Memories...Are Just That" in *Ingram's* (Vol. 28, No. 9, September 2002, pp. 37)
Pub: Show Me Publishing, Inc.
Ed: Chris Becicka. **Description:** Schools for higher education are providing students with advantages never before offered by older ones, and that difference is due to the new technologies introduced in education.

42342 ■ "Military leave" in *Ingram's* (Vol. 27, No. 12, December 2001, pp. 24)
Pub: Show Me Publishing, Inc.
Description: The obligations to both the employer and employee regarding military leave are discussed. The Uniformed Employment and Re-employment Act of 1994 is explained in detail.

42343 ■ "Misclassifying Workers Can Cost You, Big Time" in *Inc.* (November 2000, pp. 97)
Pub: The Goldhirsh Group
Description: State and national authorities are auditing employee misclassification more and more. Employment-law experts stress the importance of interviewing and keeping thorough records of freelancers and contractors doing business with a company.

42344 ■ "Money-Preneuring" in *Small Business Opportunities* (Vol. 17, September 2005, No. 5, pp. 68, 128)
Pub: Harris Publications Inc.
Ed: Robert A. Adelson. **Description:** Three strategies to give non-family executives a share in the rewards of ownership without transferring any company stock are shared: offering a non-voting stock plan, a non-qualified deferred compensation plan, or a phantom stock plan.

42345 ■ "Monthly Report - December 1999" in *Small Business Economic Trends* (December 1999, pp. COV)
Pub: National Federation of Independent Business
Description: A survey of small and independent business owners shows some 20 percent of small businesses are having trouble recruiting qualified staff, while 28 percent reported higher labor costs for November 1999. The Small Business Optimism Index rose by 2 points in November 1999 to 103.2.

42346 ■ "Monthly Report - January 2000" in *Small Business Economic Trends* (January 2000, pp. COV)
Pub: National Federation of Independent Business
Description: The Index of Small Business Optimism dropped two points to 103.0 in December 1999. Some 22 percent of companies expect to increase their workforce in the next few months, and 23 percent cited finding skilled labor their main problem at the moment.

42347 ■ "Monthly Report - June 2000" in *Small Business Economic Trends* (June 2000, pp. 1)
Pub: National Federation of Independent Business
Description: Small firms' compensation for employees increased for 34 percent of the firms surveyed, while a definite skilled labor shortage was a problem for 24 percent of firms surveyed.

42348 ■ "Monthly Report - March 2000" in *Small Business Economic Trends* **(March 2000, pp. COV)**
Pub: National Federation of Independent Business
Description: A survey of small and independent business owners. The Index of Small Business Optimism fell three points to 100.6 in February 2000, compared to January 2000. Some 16 percent of companies expected to boost their workforce in the coming months.

42349 ■ "More Fun for the Money; ASC Lures "Car Nuts" to Reshape the Company" in *Crain's Detroit Business* **(Vol. 19, No. 49, December 8, 2003)**
Pub: Crain Communications Inc., Detroit
Ed: Terry Kosdrosky. Description: ASC Inc. has hired executives from larger auto suppliers such as Johnson Controls Automotive Group, Lear Corporation and Owens Corning, by playing up the company's fun aspects.

42350 ■ "More Minority Portfolio Managers Sought" in *Sacramento Bee* **(November 13, 2005)**
Pub: The Sacramento Bee
Ed: Gilbert Chan. Description: Most private equity senior staff are white males from Ivy League schools; women and minorities continue to be ignored by money management companies. Many of the major money manager firms have paid millions in damages to settle sex-discrimination cases.

42351 ■ "Motorola Foundation Funds 'Road Map' for Employers Who Hire People With Disabilities" in *Long Island Business News* **(February 6, 2004)**
Pub: Dolan Media Newswires
Ed: Ryan McCormick. Description: Motorola Foundation provides a grant for the National Center for Disability Services to develop and publish a 'road map' for employers who hire persons with disabilities.

42352 ■ "Multiculturalism Grows Up" in *Hispanic Business* **(Vol. 24, No. 4, April 2002, pp. 58, 60)**
Pub: Hispanic Business Inc.
Description: An interview with Gustavo De La Torre, manager of Worldwide Diversity & Multiculture at Intel Corporation, about diversity in the workplace.

42353 ■ "Multilingual Execs in Demand" in *Hispanic Business* **(March 2005, pp. 15)**
Pub: Hispanic Business
Description: According to Korn/Ferry International, the need for multilingual executives is growing in the U.S. Statistical data included.

42354 ■ "MySay: Hiring Help" in *My Business* **(December/January 2003, pp. 49)**
Pub: My Business Magazine
Ed: Kathi Purnell. Description: The owner of a self-storage company discusses issues faced when she hired her best employee's mother so the two could work as a mother-daughter team for the business.

42355 ■ "National Survey Finds More Small-Business Owners Planning to Increase Their Staffs" in *Long Island Business News* **(January 30, 2004)**
Pub: Dolan Media Newswires
Ed: Ben Abelson. Description: According to a study done by the National Federation of Independent Business, 20 percent of U.S. small businesses plan to increase staff this year, a number higher than at any other point in the past 3-1/2 years. The financial services sector is leading the way in this trend.

42356 ■ "A New Breed of Entrepreneurs" in *Black Enterprise* **(Vol. 37, November 2006, No. 4, pp. 16)**
Pub: Earl G. Graves Publishing Co. Inc.
Description: Black entrepreneurs are an important part of the chain for providing economic opportunities within the community. Many black business owners are more likely to hire black employees and apply innovative strategies in building their businesses rather than taking the traditional route.

42357 ■ "A New Game Plan for C Players" in *Harvard Business Review* **(Vol. 80, No. 1, January 2002, pp. 81)**
Pub: Harvard Business School Press
Ed: Beth Axelrod, Helen Handfield-Jones, Ed Michaels. Description: Corporate managers must find means to hire and retain quality managers, while finding an efficient means for dealing with managers that do not perform at needed levels; also important is improving the quality of existing managers.

42358 ■ "New Jersey Firm Busy Westbrook, Maine, Online Classified Company" in *Portland Press Herald* **(December 7, 2005)**
Pub: Blethen Maine Newspapers, Inc.
Ed: Matt Wickensheiser. Description: The Journal Register has purchased JobsInTheUS, an online employment classifieds company. The Journal Register owns papers in Connecticut, Pennsylvania, Ohio, Rhode Island, New York, and Michigan.

42359 ■ "New Jersey Jobless Rate Down, But Jobs Lost" in *The Record* **(November 18, 2005)**
Pub: New Jersey Media Group
Ed: Michael L. Diamond. Description: According to the New Jersey Department of Labor and Workforce Development office, the state's unemployment rate fell to 3.9 percent in October 2005. However, the state's economy lost 4,700 jobs during the month. The pattern shows that New Jersey private-sector firms are hiring workers cautiously.

42360 ■ "Newbie Rules" in *Entrepreneur* **(Vol. 28, No. 8, August 2000, pp. 34)**
Pub: Entrepreneur Media Inc.
Ed: Ellen Paris. Description: The varying requirements to be followed when reporting new hires and how they affect small businesses are examined.

42361 ■ "News Blog Highlights Women's Careers" in *Marketing to Women* **(Vol. 19, November 2006, No. 11, pp. 5)**
Pub: EPM Communications, Inc.
Description: NewsonWomen.com, a news blog for businesswomen and their career achievements, has added executive job postings to its content.

42362 ■ "90 percent of laid-off hotel workers back on the job" in *Boston Business Journal* **(Vol. 22, No. 16, May 24, 2002, pp. 7)**
Pub: MCP, Inc.
Ed: Donna L. Goodison. Description: Boston hotels rehired 900 workers in May 2002, out of the 1,000 that were laid off after the September 11, 2001, terrorist attacks. Hotel occupancy rates have also rebounded.

42363 ■ "No experience necessary" in *Entrepreneur* **(Vol. 30, No. 12, December 2002, pp. 109)**
Pub: Entrepreneur Media Inc.
Ed: Kimberly L. McCall. Description: Entrepreneurs are finding that untrained, fresh sales talent can be a powerful means to build a sales force. Tips for hiring novice sales personnel are presented.

42364 ■ "No Recovery for Disabled?" in *Wall Street Journal* **(April 16, 2002, pp. B1)**
Pub: Wall Street Journal
Ed: Carlos Tejada. Description: Workers with disabilities fear they will be snubbed from employers as the economy recovers.

42365 ■ "Not hiring" in *Entrepreneur* **(Vol. 30, No. 12, December 2002, pp. 103)**
Pub: Entrepreneur Media Inc.
Ed: Chris Penttila. Description: Simple steps to follow to develop a rejection process for job candidates are listed. The importance of putting closure to rejected resumes is stressed.

42366 ■ "The NSA" in *Business Week* **(January 23, 2006, No. 3968, pp. 62)**
Pub: McGraw-Hill Companies
Description: The National Security Agency, the nation's top techno-spy agency, is competing against Web giants such as Google and Yahoo! in order to recruit and hire math teams.

42367 ■ "Oakdale Based Skills Unlimited Helps Long Island's Disabled Develop Skills and Find Work" in *Long Island Business News* **(Feb.20, 2004)**
Pub: Dolan Media Newswires
Ed: Ken Cerini. Description: Richard Kassnove, executive director of Skills Unlimited, helps disabled individuals find employment with Long Island, New York area businesses.

42368 ■ "Of One Mind: Keep Employees by Getting on the Same Page From the Get-Go" in *Entrepreneur* **(Vol. 31, No. 8, August 2003, pp. 23)**
Pub: Entrepreneur Media, Inc.
Ed: David Newton. Description: The key to retaining good employees is to keep promises made during the recruiting process. According to a recent study, salary rewards, bonuses and perks were not as important to prospective employees as autonomy and personal growth, and job security and responsibility were more important than benefits.

42369 ■ "On the Hunt for High-End Hires" in *Crain's Detroit Business* **(Vol. 21, October 31, 2005, No. 44, pp. 1)**
Pub: Crain Communications Inc. - Detroit
Ed: Andrew Dietderich. Description: John Bukowicz, CEO of Corporate Consulting Associates Inc. in Bloomfield Hills, Michigan, reports business is up 15 percent for the executive recruitment and job placement firm.

42370 ■ "One Big Reason to Expect a Decent Year for Jobs" in *Business Week* **(January 23, 2006, No. 3968, pp. 27-28)**
Pub: McGraw-Hill Companies
Ed: James C. Cooper. Description: Companies can no longer meet the demand with existing workers. The Labor Department reported a 4.9 percent jobless rate. Statistical data included.

42371 ■ "One Man's Alien is Another's Employee" in *Inc.* **(October 2005, pp. 32)**
Pub: Inc. Magazine
Ed: Darren Dahl. Description: Iowa reports a 26 percent hike in Hispanics living in the state and reports that these foreign-born workers are vital to its growing economy.

42372 ■ "Orders Up; Jobs Below Forecast" in *Charlotte Observer* **(February 2, 2007)**
Pub: Knight-Ridder/Tribune Business News
Ed: Kerry Hall. Description: U.S. Labor Department reported unemployment rates at 4.6 percent, up one-tenth of a percent. Economists had predicted 170,000 new jobs, but only 111,000 were created.

42373 ■ "Our Rankings Are Derived From 3-Month Rolling Averages of US Bureau of Labor Statistics Unadjusted Employment Data" in *Inc.* **(May1,2006)**
Pub: Inc. Magazine
Ed: Michael A. Shires. Description: Data reported September 1994 to September 2004 from the U.S. Bureau of Labor Statistics is presented. Statistical data included.

42374 ■ "Parent Trap?" in *Entrepreneur* **(Vol. 33, March 2005, No. 3, pp. 96)**
Pub: Entrepreneur Media Inc.
Ed: Mark Henricks. Description: Jay Oxenbhorn tells how he employs his 70-ish mother to fill orders for his company. Parents can offer entrepreneurs skill and expertise from their life experiences to help build a company.

42375 ■ "Parents for hire" in *Entrepreneur* **(Vol. 31, No. 4, April 2003, pp. 76)**
Pub: Entrepreneur Media Inc.
Ed: Patricia Schiff Estess. Description: Entrepreneurs often hire parents for their new companies because of their trust, savvy and availability, but it takes time to work out the role reversals in the new relationship.

42376 ■ "Part-Time Assignments" in *Black Enterprise* (Vol. 37, December 2006, No. 5, pp. 70)
Pub: Earl G. Graves Publishing Co. Inc.
Description: During critical change initiatives interim management, an employment model which uses senior-level executives to manage a special project or specific business function on a temporary basis, can have many benefits.

42377 ■ "Peering In" in *Entrepreneur* (Vol. 33, January 2005, No. 1, pp. 70)
Pub: Entrepreneur Media Inc.
Ed: Chris Penttila. **Description:** Peer-to-peer interviewing can help small companies; the applicant learns more about the company, employees help select future co-workers, and management can gain more insight into the applicant's personality.

42378 ■ *People Investment: How to Make Your Hiring Decisions Pay off for Everyone*
Pub: Oasis Press
Ed: E. R. Worthington. **Released:** 1993. **Price:** $39.95 (ringbound); $19.95 (paper).

42379 ■ "Playing e-Detective" in *Entrepreneur* (Vol. 30, No.)
Pub: Entrepreneur Media Inc.
Ed: Chris Penttila. **Description:** The pros and cons of using the Internet for background checks on potential employees is discussed.

42380 ■ "The Power of the Pack" in *Sales & Marketing Management* (Vol. 159, January-February 2007, No. 1, pp. 45)
Pub: VNU Business Media
Description: Root Learning, a learning solutions company, informs applicants of the firm's sense of hierarchy. Prospective employees are informed about the policy whereby employees are called roosters or rootizens.

42381 ■ "Power to the People" in *Incentive* (Vol. 174, No. 8, August 2000, pp. 18)
Pub: Bill Communications
Ed: Don Mogelefsky. **Description:** To effectively recruit and retain employees in the tight job market, companies are treating workers with a lot more respect.

42382 ■ "Priority" in *Inc.* (Volume 27, March 2005, No. 3, pp. 23-26, 28, 30)
Pub: Inc. Magazine
Description: Business information discussed includes information about the SEC looking into unlicensed investment brokers, the economy, freight co-ops to help shippers ease costs, hiring, Google, education, SBA assistance to women entrepreneurs, and new inventions.

42383 ■ "Prospects are dim for entry-level employment" in *Atlanta Business Chronicle* (Vol. 25, No. 21, November 1, 2002, pp. 13C)
Pub: American City Business Publications, Inc.
Ed: Tony Heffernan. **Description:** A majority of commercial real estate companies have not been hiring new employees, and others are careful about who they are hiring. CB Richard Ellis, in Atlanta, Georgia, has revealed that it does not plan to hire new staff at this time, but Grubb & Ellis Company's Atlanta office intends to hire a small number.

42384 ■ "Protecting your company from high turnover" in *Women in Busines s* (Vol. 53, No. 2, March-April, 2001, pp. 30)
Pub: The ABWA Co. Inc.
Ed: Melissa Will. **Description:** Strategies to attract and retain good caliber employees are addressed. Ways of reducing staff turnover through the use of flexible working hours, employee involvement and fair management practices are explored.

42385 ■ "Put a Hacker to Work" in *Inc.* (Volume 28, January 2006, No. 1, pp. 39, 42)
Pub: Inc. Magazine
Ed: Darren Dahl. **Description:** Profile of software developer, TopCoder, shares its strategy to find and register the world's best programmers through codewriting contests where they have hackers solve tricky math problems or algorithms. The Connecticut firm employs 65,000 coders globally.

42386 ■ *Quality Interviewing*
Pub: Crisp Publications, Inc.
Ed: Robert B. Maddux. **Released:** Third edition. **Price:** $10.95.

42387 ■ "Quarterly Report - February 2000" in *Small Business Economic Trends* (February 2000, pp. COV)
Pub: National Federation of Independent Business
Description: The Index of Small Business Optimism rose to 103.6 in January 2000, representing the highest reading since October 1997. Around one percent of companies expect to increase their workforce over the coming months, although 21 percent report that finding skilled labor is one of their main problems.

42388 ■ "Race Matters: Studies Show Race, Even Black-Sounding Names, Causes Doors To Shut" in *Black Enterprise* (Vol. 34, February 2004)
Pub: Earl Graves Publishing Co.
Ed: Marie Evan. **Description:** According to a study conducted by a sociologist at Northwestern University in Evanston, Illinois, 17 percent of white ex-cons were called back for job interviews from applications filed, while only 14 percent of crime-free Blacks were called. A study by the University of Chicago on hiring discrimination is also cited. Statistical data included.

42389 ■ "Recreation" in *Inc.* (Volume 27, July 2005, No. 7, pp. 57-58)
Pub: Inc. Magazine
Ed: Patrick J. Sauer. **Description:** A well-planned company barbeque can be used as a business opportunity for recruitment, marketing, worker and customer loyalty, employee motivation, and finding new customers. Barbeque sauce recipe included.

42390 ■ "Recruit From Another Industry" in *Sales & Marketing Management* (Vol. 157, February 2005, No. 2, pp. 16)
Pub: VNU Business Media
Description: Recruiting a top salesperson from another industry does not guarantee the same results when selling in a new sector.

42391 ■ "Recruiting and Retaining Top Talent" in *Success* (Vol. 47, No. 4, September 2000, pp. 84)
Pub: Success Publishing, Inc.
Ed: Jane Shealy. **Description:** In a recent poll of human resource executives, 80 percent characterized the labor shortage as bad, but manageable. Ten percent reported the situation so severe that they were turning business away.

42392 ■ "Recruiting Tool for Corporate Companies" in *Black Enterprise* (Vol. 35, January 2005, No. 6, pp. 53)
Pub: Earl G. Graves Publishing Co. Inc.
Ed: Sonia Alleyne. **Description:** Richard Bamsey reports his organization, LEAD (Leadership and Education Development), offers companies access to its database of the school's alumni. Students are from diverse and underserved communities and are interested in pursuing a career in business.

42393 ■ "Recruitment Contacts" in *Hispanic Business* (Vol. 24, No. 1/2, January/February 2002, pp. 62)
Pub: Hispanic Business Inc.
Description: A listing of corporations seeking multicultural and bilingual candidates is presented.

42394 ■ "Recruitment: Hispanic Employment Program Managers" in *Hispanic Business* (December 2002, pp. FRG6-FRG8)
Pub: Hispanic Business
Description: Contact information is provided from the Hispanic Employment Program Manager's Directory (HEPM); these managers are responsible with improving the representation of Hispanics in the work force.

42395 ■ "Reference Library" in *Small Business Opportunities* (Vol. 17, May 2005, No. 3, pp. 54, 56)
Pub: Harris Publications Inc.

Ed: Lin Grensing-Pophal. **Description:** Problems to avoid when offering or receiving employee references are outlined.

42396 ■ "Respect Your Elders" in *Inc.* (September 1, 2003)
Pub: Gruner & Jahr USA Publishing
Ed: Donna Fenn. **Description:** Small companies are finding smart, reliable employees by hiring individuals over the age of 65.

42397 ■ "Restaurants are Hiring Workers Faster than Other Economic Sectors" in *The Record* (November 19, 2005)
Pub: New Jersey Media Group
Ed: Kathleen Lynn. **Description:** New Jersey-based restaurants are hiring new workers three times the rate of the overall job market. The state reported 215,000 restaurants in October 2005, up nearly 3 percent of same time last year. Statistical data included.

42398 ■ "Restaurants Watch Helplessly As Wait Staff Applications Dry Up" in *Bradenton Herald* (January 31, 2005)
Pub: Bradenton Herald
Ed: Tilde Herrera. **Description:** Restaurant owners in the Bradenton area are having difficulty hiring professional wait staff. Sean Murphy, owner of Beach Bistro and Mangrove Grill, believes waiting tables has become less attractive because of the tip reporting system used by the Internal Revenue Service.

42399 ■ "Retiring Minds" in *Hispanic Business* (March 2005, pp. 50)
Pub: Hispanic Business
Ed: Joel Russell. **Description:** The large number of federal managers retiring is creating new opportunities for Hispanics. Federal agencies and mid-career outreach agencies are listed.

42400 ■ "Rewards For Recruiting: Incentivize Your Reps For Bringing In New Hires" in *Sales & Marketing Management* (Vol. 157, February 2005)
Pub: VNU Business Media
Ed: Julia Chang. **Description:** Referrals from current sales staff help attract top sales people. Some companies are using incentives to encourage salespeople to bring qualified candidates on board.

42401 ■ "Risky Business: Staff Smarts" in *Entrepreneur* (Vol. 31, No. 9, September 2003, pp. 78)
Pub: Entrepreneur Media, Inc.
Ed: Chris Penttila. **Description:** Employers are running credit checks on job applicants, and can by law, reject prospective employees on the basis of personal credit history. Information to assess a credit report is included.

42402 ■ "Romney Set To Unveil Jobs Program" in *Boston Globe* (February 3, 2005)
Pub: New York Times Company
Ed: Sasha Talcott. **Description:** Massachusetts State has partnered with Citizens Financial Group to create jobs. The new program is funded by Citizens and will be administered by the State's Department of Business and Technology.

42403 ■ "Sacramento, Calif.-Area Small Businesses Remain Optimistic for Year Ahead" in *Sacramento Bee* (October 21, 2005)
Pub: The Sacramento Bee
Ed: Thuy-Doan Le. **Description:** Despite the recent hurricanes and rising gas prices, local small businesses remain optimistic for 2006. According to a recent survey conducted by American Express, 59 percent of West Coast small business owners said they will hire new employees within the next six months.

42404 ■ "Sales & Marketing Employment Market Remains Strong" in *Hispanic Business* (Vol. 23, No. 5, May 2001, pp. 80)
Pub: Hispanic Business
Description: According to a recent survey by a national recruitment firm, sales and marketing positions remain strong, particularly in the telecommunications industry, pharmaceuticals, transportation, and information technology.

42405 ■ "San Francisco Job Applicants Do Not Have to Admit to Former Convictions" in *Sacramento Bee* **(October 26, 2005)**
Pub: The Sacramento Bee
Ed: Rachel Osterman. **Description:** The city of San Francisco has adopted a ruling that allows applicants with criminal records to apply for jobs without disclosing that information. The move was made in order to help erase the stigma faced by felons applying for public sector positions.

42406 ■ "Scenes From the Talent Wars" in *Inc.* **(Volume 28, January 2006, No. 1, pp. 29-31)**
Pub: Inc. Magazine
Ed: Scott Westcott. **Description:** Employers are willing to go to extra lengths to recruit and retain talented workers. A list of business jargon used in human resources is included.

42407 ■ "School Career Centers Think Outside the Box" in *Long Island Business News* **(February 27, 2004)**
Pub: Dolan Media Newswires
Ed: Claude Solnik. **Description:** Stony Brook University in New York has created a business etiquette program where potential employers meet with job-seeking students for a three-course meal and networking.

42408 ■ "Scouting employment in the major leagues" in *BlackEnterprise* **(Vol. 32, No. 2, September 2001, pp. 66)**
Pub: Earl Graves Publishing Co.
Ed: Milca Esdaille. **Description:** Information to assist employers and job hunters when using an employment recruiting service is covered. Pointers are listed including, what to look for in a recruiting agency.

42409 ■ "The Search for Top Talent" in *Success* **(Vol. 47, No. 4, September 2000, pp. 90)**
Pub: Success Publishing, Inc.
Description: Talent founders and husband-wife team, Kimberly and Doug Rath, offer advice to small and large businesses that are having a difficult time finding employees.

42410 ■ "Security at the Forefront" in *Women in Business* **(Vol. 54, No. 3, May-June 2002, pp. 38)**
Pub: The ABWA Co Inc.
Ed: Kate Link. **Description:** The importance of pre-employment screening is discussed.

42411 ■ *Seven Imperatives for Fair, Legal & Productive Interviewing: A Guide for Anyone Who Makes or Influences Hiring Decision*
Pub: DBM Publishing
Ed: Drake Beam Morin, Inc. staff. **Released:** Rep Ed, 1993. **Price:** $10.95 (paper).

42412 ■ "Should you take the money...and run?" in *Women in Business* **(Vol. 54, No. 3, May-June 2002, pp. 40)**
Pub: The ABWA Co Inc.
Ed: Mia Katz. **Description:** Negotiating the salary and benefits for a new job are discussed.

42413 ■ "Small businesses holding out on panic attack" in *Atlanta Business Chronicle* **(Vol. 24, No. 13, August 31, 2001, pp. 2B)**
Pub: American City Business Journals Inc.
Ed: David Mildenberg. **Description:** Small business owners are keeping an eye on the slowing economy, but are not panicky about it, according to a Small Business InSight quarterly survey, which shows an overall score of 127, versus 130 in the previous quarter. Although the general economic slowdown is now the second-most pressing concern of small business owners, work force issues like finding qualified employees remains the top concern.

42414 ■ "Small Business Advisor: Focus effort on receptive audience" in *Crain's Chicago Business* **(Vol. 23, December 11, 2000, pp. SB17)**
Pub: Crain Communications, Inc. Crain
   Communications, Inc.

Ed: R. Wendell Williams. **Description:** Employee selection techniques are probed.

42415 ■ *The Small Business Owner's Manual: Everything You Need to Know to Start Up and Run Your Business*
Pub: Career Press, Incorporated
Ed: Joe Kennedy. **Released:** June 2005. **Price:** $19.99 (US), $26.95 (Canadian). **Description:** Comprehensive guide for starting a small business, focusing on twelve ways to obtain financing, business plans, selling and advertising products and services, hiring and firing employees, setting up a Web site, business law, accounting issues, insurance, equipment, computers, banks, financing, customer credit and collection, leasing, and more.

42416 ■ "Small firms cut hires, inventory, capital plans" in *Wall Street Journal* **(November 15, 2000, pp. B17)**
Pub: Dow Jones & Co., Inc.
Description: A survey by the National Federation of Independent Business is examined.

42417 ■ *Smart Hiring for Your Business: Everything You Need to Know to Find & Hire the Best Employees*
Pub: Sourcebooks, Inc.
Ed: Robert W. Wendover. **Released:** 1993. **Price:** $17.95; $8.95 (paper).

42418 ■ "The Smart Way to Hire Superstars" in *Fortune* **(Vol. 142, No. 2, July 10, 2000, pp. 200V+)**
Pub: Time Inc.
Description: Brad Smart, author of the book "Topgrading" explains how to recruit "A" players to work for your company.

42419 ■ "Snatching Victory from Defeat" in *Hispanic Business* **(September 2006, pp. 58, 60, 62)**
Pub: Hispanic Business
Ed: Holly Ocasio-Rizzo. **Description:** Impacts felt by setbacks in affirmative action for Hispanics are discussed.

42420 ■ "Soaring Salaries: It's Payback Time" in *Business Week* **(No. 3702, October 9, 2000, pp. F24)**
Pub: McGraw-Hill, Inc.
Description: Executive salaries are reaching record levels. Entrepreneurs are forced to offer as much as 40%-60% increases for new hires and better expand benefits for those already on the payroll. Statistical data included.

42421 ■ "Someone switching careers could be the perfect match" in *Atlanta Business Chronicle* **(Vol. 24, No. 8, July 27, 2001, pp. 6B)**
Pub: American City Business Journals Inc.
Ed: Emory Mulling. **Description:** Employers might consider hiring someone who is in the process of changing careers. If employers are too focused on finding an exact match, they can actually pass up quality people. Several hiring myths are explored.

42422 ■ "Spy Games" in *Entrepreneur* **(Vol. 33, February 2005, No. 2, pp. 71)**
Pub: Entrepreneur Media Inc.
Ed: Chris Penttila. **Description:** Amendment to the Fair Credit Reporting Act (FCRA), employers are now able to conduct third-party investigations on employees without getting their written permission, or even informing them of the investigation.

42423 ■ "Staffing" in *Inc.* **(November 15, 2000, pp. 110)**
Pub: The Goldhirsh Group
Description: Small recruiters are turning the Internet inside out in search of employees. The article shares insights for employee recruitment on the Internet.

42424 ■ "Staffing Woes: The 404 Talent War" in *Journal of Accountancy* **(Vol. 198, December 2004, No. 6, pp. 62)**
Pub: American Institute of Certified Public
   Accountants

Ed: Barbara Vigilante. **Description:** Section 404 of the Sarbanes-Oxley Act is discussed. Rule 404 requires companies to hire more certified public accountants to implement and manage these new internal controls.

42425 ■ "Standing pat. Most employers not changing size of work force" in *Crain's Detroit Business* **(Vol. 19, No. 9, March 3, 2003, pp. 1)**
Pub: Crain Communications Inc., Detroit
Description: Results of a survey conducted by Manpower Inc. regarding employers' expectations for April-June 2002 employment are presented.

42426 ■ "State OKs Minimum Wage Boost" in *Altanta Journal-Constitution* **(February 2, 2007)**
Pub: Cox Newspapers, Inc.
Ed: Marilyn Geewax. **Description:** Senate voted in favor of raising the minimum wage from $5.15 to $7.25 an hour over two years, but the deal is not completed. Complex negotiations will take place between the House and Senate.

42427 ■ "Student Loan Firm Will Add 170 Jobs" in *Tampa Tribune* **(November 29, 2005)**
Pub: Media General, Inc.
Ed: Dave Simanoff. **Description:** Academic Financial Services in Tampa Bay, Florida is hiring 170 more workers for its new office space. The firm will receive $510,000 in tax rebates, $3,000 for each new job created and maintained.

42428 ■ "Student Teachers" in *Inc.* **(November 2006, pp. 44,46)**
Pub: Gruner & Jahr USA Publishing
Ed: Max Chafkin. **Description:** Hiring college undergraduates give fresh eyes approach at low investment. Many universities have programs that work with smaller local businesses as part of their hands on education programs. Large savings can accumulate without the cost of expensive consultant fees.

42429 ■ "Sun Sets on H-1B Visa Provision" in *Hispanic Business* **(December 2003, pp. 12)**
Pub: Hispanic Business
Description: The economic downturn, especially in the high-tech sector, has caused the number of H-1B visas in America to fall.

42430 ■ "Talented work force credited for right ideas" in *Crain's Detroit Business* **(Vol. 19, No. 13, March 31, 2003, pp. 14)**
Pub: Crain Communications Inc., Detroit
Description: Profile of Menlo Institute LLC, the software development services company. Rick Sheridan, co-founder and instructor believes the success of the firm lies in having the right product at the right time developed by the right people.

42431 ■ "Tapping the Potential of Employee Ranks; Human Resources" in *Crain's New York Business* **(Vol. 22, November 13, 2006, No. 46, pp. 32)**
Pub: Crain Communications, Inc.
Description: Listing of organizations that provide counseling and research on human resources issues, as well as providing employee recruitment and training, oftentimes with tax break incentives.

42432 ■ "Tech futures: Need a map for where business goes from here?" in *Entrepreneur* **(Vol. 30, No. 1, January 2002, pp. 27)**
Pub: Entrepreneur Media Inc.
Ed: Mark Henricks. **Description:** Book reviews of the title, "The Internet Galaxy", which suggests that the Internet's influence on commerce has just begun; and "The War for Talent", which offers five imperatives that can help hire the best people for a business.

42433 ■ "The Tech Track" in *Hispanic Business* **(January/February 2005, pp. 56, 58)**
Pub: Hispanic Business
Ed: Anthony Limon. **Description:** The Information Technology Association of America reports a 2 per-

cent increase in employment for first quarter periods of 2003 and 2004. The technology sector is slowly re-absorbing displaced workers, however banking, finance, manufacturing, food service and transportation accounted for 89 percent of new IT jobs. Statistical data included.

42434 ■ "Temp Hiring Signals Economic Recovery" in *Inc.* **(January 1, 2004)**
Pub: Gruner & Jahr USA Publishing
Ed: Nadine Heintz. **Description:** Demand for temporary employees, especially in the manufacturing industry, has been a sign of economic recovery in the past. With an increase in demand for temps, agencies may see a double-digit revenue growth for 2004.

42435 ■ "That'll never work!" in *Entrepreneur* **(Vol. 30, No. 2, February 2002, pp. 62)**
Pub: Entrepreneur Media Inc.
Ed: Chris Sandlund. **Description:** Interview with author Robert Sutton on counterintuitive management techniques. In his book "Weird Ideas That Work: 11 1/2 Practices for Promoting, Managing and Sustaining Innovation", Sutton explores such counterintuitive techniques as getting happy people to fight and hiring people you don't need.

42436 ■ "Think Tech; Automation Alley" in *Crain's Detroit Business* **(Vol. 21, October 3, 2005, No. 43, pp. 1)**
Pub: Crain Communications Inc. - Detroit
Ed: Andrew Dietderich, Sheena Harrison. **Description:** Two technology companies are working to keep and attract technology companies and jobs to Southeastern Michigan. The state lost 17,600 tech jobs between 2002 and 2003. Automation Alley of Troy and Sparks of Ann Arbor hope to double the number of tech companies and triple the number of tech workers by 2010.

42437 ■ "Third Base: Hiring Employees Can Free Owner to Help Business Grow" in *Crain's Detroit Business* **(Vol. 19, No. 49, December 8, 2003)**
Pub: Crain Communications Inc., Detroit
Ed: Laura Bailey. **Description:** One of the most crucial decisions a small business owner can make, is to hire the correct employee at the correct time.

42438 ■ "This is a Test: Just How Effective are Puzzle Interviews When It Comes to Singling Out the Best Candidates for the Job?" in *Entrepreneur*
Pub: Entrepreneur Media Inc.
Ed: Chris Penttila. **Description:** Puzzle interviews put job applicants through a test of questions during an intense, multi-round interview process. Many large companies, like Microsoft have instituted this process. Critics believe puzzle questions only tell employer that a candidate is good at solving puzzles, not if they fit the position.

42439 ■ "Ties That Bind" in *Entrepreneur* **(Vol. 31, No. 10, October 2003)**
Pub: Entrepreneur Media, Inc.
Ed: Jane Easter Bahls. **Description:** Many companies require employees to sign an agreement waiving their right to sue over employment disputes, rather using a panel of arbitrators.

42440 ■ "Time To Hire" in *Home Office Computing* **(Vol. 18, No. 9, September 2000, pp. 52)**
Pub: Scholastic Inc.
Ed: Todd W. Carter. **Description:** Many home-based businesses face the issue of when and whether to hire help. Questions regarding recruiting and hiring qualified workers for the home business are answered.

42441 ■ "Top Area Staffing Agencies" in *Ingram's* **(Vol. 29, No. 1, January 2003, pp. 32)**
Pub: Show Me Publishing, Inc.
Description: The top staffing agencies in Kansas City, Missouri, according to number of consultants, are listed. Heading the list is Spencer Reed Group Inc., Tri-Com Technical Services, and Trac-Excel Staffing.

42442 ■ "Top-Heavy: The Pitfalls of Overhiring" in *My Business* **(October/November 2003, pp. 56)**
Pub: My Business Magazine
Ed: Peter Provenzano. **Description:** Hiring too large a staff, especially at management level, can be detrimental to a company's ability to grow.

42443 ■ "Tough choices" in *Entrepreneur* **(Vol. 31, No. 5, May 2003, pp. 70)**
Pub: Entrepreneur Media Inc.
Ed: Chris Penttila. **Description:** A big dilemma facing entrepreneurs these days is hiring fresh new talent. Ways to handle having to hire new employees at higher wages than existing employees are discussed.

42444 ■ "Tough Sell" in *Black Enterprise* **(Vol. 37, October 2006, No. 3, pp. 92)**
Pub: Earl G. Graves Publishing Co. Inc.
Ed: Sonia Alleyne. **Description:** Career coaches can evaluate your talents and skills. In an era where more companies are downsizing a coach can help you decide if you are suited for your industry or should try switching careers.

42445 ■ "Tracing It" in *Pittsburgh Business Times* **(Vol. 22, No. 51, July 4, 2003, pp. 17)**
Pub: Pittsburgh Business Times
Ed: Maria Guzzo. **Description:** Profile of TraceEvidence Inc., led by Joe Schwera, and located in Sewickley, Pennsylvania. The firm provides assistance to companies that are seeking in-depth information on employees, and often gets involved when civil or criminal investigations are underway.

42446 ■ "Trucking Industry Faces Driver Shortage" in *Inc.* **(November 1, 2004)**
Pub: Inc. Magazine
Ed: Matt Quinn. **Description:** The trucking industry is facing driver shortages that may threaten holiday sales.

42447 ■ "U.S. CFOs Bullish on Hiring" in *Long Island Business News* **(February 27, 2004)**
Pub: Dolan Media Newswires
Ed: Ben Abelson. **Description:** Second quarter 2004 saw chief financial officers of companies across the U.S. more optimistic about hiring new employees, but 90 percent were still reluctant to begin the process at present time.

42448 ■ "Up Front: Seeking Help" in *My Business* **(February/March 2004, pp. 10-11)**
Pub: My Business Magazine
Ed: Gary M. Stern. **Description:** Creative recruiting is sometimes required in order to find the right employees. Hiring senior citizens, internships, looking at local church bulletins are a few of the recruiting tips listed.

42449 ■ "Upping the Minimum Wage: Small Business Bust or Low-Income Boost?" in *Black Enterprise* **(Vol. 35, October 2004, No. 3, pp. 60)**
Pub: Earl G. Graves Publishing Co. Inc.
Ed: Cliff Hocker. **Description:** Legislation sponsored by Senator Edward M. Kennedy could raise the federal minimum wage from $5.15 per hour to $5.85 within 60 days of the bill's passage. Hikes in the minimum wage could hurt small businesses.

42450 ■ "The Use of Criminal Record in Employment Decisions" in *Journal of Business Ethics* **(Vol. 47, No. 3, Oct. 15, 2003, pp. 237)**
Pub: Kluwer Academic Publishers Group
Ed: Helen Lam, Mark Harcourt. **Description:** Evidence suggests that employers discriminate against ex-offenders in the labor market.

42451 ■ "Vets, Your Best Bet?" in *Entrepreneur* **(Vol. 31, No. 11, November 2003, pp. 92)**
Pub: Entrepreneur Media, Inc.
Ed: Joanne Cleaver. **Description:** Entrepreneurs are hiring ex-military personnel because they are highly skilled and highly motivated workers.

42452 ■ "Want to Improve Your Hiring and Promotion Odds?" in *Kansas City Star* **(February 6, 2005)**
Pub: Knight-Ridder/Tribune Business News
Ed: Diane Stafford. **Description:** Suggestions to help employees improve chances for being hired or promoted are given.

42453 ■ "Wanted: African American Professional for Hire" in *Black Enterprise* **(Vol. 37, November 2006, No. 4, pp. 93)**
Pub: Earl G. Graves Publishing Co. Inc.
Ed: Joe Watson. **Description:** Excerpt from the book, Without Excuses: Unleash the Power of Diversity to Build Your Business, speaks to the lack of diversity in the corporate arena and why executives, recruiters, and HR professionals claim they are unable to find qualified individuals of different races when hiring.

42454 ■ "Wanted: Brainy in Business" in *Sales & Marketing Management* **(Vol. 158, October 2006, No. 10, pp. 18)**
Pub: VNU Business Media
Ed: Michel Marchetti. **Description:** Eric McMath, SerachLogix Group, offers tips and techniques for hiring a successful sales team for any business.

42455 ■ "Wanted" in *Milwaukee Journal Sentinel* **(December 11, 2005)**
Pub: Journal Sentinel, Inc.
Description: Manufacturers are facing a shortage of skilled workers. Pay and global competition are among the issues facing manufacturers and the National Association of Manufacturers reports the human capital performance gap as a threat to U.S. competitiveness and the nation's most critical business issue.

42456 ■ "Warp Speed" in *Sales & Marketing Management* **(Vol. 157, Jan. 20, 2005)**
Pub: VNU Business Media
Ed: Michele Marchetti. **Description:** According to Patricia Gardner, founder of Maximum Sales, sales and management consulting firm in Sparks, Maryland, the most important thing small companies neglect during a high-growth period, is to write job descriptions for its sales staff and other employees.

42457 ■ "Watch Out For Career Scams" in *Black Enterprise* **(Vol. 34, No. 3, October 2003, pp. 53)**
Pub: Earl Graves Publishing Co.
Ed: Laura Egodigwe. **Description:** Ways to distinguish a career counselor when seeking professional career advice is explained. Career counselors must meet a minimum education requirement of a master's degrees and be licensed by the state in which they practice. Many also seek certification from professional bodies.

42458 ■ "We've Got To Get Our Hands on Some Workers" in *Business Week* **(No. 3666, January 31, 2000, pp. 4)**
Pub: McGraw-Hill, Inc.
Description: The impact of the labor market on small business in the year 2000 is investigated.

42459 ■ "What to Pay" in *My Business* **(November/December 2001, pp. 47)**
Pub: My Business Magazine
Ed: Description: Considerations to address when hiring and compensating employees are discussed, such as linking compensation of executives to performance and salary surveys for what other companies are paying in salaries.

42460 ■ "What Works and What Doesn't - A Job Hunter's Primer to Looking for a Job on the Internet" in *Women in Business* **(Vol.54, No.3 May-Jun.)**
Pub: The ABWA Co Inc.
Ed: Kathleen Isaacson. **Description:** Job hunting and resume placement on the Internet are discussed.

42461 ■ "What You Look Like Online" in *Black Enterprise* **(Vol. 37, January 2007, No. 6, pp. 56)**
Pub: Earl G. Graves Publishing Co. Inc.
Ed: Marcia A. Reed-Woodard. **Description:** Of 100 executive recruiters 77 percent stated that they use

search engines to check the backgrounds of potential job candidates, according to a survey conducted by ExecuNet. Of those surveyed 35 percent stated that they eliminate potential candidates based on information they find online so it is important to create a positive Web presence which highlights professional image qualities.

42462 ■ "When Will 'Content of Character' Count?" in *Black Enterprise* **(Vol. 34, No. 6, January 2004, pp. 12)**
Pub: Earl Graves Publishing Co.
Ed: Earl G. Graves, Sr. **Description:** Despite the good news on the economic front, diversity remains a priority in the upper echelons of major corporations, however the large majority of black Americans still face racism in the pursuit of employment.

42463 ■ "When Wolfe Hires Someone for a Job Working a Cash Register or Cutting Meat, odds are, that Person was a Customer First" in *Inc.* **(May 2000)**
Pub: The Goldhirsh Group
Description: The challenges of hiring, retaining, and training employees in the inner city are explored.

42464 ■ "When You're no Longer Home Alone" in *Inc.* **(December 1999, pp. 92)**
Pub: The Goldhirsh Group
Description: An overview of the legal issues regarding hiring employees for home-based business.

42465 ■ "Where the Jobs Are" in *Business Week* **(January 16, 2006, No. 3967, pp. 42-43)**
Pub: McGraw-Hill Companies
Ed: Nandini Lakshman. **Description:** The number of foreign workers at Indian information technology and outsourcing companies has tripled to 30,000 in two years. Foreign workers earn about $350 per month.

42466 ■ "Where Jobs Are Plenty, Challenge is Finding Right People" in *Crain's Detroit Business* **(Vol. 22, November 27, 2006, No. 48, pp. 17)**
Pub: Crain Communications Inc. - Detroit
Ed: Anjali Fluker. **Description:** The environmental industry in Southeast Michigan has many job openings, but has difficulty finding educated and experienced workers. Part of the reason is most of the people working in that industry are content, and are not looking around.

42467 ■ "Why You're Hiring All Wrong" in *Inc.* **(February 1, 2002)**
Pub: Inc. Magazine
Ed: Kate O'Sullivan. **Description:** Advice is offered for creating a long-range career plan for every employee hired, including the use of a consulting firm to review these plans annually.

42468 ■ "Wisconsin Job Market Continues to Grow Despite Shrinking Labor Force" in *Milwaukee Journal Sentinel* **(December 16, 2005)**
Pub: Journal Sentinel, Inc.
Ed: Joel Dresang. **Description:** Continued job growth, despite a shrinking labor force, is reported by a Wisconsin labor analyst. Statistical data from Wisconsin's Department of Workforce Labor is included.

42469 ■ "The Work-at-Home Hook" in *Home Office Computing* **(Vol. 18, No. 11, November 2000, pp. 92)**
Pub: Scholastic Inc.
Ed: Lisa Roberts. **Description:** Ways in which companies are using telework to recruit and retain employees is discussed.

42470 ■ "Workforce Diversity in Small Business" in *Journal of Small Business Management* **(Vol. 38, No. 3, July 2000, pp. 27)**
Pub: West Virginia University
Ed: Don Gudmundson, Linda S. Hartenian. **Description:** While it would seem that hiring a diverse workforce would be advantageous to any firm that wants to compete globally, such diversity in fact entails costs

as well as benefits for the small firm. This study explores the relationship between workforce diversity in small businesses and the small business owner/manager's motivation to diversify, the owner/manager's personal characteristics (ethnicity, age, education, and gender), and the number of family members employed in the small business.

42471 ■ "Working It: A Surge in Part-Time Workers Can Pay Off for Your Business" in *Entrepreneur* **(Vol. 32, December 2004, No. 12, pp. 22)**
Pub: Entrepreneur Media Inc.
Ed: Mark Henricks. **Description:** The number of persons working part-time in the U.S. grew from 24.3 million to 25.5 million in the first half of 2004. Employers rarely offer employer-paid health insurance and other benefits, thus making part-time hiring attractive to small companies.

42472 ■ "The workplace: learn to do more with less" in *Atlanta Business Chronicle* **(Vol. 25, No. 20, October 25, 2002, pp. 12B)**
Pub: American City Business Publications, Inc.
Ed: Emory Mulling. **Description:** Suggestions are given to improve workplace performance in these trying economic times. Training and matching the right person with the right skills for each job is important. Additionally, it is important to recognize that employees want to be developed and to increase their work skills base.

42473 ■ "Y Stay Put? Generation Y Bounces From Job to Job" in *The Record* **(November 13, 2005)**
Pub: New Jersey Media Group
Ed: Catherine Holahan. **Description:** Americans born between 1977 and 1994 are known as Generation Y; these individuals do not consider long-term commitments in any one position. Generation Y saw too many of their baby boomer parents, who depended on job security, lose their jobs. Statistical data included.

42474 ■ "Young Guns" in *Success* **(Vol. 47, No. 1, January 2000, pp. 24)**
Pub: Success Publishing, Inc.
Ed: Sarah Duran. **Description:** Don't sweat the little stuff this summer. Get cash-hungry students to work for your business.

42475 ■ "Young is old" in *Entrepreneur* **(Vol. 30, No. 9, September 2002, pp. 28)**
Pub: Entrepreneur Media Inc.
Ed: Nichole L. Torres. **Description:** Profile of Riegsecker Marketplace Inc., a combination retailer, restaurant and furniture manufacturing company located in Sheshewana, Indiana. Riegsecker hires individuals over the age of 50 for their experience, skills and solid work ethic.

42476 ■ "Your Business" in *Entrepreneur* **(Vol. 27, No. 12, December 1999, pp. 119)**
Pub: Entrepreneur Media Inc.
Ed: Jacquelyn Lynn. **Description:** The best workers for your business aren't necessarily in your neighborhood. They may not even be on your continent.

42477 ■ "Your career can still thrive in an age of flux" in *Black Enterprise* **(Vol. 33, No. 3, October 2002, pp. 163)**
Pub: Earl Graves Publishing Co.
Description: Despite reports of layoffs, corporate bankruptcies, and stagnant raises along with a volatile stock market, this can also be an exciting time in the labor market. Companies are competing for the best talent available, with the proper skills, opportunities abound.

42478 ■ "Your space is the place" in *Fast Company* **(May 2001, pp. 60)**
Pub: Fast Company
Ed: Alison Wellner. **Description:** According to Stephen Roulac, founder and CEO of the Roulac Group Inc., a consulting firm based in San Rafael, California that specializes in real estate, states that people are now selecting where they want to live, then seeking employment, whereas in the past it was the opposite.

42479 ■ "You're Fired!" in *Forbes* **(Vol. 174, December 13, 2004, No. 12, pp. 89)**
Pub: Forbes Magazine Inc.
Ed: Christopher Steiner. **Description:** Profile of Achilles Group, a firm that assists businesses with personnel matters such as firings, discrimination suits, personality conflicts, threatened lawsuits, EEOC claims, and hiring.

42480 ■ *You're Hired: Employers Give Tips For Successful Interviewing*
Pub: JIST Works, Inc.
Released: 1997. **Price:** $239.00 (VHS). **Description:** Real people in charge of hiring others give their thoughts on a dozen different questions about the interview process.

TRADE PERIODICALS

42481 ■ *Affirmative Action Register*
Pub: Affirmative Action Register
Ed: Joyce R. Green, Editor. **Released:** Monthly. **Price:** Free to qualified subscribers; $15 by mail. **Description:** Journal for business, academia, non-profit organizations and the government to use in recruiting females, Native Americans, minorities, veterans, and persons with disabilities.

42482 ■ *Hiring & Firing*
Pub: Thomson Carswell
Ed: Cindy Moser, Editor, mnredit@nexicom.net. **Released:** Monthly. **Description:** Monitors hiring and firing issues as they relate to the law. Covers such topics as sexual harassment, discrimination, and labor relations. Recurring features include columns titled Current Cases, Legal Corner, Human Rights, News in Brief, and Professional Practices.

VIDEOCASSETTES/ AUDIOCASSETTES

42483 ■ *Brief Encounters*
Excellence in Training Corp.
1303 Marsh Ln.
Carrollton, TX 75006
Free: 800-747-6569
Released: 1991. **Price:** $695.00. **Description:** A presentation on 10 techniques to help interviewers select the best-qualified job applicant. **Availability:** VHS; 3/4U; Special order formats.

42484 ■ *Chinese for Affirmative Action*
Chinese for Affirmative Action
The Kuo Bldg.
17 Walter U. Lum Pl.
San Francisco, CA 94108
Ph:(415)274-6750
Fax:(415)397-8770
Co. E-mail: caa@caasf.org
URL: http://www.caasf.org
Released: 1974. **Description:** "Chinese for Affirmative Action" is a promotional program about the civil rights organization based in San Francisco's Chinatown. **Availability:** 3/4U.

42485 ■ *Communication Series: Interviewing*
Michigan State University
Instructional Media Center
PO Box 710
East Lansing, MI 48826-0710
Ph:(517)353-3960
Fax: (517)432-2650
Co. E-mail: imcclass@msu.edu
URL: http://www.msu.edu/unit/imc
Released: 1981. **Description:** Mike Wallace, George Gallup and John Shingleton are interviewed about the techniques they use for interviewing. **Availability:** VHS; 3/4U.

42486 ■ *The Effective Manager*
Nightingale-Conant Corp.
6245 W. Howard St.
Niles, IL 60714

Ph:(847)647-0300
Free: 800-560-6081
URL: http://www.nightingale.com
Price: $95.00. **Description:** A series of award-winning programs designed to promote effective management and help increase sales. Audio tapes and booklets are included, and the series can be purchased individually or as a set. **Availability:** VHS.

42487 ■ *Equal Opportunity*
Mercedes Maharis Productions
3066 El Camino Ave.
Las Vegas, NV 89102
Ph:(702)221-9337
Fax: (702)221-9079
Co. E-mail: cruiser@skylink.net
URL: http://www.seaspirit.com
Released: 1983. **Description:** This program explores the meaning of equal opportunity within the context of affirmative action, racial discrimination, past discrimination, union contracts, seniority, fairness and the Bill of Rights. **Availability:** VHS; 3/4U.

42488 ■ *Equal Treatment/Equal Opportunity*
Gulf Publishing Co.
PO Box 2608
Houston, TX 77252-2608
Ph:(713)520-4448
Free: 800-231-6275
Fax: (713)204-4433
Co. E-mail: csv@gulfpub.com
URL: http://www.gulfpub.com
Released: 1984. **Price:** $375.00. **Description:** This program is designed to help the workforce to understand what comprises discrimination. **Availability:** VHS; 3/4U.

42489 ■ *Man Hunt*
Video Arts, Inc.
c/o Aim Learning Group
8238-40 Lehigh
Morton Grove, IL 60053-2615
Free: 877-444-2230
Fax: (416)252-2155
Co. E-mail: service@aimlearninggroup.com
URL: http://www.aimlearninggroup.com
Released: 1974. **Price:** $790.00. **Description:** Often, managers feels that they know the person they want for a job just by seeing them. The purpose of this program is to make managers realize this is not so. It shows where and how the principal faults occur: failure to prepare for the interview, failure to draw the candidate out and get him to talk freely, and failure to come out with direct, probing questions. **Availability:** VHS; 8mm; 3/4U; Special order formats.

42490 ■ *Managing Frontline Service*
Video Arts, Inc.
c/o Aim Learning Group

8238-40 Lehigh
Morton Grove, IL 60053-2615
Free: 877-444-2230
Fax: (416)252-2155
Co. E-mail: service@aimlearninggroup.com
URL: http://www.aimlearninggroup.com
Released: 1989. **Price:** $730.00. **Description:** Through case studies in two highly successful corporations, this video shows how to improve performance by selecting, training, and motivating the right people. **Availability:** VHS; 8mm; 3/4U; Special order formats.

42491 ■ *More Than a Gut Feeling 2*
Excellence in Training Corp.
1303 Marsh Ln.
Carrollton, TX 75006
Free: 800-747-6569
Released: 1991. **Price:** $695.00. **Description:** This follow-up to "More Than a Gut Feeling" shows how to gauge a job candidate's future performance by getting her or him talk about past job experience. A leader's guide, desk reminder card, and charts of legal and illegal questions are included. **Availability:** VHS; 3/4U; Special order formats.

CONSULTANTS

42492 ■ Barada Associates Inc.
130 E 2nd St.
Rushville, IN 46173
Ph:(765)932-5917
Fax: (765)932-2938
Co. E-mail: assignments@baradainc.com
URL: http://www.baradainc.com

E-mail: assignments@baradainc.com
Scope: Professional employment screening services & provides client companies with independent and objective reference reports on candidates for salaried and hourly employment. **Publications:** "Don't Overlook Reference Checks," The School Administrator (May 1992); "Check References With Care," Nation's Business (May 1993); "Honest References," Human Resource Executive (September 1993); "Reference Checking More Critical Than Ever," Association of Executive Search Consultants, Inc. (December 1993/January 1994); "Reference Checking.Increased Necessity to Exercise 'Reasonable Care'," Kincannon & Reed (1994); "Check It Out-Hiring? What You Don't Know Could Hurt You," The American School Board Journal (1994). "Reference Checking Is More Than Ever," Human Resource Magazine (1996); "The Paper Chase," Indianapolis Monthly (1995).

42493 ■ Gately Consulting
115 Dutcher St.
Hopedale, MA 01747-1006

Ph:(508)634-7748
Fax: (508)634-0670
Co. E-mail: gately@compuserve.com

E-mail: gately@compuserve.com
Scope: Provides the PofileXT assessment, an innovative assessment technology, for personnel and pre-employment evaluations, and ensuring success in matching people to jobs and 360's. **Publications:** "The Employer's Advantage Newsletter". **Seminars:** The new art of hiring smart a three-hour introduction to recruiting, interviewing, and hiring top performers.

42494 ■ Edward M. Hepner & Associates
1200 Quail St., Ste. 275
Newport Beach, CA 92660-2720
Ph:(949)250-0818
Fax: (949)553-8437
Scope: A immigration consultant and labor certification specialist. Assists in obtaining Visa's for work, immigration and business development within the United States and Canada.

COMPUTERIZED DATABASES

42495 ■ *ABI/INFORM*
ProQuest
300 N Zeeb Rd.
PO Box 1346
Ann Arbor, MI 48106
Ph:(734)761-4700
Free: 800-521-0600
Fax: (734)761-6450
Co. E-mail: info@il.proquest.com
URL: http://www.proquest.com
Description: Provides full text access or bibliographic citations to articles in publications in business and management information worldwide. Includes 2.7 million indexes and abstracts. Comprised of three editions on CD-ROM:; ABI/INFORM Global covers more than 1600 sources, including more than 350 titles from outside the United States.; ABI/INFORM Research covers more than 700 sources.; ABI/INFORM Select covers about 350 sources with coverage beginning in 1991. **Availability:** Online: Ovid Technologies Inc., ProQuest, Thomson Dialog, Questel; Orbit, Gesellschaft fur Betriebswirtschaftliche Information mbH, STN International, Colorado Alliance of Research Libraries, Financial Times, Online Computer Library Center Inc. (OCLC), LexisNexis, EINS - European Information Network Services, Thomson Dialog; Batch: Nerac Inc. **Type:** Full text; Bibliographic; Image.

START-UP INFORMATION

42496 ■ *101 Businesses You Can Satrt at with Less Thank One Thousand Dollars: For Retirees*
Pub: Atlantic Publishing Company
Ed: Christina Bultinck. **Released:** December 2006. **Price:** $21.95. **Description:** Business ideas to help retirees start a home-based business on a low budget.

42497 ■ *101 Businesses You Can Start at with Less Than One Thousand Dollars: For Stay-At-Home Moms and Dads*
Pub: Atlantic Publishing Company
Ed: Christina Bultinck. **Released:** December 2006. **Price:** $21.95. **Description:** Business ideas to help stay-at-home moms and dads start a home-based business on a low budget.

42498 ■ *101 Internet Businesses You Can Start from Home: How to Choose and Build Your Own Successful E-Business*
Pub: Maximum Press
Ed: Susan Sweeney. **Released:** June 2006. **Price:** $29.95. **Description:** Guide for starting and growing an Internet business; information for developing a business plan, risk levels, and promotional techniques are included.

42499 ■ "250 Unleash the Entrepreneur Within You!" in *Home Business* (Vol. 12, March/April 2005, No. 2, pp. 16, 20-23, 26-29, 100-101, 104-105)
Pub: Home Business Magazine
Ed: Sandy Larson. **Description:** Directory of 250 companies offering home-based businesses, franchises, and opportunities.

42500 ■ "The ABCs of setting up a home office" in *Women in Business* (Vol. 54, No. 5, September-October 2002, pp. 23)
Pub: The ABWA Company, Inc.
Ed: Kathleen Isaacson. **Description:** Necessary equipment, possible financing and requisite legislation for home offices are discussed.

42501 ■ "At Your Service" in *Small Business Opportunities* (Vol. 12, No. 3, May 2000, pp. 70, 72, 74, 76, 78, 80-82, 84)
Pub: Harris Publications, Inc.
Description: Service businesses sell the commodities of time and convenience. The article presents the 15 best businesses to start and run from the home, including landscape/gardening, computer/internet tutor, e-commerce specialist, elder care, window washing, reunion planner, bookkeeper, children's party planner, personalized products, errand service, food delivery service, children's taxi service, personal chef, and repair/restoration services.

42502 ■ "Book Publishing for Entrepreneurs" in *Home Business* (Vol. 12, October 2005, No. 5, pp. 68)
Pub: Home Business Magazine
Ed: Stephanie Chandler. **Description:** Most publishing houses will not consider publishing a book unless it is written by a celebrity or there is already an eager audience. Things to consider before publishing your own successful book are outlined.

42503 ■ "Build Your Dream Home Business" in *Home Business* (Vol. 12, October 2005, No. 5, pp. 16, 18-22, 102, 104)
Pub: Home Business Magazine
Ed: Sandy Larson. **Description:** Ten steps to starting a home-based business, starting from the initial planning phase to financing a venture as well as marketing strategies.

42504 ■ "Cash In At Home" in *Small Business Opportunities* (Vol. 16, No. 2, March 2004, pp. 22)
Pub: Harris Publications, Inc.
Description: Seventy-five businesses that can be started and run from a home-based business are profiled, along with the top ten things anyone considering a home-based business should do before starting. Important questions are answered before pursuing a particular opportunity, as well as a listing of free resources and loan programs available from the U.S. Small Business Administration. Strategies for organizing paperwork for entrepreneurs are also presented.

42505 ■ *The Complete Guide to Making Money at Home: Everything You Need to Know to Earn Riches at Home*
Pub: Ridgewood Press
Ed: Gary J. Fuller. **Released:** January 2006. **Price:** $19.95. **Description:** Guide for starting and running an at-home business.

42506 ■ "Conference Helps Moms Jumpstart Home-Based Business Careers" in *Orange County Register* (January 28, 2005)
Pub: Freedom Communications Inc.
Ed: Nancy Luna. **Description:** The top ten home-based businesses are listed: Internet sales and marketing, Web and graphic design, online research, technical support, virtual assistant, business coach, event planner, children's product development, home services, and direct sales.

42507 ■ *The Craft Business Answer Book: Starting, Managing, and Marketing a Home-Based Art, Crafts, Design Business*
Pub: M. Evans and Company, Incorporated
Ed: Barbara Brabec. **Released:** August 2006. **Price:** $16.95. **Description:** Expert advice for starting a home-based art or crafts business is offered.

42508 ■ "Designs on Success" in *Small Business Opportunities* (Vol. 13, No. 6, November 2001, pp. 48, 50, 122)
Pub: Harris Publications, Inc.
Description: Profile of Tamotsu, who launched his own design firm with a sewing machine in his New York City apartment, and grew his company into a $20-million-a-year successful small business. Tamotsu offers his insights into running a successful small company.

42509 ■ "Doing Your Homework" in *Home Business* (Vol. 12, October 2005, No. 5, pp. 62)
Pub: Home Business Magazine
Ed: Kurt English, Esq. **Description:** Questions to ask before starting a home-based business are discussed. The importance of researching key issues is stressed.

42510 ■ "Drawing Attention" in *Small Business Opportunities* (Vol. 16, No. 3, May 2004, pp. 92, 130)
Pub: Harris Publications, Inc.
Description: Profile of Young Rembrandts, a franchised home-based business that teaches a drawing program to preschool and elementary children. The program offers parents an alternative before and after school educational program for children interested in art.

42511 ■ "Dressed for Success" in *Small Business Opportunities* (Vol. 12, No. 3, May 2000, pp. 86, 130)
Pub: Harris Publications, Inc.
Ed: Annette Wood. **Description:** Owners share insight into their $20 million a year home-based men's pants business.

42512 ■ *Earn Cash Crafting at Home: An MBA At-Home Mom Explains Step-by-Step Her Fun, Proven, Money-Making, Own-Your-Own Business Formula*
Pub: Dark Horse, Incorporated
Ed: Maria Colman. **Released:** March 2006. **Price:** $10.00. **Description:** Manual offering advice to start and run an at-home craft business.

42513 ■ "Entrepreneur Column" in *Entrepreneur.com* (October 12, 2006)
Pub: Entrepreneur Media Inc.
Ed: Lisa Druxman. **Description:** Choice of a home-based business is critical to its success. Besides the many start up items such as permits, licenses, etc., make sure you have a passion for what you plan to do. Not all businesses can build upon past training and experience but there are those that lend themselves well to home based businesses like accounting, writing, editing, and others.

42514 ■ "Finding Investors" in *Home Business* (Vol. 12, March/April 2005, No. 2, pp. 74)
Pub: Home Business Magazine
Ed: Nora Caley. **Description:** Home business startups need partners, rather than investors, to help with startup costs. And these partners expect to play a role in the business.

42515 ■ *Going Solo: Developing a Home-Based Consulting Business from the Ground Up*
Pub: McGraw-Hill Companies Incorporated
Ed: William J. Bond. **Released:** January 1997. **Price:** $14.95. **Description:** Ways to turn specialized knowledge into a home-based successful consulting firm, focusing on targeting client needs, business plans, and growth.

42516 ■ "Grassroots Marketing" in *Home Business* **(Vol. 12, March/April 2005, No. 2, pp. 58)**
Pub: Home Business Magazine
Ed: Rich Sloan. Description: Finding unconventional ways to attract customers to a startup home-based business, called grassroots marketing, can cost much less than traditional advertising.

42517 ■ "Hanging tough: Wilhelmina Bell-Taylor overcame cancer to launch a successful business" in *Black Enterprise* **(Oct. 2002, pp. 55)**
Pub: Earl Graves Publishing Co.
Ed: Phaedra Brotherton. Description: Profile of Wilhelmina Bell-Taylor, who was diagnosed with Hodgkin's disease when she was only 19 years old. At age 54, Bell-Taylor is the founder and president of BETAH Associates Inc., a management counseling, communications, information, and administrative services firm located in Bethesda, Maryland. The company started as a home-based operation, incorporated in 1994.

42518 ■ "Health Crisis Inspires Medesto, Calif. Woman to Open Needlework Store" in *Modesto Bee* **(January 22, 2003)**
Pub: Knight-Ridder/Tribune Business News
Ed: Tim Moran. Description: Lois Mouriski Bear tells how she went from legal secretary to owner of the Elegant Stitch in Modesto, California. Mouriski Bear was diagnosed with breast cancer in 1997 and started her Internet business at home selling high-end needlework patterns and supplies.

42519 ■ "Home Alone: Make an Effort to Fight Loneliness" in *My Business* **(October/November 2002, pp. 45)**
Pub: My Business Magazine
Ed: Doug McPherson. Description: Loneliness is a big factor to consider with deciding to start a home-based business; one such owner started a consultants group that meets monthly for breakfast, another takes time out for yoga classes and tennis.

42520 ■ "Home-Based Entrepreneurs Still Rely Most on the 4 F's" in *Home Business* **(Vol. 12, March/April 2005, No. 2, pp. 78)**
Pub: Home Business Magazine
Description: According to the Global Entrepreneurship Monitor, a recent study shows that founders, family, friends, and foolhardy strangers continue to fund small startup companies.

42521 ■ "Home-Based Microbiz" in *Small Business Opportunities* **(Vol. 16, No. 2, March 2004, pp. 12, 168)**
Pub: Harris Publications, Inc.
Description: Ways to turn a hobby or talent into a home microbusiness are discussed. A microbusiness is a small business with low startup costs, usually home-based, can be run by one person, offers flexible hours, and tends to be personally fulfilling as well as profitable.

42522 ■ *Home-Based Travel Agent, 5th Edition*
Pub: The Intrepid Traveler
Ed: Kelly Monaghan. Released: March 2006. Price: $59.95. Description: Advice for starting and running a home-based travel agency is given.

42523 ■ "Home: Where the Money Is!" in *Small Business Opportunities* **(Vol. 12, No. 2, March 2000, pp. 22)**
Pub: Harris Publications, Inc.
Description: A listing of 75 home-based businesses that can be started for less than $500.

42524 ■ "Home Work" in *Black Enterprise* **(Vol. 37, October 2006, No. 3, pp. 78)**
Pub: Earl G. Graves Publishing Co. Inc.
Ed: James C. Johnson. Description: Information on starting a resume-writing service is profiled.

42525 ■ "Homebased Moneymakers" in *Small Business Opportunities* **(Vol. 12, No. 5, September 2000, pp. 74, 76)**
Pub: Harris Publications, Inc.
Description: Ten quick and easy businesses that can be started from home for less than $100, including an inventory service, apartment preparation service, summer snack shop, plant watering service, messenger/fast errand service, bartender for private parties, framing service, online auction business, gardening consultant, and making scrapbooks for clients.

42526 ■ "Honey Rhymes with Money" in *Small Business Opportunities* **(Vol. 12, No. 2, March 2000, pp. 104)**
Pub: Harris Publications. Description: A profile of Robin Bunting, owner of a honey-making company in Tangerine, Florida. Ms. Bunting tends her hives in her backyard on weekends and earns $30,000 or more annually.

42527 ■ *How to Make Money While You Look for a Job*
Pub: Booklocker.com, Incorporated
Ed: Donna Boyette. Released: March 2005. Price: $11.95. Description: Six steps to make money while searching for employment are outlined, from setting up a home-based office to selling a service.

42528 ■ *How to Start a Home-Based Craft Business*
Pub: Globe Pequot Press
Ed: Kenn Oberrecht. Released: January 2004. Price: $17.95. Description: Step-by-step guide for starting and growing a home-based craft business.

42529 ■ *How to Start a Home-Based Craft Business, 5th Edition*
Pub: Globe Pequot Press
Ed: Kenn Oberrecht. Released: July 2007. Price: $18.95. Description: Advice for starting a home-based craft business is given, including sources for finding supplies on the Internet, writing a business plan, publicity, zoning ordinances, and more.

42530 ■ *How to Start a Home-Based Event Planning Business*
Pub: Globe Pequot Press
Ed: Jill Moran. Released: April 2004. Price: $17.95. Description: Guide to starting and growing a business planning events from a home-based firm.

42531 ■ *How to Start a Home-Based Interior Design Business*
Pub: Globe Pequot Press
Ed: Nita Phillips. Released: January 2006.

42532 ■ *How to Start a Home-Based Landscaping Business*
Pub: Globe Pequot Press
Ed: Owen E. Dell. Released: February 2005. Price: $34.95. Description: Guide to starting and running a home-based landscaping business.

42533 ■ *How to Start a Home-Based Mail Order Business*
Pub: Globe Pequot Press
Ed: Georganne Fiumara. Released: January 2005. Price: $17.95. Description: Step-by-step guide for starting and growing a home-based mail order business. Information about equipment, pricing, online marketing, are included along with worksheets and checklists for planning.

42534 ■ *How to Start a Home-Based Online Retail Business*
Pub: Globe Pequot Press
Ed: Jeremy Shepherd. Released: February 2007. Price: $18.95. Description: Information for starting an online retail, home-based business is shared.

42535 ■ *How to Start a Home-Based Personal Chef Business*
Pub: Globe Pequot Press
Ed: Denise Vivaldo. Released: December 2006. Price: $18.95. Description: Everything needed to know to start a personal chef business is featured.

42536 ■ *How to Start a Home-Based Professional Organizing Business*
Pub: Globe Pequot Press
Ed: Dawn Noble. Released: March 2007. Price: $18.95. Description: Tips for starting a home-based professional organizing business are presented.

42537 ■ *Interior Design Business*
Pub: Globe Pequot Press
Ed: Suzanne DeWalt; Nita B. Phillips. Released: January 2006. Price: $18.95. Description: Tips for starting and running a home-based interior design business are given.

42538 ■ "La Habra, Calif., Resident Builds Needlework Empire" in *Orange County Register* **(February 12, 2001)**
Pub: Knight-Ridder/Tribune Business News
Ed: Jan Norman. Description: Profile of Candamar Designs, maker of art needlework, including cross-stitch, needlepoint and embroidery kits, both retail and through mail order catalogs and the Internet. Candi Martin began her business venture as a means to stay home with her three daughters.

42539 ■ *Landscaping Business*
Pub: Globe Pequot Press
Ed: Owen E. Dell. Released: December 2005. Price: $18.95. Description: Guide to starting and running a successful home-based landscaping business, including tips for marketing on the Internet.

42540 ■ "License to Bill?" in *Black Enterprise* **(Vol. 34, No. 4, November 2003, pp. 48)**
Pub: Earl Graves Publishing Co.
Ed: Alan Hughes. Description: Information for starting a home-based business and licensing processes are discussed.

42541 ■ "Mail Order 500" in *Small Business Opportunities* **(Vol. 17, September 2005, No. 5, pp. 22, 24, 26, 28, 30, 32, 36, 38, 40, 42, 120)**
Pub: Harris Publications Inc.
Description: Mail order has reached $2.4 trillion in sales. Steps to plan a mail order startup business are outlined, most starting with $100 in startup expenses.

42542 ■ "Maine Lawyer Launches Personal Chef and Catering Service" in *Portland Press Herald* **(August 9, 2002)**
Pub: Knight Ridder/Tribune Business News
Ed: Mark Shanahan. Description: Profile of Carrie Yardley, former attorney turned caterer. Yardley started Add More Thyme, a personal chef and catering service, from her home in Yarmouth, Maine.

42543 ■ "Market Planning 101" in *Home Business* **(Vol. 12, October 2005, No. 5, pp. 42, 44-45)**
Pub: Home Business Magazine
Ed: Christopher J. Bachler. Description: A quick marketing plan for any small business is presented and includes all the basic information required to attract loans, partners, business services and even Small Business Administration assistance.

42544 ■ "Marketing Strategies for Your New Home-Based Business" in *Home Business* **(Vol. 12, October 2005, No. 5, pp. 24, 26-27, 54-55)**
Pub: Home Business Magazine
Ed: Steven D. Strauss. Description: Cost-effective strategies for marketing a home-based business are explored. The importance of reaching a target audience is stressed.

42545 ■ "Millinery Magic" in *Small Business Opportunities* **(Vol. 13, No. 6, November 2001, pp. 62, 122)**
Pub: Harris Publications, Inc.
Description: Profile of Laura Daly, the home-based entrepreneur who designs and manufactures her own line of one-of-kind hats. In less than one year Ms. Daly is selling her designs at famed Henri Bendel's on Fifth Avenue, New York.

42546 ■ "Prescription for Profit" in *Small Business Opportunities* **(Vol. 13, No. 6, November 2001, pp. 84, 86, 138)**
Pub: Harris Publications, Inc.
Description: Electronic medical claims processing is the cutting edge of home-based businesses that can be grown as a home-based business, and offers a flexible schedule.

42547 ■ *Scrapbooking for Profit: Cashing in on Retail, Home-Based and Internet Opportunities*
Pub: Allworth Press
Ed: Rebecca Pittman. **Released:** June 2005. **Price:** $19.95 (US), $22.95 (Canadian). **Description:** Eleven strategies for starting a scrapbooking business, including brick-and-mortar stores, home-based businesses, and online retail and wholesale outlets.

42548 ■ "Selling Yourself" in *Kiplinger's Personal Finance Magazine* **(Vol. 54, No. 12, December 2000, pp. 94)**
Pub: The Kiplinger Washington Editors, Inc.
Ed: Kimberly Lankford, Justin Wiser. **Description:** The Internet opens up a world of opportunities for freelancers.

42549 ■ "Separation Anxiety" in *Entrepreneur* **(Vol. 28, No. 6, June 2000, pp. 170)**
Pub: Entrepreneur Media Inc.
Ed: Paul Edwards and Sarah Edwards. **Description:** Should a photography studio and home be in different structures? Editors probe that question.

42550 ■ "Setting Up a Productive Home Office" in *Home Business* **(Vol. 12, October 2005, No. 5, pp. 82, 84)**
Pub: Home Business Magazine
Ed: Aliza Pilar, Sherman Risdahl. **Description:** Things to consider when purchasing furniture, hardware, software and electronics for a small home-based business are examined.

42551 ■ "Show Me the Money" in *Home Office Computing* **(Vol. 18, No. 11, November 2000, pp. 85)**
Pub: Scholastic Inc.
Ed: Steven Van Yoder. **Description:** Raising capital for a small business is a challenge that Robert Luster, who started a home-based construction company, knows firsthand. The article tells how to tap the right resources to find the cash needed to start and grow a business.

42552 ■ "Silver (and Gold) in Senior Services" in *Home Business* **(Vol. 13, January/February 2006, No. 1, pp. 32, 34, 66, 68)**
Pub: Home Business Magazine
Ed: Priscilla Y. Huff. **Description:** Fifteen home-based businesses targeting senior citizens include medical claims assistance, senior care consulting, nutrition, in-home care, money managers, seamstress/tailoring, handyman services, financial planning, home business consulting, home delivery, exercise, computer consulting, antique appraisals, lawn and garden services, and transcription and/or video services.

42553 ■ "Start a Business at Home? You've Got to be Kidding" in *Inc.* **(December 1999, pp. 92)**
Pub: The Goldhirsh Group
Description: After running his business from home for two weeks, the owner of a $65 million a year business argues against running a home-based business.

42554 ■ "Start-Up Funding Options" in *Home Business* **(Vol. 12, October 2005, No. 5, pp. 28, 30-31, 78-79)**
Pub: Home Business Magazine
Ed: Jim R. Sapp. **Description:** Alternatives for funding a start-up home-based business include using your savings account, credit cards, 401(k) or Keogh retirement plans, life insurance, second mortgage line of credit, pawn shop, or selling accumulated items no longer needed.

42555 ■ "Stress free home office" in *WorkingWoman* **(Vol. 25, No. 8, September 2000, pp. 72)**
Pub: Lang Communications Inc.
Ed: Lisa Kanarek. **Description:** Advice on how to set up a home office and how to create a working environment within a home is presented.

42556 ■ *Ultimate Homebased Business Handbook: How to Start, Run, and Grow Your Own Profitable Business*
Pub: Entrepreneur Press
Ed: James Stephenson. **Released:** July 2004. **Price:** $23.95 (US), $34.95 (Canadian). **Description:** Detailed information for anyone wanting to start a home-based business. Topics include how-to tips, ideas, tools, and print and online resources.

42557 ■ "Want New Customers? Go Guerrilla: Ad campaigns can be expensive" in *Business Week Online* **(April 29, 2002)**
Pub: McGraw-Hill, Inc.
Ed: Karen E. Klein. **Description:** Advice is offered to a start-up, home-based, independent agent for a long-distance company.

42558 ■ *Web Design Business*
Pub: Globe Pequot Press
Ed: Jim Smith. **Released:** January 2007. **Price:** $18.95. **Description:** Information for starting a home-based Web design firm is given.

42559 ■ "Web.Preneuring" in *Small Business Opportunities* **(Vol. 12, No. 3, May 2000, pp. 88, 90)**
Pub: Harris Publications, Inc.
Ed: Marie Sherlock. **Description:** A website designer shares tips on how to start a lucrative business from home.

42560 ■ "What's Your Problem?" in *Entrepreneur.com* **(Vol. 34, February 2006, No. 2, pp. 102)**
Pub: Entrepreneur Media Inc.
Ed: Sarah Edwards, Paul Edwards. **Description:** Entrepreneur asks whether he should us zero percent credit cards to finance his home-based business.

42561 ■ "Work At Home" in *Black Enterprise* **(Vol. 34, July 2004, No. 12, pp. 145)**
Pub: Earl G. Graves Publishing Co. Inc.
Ed: Tanisha A. Sykes. **Description:** Work at home Websites are presented to help entrepreneurs seeking work-at-home opportunities, including the International Telework Association & Council, a non-profit that holds seminars in telecommuting; work-at-home.com, presents a listing of telecommuter-friendly companies; and IDC, an advisory firm offering information about information technology and telecommuting industries.

42562 ■ *Work@home: A Practical Guide for Women Who Want to Work from Home*
Pub: Woman's Missionary Union
Ed: Glynnis Whitwer. **Released:** March 2007. **Price:** $15.99. **Description:** Fifty-three percent of all small business are home-based. The book provides tips to women for starting a home-based business.

ASSOCIATIONS AND OTHER ORGANIZATIONS

42563 ■ American Association of Home Based Businesses
285 Red Run Heights Rd.
Oakland, MD 21550-7907
Co. E-mail: bevspeaks@earthlink.net
URL: http://www.jbsba.com/content/suites/hb_
  teleworking/index.shtml
Contact: Beverley Williams, Founder
Membership: Works to support, encourage and advocate for home-based businesses. TCB (Taking Care of Business), Tip Sheets, 15 topics.

42564 ■ American Home Business Association
1981 Murray Holladay Rd., Ste. 225
Salt Lake City, UT 84117
Ph:(801)273-2350
Free: 800-664-2422
Fax: (801)273-2399
Co. E-mail: info@homebusiness.com
URL: http://www.homebusiness.com
Contact: Bonnie Brijs, Pres./COO
Description: Offers benefits and services dedicated to supporting the needs of home business, small business and entrepreneurs. Benefits include health-auto-home insurance, legal, low long distance and 800 numbers, business line of credit, merchant accounts, tax programs, office supply and travel discounts and more. Seeks to provide members access to the best traditional benefits and timely information that is critical to conduct a successful home, small or Internet business. **Publications:** *AHBA Hotline Newsletter* (bi-monthly).

42565 ■ Canadian Federation of Independent Business–Federation Canadienne de l'Entreprise Independante
4141 Yonge St., Ste. 401
Willowdale, ON, Canada M2P 2A6
Ph:(416)222-8022
Fax: (416)222-7593
Co. E-mail: cfib@cfib.ca
URL: http://www.cfib.ca
Contact: Catherine Swift, Pres./CEO
Membership: Independent businesses. **Purpose:** Promotes economic well-being of members and seeks to maintain a healthy domestic business climate. Represents members' interests before government agencies, labor and industrial organizations, and the public.

42566 ■ Home Office Association of America
909 3rd Ave., Ste. 990
New York, NY 10022
Ph:(212)980-4622
Contact: Bileen Jaffe
Purpose: Works to support people with home-based businesses. Lobbies for changes in tax regulations to benefit home-based workers. Conducts educational programs has monthly newsletter Home Office Connections, discounts on health insurance, telephone, and travel, business insurance. Bestows Home Office Association seal of approval upon selected products. **Publications:** *Home Office Connections* (bimonthly).

42567 ■ National Association for Business Organizations
3 Woodthorne Ct., No. 12
Owings Mills, MD 21117
Ph:(410)363-3698
Co. E-mail: nahbb@msn.com
Contact: Rudolph Lewis, Pres.
Purpose: Business organizations that develop and support small businesses that have the capability to provide their products or services on a national level. Promotes small business in a free market system; represents the interests of small businesses to government and community organizations on small business affairs; monitors and reviews laws that affect small businesses; promotes a business code of ethics. Supplies members with marketing and management assistance; encourages joint marketing services between members. Operates a Home Based Business Television Network that provides an affordable audio/visual media for small and home based businesses. **Publications:** Newsletter (periodic).

42568 ■ National Association of Home Based Businesses
10451 Mill Run Cir., Ste. 400
Owings Mills, MD 21117
Ph:(410)363-3698
Co. E-mail: nahbb@msn.com
URL: http://www.usahomebusiness.com
Contact: Rudolph Lewis, Pres.
Description: Provides support and development services to home based businesses. Offers business models and franchise development and marketing

services. **Publications:** *E-Mail Newsletter* (monthly); *National Register of U.S. Home Based Business* (annual). **Telecommunication Services:** electronic bulletin board, includes trade, national news, national register, HBB source books, how-to books, community business, business opportunity, and home business computer; electronic mail, nahbb1@comcast.net.

42569 ■ SOHO America
PO Box 941
Hurst, TX 76053-0941
Free: 800-495-SOHO
Fax: 800-841-4445
Co. E-mail: soho@1sas.com
URL: http://www.soho.org
Description: Provides virtual community for small business and home office professionals with information pertaining to small and home-based businesses.

REFERENCE WORKS

42570 ■ *201 Great Tips for Your Small Business: Increase Your Profit and Joy in Your Work*
Pub: Dundren Press Limited
Ed: Julie V. Watson. **Released:** April 2006. **Price:** $24.99. **Description:** Tips and hints for home-based, micro, and small businesses are presented.

42571 ■ "2005 Standard Mileage Rates" in *Home Business* (Vol. 12, March/April 2005, No. 2, pp. 78)
Pub: Home Business Magazine
Description: Starting January 1, 2005, standard mileage rates were increased by the Internal Revenue Service. The costs for operating an automobile for business, charitable, medical or moving expenses are: 40.5 cents a mile for all business miles driven, 15 cents a mile when figuring deductible medical or moving expenses, and 14 cents a mile when providing services to a charity.

42572 ■ "Add An 'Inc' And Get Some Respect" in *Home Office Computing* (Vol. 19, No. 1, January 2001, pp. 24)
Pub: Scholastic Inc.
Ed: Jon Halpin. **Description:** The article discusses the fact that more small businesses are incorporating. Profiles of online incorporation services are provided.

42573 ■ "Add Some Magic to Your Marketing" in *Home Business* (Vol. 12, March/April 2005, No. 2, pp. 46, 94)
Pub: Home Business Magazine
Ed: Sandy Larson. **Description:** Ways an entrepreneur can use marketing strategies to grow a home business are shared by an executive coach and professional speaker.

42574 ■ "Back in the Saddle" in *Home Business* (Vol. 12, March/April 2005, No. 2, pp. 48)
Pub: Home Business Magazine
Ed: Sandy Larson. **Description:** Profile of Jim Stewart who runs his strategic project management business from his home.

42575 ■ "Balancing Act" in *My Business* (October/November 2002, pp. 42)
Pub: My Business Magazine
Ed: Tamara Holmes. **Description:** Candace Giles, owner of Candace Giles & Associates, a home-based real estate appraisal firm in Maryland, explains how she learned to balance her business and personal life.

42576 ■ "Beauty and the Bugs" in *Home Business* (Vol. 12, March/April 2005, No. 2, pp. 81)
Pub: Home Business Magazine
Ed: Sandy Larson. **Description:** Profile of Genma Stringer Holmes, founder of a home-based pest control company.

42577 ■ "Bed, Breakfast House in Arcadia, Miss., Reopens with New Owner" in *Sun Herald* (January 11, 2004)
Pub: Knight-Ridder/Tribune Business News
Ed: Dawn Krebs. **Description:** Profile of Audra McMurray, owner of Arcadia's Magnolia House Bed & Breakfast. McMurray always loved staying at bed and breakfasts when traveling and decided it was the right home-based business for her.

42578 ■ *Being Self-Employed: How to Run a Business Out of Your Home, Claim Travel and Depreciation and Earn a Good Income Well into Your 70s or 80s*
Pub: Allyear Tax Guides
Ed: Holmes F. Crouch, Irma Jean Crouch, Barbara J. MacRae. **Released:** September 2004. **Price:** $24.95 (US), $37.95 (Canadian). **Description:** Guide for small business to keep accurate tax records.

42579 ■ *Best Home-Based Franchises*
Pub: Doubleday & Co., Inc.
Ed: Compiled by Philip Lief Group, Inc., staff. **Released:** 1992. **Price:** $15.00 (paper).

42580 ■ *Best Home Businesses for the 90's*
Pub: Jeremy P. Tarcher Inc.
Ed: Sarah Edwards. **Released:** 1995. **Price:** $13.95 (paper).

42581 ■ "The Best of the Web" in *Inc.* (December 1999, pp. 92)
Pub: The Goldhirsh Group
Description: Finding useful information for home-based businesses on the Internet, along with short reviews of specific Web sites are included in this informative article.

42582 ■ "Bigger Office, Bigger Breaks" in *Home Office Computing* (Vol. 18, No. 10, October 2000, pp. 19)
Pub: Scholastic Inc.
Ed: Jeffery D. Zbar. **Description:** Home-business tax deductions are covered.

42583 ■ "Bring the New Economy Home" in *Home Office Computing* (Vol. 18, No. 12, December 2000, pp. 66)
Pub: Scholastic Inc.
Ed: William Van Winkle. **Description:** A guide to so-called New Economy concepts that can benefit a small business is presented. Small and home-based firms can seldom afford in-house expert help, and outsourcing is a viable option for a variety of business processors. Experts recommend that companies outsource to providers with other clients in the same line of business.

42584 ■ "Business by the Book" in *Home Office Computing* (Vol. 18, No. 12, December 2000, pp. 99)
Pub: Scholastic Inc.
Description: An explanation of licenses and permits needed to get a small business up and running.

42585 ■ "Business is Bouncin'" in *Home Business* (Vol. 12, October 2005, No. 5, pp. 71)
Pub: Home Business Magazine
Ed: Sandy Larson. **Description:** Profile of Jill Plumb, former teacher who rents out inflatable play structures from her home-based business in Northern California.

42586 ■ "Business to E-Business" in *Home Office Computing* (Vol. 18, No. 11, November 2000, pp. 52)
Pub: Scholastic Inc.
Ed: Amee Abel. **Description:** Guidelines are provided for setting up a Web site for a home-based business. The Web site should function as a kind of electronic brochure, providing potential customers with an attractive and inviting preview of the company's available products and services. The Web site should also provide links to related sites, and support associated marketing tasks.

42587 ■ *Business Know-How: An Operational Guide for Home-Based and Micro-Sized Businesses with Limited Budgets*
Pub: Adams Media Corporation
Ed: Janet Attard. **Price:** $17.95.

42588 ■ "Business Services" in *Entrepreneur* (Vol. 31, No. 5, May 2003, pp. 8)
Pub: Entrepreneur Media Inc.
Description: A directory of business services is presented, listing such services as franchise consultation, attorneys, entrepreneurial information radio shows, sales and marketing plans, business startup information, home-based businesses, raising business capital, e-businesses, B2B sales leads, and software.

42589 ■ *Buying Your First Franchise*
Pub: Crisp Publications, Inc.
Ed: Rebecca Luhn. **Released:** 1994. **Price:** $15.95. **Description:** Part of the Small Business & Entrepreneurship Series.

42590 ■ "Call Centers In the Rec Room" in *Business Week* (January 23, 2006, No. 3968, pp. 76-77)
Pub: McGraw-Hill Companies
Ed: Michelle Conlin. **Description:** Homeshoring provides an alternative to offshoring, whereby American companies are finding a cheap alternative to overseas call centers in the form of stay-at-home moms, the disabled, retirees, and others. Statistical data included.

42591 ■ *Careers for Homebodies and Other Independent Souls*
Pub: McGraw-Hill
Ed: Jan Goldberg. **Released:** March 2007. **Price:** $13.95. **Description:** The books offers insight into choosing the right career for individuals. Jobs range from office to outdoors, job markets, and levels of education requirements.

42592 ■ "Chocolate Makes a Success Story for Boca Raton Fla. Shop" in *South Florida Sun-Sentinel* (December 23, 2002)
Pub: Knight Ridder/Tribune Business News
Ed: Joan Fleischer Tamen. **Description:** Profile of Yael Cambi and her European-style chocolate shop in Boca Raton, Florida. Cambi started Success Chocolatier Inc in 1995 as a mail-order business out of her home.

42593 ■ "Competing with the Big Guys" in *Home Business* (Vol. 13, January/February 2006, No. 1, pp. 71)
Pub: Home Business Magazine
Ed: Sandy Larson. **Description:** Profile of Seema Matia who runs a marketing research firm from her home in Calabasas, California. Matia offers services to small and medium-sized businesses.

42594 ■ *The Complete Small-Business Sourcebook: Information, Services & Experts Every Small & Home-Based Business Needs*
Pub: Random House, Inc.
Ed: Carl Hausman and Wilbur Cross. **Released:** 1999. **Price:** $27.50.

42595 ■ *Computer Consulting on Your Home-Based PC*
Pub: The McGraw-Hill Companies
Ed: Herman Holtz. **Released:** 1994. **Price:** $24.95; $14.95 (paper).

42596 ■ "Covering Home Base: Insuring Your Homebased Business is Easier than Ever" in *Entrepreneur* (Vol. 33, March 2005, No. 3, pp. 64)
Pub: Entrepreneur Media Inc.
Ed: Jacquelyn Lynn. **Description:** Tips for insuring a home-based business are shared. Buying an endorsement to an existing homeowners' policy will increase business property coverage with a minimal costs. An in-home business policy provides greater comprehensive coverage for business equipment as well as liability.

42597 ■ "The Crash of 2006" in *Home Business* (Vol. 13, January/February 2006, No. 1, pp. 16, 18-22, 102, 104)
Pub: Home Business Magazine
Ed: Richard Henderson. **Description:** Home business owners can find opportunity in bad economic times. The home-based advantage in a touch economy is discussed.

42598 ■ "A Crash Diet for Dot-Coms" in *Kiplinger's Personal Finance Magazine* (Vol. 54, No. 8, August 2000, pp. 21)
Pub: The Kiplinger Washington Editors, Inc.
Ed: Melynda Dovel Wilcox. **Description:** With Web downsizing, the Internet superhighway is no longer the road to riches. But, high-tech employees still have a ticket to ride.

42599 ■ "Cultivating Teleworkers" in *Home Office Computing* (Vol. 18, No. 12, December 2000, pp. 102)
Pub: Scholastic Inc.
Ed: William Van Winkle. **Description:** Mutual fund company Putnam Investments used to be able to find qualified employees at job fairs. When that resource started to dry up they discovered that there is a ripe market for those workers that want to telecommute. This article takes a look at Putnam Investment's efforts and how well they have succeeded in their telecommuting program.

42600 ■ "Dare to Disconnect" in *Home Office Computing* (Vol. 19, No. 1, January 2001, pp. 92)
Pub: Scholastic Inc.
Ed: Jeffery D. Zbar. **Description:** The article explores the fact that most teleworkers take their offices with them when traveling.

42601 ■ "Decorating Dollars" in *Small Business Opportunities* (Vol. 16, No. 2, March 2004, pp. 110, 112)
Pub: Harris Publications, Inc.
Description: Profile of Karen Price and Josie Cicerale, founders of Decor & You, a home-based decorating franchise. Professionally trained interior decorators go to client's homes and change the looks of rooms using wall and window coverings, furnishings, carpets and other elements. Currently 24 franchises are operating.

42602 ■ "Discovering a Spin-Off Business" in *Home Business* (Vol. 12, March/April 2005, No. 2, pp. 40, 42-43)
Pub: Home Business Magazine
Ed: Priscilla Y. Huff. **Description:** Entrepreneurs share ways they used spin-off ventures to attract new customers and revitalize old ones.

42603 ■ "The Doll Maker: Cozbi Cabrera Breaks the Mold" in *Black Enterprise* (Vol. 35, October 2004, No. 3, pp. 203)
Pub: Earl G. Graves Publishing Co. Inc.
Ed: Sonia Alleyne. **Description:** Profile of Cozbi A. Cabrera, who turned her love for crafts into a home-based business that grew into a boutique in Brooklyn, New York. Her one-of-a-kind dolls are dressed with detailed beading, paint and hand-rolled hems. Cabrera shares information for doll collectors.

42604 ■ "Don't Fall for these Numbers" in *Kiplinger's Personal Finance Magazine* (Vol. 55, No. 1, January, 2001, pp. 28)
Pub: The Kiplinger Washington Editors, Inc.
Description: Investigators are cracking down on work-at-home schemes that cost consumers more than they'll ever earn.

42605 ■ "DSL Users Brace for Bumpy Ride" in *Home Office Computing* (Vol. 18, No. 11, November 2000, pp. 19)
Pub: Scholastic Inc.
Ed: Bonny L. Georgia. **Description:** Tips for protecting yourself when dealing with DSL providers are given.

42606 ■ "Dulling the Tax Bite" *Fortune* (Vol. 141, No. 9, May 1, 2000)
Pub: Time Inc.
Ed: Daniel Akst. **Description:** The IRS has cut small businesses some slack in three areas, but in doing so is conducting tougher audits.

42607 ■ *Easy Financials for Your Home-Based Business: The Friendly Guide to Successful Management Systems for Busy Home Entrepreneurs*
Pub: Rayve Publications, Inc.
Ed: Norm Ray. **Released:** 1993. **Price:** $19.95 (paper).

42608 ■ *Easy to Start, Fun to Run, & Highly Profitable Home Businesses*
Pub: Adams Media Corp.
Ed: Katina Z. Jones. **Released:** 1998. **Price:** $9.95.

42609 ■ *Eighty-Plus Great Ideas for Making Money at Home: A Guide for the First-Time Entrepreneur*
Pub: Walker & Co.
Ed: Erica Barkemeyer. **Released:** 1992. **Price:** $24.95; $5.95 (paper).

42610 ■ "Employee Matters" in *Home Business* (Vol. 12, March/April 2005, No. 2, pp. 90)
Pub: Home Business Magazine
Ed: Kurt English. **Description:** Home-based businesses face unique challenges when hiring additional employees.

42611 ■ "Entrepreneur Column" in *Entrepreneur.com* (September 21, 2006)
Pub: Entrepreneur Media Inc.
Ed: Nichole L. Torres. **Description:** Women starting a business with younger children deal with special issues and concerns. It is difficult to balance the family and the business, but assistance is available and discussed to make this more manageable.

42612 ■ "Farming IT Out" in *Home Office Computing* (Vol. 18, No. 10, October 2000, pp. 16)
Pub: Scholastic Inc.
Ed: Mark Kakkuri. **Description:** Information Technology (IT) outsourcing services are ready to help home office workers with everything from setting up a computer to building a broadband LAN.

42613 ■ "Fast Learner" in *My Business* (April/May 2004, pp. 48)
Pub: My Business Magazine
Ed: Lena Basha. **Description:** Profile of Louise Creager, owner of a gift-basket business she operates from her home in Bellvue, Colorado. Creager addresses inventory issues, assets and balance sheets.

42614 ■ "Fattah's Plan for Small Business" in *Philadelphia Inquirer* (February 6, 2007)
Pub: Philadelphia Newspapers LLC
Ed: Michael Currie Schaffer. **Description:** Philadelphia Mayoral candidate, Chaka Fattah, plans to create an emergency loan fund for small business in the city, if elected. The micro-loans would be available for small and home-based businesses.

42615 ■ "Find Anything on the Web" in *Home Office Computing* (Vol. 18, No. 7, July 2000, pp. 48)
Pub: Scholastic Inc.
Ed: Susan Glinert. **Description:** Tips for using Web research tools effectively are presented. Government sites have some of the best information for anyone planning to start a home-based business, as do sites geared for particular industries.

42616 ■ "Fitting Home Offices Into Small Spaces" in *Home Business* (Vol. 12, March/April 2005, No. 2, pp. 82, 84-87)
Pub: Home Business Magazine
Ed: Aliza Sherman. **Description:** Efficient furniture and equipment is the key to outfitting a small home-based office.

42617 ■ "For Sale by (Home Office) Owner" in *Home Office Computing* (Vol. 18, No. 9, September 2000, pp. 13)
Pub: Scholastic Inc.
Ed: Lisa Roberts. **Description:** According to a National Association of Realtors (NAR) survey, of the 5.2 million homes purchased in 1999, just one percent were bought with a home office in mind.

42618 ■ "Fredericksburg, Va., Administrative Services Company Lends Firms a Virtual Hand" in *Free Lance-Star* (November 6, 2004)
Pub: Free Lance-Star Publishing Co.
Ed: Portsia Smith. **Description:** Profile of Kathy McHenry, owner of Your Virtual Advantage, a home-based company. McHenry, a former legal assistant, office manager and loan collector started her company in 2001 and provides services to clients in Virginia, Washington and Chicago.

42619 ■ "Free Reign" in *Home Office Computing* (Vol. 18, No. 12, December 2000, pp. 45)
Pub: Scholastic Inc.
Ed: Douglas Gantenbein. **Description:** Many companies now offer free E-mail and Internet access service based on an advertiser-supported model. Home-based workers will find such free ISPs useful mainly as backups to a paid account.

42620 ■ "From Tee to Green" in *Home Business* (Vol. 12, March/April 2005, No. 2, pp. 96)
Pub: Home Business Magazine
Ed: Sandy Larson. **Description:** Profile of Dr. Venanzio Cardarelli, the dentist who invented the Aero-tee, a tooth-shaped polycarbonate golf tee from his home-based business. The tee is designed to last longer than traditional plastic golf tees.

42621 ■ "Generate More Revenue with a Bottom-Up Marketing Plan" in *Home Business* (Vol. 12, March/April 2005, No. 2, pp. 32, 34-35)
Pub: Home Business Magazine
Ed: Sonya Carmichael Jones. **Description:** Marketing to grow a home business is discussed using a bottom-up plan.

42622 ■ "Get in the Zone: Checking Local Zoning Ordinances First Stops Problems Later" in *My Business* (October/November 2002, pp. 43)
Pub: My Business Magazine
Ed: Joan E. Lisante. **Description:** It is advised to check with the local municipality for zoning laws regarding home-based businesses before setting up shop.

42623 ■ "Going Global" in *Home Office Computing* (Vol. 18, No. 10, October 2000, pp. 87)
Pub: Scholastic Inc.
Ed: David Harvey. **Description:** Small and home-based business are increasingly able to do business abroad by leveraging the power of the Internet and locating online tools and resources for tapping overseas markets. Steps to building an effective Web site are covered.

42624 ■ *Greater Phoenix Chamber Membership List—Home-Based Businesses*
Pub: Greater Phoenix Chamber of Commerce
Price: $13, members; $15, nonmembers; $15, members diskette; $17, nonmembers diskette; all prices include shipping. **Covers:** 67 home-based businesses in the greater Phoenix, Arizona area. **Entries Include:** Contact details.

42625 ■ "Grow Your Client BASE" in *Home Office Computing* (Vol. 18, No. 8, August 2000, pp. 54)
Pub: Scholastic Inc.
Ed: Jeffery D. Zbar. **Description:** Five simple strategies are provided for finding new customers and generating repeat business for home-based companies.

42626 ■ "Grow Your Technology" in *Home Office Computing* (Vol. 18, No. 10, October 2000, pp. 52)
Pub: Scholastic Inc.
Ed: David Haskin. **Description:** Strategies for supporting a home business with best tech resources and support while staying within the budget are presented. The first step is to evaluate the existing tech set up, using a consultant, if necessary. Other tech strategies include developing a professional Web presence, providing adequate customer support and handling remote workers. Products and services for home office administration are listed.

42627 ■ "Growing Pains" in *Home Business* (Vol. 13, January/February 2006, No. 1, pp. 88, 90-91)
Pub: Home Business Magazine
Ed: Jodi Helmer. **Description:** Home-based business owners can hire employees to help grow a company. Tips to discover if your home-based firm is ready to hire an employee are included.

42628 ■ *Growing Your Home-Based Business: A Complete Guide to Proven Sales and Marketing Communications Strategies*
Pub: Prentice Hall
Ed: Kim T. Gordon. **Released:** 1992. **Price:** $12.95 (paper).

42629 ■ "Healthcare Insurance" in *Black Enterprise* (Vol. 34, No. 2, September 2003, pp. 48)
Pub: Earl Graves Publishing Co.
Ed: Alan Hughes. **Description:** Healthcare insurance is becoming increasingly more difficult for small business owners to provide to employees, especially for a small home-based business wishing to expand. The House Small Business Committee introduced the Self-Employed Health Care Affordability Act of 2003 (H.R. 1873) in April 2003, this bill allows self-employed business owners to deduct health insurance costs when calculating payroll taxes, thus effectively reducing those costs by more than 15 percent.

42630 ■ "The Healthy Home Office" in *Home Office Computing* (Vol. 18, No. 10, October 2000, pp. 58)
Pub: Scholastic Inc.
Ed: William Van Winkle. **Description:** According to the Occupational Safety & Health Administration (OSHA), approximately 1.8 million U.S workers suffer from repetitive strain injuries (RSIs) each year. A guide to home office ergonomics is provided to prevent such injuries. Web sites describing news, products and services are included.

42631 ■ "Healthy, Wealthy and Wise" in *Home Business* (Vol. 12, October 2005, No. 5, pp. 94)
Pub: Home Business Magazine
Description: Ways to maintain a healthy work style while running a home-based business are examined.

42632 ■ "Hello, can we take photos of your home office today?" in *Business First Columbus* (Vol. 18, No. 26, February 15, 2002, pp. 48)
Pub: Business First Columbus, Inc.
Ed: Robin Hepler. **Description:** Presentations of home office design are presented.

42633 ■ *The Home-Based Entrepreneur: The Complete Guide to Working at Home*
Pub: Upstart Publishing Co., Inc.
Ed: Linda Pinson and Jerry Jinnett. **Released:** Second edition, 1993. **Price:** $19.95 (paper). **Description:** Step-by-step guide to starting a home-based business, including zoning and licenses, tax information, advertising, recordkeeping, pricing, and sources of government and private financial assistance.

42634 ■ "Home-Based Resources" in *Small Business Opportunities* (Vol. 16, No. 2, March 2004, pp. 184)
Pub: Harris Publications, Inc.
Description: Twenty resources to help run a home-based business, including information about the U.S. Small Business Administration small business programs.

42635 ■ *Home Business to Big Business: How to Launch Your Home Business and Make it a Success*
Pub: Macmillan Publishing Co., Inc.
Ed: Mel Cook. **Released:** 1992. **Price:** $14.95 (paper).

42636 ■ *Home Business Made Easy: How to Select & Start a Home Business That Fits Your Interests, Lifestyles & Pocketbook*
Pub: Oasis Press
Ed: David Hanania. **Released:** 1992. **Price:** $19.95 (paper). **Description:** Provides information on how to choose and start a full- or part-time home business. Includes start-up sets, worksheets, and descriptions of 150 possible home businesses.

42637 ■ *Home Business Tax Deductions: Keep What You Earn*
Pub: NOLO
Ed: Stephen Fishman. **Released:** November 2006. **Price:** $34.99. **Description:** Home business tax deductions are outlined. Basic information on the ways various business structures are taxed and how deductions work is included.

42638 ■ *Home Computer Business Guide*
Pub: Entrepreneur, Inc.
Price: $8.99 (includes business guide and financial software). **Description:** Contains step-by-step instructions on how to make money with a home computer. Includes information on choosing a computer-based business, finding customers, rates, equipment, and advertising.

42639 ■ "Home Invasion" in *Business Week* (No. 3666, January 31, 2000, pp. F8)
Pub: McGraw-Hill, Inc.
Description: Employer responsibility for at-home workers' safety is explored.

42640 ■ "The Home Office Deduction" in *My Business* (October/November 2002, pp. 46)
Pub: My Business Magazine
Ed: Milton Zall. **Description:** Requirements for using home office tax deductions are discussed.

42641 ■ *The Home Office Money and Tax Guide: Bringing Professional Business Practices Home*
Pub: Probus Publishing Co., Inc.
Ed: Robert W. Wood. **Released:** 1992. **Price:** $21.95 (paper).

42642 ■ "Home Office, Simplified" in *Home Office Computing* (Vol. 18, No. 7, July 2000, pp. 54)
Pub: Scholastic Inc.
Ed: Jeffery D. Zbar. **Description:** Home-based workers often develop bad habits that lead to disorganization and reduce productivity. It is important to take control of a home office and manage the workspace effectively. Three home workers teamed with organizational experts to discuss their own weaknesses.

42643 ■ *The Home Office and Small Business Answer Book: Solutions to the Most Frequently Asked Questions about Starting and Running Home Offices*
Pub: Henry Holt & Co., Inc.
Ed: Janet Attard. **Released:** 1993. **Price:** $40.00; $19.95 (paper).

42644 ■ "Home Office vs. the Field" in *Sales & Marketing Management*
Pub: VNU Business Media
Description: Incentives for sales teams are debated by a salesperson and sales manager.

42645 ■ "Home Offices as Status Symbol" in *Home Office Computing* (Vol. 18, No. 12, December 2000, pp. 24)
Pub: Scholastic Inc.
Ed: Lisa Roberts. **Description:** The article tells how people are spending large amounts of money on home offices.

42646 ■ "Home Rules" in *Business Week* (No. 3667, February 7, 2000, pp. 53)
Pub: McGraw-Hill, Inc.
Description: Representative Thomas M. Davis (R-Va.) supports the law to keep government from regulating home offices.

42647 ■ "Home, Sweet Office" in *Entrepreneur* (Vol. 31, No. 11, November 2003, pp. 72)
Pub: Entrepreneur Media, Inc.
Ed: Jennifer Pellet. **Description:** Internal Revenue Service tax laws regarding the sale of a home that is also used as a home business are explained.

42648 ■ "Home Sweet Office: Stress Relievers" in *Sales and Marketing.com* (Vol. 156, No. 3, March 2004, pp. 66)
Pub: VNU eMedia, Inc.
Ed: Julia Chang. **Description:** Telecommuters and home based-business owners can incorporate stress relieving techniques that cannot be done in a corporate office, including the use of aromatherapy candles.

42649 ■ "Home Sweet Office: The Pitch for Telecommuting" in *Sales and Marketing.com* (Vol. 153, No. 3, March 2004, pp. 50)
Pub: VNU eMedia, Inc.
Description: Tips to convince management that telecommuting will benefit the company are presented, including detailing ways the lines of communication will be open.

42650 ■ *The Homebased Business Book*
Pub: Entrepreneur, Inc.
Released: 1994. **Description:** Guide to building a home-based business. Covers setting up an office, marketing products and services, assessing your potential, and other related data.

42651 ■ *Homemade Business*
Pub: Focus on the Family Publishing
Ed: Donna Partow. **Released:** 1999. **Price:** $10.99.

42652 ■ *Homemade Money*
Pub: M. Evans & Company Inc.
Contact: Barbara Brabec, Author
Released: Published in two volumes. **Publication Includes:** A special 76 page, updated "A-Z Crash Course" on business basics and a directory of 300 listings. **Entries Include:** Supplier name, address, description of information, price, order information. Principal content of the book is editorial matter on beginning and developing a home-based business. **Arrangement:** Classified by subject. **Indexes:** Alphabetical.

42653 ■ "Homework 2001" in *Small Business Opportunities* (Vol. 13, No. 5, September 2001, pp. 72-73)
Pub: Harris Publications, Inc.
Description: It is estimated that every week 8,000 people decide to work at home, equating to nearly 55 million people with home-based offices. This increase is making a positive impact on home design, floor plans and building materials.

42654 ■ *How to Build a Successful One-Person Business: A Common-Sense Guide to Starting & Growing a Company*
Pub: Bookhaus Publishers
Ed: Veltisezar B. Bautista. **Released:** 1995. **Price:** $24.95.

42655 ■ *How to Create an Unlimited Income Sitting at Home in Your Pajamas*
Pub: PublishAmerica, Incorporated
Ed: Michael Klisouris. **Released:** April 2006. **Price:** $19.95. **Description:** Step-by-step guide for starting, operating and expanding a home-based business is featured.

42656 ■ *How to Make 1000 Mistakes in Business & Still Succeed: The Guide to Crucial Decisions in the Small Business, Home-Based Business*
Pub: Wright Track

Ed: Harold L. Wright. **Released:** 1995. **Price:** $14.95.

42657 ■ How to Raise a Family & a Career under One Roof: A Personal Guide to Home Business for Parents
Pub: Bookhaven Press
Ed: Lisa M. Roberts; edited by Marla Olson; illustrated by Wendy Simon and George Foster. **Released:** 1997. **Price:** $15.95.

42658 ■ How to Run Your Own Home Business
Pub: NTC Business Books
Ed: Coralee Smith Kern and Tammara Hoffman Wolfgram. **Released:** 1994. **Price:** $9.95 (paper). **Description:** Covers choosing a product or service, setting up a work environment, and zoning and tax laws.

42659 ■ How to Start a Home-Based Writing Business, 5th Edition
Pub: Globe Pequot Press
Ed: Lucy Parker. **Released:** December 2007. **Price:** $18.95. **Description:** Guide for starting and running a home-based writing business.

42660 ■ How to Start a Home Business
Pub: Avon Books
Ed: Michael Antoniak. **Released:** 1995. **Price:** $12.50.

42661 ■ How to Start a Successful Home Business
Pub: Warner Books, Inc.
Ed: Karen Cheney. **Released:** 1997. **Price:** $10.99.

42662 ■ "How to Vitalize a Home-Based Operation" in Home Business (Vol. 12, October 2005, No. 5, pp. 32, 34, 95)
Pub: Home Business Magazine
Ed: Alan Stewart. **Description:** In order to be successful, home-based business owners must continue to refine and improve operations, be ready to take on new projects, new customers and new marketplaces.

42663 ■ "In the Family Way" in Home Office Computing (Vol. 18, No. 10, October 2000, pp. 86)
Pub: Scholastic Inc.
Ed: Marshall F. Lager. **Description:** Alexis D. Gutzman, e-commerce columnist for the news Web site Internet.com, tells how she has established her home network based on family security and closeness.

42664 ■ "Interiors By Design" in Black Enterprise (Vol. 35, October 2004, No. 3, pp. 54)
Pub: Earl G. Graves Publishing Co. Inc.
Ed: Virginia Myers Kelly. **Description:** Profile of Dennese Guadeloupe Rojas, a laid off direct mail worker, who earned a degree in interior design and is now the successful owner of Interiors By Design. Rojas offers interior and exterior design as well as home accessories to her clients. She started out working from home, but soon found she needed more space.

42665 ■ "Internet Firewalls" in Home Business (Vol. 12, March/April 2005, No. 2, pp. 88)
Pub: Home Business Magazine
Ed: David P. Hunter. **Description:** Importance for a home-based business to use a good firewall to protect their computers is stressed. Information is offered to help choose the best firewall for a business.

42666 ■ Iowa Home-based Business Directory
Pub: Integrity Communications
Contact: Clare Bills
Released: Annual, June/July. **Covers:** 110 products and services offered by home-based businesses in Iowa, such as computer specialists, accountants, management experts, furniture, health products, etc. **Entries Include:** Company name, address, phone, descriptions of product/service. **Arrangement:** Product/service. **Indexes:** Company name; geographical by county.

42667 ■ "It's Tax Time - Again" in Home Business (Vol. 12, March/April 2005, No. 2, pp. 76)
Pub: Home Business Magazine
Description: A listing of tax benefits and deductions allowable for small, home-based businesses are explained.

42668 ■ "Joining Forces" in Home Business (Vol. 12, October 2005, No. 5, pp. 64, 66)
Pub: Home Business Magazine
Ed: Priscilla Y. Huff. **Description:** Through the use of the Internet and affordable technology, home-based business owners are forming virtual alliances to help one another grow their businesses.

42669 ■ "Keep It Professional" in Home Office Computing (Vol. 18, No. 10, October 2000, pp. 89)
Pub: Scholastic Inc.
Ed: Joanne Cleaver. **Description:** Operating a business from home raises many thorny issues of how to separate work and personal life in order to keep the business professional in appearance. Defining the office involves examining traffic patterns employees, customers and delivery people must take to reach the home office. Once the office is clearly defined protecting the home is important, as is investing in top-notch technology to make the home office look professional.

42670 ■ "Kick the Habit" in Home Office Computing (Vol. 17, No. 1, January 1999, pp. 67)
Pub: Line56 Media
Ed: Joanne Cleaver. **Description:** A guide to using technology for more efficient time management in home offices is presented. A good filing system can make a difference when organizing an office. A service called Paper Tiger combines the assistance of a professional organizer with maintenance software.

42671 ■ "Kids @ Work" in My Business (October/November 2002, pp. 42)
Pub: My Business Magazine
Description: Multi-tasking is the key to running a successful business from home, while attending to a young family. Tips for working from home with young children are offered.

42672 ■ The Kitchen Table Millionaire: Home-Based Money-Making Strategies to Build Financial Independence Today
Pub: The McGraw-Hill Companies
Ed: Patrick W. Cochrane. **Released:** 1997.

42673 ■ "Know the Rules" in Black Enterprise (Vol. 35, December 2004, No. 5, pp. 56)
Pub: Earl G. Graves Publishing Co. Inc.
Ed: Arlene McKanic. **Description:** Rules and regulations governing home-based businesses have become more complex, especially tax laws. The Internal Revenue Service is unfair to home-based companies when it comes to deductions, while zoning codes create other barriers.

42674 ■ "Lending a Helping Hand Even When Off Duty" in Home Business (Vol. 12, March/April 2005, No. 2, pp. 62)
Pub: Home Business Magazine
Ed: Sandy Larson. **Description:** Profile of Randy Gabel and Scott Mullins, licensed paramedics, who run a home-based company offering emergency training courses.

42675 ■ "Magic Moments" in Home Business (Vol. 13, January/February 2006, No. 1, pp. 70)
Pub: Home Business Magazine
Description: Profile of Steve Petroff who runs a successful network marketing business from his home in Indianapolis, Indiana. Petroff offers fee-for-service plans and shares his formula for success.

42676 ■ Make Your Business Survive and Thrive! 100+ Proven Marketing Methods to Help You Beat the Odds
Pub: John Wiley & Sons, Incorporated

Ed: Priscilla Y. Huff. **Released:** December 2006. **Price:** $19.95. **Description:** Small business and entrepreneurial expert gives information to help small and home-based businesses grow.

42677 ■ "Managing Creativity in a Progressive Home Business" in Home Business (Vol. 13, January/February 2006, No. 1, pp. 28, 30-31, 95)
Pub: Home Business Magazine
Ed: Alan Stewart. **Description:** Identification and solutions to solving home-based business issues is examined. ▪

42678 ■ "Many happy returns" in WorkingWoman (Vol. 25, No. 2, February 2000, pp. S8)
Pub: Lang Communications Inc.
Ed: Rebecca Reisner. **Description:** Questions regarding income tax return preparation, including personal income tax exemptions and home office expense deductions, are answered.

42679 ■ "Microsoft Windows Millennium Edition" in Home Office Computing (Vol. 18, No. 10, October 2000, pp. 26)
Pub: Scholastic Inc.
Ed: Eric Grevstad. **Description:** Microsoft Windows Millenium Edition (Windows ME) is a better and more useful product for home users than Windows 2000, which needs faster, newer hardware for full performance. WindowsME comes with multimedia enhancements including Windows Movie Maker and Windows Image Acquisition programming interface. Also, users can download, free of cost, Internet Explorer 5.5 and Windows Media Player 7.

42680 ■ "More home-based businesses are leaving home" in Atlanta Business Chronicle (Vol. 24, No. 8, July 27, 2001, pp. 9B)
Pub: American City Business Journals Inc.
Ed: Eileen Brill Wagner. **Description:** Home-based businesses are no longer confined to home, as technology enables small business owners to do business anywhere and anytime. Home-based business owners have also formed support groups that meet in local coffee shops. Being mobile is an important way for home business owners to get an advantage over their traditional competition.

42681 ■ "More Women Than Men Have Home Offices" in Marketing to Women (Vol. 19, October 2006, No. 10, pp. 12)
Pub: EPM Communications, Inc.
Description: A survey of business professionals by Intellicontact reflects that women are more likely than men to have home offices. The survey also shows that while men and women both check their e-mail frequently, the two sexes manage their inboxes differently.

42682 ■ "Mrs., Mom, and CEO" in Black Enterprise (Vol. 32, No. 9, April 2)
Pub: Earl Graves Publishing Co.
Ed: Monique R. Brown. **Description:** Profile of Vickie Clark, owner and founder of a family owned, home-based business that transports kids back and forth to various activities.

42683 ■ "MyTechTool" in My Business (June/July 2002, pp. 24)
Pub: My Business Magazine
Description: Profile of Susan Soros, owner of Soap Goddess, a home-based business that makes and sells all-natural handmade soap online.

42684 ■ "The Need for Tort Reform" in My Business (October/November 2002, pp. 49)
Pub: My Business Magazine
Ed: Hilda Bankston. **Description:** The former owner of a Fayette, Mississippi family-owned drug store tells how her and her pharmacist husband were named in a class action lawsuit over the prescription drug Fen-Phen. The lawsuit has devastated the family as well as the community and its small businesses.

42685 ■ "The Networked Home" in *Home Office Computing* **(Vol. 18, No. 12, December 2000, pp. 89)**
Pub: Scholastic Inc.
Ed: Bonny L. Georgia. **Description:** This article tells what the home-based worker can do to automate their house and how to set up security systems. One such product mentioned is home automation software that helps to automate different functions such as turning on lights and appliances.

42686 ■ "New OSHA Rules to Reduce Injuries" in *Home Office Computing* **(Vol. 18, No. 8, August 2000, pp. 15)**
Pub: Scholastic Inc.
Ed: William Van Winkle. **Description:** Being ergonomically correct is about to become the law of the land; The Occupational Safety & Health Administration (OSHA) is set to implement new ergonomic rules that could send businesses, both large and small, hurrying for compliance, including companies with teleworkers in home offices.

42687 ■ "Newsstand" in *Home Business* **(Vol. 12, October 2005, No. 5, pp. 38-39)**
Pub: Home Business Magazine
Description: Various topics are covered, including information about home-based business tax deductions, the link between home computers and entrepreneurship, income gaps, demographics of home-based business owners, creation of more home-based businesses due to merger-related job cuts, and frivolous lawsuits against home-based entrepreneurs.

42688 ■ "Nikon's Newly Created Long Island Unit to Scout Tech Trends for the Home Office" in *Long Island Business News* **(March 12, 2004)**
Pub: Dolan Media Newswires
Ed: Ken Schachter. **Description:** Nikon is developing a new division to scout technology, products and market trends for the home office.

42689 ■ "No Bad Days: Sherry Williams excels as a Mary Kay sales pro while battling breast cancer" in *Black Enterprise* **(Oct. 2002, pp. 175)**
Pub: Earl Graves Publishing Co.
Ed: Shani Smothers. **Description:** Profile of Sherry B. Williams, an independent senior sales director for Mary Kay Cosmetics in Phoenix, Arizona. Williams, diagnosed with cancer for the third time in 2002, says that her business has survived her illnesses, because of its mobility. She can do business from home using the phone, mail and the Internet.

42690 ■ "No Brainer: Simple Ways to Solve Your Own Tech Problems" in *My Business* **(October/November 2002, pp. 44)**
Pub: My Business Magazine
Ed: Melany Klinck. **Description:** Prevention is the key to keeping computers up and working for small home-based businesses; a listing of free tech Web sites offering repair, support and other services, is included.

42691 ■ *No Place Like Home: Organizing Home-Based Labor in the Era of Structural Adjustment*
Pub: Routledge Inc.
Ed: David Staples. **Released:** November 2006. **Price:** $70.00. **Description:** The book examines the role of home-based women workers in contemporary capitalism.

42692 ■ "Nothing is Unworkable" in *Home Office Computing* **(Vol. 19, No. 1, January 2001, pp. 11)**
Pub: Scholastic Inc.
Ed: Eric Grevstad. **Description:** The advantages to working at home are explored.

42693 ■ "Office Down Below" in *Home Office Computing* **(Vol. 18, No. 8, August 2000, pp. 42)**
Pub: Scholastic Inc.
Ed: Marilyn Zelinsky Syarto. **Description:** Ideas for converting a basement into a home office are offered.

42694 ■ "An Office of One's Own" in *Entrepreneur* **(Vol. 31, No. 9, September 2003, pp. 105)**
Pub: Entrepreneur Media, Inc.
Description: Advice for setting up a home office without an actual office area is given by Susan Silver, president of Positively Organized, a firm located in Los Angeles, California. Location, space saving ideas, file cabinets, and storage is discussed.

42695 ■ "An Office With Ambiance" in *Home Office Computing* **(Vol. 18, No. 10, October 2000, pp. 64)**
Pub: Scholastic Inc.
Ed: Marilyn Zelinsky Syarto. **Description:** Two steps to transform a dreary home office into a comfortable retreat that is conducive to creativity are, replacing junk with objects that bring joy, and adding lighting, color, sound, and air circulation to the area. Products for creating such an environment are showcased.

42696 ■ "On a role" in *WorkingWoman* **(Vol. 25, No. 7, August 2000, pp. 79)**
Pub: Lang Communications Inc.
Ed: Russell Wild. **Description:** Acting classes can improve the performance of top executives who regularly have to make important speeches or give seminars to large groups of people.

42697 ■ *101 Best Home-Based Success Secrets for Women*
Pub: Prima Publishing
Ed: Priscilla Y. Huff. **Released:** 1999.

42698 ■ *101 Best Home Businesses*
Pub: Career Press, Inc.
Ed: Dan Ramsey. **Released:** 1997. **Price:** $14.99.

42699 ■ *101 Great Home-Based Businesses for Women: Everything You Need to Know about Getting Started on the Road to Success*
Pub: Prima Publishing & Communications
Ed: Priscilia Y. Huff. **Released:** 1995. **Price:** $10.95.

42700 ■ *One Thousand One Businesses You Can Start from Home*
Pub: John Wiley & Sons, Inc.
Ed: Daryl Allen Hall. **Released:** 1992. **Price:** $14.95 (paper).

42701 ■ *Organizing Your Home Office for Success: Expert Strategies That Can Work for You*
Pub: NAL Dutton
Ed: Lisa Kanarek. **Released:** 1993. **Price:** $10.00. **Description:** Guide to setting up or improving a home-based business, covering organization, selecting work space, and paper and time management.

42702 ■ "OSHA Ushers Itself Out" in *Business Week* **(March 27, 2000, pp. F6)**
Pub: McGraw-Hill, Inc.
Description: The Occupational Health and Safety Administration announces that it won't inspect home offices.

42703 ■ "OSHA's Proposed Ergonomic Standard and Clarification on Home Work Policy" in *Employment Relations Today* **(Vol. 27, No. 1, Spring 2000)**
Pub: John Wiley & Sons, Inc.
Ed: John J. Gallagher and Gregory R. Watchman. **Description:** Several federal regulations that impacted US workers in 1999 are discussed, focusing on home work, foreign worker, and overtime policies. Topics addressed include the US Occupational Safety and Health Administration's ergonomic standards, protection for illegal aliens, and the calculation of overtime under the Fair Labor Standards Act.

42704 ■ "Out of the Zone" in *Home Office Computing* **(Vol. 18, No. 12, December 2000, pp. 97)**
Pub: Scholastic Inc.
Ed: Steven Van Yoder. **Description:** This article takes a look at home-based business and zoning laws. The author contends that many home business workers are violating zoning laws with or without knowing it. Advice is given to avoid this problem.

42705 ■ "The outside advantage" in *My Business* **(April/May 2002, pp. 48)**
Pub: My Business Magazine
Ed: Marcia Jablonski. **Description:** Things to consider when moving a home business to a space away from the house are presented, including trying to control additional costs for the move.

42706 ■ *Partners at Work and at Home: How Couples Can Build a Successful Business Together without Killing Each Other*
Pub: Self-Counsel Press, Inc.
Ed: Annette O'Shea-Roche and Sieglinde Malmberg. **Released:** 1994, first edition. **Price:** $8.95 (paper).

42707 ■ "People Growers Deals With Personal Growing Pains" in *Business Journal-Portland* **(Vol. 20, No. 22, August 1, 2003, pp. 3)**
Pub: American City Business Journals, Inc.
Ed: Robin J. Moody. **Description:** Profile of Windy Baty, owner of People Growers. The home-based firm helps companies organize on-site health fairs and promotes wellness among employees.

42708 ■ "Perdue's home-work plan has failed past" in *Atlanta Business Chronicle* **(Vol. 25, November 29, 2002, No. 25, pp. 1A)**
Pub: American City Business Publications, Inc.
Ed: Sarah Rubenstein. **Description:** In an effort to reduce traffic congestion in Atlanta, Georgia, Governor-elect Sonny Perdue intends to persuade more companies to use telecommuting. Additionally, Perdue plans to identify 25,000 government employees who could telecommute at least part time.

42709 ■ "Post It and They Will Come" in *Home Office Computing* **(Vol. 18, No. 11, November 2000, pp. 40)**
Pub: Scholastic Inc.
Ed: Eileen Bien Calabro. **Description:** Ways to use message boards to expand your business are highlighted.

42710 ■ "The Public Library: Technology Lets You Browse the Stacks from Your Home Office" in *Black Enterprise* **(Vol. 34, No. 4, Nov. 2003)**
Pub: Earl Graves Publishing Co.
Ed: Jennifer L. Smith. **Description:** More than 3,000 libraries offer programs offering E-books, databases and online classes that can be accessed via computers for small and home businesses searching for materials on marketing and management topics.

42711 ■ "Q&A" in *Home Office Computing* **(Vol. 18, No. 9, September 2000, pp. 13)**
Pub: Scholastic Inc.
Ed: Marilyn Zelinsky Syarto. **Description:** Anna Bernstein, founder of Voice Success, a New York City-based consulting firm, discusses using your voice as a business tool.

42712 ■ "R-E-S-P-E-C-T: The Changing Attitudes Toward Home-Based Businesses" in *My Business* **(October/November 2002, pp. 45)**
Pub: My Business Magazine
Ed: Mardy Fornes. **Description:** The importance of developing a strong business plan is key to running a successful home business. Some of the obstacles faced by those operating a home-based company are discussed.

42713 ■ "Ramps to Riches" in *Small Business Opportunities* **(Vol. 17, May 2005, No. 3, pp. 66)**
Pub: Harris Publications Inc.
Description: Gator Ramps are compact ramps that are installed on pick-up trucks. The franchise provides a good home-based opportunity.

42714 ■ "Remote Control" in *Home Office Computing* **(Vol. 18, No. 10, October 2000, pp. 46)**
Pub: Scholastic Inc.
Ed: Jeffrey D. Zbar. **Description:** Organization strategies for telemanagers who work remotely, while the

staff remains on-site at the corporate campus are outlined. Views of three telemanagers on such strategies, including keeping the office working seamlessly, tackling staff problems and maintaining morale are presented.

42715 ■ "Report From Las Vegas: Inside the Home Office Of the Future" in *Fortune* **(Vol. 141, No. 3, February 7, 2000, pp. 56)**
Pub: Time Inc.
Ed: Joel Dreyfuss. **Description:** Information from the Consumer Electronics Show held each year in Las Vegas tell that the use of high technology in the home has extended into the creation of the home office.

42716 ■ "Restored 1948 warehouse home to studio, architects" in *Business First Columbus* **(Vol. 18, No. 26, Febr)**
Pub: Business First Columbus, Inc.
Ed: Lori Murray. **Description:** Architects show how they designed a business and home to fit a perfect balance.

42717 ■ "Rich in Tradition" in *Home Business* **(Vol. 12, March/April 2005, No. 2, pp. 63)**
Pub: Home Business Magazine
Ed: Sandy Larson. **Description:** Profile of Michele Ogden, who creates heirloom-type keepsakes for families from her home.

42718 ■ "Right at Home with Telecommuting" in *Business Week* **(No. 3761, December 10, 2001, pp. SB4)**
Pub: McGraw-Hill Inc.
Description: According to a survey of small business executives, conducted by Sales & Marketing Management, 86 percent believe that a sales staff can work as productively from home as in the office.

42719 ■ *Save $2000 to $8000 in Taxes with a Home-Based Business*
Pub: TKG Publishing
Ed: Greco Garcia. **Released:** February 2007. **Price:** $16.99. **Description:** Tax advice for a home-based business is given.

42720 ■ *Secrets to Running a Successful Business*
Ed: Jeanette L. Rosenberg. **Released:** 1994. **Price:** $19.95. **Description:** This book contains information on building a successful small business or home-based business. It covers all facets of business development, including the creation of a business plan, customer satisfaction, communication skills, goal setting, and time management. The information is based on interviews with CEOs and other successful business owners, as well as the author's own experience in the field of business advertising.

42721 ■ "Shock Treatment" in *My Business* **(April/May 2002, pp. 46)**
Pub: My Business Magazine
Ed: Joel Ostroff. **Description:** Ways to protect home business equipment from temporary power surges are explored, including surge protectors or protecting an entire house with a meter socket surge arrestor at the electric meter, and indoor and outdoor panel-mounted next to the circuit breaker panel.

42722 ■ "Signing Internet Noncompetes And Working From Home" in *Fortune* **(Vol. 141, No. 5, March 6, 2000, pp. 430)**
Pub: Time Inc.
Ed: Anne Fisher. **Description:** Questions answered by the editor concern signing noncompete contracts, working from home, and job interviews.

42723 ■ "Site Watch for Home Workers" in *Home Office Computing* **(Vol. 18, No. 8, August 2000, pp. 20)**
Pub: Scholastic Inc.
Ed: Cristina Gair, Sonya Donaldson. **Description:** Web sites offering services to home based workers, including financenter.com, midnightmac.com, fatbrain.com, and webentrepreneurs.com are profiled.

42724 ■ "Small Office/Home Office" in *Hispanic Business* **(Vol. 22, No. 1/2, January/February, pp. 92)**
Pub: Hispanic Business
Description: The feature is designed to provide emerging entrepreneurs with practical tips for operating a small or home office. Home-based business insurance, business licensing, and next-generation scanners are discussed.

42725 ■ "The Spirit of Independence" in *Home Office Computing* **(Vol. 18, No. 7, July 2000, pp. 42)**
Pub: Scholastic Inc.
Ed: Dave Johnson. **Description:** An annotated list of 76 home-office Web site-based resources is presented. Categories include the following: Application Service Providers (ASP), finding clients, your business, your business plans, communications, education, finance/banking, finance/taxes, government, home networking, home office, Internet, legal, marketing, mobile, online storage, online support, reference library, shipping, shopping, telecommuting, tools, travel, and bookmarks.

42726 ■ "Spy Moms" in *Home Business* **(Vol. 12, October 2005, No. 5, pp. 92)**
Pub: Home Business Magazine
Ed: Sandy Larson. **Description:** Profile of private investigators, Mollie Carman and Valerie Agosta, who run a private investigation firm from their homes in Boise, Idaho.

42727 ■ *Start and Run a Profitable Home-Based Business*
Pub: Self-Counsel Press, Inc.
Ed: Edna Sheedy. **Released:** 1994, second edition (print); 1995 (audiocassette). **Price:** $12.95 (paper); $16.95 (audiocassette).

42728 ■ "Street Smarts: Ya Gotta Love It" in *Inc.* **(November 1, 2003)**
Pub: Gruner & Jahr USA Publishing
Ed: Norm Brodsky. **Description:** Bobby and Helene Stone believe heartfelt enthusiasm can help create a successful business. The Stones run Data-Link Associates out of their basement, selling a range of computer supplies, from magnetic media to PC cleaning kits from their basement, and employ 6 people. The company reports $2.6 million in sales.

42729 ■ "Stretching Room" in *Home Office Computing* **(Vol. 18, No. 10, October 2000, pp. 42)**
Pub: Scholastic Inc.
Ed: Lisa Kanarek. **Description:** A description of how Georgia's Creations' principal, Georgia Cox, used her design skills to create a two-story home office in the middle of her three-level house. Unique features of the home office, analysis of her business and computer hardware and software used in the business are presented.

42730 ■ "Tap Into the Corporate LAN" in *Home Office Computing* **(Vol. 18, No. 9, September 2000, pp. 79)**
Pub: Scholastic Inc.
Ed: Wayne Kawamoto. **Description:** Technologies for accessing office LANs from home are discussed.

42731 ■ "Tapping Foreign Markets" in *Home Office Computing* **(Vol. 18, No. 10, October 2000, pp. 18)**
Pub: Scholastic Inc.
Ed: Sonya Donaldson. **Description:** Small and home-based businesses are doing big business abroad. According to a recent study by the National Association for the Self-Employed, or NASE, more than 22 percent of its members have sold goods or services abroad, while one in 10 focuses solely on selling abroad. And of those who don't sell goods overseas, 20 percent said they would like to.

42732 ■ "Tax Breaks: Don't Forget Your Home Office" in *Business Week* **(No. 3666, January 31, 2000, pp. 124E4)**
Pub: McGraw-Hill, Inc.

Description: Home office deductions are probably the most overlooked federal income tax deduction. The article contains information to help home businesses take advantage of the much needed tax breaks they are entitled to.

42733 ■ "Taxing Matters" in *Inc.* **(December 1999, pp. 92)**
Pub: The Goldhirsh Group
Description: Tax deductions for home-based businesses are discussed.

42734 ■ "Tech Jobs Look Up" in *Crain's Detroit Business* **(Vol. 22, September 25-October 1, 2006, No. 39, pp. 1, 39)**
Pub: Crain Communications Inc. - Detroit
Ed: Andrew Dietderich. **Description:** New Products and recent retirements have resulted in a shortage of Information Technology and other high tech areas. Significant percentage of growth is in Southeastern Michigan.

42735 ■ *Telecom Made Easy: Money-Saving, Profit-Building Solutions for Home Businesses, Telecommuters & Small Organizations*
Pub: Aegis Publishing Group, Ltd.
Ed: June Langhoff; foreward by Terri Lonier. **Released:** 3rd ed. 1998. **Price:** $19.95. **Description:** Basic, easy to understand information about the latest telephone products and services for the small business and home office markets. Learn how to benefit from the latest technology, including basic wiring options, answering devices, and online services.

42736 ■ *The Telecommuter's Advisor: Working in the Fast Lane*
Pub: Aegis Publishing Group, Ltd.
Ed: June Langhoff. **Released:** 1996. **Price:** $14.95. **Description:** Provides valuable insights and strategies for working effectively from any remote location. Includes tips and suggestions for setting up a home office; improving productivity by utilizing the latest communications equipment; and handling e-mail accounts.

42737 ■ "Telework Lowers Office Expense" in *Home Office Computing* **(Vol. 19, No. 1, January 2001, pp. 18)**
Pub: Scholastic Inc.
Ed: Jeffery D. Zbar. **Description:** All the attention given to the human resources benefits of telework - increased employee satisfaction and enhanced recruitment, retention, and flexibility - ignores another significant upside of moving workers out of the corporate office: decreased real estate costs.

42738 ■ *The Ten Best Opportunities for Starting a Home Business Today*
Pub: Live Oak Publications
Ed: Reed Glenn and New Careers Center, Inc. staff. **Released:** 1993. **Price:** $14.95. **Description:** Provides information on ten home business opportunities that can be started with little start-up money.

42739 ■ "Time To Hire" in *Home Office Computing* **(Vol. 18, No. 9, September 2000, pp. 52)**
Pub: Scholastic Inc.
Ed: Todd W. Carter. **Description:** Many home-based businesses face the issue of when and whether to hire help. Questions regarding recruiting and hiring qualified workers for the home business are answered.

42740 ■ "Tips & Trends" in *Small Business Opportunities* **(Vol. 17, September 2005, No. 5, pp. 14)**
Pub: Harris Publications Inc.
Description: Tips and trends important to small business include the addition of a coffeemaker that also makes soup, tea or cocoa; paper shredders; headsets; a sales resource guide for retailers; information for the Federal Citizen Information Center; and Creative Colors, the franchise offering mobile equipment to home-based businesses.

42741 ■ "Top 25 Overlooked Tax Deductions" in *Home Business* (Vol. 12, March/April 2005, No. 2, pp. 78)
Pub: Home Business Magazine
Description: The top 25 most-overlooked tax deductions for small businesses are listed.

42742 ■ "Tuning In to Telework" in *Home Office Computing* (Vol. 18, No. 12, December 2000, pp. 107)
Pub: Scholastic Inc.
Ed: Marilyn Zelinsky Syarto. **Description:** Telecommuting has reached even radio broadcasters. This article looks at one telecommuter who works for a New York radio station, but works out of his home in Connecticut. He maintains that it is important to still go into the office a few times a week and to have reliable technology.

42743 ■ "Twice as Nice" in *Home Office Computing* (Vol. 18, No. 8, August 2000, pp. 40)
Pub: Scholastic Inc.
Ed: Dan Costa. **Description:** Reasons are listed for adding a second line to a home office.

42744 ■ *203 Home-Based Businesses That Will Make You Rich*
Pub: Prima Publishing
Ed: Tyler G. Hicks. **Released:** 1998. **Price:** $14.95.

42745 ■ "2001 : A Home Office Odyssey" in *Home Office Computing* (Vol. 18, No. 9, September 2000, pp. 44)
Pub: Scholastic Inc.
Ed: David Haskin. **Description:** A guide to upcoming products and technologies of interest to home office users is presented.

42746 ■ "Unforgettable as Usual" in *Home Business* (Vol. 12, October 2005, No. 5, pp. 36, 100)
Pub: Home Business Magazine
Ed: Sandy Larson. **Description:** Patricia Fripp, an award-winning keynote speaker and sales trainer, explains ways to make each sales presentation unforgettable. The twelve biggest mistakes made by salespeople when making presentations are included.

42747 ■ "Use Webcasting to Grow Your Home Business" in *Home Business* (Vol. 12, March/April 2005, No. 2, pp. 36, 38, 60-61)
Pub: Home Business Magazine
Ed: Dr. Jeffrey Lant. **Description:** Online marketing is a good way for a home business to increase sales. Webcasting allows entrepreneurs to speak live to people through a computer.

42748 ■ "Virtual Company Achieves Actual Savings" in *Home Business* (Vol. 12, March/April 2005, No. 2, pp. 48)
Pub: Home Business Magazine
Ed: Sandy Larson. **Description:** Profile of Karlin Sloan, who runs her executive coaching firm from her home using a telecommuting program.

42749 ■ "VPNs Go Mainstream" in *Home Office Computing* (Vol. 18, No. 12, December 2000, pp. 16)
Pub: Scholastic Inc.
Ed: Mark Kakkuri. **Description:** As more firms tire of costly dial-in equipment and toll-free lines, or even costlier leased-line wide area networks, virtual private networks (VPNs) are becoming the hottest trends in telework technology.

42750 ■ "W. Alabama a Sweet Home - and Office - for Retailers" in *Houston Business Journal* (Vol. 34, No. 16, August 29, 2003, pp. 2)
Pub: American City Business Journals
Ed: Nancy Sarnoff. **Description:** Several retailers on West Alabama in Houston, Texas are establishing their shops on the ground floor, or next door to, their homes.

42751 ■ "Wearing Her Work on Her Sleeve" in *Home Business* (Vol. 13, January/February 2006, No. 1, pp. 80)
Pub: Home Business Magazine
Ed: Sandy Larson. **Description:** Profile of Eileen Parzek who sells work-at-home related merchandise including t-shirts, caps, mugs, mouse pads, and clocks.

42752 ■ "Web-based Accounting" in *Home Office Computing* (Vol. 18, No. 11, November 2000, pp. 71)
Pub: Scholastic Inc.
Ed: Wayne Kawamoto. **Description:** A software buyer's guide featuring integrated accounting software packages and Web-based services of value to the home office user. Among the featured products are BAport Accounting from BAport, the eLedger 2.0 application from Application Service Provider (ASP) eLedger, Peachtree Software's ePeachtree 2.0, Intacct, an online service that offers general ledger, accounts payable, accounts receivable, and human resources functions, NetLedger 4.0, and Bizfinity.

42753 ■ "Web.Preneuring" in *Small Business Opportunities* (Vol. 17, November 2005, No. 6, pp. 90, 94)
Pub: Harris Publications Inc.
Ed: Chuck Green. **Description:** Profile of Scott Kolbe and Mike Stout, entrepreneurs who started Icon Digital Design in a basement. The partners base their success on being graphic designers with strong work ethics.

42754 ■ "What Price Time?" in *Home Office Computing* (Vol. 18, No. 10, October 2000, pp. 14)
Pub: Scholastic Inc.
Ed: William Van Winkle. **Description:** A list of new companies bringing service providers and users together to help save time is provided.

42755 ■ "What To Do When Your Client Declares Bankruptcy" in *Home Business* (Vol. 13, January/February 2006, No. 1, pp. 76)
Pub: Home Business Magazine
Ed: Kurt English, Esq. **Description:** In a slow economy, small and home-based businesses should collect money in advance from clients whenever possible. Legal steps to take when accounts become delinquent are discussed.

42756 ■ "What's your problem?" in *Entrepreneur* (Vol. 30, No. 10, October 2002, pp. 146)
Pub: Entrepreneur Media Inc.
Description: The owner of a home-based residential design firm is offered advice to market the business, including the use of The Blue Book of Building and Construction which covers contractors nationwide.

42757 ■ "What's Your Problem?" in *Entrepreneur* (Vol. 31, No. 11, November 2003, pp. 124)
Pub: Entrepreneur Media, Inc.
Ed: Paul Edwards, Sarah Edwards. **Description:** Tax benefits of running a home-based business are investigated.

42758 ■ "What's Your Problem? When to Tell Customers You Work From Your Home" in *Entrepreneur* (Vol. 32, December 2004, No. 12, pp. 104)
Pub: Entrepreneur Media Inc.
Description: Five factors to consider before telling a customer you work from a home-based business are explored.

42759 ■ "When Your Job Really Makes You Sick" in *Black Enterprise* (Vol. 34, No. 5, December 2003, pp. 63)
Pub: Earl Graves Publishing Co.
Ed: Lee Anna Jackson. **Description:** Profile of Erica Benson, owner of A-Solution, her home-based consulting service offering job coaching among professional and business services.

42760 ■ "When Your Job Really Makes You Sick: Why You Need to Develop a High Adversity Quotient" in *Black Enterprise* (Vol. 34, December 2003)
Pub: Earl Graves Publishing Co.
Ed: Lee Anna Jackson. **Description:** Profile of Erica Benson, owner of A-Solution, her home-based consulting service offering job coaching among professional and business services.

42761 ■ "When You're no Longer Home Alone" in *Inc.* (December 1999, pp. 92)
Pub: The Goldhirsh Group
Description: An overview of the legal issues regarding hiring employees for home-based business.

42762 ■ "Why Do So Many Salespeople Fail to Get It?" in *Home Business* (Vol. 12, March/April 2005, No. 2, pp. 54)
Pub: Home Business Magazine
Ed: Bill Brooks. **Description:** The importance for home-based business owners to understand the keys to successful selling is stressed.

42763 ■ "Window of Opportunity" in *Small Business Opportunities* (Summer 2005)
Pub: Harris Publications Inc.
Description: Profile of Philip Bregstone, founder of Dr. Glass, a window washing business that can be run as a home-based business.

42764 ■ "Wireless Web Boom" in *Home Office Computing* (Vol. 18, No. 11, November 2000, pp. 37)
Pub: Scholastic Inc.
Ed: Dan Costa. **Description:** Thanks in part to the emergence of WAP, wireless Web services are poised to take off in the business world. WAP-based applications are expected to dramatically increase the efficiency of home-based workers, according to Joseph Fung, chief technology officer of Blueflame, a Hackensack, New Jersey-based wireless technology consulting firm. More than any other application, e-mail access is driving the wireless boom. WAP will also be used to bring Internet Protocol-based instant messaging to wireless devices.

42765 ■ "The Work-At-Home Diaries" in *Inc.* (February 1, 2002)
Pub: Inc. Magazine
Ed: Joseph Rosenbloom. **Description:** Chronicle of what happened when the author tried to take advantage of an advertised work-at-home money-making opportunity. At the end of nearly two months of work, Rosenbloom calculated that instead of earning the $2,400 promised in the advertising, he was out $261.55.

42766 ■ "The Work-at-Home Hook" in *Home Office Computing* (Vol. 18, No. 11, November 2000, pp. 92)
Pub: Scholastic Inc.
Ed: Lisa Roberts. **Description:** Ways in which companies are using telework to recruit and retain employees is discussed.

42767 ■ "Work-At-Home Scheme" in *Black Enterprise* (Vol. 35, October 2004, No. 3, pp. 200)
Pub: Earl G. Graves Publishing Co. Inc.
Ed: Tanisha A. Sykes. **Description:** Before committing to a work-at-home operation, it is important to investigate the company by requesting written materials by mail which include product and service information and information about the company. Information to file a complaint with the Federal Trade Commission is provided.

42768 ■ *Work From Home Jobs Directory*
Pub: Lulu.com
Ed: Debra Mundell. **Released:** May 2006. **Price:** $18.00. **Description:** Resources for starting and growing a home-based business are listed.

42769 ■ "Work at Home? First, Get Real" in *Business Week* **(No. 3699, September 18, 2000, pp. 112)**
Pub: McGraw-Hill, Inc.
Description: The article lists 10 tips for the prospective at-home working parent.

42770 ■ "Work at Home-More bandwidth means better performance for an important business tool called a virtual private network" in *PC Magazine*
Pub: Ziff-Davis Publishing Company
Ed: Frank J. Derfler, Jr. **Description:** Virtual private network (VPN) solutions are reviewed.

42771 ■ "Workers Simply Want to Be Organized" in *Home Office Computing* **(Vol. 18, No. 12, December 2000, pp. 23)**
Pub: Scholastic Inc.
Ed: Marilyn Zelinsky Syarto. **Description:** FileMaker's database software is helping home-based workers get organized with digital file cabinets.

42772 ■ *Working from Home: Everything You Need to Know about Living and Working Under the Same Roof*
Pub: Jeremy P. Tarcher Inc.
Ed: Paul and Sarah Edwards. **Released:** Third edition, 1990. **Price:** $15.95. **Description:** Provides information on home-based businesses, such as making the home professional, zoning and licensing, marketing, and the effects of tax reform.

42773 ■ "Workspace Wonders" in *Small Business Opportunities* **(Vol. 16, No. 2, March 2004, pp. 80)**
Pub: Harris Publications, Inc.
Description: Affordable and stylish products to equip a home office are presented by TOPDEQ (Tomorrow's Office Products Delivered Extremely Quickly), whose U.S. office is located in Cranbury, New Jersey. TOPDEQ offers a 120-page catalog of European designed office and home furnishings now available in the U.S.

42774 ■ "Write Stuff" in *Crain's New York Business* **(Vol. 23, January 15, 2007, No. 3, pp. 47)**
Pub: Crain Communications, Inc.
Ed: Elisabeth Butler. **Description:** Profile of Karen Levy, a calligrapher, and her company Writer's Camp, a business that inscribes place cards, invitations and menus for individual clients as well as large companies including Saks Fifth Avenue and J.P. Morgan Chase.

TRADE PERIODICALS

42775 ■ *At-Home Dad*
Pub: Peter Baylies
Contact: Peter Baylies, Editor & Publisher
Released: Monthly. **Price:** $15, U.S.; $18, Canada; $24, elsewhere. **Description:** Promotes the concept of fathers staying home to raise the children. Includes stories from at-home-dads, home business stories, recipes, lists of resources, and playgroups to join. Recurring features include letters to the editor, interviews, news of research, book reviews, notices of publications available, and a column titled Dr. Bob.

42776 ■ *Home-Based Working Moms*
Pub: Home-Based Working Moms
Contact: Lesley Spencer
Ed: Lesley Spencer, Editor, lesley@hbwm.com. **Released:** Monthly. **Price:** $49; $54, Canada; $65, other countries. **Description:** Directed toward parents working at home and those interested in doing so. Designed to provide support, networking, and information related to working at home with children. Recurring features include interviews, job listings, marketing tips, and a column titled Home Business Ideas.

42777 ■ *The Home Business Report*
Pub: The Kerner Group Inc.

Ed: Rick Kerner, Editor. **Released:** Monthly. **Description:** Provides information on how to operate a home-based business or work from home. Features real life success stories, "how-to" articles on marketing, and strategies to keep focused on goals. Recurring features include letters to the editor, interviews, news of research, job listings, book reviews, and notices of publications available.

42778 ■ *Our Place*
Pub: Home-Based Working Moms
Contact: Lesley Spencer
Ed: Lesley Spencer, Editor, lesley@hbwm.com. **Released:** Biweekly, 10/year. **Price:** $49, U.S.; $54, Canada; $65, elsewhere. **Description:** Advocates home employment and home businesses to allow parents more time with their children. Offers ideas, marketing tips, member profiles to promote successful employment at home. Recurring features include interviews, job listings, and book reviews.

42779 ■ *Working Moms & Dads Magazine*
Pub: Corporate Marketing & Publishing
Ed: Patrick McGuire, Editor. **Released:** Monthly. **Description:** Contains national and local news on parenting, childcare, education, and work issues. For professional and working parents.

VIDEOCASSETTES/ AUDIOCASSETTES

42780 ■ *Alternate Work Sites: At Home, at Work*
Encyclopedia Britannica
331 N. LaSalle St.
Chicago, IL 60610
Ph:(312)347-7159
Free: 800-323-1229
Fax: (312)294-2104
URL: http://www.britannica.com
Released: 1988. **Price:** $395.00. **Description:** This film features Control Data Corporation of Minneapolis and workers in an Alpine Swiss village showing how to create a work site. **Availability:** VHS; 3/4U.

42781 ■ *American Institute of Small Business: Setting Up a Home-Based Business*
American Institute of Small Business (AISB)
7515 Wayzata Blvd., Ste. 126
Minneapolis, MN 55426
Ph:(612)545-7001
Free: 800-328-2906
Fax: (612)545-7020
Co. E-mail: AISBOFMN@AOL.COM
URL: http://www.accessil.com/aisb
Released: 199?. **Price:** $69.95. **Description:** Step-by-step guide to operating a business out of your home. **Availability:** VHS.

42782 ■ *Inc. Magazine Business Success Programs*
Cambridge Educational
c/o Films Media Group
PO Box 2053
Princeton, NJ 08843-2053
Free: 800-257-5126
Fax: (609)671-0266
Co. E-mail: custserve@filmsmediagroup.com
URL: http://www.cambridgeol.com
Released: 1987. **Price:** $99.95. **Description:** These four programs contain a step-by-step explanation of what must be done to succeed in business. **Availability:** VHS; CC.

TRADE SHOWS AND CONVENTIONS

42783 ■ National Association of Home Based Businesses Convention
National Association of Home Based Businesses
PO Box 30220
Baltimore, MD 21270

Ph:(410)581-1373
Fax: (410)356-1672
Co. E-mail: nahbb@msn.com
URL: http://www.usahomebusiness.com
Released: Annual. **Audience:** Trade buyers and general public. **Principal Exhibits:** Home based business products and services, support associations, trade supplies, and related equipment.

CONSULTANTS

42784 ■ Joanne H. Pratt Associates
3520 Routh St.
Dallas, TX 75219-4730
Ph:(214)528-6540
Fax: (214)528-5730
Co. E-mail: joannepratt@post.harvard.edu
URL: http://www.joannepratt.com

E-mail: joannepratt@post.harvard.edu
Scope: Performs market research and advising on the virtual office, including telecommuting and home-based businesses. Helps organizations implement teleworking and telecommuting. Recent emphasis on related topics such as e-commerce and personnel productivity. Also helps employees obtain permission to telework. Serves private industries as well as government agencies worldwide. **Publications:** "The Impact of Location on Net Income: A Comparison of Homebased and Non-homebased Sole Proprietors," 2006; "Telework: The Latest Figures and what they Mean," 2005; "Teleworking Comes of Age with Broadband," Apr, 2003; "Telework Trends in the United States," 2003; "Strategies for Small Business Success," 2002; "Teleworkers, Trips and Telecommunications: Technology drives telework-but does it reduce trips?," 2002; "Telework and Society-Implications for Corporate and Societal Cultures, in Telework: The New Workplace of the 21st Century," Oct, 2000. **Seminars:** The Connected Home: Paradise or Poison; Equipping for Telework Success; Myths and Realities of Working at Home; Using Telemanagement to Increase Staff Productivity; Meet Your Home Office Customers; Telecommuting: What is it? Will it Work for Me?; Telemanaging a Remote Workforce.

FRANCHISES AND BUSINESS OPPORTUNITIES

42785 ■ AIS Media
130 Fifth Ave., 10th Fl.
New York, NY 10011-4399
Ph:(212)242-4399
Description: Internet services and consulting business. **Equity Capital Needed:** $19,995-$29,995 total investment; $19,995 cash required. **Franchise Fee:** None. **Royalty Fee:** None. **Training:** Yes.

42786 ■ Asheville Note Brokers
Asheville Note Brokers
PO Box 391
Skyland, NC 28776
Ph:(828)299-8568
Fax: 800-731-5073
No. of Franchise Units: 3. **No. of Company-Owned Units:** 1. **Founded:** 1994. **Description:** Buy and sell financial notes. **Equity Capital Needed:** Basic home office. **Franchise Fee:** $3,600. **Financial Assistance:** Yes. **Training:** Yes.

42787 ■ Brazilian Springs Bottled Water
Ecostreams International
130 Fifth Ave., 10th Fl.
New York, NY 10011-4399
Ph:(212)242-4399
Description: Distribution of Brazilian Springs Bottled Water, the purest, healthiest, and first eco-friendly water. Ecostreams International is exclusively licensed to import and distribute Brazilian Springs' unique water around the world. We are already sold in many Walgreens and Whole Food Stores. **Equity Capital Needed:** $10,000 cash required. **Training:** Complete training and support from Ecostreams International.

42788 ■ Business Alliance Inc.
130 Fifth Ave., 10th Fl.
New York, NY 10011-4399
Ph:(212)242-4399
Description: Home-based business franchise consultant, helping others find the ideal business. No previous business ownership experience is necessary. **Equity Capital Needed:** $20,000-$24,999 cash required. **Managerial Assistance:** Offers consultants a private website with all the forms and information, multiple conference calls each week, where consultants can learn more about the franchise concepts in their portfolio, plus the home office of the Business Alliance does all the negotiating with franchisors, so consultants can focus on matching prospective with franchisees. **Training:** Provides training and ongoing support.

42789 ■ Celsius Tannery
Celsius Franchising, Inc.
12142A State Line Rd.
Leawood, KS 66209
Free: 800-816-5158
Fax: (913)451-7001
URL: http://www.celsiustannery.com
No. of Franchise Units: 19. **No. of Company-Owned Units:** 4. **Founded:** 1995. **Franchised:** 2000. **Description:** Indoor tanning franchise. **Equity Capital Needed:** Franchise $300,000-$598,000; area development $600,000 and up. **Franchise Fee:** $20,000-$35,000. **Financial Assistance:** Third party financing. **Training:** Offers professional training.

42790 ■ Children's Technology Workshop
109 Vanderhoof Ave., Ste. 101A
Toronto, ON, Canada M4G 2H7
Ph:(416)425-2289
Free: (866)704-2267
Fax: (647)439-0890
Co. E-mail: len@ctworkshop.com
URL: http://www.ctworkshop.com
No. of Franchise Units: 39. **No. of Company-Owned Units:** 1. **Founded:** 1997. **Franchised:** 2004. **Description:** Focused on the development and delivery of hands-on, applied-technology curriculum. We believe that technology can empower all children to explore, invent and to be creative using the right applications with the right direction. Offers a variety of programs, including after school, camp, academic and group workshops. Programs are divided by age and are available in different formats to meet scheduling needs of parents and group facilitators. Opportunities are available to qualified applicants who are interested in investing in home based, single unit and area development agreements. **Equity Capital Needed:** $100,000. **Franchise Fee:** $5,000-$25,000. **Training:** 5 days at head office in Toronto.

42791 ■ CMIT Solutions
537 Woodward St., No. D
Austin, TX 78704-7324
Ph:(512)477-6667
Free: 800-710-2648
Fax: (512)692-3711
Co. E-mail: sara@cmit.biz
URL: http://www.cmitsolutions.com
No. of Franchise Units: 125. **Founded:** 1994. **Franchised:** 1998. **Description:** Offers IT service and computer support to small businesses. Franchise can be home-based, as we service the client at their place of business. **Equity Capital Needed:** $100,000-$150,000. **Franchise Fee:** $39,500. **Royalty Fee:** 6%. **Financial Assistance:** No. **Training:** Offers 1 week training.

42792 ■ DEI Franchising Systems
888 7th Ave., 9th Fl.
New York, NY 101006
Ph:(212)581-7390
Free: 800-224-2140
Co. E-mail: franchise@dei-sales.com
URL: http://www.dei-sales.com
No. of Franchise Units: 31. **No. of Company-Owned Units:** 1. **Founded:** 1979. **Franchised:** 2003. **Description:** Sales training industry. **Equity Capital Needed:** $60,000-$75,000. **Franchise Fee:** $50,000.

Royalty Fee: 7%. **Financial Assistance:** No. **Training:** Offers 2 weeks home-based training and 2 weeks at headquarters with ongoing support.

42793 ■ DNA Services of America
130 Fifth Ave., 10th Fl.
New York, NY 10011-4399
Ph:(212)242-4399
Description: Own a high-demand, innovative business that serves the growing needs of Americans by offering members of your community peace of mind through evidence provided by DNA identification test results for paternity, family relationship establishment, infidelity testing and forensic DNA. **Equity Capital Needed:** $39,150-$101,400 total investment; $12,500 cash required. **Training:** Offers a complete, proven business system, ongoing support, and thorough training.

42794 ■ The Drug Test Consultant
130 Fifth Ave., 10th Fl.
New York, NY 10011-4399
Ph:(212)242-4399
Description: Home drug testing. **Equity Capital Needed:** $2,995 total investment; $2,995 cash required. **Training:** Provides all the training, mentoring and written materials.

42795 ■ Global Broker Training Systems Inc.
130 Fifth Ave., 10th Fl.
New York, NY 10011-4399
Ph:(212)242-4399
Description: Offer clients a complete range of business financing and equipment leasing services. **Equity Capital Needed:** $19,950 total investment. **Financial Assistance:** Upon completing training program, supplied with a list of lenders that you are approved to do business with. **Managerial Assistance:** Manuals, customized stationery package and website. **Training:** Provides 3 days of intensive training in our New York offices and ongoing support.

42796 ■ Health Career Agents
12977 North Forty Dr., Ste. 100
St. Louis, MO 63141
Ph:(314)628-9893
Free: 800-209-7197
Fax: (314)523-1362
Co. E-mail: info@healthcareeragents.com
URL: http://www.healthcareeragents.com
Description: Healthcare recruiting business. **Equity Capital Needed:** $49,900. **Financial Assistance:** Internal financing up to 40%. **Managerial Assistance:** Technology solutions (worth more than $20,000) including research software, email tracking tools, candidate management software, and healthcare news clipping software, website development, logo design, starter marketing material and a PC with all software pre-loaded. **Training:** Offers 30 days of remote training where owners learn the healthcare recruiting process, educated on terms, specialties and procedures and how to use the various software tools, 2 days on-site, detailed 90 day start-up plan, 4 days of hands-on instruction at training offices with experienced recruiters, and ongoing healthcare recruiting support and assistance in making placements for the life of your business.

42797 ■ The Homesteader
Homesteader Enterprises, Inc.
130 Fifth Ave.
New York, NY 10011-4399
Ph:(212)242-8000
Founded: 1990. **Description:** Home-based monthly newspaper directly mailed to new homeowners. **Equity Capital Needed:** Less than $10,000. **Franchise Fee:** $5,000-$25,000. **Royalty Fee:** 10%. **Managerial Assistance:** Training CDs, email, and phone support are included. **Training:** Offers 2 days classroom training in Concord, Massachusetts.

42798 ■ Interiors by Decorating Den
8659 Commerce Dr.
Easton, MD 21601
Ph:(410)822-9001
Free: 800-DEC-DENS
Fax: (410)820-5131

Co. E-mail: decden@decoratingden.com
URL: http://www.decoratingden.com
No. of Franchise Units: 501. **Founded:** 1969. **Franchised:** 1970. **Description:** Interiors by Decorating is one of the oldest, international, shop-at-home interior decorating franchises in the world. Our company-trained interior decorators bring 1000's of samples including window coverings, wall coverings, floor coverings, furniture & accessories to their customer's home in our uniquely equipped ColorVan. Special business features include: home-based, marketing systems, business systems, training, support, and complete sampling. **Equity Capital Needed:** $20,000. **Franchise Fee:** $24,900. **Financial Assistance:** Financing available for a portion of franchise fee to those who qualify. **Training:** Training combines classroom work, home study, meetings, seminars and on-the-job experience including working with an experienced interior decorator. Secondary, advanced and graduate certification training continue throughout the franchise owner's career with Interiors by Decorating Den.

42799 ■ Medical Staffing Consultants (MSC)
130 Fifth Ave., 10th Fl.
New York, NY 10011-4399
Ph:(212)242-4399
Description: Medical staffing company. **Equity Capital Needed:** $20,000-$60,000 total investment. **Royalty Fee:** None. **Financial Assistance:** Assists with financing. **Managerial Assistance:** Provides assistance with insurance, licensure and registration. **Training:** Provides on-site, turn-key training programs and support services.

42800 ■ Mr. Plant
1106 2nd St.
Encinitas, CA 92024
Free: 888-677-5268
Fax: (760)295-5629
Co. E-mail: mcplant@adnc.com
URL: http://www.mrplant.com
No. of Franchise Units: 40. **No. of Company-Owned Units:** 2. **Founded:** 1980. **Franchised:** 1990. **Description:** provides plants, trees and containers for commercial and residential use. **Equity Capital Needed:** $18,500-$25,000. **Franchise Fee:** $12,500. **Royalty Fee:** Varies. **Financial Assistance:** No. **Training:** Provides 5 days training at headquarters, home study course with ongoing support.

42801 ■ The Original Basket Boutique
363 Sioux Rd., Ste. 16
Sherwood Park, AB, Canada T8A 4W7
Ph:(780)416-2530
Fax: (780)416-2531
Co. E-mail: info@originalbasketboutique.com
URL: http://www.originalbasketboutique.com
No. of Franchise Units: 36. **Founded:** 1989. **Franchised:** 1989. **Description:** The Original Basket Boutique, Canada's exclusive custom gift basket franchise **Equity Capital Needed:** $27,000. **Franchise Fee:** $20,000. **Training:** Offers 3 days training.

42802 ■ Par-T-Perfect Party Planners
T-20 1733 Bowen Bay Rd.
Bowen Island, BC, Canada V0N 1G0
Ph:(604)947-0274
Co. E-mail: michellegib@shaw.ca
URL: http://www.par-t-perfect.com
No. of Franchise Units: 20. **Founded:** 1988. **Franchised:** 2001. **Description:** Par-T-Perfect is a unique children's party and event service. A great home-based business opportunity! **Equity Capital Needed:** $29,000-$40,000. **Franchise Fee:** $24,500. **Financial Assistance:** No. **Training:** 2 weeks and ongoing.

42803 ■ SeaMaster Cruises
Carlson Travel Franchise Group
130 Fifth Ave., 10th Fl.
New York, NY 10011-4399
Ph:(212)242-4399
Description: Home-based cruise travel agency. **Equity Capital Needed:** $9,500. **Franchise Fee:** $9,500. **Training:** Provides extensive new agent training and a detailed introduction to our programs and services conducted by our Education and Training team. Thereafter, the team works year-round to host seminars, conduct net-conferencing training, plan regional and national meetings and training.

42804 ■ Suburban Cylinder Express
Suburban Franchising, Inc.
240 Rte. 10 W
Whippany, NJ 07981
Ph:(770)518-9948
Free: (866)218-7026
Co. E-mail: dzabkar@suburbanpropane.com
URL: http://www.suburbancylinderexpress.com
No. of Company-Owned Units: 21. **Founded:** 2001.
Franchised: 2002. **Description:** The franchise is a
home-based business opportunity center. It provides
propane cylinders to residential and commercial customers. **Equity Capital Needed:** $64,000-$171,400.
Franchise Fee: $34,900. **Financial Assistance:**
Commercial loans for delivery vehicle. **Training:** Provides initial start-up training, ongoing business consultation, customized business software, scheduling and
route optimization software, national phone customer
sales center, technology help desk, a consumer website, brochures, flyers, coupons and other direct mail
and mass marketing tools and materials.

42805 ■ TruePresence
130 Fifth Ave., 10th Fl.
New York, NY 10011-4399
Ph:(212)242-4399
Founded: 1995. **Description:** Home-based business
providing web services to small and medium size businesses. Services include website design, application
development, content management, e-commerce solutions, search marketing, email marketing, web advertising, site hosting and technical support. **Equity
Capital Needed:** $43,250-$106,300. **Franchise Fee:**
$29,900. **Managerial Assistance:** Provides website
development, online marketing and hosting services.
Training: Offers comprehensive training and round
the clock support.

42806 ■ Two Blonds & A Brunette Gift Co.
56 Scarborough Rd.
Toronto, ON, Canada M4E 3M5
Ph:(416)662-6276
Fax: (416)693-6229
Co. E-mail: lauramcdonald@twoandb.com
URL: http://www.twoblondsandabrunettegiftco.com

No. of Franchise Units: 7. **Founded:** 2002. **Franchised:** 2006. **Description:** Initial home-based gift-
giving business. **Equity Capital Needed:** None initially. **Franchise Fee:** $15,000-$40,000, includes
inventory, training and materials. **Training:** 1 weekend; airfare and hotel paid.

42807 ■ Worldwide Merchandise
130 Fifth Ave., 10th Fl.
New York, NY 10011-4399
Ph:(212)242-4399
Description: Business of wholesaling with over 7 different marketing programs to wholesale merchandise
including Internet sales from Cyberstore, rack merchandising, mail order, flea markets, wholesaling to
retail stores, catalog sales and general merchandising. **Equity Capital Needed:** $140.00-$900.00. **Managerial Assistance:** Custom designed website
featuring your merchandise displayed worldwide, full
color catalogs imprinted with your company name.
Training: Provides unlimited consultation and assistance from support staff.

ASSOCIATIONS AND OTHER ORGANIZATIONS

42808 ■ ASTD
Box 1443
1640 King St.
Alexandria, VA 22313-2043
Ph:(703)683-8100
Free: 800-628-2783
Fax: (703)683-8103
Co. E-mail: customercare@astd.org
URL: http://www.astd.org
Contact: Tony Bingham, Pres./CEO
Description: Represents workplace learning and performance professionals. **Publications:** *ASTD Buyer's Guide* (annual); *Info-Line: Tips, Tools, and Intelligence for Trainers* (monthly); *T&D Magazine* (monthly).

42809 ■ Canadian Society for Training and Development–Societe Canadienne pour la Formation et le Perfectionnement
720 Spadina Ave., Ste. 315
Toronto, ON, Canada M5S 2T9
Ph:(416)367-5900
Free: (866)257-4275
Fax: (416)367-1642
Co. E-mail: info@cstd.ca
URL: http://www.cstd.ca
Contact: Lynn Johnston, Pres.
Description: Works for the profession of training, workplace learning and human resources development. **Publications:** *Canadian Learning Journal* (semiannual). **Telecommunication Services:** electronic mail, ljohnston@cstd.ca; information service, NetGems.

42810 ■ Human Resource Planning Society
317 Madison Ave., Ste. 1509
New York, NY 10017
Ph:(212)490-6387
Fax: (212)682-6851
Co. E-mail: info@hrps.org
URL: http://www.hrps.org
Contact: Walter J. Cleaver, Pres./CEO
Membership: Human resource planning professionals representing 160 corporations and 3000 individual members, including strategic human resources planning and development specialists, staffing analysts, business planners, line managers, and others who function as business partners in the application of strategic human resource management practices. **Purpose:** Seeks to increase the impact of human resource planning and management on business and organizational performance. Sponsors program of professional development in human resource planning concepts, techniques, and practices. Offers networking opportunities. **Publications:** *Human Resource Planning* (quarterly); *Human Resource Planning Society—Membership Directory* (annual). Also publishes educational materials on best practices.

42811 ■ Human Resources Research Organization
66 Canal Center Plz., Ste. 400
Alexandria, VA 22314
Ph:(703)549-3611
Fax: (703)549-9025
Co. E-mail: network@humrro.org
URL: http://www.humrro.org
Contact: Laurie Wise PhD, Pres.
Description: Behavioral and social science researchers seeking to improve human performance, particularly in organizational settings, through behavioral and social science research, development, consultation and instruction. Promotes research and development to solve specific problems in: training and education; development, refinement, and instruction in the technology of training and education; studies and development of techniques to improve the motivation of personnel in training and on the job; research of leadership and management, and development of leadership programs; criterion development, individual assessment, and program evaluation in training and operating systems; measurement and evaluation of human performance under varying circumstances; organizational development studies, including performance counseling, group decision-making, and factors that affect organizational competence; development of manpower information systems and the application of management science on personnel systems. Encourages use of high technology for instructional purposes by means of computer assisted instruction, interactive video, and computer literacy. Offers technical publication services including data analysis and editorial, word processing, production, and printing services. **Publications:** Bibliography (periodic). Also publishes technical reports and professional papers.

42812 ■ International Personnel Management Association - Canada–L'Association internationale de la gestion du personnel - Canada
14868 41 Ave.
Edmonton, AB, Canada T6H 5N7
Ph:(780)433-0234
Free: (866)433-0234
Fax: (780)433-0295
Co. E-mail: info@ipma-aigp.ca
URL: http://www.ipma-aigp.ca
Contact: Linda Fields, Exec. Dir.
Membership: Human resources professionals employed by public agencies. **Purpose:** Seeks to advance the practice of personnel management. Facilitates ongoing professional development of members; sponsors research and educational programs. **Telecommunication Services:** electronic mail, fields@shaw.ca.

42813 ■ National Association for Industry-Education Cooperation
235 Hendricks Blvd.
Buffalo, NY 14226-3304
Ph:(716)834-7047
Fax: (716)834-7047
Co. E-mail: naiec@pcom.net
URL: http://www2.pcom.net/naiec

Contact: Dr. Donald M. Clark, Pres./CEO
Description: Representatives of business, industry, education, government, labor, and the professions. Fosters industry-education collaboration in continuous school improvement and workforce preparation in order to develop responsive academic and vocational programs which will more effectively serve the needs of both the students and employers as well as further human resources and economic development. Provides technical assistance to schools implementing industry-education councils, high-performance sustainable education systems and business- or industry-sponsored programs. Promotes improved career and entrepreneurship education and supports school-based job placement. Provides staff development programs to improve instruction and curricula and the efficiency and effectiveness of educational management through use of corporate and volunteer services. Acts as national clearinghouse for information on industry involvement in education; serves as liaison between organizations involved in industry-education cooperation, including American Association for Career Education, National Research Center for Career and Technical, and American Society for Training and Development. Conducts research and policy studies. **Publications:** Newsletter (bimonthly).

42814 ■ Public Risk Management Association
500 Montgomery St., Ste. 750
Alexandria, VA 22314
Ph:(703)528-7701
Fax: (703)739-0200
Co. E-mail: info@primacentral.org
URL: http://www.primacentral.org
Contact: Marshall Davies, Interim Exec.Dir.
Description: Public agency risk, insurance, human resources, attorneys, and/or safety managers from cities, counties, villages, towns, school boards, and other related areas. Provides an information clearinghouse and communications network for public risk managers to share resources, ideas, and experiences. Offers information on risk, insurance, and safety management. Monitors state and federal legislative actions and court decisions that deal with immunity, tort liability, and intergovernmental risk pools. Maintains library containing current reports from governmental units on their insurance procedures, self-insurance plans, and loss control and safety programs; and copies of policy statements, job descriptions, contractual arrangements, and indemnification clauses. **Publications:** *Public Risk* (monthly).

42815 ■ Recruiting and Staffing Focus Area
1800 Duke St.
Alexandria, VA 22314
Ph:(703)548-3440
Free: 800-283-SHRM
Fax: (703)535-6490
Co. E-mail: shrm@shrm.org
URL: http://www.shrm.org/ema
Description: Provides employment-related programs, services and networking opportunities to members with staffing-related accountabilities. **Publications:** *Global Perspectives*; *iLinX Newsletter*.

EDUCATIONAL PROGRAMS

42816 ■ AMA's Employment Law Course: Avoiding the Legal Pitfalls of EEO, FMLA and ADA
American Management Association
1601 Broadway
New York, NY 10019
Ph:(212)586-8100
Free: 800-262-9699
Fax: (212)903-8168
Co. E-mail: customerservice@amanet.org
URL: http://www.amanet.org
Price: $1,695 for non-members; $1,495 for AMA members. **Description:** Covers employee discrimination, the Family Medical Leave Act, and the Americans with Disabilities Act and how they effect your business decisions. **Locations:** San Francisco CA; Chicago, IL; and New York, NY.

42817 ■ Behavioural Interviewing (Canada)
Canadian Management Centre
150 York St., 5th Fl.
Toronto, ON, Canada M5H 3S5
Ph:(416)214-5678
Free: 800-262-9699
Fax: (416)313-4985
Co. E-mail: cmcinfo@cmctraining.org
URL: http://cmcamai.org
Price: $1,595.00 Canadian. **Description:** Covers skills for effective interviewing techniques that improve the quality and success of new hires. **Locations:** Toronto, ON; Ottawa, ON.

42818 ■ Fundamentals of Human Resources Management (Canada)
Canadian Management Centre
150 York St., 5th Fl.
Toronto, ON, Canada M5H 3S5
Ph:(416)214-5678
Free: 800-262-9699
Fax: (416)313-4985
Co. E-mail: cmcinfo@cmctraining.org
URL: http://cmcamai.org
Price: $2,195.00 Canadian. **Description:** Covers HR planning and administration, staffing, training, technology, compensation, and legal issues. **Locations:** Calgary, AB; Vancouver, BC; and Toronto, ON.

42819 ■ Fundamentals of Total Rewards Management
American Management Association
1601 Broadway
New York, NY 10019
Ph:(212)586-8100
Free: 800-262-9699
Fax: (212)903-8168
Co. E-mail: customerservice@amanet.org
URL: http://www.amanet.org
Price: $1,895 for non-members; $1,695 for AMA members. **Description:** Covers creating a work environment through a reward system that delivers performance. **Locations:** New York, NY; Atlanta, GA; Washington, DC; and San Francisco, CA.

42820 ■ How to Use a Total Rewards System to Strengthen Performance and Organizational Results
American Management Association
1601 Broadway
New York, NY 10019
Ph:(212)586-8100
Free: 800-262-9699
Fax: (212)903-8168
Co. E-mail: customerservice@amanet.org
URL: http://www.amanet.org
Price: $1,895 for non-members; $1,695 for AMA members. **Description:** Covers a strategic method through a rewards program, including compensation, benefits, and work environments. **Locations:** New York, NY; Chicago, IL; Atlanta, GA; Washington, DC; and San Francisco, CA.

42821 ■ How to Write an Affirmative Action Plan
American Management Association
1601 Broadway
New York, NY 10019

Ph:(212)586-8100
Free: 800-262-9699
Fax: (212)903-8168
Co. E-mail: customerservice@amanet.org
URL: http://www.amanet.org
Price: $1,645.00 for non-members; $1,545.00 for AMA members. **Description:** Two-day seminar for human resources and personnel managers; covers analyzing for compliance, identifying compliant activities, preparing for audits, and avoiding liability. **Locations:** New York, NY.

42822 ■ Recruiting, Interviewing and Selecting Employees
American Management Association
1601 Broadway
New York, NY 10019
Ph:(212)586-8100
Free: 800-262-9699
Fax: (212)903-8168
Co. E-mail: customerservice@amanet.org
URL: http://www.amanet.org
Price: $1,695.00 for non-members; $1,595.00 for AMA members. **Description:** Covers recruitment sources, filtering applicants, interview techniques and questions, and EEO and affirmative action guidelines. **Locations:** Washington, DC; Atlanta, GA; Chicago, IL; and New York, NY.

42823 ■ Succession Planning that Works (Canada)
Canadian Management Centre
150 York St., 5th Fl.
Toronto, ON, Canada M5H 3S5
Ph:(416)214-5678
Free: 800-262-9699
Fax: (416)313-4985
Co. E-mail: cmcinfo@cmctraining.org
URL: http://cmcamai.org
Price: $1,595.00 Canadian. **Description:** Covers the value of offering employees a career path, and techniques for implementing succession planning. **Locations:** Toronto, ON.

42824 ■ Today's HR Professional: From Technician to Strategist (Canada)
Canadian Management Centre
150 York St., 5th Fl.
Toronto, ON, Canada M5H 3S5
Ph:(866)400-4941 ext. 2252
Free: 877-CMC-2500
Fax: (416)313-4985
Co. E-mail: cmcinfo@cmctraining.org
URL: http://www.cmcamai.org
Price: $1,695 Canadian. **Description:** For human resource managers and professionals with three or more years of experience; covers the multi-task functions of today's human resource professionals. **Locations:** Toronto, ON.

REFERENCE WORKS

42825 ■ *365 Answers about Human Resources for the Small Business Owner: What Every Manager Needs to Know about Work Place Law*
Pub: Atlantic Publishing Company
Ed: Mary Holihan. **Released:** June 2006. **Price:** $21.95. **Description:** Common questions employers ask about employees and the law are answered.

42826 ■ "Adults Fueling Back To School Movement" in *Crain's Detroit Business* (Vol. 23, January 15, 2007, No. 3, pp. 9)
Pub: Crain Communications Inc. - Detroit
Ed: Mary Kramer. **Description:** Dramatic increase in enrollments by older workers. Early retirements and auto worker buyouts, which include substantial tuition assistance, are contributing to the increase in 50-plus age group returning to college for additional education.

42827 ■ *The AMA Handbook for Employee Recruitment and Retention*
Pub: AMACOM

Ed: Mary F. Cook. **Released:** 1992. **Price:** $75.00. **Description:** Guide to recruiting and retaining quality employees. Coverage includes planning, recruitment and selection programs, performance management, compensation and benefits, and training.

42828 ■ "Are Your Staffers Stealing" in *Inc.* (November 2006, pp. 33-35)
Pub: Gruner & Jahr USA Publishing
Ed: Scott Wescott. **Description:** Internal theft is a significant drain on resources and easier to prevent than amend. Selecting the right people, clear cut policies on theft, simplified accounting systems, all contribute to reducing this common problem in small companies.

42829 ■ "Ask Inc." in *Inc.* (Volume 28, January 2006, No. 1, pp. 51-52)
Pub: Inc. Magazine
Description: Advice is offered regarding noncompete agreements, factoring companies that pay businesses up-front for outstanding bills and collect payments from customers, and a pet accessory business.

42830 ■ "Bad credit and employment" in *Black Enterprise* (Vol. 31, No. 5, December 2000, pp. 172)
Pub: Earl Graves Publishing Co.
Ed: Bevolyn Williams-Harold. **Description:** The issue of screening job applicants based on credit history is discussed.

42831 ■ "BofA Cutting 70 Charlotte Tech Jobs" in *Charlotte Observer* (January 31, 2007)
Pub: Knight-Ridder/Tribune Business News
Ed: Rick Rothacker. **Description:** Bank of America announced the elimination of 70 technology positions at their Charlotte, North Carolina facility. The move is part of the company's effort to increase efficiency.

42832 ■ *Business Warrior: Strategy for Entrepreneurs*
Pub: Clearbridge Publishing
Ed: Sun Tzu. **Released:** September 2006. **Price:** $19.95. **Description:** Advice to help entrepreneurs understand competitive strategies in order to succeed, focusing on sales, marketing, and personnel management.

42833 ■ "C2G-Network" in *Entrepreneur.com* (Vol. 34, January 2006, No. 1, pp. 6)
Pub: Entrepreneur Media Inc.
Ed: Steve Cooper. **Description:** College students can be certified and placed on C2G-Network that puts them in contact with fast-growing small businesses. Students have backgrounds in technology, engineering, marketing and sales, human resources, finance, communications and more.

42834 ■ "Can Spending A Day Stuck To A Velcro Wall Help Build A Team" in *Wall Street Journal* (Vol. 248, December 2006, No. 149, pp. B1)
Pub: Dow Jones & Co. Inc.
Ed: Jared Sandberg **Description:** Profiles of several companies offering office and corporate team-building exercise outings and events. Alternative methods of company employee bonding are covered.

42835 ■ "Cautious Hiring in January Report" in *Charlotte Observer* (February 3, 2007)
Pub: Knight-Ridder/Tribune Business News
Ed: Kerry Hall. **Description:** U.S. Labor Department released a report that shows 111,000 new positions in January 2007, compared to 206,000 in December 2006. Employers remain cautious about hiring.

42836 ■ "Changing hands" in *WorkingWoman* (Vol. 25, No. 2, February 2000, pp. 38)
Pub: Lang Communications Inc.
Ed: Carol Leonetti Dannhauser. **Description:** Several corporate leaders offer advice for employees to maintain a flexible job description in order to be a viable through a company merger.

42837 ■ "Clearer Regs on Wellness Programs in the Workplace" in *Kiplinger Letter* (Vol. 78, January 19, 2007, No. 2)
Pub: Kiplinger
Description: Employers are creating employee incentives through wellness programs in order cut healthcare costs. Such programs can give employees rewards in the form of a discount or rebate in premiums; a waiver of deductibles, copays or coinsurance; or perhaps a gym membership.

42838 ■ "Clocking In: For Low-Wage Workers, Overtime May Get More Lucrative" in *Entrepreneur* (Vol. 31, No. 7, July 2003, pp. 22)
Pub: Entrepreneur Media, Inc.
Ed: Stephen Barlas. **Description:** The U.S. Labor Department has proposed changes to the law dictating overtime pay. The changes to the "white collar exemptions" of the Fair Labor Standards Act would entitle more hourly employees to time and half and further clarifies provisions that have allowed salaried employees to sue employers for overtime.

42839 ■ *A Company Policy and Personnel Workbook*
Pub: Oasis Press
Ed: Ardella Ramey and Carl R. J. Sniffen. **Released:** 1991. **Price:** $49.95 (ringbound); $29.95 (paper). **Description:** Provides information on writing company policies covering sexual harassment, privacy, AIDS, and other sensitive topics. Includes 65 written model policies and 20 forms.

42840 ■ *Complete Employee Handbook: A Step-by-Step Guide to Create a Custom Handbook That Protects Both the Employer and the Employee*
Pub: Moyer Bell
Ed: Michael A. Holzschu. **Released:** August 2007. **Price:** $39.95. **Description:** Comprehensive guide for employers deal with personnel issues; CD-ROM contains sample employee handbooks, federal regulations and laws, forms for complying with government programs and worksheets for assessing personnel needs and goals.

42841 ■ "Consequences of Information Technology on Work in the Twenty-First Century" in *Employment Relations Today* (Vol.26, No. 4, Winter 2000)
Pub: John Wiley & Sons, Inc.
Ed: Joseph F. Coates. **Description:** The implications of information technology advances for human resource management are discussed. Topics addressed include globalization and employee wages, job automation and the management of the labor supply, and training workers in computer skills.

42842 ■ "Counter-Intuitive Offers" in *Business Week* (No. 3658, December 6, 1999, pp. F8)
Pub: McGraw-Hill, Inc.
Description: The issue of making counter offers to departing employees may be a wrong move for small business.

42843 ■ *Create Your Own Employee Handbook: A Legal and Practical Guide*
Pub: NOLO
Ed: Amy DelPo, Lisa Guerin. **Released:** May 2005. **Price:** $49.99. **Description:** Information for business owners to develop an employee handbook that covers company benefits, policies, procedures, and more.

42844 ■ *The Creative Business Guide to Running a Graphic Design Business*
Pub: W.W. Norton & Company, Incorporated
Ed: Cameron S. Foote. **Released:** April 2004. **Price:** $29.95 (US); $45.00 (Canadian). **Description:** Advice for running a graphic design firm, focusing on organizations, marketing, personnel and operations.

42845 ■ "The Dark Art of Letting People Go" in *Business Week Online* ()
Pub: McGraw-Hill, Inc.
Description: Laying off employees is a difficult task, and the importance of establishing policies and procedures is covered.

42846 ■ *The Department of Labor's Overtime Regulations Effect on Small Business: Congressional Hearing*
Pub: DIANE Publishing Company
Ed: W. Todd Akin. **Released:** April 2006. **Price:** $20.00. **Description:** An overview of the Congressional hearing regarding the Department of Labor's regulations governing overtime and how they impact small business.

42847 ■ *Employee Management for Small Business*
Pub: Self-Counsel Press, Incorporated
Ed: Lin Grensing-Pophal. **Released:** August 2005. **Price:** $17.95. **Description:** Management tools to help entrepreneurs maintain an effective human resources plan for a small company.

42848 ■ "Employee Organizations: Tomorrow's Possibilities" in *Employment Relations Today* (Vol. 26, No. 4, Winter 2000, pp. 53)
Pub: John Wiley & Sons, Inc.
Ed: Arthur B. Shostak. **Description:** An investigation into the future of employees' organizations within corporations, focusing on the structure of corporate culture in the 21st century. The article identifies five factors that will influence employee groups in the future, which include economic expansion, communication systems, artificial intelligence, smart technology, and genetic engineering.

42849 ■ "Employers Can Expect More Legal Challenges from Workers" in *Kiplinger Letter* (Vol. 84, January 26, 2007, No. 4)
Pub: Kiplinger
Description: Employers may be faced will legal challenges concerning issues of overtime and The Family and Medical Leave Act since the Supreme Court broadened the definition of retaliation to include words and actions by supervisors outside the workplace.

42850 ■ "Employing Her Literary Skills" in *San Diego Business Journal* (Vol. 28, January 8, 2007, No. 2, pp. 10)
Pub: San Diego Business Journal Associates
Ed: Michelle Mowad. **Description:** Profile of Professor Susan Bisom-Rapp, author of a new book on international and comparative employment law. The book covers laws in nine countries, including labor and employment law regulations.

42851 ■ "Entrepreneur Column" in *Entrepreneur* (August 25, 2005)
Pub: Entrepreneur Media Inc.
Ed: David G. Javitch. **Description:** Guidelines and tips to assist employers in the firing process are presented.

42852 ■ *Fast-Track Business Start-Up Kit: California*
Pub: DP Group, Incorporated
Ed: Carolyn Usinger. **Released:** September 2006. **Price:** $29.00. **Description:** Step-by-step guide for starting and running a business in California, including information on sole proprietors, partnerships, limited liability companies, S and C corporations, as well as details concerning business entities, sales taxes, environmental issues, human resources, and more.

42853 ■ "From Mushing to Management" in *Inc.* (January 1, 2005)
Pub: Inc. Magazine
Ed: Nicole Gull. **Description:** Lisa Wehl learned how to manage her 22 employees through a group of Alaskan husky dogs while competing in competitions such as the Knik 200 and the Klondike 300.

42854 ■ "From the Recruiter: Enliven Your Resume" in *Sales & Marketing Management* (Vol. 157, January 2005, No. 1, pp. 51)
Pub: VNU Business Media
Ed: Dan Martin. **Description:** Because employers do not have the time to read through every resume, it is imperative to design a resume with something that captures attention quickly.

42855 ■ "The Future of Cyberwork" in *Employment Relations Today* (Vol. 26, No. 4, pp. 61)
Pub: John Wiley & Sons, Inc.
Description: Studies labor trends in Internet technology, focusing on how cyberwork will impact the decisions of managers and human resource departments by 2025. Topics addressed include the work and challenges of Internet-related professionals, as well as the changes the Internet will bring to the labor market.

42856 ■ *Gender & Successful Human Resource Decisions in Small Businesses*
Pub: Garland Publishing, Inc.
Ed: Deborah C. Good. **Released:** 1998. **Price:** $50.00 (cloth).

42857 ■ "Going by the Handbook" in *Success* (Vol. 47, No. 4, September 2000, pp. 69)
Pub: Success Publishing, Inc.
Ed: Michael Barrier. **Description:** Guidelines are given for effective employee information.

42858 ■ "Guest Speaker. The Saltshaker Theory" in *Inc.* (November 2006, pp. 69-70)
Pub: Gruner & Jahr USA Publishing
Ed: Danny Meyer. **Description:** Constant gentle pressure is invaluable in a growing company. Not so much to avoid problems, but to encourage participation and imaginative solutions to resolve those problems. Coaching and Communication are the two central keys to building consensus to resolve problems that arise.

42859 ■ *Guide to Employee Handbooks*
Pub: Warren, Gorham & Lamont, Inc.
Ed: Robert J. Nobile. **Price:** $158.00.

42860 ■ "Help Wanted" in *Small Business Opportunities* (Vol. 12, No. 5, September 2000, pp. 10, 130)
Pub: Harris Publications, Inc.
Ed: John Orth. **Description:** Outsourcing human resources functions to a Professional Employer Organization (PEO) allows entrepreneurs to focus on their core competencies, knowing that trained professionals are handling the administrative and HR activities of the business. The article offers a questionnaire to determine if it is time to outsource and a guideline for choosing the right PEO.

42861 ■ "Hickory Unemployment Stays Steady" in *Charlotte Observer* (February 2, 2007)
Pub: Knight-Ridder/Tribune Business News
Ed: Jen Aronoff. **Description:** Unemployment rates remained unchanged in Hickory, North Carolina area; the region reported 6.1 percent unemployment.

42862 ■ *The Hiring, Firing and Everything in Between Personnel Forms Book*
Pub: Round Lake Publishing Co.
Ed: James M. Jenks. **Released:** 1992. **Price:** $19.95 (paper).

42863 ■ "Hold On Tight" in *Entrepreneur* (Vol. 31, No. 8, August 2003, pp. 66)
Pub: Entrepreneur Media, Inc.
Ed: Chris Penttila. **Description:** During an economic downturn, it is recommended that company's begin maximizing loyalty in the workplace while it's still an employer's market. Look for ways to maintain a staff before they are enlisted by headhunters when the economy turns.

42864 ■ *The HR Book: Human Resources Management for Small Business*
Pub: Self-Counsel Press, Incorporated
Ed: Lin Grensing-Pophal. **Released:** September 2004. **Price:** $22.95. **Description:** Keys to hiring and maintaining productive workforce are outlined.

42865 ■ *HRD in Small Organizations: Research and Practice*
Pub: Routledge
Ed: Jim Steward, Graham Beaver. **Released:** February 2004. **Price:** $124.95 (US), $165.00 (Canadian). **Description:** Approaches to human resource development in small organizations are evaluated.

42866 ■ *Human Resource Development: The Field*
Pub: Prentice Hall
Ed: Pace. **Released:** 1991. **Price:** $38.29 (paper).

42867 ■ *Human Resource Executive's Market Resource*
Pub: LRP Publications
Contact: William E. Corsini, HR Products, Publisher
Released: Annual, November. **Covers:** Approximately 100 vendor companies and associations serving all aspects of human resources administration, including benefits, consulting and information services, software, employee assistance programs, health care, meeting and conference facilities, out placement and recruitment services, pension and retirement, recognition awards and incentives, relocation services, safety and security, temporary services, testing and assessment, training and development, and other services. **Entries Include:** Company name, address, phone, product/service, company philosophy, facilities, literature available, etc. **Arrangement:** Classified by product/service. **Indexes:** Name.

42868 ■ *Human Resources for Small Business Made Easy*
Pub: Skilled Learning Incorporated
Ed: Ruth Zimmerman. **Released:** November 2006. **Description:** Guide for human resource development for small businesses.

42869 ■ "Independent Testing" in *Inc.* (November 2000, pp. 97)
Pub: The Goldhirsh Group
Description: Rules vary from state to state, so it is recommended to talk to a Human Resources expert in order to comply with state and federal regulations when hiring contractors.

42870 ■ "The Ire Next Time" in *Business Week* (March 27, 2000, pp. F28)
Pub: McGraw-Hill, Inc.
Description: Ticket to Work and Work Incentives Improvement Act of 1999 are discussed.

42871 ■ "Is Employer-Sponsored Health Insurance On Its Way Out?" in *Kiplinger Letter* (Vol. 84, January 26, 2007, No. 4)
Pub: Kiplinger
Description: Congress is not expected to pass a bill that would count employer-provided health benefits as income, making them subject to taxes.

42872 ■ "It's Not Personal" in *Entrepreneur* (Vol. 33, September 2005, No. 9, pp. 94)
Pub: Entrepreneur Media Inc.
Ed: Jane Easter Bahls. **Description:** Most state and federal laws entitle employees to review personnel files and also make copies of them. Documents that should be kept in a personnel file are listed.

42873 ■ "Laws Mandating Paid Sick Leave Will Pass in Several States" in *Kiplinger Letter* (Vol. 78, January 19, 2007, No. 2)
Pub: Kiplinger
Description: Massachusetts, Wisconsin, Washington, Main, Montana, Vermont, and Maryland are among the states considering a law to mandate paid sick leave to employees.

42874 ■ "Lawyers on War-Path Filing Wage and Hour Lawsuits" in *Kiplinger Letter* (Vol. 78, January 19, 2007, No. 2)
Pub: Kiplinger
Description: Attorneys are targeting clients with the use of Websites to looking for disgruntled employees. Major settlements are discussed.

42875 ■ "Matchmaker" in *Forbes* (Vol. 175, February 28, 2005, No. 4, pp. 48)
Pub: Forbes Magazine Inc.
Ed: Joanne Gordon. **Description:** Profile of Debra Feldman, a job coach who helps individuals find employment.

42876 ■ "New Career Center Opens at Right Time: Laid-Off Freightliner Workers Will Need Help" in *Charlotte Observer* (February 1, 2007)
Pub: Knight-Ridder/Tribune Business News
Ed: Gail Smith-Arrants. **Description:** Rowan-Cabarrus Community College announced the opening of its new career development center that will help area workers train for new careers.

42877 ■ "News and Reviews" in *Home Business* (Vol. 13, January/February 2006, No. 1, pp. 98)
Pub: Home Business Magazine
Description: Information for closing business deals online, Web-based human resources small business software, noise canceling audio headphones, and tips for launching and marketing new products is given.

42878 ■ "Opportunity Knocks" in *Rough Notes* (Vol. 145, No. 9, September 2002, pp. 110)
Pub: Rough Notes
Ed: Michael J. Moody. **Description:** Health insurance for employees is now the number one challenge for human resources departments, chief financial officers and upper management because rates are rising, capacities are shrinking and customers are feeling dissatisfied about coverage.

42879 ■ "Orders Up; Jobs Below Forecast" in *Charlotte Observer* (February 2, 2007)
Pub: Knight-Ridder/Tribune Business News
Ed: Kerry Hall. **Description:** U.S. Labor Department reported unemployment rates at 4.6 percent, up one-tenth of a percent. Economists had predicted 170,000 new jobs, but only 111,000 were created.

42880 ■ *Personnel - HR Management in Small Organizations & Growing Companies*
Pub: Society for Human Resource Management
Released: 1997. **Price:** $99.00 (paper).

42881 ■ *Personnel Policy Handbook: How to Develop a Manual That Works*
Pub: The McGraw-Hill Companies
Ed: William S. Hubbartt. **Released:** 1995. **Price:** $74.95. **Description:** Provides instructions and examples for creating human resource policy manuals. Includes sample policies and checklists.

42882 ■ "The Postmodern Shift in Values and Jobs and the Implications for HR" in *Employment Relations Today* (Vol. 26, No. 4, Winter 2000)
Pub: John Wiley & Sons, Inc.
Ed: Andy Himes. **Description:** A report concerning the impact of postmodern social values on corporate culture and human resource management. Topics addressed include industrial psychology, attracting and retaining postmodern workers, and the relationship between management and workers in a postmodern society.

42883 ■ "Prices, Wages in 2007" in *Kiplinger Letter* (Vol. 84, January 26, 2007, No. 4)
Pub: Kiplinger
Description: Economic growth is expected to slow to 2.5 percent in 2007, keeping prices level and company profits lower.

42884 ■ "The Problem of Perceptions: Reasons for Outsourcing the Sexual Harassment Investigation" in *Employment Relations Today* (Vol.27, No.1)
Pub: John Wiley & Sons, Inc.
Ed: Jonathan Day. **Description:** Management of sexual harassment allegations by human resource departments are explored. Topics addressed include employee perceptions of harassment cases, and the outsourcing of an investigation to an independent third party.

42885 ■ "Recharge Life and Business With a Vacation" in *Crain's Detroit Business* (Vol. 22, December 18, 2006, No. 51, pp. 14)
Pub: Crain Communications Inc. - Detroit
Ed: Sheena Harrison. **Description:** Getting away from the office for a vacation offers a chance to balance home and business as well as the opportunity to explore new ideas from afar while refreshed. It's also an excellent chance to let employees develop new management skills and motivate them with the new challenges and responsibilities.

42886 ■ *Recruitment, Retention, and Employee Relations: Field-Tested Strategies for the '90s*
Pub: Greenwood Publishing Group, Inc.
Ed: D. Keith Denton. **Released:** 1992. **Price:** $49.95. **Description:** Provides information on three phases of a human resources program—recruitment, retention, and employee relations.

42887 ■ "The Regenerative Organization" in *Employment Relations Today* (Vol. 27, No. 1, Spring 2000, pp. 19)
Pub: John Wiley & Sons, Inc.
Ed: Randall J. Alford. **Description:** Issues discussed concern organizational change and management in US companies attempting to compete in a globalized marketplace. Topics addressed include how to integrate human resource management with strategic planning and how to build company vision, purpose, and community.

42888 ■ "Right in Sight" in *Entrepreneur* (Vol. 33, August 2005, No. 8, pp. 40)
Pub: Entrepreneur Media Inc.
Ed: Amanda C. Kooser. **Description:** Affordable video surveillance is available for small businesses using the Internet and video cameras.

42889 ■ "Scenes From the Talent Wars" in *Inc.* (Volume 28, January 2006, No. 1, pp. 29-31)
Pub: Inc. Magazine
Ed: Scott Westcott. **Description:** Employers are willing to go to extra lengths to recruit and retain talented workers. A list of business jargon used in human resources is included.

42890 ■ *Selection Interviews: Process Perspectives*
Pub: South-Western Publishing Co.
Ed: Robert Dipboye. **Released:** 1992. **Price:** $34.50. **Description:** Reviews developments in theory and research of the interviewing process.

42891 ■ "Six Sigma: New Opportunites for HR, New Career Growth for Employees" in *Employment Relations Today* (Vol. 27,No. 2, Summer 2000, pp. 1)
Pub: John Wiley & Sons, Inc.
Ed: Joseph A. DeFeo. **Description:** It is essential that Human Resources managers understand their role in improving efficiency and competitiveness with regard to products and all customer services. The six sigma quality concept for measuring the effectiveness of business processes is described.

42892 ■ *Six SIGMA for Small Business*
Pub: Entrepreneur Press
Ed: Greg Brue. **Released:** October 2005. **Price:** $19.95 (US), $26.95 (Canadian). **Description:** Jack Welch's Six SIGMA approach to business covers accounting, finance, sales and marketing, buying a business, human resource development, and new product development.

42893 ■ *Smart Hiring for Your Business: Everything You Need to Know to Find & Hire the Best Employees*
Pub: Sourcebooks, Inc.
Ed: Robert W. Wendover. **Released:** 1993. **Price:** $17.95; $8.95 (paper).

42894 ■ "State OKs Minimum Wage Boost" in *Altanta Journal-Constitution* (February 2, 2007)
Pub: Cox Newspapers, Inc.
Ed: Marilyn Geewax. **Description:** Senate voted in favor of raising the minimum wage from $5.15 to $7.25 an hour over two years, but the deal is not completed. Complex negotiations will take place between the House and Senate.

42895 ■ **"Tapping the Potential of Employee Ranks; Human Resources" in** *Crain's New York Business* **(Vol. 22, November 13, 2006, No. 46, pp. 32)**
Pub: Crain Communications, Inc.
Description: Listing of organizations that provide counseling and research on human resources issues, as well as offering employee recruitment and training, oftentimes with tax break incentives.

42896 ■ **"The A List" in** *Entrepreneur* **(Vol. 31, No. 8, August 2003, pp. 65)**
Pub: Entrepreneur Media, Inc.
Ed: Joanne Cleaver. **Description:** Kim Radeback, human resources manager for Spring Engineering and Manufacturing Corporation in Canton, Michigan, finds inexpensive ways to reward employees and bolster morale during a slumping economy. This practice won the company a spot on one of the Detroit, Michigan area's "101 Best and Brightest Companies to Work For" in the city's 2001 list.

42897 ■ **"They're not employees, they're people" in** *Harvard Business Review* **(Vol. 80, No. 2, February 2002, pp. 70)**
Pub: Harvard Business School Press
Ed: Peter F. Drucker. **Description:** Two fast-moving trends that are changing the way companies manage talent, the number of employees who are not longer traditional employees, and the growing number of companies that have outsourced employee relations is featured.

42898 ■ **"Top-Heavy: Is it Time to Thin Out Your Management Pool" in** *Entrepreneur* **(Vol. 32, No. 1, January 2004, pp. 30)**
Pub: Entrepreneur Media, Inc.
Ed: Nichole L. Torres. **Description:** Cynthia Shapiro, human resource consultant, recommends letting go unnecessary management. Tips for deciding which managers to pink slip are included.

42899 ■ **"Transforming Business Structures to Hyborg" in** *Employment Relations Today* **(Vol. 26, No. 4, Winter 2000, pp. 5)**
Pub: John Wiley & Sons, Inc.
Ed: Arnold Brown. **Description:** The organizational structure and corporate culture at the turn of the 21st century are studied. Topics addressed include international economic relations, competition, corporate values, employer-employee relations, and human resource management.

42900 ■ **"Wanted: African American Professional for Hire" in** *Black Enterprise* **(Vol. 37, November 2006, No. 4, pp. 93)**
Pub: Earl G. Graves Publishing Co. Inc.
Ed: Joe Watson. **Description:** Excerpt from the book, Without Excuses: Unleash the Power of Diversity to Build Your Business, speaks to the lack of diversity in the corporate arena and why executives, recruiters, and HR professionals claim they are unable to find qualified individuals of different races when hiring.

42901 ■ **"What's Next? Mistakes Were Made" in** *Inc.* **(November 2006, pp. 65-66)**
Pub: Gruner & Jahr USA Publishing
Ed: David H. Friedman. **Description:** Never hide mistakes made by a company. Communicate the event in order to develop an atmosphere of openness and of learning by mistakes, rather than that mistakes are shameful and attempts are made to cover them up.

42902 ■ **"Workers' Comp Claims Filed Have Decreased in Okla., Statistics Show" in** *Journal Record (Oklahoma City, OK)* **(February 8, 2007)**
Pub: Journal Record
Ed: Marie Price. **Description:** Workers' compensation reform has reduced the number of claims filed in Oklahoma. Statistical data included.

42903 ■ **"You're Fired!" in** *Forbes* **(Vol. 174, December 13, 2004, No. 12, pp. 89)**
Pub: Forbes Magazine Inc.
Ed: Christopher Steiner. **Description:** Profile of Achilles Group, a firm that assists businesses with personnel matters such as firings, discrimination suits, personality conflicts, threatened lawsuits, EEOC claims, and hiring.

42904 ■ **"ZoomInfo" in** *Entrepreneur* **(Vol. 33, September 2005, No. 9, pp. 6)**
Pub: Entrepreneur Media Inc.
Ed: Steve Cooper. **Description:** ZoomInfo offers a people-summarization search engine that provides personnel information such as employment history and contact information for free; a premium search engine will also narrow the search by geographic location, title and education level for $99 annually.

TRADE PERIODICALS

42905 ■ *EMA Reporter*
Pub: Society for Human Resource Management
Ed: Ann Pomeroy, Editor. **Released:** Bimonthly. **Price:** Included in membership. **Description:** Facilitates the exchange of information and ideas among members of the Association, which aims to "advance professionalism within the area of employment and associated human resources functions." Alerts members to employment trends and issues and to employment litigation. Recurring features include member and Association news and meeting reports.

42906 ■ *Employee Benefit Plan Review*
Pub: Aspen Publishing Inc.
Contact: Barbara Williams, Advertising Mgr
Ed: Bruce F. Spencer, Editor. **Released:** Monthly. **Price:** $85. **Description:** Magazine serving decision-makers who administer, design, install, and service employee benefit plans.

42907 ■ *Employee Terminations Law Bulletin*
Pub: Quinlan Publishing Co.
Ed: Elizabeth A. Wheeler, Esq., Editor. **Released:** Monthly. **Price:** $147. **Description:** Advises employers on preventable errors and lawful procedure regarding employee dismissal. Reports on court decisions involving employee terminations.

42908 ■ *FERA—Focus*
Pub: FERA Inc.
Ed: John A. Seeley, Editor. **Released:** 3/year. **Price:** Free. **Description:** Discusses consulting work and research on evaluation of corporate training, human resource development programs, community-based social services, and educational programs.

42909 ■ *Hiring & Firing*
Pub: Thomson Carswell
Ed: Cindy Moser, Editor, mnredit@nexicom.net. **Released:** Monthly. **Description:** Monitors hiring and firing issues as they relate to the law. Covers such topics as sexual harassment, discrimination, and labor relations. Recurring features include columns titled Current Cases, Legal Corner, Human Rights, News in Brief, and Professional Practices.

42910 ■ *HR Manager's Legal Reporter*
Pub: Ransom & Benjamin Publishers L.L.C.
Ed: Maureen Gallagher, Editor. **Released:** Monthly. **Price:** $179.95, individuals; $320.88, two years. **Description:** Provides information, news, and how-to articles on employment law. Recurring features include columns titled Washington Watch, You Be the Judge, From the States, and In Brief.

42911 ■ *HRMagazine*
Pub: Society for Human Resource Management
Contact: Leon Rubis, Exec. Ed.
E-mail: leon@shrm.org
Released: Monthly. **Price:** $125. **Description:** Magazine for human resource management professionals.

42912 ■ *Human Factors in Ergonomics and Manufacturing*
Pub: John Wiley & Sons Inc.
Ed: Waldemar Karwoski, Editor. **Released:** 4/yr. **Price:** $205; $205 Canada and Mexico in Canada, add 7% GST; $229 other countries; $780 institutions; $820 institutions, Canada and Mexico in Canada, add 7% GST; $854 institutions, other countries. **Description:** International journal focusing on the design, management, and operation of advanced manufacturing systems. Covers human resource management, social and organizational issues, cognitive engineering, human factors, and safety and health.

42913 ■ *Human Resources Management: Ideas and Trends Newsletter*
Pub: CCH Inc.
Contact: Nancy Kaylor, Managing Editor
Released: Biennial. **Price:** $275. **Description:** Covers general human resources management issues.

42914 ■ *Human Resources Measurements*
Pub: Wonderlic Inc.
Ed: Paul G. Coutre, Editor. **Price:** Free. **Description:** Presents information on hiring and employee testing. Covers recruiting, technology, and hiring techniques. Recurring features include news of research. Remarks: Available online only.

42915 ■ *Journal of Individual Employment Rights*
Pub: Baywood Publishing Company Inc.
Contact: Claire Meirowitz
Ed: Charles J. Coleman, Editor. **Released:** Quarterly, 4/yr. **Description:** Journal covering employee and employer rights in the workplace.

42916 ■ *Personnel Management*
Pub: Bureau of National Affairs Inc.
Contact: Jeff Day, Managing Editor
Released: Weekly. **Price:** $683. **Description:** Provides legal clarification and practical advice on employers' pay and benefit policies, including detailed discussions of pertinent federal and state laws. Discusses such topics as health care compensation laws, pension law (ERISA), job evaluation, benefit plans, compensation administration, incentive systems, and independent contractors. Part of the BNA Policy and Practice Series; can be purchased alone or in any combination with other binder sets titled Compensation, Fair Employment Practices, Wages and Hours, and Labor Relations.

42917 ■ *Smart Workplace Practices*
Pub: Independent Small Business Employers of America
Ed: Jim Collison, Editor. **Released:** Monthly. **Description:** Helps employers, managers, and supervisors stay out of trouble by adopting and maintaining the best possible workplace policies and practices to achieve more with their employees.

42918 ■ *Supervisor's Guide to Employment Practices*
Pub: Clement Communications Inc.
Contact: Robi L. Garthwait, Managing Editor
Released: Biweekly. **Price:** $149.50, single issue. **Description:** Provides information to managers and supervisors regarding sensitive human resource issues.

42919 ■ *What's Working in Human Resources*
Pub: Progressive Business Publications
Contact: Ron McRae, Editor-in-Chief
Released: Semimonthly. **Price:** $299, individuals. **Description:** Reports on the latest trends in Human Resources, including the latest employment law rulings. Recurring features include interviews, news of research, a calendar of events, news of educational opportunities, and a column titlted Sharpen Your Judgment.

42920 ■ *Workforce Diversity*
Pub: Kennedy Information Inc.
Ed: Catherine Davis, Editor. **Released:** Monthly. **Price:** $170. **Description:** Reports on innovative diversity programs, surveys, and resources used to develop or enhance efforts to meet the challenges of today's changing workforce and global workplace.

42921 ■ *Workforce Stability Alert*
Pub: M. Lee Smith Publishers L.L.C.
Ed: Roger Herman, Editor. **Released:** Monthly. **Price:** $87, individuals. **Description:** Provides information on employee recruitment and retention, management techniques, and human resource issues. Recurring features include book reviews and columns titled Crazy Idea of the Month, Leadership, Ask HR Henrietta, Recruitment, and Best Corporate Practices.

VIDEOCASSETTES/ AUDIOCASSETTES

42922 ■ *Conducting an Effective Job Interview*
Phoenix Learning Group
2349 Chaffee Dr.
St. Louis, MO 63146
Ph:(314)569-0211
Free: 800-221-1274
Fax: (314)569-2834
URL: http://www.phoenixlearninggroup.com
Released: 1988. **Price:** $450.00. **Description:** This video teaches you how to interview effectively. **Availability:** VHS; 8mm; 3/4U.

42923 ■ *Conflicts, Conflicts!*
University of Washington Educational Media
 Collection
Kane Hall, Rm. 35
Campus Box 353095
Seattle, WA 98195
Ph:(206)543-9907
Fax: (206)616-6501
Released: 1985. **Description:** This is a management training film demonstrating techniques for avoiding conflicts. **Availability:** VHS; 3/4U.

42924 ■ *Creating Effective Workshops: The Design Doctor Is In*
American Society for Training and Development
 (ASTD)
1640 King St.
Box 1443
Alexandria, VA 22313-2043
Ph:(703)683-8100
Free: 800-628-2783
Fax: (703)683-8103
URL: http://www.astd.org
Released: 1989. **Description:** The successes and failures of others can help you plan your next training sessions. From start to finish, expert trainer and Human Resource Development manager Susan Warshauer shows how to control fears associated with learning new skills, how to ensure new skills make it back to the workplace, and how to move smoothly through a variety of topics. **Availability:** VHS; 3/4U.

42925 ■ *Fair & Effective Discipline*
Business & Legal Reports, Inc.
141 Mill Rock Rd. E.
Old Saybrook, CT 06475
Ph:(860)510-0100
Free: 800-727-5257
Fax: (860)510-7220
Co. E-mail: service@blr.com
URL: http://www.blr.com
Released: 1986. **Description:** A training film for managers in handling employee problems-absenteeism, poor performance, etc. **Availability:** VHS; 3/4U.

42926 ■ *Flexible Working Time: More Time to Live*
Encyclopedia Britannica
331 N. LaSalle St.
Chicago, IL 60610
Ph:(312)347-7159
Free: 800-323-1229
Fax: (312)294-2104
URL: http://www.britannica.com
Released: 1988. **Price:** $395.00. **Description:** A look at the Dutch postal service and a German department store, two places where the employees have flexible working hours. **Availability:** VHS; 3/4U.

42927 ■ *Hiring and Firing*
Aspen Publishers
7201 McKinney Circ.
Frederick, MD 21704
Ph:(301)644-3599
Free: 800-638-8437
Fax: (301)644-3550
URL: http://www.aspenpublishers.com
Released: 1985. **Description:** For business supervisors, a film on how to decide when to terminate and hire personnel. **Availability:** VHS; 3/4U; Special order formats.

42928 ■ *How to Interview Clients Effectively*
American Law Institute
American Bar Association Committee on Continuing
 Education
4025 Chestnut St.
Philadelphia, PA 19104
Ph:(215)243-1600
Free: 800-CLE-NEWS
Fax: (215)243-1664
Co. E-mail: PHunt@ali.org
URL: http://www.ali.org
Released: 1993. **Price:** $95. **Description:** Studies the interviewing process, offering advice on opening the interview, probing for details, testing theories, and closing the interview. Includes study guide. **Availability:** VHS.

42929 ■ *Looking Ahead: Preparing to Meet the Future*
Government VideoSource, Inc.
461 Miller Dr.
Elgin, IL 60123-7232
Ph:(847)931-1955
Price: $995. **Description:** Offers managers and supervisors tips on terminating employees and hleping them find new jobs. **Availability:** VHS.

42930 ■ *Performance Appraisal*
Lippincott Williams & Wilkins
Department of Audiovisual Media
530 Walnut St.
Philadelphia, PA 19106
Ph:(215)521-8300
Fax: (215)521-8902
Co. E-mail: info@lww.com
URL: http://www.lww.com
Released: 1985. **Description:** Managers and supervisors learn how to conduct effective and productive performance evaluation interviews. **Availability:** VHS; 3/4U.

42931 ■ *Performance Improvement Program*
Professional Development, Inc.
27955 Clemens Rd.
Westlake, OH 44145
Ph:(216)892-0770
Fax: (216)892-0105
Released: 1986. **Description:** Each of these four programs delineates an aspect of proper employee relations and performance appraisals. **Availability:** VHS; 3/4U.

42932 ■ *The Power of Positive and Effective Communication*
Aspen Publishers
7201 McKinney Circ.
Frederick, MD 21704
Ph:(301)644-3599
Free: 800-638-8437
Fax: (301)644-3550
URL: http://www.aspenpublishers.com
Released: 1987. **Price:** $495.00. **Description:** A program which teaches supervisors how to be sure to give clear instructions to their subordinates. **Availability:** VHS; 3/4U; Special order formats.

42933 ■ *Supervising the Drug-Free Workplace*
Altschul Group Corp.
Health Division
1560 Sherman Ave., Ste. 100
Evanston, IL 60201
Ph:(847)328-6700
Free: 800-323-9084
Fax: (847)328-6706
Price: $475.00. **Description:** A look at the importance of documentation, intervention confrontation and follow-up when dealing with employees who use drugs. Produced in compliance with the Federal Drug-Free Workplace Act. **Availability:** VHS; 3/4U; Special order formats.

42934 ■ *Take This Job and Love It*
Government VideoSource, Inc.
461 Miller Dr.
Elgin, IL 60123-7232
Ph:(847)931-1955

Price: $595. **Description:** Offers guidelines for changing your work without changing your job by understanding what challenges and motivates you. **Availability:** VHS.

42935 ■ *The Trouble with Words*
Film Library/Greater Los Angeles Safety Council
600 Wilshire Blvd., No. 1263
Los Angeles, CA 90017
Ph:(213)385-6461
Free: 800-421-9585
Fax: (213)385-8405
URL: http://www.lasafety.org
Released: 198?. **Description:** Provides some suggestions for creating better communication and higher productivity among employees. **Availability:** VHS; 3/4U.

42936 ■ *Understanding EEOC, Part 1-3*
RMI Media
1365 N. Winchester
Olathe, KS 66061
Ph:(913)768-1696
Fax: (913)768-0184
Co. E-mail: actmedia@act.org
URL: http://www.rmimedia.com
Released: 1987. **Price:** $80.00. **Description:** In this three-part series, equal employment opportunity laws are explained and followed by suggestions for companies seeking to develop practices, policies, and procedures in this area. **Availability:** VHS; 3/4U.

42937 ■ *Who Wants to Play God?*
Film Library/Greater Los Angeles Safety Council
600 Wilshire Blvd., No. 1263
Los Angeles, CA 90017
Ph:(213)385-6461
Free: 800-421-9585
Fax: (213)385-8405
URL: http://www.lasafety.org
Released: 198?. **Description:** This is an examination of why many performance reviews fail to increase employee effectiveness. **Availability:** VHS; 3/4U.

CONSULTANTS

42938 ■ Advanced Benefits & Human Resources
9350-F Snowden River Pky., Ste. 222
Columbia, MD 21045
Ph:(410)290-9037
Fax: (410)740-2568
Co. E-mail: hrb@abhr.com

E-mail: hrb@abhr.com
Scope: Provides human resource consulting to high technology businesses. Offers services in the areas of human resources, benefits, and training. Creates, maintains, or updates current human resource functions.

42939 ■ Allyson Management Services
837 Wakefield Dr.
Cincinnati, OH 45226
Ph:(513)871-5648
Fax: (513)871-5648
Co. E-mail: ams45226@ix.netcom.com

E-mail: ams45226@ix.netcom.com
Scope: A human resources consultancy providing management services in organizational design, quality improvement, and public speaking.

42940 ■ Arnold Consulting Group
1005 Raccoon Run
Victor, NY 14564-9105
Ph:(585)924-3304
Co. E-mail: acg4u@aol.com

E-mail: acg4u@aol.com
Scope: A management consulting firm whose mission is to help companies address their human resource and organizational improvement initiatives. Firm's consultants provide customer support in key functions

of human resource management: staffing and selection, training and management development, performance management and compensation, communications, and organization design/structure and development. Specialties include employee opinion surveys, management candidate assessment executive coaching, outplacement and succession planning. Industries served: retail food, pharmaceuticals, newspaper, electronics, utility, banking, and heavy equipment manufacturing. **Seminars:** Negotiation Strategies; Leadership Development; Competency Design, High Performance Teams Development; Management of Conflict; Employee Empowerment; Team Building; Job Search.

42941 ■ Assessment Strategies
7103 Interlachen Ct.
Eden Prairie, MN 55346
Ph:(952)949-9431
Free: 877-836-8325
Fax: (952)975-3885
Co. E-mail: dougtripp@mindspring.com

E-mail: dougtripp@mindspring.com
Scope: Assessment and organizational development experts helping clients implement sound, useful and actionable multi-source, employee opinion, and team assessment programs. As an independent vendor, the firm makes objective recommendations for surveys to be included in human resource development programs. They work with normed surveys, normed surveys which can be modified, or can completely customize the assessment program.

42942 ■ Barker & Associates
1974 Wexford Cir.
Wheaton, IL 60187-6166
Ph:(630)476-9927
Fax: (630)260-9928
Scope: Consulting, training, and coaching firm specializing in providing human resource assessment, selection and development services focused primarily on people skills. Serves small, mid, and large-size organizations in both private industry and not-for-profit associations. **Seminars:** Offers numerous seminars and workshops in the field of professional development, such as Strategic Marketing; Consultative Selling and Customer Service; From Hiring to Appraising - Developing Your Employees; Increased Productivity Through Managed Stress; Producing People Results Through Teambuilding; Conflict Management; Communications, Managing Transition and Change; and Creative Problem Solving.

42943 ■ BeamPines Inc.
600 3rd Ave.
New York, NY 10016
Ph:(212)476-4100
Fax: (212)986-7798
Co. E-mail: info@beamgroup.com
URL: http://www.beampines.com

E-mail: info@beamgroup.com
Scope: A human resource consultancy with expertise in employment and employee development. Serves businesses in the United States Provides comprehensive talent management services to help organizations attract, retain, and continuously develop the best people. **Special Services:** 720 degree Profile®.

42944 ■ Benefit Dynamics Inc.
8 Ranoldo Ter.
Cherry Hill, NJ 08034
Ph:(856)616-1400
Fax: (856)616-1401
Co. E-mail: benefit@benefitdynamics.com
URL: http://www.benefitdynamics.com

E-mail: benefit@benefitdynamics.com
Scope: A full service employee benefit, record keeping consultant and outsourcing organization. provides pension consulting, administration and actuarial services, cafeteria and flexible benefit plans, human resource systems outsourcing, interactive voice-response systems, electronic employee benefit enrollment, transportation plans.

42945 ■ Benefit Partners Inc.
363 Falconbridge Rd.
Sudbury, ON, Canada P3A 5K5
Ph:(705)524-1559
Free: 800-461-6326
Fax: (705)524-5553
Co. E-mail: info@benefitpartners.com
URL: http://www.benefitpartners.com

E-mail: info@benefitpartners.com
Scope: Services include Employee Benefits, Pension, Executive Compensation, Human Resources and Finacial Management.

42946 ■ Blankinship & Associates Inc.
322 C St.
Davis, CA 95616
Ph:(530)757-0941
Fax: (530)757-0940
Co. E-mail: blankinship@envtox.com
URL: http://www.envtox.com

E-mail: blankinship@envtox.com
Scope: A human resource management and development consulting firm specializing in small to medium size businesses.

42947 ■ Brown Associates Inc.
65 Birch Hill Rd.
Belmont, MA 02478-1730
Ph:(617)489-2500
Fax: (617)484-6611
Scope: Firm provides a full range of outsourced human resources consulting and training services to business, educational, and municipal clients, with special emphasis on new start-ups and new international business ventures. Services include consulting and training in the following areas: sexual harassment prevention; ADA compliance; equal employment and affirmative action; HR benefits, policies, and procedures; employee handbooks and manuals; OSHA compliance, HazCom, and safety programs; manpower planning, recruiting, and staffing; legal compliance (federal and state); compensation, performance evaluation, and job descriptions; and a full-range of HR support services. For international clients, the firm offers expatriate recruiting and hiring programs; overseas compensation and benefits plan development; and international HR policy and procedure planning. **Publications:** "The Legal Evolution of Sexual Harassment;" "Top 10 Human Resource Mistakes and How to Avoid Them," "Do You Need a Consultant?" **Seminars:** Preventing Sexual Harassment in the Workplace; Employment Law: All You Need to Know From A to Z; Selecting and Preparing Employees for International Assignments; Outplacement-How to Humanely Handle a Reduction in Force. **Special Services:** Human Resource Information System implementation, installation and training.

42948 ■ Business Resource Services Inc.
3101 Pheasant Run
Ijamsville, MD 21754
Ph:(301)865-6994
Co. E-mail: thonse@brs-bridge.com
URL: http://www.brs-bridge.com

E-mail: thonse@brs-bridge.com
Scope: A human resources company. Affirmative Action plans that comply with federal regulations benefits consulting, job descriptions, recruitment, compensation plans, employee handbooks, and performance appraisals. Special projects such as open enrollment and communicating benefits packages.

42949 ■ Carelli & Associates
17 Reid Pl.
Delmar, NY 12054
Ph:(518)439-0233
URL: http://www.carelli.com
Scope: Provides training and writing/editing services to industry and businesses, health care and educational institutions, and government agencies, and not-for-profit organizations. **Publications:** "The Truth About Supervision", 2004.

42950 ■ The Center for Organizational Excellence
15200 Shady Grove Rd., Ste. 400
Rockville, MD 20850
Ph:(301)948-1922
Free: 877-674-3923
Fax: (301)948-2158
Co. E-mail: results@center4oe.com
URL: http://www.center4oe.com

E-mail: results@center4oe.com
Scope: An organizational effectiveness consulting firm specializing in helping organizations achieve results through people, process, and performance. Service areas include organizational performance systems, leadership systems, customer systems, and learning systems.

42951 ■ CFI Group USA L.L.C.
625 Avis Dr.
Ann Arbor, MI 48108
Ph:(734)930-9090
Fax: (734)930-0911
Co. E-mail: contactcfi@cfigroup.com
URL: http://www.cfigroup.com

E-mail: contactcfi@cfigroup.com
Scope: Management consulting firm that helps its clients worldwide to maximize shareholder value by optimizing customer and employee satisfaction. **Publications:** "Consumers Rate the Post-Boom Industry," Mortgage Banking, Jan, 2005"; "Interview with a Customer Satisfaction Guru," Rotman Magazine, 2005".

42952 ■ Cole Financial Services Inc.
65 Cadillac Sq., Ste. 2850
Detroit, MI 48226
Ph:(313)962-7055
Free: 877-972-7055
Fax: 877-962-7815
Co. E-mail: colefinancial1@ameritech.net
URL: http://www.colefinancial1.net

E-mail: colefinancial1@ameritech.net
Scope: Offers services in business and human resource management and employee motivation. Industries served: engineering, construction, government, and other business entities. **Seminars:** How to Tap Your Potential and Discover Your Genius; What Every Woman Should Know before She Goes into Business; Four Phases of Business Ownership; Total Quality Management From the Bottom Up.

42953 ■ Compensation and Performance Management Inc.
610 Newport Ctr. Dr.
Newport Beach, CA 92660
Ph:(949)640-9800
Fax: (949)640-1006
Co. E-mail: cpm@cpmnet.com

E-mail: cpm@cpmnet.com
Scope: Helps organizations allocate financial capital to their human capital. Assists with employee performance and reward management issues within a business-based framework emphasizing strategic, financial, and behavioral issues over traditional human resources concepts.

42954 ■ Consulting & Conciliation Service
3405 I St., Ste. 2
Sacramento, CA 95816
Ph:(916)396-0480
Free: 888-898-9780
Co. E-mail: peace@conciliation.org
URL: http://www.conciliation.org

E-mail: peace@conciliation.org
Scope: Offers consulting and conciliation services. Provides pre-mediation counseling, training and research on preparing for a peaceful society, mediation and facilitation, and preparation for shifts in structure, policy and personnel. Offers sliding scale business rates and free individual consultation.

42955 ■ Controlled Resources
1021 E 1st Ave., Apt. 822
Broomfield, CO 80020
Ph:(303)798-2978
Fax: (303)798-2979
Scope: Strategic planning, with focus on human performance and financial issues. Also offers institutional ergonomics.

42956 ■ The Devine Group Inc.
10200 Alliance Rd., Ste. 310
Cincinnati, OH 45242
Ph:(513)792-7500
Free: (866)792-7500
Fax: (513)793-8535
Co. E-mail: sales@devinegroup.com
URL: http://www.devinegroup.com

E-mail: sales@devinegroup.com
Scope: A human resource consulting company devoted to providing reliable and responsive information focusing on performance issues and answers. Dedicated to analyzing and enhancing job performance. Custom design and implement programs and workshops that will result in demonstrable behavior change on the job. Assist clients enhance their productivity via behavior analysis. **Seminars:** The Devine Inventory™ Level One Training, Feb, 2006. **Special Services:** Devine Inventory®.

42957 ■ DiversityWorks
1924 Franklin St., Ste. 201
Oakland, CA 94612
Ph:(510)763-9300
Fax: (510)763-9311
Co. E-mail: mail@diversityworks.org
URL: http://www.diversityworks.org

E-mail: mail@diversityworks.org
Scope: Two main focus areas include (1)Working with young people directly, training and empowering them to become peer to peer diversity trainers and (2)Working with schools, community groups and progressive corporations to increase diversity awareness. Offers workshops, staff trainings, focus group facilitation and diversity program management. **Publications:** "DiversityWords".

42958 ■ DJT Consulting Group L.L.C.
2900 Sonoma Blvd., Ste. C
PO Box 6652
Vallejo, CA 94591
Ph:(707)674-0174
Fax: (707)638-0499
Co. E-mail: info@djtconsulting.com
URL: http://www.djtconsulting.com

E-mail: info@djtconsulting.com
Scope: Offers a range of grant management services including contract monitoring, research, grant writing, evaluation and project management. **Seminars:** Finding and Winning Government Grants.

42959 ■ Dorn & Associates Inc.
8506 Bass Lake Rd., Ste. 140
New Hope, MN 55428
Ph:(763)533-7689
Fax: (763)533-1143
Scope: Services include accounting, marketing, employment/partnership, new doctor agreements, personnel issues and human resources assessment, practice management, practice merger/acquisition/sale and/or liquidation, practice surveys and valuation, staff development and training.

42960 ■ Eastern Point Consulting Group Inc.
75 Oak St.
Newton, MA 02464
Ph:(617)965-4141
Fax: (617)965-4172
Co. E-mail: info@eastpt.com
URL: http://www.eastpt.com

E-mail: info@eastpt.com
Scope: Specializes in bringing practical solutions to complex challenges. Provides consultation and train-ing in managing diversity; comprehensive sexual-harassment policies and programs; organizational development; benchmarks 360 skills assessment; executive coaching; strategic human resource planning; team building; leadership development for women; mentoring programs; and gender issues in the workplace. **Seminars:** Leadership Development for Women.

42961 ■ Effective Compensation Inc.
3609 S Wadsworth Blvd., Ste. 260
Lakewood, CO 80235
Ph:(303)854-1000
Free: 877-746-4324
Fax: (303)854-1030
Co. E-mail: eci@effectivecompensation.com
URL: http://www.effectivecompensation.com

E-mail: eci@effectivecompensation.com
Scope: Helps organizations determine how to competitively pay their employees. Provides quality, culture sensitive, compensation consulting assistance to all types of employers. **Publications:** Industry Compensation Surveys.

42962 ■ Effective Resources Inc.
2803 Southfield Ct.
Holiday, FL 34691-2505
Ph:(727)944-2507
Free: 800-288-6044
Fax: (727)944-2607
Co. E-mail: customerservice@effectiveresources.com
URL: http://www.effectiveresources.com

E-mail: customerservice@effectiveresources.com
Scope: Concerned with technical aspects of human resource management. Specializes in compensation and incentive plans; performance appraisals; team building; and personnel policies and procedures; affirmative action plan preparation.

42963 ■ Executive Directions International Inc.
1536 NW 97th St.
Clive, IA 50325-6402
URL: http://www.workwise.net
Scope: A consultant on message management in the media. **Seminars:** Getting the Right Media Attention. **Special Services:** WorkWise®.

42964 ■ The Executive Group
1645 Parkhill Dr., Ste. 4
Billings, MT 59102
Ph:(406)252-7770
Free: 800-755-5161
Fax: (406)255-7478
Co. E-mail: exgzinfo@wtp.net
URL: http://www.exegrp.net

E-mail: exgzinfo@wtp.net
Scope: The company provides executive recruitment. Services include Geographic Searches, Interviewing Assistance ,Screening/Referencing ,Travel Arrangements ,Final Offer Negotiation, Company and Candidate Follow-Up. **Seminars:** Hiring, recruitment and management seminars.

42965 ■ Fox Lawson & Associates L.L.C.
1335 County Rd. D E
Saint Paul, MN 55109-5260
Ph:(651)635-0976
Free: 800-383-0976
Fax: (651)635-0980
URL: http://www.foxlawson.com
Scope: A compensation and human resources consulting firm. Provides services to businesses of all sizes including finance, manufacturing, high tech, software development, food, retail, wholesale trade, communications, transportation, service, not-for-profit and education. **Publications:** "Effective Bonus Plans," Ventures Magazine, Feb, 2000; "Split Dollar Insurance," Ventures Magazine, Jan, 2000; "Compensating Contractors and Vendors," Ventures Magazine, Dec, 1999. **Seminars:** Compensation Strategies - Not Having a Plan Could Break the Bank.

42966 ■ Stephen J. Gill Consulting
3051 Geddes Ave.
Ann Arbor, MI 48104
Ph:(734)665-7728
Fax: (734)665-7864
Co. E-mail: sjgill@stephenjgill.com
URL: http://www.stephenjgill.com

E-mail: sjgill@stephenjgill.com
Scope: Assesses needs and evaluates human performance improvement programs. Assists companies in planning effective learning programs. Industries served: automobile manufacturing, furniture manufacturing, software development, health-care, utilities, colleges and universities, nonprofits and philanthropic foundations. **Publications:** "The Learning Alliance: Systems Thinking in Human Resource Development"; "Organizational Learning"; "Myth and Reality of E-Learning," Educational Technology, 2003; "Broaden Your View," Quirk's Marketing Research Review, Oct, 2004. **Seminars:** Organizational Learning; High Impact Training; Training Evaluation; Survey Design; Outcomes and Impact Assessment.

42967 ■ Global Business Consultants
120 Market Sq.
PO Box 776
Pinehurst, NC 28374-0776
Ph:(910)295-5991
Free: 800-991-4990
Fax: (910)295-5908
Co. E-mail: info@yourculturecoach.com

E-mail: info@yourculturecoach.com
Scope: Firm specializes in human resources management; project management; software development; and international trade. Offers litigation support.

42968 ■ Goren and Associates Inc.
32000 Northwestern Hwy., Ste. 128
Farmington Hills, MI 48334
Ph:(248)851-0824
Free: 800-851-0824
Fax: (248)851-9751
Co. E-mail: info@gorentrain.com
URL: http://www.gorentrain.com

E-mail: info@gorentrain.com
Scope: Provides customized, organizational, and human resources development and training programs. Industries served: primarily manufacturing. **Seminars:** Instituting Change; Adjusting to Stress and Change; Initiating and Managing Change For Leaders.

42969 ■ The Greystone Group Inc.
678 Front St., Ste. 159
Grand Rapids, MI 49504
Ph:(616)451-8880
Fax: (616)451-9180
Co. E-mail: consult@greystonegp.com
URL: http://www.greystonegp.com

E-mail: consult@greystonegp.com
Scope: Firm specializes in strategic planning and communications; organizational development; start-up businesses; business management; mergers and acquisitions; joint ventures; divestitures; business process re-engineering.

42970 ■ Edward M. Hepner & Associates
1200 Quail St., Ste. 275
Newport Beach, CA 92660-2720
Ph:(949)250-0818
Fax: (949)553-8437
Scope: A immigration consultant and labor certification specialist. Assists in obtaining Visa's for work, immigration and business development within the United States and Canada.

42971 ■ C. W. Hines and Associates Inc.
344 Churchill Cir., Sanctuary Bay
White Stone, VA 22578
Ph:(804)435-8844
Fax: (804)435-8855
Co. E-mail: turtlecwh@aol.com
URL: http://www.cwhinesassociates.org

E-mail: turtlecwh@aol.com

Scope: Management consultants with expertise in the following categories: advertising and public relations, health and human resources, management sciences, organizational development, computer sciences, financial management, behavioral sciences, environmental design, technology transfer, project management, facility management, program evaluation, and business therapy. Also included are complementary areas such as sampling procedures, job training, managerial effectiveness, corporate seminars, gender harassment, training for trainers, and leadership and management skills development. **Publications:** Money Muscle, 120 Exercises To Build Spiritual And Financial Strength, 2004; Inside Track: Executives Coaching Executives. **Seminars:** Career Development; Coaching and Counseling for Work Success; Communicating More Effectively in a Diverse Work Environment; Communications 600: Advanced Skills for Relationship Building; Customer Service: Building a Caring Culture.

42972 ■ HR Advice.com
PO Box 313
Mountain Lakes, NJ 07046
Free: 877-854-0469
Co. E-mail: hrpro@hradvice.com
URL: http://www.hradvice.com

E-mail: hrpro@hradvice.com
Scope: Specializes in the areas of employee relations, business planning and strategy, recruiting, human resources policy, compensation and benefits, training, development and performance systems.

42973 ■ HR Answers Inc.
7659 SW Mohawk St.
Tualatin, OR 97062
Ph:(503)885-9815
Free: 877-287-4476
Fax: (503)885-8614
Co. E-mail: info@hranswers.com
URL: http://www.hranswers.com

E-mail: info@hranswers.com
Scope: Provides all types of human resource management consulting services, either on a retained or project basis. Services include compensation program design or support, benefit plan assessment, policy and procedure development, AAP and EEO/OFCCP compliance, human resource function audits, supervisory, managerial and employee training, employee relation issues/assistance, employment law compliance, employee handbooks, risk management, performance management design and information and organizational development and transition strategies. **Seminars:** Creating Your Safety Committee, Oct, 2006; Top Ten Best Practices for I-9's, Oct, 2006; Sailing the Rough C's - Communication, Counseling & Conflict Resolution; Breaking the Secret Codes of Communication; Can We Talk; Coach or Discipline - What Action is Appropriate; Catch Your Employees Doing Something Right; The Future of Human Resources.

42974 ■ The HR Dept.
22 W Pennsylvania Ave.
PO Box 1094
Bel Air, MD 21014
Ph:(410)893-0901
Fax: (410)893-0901
Co. E-mail: info@hrdept.com
URL: http://www.hrdept.com

E-mail: info@hrdept.com
Scope: Provides human resources management support to small business employers on a part-time basis. Standard support services include the review of the human resources functions, compliance issues, performance appraisal programs, handbooks and policy manuals, annual human resources calendar, quarterly human resources reports, formal compensation structure, benefit plans analysis, manager training, human resources training, day-to-day employee issues, and human resources advice, and augmenting functioning HR departments.

42975 ■ Human Networks Inc.
210 Crest St.
Ann Arbor, MI 48103-4316
Ph:(734)665-1220
Fax: (734)665-1220
Co. E-mail: aa@exclte.com

E-mail: aa@exclte.com
Scope: Provides the following consulting services: training in the areas of stress management, team building, supervisory skills, and leadership skills; and consultation regarding organizational climate assessment and improvement. Industries served include automotive, banking, small business, school, universities, and human service agencies. **Seminars:** Mind Over Matter; How Things Work at Work; The Internal Consultant: Special Skills; The External Consultant: Skills.

42976 ■ Human Resource Specialties Inc.
3 Monroe Pky., Ste. 900
PO Box 1733
Lake Oswego, OR 97035
Ph:(503)697-3329
Free: 800-354-3512
Fax: (503)636-1594
Co. E-mail: info@hrspecialties.com
URL: http://www.hrspecialties.com

E-mail: info@hrspecialties.com
Scope: Provides human resources assistance to organizations. Offers preparation of affirmative action plans, support documents, and adverse impact studies of personnel activities. Also offers customized consultations in small business services, diversity and discrimination, and investigations, complaints and grievances.

42977 ■ I.H.R. Solutions
3333 E Bayaud Ave., Ste. 219
Denver, CO 80209
Ph:(303)588-4243
Fax: (303)978-0473
Co. E-mail: dhollands@ihrsolutions.com
URL: http://www.ihrsolutions.com

E-mail: dhollands@ihrsolutions.com
Scope: Provides joint-venture and start-up human resource consulting services as well as advice on organization development for international human capital. Industries Served: high-tech and telecommunications.

42978 ■ In Plain English
14501 Antigone Dr.
PO Box 3300
North Potomac, MD 20878
Ph:(301)340-2821
Free: 800-274-9645
Fax: (301)279-0115
Co. E-mail: rwohl@inplainenglish.com
URL: http://www.inplainenglish.com

E-mail: rwohl@inplainenglish.com
Scope: Management consultants helping government and businesses research, design, write and produce user-oriented management information for human resources, employee benefits, business process, corporate and marketing needs. Employee benefits services include summary plan descriptions, employee benefit booklets, plan documents, communication of employee benefit highlights, pay for performance systems, and Section 125 cafeteria benefit enrollment. Human resources services include producing employee handbooks, employee handbook audits, training manuals, writing training, and personnel policy and policy audits. Consultants also assist clients to re-humanize their business, human resource department, recruitment, and employee benefit program. **Publications:** The Benefits Communication Edge newsletter; The Employee Benefits Communication ToolKit, published by Commerce Clearinghouse. Benefits Communicat ion; a guide published by business & legal reports. **Seminars:** Plain English Writing Training; Summary Plan Description Compliance workshops; Re-Humanizing the Corporation, Human Resources and Employee Benefits Communication

Workshop. **Special Services:** Electronic materials; Electronic summary plan descriptions; electronic reference manuals.

42979 ■ Incentive Solutions Inc.
2337 Perimeter Park Dr., Ste. 220
Atlanta, GA 30341
Ph:(770)457-4597
Free: 888-504-1231
Fax: (770)457-4994
Co. E-mail: info@incentivesolutions.com
URL: http://www.incentivesolutions.com

E-mail: info@incentivesolutions.com
Scope: Corporate incentive and motivation programs from group travel to incentive debit cards and merchandise gift certificates. Specializes in business meeting planning, audio/visual services, and Internet development to support business communications.

42980 ■ KEYGroup
1800 Sainte Claire Plz.
1121 Boyce Rd.
Pittsburgh, PA 15241-3918
Ph:(724)942-7900
Free: 800-456-5790
Fax: (724)942-4648
Co. E-mail: info@keygrp.com
URL: http://www.keygrp.com

E-mail: info@keygrp.com
Scope: A management consulting and training firm providing expertise in the areas of creativity, influencing skills, leadership, teambuilding, assessment and organizational effectiveness. Industries served: Fortune 500 executives, healthcare administrators, manufacturing managers, government/military supervisors, insurance, financial and service industry managers, educational administrators, small business owners and community leaders. **Publications:** The Power of Partnering (book). The Keys to Conquering Change: 100 Tales of Success (book), The Keys to Putting Change in Your Pocket (book), The Keys to Mastering Leadership (book), Training Games for Managing Change (book). Private Sector: We get you! Make work cultures fit the needs and aspirations of young adults, and they will stay here(sept 2005) **Seminars:** Performance Management, Enhancing Creativity Leading Others; Coaching for Improved Performance; Team-Building; Supervisory Development; Train-the-Trainer; Stress Management; Presentation Skills; Think-on-Your-Feet.

42981 ■ William E. Kuhn & Associates
234 Cook St.
Denver, CO 80206-5305
Ph:(303)322-8233
Fax: (303)322-9032
Co. E-mail: billkuhn1@cs.com

E-mail: billkuhn1@cs.com
Scope: Firm specializes in strategic planning; profit enhancement; small business management; mergers and acquisitions; joint ventures; divestitures; human resources management; performance appraisals; team building; sales management; appraisals and valuations.

42982 ■ LRP Publications
747 Dresher Rd., Ste. 500
PO Box 980
Horsham, PA 19044
Ph:(215)784-0860
Free: 800-341-7874
Fax: (215)784-9639
Co. E-mail: custserv@lrp.com
URL: http://www.lrp.com

E-mail: custserv@lrp.com
Scope: Multi-faceted publisher of business-to-business newsletters, magazines, loose-leaf publications, videos, software and on-line services covering various professional markets, such as education, employment law, federal-sector employment, bankruptcy, health, disability, eldercare, workers' compensation and personal injury verdicts and settlements.

42983 ■ JG Manley and Associates

1403 Sneed Rd. W
Franklin, TN 37069
Ph:(615)309-6999
Fax: (615)309-8874
Co. E-mail: manleyjg@aol.com
URL: http://www.tallent.com/jgmanley

E-mail: manleyjg@aol.com
Scope: Consulting firm whose services include labor relations and law, collective bargaining, employment law, benefits and compensation and training for businesses. Specializes in labor relations, employment law, organizational planning, administration, healthcare and employee benefit plans, compensation, training, safety, and human resources.

42984 ■ McCreight & Company Inc.

36 Grove St.
New Canaan, CT 06840
Ph:(203)801-5000
Fax: (203)801-5013
Co. E-mail: roc@implementstrategy.com
URL: http://www.implementstrategy.com

E-mail: roc@implementstrategy.com
Scope: We assist our global clients with strategy implementation involving large-scale change, including mergers, divestitures, alliances, and new business launches. Along with our alliance partners, we focus on issues that energize or constrain strategic change including: plans and goals; transition design; management competence; organization structure, effectiveness, and staffing; roles and responsibilities; management processes; information management and technology; and change management effectiveness. **Publications:** Strategy Implementation Insights; ePerspective; Board Effectiveness Insights; and Information Technology Insights. **Seminars:** Successful Mergers and Acquisitions - An Implementation Guide; Global 100 - One-Face-to-the-Customer; Implementation of Strategic Change.

42985 ■ Harvey A. Meier Co.

9 S Washington, Ste. 512, The Hutton Bldg.
Spokane, WA 99201-3709
Ph:(509)458-3210
Fax: (509)458-3216
Co. E-mail: hamco@harveymeier.com
URL: http://www.harveymeier.com

E-mail: hamco@harveymeier.com
Scope: Consulting firm specializes in Interim Management, Strategic Planning, Financial Planning and Organization Governance.

42986 ■ Dawn Miller and Associates

1486 Bonniebrook Heights Rd.
Gibsons, BC, Canada V0N 1V5
Ph:(604)886-8278
Fax: (604)886-5313
Co. E-mail: dawn@dmateam.com
URL: http://www.dmateam.com

E-mail: dawn@dmateam.com
Scope: Provides human resources development, planning, consulting and training for small businesses. **Publications:** "10 keys to Thriving in Changing Times".

42987 ■ R.E. Moulton Inc.

50 Doaks Ln.
Marblehead, MA 01945
Ph:(781)631-1325
Fax: (781)631-2165
Co. E-mail: mike_lee@remoultoninc.com
URL: http://www.remoultoninc.com

E-mail: mike_lee@remoultoninc.com
Scope: Health Risk Management for employees with 20 or more employees. Specialize in Plan Design and Third Party Administration Services.

42988 ■ The Murdock Group Holding Corp.

PO Box 625
Centerville, UT 84014-0625
Ph:(801)268-3232

Free: 888-888-0892
Fax: (801)268-3289
Scope: Specializes in providing full service career services and seminars for individuals and companies, including outplacements, 'The Hiring Series' and career expos. **Publications:** "The Job Seekers Bible" **Seminars:** Networking; Interviewing, Negotiating; Marketing Yourself, Effective Hiring Fundamentals On-site Training Topics.

42989 ■ New England Human Resource Group

35 Belver Ave., Ste. 107
North Kingstown, RI 02852
Ph:(401)295-2754
Fax: (401)295-2619
Co. E-mail: info@nehrg.com
URL: http://www.nehrg.com

E-mail: info@nehrg.com
Scope: Firm specializes in compensation systems, benefits, legal compliance, personnel policies and resources, employee relations law, safety and risk management, training and development, continuous improvement, career management, organizational change, strategic planning, human resource audits, ISO 9000 & QS 9000, professional development, financial planning, staffing, and executive development.

42990 ■ Nightingale Associates

7445 Setting Sun Way
Columbia, MD 21046-1261
Ph:(410)381-4280
Fax: (410)381-4280
Co. E-mail: fcnight@aol.com
URL: http://www.members.aol.com/fcnight

E-mail: fcnight@aol.com
Scope: Nightingale Associates is an international management training and consulting firm. Their concentration is on improving operational performance through the utilization of the most effective modern management techniques, executive and organizational assessment, reengineering of business processes, creative strategic thinking and focusing of the energies of all organizational participants. In addition they also work in the area of supply chain management and cost reduction through the utilization of the optimum purchasing, inventory management and distribution practices. **Seminars:** Advanced Management; Business Process Reengineering; Strategic Thinking; Creative Problem Solving; Customer Service; International Purchasing and Materials Management; Fundamentals of Purchasing.

42991 ■ Organizational Synergies

10497 Town & Country Way, Ste. 950
Houston, TX 77024
Ph:(713)461-2203
Free: 888-461-2225
Fax: (713)461-5024
Scope: Offers services in organizational effectiveness, outplacement and outsourcing. Specific services include employee development, business effectiveness analysis, business plans, climate analysis, corporate culture, departmental effectiveness analysis, management assessment, organizational effectiveness, organizational planning/design, strategic planning/direction, succession planning, work process analysis, visioning, measuring employee and management perceptions, management planning for shared vision and purpose, strategic planning/business unit planning, structure and work flow process analysis, management assessment and support services, skill and competency assessment, staff selection, alternative work arrangements, culture analysis compensation, and employee benefit plan analysis.

42992 ■ Palmetto Business Group

1531 Blanding St
PO Box 11474
Columbia, SC 29201
Ph:(803)252-4411
Fax: (803)252-3080
Co. E-mail: tchaffin@palmettobusinessgroup.com

URL: http://www.palmettobusinessgroup.com

E-mail: tchaffin@palmettobusinessgroup.com
Scope: Human resources services include employee opinion surveys, human resources function assessment, human resources management, performance management, productive practices survey, TQM, training needs assessment, wage and benefit surveys, human resources training, communications, conflict resolution, diversity, interviewing, leadership, managing within the law, management skills, performance management, remaining union free, sexual harassment, supervising people, and team-building.

42993 ■ Papa & Associates Inc.

200 Consumers Rd., Ste. 305
Toronto, ON, Canada M2J 4R4
Ph:(416)512-7272
Fax: (416)512-2016
Co. E-mail: ppapa@papa-associates.com
URL: http://www.papa-associates.com

E-mail: ppapa@papa-associates.com
Scope: Firm provides broad based management consulting services in the areas of quality assurance, environmental, health and safety and integrated management systems.

42994 ■ PATH Associates

19 Coldwater Ct., Ruxton Crossing
Towson, MD 21204
Ph:(410)821-0538
Fax: (410)821-0538
Co. E-mail: pathassoc@aol.com
URL: http://www.pathassociatesonline.com

E-mail: pathassoc@aol.com
Scope: Provides keynote talks and workshops to associations, corporations, high growth industries, hospitals, and government agencies. Emphasis is on effective programs to prevent stress and develop mental potential to increase effectiveness on the job and in life management. Also active in the areas of management training, health education, human energy and power, and youth leadership development. Offers individual consultation and coaching sessions on motivation, career goals and stress management. **Publications:** "Sponsor Success: A Workbook for Turning Good Intentions Into Positive Results," American Literature Press, 2001; "Don't Let THEM Push Your HOT BUTTON"; "When will you get a Round Tuit?".

42995 ■ Norman Peterson & Associates

287 4th St., Ste. 4
Ashland, OR 97520
Ph:(541)488-0162
Free: 800-497-1368
Co. E-mail: returntowork@ccountry.net
URL: http://www.returntowork.com

E-mail: returntowork@ccountry.net
Scope: Assists organizations in addressing workers' compensation and ADA issues. Primary service is implementation of a copyrighted transitional work program, which documents productive temporary assignments for injured employees. Industries served: governmental units, hospitals, school districts, manufacturers, food and beverage distribution, construction, printing and others. **Publications:** "Planning Pays Off in Back to Work Programs," Ohio Association of School Business Officials Chronicle; "Diving into a pool Return-to-Work program," Public Risk Magazine. **Seminars:** Safety Council for Southeast Michigan Fall Conference; Ohio County Boards Annual Conference; Michigan Association of Pupil Transportation Conference; State of Michigan Disability Management. **Special Services:** Offers database of transitional assignments to claims adjusters and claims tracking software to employers.

42996 ■ The Plotkin Group

5650 El Camino Real, Ste. 215
Carlsbad, CA 92008
Ph:(760)603-8791
Free: 800-877-5685
Fax: (760)603-8570

Co. E-mail: buytests@plotkingroup.com
URL: http://www.plotkingroup.com

E-mail: buytests@plotkingroup.com
Scope: Employee testing and training organization offering pre-employment honesty, altitude, aptitude and skills tests; and past employment, 360 degree assessments, behavior, style and communication tests by phone, paper and pencil, computers, the web, employee attitude surveys, customer service, sales, and management training. **Publications:** "Above and Beyond". **Seminars:** Building a Winning Team; Above and Beyond Customer Service Training; Taking the Guess Work Out of Hiring and Promoting.

42997 ■ The Shannon Management Group.
415 Walnut St.
PO Box 702
Coshocton, OH 43812
Ph:(740)622-2600
Fax: (740)622-9638
Co. E-mail: info@shannonmanagementgroup.com
URL: http://www.shannonmanagementgroup.com

E-mail: info@shannonmanagementgroup.com
Scope: Serving broad range of industries and public sector organizations and foundations. Specializing in human resources recruiting and outplacement counseling on international scale for businesses of all sizes. Offers expertise in human resources policies and procedures, supervisor development, manager leadership style development, interview training, etc. Provides consulting to small business in human resources, advertising, marketing, sales, public relations and community relations. **Seminars:** Time Management workshop.

42998 ■ Siebrand-Wilton Associates Inc.
PO Box 337
Marlboro, NJ 07746-0337
Ph:(732)972-1456
Fax: (732)972-0214
Co. E-mail: clientsvcs@s-wa.com
URL: http://www.swausa.com

E-mail: clientsvcs@s-wa.com
Scope: Firm assesses, plans and implements human resources aspects of mergers/acquisitions. Offers human resources consulting in compensation and benefit plan design, mergers and acquisitions (HR aspects), business ethics assessment and development, editing, writing and association management services, and contract professionals and interim executives. **Publications:** "Should Government or Business Try to Save Medicare?," HR News; "Executive Temping," HR Horizons; "When is an Employee Truly an Employee?," HR Magazine; "Examining Your Insurance Carrier," HR Magazine.

42999 ■ STAR Associates Inc.
The BeuMar Bldg., 12 W Montgomery St.
Baltimore, MD 21230
Ph:(410)727-1558
Free: 877-708-7827
Fax: (410)752-2579
Co. E-mail: barbara@starassociatesinc.com
URL: http://www.starassociatesinc.com

E-mail: barbara@starassociatesinc.com
Scope: Provide In-home aide health care to the senior population. Also provide transportation services for the Department of Aging. Provide training for all related healthcare industry needs. Provide residential group homes for youth between the ages of 13 and 18 years. Diversity and leadership training and development programs for women. **Publications:** "Yes You Can"; "Eyes of the Beholder"; "And Still, I Cry," 1993. **Seminars:** Supervisory or Management Practices; Team Playing and Group Dynamics; Time and Stress Management; Effective Communication: One Minute Management; Progressive Discipline; Project Management; Creative Decision Making and Problem Solving; Leadership Development; Absenteeism Reduction; Sales Training; Marketing Strategies.

43000 ■ Stier Associates
4 Dunellen
Cromwell, CT 06416-2702

Ph:(860)635-1590
Fax: (860)635-1591
Co. E-mail: s.stier@worldnet.att.net

E-mail: s.stier@worldnet.att.net
Scope: Personal development consulting. Subspecialty in Family-Owned businesses. Services include succession planning, executive coaching, strategic management, team building, board development. Consulting services for public companies include process consulting, team building, executive coaching, diversity management, and strategic management. Consulting to religious institutions.

43001 ■ Sylvia M. Sultenfuss
The Buckhead Ctr. For Health, 3098 Piedmont Rd. NE, Ste. 430
Atlanta, GA 30305
Ph:(404)237-7130
Fax: (404)237-6654
Co. E-mail: sylvia@sylviasays.com
URL: http://www.joyofadulthood.com

E-mail: sylvia@sylviasays.com
Scope: Offers organizational consultation and programs such as specialized management training, excellence in productivity, stress management program team building working together with different styles of communication, stress reduction program, leadership effectiveness, team building, conflict resolution, corporate wellness programs, and employee assistance programs. The focus is on small businesses or divisions where personnel issues/development are the target need. Serves private industries as well as government agencies. **Publications:** "Take the time to make time for yourself," AJC Pulse, May, 2005; "The Joy of Adulthood: A Crash Course in Designing the Life You Want," Palladium Productions, 2004; "Wake Up and Live the Life You Love: Finding Your Life's Passion," Little Seed Publishing, 2004; "Going Home for the Holidays," Labrys Atlanta, Dec, 2004; "Strategies to help resolve conflicts that arise," AJC Pulse, Feb, 2003; "On forgiveness," AJC Pulse, May, 2002; "The healer's grief: Learning to let go, say goodbye," AJC Pulse, Dec, 2001; "A way toward healing of the nation's post-traumatic grief," AJC Pulse, Dec, 2001. **Seminars:** Leadership: What it Is and Isn't; Bringing Passion and Spirit to Leadership; Gender Communication in the Workplace: The Hormones Do Make a Difference; Communicating with Difficult People; Having What You Want Without Controlling Life; Sustaining Balance in the Midst of Chaos; Who's Speaking? Who's Listening? Bring Power to Your Communication; Breaking the Love Patterns that Bind; Discovering, Sustaining and Building your Spiritual Relationships; Healing Significant Woundings of Life; Living Life Like it Matters; Love and Honor; Trust and Forgiveness.

43002 ■ Vaccari & Associates Inc.
17 Cypress St.
Marblehead, MA 01945
Ph:(781)639-0946
Fax: (781)639-0946
Co. E-mail: rvaccari1@verizon.net
URL: http://www.vaccari-associates.com

E-mail: rvaccari1@verizon.net
Scope: A provider of appraisals for primary and secondary mortgages; mortgage refinancing; employee relocation; private mortgage insurance removal; estate planning and divorce settlement.

43003 ■ Verbit & Co.
19 Bala Ave.
Bala Cynwyd, PA 19004
Ph:(610)668-9840
Scope: The management consulting services of Verbit & Company apply to practically every facet of a business, from operations and administration to financial and information systems management. These services include: general management - to assist executives and managers fulfill their mission and to assure that adequate planning of day-to-day operations occurs; that controls are sufficient to safeguard valuable resources; and that results of decisions are re-

viewed in sufficient time to effect continuing action. Financial planning and control - to develop accounting, budgeting, forecasting, and other information systems for the management of resources and evaluation of strategies. Information systems and electronic data processing - to promote efficient and effective use of computers in company operations; operations planning and control - to design systems to promote effective management of production facilities; cost accounting and management - to design systems to record and report costs of operations; and human resources - to review organizational structures, personnel planning and compensation programs. Other services include: evaluation of desk-top computer systems for small firms; CAD/CAM implementation plan and orderly introduction of CAD/CAM to client company; and public sector services to assist with evaluation and implementation of governmental accounting systems and law enforcement information systems. Industries served: manufacturing, distribution, metals casting, equipment and components, professional services, healthcare, retail, nonprofit, and government. **Seminars:** Presents seminars on Integrating Manufacturing Management Systems with Business Systems; Negotiating Information Systems Agreements with Suppliers. **Special Services:** Low volume document/image scanning; low volume document scanning -OCR editing.

43004 ■ Wheeler & Associates
13902 N Dale Mabry Hwy.
Tampa, FL 33618
Ph:(813)264-4977
Scope: Provides services in human resource development and training and managerial development assistance for all levels of management, specifically developed for the clients' unique needs. Offers organizational effectiveness studies and organizational design assistance for private and public enterprises. Expertise in conducting needs assessments, development of training plans, instructional design, and training assessment for all types of training and education, both technical and non-technical. Industries served: educational institutions and training schools, small businesses, and engineering firms. **Seminars:** Offers interviewer skills workshops, performance assessment and appraisal seminars and workshops, communication skills workshops and seminars, and management transition process planning services.

43005 ■ Workplace Dimensions Inc.
7004 Lakewood Dr.
PO Box 18363
Richmond, VA 23229
Ph:(804)673-8777
Fax: (804)673-8178
Co. E-mail: hr@workplacedimensions.com
URL: http://www.workplacedimensions.com

E-mail: hr@workplacedimensions.com
Scope: Offers a variety of services, including designing salary programs and performance management systems, customizing employee handbooks and personnel policy manuals, conducting employee and management training on harassment prevention and other relevant topics, reviewing business practices for compliance.

COMPUTERIZED DATABASES

43006 ■ *Human Resources Report*
The Bureau of National Affairs Inc.
1231 25th St. NW
Washington, DC 20037
Ph:(202)452-4200
Free: 800-372-1033
Fax: (202)452-4226
Co. E-mail: customercare@bna.com
URL: http://www.bna.com
Description: Contains detailed reporting and news of developments and trends affecting human resources and employee relations. Covers relevant national news, legislative and regulatory developments, labor

economics, developments in training and technology, health benefits, employee-management relations, compensation, and legal developments. Provides conference reports, status reports on legislation and regulations, and state, local, and international news. Covers issues such as grievances, EEO/diversity, compensation and benefits, comparable worth, job security, flexible employment, right-to-know, maternity/paternity benefits, employment at will, employee privacy rights, pay equity, drug screening, child care benefits, smoking restrictions, early retirement, immigration reform, benefits taxation, and healthcare cost containment. **Availability:** Online: The Bureau of National Affairs Inc. **Type:** Full text.

LIBRARIES

43007 ■ American Society for Training and Development (ASTD)–Information Center
1640 King St.
PO Box 1443
Alexandria, VA 22313-2043
Ph:(703)683-8100
Fax: (703)683-1523
Co. E-mail: customercare@astd.org
URL: http://www.astd.org
Contact: Debbie Wise, Proj.Mgr.
Scope: Human resource development - general, management, training, career development, Organization development, consulting skills. **Services:** Library open to national members of the Society. **Holdings:** 3000 bound volumes. **Subscriptions:** 60 journals and other serials.

43008 ■ Towers Perrin–Information Centre
1100 Melville St., Ste. 1600
Vancouver, BC, Canada V6E 4A6
Ph:(604)691-1034
Fax: (604)691-1062
Scope: Actuarial science, employee benefits, compensation, human resources. **Holdings:** Figures not available.

43009 ■ Towers Perrin–Western Canada Information Centre
3700, 150 - 6 Ave., SW
Calgary, AB, Canada T2P 3Y7
Ph:(403)261-1432
Fax: (403)237-6733
Co. E-mail: val.ward@towers.com
Contact: Val Ward
Scope: Human resource management, total rewards, pensions, employee benefits, executive compensation, employee communications, pension and benefits administration services, pension fund asset management. **Services:** Interlibrary loan. **Holdings:** 1000 books. **Subscriptions:** 100 journals and other serials; 4 newspapers.

43010 ■ Walgreen Performance Development Library
300 Wilmot Rd.
MS No. 3B55
Deerfield, IL 60015
Ph:(847)914-8172
Fax: (847)914-8492
Contact: Norma Leonard
Scope: Human resources, performance technology. **Services:** Library not open to the public. **Holdings:** 1000 books; 200 archival items. **Subscriptions:** 80 journals and other serials.

43011 ■ Walt Disney World–Information Services Technical Resource Center
IS/Team Disney 336-N
PO Box 10,000
1375 Buena Vista Dr.
Lake Buena Vista, FL 32830-1000
Ph:(407)828-4250
Fax: (407)827-8260
Co. E-mail: david.w.hartman@disney.com
Contact: David Hartman, Adm.
Scope: Computer science, human resources, general business. **Services:** Center not open to the public. **Holdings:** 1500 books; 100 microfiche; 4000 comput-

er documents; 25 audio/visual materials. **Subscriptions:** 150 journals and other serials; 2 newspapers.

RESEARCH CENTERS

43012 ■ Rollins College–Center for Enterprise Management
Crummer Graduate School of Business
1000 Holt Ave.
Winter Park, FL 32789
Ph:(407)628-6373
Fax: (407)646-1503
Co. E-mail: mstarr@rollins.edu
Contact: Prof. Martin K. Starr, Dir.
E-mail: mstarr@rollins.edu
Scope: Operations management, including demographic profiles, human resource management, production flow management, fast response systems, and product quality. Investigates production methods and performance of Japanese-owned firms in America, foreign-affiliated firms in America, and performance of white collar and knowledge workers in manufacturing and service firms. **Educational Activities:** Conferences and seminars.

43013 ■ University of British Columbia–Bureau for Research on Applications of Information Technology
2053 Main Mall
Faculty of Commerce & Business Administration
Vancouver, BC, Canada V6T 1Z2
Ph:(604)822-8390
Fax: (604)822-0045
Co. E-mail: carson.woo@ubc.ca
URL: http://mis.commerce.ubc.ca/brite/
Contact: Prof. Carson Woo PhD, Dir.
E-mail: carson.woo@ubc.ca
Scope: Corporate information systems development and human issues.

REFERENCE WORKS

43014 ■ **"Coca-Cola Bottler Up for Sale: CEO J. Bruce Llewellyn Seeks Retirement" in** *Black Enterprise* **(Vol. 37, December 2006, No. 5, pp. 31)**
Pub: Earl G. Graves Publishing Co. Inc.
Ed: Marcia A. Wade. **Description:** J. Bruce Llewellyn of Brucephil Inc., the parent company of the Philadelphia Coca-Cola Bottling Co. has agreed to sell its remaining shares to Coca-Cola Co., which previously owned 31 percent of Philly Coke. Analysts believe that Coca-Cola will eventually sell its shares to another bottler.

43015 ■ **"Denbury Selects Digital Oilfield" in** *Mississippi Business Journal* **(Vol. 29, January 2007, No. 2, pp. 13)**
Pub: Venture Publications, Inc.
Ed: Wally Northway **Description:** Independent oil and gas company Denbury Resources Inc. has signed a multi-year license agreement with Digital Oilfield Inc. 's OpenInvoice Image and OpenContract PriceBook solutions to automate and streamline its invoicing processes.

43016 ■ *The Essential Corporation Handbook*
Pub: Oasis Press
Ed: Carl R. Sniffen. **Released:** 1992. **Price:** $21.95 (paper).

43017 ■ *Forming Corporations and Partnerships*
Pub: TAB Books, Inc.
Ed: John Cotton Howell. **Released:** 1991. **Price:** $14.95. **Description:** Provides information on corporations and partnerships, covering special corporate tax and insurance, pros and cons of various business entities, duties and responsibilities of corporate officers, and rights, duties, and obligations of parties in joint ventures.

43018 ■ *How to Form Your Own Indiana Corporation Before the Inc. Dries!*
Pub: P. Gaines Co.
Ed: Phillip G. Williams. **Released:** 2nd ed. 1997. **Price:** $31.95 (diskette; paper) Vol. 4.

43019 ■ *How to Form Your Own Michigan Corporation Before the Inc. Dries!: A Stepby-Step Guide, with Forms*
Pub: P. Gaines Co.
Ed: Phillip G. Williams. **Released:** 3rd ed. 1999. **Price:** $31.95.

43020 ■ *How to Incorporate & Start a Business in Colorado*
Pub: Adams Media Corp.
Ed: J. W. Dicks. **Released:** 1998. **Price:** $16.95.

43021 ■ *How to Incorporate & Start a Business in Georgia*
Pub: Adams Media Corp.
Ed: J. W. Dicks. **Released:** 1997. **Price:** $16.95.

43022 ■ *How to Incorporate & Start a Business in Indiana*
Pub: Adams Media Corp.
Ed: J. W. Dicks. **Released:** 1997. **Price:** $16.95.

43023 ■ *How to Incorporate & Start a Business in Minnesota*
Pub: Adams Media Corp.
Ed: J. W. Dicks. **Released:** 1997. **Price:** $16.95.

43024 ■ *How to Incorporate & Start a Business in Nevada*
Pub: Adams Media Corp.
Ed: J. W. Dicks. **Released:** 1997. **Price:** $16.95.

43025 ■ *How to Incorporate & Start a Business in Oregon*
Pub: Adams Media Corp.
Ed: J. W. Dicks. **Released:** 1997. **Price:** $16.95.

43026 ■ *How to Incorporate & Start a Business in Tennessee*
Pub: Adams Media Corp.
Ed: J. W. Dicks. **Released:** 1997. **Price:** $16.95.

43027 ■ *How to Incorporate & Start a Business in Virginia*
Pub: Adams Media Corp.
Ed: J. W. Dicks. **Released:** 1997. **Price:** $16.95.

43028 ■ *How to Incorporate & Start a Business in Washington*
Pub: Adams Media Corp.
Ed: J. W. Dicks. **Released:** 1997. **Price:** $16.95.

43029 ■ **"Pay as You Click" in** *Crain's New York Business* **(Vol. 22, December 11, 2006, No. 50, pp. 19)**
Pub: Crain Communications, Inc.
Description: Google Inc. started an online payment service, Google Checkout. It developed the service at its New York office. Google Checkout, which launched in June 2006, aims to compete with PayPal.

43030 ■ **"Putting Focus on 4 Famed Firms" in** *Crain's New York Business* **(Vol. 22, November 27, 2006, No. 48, pp. 17)**
Pub: Crain Communications, Inc.
Ed: Aaron Elstein. **Description:** Crain's spotlight on key statistics of four well-known businesses in the New York area includes information on Eileen Fisher Inc., Key Food Stores Co-Operative Inc., Ziff Davis Holdings Inc., and Publishers Clearing House.

43031 ■ **"Real Estate on New York Business. com" in** *Crain's New York Business* **(Vol. 22, December 4, 2006, No. 49, pp. 22)**
Pub: Crain Communications, Inc.
Description: Crain Communications, Inc. offers a number of services on their website, business.com. Features include back issues, current events, company alerts, breaking news, resources to government agencies and industry groups involved in New York real estate, and information on residential properties.

43032 ■ **"SoBran Partners with U.S. Navy" in** *Black Enterprise* **(Vol. 37, October 2006, No. 3, pp. 38)**
Pub: Earl G. Graves Publishing Co. Inc.
Ed: Glenn Townes. **Description:** SoBran Inc., partnered with Lockheed Martin and signed a three-Tear production service contract with the Naval Aviation Depot in Jacksonville, Florida. The $44 million contract will allow SoBran to transport and warehouse materials for Navy facilities.

43033 ■ **"World Wide Technology Expands" in** *Black Enterprise* **(Vol. 37, December 2006, No. 5, pp. 34)**
Pub: Earl G. Graves Publishing Co. Inc.
Ed: Marcia A. Wade. **Description:** World Wide Technology Inc. opened a streamlined, higher capacity 12,000-square-foot Integration Technology Center near its corporate headquarters in St. Louis. The new venture will transfer lower costs to customers.

START-UP INFORMATION

43034 ■ **"Alameda high-tech incubator is expanding"** in *Kiplinger California Letter* (Vol. 38, No. 17, September 4, 2002)
Pub: Kiplinger Washington Editors, Inc.
Description: Profile of Advancing California's Emerging Technologies high-tech incubator. The high-tech incubator will construct a 40,000 square foot laboratory and offices with $6.5 million in federal money.

43035 ■ **"Beacon Telco Aims To Jumpstart Optics"** in *Venture Capital Journal* (Vol. 40, No. 10, November 2000, pp. 6, 8)
Pub: Venture Economics
Description: Beacon Telco, a venture capital development company, was launched in mid-September 2000, to focus on optical networking and broadband communications. The venture capital firm will provide its portfolio companies with $1 million to $3 million in funding, noting that companies which choose to participate in the incubation program will also need to pay a program cost for incubator services.

43036 ■ **"Choosing an Incubator for your Business Baby"** in *Ingram's* (Vol. 28, No. 6, June 2002, pp. 49)
Pub: Show Me Publishing, Inc.
Description: Small business management techniques are featured. An outline and review of some of the 900 business incubator programs offered by federal and state agencies to assist in the development of small businesses is presented.

43037 ■ **"Co-production of business assistance in business incubators: An exploratory study"** in *Journal of Business Venturing* (Vol. 17, No. 2)
Pub: Elsevier Science, Inc.
Ed: Mark P. Rice. **Description:** This study examines the role of a business incubator and the role of the entrepreneurial ventures located within the incubator. The incubator is described as the producer of business assistance programs, while the venture holds a co-producer role. Both roles are discussed.

43038 ■ **"Entrepreneurs should be wary of incubators"** in *Red Herring* (No. 76, March 2000, pp. 86)
Pub: Herring Communications, Inc.
Ed: Alex Gove. **Description:** Not all incubators are created equal. Some incubators may offer infrastructure benefits, but the true test concerns those who run them.

43039 ■ **"Incubators that actually work? You won't find them only in Internet space"** in *Inc.* (November 2000, pp. 64)
Pub: The Goldhirsh Group
Description: In an Inc. survey of more than 30 incubator-savvy CEOs and experts in the field, eight nonprofit incubators throughout the nation stood out.

43040 ■ **"Making Ideas Fly"** in *Internet World* (Vol. 6, No. 12, June 15, 2000, pp. 31)
Pub: Mecklermedia Corporation
Ed: David Lipschultz. **Description:** Despite some setbacks, dot-com companies continue to pop up. Sometimes a start-up company would do well to go with a business incubator. These incubators can offer all manner of services from business to Web site development, but often take a large part of the company. Some start-ups work with venture capital companies who are eager to invest in Internet companies.

43041 ■ **"Minneapolis"** in *Entrepreneur* (Vol. 28, No. 4, April 2000, pp. 162)
Pub: Entrepreneur Media Inc.
Ed: Cynthia E. Griffin. **Description:** Use this incubator to hatch your business in 90 days or less. Entrenaut, a Minneapolis incubator is profiled.

43042 ■ **"Should You Get Incubated?"** in *E-business Advisor* (Vol. 18, No. 10, October 2000, pp. 18)
Pub: Advisor Media, Inc.
Ed: Kim M. Bayne. **Description:** Incubators, firms that take an idea and hatch it into a company, are on the increase. This article tells how to choose one and what to look for.

43043 ■ **"Sky Dayton"** in *Internet World* (Vol. 6, No. 7, April 1, 2000, pp. 94)
Pub: Mecklermedia Corporation
Ed: Brian Caulfield. **Description:** EarthLink Network founder Sky Dayton plans to launch more new Web-based businesses, now that EarthLink has merged with rival MindSpring. Jake Winebaum's and Dayton's eCompanies, a business incubator for new Web companies, generates efficient Web start-ups within 180 days, including funding. Dayton looks for companies that blend commerce, community, and content.

43044 ■ **"A Talk With the Net's Financiers"** in *Internet World* (Vol. 6, No. 6, March 15, 2000, pp. 60)
Pub: Mecklermedia Corporation
Ed: David Lipschultz. **Description:** An interview with five leading venture capitalists to answer questions on the state of the Internet revolution. Questions are related to topics such as the types of businesses that venture capitalists are looking for and the possibility of emergence of another Yahoo or Cisco. The venture capitalists were also asked about the importance of the CEO in a company and predictions regarding when the Internet explosion was likely to end.

43045 ■ **"This VC Firm's Motto: Make Money, Not War"** in *Fortune* (Vol. 142, No. 3, July 24, 2000, pp. 54)
Pub: Time Inc.
Ed: Jane M. Folpe. **Description:** Military Commercial Technologies, an Orlando venture capital firm and high-tech incubator, has a winning formula for bringing defense technology to the public sector.

43046 ■ **"When It's Time to Market that Matters Most"** in *Inc.* (July 2000, pp. 92)
Pub: The Goldhirsh Group

Ed: Thea Singer. **Description:** Business incubators for Internet start-ups are examined.

43047 ■ **"Yours, Mine, Ours"** in *My Business* (October/November 2002, pp. 35-37)
Pub: My Business Magazine
Ed: Kathleen Landis. **Description:** The benefits of sharing office space by small businesses are discussed. This method works especially well for startups and home offices that are expanding. Various firms successfully using this concept are profiled.

REFERENCE WORKS

43048 ■ **"Arlington, Texas, High-Tech Incubator Gets $2.85 Million Boost"** in *Dallas Morning News* (October 27, 2002)
Pub: Knight Ridder/Tribune Business News
Ed: Jenni Smith. **Description:** The Arlington Technology Incubator, a joint venture of the University of Texas at Arlington and the Arlington Chamber of Commerce, received a $150,000 technical assistance grant from the U.S. Economic Development Administration and will get another $2.7 million from the research portion of the defense bill signed by President Bush in October.

43049 ■ **"Central Indiana's High-Tech Incubator Lands First Tenant"** in *Indianapolis Star* (September 24, 2002)
Pub: Knight Ridder/Tribune Business News
Ed: Jack Naudi. **Description:** Profile of central Indiana's newest high-tech incubator, the Haelan Group, a small company with a big high-tech vision to improve health care. The startup firm is geared toward life sciences, and will be run by Indiana University's Advanced Research and Technology Institute.

43050 ■ **"Directors of High-Tech Incubator in Tampa, Fla., Vote to Shut Down"** in *Tampa Tribune* (October 4, 2002)
Pub: Knight Ridder/Tribune Business News
Ed: Frank Witsil. **Description:** Profile of TechVillage Tampa Bay, a one year old high-tech incubator, announced its closing in October 2002. The incubator had a budget of $120,000, but after nine months encountered financial problems.

43051 ■ *Directory of Operating Small Business Investment Companies*
Pub: DIANE Publishing Co.
Ed: John Wilmeth. **Released:** 1998. **Price:** $20.00.
Description: An alphabetical listing by state of SBICs including branch offices. The listed companies received licenses from the U.S. Small Business Administration (SBA) & their licenses remain outstanding. This list does not include currently licensed SBICs in the process of surrendering their licenses or subject to legal proceedings that might terminate their licenses. The report includes SBIC program information & statistics: how to seek SBIC financing, explanation of directory information, portfolio stages of development, licenses outstanding & capital resources (1990-1995) & new regular & specialized SBICs licensed (1987-1995).

43052 ■ "Down Economy Helps Incubate Small Businesses" in *Crain's Detroit Business* (Vol. 19, No. 45, November 10, 2003, pp. 11)
Pub: Crain Communications Inc., Detroit
Ed: Laura Bailey. Description: The State of Michigan reported 8,432 new business entities in 2003, and expects the trend to grow in 2004.

43053 ■ "The Eparty's Over" in *Forbes* (December 11, 2000, pp. 144)
Pub: Forbes Magazine
Ed: Dorothy Pomerantz. Description: Of all the overhyped incubators launched during the heady days of 1999, Ecompanies and its two young founders seemed like a sure bet.

43054 ■ "Hatching a Better Incubator" in *Red Herring* (No. 87, December 18, 2000, pp. 88-92, 94)
Pub: Herring Communications, Inc.
Ed: Dean Takahashi. Description: A profile of Raza Foundries, a venture capital incubator that continues to have tremendous success.

43055 ■ "Internet Incubators Rethink Strategies, Become Pickier" in *Wall Street Journal* (May 2, 2000, pp. B2)
Pub: Dow Jones & Co., Inc.
Ed: Eleena De Lisser. Description: Incubators are being more cautious in their strategies.

43056 ■ "Mining Mars" in *CMA Management* (Vol. 76, No. 6, Sept. 2002, pp. 38)
Pub: Society of Management Accountants of Canada
Ed: John Cooper. Description: Information regarding high-tech incubators in Ontario, Canada is presented, examining the possibilities for space firms.

43057 ■ "Networked incubators: Hothouses of the new economy" in *Harvard Business Review* (Vol. 78, No. 5, September-October 2000, pp. 51)
Pub: Harvard Business School Publishing Corp.
Ed: Donald N. Nitin, Henry W. Sull, Mortin T. Nohria, Hansen Chesbrough. Description: Presented are the findings of a survey of 169 of the more than 350 business incubators now operating throughout the world. The authors found that the most effective incubators offered networks of business connections along with office space and funding. The article includes graphs.

43058 ■ "Papermaster in startup mode" in *Austin Business Journal* (Vol. 22, No. 28, September 27, 2002, pp. 1)
Pub: Austin Business Journal Inc.
Ed: Spacey Higginbotham. Description: Steve Papermaster's software company Agillion Inc. was sold at auction when dot-com companies crashed. He is back now as chairman of a high tech business company formed through incubator Powershift Ventures

LLP, and co-investor with Azure Capital Partners LP, called CooperaTech Inc., which develops risk and opportunity management software.

43059 ■ "The Reverse Greenhouse Effect: Why pay another to gardener to cultivate your stock?" in *Fortune* (Vol.141, No.7, Apr. 3, 2000, pp.302)
Pub: Time Inc.
Ed: Adam Lashinsky. Description: Incubators are a lot like venture capital firms, at least in what they set out to accomplish. But incubators take a holistic approach by anticipating all of a startup's needs from the get-go.

43060 ■ *Small Business Investment Company Directory & Handbook*
Pub: International Wealth Success, Inc.
Ed: Tyler G. Hicks. Released: 10th ed. 1999. Price: $15.00.

43061 ■ "When an Incubator Goes Cold" in *Business Week Online* ()
Pub: McGraw-Hill, Inc.
Description: Investors in Idealab! want to liquidate the Pasadena high tech incubator, but instead feel they are being offered a fraction of what their shares of stock are worth.

Insurance

START-UP INFORMATION

43062 ■ "Healthcare Options" in *Small Business Opportunities* (Vol. 12, No. 3, May 2000, pp. 10, 130)
Pub: Harris Publications, Inc.
Ed: Marie Sherlock. **Description:** As a new business owner, the question of availability and cost of health insurance is vital. This article examines affordable, quality options.

43063 ■ "Learning the Ropes" in *Entrepreneur* (Vol. 33, October 2005, No. 10, pp. 99)
Pub: Entrepreneur Media Inc.
Description: A.D. Banker & Company helps individuals wishing to buy a franchise obtain licenses in the insurance, security, legal and accounting industries through classroom, online and self-study courses.

ASSOCIATIONS AND OTHER ORGANIZATIONS

43064 ■ National Council of Self-Insurers
1253 Springfield Ave.
PMB 345
New Providence, NJ 07974
Ph:(908)665-2152
Fax: (908)665-4020
Co. E-mail: natcouncil@aol.com
URL: http://www.natcouncil.com
Contact: Lawrence J. Holt, Exec.Dir.
Description: State associations, individual companies, associate members, and professional members concerned with self-insurance under the workmen's compensation laws. Promotes and protects, at all governmental levels, the interests of self-insurers or legally non-insured employers and their employees in matters of legislative and administrative activity affecting workmen's compensation; assists, advises, and uses its resources in developing and implementing common objectives among self-insurers. Current goals are: a workmen's compensation program that is just, both to the individual and to the employer; equitable distribution of the compensation dollar; strong vocational rehabilitation incentives for the injured employee. **Publications:** *Officers, Membership, and By-Laws* (bimonthly); *Self-Insurance Requirements of the States* (periodic). Also publishes self-insurance requirements of all states.

EDUCATIONAL PROGRAMS

43065 ■ Fundamentals of Risk Management and Insurance for Non-insurance Executives
American Management Association
1601 Broadway
New York, NY 10019
Ph:(212)586-8100
Free: 800-262-9699

Fax: (212)903-8168
Co. E-mail: customerservice@amanet.org
URL: http://www.amanet.org
Price: $1,195.00 for non-members; $1,095.00 for AMA members. **Description:** For executives with financial responsibilities; covers identifying insurance needs, learning insurance jargon, future planning, and an overview of the insurance market. **Locations:** Atlanta, GA; and Boston, MA.

REFERENCE WORKS

43066 ■ "Account Balances Indicate That 401(k) Participants Have Heard The Long-Term Investor Message" in *Employee Benefit Plan Review* (Vol. 55)
Pub: Charles D. Spencer & Associates, Inc.
Ed: Sue Burzawa. **Description:** Lincolnshire, Illinois-based Hewitt Associates LLC, the health benefit plan consulting company, tracks pension fund activity through its 401(k) Index. Industry analysts said that institutional investors are remaining calm as the country suffers from a period of economic upheaval.

43067 ■ "Accountants on the Move" in *Rough Notes* (Vol. 146, No. 3, March 2003, pp. 30)
Pub: Rough Notes
Ed: Gene Mason. **Description:** In the light of recent accounting scandals, many accountants are on the move and taking clients with them. Asset/professional liability policies needed by these workers are being carefully underwritten and provided by insurers.

43068 ■ "Aetna to Expand to Pompano Beach" in *Miami Herald* (March 10, 2005)
Pub: Knight-Ridder/Tribune Business News
Ed: Patrick Danner. **Description:** Aetna healthcare will open a new prescription mail order facility in Pompano Beach, Florida. The new facility will employ about 800 people. Another facility in Kansas City, Missouri, owned by Aetna, fills nearly 6 million prescriptions annually.

43069 ■ "Agent of Change" in *Rough Notes* (Vol. 145, No. 9, September 2002, pp. 38)
Pub: Rough Notes
Ed: Elaine Tolen. **Description:** Dick Fournier, owner of Oregon Insurance Agency, attributes the independent insurance agency's success to former owner Martin K. Bowes, and his staff. He also favors updating the agency with technology and continuing education.

43070 ■ *Agents and Buyer's Guide Marketing Service*
Pub: National Underwriter Co.
Released: Annual. **Price:** $249 looseleaf with quarterly updates. **Covers:** Insurance companies and special agencies providing placement for unusual or difficult to place risks. **Entries Include:** Address, telephone and telex numbers.

43071 ■ "Agents Urged to Answer the Call" in *Rough Notes* (Vol. 145, No. 12, December 2002, pp. 127)
Pub: Rough Notes
Ed: John Chivvis. **Description:** During the conference of the Independent Insurance Agents and Brokers of America, a call to action for interface improvements was made. These improvements will streamline the insurance buying and selling process.

43072 ■ "AIG Plans to Cut 27 Jobs at Neptune, N.J., Offices" in *The Record* (November 8, 2005)
Pub: New Jersey Media Group
Ed: Dennis P. Carmody. **Description:** AIG American General will cut a total of 250 employees from its group benefits workforce over the next 18 months. The group benefits division administers health insurance plans sponsored by employers.

43073 ■ "Ailing Wellness Plan considers job cuts" in *Crain's Detroit Business* (Vol. 19, No. 9, March 3, 2003, pp. 3)
Pub: Crain Communications Inc., Detroit
Ed: Katie Merx. **Description:** The State of Michigan's largest Medicaid health maintenance organization is considering laying off workers in an attempt to save money.

43074 ■ "All Offices Are Not Created Equal" in *Rough Notes* (Vol. 146, No. 3, March 2003, pp. 54)
Pub: Rough Notes
Ed: Linda Ferguson. **Description:** As exposures are not the same in all offices, potential liability would vary. Risks and exposures should be classified, premiums correspondingly adjusted, amendments and exclusions should be attached to the policy.

43075 ■ "Alternative Market Grows As Rates Harden" in *Rough Notes* (Vol. 146, No. 3, March 2003, pp. 38)
Pub: Rough Notes
Ed: Len Strazewski. **Description:** As agents find it more difficult to place their risks because of the increasingly hard market, they have turned to the alternative risk market. These are the captive insurance companies or risk retention groups like Arthur J. Gallagher and Company that accept risks at premium rates based on the agent's loss experience.

43076 ■ "Alternative Markets and Risk Financing" in *Rough Notes* (Vol. 145, No. 9, September 2002, pp. 82)
Pub: Rough Notes
Ed: Donald J. Riggin. **Description:** The alternative market in insurance is used to describe a variety of risk transferring financing options that are not normally available from the standard multi-line insurance companies. These usually take the form of reinsurances, in excess of a self-insured retention.

43077 ■ "Anatomy of a Merger" in *Rough Notes* (Vol. 145, No. 2, February 2003, pp. 66)
Pub: Rough Notes
Ed: Paul J. DiStefano. **Description:** When insurance agencies merge, the principals should address the is-

sues of equity allocation, compensations, and the assumption of roles and responsibilities.

43078 ■ "Answer the phone and have a good time" in *Rough Notes* **(Vol. 146, No. 4, April 2003, pp. 18)**
Pub: Rough Notes
Ed: Dennis Pillsbury. **Description:** Mike Heffernan is the CEO of Heffernan Group, which includes Heffernan Insurance Brokers, an insurance retail agency and Presidio and Advanced Risk Technologists. Nearly 50 percent of business is derived from niche practices and programs such as nonprofits, healthcare, property owners, construction and technology.

43079 ■ "Appraising The Agency" in *Rough Notes* **(Vol. 145, No. 2, February 2002, pp. 50)**
Pub: Rough Notes
Ed: Len Strazewski. **Description:** Marsh-Berry Services Inc., in Concord, Ohio, renders agency assessment and performance consulting services. It reports on the value of an insurance agency as a measure of its overall performance.

43080 ■ "Area HMOs get the point about acupuncture" in *San Francisco Business Times* **(Vol. 15, No. 2, August 18, 2000, pp. 29)**
Pub: American City Business Journals, Inc.
Ed: Brendan Doherty. **Description:** Long derided as quackery, acupuncture is stepping out of medicine's fringe and gaining acceptance in the San Francisco Bay area, and PacificCare and Health Net began offering employer group coverage as a benefit for acupuncture in 2000.

43081 ■ "Arris trades road shows for online presentations" in *Atlanta Business Chronicle* **(Vol. 25, No. 19, October 18, 2002, pp. 8B)**
Pub: American City Business Publications, Inc.
Ed: Lee Hall. **Description:** Arris Group Inc., in Duluth, Georgia, has shifted most of its employee benefits education efforts onto the Internet, and away from putting its executives on the road. Initially intended to save the company money, the program also proved to be very effective and more popular with employees who found that they did not need to attend meetings. In addition, the program has encouraged employees to participate, due to the confidentiality afforded by the program.

43082 ■ "Atlanta Life to Manage MetLife Assets" in *Black Enterprise* **(Vol. 35, November 2004, No. 4, pp. 32)**
Pub: Earl G. Graves Publishing Co. Inc.
Ed: Aisha Jefferson. **Description:** Atlanta Life Investment Advisors, the nation's largest African-American owned, privately held stock insurance company, agreed with MetLife to manage $50 million of MetLife's assets.

43083 ■ "Attention to Nonmedical Factors Can Facilitate Return-To-Work For Workers' Comp Claimants" in *Employee Benefit Plan Review* **(Vol. 55)**
Pub: Charles D. Spencer & Associates, Inc.
Ed: Jay E. Betz. **Description:** Workers' compensation insurance is the focus of an interview with Jay E. Betz, an executive at Milwaukee, Wisconsin-based CareNetwork Inc. The goal of workers' compensation services is to return the injured employee to work in a safe and timely manner.

43084 ■ "Auto insurer files for $350 million initial public offering" in *Atlanta Business Chronicle* **(Vol. 25, No. 19, Oct. 18, 2002, pp. 3A)**
Pub: American City Business Publications, Inc.
Ed: Lisa R. Schoolcraft. **Description:** Infinity Property and Casualty Corporation, located in Alpharetta, Georgia, will be the second company in the metropolitan Atlanta, Georgia area to file for an initial public offering in the previous two months. An insurer of high-risk drivers and a unit of the American Financial Group Inc., Infinity is looking to raise $350 million from the move, according to a filing with the U.S. Securities and Exchange Commission.

43085 ■ "Bad Judgment? Even Top Execs Can Make Mistakes" in *Entrepreneur* **(Vol. 31, No. 9, September 2003, pp. 79)**
Pub: Entrepreneur Media, Inc.
Ed: Jacquelyn Lynn. **Description:** The importance of carrying directors and officers (D&O) liability insurance for a small business is emphasized. This insurance covers directors and officers against wrongful acts typically described as bad business judgment.

43086 ■ "A Balancing Act" in *Rough Notes* **(Vol. 145, No. 1, January 2003, pp. 84)**
Pub: Rough Notes
Ed: Phil Zinkewicz. **Description:** Metro Insurance Services Inc., headed by Steven R. Gross, chairman and CEO, started out as a retail insurance agent and evolved into a wholesaler for retail agents representing United National, Lloyds of London, and Burlington Insurance Group.

43087 ■ "Battle brews against tort reform" in *Atlanta Business Chronicle* **(Vol. 25, Dec. 13, 2002, No. 27, pp. A1)**
Pub: American City Business Publications, Inc.
Ed: Julie Bryant. **Description:** As political move towards tort reform in Georgia gathers strength with the election of Sonny Perdue, trial attorneys and the victims they represent are presenting data indicating that such reforms do not halt medical malpractice insurance premium hikes. Caps on jury awards are, however, sought by physicians as they face mounting insurance premiums.

43088 ■ "Battle of the Sexes" in *Kiplinger's Personal Finance Magazine* **(Vol. 55, No. 1, January, 2001, pp. 24)**
Pub: The Kiplinger Washington Editors, Inc.
Ed: Catherine Siskos. **Description:** An investigation into how changes of life expectancy affect the purchase of different types of insurance. Women have always enjoyed an edge over men on the cost of life insurance because of their longer life expectancy, but lately the gap has narrowed.

43089 ■ "Becoming a Great Agency: Part One" in *Rough Notes* **(Vol. 145, No. 9, September 2002, pp. 62)**
Pub: Rough Notes
Ed: Roger Sitkins. **Description:** Guidelines for insurance companies to develop into what is termed a Great Agency are offered.

43090 ■ "Behind the Scenes" in *Washington Business Journal* **(Vol. 22, No. 12, July 25, 2003, pp. 18)**
Pub: Washington Business Journal
Ed: Tim Mazzucca. **Description:** Shane Chalke, CEO of Herndon, Virginia-based AnnuityNet, markets software products to investment and insurance firms. AnnuityNet acquired a subsidiary of Wachovia Bank for an undisclosed price.

43091 ■ "The Belt and Suspenders Approach to Contractual Liability Coverage" in *Rough Notes* **(Vol. 146, No. 9, September 2003, pp. 70)**
Pub: Rough Notes
Ed: Donald S. Malecki. **Description:** Information on standard interpretations of liability insurance and liability waivers, including liability insurance policies, indemnity, and applicable contract laws is presented.

43092 ■ "Benefits Costs Averaged 36.8 Percent Of Payroll In 1999" in *Employee Benefit Plan Review* **(Vol. 55, No. 10, April 2001 pp. 14)**
Pub: Charles D. Spencer & Associates, Inc.
Description: The U.S. Chamber of Commerce annual survey, "The 2000 Employee Benefits Study", shows the most costly company benefit in 1999 was still paid time off at 30 percent. The second most expensive was medical benefits, which accounted for 26 percent of the benefit dollar.

43093 ■ "Better Safe: Does Your Product Need a Warning Label?" in *Entrepreneur* **(Vol. 31, No. 9, July 2003, pp. 76)**
Pub: Entrepreneur Media, Inc.

Ed: Jane Easter Bahls. **Description:** When injured, a consumer can sue not only the manufacturer, but also the supplier, dealer, distributor or rental yard.

43094 ■ "Bill Would Boost Small Businesses" in *Bradenton Herald* **(February 13, 2007)**
Pub: Bradenton Herald
Ed: Brian Neill. **Description:** U.S. Representative Vern Buchanan has introduced a bill in Congress that includes a provision that would enable small businesses to offer health insurance more readily through the formation of associations. The bill would also benefit small business owners by allowing them to deduct a larger portion of taxes for labor and capital expenditures.

43095 ■ "Blue Cross Ties Healthy Living to Lower Rates" in *Providence Business News* **(Vol. 18, No. 23, September 22, 2003, pp. 1)**
Pub: Providence Business News, Inc.
Ed: Mike Colias. **Description:** Rhode Island's Blue Cross and Blue Shield offers lower premium rates to customers agreeing to stay in shape. Currently, this is the only program that actually ties consumer action to premium rates.

43096 ■ "Blue Cross to cut benefits for its workers" in *Crain's Detroit Business* **(Vol. 19, No. 16, April 21, 2003, pp. 1)**
Pub: Crain Communications Inc., Detroit
Ed: Katie Merx. **Description:** Blue Cross Blue Shield of Michigan plans to cut health benefits for salaried workers and retirees in order to cut costs.

43097 ■ "Blues' exclusive deals under fire" in *Crain's Detroit Business* **(Vol. 18, No. 44, Nov. 4, 2002, pp. 1)**
Pub: Crain Communications Inc., Detroit
Ed: Robert Ankeny. **Description:** Blue Cross and Blue Shield of Michigan and the Detroit Regional Chamber are hoping to retain their exclusive contract for supplying small businesses with group rate insurance. A Michigan State Representative has introduced a package of small-business health insurance reforms, including a provision that would prohibit the Blues from entering into exclusive contracts with chambers and associations.

43098 ■ "Blues offer grant to study nurse shortage" in *Crain's Detroit Business* **(Vol. 19, No. 15, April 14, 2003, pp. 14)**
Pub: Crain Communications Inc., Detroit
Ed: Ian McClure. **Description:** Blue Cross Blue Shield of Michigan Foundation, located in Detroit, Michigan, is providing grant opportunities for new programs and research to help ease the nursing shortage facing the state.

43099 ■ "Blues' Small-Biz Rates to Rise 10% in 2004" in *Crain's Detroit Business* **(Vol. 19, No. 40, October 13, 2003, pp. 1)**
Pub: Crain Communications Inc., Detroit
Ed: Katie Merx. **Description:** Despite the fact that Blue Cross Blue Shield of Michigan is cutting costs internally, small business customers will see an average 10 percent rise in premiums.

43100 ■ "Blues' Small-Biz Rates to Rise 10% in 2004; Insurer Cuts Costs with Lower Commissions" in *Crain's Detroit Business* **(Vol. 19, No. 40)**
Pub: Crain Communications Inc., Detroit
Ed: Katie Merx. **Description:** Despite the fact that Blue Cross Blue Shield of Michigan is cutting costs internally, small business customers will see an average 10 percent rise in premiums.

43101 ■ "Blues losses decline for small-group business coverage" in *Crain's Detroit Business* **(Vol. 18, No. 17, April 29, 2002, pp. 22)**
Pub: Crain Communications Inc. - Detroit
Ed: David Barkholz. **Description:** Blue Cross and Blue Shield of Michigan has cut underwriting losses in its troubled small-group business at a time when legislation is aimed at changing Blues governance and health insurance in Michigan.

43102 ■ "Blues reforms raise cost worries" in *Crain's Detroit Business* (Vol. 18, No. 19, May 13, 2002,)
Pub: Crain Communications Inc. - Detroit
Ed: David Barkholz. Description: Rising healthcare costs worry area small businesses.

43103 ■ "Boosting Morale with Work/Life Benefits" in *Rough Notes* (Vol. 145, No. 12, December 2002, pp. 110)
Pub: Rough Notes
Ed: Len Strazewski. Description: Insurance agents can deepen business relations with clients by offering and explaining the issues that occupy them regarding health care benefits to employees.

43104 ■ "Brent Bannerman" in *Entrepreneur* (Vol. 31, No. 6, June 2003, pp. 23)
Pub: Entrepreneur Media Inc.
Ed: April Y. Pennington. Description: Profile of Brent Bannerman, founder of IE-Engine, the Waltham, Massachusetts business insurance and benefits software developer; Bannerman has projected 2003 sales of $10 million for his company that was founded in 2000.

43105 ■ "Bryson Buys Two Agencies" in *Mississippi Business Journal* (Vol. 29, January 2007, No. 2, pp. 8)
Pub: Venture Publications, Inc.
Ed: Wally Northway Description: Bryson Insurance acquires Banks Insurance and Shackleford Brothers & Fortenberry.

43106 ■ "Buck's Annual 401(k) Survey Shows Dramatic Growth In Web Administration" in *Employee Benefit Plan Review* (Vol. 55, No. 7, Jan. 2001)
Pub: Charles D. Spencer & Associates, Inc.
Description: Buck Consultant's 11th annual survey reports a dramatic increase in the number of employers who make use of Web technology to administer 401(k) plans.

43107 ■ "Business Briefs" in *News Tribune* (March 10, 2005)
Pub: News Tribune
Description: Mega Life and Health Insurance Company of Oklahoma has been ordered to stop selling health insurance that violates Washington law. Washington state law requires group insurance policies to include emergency services, mammograms, maternity care stays, newborn coverage and reconstruction breast surgery.

43108 ■ *Business Insurance—Agent/Broker Profiles Issue*
Pub: Business Insurance
Contact: Paul D. Winston, Editorial Director
E-mail: pwinston@businessinsurance.com
Released: Annual, July. Publication Includes: List of approximately 200 insurance agents and brokers specializing in commercial insurance. Entries Include: Firm name, address, phone, fax, branch office locations, year established, names of subsidiaries, gross revenues, premium volume, number of employees, principal officers, percent of revenue generated by commercial retail brokerage, acquisitions. Arrangement: Alphabetical, by company. Indexes: Geographical.

43109 ■ "Business Interruption Insurance Required Rethinking" in *Rough Notes* (Vol. 146, No. 3, March 2003, pp. 82)
Pub: Rough Notes
Ed: Phil Zinkewicz. Description: The insurance losses from the terrorist attacks on the World Trade Center were the largest in history. According to PricewaterhouseCoopers, as the business interruption insurance loss will be extremely complex, this will influence the way insurers write future business interruption policies.

43110 ■ "Buy Now, Pay More Later: Paying Premiums Over Time Can Cost You" in *Entrepreneur* (Vol. 32, November 2004, No. 11, pp. 70)
Pub: Entrepreneur Media Inc.
Ed: Jacquelyn Lynn. Description: Making insurance payments rather than paying the premium in full can add extra costs. When considering this method it is important to consider the interest rate and what happens to any premium refunds issued.

43111 ■ "Buying Long-Term-Care Insurance: A Security Blanket for Old Age" in *Journal of Accountancy* (Vol. 199, January 2005, No. 1, pp. 78)
Pub: American Institute of Certified Public Accountants
Ed: Lesli S. Laffie. Description: The importance of choosing the right long term care insurance can be aided with the help of a certified public account (CPA). A CPA can assist individuals in planning their specific financial, medical, housing and personal needs.

43112 ■ "C-DHP: Where Is The Movement Headed" in *Rough Notes* (Vol. 145, No. 1, January 2003, pp. 108)
Pub: Rough Notes
Ed: Michael J. Moody. Description: The Consumer-Driven Healthcare Congress held a Winter Symposium on health care planning. The conference brought out communications and education as two major aspects required for employers and employees.

43113 ■ "California Commissioner Plans Hearings to Lower Title Insurance Premiums" in *Sacramento Bee* (December 16, 2005)
Pub: The Sacramento Bee
Ed: Rachel Osterman. Description: Due to lack of competition, California title insurance and escrow services are higher than other regions. Statistical data included.

43114 ■ "California Commissioner Proposes Overhaul to Auto Insurance Premiums" in *Sacramento Bee* (December 23, 2005)
Pub: The Sacramento Bee
Ed: Gilbert Chan. Description: California insurance commissioner, John Garamendi, is proposing new rules that would require auto insurance carriers to base their premiums primarily on a driver's safety record instead of the insured's residence. The move would close a major loophole to the state's Proposition 103 that allows insurers to rely heavily on zip codes when determining rates.

43115 ■ "Candidates' Take on Premiums" in *Inc.* (October 1, 2003)
Pub: Gruner & Jahr USA Publishing
Ed: Alison Stein Wellner. Description: A guide to Democratic presidential candidates' proposals, particularly regarding health insurance.

43116 ■ "Capitol Briefings" in *Crain's Detroit Business* (Vol. 16, No. 49, December 4, 2000, pp. 7)
Pub: Crain Communications, Inc.
Ed: Amy Lane. Description: Two bills that offer an alternative to mandated diabetes coverage are reviewed, as well as information about the Michigan Department of Consumer and Industry Services' new Web site, which assists architects and engineers.

43117 ■ "Capitol Coverage: A Report on Politics and Policy from NFIB" in *My Business* (October/November 2003, pp. 16-17)
Pub: My Business Magazine
Description: The National Federation of Independent Business (NFIB) addresses current issues of importance to small businesses in the U.S., including economic impact of policies, white collar overtime, health insurance, and the 2004 NFIB Summit, to be held in Washington, DC in June 2004.

43118 ■ "Capitol Coverage" in *My Business* (December/January 2004, pp. 16-17)
Pub: My Business Magazine
Ed: Description: The National Federation of Independent Business (NFIB) addresses current issues of importance to small businesses in the U.S., including unemployment insurance benefits, unfair trade regulation, health insurance, and taxes.

43119 ■ "Captive Agents Face Off Against Their Captors" in *Rough Notes* (Vol. 145, No. 1, January 2003, pp. 78)
Pub: Rough Notes
Ed: Phil Zinkewicz. Description: Captive insurance agents who either remained as independent agents or released by Allstate Insurance Company or State Farm Insurance Company, are involved in litigation with former companies.

43120 ■ "Captives Should Broaden their Focus" in *Rough Notes* (Vol. 146, No. 9, September 2003, pp. 16)
Pub: Rough Notes
Ed: Michael J. Moody. Description: Overview of past and current trends in the captive insurance industry, including risk management, employee benefits, and funding programs.

43121 ■ "Carrier Services Centers" in *Rough Notes* (Vol. 146, No. 3, March 2003, pp. 98)
Pub: Rough Notes
Ed: Dave Willis. Description: Travelers Property Casualty, Hartford, and SAFECO are three insurance companies that have built service centers to support independent insurance agents in writing their business.

43122 ■ "Chamber, Blues team up for expo" in *Crain's Detroit Business* (Vol. 18, No. 44, November 4, 2002, pp. 39)
Pub: Crain Communications Inc., Detroit
Description: Information about the Small Business Expo held by the Detroit Regional Chamber and Blue Cross and Blue Shield of Michigan is provided.

43123 ■ "The Changing World of Crisis Management" in *Rough Notes* (Vol. 145, No. 12, December 2002, pp. 74)
Pub: Rough Notes
Ed: Deborah M. Hampton. Description: Crisis management, once used particularly for natural disaster management, has now expanded to market fluctuations, fuel prices, and terrorism.

43124 ■ "Cheap labor: Insurance: How to get a lower workers' comp premium" in *Entrepreneur* (Vol. 30, No. 3, March 2002, pp. 84)
Pub: Entrepreneur Media Inc.
Ed: Jacquelyn Lynn. Description: Most states require firms with three or more employees to carry workers' compensation insurance. Tips for finding the most reasonable rates are offered.

43125 ■ "Chicago Tribune Inside Health Care" in *Chicago Tribune* (March 3, 2005)
Pub: Knight-Ridder/Tribune Business News
Ed: Bruce Japsen. Description: The Leapfrog Group is helping employers in the Chicago area to determine if hospitals are providing quality care to their employees. The measures will recommend that hospitals adopt three primary safety practices.

43126 ■ "Citizens Rates Set to Rise Yet Again" in *Tampa Tribune* (December 15, 2005)
Pub: Media General, Inc.
Ed: Randy Diamond. Description: Citizens Property Insurance Company raised its homeowner rates from residents in Pasco, Pinellas and Hernando, Florida counties. Increases will rise between 52 and 112 percent for homeowners due to the massive losses incurred from the recent hurricanes hitting the region.

43127 ■ "A classical gas" in *Rough Notes* (Vol. 146, No. 4, April 2003, pp. 58)
Pub: Rough Notes
Ed: Elisabeth Boone. Description: McKeel Hagerty is the president of Hagerty Collector Car and Boat Insurance which insures collectible vehicles and boats.

43128 ■ "Clear as mud" in *Rough Notes* (Vol. 146, No. 4, April 2003, pp. 104)
Pub: Rough Notes
Ed: Donald S. Malecki. Description: Policy endorsement change the policies in ways that effect the insured. Insurers should be careful in preparing them and insurance agents must explain their significance and meaning to the client.

43129 ■ "Cochran Firm Wins Record $1.62 Billion Insurance Fraud Case" in *Black Enterprise* (Vol. 34, July 2004, No. 12, pp. 21)
Pub: Earl G. Graves Publishing Co. Inc.
Ed: Carolyn M. Brown. Description: The Cochran Firm's record winning insurance fraud case could help bring about reform in the insurance industry. The verdict has impacted the way insurance agents are being hired and trained.

43130 ■ "Committed to Independence" in *Rough Notes* (Vol. 145, No. 9, September 2002, pp. 18)
Pub: Rough Notes
Ed: Dennis Pillsbury. Description: The Mahoney Group, an agency whose various offices are staffed by local individuals, run the insurance and real estate businesses as the largest independent agency in Arizona.

43131 ■ "Competition to Heat Up Among Health Insurers" in *Pittsburgh Business Times* (Vol. 23, No. 1, July 25, 2003, pp. 1)
Pub: Pittsburgh Business Times
Ed: Lynne Glover. Description: United Healthcare, the largest health insurance company in the U.S., will expand to the Sacramento area.

43132 ■ "Competitors, biz groups worry bills would help Blues too much" in *Crain's Detroit Business* (Vol. 19, No. 11, March 17, 2003, pp. 23)
Pub: Crain Communications Inc., Detroit
Ed: Katie Merx. Description: House Bills 4278 through 4282 are examined. The newly introduced legislation would help Blue Cross Blue Shield of Michigan add more healthy residents to its insurance rolls, a move that has BCBS of Michigan competitors upset.

43133 ■ "A Consistent Social Services Market For Over 20 Years" in *Rough Notes* (Vol. 145, No. 1, January 2003, pp. 54)
Pub: Rough Notes
Ed: Dennis H. Pillsbury. Description: The Great American Group, headed by John Sullivan, extends insurance coverage and services relevant to social services agencies and nonprofit organizations.

43134 ■ "Construction Defect Bill Is Progressing in Nevada, Lobbyist Says" in *Las Vegas Review-Journal* (April 11, 2003)
Pub: Knight-Ridder/Tribune Business News
Ed: Hubble Smith. Description: According to a lobbyist for the construction industry in Nevada, legislation aimed at reforming construction defect laws could help lower liability insurance rates.

43135 ■ "Consumers Hit Harder by Medicine Copayments" in *Boston Globe* (February 8, 2005)
Pub: New York Times Company
Ed: Christopher Rowland. Description: Consumers reported the biggest change in health insurance for 2004 was the increase in co-payments for prescription drugs. Statistical data included.

43136 ■ "Contractors Market" in *Rough Notes* (Vol. 145, No. 1, January 2003, pp. 64)
Pub: Rough Notes
Ed: Larry G. France. Description: Specialty lines markets deal with the tightening market on insurance needed by contractors and subcontractors on contractors' risks. A directory of insurance agents providing contractors insurance is included.

43137 ■ "Convenience pushes pendulum back to PPO coverage" in *Crain's Detroit Business* (Vol. 18, No. 16, April 22)
Pub: Crain Communications Inc. - Detroit
Ed: David Barkholz. Description: An interview with Kay Farnell, vice president of the family-owned Farnell Equipment Co. Farnell tells how her company's experiment with a health maintenance organization lasted only a year, only to return to a PPO.

43138 ■ "Court Decisions - Privacy coverage differs from patent infringement" in *Rough Notes* (Vol. 145, No. 1, January 2003, pp. 10)
Pub: Rough Notes
Description: In a suit for breach of contract filed by Konami (America) Inc. against Hartford Insurance Company of Illinois, the Appellate Court of Illinois, held that piracy differed from, and that the case did not involve, patent infringement.

43139 ■ "Covering Contractors" in *Rough Notes* (Vol. 145, No. 9, September 2002, pp. 52)
Pub: Rough Notes
Ed: Linda D. Ferguson. Description: In insuring contracts, the correct classification would depend on the scope of the jobs and which type of contractors, whether general or independent, is used.

43140 ■ "Covering Home Base: Insuring Your Homebased Business is Easier than Ever" in *Entrepreneur* (Vol. 33, March 2005, No. 3, pp. 64)
Pub: Entrepreneur Media Inc.
Ed: Jacquelyn Lynn. Description: Tips for insuring a home-based business are shared. Buying an endorsement to an existing homeowners' policy will increase business property coverage with a minimal costs. An in-home business policy provides greater comprehensive coverage for business equipment as well as liability.

43141 ■ "Crain's seeks benefits vendors for buyer's guide" in *Crain's Detroit Business* (Vol. 19, No. 15, April 14, 2003, pp. 12)
Pub: Crain Communications Inc., Detroit
Description: Crain's Detroit Business publication is looking for companies to list in its Employee Benefits Buyers Guide, including employee-benefit consultants; 401(k) plan sellers, administrators, providers; group health care providers; health insurance carriers; dental insurance carriers; and third-party administrators of health care.

43142 ■ "Crash and Burn. Wrecked Insurance Industry Sees 'Leveling' Out in Uphill Road" in *Memphis Business Journal* (Vol. 25, August 22, 2003)
Pub: American City Business Journals
Ed: Scott Shepard. Description: Recent figures for the insurance industry suggest that it is recovering from the recession. However, the recovery is not being felt throughout the industry with biggest gains seen in the property and casualty insurance sector.

43143 ■ "A Cure for Health Concerns" in *Black Enterprise* (Vol. 35, November 2004, No. 4, pp. 141)
Pub: Earl G. Graves Publishing Co. Inc.
Ed: James A. Anderson. Description: Without long-term care insurance, families will have trouble providing health care later in life.

43144 ■ "Cyber Theft" in *Rough Notes* (Vol. 145, No. 2, February 2003, pp. 40)
Pub: Rough Notes
Ed: Phil Zinkwicz. Description: There has been a rise in cyber crimes involving breaches of computer systems, invasion by computer viruses, and loss of confidential information, intellectual property and financial losses. Insurance companies can provide appropriate coverage.

43145 ■ "Cybersecurity: Opportunities for Agents" in *Rough Notes* (Vol. 145, No. 1, January 2003, pp. 110)
Pub: Rough Notes
Ed: G. Edward Kalbaugh. Description: Any product or action to secure a wired or wireless work constitutes CyberSecurity, such as virus protection for computers, risk identification, insurance, risk assessment, and liability insurance. CyberSecurity promises to be one of the fastest growing businesses of the future, as more than $330 billion have been earmarked for the Department of Homeland Security.

43146 ■ "D&O: Hard and Getting Harder" in *Rough Notes* (Vol. 145, No. 9, September 2002, pp. 71)
Pub: Rough Notes
Ed: Phil Zinkewicz. Description: After Enron Corporation, Global Crossing, and WorldCom admitted to having overstated cash flow or profits, several insurance companies involved in potential directors and officers, liability policies are seeking protection against suits owing to alleged misrepresentations in the procurement of policies.

43147 ■ "Deal Jitters?" in *Inc.* (October 2005, pp. 48)
Pub: Inc. Magazine
Ed: Dalia Fahmy. Description: Many firms are now purchasing insurance when acquiring a company. Purchase protection cover financial losses if a seller makes false claims in a sale contract, and should be used in deals valued at least $10 million.

43148 ■ "Debate Over Credit Scoring May Head to Court" in *Crain's Detroit Business* (Vol. 21, January 24, 2005, No. 4, pp. 6)
Pub: Crain Communications Inc. - Detroit
Ed: Amy Lane. Description: A proposed new law in Michigan would prohibit insurance companies from using credit scores for setting insurance rates.

43149 ■ "Debate Over State-Mandated Costs Threatens Georgia Health Insurance Measures" in *Atlanta Journal-Constitution* (March 2, 2005)
Pub: Knight-Ridder/Tribune Business News
Ed: Andy Miller. Description: Georgia legislation that aims to bring health insurance to the uninsured by removing some or all benefits required by the state is examined. Meanwhile, Senate Bill 174 offers business owners the choice of offering employees a policy with all coverages or one with fewer benefits.

43150 ■ "Demand For Flood Insurance Swells Locally" in *Sacramento Bee* (December 31, 2005)
Pub: The Sacramento Bee
Ed: Jon Ortiz. Description: Homeowners and renters are increasingly buying flood insurance along rivers in the Sacramento area. Experts believe the recent flooding in New Orleans triggered fears to residents of the region.

43151 ■ "Dental, vision plan vendors use the Web to administer, communicate, market benefits" in *Employee Benefit Plan Review* (Vol. 55, No. 6)
Pub: Charles D. Spencer & Associates, Inc.
Ed: Robert Pruter. Description: Dental and vision insurance plan providers are redesigning their Web sites to offer better services to employers and to better market themselves to small businesses.

43152 ■ "Detroit Free Press Wayne Small Business Column" in *Detroit Free Press* (July 28, 2005)
Pub: Knight-Ridder/Tribune Business News
Ed: Carol Cain. Description: Profile of Dawn McAllister, owner of Designer's Choice. The firm's studio offers four employees who focus on custom design, while the company's warehouse offers discounts up to 30 percent. The warehouse showcases cabinets, lighting, sofas, artwork and other products.

43153 ■ *Dictionary of Real Estate Terms*
Pub: Barron's Educational Series, Incorporated
Ed: Jack P. Friedman, Jack C. Harris. Released: March 2004. Price: $13.95. Description: More than 2,500 real estate terms relating to mortgages and financing, brokerage law, architecture, rentals and leases, property insurance, and more.

43154 ■ "Diving In; New Owner Plans to Use PPOM as Platform for National Network, Fast Growth" in *Crain's Detroit Business* (January 10, 2005)
Pub: Crain Communications Inc. - Detroit
Ed: Katie Merx. Description: Plans to double PPOM's market share in Michigan are discussed with president and CEO, Jeffrey Connolly. The move would more than triple the health care provider network's membership.

43155 ■ **"Do I Have a Choice?"** in *Inc.* (September 2005, pp. 40)
Pub: Inc. Magazine
Ed: Stephanie Clifford. **Description:** Greg Roderick's firm offers three health plans to his employees, which encourages competition among providers. Statistical data included.

43156 ■ **"Do-It-Yourself Insurance"** in *Inc.* (Volume 27, December 2005, No. 12, pp. 39-40, 42)
Pub: Inc. Magazine
Ed: Alison Stein Wellner. **Description:** Individual insurance policies are becoming more popular, but premiums vary from state to state. The pros of cons of a small business replacing group health plans in favor for individual policies are discussed.

43157 ■ **"Do You Need E-Business Insurance"** in *E-business Advisor* (Vol. 18, No. 9, September 2000, pp. 28)
Pub: Advisor Media, Inc.
Ed: Bernard P. Bell. **Description:** New types of insurance coverage are required to protect Internet businesses against new liabilities, such as system damage and intellectual property damage. For example, e-commerce is vulnerable to business interruptions caused by security breaches, natural disasters, internal systems problems, and failure of third parties.

43158 ■ **"Docs Face Big Financial Hit"** in *Pittsburgh Business Times* (Vol. 23, No. 9, September 19, 2003, pp. 1)
Pub: Pittsburgh Business Times
Ed: Lynne Glover. **Description:** Diane Koken, the Pennsylvania insurance commissioner, ordered insurance companies to follow new billing procedures when issuing medical malpractice insurance. The new billing procedures are mandated under the 2003 Medical Care Availability and Reduction of Error Fund (MCARE).

43159 ■ **"The Doctor Will E-Mail You Now"** in *Black Enterprise* (Vol. 36, February 2006, No. 7, pp. 168)
Pub: Earl G. Graves Publishing Co. Inc.
Ed: Leslie E. Royal. **Description:** Many physicians across the nation are offering their patients online visits and several major insurance carriers are providing coverage for the service.

43160 ■ **"Doctors Form Insurance Company"** in *South Florida Business Journal* (Vol. 23, No. 52, August 1, 2003, pp. 1)
Pub: American City Business Journals
Ed: Stephen Van Drake. **Description:** Florida physicians plan to introduce and own the Healthcare Underwriters Group of Florida, offering medical malpractice insurance.

43161 ■ **"Doing well by doing good: Latino Health Care"** in *Hispanic Business* (Vol. 22, No. 7-8, July-August 2000, pp. 24)
Pub: Hispanic Business
Ed: Kathleen O'Connor. **Description:** Long Beach-based health maintenance organization Latino Health Care has grown from nothing to more than 35,000 members with 25 hospitals and 2,300 doctors in just three and a half years.

43162 ■ **"Domestic Dispute: The Debate Over Benefits For Same-Sex Couples Heats Up"** in *Entrepreneur* (Vol. 32, September 2004, No. 9, pp. 34)
Pub: Entrepreneur Media Inc.
Ed: Chris Penttila. **Description:** The issues involved for providing benefits to same-sex couples is discussed.

43163 ■ **"Don't Bet Your Life On It"** in *Inc.* (August 2005, pp. 24-25)
Pub: Inc. Magazine
Description: The Internal Revenue Service is cracking down on split-dollar insurance, a common benefit given to company executives.

43164 ■ **"Downshift"** in *Entrepreneur* (Vol. 33, October 2005, No. 10, pp. 60)
Pub: Entrepreneur Media Inc.
Ed: Jacquelyn Lynn. **Description:** Tips to help small businesses reduce company vehicle insurance costs are covered.

43165 ■ **"Employee theft on the rise - Fidelity coverage is crucial"** in *Rough Notes* (Vol. 146, No. 4, April 2003, pp. 30)
Pub: Rough Notes
Ed: Roy C. McCormick. **Description:** Embezzlement and property theft by employees is on the rise. Background checks, security cameras, as well as employee dishonest insurance should be obtained by management.

43166 ■ **"Employees still rate health care No. 1 benefit"** in *Atlanta Business Chronicle* (Vol. 25, No. 19, October 18, 2002, pp. 13C)
Pub: American City Business Publications, Inc.
Ed: Tom Barry. **Description:** Employees still consider health care coverage as the most important benefit, according to a national study conducted by the Employee Benefit Research Institute. Statistical data included.

43167 ■ **"Employers important in shaping health care"** in *Atlanta Business Chronicle* (Vol. 25, November 15, 2002, No. 23 pp. 37A)
Pub: American City Business Publications, Inc.
Ed: Julie Bryant. **Description:** According to the National Business Coalition on Health, employers are in a unique position to influence health care's direction by acting as an advocate for high-quality health care and as a prudent purchaser. Steps taken by the Coca Cola Company and American Greetings Corporation are discussed.

43168 ■ **"Employers Get Personal with Doctors in Push for More Generic Use"** in *Crain's Detroit Business* (Vol. 19, No. 15, April 14, 2003)
Pub: Crain Communications Inc., Detroit
Ed: Roberto Ceniceros. **Description:** In an effort to cut costs, large employers and health plans are trying to persuade doctors to prescribe generic drugs whenever possible, while drug company's have their salespeople persuading doctors to prescribe brand name drugs.

43169 ■ **"Enrolling online is No. 1 choice among workers, survey finds"** in *Crain's Detroit Business* (Vol. 18, No. 18, May 6, 2002, pp. 12)
Pub: Crain Communications Inc. - Detroit
Ed: Jerry Geisel. **Description:** The Internet has become the dominant way for workers to enroll into benefits programs offered by employers.

43170 ■ **"Enterprise Risk Management-A Fading Fad?"** in *Rough Notes* (Vol. 145, No. 5, May 2002, pp. 53)
Pub: Rough Notes
Ed: Michael J. Moody. **Description:** The Enterprise Risk Management concept was developed about two years ago for a market that is only recently starting to emerge, and which is expected to grow over time in banks, insurance companies and financial institutions.

43171 ■ **"Equipment Maintenance Insurance Coverage"** in *Rough Notes* (Vol. 145, No. 1, January 2003, pp. 44)
Pub: Rough Notes
Ed: Dennis Pillsbury. **Description:** The Flanders Group, headed by Lou Ricci, offers equipment maintenance insurance coverage and uses Specialty Underwriters and REMI as support for their services.

43172 ■ **"Everything designed with the customer in mind"** in *Rough Notes* (Vol. 146, No. 3, March 2003, pp. 18)
Pub: Rough Notes
Ed: Dennis Pillsbury. **Description:** Roach Howard Smith and Hunter of Dallas/Fort Worth, Texas, is an insurance agency founded by Richard Roach in 1955 that specializes in commercial lines. The firm is now run by Karen K. Farris, who says the firm employs a customer-focused staff.

43173 ■ **"The Fast Track to CE Credits"** in *Rough Notes* (Vol. 145, No. 2, February 2003, pp. 84)
Pub: Rough Notes
Ed: Barbara Morris. **Description:** Insurance agents can have their continuing education with online CE education, such as WEBCE.com or CEU.com with convenience, flexibility and speed.

43174 ■ **"Federal suit alleges MVM overbilled"** in *Washington Business Journal* (Vol. 21, No. 50, April 11, 2003, pp. 1)
Pub: Washington Business Journal
Ed: Sean Madigan. **Description:** A civil suit has been filed against MVM Inc. by the U.S. Department of Justice, alleging that MVM submitted 44 false invoices on a security services contract. MVM is alleged to have invoiced for 4 security guards in supervisory positions, before they were actually trained.

43175 ■ **"Finding Prospects By Using The Internet"** in *Rough Notes* (Vol. 145, No. 9, September 2002, pp. 46)
Pub: Rough Notes
Ed: Steve Anderson. **Description:** Marketing for agencies has been helped by access to the Internet. There are business databases like Dun and Bradstreet and R.H. Donnelley from which lists of prospects are available.

43176 ■ **"Fire Loss Illustrates Adjustment Terms"** in *Rough Notes* (Vol. 146, No. 9, September 2003, pp. 50)
Pub: Rough Notes
Ed: LeRoy H. Utschig. **Description:** Methods to interpret terms of commercial property and casualty insurance policies involving loss due to fires are presented; business losses, depreciation considerations, and proof of loss are covered.

43177 ■ **"Fly By Night? Don't Fall for a Scam-Use These Tips Before You Buy Health Insurance"** in *Entrepreneur* (Vol. 31, No. 10, October 2003)
Pub: Entrepreneur Media, Inc.
Ed: Jacquelyn Lynn. **Description:** Health insurance scams targeting small businesses and their employees often collect millions of dollars before vanishing when claims start coming in. Tips to avoid fraudulent insurance companies are listed.

43178 ■ **"For Truckers, Insurance Barrels Out of Control"** in *Business Journal-Portland* (Vol. 20, No. 26, August 29, 2003, pp. 16)
Pub: American City Business Journals, Inc.
Ed: Robert Goldfield. **Description:** Many trucking companies are facing significant increases in insurance premiums.

43179 ■ **"Furry Friends"** in *Entrepreneur. com* (Vol. 34, February 2006, No. 2, pp. 52)
Pub: Entrepreneur Media Inc.
Ed: Jacquelyn Lynn. **Description:** With the cost of veterinary care rising, more insurance companies are offering health insurance coverage for pets and a growing number of firms are offering it in their voluntary insurance offerings to employees.

43180 ■ **"Gaining Access to Middle Market Environmental Business"** in *Rough Notes* (Vol. 146, No. 3, March 2003, pp. 28)
Pub: Rough Notes
Ed: Phil Zinkewicz. **Description:** Through its Program Brokerage Corporation, the Hub International Ltd. has formed PBC Environmental, a specialized insurance facility for agents and brokers with needs for pollution liability coverage for small or mid-sized companies.

43181 ■ **"GEICO Pays 24.2 Percent In Worker Bonuses"** in *Ledger* (February 26, 2005)
Pub: Knight-Ridder/Tribune Business News
Ed: Kyle Kennedy. **Description:** GEICO, the nation's fifth largest auto insurer, handed employees annual profit-sharing checks at 24.2 percent, up from 17.7 percent in 2004. An employee earning $30,000 collected $7,260 in bonus. Statistical data included.

43182 ■ "Georgia Insurer Riles Its Rivals" in *Crain's Detroit Business* **(Vol. 19, No. 43, October 27, 2003, pp. 3)**
Pub: Crain Communications Inc., Detroit
Ed: Katie Merx. **Description:** Palmer and Cay Inc., based in Savannah, Georgia, has expanded into the Detroit, Michigan market. The firm hired 22 area insurance professionals as part of the expansion. These hirings have prompted Marsh, the parent company, to sue Palmer and Cay Inc.

43183 ■ "Georgia Insurer Riles Its Rivals; Palmer & Cay's Moves In Detroit Prompt Marsh USA to Sue" in *Crain's Detroit Business* **(Vol. 19)**
Pub: Crain Communications Inc., Detroit
Ed: Katie Merx. **Description:** Palmer and Cay Inc., based in Savannah, Georgia, has expanded into the Detroit, Michigan market. The firm hired 22 area insurance professionals as part of the expansion. These hirings have prompted Marsh, the parent company, to sue Palmer and Cay Inc.

43184 ■ "Get With the Program! Save Money with a New Approach to Managing Disability Benefits" in *Entrepreneur* **(Vol. 31, No. 7, July 2003)**
Pub: Entrepreneur Media, Inc.
Ed: Jacquelyn Lynn. **Description:** The Integrated Disability Management (IDM) program, a coordination of benefits delivery across traditional programs, helps an employee who becomes disabled to recover and return to work as quickly as possible, thus reducing the economic and emotional impact on the employee and cut costs to the small business owner.

43185 ■ "Give Advice? Get Protected!" in *Small Business Opportunities* **(Vol. 13, No. 5, September 2001, pp. 18)**
Pub: Harris Publications, Inc.
Ed: Carla Vincent. **Description:** Concise information regarding professional liability insurance is presented. A brief profile of Nolo Press, a provider of self-help legal solutions for consumers and small businesses is also included.

43186 ■ "Global financing options" in *BlackEnterprise* **(Vol. 31, No. 8, March 2001, pp. 48)**
Pub: Earl Graves Publishing Co.
Ed: Paula McCoy-Pinderhughes. **Description:** Small business services provided by the Export-Import Banks of the United States, are profiled. The Export-Import (Ex-Im) Bank of the U.S. is an independent government agency that offers a number of financing options to minority- and women-owned export companies, including credit insurance and working capital guarantees on commercial loans.

43187 ■ "Going Public: A Public Insurance Adjuster Could Help You Get What You Deserve" in *Entrepreneur* **(Vol. 32, July 2004, No. 7, pp. 54)**
Pub: Entrepreneur Media Inc.
Ed: Jacquelyn Lynn. **Description:** Small business might consider retaining a public insurance adjuster to handle insurance claims for property loss or damage.

43188 ■ "Going Separate Ways: In a Law Suit, You and an Employee Could Be Sent Down Different Paths" in *Entrepreneur* **(Vol. 32, August 2004)**
Pub: Entrepreneur Media Inc.
Ed: Jacquelyn Lynn. **Description:** Business owners need to analyze insurance coverage in the event of a law suit that includes multiple defendants.

43189 ■ "Good intentions, bad policy" in *Crain's Detroit Business* **(Vol. 16, No. 49, December 4, 2000, pp. 8)**
Pub: Crain Communications, Inc.
Description: Mandating the coverage of diabetes will boost the cost of providing insurance to Michigan workers, thus setting a precedent for future mandates for other diseases.

43190 ■ "Got It Covered?" in *Entrepreneur* **(Vol. 32, December 2004, No. 12, pp. 47)**
Pub: Entrepreneur Media Inc.
Ed: Jill Amadio. **Description:** Extended warranties allow companies to hold onto vehicles longer.

43191 ■ "Granholm Criticized for HMO Bill Inaction" in *Crain's Detroit Business* **(Vol. 21, January 3, 2005, No. 1, pp. 20)**
Pub: Crain Communications Inc. - Detroit
Ed: Amy Lane. **Description:** Governor Jennifer Granholm killed a bill that would give health maintenance organizations greater pricing flexibility because of concerns the ruling would increase the health care costs of patients.

43192 ■ "Grassley Offers Discussion Draft on COLI Policies" in *Tax Notes* **(Vol. 102, No. 3, January 19, 2004, pp. 323-325)**
Pub: Tax Notes International
Ed: Patti Mohr, Christine Harris. **Description:** Discussion with Senate Finance Committee Chair, Charles E. Grassley, regarding corporate-owned life insurance.

43193 ■ "Gulf Team With Corpedia on Ethics Course" in *Rough Notes* **(Vol. 146, No. 9, September 2003, pp. 44)**
Pub: Rough Notes
Ed: Dennis H. Pillsbury. **Description:** Profile of Gulf Insurance Group's underwriting division, including Internet marketing, importance of teamwork, and management of debt and business losses.

43194 ■ "Hands On" in *Inc.* **(August 2000, pp. 127)**
Pub: The Goldhirsh Group
Ed: Ilan Mochari. **Description:** Managing insurance costs is a nuisance for every small business owner. This article shows how vigilance with your broker can lower insurance costs.

43195 ■ "HAP boosts employee-pay plans" in *Crain's Detroit Business* **(Vol. 19, No. 6, Feb. 10, 2003, pp. 3)**
Pub: Crain Communications Inc., Detroit
Ed: Katie Merx. **Description:** Henry Ford Health System's insurance sector is promoting its product line that will help cut the increasing costs of health care to employers.

43196 ■ "A Happy Ending" in *Entrepreneur*
Pub: Entrepreneur Media Inc.
Ed: Nichole L. Torres. **Description:** Profile of Karen and Roger Sandau, founders of WedSafe, a company providing wedding insurance to brides and grooms. The insurance covers unforeseen circumstances such as severe weather emergencies, damaged or stolen wedding gown, and lost or damaged wedding rings.

43197 ■ "A Hard Sell" in *Entrepreneur* **(Vol. 31, No. 8, August 2003, pp. 76)**
Pub: Entrepreneur Media, Inc.
Ed: Jerry Fisher. **Description:** Ways advertising can convince tradition-bound prospects to switch to e-commerce are explored. Insure.com challenged parents to purchase insurance online, facing this issue head-on.

43198 ■ "Hartford Expands Small Commercial Offerings" in *Rough Notes* **(Vol. 145, No. 6, June 2002, pp. 50)**
Pub: Rough Notes
Ed: Dennis Pillsbury. **Description:** The Hartford, an insurance company, is committed to serve the insurance needs of small commercial businesses. Its share in the market is around 4.2 percent of a $30 billion small business market.

43199 ■ "Harvard Pilgrim Purchases Medical Benefits Company" in *Boston Globe* **(March 8, 2005)**
Pub: New York Times Company
Ed: Liz Kowalczyk. **Description:** Health Plans Inc. has been purchased by Harvard Pilgrim Health Care. The move will help position Harvard Pilgrim, the second-largest health insurer in Massachusetts, to compete with Blue Cross and Blue Shield of Massachusetts. Harvard Pilgrim is also considering a move into the self-insured market.

43200 ■ "Head Games" in *Entrepreneur* **(Vol. 30, No. 3, March 2002, pp. 78)**
Pub: Entrepreneur Media Inc.
Ed: Chris Sandlund. **Description:** Attempts to mandate mental health insurance coverage are examined; this provision would not affect small businesses with fewer than 50 employees.

43201 ■ "Health Alliance Plan offers discounts on alternative therapies, medicines" in *Crain's Detroit Business* **(Vol. 16, No. 49, Dec. 4, 2000)**
Pub: Crain Communications, Inc.
Ed: Mike Scott. **Description:** Detroit-based Health Alliance Plan, along with Blue Cross Blue Shield and other managed care companies, are offering discounts on alternative medicines and services such as chiropractic care, acupuncture, and massage therapy.

43202 ■ "Health Care Battle Heats Up" in *San Francisco Business Times* **(Vol. 17, No. 50, July 18, 2003, pp. 1)**
Pub: American City Business Journals
Ed: Meg Walker. **Description:** Growing competition between Sutter Health and Kaiser Permanente in Marin, California is examined. Topics include marketing strategy, membership prices and rates, and market share.

43203 ■ "Health Care Coverage Reform Introduced in Congress" in *My Business* **(April/May 2003, pp. 18)**
Pub: My Business Magazine
Description: Legislation that could help small businesses with health care costs using association health plans (AHPs) is presented.

43204 ■ "The Health Care Crisis" in *Business Week* **(No. 3689, July 10, 2000, pp. F18)**
Pub: McGraw-Hill, Inc.
Description: A study done by the National Federation of Independent Business says that small business owners now rank health care as their number one priority for legislative reform.

43205 ■ "Health-care foundation awards its first grants" in *Atlanta Business Chronicle* **(Vol. 25, January 10, 2003, No. 31, pp. 7A)**
Pub: American City Business Publications, Inc.
Ed: Julie Bryant. **Description:** The Healthcare Georgia Foundation has finalized its first round of grants. The foundation, its genesis brought about as part of a judgment against Blue Cross and Blue Shield of Georgia, awarded grants totaling $4.3 million. Serologicals Corporation's CEO, David Dodd, assumes the duties of Georgia Biomedical Partnership chairman.

43206 ■ "Health and Happiness" in *My Business* **(April/May 2003, pp. 17)**
Pub: My Business Magazine
Ed: Wayne Ragland. **Description:** Ways to help small businesses find options to lower insurance costs are examined. Web sites are included for finding information about legislative updates and additional resources.

43207 ■ "Health Insurance Crisis: How Did We Get Here?" in *My Business* **(April/May 2003, pp. 15)**
Pub: My Business Magazine
Ed: Carolyn Denny. **Description:** Factors that have contributed to the nation's current health care crisis are sighted, including information about mandates, limited competition, litigation, and administrative costs.

43208 ■ "Health Insurance Rates Still Rising as Hospitals Struggle" in *Crain's Detroit Business* **(Vol. 19, No. 45, November 10, 2003, pp. 25)**
Pub: Crain Communications Inc., Detroit
Ed: Katie Merx. **Description:** Health insurance rate increases have slowed but continue to rise at double-digit rates and the number of working people without insurance is expected to grow, according to the Small Business Association of Michigan.

43209 ■ "Health care needs some strong medicine" in *Crain's Detroit Business* (Vol. 18, No. 19, May 13, 2002, pp. 9)
Pub: Crain Communications Inc. - Detroit
Ed: Gail Warden. **Description:** Issues facing the health care and insurance industries are discussed.

43210 ■ "Health of a Nation" in *Entrepreneur* (Vol. 33, March 2005, No. 3, pp. 70)
Pub: Entrepreneur Media Inc.
Ed: Joshua Kurlantzick. **Description:** Insurance premium costs have risen 10 to 15 percent annually over the past six years for high tech firms employing young employees who are getting married and starting families.

43211 ■ "Health Savings Accounts Not Getting Much Attention from Garden City-Area Employers" in *Long Island Business News* (January 30, 2004)
Pub: Dolan Media Newswires
Ed: Ben Abelson. **Description:** Health savings accounts could impact the health insurance industry in the U.S. These accounts allow employees with high health-insurance deductibles to set aside pre-tax income to cover the balance of deductibles.

43212 ■ "Healthcare Insurance" in *Black Enterprise* (Vol. 34, No. 2, September 2003, pp. 48)
Pub: Earl Graves Publishing Co.
Ed: Alan Hughes. **Description:** Healthcare insurance is becoming increasingly more difficult for small business owners to provide to employees, especially for a small home-based business wishing to expand. The House Small Business Committee introduced the Self-Employed Health Care Affordability Act of 2003 (H.R. 1873) in April 2003, this bill allows self-employed business owners to deduct health insurance costs when calculating payroll taxes, thus effectively reducing those costs by more than 15 percent.

43213 ■ "Healthy Habits" in *My Business* (June/July 2004, pp. 35)
Pub: My Business Magazine
Ed: Robin Warshaw. **Description:** Small businesses can save money on health insurance costs by encouraging employees to join wellness programs.

43214 ■ "He's Boss of the Blues; Phillip Pope Stays a Fiscally Prudent Course" in *Birmingham Business Journal* (Vol. 20, October 3, 2003)
Pub: American City Business Journals, Inc.
Ed: Tom Bassing. **Description:** Profile of Phillip Pope, who was promoted from within the ranks of Blue Cross and Blue Shield of Alabama. The company is successful at membership retention, investments and growth and is planning strategies to offer services to aging baby boomers.

43215 ■ "HIPAA hysteria" in *Atlanta Business Chronicle* (Vol. 25, November 29, 2002, No. 25, pp. 1C)
Pub: American City Business Publications, Inc.
Ed: Julie Bryant. **Description:** The Health Insurance Portability and Accountability Act has caused disorder and confusion in health care and insurance industries. The new privacy and security regulations were added to protect electronic patient information.

43216 ■ "Home2NetServices Announces a Revolutionary New Way of Insuring Personal Property" in *PR Newswire* (January 20, 2005)
Pub: PR Newswire Association LLC
Description: Stephen Temple, founder of Home2NetServices, has developed a new method that creates trust in the insurance transaction in the personal lines insurance industry. The method helps carriers, the insured, and agents to establish trust using a combination of in-field resources, shared property databases, and secure trust-utility technology.

43217 ■ "Hospitality Industry" in *Rough Notes* (Vol. 146, No. 4, April 2003, pp. 84)
Pub: Rough Notes
Ed: Larry G. France. **Description:** Since the World Trade Center terrorist attacks, tall hotel buildings in the hospitality industry are subject to potential loss if attacked and so insurance providers should explain to clients the various significant changes in the property and liability insurance policies being purchased.

43218 ■ "Hot Property" in *Entrepreneur* (Vol. 31, No. 8, August 2003, pp. 57)
Pub: Entrepreneur Media, Inc.
Ed: Jennifer Pellet. **Description:** Karen Gallagher, president of Stillwater, an Oklahoma-based National Student Services, provides students with personal property insurance policies at schools nationwide. The policies cover equipment and appliances such as laptops, cell phones, stereos, camera equipment, and other items in the dorm room.

43219 ■ "House Rules: Before You Let Your People Work at Home, Find Out What You're Liable For-And Cover Your Bases" in *Entrepreneur* (Vol. 32)
Pub: Entrepreneur Media Inc.
Ed: Jane Easter Bahls. **Description:** Safety and liability issues involved in allowing employees to work from home are examined. It is critical for a small business owner to have a policy that addresses office arrangements, hours, responsibilities and who pays for what, as well as safety, security of company property and proprietary information, workers' compensation and insurance.

43220 ■ "How to Cover America's Uninsured" in *Business Week* (No. 3694, August 14, 2000, pp. 72)
Pub: McGraw-Hill, Inc.
Description: The failure of the country's health system is discussed at length.

43221 ■ "How Good Is Your Online Nurse?" in *Business Week* (February 20, 2006, No. 3972, pp. 88)
Pub: McGraw-Hill Companies
Ed: Arlene Weintraub. **Description:** WellPoint, UnitedHealth Group, and Aetna offer patient Internet portals with tools to help manage health issues.

43222 ■ "How Much Of A Good Thing?" in *Entrepreneur* (Vol. 28, No. 9, September 2000, pp. 33)
Pub: Entrepreneur Media Inc.
Ed: Pamela Rohland. **Description:** Insurance may one day be the only thing that prevents you from having your life's work destroyed.

43223 ■ "How to Prepare Your Home Business for a Natural Disaster" in *Home Business* (Vol. 13, January/February 2006, No. 1, pp. 82, 84)
Pub: Home Business Magazine
Ed: William J. Lynott. **Description:** Keys to reducing risk in the event of a natural disaster include a preparation and recovery plan, off-site back-up records, insurance coverage, backup power sources, and customer contact.

43224 ■ "HSAs-A Growing Trend In Health Benefits for Businesses and Individuals" in *Entrepreneur* (Vol. 32, December 2004, No. 12, pp. 67)
Pub: Entrepreneur Media Inc.
Description: Health savings accounts (HSAs) allow individuals with high-deductible health plans to put pre-tax money aside, spend it tax-free on qualified health expenses, earn interest tax-free and also save the money for health-care expenses in retirement. HSAs may be a way for small companies to manage health benefits costs by exchanging higher deductibles for lower premiums and tax advantages.

43225 ■ "HSB Sees Growth in Monoline Equipment Breakdown Due to Hard Market" in *Rough Notes* (Vol. 145, No. 9, September 2002, pp. 14)
Pub: Rough Notes
Description: The Hartford Steam Boiler Inspection and Insurance Company, a unit of American Insurance Group, suggests that equipment breakdown coverage on a monoline basis is being sold along with services relating to risk evaluation.

43226 ■ "Humana battles for growth" in *Atlanta Business Chronicle* (Vol. 25, January 3, 2003, No. 30, pp. 3A)
Pub: American City Business Publications, Inc.
Ed: Julie Bryant. **Description:** Alan Guzzino is the new Georgia market president of Humana Inc. Guzzino was retained to manage the introduction of the company's consumer-driver health benefit plans. This rollout aims to increase the company's competitive edge in the market place.

43227 ■ "The Hungry Wolf Syndrome" in *Rough Notes* (Vol. 145, No. 1, January 2003, pp. 92)
Pub: Rough Notes
Ed: Donald S. Malecki. **Description:** Insurance agents sometimes add information on certificates or insurance, broaden contractual liability coverage, and misrepresent the truth to preserve a client whose demands are unreasonable.

43228 ■ "Illinois Regulators Investigate Possible Title Insurance Kickbacks" in *Chicago Tribune* (February 23, 2005)
Pub: Knight-Ridder/Tribune Business News
Description: State regulators across the nation are investigating a kickback scheme whereby housing developers and lenders direct title insurance business to particular companies, causing higher closing costs for homeowners.

43229 ■ "IMMS lessens market woes" in *Rough Notes* (Vol. 146, No. 4, April 2003, pp. 40)
Pub: Rough Notes
Ed: G. Barry Klein. **Description:** The Insurance Marketing and Management, headed by CEO George Nordhaus, is composed of many members who can access the service though the IMMS CompleteMarkets Website for insurance products and services.

43230 ■ "The Innovator" in *Forbes* (Vol. 175, January 10, 2005, No. 1, pp. 150)
Pub: Forbes Magazine Inc.
Ed: Carrie Coolidge. **Description:** Progressive Insurance is the third-largest auto insurer in the U.S.; earnings for the company have grown an average of 23.7 percent in the last five years. Progressive management attributes their success to innovation in claims management.

43231 ■ "Inside the Care Crisis" in *Hispanic Business* (June 2002, pp. 24, 26, 28)
Pub: Hispanic Business
Ed: Gina Binole. **Description:** Minorities are caught in the middle of a battle between insurance companies and hospitals. Hispanic business owners make up 1.5 million companies of the most vulnerable to increased healthcare costs.

43232 ■ "Inspection By Insurer Is Valuable But Doesn't Constitute A Warranty" in *Rough Notes* (Vol. 145, No. 1, January 2003, pp. 38)
Pub: Rough Notes
Ed: Roy C. McCormick. **Description:** Inspection conducted by an insurance company is for underwriting purposes only and should not be construed as a guarantee in the contract that the property be maintained in a safe condition.

43233 ■ "Insurance" in *Business Week* (January 16, 2006, No. 3967, pp. 30-31)
Pub: McGraw-Hill Companies
Ed: Peter Coy. **Description:** Although Hurricane Katrina wiped out more insurance capital than any past disaster, hedge funds are allowing businesses and families to buy coverage. Three ways hedge funds investors are gambling against natural disaster include: industry loss warranty, catastrophe bonds, and reinsurance.

43234 ■ "Insurance Carriers Leery of Paying for Bariatric Surgery" in *Business Journal-Portland* (Vol. 20, No. 25, August 22, 2003, pp. 3)
Pub: American City Business Journals, Inc.
Ed: Robin J. Moody. **Description:** Kaiser Northwest has denied a patient the right to undergo surgery for obesity, a trend being seen in the insurance industry.

43235 ■ **"Insurance Firms Forecast Profitable Year"** in *Pacific Business News* (Vol. 41, No. 19, July 18, 2003, pp. 12)
Pub: American City Business Journals
Ed: Eddy Conway. **Description:** Profile and forecasts of Hawaii's insurance industry are presented. Topics include economic conditions, profits and losses, and business forecasts.

43236 ■ **"Insurance premiums may skyrocket"** in *Crain's Detroit Business* (Vol. 17, No. 44, October 22, 2001, pp. 5)
Pub: Crain Communications, Inc.
Ed: Katie Merx. **Description:** Insurance premiums may rise as much as 30 percent since the 9-11 terrorist attack, and some with more losses or risk might face between 50-500 percent increases. Property and casualty rates for airplanes, skyscrapers and landmarks will be the hardest hit.

43237 ■ **"Insurance System Changes Would Raise Rates of Bad Drivers"** in *Boston Globe* (January 27, 2005)
Pub: New York Times Company
Ed: Bruce Mohl. **Description:** Massachusetts is proposing changes to the state's safe driving insurance plan. The change would lower the rates of good drivers, while increasing the rates of bad drivers and remove surcharges from driving records faster.

43238 ■ **"Insurer State Farm Closes Buffalo, N.Y.-Area Claims Offices; 30 Jobs to Be Cut"** in *Buffalo News* (February 17, 2004)
Pub: Knight-Ridder/Tribune Business News
Ed: Jonathan D. Epstein. **Description:** Although State Farm Mutual Insurance Company is expanding its injury claims central office in Rochester, New York, it is closing four offices in the Buffalo, New York area.

43239 ■ **"Intention, adaptation and annexation"** in *Rough Notes* (Vol. 146, No. 4, April 2003, pp. 74)
Pub: Rough Notes
Ed: LeRoy H. Utschig. **Description:** The responsibility of landlord or tenant according to the lease contract wording has to be completely understood in order for the provisions of the insurance policy to be correctly applied.

43240 ■ **"Internet Facilities Defined Contribution Model For Employer-Sponsored Health Benefits"** in *Employee Benefit Plan Review* (Vol. 55, No.12)
Pub: Charles D. Spencer & Associates, Inc.
Ed: Miriam Basch Scott. **Description:** Defined contribution health benefits plans have been transformed through the advent of the Internet. Regence Blue Cross Blue Shield of Oregon, working with Portland, Oregon-based Myhealthbank Inc., offers self-directed health benefit services.

43241 ■ **"Investigations"** in *Business Week* (January 16, 2006, No. 3967, pp. 34, 36, 38)
Pub: McGraw-Hill Companies
Ed: Arlene Weintraub, Amy Barrett. **Description:** A radical dental treatment spurs a lawsuit brought about by Aetna Insurance, while raising questions about the insurance and the Federal Drug Administrations' device-clearance process. Statistical data included.

43242 ■ **"IRS changes and finalizes 2000 cafeteria plan rules"** in *Employee Benefit Plan Review* (Vol. 55, No. 8, February 2001, pp. 13)
Pub: Charles D. Spencer & Associates, Inc.
Description: The changes made by the Internal Revenue Service regarding the status change, cost and coverage rules for cafeteria plans, and published in March 2000, are covered. These changes will be effective for cafeteria plan years beginning on or after January 1, 2001.

43243 ■ **"IRS Will Remove Tax Trap for One-Person S Corporations"** in *Kiplinger Letter* (Vol. 82, January 12, 2007, No. 1)
Pub: Kiplinger
Description: Internal Revenue Service is developing a new system that will clarify S corporation owners in states that are not allowed to deduct one-participant group health insurance plans, however, to get the deduction, the S firm must pay the medical premium.

43244 ■ **"Is Anyone Listening?"** in *Fortune* (Vol. 142, No. 2, July 10, 2000, pp. 200B+)
Pub: Time Inc.
Description: All small business owners agree that taxes are too high and complicated, health insurance is too expensive, and Washington has ignored these issues until this year. Washington seems to be learning the influence and power small businesses have in America.

43245 ■ **"Is Employer-Sponsored Health Insurance On Its Way Out?"** in *Kiplinger Letter* (Vol. 84, January 26, 2007, No. 4)
Pub: Kiplinger
Description: Congress is not expected to pass a bill that would count employer-provided health benefits as income, making them subject to taxes.

43246 ■ **"Is There a Cure?"** in *My Business* (June/July 2004, pp. 30-34)
Pub: My Business Magazine
Ed: Karen J. Bannan. **Description:** Small business owners are struggling with the high cost of providing health insurance coverage to employees. Some solutions for small employers are offered.

43247 ■ **"It's Business...and Personal"** in *Black Enterprise* (Vol. 34, July 2004, No. 12, pp. 38)
Pub: Earl G. Graves Publishing Co. Inc.
Ed: Aissatou Sidime. **Description:** Anthony Harris, owner of Popular Demand clothing store and Popular Demand Unisex Salon in Cleveland, Ohio, reports how he has formed a retirement savings account by investing in mutual funds and government bonds through a financial advisor who also helped Harris find personal medical coverage and life insurance.

43248 ■ **"It's Important to Be Proactive about Risk Issues"** in *Atlanta Business Chronicle* (Vol. 24, No. 9, August 3, 2001, pp. 9B)
Pub: American City Business Journals Inc.
Description: Major factors resulting in business failure include customer demand shortage, irregularities in accounting, issues concerning supply chain and competitive pressures. In protecting a business from risk of failure, in addition to purchasing insurance, a culture and organizational structure where risk management is seen as everyone's job, is essential.

43249 ■ **"It's really Pretty Simple"** in *Rough Notes* (Vol. 146, No. 3, March 2003, pp. 49)
Pub: Rough Notes
Ed: Roger Sitkins. **Description:** Preparation and planning are necessary for successful prospecting in insurance marketing.

43250 ■ **"The job site evolution"** in *Rough Notes* (Vol. 146, No. 3, March 2003, pp. 173)
Pub: Rough Notes
Ed: George Rusty Capulet. **Description:** Michael P. Tornesello, president of InsuranceJobChannel.com is an online career site available to the insurance industry. Nationwide Insurance is one of its customers.

43251 ■ **"Judge Halts Initial Step in Auto-Insurance Revamp"** in *Boston Globe* (February 2, 2005)
Pub: New York Times Company
Ed: Bruce Mohl. **Description:** Governor Mitt Romney's bid to revamp Massachusetts' auto insurance system was halted by a Superior Court judge. The judge deemed the initiative would cause discount insurance to stop and leave as many as 800,000 drivers in the state uninsured.

43252 ■ **"Judge Stays Implementation of Massachusetts Governor's Auto Insurance Plan"** in *Boston Globe* (February 2, 2005)
Pub: New York Times Company
Ed: Bruce Mohl. **Description:** Judge Raymond J. Brassard stayed the initial implementation of Governor Mitt Romney's proposed changes to the way high-risk drivers are apportioned among the state's insurance companies.

43253 ■ **"Katrina's Impact On Insurance Rippling Northward From Coast"** in *Mississippi Business Journal* (Vol. 29, January 2007, No. 4, pp. 3)
Pub: Venture Publications, Inc.
Ed: Richard Cotton **Description:** Due to massive devastation of Hurricane Katrina, and a very high number of insurance claims, most insurance companies are raising rates and electing to now renew existing policies or write any new ones.

43254 ■ **"Keep The Ball Rolling"** in *Rough Notes* (Vol. 145, No. 2, February 2002, pp. 79)
Pub: Rough Notes
Ed: Roger Sitkins. **Description:** For an agency to keep moving forward, agents should have an attitude of looking for improvement in themselves and their agency, have a prospect pipeline, a proactive sales management, training and education program.

43255 ■ **"The language of safety"** in *Rough Notes* (Vol. 146, No. 4, April 2003, pp. 24)
Pub: Rough Notes
Ed: Elisabeth Boone. **Description:** Accidents and injuries sustained by non-English speaking workers can be reduced or avoided when they learn by doing. Training industrial workers has been a success with Best Institute Inc., headed by Joseph E. Harcarz, Sr., CEO.

43256 ■ **"Latinocare Goes Public"** in *Hispanic Business* (June 2002, pp. 28)
Pub: Hispanic Business
Description: LatinoCare Management Corporation, a medical manager network, has become a publicly traded company. The Hispanic firm is located in Southern California.

43257 ■ **"Lawmakers Working on Insurance Issues"** in *Miami Herald* (March 10, 2005)
Pub: Knight-Ridder/Tribune Business News
Ed: Beatrice E. Garcia. **Description:** The Senate Banking and Insurance Committee approved a bill that will require insurers to offer multiple deductibles for policies covering commercial properties, including condominium associations.

43258 ■ **"Less than Half of Small Firms Offer Health Plans"** in *Wall Street Journal* (November 4, 2003, pp. B9)
Pub: Dow Jones & Co. Inc.
Ed: Richard C. Breeden. **Description:** It is estimated that less than half of all small businesses are able to offer health care plans to employees.

43259 ■ **"LifeSecure Goes National"** in *Crain's Detroit Business* (Vol. 23, January 29, 2007, No. 5, pp. 17)
Pub: Crain Communications Inc. - Detroit
Ed: Tom Henderson. **Description:** Small Brighton firm that specializes in long term insurance care Purchased a Dallas company to get licenses to sell in 41 states. Acquisition was the key to success in growing nationally and rapidly.

43260 ■ **"Lifestyle, research drugs cloud benefit decisions"** in *Business First Columbus* (Vol. 18, No. 40, May 24, 2002, pp. B8)
Pub: Business First Columbus, Inc.
Ed: Michael Nikunen, Timothy Dickman. **Description:** Companies will continue to find challenges with offering medical coverage to their employees.

43261 ■ **"Little Extras: Get More From Your Insurance Company than Just Coverage"** in *Entrepreneur* (Vol. 33, January 2005, No. 1, pp. 52)
Pub: Entrepreneur Media Inc.
Ed: Jacquelyn Lynn. **Description:** Most insurance agencies offer a variety of free services to save money and improve business while reducing risks.

43262 ■ **"Little urgency seen over HIPAA"** in *Crain's Detroit Business* (Vol. 18, No.)
Pub: Crain Communications Inc. - Detroit
Ed: David Barkholz, Andrew Dietderich. **Description:** Profile of the Health Insurance Portability and Accountability Act, which is intended to standardize and simplify security and privacy in health care.

43263 ■ "Live Long and Prosper: New Life Insurance Policies Offer Refunds" in *Entrepreneur* **(Vol. 32, December 2004, No. 12, pp. 66)**
Pub: Entrepreneur Media Inc.
Ed: Jacquelyn Lynn. **Description:** Return on Premium (ROP) insurance policies can be used as an alternative to traditional forms of life insurance. Small companies insuring key employees or buysell agreement might consider this type of policy.

43264 ■ "Long-Term Care Insurance is Growing Option Among Munster, Ind.-Area Families" in *The Times* **(July 4, 2004)**
Pub: The Times
Ed: Dan Rafter. **Description:** The State of Indiana has partnered with private insurance companies to offer residents long-term care policies to help them protect their assets and life savings should they ever require long-term care.

43265 ■ "Lose Weight, Get a Toaster" in *Inc.* **(January 1, 2005)**
Pub: Inc. Magazine
Ed: Bobbie Gossage. **Description:** Destiny Health offers consumer-driven health plans for small businesses. The insurer offers the Vitality program that awards points to participants who take care of themselves. The points can be converted into frequent-flier miles on three airlines.

43266 ■ "MACM To Issue Refunds" in *Mississippi Business Journal* **(Vol. 29, January 2007, No. 3, pp. A8)**
Pub: Venture Publications, Inc.
Description: Board of directors of the Medical Assurance Company of Mississippi has voted to issue a refund equivalent to 20-percent of the portion paid by each MACM insured for the first $1 million of coverage for this year.

43267 ■ "Magna Rating Adjusted" in *Mississippi Business Journal* **(Vol. 29, January 2007, No. 2, pp. 8)**
Pub: Venture Publications, Inc.
Ed: Wally Northway **Description:** Magna Insurance Company has had its financial strength rating downgraded from B to B by A.M. Best Co.

43268 ■ "Management Liability at the Speed of Light" in *Rough Notes* **(Vol. 145, No. 38, June 2002, pp. 38)**
Pub: Rough Notes
Ed: Elisabeth Boone. **Description:** The Royal and Sun Alliance USA, headed by Chris Mower, offers directors and officers liability insurance through its Business Assurance Center, both directly or online.

43269 ■ *Managing Health Benefits in Small and Mid-Sized Organizations*
Pub: Amacom
Ed: Patricia Halo. **Released:** July 1999. **Price:** $35.00. **Description:** Comprehensive guide for developing health care plans for companies employing between 50 and 5,000 employees in order to provide employees with better health care at lower prices.

43270 ■ "Many firms don't know they can deduct premiums" in *Birmingham Business Journal* **(Vol. 17, No. 36, September 8, 2000, pp. 14)**
Pub: American City Business Journals, Inc.
Description: A new survey of small businesses, conducted by Blue Cross and Blue Shield Association and the Employee Benefit Research Institute, found that 57 percent were not aware they could deduct all of the health insurance premiums they pay for their employees. Statistical data is included.

43271 ■ "Many Ways to Lose" in *Kiplinger's Personal Finance Magazine* **(Vol. 54, No. 11, November 2000, pp. 98)**
Pub: The Kiplinger Washington Editors, Inc.
Ed: Kimberly Lankford. **Description:** Federal and state investigators are working overtime to combat fraud in deals that let investors collect on a stranger's life insurance policy.

43272 ■ "Marsh Mac Settles Up" in *Business Week* **(February 14, 2005, No. 3920, pp. 42)**
Pub: McGraw-Hill Companies
Ed: Monica Gagnier. **Description:** Marsh & McLennan, the largest insurance broker in the world, settled civil fraud charges brought on by New York Attorney General Eliot Spitzer. Marsh will ban 'contingency fees' and other practices such as 'tying' as part of the settlement.

43273 ■ "Med Mal in Crisis Mode" in *Rough Notes* **(Vol. 145, No. 9, September 2002, pp. 66)**
Pub: Rough Notes
Ed: Phil Zinkewicz. **Description:** When St. Paul Companies, the largest writer of medical malpractice insurance in the U.S., pulled out of the line and was followed by others, physicians and doctors closed practices due to premium rates jumping to unaffordable levels.

43274 ■ "Medicaid HMOs seek cure for what ails them" in *Crain's Detroit Business* **(Vol. 19, No. 15, April 14, 2003, pp. 13)**
Pub: Crain Communications Inc., Detroit
Ed: Katie Merx. **Description:** Although most of Michigan's Medicaid HMO's are reporting profits, the largest are struggling. Information about The Wellness Plan, Great Lakes Health Plan Inc., and OmniCare Health Plan is covered. Statistical data included.

43275 ■ "Medical Coverage Options for the Self-Employed" in *Home Business* **(Vol. 13, January/February 2006, No. 1, pp. 94)**
Pub: Home Business Magazine
Ed: Tim McNeill, RN. **Description:** Government-funded alternative health coverage plans are becoming a popular choice for small businesses. Information about health savings accounts and state-funded children's health insurance programs is included.

43276 ■ "Medical Lessons: What Can Collision Repair Shops Learn About Insurance From the Health Care Industry?" in *Automotive Body Repair News*
Pub: Advanstar Communications Inc.
Ed: Mark Johnson. **Description:** Insurance companies have announced a decrease in the amount of money they will pay for certain glass replacements, including a 66 percent decrease off the CCC information system (NAGS) price. Automotive collision repair shops are being forced to lower prices. The industry is looking into the way doctors, clinics and hospitals are dealing with similar insurance pressures.

43277 ■ "Medicine Man" in *Forbes* **(June 10, 2002, p. 146)**
Pub: Forbes Magazine
Ed: Matthew Swibel. **Description:** Profile of Michael Caradimitropoulo of health discount-card seller Pinnacle Choice; Caradimitropoulo discusses ways selling discount health care cards to the uninsured can work.

43278 ■ "Minding the Money" in *Hispanic Business* **(May 2005, pp. 16)**
Pub: Hispanic Business
Description: Results of a study conducted by Roper Public Affairs showed that 74 percent of Hispanics aged 45 to 64 with household incomes of at least $45,000 feel they are financially successful. Fifty-eight percent of Hispanics find life insurance policies confusing.

43279 ■ "The Mini-K Advantage" in *Rough Notes* **(Vol. 144, No. 12, December 2001, pp. 80)**
Pub: Rough Notes
Description: Information about the new tax laws that benefit small business 401(k) retirement plans is given. Under the new tax laws, an individual making $100,000 per year can contribute $28,000 to a 401(k) plan.

43280 ■ "Money well spent" in *Rough Notes* **(Vol. 146, No. 3, March 2003, pp. 148)**
Pub: Rough Notes
Ed: John Ashenhurst. **Description:** One in four insurance agencies have a Web site, and those Web sites should attract prospects, obtain inexpensive advertising, and find customers.

43281 ■ "Monitoring Your Carriers" in *Rough Notes* **(Vol. 145, No. 2, February 2003, pp. 72)**
Pub: Rough Notes
Ed: Susan Hodges. **Description:** Guidelines for finding "red flags" when monitoring insurance carriers are presented. A.M. Best, Standard & Poor's, and Moody's are suggested as good sources to rely upon.

43282 ■ "More limited form of mold insurance emerges" in *Wall Street Journal* **(February 5, 2003, pp. B10)**
Pub: Dow Jones & Co. Inc.
Ed: Ray A. Smith. **Description:** Some insurers will offer more limited mold insurance coverage within indoor air quality policies.

43283 ■ "MSA Withdrawals: Rules on Tax Exclusion" in *Employee Benefit Plan Review* **(Vol. 55, No. 12, June 2001, pp. 8)**
Pub: Charles D. Spencer & Associates, Inc.
Description: Questions and answers focus on Cobra rules and tax rules for employee health plans. Employees are advised that they may pay medical bills by using an employer's medical savings account, which are known as Archer MSAs.

43284 ■ "The Mystery of ERM" in *Rough Notes* **(Vol. 145, No. 1, January 2003, pp. 52)**
Pub: Rough Notes
Ed: Michael J. Moody. **Description:** Enterprise Risk Management enables firms to focus on serious risks so they may develop ways to mitigate.

43285 ■ "Named Insured Wording: Doing It Right" in *Rough Notes* **(Vol. 146, No. 3, March 2003, pp. 78)**
Pub: Rough Notes
Ed: G. Barry Klein. **Description:** The Named Insured should be properly worded and written on the declarations page, or better still, on a Named Insured Endorsement. Done professionally, it puts the insurance agent ahead of the competition.

43286 ■ "Nervous About Bidding on eBay?" in *New York Times* **(November 17, 2003, pp. C7)**
Pub: The New York Times
Ed: Bob Tedeschi. **Description:** Hartford Financial Services Group and BuySafe have partnered to offer a buyer protection plan for eBay shoppers.

43287 ■ "A New Abacus for Pensions" in *Business Week* **(January 9, 2006, No. 3966, pp. 91)**
Pub: McGraw-Hill Companies
Description: New Financial Accounting Standards Board rules on post-retirement accounting will change how companies account for pensions and other employee benefits, especially retiree health insurance.

43288 ■ "New Campaign Aims to Educate Californians About Fake Insurance Policies" in *Sacramento Bee* **(October 1, 2005)**
Pub: The Sacramento Bee
Ed: Andrew McIntosh. **Description:** California's insurance commissioner has started a statewide campaign to educate the state's businesses and consumers about fraudulent insurance policies. Commissioner John Garamendi recommends that consumers contact his office before purchasing business insurance, or personal car, health or life insurance policies.

43289 ■ "New Group Plan Offers 'Free-Agent' Workers Affordable Health Benefits" in *Boston Globe* **(March 3, 2005)**
Pub: New York Times Company
Ed: Diane E. Lewis. **Description:** National Health Access is offering a program that provides lower cost health insurance to part-time, temporary, seasonal, and contract workers.

43290 ■ "New Law Likely to Save Businesses Money on Terrorism Insurance" in *Crain's Detroit Business* **(Vol. 19, No. 1, Jan. 6, 2003, pp. 16)**
Pub: Crain Communications Inc., Detroit

Ed: Katie Merx. **Description:** Investigation into terrorism risk insurance coverage for small businesses is presented. Passage of the Terrorism Risk Insurance Act should help save businesses money because the government will assume most of the risk for coverage.

43291 ■ "New NAPSLO President Helm" in *Rough Notes* **(Vol. 145, No. 1, January 2003, pp. 40)**
Pub: Rough Notes
Ed: Phil Zinkewicz. **Description:** Nicholas D. Cortezi, president of the National Association of Professional Surplus Lines Offices, finds that risks that should not be in the standard insurance market are finding their way into the surplus lines market where they belong.

43292 ■ "New Plus President Has Unique Perspective" in *Rough Notes* **(Vol. 145, No. 1, January 2003, pp. 18)**
Pub: Rough Notes
Ed: Phil Zinkewicz. **Description:** Peter Cottrell is the new president of the Professional Liability Underwriting Society. Cottrell proposes information, opportunities and solutions for members and their employees in an increasingly hostile environment.

43293 ■ "Nine Ways to Slash Your Insurance Costs, From Health Savings Accounts to Getting Tough With Your Broker To Joining Purchasing Pools" in *Inc.*
Pub: Inc. Magazine
Ed: Jennifer Gill. **Description:** Nine steps to cut small business insurance costs are covered.

43294 ■ "Nine Ways to Slash Your Insurance Costs" in *Inc.* **(April 1, 2005)**
Pub: Inc. Magazine
Ed: Jennifer Gill. **Description:** Nine steps to cut small business insurance costs are covered.

43295 ■ "No Boundaries" in *Rough Notes* **(Vol. 145, No. 9, September 2002, pp. 54)**
Pub: Rough Notes
Ed: Elisabeth Boone. **Description:** Health care or medical insurance that adequately covers the insured globally, is the main product of International Medical Group, a one-stop shop for insurance agents.

43296 ■ "Nobody's Fool? Health Insurance Scams Target Entrepreneurs" in *Entrepreneur* **(Vol. 32, August 2004, No. 8, pp. 21)**
Pub: Entrepreneur Media Inc.
Ed: Joan Szabo. **Description:** Phony health insurance plan promoters are preying on entrepreneurs promising coverage at premiums below charges by licensed insurers. These fraudulent plans escape state regulators with false claims of federally regulated plans under the Employee Retirement Income Security Act (ERISA), a law that pre-empts states from regulating ERISA-covered employee benefit plans sponsored by private employers.

43297 ■ "Not Your Typical Agency" in *Rough Notes* **(Vol. 145, No. 2, February 2003, pp. 18)**
Pub: Rough Notes
Ed: Dennis H. Pillsbury. **Description:** Profile of Brewer and Lord LLC, owned by Citizens Bank of Massachusetts. The firm is a property and casualty insurance agency that was formed 150 years ago and prides itself on providing the best service to clients.

43298 ■ "Oklahoma Insurance Commissioner Orders Tribal Companies Out of State" in *Journal Record* **(February 5, 2004)**
Pub: Dolan Media Company
Description: Carroll Fisher, Oklahoma Insurance Commissioner, ordered a group of companies claiming tribal sovereignty to stop doing business in the state. Fisher alleges the companies are required to be licensed by the Oklahoma Insurance Department, while the companies claim tribal sovereignty since they are affiliated with the Ponca Tribe of Nebraska.

43299 ■ "On the Disabled List? Save Employees (and Your Business) a World of Hurt With Disability Insurance" in *Entrepreneur* **(Vol. 32)**
Pub: Entrepreneur Media Inc.
Ed: Jacquelyn Lynn. **Description:** Because the average American worker stands a 1 in 3 chance of becoming disabled for 90 days or more, it is important to include disability insurance as an employee benefit.

43300 ■ "On the Job" in *Entrepreneur* **(Vol. 31, No. 8, August 2003, pp. 67)**
Pub: Entrepreneur Media, Inc.
Ed: Jacquelyn Lynn. **Description:** When hiring independent contractors, be sure they have the correct liability insurance. Alejandra Soto of the Insurance Information Institute states that the type of insurance needed will depend on the type of work being done by the contractor and lists various insurance coverages that me be required, including workers' compensation, general liability, completion bond, and intellectual property coverage.

43301 ■ "On The Board" in *Inc.* **(October 1, 2004)**
Pub: Inc. Magazine
Ed: Patrick J. Sauer. **Description:** Profile of Benecard Services, the New Jersey company that processes and administers prescription drug and vision programs for health plans. The firm sponsors a New Jersey State Prison chess tournament by donating boards, pieces, clocks, and books.

43302 ■ "One More For the Road" in *Sales & Marketing Management* **(January 2005)**
Pub: VNU Business Media
Ed: Denis Jensen. **Description:** Sales executives, as well as management, should avoid the pitfalls of drinking when entertaining business clients. One accident involving an employee under the influence will cause insurance rates to go up.

43303 ■ "Online APPS and Quotes for E&O" in *Rough Notes* **(Vol. 145, No. 9, September 2002, pp. 49)**
Pub: Rough Notes
Ed: Len Strazewski. **Description:** Frederick J. Fisher, president of Executive Liability Managers Insurance Brokers Inc., discusses professional liability coverage.

43304 ■ "Online Insurance Exchanges Fail to Connect" in *Atlanta Business Chronicle* **(Vol. 25, No. 19, October 18, 2002, pp. 6C)**
Pub: American City Business Publications, Inc.
Ed: Lee Hall. **Description:** Online business-to-business insurance exchanges, once viewed as offering the insurance industry savings in time and money, have not gotten far beyond the conceptual stage, and may be as far as ten years away from completion.

43305 ■ "Opportunity Knocks" in *Rough Notes* **(Vol. 145, No. 9, September 2002, pp. 110)**
Pub: Rough Notes
Ed: Michael J. Moody. **Description:** Health insurance for employees is now the number one challenge for human resources departments, chief financial officers and upper management because rates are rising, capacities are shrinking and customers are feeling dissatisfied about coverage.

43306 ■ "Optional benefits aren't always a positive" in *Rough Notes* **(Vol. 146, No. 4, April 2003, pp. 126)**
Pub: Rough Notes
Ed: Len Strazewski. **Description:** In the prevailing competition and struggling economy, employers can hardly afford a broad package of benefits to employees. Brokers and agents should survey the client's employees and ascertain the interest and need for voluntary supplemental benefits, offering the most-needed and valuable coverage.

43307 ■ "Pacific Life Insurance Committed to Secondaries" in *Venture Capital Journal* **(Vol. 41, No. 8, August 2000, pp. 41)**
Pub: Venture Economics
Ed: Alistair Christopher. **Description:** Profile of Pacific Life Insurance located in Newport Beach, California,

whose private equity portfolio consisting of 32 percent buyout/growth capital funds, 30 percent venture vehicles, 20 percent international funds, 12 percent specialty sector funds vehicles, and 6 percent mezzanine funds.

43308 ■ "Partnering for Success" in *Rough Notes* **(Vol. 146, No. 4, April 2003, pp. 32)**
Pub: Rough Notes
Description: Robyn Holt is the manager of Fraser, Yamor, Jacob and Young, the firm that has entered into a partnership with Western Valley Insurance Associates Inc.

43309 ■ "Paving the Cow Path" in *Rough Notes* **(Vol. 146, No. 9, September 2003, pp. 40)**
Pub: Rough Notes
Ed: John Ashenburst. **Description:** Overview of changes and future trends in the insurance industry. Topics covered include risk management services, Internet marketing of services, and insurance services offered through banks.

43310 ■ "The Perfect Storm? Employers Need Navigation Tools For The Newest Set of Health Cost Waves" in *Employee Benefit Plan Review* **(Vol. 55)**
Pub: Charles D. Spencer & Associates, Inc.
Ed: Stephen A. Huth. **Description:** Reports from the Department of Labor show that, for the year ended September 30, 2000, benefits costs for private industry workers rose to 6 percent. The largest portion was for health care, and employers will try many strategies to reduce costs, including passing some on to their employees.

43311 ■ "Perfect Storm Strikes CEOs" in *Hispanic Business* **(Vol. 24, No. 4, April 2002, pp. 16, 18)**
Pub: Hispanic Business Inc.
Ed: Derek Reveron. **Description:** A new study shows that insurance premiums will rise during the next few years, squeezing profits and swelling the ranks of the uninsured, and small Hispanic-owned businesses and their employees are said to be among those hardest hit.

43312 ■ "Pharmacies Fight Mail-Order Purchases, Medicaid Tax" in *Crain's Detroit Business* **(Vol. 19, No. 43, October 27, 2003, pp. 6)**
Pub: Crain Communications Inc., Detroit
Description: Michigan legislators are debating a bill that would restrict mail-order drug purchases for unions, businesses and health plans, as well as imposing a self-assessment tax in Medicaid reimbursement.

43313 ■ "The Pivotal roles of Customer Service Professionals" in *Rough Notes* **(Vol. 145, No. 2, February 2003, pp. 88)**
Pub: Rough Notes
Ed: Jim Cuprisin. **Description:** The role of the insurance customer service professional is the most customer critical in an insurance agency because the position plays a vital role in the company's growth and profitability.

43314 ■ "Plant Manager Urges Lockheed Martin Employees Not to Strike" in *Atlanta Journal-Constitution* **(March 5, 2005)**
Pub: Knight-Ridder/Tribune Business News
Ed: Dave Hirschman. **Description:** International Association of Machinists Local 709's 2,800 members are poised to reject a tentative three-year contract and authorize a strike. The Lockheed Martin's plant in Marietta, Georgia builds F/A-22 Raptor fighters and C-130J transports. Employees are unhappy about rising health care and retirement insurance costs.

43315 ■ "Poor Health" in *Entrepreneur* **(Vol. 28, No. 4, April 2000, pp. 114)**
Pub: Entrepreneur Media Inc.
Ed: Ellen Paris. **Description:** Buying health insurance for a small business.

43316 ■ "Portfolio D&O Insurance Can Leave Outside Directors in the Cold" in *Venture Capital Journal* **(October 1, 2005)**
Pub: Thomason Financial Inc.
Description: The need for liability insurance to cover directors of public and private portfolio companies is stressed. The article sites a lawsuit against Benchmark Capital.

43317 ■ "Preferred Club Program Sits Atop The Leader Board" in *Rough Notes* **(Vol. 146, No. 3, March 2003, pp. 90)**
Pub: Rough Notes
Ed: Dennis Pillsbury. **Description:** Preferred Club Program provides risk analysis, loss control and loss mitigation, claims handling, as well as golf and club industry insurance. The firm has no capacity concerns and offers specialized insurance to the industry.

43318 ■ "Premium pain" in *Boston Business Journal* **(Vol. 22, No. 16, Ma)**
Pub: MCP, Inc.
Ed: Allison Connolly, Jill Lerner. **Description:** Small business in the Boston, MA area have had their health insurance premiums increased dramatically. Health insurance premiums increased by 12-15 percent in Massachusetts in 2002.

43319 ■ "Premium Pain Relief" in *Business Week* **(June 12, 2000, pp. F14)**
Pub: McGraw-Hill, Inc.
Description: Association health plans for small businesses to help fight the soaring health-care costs.

43320 ■ "Premium RX? Consumer-driven health plans" in *Atlanta Business Chronicle* **(Vol. 25, No. 19, October 18, 2002, pp. 5C)**
Pub: American City Business Publications, Inc.
Ed: Tom Barry. **Description:** Consumer-driven health plans are increasingly being considered by companies as a means to counter the effects of double-digit health insurance premium rates, by trimming the demand for healthcare services. These plans are the other side of the managed care health plan which attempts to control health care costs through the supply side. The consumer-driven health care plans establish medical savings accounts, creating an inducement by the user to consider cost-saving options.

43321 ■ "Prescription Drug Cost Containment" in *Rough Notes* **(Vol. 145, No. 2, February 2003, pp. 76)**
Pub: Rough Notes
Ed: Len Strazewski. **Description:** As employer health care costs overwhelm small to medium-sized businesses, they can turn to pharmacy benefits management companies, such as AdvancePCS Inc., Caremark Rx Inc., and Express Scripts, Inc.

43322 ■ "Preserving Tradition, Embracing Progress" in *Rough Notes* **(Vol. 145, No. 2, February 2003, pp. 26)**
Pub: Rough Notes
Ed: Elaine Tolen. **Description:** Profile of Trey Sherwood, a partner in Valdosta Insurance Services. The independent agency provides for the insurance needs of 98 percent of Lowndes County, Valdosta, Georgia.

43323 ■ "Pressure mounting for terrorism insurance relief" in *Atlanta Business Chronicle* **(Vol. 25, No. 21, November 1, 2002, pp. 5C)**
Pub: American City Business Publications, Inc.
Ed: Jan R. Costello. **Description:** The U.S. House of Representatives and the U.S. Senate are both working on terrorism insurance reform legislation. Terrorism coverage costs have risen tremendously and a majority of policies launched after the September 11, 2001 terrorist attacks do not cover terrorism.

43324 ■ "Producer compensation linked to agency size" in *Rough Notes* **(Vol. 146, No. 3, March 2003, pp. 16)**
Pub: Rough Notes
Ed: Phil Zinkewicz. **Description:** The Business Management Group has released its 2002 Owner, Executive and Producer Compensation Survey. The survey shows that the level of compensation for producers is related to agency size and individual production.

43325 ■ "Producers as Consultants" in *Rough Notes* **(Vol. 145, No. 12, December 2002, pp. 124)**
Pub: Rough Notes
Ed: Donald S. Malecki. **Description:** Insurance agents can go beyond just their role as order-taker by being consultants in risk management and other more difficult coverage for the client.

43326 ■ "Profit is no accident" in *Crain's Detroit Business* **(Vol. 18, No.)**
Pub: Crain Communications Inc. - Detroit
Ed: David Barkholz. **Description:** Profile of James Epolito, CEO of the Lansing, Michigan-based Accident Fund Co.

43327 ■ "Promoting agency wellness" in *Rough Notes* **(Vol. 146, No. 3, March 2003, pp. 171)**
Pub: Rough Notes
Ed: Wanda Shumaker. **Description:** Wellness programs for the staff contributes to the morale and mental health of the employees, creativity, production and reduced medical costs.

43328 ■ "Protecting What's Yours" in *Hispanic Business* **(Vol. 23, No. 7/8, July/August 2001, pp. 110)**
Pub: Hispanic Business
Ed: Milton Zall. **Description:** Under deferred compensation plans, key employees are promised future rewards, bankruptcy insurance may be the best insurance to protect deferred compensation plans.

43329 ■ "Rapid Response" in *Rough Notes* **(Vol. 145, No. 9, September 2002, pp. 74)**
Pub: Rough Notes
Description: Christina Nelson, President and CEO of SilverPlume, a broad-based online insurance company, agrees with the Insurance Services Office to distribute online insurance industry information services.

43330 ■ "Rate Increases Nail Homebuilding Sector" in *Business Journal-Portland* **(Vol. 20, No. 26, August 29, 2003, pp. 18)**
Pub: American City Business Journals, Inc.
Ed: Robert Goldfield. **Description:** Insurance companies have doubled or tripled premiums for building contracts for various reasons, including the appearance of toxic mold in homes and resulting lawsuits.

43331 ■ "Reaching Their Potential" in *Rough Notes* **(Vol. 146, No. 3, March 2003, pp. 42)**
Pub: Rough Notes
Ed: Dennis Pillsbury. **Description:** Doug Witcher, president of Worldwide Insurance Network Inc., started Smart Choice Agents which contracts with insurance companies and provides access to markets.

43332 ■ "Ready To Go: How An Online Tool Helped One Company Speed Distribution of Marketing Materials To Reps" in *Sales & Marketing Management*
Pub: VNU Business Media
Ed: Alan Horowitz. **Description:** Allstate Insurance, is providing its sales reps access to thousands of sales and marketing materials via a Web-hosted service that automates order fulfillment and inventory management of sales and marketing materials. Research indicates that without this type of service, sales reps spend 25 percent of their time searching for and assembling information for sales calls.

43333 ■ "Recipe for Disaster?" in *Entrepreneur* **(Vol. 32, November 2004, No. 11, pp. 75)**
Pub: Entrepreneur Media Inc.
Ed: Scott Bernard Nelson. **Description:** Natural disasters serve as reminders to everyone to review insurance policies.

43334 ■ "Recreational/Personal Watercraft Market" in *Rough Notes* **(Vol. 145, No. 2, February 2003, pp. 48)**
Pub: Rough Notes
Ed: Larry G. France. **Description:** The watercraft insurance market has been declining as it is an industry that depends largely on the economy. Boat insurance is provided by agencies listed, including American Modern Insurance Group, American Reliable Insurance Company, and BAT Insurance Corporation.

43335 ■ "Regional Insurers Thrive" in *Rough Notes* **(Vol. 145, No. 2, February 2003, pp. 78)**
Pub: Rough Notes
Ed: Phil Zinkewicz. **Description:** Despite predictions of observers, experts and analysts, small and regional insurers increased direct written premiums nearly twice the growth achieved by large insurers between 1996-2000.

43336 ■ "Reinsurance" in *Rough Notes* **(Vol. 146, No. 9, September 2003, pp. 94)**
Pub: Rough Notes
Ed: Lori Widmer. **Description:** A review of the idea of making reinsurance available directly to customers is presented.

43337 ■ "A Remedy for Malpractice Malaise" in *Business Week* **(February 7, 2005, No. 3919, pp. 38)**
Pub: McGraw-Hill Companies
Ed: Arlene Weintraub. **Description:** In order to retain physicians, hospitals are offering malpractice insurance through not-for-profit entities known as captives. Statistical data included.

43338 ■ "Renovations of old buildings" in *Rough Notes* **(Vol. 145, No. 1, January 2003, pp. 16)**
Pub: Rough Notes
Ed: LeRoy H. Utschig. **Description:** The extensive remodeling of an old building requires comprehensive insurance coverage for contractors, project owners, and subcontractors. There are also subrogation issues, coverage on business income, and on the operation of building laws and builder's risk.

43339 ■ "Rep. Israel: Extend Terrorism Reinsurance Program Through '06" in *Long Island Business News* **(May 7, 2004)**
Pub: Dolan Media Newswires
Description: Legislatures will introduce legislation to extend the government's terrorism reinsurance program. The program is set to expire in 2006, and makes certain that insurance for terrorist attacks remain available to businesses.

43340 ■ "Resolving Owner Conflicts" in *Rough Notes* **(Vol. 145, No. 9, September 2002, pp. 26)**
Pub: Rough Notes
Ed: Paul J. DiStefano. **Description:** Lack of communications between owners of the insurance agency often results in disagreements. Unresolved conflict among owners can impede the future of an agency, whether the issue relates to money or operating philosophy.

43341 ■ "Retirees face waning insurance contributions" in *Atlanta Business Chronicle* **(Vol. 25, No. 19, October 18, 2002, pp. 7C)**
Pub: American City Business Publications, Inc.
Ed: Tom Barry. **Description:** Retirees in the future are seen as taking over a greater portion of the costs associated with healthcare benefits. By the year 2031, support by employers for retiree health benefits are forecast to shrink to less than 10 percent versus the more than 50 percent that is currently typical for larger companies. According to the study conducted by Watson Wyatt Worldwide, many companies have already eliminated or cut retiree health benefits, and the most vulnerable group targeted are those between the ages of 55 and 64.

43342 ■ "Retirement-Plan Administer To Be Bought For $115 Million" in *Wall Street Journal* **(Vol. 248, December 2006, No. 149, pp. C5)**
Pub: Dow Jones & Co. Inc.
Ed: Wall Street Journal News **Description:** Charles Schwab Corp. acquires 401(K) Co. for $115 million. 401(K) overseas $22 billion in retirement assets.

43343 ■ "Rewarding Bad Behavior" in *Rough Notes* **(Vol. 145, No. 12, December 2002, pp. 118)**
Pub: Rough Notes
Description: The National Conference of State Legislatures, using the National Association of Insurance

Commissioners, has much influence in contributing to state revenues; they are now involved in preserving state regulations and dealing with federal government pressures.

43344 ■ "Richard Whitmer" in *Crain's Detroit Business* **(Vol. 19, No. 1, January 6, 2003, pp. 12)**
Pub: Crain Communications Inc., Detroit
Ed: Katie Merx. **Description:** Profile of Richard Whitmer, who works to prevent changes to laws regarding health insurance and Blue Cross and Blue Shield of Michigan.

43345 ■ "Rising health premiums mean more uninsured" in *Atlanta Business Chronicle* **(Vol. 25, No. 19, October 18, 2002, pp. 10C)**
Pub: American City Business Publications, Inc.
Ed: Anya Martin. **Description:** The number of individuals in the state of Georgia without health care insurance is expected to rise because small businesses are having a harder time finding affordable coverage and the slowing economy has forced many small firms to eliminate or cut back coverage.

43346 ■ "Risk is His Business" in *Fortune* **(Vol. 152, October 3, 2005, No. 7, pp. 61)**
Pub: Time Inc.
Ed: David Stipp. **Description:** Risk Management Solutions (RMS) of Newark, California projects damages from hurricanes, earthquakes and other disasters for insurance companies. Robert Muir-Wood, RMS research chief, offers perspectives on New Orleans.

43347 ■ "Risk Management on the Farm" in *Hispanic Business* **(November 2002, pp. 33)**
Pub: Hispanic Business
Ed: Scott Williams. **Description:** Profile of Jim Baldonado, CEO of The Home Agency of Elwood, Nebraska. Baldonado sells crop insurance, particularly crop revenue coverage to rural farmers in the area.

43348 ■ "Risky business: on the lookout for business insurance?" in *Entrepreneur* **(Vol. 31, No. 6, June 2003, pp. 73)**
Pub: Entrepreneur Media Inc.
Ed: Mark Henricks. **Description:** According to the Insurance Information Institute, fifteen percent of small businesses do not buy business insurance to cover their enterprises because it is harder to find, less affordable, and provides less protection.

43349 ■ "Role of Coach Critical to Success of New Producer" in *Rough Notes* **(Vol. 145, No. 9, September 2002, pp. 30)**
Pub: Rough Notes
Ed: Bud Antrim. **Description:** Trainees at insurance agencies like Rue Insurance, Trenton, New Jersey; JWF Companies, Indianapolis, Indiana; Johnson, Kendall and Johnson, Langhorne, Pennsylvania, who learn from coaches are able to produce earlier in their career. Mentors serve as models and training has become an important component in the company development program.

43350 ■ "Rough Notes presents Community Service Award" in *Rough Notes* **(Vol. 146, No. 4, April 2003, pp. 98)**
Pub: Rough Notes
Ed: Bob Bloss. **Description:** The Rough Notes publication awards the Giroux-Audet-Rua Insurance Agency the 2003 Community Service Award for volunteerism.

43351 ■ "Rumblings" in *Crain's Detroit Business* **(Vol. 19, No. 1, January 6, 2003, pp. 22)**
Pub: Crain Communications Inc., Detroit
Description: Crain's Detroit Business and WJR AM 760 radio station along with the Rehabilitation Institute of Michigan have launched a competition to find the '50 Fittest CEOs' in metropolitan Detroit. According to an investment banker, Compuware Corporation is being targeted for acquisition. A listing of the top six law firms in the Detroit area making The National Law Journal 250 for 2002 is presented.

43352 ■ "Safety Dance: Get Policies in Place Now, and Avoid Liability Later" in *Entrepreneur* **(Vol. 31, No. 11, November 2003, pp. 93)**
Pub: Entrepreneur Media, Inc.
Ed: Jacquelyn Lynn. **Description:** Insurance policies designed to address potentially risky situations are important to most small businesses. Procedural policies should include employment practices, equipment management, Internet use, cell phone use, vehicles and workplace safety.

43353 ■ "School-related Risks: Don't Trip Over Those Footnotes" in *Rough Notes* **(Vol. 145, No. 1, January 2003, pp. 58)**
Pub: Rough Notes
Ed: Linda D. Ferguson. **Description:** Insurance coverage on students or schools and definitions in the policy contracts have to be carefully understood and explained because a mistake even in classification could lead to confusion and denial of any claim.

43354 ■ "Selling homeowners insurance" in *Rough Notes* **(Vol. 146, No. 3, March 2003, pp. 158)**
Pub: Rough Notes
Ed: Troy Korsgaden. **Description:** At a time when the homeowners' insurance market is tightening, insurance agents should learn to maintain and win new customers. Seven suggestions are offered.

43355 ■ "Service that truly makes a difference" in *Rough Notes* **(Vol. 146, No. 4, April 2003, pp. 114)**
Pub: Rough Notes
Ed: Suellyn Boastick. **Description:** Customer satisfaction and customer relationships require anticipation of needs, communication with clients and outreach services to the community.

43356 ■ "Severe Storm Watch" in *Inc.* **(August 1, 2003)**
Pub: Gruner & Jahr USA Publishing
Ed: Rod Kurtz. **Description:** Small business owners must understand the need to protect companies from potential storm damage if they are in an area prone to hurricanes. The U.S. Small Business Administration paid out 5,458 business recovery loans for more than $257 million from small business losses due to Hurricane Andrew.

43357 ■ "Sharing Marketing Expenses" in *Rough Notes* **(Vol. 145, No. 9, September 2002, pp. 80)**
Pub: Rough Notes
Ed: Michael J. Weinberg. **Description:** Information about marketing expenses related to sales which insurance agents and agencies can share, include business meals, contributions to community organizations, direct mail, and telemarketing.

43358 ■ "Sharp Turn" in *Puget Sound Business Journal* **(Vol. 21, No. 3, May 26, 2000, pp. 20)**
Pub: American City Business Journals, Inc.
Ed: Sean Robinson. **Description:** Once considered too experimental, acupuncture is now regarded as a viable treatment option, and health insurers are beginning to cover treatments.

43359 ■ "A Silver Lining For the Nursing Home Industry" in *Rough Notes* **(Vol. 145, No. 2, February 2003, pp. 44)**
Pub: Rough Notes
Ed: Elisabeth Boone. **Description:** Carole Fleischman, president of Arrowhead General Agency's Managed Insurance Programs Division, has developed a risk management and insurance program for the nursing home industry called Silver Lining.

43360 ■ "Small and midsize concerns are facing boosts up to 15 percent for their insurance" in *Wall Street Journal* **(March 20, 2000, pp. A2)**
Pub: Dow Jones & Co., Inc.
Ed: Deborah Lohse. **Description:** The soaring cost of insurance faced by small businesses is confronted.

43361 ■ *Small Business Access and Alternatives to Health Care: Congressional Hearing*
Pub: DIANE Publishing Company
Ed: Donald A. Manzullo. **Released:** July 2006. **Price:** $35.00. **Description:** Congressional hearings regarding the health care crisis facing America's small businesses is discussed.

43362 ■ *Small Business Desk Reference*
Pub: Penguin Books (USA) Incorporated
Ed: Gene Marks. **Released:** December 2004. **Price:** $29.95 (US), $44.00 (Canadian). **Description:** Comprehensive guide for starting or running a successful small business, focusing on buying a business or franchise, writing a business plan, financial management, accounting, legal issues, human resources management, operations, marketing, sales, customer service, taxes, insurance, and ethics. Information for launching a restaurant, property management firm, retail outlet, consulting firm, and service business is included.

43363 ■ "Small Business Gets Big Squeeze From Property Insurance Rates" in *Tampa Tribune* **(February 6, 2007)**
Pub: Media General Inc.
Ed: Dave Simanoff. **Description:** Rising costs for property insurance is making it harder for small companies to remain competitive.

43364 ■ "Small Business Strains to Provide Health Care" in *Bradenton Herald* **(December 6, 2006)**
Pub: Bradenton Herald
Ed: Robin Roger. **Description:** Florida's small businesses want to provide their employees health insurance but find that the expense is too prohibitive. According to a survey conducted by the National Federation of Independent Business, the number of small businesses in Florida that offer health insurance has declined.

43365 ■ "Small Firms, Consumers Have PWBA Health Care Benefit Tools" in *Employee Benefit Plan Review* **(Vol. 55, No. 8, February 2001, pp. 40)**
Pub: Charles D. Spencer & Associates, Inc.
Description: A discussion regarding online and paper publications of the Pension and Welfare Benefits Administration of the Department of Labor. These tools for helping individuals and small businesses in making decisions about health care benefits have resulted from the Health Benefits Education Campaign.

43366 ■ "Small-Group Reform, Blue Changes on Hold" in *Crain's Detroit Business* **(Vol. 18, No. 50, December 16, 2002, pp. 6)**
Pub: Crain Communications Inc., Detroit
Ed: Amy Lane. **Description:** Small-group insurance reform and Michigan's item-pricing law, and how businesses must deal with unclaimed property, as well as the single-business-tax credit for redeveloping blighted or contaminated property are examined.

43367 ■ "Small-group insurance reforms are in works" in *Crain's Detroit Business* **(Vol. 19, No. 16, April 21, 2003, pp. 7)**
Pub: Crain Communications Inc., Detroit
Ed: Amy Lane. **Description:** Blue Cross Blue Shield of Michigan is seeking the 75 percent rule, whereby carriers have the option of denying coverage to employers who don't enroll 75 percent of their employees with the insurer.

43368 ■ "Small Office/Home Office" in *Hispanic Business* **(Vol. 22, No. 1/2, January/February, pp. 92)**
Pub: Hispanic Business
Description: The feature is designed to provide emerging entrepreneurs with practical tips for operating a small or home office. Home-based business insurance, business licensing, and next-generation scanners are discussed.

43369 ■ "A Small Price to Pay" in *Inc.* **(September 1, 2003)**
Pub: Gruner & Jahr USA Publishing
Ed: Alison Stein. **Description:** Reasons long-term care insurance coverage makes sense is discussed.

43370 ■ **"Smaller firms see biggest jump in health-care costs"** in *Wall Street Journal* (August 29, 2000, pp. B2)

Pub: Dow Jones & Co., Inc.

Ed: Joshua Harris Prager. **Description:** An update on the soaring cost of health care faced by small businesses in the U.S. is covered.

43371 ■ **"Some "Unlikely" Losses Worth Mentioning To Business Owners"** in *Rough Notes* (Vol. 145, No. 9, September 2002, pp. 86)

Pub: Rough Notes

Ed: LeRoy H. Uschig. **Description:** Owners of businesses often neglect to update ownership, property, underground wiring and pipes, in insurance policies and this omission could jeopardize insurance claims.

43372 ■ **"Specialty Lines Annual Outlook"** in *Rough Notes* (Vol. 146, No. 3, March 2003, pp. 96)

Pub: Rough Notes

Ed: Larry G. France. **Description:** Because of a negative evaluation of the insurance industry, Rough Notes Company and the Insurance Market Place will sponsor two Specialty Lines seminars to help agencies cope with the growing uncertainty of the market.

43373 ■ **"Spectacular growth forces Accident Fund to limit new biz"** in *Crain's Detroit Business* (Vol. 18, No. 22, June 3, 2002, pp. 37)

Pub: Crain Communications Inc. - Detroit

Ed: David Barkholz. **Description:** The Accident Fund Company grew so fast in the first quarter of 2002, the management of workers' compensation insurer, has struggled to keep independent agents from writing new business.

43374 ■ **"The Spotlight's on Health Care"** in *Fortune* (Vol. 142, No. 2, July 10, 2000, pp. 200J)

Pub: Time Inc.

Ed: Daniel Kadlec. **Description:** While the cost of health care has risen about 10 percent per year, the cost to small businesses has risen at about twice that rate. Politicians are finally taking notice of the problem.

43375 ■ **"SRS leads the crane and rigging field"** in *Rough Notes* (Vol. 146, No. 4, April 2003, pp. 52)

Pub: Rough Notes

Ed: Dennis Pillsbury. **Description:** Kevin Cunningham is the CEO of Special Risk Services Group LLC which specializes in insuring heavy equipment and crane rentals; the business is backed up by Lloyds of London and AIG.

43376 ■ **"Stake a Claim: With Liability Insurance, Timing is Everything"** in *Entrepreneur* (Vol. 33, February 2005, No. 2, pp. 52)

Pub: Entrepreneur Media Inc.

Ed: Jacquelyn Lynn. **Description:** Claims-made policies protect against claims or incidents reported while a policy is in force, regardless of date; occurrence policies cover claims for incidents occurring during the policy period, regardless of when claims are reported.

43377 ■ **"State Farm Rate Boost Approved"** in *Tampa Tribune* (November 24, 2005)

Pub: Media General, Inc.

Ed: Randy Diamond. **Description:** State Farm Florida Insurance Company was given approval to raise homeowner insurance rates by 39 percent in Hernando County, 22 percent in Hillsborough County, and 15 percent in Pinellas County. Sinkholes, hurricanes and rising constructions costs are blamed for the increases.

43378 ■ **"State Farm Signs On As Host"** in *Black Enterprise* (Vol. 36, December 2005, No. 5, pp. 166)

Pub: Earl G. Graves Publishing Co. Inc.

Ed: Alysha N. Cryer. **Description:** State Farm Insurance Company has partnered with Black Enterprise to launch the inaugural Women of Pow4er Summit. The professional leadership conference is designed exclusively for women of color executives.

43379 ■ **"Storms"** in *Business Week* (January 16, 2006, No. 3967, pp. 28-31)

Pub: McGraw-Hill Companies

Ed: Adam Aston, Joseph Weber. **Description:** Science is helping insurance companies and other firms plan for hurricanes. The 2006 storm season is predicted to be filled with more hurricanes. Statistical data included.

43380 ■ **"Strong Medicine"** in *Hispanic Business* (June 2005, pp. 40, 42)

Pub: Hispanic Business

Ed: Felix Sanchez. **Description:** A focus on primary care helps Molina Healthcare manage Medicaid; the company's core business concentrates on government programs.

43381 ■ **"Study: Insurance Fraud Thriving"** in *Orlando Business Journal* (Vol. 20, No. 13, September 12, 2003, pp. 1)

Pub: American City Business Journals, Inc.

Ed: Susan Lundine. **Description:** Researchers at the Health Policy Institute of Georgetown University reported that Florida has a disproportionate number of health insurance fraud cases. Nearly 30,000 Florida residents have been left with $6 million in unpaid medical bills by fraudulent companies.

43382 ■ **"Study: Language Worsens Hispanic Healthcare Crisis"** in *Hispanic Business* (March 2003, pp. 12)

Pub: Hispanic Business

Description: The results of a survey conducted by The Commonwealth Fund, a national foundation that supports independent healthcare research, found that Hispanics who speak little or no English are often discouraged from seeking medical care. Statistical data included.

43383 ■ **"Study Looks at Benefits of Nonprofits Teaming Up to Buy Health Insurance"** in *Pittsburgh Business Times* (Vol. 23, August 8, 2003)

Pub: Pittsburgh Business Times

Ed: Lynne Glover. **Description:** The increasing price of health insurance may force nonprofit organizations to join together in a group buying plan. Dewey and Kaye, a management consulting firm, will conduct a feasibility study of the option.

43384 ■ **"Take Cover: No Need to Panic-We've Got Tips to Help You Cut Your Car Insurance Costs"** in *Entrepreneur* (Vol. 33, March 2005, No. 3)

Pub: Entrepreneur Media Inc.

Ed: Jill Amadio. **Description:** Ways to reduce insurance costs for a small business are listed. It is important to check a state's minimum insurance requirements, comparison shop online, and check for discounts.

43385 ■ **"Take Note: Document Incidents Now, and Avoid Lawsuits Later"** in *Entrepreneur* (Vol. 32, October 2004, No. 10, pp. 64)

Pub: Entrepreneur Media Inc.

Ed: Jacquelyn Lynn. **Description:** Proper documentation at the time of an injury or property damage occurring at a small company will give the firm a stronger position in litigation. If possible, take photographs, save security tapes and store documents in a safe place.

43386 ■ **"Take your pick"** in *Entrepreneur* (Vol. 31, No. 5, May 2003, pp. 69)

Pub: Entrepreneur Media Inc.

Ed: Mark Henricks. **Description:** Cafeteria health insurance plans let employees preset an amount to pay for selections from various insurances and other benefit providers. Employers prefer cafeteria-style packages because they shift some of the healthcare costs onto employees.

43387 ■ **"Taking a Dive: A Federally Chartered Insurer of Pensions has Fallen on Hard Times. Taxpayers, Beware"** in *Barron's* (July 21, 2003)

Pub: Barron's

Ed: Jim McTague. **Description:** The government-run Pension Benefit Guaranty Corporation, which insures more than 30,000 defined-benefit plan payments comprising more than 40 million workers, could be bankrupt in ten years, according to Congress. A bailout would tax citizens in the tens of billions.

43388 ■ **"Tap into Expert Input"** in *Black Enterprise* (Vol. 30, No. 12, July 2000, pp. 47)

Pub: Earl Graves Publishing Co.

Ed: Craig Owen White. **Description:** Learn how a board of advisors can benefit your firm with regard to employment policies, insurance coverage and strategic alliances.

43389 ■ **"Tax-Free Bill of Health: Health-Care Accounts with Tax Benefits"** in *Entrepreneur* (Vol. 33, January 2005, No. 1, pp. 50)

Pub: Entrepreneur Media Inc.

Ed: Joan Szabo. **Description:** Health Savings Accounts (HSAs), Health Reimbursement Arrangements (HRAs), Flexible Spending Accounts (FSAs), and Medical Savings Accounts (MSAs) are health-care spending accounts designed to help employees pay for health costs, while saving on taxes.

43390 ■ **"Terrorism Backup Legislation Raises Many Questions"** in *Rough Notes* (Vol. 145, No. 2, February 2003, pp. 34)

Pub: Rough Notes

Ed: Phil Zinkewicz. **Description:** Terrorism insurance, its back up legislation, and obligations of agents and insurance companies in regard to disclosure requirements has turned out to be so complex it raises serious questions on compliance.

43391 ■ **"Terrorism Insurance"** in *The Economist* (Vol. 376, July 16-22, 2005, No. 8435, pp. 71)

Pub: The Economist Newspaper Ltd.

Description: In the aftermath of the terrorist bombings in London, England, American insurers are looking at the Congressional scheme called TRIA, which offers a back-stop to private insurers in the event of a terrorist incident in the nation.

43392 ■ **"That Bites"** in *Entrepreneur* (Vol. 33, January 2005, No. 1, pp. 69)

Pub: Entrepreneur Media Inc.

Ed: Joshua Kurlantzick. **Description:** Ninety percent of small companies are not compliant with new COBRA regulations. Employers with more than 20 employees must now give written notice explaining COBRA. Brokers can assist small business owners with COBRA compliance.

43393 ■ **"That's entertainment!"** in *Rough Notes* (Vol. 146, No. 4, April 2003, pp. 48)

Pub: Rough Notes

Ed: Lonni Swanson. **Description:** Lance J. Ewing, Randy Thurman and Bradley R. Wood are risk managers in the hospitality and entertainment industries. In an interview, the three talk about the effect of terrorism on risk management and the hard market that followed.

43394 ■ **"Thinking Ahead"** in *Entrepreneur* (Vol. 33, September 2005, No. 9, pp. 62)

Pub: Entrepreneur Media Inc.

Ed: Jacquelyn Lynn. **Description:** Long term care insurance may be the most important insurance product on the market today. The coverage offers advantages to both the employer and employee, because they are usually tax-deductible, benefits are tax-free, and employees can take their coverage with them if they retire or leave the firm.

43395 ■ **"Tiered pricing plans have benefits and disadvantages"** in *Business First Columbus* (Vol. 18, No. 40, May 24, 2002, pp. B11)

Pub: Business First Columbus, Inc.

Ed: David Miller. **Description:** Tiered pricing is a new idea within the health insurance industry that allows customers to pay a fixed price for services regardless of the actual cost of the service.

43396 ■ "Tiger Power" in *Rough Notes* (Vol. 146, No. 9, September 2003, pp. 32)
Pub: Rough Notes
Ed: Elisabeth Boone. **Description:** Profile of Princeton Risk Managers Inc., covering risk management services, management styles, and market development.

43397 ■ "The time for talk is over" in *Rough Notes* (Vol. 146, No. 4, April 2003, pp. 16)
Pub: Rough Notes
Ed: Michael J. Moody. **Description:** After Enron's collapse, enterprise risk management has become more important in corporate governance. Pricewaterhouse-Coopers Inc.'s research indicates that consumer trust can be regained by financial institutions through checks and balances in top managers.

43398 ■ "The Time is Right For A Binder Authority Review" in *Rough Notes* (Vol. 145, No. 9, September 2002, pp. 78)
Pub: Rough Notes
Ed: Roy C. McCormick. **Description:** Agents and insurers should review agency contracts and provisions relating to binding coverage, especially as to scope, exclusions, and limitations.

43399 ■ "Tips to Keep Your Medical Renewal Cost Under Control" in *Ingram's* (Vol. 29, No. 9, September 2003, pp. 52)
Pub: Show Me Publishing, Inc.
Ed: Matt Krull. **Description:** Ways to reduce insurance costs for small businesses in the Greater Kansas City, Missouri area are covered. Topics include employment practices liability insurance, employee medical coverage, and long-term planning.

43400 ■ "TMPAA puts retail agents in touch with new markets" in *Rough Notes* (Vol. 146, No. 4, April 2003, pp. 78)
Pub: Rough Notes
Ed: Phil Zenkewicz. **Description:** Target Markets Program Administrators Association founded by Glenn Clark and headed by Ray Scotto finds just the right program administrator with a program that matches the retailer's need using a Website designed by Insuranceworkz.

43401 ■ "To your health: an old health insurance bill gets a second chance at life" in *Entrepreneur* (Vol. 31, No. 6, June 2003, pp. 26)
Pub: Entrepreneur Media Inc.
Ed: Stephen Barlas. **Description:** The Small Business Health Fairness Act (H.R. 660) would allow trade associations to create federally regulated national health insurance plans for small businesses, but Congressional Democrats are strongly opposed to the bill.

43402 ■ "To Your Health" in *Entrepreneur* (Vol. 32, July 2004, No. 7, pp. 35)
Pub: Entrepreneur Media Inc.
Description: Thirty-seven percent of U.S. entrepreneurs are taking steps to minimize health care costs. Statistical data included.

43403 ■ "TPA business for self-funded plans balanced in 2000" in *Employee Benefit Plan Review* (Vol. 56, No. 1, July 2001, pp. 18)
Pub: Charles D. Spencer & Associates, Inc.
Description: The use of third party administrators for self-funded health insurance programs is discussed, including such topics as fees paid and programs provided.

43404 ■ "Trade Group Endorsements For Every Specialty" in *Rough Notes* (Vol. 145, No. 9, September 2002, pp. 88)
Pub: Rough Notes
Ed: Dennis Pillsbury. **Description:** The Lighthouse Underwriters LLC was founded by Arthur Seifert and underwrites insurance only after developing a relationship with the association or trade group it will be insuring.

43405 ■ "Travel Plans Gone Awry; How to Prepare for Emergencies" in *Black Enterprise* (Vol. 35, February 2005, No. 7, pp. 161)
Pub: Earl G. Graves Publishing Co. Inc.
Ed: Jennifer L. Smith. **Description:** Whether traveling for business or vacation, travel insurance will protect individuals in case of emergency.

43406 ■ "Tripped up" in *Atlanta Business Chronicle* (Vol. 25, No. 19, October 18, 2002, pp. 1C)
Pub: American City Business Publications, Inc.
Ed: Charles Davidson. **Description:** Rising worker's compensation rates are up and company assessments by insurers are getting tougher.

43407 ■ "Tulsa Insurance Company Sues Kansas-based Bank" in *Journal Record (Oklahoma City, OK)* (February 8, 2007)
Pub: Journal Record
Ed: Ginger Shepherd. **Description:** Details of International Insurance Brokers Ltd. Lawsuit against Team Bank NA, Team Financial Inc., and Mystic Capital Advisors Group LLC are profiled. The suit alleges conspiracy, fraud, misrepresentation and breach of contract relating to the same of Team Insurance Group.

43408 ■ "2001 Brought Steep Increase in Uninsured" in *Business First Columbus* (Vol. 18, No. 26, Feb. 15, 2002, pp. A16)
Pub: Business First Columbus, Inc.
Ed: Kent Hoover. **Description:** Nearly two million Americans lost their health care insurance in 2001.

43409 ■ "Two Views on 2003" in *Rough Notes* (Vol. 145, No. 1, January 2003, pp. 204)
Pub: Rough Notes
Ed: Samuel Schiff. **Description:** The Conning Research and Consulting's Jack Gohsler believes the insurance industry's outlook will improve slightly in 2003. Dr. Robert Hartwig of the Insurance Information Institute says that credit information will now be used in insurance underwriting.

43410 ■ "Understanding Your Risk Portfolio" in *Rough Notes* (Vol. 145, No. 9, September 2002, pp. 58)
Pub: Rough Notes
Ed: Michael J. Moody. **Description:** Steve Saporito, Senior Vice President of Zurich IC discusses an enterprise-wide risk management in which the board of directors becomes ultimately involved.

43411 ■ "Unhealthy Costs" in *Hispanic Business* (November 2006, pp. 58, 60, 62)
Pub: Hispanic Business
Ed: Jenn Holmes. **Description:** Small business owners are having difficulty paying high insurance premiums for their employees.

43412 ■ "Uninsured: a Vexing Problem" in *Crain's New York Business* (Vol. 23, January 15, 2007, No.3, pp. 12)
Pub: Crain Communications, Inc.
Description: Health insurance costs are so high that many employers cannot afford to insure their employees. A major hospital group and New York's leading insurer proposed modest plans to expand existing programs.

43413 ■ "Union Paychecks Could Be Bigger in 2005, But At a Cost" in *Kansas City Star* (February 22, 2005)
Pub: Knight-Ridder/Tribune Business News
Ed: Randolph Heaster. **Description:** Employers that are willing to raise wages during union negotiations will most likely cut health benefits at the same time. According to a recent survey, 60 percent of employers would consider wage hikes, while 69 percent reported health insurance and related benefits were top priority in concession gains.

43414 ■ "Ups & downs" in *Entrepreneur* (Vol. 30, No. 2, February 2002, pp. 66)
Pub: Entrepreneur Media Inc.
Ed: Jacquelyn Lynn. **Description:** Four tips for getting insurance rates on the same tract as the economy are presented.

43415 ■ "Vendors Help Seniors Sort Out Medicare Options" in *Tampa Tribune* (November 17, 2005)
Pub: Media General, Inc.
Ed: Susan Hemmingway Johnson. **Description:** Medicare insurance vendors offered advice to seniors at the Senior Extravaganza held at Tropicana Field.

43416 ■ "Voting With Their Pocketbooks" in *Fortune* (Vol. 141, No. 10, May 15, 2000, pp. F372P)
Pub: Time Inc.
Ed: Edward Robinson. **Description:** A scorecard featuring the issues affecting small business owners in the 2000 election campaign.

43417 ■ "Warren Buffet's Still-Golden Touch: The Wizard of Omaha's Magic is Alive and Well" in *Barron's* (August 11, 2003, pp. 17)
Pub: Barron's
Ed: Andrew Bary. **Description:** Berkshire Hathaway Life Insurance Company has analysts and investors troubled over the uncertainty about who will replace Warren Buffet, the company's CEO for 38 years.

43418 ■ "What Comes Next" in *Business Week* (No. 3658, December 6, 1999, pp. F30)
Pub: McGraw-Hill, Inc.
Description: According to experts, small businesses will face similar problems over the next decade: low unemployment rates will continue, which means workers will be choosier; increasing health care costs; regulations; and work-family balancing. But the good news is that the trend seems to show these workers will still prefer working for small companies over large ones. Data from the U.S. Department of Labor is included.

43419 ■ "What Eliot Spitzer's Investigations Mean For You" in *Inc.* (May 1, 2005)
Pub: Inc. Magazine
Ed: Stephanie Clifford. **Description:** If a 401(k) provider or insurance company overcharges employees, a small business owner may be held liable. It is recommended that employers check fees, commission structures, and overrides with health care providers carefully.

43420 ■ "What Works For You?" in *My Business* (April/May 2003, pp. 16)
Pub: My Business Magazine
Ed: Mardy Fones. **Description:** Solutions to help small businesses with health insurance options are presented, including Association Health Plans, Health Reimbursement Arrangements, Medical Savings Accounts, and Flexible Spending Accounts.

43421 ■ "When Life Happens: A New Trend In Employee Benefits" in *Rough Notes* (Vol. 145, No. 1, January 2003, pp. 46)
Pub: Rough Notes
Ed: Elisabeth Boone. **Description:** Fortis Benefits Insurance Company and Work and Family Benefits, are the two companies dealing with broadened benefits packages that help employees balance their work and family responsibilities since 47 percent of them have a dependent care need.

43422 ■ "Who is an Insured" in *Rough Notes* (Vol. 145, No. 9, September 2002, pp. 16)
Pub: Rough Notes
Ed: Donald S. Malecki. **Description:** When the designation of the insured in commercial insurance applications is unclear, whether an individual or other, this can be costly when claims occur. Thus, applicants and producers should avoid problems beforehand by reviewing the information submitted to the underwriters.

43423 ■ "Who's Minding the Store?" in *Rough Notes* (Vol. 146, No. 3, March 2003, pp. 72)
Pub: Rough Notes
Ed: Nancy Doucette. **Description:** Afni Insurance Services provides customer services 24/7, including the use of online facilities. This is especially important during emergencies or when disasters occur for maintaining or business recovery.

43424 ■ "Woodbury-Based Bankers Life of New York Reports Record Sales" in *Long Island Business News* **(February 20, 2004)**
Pub: Dolan Media Newswires
Ed: Ben Abelson. **Description:** Bankers Life of New York reported life insurance sales of $24.9 million in 2003, an 8 percent increase over 2002. Bankers Life of New York, located in Woodbury, New York was founded in 1958.

43425 ■ "Workers' Comp Rates to Fall" in *Sacramento Bee* **(November 29, 2005)**
Pub: The Sacramento Bee
Ed: Gilbert Chan. **Description:** California's State Compensation Insurance Fund announced a reduction in rates by an average 16 percent beginning January 1, 2006. Other carriers are reducing rates from 13 percent to 15 percent.

43426 ■ *Workers Compensation Insurance: Profiles of the State Systems*
Pub: Alliance of American Insurers (AAI)
Ed: Alliance of American Insurers staff. **Released:** 1995. **Price:** $35.00.

43427 ■ *Worker's Compensation Insurance: The Survival Guide for Business*
Pub: LEXIS Law Publishing
Ed: Joseph P. Bacarro. **Released:** 1997. **Price:** $85.00 (ringbound); Vol. Issue 6.

43428 ■ "Worth the Drive? Your Company Cars Could Be Gulping More than Just Gas if You Don't Know What Your Ownership Costs Are" in *Entrepreneur*
Pub: Entrepreneur Media Inc.
Ed: Jill Amadio. **Description:** Four major fixed cost factors are involved when determining the cost of owning a company car: depreciation, state fees, financing and insurance.

43429 ■ "Writing the big ones: Part Two" in *Rough Notes* **(Vol. 146, No. 4, April 2003, pp. 46)**
Pub: Rough Notes
Ed: Michael J. Weinberg. **Description:** Acquiring big clients for your insurance business involves going to places and meeting them; joining trade groups, association meetings, conventions, civic and charitable organizations, sports activities and referrals are among possible resources.

43430 ■ "Writing the big ones" in *Rough Notes* **(Vol. 146, No. 3, March 2003, pp. 126)**
Pub: Rough Notes
Ed: Michael J. Weinberg. **Description:** Big sales goals can be achieved by visualization and customer relationship management, as well as knowledge and expertise of the product or service to the prospective target market.

43431 ■ "Your Safety Is What Drives Us: Auto Safety Tips from Allstate" in *Black Enterprise* **(Vol. 34, No. 6, January 2004, pp. 59)**
Pub: Earl Graves Publishing Co.
Description: Safety tips and money saving discounts offered by Allstate Insurance through its "Allstate Safety Connection" (TM) program are discussed.

43432 ■ "You've Got to DISTURB 'EM" in *Rough Notes* **(Vol. 145, No. 2, February 2003, pp. 96)**
Pub: Rough Notes
Ed: Francis W. Potter. **Description:** Ways to sell insurance by using vivid illustrations are presented.

43433 ■ "Zurich Canada Alliance with ING Brings Efficiencies" in *Rough Notes* **(Vol. 145, No. 12, December 2002, pp. 114)**
Pub: Rough Notes
Ed: Phil Zinkewicz. **Description:** ING Canada acquired Zurich's Canadian personal and small business Property Casualty business and Zurich will renew large accounts of both companies. Robert Landry is the president and CEO of Zurich North American Canada.

TRADE PERIODICALS

43434 ■ *The John Liner Letter*
Pub: Standard Publishing Corp.
Contact: Robert Montgomery
Ed: Robert Montgomery, Editor. **Released:** Monthly. **Price:** $219, U.S.; $269.10, elsewhere. **Description:** Provides risk management and technical insurance advice for business firms, such as broadening coverage, cutting costs, and anticipating special insurance problems.

43435 ■ *The Journal*
Pub: Society of Insurance Trainers and Educators
Contact: Lois Markovich, Exec. Dir.
Released: Annual. **Price:** Included in membership. **Description:** Provides information on training and education within the insurance industry. Recurring features include book reviews.

43436 ■ *Professional Agent*
Pub: National Association of Professional Insurance Agents
Released: Monthly. **Description:** Professional magazine for property/casualty insurance agents.

43437 ■ *Risk & Insurance Magazine's Managing Risk for Loss Prevention and Cost Control*
Pub: LRP Publications
Ed: Donald R. Kinsley, Esq, Editor. **Released:** Bi-weekly. **Description:** Discusses the function of loss prevention and risk management for businesses. Contains articles on responsibility to employees and the public, product liability and safety, worker's compensation, and computer security. Includes advice on both insurance and non-insurance methods of loss prevention.

43438 ■ *Unemployment Insurance Reports with Social Security*
Pub: CCH Inc.
Contact: Jan Gerstein, Manager
Released: Weekly. **Price:** $359, individuals Internet; $3,459, individuals CD-ROM. **Description:** Issues of CCH's Unemployment Insurance Reports with Social Security provide timely information on social security and federal/state unemployment insurance taxes, coverage, and benefits. Pertinent federal and state laws are reported promptly and reflected in place in the explanatory guides, as are regulations, judicial and administrative decisions, rulings, releases, and forms. Explanatory guides include examples showing how rules apply and offer practical information regarding the tax management, coverage, and benefit aspects of the social security and unemployment insurance systems. Each issue starts off with an informative Report Letter summarizing recent developments in these areas.

VIDEOCASSETTES/ AUDIOCASSETTES

43439 ■ *Going Bare: Crisis in Insurance*
New Jersey Network
25 S. Stockton St.
Trenton, NJ 08625-0777
Ph:(609)777-5000
Free: 800-792-8645
Fax: (609)633-2920
Co. E-mail: njnvideo@njn.org
URL: http://www.njn.net
Released: 1988. **Description:** Examines the history of the insurance industry, price wars between insurance companies, and small businesses who are without liability insurance because of extremely high premiums. **Availability:** VHS; 3/4U.

CONSULTANTS

43440 ■ Leonard R. Friedman Risk Management Inc.
170 Great Neck Rd., Ste. 140
Great Neck, NY 11021-3337
Ph:(516)466-0750
Fax: (516)466-0997
Scope: Provides risk and insurance management, and safety and claims managements services to corporations across the country. Analyzes exposure to loss, audits insurance contracts, structures competitive bidding, reviews contracts and leases, implements and monitors safety and claims management programs, and recommends risk transfer programs to reduce exposure to loss. Industries served: profit and nonprofit companies engaged in retail, manufacturing, distributing, hospitality, real estate, and service.

43441 ■ Health Insurance Specialists Inc.
17620A Redland Rd.
Rockville, MD 20855
Ph:(301)590-0006
Fax: (301)590-0661
Co. E-mail: info@his-inc.com
URL: http://www.his-inc.com

E-mail: info@his-inc.com
Scope: Serves a wide variety of businesses and individuals by designing comprehensive insurance packages and benefit plans, full service insurance and financial services firm, third party administration, human resources outsourcing.

43442 ■ A.E. Roberts Co.
11490 Xeon St. NW, Ste. 200
Coon Rapids, MN 55448
Ph:(763)757-5119
Free: 800-486-4585
Fax: (413)215-6877
Co. E-mail: info@aeroberts.com
URL: http://www.aeroberts.com

E-mail: info@aeroberts.com
Scope: A human resource and employee benefits consultant. Specializes in compliance training, focusing on regulatory compliance and human resource management issues.

43443 ■ Siver Insurance Consultants
9400 4th St. N, Ste. 119
PO Box 21343
Saint Petersburg, FL 33702
Ph:(727)577-2780
Fax: (727)579-8692
Co. E-mail: gerickson@siver.com
URL: http://www.siver.com

E-mail: gerickson@siver.com
Scope: Provides advice and counsel (no sales) on matters involving insurance, including property, casualty, life, disability, health and title insurance plus risk management, employee welfare benefits and managed care.

43444 ■ United Insurance Consultants Inc.
1 Pky.
Upper Saddle River, NJ 07458
Ph:(201)661-5000
Fax: (201)661-5001
Co. E-mail: info@uici.com
URL: http://www.uici.com

E-mail: info@uici.com
Scope: An independent insurance consulting firm that informs and educates clients of the importance of properly protecting the value of their business. Helps companies understand their insurance contracts, costs involved in properly protecting their assets and liability exposures.

FRANCHISES AND BUSINESS OPPORTUNITIES

43445 ■ Direct Car Rentals Limited
166 Toryork Dr., Ste. 1
North York, ON, Canada M9L 1X6
Ph:(416)744-6989
Free: 888-835-0338
Fax: (416)744-6987
Co. E-mail: northyork@directcarrentals.com
URL: http://www.directcarrentals.com
No. of Franchise Units: 4. **No. of Company-Owned Units:** 1. **Founded:** 1998. **Franchised:** 1999. **Description:** Direct Car Rentals are pioneers in insurance services. Provides a wide selection of import and domestic vehicles, body shops and dealerships. **Equity Capital Needed:** $50,000-$150,000. **Franchise Fee:** $15,000-$40,000. **Training:** Provides full training, operations manual, and field support.

43446 ■ Dr. Glass Window Washing
885 Sparta Dr.
Lafayette, CO 80026
Ph:(303)499-7759
Fax: (303)499-0855
No. of Franchise Units: 10. **No. of Company-Owned Units:** 3. **Founded:** 1978. **Franchised:** 2001. **Description:** Window cleaning. **Equity Capital Needed:** $4,600. **Franchise Fee:** $3,000. **Royalty Fee:** 10%. **Financial Assistance:** No. **Training:** Offers 1 week training at headquarters and ongoing support.

43447 ■ FedUSA Insurance & Financial Services
Affirmative Holdings Inc.
3690 Davie Blvd.
Ft. Lauderdale, FL 33312
Ph:(954)583-3213
Free: 888-440-6875
Fax: (954)583-3205
No. of Franchise Units: 36. **No. of Company-Owned Units:** 180. **Founded:** 1983. **Franchised:** 2001. **Description:** Insurance/property and casualty. **Equity Capital Needed:** $49,450-$71,450 total investment. **Franchise Fee:** $19,950. **Financial Assistance:** No. **Training:** Yes.

43448 ■ Paul Davis Restoration
One Independent Dr., Ste. 2300
Jacksonville, FL 32202
Free: 800-722-5066
Fax: (904)737-4204
Co. E-mail: sales@pdrestoration.com
URL: http://www.pdrestoration.com
No. of Franchise Units: 220+. **Founded:** 1966. **Franchised:** 1971. **Description:** Computerized contracting and cleaning services to the insurance industry. **Equity Capital Needed:** $150,000-$250,000 + franchise fee. **Franchise Fee:** $25,000 or $52,500. **Managerial Assistance:** Ongoing telephone support available. **Training:** 4 week training at corporate headquarters, followed by 1 week of on-site training at new franchise location.

43449 ■ Paul's Professional Window Washing Franchise Inc.
Paul's Prof. Window Washing Inc.
2707 Foothill Blvd.
La Cresenta, CA 91214
Ph:(818)249-7917
Fax: (818)249-7806
No. of Company-Owned Units: 1. **Founded:** 1981. **Franchised:** 2004. **Description:** Residential window cleaning company. **Equity Capital Needed:** $42,500-$78,000 initial investment. **Franchise Fee:** $17,500. **Financial Assistance:** No. **Training:** Yes.

43450 ■ Paul's Restorations
Paul's Restorations Management Inc.
1640 Upper Ottawa St.
Hamilton, ON, Canada L8W 3P2
Free: 800-363-7285
No. of Franchise Units: 8 **No. of Company-Owned Units:** 3. **Founded:** 1980. **Franchised:** 1995. **Description:** Insurance claim repairs and cleaning. **Equity Capital Needed:** $20,000-$80,000 or existing restoration company. **Franchise Fee:** Variable. **Financial Assistance:** No. **Training:** Yes.

43451 ■ Puroclean - The Paramedics of Property Damage
PuroSystems, Inc.
6001 Hiatus Rd., Ste. 13
Tamarac, FL 33321
Free: 800-351-2282
Fax: 800-995-8527
Co. E-mail: sales@puroclean.com
URL: http://www.purocleanopportunity.com
No. of Franchise Units: 136+. **Founded:** 1989. **Franchised:** 1990. **Description:** Property damage restoration. **Equity Capital Needed:** $81,450-$122,400 total initial investment range. **Franchise Fee:** $35,000. **Financial Assistance:** Offers assistance to secure financing with outside lending institutions, including SBA. **Training:** Provides 3 weeks at corporate training center & 1 week field training covering customer service, marketing/advertising, computer software, product knowledge, management, & hands-on application with ongoing 24 hour support.

43452 ■ The United Insurance Group
PO Box 2185
Greenville, SC 29602
Ph:(864)235-6100
Fax: (864)235-6880
Founded: 1999. **Description:** Franchise insurance and benefits.

COMPUTERIZED DATABASES

43453 ■ *Business Insurance*
Crain Communications Inc.
1155 Gratiot Ave.
Detroit, MI 48207
Ph:(313)446-6000
Free: 800-678-2427
Fax: (313)446-0361
Co. E-mail: info@crain.com
URL: http://www.crain.com
Description: Contains the complete text of *Business Insurance*, a newspaper providing information on the purchase and administration of corporate insurance and self-insurance programs, including property and liability insurance, reinsurance, and employee benefit and risk management programs. Includes reports on major commercial insurance claim settlements, legal and regulatory developments affecting the industry, and major losses resulting from fires, explosions, natural disasters, and litigation. Also includes analyses of industry issues and state, national, and international news. **Availability:** Online: Crain Communications Inc., LexisNexis, Dow Jones & Co. Inc., ProQuest, Thomson Dialog, Reuters Group PLC. **Type:** Full text.

43454 ■ *Manitoba Automobile Injury Compensation Appeal Commission Decisions*
LexisNexis Quicklaw
2 Gore St.
PO Box 2080
Kingston, ON, Canada K7L 5J8
Ph:(613)549-4611
Free: 800-267-9470
Fax: (613)548-4260
Co. E-mail: sales@quicklaw.com
URL: http://www.quicklaw.com
Description: Provides access to rulings on appeals from Manitoba Public Insurance Officers involving compensation for auto accident injuries. **Type:** Full text.

LIBRARIES

43455 ■ Anderson, Kill & Olick, LLP–Library
2100 M St. NW, Ste. 650
Washington, DC 20005
Ph:(202)218-0045
Fax: (202)218-0055
Co. E-mail: akodc@andersonkill.com
URL: http://www.andersonkill.com
Contact: Lisa Benjamin, Libn.
Scope: Insurance - property, fire, medical disability, casualty; law - civil, insurance. **Services:** Interlibrary loan; Library not open to the public. **Holdings:** Books and periodicals. **Subscriptions:** 15 journals and other serials; 4 newspapers.

43456 ■ Buffalo & Erie County Public Library–Business, Science & Technology
1 Lafayette Sq.
Buffalo, NY 14203
Ph:(716)858-8900
Fax: (716)858-7237
Co. E-mail: bst@buffalolib.org
URL: http://www.buffalolib.org
Contact: Kate Weeks, Div.Mgr.
Scope: Investments, real estate, economics, marketing, engineering, computer science, technology, medical information for laymen, consumer information, automotive repair. **Services:** Interlibrary loan; copying; Library open to the public. **Holdings:** 312,916 books; 60,516 bound periodical volumes. **Subscriptions:** 2908 journals and other serials; 4 newspapers.

43457 ■ Long & Levit–Library
601 Montgomery St., Ste. 900
San Francisco, CA 94111
Ph:(415)397-2222
Fax: (415)397-6392
Contact: Holly Mohler, Libn.
Scope: Insurance, environmental, professional liability, construction. **Services:** Interlibrary loan; copying; Library open to the public at librarian's discretion. **Holdings:** 10,000 books. **Subscriptions:** 75 journals and other serials; 4 newspapers.

43458 ■ National Association of Professional Insurance Agents–Library
400 N. Washington St.
Alexandria, VA 22314
Ph:(703)836-9340
Fax: (703)836-1279
Co. E-mail: patbo@pianet.org
URL: http://www.pianet.com
Contact: Patricia A. Barowski, Sr.VP
Scope: Anti-Semitism, insurance, insurance law. **Services:** Library not open to the public. **Holdings:** 1400 volumes; CD-ROMs.

RESEARCH CENTERS

43459 ■ Ohio Insurance Department–Research and Policy
2100 Stella Ct.
Columbus, OH 43215-1067
Ph:(614)719-1551
Fax: (614)644-3743
Co. E-mail: david.fogarty@ins.state.oh.us
Contact: David Fogarty, Ch.
E-mail: david.fogarty@ins.state.oh.us
Scope: Insurance.

START-UP INFORMATION

43460 ■ *Canadian Small Business Kit for Dummies*
Pub: CDG Books Canada, Incorporated
Ed: Margaret Kerr, JoAnn Kurtz. **Released:** August 2004. **Price:** $37.99 (Canadian). **Description:** Entrepreneurial guide to starting and running a small business in Canada.

43461 ■ *The Canadian Small Business Survival Guide: How to Start and Operate Your Own Successful Business*
Pub: Dundurn Group
Ed: Benjamin Gallander. FRQ September 2004. **Price:** $18.99. **Description:** Ideas for starting and running a successful small business. Topics include selecting a business, financing, government assistance, locations, franchises, and marketing ideas.

43462 ■ "Home base and knowledge management in international ventures" in *Journal of Business Venturing* (Vol. 17, No. 2, March 2002, pp. 99)
Pub: Elsevier Science, Inc.
Ed: Walter Kuemmerle. **Description:** Research paper detailing the broad range of international activities undertaken by start-up international ventures. Particular attention is given to the area of cross-border activities and their role in knowledge management.

43463 ■ "Instantly International" in *Inc.* (Volume 27, June 2005, No. 6, pp. 44)
Pub: Inc. Magazine
Ed: Darren Dahl. **Description:** Profile of John Buckman, owner of an email list-management company in Berkeley, California. Buckman also launched Magnatune.com, a global online music label. The entrepreneur started Magnatune.com after his wife, a composer of electronic music, had been dropped from her music label.

43464 ■ "The Quebec Story: Low Cost, Low Risk, Tremendous Opportunity" in *Venture Capital Journal* (Vol. 42, No. 5, May 2002, pp. 48, 50)
Pub: Thomas Venture Economics
Ed: Peter Diekmeyer. **Description:** Canada's venture capital center has become a hotbed of technology startups because of the unique incentives, including tax incentives, low business costs, Montreal's close ties to Europe, and an educated workforce focused on technology.

43465 ■ "Quebec's Competitive Edge" in *Venture Capital Journal* (Vol. 42, No. 5, May 2002, pp. 51-52)
Pub: Thomas Venture Economics
Description: U.S. venture capital firms that invest in Quebec, Canada may have a head start on the competition. Statistical data included.

43466 ■ *Strengthening Technology Incubation System for Creating High Technology-Based Enterprises in Asia and the Pacific*
Pub: United Nations Publications
Released: January 2005. **Price:** $75.00. **Description:** Report reviewing policy guidelines and practices to establish technology incubators that will help entrepreneurs develop small technology-based enterprises in different national economies.

ASSOCIATIONS AND OTHER ORGANIZATIONS

43467 ■ **Albanian-American Trade and Development Association**
159 E 4th St.
Dunkirk, NY 14048
Ph:(954)802-3166
Fax: (716)366-1516
Co. E-mail: aatda@engl.com
URL: http://www.albaniabiz.org
Contact: James V. Elias, Chm./CEO
Membership: Businesses and individuals engaged in trade involving the U.S. and Albania. **Purpose:** Promotes expansion of trade between Albania and the United States. Facilitates establishment of international contacts by members; lobbies for removal of barriers to trade.

43468 ■ **America-Israel Chamber of Commerce and Industry**
366 Amsterdam Ave.
PMB No. 171
New York, NY 10024
Ph:(212)819-0430
Fax: (212)819-0431
Co. E-mail: info@aicci.org
URL: http://www.aicci.org
Contact: Ronny Bassan, Exec.VP
Description: Promotes the interests of the U.S.-Israel business community; provides educational programs on trade expansion, bilateral investment, marketing and regional development; maintains close ties with the U.S. and Israeli governments and business leaders and actively participates in forums to advance bilateral trade and investment. **Publications:** *Economic Horizons* (semiannual) ; *Israel Quality* (quarterly).

43469 ■ **American Association of Exporters and Importers**
1050 17th St. NW, Ste. 810
Washington, DC 20036
Ph:(202)857-8009
Fax: (202)857-7843
Co. E-mail: hq@aaei.org
URL: http://www.aaei.org
Contact: Hallock Northcott, Pres./CEO
Description: Exporters and importers of goods, products, and raw materials; wholesalers and retailers; customs brokers and forwarders; banks; insurance underwriters; steamship companies; customs attorneys and others engaged directly or indirectly in dealing with exports and imports. Seeks fair and equitable conditions for world trade. Anticipates problems of interpretation of laws and regulations affecting members' businesses; gathers and disseminates data on world trade; supports and creates legislation promoting balanced international trade; works for fair administration of policy. Maintains liaison with government committees, agencies, and other trade policy groups. Testifies for exporters and importers before government and other official bodies. Studies problems concerning export and import; offers advice and support to members facing problems in their businesses; conducts forums and workshops on timely topics and developments; holds exporting and importing seminars. Operates extensive library of research information and government data, and records legal precedents. **Publications:** *International Trade Alert* (weekly); Newsletter (weekly); Newsletter (quarterly). Also publishes broad range of import/export-related documents.

43470 ■ **American Hellenic Institute**
1220 16th St. NW
Washington, DC 20036
Ph:(202)785-8430
Fax: (202)785-5178
Co. E-mail: nlarigakis@ahiworld.org
URL: http://www.ahiworld.org
Contact: Nicholas Larigakis, Exec.Dir.
Description: Seeks to strengthen political, cultural, trade, commerce, and related matters between the U.S. and Greece, Cyprus, and the American Hellenic community. Conducts research on issues such as Turkish threats to the Aegean, Cyprus, the rule of law, and human rights. Sponsors internship program and seminars. **Publications:** *AHI Report* (3/year); *American Hellenic Who's Who*; *Doing Business in Greece*; *General News*; *Greece's Pivotal Role in World War II and its Importance to the U.S. Today*; *Handbook on United States Relations with Greece and Cyprus*; *Rule of Law and Conditions on Foreign Aid to Turkey* ; *United States Foreign Policy Regarding Greece, Turkey and Cyprus - The Rule of Law and American Interests*; Annual Report (annual).

43471 ■ **American Indonesian Chamber of Commerce**
317 Madison Ave., Ste. 1619
New York, NY 10017
Ph:(212)687-4505
Fax: (212)687-5844
Co. E-mail: aiccny@bigplanet.com
URL: http://www.aiccusa.org
Contact: Wayne Forrest, Pres./Sec./Exec.Dir.
Description: Holds briefings on new trade policies in Indonesia and offers orientation workshops to company personnel traveling to Indonesia. **Publications:** *American Business Directory for Indonesia* (periodic); *Executive Diary* ; *Indonesia's Countertrade Experience*; *Members Bulletin* (periodic); *Outlook Indonesia* (quarterly); *Sourcing Products in Indonesia: A Guide for Importers*. Also publishes an index of articles to Indonesia appearing in major Asian publications.

43472 ■ American Israel Chamber of Commerce - Southeast Region
1150 Lake Hearn Dr., Ste. 130
Atlanta, GA 30342
Ph:(404)843-9426
Fax: (404)843-1416
Co. E-mail: aiccse@aiccse.org
URL: http://www.aiccse.org
Contact: Tom Glaser, Pres.
Membership: American and Israeli companies. **Purpose:** Promotes increased trade between Israel and the United States, with emphasis on increasing Israeli-American trade involving companies in the southeastern U.S. Facilitates networking and contact development involving Israeli and U.S. corporations; makes available trade mentoring and matchmaking services; sponsors educational programs. **Publications:** *Latest Southeast-Israel Business News* (monthly).

43473 ■ American-Southern Africa Chamber of Trade and Industry
1080 Park Ave., Ste. 4W
New York, NY 10128-1167
Ph:(212)410-6560
Contact: Dr. Robert John, Dir.Gen.
Description: Corporations involved in trade with and within Angola, Botswana, Lesotho, Malawi, Mozambique, South Africa, Swaziland, Zambia, and Zimbabwe. Furthers the development of trade and investment between the U.S. and the countries of southern Africa; gathers and disseminates information; examines questions pertaining to commercial and industrial relations; promotes and facilitates economic relations between the countries concerned.

43474 ■ American-Uzbekistan Chamber of Commerce
1717 N St. NW
Washington, DC 20036
Ph:(202)828-4111
Fax: (202)659-7010
Co. E-mail: aucc@verizon.net
URL: http://www.aucconline.com
Contact: Robert S. Pace, Exec. Dir.
Description: Brings together companies and individual professionals interested in promoting trade and investment between Uzbekistan and the United States. Represents business and industry to promote growth in interest of the U.S. business community in Uzbekistan. **Publications:** *AUCC Board Report* (monthly).

43475 ■ Association for International Business
725 G St.
Salida, CO 81201
Ph:(719)539-0500
Free: 800-359-5166
Fax: (719)539-6925
Co. E-mail: director@aibcenter.com
URL: http://www.creditman.co.uk/internat/aiblink.html
Contact: Ray Gabriel, Managing Dir.
Description: Global business community whose members are in all areas of International business. Provides a network for the international business community where members can provide and share information, resources, and help with problem solving. Hosts in 70 countries to assist visitors. Conducts a mentorship program. **Publications:** *International Business Discussion Group* (daily).

43476 ■ Australian Trade Commission
150 E 42nd St., 34th Fl.
New York, NY 10017-5612
Ph:(212)351-6560
Fax: (212)867-7710
Co. E-mail: info@austrade.gov.au
URL: http://www.austrade.gov.au
Contact: Chris Knepler, Business Development Mgr.
Description: Works in the promotion of Australian products and investments in the U.S. **Publications:** *Export Update* (monthly); *Trademark* (monthly).

43477 ■ Austrian Trade Commission
120 W 45th St., 9th Fl.
New York, NY 10036
Ph:(212)421-5250
Free: 800-847-2478

Fax: (212)421-5251
Co. E-mail: newyork@austriantrade.org
URL: http://www.austriantrade.org/usa
Contact: Bruno Freytag, Trade Commissioner
Description: Promotes U.S.-Austrian trade with particular emphasis on Austrian exports to the U.S.; identifies Austrian trade sources to meet U.S. commercial demand. Handles inquiries related to trade between the two nations and deals with issues such as customs duties, trade laws, and licensing. Compiles statistics. Sponsors trade exhibits. Conventions/Meetings: none.

43478 ■ Austrian Trade Commissions in the United States
11601 Wilshire Blvd., Ste. 2420
Los Angeles, CA 90025
Ph:(310)477-9988
Fax: (310)477-1643
Co. E-mail: losangeles@austriantrade.org
URL: http://www.austriantrade.org/usa/en
Contact: Christian Kuegerl, Commissioner
Membership: Corporations in Austria, Canada and the United States. **Purpose:** Promotes increased trade between the U.S., Canada, and Austria. Works to remove legislative barriers to international trade; represents members before international trade organizations and agencies; facilitates establishment of joint ventures and other international business connections involving members.

43479 ■ Brazilian-American Chamber of Commerce
509 Madison Ave., Ste. 304
New York, NY 10022
Ph:(212)751-4691
Fax: (212)751-7692
Co. E-mail: info@brazilcham.com
URL: http://www.brazilcham.com
Contact: Sueli C. Bonaparte, Exec.Dir
Description: Corporations, partnerships, financial institutions, and individuals either in the U.S. or Brazil interested in fostering two-way trade and investment between the countries. Compiles statistics and provides special mailings, press releases, information, and business contacts. Maintains files on business and trade information. Sponsors breakfast briefings, luncheons, seminars, and gala dinners. **Publications:** *Brazilian-American Business Review/Directory* (annual) ; *News Bulletin* (bimonthly).

43480 ■ Brazilian Government Trade Bureau of the Consulate General of Brazil in New York
1185 Ave. of the Americas, 21st Fl.
New York, NY 10036
Ph:(917)777-7777
Fax: (212)827-0225
Co. E-mail: trade@brazilny.org
URL: http://www.brazilny.org
Contact: Fred Arruda, Dir.
Description: Commercial Office of the Brazil Consulate in New York. Offers online match between Brazilian exporters of goods and services and U.S. importers. Publishes information on Brazilian trade shows and investments.

43481 ■ British Trade Office at Consulate-General
845 3rd Ave., 9th Fl.
New York, NY 10022
Ph:(212)745-0200
Fax: (212)754-3062
Co. E-mail: trade@uktradeinvestcanada.org
URL: http://www.uk-canada-trade.org
Contact: Kerry Appleton
Description: British government office that promotes trade with the U.S.; assists British companies selling in the U.S.; aids American companies that wish to import goods from or invest in Britain. **Telecommunication Services:** electronic mail, uktiny@fco.gov.uk.

43482 ■ BritishAmerican Business Inc. of New York and London
52 Vanderbilt Ave., 20th Fl.
New York, NY 10017
Ph:(212)661-4060

Fax: (212)661-4074
Co. E-mail: mallen@babinc.org
URL: http://www.babinc.org
Contact: Richard Fursland, CEO
Purpose: Works to increase the trade and investment between the U.S. and the U.K. by offering member companies a full range of transatlantic business services, information, and contacts. **Publications:** *American British Business Handbook* (annual); *British American Business Handbook* (annual); *BritishAmerican Business Inc. - Membership Directory* (annual); *Investment News* (monthly); *Issue Insight* (bimonthly); *Network London* (quarterly); *Network New York* (quarterly).

43483 ■ Canada-United States Business Association
600 Renaissance Ctr., Ste. 1100
Detroit, MI 48243
Ph:(313)446-7013
Fax: (313)567-2164
Co. E-mail: cheryl.clark@international.gc.ca
URL: http://www.dfait-maeci.gc.ca/can-am/detroit/ home_page/cusba-en.asp
Contact: Cheryl Clark, Coor.
Membership: Consists of supporters of business such as labor, banking, consulting, government, and academia. **Purpose:** Promotes stronger business and trading lineages between the U.S. and Canada by providing a forum to exchange information and ideas and to build relationships. Conducts educational programs; maintains speakers' bureau, panels, and special events.

43484 ■ Canadian-American Business Council
1900 K St. NW
Washington, DC 20006
Ph:(202)496-7430
Fax: (202)496-7756
Co. E-mail: sgreenwood@mckennalong.com
URL: http://www.canambusco.org
Contact: Maryscott Greenwood, Exec.Dir.
Membership: Individuals, corporations, institutions, and organizations with an interest in trade between the United States and Canada. **Purpose:** Promotes free trade. Gathers and disseminates information; maintains speakers' bureau. **Publications:** *CABCommunique* (bimonthly).

43485 ■ Chinese American Association of Commerce
778 Clay St., Ste. C
San Francisco, CA 94108
Ph:(415)362-4306
Fax: (415)362-1478
Contact: Charlie Chang, Pres.
Purpose: Individuals interested in improving trade between U.S. and the People's Republic of China. Promotes commerce, industry, business interests, and the welfare of the Chinese community in the U.S. Co-organizes small commodity exhibitions; researching the import and export trade between U.S. and the People's Republic of China; offers interpretation services for business tours; assists members in channeling trade complaints and problems to proper authorities in China; provides current trade opportunities and information on commodities and raw material requirements desired by the American market. Holds regular meetings with the Chinese Consulate General; makes available Chinese trade catalogs and export and import statistics. Sponsors cultural exchange program; assists U.S. business people who wish to visit the Canton Fair. Fosters closer relations among Chinese-American communities through joint outreach ventures in New York City, St. Louis, MO, Houston, TX, Boston, MA, and Los Angeles, CA. Organizes social gatherings. **Publications:** Brochure (quarterly); Newsletter (periodic).

43486 ■ Colombian American Association
30 Vesey St., Ste. 506
New York, NY 10007
Ph:(212)233-7776
Fax: (212)233-7779
Co. E-mail: andean@nyct.net
URL: http://www.colombianamerican.org

Contact: Linda A. Calvet, Sec.
Description: Facilitates commerce and trade between the Republic of Colombia and the U.S. Fosters and advances cultural relations and goodwill between the two nations. Encourages sound investments in Colombia by Americans and in the U.S. by Colombians. Disseminates information in the U.S. concerning Colombia. **Publications:** *Colombian Newsletter* (monthly).

43487 ■ Commercial Office of Spain
405 Lexington Ave., 44th Fl.
New York, NY 10174-0331
Ph:(212)661-4959
Fax: (212)972-2494
Co. E-mail: bony@mcx.es
Contact: Luis De Velasco, Trade Commissioner
Membership: Promotes the products of Spain in the U.S. Acts as information clearinghouse. Promotes US investment in Spain, and presence of corporations from Spain in USA. **Publications:** *Foods from Spain* (quarterly); *From Spain* (biennial); *Spain Gourmetour* (semiannual); *Wines from Spain.*

43488 ■ Committee for the Economic Growth of Israel
PO Box 2053
Milwaukee, WI 53217
Ph:(414)906-6250
Fax: (414)906-7878
Co. E-mail: elmer.winter@na.manpower.com
URL: http://www.cegi.org
Contact: Elmer L. Winter, Chm.
Description: Businessmen and women. Seeks to expand business relationships between Israel and the U.S. by promoting investment and joint venture opportunities for U.S. and Israeli companies. Promotes the exchange of technology, research and development, and products from Israel. **Publications:** *CEGI Newsletter* (semimonthly). Also publishes brochures.

43489 ■ Council of the Americas
680 Park Ave.
New York, NY 10021
Ph:(212)628-3200
Fax: (212)249-1880
Co. E-mail: inforequest@as-coa.org
URL: http://www.counciloftheamericas.org
Contact: Susan L. Segal, Pres./CEO
Purpose: Promotes on behalf of its members, policies and practices favoring free trade and investment, market economies and the rule of law in West Hemisphere. Provides a forum for its members to discuss economic, political and social issues relevant to the Hemisphere with public and private sector leaders. Represents the membership in public policy discussions. Assists members in the achievement of their business objectives in the region. **Publications:** Annual Report (annual).

43490 ■ Council for International Tax Education
PO Box 1012
White Plains, NY 10602
Ph:(914)328-5656
Fax: (914)328-5757
Co. E-mail: info@citeusa.org
URL: http://www.citeusa.org
Contact: William H. Green, Exec. Dir.
Description: Corporations, professional firms, and individual tax advisors. Works to maximize members' understanding of U.S. tax incentives and other offshore benefits available to exporters. Conducts educational programs for companies that generate tax incentives for the export of U.S. goods. Holds seminars on international tax, export and cross-border lease finance, and incentives offered companies that set up manufacturing or operating sites abroad. **Publications:** *International Tax News* (quarterly).

43491 ■ Danish American Chamber of Commerce
1 Dag Hammerskjold Plz.
885 2nd Ave., 18th Fl.
New York, NY 10017
Ph:(212)705-4945
Fax: (212)754-1904

Co. E-mail: daccny@daccny.com
URL: http://www.daccny.com
Contact: Nargis McGuinness, Exec.Dir.
Membership: Danish and American business leaders; firms and institutions. **Purpose:** Functions as an advisory board to support and promote commercial relations between the United States and Denmark, in both directions; makes itself available for consultation with the Danish diplomatic representatives in the U.S. and to the U.S. Department of Commerce, as well as to trade groups and members in Denmark and the U.S. Attempts to avoid duplication of governmental activities. **Publications:** Newsletter (bimonthly).

43492 ■ Engineering Export Promotion Council of India
333 N Michigan Ave., Ste. 2014
Chicago, IL 60601
Ph:(312)236-2162
Fax: (312)236-4625
Co. E-mail: eepcchicago@worldnet.att.net
Contact: Mr. Ashish Mehra, Dir.
Description: Manufacturers of engineering products in India. Aids members in sales and product promotion, marketing research, advertising, and importation of engineering products into the Canadian and American markets. Provides service to importers in the U.S. on the selection and choice of products from India. **Publications:** *Directory of Indian Engineering Exporters* (triennial); *Indian Engineering Exporter* (quarterly); *Turnkey Offers From India* (biennial).

43493 ■ European - American Business Council
1331 Pennsylvania Ave. NW, No. 600
Washington, DC 20004-1790
Ph:(202)637-3444
Fax: (202)637-3182
Co. E-mail: eabc@eabc.org
URL: http://www.eabc.org
Contact: Michael C. Maibach, Pres./CEO
Description: Represents over 50 major European and North American companies with a focus on promoting trans-Atlantic growth, bilateral trade, and investment in order to foster prosperity and stability between the US and Europe. Committed to fortifying EU-US economic integration, growth and competitiveness.

43494 ■ European-American Chamber of Commerce in the United States
12 E 49th St., 24th Fl.
New York, NY 10017
Ph:(212)315-2196
Fax: (212)315-2183
Co. E-mail: lorth@gaccny.com
Contact: Manfred Dransfeld, Pres./CEO
Membership: American and European corporations and member chambers concerned with trade and economic issues that affect all trade across the Atlantic. **Purpose:** Works to enhance the awareness of new opportunities available for both American and European businesses and represents corporations engaged in transatlantic trade. Provides information about the European Single Market. Organizes public events.

43495 ■ Fashion Exports New York
275 7th Ave., 9th Fl.
New York, NY 10001
Ph:(212)366-6160
Fax: (212)366-6162
Co. E-mail: info@nyfi.org
URL: http://www.fashionexportsny.org
Description: Fashion manufacturers. Works to assist New York manufacturers to export overseas and promote New York fashion internationally. Conducts foreign market research; organizes exhibitions.

43496 ■ Federation of International Trade Associations
11800 Sunrise Valley Dr., Ste. 210
Reston, VA 20191
Ph:(703)620-1588
Free: 800-969-3482
Fax: (703)620-4922
Co. E-mail: info@fita.org
URL: http://www.fita.org

Contact: Mr. Nelson T. Joyner, Chm.
Description: Fosters international trade by strengthening the role of local, regional, and national associations throughout the United States, Mexico, and Canada that have an international mission; affiliates are 450 independent international associations. **Publications:** *Directory of North American Trade Association* (annual); *FITA's Really Useful Sites* (biweekly).

43497 ■ Finnish American Chamber of Commerce
866 UN Plz., Ste. 250
New York, NY 10017
Ph:(212)821-0225
Fax: (212)750-4418
Co. E-mail: info@finlandtrade.com
URL: http://www.finlandtrade.com
Contact: Ann-Christine Westerlund, Pres.
Description: Maintains liaison with similar groups abroad; conducts seminars; arranges meetings with speakers. **Publications:** Newsletter (bimonthly).

43498 ■ French-American Chamber of Commerce
122 E 42nd St., Ste. 2015
New York, NY 10168
Ph:(212)867-0123
Fax: (212)867-9050
Co. E-mail: info@faccnyc.org
URL: http://www.faccnyc.org
Contact: Serge Bellanger, Pres.
Purpose: Promotes trade between the U.S. and France and fosters economic, commercial, and financial relations between the two countries. Functions in an advisory and informative capacity and assists in organizing business contacts for its members. Holds roundtable discussions, business card exchanges, and other events. Sponsors educational programs. **Publications:** *French-American Chamber of Commerce—Membership Directory* (annual); *French-American News* (5/year).

43499 ■ Global Offset and Countertrade Association
818 Connecticut Ave. NW, 12th Fl.
Washington, DC 20006
Ph:(202)887-9011
Fax: (202)872-8324
Co. E-mail: goca@globaloffset.org
URL: http://www.globaloffset.org
Contact: Mary O. Fromyer, Exec. Dir.
Description: Promotes trade and commerce between companies and their foreign customers who engage in reciprocal trade, including offset and countertrade, as a form of doing business. **Publications:** *ACA Newsletter* (periodic).

43500 ■ Guam Chamber of Commerce
Ada Plaza Ctr.
173 Aspinall Ave., Ste. 101
Hagatna, GU 96910
Ph:(671)472-6311
Fax: (671)472-6202
Co. E-mail: gchamber@guamchamber.com.gu
URL: http://www.guamchamber.com.gu
Contact: Eloise R. Baza, Pres.
Membership: Businesses and trade organizations. **Purpose:** Promotes increased international trade and tourism. Gathers and disseminates information; conducts promotional activities; represents members' interests. **Publications:** *Mailing Labels*; *The President's Report* (monthly).

43501 ■ Hellenic-American Chamber of Commerce
960 Avenue of the Americas, Ste. 1008
Atlantic Bank Bldg.
New York, NY 10001-2112
Ph:(212)629-6380
Fax: (212)564-9281
Co. E-mail: hellenicchamber-nyc@att.net
URL: http://www.hellenicamerican.cc
Contact: Andre Gregory, Pres.
Description: Promotes commerce and trade; represents members' interests. **Publications:** Journal (annual); Newsletter (quarterly).

43502 ■ Hong Kong Trade Development Council
219 E 46th St.
New York, NY 10017
Ph:(212)838-8688
Free: 800-832-4583
Fax: (212)838-8941
Co. E-mail: new.york.office@tdc.org.hk
URL: http://www.tdctrade.com
Contact: Louis Ho, Dir.
Description: Quasi-governmental body responsible for promoting Hong Kong trade with the rest of the world and creating a favorable image for Hong Kong as a trading partner and international trade center. Sponsors trade missions and participates in major trade shows around the world. Maintains library of trade publications in both Hong Kong and its North American offices. Compiles statistics. Convention/ Meeting: none. **Publications:** *Hong Kong Apparel* (quarterly); *Hong Kong Electronics* (semiannual); *Hong Kong Enterprise* (monthly); *Hong Kong for the Business Visitor; Hong Kong Gifts & Premiums* (annual).

43503 ■ Innovation Norway - United States
655 3rd Ave., Rm. 1810
New York, NY 10017-9111
Ph:(212)885-9700
Fax: (212)885-9710
Co. E-mail: newyork@invanor.no
URL: http://www.innovanor.no/usa
Contact: Arne Hjeltnes, Dir. for Tourism Americas
Description: U.S. branch of the Export Council of Norway. Assists Norwegian companies in marketing their goods and services in the U.S. Provides information to Norwegian exporters on U.S. markets, tariffs and statistics, trade constraints, and distribution channels. Establishes contacts with U.S. authorities, marketing and manufacturing firms, local lawyers, accountants, banks, patent offices, advertising and public relations agencies, consultants, and credit and debt collection agencies. Aids in establishing Norwegian subsidiaries in the U.S. **Publications:** *Norway Exports.*

43504 ■ International Association for Business Organizations
3 Woodthorn Ct., Ste. 12
Owings Mills, MD 21117
Ph:(410)581-1373
Co. E-mail: nahbb@msn.com
Contact: Rudolph Lewis, Exec. Officer
Description: Business organizations that develop and support small businesses that have the capability to provide their products or services on an international level. Establishes international business training institutions; promotes a business code of ethics for members. Conducts market studies; supplies member organizations with management assistance. Encourages joint marketing services and international trade assistance among members. Certifies international traders. **Publications:** Newsletter (periodic).

43505 ■ International Trade Council
3114 Circle Hill Rd.
Alexandria, VA 22305-1606
Ph:(703)548-1234
Fax: (703)548-6216
Contact: Dr. Peter T. Nelsen, Pres.
Description: Companies and organizations that import and export products, commodities, and services in 300 major industries including agricultural commodities, livestock, food, farm implements, and food machinery; agencies dealing with health and medicine, housing, energy, communications, transportation, forestry, water, and sanitation. Promotes free trade and the elimination of trade barriers and facilitates logistics, research, and marketing for members. Maintains legislative and educational services to develop world trade. Conducts management, technical, and educational programs; conducts financial studies of export banking, insurance, performance bonds, and transportation costs to enable exporters to be more competitive; offers speakers' bureau. Sponsors International Development Institute; offers Opportunity/Risk Analysis Service to help members find new or

expandable overseas markets for their commodities, products, services, and investments. **Publications:** *Geo Economic Review* (quarterly); *Research Report* (monthly); *World Opportunity/Risk Review* (quarterly); *World Source Directory* (annual); *World Trade Directory* (periodic); *World Trade Review* (quarterly); *Worldbusiness Directory* (annual); *Worldbusiness Review* (quarterly); *Worldbusiness Weekly;* Membership Directory (annual).

43506 ■ Italian-American Chamber of Commerce
30 S Michigan Ave., Ste. 504
Chicago, IL 60603
Ph:(312)553-9137
Fax: (312)553-9142
Co. E-mail: info@italianchamber.us
URL: http://www.italianchamber.us
Contact: Fulvio Calcinardi, Exec.Dir.
Description: Promotes trade between Italy and the U.S. and aids Italian organizations and companies to promote their products and/or services in the U.S. Organizes trade missions to Italian trade shows and trade delegations of U.S. businesses in Italy to meet with companies and organizations. Represents CASIC-BIC Sardinia to promote foreign investments in the industrial area of Cagliari, Sardinia. **Publications:** *The Bulletin* (quarterly).

43507 ■ Italy-America Chamber of Commerce
730 5th Ave., Ste. 600
New York, NY 10019
Ph:(212)459-0044
Fax: (212)459-0090
Co. E-mail: info@italchamber.org
URL: http://www.italchamber.org
Contact: Franco De Angelis, Sec.Gen.
Description: Brings together businesses ranging from individual entrepreneurs to large corporations. Advances the interests of its members through contacts and interaction with government agencies, trade associations and leading international organizations. **Publications:** *IACC Inform* (monthly); *Trade With Italy* (bimonthly); *United States - Italy Trade Directory* (annual). US - Italy Trade Directory CD-ROM.

43508 ■ Japan External Trade Organization
1221 Avenue of the Americas
McGraw Hill Bldg., 42nd Fl.
New York, NY 10020
Ph:(212)997-0400
Fax: (212)944-8808
Co. E-mail: jetrony@jetro.go.jp
URL: http://www.jetro.org
Contact: Ryohei Yamamoto
Description: Supports foreign companies in export and/or investment to Japan-related business ventures. Disseminates comprehensive information on the Japanese economy and market through surveys, reports, publications, and newsletters. Conducts trade and investment promotion seminars and symposia. Sponsors trade shows and exhibitions. Provides professional business consultation services and handles trade-related inquiries and provides opportunities for international exchange. **Publications:** *Directory of Japanese Affiliated Companies* (biennial) ; *Japan Trade Directory* (annual); *JETRO Spotlight USA* (monthly).

43509 ■ Japanese Chamber of Commerce and Industry of New York
145 W 57th St.
New York, NY 10019
Ph:(212)246-8001
Fax: (212)246-8002
Co. E-mail: info@jcciny.org
URL: http://www.jcciny.org
Contact: Motoatsu Sakurai, Pres.
Membership: Japanese and non-Japanese corporations. **Purpose:** Fosters improved trade relations between the U.S. and Japan. Conducts seminars and surveys. **Publications:** *Japan's Industries and Trade: Profiles and Interrelationships with the United States; JCCI Weekly Report, What America Needs to Know About Changing Japan* (weekly); *Joining In! A Handbook for Better Corporate Citizenship in the U.S.;* Membership Directory (annual).

43510 ■ Joint Industry Group
1620 I St. NW, Ste. 615
Washington, DC 20006
Ph:(202)466-5490
Fax: (202)463-8497
Co. E-mail: jig@moinc.com
URL: http://www.jig.org
Contact: James B. Clawson, Sec.
Description: Trade associations and business and professional firms engaged in international trade. Seeks to influence administration of customs and related trade laws to facilitate trade and encourage compliance. **Publications:** *JIG News* (monthly).

43511 ■ Korea Trade Promotion Center
460 Park Ave., Ste. 402
New York, NY 10022
Ph:(212)826-0900
Fax: (212)888-4930
Co. E-mail: kotrany@ix.netcom.com
URL: http://nyc.kotra.or.kr
Contact: Woo Jae Ryang, Pres.
Description: Works as an agency of the Korean government. Provides information about Korean export commodities and exporters, and import commodities and importers. Sponsors visits of foreign businesspersons to the Republic of Korea; arranges introductions of potential traders to Korean manufacturers and sales and buying missions of traders with the Republic of Korea. Compiles statistics; conducts economic and marketing research for distribution to Korean industry, business, and government; participates in U.S. trade shows. Maintains 35,000 volume international trade library. **Publications:** *Daily KOTRA Marketing News; Korea Trade* (5/year); *Korea Trade and Investment* (monthly).

43512 ■ Latin Chamber of Commerce of U. S.A.
1417 W Flagler St., 3rd Fl.
Miami, FL 33135
Ph:(305)642-3870
Fax: (305)642-0653
Co. E-mail: info@camacol.org
URL: http://www.camacol.org
Contact: William Alexander, Pres.
Description: Provides placement services; compiles statistics. Maintains information and referral service. **Publications:** *Revista Camacol* (monthly).

43513 ■ Mexican Arts and Technology Network
79 Central St. No.2
Waltham, MA 02453
Ph:(781)893-0125
Fax: (781)893-0125
Co. E-mail: lauragrub@comcast.net
Contact: Laura Grub, Founder & Pres.
Description: Encourages the exchange of ideas in the fields of arts, technology, and business between Mexico and other countries. Promotes innovation and development in arts, technology, and business. **Publications:** *Mexican Journals Partnerships.*

43514 ■ Moroccan American Business Council
1085 Commonwealth Ave., Ste. 194
Boston, MA 02215
Ph:(508)230-9943
Fax: (508)230-9943
Co. E-mail: mission@usa-morocco.org
URL: http://www.usa-morocco.org
Contact: Moulay M. Alaoui, Chm./Pres.
Description: Promotes commerce and business between Morocco and the United States. **Telecommunication Services:** electronic mail, moulay@usa-morocco.org.

43515 ■ National Association of Export Companies
PO Box 3949
Grand Central Station
New York, NY 10163
Free: 877-291-4901
Fax: (646)349-9628
Co. E-mail: director@nexco.org
URL: http://www.cmiregistration.com/user/splash.jxp?org=191

Contact: Ms. Gerri Cristantiello, Exec. Dir.
Membership: Established independent international trade firms, bilateral chambers of commerce, banks, law firms, accounting firms, trade associations, insurance companies, and product/service providers; export trading companies; export management companies. Promotes expansion of U.S. trade. Promotes the participation of members in international trade. Conducts educational programs.

43516 ■ National Association of Foreign-Trade Zones
1001 Connecticut Ave. NW, Ste. 350
Washington, DC 20036
Ph:(202)331-1950
Fax: (202)331-1994
Co. E-mail: info@naftz.org
URL: http://www.naftz.org
Contact: Dr. Willard M. Berry, Exec. Dir.
Description: Foreign-trade zone grantees, operators, and users; law firms, automobile manufacturers, port authorities, customs brokers, industrial firms, chambers of commerce, magazine and newspaper firms, development corporations, and concerned individuals. Aims to promote, stimulate, and improve foreign-trade zones and their utilization as integral and valuable tools in the international commerce of the U.S.; to encourage the establishment of foreign-trade zones to foster investment and the creation of jobs in the US. Sponsors seminars. **Publications:** *FTZs: A Positive Force in Trade and Economic Development*; *The Impact of Foreign Trade Zones on the 50 States and Puerto Rico*; *U.S. Foreign Trade Zones*; *Zones Report* (periodic).

43517 ■ National Association of State Development Agencies
12884 Harbor Dr.
Woodbridge, VA 22192
Ph:(703)490-6777
Fax: (703)492-4404
Co. E-mail: mfriedman@nasda.com
URL: http://www.nasda.com
Contact: Miles Friedman, Pres./CEO
Description: Provides consultation and field services in the area of state economic development. Sponsors International Trade Specialist Training Program in conjunction with American Graduate School of International Management, Glendale, AZ. Monitors hearings and legislation in Congress and interprets national events for members. Serves as clearinghouse for all member agencies. **Publications:** *Analysis of Innovative State Economic Development Financing Programs*; *Coordination of Employment and Training and Economic Development: A Resource Book*; *Directory of Incentives for Business Investment in the U.S.: A State by State Guide*; *NASDA Letter*; *NASDA State Economic Development Expenditure Survey* (semiannual) ; *Report on State Responses to the State Volume Limit on Private Activity Bonds*; *State Ed Agency*; *State Enterprise Zone Roundup* (annual); *Trade Development Catalog*.

43518 ■ National Council on International Trade Development
1001 Connecticut Ave. NW, Ste. 1110
Washington, DC 20036
Ph:(202)872-9280
Fax: (202)293-0495
Co. E-mail: cu@ncitd.org
URL: http://www.ncitd.org
Contact: Mary Fromyer, Exec. Dir.
Description: Exporters, importers, freight forwarders and brokers, ocean and airline carriers, banks, attorneys, trade groups, and consulting firms. Aims to identify impediments to all aspects of international commerce and to provide solutions to facilitating the global trade process.

43519 ■ Netherlands Chamber of Commerce in the United States
267 5th Ave., Ste. 301
New York, NY 10016
Ph:(212)265-6460
Fax: (212)265-6402
Co. E-mail: newyork@nlcoc.com
URL: http://www.netherlands.org

Contact: Kersen J. de Jong, Sec.
Description: Aims to maintain and expand business relations between The Netherlands and the United States. **Publications:** Newsletter (monthly); Annual Report (annual).

43520 ■ North American-Chilean Chamber of Commerce
30 Vasay St., Ste. 506
New York, NY 10007
Ph:(212)233-7776
Fax: (212)233-7779
Co. E-mail: andean@nyct.net
Contact: David Spencer, Exec. Dir./Sec.
Purpose: Fosters expanded trade and commerce between businesses in Chile, and the U.S.

43521 ■ Norwegian American Chamber of Commerce - New York City
825 3rd Ave., 38th Fl.
New York, NY 10022
Ph:(212)421-1653
Co. E-mail: nacc@ntcny.org
URL: http://www.nacc.no
Contact: Inger Tallaksen, Gen.Mgr.
Description: Promotes business and trade among members and between Norway and the United States. Networking opportunities, source of information. **Publications:** *Norwegian Trade Bulletin* (quarterly).

43522 ■ Organization of Women in International Trade
1001 Connecticut Ave. NW, Ste. 1110
Washington, DC 20036-5550
Co. E-mail: moniquemr@earthlink.net
URL: http://www.owit.org
Contact: Monique Roske, Pres.
Membership: International trade organizations in the United States. **Purpose:** Seeks to enhance "the visibility of and opportunities for women in the field of international trade." Makes available educational and networking opportunities for women pursuing careers in international trade.

43523 ■ Philippine-American Chamber of Commerce
1130 Connecticut Ave., Ste. 310
Washington, DC 20036
Ph:(202)835-0875
Fax: (202)835-1464
Co. E-mail: twusa1pta@aol.com
Contact: Celia P. Donahue, Pres.
Purpose: Promotes trade and investment between the U.S. and the Philippines. Provides information and services on doing business in the Philippines. **Publications:** *Living in the Philippines*; *Network* (quarterly); *Philamcham News* (biweekly); *Philippine Business Quarterly*.

43524 ■ Portuguese Trade Commission
590 5th Ave., 3rd Fl.
New York, NY 10036
Ph:(212)354-4610
Fax: (212)575-4737
Co. E-mail: webmaster@portugal.org
URL: http://www.portugal.org
Contact: Eduardo Souto Moura, Head
Description: Promotes exports from Portugal to the U.S. and helps American importers and businesses find sources in Portugal. Convention/Meeting: none. **Publications:** *Export Directory of Portugal* (annual). Also publishes fact sheets, catalogs, and industry brochures.

43525 ■ Romanian-U.S. Business Council
1615 H St. NW
Washington, DC 20062-2000
Ph:(202)659-6000
Free: 800-638-6582
Fax: (202)463-3173
URL: http://www.uschamber.com
Contact: Thomas J. Donahue, Pres./CEO
Description: Advocates American business interests with respect to U.S. Romanian trade and investments. Provides the American and Romanian business communities with a means of discussing bilateral trade

and investment issues and the formulation of policy positions that will promote and expand economic relations between the two countries. Facilitates appropriate legislation and policies regarding trade between the U.S. and Romania. Has sponsored seminars on topics such as possibilities for cooperative commercial efforts in other countries and cooperation in energy development. **Publications:** *Bridging the Atlantic*; *The Eurasia Business Committee Dispatch* (weekly).

43526 ■ Society of International Business Fellows
One Georgia Ctr.
600 W Peachtree St., Ste. 490
Atlanta, GA 30308
Ph:(404)525-7423
Fax: (404)525-5331
Co. E-mail: info@sibf.org
URL: http://www.sibf.org
Contact: Nancy Haselden, Exec. Dir.
Membership: Businesspeople active or with an interest in international trade. **Purpose:** Promotes "enhancement of the international competitiveness and prosperity of its members and the growth of the South as a vital region for global business." Works to strengthen personal and professional relations among members; conducts educational programs in international business and trade.

43527 ■ Spain-United States Chamber of Commerce
The Empire State Bldg.
350 5th Ave., Ste. 2600
New York, NY 10118
Ph:(212)967-2170
Fax: (212)564-1415
Co. E-mail: info@spainuscc.org
URL: http://www.spainuscc.org
Contact: Bisilia Bokoko, Exec. Dir.
Description: Spanish and U.S. business persons dedicated to the expansion of Spanish-American trade and goodwill. **Publications:** *Business Directories*; *Spain: The Business Link* (semiannual); *Visa and Work Permits for the USA*.

43528 ■ Swedish Trade Council
150 N Michigan Ave., Ste. 1950
Chicago, IL 60601
Ph:(312)781-6222
Free: 888-275-7933
Fax: (312)276-8606
Co. E-mail: usa@swedishtrade.se
URL: http://www.swedishtrade.com/usa
Contact: Gudrun Pettersson, Sr. Project Leader
Description: Promotes Swedish exports and assists American companies in contacting Swedish suppliers. Performs market developments studies and research, partner searches, cross-cultural training, and project management. **Publications:** *Swedish Export Directory* (annual).

43529 ■ U.S. Austrian Chamber of Commerce
165 W 46th St., Ste. 1112
New York, NY 10036
Ph:(212)819-0117
Fax: (212)819-0345
Co. E-mail: memberservices@usatchamber.com
URL: http://www.usatchamber.com
Contact: Johannes P. Hofer, Pres.
Description: Hosts receptions and luncheons. Sponsors Viennese Opera Ball, panel discussions, and business assistance. **Publications:** Newsletter (quarterly).

43530 ■ United States Council for International Business
1212 Ave. of the Americas
New York, NY 10036
Ph:(212)354-4480
Fax: (212)575-0327
Co. E-mail: info@uscib.org
URL: http://www.uscib.org
Contact: William G. Parrett, Chm.
Purpose: Serves as the U.S. National Committee of the International Chamber of Commerce. Enables

multinational enterprises to operate effectively by representing their interests to intergovernmental and governmental bodies and by keeping enterprises advised of international developments having a major impact on their operations. Serves as: U.S. representative to the International Organization of Employers; national affiliate to the U.S.A. - Business and Industry Advisory Committee to the BIAC. Operates ATA Carnet export service, which enables goods to be shipped overseas duty-free for demonstration and exhibition. Sponsors seminars and luncheon briefings. **Publications:** *Business and Environment* (periodic); *Corporate Handbook Series*; *USCIB Newsletter* (monthly).

43531 ■ United States-Mexico Chamber of Commerce
1300 Pennsylvania Ave. NW, Ste. G-0003
Washington, DC 20004-3021
Ph:(202)312-1520
Fax: (202)312-1530
Co. E-mail: news-hq@usmcoc.org
URL: http://www.usmcoc.org
Contact: Albert Zapanta, Pres./CEO
Description: U.S. businessmen and chambers of commerce in Mexico representing 350,000 companies. Works to promote private sector trade and investment between the United States and Mexico. Offers advice on economic, legal, and trade issues; informs members of long-range advantages of alternative plant locations. Works with both governments on the executive, legislative, and federal levels. Monitors legislation and regulations concerning trade issues critical to business development in both countries. Conducts seminars and luncheons. **Publications:** *Chamber News* (quarterly); *United States-Mexico Chamber of Commerce—Regional Newsletters* (periodic); *United States-Mexico Chamber of Commerce— Special Report* (periodic); Newsletter (periodic) ; Membership Directory (annual). Also publishes reference materials.

43532 ■ U.S. Pan Asian American Chamber of Commerce
1329 18th St. NW
Washington, DC 20036
Ph:(202)296-5221
Free: 800-696-7818
Fax: (202)296-5225
Co. E-mail: administrator@uspaacc.com
URL: http://www.uspaacc.com
Contact: Susan Au Allen, Natl. Pres./CEO
Description: Businesspersons and professionals united to promote contract, education and other opportunities for Asian American businesses and their partners in corporate America and government agencies. Promotes programs and activities to help members pursue owning and growing their business; enter mainstream society; and participate in procurement, commerce, trade, investment and employment opportunities in corporate America and government. Conducts educational and networking activities. Maintains scholarship fund. Holds business colloquies. Sponsors speakers' bureau. Conducts research and charitable programs. Bestows achievement awards. **Publications:** *East-West Report* (bimonthly); *Guide* (annual); *National Directory of Asian American Organizations and Resource Guide*.

43533 ■ U.S.-Russia Business Council
1701 Pennsylvania Ave. NW, Ste. 520
Washington, DC 20006
Ph:(202)739-9180
Fax: (202)659-5920
Co. E-mail: info@usrbc.org
URL: http://www.usrbc.org
Contact: Eugene K. Lawson, Pres.
Membership: U.S. corporations doing business in Russia. **Purpose:** Promotes adoption of public policies conducive to international trade in both the United States and Russia. Conducts lobbying activities; facilitates establishment of joint ventures involving U.S. and Russian companies; maintains bank of job listings; compiles trade statistics. Gathers and disseminates information on political, economic, and social issues affecting trade with Russia. **Publications:** *Event Transcript* (periodic); *Russia Business Watch* (quarterly).

43534 ■ U.S.A. - Business and Industry Advisory Committee to the OECD
1212 Ave. of the Americas
New York, NY 10036
Ph:(212)354-4480
Fax: (212)575-0327
Co. E-mail: info@uscib.org
URL: http://www.uscib.org
Contact: Thomas Niles, Pres.
Description: Sponsored by United States Council for International Business. Represents the United States on the Business and Industry Advisory Committee to the Organisation for Economic Co-Operation and Development. Acts as the official channel for conveying the views of the business community to the OECD in the fields of economics, finance, international trade, industrial relations, information and telecommunications policy investment, and taxation. Also distributes information on OECD activities. **Telecommunication Services:** electronic mail, membership@uscib.org.

43535 ■ Venezuelan American Association of the United States
30 Vesey St., Ste. 506
New York, NY 10007
Ph:(212)233-7776
Fax: (212)233-7779
Co. E-mail: andean@nyct.net
URL: http://venezuelanamerican.org
Contact: Montserrat Hernandez, Program Dir.
Description: Financial institutions, businesses, organizations, and individuals interested in the expansion and improvement of trade and trade relations between Venezuela and the United States. Fosters cultural and commercial relations, facilitates investment between the U.S. and Venezuela, and promotes improved understanding between businesspersons of the two nations. Conducts informal meetings with speakers and discussions. **Publications:** *Venezuela News Bulletin* (monthly).

EDUCATIONAL PROGRAMS

43536 ■ Export/Import Procedures and Documentation
1601 Broadway
PO Box 169
New York, NY 12983
Ph:(518)891-1500
Free: 800-262-9699
Fax: (518)891-0368
Co. E-mail: customerservice@amanet.org
URL: http://www.amanet.org
Price: $1795.00 ($1595.00 for AMA members). **Description:** Seminar for export/import managers and managers of international corporations, covering selecting foreign freight forwarders and bankers, marking merchandise effectively, special services of bonded and general warehouses, and using forms, licenses, and insurance documents. **Locations:** Atlanta, GA; Los Angeles, CA; Boston, MA; San Diego, CA; Chicago, IL; New Orleans, LA; Dallas, TX; New York, NY.

REFERENCE WORKS

43537 ■ "Abraham Lincoln and the Global Economy" in *Harvard Business Review* (Vol. 81, No. 8, August 2003, pp. 58)
Pub: Harvard Business School Press
Ed: Robert D. Hormats. **Description:** Ways the economic developments during the early 1800s helped the U.S. develop a national economy, and might be a possible blueprint for globalization.

43538 ■ "An African American in Paris: Ricki Stevenson's Entree to the City of Light" in *Black Enterprise* (Vol. 35, January 2005, No. 6)
Pub: Earl G. Graves Publishing Co. Inc.
Ed: Maureen Jenkins. **Description:** Profile of Paris as a city that attracts African Americans for business and pleasure. Many black entrepreneurs are enjoying Paris as a great place to grow their business.

43539 ■ "Alcoa's Results Could Hint at Manufacturers' Outlook" in *Wall Street Journal* (Vol. 249, January 2007, No. 5, pp. B4)
Pub: Dow Jones & Co. Inc.
Ed: Laura Mandaro. **Description:** Due to growth overseas balancing the decline in U.S. growth, raw materials companies such as Alcoa Inc., which produces more aluminum than any other company in the world, is expected to post higher earnings this quarter.

43540 ■ "Am. Axle Plans China, Europe Plants" in *Crain's Detroit Business* (Vol. 21, October 31, 2005, No. 44, pp. 4)
Pub: Crain Communications Inc. - Detroit
Ed: Terry Kosdrosky. **Description:** American Axle & Manufacturing Holdings Inc. will open its first manufacturing plant in China in late 2007 or early 2008, followed by a new plant in Central or Eastern Europe soon after.

43541 ■ *American Chambers of Commerce Abroad*
Pub: U.S. Chamber of Commerce
Covers: 94 American chambers of commerce in 82 countries. **Entries Include:** Name, address, phone, fax, title, telex, E-mail and web addresses, geographical area served, and subsidiary and branch names and locations. **Arrangement:** Geographical.

43542 ■ *The American Keiretsu: A Strategic Weapon for Global Competitiveness*
Pub: Irwin Professional Publishing
Ed: David N. Burt and Michael F. Doyle. **Released:** 1993. **Price:** $25.00. **Description:** Adapts the Japanese strategy of "keiretsu" to U.S. business to eliminate incoming defects, reduce costs, and cut product time-to-market. Also discusses strategic supply management.

43543 ■ "American Outcast" in *Entrepreneur.com* (Vol. 34, February 2006, No. 2, pp. 81)
Pub: Entrepreneur Media Inc.
Ed: Laurel Delaney. **Description:** In order to compete in a global market, small American companies must position their brands as local in order market a good brand strategy, as well as to promote a new brand with cultural sensitivity.

43544 ■ "Are Portals Just Another Integration Problem?" in *E-business Advisor* (Vol. 18, No. 7, July 2000, pp. 40)
Pub: Advisor Media, Inc.
Ed: Rik Drummund. **Description:** While portals, or e-marketplaces, expand relationships with trading partners, no single integration standard has been defined. The standard that is being proposed is ebXML. With ebXML, implementing worldwide e-commerce can be done cost-effectively; with no standard, the amount of work is 500 times greater.

43545 ■ "Area Arab-Americans can help rebuild Iraq" in *Crain's Detroit Business* (Vol. 19, No. 15, April 14, 2003, pp. 8)
Pub: Crain Communications Inc., Detroit
Description: Arab-American professionals and companies owned by Arab-Americans can act as a bridge to rebuilding not only Iraq, but also the American image in the Middle East.

43546 ■ *Arizona USA International Trade Directory*
Pub: Arizona Office of Economic Planning & Development
Released: every 1.5 years. **Price:** Free. **Covers:** 370 Arizona companies involved in international trade. **Entries Include:** name, address, phone, products or services and countries traded with.

43547 ■ *Arthur Andersen European Community Sourcebook*
Pub: Triumph Books
Ed: Arthur Andersen. **Released:** 1991. **Price:** $150.00. **Description:** Provides information for business executives on European Community (EC) rules and regulations. Includes profiles each of the 12 EC member states.

43548 ■ "Asia Rising" in *Black Enterprise*
(Vol. 35, October 2004, No. 3, pp. 46)
Pub: Earl G. Graves Publishing Co. Inc.
Ed: Donald Jay Korn. **Description:** China and India
are two emerging global economies making them attractive for investing. Manufacturing and high tech
jobs are being outsourced to both countries. It is important to research before investing in China and
India, as well as any international funds.

**43549 ■ "Asia: The VC sum rises in the
East" in** *Red Herring* **(No. 99, June 15 & July
1, 2001, pp. 35-36)**
Pub: Herring Communications
Ed: Rebecca Fannin. **Description:** Established U.S.
venture capital firms have begun to invest in Asian
companies. Cisco Systems, along with Japan's Softbank, raised $2 billion to invest in broadband, wire-
less, optical networking, and the Internet in Asia.

43550 ■ *Asian Markets: A Guide to Company
and Industry Sources*
Pub: Washington Researchers, Ltd.
Released: Third edition. **Price:** $335.00 (paper). **De-
scription:** Provides information sources on 11 Asian
countries. Includes government offices, publications,
databases, and industry experts.

43551 ■ "Ask the attorney" in *Red Herring*
(March 2003, pp. 73)
Pub: Herring Communications Inc.
Description: Legal issues are addressed that include
the following topics, pharmaceutical patents, government support for research and development, global
commerce, intellectual property rights, the transfer of
customer lists from European subsidiary to its U.S.
parent company, trademark dilution, venture financing, selling a business, stock options, corporate tax
deductions, small business patent methods, and employee use of Instant Messaging with clients.

43552 ■ "Ask Inc. Importing" in *Inc.*
(September 2006, pp. 53-54)
Pub: Gruner & Jahr USA Publishing
Description: Importing has become more involved
and difficult in recent years. Many things can be done
to expedite that prior to receipt of the items at US Customs. Necessary steps are covered in this article.

**43553 ■ "Authors Defend Study on Great
Lakes Shipping Value" in** *Milwaukee Journal
Sentinel* **(December 1, 2005)**
Pub: Journal Sentinel, Inc.
Ed: Dan Egan. **Description:** Details of a controversial
study conducted by two Michigan transportation ex-
perts and funded by a grant from Chicago, Illinois
Joyce Foundation values overseas shipping in the
Great Lakes at $55 million annually.

**43554 ■ "Auto suppliers: Steel tariffs kill
U.S. jobs permanently" in** *Crain's Detroit
Business* **(Vol. 19, No. 14, April 7, 2003, pp.
34)**
Pub: Crain Communications Inc., Detroit
Ed: Harry Stoffer. **Description:** Automotive suppliers
are focusing on a midterm review of the three-year tar-
iff program that effects steel users in the U.S.

**43555 ■ "Backers of border projects press
on despite split decision" in** *Crain's Detroit
Business* **(Vol. 19, No. 1, January 6, 2003, pp.
19)**
Pub: Crain Communications Inc., Detroit
Ed: Michael Strong. **Description:** In efforts to relieve
the truck congestion in Windsor, Ontario, Canada, a
truck-only parkway is being considered by business
and government leaders in the area.

43556 ■ "Bar None" in *Entrepreneur* **(Vol. 32,
December 2004, No. 12, pp. 24)**
Pub: Entrepreneur Media Inc.
Ed: Amanda C. Kooser. **Description:** New bar code
regulations affecting retailers and suppliers, called
Sunrise 2005, go into effect January 1, 2005. This pro-
cess allows businesses to scan different types of
codes used worldwide, and ultimately, the 14-digit
Global Trade Item Number.

43557 ■ "Bar None" in *My Business*
(December/January 2004, pp. 11)
Pub: My Business Magazine
Ed: Tamara E. Holmes. **Description:** The 2005 Sunrise mandate, instituted by the Uniform Code Council
Inc., will require all retailers to have systems able to
read 13-digit bar codes in addition to the 12-digit bar
code numbers already standard in the U.S. The
change is required EAN International, the global body
that issues product codes overseas, currently uses an
8-digit and 13-digit system.

43558 ■ *Best Practice in Business Advisory,
Counseling and Information Services*
Pub: United Nations Publications
Ed: United Nations, Economic Commission for Eu-
rope Staff. **Released:** January 2005. **Price:** $20.00.
Description: Second book in a series promoting en-
trepreneurship in small and medium-sized companies
(SMEs) throughout United Nation's Economic Com-
mission for Europe (UNECE) member states.

43559 ■ *Best Practice in Development of
Entrepreneurship and SMEs in Countries in
Transition: The Belarusian Experience*
Pub: United Nations Publications
Ed: United Nations, Economic Commission for Eu-
rope Staff. **Released:** January 2005. **Price:** $22.00.
Description: Compilation of papers presented at the
Forum on Best Practice in the Development of Entre-
preneurship and Small and Medium-sized Enterprises
(SMEs) in Countries in Transition: The Belarussian
Experience, a forum organized by the United Nations
Economic Commission for Europe. The book helps to
assist Belarus with transitioning to a market economy.

**43560 ■ "Big Plans on the Drawing Board"
in** *Boston Business Journal* **(Vol. 22, No. 16,
May 24, 200)**
Pub: MCP, Inc.
Ed: Bill Archambeault. **Description:** Profile of Steffian
Bradley, CEO of Kurt Rockstroh, who is managing the
company's international expansion.

43561 ■ *Blunders in International Business*
Pub: Blackwell Publishers
Ed: David A. Ricks. **Released:** 1993. **Price:** $18.95.
Description: Examines mistakes businesses make
when competing globally.

**43562 ■ "The Blush Is Off As Consumers
Pick Variety in Flowers for Valentine's Day"
in** *Boston Globe* **(February 11, 2005)**
Pub: New York Times Company
Ed: Chris Reidy. **Description:** Roses are no longer
the first choice for Valentine's Day flowers. Consumers are choosing tulips, orchids, or mixed arrangements in favorite colors. Imports account for 70
percent of fresh flowers sold in the U.S. and account
for the new choices.

**43563 ■ "Boost staff morale with rewards
and motivation" in** *Women In Business* **(Vol.
52, No. 3, May 2000, pp. 35)**
Pub: The ABWA Co., Inc.
Ed: Dawn J. Grubb. **Description:** A number of firms
understand the importance of recognizing their employees for good work by awarding them not only with
money, but by giving them special benefits, or by acknowledging their contribution.

**43564 ■ "Border-Crossing Backers Could
Lose Own Plans" in** *Crain's Detroit Business*
(Vol. 19, No. 40, October 13, 2003, pp. 10)
Pub: Crain Communications Inc., Detroit
Ed: Michael Strong. **Description:** Current proposals
to build a proposed new border crossing between
Michigan and Canada by three firms could be lost to
a new firm with a lower bid once the project is ap-
proved. The five corridors being considered are dis-
cussed.

43565 ■ *Brazilian-American Business
Review/Directory*
Pub: Brazilian-American Chamber of Commerce Inc.
Contact: Sueli Bonaparte, Exec. Dir.
Released: Annual, March. **Price:** $50, nonmembers
shipping and tax extra; $25, members shipping extra.

Covers: Brazilian and American businesses interested in developing trade and investment between the
two countries. **Entries Include:** Company name, address, phone, fax, key personnel, Standard Industrial
Classification (SIC) code.

**43566 ■ "Built For Speed: Baba Garba Looks
to Take His Broadband Business Abroad" in**
Black Enterprise **(Vol. 34, No. 5, December
2003, pp. 50)**
Pub: Earl Graves Publishing Co.
Ed: Zakiyyah El-Amin. **Description:** Profile of Baba
Garba, founder of Infonit LLC, launched in 2000 and
located in Niles, Michigan. The firm provides broadband installation and information technology consulting.

43567 ■ "The Business Week" in *Business
Week* **(January 16, 2006, No. 3967, pp. 26-27)**
Pub: McGraw-Hill Companies
Ed: Harry Maurer. **Description:** Topics include Fed-
eral Reserve rate hikes, management at BASF, Hilton
Hotels, China's economy, issues facing the airline in-
dustry, and more.

**43568 ■ "The Business Week News You
Need To Know" in** *Business Week* **(January
9, 2006, No. 3966, pp. 24-25)**
Pub: McGraw-Hill Companies
Ed: Harry Maurer. **Description:** Information of 2005
holiday sales, interest rates, a medical device lawsuit,
television cable news programming, the retailer Wal-
Mart, Albertson's grocery stores, Alaska drilling,
Microsoft's European business, and other issues is of-
fered.

**43569 ■ "Businesses hope comments don't
mean a tense border" in** *Crain's Detroit
Business* **(Vol. 19, No. 14, April 7, 2003, pp.
39)**
Pub: Crain Communications Inc., Detroit
Ed: Michael Strong. **Description:** U.S. companies
bordering Canada fear that Canada's lack of support
for the U.S.-led war on Iraq will affect business relations.

**43570 ■ "By Gum!...It Is Possible to Beat
Everyone-Even Big Companies-To Market..."
in** *Entrepreneur* **(Vol. 32, November 2004, No.
11, pp. 26)**
Pub: Entrepreneur Media Inc.
Ed: Geoff Williams. **Description:** Profile of Art Baer,
who invested $20,000 of his own money to launch Im-
press Gum. Baer recognized the opportunity when
Singapore lifted its ban on chewing gum, where residents chew gum for medicinal purposes.

43571 ■ "CAFTA Action" in *Hispanic
Business* **(September 2006, pp. 14)**
Pub: Hispanic Business
Ed: Patricia Guadalupe. **Description:** Guatemala has
implemented the Central America Free Trade Agreement (CAFTA-DR) joining several Central American
countries and the United States. The agreement removes barriers to trade while expanding U.S. export
opportunities.

**43572 ■ "Canada mum on funding for border
projects" in** *Crain's Detroit Business* **(Vol.
18, No. 50, December 16, 2002, pp. 5)**
Pub: Crain Communications Inc., Detroit
Ed: Michael Strong. **Description:** Proposals for projects aimed at easing truck congestion at the Windsor/
Detroit border are presented by CenTra Inc., owner of
the Ambassador Bridge; the Detroit River Tunnel Partnership; and the City of Windsor, Ontario, Canada.

**43573 ■ "Canada Rx offers access to
Canadian pharmacies" in** *Atlanta Business
Chronicle* **(Vol. 25, January 10, 2003, No. 31,
pp. 17A)**
Pub: American City Business Publications, Inc.
Ed: Melissa Fowler. **Description:** Canada Rx Shop is
described as an entity that supplies a Web-based ordering connection between clients in the U.S. and the
pharmaceutical market in Canada. Tom Connell,
owner of the company, stated that he and his wife be-

came Rx affiliates to offer clients another way to manage their finances. Increasing prescription costs in the U.S. have sent many Americans, though primarily senior citizens, north of the border seeking cheaper drug prices. The article provides information on the service, the risks and the legal implications.

43574 ■ *Canadian Entrepreneurship and Small Business Management*
Pub: McGraw-Hill Ryerson, Limited
Ed: D. Wesley Balderson. **Released:** February 2005. **Price:** $79.95. **Description:** Successful entrepreneurship and small business management is shown through the use of individual Canadian small business experiences.

43575 ■ "Caribbean Connection: This Shipping Professional is Taking His Company Overseas" in *Black Enterprise* (Vol. 34, July 2004, No. 12)
Pub: Earl G. Graves Publishing Co. Inc.
Ed: Arlene McKanic. **Description:** Franklin Vieira, CEO of minority owned Caribbean Cargo & Package Services, a shipping firm headquartered at John F. Kennedy International Airport in New York City, is expanding his company overseas. The company's Brooklyn, New York branch also helps individuals and small businesses shipping merchandise to the Caribbean.

43576 ■ *Cases in Corporate Acquisitions, Buyouts, Mergers & Takeovers*
Pub: Thomson Gale
Released: Published December, 1999. **Price:** $415, individuals. **Covers:** Approximately 300 significant acquisitions, mergers, and takeovers that involved at least one U.S.-based corporation during the 20th century. **Entries Include:** Company name, background information, financial data, transaction details, evaluation of outcome.

43577 ■ "Central command" in *Crain's Detroit Business* (Vol. 19, No. 14, April 7, 2003, pp. 38)
Pub: Crain Communications Inc., Detroit
Ed: David Sedgwick. **Description:** Delphi Corporation created a war room in 2000 as a means to help the company better manage the vast flow of information to and from its 194 factories around the world.

43578 ■ "Champagne Toasts: Brian Nembhard Schools Us On the Best of the Bubbly" in *Black Enterprise* (Vol. 34, July 2004, No. 12, pp. 138)
Pub: Earl G. Graves Publishing Co. Inc.
Ed: Sean Drakes. **Description:** Brian Nembhard, president and CEO of Nembo Imports Ltd., a New York and Caribbean-based importer and distributor of fine wines and champagne, has been commissioned by the Ritz Carleton Hotel in Montego Bay, Jamaica to reconstruct the resort's wine list.

43579 ■ "Cherry to Move 100 Jobs to Mexico" in *Milwaukee Journal Sentinel* (December 21, 2005)
Pub: Journal Sentinel, Inc.
Ed: Avrum D. Lank. **Description:** Cherry Electrical Products, a division of Cherry Corporation, reports it is moving 100 jobs to Mexico in 2006. The company makes electrical components for manufacturers.

43580 ■ "China" in *Business Week* (January 23, 2006, No. 3968, pp. 44-45)
Pub: McGraw-Hill Companies
Ed: Brian Bremner. **Description:** Citibank has been out-hustled by rivals HSBC, Bank of America, and Goldman Sachs in making deals with large Chinese banking firms. Acquisitions, consumer banking, and corporate clients could help Citi compete.

43581 ■ "China Presents Opportunities, Risks for Investors" in *Sacramento Bee* (December 27, 2005)
Pub: The Sacramento Bee
Ed: Gilbert Chan. **Description:** China's capitalist economy ruled by a communist government makes investments risky. California's Public Employee's Retirement System is discussing plans on whether to invest in China, now one of the world's fastest growing economies.

43582 ■ "China Syndrome" in *Boston Business Journal* (V)
Pub: MCP, Inc.
Ed: Tom Witkowski. **Description:** Massachusetts-based semiconductor device firms are establishing operations in China.

43583 ■ *China's Rational Entrepreneurs: The Development of the New Private Business Sector*
Pub: Routledge
Ed: Barbara Krug. **Released:** March 2004. **Price:** $104.95 (US), $149.95 (Canadian). **Description:** Difficulties faced by entrepreneurs in China are discussed, including analysis for understanding their behavior and relations with local governments in order to secure long-term business success.

43584 ■ "China's cheap labor is next threat to suppliers" in *Crain's Detroit Business* (Vol. 19, No. 2, January 13, 2003, pp. 13)
Pub: Crain Communications Inc., Detroit
Ed: Terry Kosdrosky. **Description:** U.S. auto suppliers are facing yet another threat, the growing Chinese economy. China's large supply of educated workers earning low incomes threaten the security of small to mid-size manufacturers in the U.S., especially the tool and die industry.

43585 ■ "The Chinese Are Coming" in *Inc.* (Volume 27, July 2005, No. 7, pp. 32)
Pub: Inc. Magazine
Ed: Darren Dahl. **Description:** Chinese companies acquired 649 U.S. firms in 2004, focusing on textile, appliance, electronics, and auto parts manufacturing sectors.

43586 ■ *Chinese Ethnic Business*
Pub: Routledge Inc.
Ed: Eric Fong; Chiu Ming Luk. **Released:** October 2006. **Description:** Impact of globalization on Chinese ethnic small businesses is covered, focusing on U.S., Australia, and Canada.

43587 ■ "The Chinese Negotiation" in *Harvard Business Review* (Vol. 81, No. 10, October 2003, pp. 82)
Pub: Harvard Business School Press
Ed: John L. Graham, N. Mark Lam. **Description:** Suggestions for multinational firms looking to conduct negotiations in China are presented. Cultural differences are a critical factor that can make or break an effective negotiation.

43588 ■ "Chip Demand Worldwide Drives Up 1Q Earnings for Intel" in *San Jose Mercury News* (March 11, 2005)
Pub: Knight-Ridder/Tribune Business News
Ed: Dean Takahashi. **Description:** International sales will drive first quarter earnings for Intel higher than projected. Statistical data included.

43589 ■ "Colorado Man Helped Contribute to Overseas Tech Development" in *Colorado Springs Business Journal* (February 28, 2003)
Pub: Dolan Media Newswires
Ed: Marylou Doehrman. **Description:** Profile of Chet Sulewski, who retired from Johns Manville, after spending 35 years as senior vice president, promoting overseas technological development. Sulewski now owns a liquor store that is co-managed by his two sons.

43590 ■ "Commentary: Is America Ill Positioned for Global Economy?" in *Long Island Business News* (February 6, 2004)
Pub: Dolan Media Newswires
Ed: Jerry Kremer. **Description:** Two million jobs have been lost to overseas workers since 2000. Many of these positions went overseas to countries such as China, India, Japan, as well as others. Major American corporations are able to save money by outsourcing to these countries.

43591 ■ "Commentary: Turning Job Losses to Indian Into Gains" in *Long Island Business News* (January 30, 2004)
Pub: Dolan Media Newswires
Description: An alternative strategy that might benefit the loss of jobs in the U.S. that are going to India, would be to utilize each nation's proven capabilities in homeland security by expanding defense co-production opportunities.

43592 ■ "Conference to Examine Doing Business in China" in *Crain's Detroit Business* (Vol. 21, October 31, 2005, No. 44, pp. 29)
Pub: Crain Communications Inc. - Detroit
Ed: Laura Bommarito. **Description:** Experts will meet at a conference set for December to discuss the risks and rewards of doing business with Chinese companies.

43593 ■ "Conflicts and Conflict Resolution in International Anti-trust: Do We Need International Competition Rules?" in *World Economy* (Vol. 24)
Pub: Blackwell Publishers, Inc.
Ed: Henning Klodt. **Description:** The wave of company mergers and acquisitions in the world which are driven by globalization and deregulation could lead to oligopolies in national markets and the world. This paper looks into solutions such as national anti-trust laws applying internationally, or establishing an international competition policy.

43594 ■ "Contacts for Contracts" in *Hispanic Business* (November 2003, pp. 73)
Pub: Hispanic Business
Description: Construction and engineering firms present minority vendors with opportunities both at home and abroad. A listing of procurement contacts is offered.

43595 ■ "Controversial Ruling on Cuban Trade" in *Hispanic Business* (April 2005, pp. 12)
Pub: Hispanic Business
Ed: Patricia Guadalupe. **Description:** A ruling by the U.S. Treasury Department requires all agricultural goods sent to Cuba to paid for in cash by the Cuban government before they can be shipped.

43596 ■ "Coordination of Overseas Efforts is Sought" in *Detroit Free Press* (October 23, 2006)
Pub: Knight-Ridder/Tribune Business News
Ed: Carol Cain. **Description:** Michigan Economic Development Corporation is planning to organize the efforts of the state's small businesses and organizations wishing to expand into foreign markets such as China, Japan, Germany and other countries.

43597 ■ "Costs in international commercial arbitration" in *Dispute Resolution Journal* (Vol. 56, No. 1, February-April 2001, pp. 30)
Pub: American Arbitration Association
Ed: Murray L. Smith. **Description:** Questions regarding legal costs in commercial arbitration when practice and laws vary depending on countries involved, are addressed.

43598 ■ *Council of Asian American Business Associations of California—Directory*
Pub: Council of Asian American Business Associations of California
Ed: Darlene Mar, Editor, darlenemar@worldnet.att.net. **Released:** Annual, April. **Price:** $50, individuals plus $5.00 shipping or donation requested. **Covers:** over 2,000 Asian-American professional, commercial, and industrial firms; 10 plus trade associations. **Entries Include:** Company name, address, phone, name of contact, product or service provided, number of employees, whether minority certified, market area, licenses; some listings include clients. **Arrangement:** Classified by Standard Industrial Classification (SIC) code, alphabetical. **Indexes:** Company name, association name, SIC number.

43599 ■ "The Counterfeit Catastrophe; Curbing Piracy Is As Urgent As Taking Down Trade Barriers" in *Business Week* **(February 7, 2005, pp. 96)**
Pub: McGraw-Hill Companies
Description: Issues involved with email spam, both nationally and internationally, are discussed, especially as it relates to international trade.

43600 ■ *Country Studies in Entrepreneurship: A Historical Perspective*
Pub: Palgrave Macmillan
Ed: Ioanna Minoglou; Cassis Youssef. **Released:** July 2006. **Price:** $80.00. **Description:** Comparison of eight national entrepreneurial ventures, covering three continents, is discussed.

43601 ■ "Cracks in the Melting Pot" in *Inc.* **(Volume 27, December 2005, No. 12, pp. 27-29)**
Pub: Inc. Magazine
Ed: Stephanie Clifford. **Description:** Because of stiff Visa restrictions, entrepreneurial immigrants are finding opportunities overseas. Statistical data included.

43602 ■ *Creating Capitalism Joint-Stock Enterprise in British Politics and Culture, 1800-1870*
Pub: Royal Historical Society
Ed: James Taylor. **Released:** October 2006. **Price:** $80.00. **Description:** The growth of joint-stock business in Victorian Britain is discussed, particularly the resistance to it.

43603 ■ "Critics: Free Trade Comes at a Price" in *Business First Buffalo* **(Vol. 19, No. 44, July 25, 2003, pp. 1)**
Pub: American City Business Journals, Inc.
Ed: Joe Iannarelli. **Description:** Industry analysts state that small manufacturing firms are being hurt by new international free trade agreements. Local companies, such as I Squared R Element Company Inc., have been forced to reduce manufacturing capacity due to these agreements.

43604 ■ "Cross Atlantic Capital Partners" in *Venture Capital Journal* **(Vol. 40, No. 10, November 2000, pp. 56-57)**
Pub: Venture Economics
Description: Gerry McCrory, an Irish entrepreneur came to America in 1998 to visit venture capitalists in Silicon Valley, California and Boston, Massachusetts. Mr. McCrory presented his plans for a strategic partnership between a seed-stage fund based in Ireland and a U.S. venture capital firm. The results of that visit are explored, along with a listing of some of the Cross Atlantic Partners portfolio companies.

43605 ■ "Cross-Border Property Deals" in *The Economist* **(Vol. 376, July 30-August 5, 2005, No. 8437, pp. 67)**
Pub: The Economist Newspaper Ltd.
Description: Property investors are ready to buy and to sell abroad. Property deals by region, including North America, Europe and Asia-Pacific are presented.

43606 ■ "Cuba's prosperous future" in *Hispanic Business* **(Vol. 22, No. 4, April 2000, pp. 38)**
Pub: Hispanic Business
Ed: Christopher D. Lancette. **Description:** The eventual total opening of the Cuban market will result in large profits for many U.S. businesses. Certain industries are already open to U.S. companies and the U.S.-Cuba Trade & Economic Council estimate the $750 million of business was completed between 1994 and 1999.

43607 ■ "Culture Shock" in *Entrepreneur* **(Vol. 31, No. 9, July 2003, pp. 77)**
Pub: Entrepreneur Media, Inc.
Ed: Marc Diener. **Description:** With increasing numbers of international, multinational and transnational corporations, culture is playing a major role in negotiations.

43608 ■ "Customs dictates" in *Entrepreneur* **(Vol. 30, No. 3, March 2)**
Pub: Entrepreneur Media Inc.
Ed: Michelle Prather. **Description:** Since September 11, 2001, importers and exporters can expect to experience greater unpredictability and harsher penalties for violating import/export regulations.

43609 ■ "Customs Expansion Would Hurt Riverfront" in *Crain's Detroit Business* **(Vol. 21, October 24, 2005, No. 43, pp. 8)**
Pub: Crain Communications Inc. - Detroit
Ed: Description: Plans for a new customs inspection area in Detroit would improve international crossings for both freight and vehicle traffic. The plan might also include major retail shops. Some experts fear the plan, which calls for a new road in the middle of downtown, would hurt the new pedestrian-friendly promenade which is bringing visitors to the area.

43610 ■ "Customs plan riles shippers, auto industry" in *Crain's Detroit Business* **(Vol. 19, No. 11, March 17, 2003, pp. 1)**
Pub: Crain Communications Inc., Detroit
Ed: Michael Strong. **Description:** The requirements to file cargo manifests before trucks can cross the U.S. border will costs millions of dollars and add to the cost of purchasing an automobile.

43611 ■ "Cyber-battle for a piece of the pie" in *Hispanic Business* **(Vol. 22, No. 11, November 2000, pp. 44)**
Pub: Hispanic Business
Ed: Andrea Siedsma. **Description:** An overview of the influence of the Internet on the globalization of trade. The need for businesses to offer electronic commerce as a means of trading is discussed.

43612 ■ *D & B Principal International Businesses: The World Marketing Directory*
Pub: Dun & Bradstreet Corp.
Contact: Joan Lehman
Released: Annual. **Price:** $595 commercial & library price. **Covers:** approximately 50,000 leading businesses in all lines, outside of the U.S., in 140 countries. **Entries Include:** Company name, address, phone, fax, D&B number, telex, up to six Standard Industrial Classification (SIC) code, line of business, sales volume (in U.S. currency), number of employees, parent company and location, executive name and title, year established, and import/export designation. **Arrangement:** Geographical. **Indexes:** Geographical, cross-referenced alphabetical, industry classification.

43613 ■ "DCM Nears Final Close" in *Venture Capital Journal* **(Vol. 40, No. 10, October 2000, pp. 22)**
Pub: Venture Economics
Description: Doll Capital plans to invest 20-25 percent of its new fund internationally, with focus in Asia.

43614 ■ "De-Vine Tragedy" in *Forbes* **(Vol. 175, February 14, 2005, No. 3, pp. 56)**
Pub: Forbes Magazine Inc.
Ed: Dirk Smillie. **Description:** Interview with filmmaker, Jonathan Nossiter, where he speaks about his new wine documentary that attacks the globalization of the wine trade and defends small wine producers.

43615 ■ "A Decade of NAFTA" in *Hispanic Business* **(July/August 2004, pp. 42, 44)**
Pub: Hispanic Business
Ed: Debra Beachy. **Description:** Successes and frustrations that have created the new platform for future growth are discussed. Trade investments have increased but there is still controversy over NAFTA's impact.

43616 ■ "Delivering At Domino's Pizza" in *Fortune* **(Vol. 151, February 7, 2005, No. 3, pp. 28)**
Pub: Time Inc.
Ed: Julia Boorstin. **Description:** Domino's Pizza has seen its stock climb 26 percent since going public in July 2004. In an interview with Domino's CEO, David Brandon, he tells how he helped overhaul the company's training program and dropped the employee turnover rate by 60 percent. The franchiser has also opened 1,200 new stores in the past five years, two-thirds of them overseas.

43617 ■ *Democratization Without Representation: The Politics of Small Industry in Mexico*
Pub: Pennsylvania State University Press
Ed: Kenneth C. Shalden. **Released:** July 2005. **Price:** $27.00. **Description:** Opportunities for individuals to participate in Mexico's democracy and how it is affecting the way industries do business.

43618 ■ "Despite Flaws, Franchise System is Solid" in *Automotive News* **(Vol. 79, January 31, 2005, No. 6132, pp. 12)**
Pub: Crain Communications Inc.
Ed: Keith Crain. **Description:** Franchising is still the best method for selling and distributing vehicles in the U.S.

43619 ■ *Destination Japan: A Business Guide for the 90s*
Pub: Superintendent of Documents
Ed: Eric Kennedy. **Released:** 1991. **Price:** $30.00. **Description:** Provides information for U.S. businesses interested in exporting products to Japan, including export financing assistance programs, customs clearance documentation, foreign trade barriers, and property protection rights in Japan.

43620 ■ "Detroit Free Press Small Business Column" in *Detroit Free Press* **(June 13, 2005)**
Pub: Knight-Ridder/Tribune Business News
Ed: Carol Cain. **Description:** Profile of Paul Sowinski, 19-year-old entrepreneur, who sells computer supplies to 2,100 Michigan customers, with growth projected as far away as Guam and Antigua.

43621 ■ "Detroit Free Press Wayne Small Business Column" in *Detroit Free Press* **(June 9, 2005)**
Pub: Knight-Ridder/Tribune Business News
Ed: Carol Cain. **Description:** Brian Kruger, owner of the Dutch software firm specializing in publishing products, has chosen the Ford Building in Downtown Detroit to locate WoodWing USA Inc. The firm has grown to eight employees since opening in 2003.

43622 ■ "Detroiters eye Iraq contracts" in *Crain's Detroit Business* **(Vol. 19, No. 15, April 14, 2003, pp. 1)**
Pub: Crain Communications Inc., Detroit
Ed: Jennette Smith, Brent Snavely. **Description:** Many metropolitan Detroit companies are hoping to win contracts to help rebuild Iraq. U.S. Representative John Dingell is calling for the General Accounting Office to investigate the process of contracting awards.

43623 ■ *Developmental Entrepreneurship: Adversity, Risk, and Isolation*
Pub: Elsevier Science and Technology Books
Ed: Craig Galbraith. **Released:** August 2006. **Price:** $99.95. **Description:** Volume five of the series, this book focuses on the fields of entrepreneurship, sociology, and economics. Fifteen articles related to entrepreneurship and small business development within a global environment are included.

43624 ■ "Diplomat Sells Trade with China at Tacoma, Wash., Symposium" in *News Tribune* **(April 11, 2003)**
Pub: Knight-Ridder/Tribune Business News
Ed: Al Gibbs. **Description:** According to Wang Yunxiang, China's consul general in San Francisco, increasing interaction between the United States and China will benefit both sides. Wang is in Tacoma, Washington speaking at a three-day symposium sponsored by the Wang Center for International Programs at Pacific Lutheran University.

43625 ■ *Directory of American Firms Operating in Foreign Countries*
Pub: Uniworld Business Publications Inc.
Ed: Barbara D. Fiorito, Editor. **Released:** Biennial, odd years; latest edition 17, January 2003. **Price:** $400, individuals hardcover, plus shipping charges; $975, individuals CD-ROM. **Covers:** about 3,000 American corporations with 36,300 subsidiaries or af-

filiates outside the United States. **Entries Include:** Company name, address, phone; names and titles of key personnel; number of employees, annual sales, NAICS code, web address, locations and types of facilities in foreign countries, number of employees, product/service. Separate country editions also available. **Arrangement:** Alphabetical. **Indexes:** Foreign operation by country.

43626 ■ *Directory of North American International Trade Associations*
Pub: Federation of International Trade Associations
Contact: Nelson T. Joyner
Price: Free. **Covers:** 450 member trade associations in the U.S., Canada, and Mexico. **Entries Include:** Association name, address, phone, fax, e-mail, web, President/Exec. Dir. **Arrangement:** Geographical, alphabetical, categorical.

43627 ■ *Doing Business in Asia: A Small Business Guide to Success in the World's Most Dynamic Market*
Pub: F & W Publications
Ed: David L. James. **Released:** 1993. **Price:** $18.95 (paper). **Description:** Provides information for small and medium-sized companies on doing business in Asia's principal markets.

43628 ■ "Dollars in the Deals" in *Hispanic Business* (Vol. 23, No. 11, November 2001, pp. 52, 54)
Pub: Hispanic Business Inc.
Ed: Jonathan J. Higuera. **Description:** The top 50 exporters in the United States realize that a strong dollar hurts markets overseas and focus on marketing strategies to overcome it. Uncertainties faced by various exporters are discussed.

43629 ■ "Drug Importation and the Capital Markets" in *Venture Capital Journal* (November 1, 2004)
Pub: Thomason Financial Inc.
Description: Issues involving the importation of prescription drugs are covered. An examination of the economics behind cross-border shipment of drugs is essential in order to understand the affects of importation. Canadian and European governments are able to name the price they will pay for a particular drug and the Canadian government pays only the cost of manufacturing with a small markup, while American consumers not only pay manufacturing costs, but also research and development, administrative along with a markup.

43630 ■ "Economics Focus" in *The Economist* (Vol. 377, October 22-28, 2005, No. 8449, pp. 81)
Pub: The Economist Newspaper Ltd.
Description: Inflation is being determined by global rather than local economic forces. Statistical data included.

43631 ■ *The Economics and Management of Small Business: An International Perspective*
Pub: Routledge
Ed: Graham Bannock. **Released:** April 2005. **Price:** $132.00 (US), $190.00 (Canadian). **Description:** International perspectives on the economics and management of small business, featuring case studies and empirical research.

43632 ■ "Economist Says Focus on Emerging Markets to Boost Foreign Trade" in *Portland Press Herald* (June 17, 2005)
Pub: Blethen Maine Newspapers, Inc.
Ed: Edward D. Murphy. **Description:** Emerging economies present the greatest opportunity for businesses looking to increase foreign trade. Maine ranked ninth among states in export growth from 2000 to 2004. Statistical data included.

43633 ■ "Education" in *Business Week* (January 9, 2006, No. 3966, pp. 40-43)
Pub: McGraw-Hill Companies
Ed: Louis Lavelle. **Description:** China will require 75,000 business executives with international experience by year 2010, 70,000 more than exist today. The country is equipping its schools with programs offering Western management ideas to better serve its growing global economy.

43634 ■ *Effect of the Overvalued Dollar on Small Exporters: Congressional Hearing*
Pub: DIANE Publishing Company
Ed: Donald Manzullo. **Released:** October 2004. **Price:** $30.00. **Description:** Congressional hearing: Witnesses: Dr. Lawrence Chimerine, Economist; Tony Raimondo, President and CEO, Behlen Manufacturing Company; Robert J. Weskamp, President, Wes-Tech, Inc.; Wayne Dollar, President, Georgia Farm Bureau; and Vargese George, President and CEO, Westex International, Inc. Appendix includes correspondence sent to committee on the overvalued dollar.

43635 ■ "Effects of SARS Hit Colorado Firms' Dealings with Asia" in *Denver Post* (April 11, 2003)
Pub: Knight-Ridder/Tribune Business News
Ed: Marsha Austin. **Description:** The SARS epidemic hitting China has caused many Colorado companies to ban business travel to China, Hong Kong and other Asian countries.

43636 ■ "Embrace the Deficit" in *Wall Street Journal* (Vol. 248, January 2007, No. 146, pp. B1-B3)
Pub: Dow Jones & Co. Inc.
Ed: David Malpass **Description:** U.S. trade deficit may not be as weak and unbalanced as it seems at first glance.

43637 ■ "Employing Her Literary Skills" in *San Diego Business Journal* (Vol. 28, January 8, 2007, No. 2, pp. 10)
Pub: San Diego Business Journal Associates
Ed: Michelle Mowad. **Description:** Profile of Professor Susan Bisom-Rapp, author of a new book on international and comparative employment law. The book covers laws in nine countries, including labor and employment law regulations.

43638 ■ "The End of Corporate Imperialism" in *Harvard Business Review* (Vol. 81, No. 8, August 2003, pp. 109)
Pub: Harvard Business School Press
Ed: C.K. Prahalad, Kenneth Lieberthal. **Description:** Western business models have been shown to be of minimal value outside of Europe and Northern America when companies consider foreign operations.

43639 ■ "End of Some Tariffs a Boon to Suppliers" in *Crain's Detroit Business* (Vol. 22, December 18, 2006, No. 51, pp. 6)
Pub: Crain Communications Inc. - Detroit
Ed: Brent Snavely. **Description:** Relaxation of tariffs on corrosion resistant steels will reduce supply costs for automotive suppliers. Tariffs were removed for imports from France, Canada, Australia, and Japan but remain in effect for Korea and Germany.

43640 ■ "Enhance your people skills" in *Women In Business* (Vol. 52, No. 5, September-October 2000, pp. 34)
Pub: The ABWA Co., Inc.
Ed: Diane Domeyer. **Description:** Issues are presented concerning the benefits of implementing a team-based business environment. The skills that are required by personnel involved in team-based projects are explored.

43641 ■ *The Entrepreneurial Culture Network Advantage Within Chinese and Irish Software Firms*
Pub: Edward Elgar Publishing, Incorporated
Ed: Tsang. **Released:** October 2006. **Price:** $95.00. **Description:** Ways national cultural heritage influences entrepreneurial ventures are discussed.

43642 ■ *Entrepreneurial Strategies: New Technologies and Emerging Markets*
Pub: Blackwell Publishing Limited
Ed: Arnold Cooper; Sharon Alvarez; Alejandro Carrera; Luiz Mesquita; Robert Vassolo. **Released:** August 2006. **Price:** $69.95. **Description:** Ideas to help a small business expand into emerging market economies (EMEs) are discussed. Despite the high failure rate, this book helps a small firm develop a successful plan.

43643 ■ *Entrepreneurship: Frameworks and Empirical Investigations from Forthcoming Leaders of European Research*
Pub: Elsevier Science and Technology Books
Ed: Johan Wiklund; Dimo Dimov; Jerome A. Katz; Dean Shepherd. **Released:** July 2006. **Price:** $99.95. **Description:** Entrepreneurial research and theory cover the early growth of research-based startups and the role of learning in international entrepreneurship, focusing on Europe.

43644 ■ *Entrepreneurship, Investment and Spatial Dynamics Lessons and Implications for an Enlarged EU*
Pub: Edward Elgar Publishing, Incorporated
Ed: Nijkamp. **Released:** September 2006. **Price:** $100.00. **Description:** Understanding the impact and interaction between investment, knowledge and entrepreneurship with an expanding European Union.

43645 ■ *Entrepreneurship and Small Business*
Pub: Palgrave Macmillan
Ed: Paul Burns. **Released:** January 2007. **Price:** $74.95. **Description:** Entrepreneurial skills, focusing on good management practices are discussed. Topics include family businesses, corporate, international and social entrepreneurship.

43646 ■ *Entrepreneurship and SMEs in the Euro-Zone*
Pub: Imperial College Press
Ed: Dana. **Released:** May 2006. **Price:** $48.00. **Description:** Information regarding entrepreneurship and SMEs in Europe is presented.

43647 ■ *European Marketing: A Strategic Guide to the New Opportunities*
Pub: Irwin Professional Publishing
Ed: Richard Lynch. **Price:** $35.00. **Description:** Discusses development and implementation of an effective pan-European marketing strategy. Includes specific suggestions and examples of North American companies that have opened the global doors.

43648 ■ "The Explosion of Chinese Imports Has Changed U.S. Manufacturers In Many Ways" in *Inc.* (May 1, 2005)
Pub: Inc. Magazine
Ed: Darren Dahl. **Description:** The need for a policy that does not allow the U.S. to be abused by liberalized trade is discussed, focusing on Chinese competitors.

43649 ■ "The Explosion of Chinese Imports Has Changed US Manufacturers In Many Ways-Including How They Lobby in Washington" in *Inc.* (May1,2005)
Pub: Inc. Magazine
Ed: Darren Dahl. **Description:** The need for a policy that does not allow the U.S. to be abused by liberalized trade is discussed, focusing on Chinese competitors.

43650 ■ "Export Advice" in *Entrepreneur* (Vol. 33, January 2005, No. 1, pp. 72)
Pub: Entrepreneur Media Inc.
Ed: Joshua Kurlantzick. **Description:** Small business exporters are among the fastest-growing sectors of American entrepreneurs in the U.S. The Department of Commerce has developed a new Website geared to assist smaller American export companies.

43651 ■ "The Export Engine Is Shifting Into High Gear" in *Business Week* (January 16, 2006, No. 3967, pp. 23-24)
Pub: McGraw-Hill Companies
Ed: James C. Cooper. **Description:** U. S. exporters are expected to benefit from the growing world economy despite a drop in the U.S. dollar. Recent studies show more balance in the growing global economy. Statistical data included.

43652 ■ *Export Profits: A Guide for Small Business*
Pub: Upstart Publishing Co., Inc.
Ed: Jack S. Wolf. **Released:** 1992. **Price:** $19.95 (paper). **Description:** Discusses finding the right for-

eign markets for a product, minimizing currency risks and red tape, and seeking expert assistance. Includes a glossary, and lists of resources and sample documents.

43653 ■ *Export Sales and Marketing Manual*
Pub: Export Institute
Contact: John R. Jagoe, Dir.
E-mail: jrj@exportinstitute.com
Released: Annual, January. **Publication Includes:** List of approximately 4,000 international trade contacts, including World Trade Centers, U.S. Department of Commerce Trade Specialists and Country Desk Officers, State International Trade offices, small business development centers, U.S. Customs services, U.S. Port Authorities, U.S. embassies, foreign trade associations in the U.S., and chambers of commerce in foreign countries, and foreign embassies and chambers of commerce in the U.S. **Entries Include:** Name, address, phone, fax, name and title of contact, geographical area served, products covered, description of services, and 1,200 internet addresses of export-related sites. Principal content of publication is a step-by-step program showing U.S. companies and entrepreneurs how to begin exporting or increase their existing overseas sales. **Arrangement:** Classified by product/service and export marketing funcions. **Indexes:** General, international trade or export/import.

43654 ■ "The Exporting Advantage" in *Inc.* (August 2005, pp. 40, 42)
Pub: Inc. Magazine
Ed: Jeff Bailey. **Description:** Brothers Jon, Keith and Mark Pavlansky sell rubber dirt to Mexican growers. Their company, Hibco Plastics transformed their company while increasing sales by marketing their products in Mexico.

43655 ■ "Eyes on Iraq; 'I'd rather go with a Michigan company'" in *Crain's Detroit Business* (Vol. 19, No. 16, April 21, 2003, pp. 3)
Pub: Crain Communications Inc., Detroit
Ed: Michael Strong. **Description:** An Iraqi-born scientist living in the metropolitan Detroit area, and owner of an environmental consulting business, feels American companies should be a part of rebuilding the country of Iraq.

43656 ■ "February sales at Claire's jump 6 percent" in *Daily Business Review* (Vol. 77, No. 187, March 7, 2003)
Pub: American Lawyer Media LP
Ed: AnaMaria Colmenares. **Description:** Claire's Stores sales rose 6 percent despite a plunge in consumer confidence and a drop in national retail sales. The company currently operates 2,900 stores worldwide and is looking to expand into Spain. Statistical data included.

43657 ■ "For U.S. Small Biz, Fertile Soil in Europe" in *Business Week Online* (April 3, 2002)
Pub: McGraw-Hill, Inc.
Description: This year 2002 is turning out to be a great year for many small and midsize American companies selling to or operating in Europe, especially high-tech companies.

43658 ■ "Foreign Affairs" in *Entrepreneur* (Vol. 33, March 2005, No. 3, pp. 56)
Pub: Entrepreneur Media Inc.
Ed: C.J. Prince. **Description:** Strategies to help small businesses begin exporting products to overseas markets are given.

43659 ■ "Foreign currency" in *Entrepreneur* (Vol. 30, No. 10, October 2002, pp. 58)
Pub: Entrepreneur Media Inc.
Ed: Crystal Detamore-Rodman. **Description:** Profile of Steve Lamond, who launched International Turbine Systems Inc. in 1992; Lamond tells how he was able to borrow capital through government-guaranteed loans to start his firm.

43660 ■ "Foreign expansion of small firms: the impact of domestic alternatives" in *Journal of Business Venturing* (Vol. 16, No. 6, Nov. 2001)
Pub: Elsevier Science, Inc.
Ed: Rongxin Chen, Marc J. Martin. **Description:** Research investigating factors influencing small foreign expansion plans of small firms is presented. It is concluded that the types of products offered and the domestic size of the small company tend to influence the success of its foreign expansion.

43661 ■ "Foreign Targets" in *Hispanic Business* (July/August 2004, pp. 48)
Pub: Hispanic Business
Ed: Michael Caplinger. **Description:** Wholesalers and manufactures share insight into winning in a competitive global market. Statistical data included.

43662 ■ "The Forgotten Strategy" in *Harvard Business Review* (Vol. 81, No. 11, November 2003, pp. 76)
Pub: Harvard Business School Press
Ed: Pankaj Ghemawat. **Description:** Potential changes in business globalization strategies are examined.

43663 ■ "Franklin pitches Atlanta to free-trade delegates" in *Atlanta Business Chronicle* (Vol. 25, November 8, 2002, No. 22 pp. 1A)
Pub: American City Business Publications, Inc.
Ed: Walter Woods. **Description:** Atlanta Mayor, Shirley Franklin, is trying to persuade the Free Trade Area of the Americas (FTAA) to locate its headquarters in Atlanta, Georgia. FTAA is a trade federation of 34 Western democracies that is slated to take effect by 2005.

43664 ■ "From Feast to Famine?" in *Hispanic Business* (Vol. 23, No. 11, November 2001, pp. 42, 44, 46, 48-49)
Pub: Hispanic Business Inc.
Ed: Scott Williams. **Description:** Export revenues for Hispanic companies grew in 2000, but the slowing economy may halt further growth in certain sectors. Statistics on the fastest-growing top 50 exporters, top 50 exporters by state and by sector is included.

43665 ■ "GlitzyShow, Worry Galore" in *Wall Street Journal* (Vol. 249 January 2007, No. 5, pp. A2)
Pub: Dow Jones & Co. Inc.
Ed: Associated Press. **Description:** Despite the glitzy displays of the North American Auto Show, auto-industry executives worry that 2007 may be one of the weakest years in more than a decade. Emerging markets in India and Eastern Europe are still relatively small and in the case of China, increasingly competitive.

43666 ■ *Global E-Commerce: Impacts of National Environment and Policy*
Pub: Cambridge University Press
Ed: Kenneth L. Kraemer; Jason Dedrick; Nigel P. Melville; Kevin Zhu. **Released:** August 2006. **Price:** $75.00. **Description:** Global assessment of the impact of e-business on companies as well as countries.

43667 ■ "Global Economy Reaches Into Your Wallet" in *Hispanic Business* (March 2005, pp. 6)
Pub: Hispanic Business
Ed: Jesus Chavarria. **Description:** Although the U.S. continues to increase its exports the growth of imports remains larger, hurting the U.S. economy.

43668 ■ *Global Electronic Business Research: Opportunities and Directions*
Pub: Idea Group Publishing
Ed: Nabeel A.Y. Al-Qirim. **Released:** October 2005. **Description:** Importance electronic commerce research plays in small to medium-sized enterprises in various countries.

43669 ■ "Global Entrepreneur" in *Inc.* (September 2005, pp. 48, 50)
Pub: Inc. Magazine

Ed: Lora Kolodny. **Description:** Chuck Foley, CEO of Tacit Networks, explains how he expanded his firm globally. Tacit makes software that enables instant file sharing between networks no matter the distance.

43670 ■ *Global Guide To International Business*
Pub: Facts on File, Inc.
Ed: David Hoopes and Kathleen R. Hoopes. **Price:** $180.00. **Description:** Provides information on international business operations. Organized into geographic regions and countries.

43671 ■ *The Global Learning Organization: Gaining Competitive Advantage through Continuous Learning*
Pub: Irwin Professional Publishing
Ed: Michael Marquardt and Angus Reynolds. **Price:** $32.50. **Description:** Provides instruction on how organizations can become learning organizations in the global context.

43672 ■ *Global Quality: A Synthesis of the World's Best Management Methods*
Pub: Irwin Professional Publishing
Ed: Richard Tabor Greene. **Released:** 1994. **Price:** $75.00. **Description:** Co-published with ASQC Quality Press. Offers 24 management approaches used worldwide, plus seven new quality improvement techniques being used in Japan.

43673 ■ "Global Trade" in *Entrepreneur.com* (Vol. 34, February 2006, No. 2, pp. 120)
Pub: Entrepreneur Media Inc.
Ed: Nichole L. Torres. **Description:** Careful research and planning are required to start an international business. Many colleges are offering international business courses to help entrepreneurs understand issues concerning taxes, trade law, currency conversion, language translation and cultural understanding.

43674 ■ "Global Trader" in *Hispanic Business* (April 2005, pp. 40, 42)
Pub: Hispanic Business
Ed: Luisa Beltran. **Description:** Profile of Carmen Suro-Bredie, Assistant U.S. Trade Representative for Policy Coordination. Suro-Bredie believes women are natural negotiators with a commitment to the peace process that ensures a more Democratic trade agreement.

43675 ■ *Global Training: How to Design a Program for the Multinational Corporation*
Pub: Irwin Professional Publishing
Ed: Sylvia B. Odenwald. **Price:** $30.00. **Description:** Co-published with the American Society for Training and Development. Provides tips and advice for researching, developing, and implementing an international training program.

43676 ■ "Globalized Economy a Double-Edged Sword for Americans" in *Altanta Journal-Constitution* (January 18, 2007)
Pub: Cox Newspapers, Inc.
Ed: Michael E. Kanell. **Description:** Foreign investment and trade is impacting Americans in various ways and widening the gap between the rich and middle class.

43677 ■ "Go South" in *Entrepreneur* (Vol. 33, October 2005, No. 10, pp. 26)
Pub: Entrepreneur Media Inc.
Ed: Stephen Barlas. **Description:** The new free-trade agreement with five Central American countries includes Costa Rica, the Dominican Republic, El Salvador, Guatemala, Honduras and Nicaragua. The new agreement will expand small business exports to the area. Statistical data included.

43678 ■ "Going Global" in *Home Office Computing* (Vol. 18, No. 10, October 2000, pp. 87)
Pub: Scholastic Inc.
Ed: David Harvey. **Description:** Small and home-based business are increasingly able to do business abroad by leveraging the power of the Internet and locating online tools and resources for tapping overseas markets. Steps to building an effective Web site are covered.

43679 ■ **"Going Global: International Business Tips Make a World of Difference"** in *Entrepreneur* (Vol. 32, December 2004, No. 12, pp. 34)
Pub: Entrepreneur Media Inc.
Ed: Aliza Pilar Sherman. **Description:** Tips for women business owners to follow when expanding markets and increasing sales by doing business with overseas vendors and clients.

43680 ■ *Grassroots NGOs by Women for Women: The Driving Force of Development in India*
Pub: SAGE Publications, Incorporated
Ed: Femida Handy; Meenaz Kassam; Suzanne Feeney; Bhagyashree Ranade. **Released:** July 2006. **Price:** $29.95. **Description:** Understanding the role of non-governmental organizations in women's development is offered through interviews with twenty women in India who have founded NGOs serving women.

43681 ■ **"The Great Transition"** in *Harvard Business Review* (Vol. 81, No. 10, October 2003, pp. 70)
Pub: Harvard Business School Press
Ed: Kenneth Kieberthal, Geoffrey Lieberthal. **Description:** Opportunities and perils faced by multinational corporations in the U.S. planning to set up operations in China are discussed. Specific suggestions are offered to help avoid or minimize problems.

43682 ■ *Greater Phoenix Chamber Membership List—International Trade Businesses*
Pub: Greater Phoenix Chamber of Commerce
Price: $23, members; $28, nonmembers; $25, members disk; $30, nonmembers disk. **Covers:** 222 businesses involved in international trade in the greater Phoenix, Arizona area. **Entries Include:** Contact details.

43683 ■ **"'Gridlock' Guru Studies Border Crossings; Report May Recharge Political Discussions"** in *Crain's Detroit Business* (Vol. 21)
Pub: Crain Communications Inc. - Detroit
Ed: Michelle Martinez. **Description:** The need for another border crossing between Detroit, Michigan and Windsor, Ontario, Canada is being discussed again. Three groups are vying for constructing a second crossing.

43684 ■ **"Group Quietly Pushes for New Bridge to Canada"** in *Crain's Detroit Business* (Vol. 19, No. 45, November 10, 2003, pp. 1)
Pub: Crain Communications Inc., Detroit
Ed: Michael Strong. **Description:** Proposal for a new crossing between Detroit, Michigan and Windsor, Ontario, Canada are discussed.

43685 ■ *Growing Your Business International*
Pub: Probus Publishing Co., Inc.
Ed: M. Bedward and M. Anderson. **Released:** 1992. **Price:** $24.95 (paper); $34.95 (Canada). **Description:** Covers how to form partnerships and joint ventures overseas.

43686 ■ *Growth Oriented Women Entrepreneurs and Their Businesses: A Global Research Perspective*
Pub: Edward Elgar Publishing, Incorporated
Ed: Candida G. Brush. **Released:** June 2006. **Price:** $135.00. **Description:** Roles women play in entrepreneurship globally and their economic impact are examined.

43687 ■ **"The Hague: Laws without Borders"** in *Red Herring* (No. 106, October 15, 2001, pp. 25-26)
Pub: Herring Communications
Ed: Julia Lawlor. **Description:** Important information regarding the Hague Convention on Jurisdiction and Foreign Judgments in Civil Matters is covered. The Hague treaty would deal with civil lawsuits and would require that laws regarding matters like libel, copyright, patents, and trademarks - which differ among countries - be enforced uniformly in the 53 nations participating in treaty talks.

43688 ■ **"Handicapping the Hispanic Economy"** in *Hispanic Business* (November 2002, pp. 18-20)
Pub: Hispanic Business
Description: The future trends in elections, labor, international trade, technology education and banking access to loans are discussed by experts.

43689 ■ **"Hands On"** in *Inc.* (Volume 27, July 2005, No. 7, pp. 31-32)
Pub: Inc. Magazine
Ed: Jeff Bailey. **Description:** Profile of Terry Noon, owner of Capacitor Industries, importer of low-cost electronic components from China and sells them to motor makers and other manufacturers in the U.S. and abroad.

43690 ■ **"Help Wanted"** in *Entrepreneur.com* (Vol. 34, February 2006, No. 2, pp. 80)
Pub: Entrepreneur Media Inc.
Ed: Chris Penttila. **Description:** Globalization, outsourcing and competition for capital are putting pressure on small companies to operate more like large businesses. Ideas for hiring CEOs for a small firm are included.

43691 ■ **"Helping Hands Overseas"** in *Hispanic Business* (November 2003, pp. 52, 54)
Pub: Hispanic Business
Ed: Scott Williams. **Description:** Companies on the Hispanic Business Top 50 Exporters directory look to federal programs to help in foreign markets. Statistical data included.

43692 ■ **"The hidden challenge of cross-border negotiations"** in *Harvard Business Review* (Vol. 80, No. 3, March 2002, pp. 76)
Pub: Harvard Business School Press
Ed: James K. Sebenius. **Description:** A discussion of how national culture can influence decision-making and governance in business. Strategies for how businesses can conduct themselves are examined.

43693 ■ **"The Hidden Dragon"** in *Harvard Business Review* (Vol. 81, No. 10, October 2003, pp. 92)
Pub: Harvard Business School Press
Ed: Ming Zeng, Peter J. Williamson. **Description:** Multinational corporations should give up preconceived notions about China and Chinese products and being prepared for exports of consumer goods from China that are already competing in the U.S. and globally, to the disadvantage of many multinationals and taking away market share.

43694 ■ **"A Hidden Gem? Quebec Looks To Flex Muscle"** in *Venture Capital Journal* (Vol. 42, No. 5, May 2002, pp. 44-45)
Pub: Thomas Venture Economics
Ed: Danielle Fugazy. **Description:** American venture capitalists have not invested much in Quebec's industry in the past, but the continuous growth Quebec is seeing in the fields of engineering, transportation, telecommunications, aeronautics and aerospace technology, medical research, computer science and biotechnology, has American VCs taking a second look.

43695 ■ **"The Hispanic Business 2002 Top 50 Exporters"** in *Hispanic Business* (November 2002, pp. 38-39)
Pub: Hispanic Business
Description: A listing of the top 50 Hispanic companies exporting goods includes ranking, company name and location, CEO, number of employees, number of Hispanic employees, 2001 revenues, revenue from exports, 2001 export sales, 2000 export sales, 2000-2001 export sales growth percentages, products or services, and destination.

43696 ■ **"How Can I Find the Right Business Contacts in China?"** in *Inc.* (Volume 27, June 2005, No. 6, pp. 48)
Pub: Inc. Magazine
Description: Information for starting an export-import business with Chinese businesses is offered. The U.S. Department of Commerce arranges meetings between American companies and foreign agents through its Gold Key Matching Service.

43697 ■ **"How China Will Change Your Business"** in *Inc.* (Volume 27, March 2005, No. 3, pp. 70-80, 84)
Pub: Inc. Magazine
Ed: Ted C. Fishman. **Description:** Fourteen important issues for entrepreneurs regarding China's economic expansion are covered.

43698 ■ **"How to Improve Georgia's Economy"** in *Atlanta Business Chronicle* (Vol. 25, December 6, 2002, No. 26, pp. 35A)
Pub: American City Business Publications, Inc.
Ed: Georgia **Description:** Governor-elect, Sonny Perdue, should back the Metro Atlanta Chamber of Commerce's attempts to attract the secretariat of the Free Trade Area of the Americas to the city. He should also consider opening field offices of the Georgia Department of Industry, Trade and Tourism in Latin American cities.

43699 ■ *How to Succeed in Exporting and Doing Business Internationally*
Pub: John Wiley & Sons, Inc.
Ed: Eric Sletten. **Released:** 1994. **Price:** $45.00; $17.95 (paper).

43700 ■ **"I'd Like to Buy Machinery From China"** in *Inc.* (September 2005, pp. 53)
Pub: Inc. Magazine
Description: When purchasing equipment from China, can American businesses hold Chinese manufacturers responsible if machines violate patent laws?

43701 ■ **"Illicit Affairs?"** in *Entrepreneur* (Vol. 32)
Pub: Entrepreneur Media Inc.
Ed: Jane Easter Bahls. **Description:** The Foreign Corrupt Practice Act (FCPA), enacted by Congress in 1977, prohibits the use of bribery of officials in other countries in order to do business overseas. It is illegal to make payments, promises, or offers of anything of value to foreign officials to obtain or retain business, or to make payments to a third party.

43702 ■ **"Immigration Reform, Latin American Trade Issues Piled on Congress's Plate"** in *Hispanic Business* (November 2006, pp. 24)
Pub: Hispanic Business
Ed: Patricia Guadalupe. **Description:** Immigration and trade issues with Latin American countries and Mexico are discussed.

43703 ■ **"Improvements, Programs May Help Speed Traffic Over Ambassador Bridge"** in *Crain's Detroit Business* (Vol. 19, November 10, 2003)
Pub: Crain Communications Inc., Detroit
Ed: Michael Strong. **Description:** The Detroit International Bridge Company is building a larger truck inspection area that will accommodate 45 more trucks, as well as building four new customs inspections booths. The expanded area will help ensure trucks getting across as quickly as possible.

43704 ■ **"In Search of Global Leaders"** in *Harvard Business Review* (Vol. 81, No. 8, August 2003, pp. 38)
Pub: Harvard Business School Press
Description: Stephen Green (CEO of HSBC), Fred Hassan (Chairman and CEO of Shering-Plough), Jeffrey Immelt (Chairman and CEO of General Electric), Michael Marks (CEO of Flextronics), and Daniel Meiland (Executive Chairman of Egon Zdhndr International) all express views about what global means, within an economic framework.

43705 ■ **"India Set to Enter U.S. Auto Market"** in *Altanta Journal-Constitution* (February 4, 2007)
Pub: Cox Newspapers, Inc.
Ed: Dan Chapman. **Description:** India is set to sell utility vehicles in the U.S. by 2009. The vehicles include Indian SUVs, crossovers and pickup trucks.

43706 ■ "Indian Retail Reform" in *The Economist* **(Vol. 376, July 16-22, 2005, No. 8435, pp. 39-40)**
Pub: The Economist Newspaper Ltd.
Description: Wal-Mart and other American companies are working to break into India's retail sector, which has been closed to outsiders for a long time. Many large retailers are using India as a significant source of supplies to support their efforts.

43707 ■ "Innovation drain" in *Crain's Detroit Business* **(Vol. 19, No. 1, Jan. 6, 2003, pp. 3)**
Pub: Crain Communications Inc., Detroit
Ed: Terry Kosdrosky. **Description:** Automotive industry analysts are predicting that cost reductions demanded by the Big Three on suppliers could result in business going to foreign competitors.

43708 ■ "Innovation and Incentives: VCs Find Partner in Quebec" in *Venture Capital Journal* **(Vol. 42, No. 5, May 2002, pp. 47)**
Pub: Thomas Venture Economics
Ed: Alistair Christopher. **Description:** The Quebec government offers a research and development tax credit to local businesses, which is attracting the attention of U.S. venture capitalists.

43709 ■ *International Business*
Pub: American Institute of Certified Public Accountants (AICPA)
Ed: Mark F. Murray. **Released:** 1993. **Price:** $11.25. **Description:** Booklet covering payment arrangements, exporting, and foreign currency risk.

43710 ■ *International Business Handbook*
Pub: The Haworth Press, Inc.
Ed: Vishnu H. Kirpalani, editor. **Released:** 1990. **Price:** $89.95.

43711 ■ *International Business Resource Guide DFW: Free Low cost Assistant to Start or Expand Your International Business*
Pub: Sinclair International Business Resources
Released: 1997. **Price:** $20.00.

43712 ■ *International Directory of Importers*
Pub: Interdata
Released: Annual, latest edition 2004-2005. **Price:** $485, individuals "Europe" (three volumes); postpaid; $385, individuals "Asia/Pacific" (two volumes); postpaid; $250, individuals Middle East printed edition - regular mail; $1,345, individuals Middle East printed edition - airmail. **Description:** A nine-volume series that covers over 150,000 importers and distributors in 178 countries throughout the world. Separate volumes or regional editions: "Asia/Pacific (two volumes)," 30,000 importers in Australia, Bangladesh, China, Hong Kong, India, Indonesia, Kazakhstan, Malaysia, Mauritius, Nepal, New Zealand, Pakistan, Philippines, Singapore, South Korea, South Pacific Islands, Sri Lanka, Taiwan, and Thailand; "Europe" (three volumes), 54,000 importers in Austria, Belgium, Belarus, Bulgaria, Croatia, Czech Republic, Estonia, Denmark, Finland, France, Germany, Greece, Hungary, Iceland, Ireland, Italy, Latvia, Lithuania, Macedonia, Netherlands, Norway, Poland, Portugal, Romania, Russia, Slovakia, Spain, Sweden, Switzerland, Ukraine Republic, and the United Kingdom; "Middle East," 14,000 importers in Bahrain, Egypt, Iran, Israel, Jordan, Kuwait, Lebanon, Malta, Oman, Qatar, Saudi Arabia, Syria, Turkey, United Arab Emirates, and Yemen; "North America," 20,000 United States and Ca **Arrangement:** Classified by product. **Indexes:** Geographical, product.

43713 ■ "International E-Commerce: The Time is Now" in *E-business Advisor* **(Vol. 18, No. 10, October 2000, pp. 28)**
Pub: Advisor Media, Inc.
Ed: Donald DePalma. **Description:** Internet usage is not just limited to the United States. It is exploding worldwide, and therefore, offers the opportunity to gain international customers. It is important for Web sites to be designed to entice these international "visitors", while being aware of customs, laws and politics specific to the potential customer's country.

43714 ■ *International Entrepreneurship*
Pub: Edward Elgar Publishing, Incorporated
Ed: Oviatt. **Released:** March 2007. **Price:** $295.00. **Description:** Universities are focusing research efforts on international entrepreneurship. The book features critical articles on the topic.

43715 ■ *International Entrepreneurship Education Issues and Newness*
Pub: Edward Elgar Publishing, Incorporated
Ed: Fayolle. **Released:** August 2006. **Price:** $120.00. **Description:** Entrepreneurial education, focusing on economic, political and social needs of a changing world; ideas for reassessing, redeveloping, and renewing curricula and methods for teaching entrepreneurship are offered.

43716 ■ *International Entrepreneurship in Small and Medium Size Enterprises: Orientation, Environment and Strategy*
Pub: Edward Elgar Publishing, Incorporated
Ed: Hamid Etemad. **Released:** November 2004. **Price:** $110.00. **Description:** Issues involved in internationalizing small and medium sized (SME) businesses. Topics include an investigation into the emerging patterns of SME growth and international expansion in response to the changing competitive environment, dynamics of competitive behavior, entrepreneurial processes and a formulation of strategy.

43717 ■ *International Handbook of Women and Small Business Entrepreneurship*
Pub: Edward Elgar Publishing, Incorporated
Ed: Sandra L. Fielden. **Released:** June 2005. **Price:** $165.00. **Description:** The number of women entrepreneurs is growing at a faster rate than male counterparts worldwide. Insight into the phenomenon is targeted to scholars and students of women in management and entrepreneurship as well as policymakers and small business service providers.

43718 ■ *International Herald Tribune: Doing Business in Today's Western Europe*
Pub: NTC Business Books
Ed: Alan Tillier. **Released:** 1993. **Price:** $21.95; $17.95 (paper). **Description:** Provides information on investments and business practices in Western Europe. Also analyzes national and regional market opportunities, communication systems, property costs, and work force capabilities.

43719 ■ "The International Process of Small and Medium-sized Enterprises" in *Journal of Small Business Management* **(Vol. 38, No. 4, Oct. 2000)**
Pub: West Virginia University
Ed: Harold G.J. Gankema, Henoch R. Snuif, Peter S. Zwart. **Description:** The aim of this study is to provide better insight into the internationalization process of small and medium-sized enterprises (SMEs).

43720 ■ *International Trade and Trade Policy*
Pub: MIT Press
Ed: Elhanan Helpman and Assaf Razin. **Released:** 1991. **Price:** $35.00.

43721 ■ *The Internationalization of Asset Ownership in Europe*
Pub: Cambridge University Press
Ed: Harry Huizinga, Lars Jonung. **Released:** October 2005. **Price:** $100.00. **Description:** Ten financial experts provide analysis of the growth and the implications of foreign ownership in Europe's financial markets.

43722 ■ "The Internationalization of new and small firms" in *Journal of Business Venturing* **(Vol. 16, No. 4, July 2001, pp. 333)**
Pub: Elsevier Science, Inc.
Ed: Paul Westhead, Mike Wright, Deniz Ucbasaran. **Description:** A comparative study of the parameters affecting the success or failure of small exporting and non-exporting firms is presented. In particular, the assumption that positive benefits will accrue from exporting is investigated.

43723 ■ *The Irwin International Almanac 1994*
Pub: Irwin Professional Publishing
Ed: Sumner N. Levine and Caroline Levine, editors. **Released:** 1994. **Price:** $95.00. **Description:** Provides financial and economic data on international business and investment management. Includes performance of world securities markets and a guide to international and global funds.

43724 ■ *ISO 9000: Meeting the New International Standards*
Pub: The McGraw-Hill Companies
Ed: Perry Johnson. **Released:** 1995. **Price:** $40.00. **Description:** Provides guidance and information on how to obtain ISO 9000 product certification in Europe. Includes individual case studies and detailed techniques for satisfying the ISO's 20 subsections.

43725 ■ "It's Son of NAFTA" in *Inc.* **(Volume 27, July 2005, No. 7, pp. 26-27)**
Pub: Inc. Magazine
Ed: Darren Dahl. **Description:** Will the new Central America Free Trade Agreement (CAFTA), which eliminates duties on trade between the U.S. and six Central American countries, help American businesses stay competitive?

43726 ■ "Job Flight: Is it Real: Evidence is Scant, but a Shift Would be Welcome" in *Barron's* **(August 11, 2003, pp. 26)**
Pub: Barron's
Ed: Gene Epstein. **Description:** Forecasts of a mass migration overseas of U.S. white collar jobs, representing nearly $150 billion in wages, may be fresh meat for a media frenzy, but are not supported by the data.

43727 ■ "Jordanian delegation looks to expand business ties" in *Crain's Detroit Business* **(Vol. 18, No. 50, December 16, 2002, pp. 22)**
Pub: Crain Communications Inc., Detroit
Ed: Robert Ankeny. **Description:** A Jordanian delegation arrived in Detroit in December 2002 in an attempt to expand business relations with Jordan and Southeast Michigan.

43728 ■ "Kelly Thinks Globally and Earns Locally; International Sales Up 50 Percent Over 2 Years" in *Crain's Detroit Business* **(Vol. 21)**
Pub: Crain Communications Inc. - Detroit
Ed: Brent Snavely. **Description:** Kelly Services Inc. reports a 50 percent rise in sales over the last two years, mainly due to the implementation of its international growth strategy. Net income from international sales increased to $12.8 million in 2004.

43729 ■ *Kocham Business Directory*
Pub: Korean Chamber of Commerce & Industry in USA Inc.
Released: Annual. **Covers:** about 700 offices of leading Korean companies operated by Korean nationals located throughout the United States. Other Korean service firms (banks, trade organizations, etc.) are also listed. **Entries Include:** Firm name, address, phone, cable address, telex, name of United States representative or president. Exporter listings include above information for headquarters' address and product line. Importer listings include products. **Arrangement:** Exporters and importers are alphabetical; service firms are classified by type of service.

43730 ■ "Lafayette 148 Had High Hopes For Its New Chinese Factory" in *Inc.* **(Volume 27, December 2005, No. 12, pp. 62, 66)**
Pub: Inc. Magazine
Ed: Catherine Curan. **Description:** Profile of Deirdre Quinn and her fashion business, Lafayette 148. Quinn discusses how she and partner, Shun Yen Siu were able to get her warehouse full of fine women's apparel from China to the U.S.

43731 ■ "The Language of Business" in *My Business* **(November/December 2001, pp. 17)**
Pub: My Business Magazine

Ed: Linda Formichelli. **Description:** Translation options for small businesses targeting international customers are covered, including free online translation services, business translation software, and translator/translation agencies.

43732 ■ *Latin American Markets: A Guide to Company and Industry Sources*
Pub: Washington Researchers, Ltd.
Released: First edition. **Price:** $335.00. **Description:** Provides domestic and foreign business information sources on all Latin American and Caribbean countries.

43733 ■ "Let's Make a Deal" in *Business Journal-Milwaukee* (Vol. 20, No. 47, August 8, 2003, pp. A23)
Pub: American City Business Journals, Inc.
Ed: Becca Mader. **Description:** A growing trend among Milwaukee-based manufacturers is to acquire German companies. Topics include strategic planning, market development, and foreign operations.

43734 ■ "Life Sciences Span The Globe: U.S. VCs Like to Spend Money in their Backyards" in *Venture Capital Journal* (October 1, 2004)
Pub: Thomason Financial Inc.
Ed: Matthew Sheahan. **Description:** U.S. life science companies took about $3.6 billion in venture capital funding in 2004, more than 70 percent of the worldwide total, but Europe and Canada are working to attract these same companies. The cost advantages in both Canada and Europe are discussed.

43735 ■ *Local Enterprises in the Global Economy: Issues of Governance and Upgrading*
Pub: Edward Elgar Publishing, Incorporated
Ed: Hubert Schmitz. **Released:** April 2004. **Price:** $35.00 (soft cover), $110.00 (hard bound). **Description:** Examination of the relationships between globalization, corporate governance, and the economic performance of small businesses and local enterprises.

43736 ■ "Localizing the Brand" in *Inc.* (October 2005, pp. 54-56)
Pub: Inc. Magazine
Ed: Allen P. Roberts Jr. **Description:** Henry Estate shares insight into marketing and exporting and selling his wine in China. The global entrepreneur may also look into expanding not only to China, but also Guatemala, Honduras, Dominican Republic, El Salvador, Costa Rica, and Nicaragua with the Central American Free Trade Agreement in place.

43737 ■ "The Long Road to Free Trade" in *Hispanic Business* (July/August 2004, pp. 46)
Pub: Hispanic Business
Ed: Debra Beachy. **Description:** An overview of the Central American Free Trade Agreement and the Free Trade Area of the Americas pact is presented.

43738 ■ "Loud and Clear: CEO Hopes to Find International Audience For Multimedia Services" in *Black Enterprise* (Vol. 35, September 2004)
Pub: Earl G. Graves Publishing Co. Inc.
Ed: Anthony Calypso. **Description:** Ken Lipscomb is launching his virtual broadcasting network which will feature more than 100 Web channels of music, movies, sports and video content that can be enjoyed from computers, televisions, or stereo systems. DAVE Networks also offers in-house multimedia Web-casting production and post-production services to corporate as well as private individuals.

43739 ■ "The Lure of Bay State Technology" in *Boston Globe* (February 7, 2005)
Pub: New York Times Company
Ed: Robert Weisman. **Description:** Overseas investors are seeking acquisitions in Massachusetts, focusing on the state's high-technology and life sciences start-ups. Two deals are presented.

43740 ■ "Made in America?" in *Entrepreneur* (Vol. 31, No. 10, October 2003, pp. 72)
Pub: Entrepreneur Media, Inc.
Ed: Joshua Kurlantzick. **Description:** The consequences of U.S. businesses using overseas labor to produce products and reduce costs to small U.S. manufacturers are examined.

43741 ■ "Maine International Trade Center Adds China Desk" in *Portland Press Herald* (September 23, 2005)
Pub: Blethen Maine Newspapers, Inc.
Ed: Tux Turkel. **Description:** The Maine International Trade Center has opened a China Desk to assist businesses connect with China, Hong Kong and Taiwan. The center receives most inquiries from Canada, followed closely by China.

43742 ■ "Make Them Pay!" in *Inc.* (August 1, 2003)
Pub: Gruner & Jahr USA Publishing
Description: Dealing with a deadbeat client, the good and bad for small firms operating in Mexico, and a twist on the personal asset loan guarantee are among the issues discussed.

43743 ■ "Making Life Easier Overseas; Export Assistance" in *Crain's New York Business* (Vol. 22, November 13, 2006, No. 46, pp. 22)
Pub: Crain Communications, Inc.
Description: Listing of agencies that provide financial assistance and technical information for companies that sell goods overseas.

43744 ■ *A Manager's Guide to Globalization: Six Keys to Success in a Changing World*
Pub: Irwin Professional Publishing
Ed: Stephen H. Rhinesmith. **Price:** $29.95. **Description:** Co-published with the American Society for Training and Development. Provides step-by-step action plan to help organizations adapt to and succeed in the global marketplace.

43745 ■ *Managing Complexity and Change in SMEs Frontiers in European Research*
Pub: Edward Elgar Publishing, Incorporated
Ed: Christensen. **Released:** December 2006. **Price:** $120.00. **Description:** Complexities faced by entrepreneurs in an expanding marketplace are discussed.

43746 ■ *Managing Globally: A Complete Guide to Competing Worldwide*
Pub: Irwin Professional Publishing
Ed: Carl A. Nelson. **Price:** $65.00. **Description:** Provides information on global strategic management, including analysis of changing country policies, markets, and products.

43747 ■ *Managing India's Small Industrial Economy: The Catalytic Role of Industrial Counselors and Policy Makers*
Pub: Sage Publications, Incorporated
Ed: V. Padmanand, V.G. Patel. **Released:** June 2004. **Price:** $28.95. **Description:** Case studies and methodology are used to discuss the areas where industrial consultants are influencing sustainability and growth of small businesses in India's industrial economy.

43748 ■ *Managing International Teams*
Pub: Irwin Professional Publishing
Ed: Nicola Phillips. **Price:** $35.00. **Description:** Provides successful techniques for resolving business issues worldwide.

43749 ■ "Meet Your Customers' Needs Through Cultural Marketing" in *E-business Advisor* (Vol. 18, No. 8, August 2000, pp. 18)
Pub: Advisor Media, Inc.
Ed: Donald DePalma. **Description:** Few U.S. online businesses are focusing on the needs of culturally diverse groups of users. Cultural, or ethnic, marketing targets a specific national or linguistic group and includes such cross-border issues as currency conversion, shipping concerns, and export-import compliance. Statistical information is included.

43750 ■ "Merger Fever" in *Hispanic Business* (Vol. 23, No. 10, October, 2001, pp. 42, 44)
Pub: Hispanic Business
Ed: Derek Reveron. **Description:** Hispanic advertising agencies are becoming increasingly attractive takeover targets for international conglomerates, because of the growing confidence in the market. It is predicted that the Spanish-speaking population will become a more powerful force in industry growth.

43751 ■ "Miami strikes back in bid for trade capital" in *Atlanta Business Chronicle* (Vol. 25, No. 19, October 18, 2002)
Pub: American City Business Publications, Inc.
Description: Miami, Florida business leaders are initiating a new lobbying effort to become the headquarters for the Free Trade Area of the Americas (FTAA) trade federation. The move has been sparked by a similar move by the city of Atlanta, Georgia to become the headquarters for the FTAA. Other cities competing for the honor include cities in Panama and Mexico.

43752 ■ "Mind Your Manners" in *Inc.* (September 2005, pp. 51)
Pub: Inc. Magazine
Ed: Allen P. Roberts Jr. **Description:** Norine Dresser has re-released her book, Multicultural Manners, which offers tips for American companies when negotiating with overseas firms.

43753 ■ "Minority Business Group Looks to Cement Ties with Foreign Automakers" in *Crain's Detroit Business* (Vol. 19, No. 40, October 13, 2003)
Pub: Crain Communications Inc., Detroit
Ed: Terry Kosdrosky. **Description:** The Michigan Minority Business Development Council has changed its by-laws to include foreign-owned automakers as board members. The change is hoped to forge closer ties between member auto suppliers and foreign-owned automakers.

43754 ■ "Mitch Siegler: 41 President of Sovietski collection in San Diego" in *Entrepreneur* (Vol. 30, No. 1, January 2002, pp. 19)
Pub: Entrepreneur Media Inc.
Ed: April Pennington. **Description:** Profile of the catalog marketer of gear, gifts and collectibles from Russia and Eastern Europe, Mitch Siegler.

43755 ■ "Mobile Situation UT Starcom Soars" in *Barron's* (July 21, 2003, pp. 16)
Pub: Barron's
Ed: Leslie P. Norton. **Description:** Alameda, California-based UT Starcom is welcoming a 75 percent increase in second-quarter revenue, to more than $400 million, based on increased demand from China for its wireless local-loop equipment.

43756 ■ "Money that Binds from Afar" in *Hispanic Business* (November 2003, pp. 60, 62, 64)
Pub: Hispanic Business
Ed: Derek Reveron. **Description:** Remittances and direct investment connect the U.S. Hispanic economy to hemispheric financial development. Statistical data included, along with average transfer costs for $200 and Latin American remittances.

43757 ■ "Money Talks; Here's Message to Michigan" in *Crain's Detroit Business* (Vol. 22, November 20, 2006, No. 47, pp. 9)
Pub: Crain Communications Inc. - Detroit
Ed: William Watch **Description:** Capital moves quickly away from troubled areas. International markets such as Mexico and Brazil are more attractive to investors than Detroit.

43758 ■ "New disease has businesses cautious, but few effects seen" in *Crain's Detroit Business* (Vol. 19, No. 14, April 7, 2003, pp. 46)
Pub: Crain Communications Inc., Detroit
Ed: Michael Strong. **Description:** Businesses in the metropolitan Detroit, Michigan area are keeping an eye on the progression of severe acute respiratory syndrome and keeping travel to China for business-critical issues only.

43759 ■ "The New China?" in *Entrepreneur.com* **(Vol. 34, February 2006, No. 2, pp. 17)**
Pub: Entrepreneur Media Inc.
Ed: Mark Henricks. Description: Manufacturing opportunities overseas, especially in China and Vietnam are explored.

43760 ■ "New frontiers" in *Entrepreneur* **(Vol. 31, No. 6, June 2003, pp. 34)**
Pub: Entrepreneur Media Inc.
Ed: Geoff Williams. Description: In an interview, career consultant John Bradley offers insight into expanding a small business into Afghanistan.

43761 ■ *New Technology-Based Firms in the New Millennium, Volume 3*
Pub: Elsevier Science & Technology Books
Ed: Ray Oakey, Wim During, Seleema Kauser. Released: June 2004. Price: $110.00. Description: Collection of papers from the Annual International High Technology Firms (HTSFs) Conference covering issues of importance to governments as they develop technological program. Papers are grouped into three sections: strategy, spin-off firms, clusters, networking, and global issues.

43762 ■ *New Technology-Based Firms in the New Millennium, Volume 4*
Pub: Elsevier Science & Technology Books
Ed: Ray Oakey, Wim During, Seleema Kauser. Released: December 2005. Price: $135.00. Description: Collection of papers from the Annual International High Technology Firms (HTSFs) Conference cover issues of importance to governments as they develop technological program. Papers are grouped into three sections: theory, strategy and clustering, and spin-off firms.

43763 ■ "The New World Disorder" in *Harvard Business Review* **(Vol. 81, No. 8, August 2003, pp. 70)**
Pub: Harvard Business School Press
Ed: Nicolas Checa, John Maguire, Jonathan Barney. Description: The efforts of U.S. Presidents George Bush, Sr. and Bill Clinton to develop globalization have been largely wiped out by the following: George W. Bush's overriding concern with combating terrorism, the 1997 financial crisis in Thailand, how the IMF responded to the Thailand problem, and how financial industries have responded to the above.

43764 ■ "New World Order: the European Union Will Soon be a Bigger Cash Cow" in *Entrepreneur* **(Vol. 32, No. 4, April 2004, pp. 19)**
Pub: Entrepreneur Media, Inc.
Ed: Joshua Kurlantzick. Description: Entrepreneurs should not overlook overseas markets in central and Eastern Europe when expanding international business.

43765 ■ "A Night's Sleep, Ultracheap" in *Business Week* **(January 23, 2006, No. 3968, pp. 73)**
Pub: McGraw-Hill Companies
Ed: Pete Engardio. Description: Bangalore's indiOne hotel offers rooms for business travels for $22 per night.

43766 ■ "North-South Power Balance" in *Hispanic Business* **(November 2003, pp. 58, 64)**
Pub: Hispanic Business
Ed: Derek Reveron. Description: Brazil wants more influence as ministers meet in November 20-21, 2003, in Miami to plan the Free Trade Area of the Americas.

43767 ■ "Northern Exposure: American Entrepreneurs are Finding Success by Heading for the Border" in *Entrepreneur* **(Vol. 31, August 2003)**
Pub: Entrepreneur Media, Inc.
Ed: Joshua Kurlantzick. Description: Canada is becoming more attractive to entrepreneurs because Canada has recorded the strongest economic growth of any industrialized nation in the past two years. Venture capitalists in Canada are usually more generous than those in the U.S.

43768 ■ "Northern Trust Close To an Outsourcing Foothold in Britain" in *American Banker* **(Vol. 170, February 3, 2005, No. 23, pp. 2)**
Pub: Thomson Financial Media Inc.
Ed: Laurie Kulikowski. Description: Northern Trust, headquartered in Chicago, Illinois, is close to closing an outsourcing deal with Insight Investment Management Ltd of London, England. Northern Trust would provide back- and middle-office services, including record keeping and trade matching, confirmation, and settlement to the firm. Insight Investment manages $140.5 billion of assets.

43769 ■ "Now Boarding" in *Inc.* **(Volume 28, January 2006, No. 1, pp. 66)**
Pub: Inc. Magazine
Ed: Larry Olmsted. Description: More than 100 discount airlines have been launched globally since 2004. A few of the best budget carriers are listed for the business traveler going overseas to India, the Mediterranean, Southeast Asia, South America, and Eastern Europe.

43770 ■ "Oakland, Calif., Port Agrees to Manage West Sacramento Shipping Facility" in *Sacramento Bee* **(December 21, 2005)**
Pub: The Sacramento Bee
Ed: Jim Wasserman. Description: The Bay Area Port has agreed to manage the inland Port of Sacramento in order to restore long-term financial stability to the port. The move will also offer the Port of Oakland new options to deal with the increasing amount of cargo coming in from Asia.

43771 ■ "Officials Hope Testing Center Spurs More International Investment" in *Crain's Detroit Business* **(Vol. 21, October 10, 2005, No. 43)**
Pub: Crain Communications Inc. - Detroit
Ed: Sheena Harrison. Description: Economic development officials in Livingston County, Michigan are hoping the move by Aisin Holdings of America Inc. to open its first test track and providing ground in the U.S. will attract more foreign investment to the region.

43772 ■ "Offshoring Could Boost Your Career" in *Fortune* **(Vol. 151, January 24, 2005, No. 2, pp. 36)**
Pub: Time Inc.
Ed: Anne Fisher. Description: According to a study conducted by Duke University's Fuqua School of Business and Archstone Consulting, American businesses with offshore operations will ship 81 percent more research jobs, 55 percent more engineering, and 75 percent more human resources overseas (69 percent of which are already in India). American managers will be needed to oversee these operations.

43773 ■ "Offshoring Isn't Such a Sure Thing" in *Inc.* **(September 2005, pp. 32, 34)**
Pub: Inc. Magazine
Ed: Lora Koldony. Description: According to a new survey conducted by DiamondCluster International, a Chicago, Illinois management consulting firm, U.S. companies are finding that sending work overseas can be more difficult than it is worth.

43774 ■ "On the Radar" in *E-business Advisor* **(Vol. 18, No. 4, April 2000, pp. 8)**
Pub: Advisor Media, Inc.
Description: Several vendors have come up with products and services to help companies with e-business strategy. Bolero.net is aimed at helping multinational companies with international commerce. RadView Software's WebLoad Resource Manager and WebLoad Workstation electronic commerce software products are designed to test, analyze, and verify e-business applications. Other companies offering products and services are Primix Solutions, IBM and CyberTrust.

43775 ■ "Opening Up the Baghdad Office" in *Inc.* **(November 1, 2004)**
Pub: Inc. Magazine
Ed: Nicole Gull. Description: Profile of Chris Exline, founder of Home Essentials, and one of the first entrepreneurs to set up a shop in Iraq after American troops swept the country in 2003. Exline, who speaks no Arabic, discusses the challenges and risks of working in Baghdad.

43776 ■ "Out of Work from Offshoring, California Software Programmers Turn to eBay" in *San Jose Mercury News* **(March 26, 2004)**
Pub: Knight-Ridder/Tribune Business News
Ed: Matt Marshall. Description: Software programmers in California who have lost their jobs offshore, have listed themselves on eBay's auction site.

43777 ■ "Over the Wall" in *Entrepreneur.com* **(Vol. 34, February 2006, No. 2, pp. 58)**
Pub: Entrepreneur Media Inc.
Ed: Scott Bernard Nelson. Description: Smart ways to invest in China's growing economy are presented. Mutual funds or exchange-traded funds with exposure to China are considered the best strategy.

43778 ■ "Overseas Lender of First Resort" in *Hispanic Business* **(March 2003, pp. 40-41)**
Pub: Hispanic Business
Ed: Derek Reveron. Description: Profile of the Export-Import Bank and its services to exporters is presented, including contact information.

43779 ■ "Parlez-vous e-Commerce? Here's How To Give Your Website International Appeal" in *Black Enterprise* **(Vol. 35, October 2004, No. 3)**
Pub: Earl G. Graves Publishing Co. Inc.
Ed: Carolyn M. Brown. Description: According to a recent study, more than $900 billion in Internet spending is expected to take place outside the U.S. It is advised for companies using the Internet to market a product or service to offer one or two foreign languages.

43780 ■ *Passport to International Detroit-Services*
Pub: Greater Detroit Chamber of Commerce
Contact: Angela Ladetto, Dir.
E-mail: aladetto@yahoo.com
Released: Biennial. Covers: More than 500 services involved in international trade in Metro Detroit, Michigan. Entries Include: Company name, address, phone, fax, service, employment. Arrangement: Business category. Indexes: Alphabetical.

43781 ■ "Pendleton Braces for Fight." in *Business Journal-Portland* **(Vol. 20, No. 26, August 29, 2003, pp. 1)**
Pub: American City Business Journals, Inc.
Ed: Robin J. Moody. Description: Pendleton Woolen Mills Inc. is preparing for China's entry into the World Trade Organization. The company has upgraded the mill and its products.

43782 ■ "Personal Business" in *Business Week* **(January 9, 2006, No. 3966, pp. 94)**
Pub: McGraw-Hill Companies
Ed: Mara der Hovanesian. Description: Topics include a takeover of auto lender Americredit, overseas shipping, and retail shopping in China.

43783 ■ *Petty Capitalists and Globalization: Flexibility, Entrepreneurship, and Economic Development*
Pub: State University of New York Press
Ed: Alan Smart, Josephine Smart. Released: March 2005. Price: $70.00. Description: Investigation into ways small businesses in Europe, Asia, and Latin America are required to operate and compete in the fast-growing transnational economy.

43784 ■ "Pinstriped Populist" in *New York Times* **(November 12, 2006, pp. 15)**
Pub: New York Times Company
Ed: David Sirota. Description: Profile of Lou Dobbs, author of How the Government, Big Business, and Special Interest Groups Are Waging War on the American Dream and How to Fight Back. Dobbs, a financial journalist, examines wages, corruption, trade, outsourcing, immigration and health care.

43785 ■ **"Port of Call? Port Authority in Talks to Reopen Detroit Marine Terminal"** in *Crain's Detroit Business* (Vol. 21, February 7, 2005)

Pub: Crain Communications Inc. - Detroit

Ed: Michelle Martinez. **Description:** Nicholson Terminal & Dock Company and the Detroit International Bridge Company are being considered to operate the Detroit Marine Terminal if plans to reopen the terminal by the Detroit-Wayne County Port Authority are successful.

43786 ■ **"Preparation key to conquering overseas exhibits"** in *Atlanta Business Chronicle* (Vol. 24, No. 14, September 7, 2001, pp. S16)

Pub: American City Business Journals Inc.

Ed: Jonathan Kalstrom. **Description:** Maren Christensen of the Minnesota Trade Office, Liz DeLuca of Skyline Displays Inc., and Allen Konopacki of Incomm International discuss how to plan overseas tradeshows. Factors to keep in mind are customs and postal regulations, language differences, and freight-forwarding services.

43787 ■ **"Pringle to Chinese: Bring It On"** in *Business Journal-Milwaukee* (Vol. 20, No. 44, July 18, 2003, pp. A9)

Pub: American City Business Journals, Inc.

Ed: Rich Rovito. **Description:** Profile of John Pringle, new president and CEO of NuTone. Pringle is convinced that by using automation and patents, his company will evolve into a stronger force within the residential ventilation products industry.

43788 ■ **"Profit Globally, Give Globally"** in *Harvard Business Review* (Vol. 81, No. 12, December 2003, pp. 16)

Pub: Harvard Business School Press

Ed: John Quelch, V. Kasturi Rangan. **Description:** An overview of ways corporations can and should increase non-domestic philanthropic aid is presented. Topics include sensitivity and diplomacy involved in international economic relations, and issues such as tax breaks and local law.

43789 ■ **"Promised Land"** in *Entrepreneur* (Vol. 33, August 2005, No. 8, pp. 26)

Pub: Entrepreneur Media Inc.

Ed: Mark Henricks. **Description:** As the Israeli-Palestinian conflict abates American entrepreneurs, particularly in technology areas, are looking to Israel as a new business opportunity.

43790 ■ **"Prospecting in Cuba"** in *Hispanic Business* (October 2006, pp. 28, 30)

Pub: Hispanic Business

Ed: Jenn Holmes. **Description:** Although the U.S. embargo on trade with Cuba still exists, American businesses are preparing for a post-Castro era.

43791 ■ **"Reaching Out to Low-Wage Countries"** in *Washington Business Journal* (Vol. 22, September 26, 2003)

Pub: Washington Business Journal

Ed: Tania Anderson. **Description:** Outsourcing of work overseas by engineering and computer firms has increased during the economic recession.

43792 ■ **"The Real Deal"** in *Entrepreneur* (Vol. 33, September 2005, No. 9, pp. 74)

Pub: Entrepreneur Media Inc.

Ed: April Y. Pennington, Nichole L. Torres, Geoff Williams, Sara Wilson. **Description:** Entrepreneurs discuss the highs and lows of business ownership, from embezzlement, international trade, and selling a product to Target.

43793 ■ **"Real Estate Insiders to Reveal Forecasts for the Coming Year"** in *Crain's Detroit Business* (Vol. 19, No. 1, January 6, 2003, pp. 6)

Pub: Crain Communications Inc., Detroit

Ed: Jennette Smith. **Description:** The Commercial Real Estate Trends and Forecasts Seminar will be held January 17, 2003. The seminar will highlight keynote speaker, Bradley Olsen, president of Atlantic Partners Ltd.; Bradley will discuss the impact international capital markets will have on the Motor City in 2003.

43794 ■ **"The Regenerative Organization"** in *Employment Relations Today* (Vol. 27, No. 1, Spring 2000, pp. 19)

Pub: John Wiley & Sons, Inc.

Ed: Randall J. Alford. **Description:** Issues discussed concern organizational change and management in US companies attempting to compete in a globalized marketplace. Topics addressed include how to integrate human resource management with strategic planning and how to build company vision, purpose, and community.

43795 ■ **"Rescue Mission"** in *Entrepreneur* (Vol. 33, August 2005, No. 8, pp. 15)

Pub: Entrepreneur Media Inc.

Ed: Joshua Kurlantzick. **Description:** Since 2000, U.S. entrepreneurs have focused on taking social enterprise overseas. Net Impact, the San Francisco clearinghouse for social enterprise has more than doubled membership in the last six years. Some foreign governments are seeking American small business owners to offer expertise and capital.

43796 ■ **"Resources: Web Sites, Organizations, Events and More to Grow Your Business"** in *Entrepreneur* (Vol. 32, August 2004, No. 8, pp. 8)

Pub: Entrepreneur Media Inc.

Ed: Steve Cooper. **Description:** Showcase of information to help small business include: Global Advisor offers services from United Parcel Service to help companies learn ways to conduct business overseas, including trade tools and terminology, a global time clock and HAP, supply chain management, and a guide to international shipping; a CAN-SPAM Act of 2003 summary; RE:INVENTION INC is a daily blog dedicated to women entrepreneurs; and a directory of venture capital and private equity firms.

43797 ■ **"Resources: Web Sites, Organizations, Events and More To Grow Your Business"** in *Entrepreneur* (Vol. 32, September 2004, No. 9, pp. 8)

Pub: Entrepreneur Media Inc.

Ed: Steve Cooper. **Description:** Resources to help small business are featured including the Small Business Administration's effort to help teen entrepreneurs launch a business; KnockNow an online community of entrepreneurs, executives, venture capitalists, angel investors, service sector companies, and government; the SBA's business Website offering information on small business development, financial assistance, taxes, laws and regulations, international trade, workplace issues, buying and selling and federal forms.

43798 ■ **"The Return of the Global Brand"** in *Harvard Business Review* (Vol. 81, No. 8, August 2003, pp. 22)

Pub: Harvard Business School Press

Ed: John Quelch. **Description:** Since Theordore Levitt published The Globalization of Markets in the Harvard Business Review twenty years ago, the world's economic development has adapted accordingly. International companies are finding that standardized products marketed globally have been widely accepted. This is contrary to previous efforts to develop products for regional markets. Today, China is poised to duplicate Japan's global branding successes, cutting into U.S. business sales.

43799 ■ *Riding the Waves of Culture: Understanding Diversity in Global Business*

Pub: Irwin Professional Publishing

Ed: Fons Trompenaars. **Price:** $30.00. **Description:** Provides instruction on how to build skills, sensitivity, and cultural awareness to improve management effectiveness across cultural borders. Includes graphs, examples, and other comparisons.

43800 ■ **"Rise of China's Consumer Class Excites California Ag Industry"** in *Sacramento Bee* (December 19, 2005)

Pub: The Sacramento Bee

Ed: Jim Wasserman. **Description:** China's recent growth in the world's food markets may pose the largest challenge to California's agricultural industry. Statistical data included.

43801 ■ **"Rising Drug Costs"** in *Venture Capital Journal* (October 1, 2204)

Pub: Thomason Financial Inc.

Ed: Alastair Goldfisher. **Description:** With the rising costs of conducting clinical trials of new drugs, technology companies may choose offshore outsourcing of research and development to save money. However, the cost of new drug development is rising worldwide. Statistical data included.

43802 ■ **"Road Weary No More"** in *Hispanic Business* (Vol. 24, No. 1/2, January/February 2002, pp. 10)

Pub: Hispanic Business Inc.

Ed: Tim Dougherty. **Description:** Two constitutional amendments approved by Texas voters will benefit cross-border trade and the state's Hispanic population. Proposition 2 will improve local roads along the Mexican border, while Proposition 15 provides for the creation of the Texas Mobility Fund to finance state highway and other transportation projects.

43803 ■ **"Run for the border"** in *Entrepreneur* (Vol. 30, No. 3, March 2002, pp. 123)

Pub: Entrepreneur Media Inc.

Ed: Don Debelak. **Description:** Some inventors are setting up deals with U.S. manufacturers to produce a new product, but when that fails, they are turning to foreign manufacturers to save money; risks involved in doing so are also discussed.

43804 ■ **"Sacramento, Calif., Light-Rail Plant Gets $84 Million Deal"** in *Sacramento Bee* (October 21, 2005)

Pub: The Sacramento Bee

Ed: Dale Kasler. **Description:** Siemens Transportation Systems Inc. in Sacramento, California has secured a contract with the city of Edmonton, Alberta, Canada to produce 26 light-rail cars for the city's transit system. The company plans to add 75 new jobs in order to assemble the outer shells of the rail cars.

43805 ■ **"Safer Harbors, Higher Fees"** in *Inc.* (January 1, 2004)

Pub: Gruner & Jahr USA Publishing

Ed: Rod Kurtz. **Description:** New U.S. Coast Guard rules could make shipping more expensive.

43806 ■ **"Safety Measures"** in *Washington Business Journal* (Vol. 22, No. 16, August 22, 2003, pp. 18)

Pub: Washington Business Journal

Ed: Tim Pappa. **Description:** Gary Noesner, from Control Risks Groups, points out the importance of travel information. Control Risks offers software and services to make data acquisition easier. Such information can result in saving the lives of employees of international businesses or government officials in the field.

43807 ■ **"San Diego to Host Tech Summit"** in *Hispanic Business* (Vol. 24, No. 5, May 2002, pp. 42)

Pub: Hispanic Business Inc.

Description: Technology and cross-border trade were among the issues of focus at the Hispanic Business Tech Summit held in November, 2001. Specific seminars included, B2B E-Commerce, E-Business Expansion, Strategic Online Alliances, Cross-Border Trends, and NAFTA.

43808 ■ **"Secrets of the Great White North-The world's hush-hush 3-commerce powerhouse is just a few miles away"** in *PC Computing* (April 2000)

Pub: Ziff-Davis Inc.

Ed: Jim Conley. **Description:** Canadian retailers saw a banner year in 1999, with record sales both online and offline. Exchange rates, shipping costs, and support concerns have kept many U.S. companies from expanding into the Canadian market, but the article suggests the savvy retailer will realize the opportunity.

43809 ■ **"Serving the world's poor, profitably"** in *Harvard Business Review* (Vol. 80, No. 9, September 2002, pp. 48)

Pub: Harvard Business School Press

Ed: C.K. Prahalad, Allen Hammond. **Description:** Current belief's regarding the current challenges for doing business in underdeveloped regions of the world are investigated, using a hypothetical reference.

43810 ■ "Set Up Shop in Europe" in E-business Advisor (Vol. 18, No. 2, February 2000, pp. 16)
Pub: Advisor Media, Inc.
Ed: Lars Hakan Sjoo. **Description:** The European e-commerce industry is estimated to be from one to four years behind the U.S., thus creating a myriad of opportunities for enterprising companies.

43811 ■ Shrinking the Globe into Your Company's Hands: The Step-by-Step International Trade Guide for Small Businesses
Pub: Rayve Productions, Inc.
Ed: Sidney R. Lawrence. **Released:** 1997. **Price:** $24.95.

43812 ■ "Small Biz Barges into Cuba" in Inc. (October 1, 2003)
Pub: Gruner & Jahr USA Publishing
Ed: Anton Piach. **Description:** Profile of Maybank Shipping, the small South Carolina company that shipped goods to Cuba via chartered foreign vessels. Cuba licensed a large shipper called Crowley, in Oakland, California, to import goods on foreign vessels.

43813 ■ "Small Biz Braces for Life on the High (Priced) Seas" in Inc. (September 1, 2004)
Pub: Inc. Magazine
Ed: Rod Kurtz. **Description:** The high cost of security facing importers and exporters is discussed. Statistical data included.

43814 ■ "Small Businesses Driving for 'Fast Track' on Trade" in Atlanta Business Chronicle (Vol. 24, No. 9, August 3, 2001, pp. 11B)
Pub: American City Business Journals Inc.
Ed: Kent Hoover. **Description:** Small businesses in the U.S. want Congress to grant President Bush trade promotion authority, which is the ability to negotiate trade agreements with countries outside of the U.S. These agreements would be brought back to Congress for a vote of 'yes' or 'no', with no amendments.

43815 ■ "Small Exporters in a Big World" in Hispanic Business (November 2003, pp. 42-43, 46, 48, 50)
Pub: Hispanic Business
Ed: Jennifer Riley. **Description:** Hispanic firms that have succeeded abroad show they can compete in the large and profitable markets of the global economy. Statistical data included.

43816 ■ "Small Firms' Motivation for Exporting" in Journal of Small Business Management (Vol. 38, No. 4, October 2000, pp. 1)
Pub: West Virginia University
Ed: William J. Burpitt, Dennis A. Rondinelli. **Description:** Most small firms see exporting as a risky venture and many do not obtain immediate financial returns. Statistical data included.

43817 ■ Small and Medium-Sized Enterprises in Countries in Transition
Pub: United Nations Publications
Released: January 2005. **Price:** $18.00. **Description:** Characteristics of small and medium enterprise (SME) sector in transition countries and emerging market economies.

43818 ■ SME Cluster Development: A Dynamic View on Survival Clusters in Developing Countries
Pub: Palgrave Macmillan
Ed: Mario Davide Parrilli. **Released:** April 2007. **Price:** $90.00. **Description:** Survival clustering in developing countries is discussed in order to increase effectiveness of policy-making and development operations in local contexts.

43819 ■ Snowdon's Official International Protocols: The Definitive Guide to the Business and Social Customs of the World
Pub: Irwin Professional Publishing
Ed: Sondra Snowdon. **Price:** $75.00. **Description:** Provides protocols of 60 nations, their business climates, history, and politics.

43820 ■ Social Enterprise in Europe
Pub: Routledge Inc.
Ed: Marthe Nyssens. **Released:** August 2006. **Price:** $145.00 hardcopy; $46.95 paperback. **Description:** Social enterprises in Europe are examined through three ideas: that they have a complex mixture of goals, that they mobilize various kinds of markets and non-market resources, and that they are embedded in the political context.

43821 ■ Sociopolitical Aspects of International Marketing
Pub: The Haworth Press, Inc.
Ed: Erdener Kaynak, editor. **Released:** 1991. **Price:** $24.95; $69.95 (paper). **Description:** Provides information on international marketing, focusing on macro international marketing issues, sociopolitical marketing issues, international marketing strategies, and special international marketing topics.

43822 ■ "Some Suppliers Expanding Biz" in Crain's Detroit Business (Vol. 22, January 16, 2006, No. 3, pp. 3)
Pub: Crain Communications Inc. - Detroit
Ed: Brent Snavely. **Description:** More than six local automotive suppliers are planning to spend millions in capital expenditures in 2006. A listing of announced initiatives is included.

43823 ■ "Spanish Firm Hopes U.S. Is In the Bag" in Crain's Chicago Business (Vol. 26, No. 51, December 22, 2003, pp. 14)
Pub: Crain Communications, Inc.
Ed: Sandra Jones. **Description:** Profile of Frag Comercio Internacional, one of Spain's biggest handbag makers. The firm has opened a store in Chicago, Illinois and hopes to expand retail operations to 100 stores across the nation. The store offers an ever-changing choice of purses and totes, all priced at $32. The handbags will be displayed museum-style, using a minimalist concept.

43824 ■ "Special Opps" in Entrepreneur (Vol. 32, October 2004, No. 10, pp. 38)
Pub: Entrepreneur Media Inc.
Ed: Geoff Williams. **Description:** Profile of Mark Wilson, former Marine, who has restructured his company in order to tap into a new market in Iraq. Wilson is a franchisee of The Growth Coach, which works with self-employed and small business owners. He has created a Web site for entrepreneurs who are military reservists searching for strategies to keep their businesses operating while deployed in Iraq. Chris Exline, CEO of Home Essentials, generated $3.5 billion in revenue for 2003, by renting home essentials to individuals working in foreign countries.

43825 ■ "Special Report" in The Economist (Vol. 376, July 30-August 5, 2005, No. 8437, pp. 61-63)
Pub: The Economist Newspaper Ltd.
Description: China is becoming the determiner of issues affecting workers, companies, financial markets and economies worldwide.

43826 ■ "Status Quota? Without Trade Quotas, U.S. Textile-Makers Struggle" in Entrepreneur (Vol. 33, September 2005, No. 9, pp. 23)
Pub: Entrepreneur Media Inc.
Ed: Scott Bernard Nelson. **Description:** When a global system of trade quotas expired in 2004, Chinese imports flooded the U.S. market, as high as 1,000 percent increase in some markets. In May 2005, the U.S. imposed a new quota limiting year-over-year increases in China's textile imports to 7.5 percent, providing only temporary relief. The U.S. textile industry must find new ways in which to compete with foreign competitors.

43827 ■ Stop Working: Start a Business, Globalize It, and Generate Enough Cash Flow to Get Out of the Rat Race
Pub: Eye Contact Media
Ed: Rohan Hall. **Released:** November 2004. **Price:** $19.99. **Description:** Advice is given to small companies to compete in the global marketplace by entrepreneur using the same strategy for his own business.

43828 ■ "The Struggle for Sales Overseas" in Hispanic Business (November 2002, pp. 36)
Pub: Hispanic Business
Ed: Joel Russell. **Description:** Statistics are shared regarding Hispanic companies exporting products are featured. Overall exports for the first seven months of 2002 were down 8 percent from same period in 2001.

43829 ■ Studies of Entrepreneurship, Business and Government in Hong Kong: The Economic Development of a Small Open Economy
Pub: Edwin Mellen Press
Ed: Fu-Lai Tony Yu. **Released:** November 2006. **Price:** $109.95. **Description:** Institutional and Austrian theories are used to analyze the transformation taking place in Hong Kong's economy.

43830 ■ "Study Foresees End of Boeing's Commercial Work; Company Calls Report Flawed" in News Tribune (April 11, 2003)
Pub: Knight-Ridder/Tribune Business News
Ed: John Gillie. **Description:** According to a study written by two State University of New York at Buffalo researchers, the growing expertise of overseas aerospace companies along with the demand for higher profits could prompt Boeing to leave the commercial airplane business within the next ten years.

43831 ■ Sustainable Growth and Performance in East Asia, Book III
Pub: Edward Elgar Publishing, Incorporated
Released: June 2005. **Price:** $145.00. **Description:** Ways small and medium sized enterprises contribute to achieving and sustaining growth and performance in their particular economies along with ways in which governments can assist and enhance that contribution.

43832 ■ Swedish-American Chamber of Commerce of the United States—Directory
Pub: Swedish-American Chamber of Commerce
Released: Annual, summer. **Covers:** about 1,800 United States and 200 Swedish members of the chamber, concerned with promoting commercial relations between the two countries. **Entries Include:** Company name, address, phone, fax. **Arrangement:** Separate alphabetical lists by country. **Indexes:** Classified.

43833 ■ "Table Talk" in Sales & Marketing Management (Vol. 159, January-February 2007, No. 1, pp. 33)
Pub: VNU Business Media
Description: Marketing leaders focus on the impacts of globalization of business, customers and products.

43834 ■ "Tackle Your International Logistics Obstacles" in E-business Advisor (Vol. 18, No. 12, December 2000, pp. 22)
Pub: Advisor Media, Inc.
Ed: Beth Peterson. **Description:** International e-commerce offers excellent revenue opportunities and the Internet offers the needed business infrastructure, but shipping goods across international borders can be a problems. Logistics marketplaces are emerging to aid this process, but there are other challenges. The choice of the right Internet business infrastructure is critical for the success of global e-commerce.

43835 ■ Taking Your Business Global: Your Small Business Guide to Successful International Trade
Pub: Career Press, Inc.
Ed: James Wilfong and Toni Seger. **Released:** 1997. **Price:** $18.99.

43836 ■ "Tapping Foreign Markets" in *Home Office Computing* (Vol. 18, No. 10, October 2000, pp. 18)
Pub: Scholastic Inc.
Ed: Sonya Donaldson. **Description:** Small and home-based businesses are doing big business abroad. According to a recent study by the National Association for the Self-Employed, or NASE, more than 22 percent of its members have sold goods or services abroad, while one in 10 focuses solely on selling abroad. And of those who don't sell goods overseas, 20 percent said they would like to.

43837 ■ "Tapping the Talent Pool of Hispanic Affluence" in *Hispanic Business* (Vol. 24, No. 1/2, January/February 2002, pp. 6)
Pub: Hispanic Business Inc.
Ed: Jesus Chavarria. **Description:** A brief overview of the growth of Hispanic affluence in America and the important role that plays for Hispanic entrepreneurs and marketers. Hispanic Business magazine plans to organize training and educational events with sessions on Latin American trade, B2B e-commerce strategies, Hispanic online consumers, and cross-border banking.

43838 ■ "Technology is Biggest Export" in *Hispanic Business* (November 2002, pp. 25-26, 30)
Pub: Hispanic Business
Ed: Jonathan J. Higuera. **Description:** Predications are made concerning future exports; the list of winners included information technology, auto parts, medical devices, services, processed foods, and chemicals. Statistical data includes largest U.S. export products, top purchasers of U.S. exports. Government Web sites providing foreign market research to small companies are listed.

43839 ■ "That Trade Deficit Is No Debacle" in *Business Week* (January 31, 2005, pp. 30)
Pub: McGraw-Hill Companies
Ed: Peter Coy. **Description:** Imports exceeded exports in November 2004 by a record $60 billion, the trade deficit now stands at around 6 percent of gross domestic product, the highest level in history.

43840 ■ "The Hispanic Business 2003 Top 50 Exporters" in *Hispanic Business* (November 2003, pp. 56-57)
Pub: Hispanic Business
Description: A listing of the top 50 Hispanic Business 2003 top 50 exporters, including the company number of employees, how many are Hispanic, 2002 revenues, revenue from exports, export sales, export sales growth, products or services, and destination.

43841 ■ "The U.S. Commercial Service: www.export.gov/comm_svc" in *Entrepreneur* (Vol. 32, November 2004, No. 11, pp. 6)
Pub: Entrepreneur Media Inc.
Ed: Steve Cooper. **Description:** U.S. Commercial Service offers global business solutions in the areas of market research, trade events to promote businesses and services, introductions between buyers and distributors, and export counseling.

43842 ■ "Those China Franchises are Risky" in *Automotive News* (Vol. 78, July 5, 2004, No. 6101, pp. 12)
Pub: Crain Communications Inc.
Ed: Keith Crain. **Description:** Entrepreneurs are warned about vehicle franchises being offered to sell cars manufactured in China.

43843 ■ "A time of lower returns" in *Hispanic Business* (Vol. 22, No. 11, November 2000, pp. 36)
Pub: Hispanic Business
Ed: Joel Russell. **Description:** The performance of the top 50 Hispanic American businesses whose export trade was worth $592.11-million in 1999, a drop of 38 percent on the previous year is examined. The effect of globalization on exports is discussed.

43844 ■ "Timing is Everything" in *Crain's New York Business* (Vol. 22, December 4, 2006, No. 49, pp. 20)
Pub: Crain Communications, Inc.
Description: Despite the decline in China's market due to their own professionals taking over the work, New York building-related firms are tapping into other regions that are providing development money. Latin America, Eastern Europe, and the Middle East are new markets that are lucrative for U.S. firms. Morocco will soon have a project pipeline exceeding $10 billion that American construction firms will win over due to their expertise, know-how, and extensive experience.

43845 ■ "Top 50 Exporters" in *Hispanic Business* (July/August 2004, pp. 50, 51)
Pub: Hispanic Business
Description: Of the top fifty exporters in the U.S., thirty-five of them are wholesalers and manufacturers, accounting for $1.7 billion in export sales. The fastest growing exporter was Latin Node Inc., with a 400-percent increase in export sales.

43846 ■ "Trade Mission to France Nets $5 Million in Projected Sales" in *Portland Press Herald* (November 22, 2005)
Pub: Blethen Maine Newspapers, Inc.
Ed: Matt Wickenheiser. **Description:** According to an official of the Maine International Trade Center, the states new trade mission to France has generated more than $5 million projected first-year sales. The trade center plans to focus on overseas trade shows in 2006.

43847 ■ "Trade Policy" in *The Economist* (Vol. 376, July 30-August 5, 2005, No. 8437, pp. 66)
Pub: The Economist Newspaper Ltd.
Description: Details of the Central American Free Trade Agreement (CAFTA), passed July 28, 2005, are presented.

43848 ■ "Trading For Success" in *Business First Buffalo* (Vol. 19, No. 46, August 8, 2003, pp. 17)
Pub: American City Business Journals, Inc.
Ed: Joe Iannarelli. **Description:** Integrated Thermal Solutions, led by president Richard Perez, faces an array of new regulations for pallets and other shipping products. The Buffalo, New York region is a hub for international trade, prompting local companies to seek assistance to boost their operations.

43849 ■ *Trading Places: SMEs in the Global Economy, A Critical Research Handbook*
Pub: Edward Elgar Publishing, Incorporated
Ed: Lloyd-Reason. **Released:** September 2006. **Price:** $110.00. **Description:** An overview of international research for small and medium-sized companies wishing to expand in the global economy.

43850 ■ "Traffic Turn Says Downriver Site, Public Money Best for Border" in *Crain's Detroit Business* (Vol. 21, January 31, 2005, No. 5, pp. 42)
Pub: Crain Communications Inc. - Detroit
Ed: Michelle Martinez. **Description:** Details of a study recommending a bridge location for a second border crossing between Windsor, Ontario, Canada, and Detroit, Michigan are reported.

43851 ■ "Transforming Business Structures to Hyborg" in *Employment Relations Today* (Vol. 26, No. 4, Winter 2000, pp. 5)
Pub: John Wiley & Sons, Inc.
Ed: Arnold Brown. **Description:** The organizational structure and corporate culture at the turn of the 21st century are studied. Topics addressed include international economic relations, competition, corporate values, employer-employee relations, and human resource management.

43852 ■ "Transforming TV" in *Hispanic Business* (Vol. 22, No. 7-8, July-August 2000, pp. 14)
Pub: Hispanic Business
Ed: Vivienne Heines. **Description:** Houston-based International eCommerce hopes that Hispanic families

will use its new NetForAll interactive TV, Internet and e-mail service. The company expects to have up to 20,000 customers in Mexico, plus a further 15,000-plus in the U.S., by the end of the year 2000.

43853 ■ *The Transnational Activities of Small & Medium-Sized Enterprises*
Pub: Kluwer Academic Publishers
Ed: Masataka Fujita. **Released:** 1998.

43854 ■ *Transnational Business Information: A Manual of Needs and Sources*
Pub: United Nations Center on Transnational Corporations
Released: 1991. **Price:** $45.00. **Description:** Manual providing information for individuals interested in transnational business or developing countries.

43855 ■ "The Trouble With Lifestyle Entrepreneurs" in *Inc.* (Volume 27, July 2005, No. 7, pp. 21-23)
Pub: Inc. Magazine
Ed: Daniel McGinn. **Description:** New Zealand business owners are able to enjoy a work-life balance, but this trend is becoming a national crisis. American entrepreneurs can take note that growing a business in the U.S. requires a fast-paced, stressed lifestyle. The American economy is fueled by small business.

43856 ■ "Truck stop" in *Crain's Detroit Business* (Vol. 19, No. 12, March 24, 2003, pp. 1)
Pub: Crain Communications Inc., Detroit
Ed: Michael Strong, Terry Kosdrosky. **Description:** Detroit-based automakers are lobbying the United States Customs and Border Protection officials in an effort to ease restrictions on certain trucks entering the U.S. from Canada.

43857 ■ "Trucking firms hope bridge lanes cut shipping costs" in *Crain's Detroit Business* (Vol. 18, No. 19, May 13, 2002, pp. 28)
Pub: Crain Communications Inc. - Detroit
Ed: Michael Strong. **Description:** Transporters hope to see fewer delays and lower shipping costs associated with coming into the United States from Canada via the Ambassador Bridge with the creation of 'fast lanes' for regular bridge crossers.

43858 ■ "$25M to Aid Slow Border Crossings on Fast Track" in *Crain's Detroit Business* (V. 17, No. 44, 10/22/2001)
Pub: Crain Communications, Inc.
Ed: Terry Kosdrosky. **Description:** Forty percent of all trade between Canada and the U.S. occurs at the Detroit-Windsor border. A new proposal would give the U.S. Customs Service an additional $25 million for more officers in order to ease delays at the border crossings since the 9-11 terrorist attack.

43859 ■ "Ukraine" in *Business Week* (January 9, 2006, No. 3966, pp. 44)
Pub: McGraw-Hill Companies
Ed: Rose Brady, Jason Bush. **Description:** Investing in the Ukraine could be risky business for foreign investors.

43860 ■ "U.S.-Canada Agricultural Trade to Get Stickier in 2007" in *Kiplinger Letter* (Vol. 78, January 19, 2007, No. 2)
Pub: Kiplinger
Description: Border security, U.S. corn subsidies, USDA proposed fees and inspections of farm goods from Canada along with country-of-origin rules on meat products are expected to make trade between the U.S. and Canada more difficult.

43861 ■ "U.S. Cotton Farmers Waiting Out the Market for Better Prices" in *Kiplinger Letter* (Vol. 78, January 19, 2007, No. 4)
Pub: Kiplinger
Description: U.S. cotton exports fell nearly 45 percent in 2006. China and India are expected to turn to U.S. cotton suppliers due to depletion of their crops.

43862 ■ "U.S. Exports in 2007" in *Kiplinger Letter* **(Vol. 78, January 5, 2007, No. 1)**
Pub: Kiplinger
Description: U.S. export growth is expected to drop by nearly 5 percent in 2007, reflective of slow growth in countries such as Canada, Mexico, parts of Europe, China, Japan, and South Korea.

43863 ■ "U.S. Hispanic Market Has Special Character" in *Hispanic Business* **(January/February 2005, pp. 8)**
Pub: Hispanic Business
Ed: Jesus Chavarria. **Description:** Latin American and U.S. Hispanics have become one in the eyes of corporations, investors and executives, and the same holds true with global economies. Statistical data included.

43864 ■ "U.S.-Mexico Relations Remain on Front Burner" in *Hispanic Business* **(Vol. 23, No. 11, November 2001, pp. 20)**
Pub: Hispanic Business Inc.
Ed: Patricia Guadalupe. **Description:** Despite the September 11 attacks, the U.S.-Mexico agenda will continue to work on issues of trade, immigration, and other issues of interest to both countries.

43865 ■ "Unrealized Potential" in *Hispanic Business* **(July/August 2002, pp. 58, 60, 62)**
Pub: Hispanic Business
Ed: Jonathan J. Higuera. **Description:** Reasons for the U.S.-Mexico border trade has failed to live up to some expectations of the North American Free Trade Agreement (NAFTA). Statistical data included.

43866 ■ "Up Front: Stacking Up Sales Overseas" in *My Business* **(December/January 2004, pp. 10-11)**
Pub: My Business Magazine
Ed: Mike Doser. **Description:** U.S. entrepreneurs are finding success selling beverages overseas. Advice is given to research the market, utilize foreign links, and understand it takes more time to build a long-term relationship with an overseas firm.

43867 ■ "UPS to Buy 27 Boeing Craft" in *Altanta Journal-Constitution* **(February 6, 2007)**
Pub: Cox Newspapers, Inc.
Ed: Matt Kempner. **Description:** UPS announced plans to purchase 27 new Boeing 767-300ER freighters in order to expand international markets and provide flexibility in its air fleet.

43868 ■ "U.S.: Signs That Inflation Is Losing Its Fangs" in *Business Week* **(February 7, 2005, No. 3919, pp. 25)**
Pub: McGraw-Hill Companies
Ed: James C. Cooper, Kathleen Madigan. **Description:** Global competition and information technology should help curb inflation in 2005. Statistical data included.

43869 ■ "Vancouver Vanguard" in *Fast Company* **(September 2001, pp. 36)**
Pub: Fast Company
Description: Fast Company's Heath Row will embark on the third-annual CoF Roadshow through North America. While spending time in Vancouver, British Columbia, Canada, Row will address ways Canada is competing in the global market.

43870 ■ "VAT Facts" in *Entrepreneur* **(Vol. 31, No. 10, October 2003, pp. 52)**
Pub: Entrepreneur Media, Inc.
Ed: Amanda C. Kooser. **Description:** The Value Added Tax (VAT), required for purchases made in the European Union, now includes non-EU companies, and ranges from 15-25 percent.

43871 ■ "A Very British Compromise" in *Red Herring* **(No. 105, October 1, 2001, pp. 50-53)**
Pub: Herring Communications
Ed: Guy Paisner. **Description:** The United Kingdom's largest venture capital company, 3i, has global ambitions. It aims to succeed where Silicon Valley firms fear to tread. 3i has a network of offices in 43 offices, including locations in the United States. The firm plans to overtake its rivals, especially those in the U.S., by providing risk capital to technology startups.

43872 ■ "Vietnam Primed for VC Growth" in *Venture Capital Journal* **(February 1, 2006)**
Pub: Thomason Financial Inc.
Description: Many experts predict that Vietnam is the next Southeast Asian country to emerge to become an economic powerhouse. The country has 6,000 publicly held companies. Statistical data included.

43873 ■ "What is a Global Manager?" in *Harvard Business Review* **(Vol. 81, No. 8, August 2003, pp. 101)**
Pub: Harvard Business School Press
Ed: Christopher A. Bartlett, Sumantra Ghoshal. **Description:** An effective global manager is not one person. He/she will be one of three types: a business manager, a country manager, and a function manager. For companies to utilize these managers, a set of senior executives will need to nurture and coordinate these specialists. Corning Glass' effort to develop a global market is used to illustrate the point.

43874 ■ "What Goes Up: Now There's a New Way to Track Small Business's Ups and Downs" in *Entrepreneur* **(Vol. 32, No. 1, January 2004, pp. 30)**
Pub: Entrepreneur Media, Inc.
Description: The Small Business Index (SBI) will help entrepreneurs track 19 economic indicators affecting small businesses. The indicators are grouped in four categories: costs factors, credit conditions, industry metrics, and trade competitiveness.

43875 ■ "What Makes Global Firms Resilient?" in *Harvard Business Review* **(Vol. 81, No. 7, July 2003, pp. 14)**
Pub: Harvard Business School Press
Ed: Gardiner Morse. **Description:** The economic importance of globalization is discussed by author, Daniel Yergin.

43876 ■ "Why Democracy is America's Second Most Valuable Export" in *Inc.* **(September 2005, pp. 23)**
Pub: Inc. Magazine
Ed: Carl Schramm, Robert Litan. **Description:** If entrepreneurship is exported to China, democracy is sure to follow.

43877 ■ "Why Must China Die?" in *Minority Business Journal* **(Vol. 17, No. 5, September/October 2001, pp. 4)**
Pub: Minority Business Journal
Description: Foreign investment in China and China's hardline business arrangements are discussed.

43878 ■ *Winning in Foreign Markets*
Pub: Crisp Publications, Inc.
Ed: Michele D. Forzley. **Price:** $9.95; $35.00 (three audiocassettes).

43879 ■ "Wiring the border" in *Hispanic Business* **(Vol. 22, No. 7-8, July-August 2000, pp. 70)**
Pub: Hispanic Business
Ed: Scott Williams. **Description:** The U.S.-Mexico Chamber of Commerce is backing a program that will help 200 companies along the Mexican-U.S. border to be part of the Internet revolution. The public-private partnership, known as Wiring the Border, will provide hardware, software, training and Internet access, plus business-to-business connections with major companies.

43880 ■ "With Revenue Flattening, David Galbenski Needed a Bold New Plan" in *Inc.* **(Volume 28, January 2006, No. 1, pp. 44-46)**
Pub: Inc. Magazine
Ed: Darren Dahl. **Description:** David Galbenski, owner of a temporary, contract legal firm discusses whether outsourcing to India was a smart move for his firm located in Royal Oak, Michigan.

43881 ■ *World Business Desk Reference: How to Do Business with 192 Countries by Phone, Fax, and Mail*
Pub: Irwin Professional Publishing
Ed: Alice A. Gelder with Rudy Yuly. **Price:** $75.00.
Description: Provides information on forms of address, time zones, phone codes, airports, business etiquette, and other topics regarding international business.

43882 ■ "World Cities Alliance: www.worldcitiesalliance.com" in *Entrepreneur* **(Vol. 31, No. 12, December 2003, pp. 8)**
Pub: Entrepreneur Media Inc.
Ed: Steve Cooper. **Description:** Ways to expand a small business internationally are highlighted using a Web site that covers information on labor costs, site location, taxation, start-up assistance, employee orientation and more.

43883 ■ "The world in your backyard" in *WorkingWoman* **(Vol. 25, No. 2, February 2000, pp. 72)**
Pub: Lang Communications Inc.
Ed: Caitlin Kelly. **Description:** There are 617 consulates in the U.S., offering services in international marketing, labor and culture.

43884 ■ *The World Markets Desk Book: A Region-by-Region Survey of Global Trade Opportunities*
Pub: The McGraw-Hill Companies
Ed: Lawrence W. Tuller. **Released:** 1992. **Price:** $29.95. **Description:** Guide to doing business globally providing information on exporting and setting up foreign offices.

43885 ■ *The World's Largest Market: A Business Guide to Europe 1992*
Pub: AMACOM
Ed: Robert Williams, Mark Teagan, and Jose Beneyto. **Released:** 1991. **Price:** $19.95 (paper); ($17.95 for AMA members). **Description:** Covers the effects changing Europe has on business. Provides information on exporting, relocation, trade law, GATT, and the European monetary system.

43886 ■ "Wrestling for Web dominance" in *Hispanic Business* **(Vol. 22, No. 7-8, July-August 2000, pp. 106)**
Pub: Hispanic Business
Ed: Vaughn Hagerty. **Description:** Global consolidation is taking place among the Internet's Hispanic-targeted Web sites. Among the companies set to gain a dominant position in the sector is Spanish telecom provider Terra Networks with its proposed $12.5 billion acquisition of Web service provider Lycos.

43887 ■ "XML: The Only Chance for a Worldwide Standard" in *E-business Advisor* **(Vol. 18, No. 4, April 2000, pp. 10)**
Pub: Advisor Media, Inc.
Ed: Rik Drummond. **Description:** The second meeting of the Electronic Business XML (ebXML) Initiative to produce a global standard for e-commerce was held in February 2000. There are eight project teams in ebXML. Activities of the project teams, are presented with special emphasis on the Transport/Routing and Packaging team, aimed at developing technical specifications for the e-commerce server intercommunications architecture are presented.

43888 ■ "Yamaha Sued Over Imports" in *Sacramento Bee* **(December 20, 2005)**
Pub: The Sacramento Bee
Ed: Dale Kasler. **Description:** The State of California's Air Resources Board is suing Yamaha Motor Corporation USA and two dealers in San Jose and Honolulu over claims they imported over 400 motorcycles not meeting the state's air pollution standards.

43889 ■ "You Can Take It With You: Use Your Mobile Phone Even While Abroad" in *Entrepreneur* **(Vol. 32, July 2004, No. 7, pp. 43)**
Pub: Entrepreneur Media Inc.
Ed: Amanda C. Kooser. **Description:** Entrepreneurs who travel outside of the U.S. are able to use their mobile phones while abroad. Dual-network phones work over both CDMA and GMS networks so a personal phone can be used with an international calling plan.

SOURCES OF SUPPLY

43890 ■ *Importers Manual USA*
Pub: World Trade Press
Contact: Edward Hinkelman, Author
Released: Biennial, latest edition 4, 2003. **Price:** $108.75, individuals. **Publication Includes:** Lists of trade fairs, embassies, chambers of commerce, banks, and other sources of information on various aspects of international trade. **Entries Include:** Source name, address, phone, telex, description. Principal content of publication is information on importing to the U.S. , including coverage of U.S. Customs, banking, laws, shipping, and insurance. **Indexes:** Product/service, geographical, source name.

TRADE PERIODICALS

43891 ■ *Bacard's Global Investor*
Pub: Ferney Scribes Inc.
Ed: Andre Bacard, Editor. **Released:** Monthly. **Price:** $129, U.S.. **Description:** Provides monthly updates of select no-load global and international funds, model portfolios, foreign market graphs, monthly analysis and current recommendations. Recurring features include news of research and a column titled Mutual Fund in the Spotlight.

43892 ■ *Brazilian-American Chamber of Commerce—News Bulletin*
Pub: Brazilian-American Chamber of Commerce Inc.
Contact: Monica Rocha
Ed: Monica Rocha, Editor. **Released:** Monthly. **Price:** $138, Included in membership; $85, nonmembers; $75 educational institutions. **Description:** Provides up-to-date information on the economy of Brazil and on Brazil's economic relations with the U.S. Concerned with economic data, energy, imports/exports, industry, shipping, and agriculture. Recurring features include topical articles and an executive summary.

43893 ■ *China Telecom*
Pub: Information Gatekeepers Inc.
Contact: Hui Pan
Ed: Hui Pan, Editor, editor@igigroup.com. **Released:** Monthly. **Price:** $695, U.S. and Canada; $745, elsewhere; $695 email, one user. **Description:** Reports on current events in telecommunications developments occuring in China. Recurring features include a calendar of events.

43894 ■ *CUBANEWS*
Pub: Target Research
Ed: Larry Luxner, Editor. **Released:** Monthly. **Price:** $429, individuals; $199 academic institutions. **Description:** Covers business and economic issues involving Cuba, including an economic overview, monthly developments, and industrial analysis.

43895 ■ *Export Communications*
Pub: ARISTO Marketing Corp.
Ed: Patricia J. Epple, Editor, patricia@aristonet.com. **Released:** Quarterly. **Price:** $125, U.S.; $150, Canada. **Description:** Provides practical information and trade leads on export opportunities and developments in foreign markets. Recurring features include letters to the editor, a calendar of events, job listings, and a column titled Internet Resource Guide.

43896 ■ *The Exporter*
Pub: Trade Data Reports Inc.
Released: Monthly. **Price:** $218 year. **Description:** Covers export operations, markets, training resources, and world trade information.

43897 ■ *Global Voice*
Pub: Berlitz International Inc.
Contact: Erin Giordano
Ed: Erin Giordano, Editor, erin.giordano@berlitz.com. **Released:** Quarterly. **Price:** Free. **Description:** Carries information on the importance of language fluency and cross-cultural understanding in international business.

43898 ■ *The International Trade Journal*
Pub: Taylor & Francis
Ed: Antonio J. Rodriguez, Editor, rodriguez@tamiu.edu. **Released:** Quarterly. **Description:** Professional journal dealing with theoretical and practical aspects of business and economic issues in the Western Hemisphere.

43899 ■ *International Trade Reporter*
Pub: Bureau of National Affairs Inc.
Contact: Linda G. Botsford, Managing Editor
Released: Weekly. **Price:** $1,159. **Description:** Covers current international trade policies of the U.S. and of major U.S. trading partners. Topics include bilateral negotiations, customs, export/import policy, foreign investment, standards, taxation, and other related issues. Recurring features include a calendar of events, reports of meetings, and notices of publications available. .

43900 ■ *International Trade Reporter Decisions*
Pub: Bureau of National Affairs Inc.
Ed: Linda G. Botsford, Editor, lbotsford@bna.com. **Released:** Biweekly. **Price:** $1330. **Description:** Carries digested, classified, and indexed judicial and administrative decisions dealing with legal issues arising from U.S. trade law.

43901 ■ *The International Trader*
Pub: GMS Publications
Ed: Warren Hasting, Editor. **Released:** Monthly. **Price:** $119, individuals; Included in membership. **Description:** Devoted to international trade, finance, transportation, and logistics. Provides current information on import/export matters, plus new ways to finance and market them. Recurring features include listings and details of the new members of the Centre for International Trade.

43902 ■ *International Traders' Mailbag*
Pub: IBIS/Business Information Services, International
Ed: Adair Wyett, Editor. **Released:** Monthly. **Description:** Focuses on international trade. Covers new trade regulations, restrictions, and opportunities. Offers management tips, business contacts, and other information of use to professionals in the field.

43903 ■ *International Traders Newsletter*
Pub: International Business Information Service
Released: Monthly, plus special issues. **Price:** $150, individuals in the U.S.. **Description:** Offers current information and ideas for active international traders. Recurring features include letters to the editor, news of research, a calendar of events, book reviews, notices of publications available, and columns titled Q & A and JUST IN.

43904 ■ *Internationalist*
Pub: Assist International
Ed: Peter J. Robinson, Jr., Editor. **Released:** 3x/yr. **Price:** $15, individuals. **Description:** Communicates international trade events, conferences, seminars, and trade shows occuring in the New York/Connecticut/New Jersey region. Recurring features include a calendar of events and a listing of international trade resources available in the tri-state region.

43905 ■ *Journal of Asia-Pacific Business*
Pub: The Haworth Press Inc.
Ed: Ugur Ugur Yavas, MBA, Editor, raxyavas@etsu.edu. **Released:** Quarterly. **Price:** $75 USA; $125 institutions USA; $225 libraries Agencies, USA; $101 Canada; $169 institutions, Canada; $304 libraries Agencies, Canada; $109 other countries; $181 institutions, other countries; $326 libraries Agencies, other countries. **Description:** Journal featuring managerially oriented as well as academic articles centered on the Asia-Pacific region.

43906 ■ *Journal of East-West Business*
Pub: The Haworth Press Inc.
Contact: Bill Cohen, Publisher
Ed: Erdener Kaynak, Editor, k9x@psu.edu. **Released:** Quarterly. **Price:** $85 U.S.; $175 institutions U.S.; $315 libraries agencies, U.S.; $115 Canada; $236 institutions, Canada Canada; $425 libraries agencies, Canada; $123 other countries; $254 institutions, other countries Canada; $457 libraries agencies, other countries. **Description:** Journal dealing with contemporary and emerging topics of business studies, strategies, development, and practice relating to Eastern Europe and Asia.

43907 ■ *Mexico Consensus Economic Forecast*
Pub: Bank One Economic Outlook Center
Ed: Lee R. McPheters, Editor. **Released:** Quarterly. **Price:** $20, individuals print version; $5, single issue print version; Free. **Description:** Provides forecasts and an analysis of the Mexico economy. **Remarks:** Available online or in print format.

43908 ■ *Ottawa Letter*
Pub: CCH Canadian Ltd.
Contact: Anna Wong
E-mail: awong@cch.ca
Released: Biweekly. **Price:** $650. **Description:** Reports on current events and topics of Canada, such as free trade, human rights, employment, and defense. Also provides statistics, lending, and foreign exchange rates.

43909 ■ *Political Risk Letter*
Pub: The PRS Group
Contact: Diana Spinner
E-mail: bmcternan@prsgroup.com
Ed: William D. Coplin, Editor. **Released:** Monthly, 12/year. **Price:** $415, U.S. and Canada. **Description:** Offers concise political and economic forecasts for both 18 month and 5 year time spans. Provides country risk forecasts and analysis on 100 countries around the world and provides indepth coverage on 20 countries.

43910 ■ *Puerto Rico Business Review*
Pub: Government Development Bank for Puerto Rico
Ed: Maria Socorro Rosario-Claudio, Editor. **Released:** Quarterly. **Price:** Free. **Description:** Covers business and finance related to Puerto Rico. Carries research articles from government and business leaders and government agencies on the Puerto Rican economy. Reports on activity in agricultural industries, import and export trade, retail trade, banking, tourism, manufacturing, and other enterprises. Recurring features include a column titled In Focus and a supplement called Puerto Rico Mon. Economic Indicators.

43911 ■ *SACC NYChronicle*
Pub: Swedish-American Chamber of Commerce
Ed: Veronica Stolt, Editor. **Released:** Monthly. **Price:** Included in membership. **Description:** Concerned with developments in the Swedish and U.S. business communities: unemployment rates, industry plans and investments, exports, government measures to stimulate the economy, and similar subjects. Covers the membership activities of the SACC. Recurring features include interviews with Swedish and U.S. executives.

43912 ■ *Washington Tariff & Trade Letter*
Pub: Gilston-Kalin Communications, LLC
Contact: Elayne Gilston
Ed: Samuel M. Gilston, Editor. **Released:** Weekly. **Price:** $597 print or electronic. **Description:** Reports on U.S. trade policies, negotiations, regulations, and legislation.

43913 ■ *Weekly Outlook*
Pub: University of Illinois at Urbana-Champaign
Contact: Darrel Good, Coordinator
Released: Weekly (Mon.), 50/year. **Price:** $50. **Description:** Anticipates, reports, and interprets current market information, supply, demand, and price outlook for agricultural products, including corn, soybeans, wheat, cattle, and hogs.

43914 ■ *World Trade Connection*
Pub: Consumers for World Trade
Ed: Doreen L. Brown, Editor, dbrown@cwt.org. **Released:** Quarterly. **Price:** Included in membership.

Description: Supplies information on trade issues following the issues through the legislative process to conclusion. Reports on International Trade Commission actions, carries interviews with trade leaders, and provides news of organization activities. Recurring features include letters to the editor and columns titled In Brief and New Publications.

VIDEOCASSETTES/ AUDIOCASSETTES

43915 ■ *Building the Trans-National Team*
Videolearning Systems, Inc.
38 Discovery, Ste. 250
Irvine, CA 92618
Free: 800-622-3610
Co. E-mail: sales@videolrn.com
URL: http://www.videolrn.com
Released: 1994. **Price:** $495.00. **Description:** Underlines the difficulties of doing business with people of various nationalities including French, Spanish, German, and British. Focusses on cultural differences. Comes with guide. **Availability:** VHS.

43916 ■ *The Dollars and Sense of Exporting: How to Navigate the Global Market*
PBS Home Video
Catalog Fulfillment Center
PO Box 751089
Charlotte, NC 28275-1089
Ph:800-531-4727
Free: 800-645-4PBS
Co. E-mail: info@pbs.org
URL: http://www.pbs.org
Released: 1989. **Price:** $300.00. **Description:** Helpful information for companies that wish to enter or expand in the international marketplace. Includes tips on assistance offered by various levels of government. **Availability:** VHS; 3/4U.

CONSULTANTS

43917 ■ 2010 Fund 5
24351 Spartan St., Ste. 120
Mission Viejo, CA 92691
Ph:(949)583-1992
Scope: Funds in formation that will invest in technologies licensed from 30 universities. **Seminars:** Chair, Corporate Investment and Strategic Alliance Conferences.

43918 ■ Americas Consulting Group Inc.
741 Riversville Rd.
Greenwich, CT 06831
Ph:(203)863-9168
Fax: (203)863-9161
Co. E-mail: acg03@sprynet.com
URL: http://www.americasconsult.com

E-mail: acg03@sprynet.com
Scope: A consultant whose expertise is in assisting companies in developing growth strategies within the Western hemisphere. We are experts in international business with a special focus on marketing, information acquisition and investigations.

43919 ■ Banfinanz Ltd.
1 Eab Plz.
Uniondale, NY 11555
Ph:(516)227-2205
Fax: (516)522-2835
Scope: International business consultants specializing in economics and accounting.

43920 ■ Cohen & Associates
1625 Holly Ln.
Munster, IN 46321
Ph:(219)923-2622
Fax: (219)923-3133
Scope: Domestic and international business development. Counsels companies from the start-up stage through the opening of foreign markets. Import/Export strategies; general management consulting; marketing planning; business development.

43921 ■ Dubuc Lucke & Co.
414 Walnut St., Ste607
Cincinnati, OH 45202
Ph:(513)579-8330
Fax: (513)241-6669
Scope: Consulting services in the areas of profit enhancement; small business management; mergers and acquisitions; joint ventures; divestitures; interim management; crisis management; turnarounds; appraisals; valuations; due diligence; and international trade.

43922 ■ First Washington Associates Ltd.
1501 Lee Hwy., Ste. 302
Arlington, VA 22209
Ph:(703)525-0966
Fax: (703)276-8851
Co. E-mail: fwa@mindspring.com

E-mail: fwa@mindspring.com
Scope: Provides technical assistance in all aspects of international trade finance, small business development and related disciplines, including feasibility studies, market research, design and implementation of export credit, guarantee and insurance programs, formulation of policies, procedures and programs for public and private sector clients. **Publications:** The FWA Quarterly distributed to managers of export credit agencies in all countries; The Trade & Export Finance Handbook, with Euromoney Publications. **Seminars:** Workshops on trends and innovations in export trading incentives and financial programs and training courses in international trade finance.

43923 ■ Global Business Consultants
120 Market Sq.
PO Box 776
Pinehurst, NC 28374-0776
Ph:(910)295-5991
Free: 800-991-4990
Fax: (910)295-5908
Co. E-mail: info@yourculturecoach.com

E-mail: info@yourculturecoach.com
Scope: Firm specializes in human resources management; project management; software development; and international trade. Offers litigation support.

43924 ■ Great Lakes Consulting Group Inc.
1217 S Walnut St.
South Bend, IN 46619-4305
Ph:(574)287-4500
Fax: (574)234-8207
Scope: Provides consulting services in the areas of strategic planning; feasibility studies; start-up businesses; small business management; mergers and acquisitions; joint ventures; divestitures; interim management; crisis management; turnarounds; business process re-engineering; venture capital; and international trade.

43925 ■ Idi-Supply Inc.
3866 N Fratney St.
PO Box 12050
Milwaukee, WI 53212
Ph:(414)961-2365
Fax: (414)961-1582
Scope: Firm specializes in start-up businesses; small business management; mergers and acquisitions; joint ventures; divestitures; venture capital; appraisals; valuations; and international trade.

43926 ■ Intex Exhibit Systems L.L.C.
7018 NE 40th Ave.
Vancouver, WA 98661
Ph:(360)713-0300
Free: 800-331-6633
Fax: (360)713-0327
Co. E-mail: info@intexexhibits.com
URL: http://www.intexexhibits.com

E-mail: info@intexexhibits.com
Scope: Firm specializes in the design and production of exhibits, displays and pavilions for world fairs, tradeshows and similar events. Services include product design, industrial and engineering design for edu-

cational exhibits, museum exhibits and science and technology museology. Serves private industry as well as government agencies. **Publications:** "Trade Show Marketing"; "Exhibitor Times". **Special Services:** Fastpack™; Panelflo™; affordable-1™; the graphic arm™; Expression™; TigerMark™.

43927 ■ Marringa International Co.
2520 W Dean Rd.
Milwaukee, WI 53217-2019
Ph:(414)351-5388
Scope: International business development through identification of priority foreign markets and formulation of strategies for distribution, start-up, alliances, and acquisitions. Industries served: small to mid-sized manufacturing companies.

43928 ■ Nightingale Associates
7445 Setting Sun Way
Columbia, MD 21046-1261
Ph:(410)381-4280
Fax: (410)381-4280
Co. E-mail: fcnight@aol.com
URL: http://www.members.aol.com/fcnight

E-mail: fcnight@aol.com
Scope: Nightingale Associates is an international management training and consulting firm. Their concentration is on improving operational performance through the utilization of the most effective modern management techniques, executive and organizational assessment, reengineering of business processes, creative strategic thinking and focusing of the energies of all organizational participants. In addition they also work in the area of supply chain management and cost reduction through the utilization of the optimum purchasing, inventory management and distribution practices. **Seminars:** Advanced Management; Business Process Reengineering; Strategic Thinking; Creative Problem Solving; Customer Service; International Purchasing and Materials Management; Fundamentals of Purchasing.

43929 ■ Plans and Solutions Inc.
PO Box 8905
Gaithersburg, MD 20898-8905
Ph:(301)947-8150
Fax: (240)525-5601
Co. E-mail: info@plansandsolutions.com
URL: http://www.plansandsolutions.com

E-mail: info@plansandsolutions.com
Scope: Business and strategic planning, market research and development. Most clients are minority-owned businesses in the USA and companies overseas that want to begin or increase exports to the United States and Canada. **Publications:** "Building an Import/Export Business," John Wiley & Sons, 2002.

43930 ■ Ralph J. Sigona, Associates
1575 Center Ave.
Fort Lee, NJ 07024-4644
Ph:(201)461-3067
Scope: International business consultants offering these services: formulation and execution of commercial and marketing programs for imported and/or exported products in the United States, in Europe, and in other major world markets; search for and selection of importers and distributors for the introduction of manufactured products in foreign markets; market research and market intelligence services; evaluation and implementation of business and product opportunities on behalf of qualified clients. Serves private industries as well as government agencies. **Seminars:** How to Sell Overseas, International Marketing Procedures and Practices (annually).

COMPUTERIZED DATABASES

43931 ■ *Antitrust & Trade Regulation Report*
The Bureau of National Affairs Inc.
1231 25th St. NW
Washington, DC 20037

Ph:(202)452-4200
Free: 800-372-1033
Fax: (202)452-4226
Co. E-mail: customercare@bna.com
URL: http://www.bna.com
Description: Contains the complete text of *Antitrust & Trade Regulation Report*, covering legislative, regulatory, and judicial activities related to laws on enforcement of competition and deceptive trade practices. Covers litigation, negotiations, and civil and criminal investigations. Provides news and commentary on actions by the Department of Justice, Federal Trade Commission, state attorneys general, foreign countries, consumer groups, and manufacturers. Covers such areas as franchising and franchise regulations, compliance programs, dealing with trade associations and competitors, engaging in joint ventures, and marketing and distributing goods and services. **Availability:** Online: LexisNexis, Thomson West, The Bureau of National Affairs Inc. **Type:** Full text.

43932 ■ *Business Browser U.S.*
OneSource Information Services Inc.
300 Baker Ave.
Concord, MA 01742
Ph:(978)318-4300
Fax: (978)318-4690
Co. E-mail: sales@onesource.com
URL: http://www.onesource.com
Description: Provides integrated industry information on more than 640,000 public and private companies in the United States and Canada. Contains detailed business and biographical information on more than 3.2 million executives, including name, position, and contact data. Includes company (public and private) profiles, news, client lists and rankings, industry intelligence, business and trade articles, biographical information on executives, and financial data (including annual reports and shareholding details). Allows all tabular information to be imported to spreadsheets. Provides in-depth information use in general business research, new business development, competitor analysis, marketing and sales, and monitoring companies and industries. **Availability:** Online: OneSource Information Services Inc. **Type:** Directory; Numeric; Statistical; Full text.

43933 ■ *The Eastern Europe Business Database CD-ROM*
American Directory Corp.
PO Box 7426
New York, NY 10116
Fax: (212)596-4852
Co. E-mail: eebd@didik.com
URL: http://www.didik.com/dcd.htm
Released: Annual. **Price:** $395, individuals. **Covers:** 200,000 companies and other businesses in Eastern Europe and the former Soviet Union. **Entries Include:** Company name, product location, contact information, and other criteria.

43934 ■ *EIU ViewsWire*
The Economist Group
26 Red Lion Sq.
London WC1R 4HQ, United Kingdom
Ph:44 20 75768181
Fax: 44 20 75768476
Co. E-mail: london@eiu.com
URL: http://www.eiu.com
Description: Provides up to 150 articles daily covering practical business intelligence, including key events, market issues, impending crises, and the business and regulatory environment in emerging and International markets. Covers information from more than 195 countries. Includes: Briefings: critical political, economic, and business changes around the world organized by the topics of company, economy, finance, politics, regulations, and industry. Forecasts: Country updates-continuously updated overviews of GDP, inflation, demand, investment, fiscal policy, interest rates, currency, external accounts, and the political scene in more than 190 countries.; Consensus forecasts-monthly currency, interest rate, and equity market short-term outlooks provided by multinational companies and investment banks.; Country risk sum-

mary-political and credit risk ratings and analysis for 100 countries.; Five-year forecasts—quarterly growth, inflation, and trade indicators for 60 countries.; Forecast summaries—quarterly key economic indicators and business watchlist. Background: facts and figures on current conditions in more than 190 countries.; Key economic indicators—quarterly statistics on growth, trade, reserves, and currencies.; Basic data and country fact sheet-population data, per capita GDP, political structure, taxes, foreign trade and policy issues.; Trade, tax and forex regulations-Connecticut updated full regulatory profiles on 60 countries. **Availability:** Online: The Economist Group, Thomson Financial, Financial Times, LexisNexis. **Type:** Full text; Numeric.

43935 ■ *Global Business Browser*
OneSource Information Services Inc.
300 Baker Ave.
Concord, MA 01742
Ph:(978)318-4300
Fax: (978)318-4690
Co. E-mail: sales@onesource.com
URL: http://www.onesource.com
Description: Provides integrated industry information on approximately 100,000 global companies and markets, including both established and emerging markets. Contains detailed business and biographical information on approximately 1 million executives, including name, position, and contact data. Includes company profiles, news, industry intelligence, business and trade articles, and financial data. Allows tabular information to be imported to spreadsheets. Provides in-depth information for use in general business research, new business development, competitor analysis, marketing and sales, and monitoring companies and industries. **Availability:** Online: OneSource Information Services Inc. **Type:** Directory; Numeric; Statistical; Full text.

43936 ■ *International Trade Reporter*
The Bureau of National Affairs Inc.
1231 25th St. NW
Washington, DC 20037
Ph:(202)452-4200
Free: 800-372-1033
Fax: (202)452-4226
Co. E-mail: customercare@bna.com
URL: http://www.bna.com
Description: Contains current information on developments in international trade and actions of U.S. courts and federal agencies related to imports and exports. Covers import competition and restrictions, export financing, trade agreements and negotiations, and foreign investment in the United States. Provides current information on the World Trade Organization, APEC, the European Union, and NAFTA. Covers such topics as export incentives, import relief, agricultural trade, financing, trade in services, taxation, balance of trade, foreign investments and more. **Availability:** Online: Thomson West, The Bureau of National Affairs Inc. **Type:** Full text.

43937 ■ *PIERS Exports (Latin America)*
PIERS
33 Washington St., 13th Fl.
Newark, NJ 07102-3107
Ph:(973)848-7051
Free: 800-952-3839
Fax: (973)848-7043
Co. E-mail: info@piers.com
URL: http://www.piers.com
Description: Contains financial and statistical information on exports from Latin America. Represents a compilation of manifests of vessels carrying International cargo departing from seaports in Mexico. Lists name, city, and state of exporter; product description as shown on manifest; standardized commodity description; harmonized product code; packaging; cargo weight in pounds; port name and code; overseas port name and code; overseas country name and code; and date of departure from port. **Availability:** Online: Thomson Dialog. **Type:** Directory; Numeric.

43938 ■ *PIERS Imports (Latin America)*
PIERS
33 Washington St., 13th Fl.
Newark, NJ 07102-3107

Ph:(973)848-7051
Free: 800-952-3839
Fax: (973)848-7043
Co. E-mail: info@piers.com
URL: http://www.piers.com
Description: Contains financial and statistical information on imports to Latin America. Represents a compilation of manifests of vessels discharging International cargo at seaports in Mexico. Lists name and location of overseas shipper; name and city of consignee; product description as shown on manifest; standardized commodity description; harmonized product code; date of arrival at port; cargo weight in pounds; port name and code; overseas port name and code; overseas country name and code; and packaging. **Availability:** Online: Thomson Dialog. **Type:** Directory; Numeric.

43939 ■ *United States International Trade in Goods and Services*
U.S. Census Bureau
4700 Silver Hill Rd.
Washington, DC 20233-0001
Ph:(301)457-4100
Fax: (301)457-4714
Co. E-mail: webmaster@census.gov
URL: http://www.census.gov
Description: Contains data from the Foreign Trade Statistics department of the U.S. Bureau of the Census on trade in goods and services. Delineates total exports, imports, and goods trade balances. Provides monthly Bureau of Economic Analysis statistics on U.S. trade balance. Includes information on goods by category and geographic area. Addresses trade deficits in goods and services. Includes imports and exports of domestic and foreign merchandise and petroleum. Includes trade balance using general imports c.i.f. value. **Availability:** Online: U.S. Census Bureau. **Type:** Statistical.

43940 ■ *Ward's Business Directory of U.S. Private and Public Companies*
Thomson Gale
27500 Drake Rd.
Farmington Hills, MI 48331-3535
Ph:(248)699-4253
Free: 800-877-GALE
Fax: (248)699-8069
Co. E-mail: gale.galeord@thomson.com
URL: http://www.gale.com
Description: Contains nearly 300,000 private and public companies in the United States. Used to identify market participants and study market share, locate potential clients and create targeted mailing lists, to determine parent/subsidiary relationships, and to analyze market position and find specific data on targeted companies. Corresponds to the 12-volume print version of *Ward's Business Directory of U.S. Private and Public Companies*, whose databases are available by special arrangement on disk. **Availability:** CD-ROM: Thomson Gale; Diskette: Thomson Gale. **Type:** Directory; Numeric.

LIBRARIES

43941 ■ Canada - Department of Foreign Affairs and International Trade–Main Library
Lester B. Pearson Bldg.
125 Sussex Dr.
Ottawa, ON, Canada K1A 0G2
Ph:(613)992-6150
Fax: (613)944-0222
Co. E-mail: infotech@dfait-maeci.gc.ca
URL: http://www.dfait-maeci.gc.ca/link/
Contact: Patricia Gibson, Dep.Dir. & Chf.Libn.
Scope: International relations, international law, international economics, trade, investment, international organizations. **Services:** Interlibrary loan; copying; Library open to the public with restrictions. **Holdings:** 50,000 monographs; 30,000 bound periodical volumes; 550,000 documents; 200,000 microforms; 800 maps.

43942 ■ Canadian International Trade Tribunal–Library
333 Laurier Ave. W., 15th Fl.
Ottawa, ON, Canada K1A 0G7
Ph:(613)990-2418
Fax: (613)990-2439
Co. E-mail: uschultz@citt-tcce.gc.ca
URL: http://www.citt.gc.ca
Contact: Ursula Schultz, Chf.Libn.
Scope: Trade, tariffs, customs and excise, Canadian law, commerce, economics. **Services:** Interlibrary loan; copying; Library open to the public at librarian's discretion. **Holdings:** 6000 books; 1000 bound periodical volumes. **Subscriptions:** 300 journals and other serials; 12 newspapers.

43943 ■ Ontario Ministry of Economic Development and Trade–InfoSource
900 Bay St.
Hearst Block, 6th Fl.
Toronto, ON, Canada M7A 2E1
Ph:(416)325-6626
Fax: (416)325-6825
Co. E-mail: janice.somers@edt.gov.on.ca
Scope: Trade, industry, small business, technology, management, company information. **Services:** Copying; scanning. **Holdings:** 200 books; microfiche; 20 CD-ROMs.

43944 ■ Woodbury University–Library
7500 N. Glenoaks Blvd.
PO Box 7846
Burbank, CA 91510-7846
Ph:(818)767-0888
Fax: (818)767-4534
Co. E-mail: barbara.bowley@woodbury.edu
URL: http://www.woodbury.edu/
Contact: Barbara Bowley, Dir.
Scope: Business and management, International business, art, architecture, interior design, fashion marketing and design, psychology, animation. **Ser-**

vices: Interlibrary loan; copying; Library open to the public for reference use only. **Holdings:** 58,827 books; 3070 bound periodical volumes; 92,511 microforms; 17,401 slides; 1044 videotapes; 117 CD-ROMs; 77 DVDs. **Subscriptions:** 436 journals and other serials; 5 newspapers.

RESEARCH CENTERS

43945 ■ Georgia Institute of Technology–Enterprise Innovation Institute
760 Spring St. NW, Ste. 330
Atlanta, GA 30332-0640
Ph:(404)894-2272
Fax: (404)894-1192
Co. E-mail: tisrael@gatech.edu
URL: http://www.innovate.gatech.edu
Contact: Timothy Israel, Gp.Mgr.
E-mail: tisrael@gatech.edu
Scope: International standards and quality, particularly exporting to European Community and Asian markets. Provides information, training and technical assistance and conducts research for southeastern firms interested in exporting. **Services:** Market Analysis; Product Analysis; Quality Assessments; Re-engineering and Design Services; Standards Interpretation; Standards Updating Service. **Publications:** European Market Bulletin; European Standards Directory (annually); Standards Newsletter. **Educational Activities:** Seminars and workshops on standards-related topics; Training Seminars and Workshops.

43946 ■ Georgia Southern University–Center for Global Business
College of Business Administration
PO Box 8140
Statesboro, GA 30460-8140
Ph:(912)681-5605
Fax: (912)486-7825
Co. E-mail: cswift@georgiasouthern.edu

URL: http://coba.gasou.edu/cgb
Contact: Dr. Cathy Swift, Dir.
E-mail: cswift@georgiasouthern.edu
Scope: Trade and service based commerce between Georgia companies and other nations, focusing on the impact of international trade in the southeastern U.S.

43947 ■ University of Maryland at College Park–Center for Global Business
Van Munching Hall, Rm. 3445
Robert H. Smith School of Business
College Park, MD 20742
Ph:(301)405-2198
Fax: (301)314-9526
Co. E-mail: info@rhsmith.umd.edu
URL: http://www.rhsmith.umd.edu/global
Contact: Dr. Bob Krapfel, Dir.
E-mail: info@rhsmith.umd.edu
Scope: Global business and management. **Educational Activities:** Conferences and workshops (occasionally).

43948 ■ University of Maryland at College Park–International Communications and Negotiations Simulations
3140 Tydings Hall
Department of Government and Politics
College Park, MD 20742
Ph:(301)405-4172
Fax: (301)314-9301
Co. E-mail: icons@gvpt.umd.edu
URL: http://www.icons.umd.edu
Contact: Elizabeth Kielman, Dep.Dir.
E-mail: icons@gvpt.umd.edu
Scope: Focuses on the critical connections between international issues and the perspectives that different cultures bring to negotiations. Also teaches cross cultural negotiation and develops international economic, environmental, and political scenarios/curriculum materials for university and high school students.

START-UP INFORMATION

43949 ■ **"Conversation with Randy Hinrichs"** in *Inc.* **(November 15, 2000, pp. 83)**
Pub: The Goldhirsh Group
Description: An intranet is no less than the foundation for a company's success. Advice to create powerful virtual spaces is offered by the author.

REFERENCE WORKS

43950 ■ **"Break It Down"** in *Entrepreneur* **(Vol. 28, No. 1, January 2000, pp. 116)**
Pub: Entrepreneur Media Inc.
Ed: Jacquelyn Lynn. **Description:** Would your managers take more interest in their departments' success if it were their company? Through a management method called "intrepreneurship", a concept first developed in big companies about a decade ago as a response to declining morale and productivity, might be an option.

43951 ■ **"Job Inside"** in *Fast Company* **(September 2001, pp. 177)**
Pub: Fast Company

Ed: George Anders. **Description:** The intranet is intended for internal use, but for small and mid-size companies outsourcing may be the best option for this technology.

43952 ■ **"Navy assesses small-biz impact of intranet deal"** in *Network World* **(April 3, 2000, pp. NA)**
Pub: Network World Inc.
Ed: Dan Verton. **Description:** The Small Business Administration has urged the Navy to disclose the number of small businesses that could be cut off from future Navy business once the service awards its $16 billion Intranet contract.

43953 ■ **"QEK's Intranet keeps life organized"** in *Crain's Detroit Business* **(Vol. 16, No. 34, August 21, 2000, pp. E-8)**
Pub: Crain Communications, Inc.
Ed: Jewel Gopwani. **Description:** QEK Global Solutions uses the Internet to keep up with its employees and keep track of its products.

43954 ■ **"Who Owns Your Intranet?"** in *Fast Company* **(September 2001, pp. 192)**
Pub: Fast Company
Ed: George Anders. **Description:** Ways to set up and manage a company's intranet are explored.

VIDEOCASSETTES/ AUDIOCASSETTES

43955 ■ *Fostering Creativity and Innovation*
J. Miller Associates
15669 Live Oak Springs Rd.
Santa Clarita, CA 91351-4712
Ph:(805)251-9310
Fax: (805)251-9192
Price: $99.00. **Description:** Part of the Management Speaks Series. Outlines how the success of a business is affected by its viewpoint on creativity and innovation. **Availability:** VHS.

43956 ■ *Inspiring Innovation*
American Management Association
9 Galen St.
PO Box 9119
Watertown, MA 02472
Ph:(617)926-4600
Free: 800-225-3215
Fax: (617)923-1875
URL: http://www.amanet.org
Price: $545.00. **Description:** Contains information on how to get started with the idea of innovation. **Availability:** VHS; CC.

Inventions, Licensing, and Patents

START-UP INFORMATION

43957 ■ *Entrepreneurship Strategy: Changing Patterns in New Venture Creation, Growth, and Reinvention*
Pub: SAGE Publications, Incorporated
Ed: Lisa K. Gundry; Jill R. Kickul. **Released:** August 2006. **Price:** $69.95. **Description:** Entrepreneurial strategies that incorporate new venture emergence, early growth, and reinvention and innovation are examined.

43958 ■ "Finding Success in a Haystack" in *Success* (Vol. 47, No. 5, October 2000, pp. 34)
Pub: Success Publishing, Inc.
Ed: Thomas Melville. **Description:** The article shows how Kathy Cunningham became a toy inventor at Haystack Toys.

43959 ■ "A Fitting Memorial" in *Entrepreneur* (Vol. 32, No. 5, May 2004, pp. 130)
Pub: Entrepreneur Media,, Inc.
Ed: Nichole L. Torres. **Description:** Profile of Mary Hickey and Bob Wheeler, founders of Renaissance Urn Company. The partners design and manufacturer decorative urn covers that allow families and friends to personalize funeral urns. Renaissance reported $100,000 in sales for 2003.

43960 ■ "For Love of the Game" in *Success* (Vol. 47, No. 6, November 2000, pp. 46)
Pub: Success Publishing, Inc.
Ed: Patrick Hoss. **Description:** Profile of Tim Walsh, a semi-professional baseball player in Mexico and exercise therapist, Walsh is also a board-game creator. As one of the creators of TriBond and the creator of Blurt, he shares the five things every entrepreneur should know in order to succeed.

43961 ■ "From Idea to Marketplace" in *Small Business Opportunities* (May 2005)
Pub: Harris Publications Inc.
Description: Every inventor must learn information about patenting, manufacturing, packaging, marketing and shipping when planning to take an invention from idea to the marketplace.

43962 ■ "Join the club: launching your first product" in *Entrepreneur* (Vol. 31, No. 5, May 2003, pp. 132)
Pub: Entrepreneur Media Inc.
Ed: Don Debelak. **Description:** An inexperienced inventor can gain valuable knowledge and insight by joining an inventor's club. Steps to help find the right group and make the most of a membership are listed.

43963 ■ "Just Do It" in *Entrepreneur* (Vol. 28, No. 17, July 2000, pp. 162)
Pub: Entrepreneur Media Inc.
Ed: Don Debelak. **Description:** Putting off applying for that patent? You may regret it later. The 1999 Supreme Court ruling (Pfaff v. Wells Electronics Inc.) is expected to have a huge impact on how quickly inventors apply for a patent.

43964 ■ *Legal Guide for Starting and Running a Small Business*
Pub: NOLO
Ed: Fred Steingold, Lisa Guerin. **Released:** March 2005. **Price:** $34.99. **Description:** Information for starting a new business focusing on choosing a business structure, taxes, employees and independent contractors, trademark and service marks, licensing and permits, leasing and improvement of commercial space, buying and selling a business, and more.

43965 ■ "A matter of safety" in *Black Enterprise* (Vol. 32, No. 9, April 2002)
Pub: Earl Graves Publishing Co.
Ed: Alan Hughes. **Description:** Orlando Robinson tells how a tragic event in his life prompted him to launch his own company, D&D Innovations Inc. His first product is the Seatbelt Shifter Lock, which requires the seatbelt to be locked before the car can be taken out of the park position.

43966 ■ "One of a kind? Make your product conform to break away from the norm" in *Entrepreneur* (Vol. 30, No. 12, December 2002, pp. 144)
Pub: Entrepreneur Media Inc.
Ed: Don Debelak. **Description:** One of the challenges facing entrepreneurs when developing a new invention is making sure it is a product consumers will accept.

43967 ■ "Patent Chutzpah" in *Forbes* (November 13, 2000, pp. 58)
Pub: Forbes Magazine
Ed: Krysten A. Crawford. **Description:** An Example of the ways dubious patents for ideas, rather than a physical invention, are being deployed to extract ransom from companies.

43968 ■ "Protecting Your Idea From Bigmouths, and Calling All CFOs" in *Fortune* (Vol. 142, No. 7, October 2, 2000, pp. 284)
Pub: Time Inc.
Ed: Anne Fisher. **Description:** Editor advises two partners to file for a patent on their idea and have potential investors sign nondisclosure agreements.

43969 ■ "Sky's the Limit: Think Your Product has Limited Appeal?" in *Entrepreneur* (Vol. 32, No. 4, April 2004, pp. 132)
Pub: Entrepreneur Media, Inc.
Ed: Don Debelak. **Description:** Profile of Dan Grace and Jeff Polke, two friends who invented The Everywhere Chair in 1996. The product is an outdoor chair with an adjustable back and seat and can be used on sloping surfaces. The startup cost the partners $10,000 for a patent and prototype, procured a $25,000 line of credit, and reported $2 million in sales in 2003, with projected sales close to $3 million in 2004.

43970 ■ "Success line" in *Success* (Vol. 47, No. 3, July 2000, pp. 78)
Pub: Success Publishing, Inc.
Description: Questions are answered on starting a business, including loans and grants, patents, and

federal certification for minority- or woman-owned business.

43971 ■ "Words to the Wise" in *Entrepreneur* (Vol. 28, No. 6, June 2000, pp. 180)
Pub: Entrepreneur Media Inc.
Ed: Don Dedelak. **Description:** One criterion that should be used in any evaluation of an invention is whether a meaningful patent can be obtained for a particular innovation.

43972 ■ "You're the Inspiration" in *Entrepreneur* (Vol. 33, September 2005, No. 9, pp. 96)
Pub: Entrepreneur Media Inc.
Ed: Nichole L. Torres. **Description:** Ways to patent and market a new product are shared by StartupNation.com. A business-advice Website that is run by small business experts, Jeff and Rich Sloan is highlighted.

ASSOCIATIONS AND OTHER ORGANIZATIONS

43973 ■ American Society of Inventors
PO Box 58426
Philadelphia, PA 19102
Ph:(215)546-6601
Co. E-mail: info@asoi.org
URL: http://www.asoi.org
Contact: Henry Skillman, Treas.
Membership: Engineers, scientists, businessmen, and others who are interested in a cooperative effort to serve both the short- and long-term needs of the inventor and society. **Purpose:** Works with government and industry to improve the environment for the inventor. Aims to encourage invention and innovation; help the independent inventor become self-sufficient. Establishes a networking system for inventors and businessmen to solve problems. Sponsors educational programs. **Publications:** *ASI Informer* (bimonthly); *Inventors Digest* (annual).

43974 ■ Brand Names Education Foundation
1133 Ave. of the Americas
New York, NY 10036-6710
Ph:(212)768-9885
Fax: (212)768-7796
Co. E-mail: info@bnef.org
URL: http://www.bnef.org
Contact: David Gooder, Chm.
Description: Promotes education in the trademark field; advances the brand name concept. Conducts annual Saul Lefkowitz Moot Court Competition. Promotes consumer education about the value and importance of brand names. Produces and distributes television public service announcements. **Telecommunication Services:** electronic mail, bnef@inta.org.

43975 ■ International Licensing Industry Merchandisers' Association
350 5th Ave., Ste. 1408
New York, NY 10118
Ph:(212)244-1944
Fax: (212)563-6552
Co. E-mail: info@licensing.org
URL: http://www.licensing.org
Contact: Charles M. Riotto, Pres.
Membership: Companies and individuals engaged in the marketing and servicing of licensed properties, both as agents and as property owners; manufacturers and retailers in the licensing business; supporters of the licensing industry. **Purpose:** Professional association for the licensing industry worldwide. Objectives are to establish a standard reflecting a professional and ethical management approach to the marketing of licensed properties; to become the leading source of information in the industry; to communicate this information to members and others in the industry through publishing, public speaking, seminars, and an open line; to represent the industry in trade and consumer media and in relationships with the government, retailers, manufacturers, other trade associations, and the public. Conducts research programs. Compiles statistics; maintains hall of fame and placement service. **Publications:** *BottomLine* (quarterly); *Worldwide Licensing Resource Directory* (annual).

43976 ■ International Trademark Association
655 3rd Ave., 10th Fl.
New York, NY 10017-5617
Ph:(212)768-9887
Fax: (212)768-7796
Co. E-mail: info@inta.org
URL: http://www.inta.org
Contact: Paul W. Reidl, Pres.
Membership: Trademark owners; associate members are lawyers, law firms, advertising agencies, designers, market researchers, and others in the trademark industries. **Purpose:** Seeks to: protect the interests of the public in the use of trademarks and trade names; promote the interests of members and of trademark owners generally in the use of their trademarks and trade names; disseminate information concerning the use, registration, and protection of trademarks in the United States, its territories, and in foreign countries. Maintains job bank and speakers' bureau. **Publications:** *INTA Bulletin* (biweekly); *Trademark Checklist*; *The Trademark Reporter* (bimonthly) ; Membership Directory (annual).

43977 ■ Invent America!
PO Box 26065
Alexandria, VA 22313
Ph:(703)942-7121
Fax: (703)461-0068
Co. E-mail: inquiries@inventamerica.org
URL: http://www.inventamerica.org
Contact: Nancy Metz, Exec. Dir.
Description: Aims to stimulate American inventiveness and productivity. Seeks to enhance public awareness of American inventions, both past and present. Works to recover many patent models of the 19th century, most of which were sold at public auction by the U.S. Patent Office in 1925; plans to donate these models to the Smithsonian Institution. (Patent models are working replicas of devices for which patents are sought.) Provides training seminars for teachers involved in the program. Develops curriculum materials. Compiles statistics. **Publications:** *Invent America! Creative Resource Guide*; Newsletter (quarterly).

43978 ■ Inventors Assistance League
403 S Central Ave.
Glendale, CA 91204
Ph:(818)246-6546
Free: 877-433-2246
Fax: (818)244-1882
Co. E-mail: rustyr@earthlink.net
URL: http://www.inventions.org
Contact: Rusty Ruscetta, Dir. of Operations
Description: Inventors and manufacturers. Helps inventors get their products into the marketplace and assists manufacturers in finding new products to make

and market. Brings together inventors and manufacturers for mutual benefit. Maintains speakers' bureau, small museum, and hall of fame. Convention/Meeting: none. **Publications:** *Inventor's Advisory*.

43979 ■ Inventors Workshop International Education Foundation/Entrepreneurs Workshop
PO Box 285
Santa Barbara, CA 93102-0285
Ph:(805)969-9250
Fax: (805)899-4927
Co. E-mail: alan@inventorsworkshop.org
URL: http://inventorsworkshop.org
Contact: Alan A. Tratner, Pres.
Description: Amateur and professional inventors in the U.S. Provides instruction, assistance, and guidance in areas including: patent protection; patent searches for inventions; offering inventions for sale; getting inventions and products designed, produced, and manufactured; choosing experts when required; performing as many of these vital actions as capabilities and resources provide. Organizes seminars and semiannual programs on invention promotion and "Reduction to Practice." Conducts research. Works in cooperation with Entrepreneurs Workshop International, which was formed to help inventor/members sell, market, or license their products. Offers children's services. Operates Green2Gold Incubator and workshops for energy and environmental technologies. **Publications:** *Complete Guide to Making Money With Your Inventions*; *Eco Expo Resources Guide*; *Invent!: The Magazine of Creativity, Invention and Entrepreneurship and The Lightbulb Journal* (bimonthly); *Inventors Bookshop*; *Inventor's Guidebook*; *Inventor's Journal*; *The Lightbulb/Pathfinder Newsletter* (periodic); *Little Inventions That Made Big Money*; *Membership Resources Directory*.

43980 ■ National Inventors Foundation
403 S Central Ave.
Glendale, CA 91204
Ph:(818)246-6546
Free: 877-433-2246
Fax: (818)244-1882
Co. E-mail: rustyr@earthlink.net
URL: http://www.inventions.org
Contact: Ted DeBoer, Founder/Pres.
Membership: Independent inventors united to educate individuals regarding the protection and promotion of inventions and new products. **Purpose:** Instructs potential inventors on patent laws and how to protect their inventions through methods developed by the foundation. Teaches advertising, sales and marketing techniques to get ideas into the marketplace to determine their commercial value. Assists individuals throughout the U.S. and in 44 other countries. Maintains speakers' bureau, hall of fame, and museum. Convention/Meeting: none. **Publications:** *Advisory* (quarterly).

REFERENCE WORKS

43981 ■ "20 Steps for Pricing a Patent: To Value an Invention You Have to Understand It" in *Journal of Accountancy* (Vol. 198, November 2004)
Pub: American Institute of Certified Public Accountants
Ed: J. Timothy Cromley. **Description:** Twenty steps to help certified public accounts and valuators determine the value of a patent are explained.

43982 ■ "A Market for Ideas" in *The Economist* (Vol. 377, October 22-28, 2005, No. 8449, pp. 3-6, 8-10, 12-18)
Pub: The Economist Newspaper Ltd.
Description: The magazine presents information collected from a survey conducted on issues of patents and technology. Protection of intellectual property can be good for both the technology industry and its customers. The patent system, companies preparing for intellectual-property battles, a new intellectual-property business model, sharing intellectual property, Indian and Chinese competition in innovation, and new markets for intellectual property are among issues investigated.

43983 ■ "Ad Time Firm Expands" in *San Fernando Valley Business Journal* (Vol. 11, December 2006, No. 25, pp. 28)
Pub: San Fernando Valley Business Journal Associates
Description: Bid4Spots.com, an online advertising firm, will expand its unique reverse auction method of selling unused radio ad time to independent online radio. Bid4Spots has a patent pending for this unique advertising method.

43984 ■ "Addressing the Inhibitors" in *Washington Business Journal* (Vol. 21, No. 50, April 11, 2003, pp. 28)
Pub: Washington Business Journal
Ed: Chris Silva. **Description:** Drugs designed to bolster viral fusion inhibitors are being developed by Panacos Pharmaceuticals Inc. An anti-HIV drug was approved by the U.S. Food and Drug Administration in March, which offers opportunities for a new type of drug.

43985 ■ "Agenda Items" in *Fast Company* (June 2001, pp. 147)
Pub: Fast Company
Description: A collection of the best-of-the-best innovations and technologies that set the business agenda are listed, including the bar code scanning device, the Honda Insight, the lab mouse, the catalytic converter, Perl programming language, and the Hertz Number One Gold Program.

43986 ■ "Amortization of Certain Intangible Assets" in *Journal of Accountacncy*
Pub: American Institute of Certified Public Accountants
Ed: Jennifer M. Mueller. **Description:** Intangible assets that are the result of contractual or legal rights are explained, including patents, licenses, trademarks, franchise and servicing rights.

43987 ■ "Armed for Profit-Taking" in *Small Business Opportunities* (Vol. 16, November 2004, No. 6, pp. 90)
Pub: Harris Publications Inc.
Description: Profile of Cactus Jack Barringer, inventor, entrepreneur, and marketer. Barringer's latest invention is The Enforcer, an arm wrestling machine.

43988 ■ "ArvinMeritor wins patent case" in *Crain's Detroit Business* (Vol. 19, No. 14, April 7, 2003, pp. 40)
Pub: Crain Communications Inc., Detroit
Ed: Terry Kosdrosky, Bob Ankeny. **Description:** The U.S. Court of Appeals ruled that ArvinMeritor Inc. did not infringe on Eaton Corporation's truck transmission, however ArvinMeritor wasn't able to sell a new product for several years because the lower-court judge issued an injunction for the duration of the trial and the firm was not able to recoup its investment in research and development.

43989 ■ "ArvinMeritor Rival Files New Patent Suit" in *Crain's Detroit Business* (Vol. 19, No. 49, December 8, 2003, pp. 4)
Pub: Crain Communications Inc., Detroit
Ed: Terry Kosdrosky. **Description:** Overview of a patent-infringement lawsuit against ArvinMeritor Inc. regarding a truck transmission is presented.

43990 ■ "Ask the attorney" in *Red Herring* (March 2003, pp. 73)
Pub: Herring Communications Inc.
Description: Legal issues are addressed that include the following topics, pharmaceutical patents, government support for research and development, global commerce, intellectual property rights, the transfer of customer lists from European subsidiary to its U.S. parent company, trademark dilution, venture financing, selling a business, stock options, corporate tax deductions, small business patent methods, and employee use of Instant Messaging with clients.

43991 ■ "Ask Inc. Importing" in *Inc.* (September 2006, pp. 53-54)
Pub: Gruner & Jahr USA Publishing
Description: Importing has become more involved and difficult in recent years. Many things can be done to expedite that prior to receipt of the items at US Customs. Necessary steps are covered in this article.

43992 ■ "AT&T Sues eBay and PayPal" in *Cardline* **(Vol. 3, No. 48, November 28, 2003, pp. 1)**
Pub: Thomson Media
Description: AT&T Corporation has filed a patent infringement lawsuit against eBay and its subsidiary PayPal Inc over failure to reach a licensing agreement. EBAY PRODUCT/EBAY SERVICE

43993 ■ "Avoiding Invention Scams" in *Black Enterprise* **(Vol. 37, January 2007, No. 6, pp. 46)**
Pub: Earl G. Graves Publishing Co. Inc.
Ed: James C. Johnson. **Description:** Invention promotion firms provide inventors assistance in developing a prototype for product development. It is important to research these companies before making a commitment to work with them because there are a number of these firms that are not legitimate and have caused independent inventors to lose thousands of dollars by making false claims as to the market potential of the inventions.

43994 ■ "Bad image may keep patent board away" in *Crain's Detroit Business* **(Vol. 16, No. 12, March 20, 2000, pp. 53)**
Pub: Crain Communications, Inc.
Ed: Matt Roush. **Description:** Birmingham, Michigan attorney, Eric Dobrusin, has been instrumental in establishing the year-old National Patent Board, a nonprofit alternative dispute mechanism for intellectual property cases.

43995 ■ "Best Ideas" in *Business Week* **(December 19, 2005, No. 3964, pp. 74-78, 80-82)**
Pub: McGraw-Hill Companies
Ed: Diane Brady. **Description:** Concepts that came to the forefront in 2005 may have a great impact on the future.

43996 ■ "Best Products" *Business Week* **(December 19, 2005, No. 3964, pp. 84-88, 90-92)**
Pub: McGraw-Hill Companies
Ed: Larry Armstrong. **Description:** Best products introduced in 2005 are highlighted, from the cellular phones, kitchen, Internet, even medicine.

43997 ■ "The Better Mousetrap: Detroit holds its own nationally in gaining new patents" in *Crain's Detroit Business* **(Vol.16, Mar. 20, 2000)**
Pub: Crain Communications, Inc.
Ed: Matt Roush. **Description:** Although auto companies still hold the most patents in Michigan, the Detroit area innovation is getting more diverse.

43998 ■ "A Better Way to Innovate" in *Harvard Business Review* **(Vol. 81, No. 7, July 2003, pp. 12)**
Pub: Harvard Business School Press
Ed: Henry W. Chesbrough. **Description:** Companies can profit not only from accepting innovations from other firms, but also from sharing innovations with other firms.

43999 ■ "Beyond the Big Idea: You've Got a Million-Dollar Idea; Now All You Need is a Strategy To Make It Marketable" in *Entrepreneur* **(Vol. 32)**
Pub: Entrepreneur Media Inc.
Ed: Karen E. Spaeder. **Description:** Inventors who were able to bring their ideas to life share their successes.

44000 ■ "The Big Disconnect" in *Barron's* **(Vol. 82, No. 59, February 24, 2003, pp. T1)**
Pub: Barron's
Ed: Eric J. Savitz. **Description:** The technology industry is fundamentally weak, and a recent rally is not likely to provide long-term relief to the industry. Several inventions introduced at a February 2003 Demo conference are described.

44001 ■ "Big Pharma Eyeing Startups" in *Venture Capital Journal* **(October 1, 2204)**
Pub: Thomason Financial Inc.

Ed: Tom York. **Description:** Larger pharmaceutical companies are seeking more investment deals and partnerships with emerging companies due to patent expirations and new drugs going to market.

44002 ■ "The Big Picture" in *Entrepreneur* **(Vol. 31, No. 10, October 2003, pp. 144)**
Pub: Entrepreneur Media, Inc.
Ed: Don Debelak. **Description:** Profile of Marlene Carlson, inventor of Puzzle Toes, shoes that feature a picture of a dinosaur, using the right shoe as the dinosaur's front half and the left as its back. Carlson invested about $12,000 in her company and expects sales to reach $1 million in 2003.

44003 ■ "BountyQuest Introduces New Service to Help Strengthen U.S. Patent System" in *Information Today* **(Vol. 17, No. 11, December 2000, pp. 6)**
Pub: Information Today, Inc.
Ed: Nancy Lambert. **Description:** An overview of a new Web site launched by Boston based startup, BountyQuest Corporation. Via the site, interested companies offer a minimum $10,000 reward to the first "Bounty Hunter" who can provide the prior art (patents or published references) to invalidate specified new patent submissions.

44004 ■ "Breaking the Ice: Want Skeptical Customers to Warm Up to Your Product?" in *Entrepreneur* **(Vol. 33, February 2005, No. 2, pp. 120)**
Pub: Entrepreneur Media Inc.
Ed: Don Debelak. **Description:** Peter Lerman, inventor, and marketer, Lou Matinale have partnered to license and market Lerman's invention, the Sno-Easy. The Sno-Easy is an ergonomic shovel that allows users to shovel snow without bending or twisting.

44005 ■ "Breath of Fresh Air: How Do You Sell Buyers On an Invention That Creates a New Product Category?" in *Entrepreneur* **(October 2004)**
Pub: Entrepreneur Media Inc.
Ed: Don Debelak. **Description:** Profile of Dr. Robert Pincus and Dr. Scott Gold, founders of SaltAire, a drug-free, pH-balanced saline nasal rinse. The spray is used to moisturize nasal passages and flush out irritants. The doctors share how they started with $150,000 in 1997 and 1998 and project sales of $1.1 million for 2004.

44006 ■ "BresaGen moves slowly to grow stem cell work" in *Atlanta Business Chronicle* **(Vol. 25, November 8, 2002, No. 22 pp. 1A)**
Pub: American City Business Publications, Inc.
Ed: Julie Bryant. **Description:** BresaGen Inc., located in Athens, Georgia, is working with stem cells to find treatments for various human conditions. BresaGen has received $1.6 million in U.S. government grants and has entered into various licensing and distribution accords with the National Institutes of Health.

44007 ■ "Bright Ideas" in *Entrepreneur* **(Vol. 27, No. 12, December 1999, pp. 170)**
Pub: Entrepreneur Media Inc.
Ed: Don Debelak. **Description:** The success story of Karen Alvarez and her invention of the Baby Comfort Strap, that safely secures a baby in a shopping cart.

44008 ■ "Bringing Back a Classic" in *Inc.* **(August 1, 2003)**
Pub: Gruner & Jahr USA Publishing
Ed: Leigh Buchanan. **Description:** Profile of Betty Morris, the woman who founded Shrinky Dinks in 1973 and by the 1980s the products were seen everywhere.

44009 ■ "Bruce Sunstein: Inventor Defender" in *Boston Business Journal* **(Vol. 23, No. 27, August 8, 2003, pp. 1)**
Pub: American City Business Journals
Ed: Sheri Qualters. **Description:** Interview with intellectual property attorney, Bruce Sunstein, in which he discusses his practice.

44010 ■ "Business by the Book" in *Home Office Computing* **(Vol. 18, No. 12, December 2000, pp. 99)**
Pub: Scholastic Inc.
Description: An explanation of licenses and permits needed to get a small business up and running.

44011 ■ "Buying Tunes Online" in *Kiplinger's Personal Finance Magazine* **(Vol. 54, No. 12, December 2000, pp. 28)**
Pub: The Kiplinger Washington Editors, Inc.
Ed: Kathy Jones. **Description:** Digital-music subscriptions may be the answer for record companies for making music available through the Internet.

44012 ■ "Can You Patent Your Business Model?" in *Harvard Business Review* **(Vol. 78, No. 4, July 2000, pp. 16)**
Pub: Harvard Business School Publishing Corp.
Description: The U.S. Patent and Trademark Office is hearing a high-profile court case over Amazon.com Inc.'s patent on its one-click shopping method and Priceline.com Inc.'s reverse auction patent. These cases are changing common views of patenting business methods.

44013 ■ "Cancer Drug May Hold Key to Company's Survival" in *Crain's Detroit Business* **(Vol. 18, No. 21, May 27, 2002, pp. 3)**
Pub: Crain Communications Inc. - Detroit
Ed: Andrew Dietderich. **Description:** Profile of Biotherapies, Inc., located in Ann Arbor, Michigan. The 7-year-old privately held firm has developed a patented drug to treat breast cancer, and has pending patents in the treatment of ovarian, colon, prostate and lung cancers.

44014 ■ "Chili Shack Draws Interest" in *Kansas City Star* **(February 15, 2005)**
Pub: Knight-Ridder/Tribune Business News
Ed: Joyce Smith. **Description:** Profile of John David DiCapo's new Chili Shack restaurant. DiCapo promotes his food products through his restaurants and hopes to open 10 franchise or license operations by 2006. He is also offering a line of hot sauces.

44015 ■ "Chip legend Carver Mead mixes analog and digital" in *Red Herring* **(No. 106, October 15, 2001, pp. 26)**
Pub: Herring Communications
Ed: Dean Takahashi. **Description:** Carver Mead, a pioneer of the chip industry, has started his 26th company with a former student. The Seattle-based communications chip start-up called Impinj, has patented a technique that uses a standard chip-manufacturing process to put analog components into digital chips, with a broad reach from cell phones to microprocessors.

44016 ■ *Clicking Through: A Survival Guide for Bringing Your Company Online*
Pub: Bloomberg Press
Ed: Jonathan I. Ezor. **Released:** January 2000. **Price:** $19.95. **Description:** Summary of legal compliance issues faced by small companies doing business on the Internet, including copyright and patent laws.

44017 ■ "A Conversation With Robin Asher, Clark Hill, LLC" in *Crain's Detroit Business* **(Vol. 23, February 5, 2007, No. 6, pp. 11)**
Pub: Crain Communications Inc. - Detroit
Ed: Tom Henderson. **Description:** Patent attorney discusses new patent process rules expected to be in effect later this year that would streamline the patent process. Supreme Court decision could help define what makes an idea obvious and not rely on technicalities and fine print.

44018 ■ *Copyrights, Patents and Trademarks*
Pub: The McGraw-Hill Companies
Ed: Hoyt L. Barber. **Released:** 1995. **Price:** $32.95.

44019 ■ "Court Battle Pits Fridge Pack vs. FridgeMaster" in *Atlanta Business Chronicle* **(Vol. 26, No. 10, August 15, 2003, pp. 1)**
Pub: American City Business Publications, Inc.

Ed: Charles Davidson. **Description:** Lawsuit filed by Riverwood International Corporation against Mead-Westvaco Corporation for patent infringement over the use of the terms FridgeMaster and Fridge Pack in advertising is examined.

44020 ■ **"Court Battles" in** *Business Week* **(December 19, 2005, No. 3964, pp. 33-34)**
Pub: McGraw-Hill Companies
Ed: Catherine Yang. **Description:** A settlement of the patent fight could net $1 billion for the late Tom Campana's NTP.

44021 ■ **"Court Decisions - Privacy coverage differs from patent infringement" in** *Rough Notes* **(Vol. 145, No. 1, January 2003, pp. 10)**
Pub: Rough Notes
Description: In a suit for breach of contract filed by Konami (America) Inc. against Hartford Insurance Company of Illinois, the Appellate Court of Illinois, held that piracy differed from, and that the case did not involve, patent infringement.

44022 ■ **"A Crisis of Content: It's not just pop music." in** *Time* **(Vol. 156, No. 14, October 2, 2002, pp. 68)**
Pub: Time Inc.
Description: Every industry that trades in intellectual property, from publishing to needlework patterns, could get Napsterized. Jim Hedgepath, president of Pegasus Originals, discusses problems encountered to protect his copyrighted cross-stitch needlework patterns.

44023 ■ **"Damages Aren't Always Patently Obvious" in** *Journal of Accountancy*
Pub: American Institute of Certified Public Accountants
Ed: Glenn Newman, Richard J. Gering. **Description:** CPA litigation consultants assist patent holders in patent infringement disputes; quantifying damages in these cases can be the focus of a forensic and litigation services practice.

44024 ■ **"Dartfish swimming in bigger pool" in** *Atlanta Business Chronicle* **(Vol. 24, No. 13, August 31, 2001, pp. 3A)**
Pub: American City Business Journals Inc.
Ed: Mary Jane Credeur. **Description:** Atlanta, Georgia-based Dartfish has developed a patent-pending software that has been ordered by such companies as ESPN, NBC and ABC. The technology enables the reconstruction, frame by frame, of a sporting performance, allowing coaches and athletes to notice any moves or plays that could use adjustment. Dartfish president and co-founder Victor Bergonzoli is planning on developing partnerships for the company, with hopes of gaining more success.

44025 ■ **"Dayton, Ohio, Inventor of Garden Tool Organizer Looks to Expand Business" in** *Dayton Daily News* **(July 29, 2004)**
Pub: Dayton Daily News
Ed: LaToya Thompson. **Description:** Profile of Fred Utzinger III, founder and owner of Functional Fabrics Inc., which operates within his other business, Independent Awning and Canvas Co., a fourth-generation family business. Utzinger has invented a garden tool organizer.

44026 ■ **"Detroit Free Press Macomb Small Business Column" in** *Detroit Free Press* **(September 29, 2005)**
Pub: Knight-Ridder/Tribune Business News
Ed: Carol Cain. **Description:** Former police officer, Steve Russ, describes his new product invention, Flak Vest Hangars. The hangars are designed to hold bulletproof vests.

44027 ■ **"Detroit Free Press Oakland Small Business Column" in** *Detroit Free Press* **(May 26, 2005)**
Pub: Knight-Ridder/Tribune Business News
Ed: Carol Cain. **Description:** Stephen Wiesman worked as a firefighter until being injured in 2002. Wiesman plans to introduce a new product he developed that will make stoves safer to use. Also featured: David Moncur's marketing, creative and technology consulting company.

44028 ■ **"Detroit Free Press Small Business Column" in** *Detroit Free Press* **(May 23, 2005)**
Pub: Knight-Ridder/Tribune Business News
Ed: Carol Cain. **Description:** Profile of Detroit-based Mobius Microsystems Inc., a firm that designs and sells patented intellectual property to microchip makers. Co-owners are looking to raise $5.5 million in venture capital to grow the firm.

44029 ■ **"Detroit Free Press Wayne Small Business Column" in** *Detroit Free Press* **(June 23, 2005)**
Pub: Knight-Ridder/Tribune Business News
Ed: Carol Cain. **Description:** Robert Mazur invented a handheld tool for opening medicine bottles, soup cans and plastic packaging after watching his grandmother struggle to open her medicine bottles.

44030 ■ **"The Digital Disruptors" in** *Red Herring* **(No. 102, August 15, 2001, pp. 58-59)**
Pub: Herring Communications
Ed: Jon Maples. **Description:** Profile of the ten companies, and the sector they represent, that stand to upend the entertainment markets, including Anonymous Content, advertising; News Corporation, television; Clear Channel, radio; Realnetworks, streaming media; Microsoft, gaming; Adobe Systems, publishing; NTT Docomo, wireless; Nothing Real, film; Loudeye, digital-rights management; and Audiogalaxy, music.

44031 ■ **"Don't call your doctor, send your symptoms over the Web" in** *Crain's Detroit Business* **(Vol. 16, No. 24, June 12, 2000, pp. 1)**
Pub: Crain Communications, Inc.
Ed: Matt Roush. **Description:** Ann Arbor-based Cybernet Systems Inc. received a broad patent on transmitting medical information from patient monitoring devices over the Internet. Cybernet is also incorporating the patent into a launch of a centralized, national outpatient monitoring network for remote data capture, analysis, archive and display.

44032 ■ **"Duly noted; Sheet-music company doesn't rest in copyright fight" in** *Crain's Detroit Business* **(Vol. 19, No. 10, March 10, 2003)**
Pub: Crain Communications Inc., Detroit
Ed: Andrew Dietderich. **Description:** Profile of Arthur Luck, owner of the firm Luck's Music Library Inc.; the family business is the subject of two lawsuits filed by Luck's grandsons over copyrighted work becoming part of the public domain.

44033 ■ **"Engine of Progress" in** *Fast Company* **(November 2001, pp. 144)**
Pub: Fast Company
Ed: Fara Warner. **Description:** General Motors is developing vehicles that will use a hybrid gasoline-electric engine that can be used in the traditionally styled vehicles that consumers love.

44034 ■ *Enterprise, Entrepreneurship and Innovation: Concepts, Context and Commercialization*
Pub: Elsevier Science and Technology Books
Ed: Robin Lowe, Sue Marriott. **Released:** June 2006. **Price:** $39.95. **Description:** Application of enterprise, innovation and entrepreneurship are discussed to help companies grow.

44035 ■ *Enterprise Planning and Development: Small Business and Enterprise Start-Up Survival and Growth*
Pub: Elsevier Science and Technology Books
Ed: David Butler. **Released:** August 2006. **Price:** $42.95. **Description:** Innovation, intellectual property, and exit strategies are among the issues discussed in this book involving current entrepreneurship.

44036 ■ **"Entrepreneur Column" in** *Entrepreneur.com* **(February 16, 2006)**
Pub: Entrepreneur Media Inc.
Ed: Tamara Monosoff. **Description:** Five steps to help license a new product or invention are outlined.

44037 ■ **"Entrepreneurs bring Michigan biz to Web" in** *Crain's Detroit Business* **(Vol. 16, No. 12, March 20, 2000, pp. 42)**
Pub: Crain Communications, Inc.
Ed: Matt Roush. **Description:** The founder of Amazon.com Inc. has patented his system for "one-click" online ordering, leading to litigation among e-commerce providers.

44038 ■ *Entrepreneurship, Innovation and Economic Growth*
Pub: Edward Elgar Publishing, Incorporated
Ed: David B. Audretsch. **Released:** July 2006. **Price:** $145.00. **Description:** Links between entrepreneurship, innovation and economic growth are examined.

44039 ■ **"Ex-Breed exec sues automakers, suppliers over sensor patent" in** *Crain's Detroit Business* **(Vol. 19, No. 9, March 3, 2003, pp. 28)**
Pub: Crain Communications Inc., Detroit
Ed: Terry Kosdrosky. **Description:** David Breed, inventor and former executive at Breed Technologies Inc., is suing global automakers and several parts suppliers over a patent-infringement for a side-impact airbag sensor.

44040 ■ *Fast Company's Greatest Hits: Ten Years of the Most Innovative Ideas in Business*
Pub: Penguin Group Incorporated
Ed: John Byrne; David Lidsky; Mark N. Vamos. **Released:** July 2006. **Price:** $24.95. **Description:** Offering of Fast Company's best articles covering business ideas and profiles of successful firms and their leaders.

44041 ■ **"Faster Tech Transfer" in** *Inc.* **(July 1, 2003)**
Pub: Gruner & Jahr USA Publishing
Description: Technology transfer from colleges to private sector is discussed, using examples of universities tech transfer that fueled 450 business and 4,000 licenses in 2002. Transferring innovation from college laboratories to the private sector has startups and schools arguing over licensing and royalty deals.

44042 ■ **"Flight of Fancy? Launching a High-Tech Product Can be a Technical and Financial Challenge" in** *Entrepreneur* **(Vol. 32, August 2004)**
Pub: Entrepreneur Media Inc.
Ed: Don Debelak. **Description:** Profile of William J. Boyer Jr. and partner and co-founder Ray Henson, who helped Boyer with the technical aspects of their digEplayer, a portable battery-operated in-flight entertainment system used on passenger tray tables. The company saw $1 millions in sales, first quarter 2004.

44043 ■ **"For-Your-Own-Good Innovation" in** *Inc.* **(September 1, 2003)**
Pub: Gruner & Jahr USA Publishing
Ed: Rod Kurtz. **Description:** The California firm, Payment Protection Systems, sells a dashboard device called On Time to used car dealers. The device disables a vehicle if the owner does not make a scheduled payment. Flexplay Technologies in New York has invented a disc to curb software and copyright piracy.

44044 ■ **"Forward: Patents" in** *Red Herring* **(No. 99, June 15 & July 1, 2001, pp. 34-35)**
Pub: Herring Communications
Ed: Stephan Herrera. **Description:** Overview of the biotech legal case, Festo, a recent patent-infringement decision that has fundamentally changed the balance of power that has long favored patent holders over those who deliberately or incidentally design products based on similar science.

44045 ■ **"From Dream to Reality: Inventor Takes Invention from Prototype to Product" in** *Small Business Opportunities* **(Vol. 17, May 2005, No. 3)**
Pub: Harris Publications Inc.
Description: Profile of Kurt Kirckof of Minnesota. Kirckof invented a colorful, educational board game for children. The game is presently being sold in sixteen states and Canada.

44046 ■ **"From Idea to Marketplace"** in *Small Business Opportunities* (Vol. 17, May 2005, No. 3, pp. 62, 64, 130)
Pub: Harris Publications Inc.
Ed: Kurt Kirckof. Description: Ideas to help inventors decide what to do with a newly developed product are shared.

44047 ■ *From Patent to Profit*
Pub: Inventions, Patents & Trademarks Co.
Ed: Bob DeMatteis. Released: 1997. Price: $29.95.

44048 ■ *From Patent to Profit: Secrets & Strategies for Success*
Pub: Inventions, Patents & Trademarks Co.
Ed: Bob DeMatteis; read by Bob DeMatteis. Released: 1997. Price: $39.95 (analog audio cassette; 4 cassettes). Description: Includes all about Patents; Writing Patents & Marketing Strategies; Finding Manufacturing & Marketing Partners; & All about Licensing

44049 ■ **"From Tee to Green"** in *Home Business* (Vol. 12, March/April 2005, No. 2, pp. 96)
Pub: Home Business Magazine
Ed: Sandy Larson. Description: Profile of Dr. Venanzio Cardarelli, the dentist who invented the Aero-tee, a tooth-shaped polycarbonate golf tee from his home-based business. The tee is designed to last longer than traditional plastic golf tees.

44050 ■ **"Game On! Game-Makers are Definitely not Sleeping in Seattle"** in *Entrepreneur* (Vol. 32, No. 4, April 2004, pp. 22)
Pub: Entrepreneur Media, Inc.
Ed: Nichole L. Torres. Description: Game manufacturers are catching the eyes of venture capitalists in the Seattle, Washington area. Profiles of Cranium Inc. (Cranium) founders Richard Tait and Whit Alexander, Screenlife LLC (Scene It) founders Dave Long and Craig Kinzer, and Entspire (Derivation) founders Brad Chase.

44051 ■ *Global Licensing Handbook: A Guide to Success*
Pub: South-Western Publishing Co.
Released: 1997. Price: $29.95.

44052 ■ *The Great American Idea Book - Make Money from Your Ideas: Movies, Music, Books, Inventions, Businesses, & Almost Anything Else!*
Pub: DIANE Publishing Co.
Ed: Bob Coleman and Deborah Neville. Released: 1998. Price: $23.00. Description: Explains in detail the five steps to turning your idea into an income. The authors show you how to secure the legal rights to your idea, develop it to the point where others will invest in it, promote it effectively, defend it legally and financially, and profit by making the right deals.

44053 ■ **"Greed Is Bad"** in *Red Herring* (No. 106, October 15, 2001, pp. 92)
Pub: Herring Communications
Ed: Dan Briody. Description: The entire semiconductor has slumped over the past 12 months, but shares of Rambus have been hit particularly hard due to critical losses in patent litigation lawsuits. Rambus, a semiconductor designer, depends on the aggressive pursuit and defense of its patented intellectual property.

44054 ■ **"Guilford Pharmaceuticals gets dose of health news"** in *Washington Business Journal* (Vol. 22, No. 3, May 23, 2003, pp. 25)
Pub: Washington Business Journal
Ed: Robert J. Terry. Description: An examination into the growing success of Guilford Pharmaceuticals Inc., including new contracts with Pfizer Inc., U.S. Food and Drug Administration approval of new products and research and development efforts.

44055 ■ **"The Hague: Laws without Borders"** in *Red Herring* (No. 106, October 15, 2001, pp. 25-26)
Pub: Herring Communications

Ed: Julia Lawlor. Description: Important information regarding the Hague Convention on Jurisdiction and Foreign Judgments in Civil Matters is covered. The Hague treaty would deal with civil lawsuits and would require that laws regarding matters like libel, copyright, patents, and trademarks - which differ among countries - be enforced uniformly in the 53 nations participating in treaty talks.

44056 ■ **"He Came. He Saw. He Took On the Whole Power-Tool Industry"** in *Inc.* (Volume 27, July 2005, No. 7, pp. 86-91)
Pub: Inc. Magazine
Ed: Melba Newsome. Description: Profile of Stephen Gass, inventor of the new SawStop, a power saw whose blade stops immediately when it comes into contact with the user's body.

44057 ■ **"Hollywood, Silicon Valley at odds over digital piracy bills"** in *Atlanta Business Chronicle* (Vol. 25, No. 21, Nov. 1, 2002, pp. 10B)
Pub: American City Business Publications, Inc.
Ed: Kent Hoover. Description: H.R. 5211, a bill introduced by California Democratic Representative Howard Berman, supports copyright owners in their efforts to stop unauthorized use of online music and movie materials. The bill permits copyright owners to use hacking as long as computer files are not damaged.

44058 ■ *How to Avoid Patent, Marketing and Invention Company Scams: Wow! What a Great Idea. Now What?*
Pub: Rainbow Books, Inc.
Ed: Martin C. Smith. Released: 1995. Price: $9.95.

44059 ■ *How to Develop & Market Creative Business Ideas*
Pub: Oasis Press
Price: $14.95 (paper). Description: Provides step-by-step information on new product development, including patenting, constructing prototypes, test marketing, finding licensees, financing, and distribution. Also lists prototype resources, trade shows, and funding sources.

44060 ■ **"How to Pitch a Brilliant Idea"** in *Harvard Business Review* (Vol. 81, No. 9, September 2003, pp. 117)
Pub: Harvard Business School Press
Ed: Kimberly D. Elsbach. Description: Ways screenwriters propose ideas to producers can be applied to business marketing are highlighted. An ongoing study of how products are presented to the U.S. film and television industry (Hollywood) from screenwriters is presented; from this research various self-destructive and effective personality types emerged and are described.

44061 ■ *How to Start an Internet Sales Business*
Pub: Lulu.com
Ed: Dan Davis. Released: August 2005. Price: $19.95. Description: Small business guide for launching an Internet sales company. Topics include business structure, licenses, and taxes.

44062 ■ **"I'd Like to Buy Machinery From China"** in *Inc.* (September 2005, pp. 53)
Pub: Inc. Magazine
Description: When purchasing equipment from China, can American businesses hold Chinese manufacturers responsible if machines violate patent laws?

44063 ■ **"If BlackBerry Gets Smushed..."** in *Business Week* (January 9, 2006, No. 3966, pp. 16)
Pub: McGraw-Hill Companies
Ed: Stephen H. Wildstrom. Description: Alternatives to using BlackBerry email services are discussed in the event of the service being shut down by patent infringement charges. GoodLink from Good Technology offers similar services as does Microsoft with its Exchange email system which is being upgraded.

44064 ■ **"The Importance of Well-Crafted Terms"** in *Law Firm Inc.* (August 2004)
Pub: American Lawyer Media LP
Ed: Mark Hanchet, Edward Hansen. Description: Agreements involving complex technology relationships should be negotiated and drafted with the idea of avoiding future litigation because of the long-term partnerships they create. These contracts cover such issues as outsourcing and enterprise resources planning (ERP) licensing and implementation agreements; risk avoidance, scope of services, service levels and cost need to be agreed upon before the contract is signed.

44065 ■ **"In Hot Water? Take a Closer Look at Your Marketing Materials, Or You May Get Burned"** in *Entrepreneur* (Vol. 32, September 2004)
Pub: Entrepreneur Media Inc.
Ed: Catherine Seda. Description: Although not illegal, using another company's trademark or logo on a Website, banner ad, or newsletter could get a small company into legal trouble. Internet marketing law includes copyrights, privacy rights, trademark usage and order fulfillment and more aggressive legal action to protect brands is taking place.

44066 ■ *Innov and Entrepren in Biotech*
Pub: Edward Elgar Publishing, Incorporated
Ed: Hine. Released: April 2006. Price: $100.00. Description: Innovation processes underlying successful entrepreneurship in the biotechnology sector are explored.

44067 ■ **"The Innovation Conversation"** in *Fast Company* (July 2001, pp. 70)
Pub: Fast Company
Description: Fast Company gathered ten business leaders for a 90-minute roundtable discussion in San Francisco, California. The following questions were addressed: What is the state of innovation? How are leaders competing on innovation?

44068 ■ *Innovation and Entrepreneurship*
Pub: HarperCollins Publishers, Inc.
Ed: Peter F. Drucker. Released: May 2006. Price: $16.95. Description: Presentation of entrepreneurship and innovation and a purposeful and systematic discipline and the challenges and opportunities of the American entrepreneurial economy.

44069 ■ *Innovation and Entrepreneurship: Practice and Principles*
Pub: Elsevier Science & Technology Books
Ed: Peter F. Drucker. Released: November 2004. Description: Profile of entrepreneurial innovation.

44070 ■ *Innovation Methodologies in Enterprise Research*
Pub: Edward Elgar Publishing, Incorporated
Ed: Hine. Released: December 2006. Price: $75.00. Description: The importance of qualitative, interpretist research in the field of enterprise research is discussed. The book stresses how enterprise research is a new method and permits a wide scope for new and innovative research studies.

44071 ■ **"Innovators ride rough road in Detroit area"** in *Crain's Detroit Business* (Vol. 16, No. 21, May 22, 2000, pp. 9)
Pub: Crain Communications, Inc.
Ed: Mary Kramer. Description: Forty inventors were invited to a celebration at Lawrence Technological University in Southfield, Michigan to honor "The Creators".

44072 ■ **"The Innovator's Next Bestseller?"** in *Inc.* (September 1, 2004)
Pub: Inc. Magazine
Ed: Mike Hofman. Description: Clayton M. Christensen, Harvard Business School professor and author, explains how to spot industry-changing innovations.

44073 ■ "Intellectual property rights are cyberspace issue" in *Crain's Detroit Business* (Vol. 16, No. 12, March 20, 2000, pp. 23)
Pub: Crain Communications, Inc.
Ed: Joseph Serwach. Description: When it comes to intellectual property cases, even a hyphen can make a big difference. The Internet explosion is accelerating the concern about maximizing the value of knowledge assets.

44074 ■ "Intellectual Property and Licensing Pitfalls" in *Venture Capital Journal* (December 1, 2004)
Pub: Thomason Financial Inc.
Description: Intellectual property and licensing issues can result in restrictions on a company's operations and profitability, as well as reduced flexibility in undertaking liquidity events and impair the value of an investment. Intellectual property and licensing pitfalls are outlined.

44075 ■ *Intellectual Property Litigation Guide: Patents and Trade Secrets*
Pub: Clark Boardman Callaghan
Ed: Gregory E. Upchurch. Released: 1995. Price: $425.00.

44076 ■ *Intellectual Property—Patents, Trademarks and Copyrights—in a Nutshell*
Pub: West Publishing Co.
Ed: Arthur R. Miller and Michael H. Davis. Released: Second edition, 1990. Price: $17.00 (paper).

44077 ■ "Invention: Scientist puts circuits on paper" in *Red Herring* (No. 102, August 15, 2001, pp. 25)
Pub: Herring Communications
Ed: Avi Machlis. Description: Profile of Andrew Shipway, the scientist who invented the patent-pending process which allows electrical circuits to be created using a standard laser printer.

44078 ■ *Inventions! Inventions!*
Pub: E C S Learning Systems
Ed: Marian D. Costello. Released: 1996. Price: $14.95.

44079 ■ *The Inventor's Cookbook: Your Recipe for Success, How to Patent, Protect, Produce and Profit from Your Ideas and Inventions Yourself!*
Pub: Vic-Vincent Game Co.
Ed: Victor N. Vic-Vincent. Released: 1995. Price: $14.95.

44080 ■ "It's all mine" in *Black Enterprise* (Vol. 32, No. 6, January 2002, pp. 42)
Pub: Earl Graves Publishing Co.
Ed: Quincy L. Lewis. Description: The four key types of intellectual property are discussed: trademarks, copyrights, patents, and trade secrets. Sources for further research are included.

44081 ■ "Jeff Jonas" in *Entrepreneur* (Vol. 32, September 2004, No. 9, pp. 24)
Pub: Entrepreneur Media Inc.
Ed: Sara Wilson. Description: Profile of Jeff Jonas, founder of SRD, a company specializing in the large-scale identification of individuals and their relationships with others. SRD focuses on the production of patent-pending technologies and software products, particularly with the government to address issues of national concern while protecting individual's privacy.

44082 ■ "Join Hands" in *Entrepreneur* (Vol. 33, September 2005, No. 9, pp. 138)
Pub: Entrepreneur Media Inc.
Ed: Don Debelak. Description: Profile of Shawn Donegan, founder of Trac Tool Inc., Cleveland, Ohio. Donegan signed a licensing deal with inventor Mike Puczkowski to sell the Speed Rollers paint applicator system to professional painting contractors. Steps for entrepreneurs to market inventions are examined.

44083 ■ *Jump Start Your Business Brain: Ideas, Advice and Insights for Immediate Marketing and Innovation Success*
Pub: Emmis Books
Ed: Doug Hall. Released: April 2005. Price: $23.99.
Description: Strategies to improve sales, marketing, and business development.

44084 ■ "Just Woo It: It's Possible to Flirt with Success After All" in *Entrepreneur* (Vol. 32, No. 4, April 2004, pp. 29)
Pub: Entrepreneur Media, Inc.
Ed: Sara Wilson. Description: Techniques and tools to help market a small business are listed, including the use of free samples and patents.

44085 ■ "License to Thrive" in *Entrepreneur* (Vol. 33, October 2005, No. 10, pp. 22)
Pub: Entrepreneur Media Inc.
Ed: Mark Henricks. Description: Today large companies are willing to license their patents, trademarks and other intellectual property to small companies that can profitably bring them to market.

44086 ■ "License To Thrive" in *Inc.* (August 2005, pp. 38)
Pub: Inc. Magazine
Ed: Erik Sherman. Description: The right partnership can drive sales, while it also reduces workload. The art of the alliance is outlined.

44087 ■ "License to Upgrade" in *Entrepreneur* (Vol. 32, September 2004, No. 9, pp. 44)
Pub: Entrepreneur Media Inc.
Description: CDW offers a free Software License Tracker geared to a growing business.

44088 ■ "Linking Policies for Public Web Sites" in *Information Today* (Vol. 17, No. 10, November 2000, pp. 42)
Pub: Information Today, Inc.
Ed: Shirley Duglin Kennedy. Description: The article recommends information sites offering guidelines for setting up a Web site to avoid litigation.

44089 ■ "Local Labs are Working to Perfect DNA Probes" in *Kansas City Star* (March 8, 2005)
Pub: Knight-Ridder/Tribune Business News
Ed: Julius A. Karash. Description: Children's Mercy Hospital and Phylogenetix Laboratories Inc. have partnered to complete the development of patented DNA probes for detecting diseases; when completed the probes will be brought to market.

44090 ■ "Long Island's Patent Production Falls Nearly 20 Percent Since 1988" in *Long Island Business News* (March 5, 2004)
Pub: Dolan Media Newswires
Ed: Ken Schachter. Description: Long Island's future economic health is tied to industries such as life sciences, software development and defense-industry prototyping and design rather than large-scale manufacturing. Patent growth is used to gauge the economic progress of the area.

44091 ■ "Longislandwinecountry.com Challenges the Long Island Wine Council's Trademark" in *Long Island Business News* (January 30, 2004)
Pub: Dolan Media Newswires
Description: Profile of the Website Longislandwine-country.com. The firm has challenged the Long Island Wine Council's trademark on the term "Long Island wine country" and has turned down a licensing agreement with the Council that would allow it to use the "Longislandwinecountry" domain name for five years free of charge, with no right to retain it after those five years.

44092 ■ "Losing the race: is the Patent Office's slowness putting U.S. innovation at risk?" in *Entrepreneur* (Vol. 31, No. 5, May 2003)
Pub: Entrepreneur Media Inc.
Ed: Joshua Kurlantzick. Description: The U.S. Patent and Trademark Office is no longer able to keep pace with the number of patent applications it receives.

44093 ■ "Making Lemonade" in *Entrepreneur* (Vol. 33, October 2005, No. 10, pp. 83)
Pub: Entrepreneur Media Inc.
Ed: Gwen Moran. Description: When the owner of a bird-cage and accessories company suffers from a legal battle, she found a way to turn adversity into opportunity.

44094 ■ "Manny, Moe, & Jack Are In the Driver's Seat" in *License!* (Vol. 6, No. 6, July 2003, pp. 22)
Pub: Advanstar Communications, Inc.
Ed: Teresa Andreoli. Description: Pep Boys, the auto aftermarket retail and service chain, will begin licensing property for apparel, accessories, and toys for kids, as well as novelty collectibles and how-to books for car maintenance and repair for adults.

44095 ■ *Marketing Your Invention*
Pub: Upstart Publishing Co., Inc.
6 Ed: Thomas E. Mosley, Jr. Released: 1992. Price: $22.95 (paper). Description: Provides information for inventors on how to successfully bring inventions to market. Covers protecting an idea, invention positioning, locating financing, and licensing.

44096 ■ "Melville-Based DealerTrack Inc. Sue Rival Mich.-Based RouteOne" in *Long Island Business News* (February 6, 2004)
Pub: Dolan Media Newswires
Ed: Ken Schachter. Description: DealerTrack Inc. has filed a patent lawsuit against Michigan-based RouteOne, a joint venture between DaimlerChrysler Service, Ford Motor Credit Company, General Motors Acceptance Corporation, and Toyota Financial Services. The lawsuit charges RouteOne of infringing on two patents related to a routing system, method and computer program for analyzing credit applications.

44097 ■ "Music-Go-Round: Webcasters Reach Tentative Agreement with RIAA, DiMA" in *Black Enterprise* (Vol. 34, No. 4, November 2003, pp. 52)
Pub: Earl Graves Publishing Co.
Ed: Anthony Calypso. Description: A joint-royalty rate proposal between BlakeRadio.com, the Recording Industry Association of America, and the Digital Media Association has been submitted to the U.S. Copyright Office. The proposal would keep both sides from going through expensive and lengthy arbitration processes to determine appropriate royalty fees.

44098 ■ "Music Like Water" in *Forbes* (Vol. 175, January 31, 2005, No. 2, pp. 42)
Pub: Forbes Magazine Inc.
Ed: David Kusek. Description: Development of a music utility to distribute and market interactive digital music is discussed. The system would work like water, gas and utility systems.

44099 ■ "Music To Your Ears" in *Entrepreneur.com* (Vol. 34, February 2006, No. 2, pp. 113)
Pub: Entrepreneur Media Inc.
Ed: James Park. Description: Profile of Mindy and Jerry Harvey, founders of Ultimate Ears, custom-made, high-end earpieces for professional musicians and music lovers.

44100 ■ "Musical cases" in *Crain's Detroit Business* (Vol. 19, No. 10, March 10, 2003, pp. 34)
Pub: Crain Communications Inc., Detroit
Description: Information on two pending lawsuits faced by Luck's Music Library regarding copyright laws affecting all works of authorship and not just music is examined.

44101 ■ "My Kind of Town" in *Entrepreneur* (Vol. 33, January 2005, No. 1, pp. 27)
Pub: Entrepreneur Media Inc.
Description: According to the Visa Entrepreneurial Index, Austin, Texas scored 95 points out of 100 as the most entrepreneurial city in the U.S. The study was based on the following two main criteria: average number of new business licenses and DBA registrations, and the number of utility patents issued.

44102 ■ "Name Grab-Cypersquaters, once a mere nuisance, now can go to prison for violating your trademark" in *PC Computing* **(April 2000, pp. 40)**

Pub: Ziff-Davis Inc.

Ed: Christopher Null. **Description:** The U.S. Anti-Cypersquatting Consumer Protection Act (ACPA), which was signed into law on November 29, 1999, has triggered a rash of lawsuits targeting cybersquatters. The most notable filing so far is the Coalition to Advance the Protection of Sports logos' (CAPS) case against FlairMail.com, which offers free e-mail addresses from sports domains like goavalanche.net and mightyducks1.com. Domain names have become very expensive commodities, as evidenced by the $7.5 million Business.com domain name.

44103 ■ *Naming Your Business and Its Products and Services*

Pub: P. Gaines Co.

Ed: Phillip G. Williams. **Released:** 1991. **Price:** $19.95 (paper). **Description:** Provides legal information on creating trade names, trademarks, and service marks for your company.

44104 ■ "Next step: Bricks and mortar" in *Crain's Detroit Business* **(Vol. 19, No. 10, March 10, 2003, pp. 11)**

Pub: Crain Communications Inc., Detroit

Ed: Laura Bailey. **Description:** Howard Bell, the newly appointed head of Wayne State University's Research and Technology Park is working towards a 10-20 year project that will result in a mix of emerging companies with satellite offices of Wayne State's largest industry partners.

44105 ■ "Nonstop Innovation" in *Inc.* **(Volume 27, July 2005, No. 7, pp. 34)**

Pub: Inc. Magazine

Ed: Larry Olmsted. **Description:** The firm Book 'em works to transform employees into entrepreneurs by having them develop ideas for innovative products and services.

44106 ■ "Now Showing: Win Partners by Letting Them See What You're Made Of" in *Entrepreneur* **(Vol. 31, No. 9, September 2003)**

Pub: Entrepreneur Media, Inc.

Ed: David Newton. **Description:** Ways to expand a business beyond current markets, using alliances with larger businesses, licensing of technology to others or spending resources for more internal development, are explored.

44107 ■ "OASIS Overhauls Intellectual Property Rights Policy" in *eWeek* **(February 7, 2005)**

Pub: Ziff Davis Media Inc.

Description: According to president and CEO of OASIS, Patrick Gannon, the Organization for the Advancement of Structured Information Standards (OASIS) announced a revision to its intellectual property rights policy. Under the new policy, members working on specifications can choose to license their submissions under either a RAND (Reasonable and Non-Discriminatory) mode, an RF (Royalty-Free) on RAND mode or a Royalty-Free on Limited Terms mode.

44108 ■ "One To Watch: Danger looms large for the Blackberry" in *Red Herring* **(No. 99, June 15 & July 1, 2001, pp. 36, 38)**

Pub: Herring Communications

Description: Information regarding the various companies building wireless email devices that may replace the Research In Motion's Blackberry device.

44109 ■ "Orthodontist turns inventor of breast prothesis" in *Atlanta Business Chronicle* **(Vol. 25, November 29, 2002, No. 25, pp. 4C)**

Pub: American City Business Publications, Inc.

Ed: Leslie Williams Johnson. **Description:** Terry Ferguson created Radiant Impressions, a breast prosthesis, when his wife struggled to find comfortable prosthetic options after her mastectomy. The new breast prosthesis, which features a silicon foam core, is 40-50 percent lighter than the typical prosthesis.

44110 ■ "Pain-Free Patching" in *Entrepreneur* **(Vol. 32, November 2004, No. 11, pp. 62)**

Pub: Entrepreneur Media Inc.

Ed: Liane Cassavoy. **Description:** Executive Software's Sitekeeper 3 allows information technology employees to determine hardware and software configuration throughout a company and lets you know if all products are licensed.

44111 ■ *Patent Attorneys and Agents Registered to Practice before the United States Patent and Trademark Office*

Pub: Superintendent of Documents

Released: Annual. **Price:** $415, individuals per year; $20, individuals single copies available. **Covers:** about 7224 active agents and 22635 attorneys. **Entries Include:** Name, address, phone, registration number. **Arrangement:** Geographical. **Indexes:** Alphabetical (with city, state, zip).

44112 ■ "Patent a key victory for Catuity, but smart-card wait continues" in *Crain's Detroit Business* **(Vol. 19, No. 3, Jan. 20, 2003, pp. 12)**

Pub: Crain Communications Inc., Detroit

Ed: Andrew Dietderich. **Description:** Profile of Catuity Inc., a Detroit-based company that makes loyalty software used by banks, processors of bankcards and retailers. Catiuity was awarded a patent by the U.S. Patent Office for the firms smart-card memory system, which includes the way memory is stored on the cards and how card readers communicate with other devices.

44113 ■ "The Patent Epidemic" in *Business Week* **(January 9, 2006, No. 3966, pp. 60-62)**

Pub: McGraw-Hill Companies

Ed: Michael Orey. **Description:** Defeating suspicious patents can take years, cost millions, and slow innovation, however, the Supreme Court may reshape patent law.

44114 ■ "Patent expiration to hit MSU" in *Crain's Detroit Business* **(Vol. 19, No. 14, April 7, 2003, pp. 3)**

Pub: Crain Communications Inc., Detroit

Ed: Laura Bailey. **Description:** Michigan State University Foundation will lose $25 million annually when patents on two cancer drugs the university holds expire.

44115 ■ "Patent Pending" in *Entrepreneur* **(Vol. 33, October 2005, No. 10, pp. 28)**

Pub: Entrepreneur Media Inc.

Ed: Chris Penttila. **Description:** The U.S. Federal Trade Commission is recommending stiffer qualification standards for patents, allowing competitors to challenge patents early in the application process, to make is simpler for competitors to review each other's patents, and to limit damage awards in cases of willful infringement.

44116 ■ "Patent Pitfalls for Early Stage Investors" in *Venture Capital Journal* **(November 1, 2004)**

Pub: Thomason Financial Inc.

Ed: M. Sharon Webb. **Description:** Investors need to understand that a company's patent portfolio might include patents that are not necessarily owned by the firm. It is important for the investor to be sure all patents presented in a portfolio are actually owned by the company they will be investing in.

44117 ■ *Patent Reexamination and Small Business Innovation: Congressional Hearing*

Pub: DIANE Publishing Company

Ed: Howard Coble. **Released:** February 2004. **Price:** $25.00. **Description:** Congressional hearing: Witness: Peter Theis, President, Theis Research, Inc.; Paul Heckel, Independent Inventor; Nancy Linck, Senior Vice President, General Counsel and Secretary, Guilford Pharmaceuticals, Inc.; and Mark H. Webbink, Senior Vice President and General Counsel, Red Hat, Inc.

44118 ■ *Patent Term & Patent Disclosure Legislation: Hearing Before the Committee on Small Business, U.S. House of Representatives*

Pub: DIANE Publishing Co.

Released: 1998. **Price:** $45.00. **Description:** Presents testimony on the issues of patent term & patent disclosure legislation by representatives from: Esquire, Banner & Allegretti, LTD.; National Association for the Self-Employed; Finnegan, Henderson, Farabow, Garrett & Dunnier; Molecular Biosystems, Inc.; American Intellectual Property Law Association; & The Alliance for American Innovation. Includes submitted letters & materials from the Chief Council for Advocacy U.S. Small Business Administration; Bruce A. Lehman, Secretary of Commerce & Commissioner of Patents & Trademarks; & the White House Conference on Small Business.

44119 ■ "A Patently Obvious Strategy" in *Success* **(Vol. 47, No. 3, July 2000, pp. 61)**

Pub: Success Publishing, Inc.

Ed: Karen Fuller. **Description:** Protect your intellectual property with a business-method patent, exclusivity makes your business worth more. The article answers business-strategy patent questions.

44120 ■ *Patents Handbook*

Pub: McFarland & Company Inc., Publishers

Contact: Fred K. Carr, Author

Released: latest edition 1995. **Price:** $49.95, individuals. **Publication Includes:** List of information sources for researching patents and inventorship. Principal content of publication is an overview of the patent system in the United States. **Arrangement:** Overview. **Indexes:** Master.

44121 ■ *Patents Handbook: A Guide for Inventors and Researchers to Searching Patent Documents and Preparing and Making an Application*

Pub: McFarland & Co., Inc.

Ed: Fred K. Carr. **Released:** 1995. **Price:** $38.00.

44122 ■ "Pattern Behavior" in *Entrepreneur* **(Vol. 28, No. 11, November 2000, pp. 22)**

Pub: Entrepreneur Media Inc.

Ed: Geoff Williams. **Description:** Cross-stitch companies plan legal action to halt online sharing of patterns.

44123 ■ "Personal Business" in *Business Week* **(December 19, 2005, No. 3964, pp. 95)**

Pub: McGraw-Hill Companies

Ed: Gene G. Marcial. **Description:** Profile of Expeditors International of Seattle, Washington, a freight forwarder and customs broker; licensing and patents for intellectual property; and biotech firm Sonus Pharaceuticals.

44124 ■ "Personal Style" in *Hispanic Business* **(April 2005, pp. 62)**

Pub: Hispanic Business

Ed: Leslie A. Westbrook. **Description:** James Alvarez, successful executive and entrepreneur found himself unable to putt after an accident. Alvarez designed a putter with a longer grip and angled shaft that promotes a more open stance, allowing golfers to see the putting line with both eyes, optimizing accuracy.

44125 ■ "The Power of Spin" in *The Economist* **(Vol. 377, October 1-7, 2005, No. 8446, pp. 76-77)**

Pub: The Economist Newspaper Ltd.

Description: Canadian engineer, Louis Michaud, has developed a way to create artificial whirlwinds like a tornado, these whirlwinds can be controlled and harnessed in order to generate power. Michaud calls his invention the 'atmospheric vortex engine'.

44126 ■ "Pringle to Chinese: Bring It On" in *Business Journal-Milwaukee* **(Vol. 20, No. 44, July 18, 2003, pp. A9)**

Pub: American City Business Journals, Inc.

Ed: Rich Rovito. **Description:** Profile of John Pringle, new president and CEO of NuTone. Pringle is convinced that by using automation and patents, his company will evolve into a stronger force within the residential ventilation products industry.

44127 ■ **"Priority" in** *Inc.* **(Volume 27, March 2005, No. 3, pp. 23-26, 28, 30)**
Pub: Inc. Magazine
Description: Business information discussed includes information about the SEC looking into unlicensed investment brokers, the economy, freight co-ops to help shippers ease costs, hiring, Google, education, SBA assistance to women entrepreneurs, and new inventions.

44128 ■ **"Profiting from Copyrighted Materials" in** *Rough Notes* **(Vol. 146, No. 3, March 2003, pp. 104)**
Pub: Rough Notes
Ed: G. Edward Kalbaugh. **Description:** Owners of Internet sites with public access should understand copyright laws to protect information and themselves.

44129 ■ **"Protecting Ideas" in** *Black Enterprise* **(Vol. 35, February 2005, No. 7, pp. 54)**
Pub: Earl G. Graves Publishing Co. Inc.
Ed: James C. Johnson. **Description:** U.S. Patent and Trademark Office has a Website offering facts about patents, how to get one, and a list of registered patent attorneys and agents. It is best to use a nondisclosure agreement to protect an idea or invention.

44130 ■ **"Recipe for Growth" in** *Fast Company* **(November 2001, pp. 40)**
Pub: Fast Company
Ed: Fara Warner. **Description:** How does Whirlpool cook up great ideas to get back on the fast track? By turning people loose on the challenge of innovation, and then turning up the heat on their best ideas.

44131 ■ **"Recipe for Success: Smart Partnering Can Transform a Lone Inventor Into a Market Force" in** *Entrepreneur* **(Vol. 32, September 2004)**
Pub: Entrepreneur Media Inc.
Ed: Don Debelak. **Description:** Profile of Michael Karyo, founder of SiliconZone USA in New York, New York. The company produces a line of silicone bakeware cooking tools with heat transfer and nonstick properties. Karyo used nearly $80,000 for his startup and projects sales to reach $12 million for 2004.

44132 ■ **"Report proposes update of copyright act: panel seeks liability for violations by Internet access services" in** *The New York Times*
Pub: The New York Times Company
Ed: Jeri Clausing. **Description:** The Progressive Policy Institute is releasing a report discussing the need for privacy on the Internet, specifically in the area of copyright infringement. The report states the sites like Napster should not be allowed to offer Internet users free trade of music and MP3 files. A House Small Business Committee meeting is scheduled to discuss the problems of copyright in the Internet music industry.

44133 ■ **"Research's reward" in** *Crain's Detroit Business* **(Vol. 18, No. 51, Dec. 23, 2002, pp. 1)**
Pub: Crain Communications Inc., Detroit
Ed: Laura Bailey. **Description:** Since starting their firm in 1991, James Downward and Judith Erb, have developed six patents and have 6 patents pending. Their company IA Inc, and its subsidiary Threefold Sensors, has developed the Endotect biosensor for widespread detection of compounds that mimic estrogen and appear to cause birth defects.

44134 ■ **"Resources: Web Sites, Organizations, Events and More to Grow Your Business" in** *Entrepreneur* **(Vol. 32, July 2004, No. 7, pp. 8)**
Pub: Entrepreneur Media Inc.
Ed: Steve Cooper. **Description:** Online printing and mailing services are offered by Mailersclub; Auction-Bytes is a free email newsletter that covers online auctions; Microsoft's Software Asset Management programs alerts companies when licenses are expiring and standardizes and centralizes the licensing process; U.S. Census Bureau's American Community Survey provides statistical data for small business marketing; Retailwire, provides news to retail professionals; Daypop is a specialized search engine; StumbleUpon is a free browser toolbar; and CoolSiteoftheDay spotlights good Web sites.

44135 ■ **"Rhino Products Device Keeps Ladders Stationary" in** *Journal Record* **(June 24, 2003)**
Pub: Dolan Media Company
Ed: Darren Currin. **Description:** Profile of Scott Walker, inventor of Secure Ladder, a device that attaches onto standard extension ladders to keep them stationery.

44136 ■ **"Romar Group Newest NASCAR Licensee" in** *Black Enterprise* **(Vol. 35, November 2004, No. 4, pp. 32)**
Pub: Earl G. Graves Publishing Co. Inc.
Ed: Nicole M. Richardson. **Description:** Romar Group Inc., one of the nation's largest black-owned apparel companies, received a promotional licensee deal from NASCAR.

44137 ■ **"A Rose With Another Name" in** *Forbes* **(Vol. 174, December 27, 2004, No. 13, pp. 51)**
Pub: Forbes Magazine Inc.
Ed: David Serchuk. **Description:** Profile of Speaking Roses International, the Salt Lake City firm that patented a technology to laser-print messages onto rose petals. Bouquets are available nationwide from Albertsons and Jewel-Osco supermarkets.

44138 ■ **"Rosetta, Random House settle e-book lawsuit" in** *Publishers Weekly* **(Vol. 249, No. 49, Dec. 9, 2002, pp. 9)**
Pub: Reed Business Information
Ed: Steven Zeitchik. **Description:** Random House and e-book publisher Rosetta Books have reached an out-of-court settlement that will end copyright infringement charges Random House brought against Rosetta when the e-book publisher released electronic editions of eight Random House novels. This case has created a rough blueprint for e-book licensing agreements and much legal work ahead.

44139 ■ **"Round Two: Microsoft Appeals $140M Judgment For Local Inventor" in** *Crain's Detroit Business* **(Vol. 23, January 8,2007, No. 2, pp. 1)**
Pub: Crain Communications Inc. - Detroit
Ed: Tom Henderson. **Description:** Local Inventor prepares for appeal of judgment against Microsoft for $140M. Patent infringement for a process to combat software piracy is the central issue.

44140 ■ **"Run for the border" in** *Entrepreneur* **(Vol. 30, No. 3, March 2002, pp. 123)**
Pub: Entrepreneur Media Inc.
Ed: Don Debelak. **Description:** Some inventors are setting up deals with U.S. manufacturers to produce a new product, but when that fails, they are turning to foreign manufacturers to save money; risks involved in doing so are also discussed.

44141 ■ **"Safekeeping for Software" in** *Business 2.0* **(Vol. 7, January/February 2006, No. 1, pp. 30)**
Pub: Time, Inc.
Ed: Daniel Del Re. **Description:** Source codes should be kept in a safe place; an estimated 75 percent of licensing deals require putting source codes in escrow.

44142 ■ **"Sci-Finance" in** *Entrepreneur* **(Vol. 30, No. 2, February 2002)**
Pub: Entrepreneur Media Inc.
Ed: Joshua Kurlantzick. **Description:** Because the National Science Foundation (NSF) has fallen behind the National Institutes of Health (NIH) in funding, there is less money to finance business innovations. The NIH focuses their research into biomedical sciences.

44143 ■ **"Send in the Clones" in** *Entrepreneur* **(Vol. 31, No. 9, September 2003, pp. 128)**
Pub: Entrepreneur Media, Inc.

Ed: Don Debelak. **Description:** Developing an innovative produce is the dream of every entrepreneur, but being able to market a new product is key. Jay Sorenson, founder of Java Jacket in Portland, Oregon patented the Jay Jacket, an insulating sleeve designed to keep beverages in a paper cup warm, shares advice on marketing an invention.

44144 ■ **"'Serial Inventor' Seeks Patent for Wireless Directory Network" in** *Portland Press Herald* **(August 2, 2005)**
Pub: Blethen Maine Newspapers, Inc.
Ed: Edward D. Murphy. **Description:** Profile of inventor, Jeff Strunk, who founded Wireless Directory Network. Strunk hopes to add cell phone numbers to his wireless directory. Currently, the directory assistance business generates nearly $8.5 billion in annual revenue.

44145 ■ **"A Sharp Focus on Fuzzy Thinking" in** *Business Week Online* **(February 2)**
Pub: McGraw-Hill, Inc.
Description: Advice for targeting a market for its services is offered to a new business consulting firm. The firm prepares business plans, writes proposals, assists recording artists and actors with PR and industry agreements, as well as outsourcing registration and licensing for insurance and securities brokers, and prepares trademark and copyright applications.

44146 ■ **"Silvana, Wash., Entrepreneur Designs Coffeepot-Shaped Kiosk" in** *Seattle Times* **(February 18, 2004)**
Pub: Knight-Ridder/Tribune Business News
Ed: Peyton Whitely. **Description:** Profile of Michael Berg, who uses a 12-foot-tall rolling replica of a 1950s aluminum coffee percolator to sell coffee; the kiosk is outfitted with all the equipment necessary to be a stand-alone coffee-selling kiosk. Berg is has trademarked his Hotspot Coffee.

44147 ■ **Small Business Legal Tool Kit**
Pub: Entrepreneur Press
Ed: Ira Nottonson; Theresa A. Pickner. **Released:** May 2007. **Price:** $36.95. **Description:** Legal expertise is provided by two leading entrepreneurial attorneys. Issues covered include forming and operating a business: taxes, contracts, leases, bylaws, trademarks, small claims court, etc.

44148 ■ **"Small Office/Home Office" in** *Hispanic Business* **(Vol. 22, No. 1/2, January/February, pp. 92)**
Pub: Hispanic Business
Description: The feature is designed to provide emerging entrepreneurs with practical tips for operating a small or home office. Home-based business insurance, business licensing, and next-generation scanners are discussed.

44149 ■ **"Smart patents" in** *Harvard Business Review* **(Vol. 80, No. 4, April 2002, pp. 18)**
Pub: Harvard Business School Press
Ed: Robert Maxwell. **Description:** Information is presented about the little-used legal device known as the continuation patent. This 'child' patent allows a company to extend the examination period and make changes in the language of the 'parent' patent.

44150 ■ **"The Software Patent Conundrum" in** *eWeek* **(February 3, 2005)**
Pub: Ziff Davis Media Inc.
Description: According to Greg Aharonian, patents are the best way to protect and support real innovation in the software industry. Software patent issues in both the U.S. and the European Union are discussed.

44151 ■ **"Stake A Claim" in** *Entrepreneur* **(Vol. 28, No. 1, January 2000, pp. 20)**
Pub: Entrepreneur Media Inc.
Ed: Laura Tiffany. **Description:** In the Internet gold rush, the United States Patent and Trademark Office is the lone barrier to technology infringement. Does it know what it's doing?

44152 ■ *The Stand-Alone Inventor: A Bible for Builders of Better Mousetraps*
Pub: Lee Publishing Co.
Ed: Robert G. Merrick. **Released:** 1995. **Price:** $19.95.

44153 ■ "Strategies" in *Business Week* (December 19, 2005, No. 3964, pp. 44-45)
Pub: McGraw-Hill Companies
Ed: Kenji Hall, Peter Burrows. **Description:** Toshiba Corporation is able to keep innovations out of the hands of competitors.

44154 ■ "Strather Launches Hitsville Gaming-But Not in U.S." in *Crain's Detroit Business* (Vol. 22, December 18, 2006, No. 5, pp. 3)
Pub: Crain Communications Inc. - Detroit
Ed: Robert Ankeny **Description:** Innovative entrepreneur capitalizes on Motown heritage for his online casino. Only international wagers can be placed as internet gambling is illegal in the U.S. Hitsville name used due to copyright laws not permitting the use of Motown.

44155 ■ "Suit May Cost Post Unit its Trademark" in *Washington Business Journal* (Vol. 22, No. 15, August 15, 2003, pp. 3)
Pub: Washington Business Journal
Ed: Greg A. Lohr. **Description:** Information regarding the Washington Post's lawsuit against PRIMEDIA Inc. for trademark infringement. Topics include trademark law and competition.

44156 ■ *A Summary of the Law of Patents for Useful Inventions with Forms*
Pub: Fred B. Rothman and Co.
Ed: William E. Simonds. **Released:** 1995. **Price:** $45.00.

44157 ■ "Sun CTO: New License Protects Developer Rights" in *eWeek* (February 7, 2005)
Pub: Ziff Davis Media Inc.
Description: Profile of Greg Papadopoulos, chief technical officer of Sun Microsystems Inc. Papadopoulos explains the company's use of the newly created Common Development and Distribution License for its Open Solaris project.

44158 ■ "Symbol Technologies Wins Landmark Lawsuit in Nevada Federal Court" in *Long Island Business News* (January 30, 2004)
Pub: Dolan Media Newswires
Description: A federal judge in Nevada has ruled that a coalition of bar code companies did not infringe on patents of the Lemelson Foundation, saving retail chains hundreds of millions in royalties.

44159 ■ "Taking License: It Pays to Do Your Homework Before Signing a Licensing Agreement" in *Entrepreneur* (Vol. 32, December 2004, No. 12)
Pub: Entrepreneur Media Inc.
Ed: Don Debelak. **Description:** Kevin O'Rourke chronicles his journey from product development to achieving $10 million in projected sales in 2004. O'Rourke licensed the ElectraTrac, an extension cord with electric plugs located at every eight feet, used by consumers, creators of lighting shows, and electrical and construction contractors.

44160 ■ "Taking Stock of Your Intellectual Property Assets" in *My Business* (December/January 2003, pp. 17)
Pub: My Business Magazine
Ed: John C. Borden. **Description:** It is important to include intellectual capital when valuing a small company. The need to protect these assets is discussed.

44161 ■ "A Team Sport" in *Entrepreneur* (Vol. 31, No. 9, September 2003, pp. 27)
Pub: Entrepreneur Media, Inc.
Ed: Mark Henricks. **Description:** Review of the book, "How Breakthroughs Happen", describing technology brokering, the processes that occurs when inventors borrow existing ideas from one or more fields and gather the people, funding and other assets needed to assemble and apply those ideas elsewhere.

44162 ■ "Tech Talk" in *St. Louis Post-Dispatch* (December 31, 2004)
Pub: Knight-Ridder/Tribune Business News
Ed: David Sheets. **Description:** Joseph E. Walsh Jr., patent attorney, explains how he nearly fell prey to techno-fraud in the form of an email that appeared to be from his bank. Phishing, carding or spoofing are techniques that try to extract important information from individuals using fake emails that appear to be authentic.

44163 ■ *Technological Entrepreneurship*
Pub: Edward Elgar Publishing, Incorporated
Ed: Donald Siegel. **Released:** October 2006. **Price:** $230.00. **Description:** Technological entrepreneurship at universities is discussed. The book covers four related topics: university licensing and patenting; science parks and incubators; university-based startups; and the role of academic science in entrepreneurship.

44164 ■ "They Almost Changed the World" in *Forbes* (Vol. 170, No. 13, December 23, 2002, pp. 217)
Pub: Forbes Magazine
Ed: Michael Maiello. **Description:** Failed inventions and the entrepreneurial spirit to never give up are highlighted.

44165 ■ "Think Ahead" in *Entrepreneur* (Vol. 32, October 2004, No. 10, pp. 40)
Pub: Entrepreneur Media Inc.
Ed: Mark Henricks. **Description:** Review of Seeing What's Next, written by Clayton M. Christensen, Scott D. Anthony, and Erik A. Roth. The book shows entrepreneurs ways to spot upcoming disruptive innovations that could threaten a company's success. A three-step process for predicting industry change is presented.

44166 ■ "Thinking Out of the Clamshell" in *Business 2.0* (Vol. 6, July 2005, No. 6, pp. 58)
Pub: Time, Inc.
Ed: Siri Schubert. **Description:** Thomas Perlmutter invented a tool designed to open clamshell packages. The OpenX tool opens the plastic packaging used to hold products and offer theft protection to retailers while displaying the item inside.

44167 ■ *The Tipping Point: How Little Things Can Make a Big Difference*
Pub: Little Brown & Company
Ed: Malcolm Gladwell. **Released:** January 2002. **Price:** $14.95. **Description:** Correlation between societal changes and marketing and business trends.

44168 ■ "Tips & Trends" in *Small Business Opportunities* (Vol. 16, November 2004, No. 6, pp. 14)
Pub: Harris Publications Inc.
Description: Allsteel features the Landscape Surfaces program for outfitting an office; Debugit Computer Services franchise provides computer maintenance services to homes; franchising for a children's entertainment service; and information for nationwide toy inventions are featured.

44169 ■ "A Toast to Innovation" in *Small Business Opportunities* (Vol. 16, November 2004, No. 6, pp. 48, 50)
Pub: Harris Publications Inc.
Description: Profile of Bill and Ann Rosenberg who have founded Let's Make Wine franchise. Customers can select a wine and personally bottle it and also request a special label to celebrate events.

44170 ■ "Tollhouses & cookies" in *Entrepreneur* (Vol. 30, No. 2,)
Pub: Entrepreneur Media Inc.
Ed: Amanda C. Kooser. **Description:** The World Wide Web Consortium (W3C), the standards-making body for the Internet, has proposed allowing patent holders to charge fees for technologies that become part of the Web standards.

44171 ■ "Trademarks: A Primer" in *Small Business Opportunities* (Vol. 16, No. 1, January 2004, pp. 10)
Pub: Harris Publications, Inc.
Ed: Therese B. Varndell, Esq. **Description:** Because trademarks are important assets to businesses, it is critical to avoid pitfalls when developing a trademark. Trademarks can be registered prior to starting a business based on an "intent-to-use".

44172 ■ *Trademarkscan—International Register*
Pub: Thomson & Thomson
Released: Semimonthly. **Entries Include:** Trademark word and/or design reference, current status, international class(es), description of product/service, registration number, publication details, owner name/location. **Database Covers:** Over 445,000 active registered trademarks on file at the World Intellectual Property Organization. Also included are inactive records from the last 3 years.

44173 ■ "Under Pressure" in *Entrepreneur* (Vol. 31, No. 8, August 2003, pp. 68)
Pub: Entrepreneur Media, Inc.
Ed: Juanita Weaver. **Description:** It is essential to provide a safe environment for employees asked to create something innovative. Communicate to these employees the knowledge of an uncertain outcome, provide necessary time and resources, and define the desired parameters of the outcome for measuring success of the new creation.

44174 ■ *Understanding Novelty: Information, Technological Change, and the Patent System*
Pub: Ablex Publishing Co.
Ed: Thomas Mandeville. **Released:** 1995. **Price:** $73.25.

44175 ■ "U.S. District Court Issues Injunction to Prevent Hi-Tech Pharmacal..." in *Long Island Business News* (March 5, 2004)
Pub: Dolan Media Newswires
Description: A preliminary injunction has been issued against Hi-Tech Pharmacal Company Inc. for selling Tannate 12d S, a generic form of MedPoint's Tussi-12d S cough medication. MedPoint claims Hi-Tech is violating its patent on the cough drug.

44176 ■ "When It Comes to Shopping, Safety Comes First" in *Home Business* (Vol. 13, January/February 2006, No. 1, pp. 56)
Pub: Home Business Magazine
Ed: Sandy Larson. **Description:** Profile of Tracy Richter, inventor of a safety strap that secures infant car seats to shopping carts. Mother of three is dedicated to promoting awareness of the safety issues when using infant seats in shopping carts.

44177 ■ "Where Segway Finds Traction" in *Inc.* (September 1, 2003)
Pub: Gruner & Jahr USA Publishing
Ed: Rod Kurtz. **Description:** Profile of Segway LLC, maker of the human transporter, a self-balancing personal transportation device designed to go anywhere people do. It gives people everywhere the ability to move faster and carry more, allowing them to commute, shop, and run errands more efficiently while also having fun.

44178 ■ "Whose drug is it, anyway?" in *Washington Business Journal* (Vol. 21, No. 44, Feb. 28, 2003, pp. 2,6)
Pub: Washington Business Journal
Ed: Jennifer Taylor. **Description:** Alleged legal loopholes abound keeping generic drug companies from getting their products to market faster. President Bush has proposed new rules that might fix one of those loopholes. Large companies with costly employee benefit plans are getting involved also. Drug companies with blockbuster drugs try to keep patents in effect as long as possible, claiming that research and development costs are astronomical.

44179 ■ "A Work of Art" in *Entrepreneur* (Vol. 32, December 2004, No. 12, pp. 24)
Pub: Entrepreneur Media Inc.
Ed: Mark Henricks. **Description:** Business consultant, Frans Johansson has written a book called, The Medici Effect. Johansson gathered a team of individuals with various ideas, viewpoints and experiences to study successful idea-generators, or inventors, from business, science, the arts and elsewhere.

44180 ■ "The World Bank's Innovation Market" in *Harvard Business Review* (Vol. 80, No. 11, November 2002, pp. 104)
Pub: Harvard Business School Press
Ed: Gary Robert Chapman, Hamel Wood. **Description:** A description of ways a new-products team at the World Bank created an Innovation Marketplace, a forum that allowed people to present ideas for alleviating poverty to potential funding sources.

44181 ■ "Year to Success" in *Small Business Opportunities* (Vol. 17, May 2005, No. 3, pp. 126)
Pub: Harris Publications Inc.
Description: Review of Year to Success, written by Bo Bennett. The book shares the wisdom and words of success stories and the insight of political leaders, CEOs, entrepreneurs, inventors and celebrities. The author highlights ways to handle mistakes, make a strong impression, make decisions, and create good situations from bad ones.

TRADE PERIODICALS

44182 ■ *BNA's Patent, Trademark & Copyright Journal*
Pub: Bureau of National Affairs Inc.
Contact: James D. Crowne, Managing Editor
Released: Weekly. **Price:** $1,289. **Description:** Monitors developments in the intellectual property field, including patents, trademarks, and copyrights. Covers proposed and enacted legislation, litigation, Patent and Trademark Office decisions, Copyright Office practices, activities of professional associations, government contracting, and international developments.

44183 ■ *The Entrepreneur Network*
Pub: Edward Zimmer
Contact: Ed Zimmer
Ed: Edward Zimmer, Editor, edzimmer@tenonline.org. **Description:** Provides information on private investors and other resources seeking growth-business opportunities. Remarks: Available online only.

44184 ■ *Eureka! The Canadian Invention & Innovation Newsletter*
Pub: Canadian Innovation Centre
Ed: Carolyn Parks, Editor. **Released:** Quarterly. **Price:** Free. **Description:** Serves as a forum for Canadian inventors and innovators.

44185 ■ *The Journal of Proprietary Rights*
Pub: Aspen Publishers Inc.
Ed: Michael A. Epstein, Editor. **Released:** Monthly. **Price:** $374. **Description:** Covers trends involving patent, trade secret, trademark, and intellectual property protection issues, including practical solutions.

44186 ■ *The Lightbulb/Invent! Journal*
Pub: Inventors Workshop International
Released: Bimonthly. **Description:** Journal for inventors, entrepreneurs, product developers, and creative individuals.

44187 ■ *TMP Bulletin*
Pub: AGIP - Abu-Ghazaleh Intellectual Property
Ed: May T. Abu-Ghazaleh, Editor. **Description:** Covers issues related to international patents, trademarks, designs and copyrights.

44188 ■ *United States Patents Quarterly*
Pub: Bureau of National Affairs Inc.
Contact: William R. McKey, Managing Editor
Released: Weekly. **Price:** $1,539. **Description:** Reports important decisions dealing with patents, trademarks, copyrights, unfair competition, trade secrets, and computer chip protection.

VIDEOCASSETTES/ AUDIOCASSETTES

44189 ■ *Entrepreneurs Series, Part 1: The Entrepreneurs*
Instructional Video
2219 C St.
Lincoln, NE 68502
Ph:(402)475-6570
Free: 800-228-0164
Fax: (402)475-6500
Co. E-mail: feedback@insvideo.com
URL: http://www.insvideo.com
Price: $19.98. **Description:** Part one of the six-part Entrepreneurs Series. Profiles King Gillette, Wally Amos, John H. Johnson, Charles Darrow, Thomas Edison, and others. **Availability:** VHS.

44190 ■ *Entrepreneurs Series, Part 2: The Land & Its People*
Instructional Video
2219 C St.
Lincoln, NE 68502
Ph:(402)475-6570
Free: 800-228-0164
Fax: (402)475-6500
Co. E-mail: feedback@insvideo.com
URL: http://www.insvideo.com
Price: $19.98. **Description:** Part 2 of the six-part Entrepreneurs Series. Profiles Cyrus McCormick, Harland Sanders, John D. Rockefeller, Gustavius Swift, and others. **Availability:** VHS.

44191 ■ *Entrepreneurs Series, Part 3: Expanding America*
Instructional Video
2219 C St.
Lincoln, NE 68502
Ph:(402)475-6570
Free: 800-228-0164
Fax: (402)475-6500
Co. E-mail: feedback@insvideo.com
URL: http://www.insvideo.com
Price: $19.98. **Description:** Part three of the six-part Entrepreneurs Series. Profiles DeWitt Clinton, Henry Ford, Deke Slayton, James Hill, Charles Lindbergh, and others. **Availability:** VHS.

44192 ■ *Entrepreneurs Series, Part 4: Made in America*
Instructional Video
2219 C St.
Lincoln, NE 68502
Ph:(402)475-6570
Free: 800-228-0164
Fax: (402)475-6500
Co. E-mail: feedback@insvideo.com
URL: http://www.insvideo.com
Price: $19.98. **Description:** Fourth part of the six-part Entrepreneurs Series. Profiles Andrew Carnegie, Eli Whitney, Samuel Colt, Henry Kaiser, and others. **Availability:** VHS.

44193 ■ *Entrepreneurs Series, Part 5: Giving 'Em What They Want*
Instructional Video
2219 C St.
Lincoln, NE 68502
Ph:(402)475-6570
Free: 800-228-0164
Fax: (402)475-6500
Co. E-mail: feedback@insvideo.com
URL: http://www.insvideo.com
Price: $19.98. **Description:** Part five of the six-part Entrepreneurs Series. Profiles P.T. Barnum, Richard Sears, Lillian Vernon Katz, Victor Kiam, Lee Iacocca, and others. **Availability:** VHS.

44194 ■ *Entrepreneurs Series, Part 6: Instant America*
Instructional Video
2219 C St.
Lincoln, NE 68502
Ph:(402)475-6570
Free: 800-228-0164
Fax: (402)475-6500
Co. E-mail: feedback@insvideo.com
URL: http://www.insvideo.com
Price: $19.98. **Description:** Part six of the six-part Entrepreneurs Series. Profiles Samuel Morse, Alexander Graham Bell, Adolph Zukor, David Sarnoff, George Eastman, and others. **Availability:** VHS.

44195 ■ *From Mind to Market: The Patent Process*
Instructional Video
2219 C St.
Lincoln, NE 68502
Ph:(402)475-6570
Free: 800-228-0164
Fax: (402)475-6500
Co. E-mail: feedback@insvideo.com
URL: http://www.insvideo.com
Price: $34.95. **Description:** Outlines the patent process, covering ways to protect your ideas, innovation, disclosure documents, prototypes, patent types, patent searches, marketing, and inventor show information. **Availability:** VHS.

44196 ■ *Handling Trademark Registrations under the New Law*
American Law Institute
American Bar Association Committee on Continuing Education
4025 Chestnut St.
Philadelphia, PA 19104
Ph:(215)243-1600
Free: 800-CLE-NEWS
Fax: (215)243-1664
Co. E-mail: PHunt@ali.org
URL: http://www.ali.org
Released: 1989. **Price:** $95. **Description:** Discusses the result of the 1989 changes in the U.S. Trademark Law. Complete with study guide. **Availability:** VHS.

CONSULTANTS

44197 ■ **ARK Services Corp.**
6118 W 123rd St.
Palos Heights, IL 60463
Ph:(708)371-3674
Fax: (708)371-2926
Co. E-mail: sales@arksvc.com
URL: http://www.arksvc.com

E-mail: sales@arksvc.com
Scope: Offers counsel on machine design and development (concept through turnkey or anywhere in between), especially for packaging, medical products manufacturers and food processing industries. Also offers product and manufacturing engineering and engineering management consulting. Forensic and expert witness services are provided, especially for cases involving mechanical engineering or machinery. Helps clients profit from online services and Internet. Serves private industries. Internet/Online services consulting design, development, installation, maintenance and promotion of web sites. **Seminars:** Design Management for Small Businesses; Finding and Screening New Product Ideas; Machine Design Project Management; New Product Development; Inventions, Patents and Product Development (How to Profit from Your Ideas).

44198 ■ **John S. Child Jr.**
1601 Market St., Ste. 2400
Philadelphia, PA 19103-2301
Ph:(215)563-4100
Fax: (215)563-4044
Scope: Provide solutions in the area of patent trademark and copyright laws. Technical area of expertise is chemistry. Legal matters relating to trade secrets.

44199 ■ **Direct Information Access Corp.**
8928 Maurice Ln.
PO Box 721
Annandale, VA 22003
Ph:(703)978-9428
Fax: (703)978-5740
Scope: Virtual corporation providing consulting and research assistance for mergers and acquisitions; pa-

tent infringement; fraud or money movement; and for overseas site selection. The company also provides investigative follow-up through an associated firm for corporate counter-intelligence. Serves the airline, electronics, telecommunications, law, finance, space, and aeronautics industries. Works in North America, Latin America, Europe, Asia, and the Middle East. **Special Services:** Cyber Security, Red Team/ Blue Team.

44200 ■ Jordan Driks
284 Melrose Ave.
Merion Station, PA 19066
Ph:(610)664-0290
Fax: (610)664-0292
Scope: Extensive background in all phases of patent practice including negotiation and drafting of agreements, Preparation and prosecution of patent applications, negotiating with the government and designing licensing programs.

44201 ■ Information First
9931 First St. E
Treasure Island, FL 33706-1364
Ph:(727)363-6767
Free: 800-995-1795
Fax: (727)363-6868
Co. E-mail: first1@ix.netcom.com

E-mail: first1@ix.netcom.com
Scope: Specialists in name availability and trademark searching.

44202 ■ Invent Resources Inc.
PO Box 548
Lexington, MA 02420-0005
Ph:(781)862-0200
Fax: (781)721-2300
Co. E-mail: rsilver@world.std.com
URL: http://www.inventresources.com

E-mail: rsilver@world.std.com
Scope: An organization comprised of four scientists and engineers that have helped to develop more than 200 products for their clients. After accepting a request for an invention, Invent Resources offers a license to the intellectual property and negotiates a royalty arrangement. Provides support in developing and prototyping the product.

44203 ■ Inventors Resource Consultants
3328 Lakeview Blvd.
Lake Oswego, OR 97035-5540
Ph:(503)635-6333
Fax: (503)697-7123
Co. E-mail: info@terracegames.com

E-mail: info@terracegames.com
Scope: Advises inventors and entrepreneurs regarding new products and/or business. Assists in related design, patenting, development, marketing, distribution, licensing and funding. Serves all industries in the U.S. and Canada.

44204 ■ Kessler Associates
1242 Crestview Ln.
Eagan, MN 55123
Ph:(651)905-9669
Fax: (651)905-1243
Co. E-mail: debrakessler@mindspring.com

E-mail: debrakessler@mindspring.com

44205 ■ Margiloff & Associates
621 Royalview St.
Duarte, CA 91010-1346
Ph:(626)303-1266
Fax: (626)303-0127
Co. E-mail: margiloff@compuserve.com

E-mail: margiloff@compuserve.com
Scope: Energy and water conservation studies, analysis of research and development, licensing, economics and project management. Projects involve development, training, utility review, cost analysis, manufacturing system improvement, process model-

ing and expert witness services. Clients are in the food, chemical, fermentation, energy, financial and legal services, government and general manufacturing fields.

44206 ■ Jerome W. McGee & Associates
7826 Eastern Ave. NW, Ste. 30
Washington, DC 20012-1324
Ph:(202)726-7272
Fax: (202)726-2946
Scope: Business consultants experienced in office automation, small business management, invention and patent counseling, technology commercialization, loan packaging and business plan development. **Seminars:** Marketing Research for the High-Technology Business; Introduction to Microcomputers; Marketing Technological Products to Industry; How to Evaluate Your Technical Idea; Patenting Your Own Invention.

44207 ■ National Congress of Inventor Organizations
PO Box 931881
Los Angeles, CA 90093-1881
Ph:(323)878-6952
Free: 800-458-5624
Fax: (213)947-1079
Co. E-mail: ncio@inventionconvention.com
URL: http://www.inventionconvention.com

E-mail: ncio@inventionconvention.com
Scope: Offers group and one-on-one consultations to independent inventors and small companies to guide them towards self reliance and responsibility in getting products into the marketplace. Customized evaluation and strategy along with matchmaking, networking and support services are personalized to help companies and individuals speed up the process of launching new products and technologies into the marketplace. Industries served: independent inventors, engineers, research and development labs, invent-to-order job shops, innovation and technology centers, universities, as well as small businesses, legal professions, manufacturing, distributors, sales and marketing professionals, inventor groups, and government agencies. **Publications:** "Invention Connections". **Seminars:** Exhibitor Excellence, Boothmanship - maximizing tradeshow performances; Masters of the Invention Process™.

COMPUTERIZED DATABASES

44208 ■ *Canadian Patent Reporter Plus*
Canada Law Book Inc.
240 Edward St.
Aurora, ON, Canada L4G 3S9
Ph:(905)841-6472
Free: 800-263-3269
Fax: (905)841-5085
Co. E-mail: sales@canadalawbook.ca
URL: http://www.canadalawbook.ca
Description: Contains the complete text and headnotes of approximately 12,157 decisions covered in *Canadian Patent Reporter.* Covers significant cases on patents, industrial design, copyrights, and trademarks from the Commissioner of Patents, Registrar of Trade Marks, and various Canadian courts. Also includes cases tried under the Combines Investigation Act and the Competition Act. Provides cross-references to other Canada Law Book databases. **Availability:** Online: LexisNexis Quicklaw, LexisNexis, Canada Law Book Inc; CD-ROM: Canada Law Book Inc. **Type:** Full text.

44209 ■ *CLAIMS /CITATION (1947-1970)*
IFI Claims Patent Services
3202 Kirkwood Hwy., Ste. 203
Wilmington, DE 19808
Ph:(302)633-7200
Free: 800-331-4955
Fax: (302)998-0733
Co. E-mail: info@ificlaims.com
URL: http://www.ificlaims.com
Description: Contains information on every U.S. and non-U.S. patent (over 5 million patent numbers) cited

in U.S. patents granted after 1947. Each of the more than 3.8 million records identifies, by patent number, all later U.S. patents that cite the earlier patent. NOTE: On DIALOG, the CLAIMS/Citation database is divided into three files by dates of coverage: 222 (1971 to date); 221 (1947-1970); 220 (citing patients only, from 1790-1946). **Availability:** Online: Thomson Dialog, Questel; Orbit, STN International. **Type:** Bibliographic.

44210 ■ *Federal Licensable Technologies and Patents*
Wheeling Jesuit University
316 Washington Ave.
Wheeling, WV 26003
Ph:(304)243-4341
Free: 800-678-6882
Fax: (304)243-4388
Co. E-mail: technology@nttc.edu
URL: http://www.nttc.edu
Description: Lists patents and technologies available for licensing from 17 federal agencies, including NASA and the departments of Defense, Commerce, Energy, and Health & Human Services. Includes contact information. **Availability:** Online: Wheeling Jesuit University. **Type:** Directory.

44211 ■ *Health & Wellness InSite*
Thomson Dialog
11000 Regency Pky., Ste. 10
Cary, NC 27511
Ph:(919)462-8600
Free: 800-3-DIALOG
Fax: (919)468-9890
Co. E-mail: intelligence.data@tfn.com
URL: http://www.dialog.com/sources/intelligence_
      data
Description: Contains complete information about health, medicine, fitness, and nutrition. Provides access to 170 of the world's leading professional and consumer health publications, including *The Lancet* and *Nutrition Today;* 550 health and medical pamphlets; 200,000 health-related articles from more than 3000 other publications; and 1800 overviews of different diseases and medical conditions published by Clinical Reference Systems, Ltd. Includes six medical reference books: *Columbia University College of Physicians & Surgeons Complete Home Medical Guide; Mosby's Medical, Nursing, and Allied Health Dictionary; Consumer Health Information Source Book; The People's Book of Medical Tests; USP DI-Vol. II Advice for the Patient; Drug Information in Lay Language;* and *The Complete Directory for People With Chronic Illness..* Allows searches by article title, article type, author, company name, person discussed in the article, publication name, publication date range, publication type, target audience, ticker symbol, words in the title, and words that appear anywhere in the article. **Availability:** Online: Thomson Dialog. **Type:** Full text.

44212 ■ *Industrial Patent Activity in the United States Parts 1 and 2, 1974-1998*
U.S. Patent and Trademark Office (PTO)
Crystal Plaza 3, Rm. 2C02
600 Dulany St.
PO Box 1450
Alexandria, VA 22313-1450
Ph:(703)308-4357
Free: 800-786-9199
Fax: (703)306-2737
Co. E-mail: usptoinfo@uspto.gov
URL: http://www.uspto.gov
Description: Provides information on the activity, ownership, and National origin of utility Patents granted by the U.S. Patent and Trademark Office. Part 1, Time Series Profile by Company and Country of Origin, 1974-1998, covers ownership and national origin of patents granted ty U.S. Patent Office between 1974 and 1998. Includes list of more than 8500 corporations, universities, Government agencies,and other businesses that received patents, ranked by degree of activity. Part 2, Alphabetical Listing by Company, 1974-1998, contains alphabetical list of every U.S. and foreign organization that was granted five or more U.S. patents between 1974 and 1998. **Availability:** CD-ROM: U.S. Department of Commerce. **Type:** Patents/Trademarks.

44213 ■ *LexisNexis Patent & Trademark File History Services*
LexisNexis
PO Box 933
Dayton, OH 45401-0933
Ph:(937)865-6800
Free: 800-227-9597
URL: http://www.lexisnexis.com
Description: Contains patent and trademark file histories — the official, authoritative government documents of patent or trademarks prosecution through the USPTO. **Availability:** Online: LexisNexis; CD-ROM: LexisNexis. **Type:** Full text.

44214 ■ *MarkSearch*
Information Holdings Inc.
250 Dodge Ave.
East Haven, CT 06512
Ph:(203)466-5055
Free: 800-648-6787
Fax: (203)466-5054
Co. E-mail: info@micropat.com
URL: http://www.micropat.com
Description: Contains text and images of more than 1.5 million trademarks. Provides federal trademark information, including applications and active registrations from 1884 to date; inactive records since 1984; and updates within 8 hours of receipt from the USPTO. Useful for determining whether a particular trademark has already been registered, searching for new trademarks that might infringe on the user's, and gaining advance notice of new products coming to market. The database offers many searchable fields, including word mark, international and U.S. classes, goods and services, last reported owner, last reported assignment, and proceedings of the U.S. Patent and Trademark Office (PTO) Trademark Trial and Appeal Board. Boolean operators, wildcards, range and adjacency searching, and 'nesting' allow very complex search strategies (which may be saved for future use). The PTO's Design Search Code Manual is included as a browse index, allowing users to pick search code numbers or design terms to find marks with similar design patterns. Trademarked images can be viewed on screen, printed, or transferred to other applications. Also features a simple interface and is designed to be a simplified version of MarkSearch Pro (described in a separate entry). **Type:** Patents/Trademarks; Bibliographic.

44215 ■ *Patent, Trademark & Copyright Journal*
The Bureau of National Affairs Inc.
1231 25th St. NW
Washington, DC 20037
Ph:(202)452-4200
Free: 800-372-1033
Fax: (202)452-4226
Co. E-mail: customercare@bna.com
URL: http://www.bna.com
Description: Contains the complete text of BNA's *Patent, Trademark & Copyright Journal*. Provides detailed reporting and coverage of legislation, committee reports, international developments (e.g., treaties, conventions), and court and federal agency rulings on patents, trademarks, copyright, and unfair competition. Provides particular coverage of the Supreme Court and intellectual property cases decided by the court. Includes rules from the U.S. Copyright Office, the PTO, the International Trade Commission, and related agencies. Covers policy statements issued by such associations as the American Intellectual Property Association and the U.S. Trademark Association. Covers the latest proposals, amendments, congressional debates, and pending litigation. **Availability:** Online: Thomson West, The Bureau of National Affairs Inc. **Type:** Full text.

44216 ■ *U.S. PatentImages*
Information Holdings Inc.
250 Dodge Ave.
East Haven, CT 06512
Ph:(203)466-5055
Free: 800-648-6787
Fax: (203)466-5054
Co. E-mail: info@micropat.com

URL: http://www.micropatent.com
Description: Contains full-text images of all U.S. patents, including drawings. Issued within two weeks of the U.S. Patent and Trademark Office (PTO) issue date. For each image, provides patent number, issue year, patent assignee, state/country, patent classification codes, title, text, and image. Enables the user to retrieve patents by searching by keyword in title or abstract. Also features 11 additional search fields. Backfile of patents 1964 to date is also available, but provides image-only records. A subset file, the U.S. PatentImages : Chemical database, is also available on CD-ROM (described in a separate entry). **Type:** Image; Bibliographic; Full text; Patents/Trademarks.

44217 ■ *University Licensable Technologies and Patents*
Wheeling Jesuit University
316 Washington Ave.
Wheeling, WV 26003
Ph:(304)243-4341
Free: 800-678-6882
Fax: (304)243-4388
Co. E-mail: technology@nttc.edu
URL: http://www.nttc.edu
Description: Lists patents and licensable technologies from more than 100 universities and research institute, including Massachusetts Institute of Technology, Stanford University, Johns Hopkins University, and Georgia Institute of Technology. Includes contact information. **Availability:** Online: Wheeling Jesuit University. **Type:** Directory.

LIBRARIES

44218 ■ Chicago Public Library Central Library–Business/Science/Technology Division
Harold Washington Library Center
400 S. State St., 4th Fl.
Chicago, IL 60605
Ph:(312)747-4450
Fax: (312)747-4975
URL: http://www.chipublib.org/001hwlc/hwbst.html
Contact: Marcia Dellenbach, BST Div.Chf.
Scope: Small business, marketing, technology, corporate reports, investments, management, personnel, patents, physical and biological sciences, medicine, health, computer science, careers, environmental information, gardening, cookbooks. **Services:** Interlibrary loan; copying; division open to the public. **Holdings:** 415,000 books; 52,100 bound periodical volumes; 33,000 reels of microfilm; Securities and Exchange Commission (SEC) reports; federal specifications and standards; American National Standards Institute standards; corporate Annual reports. **Subscriptions:** 4000 journals and other serials; 8 newspapers.

44219 ■ Derwent–Patent Agency
1725 Duke St., Ste. 250
Alexandria, VA 22314
Ph:(703)706-4220
Free: 800-336-5010
Fax: (703)519-5838
Co. E-mail: custserv@derwentus.com
URL: http://www.derwent.com
Contact: Jane Lehrman
Scope: Patents - United States, international, documentation. **Services:** Copying; translations; document delivery; agency not open to the public. **Holdings:** United States patents (on microfilm and CD-ROM; 1908 to present); international patents (on microfilm and CD-ROM; 1970 to present).

44220 ■ Finnegan, Henderson, Farabow, Garrett and Dunner–Library
901 New York Ave., NW
Washington, DC 20001-4413
Ph:(202)408-4290
Fax: (202)408-4400
Co. E-mail: virginia.mcnitt@finnegan.com
Contact: Virginia McNitt, Mgr., Lib.Svcs.
Scope: Patent law, trademark law, federal procedure.
Services: Interlibrary loan; Library not open to the

public. **Holdings:** 11,000 books; 200 bound periodical volumes. **Subscriptions:** 700 journals and other serials; 6 newspapers.

44221 ■ O'Melveny & Myers LLP–Library
Embarcadero Center W.
275 Battery St.
San Francisco, CA 94111-3305
Ph:(415)984-8700
Fax: (415)984-8701
Co. E-mail: hriccio@omm.com
URL: http://www.omm.com
Contact: Holly Riccio, Hd.Libn.
Scope: Law. **Services:** Library not open to the public. **Holdings:** 8000 books. **Subscriptions:** 75 journals and other serials; 10 newspapers.

44222 ■ Public Library of Cincinnati and Hamilton County–Public Documents and Patents Department
800 Vine St.
Cincinnati, OH 45202-2009
Ph:(513)369-6971
Fax: (513)369-3123
Co. E-mail: pubdocs@cincinnatilibrary.org
URL: http://www.cincinnatilibrary.org/main/pd.asp
Contact: John W. Graham, Dept.Mgr.
Scope: Federal government, patents. **Services:** Interlibrary loan; copying; Library open to the public. **Holdings:** 250,000 public documents; 1,064,000 pieces of microfiche; 6 million patents; 9550 reels of microfilm; 95,000 maps; 3574 CD-ROMs. **Subscriptions:** 300 journals and other serials.

44223 ■ Sentron Medical Inc.–Senmed Medical Ventures Library
4445 Lake Forest Dr., No. 600
Cincinnati, OH 45242-3798
Ph:(513)563-3244
Contact: Rosanne Wohlwender
Scope: Biotechnology, medical devices and diagnostics, technology transfer, pharmaceuticals, venture capital, licensing. **Services:** Library not open to the public. **Holdings:** 800 books; 50 reports. **Subscriptions:** 100 journals and other serials; 2 newspapers.

RESEARCH CENTERS

44224 ■ Indiana State University–Sponsored Programs
Erickson 114
Terre Haute, IN 47809
Ph:(812)237-3088
Fax: (812)237-3092
Co. E-mail: dunderwood@isugw.indstate.edu
URL: http://www.indstate.edu/osp/
Contact: Dawn Underwood, Assoc.Dir.
E-mail: dunderwood@isugw.indstate.edu
Scope: Coordinates pre-award activities associated with external funding and supports research and proposal development. Assists with patents, licensing, and technology transfer. Also facilitates the administrative review and approval of proposals. **Services:** Offers individual assistance, in the preparation and submission of proposals. **Publications:** Creating a Grant Proposal Budget; Finding Money for Your Project; Preparing a Winning Grant Proposal. **Educational Activities:** Seminars and workshops.

44225 ■ University of Wisconsin—Whitewater–Wisconsin Innovation Service Center
402 McCutchan Hall
Whitewater, WI 53190
Ph:(262)472-1365
Fax: (262)472-1600
Co. E-mail: innovate@uww.edu
URL: http://academics.uww.edu/business/innovate
Contact: Debra Malewicki, Dir.
E-mail: innovate@uww.edu
Scope: Performs early-stage market research for independent inventors and manufacturers. **Services:** Market information to clients; Technical reviews.

Inventory

START-UP INFORMATION

44226 ■ **"Do This, Get Rich"** in *Business 2.0* (Vol. 6, May 2005, No. 4, pp. 78-86)
Pub: Time, Inc.
Ed: Michael V. Copeland, Om Malik, Erick Schonfeld. **Description:** Profiles of the eleven hottest business opportunities are presented, including computer upgrades, advertising on the Web, specialty baby furniture, professional medical employment services, interior design for hotels, Web-enabled subscription and service monitoring, search engines for podcasts, RFID tags to track drugs and supplies in hospitals, software to save energy in homes and businesses, software and hardware to monitor and control a boat's onboard systems.

EDUCATIONAL PROGRAMS

44227 ■ **Inventory Management Techniques: Planning, Replenishing, and Control (Canada)**
Canadian Management Centre
150 York St., 5th Fl.
Toronto, ON, Canada M5H 3S5
Ph:(416)214-5678
Free: 800-262-9699
Fax: (416)313-4985
Co. E-mail: cmcinfo@cmctraining.org
URL: http://cmcamai.org
Price: $1,695.00 Canadian. **Description:** Covers material and inventory control techniques, inventory planning, management of inventory processes, and inventory accuracy. **Locations:** Mississauga, ON; and Toronto, ON.

REFERENCE WORKS

44228 ■ **"The case of the obsolete inventory"** in *Red Herring* (March 2003, pp. 34)
Pub: Herring Communications Inc.
Ed: Justin Hibbard. **Description:** In February 2002, Solectron, an electronics manufacturer pressured an employee to write off outdated company inventory. The employee was fired seven months later, now his lawsuit could benefit honest employees throughout the U.S.

44229 ■ **"Chaos, Inc."** in *Red Herring* (January 2003, pp. 38)
Pub: Herring Communications Inc.
Ed: Mitchell M. Waldrop. **Description:** Profile of Santa Fe-based BiosGroup, a 20 year old startup, that recently ran a simulation to help Procter & Gamble achieve an inventory reduction of 25 percent.

44230 ■ **"Control your inventory in a world of lean retailing"** in *Harvard Business Review* (Vol. 78, No. 6, November-December 2000, pp. 169)
Pub: Harvard Business School Publishing Corp.
Description: The production schedules and sourcing strategies of manufacturers is probed, offering a new approach as to how companies can predict their inventory requirements more accurately.

44231 ■ **"First Data: New Terminal POS Lift for Small Outfits"** in *American Banker* (Vol. 172, January 17, 2006, No. 11, pp. 17)
Pub: SourceMedia, Inc.
Ed: David Breitkopf. **Description:** First Data Corporation has partnered with Microsoft Corporation and Hewlett Packard Company to devise a more complete point of sale terminal for small retailers. The terminal will accept most transactions and will track account information, track inventory, and work with customer relationship software.

44232 ■ **"Hot Kicks, Cool Price"** in *Black Enterprise* (Vol. 37, December 2006, No. 5, pp. 34)
Pub: Earl G. Graves Publishing Co. Inc.
Ed: Topher Sanders. **Description:** Stephon Marbury of the New York Nicks introduced a new basketball shoe, the Starbury One, costing $14.98. The shoes are an addition to the Starbury clothing line and although the privately owned company would not disclose figures; stores sold out of a month's worth of inventory in merely three days.

44233 ■ **"Knock on Wood: Lumber Prices Uncertain after 'inventory rally'"** in *Barron's* (July 7, 2003, pp. MW11)
Pub: Barron's
Ed: Lester Aldrich. **Description:** Overproduction, and the subsequent havoc it plays on prices, is always a concern in the lumber sector. Analysts will keep close watch on producers, despite a healthy housing market.

44234 ■ **"Leading the Way"** in *Black Enterprise* (Vol. 35, February 2005, No. 7, pp. 57)
Pub: Earl G. Graves Publishing Co. Inc.
Ed: Bridget McCrea. **Description:** Profile of Lisa Williams, one of a few African American women leaders in the high-tech logistics and supply management field. Williams' firm conducts original research and offers technology services to help clients move information, goods, and capital within and between organizations.

44235 ■ **"National Association for the Exchange of Industrial Resources"** in *Entrepreneur* (Vol. 33, August 2005, No. 8, pp. 4)
Pub: Entrepreneur Media Inc.
Ed: Steve Cooper. **Description:** The National Association for the Exchange of Industrial Resources assists U.S. businesses in the donation of excess inventory to the ill, needy or minors. These donations earn federal income tax deductions.

44236 ■ **"Out with the bad, in with the good"** in *Entrepreneur* (Vol. 30, No. 12, December 2002, pp. 83)
Pub: Entrepreneur Media Inc.
Ed: Joan Szabo. **Description:** Investigation into the last-in, first-out method of inventory accounting and the first-in, first-out method are explained, along with their potential tax impact.

44237 ■ **"A pain in the supply chain"** in *Harvard Business Review* (Vol. 80, No. 5, May 2002, pp. 31)
Pub: Harvard Business School Press
Ed: John Butman. **Description:** Four experts offer their opinions on the aggressive promotion strategy of a fictional manufacturer that is trying to meet the wildly ambitious sales goals set by its CEO.

44238 ■ *Production and Inventory Control Handbook*
Pub: The McGraw-Hill Companies
Ed: James H. Greene. **Released:** 1995. **Price:** $89.50.

44239 ■ *Production and Inventory Management*
Pub: South-Western Publishing Co.
Ed: Donald W. Fogarty. **Released:** 1997. **Price:** $75.95.

44240 ■ **"Quid Pro Quo: Bartering Is a Cashless Alternative to Conducting Business"** in *Black Enterprise* (Vol. 35, September 2004, No. 2)
Pub: Earl G. Graves Publishing Co. Inc.
Ed: Zakiyyah El-Amin. **Description:** Bartering has become a popular way for small businesses with a surplus of inventory, unsold goods, and unused labor to do business. Advice is offered for small business owners wishing to join a barter exchange group.

44241 ■ **"Radio Frequency Identification"** in *Journal of Accountancy*
Pub: American Institute of Certified Public Accountants
Ed: Harold E. Davis, Michael S. Luehlfing. **Description:** Radio frequency identification (RFID) consists of tags, transceivers and a computer system that share the characteristics, location, arrival/shipment time and other information about inventories. RFID is expected to reduce costs and improve efficiency for managing and accounting inventory.

44242 ■ **"Reward Me: Rebates and Incentives Make Buying all the More Appealing"** in *Entrepreneur* (Vol. 32, December 2004, No. 12, pp. 39)
Pub: Entrepreneur Media Inc.
Ed: Jill Amadio. **Description:** Rebates and incentives can help clear inventory. New car dealers use this approach often near the end of a model year.

44243 ■ **"RFID: Plenty of Mixed Signals"** in *Business Week Online* (January 31, 2005)
Pub: McGraw-Hill Companies
Ed: Sarah Lacy. **Description:** Suppliers remain skeptical of radio-frequency identification technology to manage inventories.

44244 ■ **"Setting Up Shop"** in *Home Office Computing* (Vol. 18, No. 10, October 2000, pp. 90)
Pub: Scholastic Inc.
Ed: William Van Winkle. **Description:** Online hosting companies have gone far beyond building Web storefronts and are evolving into E-business service providers (eBSPs) with wide assortments of front-end and back-end office tools. They often provide basics such as Web site setup and hosting free and generate revenue with premium value-added services such as marketing, site traffic monitoring, credit-card processing and inventory management. Tips for choosing a service provider are included.

44245 ■ *Small Business Management*
Pub: John Wiley & Sons, Incorporated
Ed: Margaret Burlingame. **Released:** March 2007. **Price:** $44.95. **Description:** Advice for starting and running a small business as well as information on the value and appeal of small businesses, is given. Topics include budgets, taxes, inventory, ethics, e-commerce, and current laws.

44246 ■ **"Small firms cut hires, inventory, capital plans"** in *Wall Street Journal* (November 15, 2000, pp. B17)
Pub: Dow Jones & Co., Inc.
Description: A survey by the National Federation of Independent Business is examined.

44247 ■ **"Smaller companies plan to build up inventories"** in *Wall Street Journal* (February 15, 2002, pp. B6)
Pub: Wall Street Journal
Description: According to a January survey conducted by the National Federation of Independent Businesses, small companies are planning to build their inventories.

44248 ■ **"Strong Demand Is Firing Up U.S. Factories"** in *Business Week* (January 31, 2005, pp. 23)
Pub: McGraw-Hill Companies
Ed: James C. Cooper, Kathleen Madigan. **Description:** Spending by U.S. consumers, businesses, and governments for all goods and services grew 4.9 percent in the third quarter of 2004 and is expected to grow at the same rate for the fourth quarter.

44249 ■ **"Technology Evolving At Beall's"** in *Bradenton Herald* (February 14, 2005)
Pub: Bradenton Herald
Ed: Dana Sanchez. **Description:** Profile of Don Keller, production manager of one of Beall's Inc.'s two large distribution centers. Keller is phasing in voice recognition technology in its warehouses to increase efficiency in handling inventories.

44250 ■ **"The thrifty boss"** in *Forbes* (Vol. 6, No. 5, March 2003, pp. 46)
Pub: Forbes Magazine
Ed: Victoria Murphy. **Description:** Profile of purchasing software from Ariba. Statistical data included.

44251 ■ **"Tips for cutting costs"** in *Crain's Detroit Business* (Vol. 18, No. 32, August 12, 2002, pp. 12)
Pub: Crain Communications Inc., Detroit
Description: The Small Business Administration offers advice to small businesses for cutting business expenses, including inventory, payments, overhead, management compensation, equipment costs, expansion, joint ventures, risk management, and the use of buying groups.

44252 ■ **"'Tis the Season"** in *Entrepreneur* (Vol. 32, October 2004, No. 10, pp. 52)
Pub: Entrepreneur Media Inc.
Ed: Melissa Campanelli. **Description:** It's never too early for online retailers to prepare for the holiday season. Fulfillment and inventory operations need to be assessed.

44253 ■ **"Valuable Cargo"** in *Small Business Opportunities* (Vol. 16, November 2004, No. 6, pp. 122)
Pub: Harris Publications Inc.
Ed: Chuck Green. **Description:** Profile of Carolyn Gable, owner of New Age Transportation & Warehousing. The firm helps businesses ship and warehouse inventory.

44254 ■ **"We Must Lose the Entitlement Mentality"** in *Crain's Detroit Business* (Vol. 21, October 17, 2005, No. 43, pp. 9)
Pub: Crain Communications Inc. - Detroit
Ed: Mary Kramer. **Description:** Thomas Friedman, New York Times columnist, has written a book that identifies ten trends that are making the global economic playing field more level. Friedman offers advice, although not specifically focused on Michigan manufacturing, in the areas of outsourcing, offshoring and new supply-chain systems.

44255 ■ **"What Do Your Customers See?"** in *Inc.* (February 1, 2002)
Pub: Inc. Magazine
Ed: Bo Burlingame. **Description:** Ways to market a product, inventory, finding a niche for the product, and responding to the loss of a key supplier are the issues addressed.

44256 ■ **"When Is the Price Right?"** in *Black Enterprise* (Vol. 34, July 2004, No. 12, pp. 42)
Pub: Earl G. Graves Publishing Co. Inc.
Ed: Bridget McCrea. **Description:** When a small business is forced to cut prices to maintain market share and reduce inventory, it is important to reduce prices enough to attract customers without cutting too deeply into the company's profit margin.

44257 ■ **"Winter has Me Down. What Can I Do at Work"** in *Crain's New York Business* (Vol. 23, January 29, 2007, No. 5, pp. 47)
Pub: Crain Communications, Inc.
Description: Getting enough sunlight is important to a person's health. If you are not getting enough sunlight due to long days at the office, a good remedy is light therapy, products can be purchased as inexpensive as $89.

44258 ■ *World Class Production and Inventory Management*
Pub: John Wiley & Sons, Inc.
Released: 1995. **Price:** $45.00.

VIDEOCASSETTES/ AUDIOCASSETTES

44259 ■ *Inventory Observation and Valuation*
Center for Video Education
56 Lafayette Ave.
North White Plains, NY 10603
Ph:(914)428-9620
Free: 800-621-0043
Fax: (914)428-0180
Released: 1991. **Description:** A review of inventory observation for staff accountants. **Availability:** VHS; 3/4U.

CONSULTANTS

44260 ■ **R.J. Levulis & Associates**
601 Sequoia Trl.
Roselle, IL 60172
Ph:(630)924-9494
Fax: (630)924-9507
Co. E-mail: rjl@levulis.com
URL: http://www.levulis.com

E-mail: rjl@levulis.com
Scope: Aids manufacturing and distribution clients in securing lasting benefits through cost and investment containment, customer service improvement, cycle time reduction, factory and warehouse space layout,

and similar operations and distribution activities. **Publications:** "Finite Scheduling"; "Warehouse Management Systems"; "Materials Handling An Overlooked Weapon"; "The ABC of Inventory Management". **Seminars:** World Class Manufacturing; Better Warehousing; Basic Principles of Commercial Activities.

44261 ■ **Williamson Imagineering**
621 NE 162nd Ave., Ste. 19
Portland, OR 97230-5750
Co. E-mail: stevew@teleport.com

E-mail: stevew@teleport.com
Scope: Database developer specializing in retail quoting and inventory control applications in the PC environment. Provides system analysis of existing procedures and/or applications, and offers consultation for efficiency recommendations. Provides user training on developed applications as well as off-the-shelf software and operating systems. Industries served: small business, municipal, and light industrial. **Publications:** Publisher of The Imagineer, an informational newsletter focusing on the use of PCs in business, municipal, and light industrial environments; SAVING MONEY ON BACKPACKING FOOD article on dehydrated foods **Special Services:** Specializes in Windows relational database software, Paradox, and office automation utilizing computer technology.

FRANCHISES AND BUSINESS OPPORTUNITIES

44262 ■ **AccuTrak Inventory Specialists**
PO Box 14782
Surfside Beach, SC 29587
Ph:(843)293-8274
Fax: (843)293-5075
No. of Franchise Units: 28. **No. of Company-Owned Units:** 1. **Founded:** 1993. **Franchised:** 2000. **Description:** Inventory consultants. **Equity Capital Needed:** $49,000-$58,000. **Franchise Fee:** $32,500. **Royalty Fee:** 7%. **Financial Assistance:** No. **Training:** Provides 4 days at headquarters, 4 days at approved franchisee training site with ongoing support.

44263 ■ **Bevinco**
505 Consumers Rd., Ste. 510
Toronto, ON, Canada M2J 4V8
Ph:(416)490-6266
Free: 888-238-4626
Fax: (416)490-6899
Co. E-mail: info@bevinco.com
URL: http://www.bevinco.com
No. of Franchise Units: 250+. **No. of Company-Owned Units:** 1. **Founded:** 1987. **Franchised:** 1991. **Description:** Liquor inventory control system for bars, restaurants, hotels, clubs, etc. **Equity Capital Needed:** $40,000. **Franchise Fee:** $40,000. **Financial Assistance:** Up to $10,000 for qualified candidates. **Training:** 7 days corporate training in Toronto, 5-10 days regional training with state master franchise.

COMPUTERIZED DATABASES

44264 ■ *Atlantic Provinces Reports*
Maritime Law Book Ltd.
PO Box 302
Fredericton, NB, Canada E3B 4Y9
Ph:(506)453-9921
Free: 800-561-0220
Fax: (506)453-9525
Co. E-mail: help@mlb.nb.ca
URL: http://www.mlb.nb.ca
Description: Contains headnotes of selected judicial decisions of the courts of New Brunswick, Nova Scotia, Newfoundland, and Prince Edward Island. Also includes decisions of the Supreme Court of Canada on appeals from these provincial courts. Corresponds to *New Brunswick Reports* (2d Series), *Nova Scotia Reports* (2d Series), and *Newfoundland and Prince Edward Island Reports*. **Availability:** Online: LexisNexis Quicklaw; CD-ROM: Maritime Law Book Ltd; Diskette: Maritime Law Book Ltd. **Type:** Bibliographic.

COMPUTER SYSTEMS/ SOFTWARE

44265 ■ PCINV: Inventory Control
Computer Related Services, Inc.
Pembroke 5, Ste. 108
Virginia Beach, VA 23462

Ph:(757)499-8911
Fax: (757)490-5932
Co. E-mail: crsweb@crsva.com
URL: http://www.crsva.com
Description: Available for IBM computers. System provides inventory data management for various businesses.

START-UP INFORMATION

44266 ■ "Getting off to the Right Start" in *Venture Capital Journal* **(Vol. 40, No. 10, November 2000, pp. 40-41)**
Pub: Venture Economics
Ed: Jay K. Hachigian. **Description:** Advice for entrepreneurs to avoid start-up problems, including ways to lay a proper foundation - setting up a common sense capital structure; ways to protect intellectual property; and good operating procedures.

44267 ■ "Home base and knowledge management in international ventures" in *Journal of Business Venturing* **(Vol. 17, No. 2, March 2002, pp. 99)**
Pub: Elsevier Science, Inc.
Ed: Walter Kuemmerle. **Description:** Research paper detailing the broad range of international activities undertaken by start-up international ventures. Particular attention is given to the area of cross-border activities and their role in knowledge management.

ASSOCIATIONS AND OTHER ORGANIZATIONS

44268 ■ Society of Competitive Intelligence Professionals
1700 Diagonal Rd., Ste. 600
Alexandria, VA 22314
Ph:(703)739-0696
Fax: (703)739-2524
Co. E-mail: info@scip.org
URL: http://www.scip.org
Contact: Alexander T. Graham, Exec. Dir.
Purpose: Acts as a forum for the exchange of news and ideas among professionals involved in competitive intelligence and analysis. Addresses legal and ethical concerns; provides opportunities for improving professional expertise. Conducts programs of interest to members. **Publications:** *CI Review*; *Competitive Intelligence Magazine* (bimonthly); *Journal of Competitive Intelligence and Management* (quarterly); *SCIP.online* (semimonthly); *SCIP.ORG In-box* (weekly). Also publishes proceedings documents and books. **Telecommunication Services:** electronic mail, mbrsrv@scip.org.

REFERENCE WORKS

44269 ■ "A Market for Ideas" in *The Economist* **(Vol. 377, October 22-28, 2005, No. 8449, pp. 3-6, 8-10, 12-18)**
Pub: The Economist Newspaper Ltd.
Description: The magazine presents information collected from a survey conducted on issues of patents and technology. Protection of intellectual property can be good for both the technology industry and its customers. The patent system, companies preparing for intellectual-property battles, a new intellectual-property business model, sharing intellectual property, Indian and Chinese competition in innovation, and new markets for intellectual property are among issues investigated.

44270 ■ "Analyze This" in *Forbes* **(April 1, 2002, p. 96)**
Pub: Forbes Magazine
Ed: Erika Brown. **Description:** Sales for business intelligence software are booming. Business intelligence software is designed to make all company data from all divisions compatible with each other.

44271 ■ "Ask the attorney" in *Red Herring* **(March 2003, pp. 73)**
Pub: Herring Communications Inc.
Description: Legal issues are addressed that include the following topics, pharmaceutical patents, government support for research and development, global commerce, intellectual property rights, the transfer of customer lists from European subsidiary to its U.S. parent company, trademark dilution, venture financing, selling a business, stock options, corporate tax deductions, small business patent methods, and employee use of Instant Messaging with clients.

44272 ■ "Avienda: A New Avenue for Communications" in *Venture Capital Journal* **(Vol. 40, No. 10, November 2000, pp. 38)**
Pub: Venture Economics
Description: Profile of Avienda, the Internet technology company co-founded by former Columbia University Business School classmates, Aaron Shapiro and David Bloom. The company is a global point-to-point delivery network, that is, it provides a content delivery and storage solution for personalized data and perishable information.

44273 ■ "Bad image may keep patent board away" in *Crain's Detroit Business* **(Vol. 16, No. 12, March 20, 2000, pp. 53)**
Pub: Crain Communications, Inc.
Ed: Matt Roush. **Description:** Birmingham, Michigan attorney, Eric Dobrusin, has been instrumental in establishing the year-old National Patent Board, a nonprofit alternative dispute mechanism for intellectual property cases.

44274 ■ "Balancing Act: How to Capture Knowledge Without Killing It" in *Harvard Business Review* **(Vol. 78, No. 3, May 2000, pp. 73)**
Pub: Harvard Business School Publishing Corp.
Ed: John Seely Brown, Paul Duguid. **Description:** Top-down processes designed to institutionalize new ideas can have a chilling effect on creativity. This article shows managers how they can learn to walk the fine line between rigidity and chaos.

44275 ■ "Bar the door; New threats from viruses" in *Crain's Detroit Business* **(Vol. 19, No. 3, Jan. 20, 2003, pp. 11)**
Pub: Crain Communications Inc., Detroit
Ed: Andrew Dietderich. **Description:** The importance of data security is discussed. An interview with Ken Farmer, president of DataManagement Inc., is expecting a 40 percent increase in business in 2003 as firms are increasing data security efforts. Various methods to protect computers from hackers and viruses are examined, including alternative lines, firewall systems, disaster-recovery plans, anti-virus software.

44276 ■ "Be Prepared" in *Harvard Business Review* **(Vol. 81, No. 11, November 2003, pp. 20)**
Pub: Harvard Business School Press
Ed: Leonard Fuld. **Description:** Utilization of business intelligence tools can aid companies in planning for the future.

44277 ■ "Beyond the resume" in *Women In Business* **(Vol. 52, No. 4, July 2000, pp. 36)**
Pub: The ABWA Co., Inc.
Ed: Diane Domeyer. **Description:** Issues regarding the recruitment of personnel are presented. The importance of interpersonal skills, knowledge technology, enthusiasm, and adaptability are discussed.

44278 ■ "Bruce Sunstein: Inventor Defender" in *Boston Business Journal* **(Vol. 23, No. 27, August 8, 2003, pp. 1)**
Pub: American City Business Journals
Ed: Sheri Qualters. **Description:** Interview with intellectual property attorney, Bruce Sunstein, in which he discusses his practice.

44279 ■ "Chatting With the Enemy" in *My Business* **(April/May 2004, pp. 49)**
Pub: My Business Magazine
Ed: Michael Helfand. **Description:** Profile of Michael Helfand, co-founder of www.FindGreatLawyers.com, an online attorney-referral business. Helfand discusses information management.

44280 ■ "Communities of Practice: The Organizational Frontier" in *Harvard Business Review* **(Vol. 78, No. 1, January 2000, pp. 139)**
Pub: Harvard Business School Publishing Corp.
Ed: Etienne C. Wenger, William M. Snyder. **Description:** Communities of practice are gaining recognition as business aids well suited to companies that depend heavily upon knowledge. These groups offer a forum of groups of people within an industry or field of expertise to exchange and develop ideas and formulate new approaches to problems.

44281 ■ "Companies Embrace Modern Ways of Communicating" in *San Diego Business Journal* **(Vol. 21, No. 8, February 21, 2000, pp. 16)**
Pub: San Diego Business Journal
Ed: Curt Nelson. **Description:** An in-depth discussion of the ways that knowledge management is affecting morale and competitiveness in the workplace.

44282 ■ "Conflict of interest" in *Red Herring* **(January 2003, pp. 23)**
Pub: Herring Communications Inc.
Ed: Stacy Lawrence. **Description:** Most large U.S. firms still pay two-thirds of the money to auditors on non-audit services, however there is a shift toward spending their IT consulting budget elsewhere.

44283 ■ *Conquering Information Chaos in the Growing Business: IBM Solutions for Managing Information in an On Demand World*
Pub: Maximum Press
Ed: Jim Hoskins. **Released:** April 2005. **Price:** $29.95. **Description:** Information management is critical to any business.

44284 ■ "The costs of e-commerce" in *Hispanic Business* (Vol. 22, No. 4, April 2000, pp. 78)
Pub: Hispanic Business
Ed: Vaughn Hagerty. **Description:** The rapidly changing composition of businesses on the Internet makes it difficult for Internet-based companies to keep track of their competitors. The effects on business success of a lack of knowledge of competitors are discussed.

44285 ■ "A Crisis of Content: It's not just pop music." in *Time* (Vol. 156, No. 14, October 2, 2002, pp. 68)
Pub: Time Inc.
Description: Every industry that trades in intellectual property, from publishing to needlework patterns, could get Napsterized. Jim Hedgepath, president of Pegasus Originals, discusses problems encountered to protect his copyrighted cross-stitch needlework patterns.

44286 ■ "Damages Aren't Always Patently Obvious" in *Journal of Accountancy*
Pub: American Institute of Certified Public Accountants
Ed: Glenn Newman, Richard J. Gering. **Description:** CPA litigation consultants assist patent holders in patent infringement disputes; quantifying damages in these cases can be the focus of a forensic and litigation services practice.

44287 ■ "Detroit Free Press Small Business Column" in *Detroit Free Press* (May 23, 2005)
Pub: Knight-Ridder/Tribune Business News
Ed: Carol Cain. **Description:** Profile of Detroit-based Mobius Microsystems Inc., a firm that designs and sells patented intellectual property to microchip makers. Co-owners are looking to raise $5.5 million in venture capital to grow the firm.

44288 ■ "Digital Content Wars: Can't We All Just Get Along?" in *Red Herring* (No. 87, December 18, 2000, pp. 19-20)
Pub: Herring Communications, Inc.
Ed: Anthony B. Perkins. **Description:** The way the Internet has changed how we look at intellectual property is discussed, citing current court cases.

44289 ■ "Digital Defenses: A Business's Network Is its Castle" in *Red Herring* (January 2003, pp. 52)
Pub: Herring Communications Inc.
Ed: Lee Bruno. **Description:** The challenge for most small companies is to be able to keep the line of communication and commerce open, while securing and protecting critical business information.

44290 ■ "Discovering New Value in Intellectual Property" in *Harvard Business Review* (Vol. 78, No. 1, January 2000, pp. 54)
Pub: Harvard Business School Publishing Corp.
Ed: Kevin G. Rivette, David Kline. **Description:** This article presents the thinking of Richard Thoman, CEO of Xerox Corporation, whose strategic focus is on intellectual property. The discussion includes think clustering, bracketing, and mapping.

44291 ■ "Don't Junk Property Rights" in *Forbes* (Vol. 174, December 27, 2004, No. 13, pp. 25)
Pub: Forbes Magazine Inc.
Ed: Steve Forbes. **Description:** The U.S. Supreme Court will issue two critical rulings on property rights in the next few months.

44292 ■ *Enterprise Planning and Development: Small Business and Enterprise Start-Up Survival and Growth*
Pub: Elsevier Science and Technology Books
Ed: David Butler. **Released:** August 2006. **Price:** $42.95. **Description:** Innovation, intellectual property, and exit strategies are among the issues discussed in this book involving current entrepreneurship.

44293 ■ *Entrepreneurship and Technology Policy*
Pub: Edward Elgar Publishing, Incorporated
Ed: Link. **Released:** August 2006. **Price:** $190.00. **Description:** Journal articles focusing how and the ways small businesses' technical contributions are affecting business. The book is divided into four parts: Government's Direct Support of R&D, Government's Leveraging of R&D, Government's Infrastructure Policies; and Knowledge Flows from Universities and Laboratories.

44294 ■ "Exxon Damages for Valdez Spill Are Cut In Half" in *Wall Street Journal* (Vol. 248, December 2006, No. 149, pp. A2)
Pub: Dow Jones & Co. Inc.
Ed: Associated Press **Description:** A federal appeals court cut in half a $5 billion jury award for punitive damages against Exxon Mobil Corp. for the 1989 Valdez oil spill in Alaska.

44295 ■ "Facing the Online Music" in *Inc.* (July 1, 2003)
Pub: Gruner & Jahr USA Publishing
Description: Entrepreneurs have a stake in the debate over downloading online music and are skeptical of the recording industry's attempts to rewrite intellectual property law.

44296 ■ "Fact and Comment" in *Forbes Global* (Vol. 7, December 20, 2004, No. 22, pp. 9)
Pub: Forbes Magazine Inc.
Ed: Steve Forbes. **Description:** Two critical issues on property rights will be addressed by the U.S. Supreme Court.

44297 ■ "Faster Tech Transfer" in *Inc.* (July 1, 2003)
Pub: Gruner & Jahr USA Publishing
Description: Technology transfer from colleges to private sector is discussed, using examples of universities tech transfer that fueled 450 business and 4,000 licenses in 2002. Transferring innovation from college laboratories to the private sector has startups and schools arguing over licensing and royalty deals.

44298 ■ "Former Information Warrior D'Amico Now Fighting Cyberwarfare" in *Long Island Business News* (March 12, 2004)
Pub: Dolan Media Newswires
Ed: Ken Schachter. **Description:** Profile of Anita D'Amico, director of the 18-person company, Secure Decisions. The firm developed software used by the Navy Command and Control ship USS Blue Ridge for war games. A new initiative calls for the sale of the system to new markets, including epidemiology to track disease and outbreaks, and law enforcement to track crime patterns.

44299 ■ "A Galaxy of Knowledge" in *Business Week* (No. 3699, September 18, 2000, pp. 104)
Pub: McGraw-Hill, Inc.
Description: An overview of the knowledge management project Cap Gemini Ernest & Young, that shares employee expertise.

44300 ■ "Genzyme Battles An Old Adversary" in *Boston Globe* (January 25, 2005)
Pub: New York Times Company
Ed: Jeffrey Krasner. **Description:** A new battle over intellectual property has erupted between Genzyme Corporation and Transkaryotic Therapies Inc. (TKT) of Cambridge, Massachusetts. Genzyme has sued TKT claiming that the firm's method of purifying a treatment for a particular disease infringed on Genzyme's proprietary technology.

44301 ■ "Getting It Right the Second Time" in *Harvard Business Review* (Vol. 80, No. 1, January 2002, pp. 62)
Pub: Harvard Business School Press
Ed: Gabriel Szulanski, Sidney Winter. **Description:** Research has shown the difficulty with which businesses have had in transferring management successes from one division to another. Effective knowledge management transfer is critical, as is understanding why a procedure initially succeeded.

44302 ■ "Gold Diggers" in *PC Magazine* (February 20, 2001, pp. 7a)
Pub: Ziff-Davis Publishing Company
Ed: Sarah L. Roberts-Witt. **Description:** The need for advanced E-business intelligence is driving the adoption of data warehousing and advanced analytical tools using such technologies as OLAP. Businesses who previously kept a tight hold on competitive information assets are now feeling compelled to share the information in order to retain market share. A few forward-thinking organizations now extend access to business-critical data to organizations outside their companies because they see information as an asset to be made widely available and tapped for profit.

44303 ■ "Got Ideas? Book 'Em" in *Success* (Vol. 47, No. 6, November 2000, pp. 68)
Pub: Success Publishing, Inc.
Ed: Karen Fuller. **Description:** Profile of Firstuse.com, the world's central online registry for records, that could save your business millions.

44304 ■ "Government Hooks Man for Phishing" in *Cardline* (Vol. 4, No. 13, March 26, 2004, pp. 1)
Pub: Thomson Media Inc.
Description: An identity-theft scam has been shut down. Zachary Keith Hill used the logos of Internet service provider America Online (AOL) and the online payment service, PayPal to scam consumers into revealing credit card numbers and other confidential information.

44305 ■ "Greed Is Bad" in *Red Herring* (No. 106, October 15, 2001, pp. 92)
Pub: Herring Communications
Ed: Dan Briody. **Description:** The entire semiconductor has slumped over the past 12 months, but shares of Rambus have been hit particularly hard due to critical losses in patent litigation lawsuits. Rambus, a semiconductor designer, depends on the aggressive pursuit and defense of its patented intellectual property.

44306 ■ "He drills for knowledge" in *Fast Company* (September 2001, pp. 186)
Pub: Fast Company
Ed: Fara Warner. **Description:** The importance of intellectual assets and ways to manage knowledge are discussed including an overview of information management at Texaco Inc. is included.

44307 ■ "A heritage of success" in *Hispanic Business* (Vol. 22, No. 3, March 2000, pp. 18)
Pub: Hispanic Business
Ed: Patricia Guadalupe. **Description:** The forward planning and management information techniques put in place by Ed Fernandez, founder of Sherikon Inc., enabled the company to continue trading successfully following his sudden death in a plane crash. The importance of management information systems are discussed.

44308 ■ "Hey, you can't do that!" in *BlackEnterprise* (Vol. 31, No. 7, February 2001, pp. 57)
Pub: Earl Graves Publishing Co.
Ed: Bridget McCrea. **Description:** Profile of Edward Russell and Nicholas Stracick, partners in the company All Pro Sports Camps, Inc. After two years of presentations to the Walt Disney Company, Disney rejected the partners plans for a multi-use sports complex to be built in Orlando, Florida. The article shows how this small business went up against Disney and won.

44309 ■ "Hoover's Introduces Competitive Intelligence and Media Monitoring Service" in *Information Today* (Vol. 17, No. 11, Dec. 2000, pp. 31)
Pub: Information Today, Inc.
Description: Hoover's announces its Intelligence Monitor, a Web service for businesses that need timely market and competitive intelligence information.

44310 ■ "The House That Knowledge Built" in *Fortune* (Vol. 142, No. 7, October 2, 2000, pp. 278+)
Pub: Time Inc.
Ed: Thomas A. Stewart. **Description:** Knowledge sharing may be human nature, but the companies that do it best have a forcing mechanism that oils the jaw of the Tin Woodsman, something that lends urgency to the task.

44311 ■ "How ASPs Can Accelerate Your E-Business" in *E-business Advisor* (Vol. 18, No. 3, March 2000, pp. 20)
Pub: Advisor Media, Inc.
Ed: Lewis Ward. **Description:** E-commerce issues, including return policies, scalability and customer service are explored.

44312 ■ "How to Fix Knowledge Management" in *Harvard Business Review* (Vol. 81, No. 10, October 2003, pp. 16)
Pub: Harvard Business School Press
Ed: David Gilmour. **Description:** Businesses should stop trying to capture knowledge, and concentrate on improving employee connections.

44313 ■ "How I Did It" in *Inc.* (August 2005, pp. 88-90)
Pub: Inc. Magazine
Ed: Lora Koldny. **Description:** In an interview, Paul Frank discusses his $100 million design business he launched in 1995 with a sock puppet monkey. Paul Frank Industries employs 130 people and 200 cartoon characters. Intellectual property is a focus of the discussion.

44314 ■ "How Much Cash Does Your Company Need?" in *Harvard Business Review* (Vol. 81, No. 11, November 2003, pp. 119)
Pub: Harvard Business School Press
Ed: Richard Passov. **Description:** The economic benefits of wise knowledge management are discussed.

44315 ■ "IBM gives Lotus the muscle to punch above its weight" in *PC Magazine* (Vol. 9, No. 5, May 2000, pp. 34)
Pub: Ziff-Davis Publishing Company
Ed: Geoff Einon. **Description:** Profile of Raven, the new software that will be able to extend its searches beyond Notes databases to encompass company-wide data stores. Its information will be made available through a personalized Knowledge Portal that encapsulates any individual as a collection of contacts, tasks, interests and job focus.

44316 ■ "Identity crisis" in *Entrepreneur* (Vol. 31, No. 4, April 2003, pp. 24)
Pub: Entrepreneur Media Inc.
Ed: Nichole L. Torres. **Description:** An estimated 52,400 businesses were affected by identity theft as of June 2002. Tips to avoid identity theft, as well as two Web sites offering more advice is included.

44317 ■ "Identity Theft" in *The Economist* (Vol. 376, July 16-22, 2005, No. 8435, pp. 59)
Pub: The Economist Newspaper Ltd.
Description: Profile of Harold Kraft, the entrepreneur who started MyPublicInfo. The firm helps people look at personal public records.

44318 ■ "In Praise of Privacy" in *Inc.* (Volume 27, March 2005, No. 3, pp. 116)
Pub: Inc. Magazine
Ed: Adam Hanft. **Description:** Workplace information must be carefully rationed by company leadership.

44319 ■ "Intellectual property rights are cyberspace issue" in *Crain's Detroit Business* (Vol. 16, No. 12, March 20, 2000, pp. 23)
Pub: Crain Communications, Inc.
Ed: Joseph Serwach. **Description:** When it comes to intellectual property cases, even a hyphen can make a big difference. The Internet explosion is accelerating the concern about maximizing the value of knowledge assets.

44320 ■ "Intellectual Property and Licensing Pitfalls" in *Venture Capital Journal* (December 1, 2004)
Pub: Thomason Financial Inc.
Description: Intellectual property and licensing issues can result in restrictions on a company's operations and profitability, as well as reduced flexibility in undertaking liquidity events and impair the value of an investment. Intellectual property and licensing pitfalls are outlined.

44321 ■ "Interviews with Part-Time MBAs Point the Way for Retaining Executive Track Managers" in *Employment Relations Today* (Vol. 27, No. 1)
Pub: John Wiley & Sons, Inc.
Ed: Dan Sandweiss and David Lewin. **Description:** Issues discussed concern the retention of knowledge workers with MBA degrees from top colleges. Several part-time MBA students were surveyed, and results indicate that these students believed management development and advancement opportunities were key issues relating to retention. Statistical data included.

44322 ■ "It's all mine" in *Black Enterprise* (Vol. 32, No. 6, January 2002, pp. 42)
Pub: Earl Graves Publishing Co.
Ed: Quincy L. Lewis. **Description:** The four key types of intellectual property are discussed: trademarks, copyrights, patents, and trade secrets. Sources for further research are included.

44323 ■ "James L. McNeil" in *Entrepreneur* (Vol. 31, No. 10, October 2003, pp. 30)
Pub: Entrepreneur Media, Inc.
Ed: April Y. Pennington. **Description:** Profile of James L. McNeil, founder and CEO of McNeil Technologies Inc., in Springfield, Virginia. The firm offers language services, consulting services, information and securities services, and operates a subsidiary that publishes books, dictionaries and glossaries.

44324 ■ "Jonathan Hoffman Was Sure a Former Staffer Had Stolen His Company's Ideas" in *Inc.* (September 2005, pp. 55-56)
Pub: Inc. Magazine
Ed: Lora Kolodny. **Description:** Jonathan Hoffman, CEO of School Zone Publishing, maker of educational media; Hoffman discusses the way the family business handled litigation when a former employee stole his company's ideas.

44325 ■ "Just Zip It: A Confidentiality Agreement Can Give You the Upper Hand" in *Entrepreneur* (Vol. 32, November 2004, No. 11, pp. 96)
Pub: Entrepreneur Media Inc.
Ed: Marc Diener. **Description:** When planning a confidentiality agreement it is essential to determine what information is confidential, to whom information can be disclosed, and how long it is to remain confidential. Always make the confidentiality agreement a separate document from other contracts.

44326 ■ "Keeping America safe" in *Black Enterprise* (Vol. 32, No. 5, Decembe)
Pub: Earl Graves Publishing Co.
Ed: Michelle Buckley. **Description:** Profile of Reginald Daniel and his 1996 startup, Scientific & Engineering Solutions Information Technology consulting firm. Daniel was designated this year's Ernst & Young's IT Consulting Entrepreneur of the Year from Maryland, and National Black Chamber of Commerce name him Entrepreneur of the Year.

44327 ■ *Know-Who Based Entrepreneurship from Knowledge Creation to Business Implementation*
Pub: Edward Elgar Publishing, Incorporated
Ed: Harryson. **Released:** August 2006. **Price:** $130.00. **Description:** Analysis of the knowledge and interconnected areas of entrepreneurship and networking across various levels is presented. Best practice companies are profiled.

44328 ■ "Knowledge Management: Know What You Know" in *PC Magazine* (July 1, 2000, pp. 165)
Pub: Ziff-Davis Publishing Company
Ed: Sarah L. Roberts-Wilt. **Description:** Knowledge management encompasses an overarching business strategy to enable a company to make full use of the information, experience, and expertise resident in the company to serve customers better. Knowledge management needs data warehouses reporting engines, report-building software and ad-hoc query tools. In addition, tools are required to manage information from "soft" knowledge assets buried in text documents, spreadsheets, Web pages, and e-mail.

44329 ■ "Knowledge Networks: Making the Brand" in *Venture Capital Journal* (Vol. 41, No. 8, August 2000, pp. 18)
Pub: Venture Economics
Ed: Alistair Christopher. **Description:** Profile of Knowledge Networks, a marketing intelligence system firm, claims they offer an exclusive service to businesses that shows a concise view of consumers and their behavior toward advertising, brands, and buying.

44330 ■ "Knowledge is power" in *The Economist* (Vol. 356, No. 8189, September 23, 2000, pp. NA)
Pub: Economist Newspaper Ltd.
Description: The issue as to whether we need a new competition policy for the new economy is addressed.

44331 ■ "Law-Less Approach" in *Pittsburgh Business Times* (Vol. 23, No. 9, September 19, 2003, pp. 1)
Pub: Pittsburgh Business Times
Ed: Christopher Davis, Patty Tascarella. **Description:** Eckert Seamonas Cherin and Mellott LLC has assigned Arnie Silverman to head up the intellectual property team charged with handling the law firm's Alcoa contract. Eckert Seamans is the fourth largest law firm in the Pittsburgh, Pennsylvania area.

44332 ■ "Learning to lead" in *Incentive* (Vol. 174, No. 9, September 2000, pp. 32)
Pub: Bill Communications
Ed: Stephen Covey. **Description:** In strong organizations, leaders teach what they have learned to others so that knowledge is retained and recruits quickly learn to appreciate teamwork.

44333 ■ "Lock it Away" in *Entrepreneur* (Vol. 31, No. 11, November 2003, pp. 62)
Pub: Entrepreneur Media, Inc.
Ed: Amanda C. Kooser. **Description:** California law S.B. 1386 requires public disclosure of any computer security breach that affects a California resident's private information, such as social security number or credit card numbers. The new privacy law will reduce identity theft, but also encourages data security to small companies.

44334 ■ "Looking for Leverage" in *Hispanic Business* (Vol. 23, No. 5, May 2001, pp. 32, 34, 36)
Pub: Hispanic Business
Ed: Scott Williams. **Description:** Companies looking to grow have a variety of high-tech options. Advice is given from Omni/Strat, a Miami-based consulting firm that helps companies leverage technology to improve customer relationships, business intelligence, and e-commerce. The Web Head Group, located in San Antonio, Texas, also offers technology advice to small businesses.

44335 ■ "Making Lemonade" in *Entrepreneur* (Vol. 33, October 2005, No. 10, pp. 83)
Pub: Entrepreneur Media Inc.
Ed: Gwen Moran. **Description:** When the owner of a bird-cage and accessories company suffers from a legal battle, she found a way to turn adversity into opportunity.

44336 ■ "Market Orientation and Other Potential Influences on Performance..." in *Journal of Small Business Management* (Vol. 38, No.1, Jan. 2000)
Pub: West Virginia University
Ed: Alfred M. Pelham. **Description:** Research to provide managers in small manufacturing firms with results regarding significant factors related to performance is reported.

44337 ■ "Mind over Matter" in *Entrepreneur* (Vol. 28, No. 9, September 2000, pp. 42)
Pub: Entrepreneur Media Inc.
Ed: Robert McGarvey. **Description:** Web-based intellectual property exchanges are explored. The editor emphasizes the importance of doing a thorough investigation before sacrificing the control over your idea.

44338 ■ "Mining a Company's Mother Lode of Talent" in *Business Week* (No. 3696, August 28, 2000, pp. 135)
Pub: McGraw-Hill, Inc.
Description: An informative article discussing the ways companies are using knowledge management projects.

44339 ■ "Missouri's System of Higher Education: the New Rules for the Knowledge Economy" in *Ingram's* (Vol. 29, No. 8, August 2003, pp. 75)
Pub: Show Me Publishing, Inc.
Ed: Quentin Wilson. **Description:** The changes Missouri's colleges and universities are offering to meet the demands of potential students are presented.

44340 ■ "More tech firms feed off federal defense, IT spending growth" in *Boston Business Journal* (Vol. 22, No. 14, May 10, 2002, pp. 1)
Pub: MCP, Inc.
Description: Defense contractors are relying on increased spending by the government on defense, information technology and homeland security.

44341 ■ "The More, the Merrier" in *Inc.* (September 2005, pp. 65-66)
Pub: Inc. Magazine
Ed: Norm Brodsky. **Description:** The new privacy laws have encouraged more entrepreneurs to launch document-destruction firms. The author addresses why competition is good for any industry.

44342 ■ "MSCI-Red Herring Index" in *Red Herring* (January 2003, pp. 72)
Pub: Herring Communications Inc.
Description: An index comparison is presented, highlighting the following industries: communications equipment, Internet software & services, semiconductor equipment and products, wireless telecom services, electronic equipment and instruments, IT consulting and services, computers and peripherals, broadcasting and cable TV, software, diversified telecom services, and publishing.

44343 ■ "New Laws Take On Delaware Subsidiaries" in *Inc.* (January 1, 2005)
Pub: Inc. Magazine
Ed: Lora Kolodny. **Description:** New York Tax Courts have imposed taxes on revenue derived from intellectual property.

44344 ■ "OASIS Overhauls Intellectual Property Rights Policy" in *eWeek* (February 7, 2005)
Pub: Ziff Davis Media Inc.
Description: According to president and CEO of OASIS, Patrick Gannon, the Organization for the Advancement of Structured Information Standards (OASIS) announced a revision to its intellectual prop-

erty rights policy. Under the new policy, members working on specifications can choose to license their submissions under either a RAND (Reasonable and Non-Discriminatory) mode, an RF (Royalty-Free) on RAND mode or a Royalty-Free on Limited Terms mode.

44345 ■ "Office tech allows 'knowledge management'" in *Kansas City Business Journal* (Vol. 18, No. 21, January 28, 2000, pp. 4)
Pub: American City Business Journals, Inc.
Ed: Leslie Zganjar. **Description:** Companies are striving to improve their internal communications with what is known as knowledge management, an electronic document storing and retrieval system. In regard to improving internal communications, businesses are trying to capture knowledge before it leaves with employees who leave their companies.

44346 ■ "OKC Man Charged in Connection With Identity Theft Ring" in *Journal Record (Oklahoma City, OK)* (February 5, 2007)
Pub: Journal Record
Ed: Marie Price. **Description:** Oklahoma City man is charged with identity theft. The man is part of a group stealing credit cards in order to open accounts and purchase good from Advance Auto Parts in Oklahoma City.

44347 ■ "On Guard: What Does it Take to Keep Your Computers and Intellectual Property Safe?" in *Entrepreneur* (Vol. 31, No. 11, November 2003)
Pub: Entrepreneur Media, Inc.
Ed: Eric Bender. **Description:** The importance of information security is stressed, along with ways for small companies to protect computer and information property.

44348 ■ "Online Publisher Seeks Dismissal of Apple's Trade-Secret Lawsuit" in *San Jose Mercury News* (March 8, 2005)
Pub: Knight-Ridder/Tribune Business News
Ed: Dawn C. Chmielewski. **Description:** Website Think Secret has requested the court dismiss the computer company's trade-secret lawsuit with online publishers and Apple Computer. Apple sued Think Secret's creator of misappropriating trade secrets in his online posts about some of Apple's products.

44349 ■ "Oracle's Security Guard. Exec Vying to Put Lock on Hot Market" in *San Francisco Business Times* (Vol. 17, No. 48, July 4, 2003, pp. 1)
Pub: American City Business Journals
Ed: Lizette Wilson. **Description:** Mary Ann Davidson, chief security officer at Oracle has been responsible for maintaining data security for the company's clients since 2001. Oracle, like other large software companies, is concerned with data security.

44350 ■ "A Patently Obvious Strategy" in *Success* (Vol. 47, No. 3, July 2000, pp. 61)
Pub: Success Publishing, Inc.
Ed: Karen Fuller. **Description:** Protect your intellectual property with a business-method patent, exclusivity makes your business worth more. The article answers business-strategy patent questions.

44351 ■ "People Smarts: Human touch needed to manage knowledge" in *Atlanta Business Chronicle* (Vol. 25, No. 21, November 1, 2002, pp. 3B)
Pub: American City Business Publications, Inc.
Ed: Emory Mulling. **Description:** Making sure a business shares knowledge among the correct employees is recommended. Areas in which knowledge is important are discussed.

44352 ■ "A Perfect Visual PIM-for Some" in *PC Magazine* (February 20, 2001, pp. 52)
Pub: Ziff-Davis Publishing Company
Ed: Alfred Poor. **Description:** A profile of Info Select 6, a new personal information manager (PIM).

44353 ■ "A Pluralistic Account of Intellectual Property" in *Journal of Business Ethics* (Vol. 46, No. 4, September 15, 2003, pp. 319)
Pub: Kluwer Academic Publishers Group
Ed: David B. Resnik. **Description:** Reviews of six different approaches to intellectual property are presented.

44354 ■ "Practice List Hygiene for Healthy Business" in *Folio: the Magazine for Magazine Management* (Vol. 30, No. 1, January 2001, pp. 9)
Pub: Intertec Publishing Corp.
Description: A company's database comprises its "crown jewels" because it can outdraw outside lists by a factor of up to 10, points out Michael Hough, author of The Profitable Trade Show. He offers fives ways to keep it clean.

44355 ■ "Protect Company Info" in *Small Business Opportunities* (Vol. 16, No. 2, March 2004, pp. 86)
Pub: Harris Publications, Inc.
Ed: John DiFrances. **Description:** Ways to protect a small business' proprietary information while remaining within the U.S. law. Three written policies to protect information include one regarding the exchange of technical data between an organization's U.S. and offshore company owned or representative offices and personnel; another regarding employees taking technical and business data, both hard copy and electronic, home or downloading it remotely after company hours; and lastly one regarding what types of technical and business data may be carried on laptop computers and/or downloaded when outside the U.S.

44356 ■ "Protecting your intellectual property" in *Ingram's* (Vol. 28, No. 6, June 2002, pp. 22)
Pub: Show Me Publishing, Inc.
Description: Information and management techniques for intellectual property protection is outlined, including ways to protect intellectual property from competitors and the technologies developed for such protection.

44357 ■ "Resources for employee classes" in *Incentive* (Vol. 174, No. 9, September 2000, pp. 103)
Pub: Bill Communications
Ed: Richard G. Einsman. **Description:** How to keep current with the constantly changing knowledge in today's business management and technology, and tips for finding the right sources for training is offered.

44358 ■ "Resources: Web Sites, Organizations, Events and More to Grow Your Business" in *Entrepreneur* (Vol. 32, No. 2, February 2004, pp. 8)
Pub: Entrepreneur Media, Inc.
Ed: Steve Cooper. **Description:** Profiles of Websites to help grow a small business include Zagat Survey covering 2003 restaurants and hotels offering Wi-Fi to customers; NewIdeaTrade, an online forum for buying and selling inventions, patents, copyrights and other intellectual property; Yahoo's small business Merchant Solutions, with shopping carts, coupons and 24-hour toll-free phone support; WordBiz Report, an e-newsletter focusing on online copywriting and content; Plan-Alyzer, evaluates outcomes of marketing plans; Bob Ely, an independent copywriter and consultant; Meeting & Event Planning for Dummies; and Business Matchmaking, a service to help small business procure government contracts.

44359 ■ "S-A-P Eyes O-L-A-P" in *PC Magazine* (February 20, 2001, pp. 5a)
Pub: Ziff-Davis Publishing Company
Ed: Sarah L. Roberts-Witt. **Description:** A profile of the new business intelligence and data-warehousing products.

44360 ■ "Safeguarding your critical business information" in *Harvard Business Review* (Vol. 80, No. 2, February 2002, pp. 20)
Pub: Harvard Business School Press
Ed: Jonathan Rosenoer. **Description:** How companies can safeguard their critical business information

through the development of encryption technologies. Digital rights management (DRM) may help companies protect themselves against the loss of important information during digital attacks.

44361 ■ "The Shadow Knows" in *Entrepreneur* **(Vol. 28, No. 1, January 2000, pp. 110)**
Pub: Entrepreneur Media Inc.
Ed: Mark Henricks. Description: Are you clued in to what's really going on in your company? According to experts, the real deal can be found lurking in a shadow organization.

44362 ■ "Shh...It's a Secret" in *Entrepreneur. com* **(Vol. 34, February 2006, No. 2, pp. 82)**
Pub: Entrepreneur Media Inc.
Ed: Jane Easter Bahls. Description: When employees leave to work for a competitor, it is essential they understand the confidentiality of your company's trade secrets. Steps to ensure legal protection of company knowledge are covered.

44363 ■ "Small Firm Bankruptcy" in *Journal of Small Business Management* **(Vol. 44, October 2006, No. 4, pp. 493)**
Pub: Blackwell Publishing, Inc.
Ed: Richard Carter; Howard Van Auken. Description: Results of a survey attempt to identify the root causes of bankruptcy in firms. Statistical data included.

44364 ■ "Smart patents" in *Harvard Business Review* **(Vol. 80, No. 4, April 2002, pp. 18)**
Pub: Harvard Business School Press
Ed: Robert Maxwell. Description: Information is presented about the little-used legal device known as the continuation patent. This 'child' patent allows a company to extend the examination period and make changes in the language of the 'parent' patent.

44365 ■ "Software Preserves Knowledge, People Pass It On" in *Fortune* **(Vol. , No. , pp.)**
Pub: Time Inc.
Ed: Description:

44366 ■ "The Spies Have It" in *Business Week* **(June 12, 2000, pp. F26)**
Pub: McGraw-Hill, Inc.
Description: Excerpts from an interview with CIA Officer Pamela J. Noe, who teaches the use of competitive intelligence at George Washington University and to small businesses.

44367 ■ "Spies Like Us" in *Business Week* **(June 12, 2000, pp. F24)**
Pub: McGraw-Hill, Inc.
Description: The growing importance of competitive intelligence for small business is investigated.

44368 ■ "Spy Away" in *Entrepreneur* **(Vol. 28, No. 3, March 2000, pp. 98)**
Pub: Entrepreneur Media Inc.
Ed: Mark Henricks. Description: Informative article about competitive intelligence for small companies. What you don't know can hurt you.

44369 ■ *Strategies for Growth in SMEs: The Role of Information and Information Systems*
Pub: Elsevier Science & Technology Books
Ed: Margi Levy, Philip Powell. Released: November 2004. Price: $49.95. Description: Role of information and information systems in the growth of small and medium-sized enterprises in the U.S.

44370 ■ *Successful Proposal Strategies for Small Business: Using Knowledge Management to Win Government, Private-Sector, and International Contracts, Fourth E*
Pub: Artech House, Incorporated
Ed: Robert S. Frey. Released: February 2005. Price: $99.00. Description: Front-end proposal planning and storyboarding, focusing on the customer mission in proposals, along with the development of grant proposals.

44371 ■ "Survey Projects that Nation's Banks Will Spend More on Information Technology in 2004" in *Long Island Business News* **(Feb. 13, 2004)**
Pub: Dolan Media Newswires
Ed: Claude Solnik. Description: According to a survey conducted by the American Bankers Association and Tower Group, U.S. banks will spend more money on information technology in 2004 than previous years. It is estimated that $21.2 billion will be spent on information technology this year.

44372 ■ "Taking Stock of Your Intellectual Property Assets" in *My Business* **(December/ January 2003, pp. 17)**
Pub: My Business Magazine
Ed: John C. Borden. Description: It is important to include intellectual capital when valuing a small company. The need to protect these assets is discussed.

44373 ■ "TechTalk: Big Bargain: 'Chipless' Semiconductor Startups" in *Venture Capital Journal* **(Vol. 42, No. 10, October 2002, pp. 38-39)**
Pub: Thomas Venture Economics
Ed: Ravi Chiruvolu. Description: The 'soft silicon' approach to manufacturing chips give customers absolute control over intellectual property, allowing for a faster time to market, and if there is an error in the chip, it can be corrected quickly and inexpensively.

44374 ■ "This Just In" in *Crain's Detroit Business* **(Vol. 19, No. 1, January 6, 2003, pp. 1)**
Pub: Crain Communications Inc., Detroit
Description: The possible acquisition of Rootlevel Inc. by Carriersnet Group Inc. is covered. Rootlevel is a Web application and database development company while Carriersnet, is an electronic-logistics company in international shipping. The deal was triggered by the need to develop a system that connects the shipping industry via the Internet.

44375 ■ "Tracing It" in *Pittsburgh Business Times* **(Vol. 22, No. 51, July 4, 2003, pp. 17)**
Pub: Pittsburgh Business Times
Ed: Maria Guzzo. Description: Profile of TraceEvidence Inc., led by Joe Schwera, and located in Sewickley, Pennsylvania. The firm provides assistance to companies that are seeking in-depth information on employees, and often gets involved when civil or criminal investigations are underway.

44376 ■ "Trading in intelligence" in *Ingram's* **(Vol. 28, No. 6, June 2002, pp. 25)**
Pub: Show Me Publishing, Inc.
Description: The increasing importance of business intelligence protection is stressed; one third of Fortune 500 companies fund and staff business intelligence departments, which is triple the number from 1996.

44377 ■ "Using a Reverse RFP Process to Assess Your Outsourcing Options" in *Employment Relations Today* **(Vol. 27, No. 2, Summer 2000, pp. 7)**
Pub: John Wiley & Sons, Inc.
Ed: Jay F. Stright and Frank J. Candio. Description: Outsourcing is becoming a general principle of the knowledge economy as people focus on their competencies and engage specialists in other fields. The Reverse Request for Proposals approach to assessing outsourcing possibilities is presented.

44378 ■ "The Walking Time Bomb" in *Inc.* **(December 1, 2003)**
Pub: Gruner & Jahr USA Publishing
Description: How to defuse an abusive partner, intellectual property issues, and renting property rather than buying are topics discussed.

44379 ■ "Wanted: Chief Ignorance Officer" in *Harvard Business Review* **(Vol. 81, No. 11, November 2003, pp. 22)**
Pub: Harvard Business School Press
Ed: David Gray. Description: The value of finding new solutions to old problems is discussed.

44380 ■ "Weblining" in *Business Week* **(No. 3675, April 3, 2000, pp. EB22)**
Pub: McGraw-Hill, Inc.
Description: Tracking personal information using Web technology is discussed.

44381 ■ "Where is the new frontier of innovation?" in *Fast Company* **(September 2001, pp. 128)**
Pub: Fast Company
Ed: Fara Warner. Description: Fast-paced experimentation, distributed intelligence, total teamwork: the scientific formulation behind the new economy is still disrupting the status quo. In this case, 20,000 leagues under the sea; to appreciate the world-changing impact of digital technology, explore the world of the Monterey Bay Aquarium Research Institute.

44382 ■ "Who Knows?" in *Entrepreneur* **(Vol. 28, No. 4, April 2000, pp. 138)**
Pub: Entrepreneur Media Inc.
Ed: Chris Penttila. Description: Employees come and go, but how do you get their knowledge to stay when they leave? Suggestions are offered to help small businesses.

CONSULTANTS

44383 ■ VenturEdge Corp.
4711 Yonge St., Ste. 1105
Toronto, ON, Canada M2N 6K8
Ph:(416)224-2000
Fax: (416)224-2376
Co. E-mail: info@venturedge.com
URL: http://www.venturedge.com

E-mail: info@venturedge.com
Scope: Services include strategy formulation; performance improvement; business coaching; competitive intelligence; business planning; acquiring capital; financial management; and succession planning in mergers and acquisitions.

START-UP INFORMATION

44384 ■ "The $50 Million Giveaway" in *Business 2.0* (Vol. 6, September 2005, No. 8, pp. 76)
Pub: Time, Inc.
Ed: Michael V. Copeland. **Description:** The visions of eleven venture capital firms are examined; each firm is looking for the right startup to fulfill these visions.

44385 ■ "2005: A Quiet, But Critical Year for Venture Capital" in *Venture Capital Journal* (January 1, 2005)
Pub: Thomason Financial Inc.
Description: Some industry experts are predicting a transformation in the venture capital industry for 2005, with a shift toward seed and early stage investing.

44386 ■ "Angel Investing Still Alive, Barely, in Chicago Area" in *Chicago Tribune* (November 10, 2002)
Pub: Knight Ridder/Tribune Business News
Ed: Rob Kaiser. **Description:** Profile of Bill Maulsby, founder of the Chicago-based BusBank charter bus service, tells how he was able to secure angel investments. The decline in angels to invest in startups is discussed.

44387 ■ *The Art of the Start: The Time-Tested, Battle-Hardened Guide for Anyone Starting Anything*
Pub: Penguin Books (USA) Incorporated
Ed: Guy Kawasaki **Released:** September 2004.
Price: $26.95. **Description:** Advice for someone starting a new business covering topics such as hiring employees, building a brand, business competition, and management.

44388 ■ "Atlantis Group Plans to Back Start-ups" in *Venture Capital Journal* (Vol. 40, No. 10, November 2000, pp. 14)
Pub: Venture Economics
Description: Profile of Robbie Hardy, angel investor and entrepreneur, who founded The Atlantis Group LLC, to back seed-stage companies.

44389 ■ "Borrowing From Dad: Financing From Relatives and Friends Has Risks and Rewards" in *Black Enterprise* (Vol. 35, January 2005, No. 6)
Pub: Earl G. Graves Publishing Co. Inc.
Ed: Carolyn M. Brown. **Description:** More than half of U.S. small businesses are started with money borrowed from family or friends. Banks do not like to make business loans in amounts less than $30,000. Borrowing from family and friends runs the risk of hurting relationships.

44390 ■ "Build Your Dream Home Business" in *Home Business* (Vol. 12, October 2005, No. 5, pp. 16, 18-22, 102, 104)
Pub: Home Business Magazine
Ed: Sandy Larson. **Description:** Ten steps to starting a home-based business, starting from the initial planning phase to financing a venture as well as marketing strategies.

44391 ■ "Building on experience" in *Black Enterprise* (Vol. 33, No. 6, Jan. 2003, pp. 39)
Pub: Earl Graves Publishing Co.
Ed: Bridget McCrea. **Description:** Profile of Angelo R. Perryman, who used his 22 years of experience in the construction industry to launch his own firm. Perryman used personal savings and loans from family members for his startup.

44392 ■ *The Canadian Small Business Survival Guide: How to Start and Operate Your Own Successful Business*
Pub: Dundurn Group
Ed: Benjamin Gallander. FRQ September 2004.
Price: $18.99. **Description:** Ideas for starting and running a successful small business. Topics include selecting a business, financing, government assistance, locations, franchises, and marketing ideas.

44393 ■ *Cash In On Cash Flow*
Pub: Simon & Schuster, Incorporated
Ed: Lawrence J. Pino. **Released:** July 2005. **Price:** $14.95. **Description:** Guide to assist entrepreneurs with starting a new business as a cash flow specialist.

44394 ■ "Charging Ahead" in *Inc.* (January 1, 2004)
Pub: Gruner & Jahr USA Publishing
Ed: Bobbie Gossage. **Description:** Nearly 50 percent of all small business startups are financed with credit cards.

44395 ■ "Coming to America" in *Inc.* (November 1, 2004)
Pub: Inc. Magazine
Ed: David J. Dent. **Description:** Profile of StartSmart a program designed to help immigrants become entrepreneurs. The program is run by the not-for-profit economic development agency called Coastal Enterprises, and offers classes in entrepreneurship, one-on-one coaching, and start-up loans to immigrants and refugees. Five people helped by the program are highlighted.

44396 ■ "Commercialization gets attention in life-science funding" in *Crain's Detroit Business* (Vol. 19, No. 1, January 6, 2003, pp. 16)
Pub: Crain Communications Inc., Detroit
Ed: Laura Bailey. **Description:** The Michigan Economic Development Corporation created the Life Sciences Corridor that will distribute up to $1 billion in settlement money from tobacco companies over 20 years to develop the life-science industry. Startup firms feel that the funding guideline proposals favor funds for research over those for commercialization.

44397 ■ *The Complete Small Business Start-up Guide*
Pub: John Wiley & Sons, Incorporated
Ed: Lisa Rogak. **Released:** November 2004. **Price:** $14.95. **Description:** Guide to starting a small company, focusing on development of a business plan, organizational structure, advertising, hiring, selection of suppliers, and using the Internet to market your firm.

44398 ■ "David Nicklaus Column" in *St. Louis Post-Dispatch* (September 19, 2004)
Pub: Knight-Ridder/Tribune Business News
Ed: David Nicklaus. **Description:** Profile of Arch Angel Investor Network, a group led by the St. Louis Regional Chamber & Growth Association and the Nidus Center for Scientific Enterprise. The group is looking for investors willing to back startup companies in the St. Louis area.

44399 ■ "Dealflow: the most intriguing recent VC fundings" in *Red Herring* (January 2003, pp. 68)
Pub: Herring Communications Inc.
Description: A listing of the ten most intriguing venture fundings is presented, including the company, funding amount and round of funding, prior funding, and monthly burn rate.

44400 ■ "Detroit Free Press Macomb Small Business Column" in *Detroit Free Press* (July 28, 2005)
Pub: Knight-Ridder/Tribune Business News
Ed: Carol Cain. **Description:** Michelle Beaudette-Grates, owner of Girlie Girl, offers makeup, spa treatments and other retail products for women, such as lingerie and jewelry. Beaudette-Grates found a family friend to lend her money to start her new venture.

44401 ■ *The Entrepreneur and Small Business Problem Solver*
Pub: John Wiley & Sons, Incorporated
Ed: William A. Cohen. **Released:** December 2005.
Price: $24.95 (US), $31.99 (Canadian). **Description:** Revised edition of the resource for entrepreneurs and small business owners that covers everything from start-up financing and loans to new product promotion and more.

44402 ■ "Entrepreneur of the Year: Frank Altman" in *Inc.* (January 1, 2005)
Pub: Inc. Magazine
Ed: Jess McCuan. **Description:** Profile of Frank Alman, founder of Community Reinvestment Fund in Minneapolis, Minnesota. The company provides funding to small businesses in impoverished communities.

44403 ■ "Entrepreneurs test start-ups-on the side" in *Wall Street Journal* (May 7, 2002, pp. B6)
Pub: Wall Street Journal
Ed: Jeff Bailey. **Description:** Many entrepreneurs are working fulltime jobs in order to finance their start-ups since venture capital and start-up funding has become more difficult to acquire.

44404 ■ *Entrepreneurship*
Pub: John Wiley and Sons Inc.
Ed: William D. Bygrave; Andrew Zacharakis. **Released:** March 2007. **Price:** $115.95. **Description:** Information for starting a new business is shared, focusing on marketing and financing a product or service.

44405 ■ "Financing" in *Crain's Detroit Business* (Vol. 19, No. 49, December 8, 2003, pp. 13)
Pub: Crain Communications Inc., Detroit
Description: Sources of money for startup firms are listed.

44406 ■ "Financing First Steps" in *Entrepreneur* (Vol. 33, October 2005, No. 10, pp. 94)
Pub: Entrepreneur Media Inc.
Ed: Nichole L. Torres. **Description:** The importance of writing a good business plan before seeking startup financing is stressed.

44407 ■ "Finding Cash for Your Business" in *Black Enterprise* (Vol. 35, February 2005, No. 7, pp. 82)
Pub: Earl G. Graves Publishing Co. Inc.
Ed: Donald Jay Korn. **Description:** Financing alternatives to banks and venture capitalists are available to small businesses in the form of a micro-loan from a lender, family or friends.

44408 ■ "Finding financing" in *Black Enterprise* (Vol. 32, No. 6, January 2002, pp. 8)
Pub: Earl Graves Publishing Co.
Ed: Bevolyn Williams-Harold. **Description:** Minority entrepreneurs may need to look for more innovative capital resources, such as minority-focused venture capital funds or community-based securitization programs, to maintain cash flow.

44409 ■ "Finding Funding" in *Black Enterprise* (Vol. 34, No. 7, February 2004, pp. 48)
Pub: Earl Graves Publishing Co.
Ed: Alan Hughes. **Description:** An overview of government grants offered to minority startup businesses is presented, along with information about the U.S. Small Business Association's resources.

44410 ■ "Finding Investors" in *Home Business* (Vol. 12, March/April 2005, No. 2, pp. 74)
Pub: Home Business Magazine
Ed: Nora Caley. **Description:** Home business startups need partners, rather than investors, to help with startup costs. And these partners expect to play a role in the business.

44411 ■ "First Base: Finding Ways to Finance Your Venture" in *Crain's Detroit Business* (Vol. 19, No. 49, December 8, 2003, pp. 13)
Pub: Crain Communications Inc., Detroit
Ed: Laura Bailey. **Description:** Most entrepreneur's use their own money, or borrow from family and friends when starting a new business, others might use a more risky method of using a home-equity loan on their home.

44412 ■ "Five Ways to Finance Your Business" in *Black Enterprise* (Vol. 31, No. 3, October 2000, pp. 43)
Pub: Earl Graves Publishing Co.
Ed: Glenn Townes. **Description:** The five best ways to find the cash to make your dream a reality are identified as: personal savings, trade credit, commercial banks, second mortgages, and angel investors.

44413 ■ "Forget About Bartering. For Start-Ups, It's All About the Freebies" in *Inc.* (May 1, 2005)
Pub: Inc. Magazine
Ed: Stephanie Clifford. **Description:** Dave Morgan, founder of the Internet marketing firm Real Media shares ideas for starting a company with a minimal cash investment by offering employees benefits for working for him for free. Morgan recruited two recent college graduates to work unpaid for six months.

44414 ■ "The Four Questions" in *Home Business* (Vol. 12, March/April 2005, No. 2, pp. 64)
Pub: Home Business Magazine
Ed: Dr. Paul E. Adams. **Description:** Four questions to ask before applying to a bank for a new small business loan. It is important for entrepreneurs to understand their customer base.

44415 ■ "From the Ground Floor: The business paths to nanotech" in *Red Herring* (No. 99, June 15 & July 1, 2001, pp. 42, 44)
Pub: Herring Communications
Ed: Steve Jurvetson. **Description:** A discussion involving nanotechnology and the startup opportunities, which paths will receive U.S. government grants, and which are market-driven businesses that attract venture capital.

44416 ■ "Funding a Franchise Startup" in *Hispanic Business* (Vol. 23, No. 5, May 2001, pp. 52, 54)
Pub: Hispanic Business
Ed: Barbara Beckley. **Description:** Funding sources available for franchise start-ups are presented. The Certified Development Company, a private, non-profit organization licensed by the SBA; the Small Business Investment Companies (SBICs), which provide equity capital and long-term debt financing; and the Community Development Corporations (CDCs) are among the resources profiled.

44417 ■ "Hold'Em" in *Entrepreneur* (Vol. 28, No. 7, July 2000, pp. 78)
Pub: Entrepreneur Media Inc.
Ed: Cynthia Harrington. **Description:** Takes a look at two entrepreneurs balancing the eternal choice between selling equity or borrowing.

44418 ■ "Hollister priorities: Loan, training programs" in *Crain's Detroit Business* (Vol. 19, No. 3, January 20, 2003, pp. 24)
Pub: Crain Communications Inc., Detroit
Ed: Amy Lane. **Description:** David Hollister was named by Jennifer Granholm, Michigan's new governor, to head the new Department of Labor, Economic Growth and Urban Development. The Department will provide low interest loans to entrepreneurs in targeted redevelopment areas of the state. The extension of the Michigan Economic Growth Authority is also discussed.

44419 ■ "Home-Based Entrepreneurs Still Rely Most on the 4 F's" in *Home Business* (Vol. 12, March/April 2005, No. 2, pp. 78)
Pub: Home Business Magazine
Description: According to the Global Entrepreneurship Monitor, a recent study shows that founders, family, friends, and foolhardy strangers continue to fund small startup companies.

44420 ■ *How to Get the Financing for Your New Small Business: Innovative Solutions from the Experts Who Do It Every Day*
Pub: Atlantic Publishing Company
Ed: Sharon L. Fullen. **Released:** August 2005. **Price:** $39.95, includes companion CD-Rom. **Description:** Ready capital is essential for starting and expanding a small business. Topics include traditional financing methods, financial statements, and a good business plan.

44421 ■ "In for the Count" in *Entrepreneur* (Vol. 28, No. 9, September 2000, pp. 60)
Pub: Entrepreneur Media Inc.
Ed: Cynthia E. Griffin. **Description:** Iris J. Burnett and Nell Merlino, developers of the innovative program called Count-Me-In had revolutionized business loans for women.

44422 ■ "It's in the card" in *BlackEnterprise* (Vol. 31, No. 12, July 2001, pp. 50)
Pub: Earl Graves Publishing Co.
Ed: Paula McCoy-Pinderhughes. **Description:** American Express launches the Community Business Card, a new source of funding for entrepreneurs and small business owners who want to start and grow their companies. The program, called AmEx Community Business Credit Card, is designed for microenterprises with less than five employees and a capital need of less than $35,000 a year. Each time the business owner uses the card, AmEx will contribute one percent of that purchase to one of three select Microenterprise Development Organizations (MDO), which in turn provide loans and technical assistance to the microenterprise requesting the capital.

44423 ■ "It's Not the First Time" in *Entrepreneur* (Vol. 30, No. 2, February 2002, pp. 53)
Pub: Entrepreneur Media Inc.
Ed: Jennifer Pellet. **Description:** Venture capitalists are looking for leadership experience when investing in startup companies.

44424 ■ "Learning business was key" in *Crain's Detroit Business* (Vol. 19, No. 13, March 31, 2003, pp. 13)
Pub: Crain Communications Inc., Detroit
Description: Profile of David Fry, president and CEO of Fry Inc. Fry, a former Harvard University professor, started his firm with financing from family members. The company tripled in size in a short period of time, and Fry shares his experiences of learning about his business as it grew.

44425 ■ "Maine Women's Fund Makes a Difference With Women Entrepreneurs" in *Portland Press Herald* (April 26, 2005)
Pub: Blethen Maine Newspapers, Inc.
Ed: Tux Turkel. **Description:** Maine Women's Fund helps fund startup businesses for women as well as supporting programs to stop domestic violence. The association works with 125 centers in the U.S. that support entrepreneurial development among women.

44426 ■ "Market Planning 101" in *Home Business* (Vol. 12, October 2005, No. 5, pp. 42, 44-45)
Pub: Home Business Magazine
Ed: Christopher J. Bachler. **Description:** A quick marketing plan for any small business is presented and includes all the basic information required to attract loans, partners, business services and even Small Business Administration assistance.

44427 ■ "The Million-Dollar Post-it Note" in *Inc.* (February 1, 2002)
Pub: Inc. Magazine
Ed: George Gendron. **Description:** Ways to make money stretch for a business startup, sometimes called entrepreneurial bootstrapping, are discussed.

44428 ■ "Mining venture capital" in *Black Enterprise* (Vol. 32, No. 7, February 2002,)
Pub: Earl Graves Publishing Co.
Ed: Derek T. Dingle. **Description:** Strategies are given to entrepreneurs about finding capital to fund start-ups in today's economy. Statistical data included.

44429 ■ "New Group Creating Opportunities for Women" in *Atlanta Business Chronicle* (Vol. 25, November 15, 2002, No. 23 pp. 10A)
Pub: American City Business Publications, Inc.
Ed: Wendy Bowman-Littler. **Description:** Project Tsunami Inc., a nonprofit organization launched with a seed grant from the Ewing Marion Kaufmann Foundation in 2002, aims to provide women entrepreneurs with economic opportunities around the world.

44430 ■ "New mortgage company looks past the numbers" in *Pueblo Business Journal* (February 28, 2003)
Pub: Dolan Media Newswires
Ed: William Dagendesh. **Description:** Profile of Southern Colorado Mortgages, and the family that started the firm that is designed to provide prime (good credit) and sub-prime (bad credit) services.

44431 ■ "New Venture-Capital Group Wants to Keep Entrepreneurs in State" in *Crain's Detroit Business* (Vol. 18, No. 2, June 3, 2002, pp. 43)
Pub: Crain Communications Inc. - Detroit
Ed: Katie Merx. **Description:** Investors from across the state of Michigan hope that the Michigan Venture Capital Association will attract more venture capitalists to the state and keep entrepreneurs from leaving.

44432 ■ "The opposite sex: women in search of money still face a man's world" in *Entrepreneur* (Vol. 30, No. 9, September 2002, pp. 36)
Pub: Entrepreneur Media Inc.

Ed: Aliza Pilar Sherman. **Description:** Three women discuss the specific issues women encounter when trying to secure financing for a startup business.

44433 ■ "Pilot program to assist young entrepreneurs" in *Black Enterprise* (Vol. 32, No. 6, January 2002, pp. 37)
Pub: Earl Graves Publishing Co.
Ed: Paula McCoy-Pinderhughes. **Description:** Profile of the Prudential Young Entrepreneur Program, a three-year pilot entrepreneurial development project funded by the Prudential Foundation, a nonprofit, grant-making organization of the Newark, New Jersey-based Prudential Insurance Company of America. The program is designed to offer young adults in urban areas opportunity to train to become a small business owner.

44434 ■ "A Plan for Today's Money Market" in *Hispanic Business* (March 2003, pp. 42, 44)
Pub: Hispanic Business
Ed: Andrea Siedsma. **Description:** A well-crafted business plan is essential for an entrepreneur to obtain capital. The plan must emphasize honesty, credibility, and the details of marketing. Sandra Delarosa, a California female entrepreneur, outlines the details of her business plan for procuring capital. Web sites to assist in writing a business plan are included.

44435 ■ "Rising money" in *Entrepreneur* (Vol. 30, No. 1, January 2002, pp. 36)
Pub: Entrepreneur Media Inc.
Ed: Steve Cooper. **Description:** A listing of financial sources used by entrepreneurs in 2001, information about customer trust, and other areas of interest to small business is presented. Statistical data included.

44436 ■ "Seed Capital for Farm Communities" in *Inc.* (October 1, 2004)
Pub: Inc. Magazine
Ed: Jess McCuan. **Description:** In June, 2004, the U.S. Department of Agriculture along with the Small Business Administration, launched the Rural Business Investment Program, providing $60 million in early stage funding to companies in small rural communities.

44437 ■ "Show Me the Money" in *Black Enterprise* (Vol. 34, No. 3, October 2003, pp. 40)
Pub: Earl Graves Publishing Co.
Ed: Alan Hughes. **Description:** The U.S. Small Business Administration (SBA) offers the 7(a) Loan Guaranty Program to small startup companies. Private lenders make loans to a business, up to $150,000 and the SBA will guarantee up to 85 percent, or 75 percent on loans for more than $150,000. For loans under $150,000, the SBALowDoc (low documentation) loans are available, or the SBA Microloan Program for loans $35,000 or less.

44438 ■ "Show Me the Money" in *Entrepreneur* (Vol. 33, September 2005, No. 9, pp. 102)
Pub: Entrepreneur Media Inc.
Ed: April Y. Pennington. **Description:** Franchise ownership is not as costly as perceived. Stan Harris tells how he secured a loan from a bank to fund his wrap-sandwich restaurant, while a Hawaiian couple secured two loans, one from franchisee and one from a bank, to start their smoothie franchise that promotes healthy eating and living.

44439 ■ *The Small Business Owner's Manual: Everything You Need to Know to Start Up and Run Your Business*
Pub: Career Press, Incorporated
Ed: Joe Kennedy. **Released:** June 2005. **Price:** $19.99 (US), $26.95 (Canadian). **Description:** Comprehensive guide for starting a small business, focusing on twelve ways to obtain financing, business plans, selling and advertising products and services, hiring and firing employees, setting up a Web site, business law, accounting issues, insurance, equipment, computers, banks, financing, customer credit and collection, leasing, and more.

44440 ■ "So Close...Yet so Far" in *Entrepreneur* (Vol. 28, No. 10, October 2000, pp. 38)
Pub: Entrepreneur Media Inc.
Ed: Doug Hood and Marilea S. Hood. **Description:** You're buying a business, but your banker won't loan you the full amount, this article will help you find capital for your small business.

44441 ■ "The stages of investment" in *Crain's Detroit Business* (Vol. 19, No. 12, March 24, 2003, pp. 12)
Pub: Crain Communications Inc., Detroit
Description: The five stages of venture capital investment include the initial/seed money, first stage financing, follow-on stages financing, bridge/mezzanine stage, then the Initial Public Offering, when the company is successfully listed and traded on a stock exchange or market.

44442 ■ "Start-Up Funding Options" in *Home Business* (Vol. 12, October 2005, No. 5, pp. 28, 30-31, 78-79)
Pub: Home Business Magazine
Ed: Jim R. Sapp. **Description:** Alternatives for funding a start-up home-based business include using your savings account, credit cards, 401(k) or Keogh retirement plans, life insurance, second mortgage line of credit, pawn shop, or selling accumulated items no longer needed.

44443 ■ "Stump the slump" in *Entrepreneur* (Vol. 30, No. 2, February 2002, pp. 90)
Pub: Entrepreneur Media Inc.
Ed: Michele Marrinan. **Description:** Many entrepreneurs are taking advantage of the economic downturn to start new businesses. Ways to work the economy to find financing are discussed, including the importance of a solid business plan.

44444 ■ "Technology makes a comeback: fizzling dotcoms were last year's news" in *Black Enterprise* (Vol. 32, No. 8, March 2002, pp. 87)
Pub: Earl Graves Publishing Co.
Ed: Sonya A. Donaldson. **Description:** How African Americans fit into the discussion of venture capitalists, startups, and the technology industry is discussed. Interviews with various experts tell how African Americans can find the capital needed to fund a business venture.

44445 ■ "Touched by an Angel" in *BlackEnterprise* (Vol. 31, No. 11, June 2001, pp. 242)
Pub: Earl Graves Publishing Co.
Ed: Roger Barnes. **Description:** In-depth coverage of venture capital funding programs for African American businesses.

44446 ■ "Venture investors start lending a hand" in *Red Herring* (January 2003, pp. 68)
Pub: Herring Communications Inc.
Ed: Julie Landry. **Description:** Entrepreneurs are finding it hard to procure seed money for new ventures. Venture Credit, a New York firm, is one of many venture lenders that went out of business in 2002.

44447 ■ "Wanted" in *Black Enterprise* (Vol. 32, No. 6, January 2002, pp. 3)
Pub: Earl Graves Publishing Co.
Ed: Bridget McCrea. **Description:** Profile of David Vinson's company, Optate Inc, a Michigan-based online employee-relationship management firm. Vinson explains how his approach to staffing paid off when it came time to seek financing.

44448 ■ "We Found It! The Venture Rebound" in *Fortune* (Vol. 149, No. 9, May 3, 2004, pp. 115)
Pub: Time, Inc.
Ed: Ellen Florian. **Description:** Using data from VentureOne, a research firm that tracks over 100 sectors, the article picked the five most funded sectors, proving that VC funding is good in a few key sectors.

44449 ■ "What is venture capital?" in *Crain's Detroit Business* (Vol. 19, No. 12, March 24, 2003, pp. 12)
Pub: Crain Communications Inc., Detroit
Description: Venture capital is defined by the National Venture Capital Association as "money provided by professionals who invest alongside management in young companies that have the potential to develop into significant economic contributors."

44450 ■ "What's Your Problem?" in *Entrepreneur.com* (Vol. 34, February 2006, No. 2, pp. 102)
Pub: Entrepreneur Media Inc.
Ed: Sarah Edwards, Paul Edwards. **Description:** Entrepreneur asks whether he should us zero percent credit cards to finance his home-based business.

44451 ■ "Where Seed Money Really Comes From" in *Inc.* (August 1, 2003)
Pub: Gruner & Jahr USA Publishing
Ed: Cara Cannella. **Description:** The four "F's" for small business financing are explored: founders, family, friends and foolhardy investors.

44452 ■ *Working for Yourself: An Entrepreneur's Guide to the Basics*
Pub: Kogan Page, Limited
Ed: Jonathan Reuvid. **Released:** September 2006. **Description:** Guide for starting a new business venture, focusing on raising financing, legal and tax issues, marketing, information technology, and site location.

44453 ■ "You better shop around" in *Atlanta Business Chronicle* (Vol. 23, No. 46, April 20, 2001, pp. 65A)
Pub: American City Business Journals Inc.
Ed: Jean Capriotti. **Description:** The founders of Front Page News restaurant in the Atlanta area offer an example of the work needed to find a bank willing to work with risky new enterprises. They finally went to a bank in New Orleans for their loan. Capitol City Bank of Atlanta does specialize in small business loans, and is willing to lend up to 80 percent of the money needed by a start-up company. Charles Anderson of the Small Business Administration says that his agency can help entrepreneurs obtain loans and can provide assistance on how to run a business.

ASSOCIATIONS AND OTHER ORGANIZATIONS

44454 ■ Commercial Finance Association
225 W 34th St., Ste. 1815
New York, NY 10122
Ph:(212)594-3490
Fax: (212)564-6053
Co. E-mail: info@cfa.com
URL: http://www.cfa.com
Contact: Bruce H. Jones, Exec. Dir.
Membership: Organizations engaged in asset-based financial services including commercial financing and factoring and lending money on a secured basis to small- and medium-sized business firms. **Purpose:** Acts as a forum for information and consideration about ideas, opportunities, and legislation concerning asset-based financial services. Seeks to improve the industry's legal and operational procedures. Offers job placement and reference services for members. Sponsors School for Field Examiners and other educational programs. Compiles statistics; conducts seminars and surveys; maintains Speaker's Bureau and 21 committees. **Publications:** *Secured Lender: Magazine of the Asset-Based Financial Services Industry* (bimonthly).

44455 ■ National Association of Development Companies
6764 Old McLean Village Dr.
McLean, VA 22101
Ph:(703)748-2575
Fax: (703)748-2582
Co. E-mail: merril@nadco.org
URL: http://www.nadco.org

Contact: Christopher L. Crawford, Pres./CEO
Description: Small Business Administration Section 504 certified development companies. Provides long-term financing to small and medium-sized businesses. Represents membership in negotiations with the SBA, Congress, and congressional staff members; negotiates changes in legislation, regulations, operation procedures, and other matters such as prepayments problems, reporting requirements, and loan servicing procedures. Provides technical assistance and information regarding special training programs, marketing techniques, audit checklists, and loan closing and processing procedures. Compiles statistics. **Publications:** *NADCO News* (monthly). Also publishes information packages.

44456 ■ Risk Management Association
1801 Market St., Ste. 300
Philadelphia, PA 19103-1628
Ph:(215)446-4000
Free: 800-677-7621
Fax: (215)446-4101
Co. E-mail: member@rmahq.org
URL: http://www.rmahq.org/RMA
Contact: Maurice H. Hartigan II, Pres./CEO
Membership: Commercial and savings banks, and savings and loan, and other financial services companies. Conducts research and professional development activities in areas of loan administration, asset management, and commercial lending and credit to increase professionalism. **Publications:** *Member Roster* (annual); *RMA Annual Statement Studies* (annual); *The RMA Journal* (10/year).

REFERENCE WORKS

44457 ■ "7(a) Program Restored" in *Black Enterprise* **(Vol. 35, October 2004, No. 3, pp. 36)**
Pub: Earl G. Graves Publishing Co. Inc.
Ed: Joyce Jones. **Description:** Funding for the Small Business Administration's 7(a) program has been restored, with $79.1 million reallocated to the program after it ran out of money in January 2004.

44458 ■ "The 2003 Teenpreneur Money Guide" in *Black Enterprise* **(Vol. 34, No. 2, September 2003, pp. S10)**
Pub: Earl Graves Publishing Co.
Ed: Tanisha A. Sykes. **Description:** Online resources for young entrepreneurs that will teach them how to be financially literate.

44459 ■ "The ABCs of setting up a home office" in *Women in Business* **(Vol. 54, No. 5, September-October 2002, pp. 23)**
Pub: The ABWA Company, Inc.
Ed: Kathleen Isaacson. **Description:** Necessary equipment, possible financing and requisite legislation for home offices are discussed.

44460 ■ "Access to Capital: Closing the 'Gap'" in *Hispanic Business* **(September 2004, pp. 46)**
Pub: Hispanic Business
Description: Increasing access to capital for Hispanic companies will require a broad infrastructure along with policy changes. A number of Hispanic organizations are eager to help define strategies.

44461 ■ "Access to Capital: Government Financiers" in *Hispanic Business* **(September 2004, pp. 44)**
Pub: Hispanic Business
Description: Growing affluence has created opportunities for Hispanics to participate in public policy issues affecting the finance industry. Brief profiles of 16 leaders are highlighted.

44462 ■ "Access to Capital: Money to Grow" in *Hispanic Business* **(October 2004, pp. 98-100)**
Pub: Hispanic Business
Ed: Joel Russell. **Description:** Commercial bank loans are a popular choice for Hispanic entrepreneurs. Most Hispanic-owned firms use commercial bank loans and personal savings to start or expand their businesses. Statistical data included.

44463 ■ "An Acquired Taste" in *Entrepreneur* **(Vol. 32, October 2004, No. 10, pp. 62)**
Pub: Entrepreneur Media Inc.
Ed: Crystal Detamore-Rodman. **Description:** Tim Johnstone is a former division manager for a large bank working on the due-diligence team that analyzed companies the bank wanted to buy. Johnstone's experience helped him when he decided to purchase the Anywear Shoe Company in Seattle, Washington. The firm manufactures and distributes professional footwear.

44464 ■ "After the Gold Rush" in *Crain's Chicago Business* **(Vol. 26, No. 50, December 15, 2003, pp. 13)**
Pub: Crain Communications, Inc.
Ed: Steven R. Strahler. **Description:** Profile of Madison Dearborn Partners Inc., the largest private-equity firm in Chicago, Illinois. John A. Canning, Jr., CEO, speaks confidently about a rebound in deal flow, however a survey by Thomson Venture Economics, an equity information service, and the National Venture Capital Associations do not agree.

44465 ■ "Alternative Capital Sourcing" in *My Business* **(September/October 2001, pp. 42)**
Pub: My Business Magazine
Ed: Al Hattal. **Description:** Profile of the Small Business Administration (SBA) program, Small Business Investment Company (SBIC). The SBIC assists both high-risk small businesses and start-ups that might not otherwise receive funding.

44466 ■ "Analysts Mixed on WNY Economy" in *Business First Buffalo* **(Vol. 19, No. 44, July 25, 2003, pp. 1)**
Pub: American City Business Journals, Inc.
Ed: Tom Hartley. **Description:** Industry analysts report that economic conditions in western New York remain flat, but are showing some signs of economic revival with stronger financial performance at M and T Bank. The bank reported a 4.4 percent increase in commercial and industrial lending.

44467 ■ "Angel Investors Take a Plunge" in *Milwaukee Journal Sentinel* **(December 20, 2005)**
Pub: Journal Sentinel, Inc.
Ed: Kathleen Gallagher. **Description:** AquaSensors has obtained $360,000 from angel investors for its equipment that can calculate the amount of oxygen in beer or measure bacterial levels for wastewater treatment plants. Details of the deal are presented.

44468 ■ "'Angels' Seek to Expand Territory; Investors Begin to Target Waukesha County" in *Milwaukee Journal Sentinel* **(December 12, 2005)**
Pub: Journal Sentinel, Inc.
Ed: Kathleen Gallagher. **Description:** IQ Corridor Angel Network is targeting Waukesha County to help develop a series of high-tech companies from Chicago through Milwaukee and Madison onto Minneapolis. The firm is seeking ideas related to manufacturing equipment needed by biotech and other high-tech companies, especially those in Madison, Wisconsin.

44469 ■ "Anxious lenders fail to bait Florida borrowers" in *Atlanta Business Chronicle* **(Vol. 25, December 6, 2002, No. 26, pp. 29C)**
Pub: American City Business Publications, Inc.
Ed: Jane Bennett. **Description:** In the Northeast Florida commercial real estate market, lenders are looking for borrowers seeking quality developers competing for loans. However, many developers and construction companies are not looking for money. It seems the banks want to do business with developers with their own equity invested.

44470 ■ "Applebee Int'l Sets Up Loans for Remodeling by Franchises" in *Long Island Business News* **(March 12, 2004)**
Pub: Dolan Media Newswires
Description: Applebee's International has instituted a new loan program for its franchisees in order to remodel stores. The Overland Park, Kansas-based Applebee's will allow franchisees to draw on a credit line up to $75 million. Statistical data included.

44471 ■ "Arrested Development?" in *Entrepreneur* **(Vol. 32, November 2004, No. 11, pp. 75)**
Pub: Entrepreneur Media Inc.
Description: Small businesses backed by venture capital may soon be eligible for the Small Business Administration's Small Business Innovation Research Program.

44472 ■ "Ask the Attorney" in *Red Herring* **(No. 105, October 1, 2001, pp. 105)**
Pub: Herring Communications
Description: Legal questions are answered, including issues of venture financing, venture capital, software protection, equity, patents, insider trading, and strategic financing.

44473 ■ *Bank Directory of South Carolina*
Pub: Accuity
Released: Annual. **Covers:** Head offices and branches of every bank in the state of South Carolina. **Entries Include:** Name, address, phone, fax, key bank officers by functional title, directors, date established, detailed financial data, association's membership, attorney or counsel, correspondent banks, out-of-town branches, holding company affiliation, ABA Transit Number and Routing Symbol, MICR number with check digit, credit cards issued, trust powers, type of charter. **Arrangement:** Geographical. **Indexes:** Alphabetical.

44474 ■ *Bank Directory of South Dakota*
Pub: Accuity
Released: Annual. **Covers:** Head offices and branches of every bank in the state of South Dakota. **Entries Include:** Name, address, phone, fax, key bank officers by functional title, directors, date established, detailed financial data, association's membership, attorney or counsel, correspondent banks, out-of-town branches, holding company affiliation, ABA Transit Number and Routing Symbol, MICR number with check digit, credit cards issued, trust powers, type of charter. **Arrangement:** Geographical. **Indexes:** Alphabetical.

44475 ■ *Bank Directory of Virginia*
Pub: Accuity
Released: Annual. **Covers:** Head offices and branches of every bank in the state of Virginia. **Entries Include:** Name, address, phone, fax, key bank officers by functional title, directors, date established, detailed financial data, association's membership, attorney or counsel, correspondent banks, out-of-town branches, holding company affiliation, ABA Transit Number and Routing Symbol, MICR number with check digit, credit cards issued, trust powers, type of charter. **Arrangement:** Geographical. **Indexes:** Alphabetical.

44476 ■ "Bank Reform: Should You Be Celebrating?" in *Business Week* **(No. 3658, December 6, 1999, pp. F8)**
Pub: McGraw-Hill, Inc.
Description: Lists ways in which financial services deregulation will affect small business.

44477 ■ "Banks: Big vs. Small" in *Hispanic Business* **(October 2002, pp. 36, 38)**
Pub: Hispanic Business
Ed: Derek Reveron. **Description:** Entrepreneurs have traditionally had to choose between local lenders for customized service or larger institutions for more services, but statistics show that the margin difference between the two is narrowing.

44478 ■ "Banks May Sell Off Your Loans" in *Inc.* **(September 1, 2003)**
Pub: Gruner & Jahr USA Publishing
Ed: Amy Gunderson. **Description:** According to the U.S. Small Business Administration, a secondary market for small business loans could actually benefit entrepreneurs by increasing the overall amount of lending.

44479 ■ "Banks' distressed loans are on the rise" in *Atlanta Business Chronicle* **(Vol. 24, No. 9, August 3, 2001, pp. 3A)**
Pub: American City Business Journals Inc.

Ed: Meredith Jordan. **Description:** Across the nation, large banks are noticing an increase in non-performing loans. From the first quarter of 2000 to the first quarter of 2001, Bank of America, the largest bank in Georgia, has recorded an increase of non-performing loans of 61.4 percent. Non-performing loans are hose that demonstrate signs of negativity that could indicate a strong chance they will not be re-paid in the future.

44480 ■ "Been there, done that: growing an entrepreneurial empire?" in *Entrepreneur* **(Vol. 30, No. 9, September 2002, pp. 25)**
Pub: Entrepreneur Media Inc.
Ed: Joshua Kurlantzick. **Description:** Many venture capital entrepreneurs are seeking businesses that have the same qualities that made their own companies successful.

44481 ■ "Black Firm Sues SBA, Alleges Funding Bias" in *Boston Business Journal* **(Vol. 23, No. 30, August 29, 2003, pp. 18)**
Pub: American City Business Journals
Ed: Kent Hoover. **Description:** The racial discrimination lawsuit filed by minority-owned Small Business Investment Corporation against the U.S. Small Business Administration is addressed. Topics include management teams, funding of minority business, and business start-up loans.

44482 ■ "Bonus Round" in *Entrepreneur* **(Vol. 31, No. 7, July 2003, pp. 52)**
Pub: Entrepreneur Media, Inc.
Ed: David Worrell. **Description:** Venture debt is a loan that earns the lender a small pledge of stock warrants. VC lenders are willing to work with risky, early-stage companies because that small equity gives them a potential to a large upside.

44483 ■ "Bradenton Central CRA To Launch New Business Development Center" in *Bradenton Herald* **(January 29, 2005)**
Pub: Bradenton Herald
Ed: Tim W. McCann. **Description:** The Bradenton Central Community Redevelopment Agency is working to grow the economy of the area. The Agency will create a small business center with a professional counselor to assist small business owners in applying for a business loan, advertising, marketing and legal issues.

44484 ■ "British Virgin Islands firm finances Miami apartments" in *Daily Business Review* **(Vol. 77, No. 146, January 7, 2003, pp. A4)**
Pub: American Lawyer Media LP
Ed: Charles Kimball. **Description:** The British Virgin Islands company, Vilamoura International Corporation, has provided $8.5 million in financing for a new apartment complex in Miami, Florida.

44485 ■ "Broadband agency makes its first loan" in *Crain's Detroit Business* **(Vol. 19, No. 12, March 24, 2003, pp. 6)**
Pub: Crain Communications Inc., Detroit
Ed: Amy Lane. **Description:** The Michigan Broadband Development Authority has approved its first loan to the mid-Michigan wireless provider ISP Wireless Group Inc., located in Alma. The company intends to install wireless broadband antennae and equipment in small towns from Clare to Ithaca.

44486 ■ "The Bucks Start Here" in *Business Week* **(No. 3658, December 6, 1999, pp. F10)**
Pub: McGraw-Hill, Inc.
Description: Small, fast growing companies are investing in their businesses without taking out new bank loans to do it. As bank rates rise and profit margins remain strong, these companies are choosing to finance growth from their own cash flow.

44487 ■ "The burden of borrowing" in *Entrepreneur* **(Vol. 31, No. 4, April 2003, pp. 53)**
Pub: Entrepreneur Media Inc.
Ed: Crystal Detamore-Rodman. **Description:** Many times the indirect costs of borrowing, such as collateral conditions, may have more impact on a growing business than the loan itself.

44488 ■ "Business Owners: Are You Getting Your Share of Investment Capital?" in *Women in Business* **(Vol. 54, No. 5, Sept.-Oct. 2002, pp. 28)**
Pub: The ABWA Company, Inc.
Ed: Mary-Lane Kamberg. **Description:** Sources of funding and techniques to obtain funding are discussed.

44489 ■ "Caps off to you!" in *Entrepreneur* **(Vol. 31, No. 6, June 2003, pp. 51)**
Pub: Entrepreneur Media Inc.
Ed: C.J. Prince. **Description:** The U.S. Small Business Administration has restored the maximum loan amount of its 7(a) small business loan program to $2 million.

44490 ■ "Captains of Capital" in *Hispanic Business* **(March 2003, pp. 30-34, 36-38)**
Pub: Hispanic Business
Description: Ways in which the Hispanic Business 500 are finding growth capital are presented. Three Hispanic entrepreneurs are featured, showing how they met this investment challenge. Statistical data included.

44491 ■ "Cash crunch" in *Entrepreneur* **(Vol. 30, No.2 February 2002, pp. 53)**
Pub: Entrepreneur Media Inc.
Ed: Jennifer Pellet. **Description:** When judging the benefit of potential funding, beware of certain terms demanded by banks and other financing sources.

44492 ■ "Charter One Leads State Banks in Small-Biz Loans" in *Crain's Detroit Business* **(Vol. 21, October 24, 2005, No. 43, pp. 24)**
Pub: Crain Communications Inc. - Detroit
Ed: Tom Henderson. **Description:** Charter One Bank was reported as the number one small business lender in both Michigan and the Midwest by the U.S. Small Business Administration. Statistical data included.

44493 ■ "Citizens Bank To Lend Low-Interest Loans to Firms Relocating to Massachusetts" in *Boston Globe* **(February 4, 2005)**
Pub: New York Times Company
Ed: Sasha Talcott. **Description:** A partnership between Citizens Bank and the State of Massachusetts will offer loans to companies expanding or relocating to the state. The loans will be set at a fixed rate of 3.5 percent and for every $400,000 borrowed, the company will be required to create one new job.

44494 ■ "Columbia Credit Union branch targets 21st-century crowd" in *Vancouver, WA Business Journal* **(February 28, 2003)**
Pub: Dolan Media Newswires
Ed: Cami Joner. **Description:** The Columbia Credit Unions new branch is designed to appeal to Clark County's high tech community.

44495 ■ "Commercial Break" in *Entrepreneur* **(Vol.32)**
Pub: Entrepreneur Media Inc.
Ed: Crystal Detamore-Rodman. **Description:** Priceton Laundry, catering to New York City Hotels, found the answer to financial issues by securing a loan from a commercial finance company after traditional banks refused.

44496 ■ "Common Cents" in *Entrepreneur* **(Vol. 32, November 2004, No. 11, pp. 72)**
Pub: Entrepreneur Media Inc.
Ed: David Worrell. **Description:** Angel investors tend to invest in industries of similar interest. Angel Strategies coaches entrepreneurs to look for affinity investors.

44497 ■ *The Commonsense Way to Build Wealth: One Entrepreneur Shares His Secrets*
Pub: Griffin Publishing Group
Ed: Jack Chou. **Released:** September 2004. **Price:** $19.95. **Description:** Entrepreneurial tips to accumulate wealth, select the proper business or franchise, choose and manage rental property, and how to negotiate a good lease.

44498 ■ "Congress rejects plan to raise SBA loan fees" in *Atlanta Business Chronicle* **(Vol. 24, No. 7, July 20, 2001, pp. 5A)**
Pub: American City Business Journals Inc.
Ed: Ken Hoover. **Description:** The U.S. House Appropriations Committee has approved a $728 million budget for the Small Business Administration, adding 40 percent to the $539 million budget proposed by the Bush Administration, but still $130 million less than the 2001 budget. The increase means the agency does not need to raise fees for its flagship 7(a) loans and charge for consultation services at its Small Business Development Centers.

44499 ■ "Copy Cop Fights Back, Takes the Digital Plunge" in *Boston Business Journal* **(Vol. 23, No. 30, August 29, 2003, pp. 4)**
Pub: American City Business Journals
Ed: Jill Lerner. **Description:** Efforts by Boston, Massachusetts-based Copy Cop to recapture lost market share is examined. Topics include making capital investments in the company, developing new markets, and taking on competition.

44500 ■ "Corporate Collateral" in *Entrepreneur* **(Vol. 28, No. 7, July 2000, pp. 38)**
Pub: Entrepreneur Media Inc.
Ed: Cynthia E. Griffin. **Description:** Where to get money to grow your company, including big companies as resources.

44501 ■ "Credit crunch unlikely for most small businesses" in *Atlanta Business Chronicle* **(Vol. 23, No. 51, May 25, 2001, pp. 8A)**
Pub: American City Business Journals Inc.
Ed: Kent Hoover. **Description:** According to a survey by the National Federation of Independent Business and the Federal Reserve Board, small businesses should not have problems obtaining financing despite the tightening of standards by banks. Only 5 percent of small businesses that responded to the survey reported that obtaining loans was more difficult. Only 3 percent of NFIB members reported credit as their top problem.

44502 ■ "Cutting the Corporate Purse Strings" in *Ingram's* **(Vol. 27, No. 7, July 2001, pp. 20)**
Pub: Show Me Publishing, Inc.
Description: Techniques and management theory for women small business owners is outlined. Topics include clarifying objectives, refining business ideas, research ideas, budgeting, concept testing, developing a business plan, and securing financing.

44503 ■ "DCM Nears Final Close" in *Venture Capital Journal* **(Vol. 40, No. 10, October 2000, pp. 22)**
Pub: Venture Economics
Description: Doll Capital plans to invest 20-25 percent of its new fund internationally, with focus in Asia.

44504 ■ "Deal of the Day" in *Daily Business Review* **(Vol. 77, No. 146, January 7, 2003, pp. A4)**
Pub: American Lawyer Media LP
Ed: Charles Kimball. **Description:** Union Planters Bank loaned an additional $14.24 million to Pelican Beach Hotel Ltd., for resort development.

44505 ■ "Despite Smaller Loans, SBA Breaks Records" in *Inc.* **(November 1, 2004)**
Pub: Inc. Magazine
Ed: Darren Dahl. **Description:** The U. S. Small Business Administration backed a record number of loans in 2004, providing $15 billion in loans to businesses. These loans have helped small and family-owned small business to create 1.5 million jobs.

44506 ■ "'Devil in the Details' of Chase/J.P. Morgan Merger" in *Venture Capital Journal* **(Vol. 40, No. 10, October 2000, pp. 26)**
Pub: Venture Economics
Description: An overview of the proposed merger between J.P. Morgan Capital Corporation and Chase Capital Partners, is presented.

44507 ■ "Dotcom Damage" in *Entrepreneur* (Vol. 30, No. 1, January 200)
Pub: Entrepreneur Media Inc.
Ed: Aliza Pilar Sherman. **Description:** Gender issues following the dotcom crash are discussed. Despite what financiers may say, it seems women are still considered an investment risk.

44508 ■ "E-Cognita founders to lead group at Miller, Canfield" in *Crain's Detroit Business* (Vol. 19, No. 15, April 14, 2003, pp. 25)
Pub: Crain Communications Inc., Detroit
Ed: Jennette Smith. **Description:** Founders of the technology company E-Cognita, will be working with the newly formed capital-markets lending group at the Detroit law firm Miller, Canfield, Paddock and Stone PLC. E-Cognita Technologies Inc. developed software called StreamLoaner and Lexicon to manage transactions and automate documents and is used by lenders, lawyers, and other parties involved in loan closings.

44509 ■ "E-Cognita plots Web software for commercial real estate loans" in *Crain's Detroit Business* (Vol. 16, No. 46, Nov. 13, 2000, pp. 32)
Pub: Crain Communications, Inc.
Ed: Jennette Smith. **Description:** The Birmingham, Michigan-based E-Cognita Technologies Inc. has developed software and services to automate commercial real estate lending.

44510 ■ "E-Loan Exec Chides Lenders" in *American Banker* (Vol. 170, February 1, 2005, No. 270, pp. 9)
Pub: Thomson Financial Media Inc.
Ed: Isabelle Lindenmayer. **Description:** Mortgage lenders have been slow to develop end-to-end systems that reduce costs. The importance of implementing common technology standards is stressed for the industry.

44511 ■ "Earning Your Wings" in *Inc.* (January 1, 2005)
Pub: Inc. Magazine
Ed: Darren Dahl. **Description:** It's becoming more difficult to obtain seed money from angel investors, who pick up the slack from venture capital funds.

44512 ■ "Entrepreneur Column" in *Entrepreneur.com* (September 22, 2005)
Pub: Entrepreneur Media Inc.
Ed: James Casparie. **Description:** Strategies for raising money to startup or grow a business are shared with the founder and CEO of The Venture Alliance.

44513 ■ "Entrepreneurial Event at Automation Alley Jan. 12" in *Crain's Detroit Business* (Vol. 22, January 2, 2006, No. 1, pp. 17)
Pub: Crain Communications Inc. - Detroit
Ed: Joanne Scharich. **Description:** Three emerging technology companies, IMX, Check the Crib, and Secure Crossing, are scheduled to present business plans during the fourth Entrepreneurial Initiative of Southeast Michigan. Venture capitalists, bankers, and angel investors will provide feedback after the presentations.

44514 ■ "Exchange may improve small-business lending" in *Atlanta Business Chronicle* (Vol. 23, No. 36, February 9, 2001, pp. 52A)
Pub: American City Business Journals Inc.
Ed: Jean Capriotti. **Description:** Equifax Inc. and 19 lenders have started a database to help evaluate small business loan applications. The database will help protect lenders from extending loans to businesses that may already be overextended on other loans, and will help small businesses by taking some of the guesswork out of the loan process, thus increasing the amount of money available in some cases. The service will be tested beginning in March, and will be available in June 2001.

44515 ■ "Exposed!" in *Red Herring* (Jan. 2003, pp. 42)
Pub: Herring Communications Inc.
Ed: Tom Stein. **Description:** Venture capital will no longer be the secret society of the past because public opinion demands it of the industry. Pension funds are the largest source of cash for venture capital firms. Statistical data included.

44516 ■ "Fattah's Plan for Small Business" in *Philadelphia Inquirer* (February 6, 2007)
Pub: Philadelphia Newspapers LLC
Ed: Michael Currie Schaffer. **Description:** Philadelphia Mayoral candidate, Chaka Fattah, plans to create an emergency loan fund for small business in the city, if elected. The micro-loans would be available for small and home-based businesses.

44517 ■ "Federal Reserve Raises Key Interest Rate by Quarter Point" in *Boston Globe* (February 3, 2005)
Pub: New York Times Company
Ed: Robert Gavin. **Description:** The Federal Reserve raised key interest rates which will lead to higher charges on credit cards, home equity lines of credit, and other short-term loans. Savings and money market accounts are not expected to see a rise in interest rates.

44518 ■ "Fees of Danger" in *Entrepreneur* (Vol. 33, February 2005, No. 2, pp. 50)
Pub: Entrepreneur Media Inc.
Ed: Crystal Detamore-Rodman. **Description:** Origination fees for loans from a bank can be very costly to a small business.

44519 ■ "Finally, Credit Where Credit is Due" in *Business Week* (No. 3687, June 26, 2000, pp. 250)
Pub: McGraw-Hill, Inc.
Description: More and more banks are taking note of the unique characteristics and needs of women business owners, and it is getting easier for them to obtain loans.

44520 ■ "Finance vets bank on bypassed businesses" in *Houston Business Journal* (Vol. 33, No. 48, April 11, 2003, pp. 1A)
Pub: Houston Business Journal
Ed: Jim Greer. **Description:** Briar Capital LP has been formed by Frank Goldberg and Steve Rosencranz, to provide financing to small businesses which have been bypassed by banks.

44521 ■ "Finance with Plastic?" in *My Business* (September/October 2001, pp. 41)
Pub: My Business Magazine
Ed: Shannon Scully. **Description:** Nearly one-half of all small business owners with ten or less employees used credit cards to finance their business in 1998. The pros and cons of such practice are presented.

44522 ■ *Financing Your Business: Get a Grip on Finding the Money*
Pub: Self-Counsel Press, Incorporated
Ed: Angie Mohr. **Released:** September 2004. **Price:** $14.95 (US), $19.95 (Canadian). **Description:** Recommendations to help raise capital for a new or expanding small company.

44523 ■ *Financing Your Small Business*
Pub: Barron's Educational Series, Incorporated
Ed: Robert Walter. **Released:** March 2004. **Price:** $18.95 (US), $27.50 (Canadian). **Description:** Tips for raising venture capital, dealing with bank officials, and initiating public offerings of stock shares for small business.

44524 ■ "First to the Starting Line" in *Black Enterprise* (Vol. 36, December 2005, No. 5, pp. 32)
Pub: Earl G. Graves Publishing Co. Inc.
Ed: Cliff Hocker. **Description:** According to a report by Florida International University, blacks are more inclined to start their own businesses than whites with the same educational backgrounds. However, blacks and Hispanics have more difficulties maintaining a new firm than their white counterparts.

44525 ■ "Five Angels With Angles" in *Inc.* (Volume 27, July 2005, No. 7, pp. 92-99)
Pub: Inc. Magazine
Ed: Jim Melloan. **Description:** Today's early stage angel investors are tougher and smarter than their predecessors. Tips to help work with angel investors are presented.

44526 ■ "FNC, HomeSafe Team Up" in *Mississippi Business Journal* (Vol. 29, January 2007, No. 2, pp. 19)
Pub: Venture Publications, Inc.
Description: Mississippi technology companies FNC Inc., and HomeSafe Inspection Inc. are teaming up to help provide lenders with easy access to advanced home inspection technologies.

44527 ■ "Focused Fundraising" in *Entrepreneur.com* (Vol. 34, February 2006, No. 2, pp. 49)
Pub: Entrepreneur Media Inc.
Ed: David Worrell. **Description:** Phil Libin discusses his experiences when seeking venture capital for his national security technology firm; Libin also secured million-dollar contracts with the Department of Defense.

44528 ■ "Follow the Banker" in *Black Enterprise* (Vol. 34, July 2004, No. 12, pp. 35)
Pub: Earl G. Graves Publishing Co. Inc.
Ed: Donald Jay Korn. **Description:** According to a mutual fund research company, the bank-loan fund category has shown positive returns annually for more than ten years. Bank funds are recommended for those wishing to own an investment that produces income, involves moderate risk, and is less susceptible to interest rate increases.

44529 ■ "Former Nortel VP Joins Enterprise" in *Venture Capital Journal* (Vol. 40, No. 10, October 2000, pp. 36)
Pub: Venture Economics
Description: Enterprise Partners Venture Capital recently hired Naser Partovi as a general partner. Partovi will focus on telecommunications, specifically the optical and wireless spaces.

44530 ■ "Franchise Financing" in *Black Enterprise* (Vol. 35, September 2004, No. 2, pp. 50)
Pub: Earl G. Graves Publishing Co. Inc.
Ed: Alan Hughes. **Description:** Many times franchisors offer financing for new franchisees, or help them find an independent firm that provides loans.

44531 ■ "Free rein" in *Entrepreneur* (Vol. 31, No. 5, May 2003, pp. 23)
Pub: Entrepreneur Media Inc.
Ed: Stephen Barlas. **Description:** President Bush's proposed Fiscal 2004 Budget, while tightening the SBA's 7(a) loan program, would provide more in the way of the 504 Certified Development Loan Program.

44532 ■ "Gabriel Venture Partners Fund II Targets $300M" in *Venture Capital Journal* (Vol. 40, No. 10, November 2000, pp. 18, 20)
Pub: Venture Economics
Description: Gabriel Venture Partners plans to back 30-35 communications networking, and information technology companies with it second fund with the target $300M.

44533 ■ *Georgia Financial Institutions Directory & Fact Book*
Pub: Accuity
Contact: B. Gordon Cunningham
Ed: B. Gordon Cunningham, Editor. **Released:** Annual. **Price:** $22 not sold to the public. **Covers:** Head offices and branches of every bank, thrift, and all credit unions over $5 million in the state of Georgia. **Entries Include:** Name, address, phone, fax, key bank officers by functional title, directors, date established, detailed financial data, association's membership, attorney or counsel, correspondent banks, out-of-town branches, holding company affiliation, ABA Transit Number and Routing Symbol, MICR number with check digit, credit cards issued, trust powers, type of charter. **Arrangement:** Geographical. **Indexes:** Alphabetical.

44534 ■ "Get that SBA Loan" in *My Business* (September/October 2001, pp. 40)
Pub: My Business Magazine
Ed: Juan Hovey. **Description:** The essential elements needed to procure a small business loan are profiled.

44535 ■ "Give 'Em Credit" in *Entrepreneur* (Vol. 31, No. 8, August 2003, pp. 55)
Pub: Entrepreneur Media, Inc.
Ed: Crystal Detamore-Rodman. **Description:** Credit unions are now offering loans to small businesses. Many entrepreneurs suggest that credit unions offer better rates, as well as better service than dealing with banks.

44536 ■ "Global financing options" in *BlackEnterprise* (Vol. 31, No. 8, March 2001, pp. 48)
Pub: Earl Graves Publishing Co.
Ed: Paula McCoy-Pinderhughes. **Description:** Small business services provided by the Export-Import Banks of the United States, are profiled. The Export-Import (Ex-Im) Bank of the U.S. is an independent government agency that offers a number of financing options to minority- and women-owned export companies, including credit insurance and working capital guarantees on commercial loans.

44537 ■ *Golden States Financial Directory*
Pub: Accuity
Contact: Marideth Johnson
Released: Semiannual, January and July. **Covers:** Holding companies, head offices and branches of all commercial banks, savings and loans, and credit unions with assets over $5 million in Alaska, Arizona, California, Colorado, Hawaii, Idaho, Montana, New Mexico, Oregon, Utah, Washington, and Wyoming. **Entries Include:** Name, address, phone, fax, key bank officers by functional title, directors, date established, detailed financial data, association's membership, correspondent banks, out-of-town branches, holding company affiliation, ABA Transit Number and Routing Symbol, MICR number with check digit, type of charter. **Arrangement:** Geographical. **Indexes:** Alphabetical.

44538 ■ "Good relationships cement requests for business loans" in *Crain's Detroit Business* (Vol. 16, No. 50, December 11, 2000, pp. E-1)
Pub: Crain Communications, Inc.
Ed: Jeffrey Kosseff. **Description:** A profile of Mt. Morris Construction, located in Ypsilanti, Michigan. Owner Darryl Morris tells how he was able to get business loans for his business.

44539 ■ "Guardian Angel" in *Entrepreneur* (Vol. 33, March 2005, No. 3, pp. 58)
Pub: Entrepreneur Media Inc.
Ed: David Worrell. **Description:** Profile of the ACE-Net, the Angel Capital Electronic Network, which helps entrepreneurs with angel capital. Since it began in 1995, ACE-Net has helped entrepreneurs raise over $100 million.

44540 ■ "A Hand Up: Urban, Minority Entrepreneurs are Hotter Than Ever-So Where is Their Funding?" in *Entrepreneur* (Vol. 31, Sept. 2003)
Pub: Entrepreneur Media, Inc.
Ed: Joshua Kurlantzick. **Description:** Venture capitalists and large financial institutions are investing in minority-owned companies, although smaller banks are cutting commitments to African-American owned firms.

44541 ■ "Handicapping the Hispanic Economy" in *Hispanic Business* (November 2002, pp. 18-20)
Pub: Hispanic Business
Description: The future trends in elections, labor, international trade, technology education and banking access to loans are discussed by experts.

44542 ■ "Healthy prospects" in *Black Enterprise* (Vol. 32, No. 9, April 2002, pp.)
Pub: Earl Graves Publishing Co.
Ed: Wendy Pelle-Beer. **Description:** Profile of Juanita Simmons, owner of an exercise studio, who worked through the StoreWorks program to purchase a new building for her studio. StoreWorks is a collaborative partnership between the Neighborhood Housing Services Community Development Corp., the City of New York's Department of Housing Preservation and Development, the Department of Housing and Urban Development, and participating private lenders; available only in New York City.

44543 ■ "Helping the Economy, One Snip at a Time" in *New York Times* (November 2, 2003, pp. 1)
Pub: The New York Times
Ed: Joseph P. Fried. **Description:** Profile of a hair salon owner who has grown her business by borrowing from people close to her, as well as loans from the Small Business Administration and the Women's Venture Fund, a nonprofit group.

44544 ■ "Hennessey VC company looks for small business" in *Crain's Detroit Business* (Vol. 18, No. 23, June 1)
Pub: Crain Communications Inc. - Detroit
Ed: Michael Strong. **Description:** Owners of small businesses in search of capital may be able to tap a new source: Hennessey Capital LLC, located in Troy, MI. The company provides management services for small businesses with annual revenue ranging from $500,000 to $5 million.

44545 ■ "He's Still Standing" in *Black Enterprise* (Vol. 34, No. 2, September 2003, pp. 43)
Pub: Earl Graves Publishing Co.
Ed: Nicole Lewis. **Description:** Profile of William Burton, owner of Professional Systems Inc., a firm that consults, implements, and customizes computer software and hardware for clients in the Chicago, Illinois area. Burton has been successful despite rejections for loans.

44546 ■ "Hidden treasure" in *Entrepreneur* (Vol. 30, No. 2, February 2002, pp. 56)
Pub: Entrepreneur Media Inc.
Ed: Sean P. Melvin. **Description:** In a tightened economy, entrepreneurs can look for capital in the nooks, crannies, equipment and real estate the business already owns.

44547 ■ "Hispanic Banking Initiatives" in *Hispanic Business* (October 2002, pp. 14)
Pub: Hispanic Business
Description: Harris Bank, in the Chicago, Illinois area, is piloting a new program to assist Hispanic customers who are seeking loans, but have no credit history.

44548 ■ "Hot or Not?" in *Inc.* (Volume 28, January 2006, No. 1, pp. 102-105)
Pub: Inc. Magazine
Description: The most and least valuable industries in today's marketplace are discussed. Investors are putting more capital into entrepreneurial firms, but it is important to understand the hottest sectors. Statistical data included.

44549 ■ *How to Raise Capital: Techniques and Strategies for Financing and Valuing Your Small Business*
Pub: McGraw-Hill Companies
Ed: Jeffrey A. Timmons, Stephen Spinelli, Andrew Zacharakis. **Released:** September 2004. **Price:** $16.95 (US), $24.95 (Canadian). **Description:** Small business financing process is examined. Tips for identifying the financial life cycle of new ventures, developing a framework for financial strategies, and understanding an investor's prospective.

44550 ■ *The Illinois Financial Institutions Directory & Fact Book*
Pub: Accuity
Contact: Marideth Frazee

E-mail: marideth.johnson@tfp.com
Released: Annual. **Price:** $56, individuals 1-5 copies, one-time order; $49, individuals 1-5 copies, standing order. **Covers:** Head offices and branches of every bank, thrift, and all credit unions over $5 million in the state of Illinois. **Entries Include:** Name, address, phone, fax, key bank officers by functional title, directors, date established, detailed financial data, association's membership, attorney or counsel, correspondent banks, out-of-town branches, holding company affiliation, ABA Transit Number and Routing Symbol, MICR number with check digit, credit cards issued, trust powers, type of charter. **Arrangement:** Geographical. **Indexes:** Alphabetical.

44551 ■ "In the Balance: Learn the Factors Banks Really Weight When Setting Loan Terms" in *Entrepreneur* (Vol. 31, No. 7, July 2003, pp. 30)
Pub: Entrepreneur Media, Inc.
Ed: David Newton. **Description:** The size of a small company is not the most important issue banks look at when setting loan terms. When a small firm is seeking a bank loan, it should focus on the development and maintenance of good banking relationships, working with more than one bank.

44552 ■ "In Brief: SBA Assesses Role Of Scores in Lending" in *American Banker* (Vol. 171, November 17, 2006, No. 222, pp. 8)
Pub: SourceMedia, Inc.
Ed: Alan Kline. **Description:** Small Business Administration's Office of Advocacy reported 47 percent of banks responding to a survey say they use credit scoring to aid in small business lending decisions. Statistical data included.

44553 ■ "InterWest Fund VIII Nears $750M Mark" in *Venture Capital Journal* (Vol. 40, No. 10, October 2000, pp. 16)
Pub: Venture Economics
Description: InterWest Partners is aiming for a post-Labor Day final close on $750 million for the firm's latest vehicle, InterWest Partners VIII. The fund will back companies in the telecommunications/communications infrastructure space, medical technology and the Internet economy.

44554 ■ "Invoice-buying deals thrive on one thing: The cash factor" in *Crain's Detroit Business* (Vol. 17, No. 44, October 22, 2001, pp. 22)
Pub: Crain Communications, Inc.
Ed: Katie Merx. **Description:** Often called last-resort financing, factoring will become increasingly popular as more traditional forms of financing become difficult obtain. Factoring is the practice of selling invoices in order to get money quickly. A list of firms with factoring programs is listed.

44555 ■ "IPO Review" in *Red Herring* (No. 99, June 15 & July 1, 2001, pp. 61)
Pub: Herring Communications
Ed: Debbie Gravitz. **Description:** A look at last year's top Initial Public Offerings (IPOs), venture capital firms, and banks, before and after the fall of the economy.

44556 ■ "It's Not Enough" in *Entrepreneur* (Vol. 28, No. 8, August 2000, pp. 30)
Pub: Entrepreneur Media Inc.
Ed: Doug Hood and Marilea S. Hood. **Description:** How small businesses can obtain additional funding from banks is answered.

44557 ■ "It's a Stretch" in *Entrepreneur* (Vol. 30, No. 1, January 2002, pp. 48)
Pub: Entrepreneur Media Inc.
Ed: Mark Henricks. **Description:** The difficulty for small businesses to bridge the gap between a good product and enough capacity to fulfill the needs of big customers who can help grow a business. Expansion loans are difficult to procure for small businesses, especially in new technologies areas.

44558 ■ "Junkyard Blues" in *Forbes* **(October 30, 2000, pp. 282)**
Pub: Forbes Magazine
Ed: Michael Freedman. Description: The difficulties small companies face trying to obtain financing are examined.

44559 ■ "Just a Mirage? Proposed Legislation May Expand SBIC Financing-Someday" in *Entrepreneur* **(Vol. 31, No. 8, August 2003, pp. 24)**
Pub: Entrepreneur Media, Inc.
Ed: Stephen Barlas. Description: Profile of the Small Business Investment Company (SBIC) loan enhancement bill proposed by Senator Olympia Snowe (R-Maine) is presented. The bill would increase the stream of capital into Debenture SBICs. Money from these loans could be used by small companies to finance inventories, accounts receivable and more, the only exception would be real estate.

44560 ■ "Keep it coming" in *Entrepreneur* **(Vol. 30, No. 3, March)**
Pub: Entrepreneur Media Inc.
Ed: Michelle Prather. Description: The SBA has received a special grant of funds to meet the additional needs of the disaster loan program.

44561 ■ "Keep It Simple" in *Forbes* **(Vol. 171, No. 2, January 20, 2003, pp. 108)**
Pub: Forbes Magazine
Ed: John W. Rogers, Jr. Description: It is best to present a straightforward business plan in order to procure investments. Information about companies with clear missions, and straightforward business models is presented.

44562 ■ *Kentucky Financial Institutions Directory*
Pub: Accuity
Released: Annual. Covers: Head offices and branches of every bank, savings and loan, and all credit unions over $5 million in the state of Kentucky. Entries Include: Name, address, phone, fax, key bank officers by functional title, directors, date established, detailed financial data, association's membership, attorney or counsel, correspondent banks, out-of-town branches, holding company affiliation, ABA Transit Number and Routing Symbol, MICR number with check digit, credit cards issued, trust powers, type of charter. Arrangement: Geographical. Indexes: Alphabetical.

44563 ■ "KeyCorp Named Top SBA Lender" in *Hispanic Business* **(January/February 2003, pp. 14)**
Pub: Hispanic Business
Description: KeyCorp was named top minority business lender by the Cleveland District Office of the U.S. Small Business Administration for fiscal year ending September 30, 2002.

44564 ■ "Kleiner Perkins Adds Lane As New GP" in *Venture Capital Journal* **(Vol. 40, No. 10, October 2000, pp. 34)**
Pub: Venture Economics
Description: Raymond Lane, former chief operating officer at Oracle Corporation, has joined Kleiner, Perkins, Caufield & Byers. Lane will invest in all sectors, especially business-to-business, focusing on supply chain management.

44565 ■ "Lawmakers Tackle Loan Lender Rates" in *Atlanta Journal-Constitution* **(March 4, 2005)**
Pub: Knight-Ridder/Tribune Business News
Ed: Carrie Teegardin. Description: Georgia lawmakers are considering a bill that would cap the annual interest charged allowed for car title loans. Under current law annual percentage rates can be as high as 300 percent.

44566 ■ "Leading Lenders Shift as 2006 Activity Slows" in *Crain's New York Business* **(Vol. 22, December 11, 2006, No. 50, pp. 28)**
Pub: Crain Communications, Inc.
Description: HSBC, leader of last year's SBA loans, recorded steep declines in both the value and number of its SBA loans. Bank of America took first place in the number of SBA loans for 2006, while J.P. Morgan Chase captured second place.

44567 ■ "Lenders rebuke SBA plan to address 7(a) shortfall" in *Business First Columbus* **(Vol. 18, No. 18, March 1, 2002, pp. A14)**
Pub: Business First Columbus, Inc.
Ed: Kent Hoover. Description: Small Business Administration lenders dispute the loan program cuts. Statistical data included.

44568 ■ "Lenders wary of plan to make up SBA program shortfall" in *Wall Street Journal* **(March 19, 2002, pp. B2)**
Pub: Wall Street Journal
Ed: Jeff Bailey. Description: The requirements of the SBA's new loan program are complicating the use of funding authority from another loan category. Statistical data included.

44569 ■ "Lessons From the Past: Entrepreneur Takes the Old World Approach to Business" in *Black Enterprise* **(Vol. 34, No. 3, October 2003)**
Pub: Earl Graves Publishing Co.
Ed: Marcia A. Wade. Description: Profile of George Banks, founder of Sentry Security International Inc. Banks used loans from friends and his own savings to start his security company in 1999. The firm generated $328,000 in revenue in 2002.

44570 ■ "A Little Bit Goes a Long Way" in *My Business* **(September/October 2001, pp. 46)**
Pub: My Business Magazine
Ed: Shannon Scully. Description: Profile of microloan programs, which provide funding to small companies that don't qualify for conventional bank loans. The article includes sources to learn more about microloans, and lists Web sites of lenders.

44571 ■ "Loan guarantees: costs of default and benefits to small firms" in *Journal of Business Venturing* **(Vol. 16, No. 6, Nov. 2001, pp. 595)**
Pub: Elsevier Science, Inc.
Ed: Allan L. Riding, George Haines, Jr. Description: Research examining types of loan guarantees for the development of small firms is presented. Particular attention is given to international variations in default rates and cost benefits, with focus on the Canadian policy of loan guarantees.

44572 ■ "Loan Stars" in *Hispanic Business* **(March 2004, pp. 38, 40)**
Pub: Hispanic Business
Ed: Johanna Knapschaefer. Description: From micro-loans to Small Business Administration (SBA) programs, banks are slowly waking up to the possibilities of the Hispanic market.

44573 ■ "A Loan Time" in *Entrepreneur* **(Vol. 32, November 2004, No. 11, pp. 69)**
Pub: Entrepreneur Media Inc.
Ed: C.J. Prince. Description: Compared to 2003, the number of banks lending to small business is up. Wells Fargo has reported a 17 percent growth in lending so far this year and the Small Business Administration has already backed more than 9,000 loans than it did in 2003.

44574 ■ "Loans, grants, and more" in *BlackEnterprise* **(Vol. 32, No. 2, September 2001, pp. 46)**
Pub: Earl Graves Publishing Co.
Ed: Paul McCoy-Pinderhughes. Description: A list of government-sponsored programs, small business loans, and grants for small business are highlighted, including the Commerce Business Daily lists of government-awarded contracts; the Federal Procurement Data System; the U.S. Department of Housing and Urban Development; the 7(a) loan program; and the Small Business Innovation Research program.

44575 ■ "Loans can be more than just the numbers" in *Atlanta Business Chronicle* **(Vol. 23, No. 52, June 1, 2001, pp. 52A)**
Pub: American City Business Journals Inc.
Ed: Linda Kercher. Description: Nationwide, the top small business lenders use Fair Issac's credit-scoring models, but in Atlanta, Georgia, lenders do not use the automated process, opting for a one-on-one relationship between the banker and borrower.

44576 ■ "Loanworthy Women" in *Business Week* **(June 12, 2000, pp. F8)**
Pub: McGraw-Hill, Inc.
Description: The conditions are favorable for loans for small women-owned companies.

44577 ■ "Lockport, N.Y.-Based First Niagara Financial to Open More Branches, Buy Bank" in *The Buffalo News* **(April 11, 2203)**
Pub: Knight-Ridder/Tribune Business News
Ed: Chet Bridger. Description: First Niagara Financial Groups intends to open new branches in Buffalo, Rochester and Syracuse, New York markets and is looking for a bank acquisition in Pennsylvania.

44578 ■ "Long Island Development Corp. Steps Up Loan Programs in 2003" in *Long Island Business News* **(March 5, 2004)**
Pub: Dolan Media Newswires
Ed: Nick Anastasi. Description: The Long Island Development Company has provided 86 loans in the amount of $36.8 million from October 1, 2002 to September 30, 2003. The firm also assisted companies obtain $302 million in government and big business contracts through its Procurement Technical Assistance Program. Statistical data included.

44579 ■ "Love of Country" in *Entrepreneur* **(Vol. 33, March 2005, No. 3, pp. 62)**
Pub: Entrepreneur Media Inc.
Ed: Jennifer Pellet. Description: The Rural Business Investment Program (RBIP), a joint effort of the Department of Agriculture and the Small Business Administration are working to make $60 million available to rural entrepreneurs for equity investing and $3 million in grant-funded technical assistance for businesses.

44580 ■ "LPs Give Redpoint $1.25B Green Light" in *Venture Capital Journal* **(Vol. 40, No. 10, October 2000, pp. 16, 17)**
Pub: Venture Economics
Description: Redpoint Ventures announced in August that it held a $1.25 billion final close on its second investment vehicle. The fund will focus on the type of Internet infrastructure plays that make up approximately 60 percent of Redpoint's current investments.

44581 ■ "Maine Program Helps Businesses Apply for Federal Grants" in *Portland Press Herald* **(September 23, 2005)**
Pub: Blethen Maine Newspapers, Inc.
Ed: Matt Wickenheiser. Description: Maine's Technology Institute program helps small businesses with the grant application process.

44582 ■ "Maine Thing: Camden Tries New Approach" in *American Banker* **(Vol. 172, January 18, 2007, No. 12, pp. 1)**
Pub: SourceMedia, Inc.
Ed: Bonnie McGeer. Description: Camden National Bank, located in Maine, is offering small business financial centers in order to expand business. The centers target small and medium-sized firms, relying on referrals from accountants and attorneys. Statistical data included.

44583 ■ "Make Over Magic" in *Entrepreneur* **(Vol. 31, No. 7, July 2003, pp. 49)**
Pub: Entrepreneur Media, Inc.
Ed: C.J. Prince. Description: The U.S. Small Business Administration's 504 Certified Development Company Program offers below-market, fixed-rate loans to small businesses for real estate and heavy equipment purchases, yet few small firms use the program.

44584 ■ **"Make Them Pay!"** in *Inc.* (August 1, 2003)
Pub: Gruner & Jahr USA Publishing
Description: Dealing with a deadbeat client, the good and bad for small firms operating in Mexico, and a twist on the personal asset loan guarantee are among the issues discussed.

44585 ■ **"The Master Negotiator: How To Use the Power of Persuasion to Raise Dollars"** in *Black Enterprise* (Vol. 34, No. 2, September 2003)
Pub: Earl Graves Publishing Co.
Ed: Sonya Kimble-Ellis. **Description:** Profile of 17-year-old Amelia Landreth, who negotiated funds to pay for varsity and junior high basketball teams. Landreths power of persuasion can help all entrepreneurs to raise money.

44586 ■ **"Microlending - Arizona Style"** in *Hispanic Business* (March 2002, pp. 16)
Pub: Hispanic Business
Ed: Jonathan J. Higuera. **Description:** Profile of Frank Ballesteros, who borrows from the U.S. Small Business Administration and other financial institutions and lends to the working poor.

44587 ■ **"Microloans Face Budgetary Ax"** in *Black Enterprise* (Vol. 35, November 2004, No. 4, pp. 60)
Pub: Earl G. Graves Publishing Co. Inc.
Ed: Tamara E. Holmes. **Description:** Profile of the Small Business Association's Microloan Program, designed to loan startup businesses loans under $35,000.

44588 ■ *Million-Dollar Guide to Business & Real Estate Loan Sources*
Pub: International Wealth Success, Inc.
Ed: Tyler G. Hicks. **Released:** 10th ed. 1999. **Price:** $25.00.

44589 ■ **"Milwaukee Harley Shifts Gears"** in *Business Journal-Milwaukee* (Vol. 20, No. 46, August 1, 2003, pp. A3)
Pub: American City Business Journals, Inc.
Ed: Rich Rovito. **Description:** Milwaukee, Wisconsin's Harley-Davidson and Buell, operated by owner Bob Michel, is housed in a 36,000-square foot motorcycle dealership. Michel has acquired the business from his partner Paul Kegel, for $4 million with a financing package from Associated Bank.

44590 ■ *Minnesota Bank Directory*
Pub: Accuity
Released: Annual. **Covers:** Head offices and branches of every bank in the state of Minnesota. **Entries Include:** Name, address, phone, fax, key bank officers by functional title, directors, date established, detailed financial data, association's membership, attorney or counsel, correspondent banks, out-of-town branches, holding company affiliation, ABA Transit Number and Routing Symbol, MICR number with check digit, credit cards issued, trust powers, type of charter. **Arrangement:** Geographical. **Indexes:** Alphabetical.

44591 ■ **"Model behavior"** in *Entrepreneur* (Vol. 30, No. 3, March 2002, pp. 68)
Pub: Entrepreneur Media Inc.
Ed: David Newton. **Description:** Raising money for a growing company has taken a turn back to basics, opportunity and market share are no longer enough to secure capital; the business model, once again, plays a major role.

44592 ■ *The Money Connection: Where & How to Apply for Business Loans & Venture Capital*
Pub: PSI Research
Ed: Lawrence Flanagan. **Released:** 2nd ed. 1997. **Price:** $24.95.

44593 ■ **"Money Matters"** in *Small Business Opportunities* (Vol. 13, No. 5, September 2001, pp. 10)
Pub: Harris Publications, Inc.
Ed: Carla Vincent. **Description:** Ways for small businesses to generate venture capital are explored, including a list of government agencies that provide small business funding.

44594 ■ **"Money Rules"** in *Hispanic Business* (September 2004, pp. 34-36, 38, 40, 42)
Pub: Hispanic Business
Ed: Joel Russell. **Description:** Profile of Roel Campos, the first Hispanic to serve on the Securities and Exchange Commission. Campos wants major investment banks to provide more business loans to minority-owned small businesses in the U.S.

44595 ■ **"More than friends"** in *Entrepreneur* (Vol. 30, No. 3, March 2002, pp. 66)
Pub: Entrepreneur Media Inc.
Ed: Jennifer Pellet. **Description:** Profile of Circle Lending, an online service that enables would-be borrowers to create and administer business loans with family and friends.

44596 ■ **"More Money: Bankers focus on follow-ons"** in *Red Herring* (No. 105, October 1, 2001, pp. 94)
Pub: Herring Communications
Ed: Eric Moskowitz. **Description:** A rise in follow-on offerings, also known as secondary offerings, can be attributed to the downturn in the IPO market. The first seven months of 2001 saw $50 billion of completed follow-ons in the United States, and is predicted to reach $104 billion this year.

44597 ■ **"Mortgage Limit Up $417,000"** in *Sacramento Bee* (November 30, 2005)
Pub: The Sacramento Bee
Ed: Andrew Lepage. **Description:** Fannie Mae and Freddie Mac are increasing the dollar terms, loan limits, and promising lower financing costs for U.S. home buyers. The limit on single-family home loans rose by $57,350 to $417,000.

44598 ■ **"Mr. Cashman, You're On"** in *Inc.* (Volume 27, July 2005, No. 7, pp. 100-102, 104)
Pub: Inc. Magazine
Ed: Jim Melloan. **Description:** Entrpreneur, Chris Cashman, is looking for $500,000 in venture capital for his Protez Pharmaceuticals firm. Protez is currently working on four different drug technologies.

44599 ■ **"NEA Fund 10 $2B Hard Cap"** in *Venture Capital Journal* (Vol. 40, No. 10, October 2000, pp. 18, 20, 22)
Pub: Venture Economics
Description: NEA will continue targeting start-up companies in the information technology, communications, software, B-to-B e-commerce and semiconductor sectors, as well as medical, biotech and life sciences companies.

44600 ■ **"Networking Provides Partnership's Funding"** in *Wall Street Journal* (October 14, 2003, pp. B4)
Pub: Dow Jones & Co. Inc.
Ed: Paulette Thomas. **Description:** Case study of William G. Nelson showing ways to move from a career in finance to an entrepreneurial life on a shoestring budget through networking.

44601 ■ *New Mexico Bank Directory*
Pub: Accuity
Contact: B. Gordon Cunningham
Ed: B. Gordon Cunningham, Editor. **Released:** Annual. **Price:** $22 not sold to the public. **Covers:** Head offices and branches of every bank in the state of New Mexico. **Entries Include:** Name, address, phone, fax, key bank officers by functional title, directors, date established, detailed financial data, association's membership, attorney or counsel, correspondent banks, out-of-town branches, holding company affiliation, ABA Transit Number and Routing Symbol, MICR number with check digit, credit cards issued, trust powers, type of charter. **Arrangement:** Geographical. **Indexes:** Alphabetical.

44602 ■ **"A new venue for seeking capital"** in *BlackEnterprise* (Vol. 32, No. 3, October 2001, pp. 56)
Pub: Earl Graves Publishing Co.
Ed: Paula McCoy-Pinderhughes. **Description:** The first-ever three-day conference aimed at helping Afri-can American and other minority technology-based businesses was held in Chantilly, Fairfax County, Virginia, from July 11-13, 2001. The Emerging Business Forum (EBF) will host its second conference next fall.

44603 ■ **"New Way to 7(a)"** in *Entrepreneur* (Vol. 33, February 2005, No. 2, pp. 49)
Pub: Entrepreneur Media Inc.
Ed: C.J. Prince. **Description:** Information regarding the bill that will eliminate the $79 million federal subsidy for the Small Business Administration's loan guarantee program is presented. The bill is supposed to make the program self-sustaining.

44604 ■ **"New to You?"** in *Entrepreneur* (Vol. 28, No. 9, September 2000, pp. 50)
Pub: Entrepreneur Media Inc.
Ed: Doug Hood and Marilea S. Hood. **Description:** The Small Business Administration 504 Certified Development Companies program, a new government-guaranteed loan program with a fixed rate-separate from the SBA, is outlined in question/answer format.

44605 ■ **"NextEnergy gets $2M from feds"** in *Crain's Detroit Business* (Vol. 19, No. 10, March 10, 2003, pp. 29)
Pub: Crain Communications Inc., Detroit
Ed: Laura Bailey. **Description:** The state of Michigan's alternative-fuel research center, NextEnergy, received $2 million from an appropriations bill signed by President George W. Bush.

44606 ■ **"No Husband, No Loan"** in *Entrepreneur* (Vol. 28, No. 11, November 2000, pp. 40)
Pub: Entrepreneur Media Inc.
Ed: Doug Hood. **Description:** The successful owner of a twenty year old woman-owned business was told her husband would have to guarantee a business loan. Spousal agreements and business loans are discussed.

44607 ■ **"Nonprofit groups provide banking for bankless"** in *Wall Street Journal* (October 3, 2000, pp. B1)
Pub: Dow Jones & Co., Inc.
Ed: Jeffrey A. Tannenbaum. **Description:** An overview of community development financial institutions. Statistical data is included.

44608 ■ *The North Dakota Financial Institutions Directory*
Pub: Accuity
Contact: B. Gordon Cunningham
Ed: B. Gordon Cunningham, Editor. **Released:** Annual. **Price:** $30 not sold to the public. **Covers:** Head offices and branches of every bank, savings and loan, and all credit unions over $5 million in the state of North Dakota. **Entries Include:** Name, address, phone, fax, key bank officers by functional title, directors, date established, detailed financial data, association's membership, attorney or counsel, correspondent banks, out-of-town branches, holding company affiliation, ABA Transit Number and Routing Symbol, MICR number with check digit, credit cards issued, trust powers, type of charter. **Arrangement:** Geographical. **Indexes:** Alphabetical.

44609 ■ **"Not So Fast! Raising Money: Seeking an Investor?"** in *Entrepreneur* (Vol. 31, No. 9, September 2003, pp. 55)
Pub: Entrepreneur Media, Inc.
Ed: David Worrell. **Description:** Profile of Bob Shallenberger, owner of Highland Homes of Saint Louis, who never needed an investor until 2003. Shallenberger stresses the need to take time when finding an investor.

44610 ■ **"Of Growing Interest"** in *Ingram's* (Vol. 28, No. 1, January 2002, pp. 35)
Pub: Show Me Publishing, Inc.
Ed: Judy Z. Ellett. **Description:** The state of commercial loans and interest rates in the U.S. is discussed.

44611 ■ *The Ohio Financial Institutions Directory & Fact Book*
Pub: Accuity
Contact: Marideth Johnson

Ed: Sarah Frazee, Editor. **Released:** Annual. **Price:** $54 per issue; $45 annual subscription. **Covers:** Head offices and branches of every bank, thrift, and all credit unions over $5 million in the state of Ohio. **Entries Include:** Name, address, phone, fax, key bank officers by functional title, directors, date established, detailed financial data, association's membership, attorney or counsel, correspondent banks, out-of-town branches, holding company affiliation, ABA Transit Number and Routing Symbol, MICR number with check digit, credit cards issued, trust powers, type of charter. **Arrangement:** Geographical. **Indexes:** Alphabetical.

44612 ■ "On Good Terms" in *Entrepreneur. com* **(Vol. 34, February 2006, No. 2, pp. 51)**
Pub: Entrepreneur Media Inc.
Ed: Crystal Detamore-Rodman. **Description:** Interest rates have been rising steadily since 2004. Now might be the time for small business owners to consider refinancing loans.

44613 ■ "OneLiberty Ventures Wraps On $200M" in *Venture Capital Journal* **(Vol. 40, No. 10, October 2000, pp. 26)**
Pub: Venture Economics
Description: OneLiberty Ventures held a $200 million final close in June on OneLiberty Ventures 2000 LP, and will back early-stage information technology and medical technology companies.

44614 ■ "Opening the Door to VC" in *Hispanic Business* **(Vol. 23, No. 7/8, July/ August 2001, pp. 66)**
Pub: Hispanic Business
Ed: Christopher D. Lancette. **Description:** I-DealFlow, a national coalition of business and organizations, will sponsor a venture capital fair November 2, 2001 in Atlanta, Georgia. The coalition includes such members as AOL Time Warner, the Wall Street Project, the U.S Hispanic Chamber of Commerce (USHCC), and the Telecommunications Development Fund.

44615 ■ "Overseas Lender of First Resort" in *Hispanic Business* **(March 2003, pp. 40-41)**
Pub: Hispanic Business
Ed: Derek Reveron. **Description:** Profile of the Export-Import Bank and its services to exporters is presented, including contact information.

44616 ■ "Owners find credit a bit harder to get" in *Wall Street Journal* **(April 30, 2002, pp. B6)**
Pub: Wall Street Journal
Description: Small business owners are having more difficulty procuring loans. Statistical data included.

44617 ■ "Panel Chief Set To Reopen SBA Budget Debate" in *American Banker* **(Vol. 171, November 30, 2006, No. 229, pp. 1)**
Pub: SourceMedia, Inc.
Ed: Ben Jackson. **Description:** New York Democrat, Nydia Velazquez, is committed to changing the Small Business Administration's loan programs. Her plan would lower user fees for borrowers as well as lenders.

44618 ■ "Partners in Style" in *Hispanic Business* **(May 2005, pp. 64, 66)**
Pub: Hispanic Business
Ed: Jaime Adame. **Description:** Luis Delgado, co-founder and CEO of Samy Salon Collections, the top-selling hair care brand on the Home Shopping Network, discusses his plan to fund his company's expansion.

44619 ■ "Paying Your Dues" in *Entrepreneur* **(Vol. 32)**
Pub: Entrepreneur Media Inc.
Ed: David Worrell. **Description:** Stephen Forte, founder and president of Ascendent, a telecommunication technology company that connects wireless phones to traditional phone systems. Forte addresses the issue of due-diligence, an investor's process of fact-finding.

44620 ■ *The Pennsylvania Financial Institutions Directory & Fact Book*
Pub: Accuity
Contact: Marideth Johnson
Ed: Sarah Frazee, Editor. **Released:** Annual. **Price:** $54 per issue; $45 annual subscription. **Covers:** Head offices and branches of every bank, thrift, and all credit unions over $5 million in the state of Pennsylvania. **Entries Include:** Name, address, phone, fax, key bank officers by functional title, directors, date established, detailed financial data, association's membership, attorney or counsel, correspondent banks, out-of-town branches, holding company affiliation, ABA Transit Number and Routing Symbol, MICR number with check digit, credit cards issued, trust powers, type of charter. **Arrangement:** Geographical. **Indexes:** Alphabetical.

44621 ■ "Pond Venture Partners Closes $78M Fund II" in *Venture Capital Journal* **(Vol. 40, No. 10, October 2000, pp. 24, 26)**
Pub: Venture Economics
Description: Pond Venture Partners Ltd. will focus its investments into early-stage communications companies, including firms in Western Europe.

44622 ■ "Primus Fund V Eyes $250M Close" in *Venture Capital Journal* **(Vol. 40, No. 10, October 2000, pp. 22, 24)**
Pub: Venture Economics
Description: The Primus Fund V will focus on four industry sectors: telecommunications, Internet/e-commerce, out-sourced business services, and health care.

44623 ■ "QA: Shopping for Capital" in *Black Enterprise* **(Vol. 35, January 2005, No. 6, pp. 44)**
Pub: Earl G. Graves Publishing Co. Inc.
Ed: James C. Johnson. **Description:** Finding capital for a small, black-owned media company might be attained from private equity firms. Equity financing allows a business to obtain funds without incurring debt or repaying a specific amount of money at a particular time.

44624 ■ "A Question of Character" in *Entrepreneur* **(Vol. 28, No. 8, August 2000, pp. 30)**
Pub: Entrepreneur Media Inc.
Ed: Doug Hood and Marilea S. Hood. **Description:** Character is a very important criterion when applying for a business loan.

44625 ■ "Quick Fix: Do SBA Express Loans Really Shortchange Entrepreneurs?" in *Entrepreneur* **(Vol. 32, No. 4, April 2004, pp. 27)**
Pub: Entrepreneur Media, Inc.
Ed: Julie Monahan. **Description:** Profile of the U.S. Small Business Administration's Express program that guaranteed loans to thousands of entrepreneurs. Retailers with gross sales of $6 million or less, wholesalers with 100 employees or less, and manufacturers with 500 employees or less, are eligible for Express Loans.

44626 ■ *Raising Capital*
Pub: Raising Capital
Ed: Andrew J. Sherman. **Price:** $34.95.

44627 ■ "R&D comes to services: Bank of America's pathbreaking experiments" in *Harvard Business Review* **(Vol. 81, No. 4, April 2003, pp. 70)**
Pub: Harvard Business School Press
Ed: Stefan Thomke. **Description:** A description of the process that Bank of America has used to create new service concepts for retail banking is presented. A group of the company's branches have become a laboratory where a research team conducts service experiments with actual customers. The program shows what a true Research and Development operation might look like in a service business.

44628 ■ "Ray of hope?" in *Entrepreneur* **(Vol. 31, No. 5, May 2003, pp. 45)**
Pub: Entrepreneur Media Inc.

Ed: C.J. Prince. **Description:** With $21.2 billion of venture capital invested in 2002, the year finished at the same level as 1998. A greater number of later-stage companies and those seeking expansion capital, rather than startups, received funding.

44629 ■ "Rebuilding Interest; Bank One Brings in New Credit Chief to Ease Lending Rules, Win Back Middle-Market Business" in *Crain's Detroit Business*
Pub: Crain Communications Inc., Detroit
Ed: Katie Merx. **Description:** Bank One's new chief credit officer, is charged with bringing middle-market business to the firm.

44630 ■ "Rebuilding Interest" in *Crain's Detroit Business* **(Vol. 19, No. 45, November 10, 2003, pp. 1)**
Pub: Crain Communications Inc., Detroit
Ed: Katie Merx. **Description:** Bank One's new chief credit officer, is charged with bringing middle-market business to the firm.

44631 ■ *Registry of Utah Financial Institutions*
Pub: Accuity
Contact: B. Gordon Cunningham
Ed: B. Gordon Cunningham, Editor. **Released:** Annual. **Price:** $15 not sold to the public. **Covers:** Head offices and branches of every bank, savings and loan, and all credit unions over $5 million in the state of Utah. **Entries Include:** Name, address, phone, fax, key bank officers by functional title, directors, date established, detailed financial data, association's membership, attorney or counsel, correspondent banks, out-of-town branches, holding company affiliation, ABA Transit Number and Routing Symbol, MICR number with check digit, credit cards issued, trust powers, type of charter. **Arrangement:** Geographical. **Indexes:** Alphabetical.

44632 ■ "Reliant's refinancing package could be a model for industry" in *Houston Business Journal* **(Vol. 33, No. 48, April 11, 2003, pp. 10A)**
Pub: Houston Business Journal
Ed: Monica Perin. **Description:** Reliant Resources Inc. received a $6.2 billion refinancing deal from Barclays Bank PLC, BankAmerica Corporation, and Deutsche Bank AG. The banks agreed to lower interest rates, offer a longer term, and payment deadline extensions.

44633 ■ "Repaying the Loan Isn't Enough" in *Business Week* **(No. 3779, April 22, 2002, pp. 16)**
Pub: McGraw-Hill Inc.
Description: Banks are pressuring small companies in need of short-term credit to also use other banking services such as checking, savings and investment accounts for loans less than one year.

44634 ■ "Resources: Web Sites, Organizations, Events and More To Grow Your Business" in *Entrepreneur* **(Vol. 32, September 2004, No. 9, pp. 8)**
Pub: Entrepreneur Media Inc.
Ed: Steve Cooper. **Description:** Resources to help small business are featured including the Small Business Administration's effort to help teen entrepreneurs launch a business; KnockNow an online community of entrepreneurs, executives, venture capitalists, angel investors, service sector companies, and government; the SBA's business Website offering information on small business development, financial assistance, taxes, laws and regulations, international trade, workplace issues, buying and selling and federal forms.

44635 ■ "Richmond Times-Dispatch, Va., Business Briefs Column" in *Knight-Ridder/ Tribune Business News* **(October 23, 2001, pp. ITEM01296031)**
Pub: Knight-Ridder/Tribune Business News
Description: The Richmond Economic Development Corporation in Virginia, has been awarded $450,000 by the U.S. Treasury Department to create a loan source for small businesses lacking access to traditional financing.

44636 ■ "Riding the Greenback" in *Business Week* **(No. 3678, April 24, 2000, pp. F10)**
Pub: McGraw-Hill, Inc.
Description: Small companies now comprise 97 percent of those selling overseas, according to the Small Business Administration. International finance for small business is covered.

44637 ■ "The Right Fit" in *Entrepreneur* **(Vol. 33, September 2005, No. 9, pp. 58)**
Pub: Entrepreneur Media Inc.
Ed: Description: Word-of-mouth through networking with angel investors, venture capitalists and larger private equity groups will help entrepreneurs to learn about these boutiques who partner with small companies.

44638 ■ "Running Dry" in *Entrepreneur* **(Vol. 33, August 2005, No. 8, pp. 20)**
Pub: Entrepreneur Media Inc.
Ed: Crystal Detamore-Rodman. **Description:** The U.S. government's Small Business Investment Company (SBIC) provides equity capital to entrepreneurs. Currently the SBIC Participating Securities Program provides as much as $2 for every $1 of capital raised by venture funds licensed by the SBA; this program is in jeopardy of being discontinued.

44639 ■ "The SBA All-Stars" in *Inc.* **(August 2005, pp. 22)**
Pub: Inc. Magazine
Ed: Mina Azodi. **Description:** Listing of the top ten Small Business Administration's field offices is presented, with San Diego, California making the number one spot, followed by Utah.

44640 ■ "SBA Bad Loans on the Rise" in *Hispanic Business* **(January/February 2003, pp. 12)**
Pub: Hispanic Business
Description: The number of bad loans the Small Business Administration has been required to cover have nearly doubled from 1995 to 2002.

44641 ■ "SBA Chief: Storm Relief Advances" in *American Banker* **(Vol. 172, February 2, 2007, No. 23, pp. 3)**
Pub: SourceMedia, Inc.
Ed: Derek Klobucher. **Description:** The Small Business Administration has disbursed more than $5 billion in disaster relief loans to individuals and small business owners affected by the 2005 Gulf Coast hurricanes. The SBA also reports an additional $2 billion in funding available.

44642 ■ "SBA Finds Another Billion for Loans" in *Inc.* **(August 1, 2003)**
Pub: Gruner & Jahr USA Publishing
Ed: Bobbie Gossage. **Description:** The U.S. Small Business Administration has created an additional $1.4 billion lending authority for its primary 7(a) loan program for fiscal 2003, increasing total lending authority to more than $11 billion.

44643 ■ "SBA Includes Area Banks in Community Investment" in *Bradenton Herald* **(November 5, 2006)**
Pub: Bradenton Herald
Ed: Tilde Herrera. **Description:** Small Business Administration loans have changed in the last decade allowing local banks to tap a market of businesses not able to receive conventional financing because they do not have the collateral or are too new.

44644 ■ "SBA urged to tighten oversight of lenders" in *Atlanta Business Chronicle* **(Vol. 25, January 10, 2003, No. 31, pp. 4B)**
Pub: American City Business Publications, Inc.
Ed: Kent Hoover. **Description:** A report from the General Accounting Office claims that the Small Business Administration needs tighter oversight with respect to private-sector lenders who make government-guaranteed loans. Existing reviews of private-sector lenders have been criticized for their cursory nature.

44645 ■ "SBA Loan Lenders Ranked by Value of 7(a) Loans" in *American Banker* **(Vol. 170, February 1, 2005, No. 270, pp. 6)**
Pub: Thomson Financial Media Inc.
Description: Listing of Small Business Administration's loan lenders, ranked by value of 7(a) loans.

44646 ■ *SBA Loans*
Pub: John Wiley & Sons Inc.
Contact: Patrick D. O'Hara, Author
Released: latest edition 4th; Published April, 2002.
Price: $27.95, individuals List price. **Publication Includes:** A directory of Small Business Association field offices and a directory of services offered by the SBA. Principal content of publication is Step-by-step information of locating and securing a small business loan, including developing a business plan, researching finance options, recent lending statistics, eligibility requirements and other details.

44647 ■ "SBA Preferred Lenders" in *Crain's Detroit Business* **(Vol. 19, No. 42, October 20, 2003, pp. 18)**
Pub: Crain Communications Inc., Detroit
Description: A listing of the U.S. Small Business Administration's preferred lenders is presented. These banks are SBA approved to review and process loans with contacts in Southeast Michigan.

44648 ■ "SBA limits program's loan amounts to $500,000" in *Crain's Detroit Business* **(Vol. 18, No. 40, October 7, 2002, pp. 43)**
Pub: Crain Communications Inc., Detroit
Ed: Laura Bailey. **Description:** The U.S. Small Business Administration has lowered the amount of loans falling under the 7(a) program from $2 million to $500,000. This move could cost the State of Michigan 4,663 jobs over a year's time.

44649 ■ "SBA Raises Size Standards for Small-Business Eligibility" in *Business First Columbus* **(Vol. 18, No. 25, February 8, 2002, pp. A17)**
Pub: Business First Columbus, Inc.
Ed: Ken Hoover. **Description:** Recent changes in the Small Business Administration's size standards for small business eligibility is explained.

44650 ■ "SBA's main loan program faces deep cut for fiscal 2003" in *Wall Street Journal* **(March 12, 2002, pp. B2)**
Pub: Wall Street Journal
Ed: Jeff Bailey. **Description:** Information is presented regarding the impending cuts in the SBA's main loan program for fiscal year 2003.

44651 ■ "Score Savvy: Business Credit Scores are on the Horizon" in *Entrepreneur* **(Vol. 31, Oct. 2003)**
Pub: Entrepreneur Media, Inc.
Ed: Joanne Cleaver. **Description:** Lenders will begin using credit scores, similar to those assigned to most consumers, by summer 2004, making the loan process difficult for businesses with complicated credit histories.

44652 ■ "Second Bank Set To Offer Small-Business Job Incentives" in *Boston Globe* **(February 13, 2005)**
Pub: New York Times Company
Ed: Sasha Talcott. **Description:** Sovereign Bancorp is developing a low-interest program that will help small businesses add jobs in Massachusetts.

44653 ■ "Seeing Green" in *Entrepreneur*
Pub: Entrepreneur Media Inc.
Ed: Tracy T. Lefteroff. **Description:** An overview of Entrepreneur's 4th Annual Venture Capital 100 is presented. The listing will help entrepreneurs find the best investor for their businesses.

44654 ■ "Senkbeil: increasing equity will mean stable markets" in *Atlanta Business Chronicle* **(Vol. 24, No. 9, August 3, 2001, pp. 9C)**
Pub: American City Business Journals Inc.
Description: Tom Senkbeil, president and CEO of Carter and Associates is a long-time prominent figure in the Atlanta, Georgia real estate industry. In this interview, Senkbeil discusses his personal professional history and the changes in financing he has observed in the past five years. The largest change, according to Senkbeil, is the rise in the equity versus debt.

44655 ■ "Small is Bountiful" in *Business Week* **(May 22, 2000, pp. 126)**
Pub: McGraw-Hill, Inc.
Description: Merrill Lynch is making inroads into the banking industry through its programs for small businesses.

44656 ■ "Small-Business e-Loan" in *Hispanic Business* **(March 2002, pp. 60)**
Pub: Hispanic Business
Ed: Roger Harris. **Description:** The Small Business Administration has launched a new Web-hosted system that aids in the origination and management of SBA-backed and other traditional small-business loans.

44657 ■ *Small Business Loan Program Kit*
Pub: International Wealth Success, Incorporated
Ed: Tyler G. Hicks. **Released:** 2006. **Price:** $100.00.
Description: Guide to the Small Business Loan Program that offers loans to small and minority-owned companies doing work for government agencies, large corporations, hospitals, universities, and similar organizations.

44658 ■ *Small Business Management*
Pub: John Wiley and Sons Inc.
Ed: Margaret Burlingame; Don Gulbrandsen; Richard M. Hodgetts; Donald F. Kuratko. **Released:** March 2007. **Price:** $44.95. **Description:** Tips for starting and running a successful small business are given, including advice on writing a business plan, financing, and the law.

44659 ■ "Small Business Protests Loan Program Shift" in *Long Island Business News* **(March 12, 2004)**
Pub: Dolan Media Newswires
Ed: Adina Genn. **Description:** The U.S. Small Business Administration did not request funding for the Centereach-based Community Development Corporation of Long Island for 2005. Advocates of microloans say the cut in funding would hurt small businesses and slow job creation.

44660 ■ "Small Firms Seeking Government Contracts Will Get More Help" in *Kiplinger Letter* **(Vol. 78, January 19, 2007, No. 2)**
Pub: Kiplinger
Description: Business Matchmaking program run by the Small Business Administration, along with new rules to do away with unfair competition for government contracts, will help small companies compete for government work. The Small Business Administration will also lower fees for new loans to small companies.

44661 ■ "Soaring Angels" in *Entrepreneur. com* **(Vol. 34, February 2006, No. 2, pp. 58)**
Pub: Entrepreneur Media Inc.
Description: Tax incentives for individuals investing in young companies is increasing angel activity. Statistical data included.

44662 ■ *Southwestern Financial Directory*
Pub: Accuity
Contact: Marideth Johnson
E-mail: marideth.johnson@tfp.com
Released: Semiannual, January and July. **Price:** $155, individuals. **Covers:** Holding companies, head offices and branches of every commerical bank, Savings & Loan, and credit union over $5 million in the states of Arkansas, Louisiana, New Mexico, Oklahoma, and Texas. **Entries Include:** Name, address, phone, fax, key bank officers by functional title, directors, date established, detailed financial data, association's membership, correspondent banks, out-of-town branches, holding company affiliation, ABA Transit Number and Routing Symbol, MICR number with check digit, type of charter. **Arrangement:** Geographical. **Indexes:** Alphabetical.

44663 ■ **"Spinoff Doctors"** in *Entrepreneur* (Vol. 32, November 2004, No. 11, pp. 18)
Pub: Entrepreneur Media Inc.
Ed: David Worrel. **Description:** Trends in the venture capital industry are spotlighted.

44664 ■ **"Sterling Venture, Set to Close Fund I"** in *Venture Capital Journal* (Vol. 40, No. 10, October 2000, pp. 24)
Pub: Venture Economics
Description: Sterling Venture prefers to be the first to back a company and work with entrepreneurs.

44665 ■ **"Sticky Money"** in *Entrepreneur* (Vol. 28, No. 11, November 2000, pp. 38)
Pub: Entrepreneur Media Inc.
Ed: Cynthia E. Griffin. **Description:** A growing number of Web sites connect business owners with financing resources ranging from banks and venture capitalists to private investors looking to purchase stock in direct public offerings.

44666 ■ **"Student Loan Firm Will Add 170 Jobs"** in *Tampa Tribune* (November 29, 2005)
Pub: Media General, Inc.
Ed: Dave Simanoff. **Description:** Academic Financial Services in Tampa Bay, Florida is hiring 170 more workers for its new office space. The firm will receive $510,000 in tax rebates, $3,000 for each new job created and maintained.

44667 ■ **"Take It For Granted"** in *Entrepreneur* (Vol. 33, January 2005, No. 1, pp. 50)
Pub: Entrepreneur Media Inc.
Ed: David Worrell. **Description:** U.S. Small Business Innovative Research grants and contracts provide funding for small companies to develop high tech products. The programs are divided into two phases: one is to study the feasibility of a new technology or idea, the second to encourage commercialization of a particular technology.

44668 ■ **"Taking Flight: Angel Investors are Flocking Together to Your Advantage"** in *Entrepreneur* (Vol. 32, October 2004, No. 10, pp. 34)
Pub: Entrepreneur Media Inc.
Ed: David Worrell. **Description:** Angel investors are partnering to help screen deals and mentor entrepreneurs. Thirty member groups of the Angel Capital Association have put an average of $1.85 million into an average of 5.3 investments annually, with each group averaging about 50 individual angels. Deal terms vary, but many report purchasing 20 to 30 percent of a company's stock when investing.

44669 ■ **"Tapping Into Your Warm Market"** in *Home Business* (Vol. 13, January/February 2006, No. 1, pp. 72, 74-75)
Pub: Home Business Magazine
Ed: Nora Caley. **Description:** According to Circle Lending, family and friends account for more than half of investment dollars for start-up companies, this funding is called a warm market. Websites offering start-up funding are included.

44670 ■ *Thomson World Bank Directory*
Pub: Acuity
Contact: Marideth Johnson
E-mail: marideth.johnson@tfp.com
Released: Annual, Published September. **Covers:** Over 10,000 international banks and their branches in around 200 countries around the globe, including the top 1,000 U.S. Banks. **Entries Include:** Institution name, address, phone, fax, key banking officers by functional title, directors, data established, expanded statement of condition, including a profit and loss account and historic performance ratios. **Arrangement:** Geographical. **Indexes:** Alphabetical.

44671 ■ **"The Thrill of the Chase"** in *Entrepreneur* (Vol. 31, No. 7, July 2003, pp. 56)
Pub: Entrepreneur Media, Inc.
Ed: Tracy T. Lefteroff. **Description:** Despite the drop in venture capital spending in 2002, the trend actually

represents a return to historical norms. According to Roger Novak, general partner of Novak-Biddle in McLean, Virginia, entrepreneurs are putting together good business plans with less competitors, making this a good time for VCs.

44672 ■ **"Tight-Lipped Banks"** in *Entrepreneur* (Vol. 28, No. 7, July 2000, pp. 40)
Pub: Entrepreneur Media Inc.
Ed: Doug Hood and Marilea Hood. **Description:** Information about SBA loans is shared.

44673 ■ **"Tips on getting a loan"** in *Crain's Detroit Business* (Vol. 16, No. 50, December 11, 2000, pp. E-1)
Pub: Crain Communications, Inc.
Description: An outline covering all of the information required for a well-written loan proposal.

44674 ■ **"To lend or not to lend"** in *Atlanta Business Chronicle* (Vol. 24, No. 13, August 31, 2001, pp. 1B)
Pub: American City Business Journals Inc.
Ed: Linda Kercher. **Description:** Small business loan activity may be slowing, either due to tightening loan standards or reduced demand from small business owners, as both groups deal with an uncertain future. Lower interest rates have helped buoy demand for loans, and Small Business Administration loan guarantees help ensure that lenders will be interested in making loans. The article provides opinions from several lenders and from the National Federation of Independent Business.

44675 ■ **"Too Much Information?"** in *Black Enterprise* (Vol. 37, December 2006, No. 5, pp. 59)
Pub: Earl G. Graves Publishing Co. Inc.
Ed: James C. Johnson. **Description:** African American business owners often face the dilemma of whether or not to divulge their minority status when soliciting new customers and financial institutions. The quality of the products or services is always the key factor and race should never define one's business; however, it is appropriate to market oneself as a minority or women-owned business, especially if the company is in an industry where those clients are offered top-tier contracts.

44676 ■ **"The Top 25 Investment Banks of 2000"** in *Red Herring* (No. 99, June 15 & July 1, 2001, pp. 72, 74)
Pub: Herring Communications
Ed: Stasia Bochnowski. **Description:** The top 25 investment banks of 2000, ranked by money raised through lead-managed tech IPOs, including rank, manager, proceeds, and number of tech IPOs.

44677 ■ **"The Top 25 IPOs of 2000"** in *Red Herring* (No 99, June 15 & July 1, 2001, pp. 62, 64)
Pub: Herring Communications
Ed: Lorraine Fry. **Description:** After a wild ride, the IPO market gets back to basics. The number of tech IPOs fell in the fourth quarter. The article includes a listing of the top 25 IPOs of 2000, including rank, issuer, ticker, issue month, IPO size, and percent change since December.

44678 ■ **"Trendy VC providers still overlooking Central Ohio"** in *Business First Columbus* (Vol. 18, No. 40, May 24, 2002, pp. A6)
Pub: Business First Columbus, Inc.
Ed: Laura Newpoff. **Description:** In a comparison between the Cincinnati and Columbus areas, Columbus is not attracting as much private venture capital.

44679 ■ **"Two Companies Find Investment at Long Island VC Forum"** in *Long Island Business News* (February 13, 2004)
Pub: Dolan Media Newswires
Description: Consolidated Billing Solutions and Motion Imagine Inc. have received venture capital funding as a result of the Long Island Capital Alliance forum.

44680 ■ *The Ultimate Insider's Guide to SBA and Other Loans*
Pub: Entrepreneur Press
Ed: Dan M. Koehler. **Released:** July 2004. **Price:** $23.95. **Description:** Guide to understanding Small Business Administration government small business loans.

44681 ■ *Underwriting the Self-Employed Borrower Correspondence Course*
Pub: Mortgage Bankers Association of America
Released: 1998. **Price:** $260.00 (paper).

44682 ■ **"Vacancies up but investors still high on retail"** in *Atlanta Business Chronicle* (Vol. 25, December 13, 2002, No. 27, pp. A5)
Pub: American City Business Publications, Inc.
Ed: Lisa R. Schoolcraft. **Description:** Despite lower retail rents and more empty stores in 2002 than 2001, real estate investors continue to buy Atlanta, Georgia area retail properties, largely due to the fact that investment funds are available. The market for small investors who pool funds continues to drive this trend. A report by Marcus and Millichap provides some hope that rents will recover some of the losses as 2003 progresses.

44683 ■ **"The VC Process"** in *Hispanic Business* (March 2004, pp. 36-37)
Pub: Hispanic Business
Ed: Joel Russell. **Description:** Hispanics have lagged behind in the private-equity market, but experts offer ways for them to improve acquiring venture financing.

44684 ■ **"Venture Capital is Not For Girlie Men"** in *Fortune* (Vol. 152, October 17, 2005, No. 8, pp. 38)
Pub: Time Inc.
Ed: Adam Lashinsky. **Description:** Profile of Tim Draper, whose firm currently has a network of affiliated funds in 28 cities worldwide and 75 partners managing $3.4 billion investing in nearly 500 companies.

44685 ■ *Where to Go When the Bank Says No: Alternatives for Financing Your Business*
Pub: Bloomberg Press
Ed: David R. Evanson. **Released:** 1998. **Price:** $24.95 (cloth).

44686 ■ **"Who's small enough to get SBA aid? Some ceilings are raised"** in *Wall Street Journal* (July 18, 2000, pp. B2)
Pub: Dow Jones & Co., Inc.
Ed: Jeffrey A. Tannenbaum. **Description:** An update on the new requirements for obtaining SBA loans.

44687 ■ **"Women Business Owners Seek Financing"** in *Marketing to Women* (Vol. 19, December 2006, No. 2, pp. 8)
Pub: EPM Communications, Inc.
Description: A study by the Center for Women's Business Research shows that women business owners have become more savvy when seeking financial support for their business ventures. Statistical data included.

44688 ■ **"Women"** in *Entrepreneur* (Vol. 27, No. 12, December 1999, pp. 44)
Pub: Entrepreneur Media Inc.
Ed: Cynthia E. Griffin. **Description:** A new study underscores the old adage that the most important thing in business is location, location, location. In the top 50 U.S. metropolitan areas, the number of women-owned firms has increased 33 to 59 percent in the past seven years, according to a 1999 report by the National Foundation for Women Business Owners (NFWBO).

44689 ■ *Women Entrepreneurs*
Pub: Edward Elgar Publishing, Incorporated
Ed: Andrea Smith-Hunter. **Released:** October 2006. **Price:** $120.00. **Description:** Focus is on women entrepreneurs; information includes human capital, network structures and financial capital, with comparative analysis across racial lines.

44690 ■ "Won't You Be My Neighbor?" in *Entrepreneur* (Vol. 32, August 2004, No. 8, pp. 52)

Pub: Entrepreneur Media Inc.
Ed: Jennifer Pellet. **Description:** Community development funds invest in companies that will benefit low-income workers in distressed communities.

44691 ■ "The World Bank's Innovation Market" in *Harvard Business Review* (Vol. 80, No. 11, November 2002, pp. 104)

Pub: Harvard Business School Press
Ed: Gary Robert Chapman, Hamel Wood. **Description:** A description of ways a new-products team at the World Bank created an Innovation Marketplace, a forum that allowed people to present ideas for alleviating poverty to potential funding sources.

44692 ■ "Yazam Taps Coleman, Opens DC Office" in *Venture Capital Journal* (Vol. 40, No. 10, October 2000, pp. 36)

Pub: Venture Economics
Description: Yazam hired Sean Coleman as a managing director to head up the firm's new Washington, DC office.

TRADE PERIODICALS

44693 ■ *Mortgage Technology*

Pub: Thomson Financial
Contact: Timothy Murphy, Group Publisher
E-mail: tim.murphy@thomsonmedia.com
Released: Bimonthly, 8/yr. **Price:** $78 U.S.; $88 Canada; $108 other countries. **Description:** Magazine covering technological trends and developments within the mortgage industry.

CONSULTANTS

44694 ■ **Pioneer Business Consultants**

9042 Garfield Ave., Ste. 312
Huntington Beach, CA 92646
Ph:(714)964-7600
Fax: (714)962-6585
Scope: Offers general management consulting specializing in business acquisitions, tax and business planning, cash flow analyses, business valuations and business sales and expert witness court testimony regarding business sales, valuations and accounting.

FRANCHISES AND BUSINESS OPPORTUNITIES

44695 ■ **Cash-X Inc.**

130-3044 Bloor St. W
Toronto, ON, Canada M8X 2Y8
Ph:(416)234-8657
Free: (866)462-2749
Fax: (866)606-8364
Co. E-mail: steveceo@cashx.ca
URL: http://www.cashxsolutions.ca
No. of Franchise Units: 4. **No. of Company-Owned Units:** 1. **Founded:** 2001. **Franchised:** 2001. **Description:** Offers financial services. Operates a retail store model, a virtual storefront (unmanned Kiosk) model, as well as an Internet business model. **Equity Capital Needed:** $50,000. **Franchise Fee:** $25,000-$50,000. **Training:** Provides 5 days business management training.

44696 ■ **National Home Buyers Assistance - NHBA**

6600 E Hampden Ave.
Denver, CO 80224
Ph:(303)703-6422
Fax: (303)779-6422

No. of Franchise Units: 74. **Founded:** 2001. **Franchised:** 2002. **Description:** Helping America achieve home ownership. **Equity Capital Needed:** $105,000. **Franchise Fee:** $30,000. **Financial Assistance:** No. **Training:** Yes.

44697 ■ **Stop 'N' Cash 1000 Inc.**

809 Victoria St. N
Kitchener, ON, Canada N2B 3C3
Ph:(519)896-8088
Fax: (519)576-8853
Co. E-mail: gdavey@stopncash.com
URL: http://www.stopncash.com
No. of Franchise Units: 64. **No. of Company-Owned Units:** 9. **Founded:** 1998. **Franchised:** 1999. **Description:** The franchise provides a payday loan scheme and a solid investment return. **Equity Capital Needed:** $150,000-$200,000. **Franchise Fee:** $30,000. **Training:** 1 week of in-house in Kitchener, and ongoing support.

RESEARCH CENTERS

44698 ■ **University of Nebraska at Kearney–Nebraska Business Development Center**

West Center Bldg., Rm. 135
1917 West 24th St.
Kearney, NE 68841-4440
Ph:(308)865-8344
Fax: (308)865-8153
Co. E-mail: nbdcunk@unk.edu
URL: http://www.unk.edu/acad/nbdc/home.html
Contact: Odee Ingersoll, Dir.
E-mail: nbdcunk@unk.edu
Scope: Management education, market research, business and marketing plans, strategic planning, financial planning, cash flow budgeting, capital budgeting and loan packaging. **Services:** Consulting. **Publications:** NBDC Business Calendar (quarterly). **Educational Activities:** Continuing education programs.

START-UP INFORMATION

44699 ■ "Charting Your Course" in *Black Enterprise* **(Vol. 34, July 2004, No. 12, pp. 65)**
Pub: Earl G. Graves Publishing Co. Inc.
Ed: Sonia Alleyne. **Description:** Discussion revolving around a business professional choosing an industry in which to direct him or her to a leadership position.

44700 ■ "Digital Rules" in *Forbes* **(February 19, 2001, pp. 51)**
Pub: Forbes Magazine
Ed: Rich Karlgaard. **Description:** The article proves that, despite the New Economy, it still takes brains, salesmanship, guts and a whole lot of persistence to launch and run a startup.

44701 ■ *Essentials of Entrepreneurship and Small Business Management*
Pub: Prentice Hall PTR
Ed: Thomas W. Zimmerer; Norman M. Scarborough; Doug Wilson. **Released:** February 2007. **Price:** $106. 67. **Description:** New venture creation and the knowledge required to start a new business are shared. The challenges of entrepreneurship, business plans, marketing, e-commerce, and financial considerations are explored.

44702 ■ "Peer to peer" in *Harvard Business Review* **(Vol. 78, No. 5, September-October 2000, pp. 32)**
Pub: Harvard Business School Publishing Corp.
Ed: Roberta Fusaro. **Description:** Two peer groups for CEOs, offered in the Boston area, and conducted by the Catlin Group and the Commonwealth Institute, help CEOs of start-up high tech companies deal with the challenges of their new position.

44703 ■ *Small Business Management*
Pub: John Wiley & Sons, Incorporated
Ed: Margaret Burlingame. **Released:** March 2007. **Price:** $44.95. **Description:** Advice for starting and running a small business as well as information on the value and appeal of small businesses, is given. Topics include budgets, taxes, inventory, ethics, e-commerce, and current laws.

44704 ■ *Small Business Management: Launching and Managing New Ventures*
Pub: Nelson Thomson Learning
Ed: Justin G. Longenecker. **Released:** March 2006. **Price:** $78.95. **Description:** Tips for starting and running a successful new company are provided.

44705 ■ "Starting a business? Then get with the plan" in *Crain's Detroit Business* **(Vol. 18, No. 49, December 9, 2002, pp. 17)**
Pub: Crain Communications Inc., Detroit
Ed: Laura Bailey. **Description:** When starting a new company, it is imperative to have a good business plan.

ASSOCIATIONS AND OTHER ORGANIZATIONS

44706 ■ American Management Association
1601 Broadway
New York, NY 10019-7420
Ph:(212)586-8100
Free: 800-262-9699
Fax: (212)903-8168
Co. E-mail: customerservice@amanet.org
URL: http://www.amanet.org
Contact: Roger Kelleher, Public Relations Mgr.
Purpose: Maintains a publishing program providing tools individuals use to extend learning beyond the classroom in a process of life-long professional growth and development through education. **Publications:** *HR Focus* (monthly); *Management Review* (monthly); *Organizational Dynamics: A Quarterly Review of Organizational Behavior for Professional Managers*; *The Take-Charge Assistant* (monthly).

44707 ■ Association for Corporate Growth - Toronto Chapter
390 Bay St., Ste. 2701
Toronto, ON, Canada M5H 2Y2
Ph:(416)868-1881
Fax: (416)860-0580
Co. E-mail: acgtoronto@baystco.com
URL: http://www.acg.org/toronto
Contact: Ms. Sue Anderson, Chapter Administrator
Membership: Professionals with a leadership role in strategic corporate growth. **Purpose:** Seeks to facilitate the professional advancement of members, and the practice of corporate growth management. Fosters communication and cooperation among members; conducts continuing professional education programs. **Publications:** *Mergers & Acquisitions - The Dealmaker's Journal* (monthly).

44708 ■ Business Modeling and Integration Domain Task Force
Bldg. A, Ste. 300
140 Kendrick St.
Needham, MA 02494
Ph:(781)444-0404
Fax: (781)444-0320
Co. E-mail: info@omg.org
URL: http://www.bpmi.org
Contact: Mr. Fred A. Cummins EDS, Co-Chair
Description: Aims to empower all companies, across all industries, to develop and operate business processes that span multiple applications and business partners, behind the firewall and over the Internet.

44709 ■ Canadian Institute of Management–Institut Canadien de Gestion
15 Collier St., Lower Level
Barrie, ON, Canada L4M 1G5
Ph:(416)493-0155
Free: 800-387-5774
Fax: (416)493-0155
Co. E-mail: office@cim.ca
URL: http://www.cim.ca
Contact: Ms. Deb Johnstone CIM, Natl. Pres.

Membership: Management personnel. **Purpose:** Seeks to advance the practice of business management; promotes continuing professional development of members. Serves as a clearinghouse on management and related topics; facilitates exchange of information among members; makes available educational and training programs. **Publications:** *Canadian Manager* (quarterly).

44710 ■ Canadian Management Centre
150 York St., 5th Fl.
Toronto, ON, Canada M5H 3S5
Ph:(416)214-5678
Free: 877-CMC-2519
Fax: (416)313-4985
Co. E-mail: cmcinfo@cmctraining.org
URL: http://www.cmcamai.org
Contact: Bruce Peer, Pres./Managing Dir.
Membership: Managers of corporations and organizations. **Purpose:** Promotes excellence in management. Conducts educational and training programs for management personnel.

44711 ■ Chief Executive Officers Club
47 West St., Ste. 5C
New York, NY 10006
Ph:(212)925-7911
Fax: (212)925-7463
Co. E-mail: main@ceoclubs.org
URL: http://ceoclubs.org
Contact: Joseph R. Mancuso, Pres.
Purpose: Serves as a management resource for entrepreneurial managers and their professional advisers. Selects and makes available publications on developing business plans, organizing an entrepreneurial team, attracting venture capital, and obtaining patents, trademarks, and copyrights. Develops, collects, and disseminates information on business trends, new laws and regulations, and tax guidance. Conducts intensive-study courses and seminars. Has identified stages of the entrepreneurial process and, through essays and audiocassettes, addresses problems pertinent to each stage. **Publications:** *Entrepreneurial Manager: The Entrepreneur's Source of Useful Information* (monthly).

44712 ■ International Council for Small Business
The George Washington University
Scholarship of Business
2201 G St. NW, Funger 315
Washington, DC 20052
Ph:(202)994-0704
Fax: (202)994-4930
Co. E-mail: icsb@gwu.edu
URL: http://www.icsb.org
Contact: Rob Van der Horst, Pres.
Membership: Management educators, researchers, government officials, and professionals in 80 countries. **Purpose:** Fosters discussion of topics pertaining to the development and improvement of small business management. **Publications:** *ICSB Bulletin* (quarterly); *Journal of Small Business Management* (quarterly); Membership Directory (annual); Proceedings (annual).

44713 ■ Machinery Information Management Open Systems Alliance
2704 8th St.
Tuscaloosa, AL 35401
Ph:(949)625-8616
Fax: (949)625-8616
Co. E-mail: info@mimosa.org
URL: http://www.mimosa.org
Contact: Alan T. Johnston, Pres.
Description: Develops and encourages the adoption of open information standards for Operations and Maintenance and Collaborative Asset Lifecycle Management in commercial and military applications. Provides a forum for the members, bringing together subject matter experts in cross disciplinary technologies, to enable complex solutions for Equipment Operators, Maintainers and Fleet Managers.

44714 ■ National Management Association
2210 Arbor Blvd.
Dayton, OH 45439
Ph:(937)294-0421
Fax: (937)294-2374
Co. E-mail: nma@nma1.org
URL: http://www.nma1.org
Contact: K. Stephen Bailey CM, Pres.
Description: Business and industrial management personnel; membership comes from supervisory level, with the remainder from middle management and above. Seeks to develop and recognize management as a profession and to promote the free enterprise system. Prepares chapter programs on basic management, management policy and practice, communications, human behavior, industrial relations, economics, political education, and liberal education. Maintains speakers' bureau and hall of fame. Maintains educational, charitable, and research programs. Sponsors charitable programs. **Publications:** *Board of Directors' Directory* (annual); *Manage* (quarterly); *National Speakers' Directory* (periodic).

44715 ■ Organization Design Forum
5713 Carriage House Ct.
Apex, NC 27539
Ph:(919)662-8548
Fax: (919)662-9751
Co. E-mail: contact@organizationdesignforum.org
URL: http://www.organizationdesignforum.org
Contact: Brenda Price, Admin.
Membership: Academics, practitioners, consultants, and human resource professionals. **Purpose:** Works to promote the knowledge and practice of organizational design. Focuses on the effect organization structure and processes have on the performance of individuals, groups, and the organization itself. Offers basic and advanced training in organization design techniques. **Publications:** *Designer's Forum* (quarterly); *Organization Design*; Membership Directory (annual). Also publishes monographs on organization design.

44716 ■ SCORE
409 3rd St. SW, 6th Fl.
Washington, DC 20024
Ph:(202)205-6762
Free: 800-634-0245
Fax: (202)205-7636
Co. E-mail: media@score.org
URL: http://www.score.org
Contact: W. Kenneth Yancey Jr., CEO
Description: Serves as volunteer program sponsored by U.S. Small Business Administration in which working and retired business management professionals provide free business counseling to men and women who are considering starting a small business, encountering problems with their business, or expanding their business. Offers free one-on-one counseling, online counseling and low cost workshops on a variety of business topics. **Publications:** *SCORE eNews* (monthly) ; *SCORE Expert Answers* (monthly); *SCORE Today* (monthly) ; Annual Report (annual).

44717 ■ Society for Advancement of Management
Texas A&M University - Corpus Christi
College of Business
6300 Ocean Dr. - FC 111
Corpus Christi, TX 78412

Ph:(361)825-6045
Free: 888-827-6077
Fax: (361)825-2725
Co. E-mail: moustafa@cob.tamucc.edu
URL: http://www.cob.tamucc.edu/sam
Contact: Dr. Moustafa H. Abdelsamad, Pres./CEO
Description: Represents management executives in industry commerce, government, and education. Fields of interest include management education, policy and strategy, MIS, international management, administration, budgeting, collective bargaining, distribution, incentives, materials handling, quality control, and training. **Publications:** *Management in Practice* (quarterly); *SAM Advanced Management Journal* (quarterly); *The SAM News International* (quarterly); *Society for Advancement of Management—International Management Conference Proceedings* (annual).

44718 ■ Women in Management
PO Box 1032
Dundee, IL 60118-7032
Ph:(708)386-0496
Free: 877-946-6285
Fax: (847)683-3751
Co. E-mail: nationalwim@wimonline.org
URL: http://www.wimonline.org
Description: Supports network of women in professional and management positions that facilitate the exchange of experience and ideas. Promotes self-growth in management; provides speakers who are successful in management; sponsors workshops and special interest groups to discuss problems and share job experiences. **Publications:** *WIM National Newsletter* (quarterly); *Women in Management—National Directory* (annual).

44719 ■ World Confederation of Productivity Science
500 Sherbrooke St. W, Ste. 900
Montreal, QC, Canada H3A 3C6
Ph:(514)282-3838
Fax: (514)844-7556
Co. E-mail: secretariat@wcps.info
URL: http://www.wcps.info
Contact: Linda Carbone, Exec. Dir.
Membership: Fraternal association of manufacturing and commercial enterprises and employees, government agencies, professional institutions, and researchers. **Purpose:** Goals are to promote productivity science, advance management techniques, and improve the quality of working life and environment. **Publications:** *OPM (Quality and Productivity Management)* (quarterly); *World Congress* (periodic).

EDUCATIONAL PROGRAMS

44720 ■ 10 Tools for Resilience and Wellness in the Workplace (Canada)
Canadian Management Centre
150 York St., 5th Fl.
Toronto, ON, Canada M5H 3S5
Free: 877-CMC-2500
Fax: (416)313-4985
Co. E-mail: cmcinfo@cmctraining.org
URL: http://www.cma.org
Price: $695 Canadian. **Description:** Seminar covers stress strategies you can use anywhere, controlling psychological stress, control the four engines of change, set boundaries and say no without feeling guilty, and recognize the signs of "burn-out" before it happens. **Locations:** Toronto, ON.

44721 ■ AMA's 5-Day MBA Program
American Management Association
1601 Broadway
New York, NY 10019
Ph:(212)586-8100
Free: 800-262-9699
Fax: (212)903-8168
Co. E-mail: customerservice@amanet.org
URL: http://www.amanet.org
Price: $2,995.00 for non-members; $2,695.00 for AMA members. **Description:** Five-day seminar; cov-

ers a broad overview of business concepts typically covered in university-level MBA programs. **Locations:** San Francisco, CA; Washington, DC; and New York, NY.

44722 ■ AMA's Course for Presidents and CEOs
American Management Association
1601 Broadway
New York, NY 10019
Ph:(212)586-8100
Free: 800-262-9699
Fax: (212)903-8168
Co. E-mail: customerservice@amanet.org
URL: http://www.amanet.org
Price: $4,5950.00 for non-members; $4,195.00 for AMA members. **Description:** Covers key elements for strategic growth, methods for increasing productivity and performance, working with a company board, attracting talent, and includes relaxed discussions with other presidents.

44723 ■ AMA's Course on Supply Chain Management
American Management Association
1601 Broadway
New York, NY 10019
Ph:(212)586-8100
Free: 800-262-9699
Fax: (212)903-8168
Co. E-mail: customerservice@amanet.org
URL: http://www.amanet.org
Price: $1,995.00 for non-members; $1,795.00 for AMA members. **Description:** Covers various aspects of supply chain management including e-commerce, management issues, IT and decision support systems, and the future of supply chain management. **Locations:** Chicago, IL.

44724 ■ AMA's Leading with Emotional Intelligence
American Management Association
1601 Broadway
New York, NY 10019
Ph:(212)586-8100
Free: 800-262-9699
Fax: (212)903-8168
Co. E-mail: customerservice@amanet.org
URL: http://www.amanet.org
Price: $2,095.00 for non-members; $1,895.00 for AMA members. **Description:** Covers the importance of emotional intelligence in the workplace, and developing a style to effectively communicate and use emotions positively. **Locations:** San Francisco, CA; and Washington, DC.

44725 ■ Best Practices for Effective Operations, Production and Plant Management
American Management Association
1601 Broadway
New York, NY 10019
Ph:(212)586-8100
Free: 800-262-9699
Fax: (212)903-8168
Co. E-mail: customerservice@amanet.org
URL: http://www.amanet.org
Price: $2,895.00 for non-members; $2,595.00 for AMA members. **Description:** Four-day seminar topics include all aspects of effective plant management. **Locations:** San Francisco, CA; and Chicago, IL.

44726 ■ Best Practices for Effective Operations, Production and Plant Management (Canada)
Canadian Management Centre
150 York St., 5th Fl.
Toronto, ON, Canada M5H 3S5
Ph:(416)214-5678
Free: 800-262-9699
Fax: (416)313-4985
Co. E-mail: cmcinfo@cmctraining.org
URL: http://cmcamai.org
Price: $1,895.00 Canadian. **Description:** Four-day seminar topics include all aspects of effective plant management. **Locations:** Mississauga, ON; and Toronto, ON.

44727 ■ Best Practices for the Multi-project Manager

American Management Association
1601 Broadway
New York, NY 10019
Ph:(212)586-8100
Free: 800-262-9699
Fax: (212)903-8168
Co. E-mail: customerservice@amanet.org
URL: http://www.amanet.org
Price: $1,795.00 for non-members; $1,695.00 for AMA members. **Description:** Covers balancing work load, reducing risk and conflict, time management, prioritizing, and monitoring and reporting on multiple projects. **Locations:** San Diego, CA; Atlanta, GA; Chicago, IL; Boston, MA; and New York, NY.

44728 ■ Best Practices for the Multi-Project Manager (Canada)

Canadian Management Centre
150 York St., 5th Fl.
Toronto, ON, Canada M5H 3S5
Ph:(866)400-4941 ext. 2252
Free: 877-CMC-2500
Fax: (416)313-4985
Co. E-mail: cmcinfo@cmctraining.org
URL: http://www.cmcamai.org
Price: $1,395 Canadian. **Description:** Covers the communication skills needed to organize and prioritize projects, including time management and budgeting. **Locations:** Toronto, ON.

44729 ■ The Brain Power Course: Learn to Develop Your Thinking Skills

American Management Association
1601 Broadway
New York, NY 10019
Ph:(212)586-8100
Free: 800-262-9699
Fax: (212)903-8168
Co. E-mail: customerservice@amanet.org
URL: http://www.amanet.org
Price: $1,795.00 for non-members; $1,695.00 for AMA members. **Description:** Covers thinking styles, using brainmaps and brainscripts, ten key factors to effective thinking, and thinking as a team. **Locations:** San Francisco, CA.

44730 ■ Business Systems Analysis and Design (Canada)

Canadian Management Centre
150 York St., 5th Fl.
Toronto, ON, Canada M5H 3S5
Ph:(866)400-4941 ext. 2252
Free: 877-CMC-2500
Fax: (416)313-4985
Co. E-mail: cmcinfo@cmctraining.org
URL: http://www.cmcamai.org
Price: $1,395 Canadian. **Description:** Covers an understanding the business systems development process from the view of the client (user) and the IT, including, overseeing the overall project through completion. **Locations:** Toronto, ON.

44731 ■ Canadian Management Centre's 5-Day "MBA"(Canada)

Canadian Management Centre
150 York St., 5th Fl.
Toronto, ON, Canada M5H 3S5
Free: 877-CMC-2500
Fax: (416)313-4985
Co. E-mail: cmcinfo@cmctraining.org
URL: http://www.cma.org
Price: $2,695 Canadian. **Description:** Seminar that covers how the various components of a business must be linked, aligned and integrated into a successful business system, including business competencies, finance and accounting, marketing strategies, and leadership. **Locations:** Toronto, ON.

44732 ■ Canadian Management Centre's Course in Supply Chain Management (Canada)

Canadian Management Centre
150 York St., 5th Fl.
Toronto, ON, Canada M5H 3S5
Ph:(866)400-4941 ext. 2252

Free: 877-CMC-2500
Fax: (416)313-4985
Co. E-mail: cmcinfo@cmctraining.org
URL: http://www.cmcamai.org
Price: $1,395 Canadian. **Description:** Covers the influence of e-commerce on supply chains, inventory control and cost reduction, partnering, use the technology, and oversee the entire chain. **Locations:** Toronto, ON.

44733 ■ CMC's Course in Mergers and Acquisitions (Canada)

Canadian Management Centre
150 York St., 5th Fl.
Toronto, ON, Canada M5H 3S5
Ph:(416)214-5678
Free: 800-262-9699
Fax: (416)313-4985
Co. E-mail: cmcinfo@cmctraining.org
URL: http://cmcamai.org
Price: $1,950.00 Canadian. **Description:** Three-day seminar for executive managers; covers organizational, financial, planning, tax, and risk aspects of mergers and acquisitions. **Locations:** Toronto, ON.

44734 ■ Coaching: A Strategic Tool for Effective Leadership (Canada)

Canadian Management Centre
150 York St., 5th Fl.
Toronto, ON, Canada M5H 3S5
Ph:(866)400-4941 ext. 2252
Free: 877-CMC-2500
Fax: (416)313-4985
Co. E-mail: cmcinfo@cmctraining.org
URL: http://www.cmcamai.org
Price: $1,695 Canadian. **Description:** Covers effective coaching skills, including confidence to meet difficult situations head-on, constructive listening, and building trust. **Locations:** Toronto, ON.

44735 ■ Coaching: A Strategic Tool for Effective Leadership and Counselling for Outstanding Job Performance (Canada)

Canadian Management Centre
150 York St., 5th Fl.
Toronto, ON, Canada M5H 3S5
Ph:(416)214-5678
Free: 800-262-9699
Fax: (416)313-4985
Co. E-mail: cmcinfo@cmctraining.org
URL: http://cmcamai.org
Price: $1,695.00 Canadian. **Description:** Covers creating a successful environment, problem resolution, teamwork, soliciting valuable feedback, and models for successful coaching. **Locations:** Toronto, ON.

44736 ■ Coaching and Counseling for Outstanding Job Performance

American Management Association
1601 Broadway
New York, NY 10019
Ph:(212)586-8100
Free: 800-262-9699
Fax: (212)903-8168
Co. E-mail: customerservice@amanet.org
URL: http://www.amanet.org
Price: $1,595.00 for non-members; $1,495.00 for AMA members. **Description:** Covers creating a successful environment, problem resolution, teamwork, soliciting valuable feedback, and models for successful coaching. **Locations:** San Francisco, CA; Chicago, IL; and New York, NY.

44737 ■ Confronting the Tough Stuff: Advanced Management Skills for Supervisors

American Management Association
1601 Broadway
New York, NY 10019
Ph:(212)586-8100
Free: 800-262-9699
Fax: (212)903-8168
Co. E-mail: customerservice@amanet.org
URL: http://www.amanet.org
Price: $1,695.00 for non-members; $1,495.00 for AMA members. **Description:** Covers diffusing potential legal situations, dealing with challenges, writing performance evaluations, enhancing productivity, and managing diversity. **Locations:** Washington, DC.

44738 ■ Confronting the Tough Stuff: Advanced Management Skills for Supervisors (Canada)

Canadian Management Centre
150 York St., 5th Fl.
Toronto, ON, Canada M5H 3S5
Ph:(866)400-4941 ext. 2252
Free: 877-CMC-2500
Fax: (416)313-4985
Co. E-mail: cmcinfo@cmctraining.org
URL: http://www.cmcamai.org
Price: $1,395 Canadian. **Description:** For supervisors with three to five years of experience; covers techniques that solve disputes and create unity, defeat communication obstacles that hinder productivity, and be able to work through the impact of "survivor" shock from layoffs and mergers. **Locations:** Toronto, ON.

44739 ■ Confronting the Tough Stuff: Turning Managerial Challenges into Positive Results (Canada)

Canadian Management Centre
150 York St., 5th Fl.
Toronto, ON, Canada M5H 3S5
Free: 877-CMC-2500
Fax: (416)313-4985
Co. E-mail: cmcinfo@cmctraining.org
URL: http://www.cma.org
Price: $1,495 Canadian. **Description:** Seminar that covers the challenges and the problem-solving skills in the workplace, including coaching uncooperative employees, constructive and destructive conflict, techniques for using conflict to increase cohesion, four stages of mediation and techniques to mediate disputes between employees, and avoid potentially litigious situations. **Locations:** Toronto, ON.

44740 ■ Critical Thinking: New Paradigm for Peak Performance (Canada)

Canadian Management Centre
150 York St., 5th Fl.
Toronto, ON, Canada M5H 3S5
Ph:(866)400-4941 ext. 2252
Free: 877-CMC-2500
Fax: (416)313-4985
Co. E-mail: cmcinfo@cmctraining.org
URL: http://www.cmcamai.org
Price: $1,795 Cdn. **Description:** Covers new thinking strategies that will enable you to see the overall view, including problem solving, influencing others through a clear thought pattern, and promote innovation. **Locations:** Toronto, ON.

44741 ■ Criticism and Discipline Skills for Managers

Fred Pryor Seminars
9757 Metcalf Ave.
Overland Park, KS 66212
Free: 800-944-8503
Fax: (913)967-8849
Co. E-mail: customerservice@pryor.com
URL: http://www.careertrack.com
Description: Covers effective and constructive methods of dealing with problem employees. **Locations:** Cities throughout the United States.

44742 ■ Dealing with Competing Demands: Mastering the Managerial Balancing Act

American Management Association
1601 Broadway
New York, NY 10019
Ph:(212)586-8100
Free: 800-262-9699
Fax: (212)903-8168
Co. E-mail: customerservice@amanet.org
URL: http://www.amanet.org
Price: $1,795 for non-members; $1,595 for AMA members. **Description:** Covers setting realistic goals as they pertain to scheduling, techniques to build team effort, and stress-free prioritizing. **Locations:** New York, NY; Atlanta, GA; Chicago, IL; Washington, DC; and San Francisco, CA.

44743 ■ Dealing with Competing Demands: Mastering the Managerial Balancing Act (Canada)
Canadian Management Centre
150 York St., 5th Fl.
Toronto, ON, Canada M5H 3S5
Ph:(866)400-4941 ext. 2252
Free: 877-CMC-2500
Fax: (416)313-4985
Co. E-mail: cmcinfo@cmctraining.org
URL: http://www.cmcamai.org
Price: $1,695 Canadian. **Description:** Covers the skills necessary to manage your objectives with success, including prioritizing, realistic objectives, effective use of communication to meet your goals, and utilize control stress. **Locations:** Toronto, ON.

44744 ■ Developing Executive Leadership (Canada)
Canadian Management Centre
150 York St., 5th Fl.
Toronto, ON, Canada M5H 3S5
Free: 877-CMC-2500
Fax: (416)313-4985
Co. E-mail: cmcinfo@cmctraining.org
URL: http://www.cma.org
Price: $1,895 Canadian. **Description:** Seminar that covers leadership in today's business environment, including techniques to improve effectiveness, leading individuals and groups, keys to developing influence, and how to create your own leadership development plan. **Locations:** Toronto, ON.

44745 ■ Developing and Leading Dynamic Teams (Canada)
Canadian Management Centre
150 York St., 5th Fl.
Toronto, ON, Canada M5H 3S5
Ph:(866)400-4941 ext. 2252
Free: 877-CMC-2500
Fax: (416)313-4985
Co. E-mail: cmcinfo@cmctraining.org
URL: http://www.cmcamai.org
Price: $1,850 Canadian. **Description:** Covers the leadership skills needed to influence, and advance your team towards the organizations goals. **Locations:** Toronto, ON.

44746 ■ Disaster Recovery Planning: Insuring Business Continuity
American Management Association
1601 Broadway
New York, NY 10019
Ph:(212)586-8100
Free: 800-262-9699
Fax: (212)903-8168
Co. E-mail: customerservice@amanet.org
URL: http://www.amanet.org
Price: $1,795 for non-members; $1,595 for AMA members. **Description:** Covers setting up of an emergency response team in the event of an emergency, including the recovery plan. **Locations:** Atlanta, GA; New York, NY; Las Vegas, NV; Chicago, IL; and San Francisco, IL.

44747 ■ Earned Value Management Systems (EVMS) for Project Managers
EEI Communications
66 Canal Ctr. Plz., Ste. 200
Alexandria, VA 22314-5507
Ph:(703)683-7453
Free: 888-253-2762
Fax: (703)683-7310
Co. E-mail: train@eeicommunications.com
URL: http://www.eeicommunications.com/training
Price: $695. **Description:** Seminar based on ANSI/EIA-748-A, Earned Value Management Systems, and the Project Management Institute's (PMI) Project Management Body of Knowledge (PMBOK) that covers resource planning and estimating, project budgeting, EVM (Earned Value Management) performance metrics, variance analyses, and EVMS reports. **Locations:** Alexandria, VA; Silver Spring, MD; and Washington, DC.

44748 ■ Effective Project Leadership: Building High Commitment Through Superior Communication
American Management Association
1601 Broadway
New York, NY 10019
Ph:(212)586-8100
Free: 800-262-9699
Fax: (212)903-8168
Co. E-mail: customerservice@amanet.org
URL: http://www.amanet.org
Price: $1,895 for non-members; $1,695 for AMA members. **Description:** Covers building relationships within the organization through strong communication skills, including conflict management, and negotiation. **Locations:** New York, NY; Atlanta, GA; Washington, DC; and San Francisco, CA.

44749 ■ Effective Project Leadership: Building High Commitment Through Superior Communication (Canada)
Canadian Management Centre
150 York St., 5th Fl.
Toronto, ON, Canada M5H 3S5
Free: 877-CMC-2500
Fax: (416)313-4985
Co. E-mail: cmcinfo@cmctraining.org
URL: http://www.cma.org
Price: $1,895 Canadian. **Description:** Seminar that develops skills to build team commitment creating a predictable project environment that leads to completion of projects on time and within the budget. **Locations:** Toronto, ON.

44750 ■ Effective Purchasing Negotiations Workshop: Techniques and Tools for Today's Competitive Environment
American Management Association
1601 Broadway
New York, NY 10019
Ph:(212)586-8100
Free: 800-262-9699
Fax: (212)903-8168
Co. E-mail: customerservice@amanet.org
URL: http://www.amanet.org
Price: $1,895 for non-members; $1,695 for AMA members. **Description:** Covers an understanding of the suppliers' techniques for successful negotiation. **Locations:** Chicago, IL; Las Vegas, NV; Washington, DC; Garden Grove, CA; and Atlanta, GA.

44751 ■ The Essential Administrative Professional: The Skills and Know-How to Make You Invaluable
American Management Association
1601 Broadway
New York, NY 10019
Ph:(212)586-8100
Free: 800-262-9699
Fax: (212)903-8168
Co. E-mail: customerservice@amanet.org
URL: http://www.amanet.org
Price: $1,545 for non-members; $1,395 for AMA members. **Description:** Covers effective communication skills, hands-on learning, prioritizing and scheduling techniques. **Locations:** Washington, DC; and Atlanta GA.

44752 ■ Essentials of Management (Canada)
Canadian Management Centre
150 York St., 5th Fl.
Toronto, ON, Canada M5H 3S5
Ph:(866)400-4941 ext. 2252
Free: 877-CMC-2500
Fax: (416)313-4985
Co. E-mail: cmcinfo@cmctraining.org
URL: http://www.cmcamai.org
Price: $1,495 Canadian. **Description:** Covers positioning your workforce up for success, including time management, communication skills, setting goals, and take risks. **Locations:** Toronto, ON.

44753 ■ Executive Effectiveness Course
American Management Association
1601 Broadway
New York, NY 10019
Ph:(212)586-8100

Free: 800-262-9699
Fax: (212)903-8168
Co. E-mail: customerservice@amanet.org
URL: http://www.amanet.org
Price: $4,350.00 for non-members; $3,950.00 for AMA members. **Description:** Nine-day, two-unit seminar for senior executives and managers; covers core values, determining your management style, creating personal goals, and improving key management skills. **Locations:** San Francisco, CA; and New York, NY.

44754 ■ The First 90 Days Workshop (Canada)
Canadian Management Centre
150 York St., 5th Fl.
Toronto, ON, Canada M5H 3S5
Free: 877-CMC-2500
Fax: (416)313-4985
Co. E-mail: cmcinfo@cmctraining.org
URL: http://www.cma.org
Price: $2,250 Canadian. **Description:** Seminar that covers a set of activities that help new leaders diagnose their situations, identify potential vulnerabilities, and develop a plan for building momentum during the transition. **Locations:** Toronto, ON.

44755 ■ Fundamentals of Business Strategy
American Management Association
1601 Broadway
New York, NY 10019
Ph:(212)586-8100
Free: 800-262-9699
Fax: (212)903-8168
Co. E-mail: customerservice@amanet.org
URL: http://www.amanet.org
Price: $1,695 for non-members; $1,495 for AMA members. **Description:** Covers the understanding of the overall strategy process within an organization, and how to enhance its overall success. **Locations:** New York, NY; Washington, DC; Atlanta, GA; Chicago, IL; and San Francisco, CA.

44756 ■ Getting the Most from Change (Canada)
Canadian Management Centre
150 York St., 5th Fl.
Toronto, ON, Canada M5H 3S5
Free: 877-CMC-2500
Fax: (416)313-4985
Co. E-mail: cmcinfo@cmctraining.org
URL: http://www.cma.org
Price: $995 Canadian. **Description:** Seminar that covers adapting to change and how to seize change as on opportunity, including a tool box of ideas for encouraging and supporting change. **Locations:** Toronto, ON.

44757 ■ Getting Results Without Authority (Canada)
Canadian Management Centre
150 York St., 5th Fl.
Toronto, ON, Canada M5H 3S5
Ph:(416)214-5678
Free: 800-262-9699
Fax: (416)313-4985
Co. E-mail: cmcinfo@cmctraining.org
URL: http://cmcamai.org
Price: $1,895.00 Canadian. **Description:** Covers how to achieve results via other employees despite not having direct authority over them. **Locations:** Mississauga, ON; and Toronto, ON.

44758 ■ How to Build a More Positive Work Environment (Canada)
Canadian Management Centre
150 York St., 5th Fl.
Toronto, ON, Canada M5H 3S5
Free: 877-CMC-2500
Fax: (416)313-4985
Co. E-mail: cmcinfo@cmctraining.org
URL: http://www.cma.org
Price: $1,650 Canadian. **Description:** Seminar that covers the causes of negativity and its impact on individuals, teams and organizations, including ways of reducing employee turnover and absenteeism, strate-

gies for handling complainers, challengers, and victims, effective approaches to overcoming negativity, and how to respond when top management is the cause of organization-wide negativity. **Locations:** Toronto, ON.

44759 ■ How to Build Resilience in Your Staff and Yourself

American Management Association
1601 Broadway
New York, NY 10019
Ph:(212)586-8100
Free: 800-262-9699
Fax: (212)903-8168
Co. E-mail: customerservice@amanet.org
URL: http://www.amanet.org
Price: $1,695 for non-members; $1,495 for AMA members. **Description:** Covers communication skills that deliver results, build confidence and trust, adapting to change, and building a productive work environment. **Locations:** New York, NY; Chicago, IL; Atlanta, GA; Washington, DC; and San Francisco, CA.

44760 ■ How to Manage and Organize Accounts Payable

Fred Pryor Seminars
9757 Metcalf Ave.
Overland Park, KS 66212
Free: 800-944-8503
Fax: (913)967-8849
Co. E-mail: customerservice@pryor.com
URL: http://www.careertrack.com
Description: Covers streamlining the AP process, controlling paperwork, eliminating AP errors, and maximizing cash flow. **Locations:** Cities throughout the United States.

44761 ■ How to Manage Workplace Negativity (Canada)

Canadian Management Centre
150 York St., 5th Fl.
Toronto, ON, Canada M5H 3S5
Ph:(416)214-5678
Free: 800-262-9699
Fax: (416)313-4985
Co. E-mail: cmcinfo@cmctraining.org
URL: http://cmcamai.org
Price: $1,650.00 Canadian. **Description:** Covers enhancing team performance; dealing with complainers, blamers, and victims; handling negative perceptions of upper management; motivating employees to change attitude and behavior, and overcoming workplace negativity. **Locations:** Toronto, ON.

44762 ■ How to Overcome Workplace Negativity

Fred Pryor Seminars
9757 Metcalf Ave.
Overland Park, KS 66212
Free: 800-944-8503
Fax: (913)967-8849
Co. E-mail: customerservice@pryor.com
URL: http://www.careertrack.com
Description: Covers recognizing the warning signs of negative behavior, and techniques for diffusing negativity. **Locations:** Cities throughout the United States.

44763 ■ Improving Your Managerial Effectiveness (Canada)

Canadian Management Centre
150 York St., 5th Fl.
Toronto, ON, Canada M5H 3S5
Ph:(416)214-5678
Free: 800-262-9699
Fax: (416)313-4985
Co. E-mail: cmcinfo@cmctraining.org
URL: http://cmcamai.org
Price: $1,995.00 Canadian. **Description:** Addresses issues faced by most management professionals, including personal, operational, organizational, and interpersonal effectiveness in today's workplace. **Locations:** Toronto, ON.

44764 ■ Improving Your Project Management Skills: The Basics for Success

American Management Association
1601 Broadway
New York, NY 10019

Ph:(212)586-8100
Free: 800-262-9699
Fax: (212)903-8168
Co. E-mail: customerservice@amanet.org
URL: http://www.amanet.org
Price: $1,895.00 for non-members; $1,695.00 for AMA members. **Description:** Covers the basic principles of project management, including setting goals and schedules, managing a project plan, estimating, and budgeting. **Locations:** Cities throughout the United States.

44765 ■ Improving Your Project Management Skills: The Basics for Success (Canada)

Canadian Management Centre
150 York St., 5th Fl.
Toronto, ON, Canada M5H 3S5
Ph:(416)214-5678
Free: 800-262-9699
Fax: (416)313-4985
Co. E-mail: cmcinfo@cmctraining.org
URL: http://cmcamai.org
Price: $1,895.00 Canadian. **Description:** Topics include understanding project management, project planning and scheduling, documentation and reporting, and quality control. **Locations:** Calgary, AG; Vancouver, BC; Mississauga, ON; and Toronto, ON.

44766 ■ Information Systems Project Management (Canada)

Canadian Management Centre
150 York St., 5th Fl.
Toronto, ON, Canada M5H 3S5
Ph:(416)214-5678
Free: 800-262-9699
Fax: (416)313-4985
Co. E-mail: cmcinfo@cmctraining.org
URL: http://cmcamai.org
Price: $1,650.00 Canadian. **Description:** Covers key project management techniques, proven characteristics of successful IT projects, estimating and evaluating risks, and establishing project closure. **Locations:** Toronto, ON.

44767 ■ Information Technology Project Management

American Management Association
1601 Broadway
New York, NY 10019
Ph:(212)586-8100
Free: 800-262-9699
Fax: (212)903-8168
Co. E-mail: customerservice@amanet.org
URL: http://www.amanet.org
Price: $1,895 for non-members; $1,695 for AMA members. **Description:** Covers the entire information systems process from start to finish, including budgeting, software tools, and scheduling. **Locations:** Cities throughout the United States.

44768 ■ Introduction to Project Management

EEI Communications
66 Canal Center Plaza, Ste. 200
Alexandria, VA 22314
Ph:(703)683-0683
Fax: (703)683-4915
Co. E-mail: info@eeicommunications.com
URL: http://www.eeicommunications.com
Price: $695.00. **Description:** Topics include understanding project management, characteristics of an effective manager, documentation, and quality control. **Locations:** Silver Spring, MD; and Alexandria, VA.

44769 ■ Leadership Skills for Supervisors (Canada)

Canadian Management Centre
150 York St., 5th Fl.
Toronto, ON, Canada M5H 3S5
Ph:(416)214-5678
Free: 800-262-9699
Fax: (416)313-4985
Co. E-mail: cmcinfo@cmctraining.org
URL: http://cmcamai.org
Price: $1,750.00 Canadian. **Description:** Covers empowering supervisors and staff; using flow chart tech-

niques as a means of assessing work flow and streamlining processes; coaching, mentoring, and providing feedback; organizing and leading productive meetings; and using brainstorming to cultivate ideas. **Locations:** Mississauga, ON; and Toronto, ON.

44770 ■ Leadership and Team Development for Managerial Success

American Management Association
1601 Broadway
New York, NY 10019
Ph:(212)586-8100
Free: 800-262-9699
Fax: (212)903-8168
Co. E-mail: customerservice@amanet.org
URL: http://www.amanet.org
Price: $1,445.00 for non-members; $1,345.00 for AMA members. **Description:** Covers the difference between managing and leading, developing and communicating goals, motivating a team, and various team concepts. **Locations:** Anaheim, CA; San Francisco, CA; Washington, DC; Chicago, IL; and New York, NY.

44771 ■ Leading Virtual and Remote Teams

American Management Association
1601 Broadway
New York, NY 10019
Ph:(212)586-8100
Free: 800-262-9699
Fax: (212)903-8168
Co. E-mail: customerservice@amanet.org
URL: http://www.amanet.org
Price: $1,595.00. **Description:** Covers leadership models, communication between teams, virtual team development, measuring performance, and utilizing technology effectively. **Locations:** San Francisco, CA; Chicago, IL; and New York, NY.

44772 ■ Leading With Emotional Intelligence (Canada)

Canadian Management Centre
150 York St., 5th Fl.
Toronto, ON, Canada M5H 3S5
Ph:(866)400-4941 ext. 2252
Free: 877-CMC-2500
Fax: (416)313-4985
Co. E-mail: cmcinfo@cmctraining.org
URL: http://www.cmcamai.org
Price: $1,595 Canadian. **Description:** Covers building an environment that is productive through the use of positive reinforcement. **Locations:** Toronto, ON.

44773 ■ Making the Transition to Management

American Management Association
1601 Broadway
New York, NY 10019
Ph:(212)586-8100
Free: 800-262-9699
Fax: (212)903-8168
Co. E-mail: customerservice@amanet.org
URL: http://www.amanet.org
Price: $1,375.00 for non-members; $1,275.00 for AMA members. **Description:** Covers various aspects of the transition to manager, understanding what managers do, effective communication and coaching skills, setting attainable goals, and creating a positive atmosphere. **Locations:** San Francisco, CA; Atlanta, GA; Chicago, IL; and New York, NY.

44774 ■ Making the Transition to Management (Canada)

Canadian Management Centre
150 York St., 5th Fl.
Toronto, ON, Canada M5H 3S5
Ph:(866)400-4941 ext. 2252
Free: 877-CMC-2500
Fax: (416)313-4985
Co. E-mail: cmcinfo@cmctraining.org
URL: http://www.cmcamai.org
Price: $1,595 Canadian. **Description:** Covers the skills needed to take on the new managerial position, including planning, organizing, leading, and taking charge. **Locations:** Toronto, ON.

44775 ■ Making the Transition from Staff Member to Supervisor
American Management Association
1601 Broadway
New York, NY 10019
Ph:(212)586-8100
Free: 800-262-9699
Fax: (212)903-8168
Co. E-mail: customerservice@amanet.org
URL: http://www.amanet.org
Price: $1,345.00 for non-members; $1,245.00 for AMA members. **Description:** Covers various aspects of taking on a management position, setting goals, motivation, behavior styles, and time management. **Locations:** San Francisco, CA; Washington, DC; Fort Lauderdale, FL; Atlanta, GA; Chicago, IL; Las Vegas, NV; New York, NY; and Philadelphia, PA.

44776 ■ Making the Transition from Staff Member to Supervisor (Canada)
Canadian Management Centre
150 York St., 5th Fl.
Toronto, ON, Canada M5H 3S5
Ph:(416)214-5678
Free: 800-262-9699
Fax: (416)313-4985
Co. E-mail: cmcinfo@cmctraining.org
URL: http://cmcamai.org
Price: $1,650.00 Canadian. **Description:** Covers various aspects of the transition to manager, understanding what managers do, effective communication and coaching skills, setting attainable goals, and creating a positive atmosphere. **Locations:** Calgary, AB; Vancouver, BC; Mississauga, ON; and Toronto, ON.

44777 ■ The Management Course (Canada)
Canadian Management Centre
150 York St., 5th Fl.
Toronto, ON, Canada M5H 3S5
Ph:(416)214-5678
Free: 800-262-9699
Fax: (416)313-4985
Co. E-mail: cmcinfo@cmctraining.org
URL: http://cmcamai.org
Price: $8,000.00 Canadian. **Description:** Four-week, four-unit seminar for experienced executives; covers overviews of management, finance, marketing, and leadership. **Locations:** Vancouver, BC; and Toronto, ON.

44778 ■ The Management Course: Finance
American Management Association
1601 Broadway
New York, NY 10019
Ph:(212)586-8100
Free: 800-262-9699
Fax: (212)903-8168
Co. E-mail: customerservice@amanet.org
URL: http://www.amanet.org
Price: $2,195.00 for non-members; $1,995.00 for AMA members. **Description:** Covers financial knowledge crucial for managers, financial and accounting vocabulary, communicating with financial executives, financial planning, and cash flow. **Locations:** San Francisco, CA; Sanibel, FL; and Atlanta, GA.

44779 ■ The Management Course: Leadership
American Management Association
1601 Broadway
New York, NY 10019
Ph:(212)586-8100
Free: 800-262-9699
Fax: (212)903-8168
Co. E-mail: customerservice@amanet.org
URL: http://www.amanet.org
Price: $2,195.00 for non-members; $1,995.00 for AMA members. **Description:** Covers using leadership skills to motivate and inspire teams. **Locations:** Chicago, IL; and Hilton Head, SC.

44780 ■ The Management Course: Marketing
American Management Association
1601 Broadway
New York, NY 10019
Ph:(212)586-8100
Free: 800-262-9699

Fax: (212)903-8168
Co. E-mail: customerservice@amanet.org
URL: http://www.amanet.org
Price: $2,195.00 for non-members; $1,995.00 for AMA members. **Description:** Covers the value of marketing to an organization, marketing tools and analysis, positive communication with marketing professionals, and using marketing to improve profits. **Locations:** San Francisco, CA; and Washington, DC.

44781 ■ Management Course for Supervisors (Canada)
Canadian Management Centre
150 York St., 5th Fl.
Toronto, ON, Canada M5H 3S5
Ph:(416)214-5678
Free: 800-262-9699
Fax: (416)313-4985
Co. E-mail: cmcinfo@cmctraining.org
URL: http://cmcamai.org
Price: $1,795.00 Canadian. **Description:** Covers emotional intelligence, organizational structures, diversity initiatives, leadership styles, delegation techniques, team building, and motivating staff. **Locations:** Toronto, ON.

44782 ■ Management Mastery: Accelerating Your Management Potential (Canada)
Canadian Management Centre
150 York St., 5th Fl.
Toronto, ON, Canada M5H 3S5
Ph:(866)400-4941 ext. 2252
Free: 877-CMC-2500
Fax: (416)313-4985
Co. E-mail: cmcinfo@cmctraining.org
URL: http://www.cmcamai.org
Price: $2,495 Canadian. **Description:** Covers the key components for successful business practice, including finance, marketing, and leadership. **Locations:** Toronto, ON.

44783 ■ Management Problems of the Technical Person in a Leadership Role
Fred Pryor Seminars
9757 Metcalf Ave.
Overland Park, KS 66212
Free: 800-944-8503
Fax: (913)967-8849
Co. E-mail: customerservice@pryor.com
URL: http://www.careertrack.com
Description: Seminar for technical professionals who have recently been assigned a supervisory role; covers task delegation, conflict resolution, problem solving, and issues faced by many technical professionals who must learn to work with non-technical staff members. **Locations:** Cities throughout the United States.

44784 ■ Management Skills for Administrative Professionals
American Management Association
1601 Broadway
New York, NY 10019
Ph:(212)586-8100
Free: 800-262-9699
Fax: (212)903-8168
Co. E-mail: customerservice@amanet.org
URL: http://www.amanet.org
Price: $1,495.00 for non-members; $1,395.00 for AMA members. **Description:** Geared towards the experienced administrative professional, this seminar covers effective communication skills, conflict resolution, organizational skills, partnering with your boss, and setting attainable goals. **Locations:** Cities throughout the United States.

44785 ■ Management Skills for Administrative Professionals (Canada)
Canadian Management Centre
150 York St., 5th Fl.
Toronto, ON, Canada M5H 3S5
Ph:(866)400-4941 ext. 2252
Free: 877-CMC-2500
Fax: (416)313-4985
Co. E-mail: cmcinfo@cmctraining.org
URL: http://www.cmcamai.org
Price: $1,395 Canadian. **Description:** Covers strategies for moving your company forward with the use of

teamwork, including delegating, effective communication, positioning priorities, influence, motivate, and problem solving skills. **Locations:** Toronto, ON.

44786 ■ Management Skills for New Managers (Canada)
Canadian Management Centre
150 York St., 5th Fl.
Toronto, ON, Canada M5H 3S5
Ph:(866)400-4941 ext. 2252
Free: 877-CMC-2500
Fax: (416)313-4985
Co. E-mail: cmcinfo@cmctraining.org
URL: http://www.cmctraining.org
Price: $1,895 Canadian. **Description:** Covers effective strategies to keep up with corporate change or trends, including communication, motivation of employees to drive performance, and the ability to handle diverse situations. **Locations:** Toronto and Mississauga, ON.

44787 ■ Management Skills for New Supervisors
American Management Association
1601 Broadway
New York, NY 10019
Ph:(212)586-8100
Free: 800-262-9699
Fax: (212)903-8168
Co. E-mail: customerservice@amanet.org
URL: http://www.amanet.org
Price: $1,795 for non-members; $1,595 for AMA members. **Description:** For new supervisors with one or two years of supervisory experience; covers organization, communication, time management skills, and problem solving within the business environment. **Locations:** Cities throughout the United States.

44788 ■ Management Skills for New Supervisors (Canada)
Canadian Management Centre
150 York St., 5th Fl.
Toronto, ON, Canada M5H 3S5
Ph:(416)214-5678
Free: 800-262-9699
Fax: (416)313-4985
Co. E-mail: cmcinfo@cmctraining.org
URL: http://cmcamai.org
Price: $1,795.00 Canadian. **Description:** Covers management skills, including planning, organizing, communication, constructive criticism, motivation, and coaching. **Locations:** Calgary, AB; Vancouver, BC; Mississauga, ON; and Toronto, ON.

44789 ■ Managerial Skills of the New Supervisors
1601 Broadway
New York, NY 12983
Ph:(518)891-1500
Free: 800-262-9699
Fax: (518)891-0368
Co. E-mail: customerservice@amanet.org
URL: http://www.amanet.org
Price: $1795.00 ($1595.00 for AMA members). **Description:** Program topics include handling managerial responsibilities; utilizing leadership style; facilitating communication; motivating staff; coaching staff; delegating responsibilities; doing performance appraisals; and time management. **Locations:** Cities throughout the United States.

44790 ■ Managerial and Team-building Skills for Project Managers
American Management Association
1601 Broadway
New York, NY 10019
Ph:(212)586-8100
Free: 800-262-9699
Fax: (212)903-8168
Co. E-mail: customerservice@amanet.org
URL: http://www.amanet.org
Price: $1,895.00 for non-members; $1,695.00 for AMA members. **Description:** Covers improving people skills in order to create a powerful, cooperative project team. **Locations:** Atlanta, GA; and New York, NY.

44791 ■ Managerial and Team-building Skills for Project Managers (Canada)
Canadian Management Centre
150 York St., 5th Fl.
Toronto, ON, Canada M5H 3S5
Ph:(416)214-5678
Free: 800-262-9699
Fax: (416)313-4985
Co. E-mail: cmcinfo@cmctraining.org
URL: http://cmcamai.org
Price: $1,750.00 Canadian. **Description:** Covers improving people skills in order to create a powerful, cooperative project team. **Locations:** Mississauga, ON; and Toronto, ON.

44792 ■ Managing Chaos: Dynamic Time Management, Recall, Reading, and Stress
American Management Association
1601 Broadway
New York, NY 10019
Ph:(212)586-8100
Free: 800-262-9699
Fax: (212)903-8168
Co. E-mail: customerservice@amanet.org
URL: http://www.amanet.org
Price: $1,445.00 for non-members; $1,295.00 for AMA members. **Description:** Covers Management Skills for Administrative Professionals learning techniques, productive planning, setting goals, and methods of controlling stress. **Locations:** Cities throughout the United States.

44793 ■ Managing Chaos: How to set Priorities And Make Decisions Under Pressure
American Management Association
1601 Broadway
New York, NY 10019
Ph:(212)586-8100
Free: 800-262-9699
Fax: (212)903-8168
Co. E-mail: customerservice@amanet.org
URL: http://www.amanet.org
Price: $1,695.00 for non-members; $1,495.00 for AMA members. **Description:** Covers practical tools to prepare for unpredictable demands and balance changing priorities.

44794 ■ Managing Chaos: How to set Priorities and make Decisions Under Pressure (Canada)
Canadian Management Centre
150 York St., 5th Fl.
Toronto, ON, Canada M5H 3S5
Ph:(416)214-5678
Free: 800-262-9699
Fax: (416)313-4985
Co. E-mail: cmcinfo@cmctraining.org
URL: http://cmcamai.org
Price: $1,395.00 Canadian. **Description:** Covers techniques for prioritizing, improving mental focus, developing memory skills, and reducing stress. **Locations:** Toronto, ON and Ottawa, ON.

44795 ■ Managing Chaos: How to Set Priorities and Make Decisions Under Pressure
American Management Association
1601 Broadway
New York, NY 10019
Ph:(212)586-8100
Free: 800-262-9699
Fax: (212)903-8168
Co. E-mail: customerservice@amanet.org
URL: http://www.amanet.org
Price: $1,695 for non-members; $1,495 for AMA members. **Description:** Covers making the critical decisions under stress, direct the effort of others through knowledgeable information, and keep focused to move forward. **Locations:** New York, NY; Atlanta, GA; Chicago, IL; Washington, DC; Las Vegas, NV; and San Francisco, CA.

44796 ■ Managing Chaos: How to Set Priorities and Make Decisions Under Pressure (Canada)
Canadian Management Centre
150 York St., 5th Fl.
Toronto, ON, Canada M5H 3S5

Ph:(866)400-4941 ext. 2252
Free: 877-CMC-2500
Fax: (416)313-4985
Co. E-mail: cmcinfo@cmctraining.org
URL: http://www.cmcamai.org
Price: $1,395 Canadian. **Description:** Covers getting results in an ever changing work environment, including prioritizing, listening skill techniques, asking the right questions that offer you the feedback you need, how to remain focused, and effective decision making under pressure. **Locations:** Toronto, ON.

44797 ■ Managing Communications in a Crisis
EEI Communications
66 Canal Ctr. Plz., Ste. 200
Alexandria, VA 22314-5507
Ph:(703)683-7453
Free: 888-253-2762
Fax: (703)683-7310
Co. E-mail: train@eeicommunications.com
URL: http://www.eeicommunications.com/training
Price: $595. **Description:** Seminar for middle to senior management, public relations and marketing staff. Covers the basic principles of effective crisis management, including defining a crisis, the crisis team and plan, when to act and when to talk, crisis communications, the 10 commandments, news briefing and the working manual. **Locations:** Alexandria, VA; Silver Spring, MD; and Washington, DC.

44798 ■ Managing the Distributor Sales Network
American Management Association
1601 Broadway
New York, NY 10019
Ph:(212)586-8100
Free: 800-262-9699
Fax: (212)903-8168
Co. E-mail: customerservice@amanet.org
URL: http://www.amanet.org
Price: $1,795.00 for non-members; $1,695.00 for AMA members. **Description:** Three-day workshop covers distributors and their role in sales channels, motivating the distributor, developing performance measures, and distributor training. **Locations:** San Francisco, CA; Washington, DC; Fort Lauderdale, FL; and Chicago, IL.

44799 ■ Managing the Distributor Sales Network (Canada)
Canadian Management Centre
150 York St., 5th Fl.
Toronto, ON, Canada M5H 3S5
Ph:(416)214-5678
Free: 800-262-9699
Fax: (416)313-4985
Co. E-mail: cmcinfo@cmctraining.org
URL: http://cmcamai.org
Price: $1,695.00 Canadian. **Description:** Three-day workshop covers distributors and their role in sales channels, negotiating agreements, designing a sales program, and legal issues. **Locations:** Toronto, ON.

44800 ■ Managing Enterprise-wide Projects
American Management Association
1601 Broadway
New York, NY 10019
Ph:(212)586-8100
Free: 800-262-9699
Fax: (212)903-8168
Co. E-mail: customerservice@amanet.org
URL: http://www.amanet.org
Price: $1,895 for non-members; $1,695 for AMA members. **Description:** Covers the overall completion and importance of projects, including risk management, global projects, and fundamentals of project control systems. **Locations:** New York, NY; San Francisco, CA; Chicago, IL.

44801 ■ Managing Managers: Bridging Strategy and Implementation
American Management Association
1601 Broadway
New York, NY 10019
Ph:(212)586-8100
Free: 800-262-9699

Fax: (212)903-8168
Co. E-mail: customerservice@amanet.org
URL: http://www.amanet.org
Price: $1,995.00 for non-members; $1,795.00 for AMA members. **Description:** Covers how to effectively manage managers, characteristics of managers, delegation, communication, coaching, and motivation. **Locations:** Atlanta, GA; Chicago, IL; and New York, NY.

44802 ■ Managing Scientists in Industry
American Management Association
1601 Broadway
New York, NY 10019
Ph:(212)586-8100
Free: 800-262-9699
Fax: (212)903-8168
Co. E-mail: customerservice@amanet.org
URL: http://www.amanet.org
Price: $1,795.00 for non-members; $1,695.00 for AMA members. **Description:** Covers the scientific function of organizations, building successful relationships with scientific units, and skills for managing science professionals. **Locations:** Washington, DC.

44803 ■ Managing Technical Professionals (Canada)
Canadian Management Centre
150 York St., 5th Fl.
Toronto, ON, Canada M5H 3S5
Ph:(416)214-5678
Free: 800-262-9699
Fax: (416)313-4985
Co. E-mail: cmcinfo@cmctraining.org
URL: http://cmcamai.org
Price: $1,795.00 Canadian. **Description:** Seminar for technical professionals who have been recently assigned a managerial role; covers developing and implementing a management style, motivating employees to increase productivity, assessing the performance of technical staff, and related issues. **Locations:** Toronto, ON.

44804 ■ Managing Today's IT and Technical Professionals (Canada)
Canadian Management Centre
150 York St., 5th Fl.
Toronto, ON, Canada M5H 3S5
Free: 877-CMC-2500
Fax: (416)313-4985
Co. E-mail: cmcinfo@cmctraining.org
URL: http://www.cma.org
Price: $1,895 Canadian. **Description:** Seminar that covers aligning goals with overall business goals, identify needed competencies before staffing, managing meetings, establishing individual and departmental goals, coaching and providing constructive feedback. **Locations:** Toronto, ON.

44805 ■ Managing a World-Class IT Department
American Management Association
1601 Broadway
New York, NY 10019
Ph:(212)586-8100
Free: 800-262-9699
Fax: (212)903-8168
Co. E-mail: customerservice@amanet.org
URL: http://www.amanet.org
Price: $1,795.00 for non-members; $1,695.00 for AMA members. **Description:** Three-day seminar for new or prospective IT managers; covers leadership techniques, common challenges, budgeting, planning, testing, and decision making. **Locations:** Anaheim, CA; San Francisco, CA; Atlanta, GA; New York, NY; and Dallas, TX.

44806 ■ Managing a World-Class IT Department (Canada)
Canadian Management Centre
150 York St., 5th Fl.
Toronto, ON, Canada M5H 3S5
Ph:(866)400-4941 ext. 2252
Free: 877-CMC-2500
Fax: (416)313-4985
Co. E-mail: cmcinfo@cmctraining.org
URL: http://www.cmcamai.org

Price: $1,395 Canadian. **Description:** Covers all the skills necessary to operate the IT department, including selection of vendors, decision making skills, positive teamwork performance, and a course of action. **Locations:** Toronto, ON.

44807 ■ Managing Your Marketing Communications Mix for Better Bottom-Line Results
American Management Association
1601 Broadway
New York, NY 10019
Ph:(212)586-8100
Free: 800-262-9699
Fax: (212)903-8168
Co. E-mail: customerservice@amanet.org
URL: http://www.amanet.org
Price: $1,795.00 for non-members; $1,595.00 for AMA members. **Description:** Covers the complete marketing program, increasing profits through marketing, different types of media, and evaluating your program. **Locations:** San Francisco, CA; and Chicago, IL.

44808 ■ Managing Your Marketing Communications Mix for Better Bottom Line Results (Canada)
Canadian Management Centre
150 York St., 5th Fl.
Toronto, ON, Canada M5H 3S5
Ph:(416)214-5678
Free: 800-262-9699
Fax: (416)313-4985
Co. E-mail: cmcinfo@cmctraining.org
URL: http://cmcamai.org
Price: $1,750.00 Canadian. **Description:** Covers the complete marketing program, increasing profits through marketing, different types of media, and evaluating your program. **Locations:** Toronto, ON.

44809 ■ Master Organizational Politics, Influence and Alliances
American Management Association
1601 Broadway
New York, NY 10019
Ph:(212)586-8100
Free: 800-262-9699
Fax: (212)903-8168
Co. E-mail: customerservice@amanet.org
URL: http://www.amanet.org
Price: $1,795.00 for non-members; $1,695.00 for AMA members. **Description:** Three-day seminar for experienced supervisors; covers driving high performance, relationship management, coaching, delegating, and your political image. **Locations:** Chicago, IL.

44810 ■ Mastering Organizational Politics, Influence and Alliance: The Winning Formula for Experienced Managers (Canada)
Canadian Management Centre
150 York St., 5th Fl.
Toronto, ON, Canada M5H 3S5
Ph:(866)400-4941 ext. 2252
Free: 877-CMC-2500
Fax: (416)313-4985
Co. E-mail: cmcinfo@cmctraining.org
URL: http://www.cmcamai.org
Price: $1,595 Canadian. **Description:** Covers techniques to manage throughout the organization, skills to tackle negative political issues, distinguish between politics and influence, and improve operations through team effort. **Locations:** Toronto, ON.

44811 ■ Mastering Organizational Politics, Influence and Alliances: The Winning Formula for Experienced Managers
American Management Association
1601 Broadway
New York, NY 10019
Ph:(212)586-8100
Free: 800-262-9699
Fax: (212)903-8168
Co. E-mail: customerservice@amanet.org
URL: http://www.amanet.org
Price: $1,895 for non-members; $1,695 for AMA members. **Description:** Covers integration of team performance to gain end results. **Locations:** Cities throughout the United States. .

44812 ■ Maximum Performance Leadership (Canada)
Canadian Management Centre
150 York St., 5th Fl.
Toronto, ON, Canada M5H 3S5
Ph:(416)214-5678
Free: 800-262-9699
Fax: (416)313-4985
Co. E-mail: cmcinfo@cmctraining.org
URL: http://cmcamai.org
Price: $1,995.00 Canadian. **Description:** Covers advanced leadership skills for managers with several years of experience. **Locations:** Vancouver, BC; and Toronto, ON.

44813 ■ Mentoring: Building Employee Relationships and Increasing Productivity (Canada)
Canadian Management Centre
150 York St., 5th Fl.
Toronto, ON, Canada M5H 3S5
Ph:(416)214-5678
Free: 800-262-9699
Fax: (416)313-4985
Co. E-mail: cmcinfo@cmctraining.org
URL: http://cmcamai.org
Price: $1,595.00 Canadian. **Description:** Covers the design and implementation of an effective mentoring program in order to improve employee output and performance. **Locations:** Toronto, ON.

44814 ■ Moving from an Operational Manager to a Strategic Leader
American Management Association
1601 Broadway
New York, NY 10019
Ph:(212)586-8100
Free: 800-262-9699
Fax: (212)903-8168
Co. E-mail: customerservice@amanet.org
URL: http://www.amanet.org
Price: $1,795.00 for non-members; $1,695.00 for AMA members. **Description:** Covers strategic leadership approaches, instigating positive change, risk taking, and effective leadership styles and communication. **Locations:** San Francisco, CA; Orlando, FL; Atlanta, GA; Chicago, IL; Las Vegas, NV; and New York, NY.

44815 ■ Moving from an Operational Manager to a Strategic Thinker
American Management Association
1601 Broadway
New York, NY 10019
Ph:(212)586-8100
Free: 800-262-9699
Fax: (212)903-8168
Co. E-mail: customerservice@amanet.org
URL: http://www.amanet.org
Price: $1,895 for non-members; $1,695 for AMA members. **Description:** For managers with two or more years of experience; covers influential strategic thinking to move your team into action, build good customer relations, and know when to take risks to advance your goals. **Locations:** Cities throughout the United States.

44816 ■ Moving from Operational Manager to Strategic Thinker (Canada)
Canadian Management Centre
150 York St., 5th Fl.
Toronto, ON, Canada M5H 3S5
Ph:(866)400-4941 ext. 2252
Free: 877-CMC-2500
Fax: (416)313-4985
Co. E-mail: cmcinfo@cmctraining.org
URL: http://www.cmcamai.org
Price: $1,995 Canadian. **Description:** Covers the key components of a strategic leader, including effective communication skills, ability to recognize opportunity, and adapting to change. **Locations:** Toronto, ON.

44817 ■ The Newly Promoted African-American Manager and Supervisor: Making the Transition
American Management Association
1601 Broadway
New York, NY 10019

Ph:(212)586-8100
Free: 800-262-9699
Fax: (212)903-8168
Co. E-mail: customerservice@amanet.org
URL: http://www.amanet.org
Price: $1,575.00 for non-members; $1,475.00 for AMA members. **Description:** Covers overcoming psychological barriers, developing a personal action plan, office politics, and motivating your team. **Locations:** Atlanta, GA; and Chicago, IL.

44818 ■ Outrageous Confidence for Administrative Excellence (Canada)
Canadian Management Centre
150 York St., 5th Fl.
Toronto, ON, Canada M5H 3S5
Free: 877-CMC-2500
Fax: (416)313-4985
Co. E-mail: cmcinfo@cmctraining.org
URL: http://www.cma.org
Price: $695 Canadian. **Description:** Seminar covering strategies to tackle anything that comes your way, including speaking with greater clarity, confidence and professionalism, coping with changing priorities, effectively manage deadlines, and improve your self-image and the way others view you. **Locations:** Toronto, ON.

44819 ■ Performance Development and Appraisal: A Manager's Plan for Action
American Management Association
1601 Broadway
New York, NY 10019
Ph:(212)586-8100
Free: 800-262-9699
Fax: (212)903-8168
Co. E-mail: customerservice@amanet.org
URL: http://www.amanet.org
Price: $1,695 for non-members; $1,495 for AMA members. **Description:** Covers the skills necessary to develop overall performance, including the preparation, and delivery of the organizations year-end review. **Locations:** New York, NY; Atlanta, GA; Chicago, IL; Washington, DC; and San Francisco, CA.

44820 ■ The Performance Driven Leader (Canada)
Canadian Management Centre
150 York St., 5th Fl.
Toronto, ON, Canada M5H 3S5
Ph:(866)400-4941 ext. 2252
Free: 877-CMC-2500
Fax: (416)313-4985
Co. E-mail: cmcinfo@cmctraining.org
URL: http://www.cmcamai.org
Price: $1,895 Canadian. **Description:** Covers the expectations of leadership that your team expects, including time management, guide with the use of skill and progression, and be able to praise for a job well done. **Locations:** Toronto, ON.

44821 ■ Personnel Law for Managers and Supervisors
Fred Pryor Seminars
9757 Metcalf Ave.
Overland Park, KS 66212
Free: 800-944-8503
Fax: (913)967-8849
Co. E-mail: customerservice@pryor.com
URL: http://www.careertrack.com
Description: Covers personnel laws, pending legal actions, and how to handle legal difficulties. **Locations:** Cities throughout the United States.

44822 ■ Planning and Managing Organizational Change
American Management Association
1601 Broadway
New York, NY 10019
Ph:(212)586-8100
Free: 800-262-9699
Fax: (212)903-8168
Co. E-mail: customerservice@amanet.org
URL: http://www.amanet.org
Price: $1,695 for non-members; $1,495 for AMA members. **Description:** For managers responsible for

the changing environment within the organization; covers adapting to change in a positive way, effective communication skills, and the ability to obtain positive results. **Locations:** New York, NY; Chicago, IL; Atlanta, GA; Washington, DC; and San Francisco, CA.

44823 ■ Preparing for Leadership: What It Takes to Take the Lead (Canada)

Canadian Management Centre
150 York St., 5th Fl.
Toronto, ON, Canada M5H 3S5
Ph:(416)214-5678
Free: 800-262-9699
Fax: (416)313-4985
Co. E-mail: cmcinfo@cmctraining.org
URL: http://cmcamai.org
Price: $1,650.00 Canadian. **Description:** Covers leadership roles, the characteristics of leaders, dealing with organizational politics, and creating an action plan. **Locations:** Toronto, ON.

44824 ■ Problem Solving and Decision Making Workshop

American Management Association
1601 Broadway
New York, NY 10019
Ph:(212)586-8100
Free: 800-262-9699
Fax: (212)903-8168
Co. E-mail: customerservice@amanet.org
URL: http://www.amanet.org
Price: $1,695 for non-members; $1,495 for AMA members. **Description:** Covers recognizing a problem and implementing your solving skills, strategies to move through the barriers, and effective decision making to guide you through the process. **Locations:** New York, NY; Atlanta, GA; Washington, DC; and San Francisco, CA.

44825 ■ Process Management: Applying Process Mapping to Analyze and Improve

American Management Association
1601 Broadway
New York, NY 10019
Ph:(212)586-8100
Free: 800-262-9699
Fax: (212)903-8168
Co. E-mail: customerservice@amanet.org
URL: http://www.amanet.org
Price: $1,895 for non-members; $1,695 for AMA members. **Description:** Covers process mapping skills, an understanding of the process, and techniques to improve overall performance. **Locations:** New York, NY; Chicago, IL; Washington, DC; Atlanta, GA; and San Francisco, CA.

44826 ■ Process Management: Applying Process Mapping to Analyze and Improve Your Operation (Canada)

Canadian Management Centre
150 York St., 5th Fl.
Toronto, ON, Canada M5H 3S5
Free: 877-CMC-2500
Fax: (416)313-4985
Co. E-mail: cmcinfo@cmctraining.org
URL: http://www.cma.org
Price: $1,995 Canadian. **Description:** Seminar that covers process mapping techniques, and application and documentation of standard operation procedures, including work simplification analysis and value added versus non-value added activity analysis. **Locations:** Toronto, ON.

44827 ■ Process Management Process Mapping and Work Simplification

American Management Association
1601 Broadway
New York, NY 10019
Ph:(212)586-8100
Free: 800-262-9699
Fax: (212)903-8168
Co. E-mail: customerservice@amanet.org
URL: http://www.amanet.org
Price: $1,895 for non-members; $1,695 for AMA members. **Description:** Covers methods of improving productivity, including recognizing cost cutting factors

followed by course of action, and gain understanding of how each procedure interacts into the entire operation. **Locations:** New York, NY; Atlanta, GA; Chicago, IL; and San Francisco, CA.

44828 ■ Project Change Management

EEI Communications
66 Canal Ctr. Plz., Ste. 200
Alexandria, VA 22314-5507
Ph:(703)683-7453
Free: 888-253-2762
Fax: (703)683-7310
Co. E-mail: train@eeicommunications.com
URL: http://www.eeicommunications.com/training
Price: $695. **Description:** Seminar based on the Project Management Institute's (PMI) Project Management Body of Knowledge (PMBOK) that covers the principles of change management as applied to project management and products, including change control system, configuration management, coordinating changes throughout the project, and change management and project closure. **Locations:** Alexandria, VA; Silver Spring, MD; and Washington, DC.

44829 ■ Project Management for Administrative Professionals

American Management Association
1601 Broadway
New York, NY 10019
Ph:(212)586-8100
Free: 800-262-9699
Fax: (212)903-8168
Co. E-mail: customerservice@amanet.org
URL: http://www.amanet.org
Price: $1,545.00 for non-members; $1,395.00 for AMA members. **Description:** Covers methods for planning, controlling, organizing, and tracking projects; problem solving techniques; and time management. **Locations:** Washington, DC; Atlanta, GA; and New York, NY.

44830 ■ Project Management for Administrative Professionals (Canada)

Canadian Management Centre
150 York St., 5th Fl.
Toronto, ON, Canada M5H 3S5
Ph:(866)400-4941 ext. 2252
Free: 877-CMC-2500
Fax: (416)313-4985
Co. E-mail: cmcinfo@cmctraining.org
URL: http://www.cmcamai.org
Price: $1,550 Canadian. **Description:** Covers the effective use of project management tools to take your project through to completion, including problem-solving skills, and teamwork. **Locations:** Toronto, ON.

44831 ■ Project Management for Multimedia

EEI Communications
66 Canal Center Plaza, Ste. 200
Alexandria, VA 22314
Ph:(703)683-0683
Fax: (703)683-4915
Co. E-mail: info@eeicommunications.com
URL: http://www.eeicommunications.com
Price: $395.00. **Description:** Covers the steps involved in producing a CD-ROM or multimedia project. **Locations:** Silver Spring, MD; and Alexandria, VA.

44832 ■ The Project Management Office: A Modern Tool for Successful Projects

American Management Association
1601 Broadway
New York, NY 10019
Ph:(212)586-8100
Free: 800-262-9699
Fax: (212)903-8168
Co. E-mail: customerservice@amanet.org
URL: http://www.amanet.org
Price: $1,895 for non-members; $1,695 for AMA members. **Description:** Covers six levels of project management potential, including integrating the project manager into the organization, and calculation of costs. **Locations:** New York, NY; Atlanta, GA; Chicago, IL; and San Francisco, CA.

44833 ■ Project Management for Publications

EEI Communications
66 Canal Center Plaza, Ste. 200
Alexandria, VA 22314
Ph:(703)683-0683
Fax: (703)683-4915
Co. E-mail: info@eeicommunications.com
URL: http://www.eeicommunications.com
Price: $395.00. **Description:** Covers project management techniques for publications. **Locations:** Silver Spring, MD; and Alexandria, VA.

44834 ■ Project Management Status Reporting: How Creating More Effective Status Reports Can Improve Project Quality and Success

American Management Association
1601 Broadway
New York, NY 10019
Ph:(212)586-8100
Free: 800-262-9699
Fax: (212)903-8168
Co. E-mail: customerservice@amanet.org
URL: http://www.amanet.org
Price: $1,595.00 for non-members; $1,495.00 for AMA members. **Description:** Covers project tracking, providing feedback to project teams, and planning and implementing a system for project status reporting and communicating. **Locations:** Atlanta, GA.

44835 ■ Project Management for Streaming DVD, and Multimedia

EEI Communications
66 Canal Ctr. Plz., Ste. 200
Alexandria, VA 22314-5507
Ph:(703)683-7453
Free: 888-253-2762
Fax: (703)683-7310
Co. E-mail: train@eeicommunications.com
URL: http://www.eeicommunications.com/training
Price: $395. **Description:** Covers an overview of the steps involved in bringing a multimedia or CD-ROM project to completion, including audience and purpose analysis, information and graphic design, planning and resources, managing the creative process, scheduling and budgeting, quality control, and video and sound options. **Locations:** Alexandria, VA; Silver Spring, MD; and Washington, DC.

44836 ■ Project Management for Web Development

EEI Communications
66 Canal Center Plaza, Ste. 200
Alexandria, VA 22314
Ph:(703)683-0683
Fax: (703)683-4915
Co. E-mail: info@eeicommunications.com
URL: http://www.eeicommunications.com
Price: $395.00. **Description:** Covers the basics of managing and maintaining the development of a website. **Locations:** Silver Spring, MD; and Alexandria, VA.

44837 ■ Project Office Development (Canada)

Canadian Management Centre
150 York St., 5th Fl.
Toronto, ON, Canada M5H 3S5
Free: 877-CMC-2500
Fax: (416)313-4985
Co. E-mail: cmcinfo@cmctraining.org
URL: http://www.cma.org
Price: $995 Canadian. **Description:** Covers how to develop a framework to establish a more effective project management processes and tools, including objectives, costs and benefits, preparing for a project office, functions, matching function needs, goal setting, and delivering key projects on time. **Locations:** Toronto, ON.

44838 ■ Risk Management for Project Managers

American Management Association
1601 Broadway
New York, NY 10019
Ph:(212)586-8100

Free: 800-262-9699
Fax: (212)903-8168
Co. E-mail: customerservice@amanet.org
URL: http://www.amanet.org
Price: $1,695.00 for non-members; $1,595.00 for AMA members. **Description:** Covers the importance of risk management, identifying risk, and techniques for planning for and dealing with project risks. **Locations:** San Francisco, CA.

44839 ■ Senior Project Management
American Management Association
1601 Broadway
New York, NY 10019
Ph:(212)586-8100
Free: 800-262-9699
Fax: (212)903-8168
Co. E-mail: customerservice@amanet.org
URL: http://www.amanet.org
Price: $1,895 for non-members; $1,795.00 for AMA members. **Description:** Covers project management basics, measuring project accomplishments, trends, human factors, and automated and administrative project support. **Locations:** San Francisco, CA; Washington, DC; Atlanta, GA; Chicago, IL; and New York, NY.

44840 ■ Senior Project Management (Canada)
Canadian Management Centre
150 York St., 5th Fl.
Toronto, ON, Canada M5H 3S5
Ph:(416)214-5678
Free: 800-262-9699
Fax: (416)313-4985
Co. E-mail: cmcinfo@cmctraining.org
URL: http://cmcamai.org
Price: $2,195.00 Canadian. **Description:** Covers project management basics, measuring project accomplishments, trends, human factors, and automated and administrative project support. **Locations:** Toronto, ON.

44841 ■ Seven Steps to a Successful Business Plan (Canada)
Canadian Management Centre
150 York St., 5th Fl.
Toronto, ON, Canada M5H 3S5
Ph:(866)400-4941 ext. 2252
Free: 877-CMC-2500
Fax: (416)313-4985
Co. E-mail: cmcinfo@cmctraining.org
URL: http://www.cmcamai.org
Price: $1,795 Canadian. **Description:** Covers the processes of implementing an effective business plan to meet your overall objectives, including exploring the main reason for a business plan, and putting it to use. **Locations:** Toronto, ON.

44842 ■ Situational Leadership II Workshop
American Management Association
1601 Broadway
New York, NY 10019
Ph:(212)586-8100
Free: 800-262-9699
Fax: (212)903-8168
Co. E-mail: customerservice@amanet.org
URL: http://www.amanet.org
Price: $1,895 for non-members; $1,695 for AMA members. **Description:** Covers examining the concept of a situational leader, managing change and diversity in the workplace, flexibility, and incorporating various skills to get performance. **Locations:** New York, NY; Washington, DC; San Francisco, CA; Chicago, IL; and Atlanta, GA.

44843 ■ A Six Sigma Approach to Achieving Project Management Quality
American Management Association
1601 Broadway
New York, NY 10019
Ph:(212)586-8100
Free: 800-262-9699
Fax: (212)903-8168
Co. E-mail: customerservice@amanet.org
URL: http://www.amanet.org
Price: $1,895 for non-members; $1,695 for AMA members. **Description:** Covers the basic principals of

project management, including constructive communication, and managing a successful project through the use of delegating. **Locations:** New York, NY; Atlanta, GA; Chicago, IL; and Washington, DC.

44844 ■ Stepping Up to Leadership: A Course for Administrative Professionals
American Management Association
1601 Broadway
New York, NY 10019
Ph:(212)586-8100
Free: 800-262-9699
Fax: (212)903-8168
Co. E-mail: customerservice@amanet.org
URL: http://www.amanet.org
Price: $1,545 for non-members; $1,395 for AMA members. **Description:** Covers strategies to influence and lead within the organization, building confidence, and coaching skills. **Locations:** Washington, DC.

44845 ■ Stepping Up to Leadership: A Course for Administrative Professionals (Canada)
Canadian Management Centre
150 York St., 5th Fl.
Toronto, ON, Canada M5H 3S5
Free: 877-CMC-2500
Fax: (416)313-4985
Co. E-mail: cmcinfo@cmctraining.org
URL: http://www.cma.org
Price: $1,695 Canadian. **Description:** Seminar that covers the role of leadership, including attitudes and barriers that prevent you from taking a leadership role, create partnerships that get you the information you need, team leading without the authority, Emotional Intelligence (EI), and career development strategies. **Locations:** Toronto, ON.

44846 ■ Strategic Planning: Processes for Formulating Winning Strategies
American Management Association
1601 Broadway
New York, NY 10019
Ph:(212)586-8100
Free: 800-262-9699
Fax: (212)903-8168
Co. E-mail: customerservice@amanet.org
URL: http://www.amanet.org
Price: $1,995 for non-members; $1,795 for AMA members. **Description:** Covers the structure of strategy, including integration and objectives. **Locations:** Cities throughout the United States.

44847 ■ Strategic Planning Tools: Analytical Applications and Concepts to Enhance Your Plan
American Management Association
1601 Broadway
New York, NY 10019
Ph:(212)586-8100
Free: 800-262-9699
Fax: (212)903-8168
Co. E-mail: customerservice@amanet.org
URL: http://www.amanet.org
Price: $1,795 for non-members; $1,595 for AMA members. **Description:** Covers strategies for generating growth within your company, including how strategic opportunities are recognized and impacted. **Locations:** New York, NY; Washington, DC; Chicago, IL; Atlanta, GA; and San Francisco, CA.

44848 ■ Strategies for Effective Problem Solving and Decision Making: Good Decisions, Good Solutions
American Management Association
1601 Broadway
New York, NY 10019
Ph:(212)586-8100
Free: 800-262-9699
Fax: (212)903-8168
Co. E-mail: customerservice@amanet.org
URL: http://www.amanet.org
Price: $1,695.00 for non-members; $1,495.00 for AMA members. **Description:** Three-day seminar for experienced managers and executives; covers effective problem solving and decision making skills. **Locations:** Atlanta, GA; New York, NY; and Chicago, IL.

44849 ■ Successful Management of Laboratories
American Management Association
1601 Broadway
New York, NY 10019
Ph:(212)586-8100
Free: 800-262-9699
Fax: (212)903-8168
Co. E-mail: customerservice@amanet.org
URL: http://www.amanet.org
Price: $1,595.00 for non-members; $1,495.00 for AMA members. **Description:** Covers maximizing laboratories' contributions to a company by effective management of resources, projects, and work environment. **Locations:** San Francisco, CA.

44850 ■ Successfully Managing People
American Management Association
1601 Broadway
New York, NY 10019
Ph:(212)586-8100
Free: 800-262-9699
Fax: (212)903-8168
Co. E-mail: customerservice@amanet.org
URL: http://www.amanet.org
Price: $1,695.00 for non-members; $1,595.00 for AMA members. **Description:** Covers negotiation, motivation, confidence, leadership skills, and dealing with various types of employees. **Locations:** San Francisco, CA; Washington, DC; Orlando, FL; Atlanta, GA; Chicago, IL; New York, NY; and Dallas, TX.

44851 ■ Successfully Managing People (Canada)
Canadian Management Centre
150 York St., 5th Fl.
Toronto, ON, Canada M5H 3S5
Ph:(416)214-5678
Free: 800-262-9699
Fax: (416)313-4985
Co. E-mail: cmcinfo@cmctraining.org
URL: http://cmcamai.org
Price: $1,895.00 Canadian. **Description:** Covers negotiation, motivation, confidence, leadership skills, and dealing with various types of employees. **Locations:** Calgary, AB; Mississauga, ON; and Toronto, ON.

44852 ■ Survival Skills for Supervisors
American Management Association
1601 Broadway
New York, NY 10019
Ph:(212)586-8100
Free: 800-262-9699
Fax: (212)903-8168
Co. E-mail: customerservice@amanet.org
URL: http://www.amanet.org
Price: $1,695 for non-members; $1,495 for AMA members. **Description:** Covers developing skills that allow you to adapt to the daily challenges within the organization, including fostering trust with your employees' in order to meet your objectives. **Locations:** New York, NY; Washington, DC; and Chicago, IL.

44853 ■ Taking on Greater Responsibility Step-up Skills for Nonmanagers
American Management Association
1601 Broadway
New York, NY 10019
Ph:(212)586-8100
Free: 800-262-9699
Fax: (212)903-8168
Co. E-mail: customerservice@amanet.org
URL: http://www.amanet.org
Price: $1,445 for non-members; $1,295 for AMA members. **Description:** For anyone who wants to advance in the ever changing corporate environment; covers adapting to change, confidence in performing new tasks, effective communication, and developing a positive attitude. **Locations:** New York, NY; Chicago, IL; Atlanta, GA; Washington, DC; and San Francisco, CA.

44854 ■ Technical Project Management
American Management Association
1601 Broadway
New York, NY 10019

Ph:(212)586-8100
Free: 800-262-9699
Fax: (212)903-8168
Co. E-mail: customerservice@amanet.org
URL: http://www.amanet.org
Price: $1,895.00 for non-members; $1,695.00 for AMA members. **Description:** Covers defining cost, time, and scope; project leadership; utilizing status reports; and scheduling with milestones. **Locations:** San Francisco, CA; Chicago, IL; and New York, NY.

44855 ■ Technical Project Management (Canada)
Canadian Management Centre
150 York St., 5th Fl.
Toronto, ON, Canada M5H 3S5
Ph:(416)214-5678
Free: 800-262-9699
Fax: (416)313-4985
Co. E-mail: cmcinfo@cmctraining.org
URL: http://cmcamai.org
Price: $1,595.00 Canadian. **Description:** Covers defining cost, time, and scope; project leadership; utilizing status reports; and technical project control systems. **Locations:** Toronto, ON.

44856 ■ The Voice of Leadership: How Leaders Inspire, Influence, and Achieve Results
American Management Association
1601 Broadway
New York, NY 10019
Ph:(212)586-8100
Free: 800-262-9699
Fax: (212)903-8168
Co. E-mail: customerservice@amanet.org
URL: http://www.amanet.org
Price: $1,775.00 for non-members; $1,675.00 for AMA members. **Description:** Covers managing change, how to inspire and influence, effective communication skills, coaching, and addressing conflict. **Locations:** San Francisco, CA; Washington, DC; Atlanta, GA; Chicago, IL; New York, NY; and Dallas, TX.

44857 ■ The Voice of Leadership: How Leaders Inspire, Influence and Achieve Results (Canada)
Canadian Management Centre
150 York St., 5th Fl.
Toronto, ON, Canada M5H 3S5
Ph:(866)400-4941 ext. 2252
Free: 877-CMC-2500
Fax: (416)313-4985
Co. E-mail: cmcinfo@cmctraining.org
URL: http://www.cmcamai.org
Price: $1,895 Canadian. **Description:** Covers influential leadership skills that send a clear message. **Locations:** Toronto, ON.

44858 ■ What Every Manager Needs to Know: AMA's Tool Kit for Success
American Management Association
1601 Broadway
New York, NY 10019
Ph:(212)586-8100
Free: 800-262-9699
Fax: (212)903-8168
Co. E-mail: customerservice@amanet.org
URL: http://www.amanet.org
Price: $1,895 for non-members; $1,695 for AMA members. **Description:** Covers the overall understanding and responsibility of a managers role; including leadership skills, hiring of employees that best fit your needs, project management, and time management. **Locations:** New York, NY; Chicago, IL; Atlanta, GA; Washington, DC; and San Francisco, CA.

44859 ■ When Good Projects go Bad...and How to Fix Them (Canada)
Canadian Management Centre
150 York St., 5th Fl.
Toronto, ON, Canada M5H 3S5
Free: 877-CMC-2500
Fax: (416)313-4985
Co. E-mail: cmcinfo@cmctraining.org
URL: http://www.cma.org
Price: $1,650 Canadian. **Description:** Covers how to recognize, diagnose and turn around a problem situa-

tion, including why projects get into trouble, how team management affect project effectiveness, evaluating the status of the project work plan, and modifying the project work plan. **Locations:** Toronto, ON.

44860 ■ When Good Projects Go Bad...and How to Fix Them
American Management Association
1601 Broadway
New York, NY 10019
Ph:(212)586-8100
Free: 800-262-9699
Fax: (212)903-8168
Co. E-mail: customerservice@amanet.org
URL: http://www.amanet.org
Price: $1,695 for non-members; $1,495 for AMA members. **Description:** Covers recognizing the warning signs that a project may be in trouble, and be able to evaluate, and correct the problem. **Locations:** New York, NY; Atlanta, GA; Chicago, IL; Washington, DC; and San Francisco, CA.

REFERENCE WORKS

44861 ■ "3-D Negotiation: Playing the Whole Game" in *Harvard Business Review* **(Vol. 81, No. 11, November 2003, pp. 64)**
Pub: Harvard Business School Press
Ed: David A. Lax, James K. Sebenius. **Description:** Business negotiations require thorough planning and development in order to be successful.

44862 ■ "20 Keys to Leadership" in *Small Business Opportunities* **(Vol. 16, No. 1, January 2004, pp. 12, 20)**
Pub: Harris Publications, Inc.
Ed: Joanne G. Sujansky. **Description:** Joanne G. Sujansky, Certified Speaking Professional, shares twenty keys to help entrepreneurs and small business owners to become effective leaders.

44863 ■ "50 Most Powerful Black Women in Business" in *Black Enterprise* **(Vol. 36, February 2006, No. 7, pp. 124)**
Pub: Earl G. Graves Publishing Co. Inc.
Ed: Carolyn M. Brown. **Description:** Profiles of Black Enterprise's fifty most powerful black women in business are highlighted. The women represent senior managers of multinational corporations to founders of the largest black-owned businesses in the U.S.

44864 ■ "The 90-Day Difference" in *Inc.* **(October 1, 2003)**
Pub: Gruner & Jahr USA Publishing
Ed: Mike Hofman. **Description:** Why do some managers succeed while others fail? It all depends on the first three months.

44865 ■ "The 100 Best Companies To Work For" in *Fortune* **(Vol. 151, January 24, 2005, No. 2, pp. 72)**
Pub: Time Inc.
Ed: Robert Levering, Milton Moskowitz, Ann Harrington, Nadira A. Hira, Christopher Tkaczyk. **Description:** Complete listing of the best 100 companies to work for in the U.S. is presented. Businesses are categorized by large company, 10,000-plus employees; midsize, 2,500 to 10,000 employees; and small, 1,000 to 2,500 employees. Republic Bancorp topped out as number one small company, followed by Xilinx and Griffin Hospital.

44866 ■ *365 Answers about Human Resources for the Small Business Owner: What Every Manager Needs to Know about Work Place Law*
Pub: Atlantic Publishing Company
Ed: Mary Holihan. **Released:** June 2006. **Price:** $21.95. **Description:** Common questions employers ask about employees and the law are answered.

44867 ■ "2004 Corporate Elite Directory" in *Hispanic Business* **(January/February 2004, pp. 36, 38, 40, 42, 44, 46)**
Pub: Hispanic Business
Description: A listing of the Hispanic Business 2004 Corporate Elite Directory, with a brief profile of each winner.

44868 ■ "2005 Corporate Elite Directory" in *Hispanic Business* **(January/February 2005, pp. 22)**
Pub: Hispanic Business
Description: Profile of George Reyes, CFO at Google. Reyes helped to stage Google's $1.67 billion IPO. The trend for Hispanic men and women to hold high level positions continues to grow.

44869 ■ "2005 Elite Women" in *Hispanic Business* **(April 2005, pp. 54)**
Pub: Hispanic Business
Ed: Nydia Velazquez. **Description:** Strategies and tips for success are shared by elite women business leaders.

44870 ■ "About His Life: Bob Dallmeyer" in *Tradeshow Week* **(Vol. 34, December 20, 2004, No. 51, pp. S4)**
Pub: Reed Business Information
Ed: Gary Tufel. **Description:** Profile of Bob Dallmeyer, exhibitor, show manager, author, teacher, lecturer, and mentor in the exhibition industry. Tradeshow Week named him one of the industry's 100 Most Influential People and one of its Top Five Industry Entrepreneurs in 2003.

44871 ■ "About My Raise...How To Ask For and Get More Money" in *Black Enterprise* **(Vol. 34, July 2004, No. 12, pp. 65)**
Pub: Earl G. Graves Publishing Co. Inc.
Ed: Carla Thompson. **Description:** In order to get an overview of wages for a particular position, research must be done into companies within an industry sector, taking into consideration a firm's size and location.

44872 ■ "About the Power Breakfast series" in *Crain's Detroit Business* **(Vol. 19, No. 1, January 6, 2003, pp. 3)**
Pub: Crain Communications Inc., Detroit
Description: Crain's Detroit Business is playing host to private roundtable discussions with executives and experts in the Detroit area. Key issues will focus on Southeast Michigan businesses, including suppliers, ethics, governance, and more.

44873 ■ "Accentuating the accent" in *The New York Times* **(September 3, 2000, pp. BU10)**
Pub: The New York Times Company
Ed: Mickey Meece. **Description:** Research by Dianne Markley and Patricia Cukor-Avila shows that employers base hiring decisions on the way they judge a candidate's regional accent.

44874 ■ "Accountability key factor in family business success" in *Business First Columbus* **(Vol. 18, No. 25, February 8, 2002, pp. B3)**
Pub: Business First Columbus, Inc.
Ed: Susan Pavilkey. **Description:** Management style, and the importance of personal accountability when running and working for a family business are discussed.

44875 ■ "Acquire and Rewire" in *Memphis Business Journal* **(Vol. 25, No. 16, August 15, 2003, pp. 31)**
Pub: American City Business Journals
Ed: Rob Robertson. **Description:** First Tennessee Bank Memphis, led by president Charles Burkett, encourages managers to become involved in community affairs. The bank is the 31st largest bank in the U.S. and is expanding into Virginia.

44876 ■ "The Activist Ingredient" in *Inc.* **(July 1, 2003)**
Pub: Gruner & Jahr USA Publishing
Ed: Bobbie Gossage. **Description:** Paul Osterman of the Sloan School of Management at MIT suggests that managers take lessons from grassroots political groups to avoid employee burnout while maintaining growth.

44877 ■ *Adapting to Change: Making It Work for You*
Pub: Crisp Publications, Inc.
Ed: Carol K. Goman. **Released:** 1993. **Price:** $12.95 (paper). **Description:** Part of the Small Business and Entrepreneurship series. Discusses organizational change in business.

44878 ■ "Adriane Brown: Driven To Succeed At Honeywell" in *Business Week* **(February 14, 2005, No. 3920, pp. 10)**
Pub: McGraw-Hill Companies
Ed: Olga Kharif, Ira Sager. **Description:** Profile of Adriane Brown, newly appointed chief executive at Honeywell who is committed to growing the division. Brown's unit produces everything from engine parts to antifreeze.

44879 ■ "Aetna" in *Business Week* **(January 16, 2006, No. 3967, pp. 47-48)**
Pub: McGraw-Hill Companies
Ed: Jessi Hempel. **Description:** Profile of incoming CEO at Aetna, Ron Williams, responsible for the firm's growth. Williams plans to cut operating costs, increase offerings, target baby boomers, and build the company's merger and acquisitions.

44880 ■ "Agent flips over high-flying sport" in *Atlanta Business Chronicle* **(Vol. 25, January 10, 2003, No. 31, pp. 28A)**
Pub: American City Business Publications, Inc.
Ed: Lisa R. Schoolcraft. **Description:** Heather Williams, a 28-year-old agent for Re/Max Realty Group, has an unusual hobby. Williams is a freestyle motocross jumper who has competed in the X-games XIII in Philadelphia, Pennsylvania.

44881 ■ "All in a day's work" in *Harvard Business Review* **(Vol. 79, No. 11, December 2001, pp. 54)**
Pub: Harvard Business School Press
Description: A roundtable discussion with six experts from the corporate world, the nonprofit sector, and academia on tough questions about leadership is presented. Three common themes emerged: the need for a leader to formulate and communicate a vision for the organization, the need for the leader to add value to an enterprise and the organizational imperative for the leader to motivate followers.

44882 ■ "Along For the Ride: Losing Touch With Your Reps?" in *Entrepreneur* **(Vol. 31, No. 10, October 2003, pp. 87)**
Pub: Entrepreneur Media, Inc.
Ed: Kimberly L. McCall. **Description:** Managers should occasionally go on field visits with reps in order to keep a sales staff at its best.

44883 ■ "The American Cancer Society's Next Crusade" in *Fast Company* **(November 2001, pp. 58)**
Pub: Fast Company
Ed: Bill Breen. **Description:** For nearly 90 years, the American Cancer Society has led the war against cancer, now the society faces another do-or-die challenge: to identify the next generation of leaders who will continue the battle.

44884 ■ "Analyze This" in *Black Enterprise* **(Vol. 34, No. 6, January 2004, pp. 41)**
Pub: Earl Graves Publishing Co.
Ed: Ashley Gibson. **Description:** Profile of Charles Phillips, technology expert and rated America's best software analyst, has been appointed new executive vice president of Oracle Corporation.

44885 ■ "Analyze This: Charles Phillips Makes Bold Career Move to Oracle as Executive Vice President" in *Black Enterprise* **(Vol. 34, No. 6)**
Pub: Earl Graves Publishing Co.
Ed: Ashley Gibson. **Description:** Profile of Charles Phillips, technology expert and rated America's best software analyst, has been appointed new executive vice president of Oracle Corporation.

44886 ■ "Andrea Electronics Completes Stage 1 of Restructuring" in *Long Island Business News* **(February 27, 2004)**
Pub: Dolan Media Newswires
Ed: Ken Schachter. **Description:** Andrea Electronics has completed Phase One of a three-phase restructuring effort. Profile of the electronics firm and an interview with its chief executive, Paul Donofrio, are included.

44887 ■ "Andy Pearson Finds Love" in *Fast Company* **(August 2001, pp. 78)**
Pub: Fast Company
Ed: David Dorsey. **Description:** Profile of Andy Pearson, CEO of PepsiCo. Pearson shares his management skills and his new approach to leadership.

44888 ■ "Annual meetings an extension of nonprofit mission" in *Atlanta Business Chronicle* **(Vol. 24, No. 14, September 7, 2001, pp. S12)**
Pub: American City Business Journals Inc.
Ed: Anya Martin. **Description:** Various executives from non-profit organizations talk about annual meetings and key factors to consider.

44889 ■ "Apache on the Rise, Anadarko in Decline" in *Houston Business Journal* **(Vol. 34, No. 13, August 8, 2003, pp. 1)**
Pub: American City Business Journals
Ed: Monica Perin. **Description:** Business and management styles of Apache Corporation and Anadarko Petroleum Company are compared, including strategic planning and profit margins.

44890 ■ "Aramark executive joins VIPdesk.com" in *Washington Business Journal* **(Vol. 19, No. 17, September 1, 2000, pp. 22)**
Pub: American City Business Journals, Inc.
Ed: Christine Cube. **Description:** The Alexandria online concierge service VIPdesk.com has hired Kelly Christiano as vice president of sales. VIPdesk is a concierge service that provides personal and real-time assistance from local concierge agents.

44891 ■ "Are CIOs Obsolete?" in *Harvard Business Review* **(Vol. 78, No. 2, March 2000, pp. 55)**
Pub: Harvard Business School Publishing Corp.
Ed: Regina Fazio Maruca. **Description:** Are information technology and strategy now so much a part of each other that all senior managers are, or should be, obsolete?

44892 ■ "Are you picking the right leaders?" in *Harvard Business Review* **(Vol. 80, No. 2, February 2002, pp. 58)**
Pub: Harvard Business School Press
Ed: Melvin Sorcher, James Brant. **Description:** Advice is given to help executives choose the right leaders for their firms. Executives often overvalue certain traits and skills while overlooking more leadership-related ones.

44893 ■ "Are You In With the In Crowd?" in *Harvard Business Review* **(Vol. 81, No. 7, July 2003, pp. 86)**
Pub: Harvard Business School Press
Ed: Art Kleiner. **Description:** The influence of a select group of managers upon all facets of a company's operations is discussed.

44894 ■ "Are You Ready for Some Football Cliches?" in *Inc.* **(October 1, 2003)**
Pub: Gruner & Jahr USA Publishing
Ed: Patrick J. Sauer. **Description:** Ways the management of the New York Jets can benefit any small business are discussed.

44895 ■ "Are Your Employees Job Hunting?" in *Women In Business* **(Vol. 52, No. 3, May 2000, pp. 42)**
Pub: The ABWA Co., Inc.
Ed: Diane Domeyer. **Description:** Managers should be aware of changes in behavior of their staff, such as sudden requests for extra days off or an unwillingness to commit to future projects, which may indicate they are planning to change jobs.

44896 ■ "Are Your Staffers Stealing" in *Inc.* **(November 2006, pp. 33-35)**
Pub: Gruner & Jahr USA Publishing
Ed: Scott Wescott. **Description:** Internal theft is a significant drain on resources and easier to prevent than amend. Selecting the right people, clear cut policies on theft, simplified accounting systems, all contribute to reducing this common problem in small companies.

44897 ■ "The Art of the Real" in *Inc.* **(September 1, 2003)**
Pub: Gruner & Jahr USA Publishing
Ed: Jess McCuan. **Description:** Profile of NBC's new reality show featuring Donald Trump. The show features contestants vying for an executive job with Trump that pays in the six figures. Street-smart entrepreneurs are expected to compete.

44898 ■ "The Art of the Woman Warrior" in *Inc.* **(August 2005, pp. 26)**
Pub: Inc. Magazine
Description: Two former Marines offer management training exclusively for businesswomen. The two sisters have created leadership workshops focusing on ten concepts they learned from the Marines.

44899 ■ "Ask Inc." in *Inc.* **(September 1, 2004)**
Pub: Inc. Magazine
Description: A small stationery shop in Kansas is looking for new investors and the vice president of a residential mortgage brokerage wants to hire a coach or trainer to work with the firm's CEO.

44900 ■ "Ask Inc. Profit Sharing" in *Inc.* **(September 2006, pp. 53)**
Pub: Gruner & Jahr USA Publishing
Description: Profit sharing plans can be changed without upsetting your employees. Numerous hints and strategies are provided to address this question

44901 ■ "Asking For It: You Can't Always Get What You Want, But Chances are Better If You Learn How To Ask" in *Entrepreneur* **(August 2004)**
Pub: Entrepreneur Media Inc.
Ed: Romanus Wolter. **Description:** Advice is offered to entrepreneurs when making requests in order to get the desired response.

44902 ■ "Asking Too Much? Not a Chance. Questions Are One of the Best Tools for Unlocking Creativity" in *Entrepreneur* **(Vol. 31, October 2003)**
Pub: Entrepreneur Media, Inc.
Ed: Juanita Weaver. **Description:** Ways to learn to be creative is answered using the "Seven Whys".

44903 ■ "Aspirations for '05" in *Inc.* **(January 1, 2005)**
Pub: Inc. Magazine
Ed: Darren Dahl, Lora Kolodny. **Description:** Various entrepreneurs of growing companies talk about what they hope to accomplish in 2005.

44904 ■ "Assemble Your E-Business Team" in *E-business Advisor* **(Vol. 17, No. 12, December 1999, pp. 30)**
Pub: Advisor Media, Inc.
Ed: Zachary W. Esper. **Description:** Electronic business projects must be carefully staffed and managed. Traditional project structures work well, consisting of steering committee, project leader and supporting management team. Business-to-business projects can be led by operations or procurement managers. MIS managers, who traditionally maintain corporate Web sites, make good leaders for non-transactional Internet projects.

44905 ■ "Assembling a Crack Sales Team" in *Hispanic Business* **(October 2003, pp. 92, 94, 96)**
Pub: Hispanic Business
Ed: Teresa Talerico. **Description:** Doing it well and then training and retaining new recruits can make all the difference to a sales operation.

44906 ■ *Assertiveness for Managers: Learning Effective Skills for Managing People*
Pub: Self-Counsel Press, Inc.
Ed: Diana Cawood. **Released:** 1992, third edition. **Price:** $12.95 (paper).

44907 ■ "Attention Readers!" in *Fast Company* **(July 2001, pp. 50)**
Pub: Fast Company

Ed: Polly LaBarre. **Description:** Review of the book titled, 'The Attention Economy: Understanding the New Currency of Business'. The book explores human attention factors and offers ways of capturing and holding the attention of customers, employees, and shareholders.

44908 ■ "Avoid the four perils of CRM" in *Harvard Business Review* **(Vol. 80, No. 2, February 2002, pp. 101)**
Pub: Harvard Business School Press
Ed: Darrell K. Rigby, Frederick F. Reichheld, Phil Schefter. **Description:** Advice is given to companies on how they can have successful customer relationship management (CRM) programs.

44909 ■ "Avoiding a Communication Breakdown: Keeping Employees Informed Benefits Business" in *Black Enterprise* **(Vol. 34, September 2003)**
Pub: Earl Graves Publishing Co.
Ed: John G. Clemons. **Description:** Profile of Ariel Capital Management Inc., an investment management company in the Chicago, Illinois area. The firm was rated Number One on Black Enterprise's Asset Managers list. The firm conducts a weekly Breakfast Club for employees to help them learn about the company's operations and services portfolio, honing presentation skills, and building professional skills. Ariel employs 67 people.

44910 ■ "B-School Gets Stamp of Approval" in *Black Enterprise* **(Vol. 34, July 2004, No. 12, pp. 26)**
Pub: Earl G. Graves Publishing Co. Inc.
Ed: Tamara E. Holmes. **Description:** Medgar Evers College School of Business has achieved accreditation. The historically black college plans to contact alumni within a few years of graduation to track the success of its graduates in the business world.

44911 ■ "Bad Apples: Business Owners Share their Hiring Horror Stories" in *Entrepreneur* **(Vol. 32, No. 2, February 2004, pp. 26)**
Pub: Entrepreneur Media, Inc.
Ed: Nichole L. Torres. **Description:** Three entrepreneurs share bad hiring experiences and offer advice for managers when hiring.

44912 ■ "Balancing Act" in *Crain's Detroit Business* **(Vol. 22, January 30, 2006, No. 5, pp. 3)**
Pub: Crain Communications Inc. - Detroit
Ed: Sheena Harrison. **Description:** Small business leaders often take on more responsibilities than counterparts at large corporations. According to a recent study, high-level executives at successful small companies focus on teamwork, innovation, and strategic thinking.

44913 ■ *Balls!: 6 Rules for Winning Today's Business Game*
Pub: John Wiley & Sons, Incorporated
Ed: Alexi Venneri. **Released:** January 2005. **Price:** $19.95. **Description:** In order to be successful business leaders must be brave, authentic, loud, lovable, and spunky and they need to lead their competition.

44914 ■ "Bankable Skills" in *Hispanic Business* **(October 2004, pp. 126)**
Pub: Hispanic Business
Ed: Anthony Limon. **Description:** With a growing global economy, financial institutions need more Hispanic executives representing them.

44915 ■ "Banker Right on the Money with Financial Powerhouse" in *Houston Business Journal* **(Vol. 34, No. 13, August 8, 2003, pp. 2)**
Pub: American City Business Journals
Ed: Jim Greer. **Description:** The growing success of Southwest Bank of Texas is presented. Topics include market development, strategic planning, and management styles.

44916 ■ "Barduous journey" in *Entrepreneur* **(Vol. 30, No. 1, Januar)**
Pub: Entrepreneur Media Inc.
Ed: Geoff Williams. **Description:** Richard Olivier, of Olivier Mythodrama Associates, son of the late Sir Laurence Olivier, uses Shakespeare to teach business executives and entrepreneurs about leadership. Olivier combines four elements to the seminars: theater skills, mythology, psychology and organizational development.

44917 ■ "Bargaining a good-bye" in *BlackEnterprise* **(Vol. 32, No. 2, September 2001, pp. 61)**
Pub: Earl Graves Publishing Co.
Ed: Robyn D. Clarke. **Description:** Strategies to negotiate a job departure deal are examined.

44918 ■ "Bargaining Power" in *Sales & Marketing Management* **(Vol. 157, February 2005, No. 2, pp. 20)**
Pub: VNU Business Media
Description: According to a recent survey, nearly 48 percent of managers have to coach sales reps on negotiation skills because many are afraid to risk ruining a client relationship they worked hard to build.

44919 ■ "The bargaining table: check your ego at the door." in *Atlanta Business Chronicle* **(Vol. 25, Jan. 10, 2003, No. 31, pp. 1B)**
Pub: American City Business Publications, Inc.
Ed: Tom Barry. **Description:** Negotiation skills are very valuable in today's business world; qualities of an effective negotiator, as well as how to negotiate effectively, as discussed.

44920 ■ *Be an Even Better Manager: Improve Performance, Profits, and Productivity*
Pub: Self-Counsel Press, Inc.
Ed: Michael Armstrong. **Released:** 1990, second edition. **Price:** $9.95 (paper).

44921 ■ "Be Prepared" in *Harvard Business Review* **(Vol. 81, No. 11, November 2003, pp. 20)**
Pub: Harvard Business School Press
Ed: Leonard Fuld. **Description:** Utilization of business intelligence tools can aid companies in planning for the future.

44922 ■ "B.E. Successpert Speaks" in *Black Enterprise* **(Vol. 34, No. 5, December 2003, pp. 139)**
Pub: Earl Graves Publishing Co.
Ed: Keisha Gaye-Anderson. **Description:** A lawyer and author offers advise to help others build their careers.

44923 ■ "Beating Strong" in *Houston Business Journal* **(Vol. 34, No. 14, August 15, 2003, pp. 17)**
Pub: American City Business Journals
Ed: Allison Wollam. **Description:** Profile of American Medical Equipment, Houston, Texas, as it prepares to move into new facilities in the Texas Medical Center. Topics include business planning, management styles, and medical equipment product lines.

44924 ■ "Behave yourself" in *Harvard Business Review* **(Vol. 80, No. 10, October 2002, pp. 22)**
Pub: Harvard Business School Press
Ed: Gardiner Morse. **Description:** Marshall Goldsmith is a successful executive coach. He answers 7 questions designed to help executives become more effective leaders. The most important advice he offers is to overcome behavior problems.

44925 ■ "Behind the Boards" in *Forbes* **(Vol. 170, No. 9, October 28, 2002, pp. 252)**
Pub: Forbes Magazine
Ed: Michael K. Ozanian. **Description:** The importance of corporate governance is discussed, along with growth value of a company when choosing stocks.

44926 ■ "Best of 2005" in *Business Week* **(December 19, 2005, No. 3964, pp. 58-64, 66, 68, 72)**
Pub: McGraw-Hill Companies
Ed: Bruce Nussbaum. **Description:** Profiles of the best and most innovative business leaders in 2005.

44927 ■ "Best of the Best" in *Hispanic Business* **(June 2002, pp. 32, 34, 36)**
Pub: Hispanic Business
Ed: Holly Ocasio Rizzo. **Description:** The Hispanic Business 500 listing of the 500 largest Hispanic firms in the U.S. shows how managers have achieved success, despite the social barriers facing minority entrepreneurs.

44928 ■ "The Best" in *Forbes* **(May 13, 2002, p. 104)**
Pub: Forbes Magazine
Description: A listing of the best chief executive officers, executive salaries and shareholder returns is featured.

44929 ■ "The best-laid incentive plans" in *Harvard Business Review* **(Vol. 81, No. 1, January 2003, pp. 27)**
Pub: Harvard Business School Press
Ed: Steve Kerr. **Description:** A case study is presented where a CFO and chief administrative officer of a consumer durables manufacturer has instituted a performance management system that seemed successful to him, but had negative results for employee morale and customer service. Four experts offer advice on ways the company should proceed.

44930 ■ "A better way to deliver bad news" in *Harvard Business Review* **(Vol. 80, No. 9, Sept. 2002, pp. 114)**
Pub: Harvard Business School Press
Ed: Jean-Francois Manzoni. **Description:** Managerial methods for the effective delivery of bad news to employees are examined.

44931 ■ "Between Right And Right" in *Fortuneit* **(Vol. 146, No. 9, November 11, 2002, pp. 66)**
Pub: Time Inc.
Ed: Geoffrey Colvin. **Description:** Three specific corporate ethics issues are examined.

44932 ■ "Beware the busy manager" in *Harvard Business Review* **(Vol. 80, No. 2, February 2002, pp. 62)**
Pub: Harvard Business School Press
Ed: Heike Bruch, Sumantra Ghoshal. **Description:** The business of executives and how the busiest ones may not necessarily be accomplishing that much work is discussed.

44933 ■ "Beyond empowerment: Building a company of citizens" in *Harvard Business Review* **(Vol. 81, No. 1, January 2003, pp. 48)**
Pub: Harvard Business School Press
Ed: Brook Manville, Josiah Ober. **Description:** The ancient Greek city-state of Athens is used as a model for a democratic business organization suited to the knowledge economy of today. The Athenian model does not provide a simple set of prescriptions, but offers a window into how companies can create an atmosphere of dignity and trust without resorting to a stifling bureaucracy.

44934 ■ *Beyond Entrepreneurship: Turning Your Business into an Enduring Great Company*
Pub: Prentice Hall
Ed: James C. Collins and William C. Lazier. **Released:** 1992. **Price:** $19.95.

44935 ■ "Beyond the resume" in *Women In Business* **(Vol. 52, No. 4, July 2000, pp. 36)**
Pub: The ABWA Co., Inc.
Ed: Diane Domeyer. **Description:** Issues regarding the recruitment of personnel are presented. The importance of interpersonal skills, knowledge technology, enthusiasm, and adaptability are discussed.

44936 ■ "The Big Comeback. How do you get a faltering team back on track?" in *Harvard Business Review* (Vol. 80, No. 1, January 2002, pp. 20)
Pub: Harvard Business School Press
Ed: Roberta Fusaro. **Description:** Al Skinner, coach of the Boston College Basketball team, answered questions about how he turned around a losing team, which has implications for business.

44937 ■ "Big pay for directors of small companies comes to light in a new study" in *Wall Street Journal* (March 9, 2000, pp. A1)
Pub: Dow Jones & Co., Inc.
Ed: Pamela Sebastian Ridge. **Description:** A survey of the National Association of Corporate Directors is examined.

44938 ■ "Big Switch: Walk a Mile In Your Employees' Shoes-You Could Learn a Lot" in *Entrepreneur* (Vol. 32, August 2004, No. 8, pp. 32)
Pub: Entrepreneur Media Inc.
Ed: April Y. Pennington. **Description:** Six corporate leaders switched places with employees in order to gain new perspectives, and respect for the people who work for them.

44939 ■ "Billy Mitchell outstanding in industry and community" in *Atlanta Business Chronicle* (Vol. 25, December 6, 2002, No. 26, pp. 3C)
Pub: American City Business Publications, Inc.
Ed: Martin Sinderman. **Description:** Carter & Associates chairman, William A. "Billy" Mitchell has won The Carter/Mathis Award from the Georgia Chapter of the National Association of Industrial and Office Properties. The award recognizes a person or company that has made a lasting contribution to the real estate industry and the community.

44940 ■ "Black Board Directors Form Network" in *Black Enterprise* (Vol. 35, December 2004, No. 5, pp. 38)
Pub: Earl G. Graves Publishing Co. Inc.
Ed: K. Terrell Reed. **Description:** According to the Investor Research Center, nearly 185 blacks sit on corporate boards, sharing 321 board seats out of 3,447. A recent gathering brought top black executives together to address a diversity agenda in board rooms.

44941 ■ "Black Hawk down at work" in *Harvard Business Review* (Vol. 81, No. 1, January 2003, pp. 16)
Pub: Harvard Business School Press
Ed: Thomas W. Britt. **Description:** U.S. soldiers compare experiences in Somalia in 1992 with morale issues in business. In both situations ambiguity about work roles, inadequate resources and overwork lead to dissatisfaction and, in the business context, the defection of the best workers.

44942 ■ "A Blogger in Their Midst" in *Harvard Business Review* (Vol. 81, No. 9, September 2003, pp. 30)
Pub: Harvard Business School Press
Ed: Halley Suitt. **Description:** A hypothetical situation is presented where an indiscreet employee provides an online endorsement of a product that results in dramatically increased sales. Experts discuss how the CEO should deal with the matter.

44943 ■ "Bloopers & Blunders" in *Small Business Opportunities* (Vol. 16, November 2004, No. 6, pp. 72)
Pub: Harris Publications Inc.
Ed: Joanne G. Sujansky. **Description:** Seven mistakes made by company leaders and ways to avoid them are explained: lack of trust, failure to shape and share vision, unclear expectations, insufficient modeling of desire behaviors, too little partnering, failure to retain top talent, and too little celebration of success.

44944 ■ "Board certified" in *Black Enterprise* (Vol. 33, No. 6, Jan. 2003, pp. 45)
Pub: Earl Graves Publishing Co.
Ed: Phaedra Brotherton. **Description:** Landing a seat on a corporate board is an excellent opportunity to meet and network with high-level executives and industry leaders, as well as earning cash and stocks.

44945 ■ "The board's missing link" in *Harvard Business Review* (Vol. 81, No. 3, March 2003, pp. 86)
Pub: Harvard Business School Press
Ed: Cynthia A. Montgomery, Rhonda Kaufman. **Description:** The relationship between boards of directors and shareholders is examined. Exchange of information is poor and shareholders fail to exert much influence over boards.

44946 ■ "Bonus Round" in *Entrepreneur* (Vol. 32, December 2004, No. 12, pp. 97)
Pub: Entrepreneur Media Inc.
Ed: Chris Penttila. **Description:** Alternatives to offer employees who reach the top of their pay scale include gift certificates, equity, tuition reimbursements, bonuses, job title enhancement, more benefits such as extra vacation days, or assigning high-profile projects to them.

44947 ■ *The Book of Hard Choices: Making the Right Decisions at Work without Losing Your Self-Respect*
Pub: Broadway Books
Ed: Peter Roy; James A. Autry. **Released:** December 2006. **Price:** $23.95.

44948 ■ "Boost staff morale with rewards and motivation" in *Women In Business* (Vol. 52, No. 3, May 2000, pp. 35)
Pub: The ABWA Co., Inc.
Ed: Dawn J. Grubb. **Description:** A number of firms understand the importance of recognizing their employees for good work by awarding them not only with money, but by giving them special benefits, or by acknowledging their contribution.

44949 ■ "Boosting Corporate Diversity" in *Hispanic Business* (April 2005, pp. 14)
Pub: Hispanic Business
Description: Many corporate managers believe that diversity programs provide a competitive edge because they improve a company's performance and leadership. The University of Texas, Austin started a program to expand the number of diverse students for their MBA program.

44950 ■ "Boosting moral" in *Black Enterprise* (Vol. 32, No. 9, April 2002, pp. 43)
Pub: Earl Graves Publishing Co.
Ed: Bridget McCrea. **Description:** Suggestions are offered to managers to help boost company morale.

44951 ■ "Bored Meeting" in *Entrepreneur* (Vol. 31, No. 9, September 2003, pp. 78)
Pub: Entrepreneur Media, Inc.
Description: Business owners serving on commissions quickly find out it is not a way to gather intelligence about competitors, rather they should cultivate relationships with commercial real estate brokers and landlords.

44952 ■ "A Boss's Toughest Job; Grace was my first employee" in *Business Week Online* (November 7, 2002)
Pub: McGraw-Hill Inc.
Ed: Gloria Washington. **Description:** An entrepreneur discusses the difficulties faced when having to fire an employee. Her experience was when her first employee hired, after many years of service, began alienating customers.

44953 ■ "Bottom feeding for blockbuster businesses" in *Harvard Business Review* (Vol. 81, No. 3, March 2003, pp. 52)
Pub: Harvard Business School Press
Ed: David Rosenblum, Doug Tomlinson, Larry Scott. **Description:** Research shows that companies can make profits from customers that are momentarily unprofitable and executives should ask themselves how they can make money from customers shunned by others, such as by serving small businesses that can't afford expensive services.

44954 ■ *Bradford's International Directory of Marketing Research Agencies*
Pub: Business Research Services Inc.

Released: Biennial, latest edition 28. **Price:** $95, individuals paperback; $125, individuals diskette. **Covers:** over 1,700 marketing research agencies worldwide. Includes domestic and international demographic data and professional association contacts. **Entries Include:** Company name, address, phone, name and title of contact, date founded, number of employees, description of products or services, e-mail, URL. **Arrangement:** Geographical. **Indexes:** Alphabetical by company.

44955 ■ "A Brand New Day" in *Entrepreneur* (Vol. 33, March 2005, No. 3, pp. 134)
Pub: Entrepreneur Media Inc.
Ed: Romanus Wolter. **Description:** Tips to help motivate entrepreneurs on a daily basis.

44956 ■ "Break It Down" in *Entrepreneur* (Vol. 28, No. 1, January 2000, pp. 116)
Pub: Entrepreneur Media Inc.
Ed: Jacquelyn Lynn. **Description:** Would your managers take more interest in their departments' success if it were their company? Through a management method called "intrepreneurship", a concept first developed in big companies about a decade ago as a response to declining morale and productivity, might be an option.

44957 ■ "Breaking Through Excuses" in *Business 2.0* (Vol. 6, May 2005, No. 4, pp. 76)
Pub: Time, Inc.
Ed: Jeffrey Pfeffer. **Description:** Most managers are good at explaining why something can't be done; allowing excuses to inhibit change results in failure to improve.

44958 ■ "Bright lights" in *Entrepreneur* (Vol. 30, No. 2, Feb)
Pub: Entrepreneur Media Inc.
Ed: Amanda C. Kooser. **Description:** Information about various portable projectors to help with presentations is offered, including a shopping list for Epson PowerLite 600p, Hitachi CP-X270W, InFocus LP280, Optoma ExPro750, and Sharp PG-C20XU.

44959 ■ "Broaddus Opens Office" in *Mississippi Business Journal* (Vol. 28, September 2006, No. 36, pp. 23)
Pub: Venture Publications, Inc.
Description: Profile of Broaddus & Associates, construction planning and management firm. Broaddus & Associates has opened an office in the Mississippi Gulf Coast area, its first office outside of Texas, to aid in the vast need in rebuilding management and planning.

44960 ■ "Bucking the Odds at Amylin" in *Business Week* (January 9, 2006, No. 3966, pp. 64, 66)
Pub: McGraw-Hill Companies
Ed: Arlene Weintraub. **Description:** Profile of Ginger Graham, chief executive at Amylin Pharmaceuticals Inc., who was considering retirement before taking the reins at Amylin. Graham, who is a diabetic, has helped the company attain government approval on two diabetes drugs.

44961 ■ "Building Character" in *Black Enterprise* (Vol. 35, January 2005, No. 6, pp. 41)
Pub: Earl G. Graves Publishing Co. Inc.
Ed: Glenn Townes. **Description:** Mike Jones has launched, Discover Leadership Training, providing weekend training and development seminars designed to develop and improve leadership skills.

44962 ■ "Building a Good Rep" in *Black Enterprise* (Vol. 36, December 2005, No. 5, pp. 136)
Pub: Earl G. Graves Publishing Co. Inc.
Ed: Scott Westcott. **Description:** According to Jerome Henderson, former football star and manager of a team of mortgage bankers, reputation is the most important key to business success.

44963 ■ "Building a Professional Pipeline" in *Hispanic Business* (March 2004, pp. 44-45)
Pub: Hispanic Business
Ed: Janet Perez. **Description:** A new report finds schools need to do more to prepare Hispanics for business careers.

44964 ■ "Building visibility" in *Women in Business* (Vol. 54, No. 2, March-April 2002, pp. 32)
Pub: The ABWA Co Inc.
Ed: Liz Hughes. **Description:** Techniques for building visibility and creating business success are provided, including the avoidance of gossip and increased communication skills.

44965 ■ "Bulking up; Dollar Castle's ruler plans retailing, distribution kingdom" in *Crain's Detroit Business* (Dec. 9, 2002, pp. 3)
Pub: Crain Communications Inc., Detroit
Ed: Laura Bailey. **Description:** Profile of Dollar Castle's owner Eddie Denha and his successful management style.

44966 ■ "Bullied by the Big Guys? Try Fighting Back!" in *Fortune* (Vol. 142, No. 2, July 10, 2000, pp. 200T)
Pub: Time Inc.
Description: Techniques for dealing with clients that are trying to take advantage because of your size. Big perks, a Web prospectus, and how to value a business are discussed.

44967 ■ "Business, Employee Short-Term Focus Is on Survival" in *Atlanta Business Chronicle* (Vol. 25, November 15, 2002, No. 23 pp. 2B)
Pub: American City Business Publications, Inc.
Ed: Emory Mulling. **Description:** As companies try to streamline, many are doing more work with fewer employees. Despite a tight market, employers should not assume that workers will tolerate miserable conditions. Maintaining spending on key areas and providing strong leadership remain vital to the health of a company.

44968 ■ "Business Prophet" in *Business Week* (January 23, 2006, No. 3968, pp. 68-73)
Pub: McGraw-Hill Companies
Ed: Description: C.K. Prahalad shares lessons for executives in order to run their companies successfully. Prahalad's strategy suggests that the ingenuity used at work in poor nations, where success depends on brilliant deployment of minimal resources, has strong implications for executives worldwide.

44969 ■ *Business Warrior: Strategy for Entrepreneurs*
Pub: Clearbridge Publishing
Ed: Sun Tzu. **Released:** September 2006. **Price:** $19.95. **Description:** Advice to help entrepreneurs understand competitive strategies in order to succeed, focusing on sales, marketing, and personnel management.

44970 ■ "The Business Week News You Need to Know" in *Business Week* (January 23, 2006, No. 3968, pp. 30-31)
Pub: McGraw-Hill Companies
Ed: Harry Maurer. **Description:** News about the Detroit Auto Show, job growth, Home Depot's expansion plans, Internet search engines, new executive pay rules, the stock market, and more.

44971 ■ "Buyer's Mentality" in *Sales & Marketing Management* (Vol. 159, January-February 2007, No. 1, pp. 45)
Pub: VNU Business Media
Ed: John Boe. **Description:** Sales managers should approach hiring interviews with the same logic as a buyer's mentality.

44972 ■ "By the Book" in *Entrepreneur.com* (Vol. 34, February 2006, No. 2, pp. 77)
Pub: Entrepreneur Media Inc.
Ed: Kimberly L. McCall. **Description:** Reviews of three new books to help managers motivate sales

teams include, In Selling To Big Companies, by Jill Konrath; Jack, You're Fired! The Top 66 Reasons for Firing Sales Professionals...and How You Can Avoid Every Single One of Them, by Jack Perry; and Leading Leaders: How to Manage Smart, Talented, Rich and Powerful People, by Jeswald Salacuse.

44973 ■ "By Degrees" in *Entrepreneur* (Vol. 32, December 2004, No. 12, pp. 98)
Pub: Entrepreneur Media Inc.
Ed: Chris Penttila. **Description:** According to the Bureau of Labor Statistics, the number of jobs filled, between 2000 to 2010, by PhDs will increase by nearly 25 percent. It is important for employers to understand how to meld MBAs and PhDs in the workplace.

44974 ■ "C2G-Network" in *Entrepreneur.com* (Vol. 34, January 2006, No. 1, pp. 6)
Pub: Entrepreneur Media Inc.
Ed: Steve Cooper. **Description:** College students can be certified and placed on C2G-Network that puts them in contact with fast-growing small businesses. Students have backgrounds in technology, engineering, marketing and sales, human resources, finance, communications and more.

44975 ■ "Cadence Bank" in *Mississippi Business Journal* (Vol. 29, January 2007, No. 3, pp. A6)
Pub: Venture Publications, Inc.
Description: Profile of Jim McAlexander, president of Cadence Bank's Columbus Banking Center. McAlexander has been with Cadence Bank since 1973.

44976 ■ "Calling in Sick" in *Fortune* (Vol. 152, August 8, 2005, No. 3, pp. 96H)
Pub: Time Inc.
Ed: Kevin Kelly. **Description:** The importance for a company to have a backup plan in the event the CEO is too ill to report to work is stressed.

44977 ■ "Campaign Close-Up: Cargill" in *Sales & Marketing Management* (Vol. 158, November-December 2006, No. 11, pp. 15)
Pub: VNU Business Media
Ed: Jackie Hunzinger. **Description:** Profile of Cargill whose current advertising campaign shows how the company delivers its food from the processing plant to the dinner table.

44978 ■ "Can everyone contribute?" in *Black Enterprise* (Vol. 33, No. 3, Oct. 2002, pp. 71)
Pub: Earl Graves Publishing Co.
Ed: Christina Morgan. **Description:** Management strategies are covered by Tony Manning, business consultant and author; Manning suggests that managers need to do more than concentrate on the bottom line during a down economy and pay attention to the future needs of the company when the economy changes as well.

44979 ■ "Can Firms Ban Weapons?" in *St. Louis Post-Dispatch* (December 6, 2004)
Pub: Knight-Ridder/Tribune Business News
Ed: Repps Hudson. **Description:** Potential for workforce violence and the fight over whether employees should have the right to carry firearms at work is examined.

44980 ■ "Can Loyalty Be Leased?" in *Harvard Business Review* (Vol. 80, No. 9, Sept. 2002, pp. 24)
Pub: Harvard Business School Press
Ed: Elizabeth Craig, John Kimberly, Hamid Bouchikhi. **Description:** Research involving 400 mid-level executives from various companies throughout the world has shown that executive education that improve an executive's marketable talents, resulted in more executives staying with a company.

44981 ■ "Can a Nice Guy Finish First?" in *Washington Business Journal* (Vol. 22, No. 3, May 23, 2003, pp. 28)
Pub: Washington Business Journal
Ed: Suzanne White. **Description:** Profile of Daniel Bruce Karchem, president of Washington, DC area Karchem Properties. Topics include real estate development, management styles, and lifestyles.

44982 ■ "Can Spending A Day Stuck To A Velcro Wall Help Build A Team" in *Wall Street Journal* (Vol. 248, December 2006, No. 149, pp. B1)
Pub: Dow Jones & Co. Inc.
Ed: Jared Sandberg **Description:** Profiles of several companies offering office and corporate team-building exercise outings and events. Alternative methods of company employee bonding are covered.

44983 ■ "Can You Manage? Should the Office Hotshot Be Your Next Manager?" in *Entrepreneur* (Vol. 31, No. 7, July 2003)
Pub: Entrepreneur Media, Inc.
Ed: Chris Penttila. **Description:** Profile of Erika Mangrum, co-founder and president of Iatria Day Spa and Health Center in Raleigh, North Carolina. Mangrum realized she had promoted the wrong person to a management position, creating big problems as the company grew.

44984 ■ "Can You 'Pass' on Passion?" in *Women in Business* (Vol. 53, No. 5, September-October, 2001, pp. 12)
Pub: The ABWA Co. Inc.
Ed: Mary-Lane Kamberg. **Description:** Ways to ensure that the passion within an organization is pervasive throughout the company are to get employees involved, acknowledge employee contributions to the company, and reward top performing employees.

44985 ■ *Canadian Entrepreneurship and Small Business Management*
Pub: McGraw-Hill Ryerson, Limited
Ed: D. Wesley Balderson. **Released:** February 2005. **Price:** $79.95. **Description:** Successful entrepreneurship and small business management is shown through the use of individual Canadian small business experiences.

44986 ■ "Career Guide" in *Black Enterprise* (Vol. 33, No. 7, February 2003, pp. 6)
Pub: Earl Graves Publishing Co.
Description: Black Enterprise magazine offers a Web site that provides information to guide individuals through various stages of their career, tools to help assist career advancement with links to job search engines, interviewing tips, and a resume guide. Additional topics include management, COBRA, plus the top ten cities for African Americans to live, work and play.

44987 ■ "Casino Case Hits Legal Jackpot" in *Inc.* (August 1, 2003)
Pub: Gruner & Jahr USA Publishing
Ed: Bobbie Gossage. **Description:** A new ruling against Caesars Palace in Las Vegas, Nevada, will affect all companies when firing employees. The Supreme Court affirmed that circumstantial evidence in the casino's firing of an employee would suffice for a female warehouse worker fired for brawling with a co-worker.

44988 ■ "The CEO's Secret Handbook" in *Business 2.0* (Vol. 6, July 2005, No. 6, pp. 68-74)
Pub: Time, Inc.
Ed: Paul Kaihla. **Description:** Accidental guru, Bill Swanson, CEO at Raython shares a lifetime's worth of executive wisdom in his 760-page spiral-bound guidebook, Swanson's Unwritten Rules of Management.

44989 ■ "CFO's Exit Returns CPI Aerostructures Inc. to Recruiting Market" in *Long Island Business News* (February 6, 2004)
Pub: Dolan Media Newswires
Ed: Ken Schachter. **Description:** Profile of CPI Aerostructures Inc., the defense contractor; CPI is looking for a new chief financial officer, and Edward Fred, CPI's president and chief executive said he will resume duties as the CFO until a new manager is hired.

44990 ■ **"Change the way you persuade"** in *Harvard Business Review* (Vol. 80, No. 5, May 2002, pp. 65)
Pub: Harvard Business School Press
Ed: Robert B. Miller, Gary A. Williams. **Description:** Suggestions are offered for tailoring one's style of persuasion to the type of executive making the business decision. There are five types of decision makers: charismatics, thinkers, skeptics, followers and controllers.

44991 ■ **"Changing for the better through conferences and conventions"** in *Women in Business* (Vol. 54, No. 2, March-April 2002, pp. 24)
Pub: The ABWA Co Inc.
Ed: Mary-Lane Kamberg. **Description:** American Business Women's Association members can change their work lives when attending association conventions. Courses and get-togethers with other members can prove to be beneficial.

44992 ■ **"Changing Times Require Changes in Recruiting Styles"** in *Rough Notes* (Vol. 145, No. 2, February 2003, pp. 65)
Pub: Rough Notes
Ed: Troy Korsgaden. **Description:** The insurance and financial services industry must create deliberate recruitment processes to maintain seamless and expert service to customers.

44993 ■ **"Channel Surfing"** in *Sales and Marketing.com* (Vol. 156, No. 3, March 2004, pp. 7)
Pub: VNU eMedia, Inc.
Ed: Jennifer Gilbert. **Description:** According to a report from Mercer Management Consulting, called "Do You Know Who Your Profitable Channel Partners Are?", smaller channels can provide higher growth potential, leading to higher profit margins, despite the common belief that larger channels such as retailers and distributors are the most profitable.

44994 ■ **"Charmed, I'm Sure: Proper Business Etiquette Goes Beyond the Salad Fork"** in *Black Enterprise* (Vol. 35, February 2005, No. 7, pp. 64)
Pub: Earl G. Graves Publishing Co. Inc.
Ed: Lee Anna Jackson. **Description:** Proper business etiquette is examined, offering a list of several things that develop effective business skills.

44995 ■ **"Checking Inn at the Office"** in *Home Office Computing* (Vol. 18, No. 10, October 2000, pp. 92)
Pub: Scholastic Inc.
Ed: William Van Winkle. **Description:** While sending workers home lets a company move to smaller quarters, thus saving money, the firm still needs to accommodate telecommuters and mobile workers when they do come in, whether its for two days, a week, or only one day per month. Firms are looking to a practical solution: hoteling. Most hoteling spaces are designed by architectural and planning firms to make the workplace comfortable and inviting for transient workers.

44996 ■ **"Chicago Defender"** in *Black Enterprise* (Vol. 35, December 2004, No. 5, pp. 86)
Pub: Earl G. Graves Publishing Co. Inc.
Description: Roland S. Martin has been named executive editor of the Chicago Defender. The black newspaper was founded in 1905.

44997 ■ **"Chief concern"** in *Entrepreneur* (Vol. 31, No. 4, April 2003, pp. 51)
Pub: Entrepreneur Media Inc.
Ed: David Lipschultz. **Description:** The need for hiring a chief financial officer for companies is examined; one question to ask in making a determination is whether the bill from an accounting firm is higher than the salary of a seasoned financial manager.

44998 ■ **"Chief Risk Officer No Solution"** in *American Banker* (Vol. 170, February 4, 2005, No. 24, pp. 11)
Pub: Thomson Financial Media Inc.
Description: Separating business operations from risk management can lead to disjointed decision-making for a company. Ways to make risk management a business support function are critiqued.

44999 ■ **"Chip Shot. Teradyne's New President is Crafting a Comeback after an Industry Slump"** in *Boston Business Journal* (Vol. 23, Jul. 4, 03)
Pub: American City Business Journals
Ed: Tom Witkowski. **Description:** Biography of Michael A. Bradley, the new president of Teradyne Inc. is presented. Teradyne Inc. manufactures automatic test equipment and interconnection systems to semiconductor, electronics and network systems companies.

45000 ■ **"Clarence Otis Named CEO of Darden Restaurants"** in *Black Enterprise* (Vol. 35, November 2004, No. 4, pp. 28)
Pub: Earl G. Graves Publishing Co. Inc.
Ed: Tamara E. Holmes. **Description:** Profile of Clarence Otis Jr., executive vice president of Darden Restaurants Inc., who will become the seventh black American leading a Fortune 500 company. Otis joined Darden in 1995 and became president of Smokey Bones in 2002. Statistical data included.

45001 ■ **"A Class Act"** in *Entrepreneur* (Vol. 32, December 2004, No. 12, pp. 61)
Pub: Entrepreneur Media Inc.
Ed: C.J. Prince. **Description:** Increasingly, entrepreneurs are taking courses designed to assist in running a business, including leadership, finance, accounting and economics.

45002 ■ **"A Clean Slate"** in *Entrepreneur* (Vol. 31, No. 11, November 2003, pp. 94)
Pub: Entrepreneur Media Inc.
Ed: Juanita Weaver. **Description:** Entrepreneurial creativity can be hampered by those unwilling to make room for new ideas. Starting fresh can lead to new innovations.

45003 ■ **"The Clear Leader: Marcus Buckingham Has Spent a Lot of Time Watching Leadership At Its Best"** in *Fast Company* (March 2005, No. 92)
Pub: Gruner & Jahr USA Publishing
Ed: Bill Breen. **Description:** Marcus Buckingham, researcher, discusses the heart of true leadership. Buckingham has authored a book that explains how strong, successful leaders are compelled by the future.

45004 ■ **"Clear leadership"** in *Women in Business* (Vol. 54, No. 5, September-October 2002, pp. 41)
Pub: The ABWA Company, Inc.
Ed: Andrew Harvey. **Description:** Leadership requires a vision of where an organization will be taken.

45005 ■ **"Clone yourself"** in *WorkingWoman* (Vol. 25, No. 5, May 2000, pp. 79)
Pub: Lang Communications Inc.
Ed: Russell Wild. **Description:** Planning for a successor is a good strategy for career development and makes good sense. Issues concerning the training of a replacement and the ability to delegate are presented.

45006 ■ **"Close to Finding RedZone's Niche"** in *Pittsburgh Business Times* (Vol. 4, August 15, 2003, pp. 14)
Pub: Pittsburgh Business Times
Ed: Maria Guzzo. **Description:** Profile of Pittsburgh, Pennsylvania-based RedZone Robotics Inc.; topics include market development, management styles, and management of small business.

45007 ■ **"Co-Ed Management"** in *Entrepreneur* (Vol. 28, No. 2, February 2000, pp. 34)
Pub: Entrepreneur Media Inc.
Ed: Cynthia E. Griffin. **Description:** Diversity in your management team can help your Initial Public Offering (IPO) soar.

45008 ■ **"The coach who got poached"** in *Harvard Business Review* (Vol. 80, No. 3, March 2002, pp. 31)
Pub: Harvard Business School Press
Ed: Idalene F. Kesner. **Description:** A case study about a manager who develops excellent people only to see them stolen away by other divisions.

45009 ■ *Coaching Through Effective Feedback: Successful Communication*
Pub: Pfeiffer & Co.
Ed: Paul J. Jerome. **Price:** $12.95 (paper). **Description:** Part of the Management Skills Series.

45010 ■ **"Coevolving At Last, a Way to Make Synergies Work"** in *Harvard Business Review* (Vol. 78, No. 1, January 2000, pp. 91)
Pub: Harvard Business School Publishing Corp.
Ed: Kathleen M. Eisenhardt, D. Charles Galunic. **Description:** Cross-business synergies as a strategy is the challenge most companies are trying to capture. The process of coevolution, whereby companies collaborate to achieve a specific goal, is one that can help managers direct the company.

45011 ■ **"Collaboration is the Hottest Buzzword in Business Today. Too Bad it doesn't work."** in *Inc.* (September 2006, pp. 61-62)
Pub: Gruner & Jahr USA Publishing
Ed: David H. Freedman. **Description:** Individual decision making, although frowned on in business circles today, is usually frowned upon when a consensus is bypassed in making that decision. Both strategies are important if properly used.

45012 ■ **"A College Lockout?"** in *Hispanic Business* (October 2002, pp. 30-32, 34)
Pub: Hispanic Business
Ed: Scott Williams. **Description:** An investigation into the issues involving the low national average of Hispanics achieving postsecondary degrees. Statistical data included showing degrees earned by Hispanics, including associate's, bachelor's, master's, and doctorate degrees.

45013 ■ **"Commentary: For Women in Management, Communication is King"** in *Long Island Business News* (March 12, 2004)
Pub: Dolan Media Newswires
Ed: Natalie Canavor. **Description:** Reasoning behind women's management skills versus men's are discussed; research studies are used to document opinions.

45014 ■ **"Commentary: Three Steps to Becoming a Business Leader in Your Field"** in *Long Island Business News* (February 13, 2004)
Pub: Dolan Media Newswires
Description: Interview with Martha Ann Walther, one of the most impressive women in business today. Walther is vice president of operations for Triborough Bridge and Tunnel Authority and believes that being perceived as a leader can be a career-making factor for women in every industry at any stage of her career.

45015 ■ **"Community"** in *Inc.* (September 2005, pp. 88)
Pub: Inc. Magazine
Ed: Darren Dahl. **Description:** Entrepreneurs, lawyers, MBAs and PhDs meet monthly in Newburyport, Massachusetts to discuss ways to apply business lessons learned from the book club's monthly selection.

45016 ■ **"Companies spiff up dress codes in recession"** in *Atlanta Business Chronicle* (Vol. 25, No. 19, October 18, 2002, pp. 4C)
Pub: American City Business Publications, Inc.
Ed: Ray Glier. **Description:** Casual dress codes at companies are becoming a casualty of the current economic recession, as businesses become more serious about doing business.

45017 ■ **"Company Crisis: CEO Under Fire"** in *Hispanic Business* (March 2003, pp. 54-56)
Pub: Hispanic Business
Ed: Scott Williams. **Description:** Crisis management guidelines for CEOs and other top management executives are presented for times when a company is faced with an emergency.

45018 ■ **"Competition Keeps Athletic Execs Stoked"** in *Crain's Detroit Business* (Vol. 21, October 3, 2005, No. 43, pp. 27)
Pub: Crain Communications Inc. - Detroit

Ed: Scott Cendrowski. **Description:** Clubs and competitive sports leagues contribute to keeping executives competitive.

45019 ■ "A Confidence Boost" in *Sales & Marketing Management* **(Vol. 158, November-December 2006, No. 11, pp. 17)**
Pub: VNU Business Media
Ed: Keith Ferrazzi. **Description:** Tips for motivating a sales team are presented.

45020 ■ "The Confidence Game" in *Forbes* **(Vol. 170, No. 13, December 23, 2002, pp. 234)**
Pub: Forbes Magazine
Ed: George Gilder. **Description:** The entire makeup of a successful company is based wholly on trust.

45021 ■ "Convention Calendar" in *Black Enterprise* **(Vol. 37, November 2006, No. 4, pp. 76)**
Pub: Earl G. Graves Publishing Co. Inc.
Description: Listing of conferences targeted at African American executives and business owners.

45022 ■ "Cooking Up a Winner in Manny Garcia's Kitchen" in *Orlando Business Journal* **(Vol. 20, No. 2, June 27, 2003, pp. 26)**
Pub: American City Business Journals, Inc.
Ed: Bob Mervine. **Description:** Profile of Manny Garcia's Culinary Concepts Inc., including profit levels, strategic planning, and management style.

45023 ■ "Coordinating Staff With IT Technology" in *Ingram's* **(Vol. 27, No. 8, August 2001, pp. 23)**
Pub: Show Me Publishing, Inc.
Ed: Michael May. **Description:** The management of employees use of information technology is discussed. Advice is given on software training and Internet usage monitoring.

45024 ■ "COOs: Less Room At the Top" in *Business Week* **(January 31, 2005, pp. 11)**
Pub: McGraw-Hill Companies
Ed: Louis Lavelle, Ira Sager. **Description:** Since the dot.com demise, a number of companies are eliminating the position of Chief Operating Officer from their executive teams.

45025 ■ *Corporate Crisis and Risk Management: Modeling, Strategies and SME Application*
Pub: Elsevier Science and Technology Books
Ed: M. Aba-Bulgu; S.M.N. Islam. **Released:** December 2006. **Price:** $115.00. **Description:** Methods and tools for handling corporate risk and crisis management are profiled for small to medium-sized businesses.

45026 ■ "Corporate Elite" in *Hispanic Business* **(January/February 2005, pp. 30, 32, 34, 38, 40, 42)**
Pub: Hispanic Business
Description: Profiles of leading Hispanic corporate leaders include Richard A. Gonzalez, Abbott Laboratories; Carolos M. Morales, Merrill Lynch; James J. Padilla, Ford Motor Co.; William D. Perez, Nike; Marie Quintana Cummiskey, PepsiCo; and Felicia D. Thornton, Albertsons Inc., as well as others.

45027 ■ *Corporate Entrepreneurship: Top Managers and New Business Creation*
Pub: Cambridge University Press
Ed: Vijay Sathe. **Released:** February 2007. **Price:** $35.00. **Description:** Studies covering entrepreneurship and business growth are examined.

45028 ■ "Corporate Governance" in *Atlanta Business Chronicle* **(Vol. 25, Nov. 8, 2002, No. 22 pp. S1)**
Pub: American City Business Publications, Inc.
Description: A panel discussion concerning corporate governance modifications resulting from the Sarbanes-Oxley Act of 2002 and various proposed regulations is presented. General counsels involved in the discussion came from Atlanta-based firms, including Acuity Brands Inc., ChoicePoint Inc., and Turner Broadcasting System Inc.

45029 ■ "The cost center that paid its way" in *Harvard Business Review* **(Vol. 80, No. 4, April 2002, pp. 31)**
Pub: Harvard Business School Press
Ed: Julia Kirby. **Description:** A case study where four commentators review the workings of a fictional company's marketing communications department. Advice is offered on how its leader could have avoided the discontent within other departments.

45030 ■ "Counter-Intuitive Offers" in *Business Week* **(No. 3658, December 6, 1999, pp. F8)**
Pub: McGraw-Hill, Inc.
Description: The issue of making counter offers to departing employees may be a wrong move for small business.

45031 ■ "Crafting the most productive and efficient work force" in *Fairfield County Business Journal* **(Vol. 42, No. 3, Jan. 20, 2003, pp. 4)**
Pub: Westfair Communications, Inc.
Ed: Steven Drexel. **Description:** The importance of using both long-term and short-term recruitment strategies during slow economic times is discussed.

45032 ■ "Cream of the Crop" in *Hispanic Business* **(March 2002, pp. 36)**
Pub: Hispanic Business
Description: Advice is given for choosing a business or law school, with information geared toward Hispanic students.

45033 ■ "Create a Client Loyalty Program" in *Rough Notes* **(Vol. 146, No. 3, March 2003, pp. 52)**
Pub: Rough Notes
Ed: Steve Andersen. **Description:** Pareto's Principle, the 80/20 Rule, can be used in managing an insurance agency by focusing 80 percent of time and energy on 20 percent of its clients.

45034 ■ "Creative Control" in *Washington Business Journal* **(Vol. 22, No. 9, July 4, 2003, pp. 16)**
Pub: Washington Business Journal
Ed: Chris Silva. **Description:** Management style, marketing and strategic planning of Washington, DC-based Healthcare Ventures LLC is discussed.

45035 ■ "Crisis Mode" in *Entrepreneur* **(Vol. 32, December 2004, No. 12, pp. 32)**
Pub: Entrepreneur Media Inc.
Ed: Geoff Williams. **Description:** When a personal crisis hits a small business owner, experts recommend giving full disclosure to employees.

45036 ■ "Critical Mass" in *Small Business Opportunities* **(Summer 2005)**
Pub: Harris Publications Inc.
Ed: Dave Anderson. **Description:** Five key issues to run a successful small business are outlined.

45037 ■ "Crucibles of leadership" in *Harvard Business Review* **(Vol. 80, No. 9, September 2002, pp. 39)**
Pub: Harvard Business School Press
Ed: Warren G. Bennis, Robert J. Thomas. **Description:** Various incidents recount the ways executives have successfully coped with adversity.

45038 ■ "CSFB Repositions Top Exec" in *Black Enterprise* **(Vol. 35, November 2004, No. 4, pp. 30)**
Pub: Earl G. Graves Publishing Co. Inc.
Ed: K. Terrell Reed. **Description:** Credit Suisse First Boston has appointed Adebayo Bayo Ogunlesi as its newly created chief client officer and executive vice chairman. Ogunlesi will devote his time working with clients.

45039 ■ "Culture Shock" in *Entrepreneur* **(Vol. 31, No. 9, July 2003, pp. 77)**
Pub: Entrepreneur Media, Inc.
Ed: Marc Diener. **Description:** With increasing numbers of international, multinational and transnational corporations, culture is playing a major role in negotiations.

45040 ■ "The Curse of the superstar CEO" in *Harvard Business Review* **(Vol. 80, No. 9, September 2002, pp. 60)**
Pub: Harvard Business School Press
Ed: Rakesh Khurana. **Description:** Recent examples are used to show how destructive the process for recruiting for a CEO can be, especially if the CEO is charismatic, yet prone to crucial errors.

45041 ■ "Cycles teach you patience" in *Fast Company* **(May 2001, pp. 88)**
Pub: Fast Company
Ed: Warren Bennis. **Description:** Leadership guru Warren Bennis, discusses economic cycles and how these cycles teach patience to business owners.

45042 ■ "Dangle Carrots: How To Keep Your Sales Force Hopping" in *My Business* **(October/November 2003, pp. 45)**
Pub: My Business Magazine
Ed: Lena Basha. **Description:** Four tips to help motive a sales team are listed, including sales strategies that involve team efforts, providing the necessary tools to a sales force, setting realistic goals, and the use of rewards to motivate.

45043 ■ "The Dark Art of Letting People Go" in *Business Week Online* **()**
Pub: McGraw-Hill, Inc.
Description: Laying off employees is a difficult task, and the importance of establishing policies and procedures is covered.

45044 ■ "Dawson on Board at Melville-based Fala Direct Marketing" in *Long Island Business News* **(March 12, 2004)**
Pub: Dolan Media Newswires
Ed: Ryan McCormick. **Description:** Profile of Terrence Dawson, newly appointed COO of Fala Direct Marketing; Dawson attributes his success to the philosophy of knowing your role in the company in which you are working.

45045 ■ "Day's 'lean' philosophy to face new test at Venture Holdings" in *Crain's Detroit Business* **(Vol. 19, No. 14, April 7, 2003, pp. 41)**
Pub: Crain Communications Inc., Detroit
Ed: Rhoda Miel. **Description:** Profile of Joseph Day, the new leader of Venture Holdings Company LLC, who will be able to test his lean-manufacturing ideas since Venture Holdings has filed for Chapter 11 bankruptcy protection.

45046 ■ "Dealing With Bonus Backlash" in *Sales and Marketing.com* **(Vol. 147, No. 2, February 2004, pp. 7)**
Pub: VNU eMedia, Inc.
Ed: Melinda Ligos. **Description:** Three steps to help motivate a sales staff in a year of lower commissions and bonuses are listed, including short term rewards, holding a compensation seminar, and convincing the staff that management is committed to helping them increase their income.

45047 ■ "Dealing With a Slumping Rep" in *Sales and Marketing.com* **(Vol. 156, No. 3, March 2004, pp. 12)**
Pub: VNU eMedia, Inc.
Description: David MacDonald, senior sales director at SAS, a software firm in Cary, North Carolina, prefers to work with a sales rep in a slump, rather than giving up on him or her.

45048 ■ "Deals Unplugged" in *Entrepreneur* **(Vol. 31, No. 8, August 2003, pp. 69)**
Pub: Entrepreneur Media, Inc.
Ed: Marc Diener. **Description:** When negotiating deals it is time to leave the table when the other side's last best offer isn't good enough, there's a better alternative, or it is discovered that the opponent is unethical, however there are also more subtle signs to look for, such as a difficult opponent or the fact that transactional costs will be too expensive.

45049 ■ "Dear white boss; What it's really like to be a black manager" in *Harvard Business Review* **(Vol. 80, No. 11, November 2002, pp. 76)**
Pub: Harvard Business School Press
Description: This fictional letter describes what it is like to be different in the workplace and sheds light on the sometimes subtle and often systemic racial biases in the corporate world.

45050 ■ "Deciding Factors" in *Journal of Business Strategies* **(Vol. 21, No. 5, September 2000, pp. 4)**
Pub: Center for Business and Economic Research
Description: A survey by management consulting firm Kepner-Tregoe found that most managers and workers believe that the number of decisions they must make each day has increased in the last three years, and they feel they have less time to make the decisions than in the past.

45051 ■ "Decisions, decisions: This book lets you be the judge" in *Entrepreneur* **(Vol. 30, No. 2, February 2002, pp. 22)**
Pub: Entrepreneur Media Inc.
Ed: Mark Henricks. **Description:** Review of the book entitled, "Why Didn't I Think of That?", by Charles W. McCoy Jr. The book is full of innovative-thinking exercises, checklists, anecdotes, challenges, puzzles and more.

45052 ■ *The Definitive Drucker: The Final Word from the Father of Modern Management*
Pub: McGraw-Hill
Ed: Elizabeth Haas Edersheim; A.G. Lafley. **Released:** December 2006. **Price:** $27.95.

45053 ■ "Delicate Deliveries" in *Birmingham Business Journal* **(Vol. 20, No. 33, August 15, 2003, pp. 13)**
Pub: American City Business Journals, Inc.
Ed: Leslie Zganjar. **Description:** Profile of Birmingham, Alabama florist, Masterpiece Flowers; topics cover management of a small business, marketing and advertising, and average annual sales.

45054 ■ "Delta Industries Inc" in *Mississippi Business Journal* **(Vol. 29, January 2007, No. 4, pp. 6)**
Pub: Venture Publications, Inc.
Description: Profile of Les Howell Jr., vice president of Delta Industries Inc. Howell has been chief engineer of Delta for seven years.

45055 ■ "Delusions of Success: How Optimism Undermines Executives' Decisions" in *Harvard Business Review* **(Vol. 81, No. 7, July 2003, pp. 56)**
Pub: Harvard Business School Press
Ed: Dan Lovallo, Daniel Kahneman. **Description:** Realistic business forecasting is discussed.

45056 ■ "Departures Raise Questions About Loss of Women" in *Crain's Detroit Business* **(Vol. 22, November 27, 2006, No. 48, pp. 12)**
Pub: Crain Communications Inc. - Detroit
Ed: Brent Snaveley. **Description:** Female executives are leaving a void behind them in business and industry when they leave. Most of them leave the auto industry entirely and a few move to tier one and tier two suppliers. Strong message is sent to other women in the organization of the unrest.

45057 ■ *Design Your Own Effective Employee Handbook: How to Make the Most of Your Staff with Companion CD-ROM*
Pub: Atlantic Publishing Company
Ed: Michelle Devon. **Released:** June 2006. **Price:** $39.95. **Description:** An employee handbook should include clearly written policies covering the rights and responsibilities of workers.

45058 ■ "Desperate Measures" in *Entrepreneur* **(Vol. 31, No. 8, August 2003, pp. 25)**
Pub: Entrepreneur Media, Inc.
Ed: Karen Axelton. **Description:** The Creative Group, an employment service located in Menlo Park, Califor-

nia, conducted a survey that asked executives to describe the most unusual maneuver they had seen job candidates use to get their attention. The results of that survey are presented.

45059 ■ "Devalued by Diversity" in *Black Enterprise* **(Vol. 35, January 2005, No. 6, pp. 53)**
Pub: Earl G. Graves Publishing Co. Inc.
Description: Key factors to determine whether diversity is managed effectively in a company are presented.

45060 ■ "Developing performers" in *Women in Business* **(Vol. 53, No. 3, May-June, 2001, pp. 8)**
Pub: The ABWA Co. Inc.
Ed: Rachel Warbington. **Description:** Small business owners need to find reliable staff whose skills can be developed to help ease some of the owner's workload. The business owner needs to recognize, develop and monitor their employees' potential.

45061 ■ "Developing a working relationship with your supervisor" in *Wome n in Business* **(Vol. 53, No. 1, January-February 2001, pp. 42)**
Pub: The ABWA Co. Inc.
Description: Ways to develop a working relationship with supervisors are discussed.

45062 ■ "Developing Your Leadership Pipeline" in *Harvard Business Review* **(Vol. 81, No. 12, December 2003, pp. 76)**
Pub: Harvard Business School Press
Ed: Jay A conger, Robert M. Fulmer. **Description:** Key guidelines for effective leadership communication in succession management are examined, including identification of linchpin positions, making the transition process transparent, assessment of progress on a regular basis, and maintaining flexibility.

45063 ■ "Differentiating Legal Issues by Business Type" in *Journal of Small Business Management* **(Vol. 44, October 2006, No. 4, pp. 563)**
Pub: Blackwell Publishing, Inc.
Ed: Sandra Malach; Peter Robinson; Tannis Radcliffe. **Description:** A fundamental issue when forming a business and its strategic operation is developing legal strategies to better protect the assets of the business and entrepreneur. An analysis of data indicated that certain legal issues are relevant to specific types of new ventures while certain legal issues are important to all new ventures. Depending on the category of business, the relevancy of individual legal issues will vary. Statistical data included.

45064 ■ *Directory of Management Consultants*
Pub: Kennedy Information
Released: Biennial, latest edition 2004. **Covers:** 2,859 management consulting firms in North America. **Entries Include:** Firm name, address, phone, fax, e-mail, name of principal executive, date founded, staff size and revenue (in range), services offered, SIC numbers of industries served, plus brief description of firm. For commercial use requests, please contact publisher. **Arrangement:** Alphabetical. **Indexes:** Geographical, key contacts, services, industries.

45065 ■ "Disgruntled Workers Were Driving Vance Patterson Crazy" in *Inc.* **(Volume 27, July 2005, No. 7, pp. 42-43)**
Pub: Inc. Magazine
Ed: Stephanie Clifford. **Description:** Vance Patterson, CEO of Patterson Fan, discusses the way he handled disgruntled employees he felt were destroying his company.

45066 ■ "Disruptive change: When trying harder is part of the problem" in *Harvard Business Review* **(Vol. 80, No. 5, May 2002, pp. 94)**
Pub: Harvard Business School Press
Ed: Joseph L. Clark, Bower Gilbert. **Description:** How executives react to disruptions in their markets, such as to new technology, should be regarded as both a threat and an opportunity.

45067 ■ "Distance Makes a Difference" in *Home Office Computing* **(Vol. 18, No. 8, August 2000, pp. 20)**
Pub: Scholastic Inc.
Ed: Cynthia Froggatt. **Description:** As increasing numbers of workers are working at home, bosses are discovering that traditional management practices may no longer apply. The three basic distinctions in telemanagment vs. traditional management methods are described.

45068 ■ "Do ask. Do Tell" in *Folio: the Magazine for Magazine Management* **(Vol. 30, No. 1, January 2001, pp. 2)**
Pub: Intertec Publishing Corp.
Description: The things to ask when looking for a new supplier are outlined.

45069 ■ "Do Something - He's About to Snap" in *Harvard Business Review* **(Vol. 81, No. 7, July 2003, pp. 23)**
Pub: Harvard Business School Press
Ed: Eileen Roche. **Description:** It is difficult to discipline an employee who has not committed any transgressions but who's behavior has other employees concerned.

45070 ■ "Do you have a well-designed organization?" in *Harvard Business Review* **(Vol. 80, No. 3, March 2002, pp. 117)**
Pub: Harvard Business School Press
Ed: Michael Goold, Andrew Campbell. **Description:** An executive's job of creating a new organizational design and the nine tests of organization design, which can either evaluate an existing structure or create a new one are discussed.

45071 ■ "Do You Love What You Do?" in *Fast Company* **(March 2005, No. 92, pp. 88)**
Pub: Gruner & Jahr USA Publishing
Ed: Marshall Goldsmith. **Description:** Profile of Warren Bennis, founding chairman of the Leadership Institute at the University of Southern California. Bennis discusses job satisfaction.

45072 ■ "Does Your Sales Management Stink?" in *Sales & Marketing Management* **(Vol. 159, January-February 2007, No. 1, pp. 12)**
Pub: VNU Business Media
Description: Tips for build and assess a successful sales team are explored.

45073 ■ "Does Your Team Need a Hug or a Prod?" in *Sales and Marketing.com* **(Vol. 147, No. 2, February 2004, pp. 14)**
Pub: VNU eMedia, Inc.
Ed: Michele Marchetti. **Description:** Finding the right style that works for managing a staff requires a quick lesson in behavioral science, according to Hellen Davis, president and CEO of a management counseling and training firm in Pennsylvania. Unless a manager uses the correct style, employees will not be motivated.

45074 ■ "Dollars for Scholars" in *Hispanic Business* **(September 2003, pp. 64, 66, 68)**
Pub: Hispanic Business
Description: A select guide to scholarships for the study of business or law is presented.

45075 ■ "Don't Get Mad, Get Practical" in *My Business* **(April/May 2004, pp. 39)**
Pub: My Business Magazine
Description: Ways to diffuse any difficult situation are listed in order to use conflict as a means for business growth.

45076 ■ "Don't Go Changing" in *Entrepreneur* **(Vol. 28, No. 3, March 2000, pp. 122)**
Pub: Entrepreneur Media Inc.
Description: Limiting change in business is the topic of this discussion.

45077 ■ "Don't Hire the Wrong CEO" in *Harvard Business Review* **(Vol. 78, No. 3, May 2000, pp. 170)**
Pub: Harvard Business School Publishing Corp.
Ed: Warren Bennis, James O'Toole. **Description:** The right CEO can make or break a company, yet boards often go about CEO selection all wrong. Several guidelines are presented to help boards find the best leader for their company.

45078 ■ "Don't Tell It To The Judge" in *Entrepreneur* **(Vol. 28, No. 6, June 2000, pp. 127)**
Pub: Entrepreneur Media Inc.
Ed: Steven C. Bahls and Jane Aster Bahls. **Description:** It's good to fire bad employees. It's not so good to talk about how bad they were at unemployment hearings.

45079 ■ "Drawing the Line: The Right Way To Do Business With Friends" in *Sales & Marketing Management* **(Vol. 157, February 2005, No. 2, pp. 18)**
Pub: VNU Business Media
Ed: Sara Calabro. **Description:** The best way to handle business relationships with friends is to use the same client-customer principles of other deals, including putting everything in writing.

45080 ■ "The Dress Code: How Business Style is Communicated" in *Black Enterprise* **(Vol. 34, No. 2, September 2003, pp. 60)**
Pub: Earl Graves Publishing Co.
Ed: Laura Egodigwe. **Description:** Women business leaders tend to set standards by their business style. The basis of any executive's wardrobe is a great suit and wearing the best affordable quality.

45081 ■ "Drumming Up Business For the Democrats" in *Business Week* **(January 9, 2006, No. 3966, pp. 39)**
Pub: McGraw-Hill Companies
Ed: Richard S. Dunham. **Description:** Heath Shuler is among the new recruits running as candidates for Democratic seats; these new recruits are business executives offering financial experience that will make the party stronger.

45082 ■ "The Dubious Dole" in *Entrepreneur* **(Vol. 28, No. 10, October 2000, pp. 123)**
Pub: Entrepreneur Media Inc.
Ed: Jacquelyn Lynn. **Description:** Unemployment compensation is an insurance program designed to provide income to people who are out of work. Don't treat claims for unemployment compensation by former employees lightly, and the reasons why are covered.

45083 ■ *The Dynamic Small Business Manager*
Pub: Lulu.com
Ed: Frank Vickers. **Released:** March 2006. **Price:** $39.99. **Description:** Practical advice is given to help small business owners successfully manage their company.

45084 ■ "The dynamics of team interaction" in *Women in Business* **(Vol. 53, No. 2, March-April, 2001, pp. 42)**
Pub: The ABWA Co. Inc.
Ed: Mary-Lane Kamberg. **Description:** Guidance on how to work effectively as a member of a team is presented. The effect of group dynamics, the management of conflict within a team and useful and counterproductive behavior within a team are explored.

45085 ■ *E-Myth Mastery: The Seven Essential Disciplines for Building a World Class Company*
Pub: HarperCollins Publishers Inc.
Ed: Michael E. Gerber. **Released:** March 2007. **Price:** $16.95. **Description:** Leadership, marketing, money, management, lead conversion, lead generation, client fulfillment are the seven keys to successful entrepreneurship.

45086 ■ "E-Train" in *Sales and Marketing. com* **(Vol. 156, No. 3, March 2004, pp. 19)**
Pub: VNU eMedia, Inc.
Description: Profile of Ninth House Inc.'s Instant Advice E-Learning Solution. Using an online library of 500 business topics, users receive coaching from notable management gurus such as Tom Peters and Ken Blanchard.

45087 ■ "Easy Does It" in *Entrepreneur* **(Vol. 28, No. 6, June 2000, pp. 22)**
Pub: Entrepreneur Media Inc.
Ed: Mark Henricks. **Description:** Michelle Paster's education business has no debt, more customers than it can handle, and a hands-on owner whose concern for quality requires her to do virtually everything herself.

45088 ■ "The Economic Ground War" in *Hispanic Business* **(March 2003, pp. 18)**
Pub: Hispanic Business
Ed: Joel Russell. **Description:** Small business executives and economic experts are predicting a slowdown for the first half of 2003. It is hoped that spending will increase when global political threats are stabilized.

45089 ■ *The Economics and Management of Small Business: An International Perspective*
Pub: Routledge
Ed: Graham Bannock. **Released:** April 2005. **Price:** $132.00 (US), $190.00 (Canadian). **Description:** International perspectives on the economics and management of small business, featuring case studies and empirical research.

45090 ■ "Education" in *Business Week* **(January 9, 2006, No. 3966, pp. 40-43)**
Pub: McGraw-Hill Companies
Ed: Louis Lavelle. **Description:** China will require 75,000 business executives with international experience by year 2010, 70,000 more than exist today. The country is equipping its schools with programs offering Western management ideas to better serve its growing global economy.

45091 ■ "Educational-software concern is cutting work force by 20 percent" in *Wall Street Journal* **(May 20, 2002, pp. C9)**
Pub: Wall Street Journal
Description: Docent Inc, the educational software company, is planning to cut its workforce by 20 percent this year.

45092 ■ "The Effect of Social Style on Peer Evaluation Ratings in Project Teams" in *Journal of Business Communications* **(Vol. 43, January 2006)**
Pub: Association for Business Communication
Ed: Gary L. May, Lisa E. Gueldenzoph. **Description:** A study of peer-to-peer performance appraisals in the team context is presented.

45093 ■ *Effective Small Business Management*
Pub: Macmillan Publishing Co., Inc.
Ed: Thomas W. Simmerer. **Price:** $29.70

45094 ■ "Efficiency Creates Opportunity" in *Hispanic Business* **(June 2002, pp. 74)**
Pub: Hispanic Business
Ed: Scott Williams. **Description:** Efficiency experts agree that companies can become more efficient by fostering an environment of improvement.

45095 ■ "The 80-20 Rule: It's Not Just a Glib Remark" in *Barron's* **(Vol. 82, No. 57, February, 10, 2003, pp. 39)**
Pub: Barron's
Ed: Thomas G. Donlan. **Description:** Goldman Sachs CEO, Henry M. Paulson, Jr. was correct in citing the 80-20 rule, which is one of the most true management aphorisms ever invented. A small proportion of people almost always produce most of the work, innovation, and results in most organizations.

45096 ■ "Elbows Off the Table" in *My Business* **(February/March 2004, pp. 14)**
Pub: My Business Magazine
Ed: Julie Bawden Davis. **Description:** Rules of etiquette that still apply to be successful are listed. Manners are critical to business success.

45097 ■ "Electronic Arts to Convert Some of Its Salaried Employees to Hourly Pay" in *San Jose Mercury News* **(March 10, 2005)**
Pub: Knight-Ridder/Tribune Business News
Description: Electronic Arts has transitioned some of its salaried workers to hourly wage earners. The employees will be allowed to collect overtime pay, but will no longer be eligible for company stock options or bonuses. The video game firm's move is one example of the changing nature of the tech economy since the dot-com collapse.

45098 ■ "The emancipates organization. Insights on gender, leadership, and power" in *Harvard Business Review* **(Vol. 80, Sept. 2002, pp. 20)**
Pub: Harvard Business School Press
Ed: Gardiner Morse. **Description:** In an interview with Kim Campbell, former Canadian Prime Minister, Campbell answers questions about being a female in male-dominated managerial jobs.

45099 ■ "The empire strikes back; Counterrevolutionary strategies for industry leaders" in *Harvard Business Review* **(Vol. 80, Nov. 2002, pp. 66)**
Pub: Harvard Business School Press
Ed: Richard D'Aveni. **Description:** Five ways that industry leaders can respond to revolutionary business models or disruptive technologies. The strategies are containment, shaping, absorption, neutralization and annulment.

45100 ■ "Employee theft on the rise - Fidelity coverage is crucial" in *Rough Notes* **(Vol. 146, No. 4, April 2003, pp. 30)**
Pub: Rough Notes
Ed: Roy C. McCormick. **Description:** Embezzlement and property theft by employees is on the rise. Background checks, security cameras, as well as employee dishonest insurance should be obtained by management.

45101 ■ *Employee Management for Small Business*
Pub: Self-Counsel Press, Incorporated
Ed: Lin Grensing-Pophal. **Released:** August 2005. **Price:** $17.95. **Description:** Management tools to help entrepreneurs maintain an effective human resources plan for a small company.

45102 ■ "The enemies of trust" in *Harvard Business Review* **(Vol. 81, No. 2, February 2003, pp. 88)**
Pub: Harvard Business School Press
Ed: Robert Galford, Ann Siebold Drapeau. **Description:** The relationship between a business and its client and a company's relationship with its employees is contrasted showing that the business/client relationship allows for trust to develop easier than that of the company/managers/employees relationships.

45103 ■ "Enjoy the Silence" in *Black Enterprise* **(Vol. 36, November 2005, No. 4, pp. 162)**
Pub: Earl G. Graves Publishing Co. Inc.
Ed: Robyn D. Clarke. **Description:** Silence can be used as a useful communication tool. Gestures, nods and smiles can also communicate a point in business communications.

45104 ■ *Enlightened Leadership: Best Practice Guidelines and Timesaving Tools for Easily Implementing Learning Organizations*
Pub: Learning House Publishing, Incorporated
Ed: Alan G. Thomas; Ralph L. LoVuolo; Jeanne C. Hillson. **Released:** September 2006, printable 3 times/year. **Price:** $21.00. **Description:** Book provides the tools required to create a learning organiza-

tion management model along with a step-by-step guide for team planning and learning. The strategy works as a manager's self-help guide as well as offering continuous learning and improvement for company-wide success.

45105 ■ "Enter the Limelight" in
Entrepreneur (Vol. 28, No. 8, August 2000,
pp. 36)
Pub: Entrepreneur Media Inc.
Description: Five sure ways to be a successful business manager are cited.

45106 ■ "Entrepreneur Column" in
Entrepreneur (August 25, 2005)
Pub: Entrepreneur Media Inc.
Ed: David G. Javitch. **Description:** Guidelines and tips to assist employers in the firing process are presented.

45107 ■ "Entrepreneur Column" in
Entrepreneur.com (January 12 2006)
Pub: Entrepreneur Media Inc.
Ed: David Javitch. **Description:** Ways to recognize and help prevent and rescue employees showing signs of being burnt-out on the job. Many factors in the workplace environment can cause employee burnout. Tardiness, absenteeism, apathy, moping, backstabbing, decreased quality, decreased productivity, increased errors, accidents or injuries are all signs of burnout.

45108 ■ Entrepreneurial Decision-Making
Individuals, Tasks and Cognitions
Pub: Edward Elgar Publishing, Incorporated
Ed: Gusfafsson. **Released:** December 2006. **Price:** $85.00. **Description:** Entrepreneurial decision-making is examined by comparing various individuals with differing levels of expertise and potential.

45109 ■ The Entrepreneur's Strategy Guide:
Ten Keys for Achieving Marketplace
Leadership
Pub: Greenwood Publishing Group, Incorporated
Ed: Tom Cannon. **Released:** September 2006. **Price:** $44.95. **Description:** Ten principles of marketplace leadership are explored. The book provides a plan for small businesses, including diagnostics, checklists, and other interactive exercises to study both external and internal principles.

45110 ■ Entrepreneurship and Small
Business
Pub: Palgrave Macmillan
Ed: Paul Burns. **Released:** January 2007. **Price:** $74.95. **Description:** Successful management practices are examined to encourage and develop entrepreneurial skills.

45111 ■ Entrepreneurship & Small Business
Management
Pub: Glencoe McGraw-Hill
Ed: Earl C. Meyer. **Released:** 1999. **Price:** $8.10.

45112 ■ "ERM to the rescue" in Rough
Notes (Vol. 146, No. 3, March 2003, pp. 116)
Pub: Rough Notes
Ed: Michael J. Moody. **Description:** After the recent passage of the Sarbanes-Oxley Act, regulations on corporate governance, as well as the PricewaterhouseCoopers study on risk management programs, management concerns are for renewed interest in enterprise risk management.

45113 ■ "The ethical leader's decision tree."
in Harvard Business Review (Vol. 81, No. 2,
February 2003, pp. 18)
Pub: Harvard Business School Press
Ed: Constance E. Bagley. **Description:** The idea of a decision tree to help executives choose to continue an action is presented. The tree takes into consideration legal ramifications, shareholder value, and ethics.

45114 ■ "Ethics of Justice and Care in
Corporate Crisis Management" in Journal of
Business Ethics (Vol. 46, No. 4, Sept. 15,
2003, pp. 351)
Pub: Kluwer Academic Publishers Group
Ed: Sheldene Simola. **Description:** The importance of ethics in corporate crisis management is discussed.

45115 ■ "Everyone's a CFO" in Inc.
(September 2005, pp. 42, 45)
Pub: Inc. Magazine
Ed: Nadine Heintz. **Description:** DCI CEO, Andrew Levine, assigns employees to present monthly financial reports, teaches them to spot trends and anomalies in the numbers, and has them focus on accounting basics.

45116 ■ Excellence in Management
Pub: Crisp Publications, Inc.
Ed: Rick Conlow. **Price:** $12.95. **Description:** Provides six keys to management excellence, examples of best and worst managers, exercises, and case studies designed to help managers succeed.

45117 ■ "Excellent leadership is all in the
people leading" in Atlanta Business
Chronicle (Vol. 24, No. 14, September 7,
2001, pp. 9B)
Pub: American City Business Journals Inc.
Ed: Michael H. Mescon, Timothy S. Mescon. **Description:** Dr. Timothy S. Mescon and Dr. Michael H. Mescon discuss leadership, and what makes good leaders. They use the business EBC Office Centers as an example of good leadership, with EBC employees and executives performing their jobs as professionals. Both doctors comment that a business is built from top to bottom, and from inside out.

45118 ■ "Execs Offer Coaching For New
Tigers Manager; Advice" in Crain's Detroit
Business (Vol. 21, October 10, 2005, No. 43,
pp. 7)
Pub: Crain Communications Inc. - Detroit
Ed: Andrew Dietderich. **Description:** Local executives share insight into good leadership to new Detroit Tigers manager, Jim Leyland.

45119 ■ "Executive women and the myth of
having it all" in Harvard Business Review
(Vol. 80, No. 4, April 2002, pp. 66)
Pub: Harvard Business School Press
Ed: Sylvia Ann Hewlett. **Description:** The results of research into the professional and private lives of highly-educated and high-earning women. The research reveals that, while high-achieving men continue to 'have it all', high-achieving women tend to be unable to combine career success and having children.

45120 ■ "Executive pay off?" in Washington
Business Journal (Vol. 22, No. 3, May 23,
2003, pp. 23)
Pub: Washington Business Journal
Ed: Roger Hughlett. **Description:** The results of a salary survey of executive compensation of companies in the greater Washington, DC area, including bonuses and stock options are presented.

45121 ■ "An Executive Risk Handbook" in
Fortune (Vol. 152, October 3, 2005, No. 7, pp.
69)
Pub: Time Inc.
Ed: Geoffrey Colvin. **Description:** Contingency planning for natural disasters is covered. Understanding corporate risk has companies adopting risk management programs that include the appointment of a chief risk officer.

45122 ■ "Exit interviews can reveal wealth of
information" in Crain's Detroit Business (Vol.
18, No. 49, December 9, 2002, pp. 13)
Pub: Crain Communications Inc., Detroit
Ed: Laura Bailey. **Description:** The pros and cons of hiring outside a company are explored.

45123 ■ Expanding Leadership Impact:
Managing People and Processes
Pub: Pfeiffer & Co.

Ed: Kevin R. Kehoe. **Price:** $12.95 (paper). **Description:** Part of the Management Skills Series.

45124 ■ "Experimental Games for the Design
of Reputation Management Systems" in IBM
Systems Journal (Vol. 42, No. 3, September
2003, pp. 498)
Pub: IBM Technical Journals
Ed: C. Keser. **Description:** Trust between people engaging in economic transactions affects the economic growth of their community. Reputation management systems, such as the Feedback Forum of eBay Inc., can increase the trust level of the participants. The paper shows that experimental economics can be used in a controlled laboratory environment to measure trust and trust enhancement. Emerging issues in the design of reputation management systems are discussed.

45125 ■ "Expert Help" in Entrepreneur (Vol.
28, No. 8, August 2000,pp. 135)
Pub: Entrepreneur Media Inc.
Ed: Cynthia E. Griffin. **Description:** The President's Resource Organization helps small businesses form boards of advisors.

45126 ■ "Experts Advise Office Workers on
the Fine Art of Holiday Gift-Giving" in
Portland Press Herald (December 16, 2005)
Pub: Blethen Maine Newspapers, Inc.
Ed: Matt Wickenheiser. **Description:** Pitfalls to avoid for company gift giving should include the avoidance of gag gifts and personal items; and it is essential to follow a company's gift-giving policy.

45127 ■ "The Extra Mile: Customer Service
That's a Step Beyond" in Sales & Marketing
Management (Vol. 157, February 2005, No. 2,
pp. 18)
Pub: VNU Business Media
Description: SecureWorks, an Internet security firm based in Atlanta, Georgia had its vice president of sales successfully handle a miscommunication between sales reps and customers. He was also able to refer seven new clients to the company in the process.

45128 ■ "Extra scrutiny" in Crain's Detroit
Business (Vol. 19, No. 11, March 17, 2003,
pp. 14)
Pub: Crain Communications Inc., Detroit
Description: Robert Verdun presents his list of recovery methods for struggling companies.

45129 ■ "Eyes Wide Shut? The Inspiration
You Need Could Be Right Under Your Nose"
in Entrepreneur (Vol. 31, No. 9, July 2003, pp.
76)
Pub: Entrepreneur Media, Inc.
Ed: Juanita Weaver. **Description:** Tips to broaden entrepreneurial perspective and to find inspiration are presented.

45130 ■ "Failure of Genius" in Inc. (August
1, 2003)
Pub: Gruner & Jahr USA Publishing
Ed: Jess McCuan. **Description:** Profile of Future Beef. The founders of Future Beef were the smartest, most forward-thinking individuals in the beef business, yet the company did not succeed.

45131 ■ "Fair process: Managing in the
knowledge economy" in Harvard Business
Review (Vol. 81, No. 1, January 2003)
Pub: Harvard Business School Press
Ed: W. Chan Kim, Renee Mauborgne. **Description:** A discussion of "fair process" is presented, pointing out that employees will commit to a management decision, even if they disagree, if they believe that the process used in arriving at the decision was fair.

45132 ■ "Falling Flat? How Flat is Too Flat
When It Comes to Management?" in
Entrepreneur (Vol. 33, January 2005, No. 1,
pp. 69)
Pub: Entrepreneur Media Inc.
Ed: Mark Henricks. **Description:** The importance of a proper management hierarchy is highlighted.

45133 ■ "Family-Biz Circle" in *Business Week Online* (February 17, 2006)
Pub: McGraw-Hill Companies
Description: Entrepreneurs must develop a business plan to pass the family-owned business to the next generation. Consultants at the Family Business Institute can help small business owners construct a plan designed for their small business.

45134 ■ "Fast Track Business" in *Hispanic Business* (March 2002, pp. 60-62)
Pub: Hispanic Business
Ed: John H. Sullivan. **Description:** Profile of Hispanic businessman, Adrian Fernandez, who not only credits 150 race starts to his career, but is the only Championship Auto Racing Team (CART) driver who owns his own race team.

45135 ■ "Fear of feedback" in *Harvard Business Review* (Vol. 81, No. 4, April 2003, pp. 101)
Pub: Harvard Business School Press
Ed: Jay M. Jackman, Myra H. Strober. **Description:** The negative effects of the fear of feedback for workers and bosses are addressed. Ways to overcome that fear so employees can bring work into better alignment with organizational goals are discussed.

45136 ■ "Feedback Needed" in *Sales and Marketing.com* (Vol. 156, No. 3, March 2004, pp. 63)
Pub: VNU eMedia, Inc.
Ed: Julia Chang. **Description:** According to a recent S&MM Equation Research Survey, many successful managers seek out criticism, however 44 percent reported avoiding this strategy.

45137 ■ "Fellowship of the rings" in *Atlanta Business Chronicle* (Vol. 25, No. 19, October 18, 2002, pp. 1B)
Pub: American City Business Publications, Inc.
Ed: Lee Hall. **Description:** Innovative Service Technology Management Services Inc., located in Atlanta, Georgia, honors its 150 employees for a job well done with gifts of Godiva Chocolates, company rings, money and leather jackets emblazoned with the company logo, resulting in a more stable and efficient workforce.

45138 ■ "The 50 Most Powerful Women In Business: Secrets of the Fastest-Rising Stars" in *Fortune* (No. 9, Oct. 16, 2000, pp. 13)
Pub: Time Inc.
Description: In-depth profile of some of the top businesswomen in America, with interviews sharing insight into their secrets of success.

45139 ■ "Filling big shoes at Adobe" in *Harvard Business Review* (Vol. 81, No. 3, March 2003, pp. 20)
Pub: Harvard Business School Press
Ed: Gardiner Morse. **Description:** Bruce Chizen, CEO of Adobe Systems, discusses how he took over leadership from the company's founders and used humility to win converts among the company's employees.

45140 ■ "Financial bootstrapping in small businesses" in *Journal of Business Venturing* (Vol. 16, No. 3, May 2001, pp. 235)
Pub: Elsevier Science, Inc.
Ed: Joakim Winborg, Hans Landstrom. **Description:** Research into the financial bootstrapping methods used by managers of small businesses to acquire resources is presented.

45141 ■ *Financial Times Guide to Business Start Up 2007*
Pub: Pearson Education, Limited
Ed: Sara Williams; Jonquil Lowe. **Released:** November 2006. **Price:** $52.50. **Description:** Guide for starting and running a new business is presented. Sections include ways to get started, direct marketing, customer relations, management and accounting.

45142 ■ "Finding and Keeping Good Employees" in *Ingram's* (Vol. 28, No. 1, January 2002, pp. 69)
Pub: Show Me Publishing, Inc.
Description: Strategies for retaining valued employees are presented.

45143 ■ "Firms rate terrorist attack as No. 1 concern" in *Wall Street Journal* (December 17, 2002, pp. B7)
Pub: Dow Jones & Co. Inc.
Ed: Richard C. Breeden. **Description:** A poll of small business executives, taken by TEC International Inc., shows that firms rate terrorist attacks as their number one concern.

45144 ■ *First, Break All the Rules: What the World's Greatest Managers Do Differently*
Pub: Simon & Schuster, Incorporated
Ed: Marcus Buckingham, Curt Coffman. **Released:** May 1999. **Price:** $27.00. **Description:** Great managers break virtually every rule revered by conventional wisdom.

45145 ■ "First Impressions" in *Black Enterprise* (Vol. 36, December 2005, No. 5, pp. 62)
Pub: Earl G. Graves Publishing Co. Inc.
Description: Sonya Lowerey, author of The Secret Language of Business Cards, discusses the eight common business card mistakes made by small companies.

45146 ■ *The First-Time Manager: A Survival Guide*
Pub: Self-Counsel Press, Inc.
Ed: Theodore G. Tyssen. **Released:** 1992 (print); 1995 (audiocassette). **Price:** $7.95 (paper); $16.95 (audiocassette).

45147 ■ *The Five Dysfunctions of a Team: A Leadership Fable*
Pub: John Wiley & Sons, Incorporated
Ed: Patrick M. Lencioni. **Released:** April 2002. **Price:** $22.95. **Description:** Analysis of a hypothetical tale of the CEO of a struggling, high-profile firm with a dysfunctional executive team.

45148 ■ "5 Honeymoon Hints" in *My Business* (November/December 2001, pp. 46)
Pub: My Business Magazine
Description: The first few weeks in a new position are critical to small companies when hiring new employees. Five ways to assist new hires to adjust to working at a new company are listed.

45149 ■ "The Five Minds of a Manager" in *Harvard Business Review* (Vol. 81, No. 11, November 2003, pp. 54)
Pub: Harvard Business School Press
Ed: Jonathan Gosling, Henry Mintzberg. **Description:** The reflective, action, analytical, global and collaborative management styles are examined.

45150 ■ "The 5 Pitfalls Of CEO Succession" in *Fortune* (Vol. 146, No. 10, November 18, 2002, pp. 78)
Pub: Time Inc.
Ed: Ram Charan, Jerry Useem. **Description:** The five largest mistakes for grooming potential CEOs are listed. Succession planning is the key.

45151 ■ "Five Questions: Diane Primo, Vice President, Chief Marketing Office, CDW" in *Sales & Marketing Management* (Vol. 157, February 2005)
Pub: VNU Business Media
Description: Dian Primo, vice president and chief marketing officer for CDW answers questions regarding brand loyalty, marketing and sales functions, innovation, and more.

45152 ■ "Five Questions" in *Sales and Marketing.com* (Vol. 156, No. 3, March 2004, pp. 11)
Pub: VNU eMedia, Inc.
Description: Jay Fiore answers questions about his newest eBay campaign that targets small businesses.

45153 ■ "Flaw and Order: Are You Apt to Make Mistakes? You're Not Alone" in *Entrepreneur* (Vol. 32)
Pub: Entrepreneur Media Inc.
Ed: Mark Henricks. **Description:** Eight strategy flaws identified by Charles Roxburgh, a director of consulting firm McKinsey & Company, are cited, with overconfidence being number one followed by mental accounting.

45154 ■ "Focused Vision" in *Hispanic Business* (April 2005, pp. 34, 36)
Pub: Hispanic Business
Ed: Janet Perez. **Description:** Profile of Janet Murguia, president and CEO of the National Council of La Raza (NCLR). Murguia works to advance the organization's presence and advocacy among policymakers and constituents. NCLR is committed to improving the lives of Hispanics.

45155 ■ "Follow the Market Cues" in *Harvard Business Review* (Vol. 80, No. 5, May 2002, pp. 20)
Pub: Harvard Business School Press
Ed: Peter Navarro. **Description:** Knowledge of stock market cycles can help executives make broad strategic decisions as well as more tactical ones. Companies must be aware of their sector's place in the business cycle.

45156 ■ "Follow the flight plan" in *Entrepreneur* (Vol. 30, No. 1,)
Pub: Entrepreneur Media Inc.
Ed: Geoff Williams. **Description:** The author suggests that learning to think like a fighter pilot will help entrepreneurs be successful. Many top managers from companies like Home Depot and FedEx have followed that trend.

45157 ■ "Follow Your Leader" in *Entrepreneur* (Vol. 32, No. 4, April 2004, pp. 124)
Pub: Entrepreneur Media, Inc.
Ed: Romanus Wolter. **Description:** Ways an entrepreneur can find someone to mentor them with business issues are listed. Mentors can help aspiring entrepreneurs to increase sales, create a business plan, as well as handling other challenges.

45158 ■ "Following the Leader: Learn these Laws, and Employees Won't Be Far Behind You" in *Entrepreneur* (Vol. 32, July 2004, No. 7, pp. 34)
Pub: Entrepreneur Media Inc.
Description: Review of Michael Feiner's book, The Feiner Points of Leadership. The book offers insight into motivating employees and creating loyalty.

45159 ■ "Forbes Keeps Track In It's Upscale Or Hot on the Lot" in *Sacramento Bee* (November 16, 2005)
Pub: The Sacramento Bee
Ed: Mark Glover. **Description:** Forbes magazine has launched a new website designed to attract successful business people. The Website, www.forbesautos. com is geared for the luxury automotive buyer. Tips for negotiating with automobile dealers, tests drives, financing and insurance are also included on the site.

45160 ■ "Forget vive la difference" in *Incentive* (Vol. 174, No. 8, August 2000, pp. 16)
Pub: Bill Communications
Ed: Jean Jaworek. **Description:** Managing in a gender-integrated environment is tough for some male managers. But with the right approach, they can come out smelling like a rose.

45161 ■ "Frank Otto Named EDO's COO" in *Long Island Business News* (February 27, 2004)
Pub: Dolan Media Newswires
Description: Profile of Frank Otto, newly appointed COO of defense contractor, Long Island Forum for Technology.

45162 ■ "Fred Smith" in *Fast Company* (June 2001, pp. 64)
Pub: Fast Company
Ed: Charles Fishman. Description: An interview with Fred Smith, founder of Federal Express, the creator of overnight delivery.

45163 ■ "Friendly firing" in *WorkingWoman* (Vol. 25, No. 4, April 2000, pp. 36)
Pub: Lang Communications Inc.
Ed: Carol Leonetti Dannhauser. Description: Expert advice is given for dismissing an employee without incurring a legal action.

45164 ■ "From Barracks to Boardroom" in *Hispanic Business* (Vol. 24, No. 1/2, January/February 2002, pp. 59-60)
Pub: Hispanic Business Inc.
Ed: Vivienne Heines. Description: Because of the technical training and education received during military service, many recruits are developing a work ethic proven to improve employment prospects.

45165 ■ "From Fifth Hire to Top Exec, New CEO to Lead SurePayroll" in *Crain's Chicago Business* (Vol. 26, No. 50, December 15, 2003, pp. 12)
Pub: Crain Communications, Inc.
Ed: Julie Johnsson. Description: Profile of Michael Alter, newly appointed CEO of SurePayroll. The firm, started in 1999, provides payroll checks to companies with fewer than 100 employees. The process is simpler than traditional payroll services with everything done online, and costs 30-50 percent less than competitors.

45166 ■ "From office catnaps to lunchtime jogs" in *Wall Street Journal* (May 16, 2002, pp. D1)
Pub: Wall Street Journal
Ed: Sue Shellenbarger. Description: The art of balancing work and life is explored. Statistical data included.

45167 ■ "From Mushing to Management" in *Inc.* (January 1, 2005)
Pub: Inc. Magazine
Ed: Nicole Gull. Description: Lisa Wehl learned how to manage her 22 employees through a group of Alaskan husky dogs while competing in competitions such as the Knik 200 and the Klondike 300.

45168 ■ "Full Esteem Ahead: Act Like an Executive-And Get the Respect You Deserve" in *Entrepreneur* (Vol. 31, No. 9, September 2003, pp. 104)
Pub: Entrepreneur Media, Inc.
Description: Ways new entrepreneurs can learn to have the presence of a seasoned pro are listed, including the technique of talking slowly, standing with confidence, body language, and more.

45169 ■ "The Future of Cyberwork" in *Employment Relations Today* (Vol. 26, No. 4, pp. 61)
Pub: John Wiley & Sons, Inc.
Description: Studies labor trends in Internet technology, focusing on how cyberwork will impact the decisions of managers and human resource departments by 2025. Topics addressed include the work and challenges of Internet-related professionals, as well as the changes the Internet will bring to the labor market.

45170 ■ *Gambling on Growth: How to Manage the Small High-Tech Firm*
Pub: John Wiley & Sons, Inc.
Ed: Stuart Slatter. Released: 1992. Price: $72.00.

45171 ■ "A Gambling Man: Career Transitions that Put a Vegas Hotshot on Top" in *Black Enterprise* (Vol. 37, October 2006, No. 3, pp. 89)
Pub: Earl G. Graves Publishing Co. Inc.
Ed: Laura Egodigwe. Description: Interview with Lorenzo Creighton, president and chief operating officer of MGM Mirage's New York-New York Hotel and Casino. Creighton talks about his history and the challenges he faced since he didn't come from the casino industry.

45172 ■ "Gates Plans to Challenge Schnitzers" in *Business Journal-Portland* (Vol. 20, No. 25, August 22, 2003, pp. 1)
Pub: American City Business Journals, Inc.
Ed: Shelly Strom. Description: Bill Gates is attempting to reform the board of directors at Portland, Oregon-based Schnitzer Steel Industries. Gates, who has obtained support of shareholders for his proposal, is seeking to create a more independent board at the family-dominated company.

45173 ■ "Gearing Up For Expansion" in *Fast Company* (March 2005, No. 92, pp. 90)
Pub: Gruner & Jahr USA Publishing
Ed: Shonan Noronha. Description: Profile of Adobe's Acrobat 7 business software designed to allow users to take total control over the creation and distribution of important documents, as well as making them more accessible to clients, coworkers, and strategic partners.

45174 ■ "Gender Inequity at Top" in *Crain's Detroit Business* (Vol. 19, No. 42, October 20, 2003, pp. 8)
Pub: Crain Communications Inc., Detroit
Description: Fewer than 10 percent of the top positions and board seats in the Michigan Index 100, are held by women. The index is a collaboration of the Center for the Education of Women at University of Michigan and the Women's Leadership Forum, a nonprofit affiliated with the Women's Economic Club in Detroit and supported financially by Ford Motor Company, General Motors Corporation and the forum.

45175 ■ "Generation Gap at the Office" in *Hispanic Business* (November 2002, pp. 58, 60, 62)
Pub: Hispanic Business
Ed: Rosa Antonia Carrillo, Rachel Michelson. Description: Ways in which communication and a comprehensive transition plan can help family-owned businesses survive into the second generation and beyond.

45176 ■ "Get In Sync: To Spark Business Growth, Follow the Leader In Your Industry" in *Entrepreneur* (Vol. 31, No. 10, October 2003, pp. 38)
Pub: Entrepreneur Media, Inc.
Ed: David Newton. Description: Coordinating business strategy with a wide range of administrative and managerial processes is a major key to growing a company.

45177 ■ "Get Inspired!" in *My Business* (April/May 2003, pp. 44)
Pub: My Business Magazine
Ed: Mardy Fones. Description: Renewal strategies for small business leaders to keep creative and productive are presented.

45178 ■ "Get Moving 7" in *Incentive* (Vol. 174, No. 9, September 2000, pp. 40)
Pub: Bill Communications
Ed: Jeanie Casison. Description: Take control of these seven key forces for efficient management that, if left unchecked, can keep your company from staying ahead of the game.

45179 ■ "Get organized" in *Black Enterprise* (Vol. 33, No. 6, January 2003, pp. 10)
Pub: Earl Graves Publishing Co.
Description: Online advice is offered to get a career on track, tips for getting organized at work, and moving up the corporate ladder, are just a few of the issues addressed at this Web site.

45180 ■ "Get the Raise You Deserve: A Step-by-Step Guide to Negotiating the Right Pay Package" in *Journal of Accountancy* (October 2004)
Pub: American Institute of Certified Public Accountants
Ed: Anita Dennis. Description: According to experts, there are several steps that certified public accountants can take to receive the pay they feel they are worth.

45181 ■ "Get Tough: No More Mr. Nice Guy." in *Entrepreneur* (Vol. 33, January 2005, No. 1, pp. 28)
Pub: Entrepreneur Media Inc.
Ed: Mark Henricks. Description: Review of the book, Hardball: Are You Playing to Play or Playing to Win?, by George Stalk and Rob Lachenauer. The authors explain how to gain and maintain a competitive advantage by enticing competitors into retreat.

45182 ■ "Getting 360 degree feedback right" in *Harvard Business Review* (Vol. 79, No. 1, January 2001, pp. 142)
Pub: Harvard Business School Publishing Corp.
Ed: Maury A. Peiperl. Description: Recognizing the four paradoxes of peer appraisal by managers can make the 360-degree feedback process more effective.

45183 ■ "Getting Beyond a Bachelor's Degree" in *Hispanic Business* (December 2002, pp. 44, 46, 48)
Pub: Hispanic Business
Ed: Scott Williams. Description: Despite the fact that more Hispanics are attending colleges and universities in record numbers, very few are continuing on to graduate school.

45184 ■ "Getting on Board" in *Hispanic Business* (March 2003, pp. 62)
Pub: Hispanic Business
Description: Career development advice is given for Hispanic professionals wishing to increase their professional profile through board directorships.

45185 ■ "Getting the Corner Office" in *Black Enterprise* (Vol. 35, August 2004, No. 1, pp. 78)
Pub: Earl G. Graves Publishing Co. Inc.
Ed: Maureen Jenkins. Description: Profiles of African American women who have been successful in various businesses.

45186 ■ "Getting It Right the Second Time" in *Harvard Business Review* (Vol. 80, No. 1, January 2002, pp. 62)
Pub: Harvard Business School Press
Ed: Gabriel Szulanski, Sidney Winter. Description: Research has shown the difficulty with which businesses have had in transferring management successes from one division to another. Effective knowledge management transfer is critical, as is understanding why a procedure initially succeeded.

45187 ■ *Getting Things Done: The Art of Stress-Free Productivity*
Pub: Penguin Books (USA) Incorporated
Ed: David Allen. Released: December 2002. Price: $15.00. Description: Coach and management consultant recommends methods for stress-free performance under the premise that productivity is directly related to our ability to relax.

45188 ■ "Getting To No" in *Inc.* (October 1, 2003)
Pub: Gruner & Jahr USA Publishing
Ed: Nicole Gull. Description: Sales strategy of Y2 Marketing, the firm that is selective about its customers, is profiled.

45189 ■ *Getting to Yes: Negotiating Agreement Without Giving In*
Pub: Penguin Books (USA) Incorporated
Ed: Roger Fisher, William L. Ury, Bruce Patton. Released: December 1991. Price: $15.00. Description: Strategies for negotiating mutually acceptable agreements in all types of conflict.

45190 ■ *The Girl's Guide to Being a Boss (Without Being a Bitch): Valuable Lessons, Smart Suggestions, and True Stories for Succeeding*
Pub: Random Housing Publishing Group
Ed: Caitlin Friedman; Kimberly Yorio. Released: April 2006.

45191 ■ "Glass Ceiling Persists in the Board Room" in *Marketing to Women* **(Vol. 19, December 2006, No. 2, pp. 8)**
Pub: EPM Communications, Inc.
Description: A study by search firm Heidrick & Struggles and Women Corporate Directors shows that executive inequality remains high despite the number of women who hold board seats. Although these women tend to mentor and recommend other women for candidates, only 54 percent say that at least one of the women recommended was actually elected to the board. Despite the meager statistics, 76 percent of women on boards surveyed stated that they oppose a legal quota that would mandate an increase of women occupying board seats.

45192 ■ "Gluttons for Punishment" in *Success* **(Vol. 47, No. 1, January 2000, pp. 30)**
Pub: Success Publishing, Inc.
Ed: Jeff Wise. **Description:** Platinum Capital achieved success despite defections, market downturns, and a killer opossum attack.

45193 ■ "Go With the Flow" in *Entrepreneur* **(Vol. 32, August 2004, No. 8, pp. 32)**
Pub: Entrepreneur Media Inc.
Ed: Mark Henricks. **Description:** Review of the book, Good Business: Leadership, Flow and the Making of Meaning, is presented. The author shows that setting clear goals, giving feedback and matching challenges to skills can make an entrepreneur successful.

45194 ■ "Godwin Group" in *Mississippi Business Journal* **(Vol. 29, January 2007, No. 3, pp. A6)**
Pub: Venture Publications, Inc.
Description: Profile of Joey Lee, vice president, coastal region of Godwin Group. Lee has previously served as Godwin Group's account manager, strategic communications.

45195 ■ "Going by the Handbook" in *Success* **(Vol. 47, No. 4, September 2000, pp. 69)**
Pub: Success Publishing, Inc.
Ed: Michael Barrier. **Description:** Guidelines are given for effective employee information.

45196 ■ "Gonzales Names PepsiCo VP" in *Hispanic Business* **(Vol. 23, No. 11, November 2001, pp. 20)**
Pub: Hispanic Business Inc.
Ed: Teresa Talerico. **Description:** Profile of David Gonzales, vice president of community affairs at PepsiCo. Throughout his career, Gonzales has worked to ensure that minority-owned businesses have contract and vending opportunities with PepsiCo.

45197 ■ "GOOD business and good BUSINESS" in *Harvard Business Review* **(Vol. 81, No. 3, March 2003, pp. 10)**
Pub: Harvard Business School Press
Ed: Thomas A. Stewart. **Description:** The editor of Harvard Business Review discusses stock options as too much of a good thing. Originally intended to link managers' interest with those of owners, they now create a means for executives to maximize their profit at the owners' expense.

45198 ■ "The Good Fire" in *Entrepreneur* **(Vol. 28, No. 3, March 2000, pp. 127)**
Pub: Entrepreneur Media Inc.
Ed: Jacquelyn Lynn. **Description:** Try a kinder, gentler termination to help avoid workplace violence.

45199 ■ *Good to Great: Why Some Companies Make the Leap...and Others Don't*
Pub: HarperInformation
Ed: Jim Collins. **Released:** October 2001. **Price:** $27.50. **Description:** Management styles for growing a modern business.

45200 ■ "The Good Manager-A Moral Manager?" in *Journal of Business Ethics* **(Vol. 27, No. 3, October 1, 2000, pp. 247)**
Pub: Kluwer Academic Publishers
Ed: Per Sundman. **Description:** Two problems associated with the recently developed "practice or virtue approach" to business ethics are discussed. The first problem concerns an alleged harmony between common demands of morality and the internal goods of actual business practice. The second problem is related to the first and concerns the alleged relevance of a virtue perspective for business ethics.

45201 ■ "Got anything smaller?" in *Entrepreneur* **(Vol. 30, No. 10, October 2002, pp. 83)**
Pub: Entrepreneur Media Inc.
Ed: Chris Sandlund. **Description:** A new trend shows that two out of three corporate executives prefer to work for smaller firms.

45202 ■ "Great Expectation" in *Entrepreneur* **(Vol. 33, February 2005, No. 2, pp. 72)**
Pub: Entrepreneur Media Inc.
Ed: Chris Penttila. **Description:** According to a recent study conducted by the Corporate Leadership Council, 40 percent of newly hired employees will be fired within their first year and half with a company.

45203 ■ "Grist: Beyond the Vale of Smiles" in *Inc.* **(July 1, 2004)**
Pub: Inc. Magazine
Ed: Adam Hanft. **Description:** Issues involved when encouraging employees to challenge their boss are addressed.

45204 ■ "Grist: Micromanagers, Unite!" in *Inc.* **(December 1, 2004)**
Pub: Inc. Magazine
Ed: Adam Hanft. **Description:** Micromanagement is considered meddling, but small companies can benefit from micromanagers.

45205 ■ *Groups in Context: Leadership and Participation in Small Groups*
Pub: McGraw-Hill Companies
Ed: Gerald L. Wilson. **Released:** June 2004. **Price:** $70.00 (US), $105.95 (Canadian). **Description:** Small group communication skills for the workplace, in churches, social groups, or civic organizations.

45206 ■ "Grow Up: Teach Employees to Lead" in *My Business* **(April/May 2003, pp. 44)**
Pub: My Business Magazine
Ed: Melany Klink. **Description:** The importance of small business owners in hiring a team of leaders to run a company is stressed, using three key actions.

45207 ■ "Grow Your Own Executive Team" in *Journal of Accountancy* **(Vol. 199, January 2005, No. 1, pp. 108)**
Pub: American Institute of Certified Public Accountants
Ed: Stanley Zarowin. **Description:** Experts advise small business to establish a management incubator in order to promote present staff into key positions.

45208 ■ *Growing Business Handbook: Inspirational Advice from Successful Entrepreneurs and Fast-Growing UK Companies*
Pub: Kogan Page, Limited
Ed: Adam Jolly. **Released:** February 2007. **Price:** $49.95. **Description:** Tips for growing and running a successful business are covered, focusing on senior managers in middle market and SME companies.

45209 ■ "Growing Concern" in *Pittsburgh Business Times* **(Vol. 23, No. 4, August 15, 2003, pp. 19)**
Pub: Pittsburgh Business Times
Ed: Patty Tascarella. **Description:** The growing success of Pittsburgh, Pennsylvania-based EZ-FLO Inc. is presented. Topics include managing a small business, marketing strategy, and sales volume.

45210 ■ *Growing and Managing a Small Business: An Entrepreneurial Perspective*
Pub: Houghton Mifflin College Division
Ed: Kathleen R. Allen. **Released:** July 2006. **Price:** $105.27. **Description:** Introduction to business ownership and management from startup through growth.

45211 ■ "The Growing Number of Female Managers in VC-backed Firms means that Women are seen as Less Risky" in *Inc.* **(September 2000, pp. 60)**
Pub: The Goldhirsh Group
Ed: D.M. Osborne. **Description:** Catherine Muther created not a separate, women-only network but rather a system for ushering women into the larger venture landscape. Managers of venture funds targeting women stress that they're not interested in special-needs cases.

45212 ■ "Growth Guru: How to Turn Your Business Into a Hot Commodity" in *Entrepreneur* **(Vol. 31, No. 7, July 2003, pp. 27)**
Pub: Entrepreneur Media, Inc.
Ed: Mark Henricks. **Description:** Reviews of the books, "What I Learned Before I Sold to Warren Buffett", which deals with hiring, leading, communicating, decision-making and general management issues; and "What's The Big Idea", which deals with management ideas, are presented.

45213 ■ *Growth/Management of Entrepreneur Businesses*
Pub: Houghton Mifflin Co.
Ed: Allen. **Released:** 1998. **Price:** $52.17.

45214 ■ "Guest Speaker. The Saltshaker Theory" in *Inc.* **(November 2006, pp. 69-70)**
Pub: Gruner & Jahr USA Publishing
Ed: Danny Meyer. **Description:** Constant gentle pressure is invaluable in a growing company. Not so much to avoid problems, but to encourage participation and imaginative solutions to resolve those problems. Coaching and Communication are the two central keys to building consensus to resolve problems that arise.

45215 ■ "Hand In Hand" in *Entrepreneur* **(Vol. 31, No. 8, August 2003, pp. 68)**
Pub: Entrepreneur Media, Inc.
Ed: Jane Easter Bahls. **Description:** If you negotiate well, joining forces with a big firm can be the smart way to get a new product to the marketplace. The product may be just what a big company needs to boost slumping sales.

45216 ■ "Handling conflict" in *Black Enterprise* **(Vol. 33, No. 7, February 2003, pp. 14)**
Pub: Earl Graves Publishing Co.
Ed: Yvonne Abraham. **Description:** In response to an article about workplace conflict, a reader addresses the problems between her boss and project manager and provides a solution.

45217 ■ "Handling people with tact and skill" in *Women in Business* **(Vol. 53, No. 5, September-October, 2001, pp. 5)**
Pub: The ABWA Co. Inc.
Ed: Florence M. Stone. **Description:** Techniques for resolving work conflicts are presented. A six-step problem solving process and a conflict reduction process, are provided.

45218 ■ "Hands On" in *Inc.* **(September 2005, pp. 37-38)**
Pub: Inc. Magazine
Ed: Alison Stein Wellner. **Description:** Email, Blackberrys, and text messaging are replacing face-to-face business communication. Facial expression and body language, voice inflection, and words can help derive meaning to business discussions.

45219 ■ "Hangin' Tough: How to Beef Up Your Negotiating Game" in *Entrepreneur* **(Vol. 32, August 2004, No. 8, pp. 72)**
Pub: Entrepreneur Media Inc.
Ed: Marc Diener. **Description:** Negotiating skills out outlined, focusing on technique, not just game face. If you must give something, be sure to get something back in return.

45220 ■ **"The hard work of being a soft manager"** in *Harvard Business Review* (Vol. 79, No. 11, December 2001, pp. 99)
Pub: Harvard Business School Press
Ed: William H. Peace. **Description:** The author describes, from his own experience, what it means to be a soft manager. It does not mean being weak, but deliberate vulnerability, openness and the willingness to take the heart for unpopular positions.

45221 ■ **"The Harder They Fall"** in *Harvard Business Review* (Vol. 81, No. 10, October 2003, pp. 58)
Pub: Harvard Business School Press
Ed: Roderick M. Kramer. **Description:** Advice is given for executives, and by extension employees, wishing to avoid having careers come to an untimely end due to lapses of professional judgment.

45222 ■ **"Harding Brews Success at Anheuser-Busch"** in *Black Enterprise* (Vol. 37, February 2007, No. 7, pp. 1)
Pub: Earl G. Graves Publishing Co. Inc.
Ed: Mashaun D. Simon. **Description:** Profile of Michael S. Harding, president and CEO of Anheuser-Busch packaging Group. Harding oversees five business units, 15 facilities, and over 2,300 workers.

45223 ■ **"Harley's Leadership U-Turn"** in *Harvard Business Review* (Vol. 78, No. 4, July 2000, pp. 43)
Pub: Harvard Business School Publishing Corp.
Ed: Rich Teerlink. **Description:** Former company executive details how the company was saved from financial disaster.

45224 ■ **"Harmony and bottom line: hm..."** in *The New York Times* (February 9, 2000, pp. G1)
Pub: The New York Times Company
Ed: Jobert E. Abueva. **Description:** Feng Shui in the workplace is explored.

45225 ■ **"Hate Performance Appraisals? Here's a better way to evaluate employees"** in *My Business* (November/December 2001, pp. 43)
Pub: My Business Magazine
Description: According to small business consultant, Mary Jenkins, traditional job performance appraisals do not work for small companies. The article further suggests that the key to evaluating employees effectively is to shift responsibility for feedback and coaching from the owner to the employee.

45226 ■ **"Head to Head: How to Deal With Difficult Opponents"** in *Entrepreneur* (Vol. 32, October 2004, No. 10, pp. 96)
Pub: Entrepreneur Media Inc.
Ed: Marc Diener. **Description:** Building trust is essential when dealing with difficult people in business. Speak to an opponent's interests and make easy concessions in the beginning.

45227 ■ **"Healthy ways to handle rivalry in the workplace"** in *Atlanta Business Chronicle* (Vol. 25, December 20, 2002, No. 28, pp. 4B)
Pub: American City Business Publications, Inc.
Ed: Emory Mulling. **Description:** Managers need to know how to deal with workplace nemesis, someone who either gets in the way or is a challenge to deal with. These individuals can take a number of forms, such as those who are unknowingly annoying, to those who deliberately set out to obstruct. Whichever one the manager faces, each must be dealt with carefully. In addition, managers must be on the lookout for emerging problems, and must also understand the difference between negative friction and creative tension.

45228 ■ **"Heart of the Matter"** in *Hispanic Business* (March 2005, pp. 58, 60)
Pub: Hispanic Business
Ed: Luisa Beltran. **Description:** Jose Nino, CEO of El Nino Group, discusses cardiovascular disease, the number one cause of death. Nino shares healthy choices to decrease risk factors for busy executives.

45229 ■ **"Help Wanted"** in *Entrepreneur.com* (Vol. 34, February 2006, No. 2, pp. 80)
Pub: Entrepreneur Media Inc.
Ed: Chris Penttila. **Description:** Globalization, outsourcing and competition for capital are putting pressure on small companies to operate more like large businesses. Ideas for hiring CEOs for a small firm are included.

45230 ■ **"Helping each other - one woman at a time"** in *Women in Business* (Vol. 53, No. 7, January-February 2002, pp. 9)
Pub: The ABWA Co Inc.
Ed: Carolyn B. Elman. **Description:** The aims and objectives of the American Business Women's Association are provided. It is important for businesswomen to assist and mentor each other.

45231 ■ **"Here's what I'm thinking: you'll get your best deal if prospects see things your way"** in *Entrepreneur* (Vol. 30, No. 10, Oct. 2002)
Pub: Entrepreneur Media Inc.
Ed: Marc Diener. **Description:** Preparation is the key to the power of persuasion when negotiating a business deal. Three important tips are offered by speaker and attorney, Marc Diener, author of the book, Deal Power.

45232 ■ **"Here's a Late Resolution, But One to Be Taken Seriously"** in *St. Louis Post-Dispatch* (January 9, 2005)
Pub: Knight-Ridder/Tribune Business News
Ed: Repps Hudson. **Description:** A discussion involving politeness and consideration in the workplace is examined. Consideration of others in the work environment might improve business, boost morale and help with promotion opportunities.

45233 ■ **"A heritage of success"** in *Hispanic Business* (Vol. 22, No. 3, March 2000, pp. 18)
Pub: Hispanic Business
Ed: Patricia Guadalupe. **Description:** The forward planning and management information techniques put in place by Ed Fernandez, founder of Sherikon Inc., enabled the company to continue trading successfully following his sudden death in a plane crash. The importance of management information systems are discussed.

45234 ■ **"He's Boss of the Blues; Phillip Pope Stays a Fiscally Prudent Course"** in *Birmingham Business Journal* (Vol. 20, October 3, 2003)
Pub: American City Business Journals, Inc.
Ed: Tom Bassing. **Description:** Profile of Phillip Pope, who was promoted from within the ranks of Blue Cross and Blue Shield of Alabama. The company is successful at membership retention, investments and growth and is planning strategies to offer services to aging baby boomers.

45235 ■ **"He's Grrrreat!"** in *Hispanic Business* (January/February 2004, pp. 26, 28)
Pub: Hispanic Business
Ed: Nancie Hudson. **Description:** Profile of Carlos M. Gutierrez, CEO of the cereal maker, Kellogg; and since Gutierrez became CEO in April 1999, the firm has posted increased sales and earnings and reestablished itself as the world's top cereal seller.

45236 ■ **"Hibernia Southcoast Capital Corp."** in *Black Enterprise* (Vol. 33, No. 6, January 2003, pp. 47)
Pub: Earl Graves Publishing Co.
Description: Joseph E. Williams was named president and CEO of Hibernia Southcoast Capital Corporation, the investment-banking arm of New Orleans-based Hibernia National Bank.

45237 ■ **"Hicksville-Based KeySpan Trains Managers to Take Over Blue-Collar/Clerical Jobs..."** in *Long Island Business News* (Feb. 20, 2004)
Pub: Dolan Media Newswires
Ed: Claude Solnik. **Description:** KeySpan Corporation, an energy company in New York, trained managers to assume blue collar and clerical positions in the event of a possible strike by some 3,000 employees.

45238 ■ **"The high cost of lost trust."** in *Harvard Business Review* (Vol. 80, No. 9, September 2002, pp. 18)
Pub: Harvard Business School Press
Ed: Tony Simons. **Description:** Advice is offered for managers to maintain trust by the company's employees.

45239 ■ **"High-Quality Relationships Succeed Where Incentives Fall Short"** in *Incentive* (Vol. 174, No. 9, September 2000, pp. 76)
Pub: Bill Communications
Ed: Jim Ryan. **Description:** With today's increasingly complex marketplace, businesses have reason to be concerned about selling products and services. Warnings about consultants offering relationships, but are really selling incentive programs are investigated.

45240 ■ **"Hire for Attitude, Train for Skills"** in *Rough Notes* (Vol. 145, No. 9, September 2002, pp. 106)
Pub: Rough Notes
Ed: Nancy Doucette. **Description:** Managing employees starts with hiring them for attitude and then training them for skills. Thus, hiring is pure expense initially.

45241 ■ **"Hire Ground"** in *Entrepreneur* (Vol. 33, March 2005, No. 3, pp. 28)
Pub: Entrepreneur Media Inc.
Ed: Mark Henricks. **Description:** According to the Small Business Scoreboard, compiled by SurePayroll, a payroll services company, hiring was up, but wages were down in 2004.

45242 ■ **"Hiring, Hollywood Style"** in *Inc.* (January 1, 2004)
Pub: Gruner & Jahr USA Publishing
Ed: Bobbie Gossage. **Description:** Typecasting is used in business according to a study conducted by Ezra Zuckerman, a Massachusetts Institute of Technology professor. Zuckerman's research found that employers are more likely to hire an individual who is easily typecast into a particular role, especially early in careers. However, typecasting could be a bad policy.

45243 ■ **"His Brother's Keeper: a Mentor Learns the True Meaning of Leadership"** in *Black Enterprise* (Vol. 37, December 2006, No. 5, pp. 69)
Pub: Earl G. Graves Publishing Co. Inc.
Ed: Laura Egodigwe. **Description:** Interview with Keith R. Wyche of Pitney Bowes Management Services which discusses the relationship between a mentor and mentee as well as sponsorship.

45244 ■ **"The Hispanic Business Top 10 Business Schools"** in *Hispanic Business* (March 2002, pp. 38, 40, 42)
Pub: Hispanic Business
Description: A listing of the top 10 business schools for Hispanic students across the U.S. is presented, with University of Texas at Austin placing first.

45245 ■ **"Hold On Tight"** in *Entrepreneur* (Vol. 31, No. 8, August 2003, pp. 66)
Pub: Entrepreneur Media, Inc.
Ed: Chris Penttila. **Description:** During an economic downturn, it is recommended that company's begin maximizing loyalty in the workplace while it's still an employer's market. Look for ways to maintain a staff before they are enlisted by headhunters when the economy turns.

45246 ■ **"Hold Your Tongue"** in *Black Enterprise* (Vol. 34, No. 3, October 2003, pp. 54)
Pub: Earl Graves Publishing Co.
Ed: Sonia Alleyne. **Description:** Advice is given to the unemployed when going on a job interview, including the resources: 101 Great Answers to the Toughest Interview Questions and 101 Greatest Questions to Ask on Your Interview.

45247 ■ "Holding onto talent: the best defense is a preemptive strike" in *Wall Street Journal* (March 14, 2000, pp. B1)
Pub: Dow Jones & Co., Inc.
Ed: Carol Hymowitz and Eleena De Lisser. **Description:** An overview of corporate personnel management in a time of high labor mobility.

45248 ■ "Home Depot Offers Expensive Lesson in Curbing Execs' Pay" in *Crain's Chicago Business* (Vol. 30, January 2007, No. 3, pp. 13)
Pub: Crain Communications, Inc.
Ed: **Description:** Linking executive pay to performance is becoming a top priority for the board of directors as part of their role is compensation watchdogs. Recent departure of Home Depot's CEO, Robert Nardelli left him with a $210 million compensation package. Profile of the Home Depot debacle included.

45249 ■ "Home Office vs. the Field" in *Sales & Marketing Management*
Pub: VNU Business Media
Ed: Robin Freedman, Andy Watt. **Description:** The issue whether a sales manager should address one rep's mistake in front of the entire sales team is examined by a salesperson and a sales manager.

45250 ■ "Home Office vs. the Field" in *Sales and Marketing.com* (Vol. 156, No. 3, March 2004, pp. 13)
Pub: VNU eMedia, Inc.
Description: A salesperson and manager debate who should be responsible for handling an angry client.

45251 ■ "Home Plate: Learning How to Let Go by Delegating" in *Crain's Detroit Business* (Vol. 19, No. 49, December 8, 2003, pp. 18)
Pub: Crain Communications Inc., Detroit
Ed: Joel Golden. **Description:** Delegating effectively can help a small business owner free up time, increase employee satisfaction and increase the company's bottom line.

45252 ■ *Honest Business: A Superior Strategy for Starting & Maintaining Your Own Business*
Pub: Shambhala Publications, Inc.
Ed: Michael Phillips. **Released:** 1996.

45253 ■ "Hospitality Hobnobber" in *Crain's New York Business* (Vol. 23, January 29, 2007, No. 5, pp. F10)
Pub: Crain Communications, Inc.
Ed: Julie Satow. **Description:** Profile of Mark Gordon, investment banker and managing director of Sonnenblick-Goldman. In the past twelve years he has completed $10 billion worth of transactions.

45254 ■ "Hot Tips" in *Inc.* (May 2000, pp. 161)
Pub: The Goldhirsh Group
Description: Tips regarding hiring an executive recruiter and information regarding the Family and Medical Leave Act (FMLA) are covered.

45255 ■ "How to Be a Good Listener" in *Women in Business* (Vol. 54, No. 5, September-October 2002, pp. 17)
Pub: The ABWA Company, Inc.
Ed: Liz Hughes. **Description:** Good listening techniques for managers include paying attention and preventing interruptions.

45256 ■ *How to Be the Life of the Podium: Openers, Closers & Everything in Between to Keep Them Listening*
Pub: AMACOM
Ed: Sylvia Simmons. **Released:** 1993. **Price:** $15.95 ($14.35 for AMA members). **Description:** Guide to organizing and writing speeches. Includes openers and proverbs organized by subject area and information on operating audiovisual equipment.

45257 ■ "How Departing Staff Can Still Help You" in *My Business* (November/December 2001, pp. 46)
Pub: My Business Magazine
Ed: Drew Sullivan. **Description:** Advice for setting up exit interviews for small businesses is presented, including a listing of suggested topics to cover in the interview.

45258 ■ "How Do You Measure Up? They're Supposed to Follow, But Are You a Leader?" in *My Business* (April/May 2003, pp. 45)
Pub: My Business Magazine
Ed: Jackie Ross. **Description:** Characteristics shared by successful leaders are presented, including vision, dedication, charisma, communication, courage, intuition, and empathy.

45259 ■ "How to Fix Knowledge Management" in *Harvard Business Review* (Vol. 81, No. 10, October 2003, pp. 16)
Pub: Harvard Business School Press
Ed: David Gilmour. **Description:** Businesses should stop trying to capture knowledge, and concentrate on improving employee connections.

45260 ■ "How I Got Here" in *Sales & Marketing Management* (Vol. 157, January 2005, No. 1, pp. 50)
Pub: VNU Business Media
Ed: Kathryn Droullard. **Description:** Profile of John Fox, president of Venture Marketing, Downers Grove, Illinois. Fox shares his three principles of success in the sales and marketing industry.

45261 ■ "How Managers Can Keep From Being Ambushed by the Boss" in *Wall Street Journal* (April 9, 2002, pp. B1)
Pub: Wall Street Journal
Ed: Carol Hymowitz. **Description:** Managerial skills are discussed.

45262 ■ "How to Motivate Your Problem People" in *Harvard Business Review* (Vol. 81, No. 1, January 2003, pp. 57)
Pub: Harvard Business School Press
Description: Methods for motivating intractable employees are examined. A manager must pull solutions out of problem employees rather than pushing solutions on them. The article sites examples.

45263 ■ "How Networking Really Works" in *Black Enterprise* (Vol. 35, February 2005, No. 7, pp. 98)
Pub: Earl G. Graves Publishing Co. Inc.
Ed: Laura Egodigwe. **Description:** Networking is considered a two-way street by successful professionals and should benefit both parties.

45264 ■ "How to Plan as a Small Scale Business Owner" in *Journal of Small Business Management* (Vol. 38, No. 38, April 2000, pp. 1)
Pub: West Virginia University
Ed: Michael Frese, Marco van Gelderen, Michael Ombach. **Description:** This study takes a psychological approach to investigate the process characteristics of action strategies used by small business owners; these strategy characteristics are then related to the firms' success. The objective of the research is to deepen the understanding of how strategies are used and how the owner's strategy-relevant behavior is related to the business' success.

45265 ■ "How Presidents Persuade" in *Harvard Business Review* (Vol. 81, No. 1, January 2003, pp. 20)
Pub: Harvard Business School Press
Ed: David R. Gergen. **Description:** An advisor to four presidents discusses how U.S. presidents establish trust and use their powers of oratory to persuade. He also points out the need for true humility and strict honesty with the American people.

45266 ■ *How to Recognize and Reward Employees: 150 Ways to Inspire Peak Performance*
Pub: American Management Association

Ed: Donna Deeprose. **Released:** 2006. **Price:** $13.95.

45267 ■ "How Snapple Got Its Juice Back" in *Harvard Business Review* (Vol. 80, No. 1, January 2002, pp. 47)
Pub: Harvard Business School Press
Ed: John Deighton. **Description:** Quaker Oats bought Snapple for $1.4 million, only to sell it four years later for $300 million to Triarc. Triarc then reorganized the brand and sold it to Cadbury Schweppes for about $1 billion. Returning the company required changes in management, packaging, and products.

45268 ■ *How to Start, Finance, and Manage Your Own Small Business: Featuring Andrew Tobias' Managing Your Money Software*
Pub: Random House, Inc.
Ed: Joseph R. Mancuso. **Released:** 1993. **Price:** $20.00 (paper).

45269 ■ "How To Be a Great Boss" in *Inc.* (October 1, 2004)
Pub: Inc. Magazine
Ed: Rod Kurtz. **Description:** Management means directing workers, but a boss should also let employees know that you mean well when making decisions.

45270 ■ "How To Fire Decisively" in *Inc.* (October 1, 2004)
Pub: Inc. Magazine
Ed: Patrick J. Sauer. **Description:** Tips to assist managers in firing an employee are presented.

45271 ■ "How To Groom a No. 2 (Or, Gasp, a Successor)" in *Inc.* (October 1, 2004)
Pub: Inc. Magazine
Ed: Patrick J. Sauer. **Description:** Ways to handle choosing a successor, or second-in-command are examined, along with the decision to stay within the company or to look outside.

45272 ■ "How To Hire Wisely" in *Inc.* (October 1, 2004)
Pub: Inc. Magazine
Ed: Patrick J. Sauer. **Description:** Tips to help hire quality employees without using gimmicky tests and interview books.

45273 ■ "How To Prevent Violence At Work" in *Fortune* (Vol. 151, February 21, 2005, No. 4, pp. 42)
Pub: Time Inc.
Ed: Anne Fisher. **Description:** According to the U.S. Bureau of Labor Statistics, 18,104 injuries from assaults and 609 homicides in the workplace were reported in 2002. The U.S. Centers for Disease Control have determined workplace violence as a national epidemic.

45274 ■ "How (Un)Ethical Are You?" in *Harvard Business Review* (Vol. 81, No. 12, December 2003, pp. 56)
Pub: Harvard Business School Press
Ed: Mahzaarin R. Banaji, Max H. Bazerman, Dolly Chugh. **Description:** Four sources of unintentional bias in management decision making are examined: conflict of interest, in-group favoritism, overclaiming credit, and implicit prejudice are shown. Methods for mitigating the sources of bias include shaping one's environment to reduce external cues, broadening the hypothetical influence of decision-making processes, and remaining vigilant.

45275 ■ "How We're Fixing Up Tyco" in *Harvard Business Review* (Vol. 81, No. 12, December 2003, pp. 96)
Pub: Harvard Business School Press
Ed: Eric M. Pillmore. **Description:** An overview is presented on the management reform processes underway at Tyco International Ltd. These include aligning corporate divisions with company objectives, launching a new yearly bonus plan, capping stock-option-equity awards and severance payments, and adjusting director compensations.

45276 ■ "How resilience works" in *Harvard Business Review* (Vol. 80, No. 5, May 2002, pp. 46)
Pub: Harvard Business School Press
Ed: Diane L. Coutu. **Description:** The three characteristics of companies and individuals that enable them to bounce back from adversity are highlighted; each has the capacity to accept reality, find meaning in some aspect of life, and improvise.

45277 ■ *How to Write a Great Business Plan for Your Small Business in 60 Minutes or Less*
Pub: Atlantic Publishing
Ed: Sharon L. Fullen. **Released:** September 2005. **Price:** $39.95 includes CD-Rom. **Description:** A good business plan outlines goals and works as a company's resume to obtain funding, credit from suppliers, management of the operations and finances, promotion and marketing, and more.

45278 ■ "How Your CFO should Raise Money: What the Experts Say" in *Inc.* (April 2000, pp. 123)
Pub: The Goldhirsh Group
Description: There is a new breed of chief financial officers: those who actively network to raise money in addition to handling the paperwork. Some venture capitalists share their thoughts on this approach.

45279 ■ "Huddle Up" in *Entrepreneur* (Vol. 27, No. 12, December 1999, pp. 131)
Pub: Entrepreneur Media Inc.
Ed: Robert McGarvey. **Description:** Management techniques for motivating employees are explored.

45280 ■ "Humanizing Leaders" in *Fast Company* (March 2005, No. 92, pp. 82)
Pub: Gruner & Jahr USA Publishing
Ed: Jennifer Vilaga. **Description:** Leadership courses are previewed, including a six-day course that allows business leaders to address the larger issues of leadership, innovation and creativity.

45281 ■ "I Think I'll Pass: Do Women Have a Tougher Time Delegating Tasks?" in *Entrepreneur* (Vol. 32, October 2004, No. 10, pp. 44)
Pub: Entrepreneur Media Inc.
Ed: Aliza Pilar Sherman. **Description:** Although all entrepreneurs have trouble delegating tasks to employees, women business owners seem to have even more difficulty. Women also tend to be nurturing when delegating.

45282 ■ "Ideas on demand: you don't have to wait for inspiration" in *Entrepreneur* (Vol. 31, No. 4, April 2003, pp. 78)
Pub: Entrepreneur Media Inc.
Ed: Juanita Weaver. **Description:** The novel prompt creativity technique to promote innovation is examined. A novel prompt can be anything such as a word, a color, a fantasy, or an object that will launch thinking that will generate new ideas. Examples using the technique are given.

45283 ■ "If you want honesty, break some rules" in *Harvard Business Review* (Vol. 80, No. 4, April 2002, pp. 42)
Pub: Harvard Business School Press
Ed: Ginger L. Graham. **Description:** Profile of CEO of Advanced Cardiovascular Systems, who worked to create a culture where people were not afraid to speak the truth. Two strategies were to assign non-executive coaches to senior managers to get grass roots feedback and to tell the whole truth to the rank and file.

45284 ■ "If you want something done right, delegate it" in *Women in Business* (Vol. 53, No. 7, January-February 2002, pp. 13)
Pub: The ABWA Co Inc.
Ed: Liz Hughes. **Description:** Delegation can provide a manager with an opportunity to trust their staff and evaluate their own communication skills. Delegation allows a manager additional time for strategic planning.

45285 ■ "If You Have Rules, You Have To Be Prepared to Stick With Them-Even When It's Hard" in *Inc.* (May 1, 2005)
Pub: Inc. Magazine
Ed: Norm Brodsky. **Description:** Problems encountered when hiring an employee who has falsified his/her applications are examined.

45286 ■ "I'm Stuck. Can You Pass the Play-Doh?" in *Inc.* (August 2005, pp. 68)
Pub: Inc. Magazine
Ed: Lee Gimpel. **Description:** Meeting places designed to promote creativity are outlined. Contact information for six such sites is included.

45287 ■ "In their corner" in *Entrepreneur* (Vol. 31, No. 6, June 2003, pp. 79)
Pub: Entrepreneur Media Inc.
Ed: Kimberly L. McCall. **Description:** Reasons to devote coaching time to the elite sales performers are listed.

45288 ■ "In critical decisions, often sole adviser is kin" in *Wall Street Journal* (September 24, 2002, pp. B6)
Pub: Dow Jones & Co. Inc.
Ed: Richard C. Breeden. **Description:** Results of a survey of small business owners, conducted by Wells Fargo and National Federation of Independent Business, is presented. Statistical data included.

45289 ■ "In Defense of the CEO Chair" in *Harvard Business Review* (Vol. 81, No. 9, September 2003, pp. 24)
Pub: Harvard Business School Press
Ed: William T. Allen, William R. Berkeley. **Description:** The disadvantages to a company and its shareholders if the company separates the roles of CEO and chairman are examined.

45290 ■ "In the Hot Seat" in *Entrepreneur.com* (Vol. 34, January 2006, No. 1, pp. 19)
Pub: Entrepreneur Media Inc.
Ed: Chris Penttila. **Description:** According to a 2005 survey conducted by CareerBuilder.com, more than 56 percent of workers stated they have dated a co-worker. These office romances are becoming the stuff new legal battles are made of in the workplace. Sexual harassment suits are arising after workers lose promotions to those dating supervisors.

45291 ■ "In the 'No': Pessimistic Employees May Not Be So Bad For Your Business After All" in *Entrepreneur* (Vol. 32, September 2004, No. 9)
Pub: Entrepreneur Media Inc.
Ed: Nichole L. Torres. **Description:** Pessimists tend to make safer choices with regard to gambling than optimistic counterparts, thus making them an asset to a small business.

45292 ■ "In Praise of Boundaries: A Conversation with Miss Manners" in *Harvard Business Review* (Vol. 81, No. 12, December 2003, pp. 41)
Pub: Harvard Business School Press
Ed: Diane L. Coutu. **Description:** Judith Martin, known as the syndicated columnist Miss Manners, argues in favor of establishing formal limits to govern behavior in the office, as the personalization of business relations interferes with efficiency and in some cases, can have legal repercussions, such as sexual harassment.

45293 ■ "In Praise of Privacy" in *Inc.* (Volume 27, March 2005, No. 3, pp. 116)
Pub: Inc. Magazine
Ed: Adam Hanft. **Description:** Workplace information must be carefully rationed by company leadership.

45294 ■ "In search of hire principles" in *Incentive* (Vol. 174, No. 7, July 2000, pp. 16)
Pub: Bill Communications
Ed: Stephen Covey. **Description:** Finding a body as quickly as possible should not be a manager's top priority when trying to fill a position. Strategic recruiting and selection are vital to success.

45295 ■ "In Pursuit of a Bias-Free Workplace" in *Hispanic Business* (January/February 2003, pp. 44, 48)
Pub: Hispanic Business
Ed: Patricia Guadalupe. **Description:** A survey conducted by PricewaterhouseCoopers, called The Diversity Survey: A Nationwide Survey on the State of Workplace Diversity, shows that most respondents to the survey felt employers saw diversity as important in the workplace and that working in a diverse environment important, however most felt that during a recession, diversity programs would not be a key in employment decisions.

45296 ■ "In Search of a Leader" in *Women in Business* (Vol. 54, No. 2, March-April 2002, pp. 11)
Pub: The ABWA Co Inc.
Ed: Linda S. Demorest, Deona Grady. **Description:** Specific personality traits are exhibited by leaders; some of these traits include charisma and motivational skills.

45297 ■ "The Incredibly Unproductive Shareholder" in *Harvard Business Review* (Vol. 80, No. 1, January 2002, pp. 18)
Pub: Harvard Business School Press
Ed: Marjorie Kelly. **Description:** Stock-market investors' interests have often been put above that of the company, which has resulted in decisions that have been counterproductive.

45298 ■ *Influence without Authority*
Pub: John Wiley and Sons Inc.
Ed: Allan R. Cohen; David L. Bradford. **Released:** March 2005. **Price:** $29.95.

45299 ■ "Information Technology Software" in *Business Week* (January 23, 2006, No. 3968, pp. 65-66)
Pub: McGraw-Hill Companies
Ed: Sarah Lacy. **Description:** Profile of Oracle's John Wookey and his boss, Larry Ellison. The two are working to meld together the company's latest string of acquisitions.

45300 ■ "Inheriting business as challenging as starting one" in *Atlanta Business Chronicle* (Vol. 24, No. 13, August 24, 2001, pp. 5B)
Pub: American City Business Journals Inc.
Ed: Tara Milligan. **Description:** Taking over a business that is already operating has unique challenges. In the article is a case study of Carl Greenway's takeover of the Molly Maid franchise in Memphis five years ago, when it had six employees and eight dilapidated cars. It now has 24 employees, and competes against the national leader Merry Maids, which is also headquartered in Memphis.

45301 ■ "The innovation toolkit" in *Entrepreneur* (Vol. 31, No. 5, May 2003, pp. 52)
Pub: Entrepreneur Media Inc.
Ed: Joshua Kurlantzick. **Description:** Innovation remains the most important component of small business success. A listing of 18 how-to's of innovation every entrepreneur should know are included.

45302 ■ "Inside Intel" in *Business Week* (January 9, 2006, No. 3966, pp. 46-52, 54)
Pub: McGraw-Hill Companies
Ed: Cliff Edwards. **Description:** Profile of Paul Otellini, CEO of Intel Corporation. Otellini is taking the computer chipmaker into sectors such as consumer electronics, wireless communications, and health care.

45303 ■ "Inside Microsoft. Balancing Creativity and Discipline" in *Harvard Business Review* (Vol. 80, No. 1, January 2002, pp. 73)
Pub: Harvard Business School Press
Ed: Robert Herbold. **Description:** Microsoft's hands-off management approach began to interfere with productivity; this required rethinking the company, better integration of information, and general operations while maintaining the company's need for creative thinking.

45304 ■ "Inside Out" in *Houston Business Journal* (Vol. 34, No. 11, July 25, pp. 19)
Pub: American City Business Journals
Ed: Catherine Spaulding. Description: Profile of the design firm Batsche Design; topics include management style, business strategy, and competition.

45305 ■ *Instant Profit: Successful Strategies to Boost Your Margin and Increase the Profitability of Your Business*
Pub: McGraw-Hill Companies
Ed: Bradley J. Sugars. Released: December 2005. Price: $16.95 (US), $22.95 (Canadian). Description: Advice on management, money, marketing, and merchandising a successful small business is offered.

45306 ■ "Intel is putting its chips on the Net" in *Fast Company* (July 2001, pp. 152)
Pub: Fast Company
Ed: Cheryl Dahle. Description: Profile of Craig Barrett, Intel CEO. Barrett discusses his experiences running the Intel, after replacing former CEO Andy Grove.

45307 ■ "Intern Burn: Hired the Ultimate Intern from Hell?" in *Entrepreneur* (Vol. 32, November 2004, No. 11, pp. 96)
Pub: Entrepreneur Media Inc.
Ed: Chris Penttila. Description: Intership programs offer an inexpensive labor source, as well as a good recruiting tool. Advice for hiring interns is discussed.

45308 ■ "Interviews with Part-Time MBAs Point the Way for Retaining Executive Track Managers" in *Employment Relations Today* (Vol. 27, No. 1)
Pub: John Wiley & Sons, Inc.
Ed: Dan Sandweiss and David Lewin. Description: Issues discussed concern the retention of knowledge workers with MBA degrees from top colleges. Several part-time MBA students were surveyed, and results indicate that these students believed management development and advancement opportunities were key issues relating to retention. Statistical data included.

45309 ■ "Is Anybody in Charge?" in *Fast Company* (June 2001, pp. 52)
Pub: Fast Company
Ed: Christine Canabou. Description: The changing face of management in the new technology-driven world is explored.

45310 ■ "Is GM on the Road to a Board Fight?" in *Business Week* (January 23, 2006, No. 3968, pp. 35)
Pub: McGraw-Hill Companies
Ed: David Welch. Description: Kirk Kerkorian may nominate directors if Richard Wagoner Jr., chairman and chief executive, keeps ignoring his advice to cut dividends. Statistical data included.

45311 ■ "Is Your Mate Ready For Your Success?" in *Black Enterprise* (Vol. 34, July 2004, No. 12, pp. 139)
Pub: Earl G. Graves Publishing Co. Inc.
Ed: Robyn D. Clarke. Description: Young entrepreneurs and business leaders need support from home in order to be comfortable with their successes.

45312 ■ *The ISO 9000 Almanac, 1994-1995 Edition*
Pub: Irwin Professional Publishing
Ed: Timeplace, Inc. Released: 1994-1995 edition. Price: $75.00. Description: Provides information on ISO 9000 registration, including lists of resources, consultants, seminars, books and other references, and associations.

45313 ■ "It's Cheaper to Keep 'Em" in *Black Enterprise* (Vol. 36, February 2006, No. 7, pp. 72)
Pub: Earl G. Graves Publishing Co. Inc.
Ed: Lee Anna Jackson. Description: According to a recent study, about 22 percent of all employees leave their job within the first year. The cost of replacing an employee varies, but can run an average of $13,000 per full-time worker, up 6.8 percent from 2002.

45314 ■ "It's a Given" in *Entrepreneur* (Vol. 28, No. 9, September 2000, pp. 142)
Pub: Entrepreneur Media Inc.
Ed: Chris Penttila. Description: A discussion about the personal and business benefits derived from volunteer work.

45315 ■ "It's Important to Be Proactive about Risk Issues" in *Atlanta Business Chronicle* (Vol. 24, No. 9, August 3, 2001, pp. 9B)
Pub: American City Business Journals Inc.
Description: Major factors resulting in business failure include customer demand shortage, irregularities in accounting, issues concerning supply chain and competitive pressures. In protecting a business from risk of failure, in addition to purchasing insurance, a culture and organizational structure where risk management is seen as everyone's job, is essential.

45316 ■ "It's the Sound Bite, Stupid" in *Inc.* (Volume 27, June 2005, No. 6, pp. 128)
Pub: Inc. Magazine
Ed: Adam Hanft. Description: Business leaders must understand the importance of good communications skills when conducting business.

45317 ■ "It's Swing Time" in *Inc.* (September 1, 2004)
Pub: Inc. Magazine
Ed: Adam Hanft. Description: Corporate America is suffering from bipolar management disorder.

45318 ■ "It's a Team Thing" in *Black Enterprise* (Vol. 35, December 2004, No. 5, pp. 67)
Pub: Earl G. Graves Publishing Co. Inc.
Ed: Bridget McCrea. Description: Larry Sheffield's ability to build and motivate teams in NEC's Solutions Platform Group is examined. Sheffield oversees the company's 200 employees in the firm's mobile solutions, software, server, advanced optical, customer and high-performance computing divisions.

45319 ■ "Jack on Jack" in *Harvard Business Review* (Vol. 80, No. 2, February 2002, pp. 88)
Pub: Harvard Business School Press
Ed: Harris Collingwood, Diane L. Coutu. Description: An interview with Jack Welch, former CEO of General Electric, who stepped down from his position in September 2001. Welch's influence over future leaders is still unclear.

45320 ■ "James Bronce Henderson III" in *Crain's Detroit Business* (Vol. 19, No. 1, January 6, 2003, pp. 11)
Pub: Crain Communications Inc., Detroit
Ed: Michael Strong. Description: James Bronce Henderson III, owner of Utica Enterprises Inc. in Shelby Township, Michigan discusses his filing Chapter 11 bankruptcy and the impact it had on his employees.

45321 ■ "JBHM Education Group, LLC" in *Mississippi Business Journal* (Vol. 29, January 2007, No. 4, pp. 6)
Pub: Venture Publications, Inc.
Description: Profile of Pat Whitlock, who recently joined JBHM Education Group as human resources director. She most recently worked as a human resources manager at Time Warner Cable. JBHM Education Group provides educational management consulting to over 200 schools in Alabama, Arkansas, Louisiana and Mississippi.

45322 ■ "J.M. Neil and Associates: Primary Vendor IT and Network contract with International Communications Company" in *Ingram's* (Vol. 27,No. 7)
Pub: Show Me Publishing, Inc.
Description: Company management information about Kansas City-based J.M. Neil and Associates Inc., is discussed. The employment services company has recently made the Kansas City 100 fastest growing companies.

45323 ■ "Job Titles of the Future" in *Fast Company* (July 2001, pp. 50)
Pub: Fast Company

Ed: Erika Germer. Description: Profile of Michael Lamb, Chief Privacy Officer of AT&T Corporation; with the new title, Lamb is committed to developing privacy practices for all of AT&T's services, especially the wireless and cable services.

45324 ■ "Job Titles of the Future: Project Meanie" in *Fast Company* (September 2001, pp. 70)
Pub: Fast Company
Ed: Annie F. Pyatak. Description: Profile of Marlene Dolan, the project meanie at Company InsightShare LLC, a CRM software-and-services company based in Andover, Massachusetts.

45325 ■ "Job Training Serious Play" in *Crain's Detroit Business* (Vol. 19, No. 17, April 28, 2003, pp. 11)
Pub: Crain Communications Inc., Detroit
Ed: Laura Bailey. Description: Profile of Rachel Evans and Sue Jackson, co-founders of Rochester Hills, Michigan EnteLead Inc. The firm provides professional training based on the science of organizational development, using hands-on activities to teach, including Lego building blocks.

45326 ■ "A Job Well Done" in *My Business* (June/July 2004, pp. 46)
Pub: My Business Magazine
Ed: Robyn A. Friedman. Description: Service Net Solutions offers employees not only a career path, but also allows workers to spend more time with their families.

45327 ■ "Joining the Ranks" in *Entrepreneur* (Vol. 33, October 2005, No. 10, pp. 89)
Pub: Entrepreneur Media Inc.
Ed: Mark Henricks. Description: American entrepreneurs are finding returning military personnel to be attractive employees for their small companies due to their work experience combined with an eagerness to prove themselves.

45328 ■ "The Joy of Conflict" in *Inc.* (August 2005, pp. 112)
Pub: Inc. Magazine
Ed: Adam Hanft. Description: Workplace consensus versus workplace conflict is debated.

45329 ■ *Jump Start Your Business Brain: Ideas, Advice and Insights for Immediate Marketing and Innovation Success*
Pub: Emmis Books
Ed: Doug Hall. Released: April 2005. Price: $23.99. Description: Strategies to improve sales, marketing, and business development.

45330 ■ "The jungle" in *Wall Street Journal* (May 7, 2002, pp. B12)
Pub: Wall Street Journal
Ed: Kemba J. Dunham. Description: Executive recruiters debate the wisdom of 'parallel processing' or presenting the same candidate to two corporate clients simultaneously.

45331 ■ "Just for kicks: Every car you buy doesn't have to go to work with you" in *Entrepreneur* (Vol. 30, No. 1, January 2002, pp. 20)
Pub: Entrepreneur Media Inc.
Ed: Jill Amadio. Description: Profile of three fun cars for executives to trade their business sedans for on weekends are profiled, including BMW's Mini Cooper, Volkswagen's Cabrio GLX and the Lexus SC 430.

45332 ■ *Just Promoted: How to Survive and Thrive in Your First 12 Months as a Manager*
Pub: The McGraw-Hill Companies
Ed: Edward Betof. Released: 1992. Price: $29.95; $14.95 (paper).

45333 ■ "Keep it Simple" in *Entrepreneur.com* (Vol. 34, February 2006, No. 2, pp. 60)
Pub: Entrepreneur Media Inc.
Ed: Chris Penttila. Description: Twenty-five tips for fine tuning a small business are outlined, focusing on technology, money, banking, taxes, credit and collection, accounting systems, mergers, management, and marketing ideas.

45334 ■ "Keep The Ball Rolling" in *Rough Notes* (Vol. 145, No. 2, February 2002, pp. 79)
Pub: Rough Notes
Ed: Roger Sitkins. Description: For an agency to keep moving forward, agents should have an attitude of looking for improvement in themselves and their agency, have a prospect pipeline, a proactive sales management, training and education program.

45335 ■ "Keeping It Simple" in *Entrepreneur* (Vol. 28, No. 8, August 2000, pp. 94)
Pub: Entrepreneur Media Inc.
Ed: Mark Henricks. Description: There are three important ways to make your company more efficient and cost-effective: simple beginnings, simplifying simplified, and knowing your limits. These issues are covered in detail.

45336 ■ "Keeping Mums" in *Entrepreneur* (Vol. 33, February 2005, No. 2, pp. 71)
Pub: Entrepreneur Media Inc.
Ed: Mark Henricks. Description: Owner of an advertising agency in San Antonio, Texas tells how he hired a pregnant woman in 1995. The two worked out a plan whereby she could telecommute two days a week in order for her to be with her new baby. She has since become a partner in the ad, marketing and public relations agency that reports $30 million in annual billings.

45337 ■ "Keller Graduate School of Management of DeVry University" in *Ingram's* (Vol. 29, No. 8, August 2003, pp. 59)
Pub: Show Me Publishing, Inc.
Description: Keller Graduate School of Management of DeVry University highlights its management programs.

45338 ■ "Ken Burn's Jeffersonian Pavilion" in *Inc.* (January 1, 2002)
Pub: Inc. Magazine
Ed: John Grossmann. Description: Filmmaker Ken Burns speaks to the importance of finding a space for one's self, in order to get away from daily business pressures.

45339 ■ "Keys to Motivation" in *Small Business Opportunities* (Vol. 12, No. 2, March 2000, pp. 94, 96, 146)
Pub: Harris Publications, Inc.
Description: Fifteen ways to motivate employees in 15 days is presented by Alexander Hiam, trainer and consultant.

45340 ■ *The Kindess Revolution: The Company-Wide Culture Shift That Inspires Phenomenal Customer Service*
Pub: American Management Association
Ed: Ed Horrell. Released: 2006. Price: $23.00.

45341 ■ "Knowledge helped company bounce back" in *Crain's Detroit Business* (Vol. 19, No. 11, March 17, 2003, pp. 14)
Pub: Crain Communications Inc., Detroit
Ed: Laura Bailey. Description: Robert Verdun, head of CFI, a company specializing in software and consulting to help large companies control real estate costs, is profiled.

45342 ■ "Larry Nelson" in *Black Enterprise* (Vol. 34, No. 5, December 2003, pp. 68)
Pub: Earl Graves Publishing Co.
Description: Profile of Larry Nelson, recently named senior vice president and associate general counsel, development for Wendy's International. Nelson will oversee legal matters for the corporation, including franchising and real estate.

45343 ■ "Laugh track" in *Entrepreneur* (Vol. 30, No. 2, February 2002)
Pub: Entrepreneur Media Inc.
Ed: April Pennington. Description: Profile of Sushil Bhatia, founder of the Laughing Clubs of America. The firm offers 30-45 minute sessions of laughter that encourage a more positive attitude, relaxation and a strengthened immune system.

45344 ■ "Laughing All the Way to the Bank" in *Harvard Business Review* (Vol. 81, No. 9, September 2003, pp. 16)
Pub: Harvard Business School Press
Ed: Fabio Sala. Description: Studies conducted of executives to determine humor in management, found that those using humor intended to build bridges rather than interfere with the flow of conversation or otherwise be undermining, tended to receive more money.

45345 ■ "Law Talent" in *Entrepreneur* (Vol. 32, October 2004, No. 10, pp. 98)
Pub: Entrepreneur Media Inc.
Ed: Jane Easter Bahls. Description: Smart entrepreneurs understand the concept that lawyers can offer more than the knowledge of law to a company, they can help decision makers in terms of transitions, of what might happen in relationships.

45346 ■ "Leaders for the Long Haul" in *Fast Company* (July 2001, pp. 56)
Pub: Fast Company
Ed: Keith H. Hammonds. Description: When workers and executives from Roadway Express came together to strategize about the company's future, they made a startling discovery: everyone wanted the same things.

45347 ■ *Leadership 101: What Every Leader Needs to Know*
Pub: Nelson Business
Ed: John C. Maxwell. Released: September 2002. Price: $9.99. Description: Ways to enhance leadership skills focusing on following a vision and bringing others along.

45348 ■ "A Leadership Evolution" in *Employment Relations Today* (Vol. 26, No. 4, Winter 2000, pp. 73)
Pub: John Wiley & Sons, Inc.
Ed: Roger E. Herman. Description: Looks at the future of organizational leadership in the 21st century. Topics addressed include individual worker responsibility, participatory management, and the impact of globalization on leadership and collaboration.

45349 ■ "Leadership and followership" in *Physician Executive* (Vol. 28, No. 1, January-February 2002, pp. 91)
Pub: American College of Physician Executives
Ed: Mary Francis Lyons. Description: A discussion on leadership skills is presented. The traits highlighted include projecting a vision, being a team builder and leader, thinking strategically, understanding systems, and being able to read market forces.

45350 ■ "Leadership that Gets Results" in *Harvard Business Review* (Vol. 78, No. 2, March 2000, pp. 78)
Pub: Harvard Business School Publishing Corp.
Ed: Daniel Goleman. Description: New research suggests that the most effective executives use a collection of distinct styles, each in the right measure, at just the right time.

45351 ■ "Leadership" in *Harvard Business Review* (Vol. 79, No. 11, December 2001, pp. 121)
Pub: Harvard Business School Press
Ed: Thomas J. Peters. Description: The sloppiness of an executive's workday is discussed, stating that the sad facts of leadership such as endless interruptions can be turned into opportunities to communicate values and persuade.

45352 ■ "The leadership journey" in *Harvard Business Review* (Vol. 80, No. 10, October 2002, pp. 42)
Pub: Harvard Business School Press
Ed: Leonard D. Schaeffer. Description: Leonard D. Schaeffer, CEO of Blue Cross of California, discusses how he turned around losses at the organization. The company has changed its name to WellPoint Health Networks. Three management techniques are discussed, including the autocrat, the participative leader, and the reformer.

45353 ■ *The Leadership Secrets of Colin Powell*
Pub: McGraw-Hill Companies
Ed: Oren Harari. Released: January 2002. Price: $21.95. Description: Profile of Colin Powell, stressing his abilities as a world leader.

45354 ■ "Leadership Training" in *Black Enterprise* (Vol. 37, January 2007, No. 6, pp. 56)
Pub: Earl G. Graves Publishing Co. Inc.
Ed: Sonia Alleyne. Description: Profile of Theopolis Holman, Group Vice-President of Duke Energy, who discusses how he prepared for the merger between Duke Energy and Cinergy. Holman oversees a division of 9,000 service contractors and employees.

45355 ■ "Leadership Training in Uniform" in *Hispanic Business* (Vol. 23, No. 7/8, July/August 2001, pp. 20)
Pub: Hispanic Business
Ed: Vivienne Heines. Description: Profile of Command Sergeant Major Daniel Chavez, highlighting his leadership skills, which he compares to that of a small business manager.

45356 ■ "Leadership in a combat zone" in *Harvard Business Review* (Vol. 79, No. 11, December 2001, pp. 107)
Pub: Harvard Business School Press
Description: The similarities between leadership in the military and in business are presented. The author, a lieutenant general in the U.S. Army argues that to lead successfully a person must demonstrate both expertise and empathy, know your stuff and listen hard.

45357 ■ "Leading from the slow lane" in *Incentive* (Vol. 174, No. 9, September 2000, pp. 33)
Pub: Bill Communications
Ed: Nancy K. Austin. Description: When it comes to leadership, high-octane doesn't always mean high-performance. A new book takes the leadership role out for a new spin.

45358 ■ "Leading in Times of Trauma" in *Harvard Business Review* (Vol. 80, No. 1, January 2002, pp. 55)
Pub: Harvard Business School Press
Ed: Jane E. Dutton. Description: Using three years of research conducted at the Compassion Lab (jointly operated by the University of Michigan Business School and the University of British Columbia), recommendations are offered for dealing with trauma, disaster, and grief within a business environment.

45359 ■ "Leading for value" in *Harvard Business Review* (Vol. 81, No. 4, April 2003, pp. 41)
Pub: Harvard Business School Press
Ed: Brian Pitman. Description: The former CEO of Lloyds Bank PLC describes how he and his team transformed the bank's corporate culture by focusing on increasing shareholder value and reaching decisions through debate, the key to agreement.

45360 ■ "The Lean Service Machine" in *Harvard Business Review* (Vol. 81, No. 10, October 2003, pp. 123)
Pub: Harvard Business School Press
Ed: Cynthia Karen Swank. Description: Jefferson Pilot Financial is featured as a service company that has taken a page from management used by the manufacturing industry to cut costs.

45361 ■ *Lean Six Sigmas That Works: A Powerful Action Plan for Dramatically Improving Quality, Increasing Speed, and Reducing Waste*
Pub: American Management Association
Ed: Bill Carreira; Bill Trudell. Released: 2006. Price: $21.95.

45362 ■ "Learn to lead with a little help from your friends" in *Women In Business* (Vol. 52, No. 2, March 2000, pp. 24)
Pub: The ABWA Co., Inc.

Description: The American Business Women's Association offers a number of leadership programs to assist members with professional development.

45363 ■ "Learning business was key" in *Crain's Detroit Business* (Vol. 19, No. 13, March 31, 2003, pp. 13)
Pub: Crain Communications Inc., Detroit
Description: Profile of David Fry, president and CEO of Fry Inc. Fry, a former Harvard University professor, started his firm with financing from family members. The company tripled in size in a short period of time, and Fry shares his experiences of learning about his business as it grew.

45364 ■ "Learning to lead" in *Incentive* (Vol. 174, No. 9, September 2000, pp. 32)
Pub: Bill Communications
Ed: Stephen Covey. **Description:** In strong organizations, leaders teach what they have learned to others so that knowledge is retained and recruits quickly learn to appreciate teamwork.

45365 ■ *Learning Leadership*
Pub: Bonus Books, Inc.
Ed: Abraham Zaleznik. **Released:** 1992. **Price:** $19.95.

45366 ■ "Led poisoning" in *Entrepreneur* (Vol. 30, No. 1, January 2002, pp. 18)
Pub: Entrepreneur Media Inc.
Ed: Watts Wacker. **Description:** A brief discussion involving the qualities of leadership for the future of business.

45367 ■ "Left Unsaid: How Ignoring Internal Conflict Can Kill Your Small Business" in *My Business* (April/May 2004, pp. 36-39)
Pub: My Business Magazine
Ed: Karen J. Bannan. **Description:** Conflict is necessary and important to a small business, it sparks creativity and keeps relationships from stagnating, however most small business owners do not understand that conflict really is an impetus for change.

45368 ■ "Let Go" in *My Business* (December/January 2003, pp. 35-37)
Pub: My Business Magazine
Ed: Paul S. Howell. **Description:** A look at four small businesses that profited when their leaders learned to delegate work to employees. Owners of small companies tend to micromanage much more that managers in large corporations.

45369 ■ "Let's celebrate! Use performance evaluations as a time to praise" in *Black Enterprise* (Vol. 32, No. 6, January 2002, pp. 45)
Pub: Earl Graves Publishing Co.
Ed: Monique R. Brown. **Description:** Strategies to transform year-end reviews and provide effective feedback on performance are outlined.

45370 ■ "Let's Talk About Sexism: Do Sexist Attitudes Still Exist in Business? Women Sound Off" in *Entrepreneur* (Vol. 32, No. 4, April 2004)
Pub: Entrepreneur Media, Inc.
Ed: Aliza Pilar Sherman. **Description:** Women entrepreneurs discuss the issues of sexism in business, comparing issues today with those of the past. The article is divided with interviews with these women in each decade starting in the 1970s.

45371 ■ "A letter to the chief executive" in *Harvard Business Review* (Vol. 80, No. 10, October 2002, pp. 94)
Pub: Harvard Business School Press
Ed: Joseph Fuller. **Description:** This fictitious letter to the head of a company explores managerial faults within large companies that have recently been in the news, and that have challenged many long-held beliefs and misconceptions.

45372 ■ "Life after bankruptcy: there are still pitfalls in folding a business" in *Black Enterprise* (Vol. 33, No. 3, October 2002, pp. 58)
Pub: Earl Graves Publishing Co.
Ed: Bridget McCrea. **Description:** When filing for bankruptcy, small business owners have two choices: Chapter 7 or Chapter 11. The process for filing for bankruptcy is described, along with tips to make the processes easier.

45373 ■ "Lightening the Workload: Entrepreneurs Should Know When It's Time to Delegate" in *Black Enterprise* (Vol. 34, No. 2, September 2003)
Pub: Earl Graves Publishing Co.
Ed: Bridget McCrea. **Description:** The importance of business owners realizing they need to delegate work to employees rather than continuing to adopt the theory, "if you want a job done right, you must do it yourself."

45374 ■ "Like It or Not...Culture Matters" in *Employment Relations Today* (Vol. 27, No. 2, Summer 2000, pp. 43)
Pub: John Wiley & Sons, Inc.
Ed: Caroline J. Fisher. **Description:** The true costs of an operational business culture that leaves employees feeling dispirited, disenfranchised and unmotivated are identified. Daniel Denison's model, which identifies the connection between a productive corporate culture and the bottom line, is discussed.

45375 ■ "A Little Friendly Advice: Exhibitor Advisory Committees Can Make a Difference" in *Tradeshow Week* (Vol. 34, December 6, 2004, No. 49)
Pub: Reed Business Information
Ed: Gary Tufel. **Description:** Exhibitor advisory committees, though rare, can be very useful in creating successful tradeshows if show managers are willing to act on their recommendations.

45376 ■ "Little things mean a lot" in *Rough Notes* (Vol. 146, No. 3, March 2003, pp. 118)
Pub: Rough Notes
Ed: Robert L. Bailey. **Description:** The song, "Little Things Mean a Lot" translates into a valuable lesson in business leadership. Customers never forget the small courtesies or notes of appreciation from staff, however they never forget negative treatment either.

45377 ■ "Living the Lifestyle of the Successful Businessperson" in *Hispanic Business* (January/February 2005, pp. 63, 64)
Pub: Hispanic Business
Ed: Leslie A. Westbrook. **Description:** Victor Lopez, senior vice president at Hyatt Hotels Corporation believes balance is the key to a successful executive lifestyle. Profile of X9 GPS that allows users to map a route and upload the information onto a watch is included.

45378 ■ "Lloyd Ward: Victim or Villan?" in *Black Enterprise* (Vol. 34, No. 6, January 2004, pp. 60)
Pub: Earl Graves Publishing Co.
Ed: Matthew S. Scott. **Description:** Interview with Lloyd Ward, former U.S. Olympic Committee CEO is presented. Ward gives his side on issues regarding the campaign to discredit him citing unpopular business practices and management style to derail his career.

45379 ■ *Local Enterprises in the Global Economy: Issues of Governance and Upgrading*
Pub: Edward Elgar Publishing, Incorporated
Ed: Hubert Schmitz. **Released:** April 2004. **Price:** $35.00 (soft cover), $110.00 (hard bound). **Description:** Examination of the relationships between globalization, corporate governance, and the economic performance of small businesses and local enterprises.

45380 ■ "Locker Room Tactics" in *Hispanic Business* (October 2002, pp. 76)
Pub: Hispanic Business

Ed: Teresa Talerico. **Description:** Professional coaching is used to help individuals and companies obtain results and reach goals. Corporate diversity training can work to combat workplace discrimination.

45381 ■ "Long Live the New King of Bonds" in *Business Week* (January 16, 2006, No. 3967, pp. 68, 70)
Pub: McGraw-Hill Companies
Ed: Christopher Palmeri. **Description:** Profile of Ken Leech, chief investment officer at Western Asset Management Company (Wamco). Wamco manages about $5.5 billion in 11 mutual funds. Experts believe the key to Wamco's success has been it consistent focus on large institutional bond clients.

45382 ■ "Look before you lay off" in *Harvard Business Review* (Vol. 80, No. 4, April 2002, pp. 20)
Pub: Harvard Business School Press
Ed: Darrell Rigby. **Description:** An examination of the pitfalls inherent in layoffs during an economic downturn. Research shows that shareholders punish companies that use layoffs solely to cut costs. Graphs are included.

45383 ■ "Losing Stream: Smart Moves: Is Your Business Leaking Profits?" in *Entrepreneur* (Vol. 31, No. 9, September 2003, pp. 77)
Pub: Entrepreneur Media, Inc.
Ed: Mark Henricks. **Description:** Ways to get more sales revenue back into a small company are discussed.

45384 ■ "Low-Cost Teleconferencing" in *My Business* (February/March 2004, pp. 17)
Pub: My Business Magazine
Description: Profile of Apple's new iSight, a cylindrical camera and microphone that connects to a Macintosh computer via high-speed firewire and Apple's proprietary multimedia Internet messaging software iCath-AV, providing always-on videoconferencing.

45385 ■ "The Low Down" in *My Business* (June/July 2004, pp. 46)
Pub: My Business Magazine
Ed: Karen J. Bannan. **Description:** Pre-hire tests can give employers more insight into job candidates than a resume alone.

45386 ■ "Mad skills" in *Entrepreneur* (Vol. 31, No. 4, April 2003, pp. 79)
Pub: Entrepreneur Media Inc.
Ed: Marc Diener. **Description:** Anger can be used as another weapon in the negotiation process, but the proper use of anger is key.

45387 ■ "Maine Executives Give State's Economy 'Worst' Rating" in *Portland Press Herald* (May 27, 2005)
Pub: Blethen Maine Newspapers, Inc.
Ed: Edward D. Murphy. **Description:** Market Research Insight surveyed 502 business leaders from Maine and discovered senior managers have a negative view of the economy, the business climate, and the state's ability to handle its economic issues.

45388 ■ "Make sure that employee ranking systems are effective" in *Atlanta Business Chronicle* (Vol. 24, No. 13, August 24, 2001, pp. 6B)
Pub: American City Business Journals Inc.
Ed: Emory Mulling. **Description:** Employee ranking schemes can be used to determine which employees should be the first to be laid off and how to administer raises, but such programs must be carefully designed and managed to prevent charges of discrimination. For example, an employee who has just been promoted because of effectiveness might not achieve the same high ranking immediately in the new position, and so might be unfairly punished. Also systems that force ranking employees on a bell curve might punish some employees, while some managers might inflate the ranking of their employees to make themselves look good.

45389 ■ "Make your layoff list and check it twice" in *BlackEnterprise* **(Vol. 32, No. 3, October 2001, pp. 70)**
Pub: Earl Graves Publishing Co.
Ed: Robyn D. Clarke. **Description:** David A. Branch, an employment and civil rights attorney in Washington DC, provides four important points for businesses to consider when planning a pre-layoff checklist.

45390 ■ "Make Up Your Mind" in *Black Enterprise* **(Vol. 36, February 2006, No. 7, pp. 164)**
Pub: Earl G. Graves Publishing Co. Inc.
Ed: Marcia A. Reed-Woodard. **Description:** Seven steps for making good decisions are outlined by Dr. Spencer Johnson, author of "Yes" or "No" The Guide To Better Decisions. Dr. Johnson believes a person's status is ruled by their choices.

45391 ■ "Making a Clean Break" in *Atlanta Business Chronicle* **(Vol. 25, December 6, 2002, No. 26, pp. 1B)**
Pub: American City Business Publications, Inc.
Ed: Lee Hall. **Description:** When a business determines that it must terminate a client, being honest and sharing blame are important elements of the process. Business relationships can become strained to the point that they no longer work.

45392 ■ "Making a Comeback" in *Entrepreneur* **(Vol. 32, August 2004, No. 8, pp. 71)**
Pub: Entrepreneur Media Inc.
Ed: Joanne Cleaver. **Description:** Advantages as well as disadvantages to rehiring an employee to serve as a consultant are explored.

45393 ■ "The Making of a Corporate Athlete" in *Harvard Business Review* **(Vol. 79, No. 1, January 2001, pp. 120)**
Pub: Harvard Business School Publishing Corp.
Ed: Jim Loehr, Tony Schwartz. **Description:** Quality work is produced by executives not only because of mental attributes, but also due to spiritual, emotional and physical characteristics.

45394 ■ "Making Partner: A Mentor's Guide to the Psychological Journey" in *Harvard Business Review* **(Vol. 78, No. 2, March 2000, pp. 147)**
Pub: Harvard Business School Publishing Corp.
Ed: Herminia Ibarra. **Description:** In this era of talent wars, partners at professional firms can no longer afford to have a survival of the fittest mind-set toward consultants, investment bankers, and junior accountants aspiring to join their business. Instead, they must understand, and guide, the complex emotional transformation that every partner hopeful must go through.

45395 ■ "Male and female in organizational behavior" in *Journal of Organizational Behavior* **(Vol. 23, No. 2, March 2002, pp. 149)**
Pub: John Wiley & Sons Inc.
Ed: Lloyd E. Sandelands. **Description:** The influence of a person's sex on the operation of an organization is discussed. The lack of published information on this topic is also discussed.

45396 ■ "Manage with care" in *Black Enterprise* **(Vol. 32, No. 5, December 2001, pp. 61)**
Pub: Earl Graves Publishing Co.
Ed: Monique R. Brown. **Description:** Suggestions are offered to ensure proper support to employees in times of crisis.

45397 ■ "Management commitment to innovation and ESOP stock concentration" in *Journal of Business Venturing* **(Vol. 15, No. 5-6, Sept.-Nov. 2000)**
Pub: Elsevier Science, Inc.
Ed: John E. Gamble. **Description:** A new study investigates the ability of managers to use employee stock ownership plans to aid managerial decision control.

45398 ■ "Management Liability at the Speed of Light" in *Rough Notes* **(Vol. 145, No. 38, June 2002, pp. 38)**
Pub: Rough Notes
Ed: Elisabeth Boone. **Description:** The Royal and Sun Alliance USA, headed by Chris Mower, offers directors and officers liability insurance through its Business Assurance Center, both directly or online.

45399 ■ *Management Mess-Ups: 57 Pitfalls You Can Avoid (& Stories of Those Who Didn't)*
Pub: Career Press, Inc.
Ed: Mark Eppler. **Released:** 1997. **Price:** $12.99.

45400 ■ "Management by whose objectives?" in *Harvard Business Review* **(Vol. 81, No. 1, January 2003, pp. 107)**
Pub: Harvard Business School Press
Ed: Harry Levinson. **Description:** The argument that most performance appraisals fail because the do not take into account the aspirations of the employees is presented. Individual needs and organizational requirements must converge for self-motivation to occur.

45401 ■ "Managerial Rudeness: Bad Attitudes Can Demoralize Your Staff" in *Black Enterprise* **(Vol. 37, January 2007, No. 6, pp. 58)**
Pub: Earl G. Graves Publishing Co. Inc.
Ed: Chauntelle Folds. **Description:** Positive leadership in the managerial realm leads to a more productive workplace. Managers who are negative, hostile, arrogant, rude or fail to accept any responsibility for their own mistakes find that employees will not give their all on the job.

45402 ■ *The Manager's Guide to Rewards: What You Need to Know to Get the Best of–and from–Your Employees*
Pub: American Management Association
Ed: Doug Jensen; Tom McMullen; Mel Stark. **Released:** 2006. **Price:** $24.95.

45403 ■ *Managing Business Growth: Get a Grip on the Numbers That Count*
Pub: Self-Counsel Press, Incorporated
Ed: Angie Mohr. **Released:** September 2004. **Price:** $14.95. **Description:** Fourth book in the Numbers 101 for Small Business Series, teaches how small company owners can expand their businesses using sound financial planning.

45404 ■ "Managing in the Cappuccino Economy" in *Harvard Business Review* **(Vol. 78, No. 2, March 2000, pp. 177)**
Pub: Harvard Business School Publishing Corp.
Ed: Eileen C. Shapiro. **Description:** Chris Argyris offers an insightful diagnosis of why traditional companies don't empower their people.

45405 ■ "Managing emotional fallout" in *Harvard Business Review* **(Vol. 80, No. 2, February 2002, pp. 55)**
Pub: Harvard Business School Press
Ed: Steven E. Hyman. **Description:** The opinions of Dr. Steven E. Hyman, the former director of the National Institute of Mental Health, regarding stress and depression in the workplace, especially in the aftermath of the terrorist attacks of September 11, 2001, are presented.

45406 ■ *Managing to Have Profits: The Secret Japan Learned but the U.S. Forgot*
Pub: CashFlow Books
Ed: Arnold J. Olenick. **Released:** 1992. **Price:** $24.95: $24.95 (paper). **Description:** Topics covered include strategic planning, marketing plans, pricing issues, break-even analysis, quality control, distribution channels and costs, evaluating managerial performance, and other subjects. Includes checklists, sample forms, and worksheets; contains an index.

45407 ■ *Managing Labour in Small Firms*
Pub: Routledge
Ed: Susan Marlow, Dean Patton, Monder Ram. **Released:** December 2004. **Price:** $105.00 (US), $147.00 (Canadian). **Description:** Essays addressing conditions of workers in small business.

45408 ■ "Managing information overload" in *Women In Business* **(Vol. 52, No. 2, March 2000, pp. 20)**
Pub: The ABWA Co., Inc.
Ed: Rachel Warbington. **Description:** Information management requires skill planning. Many resources are available to assist people to analyze their behavior and to prioritize.

45409 ■ *Managing People and Organizations*
Pub: The McGraw-Hill Companies
Ed: John Gabarro. **Released:** 1992. **Price:** $29.95 (paper).

45410 ■ *Managing for Results*
Pub: HarperCollins Publishers, Inc.
Ed: Peter F. Drucker. **Released:** October 2006. **Price:** $16.95. **Description:** Entrepreneurs running successful small companies focus on opportunity rather than problems.

45411 ■ *Managing a Small Business Made Easy*
Pub: Entrepreneur Press
Ed: Martin E. Davis. **Released:** September 2005. **Price:** $19.95 (US), $26.95 (Canadian). **Description:** Examination of the essential elements for an entrepreneur running a business, including advice on leadership, customer service, financials, and more.

45412 ■ *Managing Small Businesses*
Pub: West Publishing Co.
Ed: Robert L. Anderson. **Released:** 1993. **Price:** $57.00.

45413 ■ "Managing for the next big thing" in *Harvard Business Review* **(Vol. 79, No. 1, January 2001, pp. 131)**
Pub: Harvard Business School Publishing Corp.
Ed: Paul Hemp. **Description:** Michael Ruettgers of data storage device manufacturer EMC discusses the company's success and how it has managed to stay ahead of the trends in the computer industry.

45414 ■ "Managing to Win" in *Small Business Opportunities* **(Vol. 17, November 2005, No. 6, pp. 10, 20)**
Pub: Harris Publications Inc.
Ed: Joe John Duran. **Description:** Business professional shares tips to help company leaders build championship teams. Tips to prevent identity theft are also listed.

45415 ■ "Managing Your IT Managers" in *Ingram's* **(Vol. 28, No. 5, May 2002, pp. 26)**
Pub: Show Me Publishing, Inc.
Ed: Russ Johnson. **Description:** Guidelines for developing effective information technology leadership in a small company are presented.

45416 ■ "Maneuver warfare: Can modern military strategy lead you to victory?" in *Harvard Business Review* **(Vol. 80, No. 4, April 2002, pp. 57)**
Pub: Harvard Business School Press
Ed: Jason A. Clemons, Eric K. Clemons, Santamaria Clemons. **Description:** Warfare as a metaphor for business is examined by presenting the theory of maneuver warfare by which a company, rather than destroying a competitor, renders that adversary unable to fight as an effective, coordinated whole.

45417 ■ "Marcus Buckingham Thinks Your Boss Has an Attitude Problem" in *Fast Company* **(August 2001, pp. 88)**
Pub: Fast Company
Ed: Polly LaBarre. **Description:** Marcus Buckingham is a consultant who teaches CEOs how to get the most from their employees. Buckingham has authored two books to help managers lead their employees.

45418 ■ "Market Orientation and Other Potential Influences on Performance..." in *Journal of Small Business Management* **(Vol. 38, No.1, Jan. 2000)**
Pub: West Virginia University
Ed: Alfred M. Pelham. **Description:** Research to provide managers in small manufacturing firms with results regarding significant factors related to performance is reported.

45419 ■ *The Martha Rules: 10 Essentials for Achieving Success as You Start, Build, or Manage a Business*
Pub: Rodale Press, Incorporated
Ed: Martha Stewart. **Released:** October 2005. **Price:** $24.95. **Description:** Martha Stewart offers insight into starting, building and managing a successful business.

45420 ■ *The Martha Rules: 10 Essentials for Achieving Success as You Start, Grow, or Manage a Business*
Pub: Rodale Press, Inc.
Ed: Martha Stewart. **Released:** October 2005.

45421 ■ "Master of Her Retail Space" in *Crain's New York Business* (Vol. 23, January 29, 2007, No. 5, pp. F11)
Pub: Crain Communications, Inc.
Ed: Elisabeth Butler. **Description:** Profile of Amira Yunis and her position as executive vice president of Newmark Knight Frank Retail. Ms. Yunis won the Real Estate Board of New York's Retail Deal of the Year award for putting Trader Joe's into Union Square. She brokered $10 million in business last year as well.

45422 ■ "Mastering Agency Management" in *Rough Notes* (Vol. 146, No. 9, September 2003, pp. 52)
Pub: Rough Notes
Ed: Elisabeth Boone. **Description:** Profile of the courses offered by Appalachian State University for insurance agents and industry managers. Topics include writing insurance policies, management styles and techniques, and advancement within the industry.

45423 ■ *Mastering Change Management: Turning Obstacles into Opportunities*
Pub: Pfeiffer & Co.
Ed: Richard Y. Chang. **Price:** $12.95 (paper). **Description:** Part of the Management Skills Series.

45424 ■ "Maximizing Employee Performance: Grow Your Business by Empowering Your Workforce" in *Black Enterprise* (Vol. 35, February 2005, No. 7)
Pub: Earl G. Graves Publishing Co. Inc.
Ed: Arlene McKanic. **Description:** Guild Associates developed two entry-level management courses and the Leadership Development Program designed to develop and maximize leadership skills. The program features six steps that create a supportive culture that motivates and empowers a workforce.

45425 ■ "MBA Programs That Work for the Working Professional" in *Ingram's* (Vol. 29, No. 8, August 2003, pp. 53)
Pub: Show Me Publishing, Inc.
Description: The range of business schools in the Kansas City, Missouri areas offering MBA programs is covered.

45426 ■ "MC, MMA Offering Manufacturing Management Program" in *Mississippi Business Journal* (Vol. 29, January 2007, No. 3, pp. A15)
Pub: Venture Publications, Inc.
Ed: M.R. Gorringe. **Description:** Mississippi Manufacturers Association and the School of Business at Mississippi College will offer a Certified Manager of Performance Excellence in Manufacturing Program. The program is built around the Baldridge Criteria for Performance Excellence.

45427 ■ "McMullouch Has Had Busy Telecommunications Career" in *Mississippi Business Journal* (Vol. 29, January 2007, No. 4, pp. 10)
Pub: Venture Publications, Inc.
Ed: Lynn Lofton **Description:** Interview and profile of John McCullouch. McCullouch has served as Bell-South's president of operations.

45428 ■ "Mediocre Middle Management" in *Entrepreneur* (Vol. 28, No. 2, February 2000, pp. 38)
Pub: Entrepreneur Media Inc.
Ed: Ellen Paris. **Description:** An new survey concludes that employee retention is directly linked to employee-manager relationships.

45429 ■ "Meet Your New Executives" in *Inc.* (Volume 28, January 2006, No. 1, pp. 57-58)
Pub: Inc. Magazine
Ed: David H. Freedman. **Description:** Are computers replacing executives in the business place? New, powerful software is capable of understanding data.

45430 ■ "Meeting the Challenge of Disruptive Change" in *Harvard Business Review* (Vol. 78, No. 2, March 2000, pp. 66)
Pub: Harvard Business School Publishing Corp.
Ed: Clayton M. Christensen, Michael Overdorf. **Description:** It's no wonder that innovation is so difficult for established firms. They employ highly capable workers, only to set them to work within processes and business models that doom them to failure. This article shows ways out of this dilemma.

45431 ■ "Meg Whitman" in *Fast Company* (May 2001, pp. 72)
Pub: Fast Company
Ed: Charles Fishman. **Description:** Profile of Meg Whitman, CEO of the e-commerce company eBay.

45432 ■ "Membership Privileges: How To Benefit From Joining a Professional Organization" in *Black Enterprise* (Vol. 34, July 2004, No. 12)
Pub: Earl G. Graves Publishing Co. Inc.
Ed: Lee Anna Jackson. **Description:** Belonging to an industry-related organization can help a small business owner or a company leader through the networking opportunities presented.

45433 ■ "Memo to Rex Tillerson" in *Business Week* (January 9, 2006, No. 3966, pp. 36)
Pub: McGraw-Hill Companies
Description: Advice given to Mobil Corporation's future CEO, Rex Tillerson, who will be stepping into Lee F. Raymonds position when he retires from the company.

45434 ■ *Microfinance*
Pub: Palgrave Macmillan
Ed: Mario La Torre; Gianfranco A. Vento; Philip Molyneux. **Released:** October 2006. **Price:** $80.00. **Description:** Microfinance involves the analysis of operational, managerial and financial aspects of a small business.

45435 ■ "Millennial Madness" in *Entrepreneur* (Vol. 32, August 2004, No. 8, pp. 74)
Pub: Entrepreneur Media Inc.
Ed: Joanne Cleaver. **Description:** Millennials are the newest category of workers between the ages of 18 to 20s. Unlike Gen Xers, these employees are good team players and want to be included in a firm's growth strategies. Patrick Kulesa, global research director for a research and consulting firm reports that small businesses see an immediate difference when employing Millenials.

45436 ■ "Mind Games: Jump-Start Your Problem-Solving Skills for a Better Business" in *Entrepreneur* (Vol. 31, No. 10, October 2003, pp. 34)
Pub: Entrepreneur Media, Inc.
Ed: Mark Hendricks. **Description:** Review of the book, "Retrain Your Business Brain", by Donalee Markus, Lindsey Paige Markus and Pat Taylor; the book provides visual and verbal puzzles to small business owners to become better at solving business issues and spotting problems.

45437 ■ "Mind Over Matter" in *Entrepreneur* (Vol. 33, August 2005, No. 8, pp. 37)
Pub: Entrepreneur Media Inc.
Ed: Heather Clancy. **Description:** Infoblox founder Stuart Bailey offers Tae Kwon Do classes to employees on-site. Bailey feels the classes help foster a sense of community at his firm.

45438 ■ "Mind Your Manners" in *Sales & Marketing Management*
Pub: VNU Business Media

Ed: Kathryn Droullard. **Description:** With new technologies, business communications are becoming less personal as a result of email messages and high-tech devices. A guide to help sales reps avoid 25 common mistakes when corresponding with clients is presented.

45439 ■ "Mingling at Business Holiday Parties Made Easier for Some" in *Sacramento Bee* (November 29, 2005)
Pub: The Sacramento Bee
Ed: Gilbert Chan. **Description:** Tips to ease anxiety over attending holiday business parties are shared, including the use of networking for career building.

45440 ■ "Misclassifying Workers Can Cost You, Big Time" in *Inc.* (November 2000, pp. 97)
Pub: The Goldhirsh Group
Description: State and national authorities are auditing employee misclassification more and more. Employment-law experts stress the importance of interviewing and keeping thorough records of freelancers and contractors doing business with a company.

45441 ■ "A Modest Manifesto for Shattering the Glass Ceiling" in *Harvard Business Review* (Vol. 78, No. 1, January 2000, pp. 127)
Pub: Harvard Business School Publishing Corp.
Ed: Debra E. Meyerson, Joyce K. Fletcher. **Description:** Women, who were discriminated against in the past, are steadily making progress in the corporate world as they continually hold seats on corporate boards. The article suggests that even if that statement were the case, women at the highest levels of businesses are still rare.

45442 ■ "The moonlighter" in *Harvard Business Review* (Vol. 80, No. 11, November 2002, pp. 33)
Pub: Harvard Business School Press
Ed: Bronwyn Fryer. **Description:** In this fictional case study, an employee of one company is working on a project for another company in his free time in the first company's offices. Five experts discuss how the first company's managers should handle the situation.

45443 ■ "A More Perfect Business" in *Inc.* (August 1, 2003)
Pub: Gruner & Jahr USA Publishing
Ed: Matthew Fogel. **Description:** A family-business constitution could help direct a company through crisis and change. The constitution would consist of a statement of principles designed to guide issues of ownership, performance, accountability, and compensation, though would not be legally binding.

45444 ■ "More Than Smart Talk" in *Hispanic Business* (June 2002, pp. 76)
Pub: Hispanic Business
Ed: Scott Williams. **Description:** Effective communication begins with good listening skills, this is especially important among top management.

45445 ■ "Mortgage Warehouse in Melville Announces Staffing Changes" in *Long Island Business News* (March 5, 2004)
Pub: Dolan Media Newswires
Ed: Ryan McCormick. **Description:** Jonathan Foxx and Stephen Mayer have been appointed by Mortgage Warehouse in Melville, New York. Foxx will work as compliance management consultant, while Mayer will be responsible for managing and reviewing every facet of Mortgage Warehouse's financial and accounting records as controller.

45446 ■ "Motivator Vehicles" in *Sacramento Bee* (October 31, 2005)
Pub: The Sacramento Bee
Ed: Rachel Osterman. **Description:** Experts recommend small companies reward hardworking employees with items used daily rather than a large company dinner or the like. Gift certificates to popular coffee houses or retailers motivate workers.

45447 ■ "Moving mountains" in *Harvard Business Review* **(Vol. 81, No. 1, January 2003, pp. 41)**
Pub: Harvard Business School Press
Description: Twelve business leaders, including Carly Fiorina of Hewlett-Packard and Robert Eckert of Mattel, discuss their approaches to motivating employees. Some managers stress a person's need for the rational and orderly while others speak of inspiring through example.

45448 ■ "MTDC 'speaks' for itself" in *Women In Business* **(Vol. 52, No. 4, July 2000, pp. 35)**
Pub: The ABWA Co., Inc.
Ed: Rachel Warbington. **Description:** The benefit of participating in the American Business Women's Association program of Membership Training & Development Certification are discussed.

45449 ■ "Much Higher Learning: Exploring the Benefits Of an Academic Career" in *Black Enterprise* **(Vol. 34, July 2004, No. 12, pp. 61)**
Pub: Earl G. Graves Publishing Co. Inc.
Ed: Lee Anna Jackson. **Description:** Profile of the PhD Project, an organization that is committed to increasing the diversity of business school faculty by focusing minorities in the direction of doctoral programs. The program receives contributions from numerous corporations.

45450 ■ "Multiple Stakeholder Judgments of Employee Behaviors" in *Journal of Business Ethics* **(Vol. 46, No. 3, September 2003, pp. 235)**
Pub: Kluwer Academic Publishers Group
Ed: Elizabeth D. Scott, Karen A. Jehn. **Description:** Do moral judgments made by various stakeholders in determining whether an event, caused by an organizational employee, constitute dishonesty?

45451 ■ "Must Love Wing Tips; Executives Tend to List Eyes as Their Best Feature" in *Business Week* **(February 20, 2006, No. 3972, pp. 84)**
Pub: McGraw-Hill Companies
Ed: Christopher Palmeri. **Description:** Single executives over the age of 45, making more than $100,000 annually, make up a third of all online daters; most are divorced, have dogs, and enjoy wine tasting parties and list their eyes as their best feature.

45452 ■ "My Bad! Playing the Blame Game is Out." in *Entrepreneur* **(Vol. 33, March 2005, No. 3, pp. 94)**
Pub: Entrepreneur Media Inc.
Ed: Chris Penttila. **Description:** A growing number of CEOs are concerned with credibility, and are offering apologies for mistakes.

45453 ■ "MySay: Hiring Help" in *My Business* **(December/January 2003, pp. 49)**
Pub: My Business Magazine
Ed: Kathi Purnell. **Description:** The owner of a self-storage company discusses issues faced when she hired her best employee's mother so the two could work as a mother-daughter team for the business.

45454 ■ "The Myth of the Superstar CEO" in *Venture Capital Journal* **(November 1, 2004)**
Pub: Thomason Financial Inc.
Ed: Ravi Chiruvolu. **Description:** PeopleSoft, the enterprise software company, replaced its CEO Craig Conway with founder and chairman, Dave Duffield. Whether a superstar CEO is worth the time, effort and additional equity required to retain him or her is addressed.

45455 ■ "NEC Solutions (America) Inc." in *Black Enterprise* **(Vol. 34, No. 3, October 2003, pp. 58)**
Pub: Earl Graves Publishing Co.
Description: Profile of Larry Sheffield, newly appointed senior vice president of Server and OEM Products business units at NEC Solutions (America) Inc. Sheffield will support the firm's integrated solutions and service approach.

45456 ■ "Need to Boost Morale? Try Good Food, Fitness and Communication" in *Wall Street Journal* **(May 28, 2002, pp. B1)**
Pub: Wall Street Journal
Ed: Carol Hymowitz. **Description:** Suggestions are offered to help boost employee moral in the workplace.

45457 ■ "The Need for Speed in New Millennium Leadership Styles" in *Employment Relations Today* **(Vol. 27, No. 1, Spring 2000, pp. 61)**
Pub: John Wiley & Sons, Inc.
Ed: David Cottrell. **Description:** An overview of corporate management in an era of technological change, and the need for leadership styles that rely on quick decision-making and planning. Topics addressed include incorporating speed into company culture, streamlining processes, and implementing faster communication systems.

45458 ■ "Negotiating the spirit of a deal" in *Harvard Business Review* **(Vol. 81, No. 2, February 2003, pp. 66)**
Pub: Harvard Business School Press
Ed: Ron S. Fortgang, David A. Lax, James K. Sebenius. **Description:** Negotiating a deal can succeed or fail based upon a complete understanding by all parties of issues that are implied, such as expectations and social issues, as well as what is written down.

45459 ■ "Negotiating without a net. A conversation with the NYPD's Dominick J. Misino" in *Harvard Business Review* **(Vol. 80, Oct. 2002, pp. 49)**
Pub: Harvard Business School Press
Ed: Diane L. Coutu. **Description:** Dominick J. Misino answers questions about management techniques used to run the New York City Police Department.

45460 ■ "Negotiating Tips" in *Black Enterprise* **(Vol. 37, December 2006, No. 5, pp. 70)**
Pub: Earl G. Graves Publishing Co. Inc.
Description: Sekou Kaalund, head of strategy, mergers & acquisitions at Citigroup Securities & Fund Services, states that "Negotiation skills are paramount to success in a business environment because of client, employee, and shareholder relationships". He discusses how the book by George Kohlrieser, Hostage at the Table: How Leaders Can Overcome Conflict, Influence Others, and Raise Performance, has helped him negotiate more powerfully and enhance his skills at conflict-resolution.

45461 ■ "Network for a greater good in 2002" in *Women in Business* **(Vol. 54, No. 2, March-April 2002, pp. 33)**
Pub: The ABWA Co Inc.
Ed: Donna Fisher. **Description:** Networking tools for businesswomen are provided; maintaining networks and using business cards are discussed.

45462 ■ "Networking know-how" in *Women in Business* **(Vol. 53, No. 7, January-February 2002, pp. 40)**
Pub: The ABWA Co Inc.
Description: Different networking techniques and groups are listed. Networks can be provided by professional business organizations as well as civic organizations.

45463 ■ *Never Eat Alone: And Other Secrets to Success, One Relationship at a Time*
Pub: Doubleday Broadway Publishing Group
Ed: Keith Ferrazzi, Tahl Raz. **Released:** February 2005. **Price:** $24.95. **Description:** Business networking strategies are offered.

45464 ■ "New CEO: So What is Moto, Anyway?" in *Crain's Chicago Business* **(Vol. 26, No. 51, December 22, 2003, pp. 20)**
Pub: Crain Communications, Inc.
Ed: Julie Johnsson. **Description:** Newly appointed CEO of Motorola, Edward Zander, wants to fashion a distinctive corporate image for the electronics giant. The firm reports $27 billion in revenues and Zander feels the firm needs to better define itself.

45465 ■ "A New Game Plan for C Players" in *Harvard Business Review* **(Vol. 80, No. 1, January 2002, pp. 81)**
Pub: Harvard Business School Press
Ed: Beth Axelrod, Helen Handfield-Jones, Ed Michaels. **Description:** Corporate managers must find means to hire and retain quality managers, while finding an efficient means for dealing with managers that do not perform at needed levels; also important is improving the quality of existing managers.

45466 ■ "New Leadership Breeds New Energy" in *Women In Business* **(Vol. 52, No. 3, May 2000, pp. 18)**
Pub: The ABWA Co., Inc.
Ed: Rachel Warbington. **Description:** Issues concerning the membership of the American Business Women's Association and advice on helping new members develop leadership skills are covered.

45467 ■ "A New Leaf" in *Entrepreneur* **(Vol. 32, November 2004, No. 11, pp. 95)**
Pub: Entrepreneur Media Inc.
Ed: Mark Henricks. **Description:** Consulting firm, McKinsey & Company has designed a four-step process that assists entrepreneurs when making changes to a company. The first step involves convincing people, including employees, that a change is necessary for the firm.

45468 ■ "New Lessons to Learn" in *Fortune* **(Vol. 152, October 3, 2005, No. 7, pp. 87)**
Pub: Time Inc.
Ed: Howard Schultz. **Description:** Eight Fortune 500 CEOs discuss how Hurricane Katrina changed the way they think about crisis management. Focus is on caring for employees, keeping communication lines open, and preparation for the next disaster.

45469 ■ "The New School: What to Expect from Today's MBA Program" in *Black Enterprise* **(Vol. 34, No. 4, November 2003, pp. 57)**
Pub: Earl Graves Publishing Co.
Ed: Kim Jack Riley. **Description:** Career specialists are warning against postponing a job search and pursuing a master's degree. Primary concerns of employers in today's market are listed.

45470 ■ "New Year's 2003: resolve to be a better boss" in *Atlanta Business Chronicle* **(Vol. 25, January 3, 2003, No. 30, pp. 2B)**
Pub: American City Business Publications, Inc.
Ed: Emory Mulling. **Description:** A list of ten resolutions for better business management are highlighted. These resolutions include learning to delegate, constructive criticism, information sharing, and to listen more.

45471 ■ "The Next Management Revolution" in *Inc.* **(July 1, 2004)**
Pub: Inc. Magazine
Ed: Hillary Johnson. **Description:** Running a business like a household proved successful to the editor of a small newspaper.

45472 ■ "Nice Girls Don't Ask" in *Harvard Business Review* **(Vol. 81, No. 10, October 2003, pp. 14)**
Pub: Harvard Business School Press
Ed: Linda Babcock. **Description:** Three recent studies have shown that women are less likely to engage in negotiations because they are less likely to get what they asked for.

45473 ■ "Nicknamed 'nag' she's just doing her job" in *Wall Street Journal* **(May 14, 2002, pp. B1)**
Pub: Wall Street Journal
Ed: Timothy Aeppel. **Description:** The Career Journal features issues involved in being a quality improvement manager.

45474 ■ "Nip It In the Bud" in *Entrepreneur* **(Vol. 32, November 2004, No. 11, pp. 95)**
Pub: Entrepreneur Media Inc.
Ed: Chris Penttila. **Description:** An ombudsman program can act like an insurance policy by providing a confidential resource for employees.

45475 ■ **"No More Ms. NiceGuy: Do Nice Girls Really Finish Last in the Business World"** in *Entrepreneur* (Vol. 33, February 2005, No. 2, pp. 34)
Pub: Entrepreneur Media Inc.
Ed: Alisa Pilar Sherman. **Description:** Lois P. Frankel, corporate coach and author of Nice Girls Don't Get Rich: 75 Avoidable Mistakes Women Make With Money, recommends that female entrepreneurs stand up for themselves while providing services.

45476 ■ **"No Surrender"** in *Entrepreneur* (Vol. 33, January 2005, No. 1, pp. 63)
Pub: Entrepreneur Media Inc.
Ed: Barry Farber. **Description:** Obstacles, rejections and refusals can be used as a tool to take a sales program to the next level.

45477 ■ **"Not Your Ordinary Perks"** in *My Business* (April/May 2004, pp. 14)
Pub: My Business Magazine
Description: The firm CoManage credits low employee turnover to perks such as flexible hours, free gourmet coffee, fresh-baked bread daily, and high-speed Internet connections to employee homes, as well as on-site pinball machines for de-stressing.

45478 ■ **"Note to Staff"** in *My Business* (April/May 2004, pp. 44)
Pub: My Business Magazine
Ed: Lee Gimpel. **Description:** Small business owners should create a business manual for employees, allowing the owner time away from the company.

45479 ■ **"Obits"** in *Inc.* (September 2000, pp. 29)
Pub: The Goldhirsh Group
Description: Profile that chronicles the demise of a custom boat builder due to the owners' inexperience and underbidding for contracts.

45480 ■ **"Objectivity, Consensus Key For Survival of Family Biz"** in *Crain's Detroit Business* (Vol. 21, October 10, 2005, No. 43, pp. 23)
Pub: Crain Communications Inc. - Detroit
Ed: Sheena Harrison. **Description:** Three keys to help family-owned companies survive into the fourth-generation and beyond are shared by Steve McClure of The Family Business Consulting Group Inc. The Marietta, Georgia-based consulting firm stresses objectivity, family organization and consensus on a business direction as key.

45481 ■ **"October Recap"** in *Sales & Marketing Management* (Vol. 159, January-February 2007, No. 1, pp. 48)
Pub: VNU Business Media
Description: Problems among older and younger sales representatives are discussed.

45482 ■ **"Of One Mind: Keep Employees by Getting on the Same Page From the Get-Go"** in *Entrepreneur* (Vol. 31, No. 8, August 2003, pp. 23)
Pub: Entrepreneur Media, Inc.
Ed: David Newton. **Description:** The key to retaining good employees is to keep promises made during the recruiting process. According to a recent study, salary rewards, bonuses and perks were not as important to prospective employees as autonomy and personal growth, and job security and responsibility were more important than benefits.

45483 ■ **"Offshoring Could Boost Your Career"** in *Fortune* (Vol. 151, January 24, 2005, No. 2, pp. 36)
Pub: Time Inc.
Ed: Anne Fisher. **Description:** According to a study conducted by Duke University's Fuqua School of Business and Archstone Consulting, American businesses with offshore operations will ship 81 percent more research jobs, 55 percent more engineering, and 75 percent more human resources overseas (69 percent of which are already in India). American managers will be needed to oversee these operations.

45484 ■ **"Oil Slicks"** in *Inc.* (October 1, 2003)
Pub: Gruner & Jahr USA Publishing
Ed: Tahl Raz. **Description:** Tim Marquez and Rod Eson were on their way to revolutionizing the oil industry until they ran into legal issues that tore them apart.

45485 ■ **"Ok, let's review"** in *Entrepreneur* (Vol. 30, No. 10, October 2002, pp. 91)
Pub: Entrepreneur Media Inc.
Ed: Kimberly L. McCall. **Description:** Guidelines for use during performance reviews of sales staff that praise performers and weed out low producers are given.

45486 ■ **"Older CEOs Plan to Work Past Age 65. They May Find That Harder Than They Expect"** in *Inc.* (September 2005, pp. 27-29)
Pub: Inc. Magazine
Ed: Stephanie Clifford. **Description:** The entrepreneurial revolution was part of the baby boomer phenomenon. The trend toward older CEOs planning to work past the age of 65 is growing.

45487 ■ **"On Boss Day, We Praise and Pan"** in *Sacramento Bee* (October 17, 2005)
Pub: The Sacramento Bee
Ed: Rachel Osterman. **Description:** October 16th has been held as National Boss Day since 1958. According to recent studies, many employees are unhappy with supervisors and would not want to be in charge; others feel the day is an opportunity for team building. Statistical data included.

45488 ■ **"On the road to fitness"** in *Women in Business* (Vol. 54, No. 2, March-April 2002, pp. 30)
Pub: The ABWA Co Inc.
Ed: Mary-Lane Kamberg. **Description:** Businesswomen should maintain their physical fitness routines and business travel should not interfere.

45489 ■ **"On the Road"** in *Sales and Marketing.com* (Vol. 156, No. 3, March 2004, pp. 48)
Pub: VNU eMedia, Inc.
Ed: Betsy Cummings. **Description:** Six tips for sales managers to follow when purchasing vehicles for a sales fleet are offered by fleet experts. These strategies will help save money while making sales reps more productive.

45490 ■ *On-the-Job Training and Orientation: Enhanced Performance*
Pub: Pfeiffer & Co.
Ed: Larry R. Smalley. **Price:** $12.95 (paper). **Description:** Part of the Management Skills Series.

45491 ■ **"Once Upon A Time"** in *Entrepreneur* (Vol. 28, No. 2, February 2000, pp. 20)
Pub: Entrepreneur Media Inc.
Ed: Michelle Prather. **Description:** They used to work for Disney. Now they are the happiest corporate dropouts on earth.

45492 ■ **"100 Best Companies to Work for: In Good Times They GoWild with Perks"** in *Fortuneit* (V. 146, No. 1, 1/20/03, pp. 127)
Pub: Time Inc.
Ed: Christopher Tkaczyk, Ann Harrington, Milton Moskowitz, Robert Levering. **Description:** A listing of Fortune's 100 Best Companies To Work For is presented. Criteria for selection included a sampling of employee opinion from 269 candidate companies regarding their workplaces. Statistics include information on the firm's headquarters; U.S. employees, including minority and women percentages; percent of job growth and number of new jobs; and applicants and voluntary turnover.

45493 ■ *101 Simple Things to Improve Your Business*
Pub: Crisp Publications, Inc.
Ed: Dottie and Lilly Walters. **Released:** 1995. **Price:** $12.95.

45494 ■ **"One More For the Road"** in *Sales & Marketing Management* (January 2005)
Pub: VNU Business Media
Ed: Denis Jensen. **Description:** Sales executives, as well as management, should avoid the pitfalls of drinking when entertaining business clients. One accident involving an employee under the influence will cause insurance rates to go up.

45495 ■ **"One More Time: How Do You Motivate Employees?"** in *Harvard Business Review* (Vol. 81, No. 1, January 2003, pp. 87)
Pub: Harvard Business School Press
Ed: Frederick Herzberg. **Description:** Employee motivation requires interesting work, challenge and increasing responsibility.

45496 ■ **"One Tough Lesson Plan"** in *Forbes* (Vol. 170, No. 9, October 28, 2002, pp. 238)
Pub: Forbes Magazine
Ed: Luisa Kroll. **Description:** Chosen as one of the 200 Best Companies by Forbes, co-founder and chief executive of Corinthian Colleges tells how he uses his past military career to oversee 4,800 faculty and staff and more than 34,000 students. Corinthian Colleges is one of the country's largest post-secondary education companies.

45497 ■ **"Online Employee Surveys Slow to Catch on"** in *Atlanta Business Chronicle* (Vol. 25, No. 19, October 18, 2002, pp. 12C)
Pub: American City Business Publications, Inc.
Ed: Paige Bowers. **Description:** Online employee surveys are not being used by businesses for various reasons. It is considered that paper-based surveys are easier to use when dealing with cross-country truck drivers or assembly line workers, while the slowing economy has forced other businesses to set aside company Intranet projects.

45498 ■ **"Open-market innovation"** in *Harvard Business Review* (Vol. 80, No. 10, October 2002, pp. 80)
Pub: Harvard Business School Press
Ed: Darrell Rigby, Chris Zook. **Description:** An analysis of managerial techniques used by Pitney Bowes to quickly identify and develop effective means that could help clients prevent anthrax contamination in the mail room. These ideas generally came from outside the company, and required special managerial techniques.

45499 ■ **"Open Your Books To Grow Your Business"** in *My Business* (November/December 2001, pp. 42)
Pub: My Business Magazine
Ed: Shannon Scully. **Description:** Open book management (OBM), is described by its originator, Victor Ornelas owner of a Latino marketing firm in Dallas, Texas. Open book management is a company policy that requires the business owner to share the company's financial information with its employees.

45500 ■ **"Opening the Kimono"** in *Inc.* (September 1, 2003)
Pub: Gruner & Jahr USA Publishing
Ed: Bobbie Gossage. **Description:** How much information should be revealed when negotiating with potential partners? Tips for successful negotiating are revealed.

45501 ■ **"Oracle chief puts CEOs to the test"** in *San Francisco Business Times* (Vol. 16, No. 43, May 31, 2002, pp. 1)
Pub: San Francisco Business Times Inc.
Ed: Lizette Wilson. **Description:** Former Oracle employees who have gone on to success outside the company, such as Craig Conway of PeopleSoft and Tim Siebel of Siebel Systems, are discussed along with Oracle CEO Larry Ellison's management style. More than half of all top technical firms have Oracle workers in their top ranks.

45502 ■ *Other Essentials of Business Ownership*
Pub: PublishAmerica, Incorporated
Ed: Charles Shaw. **Released:** May 2006. **Price:** $19.95. **Description:** Things a business owner, entrepreneur, or manager must be aware of in order to successfully manage a small business.

45503 ■ "Our Companies, Ourselves" in *Inc.* (November 2006, pp. 39-40)
Pub: Gruner & Jahr USA Publishing
Ed: Thea Singer. **Description:** Overidentifying with your company can become dangerous ad is best to try to separate the two. This is very difficult to do if you started the business yourself.

45504 ■ "Out of Control" in *Inc.* (September 1, 2003)
Pub: Gruner & Jahr USA Publishing
Ed: Susan Hansen. **Description:** Profile of Travis Parsons, founder of Elogex, an Internet-based software application that would enable clients to coordinate shipping and delivery services across multiple warehouses and destinations. When Parsons sold the firm he also lost his decision-making power.

45505 ■ "Out of stock" in *Entrepreneur* (Vol. 30, No. 3, March 2002, pp. 65)
Pub: Entrepreneur Media Inc.
Ed: Jennifer Pellet. **Description:** In the right circumstances, going private might be the best solution for a company. The special circumstances involved in going private are discussed.

45506 ■ "An outsider's perspective" in *Wall Street Journal* (October 28, 2002, pp. R9)
Pub: Dow Jones & Co. Inc.
Ed: Kemba J. Dunham. **Description:** Information is shared for managing a family-owned business.

45507 ■ "Over Their Shoulders" in *My Business* (November/December 2001, pp. 43)
Pub: My Business Magazine
Ed: Shannon Scully. **Description:** A brief discussion is presented involving the monitoring of employee's time spent online for personal use and email. A recent survey conducted by Vault.com found that nearly one-half of employees do not believe their employers monitor their online activity; they also stated they would not spend time online if they knew they were being monitored.

45508 ■ "Overcome E-Business Barriers" in *E-business Advisor* (Vol. 18, No. 1, January 2000, pp. 10)
Pub: Advisor Media, Inc.
Ed: Laurie Windham. **Description:** Today's e-business environment challenges managers to respond with effective online business strategies. Customers have already demonstrated their preference to do business over the Web, especially for routine tasks, and businesses that offer online services early are rewarded with customer loyalty and marketshare. Understanding how an e-business strategy influences time-to-market considerations is crucial to success.

45509 ■ *Overcoming the Five Dysfunctions of a Team: A Field Guide for Leaders, Manager, and Facilitators*
Pub: John Wiley & Sons, Incorporated
Ed: Patrick M. Lencioni. **Released:** March 2005. **Price:** $24.95. **Description:** Tools, exercises, assessment, and real-world examples for overcoming the five dysfunctions of a team.

45510 ■ "Owner of Panama Hatties in Huntington Station Plays Roles of Chef and Business Manager" in *Long Island Business News* (Feb. 13, 2004)
Pub: Dolan Media Newswires
Ed: Claude Solnik. **Description:** Profile of Matthew Hisiger, head chef and owner of Panama Hatties, a restaurant and banquet facility in Huntington Station.

45511 ■ "Owning Up" in *Entrepreneur* (Vol. 31, No. 8, August 2003, pp. 65)
Pub: Entrepreneur Media, Inc.
Ed: Mark Henricks. **Description:** Is a business better off renting or buying its location? This question is answered by looking at the benefits of purchasing property to build equity and control costs.

45512 ■ "Painting by numbers" in *Hispanic Business* (Vol. 22, No. 9, September 2000, pp. 82)
Pub: Hispanic Business
Ed: Scott Williams. **Description:** Standards in workmanship and encouraging the use of business management skills are just two of the aims of franchise operation Certa ProPainters.

45513 ■ "Parents for hire" in *Entrepreneur* (Vol. 31, No. 4, April 2003, pp. 76)
Pub: Entrepreneur Media Inc.
Ed: Patricia Schiff Estess. **Description:** Entrepreneurs often hire parents for their new companies because of their trust, savvy and availability, but it takes time to work out the role reversals in the new relationship.

45514 ■ "Part-Time Assignments" in *Black Enterprise* (Vol. 37, December 2006, No. 5, pp. 70)
Pub: Earl G. Graves Publishing Co. Inc.
Description: During critical change initiatives interim management, an employment model which uses senior-level executives to manage a special project or specific business function on a temporary basis, can have many benefits.

45515 ■ "Passing the Torch" in *Entrepreneur* (Vol. 31, No. 11, November 2003, pp. 97)
Pub: Entrepreneur Media, Inc.
Ed: Kimberly L. McCall. **Description:** Ways to hire and introduce a replacement managing a sales team are examined.

45516 ■ *A Passion for Planning*
Pub: University Press of America
Contact: Gina Vega, Author
Released: Published 2001. **Covers:** Small business topics, including growth, manufacturing, technology, sales, distribution, services, resources, networking, and business ethics. **Entries Include:** Contact details, Web sites.

45517 ■ "Past Track to the Future" in *Fast Company* (May 2001, pp. 166)
Pub: Fast Company
Ed: Harriet Rubin. **Description:** Stephen E. Ambrose has written best-selling histories of great feats of leadership and human endeavor, from World Wars to the opening of the American West, to the building of the transcontinental railroad. His insights from the past have inspired Hollywood blockbusters such as 'Saving Private Ryan'. Ambrose thinks that the past is the way to navigate the future.

45518 ■ "Pat Croce's Bottom Line" in *Inc.* (January 1, 2002)
Pub: Inc. Magazine
Ed: Leslie Brokaw. **Description:** Former president of the Philadelphia 76ers discusses the benefits of fitness, and ways to fit exercise into a busy schedule.

45519 ■ "Patrick Tisdale, Chief Information Officer" in *Law Firm Inc.* (August 2004)
Pub: American Lawyer Media LP
Description: Patrick Tisdale, chief information officer of Orrick explains how e-learning tools were made available to staff to improve skills. Tisdale also focused on increasing the help desk's level of expertise and instill the important role they play in the law firm, using a week long course in customer service skills.

45520 ■ "The Pay-for-Performance Fallacy" in *Business 2.0* (Vol. 6, July 2005, No. 6, pp. 64)
Pub: Time, Inc.
Ed: Jeffrey Pfeffer. **Description:** CEO pay and work performance are covered.

45521 ■ "Paying off in the end" in *BlackEnterprise* (Vol. 31, No. 11, June 2001, pp. 71)
Pub: Earl Graves Publishing Co.
Ed: Nancy Bearden Henderson. **Description:** Mentoring begins with a vision. The business owner who envisions his company to the next level while improving his performance and that of his employees is what the mentoring process is about. Recommendations for implementing a mentoring program for small companies, is included.

45522 ■ "Paying in Kind" in *Entrepreneur. com* (Vol. 34, February 2006, No. 2, pp. 82)
Pub: Entrepreneur Media Inc.
Ed: Mark Henricks. **Description:** Some companies send surveys to customers in order to determine the quality of customer service provided by employees.

45523 ■ "Paying your respects" in *Entrepreneur* (Vol. 31, No. 5, May 2003, pp. 70)
Pub: Entrepreneur Media Inc.
Ed: Joanne Cleaver. **Description:** Managers who show respect for employees have a much higher rate of employee satisfaction, equating to employees staying on the job.

45524 ■ "Peering In" in *Entrepreneur* (Vol. 33, January 2005, No. 1, pp. 70)
Pub: Entrepreneur Media Inc.
Ed: Chris Penttila. **Description:** Peer-to-peer interviewing can help small companies; the applicant learns more about the company, employees help select future co-workers, and management can gain more insight into the applicant's personality.

45525 ■ "Penney" in *Business Week* (January 9, 2006, No. 3966, pp. 82, 84)
Pub: McGraw-Hill Companies
Ed: Robert Berner. **Description:** Profile of Myron "Mike" Ullman III, chief executive for J.C. Penney's, who has launched new brand management techniques to boost the retailer's sales and earnings.

45526 ■ "Pension Funds Prod Firms to Show Management Compensation Packages" in *Sacramento Bee* (December 22, 2005)
Pub: The Sacramento Bee
Ed: Gilbert Chan. **Description:** Securities and Exchange Commission Chairman, Christopher Cox, is planning to perform the first changes in executive compensations rules since 1992 by ordering companies to define details of their management compensation packages.

45527 ■ "People Smarts: Human touch needed to manage knowledge" in *Atlanta Business Chronicle* (Vol. 25, No. 21, November 1, 2002, pp. 3B)
Pub: American City Business Publications, Inc.
Ed: Emory Mulling. **Description:** Making sure a business shares knowledge among the correct employees is recommended. Areas in which knowledge is important are discussed.

45528 ■ "Performance Appraisal Reappraised" in *Harvard Business Review* (Vol. 78, No. 1, January 2000, pp. 21)
Pub: Harvard Business School Publishing Corp.
Ed: Dick Grote. **Description:** Some of the freshest ideas for evaluating employees are coming from an unexpected source: the public sector.

45529 ■ "Personal histories" in *Harvard Business Review* (Vol. 79, No. 11, December 2001, pp.)
Pub: Harvard Business School Press
Description: The responses of 17 leaders in business, academia and the arts respond to a request for stories of experiences that taught them about leadership at its best and worst. Among the respondents were Michael Eisner of Disney, Ben Bradlee, former Washington Post editor, and Xerox CEO, Anne Mulcahy.

45530 ■ "Personalize your management development" in *Harvard Business Review* (Vol. 81, No. 3, March 2003, pp. 113)
Pub: Harvard Business School Press
Ed: Natalie Shope Griffin. **Description:** The problems organizations have with leadership development are explored. An outline of specific training approaches for various types of prospective leaders, such as reluctant leaders, arrogant leaders, overlooked leaders, and workaholics is presented.

45531 ■ "Perspective: Doing Well By Doing Nothing" in *Inc.* (July 1, 2004)
Pub: Inc. Magazine

Ed: Jess McCuan. **Description:** Businesses are promoting meditation at work in order to keep employees healthy and happy.

45532 ■ "Peter Drucker, still essential" in *Red Herring* (No. 102, August 15, 2001, pp. 35)
Pub: Herring Communications
Ed: Mark Williams. **Description:** A review of the book, The Essential Drucker, issued in three volumes, one on management, one on the individual in organizations, and one on society in general.

45533 ■ "Phone Home" in *My Business* (April/May 2004, pp. 44)
Pub: My Business Magazine
Ed: Marcia Layton Turner. **Description:** Ways a small business owner can get away from business and enjoy a vacation are discussed.

45534 ■ "Pick a niche and fill it" in *Hispanic Business* (Vol. 22, No. 7-8, July-August 2000, pp. 44)
Pub: Hispanic Business
Description: An analysis is presented showing how Hispanic American chief executive officers have achieved fast-growing companies in slow growing industries.

45535 ■ "Pick Your Battles" in *Entrepreneur* (Vol. 31, No. 11, November 2003, pp. 95)
Pub: Entrepreneur Media, Inc.
Ed: Marc Diener. **Description:** Ways to determine the difference between being outmaneuvered or outgunned during negotiations are presented.

45536 ■ "Picking Up the Pieces" in *Black Enterprise* (Vol. 32, No. 9, April 2002, pp. 44)
Pub: Earl Graves Publishing Co.
Ed: Bridget McCrea. **Description:** Patrick Duroseau, founder and president of Marnic Technologies, tell how he and his firm and employees are carrying on after the terrorist attacks of September 11, 2001.

45537 ■ "Pizza Schmizza Ready to Take on Puget Sound" in *Business Journal-Portland* (Vol. 20, No. 22, August 1, 2003, pp. 7)
Pub: American City Business Journals, Inc.
Ed: Robert Goldfield. **Description:** An overview of the growing success and expansion plans of Portland, Oregon-based Pizza Schmizza. Topics include management styles, competition, and long-term goals.

45538 ■ "Plan to Avoid Confusion When Passing the Torch" in *Atlanta Business Chronicle* (Vol. 23, No. 49, May 11, 2001, pp. 10B)
Pub: American City Business Journals Inc.
Ed: James Lea. **Description:** Family-owned businesses must make careful plans for passing on of ownership and management, especially when divorce has complicated the family dynamics. Co-owners must also be aware that they will not necessarily want to retire at the same time, and offspring may or may not want to continue in the family business. The economics of multiple ownership can also be complicated, especially if a business cannot support two or more families.

45539 ■ "Plan Events that Will Fill Seats" in *Women In Business* (Vol. 52, No. 2, March 2000, pp. 32)
Pub: The ABWA Co., Inc.
Ed: Jane Thomas. **Description:** Kansas City Express Network is a network for professional women which helps them to make contacts, while also considering their lack of time. The group holds 1-1/2 hour monthly lunch meetings and plans meetings quarterly.

45540 ■ "Planes, Tractors and Automobiles" in *Tradeshow Week* (Vol. 34, November 29, 2004, No. 48, pp. 64)
Pub: Reed Business Information
Ed: Heidi Genoist. **Description:** Trade show management is highlighted.

45541 ■ "Planning is everything" in *Ingram's* (Vol. 27, No. 2, February 2001, pp. 28)
Pub: Show Me Publishing, Inc.
Ed: Nancy Lauterbach. **Description:** The Small Business Advisor shows ways to use a company's annual meeting as a means of creating a sense of community among employees.

45542 ■ "Planning productive programs" in *Women In Business* (Vol. 52, No. 4, July 2000, pp. 28)
Pub: The ABWA Co., Inc.
Ed: Rachel Warbington. **Description:** Issues concerning the successful planning of programs to present to staff who are members of the American Business Women's Association are presented. The importance of choosing good educational speakers is discussed.

45543 ■ "Playbook" in *Business 2.0* (Vol. 6, May 2005, No. 4, pp. 121-122, 126-127)
Pub: Time, Inc.
Ed: Damon Darlin. **Description:** Leadership is the difference between enterprises that flourish and those that fail. Ways to turn a company into a thriving business are examined.

45544 ■ "Playing Favorites" in *Entrepreneur* (Vol. 31, Sept. 2003)
Pub: Entrepreneur Media, Inc.
Ed: Aliza Pilar Sherman. **Description:** Women entrepreneurs report favorite business Web sites they use to run their companies, with Google.com heading the list.

45545 ■ "The Plumtree Software Soap Opera" in *Forbes* (May 29, 2000, pp. 96)
Pub: Forbes Magazine
Ed: Luisa Kroll. **Description:** Profile of Plumtree Software and the problems it, like most startup companies, is facing.

45546 ■ "Pop Quiz: A Quick Test Of Your Managerial Skills" in *Sales & Marketing Management* (Vol. 157, January 2005, No. 1, pp. 17)
Pub: VNU Business Media
Description: Ways to determine whether a small business is capitalizing on its return on sales investment are presented.

45547 ■ "Pop Quiz: A Quick Test of Your Managerial Skills" in *Sales & Marketing Management* (Vol. 157, February 2005, No. 2, pp. 17)
Pub: VNU Business Media
Description: Three questions to determine whether you are an approachable or intimidating sales manager to your sales teams are asked.

45548 ■ "Pop Quiz: A Quick Test of Your Managerial Skills" in *Sales and Marketing. com* (Vol. 156, No. 3, March 2004, pp. 13)
Pub: VNU eMedia, Inc.
Description: Presentation of a quiz to help determine a new manager's skills. Answers are provided by Michael Watkins, associate professor of business administration at Harvard Business School, and author of The First 90 Days: Critical Success Strategies for New Leaders at All Levels.

45549 ■ "Position in management doesn't equal leadership" in *Atlanta Business Chronicle* (Vol. 24, No. 14, September 7, 2001, pp. 2B)
Pub: American City Business Journals Inc.
Ed: Emory Mulling. **Description:** Emory Mulling, chairman of The Mulling Companies, believes that managers are not genuine leaders until they work with employees instead of giving orders. Several ways of transforming managers into leaders are involving them in decision-making processes, putting them in true leadership positions, encouraging relations between emerging managers and executives, developing an environment that encourages innovation, and having an outlook that is long-term.

45550 ■ "Positive Peer Pressure" in *My Business* (December/January 2004, pp. 34-37)
Pub: My Business Magazine
Ed: Karen J. Bannan. **Description:** A new trend seen for small companies, has owners relying on peer groups for dealing with the pressures of running a business. Networking options can offer advice, education and camaraderie.

45551 ■ "The Power 50" in *Fortune* (Vol. 142, No. 9, October 16, 2000, pp. 139+)
Pub: Time Inc.
Ed: Grainger David, Christopher Tkaczyk, and Alynda Wheat. **Description:** Fortune's 2000 ranking of America's top women has a record 18 newcomers and each are listed with a brief description of their talents.

45552 ■ "Power Living: Teresa Kay-Aba Kennedy Says Executives Don't Get Enough S.E.X." in *Black Enterprise* (Vol. 34, No. 6, January 2004)
Pub: Earl Graves Publishing Co.
Ed: Sonia Alleyne. **Description:** Profile of Teresa Kay-Aba Kennedy, former vice president of business development operations at MTV Networks Interactive. Kennedy left her corporation position and founded a yoga center in Harlem, New York and is now president of Power Living Enterprises Inc., a lifestyle coaching company with programs that teach executives how to lead productive, healthy lives.

45553 ■ "Power is the great motivator" in *Harvard Business Review* (Vol. 81, No. 1, January 2003, pp. 117)
Pub: Harvard Business School Press
Ed: David C. McClelland, David H. Burnham. **Description:** Descriptions of three types of managers are discussed. Affiliative managers need to be liked more than they need to get things done, while personal power managers put their own achievement ahead of everything. The third group focuses on building power through influence, rather than promoting their own personal achievement, and are the most effective of the three groups.

45554 ■ "Power to the People" in *Incentive* (Vol. 174, No. 8, August 2000, pp. 18)
Pub: Bill Communications
Ed: Don Mogelefsky. **Description:** To effectively recruit and retain employees in the tight job market, companies are treating workers with a lot more respect.

45555 ■ "Practical Ideas for Improving Your Business" in *Journal of Accountancy* (Vol. 199, February 2005, No. 2, pp. 108)
Pub: American Institute of Certified Public Accountants
Ed: Stanley Zarowin. **Description:** Computers are playing a vital role in business growth. Should business managers or information technology staff be in charge of choosing the technical products and services for a company?

45556 ■ "Pre-Nups for Small Business" in *Black Enterprise* (Vol. 30, No. 7, February 2000, pp. 65)
Pub: Earl Graves Publishing Co.
Ed: Michael S. Mullman. **Description:** Plan your exit before you open the door. By writing a comprehensive shareholder agreement concerning such issues, shareholders simplify estate planning, reduce some of the risk and uncertainty inherent in any business and ensure an orderly continuation of their firm's work.

45557 ■ "Predictable surprises: The disasters you should have seen coming" in *Harvard Business Review* (Vol. 81, No. 3, March 2003, pp. 72)
Pub: Harvard Business School Press
Ed: Michael Watkins, Max Bazerman. **Description:** Many unexpected events that turn into disasters, such as financial scandals and product failures, can be foreseen and avoided, using the RPM approach: recognizing, prioritizing, and mobilizing.

45558 ■ *Prentice Hall Small Business Management Handbook*
Pub: Prentice Hall
Released: 1996. **Price:** $24.95.

45559 ■ "Preoccupied with what's working—or what's not—many CEOs see only linear paths to growth" in *Inc.* (November 2000, pp. 78)
Pub: The Goldhirsh Group
Description: A profile of a bike shop owner and the lessons he learned while trying to expand his existing business.

45560 ■ "Preparing for evil" in *Harvard Business Review* (Vol. 81, No. 4, April 2003, pp. 109)
Pub: Harvard Business School Press
Ed: Ian I. Mitroff, Murat C. Alpaslan. **Description:** The lack of preparation for crises in organizations, including Fortune 500 companies, is discussed. Crisis-prepared companies use a systematic approach to focus efforts for planning for natural disasters and two types of manmade calamities, accidental and deliberate.

45561 ■ "Preserving Tradition, Embracing Progress" in *Rough Notes* (Vol. 145, No. 2, February 2003, pp. 26)
Pub: Rough Notes
Ed: Elaine Tolen. **Description:** Profile of Trey Sherwood, a partner in Valdosta Insurance Services. The independent agency provides for the insurance needs of 98 percent of Lowndes County, Valdosta, Georgia.

45562 ■ "Primal Leadership: The hidden driver of great performance" in *Harvard Business Review* (Vol. 79, No. 11, December 2001, pp. 42)
Pub: Harvard Business School Press
Ed: Annie Richard, McKee Danile, Boyatzis Goleman. **Description:** Research into the effects of a leader's moods on the organization are presented. Leader's moods and behaviors are potent drivers of business success, since moods are literally contagious.

45563 ■ "Prince of Management" in *Entrepreneur* (Vol. 27, No. 12, December 1999, pp. 20)
Pub: Entrepreneur Media Inc.
Description: Management ideas gleaned from the story of Moses.

45564 ■ "Professionals and Professors: Substance or Style?" in *Business Communication Quarterly* (Vol. 63, No. 3, September 2000, pp. 9)
Pub: Association for Business Communication
Ed: Srivatsa Seshardri and Larry D. Theye. **Description:** The article gives an overall assessment of communication skills, standards of good writing, and writing style.

45565 ■ "Programs" in *Black Enterprise* (Vol. 34, No. 5, December 2003, pp. S8)
Pub: Earl Graves Publishing Co.
Description: Profile of Finding Leaders Among Minorities Everywhere (FLAME) program. The program is designed to build confidence and encourage professional growth.

45566 ■ *Project Management for Small Business Made Easy*
Pub: Entrepreneur Press
Ed: Sid Kemp. **Released:** April 2006. **Price:** $26.95.
Description: Strategies for implementing project management for small business are offered.

45567 ■ "Promise-keeping has lost its importance as a core value" in *Atlanta Business Chronicle* (Vol. 25, November 15, 2002, No. 23 pp. 27A)
Pub: American City Business Publications, Inc.
Ed: Ellwood F. Oakley III. **Description:** Managers consider "promise keeping" to be a lower-level ethical priority in business activity. MindSpring Enterprises Inc. is a high-profile exception; the company lives up to its commitments. Senior management must practice promise-keeping in order for it to be reintroduced into a workplace.

45568 ■ "Promotion Creativity Through the Logic of Contradiction" in *Journal of Organizational Behavior* (Vol. 23, No. 3, May 2002, pp. 321)
Pub: John Wiley & Sons Inc.
Ed: Linda Parrack Livinstone, Leslie E. Palicyh, Gary R. Carini. **Description:** The logic of contradiction which embraces paradox and contradiction as vehicles through which positive change and growth in the organization occur, is proposed and Intel Corporation of the microprocessor industry is used as an illustration. Intel crated new powerful microprocessor chips which were not yet in use so it invested in firms that promised to create need for their increased computing power.

45569 ■ "Protect Yourself: Records to store off-site" in *My Business* (April/May 2002, pp. 17)
Pub: My Business Magazine
Description: The California Society of Enrolled Agents provides a list of records a small business should store outside of the business or office to protect from disaster.

45570 ■ "Protecting your company from high turnover" in *Women in Busines s* (Vol. 53, No. 2, March-April, 2001, pp. 30)
Pub: The ABWA Co. Inc.
Ed: Melissa Will. **Description:** Strategies to attract and retain good caliber employees are addressed. Ways of reducing staff turnover through the use of flexible working hours, employee involvement and fair management practices are explored.

45571 ■ "PSI Uses Technology to Keep Call-Center Biz in U.S." in *Crain's Detroit Business* (Vol. 21, December 19, 2005, No. 51, pp. 10)
Pub: Crain Communications Inc. - Detroit
Ed: Anjali Fluker. **Description:** Larry Evans, president and owner of PSI based in West Bloomfield Township, Michigan, has invested nearly $500,000 into expanding his business. The move includes new technology and the addition of about 50 workers. Evans discusses the advantages to keeping his operations here rather than offshore outsourcing the work.

45572 ■ "The Public Library: Technology Lets You Browse the Stacks from Your Home Office" in *Black Enterprise* (Vol. 34, No. 4, Nov. 2003)
Pub: Earl Graves Publishing Co.
Ed: Jennifer L. Smith. **Description:** More than 3,000 libraries offer programs offering E-books, databases and online classes that can be accessed via computers for small and home businesses searching for materials on marketing and management topics.

45573 ■ "Publix chief leads quietly" in *Atlanta Business Chronicle* (Vol. 24, No. 13, August 31, 2001, pp. 3A)
Pub: American City Business Journals Inc.
Ed: Jarred Schenke. **Description:** Bob Moore is the president of Publix Super Markets Inc., an Atlanta company that has opened 97 stores after entering the market a decade ago. Moore, who started at Publix as a stock boy, has moved up the ranks, and has seen Publix grab 27.4 percent of the metro grocery market share. Publix has future plans of launching an online site and acquiring a grocery chain to promote further growth.

45574 ■ "Pygmalion in management" in *Harvard Business Review* (Vol. 81, No. 1, January 2003, pp. 97)
Pub: Harvard Business School Press
Ed: J. Sterling Livingston. **Description:** Ways some managers are able to inspire their subordinates to superior performance are listed. The high expectations these managers hold for themselves and their employees bring out the best in all.

45575 ■ "Quality Time: Not Getting What You Want Out of Your Sales Meeting? Here are 5 Tips to Point You in the Right Direction" in *Entrepreneur*
Pub: Entrepreneur Media Inc.

Ed: Kimberly L. McCall. **Description:** Besides confidence building, information dissemination, and company strategies, sales meetings can also be used to inspire a sales team to produce. Steps to changing dull sales meetings into creative sales meetings are listed.

45576 ■ "A Quick Test of Your Managerial Skills" in *Sales & Marketing Management* (Vol. 158, October 2006, No. 10, pp. 19)
Pub: VNU Business Media
Description: Al Siebert, director of the Resiliency Center located in Portland, Oregon discusses the need for resiliency in salespeople.

45577 ■ "QuikTrip Policy Points to Dismissal" in *Kansas City Star* (February 24, 2005)
Pub: Knight-Ridder/Tribune Business News
Ed: Diane Stafford. **Description:** Biometric systems are being used as an employee tracking system at many companies now. This system replaced traditional time clocks and records employee fingerprints rather than punching a card or filling out a time sheet.

45578 ■ "Raines Stays Cool Under Fire" in *Black Enterprise* (Vol. 35, December 2004, No. 5, pp. 34)
Pub: Earl G. Graves Publishing Co. Inc.
Ed: Hamil Harris. **Description:** Overview of the case against Franklin Raines, CEO of Fannie Mae, the nation's largest source of financing for home mortgages. Franklin has been charged with engaging in accounting violations.

45579 ■ "Rave Reviews" in *My Business* (April/May 2003, pp. 42)
Pub: My Business Magazine
Ed: Carolyn Denny. **Description:** Advice is given for setting up an employee review process.

45580 ■ "Recession session" in *Entrepreneur* (Vol. 30, No. 3, March 2002, pp.)
Pub: Entrepreneur Media Inc.
Ed: Mark Henricks. **Description:** An interview with various experts and entrepreneurs to learn how and when they recommend aggressive or defensive positions in the areas of money management, people management, marketing, and technology.

45581 ■ "Recharge Life and Business With a Vacation" in *Crain's Detroit Business* (Vol. 22, December 18, 2006, No. 51, pp. 14)
Pub: Crain Communications Inc. - Detroit
Ed: Sheena Harrison. **Description:** Getting away from the office for a vacation offers a chance to balance home and business as well as the opportunity to explore new ideas from afar while refreshed. It's also an excellent chance to let employees develop new management skills and motivate them with the new challenges and responsibilities.

45582 ■ "Recreation" in *Inc.* (Volume 27, July 2005, No. 7, pp. 57-58)
Pub: Inc. Magazine
Ed: Patrick J. Sauer. **Description:** A well-planned company barbeque can be used as a business opportunity for recruitment, marketing, worker and customer loyalty, employee motivation, and finding new customers. Barbeque sauce recipe included.

45583 ■ "Recruit From Another Industry" in *Sales & Marketing Management* (Vol. 157, February 2005, No. 2, pp. 16)
Pub: VNU Business Media
Description: Recruiting a top salesperson from another industry does not guarantee the same results when selling in a new sector.

45584 ■ "Recruiting Tool for Corporate Companies" in *Black Enterprise* (Vol. 35, January 2005, No. 6, pp. 53)
Pub: Earl G. Graves Publishing Co. Inc.
Ed: Sonia Alleyne. **Description:** Richard Bamsey reports his organization, LEAD (Leadership and Education Development), offers companies access to its database of the school's alumni. Students are from diverse and underserved communities and are interested in pursuing a career in business.

45585 ■ *Reengineering the Corporation: A Manifesto for Business Revolution*
Pub: Harper Business
Ed: Michael Hammer and James Champy. Price: $14.00. Description: Describes how to design a new process of doing business.

45586 ■ "Reference Library" in *Small Business Opportunities* (Vol. 17, May 2005, No. 3, pp. 54, 56)
Pub: Harris Publications Inc.
Ed: Lin Grensing-Pophal. Description: Problems to avoid when offering or receiving employee references are outlined.

45587 ■ "Reining In Office Rumors" in *Inc.* (November 1, 2004)
Pub: Inc. Magazine
Description: Finding sales talent and controlling office gossip are key topics discussed.

45588 ■ "Relative power and influence strategy" in *Journal of Organizational Behavior* (Vol. 23, No. 2, March 2002, pp. 167)
Pub: John Wiley & Sons Inc.
Ed: Anit Somech, Anat Drach-Zahavy. Description: Management training should provide supervisory personnel with techniques to utilize to influence their subordinates to achieve the desired results. As a result of the training, supervisory personnel should then be able to decide which techniques would work best with each subordinate.

45589 ■ "Relax Your Grip" in *Black Enterprise* (Vol. 36, February 2006, No. 7, pp. 71)
Pub: Earl G. Graves Publishing Co. Inc.
Ed: Lee Anna Jackson. Description: Profile of Cassandra Hayes, director of U.S. External Communications for Avon. Hayes offers insight to managers on ways to delegate responsibility in the organization, which in turn, frees her from worry when she is not at the workplace.

45590 ■ "The Remote Control CEO" in *Inc.* (October 2005, pp. 96-101, 144, 146)
Pub: Inc. Magazine
Ed: Donna Fenn. Description: CEO, Stephen McConnell believes a major reason for his organic meat company's success is because he works from home four days a week. The success of his firm, Applegate Farms, reinforces this strategy.

45591 ■ "Remote Control" in *Entrepreneur* (Vol. 33, February 2005, No. 2, pp. 56)
Pub: Entrepreneur Media Inc.
Ed: Mark Henricks. Description: In 2003, 54 percent of companies internationally reported telecommuting programs for their staffs, that number rose to 80 percent in 2005. Skills for managing a telecommuting workforce are defined.

45592 ■ "Remote Control" in *Home Office Computing* (Vol. 18, No. 10, October 2000, pp. 46)
Pub: Scholastic Inc.
Ed: Jeffrey D. Zbar. Description: Organization strategies for telemanagers who work remotely, while the staff remains on-site at the corporate campus are outlined. Views of three telemanagers on such strategies, including keeping the office working seamlessly, tackling staff problems and maintaining morale are presented.

45593 ■ "Reporters' Notebook; Weighing Fed's Tough-guy Tactics" in *Crain's Detroit Business* (Vol. 22, December 11, 2006, No. 50, pp. 11)
Pub: Crain Communications Inc. - Detroit
Ed: Robert Ankeny. Description: U.S. Justice Department Thompson Memorandum demands that corporations under investigation waive the attorney-client privilege and also pressures those companies to stop paying attorney fees for employees facing charges.

45594 ■ "Required reading" in *Harvard Business Review* (Vol. 79, No. 11, December 2001, pp. 15)
Pub: Harvard Business School Press
Ed: Barbara Kellerman. Description: While there is no top ten list of books on leadership whose supremacy and currency are self-evident, leadership scholar Barbara Kellerman presents a list of works which she considers universal. The list includes Totalitarianism by Hannad Arendt; The Prince, by Machiavelli; Moses and Monotheism, by Freud; and Letter from Birmingham Jail, by Martin Luther King Jr.

45595 ■ "Resolving Owner Conflicts" in *Rough Notes* (Vol. 145, No. 9, September 2002, pp. 26)
Pub: Rough Notes
Ed: Paul J. DiStefano. Description: Lack of communications between owners of the insurance agency often results in disagreements. Unresolved conflict among owners can impede the future of an agency, whether the issue relates to money or operating philosophy.

45596 ■ "Resource line" in *Black Enterprise* (Vol. 33, No. 7, February 2003, pp. 6)
Pub: Earl Graves Publishing Co.
Ed: Latif Lewis. Description: Whatever your professional or entrepreneurial needs, blackenterprise.com's Interactive Media Editor Lewis' column provides useful resources for business owners, corporate executives, and investors.

45597 ■ "Resources for employee classes" in *Incentive* (Vol. 174, No. 9, September 2000, pp. 103)
Pub: Bill Communications
Ed: Richard G. Einsman. Description: How to keep current with the constantly changing business management and technology, and tips for finding the right sources for training is offered.

45598 ■ "Retail Experts Laud Costco's Shopping Strategy" in *Business Journal-Portland* (Vol. 20, No. 22, August 1, 2003, pp. 11)
Pub: American City Business Journals, Inc.
Ed: Carol Tice. Description: Marketing strategy used by Costco Companies is examined, including management styles, U.S. economic conditions, and business planning.

45599 ■ "Retired exec finds leisure time less than idle" in *Atlanta Business Chronicle* (Vol. 25, December 6, 2002, No. 26, pp. 26A)
Pub: American City Business Publications, Inc.
Ed: Meredith Jordan. Description: Roger Scovil, retired president of Lockwood Greene International, is presently chairman of the World Trade Center Atlanta's executive committee. Scovil has written a new book, "Get Ahead, Scovil's 7 Rules for Success in Management".

45600 ■ "Retiring Minds" in *Hispanic Business* (March 2005, pp. 50)
Pub: Hispanic Business
Ed: Joel Russell. Description: The large number of federal managers retiring is creating new opportunities for Hispanics. Federal agencies and mid-career outreach agencies are listed.

45601 ■ "Reverence for radicals" in *Fast Company* (June 2001, pp. 48)
Pub: Fast Company
Ed: Rekha Balu. Description: Reverend Cecil Williams, of San Francisco's Glide Memorial United Methodist Church, is on a mission: he's teaching tradition-bound congregations how to stay vital by embracing change. The article shows how Marvin Arnpriester uses Reverend Williams as inspiration for staking out new markets and younger customers for his business.

45602 ■ "The right carrot" in *Entrepreneur* (Vol. 30, No. 2, February 20)
Pub: Entrepreneur Media Inc.
Ed: Kimberly L. McCall. Description: Ways to motivate and retain sales professionals are explored, including a discussion on the importance of a good compensation plan.

45603 ■ "Right at Home with Telecommuting" in *Business Week* (No. 3761, December 10, 2001, pp. SB4)
Pub: McGraw-Hill Inc.
Description: According to a survey of small business executives, conducted by Sales & Marketing Management, 86 percent believe that a sales staff can work as productively from home as in the office.

45604 ■ "Righting the Digital Ship" in *Black Enterprise* (Vol. 36, February 2006, No. 7, pp. 63)
Pub: Earl G. Graves Publishing Co. Inc.
Ed: Bridget McCrea. Description: Champ Mitchell, CEO and chairman of Network Solutions in Virginia, created a customer service program that replaced nearly 70 percent of its current employees, and setup a six-week intensive training program to ensure newly hired employees are highly skilled.

45605 ■ "The ROI On Your MBA" in *Business 2.0* (Vol. 6, September 2005, No. 8, pp. 99)
Pub: Time, Inc.
Ed: Rob Howe. Description: MBA candidates will find an extensive review of the top MBA schools in order to compare their return on investment.

45606 ■ "The Role of Integrity as a Mediator in Strategic Leadership" in *Journal of Business Ethics* (Vol. 46, No. 1, Aug. 2003, pp. 31)
Pub: Kluwer Academic Publishers Group
Ed: Skip Worden. Description: An examination of the role of integrity as a mediator within strategic leadership and its impact on credibility in reputational capital is discussed.

45607 ■ *The Role of the Non-Executive Director in the Small to Medium-Sized Business*
Pub: Palgrave Macmillan
Ed: John Smithson. Released: March 2004. Price: $75.00. Description: The role of the non-executive director in a small to medium-sized business is examined.

45608 ■ "Room at the table" in *Boston Business Journal* (Vol. 22, No. 14, May 10, 2002, pp. 21)
Pub: MCP, Inc.
Ed: Jill Lerner. Description: Profile of Loren Carlson, founder of CEO Roundtable LLC, a company where CEOs, presidents and company owners can converse with noncompetitive peers.

45609 ■ "Rough-Cut Dimon" in *Forbes* (May 13, 2002, p. 64)
Pub: Forbes Magazine
Ed: Mark Tatge. Description: Profile of James Dimon. Dimon rescued Bank One back from the brink after leaving Citigroup four years ago.

45610 ■ "Round Table" in *Atlanta Business Chronicle* (Vol. 25, November 15, 2002, No. 23 pp. 7B)
Pub: American City Business Publications, Inc.
Description: Five Atlanta, Georgia-area executives respond to handling three potential dilemmas, which involve ethical issues. Responses are given by Arn Rubinoff of Powell, Goldstein, Frazer & Murphy LLC; John C. Knapp of The Southern Institute for Business and Professional Ethics; Dave Brookmire of Corporate Performance Strategies Inc.; Emmett Hawkins III of Leapfrog Services Inc.; and Larry Hart of The Executive Committee.

45611 ■ "Running Into Profits" in *My Business* (June/July 2004, pp. 16)
Pub: My Business Magazine
Description: Jogging sessions fit into tight schedules may actually improve a company's profits.

45612 ■ *Running Things: The Art of Making Things Happen*
Pub: The McGraw-Hill Companies
Ed: Philip B. Crosby. Price: $27.95. Description: Provides organizational and motivational advice for management.

45613 ■ "Running a Tight Ship" in *My Business* (October/November 2002, pp. 16)
Pub: My Business Magazine
Ed: Mardy Fones. **Description:** Former Naval officer, Capt. D. Michael Abrashoff, offers insight into handling personnel issues. Abrashoff, CEO of Grassroots Leadership, Inc. in Boston, Massachusetts uses his Navy experiences to run his consulting firm.

45614 ■ "The Sales Auction: Is Bidding for Leads the Sales Trend of the Future" in *Sales and Marketing.com* (Vol. 156, No. 3, March 2004)
Pub: VNU eMedia, Inc.
Ed: Michael Schrage. **Description:** Would a more rigorous and impartial mechanism for allocating sales leads, prospects, and territories lead to a better sales force by forming an auction lot? Salespeople would be allowed to bid on prospects they feel they could turn into clients. Bids could be percentages of anticipated commissions, and a portion could come from existing clients' proceeds, or even the company's Bid4Prospects program.

45615 ■ "S&MM Pulse" in *Sales & Marketing Management* (Vol. 157, February 2005, No. 2, pp. 11)
Pub: VNU Business Media
Description: Written definitions of what constitutes a qualified sales lead are important to a sales staff.

45616 ■ *The Save Your Business Book: A Business Survival Handbook for the 1990s and Beyond*
Pub: The Free Press
Ed: John D. Goldhammer. **Released:** 1993. **Price:** $22.95.

45617 ■ "Saving money, saving lives" in *Harvard Business Review* (Vol. 78, No. 6, November-December 2000, pp. 57)
Pub: Harvard Business School Publishing Corp.
Description: Jon Meliones, the chief medical director at Duke Children's Hospital (DCH) improved the quality of care at the hospital by focusing less like a non-profit that loses money, and more like a profitable corporation.

45618 ■ "Saving your rookie managers from themselves" in *Harvard Business Review* (Vol. 80, No. 4, April 2002, pp. 97)
Pub: Harvard Business School Press
Ed: Carol A. Walker. **Description:** Employees who are promoted to managerial positions based on technical competence often have difficulty translating that competence into good managerial performance. Strategies are presented to overcome the problem areas that rookie managers face: delegating, getting support from senior staffers, projecting confidence, thinking strategically and giving feedback.

45619 ■ "Scandal 101: Lessons From Ken Lay" in *Fortuneit* (Vol. 146, No. 4, September 2, 2002, pp. 52)
Pub: Time Inc.
Ed: Julie Schlosser. **Description:** A listing of U.S. universities offering Ethics and Management Courses, starting fall 2002.

45620 ■ "School Career Centers Think Outside the Box" in *Long Island Business News* (February 27, 2004)
Pub: Dolan Media Newswires
Ed: Claude Solnik. **Description:** Stony Brook University in New York has created a business etiquette program where potential employers meet with job-seeking students for a three-course meal and networking.

45621 ■ "School Is In for Entrepreneurs: Continuing Education Courses Abound." in *Black Enterprise* (Vol. 35, October 2004, No. 3)
Pub: Earl G. Graves Publishing Co. Inc.
Ed: Bridget McCrea. **Description:** A growing number of small business owners are taking courses to help them better manage company growth, employees, financial operations, and other key issues.

45622 ■ "The science behind six degrees." in *Harvard Business Review* (Vol. 81, No. 2, Feb. 2003, pp. 16)
Pub: Harvard Business School Press
Ed: Gardiner Morse. **Description:** Duncan Watts answers questions about his research into network science and how it can help explain why products sell, and how companies effectively manage themselves. Critical elements of this field of study are human behavior, group dynamics, and perception.

45623 ■ "Screen Gems" in *Fast Company* (March 2005, No. 92, pp. 39)
Pub: Gruner & Jahr USA Publishing
Ed: Lucas Conley, Danielle Sacks. **Description:** Film industry leaders share insight into managing teams, coping with rejection and implementing the visions of others.

45624 ■ "Search" in *Inc.* (January 1, 2002)
Pub: Inc. Magazine
Description: Brief information about management advice services and general information about management are provided.

45625 ■ "Searching the sky" in *Atlanta Business Chronicle* (Vol. 25, Nov. 15, 2002, No. 23 pp. 38A)
Pub: American City Business Publications, Inc.
Ed: Jim Lovel. **Description:** Jamie Turner is One-Source Marketing's chief marketing officer and executive creative director, as well as an amateur astronomer. Turner discusses his fascination with astronomy and the peacefulness he receives from this hobby.

45626 ■ *Secrets of Entrepreneurial Leadership: Building Top Performance Through Trust & Teamwork*
Pub: Dearborn Financial Publishing, Inc.
Ed: Ted Nicholas. **Released:** 1992. **Price:** $19.95.

45627 ■ "Section 404 Compliance in the Annual Report" in *Journal of Accountancy*
Pub: American Institute of Certified Public Accountants
Ed: Michael Ramos. **Description:** Most publicly traded companies in the U.S. will be required to comply with SEC rules by reporting the effectiveness of internal controls in the annual report. The content required in this report is covered.

45628 ■ "Security Blanket: Terrorists changed your employees" in *Entrepreneur* (Vol. 30, No. 3, March 2002, pp. 19)
Pub: Entrepreneur Media Inc.
Ed: Chris Penttila. **Description:** Since the terrorist attacks, employees want a sense of security combined with the opportunity to do good; work is no longer about making money. Employees also wish to find a better balance between work and home life. Advices is offered to management to help towards this trend.

45629 ■ "Seeds of success" in *Houston Business Journal* (Vol. 33, No. 46, March 28, 2003, pp. 17A)
Pub: Houston Business Journal
Ed: Allison Wollam. **Description:** The leadership style of Suzanne Longley as president of Suzanne Longley Landscapes Inc. is profiled. The company grows its own tress and is planning to add a sprinkler system and a greenhouse in order to grow flowers.

45630 ■ "Seeing Is Believing: Creating a Vision To Guide Your Team To Success" in *Black Enterprise* (Vol. 35, September 2004, No. 2, pp. 181)
Pub: Earl G. Graves Publishing Co. Inc.
Ed: Kimberly J. Hamilton-Wright. **Description:** Small business success can be attributed to setting a vision of excellence for the entire team to follow.

45631 ■ "Seize the Day After Tomorrow" in *Harvard Business Review* (Vol. 78, No. 4, July 2000, pp. 8)
Pub: Harvard Business School Publishing Corp.
Description: A recent management conference was held in Chatham. The conference was sponsored by Harvard Business School Publishing.

45632 ■ "Sending the Right Messages: How to Make Staff Meetings More Effective" in *Black Enterprise* (Vol. 35, November 2004, No. 4, pp. 74)
Pub: Earl G. Graves Publishing Co. Inc.
Ed: Carla Thompson. **Description:** Ways to make staff meetings more effectivee are discussed using the strategy of Maria Tajil Battle, senior vice president of public affairs and marketing. Battle sees meetings as an opportunity to discern information to report to bosses about her division's activities.

45633 ■ "Sense and reliability: A conversation with celebrated psychologist Karl E. Weick" in *Harvard Business Review* (Vol. 81, No. 4, Apr. 2003)
Pub: Harvard Business School Press
Ed: Diane Coutu. **Description:** A noted psychologist examines the characteristics of high-reliability organizations, such as nuclear plants, firefighting units, and emergency rooms. Corporations can learn much from these organizations that cannot afford surprises in the workplace.

45634 ■ "September 11, 2001. A CEO's story" in *Harvard Business Review* (Vol. 80, No. 10, October 2002, pp. 58)
Pub: Harvard Business School Press
Ed: Jeffrey W. Greenberg. **Description:** Marsh & McLennan Companies' offices in the World Trade Center were destroyed on September 11, 2001. Jeffrey W. Greenberg, chairman of Marsh & McLennan Companies Inc., recounts his immediate response to the airplane attack, efforts to save lives, locate people, recapture company data, help with the healing, inspire confidence, and generally insure that the company and its employees were able to continue.

45635 ■ "Services finalists" in *Crain's Detroit Business* (Vol. 16, No. 26, June 26, 2000, pp. E-15)
Pub: Crain Communications, Inc.
Description: Profiles of service industry executives, including Edward Christian, Chairman, president and CEO of Saga Communications Inc., Grosse Pointe Farms, Michigan; Kerry Brian Budry, CEO and president, QEK Global Solutions, Bloomfield Hills, Michigan; Pam Hassevoort, CEO of Foreway Transportation Inc., Coopersville, Michigan; and William Rauwerdink, former executive vice president, CFO Lason Inc., Troy, Michigan.

45636 ■ "Shifting Into Growth Mode" in *Sales and Marketing.com* (Vol. 156, No. 3, March 2004, pp. 12)
Pub: VNU eMedia, Inc.
Ed: Michele Marchetti. **Description:** Managers will be required to makes changes to maximize productivity of sales teams as firms shift from survival mode to growth mode. Several management tactics are outlined.

45637 ■ "Shipbuilders Labor Union Threatens Management Over Layoff Plans in Bath, Maine" in *Portland Press Herald* (June 22, 2005)
Pub: Blethen Maine Newspapers, Inc.
Ed: Matt Wickenheiser. **Description:** Bath Iron Works' maintenance workers union is concerned about the firm's move to hire a private firm to clean offices, care for the grounds, run the heating and cooling systems, and perform other tasks; the move would eliminate 24 union jobs.

45638 ■ "A site full of workers that isn't so sunny? Try this: give money" in *Wall Street Journal* (May 22, 2002, pp. B1)
Pub: Wall Street Journal
Ed: Suein L. Hwang. **Description:** Ideas for posters that encourage workers to relax to reduce stress in the workplace are presented.

45639 ■ "Six IT decisions your IT people shouldn't make" in *Harvard Business Review* (Vol. 80, No. 11, November 2002, pp. 85)
Pub: Harvard Business School Press
Ed: Jeanne W. Peter, Ross Weill. **Description:** The need for senior managers to take leadership in making

six key information technology decisions is investigated. These managers should decide how much to spend on IT, which business processes should receive IT funds, and which IT capabilities need to be company wide. Decisions must also be made regarding the quality of IT services, which privacy and security risks are acceptable and whom to blame if an IT initiative fails.

45640 ■ **"60 second strategist"** in *Atlanta Business Chronicle* **(Vol. 25, January 3, 2003, No. 30, pp. 6B)**
Pub: American City Business Publications, Inc.
Ed: Jon Gordon. **Description:** Four tips for a post-holiday energy kick are presented to help get back into the work mode.

45641 ■ *Small Business Barriers & Battlefields: Adding Reality to the American Dream*
Pub: Matahari Publishing
Ed: Robert E. Fleury. **Price:** $27.95; $15.95 (paper).

45642 ■ *Small Business Clustering Technology: Applications in Marketing, Management, Finance, and IT*
Pub: Idea Group Publishing
Ed: Robert C. MacGregor; Ann Hodgkinson. **Released:** June 2006. **Description:** An overview of the development and role of small business clusters in disciplines that include economics, marketing, management and information systems.

45643 ■ *Small Business Management*
Pub: John Wiley and Sons Inc.
Ed: Margaret Burlingame; Don Gulbrandsen; Richard M. Hodgetts; Donald F. Kuratko. **Released:** March 2007. **Price:** $44.95. **Description:** Tips for starting and running a successful small business are given, including advice on writing a business plan, financing, and the law.

45644 ■ *Small Business Management: A Planning Approach*
Pub: Irwin Professional Publishing
Ed: Joel Corman. **Released:** 1995. **Price:** $57.95.

45645 ■ *Small Business Management: An Entrepreneur's Guide to Success*
Pub: Richard D. Irwin, Inc.
Ed: William L. Megginson. **Released:** 1993. **Price:** $47.95.

45646 ■ *Small Business Management Fundamentals*
Pub: The McGraw-Hill Companies
Ed: Dan Steinhoff. **Released:** Sixth edition, 1993.

45647 ■ *Small-Business Management Guide: Advice from the Brass-Tacks Entrepreneur*
Pub: Henry Holt & Company
Ed: Jim Schell. **Released:** October 1995. **Description:** Entrepreneurs offer advice for managing a small business.

45648 ■ *The Small Business Owner's Manual: Everything You Need to Know to Start Up and Run Your Business*
Pub: Career Press, Incorporated
Ed: Joe Kennedy. **Released:** June 2005. **Price:** $19.99 (US), $26.95 (Canadian). **Description:** Comprehensive guide for starting a small business, focusing on twelve ways to obtain financing, business plans, selling and advertising products and services, hiring and firing employees, setting up a Web site, business law, accounting issues, insurance, equipment, computers, banks, financing, customer credit and collection, leasing, and more.

45649 ■ *Small Business: Planning and Management*
Pub: Dryden Press
Ed: Charles Kuehl. **Released:** Second edition, 1990. **Price:** $52.00.

45650 ■ *Small Business Start-Up Workbook: A Step-by-Step Guide to Starting the Business You've Dreamed Of*
Pub: How To Books
Ed: Cheryl D. Rickman. **Released:** February 2006. **Price:** $24.75. **Description:** Book provides practical exercises for starting a small business, including marketing and management strategies.

45651 ■ *A Small Enterprise*
Pub: Lulu.com
Ed: Tsvi Reiss. **Released:** October 2005. **Price:** $16.36. **Description:** Eleven issues involved in the process of completion for Small Enterprise Management.

45652 ■ **"Small Firm Bankruptcy"** in *Journal of Small Business Management* **(Vol. 44, October 2006, No. 4, pp. 493)**
Pub: Blackwell Publishing, Inc.
Ed: Richard Carter; Howard Van Auken. **Description:** Results of a survey attempt to identify the root causes of bankruptcy in firms. Statistical data included.

45653 ■ **"Smarter Than You"** in *Inc.* **(September 2005, pp. 69, 72)**
Pub: Inc. Magazine
Ed: Michael S. Hopkins. **Description:** James Surowiecki's book, The Wisdom of Crowds, explains why so many entrepreneurial companies don't grow, or are unable to successfully produce a second product; the book also offers CEOs solutions to these challenges.

45654 ■ **"Smoke screening"** in *Entrepreneur* **(Vol. 30, No. 9, September 2002, pp. 30)**
Pub: Entrepreneur Media Inc.
Ed: Chad Scheer. **Description:** Companies nationwide are considering imposing employee restrictions, not only on smoking, but also on cholesterol levels of employees in order to cut insurance costs and improve employee productivity. The American Civil Liberties Union wants the trend to stop with smoking.

45655 ■ **"Soup's On"** in *San Francisco Business Times* **(Vol. 18, No. 2, August 22, 2003, pp. 38)**
Pub: American City Business Journals
Ed: Jessica Materna. **Description:** The growing success of the San Francisco Soup Company is examined, including sales levels, management styles, and long term plans.

45656 ■ **"Speak Easy"** in *Fast Company* **(March 2005, No. 92, pp. 30)**
Pub: Gruner & Jahr USA Publishing
Ed: Ryan Underwood. **Description:** Five key steps to overcoming the fear of speaking in public are outlined.

45657 ■ **"Speak Up: Hate to Negotiate? That's Still No Excuse to Avoid Learning This Skill"** in *Entrepreneur* **(Vol. 32, September 2004)**
Pub: Entrepreneur Media Inc.
Ed: Marc Diener. **Description:** The art of negotiating is investigated. Tips are offered to entrepreneurs to improve their skills at the bargaining table.

45658 ■ **"Speed Kills: Supply Chain Lessons From the War in Iraq"** in *Harvard Business Review* **(Vol. 81, No. 11, November 2003, pp. 16)**
Pub: Harvard Business School Press
Ed: Diane K. Morales; Steve Geary. **Description:** The supply chain management system utilized by the U.S. during the Iraq War is discussed in context to business supply chain management.

45659 ■ **"Spirit of business"** in *Boston Business Journal* **(Vol. 22, No. 11, April 19, 2002, pp. 27)**
Pub: MCP, Inc.
Description: Richard Whiteley, who founded the Whiteley Group Inc., writes and speaks about management and the corporate world. His life's purpose is to bring spirit back to business.

45660 ■ **"Spirited leadership: Carl Horton named President & CEO of Absolut"** in *Black Enterprise* **(Vol. 32, No. 9, April 2002, pp. 28)**
Pub: Earl Graves Publishing Co.
Ed: Derek T. Dingle. **Description:** Profile of Carol Horton, new president and CEO of The Absolut Spirits Company. Horton has become the industry's top-ranking African American as well as one of the most powerful black executives in corporate America. Horton views his new role as a transition from corporate execute to an entrepreneur of a start-up.

45661 ■ **"Sports Scenario: There's No Room for Ball Hogs on Your Team"** in *Small Business Opportunities* **(Vol. 16, No. 1, January 2004, pp. 54)**
Pub: Harris Publications, Inc.
Ed: Pam Mitchell. **Description:** Teamwork is imperative in order for a small business to succeed. The four major issues that cause sub-optimal teamwork are investigated. Customer value programs can become strategic planning sessions.

45662 ■ **"Spotting management fads."** in *Harvard Business Review* **(Vol. 80, No. 10, Oct. 2002, pp. 26)**
Pub: Harvard Business School Press
Ed: Danny Miller; Jon Hartwick. **Description:** Management fads for the past 40 years are used to make observations, concluding that fads are ultimately doomed because they tend to be overly simplistic and rarely change managerial techniques.

45663 ■ **"Spy Games"** in *Entrepreneur* **(Vol. 33, February 2005, No. 2, pp. 71)**
Pub: Entrepreneur Media Inc.
Ed: Chris Penttila. **Description:** Amendment to the Fair Credit Reporting Act (FCRA), employers are now able to conduct third-party investigations on employees without getting their written permission, or even informing them of the investigation.

45664 ■ **"Staring all over again"** in *BlackEnterprise* **(Vol. 31, No. 8, March 2001, pp. 50)**
Pub: Earl Graves Publishing Co.
Ed: Bridget McCrea. **Description:** Profile of Gina and Raphael Bruce, co-founders of the former Millennium 2000 Computer Consulting Group, located in Georgia. The partners tell how they had to reinvent their business after helping companies prepare for Y2K.

45665 ■ **"State Farm Signs On As Host"** in *Black Enterprise* **(Vol. 36, December 2005, No. 5, pp. 166)**
Pub: Earl G. Graves Publishing Co. Inc.
Ed: Alysha N. Cryer. **Description:** State Farm Insurance Company has partnered with Black Enterprise to launch the inaugural Women of Pow4er Summit. The professional leadership conference is designed exclusively for women of color executives.

45666 ■ **"Staying Ahead of the Curve"** in *Fortune International* **(Vol. 146, No. 4, March 3, 2003, pp. 41)**
Pub: Time Inc.
Ed: Scott Spreier; Dawn Sherman. **Description:** According to a survey conducted by the magazine, the companies most admired are those focused on addressing critical strategic issues and maintaining the capability and commitment of their workforces. Statistical data included.

45667 ■ **"Staying power"** in *Black Enterprise* **(Vol. 32, No. 9, April 2002, pp. 108)**
Pub: Earl Graves Publishing Co.
Ed: Sonia Alleyne. **Description:** Five critical factors in acquiring and maintaining a vice presidential position in a company are outlined.

45668 ■ **"Stepping down"** in *Entrepreneur* **(Vol. 30, No. 2, February 2002, pp. 64)**
Pub: Entrepreneur Media Inc.
Ed: Chris Sandlund. **Description:** Some executives are taking lower positions during the economic slump.

45669 ■ "Stiff upper lips: are your employees happy or just biding their time?" in *Black Enterprise* (Vol. 32, No. 9, April 2002, pp. 59)
Pub: Earl Graves Publishing Co.
Ed: Sonia Alleyne. **Description:** Low company morale in a downsized working environment is discussed. Suggestions to help lower stress levels in the workplace are offered by two experts.

45670 ■ "Stone to Run Hickory Farmer's Market" in *Charlotte Observer* (January 31, 2007)
Pub: Knight-Ridder/Tribune Business News
Ed: Jen Aronoff. **Description:** Betty Stone has been hired to manage the Downtown Hickory Farmers Market. The market will run from May 5 through October 6, 2007.

45671 ■ "Stop-gap Measures" in *Entrepreneur* (Vol. 28, No. 9, September 2000, pp. 89)
Pub: Entrepreneur Media Inc.
Ed: Geoff Williams. **Description:** Meet two sets of entrepreneurs, one who could successfully span the generation gap running their business, and one that could not.

45672 ■ "Stop Whining—And Start Winning" in *Success* (Vol. 47, No. 3, July 2000, pp. 40)
Pub: Success Publishing, Inc.
Description: Leadership skills are the oldest, most effective "management" tool at our disposal. Reasons why businesses fail are explored.

45673 ■ "Strategic experimentation: understanding change and performance in new ventures" in *Journal of Business Venturing* (Vol. 15, No. 5-6)
Pub: Elsevier Science, Inc.
Ed: Charlene L. Nicholls-Nixon, Arnold C. Cooper, Carolyn Y. Woo. **Description:** A new study explores the relationship between management experimentation, strategic change and final performance, focusing on new ventures.

45674 ■ "Strategies, Let's Be Friends" in *Inc.* (Volume 27, March 2005, No. 3, pp. 33-34)
Pub: Inc. Magazine
Ed: Allison Stein Wellner. **Description:** New research shows that CEOs who become friendly with competitors achieve more success than others.

45675 ■ "Street Smarts. Are You Listening to Me?" in *Inc.* (November 2006, pp. 61-62)
Pub: Gruner & Jahr USA Publishing
Ed: Norm Brodsky. **Description:** As an entrepreneur, you ultimately need to make the final decisions. Sometimes too much advice from the wrong persons on the right things or the right person on the wrong things clouds the issue and can lead to a bad final decision you may have to live with.

45676 ■ "Street Smarts: Just Say Yes" in *Inc.* (November 1, 2004)
Pub: Inc. Magazine
Ed: Norm Brodsky. **Description:** One small business owner has found that a drug testing policy started at his company six years ago because of rumors about marijuana being used on the premises. The new policy not only decreased accidents and petty theft, but also helped employees.

45677 ■ "Street Smarts. Keep Your Customers" in *Inc.* (September 2006, pp. 57-58)
Pub: Gruner & Jahr USA Publishing
Ed: Norm Brodsky. **Description:** Keeping customers is as important as recruiting new ones and much more economical. Listen to your customers input and react to their requests, complaints, and maybe even their demands, if reasonable; if that's what it takes to keep them.

45678 ■ "Street Smarts: Pennies From Heaven" in *Inc.* (December 1, 2004)
Pub: Inc. Magazine
Ed: Norm Brodsky. **Description:** Employee participation in cost control can actually motivate workers.

45679 ■ "Street Smarts: Presumed Guilty" in *Inc.* (October 1, 2004)
Pub: Inc. Magazine
Ed: Norm Brodsky. **Description:** Experts recommend that small businesses let lawyers make legal decision, but to keep business decisions with company management.

45680 ■ "Street Smarts: The Capacity Trap II" in *Inc.* (December 1, 2003)
Pub: Gruner & Jahr USA Publishing
Ed: Norm Brodsky. **Description:** Sometimes its better to let unused capacity remain unused rather than win a contract that will be too costly to meet.

45681 ■ *Streetwise Motivating and Rewarding Employees: New and Better Ways to Inspire Your People*
Pub: Adams Media Corporation
Ed: Alexander Hiam. **Released:** May 1999. **Price:** $19.95. **Description:** Ways for employers and business managers to motivate difficult employees.

45682 ■ "Strictly Business" in *Entrepreneur* (Vol. 28, No. 1, January 2000, pp. 118)
Pub: Entrepreneur Media Inc.
Ed: Patricia Schiff Estess. **Description:** The topic of managing personnel issues in the family business is covered.

45683 ■ "Stuck in Mud?" in *My Business* (October/November 2003, pp. 12)
Pub: My Business Magazine
Ed: Doug McPherson. **Description:** Ways to structure offices tasks should be structured in order for employees to become more proficient are addressed. Four tips for a more structured, smoother-running office are given.

45684 ■ "Student Teachers" in *Inc.* (November 2006, pp. 44,46)
Pub: Gruner & Jahr USA Publishing
Ed: Max Chafkin. **Description:** Hiring college undergraduates give fresh eyes approach at low investment. Many universities have programs that work with smaller local businesses as part of their hands on education programs. Large savings can accumulate without the cost of expensive consultant fees.

45685 ■ "Study: Women Executives Want Corner Office, Too" in *Miami Herald* (June 24, 2004)
Pub: Knight-Ridder/Tribune Business News
Ed: Gillian Wee. **Description:** According to a recent survey, female officials aspire to be chief executives at the same rate as male counterparts.

45686 ■ "Substitute Presenter" in *Sales & Marketing Management* (Vol. 157, February 2005, No. 2, pp. 11)
Pub: VNU Business Media
Description: Ideas for better sales leads are discussed.

45687 ■ "Success Within Your Reach" in *Home Business* (Vol. 13, January/February 2006, No. 1, pp. 36, 100)
Pub: Home Business Magazine
Ed: Sandy Larson. **Description:** Author, Jack Canfield, shares his secrets to building a successful publishing empire. Canfield is CEO of Chicken Soup for the Soul Enterprises.

45688 ■ *Successful Training Practice: A Manager's Guide to Personnel Development*
Pub: Blackwell Publishers
Ed: Alan H. Anderson. **Released:** 1993. **Price:** $44. 95 (paper).

45689 ■ "Succession Management for the Entire Organization" in *Employment Relations Today* (Vol. 27, No. 2, Summer 2000, pp. 53)
Pub: John Wiley & Sons, Inc.
Ed: Scott T. Fleischmann. **Description:** Succession Management improves employee retention, protects critical positions within a company, provides a career path for employees, maintains competitive advantages in the marketplace, and maintains a high level of product and service quality. The process of succession management for all positions within an organization is described.

45690 ■ *Supervisor's Infobank: 1000 Quick Answers to Your Toughest Problems*
Pub: The McGraw-Hill Companies
Ed: Arthur R. Pell. **Released:** 1995. **Price:** $49.95. **Description:** Provides advice on and examples of the best ways to handle the problems supervisors face.

45691 ■ "Surprise, It's the CEO" in *Sales and Marketing.com* (Vol. 156, No. 3, March 2004, pp. 9)
Pub: VNU eMedia, Inc.
Description: Steps to take when the company CEO drops into the middle of a sales presentation is outlined, including the tactic of engaging the CEO.

45692 ■ "Survey" in *Crain's Detroit Business* (Vol. 21, October 24, 2005, No. 43, pp. 1)
Pub: Crain Communications Inc. - Detroit
Ed: Tom Hdnderson. **Description:** According to the 2005 Michigan Women's Leadership Index, the number of top women executives has fallen by 20 percent over the last two years. The auto industry ranked lowest for upper-management opportunity for its female executives.

45693 ■ "...Survey Shows Employees Using Work Computers for Romantic/Sexual Activity" in *Long Island Business News* (Feb. 27, 2004)
Pub: Dolan Media Newswires
Ed: Rosamaria Mancini. **Description:** Statistics involving computer use for personal activity in the workplace are presented, with nearly 25 percent of Americans saying they or their coworkers use office computers to participate in sexually explicit online activity.

45694 ■ *Survival Skills for Supervisors*
Pub: American Management Association
Price: $1,695 for non-members; $1,495 for AMA members. **Description:** Covers developing skills that allow you to adapt to the daily challenges within the organization, including fostering trust with your employees' in order to meet your objectives. **Locations:** New York, NY; Washington, DC; and Chicago, IL.

45695 ■ "Surviving the New Economy" in *Inc.* (October 1, 2003)
Pub: Gruner & Jahr USA Publishing
Ed: Nadine Heintz. **Description:** Profile of Data Return and its management. Data Return is a Web-hosting firm sold by Sunny Vanderbeck, who is considering buying his company back.

45696 ■ "Symbol Technologies Appoints Steinberg as CTO and VP of Its Mobility Solutions Group" in *Long Island Business News* (February 6, 2004)
Pub: Dolan Media Newswires
Ed: Ryan McCormick. **Description:** Profile of Lou Steinberg, newly appointed CTO and vice president of Symbol Technologies; Steinberg will be responsible for coordinating the firm's global sales, and development of end-to-end product requirements. He will also create marketing communications around the company's mobile solutions.

45697 ■ "Symbol Technologies Inc. Hires Former IBM Executive" in *Long Island Business News* (March 5, 2004)
Pub: Dolan Media Newswires
Description: Profiles of Verlin P. Youd, vice president of retail systems for Symbol Technologies Inc., and Anthony Bartolo, vice president and general manager of wireless infrastructure division.

45698 ■ *Take Back Your Time: How to Regain Control of Work, Information and Technology*
Pub: St. Martin's Press LLC
Ed: Jan Jasper. **Released:** November 1999. **Price:** $13.95. **Description:** Strategies to become more organized and productive.

45699 ■ "Take It to the Bank" in *Washington Business Journal* (Vol. 22, No. 15, August 15, 2003, pp. 3)
Pub: Washington Business Journal

Ed: Tim Mazzucca. **Description:** Profile of Washington's newest bank, Congressional Bank, examining management goals and plans, including long term planning, market development, and management styles.

45700 ■ **"Take It Or Leave It: The Only Guide to Negotiating You Will Ever Need" in** *Inc.* **(August 1, 2003)**
Pub: Gruner & Jahr USA Publishing
Ed: Rob Walker. **Description:** In order to become a good negotiator it is important to change your mindset and your behavior. A guide to becoming a better negotiator is presented.

45701 ■ **"Take it from me" in** *Entrepreneur* **(Vol. 31, No. 4, April 2003, pp. 26)**
Pub: Entrepreneur Media Inc.
Ed: Aliza Pilar Sherman. **Description:** An interview with two women business owners offering advice in management, business growth, and business downsizing.

45702 ■ **"Take the Work Home" in** *Black Enterprise* **(Vol. 36, December 2005, No. 5, pp. 72)**
Pub: Earl G. Graves Publishing Co. Inc.
Ed: Marcia A. Reed-Woodard. **Description:** According to Jane Anderson, director of Midwest Institute of Telecommuting, there is a trend towards making jobs more mobile, which allows workers to access work from home. Statistical data included.

45703 ■ **"Take Your Life for a Spin" in** *Fast Company* **(July 2001, pp. 52)**
Pub: Fast Company
Ed: Christine Canabou. **Description:** Profile of Tony Caserta, senior vice president at Leerink Swann & Company, a Boston-based financial services firm. Caserta says a second job has helped him focus and feel in control during a stressful period of his life.

45704 ■ **"Takes the cake" in** *Black Enterprise* **(Vol. 32, No. 10, May 2002, pp. 58)**
Pub: Earl Graves Publishing Co.
Ed: Ron Childs. **Description:** Profile of Amy Hilliard, senior vice president of integrated marketing at Burrell Communications Groups Inc. Hilliard thrives on creating and launching products.

45705 ■ **"Taking charge in a new leadership role" in** *Women in Business* **(Vol. 53, No. 5, September-October, 2001, pp. 32)**
Pub: The ABWA Co. Inc.
Ed: Liz Hubler. **Description:** The pitfalls of new managers are presented. These pitfalls include micromanaging and not possessing an action plan.

45706 ■ **"Taking stock" in** *Harvard Business Review* **(Vol. 81, No. 1, January 2003, pp. 19)**
Pub: Harvard Business School Press
Ed: Roger L. Martin. **Description:** The Dean of Rotman School of Management at the University of Toronto disputes the theory that managers should be compensated with company stock or options; he suggests bonuses based on real earnings growth.

45707 ■ **"Talent" in** *Business Week* **(January 9, 2006, No. 3966, pp. 26-28)**
Pub: McGraw-Hill Companies
Ed: Jena McGregor. **Description:** Companies are questioning the value of rigid ranking systems that might hinder teamwork and innovation.

45708 ■ **"Taming of the Crew: What Lion Tamers Teach Us About Team Management" in** *Entrepreneur* **(Vol. 33, January 2005, No. 1, pp. 26)**
Pub: Entrepreneur Media Inc.
Ed: Geoff Williams. **Description:** In his book, Lion Taming: Working Successfully With Leaders, Bosses and Other Tough Customers, Steve Katz gathers insights from professional lion tamers to help entrepreneurs learn to tame suppliers, customers and competitors.

45709 ■ **"Tap into Expert Input" in** *Black Enterprise* **(Vol. 30, No. 12, July 2000, pp. 47)**
Pub: Earl Graves Publishing Co.
Ed: Craig Owen White. **Description:** Learn how a board of advisors can benefit your firm with regard to employment policies, insurance coverage and strategic alliances.

45710 ■ **"Tapping local markets can pay off" in** *Wall Street Journal* **(May 14, 2002, pp. B4)**
Pub: Wall Street Journal
Ed: Jeff Bailey. **Description:** Harvey Saltzman of Triangle Printers Inc does business locally as well as nationally, but states that his local customers often boost his firms sales at a lower operating cost.

45711 ■ **"Tapping the Talent Pool of Hispanic Affluence" in** *Hispanic Business* **(Vol. 24, No. 1/2, January/February 2002, pp. 6)**
Pub: Hispanic Business Inc.
Ed: Jesus Chavarria. **Description:** A brief overview of the growth of Hispanic affluence in America and the important role that plays for Hispanic entrepreneurs and marketers. Hispanic Business magazine plans to organize training and educational events with sessions on Latin American trade, B2B e-commerce strategies, Hispanic online consumers, and cross-border banking.

45712 ■ **"A Tasty Blend of the Old and New" in** *Hispanic Business* **(June 2002, pp. 104)**
Pub: Hispanic Business
Ed: Barbara Beckley. **Description:** San Antonio, Texas is the perfect city to mix business with pleasure. Information for contacting the San Antonio Convention and Visitors Bureau is listed.

45713 ■ **"Teacher in Chief" in** *Fast Company* **(September 2001, pp. 66)**
Pub: Fast Company
Ed: Jennifer Reingold. **Description:** Why would a CEO of a fast-growing company take time out every month to teach his new hires? He does this because he wants them to take customer service as seriously as he does.

45714 ■ **"Teamwork tips" in** *BlackEnterprise* **(Vol. 32, No. 3, October 2001, pp. 68)**
Pub: Earl Graves Publishing Co.
Ed: Quincy L. Lewis. **Description:** Book review of 'Team Troubleshoot: How To Find and Fix Team Problems', by Robert W. Barner. Team Troubleshooter presents a five-stage plan to strengthen teams by spotting and resolving problems, including identifying problems, exploring options, planning for action, gaining commitment for plans, and implementing and following up on the plans.

45715 ■ **"Tech futures: Need a map for where business goes from here?" in** *Entrepreneur* **(Vol. 30, No. 1, January 2002, pp. 27)**
Pub: Entrepreneur Media Inc.
Ed: Mark Henricks. **Description:** Book reviews of the title, "The Internet Galaxy", which suggests that the Internet's influence on commerce has just begun; and "The War for Talent", which offers five imperatives that can help hire the best people for a business.

45716 ■ **"Tech, Please: 'Next-Generation CIOs' Offer More Than Just Tech Advice" in** *Entrepreneur* **(Vol. 33, January 2005, No. 1, pp. 22)**
Pub: Entrepreneur Media Inc.
Ed: Mark Henricks. **Description:** Successful chief information officers understand the business in which they work. They should continually examine new technologies and competitors' IT practices, and bring in new products, services and process improvements.

45717 ■ **"Tech-wreck survivors" in** *Crain's Detroit Business* **(Vol. 19, No. 13, March 31, 2003, pp. 11)**
Pub: Crain Communications Inc., Detroit
Ed: Andrew Dietderich. **Description:** Information on seven metro Detroit area high tech companies that

have prospered while others have gone out of business is discussed. The CEOs of Clarity LLC, Dewpoint Inc., ePrize LLC, Fry Inc., The Menlo Institute LLC, New World Systems, and Stoneage.com are interviewed.

45718 ■ **"Technology Evolving At Beall's" in** *Bradenton Herald* **(February 14, 2005)**
Pub: Bradenton Herald
Ed: Dana Sanchez. **Description:** Profile of Don Keller, production manager of one of Beall's Inc.'s two large distribution centers. Keller is phasing in voice recognition technology in its warehouses to increase efficiency in handling inventories.

45719 ■ **"Termination reasons key to workers' comp claims" in** *Business First Columbus* **(Vol. 18, No. 40, May 24, 2002, pp. B6)**
Pub: Business First Columbus, Inc.
Ed: Brent Wilder. **Description:** The Ohio Supreme Court ruled in four cases regarding workers compensation and termination. If an employee is fired for reasons that were well documented prior to a worker being injured, the employee will receive nothing.

45720 ■ **"That'll never work!" in** *Entrepreneur* **(Vol. 30, No. 2, February 2002, pp. 62)**
Pub: Entrepreneur Media Inc.
Ed: Chris Sandlund. **Description:** Interview with author Robert Sutton on counterintuitive management techniques. In his book "Weird Ideas That Work: 11 1/2 Practices for Promoting, Managing and Sustaining Innovation", Sutton explores such counterintuitive techniques as getting happy people to fight and hiring people you don't need.

45721 ■ **"The 100 Influentials" in** *Hispanic Business* **(October 2004, pp. 38)**
Pub: Hispanic Business
Description: Hispanic Business Directory of the 100 most influential Hispanics is presented. The list focuses on politics, the financial industry, and non-profit organizations, and the growing power and influence of these leaders. Profiles of these leaders are included.

45722 ■ **"The Best for Women" in** *Crain's Detroit Business* **(Vol. 19, No. 42, October 20, 2003, pp. 30)**
Pub: Crain Communications Inc., Detroit
Description: A listing of the top-ten scoring companies on the 2003 Michigan Women's Leadership Index, with FNBH Bancorp Inc. finishing first with 24 points, followed by Compuware Corporation and Energy Conversion Devices Inc., respectively.

45723 ■ **"The Champagne Group Launches 'Manager Makeover' Program" in** *Bellingham Business Journal* **(January 2007, pp. 4)**
Pub: Sun News Inc.
Description: Twelve-year-old business and leadership coaching company, The Champagne Group, is launching their new Manager Makeover Program. The five-step, customized program equips managers with techniques on becoming leaders who can resolve conflicts and increase performance.

45724 ■ **"Their Life's Work" in** *Tampa Tribune* **(November 25, 2005)**
Pub: Media General, Inc.
Ed: Dave Simanoff. **Description:** Employees with long tenure become an integral part of any small business, creating a bond and trust between management and employee as well as customer satisfaction.

45725 ■ **"There's No Perk Like Home" in** *Inc.* **(December 1, 2003)**
Pub: Gruner & Jahr USA Publishing
Ed: Nadine Heintze. **Description:** Some small companies are offering assistance to home purchases to employees. ArchivesOne awards two low interest homes to employees annually.

45726 ■ **"They Bought In. Now They Want to Bail Out" in** *Harvard Business Review* **(Vol. 81, No. 12, December 2003, pp. 28)**
Pub: Harvard Business School Press

Ed: Eric McNulty. **Description:** A hypothetical case is presented in which a chief technology officer is required to justify a potential investment in customer relationship management software. Teaching highlights include evaluating whether the fictional company needs the software, techniques for selling an idea or project, and the importance of widespread support for the success of such ventures.

45727 ■ **"They Hate You...They Really, Really Hate You"** in *Entrepreneur* (Vol. 28, No. 8, August 2000, pp. 99)
Pub: Entrepreneur Media Inc.
Ed: Jacquelyn Lynn. **Description:** What to do when you're the target of an anti-employer Web site.

45728 ■ **"They're not employees, they're people"** in *Harvard Business Review* (Vol. 80, No. 2, February 2002, pp. 70)
Pub: Harvard Business School Press
Ed: Peter F. Drucker. **Description:** Two fast-moving trends that are changing the way companies manage talent, the number of employees who are not longer traditional employees, and the growing number of companies that have outsourced employee relations is featured.

45729 ■ **"Things I Can't Live Without: Marcy Zambelli"** in *Inc.* (July 1, 2004)
Pub: Inc. Magazine
Ed: Ian Mount. **Description:** Interview with Marcy Zambelli, CEO of Zambelli Fireworks, a third generation family business. The firm was founded in 1893 and is worth $12 million.

45730 ■ **"Think Small. No, Smaller"** in *Inc.* (January 1, 2002)
Pub: Inc. Magazine
Ed: George Gendron. **Description:** Leadership skills are discussed.

45731 ■ **"Third Base: Hiring Employees Can Free Owner to Help Business Grow"** in *Crain's Detroit Business* (Vol. 19, No. 49, December 8, 2003)
Pub: Crain Communications Inc., Detroit
Ed: Laura Bailey. **Description:** One of the most crucial decisions a small business owner can make, is to hire the correct employee at the correct time.

45732 ■ **"This is a Test: Just How Effective are Puzzle Interviews When It Comes to Singling Out the Best Candidates for the Job?"** in *Entrepreneur*
Pub: Entrepreneur Media Inc.
Ed: Chris Penttila. **Description:** Puzzle interviews put job applicants through a test of questions during an intense, multi-round interview process. Many large companies, like Microsoft have instituted this process. Critics believe puzzle questions only tell employer that a candidate is good at solving puzzles, not if they fit the position.

45733 ■ **"This job guarantees a good workout"** in *Wall Street Journal* (April 15, 2003, pp. B7)
Pub: Dow Jones & Co. Inc.
Ed: Kris Maher. **Description:** Horizon Fitness is looking for a new vice president in charge of product development.

45734 ■ **"A Thorough Assessment: Want to Evaluate Your Management Skills?"** in *Sales and Marketing.com* (Vol. 156, No. 3, March 2004)
Pub: VNU eMedia, Inc.
Ed: Julia Chang. **Description:** Profile of the Hay Group's multirater tests for technology executives. The firm rated 276 technology executives and found the most accurate performance ratings came from direct reports, followed by managers. Self and peer assessments were the poorest, citing executives tend to overrate their performance and that of colleagues.

45735 ■ **"Thoughts On the Business of Life"** in *Forbes* (Vol. 170, No. 13, December 23, 2002, pp. 396)
Pub: Forbes Magazine

Description: Thoughts gathered by several successful men from all walks of life, over some 85 years, are presented, from John D. Rockefeller, 1917 to Dennis Kozlowski, 2000.

45736 ■ **"A thousand bottles of beer on the wall"** in *Washington Business Journal* (Vol. 22, No. 3, May 23, 2003, pp. 31)
Pub: Washington Business Journal
Ed: Sean Madigan. **Description:** Profile of the management of a Washington, DC area tavern called the Brickskeller. Topics include management styles, product lines, and financial management.

45737 ■ **"Through the Grape Vine"** in *Tampa Tribune* (November 21, 2005)
Pub: Media General, Inc.
Ed: Marla Marino. **Description:** Local Florida wineries are marketing their traditional as well as their unique citrus and berry wines as novelty gifts to tourists.

45738 ■ **"Throwing Money at Technology Isn't the Solution"** in *My Business* (April/May 2002, pp. 18)
Pub: My Business Magazine
Ed: Michael Grebb. **Description:** Not all business problems can be solved by technology. Small firms must first identify and analyze an issue then break the problem down into three components: process, people, and technology.

45739 ■ **"Tiger Power"** in *Rough Notes* (Vol. 146, No. 9, September 2003, pp. 32)
Pub: Rough Notes
Ed: Elisabeth Boone. **Description:** Profile of Princeton Risk Managers Inc., covering risk management services, management styles, and market development.

45740 ■ **"Time For a Checkup"** in *Sales and Marketing.com* (Vol. 156, No. 3, March 2004, pp. 68)
Pub: VNU eMedia, Inc.
Ed: Marc S. Daner. **Description:** Executives should have a financial plan prepared every three years, and every other year within ten years of retirement. A financial planner can assist in planning long and short-term goals.

45741 ■ **"The time for talk is over"** in *Rough Notes* (Vol. 146, No. 4, April 2003, pp. 16)
Pub: Rough Notes
Ed: Michael J. Moody. **Description:** After Enron's collapse, enterprise risk management has become more important in corporate governance. Pricewaterhouse-Coopers Inc.'s research indicates that consumer trust can be regained by financial institutions through checks and balances in top managers.

45742 ■ **"The Time is Now"** in *My Business* (April/May 2004, pp. 14)
Pub: My Business Magazine
Ed: Lena Basha. **Description:** With a growing economy, it is important for small businesses to focus on employee retention; flexibility is an important incentive to employees.

45743 ■ **"A Time to Shine: Awards Celebration Spotlights Today's Successful Entrepreneurs"** in *Black Enterprise* (Vol. 34, No. 4, November 2003)
Pub: Earl Graves Publishing Co.
Description: Black Enterprise recognizes outstanding African American entrepreneurs, including small business owners and top-level executives who appear on the BE 100s lists.

45744 ■ **"Time's Up: New Laws Tell You Who Gets Overtime-And Who Doesn't"** in *Entrepreneur* (Vol. 32, October 2004, No. 10, pp. 40)
Pub: Entrepreneur Media Inc.
Ed: Chris Penttila. **Description:** New U.S. Department of Labor rules state that employees earning over $100,000 annually in executive, administrative and professional positions are no longer eligible for overtime; workers earning less than $23,660 annually are.

45745 ■ **"Tipping point leadership"** in *Harvard Business Review* (Vol. 81, No. 4, April 2003, pp. 60)
Pub: Harvard Business School Press
Ed: W. Chan Kim, Renee Mauborgne. **Description:** Profile of the career of William Bratton in law enforcement administration, and the agencies that he has helped turn around, such as the New York City Police Department. Bratton's leadership style is referred to as tipping point leadership.

45746 ■ **"Todd Brown"** in *Black Enterprise* (Vol. 34, No. 5, December 2003, pp. 68)
Pub: Earl Graves Publishing Co.
Description: Profile of Todd Brown, vice chairman of ShoreBank Corporation and chairman of the board of directors for the company's banking operations in Chicago, Illinois and Detroit, Michigan.

45747 ■ **"Too old to learn?"** in *Harvard Business Review* (Vol. 78, No. 6, November-December 2000, pp. 37)
Pub: Harvard Business School Publishing Corp.
Description: Armor Coat Insurance executives share their experiences working with 20-somethings to update their computer and Internet skills.

45748 ■ **"Top 10 Business Schools for Hispanics"** in *Hispanic Business* (September 2003, pp. 48, 50, 52, 54)
Pub: Hispanic Business
Description: A listing of the top ten business schools for Hispanic students to consider, with University of Texas at Austin's McCombs School of Business at number one, followed by Yale University's Yale School of Management.

45749 ■ **"Top ten business women of ABWA!"** in *Women in Business* (Vol. 53, No. 7, January-February 2002, pp. 14)
Pub: The ABWA Co Inc.
Ed: Rachel Warbington. **Description:** The Top Ten Businesswoman Award is one of the most prestigious in the American Business Women's Association. A profile of those members who won the award in 2002 is provided.

45750 ■ **"Top Executives Set the Tone for Treating Employees Well"** in *St. Louis Post-Dispatch* (January 16, 2005)
Pub: Knight-Ridder/Tribune Business News
Ed: Repps Hudson. **Description:** Profile of Robert Levering, co-founder of Great Place to Work Institute. Levering scores U.S. companies on how they treat employees and what employees think about the companies in which they work.

45751 ■ **"Top-Heavy: Is it Time to Thin Out Your Management Pool"** in *Entrepreneur* (Vol. 32, No. 1, January 2004, pp. 30)
Pub: Entrepreneur Media, Inc.
Ed: Nichole L. Torres. **Description:** Cynthia Shapiro, human resource consultant, recommends letting go unnecessary management. Tips for deciding which managers to pink slip are included.

45752 ■ **"Top-Heavy: The Pitfalls of Overhiring"** in *My Business* (October/November 2003, pp. 56)
Pub: My Business Magazine
Ed: Peter Provenzano. **Description:** Hiring too large a staff, especially at management level, can be detrimental to a company's ability to grow.

45753 ■ **"Top MBA Programs (MO&KS)"** in *Ingram's* (Vol. 28, No. 9, September 2002, pp. 42)
Pub: Show Me Publishing, Inc.
Description: A listing of the top Missouri and Kansas universities offerings MBA degree courses ranked according to 2001 enrollment. The top three are Webster University; Baker University, School of Professorial and Graduate Studies; and Rockhurst University.

45754 ■ *Total Improvement Management: How to Coordinate Diverse Improvement Efforts for Maximum Gain*
Pub: The McGraw-Hill Companies

Ed: H. James Harrington. **Released:** 1995. **Price:** $32.95. **Description:** Discusses strategies for organization-wide improvement, including Total Quality Management and Total Cost Management.

45755 ■ "A Touch of Class: Teaching Can Give Your Career a Boost" in *Sales and Marketing.com* **(Vol. 156, No. 3, March 2004, pp. 48)**
Pub: VNU eMedia, Inc.
Ed: Amy Moerke. **Description:** Profile of Maria Andreu, president of the North New Jersey Coach Alliance, who volunteers teaching adult education classes. The center allows professionals to design and teach their own courses, which in turn, helps them become more successful.

45756 ■ "Touchdown!" in *Rough Notes* **(Vol. 145, No. 2, February 2002, pp. 92)**
Pub: Rough Notes
Ed: Troy Korsgaden. **Description:** Like a good quarterback, running a successful insurance agency has to have the qualities of persistence which will overcome people's distrust of sales people and commitment which is backed up by assessment of a situation, visualization of the goals to be achieved and an action plan to accomplish the agency's goals.

45757 ■ *Tough Choices: A Memoir*
Pub: Penguin Group
Ed: Carly Florina. **Released:** October 2006. **Price:** $24.95. **Description:** Former woman CEO at Hewlett-Packard is profiled.

45758 ■ "Tough choices" in *Entrepreneur* **(Vol. 31, No. 5, May 2003, pp. 70)**
Pub: Entrepreneur Media Inc.
Ed: Chris Penttila. **Description:** A big dilemma facing entrepreneurs these days is hiring fresh new talent. Ways to handle having to hire new employees at higher wages than existing employees are discussed.

45759 ■ "A tough review" in *Black Enterprise* **(Vol. 32, No. 10, May 2002, pp. 107)**
Pub: Earl Graves Publishing Co.
Ed: Alfred A. Edmond, Jr. **Description:** Advice is given on things to learn from an employee performance review which will help both an employee and manager.

45760 ■ "Tough Talk" in *Entrepreneur.com* **(Vol. 34, February 2006, No. 2, pp. 100)**
Pub: Entrepreneur Media Inc.
Ed: Nichole L. Torres. **Description:** Barbara Pachter, author of The Power of Positive Confrontation: The Skills You Need to Know to Handle Conflicts at Work, Home, and in Life, offers five tips for successful business conversations.

45761 ■ "Tougher rules likely to dry up boardroom candidates" in *Crain's Detroit Business* **(Vol. 19, No. 6, February 10, 2003, pp. 14)**
Pub: Crain Communications Inc., Detroit
Ed: Katie Merx. **Description:** The impact of the Sarbanes-Oxley Act are investigated, including the affect it will have on part-time directorships.

45762 ■ *The TQM Almanac, 1994-1995 Edition*
Pub: Irwin Professional Publishing
Ed: Timeplace, Inc. **Released:** 1994-1995 edition. **Price:** $75.00. **Description:** Provides advice and information on implementing Total Quality Management in an organization successfully. Includes list of resources, consultants, seminars, books and associations.

45763 ■ "Traditional vs. On-Line Learning: It's Not an Either/or Proposition" in *Employment Relations Today* **(Vol.27, No.1, Spring 2000, pp. 47)**
Pub: John Wiley & Sons, Inc.
Ed: James H.S. Davis. **Description:** Issues discussed concern the management of corporate training programs, focusing on the use of traditional and online education techniques. Topics addressed include how to most efficiently combine classroom and Internet-based training and methodologies to offer employees the opportunity to advance their skills.

45764 ■ "Training Managers to be Better Communicators" in *Employment Relations Today* **(Vol. 27, No. 1, Spring 2000, pp. 73)**
Pub: John Wiley & Sons, Inc.
Ed: Merna Skinner. **Description:** Covers ways to train managers in effective business communication, focusing on the mistakes managers often make when communicating with their subordinates. Topics addressed include human resource management, self-awareness, and developing interpersonal skills.

45765 ■ "Training Trainers and Leaders" in *Women in Business* **(Vol. 53, No. 7, January-February 2002, pp. 30)**
Pub: The ABWA Co Inc.
Description: The American Business Women's Association provides the Membership Training and Development Certification Program and the Leadership Certificate Program for developing training and leadership skills. Organization members have used the skills they have learned in the programs at work and in volunteer situations.

45766 ■ "Triple sport star: Steve Mills scores for the Knicks, Rangers, and the Liberty" in *Black Enterprise* **(Vol.33, No.3, Oct. 2002, pp. 72)**
Pub: Earl Graves Publishing Co.
Ed: Sonia Alleyne. **Description:** Profile of Steve Mills, president of sports team operations for Madison Square Garden in New York City. Mills manages business operations, finances, and marketing for the three teams, the Knicks, Rangers, and Liberty, housed at the Garden. Mills shares ways to successfully apply what is learned in sports to a business setting.

45767 ■ "Trouble on the horizon...isn't going away" in *Fast Company* **(May 2001, pp. 85)**
Pub: Fast Company
Ed: Peter C. Peterson. **Description:** Profile of Peter C. Peterson, a former U.S. Secretary of Commerce and former Chairman and CEO of Leisman Brothers, is chairman of the Council on Foreign Relations and of the Federal Reserve Bank of New York, among other organizations. He is also founding president of the Concord Coalition, an organization devoted to fiscal responsibility, and is a special limited-advisory partner to Millennium Technology Ventures LP.

45768 ■ "The trouble I've seen" in *Harvard Business Review* **(Vol. 80, No. 3, March 2002, pp. 42)**
Pub: Harvard Business School Press
Ed: David N. James. **Description:** The experiences of crisis manager, David N. James, are profiled. James has 30 years of experience and offers advice about rescuing companies about to go under.

45769 ■ *True to Yourself: Leading a Values-Based Business*
Pub: Berrett-Koehler Publishers, Incorporated
Ed: Mark S. Albion. **Released:** June 2006. **Price:** $14.95. **Description:** Pressures faced by entrepreneurs running small companies are discussed. Advice is offered to help grow and maintain a profitable business.

45770 ■ "A Tug of War: Real Deal: You Can't Have It All." in *Entrepreneur* **(Vol. 31, No. 9, September 2003, pp. 81)**
Pub: Entrepreneur Media, Inc.
Ed: Marc Diener. **Description:** When negotiating deals, it is important to understand two critical tools: concession and the condition. A concession is what is given, the condition is the "if" clause.

45771 ■ "Turing the Page" in *Business 2.0* **(Vol. 6, July 2005, No. 6, pp. 98-100)**
Pub: Time, Inc.
Ed: John Battelle. **Description:** Xerox CEO Anne Mulcahy is digitizing the company she helped save. In an interview, Mulcahy discusses the humility that comes from turning a business around.

45772 ■ "Turn It Off!" in *Entrepreneur* **(Vol. 31, No. 9, September 2003, pp. 77)**
Pub: Entrepreneur Media, Inc.

Ed: Joanne Cleaver. **Description:** According to managers at Traq-wireless, a telecommunications consulting firm, more than half of their corporate clients are enforcing strict no cell/no PDA/no BlackBerry policies during meetings.

45773 ■ "The 2003 HBR List: Breakthrough Ideas for Tomorrow" in *Harvard Business Review* **(Vol. 81, No. 4, 4/03, pp. 92)**
Pub: Harvard Business School Press
Description: The editors consider strategy, organizations and leadership in the light of the events of the past year. They ponder the role of the leader, soft issues such as emotional intelligence and the unavoidable messiness of organizations.

45774 ■ *Ultimate Guide to Project Management*
Pub: Entrepreneurial Press
Ed: Sid Kemp. **Released:** October 2005. **Price:** $29.95 (US), $39.95 (Canadian). **Description:** Project management strategies including writing a business plan and developing a good advertising campaign.

45775 ■ *The Ultimate No B.S., No Holds Barred, Kick Butt, Take No Prisoners, and Make Tons of Money Business Success Book*
Pub: Self-Counsel Press, Inc.
Ed: Dan Kennedy. **Released:** 1993. **Price:** $16.95 (business package); $8.95 (paper); $14.95 (two audiocassettes). **Description:** Business package includes book plus audiocassettes.

45776 ■ "Uncertainty and Information Search Activities" in *Journal of Small Business Management* **(Vol. 41, No. 4, October 2003, pp. 385)**
Pub: International Council of Small Business
Ed: Jeffrey E. McGee, Olukemi O. Sawyerr. **Description:** An examination of the relationship among perceived strategic uncertainty (PSU), environmental scanning, and the information sources used by owner-managers, using 153 small high-technology manufacturing firms.

45777 ■ "Under Pressure" in *Entrepreneur* **(Vol. 31, No. 8, August 2003, pp. 68)**
Pub: Entrepreneur Media, Inc.
Ed: Juanita Weaver. **Description:** It is essential to provide a safe environment for employees asked to create something innovative. Communicate to these employees the knowledge of an uncertain outcome, provide necessary time and resources, and define the desired parameters of the outcome for measuring success of the new creation.

45778 ■ "Under Pressure: If an Employee Feels Forced to Quit, It Could Be Trouble" in *Entrepreneur*
Pub: Entrepreneur Media Inc.
Ed: Jane Easter Bahls. **Description:** Constructive discharge is the legal concept that means conditions at work had become so intolerable that any reasonable employee would have quit. An employee can sue under these conditions and an employer can be held liable.

45779 ■ "U.S. CFOs Bullish on Hiring" in *Long Island Business News* **(February 27, 2004)**
Pub: Dolan Media Newswires
Ed: Ben Abelson. **Description:** Second quarter 2004 saw chief financial officers of companies across the U.S. more optimistic about hiring new employees, but 90 percent were still reluctant to begin the process at present time.

45780 ■ "Unselfish Teamwork Helps Gibson Insurance Agency Grow" in *Rough Notes* **(Vol. 146, No. 9, September 2003, pp. 18)**
Pub: Rough Notes
Ed: Dennis H. Pillsbury. **Description:** Profile of Gibson Insurance Agency; topics include teamwork, management styles, and market share.

45781 ■ **"Up Front: Seeking Help" in** *My Business* **(February/March 2004, pp. 10-11)**
Pub: My Business Magazine
Ed: Gary M. Stern. Description: Creative recruiting is sometimes required in order to find the right employees. Hiring senior citizens, internships, looking at local church bulletins are a few of the recruiting tips listed.

45782 ■ **"Up and Running: Energize Salespeople To Get Out Of a First-Quarter Slump" in** *Sales & Marketing Management* **(Vol. 157, February 2005)**
Pub: VNU Business Media
Ed: Betsy Cummings. Description: It is critical to jump-start sales early in a new year. The importance of choosing incentives that work is addressed.

45783 ■ **"Upfront: Be Flexible or Fold" in** *My Business* **(June/July 2002, pp. 13-14)**
Pub: My Business Magazine
Ed: Karen E. Klein. Description: Sometimes a small firm needs to steer away from original business plans in order to grow. Martha C. de al Torre, Hispanic Business Woman of the Year 2000, tells how she learned to be flexible and creative with her business plan.

45784 ■ **"The Use of Criminal Record in Employment Decisions" in** *Journal of Business Ethics* **(Vol. 47, No. 3, Oct. 15, 2003, pp. 237)**
Pub: Kluwer Academic Publishers Group
Ed: Helen Lam, Mark Harcourt. Description: Evidence suggests that employers discriminate against ex-offenders in the labor market.

45785 ■ **"Using intuition at work" in** *Women in Business* **(Vol. 54, No. 3, May-June 2002, pp.)**
Pub: The ABWA Co Inc.
Ed: James Wanless. Description: Using intuition in the workplace is discussed. An excerpt from the book, 'Intuition @ Work and at Home and Play', with a quiz included to test your intuition.

45786 ■ *Value-Added Sales Management: A Guide for Salespeople and Their Managers*
Pub: Contemporary Books, Inc.
Ed: Tom Reilly. Released: 1993. Price: $12.95 (paper).

45787 ■ **"Value system" in** *Entrepreneur* **(Vol. 30, No. 3, March)**
Pub: Entrepreneur Media Inc.
Ed: Steven C. Bahls, Jane Easter Bahls. Description: Under Title VII of the Civil Rights Act of 1964, employers must make reasonable accommodations for employees' religious practices, unless doing so would impose an undue hardship on the company.

45788 ■ **"VC Goes Institutional: The Hiring of a Chief Operating Officer" in** *Venture Capital Journal* **(Vol. 40, No. 10, October 2000, pp. 41-43)**
Pub: Venture Economics
Ed: Alissa Leibowitz. Description: An overview of venture capital firms who have turned to a Chief Operating Officer to manage the firm's capital. These firms feel this move will enable them to offer more services.

45789 ■ **"A View From the Top" in** *Sales and Marketing.com* **(Vol. 156, No. 3, March 2004, pp. 19)**
Pub: VNU eMedia, Inc.
Ed: Julia Chang. Description: The importance of management team building is stressed; weekly meetings are one way to discuss each department's issues.

45790 ■ **"The virtue matrix" in** *Harvard Business Review* **(Vol. 80, No. 3, March 2002, pp. 69)**
Pub: Harvard Business School Press
Ed: Roger L. Martin. Description: Corporate ethics issues are discussed at the Aspen Institute's Initiative for Social Innovation Through Business, and the virtue matrix, an analytical tool that helps executives think about corporate responsibility, designed after the Aspen Institute discussion.

45791 ■ **"A Virtuous Cycle" in** *Forbes* **(Vol. 170, No. 13, December 23, 2002, pp. 248)**
Pub: Forbes Magazine
Ed: James Surowiecki. Description: The importance of trust and honesty in relation to capitalism is examined.

45792 ■ **"Voices carry" in** *Entrepreneur* **(Vol. 31, No. 6, June 2003, pp. 80)**
Pub: Entrepreneur Media Inc.
Ed: Elizabeth J. Goodgold. Description: Ways to improve vocal skills are listed, including improving elocution, slowing down speech, finding a perfect pitch, and using a tape recorder.

45793 ■ **"Voyage of a Lifetime" in** *Inc.* **(September 1, 2004)**
Pub: Inc. Magazine
Ed: Riza Cruz. Description: Profile of Kip Stone, owner of the T-shirt company called Artforms. Stone talks about his rethinking of his management strategy and hired managers with expertise in areas of production and inventory to accounting and sales who didn't need constant direction in order to allow him to continue to pursue his dreams of sailing.

45794 ■ **"The Walking Time Bomb" in** *Inc.* **(December 1, 2003)**
Pub: Gruner & Jahr USA Publishing
Description: How to defuse an abusive partner, intellectual property issues, and renting property rather than buying are topics discussed.

45795 ■ **"Want to Improve Your Hiring and Promotion Odds?" in** *Kansas City Star* **(February 6, 2005)**
Pub: Knight-Ridder/Tribune Business News
Ed: Diane Stafford. Description: Suggestions to help employees improve chances for being hired or promoted are given.

45796 ■ **"Wanted: African American Professional for Hire" in** *Black Enterprise* **(Vol. 37, November 2006, No. 4, pp. 93)**
Pub: Earl G. Graves Publishing Co. Inc.
Ed: Joe Watson. Description: Excerpt from the book, Without Excuses: Unleash the Power of Diversity to Build Your Business, speaks to the lack of diversity in the corporate arena and why executives, recruiters, and HR professionals claim they are unable to find qualified individuals of different races when hiring.

45797 ■ **"Wanted: Chief Ignorance Officer" in** *Harvard Business Review* **(Vol. 81, No. 11, November 2003, pp. 22)**
Pub: Harvard Business School Press
Ed: David Gray. Description: The value of finding new solutions to old problems is discussed.

45798 ■ **"Wanted: E-Business Professionals" in** *E-business Advisor* **(Vol. 17, No. 12, December 1999, pp. 6)**
Pub: Advisor Media, Inc.
Ed: Jane Falla. Description: The article offers advice for attracting the top e-business talent to your business, including Director of E-Business, E-Commerce Consultant, Director of Business Development, E-Commerce, and E-Commerce Sales Executive.

45799 ■ **"Warp Speed" in** *Sales & Marketing Management* **(Vol. 157, Jan. 20, 2005)**
Pub: VNU Business Media
Ed: Michele Marchetti. Description: According to Patricia Gardner, founder of Maximum Sales, sales and management consulting firm in Sparks, Maryland, the most important thing small companies neglect during a high-growth period, is to write job descriptions for its sales staff and other employees.

45800 ■ **"The Way he was" in** *Crain's Detroit Business* **(Vol. 19, No. 2, January 13, 2003, pp. 11)**
Pub: Crain Communications Inc., Detroit
Description: Profile of Ken Way, former CEO and chairman of Lear Seating Corporation.

45801 ■ **"Welcome aboard (but don't change a thing)" in** *Harvard Business Review* **(Vol. 80, No. 10, October 2002, pp. 32)**
Pub: Harvard Business School Press
Ed: Eric McNulty. Description: The fictitious company, Lakeland Wonders, brought in a new CEO with fresh ideas, but the company balked at implementing them. Experts analyze the scenario.

45802 ■ **"'Well dones' shouldn't be rare" in** *BlackEnterprise* **(Vol. 32, No. 3, October 2001, pp. 67)**
Pub: Earl Graves Publishing Co.
Ed: Robyn D. Clarke. Description: In a survey conducted by Office Team, 60 percent of executives polled believed that companies do a somewhat effective job of acknowledging top performers, while 33 percent believed that staff recognition efforts are inadequate. Four employee incentives are listed by Liz Hubler, executive director of Office Team.

45803 ■ **"What are you complaining about?" in** *Fast Company* **(May 2001, pp. 66)**
Pub: Fast Company
Ed: Cheryl Dahle. Description: Many companies are stuck in the gripe mode, but Harvard researchers Robert Kegan and Lisa Laskow Lahey have a prescription to turn complaints into an agenda for change.

45804 ■ **"What Are You Worth?" in** *Fortune* **(Vol. 141, No. 12, June 12, 2000, pp. 264B+)**
Pub: Time Inc.
Description: Deciding how much to pay yourself is one of the toughest and most fundamental calls a small business person has to make. Should new hires be given a share of the business? These topics are reviewed.

45805 ■ **"What Drives Inspiration?" in** *Entrepreneur* **(Vol. 32, December 2004, No. 12, pp. 20)**
Pub: Entrepreneur Media Inc.
Description: Four tips for entrepreneurs to remain flexible in managing their business include: being realistic, updating technology, customer satisfaction, and being a good boss.

45806 ■ **"What is science good for?" in** *Harvard Business Review* **(Vol. 79, No. 1, January 2001, pp. 159)**
Pub: Harvard Business School Publishing Corp.
Description: Evolutionary biologist Richard Dawkins discusses the misconceptions of science and genetics and their overuse in business management.

45807 ■ **"What is a Global Manager?" in** *Harvard Business Review* **(Vol. 81, No. 8, August 2003, pp. 101)**
Pub: Harvard Business School Press
Ed: Christopher A. Bartlett, Sumantra Ghoshal. Description: An effective global manager is not one person. He/she will be one of three types: a business manager, a country manager, and a function manager. For companies to utilize these managers, a set of senior executives will need to nurture and coordinate these specialists. Corning Glass' effort to develop a global market is used to illustrate the point.

45808 ■ **"What makes great boards great." in** *Harvard Business Review* **(Vol. 80, No. 9, Sept. 2002, pp. 106)**
Pub: Harvard Business School Press
Ed: Jeffrey A. Sonnenfeld. Description: An overview of the basic traits required to establish a good board of directors is presented.

45809 ■ **"What I Know Now" in** *Fast Company* **(March 2005, No. 92, pp. 96)**
Pub: Gruner & Jahr USA Publishing
Ed: Keith H. Hammonds. Description: Profile of Anne M. Mulcahy, chairman and CEO of Xerox Corporation. Mulcahy shares her experiences of the last four years as a leader at Xerox.

45810 ■ **"What It Takes to be a Successful Intrapreneur" in** *Black Enterprise* **(Vol. 36, December 2005, No. 5, pp.)**
Pub: Earl G. Graves Publishing Co. Inc.

Ed: Nicole Marie Richardson. **Description:** Enterprising and innovative corporate professionals are being called intrapreneurs, or corporate entrepreneurship and corporate renewal professionals.

45811 ■ **"What Leaders Really Do"** in *Harvard Business Review* (Vol. 79, No. 11, December 2001, pp. 85)
Pub: Harvard Business School Press
Ed: John P. Kotter. **Description:** Leadership is different from management. Leadership and management are two complementary systems. While management copes with complexity, leadership copes with change. Because the business world has become more competitive and demands more change, it also demands more leadership.

45812 ■ **"What to Pay"** in *My Business* (November/December 2001, pp. 47)
Pub: My Business Magazine
Ed: Description: Considerations to address when hiring and compensating employees are discussed, such as linking compensation of executives to performance and salary surveys for what other companies are paying in salaries.

45813 ■ **"What Really Works"** in *Harvard Business Review* (Vol. 81, No. 7, July 2003, pp. 42)
Pub: Harvard Business School Press
Ed: Nitin Nohria, William Joyce, Bruce Roberson. **Description:** Management practices that result in business success are examined.

45814 ■ **"What Should You Do"** in *Sales and Marketing.com* (Vol. 156, No. 3, March 2004, pp. 8)
Pub: VNU eMedia, Inc.
Description: Reorganizing sales territories can sometimes help reenergize sales reps. Solutions to this reorganization are offered to help avoid angering salespeople or disrupting client/seller relationships.

45815 ■ **"What the Titans Can Teach Us"** in *Harvard Business Review* (Vol. 79, No. 11, December 2001, pp. 70)
Pub: Harvard Business School Press
Ed: Richard S. Tedlow. **Description:** Profile of legendary leaders of American business such as Andrew Carnegie, Henry Ford and Sam Walton of Wal-Mart. While some of their traits should not be emulated, the author argues that we can all learn from them. These people had the courage to bet on their vision of market potential, they shaped their vision into a mission for the company and they delivered more than they promised.

45816 ■ **"What's the Biggest Problem in American Business? An Excess of Loyalty"** in *Inc.* (May 1, 2005)
Pub: Inc. Magazine
Ed: Adam Hanft. **Description:** The difference between loyalty and trust in the world of business are discussed.

45817 ■ **"What's the Deal?"** in *Entrepreneur* (Vol. 31, No. 10, October 2003, pp. 34)
Pub: Entrepreneur Media, Inc.
Ed: Mark Hendricks. **Description:** Book review of, "The Only Negotiating Guide You'll Ever Need", written by Peter B. Stark and Jane Flaherty. Stark and Flaherty, both business consultants, stress that negotiators must always consider the other side's needs in order to win repeat customers and develop strong vendor relationships.

45818 ■ **"What's the best way to get noticed by an executive-search firm?"** in *Wall Street Journal* (May 28, 2002, pp. B12)
Pub: Wall Street Journal
Ed: Kemba J. Dunham. **Description:** Information for executives search for employment, as well as information for prospective employers, is discussed.

45819 ■ **"What's In Your Wallet?"** in *Tradeshow Week* (Vol. 34, December 13, 2004, No. 50, pp. 1)
Pub: Reed Business Information
Description: Statistical information regarding tradeshow managers is presented. Show manager income rose an average of 3.6 percent in 2004. Statistical data included.

45820 ■ **"What's Next? Mistakes Were Made"** in *Inc.* (November 2006, pp. 65-66)
Pub: Gruner & Jahr USA Publishing
Ed: David H. Friedman. **Description:** Never hide mistakes made by a company. Communicate the event in order to develop an atmosphere of openness and of learning by mistakes, rather than that mistakes are shameful and attempts are made to cover them up.

45821 ■ **"What's That Bad Odor at Innovation Skunkworks?"** in *Fortune* (Vol. 140, No. 12, December 20, 1999, pp. 338)
Pub: Time Inc.
Ed: Michael Schrage. **Description:** When an enterprise goes skunk, what's the real message? Management launches a skunkworks because it has failed to create an organization that cannot innovate without skunks.

45822 ■ **"What's Wrong with Executive Compensation"** in *Harvard Business Review* (Vol. 81, No. 1, January 2003, pp. 69)
Pub: Harvard Business School Press
Ed: Charles Elson. **Description:** Harvard Business Review and the University of Delaware's Center for Corporate Governance convened a roundtable to discuss executive compensation. The twelve panelists discussed ways to align the interests of executives with long-term company interests and the broader questions of corporate governance and company values.

45823 ■ **"What's on Your Agenda?"** in *Fast Company* (June 2001, pp. 85)
Pub: Fast Company
Description: Fast Company asked ten senior executives and thinkers to explain the most crucial item on their particular leadership agenda.

45824 ■ **"What's Your Angle? Get Fresh Ideas When You Change Your Perspective"** in *Entrepreneur* (Vol. 31, No. 9, September 2003, pp. 81)
Pub: Entrepreneur Media, Inc.
Ed: Juanita Weaver. **Description:** Reversing current ideas and beliefs can lead to new ways to develop a business, according to a creativity coach and business consultant.

45825 ■ **"When the Boss Won't Budge"** in *Harvard Business Review* (Vol. 78, No. 1, January 2000, pp. 25)
Pub: Harvard Business School Publishing Corp.
Ed: Regina Fazio Maruca. **Description:** What happens when the top manager is holding back the company he created?

45826 ■ **"When Does Bending Rules Become Breaking Rules?"** in *Atlanta Business Chronicle* (Vol. 24, No. 10, August 10, 2001, pp. 46A)
Pub: American City Business Journals Inc.
Ed: Emory Mulling. **Description:** Management needs to be consistent with the company's rules and core values. Company values need to be reiterated in a regular basis. In addition, people should not be expected to automatically absorb a corporate culture.

45827 ■ **"When Leadership Means Letting Go"** in *Law Firm Inc.* (October 2004)
Pub: American Lawyer Media LP
Description: In law firms, it is important for the chief marketing officer to report to the firm's top leader in order for the position to be taken seriously. The chief marketing leader's expertise to handle marketing and sales efforts is critical.

45828 ■ **"When the Love is Gone: How to Reignite Passion for the Job"** in *Black Enterprise* (Vol. 35, January 2005, No. 6, pp. 54)
Pub: Earl G. Graves Publishing Co. Inc.
Ed: Lee Anna Jackson. **Description:** According to a study performed by the Conference Board, a nonprofit business leader resource, job satisfaction has been falling since 1995. Previous studies reported a direct connection between job satisfaction and top performing individuals and teams.

45829 ■ **"When to Put the Brakes on Learning."** in *Harvard Business Review* (Vol. 81, No. 2, February 2003, pp. 20)
Pub: Harvard Business School Press
Ed: J. Stuart Bunderson, Kathleen M. Sutcliffe. **Description:** Two fortune 100 companies' business units are compared to show that continued learning can reach a point of diminishing returns. Three suggestions are offered to help manage learning within a company.

45830 ■ **"When those at the Thanksgiving table are your team"** in *Business First Columbus* (Vol. 18, No. 25, February 8, 2002, pp. B6)
Pub: Business First Columbus, Inc.
Ed: Carole W. Tomko. **Description:** Tips for running a family-owned business are presented, including issues presented when managing family members.

45831 ■ **"Where Everyone's a Winner: Sure, the Annual Trip to Hawaii Is a Great Reward For Your Top Performers"** in *Sales & Marketing Management*
Pub: VNU Business Media
Ed: Julia Chang. **Description:** Motivational strategies that benefit an entire sales team, rather than rewarding only the top few salespeople, can provide greater success. In a recent survey, 68 percent of workers stated that more award opportunities would further motivate them in their jobs.

45832 ■ **"Where Fiorina Went Wrong; A Charismatic Leader, She Helped Make HP a Powerful Marketer"** in *Business Week Online* (February 10, 2005)
Pub: McGraw-Hill Companies
Ed: Cliff Edwards. **Description:** Carly Fiorina, CEO of Hewlett Packard Company, resigned February 8, 2005. Fiorina's refusal to delegate along with the loss of key leaders were responsible for the end of her six year tenure with the firm.

45833 ■ *Where to Get the Money & Management Help for New Business Start-Ups & Small Business Growth: South Atlantic Region, DE, DC, FL, GA, MD, NC, SC, VA, WV*
Pub: Special Reports, Inc.
Ed: Richard S. Guyer and Frank J. Domeracki. **Released:** 1997. **Price:** $197.00.

45834 ■ **"Wherefore Art Thou Board Member?"** in *Entrepreneur* (Vol. 31, No. 10, October 2003, pp. 64)
Pub: Entrepreneur Media, Inc.
Ed: Jennifer Pellet. **Description:** The risk and time involved in serving on company boards is discussed, along with ways to lure top notch talent to a small firm's board of directors.

45835 ■ **"Which School is Right?"** in *Hispanic Business* (September 2003, pp. 46)
Pub: Hispanic Business
Ed: Joel Russell. **Description:** For Hispanic students, selecting an MBA or a law school program involves academic, social, personal, and financial considerations.

45836 ■ **"Whipping up a great meeting"** in *Black Enterprise* (Vol. 31, No. 5, December 2000, pp. 82)
Pub: Earl Graves Publishing Co.
Ed: Robyn D. Clarke. **Description:** The ten essential ingredients for meetings that get results are explained.

45837 ■ "Who Are the Gurus' Gurus? One Thing is Clear: They're Not the Usual Suspects" in *Harvard Business Review* (Vol. 81, No. 12, Dec. 2003)
Pub: Harvard Business School Press
Ed: Lawrence Prusak, Thomas H. Davenport. **Description:** An examination of the various sources that dominate management literature and mass media; they reflect a wide range of intellectual specialties, including anthropology, history, psychology, and more. Implications of this diversity on management science and practice are briefly noted.

45838 ■ "Who Can You Trust?" in *Inc.* (October 1, 2004)
Pub: Inc. Magazine
Ed: Alison Stein Wellner. **Description:** One of the biggest problems faced by entrepreneurs is delegating responsibility to other employees.

45839 ■ "Who Knows?" in *Entrepreneur* (Vol. 28, No. 4, April 2000, pp. 138)
Pub: Entrepreneur Media Inc.
Ed: Chris Penttila. **Description:** Employees come and go, but how do you get their knowledge to stay when they leave? Suggestions are offered to help small businesses.

45840 ■ "Who Needs Budgets?" in *Harvard Business Review* (Vol. 81, No. 2, February 2003, pp. 108)
Pub: Harvard Business School Press
Ed: Jeremy Hope, Robin Fraser. **Description:** The article advocates for the abolishment of budgeting within corporations using hypothetical scenarios and real situations to show that budgets can be detrimental to companies.

45841 ■ "Who's the Boss? Business isn't a democracy" in *Fortune* (Vol. 141, No. 5, March 6, 2000, pp. 432A+)
Pub: Time Inc.
Description: Every company needs an absolute ruler. This article helps you decide if you have what it takes to be a leader.

45842 ■ "Who's bringing you hot ideas, and how are you responding?" in *Harvard Business Review* (Vol. 81, No. 2, February 2003, pp. 58)
Pub: Harvard Business School Press
Ed: Thomas H. Davenport, Laurence Prusak, H. James Wilson. **Description:** Research into business management is presented, especially regarding management and executives who suggest meaningful ideas that benefit the company and calls these individuals idea practitioners.

45843 ■ "Who's Next? Smart Moves" in *Entrepreneur* (Vol. 30, No. 3, March 2002, pp. 77)
Pub: Entrepreneur Media Inc.
Ed: Mark Henricks. **Description:** The importance of having a plan for succession is stressed for all businesses.

45844 ■ *Who's Who in the Management Sciences*
Pub: Edward Elgar Publishing Inc.
Ed: Cary L. Cooper, CBE, Editor. **Price:** $250, individuals hardback. **Covers:** Approximately 330 entries related to management academics including business and policy strategy, human resources, international management, and organizational behavior. **Entries Include:** information on management scholars.

45845 ■ "Why Bad Projects Are So Hard to Kill" in *Harvard Business Review* (Vol. 81, No. 2, February 2003, pp. 48)
Pub: Harvard Business School Press
Ed: Isabelle Royer. **Description:** Research into ways a company might continue to invest money in a technology that will never be marketable, and points out businesses don't often appreciate the need for those individuals who are willing to terminate a bad project.

45846 ■ "Why Can't We Be Friends?" in *Inc.* (January 1, 2004)
Pub: Gruner & Jahr USA Publishing
Ed: Nadine Heintz. **Description:** Small companies may be informal but it is important for management to remain formal in relationships with employees.

45847 ■ "Why Do They Keep Leaving" in *Harvard Business Review* (Vol. 81, No. 2, February 2003, pp. 14)
Pub: Harvard Business School Press
Ed: Jeffrey A. King. **Description:** Statistical analysis of companies that have not gone through a merger show that attrition rates are about 10 percent, while companies that merge have attrition rates nearly double for as long as nine years after the merger. Reasons include stress and perceived lack of advancement opportunities. Research shows that even executives hired after a merger, leave at these elevated rates.

45848 ■ "Why Employees Should Lead Themselves" in *Business 2.0* (Vol. 7, January/February 2006, No. 1, pp. 76)
Pub: Time, Inc.
Ed: Jeffrey Pfeffer. **Description:** Distributed management could help a small business become more innovative and productive.

45849 ■ "Why Executives Fail: Not Enough of the Right Info" in *Crain's Detroit Business* (Vol. 16, No. 20, May 15, 2000, pp. 1)
Pub: Crain Communications, Inc.
Ed: Matt Roush. **Description:** A new study shows that executives wish they had a little bit more information on what's really going on at their companies when they start a new job.

45850 ■ "Why Good Employees Leave" in *Rough Notes* (Vol. 145, No. 12, December 2002, pp. 121)
Pub: Rough Notes
Ed: Emily Huling. **Description:** Good employees leave for various reasons that employers may not be aware. A listing of reasons is presented which includes employees feeling undervalued, used or exploited as well as frustration over office politics or favoritism.

45851 ■ "Why Hard-Nosed Executives Should Care About Management Theory" in *Harvard Business Review* (Vol. 81, No. 9, September 2003, pp. 66)
Pub: Harvard Business School Press
Ed: Clayton M. Christensen, Michael E. Raynor. **Description:** Often, business executives use generic business plans that are in vogue at the moment; creating a sound business theory, as described, is more likely to provide the desired goals.

45852 ■ "Why Hierarchies Thrive" in *Harvard Business Review* (Vol. 81, No. 3, March 2003, pp. 96)
Pub: Harvard Business School Press
Ed: Harold J. Leavit. **Description:** Despite the fact that hardly anyone likes them, hierarchies persist in business, because they fulfill the human need for order and security. However, they are always authoritarian.

45853 ■ "Why Johnny Can't Sell...And What to Do About It" in *Sales & Marketing Management* (Vol. 158, October 2006, No. 10, pp. 54)
Pub: VNU Business Media
Ed: Tali Arbel. **Description:** Review of the book, Why Johnny Can't Sell...And What to Do About It is presented. Authors Michael J. Nick and Robert F. Kantin, sales marketing experts, share insight into tools to help salespeople to reach leads and increase sales.

45854 ■ "Why We Misread Motives" in *Harvard Business Review* (Vol. 81, No. 1, January 2003)
Pub: Harvard Business School Press
Description: Research by Stanford University professor, Chip Heath, suggests that managers tend to have

an extrinsic incentives bias by assuming that others are more driven than they are by external rewards for work. Extrinsic rewards are such things as pay and job security, while intrinsic rewards are learning new skills and contributing to an organization.

45855 ■ "Will I Lose If I Beat the Boss At Racquetball?" in *Fortune* (Vol. 151, January 24, 2005, No. 2, pp. 36)
Pub: Time Inc.
Ed: Anne Fisher. **Description:** A manager may not respect the employee that lets him win at sports. Research shows that people like those who are most like them, so the rule would be to play to win. Many managers report learning more about colleagues and bosses playing a sport with them, than ever learned in a business meeting.

45856 ■ "'Windtunnel' Vision: Air Out Some New Ideas with This Technique" in *Entrepreneur* (Vol. 31, No. 6, June 2003, pp. 76)
Pub: Entrepreneur Media Inc.
Ed: Juanita Weaver. **Description:** A technique for generating new ideas, called windtunnel, is done in pairs. This technique of brainstorming, originated by creative expert Win Wenger, is outlined.

45857 ■ "Winning at Work: What doesn't kill you will make you stronger" in *Atlanta Business Chronicle* (Vol. 25, Nov. 8, 2002, No. 22 pp. 4B)
Pub: American City Business Publications, Inc.
Ed: Connie Glaser. **Description:** Catch phrases concerning the resiliency of professional employees are presented. Suggestions for handling professional disappointments are discussed.

45858 ■ "The Wisdom of Thoughtfulness: In Tight Labor Market, Bosses Find Value in Being Nice" in *The New York Times* (May 31, 2000, pp. C1)
Pub: The New York Times Company
Ed: Amy Zipkin. **Description:** A new survey finds employees value a caring boss more than they value money or fringe benefits.

45859 ■ "With employee retention a headache, a small business builds entertainment into the work routine" in *Wall Street Journal* (March14,2000)
Pub: Dow Jones & Co., Inc.
Ed: Eleena De Lisser. **Description:** A profile of Mid-American Technologies.

45860 ■ "Women integrating workday courage" in *Women in Business* (Vol. 54, No. 2, March-April 2002, pp. 28)
Pub: The ABWA Co Inc.
Ed: Sandra Ford Walston. **Description:** Courage in the workplace is important to utilize. Businesswomen must be accountable and overcome limitations.

45861 ■ "Women Move Up In Manufacturing" in *Fortune* (Vol. 141, No. 10, May 15, 2000, pp. 137B+)
Pub: Time Inc.
Description: The future looks bright for women, because manufacturing will need even more of the kinds of people who are already in short supply: computer scientists, engineers, and design professionals as well as superb communicators and people with vision.

45862 ■ "Women mentoring women" in *Women in Business* (Vol. 53, No. 7, January-February 2002, pp. 28)
Pub: The ABWA Co Inc.
Ed: Lisa Keating. **Description:** There are psychological and professional rewards for the mentor and the person who is mentored. Women mentors can assist new businesswomen to learn how to manage job stress and plan their careers or small business.

45863 ■ "Words from the Wise" in *Entrepreneur* (Vol. 28, No. 1, January 2000, pp. 42)
Pub: Entrepreneur Media Inc.
Ed: Cynthia E. Griffin. **Description:** In Tustin, California there is a non-profit organization dedicated to helping women-owned businesses create their first board of directors or advisory board.

45864 ■ "Work, Interrupted: Think Work Distractions Are a Pain? Top CEOs Tend to Disagree" in *Entrepreneur* (Vol. 32, September 2004, No. 9)
Pub: Entrepreneur Media Inc.
Ed: Mark Henricks. **Description:** According to Stephanie Winston, an organization expert and author, top executives regard interruptions as a valuable tool for connecting with fellow workers.

45865 ■ "Work Like an Insurance Company to Save Money" in *Journal of Accountancy*
Pub: American Institute of Certified Public Accountants
Ed: Joseph A. Gerber, Elliott R. Feldman. **Description:** Financial managers can use the same practices and procedures to recover lost profits as insurance companies use: subrogation, the legal process that permits an insurance company, after paying a policyholder's claim, to sue one or more third parties responsible for causing the damage or injury to the policyholder.

45866 ■ "Work with Me! Resolving Everyday Conflicts in Your Organization" in *Dispute Resolution Journal* (Vol. 56, No. 1, February-April 2001)
Pub: American Arbitration Association
Ed: Cindy Fazzi. **Description:** Book review of the recent publication, "Work with Me! Resolving Everyday Conflicts in Your Organization", which helps management deal with problems arising with employees in small companies.

45867 ■ "The work of leadership" in *Harvard Business Review* (Vol. 79, No. 11, December 2001, pp. 131)
Pub: Harvard Business School Press
Ed: Donald Laurie, Ronald A. Heifitz. **Description:** The authors argue that the most important task for leaders is to mobilize people in their organization to do adaptive work. Six principles for leading adaptive work are presented.

45868 ■ "Workforce Diversity in Small Business" in *Journal of Small Business Management* (Vol. 38, No. 3, July 2000, pp. 27)
Pub: West Virginia University
Ed: Don Gudmundson, Linda S. Hartenian. **Description:** While it would seem that hiring a diverse workforce would be advantageous to any firm that wants to compete globally, such diversity in fact entails costs as well as benefits for the small firm. This study explores the relationship between workforce diversity in small businesses and the small business owner/manager's motivation to diversify, the owner/manager's personal characteristics (ethnicity, age, education, and gender), and the number of family members employed in the small business.

45869 ■ "Working Hard for the Money" in *Black Enterprise* (Vol. 36, February 2006, No. 7, pp. 44)
Pub: Earl G. Graves Publishing Co. Inc.
Ed: Brenda Porter. **Description:** Black women with bachelor's degrees are securing more positions than Hispanic and white women with the same education level. The trend may be a result of black women working more hours and/or working more than job.

45870 ■ "Working It: A Surge in Part-Time Workers Can Pay Off for Your Business" in *Entrepreneur* (Vol. 32, December 2004, No. 12, pp. 22)
Pub: Entrepreneur Media Inc.
Ed: Mark Henricks. **Description:** The number of persons working part-time in the U.S. grew from 24.3 million to 25.5 million in the first half of 2004. Employers rarely offer employer-paid health insurance and other benefits, thus making part-time hiring attractive to small companies.

45871 ■ "Working With Women" in *My Business* (April/May 2003, pp. 14)
Pub: My Business Magazine
Ed: Mardy Fones. **Description:** Ways in which women business owners can grow a business by effectively managing female employees are addressed in a question/answer format.

45872 ■ "Workplace" in *Business 2.0* (Vol. 6, July 2005, No. 6, pp. 109)
Pub: Time, Inc.
Ed: Michael V. Copeland. **Description:** Executives at Ventura, California's Patagonia hit the surf when the swell is good. The firm, an outdoor-gear maker, admits the outdoor recreation helps promote a dedicated staff.

45873 ■ "The workplace: learn to do more with less" in *Atlanta Business Chronicle* (Vol. 25, No. 20, October 25, 2002, pp. 12B)
Pub: American City Business Publications, Inc.
Ed: Emory Mulling. **Description:** Suggestions are given to improve workplace performance in these trying economic times. Training and matching the right person with the right skills for each job is important. Additionally, it is important to recognize that employees want to be developed and to increase their work skills base.

45874 ■ "Writing her own e-ticket" in *WorkingWoman* (Vol. 25, No. 8, September 2000, pp. 20)
Pub: Lang Communications Inc.
Ed: Susan Caminiti. **Description:** Priceline.com Chief Financial Officer (CFO) Heidi Miller talks about her plans for new role and of leaving Citigroup where she was also CFO.

45875 ■ "WSJ Honors Economist" in *Hispanic Business* (June 2005, pp. 18)
Pub: Hispanic Business
Description: Maria Fiorini Ramierez, president and CEO of her global economic and financial consulting firm of the same name, was named one of the top two economists in the U.S. in forecasting the actual rate of inflation during the last three years by The Wall Street Journal.

45876 ■ "Year to Success" in *Small Business Opportunities* (Vol. 17, May 2005, No. 3, pp. 126)
Pub: Harris Publications Inc.
Description: Review of Year to Success, written by Bo Bennett. The book shares the wisdom and words of success stories and the insight of political leaders, CEOs, entrepreneurs, inventors and celebrities. The author highlights ways to handle mistakes, make a strong impression, make decisions, and create good situations from bad ones.

45877 ■ "Yes, No, Maybe So" in *Inc.* (August 1, 2003)
Pub: Gruner & Jahr USA Publishing
Ed: John Koten. **Description:** The silent treatment is one of the oldest tactics in journalism, but can also be used in business negotiations.

45878 ■ "You can't lead without making sacrifices" in *Fast Company* (June 2001, pp. 106)
Pub: Fast Company
Ed: Randy Hopper. **Description:** Profile of the U.S. Military Academy, recognized for its Grassroots Leadership Home Base, located in West Point, New York.

45879 ■ "You First: An Opening Move May Make or Break a Deal-So Step Lightly" in *Entrepreneur* (Vol. 33, March 2005, No. 3, pp. 96)
Pub: Entrepreneur Media Inc.
Ed: Marc Diener. **Description:** Negotiation tips are offered to help close deals.

45880 ■ "You Should Be the Boss of Them" in *My Business* (June/July 2004, pp. 51)
Pub: My Business Magazine
Ed: Jackie Van Nice. **Description:** It is essential for small business owners to know and understand all employees and the jobs they perform.

45881 ■ "Your Boss is Watching" in *PC Computing* (March 2000, pp. 86)
Pub: Ziff-Davis Inc.
Description: Web monitoring software is used by 45 percent of all companies and 17 percent of Fortune 1000 companies to make sure employees are not misusing the Web while at work. The WinWhatWhere Investigator software can record every keystroke an employee enters on a PC, while Elron Software's CommandView has the Message Inspector module that filters, stores and blocks emails at the network server. The article recommends that employees should minimize non-business-related web browsing on the company's computer.

45882 ■ "Your Business needs to be E-Commerce - so what now?" in *Ingram's* (Vol. 27, No. 7, July 2001, pp. 19)
Pub: Show Me Publishing, Inc.
Description: Management techniques and theory are outlined for e-commerce management. Some techniques include treating online and offline sales the same way, organize and prioritize what the Website needs to accomplish, and consider market potential.

45883 ■ "Your Secret Weapon" in *Small Business Opportunities* (Vol. 16, No. 3, May 2004, pp. 10, 120)
Pub: Harris Publications, Inc.
Ed: Lynn A. Robinson. **Description:** Intuition can be the secret weapon used to make successful sales.

45884 ■ "You've got to keep your nose down and your fanny up" in *Fast Company* (May 2001, pp. 92)
Pub: Fast Company
Ed: Robert L. Crandall. **Description:** Former CEO for American Airlines/AMR Corporation, Robert Crandall, created a number of breakthrough programs including AAdvantage, the industry's first frequent-flier program.

45885 ■ "Zander's Chip Shot; New CEO Faces Tough Call on Semiconductor Unit" in *Crain's Chicago Business* (Vol. 26, No. 51, December 22, 2003)
Pub: Crain Communications, Inc.
Ed: Julie Johnsson. **Description:** Edward Zander, new CEO of Motorola Inc., is faced with the dilemma to sell or spin off the company's struggling semiconductor unit. The company is making plans for an initial public offering of its chip business, which saw $5 billion in revenue, but is also considering interest from rivals and private-equity firms.

45886 ■ "Zen and the Art of Management Coaching" in *Inc.* (February 1, 2002)
Pub: Inc. Magazine
Ed: Andrew Raskin. **Description:** A discussion about management coaching is presented.

TRADE PERIODICALS

45887 ■ *Chief Executive Officer's Newsletter*
Pub: Chief Executive Officers Clubs
Ed: Joe Manuso, Editor. **Released:** Monthly. **Price:** Included in membership; $96, nonmembers. **Description:** "Designed to provide accurate and authoritative information relative to subjects of concern to entrepreneurial managers." Covers management, taxes, finance, marketing, information sources, and educational programs. Recurring features include news of seminars, book reviews, news of research and survey results, and columns titled Entrepreneurs's Hall of Fame, Mind Your Own Business, Resources, Accounting, Personal, Miscellaneous, and The Business Exchange.

45888 ■ *Harvard Management Update*
Pub: Harvard Business School Publishing
Ed: Loren Gary, Editor. **Released:** Monthly. **Price:** $99, U.S.; $169, Canada and Mexico; $189, elsewhere; $210, two years in USA. **Description:** Provides information on current management techniques and trends.

45889 ■ *Human Factors in Ergonomics and Manufacturing*
Pub: John Wiley & Sons Inc.
Ed: Waldemar Karwoski, Editor. **Released:** 4/yr. **Price:** $205; $205 Canada and Mexico in Canada,

add 7% GST; $229 other countries; $780 institutions; $820 institutions, Canada and Mexico in Canada, add 7% GST; $854 institutions, other countries. **Description:** International journal focusing on the design, management, and operation of advanced manufacturing systems. Covers human resource management, social and organizational issues, cognitive engineering, human factors, and safety and health.

45890 ■ *Innovative Leader*
Pub: Winston J. Brill & Associates
Contact: Winston J. Brill
E-mail: wbrill@winstonbrill.com
Released: Monthly. **Price:** Free. **Description:** Serves as a resource for managers on creativity and productivity.

45891 ■ *Journal of Economics and Management Strategy*
Pub: MIT Press
Ed: Daniel F. Spulber, Editor. **Released:** Quarterly. **Price:** $53 print & online; $50 online only; $298 institutions print & premium online; $271 institutions print & standard online; $257 institutions premium online. **Description:** Journal providing a forum for research and discussion on competitive strategies of managers and the organizational structure of firms.

45892 ■ *Journal of Innovative Management*
Pub: GOAL/QPC
Contact: Monique Mazejka, Mktg. Mgr.
Released: Quarterly. **Price:** $99 Canada; $119 other countries; $198 Canada 2 years; $208 other countries 2 years; $99 U.S.; $168 two years U.S. **Description:** Journal focusing on news and information on quality management, systems thinking, and creativity and innovation.

45893 ■ *Journal of Management*
Pub: University of California Press
Ed: Daniel Feldman, Editor. **Released:** Bimonthly. **Price:** $165; $441 institutions. **Description:** Scholarly journal.

45894 ■ *The Journal for Quality and Participation*
Pub: American Society for Quality
Released: Quarterly, 4/yr. **Price:** $95 institutions international; $45 domestic, members; $70 international, members; $65 Canada, members; $75 domestic, non-members; $85 international, non-members; $85 Canada, non-members. **Description:** Journal covering total quality management and employee involvement processes.

45895 ■ *Journal of Small Business Management*
Pub: Bureau of Business and Economic Research
Contact: Linda Moore, Business Mgr
Ed: Patrick C. Mann, Ph.D., Editor. **Released:** Quarterly. **Price:** $20 single issue Prior to 1998 copies. **Description:** Magazine dedicated to the development of entrepreneurship and small business management through education, research, and the free exchange of ideas.

45896 ■ *Leadership Strategies*
Pub: Briefings Publishing Group
Ed: Nona Aguilar, Editor. **Released:** Monthly. **Price:** $99. **Description:** Offers information and advice for effective business leadership.

45897 ■ *Make It A Winning Life*
Pub: Wolf Rinke Associates,Inc.
Ed: Wolf J. Rinke, Ph.D., Editor, wolfrinke@aol.com. **Released:** Bimonthly. **Price:** Free. **Description:** Features ideas and strategies to help individuals succeed faster and improve the quality of their life. Remarks: America Online, Inc.

45898 ■ *Management Report for Nonunion Organizations*
Pub: John Wiley and Sons Inc.
Ed: Sarah Magee, Editor. **Released:** Monthly. **Price:** $995, U.S.; $995, Canada and Mexico; $1067, elsewhere. **Description:** Features news on current activi-

ties; employers' responses; NLRB rulings; court cases; pending legislation; government policies; and advice and opinions from Alfred T. DeMaria, "one of the country's foremost labor lawyers" representing management. Includes information on preventive tactics on how to handle human resources and labor issues without risking unionization, a campaign workshop on what the laws and regulations mean in terms of day-to-day management, white-collar organizing, and questions and answers on common problems.

45899 ■ *The Manager's Intelligence Report*
Pub: Lawrence Ragan Communications Inc.
Contact: Gretchen Eisenfelder
Ed: Steve Crescenzo, Editor. **Released:** Monthly. **Price:** $129; $159, Canada. **Description:** Provides strategies and ideas to help boost employee morale, save time on the job, and aid career advancement.

45900 ■ *The Motivational Manager*
Pub: Lawrence Ragan Communications Inc.
Contact: Gretchen Eisenfelder
Ed: Steve Crescenzo, Editor. **Released:** Monthly. **Price:** $119; $159, Canada. **Description:** Provides strategies and ideas to help inspire employees. Covers hiring, training, and recognizing and retaining strong employees through participative management.

45901 ■ *The Navigator*
Pub: Chart Your Course International
Contact: Gregory P. Smith, President
E-mail: greg@chartcourse.com
Released: Quarterly. **Price:** Free. **Description:** Publishes advice, how-to tips, and trends in business, including management, TQM, leadership, customer service. Recurring features include news of research, a calendar of events, and a column titled Improving Productivity.

45902 ■ *Positive Leadership*
Pub: Lawrence Ragan Communications Inc.
Contact: Lisa Ban
Ed: John Cowan, Editor. **Released:** Monthly. **Price:** $139; $159, Canada. **Description:** Provides information about hiring and motivating top employees, dealing with work/family issues, giving back to your community, and becoming a more respected, ethical manager.

45903 ■ *Quality Management Journal*
Pub: American Society for Quality
Contact: William Tony, Publisher
Ed: Barbara Flynn, Editor. **Released:** Quarterly. **Price:** $50 U.S. members; $80 Canada members; $74 other countries members; $75 U.S. non-members; $95 Canada non-members; $90 other countries non-members; $130 U.S. institutions; $160 Canada institutions; $150 other countries institutions. **Description:** Academic journal covering the development of quality management literature.

45904 ■ *Quality Manager's Alert*
Pub: Progressive Business Publications
Ed: Jim Giuliano, Editor. **Released:** Semimonthly. **Price:** $299, individuals. **Description:** Communicates the latest information on changing quality standards and how companies get buy-in on quality from employees. Recurring features include interviews, news of research, a calendar of events, news of educational opportunities, and a column titled Sharpen Your Judgment.

45905 ■ *Self Employment Update*
Pub: Update Publicare Co.
Contact: A. Doyle
Ed: A.C. Doyle, Editor. **Released:** Annual. **Description:** Introduces readers to the broad interest of self-employment. Carries news of relevant books. Recurring features include news of research and ideas for small businesses.

45906 ■ *Small Business Executive Report*
Pub: Charles Moore Associates Inc.
Released: Monthly. **Description:** Covers economic and commercial trends and other information related to small businesses.

45907 ■ *Small Business Taxes and Management*
Pub: A/N Group Inc.
Contact: Steven A. Hopfenmuller, Publisher
Released: Semimonthly, Daily (Mon. thru Fri.). **Price:** $49.95. **Description:** Offers current tax news, reviews of recent cases, tax saving tips, and personal financial planning for small business owners. Includes articles on issues such as finance and management. Remarks: Available online only

45908 ■ *Small Farm News*
Pub: Small Farm Center
Contact: Susan McCue
Ed: Susan McCue, Editor, semccue@ucdavis.edu. **Released:** Quarterly, 4/year. **Price:** Free. **Description:** Covers topics of interest to small farmers. Includes farmer profiles, government actions and crop information. Recurring features include letters to the editor, interviews, news of research, a calendar of events, notices of publications available, Directors' Column, resources section, news notes, and program news.

45909 ■ *Supervisors Legal Update*
Pub: Progressive Business Publications
Ed: Thomas J. Gorman, IV, Editor. **Released:** Semimonthly. **Price:** $94.56, individuals. **Description:** Supplies brief updates on employment law for supervisors. Review a column titled Sharpen Your Judgment.

45910 ■ *Utility Automation*
Pub: PennWell Corp.
Contact: Michael Grossman, Publisher
E-mail: michaelg@pennwell.com
Ed: Steven M. Brown, Editor, stevenb@pennwell.com. **Released:** 7/yr. **Description:** Trade publication addressing technology issues, innovations, and applications for the utilities industry.

45911 ■ *Your New Pryor Report Managers Edge*
Pub: Briefings Publishing Group
Ed: Joe McGavin, Editor. **Released:** Monthly. **Price:** $97, U.S.; $117, Canada; $147, elsewhere. **Description:** Features information for managers.

VIDEOCASSETTES/AUDIOCASSETTES

45912 ■ *American Business Management Series*
Instructional Video
2219 C St.
Lincoln, NE 68502
Ph:(402)475-6570
Free: 800-228-0164
Fax: (402)475-6500
Co. E-mail: feedback@insvideo.com
URL: http://www.insvideo.com
Description: Management training series offers instruction on many of today's business and management issues. **Availability:** VHS.

45913 ■ *Anticipation: Rx for Crisis Management*
Aspen Publishers
7201 McKinney Circ.
Frederick, MD 21704
Ph:(301)644-3599
Free: 800-638-8437
Fax: (301)644-3550
URL: http://www.aspenpublishers.com
Released: 1991. **Price:** $495.00. **Description:** A guide for supervisors on analyzing daily work situations in order to avoid trouble before it happens. **Availability:** VHS; 3/4U.

45914 ■ *The Art of Negotiating*
Aspen Publishers
7201 McKinney Circ.
Frederick, MD 21704
Ph:(301)644-3599
Free: 800-638-8437

Fax: (301)644-3550
URL: http://www.aspenpublishers.com
Released: 1991. **Price:** $495.00. **Description:** Supervisors and managers will learn how to get what they want with seven basic strategies in the fine art of negotiation. Hosted by master negotiator and world renowned counselor Gerard Nierenberg. **Availability:** VHS; 3/4U.

45915 ■ *Beyond Start-Up: Management Lessons for Growing Companies*
Video Arts, Inc.
c/o Aim Learning Group
8238-40 Lehigh
Morton Grove, IL 60053-2615
Free: 877-444-2230
Fax: (416)252-2155
Co. E-mail: service@aimlearninggroup.com
URL: http://www.aimlearninggroup.com
Released: 1989. **Price:** $395.00. **Description:** Don't settle for being a small company—find out what it takes to expand your business. **Availability:** VHS; 3/4U.

45916 ■ *Carl Rogers: Communication and Management*
Salenger Films, Inc.
1635 12th St.
Santa Monica, CA 90404-9988
Ph:(310)450-1300
Free: 800-775-5025
Fax: (310)450-1010
Co. E-mail: salenger@aol.com
URL: http://salengerfilms.visualnet.com
Released: 1986. **Description:** A conversation with Dr. Carl Rogers about efficient business management. **Availability:** 3/4U; Special order formats.

45917 ■ *Center on Profit*
International Dairy-Deli-Bakery Association (IDDBA)
313 Price Pl., Ste. 202
PO Box 5528
Madison, WI 53705-0528
Ph:(608)238-7908
Fax: (608)238-6330
Co. E-mail: iddba@iddba.org
Price: $160.00. **Description:** Teaches managers how to reduce unknown shrink, write effective orders and schedules, plus calculate deli items' profit and gross margin contribution to margin. **Availability:** VHS.

45918 ■ *Competing Through Information Technology*
Government VideoSource, Inc.
461 Miller Dr.
Elgin, IL 60123-7232
Ph:(847)931-1955
Released: 1994. **Price:** $1450.00. **Description:** Senior managers from companies like Corning, Becton Dickinson, Unilever and others explore applications of a transitional solution to adopting a specific management model. **Availability:** VHS.

45919 ■ *Days of Reckoning*
Film Library/Greater Los Angeles Safety Council
600 Wilshire Blvd., No. 1263
Los Angeles, CA 90017
Ph:(213)385-6461
Free: 800-421-9585
Fax: (213)385-8405
URL: http://www.lasafety.org
Released: 198?. **Description:** This film chronicles the fables of managing a small business **Availability:** VHS; 3/4U.

45920 ■ *Dealing with Difficult People Volume Two*
RMI Media
1365 N. Winchester
Olathe, KS 66061
Ph:(913)768-1696
Fax: (913)768-0184
Co. E-mail: actmedia@act.org
URL: http://www.rmimedia.com
Released: 1993. **Price:** $99.00. **Description:** Ed Greif explains how to handle very difficult problems with people. **Availability:** VHS.

45921 ■ *Delegating Responsibility*
1st Financial Training Services
1515 E. Woodfield Rd., Ste. 345
Schaumburg, IL 60173
Ph:(847)969-0900
Free: 800-442-8662
Fax: (847)969-0521
Co. E-mail: sales@1stfinancialtraining.com
URL: http://www.1stfinancialtraining.com
Released: 1987. **Price:** $150.00. **Description:** A primer for managers in dispersing and assigning work to employees. **Availability:** VHS; 3/4U.

45922 ■ *Discipline: A Matter of Judgment*
Encyclopedia Britannica
331 N. LaSalle St.
Chicago, IL 60610
Ph:(312)347-7159
Free: 800-323-1229
Fax: (312)294-2104
URL: http://www.britannica.com
Released: 1989. **Description:** This video teaches that discipline must educate, not humiliate, and urges fair, prompt, and consistent disciplinary action. **Availability:** VHS; 3/4U.

45923 ■ *Don't Keep It To Yourself*
Instructional Video
2219 C St.
Lincoln, NE 68502
Ph:(402)475-6570
Free: 800-228-0164
Fax: (402)475-6500
Co. E-mail: feedback@insvideo.com
URL: http://www.insvideo.com
Price: $150.00. **Description:** Part of the Super Vision for the '90s management training series. Discusses the importance of communication between supervisor and employees. Also provides information on how to increase productivity and decrease tension. **Availability:** VHS.

45924 ■ *Empowerment: The Attitude Opportunity*
International Training Consultants, Inc.
1838 Park Oaks
Kemah, TX 77565
Free: 800-998-8764
Co. E-mail: itc@trainingitc.com
URL: http://www.trainingitc.com
Price: $495.00. **Description:** Part of the "Empowerment: The Employee Development Series." Teaches employees to accept responsibility for their attitude problems, seeing them as opportunities for improvement, and offers them tips on how to make the transition from attitude problem to attitude opportunity. Also provides information on how to monitor and reward their progress. Comes with leader's guide, self-study instructions, and five participant booklets. **Availability:** VHS.

45925 ■ *Everything You Always Wanted to Know about Management*
American Media, Inc.
4621 121st St.
Urbandale, IA 50323-2311
Ph:(515)224-0919
Free: 888-776-8268
Fax: (515)327-2555
Co. E-mail: custsvc@ammedia.com
URL: http://www.ammedia.com
Released: 1995. **Price:** $595. **Description:** Outlines the essentials of good management, including the six steps of delegation, employee empowerment, communication, feedback, and goal achievement. Includes course guide with participant exercises and case studies. **Availability:** VHS; CC.

45926 ■ *Finding Your 15%*
RMI Media
1365 N. Winchester
Olathe, KS 66061
Ph:(913)768-1696
Fax: (913)768-0184
Co. E-mail: actmedia@act.org
URL: http://www.rmimedia.com
Description: Host Gareth Morgan tells us there is actually little we can control in our lives. So, in this video

intended for business managers trying to make changes, the narrator recommends that we work hard on percentage that we can control, and that change should come only in increments. **Availability:** VHS.

45927 ■ *Leadership Skills by Aaron Alejandro*
Cambridge Educational
c/o Films Media Group
PO Box 2053
Princeton, NJ 08843-2053
Free: 800-257-5126
Fax: (609)671-0266
Co. E-mail: custserve@filmsmediagroup.com
URL: http://www.cambridgeol.com
Released: 1991. **Price:** $79.95. **Description:** Fast-paced leadership workshop designed to develop and sharpen leadership skills. **Availability:** VHS.

45928 ■ *Looking at It from Every Angle*
American Management Association
9 Galen St.
PO Box 9119
Watertown, MA 02472
Ph:(617)926-4600
Free: 800-225-3215
Fax: (617)923-1875
URL: http://www.amanet.org
Released: 1985. **Description:** An analysis of proper business training in terms of management decision-making, problem-solving efficiency and department use. **Availability:** VHS; 3/4U.

45929 ■ *Love and Profit: The Art of Caring Leadership*
Government VideoSource, Inc.
461 Miller Dr.
Elgin, IL 60123-7232
Ph:(847)931-1955
Released: 1994. **Price:** $695.00. **Description:** James Autry, Fortune 500 executive and business consultant, reviews four basic elements of progressive leadership: trust, honesty, special treatment, and courage. Includes leader's guide and a participant workbook. **Availability:** VHS.

45930 ■ *Management Action Program*
Format International
2421 E. Washington St.
Indianapolis, IN 46201-4123
Released: 1986. **Price:** $680.00. **Description:** A series of videos that look at customer service, innovation and productivity. **Availability:** VHS; 8mm; 3/4U; Special order formats.

45931 ■ *Management: Emphasize Your Strengths*
Direct Cinema Ltd.
PO Box 10003
Santa Monica, CA 90410-1003
Ph:(310)636-8200
Free: 800-525-0000
Fax: (310)636-8228
Co. E-mail: orders@directcinemalimited.com
URL: http://www.directcinema.com
Released: 1985. **Description:** A management training program emphasizing personal strengths. **Availability:** VHS; 3/4U.

45932 ■ *Management 1*
MR Communication Consultants Inc.
340 Sheppard Ave E, Ste. 300
Toronto, ON, Canada M2N 3B4
Ph:(416)539-9520
Free: 800-263-8326
Fax: (416)539-9604
Co. E-mail: info@mrcomm.com
URL: http://www.mrcomm.com
Released: 1980. **Description:** A course intended to teach supervisors the fundamental skills to apply to their work situation. **Availability:** VHS; 3/4U.

45933 ■ *Management Techniques That Work*
Instructional Video
2219 C St.
Lincoln, NE 68502
Ph:(402)475-6570

Free: 800-228-0164
Fax: (402)475-6500
Co. E-mail: feedback@insvideo.com
URL: http://www.insvideo.com
Price: $89.95. **Description:** Three management experts discuss techniques to improve productivity while also improving the workplace environment. Also looks at participative management and other techniques. **Availability:** VHS.

45934 ■ *The Management of Work*
Resources for Education & Management, Inc.
1804 Montreal Ct., Ste. A
Tucker, GA 30084
Description: A series intended to show managers how to build the key skills of organizing, planning, directing, and controlling. **Availability:** VHS; 3/4U.

45935 ■ *MBA—Management Basics in Action*
Phoenix Learning Group
2349 Chaffee Dr.
St. Louis, MO 63146
Ph:(314)569-0211
Free: 800-221-1274
Fax: (314)569-2834
URL: http://www.phoenixlearninggroup.com
Released: 1985. **Description:** A program library for management of business. **Availability:** VHS.

45936 ■ *Nobody's Perfect: Managing the Team*
Video Arts, Inc.
c/o Aim Learning Group
8238-40 Lehigh
Morton Grove, IL 60053-2615
Free: 877-444-2230
Fax: (416)252-2155
Co. E-mail: service@aimlearninggroup.com
URL: http://www.aimlearninggroup.com
Released: 1991. **Price:** $790.00. **Description:** How to put the right people in the right position on a team, enhancing win potential and covering weak spots. **Availability:** VHS; 8mm; 3/4U; Special order formats.

45937 ■ *One Small Step*
Film Library/Greater Los Angeles Safety Council
600 Wilshire Blvd., No. 1263
Los Angeles, CA 90017
Ph:(213)385-6461
Free: 800-421-9585
Fax: (213)385-8405
URL: http://www.lasafety.org
Released: 198?. **Description:** This film looks at how managers can improve their work environments through better communication with their employees. **Availability:** VHS; 3/4U.

45938 ■ *Organizational Transactions*
Professional Development, Inc.
27955 Clemens Rd.
Westlake, OH 44145
Ph:(216)892-0770
Fax: (216)892-0105
Released: 1986. **Description:** A series of training films about optimum managerial organization. **Availability:** VHS; 3/4U; Special order formats.

45939 ■ *Performance Management: The Road to Excellence*
Aspen Publishers
7201 McKinney Circ.
Frederick, MD 21704
Ph:(301)644-3599
Free: 800-638-8437
Fax: (301)644-3550
URL: http://www.aspenpublishers.com
Released: 1985. **Price:** $495.00. **Description:** Employee work levels tend to increase when positive attributes and contributions are stressed. Learn how to implement this performance plan with these helpful tips. **Availability:** VHS; 3/4U; Special order formats.

45940 ■ *Performance Standards and Objectives*
L & K International Training
3065 Ridgeway Dr., Unit 34
Mississauga, ON, Canada L5M 5M6

Ph:(905)270-6200
Fax: (905)270-3786
Co. E-mail: inquiry@lk-intl.com
URL: http://www.lk-intl.com
Released: 1987. **Price:** $365.00. **Description:** Mike Powell talks about how objectives can be used to increase productivity. **Availability:** VHS; 3/4U.

45941 ■ *Principles of Management*
RMI Media
1365 N. Winchester
Olathe, KS 66061
Ph:(913)768-1696
Fax: (913)768-0184
Co. E-mail: actmedia@act.org
URL: http://www.rmimedia.com
Released: 1987. **Description:** These videos describe the basic skills needed for effective management. **Availability:** VHS; 3/4U.

45942 ■ *Problem Solving: A Process for Managers*
Encyclopedia Britannica
331 N. LaSalle St.
Chicago, IL 60610
Ph:(312)347-7159
Free: 800-323-1229
Fax: (312)294-2104
URL: http://www.britannica.com
Released: 1989. **Description:** This program introduces managers to a practical, efficient six-step problem solving method applicable to most management problems. **Availability:** 3/4U.

45943 ■ *Training Needs Assessment*
Aspen Publishers
7201 McKinney Circ.
Frederick, MD 21704
Ph:(301)644-3599
Free: 800-638-8437
Fax: (301)644-3550
URL: http://www.aspenpublishers.com
Released: 1986. **Price:** $495.00. **Description:** Supervisor Dave Eppinger explains the process of training needs assessment and discusses the characteristics necessary for a completely efficient system. **Availability:** VHS; 3/4U.

45944 ■ *What Went Wrong?*
Aspen Publishers
7201 McKinney Circ.
Frederick, MD 21704
Ph:(301)644-3599
Free: 800-638-8437
Fax: (301)644-3550
URL: http://www.aspenpublishers.com
Released: 1985. **Price:** $495.00. **Description:** An instructional seminar in the art of decision-making and problem-solving in business. **Availability:** VHS; 3/4U.

45945 ■ *Where There's a Will...(Leadership and Motivation)*
Video Arts, Inc.
c/o Aim Learning Group
8238-40 Lehigh
Morton Grove, IL 60053-2615
Free: 877-444-2230
Fax: (416)252-2155
Co. E-mail: service@aimlearninggroup.com
URL: http://www.aimlearninggroup.com
Released: 1988. **Price:** $790.00. **Description:** Find out how you can motivate your workers to a higher productivity level. **Availability:** VHS; 8mm; 3/4U; Special order formats.

45946 ■ *Who Does What?*
Aspen Publishers
7201 McKinney Circ.
Frederick, MD 21704
Ph:(301)644-3599
Free: 800-638-8437
Fax: (301)644-3550
URL: http://www.aspenpublishers.com
Released: 1989. **Price:** $495.00. **Description:** Supervisors will learn how to delegate authority and maximize employee productivity and time management by implementing a nine step checklist, demonstrated through a variety of workplace dramatizations. **Availability:** VHS; 3/4U.

45947 ■ *Winning Entrepreneurial Style*
Orion Home Video
MGM
2500 Broadway, 3515
Santa Monica, CA 90404-3036
Ph:(310)449-3000
Released: 1986. **Description:** A bevy of nationwide entrepreneurs share their secrets for financial success. **Availability:** VHS; CC.

TRADE SHOWS AND CONVENTIONS

45948 ■ Alliance Texas
Showorks Inc.
1325 W. 1st Ave., Ste. 312
Spokane, WA 99201
Ph:(509)838-8755
Fax: (509)838-2838
Co. E-mail: showorks@showorksinc.com
URL: http://www.showorksinc.com
Audience: Buyers and contracting officers from military bases. **Principal Exhibits:** Small business procurement opportunities.

CONSULTANTS

45949 ■ ABA Inc.
24 Wellesley St. W, Ste. 411
Toronto, ON, Canada M4Y 2X6
Ph:(416)219-8447
Fax: (416)924-4664
Co. E-mail: info@abaconsult.com
URL: http://www.abaconsult.com

E-mail: info@abaconsult.com
Scope: Firm provides management consultation to emerging and growth oriented companies in the Internet, film and television, and multimedia industries. Areas of expertise include planning and developing best practices in strategy, finance, marketing, HR, and operations. Services range from full strategy papers to business/marketing plans, and financial performance reviews. **Seminars:** Reduces Cycle Time; Cuts Costs; Improves Learning; Facilitates Accountability.

45950 ■ Advanced Benefits & Human Resources
9350-F Snowden River Pky., Ste. 222
Columbia, MD 21045
Ph:(410)290-9037
Fax: (410)740-2568
Co. E-mail: hrb@abhr.com

E-mail: hrb@abhr.com
Scope: Provides human resource consulting to high technology businesses. Offers services in the areas of human resources, benefits, and training. Creates, maintains, or updates current human resource functions.

45951 ■ Advisory Management Services Inc.
9600 E 129th St., Ste. B
Kansas City, MO 64149-1025
Ph:(816)765-9611
Fax: (816)765-7447
Co. E-mail: amsi1@mindspring.com

E-mail: amsi1@mindspring.com
Scope: A management consulting and training firm specializing in employee relations, management and staff training, organizational development, strategic planning, and continuous quality improvement.

45952 ■ Charles J. Allen and Associates
2668 Foxglove St.
Woodridge, IL 60517
Ph:(630)963-1444
Scope: Specializes in marketing, communication, advertising and promotional consulting. Also serves as business management consultants on a continuing basis.

45953 ■ The Alliance Management Group Inc.
38 Old Chester Rd., Ste. 300
Gladstone, NJ 07934
Ph:(908)234-2344
Fax: (908)234-0638
Co. E-mail: Kathy@strategicalliance.com
URL: http://www.strategicalliance.com

E-mail: Kathy@strategicalliance.com
Publications: Allocating Patent Rights in Collaborative Research Agreements; Protecting Know-how and Trade Secrets in Collaborative Research Agreements, Aug, 2006; Sourcing External Technology for Innovation, Jun, 2006.

45954 ■ Alliance Management International Ltd.
PO Box 470691
Cleveland, OH 44147-0691
Ph:(440)838-1922
Fax: (928)752-5728
Co. E-mail: bgruss@cox.net
URL: http://www.members.cox.net/bgruss

E-mail: bgruss@cox.net
Scope: A consulting company that helps to form national and international strategic alliances. Handles alliances between companies forming joint ventures. Staff specialized in small company-large company alliance, alliance assessment and analysis, and alliance strategic planning. **Seminars:** Joint Business Planning; Developing a Shared Vision; Current and New/Prospective Partner Assessment; Customer Service; Sales Training; Leader and Management Skills.

45955 ■ Allsup Inc.
300 Allsup Pl.
Belleville, IL 62223
Ph:(618)234-8434
Free: 800-854-1418
Fax: (618)236-5778
Co. E-mail: info@allsupinc.com
URL: http://www.allsupinc.com

E-mail: info@allsupinc.com
Scope: A business management consulting firm serving clients in the U.S. Social Security and Medicare reimbursement services. **Publications:** The Allsup Alternative, bi-monthly magazine.

45956 ■ AMC International Inc.
PO Box 11292
Beverly Hills, CA 90213-4292
Ph:(310)652-5620
Fax: (310)652-6709
Co. E-mail: inquiry@amcusa.com
URL: http://www.amcusa.com

E-mail: inquiry@amcusa.com
Scope: Offers day-to-day business management, business turnaround, marketing strategies, development/refinement of corporate mission, and merger and acquisition evaluations. Industries served: all.

45957 ■ The American Supplier Institute
38705 7 Mile Rd., Ste. 345
Livonia, MI 48152
Ph:(734)464-1395
Free: 800-462-4500
Fax: (734)464-1399
Co. E-mail: asi@asiusa.com
URL: http://www.amsup.com

E-mail: asi@asiusa.com
Scope: Provides business management assistance and quality control consulting to automotive and industrial clients worldwide. **Publications:** The Ice Cream Maker; Design for Six Sigma:The Revolutionary Process for Achieving Extraordinary Profits, Hardcover, 2002. **Seminars:** SIX SIGMA; ROBUST ENGINEERING; Quality Tools.

45958 ■ Anderson/Roethle Inc.
700 N Water St., Ste. 1100
Milwaukee, WI 53202
Ph:(414)276-0070

Fax: (414)276-4364
Co. E-mail: info@anderson-roethle.com
URL: http://www.anderson-roethle.com

E-mail: info@anderson-roethle.com
Scope: Provides merger, acquisition and divestiture advisory services. Offers strategic planning, valuations and specialized M&A advisory services.

45959 ■ Apex Innovations Inc.
14830 W 117th St., Ste. 200
PO Box 15208
Olathe, KS 66062
Ph:(816)561-7787
Fax: (913)254-0320
URL: http://www.apex-innovations.com
Scope: A firm of business operations and technology professionals providing solutions nationwide for business needs. Provides a bridge between operations and technology for clients in manufacturing, insurance, banking, and government. Offers services in business planning, assessment, education, business performance improvement, change management, and the planning, and implementation management of solutions. **Special Services:** i-INFO.

45960 ■ Scott Ashby Teleselling Inc.
1102 Ben Franklin Dr., Ste. 309
Sarasota, FL 34236
Ph:(941)388-4283
Fax: (941)388-5240
Co. E-mail: rscottashby@netscape.net
URL: http://www.scottashbyteleselling.com

E-mail: rscottashby@netscape.net
Scope: Provides consulting services and customized training programs that emphasize consultative telephone selling techniques. **Publications:** "How Will The Internet Affect Teleselling Programs?"; "When is Telemarketing Really Not Telemarketing?"; "The Future of Account Management Telesales".

45961 ■ Aurora Management Partners Inc.
4485 Tench Rd., Ste. 340A
Suwanee, GA 30024
Ph:(770)904-5207
Co. E-mail: rturcotte@auroramp.com
URL: http://www.auroramp.com

E-mail: rturcotte@auroramp.com
Scope: Firm specializes in turnaround management and reorganization consulting. **Publications:** Back From The Brink - Bland Farms; New Breed of Turnaround Managers; Key Performance Drivers - Bland Farms; The Missing Element in Corporate Governance Ratings.

45962 ■ Automated Accounting
13800 Heacock St.
Moreno Valley, CA 92553
Ph:(951)653-5053
Co. E-mail: autoacc@earthlink.net

E-mail: autoacc@earthlink.net
Scope: A business management consulting firm that caters to small businesses. Services include part-time chief, financial officer services. Also offers software installation services, tax preparation services and business plan advisory services.

45963 ■ Avery, Cooper & Co.
4918-50th St.
PO Box 1620
Yellowknife, NT, Canada X1A 2P2
Ph:(867)873-3441
Fax: (867)873-2353
Co. E-mail: gerry@averyco.nt.ca
URL: http://www.averyco.nt.ca

E-mail: gerry@averyco.nt.ca
Scope: Accounting and management consulting firm.

45964 ■ Bahr International Inc.
PO Box 795
Gainesville, TX 76241
Ph:(940)665-2344
Fax: (940)665-2359

Co. E-mail: info@bahrintl.com
URL: http://www.bahrintl.com

E-mail: info@bahrintl.com
Scope: Offers consulting in general management, corporate polices and culture, and strategic and long-range planning. Provides management audits and reports and profit improvement programs. High level strategic marketing, advertising strategy/tactics, turnaround consulting and management.

45965 ■ Melvin E. Barnette & Associates Inc.
805 Hopkins Ave.
Pendleton, SC 29670
Ph:(864)646-7622
Co. E-mail: melvin@mbarnette.com
URL: http://www.mbarnette.com

E-mail: melvin@mbarnette.com
Scope: A multi disciplinary management consulting firm specializing in a broad array of higher education and public sector consulting assignments, including Administrative consulting, business and financial operations reviews, crisis management, organizational restructuring, and management training.

45966 ■ Beacon Management Group Inc.
1000 W McNab Rd.
Pompano Beach, FL 33069
Ph:(954)782-1119
Free: 800-771-8721
Fax: (954)969-2566
Co. E-mail: md@beaconmgmt.com
URL: http://www.beaconmgmt.com

E-mail: md@beaconmgmt.com
Scope: Provides entrepreneurial companies with managerial and financial expertise. Services include strategic and business planning; corporate finance; franchise development services; information management; turnaround management and consulting; and joint venture, strategic alliances and acquisition services, including due diligence, market intelligence, targeted searches, valuation, negotiation, and deal structure. Provides assistance for financially-troubled companies, not-for-profits and the public sector

45967 ■ Don L. Beck Associates Inc.
10050 N Foothill Blvd.
Cupertino, CA 95014-5601
Ph:(408)973-8688
Fax: (408)973-8714
Co. E-mail: dbeck@dlba.com
URL: http://www.dlba.com

E-mail: dbeck@dlba.com
Scope: A management consulting firm specializing in building facilities planning and management worldwide.

45968 ■ Benchmark Consulting Group Inc.
110 Broad St.
Boston, MA 02110-3030
Ph:(617)482-7661
Fax: (617)423-2158
Scope: Provides financial and management services to companies. Helps companies grow through debt and equity sourcing and restructuring, business valuation, acquisition/divestiture, computer information systems, and improved operation profitability.

45969 ■ Better Bottom Lines
2365 Rebel Rd.
Cumming, GA 30041
Ph:(770)887-3450
Fax: (770)887-3450
Scope: Firm conducts management and marketing consulting. It serves all small businesses, with a concentration on electromechanical sales, service and installation companies in the U.S. and Canada. **Seminars:** List of seminars and workshops available from firm upon request.

45970 ■ Biomedical Management Resources
PO Box 521125
Salt Lake City, UT 84152-1125
Ph:(801)272-4668

Fax: (801)277-3290
Co. E-mail: SeniorManagement@
   BiomedicalManagement.com
URL: http://www.biomedicalmanagement.com

E-mail: SeniorManagement@
   BiomedicalManagement.com
Scope: Provides business development, interim management, and executive search services. Assists companies in strategic alliances, corporate partnering, business acquisition. Demonstrated success in identifying recruiting, and placing key managers in difficult to hire positions.

45971 ■ Blackford Associates
30 George Rd.
PO Box 2157
Contoocook, NH 03229
Ph:(603)225-2228
Fax: (603)225-2228
Co. E-mail: jblackfd@totalnet.net

E-mail: jblackfd@totalnet.net
Scope: Provides general management consulting to smaller manufacturing companies. Counsels chief executive officers and presidents on strategy, organization, finances and operations. Areas of expertise include the following: new products, services or markets; problems of expansion or retrenchment; financing and bank relations; morale, organization and training; budgeting and business plans; factory flow and inventory control; quality control and methods; cash flow problems; and financial information and controls.

45972 ■ Blankinship & Associates Inc.
322 C St.
Davis, CA 95616
Ph:(530)757-0941
Fax: (530)757-0940
Co. E-mail: blankinship@envtox.com
URL: http://www.envtox.com

E-mail: blankinship@envtox.com
Scope: A human resource management and development consulting firm specializing in small to medium size businesses.

45973 ■ C. Clint Bolte & Associates
809 Philadelphia Ave.
Chambersburg, PA 17201
Ph:(717)263-5768
Fax: (717)263-8945
Co. E-mail: clint@clintbolte.com
URL: http://www.clintbolte.com

E-mail: clint@clintbolte.com
Scope: Provides management consulting services to firms involved with the printing industry. Services include outsourcing studies, graphics supply chain management studies, company and equipment valuations, plant layout services, litigation support, fulfillment warehouse consulting and product development services. **Publications:** "Time to Break Through the Glass Ceiling," The Seybold Report, May, 2006; "Challenges & Opportunities Presented by Postal Rate Increases," The Seybold Report, May, 2006; "Packaging Roll Sheeting Comes of Age," The Seybold Report, May, 2006; "Diversifying With Mailing & Fulfillment Services," The Seybold Report, Jan, 2006.

45974 ■ BPT Consulting Associates Ltd.
12 Parmenter Rd., Ste. B6
Londonderry, NH 03053
Ph:(603)437-8484
Co. E-mail: bptcons@tiac.net
URL: http://www.bptconsulting.com

E-mail: bptcons@tiac.net
Scope: Provides management consulting expertise and resources to cross-industry clients with services for: Business Management consulting, People/Human Resources Transition and Training programs, and a full cadre of multi-disciplined Technology Computer experts. Virtual consultants with expertise in e-commerce, supply chain management, organizational

development, and business application development consulting. **Seminars:** Business: MRPII, DRPII, JIT/TQC. Business Requirements Analysis, Small Business Start-Up, Strategic Planning. People: Team Building, Performance Evaluation, Career Transition and Counseling Seminars. Technology: User Training for Customized Software, Internet, Full array of application development, i.e., C, Java, website development. **Special Services:** Provides a full array of computer and related user training services. Resources include application developers, database developers and managers, project management experts for a full array of industries (manufacturing, software, defense, healthcare, pharmaceutical, and small business).

45975 ■ Chip Bradley Management Advisor
543 Delaware Ave.
Delmar, NY 12054-2835
Ph:(518)475-0152
Fax: (518)475-0152
Scope: Management training specializing in personal and interpersonal skills development. Offers an array of problem-solving programs and products to meet productivity and profitability challenges. Industries served: colleges, universities, adult education centers; professional and trade associations; not-for-profit organizations; home-based entrepreneurs and independent consultants. **Seminars:** How to Begin and Build a Successful Consulting Practice; Managing Multiple Priorities in Your Work Unit; Making Time Count: How to Become a Better Manager of Yourself and Your Time; Supervisory Skills for New and Prospective Managers.

45976 ■ Bran Management Services Inc.
7116 Lupton Dr., Ste. 100
Dallas, TX 75225-1735
Ph:(214)739-2340
Fax: (214)739-2360
Scope: Offers management consulting services to companies in manufacturing, distribution and services to help them cope with growth and change. Helps small businesses create and identify product strategies. Services include developing international business opportunities; turnaround management; sales and marketing development; business planning; acquisitions and mergers.

45977 ■ BroadVision Inc.
585 Broadway
Redwood City, CA 94063
Ph:(650)542-5100
Free: (866)287-6669
Fax: (650)542-5900
Co. E-mail: info@broadvision.com
URL: http://www.broadvision.com

E-mail: info@broadvision.com
Scope: Areas of expertise include strategic services, interactive services, content and creative services and client services. Services include business planning, application strategy, ROI analysis, organization and business process consulting, building and deploying applications, content management, sourcing and workflow processes. **Special Services:** BroadVision Process; BroadVision Commerce; BroadVision Portal; BroadVision Content Services; BroadVision eMarketing; BroadVision QuickSilver; BroadVision Deployment; BroadVision Multi-Touchpoint; BroadVision Search.

45978 ■ Business Education Associates
PO Box 4
Bethel, CT 06801
Ph:(203)798-6035
Co. E-mail: bob@ashfordgrp.com
URL: http://www.ashfordgrp.com

E-mail: bob@ashfordgrp.com
Scope: Offers tailored management education programs. Has been designed to meet the business education needs of companies implementing new systems and companies to re-educate users of existing systems. **Publications:** "The Ashford Group and TQuist Partner to Provide High Impact Manufacturing Solutions"; "The Future of ERP".

45979 ■ Business Improvement Architects
33 Riderwood Dr.
Toronto, ON, Canada M2L 2X4
Ph:(416)444-8225
Free: (866)346-3242
Fax: (416)444-6743
Co. E-mail: info@bia.ca
URL: http://www.bia.ca

E-mail: info@bia.ca
Scope: Specializes in management training, project management, marketing planning, promotions and incentives.

45980 ■ Business Ventures Inc.
1650 Oakbrook Dr., Ste. 440
Norcross, GA 30093-1881
Ph:(770)729-8000
Fax: (770)729-8028
Scope: Business development consultants specializing in construction industry. Works with HVAC, plumbing, and electrical contraction who need assistance in marketing, sales and promotion, operations management or finance. Also plan, execute, and monitor the marketing, sales, and promotional activities for new product introductions. Firm also writes business plans, monitors financial health of businesses, and performs operations management. **Publications:** How to Write a Business Plan, Atlanta Business Chronicle; Ask 10 Questions Before You Begin Your Business, Income Opportunities. **Seminars:** The Seven Rules for Business Success; The Seven Greatest Lies of Small Business; Understanding the Financial Side of Business; Small Business Marketing; Strategic Business Planning.

45981 ■ ByrneMRG
22 Isle of Pines Dr.
Hilton Head Island, SC 29928
Ph:(215)630-7411
Free: 888-816-8080
Co. E-mail: info@byrnemrg.com
URL: http://www.byrnemrg.com

E-mail: info@byrnemrg.com
Scope: Firm specializes in management consulting, including department management, equipment evaluation and selection, project management, R and D planning, and database design and management. **Publications:** "Implementing Solutions to Everyday Issues".

45982 ■ Career Strategies
1150 Wilmette Ave.
Wilmette, IL 60091
Ph:(847)251-1661
Free: 800-728-1709
Fax: (847)251-5191
Co. E-mail: mmkcareer@aol.com
URL: http://www.moatskennedy.com

E-mail: mmkcareer@aol.com
Scope: Provides consulting services for a variety of associations and companies in the area of personnel and management. Speaks and consults on the following topics: office politics, leadership skills, demographics workplace issues. Serves industry as well as government agencies in the U.S. **Publications:** Seven Principles of Leadership/Management; How to Prove Your Work Makes A Difference. **Seminars:** Workshops on career planning, office politics, and cross-generational workplace issues.

45983 ■ Carelli & Associates
17 Reid Pl.
Delmar, NY 12054
Ph:(518)439-0233
URL: http://www.carelli.com
Scope: Provides training and writing/editing services to industry and businesses, health care and educational institutions, and government agencies, and not-for-profit organizations. **Publications:** "The Truth About Supervision", 2004.

45984 ■ Casino, Hotel & Resort Consultants L.L.C.
8100 Via Del Cerro Ct.
Las Vegas, NV 89117

Ph:(702)646-7200
Fax: (702)646-6680
Co. E-mail: info@hraba.com
URL: http://www.hraba.com

E-mail: info@hraba.com
Scope: Casino and hospitality industry consultants. Firm specializes in developing and implementing customized forecast and labor management control systems that deliver immediate, positive impact to the company's bottom line. We are involved in production planning, emply surveys and communication, inventory management, business process reviews, audits, development and implementation of key management reports. **Seminars:** Payroll Cost Control and Effective Staff Scheduling

45985 ■ CBIZ Inc.
6050 Oak Tree, Blvd. S, Ste. 500
Cleveland, OH 44131
Ph:(216)447-9000
Fax: (216)447-9007
Co. E-mail: info@cbiz.com
URL: http://www.cbiz.com

E-mail: info@cbiz.com
Scope: A business consulting and tax services firm providing financial, consulting, tax and business services through seven groups: financial management, tax advisory, construction and real estate, healthcare, litigation support, capital resource, and CEO outsource.

45986 ■ CEA Investments Corp.
301-2210 W 40th Ave.
Vancouver, BC, Canada V6M 1W6
Ph:(604)689-5547
Fax: (604)689-5567
Co. E-mail: info@ceainvestment.com
URL: http://www.ceainvestment.com

E-mail: info@ceainvestment.com
Scope: Specializes in strategic planning, mergers and acquisitions, and operations consulting, to mid-sized corporations. Areas of expertise include corporate planning, financial engineering, joint venture structuring, international corporate networking, identifying acquisition opportunities, locating investment partners, corporate evaluations, negotiating buy/sell agreements, business planning, markets studies and products evaluation, and outsourcing.

45987 ■ The Center for Organizational Excellence
15200 Shady Grove Rd., Ste. 400
Rockville, MD 20850
Ph:(301)948-1922
Free: 877-674-3923
Fax: (301)948-2158
Co. E-mail: results@center4oe.com
URL: http://www.center4oe.com

E-mail: results@center4oe.com
Scope: An organizational effectiveness consulting firm specializing in helping organizations achieve results through people, process, and performance. Service areas include organizational performance systems, leadership systems, customer systems, and learning systems.

45988 ■ CFI Group USA L.L.C.
625 Avis Dr.
Ann Arbor, MI 48108
Ph:(734)930-9090
Fax: (734)930-0911
Co. E-mail: contactcfi@cfigroup.com
URL: http://www.cfigroup.com

E-mail: contactcfi@cfigroup.com
Scope: Management consulting firm that helps its clients worldwide to maximize shareholder value by optimizing customer and employee satisfaction. **Publications:** "Consumers Rate the Post-Boom Industry," Mortgage Banking, Jan, 2005"; "Interview with a Customer Satisfaction Guru," Rotman Magazine, 2005".

45989 ■ CFO Service
112 Chester Ave.
Saint Louis, MO 63122
Ph:(314)757-2940
Co. E-mail: jskae@cfoservice.com
URL: http://www.cfoservice.com

E-mail: jskae@cfoservice.com
Scope: A group of professional executives that provide upper management services to companies that cannot support a full time COO or CFO. Provides clients in the areas of business planning, company policies, contract negotiations, safety policies, product and service pricing, loans management, taxes, cost analysis, loss control and budgeting.

45990 ■ Chamberlain & Cansler Inc.
2251 Perimeter Park Dr.
Atlanta, GA 30341
Ph:(770)457-5699
Scope: Firm specializes in strategic planning; profit enhancement; small business management; interim management; crisis management; turnarounds.

45991 ■ Chartered Management Co.
125 S Wacker Dr., Ste. 300
Chicago, IL 60606-4402
Ph:(312)214-2575
Scope: Operations improvement consultants. Specializes in strategic planning; feasibility studies; management audits and reports; profit enhancement; start-up businesses; mergers and acquisitions; joint ventures; divestitures; interim management; crisis management; turnarounds; business process re-engineering; venture capital; and due diligence.

45992 ■ Claremont Consulting Group
4525 Castle Ln.
La Canada, CA 91011-1436
Ph:(818)249-0584
Fax: (818)249-5811
Scope: Consulting, coaching, training, & litigation support in project management, engineering management, system engineering & cost estimating. **Publications:** Over 85 publications, including, "What Every Engineer Should Know About Project Management." **Seminars:** Project Management, System Engineering & Cost Estimating.

45993 ■ Comer & Associates L.L.C.
5255 Holmes Pl.
Boulder, CO 80303
Ph:(303)786-7986
Free: 888-950-3190
Fax: (303)473-9830
URL: http://www.comerassociates.com
Scope: Specialize in developing markets & businesses. Marketing support includes: developing & writing strategic & tactical business plans; developing & writing focused, effective market plans; researching market potential & competition; implementing targeted marketing tactics to achieve company objectives; conducting customer surveys to determine satisfaction & attitudes toward client. Maintains a network of database research specialists, market communications providers, public relations firms, internet resources, focus group facilitators, technical writers & executive recruiters to assist with any project. Organization development support includes: executive/management training programs; executive coaching; team building; developing effective organization structures & processes; management of change in dynamic & competitive environments; individual coaching for management & leadership effectiveness. **Seminars:** Developing a strategic market plan; market research: defining your opportunity; management & leadership effectiveness; team building; developing a business plan.

45994 ■ C.C. Comfort Consulting
3370 N Hayden Rd.
Scottsdale, AZ 85251
Ph:(602)483-8364
Co. E-mail: cccomfortcfe@martindalemail.com

E-mail: cccomfortcfe@martindalemail.com
Scope: Evaluates, develops and implements financial, operational and compliance management systems' strategies, programs and practices. Professional recognition as Certified Public Accountant, Internal Auditor, Cost Analyst and Fraud Examiner plus investigatory, law enforcement, and court experience ensure confidential handling of sensitive and legal matters. Works with management, audit, legal, security and outside personnel to evaluate and improve compliance, efficiency and effectiveness.

45995 ■ Consolidated Resources
PO Box 1864
Kailua, HI 96734
Scope: Firm offers marketing and management consulting.

45996 ■ Consulting & Conciliation Service
3405 I St., Ste. 2
Sacramento, CA 95816
Ph:(916)396-0480
Free: 888-898-9780
Co. E-mail: peace@conciliation.org
URL: http://www.conciliation.org

E-mail: peace@conciliation.org
Scope: Offers consulting and conciliation services. Provides pre-mediation counseling, training and research on preparing for a peaceful society, mediation and facilitation, and preparation for shifts in structure, policy and personnel. Offers sliding scale business rates and free individual consultation.

45997 ■ The Consulting Exchange
1770 Mass Ave., Ste. 288
Cambridge, MA 02140
Ph:(617)576-2100
Free: 800-824-4828
Co. E-mail: gday@cx.com
URL: http://www.cx.com

E-mail: gday@cx.com
Scope: A consultant referral service for management and technical consultants. Serves a local, regional, and international client base. **Publications:** "Getting Full Value From Consulting is in Your Hands", May 25, 1998; "Looking for a Consultant?", June 2, 2001.

45998 ■ The Corlund Group L.L.C.
101 Federal St., Ste. 310
Boston, MA 02110
Ph:(617)423-9364
Fax: (617)423-9371
Co. E-mail: info@corlundgroup.com
URL: http://www.corlundgroup.com

E-mail: info@corlundgroup.com
Scope: Boutique firms offers services in the areas of leadership, governance, and change, with a particular focus on CEO and senior executive succession planning, including assessment, development, and orchestrating succession processes with management and Boards of Directors. Also Board governance effectiveness. **Publications:** "Leadership Due Diligence: The Neglected Governance Frontier," Directorship, Sep, 2001; "Leadership Due Diligence: Managing the Risks," The Corporate Board, Aug, 2001; "Succession: The need for detailed insight," Directors and Boards, 2001; "CEO Succession: Who's Doing Due Diligence?," 2001.

45999 ■ Corporate Consulting Inc.
3333 Belcaro Dr.
Denver, CO 80209
Ph:(303)698-9292
Fax: (303)698-9292
Co. E-mail: corpcons@compuserve.com

E-mail: corpcons@compuserve.com
Scope: Specializes in feasibility studies; organizational development; small business management; mergers and acquisitions; joint ventures; divestitures; interim management; crisis management; turnarounds; financing; appraisals and valuations; and due diligence studies.

46000 ■ Corporate Impact
33326 Bonnieview, Ste. 200
Avon Lake, OH 44012-1230

Ph:(440)930-2477
Fax: (440)930-2525
Co. E-mail: inquiry@corpimpact.com
URL: http://www.corpimpact.com

E-mail: inquiry@corpimpact.com
Scope: Provides coaching, consultation, facilitation and training services to help you develop, a business that delivers sustained shareholder value and growth. Supports the development of the skills and implementation of the change programs learned in the workshop. Also, for small businesses, firm provides general consulting in the areas of strategic planning, marketing, and product and sales strategy. Industries served: all except government and nonprofit. **Publications:** 8 Lies of Teamwork. **Seminars:** Personal Productivity Management; The Challenge of Leadership; Collaborative Problem Solving; The Creative Side of Enterprise; Teamwork and Peak Performance; Winning Customers; Conflict Resolution.

46001 ■ Morton Cotlar
700 Richards St.
Honolulu, HI 96813
Ph:(808)396-0057
Co. E-mail: morton@uhunix.uhcc.hawaii.edu

E-mail: morton@uhunix.uhcc.hawaii.edu
Scope: Provides organizational management counsel including (1) surveys of effectiveness in operations, (2) training and development seminars for managers, (3) consulting in organizational operations, and (4) development of expert systems for strategic planning and operations, and assistance with implementation. Serves private industries as well as government agencies.

46002 ■ Crystal Clear Communications Inc.
8989 N Port Washington Rd., Ste. 210
Milwaukee, WI 53217-1667
Ph:(414)228-8799
Scope: Specializes in strategic planning; organizational development; small business management; mergers and acquisitions; joint ventures; divestitures; strategy implementation; executive coaching.

46003 ■ The Decision Group
7204 Penny Rd.
Raleigh, NC 27606-9321
Ph:(919)851-9679
Co. E-mail: decisiongroup@nc.rr.com
URL: http://www.decisiongroup.com

E-mail: decisiongroup@nc.rr.com
Scope: Provides comprehensive consulting services to manufacturing, distribution, and service companies in the areas of: productivity and quality improvement, performance measurement, information systems design, and operations management. Serves private industries as well as government agencies. **Publications:** "Measuring, Managing, and Maximizing Performance," Productivity Press; "Operational Performance Measurement: Increasing Total Productivity," St. Lucie Press; "Implementing Manufacturing Performance Measures - A Case Study". **Seminars:** Quality Improvement Made Simple; Measuring Performance to Increase Total Productivity.

46004 ■ Del Technology Inc.
7407 E Via Estrella Ave., Ste. 10
Scottsdale, AZ 85258
Ph:(480)483-7588
Fax: (480)483-7533
Scope: Provides services in three areas: management consulting, information technology, and micro business. Focuses on organizational assessment, business process reengineering, quality assurance program development, hardware/software evaluation and acquisition, applications software development, systems integration, LAN support, and new technology training. Industries served: all. **Publications:** "Standards for Information Systems Development and Project Administration". **Seminars:** Organization for Future Technology; Business Reengineering; Managing Successful Projects; Planning and Implementing the Information Systems Architecture; and Successfully Managing the Information Resource.

46005 ■ Delohery Associates
3214 Cedar Bluff Dr. NE
Marietta, GA 30062
Ph:(770)977-9509
Scope: Offers total quality management, business process and procedure analysis and design using current contemporary quality techniques.

46006 ■ Development Resource Consultants
PO Box 118
Rancho Cucamonga, CA 91729
Ph:(909)902-7655
Fax: (909)476-6942
Co. E-mail: info@gotodrc.com

E-mail: info@gotodrc.com
Scope: A small business advisory service specializing in office re-organization, employee training in office organization, communication skills, sales training and career counseling.

46007 ■ Directions Ltd.
4021 Albert Dr.
PO Box 40782
Nashville, TN 37204
Ph:(615)269-4043
Fax: (615)385-9559
Co. E-mail: scheuerm@bellsouth.net

E-mail: scheuerm@bellsouth.net
Scope: Works with Chief Executive Officers and companies trying to resolve problems that management and leadership have not had the time to solve due to other priorities. Areas of interest: management and leadership problems; resolving problems associated with profitability, growth, change and resources; strategic issues, under-performance issues and boards of directors issues. Experience is with publicly traded or privately owned companies in various industries.

46008 ■ donphin.com Inc.
5713 Corporate Way, Ste. 101
West Palm Beach, FL 33407
Ph:(561)688-1000
Free: 800-234-3304
Fax: (561)688-1142
Co. E-mail: inquiry@donphin.com
URL: http://www.donphin.com

E-mail: inquiry@donphin.com
Scope: Offers a comprehensive approach to understanding and applying a broad range of business principles: legal compliance issues, management concerns, health and safety, customer service, marketing, information management. Industries served: all developing small businesses. **Publications:** "Doing Business Right!". **Seminars:** Doing Business Right!; HR That Works!.

46009 ■ Dorn & Associates Inc.
8506 Bass Lake Rd., Ste. 140
New Hope, MN 55428
Ph:(763)533-7689
Fax: (763)533-1143
Scope: Services include accounting, marketing, employment/partnership, new doctor agreements, personnel issues and human resources assessment, practice management, practice merger/acquisition/sale and/or liquidation, practice surveys and valuation, staff development and training.

46010 ■ DRI Consulting
2 Otter Ln.
North Oaks, MN 55127-6436
Ph:(651)415-1400
Free: (866)276-4600
Fax: (651)415-9968
Co. E-mail: dric@dric.com
URL: http://www.dric.com

E-mail: dric@dric.com
Scope: Licensed psychologists providing organization and management consulting. developing leaders, managers and individuals through coaching, business strategy, career development, crisis management, policy consultation and technology optimization.

46011 ■ Dropkin & Co.
390 George St.
New Brunswick, NJ 08901
Ph:(732)828-3211
Fax: (732)828-4118
Co. E-mail: murray@dropkin.com
URL: http://www.dropkin.com

E-mail: murray@dropkin.com
Scope: Firm specializes in feasibility studies; business management; business process re-engineering; and team building, healthcare and housing. **Publications:** "Guide to Auditing Nonprofit Organizations"; "The Cash Flow Management Book for Nonprofits"

46012 ■ Dubuc Lucke & Co.
414 Walnut St., Ste607
Cincinnati, OH 45202
Ph:(513)579-8330
Fax: (513)241-6669
Scope: Consulting services in the areas of profit enhancement; small business management; mergers and acquisitions; joint ventures; divestitures; interim management; crisis management; turnarounds; appraisals; valuations; due diligence; and international trade.

46013 ■ The DuMond Group
5282 Princeton Ave.
Westminster, CA 92683-2753
Ph:(714)373-0610
Scope: Firm specializes in organizational development; small business management; employee surveys and communication; performance appraisals; and team building.

46014 ■ Dunelm International
14 S Bryn Mawr Ave., Ste. 206
Bryn Mawr, PA 19010-3216
Ph:(610)520-4491
Fax: (610)520-4492
Scope: Firm specializes in feasibility studies; start-up businesses; interim management; crisis management; turnarounds; business process re-engineering; sales forecasting; supply chain solution and project management.

46015 ■ Dynamic Firm Management
4570 Campus Dr., Ste. 60
Newport Beach, CA 92660
Ph:(949)640-2220
Co. E-mail: info@dynamicfirm.com
URL: http://www.dynamicfirm.com

E-mail: info@dynamicfirm.com
Scope: Management consulting to law firms and other professional service providers. Emphasis on Partnership Relations, Compensation, Strategic Planning, Increasing Revenues, Profitable Firm Operations and Effective Management and Team building. Initial work includes the determination of your objectives; quantifying measurable accomplishments and outlining the consulting requirements. Industries served: Law Firms, attorneys, professional service. **Publications:** "Why Good Partnerships Go Bad", The Journal of Law Office Economics and Management, Feb, 2006; "Perfect Union", Daily Journal, Mar, 2004; "Future Perfect", Daily Journal, Dec, 2003. **Seminars:** Facilitates Partner retreats and management workshops. Topics covered include: Partner relations; compensation; management effectiveness; team building and strategic planning.

46016 ■ Effective Resources Inc.
2803 Southfield Ct.
Holiday, FL 34691-2505
Ph:(727)944-2507
Free: 800-288-6044
Fax: (727)944-2607
Co. E-mail: customerservice@effectiveresources.
  com
URL: http://www.effectiveresources.com

E-mail: customerservice@effectiveresources.com
Scope: Concerned with technical aspects of human resource management. Specializes in compensation and incentive plans; performance appraisals; team building; and personnel policies and procedures; affirmative action plan preparation.

46017 ■ EGL Holdings

3495 Piedmont Rd., Ste. 412
Atlanta, GA 30305
Ph:(404)949-8300
Fax: (404)949-8311
URL: http://www.eglholdings.com
Scope: A management consulting team that specializes in solving the financial problems of medium sized businesses and in helping the management capitalize on business opportunities. Designs and implements remedies for shortage of working capital and low profitability. Services include strategic corporate planning, cost reduction/profit improvement, acquisition analysis, divestiture and financing. Long-term/short-term analysis of business opportunities.

46018 ■ EMS Network International

858 Longview Rd.
Burlingame, CA 94010-6974
Ph:(650)342-5259
Fax: (650)344-5005
Co. E-mail: ems@emsnetwork.com
URL: http://www.emsnetwork.com

E-mail: ems@emsnetwork.com
Scope: Helping teams to develop and implement breakthrough solutions through purpose expansion, soution-after-next, technology fiction, people participation and change management. Serves clients in all industries. Firm is an affiliate of The Center for Breakthrough Thinking Inc., the ForeSight Network, the Institute for Global Ethics, and Management Consultant Network International. **Publications:** "How to Get Value from a Management Consultant". **Seminars:** Facilitation skills; basic skills for internal consultants; entrepreneurs and champions; breakthrough thinking; building decision skills and ethical fitness.

46019 ■ Espionage Research Institute

10903 Indian Head Hwy., Ste. 304
Fort Washington, MD 20744
Ph:(240)273-8823
Fax: (301)292-4635
Co. E-mail: k3do@earthlink.net
URL: http://www.espionbusiness.com

E-mail: k3do@earthlink.net
Scope: Provides solutions to collecting and promulgating information on hostile espionage activity. Provides its members with news of espionage incidents and trends to enable them to serve their clients more effectively. **Publications:** A Guidebook For Beginning Sweepers; The Ear Volume; The Attack on Axnan Headquarters; The TSCM Threat Book.

46020 ■ Family Business Institute Inc.

904 Steffi Ct.
Lawrenceville, GA 30044
Ph:(770)952-4085
Fax: (770)432-6660
Co. E-mail: asktheexpert@family-business-experts.
  com
URL: http://www.family-business-experts.com

E-mail: asktheexpert@family-business-experts.com
Scope: A multidisciplinary consulting team established to help families in business together achieve their personal, family, and organizational goals by meeting challenges that are unique to family-owned businesses. Provides coordinated and integrated assessments and solutions for family issues and needs; for company finance; and for human resource and operational requirements. **Publications:** "Professional Intervention in the Family Owned Business"; "Building Consensus in a Family Business"; "Professionalizing Family Business Management"; "Recognizing generations - know them by their weekends"; "Succession planning tactics".

46021 ■ FCP Consulting

500 Sutter St., Ste. 507
San Francisco, CA 94102
Ph:(415)956-5558
Fax: (415)956-5722
Co. E-mail: cox@coxcmc.com
URL: http://www.coxcmc.com

E-mail: cox@coxcmc.com
Scope: Management consulting in Business-To-Business sales.

46022 ■ Federer Resources Inc.

106 E 6th St.
Austin, TX 78701-3659
Ph:(512)476-8800
Scope: Firm specializes in feasibility studies; start-up businesses; small business management; mergers and acquisitions; joint ventures; divestitures; interim management; crisis management; turnarounds; production planning; team building; appraisals and valuations.

46023 ■ Firemark Investments

200 W DeVargas St., Ste. 9
Santa Fe, NM 87501
Ph:(505)989-8384
Free: 800-530-0786
Fax: (505)989-8316
Co. E-mail: info@firemarkinv.com
URL: http://www.firemarkinv.com

E-mail: info@firemarkinv.com
Scope: Firm provides management consulting, investment advice and fund management.

46024 ■ First Strike Management Consulting Inc.

401 Loblolly Ave.
PO Box 1188
Little River, SC 29566-1188
Ph:(843)385-6338
Fax: (843)390-1004
Co. E-mail: fsmc.hq@fsmc.com
URL: http://www.fsmc.com

E-mail: fsmc.hq@fsmc.com
Scope: A management consulting firm that provides services such as proposals, enterprise systems, management systems, and staff augmentation. Specializes in new business proposals, project management support and training. **Publications:** Project Management for Executives, Project Risk Management, Project Communications Management, Winning Proposals, Four Computer Based Training (CBT) courses. **Seminars:** Preparing Winning Proposals in Response to Government RFPs.

46025 ■ The Foster Group Inc.

330 N Wabash Ave., Ste. 3500
Chicago, IL 60611
Ph:(312)609-1009
Fax: (312)609-1109
Co. E-mail: info@thefostergroup.com
URL: http://www.thefostergroup.com

E-mail: info@thefostergroup.com
Scope: Offers information systems and data security, financial accounting services, and management consulting.

46026 ■ Freese & Associates Inc.

PO Box 814
Chagrin Falls, OH 44022-0814
Ph:(440)564-9183
Fax: (440)564-7339
Co. E-mail: tfreese@freeseinc.com
URL: http://www.freeseinc.com

E-mail: tfreese@freeseinc.com
Scope: A management consulting firm offering advice in all forms of business logistics. Consulting services are in the areas of strategic planning; network analysis, site selection, facility layout and design, outsourcing, warehousing, transportation and customer service. Typical projects include 3PL marketing surveys; third party outsourcing selection; operational audits; competitive analysis; inventory management; due diligence; and implementation project management. **Publications:** "Building Relationships is Key to Motivation," Distribution Center Management, Apr, 2006; "Getting Maximum Results from Performance Reviews," WERCSheet, Oct, 2003; "SCM: Making the Vision a Reality," Supply Chain Management Review, Oct, 2003; "Contents Under Pressure," DCVelocity, Aug, 2003; "When Considering Outsourcing, It's Really a Financial Decision," Inventory Management Report, Mar, 2003. **Seminars:** Keys to Retaining & Motivating Your Associates, Mar, 2006; The Value and Challenges of Supply Chain Management, Global Supply Chain & Logistics Conference, Feb, 2006; Best Practices in Logistics in China, Jun, 2005; Keys to Motivating Associates, WERC Annual Conference, May, 2005; The Goal and the Way of International Cooperation in Logistics, Apr, 2005.

46027 ■ Gates, Moore & Co.

3340 Peachtree Rd. NE, Tower Pl. 100, Ste. 600
Atlanta, GA 30326
Ph:(404)266-9876
Fax: (404)266-2669
Co. E-mail: postmaster@gatesmoore.com
URL: http://www.gatesmoore.com

E-mail: postmaster@gatesmoore.com
Scope: Firm provides management consulting and accounting services to medical practices, hospital owned practices, staff model managed care organizations, IPAs, MSOs, PO, and PHOs. Services include comprehensive operational assessments, managed care negotiations, practice start-ups and expansion, development of MSOs, strategic planning, mergers, cost accounting analysis, practice valuations, income division plans, medical record documentation and coding reviews, expert witness testimony, patient satisfaction surveys and corporate compliance planning. **Publications:** Physicians, Dentists and Veterinarians; Insurance Portability and Accountability Act Privacy Manual; How To Guide for your Medical Practice and Health Insurance Portability and Accountability Act Security Manual; A How To Guide for your Medical Practice; Cost Analysis Made Simple: A Step by Step Guide to Using Cost Accounting to Ensure Practice Profitability; Cost Cutting Strategies for Medical Practices. **Seminars:** Implementing a Cost Accounting Analysis to Monitor Practice Profitability, Georgia Chapter-American Academy of Pediatrics, Jun, 2006; NPI Update, Saint Josephs Hospital, Jun, 2006.

46028 ■ Glass & Associates Inc.

623 5th Ave., Fl. 15
New York, NY 10022
Ph:(212)223-2002
Free: (866)452-7716
Fax: (212)223-5477
Co. E-mail: jmansell@glass-consulting.com
URL: http://www.glass-consulting.com

E-mail: jmansell@glass-consulting.com
Scope: Works with troubled companies, functioning as agents of change to help organizations deal with extraordinary needs in situations ranging from the early stages of financial decline to "life-or-death" crisis conditions. Provides in-depth analysis and strategic planning, backed up by leadership and decisive action to help under-performing companies change the way they operate and survive crisis situations. Assists management, creditors, lenders and other "parties in interest" involved with financially troubled companies; crisis management services include on-site interim crisis management, including direction of the Chapter 11 process, for insolvent companies; human resources services include personnel for temporary senior-level management and professional staff assignments; executive search, selection and placement; specialized advisory services in human resource areas such as worker's compensation and health benefits.

46029 ■ Global Business Consultants

120 Market Sq.
PO Box 776
Pinehurst, NC 28374-0776
Ph:(910)295-5991
Free: 800-991-4990
Fax: (910)295-5908
Co. E-mail: info@yourculturecoach.com

E-mail: info@yourculturecoach.com
Scope: Firm specializes in human resources management; project management; software development; and international trade. Offers litigation support.

46030 ■ Global Technology Transfer

1500 Dixie Hwy.
Covington, KY 41011
Ph:(859)431-1262
Fax: (859)431-5148
Co. E-mail: arzembrodt@worldnet.att.net

E-mail: arzembrodt@worldnet.att.net
Scope: Firm specializes in product development; quality assurance; new product development; and total quality management focusing on household chemical specialties, especially air fresheners. Utilizes latest technology from global resources. Specializes in enhancement products for home and automobile.

46031 ■ Arnold S. Goldin & Associates Inc.

5030 Champion Blvd., Ste. G-6231
Boca Raton, FL 33496
Ph:(561)994-5810
Fax: (561)994-5860
Co. E-mail: arnold@goldin.com
URL: http://www.goldin.com

E-mail: arnold@goldin.com
Scope: An accounting and management consulting firm. Serves clients worldwide. Provides management services. Handles monthly write-ups and tax returns.

46032 ■ Goldore Consulting Inc.

120-5 St. NW
PO Box 590
Linden, AB, Canada T0M 1J0
Ph:(403)546-4208
Fax: (403)546-4208
Co. E-mail: goldore@leadershipessentials.com

E-mail: goldore@leadershipessentials.com
Scope: Provides consulting service in Leadership and management skills. Industries served: primarily charities, non-profits; some businesses. **Seminars:** O Desafio de Lideranca; The Challenge Of Leadership; Le Challenge du Leadership; El Desafio de Liderazgo; Tantangan Kipeminpinan.

46033 ■ Gordian Concepts & Solutions

16 Blueberry Ln.
Lincoln, MA 01773
Ph:(617)259-8341
Co. E-mail: gordian@usa1.com

E-mail: gordian@usa1.com
Scope: An engineering and management consultancy, the firm offers a broad range of general, financial, and valuation services, civil and tax litigation support, helps clients to enter new businesses, to plan new products and services, to evaluate feasibility, and assists with their due diligence efforts. Targets industrial concerns engaged in manufacturing, assembly, warehousing, energy production, process systems and biotechnology, steel, paper, and electronics. Also services businesses such as retailing, financial services, health-care, satellite broadcasting and cable television, outdoor advertising, and professional practices.

46034 ■ Great Lakes Consulting Group Inc.

1217 S Walnut St.
South Bend, IN 46619-4305
Ph:(574)287-4500
Fax: (574)234-8207
Scope: Provides consulting services in the areas of strategic planning; feasibility studies; start-up businesses; small business management; mergers and acquisitions; joint ventures; divestitures; interim management; crisis management; turnarounds; business process re-engineering; venture capital; and international trade.

46035 ■ Great Western Association Management Inc.

7995 E Prentice Ave., Ste. 100
Greenwood Village, CO 80111
Ph:(303)770-2220
Fax: (303)770-1614
Co. E-mail: info83@gwami.com
URL: http://www.gwami.com

E-mail: info83@gwami.com
Scope: Expertise in managing not for-profit organizations. Clients select from a menu of services including association development and public relations, conferences and seminars, financial management, membership communications, and governance. Expertise also includes association strategic planning, compliance, lobbying, meeting planning, fundraising, marketing and communications.

46036 ■ Joel Greenstein & Associates

6212 Nethercombe Ct.
McLean, VA 22101
Ph:(703)893-1888
Co. E-mail: jgreenstein@contractmasters.com

E-mail: jgreenstein@contractmasters.com
Scope: Provides services to minority and women-owned businesses and government agencies. Experienced in interpreting federal and agency-specific acquisition regulations and contract terms and conditions. Offers assistance with preparing technical and cost proposals and sealed bids.

46037 ■ The Greystone Group Inc.

678 Front St., Ste. 159
Grand Rapids, MI 49504
Ph:(616)451-8880
Fax: (616)451-9180
Co. E-mail: consult@greystonegp.com
URL: http://www.greystonegp.com

E-mail: consult@greystonegp.com
Scope: Firm specializes in strategic planning and communications; organizational development; start-up businesses; business management; mergers and acquisitions; joint ventures; divestitures; business process re-engineering.

46038 ■ Grimmick Consulting Services

455 Donner Way
San Ramon, CA 94583
Ph:(925)735-9090
Fax: (925)735-1100
Co. E-mail: grimmick@pacbell.net

E-mail: grimmick@pacbell.net
Scope: Provides consulting services in the areas of strategic planning; organizational assessment; organizational development; leadership development and Baldridge Criteria.

46039 ■ Harding & Co.

9 Sommer Ave.
Maplewood, NJ 07040
Ph:(973)763-9284
Fax: (973)763-9347
Co. E-mail: fharding@hardingco.com
URL: http://www.hardingco.com

E-mail: fharding@hardingco.com
Scope: Firm specializes in sales management, client development, and employee training. **Publications:** "Rain Making: The Professional's Guide to Attracting New Clients"; "Creating Rainmakers: The Managers Guide to Training Professionals to Attract New Clients"; "Cross-Selling Success: A Rainmakers Guide to Professional Account Development".

46040 ■ Hawthorne Management Consulting Inc.

14644 Poway Mesa Dr.
Poway, CA 92064
Ph:(858)486-2571
Fax: (858)486-1580
Co. E-mail: hmcinc@compuserve.com
URL: http://ourworld.compuserve.com/homepages/hmcinc

E-mail: hmcinc@compuserve.com
Scope: Firm offers expertise in productivity improvement, business process re-engineering, methods engineering, facilities layout, logistics, work standards, planning and control, incentive programs, problem solving and project management. **Publications:** Lessons To Be Learned Just In Time, 1997; Project Management Basics, Industrial Engineering Solutions magazine, Dec, 1997; Is it Time to Turn Out the Lights, Industrial Engineering Solutions magazine, Nov, 1996; 12 Key Factors that Determine World Class J.I.T. Operations, APICS magazine, Jan, 1994. **Seminars:** Power Problem Solving, the Key to Continuous Process improvement; How to Increase Your Productivity; Just in Time Manufacturing.

46041 ■ Claude Hayes & Associates

5115 Maryland Way Frnt.
Brentwood, TN 37027-7556
Ph:(615)377-0743
Fax: (615)370-8106
Scope: Turnarounds, Re-engineering, Re-Structuring, Re-Organization, Start-ups, High profile growth, Acquisitions, Divestures, Due Diligence, Strategic/Business (Marketing/Sales) Plans, Inventory Control and Management, Cost Pricing and Control. Market Management, Demand Forecasting.

46042 ■ Hewitt Development Enterprises

1717 N Bayshore Dr., Ste. 2154
Miami, FL 33132
Ph:(305)372-0941
Free: 800-631-3098
Fax: (305)372-0941
Co. E-mail: info@hewittdevelopment.com
URL: http://www.hewittdevelopment.com

E-mail: info@hewittdevelopment.com
Scope: A manufacturing management consulting firm. Specializes in strategic planning; profit enhancement; start-up businesses; interim management; crisis management; turnarounds; production planning; Just-in-Time inventory management; and project management.

46043 ■ Hickey & Hill Inc.

1009 Oak Hill Rd., Ste. 201
Lafayette, CA 94549
Ph:(925)283-7802
Fax: (925)283-4259
Scope: Firm provides management consulting services to companies in financial distress. Expertise area: corporate restructuring and turnaround.

46044 ■ hightechbiz.com

4209 Santa Monica Blvd., Ste. 201
Los Angeles, CA 90029-3027
Ph:(818)216-9356
Free: 877-648-4753
Fax: (323)913-3355
Co. E-mail: info@hightechbiz.com
URL: http://www.hightechbiz.com

E-mail: info@hightechbiz.com
Scope: Business development, strategic planning and investing in high tech companies. Turnaround consulting and financial sort our of distressed business and start up companies with strong emphasis on technology. A full service marketing agency specializing in integrated marketing solutions. Products and services include marketing surveys; positioning surveys; strategic & tactical plans; implementation plans; management consulting; product brochures; product catalogs; product packaging; product data sheets; direct mail programs; media research; competitive research; complete creative; production and film; media placement; corporate identity; in-house creative; public relations; logos & stationary; annual reports; publications; corporate brochures; corporate videos; trade show booth graphics; concept & design; copywriting; computerized production; illustration/cartoons; computer graphics; Internet home page design; media relations; financial relations; news releases; feature length stories; new product releases; and tracking and clipping.

46045 ■ C. W. Hines and Associates Inc.

344 Churchill Cir., Sanctuary Bay
White Stone, VA 22578
Ph:(804)435-8844
Fax: (804)435-8855
Co. E-mail: turtlecwh@aol.com
URL: http://www.cwhinesassociates.org

E-mail: turtlecwh@aol.com
Scope: Management consultants with expertise in the following categories: advertising and public relations, health and human resources, management sciences, organizational development, computer sciences, financial management, behavioral sciences, environmental design, technology transfer, project management, facility management, program evaluation, and business therapy. Also included are complementary areas such as sampling procedures, job training, managerial effectiveness, corporate seminars, gender harassment, training for trainers, and leadership and management skills development. **Publications:** Money Muscle, 120 Exercises To Build Spiritual And Financial Strength, 2004; Inside Track: Executives Coaching Executives. **Seminars:** Career Development; Coaching and Counseling for Work Success; Communicating More Effectively in a Diverse Work Environment; Communications 600: Advanced Skills for Relationship Building; Customer Service: Building a Caring Culture.

46046 ■ Holt Capital
1100 Dexter Ave. N
Seattle, WA 98109
Ph:(206)676-3822
Fax: (206)789-8034
Co. E-mail: info@holtcapital.com
URL: http://www.holtcapital.com

E-mail: info@holtcapital.com
Scope: Connects companies with capital. Mergers and acquisitions, finance through debt and leasing, private equity and venture capital. Is a registered Investment Advisor. **Publications:** "Is Your First Paragraph a Turn-off?"; "Bubble Rubble: Bridging the Price Gapfor an Early-Stage Business"; "Are You Ready For The New New Economy?"; "Could I Get Money or Jail Time With That? The Sarbanes-Oxley Act Of 2002 gives early-stage companies More Risks". **Seminars:** Attracting Private Investors; Five Proven Ways to Finance Your Company.

46047 ■ Human Resource Specialties Inc.
3 Monroe Pky., Ste. 900
PO Box 1733
Lake Oswego, OR 97035
Ph:(503)697-3329
Free: 800-354-3512
Fax: (503)636-1594
Co. E-mail: info@hrspecialties.com
URL: http://www.hrspecialties.com

E-mail: info@hrspecialties.com
Scope: Provides human resources assistance to organizations. Offers preparation of affirmative action plans, support documents, and adverse impact studies of personnel activities. Also offers customized consultations in small business services, diversity and discrimination, and investigations, complaints and grievances.

46048 ■ ICOP, Business Management Consultant
5C-17/4 Estate Santa Maria
PO Box 305396
Saint Thomas, VI 00803-5396
Ph:(340)776-0581
Fax: (340)776-0581
Scope: Consultant in human relations dealing with attitudes and behavior. Racism, Workplace violence, domestic violence, child abuse, sexism and philosophical attitudes to include religion. **Publications:** Net newspaper publisher! The Simplistic Philosopher and Krim's Simplistic Philosophies, Vantage Press, W4, 1988, (OOT of Print). **Seminars:** Produce seminars unique to audience based on client perceptions.

46049 ■ Idi-Supply Inc.
3866 N Fratney St.
PO Box 12050
Milwaukee, WI 53212
Ph:(414)961-2365
Fax: (414)961-1582
Scope: Firm specializes in start-up businesses; small business management; mergers and acquisitions; joint ventures; divestitures; venture capital; appraisals; valuations; and international trade.

46050 ■ I.H.R. Solutions
3333 E Bayaud Ave., Ste. 219
Denver, CO 80209
Ph:(303)588-4243
Fax: (303)978-0473
Co. E-mail: dhollands@ihrsolutions.com
URL: http://www.ihrsolutions.com

E-mail: dhollands@ihrsolutions.com
Scope: Provides joint-venture and start-up human resource consulting services as well as advice on organization development for international human capital. Industries Served: high-tech and telecommunications.

46051 ■ IMC Consulting & Training
901 McHenry Ave., Ste. A
Modesto, CA 95350
Ph:(209)572-2271
Fax: (209)572-2862
Co. E-mail: michael@imc-1.net
URL: http://www.imc-1.net

E-mail: michael@imc-1.net
Scope: Firm helps businesses and professionals identify, develop and market their selling proposition to increase profits. Services include B-to-B surveys, direct marketing, media relations, planning and strategy, sales management, training and leadership coaching. **Publications:** "Adapting to Change - The New Competitive Advantage," Business Journal, Jul, 2004; "Consultant Earns Advanced Certificate," HCCSC Business Review, Dec, 2004. **Seminars:** Winning the 2nd Half: A 6-month Plan to Score New Customers and Profits.

46052 ■ The Impact Group L.L.C.
18 Stonewall Dr.
West Granby, CT 06090
Ph:(860)653-0757
Co. E-mail: tallen@operationalimpact.com
URL: http://www.operationalimpact.com

E-mail: tallen@operationalimpact.com
Scope: Firm specializes in business operations improvement and TQM consulting initiatives.

46053 ■ In Plain English
14501 Antigone Dr.
PO Box 3300
North Potomac, MD 20878
Ph:(301)340-2821
Free: 800-274-9645
Fax: (301)279-0115
Co. E-mail: rwohl@inplainenglish.com
URL: http://www.inplainenglish.com

E-mail: rwohl@inplainenglish.com
Scope: Management consultants helping government and businesses research, design, write and produce user-oriented management information for human resources, employee benefits, business process, corporate and marketing needs. Employee benefits services include summary plan descriptions, employee benefit booklets, plan documents, communication of employee benefit highlights, pay for performance systems, and Section 125 cafeteria benefit enrollment. Human resources services include producing employee handbooks, employee handbook audits, training manuals, writing training, and personnel policy and policy audits. Consultants also assist clients to re-humanize their business, human resource department, recruitment, and employee benefit program. **Publications:** The Benefits Communication Edge newsletter; The Employee Benefits Communication ToolKit, published by Commerce Clearinghouse. Benefits Communicat ion; a guide published by business & legal reports. **Seminars:** Plain English Writing Training; Summary Plan Description Compliance workshops; Re-Humanizing the Corporation, Human Resources and Employee Benefits Communication Workshop. **Special Services:** Electronic materials; Electronic summary plan descriptions; electronic reference manuals.

46054 ■ Institute for Management Excellence
PO Box 5459
Lacey, WA 98509-5459

Ph:(360)412-0404
URL: http://www.itstime.com
Scope: Management consulting and training focuses on improving productivity, using "best practices" and creative techniques. Practices based on company's theme, "It's time for new ways of doing business." Industries Served: Public Sector, Law Enforcement, Finance/Banking, Non-Profit, Computers/High Technology, Education, Human Resources, Utilities. **Publications:** "The Other Side of Midnight, 2000: An Executive Guide to the Year 2000 Problem" ISBN: 0-9643853-9-2, Authors: Barbara Taylor and Martha Daniel. **Seminars:** The Personality Game, Team Building and Communication Skills, Sexual Harassment and Discrimination Prevention. **Special Services:** Project management for computer systems implementations, including web/internet consulting.

46055 ■ Interax Corp.
4524 S Michigan St.
PO Box 2287
South Bend, IN 46680-2287
Ph:(574)299-0660
Free: 800-560-4489
Fax: (574)299-0683
Co. E-mail: info@interaxcorp.com
URL: http://www.interaxcorp.com

E-mail: info@interaxcorp.com
Scope: Company provides management consulting services, including training, organizational group facilitation, total quality management, participative management, and human technology interaction management. Serves all industries worldwide. **Special Services:** Interax®.

46056 ■ Interpersonal Coaching & Consulting
1516 W Lake St., Ste. 2000S
Minneapolis, MN 55408
Ph:(612)381-2494
Fax: (612)381-2494
Co. E-mail: mail@interpersonal-coaching.com
URL: http://www.interpersonal-coaching.com

E-mail: mail@interpersonal-coaching.com
Scope: Provides coaching and consulting to businesses and organizations. Assesses the interpersonal workplace through interviews, assessment instruments and individual group settings. Experienced as a therapist for over a decade.

46057 ■ JMB International
110 W 40th St., Ste. 501
New York, NY 10018
Ph:(212)575-1226
Fax: (212)575-1226
Co. E-mail: jmberanek@bellefavors.com

E-mail: jmberanek@bellefavors.com
Scope: Management consulting firm offering consultation and customized training in two divisions: business and competitive strategies and intelligence; and creating learning organizations and cross-cultural training. Industries served: telecommunications, chemical, pharmaceutical, and financial services. **Seminars:** Benchmarking; Developing Organizational Intelligence Capabilities; Coaching Skills for Managers; Effective Strategic Thinking; Competitive Analysis Techniques; Learning to Learn; Learning from Work.

46058 ■ Johnston Co.
1646 Massachusetts Ave., Ste. 22
Lexington, MA 02420
Ph:(781)862-7595
Fax: (781)862-9066
Co. E-mail: info@johnstoncompany.com
URL: http://www.johnstoncompany.com

E-mail: info@johnstoncompany.com
Scope: Firm specializes in management audits and reports; start-up businesses; small business management; mergers and acquisitions; joint ventures; divestitures; interim management; crisis management; turnarounds; cost controls; financing; venture capital.

46059 ■ Jordan International Enterprises
PO Box 487
Atlanta, GA 30303
Free: 800-672-8677

46060 ■ K & T Training
103 Greenville St.
Newnan, GA 30263-2630
Ph:(770)253-5870
Fax: (770)253-8866
Scope: Specializes in strategic planning; profit enhancement; organizational development; start-up businesses; interim management; crisis management; turnarounds; business process re-engineering; team building; cost controls.

46061 ■ Kaiser Group Inc.
237 South St.
Waukesha, WI 53186
Ph:(262)544-4971
Fax: (262)544-6271
Co. E-mail: jnitz@kaisergrp.com
URL: http://www.kaisergrp.com

E-mail: jnitz@kaisergrp.com
Scope: Management support consultants with an emphasis on service to capital and consumer goods manufacturers of under twenty million in sales. Current activity is concentrated on startup and turnaround management, executive and supervisory development, marketing and sales strategies and planning, development of capital and loan formation packages, modular housing and real estate development, employment and training activities, participative management implementation, product and service costing, active market research programs and employee involvement programs. Serves private industries as well as government agencies. **Publications:** "A Comprehensive Resource Guide for Workforce Board Staff"; "Guide to Effective Workgroups and Meetings"; "From Research to Reality"; "Business Services Team Development Guide". **Seminars:** Job Readiness and Assessment Strategies; Career Advising; Understanding Motivation; Customer Service Strategies; Developing Leadership for Supervisors; Case Management Interventions; Team Development.

46062 ■ Keiei Senryaku Corp.
19191 S Vermont Ave., Ste. 530
Torrance, CA 90502
Ph:(310)366-3331
Free: 800-951-8780
Fax: (310)366-3330
Co. E-mail: takenakaes@earthlink.net

E-mail: takenakaes@earthlink.net
Scope: Consulting services in the areas of strategic planning; feasibility studies; profit enhancement; organizational development; start-up businesses; mergers and acquisitions; joint ventures; divestitures; executive searches; sales management; competitive analysis. Entering Japanese market.

46063 ■ Kostka & Company Inc.
2114 Town Pl.
Middletown, CT 06457
Co. E-mail: mail@mmgnet.com
URL: http://www.mmgnet.com

E-mail: mail@mmgnet.com
Scope: Management consulting firm that specializes in business process re-engineering, risk management, and information technology.

46064 ■ William E. Kuhn & Associates
234 Cook St.
Denver, CO 80206-5305
Ph:(303)322-8233
Fax: (303)322-9032
Co. E-mail: billkuhn1@cs.com

E-mail: billkuhn1@cs.com
Scope: Firm specializes in strategic planning; profit enhancement; small business management; mergers and acquisitions; joint ventures; divestitures; human resources management; performance appraisals; team building; sales management; appraisals and valuations.

46065 ■ Leadership Development Center
155 Edgewood Ave. S
Jacksonville, FL 32254
Ph:(904)387-0110
Free: 800-659-1720
Fax: (904)246-9270
Co. E-mail: jbleech@no-excuses.com
URL: http://www.no-excuses.com

E-mail: jbleech@no-excuses.com
Scope: Management consulting firm offering development of leadership skills for CEOs and senior management. Specializes in issues of corporate culture and strategic planning. Industries served: all. **Publications:** "Let's Get Results, Not Excuses!"; "Knockdown!"; The On-Purpose Person; "When the Other Guy's Price Is Lower". **Seminars:** Let's Get Results!; Corporate Culture and Values: Establishing the Center; The X Predicament: Maximizing Profits through Sales Department Design.

46066 ■ Liberty Business Strategies Ltd.
The Times Bldg., Ste. 400, Suburban Sq.
Ardmore, PA 19003
Ph:(610)649-3800
Fax: (610)649-0408
Co. E-mail: info@libertystrategies.com
URL: http://www.libertystrategies.com

E-mail: info@libertystrategies.com
Scope: Management consulting firm working with clients to gain speed and agility in driving their business strategy. The consulting model builds the alignment of strategy, organization commitment, and technology.

46067 ■ Lupfer & Associates
92 Glen St.
South Natick, MA 01760
Ph:(508)655-3950
Fax: (508)655-7826
Co. E-mail: donlupfer@aol.com
URL: http://www.lupferassociates.com

E-mail: donlupfer@aol.com
Scope: Assists off shore hi-tech companies in entering United States markets and specializes in channel development for all sorts of products. Perform MARCOM support for hi-tech United States clients. **Publications:** "What's Next For Distribution-Feast or Famine?"; "The Changing Global Marketplace"; "Making Global Distribution Work". **Seminars:** How to do Business in the United States.

46068 ■ Management Growth Institute
572 Washington St.
Wellesley, MA 02482
Ph:(781)235-1520
Fax: (781)235-8881
Co. E-mail: dtbarry@ziplink.net
URL: http://www.managementgrowth.com

E-mail: dtbarry@ziplink.net
Scope: Offers assistance in the specification, design, and implementation of management development programs. Clients include individuals, small businesses, national trade associations, and government agencies. **Seminars:** Profit Enhancement; Family-Owned Businesses; Strategic Planning; Survival and Growth in a Down Economy.

46069 ■ Management House Inc.
36422 Sidewinder Rd.
PO Box 2708
Carefree, AZ 85377-2708
Ph:(480)437-9023
Fax: (480)437-9024
Co. E-mail: managementhouse@cox.net
URL: http://www.managementhouse.com

E-mail: managementhouse@cox.net
Scope: Offers management consulting that emphasizes management education and human resources programming for health service, business, military, and academic organizations. This programming is based on needs analysis and can be presented as keynote addresses, half-day or full-day programs, or

multiple-day seminars and executive retreats. Programs are specifically developed to respond to needs analysis findings. **Publications:** "Raising Standards in American Healthcare" **Seminars:** Offers the following in-house programs: The Uncommon Leader; The New American Organization; The New American Hospital; Productivity & Performance Improvement; Keys to Managerial Effectiveness; Creating Organizational Excellence; Managing Change & Conflict; Handling the Problem Employee; Gaining Power & Persuasion; Building a Winning Team; and Managing Stress, Strain, and Dis-Ease; Creating the New American Hospital: A Time For Greatness; Total Customer Satisfaction; Leading With Certainty in Uncertain Times; Raising Standards in American Health Care.

46070 ■ Management Methods Inc.
207 Johnston St. SE, Ste. 208
PO Box 1484
Decatur, AL 35602
Ph:(256)355-3896
Fax: (256)353-3140
Co. E-mail: robert@managementmethods.com
URL: http://www.managementmethods.com

E-mail: robert@managementmethods.com
Scope: Management and manufacturing consultants who specialize in showing companies how to be the low-cost, high-quality producer in their industry. Services include general management consulting, total quality management, ISO-9000/QS-9000, statistical process control, and other problem solving methods. Also speak professional for clients, trade associations, and professional groups. Clients include small businesses and Fortune 100 companies in the following industries: automotive, chemicals, textiles, utilities, petroleum, and plastics/polymers, as well as government agencies. **Publications:** "A Manager's Guide to the 10 Essentials"; "A Manager's Guide to TQM Success". **Seminars:** Statistical Process Control (SPC): Concepts and Applications; Advanced Statistical Methods; Team Problem Solving; Effective Management Methods; Measurement Systems SPC and ISO 9000; What To Do When Total Quality Management Isn't Working; Seven Golden Rules for the Best Customer Service; How To Make Quality Management a Success; Managing Without Unions; Five Techniques for Keeping Technical People From Failing as Managers; How To Stop the War Between Sales, Engineering and Manufacturing; Reengineer Your Company with Common Sense and Compassion; Having High Values in a Low Cost, High Quality Business. **Special Services:** Customized training by computer, "paperless" manufacturing. ISO, QS 9000 Registration/Documentation software, "troubleshooting" software.

46071 ■ The Management Network Group Inc.
7300 College Blvd., Ste. 302
Overland Park, KS 66210
Ph:(913)345-9315
Free: 888-480-8664
Fax: (913)451-1845
Co. E-mail: rich.nespola@tmng.com
URL: http://www.tmng.com

E-mail: rich.nespola@tmng.com
Scope: A provider of strategy, management, marketing, operational and technology consulting services to the global telecommunications industry.

46072 ■ Management Resource Partners
181 2nd Ave., Ste. 542
San Mateo, CA 94401-3813
Ph:(650)401-5850
Fax: (650)401-5850
Scope: Firm specializes in strategic planning; small business management; mergers and acquisitions; joint ventures; divestitures; interim management; crisis management; turnarounds; venture capital; appraisals and valuations.

46073 ■ Management Strategies
1000 S Old Woodward, Ste. 105
Birmingham, MI 48009
Ph:(248)258-2756
Fax: (248)258-3407

Co. E-mail: bob@hois.com

E-mail: bob@hois.com
Scope: Firm specializes in strategic planning; feasibility studies; profit enhancement; organizational studies; start-up businesses; turnarounds; business process re-engineering; industrial engineering; marketing; ecommerce.

46074 ■ Management Technology Associates Ltd.
2768 SW Sherwood Dr., Ste. 105
Portland, OR 97201-2251
Ph:(503)224-5220
Fax: (503)224-5334
Co. E-mail: lcuster@mta-ltd.com
URL: http://www.mgmt-tech.com

E-mail: lcuster@mta-ltd.com
Scope: Offers troubled company turnarounds, strategic business planning, productivity improvement, information systems, business mediation and business valuations. Industries served: manufacturing, wholesale distribution, forest products, transportation, construction, retailing, healthcare, and government. **Publications:** "What It takes to Manage in the '90's" Business Journal; Bringing Management Techniques to Small Business Clients. How to Value and Sell Your Company. **Seminars:** Strategic Business Planning; Management Control Systems, Business Dispute Resolution; Management Techniques for Small Business Clients. **Special Services:** Software and hardware selection, implementation, project management.

46075 ■ Market Focus
12 Maryland Rd.
PO Box 402
Maplewood, NJ 07040
Ph:(973)378-2470
Fax: (973)378-2470
Co. E-mail: mcss66@marketfocus.com

E-mail: mcss66@marketfocus.com
Scope: Offers advisory services to executives of corporate business units and mid-sized companies in the development and implementation of corporate and market strategies. Studies relate to business planning, new market/product entry, acquisitions and industry/competitive profiles for firms in advanced technology, business and financial services and basic industry. Projects focus on practical, effective approaches to maximizing the potential of existing operations and exploiting future growth opportunities. Practice philosophy emphasizes close client relationships, active management participation and senior consultant involvement. **Publications:** "Are Your Customers Buying What You're Selling", Constructive Strategy Newsletter; "Improving Productivity: Now More Than Ever", Constructive Strategy Newsletter; "Surviving in Hard Times", NJ Contractor. **Seminars:** Charting a Course for Future Company Growth; Marketing Planning; Construction Marketing in the 90's; Marketing and The CFO.

46076 ■ Stuart Matlins Associates
Rte. 4
PO Box 237
Woodstock, VT 05091-0237
Ph:(802)457-4000
Free: 800-962-4544
Fax: (802)457-4004
Co. E-mail: everyone@longhillpartners.com

E-mail: everyone@longhillpartners.com
Scope: Provides management consulting and research services to private and public sector clients. Services include: profit improvement; growth management; planning and organization; financial, economic and market feasibility; financial management and control; negotiations for new ventures, joint ventures and licensing of products/processes; and management training.

46077 ■ George S. May International Co.
303 S Northwest Hwy.
Park Ridge, IL 60068-4255
Ph:(847)825-8806

Free: 800-999-3020
Fax: (847)825-7937
Co. E-mail: info@georgesmay.com
URL: http://www.georgesmay.com

E-mail: info@georgesmay.com
Scope: General management consultants concentrating on the problems of medium and small-sized companies. Offers programs in organization, profit and expense control, inventory, production control, cash flow and finance, sales planning, web site development etc. Serves manufacturing, wholesale, retail, service, and healthcare businesses. **Seminars:** Break Even Analysis and Its Impact on Pricing; Health Care Facility Management.

46078 ■ McDonald Consulting Group Inc.
7701 France Ave. S, Ste. 200
Edina, MN 55435
Ph:(952)841-6357
Fax: (507)664-9389
Co. E-mail: rmcdonald@mcdonaldconsultinggroup.com
URL: http://www.mcdonaldconsultinggroup.com

E-mail: rmcdonald@mcdonaldconsultinggroup.com
Scope: A management consulting firm specializing in assisting insurance companies improve operations. Provides services in the areas of strategic planning; profit enhancement; organizational development; interim management; crisis management; turnarounds; business process re-engineering; benefits and compensation planning and total quality management (TQM).

46079 ■ Jerome W. McGee & Associates
7826 Eastern Ave. NW, Ste. 30
Washington, DC 20012-1324
Ph:(202)726-7272
Fax: (202)726-2946
Scope: Business consultants experienced in office automation, small business management, invention and patent counseling, technology commercialization, loan packaging and business plan development. **Seminars:** Marketing Research for the High-Technology Business; Introduction to Microcomputers; Marketing Technological Products to Industry; How to Evaluate Your Technical Idea; Patenting Your Own Invention.

46080 ■ MCR Capital Advisors L.L.P.
5555 San Felipe, Ste. 780
Houston, TX 77056
Ph:(713)623-6778
Fax: (713)622-0410
Co. E-mail: contact@mcrcapitaladvisors.com
URL: http://www.mcrcapitaladvisors.com

E-mail: contact@mcrcapitaladvisors.com
Scope: Valuations and strategy for mergers and acquisitions, workout agreements and development of strategic partnerships; direct business advisors to senior management and board of directors utilizing industry experience and business acumen; accounting and financial consulting for debt restructuring, outsourcing of top-side accounting services and preparation for significant financing or IPO; and consulting for IT vendor evaluations, organizational design, human performance optimization and customer relationship management strategy. Serves the unique needs of small and mid-size companies.

46081 ■ McShane Group Inc.
2345 York Rd.
Timonium, MD 21093
Ph:(410)560-0077
Fax: (410)560-2718
Co. E-mail: tmcshane@mcshanegroup.com
URL: http://www.mcshanegroup.com

E-mail: tmcshane@mcshanegroup.com
Scope: Management consulting firm specializing in helping financially troubled companies. All senior level business executives with strong operations backgrounds. Focuses on turnarounds, interim management, crisis management, debt restructuring, organizational restructuring, operating business and asset sales.

46082 ■ Medical Imaging Consultants Inc.
1037 Rte. 46 E G-2
Clifton, NJ 07013-2445
Ph:(973)574-8000
Free: 800-589-5685
Fax: (973)574-8001
Co. E-mail: info@micinfo.com
URL: http://www.micinfo.com

E-mail: info@micinfo.com
Scope: Provides management consulting services to hospitals, imaging centers, health-care companies and insurance companies. Firm specializes in interim management; crisis management; turnarounds; market research; and new product development. **Seminars:** Sectional Anatomy & Imaging Strategies; CT Cross-Trainer; CT Registry Review Program; MR Cross-Trainer; Digital Mammography Essentials for Technologists; Radiology Trends for Technologists.

46083 ■ Medical Outcomes Management Inc.
Central Street Office Pk., 132 Central St., Ste. 215
Foxborough, MA 02035-2422
Ph:(508)543-0050
Fax: (508)543-1919
Co. E-mail: info@mom-inc.com
URL: http://www.mom-inc.com

E-mail: info@mom-inc.com
Scope: A health-care management and technology consulting firm providing a specially focused group of services, such as disease management programs, pharmaco-economic studies and medical writing. Physician educational outreach. **Publications:** "Treatment of acute exacerbation's of chronic bronchitis in patients with chronic obstructive pulmonary disease: A retrospective cohort analysis or Clarithromycin extended release vs. Azithromycin," 2003; "A retrospective analysis of cyclooxygenase-II inhibitor response patterns," 2002; "The formulary management system and decision-making process at Horizon Blue Cross Blue Shield of New Jersey," Pharmacotherapy, 2001. **Seminars:** Economic Modeling as a Disease Management Tool, Academy of Managed Care Pharmacy, Apr, 2005; Integrating Disease State Management and Economics, Academy of Managed Care Pharmacy, Oct, 2004; Clinical and economic outcomes in the treatment of peripheral occlusive diseases, Mar, 2003.

46084 ■ Colmen Menard Company Inc.
The Woods, 994 Old Eagle School Rd., Ste. 1000
Wayne, PA 19087
Ph:(484)367-0300
Fax: (484)367-0305
Co. E-mail: cmci@colmenmenard.com
URL: http://www.colmenmenard.com

E-mail: cmci@colmenmenard.com
Scope: Merger and acquisition corporate finance and business advisory services for public and private companies located in North America.

46085 ■ MIIX Healthcare Group
2 Princess Rd.
Lawrenceville, NJ 08648
Ph:(609)219-1111
Free: 800-234-6449
Fax: (609)219-6727
URL: http://www.miix.com
Scope: Firm provides comprehensive healthcare consulting services and unique products designed to assist physicians, and healthcare organizations meet the challenges of a managed care environment. Consulting services range from practice management to network formation and marketing, practice valuations, practice mergers and acquisitions, and compliance.

46086 ■ Miller/Cook & Associates Inc.
1316 2nd St.
Roanoke, VA 24016
Ph:(540)345-4393
Free: 800-591-1141
Fax: (239)394-2652
Co. E-mail: ccook2412@aol.com
URL: http://www.millercook.com

E-mail: ccook2412@aol.com
Scope: Enrollment management, specializing in revenue-based enrollment: helping admissions and financial aid with the important business of balancing head count, net revenue, and quality, communications strategies. **Publications:** "Capital Gains: Surviving in an Increasingly For-Profit World"; "Making Steps to a Brighter Future".

46087 ■ Miller, Hellwig Associates
150 W End Ave.
New York, NY 10023-5713
Ph:(212)799-0471
Fax: (212)877-0186
Co. E-mail: millerhelwig@earthlink.net

E-mail: millerhelwig@earthlink.net
Scope: Consulting services in the areas of start-up businesses; small business management; employee surveys and communication; performance appraisals; executive searches; team building; personnel policies and procedures; market research. Also involved in improving cross-cultural and multi-cultural relationships, particularly with Japanese clients. **Seminars:** Objectives and standards/recruiting for boards of directors.

46088 ■ R.E. Moulton Inc.
50 Doaks Ln.
Marblehead, MA 01945
Ph:(781)631-1325
Fax: (781)631-2165
Co. E-mail: mike_lee@remoultoninc.com
URL: http://www.remoultoninc.com

E-mail: mike_lee@remoultoninc.com
Scope: Health Risk Management for employees with 20 or more employees. Specialize in Plan Design and Third Party Administration Services.

46089 ■ Mykytyn Consulting Group Inc.
185 N Redwood Dr., Ste. 200
San Rafael, CA 94903
Ph:(415)491-1770
Fax: (415)491-1251
Co. E-mail: info@mcgi.com

E-mail: info@mcgi.com
Scope: Develops structural models of new businesses and industries. Provides an interim CEO and management team at the start-up of a new business. Experienced in computer science and operations research.

46090 ■ National Bureau of Certified Consultants Inc.
1850 5th Ave.
San Diego, CA 92101
Ph:(619)239-7076
Free: 888-543-1114
Fax: (619)296-3580
Co. E-mail: nationalbureau@att.net

E-mail: nationalbureau@att.net
Scope: Referral services available to companies seeking Certified Professional Consultants to Management. These services are on a no fee basis. Industries served: Manufacturing and Services Industries. **Publications:** Consultants Bulletin published six times per year. **Seminars:** Annual conference for management consultants.

46091 ■ Navarro, Kim & Associates
529 N Charles St., Ste. 202
Baltimore, MD 21201-5043
Ph:(410)837-6317
Fax: (410)837-6294
Co. E-mail: bnavarro@sprynet.com

E-mail: bnavarro@sprynet.com
Scope: Firm specializes in bridging the gap between firms and non-traditional ethnic communities, especially in community development and institutional building.

46092 ■ The Nelson Group Ltd.
5 Milk St., Ste. 4
Portland, ME 04101

Ph:(207)775-1199
Fax: (207)775-0141
URL: http://www.nelsonltd.com
Scope: Consulting services in the areas of strategic planning; organizational development; small business management; mergers and acquisitions; joint ventures; divestitures; interim management; crisis management; turnarounds; performance appraisals; executive searches; outplacement; and team building.

46093 ■ Nightingale Associates
7445 Setting Sun Way
Columbia, MD 21046-1261
Ph:(410)381-4280
Fax: (410)381-4280
Co. E-mail: fcnight@aol.com
URL: http://www.members.aol.com/fcnight

E-mail: fcnight@aol.com
Scope: Nightingale Associates is an international management training and consulting firm. Their concentration is on improving operational performance through the utilization of the most effective modern management techniques, executive and organizational assessment, reengineering of business processes, creative strategic thinking and focusing of the energies of all organizational participants. In addition they also work in the area of supply chain management and cost reduction through the utilization of the optimum purchasing, inventory management and distribution practices. **Seminars:** Advanced Management; Business Process Reengineering; Strategic Thinking; Creative Problem Solving; Customer Service; International Purchasing and Materials Management; Fundamentals of Purchasing.

46094 ■ Oakdales Olde Towne Veterinary Hospital
144 S 1st Ave.
Oakdale, CA 95361
Ph:(209)847-9077
Fax: (209)847-4390
Scope: Provides animal agriculture management.

46095 ■ Organization Counselors Inc.
44 W Broadway, Ste. 1102
PO Box 987
Salt Lake City, UT 84101
Ph:(801)363-2900
Fax: (801)363-0861
Co. E-mail: jpanos@xmission.com

E-mail: jpanos@xmission.com
Scope: Firm specializes in organizational development; employee surveys and communication; outplacement; team building; total quality management (TQM) and continuous improvement. **Seminars:** Correcting Performance Problems; Total Quality Management; Employee Selection; Performance Management.

46096 ■ Organizational Consulting Services Inc.
230 S Bemiston Ave., Ste. 1107
Saint Louis, MO 63105-1907
Ph:(314)863-1200
Fax: (314)863-6718
Co. E-mail: info@ocs-oe.com
URL: http://www.ocs-oe.com

E-mail: info@ocs-oe.com
Scope: Services include business assessment, planning, and restructuring; team building, executive assessment and development; financial analysis and cost accounting; market analysis and customer surveys. Consultants also serve as facilitators of planning retreats, offering guidance in strategy development and goal setting. The firm works with CEO's and senior executives of privately held companies and major corporations. **Seminars:** The Integrated Executive seminars; Strategic Planning and Management; Change Management; Management Transitions; Team Building.

46097 ■ Organizational Futures
56 Pine St., Ste. 2b
Providence, RI 02903

Ph:(401)351-7110
Fax: (401)351-7158
Scope: Builder of agile human networks to champion innovation and mobilize change; to pursue business opportunities; to custom design agile organizations and communities, to foster civic engagement. **Seminars:** Facilitating for Results.

46098 ■ P2C2 Group Inc.
4101 Denfeld Ave.
Kensington, MD 20895-1514
Ph:(301)942-7985
Fax: (301)942-7986
Co. E-mail: info@p2c2group.com
URL: http://www.p2c2group.com

E-mail: info@p2c2group.com
Scope: Firm specializes in federal information technology management including capital investment management, strategic plans, policy, enterprise architecture, information security, documentation and knowledge management, OMB and NIST compliance, and IT program management. **Publications:** "How to Work with Proposal Consultants"; "Outside Reviewers for Proposals"; "The High Cost of Federal Information Technology".

46099 ■ Papa & Associates Inc.
200 Consumers Rd., Ste. 305
Toronto, ON, Canada M2J 4R4
Ph:(416)512-7272
Fax: (416)512-2016
Co. E-mail: ppapa@papa-associates.com
URL: http://www.papa-associates.com

E-mail: ppapa@papa-associates.com
Scope: Firm provides broad based management consulting services in the areas of quality assurance, environmental, health and safety and integrated management systems.

46100 ■ Parker Consultants Inc.
67 Mason St.
Greenwich, CT 06830
Ph:(203)869-9400
Scope: Firm specializes in strategic planning; organizational development; small business management; performance appraisals; executive searches; team building; and customer service audits.

46101 ■ PCS Laboratory Services Group Inc.
4750 Venture Dr., Ste. 400
Ann Arbor, MI 48108
Ph:(734)662-6363
Free: 800-860-5454
Fax: (734)662-7118
Co. E-mail: root@chilab.com

E-mail: root@chilab.com
Scope: Park City Solutions/Laboratory Services Group offers a comprehensive set of solutions to today's laboratory management challenges, such as: recruitment support, clinical laboratory operations improvement (identification and quantification of non-value added activities, workstation comparative cost analysis, etc.), advanced benchmarking methodology, multi-lab consolidation feasibility assessment, laboratory sales and marketing, regulatory compliance reviews and training, lab billing and collections consulting, and pathology staffing and compensation consulting.

46102 ■ Performance Consulting Associates Inc.
3700 Crestwood Pky., Ste. 100
Duluth, GA 30096
Ph:(770)717-2737
Fax: (770)717-7014
Co. E-mail: info@pcaconsulting.com
URL: http://www.pcaconsulting.com

E-mail: info@pcaconsulting.com
Scope: Maintenance consulting and engineering firm specializing in production planning, project management, team building, and re-engineering maintenance. **Publications:** "Asset Reliability Coordinator," Maintenance Technology; "Does Planning Pay," Plant Services; "Know What It Is You Have To Maintain," Maintenance Technology.

46103 ■ Performance Consulting Group

8535 Baymeadows Rd., Ste. 143-3
Jacksonville, FL 32202
Ph:(904)448-4473
Fax: (904)287-1244
Scope: Consulting services in the areas of strategic planning; profit enhancement; product development; production planning.

46104 ■ Pioneer Business Consultants

9042 Garfield Ave., Ste. 312
Huntington Beach, CA 92646
Ph:(714)964-7600
Fax: (714)962-6585
Scope: Offers general management consulting specializing in business acquisitions, tax and business planning, cash flow analyses, business valuations and business sales and expert witness court testimony regarding business sales, valuations and accounting.

46105 ■ Primavera Systems Inc.

3 Bala Plz. W, Ste. 700
Bala Cynwyd, PA 19004
Ph:(610)667-8600
Free: 800-423-0245
Fax: (610)667-7894
Co. E-mail: info@primavera.com
URL: http://www.primavera.com

E-mail: info@primavera.com
Scope: Provider of comprehensive project portfolio management, control and execution software.

46106 ■ Priority Process Associates Inc.

1236 E Horseshoe Bend Ct.
Rochester Hills, MI 48306
Ph:(248)608-8966
Fax: (248)608-8966
Scope: A management consulting firm with expertise in computer technology, telecommunications, and information services. Provides the following specific services: business process re-engineering-establishes correctly implemented, computer technologies that empower and accelerate work groups to act autonomously but in concert with corporate goals, document work-flow analysis-models and simulates the flow of documents through selected organizational processes, enterprise metrics-identifies unique metrics for enterprises to evaluate their continuous improvement of business processes, cost justification-identifies value using Activity Based Costing and innovative approaches to quantify time-to-market reductions, project profitability, and reduce and manage costs, proposal development-generates Requests for Proposals to solicit competitive quotations for cost effective off-the-shelf software, computer hardware, and communication products, implementation planning-negotiates implementation plans for clients through qualified software vendors, custom software integrators, and hardware, communication, and outsource suppliers, project auditing-audits the integration, installation and use of on-time, quality enterprise multi-vendor software, hardware and communications systems on computer networks, training-expands clients knowledge through information sources, and client-specific management seminars and skill building workshops. Serves manufacturing industries in the United States.

46107 ■ Professional Management Institute

4405 S Sandusky Ave.
Tulsa, OK 74135
Ph:(918)492-3007
Fax: (918)492-3009
URL: http://www.pmiimpac.com
Scope: Provides Integrated Management Planning and Control (IMPAC)® profitability improvement services, workshops, materials, and software based on the Planagement® System, a step-by-step method for organizing, planning and analyzing information so that better, more timely decisions can be made and cost effective actions developed for implementation. Programs can be specifically tailored for any industry and any size organization. **Publications:** "Planagement®-Moving Concept Into Reality; Thank God It's Monday"; "Bridging the Gap series", manuals, work-

books, video, audio, licensee traning programs, self instructional and tailored materials. **Seminars:** The continuous improvement process; Meeting the needs of the top management team with one enterprise management system; Applied intelligence information technology: How to make your sales go up faster than the market goes up and down slower than the market goes down with profits increasing faster than sales. **Special Services:** IMPACT® (Integrated Management Planning And Control) software; QMS (Quantitative Management System), a proactive financial management PC software; planagement®; PMI®.

46108 ■ Quality Specialists

13422 215th Ave. E
Sumner, WA 98390
Ph:(253)862-4937
Fax: (253)862-4937
Co. E-mail: inquiries@qualityspecialists.com
URL: http://www.qualityspecialists.com

E-mail: inquiries@qualityspecialists.com
Scope: Offers services in quality control, audit configuration control, and organizational culture change.

46109 ■ Research Applications Inc.

414 Hungerford Dr., Ste. 220
Rockville, MD 20850-4125
Ph:(301)251-6717
Free: 888-311-6221
Fax: (301)251-6719
Co. E-mail: dfriedman@researchapps.com
URL: http://www.researchapps.com

E-mail: dfriedman@researchapps.com
Scope: Offers counsel on the development and administration of job performance evaluation and assessment, cognitive ability tests, large scale survey administration, management training, logistical support for meetings and conferences, computer programming support for survey and test and measurement projects, and development of financial, auditing and training software for small business. International experts and specialists in the development of mail test decks to test United States and foreign-made postal handling equipment. Specialists in computer generated and computer adaptive achievement test design and administration. Serves private industries as well as government agencies. **Seminars:** Gender Awareness in the Workplace; Humor in the Workplace; Understanding and Using Assessments (Validity/Reliability); Diversity in the Workplace; Structured Interviews.

46110 ■ Rose & Crangle Ltd.

117 N 4th St.
PO Box 285
Lincoln, KS 67455-0285
Ph:(785)524-5050
Fax: (785)524-3130
Co. E-mail: rcltd@nckcn.com

E-mail: rcltd@nckcn.com
Scope: Firm provides evaluation, planning and policy analyses for universities, associations, foundations, governmental agencies and private companies engaged in scientific, technological or educational activities. Special expertise in the development of new institutions. Special skills in providing planning and related group facilitation workshops.

46111 ■ Rothschild Strategies Unlimited L. L.C.

PO Box 7568
Wilton, CT 06897-7568
Ph:(203)846-6898
Fax: (203)847-1426
Co. E-mail: bill@strategyleader.com
URL: http://www.strategyleader.com

E-mail: bill@strategyleader.com
Scope: Consults with senior management and business level strategy teams to develop overall strategic direction, set priorities and creates sustainable competitive advantages and differentiators. Enables organizations to enhance their own strategic thinking and

leadership skills so that they can continue to develop and implement profitable growth strategies. **Publications:** "Putting It All Together-a guide to strategic thinking"; "Competitive Advantage"; "Ristaker, Caretaker, Surgeon & Undertaker-four faces of strategic leadership". **Special Services:** StrategyLeader®.

46112 ■ David G. Schantz & Associates

29 Wood Run Cir.
Rochester, NY 14612-2271
Ph:(716)723-0760
Fax: (716)723-8724
Co. E-mail: daveschantz@yahoo.com
URL: http://www.daveschantz.freeservers.com

E-mail: daveschantz@yahoo.com
Scope: Consultant provides industrial engineering services for photofinishing labs, including amateur-wholesale, professional, commercial, school, and package.

46113 ■ Schneider Consulting Group Inc.

50 S Steele St., Ste. 390
Denver, CO 80209
Ph:(303)320-4413
Fax: (303)320-5795
Co. E-mail: info@scgfambus.com
URL: http://www.schneiderconsultinggroup.com

E-mail: info@scgfambus.com
Scope: Assists family-owned and privately-held business transition to the next generation and/or to a more professionally managed company, turnaround consulting for small and medium size companies.

46114 ■ Shealy & Associates

1100 Baker Lake Rd.
Guthrie, OK 73044
Ph:(405)282-5578
Free: 800-484-9446
Fax: (405)282-7488
Co. E-mail: lsshealy@aol.com

E-mail: lsshealy@aol.com
Scope: A network of consultants whose mission is to assist small-to-mid size organizations implement successful strategic management practices.

46115 ■ Sklar & Associates

1101 S Arlington Ridge Rd. Ste. 511
Arlington, VA 22202-1925
Ph:(202)257-5061
Fax: (202)828-4130
Co. E-mail: sklarincdc@aol.com
URL: http://www.sklarinc.com

E-mail: sklarincdc@aol.com
Scope: Provides Audit Oversight services to listed corporations on Sarbanes-Oxley compliance. **Seminars:** Financial Analysis in MBA; Emerging Company Finance; Due Diligence in Business Acquisition; Business Valuation. **Special Services:** Financial Modeling. Course titled *Understanding and Detecting Deceptive Creative Accounting Practices.*

46116 ■ Smart Ways to Work

1441 Franklin St., Ste. 301
Oakland, CA 94612
Ph:(510)763-8482
Free: 800-599-8463
Fax: (510)763-0790
Co. E-mail: odette@smartwaystowork.com
URL: http://www.smartwaystowork.com

E-mail: odette@smartwaystowork.com
Scope: A management consulting firm specializing in the training of supervisors, managers and professional staff in the area of time management, problem solving, decision making and strategic planning. Assists businesses and corporations in developing and implementing programs for increased productivity, greater profit and improved employee morale. Serves private industries as well as government agencies. **Publications:** "Surviving Information Overload: How to Find, Filter, and Focus on What's Important"; "Take Back Your Life: Smart Ways to Simplify Daily Living"; "Or-

ganizing Your Workspace: A Guide to Personal Productivity"; "365 Ways to Simplify Your Work Life". **Seminars:** Managing Multiple Demands: Surviving Ground Zero; Defending Your Life: Balancing Work And Home; Desktop Sprawl: Conquer Your Paper Pile-Up.

46117 ■ Smith, Turner & Reeves P.A.
200 E Capital St., Ste. 100
PO Box 23027
Jackson, MS 39201-2200
Ph:(601)948-6700
Fax: (601)948-6000
URL: http://www.str-cpa.com
Scope: Offers services in business advisory, merger and acquisitions, physician practice management, financial management, turnaround and operational reviews. Audit, tax and consulting services in the healthcare, utilities, telecommunications, insurance, government, lenders, manufacturing, retail/wholesale, construction, and law firm industries. **Publications:** The Spirit of Success-A Financial Guide to Starting a Business in Mississippi. **Seminars:** Workshops for Lenders - Financial Statements; Troubled Borrowers; Asset Based Lending; Bookkeeping Workshops; Tax Law Updates.

46118 ■ Stalley Associates Inc.
10635 James Cir. S
Minneapolis, MN 55431-4157
Ph:(952)888-0617
Fax: (952)888-5403
Co. E-mail: info@stalley.com
URL: http://www.stalley.com

E-mail: info@stalley.com
Scope: Advises management of companies in the areas of finance, administrative and general management, corporate objectives, policies and procedures, and management and organization audits. Firm has developed a particular expertise in advising management of young and growing companies. Advises in strategic planning, capital planning and financing strategies, securing private and public investment capital, establishing strategic alliances, management and staff organizational restructuring, working with board of directors, shareholders and serving as chief financial officer and chief operations officer on a contract basis.

46119 ■ R.F. Stengel & Company Inc.
780 Yellow Springs Rd.
Paoli, PA 19301
Ph:(610)296-8950
Fax: (610)296-8991
Scope: A management consulting and crisis management firm providing services to financially and operationally troubled companies. Develops and implements business recovery programs.

46120 ■ Herbert Stillman
21405 Woodchuck Ln.
Boca Raton, FL 33428
Ph:(561)483-0624
Co. E-mail: herb616@aol.com

E-mail: herb616@aol.com
Scope: Offers consulting services in the following areas: management, start-ups, profit maximization, world wide negotiating, interim management, corporate debt resolution.

46121 ■ Straightline Services Inc.
11 Centre St., Ste. 10
Salem, CT 06420
Ph:(860)889-7929
Fax: (860)885-1894
Co. E-mail: straitln@aol.com

E-mail: straitln@aol.com
Scope: Design and implementation of organizational infrastructure, business plans and troubleshooting. Emphasis on operations with a central and field or satellite offices. Industries Served: Construction, resorts, Indian tribes, academies, small-medium sized business- mostly privately held. **Publications:** Photos

published in "Engineering News Record," "New England Construction News." **Seminars:** Start up, Troubleshooting seminars. **Special Services:** Commercial/Industrial Photography - Member of CIPNE (Comm/Ind Photographers of New England). Also member of the National Bureau of Professional Management Consultants is a CPCM or Certified Professional Consultant to Management.

46122 ■ Strategic MindShare Consulting
1401 Brickell Ave., Ste. 640
Miami, FL 33131
Ph:(305)377-2220
Fax: (305)377-2280
Co. E-mail: dee@strategicmindshare.com
URL: http://www.strategicmindshare.com

E-mail: dee@strategicmindshare.com
Scope: Firm specializes in strategic planning; feasibility studies; profit enhancement; organizational development; start-up businesses; mergers and acquisitions; joint ventures; divestitures; interim management; crisis management; turnarounds; new product development and competitive analysis. **Publications:** "Top Ten CEO Burning Issues for 2005"; "Top Ten Consumer Behavioral Trends for 2005"; "The Influence Factors".

46123 ■ Syed Hussayn TMCI
95 October Ln.
Aurora, ON, Canada L4G 7A1
Ph:(905)949-4555
Fax: (905)949-9116
Co. E-mail: syedn.hussain@sympatico.ca

E-mail: syedn.hussain@sympatico.ca
Scope: Business process re-engineering, change management, financial restructuring & insolvency, consumer & corporate bankruptcy, financial/debt management, investments & insurance advisory services, management/executive development, marketing management, organizational development, needs assessment, financial counselling, succession planning, performance management/measurement, program evaluation, project management, strategic planning and import/export advisory. **Publications:** "Innovative Management"; "Team Building and Leadership"; "Financial Planning"; "Estate Planning"; "Risk Management"; "Export/Import Trade Finance Mechanics"; "Marketing and Sales Management"; "What Your Banker Needs to Know"; "Building A Successful Financial Plan". **Seminars:** Workplace Solutions Seminars; Export Development; Executive Education & Leadership Development; Financial Planning; Estate Planning; Succession Planning; Wealth Accumulation and Management; Strategic Planning/Competitive Positioning.

46124 ■ Tamayo Consulting Inc.
169 Saxony Rd., Ste. 112
Encinitas, CA 92024-6779
Free: 800-580-9606
Fax: (760)479-1465
Co. E-mail: info@tamayoconsulting.com
URL: http://www.tamayoconsulting.com

E-mail: info@tamayoconsulting.com
Scope: Training and consulting firm specializing in: leadership and team development. Industries served: private, non-profit, government, educational.

46125 ■ TC International Marketing Inc.
18 Blooms Corners Rd.
Warwick, NY 10990-2401
Ph:(845)258-7482
Fax: (845)986-2130
Co. E-mail: tcintl@warwick.net
URL: http://www.tcintlmarketing.com

E-mail: tcintl@warwick.net
Scope: Business expansion consulting, including feasibility studies, mergers and acquisitions, divestments, market research, and strategizing.

46126 ■ Team Focus Group
46 Pineridge Cres.
Saint Albert, AB, Canada T8N 4P7

Ph:(780)460-1625
Fax: (780)460-2003
URL: http://www.teamfocus.org
Scope: An international consultancy group, specializing in the field of value and risk management, including project management, partnering and team alignment. Services include business program re-focusing, strategy formulation, program planning, project definition, decision analysis, risk management, and team building. **Seminars:** Sharpening The Performance Edge: Project Delivery Enhancement Through Value Assurance, Nov, 2003; Results Oriented Performance Using The Project Performance Enhancement Approach, Jun, 2002; Value Is In The Eye Of The Beholder, Part 1: A Framework For Smart Project Development And Service Enhancement, May 2002; Accredited SAVE International Module I Basic Training Seminars; Team Building and Partnering training; Advanced Project Management training.

46127 ■ Trendzitions Inc.
310 Goddard, Ste. 100
Irvine, CA 92618
Ph:(949)727-9100
Free: 800-266-2767
Fax: (949)851-8444
Co. E-mail: bgeer@trendzitions.com
URL: http://www.trendzitions.com

E-mail: bgeer@trendzitions.com
Scope: Provides services in the areas of communications consulting, project management, construction management, and furniture procurement. Offers information on spatial uses, building codes, ADA compliance, and city ordinances. Also offers budget projections.

46128 ■ Turnaround Inc.
3415 A St. NW
Gig Harbor, WA 98335
Ph:(253)857-6730
Fax: (253)857-6344
Co. E-mail: info@turnround-inc.com
URL: http://www.turnaround-inc.com

E-mail: info@turnround-inc.com
Scope: Firm provides interim executive management assistance and management advisory to small, medium and family-owned businesses that are not meeting their goals. Services include acting as an interim executive or on-site manager. Extensive practices in arena of bankruptcy management. **Publications:** "How to Identify Problem and Promising Management"; "How to Tell if Your Company is a Bankruptcy Candidate"; "Signs that Your Company is in Trouble"; "The Turnaround Specialist: How to File a Petition Under 11 USC 11". **Seminars:** Competitive Intelligence Gathering.

46129 ■ TWD & Associates
431 S Patton Ave.
Arlington Heights, IL 60005-2253
Ph:(847)398-6410
Fax: (847)255-5095
Co. E-mail: tdoo@aol.com

E-mail: tdoo@aol.com
Scope: Consulting specialists in small business management particularly in the areas of personnel, training, marketing, franchising, sales, time management, budgeting, raising capital, and long-range planning. **Seminars:** Alternative Methods of Financing for Franchising; Effectiveness of Organizational Development Training Programs for Hourly-Hire Workers in Manufacturing Plants.

46130 ■ Tweed-Weber Inc.
PO Box 112
Reading, PA 19603-0112
Ph:(610)376-6615
Free: 800-999-6615
Fax: (610)376-9161
Co. E-mail: mail@tweedweber.com
URL: http://www.tweedweber.com

E-mail: mail@tweedweber.com
Scope: A consulting firm specializing in customized market research and strategic planning. Strategic

planning research: customer satisfaction surveys; employee satisfaction surveys; market assessment customer satisfaction surveys. **Seminars:** Board of Directors Retreats; Executive Retreats; Executive and Management Development.

46131 ■ Unlimited Success Enterprises
3552 Vancouver Ave., 2nd Fl.
PO Box 880885
San Diego, CA 92168-0885
Free: 888-787-0419
Co. E-mail: info@whatmakesyousmile.com
URL: http://www.whatmakesyousmile.com

E-mail: info@whatmakesyousmile.com
Scope: Personal Success Coaching and Life Skill Training. One on one, group seminars, Critical thinking with executives, CEO's, business owners. Phone or in person. **Seminars:** What Makes You Smile?, Smile Files, Have you left your distinctive mark on the world today?, Brainstorms For Sale, Is the Customer Always Right?, Make the best of your given talent, A smile is a lifetime of balance.

46132 ■ ValueNomics Value Specialists
10 Almaden Blvd., Ste. 1450
San Jose, CA 95113-2226
Ph:(408)257-8521
Fax: (408)257-1146
Co. E-mail: value@valuenomics.com
URL: http://www.valuenomics.com

E-mail: value@valuenomics.com
Scope: Specializes in valuations; appraisals; strategic planning; feasibility studies; mergers and acquisitions; joint ventures; divestitures; competitive intelligence; and due diligence. Acts as an expert witness. Offers litigation support. **Publications:** "The Business of Business Valuation and the CPA as an expert witness". **Special Services:** ValueNomics®.

46133 ■ VenturEdge Corp.
4711 Yonge St., Ste. 1105
Toronto, ON, Canada M2N 6K8
Ph:(416)224-2000
Fax: (416)224-2376
Co. E-mail: info@venturedge.com
URL: http://www.venturedge.com

E-mail: info@venturedge.com
Scope: Services include strategy formulation; performance improvement; business coaching; competitive intelligence; business planning; acquiring capital; financial management; and succession planning in mergers and acquisitions.

46134 ■ Verbit & Co.
19 Bala Ave.
Bala Cynwyd, PA 19004
Ph:(610)668-9840
Scope: The management consulting services of Verbit & Company apply to practically every facet of a business, from operations and administration to financial and information systems management. These services include: general management - to assist executives and managers fulfill their mission and to assure that adequate planning of day-to-day operations occurs; that controls are sufficient to safeguard valuable resources; and that results of decisions are reviewed in sufficient time to effect continuing action. Financial planning and control - to develop accounting, budgeting, forecasting, and other information systems for the management of resources and evaluation of strategies. Information systems and electronic data processing - to promote efficient and effective use of computers in company operations; operations planning and control - to design systems to promote effective management of production facilities; cost accounting and management - to design systems to record and report costs of operations; and human resources - to review organizational structures, personnel planning and compensation programs. Other services include: evaluation of desk-top computer systems for small firms; CAD/CAM implementation plan and orderly introduction of CAD/CAM to client company; and public sector services to assist with

evaluation and implementation of governmental accounting systems and law enforcement information systems. Industries served: manufacturing, distribution, metals casting, equipment and components, professional services, healthcare, retail, nonprofit, and government. **Seminars:** Presents seminars on Integrating Manufacturing Management Systems with Business Systems; Negotiating Information Systems Agreements with Suppliers. **Special Services:** Low volume document/image scanning; low volume document scanning -OCR editing.

46135 ■ Via Nova Consulting
1228 Winburn Dr.
Atlanta, GA 30344
Ph:(404)761-7484
Fax: (404)762-7123
Scope: Consulting services in the areas of strategic planning; privatization; executive searches; market research; customer service audits; new product development; competitive intelligence; and Total Quality Management (TQM).

46136 ■ Vision Management
149 Meadows Rd.
Lafayette, NJ 07848-3120
Ph:(973)702-1116
Fax: (201)702-8311
Scope: Firm specializes in profit enhancement; strategic planning; business process re-engineering; industrial engineering; facilities planning; team building; inventory management; and Total Quality Management (TQM).

46137 ■ WBS Western Business Services Ltd.
1269 Lindsay St.
Regina, SK, Canada S4N 3B4
Ph:(306)522-1493
Fax: (306)522-9076
Co. E-mail: wbs@accesscomm.ca
URL: http://www.wbs.bz

E-mail: wbs@accesscomm.ca
Scope: Business and management consulting services in areas such as finance, marketing, accounting, and business planning.

46138 ■ Weich & Bilotti Inc.
74 Main St.
Framingham, MA 01702
Ph:(508)879-8007
Fax: (508)879-7811
Co. E-mail: info@weich-bilotti.com
URL: http://www.weich.com

E-mail: info@weich-bilotti.com
Scope: Specializes in business plans, venture capital, computer information systems, turnaround/interim management, retail consulting, start-up process, college recruiting, and IS and IT personnel.

46139 ■ Wheeler and Young Inc.
33 Peter St.
Markham, ON, Canada L3P 2A5
Ph:(905)471-9064
Fax: (905)471-9989
Co. E-mail: wheeler@ericwheeler.ca

E-mail: wheeler@ericwheeler.ca
Scope: Business management services, including ISO 9000 implementation, software development process, and knowledge-management in organizations. Industries Served: Knowledge-based industries, including software and hardware development, medical and legal professionals, information service providers. **Seminars:** The Web, Software, and Getting it Right.

46140 ■ Donald C. Wright
3906 Lawndale Ln. N
Minneapolis, MN 55446-2940
Ph:(763)478-5595
Co. E-mail: donaldwright@compuserve.com

E-mail: donaldwright@compuserve.com
Scope: Consultant offers expertise in accounting and taxes, personal financial planning, strategic planning,

pension/profit sharing planning and administration, professional practice management and surveys. Surveys and consultations performed worldwide. **Seminars:** Qualified pension plans and employee welfare benefit plans.

46141 ■ Bruce D. Wyman Co.
6147 Poburn Landing Ct.
Burke, VA 22015-2535
Ph:(703)503-9753
Fax: (703)503-2091
Co. E-mail: bdwyman@bdwyman.com
URL: http://www.bdwyman.com

E-mail: bdwyman@bdwyman.com
Scope: Provides strategic business planning services to aid small and micro for-profit and nonprofit businesses and associations in identifying and handling challenges and opportunities in an environment of incomplete information. Services include business environmental scanning; mission, goal, and strategy identification and development; and development of integrated implementation plans to convert intentions into actions. Provide training in quality management tools, processes, and applications, as well as ASQ certification examination preparation. Industries served: all industries, with special emphasis on smaller firms and associations including micro businesses. **Seminars:** Strategic Business Planning for Small and Micro Businesses and Associations; quality management and processes consulting and training (CQ Mgr. and CQIA).

FRANCHISES AND BUSINESS OPPORTUNITIES

46142 ■ LMI Canada Inc.
205 Matheson Blvd. E, Unit 15
Mississauga, ON, Canada L4Z 3E3
Ph:(905)890-0504
Free: 877-857-4083
Fax: (905)890-2498
Co. E-mail: info@lmicanada.ca
URL: http://www.lmi-inc.com
No. of Franchise Units: 15. **No. of Company-Owned Units:** 1. **Founded:** 1980. **Franchised:** 1998. **Description:** The franchise is a well-known personal, organizational and management development company, which enhances performance, productivity and profitability of their companies. **Franchise Fee:** $38,000. **Training:** Initial and ongoing support provided.

COMPUTERIZED DATABASES

46143 ■ *Corporate Governance Library*
The Bureau of National Affairs Inc.
1231 25th St. NW
Washington, DC 20037
Ph:(202)452-4200
Free: 800-372-1033
Fax: (202)452-4226
Co. E-mail: customercare@bna.com
URL: http://www.bna.com
Description: Contains information on corporate governance. Subjects include annual meetings of shareholders, audit committees, application of the business judgment rule, compensation committees, directors' fiduciary duties, piercing the corporate veil, poison pills, insider trading, boards of directors, director indemnification, executive compensation, and minority shareholder rights. Covers highlights of significant developments in corporate governance, news and case reports, conference coverages, analysis of corporate governance topics, and worksheets. Enables users to search on an alphabetical list of subjects. **Availability:** Online: The Bureau of National Affairs Inc. **Type:** Full text.

46144 ■ *Leadership and Management in Engineering*
American Society of Civil Engineers
1801 Alexander Bell Dr.
Reston, VA 20191-4400
Ph:(703)295-6300
Free: 800-548-2723
Fax: (703)295-6222
Co. E-mail: gsd_master@asce.org
URL: http://www.asce.org
Description: Contains information on management and leadership in the field of engineering. Encompasses new stories and case studies on topics including capital accumulation and retention, project management, marketing, budgeting, strategic planning, quality control, career development, team building, performance improvement, networking, partnering, risk management, law and ethics, managing people and profits, and related topics. **Availability:** Online: American Society of Civil Engineers. **Type:** Full text.

46145 ■ *Stern's Management Review*
Stern and Associates
11260 Overland Ave., Ste. 16A
Culver City, CA 90230
Ph:(310)838-0551
Co. E-mail: info@hrconsultant.com
URL: http://www.hrconsultant.com/index.html
Description: Contains business management information and ideas from the print version of Stern's Management Review, a quarterly management newsletter. Includes the full text of editorials from the newsletter since 1992. Covers such issues as business trends, leadership, corporate downsizing, management, compensation, and much more. **Availability:** Online: Stern and Associates. **Type:** Full text.

46146 ■ *World Databases in Management*
K.G. Saur Verlag KG
Ortlerstrasse 8
Postfach 701620
D-81373 Munich, Germany
Ph:49 89 769 02 0
Fax: 49 89 769 02 150
Co. E-mail: saur.info@thomson.com
URL: http://www.saur.de/
Ed: Chris Armstrong, Editor. **Released:** Published 1995. **Price:** $198, individuals eur hardbound; $341, individuals. **Covers:** Management information on databases, including administration, advertising, consumerism, economics, marketing, and public relations. **Entries Include:** Database name, description, years of coverage, number of records held, geographical coverage, languages, search software used, search aids and manuals, type of database, provider information. **Arrangement:** Subject then alphabetically.

LIBRARIES

46147 ■ Boston University–Frederick S. Pardee Management Library
595 Commonwealth Ave.
Boston, MA 02215
Ph:(617)353-4301
Fax: (617)353-4307
Co. E-mail: ajac@bu.edu
URL: http://www.bu.edu/library/management/
Contact: Arlyne A. Jackson, Lib.Hd.
Scope: Management and management-related fields, healthcare management, public management, nonprofit management. **Services:** Library open to the public. **Holdings:** 91,446 volumes; 333,106 microforms; 20,000 e-subscriptions (journals and databases). **Subscriptions:** 436 journals and other serials.

46148 ■ Business Development Bank of Canada–Research & Information Centre
5 Place Ville Marie, Ste. 300
Montreal, QC, Canada H3B 5E7
Ph:(514)283-7632
Fax: (514)283-0439
Co. E-mail: odette.lavoie@bdc.ca

Contact: Odette Lavoie, Sr.Info.Spec.
Scope: Small business, management, Canadian business and industry, banking and finance, development banking. **Services:** Interlibrary loan; Library not open to the public. **Holdings:** 5000 books; CD-ROMs. **Subscriptions:** 100 journals and other serials; 7 newspapers.

46149 ■ Canada School of Public Service–Library
373 Sussex Dr.
Ottawa, ON, Canada K1N 6Z2
Ph:(613)943-5599
Fax: (613)943-5677
Co. E-mail: estelle.lacroix@csps-efpc.gc.ca
URL: http://www.myschool-monecole.gc.ca/main_e.html
Contact: Estelle Lacroix
Scope: Management, government, public administration, coaching, leadership, diversity. **Services:** Interlibrary loan; copying. **Holdings:** 5000 books; 450 videos; 35 audio cassettes. **Subscriptions:** 6 newspapers.

46150 ■ Carnegie Library of Pittsburgh–Library Center
Business Dept.
612 Smithfield St.
Pittsburgh, PA 15222
Ph:(412)281-7141
Fax: (412)471-1724
Co. E-mail: wernerr@carnegielibrary.org
URL: http://www.clpgh.org/locations/business/
Contact: Roye Werner, Dept.Hd.
Scope: Investments, small business, entrepreneurship, management, marketing, insurance, advertising, personal finance, accounting, real estate, job and career, international business. **Services:** Interlibrary loan; Library open to the public. **Holdings:** 14,000 business volumes; VF materials; microfilm; looseleaf services; AV cassettes. **Subscriptions:** 350 business journals, serials, and newspapers.

46151 ■ Chicago Public Library Central Library–Business/Science/Technology Division
Harold Washington Library Center
400 S. State St., 4th Fl.
Chicago, IL 60605
Ph:(312)747-4450
Fax: (312)747-4975
URL: http://www.chipublib.org/001hwlc/hwbst.html
Contact: Marcia Dellenbach, BST Div.Chf.
Scope: Small business, marketing, technology, corporate reports, investments, management, personnel, patents, physical and biological sciences, medicine, health, computer science, careers, environmental information, gardening, cookbooks. **Services:** Interlibrary loan; copying; division open to the public. **Holdings:** 415,000 books; 52,100 bound periodical volumes; 33,000 reels of microfilm; Securities and Exchange Commission (SEC) reports; federal specifications and standards; American National Standards Institute standards; corporate Annual reports. **Subscriptions:** 4000 journals and other serials; 8 newspapers.

46152 ■ Michigan (State) Financial Independence Agency–Office of Training and Staff Development–Resource Library (Grand)
Grand Tower, Ste. 301
235 S. Grand Ave.
Lansing, MI 48909
Ph:(517)335-4698
Fax: (517)241-7041
Contact: Ron Walters
Scope: Management, supervision, self-development. **Services:** Library open to governmental units, private children's agencies and private contractors. **Holdings:** 350 videotapes; 150 audiocassettes; 100 book summaries.

46153 ■ Nichols College–Conant Library
Center Rd.
Dudley, MA 01571
Ph:(508)213-2222
Free: 877-266-2681

Co. E-mail: reference@nichols.edu
URL: http://www.nichols.edu/library/
Contact: Jim Douglas, Lib.Dir.
Scope: Management, advertising, finance and accounting, small business, marketing, taxation, economics, International trade, humanities. **Services:** Interlibrary loan; copying; information service to groups; document delivery; Library open to Dudley and Webster residents. **Holdings:** 48,000 volumes; 1677 audio/visual titles; 3804 reels of microfilm. **Subscriptions:** 278 journals and electronic subscriptions.

46154 ■ Ontario Ministry of Economic Development and Trade–InfoSource
900 Bay St.
Hearst Block, 6th Fl.
Toronto, ON, Canada M7A 2E1
Ph:(416)325-6626
Fax: (416)325-6825
Co. E-mail: janice.somers@edt.gov.on.ca
Scope: Trade, industry, small business, technology, management, company information. **Services:** Copying; scanning. **Holdings:** 200 books; microfiche; 20 CD-ROMs.

46155 ■ Southeastern University–Library
501 I St., SW
Washington, DC 20024
Ph:(202)478-8272
Fax: (202)488-8093
Co. E-mail: library@seu.edu
URL: http://www.seu.edu/gen/library/default.htm
Contact: O.D. Alexander, MLS, Dir.
Scope: Management, public administration, taxes, marketing, accounting, computer science, childhood development education, health services administration, business management, information systems, nonprofit management. **Services:** Interlibrary loan; copying; Library open to the public for reference use only. **Holdings:** 40,000 books; 53 bound periodical volumes. **Subscriptions:** 150 journals and other serials; 6 newspapers.

46156 ■ Strategic Decisions Group–Information Center
735 Emerson St.
Palo Alto, CA 94301
Ph:(650)475-4400
Fax: (650)475-4401
URL: http://www.sdg.com
Contact: Robin Arnold, CEO
Scope: Business, management. **Services:** Interlibrary loan; copying; SDI; Library open to the public at librarian's discretion. **Holdings:** 700 books. **Subscriptions:** 120 journals and other serials; 5 newspapers.

46157 ■ Touro College–Lander College for Men Library
75-31 150th St.
Kew Gardens Hills, NY 11367
Ph:(718)820-4894
Fax: (718)820-4825
Co. E-mail: zhannama@touro.edu
URL: http://www.touro.edu/library/directories/Directory.asp
Contact: Zhanna S. Marina, Libn.
Scope: Biology, business, computer science, management information science, political science, psychology, social sciences, Judaica. **Holdings:** Books; diskettes; audio and video tapes; CD-ROMs; DVDs; microfiche.

46158 ■ US West Communications–Learning Systems/Employee Development–Library (2626)
2626 W. Evans Ave.
Denver, CO 80219-5506
Ph:(303)763-1252
Fax: (303)985-6496
Contact: Gaylene Pepion, Libn. Hd.
Scope: Communications, management, economics, adult education, pluralism, computer technology. **Holdings:** 3000 books; Bell Company Practices; Bell technical journals. **Subscriptions:** 40 journals and other serials.

46159 ■ Woodbury University–Library

7500 N. Glenoaks Blvd.
PO Box 7846
Burbank, CA 91510-7846
Ph:(818)767-0888
Fax: (818)767-4534
Co. E-mail: barbara.bowley@woodbury.edu
URL: http://www.woodbury.edu/
Contact: Barbara Bowley, Dir.
Scope: Business and management, International business, art, architecture, interior design, fashion marketing and design, psychology, animation. **Services:** Interlibrary loan; copying; Library open to the public for reference use only. **Holdings:** 58,827 books; 3070 bound periodical volumes; 92,511 microforms; 17,401 slides; 1044 videotapes; 117 CD-ROMs; 77 DVDs. **Subscriptions:** 436 journals and other serials; 5 newspapers.

RESEARCH CENTERS

46160 ■ Bradley University–Center for Executive and Professional Development

Foster College of Business Administration
1501 W Bradley Ave
Peoria, IL 61625
Ph:(309)677-3549
Fax: (309)677-4065
Co. E-mail: ls@bradley.edu
URL: http://www.bradley.edu/fcba/community/cepd/index.shtml
Contact: Lisa Stufflebeam, Exec.Dir.
E-mail: ls@bradley.edu
Scope: Develops executive and management programs for business needs. **Educational Activities:** Customized workshops, to meet specific needs of businesses; Public seminars, on current business topics.

46161 ■ The Conference Board, Inc.

845 3rd Ave.
New York, NY 10022
Ph:(212)339-0345
Fax: (212)336-9740
Co. E-mail: info@conference-board.org
URL: http://www.conference-board.org
Contact: Richard E. Cavanagh, Pres./CEO
E-mail: info@conference-board.org
Scope: Business management practices worldwide, especially economic, and demographic in nature. Specific concerns include: corporate citizenship, including corporate contributions, diversity, environmental policy and issues, and government relations; corporate governance, including boards of directors, role of chief executives, relations with institutional investors, and shareholder input and influence; economics, including economic and financial forecasts, consumer confidence, leading economic indicators, North American outlook and trends, and global economic environment; human resources and organizational effectiveness, including organization structure and design, compensation and benefits, training and development, and communications; and performance excellence. **Publications:** Across the Board (bimonthly); The Conference Board Newsletter (quarterly); Consumer Confidence Survey (monthly); E-mail Express (monthly); Executive Action Series (weekly); Research reports; StraightTalk (10/year). **Educational Activities:** Conferences; Forums and seminars on selected topics of business, professional, and academic interest.

46162 ■ Kansas State University–Center for Leadership

Department of Management
College of Business Administration
110 Calvin Hall
Manhattan, KS 66502
Ph:(785)532-7451
Fax: (785)532-1339
Co. E-mail: jkatz@k-state.edu
URL: http://cba.ksu.edu/leadership/
Contact: Jeffrey P. Katz PhD, Dir.
E-mail: jkatz@k-state.edu
Scope: Leadership and management issues. **Educational Activities:** Panel discussions, workshops, conferences, and seminars.

46163 ■ Organization Development Institute

11234 Walnut Ridge Rd.
Chesterland, OH 44026-1240
Ph:(440)729-7419
Fax: (440)729-9319
Co. E-mail: donwcole@aol.com
URL: http://www.odinstitute.org
Contact: Dr. Donald W. Cole, Pres.
E-mail: donwcole@aol.com
Scope: Conflict resolution technology and management, productivity improvement, improvement of quality and organization development, human resources development, means for improving the quality of life, and organizational effectiveness. Sponsors the research/study team on nonviolent large systems change. **Services:** Consulting. **Publications:** International Registry of OD Professionals and the OD Handbook (annually); Nonviolent Change Newsletter (3/year); Organization Development Journal (quarterly); Organizations and Change (monthly). **Educational Activities:** Annual International Congress; What's New in Organization Development and Human Resources Development Conference (annually), in May; Workshops for behavioral scientists and other interested parties. **Awards:** Jack Gibb Award, for the best presentation at the Annual Information Exchange, in the amount of $1000; Outstanding Organization Development Article of the Year; Outstanding Organization Development Project of the Year; Outstanding Organizational Development Consultant of the Year Award.

46164 ■ University of British Columbia–Centre for Operations Excellence

2053 Main Mall
Faculty of Commerce
Vancouver, BC, Canada V6T 1Z2
Ph:(604)822-1800
Fax: (604)822-1544
Co. E-mail: info@coe.ubc.ca
URL: http://www.coe.ubc.ca
Contact: Dr. Eric Cope, Dir.
E-mail: info@coe.ubc.ca
Scope: Issues facing operations managers, and the development of methods, tools, and techniques to shape the business environment of the future. **Services:** Industrial Partners' Program (10/year).

Manufacturing

START-UP INFORMATION

46165 ■ "Mentor Wanted" in *Black Enterprise* **(Vol. 35, January 2005, No. 6, pp. 97)**
Pub: Earl G. Graves Publishing Co. Inc.
Ed: Tanisha A. Sykes. **Description:** Young African American man is looking for a mentor to help him start his own clothing business. The entrepreneur has placed some shirts in an area store, but is unsure of marketing and manufacturing of his clothing.

46166 ■ "Minority-certified paper company sets up shop in Canton Twp." in *Crain's Detroit Business* **(Vol. 19, No. 16, April 21, 2003, pp. 6)**
Pub: Crain Communications Inc., Detroit
Ed: Michael Strong. **Description:** Twin Pines Paper LLC, paper manufacturer, has opened in Canton, Michigan. Twin Pines is the first and only minority-certified paper manufacturer in the Midwest. The startup company produces tissues, toilet paper, and paper towels.

ASSOCIATIONS AND OTHER ORGANIZATIONS

46167 ■ CAMUS International
505 Beach St., Ste. 130
San Francisco, CA 94133
Ph:(415)647-4503
Fax: (415)647-4539
Co. E-mail: info@camus.org
URL: http://www.camus.org
Contact: Jeffrey L. Milde, Exec. Dir.
Description: Provides forum for manufacturing application users to interact with and learn from each other.

46168 ■ Canadian Plastics Industry Association–Association Canadienne de l'industrie des Plastiques
5915 Airport Rd., Ste. 712
Mississauga, ON, Canada L4V 1T1
Ph:(905)678-7748
Fax: (905)678-0774
Co. E-mail: slavoie@cpia.ca
URL: http://www.cpia.ca
Contact: Serge Lavoie, Pres./CEO
Description: Plastics manufacturers, distributors, importers, and exporters in Canada. Encourages research and development programs. Represents and defends members' interests.

46169 ■ Canadian Tooling and Machining Association
140 McGovern Dr., Unit 3
Cambridge, ON, Canada N3H 4R7
Ph:(519)653-7265
Fax: (519)653-6764
Co. E-mail: info@ctma.com
URL: http://www.ctma.com
Contact: Mr. Les Payne, Exec. Dir.

Purpose: Aims to represent Canadian tooling manufacturing at all levels of governments, their departments, and agencies. **Publications:** *CTMA View.*

46170 ■ Forest Products Association of Canada–Association des Produits Forestiers du Canada
99 Bank St., Ste. 410
Ottawa, ON, Canada K1P 6B9
Ph:(613)563-1441
Fax: (613)563-4720
Co. E-mail: ottawa@fpac.ca
URL: http://www.fpac.ca
Contact: Avrim D. Lazar, Pres./CEO
Description: Forest products manufacturers. Lobbies government on legislation, taxation, and other policy matters.

46171 ■ LTD Shippers Association
1230 Pottstown Pike, Ste. 6
Glenmoore, PA 19343
Ph:(610)458-3636
Fax: (610)458-8039
URL: http://www.ltdmgmt.com
Contact: Tom Craig, Pres.
Description: Works to leverage the buying power of the members for lower ocean freight prices. Has scope that includes ocean rates from Asia to United States, to Canada, Mexico, Puerto Rico and many other destinations; also rates to the US and Canada from Brazil, the Mediterranean, India and other origins. Aims to design, develop, negotiate, implement and manage logistics or transportation programs for members.

46172 ■ Manufacturing Jewelers and Suppliers of America
45 Royal Little Dr.
Providence, RI 02904
Ph:(401)274-3840
Free: 800-444-MJSA
Fax: (401)274-0265
Co. E-mail: info@mjsa.org
URL: http://www.mjsa.org
Contact: Frank Dallahan, Pres./CEO
Description: Represents American manufacturers and suppliers within the jewelry industry. Seeks to foster long-term stability and prosperity of the jewelry industry. Provides leadership in government affairs and industry education. **Publications:** *AJM: The Authority on Jewelry Manufacturing* (monthly); *Buyers Guide* (biennial).

46173 ■ National Association of Manufacturers
1331 Pennsylvania Ave. NW
Washington, DC 20004-1790
Ph:(202)637-3000
Free: 800-248-6626
Fax: (202)637-3182
Co. E-mail: manufacturing@nam.org
URL: http://www.nam.org
Contact: Mr. John Engler, Pres./CEO
Membership: Manufacturers and cooperating non-manufacturers having a direct interest in or relation-

ship to manufacturing. **Purpose:** Represents industry's views on national and international problems to government. Maintains public affairs and public relations programs. Reviews current and proposed legislation, administrative rulings, and interpretations, judicial decisions, and legal matters affecting industry. Maintains numerous policy groups: Human Resources Policy; Small and Medium Manufacturers; Tax Policy; Resources & Environmental Policy; Regulation and Legal Reform Policy; International Economic Affairs. Affiliated with 150 local and state trade associations of manufacturers through National Industrial Council and 250 manufacturing trade associations through the Associations Council. **Publications:** *Directory of Officers, Directors and Committees* (annual); *Just in Time* (monthly); *NAM Member Focus* (monthly); *Small and Medium Manufacturers NewsLine* (monthly); *Washington 1000; Winning at Public Affairs* ; Bulletin (periodic). Also publishes legal studies, issue briefs, and specialized publications. **Telecommunication Services:** electronic bulletin board, daily legislative news brief.

46174 ■ National Council for Advanced Manufacturing
2000 L St. NW, Ste. 807
Washington, DC 20036
Ph:(202)429-2220
Fax: (202)429-2422
Co. E-mail: nacfam@nacfam.org
URL: http://www.nacfam.org
Contact: Mary Gabriel, Communications Mgr.
Membership: Companies (500), university centers, laboratories, and manufacturing extension services (250), national trade associations (18), and national technical education associations (8). **Purpose:** Seeks to "enhance the productivity, quality and competitiveness of all tiers of the U.S. domestic industrial base." Organizes public and private technology research and development projects; serves as a network linking members; conducts workforce skills standards development programs. **Publications:** *NACFAM Weekly* (weekly).

EDUCATIONAL PROGRAMS

46175 ■ 5S for Manufacturers (Canada)
Canadian Management Centre
150 York St., 5th Fl.
Toronto, ON, Canada M5H 3S5
Ph:(866)400-4941 ext. 2252
Free: 877-CMC-2500
Fax: (416)313-4985
Co. E-mail: cmcinfo@cmctraining.org
URL: http://www.cmcamai.org
Price: $1,395 Canadian. **Description:** Covers how incorporating 5S in any workplace will make for cleaner and better organized conditions, and overall improved moral. **Locations:** Toronto, ON.

46176 ■ How to Measure and Evaluate Your Warehouse Operating Performance
American Management Association
1601 Broadway
New York, NY 10019

Ph:(212)586-8100
Free: 800-262-9699
Fax: (212)903-8168
Co. E-mail: customerservice@amanet.org
URL: http://www.amanet.org
Price: $1,550.00 for non-members; $1,450.00 for AMA members. **Description:** Covers warehouse efficiency, identifying problems and determining solutions, and auditing your warehouse. **Locations:** Chicago, IL.

46177 ■ Lean Manufacturing (Canada)
Canadian Management Centre
150 York St., 5th Fl.
Toronto, ON, Canada M5H 3S5
Ph:(416)214-5678
Free: 800-262-9699
Fax: (416)313-4985
Co. E-mail: cmcinfo@cmctraining.org
URL: http://cmcamai.org
Price: $1,695.00 Canadian. **Description:** Covers reducing waste, lowering cost, and improving revenue. **Locations:** Toronto, ON.

46178 ■ Production Planning, Scheduling and Activity Control Workshop
American Management Association
1601 Broadway
New York, NY 10019
Ph:(212)586-8100
Free: 800-262-9699
Fax: (212)903-8168
Co. E-mail: customerservice@amanet.org
URL: http://www.amanet.org
Price: $1,795.00 for non-members; $1,695.00 for AMA members. **Description:** Four-day seminar for plant managers and operations engineers and managers; covers manufacturing standards, reducing lead and cycle times, working with technology, resource planning, scheduling, and prioritization. **Locations:** Las Vegas, NV.

46179 ■ Production Planning, Scheduling and Activity Control Workshop (Canada)
Canadian Management Centre
150 York St., 5th Fl.
Toronto, ON, Canada M5H 3S5
Ph:(416)214-5678
Free: 800-262-9699
Fax: (416)313-4985
Co. E-mail: cmcinfo@cmctraining.org
URL: http://cmcamai.org
Price: $1,795.00 Canadian. **Description:** Seminar for plant managers and operations engineers and managers; covers manufacturing standards, reducing lead and cycle times, working with technology, resource planning, scheduling, and prioritization. **Locations:** Toronto, ON.

46180 ■ Root Cause Analysis and Problem Solving (Canada)
Canadian Management Centre
150 York St., 5th Fl.
Toronto, ON, Canada M5H 3S5
Ph:(866)400-4941 ext. 2252
Free: 877-CMC-2500
Fax: (416)313-4985
Co. E-mail: cmcinfo@cmctraining.org
URL: http://www.cmcamai.org
Price: $1,395 Canadian. **Description:** Covers a six-step process for problem detection, review and solution, including statistical tools, and change. **Locations:** Toronto, ON.

DIRECTORIES OF EDUCATIONAL PROGRAMS

46181 ■ Business Journal's Directory of Manufacturing
Pub: Corfacts Publishing
Released: Annual. **Covers:** 10,5000 manufacturing companies located in New Jersey. **Entries Include:** Company name, address, phone, year founded, key executives by name and title. **Arrangement:** Alphabetical, then geographical with the SIC code. **Indexes:** Cross indexed by employee size and annual revenue.

46182 ■ Regional Directory: National
Pub: Manufacturers' News Inc.
Price: $3,142 print; $7,495 CD-ROM (EZ select full); $5,195 CD-ROM (EZ select with 10 plus employees); $4,195 CD-ROM (EZ select with 20 plus employees). **Covers:** Some 399,382 plants, 912,247 executives in the manufacturing sector across the U.S. **Entries Include:** Company name, address, phone, fax, toll-free numbers, email and Web addresses, executive names, annual sales, plant square footage, number of employees, distribution area, parent company information, ISO certifications and more.

46183 ■ Scott's Directories
Pub: Scott's Directories
Ed: Barbara Peard, Editor. **Released:** Annual, February; latest edition 2005 edition. **Covers:** 68,000 manufacturers throughout Canada. **Entries Include:** Company name, address, phone, fax, telex, names and titles of key personnel, number of employees, parent or subsidiary companies, North American Standard Industrial (NAICS) code, product, export interest, year established.

REFERENCE WORKS

46184 ■ "An Acquired Taste" in Entrepreneur (Vol. 32, October 2004, No. 10, pp. 62)
Pub: Entrepreneur Media Inc.
Ed: Crystal Detamore-Rodman. **Description:** Tim Johnstone is a former division manager for a large bank working on the due-diligence team that analyzed companies the bank wanted to buy. Johnstone's experience helped him when he decided to purchase the Anywear Shoe Company in Seattle, Washington. The firm manufactures and distributes professional footwear.

46185 ■ "Adventures in the Paper Trade: Boise Buys OfficeMax" in Barron's (July 21, 2003, pp. 15)
Pub: Barron's
Ed: Michael Santoli. **Description:** Boise Cascade's $9/share offer for office products retailer OfficeMax, an also-ran in its market, totals $1.2 billion. Forest products manufacturer Boise Cascade is taking the risk in the belief that diversification is key to survival.

46186 ■ "Aegis of Success" in Hispanic Business (June 2002, pp. 16)
Pub: Hispanic Business
Ed: Rick Laezman. **Description:** New York manufacturer, Aegis Electronic Systems, has procured federal contracts for aerospace and military programs.

46187 ■ "Aftermarket Technology to Move 150 N.J. Jobs to OKC" in Journal Record (June 24, 2003)
Pub: Dolan Media Company
Ed: Janice Francis-Smith. **Description:** Aftermarket Technology Corporation, a remanufacturer of transmissions and recovering of other auto parts, will consolidate its New Jersey facility into its Oklahoma City plant.

46188 ■ "Airline Slump Hurts Houston-Based Maker of Tow Tractors" in Houston Chronicle (April 11, 2003)
Pub: Knight-Ridder/Tribune Business News
Description: Houston manufacturer, Steward & Stevenson Services, reported a revision in its fourth-quarter earnings report due to the slump in airline travel. The company makes airline-equipment such as tractors that push and tow aircraft.

46189 ■ "Airport Industrial Sites in Demand" in Milwaukee Journal Sentinel (December 19, 2005)
Pub: Journal Sentinel, Inc.
Ed: Tom Daykin. **Description:** Several light large industrial buildings are being developed near Mitchell International Airport. New interest in such space used for storing and distributing products, as well as manufacturers, holds hope for the economy.

46190 ■ "AK Steel Goes Ahead with Bid for National" in Pittsburgh Post-Gazette (April 11, 2003)
Pub: Knight-Ridder/Tribune Business News
Ed: Jim McKay. **Description:** An overview of AK Steel's attempt to acquire the assets of National Steel Corporation is presented.

46191 ■ Alaska Industrial Directory
Pub: Harris InfoSource
Released: Annual, latest edition 2003. **Covers:** 2,210 manufacturing companies in Alaska. **Entries Include:** Company name, address, county, phone, fax, web site address (on CD-ROM only), number of employees, names and titles of key executives, plant size, year established, parent company, annual sales, import/export information, Standard Industrial Classification (SIC) code, and product description. **Arrangement:** Geographical. **Indexes:** Geographical, alphabetical, SIC code, product.

46192 ■ "Alcoa's Results Could Hint at Manufacturers' Outlook" in Wall Street Journal (Vol. 249, January 2007, No. 5, pp. B4)
Pub: Dow Jones & Co. Inc.
Ed: Laura Mandaro. **Description:** Due to growth overseas balancing the decline in U.S. growth, raw materials companies such as Alcoa Inc., which produces more aluminum than any other company in the world, is expected to post higher earnings this quarter.

46193 ■ "Alive with Sound of Music Selling" in Chicago Tribune (March 6, 2005)
Pub: Knight-Ridder/Tribune Business News
Ed: Mike Hughlett. **Description:** Cell phone manufacturers have developed new generation music-playing phones. Motorola's iTunes model will be among the systems offered.

46194 ■ "Am. Axle Plans China, Europe Plants" in Crain's Detroit Business (Vol. 21, October 31, 2005, No. 44, pp. 4)
Pub: Crain Communications Inc. - Detroit
Ed: Terry Kosdrosky. **Description:** American Axle & Manufacturing Holdings Inc. will open its first manufacturing plant in China in late 2007 or early 2008, followed by a new plant in Central or Eastern Europe soon after.

46195 ■ American Big Businesses Directory
Pub: infoUSA Inc.
Released: Annual. **Price:** $295; $595 both print & CD-ROM. **Covers:** 218,000 U.S. businesses with more than 100 employees, and 500,000 key executives and directors. CD-ROM version contains 160,000 top firms and 431,000 key executives. **Entries Include:** Name, address, phone, names and titles of key personnel, number of employees, sales volume, Standard Industrial Classification (SIC) codes, subsidiaries and parent company names, stock exchanges on which traded. **Arrangement:** Section 1: alphabetical by company name; Section 2: geographical by city; Section 3: classified by Standard Industrial Classification (SIC) code; Section 4: alphabetical by executive name. **Indexes:** Geographical, SIC, executive name.

46196 ■ "Amerigon, BorgWarner Fare Better Among Suppliers" in Crain's Detroit Business (Vol. 21, October 31, 2005, No. 44, pp. 4)
Pub: Crain Communications Inc. - Detroit
Ed: Terry Kosdrosky. **Description:** Despite losses reported by local auto suppliers in third quarter 2005, Amerigon Inc. and BorgWarner Inc. both posted gains in revenue and net income.

46197 ■ "Analysts: Pricing, Material Costs to Spur Supplier Mergers" in Crain's Detroit Business (Vol. 21, January 10, 2005, No. 2, pp. 19)
Pub: Crain Communications Inc. - Detroit
Ed: Julie Armstrong. **Description:** Consolidation of automotive suppliers will rise in 2005 because of high raw-material prices and pricing pressures from automakers.

46198 ■ "Army Extends Contract With Maine Company to Improve Armor On Humvees" in *Portland Press Herald* **(December 3, 2005)**
Pub: Blethen Maine Newspapers, Inc.
Ed: Bart Jansen. Description: Maine Readiness Sustainment Center's Maine Military Authority was awarded a temporary contract with the U.S. Army to improve the armor on its Humvees. The contract will save 250 local jobs for workers.

46199 ■ "ASC Pushes Niche Vehicles as Industry Cure" in *Crain's Detroit Business* **(Vol. 22, January 16, 2006, No. 3, pp. 22)**
Pub: Crain Communications Inc. - Detroit
Ed: Brent Snavely. Description: ASC Inc. announced plans to actively pursue the design and development of niche vehicles by offering low-cost exciting, profit-generating, halo-casting vehicles to original equipment manufacturers.

46200 ■ "Asia Rising" in *Black Enterprise* **(Vol. 35, October 2004, No. 3, pp. 46)**
Pub: Earl G. Graves Publishing Co. Inc.
Ed: Donald Jay Korn. Description: China and India are two emerging global economies making them attractive for investing. Manufacturing and high tech jobs are being outsourced to both countries. It is important to research before investing in China and India, as well as any international funds.

46201 ■ "Auto Consolidation Likely to Speed Up" in *Crain's Detroit Business* **(Vol. 23, January 8, 2007, No. 2, pp. 15)**
Pub: Crain Communications Inc: - Detroit
Ed: Brent Snavely. Description: Further consolidations and bankruptcies in the auto supply business are increasing. Industry is in the midst of a major restructuring.

46202 ■ "Auto Sector Leads in Investment; Michigan No. 2 State" in *Crain's Detroit Business* **(Vol. 21, October 17, 2005, No. 43, pp. 1)**
Pub: Crain Communications Inc. - Detroit
Ed: Tom Henderson. Description: Michigan's auto sector led the U.S. in major capital-investment projects that began in 2004, ranking the state second only to Texas in new project valuation.

46203 ■ "Auto suppliers: Steel tariffs kill U.S. jobs permanently" in *Crain's Detroit Business* **(Vol. 19, No. 14, April 7, 2003, pp. 34)**
Pub: Crain Communications Inc., Detroit
Ed: Harry Stoffer. Description: Automotive suppliers are focusing on a midterm review of the three-year tariff program that effects steel users in the U.S.

46204 ■ "Automaker pullback blamed for Detroit stamper's closing" in *Crain's Detroit Business* **(Vol. 19, No. 8, February 24, 2003, pp. 6)**
Pub: Crain Communications Inc., Detroit
Ed: Terry Kosdrosky. Description: Davis Tool & Engineering Company will close its doors after being open for 65 years. The Detroit stamping plant is closing as the result of price competition and the automaker's recent trend to push component production back in-house.

46205 ■ "Automaker-Union Talks Critical to State" in *Crain's Detroit Business* **(Vol. 22, November 27, 2006, No. 48, pp. 8)**
Pub: Crain Communications Inc. - Detroit
Description: Critical business issue in 2007 for the State of Michigan will be the auto contract talks between the UAW and the Big 3 US automakers. Not only will the results affect the companies themselves, but all the other manufacturers in the region and the ability to draw new manufacturers into the State.

46206 ■ "Behind the looking glass" in *Red Herring* **(March 2003, pp. 58)**
Pub: Herring Communications Inc.
Ed: Celeste Biever. Description: A listing of everyday products manufactured through nanotechnology is presented, including antibacterial products, self-cleaning glass, sunscreens, tennis balls and more.

46207 ■ *Benchmarking Global Manufacturing: Understanding International Suppliers, Customers, and Competitors*
Pub: Irwin Professional Publishing
Ed: Jeffrey G. Miller, Arnoud De Meyer and Jinichiro Nakane. Price: $47.50. Description: Provides manufacturing industry statistics and benchmarking toolkit to help your organization implement benchmarking.

46208 ■ "Bereinga Starts $150M Fund, Opens China Office" in *Crain's Detroit Business* **(Vol. 23, February 5, 2007, No. 6, pp. 25)**
Pub: Crain Communications Inc. - Detroit
Ed: Tom Henderson. Description: Tier one auto supplier acquisition or venture with Chinese is early project justifying Shanghai office; firm also hopes to help keep Southeast Michigan out front of new investments in not only auto-related commerce.

46209 ■ "The best-laid incentive plans" in *Harvard Business Review* **(Vol. 81, No. 1, January 2003, pp. 27)**
Pub: Harvard Business School Press
Ed: Steve Kerr. Description: A case study is presented where a CFO and chief administrative officer of a consumer durables manufacturer has instituted a performance management system that seemed successful to him, but had negative results for employee morale and customer service. Four experts offer advice on ways the company should proceed.

46210 ■ "Bette LaPlante & Diane Cuvelier" in *Entrepreneur* **(Vol. 31, No. 4, April 2003, pp. 17)**
Pub: Entrepreneur Media Inc.
Description: Profile of Bette LaPlante and Diane Cuvelier, co-founders of Doughmakers LLC, a manufacturer of solid aluminum bakeware with a patented pebble pattern. The two women started their company with $1,000 in 1997 and projected sales for 2003 are estimated at more than $5 million.

46211 ■ "Better Safe: Does Your Product Need a Warning Label?" in *Entrepreneur* **(Vol. 31, No. 9, July 2003, pp. 76)**
Pub: Entrepreneur Media, Inc.
Ed: Jane Easter Bahls. Description: When injured, a consumer can sue not only the manufacturer, but also the supplier, dealer, distributor or rental yard.

46212 ■ "Biddeford, Maine, Cord Business Weathers Trials of Domestic Textile Industry" in *Portland Press Herald* **(November 18, 2005)**
Pub: Blethen Maine Newspapers, Inc.
Ed: Seth Harkenss. Description: Bob Rice, entrepreneur and owner of Spurwink Cordage, discusses his success in an industry that is rapidly shrinking in the U.S. Spurwink Cordage reported nearly $1 million in annual sales, mostly to saddle manufacturers in western states.

46213 ■ "Big Projects Give Some Life to Sluggish Real Estate Sector" in *Crain's Detroit Business* **(Vol. 19, No. 45, November 10, 2003, pp. 15)**
Pub: Crain Communications Inc., Detroit
Ed: Jennette Smith. Description: Upcoming high-technology automotive projects by Hyundai Motor American, BorgWarner Inc., and Visteon Corporation will help the stalled real estate sector.

46214 ■ "A Billion in Baskets" in *Small Business Opportunities* **(Vol. 13, No. 6, November 2001, pp. 38, 40)**
Pub: Harris Publications, Inc.
Description: Profile of Longaberger Company, the largest handmade basket-making company in the United States. The company grew from a small family business to a billion-dollar empire, and is the 22nd largest woman-owned company in America.

46215 ■ "Bioigen Unchained" in *Harvard Business Review* **(Vol. 78, No. 3, May 2000, pp. 28)**
Pub: Harvard Business School Publishing Corp.
Ed: David Bovet, Joseph Martha. Description: When the biotech pioneer had to get a blockbuster drug to market fast, it joined with partners to become a virtual manufacturer.

46216 ■ "The Bleeding-Heart Rationalist: William Morris b. 1911" in *New York Times* **(December 31, 2006, pp. 14)**
Pub: New York Times Company
Ed: Walter Kirn. Description: Profile of William Norris, founder of Control Data Corporation, now defunct, but at one time, one of the nation's largest computer manufacturing companies. Norris also founded an institute that promoted education and small business growth.

46217 ■ *Blue Book of Building and Construction—North and Central Florida Edition*
Pub: Contractors Register Inc.
Contact: Jeff Fandl
Released: Annual, February. Price: Free. Covers: Architects, contractors, subcontractors, manufacturers, and suppliers of construction materials and equipment. Entries Include: Company name, address, phone, fax. Arrangement: Classified by line of business. Indexes: Alphabetical by category.

46218 ■ "Bound by the Long View" in *Business Journal-Milwaukee* **(Vol. 20, No. 48, August 15, 2003, pp. A25)**
Pub: American City Business Journals, Inc.
Ed: Becca Mader. Description: A children's book-binder and distributor, Demco Media Ltd., has moved to a new facility as part of its expansion plan. Demco Media, led by Brendan Wall, has leased a small part of a new $3 million, 200,000-square foot warehouse and manufacturing complex.

46219 ■ "Bridging the Gap" in *Sales & Marketing Management*
Pub: VNU Business Media
Ed: David Macey. Description: Retail-specific marketing solutions are becoming more important as effective ways to influence buying behavior in today's consumer market.

46220 ■ "Building on History" in *Philadelphia Inquirer* **(October 16, 2006)**
Pub: Philadelphia Newspapers LLC
Ed: Benjamin Y. Lowe. Description: Profile of Rick Skidmore, president and founder of Timberlane Inc. Skidmore, a former life insurance agent, discovered the need for custom made window shutters. The company allows employees to review the firm's financial performance on a quarterly basis.

46221 ■ "Business Briefs" in *Salt Lake Tribune* **(February 24, 2005)**
Pub: Knight-Ridder/Tribune Business News
Description: Business information involving Extra Space Storage, a real estate investment trust that owns and operates self-storage properties; Cirtran Corp. a contract manufacturer; Maxwell Publishing; Trio Restaurant Group; Raser Technologies, who received a contract to develop mobile power generation technology for the government; and Cyprus Credit Union's fundraiser for Primary Children's Medical Center, is spotlighted.

46222 ■ *The Business of Injection Molding: What It Takes to Succeed As a Custom Molder*
Pub: Abby Communications, Inc.
Ed: Clare Goldsberry. Released: 1998. Price: $59.95.

46223 ■ "The Business Week News You Need to Know" in *Business Week* **(January 23, 2006, No. 3968, pp. 30-31)**
Pub: McGraw-Hill Companies
Ed: Harry Maurer. Description: News about the Detroit Auto Show, job growth, Home Depot's expansion plans, Internet search engines, new executive pay rules, the stock market, and more.

46224 ■ "C & A Says Company Will Be Sold" in *Crain's Detroit Business* **(Vol. 22, November 20, 2006, No. 47, pp. 1)**
Pub: Crain Communications Inc. - Detroit
Ed: Brent Snavely. Description: Southfield based interior supplier has decided to go out of business in wake of reduced sales volume and difficulty in emerging from bankruptcy. Entire company or individual assets are available for sale and will be consolidated and closed as the business winds down.

46225 ■ "Canned Profits" in *Forbes* (Vol. 175, January 10, 2005, No. 1, pp. 152)
Pub: Forbes Magazine Inc.
Ed: Phyllis Berman. **Description:** Profile of Ball Corporation, best known for canning supplies. Today the company is the leading producer of beverage cans, with a 33 percent share in the U.S. and 29 percent in Europe. Shares have increased at an average of 45.3 percent annually since 1999.

46226 ■ "Car's Star Turn: August Sales Zoom-For Foreign Models. At Least U.S. Makers' Bonds are Thriving" in *Barron's* (September 8, 2003)
Pub: Barron's
Ed: Jay Palmer. **Description:** U.S. automobile manufacturers did not witness the same brisk late-summer sales as their foreign counterparts. General Motor's aggressive incentive offerings kept its falloff at only one percent, while Ford and Chrysler saw sales declines of 13 percent and six percent, respectively.

46227 ■ "Case Study" in *Inc.* (January 1, 2005)
Pub: Inc. Magazine
Ed: Patrick J. Sauer. **Description:** Magnetech Industrial Services is considering the implementation of an apprenticeship program in order to triple its work force in a slowing industry.

46228 ■ "Champion Sells Five Retail Centers, Closes 12 Others" in *Crain's Detroit Business* (Vol. 21, January 10, 2005, No. 2, pp. 22)
Pub: Crain Communications Inc. - Detroit
Ed: Jennette Smith. **Description:** Champion Enterprises Inc., a manufactured home producer, sold four retail centers in Kentucky and Texas and will sell one center in South Carolina. The company will also close 12 retail centers in seven states.

46229 ■ "Cheap Jet Update" in *Forbes* (Vol. 175, January 10, 2005, No. 1, pp. 31)
Pub: Forbes Magazine Inc.
Ed: Rich Karlgaard. **Description:** Profile of Bill Lear, creator of the Learjet, is presented. Lear is the last entrepreneur to build, certify and sell a business jet.

46230 ■ "Cheap Tricks" in *The Economist* (Vol. 377, October 1-7, 2005, No. 8446, pp. 62)
Pub: The Economist Newspaper Ltd.
Description: Nicholas Negroponte, founder of MIT Media Lab, created an idea that would give a $100 laptop to every low-income child around the world. Negroponte unveiled his idea at the World Economic Forum. The program, One Laptop Per Child, could hurt the world's computer manufacturers.

46231 ■ "Chemical Balance" in *Black Enterprise* (Vol. 34, No. 5, December 2003, pp. 38)
Pub: Earl Graves Publishing Co.
Ed: Sakina P. Spruell. **Description:** John Moten, former Deutsche Bank analyst, is recommending chemical stocks. Moten notes that chemical companies thrive when oil prices are down because they use oil for energy and production of raw materials.

46232 ■ "Cherry to Move 100 Jobs to Mexico" in *Milwaukee Journal Sentinel* (December 21, 2005)
Pub: Journal Sentinel, Inc.
Ed: Avrum D. Lank. **Description:** Cherry Electrical Products, a division of Cherry Corporation, reports it is moving 100 jobs to Mexico in 2006. The company makes electrical components for manufacturers.

46233 ■ "Chicago Tribune Business Agenda" in *Chicago Tribune* (February 28, 2005)
Pub: Knight-Ridder/Tribune Business News
Description: Economic predictions, unemployment rates, and manufacturing are issues discussed.

46234 ■ "China's cheap labor is next threat to suppliers" in *Crain's Detroit Business* (Vol. 19, No. 2, January 13, 2003, pp. 13)
Pub: Crain Communications Inc., Detroit
Ed: Terry Kosdrosky. **Description:** U.S. auto suppliers are facing yet another threat, the growing Chinese economy. China's large supply of educated workers earning low incomes threaten the security of small to mid-size manufacturers in the U.S., especially the tool and die industry.

46235 ■ "The Chinese Are Coming" in *Inc.* (Volume 27, July 2005, No. 7, pp. 32)
Pub: Inc. Magazine
Ed: Darren Dahl. **Description:** Chinese companies acquired 649 U.S. firms in 2004, focusing on textile, appliance, electronics, and auto parts manufacturing sectors.

46236 ■ "Chip Shot. Teradyne's New President is Crafting a Comeback after an Industry Slump" in *Boston Business Journal* (Vol. 23, Jul. 4, 03)
Pub: American City Business Journals
Ed: Tom Witkowski. **Description:** Biography of Michael A. Bradley, the new president of Teradyne Inc. is presented. Teradyne Inc. manufactures automatic test equipment and interconnection systems to semiconductor, electronics and network systems companies.

46237 ■ "Chocolate temperers" in *Candy Industry* (Vol. 167, No. 4, April 2002, pp. 88)
Pub: Stagnito Communications Inc.
Description: Preview of the new Chocovision chocolate temperer. The Revolation Series, produced by Chocovision Corp., Poughkeepsie, NY, represents the most efficient tabletop chocolate processing equipment that allows for the highest degree of accuracy along with ease of operation, replacing the Sinsation Series temperers.

46238 ■ "Chrysler Deal Has SET Looking at Opening New Plant In Ohio" in *Crain's Detroit Business* (Vol. 21, October 10, 2005, No. 43, pp. 42)
Pub: Crain Communications Inc. - Detroit
Ed: Terry Kosdrosky. **Description:** After winning a big contract from the Chrysler Group, SET Enterprises Inc. is planning to open a new plant in Cleveland, Ohio. SET is a Warren, Michigan metal processor. The deal will supply steel blanks for the Dodge Durango SUV and Dodge Caravan and Chrysler Town & Country minivans.

46239 ■ "Chrysler to Introduce Cleaner Diesel Engines" in *Altanta Journal-Constitution* (January 24, 2007)
Pub: Cox Newspapers, Inc.
Ed: Rob Douthit. **Description:** Chrysler will sell a heavy-duty diesel pickup truck meeting new emissions standards and a new diesel version of Jeep Grand Cherokee.

46240 ■ "Clarion Partners buys 36 buildings in Atlanta" in *Atlanta Business Chronicle* (Vol. 25, December 20, 2002, No. 28, pp. 14A)
Pub: American City Business Publications, Inc.
Ed: Jarred Schenke. **Description:** Clarion Partners has acquired a total of 36 buildings in the Atlanta, Georgia area from Crow Holdings Industrial Trust, as part of a larger, nationwide purchase of 287 industrial properties valued at $1.6 million from Crow. The total purchase covers more than 320 acres of land zoned for industry, covering over 35 million square feet.

46241 ■ "Clybourn Ave.'s PMD Corridor Leads Nowhere" in *Crain's Chicago Business* (Vol. 30, January 2007, No. 1, pp. 8)
Pub: Crain Communications, Inc.
Description: In an effort to stem the loss of manufacturing jobs the city created planned manufacturing districts. A. Finkl & Sons Co. is moving its manufacturing plant to a new location and real estate developers are clamoring to turn the site into one of Chicago's hottest neighborhoods but are not able to make the purchase since the plant sits in a PMD.

46242 ■ "Coagulating-Powder Firm Seeks Site To Build New Factory In Florida" in *Bradenton Herald* (January 6, 2005)
Pub: Bradenton Herald
Ed: Dana Sanchez. **Description:** Biolife LLC has plans to expand its coagulating-powder plant. The firm is looking to purchase land in the airport area where its existing manufacturing plan is located. The company reports annual sales of $1.7 million and employs 39 individuals.

46243 ■ "Coca-Cola Bottler Up for Sale: CEO J. Bruce Llewellyn Seeks Retirement" in *Black Enterprise* (Vol. 37, December 2006, No. 5, pp. 31)
Pub: Earl G. Graves Publishing Co. Inc.
Ed: Marcia A. Wade. **Description:** J. Bruce Llewellyn of Brucephil Inc., the parent company of the Philadelphia Coca-Cola Bottling Co. has agreed to sell its remaining shares to Coca-Cola Co., which previously owned 31 percent of Philly Coke. Analysts believe that Coca-Cola will eventually sell its shares to another bottler.

46244 ■ "Collins & Aikman Faces Risk with Futura" in *Crain's Detroit Business* (Vol. 19, No. 45, November 10, 2003, pp. 29)
Pub: Crain Communications Inc., Detroit
Ed: Robert Sherefkin. **Description:** Collins & Aikman Corporation will supply much of the interior to the 2006 Ford Futura sedan, but is facing the loss of a $1 billion contract from the Chrysler Group.

46245 ■ "Commentary: Departure of Jobs Hurts National Security" in *Long Island Business News* (February 6, 2004)
Pub: Dolan Media Newswires
Ed: John Kiernan. **Description:** The trend to send jobs overseas not only hurts America's economy, but also jeopardizes national security in the long term. National policy must be created to encourage and keep manufacturing jobs and capacity in the U.S.

46246 ■ "Company Builds Security Trailer for Feds" in *Crain's Detroit Business* (Vol. 19, No. 42, October 20, 2003, pp. 29)
Pub: Crain Communications Inc., Detroit
Ed: Michael Strong. **Description:** Profile of the Walled Lake, Michigan-based Trailer Technologies Inc. The firm manufactures customized trailers for use as a mobile command center for the U.S. Department of Homeland Security.

46247 ■ "Company Looks to Link Rural Firms with City Buyers" in *St. Louis Post-Dispatch* (February 17, 2005)
Pub: Knight-Ridder/Tribune Business News
Ed: Martin Van Der Werf. **Description:** Profile of Rural Business Consultants, led by Robert Fowler. The firm links interested buyers with rural companies, mostly manufacturers. Many of the buyers will be able to take advantage of a federal program that guarantees loans for businesses in rural areas.

46248 ■ "Company Tied to Style, Success" in *Milwaukee Journal Sentinel* (December 9, 2005)
Pub: Journal Sentinel, Inc.
Ed: Rick Barrett. **Description:** Profile of XMI Corporation located in Chippewa Falls, Wisconsin. The firm is one of a few silk-tie manufacturers remaining in the U.S. Men's ties run from $70 to $100 each and the company makes about 350,000 of the hand-sewn ties per year.

46249 ■ "Copper Prices Hover Near Record Highs" in *Milwaukee Journal Sentinel* (December 17, 2005)
Pub: Journal Sentinel, Inc.
Ed: Rick Barrett. **Description:** Manufacturers are being squeezed by the 43 percent increase in copper prices over the last year. Copper is used in the manufacture of items from toasters and electric blankets to electronics and automobiles.

46250 ■ "Cost Transparency: The Net's Real Threat to Prices and Brands" in *Harvard Business Review* (Vol. 78, No. 2, March 2000, pp. 43)
Pub: Harvard Business School Publishing Corp.
Ed: Indrajit Sinha. Description: The vast sea of information about prices, competitors, and features that is readily available on the Internet helps buyers "see through" the costs of products and services. That's bad news for manufacturers and retailers, and there are ways to fight back.

46251 ■ "Court OKs Meridian Ch. 11 Plan" in *Crain's Detroit Business* (Vol. 22, December 11, 2006, No. 50, pp. 6)
Pub: Crain Communications Inc. - Detroit
Ed: Bill Shea. Description: U.S. bankruptcy court approved reorganization plan to emerge from Chapter Eleven bankruptcy for local auto parts supplier. Management reorganization, reduced workforce, and price negotiations were part of plan filed last May.

46252 ■ "CPI Aerostructures Wins $3M Contract for Assemblies" in *Long Island Business News* (March 12, 2004)
Pub: Dolan Media Newswires
Description: CPI Aerostructures Inc. announced the procurement of a new contract worth approximately $3 million to build aircraft structural assemblies. CPI reports this contract as one of its largest ever from a non-governmental or military entity.

46253 ■ "Cracking Down On Copycats" in *Milwaukee Journal Sentinel* (December 6, 2005)
Pub: Journal Sentinel, Inc.
Ed: Rick Barrett. Description: Wisconsin marine manufacturers fear a new law that prohibits competitors from building unauthorized copies of a hull design will not be enough to stop them from hull splashing because it is not strong enough and is difficult for manufacturers to use.

46254 ■ "Critical Success Factors for Manufacturing Networks..." in *Journal of Small Business Management* (Vol. 41, No. 4, October 2003)
Pub: International Council of Small Business
Ed: Susan A. Sherer. Description: Networking among small and medium-sized manufacturing firms is increasing, but there has been little study of the factors leading to the success of these networks.

46255 ■ "Critics: Free Trade Comes at a Price" in *Business First Buffalo* (Vol. 19, No. 44, July 25, 2003, pp. 1)
Pub: American City Business Journals, Inc.
Ed: Joe Iannarelli. Description: Industry analysts state that small manufacturing firms are being hurt by new international free trade agreements. Local companies, such as I Squared R Element Company Inc., have been forced to reduce manufacturing capacity due to these agreements.

46256 ■ "Cuts in Retail, Manufacturing Hurt Northern New Jersey's Job Growth" in *The Record* (November 9, 2005)
Pub: New Jersey Media Group
Ed: Kathleen Lynn. Description: According to the federal Bureau of Labor Statistics, northern New Jersey firms are not hiring new employees. Statistical data included.

46257 ■ "Daimler deal: You can see state's offer - for $11,538" in *Atlanta Business Chronicle* (Vol. 25, November 15, 2002, No. 23 pp. 3A)
Pub: American City Business Publications, Inc.
Ed: Walter Woods. Description: According to the Department of Industry, Trade and Tourism, seeing the economic incentive package offered by the state to DaimlerChrysler AG, to bring a truck plant to Georgia, will cost $11,538 in administrative costs. The deal has not been finalized.

46258 ■ "Dana Has Cash, Looks for Ways to Spend It" in *Crain's Detroit Business* (Vol. 21, January 31, 2005, No. 5, pp. 12)
Pub: Crain Communications Inc. - Detroit
Description: Dana Corporation is considering various mergers and acquisitions of companies working in the vehicle and engine compartment sector of the industry.

46259 ■ "Day's 'lean' philosophy to face new test at Venture Holdings" in *Crain's Detroit Business* (Vol. 19, No. 14, April 7, 2003, pp. 41)
Pub: Crain Communications Inc., Detroit
Ed: Rhoda Miel. Description: Profile of Joseph Day, the new leader of Venture Holdings Company LLC, who will be able to test his lean-manufacturing ideas since Venture Holdings has filed for Chapter 11 bankruptcy protection.

46260 ■ "Death By Red Ink" in *The Economist* (Vol. 377, October 22-28, 2005, No. 8449, pp. 66, 68)
Pub: The Economist Newspaper Ltd.
Description: Problems faced by the Big Three automakers, particularly that of General Motors are discussed.

46261 ■ "Delphos Gets OK to Take $3.4B Cerberus-led offer" in *Crain's Detroit Business* (Vol. 23, January 15, 2007, No. 3, pp. 1)
Pub: Crain Communications Inc. - Detroit
Ed: Brent Snaveley. Description: US Bankruptcy judge clears way for Delphos to proceed with Cerberus investment package. GM and UAW approval is still required to proceed.

46262 ■ "Demand surges in manufacturing" in *Hispanic Business* (Vol. 22, No. 6, June 2000, pp. 106)
Pub: Hispanic Business
Ed: Christopher D. Lancette, Scott Williams, Joel Russell. Description: Hispanic-owned automotive powertrain maker UniBoring Company Inc. ranks 33rd in the Hispanic Business 500 table with revenues totaling $110 million in 1999. The company's growth is due to the strong economic climate in the U.S., says CEO Facundo Bravo.

46263 ■ "Departures Raise Questions About Loss of Women" in *Crain's Detroit Business* (Vol. 22, November 27, 2006, No. 48, pp. 12)
Pub: Crain Communications Inc. - Detroit
Ed: Brent Snaveley. Description: Female executives are leaving a void behind them in business and industry when they leave. Most of them leave the auto industry entirely and a few move to tier one and tier two suppliers. Strong message is sent to other women in the organization of the unrest.

46264 ■ "Despite Loss, Lear Has Wall Street Impressed" in *Crain's Detroit Business* (Vol. 23, January 29, 2007, No. 5, pp. 4)
Pub: Crain Communications Inc. - Detroit
Ed: Brent Snaveley. Description: Disposal of Interiors Division significantly improves restructuring plans at Lear, but accounts for large reported loss in 2006. Fourth quarter results were much stronger than forecast. Shift in Asia supply from domestic Big 3 attributed to positive outcome.

46265 ■ "Developer raises $200 million to buy buildings" in *Atlanta Business Chronicle* (Vol. 25, December 6, 2002, No. 26, pp. 3A)
Pub: American City Business Publications, Inc.
Ed: Jarred Schenke. Description: Industrial Developments International Inc. aims to use the $200 million raised to purchase warehouses and other industrial properties.

46266 ■ "The Dimensions of Ping Fu" in *Inc.* (Volume 27, December 2005, No. 12, pp. 90-97, 132, 134-135)
Pub: Inc. Magazine
Ed: John Brant. Description: Profile of Ping Fu, owner of a software firm called Geomagic in Research

Triangle Park, North Carolina. Geomagic has defined and dominated the high-tech field of digital shape sampling and processing or DSSP, which entails scanning an object with optical beams, rendering it on a computer screen three-dimensionally for manufacturing, testing, and inspection purposes.

46267 ■ "Dream Machines" in *Business Week* (January 16, 2006, No. 3967, pp. 52-56, 58)
Pub: McGraw-Hill Companies
Ed: Lee Walczak, David Welch. Description: The automobile industry is taking advantage of the competitive pressure it faces by offering new designs, technology-driven innovation, safety features, and more choices to customize vehicles.

46268 ■ "Dresser to Close Plant Eliminate 244 Jobs" in *Houston Business Journal* (Vol. 34, No. 14, August 15, 2003, pp. 3)
Pub: American City Business Journals
Description: Dresser Flow Solutions plans to close its manufacturing facility in Houston, Texas as part of a business consolidation effort. Topics include business losses, economic conditions, and layoffs.

46269 ■ "Duncan Manufacturing Firm to Receive Exemption from OSHA" in *Journal Record* (February 4, 2004)
Pub: Dolan Media Company
Description: Richard's Manufacturing, Duncan, Oklahoma, will be one of 34 businesses exempt from the Occupational Safety and Health Administration inspection. The precision machine shop has been in business since 1976.

46270 ■ "Eating Up Profits" in *Hispanic Business* (June 2005, pp. 94)
Pub: Hispanic Business
Ed: Keith Rosenblum. Description: Rising costs deter an otherwise strong 2004 for manufacturers in the U.S. Statistical data included.

46271 ■ "Economic Developers Expect a Busier Year in '03" in *Atlanta Business Chronicle* (Vol. 25, December 6, 2002, No. 26, pp. 8A)
Pub: American City Business Publications, Inc.
Ed: Jarred Schenke. Description: The Georgia Department of Industry, Trade and Tourism and Georgia Power Company, Georgia's largest economic development organizations, are working to attract more companies to the state. This trend could generate business for industrial real estate planners.

46272 ■ "Economist Upbeat About Macomb in 2005 Despite Lagging Recovery" in *Crain's Detroit Business* (Vol. 21, January 24, 2005, No. 4, pp. 5)
Pub: Crain Communications Inc. - Detroit
Ed: Anjali Fluker. Description: Macomb County, Michigan is falling behind the national economic recovery being experienced in other counties. Issues of loss in manufacturing and the domestic automobile industry were sited as factors.

46273 ■ "End of the Road" in *Entrepreneur* (Vol. 31, No. 8, August 2003, pp. 24)
Pub: Entrepreneur Media, Inc.
Ed: Joshua Kurlantzick. Description: Two Department of Commerce programs, the Advanced Technology Program (ATP) and the Manufacturing Extension Partnership (MEP) may be discontinued as part of the 2004 federal budget. The ATP program assists small firms by supporting research and development, while the MEP aids manufacturers in upgrading technology and human resources.

46274 ■ "Entrepreneur Column" in *Entrepreneur.com* (October 26, 2006)
Pub: Entrepreneur Media Inc.
Ed: Roy Williams. Description: Maximize your advertising by understanding that the type of your product may dictate the type of advertising. Using professional announcers does not always achieve the effect of being your own spokesman.

46275 ■ **"Environmental technology firm files bankruptcy" in** *Atlanta Business Chronicle* **(Vol. 25, December 20, 2002, No. 28, pp. 8A)**
Pub: American City Business Publications, Inc.
Ed: Mary Jane Credeur. **Description:** Apyron Technologies Inc., a manufacturer of commercial water, air and emissions purification and detoxification products, has filed for Chapter 7 bankruptcy in the U.S. Bankruptcy Court, Atlanta, Georgia. The eight-year-old firm has raised nearly $17 million over that same period, and lists for around $2 million in claims.

46276 ■ **"Equipment Maintenance Insurance Coverage" in** *Rough Notes* **(Vol. 145, No. 1, January 2003, pp. 44)**
Pub: Rough Notes
Ed: Dennis Pillsbury. **Description:** The Flanders Group, headed by Lou Ricci, offers equipment maintenance insurance coverage and uses Specialty Underwriters and REMI as support for their services.

46277 ■ **"Ever-Changing SUVs" in** *Business First Buffalo* **(Vol. 19, No. 44, July 25, 2003, pp. 17)**
Pub: American City Business Journals, Inc.
Ed: Dave English. **Description:** New 2004 sport utility vehicles offer consumers a broad range of styles, entertainment packages, and engine capabilities. The new models offered include Buick Rainier, Toyota Scion, Cadillac SRX, Chevrolet Equinox, Nissan Pathfinder Armada, and BMW X3.

46278 ■ **"The Explosion of Chinese Imports Has Changed U.S. Manufacturers In Many Ways" in** *Inc.* **(May 1, 2005)**
Pub: Inc. Magazine
Ed: Darren Dahl. **Description:** The need for a policy that does not allow the U.S. to be abused by liberalized trade is discussed, focusing on Chinese competitors.

46279 ■ **"The Explosion of Chinese Imports Has Changed US Manufacturers In Many Ways-Including How They Lobby in Washington" in** *Inc.* **(May1,2005)**
Pub: Inc. Magazine
Ed: Darren Dahl. **Description:** The need for a policy that does not allow the U.S. to be abused by liberalized trade is discussed, focusing on Chinese competitors.

46280 ■ **"The Exporting Advantage" in** *Inc.* **(August 2005, pp. 40, 42)**
Pub: Inc. Magazine
Ed: Jeff Bailey. **Description:** Brothers Jon, Keith and Mark Pavlansky sell rubber dirt to Mexican growers. Their company, Hibco Plastics transformed their company while increasing sales by marketing their products in Mexico.

46281 ■ **"Extreme hunter scores big with tiny funds" in** *Red Herring* **(March 2003, pp. 52)**
Pub: Herring Communications Inc.
Ed: Niall McKay. **Description:** Profile of Jonathan Trent, an astrobiologist at NASA. Trent discovered a breakthrough in 1991 that may revolutionize a segment of nanotechnology known as molecular manufacturing.

46282 ■ **"An eye for a dye" in** *Red Herring* **(March 2003, pp. 60)**
Pub: Herring Communications Inc.
Ed: Michael V. Copeland. **Description:** Optiva's nanotechnology has attracted JP Morgan Partners investment.

46283 ■ **"The fabric of consumer reality" in** *Red Herring* **(March 2003, pp. 54)**
Pub: Herring Communications Inc.
Ed: Alan Zeichick. **Description:** The economics of nanotechnology are discussed. In order for a particular consumer good to be priced competitively, the nano-scale components required must be manufactured in bulk, using techniques similar to those used in making larger-scale products.

46284 ■ **"A Family Affair" in** *Pittsburgh Business Times* **(Vol. 22, No. 52, July 11, 2003, pp. 19)**
Pub: Pittsburgh Business Times
Ed: Christopher Davis. **Description:** Profile of Delp Family Powder Coatings Inc., launched in 2002, a successful metal coatings business in Oakland, California; the firm is expanding operations due to high level of demand.

46285 ■ **"Family divisions threaten Jervis B. Webb" in** *Crain's Detroit Business* **(Vol. 19, No. 11, March 17, 2003, pp. 20)**
Pub: Crain Communications Inc., Detroit
Ed: Michael Strong. **Description:** Farmington Hills, Michigan-based Jervis B. Webb Company, manufacturer of conveyor equipment, is involved in a struggle among family members that is now being heard in Oakland County Circuit Court.

46286 ■ **"Faurecia May Buy to Grow, but Only If It Fits Plan" in** *Crain's Detroit Business* **(Vol.23, January 15, 2007, No.3, pp. 1)**
Pub: Crain Communications Inc. - Detroit
Ed: Brent Snaveley. **Description:** European interiors supplier may enter domestic supply market by purchasing acquisitions in U.S. market if they match their business plan. A global giant, but currently not in the U.S. domestic market, Faurecia was invited in by General Motors since nearly 40 percent of domestic competition is bankrupt or struggling financially.

46287 ■ **"Feeling Loaded Down? Use Partnerships to Bag New Customers" in** *My Business* **(October/November 2003, pp. 44)**
Pub: My Business Magazine
Ed: Paige Orr. **Description:** Michael Hess, president and chief executive of Road Wired, a technology travel accessory firm, partnered with Travelpro International, a luggage manufacturer and distributor. This partnership has helped Hess to grow his business.

46288 ■ **"FEI's Strategy for Reaching Big Leagues" in** *Business Journal-Portland* **(Vol. 20, No. 24, August 15, 2003, pp. 1)**
Pub: American City Business Journals, Inc.
Ed: Aliza Earnshaw. **Description:** Profile of FEI Company, manufacturer of three-dimensional inspection technology used in semiconductor manufacturing. The firm's goal is to have $1 billion in revenue.

46289 ■ **"Fleeting Moment" in** *Entrepreneur* **(Vol. 32, December 2004, No. 12, pp. 39)**
Pub: Entrepreneur Media Inc.
Ed: Jill Amadio. **Description:** Auto manufacturers, particularly the Big Three in Detroit, provide incentives to small companies to fleet lease from them. The advantages of fleet leasing include tax deductions for interest, ability to hold on to more capital, vehicles are always under warranty, and more.

46290 ■ **"Flower power" in** *Entrepreneur* **(Vol. 31, No. 5, May 2003, pp. 104)**
Pub: Entrepreneur Media Inc.
Ed: Nichole L. Torres. **Description:** Profile of Tish Ciravolo of Daisy Rock Girl Guitars LLC. Ciravolo started her manufacturing firm in 2000 to make guitars that fit little girl's fingers and have flower and heart designs.

46291 ■ **"Food for thought" in** *Black Enterprise* **(Vol. 32, No. 9, Ma rch 2002, pp. 102)**
Pub: Earl Graves Publishing Co.
Ed: James A. Anderson. **Description:** Five funds concentrating on the food industry and consumer staples are highlighted. Statistical data included.

46292 ■ **"For Some, ITC's Steel Stance a Lose-Lose Deal" in** *Pittsburgh Business Times* **(Vol. 23, No. 8, September 12, 2003, pp. 1)**
Pub: Pittsburgh Business Times
Ed: Christopher Davis. **Description:** Monaca, Pennsylvania-based Beaver Valley Alloy Foundry Company, a small steel producer, may be affected by any changes in U.S. steel tariffs. The tariffs are under review by the U.S. International Trade Commission.

46293 ■ **"Ford Backs Off Supporting Expanded Freight Terminal" in** *Crain's Detroit Business* **(Vol. 19, No. 42, October 20, 2003, pp. 2)**
Pub: Crain Communications Inc., Detroit
Ed: Michael Strong. **Description:** Ford Motor Company has declined support for an expanded freight terminal in southwest Detroit because it feels an increase in truck traffic would interfere with just-in-time delivery to its Dearborn Truck Plant.

46294 ■ **"Foreign currency" in** *Entrepreneur* **(Vol. 30, No. 10, October 2002, pp. 58)**
Pub: Entrepreneur Media Inc.
Ed: Crystal Detamore-Rodman. **Description:** Profile of Steve Lamond, who launched International Turbine Systems Inc. in 1992; Lamond tells how he was able to borrow capital through government-guaranteed loans to start his firm.

46295 ■ **"Frank Robinson Robinson Helicopter for Whipping an Entire Industry Into Shape" in** *Inc.* **(April 1, 2005)**
Pub: Inc. Magazine
Description: Profile of Frank Robinson, founder of Robinson Helicopter. Robinson outsells all other North American manufacturers, with nearly 6,000 helos worldwide.

46296 ■ **"From Idea to Marketplace" in** *Small Business Opportunities* **(May 2005)**
Pub: Harris Publications Inc.
Description: Every inventor must learn information about patenting, manufacturing, packaging, marketing and shipping when planning to take an invention from idea to the marketplace.

46297 ■ **"Frozen assets" in** *Entrepreneur* **(Vol. 31, No. 6, June 2003, pp. 114)**
Pub: Entrepreneur Media Inc.
Ed: Nichole L. Torres. **Description:** Profile of Mike Fanning and Bill Sammon of Hima Ice Towel Corporation, a manufacturer of ice-cold towels used in hot climates.

46298 ■ **"Fuel Efficiency Becomes Grail" in** *Crain's Detroit Business* **(Vol. 23, January 8, 2007, No. 2, pp. 11)**
Pub: Crain Communications Inc. - Detroit
Ed: Brent Snaveley. **Description:** Fuel efficiency, quality, and safety are primary customer concerns for vehicle and subsystems development. Many suppliers are shifting capital expenditures toward smaller fuel efficient vehicles.

46299 ■ **"Gates Plans to Challenge Schnitzers" in** *Business Journal-Portland* **(Vol. 20, No. 25, August 22, 2003, pp. 1)**
Pub: American City Business Journals, Inc.
Ed: Shelly Strom. **Description:** Bill Gates is attempting to reform the board of directors at Portland, Oregon-based Schnitzer Steel Industries. Gates, who has obtained support of shareholders for his proposal, is seeking to create a more independent board at the family-dominated company.

46300 ■ **"GlitzyShow, Worry Galore" in** *Wall Street Journal* **(Vol. 249 January 2007, No. 5, pp. A2)**
Pub: Dow Jones & Co. Inc.
Ed: Associated Press. **Description:** Despite the glitzy displays of the North American Auto Show, auto-industry executives worry that 2007 may be one of the weakest years in more than a decade. Emerging markets in India and Eastern Europe are still relatively small and in the case of China, increasingly competitive.

46301 ■ **"GM Set To Unleash $3B In IT Deals" in** *Crain's Detroit Business* **(Vol. 21, December 19, 2005, No. 51, pp. 1)**
Pub: Crain Communications Inc. - Detroit
Ed: Andrew Dietderich. **Description:** General Motors Corporation announced plans for $3 Billion worth of information technology contracts to be awarded to more than 40 technology contractors and subcontracts from the Detroit area.

46302 ■ **"GM Smiles on Local Suppliers; New Contracts Mean Big Growth for Brake Producer"** in *Crain's Detroit Business* (December 20, 2004)
Pub: Crain Communications Inc. - Detroit
Ed: Terry Kosdrosky. Description: Advics North America Inc. will supply full brake systems for GMs Hummer H3. The new supplier also won a contract to supply stability controls and a hydraulic brake actuation system for a future General Motors vehicle.

46303 ■ **"GM's Way Or the Highway"** in *Business Week* (December 19, 2005, No. 3964, pp. 48-49)
Pub: McGraw-Hill Companies
Ed: Steve Hamm. Description: With $15 billion in deals to discourse, General Motors is changing technology outsourcing business.

46304 ■ **"Going, going, gone"** in *Harvard Business Review* (Vol. 78, No. 6, November-December 2000, pp. 30)
Pub: Harvard Business School Publishing Corp.
Description: A discussion about companies using online reverse auctions to procure a variety of materials, services, and parts. Auctions force manufacturers to bid for contracts, and can produce great reductions in the cost of supplies, but they may also have risks.

46305 ■ **"Granholm wants to scrap workers' comp appeal board"** in *Crain's Detroit Business* (Vol. 19, No. 11, March 17, 2003, pp. 6)
Pub: Crain Communications Inc., Detroit
Ed: Amy Lane. Description: Michigan Governor Jennifer Granholm wants to eliminate the Workers' Compensation Appellate Commission; manufacturers feel they would lose an important place to adjudicate claims for disability benefits outside of court.

46306 ■ **"The Great Jobs Switch"** in *The Economist* (Vol. 377, October 1-7, 2005, No. 8446, pp. 13, 16)
Pub: The Economist Newspaper Ltd.
Description: Manufacturing accounts for less than 10 percent of all jobs in the U.S. However, the fall in manufacturing jobs is a sign of economic progress, not decline.

46307 ■ **"Growth of home health products industry brings liability issues"** in *Pittsburgh Business Times* (Vol. 22, No. 39, April 11, 2003)
Pub: Pittsburgh Business Times
Ed: Christopher Davis. Description: Medical equipment manufacturers must remain aware of liability issues when allowing devices to be operated in patient homes.

46308 ■ **"Guiding Light"** in *Entrepreneur* (Vol. 33, August 2005, No. 8, pp. 16)
Pub: Entrepreneur Media Inc.
Ed: Sara Wilson. Description: Profile of Frederick Bouchardy, founder of Joya candle manufacturing company. Bouchardy started his firm with $70,000 in 2003 and expects sales to reach $1 million in 2005.

46309 ■ **"The Handicapped Deserve More Help"** in *Automotive News* (Vol. 79 February 14, 2005, No. 6134, pp. 12)
Pub: Crain Communications Inc.
Ed: Keith Crain. Description: Need for special-purpose vehicles to serve the disabled population is investigated.

46310 ■ **"Hands On"** in *Inc.* (Volume 27, July 2005, No. 7, pp. 31-32)
Pub: Inc. Magazine
Ed: Jeff Bailey. Description: Profile of Terry Noon, owner of Capacitor Industries, importer of low-cost electronic components from China and sells them to motor makers and other manufacturers in the U.S. and abroad.

46311 ■ **"Hauppauge-based Spellman High Voltage Electronics Doubles the Size of Its Bohemia Facility"** in *Long Island Business News* (Jan.30,2004)
Pub: Dolan Media Newswires
Ed: Nick Anastasi. Description: The nation's largest independent manufacturer of high-voltage power conversion products, Spellman High Voltage Electronics Corporation, has doubled the size of its Bohemia facility. The expansion will include metal fabrication and machining divisions.

46312 ■ *Hawaii Industrial Directory*
Pub: Harris InfoSource
Ed: Fran Carlsen, Editor. Released: Annual, latest edition 2003. Price: $89. Covers: 2,895 manufacturing companies in Hawaii. Entries Include: Company name, address, phone, fax, web site address (on CD-ROM only), toll-free, names and titles of key personnel, number of employees, geographical area served, financial data, descriptions of product/service, Standard Industrial Classification (SIC) code, year established, annual revenues, plant size, legal structure, export/import information. Arrangement: Classified by product/service, line of business. Indexes: Product/service, name, geographical.

46313 ■ **"High Profit in Play"** in *Small Business Opportunities* (Vol. 16, No. 1, January 2004, pp. 62, 64)
Pub: Harris Publications, Inc.
Ed: Stan Roberts. Description: Profile of Ron Kaplan who took over his family's toy distribution business, Action Products International in Orlando, Florida, in 1997. Kaplan decided to shift the focus of the company from supplying toys, books and souvenirs to museums, to concentrating on manufacturing educational toys. The company now reports sales of $6 million a year.

46314 ■ **"Hiring Employees With Disabilities"** in *Inc.* (October 2005, pp. 29-32)
Pub: Inc. Magazine
Ed: Darren Dahl. Description: Habitat International, a carpet, turf and contract manufacturing firm in Chattanooga, Tennessee hires employees with disabilities. Three in four firms in the U.S. have no disabled workers employed. Statistical data included.

46315 ■ *A History of Small Business in America*
Pub: University of North Carolina Press
Ed: Mansel G. Blackford. Released: January 2003. Price: $18.95. Description: History of American small business from the colonial era to present, showing how it has played a role in the nation's economic, political, and cultural development across manufacturing, sales, services and farming.

46316 ■ **"I'd Like to Buy Machinery From China"** in *Inc.* (September 2005, pp. 53)
Pub: Inc. Magazine
Description: When purchasing equipment from China, can American businesses hold Chinese manufacturers responsible if machines violate patent laws?

46317 ■ **"Industrial Cleanser"** in *Entrepreneur* (Vol. 28, No. 1, January 2000, pp. 132)
Pub: Entrepreneur Media Inc.
Ed: Stephen Barlas. Description: The EPA is targeting small business for pollution cleanup. The environmental laws governing small manufacturing businesses is explained.

46318 ■ **"Industrial Metamorphosis"** in *The Economist* (Vol. 377, October 1-7, 2005, No. 8446, pp. 69-70)
Pub: The Economist Newspaper Ltd.
Description: Despite the drop in manufacturing jobs in America, manufacturing real output has been growing by nearly 4 percent annually since 1991, faster than overall GDP growth. Statistical data included.

46319 ■ **"Inside Intel"** in *Business Week* (January 9, 2006, No. 3966, pp. 46-52, 54)
Pub: McGraw-Hill Companies

Ed: Cliff Edwards. Description: Profile of Paul Otellini, CEO of Intel Corporation. Otellini is taking the computer chipmaker into sectors such as consumer electronics, wireless communications, and health care.

46320 ■ **"Interactive TV: What's In the Cards?"** in *Business Week* (January 31, 2005, pp. 32)
Pub: McGraw-Hill Companies
Ed: Cliff Edwards. Description: Electronics companies and cable companies are vying for control over digital services. Profile of CableCards, a device that unscrambles digital video images, is presented.

46321 ■ **"Internet Use by Manufacturers is Small for Business-to-Business Commerce"** in *Wall Street Journal* (February 23, 2000, pp. B11C)
Pub: Dow Jones & Co., Inc.
Ed: John Connor. Description: A survey by the National Association of Manufacturers regarding Internet usage by manufacturers is examined.

46322 ■ *Interstate Manufacturers and Industrial Directory*
Pub: Interstate Publishers Corp.
Ed: Frank Majorana, Editor. Released: Annual, May. Price: $60. Covers: 26,000 firms in 22 states, primarily in the East, South, and West. Entries Include: Firm name, address, phone. Arrangement: Classified by product or service.

46323 ■ **"IPOs/Recent Issues"** in *Venture Capital Journal* (Vol. 41, No. 8, August 2000, pp. 42-45)
Pub: Venture Economics
Description: Profile of seven venture-backed companies that went public during June 2001, including General Maritime Corporation, Monolithic System Technology Inc., MultiLink Technology Corporation, The Princeton Review, Torch Offshore Inc., Unilab Corporation, and United Surgical Partners International.

46324 ■ **"Is GM on the Road to a Board Fight?"** in *Business Week* (January 23, 2006, No. 3968, pp. 35)
Pub: McGraw-Hill Companies
Ed: David Welch. Description: Kirk Kerkorian may nominate directors if Richard Wagoner Jr., chairman and chief executive, keeps ignoring his advice to cut dividends. Statistical data included.

46325 ■ **"Is a Minority Share Really Worth It?"** in *Automotive News* (Vol. 79, February 28, 2005, No. 6136, pp. 12)
Pub: Crain Communications Inc.
Ed: Keith Crain. Description: Is General Motors move to own small portions of other companies better than owning the whole thing? This and other auto-related issues are discussed.

46326 ■ **"Itching to Make Your Mark?"** in *Inc.* (February 1, 2002)
Pub: Inc. Magazine
Ed: Jill Andresky Fraser. Description: Profile of a rubber-stamp and marking-device manufacturing business on the market for $575,000. The pros and cons to buying such a business are discussed.

46327 ■ **"It's a Three-Ring Circus and Then Some"** in *Crain's Detroit Business* (Vol. 22, January 16, 2006, No. 4, pp. 8)
Pub: Crain Communications Inc. - Detroit
Ed: Keith Crain. Description: Manufacturers at the 2006 North American International Auto Show continue to improve displays each year.

46328 ■ **"JCI Auto Chief"** in *Crain's Detroit Business* (Vol. 22, January 30, 2006, No. 5, pp. 35)
Pub: Crain Communications Inc. - Detroit
Description: Interview with Keith Wandell, president of Johnson Controls Automotive Group, Plymouth, Michigan. Wandell discusses the impact of increased materials costs and production cuts for automotive suppliers in the U.S. for the next few years.

46329 ■ "Jeep Adds to Legacy of Federal Program Gone Well" in *San Diego Business Journal* (Vol. 28, January 8, 2007, No. 2, pp. 12)
Pub: San Diego Business Journal Associates
Ed: Cordell Koland. Description: Profile of the Jeep Wrangler and its beginnings as a military light reconnaissance vehicle in the 1940s.

46330 ■ "Job Growth Encouraging in Silicon Valley, Nationwide" in *San Jose Mercury News* (March 5, 2005)
Pub: Knight-Ridder/Tribune Business News
Ed: Nicole C. Wong. Description: Nearly 169,400 new manufacturing jobs were created in Silicon Valley in January 2005, offering hope for a recovering economy in the area.

46331 ■ "Jobs Increase in Milwaukee Area" in *Milwaukee Journal Sentinel* (December 22, 2005)
Pub: Journal Sentinel, Inc.
Ed: Joel Dresang. Description: According to the Wisconsin Department of Workforce Development, Milwaukee showed an increase in jobs over the last year, including the manufacturing sector. From November 2004 to November 2005, 1,300 new factory jobs were created paying an average of $17.37 an hour.

46332 ■ "Joining Forces" in *Sales & Marketing Management*
Pub: VNU Business Media
Ed: Dale Buss. Description: Special-ingredient manufacturers are lending value to some food and beverage brands to attract the attention of grocery store shoppers.

46333 ■ "JPMorgan Chase Regional Economist Forecasts Long Island Growth for 2004" in *Long Island Business News* (January 30, 2004)
Pub: Dolan Media Newswires
Description: Marc Goloven, an economist for JPMorgan Chase predicts economic growth of about 4 percent nationwide and in the Long Island, New York region. Goloven attributes this in part to the fact that many small businesses suffered less economic damage in the last few years. Long Island has shifted away from the manufacturing sector to the services industry, helping the area.

46334 ■ "Lawn Tractor Manufacturer Relocates From Wisconsin to Portland, Maine" in *Portland Press Herald* (August 17, 2005)
Pub: Blethen Maine Newspapers, Inc.
Ed: Edward D. Murphy. Description: Eastman Industries is moving its lawn and garden tractor plant from Wisconsin to Portland, Maine. The new plant will add about a dozen new manufacturing jobs to the area. Details of the move are included.

46335 ■ "Lawsuit against Masco alleges predatory pricing" in *Crain's Detroit Business* (Vol. 19, No. 10, March 10, 2003, pp. 32)
Pub: Crain Communications Inc., Detroit
Ed: Michael Strong. Description: Wilson Insulation Group Inc. has filed a lawsuit against Masco Corporation for predatory pricing and monopolizing in an attempt to drive Wilson out of the Augusta, Georgia market.

46336 ■ "Leaders Make Deal on Business Taxes" in *Crain's Detroit Business* (Vol. 21, November 7, 2005, No. 45, pp. 6)
Pub: Crain Communications Inc. - Detroit
Ed: Amy Lane. Description: Michigan Governor Granholm, along with Republican legislators, agreed to a personal property tax relief plan for state manufacturers. The plan would provide any business moving workers or equipment into the state a single-business tax credit for 100 percent of personal-property taxes paid.

46337 ■ "'Lean manufacturing' consultant moves south" in *Atlanta Business Chronicle* (Vol. 25, November 29, 2002, No. 25, pp. 5A)
Pub: American City Business Publications, Inc.
Ed: Jim Lovel. Description: RWD Technologies Inc., plans to move the headquarters of its performance solutions division from Troy, Michigan to Atlanta, Georgia. The division, which has primarily been associated with the automotive industry, intends to work more closely with the textile industry and hospital systems as part of its move to the South.

46338 ■ "Lear won't take a back seat" in *Fast Company* (June 2001, pp. 179)
Pub: Fast Company
Ed: Fara Warner. Description: For decades, Lear Corporation made car seats. Today, with the help of a virtual reality and other digital technologies, Lear makes a whole lot more, and makes it faster.

46339 ■ "Learning across lines. The secret to more efficient factories" in *Harvard Business Review* (Vol. 80, No. 10, October 2002, pp. 107)
Pub: Harvard Business School Press
Ed: Michael A. Lapre, Luke N. Van Wassenhove. Description: The complexities and pitfalls associated with efforts to boost operating productivity at factories are reviewed. This effort invariably also requires employees learning new skills and transferring those skills to other parts of the factory or company.

46340 ■ "Let Them Eat Cake: When It Comes to Small Business, a New Tax-Cut Bill is Half-Baked" in *Entrepreneur* (Vol. 32, November 2004)
Pub: Entrepreneur Media Inc.
Ed: Stephen Barlas. Description: New tax incentives for U.S. manufacturers are discussed.

46341 ■ "Let's Make a Deal" in *Business Journal-Milwaukee* (Vol. 20, No. 47, August 8, 2003, pp. A23)
Pub: American City Business Journals, Inc.
Ed: Becca Mader. Description: A growing trend among Milwaukee-based manufacturers is to acquire German companies. Topics include strategic planning, market development, and foreign operations.

46342 ■ "Local Motion: For a Competitive Edge, Offer Items Made Locally" in *Entrepreneur* (Vol. 32, November 2004, No. 11, pp. 90)
Pub: Entrepreneur Media Inc.
Ed: Gwen Moran. Description: Trade shows, farmers markets, festivals, local events, as well as local business associations are good sources for locating manufacturers.

46343 ■ "Local nonprofits benefit from polluter-pay rulings" in *Crain's Detroit Business* (Vol. 19, No. 1, January 6, 2003, pp. 19)
Pub: Crain Communications Inc., Detroit
Ed: Robert Ankeny. Description: Fines issued to U.S. Liquids of Detroit Inc. will benefit two Detroit areas charities. An increasing trend towards federal courts ordering companies convicted of polluting will also help offset environmental damage.

46344 ■ "Location of Huge Development Depends on Interchange Site" in *St. Louis Post-Dispatch* (January 6, 2005)
Pub: Knight-Ridder/Tribune Business News
Ed: Maring Van Der Werf. Description: Two construction firms are competing over proposed ventures in Illinois that feature light manufacturing and large distribution warehouses. Plans by Overland-based Clayco Construction Company and Crestwood-based G.J. Grewe Inc., are outlined.

46345 ■ "Long Island's Industrial Agencies Spend $733 Million in 2003 on Economic Incentives" in *Long Island Business News* (February 20, 2004)
Pub: Dolan Media Newswires
Ed: Nick Anastasi. Description: Eight industrial development agencies in Long Island spent more than $733 million in economic incentives to draw and retain companies in the area.

46346 ■ "Long-Time Music Publisher Sings" in *San Fernando Valley Business Journal* (Vol. 11, November 2006, No. 24, pp. 26)
Pub: San Fernando Valley Business Journal Associates
Ed: Description: Profile of Alfred Publishing Co., a successful company that publishes music-related material and its acquisition of Daisy Rock Guitars, makers of acoustic and electrical guitars for women and girls.

46347 ■ "Low-key expansion expected for manufacturers" in *Atlanta Business Chronicle* (Vol. 25, January 10, 2003, No. 31, pp. 24A)
Pub: American City Business Publications, Inc.
Ed: Tony Heffernan. Description: Even though Georgia's manufacturing sector has been in a slump since 2002, the Georgia Economic Outlook 2003 survey indicated that capacity, production, and utilization will expand slightly in 2003.

46348 ■ "Low-Volume Chevy Dealers Criticize Incentive Program" in *Automotive News* (Vol. 79, February 7, 2005, No. 6133, pp. 42)
Pub: Crain Communications Inc.
Ed: K.C. Crain. Description: Many low-volume Chevy dealers have expressed dissatisfaction with the Chevrolet Standards of Excellence program, which has been in effect for six months. The sign-up fee is $30,000 regardless of franchise size.

46349 ■ "Made in America?" in *Entrepreneur* (Vol. 31, No. 10, October 2003, pp. 72)
Pub: Entrepreneur Media, Inc.
Ed: Joshua Kurlantzick. Description: The consequences of U.S. businesses using overseas labor to produce products and reduce costs to small U.S. manufacturers are examined.

46350 ■ "Made in the Shade" in *Small Business Opportunities* (Vol. 17, May 2005, No. 3, pp. 102-103)
Pub: Harris Publications Inc.
Ed: Stan Roberts. Description: Profile of Larry Ball, who launched BP International in order to create and market shade structures used to protect tennis players and individuals from the sun. The company also manufactures tennis court, athletic field and gymnasium equipment.

46351 ■ "Maine Debate Imposing Stricter Standards for Auto Emissions" in *Portland Press Herald* (October 7, 2005)
Pub: Blethen Maine Newspapers, Inc.
Ed: John Richardson. Description: Maine's Board of Environmental Protection is considering a proposal that would require new cars and trucks sold in Maine to release 30 percent less greenhouse gases by 2016.

46352 ■ "Maine Reweaves Thread of Former Textile Industry Into Artistry" in *Portland Press Herald* (September 6, 2005)
Pub: Blethen Maine Newspapers, Inc.
Ed: Edward D. Murphy. Description: Some of Maine's textile mills are returning to the state through craftspeople and artists who use the material to create art for companies wishing to stand out at trade shows, retailers to increase visibility, and architects creating a look that stands out in a crowd.

46353 ■ "Maine Tribes Express Interest in Naval Base Redevelopment Project" in *Portland Press Herald* (December 17, 2005)
Pub: Blethen Maine Newspapers, Inc.
Ed: Kevin Wack. Description: The Penobscot Indian Nation and the Passamaquoddy Tribe are interested in redeveloping the Brunswick Naval Air Station. Plans include the manufacture of environmentally friendly wood-based products, aviation maintenance and manufacturing of airplane parts, and production of renewable energy.

46354 ■ "Making Sense of Scanner Data" in *Harvard Business Review* (Vol. 78, No. 2, March 2000, pp. 24)
Pub: Harvard Business School Publishing Corp.

Ed: Peter Rossi, Phil DeLurgio, David Kantor. **Description:** A new statistical technique, called Bayesian shrinkage, can help manufacturers target their retail promotions.

46355 ■ *Managing Complexity and Change in SMEs Frontiers in European Research*
Pub: Edward Elgar Publishing, Incorporated
Ed: Christensen. **Released:** December 2006. **Price:** $120.00. **Description:** Complexities faced by entrepreneurs in an expanding marketplace are discussed.

46356 ■ "Manatee Boat Makers Are Hiring, But Workers Aren't Plentiful" in *Bradenton Herald* (February 4, 2005)
Pub: Bradenton Herald
Ed: Tilde Herrera. **Description:** Growth of the boating industry has increased significantly, with Chris-Craft reporting above 15 percent increase in sales for 2004. However, companies are having difficulty finding skilled labor to produce the growing demand.

46357 ■ "Manufacturer AmerTac Buys Night Light Maker" in *The Record* (November 8, 2005)
Pub: New Jersey Media Group
Ed: Kathleen Lynn. **Description:** AmerTac, manufacturer of lighting products, has acquired Elumina Lighting Technologies Inc., a Canadian company. The move will give AmerTack ownership of Elumina's patented safety technology for night lights and other lighting products.

46358 ■ *Manufacturer's Directory*
Pub: Detroit Regional Chamber
Released: Biennial, November. **Price:** $50, nonmembers; $35, members; $175, individuals on disk for chamber members; $200, individuals on disk for nonmembers. **Covers:** Manufacturers and industrial parks in the 10 county Detroit region. **Entries Include:** Name, address, phone, fax, Standard Industrial Classification (SIC) code, contact name and title, product description, email and website when available. **Arrangement:** Classified by Alphabetical, then Standard Industrial Classification (SIC) code. **Indexes:** SIC code.

46359 ■ "Manufacturers Group Wants End to Spam" in *Crain's Detroit Business* (Vol. 19, No. 10, March 10, 2003, pp. 6)
Pub: Crain Communications Inc., Detroit
Ed: Amy Lane. **Description:** The Michigan Manufacturers Association is fighting to stop spam on the Internet and is asking for the Michigan Legislature's help.

46360 ■ "Manufacturing History: Tales of Turning Points in Factory Jobs are Just That" in *Barron's* (July 28, 2003, pp. 30)
Pub: Barron's
Ed: Gene Epstein. **Description:** The continuing erosion of manufacturing jobs in the U.S. may have produced a nearly 40-year low, with less than 15 million factory-related jobs; and its percentage of total private employment, at less than 15 percent, may be nearly 20 percent less than the previous low; but that still does not indicate anything structurally wrong, or any harmful effect of foreign manufacturing.

46361 ■ "Manufacturing: Industrial Strength Integration" in *Microsoft Executive Circle* (Vol. 1, No. 2, Q2 2001, pp. 56-58)
Pub: Putman Media
Ed: Marty Weil. **Description:** The Internet has forced manufacturers to rethink business in order to stay competitive. One global chemical maker handles 4.5 million transactions every month with a 2-3 second response time using the Internet to transact business.

46362 ■ "Manufacturing Job Losses Hit Other Sectors" in *Crain's Detroit Business* (Vol. 22, November 20, 2006,No. 47, pp. 3)
Pub: Crain Communications Inc. - Detroit
Ed: Amy Lane. **Description:** Detroit area service industry job market is flat as a result of the decline in manufacturing job. Service sector jobs are still growing in the rest of the state, however.

46363 ■ "Manufacturing Sector Expects Improvement After Slow January" in *Journal Record (Oklahoma City, OK)* (February 1, 2007)
Pub: Journal Record
Ed: Jerry Shottenkirk. **Description:** Oklahoma manufacturing numbers fell in January 2007, but is expected to recover shortly.

46364 ■ "Manufacturing Sector Strengthening" in *Milwaukee Journal Sentinel* (December 1, 2005)
Pub: Journal Sentinel, Inc.
Ed: Thomas Content, Rick Barrett. **Description:** According to two recent reports, the manufacturing sector is seeing an increase in production while the economy in the Milwaukee, Wisconsin area rose 10 points from October to November 2005.

46365 ■ "MAPICS Implements Web-based Self Service Tool to Enhance Customer Service For High Tech Manufacturers" in *PR Newswire* (Oct. 29, 2001)
Pub: PR Newswire Association, Inc.
Description: New solutions database offers on-demand support for MAPICS' ERP for extended systems customers. MAPICS is a leading provider of collaborative, extended enterprise applications for manufacturers.

46366 ■ "Marine One, Sikorsky Zero" in *Business Week* (February 14, 2005, No. 3920, pp. 40)
Pub: McGraw-Hill Companies
Ed: Diane Brady. **Description:** United Technologies Corporation's chairman and CEO, George David, talks about losing the contract for providing the presidential Sikorsky helicopter. The U.S. Navy awarded the contract to Lockheed Martin Corporation.

46367 ■ "Market Orientation and Other Potential Influences on Performance..." in *Journal of Small Business Management* (Vol. 38, No.1, Jan. 2000)
Pub: West Virginia University
Ed: Alfred M. Pelham. **Description:** Research to provide managers in small manufacturing firms with results regarding significant factors related to performance is reported.

46368 ■ "Masco to Reduce Jobs, Businesses" in *Crain's Detroit Business* (Vol. 21, November 7, 2005, No. 45, pp. 41)
Pub: Crain Communications Inc. - Detroit
Ed: Sheena Harrison. **Description:** Masco Corporation plans to consolidate or sell many of its businesses, the move is expected to save the company $200 million by the end of 2007.

46369 ■ "MC, MMA Offering Manufacturing Management Program" in *Mississippi Business Journal* (Vol. 29, January 2007, No. 3, pp. A15)
Pub: Venture Publications, Inc.
Ed: M.R. Gorringe. **Description:** Mississippi Manufacturers Association and the School of Business at Mississippi College will offer a Certified Manager of Performance Excellence in Manufacturing Program. The program is built around the Baldridge Criteria for Performance Excellence.

46370 ■ "MEDC Showcases Michigan's Automotive Brainpower at Auto Show Symposium" in *Crain's Detroit Business* (Vol. 21, December 19, 2005)
Pub: Crain Communications Inc. - Detroit
Ed: Terry Kosdrosky. **Description:** Michigan Economic Development Corporation hosted a symposium promoting Michigan's automotive intellectual power.

46371 ■ "Meet the New Taurus" in *Atlanta Journal-Constitution* (February 7, 2007)
Pub: Cox Newspapers, Inc.
Ed: Mike Tierney. **Description:** Ford Motor Company announced the revival of the Ford Taurus. Statistical data included.

46372 ■ "Microchip Delays Start in Gresham" in *Business Journal-Portland* (Vol. 20, No. 22, August 1, 2003, pp. 1)
Pub: American City Business Journals, Inc.
Ed: Aliza Earnshaw. **Description:** Profile of Microchip Technology Inc. and production delays being encountered, as well as competition, production management, and market conditions.

46373 ■ "Minorities Push to Keep Supplier Program" in *Plastics News* (Vol. 16, July 12, 2004, No. 19, pp. 10)
Pub: Crain Communications Inc.
Ed: Terry Kosdrosky. **Description:** Minority suppliers are interviewed, discussing the U.S. automakers' purchasing program. These suppliers are urging automakers to develop more rigorous auditing policies for minority purchasing and to establish consequences for Tier 1 suppliers that fall short of goals.

46374 ■ "Minority Biz of the Year" in *Hispanic Business* (March 2002, pp. 10)
Pub: Hispanic Business
Description: A. Anthony Corp. was honored by the Upstate New York Regional Minority Purchasing Council as the Minority Supplier of the Year.

46375 ■ "Minority Business Group Looks to Cement Ties with Foreign Automakers" in *Crain's Detroit Business* (Vol. 19, No. 40, October 13, 2003)
Pub: Crain Communications Inc., Detroit
Ed: Terry Kosdrosky. **Description:** The Michigan Minority Business Development Council has changed its by-laws to include foreign-owned automakers as board members. The change is hoped to forge closer ties between member auto suppliers and foreign-owned automakers.

46376 ■ "Modine Manufacturing Unit to Provide Cooling System for Video-Game Computers" in *Milwaukee Journal Sentinel* (December 8, 2005)
Pub: Journal Sentinel, Inc.
Ed: Rick Barrett. **Description:** Thermacore International, Inc., a subsidiary of Modine Manufacturing, will provide advanced liquid cooling systems for Alienware's video game computers. The system uses liquid-to-air heat exchangers that allow computers to operate at cooler temperatures even when used at maximum power.

46377 ■ "Modular Home Center Opens in Arcadia" in *Charlotte Observer* (February 1, 2007)
Pub: Knight-Ridder/Tribune Business News
Ed: John Lawhorne. **Description:** Arcadia Home Center features modular homes constructed on a steel frame; regulations regarding the manufacture and moving of these homes are included.

46378 ■ "More Tool-and-Die Firms to Get Tax Relief" in *Crain's Detroit Business* (Vol. 22, January 2, 2006, No. 1, pp. 20)
Pub: Crain Communications Inc. - Detroit
Ed: Amy Lane. **Description:** Under a new state law, Michigan tool-and-die firms will be able to take advantage of tax breaks.

46379 ■ "Motor City Mayhem" in *Hispanic Business* (November 2006, pp. 42, 44, 46, 48)
Pub: Hispanic Business
Ed: Paul A. Eisenstein. **Description:** Hispanic consumers could help the U.S. automotive industry get back on track. Profiles of the top twenty Hispanic-owned automotive companies are included.

46380 ■ "Multifaceted Motoring" in *Sacramento Bee* (December 9, 2005)
Pub: The Sacramento Bee
Ed: Mark Glover. **Description:** Crossovers are vehicles that combine the characteristics of two or more vehicles including a wagon/minivan/SUV/car. A listing of current crossover models with profiles of each is included.

46381 ■ **"NADA Was a Success and Then Some"** in *Automotive News* (Vol. 79, February 7, 2005, No. 6133, pp. 12)
Pub: Crain Communications Inc.
Ed: Keith Crain. Description: Changes needing to take place with the National Automobile Dealers Association are discussed.

46382 ■ **"Nanotechnology sector analysis"** in *Red Herring* (March 2003, pp. 62)
Pub: Herring Communications Inc.
Description: An overview of the nanotechnology industry is presented, including information nano-based devices that can change electronics one atom at a time.

46383 ■ **"National Association for the Exchange of Industrial Resources"** in *Entrepreneur* (Vol. 33, August 2005, No. 8, pp. 4)
Pub: Entrepreneur Media Inc.
Ed: Steve Cooper. Description: The National Association for the Exchange of Industrial Resources assists U.S. businesses in the donation of excess inventory to the ill, needy or minors. These donations earn federal income tax deductions.

46384 ■ **"Needs Toner: Facing Rivals, Lexmark Shares Could Go Lower"** in *Barron's* (July 28, 2003, pp. 15)
Pub: Barron's
Ed: Sandra Ward. Description: Printer manufacturer Lexmark's recent loss of nearly 20 percent from its share price was occasioned by third-quarter earnings that were shy of estimates by only one penny. The market's extreme reaction to the near-miss betrays deeper-seated misgivings about Lexmark's competitiveness in the sector.

46385 ■ *Nevada Manufacturers Register*
Pub: Harris InfoSource
Contact: Vera Roldan
Ed: Fran Carlsen, Editor. Released: Annual, latest edition 2003. Price: $99. Covers: Approximately 2,470 manufacturers in Nevada plus names and titles of key executives. Entries Include: Company name, address, parent name/location, telephone, fax and 800 numbers, Web site address (on CD-ROM only), number of employees, year established, annual revenue, plant size, business description, Standard Industrial Classification (SIC) codes, executive names/titles, public ownership, legal structure, import/export designators, female/minority ownership. Arrangement: Classified by product/service, line of business. Indexes: Product/service, alphabetical, geographical, international trade.

46386 ■ **"The New China?"** in *Entrepreneur. com* (Vol. 34, February 2006, No. 2, pp. 17)
Pub: Entrepreneur Media Inc.
Ed: Mark Henricks. Description: Manufacturing opportunities overseas, especially in China and Vietnam are explored.

46387 ■ **"New Rochelle-Based Simone Development Increases its Long Island Holdings"** in *Long Island Business News* (February 20, 2004)
Pub: Dolan Media Newswires
Ed: Nick Anastasi. Description: Simone Development of New Rochelle, New York has purchased 150,000-square foot industrial building on South Oyster Bay Road, increasing the firm's holdings to nearly 1 million square feet of space in 27 buildings.

46388 ■ **"New Rules Cut Health Risks from Lead in Children's Jewelry"** in *Kansas City Star* (February 9, 2005)
Pub: Knight-Ridder/Tribune Business News
Ed: Paul Wenske. Description: In a move to reduce health risks for children, the U.S. Consumer Product Safety Commission has established guidelines for children's metal jewelry. New procedures for manufacturers, importers and retailers for testing lead in the jewelry have also been developed.

46389 ■ **"A new standard"** in *Entrepreneur* (Vol. 30, No. 10, October 2002, pp. 83)
Pub: Entrepreneur Media Inc.
Ed: Mark Henricks. Description: Profile of the International Organization for Standardization is presented. Currently more than 1,500 U.S. firms are certified under the ISO 14001 banner.

46390 ■ **"New Work Rules Will Help Cobo, Auto Show"** in *Crain's Detroit Business* (Vol. 21, October 10, 2005, No. 43, pp. 8)
Pub: Crain Communications Inc. - Detroit
Description: Exhibit companies for the North American International Auto Show and five skilled-trades unions adopted new work rules to govern labor for preparation and presentation of the show. The new five-year pact could cut costs through reduction in crew sizes and overtime.

46391 ■ **"Newton Gets Whiff of Success in Bottles: Glass Factory Makes Vials for Perfumes"** in *Altanta Journal-Constitution* (January 29, 2007)
Pub: Cox Newspapers, Inc.
Ed: Moni Basu. Description: Saint-Gobain Desjonqueres, a French firm operating in Covington, Georgia plans to expand its plant in order to increase production glass perfume bottles.

46392 ■ **"1999 McKinsey Awards"** in *Harvard Business* (Vol. 78, No. 1, January 2000, pp. 137)
Pub: Harvard Business School Publishing Corp.
Description: This article defines the three types of businesses companies are engaged in: customer service, operations, and product development.

46393 ■ **"NMSDC Honors PepsiCo, Toyota"** in *Hispanic Business* (January/February 2005, pp. 16)
Pub: Hispanic Business
Description: National Minority Supplier Development Council honored PepsiCo and Toyota Motor Manufacturing North America for their increased use of minority suppliers. PepsiCo increased it's partnerships with minority suppliers by 11 percent in 2003.

46394 ■ **"No Wonder Market Shares are Falling"** in *Automotive News* (Vol. 79, February 21, 2005, No. 6135, pp. 12)
Pub: Crain Communications Inc.
Ed: Keith Crain. Description: With China, and soon Europe, entering the automobile market with new models, the U.S. automakers need a plan to retain market share.

46395 ■ **"Noble International to Buy Laser Welding International"** in *Crain's Detroit Business* (January 26, 2004, pp. 20)
Pub: Crain Communications Inc., Detroit
Ed: Terry Kosdrosky. Description: Laser Welding International Inc. will soon be acquired by Noble International Ltd, a supplier of laser-welded blanks for the automotive industry.

46396 ■ **"Novel Ideas: Two Entrepreneurs Write Books About Their Experiences-And Learn Something in the Process"** in *Entrepreneur* (Vol. 32)
Pub: Entrepreneur Media Inc.
Ed: Aliza Pilar Sherman. Description: Profiles of Lisa Price, president of a manufacturing and retail company that specializes in homemade body care products and Lisa Hammons, founder and CEO of Femail Creations, a handcrafted-gift catalog and Website featuring female-focused products created by women. Both entrepreneurs wrote books about their business and personal lives and offer advice for publishing a book.

46397 ■ **"Opportunities emerge in a new age of miracle materials. (Nanotechnology)"** in *Red Herring* (March 2003, pp. 50)
Pub: Herring Communications Inc.
Ed: Lee Bruno. Description: An overview of nanotechnology, the study of materials smaller than 100 nanometers, or approximately 1/100th the width of a human hair. Nanotechnology involves two main areas of research.

46398 ■ **"Orbit International Corp. Expects $1M in UPS Orders"** in *Long Island Business News* (February 6, 2004)
Pub: Dolan Media Newswires
Description: Orbit International Corporation expects more than $1 million in orders for its MK 119 gun-control power-supply system to the U.S. Navy's Aegis Destroyers.

46399 ■ **"Out of the Ashes: This Company Faced Sure Disaster-But Came Out Shining"** in *Entrepreneur* (Vol. 31, No. 9, September 2003, pp. 104)
Pub: Entrepreneur Media, Inc.
Description: Profile of Michael Feldman and Jonathan Mafrice owners of Pyramat LLC, located in Los Angeles, California. The firm manufactures floor mats that fold into chairs for video game players. The two young men began selling their products at industry trade shows.

46400 ■ **"A pain in the supply chain"** in *Harvard Business Review* (Vol. 80, No. 5, May 2002, pp. 31)
Pub: Harvard Business School Press
Ed: John Butman. Description: Four experts offer their opinions on the aggressive promotion strategy of a fictional manufacturer that is trying to meet the wildly ambitious sales goals set by its CEO.

46401 ■ **"Passing the baton the importance of sequence, timing, technique and communication in executive succession"** in *Journal of Business Venturing*
Pub: Elsevier Science, Inc.
Ed: Bruno Dyck, Michael Mauws, Frederick A. Starke, Gary A. Mischke. Description: Four factors said to influence the process of executive succession are discussed. These factors, sequence, timing, baton-passing techniques, and communication are examined within the analogy of a relay race, and plot the executive succession in a small manufacturing company, which is family owned.

46402 ■ **"Pendleton Braces for Fight."** in *Business Journal-Portland* (Vol. 20, No. 26, August 29, 2003, pp. 1)
Pub: American City Business Journals, Inc.
Ed: Robin J. Moody. Description: Pendleton Woolen Mills Inc. is preparing for China's entry into the World Trade Organization. The company has upgraded the mill and its products.

46403 ■ **"Peter Falvey: Whiz Kid: Peter Falvey is Betting the Company on Tech Investment"** in *Boston Business Journal* (Vol. 23, July 11, 2003)
Pub: American City Business Journals
Ed: Edward Mason. Description: Revolution Partners focuses on high technology investment; profile of the investment bank's co-founder Peter Falvey is included.

46404 ■ **"Plan May Need Overhaul to Maintain Growth"** in *Crain's Detroit Business* (Vol. 21, January 17, 2005, No. 3, pp. 18)
Pub: Crain Communications Inc. - Detroit
Ed: Sheena Harrison. Description: Quality Cable has seen growth since achieving ISO 9001: 2000 certification. The company produces medical cables. William Connors discussed the firm's plans for growth.

46405 ■ **"Plan Would Share Wealth From $1B Fund"** in *Crain's Detroit Business* (Vol. 21, October 24, 2005, No. 43, pp. 26)
Pub: Crain Communications Inc. - Detroit
Ed: Amy Lane. Description: Life-sciences, technology, tourism, manufacturing, agriculture, film-production, and defense companies will all benefit from $101 million in government funds to support growing or technology-oriented businesses.

46406 ■ **"Plant Manager Urges Lockheed Martin Employees Not to Strike"** in *Atlanta Journal-Constitution* (March 5, 2005)
Pub: Knight-Ridder/Tribune Business News
Ed: Dave Hirschman. Description: International Association of Machinists Local 709's 2,800 members

are poised to reject a tentative three-year contract and authorize a strike. The Lockheed Martin's plant in Marietta, Georgia builds F/A-22 Raptor fighters and C-130J transports. Employees are unhappy about rising health care and retirement insurance costs.

46407 ■ "Plexus Finds Success in Helping Manufacturers with Cost-Cutting Software" in Crain's Detroit Business (Vol. 22, January 16, 2006)
Pub: Crain Communications Inc. - Detroit
Ed: Andrew Dietderich. **Description:** Plexus Systems LLC offers software and services that help companies operate more efficiently from inventory to accounting. The software is used at 270 manufacturing locations.

46408 ■ "PMMI Debuts Contracting Service: By Taking Over Services, PACK EXPO Intl" in Tradeshow Week (Vol. 34)
Pub: Reed Business Information
Ed: Rachelle Crum. **Description:** Packaging Machinery Manufacturers Institute 27th Expo was held in Chicago, Illinois. The show introduced PACK EXPO Services. The show drew more than 46,000 visitors and 1,600 exhibitors.

46409 ■ "Private Investors Purchase a Controlling Stake at Ecoboard Holdings" in Long Island Business News (February 13, 2004)
Pub: Dolan Media Newswires
Ed: Ben Abelson. **Description:** Ecoboard Holdings Inc., manufacturer of plastic lumber, has raised nearly $750,000 from Long Island Capital Alliance's annual venture capital forum. The company's products are used mainly for outdoor applications such as decks, bridges, and piers.

46410 ■ "Profit Comes Harder: WD-40 Co." in San Diego Business Journal (Vol. 28, January 15, 2007, No. 3, pp. 38)
Pub: San Diego Business Journal Associates
Ed: Andy Killion. **Description:** Lubricant and cleaning product manufacturer, WD-40 Company, posted first-quarter earnings up 7.1 percent.

46411 ■ "Purchase Cements Metaldyne Chassis Biz" in Crain's Detroit Business (January 26, 2004, pp. 28)
Pub: Crain Communications Inc., Detroit
Ed: Terry Kosdrosky. **Description:** Metaldyne Corporation acquired a DaimlerChrysler manufacturing plant in New Castle, Indiana. This acquisition will double Metaldyne's capacity to produce automotive chassis components. Metaldyne is one of the largest chassis component makers, with Delphi Corporation, Troy, Michigan being the largest.

46412 ■ "Quick Fix: Do SBA Express Loans Really Shortchange Entrepreneurs?" in Entrepreneur (Vol. 32, No. 4, April 2004, pp. 27)
Pub: Entrepreneur Media, Inc.
Ed: Julie Monahan. **Description:** Profile of the U.S. Small Business Administration's Express program that guaranteed loans to thousands of entrepreneurs. Retailers with gross sales of $6 million or less, wholesalers with 100 employees or less, and manufacturers with 500 employees or less, are eligible for Express Loans.

46413 ■ "Rabbit on a Run" in Business 2.0 (Vol. 7, January/February 2006, No. 1, pp. 69)
Pub: Time, Inc.
Ed: Monica Khemsurov. **Description:** Metrokane used the existing design of a popular corkscrew to jump past a competitor and sell 200,000 units in 2005. Statistical data included.

46414 ■ "Raw-Material Costs Put Squeeze on JCI" in Crain's Detroit Business (Vol. 21, January 24, 2005, No. 4, pp. 7)
Pub: Crain Communications Inc. - Detroit
Description: Keith Wandell, president of Johnson Controls Inc., discusses issues of pricing and raw-materials pressures faced by his company.

46415 ■ "Read a plant-fast" in Harvard Business Review (Vol. 80, No. 5, May 2002, pp. 105)
Pub: Harvard Business School Press
Ed: R. Eugene Goodson. **Description:** Presentation of a tool for assessing the strengths and weaknesses of factories called the Rapid Plant Assessment. This tool has been used hundreds of times with different teams touring the same plant producing consistent results.

46416 ■ "Reed Acquires Manufacturing Shows" in Tradeshow Week (Vol. 34, December 13, 2004, No. 50, pp. 3)
Pub: Reed Business Information
Description: Reed Exhibitions has acquired a series of regional manufacturing tradeshows with the purchase of Advanced Manufacturing and Productivity Exposition series from the Technical Exhibitions and Conferences. The shows focus on automated manufacturing, assembly systems and information technology.

46417 ■ "Report of Big Oil-Inventory Drop Appears To Correct An Error" in Wall Street Journal (Vol. 248, December 2006, No. 153, pp. C9)
Pub: Dow Jones & Co. Inc.
Ed: Matt Chambers **Description:** An unexpected 8.1 million barrel fall in U.S. crude-oil inventories reported by the Energy Dept. was largely due to an error correction in a previous report. The sheer magnitude of the drop sent crude prices up. Analysts provide a bleak short-term forecast.

46418 ■ "Reporter's Notebook; The Question of Private Equity" in Crain's Detroit Business (Vol. 23, January 29, 2007, No. 5, pp. 11)
Pub: Crain Communications Inc. - Detroit
Ed: Brent Snaveley. **Description:** Many smaller auto suppliers have been purchased by private equity and hedge funds. This may not be in the best interests of the supplier company or the customer, but may be necessary for survival.

46419 ■ Risk-Free Entrepreneur
Pub: Adams Media Corporation
Ed: Don Debelak. **Released:** June 2006. **Price:** $14.95. **Description:** Information is offered to help entrepreneurs to develop an idea for a product or service and have other companies provide the marketing, manufacturing and staff.

46420 ■ "Rocky Mountain Steel Mill, a decade and counting" in Colorado Springs Business Journal (March 7, 2003)
Pub: Dolan Media Newswires
Ed: Lance Gurwell. **Description:** Profile of Rocky Mountain Steel Mill in Pueblo, Colorado and the changes made in the last decade that have helped the mill succeed.

46421 ■ "A rose by any other name" in Harvard Business Review (Vol. 81, No. 3, March 2003, pp. 29)
Pub: Harvard Business School Press
Ed: Daniel Stone. **Description:** Five experts give opinions on the choices facing a fictional paper goods manufacturer. Should the fictional company become a supplier for a retailer that has decided to create its own line of party goods, or should it put its efforts behind its own brand?

46422 ■ "Rouge Industries' Russian Suitor Promises New Furnace" in Crain's Detroit Business (Vol. 19, No. 43, October 27, 2003, pp. 17)
Pub: Crain Communications Inc., Detroit
Ed: Terry Kosdrosky. **Description:** Severstal, the Russian steel manufacturer vying to purchase Dearborn, Michigan steelmaker Rouge Industries Inc., plans to build an electric arc furnace. Rouge Industries employs about 2,600 employees.

46423 ■ "Run for the border" in Entrepreneur (Vol. 30, No. 3, March 2002, pp. 123)
Pub: Entrepreneur Media Inc.

Ed: Don Debelak. **Description:** Some inventors are setting up deals with U.S. manufacturers to produce a new product, but when that fails, they are turning to foreign manufacturers to save money; risks involved in doing so are also discussed.

46424 ■ "Sacramento, Calif., Light-Rail Plant Gets $84 Million Deal" in Sacramento Bee (October 21, 2005)
Pub: The Sacramento Bee
Ed: Dale Kasler. **Description:** Siemens Transportation Systems Inc. in Sacramento, California has secured a contract with the city of Edmonton, Alberta, Canada to produce 26 light-rail cars for the city's transit system. The company plans to add 75 new jobs in order to assemble the outer shells of the rail cars.

46425 ■ "Save Your Energy" in Business First Buffalo (Vol. 19, No. 48, August 22, 2003, pp. 15)
Pub: American City Business Journals, Inc.
Ed: Joe Iannarelli. **Description:** Profile of Engergen Inc., designer, manufacturer and marketer of natural gas driven air compressors, chillers, refrigeration equipment, pump drives, and power generation equipment.

46426 ■ Scott's Directories
Pub: Scott's Directories
Released: Annual, latest edition June 2004. **Covers:** About 3,900 manufacturers and 1,500 wholesalers, distributors, and manufacturers' agents in Newfoundland, New Brunswick, Nova Scotia, and Prince Edward Island, Canada. **Entries Include:** Company name, address, phone, fax, names and titles of key personnel, number of employees, parent companies, Standard Industrial Classification (SIC) code, product, year established. **Arrangement:** Geographical. **Indexes:** Alphabetical, SIC, Web, ISO.

46427 ■ "Seizing the Sun" in Boston Business Journal (Vol. 23, No. 25, July 25, 2003, pp. 20)
Pub: American City Business Journals
Ed: Mark Micheli. **Description:** Konarka Technologies, led by CEO and president, William M. Bechenbaugh, produces solar cell material that is light and flexible; the firm states that the new product is more cost-effective than traditional hard solar cells.

46428 ■ "Semiconductor Industry's Growth Will Slow" in Kiplinger Letter (Vol. 78, January 19, 2007, No. 2)
Pub: Kiplinger
Description: Semiconductor manufacturers are expecting a 3 percent drop in sales worldwide in 2007.

46429 ■ "Semiconductors Pierre Lamond" in Venture Capital Journal (January 1, 2005)
Pub: Thomason Financial Inc.
Description: Pierre Lamond shares insight into the best and worst that could happen to the semiconductor industry for 2005. Lamond believes continued growth in the global economy is essential.

46430 ■ "Senate Debates Bill That Shields Gunmakers From Some Lawsuits" in Portland Press Herald (July 27, 2005)
Pub: Blethen Maine Newspapers, Inc.
Ed: Bart Jansen. **Description:** Debate over lawsuits filed by customers against gun manufacturers over misuse of weapons is covered.

46431 ■ "Send In the Robots!" in Fortune (Vol. 151, January 24, 2005, No. 2, pp. 140)
Pub: Time Inc.
Ed: Stuart F. Brown. **Description:** New generation industrial robots can strip paint, inspect buried gas mains, traverse desserts, and even cut grass for golf courses. Computer and navigational technology costs have fallen making these robots affordable to most small businesses.

46432 ■ **"Small Business Advisor: Toy Story: Sharon P. John's Toy Company is Relaunching the Dawn Doll"** in *Crain's Chicago Business* (Vol. 23)
Pub: Crain Communications, Inc. Crain Communications, Inc.
Ed: Barbara B. Buchholz. **Description:** A profile of Sharon P. John, Checkerboard Toys Inc., and her plans to relaunch the Dawn doll, first introduced in 1970.

46433 ■ **"Small Manufacturers Aren't Using the Internet"** in *Wall Street Journal* (July 3, 2000, pp. B6)
Pub: Dow Jones & Co., Inc.
Description: The fact that small manufacturing companies have not jumped into Internet usage is explored.

46434 ■ **"Smurfit-Stone Narrows Losses"** in *St. Louis Post-Dispatch* (January 26, 2005)
Pub: Knight-Ridder/Tribune Business News
Description: Smurfit-Stone Container Corporation reported smaller fourth-quarter and annual losses due to raising its cost for containerboard and boxes. The company has a positive outlook for the economy and expects stable demand trends in the industry.

46435 ■ **"Social Grace"** in *Entrepreneur* (Vol. 33, September 2005, No. 9, pp. 91)
Pub: Entrepreneur Media Inc.
Ed: Sara Wilson. **Description:** Profile of Jeffrey Hollender, president of Burlington, Vermont's Seventh Generation. Hollender manufactures environmentally safe household and personal-care products. The firm offers employee incentives for community involvement.

46436 ■ **"Squeezing Suppliers Can Cost Automakers, Study Says"** in *Crain's Detroit Business* (Vol. 21, January 3, 2005, No. 1, pp. 5)
Pub: Crain Communications Inc. - Detroit
Ed: Lindsay Chappell. **Description:** Big three automakers are paying about 8 percent more to suppliers because of poor relationships with vendors. John Henke Jr., president of Planning Perspectives Inc., conducted a survey covering Big Three purchasing practices.

46437 ■ **"Stakes High For Region as Big Three, UAW Sit Down to Talk."** in *Crain's Detroit Business* (Vol. 23, January 1, 2007, No. 1, pp. 3)
Pub: Crain Communications Inc. - Detroit
Ed: Brent Snaveley. **Description:** Major conflicts loom as contracts expire and must be renegotiated. Financial distress of the North American auto industry is pitted against the declining Union membership and Jobs Bank program. Strikes are possible on these major issues.

46438 ■ **"State Manufacturers Ready to Raise Voices"** in *Crain's Detroit Business* (Vol. 19, No. 49, December 8, 2003, pp. 1)
Pub: Crain Communications Inc., Detroit
Ed: Michael Strong. **Description:** More worker training and streamlined regulatory procedures are among the issues small and mid-sized manufacturers want, according to a survey of more than 1,000 manufacturers in the State of Michigan.

46439 ■ **"State Stocks Show Generally Strong 3Q, Despite Auto Woes"** in *Crain's Detroit Business* (Vol. 21, October 10, 2005, No. 43, pp. 43)
Pub: Crain Communications Inc. - Detroit
Ed: Tom Henderson. **Description:** Michigan's publicly traded companies reported a good showing for third quarter 2005. David Sowerby, portfolio manager for Loomis Sayles & Co. LP, showed a share-based gain of 3.8 percent, up a bit from Standard & Poor's index.

46440 ■ **"Status Quota? Without Trade Quotas, U.S. Textile-Makers Struggle"** in *Entrepreneur* (Vol. 33, September 2005, No. 9, pp. 23)
Pub: Entrepreneur Media Inc.

Ed: Scott Bernard Nelson. **Description:** When a global system of trade quotas expired in 2004, Chinese imports flooded the U.S. market, as high as 1,000 percent increase in some markets. In May 2005, the U.S. imposed a new quota limiting year-over-year increases in China's textile imports to 7.5 percent, providing only temporary relief. The U.S. textile industry must find new ways in which to compete with foreign competitors.

46441 ■ **"SteelSalvor Chooses Lois Paul & Partners to Kick Start Public Relations, Strategic Communications Initiative"** in *PR Newswire*
Pub: PR Newswire Association LLC
Description: SteelSalvor, the only marketing company that maintains an online auction serving the steel industry, has appointed Lois Paul & Partners LLC as its marketing and public relations partner.

46442 ■ **"Stepping On It: Will New Measures Really Rev Up U.S. Manufacturers' Engines?"** in *Entrepreneur* (Vol. 32, July 2004, No. 7, pp. 35)
Pub: Entrepreneur Media Inc.
Ed: Stephen Barlas. **Description:** Under Executive Order by President Bush, federal agencies are to emphasize manufacturing in the Small Business Innovation Research (SBIR) and Small Business Technology Transfer (STTR) programs.

46443 ■ **"Stewart & Stevenson Treads Through Tough Times"** in *Houston Business Journal* (Vol. 34, No. 19, September 19, 2003, pp. 2A)
Pub: American City Business Journals
Ed: Jim Greer. **Description:** Stewart & Stevenson Services Inc., has announced the resignation of its president and CEO Michael Grimes; the truck maker has been plagued by financial problems.

46444 ■ **"Stop Fighting Fires"** in *Harvard Business Review* (Vol. 78, No. 4, July 2000, pp. 83)
Pub: Harvard Business School Publishing Corp.
Ed: Roger Bohn. **Description:** An analysis of companies with complex research and design and manufacturing processes indicates they are likely to engage in harmful fire fighting operations to manage complex problems.

46445 ■ **"Strength in diversity"** in *Hispanic Business* (Vol. 22, No. 7-8, July-August 2000, pp. CA4)
Pub: Hispanic Business
Ed: Joel Russell. **Description:** California's biggest Hispanic businesses are active in a wide range of sectors, including auto detailing, manufacturing and health care. The combined revenue of the state's top 100 Hispanic companies amounted to $2.98 billion in 1999, with the service sector being the largest.

46446 ■ **"Stressed Industries Drive Demand for Temporary Execs"** in *Crain's Detroit Business* (Vol. 22, January 2, 2006, No. 1, pp. 22)
Pub: Crain Communications Inc. - Detroit
Ed: Terry Kosdrosky, Brent Snavely. **Description:** Due to changes in bankruptcy laws and private-equity buyers, as well as issues facing the auto industry, local firms are hiring temporary executives.

46447 ■ **"Strong Demand Is Firing Up U.S. Factories"** in *Business Week* (January 31, 2005, pp. 23)
Pub: McGraw-Hill Companies
Ed: James C. Cooper, Kathleen Madigan. **Description:** Spending by U.S. consumers, businesses, and governments for all goods and services grew 4.9 percent in the third quarter of 2004 and is expected to grow at the same rate for the fourth quarter.

46448 ■ **"Study Foresees End of Boeing's Commercial Work; Company Calls Report Flawed"** in *News Tribune* (April 11, 2003)
Pub: Knight-Ridder/Tribune Business News
Ed: John Gillie. **Description:** According to a study written by two State University of New York at Buffalo

researchers, the growing expertise of overseas aerospace companies along with the demand for higher profits could prompt Boeing to leave the commercial airplane business within the next ten years.

46449 ■ **"Summit Plastics Pursues Acquisition of Industrial Property in Bay Shore"** in *Long Island Business News* (March 5, 2004)
Pub: Dolan Media Newswires
Ed: Nick Anastasi. **Description:** Profile of Summit Plastics Inc. and its move to double the size of the firm's holdings. Summit manufactures and supplies retail displays, such as vacuum-formed menu boards and signs primarily for Coca-Cola Corporation, but is expanding into other product areas such as cosmetics for Revlon and Coty.

46450 ■ **"Suppliers Called On To Boost Minority Deals"** in *Crain's Detroit Business* (Vol. 21, October 3, 2005, No. 43)
Pub: Crain Communications Inc. - Detroit
Ed: Terry Kosdrosky. **Description:** According to Tony Brown, chairman Michigan's minority business association, many of the top auto suppliers are not purchasing from minority-owned companies.

46451 ■ **"Suppliers Picked for Pilot Program"** in *Crain's Detroit Business* (Vol. 21, January 24, 2005, No. 4, pp. 18)
Pub: Crain Communications Inc. - Detroit
Ed: Mary Connelly, Robert Sherefkin. **Description:** Johnson Controls Automotive Group has been selected by the Chrysler Group pilot program that gets suppliers involved in early product development.

46452 ■ **"Survey"** in *Crain's Detroit Business* (Vol. 21, October 24, 2005, No. 43, pp. 1)
Pub: Crain Communications Inc. - Detroit
Ed: Tom Hdnderson. **Description:** According to the 2005 Michigan Women's Leadership Index, the number of top women executives has fallen by 20 percent over the last two years. The auto industry ranked lowest for upper-management opportunity for its female executives.

46453 ■ **"Switching Gears Pays Off"** in *Crain's Detroit Business* (Vol. 21, October 10, 2005, No. 43, pp. 21)
Pub: Crain Communications Inc. - Detroit
Ed: Terry Kosdrosky. **Description:** Porsche Engineering Services Inc. has changed its strategy to working on engineering design, testing, clay modeling, computer modeling, vehicle launches, and supplier management rather than focusing on high-tech projects.

46454 ■ **"Takeover Offer Is Accepted By Parent Of Argo-Tech"** in *Wall Street Journal* (Vol. 248, December 2006, No. 152, pp. A7)
Pub: Dow Jones & Co. Inc.
Ed: Reuters News Service **Description:** Eaton Corp., is to acquire AT Holdings Corp., parent of Argo-Tech Corp. Argo-Tech makers of military and aerospace fuel pumps as well as numerous non-aerospace businesses provides 60% of all commercial airliner fuel pumps, yet these non-aerospace businesses won't be included in the transaction, leaving this vital area of commercial airliner manufacture with an uncertain future.

46455 ■ **"The Talk of the Inc. 500"** in *Inc.* (October, 2000, pp. 13)
Pub: The Goldhirsh Group
Description: Attendees at the Inc. 500 conference contended that the biggest problems facing America's fastest growing companies in 2000 were related to financing business growth. Nearly 75 percent of attendees said they would consider a merger if the right offer came along and nearly two-thirds expressed difficulty implementing e-commerce solutions and many plan to spend more money on Internet marketing than on more traditional marketing media.

46456 ■ **"A targeted approach"** in *Pittsburgh Business Times* (Vol. 22, No. 39, April 11, 2003, pp. 24)
Pub: Pittsburgh Business Times

Ed: Patty Tascarella. **Description:** Profile of Straightline Source, steel distributor, focuses on small, non-traditional steel purchasing companies.

46457 ■ "The Tech Track" in *Hispanic Business* **(January/February 2005, pp. 56, 58)**
Pub: Hispanic Business
Ed: Anthony Limon. **Description:** The Information Technology Association of America reports a 2 percent increase in employment for first quarter periods of 2003 and 2004. The technology sector is slowly re-absorbing displaced workers, however banking, finance, manufacturing, food service and transportation accounted for 89 percent of new IT jobs. Statistical data included.

46458 ■ "Things I Can't Live Without: Marcy Zambelli" in *Inc.* **(July 1, 2004)**
Pub: Inc. Magazine
Ed: Ian Mount. **Description:** Interview with Marcy Zambelli, CEO of Zambelli Fireworks, a third generation family business. The firm was founded in 1893 and is worth $12 million.

46459 ■ "Thinking Out of the Clamshell" in *Business 2.0* **(Vol. 6, July 2005, No. 6, pp. 58)**
Pub: Time, Inc.
Ed: Siri Schubert. **Description:** Thomas Perlmutter invented a tool designed to open clamshell packages. The OpenX tool opens the plastic packaging used to hold products and offer theft protection to retailers while displaying the item inside.

46460 ■ "This Just In" in *Crain's Detroit Business* **(Vol. 19, No. 40, October 13, 2003, pp. 1)**
Pub: Crain Communications Inc., Detroit
Description: Bridgewater Interiors has taken over a Johnson Controls Inc. operation, creating 600 new jobs in Warren, Michigan. The new operation is a joint-venture between Johnson Controls and Detroit-based Epsilon LLC, a minority-owned firm.

46461 ■ "Tower Automotive Plans to Cut More Jobs, Close More Plants" in *Crain's Detroit Business* **(Vol. 22, January 16, 2006, No. 4, pp.)**
Pub: Crain Communications Inc. - Detroit
Ed: Greg Migliore. **Description:** Tower Automotive Inc. filed documents to emerge from Chapter 11 reorganization. The automotive supplier plans to reduce the number of North American plants from 24 to about 15.

46462 ■ "Toyota's Opportunity Exchange" in *Hispanic Business* **(September 2002, pp. 8)**
Pub: Hispanic Business
Description: Toyota Motor Manufacturing America will hold its annual trade fair and conference for Tier I suppliers in November. Toyota's Opportunity Exchange was created to build business relationships between direct, or Tier I, suppliers and MBEs.

46463 ■ "Toyota's Plans Get Suppliers Worked Up; U.S. Expansion Drives Scramble for Business" in *Crain's Detroit Business* **(Vol. 21)**
Pub: Crain Communications Inc. - Detroit
Ed: Terry Kosdrosky. **Description:** Automotive suppliers are working to secure new contracts with Toyota Motor Manufacturing after it announced expansion plans.

46464 ■ "Training Wheels" in *Inc.* **(October 2005, pp. 51-52)**
Pub: Inc. Magazine
Ed: Nadine Heintz. **Description:** Ben Serotta developed a plan to teach retailers how to sell the bicycles he manufactures. Serotta's plan helps retailers custom-fit the bike to its buyer.

46465 ■ "Truck stop" in *Crain's Detroit Business* **(Vol. 19, No. 12, March 24, 2003, pp. 1)**
Pub: Crain Communications Inc., Detroit
Ed: Michael Strong, Terry Kosdrosky. **Description:** Detroit-based automakers are lobbying the United States Customs and Border Protection officials in an effort to ease restrictions on certain trucks entering the U.S. from Canada.

46466 ■ "The true believer" in *Red Herring* **(March 2003, pp. 56)**
Pub: Herring Communications Inc.
Ed: Lee Bruno. **Description:** Scientific developments that are transforming nanotechnology from science fiction to reality are explored, including challenges facing the nanotechnology industry and the talents and skills needed for newcomers to the industry.

46467 ■ *21st Century Manufacturing Enterprise Strategy, Vol. I: An Industry-Led View*
Pub: DIANE Publishing Co.
Ed: Roger N. Nagel and Rick Dove. **Released:** 1998. **Price:** $20.00.

46468 ■ *21st Century Manufacturing Enterprise Strategy, Vol. II: Infrastructure*
Pub: DIANE Publishing Co.
Ed: Roger N. Nagel and Rick Dove. **Released:** 1998. **Price:** $25.00.

46469 ■ "Uncertainty and Information Search Activities" in *Journal of Small Business Management* **(Vol. 41, No. 4, October 2003, pp. 385)**
Pub: International Council of Small Business
Ed: Jeffrey E. McGee, Olukemi O. Sawyerr. **Description:** An examination of the relationship among perceived strategic uncertainty (PSU), environmental scanning, and the information sources used by owner-managers, using 153 small high-technology manufacturing firms.

46470 ■ "Up Front: Supersize It? No Thanks!" in *My Business* **(October/November 2003, pp. 10-11)**
Pub: My Business Magazine
Ed: Jackie Ross. **Description:** Profile of Sarah Cohen, owner of Route 11 Potato Chips, located in Middletown, Virginia; Cohen manufactures the snacks in retro packaging. The potato chips are fried in pure, monounsaturated sunflower and peanut oils and are hand-blended with salt and seasonings in order to produce an all natural product.

46471 ■ "The Upside and Downside of Outsourcing" in *Business Week* **(February 20, 2006, No. 3972, pp. 18)**
Pub: McGraw-Hill Companies
Description: Foreign companies are outsourcing jobs to the U.S. at record rates. Eight percent of U.S. workers are employed in the service industry, 19 percent in manufacturing, and only 1 percent in farming.

46472 ■ *Utah Manufacturers Register*
Pub: Harris InfoSource
Released: Annual, latest edition 2003. **Price:** $99, individuals. **Covers:** Approximately 4,360 manufacturers in Utah, plus names of key executives. **Entries Include:** Company name, address, parent name/location, telephone, fax and 800 numbers, Web site address (on CD-ROM only), number of employees, year established, annual revenue, plant size, business description, Standard Industrial Classification (SIC) codes, executive names/titles, public ownership, legal structure, import/export designators, female/minority ownership. **Arrangement:** Classified by product/service, line of business. **Indexes:** Product/service, alphabetical, geographical, international trade.

46473 ■ "Vacaville, Calif.-Based Biotech Firm Ends Operations" in *Sacramento Bee* **(December 23, 2005)**
Pub: The Sacramento Bee
Ed: Jim Wasserman. **Description:** Large Scale Biology Corporation, manufacturer of proteins and vaccines for tobacco plants closed its operations in Vacaville, California as well as its site in Kentucky, due to lack of funds. The firm went public five years ago.

46474 ■ "Veltri, Edgcomb to close Macomb plants" in *Crain's Detroit Business* **(Vol. 19, No. 15, April 14, 2003, pp. 30)**
Pub: Crain Communications Inc., Detroit

Ed: Terry Kosdrosky. **Description:** Veltri Metal Products Inc. and Edgcomb Metals Company, both located in Macomb County, Michigan will close their plants. The closing will add 149 to the unemployment list in Michigan.

46475 ■ "Viking Adds Rangetops" in *Mississippi Business Journal* **(Vol. 28, September 2006, No. 36, pp. 24)**
Pub: Venture Publications, Inc
Description: Viking Range Corp. has added a continuous grate gas rangetop and electric rangetop stove to its Designer Series products line.

46476 ■ "Visteon CEO" in *Crain's Detroit Business* **(Vol. 21, October 3, 2005, No. 43, pp. 4)**
Pub: Crain Communications Inc. - Detroit
Ed: David Barkholz, Robert Sherefkin. **Description:** Michael Johnston, CEO at Visteon Corporation, reported the company will make more cuts in the areas that do not fit into its three core areas that include electronics, climate control and interiors.

46477 ■ "Visteon Plans to Close, Fix or Sell 23 Plants" in *Crain's Detroit Business* **(Vol. 22, January 16, 2006, No. 3, pp. 4)**
Pub: Crain Communications Inc. - Detroit
Ed: Brent Snavely. **Description:** Visteon Corporation reports plans to fix, sell or close 23 plans in a three-year restructuring effort. Statistical details included.

46478 ■ "Volvo Opens Supplier Diversity Office" in *Hispanic Business* **(July/August 2002, pp. 10)**
Pub: Hispanic Business
Description: Volvo Truck North America Inc. announced the development of a supplier diversity office to help diversity suppliers conduct business with the company.

46479 ■ "Walk the Line" in *Entrepreneur. com* **(Vol. 34, February 2006, No. 2, pp. 80)**
Pub: Entrepreneur Media Inc.
Ed: Chris Penttila. **Description:** The Supreme Court ruled in November 2005 that workers must be paid for time spent between locker rooms and workstations as well as time spent waiting in line to turn in or receive work equipment.

46480 ■ "Want List" in *Crain's Detroit Business* **(Vol. 19, No. 49, December 8, 2003, pp. 1)**
Pub: Crain Communications Inc., Detroit
Description: A list of issues Michigan manufacturers want considered when state and federal policies are formed, is presented.

46481 ■ "Wanted" in *Milwaukee Journal Sentinel* **(December 11, 2005)**
Pub: Journal Sentinel, Inc.
Description: Manufacturers are facing a shortage of skilled workers. Pay and global competition are among the issues facing manufacturers and the National Association of Manufacturers reports the human capital performance gap as a threat to U.S. competitiveness and the nation's most critical business issue.

46482 ■ "Water Wagons" in *Forbes* **(Vol. 175, January 31, 2005, No. 2, pp. 58)**
Pub: Forbes Magazine Inc.
Ed: Joann Muller. **Description:** General Motors is planning to build inexpensive cars in small quantities using hydropressure. Information about this process is described.

46483 ■ "We Must Lose the Entitlement Mentality" in *Crain's Detroit Business* **(Vol. 21, October 17, 2005, No. 43, pp. 9)**
Pub: Crain Communications Inc. - Detroit
Ed: Mary Kramer. **Description:** Thomas Friedman, New York Times columnist, has written a book that identifies ten trends that are making the global economic playing field more level. Friedman offers advice, although not specifically focused on Michigan manufacturing, in the areas of outsourcing, offshoring and new supply-chain systems.

46484 ■ "A Wealth of Choices: Automakers Try to Create Excitement with New Releases" in *San Jose Mercury News* (March 10, 2005)
Pub: Knight-Ridder/Tribune Business News
Ed: Matt Nauman. Description: Automakers released 59 all-new vehicle models in 2004 and 65 more will be launched in 2005. Consumers can choose from 316 different cars, trucks, van and sport-utilities.

46485 ■ "Welcome to the Doll Factory" in *Inc.* (Volume 28, January 2006, No. 1, pp. 26-27)
Pub: Inc. Magazine
Ed: Cara Cannella. Description: Lee Middleton's Original Dolls factory is being used to film footage for the Steven Soderbergh film, Bubble.

46486 ■ *Western Hi-Tech Companies Database*
Pub: Harris InfoSource
Ed: Fran Carlsen, Editor. Released: latest edition 2003. Price: $1,295. Entries Include: Company name, address, phone, fax, toll-free, names and titles of key personnel, number of employees, geographical area served, financial data, descriptions of product/service, Standard Industrial Classification (SIC) code, year established, annual revenues, plant size, legal structure, export/import information. Database Covers: Over 14,900 technology-based manufacturers, software developers, and other high tech companies in Alaska, Arizona, California, Colorado, Hawaii, Idaho, Kansas, Missouri, North Dakota, Nebraska, Oklahoma, South Dakota, Texas, Montana, New Mexico, Nevada, Oregon, Utah, Washington, Wyoming; names of owners, CEOs, and key executives.

46487 ■ "What's Up Doc? They May Not be Old Enough for Medical School, But Now Kids Can Look the Part" in *Entrepreneur* (Vol. 32, July 2004)
Pub: Entrepreneur Media Inc.
Ed: Nichole L. Torres. Description: Profile of Jacquelyn Aven, founder of MiniScrubs Inc. Aven's company manufactures personalized doctors' scrubs for children to wear both inside and outside the hospital setting.

46488 ■ "Who's Got the Power?" in *Business Journal-Portland* (Vol. 20, No. 24, August 15, 2003, pp. 17)
Pub: American City Business Journals, Inc.
Ed: Shelly Strom. Description: Profile of Newberg, Oregon-based SP Newsprint Company. The firm has developed a new $75 million cogeneration power facility which reduced manufacturing costs by 25 percent, while cutting energy expenditures.

46489 ■ "Women Move Up In Manufacturing" in *Fortune* (Vol. 141, No. 10, May 15, 2000, pp. 137B+)
Pub: Time Inc.
Description: The future looks bright for women, because manufacturing will need even more of the kinds of people who are already in short supply: computer scientists, engineers, and design professionals as well as superb communicators and people with vision.

46490 ■ "Would You Buy a Chinese Car From This Man?" in *Inc.* (Volume 27, July 2005, No. 7, pp. 68-72, 74)
Pub: Inc. Magazine
Ed: Darren Dahl. Description: Profile of Malcolm Bricklin, CEO of Visionary Vehicles. Bricklin is on a quest to revolutionize the auto industry.

46491 ■ "The Write Stuff: Entrepreneurs Find Success with a New Take on a Familiar Product" in *Entrepreneur* (Vol. 32, November 2004, No. 11)
Pub: Entrepreneur Media Inc.
Ed: Don Debelak. Description: Profile of Colin Roche and Bobby Ronsse, 33-year-old co-founders of Pacific Writing Instruments. The PenAgain is a writing tool shaped like a wishbone. The pair used about $15,000 to manufacture the first 5,000 units and predict sales to surpass $3 million in 2004.

46492 ■ "A Year of Advice is Prize in Woman-Owned Program" in *Crain's Detroit Business* (Vol. 21, December 12, 2005, No. 50, pp. 2)
Pub: Crain Communications Inc. - Detroit
Description: Three Detroit-area woman-owned businesses will receive professional assistance from the Athena PowerLink program. The winners must be companies that are majority-owned by a woman, operating for at least two years, have a minimum of two employees, annual revenue of $250,000 or more in manufacturing or retail, or $100,000 in service business, and have clearly defined goals.

46493 ■ "Young Millionaires: Class of 2004" in *Entrepreneur* (Vol. 32, November 2004, No. 11, pp. 77)
Pub: Entrepreneur Media Inc.
Ed: Amanda C. Kooser, April Y. Pennington, Jonathan Riggs, Nichole L. Torres, Sara Wilson. Description: Profiles of successful entrepreneurs include Cristina Bartolucci and Laura Deluisa, manufacturers of specialty makeup and body creams; Ashton Palmer and Kristy Royce, founders of an Internet-based adventure travel company; Bernard Frei, who sells soccer and rugby apparel online; Christopher Faulkner, a Web-hosting and data center infrastructure provider; Marco and Sandra Johnson, who founded an accredited medical college; Shawn Nelson, owner of modular furniture stores; a media advertising company; James P. Funderburk Jr., owner of clothing stores, a private nightclub and real estate company; and a firm that manages online sites for clothing manufacturers.

SOURCES OF SUPPLY

46494 ■ *Aquaculture Magazine Buyer's Guide & Industry Directory*
Pub: Achill River Corp.
Ed: Gregory J. Gallagher, Editor. Released: Annual, December. Price: $22; $25 outside U.S.. Covers: 2,400 manufacturers and suppliers of equipment used in aquaculture, including fish farming, production, processing, and marketing. Entries Include: Name, address, phone, URL info, and services.

STATISTICAL SOURCES

46495 ■ *RMA Annual Statement Studies*
Pub: Robert Morris Associates (RMA)
Released: Annual. Price: $175.00 2004-05 edition, $105.00. Description: Contains composite balance sheets and income statements for more than 360 industries, including the accounting, auditing, and bookkeeping industries. Also contains five years of comparative historical data for discerning trends. Includes 16 commonly used ratios, computed for most of the size groupings for nearly every industry.

TRADE PERIODICALS

46496 ■ *American Gear Manufacturers Association—News Digest*
Pub: American Gear Manufacturers Association
Ed: Mary Dee Bartolomei, Editor, marydee@agma.org. Released: Bimonthly. Price: Included in membership. Description: Carries information of interest to gear manufacturers and suppliers. Recurring features include news of research, a calendar of events, reports of meetings, news of educational opportunities, and columns titled Economic Review, President's Corner, and Executive Director's View.

46497 ■ *Automotive Design and Production*
Pub: Gardner Publications Inc.
Contact: Gary Vasilash, Editor-in-Chief
E-mail: gsv@autofieldguide.com
Released: Monthly. Description: Magazine for manufacturing professionals who are involved in key aspects of automotive production functions, from process design and development to final inspection and test. Covers equipment as well as management methods.

46498 ■ *Automotive Plastics Newsletter*
Pub: Market Search Inc.
Released: Biweekly. Price: $498, individuals. Description: Reports on news of the automotive and plastics industry. Also includes forecasts.

46499 ■ *Billet Forming*
Pub: Engineering Research Center for Net Shape Manufacturing, Ohio State University
Ed: Sabine Tonnesmann, Editor. Price: Free. Description: Discusses recent events and research into net shape manufacturing at the ERC. Includes announcements of upcoming metal forming conferences and meetings.

46500 ■ *CAMM News*
Pub: Canadian Association of Moldmakers (CAMM)
Contact: Patricia Papp
Ed: Patricia Papp, Editor. Released: Quarterly, 5-6/year. Description: Contains items of interest to members of the moldmaking industry. Recurring features include editorials, information on education and shows, letters to the editor, a calendar of events, reports of meetings, news of educational opportunities, and columns titled Technical Corner and Members in the News.

46501 ■ *Composites in Manufacturing*
Pub: Society of Manufacturing Engineers
Contact: Dianna Helka, Assoc. Ed.
E-mail: helkdia@sme.org
Released: Quarterly. Price: $72, U.S. nonmembers; $82, Canada and Mexico nonmembers; $97, elsewhere nonmembers. Description: Covers composites and advanced composite materials from development through application. Recurring features include a calendar of events, news of educational opportunities, industry news, and notices of publications available.

46502 ■ *Compoundings*
Pub: Independent Lubricant Manufacturers Association
Ed: Michael Cannizzaro, Editor, editor@ilma.org. Released: Monthly. Price: Included in membership; $900, nonmembers in the U.S.. Description: Presents timely technical and marketing news about the lubricant manufacturing industry. Covers trends, new products, legislative, and regulatory information. Also focuses on Association members and events.

46503 ■ *Die Casting*
Pub: Engineering Research Center for Net Shape Manufacturing, Ohio State University
Ed: Sabine Tonnesmann, Editor. Price: Free. Description: Covers net shape manufacturing of die casting project descriptions and plans. Also contains die casting reports. Recurring features include news of research and notices of publications available.

46504 ■ *Die & Mold Design and Manufacturing*
Pub: Engineering Research Center for Net Shape Manufacturing, Ohio State University
Ed: Sabine Toennesmann, Editor. Price: Free. Description: Covers net shape manufacturing design project descriptions and plans. Recurring features include news of research.

46505 ■ *Electrical Product News*
Pub: Business Marketing & Publishing Inc.
Ed: George B. Young, Editor, editor@epnweb.com. Released: Monthly. Description: Covers electrical products and distributor services. Provides information on new products, product applications, manufacturer programs supporting product sales, features added to existing products, special promotions and incentive programs, and marketing/sales news. Recurring features include letters to the editor, news of research, reports of meetings, and columns titled Telemarketing and Taxes.

46506 ■ *First Line Supervisor*
Pub: The Dartnell Corp.
Contact: Marceline Bunzey
Ed: Marceline Bunzey, Editor, mbunzey@lrp.com. Released: Bimonthly. Price: $286.70, individuals in-

cludes shipping / handling. **Description:** Training newsletter designed to improve performance through how-to articles on all aspects of first-line supervision in a manufacturing environment.

46507 ■ Human Factors in Ergonomics and Manufacturing

Pub: John Wiley & Sons Inc.
Ed: Waldemar Karwoski, Editor. **Released:** 4/yr. **Price:** $205; $205 Canada and Mexico in Canada, add 7% GST; $229 other countries; $780 institutions; $820 institutions, Canada and Mexico in Canada, add 7% GST; $854 institutions, other countries. **Description:** International journal focusing on the design, management, and operation of advanced manufacturing systems. Covers human resource management, social and organizational issues, cognitive engineering, human factors, and safety and health.

46508 ■ Industrial Laser Solutions

Pub: PennWell Publishing Co.
Ed: Laureen Belleville, Editor, laureenb@pennwell. com. **Released:** Bimonthly. **Price:** Free. **Description:** Devoted exclusively to the increased productivity and profitability of industrial lasers. Offers current information on the application of lasers in material processing, lasers on the production line, new systems and products, technical and economic analyses, company information, business news and more.

46509 ■ Manufacturer's Mart

Pub: Manufacturers' Mart Publications
Contact: Richard W. Cannon, Advertising Mgr
Released: Monthly. **Description:** Publication for manufacturing and production engineers.

46510 ■ Manufacturing Automation

Pub: Vital Information Publications
Contact: L. Bekker
Ed: Peter Adrian, Editor. **Released:** Monthly. **Price:** $395, individuals U.S. and Canada; $420, individuals elsewhere. **Description:** Provides global information and market analysis on manufacturing automation. Topics include CADCAM, robotics, material handling, machine tools, systems integration, automation software, and manufacturing management issues.

46511 ■ Manufacturing Market Insider

Pub: JBT Communications
Contact: John Tuck
Released: Monthly. **Price:** $420 /year; $740 /2 years. **Description:** Covers outsourcing and the contract manufacturing of electronics. Includes news of acquisitions, expansions, and contract awards.

46512 ■ The Manufacturing Report

Pub: Lionheart Publishing Inc.
Ed: David Blanchard, Editor, blanchard@lionhrtpub. com. **Released:** Monthly. **Price:** $115, U.S. and Canada; $125, elsewhere. **Description:** Provides solutions for manufacturing personnel. Includes industry news and information on specific production problems. **Remarks:** Includes ELectronic Commerce Update.

46513 ■ Manufacturing Technology

Pub: National Technical Information Service
Contact: Linda Davis
Released: Bimonthly. **Price:** $224.25, U.S., Canada, and Mexico; $299, elsewhere weekly e-mail; $125 e-mail. **Description:** Publishes abstracts of reports on computer aided design, computeraAided manufacturing, technology transfer, and other matters related to manufacturing technology. Provides information on subjects such as planning, marketing and economics, and research program administration. **Remarks:** Also available via e-mail.

46514 ■ Manufacturing and Technology News

Pub: Publishers & Producers
Ed: Richard McCormack, Editor, richard@manufacturingnews.com. **Released:** Biweekly. **Price:** $395, individuals. **Description:** Relates breaking news on manufacturing programs and policies, electronic commerce, new manufacturing technologies, and techniques. Carries guest editorials. Recurring features include letters to the editor, interviews, news of research, reports of meetings, book reviews, and notices of publications available.

46515 ■ Member Connections

Pub: Fabricators & Manufacturers Association, International
Contact: Jennifer Hoffman
Ed: Kimberly Pollard, Editor. **Released:** Bimonthly. **Price:** Included in membership. **Description:** Provides members with the latest news about the Association, including benefits and educational activities, all revolving around the metal forming and fabricating industries. Recurring features include a calendar of events, news of educational opportunities, book review, and Q & A forum.

46516 ■ The MFP Report

Pub: Bissett Communications Corp.
Contact: Brian Bissett, Editor & Publisher
E-mail: bbissett@ix.netcom.com
Released: Monthly. **Price:** $659, U.S.; $699, elsewhere. **Description:** Offers business intelligence on the latest multifunction peripherals business, market and technology issues, and their impact. Features standards, products, trade shows, and company features. Recurring features include interviews, news of research, and a collection.

46517 ■ The Packet

Pub: National Paperbox Association
Contact: R. Mickey Gorman
Ed: Scott Miller, Editor. **Released:** Biennial. **Price:** Included in membership; $50, nonmembers in the U.S.. **Description:** Spotlights Association news and related items of interest to carton manufacturers. Recurring features include news of research, a calendar of events, news of educational opportunities, and notices of publications available.

46518 ■ Processing of Polymeric Composites and Injection Molding

Pub: Engineering Research Center for Net Shape Manufacturing, Ohio State University
Ed: Sabine Toennesmann, Editor. **Price:** Free. **Description:** Covers net shape manufacturing project descriptions and plans. Contains improvement of processing techniques for manufacturing polymeric materials. Recurring features include news of research and notices of publications available.

46519 ■ REMAN Newsletter

Pub: APICS—The Association for Operations Management
Contact: David Bowman
Ed: David Bowman, Editor, d_bowman@apics-hq. org. **Released:** Quarterly. **Price:** Included in membership. **Description:** Covers production, consulting, and manufacturing in the remanufacturing, repair, and overhaul (REMAN) fields.

46520 ■ Screening Industry

Pub: Screen Manufacturers Association (SMA)
Ed: Frank S. Fitzgerald, Editor, fscottfitzgerald@compuserve.com. **Price:** Included in membership. **Description:** Covers the window and door screen industry. Recurring features include letters to the editor, news of research, a calendar of events, reports of meetings, and notices of publications available.

46521 ■ SEMA News

Pub: Specialty Equipment Market Association
Contact: Steve Campbell, Editorial Director
E-mail: stevec@sema.org
Released: Monthly. **Price:** Included in membership. **Description:** Covers the automotive specialty, performance equipment, and accessory sectors. Recurring features include news of government and legislative actions, new products, international markets, and member and Association activities.

46522 ■ Sheet Metal Forming

Pub: Engineering Research Center for Net Shape Manufacturing, Ohio State University
Ed: Sabine Toennesmann, Editor. **Price:** Free. **Description:** Covers net shape manufacturing of sheet metal forming project descriptions and plans. Recurring features include news of research and notices of publications available.

46523 ■ Small Manufacturing SIG Newsletter

Pub: APICS—The Association for Operations Management
Released: Quarterly. **Price:** Included in membership. **Description:** Covers production, consulting, and manufacturing in the small manufacturing (SM) fields.

46524 ■ Stork Technimet Topics

Pub: Stork Technimet Inc.
Contact: Barbara Tucholke
Ed: Barbara J. Tucholke, Editor. **Released:** 4/year. **Price:** Free. **Description:** Presents technical articles detailing the use of materials science to solve problems of manufacture or failure of components. Covers subjects such as machinability, weldability, and various failure mechanisms such as fatigue, corrosion, and brittle fracture.

46525 ■ Teamwork

Pub: The Dartnell Corp.
Released: Biweekly. **Price:** $286.70. **Description:** Focuses on successful teamwork in manufacturing and corporate businesses. Recurring features include columns titled What Would You Do?, Test Yourself and See, and Teamwork in Action.

VIDEOCASSETTES/ AUDIOCASSETTES

46526 ■ Competing Through Manufacturing

Video Arts, Inc.
c/o Aim Learning Group
8238-40 Lehigh
Morton Grove, IL 60053-2615
Free: 877-444-2230
Fax: (416)252-2155
Co. E-mail: service@aimlearninggroup.com
URL: http://www.aimlearninggroup.com
Released: 1989. **Price:** $2890.00. **Description:** These three 50-minute videos will help you make your company competitive through innovative manufacturing. **Availability:** VHS; 8mm; 3/4U; Special order formats.

46527 ■ Concerns Quarterly with Footage from CBS News: General Business

Harcourt Brace College Publishers
301 Commerce, Ste. 3700
Fort Worth, TX 76102
Ph:(817)334-7500
Free: 800-237-2665
Fax: (817)334-0947
Co. E-mail: info@harcourt.com
URL: http://www.harcourt.com
Released: 1995. **Price:** $80.00. **Description:** Video newsletter containing footage from such CBS programs as CBS Evening News, 48 Hours, Street Stories, and CBS This Morning. Provides information on such topics as ethical responsibilities in business, people in business, competition, manufacturing, and marketing. Comes with instructor's guide. Available at an annual subscription rate of $300.00. **Availability:** VHS.

46528 ■ Manufacturing Control in the Small Plant (7MP-J01)

Thomson National Education Training Group (NETg)
14624 N. Scottsdale Rd., Ste. 300
Phoenix, AZ 85254
Ph:(480)315-4000
Free: 800-265-1900
Fax: (480)315-4001
Co. E-mail: info@netg.com
URL: http://www.netg.com
Description: Part of an integrated course for anyone involved in the management and operation of a small company, or a small division of a large company. **Availability:** 3/4U.

TRADE SHOWS AND CONVENTIONS

46529 ■ Automated Manufacturing Exposition and Conference
TEC Inc. - Technical Expositions & Conferences
2001 Assembly St, Ste. 204
Columbia, SC 29201-2153
Ph:(803)779-7123
Free: 800-553-7702
Fax: (803)779-7167
Released: Annual. **Audience:** Managers and engineers interested in the manufacturing environment. **Principal Exhibits:** Computer and automation applications: robotics, AGV's, laser inspection and counting equipment, vision systems, quality control, and instrumentation.

46530 ■ NMW - National Manufacturing Week
Reed Exhibitions (North American Headquarters)
383 Main Ave.
Norwalk, CT 06851
Ph:(203)840-5337
Fax: (203)840-9570
Co. E-mail: export@reedexpo.com
URL: http://www.reedexpo.com
Released: Annual. **Audience:** Trade Professionals.
Principal Exhibits: Process control/automation, compressors and air equipment, computers in manufacturing, fluid power, general manufacturing, lubrication, heat treatment, lasers in manufacturing, machine tools, weighing sensors and instrumentation, drives and controls, pumps and valves, safety equipment, welding equipment, design in engineering, engineering products and materials, assembly, automation and robotics.

46531 ■ PMDS - Plant Maintenance and Design Engineering Show/Montreal
Reed Exhibitions Canada
Unit 1, 3761 Victoria Park Ave.
Toronto, ON, Canada M1W 3S2
Ph:(416)491-7565
Free: 888-322-7333
Fax: (416)491-5088
Co. E-mail: canada@reedexpo.com
URL: http://www.reedexpo.ca
Released: Biennial. **Audience:** Trade professionals.
Principal Exhibits: Original equipment manufacturing, and the aftermarket of maintenance, repair/overhaul and operating of industrial machinery and equipment. **Dates and Locations:** 2007 May 15-17, Montreal, QC.

46532 ■ Wisconsin Manufacturing and Machine Tool Expo
Expo Productions Inc.
510 Hartbrook Dr.
Hartland, WI 53029
Ph:(262)367-5500
Free: 800-367-5520
Fax: (262)367-9956
Co. E-mail: expo@execpc.com
URL: http://www.expoproductionsinc.com
Released: Biennial. **Audience:** Purchasing agents, presidents and CEOs of companies, and plant engineers. **Principal Exhibits:** Metal working machinery and related manufacturing equipment, supplies, and services machine tools. **Dates and Locations:** 2007 Oct 09-11, Milwaukee, WI.

CONSULTANTS

46533 ■ Albee-Campbell L.L.C.
2913 Windmill Rd.
PO Box 2087
Sinking Spring, PA 19608-9087
Ph:(610)678-3361
Free: 800-445-0586
Fax: (610)678-3528
Co. E-mail: office@albee-campbell.com
URL: http://www.albee-campbell.com

E-mail: office@albee-campbell.com
Scope: Provides full range of marketing services to manufacturers and manufacturers' representative agencies. Specializes in promoting product lines in specific sales territories. Albee-Campbell, Inc. is the oldest and largest representative search service in the U.S. **Seminars:** How to Succeed with Manufacturers' Representatives, conducted 3-4 times a year in various cities across the United States.

46534 ■ Anderson/Roethle Inc.
700 N Water St., Ste. 1100
Milwaukee, WI 53202
Ph:(414)276-0070
Fax: (414)276-4364
Co. E-mail: info@anderson-roethle.com
URL: http://www.anderson-roethle.com

E-mail: info@anderson-roethle.com
Scope: Provides merger, acquisition and divestiture advisory services. Offers strategic planning, valuations and specialized M&A advisory services.

46535 ■ Blackford Associates
30 George Rd.
PO Box 2157
Contoocook, NH 03229
Ph:(603)225-2228
Fax: (603)225-2228
Co. E-mail: jblackfd@totalnet.net

E-mail: jblackfd@totalnet.net
Scope: Provides general management consulting to smaller manufacturing companies. Counsels chief executive officers and presidents on strategy, organization, finances and operations. Areas of expertise include the following: new products, services or markets; problems of expansion or retrenchment; financing and bank relations; morale, organization and training; budgeting and business plans; factory flow and inventory control; quality control and methods; cash flow problems; and financial information and controls.

46536 ■ Distribution Assistance
PO Box 1418
East Dennis, MA 02641-1418
Ph:(508)470-0141
Fax: (508)385-9802
Co. E-mail: atsilk@gis.net
URL: http://www.distributionassistance.com

E-mail: atsilk@gis.net
Scope: Management logistics consultants assist client companies identify, develop and implement productivity and customer service strategies geared to bottom line profit improvement. Focus on a clients entire logistics cycle including automated or nonautomated material handling systems, cost reduction, distribution operations planning and goal setting, effective utilization of existing facilities, downsizing as necessary or planning new facilities, inventory control and warehouse workflow. Industries served: banking, consumer products, financial services, industrial products, insurance, nonprofits, paper, public warehousing, retail and wholesale distributors. wholesale distributors. Also serve as an expert witness in logistics issues at depositions, mediations and arbitration proceedings. **Publications:** "Improving Warehouse Operations"; "Fundamentals of Traffic Management"; "Advanced Transportation Management"; "Cost Effective Worldwide Product Delivery"; "Supply Chain Management". **Seminars:** Professional development Logistics and Supply Chain Operations Seminars have been developed and presented for Universities such as Clemson, Southwest Missouri State, Univ. of Alabama, Baldwin Wallace, James Madison, Rowan, San Jose State, St. John's, Southern Methodist, University of Louisville and Wright State. American Management Assn. (AMA) and International Quality and Productivity Center (IQPC) Seminars presented include: ECR/Quick Response High Efficiency Supply Chain Management and Supply Chain Management in the Nineties.

46537 ■ Obie Good & Associates
122 Lake Lure Dr.
Alma, GA 31510

Ph:(912)632-6208
Fax: (912)632-6208
Scope: Manufacturing consultant in metal working field for commercial and military products, manufacturing management and engineering.

46538 ■ Arthur Helt, Jr.
69 Alden Ln.
Lake Forest, IL 60045
Ph:(847)234-4137
Fax: (847)295-9230
Scope: Industrial consultants specializing in plant layout and design for warehouse, packing systems, cranes specifications, office layouts, and material handling and material flow systems. Additional equipment selection and appraisal, manpower assessment, order processing, and production scheduling and time motion studies. Industries served: steel service centers, and manufacturing plants. **Seminars:** Coil Processing Conference/S.S.C.I. Plate and Shapes Conference.

46539 ■ Hewitt Development Enterprises
1717 N Bayshore Dr., Ste. 2154
Miami, FL 33132
Ph:(305)372-0941
Free: 800-631-3098
Fax: (305)372-0941
Co. E-mail: info@hewittdevelopment.com
URL: http://www.hewittdevelopment.com

E-mail: info@hewittdevelopment.com
Scope: A manufacturing management consulting firm. Specializes in strategic planning; profit enhancement; start-up businesses; interim management; crisis management; turnarounds; production planning; Just-in-Time inventory management; and project management.

46540 ■ Industrial Management Services
103 Woodmancy Ln.
Fayetteville, NY 13066-1534
Ph:(315)637-8966
Fax: (315)637-8966
Scope: Assists manufacturers in minimizing their manufacturing costs by maximizing the return on investments in and expenditures for facilities and labor. This is accomplished by determining where improvements can be made, evaluating the potentials in each selected area, and developing ways of causing the potential improvement to be accomplished. Specific areas include: economic feasibility studies, labor utilization studies, work measurement, expense reduction studies, facilities planning, long range planning, management controls, profit improvement surveys, incentive systems, design of manufacturing systems, plant layout, cost improvement programs, and assistance with safety programs.

46541 ■ Institute for Management Excellence
PO Box 5459
Lacey, WA 98509-5459
Ph:(360)412-0404
URL: http://www.itstime.com
Scope: Management consulting and training focuses on improving productivity, using "best practices" and creative techniques. Practices based on company's theme, "It's time for new ways of doing business." Industries Served: Public Sector, Law Enforcement, Finance/Banking, Non-Profit, Computers/High Technology, Education, Human Resources, Utilities. **Publications:** "The Other Side of Midnight, 2000: An Executive Guide to the Year 2000 Problem" ISBN: 0-9643853-9-2, Authors: Barbara Taylor and Martha Daniel. **Seminars:** The Personality Game, Team Building and Communication Skills, Sexual Harassment and Discrimination Prevention. **Special Services:** Project management for computer systems implementations, including web/internet consulting.

46542 ■ The Manhattan Consulting Group Inc.
226 E 54th St., Ste. 600
New York, NY 10022-6207
Ph:(212)751-3000
URL: http://www.manhattanconsultinggroup.com
Scope: Management consulting firm that specializes in industry and corporate performance studies for se-

lected industries in the manufacturing sector, world-wide. Assignments include acquisitions and management team performance evaluations, corporate strategic direction, industry and competitive analysis, customer satisfaction measurement, related organization change management, benchmarking, overall marketing effectiveness, business strategy and its implementation. In addition, the firm conducts viability studies of manufacturing companies for those involved (financial institutions and investment) in the purchase of a unit or its turnaround. With its proprietary corporate performance database, it assesses relative competitive position and advantage in the context of customer satisfaction. In addition, conducts seminars and workshops in corporate performance measurement, customer satisfaction management concepts, techniques, and their applications. The firm also conducts independent research and publishes articles and studies for governments and corporate executives. Industries served: chemicals, electronics, medical devices and equipment, pharmaceuticals, food, fabricated products, government, and other related industrial, commercial, and process industries. **Publications:** T.H. Kieren and others, "Customer Satisfaction in the Electronics and Electrical Industries," Connector Technology Magazine; "Customer Satisfaction in the Chemical Industry," Chemical Week Magazine; "Customer Satisfaction in the Food Industry," Part 1, Food Processing Magazine; "Organization Change Issues for the 90s," Business Age Magazine; "Assessing the Viability of the Manufacturing Company," Commercial Lending Review; monographs available from firm. **Seminars:** Seminars and workshop in corporate performance and customer satisfaction management for industrial manufacturing companies, acquisition candidate evaluations, viability analysis for LBO firms and banks, and business strategy for a variety of institutions within the manufacturing sector. These programs are conducted at firm's location or the client's venue.

46543 ■ Northwest Trade Adjustment Assistance Center
1200 Westlake Ave. N, Ste. 802
Seattle, WA 98109
Ph:(206)622-2730
Free: 800-667-8087
Fax: (206)622-1105
Co. E-mail: info@taacenters.org
URL: http://www.taacenters.org

E-mail: info@taacenters.org
Scope: Private, nonprofit organization sponsored by the U.S. Department of Commerce which provides up to 75 percent cost paid technical assistance to help manufacturers improve their competitive position relative to imported products. Areas of expertise include website design, ISO 9000 certification, new market identification, new product introduction, business plans, marketing plans, upgrading of product design and packaging, improvement of distribution, use of new technology, inventory cost reduction, production cost reduction, development of employee incentive plans, and preparation of loan applications. Industries served: manufacturers and food processors.

46544 ■ The Walden Group
968 Main St., Ste. 8
Wakefield, MA 01880
Ph:(781)246-7599
Co. E-mail: sales@thewaldengroup.com
URL: http://www.thewaldengroup.com

E-mail: sales@thewaldengroup.com
Scope: Provides solutions for firms in the distribution and manufacturing arenas. Specializes in small-to-medium sized enterprises. Services include distribution and manufacturing operations, information system selection and implementation, and self managing team implementation. Industries served: all. **Seminars:** New Age Warehousing; How to Control Manufacturing Without Acronyms; Information Technology in Manufacturing Today; 7 Steps to a Successful Manufacturing System.

FRANCHISES AND BUSINESS OPPORTUNITIES

46545 ■ The Gutter Guys
The Gutter Guys Franchisor, Inc.
2547 Fire Rd., No. E-5
Egg Harbor Township, NJ 08234
Ph:(609)646-4888
Free: 800-8GU-TTER
Fax: (609)646-7283
URL: http://www.thegutterguys.com
No. of Franchise Units: 10. **No. of Company-Owned Units:** 4. **Founded:** 1988. **Franchised:** 2000. **Description:** Seamless gutter manufacturing, installation and maintenance. **Equity Capital Needed:** $36,500 liquid; $90,000 total investment range. **Franchise Fee:** $15,000. **Royalty Fee:** 5%. **Financial Assistance:** Yes. **Training:** 2 weeks at headquarters, 1 week on-site and ongoing.

46546 ■ Old Hippy Wood Products
2415 80 Ave.
Edmonton, AB, Canada T6P 1N3
Ph:(780)448-1163
Free: 888-464-9700
Fax: (780)435-5475
Co. E-mail: franchise@oldhippy.com
URL: http://www.oldhippy.com
No. of Franchise Units: 8. **Founded:** 1990. **Franchised:** 1992. **Description:** Manufacturers high quality solid wood furniture in Pine, Birch, Cherry, Maple and Oak. From the manufacturing centre in Edmonton, Old Hippy supplies Canadian franchise-store outlets and is proud to be an experienced exporter to Japan. Old Hippy furniture is destined to become a cherished antique. **Equity Capital Needed:** $150,000-$250,000. **Franchise Fee:** $10,000. **Training:** Initial training and ongoing support provided.

RESEARCH CENTERS

46547 ■ Bevill Manufacturing Technology Center
401 Korner St.
Gadsden, AL 35903
Ph:(256)549-8162
Fax: (256)547-5790
URL: http://www.bevillcntr.org
Contact: Gregg Bennett, Dir.
Scope: Works to increase the productivity of companies through projects aimed at solving existing problems, installing new systems and equipment, prototyping new designs, and conducting feasibility studies and simulations. Activities focus on technology related to computerized machining (CAM), industrial robotics, computer aided design and engineering (CAD), automated inspection, automated process control, manufacturing resources planning (MRP), and total quality management. **Services:** Technical literature searches; Technology transfer. **Educational Activities:** Curriculum-based programs for students; Custom-designed training for companies; Programs with elementary, secondary, post-secondary and higher education groups; Seminars; Short courses; Symposia. **Awards:** Advanced Manufacturing Technology Engineering Certification, to engineering students.

46548 ■ California State Polytechnic University, Pomona–Apparel Technology and Research Center
3801 W Temple Ave., Bldg. 45
Pomona, CA 91768
Ph:(909)869-4772
Fax: (909)869-4333
Co. E-mail: jgipe@csupomona.edu
URL: http://atrc.age.csupomona.edu
Contact: Prof. Jean Gipe, Dir.
E-mail: jgipe@csupomona.edu
Scope: Apparel manufacturing. **Services:** Consulting and technical assistance. **Educational Activities:** Seminars (monthly).

46549 ■ Center for Autonomous Control Engineering
125 EECE Bldg.
University of New Mexico
Albuquerque, NM 87131-1356
Ph:(505)277-5538
Fax: (505)277-4681
Co. E-mail: moj@cybermesa.com
URL: http://ace.unm.edu
Contact: Prof. Mo Jamshidi, Dir.
E-mail: moj@cybermesa.com
Scope: Autonomous control, space science research, intelligent agent systems, intelligent technology transfer of advanced manufacturing technology to small and medium-sized industries, satellite arrays technology. **Educational Activities:** Student conference (annually).

46550 ■ Grand Valley State University–Michigan Small Business Development Center
Seidman College of Business
510 W Fulton St.
Grand Rapids, MI 49504
Ph:(616)331-7480
Fax: (616)331-7485
Co. E-mail: sbdchq@gvsu.edu
URL: http://www.misbtdc.org/
Contact: Carol Lopucki, State Dir.
E-mail: sbdchq@gvsu.edu
Scope: Manufacturing, financing, and international business information (particularly the export process) for small businesses. Resources for the export process includes determining and detailing international feasibility, foreign market entry plans, and responding to international inquiries. Foreign market information includes business etiquette and negotiating, country demographics, detailed tax information, financing sources, industry specific information, intellectual property rights, market contracts, rules and regulations, specific market information, and tariff reduction schedules. **Services:** Business management consulting.

46551 ■ National Center for Manufacturing Sciences
3025 Boardwalk
Ann Arbor, MI 48108-3230
Free: 800—222-6267
Fax: (734)995-1150
URL: http://www.ncms.org
Contact: Richard F. Pearson, Pres./CEO
Scope: Fundamental manufacturing sciences, process technology and capabilities, behavior of materials during manufacturing, machine mechanics and components, precision manufacturing, sensor and control techniques, test and evaluation methods, quality assurance and reliability techniques, equipment and component standards, manufacturing systems design, electronic manufacturing. Technology, and environmental manufacturing (prevention, minimization, treatment, remediation and monitor control). **Publications:** NCMS at a Glance.

46552 ■ North American Manufacturing Research Institution
Society of Manufacturing Engineers
1 SME Dr.
Dearborn, MI 48121
Ph:(313)271-1500
Fax: (313)425-3416
Co. E-mail: mstratton@sme.org
URL: http://www.sme.org/namri
Contact: Mark Stratton
E-mail: mstratton@sme.org
Scope: Manufacturing research and technology development. Provides researchers and industry practitioners with a means of exchanging ideas and sharing findings with leading researchers in the field of manufacturing. **Publications:** Annual Transactions. **Educational Activities:** Annual meeting and conference; North American Manufacturing Research Conference (annually), in May.

46553 ■ **Ohio State University–Engineering Research Center for Net Shape Manufacturing**
339 Baker Systems Engineering Bldg.
College of Engineering
1971 Neil Ave.
Columbus, OH 43210-1271
Ph:(614)292-5063
Fax: (614)292-7219
Co. E-mail: altan.1@osu.edu
URL: http://nsmwww.eng.ohio-state.edu/
Contact: Dr. Taylan Altan, Dir.
E-mail: altan.1@osu.edu
Scope: Manufacturing processes, specifically the manufacture of discrete parts to net or near-net dimensions, sheet forming, precision forging, tube/sheet hydroforming, machining, die/mold manufacturing. **Services:** Consulting. **Publications:** Technical papers and presentations. **Educational Activities:** Continuing education courses.

46554 ■ **Purdue University–Dauch Center for the Management of Manufacturing Enterprises**
Krannert School of Management
403 W State St.
West Lafayette, IN 47907-2056
Ph:(765)494-4322
Fax: (765)494-9658
Co. E-mail: aiyer@mgmt.purdue.edu
URL: http://www.gscmi.org
Contact: Prof. Ananth Iyer, Dir.

E-mail: aiyer@mgmt.purdue.edu
Scope: Technology management in manufacturing environments, including lean manufacturing, Six Sigma methodologies, manufacturing strategy, advanced manufacturing planning and control systems, organizational behavior and human resource management, activity-based accounting, improvement decision support tools, total quality management, quality and enterprise integration. **Services:** Arrangement of student projects with companies for hands-on learning (semiannually). **Publications:** Working papers. **Awards:** Mike and Jo Ann Allen Graduate Award (annually).

46555 ■ **Rochester Institute of Technology–Center for Integrated Manufacturing Studies**
111 Lomb Memorial Dr.
Rochester, NY 14623-5608
Ph:(585)475-5101
Free: (866)-490-4044
Fax: (585)475-5250
Co. E-mail: info@cims.rit.edu
URL: http://www.cims.rit.edu
Contact: Dr. Nabil Nast, Dir.
E-mail: info@cims.rit.edu
Scope: Electronics, imaging, supplier integration, remanufacturing, ergonomics and simulation. Areas of study include total quality management, cycle time reduction, life cycle costs, product and process development, concurrent engineering, and integration theory.

Special emphasis is on serving groups of companies to understand common requirements such as training and ISO 9000. process development, concurrent engineering, and integration theory. Special emphasis is on serving groups of companies to understand common requirements such as training and ISO 9000. **Services:** Extension services, for small businesses. **Educational Activities:** Training programs.

46556 ■ **Tennessee Technological University–Center for Manufacturing Research**
Brown Hall 222
115 W 10th St.
PO Box 5077
Cookeville, TN 38505-0001
Ph:(931)372-3362
Fax: (931)372-6345
Co. E-mail: mfgctr@tntech.edu
URL: http://www.tntech.edu/cmr
Contact: Dr. Kenneth R. Currie, Dir.
E-mail: mfgctr@tntech.edu
Scope: Control of processes and equipment; next generation materials and manufacturing processes; integrated product/process realization; and pervasive simulation and modeling. **Services:** Material testing. **Publications:** Annual report (annually); Executive Summary (annually); Research reports. **Educational Activities:** Conferences; Industrial Study-Work Program; Seminars, workshops, and short courses, for practicing engineers.

START-UP INFORMATION

46557 ■ "Balancing Act" in *Entrepreneur*
Pub: Entrepreneur Media Inc.
Ed: Nichole L. Torres. **Description:** Art of finding new customers, while maintaining existing ones for a new company is outlined.

46558 ■ "Big Bucks in Big Mouth" in *Small Business Opportunities* (Vol. 14, No. 1, January 2002, pp. 96, 103)
Pub: Harris Publications, Inc.
Description: Profile of Reggie Smith and Ed Hughes, co-owners of Bocaza Mexican Grille, launched in 1996. As an opening promotion, they handed out free samples of food to passing motorists and pedestrians.

46559 ■ "Bigcat Systems leaves little to chance in Internet Marketing" in *Crain's Detroit Business* (Vol. , No. , pp.)
Pub: Crain Communications, Inc.
Ed: Jeffrey Kosseff. **Description:** A profile of Bigcat Systems L.L.C. the 20-employee company located in Ann Arbor, Michigan, that specializes in interactive voice response systems.

46560 ■ "Biz By the Book" in *Small Business Opportunities* (Vol. 17, September 2005, No. 5, pp. 58, 60)
Pub: Harris Publications Inc.
Ed: Vicki Gerson. **Description:** Partners, Ann Christophersen and Linda Bubon sell books for women and children. Women & Children First hosts events and book signings to promote the shop. Steps to open and market a book store are included.

46561 ■ "Build Your Dream Home Business" in *Home Business* (Vol. 12, October 2005, No. 5, pp. 16, 18-22, 102, 104)
Pub: Home Business Magazine
Ed: Sandy Larson. **Description:** Ten steps to starting a home-based business, starting from the initial planning phase to financing a venture as well as marketing strategies.

46562 ■ *The Canadian Small Business Survival Guide: How to Start and Operate Your Own Successful Business*
Pub: Dundurn Group
Ed: Benjamin Gallander. FRQ September 2004. **Price:** $18.99. **Description:** Ideas for starting and running a successful small business. Topics include selecting a business, financing, government assistance, locations, franchises, and marketing ideas.

46563 ■ "Children's stories" in *BlackEnterprise* (Vol. 32, No. 3, October 2001, pp. 56)
Pub: Earl Graves Publishing Co.
Description: Advice is given for marketing self-published books, with Web sites for three publishers to submit children's books including Scholastic Books, Houghton Mifflin, and Little, Brown & Co.

46564 ■ "Coaching Companies" in *Black Enterprise* (Vol. 31, No. 2, September 2000, pp. 56)
Pub: Earl Graves Publishing Co.
Ed: Gerda Gallop-Goodman. **Description:** Suggestions for books, articles, and online assistance designed to coach small business owners and entrepreneurs on presenting their ideas and products to large retail companies.

46565 ■ *The Complete Small Business Start-up Guide*
Pub: John Wiley & Sons, Incorporated
Ed: Lisa Rogak. **Released:** November 2004. **Price:** $14.95. **Description:** Guide to starting a small company, focusing on development of a business plan, organizational structure, advertising, hiring, selection of suppliers, and using the Internet to market your firm.

46566 ■ "Crafting a specialty: how to target a pleasant and profitable niche" in *Meetings & Conventions* (Vol. 37, No. 10, Sept. 2002, pp. 49)
Pub: NorthStar Travel Media, LLC
Ed: Sarah J.F. Braley. **Description:** Elizabeth Zielinski, shares her experiences while starting her own marketing service for independent planners.

46567 ■ "Direct Success" in *Small Business Opportunities* (Vol. 13, No. 6, November 2001, pp. 58, 60)
Pub: Harris Publications, Inc.
Ed: Patricia Gilbers. **Description:** Profile of Dennis Barnes, president of Marketing Direct, Inc. Mr. Barnes started his company with approximately $5,000 from his dining room, and grew it into a $5 million a year business.

46568 ■ *Entrepreneurship*
Pub: John Wiley and Sons Inc.
Ed: William D. Bygrave; Andrew Zacharakis. **Released:** March 2007. **Price:** $115.95. **Description:** Information for starting a new business is shared, focusing on marketing and financing a product or service.

46569 ■ *Going Solo: Developing a Home-Based Consulting Business from the Ground Up*
Pub: McGraw-Hill Companies Incorporated
Ed: William J. Bond. **Released:** January 1997. **Price:** $14.95. **Description:** Ways to turn specialized knowledge into a home-based successful consulting firm, focusing on targeting client needs, business plans, and growth.

46570 ■ "Grassroots Marketing" in *Home Business* (Vol. 12, March/April 2005, No. 2, pp. 58)
Pub: Home Business Magazine
Ed: Rich Sloan. **Description:** Finding unconventional ways to attract customers to a startup home-based business, called grassroots marketing, can cost much less than traditional advertising.

46571 ■ "Growth Strategies" in *Inc.* (November 2000, pp. 78)
Pub: The Goldhirsh Group
Description: Chris Zane's bike shop was healthy and profitable, but he needed the skills of a CEO to make it grow.

46572 ■ "Growth Tales; Key Strategies Used by Young Firms" in *Crain's New York Business* (Vol. 22, December 11, 2006, No. 50, pp. 27)
Pub: Crain Communications, Inc.
Ed: Lisa Goff. **Description:** Profile of businesses who have used innovative marketing campaigns that cost little to no capital.

46573 ■ "Hot 100" in *Entrepreneur* (Vol. 31, No. 6, June 2003, pp. 64)
Pub: Entrepreneur Media Inc.
Ed: Amanda C. Kooser. **Description:** Twenty-five of the 100 companies hitting the year's hottest industry for 2003 come from the business services sector, nine providing logistics services (such as freight-handling, trucking and transportation) and six providing marketing and advertising services.

46574 ■ *How to Start a Home-Based Mail Order Business*
Pub: Globe Pequot Press
Ed: Georganne Fiumara. **Released:** January 2005. **Price:** $17.95. **Description:** Step-by-step guide for starting and growing a home-based mail order business. Information about equipment, pricing, online marketing, are included along with worksheets and checklists for planning.

46575 ■ "The Inadvertent Entrepreneur" in *Success* (Vol. 47, No. 6, November 2000, pp. 22)
Pub: Success Publishing, Inc.
Ed: Richard E. Mueller. **Description:** Profile of Richard E. Mueller, founder and CEO of MTW Corporation. Mr. Mueller tells how, after 20 years as a CEO, he developed MTW, which began as a technical staffing company.

46576 ■ "Join the club: launching your first product" in *Entrepreneur* (Vol. 31, No. 5, May 2003, pp. 132)
Pub: Entrepreneur Media Inc.
Ed: Don Debelak. **Description:** An inexperienced inventor can gain valuable knowledge and insight by joining an inventor's club. Steps to help find the right group and make the most of a membership are listed.

46577 ■ "Learning the Game of Hard Knocks" in *Hispanic Business* (October 2003, pp. 36, 38)
Pub: Hispanic Business
Ed: Scott Williams. **Description:** A pair of aspiring marketers find out that unexpected problems are often part and parcel of starting new business ventures.

46578 ■ "Less Is More: Believe It Or Not" in *Entrepreneur* (Vol. 31, No. 8, August 2003, pp. 114)
Pub: Entrepreneur Media, Inc.
Ed: Don Debelak. Description: Melody Ross, founder of Chatterbox Inc. in Eagle, Idaho, tells how she was able to successfully market her line of products for scrapbooking. Ross projects $4 million in sales for 2003.

46579 ■ "Market Planning 101" in *Home Business* (Vol. 12, October 2005, No. 5, pp. 42, 44-45)
Pub: Home Business Magazine
Ed: Christopher J. Bachler. Description: A quick marketing plan for any small business is presented and includes all the basic information required to attract loans, partners, business services and even Small Business Administration assistance.

46580 ■ "Marketing Know-How" in *Black Enterprise* (Vol. 30, No. 5, December 1999, pp. 42)
Pub: Earl Graves Publishing Co.
Ed: Gerda Gallop-Goodman. Description: Advice is given to an entrepreneur who wants to expand a small African American ceramic statues business.

46581 ■ "Marketing Strategies for Your New Home-Based Business" in *Home Business* (Vol. 12, October 2005, No. 5, pp. 24, 26-27, 54-55)
Pub: Home Business Magazine
Ed: Steven D. Strauss. Description: Cost-effective strategies for marketing a home-based business are explored. The importance of reaching a target audience is stressed.

46582 ■ "Mentor Wanted" in *Black Enterprise* (Vol. 35, January 2005, No. 6, pp. 97)
Pub: Earl G. Graves Publishing Co. Inc.
Ed: Tanisha A. Sykes. Description: Young African American man is looking for a mentor to help him start his own clothing business. The entrepreneur has placed some shirts in an area store, but is unsure of marketing and manufacturing of his clothing.

46583 ■ "National" in *Entrepreneur* (Vol. 28, No. 10, October 2000, pp. 138)
Pub: Entrepreneur Media Inc.
Ed: Cynthia E. Griffin. Description: As the number of entrepreneurial firms grow, corporate America is taking notice of the potential market that can also benefit small business. A roundup of some of the newest offerings is featured.

46584 ■ "On the Launch Pad: Spot Runner" in *Business 2.0* (Vol. 7, January/February 2006, No. 1, pp. 30)
Pub: Time, Inc.
Ed: Michael V. Copeland. Description: Profile of Spot Runner, the startup that hopes to make television advertising as targeted as Web advertising, and affordable to small business.

46585 ■ "One of a kind? Make your product conform to break away from the norm" in *Entrepreneur* (Vol. 30, No. 12, December 2002, pp. 144)
Pub: Entrepreneur Media Inc.
Ed: Don Debelak. Description: One of the challenges facing entrepreneurs when developing a new invention is making sure it is a product consumers will accept.

46586 ■ "Ready For Launch" in *My Business* (June/July 2002, pp. 16)
Pub: My Business Magazine
Ed: Vicki Gerson. Description: Creativity is the key in successfully introducing a new product to the market.

46587 ■ "Reeling In the Big One" in *Inc.* (August 1, 2004)
Pub: Inc. Magazine
Ed: Jess McCuan. Description: Ways a startup business can land a large, brand name client are examined.

46588 ■ *The Small Business Owner's Manual: Everything You Need to Know to Start Up and Run Your Business*
Pub: Career Press, Incorporated
Ed: Joe Kennedy. Released: June 2005. Price: $19.99 (US), $26.95 (Canadian). Description: Comprehensive guide for starting a small business, focusing on twelve ways to obtain financing, business plans, selling and advertising products and services, hiring and firing employees, setting up a Web site, business law, accounting issues, insurance, equipment, computers, banks, financing, customer credit and collection, leasing, and more.

46589 ■ "Small Business Spotlight" in *Small Business Opportunities* (Vol. 14, No. 1, January 2002, pp. 110)
Pub: Harris Publications, Inc.
Description: Profiles of three franchise startups, including a Sign-A-Rama that opened in a Puerto Rican neighborhood in Chicago's north side through the Latino Economic Development Assistance Corporation (LEDAC); Hi Frequency Marketing, a Carrboro, North Carolina-based company focusing on the youth marked; and Buffalo Lube Associates, operator of 15 Valvoline Instant Oil Change centers in New York.

46590 ■ "Stake Your Claim: Contrary to Popular Belief, There's No Need to Ante Up a Fortune When You're Playing the Startup Game" in *Entrepreneur*
Pub: Entrepreneur Media Inc.
Ed: Karen E. Spaeder. Description: Three entrepreneurs share ways they started their high-cost businesses without large sums of money: Steve Bandovich, owner of Cloud 9 Specialty Car Rentals; Chi Conley, who started up with one hotel and now owns 31 hospitality businesses in Northern California; and Tom Hatten, who started Mountainside Fitness in 1991.

46591 ■ "The Starbucks Effect" in *Harvard Business Review* (Vol. 78, No. 2, March 2000, pp. 17)
Pub: Harvard Business School Publishing Corp.
Ed: Vijay Vishwanath, David Harding. Description: When a product suddenly becomes hip, the whole category can prosper.

46592 ■ "Stars of PR" in *Entrepreneur* (Vol. 30, No. 10, October 2002, pp. 91)
Pub: Entrepreneur Media Inc.
Ed: Nichole L. Torres. Description: Media stories imply credibility for a new business starting up. Strategies used for public relations by Starbucks, Red Bull, and Amazon.com are discussed.

46593 ■ "Street Smarts: The Myths About Niches" in *Inc.* (August 1, 2004)
Pub: Inc. Magazine
Ed: Norm Brodsky. Description: For a small business starting out, finding its niche is key, being prepared for it to change and keep on changing is essential.

46594 ■ "Taking the 'dis' out of disability" in *Black Enterprise* (Vol. 32, No. 9, March 2002, pp. 102)
Pub: Earl Graves Publishing Co.
Ed: Alan Hughes. Description: Profile of Carmen Jones who triumphed over a crippling car accident and built a marketing firm that serves disabled consumers.

46595 ■ "To get product on shelves, knock on a lot of doors" in *Crain's Detroit Business* (Dec. 16, 2002, pp. 18)
Pub: Crain Communications Inc., Detroit
Ed: Laura Bailey. Description: Various entrepreneurs share tips for successfully marketing new products.

46596 ■ "Turning the Tables: You Worked for Them, and Now You Want Them to 'Work' for You" in *Entrepreneur* (Vol. 32, December 2004, No. 12)
Pub: Entrepreneur Media Inc.
Ed: Laura Koss-Feder. Description: The process for landing your former employer as your first client is outlined.

46597 ■ *The Unofficial Guide to Starting a Small Business*
Pub: John Wiley & Sons, Incorporated
Ed: Marcia Layton Turner. Released: October 2004. Price: $16.99. Description: Information and tools for starting a small business, covering the start-up process, from market research, to business plans, to marketing programs.

46598 ■ "Want New Customers? Go Guerrilla: Ad campaigns can be expensive" in *Business Week Online* (April 29, 2002)
Pub: McGraw-Hill, Inc.
Ed: Karen E. Klein. Description: Advice is offered to a start-up, home-based, independent agent for a long-distance company.

46599 ■ *What No Ever Tells You About Starting Your Own Business: Real-Life Start-Up Advice from 101 Successful Entrepreneurs*
Pub: Kaplan Publishing
Ed: Jan Norman. Released: July 2004. Price: $18.95 (US), $28.95 (Canadian). Description: From planning to marketing, advice is given to entrepreneurs starting new companies. s.

46600 ■ "What's In a Name? Often Overlooked, Choosing the Right Business Moniker is Key" in *Black Enterprise* (Vol. 34, No. 4, Nov. 2003)
Pub: Earl Graves Publishing Co.
Ed: Marcia A. Wade. Description: Both private and practical issues involved in naming a new business are explored. The importance of finding a name that does not require extensive advertising to communicate a company's function is stressed.

46601 ■ "Who let the blogs out? Blogging has become one of the hottest Web trends." in *Entrepreneur* (Vol. 30, No. 10, October 2002, pp. 35)
Pub: Entrepreneur Media Inc.
Ed: Amanda C. Kooser. Description: A blog is a frequently updated, timed and dated online journal with links involved. Blogs are a good resource for entrepreneurs to promote a business and to get other people to work with you on your business.

46602 ■ *Working for Yourself: An Entrepreneur's Guide to the Basics*
Pub: Kogan Page, Limited
Ed: Jonathan Reuvid. Released: September 2006. Description: Guide for starting a new business venture, focusing on raising financing, legal and tax issues, marketing, information technology, and site location.

46603 ■ "You're the Inspiration" in *Entrepreneur* (Vol. 33, September 2005, No. 9, pp. 96)
Pub: Entrepreneur Media Inc.
Ed: Nichole L. Torres. Description: Ways to patent and market a new product are shared by StartupNation.com. A business-advice Website that is run by small business experts, Jeff and Rich Sloan is highlighted.

ASSOCIATIONS AND OTHER ORGANIZATIONS

46604 ■ Advertising and Marketing International Network
12323 Nantucket
Wichita, KS 67235
Ph:(316)531-2342
Fax: (316)722-8353
Co. E-mail: vaughn.sink@shscom.com
URL: http://www.aminworldwide.com
Contact: B. Vaughn Sink, Exec. Dir.
Membership: Comprised of cooperative worldwide network of non-competing independent advertising agencies organized to provide facilities and branch office services for affiliated agencies. Publications: *AMIN Directory* (annual).

46605 ■ American Academy of Professional Coders
2480 S 3850 W, Ste. B
Salt Lake City, UT 84120
Ph:(801)236-2200
Free: 800-626-2633
Fax: (801)236-2258
Co. E-mail: info@aapc.com
URL: http://www.aapc.com
Contact: Ms. Traci Wood, Marketing Coor.
Description: Works to elevate the standards of medical coding by providing ongoing education, certification, networking and recognition. Represents nearly 50,000 members worldwide. Promotes high standards of physician and outpatient facility coding through education and certification. **Publications:** *ACADEMY CODING EDGE* (monthly).

46606 ■ American Marketing Association
311 S Wacker Dr., Ste. 5800
Chicago, IL 60606
Ph:(312)542-9000
Free: 800-262-1150
Fax: (312)542-9001
Co. E-mail: info@ama.org
URL: http://www.marketingpower.com
Contact: Jack Weekes, Chm.
Fosters research; sponsors seminars, conferences, and student marketing clubs; provides educational placement service and doctoral consortium. **Publications:** *American Marketing Association—Proceedings* (annual); *Journal of Marketing* (quarterly); *Journal of Marketing Research* (quarterly); *Journal of Public Policy and Marketing* (semiannual) ; *The M Guide* (annual); *Marketing Academics at AMA* (bimonthly); *Marketing Health Service* (quarterly); *Marketing Management* (bimonthly); *Marketing Matters* (biweekly); *Marketing News: Reporting on the Marketing Professional and Its Association* (biennial); *Marketing Power Personalized* (biweekly); *Marketing Research* (quarterly).

46607 ■ Association of Directory Marketing
1187 Thorn Run Rd., Ste. 630
Moon Township, PA 15108-3198
Ph:(412)269-0663
Fax: (412)269-0655
Co. E-mail: adm@admworks.org
URL: http://www.admworks.org
Contact: Herb Gordon, Pres./CEO
Membership: Certified marketing representatives and agencies (61); directory publishers (27); suppliers (19). **Purpose:** Promotes use of telephone directories in marketing. Provides support and services to marketers wishing to make use of print and internet directories, telephone directories. **Publications:** *Flash* (monthly). **Telecommunication Services:** electronic mail, hgordon@admworks.org.

46608 ■ Center for Exhibition Industry Research
8111 LBJ Fwy., Ste. 750
Dallas, TX 75251
Ph:(972)687-9242
Fax: (972)692-6020
Co. E-mail: info@ceir.org
URL: http://www.ceir.org
Contact: Douglas L. Ducate, Pres./CEO
Description: Promotes the growth, awareness and value of exhibitions and other face-to-face marketing events by producing and delivering research-based knowledge tools. Consists of exhibition organizers, service providers, exhibitors, CVBs and facilities. **Publications:** *CEIR Direct* (bimonthly); *Face-to-Face Marketing*; *Guru Reports*; *The Power of Exhibitions*.

46609 ■ Council for Marketing and Opinion Research
110 National Dr., 2nd Fl.
Glastonbury, CT 06033
Ph:(860)657-1881
Fax: (860)682-1010
Co. E-mail: info@cmor.org
URL: http://www.cmor.org
Contact: Donna Gillin, Dir. of Operations
Description: Represents the marketing and opinion research industry. Addresses government affairs and respondent cooperation issues. **Publications:** *Industry Watch* (quarterly); *Legislative Watch* (monthly).

46610 ■ Direct Marketing Association
1120 Avenue of the Americas
New York, NY 10036-6700
Ph:(212)768-7277
Fax: (212)302-6714
Co. E-mail: president@the-dma.org
URL: http://www.the-dma.org
Contact: John A. Greco Jr., Pres./CEO
Membership: Manufacturers, wholesalers, public utilities, retailers, mail order firms, publishers, schools, clubs, insurance companies, financial organizations, business equipment manufacturers, paper and envelope manufacturers, list brokers, compilers, managers, owners, computer service bureaus, advertising agencies, letter shops, research organizations, printers, lithographers, creators, and producers of direct mail and direct response advertising. **Purpose:** Studies consumer and business attitudes toward direct mail and related direct marketing statistics. Offers Mail Preference Service for consumers who wish to receive less mail advertising, Mail Order Action Line to help resolve difficulties with mail order purchases, and Telephone Preference Service for people who wish to receive fewer telephone sales calls. Maintains hall of fame; offers placement service; compiles statistics. Sponsors several three-day Basic Direct Marketing Institutes, Advanced Direct Marketing Institutes, and special interest seminars and workshops. Maintains Government Affairs office in Washington, DC. Operates Direct Marketing Educational Foundation. **Publications:** *Council Newsletter* (quarterly); *Dateline: DMA* (quarterly) ; *Direct Line: The DMA Newsletter Serving the Direct Marketing Industry* (monthly); *The DMA Insider* (quarterly); *DMA Washington Report: Federal and State Regulatory Issues of Concern* (monthly); *Fact Book on Direct Marketing* (annual); *Membership Roster* (annual); *MyDMA*; *Washington Alert*; *Annual Report* (annual).

46611 ■ Electronic Retailing Association
2000 N 14th St., Ste. 300
Arlington, VA 22201
Ph:(703)841-1751
Free: 800-987-6462
Fax: (703)841-1860
Co. E-mail: contact@retailing.org
URL: http://www.retailing.org
Contact: Ms. Barbara Tulipane CAE, Pres./CEO
Description: Serves companies that use the power of electronic media to sell goods and services to the public. Its global membership includes television, radio and Internet retailers, along with expert back-end suppliers. **Publications:** *E-News Weekly* (weekly); *Electronic Retailer* (monthly); *Marketing, Meetings and Membership* (monthly); *Retailing.org* (bimonthly); *Retailing.org Daily* (daily).

46612 ■ International Internet Marketing Association
PO Box 4018
Vancouver, BC, Canada V6B 3Z4
Free: (866)281-4462
Co. E-mail: president@iimaonline.org
URL: http://www.iimaonline.org
Contact: Paula Skaper, Pres.
Description: Encourages internet and traditional marketers to use the internet as a vital component of the marketing mix. Supports members by providing networking and educational events designed to keep members informed about internet trends, changes, opportunities, and career advancement. **Publications:** Newsletter (quarterly).

46613 ■ Mailing and Fulfillment Service Association
1421 Prince St., Ste. 410
Alexandria, VA 22314-2806
Ph:(703)836-9200
Free: 800-333-6272
Fax: (703)548-8204
Co. E-mail: mfsa-mail@mfsanet.org
URL: http://www.mfsanet.org
Contact: David A. Weaver, Pres./CEO
Membership: Commercial direct mail producers, letter shops, mailing list houses, fulfillment operations, and advertising agencies. Conducts special interest group meetings. Offers specialized education; conducts research programs. **Publications:** *MFSA Wage Salary, and Fringe Benefit Survey* (semiannual); *Performance Profiles: The Financial Ratios for the Mailing Service Industry* (annual); *Postscripts* (monthly); *Who's Who: MASA's Buyers' Guide to Blue Ribbon Mailing Services* (annual). **Telecommunication Services:** electronic mail, daweaver@mfsanet.org.

46614 ■ Multi-Level Marketing International Association
119 Stanford Ct.
Irvine, CA 92612
Ph:(949)854-0484
Fax: (949)854-7687
Co. E-mail: info@mlmia.com
URL: http://www.mlmia.com
Contact: Doris Wood, Chair
Membership: Companies, support groups, and distributors. **Purpose:** Seeks to strengthen and improve the Multi-Level Marketing (also known as Network Marketing) industry in the U.S. and abroad. (Multi-Level Marketing is a method of selling products directly, independently, and usually out of the home, without the medium of a retail outlet.) Provides educational services to consumers and law enforcement agencies. Serves as an information source for the industry. Offers recommendations for start-up companies; maintains speakers' bureau; conducts training programs. **Publications:** *Connecting Point*; *Corporate Directory - Support Directory* (quarterly). **Telecommunication Services:** electronic bulletin board; electronic mail, doriswood@mlmia.com; teleconference.

46615 ■ Promotional Products Association of Canada–Association de la Publicite par l'Objet du Canada
4920 de Maisonneuve W, Ste. 305
Westmount, QC, Canada H3Z 1N1
Ph:(514)489-5359
Fax: (514)489-7760
Co. E-mail: info@promocan.com
URL: http://www.promocan.com
Contact: Kurt R. Reckziegel, Pres./COO
Description: Studies, promotes, fosters, and develops the economic interests of the participants in the promotional products industry of Canada. **Publications:** *E-Image News* (monthly); *The Idea Book* (annual); *Images* (semiannual); *promoVantage* (semiannual); *promoXpert* (semiannual).

46616 ■ Trade Show Exhibitors Association
2301 S Lake Shore Dr., Ste. 1005
Chicago, IL 60616
Ph:(312)842-8732
Fax: (312)842-8744
Co. E-mail: tsea@tsea.org
URL: http://www.tsea.org
Contact: Stephen Schuldenfrei, Pres.
Description: Exhibitors working to improve the effectiveness of trade shows as a marketing tool. Purposes are to promote the progress and development of trade show exhibiting; to collect and disseminate trade show information; conduct studies, surveys, and stated projects designed to improve trade shows; to foster good relations and communications with organizations representing others in the industry; to undertake other activities necessary to promote the welfare of member companies. Sponsors Exhibit Industry Education Foundation and professional exhibiting seminars; the forum series of educational programs on key issues affecting the industry. Maintains placement service; compiles statistics. **Publications:** *How to Develop a Successful Exhibit Marketing Plan* (periodic); *Trade Show Ideas Magazine* (monthly); Membership Directory (annual). Also publishes periodic special management reports, budget guide, salary survey, international exhibitors handbook and guide, and position statements.

46617 ■ Women's Regional Publications of America
12620-3 Beach Blvd., No. 303
Jacksonville, FL 32246
Ph:(904)992-7228
Co. E-mail: kgreen@womsdigest.net

URL: http://www.womensyellowpages.org
Contact: Karen Green, Pres.
Description: Objectives are: to provide a forum where publishers of women's publications and business directories share information and resources; increase the visibility, authority, influence and status of women's business for the purpose of promoting growth and support of women; educate the general public about the need to support women-owned businesses, including equal opportunity employers and contractors. Directories published annually to reach out to the women's business community.

EDUCATIONAL PROGRAMS

46618 ■ Advanced Strategies for Marketing Management Success
American Management Association
1601 Broadway
New York, NY 10019
Ph:(212)586-8100
Free: 800-262-9699
Fax: (212)903-8168
Co. E-mail: customerservice@amanet.org
URL: http://www.amanet.org
Price: $1,895 for non-members; $1,695 for AMA members. **Description:** Covers the understanding of marketing under current conditions; including the advantage of the Internet and e-commerce approach as it pertains to sales growth, increase the sales of the existing customer base, and develop new marketing programs. **Locations:** New York, NY; Atlanta, GA; Chicago, IL.

46619 ■ AMA's Advanced Course in Strategic Marketing
American Management Association
1601 Broadway
New York, NY 10019
Ph:(212)586-8100
Free: 800-262-9699
Fax: (212)903-8168
Co. E-mail: customerservice@amanet.org
URL: http://www.amanet.org
Price: $1,895 for non-members; $1,695 for AMA members. **Description:** Covers the strategic skills and resources necessary in the ever changing environment, including expanding on your market share, and the increased knowledge of customer care. **Locations:** New York, NY; Atlanta, GA; and Chicago, IL.

46620 ■ AMA's Course on Direct Marketing
American Management Association
1601 Broadway
New York, NY 10019
Ph:(212)586-8100
Free: 800-262-9699
Fax: (212)903-8168
Co. E-mail: customerservice@amanet.org
URL: http://www.amanet.org
Price: $1,695 for non-members; $1,495 for AMA members. **Description:** Covers the key factors to increase the sale, including planning and testing, effective communication throughout the process, measure investments, and utilization of technology. **Locations:** New York, NY; Washington, San Francisco, CA; DC; Chicago, IL.

46621 ■ Canadian Management Centre's Advanced Course in Strategic Marketing (Canada)
Canadian Management Centre
150 York St., 5th Fl.
Toronto, ON, Canada M5H 3S5
Free: 877-CMC-2500
Fax: (416)313-4985
Co. E-mail: cmcinfo@cmctraining.org
URL: http://www.cma.org
Price: $2,095 Canadian. **Description:** Covers the advanced approaches to maximize the benefits of Internet and e-commerce technology, including marketing strategies for distinct groups, moving beyond pricing as an objective, promotions and communications as an integrated process, and the seven stages of new product/service development. **Locations:** Toronto, ON.

46622 ■ Competitive Strategy: How to Develop Winning Marketing Plans and Breakthrough Strategies
American Management Association
1601 Broadway
New York, NY 10019
Ph:(212)586-8100
Free: 800-262-9699
Fax: (212)903-8168
Co. E-mail: customerservice@amanet.org
URL: http://www.amanet.org
Price: $1,695.00 for non-members; $1,595.00 for AMA members. **Description:** Covers methods for understanding and predicting changing market conditions and customer needs, and techniques for outperforming your competitors. **Locations:** San Diego, CA; Washington, DC; Chicago, IL; and New York, NY.

46623 ■ Competitive Strategy: How to Develop Winning Marketing Plans and Breakthrough Strategies (Canada)
Canadian Management Centre
150 York St., 5th Fl.
Toronto, ON, Canada M5H 3S5
Ph:(416)214-5678
Free: 800-262-9699
Fax: (416)313-4985
Co. E-mail: cmcinfo@cmctraining.org
URL: http://cmcamai.org
Price: $1,850.00; 2005 fee 1,795.00 Canadian. **Description:** Covers methods for understanding and predicting changing market conditions and customer needs, and techniques for outperforming your competitors. **Locations:** Toronto, ON.

46624 ■ E-mail Marketing
EEI Communications
66 Canal Center Plaza, Ste. 200
Alexandria, VA 22314
Ph:(703)683-0683
Fax: (703)683-4915
Co. E-mail: info@eeicommunications.com
URL: http://www.eeicommunications.com
Price: $695.00. **Description:** Covers using an e-mail newsletter to effectively market your business, including permissions, technical issues, and measuring results. **Locations:** Silver Spring, MD; and Alexandria, VA.

46625 ■ E-mail Marketing, RSS Feeds, and Blogs
EEI Communications
66 Canal Ctr. Plz., Ste. 200
Alexandria, VA 22314-5507
Ph:(703)683-7453
Free: 888-253-2762
Fax: (703)683-7310
Co. E-mail: train@eeicommunications.com
URL: http://www.eeicommunications.com/training
Price: $695. **Description:** Seminar that teaches how to reach customers and prospects by getting around the spam filters without breaking the CAN-SPAM laws by using a mix of e-mail, RSS feeds, and blogs **Locations:** Alexandria, VA; Silver Spring, MD; and Washington, DC.

46626 ■ Effective E-Mail Marketing
American Management Association
1601 Broadway
New York, NY 10019
Ph:(212)586-8100
Free: 800-262-9699
Fax: (212)903-8168
Co. E-mail: customerservice@amanet.org
URL: http://www.amanet.org
Price: $1,795 for non-members; $1,595 for AMA members. **Description:** Covers the overall skills needed for effective e-mail marketing from start to finish, and an understanding the effectiveness of the end result. **Locations:** San Francisco, CA; Chicago, IL; Washington, DC; and New York, NY.

46627 ■ Effectively Marketing to Women: Tapping into Hidden Profits
American Management Association
1601 Broadway
New York, NY 10019

Ph:(212)586-8100
Free: 800-262-9699
Fax: (212)903-8168
Co. E-mail: customerservice@amanet.org
URL: http://www.amanet.org
Price: $1,695.00 for non-members; $1,59500 for AMA members. **Description:** Covers women's buying behavior, techniques for marketing to women, customer retention, and online marketing practices. **Locations:** San Francisco, CA; and Washington, DC.

46628 ■ Fundamentals of Marketing: Your Action Plan for Success
American Management Association
1601 Broadway
New York, NY 10019
Ph:(212)586-8100
Free: 800-262-9699
Fax: (212)903-8168
Co. E-mail: customerservice@amanet.org
URL: http://www.amanet.org
Price: $1,895.00 for non-members; $1,795.00 for AMA members. **Description:** Four-day seminar for new marketing professionals and product managers; covers marketing tools, skills, and techniques. **Locations:** San Francisco, CA; Washington, DC; Atlanta, GA; Chicago, IL; New York, NY.

46629 ■ Fundamentals of Marketing: Your Action Plan for Success (Canada)
Canadian Management Centre
150 York St., 5th Fl.
Toronto, ON, Canada M5H 3S5
Ph:(416)214-5678
Free: 800-262-9699
Fax: (416)313-4985
Co. E-mail: cmcinfo@cmctraining.org
URL: http://cmcamai.org
Price: $2,095.00 Canadian; 2005 fee 1,995.00. **Description:** Four-day seminar for new marketing professionals and product managers; covers marketing tools, skills, and techniques. **Locations:** Toronto, ON.

46630 ■ Harnessing the Power in the Canadian Marketplace (Canada)
Canadian Management Centre
150 York St., 5th Fl.
Toronto, ON, Canada M5H 3S5
Ph:(866)400-4941 ext. 2252
Free: 877-CMC-2500
Fax: (416)313-4985
Co. E-mail: cmcinfo@cmctraining.org
URL: http://www.cmcamai.org
Price: $1,595 Canadian. **Description:** Covers public relations and how it interacts with the marketing goals of your company, overall effective communication, generate media coverage for your company, and coach your corporate speakers, learn how publicly-traded companies communicate with their intended audiences, and assess the influence of your public relations efforts. **Locations:** Toronto, ON.

46631 ■ Intensive Introduction to Copyediting
EEI Communications
66 Canal Center Plaza, Ste. 200
Alexandria, VA 22314
Ph:(703)683-0683
Fax: (703)683-4915
Co. E-mail: info@eeicommunications.com
URL: http://www.eeicommunications.com
Price: $895.00. **Description:** Covers basic editorial marks, style, spelling and grammar, and other details of copywriting and editing. **Locations:** Silver Spring, MD; and Alexandria, VA.

46632 ■ Managing Your Marketing Communications Mix: An Integrated Strategy
American Management Association
1601 Broadway
New York, NY 10019
Ph:(212)586-8100
Free: 800-262-9699
Fax: (212)903-8168
Co. E-mail: customerservice@amanet.org
URL: http://www.amanet.org
Price: $1,795 for non-members; $1,595 for AMA members. **Description:** Covers an understanding of

marketing strategy, including integration, implementation and evaluation. **Locations:** Newport Beach, CA; San Francisco, CA; New York, NY; and Atlanta, GA.

46633 ■ Market Research: How to Get the Right Data to Make the Right Decisions
American Management Association
1601 Broadway
New York, NY 10019
Ph:(212)586-8100
Free: 800-262-9699
Fax: (212)903-8168
Co. E-mail: customerservice@amanet.org
URL: http://www.amanet.org
Price: $1,695 for non-members; $1,495 for AMA members. **Description:** Covers the marketing tools and strategies needed to ensure the organization's performance by providing them with the competitive advantage. **Locations:** San Francisco, CA; Washington, DC; Atlanta, GA; Chicago, IL; and New York, NY.

46634 ■ Market Research: How to get the Right Data to Make the Right Decisions
American Management Association
1601 Broadway
New York, NY 10019
Ph:(212)586-8100
Free: 800-262-9699
Fax: (212)903-8168
Co. E-mail: customerservice@amanet.org
URL: http://www.amanet.org
Price: $1,695 for non-members; $1,495 for AMA members. **Description:** Covers conducting market research detailed to fit the current environment; including questionnaire design, focus groups, observational research, testing/sampling results, and statistical analysis. **Locations:** New York, NY; Atlanta, GA; Washington, DC; and San Francisco, CA.

46635 ■ Marketing Communications for Non-Marketers
EEI Communications
66 Canal Ctr. Plz., Ste. 200
Alexandria, VA 22314-5507
Ph:(703)683-7453
Free: 888-253-2762
Fax: (703)683-7310
Co. E-mail: train@eeicommunications.com
URL: http://www.eeicommunications.com/training
Price: $895. **Description:** Seminar that teaches how to sell products inside or outside the organization, including communications today, the "marketing" in communications, writing basics, the thoughtful way to write, branding, and the marketing communications plan. **Locations:** Alexandria, VA; Silver Spring, MD; and Washington, DC.

46636 ■ Marketing for Service-driven Organizations
American Management Association
1601 Broadway
New York, NY 10019
Ph:(212)586-8100
Free: 800-262-9699
Fax: (212)903-8168
Co. E-mail: customerservice@amanet.org
URL: http://www.amanet.org
Price: $1,695 for non-members; $1,495 for AMA members. **Description:** Covers marketing skills to achieve overall satisfying customer service; including positive approach's to increase business growth, implement new loyalty programs, motivate service sector to increase the customer base, and getting to know the customer. **Locations:** New York, NY; Atlanta, GA; Chicago, IL; Washington, DC; and San Francisco, CA.

46637 ■ Online Marketing and Search Engine Optimization
EEI Communications
66 Canal Ctr. Plz., Ste. 200
Alexandria, VA 22314-5507
Ph:(703)683-7453
Free: 888-253-2762
Fax: (703)683-7310
Co. E-mail: train@eeicommunications.com
URL: http://www.eeicommunications.com/training
Price: $695. **Description:** Covers how to increase traffic to your online site to market your products and

services using the Web, including creating and implementation of your plan, setting a budget, redesigning Web site for search engine optimization, tips and tricks, promotion hints, tips, and advice, and how to measure your Internet marketing results. **Locations:** Alexandria, VA; Silver Spring, MD; and Washington, DC.

46638 ■ Planning and Developing New Products (Canada)
Canadian Management Centre
150 York St., 5th Fl.
Toronto, ON, Canada M5H 3S5
Ph:(866)400-4941 ext. 2252
Free: 877-CMC-2500
Fax: (416)313-4985
Co. E-mail: cmcinfo@cmctraining.org
URL: http://www.cmcamai.org
Price: $1,895 Canadian. **Description:** For product developers; covers the differences between good and bad ideas, develop the products, isolate the markets, devise strategies to insure a successful launch. **Locations:** Toronto, ON.

46639 ■ Successful Branding: Managing Your Brand as an Asset
American Management Association
1601 Broadway
New York, NY 10019
Ph:(212)586-8100
Free: 800-262-9699
Fax: (212)903-8168
Co. E-mail: customerservice@amanet.org
URL: http://www.amanet.org
Price: $1,695.00 for non-members; $1,595.00 for AMA members. **Description:** Covers brand analysis and brand identity. **Locations:** San Francisco, CA.

46640 ■ Successful Product Management
American Management Association
1601 Broadway
New York, NY 10019
Ph:(212)586-8100
Free: 800-262-9699
Fax: (212)903-8168
Co. E-mail: customerservice@amanet.org
URL: http://www.amanet.org
Price: $2,095.00 for non-members; $1,895.00 for AMA members. **Description:** Covers Product Manager duties, finance, marketing techniques, new product development, and advertising. **Locations:** San Francisco, CA; and Chicago, IL.

46641 ■ Successful Product Management (Canada)
Canadian Management Centre
150 York St., 5th Fl.
Toronto, ON, Canada M5H 3S5
Ph:(416)214-5678
Free: 800-262-9699
Fax: (416)313-4985
Co. E-mail: cmcinfo@cmctraining.org
URL: http://cmcamai.org
Price: $1,895.00 Canadian. **Description:** Covers Product Manager duties, finance, marketing techniques, new product development, and advertising. **Locations:** Toronto, ON and Mississauga, ON.

DIRECTORIES OF EDUCATIONAL PROGRAMS

46642 ■ *O'Dwyer's New York Public Relations Directory*
Pub: J.R. O'Dwyer Company Inc.
Contact: Eileen Kelly, Sales Mgr.
Released: Annual, latest edition 2000, new edition expected 2003. **Price:** $50, individuals plus $4.00 for postage. **Covers:** Approximately 600 public relations firms, 840 corporations, 225 trade associations, and 500 public relations service firms; over 50 executive recruiters and employment agencies. **Entries Include:** Contact information.

46643 ■ *Who's Who in Direct Selling*
Pub: Direct Selling Education Foundation

Released: Quarterly. **Price:** Free. **Covers:** 100 companies involved in direct selling via person-to-person and party plan means. **Entries Include:** Company name, address, phone, fax, name and title of contact, product/service offered.

REFERENCE WORKS

46644 ■ *"5 Tips to Make Your Web Site Work"* in *My Business* (December/January 2004, pp. 45)
Pub: My Business Magazine
Ed: Lena Basha. **Description:** Tips to make a Web site more effective are listed. It is important to be able to find facts quickly and easily and to keep information current. Customers using dialup Internet services do not like to be slowed by unnecessary images on a Web site.

46645 ■ *"19th Annual Entrepreneurial Woman's Conference"* in *Entrepreneur* (Vol. 33, August 2005, No. 8, pp. 4)
Pub: Entrepreneur Media Inc.
Ed: Steve Cooper. **Description:** The Women's Business Development Center holds its annual Entrepreneurial Women's Conference for women business owners. The event presents a buyer's mart that allows the owners to market products and services to corporate and government buyers. There are also discussions and workshops addressing issues and trends affecting women-owned businesses.

46646 ■ *101 Internet Businesses You Can Start from Home: How to Choose and Build Your Own Successful E-Business*
Pub: Maximum Press
Ed: Susan Sweeney. **Released:** June 2006. **Price:** $29.95. **Description:** Guide for starting and growing an Internet business; information for developing a business plan, risk levels, and promotional techniques are included.

46647 ■ *101 Ways to Really Satisfy Your Customers: How to Keep Your Customers and Attract New Ones*
Pub: Allen & Unwin Pty., Limited
Ed: Andrew Griffiths. **Released:** April 2007. **Price:** $14.95. **Description:** Tips for providing excellent customer service that ensure loyalty and interest to a small business are examined.

46648 ■ *"112 Million Handsets Can't Be Wrong"* in *Inc.* (July 1, 2004)
Pub: Inc. Magazine
Ed: Lora Kolodny. **Description:** Direct marketing via the cell phone is proving to be a success. Cell phone users are receiving, via text messages, promotions for area businesses.

46649 ■ *"Accessing Minority Markets"* in *Hispanic Business* (Vol. 24, No. 5, May 2002, pp. 14)
Pub: Hispanic Business Inc.
Ed: Holly Ocasio Rizzo. **Description:** The U.S. Chamber of Commerce has launched a new program called, Access America, in order to gain a foothold with Hispanics and other minorities.

46650 ■ *Achieving Planned Innovation: A Proven System for Success with New Products & Services*
Pub: The Free Press
Ed: Frank R. Bacon and Thomas W. Butler. **Released:** 1998. **Price:** $29.50; $30.00.

46651 ■ *"Actioncoaching.com"* in *Entrepreneur.com* (Vol. 34, January 2006, No. 1, pp. 6)
Pub: Entrepreneur Media Inc.
Ed: Steve Cooper. **Description:** The Business Coaching Franchise has launched its new Action-Coaching.com, a franchise offering small business owners topics for growing a business, marketing, and selling products and services.

46652 ■ "Ad Companies Probe Potential of Blog World" in *Chicago Tribune* (February 22, 2005)
Pub: Knight-Ridder/Tribune Business News
Ed: Mike Hughlett. **Description:** The blog world's potential as an avenue for advertising is investigated. Blogs can provide a resource to a targeted audience.

46653 ■ "Ad firm monkeys around with its old office design" in *Washington Business Journal* (Vol. 21, No. 50, April 11, 2003, pp. 60)
Pub: Washington Business Journal
Ed: Jeanine Herbst. **Description:** Focused Image's office is housed in a traditional townhouse in Old Town Alexandria, Virginia. The company redecorated the offices with bright colors and placed stuffed monkeys in the rooms.

46654 ■ "Ad Sales Growth to Slow in 2001" in *Folio: the Magazine for Magazine Management* (Vol. 30, No. 1, January 2001, pp. 15)
Pub: Intertec Publishing Corp.
Ed: Dale Buss. **Description:** Barring an outright recession, advertising growth will remain healthy as manufacturers introduce new products and sophisticated marketers realize that advertising is never expendable.

46655 ■ "Ad Spending Heats Up" in *Hispanic Business* (December 2002, pp. 30, 32-34, 36, 38)
Pub: Hispanic Business
Description: Hispanic advertising expenditures are expected to grow at the rate of 11 percent. Statistical data includes a top 25 billing survey, 2002 Internet revenue estimates, and a listing of the nation's top Hispanic advertising agencies.

46656 ■ "Ad Time Firm Expands" in *San Fernando Valley Business Journal* (Vol. 11, December 2006, No. 25, pp. 28)
Pub: San Fernando Valley Business Journal Associates
Description: Bid4Spots.com, an online advertising firm, will expand its unique auction method of selling unused radio ad time to independent online radio. Bid4Spots has a patent pending for this unique advertising method.

46657 ■ "Ada Liquor Store Growing Through a Lighthearted Approach to Sales" in *Journal Record* (June 24, 2003)
Pub: Dolan Media Company
Ed: Janice Francis-Smith. **Description:** Profile of Townsend's Bottle Shop, Ada, Oklahoma. Townsend's wife, a former English teacher, writes the catchy sales ads for the store, which have increased sales.

46658 ■ "Adcomparator" in *Entrepreneur.com* (Vol. 34, January 2006, No. 1, pp. 6)
Pub: Entrepreneur Media Inc.
Ed: Steve Cooper. **Description:** Free ad comparisons are offered by Adcomparator's Website, which allows users to test up to 15 aspects of advertising.

46659 ■ "Add Some Magic to Your Marketing" in *Home Business* (Vol. 12, March/April 2005, No. 2, pp. 46, 94)
Pub: Home Business Magazine
Ed: Sandy Larson. **Description:** Ways an entrepreneur can use marketing strategies to grow a home business are shared by an executive coach and professional speaker.

46660 ■ "Adversity Leads to Creativity in Tourism" in *South Florida Business Journal* (Vol. 23, No. 48, July 4, 2003, pp. 1)
Pub: American City Business Journals
Ed: Alexis Muellner. **Description:** The tourism industry in Florida seems to have changed and evolved requiring more marketing effort on the part of hotels and attractions. These efforts are resulting in improved tourism for the state.

46661 ■ "Advertisers Want to Leave Their Message on Your Cell Phone" in *Crain's Detroit Business* (Vol. 23, January 15, 2007, No. 3, pp. 13)
Pub: Crain Communications Inc. - Detroit
Ed: Bill Shea. **Description:** Mobile phones are becoming more interactive with the Internet for online local information. Triggered by a voluntary request of the user, things like Google search can be used as either audio or text message advertising specifically targeted at the requestor.

46662 ■ *The Advertising Kit: A Complete Guide for Small Businesses*
Pub: Jossey-Bass, Inc.
Ed: Jeanette Smith. **Released:** 1994. **Price:** $19.95.

46663 ■ "Advertising/Marketing" in *Hispanic Business* (July/August 2002, pp. 14)
Pub: Hispanic Business
Description: A discussion of corporations now using bilingual marketing campaigns that target the Hispanic community is presented.

46664 ■ "Advisory Board Members Help Students Understand Market and Customers" in *Long Island Business News* (February 13, 2004)
Pub: Dolan Media Newswires
Ed: Adina Genn. **Description:** Suggestions for choosing people to serve on an advisory board are offered. It is important to consider the board's mission and to appoint individuals who will help the firm beyond the boardroom.

46665 ■ "Adwatcher" in *Entrepreneur.com* (Vol. 34, February 2006, No. 2, pp. 6)
Pub: Entrepreneur Media Inc.
Description: AdWatcher tracks advertising campaigns across Websites, monitors search engines, banners and newsletters.

46666 ■ "Affluence in Two Cultures" in *Hispanic Business* (December 2003, pp. 30, 32)
Pub: Hispanic Business
Description: English language skills lead to higher income and net worth for American Hispanics. Statistical data included showing income and occupation by language dominance, and more.

46667 ■ "Affordable branding 101" in *E-business Advisor* (Vol. 18, No. 10, October 2000, pp. 12)
Pub: Advisor Media, Inc.
Description: NetMediaVC helps startups and established business-to-consumer and business-to-business e-businesses plan and pay for traditional media campaigns (radio, magazines, television, etc.). Clients contribute 70 percent of the funds required and NetMedia kicks in the other 30 percent for an equity stake in the company.

46668 ■ "Against the Grain: Forget Big Marketing Budgets-Its Time to Think Outside the (Cereal) Box" in *Entrepreneur* (Vol. 32, August 2004)
Pub: Entrepreneur Media Inc.
Ed: Mark Henricks. **Description:** Review of Seth Godin's book, Free Prize Inside: The Next Big Marketing Idea. Godin suggests soft innovation that requires initiative and curiosity will help a product sell itself. The book offers techniques, tools and tricks for soft innovation.

46669 ■ "Ahead of the Law" in *Adweek* (Vol. 46, January 17, 2005, No. 3, pp. 16)
Pub: VNU Business Media
Ed: Wendy Melillo. **Description:** Laws and regulations involving television advertising are examined.

46670 ■ "All Fired Up: With the Right Marketing Plan, Your Product Will Blaze Trails Across the Globe" in *Entrepreneur* (Vol. 32, July 2004)
Pub: Entrepreneur Media Inc.
Ed: Don Debelak. **Description:** Entrepreneurs share steps to successfully market products and services. Profile of Robustion Products Inc., maker of the Java-Log for fireplaces is included.

46671 ■ "All-star performance" in *Incentive* (Vol. 174, No. 10, October 2000, pp. 126)
Pub: Bill Communications
Ed: Nancy K. Austin. **Description:** Placing only the brightest stars at the center of your business universe will eventually bring your company crashing down to earth.

46672 ■ "Almost Famous: Market Yourself as an Expert" in *My Business* (October/November 2003, pp. 45)
Pub: My Business Magazine
Ed: Nancy Mann Jackson. **Description:** The importance of establishing one's self as an expert in the particular field in which you are selling will help a salesperson stand out from competitors. Tips includes speaking at conferences, creating informational products, the use of newspapers and magazines or business publications, writing articles, or doing guest spots on television or radio shows.

46673 ■ "Ambulance Chasing, Web-Style" in *Forbes* (Vol. 174, December 27, 2004, No. 13, pp. 56)
Pub: Forbes Magazine Inc.
Ed: David Whelan. **Description:** Law firms are paying large sums to place pay-per-click ads on Internet sites. The ads take the user to a law firm's Web site or a middleman, and a lawyer pays up to $160 to the Internet service provider.

46674 ■ *American Marketing Association— The M Guide Directory*
Pub: American Marketing Association
Contact: Sally Schmitz, Production Mgr.
Released: Annual, February. **Covers:** 24,000 individual members and about 1,000 paid listings for member research and service firms. **Entries Include:** For individuals—Member name, position, home and office address, and phone numbers. For advertisers—Company name, address, phone, names of principal executives.

46675 ■ "American Urban Radio Networks" in *Black Enterprise* (Vol. 34, No. 7, February 2004, pp. 64)
Pub: Earl Graves Publishing Co.
Description: Profile of Mary Ware, regional director of marketing and new business development for American Urban Radio Networks, located in Chicago, Illinois.

46676 ■ "Amgen's Profit Up 58 Percent in 2nd Quarter" in *Providence Business News* (Vol. 18, No. 15, July 28, 2003, pp. 1)
Pub: Providence Business News, Inc.
Ed: Mike Colias. **Description:** A presentation of second-quarter profits in 2003 reported by Amgen Inc. Topics include market share, market development, and business strategy.

46677 ■ "An Attractive Site" in *Black Enterprise* (Vol. 36, November 2005, No. 4, pp. 74)
Pub: Earl G. Graves Publishing Co. Inc.
Ed: James C. Johnson. **Description:** Tips to help a Website network with African American professionals and manage the costs associated with advertising on the site are listed.

46678 ■ *Analyzing Sales Promotions*
Pub: Probus Publishing Co., Inc.
Ed: Martin P. Block. **Released:** Second edition, 1994. **Price:** $19.95 (paper); $48.95 (Canada). **Description:** Provides information for small business owners and marketing and advertising professionals on sales promotions strategy and management. Covers integrated marketing communication, characteristics of trade and sales force audiences, "fact-based" marketing, and principles of promotional strategy and analysis.

46679 ■ "And Now a Syllable From Our Sponsor" in *Inc.* (August 2005, pp. 22)
Pub: Inc. Magazine
Description: New advertising campaigns are featuring one-second television commercials to promote products.

46680 ■ "And Now, a Word From Our Sponsor" in *Harvard Business Review* **(Vol. 81, No. 10, October 2003, pp. 31)**
Pub: Harvard Business School Press
Ed: M. Ellen Peebles. **Description:** Experts discuss the question of product placement within a larger discussion of effective advertising techniques.

46681 ■ "Another Act" in *Entrepreneur* **(Vol. 31, No. 7, July 2003, pp. 40)**
Pub: Entrepreneur Media, Inc.
Ed: Liane Cassavoy. **Description:** Profile of ACT!, the contact management and sales-force automation application. The software is now available in a Web version.

46682 ■ "Applying Old Ideals to Crain's New Tasks" in *Crain's New York Business* **(Vol. 23, January 8, 2007, No. 2, pp. 11)**
Pub: Crain Communications, Inc.
Ed: Greg David. **Description:** Crain's New York Business announces its plans for the coming year which include a comprehensive website that will provide readers with daily news stories.

46683 ■ "Are Customers Selling For You?" in *Sales and Marketing.com* **(Vol. 156, No. 3, March 2004, pp. 22)**
Pub: VNU eMedia, Inc.
Ed: Michael Schrage. **Description:** Although there are three types of clients, those that willingly and effectively serve as sales references are the most valuable to a small business.

46684 ■ "Art Lover Plays Fair Game" in *Crain's New York Business* **(Vol. 23, January 29, 2007, No. 5, pp. F19)**
Pub: Crain Communications, Inc.
Ed: Miriam Kreinin Souccar. **Description:** Profile of Helen Allen and her art fairs, including Pulse, a contemporary art fair in Miami which took in more than $10 million. Numerous dealers sold out their inventory on the first day of the fair. Her art fairs which in addition to Pulse include Ramsay and Art 212 are designed for a younger generation and feature more affordable pieces of work.

46685 ■ "Art Van Shoots to Score with Yzerman, Ireland Furniture Lines" in *Crain's Detroit Business* **(Vol. 19, No. 40, October 13, 2003, pp. 1)**
Pub: Crain Communications Inc., Detroit
Ed: Brent Snavely. **Description:** Hockey star, Steve Yzerman and supermodel Kathy Ireland, have unveiled exclusive new lines for Art Van Furniture Inc.

46686 ■ "Arts and Crafts are Big with Women" in *Marketing to Women* **(Vol. 19, October 2006, No. 10, pp. 1)**
Pub: EPM Communications, Inc.
Description: Every year more women are turning to arts and crafts as an "antidote" to all the time they are spending in the virtual world of computers. Statistical data included.

46687 ■ "As seen on TV" in *Entrepreneur* **(Vol. 30, No. 2, Fe)**
Pub: Entrepreneur Media Inc.
Ed: Kim T. Gordon. **Description:** A winning formula for direct response TV advertising is presented. Entrepreneurs can create TV spots and keep costs down.

46688 ■ "Ask Inc, Marketing" in *Inc.* **(November 2006, pp. 53)**
Pub: Gruner & Jahr USA Publishing
Ed: Doug Houte **Description:** Federal "Do Not Call" registry injured much of the telemarketing business to consumer marketers, but did not affect business to business as deeply. The key is to discover who needs what you have to sell, rather than mass canvassing. Help is available online or with companies that specialize in this.

46689 ■ "AT&T Set for Expensive Branding Campaign" in *Sacramento Bee* **(December 29, 2005)**
Pub: The Sacramento Bee
Ed: Clint Swett. **Description:** Former SBC Communications' acquisition of AT&T Corporation has the firm

setting a new national identity in an expensive branding campaign. The advertising will begin New Year's Eve and run for a year.

46690 ■ "Atlanta's top promotions firms" in *Atlanta Business Chronicle* **(Vol. 25, November 15, 2002, No. 23 pp. S8)**
Pub: American City Business Publications, Inc.
Description: Atlanta's top ten promotion firms are ranked by net revenue in Atlanta in 2001. Also included is expected net revenue for 2002, number of full time staff, accounts gained and lost in 2002, significant events, major clients, chief officer, contact information, and year of establishment.

46691 ■ "The Attention Getter" in *My Business* **(June/July 2004, pp. 48)**
Pub: My Business Magazine
Ed: Jamie Roberts. **Description:** Profile of Greg Grimaud, owner of nine Precision Tune Auto Care franchises. Grimaud shares secrets to his marketing success. He advertises in both English and Spanish and promotes his stores by driving Hummer automobiles with the company logos.

46692 ■ "Attention Readers!" in *Fast Company* **(July 2001, pp. 50)**
Pub: Fast Company
Ed: Polly LaBarre. **Description:** Review of the book titled, 'The Attention Economy: Understanding the New Currency of Business'. The book explores human attention factors and offers ways of capturing and holding the attention of customers, employees, and shareholders.

46693 ■ "Attract Stragglers" in *Sales & Marketing Management* **(Vol. 159, January-February 2007, No. 1, pp. 14)**
Pub: VNU Business Media
Ed: Leo Jakobson. **Description:** Employee sales incentive programs are profiled.

46694 ■ *Attracting Investors: A Marketing Approach to Finding Funds for Your Business*
Pub: John Wiley & Sons, Incorporated
Ed: Philip Kotler, Hermawan Kartajaya, S. David Young. **Released:** August 2004. **Price:** $29.95 (US), $42.99 (Canadian). **Description:** Marketing experts advise entrepreneurs in ways to find investors in order to raise capital for their companies.

46695 ■ "Aven Hopes Portable Microscope Drives Growth" in *Crain's Detroit Business* **(Vol. 22, December 18, 2006, No. pp. 16)**
Pub: Crain Communications Inc. - Detroit
Ed: Tom Henderson. **Description:** New portable microscope and digital camera to be marketed by Ann Arbor firm. This product combines a high resolution camera, with a series of in-house developed lenses. Target markets are crime scene investigations and quality control in manufacturing.

46696 ■ "Avoiding Invention Scams" in *Black Enterprise* **(Vol. 37, January 2007, No. 6, pp. 46)**
Pub: Earl G. Graves Publishing Co. Inc.
Ed: James C. Johnson. **Description:** Invention promotion firms provide inventors assistance in developing a prototype for product development. It is important to research these companies before making a commitment to work with them because there are a number of these firms that are not legitimate and have caused independent inventors to lose thousands of dollars by making false claims as to the market potential of the inventions.

46697 ■ "Avon's anti-aging ultimate gets Anew launch" in *Brandweek* **(Vol. 43, No. 34, September 23, 2002, pp. 4)**
Pub: VNU Business Media
Ed: Christine Bittar. **Description:** Avon has launched a new ad campaign for its anti-aging product, Ultimate. The anti-aging cream moves Avon and its Anew sub-brand a bit further upscale in the cosmetic industry.

46698 ■ "Back to School" in *Inc.* **(September 1, 2003)**
Pub: Gruner & Jahr USA Publishing
Ed: Nicole Gull. **Description:** At Merkle Direct Marketing, education is not an option for its employees it is a requirement for working there.

46699 ■ "A bad rap: have you been slammed as a spammer? Here's how to fight back" in *Entrepreneur* **(Vol. 31, No. 6, June 2003, pp. 83)**
Pub: Entrepreneur Media Inc.
Ed: Catherine Seda. **Description:** Spamming is the act of sending email to individuals without their permission. SpamCop reports that it receives 9 million spam complaints monthly.

46700 ■ "Bagging the Right Customers" in *Business 2.0* **(Vol. 6, May 2005, No. 4, pp. 56-57)**
Pub: Time, Inc.
Ed: Andrew Tilin. **Description:** Bagmaker Timbuk2 is prospering through the use of exploiting the areas between niche obscurity and mass-market dullness. Big-box retailers offer a large selection within a broadly defined product category while smaller specialty stores serve a finely defined market segment with brand more important than price.

46701 ■ "Balancing Act" in *Sales and Marketing.com* **(Vol. 147, No. 2, February 2004, pp. 16)**
Pub: VNU eMedia, Inc.
Ed: Julia Chang. **Description:** Many small businesses are learning that work/life balances, as well as financial rewards, for sales and marketing employees have become increasingly important.

46702 ■ "Bald Ambition: Hell-Bent on Getting Attention? Try a Zany Marketing Stunt" in *Entrepreneur* **(Vol. 32, December 2004, No. 12, pp. 28)**
Pub: Entrepreneur Media Inc.
Ed: Geoff Williams. **Description:** Gary Arnold, owner of Gary's Uptown Restaurant and Bar, offered discounts to balding customers every Wednesday and received national press.

46703 ■ "Ballooning Riches" in *Small Business Opportunities* **(Vol. 16, No. 3, May 2004, pp. 46, 48)**
Pub: Harris Publications, Inc.
Description: Profile of Landmark Creations of Burnsville, Minnesota. The firm offers fun and affordable inflatables to attract clients, and build a company's product image or brand.

46704 ■ "Banker Boosts Community" in *Crain's New York Business* **(Vol. 23, January 29, 2007, No. 5, pp. F14)**
Pub: Crain Communications, Inc.
Ed: Tom Fredrickson. **Description:** Profile of Maurice L. Coleman, New York Market Executive for Bank of America. Under his leadership, Bank of America is becoming a major player in community development in New York City, specifically targeting affordable housing and small businesses in low-income areas. Statistical data included.

46705 ■ "Banker Right on the Money with Financial Powerhouse" in *Houston Business Journal* **(Vol. 34, No. 13, August 8, 2003, pp. 2)**
Pub: American City Business Journals
Ed: Jim Greer. **Description:** The growing success of Southwest Bank of Texas is presented. Topics include market development, strategic planning, and management styles.

46706 ■ "Banking on Culture" in *Boston Business Journal* **(Vol. 23, No. 31, September 5, 2003, pp. 3)**
Pub: American City Business Journals
Ed: Edward Mason. **Description:** Raymond K. Tung, president and CEO of Asian American Bank, reports the firm is targeting Asian Americans as a first phase of expansion strategy. Asian American, located in Boston, Massachusetts' Chinatown neighborhood, is celebrating its tenth anniversary.

46707 ■ "Banks Reaching Out to New Communities" in *San Francisco Business Times* (Vol. 18, No. 6, September 19, 2003, pp. 22)
Pub: American City Business Journals
Ed: Steven E.F. Brown. Description: Wells Fargo, Bank of America and other banks are trying to get Hispanic customers by signing them up at the Mexican consulate.

46708 ■ "Banner Year" in *Entrepreneur* (Vol. 32, September 2004, No. 9, pp. 34)
Pub: Entrepreneur Media Inc.
Description: Online advertising has seen a dramatic increase in 2004. Statistical data included.

46709 ■ "Banners Tout Development" in *Mississippi Business Journal* (Vol. 29, January 2007, No. 4, pp. 11)
Pub: Venture Publications, Inc.
Ed: Wally Northway Description: Flashy banners have been erected all over downtown Jackson's business district. The banner idea, originated by a local restaurateur, is designed to bring visual attention to many unnoticed development projects and businesses in the area.

46710 ■ *Beating the Competition: 150 Ways to Win New Customers for Your Small Business*
Pub: Madison Books
Ed: Tait Trussell. Released: 1992. Price: $10.95 (paper). Description: Discusses how to attract new customers and the importance of public relations. Includes sample press releases and communication plans.

46711 ■ "Beau Rivage Resort And Casino" in *Mississippi Business Journal* (Vol. 29, January 2007, No. 2, pp. 6)
Pub: Venture Publications, Inc.
Description: Profile of Brian J. Bork, Executive Director of Advertising for the Beau Rivage Resort and Casino in Biloxi. Bork manages a team of graphic artists, production assistants and account coordinators.

46712 ■ "Being Small, Looking Big" in *Boston Business Journal* (Vol. 23, No. 21, June 27, 2003, pp. 24)
Pub: American City Business Journals
Ed: Chelsea Lowe. Description: Nancy Michaels of Impression Impact, Inc. discusses ways small companies can market themselves in a way that makes them look large, without spending large amounts of money to do so.

46713 ■ "Best of Both Worlds" in *Entrepreneur* (Vol. 31, No. 9, July 2003, pp. 100)
Pub: Entrepreneur Media, Inc.
Ed: Nichole L. Torres. Description: Profile of Kevin D. Brewer, founder of Creative Visions Integrated Marketing Concepts, an agency producing commercials and promotional videos to TV pilots and product demonstrations.

46714 ■ "Better Ingredients for Better Ads" in *Tampa Tribune* (December 3, 2005)
Pub: Media General, Inc.
Ed: Dave Simanoff. Description: A team of University of South Florida students studied marketing research and created an advertising campaign for Papa John's pizza that targets cost-conscious consumers such as themselves.

46715 ■ "Better Methods" in *Inc.* (September 1, 2003)
Pub: Gruner & Jahr USA Publishing
Ed: Robert X. Cringely. Description: An investigation into the reasons why advertising works is highlighted.

46716 ■ "Better Off Red" in *Entrepreneur. com* (Vol. 34, February 2006, No. 2, pp. 74)
Pub: Entrepreneur Media Inc.
Ed: Gwen Moran. Description: People are moving away from traditional Valentine's gifts and buying more meaningful gifts for their loved ones. Marketing experts suggest retailers use red to merchandise products, suggest products as perfect gifts for the holiday, and use heart shaped items.

46717 ■ "Better Way for Better Made?" in *Crain's Detroit Business* (Vol. 21, October 3, 2005, No. 43, pp. 3)
Pub: Crain Communications Inc. - Detroit
Ed: Brent Snavely. Description: Better Made Snack Foods Inc. is hoping its new products will boost sales for the firm. The company has put together a new executive team and signed a new union contract.

46718 ■ "Beyond the Banner Ad" in *Business Week* (December 11, 2000, pp. 16)
Pub: McGraw-Hill, Inc.
Description: An investigation of effective advertising on the Internet.

46719 ■ "The Biggest TV Network You've Never Heard Of" in *Inc.* (Volume 27, June 2005, No. 6, pp. 110-113, 116, 117)
Pub: Inc. Magazine
Ed: Ian Mount. Description: Michael Stern discusses the theory he used when launching his PRN network. PRN shows commercials inside stores for customers to view while shopping.

46720 ■ "Billings Bonanza" in *Hispanic Business* (December 2001, pp. 41, 44, 46, 48)
Pub: Hispanic Business
Description: Most of the Top 25 Hispanic Business ad agencies enjoyed a successful 2001, and expect 2002 to be better. A listing of the top 25 agencies is presented. Statistical data included.

46721 ■ "Blog Me, Baby" in *Inc.* (November 15, 2000, pp. 145)
Pub: The Goldhirsh Group
Description: A concise list of services for Web logging, including Blogger, UserLand, and GrokSoup.

46722 ■ "A Blogger in Their Midst" in *Harvard Business Review* (Vol. 81, No. 9, September 2003, pp. 30)
Pub: Harvard Business School Press
Ed: Halley Suitt. Description: A hypothetical situation is presented where an indiscreet employee provides an online endorsement of a product that results in dramatically increased sales. Experts discuss how the CEO should deal with the matter.

46723 ■ "Blogs Can Provide Testimonials" in *Sales & Marketing Management* (Vol. 159, January-February 2007, No. 1, pp. 8)
Pub: VNU Business Media
Ed: Betsy Cummings. Description: Third party blogs are helping small companies market and promote products and services.

46724 ■ "Boldness and prudence can accelerate business growth" in *Ingram's* (Vol. 28, No. 3, March 2002, pp. 21)
Pub: Show Me Publishing, Inc.
Ed: J. Chris Snedeker. Description: Small business owners are challenged daily to balance boldness with prudence; when taking bold marketing initiatives, the company's bottom line should be kept in mind.

46725 ■ "A Bonding Experience" in *Ingram's* (Vol. 28, No. 9, September 2002, pp. 23)
Pub: Show Me Publishing, Inc.
Ed: Mike Glynn. Description: Scouting for an ad agency, Maris Brenner from The Lodge of Four Seasons, regards track record as important and so chose Kupper Parker Communications, while Bob Sullivan of Boulevard Brewing Company says that an agency should have a clear understanding of what the business is and chose CHRW Advertising. Kansas Lottery chose Barkley Evergreen and Partners because of the firm's imagination.

46726 ■ "Boom: Marketing to the Ultimate Power Consumer" in *Marketing to Women* (Vol. 20, January 2007, No. 1, pp. 6)
Pub: EPM Communications, Inc.
Ed: Mary Brown; Carol Osborn. Description: The Baby Boomer woman has emerged as a leader in driving the marketplace. Carol Osborn, the co-author of Boom explains this phenomenon.

46727 ■ *BOOM: Marketing to the Ultimate Power Consumer-The Baby-Boomer Woman*
Pub: American Management Association
Ed: Mary Brown; Carol Orsborn. Released: 2006. Price: $24.00.

46728 ■ "Boomer Women Need Financial Advisors" in *Marketing to Women* (Vol. 19, October 2006, No. 10, pp. 8)
Pub: EPM Communications, Inc.
Description: Although most financially successful Boomer women don't have financial advisors, The Wall Street Journal reports, they need them. Financial services firms are eager to reach this market as they tend to give referrals.

46729 ■ "Bovine Blues?" in *Entrepreneur* (Vol. 31, No. 8, August 2003, pp. 25)
Pub: Entrepreneur Media, Inc.
Ed: Mark Henricks. Description: Review of the book, "Purple Cow: Transform Your Business by Being Remarkable", written by Seth Godin. Godin believes every company needs something phenomenal, counterintuitive and exciting in order to take attention away from competitors.

46730 ■ "Bradenton Central CRA To Launch New Business Development Center" in *Bradenton Herald* (January 29, 2005)
Pub: Bradenton Herald
Ed: Tim W. McCann. Description: The Bradenton Central Community Redevelopment Agency is working to grow the economy of the area. The Agency will create a small business center with a professional counselor to assist small business owners in applying for a business loan, advertising, marketing and legal issues.

46731 ■ "Bradenton Firm Capitalizes On Restroom 'Downtime' With 'Captive Audience' Ads" in *Bradenton Herald* (February 14, 2005)
Pub: Bradenton Herald
Ed: Tilde Herrera. Description: Focus Indoor Media is placing slogans and ads for real estate agents, restaurants, and other companies, in bathroom stalls, tanning salons, drinking fountain areas and elevators.

46732 ■ "The Bradenton Herald, Fla., Dana Sanchez Column" in *Bradenton Herald* (January 5, 2005)
Pub: Bradenton Herald
Ed: Dana Sanchez. Description: Tourism accounted for 12.5 percent of sales taxes paid in Manatee County, Florida in 2003. Businesses in the county continue to market diversity and the numerous offerings to visitors of the area.

46733 ■ *Bradford's International Directory of Marketing Research Agencies*
Pub: Business Research Services Inc.
Released: Biennial, latest edition 28. Price: $95, individuals paperback; $125, individuals diskette. Covers: over 1,700 marketing research agencies worldwide. Includes domestic and international demographic data and professional association contacts. Entries Include: Company name, address, phone, name and title of contact, date founded, number of employees, description of products or services, e-mail, URL. Arrangement: Geographical. Indexes: Alphabetical by company.

46734 ■ "BrainWorks Advertising Announces Staff Addition" in *Journal Record* (June 24, 2003)
Pub: Dolan Media Company
Description: Leah Steward has joined BrainWorks Advertising to handle public relations and account services.

46735 ■ "Brand Aid" in *Entrepreneur* (Vol. 33, March 2005, No. 3, pp. 142)
Pub: Entrepreneur Media Inc.
Ed: Don Debelak. Description: Entrepreneur, Missy Cohen-Fyffe, founder of Babe Ease LLC is offered advice to brand and market her quilted shopping cart covers that prevent children from exposure from disease-causing bacteria.

46736 ■ *Brand Marketing: How to Build and Hold Customer Loyalty*
Pub: NTC Business Books
Ed: William M. Weilbacher. **Released:** 1993. **Price:** $39.95. **Description:** Provides information on the brand marketing process.

46737 ■ **"Brand Me: Marketing Techniques to Make You Stand Out"** in *Black Enterprise* (Vol. 35, December 2004, No. 5, pp. 78)
Pub: Earl G. Graves Publishing Co. Inc.
Ed: Lee Anna Jackson. **Description:** Branding is important when marketing a product or service. Proper branding can make a product stand out from competitors.

46738 ■ **"The Brand Report Card"** in *Harvard Business Review* (Vol. 78, No. 1, January 2000, pp. 147)
Pub: Harvard Business School Publishing Corp.
Ed: Kevin Lane Keller. **Description:** The importance of brand management transcends all industry types and companies. Brand image and consumer perception should be continually analyzed to help maintain a product's foothold in the market.

46739 ■ **"The Brand of Success"** in *Small Business Opportunities* (Vol. 16, No. 2, March 2004, pp. 118, 120)
Pub: Harris Publications, Inc.
Ed: James Feldman. **Description:** Brand image is critical to a small business' success. Marketing materials serve two purposes. Guidelines to create or design promotions materials are presented.

46740 ■ **"Brand This Way"** in *Inc.* (November 1, 2003)
Pub: Gruner & Jahr USA Publishing
Ed: Nicole Gull. **Description:** Branding ideas can be learned by today's rock stars who use innovation at a controlled rate, by not evolving too fast.

46741 ■ **"Branding in a Chicken Suit; The Marketing Game had Changed"** in *Crain's Chicago Business* (Vol. 30, January 2007, No. 3, pp. 16)
Pub: Crain Communications, Inc.
Ed: Steve Hendershot. **Description:** Marketers have had to abandon old tactics of reaching consumers in favor of online marketing. While traditional means of reaching customers are faltering online ad spending grew 31 percent nationwide in 2006, the third consecutive year that it's increased by at least 30 percent.

46742 ■ **"Branding: Not Just for Big-Budget Businesses"** in *Ingram's* (Vol. 29, No. 8, August 2003, pp. 16)
Pub: Show Me Publishing, Inc.
Ed: T. DeWayne Ables. **Description:** Basic information regarding the importance of properly branding products in order to increase sales is examined.

46743 ■ **"Brave New World"** in *Home Office Computing* (Vol. 18, No. 9, September 2000, pp. 92)
Pub: Scholastic Inc.
Ed: Jeffery D. Zbar. **Description:** Horror author Stephen King stirred the publishing world with his Riding the Bullet, an e-book that sold for $2.50 a copy online. Resources for creative professionals range from file-sharing sites that let artists post and sell content while retaining their own copyrights. Experts warn that some sites charge fees ranging from 20 to 50 percent of sales. Authors should aggressively market their works at other Web sites and e-zines. Publicity and power are much the same in the E-publishing world.

46744 ■ **"Break Through Ads"** in *My Business* (February/March 2003, pp. 13-14)
Pub: My Business Magazine
Ed: Kathleen Landis. **Description:** The use of vehicles with signs for advertising is investigated. Various options are explored, including hand-painted signs, vinyl signs, decals, magnetic signs, and adhesive vinyl wraps.

46745 ■ **"Breaking the Ice: Want Skeptical Customers to Warm Up to Your Product?"** in *Entrepreneur* (Vol. 33, February 2005, No. 2, pp. 120)
Pub: Entrepreneur Media Inc.
Ed: Don Debelak. **Description:** Peter Lerman, inventor, and marketer, Lou Matinale have partnered to license and market Lerman's invention, the Sno-Easy. The Sno-Easy is an ergonomic shovel that allows users to shovel snow without bending or twisting.

46746 ■ **"Bridging the Gap"** in *Sales & Marketing Management*
Pub: VNU Business Media
Ed: David Macey. **Description:** Retail-specific marketing solutions are becoming more important as effective ways to influence buying behavior in today's consumer market.

46747 ■ **"Bring Back Old Territories"** in *Sales & Marketing Management* (Vol. 158, November-December 2006, No. 11, pp. 13)
Pub: VNU Business Media
Description: Dave Lakhani, president of Bold Approach, offers tips to generate new business leads.

46748 ■ **"Bringing Back a Classic"** in *Inc.* (August 1, 2003)
Pub: Gruner & Jahr USA Publishing
Ed: Leigh Buchanan. **Description:** Profile of Betty Morris, the woman who founded Shrinky Dinks in 1973 and by the 1980s the products were seen everywhere.

46749 ■ **"Bringing the Noise"** in *Hispanic Business* (December 2001, pp. 54, 56)
Pub: Hispanic Business
Ed: Teresa Talerico. **Description:** Profile of the Ruido Group, the ad agency capitalizing on its understanding of Hispanic youth in order to market products such as Coca Cola.

46750 ■ **"Bromley, AHAA shine at Confab"** in *Hispanic Business* (Vol. 22, No. 11, November 2000, pp. 12)
Pub: Hispanic Business
Ed: Peter Brennan. **Description:** A description is presented of events at the 'Advertising Age' Hispanic Creative Advertising Awards held in September 2000. Bromley Communications won eight medals, three of which were gold.

46751 ■ **"Bronto Email Marketing Toolkit"** in *Entrepreneur.com* (Vol. 34, February 2006, No. 2, pp. 6)
Pub: Entrepreneur Media Inc.
Description: Free guide offered by Bronto software focuses on email marketing for small business.

46752 ■ **"Bugged out"** in *Entrepreneur* (Vol. 31, No. 5, May 2003, pp. 38)
Pub: Entrepreneur Media Inc.
Ed: Melissa Campanelli. **Description:** Information about Web bugs as a means to gather data on visitors to Web sites is presented. Most Web bugs are used through products and services from firms offering site analysis services or products.

46753 ■ **"Build a Strong Customer-Brand Relationship"** in *E-business Advisor* (Vol. 18, No. 4, April 2000, pp. 34)
Pub: Advisor Media, Inc.
Ed: Doug Barton. **Description:** The article shows how the Internet is changing marketing practices as companies focus on developing customer loyalty instead of building brand images through advertising and traditional distribution channels. The two main factors driving sales are now customer loyalty and price.

46754 ■ **"Build Your Business with eBay"** in *Home Business* (Vol. 13, January/February 2006, No. 1, pp. 58, 60)
Pub: Home Business Magazine
Description: According to the American Business Association, consumers are using online markets as a convenient way to buy products. Small companies should diversify into the online sector as a means to grow a business. Tips for opening an online shop are outlined.

46755 ■ **"Build Your Own Web Site"** in *Home Business* (Vol. 12, October 2005, No. 5, pp. 88, 90-91)
Pub: Home Business Magazine
Ed: Morgan Reed. **Description:** The importance of Internet presence for any small company is critical. A Web site gives a firm credibility, while marketing products or services.

46756 ■ **"Build Your Web Identity"** in *E-business Advisor* (Vol. 18, No. 5, May 2000, pp. 30)
Pub: Advisor Media, Inc.
Ed: Maria Szalay, James J. Datovech. **Description:** With about 800 million Web pages deployed over eight million Web sites, e-commerce companies have to follow certain fundamental design and marketing principles in their Web strategy. Key tips for such strategy are provided.

46757 ■ **"Building Downline...Online"** in *Success* (Vol. 47, No. 2, June 2000, pp. 80)
Pub: Success Publishing, Inc.
Ed: Greg Matusky, Mark Butler. **Description:** In the online world, brand is subordinate to the power of relationships. If relationships are the key to unlocking the wealth-building opportunities of multi-level marketing, then the Internet provides the electronic ways for creating the connections.

46758 ■ **"Building Your Business"** in *Small Business Opportunities* (Vol. 17, May 2005, No. 3, pp. 12)
Pub: Harris Publications Inc.
Ed: Carla Longley Vincent. **Description:** Seven ways for a small business to tap into customers and increase profits include the development of alliances, franchising, adding wholesale clients, sell to the government, work with nonprofits, market yourself, and create new goods or services.

46759 ■ **"Business Buzz"** in *Tribune* (February 3, 2004)
Pub: Knight-Ridder/Tribune Business News
Description: The City of San Luis Obispo and the county's Visitors & Conference Bureau have partnered in a statewide ad campaign promoting local tourism.

46760 ■ **"Business Challenge: Rex Bird Noticed Some Online Customers"** in *My Business* (October/November 2003, pp. 42)
Pub: My Business Magazine
Ed: Karen M. Kroll. **Description:** Profile of Rex Bird, owner of BodyTrends.com, a Web site selling fitness equipment. Bird recognized the patterns customers used while navigating his Website and offers solutions to help small business owners market successfully with Internet sites.

46761 ■ **"Business to E-Business"** in *Home Office Computing* (Vol. 18, No. 11, November 2000, pp. 52)
Pub: Scholastic Inc.
Ed: Amee Abel. **Description:** Guidelines are provided for setting up a Web site for a home-based business. The Web site should function as a kind of electronic brochure, providing potential customers with an attractive and inviting preview of the company's available products and services. The Web site should also provide links to related sites, and support associated marketing tasks.

46762 ■ **"Business Gone Wild"** in *Entrepreneur* (Vol. 32, July 2004, No. 7, pp. 69)
Pub: Entrepreneur Media Inc.
Ed: Gwen Moran. **Description:** Profile of California Tortilla restaurants in the Washington DC area; partner Pam Felix, who also co-owns a comedy club, suggested customers do silly things in order to get free food. The marketing technique has increased profits for the restaurants.

46763 ■ "Business Integrator Entrepreneur Marries Technology and Advertising to Grow Business" in *Black Enterprise* (Vol. 35, Jan. 2005, No. 6)
Pub: Earl G. Graves Publishing Co. Inc.
Ed: Nichole Lewis. **Description:** Interactive marketing strategies have helped POWERi to grow in the travel and tourism industry despite a slowdown since the terrorist attacks of 9-11. The firm operates three lines of business: technology within an advertising agency that could also provide marketing strategy and graphic design services. The firm reported revenues of $1 million in 2003.

46764 ■ *Business Marketing Association— Membership & Resource Directory*
Pub: Business Marketing Association
Contact: Rick Kean, CON
Released: Annual, January. **Covers:** over 4,500 member business communications professionals in fields of advertising, marketing communications, and marketing; their service and supply companies are listed in the "Marketing Resources" section. **Entries Include:** For individuals—Name, title, company with which affiliated, address, phone. For companies— Name, address, phone, contact, description of products or services. **Arrangement:** Individuals are alphabetical within chapter; companies are classified by product or service. **Indexes:** Alpha, company, chapter.

46765 ■ "Business Plan Helps Set Goals, Draw Investors" in *Crain's Detroit Business* (Vol. 22, November 20, 2006, No. 47, pp. 18)
Pub: Crain Communications Inc. - Detroit
Ed: Sheena Harrison. **Description:** Financial investors always require a business plan before they will commit to investment in new or expanding ventures. Sound business planning and management also include a good business plan with time phased measurable goals to monitor progress and indicate need for adjustments of the plan.

46766 ■ *Business Warrior: Strategy for Entrepreneurs*
Pub: Clearbridge Publishing
Ed: Sun Tzu. **Released:** September 2006. **Price:** $19.95. **Description:** Advice to help entrepreneurs understand competitive strategies in order to succeed, focusing on sales, marketing, and personnel management.

46767 ■ "But Wait, There's More" in *Entrepreneur* (Vol. 31, No. 11, November 2003, pp. 98)
Pub: Entrepreneur Media, Inc.
Ed: Gwen Moran. **Description:** Gift-with-purchase promotions can increase sales, build a brand and make customers feel good about shopping in your store.

46768 ■ "The buzz on buzz" in *Harvard Business Review* (Vol. 78, No. 6, November-December 2000, pp. 139)
Pub: Harvard Business School Publishing Corp.
Description: Tips on promoting products, including five common myths companies must reject in order to successfully market their products.

46769 ■ "Buzz Skill" in *Entrepreneur* (Vol. 33, October 2005, No. 10, pp. 81)
Pub: Entrepreneur Media Inc.
Ed: Gwen Moran. **Description:** Profile of Dave Balter, known as the Buzzmaster. Balter founded the Boston, Massachusetts marketing agency, BzzAgent Inc. Balter promotes word-of-mouth marketing through a network of 92,000 volunteers he calls BzzAgents.

46770 ■ "C2G-Network" in *Entrepreneur.com* (Vol. 34, January 2006, No. 1, pp. 6)
Pub: Entrepreneur Media Inc.
Ed: Steve Cooper. **Description:** College students can be certified and placed on C2G-Network that puts them in contact with fast-growing small businesses. Students have backgrounds in technology, engineering, marketing and sales, human resources, finance, communications and more.

46771 ■ "Calculating clicks" in *Entrepreneur* (Vol. 30, No. 2, February 2002, pp. 72)
Pub: Entrepreneur Media Inc.
Ed: Nichole L. Torres. **Description:** A review of the new guidelines recently released by the Interactive Advertising Bureau for selling ad space on a company's Web site.

46772 ■ "Calm After the Storm" in *Hispanic Business* (December 2001, pp. 64)
Pub: Hispanic Business
Ed: Michael Caplinger. **Description:** Spanish-language radio billings are seeing a slowdown after years of steady growth. The Spanish-language radio's top ten billers are presented.

46773 ■ "Campaign Close-Up: Cargill" in *Sales & Marketing Management* (Vol. 158, November-December 2006, No. 11, pp. 15)
Pub: VNU Business Media
Ed: Jackie Hunzinger. **Description:** Profile of Cargill whose current advertising campaign shows how the company delivers its food from the processing plant to the dinner table.

46774 ■ "Campaigns for several products are shifting their focus from 'women only' to include 'real men'" in *New York Times* (August 31, 2001)
Pub: The New York Times
Ed: Suzanne Kapner. **Description:** Many companies, including German skin care products company Nivea and U.S. yogurt-maker Dannon Company Inc., are trying to broaden their markets by including men in their new ad campaigns. Their products, formerly identified with female consumers, are now being targeted to male consumers. Another company, Hard Candy of Beverly Hills, California, which makes nail polish and makeup, has had less success appealing to men.

46775 ■ "Can Brand Management Help You Succeed?" in *Success* (Vol. 47, No. 6, November 2000, pp. 58)
Pub: Success Publishing, Inc.
Ed: Mary Jane Genova. **Description:** Branding isn't just about the perfect name—it's about how you organize and run your business. By using brand management, small businesses become household words.

46776 ■ "Can you keep a secret?" in *Fast Company* (June 2001, pp. 186)
Pub: Fast Company
Ed: George Anders. **Description:** The push for online privacy threatens to kill the dream of super-sophisticated net-driven marketing, but there are simple ways that companies can have their data and also protect it.

46777 ■ "Carb Games" in *Entrepreneur* (Vol. 32, October 2004, No. 10, pp. 42)
Pub: Entrepreneur Media Inc.
Ed: Judith Potwora. **Description:** High-carb food sellers should stress moderation when marketing their products. Graeter's Ice Cream in Cincinnati, Ohio promotes product purity; Greg Pyne of The Brookly Cafe in Atlanta, Georgia offers customers a choice of low carb pasta dishes. The American Bakers Association and North American Millers' Association are sponsoring a campaign designating bread as essential.

46778 ■ "Card Firms Try Two-Pronged Approach to Small Business" in *American Banker* (Vol. 171, November 20, 2006, No. 223, pp. 1)
Pub: SourceMedia, Inc.
Ed: H. Michael Jalili. **Description:** Obstacles faced by the credit card industry when serving the small business sector are discussed.

46779 ■ "CarsDirect.com Buys 2 Web Sites" in *American Banker* (Vol. 170, February 4, 2005, No. 24, pp. 17)
Pub: Thomson Financial Media Inc.
Ed: Erick Bergquist. **Description:** CarsDirect.com Inc. has bought a mortgage lead platform and two consumer Web sites, BestRate.com and LoanApp.com. The Los Angeles online car marketplace and lender says the move will help the company build on its business model of lead generation and mortgage brokering, along with adding the new component of subscription-based lender advertising.

46780 ■ "Case Study. Anatomy of a Business Decision" in *Inc.* (September 2006, pp. 47-48, 50)
Pub: Gruner & Jahr USA Publishing
Ed: Phaedra Hise. **Description:** Review and analysis of a downmarketing strategy is detailed in this article. Small business growth typically moves to higher end customers that are increasingly difficult to please. If it isn't cost effective, going back to the basics of the success of the growth may expand the business and increase profitability.

46781 ■ "Case Study" in *Inc.* (August 1, 2004)
Pub: Inc. Magazine
Ed: Lora Kolodny. **Description:** Kuma Reality Games talks about the controversy of its new video game based on the Iraq war. Keith Halper, CEO of the firm, believes that publicity can work as free advertising.

46782 ■ *Cash Copy: How to Offer Your Products and Services So Your Prospects Buy Them... Now!*
Pub: JLA Publications
Ed: Jeffrey Lant. **Released:** Third edition, 1992. **Price:** $35.00 (paper). **Description:** Provides information on marketing communication, including avoiding common mistakes and using testimonials.

46783 ■ "Cash In On Coupons" in *Small Business Opportunities* (Vol. 13, No. 5, September 2001, pp. 44)
Pub: Harris Publications, Inc.
Ed: Stan Roberts. **Description:** Profile of Brenda Fisher, owner and president of Super Coups, the direct mail coupon business located in Central Florida.

46784 ■ "Cash is King" in *Fast Company* (May 2001, pp. 80)
Pub: Fast Company
Ed: Walter Wriston. **Description:** Interview with Walter Wriston, former CEO of Citicorp/Citibank. Wriston advises that during economic hard times small businesses need to get back to the basics: inventory control, receivables, payables, and cash flow, the things forgotten during the new economy. Focus on generating cash, and a company will be positioned to take advantage of opportunities that the cash-strapped firms can't afford.

46785 ■ "Catalog companies show the upstarts that they know a thing or two about Internet retailing" in *The New York Times* (May 15, 2000, pp.C16)
Pub: The New York Times Company
Ed: Bob Tedeschi. **Description:** Well-established catalog firms see profits from e-commerce grow sharply, and have a high rate of success in converting online browsers into buyers.

46786 ■ "Caterpillar" in *Sales & Marketing Management* (Vol. 158, October 2006, No. 10, pp. 17)
Pub: VNU Business Media
Ed: Tali Arbel. **Description:** VSA Partners located in Chicago and Saint Louis offer marketing strategies they use to promote Caterpillar, the global leader of earth-moving equipment.

46787 ■ "The cat's meow" in *Entrepreneur* (Vol. 31, No. 5, May 2003, pp. 80)
Pub: Entrepreneur Media Inc.
Ed: Jerry Fisher. **Description:** The importance of finding an idea that is unique to market a product is discussed.

46788 ■ "Caught In the Crossfire" in *Inc.* (August 1, 2003)
Pub: Gruner & Jahr USA Publishing
Ed: Ellen Neubone. **Description:** New spam filters are making it difficult for small companies relying on email for marketing strategies.

46789 ■ "Caught in 'Tween" in *Entrepreneur* (Vol. 32, October 2004, No. 10, pp. 40)
Pub: Entrepreneur Media Inc.
Ed: Mark Henricks. **Description:** Book review of, The Great Tween Market, written by youth-market experts

David L. Siegel, Timothy J. Coffey and Gregory Livingston. Children aged 8 to 12 represent a large, profitable market for purchases influenced by them or made with their own money.

46790 ■ "Celeb-Savvy Publisher" in *Crain's New York Business* **(Vol. 23, January 29, 2007, No. 5, pp. F24)**
Pub: Crain Communications, Inc.
Ed: Matthew Flamm. Description: Profile of Jason Binn who is the founder and chief executive of Niche Media Holdings, a publisher of glossy magazines such as Gotham and Los Angeles Confidential. His innovative techniques led to a successful company which reports $40 million in annual revenues.

46791 ■ "Celebrating Business Heroes" in *Hispanic Business* **(December 2002, pp. 58-60)**
Pub: Hispanic Business
Ed: Scott Williams. Description: Hispanic CEO's share their challenges while seeing a successful market niche, including an artist who designs pools, waterfalls, and water sculptures; founders of BLVD magazine, a doctor who treats varicose veins, and a magazine offering branding advice.

46792 ■ "Celebration of Culture and Commerce" in *Hispanic Business* **(September 2003, pp. 34, 36, 38)**
Pub: Hispanic Business
Ed: Janet Perez. Description: Ethnic event marketing works throughout the year, but hits a high season during Hispanic Heritage Month. Calendar of Hispanic cultural events is included.

46793 ■ "Change, of Course" in *Entrepreneur.com* **(Vol. 34, February 2006, No. 2, pp. 79)**
Pub: Entrepreneur Media Inc.
Ed: David Worrell. Description: Profile of George Deeb, owner of iExplore Inc., a Chicago, Illinois-based adventure-travel firm with nearly $10 million in annual sales. Deeb offers his own tours and sells advertising on his Website.

46794 ■ "Change of Face: Tactics: Is Your Logo Losing Its Luster?" in *Entrepreneur* **(Vol. 31, No. 9, September 2003, pp. 87)**
Pub: Entrepreneur Media, Inc.
Ed: Kim T. Gordon. Description: The importance of a company logo is stressed, including facts on the three types of logos used. Ways to determine if a company's logo has become dated and needs to be updated are explored.

46795 ■ "The Change Up: Find New Uses for Your Products" in *My Business* **(February/March 2003, pp. 15)**
Pub: My Business Magazine
Ed: Evelyn Beck. Description: Diversification of a product can be a good tool for increasing sales, but it is imperative to do research.

46796 ■ "Chart-toppers" in *Entrepreneur* **(Vol. 30, No. 3, March 2002, pp. 88)**
Pub: Entrepreneur Media Inc.
Ed: Nichole L. Torres. Description: The use of charts in getting business publicity is explored.

46797 ■ "Chatom Offers Wines With Cause Tie-Ins" in *Marketing to Women* **(Vol. 19, November 2006, No. 11, pp. 5)**
Pub: EPM Communications, Inc.
Description: She Wines, a line of wines created to benefit heart disease and breast cancer research, was introduced by women-owned and run Chatom Vineyards. The winery is based in Calaveras County, California.

46798 ■ "Check It Out" in *Entrepreneur* **(Vol. 32, November 2004, No. 11, pp. 14)**
Pub: Entrepreneur Media Inc.
Description: Nancy Michaels latest offering, Perfecting Your Pitch: 10 Proven Strategies/or Winning the Clients Everyone Wants, shows how entrepreneurs can generate new clients or customers and close deals.

46799 ■ "Chicago Mercantile Exchange" in *Sales & Marketing Management* **(Vol. 159, January-February 2007, No. 1, pp. 10)**
Pub: VNU Business Media
Ed: Jackie Hunzinger. Description: Chicago Mercantile Exchange (CME) is focusing their 2007 advertising campaign on reaching customers from various sectors. The campaign will run in various financial journals and magazines.

46800 ■ "Chicago's Top Brands" in *Crain's Chicago Business* **(Vol. 30, January 2007, No. 3, pp. 15)**
Pub: Crain Communications, Inc.
Description: Profiles of five Chicago companies which made the list of Interbrand Corp., a global marketing firm, most powerful brands in the world.

46801 ■ "Chick magnet: How can you attract women to your business?" in *Entrepreneur* **(Vol. 30, No. 3, March 2002, pp. 93)**
Pub: Entrepreneur Media Inc.
Ed: Kim T. Gordon. Description: Nine out of ten households identify women as the primary shopper and in the past five years, women-owned businesses have increased at twice the rate of firms overall, therefore whether targeting businesses or consumers, it is important to improve ways of marketing to women in order to be successful.

46802 ■ "Chocolat flick on tap for Valentine's Day special" in *Business First Columbus* **(Vol. 18, No. 25, February 8, 2002, pp. A12)**
Pub: Business First Columbus, Inc.
Ed: Laura Newpoff. Description: A review of the movie and dinner promotions set for Valentine's Day by area restaurants is presented.

46803 ■ *Choosing and Working with Your Advertising Agency*
Pub: NTC Business Books
Ed: William M. Weilbacher. Released: 1991. Price: $39.95. Description: Describes how to establish a search group (or how to select an agency through one-on-one interviewing), write an account profile, determine selection criteria, compose a fact sheet, evaluate agency presentations, and other topics. Discusses the six basic areas of advertiser-agency interaction.

46804 ■ "City Guide for Moms Launched" in *Marketing to Women* **(Vol. 20, January 2007, No. 1, pp. 3)**
Pub: EPM Communications, Inc.
Description: ModernMom.com has launched a series of city guides on the Internet designed to highlight local businesses that offer goods and services a mother may need. Los Angeles, San Francisco, Chicago, New York City, Seattle, Austin Minneapolis, Atlanta, San Diego, Boston, Philadelphia and Washington D.C. are cities included so far in Modern Mom City Guides.

46805 ■ "Clickalyzer www.clickalyzer.com" in *Entrepreneur* **(Vol. 32, No. 1, January 2004, pp. 10)**
Pub: Entrepreneur Media, Inc.
Ed: Steve Cooper. Description: Profile of the Website that tracks and monitors advertising, Web pages, sales letters and visitors.

46806 ■ "Clicking with Hispanics" in *Hispanic Business* **(March 2004, pp. 54, 56)**
Pub: Hispanic Business
Ed: Derek Reveron. Description: Michael Dell, CEO of Dell Inc., announces a new strategy to target the Hispanic computer buyer and the Tech Know program that gives at-risk children the opportunity to take home a Dell computer.

46807 ■ "Clicks to Bricks" in *Entrepreneur* **(Vol. 33, August 2005, No. 8, pp. 44)**
Pub: Entrepreneur Media Inc.
Ed: Melissa Campanelli. Description: Following a current trend, more e-tailers are opening brick-and-mortar stores. This move will strengthen brand-name recognition, give local customers a place to shop or return merchandise, lower promotional fees, and expand a customer base.

46808 ■ "Clicks, not licks, as Green Stamps go digital" in *The New York Times* **(March 9, 2000, pp. D1, G1)**
Pub: The New York Times Company
Ed: Michelle Slatella. Description: S&H Green Stamps are back with green points, an online form of Green Stamps, given out as rewards for shopping online.

46809 ■ "Client Surveys Slow to Catch on as a Legal Marketing Tool" in *Journal Record (Oklahoma City, OK)* **(February 8, 2007)**
Pub: Journal Record
Ed: Dick Dahl. Description: Client surveys are not as successful a marketing tool for attorneys as other industries.

46810 ■ "Close to Finding RedZone's Niche" in *Pittsburgh Business Times* **(Vol. 4, August 15, 2003, pp. 14)**
Pub: Pittsburgh Business Times
Ed: Maria Guzzo. Description: Profile of Pittsburgh, Pennsylvania-based RedZone Robotics Inc.; topics include market development, management styles, and management of small business.

46811 ■ "Close to Home" in *Entrepreneur* **(Vol. 33, February 2005, No. 2, pp. 69)**
Pub: Entrepreneur Media Inc.
Ed: Catherine Seda. Description: Online advertising programs offering geographic-targeting plans can help a small business market to a specific audience. A listing of Websites offering online advertising programs is included.

46812 ■ "Club Planet Takes Off" in *Small Business Opportunities* **(Vol. 17, May 2005, No. 3, pp. 72)**
Pub: Harris Publications Inc.
Description: Profile of Andrew Fox who started Clubplanet.com from his New York City apartment. Later he and his sister founded Track Entertainment, a nightlife Website and entertainment marketing agency.

46813 ■ "Clueing in customers." in *Harvard Business Review* **(Vol. 81, No. 2, February 2003, pp. 100)**
Pub: Harvard Business School Press
Ed: Leonard L. Berry, Neeli Bendapudi. Description: Evidence management is discussed by examining how the Mayo Clinic has continually worked to provide as positive an experience as possible to its patients. As a result, word of mouth about the hospital is quite positive, along with strong customer loyalty.

46814 ■ "Coke Out to Woo Mall Rats Here With Lounge" in *Crain's Chicago Business* **(Vol. 26, No. 51, December 22, 2003, pp. 9)**
Pub: Crain Communications, Inc.
Ed: Kate MacArthur. Description: Coca-Cola has created the Coca-Cola Red Lounge for teenagers shopping at the north suburban Vernon Hills, Westfield Shoppingtown Hawthorn Center, as well as another site in Los Angeles, California. Coke is trying to build a brand with young people, separating it from being a brand for older folks. Statistical data included.

46815 ■ "Cold gold" in *Entrepreneur* **(Vol. 30, No. 3, March 2002, pp. 92)**
Pub: Entrepreneur Media Inc.
Ed: Jerry Fisher. Description: Advice is given on using true originality in advertising, spotlighting Amana Appliances in Amana, Iowa.

46816 ■ "Commentary: 'About Us' Pages Spell Good Business, Consumer Confidence" in *Long Island Business News* **(February 27, 2004)**
Pub: Dolan Media Newswires
Ed: Adina Genn. Description: Small businesses are creating About Us pages on their Websites. These provide a site where a company can share information about its history, philosophies and mission. This information can be used as a marketing tool to attract new customers.

46817 ■ "Commentary: 'Opportunity Calls': Networking With an Agenda" in *Long Island Business News* (February 20, 2004)
Pub: Dolan Media Newswires
Description: All sales leads tend to come from a close network of long-term business associates.

46818 ■ "Commentary: Testimonials-Let Your Customers Do the Talking" in *Long Island Business News* (March 12, 2004)
Pub: Dolan Media Newswires
Ed: Adina Genn. **Description:** Long Island businesses are cultivating customer testimonials on the Web, in brochures and on site. Tips for using customer praise to promote a business are included.

46819 ■ "Commentary: Testimonials-Let Your Customers Do the Talking" in *Long Island Business News* (March 12, 2004)
Pub: Dolan Media Newswires
Ed: Adina Genn. **Description:** Long Island businesses are cultivating customer testimonials on the Web, in brochures and on site. Tips for using customer praise to promote a business are included.

46820 ■ "Commerce: The bar code's high-tech sibling" in *Red Herring* (No. 105, October 1, 2001, pp. 27)
Pub: Herring Communications
Ed: Vinee Tong. **Description:** McDonalds restaurants in the Chicago area will be offering smart key chains to customers enabling them to pay for food in a wireless, cashless transaction. The devices, that use radio frequency identification (RFID), are the same as those being used by ExxonMobil gasoline stations.

46821 ■ "Commercials are music to recording artists' ears" in *Atlanta Business Chronicle* (Vol. 25, November 15, 2002, No. 23 pp. S10)
Pub: American City Business Publications, Inc.
Ed: Heather Cole. **Description:** Many local musicians in St. Louis, Missouri are able to supplement income by assisting with commercial work, and local agencies are often able to find the talent they need within the city. Computerized aspects of commercial music have allowed one-person businesses to operate.

46822 ■ "Communications initiatives vital for small business" in *Atlanta Business Chronicle* (Vol. 24, No. 14, September 7, 2001, pp. 4B)
Pub: American City Business Journals Inc.
Ed: Melissa Goehring. **Description:** Melissa Goehring, executive producer at Mountain View Productions Ltd., discusses communications initiatives. These are both external and internal communications that focus on the company vision and bolster company branding. Goehring says that this method is especially important to small businesses, and outlines ways for which corporations can develop successful communications initiatives.

46823 ■ "Company Tracks Shoppers, Issues Coupons on Tendencies" in *Tampa Tribune* (November 16, 2005)
Pub: Media General, Inc.
Ed: Richard Mullins. **Description:** Catalina Marketing, based in St. Petersburg, Florida, tracks purchases for stores like Kash n' Karry, Meijer and Safeway. The firm records the purchases through customer loyalty cards, credit cards and debit cards and offers targeted coupons to specific customers.

46824 ■ "Compare Your Clicks: www.compareyourclicks.com" in *Entrepreneur* (Vol. 32, November 2004, No. 11, pp. 6)
Pub: Entrepreneur Media Inc.
Ed: Steve Cooper. **Description:** Profile of Compare Your Clicks, an online resource that lets marketers run live comparisons of keyword bid prices at multiple search engines.

46825 ■ "Competing with the Big Guys" in *Home Business* (Vol. 13, January/February 2006, No. 1, pp. 71)
Pub: Home Business Magazine

Ed: Sandy Larson. **Description:** Profile of Seema Matia who runs a marketing research firm from her home in Calabasas, California. Matia offers services to small and medium-sized businesses.

46826 ■ "Competition Forces Malls to Redefine Marketing" in *Atlanta Business Chronicle* (Vol. 26, No. 11, August 22, 2003, pp. 3A)
Pub: American City Business Publications, Inc.
Ed: Jim Lovel. **Description:** Small shopping centers have a larger customer base than larger regional malls in the Atlanta, Georgia area.

46827 ■ *The Complete Guide to Publicity: Maximize Visibility for Your Products, Services & Organizations*
Pub: N T C Contemporary Publishing Co.
Ed: Joe Marconi. **Released:** 1999. **Price:** $39.95.

46828 ■ "Computer-Assisted Consulting" in *Hispanic Business* (Vol. 24, No. 5, May 2002, pp. 50)
Pub: Hispanic Business Inc.
Ed: Roger Harris. **Description:** BRS software products will help business consultants to become more successful. The software packages offer solid advice on everything from writing business and marketing plans to development of pricing and sales strategies.

46829 ■ "Conference Calendar" in *Marketing to Women* (Vol. 20, January 2007, No. 1, pp. 7)
Pub: EPM Communications, Inc.
Description: Calendar spotlighting women's business conferences through the month of June.

46830 ■ "A Confidence Boost" in *Sales & Marketing Management* (Vol. 158, October 2006, No. 10, pp. 19)
Pub: VNU Business Media
Ed: Bill Raymond. **Description:** Accountability is a key component of developing an effective sales staff.

46831 ■ "Consultants on their own" in *Atlanta Business Chronicle* (Vol. 24, No. 10, August 10, 2001, pp. 3A)
Pub: American City Business Journals Inc.
Ed: Jim Lovel. **Description:** An increasing number of marketing consultants are becoming independent for various reasons. As their numbers increase, the consultants have found new ways to boost their business, including formal alliances setting up a Web site devoted to independents.

46832 ■ "Consumer Control Issue is Marketing's Two-Edged Sword" in *Advertising Age* (Vol. 75, November 1, 2004, No. 44, pp. 17)
Pub: Crain Communications Inc.
Ed: Rance Crain. **Description:** Consumers have the power to alter marketing behavior and manipulating the way products are promoted.

46833 ■ "Consumer Research" in *Business 2.0* (Vol. 6, September 2005, No. 8, pp. 36)
Pub: Time Inc.
Ed: Bridget Finn. **Description:** Umbria Communications in Boulder, Colorado is turning the Internet into a marketing bonanza. The firm's software called Buzz Report searches 13 million blogs to uncover consumer's feelings about new products and trends.

46834 ■ "Consumers Look for Post-Holiday Sales" in *Sacramento Bee* (December 27, 2005)
Pub: The Sacramento Bee
Ed: Jon Ortiz. **Description:** Retailers are becoming increasingly dependent on post-holiday sales. Shoppers tend to purchase new items seen in sales and promotions while returning unwanted items.

46835 ■ "Contagious Commercials" in *Inc.* (November 2006, pp. 31-32)
Pub: Gruner & Jahr USA Publishing
Ed: Jennifer Gill. **Description:** Short videos on YouTube and MySpace can start a stream of information networks that can convey your business message. This process is known as viral video marketing and is rapidly growing on the web.

46836 ■ "Content sites find a way to keep e-tailer marketing booths on their page-without having lured their visitors away" in *The New York Times*
Pub: The New York Times Company
Ed: Bob Tedeschi. **Description:** Affiliate marketing between e-tailers and content Web sites is discussed.

46837 ■ "Contextual marketing" in *Harvard Business Review* (Vol. 78, No. 6, November-December 2000, pp. 119)
Pub: Harvard Business School Publishing Corp.
Description: Contextual marketing is examined and the ways new technologies will shift the focus of e-commerce from content to context, making many Web sites irrelevant.

46838 ■ "Cool Novelty Cups" in *Dairy Foods* (Vol. 102, No. 10, October 2001, pp. 50)
Pub: Business News Publishing Co.
Ed: Donna Berry. **Description:** Golden West Distributing is manufacturing new, 8-ounce ice cream sundaes covered with a variety of 12 different toppings ranging from Strawberry Mudslides, to kid favorites like Tart N'Tiny's, Sour Towers, and Gummi Bear Mountain. Sales have surpassed the company's expectations.

46839 ■ "Cool Tools" in *Inc.* (November 15, 2000, pp. 145)
Pub: The Goldhirsh Group
Description: If you are marketing to a special niche or need an online forum for new ideas, Web logs could be the answer. A Web log is a Web site, or a section of a Web site, whose overriding characteristic is its ever-changing list of links.

46840 ■ "Copy Cop Fights Back, Takes the Digital Plunge" in *Boston Business Journal* (Vol. 23, No. 30, August 29, 2003, pp. 4)
Pub: American City Business Journals
Ed: Jill Lerner. **Description:** Efforts by Boston, Massachusetts-based Copy Cop to recapture lost market share is examined. Topics include making capital investments in the company, developing new markets, and taking on competition.

46841 ■ "The cost center that paid its way" in *Harvard Business Review* (Vol. 80, No. 4, April 2002, pp. 31)
Pub: Harvard Business School Press
Ed: Julia Kirby. **Description:** A case study where four commentators review the workings of a fictional company's marketing communications department. Advice is offered on how its leader could have avoided the discontent within other departments.

46842 ■ "Council Promotes Banners, Tours to Publicize Super Bowl" in *Crain's Detroit Business* (Vol. 21, October 10, 2005, No. 43, pp. 33)
Pub: Crain Communications Inc. - Detroit
Ed: Jennette Smith. **Description:** Detroit's Tourism Economic Development Councils is recommending the use of banners on businesses and downtown tours as a means to publicize and market Super Bowl XL. The move is expected to help businesses after the game has departed.

46843 ■ "Counting the Eyeballs" in *Business Week* (January 16, 2006, No. 3967, pp. 84-85)
Pub: McGraw-Hill Companies
Ed: David Kiley. **Description:** Ratings for television advertising could enable networks, cable channels, and advertisers of justify campaign budgets, however new technology allows viewers to skip the advertising aired during programming. Statistical data included.

46844 ■ "Coupon mailer raises banner with an Innovative acquisition" in *Crain's Detroit Business* (Vol. 19, No. 9, March 3, 2003, pp. 24)
Pub: Crain Communications Inc., Detroit
Ed: Jennette Smith. **Description:** Marketshare Inc., a direct-mail coupon book marketing firm has purchased Innovative Media LLC, maker of large vinyl banners.

46845 ■ "Coupons Go Cellular" in *Sacramento Bee* (December 16, 2005)
Pub: The Sacramento Bee
Ed: Jim Wasserman. **Description:** Phone coupons are expected to become effective marketing tools for retailers. Users are able to download free software into cellular phones and forward the offers to friends.

46846 ■ "Court Battle Pits Fridge Pack vs. FridgeMaster" in *Atlanta Business Chronicle* (Vol. 26, No. 10, August 15, 2003, pp. 1)
Pub: American City Business Publications, Inc.
Ed: Charles Davidson. **Description:** Lawsuit filed by Riverwood International Corporation against Mead-Westvaco Corporation for patent infringement over the use of the terms FridgeMaster and Fridge Pack in advertising is examined.

46847 ■ "Cracking Jones Soda's Secret Formula" in *Fast Company* (March 2005, No. 92, pp. 74)
Pub: Gruner & Jahr USA Publishing
Ed: Ryan Underwood. **Description:** Peter van Stolk, founder and CEO of Jones Soda Company, believes his secret ingredient to his product's success is the customer.

46848 ■ *The Craft Business Answer Book: Starting, Managing, and Marketing a Home-Based Art, Crafts, Design Business*
Pub: M. Evans and Company, Incorporated
Ed: Barbara Brabec. **Released:** August 2006. **Price:** $16.95. **Description:** Expert advice for starting a home-based art or crafts business is offered.

46849 ■ "Crain's Top Lists Online, On Disk; Book of Lists" in *Crain's New York Business* (Vol. 21, January 31, 2005, No. 5, pp. 30)
Pub: Crain Communications Inc.
Description: Crain's Premium Book of Lists, a marketing tool for any company conducting business in New York, is featured.

46850 ■ "Crazy Drivers: The Clubs About To Shake Up Golf" in *Wall Street Journal* (Vol. 249, January 2007, No. 5, pp. P1-P4)
Pub: Dow Jones & Co. Inc.
Ed: Wall Street Journal **Description:** New top-of-the-line unconventional clubs by makers such as Nike and Calaway have been introduced to the marketplace. Golf traditionalists are concerned the clubs will take the challenge away.

46851 ■ "Creating An Effective Website" in *Black Enterprise* (Vol. 35, January 2005, No. 6, pp. 10)
Pub: Earl G. Graves Publishing Co. Inc.
Description: Black Enterprise offers a program that helps small companies develop Websites to sell products and services, distribute information, and market a small business.

46852 ■ *Creating Customers: An Action Plan for Maximizing Sales, Promotion and Publicity for the Small Business*
Pub: Upstart Publishing Co., Inc.
Ed: David H. Bangs, Jr., and the editors of *Common Sense*. **Released:** 1992. **Price:** $19.95 (paper). **Description:** Provides information to business owners and managers on selling and promoting. Covers inexpensive market research, pricing goods and services, writing a marketing plan, and public relations.

46853 ■ *The Creative Business Guide to Running a Graphic Design Business*
Pub: W.W. Norton & Company, Incorporated
Ed: Cameron S. Foote. **Released:** April 2004. **Price:** $29.95 (US), $45.00 (Canadian). **Description:** Advice for running a graphic design firm, focusing on organizations, marketing, personnel and operations.

46854 ■ "Creative Club Celebrates Centennial" in *Crain's Detroit Business* (Vol. 21, October , 2005, No. 43, pp. 6)
Pub: Crain Communications Inc. - Detroit
Ed: Jennette Smith. **Description:** In celebrating 100 years in advertising, Adcraft will look back on its changes and creative accomplishments over the years.

46855 ■ "Creative Control" in *Washington Business Journal* (Vol. 22, No. 9, July 4, 2003, pp. 16)
Pub: Washington Business Journal
Ed: Chris Silva. **Description:** Management style, marketing and strategic planning of Washington, DC-based Healthcare Ventures LLC is discussed.

46856 ■ "Cross-Training" in *Entrepreneur* (Vol. 31, No. 9, July 2003, pp. 83)
Pub: Entrepreneur Media, Inc.
Ed: Kim T. Gordon. **Description:** Multichannel marketing, using broadcast, direct mail, email and print campaigns, are being used to attract customers and increase sales.

46857 ■ *Crossing the Chasm: Marketing and Selling Disruptive Products to Mainstream Customers*
Pub: HarperInformation
Ed: Geoffrey A. Moore. **Released:** September 2002. **Price:** $17.95. **Description:** A guide for marketing in high-technology industries, focusing on the Internet.

46858 ■ "Crucial triad" in *Daily Business Review* (Vol. 77, No. 198, March 24, 2003, pp. AA4)
Pub: American Lawyer Media LP
Ed: David Geyer, Elizabeth Lampert. **Description:** Ways in which law firm partners can use the triad of business development, marketing and media relations to better serve clients is explained.

46859 ■ "CueCat links printed ads to Web, but skeptics are wary" in *The New York Times* (September 28, 2000, pp. D8)
Pub: The New York Times Company
Ed: Katie Hafner. **Description:** A new device called CueCat, made by Digital Convergance and distributed for free at Radio Shack, makes it possible for computer users to scan printed ad barcodes which will direct them to relevant Web sites. Critics are worried that the data will be used in turn by e-tailers to gather information on Web shoppers using the devices in violation of the privacy rights.

46860 ■ "Cultural Access Moves into Medical Research" in *Hispanic Business* (Vol. 23, No. 5, May 2001, pp. 6)
Pub: Hispanic Business
Description: Cultural Access Group, a multicultural marketing firm, hired Raul Lopez to manage its new Miami office.

46861 ■ "Culture Club: Many E-Tailers are Lining Up to Target the Growing Hispanic Market" in *Entrepreneur* (Vol. 31, No. 10, October 2003)
Pub: Entrepreneur Media, Inc.
Ed: Melissa Campanelli. **Description:** According to comScore Networks, nearly 12.5 million Hispanics are online, prompting online retailers to market to Hispanic consumers.

46862 ■ "Curves tries straight talk" in *Brandweek* (Vol. 43, No. 46, December 16, 2002, pp. 5)
Pub: VNU Business Media
Ed: Mindy Charski. **Description:** Curves International fitness centers has launched a $15-18 million national advertising campaign targeting women ages 34-54.

46863 ■ "The Customer Has Escaped" in *Harvard Business Review* (Vol. 81, No. 11, November 2003, pp. 96)
Pub: Harvard Business School Press
Ed: Paul F. Nunes, Frank V. Cespedes. **Description:** Consumer behavior and the economic benefits of the wise use of available distribution channels are discussed.

46864 ■ "Customer Loyalty" in *Small Business Opportunities* (Vol. 16, No. 3, May 2004, pp. 18, 20)
Pub: Harris Publications, Inc.
Ed: Jill Griffin. **Description:** Twelve laws of loyalty in order to develop non-customers into loyal advocates are explained.

46865 ■ "Customers as Innovators" in *Harvard Business Review* (Vol. 80, No. 4, April 2002, pp. 74)
Pub: Harvard Business School Press
Ed: Eric Stefan, von Hippel Thomke. **Description:** A radically new approach to research and development is described. Companies are now encouraging customers to design and develop their own products and advice is given on how this can be achieved.

46866 ■ "Cutting the Corporate Purse Strings" in *Ingram's* (Vol. 27, No. 7, July 2001, pp. 20)
Pub: Show Me Publishing, Inc.
Description: Techniques and management theory for women small business owners is outlined. Topics include clarifying objectives, refining business ideas, research ideas, budgeting, concept testing, developing a business plan, and securing financing.

46867 ■ "Cybersearch Specialist" in *Crain's New York Business* (Vol. 23, January 29, 2007, No. 5 ,pp. F16)
Pub: Crain Communications, Inc.
Ed: Amanda Fung. **Description:** Profile of Matthew Greitzer, director of search engine marketing for Avenue A/Razorfish. The firm has garnered more than twenty search marketing campaigns from clients such as Schering-Plough and Verizon and is the largest buyer of search advertising.

46868 ■ "The Daily Paper of Tomorrow" in *Business Week* (January 9, 2006, No. 3966, pp. 20)
Pub: McGraw-Hill Companies
Ed: Jon Fine. **Description:** A six-point list of things for the future of daily newspapers include using Google to advertise, offer a news-digest daily, put more information online, increase local coverage, redesign products for more appeal, and build communities and businesses around community-created content.

46869 ■ "Dare to Compare." in *Entrepreneur* (Vol. 33, January 2005, No. 1, pp. 43)
Pub: Entrepreneur Media Inc.
Ed: Melissa Campanelli. **Description:** Online merchants wishing to grow their business might consider placing products on comparison shopping Websites. These sites display product information in a simple format and lets buyers compare and choose the best product from a list of different retailers.

46870 ■ "Database Dollars" in *Small Business Opportunities* (Vol. 12, No. 5, September 2000, pp. 44)
Pub: Harris Publications, Inc.
Ed: Carla Vincent. **Description:** A customer database can help find new customers, increase sales, and build clientele. Ways to develop a database are outlined.

46871 ■ *Database Marketing: The Ultimate Marketing Tool*
Pub: The McGraw-Hill Companies
Ed: Edward L. Nash. **Released:** 1995. **Price:** $444.95. **Description:** Guide to developing and implementing database marketing strategies in all aspects of business.

46872 ■ "Dawson on Board at Melville-based Fala Direct Marketing" in *Long Island Business News* (March 12, 2004)
Pub: Dolan Media Newswires
Ed: Ryan McCormick. **Description:** Profile of Terrence Dawson, newly appointed COO of Fala Direct Marketing; Dawson attributes his success to the philosophy of knowing your role in the company in which you are working.

46873 ■ "Deals on Wheels" in *Kiplinger's Personal Finance Magazine* (Vol. 54, No. 12, December 2000, pp. 30)
Pub: The Kiplinger Washington Editors, Inc.
Ed: Erin Burt. **Description:** To drive home sales pitches, enterprising advertisers will pay to turn cars into billboards.

46874 ■ "Death to Cool" in *Inc.* **(July 1, 2003)**
Pub: Gruner & Jahr USA Publishing
Description: Profile of iRobot, a boutique high-tech firm reinvented itself as an appliance company and now sells new products on the Home Shopping Network.

46875 ■ "Declaring War On Wal-Mart" in *Business Week* **(February 7, 2005, No. 3919, pp. 31)**
Pub: McGraw-Hill Companies
Ed: Aaron Bernstein. **Description:** Wal-Mart has launched an ad campaign in January with the message: Wal-Mart is working for everyone. The retailer is fighting back against allegations of sex discrimination, poverty-level wages, and non-union workforce.

46876 ■ "Delicate Deliveries" in *Birmingham Business Journal* **(Vol. 20, No. 33, August 15, 2003, pp. 13)**
Pub: American City Business Journals, Inc.
Ed: Leslie Zganjar. **Description:** Profile of Birmingham, Alabama florist, Masterpiece Flowers; topics cover management of a small business, marketing and advertising, and average annual sales.

46877 ■ "Dell to offer hosting of small business Web sites" in *Wall Street Journal* **(February 22, 2000, pp. B23)**
Pub: Dow Jones & Co., Inc.
Ed: Gary McWilliams. **Description:** As part of its E-Works initiative, Dell has launched a Web site hosting service for small business called Dellhost.com. The company will resell services of some of the ISPs that buy its servers. The site hosting market is expected to grow from $2 billion in 1999 to $17 billion 2003. Interliant Inc. will provide the Internet connection for Dell customers for $18 to $300 a month.

46878 ■ "Dental, vision plan vendors use the Web to administer, communicate, market benefits" in *Employee Benefit Plan Review* **(Vol. 55, No. 6)**
Pub: Charles D. Spencer & Associates, Inc.
Ed: Robert Pruter. **Description:** Dental and vision insurance plan providers are redesigning their Web sites to offer better services to employers and to better market themselves to small businesses.

46879 ■ "Designer is Walking Ad for TIBI Line" in *Charlotte Observer* **(February 5, 2007)**
Pub: Knight-Ridder/Tribune Business News
Ed: Crystal Dempsey. **Description:** Profile of Amy Smilovic, mother of two children, and clothing designer. Smilovic wears what she designs, making her a great marketing tool for her clothing line TIBI.

46880 ■ "Designing web sites that work" in *Women in Business* **(Vol. 53, No. 3, May-June, 2001, pp. 26)**
Pub: The ABWA Co. Inc.
Ed: Mary-Lane Kamberg. **Description:** A Web site is important for many businesses and individuals today, but achieving an effective site is not always simple. Tips are provided on ways to develop a professional-looking, user-friendly site.

46881 ■ "Desperately Seeking Sales Stars" in *Sales & Marketing Management* **(Vol. 158, October 2006, No. 10, pp. 44)**
Pub: VNU Business Media
Ed: Julia Chang. **Description:** Competition to hire sales personnel is growing; companies strategic plans for recruiting successful sales teams are presented.

46882 ■ "Detergent Exhibit Cleanses Female Stereotypes" in *Official Board Markets* **(Vol. 77, No. 35, September 1, 2001, pp. 14)**
Pub: Advanstar Communications, Inc.
Description: An exhibition of washing detergent cartons, titled 'Dirty Washing', spanning 170 years, was assembled by London's Design Museum to illustrate a point about a woman's place in the home.

46883 ■ "Detroit Free Press Macomb Small Business Column" in *Detroit Free Press* **(June 30, 2005)**
Pub: Knight-Ridder/Tribune Business News
Ed: Carol Cain. **Description:** Retailers along Mack Avenue in Grosse Pointe Woods are offering employees of all St. John Health System discounts in order to increase customer activity.

46884 ■ "Detroit Free Press Oakland Small Business Column" in *Detroit Free Press* **(May 26, 2005)**
Pub: Knight-Ridder/Tribune Business News
Ed: Carol Cain. **Description:** Stephen Wiesman worked as a firefighter until being injured in 2002. Wiesman plans to introduce a new product he developed that will make stoves safer to use. Also featured: David Moncur's marketing, creative and technology consulting company.

46885 ■ "Developing a brand" in *Black Enterprise* **(Vol. 32, No. 10, May 2002, pp. 47)**
Pub: Earl Graves Publishing Co.
Ed: Fabian Robinson, Rebecca Rohan. **Description:** A brand is the relationship between product and consumer. Advice is given to market a brand online and offline and ways to protect that brand online.

46886 ■ *Developing, Implementing, & Managing an Effective Marketing Plan*
Pub: N T C Comtemporary Publishing Co.
Released: 1995. **Price:** $29.95 (paper). **Description:** Guide to developing a marketing plan. Includes case studies, worksheets, and graphs.

46887 ■ "Digging Deeper" in *Sales and Marketing.com* **(Vol. 147, No. 2, February 2004, pp. 8)**
Pub: VNU eMedia, Inc.
Ed: Betsy Cummings. **Description:** In a slowing economy, sales staff should try to sell more to existing customers. In order to achieve this goal, sales people could focus on developing a network of contacts in positions both above and below the salesperson's initial connection.

46888 ■ "The Digital Disruptors" in *Red Herring* **(No. 102, August 15, 2001, pp. 58-59)**
Pub: Herring Communications
Ed: Jon Maples. **Description:** Profile of the ten companies, and the sector they represent, that stand to upend the entertainment markets, including Anonymous Content, advertising; News Corporation, television; Clear Channel, radio; Realnetworks, streaming media; Microsoft, gaming; Adobe Systems, publishing; NTT Docomo, wireless; Nothing Real, film; Loudeye, digital-rights management; and Audiogalaxy, music.

46889 ■ "The Dilemma of CNET's Success; It Gets Top Dollar For Online Ads, Most Tech-Oriented" in *Business Week Online* **(February 9, 2005)**
Pub: McGraw-Hill Companies
Ed: Sarah Lacy. **Description:** Technology-site ad rates rose 46 percent in 2004, but are mainstream marketers willing to pay for online ads? Statistical data included.

46890 ■ "Direct Effect: Make the Most of Your Direct-Mail Campaign" in *Entrepreneur* **(Vol. 32, November 2004, No. 11, pp. 91)**
Pub: Entrepreneur Media Inc.
Ed: Nancy Michaels. **Description:** Timing of a direct-mail advertising campaign is critical to its effectiveness.

46891 ■ "Direct Hit: Can Direct Marketing Survive a Consumer Backlash?" in *Entrepreneur* **(Vol. 31, No. 9, September 2003, pp. 23)**
Pub: Entrepreneur Media, Inc.
Ed: Chris Penttila. **Description:** Congress, the states and large technology companies are taking action against telemarketing, junk mail and spam.

46892 ■ *Direct Mail Magic*
Pub: Crisp Publications, Inc.
Ed: Charles Mallory. **Price:** $9.95.

46893 ■ "The direct marketing industry hopes to get Internet retailers to see things in an old light"in *The New York Times* **(Jul. 12,2000, pp.C6)**
Pub: The New York Times Company
Ed: Bernard Stamler. **Description:** Until recently, electronic commerce conducted their ad and marketing campaigns as if they were separate from the vagaries of those who learned to choose media carefully and control the cost of campaigns. Thus, online sellers spent lavishly, ignoring less expensive and often more effective direct marketing. Electronic retailers relied on branding alone, until the Internet boom went bust. Wall Street was more interested in profits than brand recognition. Now, many e-tailers are embracing direct marketing with a passion inspired by the potential of bankruptcy.

46894 ■ *Direct Marketing: Strategy, Planning, Execution*
Pub: The McGraw-Hill Companies
Ed: Edward L. Nash. **Released:** Third edition, 1995. **Price:** $44.95. **Description:** Provides advice for marketing, including the use of infomercials, the Internet, and other databases.

46895 ■ *Direct Marketing Survival Guide for the Small Business Owner on a Budget*
Pub: U.S. Press and Graphics
Ed: Kevin Boerup. **Released:** January 2005. **Price:** $5.00. **Description:** Advice to direct market products and services. Coupons and discount offers are included in the book.

46896 ■ "Disintegrated marketing" in *Harvard Business Review* **(Vol. 81, No. 3, March 2003, pp. 18)**
Pub: Harvard Business School Press
Ed: Daniel Klein. **Description:** A senior vice president at Foote, Cone and Belding, discusses marketing campaigns and argues against dividing a campaign among external agencies and internal marketing groups operating independently and is in favor of a "systems engineered" campaign.

46897 ■ "Disney Collaboration" in *San Fernando Valley Business Journal* **(Vol. 11, December 2006, No. 25, pp. 23)**
Pub: San Fernando Valley Business Journal Associates
Ed: Barbara Sheppard. **Description:** The Walt Disney Co. will develop footwear exclusively for sale at Payless ShoeSource stores. The first products will be in stores in spring 2007.

46898 ■ "Disruptive change: When trying harder is part of the problem" in *Harvard Business Review* **(Vol. 80, No. 5, May 2002, pp. 94)**
Pub: Harvard Business School Press
Ed: Joseph L. Clark, Bower Gilbert. **Description:** How executives react to disruptions in their markets, such as to new technology, should be regarded as both a threat and an opportunity.

46899 ■ "A Diversity Plan Turns 100" in *Hispanic Business* **(September 2003, pp. 30, 32)**
Pub: Hispanic Business
Ed: Gina Binole. **Description:** Ford Motor Company has prospered for 100 years by marketing to the Hispanic market. James Padilla, president of Ford's North American production, discusses the fact that Ford Motor Company understands the power of the Hispanic consumer and the importance of the Hispanic business owner.

46900 ■ "Do it already!" in *Entrepreneur* **(Vol. 30, No. 1, January 2002, pp. 43)**
Pub: Entrepreneur Media Inc.
Ed: Amanda C. Kooser. **Description:** iBizResources. com encourages brick-and-mortar businesses to get online and use the new technologies available to small businesses. The site offers technical services, e-commerce tools, marketing, promotion and business products and services.

46901 ■ *Do-It-Yourself Advertising*
Pub: AMACOM
Ed: David F. Ramacitti. **Released:** 1992. **Price:** $18.95 (paper); ($17.05 for AMA members). **Description:** Companion to *Do-It-Yourself Publicity*. Shows small businesses, clubs, and nonprofit organizations how to compete for customers. Covers defining advertising goals, identifying the right audience, choosing where to advertise, producing both effective and creative advertising, and developing a plan. Includes illustrations, mini-cases, a glossary of terms, lists of suggested reading and organizations to contact, and sample plans and budgets.

46902 ■ *Do-It-Yourself Advertising: How to Produce Great Ads, Brochures, Catalogs, Direct Mail, and Much More*
Pub: John Wiley & Sons, Inc.
Ed: Fred E. Hahn. **Released:** 1993. **Price:** $52.50; $45.00 (paper). **Description:** Guide to creating or supervising advertising and promotion campaigns, covering magazine and newspaper advertising, flyers, brochures, direct mail, telemarketing, and conventions and tradeshows. Includes information on design, format, and production. Contains checklists.

46903 ■ *Do-It-Yourself Publicity*
Pub: AMACOM
Ed: David F. Ramacitti. **Released:** 1991. **Price:** $17.95 (paper); ($16.15 for AMA members). **Description:** Provides information on public relations, including when and how to write a press release, how to organize a press conference, how to develop a media list, and how to use trade and local publications.

46904 ■ "Do You Work for Free?" in *My Business* (February/March 2004, pp. 50)
Pub: My Business Magazine
Ed: Susan Palmquist. **Description:** When negotiating with potential clients, it is important to let a client have only a sampling of your expertise and to remain professional.

46905 ■ "Doctored Image" in *Entrepreneur* (Vol. 30, No. 3, March 2002, pp. 25)
Pub: Entrepreneur Media Inc.
Ed: Elizabeth J. Goodgold. **Description:** Often, tuning up a brand on a product, is just what the doctor ordered to increase sales.

46906 ■ "Does Your Sales Management Stink?" in *Sales & Marketing Management* (Vol. 159, January-February 2007, No. 1, pp. 12)
Pub: VNU Business Media
Description: Tips for build and assess a successful sales team are explored.

46907 ■ "Don Coleman" in *Crain's Detroit Business* (Vol. 19, No. 1, January 6, 2003, pp. 11)
Pub: Crain Communications Inc., Detroit
Ed: Jennette Smith. **Description:** Profile of Don Coleman, chairman and CEO of the GlobalHue advertising agency, a one-stop shop for all types of multicultural advertising.

46908 ■ "Done Deal: How One Sales Pro Closed a Big Customer" in *Sales & Marketing Management* (Vol. 158, October 2006, No. 10, pp. 15)
Pub: VNU Business Media
Ed: Betsy Cummings. **Description:** Sam Braunstein convinced area stores that athletic sports-support equipment is a necessary product to be sold in sporting goods stores.

46909 ■ "Done Deal: How One Sales Pro Closed a Big Customer" in *Sales and Marketing.com* (Vol. 156, No. 3, March 2004, pp. 9)
Pub: VNU eMedia, Inc.
Description: Tanya Spaulding, principal with Shea Inc., a marketing design firm in Minnesota, recalls a situation where she had to help a client in a highly desirable retail space to either rebrand the business, create a new business, or to sell the property.

46910 ■ "Don't Just Listen Connect" in *Fast Company* (August 2001, pp. 140)
Pub: Fast Company
Ed: Paul C. Judge. **Description:** An interview with John I. Sviokla, vice chairman and leader of the digital-strategy practice at DiamondCluster International Inc., a consulting firm in Chicago. Sviokla makes a series of connections when interacting with customers and compares technology today to where it must be in the future.

46911 ■ "Dot-com Seeks Firm Footing" in *Boston Business Journal* (Vol. 22, No. 11, April 19, 2002, pp. 11)
Pub: MCP, Inc.
Ed: Scott Savitz. **Description:** Shoebuy.com Inc. has 10,000 products with 220 brands and increasing numbers of customers. By sticking to a disciplined marketing style, this dot.com online retailer has been able to grow steadily.

46912 ■ "Dot your eyes" in *Entrepreneur* (Vol. 30, No. 2, February 2002, pp. 25)
Pub: Entrepreneur Media Inc.
Ed: Elizabeth J. Goodgold. **Description:** Innovated shuttle bus painting is helping off-airport parking companies increase business.

46913 ■ "Double header" in *WorkingWoman* (Vol. 25, No. 5, May 2000, pp. 38)
Pub: Lang Communications Inc.
Ed: Eilene Zimmerman. **Description:** The Female Athlete company has 70 percent of its sales generated by catlogs and 30 percent from Web sites sales. Issues concerning marketing strategies to direct customers away from traditional catalog buying to purchasing on-line are presented.

46914 ■ "Double Play: Could Sending a Paper Catalog to Customers Boost Your E-Commerce Business?" in *Entrepreneur* (Vol. 32, September 2004)
Pub: Entrepreneur Media Inc.
Ed: Melissa Campanelli. **Description:** Many e-tailers are using catalogs to increase Internet sales. Statistical data included.

46915 ■ "Downturn brings opportunities along with risks" in *Atlanta Business Chronicle* (Vol. 23, No. 49, May 11, 2001, pp. 3B)
Pub: American City Business Journals Inc.
Ed: Alf Nucifora. **Description:** If a recession does occur, small businesses should be aware of the opportunities, as well as the risks that will come along. Cutting marketing budgets can hurt a firm during and for some years after a recession, according to several studies. Ways to maintain effective marketing with minimal outlays are discussed.

46916 ■ "Doyenne of Hip Proffers Hot Tips" in *Crain's New York Business* (Vol. 23, January 29, 2007, No. 5, pp. F9)
Pub: Crain Communications, Inc.
Ed: Elisabeth Butler. **Description:** Profile of Dany Levy and her trendy business, an e-newsletter, Daily Candy. Advertisers are flocking to this Internet publication which expects to generate revenues of $25 million this year.

46917 ■ "Driving a Hard Bargain" in *Business Week* (January 16, 2006, No. 3967, pp. 66)
Pub: McGraw-Hill Companies
Description: Profiles of five cars that manufacturers marketed incorrectly on either the brand or the product. These five vehicles offer bargains based on how high customers rated them.

46918 ■ "Duck Season" in *Entrepreneur* (Vol. 33, January 2005, No. 1, pp. 67)
Pub: Entrepreneur Media Inc.
Ed: Jerry Fisher. **Description:** The AFLAC duck is used to demonstrate the power of branding through advertising.

46919 ■ *Duct Tape Marketing: The World's Most Practical Small Business Marketing Guide*
Pub: Nelson Business
Ed: John Jantsch. **Released:** January 2007. **Price:** $24.99. **Description:** Tools and tactics to successfully build a marketing plan for any small business.

46920 ■ "E-Biz Buzz" in *E-business Advisor* (Vol. 18, No. 8, August 2000, pp. 58)
Pub: Advisor Media, Inc.
Ed: Buzz Hunter. **Description:** Web users are becoming less receptive to traditional forms of marketing. E-commerce providers will find a lucrative market in small businesses by offering solid support, quick answers to questions, and easy access to other services and products.

46921 ■ "E-Commerce Market Heats Up" in *Hispanic Business* (October 2003, pp. 98, 100)
Pub: Hispanic Business
Ed: Andrea Siedsma. **Description:** New studies indicate Hispanics are ready to buy online if merchants carry the right products, a strong brand, and financial security. A listing of the top sites for Hispanic online shoppers is included. Statistical data included.

46922 ■ "E-mail Marketer Looks for More Clout" in *Atlanta Business Chronicle* (Vol. 25, December 13, 2002, No. 27, pp. A3)
Pub: American City Business Publications, Inc.
Ed: Mary Jane Credeur. **Description:** Silverpop Systems Inc. has acquired Epigraphx LLC, Redwood, California. The acquisition took place in December 2002, as part of Silverpop's initiative to grow in the e-mail marketing industry. The deal will increase staff to 55 and will triple Silverpop's revenues, which remain undisclosed. The deal also expands Silverpop's client roster and increased profits are discussed by Silverpop CEO, Bill Nussey.

46923 ■ "E-Mail Marketing" in *Small Business Opportunities* (Vol. 13, No. 5, September 2001, pp. 100, 102)
Pub: Harris Publications, Inc.
Ed: Lin Grensing-Pophal. **Description:** The pros and cons to using e-mail as part of a marketing program are outlined. Spam, permission marketing, Internet services, are discussed. A list of online resources is included.

46924 ■ "E-retailers turn to the printed page to put their wares before consumers" in *The New York Times* (July 10, 2000, pp. C12)
Pub: The New York Times Company
Ed: Bob Tedeschi. **Description:** Online retailers have started using or developing programs that will mail catalogs to consumers.

46925 ■ "East End PR Firm Helps Give Webshots One More Shot" in *Long Island Business News* (February 27, 2004)
Pub: Dolan Media Newswires
Ed: Claude Solnik. **Description:** Profile of Webshots, a company providing online digital photo services. The firm hired Vineberg Communications to provide market research and to handle media and analyst relations.

46926 ■ "Eclipse gum: Paul Chibe" in *Advertising Age* (Vol. 72, October 8, 2001, pp. S10)
Pub: Crain Communications, Inc.
Ed: Faye Brookman. **Description:** Profile of Paul Chibe, senior marketing manager for Wm. Wrigley Jr. Co., describes his successful marketing campaign for Eclipse chewing gum.

46927 ■ "Elan Frozen Yogurt returns to New York" in *Ice Cream Reporter* (Vol. 14, No. 2, January 20, 2001, pp. 2)
Pub: Howard Waxman
Description: Boston-based ice cream and frozen yogurt maker, Brigham's, has announced a new look, a new flavor, and new distribution for its Elan All Natural Frozen Yogurt line, and will now be available in northern New Jersey and Long Island at Stop & Shop and King's Supermarkets.

46928 ■ *Email Marketing by the Numbers: How to Use the World's Greatest Marketing Tool to Take Any Organization to the Next Level*
Pub: John Wiley and Sons Inc.
Ed: Chris Baggott. Released: April 2007. Price: $29.99 (CND). Description: Tips for using email to market small business products and services are provided.

46929 ■ **"Engineering the Engineer" in** *Sales & Marketing Management* **(Vol. 157, January 2005, No. 1, pp. 11)**
Pub: VNU Business Media
Description: Sales presentations by an engineer to a prospective customer can help seal the deal. Three steps to accomplish this strategy are presented.

46930 ■ **"Entrepreneur Column" in** *Entrepreneur* **(August 18, 2005)**
Pub: Entrepreneur Media Inc.
Ed: Gail F. Goodman. Description: Electronic newsletters can be a great marketing tool if done properly. Email marketing solutions should include data that allows a firm to analyze and optimize any e-newsletter campaign.

46931 ■ **"Entrepreneur Column" in** *Entrepreneur.com* **(September 15, 2005)**
Pub: Entrepreneur Media Inc.
Ed: Kim Gordon. Description: In order to develop a marketing campaign to develop referrals for a small business, you must determine whether you are marketing to the influencers or the influential. Steps for winning referrals from both groups are outlined.

46932 ■ **"EPrize Touts Small Business" in** *Detroit Free Press* **(January 17, 2007)**
Pub: Knight-Ridder/Tribune Business News
Ed: Jewel Gopwani. Description: ePrize is targeting small businesses to advertise on its new Website, www.caffeinenow.com. The company designs promotions for larger companies but is offering space for small businesses to market their businesses by placing sweepstakes and rewards programs on the site.

46933 ■ **"Escondido: Sometimes, the Best Advice is Free" in** *San Diego Business Journal* **(Vol. 28, January 8, 2007, No. 2, pp. 27)**
Pub: San Diego Business Journal Associates
Ed: Jessica Long. Description: Thursdays with Joe is a new program that offers free advice to small business owners in the Escondido, California area. Topics include marketing tips and financial planning advice.

46934 ■ *Essentials of Entrepreneurship and Small Business Management*
Pub: Prentice Hall PTR
Ed: Thomas W. Zimmerer; Norman M. Scarborough; Doug Wilson. Released: February 2007. Price: $106.67. Description: New venture creation and the knowledge required to start a new business are shared. The challenges of entrepreneurship, business plans, marketing, e-commerce, and financial considerations are explored.

46935 ■ **"Everything I know about business I learned from Monopoly" in** *Harvard Business Review* **(Vol. 80, No. 3, March 2002, pp. 51)**
Pub: Harvard Business School Press
Ed: Phil Orbanes. Description: Profile of Phil Orbanes, one of the world's prominent game designers and an executive at Winning Moves Games. Orbanes reflects on competition and winning.

46936 ■ **"Ex-BBDO Exec Forms New Agency" in** *Crain's Detroit Business* **(Vol. 21, January 24, 2005, No. 4, pp. 18)**
Pub: Crain Communications Inc. - Detroit
Ed: Jean Halliday. Description: Profile of Mike Vogel, former CEO of Omnicom Group's BBDO Detroit has left that firm in order to form RTV Communications Group. Vogel's new firm will consist of RTV Consulting, Consolidated Purchasing Partners and Vineyard Group, all located in Auburn Hills, Michigan. RTV offers marketing, strategy, consulting, creative, public relations, advertising, media, events and printing services.

46937 ■ **"The Excitable Client" in** *Adweek* **(Vol. 46, February 14, 2005, No. 7, pp. 20)**
Pub: VNU Business Media
Ed: Paul Venables. Description: Art of bringing passion and energy to an advertising campaign is featured.

46938 ■ **"Exclusive Survey Reveals Diversity Trends" in** *Hispanic Business* **(January/February 2003, pp. 34-35, 36, 38, 40-42)**
Pub: Hispanic Business
Description: According to the first Hispanic Business Corporate Diversity Survey, which focuses on public corporations among the top 60 advertisers in the Hispanic market, companies with Hispanic executives fare better in procurement and recruitment.

46939 ■ **"Exec has Firm Grip on Software Sales" in** *Crain's New York Business* **(Vol. 23, January 29, 2007, No. 5, pp. F13)**
Pub: Crain Communications, Inc.
Ed: Amanda Fung. Description: Profile of Amanda Fung and her position as business and marketing officer for Microsoft Corp's New York/New Jersey district. Her precision helped bring in revenues of more than $492 million for her region in 2006 and her team expects this year's revenues to exceed $600 million.

46940 ■ *Exhibiting at Tradeshows*
Pub: Crisp Publications, Inc.
Ed: Susan A. Friedmann. Released: 1992. Price: $10.95.

46941 ■ **"Express Personnel Exec Named American Staffing Association Committee Chair" in** *Journal Record* **(June 25, 2003)**
Pub: Dolan Media Company
Description: Profile of Linda C. Haneborg, newly named committee chair for American Staffing Association. Haneborg also serves on the U.S. Chamber of Commerce Labor Relations Board.

46942 ■ **"The Extra Mile: Customer Service That's a Step Beyond" in** *Sales & Marketing Management* **(Vol. 158, October 2006, No. 10, pp. 14)**
Pub: VNU Business Media
Description: An independent knife distributor shares the story of gifting a hunting knife to a client, resulting in increased orders.

46943 ■ **"Face-Off: Survival of the Fittest" in** *Folio: the Magazine for Magazine Management* **(Vol. 32, No. 1, January 1, 2003)**
Pub: Folio: the Magazine for Magazine Management
Description: The new trend in advertising for women is to use a softer, mind-body-and-soul approach, shifting from the hard-body mentality of previous years. Profiles of four magazines are presented, including Shape, Fitness, Health, and Self. Statistical data included.

46944 ■ **"A Family Affair-In Advertising" in** *Business Week* **(No. 3762, December 17, 2001, pp. 10)**
Pub: McGraw-Hill Inc.
Description: More companies are using family settings to promote products.

46945 ■ *Fashion & Print Directory*
Pub: Peter Glenn Publications
Ed: Gregory James, Editor. Released: Annual, November; latest edition 47 edition. Price: $39.95, individuals. Covers: advertising agencies, PR firms, marketing companies, 1000 client brand companies and related services in the U.S. and Canada. Includes photographers, marketing agency, suppliers, sources of props and rentals, fashion houses, beauty services, locations. Entries Include: Company name, address, phone; paid listingsnumbering 5000 include description of products or services, key personnel. Arrangement: Classified by line of business.

46946 ■ **"Fashion Sense Dictates Where Women Shop" in** *Marketing to Women* **(Vol. 19, October 2006, No. 10, pp. 7)**
Pub: EPM Communications, Inc.

Description: According to BIGresearch, while women overall choose value-priced retailers, fashionistas would rather shop at specialty or department stores.

46947 ■ **"Fast times at Pepsi High" in** *WorkingWoman* **(Vol. 25, No. 2, February 2000, pp. 20)**
Pub: Lang Communications Inc.
Ed: Bernice Kanner. Description: Commercials for Channel One, Domino's Pizza, Taco Bell and other enterprises are seen by millions of students in thousands of schools ten years since the ad program began.

46948 ■ **"Fast Talk" in** *Fast Company* **(September 2001, pp. 80)**
Pub: Fast Company
Description: The state of the customer economy is addressed, focusing on customer-relationship management.

46949 ■ *Fast Track Marketing: Implementing Innovative Tactics in the Global Marketplace*
Pub: Van Nostrand Reinhold Co., Inc.
Ed: John Hathaway-Bates. Released: 1993. Price: $24.95. Description: Provides information on implementing an effective marketing plan, from conceptualization through analysis.

46950 ■ **"The Father of Spam: Half of All E-Mail Sent Today is Spam" in** *Entrepreneur* **(Vol. 31, No. 10, October 2003)**
Pub: Entrepreneur Media, Inc.
Ed: Geoff Williams. Description: Internet Spam costs companies $8 billion to $10 billion annually in the form of lost productivity as entrepreneurs and employees rid email boxes of unwanted email.

46951 ■ **"Fax Attack: This Entrepreneur's Fighting Mad About Junk Faxes" in** *Entrepreneur* **(Vol. 32, No. 1, January 2004, pp. 34)**
Pub: Entrepreneur Media, Inc.
Ed: Geoff Williams. Description: Steve Kirsch, owner of a software company in San Jose, California, has filed a $2.2 trillion class-action lawsuit against Fax.com, in the hopes of ending junk fax mail.

46952 ■ **"Fax Regs Rethought" in** *Inc.* **(December 1, 2004)**
Pub: Inc. Magazine
Ed: Darren Dahl. Description: Federal regulations regarding mass faxes could hurt small businesses. The new law would allow businesses to fax any customer they have done businesses with in the last seven years.

46953 ■ **"FC Shortlist" in** *Fast Company* **(October 2001, pp. 46)**
Pub: Fast Company
Description: Review of the book "Gonzo Marketing: Winning Through Worst Practices" by Christopher Locke. The author describes micro-audiences and micro-markets as the new units of growth and competitive advantage. The book by Barbara Waugh, "The Soul in the Computer: The Story of a Corporate Revolutionary" is also reviewed. Ms. Waugh is the world-wide change manager at Hewlett-Packard and co-founder of HP's World e-Inclusion unit.

46954 ■ **"Feast or Famine" in** *Black Enterprise* **(Vol. 35, November 2004, No. 4, pp. 60)**
Pub: Earl G. Graves Publishing Co. Inc.
Ed: Alan Hughes. Description: Owner of a T-shirt business that uses heat transfers to create fashions is seeking marketing advice to balance workforce and cash flow with orders.

46955 ■ **"Feeding Frenzy" in** *Entrepreneur.com* **(Vol. 34, February 2006, No. 2, pp. 77)**
Pub: Entrepreneur Media Inc.
Ed: Catherine Seda. Description: Creative marketers are using RSS feed in order to send successful marketing email. RSS is 100 percent opt-in. Users subscribe to a reader such as Bloglines, Newsgator, or Pluck and choose the feeds they wish to receive, no spam allowed. The number of RSS users is growing quickly making it an opportunity to market products and services for small companies.

46956 ■ "The Fiberglass Menagerie" in *Inc.* (February 1, 2002)
Pub: Inc. Magazine
Ed: Ed Engel. **Description:** Profile of FAST Corporation, the manufacturer of fiberglass roadside figures used for business advertising.

46957 ■ "Find Your Niche-and Stick with It" in *Business Week Online* (March 22, 2002)
Pub: McGraw-Hill, Inc.
Description: An interview with Leslie Godwin, a career and life-transition coach located in Calabas, California, explains how narrowing focus can help small businesses to attract good customers and while better-serving that customer base.

46958 ■ "Finding a Niche Within a Niche" in *Black Enterprise* (Vol. 36, February 2006, No. 7, pp. 93)
Pub: Earl G. Graves Publishing Co. Inc.
Ed: Layton Turner. **Description:** Choosing a niche is a good strategy for businesses with fewer resources than larger competitors.

46959 ■ "Finding the Right Keyword" in *Inc.* (October 1, 2003)
Pub: Gruner & Jahr USA Publishing
Ed: Ellen Neuborne. **Description:** Marketing via search engines like Yahoo and Google is difficult and costly, but it is still a good way to market products and services if done wisely.

46960 ■ "Finding-Site search and geographic maps are an easy way to make a site more usable and useful to your visitors" in *PC Magazine* (Feb.01)
Pub: Ziff-Davis Publishing Company
Ed: Troy Dreier. **Description:** Information about site search tools and geographic maps to make a Web site more useful are examined.

46961 ■ "Finding your innovation sweet spot" in *Harvard Business Review* (Vol. 81, No. 3, March 2003, pp. 120)
Pub: Harvard Business School Press
Ed: Jacob Goldenberg, Roni Horowitz, Amnon Levav, David Mazursky. **Description:** Five innovative patterns that can be used for product innovation are presented. These patterns manipulate existing components of a product to come up with something ingenious and viable. The patterns include multiplication, subtraction, division, task unification, and attribute dependency.

46962 ■ "Firms Use Students to Study Buying Habits" in *Sacramento Bee* (November 7, 2005)
Pub: The Sacramento Bee
Ed: Rachel Osterman. **Description:** Companies and organizations are using college students for market research. EdVenture Partners works with professors from 400 U.S. colleges by creating class projects where students market to their peers, research the youth marketplace, or brainstorm marketing strategies on a client's behalf.

46963 ■ "First Impressions" in *Black Enterprise* (Vol. 36, December 2005, No. 5, pp. 62)
Pub: Earl G. Graves Publishing Co. Inc.
Description: Sonya Lowerey, author of The Secret Language of Business Cards, discusses the eight common business card mistakes made by small companies.

46964 ■ "First Impressions" in *Entrepreneur* (Vol. 33, March 2005, No. 3, pp. 90)
Pub: Entrepreneur Media Inc.
Ed: Jerry Fisher. **Description:** John Caples, author of the book, Tested Advertising Methods, offers tips for making a good first impression when advertising a product or service.

46965 ■ "First Person" in *Entrepreneur* (Vol. 28, No. 3, March 2000, pp. 146)
Pub: Entrepreneur Media Inc.
Ed: Barry Farber. **Description:** If you want to know what customers want, all you need to do is ask them.

46966 ■ "First Women's Sports Talk Show Launches" in *Marketing to Women* (Vol. 19, October 2006, No. 10, pp. 5)
Pub: EPM Communications, Inc.
Description: The Philadelphia area launches the first all-female sports talk radio show, Fantoo Girls. Greater Media's Talk 950 WPEN radio station brings the show to its area based on the popular Podcast, "Fantoo Girls: Where the Girls Talk Sports," which won "Best Sports Podcast" in 2006.

46967 ■ "Fishing for trouble" in *Entrepreneur* (Vol. 30, No. 12, December 2002, pp. 112)
Pub: Entrepreneur Media Inc.
Ed: Barry Farber. **Description:** The fine line between being persistent and being obnoxious when trying to close sales is defined, with tips showing how to be persistent without annoying prospects.

46968 ■ "Fitness Chain Curves Makes Boston Push" in *Boston Business Journal* (Vol. 23, No. 30, August 29, 2003, pp. 3)
Pub: American City Business Journals
Ed: Jill Lerner. **Description:** The growing success of Curves for Women locations in the Boston, Massachusetts area is explored. Topics include the franchise company's marketing plans, strategic planning, and market development.

46969 ■ "Five Ideas to Watch" in *Inc.* (July 1, 2004)
Pub: Inc. Magazine
Ed: Rod Kurtz. **Description:** Five new products coming to the market are profiled, including beer goggles that simulate to students how motor skills are impaired after drinking a few beers; scratch-and-sniff advertising campaigns; software that navigates users through the streets of Baghdad, Iraq; a Dick Tracy wrist communicator; and oversized plastic cases for lunchboxes.

46970 ■ "Five Questions: Diane Primo, Vice President, Chief Marketing Office, CDW" in *Sales & Marketing Management* (Vol. 157, February 2005)
Pub: VNU Business Media
Description: Dian Primo, vice president and chief marketing officer for CDW answers questions regarding brand loyalty, marketing and sales functions, innovation, and more.

46971 ■ "Five Questions" in *Sales & Marketing Management* (Vol. 157, January 2005, No. 1, pp. 15)
Pub: VNU Business Media
Description: Kim Olson, director of Brand Public Relations, answers five questions regarding marketing strategies for small, growing companies.

46972 ■ "Five Questions" in *Sales and Marketing.com* (Vol. 156, No. 3, March 2004, pp. 11)
Pub: VNU eMedia, Inc.
Description: Jay Fiore answers questions about his newest eBay campaign that targets small businesses.

46973 ■ "Food for Thought" in *Black Enterprise* (Vol. 36, February 2006, No. 7, pp. 60)
Pub: Earl G. Graves Publishing Co. Inc.
Ed: James C. Johnson. **Description:** Advice is offered to would-be entrepreneur wishing to introduce a new snack food product to Frito-Lay Corporation.

46974 ■ "For Advertisers, Super Bowl Still Holds Promise of Super Payoffs" in *Boston Globe* (February 4, 2005)
Pub: New York Times Company
Ed: Naomi Aoki. **Description:** Small advertisers can reach a large audience with a single ad during the Super Bowl. Emerald of California is advertising its snack foods during the game in the hopes of increasing sales.

46975 ■ "For the Love of the Game: How One Woman Scores in the Sports Entertainment Industry" in *Black Enterprise* (Vol. 35, August 2004)
Pub: Earl G. Graves Publishing Co. Inc.
Ed: Zakiyyah El-Amin. **Description:** Profile of Cydni Bickerstaff, founder of Bickerstaff Sports & Entertainment. Bickerstaff is a full-service sports marketing, managing, and event production company, specializing in marketing and promotions, sporting events, athlete appearances, and sponsorships.

46976 ■ "Ford to Mark 100th Anniversary This Year" in *San Jose Mercury News* (April 11, 2003)
Pub: Knight-Ridder/Tribune Business News
Ed: Matt Nauman. **Description:** Ford Motor Company will use its 100th Anniversary as a tool to market its vehicles, through reminders of Ford's impact over the past century.

46977 ■ "Forget About Bartering. For Start-Ups, It's All About the Freebies" in *Inc.* (May 1, 2005)
Pub: Inc. Magazine
Ed: Stephanie Clifford. **Description:** Dave Morgan, founder of the Internet marketing firm Real Media shares ideas for starting a company with a minimal cash investment by offering employees benefits for working for him for free. Morgan recruited two recent college graduates to work unpaid for six months.

46978 ■ "Forward Thinking" in *Sales and Marketing.com* (Vol. 156, No. 3, March 2004, pp. 32)
Pub: VNU eMedia, Inc.
Ed: Mike Beirne. **Description:** Marketing experts are predicting a decline in consumer spending starting in 2006, as baby boomers pass their peak spending years of 45 to 54. The void is expected to remain until today's teenagers reach their 30s. Marketing will need to target "best" customers only in order to reach return on investment (ROI).

46979 ■ "Found It! Building a Search-Engine Friendly Web Site" in *My Business* (December/January 2004, pp. 44)
Pub: My Business Magazine
Ed: Lee Gimpel. **Description:** Ways to improve a Web site's ranking for a small business are examined, including the use of search words and phrases and being listed in a directory of Web sites.

46980 ■ "14th Annual Rough Notes Marketing Agency of the Year Candidate" in *Rough Notes* (Vol. 145, No. 1, January 2003, pp. 20)
Pub: Rough Notes
Description: Rough Notes will send ballots to 141 firms who will vote for the marketing agency of the year. Candidates which include Oswald Trippe and Company, The Cambridge Group, and Professional Insurers Consultants Agency Inc., are named in the article.

46981 ■ "A fourth frontier that technology has now crossed enables users to receive fat video files" in *Inc.* (November 15, 2000, pp. 88)
Pub: The Goldhirsh Group
Description: Companies are already using Internet video to communicate with customers and investors.

46982 ■ "Free Agents in the Olde World" in *Fast Company* (May 2001, pp. 136)
Pub: Fast Company
Ed: Jill Rosenfeld. **Description:** Thomas Malone, a professor at MIT's Sloan School of Management and founder of the Center for Coordination Science, takes a look at the future of commerce and at the structure of how work will get done.

46983 ■ "Free-for-all on the name exchange" in *The New York Times* (March 27, 2000, pp. D3, H3)
Pub: The New York Times Company
Ed: Sue Cummings. **Description:** Internet domain names are discussed. Statistical data included.

46984 ■ "Free Reign" in *Home Office Computing* (Vol. 18, No. 12, December 2000, pp. 45)
Pub: Scholastic Inc.
Ed: Douglas Gantenbein. Description: Many companies now offer free E-mail and Internet access service based on an advertiser-supported model. Home-based workers will find such free ISPs useful mainly as backups to a paid account.

46985 ■ "Free Speech" in *Entrepreneur* (Vol. 31, No. 9, July 2003, pp. 80)
Pub: Entrepreneur Media, Inc.
Ed: Elizabeth Goodgold. Description: Sarah Victory, author of How to Double Your Business in One Year or Less, speaking to an audience can generate large returns for a business, as long as the audience is in a position to buy.

46986 ■ "Free Tuition: Win New Customers With Educational Programs" in *Sales & Marketing Management* (Vol. 157, February 2005, No. 2, pp. 20)
Pub: VNU Business Media
Ed: Julia Chang. Description: Many companies have begun offering free sales and marketing seminars in their stores to attract small business owners. Office Depot held a series of seminars that incorporated some product pitches, but the real goal was to build a relationship with its small business customers.

46987 ■ "Free! (With Purchase)" in *Business 2.0* (Vol. 7, January/February 2006, No. 1, pp. 113-115)
Pub: Time, Inc.
Ed: John Battelle. Description: Profile of Scott Mc-Nealy, CEO of Sun Microsystems. McNealy is giving away software in order to sell the company's hardware.

46988 ■ "Fresh Ideas" in *Entrepreneur* (Vol. 32, December 2004, No. 12, pp. 91)
Pub: Entrepreneur Media Inc.
Ed: Gwen Moran. Description: Anthony Shurman, president of Yosha! Enterprises was inspired by a movie to give his Momints breath mints to department store and mall Santas during the holiday. Radio stations started mentioning the promotion on their stations, giving Shurman more impact than a typical marketing campaign.

46989 ■ "Friends should never ask friends to spam-even if Big Blue says to do so" in *InfoWorld* (Vol. 22, No. 38, September 18, 2000 pp. 109)
Pub: InfoWorld
Ed: Ed Foster. Description: Internet marketers frequently use chain-letter methods to sell products and services, offering free items if a user agrees to spam friends. IBM has drawn several complaints from users by resorting to such tactics when marketing its ViaVoice speech-recognition product. Users received E-mail forms IBM titled 'How to Get ViaVoice Free' that offered a $169 copy of ViaVoice Millennium Pro at no charge if they persuaded five friends to sign up for the same small-business online newsletter. IBM asked users to forward a specific canned message to others offering an electronic Small Business Resource Guide as a bonus gift, but failed to mention that the person forwarding the message had received a bribe. Many people are appalled that IBM would stoop to spam methods.

46990 ■ "From Concept to Customer" in *Black Enterprise* (Vol. 36, November 2005, No. 4, pp. 124)
Pub: Earl G. Graves Publishing Co. Inc.
Ed: Sakina P. Spruell, James C. Johnson. Description: Six steps to bring a new product to market are outlined.

46991 ■ "From Digital Image to Document" in *Sales & Marketing Management* (Vol. 158, November-December 2006, No. 11, pp. 62)
Pub: VNU Business Media
Ed: Tali Arbel. Description: Free Web-based application, scanR.com, allows users to convert camera phone snapshots into files that can be sent to email or faxed to other locations.

46992 ■ "From Idea to Marketplace" in *Small Business Opportunities* (Vol. 17, May 2005, No. 3, pp. 62, 64, 130)
Pub: Harris Publications Inc.
Ed: Kurt Kirckof. Description: Ideas to help inventors decide what to do with a newly developed product are shared.

46993 ■ "From Managing Pills to Managing Brands" in *Harvard Business Review* (Vol. 78, No. 2, March 2000, pp. 20)
Pub: Harvard Business School Publishing Corp.
Ed: Marcel Corstjens, Marie Carpenter. Description: In the drug business, marketing is now as important as science.

46994 ■ "Frontier Country Marketing Association Gives Out Awards" in *Journal Record* (June 25, 2003)
Pub: Dolan Media Company
Description: Frontier Country Marketing Association presented awards to Oklahoma businesses at its annual meeting in Midwest City, Oklahoma. A listing of recipients is included.

46995 ■ "Fueling the Ads" in *Crain's Detroit Business* (Vol. 21, October 31, 2005, No. 44, pp. 3)
Pub: Crain Communications Inc. - Detroit
Ed: Jennette Smith. Description: Detroit ad agencies are creating new advertising campaigns for the areas automakers, hyping fuel economy and hybrid vehicles.

46996 ■ "Full-Court Press" in *Hispanic Business* (May 2005, pp. 20, 22)
Pub: Hispanic Business
Ed: Kevin Brass. Description: Business publishers are aggressively targeting the Hispanic executive market to grow circulation of their business magazines. These publications include Hispanic Business, Latin Trade, Latino Leaders, Poder, and Hispanic Trends.

46997 ■ "Full-Figured Women are Avid Online Shoppers" in *Marketing to Women* (Vol. 19, November 2006, No. 11, pp. 11)
Pub: EPM Communications, Inc.
Description: According to a study by Anderson Analytics, commissioned by lingerie retailer, GiGi's Closet, a wider range of items are purchased online by full-figured women than by women weighing less. Statistical data included.

46998 ■ "Funny Business: No Ifs, Ands or Buts" in *Entrepreneur* (Vol. 32, October 2004, No. 10, pp. 93)
Pub: Entrepreneur Media Inc.
Ed: Jerry Fisher. Description: Individuals can promote a product or service and help it to stand out from competition.

46999 ■ "Funny Stuff: Laughter is the Best Marketing, so Find Your Sense of Humor" in *Entrepreneur* (Vol. 33, February 2005, No. 2, pp. 78)
Pub: Entrepreneur Media Inc.
Ed: Nichole L. Torres. Description: Profile of Trevor Dahlen and Mary Little, husband-and-wife team who founded Babies Can't Read Clothing Company. The couple explain how they use funny slogans from the children's items sold, as marketing tools.

47000 ■ "Furniture.com stages revival, forges ties with non-com allies" in *Boston Business Journal* (Vol. 22, No. 11, April 19, 2002, pp. 1)
Pub: MCP, Inc.
Description: Furniture.com Inc., which went into bankruptcy, is making a comeback by partnering with brick-and-mortar retailers like Levitz Furniture Corporation and Seaman Furniture Company Inc.; Furniture.com is being backed by Resurgence Asset Management LLC.

47001 ■ "The Future of Advertising is Here" in *Inc.* (August 2005, pp. 70-77)
Pub: Inc. Magazine

Ed: David H. Freedman. Description: Advertising firms are targeting 'smart ads' to specific demographics. New advertising techniques affordable for small companies are outlined.

47002 ■ "Gadget Gurus" in *Entrepreneur* (Vol. 33, September 2005, No. 9, pp. 22)
Pub: Entrepreneur Media Inc.
Ed: Steve Cooper. Description: According to a study conducted by Burson-Marsteller, a global public relations agency, 86 percent of technology-driven leaders who try products and technologies first then relay their experiences online via blogs and/or discussion forums, are consulted by family and friends for advice before purchasing tech equipment.

47003 ■ "Garner Debuts New Site" in *Mississippi Business Journal* (Vol. 28, September 2006, No. 36, pp. 22)
Pub: Venture Publications, Inc.
Description: Full-service marketing firm Garner Media Inc. has launched its new Website at http://www.garnermediainc.com/.

47004 ■ "Generate More Revenue with a Bottom-Up Marketing Plan" in *Home Business* (Vol. 12, March/April 2005, No. 2, pp. 32, 34-35)
Pub: Home Business Magazine
Ed: Sonya Carmichael Jones. Description: Marketing to grow a home business is discussed using a bottom-up plan.

47005 ■ "Georgia has ad revenue on its mind" in *Atlanta Business Chronicle* (Vol. 25, December 13, 2002, No. 27, pp. A2)
Pub: American City Business Publications, Inc.
Ed: Jim Lovel. Description: The Georgia Department of Industry, Trade and Tourism is seeking a periodicals publisher for its 'Georgia On My Mind' tourist publication as well as its "Multicultural Travel Guide" which targets African-American tourists. Currently, Emmiss Communications Corporation is publishing the guides which contain approximately 30 percent advertising. The initiative is meant to increase the advertising sold, thus generating more income for the state.

47006 ■ *Get Clients Now!, 2nd Edition: A 28-Day Marketing Program for Professionals, Consultants, and Coaches*
Pub: American Management Association
Ed: C.J. Hayden. Released: 2006. Price: $19.95.

47007 ■ "Get Connected" in *Business Week* (No. 3761, December 10, 2001, pp. SB12)
Pub: McGraw-Hill Inc.
Description: Tips for bringing small business phone systems into the Internet age are offered, with focus on call centers.

47008 ■ "Get Involved in Your Association" in *Tourist Attractions and Parks* (Vol. 35, January 2005, No. 1, pp. 47)
Pub: Kane Communications Inc.
Ed: Carol Crain. Description: Profile of the International Inflatable Products and Games Association is presented. The association is committed to the survival of the inflatable industry, which can be used for advertising and marketing campaigns.

47009 ■ "Get the Scoop" in *Entrepreneur* (Vol. 28, No. 2, February 2000, pp. 142)
Pub: Entrepreneur Media Inc.
Ed: Gwen Moran. Description: When it comes to promoting your business, knowledge is power. The more you know about your market, customers, competition and prospects, the more likely you are to make smart decisions.

47010 ■ "Get Smarty" in *Entrepreneur* (Vol. 32, October 2004, No. 10, pp. 92)
Pub: Entrepreneur Media Inc.
Ed: Kim T. Gordon. Description: According to an eGrad Research Study, focusing on the 2.3 million college graduates annually, an entrepreneur could tap

into the nearly $40 billion spent on products and services by the grads as well as the 18 to 24 age group demographic. Wardrobe, automobiles, insurance, cellular phones, and credit cards are among the items purchased within the first year of graduation. Statistical data included.

47011 ■ "Get in tune: keep your site visitors dialed in and buying" in *Entrepreneur* **(Vol. 31, No. 5, May 2003, pp. 79)**
Pub: Entrepreneur Media Inc.
Ed: Catherine Seda. **Description:** Opt-in offers can provide a coupon, a free report, or a newsletter to customers.

47012 ■ "Get the Word Out" in *Small Business Opportunities* **(Vol. 12, No. 5, September 2000, pp. 12)**
Pub: Harris Publications, Inc.
Ed: Lin Grensing-Pophal. **Description:** Ways to let buyers know about a Web site and having them return are covered. Simple things such as putting the Web address on business cards, stationery, and printed materials, e-mail signature files and exchange links are explored.

47013 ■ "Getting Ink: Need Exposure?" in *Entrepreneur* **(Vol. 33, February 2005, No. 2)**
Pub: Entrepreneur Media Inc.
Ed: Kim T. Gordon. **Description:** Hiring a publicist or a public relations firm can help establish media contacts. Six practical tips to get media coverage for a small firm are listed.

47014 ■ "Getting Stars to Shine: Dawn To Dusk Image Agency has an A-List Clientele" in *Black Enterprise* **(Vol. 34, No. 4, Nov. 2003, pp. 43)**
Pub: Earl Graves Publishing Co.
Ed: Bridget McCrea. **Description:** Profile of Dawn To Dusk Image Agency based in Los Angeles and New York is presented. The 10-employee firm represents independent artists who create hairstyles, makeup, wardrobes, and overall images of stars.

47015 ■ "Getting the Word Out-Inexpensively" in *Black Enterprise* **(Vol. 34, No. 6, January 2004)**
Pub: Earl Graves Publishing Co.
Ed: Marcia A. Wade. **Description:** Profile of Niles Communications Group Inc. (NCG), a New York-based graphics communication and marketing firm. The company uses innovative marketing techniques and sponsors events to attract new business.

47016 ■ "Getting the Word Out-Inexpensively: How to Get the Most Bang Out of Your Marketing Dollars" in *Black Enterprise* **(Vol. 34, No. 6)**
Pub: Earl Graves Publishing Co.
Ed: Marcia A. Wade. **Description:** Profile of Niles Communications Group Inc. (NCG), a New York-based graphics communication and marketing firm. The company uses innovative marketing techniques and sponsors events to attract new business.

47017 ■ "Gilded and Gelded. Hard-Won Lessons From the PR Wars" in *Harvard Business Review* **(Vol. 81, No. 10, October 2003, pp. 44)**
Pub: Harvard Business School Press
Ed: Dick Martin. **Description:** The ways in which AT&T mismanaged itself into a public relations problem are evaluated.

47018 ■ "Girls Learn to Ride" in *Marketing to Women* **(Vol. 19, December 2006, No. 12, pp. 5)**
Pub: EPM Communications, Inc.
Description: Girls Learn To Ride, a company dedicated to girls involved in action sports, is broadening its reach to adult women. They have developed a new website, WomenLearnToRide.com, for women interested in action sports. The site will include news about retreats, camps, and clinics that offer sports instruction, yoga tips, and travel information.

47019 ■ "Give 'Em Liberty" in *Entrepreneur* **(Vol. 33, September 2005, No. 9, pp. 85)**
Pub: Entrepreneur Media Inc.
Ed: Kim T. Gordon. **Description:** Steps to build a winning ad campaign while offering consumers freedom of choice are outlined: Find out what the customer wants and build out a strategy.

47020 ■ "Give It a Go: A 'Hands-On' Approach to Marketing Your Product Could Be Just the Thing to Win Customers" in *Entrepreneur* **(Vol. 32)**
Pub: Entrepreneur Media Inc.
Ed: Kim T. Gordon. **Description:** Four tips to market a product are listed for using experiential marketing. This approach uses events to bring customers into one-on-one contact with a product or brand to create a memorable experience.

47021 ■ "Glam Media Launches Fashion Week Site" in *Marketing to Women* **(Vol. 19, October 2006, No. 10, pp. 5)**
Pub: EPM Communications, Inc.
Description: GlamCentral.com, a website being launched by Glam Media, offers blog hosting for fashion fans and highlights fashion-related articles. The site is designed to help fashion editorial get wider exposure and focuses on coverage of New York Fashion Week.

47022 ■ "Glass Ceiling Persists in the Board Room" in *Marketing to Women* **(Vol. 19, December 2006, No. 2, pp. 8)**
Pub: EPM Communications, Inc.
Description: A study by search firm Heidrick & Struggles and Women Corporate Directors shows that executive inequality remains high despite the number of women who hold board seats. Although these women tend to mentor and recommend other women for candidates, only 54 percent say that at least one of the women recommended was actually elected to the board. Despite the meager statistics, 76 percent of women on boards surveyed stated that they oppose a legal quota that would mandate an increase of women occupying board seats.

47023 ■ "Go major league" in *Entrepreneur* **(Vol. 31, No. 4, April 2003, pp. 81)**
Pub: Entrepreneur Media Inc.
Ed: Kimberly L. McCall. **Description:** The benefits of team selling are good for the salesperson, team and the company overall. The team concept will help to close sales, maintain the client, create a happier customer environment, and provide unity within the firm.

47024 ■ "Go West: Want a Few Business Pointers? Mosey on Over to Deadwood" in *Entrepreneur* **(Vol. 32, November 2004, No. 11, pp. 22)**
Pub: Entrepreneur Media Inc.
Ed: Steve Cooper. **Description:** HBO's new series Deadwood, based on a real-life town in South Dakota around 1876, offers insight into business leadership, contracts, property rights, marketing, managing and business expansion.

47025 ■ "Going digital for dollars" in *Black Enterprise* **(Vol. 33, No. 3, October 2002, pp. 145)**
Pub: Earl Graves Publishing Co.
Ed: Bernadette Williams. **Description:** The future of electronic commerce is discussed, including ways information technology can be used in the vision, creativity, and long-term planning for small business entrepreneurs. Security issues to protect small businesses, joint marketing between firms selling a similar product or service, and ways for African American small business owners can target their markets.

47026 ■ "Going For a Whirl: Jamail Larkin Soars, Dips, and Shows Off a Few Stunts" in *Black Enterprise* **(Vol. 35, January 2005, No. 6, pp. 103)**
Pub: Earl G. Graves Publishing Co. Inc.
Ed: Jermine Benton. **Description:** Profile of Jamail Larkins, owner of an aviation marketing group. Larkins runs his business while attending Embry-Riddle Aero-

nautic University in Daytona, Florida. The entrepreneur decided to start a small business to pay for school, rather than work for minimum wage. The company is expected to show $200,000 in earnings for 2004.

47027 ■ *The Golden Mailbox: How to Get Rich Direct Marketing Your Product*
Pub: Dearborn Financial Publishing, Inc.
Ed: Ted Nicholas. **Released:** 1993. **Price:** $39.95 (paper). **Description:** Provides information on various types of direct and client marketing. Includes sample ads, sample promotions, and type spec tables and worksheets.

47028 ■ "Golf School Caters to Women" in *Marketing to Women* **(Vol. 20, January 2007, No. 1, pp. 8)**
Pub: EPM Communications, Inc.
Description: Golf Made Simple, a golf school program with locations in California and Florida, is targeting businesswomen who would like to acquire skills in the sport. Three, five, or seven-day instruction is followed by e-mail and phone call follow-up with a professional coach.

47029 ■ "Good Marketing Moves" in *Crain's Detroit Business* **(Vol. 22, February 13, 2006, No. 7, pp. 17)**
Pub: Crain Communications Inc. - Detroit
Ed: Brent Snavely. **Description:** Robert McDonald, co-owner of Eph McNally's restaurant, attributes some of the establishment's success to its location in a small historic corner of the city of Detroit. The restaurant features New York-style deli sandwiches piled high with premium meats.

47030 ■ "Good question! Ask, and the people will read" in *Entrepreneur* **(Vol. 30, No. 10, October 2002, pp. 98)**
Pub: Entrepreneur Media Inc.
Ed: Jerry Fisher. **Description:** Ways to make an impact using smaller cost advertising are presented.

47031 ■ "Good Timing" in *Entrepreneur* **(Vol. 32, August 2004, No. 8, pp. 65)**
Pub: Entrepreneur Media Inc.
Ed: Gwen Moran. **Description:** Scott Tests, COO and co-founder of Mindbridge Software Inc. in Pennsylvania, takes advantage of slow news periods to announce the release of his company's new products.

47032 ■ "Goodbye, Retainers" in *Inc.* **(November 2006, pp. 35,38)**
Pub: Gruner & Jahr USA Publishing
Ed: Stefanie Clifford. **Description:** Pay-as-you-go, results based public relations are replaced the traditional retainer system. Significant costs are realized on a timely basis.

47033 ■ "Google Update Draws Criticism from Small Biz" in *Inc.* **(January 1, 2004)**
Pub: Gruner & Jahr USA Publishing
Ed: Rod Kurtz. **Description:** The recent upgrade at Google has small advertisers upset because ads will not longer be linked just to the specific keyword paid for. Google states the new system will help advertisers reach a wider audience, but some complain the system will also send irrelevant consumers to their sites.

47034 ■ "Gourmet G-Day" in *San Diego Business Journal* **(Vol. 28, January 15, 2007, No. 3, pp. 12)**
Pub: San Diego Business Journal Associates
Ed: Jessica Long. **Description:** Gourmet G'Day is offering Australian products to its Southern California customers.

47035 ■ *Great Ad! Low Cost, Do-It-Yourself Advertising for Your Small Business*
Pub: The McGraw-Hill Companies
Ed: Carol Wilkie Wallace. **Released:** 1990. **Price:** $32.95; $89.95 (paper).

47036 ■ "The Great Hyped Hope" in *Washington Business Journal* **(Vol. 22, No. 17, August 29, 2003, pp. 20)**
Pub: Washington Business Journal

Ed: Greg A. Lohr. **Description:** State of the advertising industry in greater Washington, DC area is presented. Topics include advertising agencies, top advertising executives, and effective advertising campaigns.

47037 ■ *The Great Marketing Turnaround*
Pub: NAL Dutton
Ed: Stan Rapp and Tom Collins. **Released:** Revised edition, 1992. **Price:** $22.95 (paper). **Description:** Provides information on marketing for entrepreneurs interested in launching or growing a national brand on a small budget. Includes tips, checklists, and examples.

47038 ■ "The Great Outdoors" in *Entrepreneur* (Vol. 31, No. 4, April 2003, pp. 82)
Pub: Entrepreneur Media Inc.
Ed: Elizabeth J. Goodgold. **Description:** With a slowing economy, outdoor advertising rates are lower and premium spaces have become available. Tips for planning a billboard advertisement are included.

47039 ■ *GreenBook Worldwide—Directory of Marketing Research Companies and Services*
Pub: New York AMA Communication Services Inc.
Released: Annual, March. **Price:** $350 both volumes; $15 shipping & handling. **Covers:** more than 2,500 marketing research companies worldwide (computer services, interviewing services, etc.) of marketing research needs; international coverage. Includes a list of computer programs for marketing research. **Entries Include:** Company name, address, phone, name of principal executive, products and services, branch offices. **Arrangement:** Alphabetical. **Indexes:** Geographical, principal executive name, research services, market/industry served, computer program name, trademark/servicemarks.

47040 ■ "Grow Your Client BASE" in *Home Office Computing* (Vol. 18, No. 8, August 2000, pp. 54)
Pub: Scholastic Inc.
Ed: Jeffery D. Zbar. **Description:** Five simple strategies are provided for finding new customers and generating repeat business for home-based companies.

47041 ■ "Grow Your Market" in *PC Computing* (April 2000, pp. 100)
Pub: Ziff-Davis Inc.
Ed: Jason Compton. **Description:** Maps of all kinds can add value to a Web site and even increase customer usage. This article gives brief evaluations of map databases that can be used.

47042 ■ "Growing Concern" in *Pittsburgh Business Times* (Vol. 23, No. 4, August 15, 2003, pp. 19)
Pub: Pittsburgh Business Times
Ed: Patty Tascarella. **Description:** The growing success of Pittsburgh, Pennsylvania-based EZ-FLO Inc. is presented. Topics include managing a small business, marketing strategy, and sales volume.

47043 ■ *Guerrilla Marketing, 4th Edition: Easy and Inexpensive Strategies for Making Big Profits from Your Small Business*
Pub: Houghton Mifflin Company
Ed: Jay Conrad Levinson. **Released:** May 2007. **Price:** $19.95. **Description:** Marketing strategies for small businesses is designed to revolutionize, expand and grow businesses. .

47044 ■ *Guerrilla Marketing During Tough Times*
Pub: Morgan James Publishing, LLC
Ed: Jay Conrad Levinson. **Released:** October 2005. **Price:** $14.00. **Description:** Ways to market a small business during slow economic times.

47045 ■ *Guerrilla Marketing Excellence: The Fifty Golden Rules for Small Business Success*
Pub: Houghton Mifflin Co.
Ed: Jay Conrad Levinson. **Released:** 1993. **Price:** $12.95.

47046 ■ *Guerrilla Marketing for the New Millennium*
Pub: Morgan James Publishing, LLC
Ed: Jay Conrad Levinson. **Released:** September 2005. **Price:** $14.00. **Description:** Steps to successfully market a small business on the Internet.

47047 ■ *Guerrilla Marketing: Put Your Advertising on Steroids*
Pub: Morgan James Publishing, LLC
Ed: Jay Conrad Levinson. **Released:** October 2005. **Price:** $14.00. **Description:** Marketing concepts to successfully advertise any Internet business, featuring the ten most successful advertising campaigns of the 20th Century.

47048 ■ *Guerrilla Marketing Weapons: 100 Affordable Marketing Methods for Maximizing Profits from Your Small Business*
Pub: NAL Dutton
Ed: Jay Conrad Levinson. **Released:** 1990. **Price:** $12.95. **Description:** Presents methods intended to help liberate cash flow, increase profits, and add potency to a marketing program.

47049 ■ "Guerrilla Tactic Targets Golfers" in *Inc.* (October 1, 2004)
Pub: Inc. Magazine
Ed: Jess McCuan. **Description:** Profile of CPRi, a staffing firm based in Chicago, Illinois, affixes its logo to golf carts at charity tournaments for publicity.

47050 ■ "Guerrillas in our Midst" in *Crain's Chicago Business* (Vol. 30, January 2007, No. 3, pp. 16)
Pub: Crain Communications, Inc.
Ed: Steve Hendershot. **Description:** Guerrilla Marketing is an innovative way of getting a company's products name to consumers by attention-grabbing antics.

47051 ■ "Guide Advises Would-Be Entrepreneurs" in *Marketing to Women* (Vol. 20, January 2007, No. 1, pp. 8)
Pub: EPM Communications, Inc.
Description: Smart Women and Small Business: How to Make the Leap from Corporate Careers to the Right Small Enterprise, a new how-to guide book for women looking to leave their corporate careers and join the entrepreneurial workforce, offers tips on getting loans, starting a business, working with business partners, and finding and closing the right deals.

47052 ■ *Guide to Marketing and Business Resources*
Pub: Ad Facs Communications Corp.
Covers: Business providers in over 100 fields of business. **Entries Include:** Name, address, phone, fax.

47053 ■ "Gulf Team With Corpedia on Ethics Course" in *Rough Notes* (Vol. 146, No. 9, September 2003, pp. 44)
Pub: Rough Notes
Ed: Dennis H. Pillsbury. **Description:** Profile of Gulf Insurance Group's underwriting division, including Internet marketing, importance of teamwork, and management of debt and business losses.

47054 ■ "Hands On" in *Inc.* (August 2005, pp. 29-30)
Pub: Inc. Magazine
Ed: Adam L. Penenberg. **Description:** Up to 35 percent of all pay-per-click Internet advertising transactions may be fraudulent. Statistical data included.

47055 ■ "Hard Cell" in *Fast Company* (May 2001, pp. 108)
Pub: Fast Company
Ed: George Anders. **Description:** Is there anything more routine than making a call (or even surfing the Web) on a wireless phone? The process of making a stylish phone is anything but routine, and the story of the Kyocera Smartphone is a case study in creativity, design and engineering. The article addresses the obstacles to launching a new product in a crowded market.

47056 ■ "A Hard Sell" in *Entrepreneur* (Vol. 31, No. 8, August 2003, pp. 76)
Pub: Entrepreneur Media, Inc.
Ed: Jerry Fisher. **Description:** Ways advertising can convince tradition-bound prospects to switch to e-commerce are explored. Insure.com challenged parents to purchase insurance online, facing this issue head-on.

47057 ■ "Has Your Company Found Its Voice?" in *Fast Company* (August 2001, pp. 40)
Pub: Fast Company
Ed: Paul C. Judge. **Description:** Some brands really talk the talk, and sophisticated technology has the power to turn a customer's interaction with an automated call center into a virtual marketing conversation.

47058 ■ "Hatred of Spam Puts Crinkle in Faxing" in *Crain's Detroit Business* (Vol. 19, No. 45, November 10, 2003, pp. 9)
Pub: Crain Communications Inc., Detroit
Ed: Mary Kramer. **Description:** New rules adopted by the Federal Communications Commission require businesses to secure written approval from recipients before sending commercial faxes.

47059 ■ "Hauppauge-Based Robert Martin Advertising Attracts Customers in the Same Way It Helps Them" in *Long Island Business News* (Mar.5,2004)
Pub: Dolan Media Newswires
Ed: Adina Genn. **Description:** Profile of Bob Salomone and Bob Beroze, senior partners at Hauppauge-based marketing firm Robert Martin Advertising. The team identifies trends, issues and leaders in a given industry and targets campaigns towards the industry's decision makers.

47060 ■ "Have It Your Way" in *Forbes* (Vol. 175, February 14, 2005, No. 3, pp. 78)
Pub: Forbes Magazine Inc.
Ed: Melanie Wells. **Description:** Companies are tapping consumers to create new products with appeal. When General Motors announces its new Hummer He3, it will feature equipment inspired by customers.

47061 ■ "Hawaii's Growers Wake Up and Sell the Coffee" in *Pacific Business News* (Vol. 41, No. 19, July 18, 2003, pp. 23)
Pub: American City Business Journals
Ed: Howard Dicus. **Description:** The success that Hawaii Coffee is experiencing with the sale of specialty coffees using celebrity endorsements is discussed. Topics include strategic planning, advertising, and market development.

47062 ■ "Head Long" in *Entrepreneur* (Vol. 31, No. 9, July 2003, pp. 84)
Pub: Entrepreneur Media, Inc.
Ed: Jerry Fisher. **Description:** When writing advertisements, it is best to keep your message short, however there are exceptions to this rule.

47063 ■ "Help! My brain's being eaten by a zillion dot-com ads!" in *The New York Times* (March 27, 2000, pp. D18, H18)
Pub: The New York Times Company
Description: A discussion about e-commerce between Sheri Baron, George Parker, David Wecal, Michael Zapolin, Roy Grace, Ellis Verdi, and Robert Bowman, moderated by Warren Berger.

47064 ■ "Helping Doctors Go Digital" in *Business 2.0* (Vol. 6, July 2005, No. 6, pp. 54-55)
Pub: Time, Inc.
Ed: Erick Schonfeld. **Description:** Epocrates Essentials grew its subscriber base by offering important medical information to doctors, and in the process is able to profit from advertisers targeting the medical industry. Subscriptions to the service start at $60 annually.

47065 ■ **"Helping Hand"** in *Crain's New York Business* (Vol. 23, January 15, 2007, No. 3, pp. 24)
Pub: Crain Communications, Inc.
Description: Bronx officials created a $6.75 million fund providing no-interest loans to businesses that make energy-saving renovations. Companies are also eligible for state and federal subsidies through the three Empire Zones and the Empowerment Zone. Bronx Overall Economic Development Corp. is also reaching out to businesses across the country trying to lure them to the region.

47066 ■ **"Helping HBO Discover Hispanics"** in *Hispanic Business* (Vol. 23, No. 5, May 2001, pp. 16)
Pub: Hispanic Business
Ed: Rick Laezman. **Description:** Profile of Bernadette Aulestia, director of target marketing for movie network, HBO. Ms. Aulestia helped launch the HBO Latino channel.

47067 ■ **"Hey, Get a Clue!"** in *Entrepreneur* (Vol. 32, No. 1, January 2004, pp. 112)
Pub: Entrepreneur Media, Inc.
Ed: Andrew A. Caffey. **Description:** Profile of the Uniform Franchise Offering Circular (UFOC), a document designed to make a franchise investment a fully informed decision. The federal franchise law has required franchisors to deliver this document to prospective franchisees a couple weeks before closing.

47068 ■ **"Hey, Got a Qpass Rookie Card?"** in *Fast Company* (November 2001, pp. 44)
Pub: Fast Company
Ed: Alison Overholt. **Description:** Profile of Seattle-based Qpass, and vice president of marketing Norman Guadagno, who launched a campaign to bring employees up to speed on the firm's restructured business model and newly designed logo using trading cards.

47069 ■ **"Hidden Assets"** in *Hispanic Business* (June 2002, pp. 68)
Pub: Hispanic Business
Ed: Derek Reveron. **Description:** Cutting sales and marketing departments are usually the first departments to be downsized in an economic downturn. Experts advise an opposite strategy.

47070 ■ **"High-Quality Relationships Succeed Where Incentives Fall Short"** in *Incentive* (Vol. 174, No. 9, September 2000, pp. 76)
Pub: Bill Communications
Ed: Jim Ryan. **Description:** With today's increasingly complex marketplace, businesses have reason to be concerned about selling products and services. Warnings about consultants offering relationships, but are really selling incentive programs are investigated.

47071 ■ **"High Tech, High Sales"** in *Small Business Opportunities* (Vol. 13, No. 5, September 2001, pp. 76, 78)
Pub: Harris Publications, Inc.
Ed: Lin Grensing-Pophal. **Description:** An overview of the use of CD-Rom's as marketing tools, including a profile of Jim O'Reilly and his software company, DCA Holdings, Inc. of Minneapolis, Minnesota.

47072 ■ *The High Tech Marketing Machine: Applying the Power of Coputers to Out-Smart the Competition*
Pub: Probus Publishing Co., Inc.
Ed: Timothy W. Powell. **Released:** 1993. **Price:** $24.95. **Description:** Provides information on how to automate marketing, covering mail-merge, contact management, database marketing management, and ad campaigns and promotions. Includes checklists and diagrams.

47073 ■ **"High-Tech Trade Shows"** in *Sales and Marketing.com* (Vol. 147, No. 2, February 2004, pp. 12)
Pub: VNU eMedia, Inc.
Ed: Megan Sweas. **Description:** A marketing strategy by Biovail Pharmaceuticals Inc. at trade shows, is

to use an interactive video game called, Race Under Pressure. The game helped to generate 900 leads at the 2003 American College of Cardiology Show, up from only 250 leads in 2002.

47074 ■ **"Highland Park, Budco are happy together"** in *Crain's Detroit Business* (Vol. 19, No. 6, Feb. 10, 2003, pp. 16)
Pub: Crain Communications Inc., Detroit
Ed: Robert Ankeny. **Description:** Profile of Budco, the growing marketing and communications company, will settle in the city of Highland Park, Michigan.

47075 ■ **"Hired Guns: Is Enlisting Bloggers the Wave of the Future in Marketing?"** in *Entrepreneur* (Vol. 31, No. 9, September 2003, pp. 30)
Pub: Entrepreneur Media, Inc.
Ed: Chris Penttila. **Description:** Blogs, Web logs or journals, are showing up all over the Internet and are being hired by companies to promote products.

47076 ■ **"The Hispanic Market Goes Wireless"** in *Hispanic Business* (March 2003, pp. 50-52)
Pub: Hispanic Business
Ed: Cindy Waxer. **Description:** Of the top 60 advertisers in the Hispanic market, four are telecommunications carriers, demonstrating the Hispanic community's interest in wireless communication. Statistical data included.

47077 ■ **"Hispanic market pioneer retires"** in *Hispanic Business* (Vol. 22, No. 1-2, January-February 2000, pp. 30)
Pub: Hispanic Business
Description: Robert W. Gray, former president of insurance group Allstate Property and Casualty, retired at the end of 1999 after 37 years with the company. Gary had a twin-track approach to marketing, incorporating Spanish-language advertising.

47078 ■ **"Hispanics Now Top Minority"** in *Hispanic Business* (March 2003, pp. 16)
Pub: Hispanic Business
Description: According to the 2000 U.S. Census, Hispanics are now the nation's largest minority group, surpassing African Americans.

47079 ■ **"Hit the Mark"** in *My Business* (August/September 2002, pp. 28-35)
Pub: My Business Magazine
Description: Seven small business trends that will position a company for success are profiled. These trends include mentoring programs, e-mail marketing, customer service, personalized products and services, employee stock ownership plans, targeting markets, and automation.

47080 ■ **"Hit the Road"** in *Entrepreneur* (Vol. 31, No. 10, October 2003, pp. 87)
Pub: Entrepreneur Media, Inc.
Ed: Elizabeth Goodgold. **Description:** The Adopt-a-Highway program also provides a means for a small business to gain visibility while doing good.

47081 ■ **"Holiday Bonus"** in *Entrepreneur* (Vol. 33, September 2005, No. 9, pp. 48)
Pub: Entrepreneur Media, Inc.
Ed: Melissa Campanelli. **Description:** According to a recent study, Websites offering a gift-idea center during the 2004 holidays were the most successful. Four ideas for adding special features to a Website for holiday 2005 are included.

47082 ■ **"Home Depot"** in *Sales & Marketing Management* (Vol. 159, January-February 2007, No. 1, pp. 15)
Pub: VNU Business Media
Ed: Sarah Boehle. **Description:** Home Depot's Web-based training program is being used as a successful case study for other firms.

47083 ■ **"Home, cheap home"** in *Entrepreneur* (Vol. 30, No. 9, September 2002, pp. 4)
Pub: Entrepreneur Media Inc.
Ed: Michelle Prather. **Description:** Nearly 18-million 20- to 34-year-olds currently live with their parents not

as a sign of failure, but as a financial opportunity. Cars, clothing, travel and entertainment are the hottest trends in purchasing for this segment of the population in America and living with parents allows them financial freedom.

47084 ■ **"Home In on Your Image"** in *My Business* (June/July 2002, pp. 15)
Pub: My Business Magazine
Ed: Lisa Waddle. **Description:** Artist, Jean Steinhardt, helps small businesses set themselves apart from large competitors by drawing owner's homes or small office buildings used for mailing and marketing materials.

47085 ■ **"Homebuilders Pony Up with Incentives for Home Buyers"** in *Memphis Business Journal* (Vol. 25, No. 19, September 5, 2003, pp. 1)
Pub: American City Business Journals
Ed: Kate Miller Morton. **Description:** Martha Fondren of Reeves-Williams LLC stated that the firm has begun offering incentives to both starter home and higher end homebuyers, following an industry trend; incentives can include appliances, interior upgrades, etc.

47086 ■ **"Hoover's Introduces Competitive Intelligence and Media Monitoring Service"** in *Information Today* (Vol. 17, No. 11, Dec. 2000, pp. 31)
Pub: Information Today, Inc.
Description: Hoover's announces its Intelligence Monitor, a Web service for businesses that need timely market and competitive intelligence information.

47087 ■ **"Hospitals Turn to Ads as the Rx for Blahs"** in *San Francisco Business Times* (Vol. 17, No. 51, July 25, 2003, pp. 20)
Pub: American City Business Journals
Ed: Meg Walker. **Description:** Advertising campaigns of San Francisco, California hospitals are discussed.

47088 ■ **"Hot Disks"** in *Entrepreneur* (Vol. 32, August 2004, No. 8, pp. 44)
Pub: Entrepreneur Media Inc.
Ed: Liane Cassavoy. **Description:** Profiles of small business tools include Avanquest's Design & Print Business Edition for creating marketing materials; Mozilla's Firefox 0.8 browser; Avidian Technologies' all-in-one Prophet 2004 that lets a business manage sales opportunities via email without switching applications; and Symantec's pcAnywhere, allows help-desk staff access the company's PCs without leaving the help desk.

47089 ■ **"Hot on Their Trail: How to Use the Net to Track Offline Customers"** in *Entrepreneur* (Vol. 32, December 2004, No. 12, pp. 94)
Pub: Entrepreneur Media Inc.
Ed: Catherine Seda. **Description:** Many small companies are using ad-tracking programs to monitor return on investment. When using the Internet to increase offline sales, be sure to offer a toll-free number, coupons, and printable order forms when designing the Website.

47090 ■ **"A House Divided"** in *Hispanic Business* (December 2003, pp. 34-36, 38, 40)
Pub: Hispanic Business
Description: The Hispanic advertising market consists of one big broadcaster and two different languages. A profile of Univision-Hispanic Broadcasting's merger is included. Statistical data regarding Hispanics advertisers is presented.

47091 ■ **"Hover craft"** in *Entrepreneur* (Vol. 30, No. 1, January 2002, pp. 18)
Pub: Entrepreneur Media Inc.
Description: Holomedia has developed an in-store device that projects full-color images that may create a faster and more lasting memory imprint than traditional advertising.

47092 ■ "How About a Little Browser Branding?" in *Sales & Marketing Management* (Vol. 159, January-February 2007, No. 1, pp. 45)
Pub: VNU Business Media
Description: Toolbars with built-in search engines can be customized to particular target markets.

47093 ■ *How to Achieve Zero-Defect Marketing*
Pub: AMACOM
Ed: Allan J. Magrath. **Released:** 1993. **Price:** $22.95 ($20.65 for AMA members). **Description:** Describes how to apply total quality management (TQM) standards to marketing. Contains more than 200 examples and action tips.

47094 ■ "How to Acquire Customers on the Web" in *Harvard Business Review* (Vol. 78, No. 3, May 2000, pp. 179)
Pub: Harvard Business School Publishing Corp.
Ed: Donna L. Hoffman, Thomas P. Novak. **Description:** Customer acquisition is one of the biggest challenges facing online companies today. Success requires a fresh approach to managing the market mix.

47095 ■ "How to Advertise with Flyers" in *Home Business* (Vol. 12, October 2005, No. 5, pp. 52)
Pub: Home Business Magazine
Ed: Terri Seymour. **Description:** Flyers provide a low-cost strategy to generate business leads. Steps for making professional-looking flyers that reach potential customers are outlined.

47096 ■ *How to Advertise a Small Business: Step by Step Guide to Starting Your Own Business*
Pub: Lewis and Renn Associates
Ed: Leslie D. Renn; Jerre G. Lewis. **Released:** 2007. **Price:** $21.95. **Description:** Step-by-step guide to help small business owners advertise products and services.

47097 ■ "How newspaper overcame loss of big advertisers" in *Wall Street Journal* (January 25, 2002, pp. A13)
Pub: Wall Street Journal
Ed: Patricka Callahan. **Description:** As the Modesto Bee faced a national loss of ad revenue and the local loss of giant ad source, Montgomery Ward, publisher Lynn Dickerson focused on small business with discount rate packages and seminars for mom-and-pop operations on the importance of newspaper advertising.

47098 ■ "How to build a blockbuster" in *Harvard Business Review* (Vol. 80, No. 10, October 2002, pp. 18)
Pub: Harvard Business School Press
Ed: Gary Lynn, Richard Reilly. **Description:** Colgate-Palmolive's debut of a new toothpaste is used as a case study to understand why the product achieved only a one percent market share.

47099 ■ "How to Create an E-Culture" in *E-business Advisor* (Vol. 18, No. 9, September 2000, pp. 16)
Pub: Advisor Media, Inc.
Ed: Shelly Wolf. **Description:** Companies can emulate an 'e-culture' model by adapting quickly to market changes, responding faster to customers and operating at the lowest possible cost. To accomplish this goal, companies' leadership teams must okay e-commerce projects and the company organization must be team-oriented.

47100 ■ "How to Develop a Marketing Plan to Sell Your E-Book" in *Web Marketing Today* (No. 121, February 5, 2003)
Pub: Wilson Internet Services
Ed: Ralph F. Wilson. **Description:** Ways to market electronic books are discussed, including e-book marketplaces, search engine positioning, pay-per-click advertising, e-zine advertising, affiliate programs and CPA advertising.

47101 ■ *How to Develop a Successful Advertising Plan*
Pub: NTC Business Books
Ed: James W. Taylor. **Released:** Second edition, 1993. **Price:** $39.95. **Description:** Guide to developing and implementing an advertising plan, including guidelines for selecting an agency to execute the plan. Also contains worksheets, planning documents, and case studies.

47102 ■ *How to Evaluate and Improve Your Marketing Department*
Pub: N T C Comtemporary Publishing Co.
Released: 1992. **Price:** $79.95.

47103 ■ "How I Did It" in *Inc.* (September 2005, pp. 140-142)
Pub: Inc. Magazine
Ed: Stephanie Clifford. **Description:** In an interview, Sidney Frank tells how he started importing a German herbal elixier called Jagermeister in 1972. Frank's unique marketing techniques are discussed.

47104 ■ "How I Got Here" in *Sales & Marketing Management* (Vol. 157, January 2005, No. 1, pp. 50)
Pub: VNU Business Media
Ed: Kathryn Droullard. **Description:** Profile of John Fox, president of Venture Marketing, Downers Grove, Illinois. Fox shares his three principles of success in the sales and marketing industry.

47105 ■ *How to Make Big Money in Your Own Small Business: Unexpected Rules Every Small Business Owner Needs to Know*
Pub: Hyperion Press
Ed: Jeffrey J. Fox. **Released:** May 2004. **Price:** $16.95. **Description:** Former sales and marketing pro offers advice on growing a small business.

47106 ■ *How to Make Your Sales Explode with Television Advertising: The Small Business Television Advertising Manual*
Pub: D. B. Carson & Co., Inc.
Ed: Dale B. Carson. **Released:** 1992. **Price:** $35.00 (paper).

47107 ■ *How to Market Your Business in the '90s: An Essential Small Business Guide*
Pub: Frugal Marketer Publishing
Ed: Warren A. Shuman. **Released:** 1995. **Price:** $19.95.

47108 ■ *How to Market Your Business: An Introduction to Tools and Tactics for Marketing Your Business*
Pub: Sourcebooks, Inc.
Ed: Ian B. Rosengarten. **Released:** 1995. **Price:** $8.95.

47109 ■ "How do you narrow your product options?" in *Wall Street Journal* (March 17, 2003, pp. R3)
Pub: Dow Jones & Co. Inc.
Ed: Carl Bialik. **Description:** Profile of DNA-testing device developers Kalyan Handique and Sundaresh Brahmasandra and the founders of HandyLab Inc.

47110 ■ "How to Pitch a Brilliant Idea" in *Harvard Business Review* (Vol. 81, No. 9, September 2003, pp. 117)
Pub: Harvard Business School Press
Ed: Kimberly D. Elsbach. **Description:** Ways screenwriters propose ideas to producers can be applied to business marketing are highlighted. An ongoing study of how products are presented to the U.S. film and television industry (Hollywood) from screenwriters is presented; from this research various self-destructive and effective personality types emerged and are described.

47111 ■ *How to Promote, Publicize and Advertise Your Growing Business: Getting the Word Out without Spending a Fortune*
Pub: John Wiley & Sons, Inc.
Ed: Kim Baker and Sunny Baker. **Released:** 1992. **Price:** $65.95; $18.95 (paper). **Description:** Provides information on how to create, manage, and produce cost effective advertising, brochures, catalogs, and public relations events. Contains charts and checklists.

47112 ■ "How Snapple Got Its Juice Back" in *Harvard Business Review* (Vol. 80, No. 1, January 2002, pp. 47)
Pub: Harvard Business School Press
Ed: John Deighton. **Description:** Quaker Oats bought Snapple for $1.4 million, only to sell it four years later for $300 million to Triarc. Triarc then reorganized the brand and sold it to Cadbury Schweppes for about $1 billion. Returning the company required changes in management, packaging, and products.

47113 ■ "How Surveys Influence Customers" in *Harvard Business Review* (Vol. 80, No. 5, May 2002, pp. 18)
Pub: Harvard Business School Press
Ed: Vicki G. Morwitz, Paul M. Dholakia. **Description:** New research indicates that a customer survey can enhance the loyalty and profitability of already satisfied customers. Surveys seem to crystallize existing opinions and focus attention on them.

47114 ■ "How To Star in an Ad (Without Looking Like an Idiot)" in *Inc.* (October 1, 2004)
Pub: Inc. Magazine
Ed: Gary Hirshberg. **Description:** The importance of hiring an ad agency that understands your business is crucial. Whether to be the star of your company's ad is discussed.

47115 ■ "How to Win a Marquee Account" in *Sales and Marketing.com* (Vol. 156, No. 3, March 2004, pp. 72)
Pub: VNU eMedia, Inc.
Ed: John Zimmer. **Description:** Profile of Toshiba America Medical Systems, which sells medical imaging products for the diagnosis and treatment of heart disease, cancer and stroke. Toshiba's marketing strategy has helped them achieve double-digit growth in an otherwise sluggish market.

47116 ■ *How to Write a Great Business Plan for Your Small Business in 60 Minutes or Less*
Pub: Atlantic Publishing
Ed: Sharon L. Fullen. **Released:** September 2005. **Price:** $39.95 includes CD-Rom. **Description:** A good business plan outlines goals and works as a company's resume to obtain funding, credit from suppliers, management of the operations and finances, promotion and marketing, and more.

47117 ■ *How to Write a Successful Advertising Plan*
Pub: N T C Comtemporary Publishing Co.
Ed: James Taylor. **Released:** 1993. **Price:** $19.95 (paper). **Description:** Explains how to stake out a marketing position, how to set an advertising budget, and how to make sure the execution stays within the objectives. Includes actual charts, storyboards, and media plans from existing companies. Also contains a section on planning for retail stores, an outline of a sample advertising plan, and examples of failed strategies.

47118 ■ "IACVB Considers Changing Its Name" in *Tradeshow Week* (Vol. 34, December 20, 2004, No. 51, pp. 3)
Pub: Reed Business Information
Description: The Board of Directors of the International Association of Convention and Visitor Bureaus is considering changing the organization's name to the Destination Marketing Association. Members and non-members are encouraged to provide feedback at a published Website.

47119 ■ "Ideal PR consultant knows to keep pitches clear and simple" in *Boston Business Journal* (Vol. 22, No. 14, May 10, 2002, pp. 44)
Pub: MCP, Inc.
Description: Guidelines for companies wishing to get their money's worth from public relations firms are presented.

47120 ■ "If Telemarketers Paid For Your Time" in *Forbes* (April 15, 2002, p. 225)
Pub: Forbes Magazine

Ed: Ian Ayres, Barry Nalebuff. **Description:** Ideas are offered to help small businesses improve processes and services to help them prosper.

47121 ■ "If You Market, They Will Come" in *Success* (Vol. 47, No. 1, January 2000, pp. 50)
Pub: Success Publishing, Inc.
Ed: Rivka Tadjer. **Description:** Three easy steps to draw customers to your online store.

47122 ■ "Image is Everything" in *Entrepreneur* (Vol. 32, September 2004, No. 9, pp. 106)
Pub: Entrepreneur Media Inc.
Description: Profile of Sandy Meyers, marketer of materials that incorporate fine art. Meyers uses the process of securing fine art prints and displaying them on items such as luggage tags, postcards, mouse pads, and coffee mugs, instead of a company's logo for marketing purposes. She also runs Visual Promotions, a firm that creates point-of-purchase and trade show banners and displays.

47123 ■ "In Brief: Discover Touting Gas Rewards" in *American Banker* (Vol. 172, January 31, 2007, No. 21, pp. 16)
Pub: SourceMedia, Inc.
Ed: H. Michael Jalili. **Description:** Discover Financial Services LLC reported a direct correlation between energy prices and small business confidence. Discover's small business program that offers cash back on gasoline purchases has been successful. Statistical data included.

47124 ■ "In the Chips; Handheld Lab Gets HandyLab $6M" in *Crain's Detroit Business* (Vol. 22, January 23, 2006, No. 4, pp. 1)
Pub: Crain Communications Inc. - Detroit
Ed: Tom Henderson. **Description:** HandyLab Inc., Ann Arbor, Michigan, will use $6 million of venture capital to hire sales and marketing teams to bring its first medical diagnostic device to market. The firm was founded in 2000 by a group of engineering graduates from University of Michigan.

47125 ■ "In Demand" in *Entrepreneur* (Vol. 32, November 2004, No. 11, pp. 89)
Pub: Entrepreneur Media Inc.
Ed: Gwen Moran. **Description:** Brother filmmakers, Gregg and Evan Spiridellis, share ways to handle overnight success with a product. After producing an animated political film on their Website Jibjab, the entrepreneurs were not prepared for the number of phone calls, emails and national media appearances that followed. Hiring temp help and including an email contact on their Website could have helped.

47126 ■ "In Entertainment Men Out-Earn Women" in *Marketing to Women* (Vol. 20, January 2007, No. 1, pp. 4)
Pub: EPM Communications, Inc.
Ed: Susan Nunziata. **Description:** Particularly among the upper ranks of the entertainment industry executives, females are paid less than male counterparts. Statistical data included.

47127 ■ "In High Spirits: How to Get Yourself and Your Business Fired up from the Inside out" in *Entrepreneur* (Vol. 31, No. 4, April 2003)
Pub: Entrepreneur Media Inc.
Ed: Barry Farber. **Description:** Four keys to help increase and maintain enthusiasm in a company include the following: learn something new everyday, revel in the smallest steps toward success, set goals and stick to them, and protect the environment around you.

47128 ■ "In Hot Water? Take a Closer Look at Your Marketing Materials, Or You May Get Burned" in *Entrepreneur* (Vol. 32, September 2004)
Pub: Entrepreneur Media Inc.
Ed: Catherine Seda. **Description:** Although not illegal, using another company's trademark or logo on a Website, banner ad, or newsletter could get a small company into legal trouble. Internet marketing law includes copyrights, privacy rights, trademark usage and order fulfillment and more aggressive legal action to protect brands is taking place.

47129 ■ "In Marketing and Sales, Know When to Back Away" in *Folio: the Magazine for Magazine Management* (Vol. 30, No. 1, January 2001, pp. 10)
Pub: Intertec Publishing Corp.
Description: Ad sales people should address these four areas with advertisers: (1) What are their concerns about ad clutter? What are their frustrations about consumer indifference? (2) What are their fears about retailer clout? (3) There is mounting pressure on margin. How can you help? (4) Discuss the pressure to maintain a real point of difference. Follow this formula to have a good start to leveraging relationships into business.

47130 ■ "In the Mood" in *Entrepreneur* (Vol. 33, October 2005, No. 10, pp. 130)
Pub: Entrepreneur Media Inc.
Ed: Don Debelak. **Description:** Overcoming retailer resistance when introducing a new product is discussed using the story of an entrepreneur who was trying to sell her interior home lighting products to retailers.

47131 ■ "In My Humble Opinion: They gathered this past spring" in *Fast Company* (September 2001, pp. 92)
Pub: Fast Company
Ed: John Ellis. **Description:** Thanks to companies such as Recipio, PlanetFeedback.com, and InsightExpress, customers can vote on existing products and services.

47132 ■ "In with the New" in *Entrepreneur* (Vol. 28, No. 10, October 2000, pp. 102)
Pub: Entrepreneur Media Inc.
Ed: Mark Henricks. **Description:** The key to fast growth lies is not only treating your existing customers well, but also in seeking new customers.

47133 ■ "In a Nutshell: Something as Unexpected as a Talking Almond Could be Just What You Need to Catch the Reader's Eye" in *Entrepreneur*
Pub: Entrepreneur Media Inc.
Ed: Jerry Fisher. **Description:** A talking almond used by the Almond Board of California is used to demonstrate the creative ways advertising can attract attention.

47134 ■ "In Praise of the 'Thank You' Note: Want to make an impression?" in *Business Week Online* (March 7, 2002)
Pub: McGraw-Hill, Inc.
Description: Handwritten thank you notes can be used as a sales and marketing tool for small businesses. A thank you note displays an attitude of gratitude no ad slogan or coffee mug can match.

47135 ■ "In Vain: What Does the Future Hold for the Once-Hot Metrosexual?" in *Entrepreneur* (Vol. 32, July 2004, No. 7, pp. 24)
Pub: Entrepreneur Media Inc.
Ed: Chris Penttila. **Description:** Entrepreneurs should target marketing to multiple audiences, rather targeting one market. Marketing to the metrosexual man in 2004 is waning.

47136 ■ "In With the New: Get Your Customers to Get Rid of Your Products-So They Can Buy More" in *Entrepreneur* (Vol. 31, No. 5, May 2003)
Pub: Entrepreneur Media Inc.
Ed: Kimberly L. McCall. **Description:** Strategies being used by entrepreneurs to embrace disposable products in order to boost income are discussed.

47137 ■ "In Your Eyes" in *Entrepreneur* (Vol. 30, No. 2, Feb)
Pub: Entrepreneur Media Inc.
Ed: Jerry Fisher. **Description:** American Express Travelers Cheques captivating advertising campaign offers lessons any small business could use to market products.

47138 ■ "In Your Face: Cross Your Fingers, Hold Your Breath...And Put Out Ads With No Holds Barred" in *Entrepreneur* (Vol. 31, October 2003)
Pub: Entrepreneur Media, Inc.
Ed: Jerry Fisher. **Description:** An examination of the advertising used for TheraSeed treatment, an alternative to surgery to treat prostate cancer is presented.

47139 ■ "In-Your-Face-Selling" in *Inc.* (November 2006, pp. 33)
Pub: Gruner & Jahr USA Publishing
Ed: Adam Bluestein. **Description:** A strong approach to closing business to business deals is to take a small group to the customer to meet with the client and show the support that's available if you're chosen. While an expensive approach due to travel expenses, the pay-offs are very lucrative in the long term. The client identifies more with your company after a face to face meeting.

47140 ■ "Inking the Deal" in *Kiplinger's Personal Finance Magazine* (Vol. 54, No. 12, December 2000, pp. 26)
Pub: The Kiplinger Washington Editors, Inc.
Ed: Catherine Siskos. **Description:** This holiday season, online retailers are publishing print catalogs to attract customers.

47141 ■ "Innovating a Classic at Airstream" in *Harvard Business Review* (Vol. 81, No. 10, October 2003, pp. 18)
Pub: Harvard Business School Press
Ed: Gardiner Morse. **Description:** Airstream trailers are once again trendy; Dicy Riegel discusses Thor Industries and how it transformed the aluminum-clad trailer into a new, trendy item. Sales have increased since Thor acquired Airstream in 1980.

47142 ■ "The ins and outs: Sales Force: Answering the eternal question" in *Entrepreneur* (Vol. 30, No. 3, March 2002, pp. 87)
Pub: Entrepreneur Media Inc.
Ed: Kimberly L. McCall. **Description:** Three myths regarding inside and outside sales teams are explored. In general, inside teams that do all their selling over the phone are generally less expensive to run and easier to manage, while outside teams working in the field establish the crucial personal link that allows a real glimpse into sales prospects.

47143 ■ *Instant Cashflow: Hundreds of Proven Strategies to Win Customers, Boost Margins and Take More Money Home*
Pub: McGraw-Hill Companies
Ed: Bradley J. Sugars. **Released:** December 2005. **Price:** $16.95 (US), $22.95 (Canadian). **Description:** Nearly 300 proven marketing and sales strategies are shared by the author, a self-made millionaire. Advice on creating the proper mindset, generating new leads, boosting the conversion rate of leads to sales, maximizing the value of the average sale, and measuring results is included.

47144 ■ *Instant Income*
Pub: McGraw-Hill Inc.
Ed: Janet Switzer. **Released:** February 2007. **Price:** $30.95 (CND). **Description:** Book covers small business advertising techniques, marketing, joint ventures, and sales.

47145 ■ *Instant Profit: Successful Strategies to Boost Your Margin and Increase the Profitability of Your Business*
Pub: McGraw-Hill Companies
Ed: Bradley J. Sugars. **Released:** December 2005. **Price:** $16.95 (US), $22.95 (Canadian). **Description:** Advice on management, money, marketing, and merchandising a successful small business is offered.

47146 ■ "Internet Companies Learn How to Personalize Service" in *The New York Times* (August 28, 2000, pp. C8(L))
Pub: The New York Times Company
Ed: Susan Stellin. **Description:** Technologies for delivering customized, individually-oriented 'one to one marketing' or 'targeted merchandising' are still in the early stages of development, but are already in use by Amazon.com.

47147 ■ "Internet Law Arena Marked by Issues About Spam, Pop-Up Ads, Domain Names, and File Sharing" in *Long Island Business News* (Feb.6, 2004)
Pub: Dolan Media Newswires
Ed: Rosmaria Mancini. **Description:** Microsoft and New York's State Attorney General have partnered and filed lawsuits against a spamming ring allegedly responsible for sending billions of deceptive and illegal emails. CAN-SPAM (Controlling the Assault of Non-Solicited Pornography and Marketing Act), is federal legislation that would require marketers to provide return addresses in emails so consumers can request being removed from mailing lists.

47148 ■ "Internet Marketing Focusing on Search Engines" in *Atlanta Business Chronicle* (Vol. 24, No. 14, September 7, 2001, pp. 4A)
Pub: American City Business Journals Inc.
Ed: Jim Lovel. **Description:** Companies such as Marketingcentral LLC and Socketware Inc. are using a new technology called search engine optimization, which moves their company to the top of the search engine list to market their Web sites. Stacy Williams, of Prominent Placement Inc. and Andrew Wetzler, of MoreVisibility.com had their companies work with Marketcentral and Socketware to remodel their Web sites. This is the latest technology in search engines, and as the demand increases, so do the companies providing these services.

47149 ■ "Internet Opens World of Sales" in *Roanoke Times* (January 21, 2005)
Pub: Roanoke Times
Ed: Jenny Kincaid. **Description:** Retailers are selling items that don't sell in their shops on eBay and other online auction sites. Libby Snider-Chittum, an eBay Internet specialist with Business Seed Capital in Roanoke, Virginia, works with small businesses that are expanding or in need of business loans. Snider-Chittum offers seminars for small companies in rural communities and individuals to teach them how to sell items, personal or business, on eBay.

47150 ■ "Intoxicating Results" in *Inc.* (Volume 27, June 2005, No. 6, pp. 38)
Pub: Inc. Magazine
Ed: Lora Kolodny. **Description:** Cisco Brewers, micro-brewer of the distilled vodka, Triple 8, built a successful brand on a small marketing budget.

47151 ■ "Invasion of the Privacy Snatchers" in *Success* (Vol. 47, No. 4, September 2000, pp. 78)
Pub: Success Publishing, Inc.
Ed: Hollis Thomases. **Description:** Profiling. It's an ugly word, with lots of growing connotation surrounding it. It means that your purchasing habits are being recorded, cataloged, analyzed, and used for further direct-marketing efforts toward you.

47152 ■ "An investigation of marketing practice by firm size" in *Journal of Business Venturing* (Vol. 15, No. 5-6, Sept.-Nov. 2000, pp. 523)
Pub: Elsevier Science, Inc.
Ed: Nicole E. Coviello, Roderick J. Brodie, Hugh J. Munro. **Description:** A new study investigates the relevance of traditional marketing practice to small firms.

47153 ■ "Irby Buys Two Companies" in *Mississippi Business Journal* (Vol. 29, January 2007, No. 4, pp. 8)
Pub: Venture Publications, Inc.
Ed: Wally Northway **Description:** Stuart C. Irby Co., a subsidiary of Sonepar USA acquires Burmeister Electric Co. and High Voltage Testing Laboratories. Profiles of both acquired companies included.

47154 ■ "It's All About the Image" in *Crain's New York Business* (Vol. 22, December 11, 2006, No. 50, pp. 26)
Pub: Crain Communications, Inc.
Description: Advantage Consulting Services, a Los Angeles-based Internet marketing consultancy, offers businesses the service of creating and maintaining their MySpace pages.

47155 ■ "It's All About Results" in *Entrepreneur* (Vol. 32, October 2004, No. 10, pp. 92)
Pub: Entrepreneur Media Inc.
Ed: Catherine Seda. **Description:** Three steps to consider before engaging in a pay-for-performance marketing program are listed. Internet marketing agencies run performance-based advertising programs.

47156 ■ "It's a New Game: Killerspin Pushes Table Tennis to Extreme Heights" in *Black Enterprise* (Vol. 37, October 2006, No. 3, pp. 73)
Pub: Earl G. Graves Publishing Co. Inc.
Ed: Bridget McCrea. **Description:** Profile of Robert Blackwell and his company Killerspin L.L.C., which is popularizing the sport of table tennis. Killerspin has hit $1 million in revenues due to product sales primarily generated through the company's website, magazines, DVDs, and event ticket sales.

47157 ■ "It's really Pretty Simple" in *Rough Notes* (Vol. 146, No. 3, March 2003, pp. 49)
Pub: Rough Notes
Ed: Roger Sitkins. **Description:** Preparation and planning are necessary for successful prospecting in insurance marketing.

47158 ■ "It's a Woman's World" in *Black Enterprise* (Vol. 36, November 2005, No. 4, pp. 80)
Pub: Earl G. Graves Publishing Co. Inc.
Ed: Tennille M. Robinson. **Description:** Miriam Muley named her company 85% Niche after the percentage of sales directly and indirectly influenced by women. The firm offers brand marketing and new product development services. Statistical data included.

47159 ■ "Jewelry Mixes Fashion and Healing Energies" in *Marketing to Women* (Vol. 19, November 2006, No. 11, pp. 5)
Pub: EPM Communications, Inc.
Description: Body Rocks combines fashion and spirituality in their new line of jewelry and accessories that harness the healing properties of specific stones.

47160 ■ "Join Hands" in *Entrepreneur* (Vol. 33, September 2005, No. 9, pp. 138)
Pub: Entrepreneur Media Inc.
Ed: Don Debelak. **Description:** Profile of Shawn Donegan, founder of Trac Tool Inc., Cleveland, Ohio. Donegan signed a licensing deal with inventor Mike Puczkowski to sell the Speed Rollers paint applicator system to professional painting contractors. Steps for entrepreneurs to market inventions are examined.

47161 ■ "Joining Forces" in *Sales & Marketing Management*
Pub: VNU Business Media
Ed: Dale Buss. **Description:** Special-ingredient manufacturers are lending value to some food and beverage brands to attract the attention of grocery store shoppers.

47162 ■ *Jump Start Your Business Brain: Ideas, Advice and Insights for Immediate Marketing and Innovation Success*
Pub: Emmis Books
Ed: Doug Hall. **Released:** April 2005. **Price:** $23.99.
Description: Strategies to improve sales, marketing, and business development.

47163 ■ "Just Ask: Use e-mail to start a conversation with online buyers" in *My Business* (October/November 2002, pp. 17)
Pub: My Business Magazine
Description: Customer emails can be a good tool to target customers for online purchases.

47164 ■ "Just down the block" in *Entrepreneur* (Vol. 30, No. 1, January 2002, pp. 18)
Pub: Entrepreneur Media Inc.
Description: Adkey software has developed a program that denies access to users who used ad-filtering software that block a company's advertising.

47165 ■ "Just for shows with a new design, these booths are gonna walk all over you" in *Entrepreneur* (Vol. 30, No. 1, January 2002, pp. 26)
Pub: Entrepreneur Media Inc.
Ed: Elizabeth J. Goodgold. **Description:** The importance of trade shows and a booth's appearance can dramatically change the perception of a business, which in turn can increase profits.

47166 ■ "Just Teasing: A Ads" in *Entrepreneur* (Vol. 31, No. 9, September 2003, pp. 88)
Pub: Entrepreneur Media, Inc.
Ed: Jerry Fisher. **Description:** Ways to create advertising that attracts customers are examined, using an ad created by LoSasso Advertising Inc., in Chicago, Illinois as an example.

47167 ■ "Just Woo It: It's Possible to Flirt with Success After All" in *Entrepreneur* (Vol. 32, No. 4, April 2004, pp. 29)
Pub: Entrepreneur Media, Inc.
Ed: Sara Wilson. **Description:** Techniques and tools to help market a small business are listed, including the use of free samples and patents.

47168 ■ "Keeping It Legal" in *Small Business Opportunities* (Vol. 12, No. 2, March 2000, pp. 76)
Pub: Harris Publications, Inc.
Ed: Lin Grensing-Pophal. **Description:** Guidelines for creating advertising to stay on the right side of the law are presented.

47169 ■ "Keeping Mums" in *Entrepreneur* (Vol. 33, February 2005, No. 2, pp. 71)
Pub: Entrepreneur Media Inc.
Ed: Mark Henricks. **Description:** Owner of an advertising agency in San Antonio, Texas tells how he hired a pregnant woman in 1995. The two worked out a plan whereby she could telecommute two days a week in order for her to be with her new baby. She has since become a partner in the ad, marketing and public relations agency that reports $30 million in annual billings.

47170 ■ "KFC Forms Moms' Advisory Board" in *Marketing to Women* (Vol. 19, October 2006, No. 10, pp. 3)
Pub: EPM Communications, Inc.
Description: Kentucky Fried Chicken has formed an advisory board, KFC Moms Matter, to consul the company on how it can best meet mother's needs. The board consists of employees who are mothers as well as moms recruited from across the country.

47171 ■ "Kids get 411 on Healthy Habits from Moms" in *Marketing to Women* (Vol. 19, October 2006, No. 10, pp. 3)
Pub: EPM Communications, Inc.
Description: Healthy habits are passed on to kids chiefly by their moms, according to a Harris Interactive study for the America On the Move Foundation. Statistical data included.

47172 ■ "Kill a Brand, Keep a Customer" in *Harvard Business Review* (Vol. 81, No. 12, December 2003, pp. 86)
Pub: Harvard Business School Press
Ed: Nirmalya Kumar. **Description:** An examination of the process of brand discontinuation and how this process can be used to improve customer loyalty. Methods include the portfolio approach, the segment approach, merging brands, and selling brands.

47173 ■ "The Killer Ad Machine" in *Forbes* (December 11, 2000, pp. 168)
Pub: Forbes Magazine
Ed: Quentin Hardy. **Description:** Yahoo has the ability to provide ad feedback to its advertisers when the ad is online.

47174 ■ *Killer Tactics: Survival Guide for Choosing, Running, Marketing a Small Business in the '90s*
Pub: J. Flores Publications
Ed: Lee Simon. **Released:** 1995. **Price:** $22.95.

47175 ■ "Kmart Makes Branding Pro Its New Chief" in *Black Enterprise* **(Vol. 35, December 2004, No. 5, pp. 33)**
Pub: Earl G. Graves Publishing Co. Inc.
Ed: Sonia Alleyne. **Description:** Kmart's appointment of Aylwin Lewis makes him the sixth African American to head a Fortune 500 company at this time, eighth to ever hold the position. Kmart believes Lewis' strong reputation for branding and team building will increase the retailer's profits. Statistical data included.

47176 ■ "Know Your Customers" in *PC Computing* **(April 2000, pp. 94)**
Pub: Ziff-Davis Inc.
Ed: Jason Compton. **Description:** Software and on-line solutions for digital mapping are reviewed. MapInfo's MapInfo Professional 5.5 offers almost unlimited options for both generating maps and analyzing information. ESRI's BusinessMap Pro, is a collection of maps with solid graphing and charting features. The Corporate version adds extra business-to-business data. Microsoft's MapPoint 2000 is very easy to use, but has fewer features than BusinessMap Pro. DemographicsNow.com is a Web-based that includes interactive maps and helps users answer crucial questions about customers and works with the Autodesk Map Guide browser plug-in, which is easy to use.

47177 ■ "Knowledge Networks: Making the Brand" in *Venture Capital Journal* **(Vol. 41, No. 8, August 2000, pp. 18)**
Pub: Venture Economics
Ed: Alistair Christopher. **Description:** Profile of Knowledge Networks, a marketing intelligence system firm, claims they offer an exclusive service to businesses that shows a concise view of consumers and their behavior toward advertising, brands, and buying.

47178 ■ "Kraft Not Alone" in *Crain's Chicago Business* **(Vol. 30, February 2007, No. 6, pp. 8)**
Pub: Crain Communications, Inc.
Description: Consumer watchdog group, The Center for Science in the Public Interest, has been putting pressure on food companies to be more truthful on their product labels. Listing of companies who have had misleading claims on their products is included.

47179 ■ "La Habra, Calif., Entrepreneur Starts Errand-Running Service for Busy Workers" in *San Gabriel Valley Tribune* **(July 8, 2004)**
Pub: San Gabriel Valley Tribune
Ed: Andrew Blazier. **Description:** Profile of Sherri Durbin, owner of Consider It Done!, a new errand service. Durbin charges $32 per hour for services performed by her team of six independent contractors. Durban also founded an international mystery shopping and staffing company that she continues to manage.

47180 ■ "Landscape shifts to exclude midsize firms" in *Atlanta Business Chronicle* **(Vol. 25, November 15, 2002, No. 23 pp. S8)**
Pub: American City Business Publications, Inc.
Ed: Randy Southerland. **Description:** Many of Atlanta's public relations firms are forming alliances with other firms that offer different services.

47181 ■ *Landscaping Business*
Pub: Globe Pequot Press
Ed: Owen E. Dell. **Released:** December 2005. **Price:** $18.95. **Description:** Guide to starting and running a successful home-based landscaping business, including tips for marketing on the Internet.

47182 ■ "Language and Markets in the U.S." in *Hispanic Business* **(December 2002, pp. 16, 18, 20)**
Pub: Hispanic Business
Description: Research shows that historically immigrants arriving to the U.S. have adopted the English language, and it is expected the same will hold true for new Hispanic individuals. However, there tend to be two Hispanic markets, one that is Spanish speaking, the other using English. Statistical data included.

47183 ■ "Language of the Middle Class" in *Hispanic Business* **(December 2003, pp. 28-30, 32)**
Pub: Hispanic Business
Description: English is the key, both for U.S. Hispanics who want to succeed in business, and the marketers wanting to appeal to them. Statistical data included.

47184 ■ "The Language of Sales" in *My Business* **(October/November 2003, pp. 43)**
Pub: My Business Magazine
Ed: Lee Gimpel. **Description:** Profile of Dr. John Beshel, a chiropractor in Burlington, North Carolina. Dr. Beshel increased his patient-base by using Spanish language advertising to draw the growing Hispanic population in the area. Beshel also hired a bilingual employee and also distributes Spanish business cards.

47185 ■ *Lateral Marketing: New Techniques for Finding Breakthrough Ideas*
Pub: John Wiley & Sons, Incorporated
Ed: Philip Kotler, Fernando Trias de Bes. **Released:** September 2003. **Price:** $24.95. **Description:** Lateral marketing complements traditional marketing by allowing marketers develop a new product for a wider audience.

47186 ■ "Latinas' Businesses and Earnings are Seeing Major Growth" in *Marketing to Women* **(Vol. 19, October 2006, No. 10, pp. 2)**
Pub: EPM Communications, Inc.
Description: According to Hispanic Business Inc., Hispanic woman-owned businesses grew 64 percent between 1997 and 2004. Latinas' median incomes also grew. Statistical data included.

47187 ■ "Lead Generator: Quick Ideas for Better Sales Leads" in *Sales and Marketing.com* **(Vol. 156, No. 3, March 2004, pp. 9)**
Pub: VNU eMedia, Inc.
Description: Three tips to promote successful lead generation by a sales staff are listed, including the creation of an internal chat room to make it easier for field offices to communicate.

47188 ■ "Lead Softly, but Carry a Big Baton" in *Fast Company* **(July 2001, pp. 46)**
Pub: Fast Company
Ed: Jill Rosenfeld. **Description:** Symphony conductor, Roger Nierenberg, knows a thing or two about creative management. How else do you get the piccolos and the percussion to stay on the same page?

47189 ■ "Learn Your Lines" in *Entrepreneur*
Pub: Entrepreneur Media Inc.
Ed: Kimberly L. McCall. **Description:** Eight steps to help sales reps improve selling techniques over the phone.

47190 ■ "Leave Me Alone!" in *Entrepreneur* **(Vol. 32, August 2004, No. 8, pp. 31)**
Pub: Entrepreneur Media Inc.
Description: Sixty-percent of consumers have a negative opinion of marketing and advertising than in the past, with 69 percent interested in products and services that help block or skip marketing promotions.

47191 ■ "Legal Eagle?" in *Entrepreneur* **(Vol. 32, October 2004, No. 10, pp. 89)**
Pub: Entrepreneur Media Inc.
Ed: Gwen Moran. **Description:** Important updates on marketing law are shared, including an amendment to telemarketing sales rules, Internet spam, and security software.

47192 ■ "Lessons from the Sandbox" in *Small Business Opportunities* **(Vol. 12, No. 5, September 2000, pp. 106)**
Pub: Harris Publications, Inc.
Description: Consulting guru and author, Alan S. Gregerman, tells how people should act more like kids in order to achieve lasting success. Mr. Gregerman believes the success of any business hinges on the ability to innovate quickly, and get the right new products, services and ideas to the right customers ahead of competitors.

47193 ■ "Lexicon Leads Advertising Pack Wireless Plans, Consumer Products Also Big" in *Hispanic Business* **(December 2006, pp. 36, 38, 40, 42)**
Pub: Hispanic Business
Ed: Jacob Beniflah. **Description:** Profiles of the fifty largest advertisers using Hispanic media.

47194 ■ "A Life Experience is Part of the Package" in *Sacramento Bee* **(November 21, 2005)**
Pub: The Sacramento Bee
Ed: Jon Ortiz. **Description:** Holiday marketing of Carnival Corporation's cruise ships is outlined. The Miami, Florida cruise line partnered with Cooper DDB to advertise its ships with images of shoppers carrying large foil-wrapped replicas of Carnival ships.

47195 ■ "Lights, Camera, Action! Do You Dream of Promoting Your Business On Oprah Or the Today Show, But Don't Know Where To Start?" in *Entrepreneur*
Pub: Entrepreneur Media Inc.
Ed: Eileen Figure Sandlin. **Description:** Lee Snijders, founder of Lee Snijders Designs, explains how, after appearing on HGTV's decorating show, Designers' Challenge, he was shocked at the response. By the next morning he had received 225 emails requesting his interior design service. Four steps to promote a business on a television show are presented.

47196 ■ "Lights, camera, action" in *Entrepreneur* **(Vol. 31, No. 4, April 2003, pp. 126)**
Pub: Entrepreneur Media Inc.
Ed: Don Debelak. **Description:** Steps to take in order to get a new product featured on a home shopping network are presented.

47197 ■ "Listen Up! If You're Not Advertising on Internet Radio, You Could Be Missing Out" in *Entrepreneur* **(Vol. 32, November 2004, No. 11)**
Pub: Entrepreneur Media Inc.
Ed: Catherine Seda. **Description:** Internet radio has an estimated audience of nearly 19 million Americans, making it a great avenue for marketing. Tips based on audience demographics and behaviors are examined.

47198 ■ "Listening Begins at Home" in *Harvard Business Review* **(Vol. 81, No. 11, November 2003, pp. 106)**
Pub: Harvard Business School Press
Ed: James R. Stengel, Andrea L. Dixon, Chris T. Allen. **Description:** The utilization of market research techniques to identify and address employee concerns is analyzed in an examination of Proctor and Gamble.

47199 ■ "Livin' la vida promo" in *Incentive* **(Vol. 174, No. 10, October 2000, pp. 28)**
Pub: Bill Communications
Ed: Libby Estell. **Description:** Marketers are targeting the growing Hispanic population in America.

47200 ■ "Living High on the Blog" in *Entrepreneur* **(Vol. 33, February 2005, No. 2, pp. 65)**
Pub: Entrepreneur Media Inc.
Ed: Gwen Moran. **Description:** Reach Communications Consulting founder, William Arruda, discovered an 800 percent hike in traffic on his firm's Website after being mentioned on an Internet blog; ways to add blogs to a public relations campaign are investigated.

47201 ■ "Local Paradox" in *Atlanta Business Chronicle* **(Vol. 23, No. 40, March 9, 2001, pp. 1B)**
Pub: American City Business Journals Inc.
Ed: Chaundra Frierson. **Description:** The Network of City Business in Atlanta, surveyed 700 small businesses in the year 2000, and discovered that 70 percent received 100 percent of their revenues from their home base. For small business owners in Atlanta, deriving the major portion of their sales from the home base has proven to be challenging. The article discusses the ways small business owners in Atlanta are searching for ways to thrive in this particular market.

47202 ■ "Local execs buy ad agency from parent" in *Crain's Detroit Business* (Vol. 19, No. 15, April 14, 2003, pp. 25)
Pub: Crain Communications Inc., Detroit
Ed: Jennette Smith. Description: Profile of the ad agency called re:group. The firm was purchased by a group of local executives at the Ann Arbor office of Fitch:Worldwide from London-based Cordiant Communications Group PLC and they've taken the business private.

47203 ■ "Location, Location, Location" in *Sales & Marketing Management* (Vol. 159, January-February 2007, No. 1, pp. 28)
Pub: VNU Business Media
Ed: Rebecca Aronauer. Description: Five best cities for marketers include, Atlanta, Las Vegas, Miami, Phoenix and San Diego.

47204 ■ "Loft, Condo Projects Planned in Birmingham, Ferndale" in *Crain's Detroit Business* (Vol. 22, December 18, 2006, No. 51, pp. 16)
Pub: Crain Communications Inc. - Detroit
Ed: Anjali Fluker. Description: Three proposed developments of lofts and condominiums by developers are targeting niches in a challenging market. Both Birmingham and Ferndale markets are open at the lower end of the current price ranges.

47205 ■ "Logged on; Moon Valley Furniture's New Owner Expanding Biz." in *Crain's Detroit Business* (Vol. 23, January 29, 2007, No. 5, pp. 3)
Pub: Crain Communications Inc. - Detroit
Ed: Sheena Harrison. Description: New business oriented owner sees growth potential in rustic furniture market by aligning with log-home builders. Growth forecast to triple in the next five years.

47206 ■ "Logos That Turn Heads" in *Inc.* (December 1, 2003)
Pub: Gruner & Jahr USA Publishing
Ed: Nicole Gull. Description: Many companies are now using people as walking, talking advertisements by displaying or tattooing their logos on them.

47207 ■ "Long Island Banks Compete for Customers by Offering 'Pay Less' ATMs" in *Long Island Business News* (February 13, 2004)
Pub: Dolan Media Newswires
Ed: Claude Solnik. Description: Many banks are offering free or low-cost ATM services in order to attract new customers.

47208 ■ "Looking for Attention" in *Entrepreneur* (Vol. 28, No. 11, November 2000, pp. 30)
Pub: Entrepreneur Media Inc.
Ed: Robert McGarvey. Description: A profile of a marketing online service that offers tools for small businesses.

47209 ■ *Low-Budget Online Marketing for Small Business*
Pub: Self-Counsel Press, Incorporated
Ed: Holley Berkley. Released: July 2005. Price: $14.95, CD-Rom. Description: Low-cost, effective online marketing tips for small companies selling products or services over the Internet.

47210 ■ "Lucky Charms" in *Small Business Opportunities* (Vol. 14, No. 1, January 2002, pp. 12)
Pub: Harris Publications, Inc.
Ed: Paul Hanlon. Description: Selling strategies to build a larger client base for small business, including prospecting, customer confidence, and learning from past mistakes are covered.

47211 ■ *Lucrative List Building*
Pub: Morgan James Publishing, LLC
Ed: Glen Hopkins. Released: July 2006. Price: $13.95. Description: List building guaranteed to double profits is outlined.

47212 ■ "Luxury for the Little People" in *Inc.* (August 1, 2003)
Pub: Gruner & Jahr USA Publishing
Ed: Mike Hofman. Description: A look at America's passion for new luxury goods.

47213 ■ "Luxury for the masses" in *Harvard Business Review* (Vol. 81, No. 4, April 2003, pp. 48)
Pub: Harvard Business School Press
Ed: Michael J. Silverstien, Neil Fiske. Description: A description of the new products called new luxury. New luxury is the result of America's middle market consumers moving to higher levels of quality and taste than ever before. These new luxury products generate high sales volumes and bring companies providing them levels of profitability beyond those of conventional competitors.

47214 ■ "A Macro View at Microsoft" in *Hispanic Business* (January/February 2005, pp. 24, 26, 28)
Pub: Hispanic Business
Ed: Judi Erickson. Description: Orlando Ayala is targeting small and mid-size companies around the world to increase the global reach of technology firm Microsoft. Orlando discusses marketing strategies for selling Microsoft Business Solutions worldwide.

47215 ■ *MadScam: Kick-Ass Advertising Without the Madison Avenue Price Tag*
Pub: McGraw-Hill Ryerson Ltd.
Ed: George Parker. Released: November 2006. Price: $24.95. Description: Effective advertising strategies for small companies on a budget are presented.

47216 ■ "Magazine Covers Anti-Aging Treatments" in *Marketing to Women* (Vol. 19, October 2006, No. 10, pp. 5)
Pub: EPM Communications, Inc.
Description: Elixir, a new consumer magazine, is distributed in spas, hotels, and gyms, as well as at newsagents and online. The magazine focuses on anti-aging treatments including hormone replacement therapy, cosmetic surgery, nutraceuticals, and staying fit.

47217 ■ "Magazines Snare More Dot-Com Ad Dollars" in *Folio: the Magazine for Magazine Management* (Vol. 30, No. 1, January 2001, pp. 7)
Pub: Intertec Publishing Corp.
Ed: Dale Buss. Description: As advertisers redirect their money to more targeted media, the magazine industry is reaping the benefits and enjoying a healthy gain over last year's share of the dot-com ad dollar distribution.

47218 ■ "Magic Markets: The Experts Use Marketing Mojo on Our Tech Makeover Winner" in *Entrepreneur* (Vol. 32, December 2004, No. 12, pp. 106)
Pub: Entrepreneur Media Inc.
Ed: Amanda C. Kooser. Description: Winner of the Interland and Entrpreneur's Website makeover contest are featured. Deborah Nail of Pursesnickety! Reports the increase in sales are due to the new marketing and Website initiatives.

47219 ■ "Magic Moments" in *Home Business* (Vol. 13, January/February 2006, No. 1, pp. 70)
Pub: Home Business Magazine
Description: Profile of Steve Petroff who runs a successful network marketing business from his home in Indianapolis, Indiana. Petroff offers fee-for-service plans and shares his formula for success.

47220 ■ "Maine Tourism Bureau Awards Account to New York Firm" in *Portland Press Herald* (September 20, 2005)
Pub: Blethen Maine Newspapers, Inc.
Ed: Tux Turkel. Description: Maine's Office of Tourism has signed a $3.2 million a year contract with New York City's Warren Kremer Paino. The firm will promote Maine's tourism.

47221 ■ *Make Your Business Survive and Thrive! 100+ Proven Marketing Methods to Help You Beat the Odds*
Pub: John Wiley & Sons, Incorporated
Ed: Priscilla Y. Huff. Released: December 2006. Price: $19.95. Description: Small business and entrepreneurial expert gives information to help small and home-based businesses grow.

47222 ■ "Making E-Mail Work" in *Sales and Marketing.com* (Vol. 156, No. 3, March 2004, pp. 18)
Pub: VNU eMedia, Inc.
Ed: Ellen Neuborne. Description: Marketers are adjusting online newsletters sent to customers with the newly established spam laws. Four ways to send successful emails to customers that will help a small business grow are examined.

47223 ■ "Making the Most Of It" in *Sales & Marketing Management*
Pub: VNU Business Media
Ed: Robin Kocina. Description: Mid-America Events & Expos Inc. specializes in bringing businesses and potential customers together in the same room. The firm is committed to teaching exhibitors how to best benefit from these face-to-face interactions.

47224 ■ "Making New Memories at Little Cheese Shop" in *Business Journal-Milwaukee* (Vol. 20, No. 45, July 25, 2003, pp. A15)
Pub: American City Business Journals, Inc.
Ed: Becca Mader. Description: Profile of Linda Lutz and brother-in-law Howard Lutz, who reopened West Allis Cheese & Sausage Shop after it closed in 2001. They have rebranded the company, expanded the line of foods it makes, began marketing the foods to local shopping malls, as well as changing the labels to make the small company profitable.

47225 ■ "Making a scene: your special event won't be so special if nobody hears about it." in *Entrepreneur* (Vol. 31, No. 5, May 2003, pp. 79)
Pub: Entrepreneur Media Inc.
Ed: Kim T. Gordon. Description: Various methods to promote a special event for a small business are covered, including the use of magazines and newspapers or television and radio.

47226 ■ "Making Your Case: Think Client Testimonials are Just Icing on the Cake?" in *Entrepreneur* (Vol. 33, January 2005, No. 1, pp. 64)
Pub: Entrepreneur Media Inc.
Ed: Kimberly L. McCall. Description: Customer testimonials can act as a case study for increasing sales.

47227 ■ "Man Power: Tips To Get Male Shoppers Spending in Your Store" in *Entrepreneur* (Vol. 32, October 2004, No. 10, pp. 91)
Pub: Entrepreneur Media Inc.
Ed: Nancy Michaels. Description: Tips for marketing to men are presented.

47228 ■ "Man With the Golden Touch" in *Black Enterprise* (Vol. 35, October 2004, No. 3, pp. 53)
Pub: Earl G. Graves Publishing Co. Inc.
Ed: Demetria Lucas. Description: Profile of Darrick Lee Warfield, owner of the Atlanta-based Goldfinger C.S., with revenues of $300,000 reported in 2003. Warfield and his three employees design album covers, Websites, logos, and advertisements. While in high school, Warfield won a national design competition for the American Can Company.

47229 ■ "Management to Go" in *Success* (Vol. 47, No. 6, November 2000, pp. 54)
Pub: Success Publishing, Inc.
Ed: Eddy Goldberg, Paul Gallagher. Description: Virtual CEO's can be your key to succeeding in the new economy. Thanks to the Internet, outsourcing business operations that used to be considered essential, even confidential, makes good business sense today.

47230 ■ **"Many Eggs, Many Baskets"** in *Crain's Chicago Business* **(Vol. 30, January 2007, No. 3, pp. 18)**
Pub: Crain Communications, Inc.
Ed: Steve Hendershot. Description: Allstate Corp. isn't giving up traditional marketing just yet. They are however, combining the traditional route of television with more innovative means. Although Allstate's TV advertising budget remained the same in 2006, it invested more in online marketing.

47231 ■ **"Many analysts think the old-style expensive portal deals deserve more scrutiny from e-tailers"** in *The New York Times* **(May 1, 2000)**
Pub: The New York Times Company
Ed: Bob Tedeschi. Description: Online retailers are re-evaluating how their advertising dollars are spent. Besides TV ads, the practice has been to buy ad space on Web portal pages. Portal companies, like Yahoo, MSN, or AOL, would create a category, then let e-tailers bid up the price for the top three slots. Often this led to $2-$3 million per year deals between the portal and e-tailer. Now online retailers are facing a cash squeeze as investors step back from Internet stocks. Also, the e-tail market is anticipating consolidation among different segments. If only 2 or 3 players remain in a given online retail category, bidding will fall off further, and portals will see a further erosion of revenue. At the same time, as portal sites gain traffic, advertisers will seek out the top 3 or 5 sites to place their ads.

47232 ■ **"Maponics: www.maponics.com"** in *Entrepreneur* **(Vol. 32, November 2004, No. 11, pp. 6)**
Pub: Entrepreneur Media Inc.
Ed: Steve Cooper. Description: A Website featuring custom mapping, geographic targeting and sales territory analysis is profiled.

47233 ■ **"Market Driver"** in *Hispanic Business* **(April 2005, pp. 30-31)**
Pub: Hispanic Business
Ed: Joel Russell. Description: Profile of Sonia Maria Green, director of Hispanic diversity marketing and sales at General Motors. Green believes that taking time to build relationships with consumers will sell cars.

47234 ■ **"Marketers Hang Their Hopes on Holiday Promotions"** in *Sacramento Bee* **(December 21, 2005)**
Pub: The Sacramento Bee
Ed: Jon Ortiz. Description: Companies depend on holiday marketing promotions in order to increase sales. Seasonal packaging plans begin during the summer before each Christmas holiday, can boost a company's sales, and increase brand recognition while making a statement about a company's self-image.

47235 ■ *Marketing for Dummies*
Pub: John Wiley & Sons Inc.
Ed: Alexander Hiam, Editor. Released: latest edition 2. Price: $21.99, individuals. Publication Includes: Marketing web sites, marketing consultants, trade associations, market researchers, and other experts. Entries Include: Individual or company name, address, phone number, web site address (where applicable). Principal content of publication is articles on marketing strategies.

47236 ■ **"Marketing for Dummies"** in *Inc.* **(October 2005, pp. 70-72)**
Pub: Inc. Magazine
Ed: Norm Brodsky. Description: It is important for marketing campaigns to be based on what a company is about, not an image fabricated by a marketer.

47237 ■ **"Marketing E-Coaches"** in *Entrepreneur* **(Vol. 28, No. 10, October 2000, pp. 30)**
Pub: Entrepreneur Media Inc.
Ed: Robert McGarvey. Description: A listing of Web sites to help improve your marketing savvy.

47238 ■ *The Marketing Glossary: Key Terms, Concepts, and Applications*
Pub: AMACOM
Ed: Mark N. Clemente. Released: 1992. Price: $34.95. Description: Reference guide focusing on the key terms, concepts, and applications of marketing. Covers marketing management, advertising, direct marketing, sales, research, public relations, and sales promotion. Includes examples, checklists, and formulas.

47239 ■ **"Marketing: How to Get Some Attention"** in *Business Week Online* **(October 18, 2002)**
Pub: McGraw-Hill Inc.
Ed: Karen E. Klein. Description: Small businesses can be at a disadvantage when it comes to publicity. Tips for getting press coverage and attracting business partners for a small Midwest cabinet shop are offered.

47240 ■ **"Marketing"** in *Inc.* **(Volume 27, March 2005, No. 3, pp. 36)**
Pub: Inc. Magazine
Ed: Lora Kolodny. Description: The art of writing a press release is investigated.

47241 ■ **"A marketing leader is made of life's experiences"** in *Atlanta Business Chronicle* **(Vol. 24, No. 9, August 3, 2001, pp. 2B)**
Pub: American City Business Journals Inc.
Ed: Alf Nucifora. Description: The fundamentals of marketing and leadership are listed. Among the traits, marketing leaders should crave learning, learn to listen, seek wisdom, and speak well and write well.

47242 ■ *Marketing Masters: Secrets of America's Best Companies*
Pub: Harper Business
Ed: Gene Walden and Edmund O. Lawler. Released: 1993. Price: $12.00. Description: Describes how to compete in a crowded market and how small businesses can use secrets of big corporations to improve marketing strategy.

47243 ■ *Marketing Myths*
Pub: Bell Springs Publishing
Ed: K. J. Clancy and R. S. Shulman. Price: $19.95. Description: Marketing, promotion, and spreading the word about your product or service is essential to every business, big or small. Here is the help you need to cut through the theories and myths, and deal with the real world of finding and keeping customers and clients.

47244 ■ *Marketing Myths That Are Killing Business: The Cure for Death Wish Marketing*
Pub: The McGraw-Hill Companies
Ed: Kevin J. Clancy and Robert S. Shulman. Released: 1995. Price: $19.95. Description: Details the most commonly used incorrect and unsuccessful marketing strategies and how to avoid, correct, eliminate and replace them.

47245 ■ *Marketing News—Software Directory*
Pub: American Marketing Association
Ed: Lisa M. Keeke, Editor. Released: Annual. Price: $35, members; $199, members Non-North American; $100, nonmembers; $130, libraries corporations and institutions. Publication Includes: Listings of suppliers of computer software for use in marketing research. Entries Include: Company name, address, phone, description of products. Arrangement: Alphabetical. Indexes: Product use or application.

47246 ■ *Marketing in the Not-for-Profit Sectors*
Pub: Butterworth-Heinemann
Ed: Margaret Kinnell-Evans and Jennifer MacDougall. Released: 1997. Price: $32.95; $34.95.

47247 ■ **"Marketing in the Portable Age"** in *Crain's Detroit Business* **(Vol. 19, No. 45, November 10, 2003, pp. 28)**
Pub: Crain Communications Inc., Detroit
Description: Incentives wireless providers will offer to maintain customers, since the new Federal Communications Commissions ruling to allow clients to maintain existing phone numbers when switching carriers are highlighted.

47248 ■ **"Marketing Quandary: VCs See a Growing Need for Differentiation"** in *Venture Capital Journal* **(Vol. 41, No. 8, August 2000, pp. 31-33)**
Pub: Venture Economics
Ed: Charles Fellers. Description: Marketing partners become a new addition to several venture capital firms by focusing on mentoring and promoting portfolio companies.

47249 ■ **"Marketing budgets may rise"** in *Atlanta Business Chronicle* **(Vol. 25, January 10, 2003, No. 31, pp. 3A)**
Pub: American City Business Publications, Inc.
Ed: Jim Lovel. Description: Industry insiders predict that major corporations will commit more dollars to marketing efforts throughout 2003. A Patrick Marketing Group surveyed marketing executives, and indicates that budgets will increase by an average of 11 percent in 2003.

47250 ■ **"Marketing and sales"** in *Boston Business Journal* **(Vol. 22, No. 14, May 10, 2002, pp. 22)**
Pub: MCP, Inc.
Ed: Ken Cook. Description: The difference between marketing and sales, and how each is important and supports the other for sustainable growth, is discussed.

47251 ■ **"Marketing Spreads Hawaiian Message"** in *Pacific Business News* **(Vol. 41, No. 22, August 8, 2003, pp. 1)**
Pub: American City Business Journals
Ed: Nina Wu. Description: Marketing campaign that supports federal self-determination legislation for Native Hawaiians and the impact of the legislation on Hawaiian businesses are discussed.

47252 ■ *Marketing Strategies for Small Businesses*
Pub: Crisp Publications, Inc.
Ed: Richard F. Gerson. Price: $15.95. Description: Part of the Small Business & Entrepreneurship Series.

47253 ■ **"Marketing: Use 2003 As a Building Year"** in *Atlanta Business Chronicle* **(Vol. 25, No. 20, October 25, 2002, pp. 10B)**
Pub: American City Business Publications, Inc.
Ed: Alf Nucifora. Description: Several suggestions are given for using the year 2003 to build marketing endeavors, including the pushing of innovation and experimentation with new products.

47254 ■ *Marketing with Video: How to Create a Winning Video for Your Small Business or Non-Profit*
Pub: Oak Tree Press
Ed: Hal Landen. Released: 1996. Price: $19.95.

47255 ■ *Marketing Without Advertising*
Pub: Bell Springs Publishing
Ed: Michael Phillips and Salli Rasberry. Price: 18.95. Description: Argues with documented proof that almost all advertising is totally ineffective and an utter waste of money and that most business owners have been successfully duped into believing that advertising is both necessary and productive in spite of obvious evidence to the contrary. Includes more than a hundred tried and tested marketing strategies that have worked for all kinds of small businesses.

47256 ■ *Marketing Without Money for Small and Midsize Businesses: 300 FREE and Cheap Ways to Increase Your Sales*
Pub: Halle House Publishing
Ed: Nicholas E. Bade. Released: July 2005. Price: $16.95. Description: Three hundred practical low-cost or no-cost strategies to increase sales, focusing on free advertising, free marketing assistance, and free referrals to the Internet.

47257 ■ *Marketing that Works: How Entrepreneurial Marketing Can Add Sustainable Value to Any Sized Company*
Pub: Wharton School Publishing
Ed: Leonard M. Lodish; Howard Morgan; Shellye Archambeau. Released: March 2007. Price: $36.99 (CND). Description: Entrepreneurial marketing techniques are shared in order to help a new company position and target products and services.

47258 ■ *Marketing Works: Unlock Big Company Strategies for Small Business*
Pub: Morgan James Publishing, LLC
Ed: Chris Lee; Daniele Lima. Released: May 2006. Price: $19.95. Description: Marketing strategies for any small business are outlined.

47259 ■ "Marketing Your Consulting Service by Elaine Biech: www.josseybass.com" in *Entrepreneur* (Vol. 31, No. 10, October 2003, pp. 6)
Pub: Entrepreneur Media, Inc.
Ed: Steve Cooper. Description: Marketing tactics to help grow a business are presented.

47260 ■ *Marketing Your Product*
Pub: Self-Counsel Press, Incorporated
Ed: Donald Cyr, Douglas Gray. Released: September 2004. Price: $18.95. Description: Tips for marketing any product in today's competitive consumer environment. One chapter focuses on using the Internet as a marketing tool.

47261 ■ *Marketing Your Small Business for Big Profits*
Pub: Morgan James Publishing, LLC
Released: September 2006. Price: $12.95. Description: Successful marketing tip to grow a small business are presented.

47262 ■ "MarketingExperiments.com: www.marketingexperiments.com" in *Entrepreneur* (Vol. 32, November 2004, No. 11, pp. 6)
Pub: Entrepreneur Media Inc.
Ed: Steve Cooper. Description: Two Web sites testing marketing programs are featured.

47263 ■ "Marketingfix: www.marketingfix.com" in *Entrepreneur* (Vol. 31, No. 10, October 2003, pp. 6)
Pub: Entrepreneur Media, Inc.
Ed: Steve Cooper. Description: E-marketing news from marketing consultant, Rick E. Bruner, is available from www.marketingfix.com.

47264 ■ "MarketingSherpa: www.marketingsherpa.com" in *Entrepreneur* (Vol. 33, February 2005, No. 2, pp. 8)
Pub: Entrepreneur Media Inc.
Description: MarketingSherpa provides marketers with statistics, case studies, and email marketing newsletters.

47265 ■ "Math Will Rock Your World" in *Business Week* (January 23, 2006, No. 3968, pp. 54-58, 60, 62)
Pub: McGraw-Hill Companies
Ed: Stephen Baker. Description: Businesses are using math experts in ways that were unthinkable years ago. They are changing personal data, trends, and online content into math, crunching the numbers, and discovering new ways to market products and services.

47266 ■ "A Matter of Opinion" in *Entrepreneur* (Vol. 31, No. 8, August 2003, pp. 72)
Pub: Entrepreneur Media, Inc.
Ed: Elizabeth Goodgold. Description: According to Jeffrey G. Jordan, market researcher for 1-on-One Marketing Associates, mystery shopping, customer comment cards, on-site intercepting, Web site evaluation and toll-free telephone numbers are great ways to get customer feedback.

47267 ■ *Maximum Marketing, Minimum Dollars: The Top 50 Ways to Grow Your Small Business*
Pub: Kaplan Books
Ed: Kim Gordon. Released: April 2006. Price: $24.00. Description: Marketing tips to increase sales are presented. Small business owners will learn to maximize marketing with 50 innovative and affordable methods, including online marketing.

47268 ■ "Measure twice, cut once" in *Incentive* (Vol. 174, No. 9, September 2000, pp. 74)
Pub: Bill Communications
Ed: John Farrell. Description: Measurable marketing is the performance industry's call to action.

47269 ■ "Measuring the Car Market" in *Hispanic Business* (November 2003, pp. 66, 68, 70)
Pub: Hispanic Business
Ed: Paul A. Eisenstein. Description: Annually, Hispanics spend more money to purchase more cars, impacting the U.S. auto industry's future. A listing of automotive expenditures by Hispanics for years 1997-2001 is presented, as well as statistical data showing percentage of Hispanic purchases by brand for 2002 and 2003.

47270 ■ "Media Habits of Working Moms" in *Marketing to Women* (Vol. 20, January 2007, No. 1, pp. 4)
Pub: EPM Communications, Inc.
Description: Working mothers are spending less time than average consumers reading newspapers and watching television. They are getting the bulk of their information through the Internet, radio, and direct mailing. Statistical data included.

47271 ■ "Media, Mid-Perm" in *Inc.* (October 1, 2003)
Pub: Gruner & Jahr USA Publishing
Ed: Nadine Heintz. Description: Entrepreneur hair stylist, Ava DuVernay, launched Urban Beauty Collective Television (UBC TV). UBC TV is a two-hour video targeting primarily African American and Hispanic women in 16 cities from Miami to Detroit. The video contains movie trailers and videos, as well as advertising by companies.

47272 ■ "Media Planning: The Seven 'Undeniable Truths'" in *Ingram's* (Vol. 28, No. 9, September 2002, pp. 27)
Pub: Show Me Publishing, Inc.
Ed: John McGuigan. Description: A guide for planning and executing integrated marketing programs for clients is provided.

47273 ■ "Medium or Marketplace?" in *Tradeshow Week* (Vol. 34, December 20, 2004, No. 51, pp. 7)
Pub: Reed Business Information
Ed: Adam Schaffer. Description: Chris Meyer of the Las Vegas Convention and Visitors Authority believes tradeshows are a good marketing tool for companies to show goods and services. Statistical data included.

47274 ■ "The Meet Market: Looking for New Business Leads? Networking Clubs on the Web Make it Easy" in *Entrepreneur* (Vol. 32, August 2004)
Pub: Entrepreneur Media Inc.
Ed: Catherine Seda. Description: Techniques that will help small business owners meet valuable contacts and secure new projects on the Internet are listed.

47275 ■ "Meet & Potatoes" in *Entrepreneur* (Vol. 30, No. 3, March 2002, pp. 89)
Pub: Entrepreneur Media Inc.
Ed: Barry Farber. Description: Ideas to help entrepreneurs to network outside of a safe, familiar circle of contracts are presented.

47276 ■ "Meet Your Customers' Needs Through Cultural Marketing" in *E-business Advisor* (Vol. 18, No. 8, August 2000, pp. 18)
Pub: Advisor Media, Inc.
Ed: Donald DePalma. Description: Few U.S. online businesses are focusing on the needs of culturally diverse groups of users. Cultural, or ethnic, marketing targets a specific national or linguistic group and includes such cross-border issues as currency conversion, shipping concerns, and export-import compliance. Statistical information is included.

47277 ■ "A Melting Pot with Flavor" in *Hispanic Business* (December 2003, pp. 20-21)
Pub: Hispanic Business
Description: Convergence of the Hispanic population with mainstream American culture has created a unique market for the future. To understand the cultural dynamics of the market, researchers have divided the population using a quadrant system; an example of the cultural matrix is provided.

47278 ■ "Memory Lane" in *Entrepreneur* (Vol. 33, September 2005, No. 9, pp. 88)
Pub: Entrepreneur Media Inc.
Ed: Jerry Fisher. Description: Nostalgia-loving baby boomers love advertising that uses memorabilia reminiscent of their younger years.

47279 ■ "Meredith Debuts Mag for Cancer Survivors" in *Marketing to Women* (Vol. 19, October 2006, No. 10, pp. 5)
Pub: EPM Communications, Inc.
Description: Meredith Corp.'s Special Interest Media Health Group debuts the first magazine geared specifically to women who have had breast cancer. Beyond: Live & Thrive After Breast Cancer includes personal stories, advice, resources, and up-to-date medical information.

47280 ■ "Merger with Advo May Mean Shift in Business for Valassis" in *Crain's Detroit Business* (Vol. 232, January 8, 2007, No. 2, pp. 4)
Pub: Crain Communications Inc. - Detroit
Ed: Bill Shea. Description: The merger of Valassis and Advo is a long term strategy to grow the business into direct mailing. Valassis has been limited solely to the insert mailings in periodicals.

47281 ■ "A Meta-Study of the Market" in *Hispanic Business* (December 2002, pp. 22, 24, 26)
Pub: Hispanic Business
Description: The results of a study on the subject of language usage among U.S. Hispanic consumers to track marketing trends are presented. The meta-study is a synthesis of earlier research and suggests that a significant number of individuals in the Hispanic market will conduct business in the English language.

47282 ■ "Middays of Thunder" in *Inc.* (January 1, 2002)
Pub: Inc. Magazine
Ed: Rebecca Dorr. Description: Robert River, founder of Spectrum Communications Cabling Services Inc., tells how he took his top customers and some employees to a race track to race cars, rather than dinner or a ball game.

47283 ■ "Might mascots" in *Entrepreneur* (Vol. 31, No. 6, June 2003, pp. 79)
Pub: Entrepreneur Media Inc.
Ed: Elizabeth J. Goodgold. Description: The use of a mascot for marketing products and services can translate into strong sales. Guidelines for creating a mascot for a small business are listed.

47284 ■ "Military Detail" in *Entrepreneur* (Vol. 32, No. 1, January 2004, pp. 26)
Pub: Entrepreneur Media, Inc.
Ed: Gwen Moran. Description: Because the armed forces is a tremendous market, many small businesses are offering discounts or incentives to military families for goods and services.

47285 ■ "Mind Over Market" in *Entrepreneur* (Vol. 33, March 2005, No. 3, pp. 66)
Pub: Entrepreneur Media Inc.
Ed: Jay Conrad Levinson, Al Lautenslager. Description: Jay Conrad Levinson shares his effective marketing strategies used to market his book, Guerrilla Marketing.

47286 ■ "Mind Your Pricing Cues" in *Harvard Business Review* (Vol. 81, No. 9, September 2003, pp. 96)
Pub: Harvard Business School Press

Ed: Eric Anderson, Duncan Simester. **Description:** Research on buying habits are documented here. Some aspects of the research includes: pricing goods that end in 9 increased sales ($34 versus $39.99), sales signs can have a positive or negative effect, and the fact that too many signs results in lower sales.

47287 ■ "Mining Online for the Bottom Line" in *Success* **(Vol. 47, No. 4, September 2000, pp. 82)**
Pub: Success Publishing, Inc.
Ed: Paul Gallagher. **Description:** Office services franchisors use the Internet to unearth more customers.

47288 ■ "The Mismanagement of Advertising" in *Harvard Business Review* **(Vol. 78, No. 1, January 2000, pp. 22)**
Pub: Harvard Business School Publishing Corp.
Ed: John Philip Jones. **Description:** This article discusses the effectiveness of advertising. The author evaluates the performance of present-day ad agencies in relation to the accomplishments of past industry leaders.

47289 ■ "The Missing Link?" in *Entrepreneur* **(Vol. 33, September 2005, No. 9, pp. 88)**
Pub: Entrepreneur Media Inc.
Ed: Catherine Seda. **Description:** The much-overlooked marketing strategy of getting links from other Websites to yours is examined. This tool will bring more visitors to a site while helping to achieve higher search engine rankings.

47290 ■ "Moms Have Their Own Generation Gap" in *Marketing to Women* **(Vol. 20, January 2007, No. 1, pp. 5)**
Pub: EPM Communications, Inc.
Description: A Johnson & Johnson study compares the mothers of today with the mothers of 1967. Statistical data included.

47291 ■ "Moms Say Missing Their Babies is Hardest Part of Returning to Work" in *Marketing to Women* **(Vol. 19, November 2006, No. 11, pp. 3)**
Pub: EPM Communications, Inc.
Description: According to a survey by Modern Mom, the hardest thing about going to work outside the home for mothers is the separation anxiety they experience with their children. This leads to problems like getting to the office on time and getting back to speed with projects.

47292 ■ "Moms Want Ads to Address Them as Women" in *Marketing to Women* **(Vol. 19, October 2006, No. 10, pp. 3)**
Pub: EPM Communications, Inc.
Description: A study by Draft Chicago found that in advertising mothers want to be spoken to as a well rounded individual instead of as only a mom. Statistical data included.

47293 ■ "More bang" in *Entrepreneur* **(Vol. 30, No. 2, February)**
Pub: Entrepreneur Media Inc.
Ed: Chris Penttila. **Description:** Presentation of twenty-five tips for under $1,000 that will make a business better, from marketing to sales, and employees to equipment.

47294 ■ "More Bang for Your Buck" in *Entrepreneur* **(Vol. 32)**
Pub: Entrepreneur Media Inc.
Ed: Nichole L. Torres. **Description:** Associated Surplus Dealers/Associated Merchandise Dealers (ASD/MD) Trade Show Las Vegas, produced by VNU Expositions, offers small business entrepreneurs and eBay resellers a cost-effective venue for selling products. The show includes 3,500 exhibitors with products ranging from dollar-store merchandise to general merchandise such as toys, gifts, electronics, health and beauty, and fashion accessories.

47295 ■ "More steady growth: Hispanic ad expenditures increase 11 percent to reach nearly $1.9 billion" in *Hispanic Business* **(Dec. 1999, pp.56)**
Pub: Hispanic Business
Ed: Tim Dougherty. **Description:** Expansion in Hispanic advertising expenditures slowed to 11 percent in 1999, from 21 percent in 1998. However, the Top 50 Advertiser total rose 30 percent to $545.97 million. The impact of the Internet on Hispanic advertising is discussed.

47296 ■ "More Women Than Men Have Home Offices" in *Marketing to Women* **(Vol. 19, October 2006, No. 10, pp. 12)**
Pub: EPM Communications, Inc.
Description: A survey of business professionals by Intellicontact reflects that women are more likely than men to have home offices. The survey also shows that while men and women both check their e-mail frequently, the two sexes manage their inboxes differently.

47297 ■ "Most Women Make Electronics Buying Choices" in *Marketing to Women* **(Vol. 19, November 2006, No. 11, pp. 11)**
Pub: EPM Communications, Inc.
Description: According to the Vertis 2006 Customer Focus Home Electronics Study, more than nine in ten women in the 35-49 age group say they are chief or equal decision-makers when shopping for home electronics. Statistical data included.

47298 ■ "The Mother of Stunt Marketers" in *Business 2.0* **(Vol. 6, July 2005, No. 6, pp. 60-61)**
Pub: Time, Inc.
Ed: Elizabeth Esfahani. **Description:** The Publicity Stunts Hall of Fame highlights the crazy things people have done as marketing tricks that generated publicity and increased sales for products.

47299 ■ "Motherhood Maternity Debuts Canadian Site" in *Marketing to Women* **(Vol. 19, November 2006, No. 11, pp. 5)**
Pub: EPM Communications, Inc.
Description: Motherhoodcanada.ca, a Website serving residents of Canadian provinces, with the exception of Quebec, was launched by Motherhood Maternity.

47300 ■ *MRA Blue Book Research Services Directory*
Pub: Marketing Research Association
Contact: Laura Cole
Released: Annual, February. **Price:** $169.95, non-members; $99.95, members. **Covers:** over 1,200 marketing research companies and field interviewing services. **Entries Include:** Company name, address, phone, names of executives, services, facilities, special interviewing capabilities. **Arrangement:** Geographical; business type. **Indexes:** geographic and by specialty.

47301 ■ "MSN Signs DIY Expert With Female Focus" in *Marketing to Women* **(Vol. 20, January 2007, No. 1, pp. 8)**
Pub: EPM Communications, Inc.
Description: MSN and the online community devoted to women, Be Jane, team up to bring the subject of women's home improvement to a broader audience via the Internet. Video clips, animated tutorials, articles, message boards, and blogs will address such varied topics as repairing holes in dry wall to painting a garage door.

47302 ■ "Muscling in on the Hispanic Market" in *Hispanic Business* **(January/February 2003, pp. 28)**
Pub: Hispanic Business
Description: General Motors is reaching out to the Hispanic market with their new car marketing plans by using Spanish language advertising.

47303 ■ "My Business Manual: Due Diligence" in *My Business* **(December/January 2003, pp. 44)**
Pub: My Business Magazine

Ed: Julie Bawden Davis. **Description:** A good customer service program ensures repeat business. Five easy ways to gain new customers are also listed.

47304 ■ "My Business Manual: One Step Ahead" in *My Business* **(December/January 2003, pp. 43)**
Pub: My Business Magazine
Ed: Alan S. Horowitz. **Description:** Customer loyalty programs are discussed, including tips on starting a frequent buyer program.

47305 ■ "My Business Manual: Open Up" in *My Business* **(December/January 2003, pp. 41-42)**
Pub: My Business Magazine
Ed: John Rubino. **Description:** Five ways to grow a business by targeting new customers are highlighted, including identification of the new target market, becoming part of the community, know the limitations of a business, getting clients interested in a product, and ways to market a new product.

47306 ■ "My Favorite Fiascos" in *Fast Company* **(November 2001, pp. 38)**
Pub: Fast Company
Description: Alberto Alessi discusses his favorite business disasters, customer savvy, and customer loyalty.

47307 ■ "My Gadget" in *My Business* **(February/March 2004, pp. 17)**
Pub: My Business Magazine
Ed: Lena Basha. **Description:** Profile of AccuCard, a self-updating address book designed for use with Microsoft Outlook. The service will send personalized quarterly emails to every small business contact, requesting updated or confirmation of correct contact information and automatically updates information every three months.

47308 ■ *My Homemade Business*
Pub: Graphico Publishing Company
Ed: Victoria Ring. **Released:** January 2005. **Price:** $39.99. **Description:** Author shares insight into ways she marketed different businesses over a 16-year period. Free Web design software included.

47309 ■ "MySpace for Business: Are You Connected?" in *Sales & Marketing Management* **(Vol. 158, November-December 2006, No. 11, pp. 20)**
Pub: VNU Business Media
Ed: Rebecca Aronauer. **Description:** Joining an online community can prove profitable to any salesperson.

47310 ■ "Mystery Shoppers Take a Second Glance at Customer Service" in *Business Record* **(Vol. 22, August 30, 2004, No. 35, pp. 1)**
Pub: Business Publication Corporation
Ed: Erin Morain. **Description:** Prairie Life Health & Fitness center in West Des Moines, Iowa uses mystery shoppers to conduct market research.

47311 ■ "Nab your Niche" in *Entrepreneur* **(Vol. 31, No. 6, June 2003, pp. 100)**
Pub: Entrepreneur Media Inc.
Ed: Nichole L. Torres. **Description:** Finding a niche in the home-remodeling market is important; according to the National Association of Home Builders, 1.35 million new single-family homes will be built in the U.S. in 2003, and remodeling is at all time highs.

47312 ■ "NAHREP Set to Host Confab" in *Hispanic Business* **(Vol. 23, No. 10, October, 2001, pp. 104)**
Pub: Hispanic Business
Description: The National Association of Hispanic Real Estate Professionals (NAHREP) will host the nation's first real estate conference dedicated exclusively to Hispanic marketing.

47313 ■ "The Name Game" in *Entrepreneur* **(Vol. 33, January 2005, No. 1, pp. 72)**
Pub: Entrepreneur Media Inc.

Ed: Jane Easter Bahls. **Description:** Under the legal doctrine, reverse confusion, small companies can file lawsuits against large corporations over trademark infringement.

47314 ■ **"National trends in Webcast advertising"** in *Crain's Detroit Business* (Vol. 16, No. 46, November 13, 2000, pp. 15)
Pub: Crain Communications, Inc.
Description: Market information and statistical data regarding online advertising, banner ads, sponsorship, e-mail, pop-ups, and buttons are discussed.

47315 ■ **"Needful things?"** in *Entrepreneur* (Vol. 30, No. 12, December 2002, pp. 109)
Pub: Entrepreneur Media Inc.
Ed: Nichole L. Torres. **Description:** Ways to sell non-essential items are examined.

47316 ■ **"Net Company: Don't Shout, Listen"** in *Fast Company* (August 2001, pp. 129)
Pub: Fast Company
Ed: Fara Warner. **Description:** The article shows how the Proctor & Gamble company has turned the Internet into a device for listening to customers, and also experiment with their brands.

47317 ■ *Network Marketing*
Pub: Crisp Publications, Inc.
Ed: Mary Averill and Bud Corkin. **Price:** $10.95.

47318 ■ **"Network Marketing or Pyramid Scheme?"** in *Black Enterprise* (Vol. 35, November 2004, No. 4, pp. 102)
Pub: Earl G. Graves Publishing Co. Inc.
Ed: Wendy Harris. **Description:** When Cameron Brickey signed up to be an independent associate for Pre-Paid Legal Services Inc., a network marketing company, he thought he would earn an easy living. The company provides affordable legal services targeted to low- and middle-income individuals and families. While many multilevel marketing companies are legitimate, also known as pyramid schemes, they can be risky.

47319 ■ **"Networking Nice"** in *Success* (Vol. 47, No. 1, January 2000, pp. 54)
Pub: Success Publishing, Inc.
Ed: Martha Visser. **Description:** A guide to making your friends and family also your client, suggesting that the approach you take selling to them needs to be crafted carefully.

47320 ■ **"Net.Working"** in *Small Business Opportunities* (Vol. 12, No. 2, March 2000, pp. 80)
Pub: Harris Publications, Inc.
Ed: Robert Spiegel. **Description:** One entrepreneur tells how net affiliations help him make an extra $250,000 a year by using them.

47321 ■ **"Neuburger Outgrows Pajamas"** in *San Francisco Business Times* (Vol. 17, No. 51, July 25, 2003, pp. 1)
Pub: American City Business Journals
Ed: Ryan Tate. **Description:** Profile of retail clothing store, Neuburger; topics include market share, market development and profits.

47322 ■ **"New Business Owners Learn the Ropes in 2006"** in *Bellingham Business Journal* (January 2007, pp.)
Pub: Sun News Inc.
Ed: Dan Hiestand. **Description:** Local business owners say that the biggest challenge of the business is getting one's name out there.

47323 ■ **"New CEO: So What is Moto, Anyway?"** in *Crain's Chicago Business* (Vol. 26, No. 51, December 22, 2003, pp. 20)
Pub: Crain Communications, Inc.
Ed: Julie Johnsson. **Description:** Newly appointed CEO of Motorola, Edward Zander, wants to fashion a distinctive corporate image for the electronics giant. The firm reports $27 billion in revenues and Zander feels the firm needs to better define itself.

47324 ■ **"The new culture of criticism is hurting you and your company"** in *Fast Company* (May 2001, pp. 102)
Pub: Fast Company
Ed: Seth Godin. **Description:** The five ways to be an unfair critic, and in turn hurt your business, are listed.

47325 ■ *The New Direct Marketing: How to Implement a Profit-Driven Database Marketing Strategy*
Pub: McGraw-Hill Professional Book Group
Released: 3rd ed. 1998. **Price:** $114.95; $79.95.

47326 ■ **"New Foundation"** in *Hispanic Business* (June 2005, pp. 20)
Pub: Hispanic Business
Description: Hispanic Advertising Agencies Foundation was created by the Association of Hispanic Advertising Agencies in an effort to fund and distribute market research related to Hispanic consumers. The foundation will also offer educational opportunities and scholarships to individuals pursuing a career in Hispanic advertising.

47327 ■ *The New How to Advertise: Expanded, Updated, and Completely Revised for the '90s*
Pub: St. Martin's Press, Inc.
Ed: Kenneth Roman. **Released:** 1992. **Price:** $22.95.

47328 ■ **"New Office Created to Market Michigan for Films"** in *Crain's Detroit Business* (Vol. 22, December 18, 2006, No. 51, pp. 19)
Pub: Crain Communications Inc. - Detroit
Ed: Bill Shea. **Description:** Michigan to organize marketing for film making in the region. New office will concentrate on luring movie companies to film in Michigan

47329 ■ **"The New Prime Time"** in *Crain's New York Business* (Vol. 23, November 20, 2006, No. 47, pp. 28)
Pub: Crain Communications, Inc.
Description: Advertisers are finding that more people are spending time on their websites during the workday. Marketers feel that the daytime hours are the new prime time and website creators are happy to supply entertainment and information to bored office workers.

47330 ■ **"New Products Hit Showfloor: Expo! Expo!"** in *Tradeshow Week* (Vol. 34, November 29, 2004, No. 48, pp. 47)
Pub: Reed Business Information
Ed: Margo McCall. **Description:** New technology products and services were unveiled at the Expo! Expo! Show. The show's highlights include Accumanage, a new software program that provides an exhibitor management system that can be used by show management or exhibitors to complete company profiles for a directory listing.

47331 ■ **"New Shade of Vodka Targets Women"** in *Marketing to Women* (Vol. 20, January 2007, No. 1, pp. 8)
Pub: EPM Communications, Inc.
Description: Pinky Vodka is a specialty vodka with a distinctive blush which is produced from a combination of botanicals. Violets, rose petals, and strawberries give this liquor its unique flavor and color.

47332 ■ **"New Site Sells Women's Self-Defense Wares"** in *Marketing to Women* (Vol. 20, January 2007, No. 1, pp. 8)
Pub: EPM Communications, Inc.
Description: WomenOnGuard.com is a website selling non-lethal self-defense products. The site is designed to teach women how to protect themselves and includes an interactive section for discussion and links to organizations that provide victim services.

47333 ■ **"The New Sounds of Selling"** in *Business 2.0* (Vol. 6, May 2005, No. 4, pp. 58, 60)
Pub: Time, Inc.
Ed: Thomas Mucha. **Description:** Smart marketers are using music clips, beeps and other sound bites to attract consumer attention quickly.

47334 ■ **"New Tacks for Tough Times"** in *Business Week Online* (Oct. 17, 2002)
Pub: McGraw-Hill Inc.
Ed: Roger Franklin. **Description:** According to a small business survey, 75 percent of the 5,000 firms responding, have a positive attitude about the future, and predict bottom-line growth. One-third of the companies expect significant expansion.

47335 ■ **"New Territory: To Get New Customers, Widen Your Ad Campaign"** in *Entrepreneur* (Vol. 32, August 2004, No. 8, pp. 67)
Pub: Entrepreneur Media Inc.
Ed: Nancy Michaels. **Description:** Owner of five travel agencies offering travelers unique, authentic experiences abroad wishes to expand advertising from local to national.

47336 ■ **"New TV Network on the Launch Pad"** in *Hispanic Business* (March 2003, pp. 14)
Pub: Hispanic Business
Description: Expresion Media Group, based in Chicago, has started sales for a new Hispanic cable television network that will launch nationally in May 2003. The network will offer both Spanish and bilingual original programming, independent films, and music features geared toward successful Hispanics between the ages of 18-49.

47337 ■ **"A New Vision for Network Marketing"** in *Success* (Vol. 47, No. 3, July 2000, pp. 80)
Pub: Success Publishing, Inc.
Ed: Karin Fuller. **Description:** Profile of New Vision, a network-marketing company, whose co-founder shares some secrets of success.

47338 ■ **"New Website for Women's Clothes"** in *Marketing to Women* (Vol. 20, January 2007, No. 1, pp. 8)
Pub: EPM Communications, Inc.
Description: FrillyGirls.com is a new website catering to women between the ages of 21-45. The site is run by three stay-at-home mothers looking to reenter the workforce and specializes in designer clothing and accessories.

47339 ■ **"New York Community Bancorp Renames All of Its Branches..."** in *Long Island Business News* (February 6, 2004)
Pub: Dolan Media Newswires
Ed: Claude Solnik. **Description:** New York Community Bancorp has rebranded its bank branches in Nassau and Suffolk in order to create a more clearly defined network of regional banks. Information regarding the bank's reorganization efforts is explained.

47340 ■ **"The New You"** in *Entrepreneur* (Vol. 32, October 2004, No. 10, pp. 100)
Pub: Entrepreneur Media Inc.
Ed: Nichole L. Torres. **Description:** According to market strategists, entrepreneurs should take a long look at their brand and focus on services or products that fit the overall brand.

47341 ■ **"News Blog Highlights Women's Careers"** in *Marketing to Women* (Vol. 19, November 2006, No. 11, pp. 5)
Pub: EPM Communications, Inc.
Description: NewsonWomen.com, a news blog for businesswomen and their career achievements, has added executive job postings to its content.

47342 ■ **"News and Reviews"** in *Home Business* (Vol. 13, January/February 2006, No. 1, pp. 98)
Pub: Home Business Magazine
Description: Information for closing business deals online, Web-based human resources small business software, noise canceling audio headphones, and tips for launching and marketing new products is given.

47343 ■ **"News on Women"** in *Marketing to Women* (Vol. 19, November 2006, No. 22, pp. 8)
Pub: EPM Communications, Inc.

Description: Various excerpts from articles and reports intended to provide information relevant to marketers targeting female consumers.

47344 ■ **"Newsletter company to nearly double in size"** in *Atlanta Business Chronicle* (Vol. 25, January 10, 2003, No. 31, pp. 5A)

Pub: American City Business Publications, Inc.

Ed: Jim Lovel. **Description:** NewRx which presently publishes 24 health and medicine-related newsletters, will double its size with the addition of 20 more publications. The Georgia International Convention Center has hired four marketing consultants to promote the grand opening of the College Park Center.

47345 ■ **"Newsstand"** in *Home Business* (Vol. 13, January/February 2006, No. 1, pp. 38-39)

Pub: Home Business Magazine

Description: Topics include marketing of office supplies and equipment, rising gas prices, toxic office environments, entrepreneurship, and online retailing.

47346 ■ **"The Next Big Idea is Already Here"** in *Automotive News* (Vol. 79, January 24, 2005, No. 79, pp. 12)

Pub: Crain Communications Inc.

Ed: Keith Crain. **Description:** According to one expert, luxury automakers could create the next best marketing idea by offering a one-price lease that includes license plates along with insurance. Although Volkswagen is testing the idea in a few states, their models do not fit the proper niche for this type of plan.

47347 ■ **"The Next Big Market"** in *Success* (Vol. 47, No. 5, October 2000, pp. 36)

Pub: Success Publishing, Inc.

Ed: Frank Solis. **Description:** According to the Census Bureau, Hispanics make up the nation's fastest-growing consumer segment, spending some $380 billion on products and services annually.

47348 ■ **"Nike Develops Brand for Women"** in *Marketing to Women* (Vol. 20, January 2007, No. 1, pp. 8)

Pub: EPM Communications, Inc.

Description: A new brand of tennis shoes for women will hit shelves in spring 2007. The brand Tailwind will combine contemporary fashion with athletic performance and is a result of marketing partnership between Payless Shoe Source and Exeter Brands Group, a subsidiary of Nike.

47349 ■ **"No Ad Recession for Hispanic Marketers"** in *Business Week Online* (February 19, 2002)

Pub: McGraw-Hill, Inc.

Description: Advertising agencies targeting Hispanic consumers are growing despite the overall decline in ad spending, with some agencies expecting ethnic-marketing budgets to more than double in 2002.

47350 ■ **"No Line At 6 a.m. Black Friday"** in *Tampa Tribune* (December 7, 2005)

Pub: Media General, Inc.

Ed: Michael Sasso. **Description:** A group of independent retailers share marketing ideas they use to increase sales during the holidays, especially on Black Friday, the day after Thanksgiving.

47351 ■ **"North market merchants selling Valentine's package"** in *Business First Columbus* (Vol. 18, No. 25, February 8, 2002, pp. A12)

Pub: Business First Columbus, Inc.

Ed: Laura Newpoff. **Description:** A preview of the Valentine's Day packages being offered by Columbus area restaurants.

47352 ■ **"Northwest Accord To Allow Flying For Other Carriers"** in *Wall Street Journal* (Vol. 248, December 2006, No. 149, pp. B2)

Pub: Dow Jones & Co. Inc.

Ed: Associated Press **Description:** Regional Pinnacle Airlines Corporation struck a 10-year agreement with Northwest Airlines Corp. to expand Pinnacle's flying to other carriers in exchange for an unsecured claim in Northwest's bankruptcy proceedings.

47353 ■ **"Not Lost in Translation"** in *Entrepreneur* (Vol. 32, December 2004, No. 12, pp. 16)

Pub: Entrepreneur Media Inc.

Ed: Kimberly L. McCall. **Description:** Suggestions for U.S. entrepreneurs wishing to adapt global marketing techniques to their business are offered.

47354 ■ **"The Not-So-Talented Tenth"** in *Sales & Marketing Management* (Vol. 158, November-December 2006, No. 11, pp. 16)

Pub: VNU Business Media

Ed: Michelle Marchetti. **Description:** New sales staff at Financial Resources of America must complete the company's five-day training program before selling to customers.

47355 ■ **"Now Playing"** in *Entrepreneur* (Vol. 33, March 2005, No. 3, pp. 87)

Pub: Entrepreneur Media Inc.

Ed: Kim T. Gordon. **Description:** Cinema advertising is the fastest growing form for marketing a product.

47356 ■ **"Now Showing: Hard At Work"** in *My Business* (April/May 2002, pp. 44)

Pub: My Business Magazine

Ed: Roseanne Hooper. **Description:** Profile of The Propel Group, a graphic design firm in Dallas, Texas. The firm purchased a 55-year-old movie theatre as a marketing tool for designing advertising, Web pages, catalogs and logos for clients.

47357 ■ **"Now you've done it! Real deal"** in *Entrepreneur* (Vol. 30, No. 3, March 2002, pp.)

Pub: Entrepreneur Media Inc.

Ed: Marc Diener. **Description:** Five basic principles to avoid during negotiations are presented.

47358 ■ **"Nurun Transforms Loews Hotels Website Into a More User-Friendly Experience"** in *Canadian Corporate News* (February 7, 2007)

Pub: Comtex News Network, Inc.

Description: Loews Hotels has updated its Website to market its properties to online users.

47359 ■ **"October Winner"** in *Sales & Marketing Management* (Vol. 159, January-February 2007, No. 1, pp. 48)

Pub: VNU Business Media

Description: Profile of Andrew M. Podner, product specialist at Southwest Region Sigma Corporation located in Houston, Texas.

47360 ■ **"On the Cheap: Creative Ways to Stretch Your Marketing Dollar"** in *Sales and Marketing.com* (Vol. 156, No. 3, March 2004, pp. 10)

Pub: VNU eMedia, Inc.

Description: Customer testimonials are a powerful way to enhance a sales rep's credibility with new clients.

47361 ■ **"On the Cheap"** in *Sales & Marketing Management* (Vol. 158, November-December 2006, No. 11, pp. 14)

Pub: VNU Business Media

Description: Clear Channel offers five-second commercial spots to help small firms afford advertising.

47362 ■ **"On the Radar"** in *E-business Advisor* (Vol. 18, No. 9, September 2000, pp. 8)

Pub: Advisor Media, Inc.

Description: Marketplace exchanges are reaching a sensitive period in their development. At present, exchange-pricing models should be overhauled to give buyers and sellers incentives to initiate business. In addition, most exchanges are not truly global, though many claim to be.

47363 ■ **"On the Same Page: Newspaper Advertising is Generally Flat"** in *Hispanic Business* (Vol. 21, No. 12, December 1999, pp. 70)

Pub: Hispanic Business

Description: Trends in newspaper advertising aimed at Hispanic Americans are examined. The dominant market is Los Angeles, California, where advertising expenditure is anticipated to be $71.44 million in 1999.

47364 ■ **"On Target: Get the Specifics on Potential Customers"** in *Entrepreneur* (Vol. 31, No. 11, November 2003, pp. 99)

Pub: Entrepreneur Media, Inc.

Ed: April Y. Pennington. **Description:** A client support/sales department can help a small business target specific customers.

47365 ■ **"On Target: You Need Market Research to Hit the Mark with Prospects"** in *Entrepreneur* (Vol. 32, August 2004, No. 8, pp. 88)

Pub: Entrepreneur Media Inc.

Ed: Isabella Trebond. **Description:** Creative, low-cost methods to identify a small company's target market are explored.

47366 ■ **"On With the Show"** in *Hispanic Business* (December 2001, pp. 60, 62)

Pub: Hispanic Business

Ed: Derek Reveron. **Description:** Although revenue is flat or down in the general-sector television market, advertising is strong among Spanish-language networks.

47367 ■ **"One More For the Road"** in *Sales & Marketing Management* (January 2005)

Pub: VNU Business Media

Ed: Denis Jensen. **Description:** Sales executives, as well as management, should avoid the pitfalls of drinking when entertaining business clients. One accident involving an employee under the influence will cause insurance rates to go up.

47368 ■ *The One to One Future*

Pub: Doubleday & Co., Inc.

Ed: Don Peppers and Martha Rogers. **Released:** 1993. **Price:** $15.95. **Description:** Provides information on the transition from transition-based marketing to relationship-based marketing.

47369 ■ **"A One-Stop Marketing Shop"** in *Entrepreneur* (Vol. 31, No. 10, October 2003, pp. 112)

Pub: Entrepreneur Media, Inc.

Description: Profile of PRstore LLC, offering franchises to former corporate marketing executives wishing to own a retail business. The firm has created more than 50 standard customizable products that franchisees use to help clients develop marketing campaigns.

47370 ■ **"1,000 Crates of Sprinkles With That"** in *The New York Times* (March 27, 2000, pp. D28, H28)

Pub: The New York Times Company

Ed: Stephen Mihm. **Description:** The structuring of business-to-business commerce online. Statistical data included.

47371 ■ *1,001 Ways to Market Yourself & Your Small Business*

Pub: Berkley Publishing Group

Ed: Lisa Shaw. **Released:** 1997. **Price:** $12.95.

47372 ■ **"Online Content Reaches Bottom Line"** in *Crain's New York Business* (Vol. 20, No. 12, March 22, 2004, pp. 4)

Pub: Crain Communications, Inc.

Ed: Anita Jain. **Description:** Online magazine publishers are seeing an increase in advertising sales as consumer confidence grows. Profiles of TheStreet.com, Nerve.com, and Slate are included, with each sharing the ways they are earning profits with online magazines.

47373 ■ **"Online Rivals' Market Plays"** in *Hispanic Business* (January/February 2003, pp. 50, 52)

Pub: Hispanic Business

Ed: Romona Padena. **Description:** Internet providers are exploring methods to target the Hispanic market, an estimated market of 10 million users. According to a report by HispanTelligence, American Hispanic purchasing power equated to $540 billion in 2002.

47374 ■ "Online Video Ads Get Ready to Grab You" in *Business 2.0* (Vol. 6, May 2005, No. 4, pp. 25-26)
Pub: Time, Inc.
Ed: Matthew Maier. **Description:** Spending for online video advertising is expected to grow from $100 million to $600 million in the next five years.

47375 ■ "The Only Question That Matters" in *Business 2.0* (Vol. 6, September 2005, No. 8, pp. 50)
Pub: Time, Inc.
Ed: Description: Companies using the net promoter technique are listed. This technique asks customers whether they would recommend a product, subtracts positive responses from neutral and negative ones giving a barometer of customer satisfaction.

47376 ■ "Onward, Christian Marketer" in *Inc.* (July 1, 2004)
Pub: Inc. Magazine
Ed: Nicole Gull. **Description:** The success of Mel Gibson's, The Passion of the Christ, proved to marketers that there is a demand for Christian-based movies, but also that Christians love the Internet.

47377 ■ "Open Your Books To Grow Your Business" in *My Business* (November/December 2001, pp. 42)
Pub: My Business Magazine
Ed: Shannon Scully. **Description:** Open book management (OBM), is described by its originator, Victor Ornelas owner of a Latino marketing firm in Dallas, Texas. Open book management is a company policy that requires the business owner to share the company's financial information with its employees.

47378 ■ "Opt-In News" in *Entrepreneur* (Vol. 31, No. 8, August 2003, pp. 6)
Pub: Entrepreneur Media, Inc.
Ed: Steve Cooper. **Description:** A Website offering email marketing trends, players and news through daily updates is featured. The firm also offers a free newsletter and a resource directory with links to sources for email marketing consultants.

47379 ■ "Optimal Marketing" in *Harvard Business Review* (Vol. 81, No. 10, October 2003, pp. 114)
Pub: Harvard Business School Press
Ed: Marcel Corstjens, Jeffrey Merrihue. **Description:** Profile of Samsung shows how the company tracks the effectiveness of its $1 billion marketing program.

47380 ■ "Orchestrating Assistance; Chambers of Commerce" in *Crain's New York Business* (Vol. 22, November 13, 2006, No. 46, pp. 38)
Pub: Crain Communications, Inc.
Description: Listing of local chapters of New York's chambers of commerce. These organizations serve as sources of information and representation for local business interest provide a number of services and a wide variety of programs for small businesses.

47381 ■ "Our World with Black Enterprise" in *Black Enterprise* (Vol. 37, February 2007, No. 7, pp. 145)
Pub: Earl G. Graves Publishing Co. Inc.
Description: Our World with Black Enterprise is a television broadcast that features roundtable discussions and interviews with important African American figures.

47382 ■ "Out of the blue into the black" in *Harvard Business Review* (Vol. 80, No. 4, April 2002, pp. 112)
Pub: Harvard Business School Press
Ed: Frank Batten. **Description:** A chronicle of the development of the Weather Channel, the brainchild of Frank Batten, chairman of Landmark Communications. Batten's new concept in cable television, twenty years after its founding, is one of the world's most trusted media brands.

47383 ■ "Overcome E-Business Barriers" in *E-business Advisor* (Vol. 18, No. 1, January 2000, pp. 10)
Pub: Advisor Media, Inc.
Ed: Laurie Windham. **Description:** Today's e-business environment challenges managers to respond with effective online business strategies. Customers have already demonstrated their preference to do business over the Web, especially for routine tasks, and businesses that offer online services early are rewarded with customer loyalty and marketshare. Understanding how an e-business strategy influences time-to-market considerations is crucial to success.

47384 ■ *The Owners Manual for Small Business*
Pub: Planning Shop
Ed: Rhonda Abrams. **Released:** December 2005. **Price:** $19.95. **Description:** Reference book offering tips for starting a small business, low-cost marketing, and communicating effectively.

47385 ■ "Pack a Punch" in *Entrepreneur* (Vol. 31, No. 11, November 2003, pp. 102)
Pub: Entrepreneur Media, Inc.
Ed: Jerry Fisher. **Description:** Attention-getting ideas to market products and services are investigated.

47386 ■ "Panasonic Tunes In Hispanic Market" in *Hispanic Business* (March 2003, pp. 24)
Pub: Hispanic Business
Description: Panasonic has started a series of print ads and television commercials featuring Spanish-language spots for their PV-DC252 Palmcorder and high-definition 42-inch plasma monitor. The article sites examples of other companies following the same trend, marketing to the Hispanic population in the U.S.

47387 ■ "Partners in Branding" in *Sales and Marketing.com* (Vol. 156, No. 3, March 2004, pp. 10)
Pub: VNU eMedia, Inc.
Ed: Jennifer Gilbert. **Description:** Marketing partnerships should be formed for brand-building as much as they are formed for increasing sales. The three main reasons for companies to partner is to bring new customers to current target markets, to extend a brand to a new product or service, and to preempt competition.

47388 ■ "Paternal Instincts" in *Entrepreneur* (Vol. 32, October 2004, No. 10, pp. 102)
Pub: Entrepreneur Media Inc.
Ed: Nichole L. Torres. **Description:** Because fathers are spending more time with their children, coupled with the growing number of single fathers in the U.S., marketing to dads is a smart move. Statistical data included.

47389 ■ "Patriot Acts: Should You Play Up the 'Made in the USA' Angle?" in *Entrepreneur* (Vol. 32, December 2004, No. 12, pp. 93)
Pub: Entrepreneur Media Inc.
Ed: Nancy Michaels. **Description:** Marketing a product that is produced in the USA can make a positive statement to consumers, especially when patriotism is running high in the country. Suggestions to use when promoting U.S. products are given.

47390 ■ "Paving the Cow Path" in *Rough Notes* (Vol. 146, No. 9, September 2003, pp. 40)
Pub: Rough Notes
Ed: John Ashenburst. **Description:** Overview of changes and future trends in the insurance industry. Topics covered include risk management services, Internet marketing of services, and insurance services offered through banks.

47391 ■ "Pay Per Sale" in *The Economist* (Vol. 377, October 1-7, 2005, No. 8446, pp. 62)
Pub: The Economist Newspaper Ltd.
Description: Microsoft launched its 'paid-search' or 'pay-per-click' advertising program which allows advertisers to bid in an online auction for the right to have their link displayed next to the results for specific search terms and pay only when a Web surfer actually links to the advertiser's site.

47392 ■ "Peachtree Data expands as clients clean databases" in *Atlanta Business Chronicle* (Vol. 24, No. 15, September 14, 2001, pp. 30A)
Pub: American City Business Journals Inc.
Ed: Douglas Jordan. **Description:** Peachtree Data has doubled its number of sales people to 10 and increased staff to 17 due to annual sales increases each of its eight years reaching $3.25 million last year. The company provides database clean-up services, obtaining correct addresses for those that have moved and finding out clients have passed away, for database marketers who maintain mailing lists of potential customers.

47393 ■ "PeopleProfileUSA" in *Entrepreneur* (Vol. 32, No. 1, January 2004, pp. 10)
Pub: Entrepreneur Media, Inc.
Ed: Steve Cooper. **Description:** PeopleProfileUSA searches consumer profiles gathered from phone directories, voter registrations and other sources to offer a projected profile and contact information, to be used as a marketing tool. The services are free.

47394 ■ "Perfect Proposals" in *Sales & Marketing Management* (Vol. 159, January-February 2007, No. 1, pp. 9)
Pub: VNU Business Media
Description: Michael McLaughlin, principal at Mind-Share Consulting LLC, offers tips for developing sales proposals, and stresses keeping it simple.

47395 ■ "The Perfect System" in *Small Business Opportunities* (Vol. 14, No. 1, January 2002, pp. 70, 104)
Pub: Harris Publications, Inc.
Ed: Paul Soltoff. **Description:** Tips on selecting the right email marketing system for small business are explored, including profitability, permission issues, and customer affinity.

47396 ■ "Perk Avenue" in *Entrepreneur* (Vol. 31, No. 8, August 2003, pp. 71)
Pub: Entrepreneur Media, Inc.
Ed: Kimberly L. McCall. **Description:** There are many ways to motivate sales reps to succeed while keeping within a budget by using perks. Lin Grensing-Pophal, author of "Motivating Today's Employees" feels that perks can help employees feel valued by the firm, which can lead to greater productivity, improved morale and loyalty. Tips are offered to motivate a sales staff.

47397 ■ "The Perks of Luxury; Automakers Work to Make the Experience Match the Vehicle" in *Crain's Detroit Business* (Vol. 19, No. 43)
Pub: Crain Communications Inc., Detroit
Ed: Michelle Krebs. **Description:** Luxury automakers are offering trips, pampering service and tickets to exclusive events to attract customers.

47398 ■ "The Perks of Luxury" in *Crain's Detroit Business* (Vol. 19, No. 43, October 27, 2003, pp. E-3)
Pub: Crain Communications Inc., Detroit
Ed: Michelle Krebs. **Description:** Luxury automakers are offering trips, pampering service and tickets to exclusive events to attract customers.

47399 ■ "Personal, Thoughtful Ways to Stay in Touch" in *Rough Notes* (Vol. 145, No. 2, February 2003, pp. 32)
Pub: Rough Notes
Description: Staying in touch with business contacts and customers is very important in marketing. This can be done with phone calls, cards, a newsletter, or a personal note.

47400 ■ *Persuasive Advertising for Entrepreneurs and Small Business Owners: How to Create More Effective Sales Messages*
Pub: The Haworth Press, Inc.
Ed: Jay P. Granat. **Released:** 1994. **Price:** $39.95; $19.95 (paper).

47401 ■ "Pick Your Startup Tool" in *Black Enterprise* **(Vol. 36, November 2005, No. 4, pp. 74)**
Pub: Earl G. Graves Publishing Co. Inc.
Ed: Sonya Donaldson. **Description:** Besides being a good business plan, financial management tools are an asset for planning a marketing strategy. Business Plan Pro Standard, QuickBooks, Peachtree, and Business Resource Software can help startups write business plans that include pricing strategy, advertising, and budgeting.

47402 ■ "A Place in the Heart" in *Ingram's* **(Vol. 28, No. 9, September 2002, pp. 32)**
Pub: Show Me Publishing, Inc.
Ed: Andrea Darr. **Description:** Profile of Rick's Place, a not-for-profit charitable organization that helps advertising colleagues head-off a career crisis.

47403 ■ "Playing games with customers" in *Harvard Business Review* **(Vol. 81, No. 4, April 2003, pp. 21)**
Pub: Harvard Business School Press
Ed: Keith Ferrazzi, Jane Chen, Zhan Li. **Description:** Many U.S. companies and the U.S. Army are using computer games to sell products and recruit soldiers.

47404 ■ "Playskool Makes Product for Moms" in *Marketing to Women* **(Vol. 20, January 2007, No. 1, pp. 3)**
Pub: EPM Communications, Inc.
Description: Playskool has linked with Sourcebooks Inc. to produce a line of parenting books designed for both new and experienced mothers.

47405 ■ "Podcast Network Focuses on Wedding Plans" in *Marketing to Women* **(Vol. 19, October 2006, No. 10, pp. 5)**
Pub: EPM Communications, Inc.
Description: The newly launched Wedding Podcast Network provides couples with programming dedicated to planning their wedding. Shows include a diversity of topics ranging from getting in shape for the big day to tips from expert wedding planners to popular wedding destinations.

47406 ■ "Pop Quiz: A Quick Test of Your Managerial Skills" in *Sales & Marketing Management* **(Vol. 158, November-December 2006, No. 11, pp. 17)**
Pub: VNU Business Media
Description: Leadership and sales coaching consultant shares tips for sales managers.

47407 ■ "Portals popping up again as links to customers" in *Atlanta Business Chronicle* **(Vol. 25, No. 21, November 1, 2002, pp. 5A)**
Pub: American City Business Publications, Inc.
Ed: Mary Jane Credeur. **Description:** Many companies are again putting considerable resources in to portals in attempts to save money. Delta Air Lines Inc., a portal user, obtains approximately 11 percent of its passenger sales via its Delta.com site that receives about 6 million visitors monthly. Other portal efforts are discussed.

47408 ■ "Portland's Small Retailers Launch 'Independents' Day' Campaign to Buy Locally" in *Portland Press Herald* **(December 23, 2005)**
Pub: Blethen Maine Newspapers, Inc.
Ed: Edward D. Murphy. **Description:** Nearly two dozen Portland, Maine retailers are planning a campaign to encourage consumers and businesses to buy from local stores and suppliers.

47409 ■ "Postcards with an Edge" in *Small Business Opportunities* **(Vol. 12, No. 5, September 2000, pp. 52-53)**
Pub: Harris Publications, Inc.
Ed: Carla Vincent. **Description:** Four ways to use postcards to boost sales for small business are explained.

47410 ■ "Postcards From The Edge" in *Forbes* **(Vol. 174, December 27, 2004, No. 13, pp. 54)**
Pub: Forbes Magazine Inc.

Ed: Andy Stone. **Description:** ShipShapes offers small businesses a direct-mail plastic postcard with a picture of a product on one side and the advertiser's message on the back. Krispy Kreme generated an 11 percent response rate with their first card, compared to the national average of 3 percent of ordinary junk mail.

47411 ■ "Power to the Buyer With Group Buying Sites" in *E-business Advisor* **(Vol. 18, No. 2, February 2000, pp. 10)**
Pub: Advisor Media, Inc.
Ed: Erica Rugullies. **Description:** Group buying practices that enable customers to lower their acquisition costs and allow the vendor to reach new audiences, test new promotions and sell excess inventory are discussed.

47412 ■ *Power Direct Marketing: How to Make It Work for You*
Pub: N T C Comtemporary Publishing Co.
Ed: Ray S. Jutkin. **Released:** 1994. **Price:** $39.95.
Description: Guide to direct marketing.

47413 ■ "The Power of Ideas" in *Ingram's* **(Vol. 27, No. 8, August 2001, pp. 20)**
Pub: Show Me Publishing, Inc.
Ed: Ron Fredman. **Description:** The importance of inspiring ideas in small business marketing is discussed.

47414 ■ *Power Marketing for Small Business*
Pub: Oasis Press
Ed: Jody Hornor. **Released:** 1993. **Price:** $19.95 (paper).

47415 ■ "PR advertising" in *Atlanta Business Chronicle* **(Vol. 25, Nov. 15, 2002, No. 23 pp. S1)**
Pub: American City Business Publications, Inc.
Ed: Jim Lovel. **Description:** Public relations is largely replacing advertising, seen as a more effective way to get things done, because a company can tell its story indirectly, giving it more credibility. Public relations costs are also lower.

47416 ■ "PR Firms Tout the Value of 'Buzz' Marketing" in *Atlanta Business Chronicle* **(Vol. 25, November 15, 2002, No. 23 pp. S12)**
Pub: American City Business Publications, Inc.
Ed: Keith Reed. **Description:** Public relations companies are using 'guerrilla' and 'buzz' marketing as a more effective, less expensive method for taking messages directly to the audience. Virtual marketing is also being used, but often these emails are associated with spam and disregarded.

47417 ■ "PR Leads www.prleads.com" in *Entrepreneur* **(Vol. 32, No. 1, January 2004, pp. 10)**
Pub: Entrepreneur Media, Inc.
Ed: Steve Cooper. **Description:** Website that directs journalists to clients based on the client's expertise. Membership can be purchased on a three-month trial basis, or annually.

47418 ■ "PR Power" in *Entrepreneur* **(Vol. 31, No. 11, November 2003, pp. 97)**
Pub: Entrepreneur Media, Inc.
Ed: Gwen Moran. **Description:** Services designed to help promote media relations for small companies are listed.

47419 ■ *Practical Marketing Research*
Pub: AMACOM
Ed: Jeffrey L. Pope. **Released:** Revised edition, 1993.
Price: $32.95. ($29.65 for AMA members). **Description:** Describes how to use research in making marketing decisions in particular areas, including product development, package design, and sales. Also covers international research, customer satisfaction research, research for service companies, choosing interviewing methods, and analyzing data.

47420 ■ "Pre-Showtime class on the art of selling space" in *Atlanta Business Chronicle* **(Vol. 25, No. 21, November 1, 2002, pp. 9C)**
Pub: American City Business Publications, Inc.
Ed: Leslie Williams Johnson. **Description:** "Marketing Commercial Real Estate 101-The Experts Talk" is being offered as a class to real estate professionals before they attend the annual Showtime tradeshow. The class, focusing on selling commercial real estate space, is available at no charge for the 1,600 members of the Atlanta Commercial Board of Realtors.

47421 ■ "Prepaid Card Benefits Breast Cancer Research" in *Marketing to Women* **(Vol. 19, November 2006, No. 11, pp. 5)**
Pub: EPM Communications, Inc.
Description: NetSpend prepaid card marketer and financial services company, ACE Cash Express partner to launch a reloadable prepaid debit card for breast cancer research. A portion of all purchases made with the pink All-Access Visa Card through October 2007 will be donated to breast cancer research and educational charities.

47422 ■ "Press Conference: You've Worked Hard to Land That Media Interview-So Don't Blow Your Opportunity" in *Entrepreneur*
Pub: Entrepreneur Media Inc.
Ed: Kim T. Gordon. **Description:** Techniques for handling print, radio and television interviews are offered. Preparation is stressed as a key to a successful interview.

47423 ■ "Priced to Sell" in *Entrepreneur.com* **(Vol. 34, February 2006, No. 2, pp. 100)**
Pub: Entrepreneur Media Inc.
Ed: Nichole L. Torres. **Description:** Ways to market products based on selling price are presented. It is essential to know where your band fits in the marketplace.

47424 ■ "Prioritizing a Hectic Schedule" in *Sales & Marketing Management* **(Vol. 157, January 2005, No. 1, pp. 52)**
Pub: VNU Business Media
Ed: Kathryn Droullard. **Description:** Profile of Brian O'Neill, marketing and communications director at Circadian Technologies in Lexington, Massachusetts; O'Neill assists managers of extended-hour, shift-work operations to build time-management skills.

47425 ■ "Productive Lessons from a Tech Meltdown" in *Hispanic Business* **(Vol. 23, No. 7/8, July/August 2001, pp. 6)**
Pub: Hispanic Business
Ed: Jesus Chavarria. **Description:** A brief look at the long-term effects of technology on the Hispanic economy, and the need to deal with Hispanics as consumers as well as entrepreneurial innovators.

47426 ■ "Professional Financial Planners in Garden City Appoints Steiger Financial..." in *Long Island Business News* **(February 20, 2004)**
Pub: Dolan Media Newswires
Ed: Ryan McCormick. **Description:** Profile of Professional Financial Planners' newly appointed financial and marketing specialist, Ronald D. Steiger. The firm is located in Garden City, New York.

47427 ■ "Profiting - Adding an affiliate program links site content to product sales" in *PC Magazine* **(February 20, 2001, pp. 133)**
Pub: Ziff-Davis Publishing Company
Ed: Neil Randall. **Description:** Banner ads are a way for Web site developers to make a profit. Placing a banner ad on the page directs interested site visitors to the advertiser's site. The affiliate network tracks the origin of the visit and pays the host of the originating site a percentage of all sales. Some pay a fee just for directing a visitor to a site. Commission Junction offers commissions from more than 1,600 companies in a wide variety of industries. LinkShare offers commissions from just over 500 companies, but they are major organizations.

47428 ■ "Progressive Dinner, Segway-Style" in *Kansas City Star* (February 4, 2005)
Pub: Knight-Ridder/Tribune Business News
Ed: Joyce Smith. **Description:** Segway Experience of Kansas City is offering a Taste of the Plaza tour. Customers will be transported to participating restaurants where some owners will offer a short presentation about their restaurant's history and distribute coupons to encourage customers to return.

47429 ■ "Promoting their own" in *Crain's Detroit Business* (Vol. 16,No. 49, December 4, 2000, pp. 25)
Pub: Crain Communications, Inc.
Ed: David Barkholz. **Description:** Championing doctors has become a popular tool in a hot year for local hospital advertising.

47430 ■ "Promoting Praise: Incorporating Client Feedback Into Your Motivation Efforts" in *Sales & Marketing Management* (Vol. 157, Jan. 2005)
Pub: VNU Business Media
Ed: Kathryn Droullard. **Description:** Positive customer feedback can be used as a tool to motivate sales teams.

47431 ■ "Promotions for Pennies; You don't need a Madison Avenue budget to turn heads" in *Business Week Online* (November 1, 2002)
Pub: McGraw-Hill Inc.
Description: Debbie Patt, owner of Clarendon Cheesecakes, explains how, despite a limited advertising budget, finds creative, low-cost marketing strategies that draw attention to her products, including the use of her products for nonprofit fundraisers.

47432 ■ *Proven Promotions for Kitchen & Bathroom Businesses*
Pub: National Kitchen & Bath Association.
Ed: Jim Krengel and Lori J. Krengel. **Released:** 1997. **Price:** $50.00.

47433 ■ "PS Cleaning Products, Lightning Join to Promote Line" in *Tampa Tribune* (December 23, 2005)
Pub: Media General, Inc.
Ed: Alan Snel. **Description:** American HomeHealth, a startup from St. Petersburg, Florida, has partnered with the St. Pete Times Forum and Tampa Bay Lightning local games to promote its PS brand of home cleaners, soaps and disinfectants. The $2 million deal will feature PS advertisements on the Forum's Zamboni ice machines, trash cans and electronic signs and PS soap will be used in the bathrooms.

47434 ■ "The Public Library: Technology Lets You Browse the Stacks from Your Home Office" in *Black Enterprise* (Vol. 34, No. 4, Nov. 2003)
Pub: Earl Graves Publishing Co.
Ed: Jennifer L. Smith. **Description:** More than 3,000 libraries offer programs offering E-books, databases and online classes that can be accessed via computers for small and home businesses searching for materials on marketing and management topics.

47435 ■ "Publicis throws a few Curves" in *ADWEEK New England Edition* (Vol. 39, No. 50, December 16, 2002, pp. 6)
Pub: VNU Business Media
Ed: Mindy Charski. **Description:** Publicis in Mid America captures the emotional power women achieve from working out at Curves International fitness centers in the client's first national television effort.

47436 ■ "Publish or Perish" in *Forbes* (November 13, 2000, pp. 252)
Pub: Forbes Magazine
Ed: Brendan Coffey. **Description:** Struggling dotcoms are seeking more traditional forms of revenue from advertising and subscriptions. At least seven Weblets have created magazines in recent months, and more are considering the same.

47437 ■ "Publishing" in *Business Week* (January 9, 2006, No. 3966, pp. 29-30)
Pub: McGraw-Hill Companies
Ed: Louise Lee. **Description:** Web magazines are launching print versions of their publications in order to increase readership and advertising sales.

47438 ■ "The Pulse" in *Sales & Marketing Management* (Vol. 159, January-February 2007, No. 1, pp. 9)
Pub: VNU Business Media
Description: According to a survey conducted by Extraprise, 63 percent of all business-to-business companies will implement marketing automation technology in 2007.

47439 ■ "Pump Up with PR" in *Small Business Opportunities* (Vol. 16, No. 2, March 2004, pp. 10)
Pub: Harris Publications, Inc.
Ed: Patricia Faulhaber. **Description:** Fourteen proven tips in public relations and publicity for small businesses. Public relations technically revolve around media relations, press releases, trade shows, brand creation, marketing communications, internal messaging, special event planning, networking and more.

47440 ■ "Putting Focus on 4 Famed Firms" in *Crain's New York Business* (Vol. 22, November 27, 2006, No. 48, pp. 17)
Pub: Crain Communications, Inc.
Ed: Aaron Elstein. **Description:** Crain's spotlight on key statistics of four well-known businesses in the New York area includes information on Eileen Fisher Inc., Key Food Stores Co-Operative Inc., Ziff Davis Holdings Inc., and Publishers Clearing House.

47441 ■ "Putting the Screws to Google" in *Business Week* (January 23, 2006, No. 3968, pp. 24)
Pub: McGraw-Hill Companies
Ed: Jon Fine. **Description:** How Old Media could take back market share of Google and Yahoo's! advertising market.

47442 ■ "Puzzleman to the Rescue" in *My Business* (December/January 2003, pp. 12-13)
Pub: My Business Magazine
Ed: Melany Klinck. **Description:** Profile of Cypriana Porter, owner of the educational toy store called The Gingerbread House. Porter invented the superhero Puzzleman to increase sales.

47443 ■ "Pyrotechnics fire up the crowd at meetings" in *Atlanta Business Chronicle* (Vol. 24, No. 14, September 7, 2001, pp. S15)
Pub: American City Business Journals Inc.
Ed: Lucy Pritchett. **Description:** Pyrotechnics, the use of indoor lighting shows, has increased in popularity in recent years. Dawna VanHook, Axxis Inc.'s production manager discusses the use of pyrotechnics and how they appeal to company employees. This technology can be used for events such as product introductions, company peak sales announcements, and company mergers.

47444 ■ "Quick pick" in *Entrepreneur* (Vol. 31, No. 6, June 2003, pp. 81)
Pub: Entrepreneur Media Inc.
Ed: Elizabeth J. Goodgold. **Description:** A new service just launched, Major Newswire, will send press releases to more than 85,000 journalists, editors and newswire services for a fee of $349.

47445 ■ "A Quick Test of Your Managerial Skills" in *Sales & Marketing Management* (Vol. 158, October 2006, No. 10, pp. 19)
Pub: VNU Business Media
Description: Al Siebert, director of the Resiliency Center located in Portland, Oregon discusses the need for resiliency in salespeople.

47446 ■ "QuickSeek" in *Entrepreneur* (Vol. 33, September 2005, No. 9, pp. 6)
Pub: Entrepreneur Media Inc.
Ed: Steve Cooper. **Description:** Online directory, QuickSeek, lists more than 16 million businesses in a database. Information includes operating hours, business descriptions, email addresses, directions and links to corporate sites. Preferred listings, which include full-page design with graphics, photos and images, run $99 per year.

47447 ■ "The Race to Reach Critical Mass" in *Hispanic Business* (Vol. 22, No. 1/2, January/February, pp. 18, 20, 22)
Pub: Hispanic Business
Ed: Derek Reveron. **Description:** By forming an alliance with his competitors, Manuel Chavez creates a new model for winning business from large corporations.

47448 ■ "Radio weaves a web of listeners; Internet helps stations build an audience and advertising" in *Crain's Detroit Business*
Pub: Crain Communications, Inc.
Ed: Katie Merx. **Description:** Local radio stations say they're not in the Internet business, but they are experimenting to see how the Web can help them win listeners and advertising revenue.

47449 ■ "Raising the Roof: Cincinnati Realtor Undaunted by Race Riots" in *Black Enterprise* (Vol. 35, November 2004, No. 4, pp. 51)
Pub: Earl G. Graves Publishing Co. Inc.
Ed: Glenn Townes. **Description:** Despite racial tension in Cincinnati, Ohio in 2001, Roosevelt Barnes launched his real estate business, using $10,000 of personal savings. Barnes shares his marketing strategy to grow his business.

47450 ■ "The Ratings Game" in *Entrepreneur* (Vol. 31, No. 8, August 2003, pp. 45)
Pub: Entrepreneur Media, Inc.
Ed: Melissa Campanelli. **Description:** Many small business e-entrepreneurs are following the lead of Amazon.com and Drugstore.com by posting uncensored reviews and ratings of products sold on the firm's Website. The pros and cons of this practice are examined.

47451 ■ "ReachLocal" in *Entrepreneur* (Vol. 33, August 2005, No. 8, pp. 4)
Pub: Entrepreneur Media Inc.
Ed: Steve Cooper. **Description:** ReachLocal is an online service that works in conjunction with Google, Overture, SuperPages.com and other sites that offer advertising channels. The service presents a business to online searchers looking for a product or service in their area. It tracks traffic, offers reports, and uses a performance-based payment system.

47452 ■ "Ready? Set? Search! Rev Up Your Sales With Comparison-Shopping Engines" in *Entrepreneur* (Vol. 31, No. 9, September 2003, pp. 87)
Pub: Entrepreneur Media, Inc.
Ed: Catherine Seda. **Description:** According to a survey conducted in January 2003, more than 50 percent of shoppers believe comparison-shopping search engines save time and money. The sites offer product descriptions, prices, and customer testimonials.

47453 ■ "Ready To Go: How An Online Tool Helped One Company Speed Distribution of Marketing Materials To Reps" in *Sales & Marketing Management*
Pub: VNU Business Media
Ed: Alan Horowitz. **Description:** Allstate Insurance, is providing its sales reps access to thousands of sales and marketing materials via a Web-hosted service that automates order fulfillment and inventory management of sales and marketing materials. Research indicates that without this type of service, sales reps spend 25 percent of their time searching for and assembling information for sales calls.

47454 ■ "The Real Deal" in *Entrepreneur* (Vol. 33, September 2005, No. 9, pp. 74)
Pub: Entrepreneur Media Inc.
Ed: April Y. Pennington, Nichole L. Torres, Geoff Williams, Sara Wilson. **Description:** Entrepreneurs discuss the highs and lows of business ownership, from embezzlement, international trade, and selling a product to Target.

47455 ■ **"The Real Pepsi Challenge"** in *New York Times* (February 4, 2007, pp. 7)
Pub: New York Times Company
Ed: Stephanie Capparell. **Description:** Special-markets sales staff of the Pepsi-Cola Company is profiled. Walter S. Mack, Jr. took over the company in 1938; Mack strengthened the company by marketing to the African American population.

47456 ■ **"Recession session"** in *Entrepreneur* (Vol. 30, No. 3, March 2002, pp.)
Pub: Entrepreneur Media Inc.
Ed: Mark Henricks. **Description:** An interview with various experts and entrepreneurs to learn how and when they recommend aggressive or defensive positions in the areas of money management, people management, marketing, and technology.

47457 ■ **"Redefining Sick Days"** in *Sales & Marketing Management* (Vol. 157)
Pub: VNU Business Media
Ed: Kathryn Droullard. **Description:** Many companies are now offering flexible time-off policies whereby an employee can use sick time for reasons other than personal illness, such as family issues, personal needs, and stress. Allowing a workforce flexible time off not only motivates a staff, but can also lead to stronger management capabilities.

47458 ■ **"Reebok Rolls Out Marketing Device"** in *Boston Globe* (February 10, 2005)
Pub: New York Times Company
Ed: Christopher Rowland. **Description:** Reebok is launching its largest marketing campaign to reach its target audience, using the signature phrase, 'I am what I am'. Reebok admits to its similarity to Popeye, but says that is just a coincidence.

47459 ■ **"Refer madness"** in *Entrepreneur* (Vol. 30, No. 3, March 2002, pp. 87)
Pub: Entrepreneur Media Inc.
Ed: Nichole L. Torres. **Description:** The impact of word-of-mouth advertising by online customers is discussed.

47460 ■ **"Reinventing the wheel"** in *Hispanic Business* (Vol. 22, No. 4, April 2000, pp. 12)
Pub: Hispanic Business
Ed: Jonathan Higuera. **Description:** The expansion of the online advertising provider Adsmart NetFuerza is discussed. The company is achieving a 30 percent per month increase in the number of Internet sites, which it serves. It has a client base of 67 companies with Internet sites in 16 countries.

47461 ■ **"Relationship-marketing ventures take toll on Valassis earnings"** in *Crain's Detroit Business* (Vol. 19, No. 9, March 3, 2003, pp. 4)
Pub: Crain Communications Inc., Detroit
Ed: Jennette Smith. **Description:** Despite Valassis Communications Inc.'s strong sales in newspaper insert advertising, the company showed fourth quarter losses because two other units of the firm are not performing as well as expected.

47462 ■ **"Release the Hounds "** in *Entrepreneur*
Pub: Entrepreneur Media Inc.
Ed: Mike Hogan. **Description:** Competition in the Web search engine sector is fierce, providing advertising opportunities for small companies.

47463 ■ **"Resources: Web Sites, Organizations, Events and More to Grow Your Business"** in *Entrepreneur* (Vol. 32, No. 2, February 2004, pp. 8)
Pub: Entrepreneur Media, Inc.
Ed: Steve Cooper. **Description:** Profiles of Websites to help grow a small business include Zagat Survey covering 2003 restaurants and hotels offering Wi-Fi to customers; NewIdeaTrade, an online forum for buying and selling inventions, patents, copyrights and other intellectual property; Yahoo's small business Merchant Solutions, with shopping carts, coupons and 24-hour toll-free phone support; WordBiz Report, an e-newsletter focusing on online copywriting and content; Plan-Alyzer, evaluates outcomes of marketing plans; Bob Ely, an independent copywriter and consultant; Meeting & Event Planning for Dummies; and Business Matchmaking, a service to help small business procure government contracts.

47464 ■ *Restaurant Marketing for Owners and Managers*
Pub: John Wiley & Sons, Incorporated
Ed: Patti J. Shock, John T. Bowen, John M. Stefanelli. **Released:** October 2003. **Price:** $30.00. **Description:** Tools for combining marketing theory to practice in a restaurant business are covered.

47465 ■ **"Retail Experts Laud Costco's Shopping Strategy"** in *Business Journal-Portland* (Vol. 20, No. 22, August 1, 2003, pp. 11)
Pub: American City Business Journals, Inc.
Ed: Carol Tice. **Description:** Marketing strategy used by Costco Companies is examined, including management styles, U.S. economic conditions, and business planning.

47466 ■ **"Retailing Experts See Rise in Label-Conscious Male Shoppers"** in *Atlanta Journal-Constitution* (February 17, 2004)
Pub: Knight-Ridder/Tribune Business News
Ed: Renee DeGross. **Description:** Male consumers are becoming an important force in retail sales.

47467 ■ **"Retailing Your Personal Lines Accounts"** in *Rough Notes* (Vol. 146, No. 9, September 2003, pp. 56)
Pub: Rough Notes
Ed: Troy Korsgaden. **Description:** Ways for insurance agents to increase personal insurance lines; topics include strategic marketing, techniques in selling, and tips on improving customer service.

47468 ■ **"Retention Rate Can Be Enhanced"** in *Morgage Servicing News* (Vol. 5, No. 10, November 2001, pp. 4)
Pub: Thompson Financial Publishing
Ed: Steve Kropper. **Description:** Interview with Steven Kropper, co-founder and CEO of Domania Inc., a Boston-based financial and marketing services software company that provides customer acquisition and retention products, shares insight into retaining customers.

47469 ■ **"The Return of the Global Brand"** in *Harvard Business Review* (Vol. 81, No. 8, August 2003, pp. 22)
Pub: Harvard Business School Press
Ed: John Quelch. **Description:** Since Theordore Levitt published The Globalization of Markets in the Harvard Business Review twenty years ago, the world's economic development has adapted accordingly. International companies are finding that standardized products marketed globally have been widely accepted. This is contrary to previous efforts to develop products for regional markets. Today, China is poised to duplicate Japan's global branding successes, cutting into U.S. business sales.

47470 ■ **"Return To Me"** in *Entrepreneur* (Vol. 33, September 2005, No. 9, pp. 28)
Pub: Entrepreneur Media Inc.
Ed: Mark Henricks. **Description:** Authors Don Peppers and Martha Rogers help small business owners capitalize on return customers for sales. They recommend a focus on assessing and tracking customer equity, lifetime customer value and specific measure to maximize those values.

47471 ■ **"Revenue Upswing"** in *Hispanic Business* (December 2002, pp. 40-41)
Pub: Hispanic Business
Description: The Spanish-language radio market is showing signs of recovery. A list of the top radio station clusters in key markets showing location/owner, percent of Hispanic ownership, and gross billing, as well as Spanish radio's ten top billings, is presented.

47472 ■ **"Reverence for radicals"** in *Fast Company* (June 2001, pp. 48)
Pub: Fast Company
Ed: Rekha Balu. **Description:** Reverend Cecil Williams, of San Francisco's Glide Memorial United Methodist Church, is on a mission: he's teaching tradition-bound congregations how to stay vital by embracing change. The article shows how Marvin Arnpriester uses Reverend Williams as inspiration for staking out new markets and younger customers for his business.

47473 ■ **"Reveries"** in *Entrepreneur* (Vol. 31, No. 8, August 2003, pp. 6)
Pub: Entrepreneur Media, Inc.
Ed: Steve Cooper. **Description:** An e-zine catering to senior-level marketers is highlighted. The daily e-newsletter offers questions and answers, surveys, roundtables, white papers and opinions focusing on strategic marketing issues.

47474 ■ **"Reward Me: Rebates and Incentives Make Buying all the More Appealing"** in *Entrepreneur* (Vol. 32, December 2004, No. 12, pp. 39)
Pub: Entrepreneur Media Inc.
Ed: Jill Amadio. **Description:** Rebates and incentives can help clear inventory. New car dealers use this approach often near the end of a model year.

47475 ■ **"Riding the Airwaves"** in *Entrepreneur.com* (Vol. 34, February 2006, No. 2, pp. 75)
Pub: Entrepreneur Media Inc.
Ed: Kim T. Gordon. **Description:** Six steps to promote a small business is to conduct a public relations radio tour are outlined. It is important to target the right media for a product or service.

47476 ■ **"Riding the Rebates; Wixom Company Grows by Hitching Itself to National Retail Trend"** in *Crain's Detroit Business* (Vol. 20)
Pub: Crain Communications Inc. - Detroit
Ed: Andrew Dietderich. **Description:** Profile of Al Goldberg, founder of The Express Group, a rebate fulfillment company. Goldberg attributes his business plan to a meeting with Kmart executives 23 years ago.

47477 ■ **"The right carrot"** in *Entrepreneur* (Vol. 30, No. 2, February 20)
Pub: Entrepreneur Media Inc.
Ed: Kimberly L. McCall. **Description:** Ways to motivate and retain sales professionals are explored, including a discussion on the importance of a good compensation plan.

47478 ■ **"Right Message, Right Time Key for Hospitality Marketing"** in *Crain's Detroit Business* (Vol. 21, October 10, 2005, No. 43, pp. 16)
Pub: Crain Communications Inc. - Detroit
Ed: Roger Slavens. **Description:** According to the Meetings & Conventions 2004 Meetings Market Report, meeting planners and hotel executives are the two most lucrative audiences for marketers looking to increase involvement in the hospitality and travel industry.

47479 ■ *Risk-Free Entrepreneur*
Pub: Adams Media Corporation
Ed: Don Debelak. **Released:** June 2006. **Price:** $14.95. **Description:** Information is offered to help entrepreneurs to develop an idea for a product or service and have other companies provide the marketing, manufacturing and staff.

47480 ■ **"Risky Business: Wacky Marketing Moves Put These Businesses on the Map"** in *Entrepreneur* (Vol. 32, August 2004, No. 8, pp. 26)
Pub: Entrepreneur Media Inc.
Ed: April Y. Pennington. **Description:** Creating controversy is a good way to build a brand.

47481 ■ **"Rivaling a Giant"** in *Boston Business Journal* (Vol. 23, No. 30, August 29, 2003, pp. 3)
Pub: American City Business Journals

Ed: Tom Witkowski. **Description:** Profile of Enterasys Networks efforts to capture market share away from rival giant Cisco Systems Inc. Topics include market development, product development, and competition.

47482 ■ **"Road Signs"** in *Entrepreneur* (Vol. 33, September 2005, No. 9, pp. 85)
Pub: Entrepreneur Media Inc.
Description: FlapMedia LLC and Targeted Media Partners are offering automobile-based media vehicles as an affordable alternative for advertising a product or service.

47483 ■ *The Royal Guide to Direct Mail for Small Businesses*
Pub: Butterworth-Heinemann
Ed: Thomas. **Released:** 1997. **Price:** $28.95.

47484 ■ **"Sage Advice"** in *Entrepreneur* (Vol. 33, September 2005, No. 9, pp. 86)
Pub: Entrepreneur Media Inc.
Ed: Kirsten Osolind. **Description:** Three mediation tools to help create a B2B marketing program are explained.

47485 ■ **"Sales"** in *Inc.* (February 1, 2002)
Pub: Inc. Magazine
Ed: Susan Greco. **Description:** An overview of ways smart companies are tackling today's toughest selling challenges in today's economic downturn.

47486 ■ **"Sales & Marketing Employment Market Remains Strong"** in *Hispanic Business* (Vol. 23, No. 5, May 2001, pp. 80)
Pub: Hispanic Business
Description: According to a recent survey by a national recruitment firm, sales and marketing positions remain strong, particularly in the telecommunications industry, pharmaceuticals, transportation, and information technology.

47487 ■ **""** in *Sales & Marketing Management* (Vol. 158, October 2006, No. 10, pp. 11)
Pub: VNU Business Media
Description: Ideas for creating a business blog are presented. Blogs can feature ideas, criticisms, and insights.

47488 ■ **"Sales & Marketing: The Power of Brand"** in *Ingram's* (Vol. 27, No. 6, June 2001, pp. 23)
Pub: Show Me Publishing, Inc.
Ed: Jean Hughes. **Description:** The answer to increasing product usage is to leverage the company's brand and to strengthen account relationships.

47489 ■ **"Sales & Marketing: Why Advertise Anyway?"** in *Ingram's* (Vol. 27, No. 5, May 2001, pp. 28)
Pub: Show Me Publishing, Inc.
Ed: Rob Pearcy. **Description:** Business plans need to include a marketing budget for advertising in order to be successful.

47490 ■ **"Sales Secrets: Persistence is key to building your brand"** in *Atlanta Business Chronicle* (Vol. 25, No. 21, November 1, 2002, pp. 2B)
Pub: American City Business Publications, Inc.
Ed: Jeffrey Gitomer. **Description:** A suggested formula for building a brand is discussed, along with branding step recommendations.

47491 ■ **"S&MM Pulse"** in *Sales & Marketing Management* (Vol. 158, October 2006, No. 10, pp. 16)
Pub: VNU Business Media
Description: Information to help small companies embrace the Intered for IT and marketing is presented.

47492 ■ **"S&MM Pulse"** in *Sales and Marketing.com* (Vol. 156, No. 3, March 2004, pp. 10)
Pub: VNU eMedia, Inc.
Description: According to S&MM's Equation Research Survey of 529 executives, business-to-business marketers are predicting economic growth in 2004. Statistical data included.

47493 ■ **"Saving the Day: Does Your Brand Need Triage? Here's Something to Help"** in *Entrepreneur* (Vol. 31, No. 9, September 2003, pp. 27)
Pub: Entrepreneur Media, Inc.
Ed: Mark Henricks. **Description:** Review of the book, "Brand Aid", to help entrepreneurs make the most out of their brand using limited resources.

47494 ■ **"Savvy Media Buying"** in *Small Business Opportunities* (Fall 2005)
Pub: Harris Publications Inc.
Ed: Peter Koeppel. **Description:** Four ways a media buyer can help increase the effectiveness of advertising are examined.

47495 ■ **"Say It Again"** in *Entrepreneur* (Vol. 33, January 2005, No. 1, pp. 66)
Pub: Entrepreneur Media Inc.
Ed: Kim T. Gordon. **Description:** Help to develop a well-rounded media program that will leave consumers remembering a particular message is provided.

47496 ■ **"Say It and Sell It"** in *Sales & Marketing Management* (Vol. 158, November-December 2006, No. 11, pp. 13)
Pub: VNU Business Media
Description: Ways to renew a contract with a price increase are defined.

47497 ■ **"Scanning For Dollars"** in *Fortune* (Vol. 151, January 10, 2005, No. 1, pp. 60)
Pub: Time Inc.
Ed: Julie Schlosser. **Description:** New technology is being used by marketers to study consumer emotions and motivations. Functional magnetic resonance imaging (fMRI) detects the flow of blood to the brain's centers of pleasure, thought or memory. Researchers suggest that blood flow increases in areas of the prefrontal cortex when an individual likes what he or she is seeing.

47498 ■ **"Scare Tactics: Creative Ways to Profit from Halloween"** in *Entrepreneur* (Vol. 32, October 2004, No. 10, pp. 90)
Pub: Entrepreneur Media Inc.
Description: Retailers thinking Halloween does not fit their brand, can apply three listed methods that will draw customers in during the holiday.

47499 ■ **"School's out; Working Moms are Worried"** in *Marketing to Women* (Vol. 20, January 2007, No. 1, pp. 5)
Pub: EPM Communications, Inc.
Description: Catalyst, a non-profit research firm dedicated to expanding workplace opportunities to women, has discovered that work productivity tends to be drained by concern over their children's after-school time activities.

47500 ■ **"The science behind six degrees."** in *Harvard Business Review* (Vol. 81, No. 2, Feb. 2003, pp. 16)
Pub: Harvard Business School Press
Ed: Gardiner Morse. **Description:** Duncan Watts answers questions about his research into network science and how it can help explain why products sell, and how companies effectively manage themselves. Critical elements of this field of study are human behavior, group dynamics, and perception.

47501 ■ **"The Science of Status"** in *Inc.* (September 1, 2003)
Pub: Gruner & Jahr USA Publishing
Ed: Nadine Heintz. **Description:** The roles that perceptions play in the marketplace are observed.

47502 ■ **"Scout New Business"** in *PC Computing* (April 2000, pp. 90)
Pub: Ziff-Davis Inc.
Ed: Jason Compton. **Description:** A guide to digital-mapping resources for scouting new markets and studying demographics is presented. IAtlas Info Lens is a free service that gathers data on various industries sorted by region, state or metropolitan area and lets users target business-oriented products closely.

Tetrad's PCensus has Profile and Target modes that output and input graphical/numerical data respectively. AnySite.com is a powerful Web-based service offering a wealth of demographic data from the U.S. Census and other sources. High-end GIS products include TTG Territory Mapper and ESRI ArcView.

47503 ■ **"Screen Play"** in *Hispanic Business* (December 2006, pp. 28-30, 32, 34)
Pub: Hispanic Business
Ed: Hildy Medina. **Description:** Advertisers and media companies are reaching the Hispanic marketing via the Internet. Statistical data included.

47504 ■ **"?Se Habla Espanol? If you don't already, it's time to start. "** in *Entrepreneur* (Vol. 31, No. 6, June 2003)
Pub: Entrepreneur Media Inc.
Ed: Kim T. Gordon. **Description:** With new economic clout, the Latino market has become an entrepreneur's dream. Over 60 percent of Latinos living in the U.S. are under the age of 28. By the year 2005, Latinos will drive nearly one-fifth of the growth in the apparel, shoe and food sectors.

47505 ■ **"Sea Change"** in *Inc.* (January 1, 2002)
Pub: Inc. Magazine
Ed: John Grossmann. **Description:** Profile of Henry Lovejoy, wholesaler of ecologically acceptable fish and shellfish; Lovejoy shares ways he was able to brand his product.

47506 ■ **"Searching the sky"** in *Atlanta Business Chronicle* (Vol. 25, Nov. 15, 2002, No. 23 pp. 38A)
Pub: American City Business Publications, Inc.
Ed: Jim Lovel. **Description:** Jamie Turner is One-Source Marketing's chief marketing officer and executive creative director, as well as an amateur astronomer. Turner discusses his fascination with astronomy and the peacefulness he receives from this hobby.

47507 ■ **"Seeing Greens"** in *Entrepreneur* (Vol. 32, November 2004, No. 11, pp. 126)
Pub: Entrepreneur Media Inc.
Ed: Nichole L. Torres. **Description:** Profile of Andy Yocom of Invision Golf Group Inc. Yocum and his brother Timmy developed the idea of placing print advertising on the flags at golf courses. Yocom describes how he beat skepticism when selling the idea to golf course managers.

47508 ■ **"Seeing the light"** in *Boston Business Journal* (Vol. 22, No. 15, May 17, 2002)
Pub: MCP, Inc.
Ed: Sean McFadden. **Description:** Profile of Rhonda Kallman, founder of New Century Brewing Co. Kallman introduced Edison Light Beer in September 2001 locally, and it will enter the national market by late 2003.

47509 ■ **"Seeing the Sites"** in *Entrepreneur* (Vol. 33, September 2005, No. 9, pp. 120)
Pub: Entrepreneur Media Inc.
Ed: Sarah Pierce. **Description:** Profile of Heritage Web Solutions. The marketing company designs and hosts Websites for small companies for $1,000.

47510 ■ **"Selling Innovation"** in *Sales and Marketing.com* (Vol. 156, No. 3, March 2004, pp. 56)
Pub: VNU eMedia, Inc.
Ed: Scott Owens. **Description:** Profile of Mike Curran, owner of U.S. Interactive. Curran created Take-Home Defensive Driving, the nation's first state-certified driving course on video. The firm has trained more than 2 million Americans to drive more safely.

47511 ■ **"Seniority Rules"** in *Entrepreneur* (Vol. 31, No. 10, October 2003, pp. 88)
Pub: Entrepreneur Media, Inc.
Ed: Elizabeth Goodgold. **Description:** Individuals aged 65 and older make up 12 percent of the population but account for more than 48 percent of discre-

tionary purchases. The director of Marketing Directions Service suggests that entrepreneurs should market to this age group as the way they wish to be seen: full of vitality and reflecting realistic aspirations.

47512 ■ "Service To A Tee" in *Entrepreneur* (Vol. 28, No. 4, April 2000, pp. 172)
Pub: Entrepreneur Media Inc.
Ed: Paul Edward and Sarah Edward. **Description:** Marketing tips for consultants.

47513 ■ "Serving Up Success: There's Something to be Said for Doing Things Your Way" in *Entrepreneur* (Vol. 31, No. 11, November 2003, pp. 86)
Pub: Entrepreneur Media, Inc.
Ed: Joshua Kurlantzick. **Description:** Profiles of Fred DeLuca, founder of Subway sandwich shops and Howard Schultz, founder of Starbucks coffee conglomerate. Each found success in his own way.

47514 ■ "Serving Your Client-And Yourself" in *Sales and Marketing.com* (Vol. 156, No. 3, March 2004, pp. 20)
Pub: VNU eMedia, Inc.
Ed: Daniel Tynan. **Description:** Profile of Craig Elias, founder of InnerSell, a firm through which salespeople can locate services for their customers, make referrals, and earn a percentage of the deal.

47515 ■ "Setting Sights on the Hispanic Buyer" in *Hispanic Business* (November 2002, pp. 49, 52, 54)
Pub: Hispanic Business
Ed: Paul A. Eisenstein. **Description:** Hispanics as a target market for the automobile industry is discussed. Statistical data covering Hispanic new and used car and truck purchases from 1994 through 2000 is presented.

47516 ■ "Setting Up Shop" in *Home Office Computing* (Vol. 18, No. 10, October 2000, pp. 90)
Pub: Scholastic Inc.
Ed: William Van Winkle. **Description:** Online hosting companies have gone far beyond building Web storefronts and are evolving into E-business service providers (eBSPs) with wide assortments of front-end and back-end office tools. They often provide basics such as Web site setup and hosting free and generate revenue with premium value-added services such as marketing, site traffic monitoring, credit-card processing and inventory management. Tips for choosing a service provider are included.

47517 ■ "7 Ways You Can Use E-Books to Build Your Business" in *Web Marketing Today* (No. 121, February 5, 2003)
Pub: Wilson Internet Services
Ed: Ralph F. Wilson. **Description:** E-books can be an excellent marketing tool to build a business.

47518 ■ "Sexton Hoping to Hit the Jackpot for Viejas Casino" in *San Diego Business Journal* (Vol. 28, January 8, 2007, No. 2, pp. 16)
Pub: San Diego Business Journal Associates
Ed: Jessica Long. **Description:** Sexton Communications was hired to promote East County's Viejas Casino.

47519 ■ "Sexy Or Sensible? What You Buy To Drive May Not Be What You're Driven To Buy" in *Business Week* (January 16, 2006, No. 3967)
Pub: McGraw-Hill Companies
Ed: David Kiley. **Description:** Marketing plays a role in consumer decisions. Profiles using left brain, right brain thinking help sort out new vehicle purchasing choices.

47520 ■ "Sharing Marketing Expenses" in *Rough Notes* (Vol. 145, No. 9, September 2002, pp. 80)
Pub: Rough Notes
Ed: Michael J. Weinberg. **Description:** Information about marketing expenses related to sales which insurance agents and agencies can share, include business meals, contributions to community organizations, direct mail, and telemarketing.

47521 ■ "Sharing the Wealth: Want to Get a Piece of the eBay Pie?" in *Entrepreneur* (Vol. 33, February 2005, No. 2, pp. 40)
Pub: Entrepreneur Media Inc.
Ed: Melissa Campanelli. **Description:** Online affiliate programs offer banner advertising for companies in exchange for a percentage of any sales referred to the advertiser; one of the most lucrative programs is operated by online retailer, eBay.

47522 ■ "Shattered Magazine: A Monthly for the Global Businesswoman" in *Marketing to Women* (Vol. 19, December 2006, No. 2, pp. 6)
Pub: EPM Communications, Inc.
Ed: Julie Ros. **Description:** Shattered is a glossy magazine distributed monthly and run by veteran financial journalist, Julie Ros. Shattered concentrates its focus on the business world and puts special emphasis on the global impact women are having in the leadership roles of the business community.

47523 ■ "Shelf-Determination" in *Forbes* (April 15, 2002, p. 130)
Pub: Forbes Magazine
Ed: Brandon Copple. **Description:** Under the leadership of Betsy Holden, Kraft Foods is winning the war of the aisles, and causing plenty of casualties along the way.

47524 ■ "Shoestring Marketing: Web Research: Is This Fantasy or Reality?" in *Atlanta Business Chronicle* (Vol. 25, No. 21, Nov. 1, 2002)
Pub: American City Business Publications, Inc.
Ed: Alf Nucifora. **Description:** The advantages and disadvantages of online research are discussed. WebSurveyor, which has experienced online survey success, has received 2,000-plus customers globally via the hosting of 50,000 surveys in which 4 million responses were processed.

47525 ■ "Shooting from the hip" in *Entrepreneur* (Vol. 31, No. 5, May 2003, pp. 75)
Pub: Entrepreneur Media Inc.
Ed: Elizabeth J. Goodgold. **Description:** Advice for marketing to teens is offered. It is important to remember that trends come and go, the importance of having a lasting market strategy is stressed.

47526 ■ "Shop Shifting" in *Hispanic Business* (April 2005, pp. 18, 20)
Pub: Hispanic Business
Ed: Joel Russell. **Description:** Hispanic advertising agencies are faced with identity issues that involve integration and specialization. As more mainstream agencies become more multicultural, Hispanic agencies will become more mainstream.

47527 ■ "Sign of the Times: Are You Missing Out on This Simple, Inexpensive Marketing Tool?" in *Entrepreneur* (Vol. 33, January 2005, No. 1)
Pub: Entrepreneur Media Inc.
Ed: Catherine Seda. **Description:** Tactics to use email messages as an inexpensive marketing tool are given.

47528 ■ "Signal Strength" in *Entrepreneur* (Vol. 33, March 2005, No. 3, pp. 18)
Pub: Entrepreneur Media Inc.
Ed: John F. Ince. **Description:** Venture capital firms are ramping up marketing efforts by hiring public relations firms to promote their portfolio companies and full-time marketing consultants to introduce their names to prospective entrepreneurs.

47529 ■ "Silent treatment: Want big buzz? keep your mouth shut" in *Entrepreneur* (Vol. 30, No. 3, March 2002, pp. 97)
Pub: Entrepreneur Media Inc.
Ed: April Pennington. **Description:** Profile of Interactive Imagination, the multimedia entertainment company that introduced the fantasy world of Magi-nation collectible cards into the game industry one piece at a time.

47530 ■ "Similac Launches Online Moms' Community" in *Marketing to Women* (Vol. 19, November 2006, No. 11, pp. 3)
Pub: EPM Communications, Inc.
Description: Similacmomsalliance.com, a Website by Abbott Laboratories who manufacture Similac baby formulas, launched the site to provide a community forum for mothers. Panel members include Itsy Bitsy Yoga founder Helen Garabedian, Pediatrician Julie Segal and Olympic swimmer and mom Summer Sanders.

47531 ■ "Simon Group Offers Cobranded Giftcard" in *Marketing to Women* (Vol. 19, October 2006, No. 10, pp. 9)
Pub: EPM Communications, Inc.
Description: Komen Foundation partners with Simon Property Group to produce a cobranded Simon Pink Ribbon Giftcard. This Visa debit card issued by Meta-Bank are sold at Simon malls nationwide and online at Simon.com. One dollar from every card purchased will be donated to the Komen Foundation.

47532 ■ "Sink or Swim" in *My Business* (February/March 2004, pp. 20-25)
Pub: My Business Magazine
Ed: Shannon Scully. **Description:** The importance of e-commerce to small business marketing is discussed. The process of building a Website in order to improve a brick-and-mortar business is critical. A Website should be easy for a customer to surf; it is suggested to stay away from fancy Flash products.

47533 ■ "Site Watch for Home Workers" in *Home Office Computing* (Vol. 19, No. 1, January 2001, pp. 20)
Pub: Scholastic Inc.
Ed: Nicholas J. DeVito. **Description:** If you're looking for one-stop shopping for all your marketing and sales needs, eSolo links to over 1,300 services from 650 pre-screened providers, including bCentral AdStore, International Trademark Association, and eCongo. The article includes information about Homestead.com, Personable.com and Bizland.com.

47534 ■ *Six SIGMA for Small Business*
Pub: Entrepreneur Press
Ed: Greg Brue. **Released:** October 2005. **Price:** $19.95 (US), $26.95 (Canadian). **Description:** Jack Welch's Six SIGMA approach to business covers accounting, finance, sales and marketing, buying a business, human resource development, and new product development.

47535 ■ "Size Matters: Does Your Product Jam a Lot of Benefits Into a Small Package? Here's How to Sell It" in *Entrepreneur* (August 2004)
Pub: Entrepreneur Media Inc.
Ed: Jerry Fisher. **Description:** Expert advertising advice is given to help sell a product. If a product offers many benefits, using a headline to set the consumer up and a footline to give the payoff, can be a key to a great sales campaign.

47536 ■ "Sizing Up the Market" in *Boston Business Journal* (Vol. 23, No. 25, July 25, 2003, pp. 3)
Pub: American City Business Journals
Ed: Paul T. Gannon. **Description:** Profile of Boston, Massachusetts-based Shaw's Supermarkets Inc. Topics include competition, strategic business planning, and market development.

47537 ■ "The Sky's the Limit" in *Hispanic Business* (December 2001, pp. 50, 52)
Pub: Hispanic Business
Ed: Teresa Talerico. **Description:** New technologies and increased advertising budgets have helped Hispanic creative directors to excel.

47538 ■ "Small Business Advisor: A Customer for All Seasons" in *Ingram's* (Vol. 27, No. 5, May 2001, pp. 25)
Pub: Show Me Publishing, Inc.
Ed: Jeff Yowell. **Description:** In order to retain customers, customer relationship management needs to be part of a company's marketing plan.

47539 ■ *The Small Business Bible: Everything You Need to Know to Succeed in Your Small Business*
Pub: John Wiley & Sons, Incorporated
Ed: Steven D. Strauss. **Released:** December 2004. **Price:** $19.95 (US), $28.99 (Canadian). **Description:** Comprehensive guide to starting and running a successful small business. Topics include bookkeeping and financial management, marketing, publicity, and advertising.

47540 ■ *Small Business Clustering Technology: Applications in Marketing, Management, Finance, and IT*
Pub: Idea Group Publishing
Ed: Robert C. MacGregor; Ann Hodgkinson. **Released:** June 2006. **Description:** An overview of the development and role of small business clusters in disciplines that include economics, marketing, management and information systems.

47541 ■ "Small business" in *Crain's Detroit Business* (Vol. 18, No. 45, November 11, 2002, pp. 23)
Pub: Crain Communications Inc., Detroit
Description: Ways to improve profits for various types of small businesses are presented, including marketing ideas and pricing.

47542 ■ *Small Business Desk Reference*
Pub: Penguin Books (USA) Incorporated
Ed: Gene Marks. **Released:** December 2004. **Price:** $29.95 (US), $44.00 (Canadian). **Description:** Comprehensive guide for starting or running a successful small business, focusing on buying a business or franchise, writing a business plan, financial management, accounting, legal issues, human resources management, operations, marketing, sales, customer service, taxes, insurance, and ethics. Information for launching a restaurant, property management firm, retail outlet, consulting firm, and service business is included.

47543 ■ *A Small Business Guide to Direct Mail: Build Your Customer Base and Boost Profits*
Pub: Self-Counsel Press, Inc.
Ed: Lin Grensing. **Released:** 1991. **Price:** $9.95 (paper). **Description:** Describes how to write, produce, and execute a high-impact direct mail marketing campaign; offers strategies for success.

47544 ■ *Small Business Marketing for Dummies*
Pub: John Wiley & Sons, Incorporated
Ed: Barbara Findlay Schenck. **Released:** February 2005. **Price:** $19.99 (US), $25.99 (Canadian). **Description:** Marketing strategies for every type of small business.

47545 ■ "Small-Business Owners in Sacramento, Calif., Area Use Web as Marketing Tool" in *Sacramento Bee* (August 25, 2004)
Pub: Sacramento Bee
Ed: Marcin Skomial. **Description:** A wedding planner and caterer share ways they've used the Internet to market their businesses.

47546 ■ *Small Business Start-Up Workbook: A Step-by-Step Guide to Starting the Business You've Dreamed Of*
Pub: How To Books
Ed: Cheryl D. Rickman. **Released:** February 2006. **Price:** $24.75. **Description:** Book provides practical exercises for starting a small business, including marketing and management strategies.

47547 ■ "Small Businesses Looking to Bolster Web Presence Are in Luck" in *Kiplinger Letter* (Vol. 84, January 26, 2007, No. 4)
Pub: Kiplinger
Description: Microsoft, Yahoo and Concentric are offering small firms advertising space on search engines that track visitors to sites.

47548 ■ "Small Deals, Big Business" in *Washington Business Journal* (Vol. 22, No. 17, August 29, 2003, pp. 17)
Pub: Washington Business Journal
Description: The growing role of small business in the software industry is discussed. Topics include growing sales, marketing strategy, and market adaptability.

47549 ■ "Small Firms Emphasize Trade-Show Marketing" in *Crain's Detroit Business* (Vol. 21, February 7, 2005, No. 6, pp. 24)
Pub: Crain Communications Inc. - Detroit
Ed: DeAnna Belger. **Description:** According to a recent survey, more small companies in Michigan rely on trade shows than their larger competitors. Most respondents reported attending trade shows to generate sales leads, increase visibility, and to network.

47550 ■ "Smaller Shopping Centers Adopt Larger Style" in *Crain's Detroit Business* (Vol. 22, December 4, 2006, No. 49, pp. 33)
Pub: Crain Communications Inc. - Detroit
Ed: Anjali Fluker. **Description:** Fancy landscaping, public gathering areas, and more attractive architecture are no longer limited to only high-end restaurants and stores. Smaller proposed developments in the suburbs are including similar features to attract more customers and improve the shopping experience.

47551 ■ "Smart Marketing Can Make Your Fortune" in *Success* (Vol. 47, No. 5, October 2000, pp. 30)
Pub: Success Publishing, Inc.
Ed: Debbie Selinsky. **Description:** A marketing guru/author tells how she wows business clients with quirky promotions.

47552 ■ "Smart Money: Where to Spend Your Marketing Dollars When a Product Isn't Selling" in *Entrepreneur* (Vol. 33, January 2005, No. 1)
Pub: Entrepreneur Media Inc.
Ed: Nancy Michaels. **Description:** Marketing tips for selling under-performing products are provided.

47553 ■ "Smithtown-based LuminNet Helps Small Businesses Design and Market Their Own Web Sites" in *Long Island Business News* (Feb. 20, 2004)
Pub: Dolan Media Newswires
Ed: Adina Genn. **Description:** Profile of Annette Galarza, owner of LuminNet, a provider of Website development for small businesses. Galarza trains clients to understand ways to use a Website as a cost-effective business tool.

47554 ■ "Soaring Sales" in *Small Business Opportunities* (Vol. 16, No. 2, March 2004, pp. 62)
Pub: Harris Publications, Inc.
Ed: Chuck Green. **Description:** Profile of Bird-X, a company that provides products to repel birds, and works on honing in on their target market to maximize sales. Ways the company markets its products are discussed.

47555 ■ "Sock It To 'Em: Can a Negative Marketing Campaign Have Positive Results?" in *Entrepreneur* (Vol. 32, November 2004, No. 11, pp. 92)
Pub: Entrepreneur Media Inc.
Ed: Kim T. Gordon. **Description:** Negative advertising can produce positive results. Comparative advertising is effective because it is more memorable.

47556 ■ "Soft Market Stall Apartments" in *Houston Business Journal* (Vol. 34, No. 11, July 25, pp. 1)
Pub: American City Business Journals
Ed: Nancy Sarnoff. **Description:** Profile of real estate sales and marketing in the greater Houston area; including real estate development, real estate prices and rates, and poor economic conditions.

47557 ■ "Some Wichita listeners misled by radio spots" in *Atlanta Business Chronicle* (Vol. 25, November 15, 2002, No. 23 pp. S10)
Pub: American City Business Publications, Inc.
Ed: Sherry Graham, Lainie Mazzullo. **Description:** A series of radio commercials intended to improve the image held by the people of Wichita, Kansas have created controversy. The people in the ads giving testimonials are fictitious, but creators of the campaign say the experiences depicted are real. Some fear the commercials could raise questions of credibility, but others feel the ads are still effective.

47558 ■ "South Carolina Duo Cashes in By Buying Ugly Houses as Fixer-Uppers" in *Sun News* (January 9, 2005)
Pub: Knight-Ridder/Tribune News
Ed: Jenny Burns. **Description:** Profile of Bennie Marshall and Jack Rockey, who bought a franchise that buys homes in need of work, renovates them, and sells them for a profit. The franchise uses billboards advertising, We Buy Ugly Houses.

47559 ■ "Speak Up! The Ins and Outs of Hiring a Spokesperson" in *Entrepreneur* (Vol. 32, No. 2, February 2004, pp. 75)
Pub: Entrepreneur Media, Inc.
Ed: Nancy Michaels. **Description:** Pros and cons to hiring a spokesperson to represent a small company are discussed. Resources are included.

47560 ■ "Specifically Speaking" in *Entrepreneur* (Vol. 28, No. 7, July 2000, pp. 150)
Pub: Entrepreneur Media Inc.
Ed: Paul Edwards and Sarah Edwards. **Description:** Finding the perfect niche for you business is discussed.

47561 ■ "Spend, Target Ad Dollars Wisely" in *Crain's Detroit Business* (Vol. 22, January 16, 2006, No. 3, pp. 16)
Pub: Crain Communications Inc. - Detroit
Ed: Sheena Harrison. **Description:** The importance of advertising and marketing for small businesses, despite industry, is stressed.

47562 ■ "Spending Spree" in *Hispanic Business* (December 2001, pp. 38, 40, 56)
Pub: Hispanic Business
Description: Overall growth in the Hispanic ad market slowed in 2001, yet Hispanic purchasing power continued to rise. A list of the top 60 advertisers in the Hispanic Market for 2001 is spotlighted. Statistical data included.

47563 ■ "Sporting Goods Web Sites, Last Year's Costly Rage, Are Turned Over tothe Professionals" in *The New York Times* (Sept. 4, 2000, pp. C5)
Pub: The New York Times Company
Ed: Bob Tedeschi. **Description:** E-commerce Web sites formed by media companies are being handed over to outside companies with retail experience.

47564 ■ "Spread the News: Communicate with Customers" in *My Business* (October/November 2003, pp. 46)
Pub: My Business Magazine
Ed: Julie Bawden Davis. **Description:** In order to create a successful newsletter for a small company the owner must know the purpose for creating the newsletter, identify the audience, determine frequency of publishing, consider outsourcing or designing it in-house, and most importantly have the newsletter be a professional extension of the business.

47565 ■ "Spread the Word" in *BlackEnterprise* (Vol. 31, No. 10, May 2001, pp. 110)
Pub: Earl Graves Publishing Co.
Ed: Holly Aguirre. **Description:** Successful ways to build a Web site for advertising a small business are shown, including search engines, links on other sites, and offline sources that include word-of-mouth and traditional advertising and marketing.

47566 ■ **"Spread the Word: Get Customers Talking and They'll Do Your Advertising For You"** in *Entrepreneur* (Vol. 33, February 2005, No. 2)
Pub: Entrepreneur Media Inc.
Ed: Jerry Fisher. **Description:** Co-authors of Creating Customer Evangelists, Ben McConnell and Jackie Huba suggest that word-of-mouth advertising is an important component to any sales program.

47567 ■ **"Spreading Viruses Can be a Good Thing"** in *Crain's Chicago Business* (Vol. 30, January 2007, No. 3, pp. 18)
Pub: Crain Communications, Inc.
Ed: Steve Hendershot. **Description:** Viral Marketing, spreading a company's message by email which directs consumers to the company's website, is another of the creative new marketing techniques finding success online. Downsides of this powerful tool are explored.

47568 ■ **"Spring cleaning"** in *Entrepreneur* (Vol. 31, No. 4, April 2003, pp. 44)
Pub: Entrepreneur Media Inc.
Ed: Melissa Campanelli. **Description:** There are a variety of software tools available to make sure a Web site is in good working order. Keynote NetMechanic spots and fixes common HTML code errors and generates a repaired file to upload to the Web host.

47569 ■ **"Stacking the Digital Deck"** in *Hispanic Business* (May 2005, pp. 32, 34, 36, 38)
Pub: Hispanic Business
Ed: Kevin Savetz. **Description:** The newest technology systems and business software can help small companies target new markets, increase productivity, and lower costs.

47570 ■ **"Starbucks Brews a New Strategy"** in *Fast Company* (August 2001, pp. 145)
Pub: Fast Company
Ed: George Anders. **Description:** Starbucks is tying its online efforts closely to its central mission: building customer loyalty around cappuccinos, lattes, and other fancy beverages.

47571 ■ **"Starbucks Gets A New Look"** in *Frozen Food Age* (Vol. 50, No. 3, October 2001, pp. 12)
Pub: VNU Business Media
Description: Enterprise IG, located in San Francisco, California, has partnered with Starbucks Ice Cream Partnership (a joint venture with Dreyer's Grand Ice Cream) in order to provide brand identity and help its product stand out on store shelves.

47572 ■ **"Start Spreading the News"** in *Business 2.0* (Vol. 6, July 2005, No. 6, pp. 40, 42)
Pub: Time, Inc.
Ed: John Heilemann. **Description:** Fred Wilson, venture capitalist and leader of the new firm, Union Square Adventures, is investing in New York. Wilson believes that as the Internet transforms the media, marketing, and finance new technologies will make investing in Internet startups profitable again.

47573 ■ **"Start Your Engines"** in *My Business* (June/July 2004, pp. 44)
Pub: My Business Magazine
Ed: Paige Orr. **Description:** Ways to show up high on a search engine's list are shared.

47574 ■ *Starting a Yahoo! Business for Dummies*
Pub: John Wiley & Sons, Incorporated
Ed: Rob Snell. **Released:** June 2006. **Price:** $24.99.
Description: Rob Snell offers advice for turning online browsers into buyers, increase online traffic, and build an online store from scratch.

47575 ■ **"State of the Banner"** in *Forbes* (December 25, 2000, pp. 273)
Pub: Forbes Magazine
Ed: John C. Dvorak. **Description:** Banner advertising, now seen as ineffective and old-fashioned, may be on its last leg. Nobody likes banners, and the frequency of people clicking on them has fallen off drastically, to 0.5 percent, indicating that people simply ignore them.

47576 ■ **"Staying Interactive: Web Presentation Success Requires More Than Just Technical Skills"** in *Sales & Marketing Management* (Vol. 157)
Pub: VNU Business Media
Ed: Julia Chang. **Description:** According to a study performed by Wainhouse Research, a market research firm in Massachusetts, forty percent of companies are expected to increased spending on Web conferencing in 2005. Webinar provides training in the technical skills required for Web conferencing, but also emphasizes ways to use voice to emphasize points and captivate an audience.

47577 ■ **"SteelSalvor Chooses Lois Paul & Partners to Kick Start Public Relations, Strategic Communications Initiative"** in *PR Newswire*
Pub: PR Newswire Association LLC
Description: SteelSalvor, the only marketing company that maintains an online auction serving the steel industry, has appointed Lois Paul & Partners LLC as its marketing and public relations partner.

47578 ■ **"Sterling Makes a Mint on Sale of Single-Family Mortgage Business"** in *Houston Business Journal* (Vol. 34, No. 11, July 25, pp. 7)
Pub: American City Business Journals
Ed: Jim Greer. **Description:** Profile of Sterling Bancshare and its fast-selling line of single-family mortgage packages. Topics include mortgage prices and rates, profits levels, and marketing strategy.

47579 ■ **"Stick to the core - or go for more?"** in *Harvard Business Review* (Vol. 80, No. 2, February 2002, pp. 31)
Pub: Harvard Business School Press
Ed: Thomas J. Waite. **Description:** A presentation of the case study of Advaark. The issue is whether or not the New York advertising agency should stick to its core competence.

47580 ■ **"Straight to Video"** in *Entrepreneur.com* (Vol. 34, January 2006, No. 1, pp. 22)
Pub: Entrepreneur Media Inc.
Ed: Amanda C. Kooser. **Description:** Microsoft's Small Business Center offers short clips to help small businesses market on the Internet. Businesses can test advertising, provide details on products and services, or show video tips to keep users returning to your site.

47581 ■ **"Striking Up the Brand Band"** in *Houston Business Journal* (Vol. 34, No. 19, September 19, 2003, pp. 17A)
Pub: American City Business Journals
Ed: Judy Rider. **Description:** Easterly and Company, Houston, Texas, is a marketing company led by Gary D. Easterly, president; the marketing firm has received new branding contract from several Enron subsidiaries.

47582 ■ **"Students help biz with marketing, consulting"** in *Crain's Detroit Business* (Vol. 18, No. 24, June 17, 2002, pp. 12)
Pub: Crain Communications Inc. - Detroit
Ed: Laura Bailey. **Description:** University of Michigan, Michigan State University, Lawrence Technological University and Oakland University have programs that place students or groups of students with companies to solve business issues.

47583 ■ **"Success a Big Seller: N. Carolina, Duke Coaches Cash in as Marketers' Dreams"** in *Charlotte Observer* (February 7, 2007)
Pub: Knight-Ridder/Tribune Business News
Ed: Ken Tysiac. **Description:** North Carolina sporting coaches are marketing goods and services in television commercials and print media.

47584 ■ **"Success Off the Shelf"** in *Hispanic Business* (October 2003, pp. 88)
Pub: Hispanic Business
Ed: Joel Russell. **Description:** Two Hispanic authors share expertise on branding and on managing money.

47585 ■ **"Success Products"** in *Black Enterprise* (Vol. 37, February 2007, No. 7, pp. 135)
Pub: Earl G. Graves Publishing Co. Inc.
Ed: Tanisha A. Sykes. **Description:** Using innovative resources that are already at your fingertips instead of trying to reach out to companies first is a great way to discover whether you have a viable idea or product. Be motivated to start an e-newsletter letting people know about your products and attend conferences like The Motivation Show, the world's largest exhibition of motivational products and services related to performance in business.

47586 ■ *The Successful Exhibitor's Handbook: Trade Show Techniques for Beginners and Pros*
Pub: Self-Counsel Press, Inc.
Ed: Barry Siskind. **Released:** 1993, second edition. **Price:** $14.95 (paper).

47587 ■ **"Summer Could Help Lick Tourism Slump"** in *Pacific Business News* (Vol. 41, No. 16, June 27, 2003, pp. 1)
Pub: American City Business Journals
Ed: Prabha Natarajan. **Description:** Hawaii experienced a poor showing in the tourism industry the first two quarters of 2003. State and private tourism marketers are marketing to Japan and airline flights have increased between Japan and Hawaii.

47588 ■ **"Support the Advocate!"** in *Bellingham Business Journal* (December 2006, pp. 3)
Pub: Sun News Inc.
Ed: Drew Graham. **Description:** The Whatcom Business Advocate is now a pull-out section of the Business Journal. One of the premier news publications the newsletter reaches more than 30,000 individual readers each month. The newsletter and journal are excellent sources for advertisers.

47589 ■ **"Survey Says...Market Research on the Cheap is Just a Click Away"** in *Entrepreneur* (Vol. 32, September 2004, No. 9, pp. 73)
Pub: Entrepreneur Media Inc.
Ed: Nancy Michaels. **Description:** Tips for using online market surveys are presented.

47590 ■ **"Survey Your Customers"** in *Home Business* (Vol. 12, March/April 2005, No. 2, pp. 50, 52-53)
Pub: Home Business Magazine
Ed: Christopher J. Bachler. **Description:** A customer survey provides important information to improve customer service as well as how to market wisely.

47591 ■ **"Sweet Reward: Reaching Out to the Media Really Does Pay Off"** in *Entrepreneur* (Vol. 31, No. 9, July 2003, pp. 81)
Pub: Entrepreneur Media, Inc.
Ed: April Y. Pennington. **Description:** Profile of Fran Bigelow, owner of Fran's Chocolates Ltd., opened in 1982. Bigelow sent letters to food editors educating them on the fine chocolates she uses and included samples. The editors published articles that gave her store more exposures and Bigelow was named The Best Chocolatier in America by The Book of Chocolate.

47592 ■ **"Sweet Rewards"** in *Entrepreneur* (Vol. 31, No. 8, August 2003, pp. 75)
Pub: Entrepreneur Media, Inc.
Ed: Kim T. Gordon. **Description:** Win over existing customers with a customer loyalty program and increase sales at the same time.

47593 ■ **"The Sweet Spot: A Sugar-Coated Pitch Paid Off Big Time"** in *Black Enterprise* (Vol. 37, November 2006, No. 4, pp. 71)
Pub: Earl G. Graves Publishing Co. Inc.
Ed: Laura Egodigwe. **Description:** In an interview with Debra Sandler, president of McNeil Nutritionals L.L.C., Sandler talks about the challenges of bringing a new product to the marketplace, how her personal experiences effect her business decisions, and the difficulties of re-entering the workforce.

47594 ■ "Sweetwoods' a man with a brand" in *Atlanta Business Chronicle* (Vol. 24, No. 14, September 7, 2001, pp. 26A)
Pub: American City Business Journals Inc.
Ed: Walter Woods. Description: John Sweetwood, part of the management committee of Bass Hotels & Resorts, has been behind advertisements such as the Energizer bunny and Purina Dog Chow. Having been hired in 1997 as president of Holiday Inn Express, he now enjoys working for the parent company. Despite the recent cutbacks in the hotel industry, Sweetwood says his company is going strong.

47595 ■ "T & E Report" in *Sales & Marketing Management* (Vol. 157, January 2005, No. 1, pp. 54)
Pub: VNU Business Media
Description: Rent-A-Wreck, headquartered in Owing, Maryland, is marketing price advantage to attract business travelers with low-cost rentals ten to twenty percent lower than larger car rental agencies.

47596 ■ "Table Talk" in *Sales & Marketing Management* (Vol. 159, January-February 2007, No. 1, pp. 33)
Pub: VNU Business Media
Description: Marketing leaders focus on the impacts of globalization of business, customers and products.

47597 ■ "Take-Aways" in *Sales & Marketing Management* (Vol. 158, October 2006, No. 10, pp. 16)
Pub: VNU Business Media
Description: Tips for using music for branding products or services are presented by Paul Anthony, CEO of Rumblefish.

47598 ■ "Take It to the Bank" in *Washington Business Journal* (Vol. 22, No. 15, August 15, 2003, pp. 3)
Pub: Washington Business Journal
Ed: Tim Mazzucca. Description: Profile of Washington's newest bank, Congressional Bank, examining management goals and plans, including long term planning, market development, and management styles.

47599 ■ "Take the Plunge" in *Entrepreneur* (Vol. 32, November 2004, No. 11, pp. 93)
Pub: Entrepreneur Media Inc.
Ed: Jerry Fisher. Description: Advertising promotions that use 'bad news' as an opener can be unusual enough to generate interest.

47600 ■ "Takes the cake" in *Black Enterprise* (Vol. 32, No. 10, May 2002, pp. 58)
Pub: Earl Graves Publishing Co.
Ed: Ron Childs. Description: Profile of Amy Hilliard, senior vice president of integrated marketing at Burrell Communications Groups Inc. Hilliard thrives on creating and launching products.

47601 ■ "Taking Our Affluence For Granted" in *Black Enterprise* (Vol. 34, No. 3, October 2003, pp. 12)
Pub: Earl Graves Publishing Co.
Ed: Earl G. Graves, Sr. Description: The importance of black consumer spending and marketing strategies directed towards African Americans is discussed.

47602 ■ "Taking Spiritual E-Path" in *Crain's New York Business* (Vol. 23, November 20, 2006, No. 47, pp. 29)
Pub: Crain Communications, Inc.
Ed: Description: Profile of Cathy O'Brien and her position at Beliefnet, a website which combines blogs, news and videos, and a free e-mail newsletter on subjects of faith, spirituality and religion. O'Brien hopes to attract advertisers to the popular eight-year-old site.

47603 ■ "Talking heads" in *Entrepreneur* (Vol. 31, No. 6, June 2003, pp. 84)
Pub: Entrepreneur Media Inc.
Ed: Jerry Fisher. Description: The use of a cartoon animal character with a word balloon still attracts the attention of consumers. The reasons these ads still work are discussed.

47604 ■ "Talking Shop: Where Should You Focus Your Online Marketing? Try the Office" in *Entrepreneur* (Vol. 31, No. 9, July 2003, pp. 83)
Pub: Entrepreneur Media, Inc.
Ed: Catherine Seda. Description: According to a study by ComScore Networks, about 60 percent of online shopping is being conducted at the workplace. Ways to market online products targeting workers are presented.

47605 ■ "Tapping local markets can pay off" in *Wall Street Journal* (May 14, 2002, pp. B4)
Pub: Wall Street Journal
Ed: Jeff Bailey. Description: Harvey Saltzman of Triangle Printers Inc does business locally as well as nationally, but states that his local customers often boost his firms sales at a lower operating cost.

47606 ■ "Tapping the Talent Pool of Hispanic Affluence" in *Hispanic Business* (Vol. 24, No. 1/2, January/February 2002, pp. 6)
Pub: Hispanic Business Inc.
Ed: Jesus Chavarria. Description: A brief overview of the growth of Hispanic affluence in America and the important role that plays for Hispanic entrepreneurs and marketers. Hispanic Business magazine plans to organize training and educational events with sessions on Latin American trade, B2B e-commerce strategies, Hispanic online consumers, and cross-border banking.

47607 ■ *Target Marketing for the Small Business: Researching, Reaching and Retaining Your Target Market*
Pub: Upstart Publishing Co., Inc.
Ed: Linda Pinson and Jerry Jinnett. Released: 1993. Price: $19.95 (paper). Description: Three step guide to developing a marketing plan for the small or micro business, covering researching the market, reaching the target market, and retaining a customer base. Contains forms and examples, a resource section, and an index.

47608 ■ "Target Practice" in *Entrepreneur* (Vol. 31, No. 8, August 2003, pp. 72)
Pub: Entrepreneur Media, Inc.
Ed: Barry Farber. Description: The key to landing a sale can sometimes lie in clearing away the obstacles that can make a salesperson miss the mark. Five practical and effective strategies to apply to sales are investigated.

47609 ■ *Target Smart: Database Marketing for the Small Business*
Pub: PSI Research
Ed: Jay Newberg and Claudio Marcus. Released: 1997. Price: $19.95.

47610 ■ "Targeting Success" in *Small Business Opportunities* (Vol. 12, No. 5, September 2000, pp. 60, 64)
Pub: Harris Publications, Inc.
Ed: Annette Wood. Description: A profile of Results Direct Marketing, a two year old company, that designs and produces mailers, brochures, and other ad material.

47611 ■ "Targeting a Tighter Audience" in *Hispanic Business* (Vol. 22, No. 1/2, January/February, pp. 90)
Pub: Hispanic Business
Ed: Vaughn Hagerty. Description: Money-focused Consejero.com represents a new breed of niche sites.

47612 ■ "Taste, Bud" in *Fast Company* (July 2001, pp. 62)
Pub: Fast Company
Ed: Cheryl Dahle. Description: Profile of John Harrison, the official taster for Edy's Grand Ice Cream, in Oakland, California. Harrison also makes regular visits to supermarkets around the country for random taste tests.

47613 ■ "Tastes Differ" in *Crain's New York Business* (Vol. 22, December 11, 2006, No. 50, pp. 24)
Pub: Crain Communications, Inc.
Description: Executives for reality shows say that the key to getting one's products on air is to be available on short notice, be patient, and have a great product. Many shows not only mention vendors by name but they also feature them on their websites.

47614 ■ "Team Players" in *Entrepreneur* (Vol. 33, October 2005, No. 10, pp. 85)
Pub: Entrepreneur Media Inc.
Ed: Catherine Seda. Description: Questions for planning an affiliate program for marketing a business are presented, focusing on hiring Internet marketers to promote your business with no up-front costs.

47615 ■ "Technically correct" in *Pittsburgh Business Times* (Vol. 22, No. 46, May 30, 2003, pp. 19)
Pub: Pittsburgh Business Times
Ed: Maria Guzzo. Description: Profiles of product lines and new product development at the Michael Baker Corporation, including business creativity, market share, and business strategy.

47616 ■ "Technophobe Help Desk" in *Sales & Marketing Management* (Vol. 158, October 2006, No. 10, pp. 22)
Pub: VNU Business Media
Description: Traditional marketing channels are based on self-reported surveys, circulation audits and promotional code tracking, however, Web analytics provide actual site traffic, including page hits, number of visits, browser usage and visitors' regional origin.

47617 ■ "Telemarketers Plan to Do-Not-Call" in *Providence Business News* (Vol. 18, No. 20, September 1, 2003, pp. 1)
Pub: Providence Business News, Inc.
Ed: Mike Colias. Description: The possible effect of the Do-Not-Call list will have on the direct marketing industry is examined. Topics include business closures, layoffs, and economic hardship.

47618 ■ *Telemarketing: Applications and Opportunities*
Pub: Crisp Publications, Inc.
Ed: Lloyd and Vivyan Finch. Released: 1995. Price: $10.95.

47619 ■ *Telemarketing Basics*
Pub: Crisp Publications, Inc.
Ed: Julie Freestone and Janet Brusse. Price: $9.95.

47620 ■ "Tell-A-Friend Wizard" in *Entrepreneur* (Vol. 33, September 2005, No. 9, pp. 6)
Pub: Entrepreneur Media Inc.
Ed: Steve Cooper. Description: Tell-a-Friend Wizard helps to add customized buttons to any Website that allow visitors to recommend a product or service. The service starts at $5.95 per month.

47621 ■ "Texas Town Changes Its Name to Dish to Get Free Satellite TV" in *Sacramento Bee* (November 17, 2005)
Pub: The Sacramento Bee
Ed: Clint Swett. Description: Residents of Clark, Texas voted to change the town's name to Dish in order to receive 10 years of free satellite television.

47622 ■ "That's the Spirit" in *Entrepreneur* (Vol. 33, October 2005, No. 10, pp. 83)
Pub: Entrepreneur Media Inc.
Ed: Kim T. Gordon. Description: Four steps to increase sales and promote customer loyalty for the 2005 holiday season are outlined, including customer rewards, holiday promotions, donations to charities, and holding a holiday party.

47623 ■ "The AdStop Inc.: www.theadstop. com" in *Entrepreneur* (Vol. 31, No. 12, December 2003, pp. 8)
Pub: Entrepreneur Media Inc.
Ed: Steve Cooper. Description: Profile of The AdStop Inc. Web site that offers resources for Internet advertising to help grow a business.

47624 ■ "The ROI Treatment: Get Better Results by Creating an ROI Model" in *Entrepreneur* **(Vol. 31, No. 11, November 2003, pp. 100)**
Pub: Entrepreneur Media, Inc.
Ed: Catherine Seda. Description: Developing a return on investment (ROI) model for a business can be done in five simple steps, starting with researching market demand.

47625 ■ "The U.S. Commercial Service: www.export.gov/comm_svc" in *Entrepreneur* **(Vol. 32, November 2004, No. 11, pp. 6)**
Pub: Entrepreneur Media Inc.
Ed: Steve Cooper. Description: U.S. Commercial Service offers global business solutions in the areas of market research, trade events to promote businesses and services, introductions between buyers and distributors, and export counseling.

47626 ■ "Theme: Marketing an E-Book" in *Web Marketing Today* **(No. 121, February 5, 2003)**
Pub: Wilson Internet Services
Description: The best ways to market electronic books are listed.

47627 ■ "There's More to E-Business Than Point and Click" in *Journal of Business Strategies* **(Vol. 21, No. 5, September 2000, pp. 11)**
Pub: Center for Business and Economic Research
Ed: Jerry Savin, Dave Silberg. Description: Companies that create an effective Web presence can streamline operations, shorten response time to customer requests, gather more market data, increase their geographic reach, and sell more goods.

47628 ■ "They clicked, they left: why aren't your web site visitors buying?" in *Entrepreneur* **(Vol. 31, No. 4, April 2003, pp. 85)**
Pub: Entrepreneur Media Inc.
Ed: Catherine Seda. Description: Business owners should evaluate the entry, or landing page of Web sites to see if their ad entices people to click for more information.

47629 ■ "They've Got Mail - From You" in *My Business* **(June/July 2004, pp. 45)**
Pub: My Business Magazine
Ed: Nancy Mann Jackson. Description: A customer newsletter can help build strong relationships with clients and attract new customers.

47630 ■ "Things I Can't Live Without" in *Inc.* **(September 1, 2004)**
Pub: Inc. Magazine
Ed: Lisa Osborne, Alex Bogusky. Description: Profile of Crispin Porter Bogusky, an award-winning advertising agency. The Florida agency is best-known for its campaigns for Mini Cooper, Ikea, Molson, Virgin Atlantic Airways, Burger King, and FX Networks show Nip/Tuck.

47631 ■ "Thinking Pink? Think Again" in *Entrepreneur* **(Vol. 32, No. 2, February 2004, pp. 12)**
Pub: Entrepreneur Media, Inc.
Ed: Rieva Lesonsky. Description: Female entrepreneurs claim a natural advantage over men when it comes to marketing to women. Because of the growing economic status of women, they have become an important and influential market.

47632 ■ "Thinking Small: Coca-Cola Shows How the 20'x20' Exhibit Is Done" in *Tradeshow Week* **(Vol. 34, December 6, 2004, No. 49, pp. S6)**
Pub: Reed Business Information
Ed: Heidi Genoist. Description: Small companies are using Coca-Cola's small tradeshow booth as a model for introducing new products to a key buyer group.

47633 ■ "Third Degree Advertising Names VP for Solomon Inc." in *Journal Record* **(June 25, 2003)**
Pub: Dolan Media Company

Description: Profile of Randy Nichols, newly named vice president for Solomon Inc., a research and branding division of Third Degree Advertising and Communications.

47634 ■ "This Marketing Pro's Aim is to Clear the Clutter" in *The Record* **(November 6, 2005)**
Pub: New Jersey Media Group
Ed: William Conroy. Description: Profile of Janice Marino-Doyle, owner of Clear Aim Marketing and Organizing LLC. Marino-Doyle operates her one-person firm by offering clients marketing services while helping them get organized.

47635 ■ "This will keep you up at night" in *E-business Advisor* **(Vol. 18, No. 10, October 2000, pp. 10)**
Pub: Advisor Media, Inc.
Description: Business intelligence agency Cyveillance, who works with Global 2000 firms to understand Internet opportunities and risks, reports the five key risks that threaten revenue, decrease market share, and detract from customer and brand loyalty.

47636 ■ "This Week: McD's Eyes Ad Plan, Shifts Breakfast Biz" in *Crain's Chicago Business* **(Vol. 30, February 2007, No. 6, pp. 1)**
Pub: Crain Communications, Inc.
Ed: Kate MacArthur. Description: McDonald's is moving its national breakfast ad account from DDB Chicago to Arnold Worldwide of Boston and Moroch of Dallas in an attempt to change its marketing strategy. It is also doing a study to keep abreast of consumer trends.

47637 ■ "This Week: McD's Tests Trans-Free Oil in 1,200 Locations" in *Crain's Chicago Business* **(Vol. 29, December 2006, No. 50, pp. 1)**
Pub: Crain Communications, Inc.
Ed: Julie Jargon. Description: Just under ten percent of McDonald's U.S. outlets are performing initial tests with trans fat-free oil in their foods. Pressure is high as rival fast food restaurants have already introduced these trans fat-free foods and New York passed the ban which takes place in July.

47638 ■ "Three questions you need to ask about your brand" in *Harvard Business Review* **(Vol. 80, No. 9, September 2002, pp. 80)**
Pub: Harvard Business School Press
Ed: Kevin Lane Keller, Brian Sternthal, Alice Tybout. Description: Successful brand positioning is not so much about differentiating a product from competitors as it is in understanding the frame of reference in which the product must compete for attention. Various companies' efforts are explored.

47639 ■ "Three Scary Words: Buy it Used" in *Inc.* **(September 2006, pp. 29-31)**
Pub: Gruner & Jahr USA Publishing
Ed: Max Chafkin. Description: Secondhand items have become more attractive to consumers. Internet auctions like eBay or listings on Crain's list have given rise to tremendous growth of these items. Manufacturers are rethinking their product life strategies as the consequences could be serious.

47640 ■ "Thumbs Up! Rave Reviews Could be All the Advertising You Need" in *Entrepreneur* **(Vol. 32, July 2004, No. 7, pp. 71)**
Pub: Entrepreneur Media Inc.
Ed: Nancy Michaels. Description: Owner of a software/Web site design business is offered advice for word-of-mouth marketing after having little success with radio and newspaper ads.

47641 ■ "Tickle Makes a Match With SendTec" in *ADWEEK Western Edition* **(December 24, 2003)**
Pub: VNU Business Media
Ed: Gregory Solman. Description: SendTec wins advertising account from online dating service Tickle.

47642 ■ "Tiger Power" in *Rough Notes* **(Vol. 146, No. 9, September 2003, pp. 32)**
Pub: Rough Notes
Ed: Elisabeth Boone. Description: Profile of Princeton Risk Managers Inc., covering risk management services, management styles, and market development.

47643 ■ "Time for marketers to grow up?" in *Wall Street Journal* **(February 27, 2003, pp. B1)**
Pub: Dow Jones & Co. Inc.
Ed: Cris Prystay, Sarah Ellison. Description: While major industrial nations are seeing increasingly aging populations, as is the case in Japan where half the population will be over 50 in the year 2025, the marketing industry has failed to respond to that market, concentrating all efforts on the younger population. Analysts argue that advertisers should take these major demographic trends into account when planning strategy.

47644 ■ "Tip of the Month" in *E-business Advisor* **(Vol. 17, No. 12, December 1999, pp. 44)**
Pub: Advisor Media, Inc.
Ed: Larry C. Whipple. Description: Tips for making banner advertisements eye-catching and effective are provided. Strategies include the correct choice of colors, keeping them simple, adding words such as 'free' and 'click here' and using small files. Programming tips are also provided for dealing with browser inconsistency in Web page creation and reducing Web graphic problems.

47645 ■ *The Tipping Point: How Little Things Can Make a Big Difference*
Pub: Little Brown & Company
Ed: Malcolm Gladwell. Released: January 2002. Price: $14.95. Description: Correlation between societal changes and marketing and business trends.

47646 ■ "To DVD or not to DVD; Multimedia advertising comes in many shapes" in *Crain's Detroit Business* **(Vol. 19, No. 10, March 10, 2003)**
Pub: Crain Communications Inc., Detroit
Ed: Jennette Smith. Description: Companies are starting to use DVD's to promote products and services.

47647 ■ "To the Extreme: Watch Sales Grow by Making a Positive Lasting Impression" in *Sales & Marketing Management* **(Vol. 157, January 2005)**
Pub: VNU Business Media
Ed: Sara Calabro. Description: Positive Response, a marketing consulting firm in Ohio, developed an extreme marketing plan to help CSi Complete gain the competitive edge to win approval to sell its customer satisfaction measurement services for collision repair companies. Positive Response created a three-step mail campaign targeted to collision repair services over six weeks.

47648 ■ "To Fax or Not to Fax?" in *My Business* **(October/November 2003, pp. 11)**
Pub: My Business Magazine
Description: Information regarding the new rules for advertising and telemarketing via fax machines is addressed, including information about the do-not-call rules, whereby companies violating the law can be fined up to $2,000 per violation.

47649 ■ "To opt or not to opt" in *Working Woman* **(Vol. 25, No. 6, June 2000, pp. 22)**
Pub: Lang Communications Inc.
Ed: Ananda Chaudhuri. Description: Internet retailers are adopting a new approach to selling goods and services to consumers, known as permission-based marketing, by asking electronic mail users to agree to opt to receive advertisements.

47650 ■ "TodaysMama.com Relaunches Website" in *Marketing to Women* **(Vol. 20, January 2007, No. 1, pp. 3)**
Pub: EPM Communications Inc.
Description: TodaysMama.com, an online resource for mothers, debuted its enhanced Website. They

have partnered with Kiva, a charitable organization, to fund microloans to entrepreneurs in developing nations.

47651 ■ "Tomboy Tools Ties in With Pink Hammer" in *Marketing to Women* (Vol. 19, October 2006, No. 10, pp. 9)
Pub: EPM Communications, Inc.
Description: The Komen Foundation partners with Tomboy Tools, manufacturer of ergonomically designed tools for women, for an exception to its "no pink tools" slogan. The "Pink for a Purpose" special-edition hammer is available through the company's website or their home-party distribution network.

47652 ■ "Too Much Information?" in *Black Enterprise* (Vol. 37, December 2006, No. 5, pp. 59)
Pub: Earl G. Graves Publishing Co. Inc.
Ed: James C. Johnson. **Description:** African American business owners often face the dilemma of whether or not to divulge their minority status when soliciting new customers and financial institutions. The quality of the products or services is always the key factor and race should never define one's business; however, it is appropriate to market oneself as a minority or women-owned business, especially if the company is in an industry where those clients are offered top-tier contracts.

47653 ■ "Top 25 Hispanic Ad Agencies" in *Hispanic Business* (December 2003, pp. 42, 44, 46, 48, 50)
Pub: Hispanic Business
Description: A listing of the top 25 Hispanic advertising agencies is presented, with 23 of the 25 agencies reporting increased billings since 2002. Statistical data included.

47654 ■ "Top Area Advertising Agencies" in *Ingram's* (Vol. 28, No. 9, September 2002, pp. 29)
Pub: Show Me Publishing, Inc.
Description: A listing of the top Kansas area advertising agencies ranked in 2001, according to capitalized billings. The top three are Bernstein-Rein Advertising Inc., Barkley Evergreen and Partners Inc., and Valentine Radford Inc.

47655 ■ "A top brand won't happen without top leadership" in *Atlanta Business Chronicle* (Vol. 24, No. 10, August 10, 2001, pp. 43A)
Pub: American City Business Journals Inc.
Ed: Michael H. Mescon, Timothy S. Mescon. **Description:** Leadership is key to building a brand. While goals, structure and people, are the basic elements in any organizational endeavor, the leader's vision and passion transforms an organization into an institution, an entity with a brand.

47656 ■ "Top-down diversity" in *Hispanic Business* (Vol. 22, No. 9, September 2000, pp. 42)
Pub: Hispanic Business
Ed: Jonathan Higuera. **Description:** Research is presented showing corporate America is benefiting from the positive use of workplace diversity and a growing number of minority group employees in management positions.

47657 ■ "Total Recall" in *Entrepreneur* (Vol. 31, No. 11, November 2003, pp. 100)
Pub: Entrepreneur Media, Inc.
Ed: Kim T. Gordon. **Description:** Methods for producing memorable ad campaigns are examined.

47658 ■ "A Touch of Class" in *Entrepreneur* (Vol. 28, No. 10, October 2000, pp. 29)
Pub: Entrepreneur Media Inc.
Ed: Amanda C. Kooser. **Description:** E-mail has evolved into a prime marketing tool for businesses. Jupiter Communications predicts the e-mail marketing industry will reach $7.3 billion by 2005.

47659 ■ "Toying with new ideas" in *Entrepreneur* (Vol. 31, No. 4, April 2003, pp. 81)
Pub: Entrepreneur Media Inc.
Ed: Elizabeth J. Goodgold. **Description:** Profile of Edward Roberts, co-founder and CEO of Zoinks!, a 7,700-square-foot toy store located in Boston, Massachusetts. Roberts and partner Thomas Brown have geared the store to singles.

47660 ■ "Toyota-eBay Deal Opens Floodgates" in *Automotive News* (Vol. 78, No. 6086, March 29, 2004, pp. 20B)
Pub: Crain Communications, Inc.
Ed: Jason Stein. **Description:** Toyota Motor Sales USA has partnered with eBay to market its vehicles on an exclusive Web page linked to the auction site.

47661 ■ *Trade Show Exhibiting: The Insider's Guide for Entrepreneurs*
Pub: The McGraw-Hill Companies
Ed: Diane K. Weintraub. **Released:** 1991. **Price:** $14.95 (paper).

47662 ■ *Trade Shows: The Small Business Guide to Successful Exhibiting*
Pub: TAB Books, Inc.
Ed: Diane K. Weintraub. **Released:** 1991. **Price:** $14.95 (paper). **Description:** Published by Liberty Hall Press.

47663 ■ *Trade Shows Worldwide*
Pub: Thomson Gale
Released: Annual, latest edition 22, Published July 2005. **Price:** $435, individuals. **Covers:** over 10,800 trade shows and exhibitions, including those held at conferences, conventions, meetings, trade and industrial events, merchandise marts, and national expositions; 6,000 trade show sponsors and organizers; of trade show facilities, services, and information sources, approximately 2,000 conference and convention centers, about 600 visitor and convention bureaus, 400 World Trade Centers; sources of information for the trade show industry, including professional associations, consulting organizations, and publications; and 1,900 trade show industry service suppliers. **Entries Include:** For shows and exhibitions—Name of convention, exhibit, or show; producer, sponsor, and/or organizer name, address, phone, e-mail, website, toll-free phone, telex, fax, name and title of contact; show frequency; founding date; audience; number of attendees; price for display space; description of exhibits; registration fees; industry programs; social events; square feet/meters of exhibition space; number of meeting rooms needed; number of hotel rooms and nights needed; publications and dates and locations of future shows. For sponsors and organizers—Company or organization name, address, phone, toll-free, e-mail, URL, fax, telex, and alphabetical listing of shows handled. For facilities, suppliers of services, and information sources— Company or organization name, address, phone, toll-free, e-mail, URL, telex, fax, name and title of contact, and description of services. **Arrangement:** Separate sections for shows and exhibitions, for sponsors/organizers, and for trade show facilities, services, and information sources. **Indexes:** Chronological (show date), geographical (show location), subject, name and keyword.

47664 ■ "Tragic taste" in *Entrepreneur* (Vol. 30, No. 1, January 2002, p)
Pub: Entrepreneur Media Inc.
Ed: Michelle Prather. **Description:** Since the September terrorist attacks, Atlanta-based Zyman Marketing Group suggests that the political climate cannot be separated from the marketing climate and as Americans strive to return to normal, marketing tactics cannot.

47665 ■ "A Trailblazer, Rediscovered" in *Inc.* (September 1, 2003)
Pub: Gruner & Jahr USA Publishing
Ed: Nadine Heintz. **Description:** Profile of Brownie Wise who built the multimillion-dollar Tupperware empire. A new documentary entitled, "In Tupperware!" will be seen on PBS in spring 2003. The film assesses Wise's marketing genius and her ouster in 1958.

47666 ■ "Trends" in *E-business Advisor* (Vol. 17, No. 12, December 1999, pp. 8)
Pub: Advisor Media, Inc.
Description: New business-to-business "e-market makers" are "reintermediaries" that enter supply chains and introduce new efficiencies and ways of buying and selling products and services. According to Dataquest, a unit of Gartner Group Inc., an e-market maker is an organization that develops a business-to-business, Internet Protocol (IP) network-based e-marketplace of buyers and sellers within a particular industry, geographic region, or affinity group.

47667 ■ "Trends in organization management" in *Hispanic Business* (Vol. 22, No. 9, September 2000, pp. 80)
Pub: Hispanic Business
Ed: Vivienne Heines. **Description:** Management issues of American non-profit organizations are explored.

47668 ■ "Tricks of the Trade" in *Small Business Opportunities* (Vol. 12, No. 5, September 2000, pp. 46, 48, 102-103)
Pub: Harris Publications, Inc.
Ed: Richard Siedlecki. **Description:** Designing a Web site like a direct marketer instead of using conventional marketing techniques can generate more profitable sales and help grow an Internet business more successfully.

47669 ■ "The Truth Is Out There" in *Entrepreneur* (Vol. 33, August 2005, No. 8, pp. 8)
Pub: Entrepreneur Media Inc.
Ed: Rieva Lesonsky. **Description:** Entrepreneurs should be wary of using bad or misleading advertising in marketing campaigns.

47670 ■ "Trying to Reach a Senior Level Executive?" in *Sales & Marketing Management* (Vol. 159, January-February 2007, No. 1, pp. 9)
Pub: VNU Business Media
Description: Ernest Nicastro, principal of Positive Response LLC, offers advice for reaching the attention of top level executives when trying to sell products or services.

47671 ■ "Turn Customer Input into Innovation" in *Harvard Business Review* (Vol. 80, No. 1, January 2002, pp. 91)
Pub: Harvard Business School Press
Ed: Anthony W. Ulwick. **Description:** A new methodology is proposed for more effectively capturing customer input for new products and services that should minimize failure when the product or service is introduced. Previous methods often failed to correctly understand customer feedback.

47672 ■ "Turn classmates into customers" in *Black Enterprise* (Vol. 33, No. 3, October 2002, pp. S2)
Pub: Earl Graves Publishing Co.
Ed: LaToya S. Foye. **Description:** Suggestions are offered for successfully marketing a business, including targeting classmates as customers. The nonprofit organization BUILD (Businesses United in Investing, Lending and Development) encourages young people to develop businesses is highlighted.

47673 ■ "Turn It Up" in *Entrepreneur* (Vol. 32, No. 1, January 2004, pp. 80)
Pub: Entrepreneur Media, Inc.
Ed: Kim T. Gordon. **Description:** Three guidelines to get the most out of radio advertising for a small business are featured.

47674 ■ "TV One Auditions District for HQ" in *Washington Business Journal* (Vol. 22, No. 9, July 4, 2003, pp. 1)
Pub: Washington Business Journal
Ed: Greg A. Lohr. **Description:** Marketing efforts and attempts to find larger office facilities for TV One are presented.

47675 ■ **"Twin Picks" in** *Entrepreneur* **(Vol. 32, December 2004, No. 12, pp. 95)**
Pub: Entrepreneur Media Inc.
Ed: Jerry Fisher. **Description:** Side-by-side comparison marketing is presented using a soluble, natural health supplement as an example.

47676 ■ **"Two Marketing Firms Called Momentum Was One Too Many" in** *Inc.* **(Volume 27, June 2005, No. 6, pp. 41-42)**
Pub: Inc. Magazine
Ed: Nicole Gull. **Description:** Brad Nierenberg discusses the risks he took when changing his business name from Momentum Marketing to Red Peg. The article also examines the way the firm marketed its new name.

47677 ■ **"Tyrannosaurus Rep?" in** *Incentive* **(Vol. 174, No. 10, October 2000, pp. 21)**
Pub: Bill Communications
Ed: Kenneth Hein. **Description:** E-commerce is transforming the process for buying and selling premiums. Does this mean ad specialty reps are headed for extinction?

47678 ■ *The Ultimate Guide to Electronic Marketing for Small Business: Low-Cost/High Return Tools and Techniques That Really Work*
Pub: John Wiley & Sons, Incorporated
Ed: Tom Antion. **Released:** June 2005. **Price:** $19.95 (US), $25.99 (Canadian). **Description:** Online marketing techniques for small business to grow and increase sales.

47679 ■ *Ultimate Small Business Marketing Guide*
Pub: Entrepreneur Press
Ed: James Stephenson. **Released:** January 2007. **Price:** $24.95. **Description:** Comprehensive information is provided to help market a small business; more than 1,500 tips are included.

47680 ■ **"Uncharted Territory" in** *Entrepreneur* **(Vol. 32, No. 1, January 2004, pp. 27)**
Pub: Entrepreneur Media, Inc.
Ed: Don Nichols. **Description:** Profile of Bill Davidson, author of Breakthrough: How Great Companies Set Outrageous Objectives-and Achieve Them. Davidson advises entrepreneurs to set outrageous objectives and to use creative thinking about customer care, cost reduction, and other issues to reach customers.

47681 ■ **"Understanding Women is Key to Biz Success, Author Says" in** *Crain's Detroit Business* **(Vol. 22, November 20, 2006, No. 47, pp. 6)**
Pub: Crain Communications Inc. - Detroit
Ed: Bill Shea. **Description:** Successful companies recognize that women make 80% of all buying decisions. Author also has advice for women-owned businesses with trend and specifics provided.

47682 ■ **"U.S. Postal Service Business Reply Mail" in** *Entrepreneur* **(Vol. 33, August 2005, No. 8, pp. 4)**
Pub: Entrepreneur Media Inc.
Ed: Steve Cooper. **Description:** Offering customers a postage-free reply can prove to be an effective marketing tool. The U.S. Postal Service charges only for those pieces of mail returned.

47683 ■ **"Up Front: Broad Brand" in** *My Business* **(April/May 2004, pp. 12-13)**
Pub: My Business Magazine
Ed: Gary M. Stern. **Description:** Ways a business can increase business by creating a fresh brand are explored. Tips for successful branding include naming a brand appropriately, generating publicity, remaining focused, creating a slogan, and integrating graphics with your mission.

47684 ■ **"Up Front: Thinking Outside the Box" in** *My Business* **(April/May 2003, pp. 8-9)**
Pub: My Business Magazine

Ed: Kathleen Landis. **Description:** One of the best ways to build a business is to ask clients for referrals; author Maribeth Kuzmeski, business consultant and author refers to client referrals as "strategic alliances", which allow two companies to create an advantage over competitors.

47685 ■ **"Upfront: Don't Say That" in** *My Business* **(April/May 2002, pp. 13-14)**
Pub: My Business Magazine
Ed: Ivan Sylvester. **Description:** Market consultant and trainer, Merrie Spaeth, believes that public communication is all about the power of negatives. Spaeth sends out a monthly e-mail known as "The Bimbo Award", that recognizes public comments that cause the listener to believe exactly the opposite of what is said. Spaeth and her employees teach big and small firms how to communicate effectively.

47686 ■ **"Use Webcasting to Grow Your Home Business" in** *Home Business* **(Vol. 12, March/April 2005, No. 2, pp. 36, 38, 60-61)**
Pub: Home Business Magazine
Ed: Dr. Jeffrey Lant. **Description:** Online marketing is a good way for a home business to increase sales. Webcasting allows entrepreneurs to speak live to people through a computer.

47687 ■ **"Valassis Buys N'West Center; Refines Plans for $30M Livonia Campus" in** *Crain's Detroit Business* **(Vol. 21, January 31, 2005, No. 5)**
Pub: Crain Communications Inc. - Detroit
Ed: Jennette Smith. **Description:** Valassis Communications Inc. Purchased Northwest Airlines old reservation center in Livonia, Michigan. The company plans to convert the building into a 300-employee post-order hub for its marketing business.

47688 ■ *Value-Added Sales Management: A Guide for Salespeople and Their Managers*
Pub: Contemporary Books, Inc.
Ed: Tom Reilly. **Released:** 1993. **Price:** $12.95 (paper).

47689 ■ **"The Value of Networking" in** *Home Business* **(Vol. 13, January/February 2006, No. 1, pp. 42, 44-45)**
Pub: Home Business Magazine
Ed: Christopher J. Bachler. **Description:** Networking skills to market and grow a business, including a list of prospects, are discussed.

47690 ■ **"Verizon Breaks New Ads" in** *Hispanic Business* **(March 2003, pp. 16)**
Pub: Hispanic Business
Description: Firms promoting the use of Spanish language ad campaigns, Web sites and media campaigns are profiled.

47691 ■ **"The Vice Squad" in** *Incentive* **(Vol. 174, No. 10, October 2000, pp. 30)**
Pub: Bill Communications
Ed: Jeanie Casison. **Description:** Marketing mavericks use savvy promotions to sell alcohol and tobacco in a culture of contradiction.

47692 ■ **"Viewpoint: Rule on Race, Gender Data Has Outlived Its Intent" in** *American Banker* **(Vol. 171, December 15, 2006, No. 240, pp. 11)**
Pub: SourceMedia, Inc.
Ed: David Lizarraga; Fred Jordan. **Description:** Information regarding the Federaladopted Regulation B is presented. The regulation bars regulated financial institutions from targeting minorities in marketing or advertising campaigns or tracking or recording lending data by race, ethnicity, or gender.

47693 ■ **"Vivid Buys Amerigos, Char" in** *Mississippi Business Journal* **(Vol. 29, January 2007, No. 3, pp. A8)**
Pub: Venture Publications, Inc.
Description: Amerigo Restaurant Corp. have transferred ownership of their five restaurants to Vivid Restaurant Concepts. Vivid will continue to operate the Jackson's Char and Amerigo restaurants as well as Tennessee's three Amerigo restaurants.

47694 ■ **"Vonage V-Phone: Use Your Laptop to Make Calls Via the Internet" in** *Black Enterprise* **(Vol. 37, January 2007, No. 6, pp. 52)**
Pub: Earl G. Graves Publishing Co. Inc.
Ed: James C. Johnson. **Description:** Overview of the Vonage V-Phone, which is small flash drive device that lets you make phone calls through a high-speed Internet connection and plugs into any computer's USB port. Business travels may find this product to be a wonderful solution as it includes 250MB of memory and can store files, digital photos, MP3s, and more.

47695 ■ **"Wacky, fake Web sites grab attention, while only slyly referring to their sponsors" in** *The New York Times* **(August 14, 2000, pp. C8)**
Pub: The New York Times Company
Ed: Allison Fass. **Description:** Companies, advertisers, and pranksters have found the fun of creating fake Web sites to enhance their image and be part of the giddy alternative to e-commerce. Sun Country Airlines, with BVK McDonald invented www.heybill.com which the company plays with for "relationship marketing" as opposed to its www.suncountry.com business site. Steve Fink and Steve Casino produced the fictional www.goblertoys.com merely for their own fancy. And Ted C. Fishman's parody site, www. FreeWhellz.com, eventually sold his domain name for his fake company for $25,000.

47696 ■ **"Wanted: Brainy in Business" in** *Sales & Marketing Management* **(Vol. 158, October 2006, No. 10, pp. 18)**
Pub: VNU Business Media
Ed: Michel Marchetti. **Description:** Eric McMath, SerachLogix Group, offers tips and techniques for hiring a successful sales team for any business.

47697 ■ **"Ward off Competitors" in** *PC Computing* **(April 2000, pp. 95)**
Pub: Ziff-Davis Inc.
Ed: Jason Compton. **Description:** Microsoft Map-Point 2000 will help a retail store use customer zip code and sales amount information to see how the proximity of a competitor will affect sales volumes.

47698 ■ **"Warm Up to Cold Calls" in** *Sales & Marketing Management* **(Vol. 158, October 2006, No. 10, pp. 15)**
Pub: VNU Business Media
Description: Shawn Greene, owner of Savage and Green, a sales training company in California, provides tips for effective telemarketing.

47699 ■ **"Warming Up to Cold Calls" in** *Inc.* **(November 1, 2004)**
Pub: Inc. Magazine
Ed: Nicole Gull. **Description:** Samantha Ettus, CEO of Ettus Media Management, a New York City public relations and branding agency spends much of her time making cold calls in order to land new accounts.

47700 ■ **"Web Connect Directory" in** *San Diego Business Journal* **(Vol. 28, January 15, 2007, No. 3, pp. 29)**
Pub: San Diego Business Journal Associates
Description: A listing of advertising agencies and their Web addresses.

47701 ■ **"Web Expertise in Novel Locales" in** *Inc.* **(June 2000, pp. 123)**
Pub: The Goldhirsh Group
Description: For companies that cannot afford the high price for a business Web site, unconventional alternatives are explored.

47702 ■ **"Web Sites Can Make You Look Bigger, Better" in** *Crain's Detroit Business* **(Vol. 21, October 17, 2005, No. 43, pp. 20)**
Pub: Crain Communications Inc. - Detroit
Ed: Sheena Harrison. **Description:** In order to compete, a small business must use its Website as a means of marketing products and services.

47703 ■ **"Web Surveys' Hidden Hazards"** in *Harvard Business Review* (Vol. 81, No. 7, July 2003, pp. 16)
Pub: Harvard Business School Press
Ed: Palmer Morrel-Samuels. Description: The advantages and disadvantages of Web-based corporate surveys are compared.

47704 ■ **"Web Wise"** in *Inc.* (November 15, 2000, pp. 130)
Pub: The Goldhirsh Group
Description: The four basic categories to address in order to make the Web work for businesses are addressed.

47705 ■ **"Web.Preneuring"** in *Small Business Opportunities* (Vol. 17, November 2005, No. 6, pp. 90, 94)
Pub: Harris Publications Inc.
Ed: Chuck Green. Description: Profile of Scott Kolbe and Mike Stout, entrepreneurs who started Icon Digital Design in a basement. The partners base their success on being graphic designers with strong work ethics.

47706 ■ **"Website Offers Family Pages and Networking"** in *Marketing to Women* (Vol. 19, October 2006, No. 10, pp. 5)
Pub: EPM Communications, Inc.
Description: MommyTalk.com, a recently launched online social community, offers family oriented services including chat groups, blogs, and family homepages.

47707 ■ **"Webvan, Microsoft, and the second-mover advantage"** in *Red Herring* (No. 102, August 15, 2001, pp. 100)
Pub: Herring Communications
Ed: Jason Pontin. Description: Discussion regarding the second-mover advantage. The rule of the second-mover advantage states that, market dominance rarely goes to the pluck startup that first releases a product, but to the second company, sometimes an established business, that most effectively markets and sells the products, and which then gives the best customer service.

47708 ■ **"The Wedding Planner"** in *Everett Business Journal* (Vol. 6, No. 12, December 2003, pp. A9)
Pub: Wenatchee Business Journal, Inc.
Ed: Myke Folger. Description: Paulette Deckers will host the first Northwest Bridal Showcase; Deckers is promoting the show to business owners throughout Snohomish, Skagit and Whatcom counties.

47709 ■ **"Weigh your opt-ins"** in *Entrepreneur* (Vol. 30, No. 10, October 2002, pp. 96)
Pub: Entrepreneur Media Inc.
Ed: Kim T. Gordon. Description: Much less costly than paper newsletters, e-mail letters can be a successful communication tool for marketing a product or service.

47710 ■ **"Welcome to the New Economy: Act III"** in *Inc.* (November 15, 2000, pp. 139)
Pub: The Goldhirsh Group
Description: Extensive review of the books "From.com to .profit" and "How Digital Is Your Business?".

47711 ■ **"What Becomes an Icon Most"** in *Harvard Business Review* (Vol. 81, No. 3, March 2003, pp. 43)
Pub: Harvard Business School Press
Ed: Douglas B. Holt. Description: Brands become icons by providing myths for the society. Ways some brands become icons and maintain the power to hold its market place for years is examined. The most successful brands create myths, most often in the U.S., by creating an intimate and credible relationship with the desire of Americans to be rebels.

47712 ■ **"What Can Consultants, Doctors, Lawyers, and Accountants do Online Besides Boast about Their Skills?"** in *Inc.* (Nov. 15, 2000, pp. 130)
Pub: The Goldhirsh Group

Description: An expert shares ideas to become interactive on the Web.

47713 ■ **"What Customer Relationship?"** in *Sales & Marketing Management* (Vol. 159, January-February 2007, No. 1, pp. 11)
Pub: VNU Business Media
Ed: Scott Horstein. Description: Customer relationship management is explained; marketing strategies using this concept are included.

47714 ■ **"What a deal!"** in *Entrepreneur* (Vol. 30, No. 2, February 2002, pp. 71)
Pub: Entrepreneur Media Inc.
Ed: Nichole L. Torres. Description: The benefits of hiring an interim marketing manager are discussed.

47715 ■ **"What is Del.icio.us and How Is It Used?"** in *Sales & Marketing Management* (Vol. 159, January-February 2007, No. 1, pp. 17)
Pub: VNU Business Media
Description: Profile of the social book-marking Web service that allows users to see saved sites of other members of the service.

47716 ■ **"What Do Your Customers See?"** in *Inc.* (February 1, 2002)
Pub: Inc. Magazine
Ed: Bo Burlingame. Description: Ways to market a product, inventory, finding a niche for the product, and responding to the loss of a key supplier are the issues addressed.

47717 ■ **"What Happened to the Paperless Society?"** in *Automotive News* (Vol. 20, December 6, 2004, No. 49, pp. 8)
Pub: Crain Communications Inc.
Ed: Keith Crain. Description: Amid the growing use of the Internet, many companies are still sending catalogs to customers in order to sell products.

47718 ■ **"What I Think of Pink"** in *Marketing to Women* (Vol. 20, January 2007, No. 1, pp. 2)
Pub: EPM Communications, Inc.
Ed: Ellen Neuborne. Description: Marketers have embraced women by using the color pink to entice them into buying their products.

47719 ■ **"What I've Learned About Women"** in *Marketing to Women* (Vol. 19, November 2006, No. 1, pp. 2)
Pub: EPM Communications, Inc.
Ed: Lisa Finn. Description: Over the years the women's marketing landscape has changed a great deal. Companies are more open to testing their ideas and doing research and women are helping marketers do their job better by expressing their opinions to companies.

47720 ■ **"What is the Most Effective Way to Advertise?"** in *Home Business* (Vol. 12, March/April 2005, No. 2, pp. 56)
Pub: Home Business Magazine
Ed: Charlie Cook. Description: In order to be effective, advertising must be directed toward the target market.

47721 ■ **"What Not To Do in a Press Release"** in *Inc.* (January 1, 2004)
Pub: Gruner & Jahr USA Publishing
Ed: Nicole Gull. Description: Entrepreneurs should double-check all information before allowing a press release to be printed.

47722 ■ ***What Self-Made Millionaires Really Think, Know and Do: A Straight-Talking Guide to Business Success and Personal Riches***
Pub: John Wiley & Sons, Incorporated
Ed: Richard Dobbins; Barrie Pettman. Released: September 2006. Price: $24.95. Description: Guide for understanding the concepts of entrepreneurial success; the book offers insight into bringing an idea into reality, marketing, time management, leadership skills, and setting clear goals.

47723 ■ **"What a Smile Means"** in *Inc.* (October 1, 2003)
Pub: Gruner & Jahr USA Publishing
Ed: Bobbie Gossage. Description: A smile can mean a lot to a small business when negotiating deals. Smiles and frowns reflect a consumer's opinion more accurately, according to facial coding research studies.

47724 ■ **"What the Titans Can Teach Us"** in *Harvard Business Review* (Vol. 79, No. 11, December 2001, pp. 70)
Pub: Harvard Business School Press
Ed: Richard S. Tedlow. Description: Profile of legendary leaders of American business such as Andrew Carnegie, Henry Ford and Sam Walton of Wal-Mart. While some of their traits should not be emulated, the author argues that we can all learn from them. These people had the courage to bet on their vision of market potential, they shaped their vision into a mission for the company and they delivered more than they promised.

47725 ■ **"What Women Want"** in *Entrepreneur* (Vol. 32, No. 2, February 2004, pp. 54)
Pub: Entrepreneur Media, Inc.
Ed: Joanne Cleaver. Description: Small business owners are targeting market strategies toward women consumers, a market once ignored. Women pay attention to detail in product design and service and require a longer selling process because they wish to understand what they are purchasing.

47726 ■ **"What Women Want at Work"** in *Marketing to Women* (Vol. 20, January 2007, No. 1, pp. 5)
Pub: EPM Communications, Inc.
Description: Men and women at different ages want different things from their workplace. According to a study by The American Business Collaboration, employers may want to factor in these differences when trying to attract and retain top female talent.

47727 ■ **"What You Look Like Online"** in *Black Enterprise* (Vol. 37, January 2007, No. 6, pp. 56)
Pub: Earl G. Graves Publishing Co. Inc.
Ed: Marcia A. Reed-Woodard. Description: Of 100 executive recruiters 77 percent stated that they use search engines to check the backgrounds of potential job candidates, according to a survey conducted by ExecuNet. Of those surveyed 35 percent stated that they eliminate potential candidates based on information they find online so it is important to create a positive Web presence which highlights professional image qualities.

47728 ■ **"Whatever it takes"** in *BlackEnterprise* (Vol. 32, No. 3, October 2001, pp. 54)
Pub: Earl Graves Publishing Co.
Ed: Mark Richard Moss. Description: Review of the publication, 'Off-the-Wall Marketing Ideas.' The book offers advice on such diverse topics as business card design, generating publicity and "Pro Bono: Civic Marketing."

47729 ■ **"What's In a Name?"** in *Entrepreneur* (Vol. 32)
Pub: Entrepreneur Media Inc.
Ed: Amanda C. Kooser. Description: The new .mail domain being considered could change the way businesses send out legitimate marketing emails, however the domain does not act as an anti-spam system.

47730 ■ **"What's In a Name?"** in *Inc.* (July 1, 2004)
Pub: Inc. Magazine
Ed: Bobbie Gossage. Description: Choosing a company or brand name is critical to success. Ways to get the name your small company deserves are outlined.

47731 ■ **"What's the Plan? Need a Marketing Plan?"** in *Entrepreneur* (Vol. 32, December 2004, No. 12, pp. 94)
Pub: Entrepreneur Media Inc.

Ed: Kim T. Gordon. **Description:** Tactics priced to fit any company when marketing a product or service are explained, broken down to fit a high-end budget, mid-range and low-range marketing budgets.

47732 ■ "What's your problem?" in *Entrepreneur* **(Vol. 30, No. 10, October 2002, pp. 146)**
Pub: Entrepreneur Media Inc.
Description: The owner of a home-based residential design firm is offered advice to market the business, including the use of The Blue Book of Building and Construction which covers contractors nationwide.

47733 ■ "What's your problem? People don't open junk mail, so send a postcard" in *Entrepreneur* **(Vol. 30, No. 3, March 2002, pp. 142)**
Pub: Entrepreneur Media Inc.
Description: Information for using postcards as a sales and marketing tool is discussed.

47734 ■ "What's Wrong with Computer-Generated Images of Perfection in Advertising?" in *Journal of Business Ethics* **(Vol. 45, No. 3, July 2003)**
Pub: Kluwer Academic Publishers Group
Ed: Earl W. Spurgin. **Description:** Advertisers often use computers to create fantastic images, however advertisers are ethically obligated to avoid certain aesthetic results that are produced by computer-generated images of perfection.

47735 ■ "When Leadership Means Letting Go" in *Law Firm Inc.* **(October 2004)**
Pub: American Lawyer Media LP
Description: In law firms, it is important for the chief marketing officer to report to the firm's top leader in order for the position to be taken seriously. The chief marketing leader's expertise to handle marketing and sales efforts is critical.

47736 ■ "When You Really Lose Customers" in *Entrepreneur* **(Vol. 30, No. 1)**
Pub: Entrepreneur Media Inc.
Ed: Melissa Campanelli. **Description:** A recent study shows that less than one-third of consumers notify regularly visited Web sites, online newsletters and discussion lists with new email addresses. Statistical data included.

47737 ■ "Where Ads Aimed at Kids Come to Life" in *The New York Times* **(December 13, 2000, pp. D14, H14)**
Pub: The New York Times Company
Ed: Dulcie Leimbach. **Description:** Cereal and toy companies use their Web sites to market to children.

47738 ■ "Where Are You Going?" in *My Business* **(April/May 2003, pp. 46)**
Pub: My Business Magazine
Ed: Karen J. Bannan. **Description:** Business visions require identifying a target market, as well as the services and products a small business intends to supply.

47739 ■ "Where to Find Business Answers; Advice and Education" in *Crain's New York Business* **(Vol. 22, November 13, 2006, No. 46, pp. 24)**
Pub: Crain Communications, Inc.
Description: Listing of organizations and agencies that provide training, financial and managerial advice, and technical expertise to current or would-be business owners.

47740 ■ "Where To Go Next" in *Adweek* **(Vol. 45, October 11, 2004, No. 38, pp. 24)**
Pub: VNU Business Media
Ed: Eleftheria Parpis. **Description:** Two recent industry confabs, the American Association of Advertising Agencies' Creative Conference in New York and Adweek's 30th Creative Seminar in San Francisco, brought creative directors from shops to discuss how to build brands, how to change creative cultures, how to succeed in increasingly difficult jobs, and how to reach consumers in a fractured media environment.

47741 ■ "Who Needs 'Em?" in *Entrepreneur* **(Vol. 28, No. 7, July 2000, pp. 160)**
Pub: Entrepreneur Media Inc.
Ed: Don Debelak. **Description:** Craig Winchell tells how he is marketing games through the Internet.

47742 ■ "Who benefits from price promotions?" in *Harvard Business Review* **(Vol. 80, No. 9, September 2002, pp. 22)**
Pub: Harvard Business School Press
Ed: Shuba Srinivasan. **Description:** Research has shown that reducing prices temporarily as part of a marketing campaign can adversely affect a retail company.

47743 ■ "Who pays to get it there? Net Profits" in *Entrepreneur* **(Vol. 3)**
Pub: Entrepreneur Media Inc.
Ed: Melissa Campanelli. **Description:** The issue of shipping and handling charges is one of the most critical facing online merchants today.

47744 ■ "Who's Talking Behind Your Back?" in *Crain's Chicago Business* **(Vol. 30, January 2007, No. 3, pp. 18)**
Pub: Crain Communications, Inc.
Ed: Steve Hendershot. **Description:** Chicago's Word of Mouth Marketing Association, Womma, cultivates, studies, and celebrates consumers telling others about a company or its products or services. Success stories included.

47745 ■ "Why Clip When You Can Clip?" in *Kiplinger's Personal Finance Magazine* **(Vol. 54, No. 9, September 2000, pp. 24)**
Pub: The Kiplinger Washington Editors, Inc.
Ed: Melynda Dovel Wilcox. **Description:** A new service links online discounts with off-line merchants, thus eliminating paper coupons.

47746 ■ "Why Image Matters" in *My Business* **(December/January 2003, pp. 28-31)**
Pub: My Business Magazine
Ed: Shannon Scully. **Description:** Solutions for building a small business' image are explored, using various companies as examples, including a home remodeling company, garage door/window sales company, retail bicycle shop, candy and snack food manufacturer and retailer, and a public relations firm.

47747 ■ "Why Johnny Can't Sell...And What to Do About It" in *Sales & Marketing Management* **(Vol. 158, October 2006, No. 10, pp. 54)**
Pub: VNU Business Media
Ed: Tali Arbel. **Description:** Review of the book, Why Johnny Can't Sell...And What to Do About It is presented. Authors Michael J. Nick and Robert F. Kantin, sales marketing experts, share insight into tools to help salespeople to reach leads and increase sales.

47748 ■ "Why the Small-Business Market is the Internet's new frontier" in *Red Herring* **(No. 76, pp. 185-186, 188, 192, 194, 198-200, 202, 204)**
Pub: Herring Communications, Inc.
Description: Why venture capitalists, retail investors, and many Internet companies think they can make large profits by targeting the small business market. Extensive statistical data is included with charts and graphs.

47749 ■ "Why There's No Escaping the Blog" in *Fortune* **(Vol. 151, January 10, 2005, No. 1, pp. 44)**
Pub: Time Inc.
Ed: David Kirkpatrick, Daniel Roth, Oliver Ryan. **Description:** Microsoft has unveiled a plan to develop a new service called MSN Spaces, an online software that allows users to easily create and maintain blogs on the Internet. The power of blogs and bloggers to make or break a product or service is examined.

47750 ■ "'Windtunnel' Vision: Air Out Some New Ideas with This Technique" in *Entrepreneur* **(Vol. 31, No. 6, June 2003, pp. 76)**
Pub: Entrepreneur Media Inc.
Ed: Juanita Weaver. **Description:** A technique for generating new ideas, called windtunnel, is done in pairs. This technique of brainstorming, originated by creative expert Win Wenger, is outlined.

47751 ■ "Winning the paper chase" in *Incentive* **(Vol. 174, No. 10, October 2000, pp. 123)**
Pub: Bill Communications
Ed: Libby Estell. **Description:** Profile of the Kelly Paper Company, that has locked in its customer base and boosted sales by using a points-based loyalty program that allows customers to choose from among a variety of rewards.

47752 ■ "Wish I'd Thought Of That! Aim small to make it big? You bet." in *Fortune* **(Vol. 141, No. 10, May 15, 2000, pp. F372C+)**
Pub: Time Inc.
Ed: Arlyn Tobias Gajilan. **Description:** Small corners of the market ignored by others can be quite lucrative. Both online and off, small players need to burrow into ever narrower niches.

47753 ■ "Women Business Owners Get Credit Easily" in *Marketing to Women* **(Vol. 19, November 2006, No. 11, pp. 12)**
Pub: EPM Communications, Inc.
Description: According to a Gallup study commissioned by Wells Fargo, women find it easier to obtain credit than men. Statistical data included.

47754 ■ "Women Business Owners Seek Financing" in *Marketing to Women* **(Vol. 19, December 2006, No. 2, pp. 8)**
Pub: EPM Communications, Inc.
Description: A study by the Center for Women's Business Research shows that women business owners have become more savvy when seeking financial support for their business ventures. Statistical data included.

47755 ■ "Women Favor Discounters for Back-to-School" in *Marketing to Women* **(Vol. 19, October 2006, No. 10, pp. 11)**
Pub: EPM Communications, Inc.
Description: When back-to-school shopping men are more likely to shop at specialty and department stores, while women are more likely to shop at drugstores and discounters, according to BIGresearch and the National Retail Federation. Statistical data included.

47756 ■ "Women Want More Info on Wellness" in *Marketing to Women* **(Vol. 19, December 2006, No. 2, pp. 8)**
Pub: EPM Communications, Inc.
Description: IVilliage.com reports that although women consider wellness a top priority in their lives, studies show that two-thirds of women surveyed feel that their lives are out of balance. Statistical data included.

47757 ■ "Women's Firms Reach Nearly $2 Trillion in Sales" in *Marketing to Women* **(Vol. 19, October 2006, No. 10, pp. 12)**
Pub: EPM Communications, Inc.
Description: According to the Center for Women's Business Research, women own a half or majority stake in 40 percent of all businesses in the U.S. and employ 12.8 million people. Statistical data included.

47758 ■ "Women's Talk Radio Network Launches" in *Marketing to Women* **(Vol. 19, October 2006, No. 10, pp. 5)**
Pub: EPM Communications, Inc.
Description: GreenStone Media launches a new talk radio network just for women. It will feature four weekday programs including a show for working moms hosted by author Lisa Birnbach. Healthcare, education, and work-family balance are among the topics covered.

47759 ■ "Words to the Wise: Has Your Marketing Copy Lost Its Punch?" in *Entrepreneur* **(Vol. 31, No. 10, October 2003, pp. 91)**
Pub: Entrepreneur Media, Inc.
Ed: Kim T. Gordon. **Description:** Herschell Gordon Lewis, author of "On the Art of Writing Copy", offers tips for fine-tuning marketing copy, whether used in print, broadcast ads, direct mail, email or even billboards.

47760 ■ "Working Wonders on the Web" in *Inc.* **(October 1, 2003)**
Pub: Gruner & Jahr USA Publishing
Ed: Leigh Buchanan. **Description:** The Internet isn't being used for decorative marketing sites only; small companies are using the Web to run some of their most strategic operations successfully.

47761 ■ "Works Great! Sales success" in *Entrepreneur* **(Vol. 30, No. 2, February 2002,)**
Pub: Entrepreneur Media Inc.
Ed: Barry Farber. **Description:** The use of customer testimonials to increase sales is examined.

47762 ■ "World Cup Kicks Print Media Into High Gear" in *Hispanic Business* **(December 2006, pp. 54)**
Pub: Hispanic Business
Ed: Mike Traphagen. **Description:** Spanish-language print media, such as magazines and newspapers, saw an increase in advertising during the 2006 World Cup series.

47763 ■ "The world in your backyard" in *WorkingWoman* **(Vol. 25, No. 2, February 2000, pp. 72)**
Pub: Lang Communications Inc.
Ed: Caitlin Kelly. **Description:** There are 617 consulates in the U.S., offering services in international marketing, labor and culture.

47764 ■ "Worth a Try" in *Entrepreneur* **(Vol. 31, No. 8, August 2003, pp. 71)**
Pub: Entrepreneur Media, Inc.
Ed: Elizabeth Goodgold. **Description:** Maureen Murphy, president of Direct Effectz, a direct-marketing consulting firm in San Diego, California recommends offering free samples, even in the service area. Direct Effectz offers a free marketing audit to interested companies.

47765 ■ "The Write Stuff: What Does it Take to Launch a Brand-New Product?" in *Entrepreneur* **(Vol. 32, December 2004, No. 12, pp. 104)**
Pub: Entrepreneur Media Inc.
Ed: Amanda C. Kooser. **Description:** Barry Farber, entrepreneur, shares tips for successfully bringing a new product to the marketplace.

47766 ■ *Writing and Implementing a Marketing Plan*
Pub: Crisp Publications, Inc.
Ed: Richard Gerson. **Price:** $9.95.

47767 ■ "Yellow Pages Association" in *Sales & Marketing Management* **(Vol. 157, February 2005, No. 2, pp. 14)**
Pub: VNU Business Media
Ed: Sara Calabro. **Description:** Yellow Pages Association is targeting national advertisers for print ads with a new log and Website.

47768 ■ "Yessian Music hires Detroit producer, wins contract for ads" in *Crain's Detroit Business* **(Vol. 18, No. 50, Dec. 16, 2002, pp. 16)**
Pub: Crain Communications Inc., Detroit
Ed: Jennette Smith. **Description:** Yessian Music, located in Farmington Hills, Michigan hired producer, Gerard Smerek, and landed contracts for a number of high-profile commercials. Yessian Music is owned by Brian Yessian, along with his brother Michael, and his father Dan.

47769 ■ "You Are What You Charge" in *Journal of Accountancy* **(Vol. 198, November 2004, No. 5, pp. 20)**
Pub: American Institute of Certified Public Accountants
Ed: Ron Baker, Paul Dunn. **Description:** The four P's of marketing include price, place, promotion, and product, of these pricing is the most complicated.

47770 ■ "You Can Count on Me: A Friend Can Make the Best Kind of Business Partner" in *Entrepreneur* **(Vol. 32, November 2004, No. 11, pp. 36)**
Pub: Entrepreneur Media Inc.
Ed: Aliza Pilar Sherman. **Description:** Profiles of friends who ventured into businesses together. Lynn Harris Medcalf and Susan Apgood teamed to launch News Generation, a public relations firm in Atlanta, Georgia. Sarah Eck and Brook Jay, partnered to create All Terrain Productions, an events-marketing firm in Chicago, Illinois.

47771 ■ "Young at Heart: Are you Making the Mistake of Lumping Older Baby Boomers with Seniors in Your Marketing Campaign?" in *Entrepreneur*
Pub: Entrepreneur Media Inc.
Ed: Kim T. Gordon. **Description:** Most marketers are overlooking American baby boomers between the ages of 54 to 64. Rather, marketing is directed at those 18 to 49 years old. Baby boomers have a different self-image of themselves than seniors and have the highest estimated average net worth than any other age group. Statistical details included.

47772 ■ "Young Professional Share Ideas" in *San Fernando Valley Business Journal* **(Vol. 12, January 2007, No. 2, pp. 1)**
Pub: San Fernando Valley Business Journal Associates
Ed: Chris Coates. **Description:** Interview with four young business professionals from various fields who talk about gaining creditability in the workplace, image, and marketing.

47773 ■ "Your Business needs to be E-Commerce - so what now?" in *Ingram's* **(Vol. 27, No. 7, July 2001, pp. 19)**
Pub: Show Me Publishing, Inc.
Description: Management techniques and theory are outlined for e-commerce management. Some techniques include treating online and offline sales the same way, organize and prioritize what the Website needs to accomplish, and consider market potential.

47774 ■ "Your New Neighborhood" in *Small Business Opportunities* **(May 2005)**
Pub: Harris Publications Inc.
Ed: Hector Ocri. **Description:** Key tips for retailers to succeed in diverse ethnic communities are shared.

47775 ■ "Your Story Here" in *Black Enterprise* **(Vol. 36, February 2006, No. 7, pp. 57)**
Pub: Earl G. Graves Publishing Co. Inc.
Ed: Kenneth Meeks. **Description:** BlackNews.com will feature a press release on its Website, an email and fax to every African American newspaper, magazine, radio station and TV station for only $150. Diversity City Media Inc., the multicultural marketing and public relations firm not only runs the Website, but also Black PR.com a press release distribution service.

47776 ■ "Yourshop@Black Enterprise.com" in *Black Enterprise* **(Vol. 31, No. 2, September 2000, pp. 215)**
Pub: Earl Graves Publishing Co.
Ed: Dorett Smith. **Description:** Small business can join the e-commerce revolution. If you are considering a Web presence to sell your company's products online, you'll need to weigh a number of factors related to e-business planning, such as productivity and functionality, advertising, sales, and service.

47777 ■ "Yule be Sorry" in *Entrepreneur* **(Vol. 28, No. 10, October 2000, pp. 56)**
Pub: Entrepreneur Media Inc.

Ed: Melissa Campanelli. **Description:** Planning for Internet business for Christmas operations is explored. LeapFrog, a California company, shares problems they encountered during the 1999 holiday season.

SOURCES OF SUPPLY

47778 ■ *Ad Source*
Pub: Walter Ketcham & Associates
Contact: Walter Ketcham, Publisher
E-mail: wketcham@adsourceonline.com
Price: Free. **Covers:** 3,500 companies in Upstate New York providing creative services, including advertising agencies, designers, illustrators, photographers, printers, video production services, multimedia and internet services, radio, television, and advertising publications. **Entries Include:** Company name, address, phone, name and title of contact, names and titles of key personnel, descriptions of services, products or services provided, email, websites. **Arrangement:** Classified by line of business, geographical by region, alphabetical by company name. **Indexes:** Name, subject, phone number, region, city, county, keywords.

47779 ■ *Aquaculture Magazine Buyer's Guide & Industry Directory*
Pub: Achill River Corp.
Ed: Gregory J. Gallagher, Editor. **Released:** Annual, December. **Price:** $22; $25 outside U.S.. **Covers:** 2,400 manufacturers and suppliers of equipment used in aquaculture, including fish farming, production, processing, and marketing. **Entries Include:** Name, address, phone, URL info, and services.

TRADE PERIODICALS

47780 ■ *Accutips*
Pub: Accudata America
Released: Monthly. **Price:** Free. **Description:** Discusses promotion and marketing issues relevant to businesses.

47781 ■ *ADM Flash*
Pub: Association of Directory Marketing
Ed: Nancy Augustine, Editor, naugustine@admworks.org. **Released:** 10/year. **Price:** Free. **Description:** Features information about marketing directories.

47782 ■ *Business Ideas Newsletter*
Pub: Dan Newman Co.
Ed: Dan Newman, Editor. **Released:** 10/year. **Price:** $50. **Description:** Publishes information for advertising and marketing executives to "increase results, returns, and profits." Reports on and interprets developments affecting the business community, including issues such as legislative and regulatory activities and tax reform. Covers new product developments, employment strategies, advertising techniques, and direct marketing potential. Recurring features include news of research, reports of meetings, news of educational opportunities, and book reviews.

47783 ■ *The Canadian Direct Marketing Association—Communicator*
Pub: The Canadian Direct Marketing Association
Contact: Elizabeth Lewis
Released: 10/year. **Price:** Included in membership; $30, Canada. **Description:** Provides information about direct marketing in Canada. Recurring features include news of research, a calendar of events, reports of meetings, news of educational opportunities, book reviews, and notices of publications available.

47784 ■ *Color Q Connection*
Pub: Color Q Inc.
Ed: Sue Viders, Editor, viders@worldnet.att.net. **Released:** 3/year. **Price:** Free. **Description:** Contains marketing information for print artists. Recurring features include letters to the editor, news of research, book reviews, interviews, columns and calendar of events.

47785 ■ Current Competition
Pub: FT Energy
Contact: Tod Sedgwick, Publisher
Ed: Patrice Hagmann, Editor. **Released:** Biweekly. **Price:** $327 in the U.S., Canada and Mexico. **Description:** Offers market opportunities and intelligence for the buying and selling of power. Recurring features include columns titled Bidding Calendar, and State Roundup.

47786 ■ E-Tactics Letter
Pub: E-Tactics Inc.
Ed: Sarah Stambler, Editor. **Released:** Monthly. **Price:** $149, U.S. and Canada email delivery; $249, elsewhere fax delivery. **Description:** Covers marketing information and techniques for businesses to increase profits and sales by using electronic delivery channels such as email, faxes, websites, and cable television. Recurring features include interviews and news of research.

47787 ■ The Gauge
Pub: Delahaye Medialink
Contact: Katharine Delahaye Paine, Publisher
E-mail: kpaine@delahaye.com
Ed: William Teunis Paarlberg, Editor, wpaarlberg@aol.com. **Released:** Bimonthly. **Price:** $75. **Description:** Provides information on and evaluates marketing communications activities of companies. Recurring features include interviews, news of research, and a calendar of events.

47788 ■ Guerilla Marketing Newsletter
Pub: Jay Conrad Levinson
Ed: William Shea, Editor. **Released:** Bimonthly. **Description:** Explores marketing trends, tips, and technology. Recurring features include news of research.

47789 ■ Helen Hecker's Hotline: Marketing Strategies for Publishers & Entrepreneurs
Pub: Twin Peaks Press
Contact: Helen Hecker, Editor & Publisher
Released: Quarterly. **Price:** Free. **Description:** Provides marketing strategies for publishers, audio and video producers, and small business owners. Recurring features include interviews, news of research, reports of meetings, news of educational opportunities, book reviews, and notices of publications available.

47790 ■ Interactive Global News
Pub: PANGAEA Communications
Contact: Beth Stone
Ed: Beth Stone, Editor, bstone@pangaea.net. **Released:** Monthly. **Price:** $36, U.S.; $48, out of country; $12, single issue. **Description:** Covers international business, global marketing trends, and consumer product and service industries. Recurring features include news of research, a calendar of events, book reviews, job listings, notices of publications available, and columns titled Bargain Travel, Country Profiles & Updates. Remarks: Daily news updates available online.

47791 ■ Internet Marketing Report
Pub: Progressive Business Publications
Ed: Alan Field, Editor. **Released:** Semimonthly. **Price:** $299, individuals. **Description:** Communicates the latest news and trends in website marketing.

47792 ■ Journal of Global Marketing
Pub: The Haworth Press Inc.
Contact: Bill Cohen, Publisher
Ed: Erdener Kaynak, Ph.D., Editor, k9x@psu.edu. **Released:** Quarterly. **Price:** $75 USA; $150 institutions USA; $480 libraries agencies, USA; $101 Canada; $203 institutions, Canada; $648 libraries agencies, Canada; $109 other countries; $218 institutions, other countries; $696 libraries agencies, other countries. **Description:** Professional journal addressing marketing challenges, opportunities, and problems encountered by firms, industries, and governments on a global scale.

47793 ■ Journal of International Consumer Marketing
Pub: The Haworth Press Inc.
Contact: Bill Cohen, Publisher

Ed: Erdener Kaynak, Ph.D., Editor, k9x@psu.edu. **Released:** Quarterly. **Price:** $75 USA; $150 institutions USA; $460 libraries agencies, USA; $101 Canada; $203 institutions, Canada; $621 libraries agencies, Canada; $109 other countries; $218 institutions, other countries; $667 libraries agencies, other countries. **Description:** Professional journal offering international managerial insights and improving understanding of cross-cultural/national aspects of consumer behavior, research, and application.

47794 ■ Journal of Marketing Channels
Pub: The Haworth Press Inc.
Contact: Dheeraj Sharma Ph.D., Assoc. Ed.
E-mail: pelton@unt.edu
Released: Quarterly. **Price:** $60 U.S.; $81 Canada; $87 other countries; $125 institutions U.S.; $169 institutions, Canada; $181 institutions, other countries; $350 libraries agencies, U.S.; $473 libraries agencies, Canada; $508 libraries agencies, other countries. **Description:** Journal for marketing executives profiling distribution systems, strategies, and management.

47795 ■ Journal of Relationship Marketing
Pub: The Haworth Press Inc.
Contact: Bill Cohen Ph.D., Publisher
Released: Quarterly, 4 issues/volume. **Price:** $60 U.S.; $81; $87 other countries; $140 institutions U.S.; $189 institutions, Canada; $203 institutions, other countries; $340 libraries agencies, U.S.; $459 libraries agencies, Canada; $493 libraries agencies, other countries. **Description:** Journal on marketing.

47796 ■ Larry Chase's Web Digest for Marketers (WDFM)
Pub: Chase Online Marketing Strategies,Inc
Contact: Larry Chase, Exec. Editor
E-mail: larry@wdfm.com
Ed: Mary Gillen, Editor. **Released:** Weekly. **Price:** Free. **Description:** Delivers 15 short reviews of business-related websites every issue. Remarks: America Online, Inc.

47797 ■ Magnet Marketing & Sales
Pub: John R. Graham Inc.
Ed: Michael Maynard, Editor, m_maynard@grahamcomm.com. **Released:** Quarterly. **Price:** Free. **Description:** Contains information and advice on marketing, sales, and public relations.

47798 ■ Marketing News
Pub: American Marketing Association
Contact: Richard Ballschmiede, Sales Dir.
E-mail: rballschmiede@ama.org
Ed: Lisa M. Keefe, Editor, lkeefe@ama.org. **Released:** 20/year. **Price:** $35 members; $100 nonmembers; $130 institutions libraries and corporations; $3 single issue individuals; $5 single issue institutions; $140 institutions, other countries extra for air delivery. **Description:** Business magazine focusing on current marketing trends.

47799 ■ The Marketing Report
Pub: Progressive Business Publications
Contact: John Walston
E-mail: walston@pbp.com
Released: Semimonthly. **Price:** $264, individuals. **Description:** Presents the latest thinking from the leading marketing experts in the world. Recurring features include interviews, news of research, a calendar of events, and columns titled Sharpen Your Judgment and Marketing Communications.

47800 ■ Meetings & Conventions
Pub: Northstar Travel Media
Contact: Bernard Shraer, Group Publisher
Released: Monthly. **Description:** Magazine focusing on meetings, conferences and trade show.

47801 ■ Most Likely to Succeed
Pub: Richard Siedlecki Consulting Inc.
Released: Bimonthly. **Price:** $49; $54, Canada. **Description:** Provides tips, techniques, and insights on managing and marketing small and growing businesses. Recurring features include interviews, news of research, book reviews, and notices of publications available.

47802 ■ MW Megawatt Markets
Pub: FT Energy
Contact: Randy Rischard, Managing Editor
Ed: Daniel Macey, Editor. **Released:** Quarterly. **Description:** Provides market insight into buying and selling power.

47803 ■ PCS Direct Marketing Newsletter
Pub: PCS Mailing List Company
Contact: Ed Nasser, Associate Editor
E-mail: ednasser@pcslist.com
Ed: Ann Guyer, Editor, aguyer@pcslist.com. **Released:** Bimonthly. **Price:** Free. **Description:** Offers research tools, publications, and other advice on legal, medical, financial & consumer, direct marketing. Also covers mailing lists, databases, and software to assist with direct mailings. Reports on news and conferences in this field as well. Recurring features include notices of publications available and book reviews.

47804 ■ PROMO
Pub: Primedia Business
Released: Monthly. **Description:** Trade publication covering information, trends, and how-to features relating to consumer and trade promotion marketing.

47805 ■ Promotion Marketing Association—Outlook
Pub: Promotion Marketing Association Inc.
Contact: Claire Rosenzweig, Exec. Dir.
E-mail: crosenzw@pmalink.org
Released: QRT. **Price:** Included in membership. **Description:** Discusses issues and trends in the field of promotion marketing. Analyzes the merits of various types of promotion programs and marketing techniques. Carries the results of surveys and studies of industry groups and premium usage conducted by the Association. Recurring features include calendar of events. Remarks: Available online only.

47806 ■ Proof
Pub: Direct Marketing Club of New York
Contact: Stuart Boysen
E-mail: stuboysen@earthlink.net
Released: 10/year. **Description:** Provides information concerning direct marketing to members of the Direct Marketing Club of New York. Recurring features include a calendar of events, news of members, news of educational opportunities, book reviews, and various columns on direct marketing techniques and advancements.

47807 ■ The Publicity Hound
Pub: Joan Stewart
Contact: Joan Stewart, Publisher
E-mail: jstewart@publicityhound.com
Released: Bimonthly. **Price:** $49.95. **Description:** Provides techniques and strategies on self-promotion and inexpensive publicity. Recurring features include letters to the editor, interviews, news of research, book reviews, news of educational opportunities, notices of publications available, and columns titled Advice From Media People, Seasonal Story Ideas, Resource Page, Success Stories, and Media Insider Secrets. Does not report public relations agency staff changes.

47808 ■ Research Alert
Pub: EPM Communications Inc.
Contact: Ira Mayer, President/Publisher
Ed: Barbara Perrin, Editor, bperrin@epmcom.com. **Released:** 24/year. **Price:** $389, individuals $369/year, U.S. and Canada; $429 elsewhere. **Description:** Summarizes the most current consumer marketing research reports. Includes complete contact, methodology, and price information.

47809 ■ Sales Automation Success
Pub: Denali Group Inc.
Ed: Steve Pokin, Editor. **Released:** 10/year. **Description:** Reviews sales automation software. Offers advice for applying technology to sales and marketing problems, and how to sell more now through effective use of high technology. Recurring features include interviews, news of research, and book reviews.

47810 ■ *Signs of the Times*
Pub: ST Media Group International Inc.
Contact: Tedd Swormstedt, President/CEO
E-mail: tedd.swormstedt@stmediagroup.com
Released: 13/yr. Price: $39 1 year, U.S.; $60 2 years, U.S.; $59 1 year, Canada (surface); $101 2 years, Canada (surface); $62 1 year, Mexico/foreign (surface); $112 2 years, Mexico/foreign (surface); $112 1 year, Central/South America (airmail); $212 2 years, Central/South America (airmail); $142 1 year, Europe (airmail); $272 2 years, Europe (airmail). Description: Signs of the Times covers the latest technological information and product news for the sign industry and also provides in-depth analyses and regular columns by top industry experts.

47811 ■ *What's Working for American Companies in International Sales & Marketing*
Pub: Progressive Business Publications
Ed: Julie Power, Editor, power@pbb.com. Released: Semimonthly. Price: $391, individuals. Description: Offers real world examples and the latest news from around the world to supply sales and marketing professionals an edge in international business. Recurring features include interviews, news of research, a calendar of events, news of educational opportunities, and a column titled Sharpen Your Judgment.

VIDEOCASSETTES/ AUDIOCASSETTES

47812 ■ *Concerns Quarterly with Footage from CBS News: General Business*
Harcourt Brace College Publishers
301 Commerce, Ste. 3700
Fort Worth, TX 76102
Ph:(817)334-7500
Free: 800-237-2665
Fax: (817)334-0947
Co. E-mail: info@harcourt.com
URL: http://www.harcourt.com
Released: 1995. Price: $80.00. Description: Video newsletter containing footage from such CBS programs as CBS Evening News, 48 Hours, Street Stories, and CBS This Morning. Provides information on such topics as ethical responsibilities in business, people in business, competition, manufacturing, and marketing. Comes with instructor's guide. Available at an annual subscription rate of $300.00. Availability: VHS.

47813 ■ *Creating a Winner: The Real Secrets of Successful Marketing*
Instructional Video
2219 C St.
Lincoln, NE 68502
Ph:(402)475-6570
Free: 800-228-0164
Fax: (402)475-6500
Co. E-mail: feedback@insvideo.com
URL: http://www.insvideo.com
Price: $59.95. Description: Award-winning program offers step-by-step techniques for improving marketing skills, including information on new product launches, product line growth, and repositioning. Availability: VHS.

47814 ■ *Finding a Niche: Determining Business Potential*
Instructional Video
2219 C St.
Lincoln, NE 68502
Ph:(402)475-6570
Free: 800-228-0164
Fax: (402)475-6500
Co. E-mail: feedback@insvideo.com
URL: http://www.insvideo.com
Price: $99.00. Description: Outlines the process of selecting an appropriate market for your product, including profile development of potential customers and planning and implementing a feasability study. Availability: VHS.

47815 ■ *Marketing*
Coast Telecourses
11460 Warner Ave.
Fountain Valley, CA 92708-2597
Ph:(714)241-6109
Free: 800-547-4748
Fax: (714)241-6286
Co. E-mail: coastlearning@cccd.edu
URL: http://www.coastlearning.org
Released: 1992. Description: A video course in marketing. Availability: VHS; 3/4U; Q.

47816 ■ *Marketing Perspectives*
RMI Media
1365 N. Winchester
Olathe, KS 66061
Ph:(913)768-1696
Fax: (913)768-0184
Co. E-mail: actmedia@act.org
URL: http://www.rmimedia.com
Released: 1987. Description: Reviews the basic concepts of marketing. Availability: VHS; 3/4U.

47817 ■ *The Name Principle*
L & K International Training
3065 Ridgeway Dr., Unit 34
Mississauga, ON, Canada L5M 5M6
Ph:(905)270-6200
Fax: (905)270-3786
Co. E-mail: inquiry@lk-intl.com
URL: http://www.lk-intl.com
Released: 1988. Price: $245.00. Description: Calling a potential customer by name is shown to have a positive effect when trying to make a sale. Availability: VHS; 3/4U.

47818 ■ *The New Selling with Service*
RMI Media
1365 N. Winchester
Olathe, KS 66061
Ph:(913)768-1696
Fax: (913)768-0184
Co. E-mail: actmedia@act.org
URL: http://www.rmimedia.com
Released: 1993. Price: $89.95. Description: Philip Wexler explains how to implement a marketing philosophy to maintain and increase customers. Availability: VHS.

47819 ■ *That's Show Business: The Rules of Exhibiting*
Video Arts, Inc.
c/o Aim Learning Group
8238-40 Lehigh
Morton Grove, IL 60053-2615
Free: 877-444-2230
Fax: (416)252-2155
Co. E-mail: service@aimlearninggroup.com
URL: http://www.aimlearninggroup.com
Released: 1991. Price: $790.00. Description: A sensible yet humorous approach to business exhibitions show the most common mistakes and how to avoid them. Availability: VHS; 8mm; 3/4U; Special order formats.

TRADE SHOWS AND CONVENTIONS

47820 ■ HSMAI - Affordable Meetings West
George Little Management, LLC (New York)
10 Bank St.
White Plains, NY 10606-1954
Ph:(914)421-3200
Free: 800-272-SHOW
Fax: (914)948-6180
Co. E-mail: cathy_steel@glmshows.com
URL: http://www.glmshows.com
Released: Annual. Audience: Trade professionals. Principal Exhibits: Equipment, supplies, and services for the hospitality and marketing industry.

CONSULTANTS

47821 ■ Sol Abrams Public Relations Counsel & Marketing Consultants
331 Webster Dr.
New Milford, NJ 07646
Ph:(201)262-4111
Fax: (201)262-7669
Scope: Independent consulting provides publicity, public relations and marketing counsel and services to management of private and public enterprises. Also serves as public relations consultants to other public relations consulting firms, advertising agencies and marketing companies. Provides expert witness services involving public relations. Also lectures, trains, teaches, and conducts seminars in public relations and marketing. Industries served: corporate management, businesses large and small including real estate, construction, entertainment, food, fashion, fundraising, automotive, aviation, franchising, government agencies, and nonprofit organizations. Seminars: How to Select a Public Relations Firm; Publicity and Promotion for Small Business Owner; Expose Yourself - Don't Be a Secret Agent -Increase Your Sales, Incomes, Images, Publicity, Profits and Prestige via Professional Public Relations.

47822 ■ Aegis Communications Inc.
2 Greenwich Plz., Ste. 100
Greenwich, CT 06830
Ph:(203)622-4944
Scope: Marketing firm specializing in using visualization tools to help clients define communication needs and develop communication strategies and plans.

47823 ■ Alden and Associates Marketing Research
2536 Via Sanchez
Palos Verdes Estates, CA 90274-2806
Ph:(310)544-6282
Free: 800-742-6076
Fax: (310)544-6285
Co. E-mail: info@aa-mr.com
URL: http://www.aa-mr.com

E-mail: info@aa-mr.com
Scope: Full-service marketing research firm specializing in custom, industrial and consumer research conducted by mailed or web-based survey, telephone/ personal interview, or focus group in North America, Latin America, Europe and Asia/Oceania. Industries served: all.

47824 ■ Charles J. Allen and Associates
2668 Foxglove St.
Woodridge, IL 60517
Ph:(630)963-1444
Scope: Specializes in marketing, communication, advertising and promotional consulting. Also serves as business management consultants on a continuing basis.

47825 ■ AMC International Inc.
PO Box 11292
Beverly Hills, CA 90213-4292
Ph:(310)652-5620
Fax: (310)652-6709
Co. E-mail: inquiry@amcusa.com
URL: http://www.amcusa.com

E-mail: inquiry@amcusa.com
Scope: Offers day-to-day business management, business turnaround, marketing strategies, development/refinement of corporate mission, and merger and acquisition evaluations. Industries served: all.

47826 ■ Anderson/Roethle Inc.
700 N Water St., Ste. 1100
Milwaukee, WI 53202
Ph:(414)276-0070
Fax: (414)276-4364
Co. E-mail: info@anderson-roethle.com
URL: http://www.anderson-roethle.com

E-mail: info@anderson-roethle.com
Scope: Provides merger, acquisition and divestiture advisory services. Offers strategic planning, valuations and specialized M&A advisory services.

47827 ■ ARG & Associates
4615 E Colt Ct.
Inverness, FL 34452
Ph:(352)341-3222
Scope: IS strategic planning and tactical implementation. **Publications:** Pre-production article on "Managerial Social Types and Why Managers Fail." Second article on "The Benefits of Organizational Diversity." **Seminars:** Offers specialized training seminars in: enterprise IT/IS Strategic Planning; Selecting and ERP solution and sales force automation. **Special Services:** Systems Integration; ISD Strategic Planning and Implementations; ERP and SFA; e-commerce.

47828 ■ The Atlanta Connection
PO Box 53114
Atlanta, GA 30355
Ph:(404)989-2577
Fax: (404)264-1203
Co. E-mail: hamilton@atlantaconnection.com
URL: http://www.atlantaconnection.com

E-mail: hamilton@atlantaconnection.com
Scope: Communications consulting firm specializing in marketing, media relations, project management, and communications.

47829 ■ Barker & Associates
1974 Wexford Cir.
Wheaton, IL 60187-6166
Ph:(630)260-9927
Fax: (630)260-9928
Scope: Consulting, training, and coaching firm specializing in providing human resource assessment, selection and development services focused primarily on people skills. Serves small, mid, and large-size organizations in both private industry and not-for-profit associations. **Seminars:** Offers numerous seminars and workshops in the field of professional development, such as Strategic Marketing; Consultative Selling and Customer Service; From Hiring to Appraising - Developing Your Employees; Increased Productivity Through Managed Stress; Producing People Results Through Teambuilding; Conflict Management; Communications, Managing Transition and Change; and Creative Problem Solving.

47830 ■ Barson Marketing Inc.
Rte. 9
PO Box 1148
Manalapan, NJ 07726
Ph:(732)446-3662
Fax: (732)446-5609
Co. E-mail: info@barsonmarketing.com
URL: http://www.barsonmarketing.com

E-mail: info@barsonmarketing.com
Scope: Specializes in the preparation of analytical market studies of various industries that are used as a basis for marketing intelligence programs. Services include advertising, marketing and public relations. Industries Served: Personal care, pharmaceutical and health, retail, consumer packaged goods. **Publications:** "Compass Magazine". **Seminars:** Marketing Intelligence for the Cosmetic and Skincare Markets; Monitoring Consumer Purchasing Trends through Marketing Intelligence; Marketing for Professionals; Marketing is No Longer a Dirty Word; Marketing is Essential; Marketing - What's It All About; Targeting Your Target Market; Setting up a marketing intelligence program; Finding Hard to Find Information; Know Thy Competition.

47831 ■ Better Bottom Lines
2365 Rebel Rd.
Cumming, GA 30041
Ph:(770)887-3450
Fax: (770)887-3450
Scope: Firm conducts management and marketing consulting. It serves all small businesses, with a concentration on electromechanical sales, service and installation companies in the U.S. and Canada. **Seminars:** List of seminars and workshops available from firm upon request.

47832 ■ Bitner Goodman
5310 NW 33rd Ave., Ste. 218
Fort Lauderdale, FL 33309-6300
Ph:(954)730-7730
Fax: (954)730-7130
Co. E-mail: info@bitner.com
URL: http://www.bitner.com

E-mail: info@bitner.com
Scope: A public relations, advertising and marketing consultancy. Serves industries including: travel, technology, telecommunications, financial services, consumer products, health-care, government, automotive, real estate and retail.

47833 ■ William Blades L.L.C.
9814 E Hidden Green Dr.
Scottsdale, AZ 85262
Ph:(480)563-5355
Fax: (480)563-0515
Co. E-mail: bill@williamblades.com
URL: http://www.williamblades.com

E-mail: bill@williamblades.com
Scope: A business consulting firm with expertise in marketing and sales. Presents seminars, workshops, and keynotes on the following topics: Re-energizing the Organization; Professional Selling/Marketing; Corporate Culture; Proactive Leadership; World-Class Customer Service; Creativity; Great Teamwork. List of publications, audios, and videos is available from firm. **Publications:** "Selling-The Mother of All Enterprise"; "Leadership Defined"; "Why Do We Make Change So Hard?"; "10 Crucial Steps for Sales Management Success". **Seminars:** Sales Leadership Culture Creativity; Sales and Management.

47834 ■ Bobrow Consulting Group Inc.
1025 5th Ave., 3 FN
New York, NY 10028-0134
Ph:(212)249-7001
Fax: (212)249-7256
Co. E-mail: edbobrow@verizon.net

E-mail: edbobrow@verizon.net
Scope: A management consulting firm specializing in: strategic planning, new product development and marketing, process development, and selling and marketing through independent representatives. **Seminars:** Consulting Skills and Practices; New Product Development: How to Establish an Ongoing Process.

47835 ■ Bourget Research Group
29 North Main St., Ste. 2
PO Box 271821
West Hartford, CT 06127
Ph:(860)561-1300
Fax: (860)561-1771
Co. E-mail: info@bourgetresearch.com
URL: http://www.bourgetresearch.com

E-mail: info@bourgetresearch.com
Scope: Offers market research and consulting service on both national and regional basis. Performs consumer and industrial research including advertising testing, market potential and market share sampling, product design tests, image studies, attitude and awareness tests and opinion polls. All qualitative and quantitative services including data processing and reports. Industries served: banking, insurance, government agencies, healthcare, utilities (gas, electric, telephone), and manufacturing.

47836 ■ Bran Management Services Inc.
7116 Lupton Dr., Ste. 100
Dallas, TX 75225-1735
Ph:(214)739-2340
Fax: (214)739-2360
Scope: Offers management consulting services to companies in manufacturing, distribution and services to help them cope with growth and change. Helps small businesses create and identify product strategies. Services include developing international business opportunities; turnaround management; sales and marketing development; business planning; acquisitions and mergers.

47837 ■ Business Improvement Architects
33 Riderwood Dr.
Toronto, ON, Canada M2L 2X4
Ph:(416)444-8225
Free: (866)346-3242
Fax: (416)444-6743
Co. E-mail: info@bia.ca
URL: http://www.bia.ca

E-mail: info@bia.ca
Scope: Specializes in management training, project management, marketing planning, promotions and incentives.

47838 ■ Camarro Research
580 Commerce Dr.
Fairfield, CT 06825
Ph:(203)336-4566
Fax: (203)331-0470
Co. E-mail: kcamarro@snet.net

E-mail: kcamarro@snet.net
Scope: Firm provides market research and business consulting. Also offers office automation product development and market research. **Publications:** "Multifunction Product and Market Trend".

47839 ■ Elizabeth Capen
27 E 95th St.
New York, NY 10128-0805
Ph:(212)427-7654
Fax: (212)876-3190
Scope: Focuses on strategic marketing planning and positioning. Identifies effective marketing tools; plans and reviews advertising and collateral materials; writes business plans; and performs secondary research and competitive analysis. Industries served: services, small businesses, and entrepreneurial ventures in northeastern and middle Atlantic regions. **Seminars:** Handling Issues of Growth; Using Published Information as a Marketing Tool.

47840 ■ Capstone Communications Group
15 Wilson St.
Markham, ON, Canada L3P 1M9
Ph:(905)472-2330
Fax: (905)294-9435
Co. E-mail: capstone@capstonecomm.com
URL: http://www.capstonecomm.com

E-mail: capstone@capstonecomm.com
Scope: Helps entrepreneurial companies reach their target markets through dynamic marketing materials and strategies. Industries served: small and medium businesses in most industry sectors. **Publications:** "Is Blogging the Next Great Thing?"; "Nice Guys Finish First"; "Why should a business have a website?"; "Too Dull? Too Sharp?" **Seminars:** How to Create Marketing Materials That Work; Facing the Challenge of the Blank Page-A Design Workshop for Non-Designers, How to Create Web Sites that Work; The Service Sellers Masters Course; The Netwriting Masters Course; The Pricing Masters Course; The Info-Product Masters Course; The Net Auction Masters Course; The Affiliate Masters Course. **Special Services:** Website Design.

47841 ■ Frederick Chin
94 Condor St.
East Boston, MA 02128-1306
Ph:(617)567-8554
Scope: Offers market research, strategic and technical development, and formation of business liaisons for both public and private sectors industries in the United States, New England and Eastern Asia.

47842 ■ Kelley Chunn & Associates
184 Dudley St., Ste. 106
PO Box 2348
Boston, MA 02119
Ph:(617)427-0997
Fax: (617)427-3997
Co. E-mail: kc4info@aol.com
URL: http://www.kelleychunn.com

E-mail: kc4info@aol.com
Scope: Helps businesses, nonprofits and individuals develop multicultural, cause-related marketing and

public relations strategies. Strategic planning, media relations, event planning and management. **Seminars:** Crisis communications; Guerrilla marketing; Ethnic marketing.

47843 ■ Clayton/Curtis/Cottrell
1722 Madison Ct.
Louisville, CO 80027
Ph:(303)665-2005
Fax: (303)665-2276
Scope: Firm specializes packaged goods, telecommunications, direct marketing & printing, & packaging industries. Services include strategic planning; profit enhancement; start-up businesses; mergers and acquisitions; joint ventures; divestitures; interim management; crisis management; turnarounds; market size, segmentation and rates of growth; competitor intelligence; image & reputation, & competitive analysis.

47844 ■ Comer & Associates L.L.C.
5255 Holmes Pl.
Boulder, CO 80303
Ph:(303)786-7986
Free: 888-950-3190
Fax: (303)473-9830
URL: http://www.comerassociates.com
Scope: Specialize in developing markets & businesses. Marketing support includes: developing & writing strategic & tactical business plans; developing & writing focused, effective market plans; researching market potential & competition; implementing targeted marketing tactics to achieve company objectives; conducting customer surveys to determine satisfaction & attitudes toward client. Maintains a network of database research specialists, market communications providers, public relations firms, internet resources, focus group facilitators, technical writers & executive recruiters to assist with any project. Organization development support includes: executive/management training programs; executive coaching; team building; developing effective organization structures & processes; management of change in dynamic & competitive environments; individual coaching for management & leadership effectiveness. **Seminars:** Developing a strategic market plan; market research: defining your opportunity; management & leadership effectiveness; team building; developing a business plan.

47845 ■ Conor Environmental Services Inc.
4 Shoppers Ln., Ste. 202
Turnersville, NJ 08012-1400
Ph:(609)589-5475
Fax: (609)589-6037
Co. E-mail: consultces@usa.net

E-mail: consultces@usa.net
Scope: Firm provides a full range of environmental and engineering consulting services for both public and private organizations. Environmental company provides assessment, engineering, and remediation services, specializing in industrial and hazardous waste management. The integrated approach-combining scientific, engineering, and management services-provides cost-effective solutions to the complex scope of environmental problems. Offers expertise in the following areas: complete engineering and environmental turnkey services; groundwater and underground storage tank services; water and wastewater treatment services; environmental review and audit services; site investigation and remediation services; risk assessment and audit programs; and spill response management and planning services. Industries served: manufacturing, petroleum, power plants, utilities, wastewater treatment facilities, pipelines, landfills, banks, financial institutions, real estate developers, law firms, insurance companies, and government. **Seminars:** Beating the Competition: Winning with Better Information. **Special Services:** Company uses more than 4,000 world-class, restricted access databases to offer exhaustive coverage of business and marketing.

47846 ■ Consolidated Resources
PO Box 1864
Kailua, HI 96734
Scope: Firm offers marketing and management consulting.

47847 ■ Corporate Expressions International Inc.
105 Main S
PO Box 1010
Hackensack, NJ 07601-7103
Ph:(201)488-1660
Fax: (201)488-6973
Scope: Conducts marketing research with a special emphasis on multicultural marketing and Seniors. Serves all industries nationwide, with a special focus on health-care, entertainment, and consumer products industries. **Seminars:** Marketing to Seniors.

47848 ■ Coyne Associates
4010 E Lake St.
Minneapolis, MN 55406
Ph:(612)724-1188
Fax: (612)722-1379
Scope: A marketing and public relations consulting firm specializing in assisting architectural, engineering, and contractor/developer firms. Services include marketing plains and audits, strategic planning, corporate identity, turnarounds, and sales training.

47849 ■ Customer Perspectives
213 W River Rd.
Hooksett, NH 03106-2628
Ph:(603)647-1300
Free: 800-277-4677
Fax: (603)647-0900
Co. E-mail: info@customerperspectives.com
URL: http://www.customerperspectives.com

E-mail: info@customerperspectives.com
Scope: A market research consultancy specializing in mystery shopping. **Special Services:** Customer Perspectives™.

47850 ■ Development Resource Consultants
PO Box 118
Rancho Cucamonga, CA 91729
Ph:(909)902-7655
Fax: (909)476-6942
Co. E-mail: info@gotodrc.com

E-mail: info@gotodrc.com
Scope: A small business advisory service specializing in office re-organization, employee training in office organization, communication skills, sales training and career counseling.

47851 ■ Devillier Communications Inc.
5335 Wisconsin Ave. NW, Ste. 440
Washington, DC 20015
Ph:(202)885-5544
Fax: (202)885-5541
Co. E-mail: info@devillier.com
URL: http://www.devillier.com

E-mail: info@devillier.com
Scope: A public relations firm and marketing consultancy. Firm develops innovative solutions for a wide range of extraordinary clients.

47852 ■ Digital Deli Inc.
3145 Geary Blvd., Ste. 532
San Francisco, CA 94118
Ph:(415)992-8077
Free: 800-557-3354
Fax: (415)217-3636
Co. E-mail: sales@thedeli.com
URL: http://www.theDeli.com

E-mail: sales@thedeli.com
Scope: Specializes in interactive marketing development. Provides strategic and tactical planning for interactive media.

47853 ■ donphin.com Inc.
5713 Corporate Way, Ste. 101
West Palm Beach, FL 33407
Ph:(561)688-1000
Free: 800-234-3304
Fax: (561)688-1142
Co. E-mail: inquiry@donphin.com
URL: http://www.donphin.com

E-mail: inquiry@donphin.com
Scope: Offers a comprehensive approach to understanding and applying a broad range of business principles: legal compliance issues, management concerns, health and safety, customer service, marketing, information management. Industries served: all developing small businesses. **Publications:** "Doing Business Right!". **Seminars:** Doing Business Right!; HR That Works!.

47854 ■ Drennan Communications
6 Robin Ln.
East Kingston, NH 03827-2000
Ph:(603)642-8002
Fax: (603)642-8002
Scope: Marketing consultants specializing in the creation of names for new products, new companies, and new processes for organizations of all sizes and for individuals. Additionally provides manuscript consultation and analysis as well as substantive editing, rewriting, copy editing, and proofreading. Also offers original writing for organizations of all sizes, government agencies, and for individuals.

47855 ■ Duncan Direct Associates
16 Elm St.
Peterborough, NH 03458
Ph:(603)924-3121
Fax: (603)924-8511
Co. E-mail: duncandirect@pobox.com
URL: http://www.duncandirect.com

E-mail: duncandirect@pobox.com
Scope: A direct marketing consultant and copywriter who provides response strategies, copy and creative support both to consultants to help them develop their own practices and to their clients as a business partner. Also specializes in sales letters and brochures to complete lead-generation campaigns. **Publications:** "Streetwise Direct Marketing", Adams Media, Jan, 2001; "Website Dynamics: The Four C's of Stickiness"; "It's For You: Telemarketing Without the Hang-ups"; "Determining Your Package Format"; "Preparing to Write: Researching the Product and the Market"; "All About Benefits"; "Writing and Designing Response Advertising"; "Alternative Print Media: The low cost route to prospecting"; "Direct Mail and the Dynamics of Response".

47856 ■ Everest Marketing
957 Ashland Ave.
Saint Paul, MN 55104
Ph:(612)581-1333
Fax: (651)221-1978
Co. E-mail: aistrup@aistrup.com
URL: http://www.aistrup.com

E-mail: aistrup@aistrup.com
Scope: Provides business-to-business marketing services including marketing plan development, marketing communications, market research and business intelligence. **Publications:** "Finding and Using Local Market Research To Improve Your Sales"; "Marketing to the Right People at the Right Time"; "Marketing in a Sales-Driven Environment"; "Money Well Spent! (Eight Steps to a successful consulting project)"; "Does this sound like you?"; "Marketing Quickies". **Seminars:** Market Research Basics for Managers; Profiting from Your Customer Database; Developing Your Strategic Marketing Plan from the Ground Up; A Team Process for Developing Your Marketing Plan; Developing a Commercialization Plan for Your SBIR (Small Business Innovation Research) Proposal; Using Marketing Strategies to Jump-Start Your Sales; Marketing in a Sales-Driven Environment & Marketing in a Technology-Driven Environment.

47857 ■ Edgar Falk Communications
301 E 78th St.
New York, NY 10021
Ph:(212)628-3314
Fax: (212)628-7606
Scope: Offers full marketing services for the smaller retailer by the author of *1,001 Ideas to Create Retail Excitement* as well as public relations and marketing services for consumer goods and services.

47858 ■ The Farnsworth Group
6640 Intech Blvd., Ste. 100, Intech Bldg. 10
Indianapolis, IN 46278
Ph:(317)241-5600
Fax: (317)227-3010
Co. E-mail: tfg@thefarnsworthgroup.com
URL: http://www.thefarnsworthgroup.com

E-mail: tfg@thefarnsworthgroup.com
Scope: Research-based marketing consulting company. Serves the home improvement/hardware and building materials industries. Specializes in assisting manufacturers, distributors, retailers, and professional supply dealers to increase product sales and develop growth strategies.

47859 ■ John C. Faulkner
27 Nearwater Ln.
Darien, CT 06820-5614
Ph:(203)656-2196
Fax: (203)656-2196
Scope: Specializes in marketing of industrial/consumer products and services, strategic planning, general management studies, and acquisition planning. Also market research, incentive sales compensation and organization. Serves private industries.

47860 ■ Steven M. Ferguson & Associates
6212 Massachusetts Ave.
Bethesda, MD 20816
Ph:(301)229-8676
Fax: (301)320-4495
Co. E-mail: sfergus@erols.com

E-mail: sfergus@erols.com
Scope: Performs general marketing consultations and writing services for small to medium-sized firms. Serves as business education advisor for entrepreneurial educational programs. Serves private industries as well as government agencies. **Publications:** S. Ferguson, Starting and Operating a Business in West Virginia, Oasis Press (1992); Starting and Operating a Business in the District of Columbia, Oasis Press (1992).

47861 ■ Flor & Associates
179 Schan Dr.
Churchville, PA 18966
Ph:(215)355-7466
Fax: (215)355-7464
Co. E-mail: fredflor@msn.com

E-mail: fredflor@msn.com
Scope: Business Development Consulting helping companies increase the value of their businesses. Services include: market development for technologies and products; product positioning strategies; technology assessment; competitive intelligence and analysis; team augmentation and facilitation; business growth strategies including acquisitions, licensing, and partnerships.

47862 ■ Russ Fons Public Relations
7509 Turtle Dove Ct.
Las Vegas, NV 89129-6032
Ph:(702)658-7654
Free: 888-658-7654
Fax: (702)658-1349
Co. E-mail: russfons@cox.net
URL: http://www.russfons.com

E-mail: russfons@cox.net
Scope: Offers corporate counseling and image development; media relations; marketing communications and product publicity; event management and special promotions; and graphic design and production. Industries served: all worldwide. Licensing and merchandising, literary services, Hispanic communications. Revenue Sharing/PI Advertising. **Publications:** The Executive Crisis Manager, a planning guide to surviving corporate crisis.

47863 ■ Freese & Associates Inc.
PO Box 814
Chagrin Falls, OH 44022-0814
Ph:(440)564-9183
Fax: (440)564-7339

Co. E-mail: tfreese@freeseinc.com
URL: http://www.freeseinc.com

E-mail: tfreese@freeseinc.com
Scope: A management consulting firm offering advice in all forms of business logistics. Consulting services are in the areas of strategic planning; network analysis, site selection, facility layout and design, outsourcing, warehousing, transportation and customer service. Typical projects include 3PL marketing surveys; third party outsourcing selection; operational audits; competitive analysis; inventory management; due diligence; and implementation project management. **Publications:** "Building Relationships is Key to Motivation," Distribution Center Management, Apr, 2006; "Getting Maximum Results from Performance Reviews," WERCSheet, Oct, 2003; "SCM: Making the Vision a Reality," Supply Chain Management Review, Oct, 2003; "Contents Under Pressure," DCVelocity, Aug, 2003; "When Considering Outsourcing, It's Really a Financial Decision," Inventory Management Report, Mar, 2003. **Seminars:** Keys to Retaining & Motivating Your Associates, Mar, 2006; The Value and Challenges of Supply Chain Management, Global Supply Chain & Logistics Conference, Feb, 2006; Best Practices in Logistics in China, Jun, 2005; Keys to Motivating Associates, WERC Annual Conference, May, 2005; The Goal and the Way of International Cooperation in Logistics, Apr, 2005.

47864 ■ John Gartner & Company, Technical Marketing Consultants
26 Chasewood Ln., Ste. 200
East Amherst, NY 14051-1813
Ph:(716)688-7876
Fax: (716)639-0747
Co. E-mail: jngartner@adelphia.net
URL: http://www.zarden.com/marketresearch/alphaj.
    html

E-mail: jngartner@adelphia.net
Scope: JGCO offers a broad range of technical marketing expertise to improve the sales and marketing effectiveness of high-tech industrial companies, professional services firms and economic development organizations. Provides market research studies and strategic marketing plans, marketing and corporate communications programs, and support for sales and marketing organization development. Located in the Niagara Region, specializes in U.S./Canadian cross-border marketing services.

47865 ■ GBA Inc.
11445 Johns Creek Pky.
Duluth, GA 30097
Ph:(770)232-1711
Fax: (770)232-1722
Co. E-mail: info@gba.com

E-mail: info@gba.com
Scope: A strategic marketing and full-service communications firm specializing in business-to-business sales and marketing consulting, design and implementation of customer strategy, strategic planning, creativity, corporate identity/positioning process, direct marketing, database design, marketing fulfillment, program metrics, performance measurement, and communications technology.

47866 ■ Geibel Marketing & Public Relations
PO Box 611
Belmont, MA 02478-0005
Ph:(617)484-8285
Fax: (617)489-3567
Co. E-mail: webquery@geibelmarketing.com
URL: http://www.geibelmarketing.com

E-mail: webquery@geibelmarketing.com
Scope: Supports clients with sales messaging, sales-based marketing programs and consulting services that are developed from a diagnosis of both successful sales and market environment. Additional services include public relations, custom market research based on executive-level interviews, customized marketing skills instruction, video development and production supervision for sales-messaging and

marketing support videos. **Publications:** "The Sick Press Release," 2006; "Applications Software Marketing: A Field Manual for Success"; "CSI Marketing-Separating Fact from Fiction"; "Blog-Where's the beef"; "Can your marketing pass the test"; "How to Leverage the Hidden Code in Your Successful Sales"; "The Sales Autopsy"; "Turning Web Prospects into Customer Profits: How To Use Sales Instruction Techniques"; "Why Your Customer Success Stories are Less than Successful Sales Tools"; "Marketing ROI: Estimating Your 'Reachable' Market Potential"; "Avoiding Product Marketing Errors: Six Tips for Using Product Review Public Relations". **Seminars:** How to Develop a Vertical Marketing Program for Software and Systems; Public Relations Techniques for Vertical Market Product Launches.

47867 ■ The Handler Group Inc.
425 W End Ave.
New York, NY 10024
Ph:(212)595-6697
Fax: (212)627-1124
Scope: Provides marketing, communication planning, and design services, specializing in development of internal and external business communications. Develops corporate identity, corporate literature, employee communications, sales promotion materials, consumer product packaging and information, brochures, annual reports, and presentation materials. Industries served: cable/television, technology software, business information, hospitality, and banking.

47868 ■ hightechbiz.com
4209 Santa Monica Blvd., Ste. 201
Los Angeles, CA 90029-3027
Ph:(818)216-9356
Free: 877-648-4753
Fax: (323)913-3355
Co. E-mail: info@hightechbiz.com
URL: http://www.hightechbiz.com

E-mail: info@hightechbiz.com
Scope: Business development, strategic planning and investing in high tech companies. Turnaround consulting and financial sort our of distressed business and start up companies with strong emphasis on technology. A full service marketing agency specializing in integrated marketing solutions. Products and services include marketing surveys; positioning surveys; strategic & tactical plans; implementation plans; management consulting; product brochures; product catalogs; product packaging; product data sheets; direct mail programs; media research; competitive research; complete creative; production and film; media placement; corporate identity; in-house creative; public relations; logos & stationary; annual reports; publications; corporate brochures; corporate videos; trade show booth graphics; concept & design; copywriting; computerized production; illustration/cartoons; computer graphics; Internet home page design; media relations; financial relations; news releases; feature length stories; new product releases; and tracking and clipping.

47869 ■ Hills Consulting Group Inc.
6 Partridge Ct.
Novato, CA 94945
Ph:(415)898-3944
Scope: Strategic marketing consulting and training firm. Specializes in strategic planning; marketing surveys; market research; customer service audits; new product development; competitive analysis; and sales forecasting.

47870 ■ C. W. Hines and Associates Inc.
344 Churchill Cir., Sanctuary Bay
White Stone, VA 22578
Ph:(804)435-8844
Fax: (804)435-8855
Co. E-mail: turtlecwh@aol.com
URL: http://www.cwhinesassociates.org

E-mail: turtlecwh@aol.com
Scope: Management consultants with expertise in the following categories: advertising and public relations, health and human resources, management sciences,

organizational development, computer sciences, financial management, behavioral sciences, environmental design, technology transfer, project management, facility management, program evaluation, and business therapy. Also included are complementary areas such as sampling procedures, job training, managerial effectiveness, corporate seminars, gender harassment, training for trainers, and leadership and management skills development. **Publications:** Money Muscle, 120 Exercises To Build Spiritual And Financial Strength, 2004; Inside Track: Executives Coaching Executives. **Seminars:** Career Development; Coaching and Counseling for Work Success; Communicating More Effectively in a Diverse Work Environment; Communications 600: Advanced Skills for Relationship Building; Customer Service: Building a Caring Culture.

47871 ■ Holcomb Gallagher Adams Advertising Inc.
300 Marconi Blvd., 3rd Fl., Ste. 303
Columbus, OH 43215
Ph:(614)221-3343
Fax: (614)221-3367
URL: http://www.hgainc.com
Scope: Consults in strategic marketing planning, and new business, brand equity, creative strategy, and media strategy development. Industries served: consumer goods and services, manufacturing, retail, business-to-business products and services, education, travel, and tourism.

47872 ■ Hornberger & Associates
1966 Lombard St., Ste. 200
San Francisco, CA 94123
Ph:(415)346-2106
Fax: (415)346-9993
Co. E-mail: info@hornbergerassociates.com
URL: http://www.hornbergerassociates.com

E-mail: info@hornbergerassociates.com
Scope: Firm specializes in Internet marketing, strategic planning; new product development; client acquisition and retention; helping banks and brokerage firms do more business with affluent clients. **Seminars:** Building a Marketing Plan Directed at Emerging Wealth Baby Boomers.

47873 ■ Ilium Associates Inc.
600 108th Ave. NE, Ste. 660
Bellevue, WA 98004
Ph:(425)646-6525
Free: 800-874-6525
Fax: (425)646-6522
Co. E-mail: ilium@ilium.com
URL: http://www.ilium.com

E-mail: ilium@ilium.com
Scope: Marketing consultants active in market research and analysis, marketing planning, product and packaging design and graphics, as well as architectural design (graphics, signage, electronics). Industries served: transportation, real estate development, architecture, manufacturing, software publishing and government agencies worldwide.

47874 ■ IMC Consulting & Training
901 McHenry Ave., Ste. A
Modesto, CA 95350
Ph:(209)572-2271
Fax: (209)572-2862
Co. E-mail: michael@imc-1.net
URL: http://www.imc-1.net

E-mail: michael@imc-1.net
Scope: Firm helps businesses and professionals identify, develop and market their selling proposition to increase profits. Services include B-to-B surveys, direct marketing, media relations, planning and strategy, sales management, training and leadership coaching. **Publications:** "Adapting to Change - The New Competitive Advantage," Business Journal, Jul, 2004; "Consultant Earns Advanced Certificate," HCCSC Business Review, Dec, 2004. **Seminars:** Winning the 2nd Half: A 6-month Plan to Score New Customers and Profits.

47875 ■ In Plain English
14501 Antigone Dr.
PO Box 3300
North Potomac, MD 20878
Ph:(301)340-2821
Free: 800-274-9645
Fax: (301)279-0115
Co. E-mail: rwohl@inplainenglish.com
URL: http://www.inplainenglish.com

E-mail: rwohl@inplainenglish.com
Scope: Management consultants helping government and businesses research, design, write and produce user-oriented management information for human resources, employee benefits, business process, corporate and marketing needs. Employee benefits services include summary plan descriptions, employee benefit booklets, plan documents, communication of employee benefit highlights, pay for performance systems, and Section 125 cafeteria benefit enrollment. Human resources services include producing employee handbooks, employee handbook audits, training manuals, writing training, and personnel policy and policy audits. Consultants also assist clients to re-humanize their business, human resource department, recruitment, and employee benefit program. **Publications:** The Benefits Communication Edge newsletter; The Employee Benefits Communication ToolKit, published by Commerce Clearinghouse. Benefits Communicat ion; a guide published by business & legal reports. **Seminars:** Plain English Writing Training; Summary Plan Description Compliance workshops; Re-Humanizing the Corporation, Human Resources and Employee Benefits Communication Workshop. **Special Services:** Electronic materials; Electronic summary plan descriptions; electronic reference manuals.

47876 ■ JF Robinson Research & Demographics
PO Box 1752
Lake Arrowhead, CA 92352
Ph:(909)337-1484
Fax: (909)337-1484
Co. E-mail: jrobi60317@aol.com

E-mail: jrobi60317@aol.com
Scope: Firm specializes in target marketing for public and private agencies and businesses, targeting consumers and voters. Reports include projections, geodemographics, market potential, and consumer lists for specific segments of the population. Also offers research and development of funding and grants for non-profits using targeting methods and government appropriations, competitive, market, and opponent intelligence about domestic and foreign competitors. **Seminars:** Offers seminars on grants and funding research for non-profits, preparation for a school bond election, and using demographics in marketing and small business development. **Special Services:** Uses numerous online sources to gather research.

47877 ■ Keck & Co.
410 Walsh Rd.
Atherton, CA 94027
Ph:(650)854-9588
Fax: (650)854-7240
Co. E-mail: info@kecko.com
URL: http://www.keckco.com

E-mail: info@kecko.com
Scope: Conducts management services nationally, focusing on strategic research, marketing, and planning for businesses involved in the packaging container and equipment industry, food processing, and related technology suppliers. Develops feasibility studies to assess the possible success or failure of entering a new market, introducing a new product or product line extension, or starting a new venture; primary market research to determine what motivates consumers/buyers, and best "positioning" for product in the marketplace; business development programs; promotional programs to differentiate client company from competitors; vertical/horizontal marketing audits; technology acceptance assessments; due diligence

for investors; and management assistance with investment issues. **Seminars:** Taking the Failure Factors Out of New Product Introductions; Introduction to Marketing for Food Manufacturing Personnel; New Product Development Workshop: Plans and Elements; Starting Your Own Consulting Business; The Marketing Plan. **Special Services:** Conducts database searches for venture and expansion capital for packaging companies and companies introducing packaging functional foods. Maintains 1600-record proprietary database of international and North American magazines available to clients for public relations placements. Serves as basis of customized press lists and analysis of media for market entry and promotional purpose.

47878 ■ The Kelsey Group Inc.
600 Executive Dr.
Princeton, NJ 08540-1528
Ph:(609)921-7200
Fax: (609)921-2112
Co. E-mail: tkg@kelseygroup.com
URL: http://www.kelseygroup.com

E-mail: tkg@kelseygroup.com
Scope: A provider of research and fact-based analysis focusing on local advertising and electronic commerce.

47879 ■ James O. Kennedy & Co.
515 Monroe Ave.
River Forest, IL 60305-1901
Ph:(708)366-6884
Fax: (708)366-7003
Co. E-mail: jimboken@aol.com

E-mail: jimboken@aol.com
Scope: Offers general marketing communications consulting, advertising, and business writing for small business. Industries served: General business.

47880 ■ Key Communications Group Inc.
5617 Warwick Pl.
Chevy Chase, MD 20815-5503
Ph:(301)656-0450
Free: 800-705-5353
Fax: (301)656-4554
Co. E-mail: mr.dm@verizon.net

E-mail: mr.dm@verizon.net
Scope: Direct marketing and publishing consultants specializing in subscriber and member acquisition for newsletters and other niche B2B publications, organizations and associations. Specialties: small and start-up businesses; mergers and acquisitions; joint ventures; divestitures; product development; employee surveys and communication; market research; customer service audits; new product development; direct marketing; and competitive intelligence.

47881 ■ Koch Group Inc.
240 E Lake St., Ste. 300
Addison, IL 60101
Ph:(630)941-1100
Free: 800-470-7845
Fax: (630)941-3865
Co. E-mail: info@kochgroup.com
URL: http://www.kochgroup.com

E-mail: info@kochgroup.com
Scope: Provides industrial marketing consulting services to small to mid-sized manufacturers. Primary assistance includes industrial market research and analysis, identification of potential markets, strategic planning and plan implementation. Most project activities focus on increasing profitable sales to existing markets, new markets or geographic areas previously unserved. Specializes in assisting manufacturers identify, recruit, and manage manufacturers agents and reps. Also develops industrial websites that generate excellent opportunities for increased sales. **Seminars:** Niche Marketing; Regional Industrial Association Recruiting; Strategic Marketing for Manufacturers; Strategic Marketing; How To Identify, Screen, Interview and Select High Quality Agents; Basics of Industrial Market Research; Elements of Industrial Marketing.

47882 ■ Krantz Marketing Services L.L.C.
31-T Mountain Blvd.
Warren, NJ 07059
Ph:(908)757-3300
Fax: (908)757-0466
Co. E-mail: info@krantzonline.com
URL: http://www.krantzonline.com

E-mail: info@krantzonline.com
Scope: Offers strategic planning for digital marketing and e-business, public relations, advertising, marketing, research, management consulting, telemarketing, and sales and management training for clients in business-to-business, and professional services. **Seminars:** Sales Management; Market Planning; Pricing; Entrepreneurial Marketing; High Technology Marketing - Creating Differentiation in Product and Services Marketing. **Special Services:** World Wide Web planning, design and hosting.

47883 ■ Kubba Consultants Inc.
801 Glendale Rd.
Glenview, IL 60025
Ph:(847)729-0051
Fax: (847)729-8765
Co. E-mail: edkubba@aol.com
URL: http://www.kubbainc.com

E-mail: edkubba@aol.com
Scope: Industrial and business-to-business marketing research and consulting. Services include new product research, new market evaluation, competitor analysis and customer value analysis.

47884 ■ Jeffrey Lant Associates Inc.
50 Follen St., Ste. 507
Cambridge, MA 02238
Ph:(617)547-6372
Fax: (617)547-0061
Co. E-mail: drjlant@worldprofit.com
URL: http://www.jeffreylant.com

E-mail: drjlant@worldprofit.com
Scope: Firm sets up businesses online, design websites and assist with marketing. **Publications:** Web Wealth: How to Turn the World Wide Web Into a Cash Hose for Your Business.Whatever Youre Selling!, 1997; The Consultants Kit: Establishing and Operating Your Successful Consulting Business. **Seminars:** Business and personal development, including Establishing and Operating Your Successful Consulting Business; Successfully Promoting Your Small Business and Professional Practice; Succeeding in Your Mail Order Business; Successfully Raising Money for Your Nonprofit Organization from Foundations, Corporations and Individuals; Money Making Marketing: Finding the People Who Need What Youre Selling and Making Sure They Buy It; Getting Corporations, Foundations, and Individuals to Give You the Money Your Nonprofit Organization Needs.

47885 ■ Liberty Business Strategies Ltd.
The Times Bldg., Ste. 400, Suburban Sq.
Ardmore, PA 19003
Ph:(610)649-3800
Fax: (610)649-0408
Co. E-mail: info@libertystrategies.com
URL: http://www.libertystrategies.com

E-mail: info@libertystrategies.com
Scope: Management consulting firm working with clients to gain speed and agility in driving their business strategy. The consulting model builds the alignment of strategy, organization commitment, and technology.

47886 ■ Lupfer & Associates
92 Glen St.
South Natick, MA 01760
Ph:(508)655-3950
Fax: (508)655-7826
Co. E-mail: donlupfer@aol.com
URL: http://www.lupferassociates.com

E-mail: donlupfer@aol.com
Scope: Assists off shore hi-tech companies in entering United States markets and specializes in channel

development for all sorts of products. Perform MAR-COM support for hi-tech United States clients. **Publications:** "What's Next For Distribution-Feast or Famine?"; "The Changing Global Marketplace"; "Making Global Distribution Work". **Seminars:** How to do Business in the United States.

47887 ■ Management Strategies
1000 S Old Woodward, Ste. 105
Birmingham, MI 48009
Ph:(248)258-2756
Fax: (248)258-3407
Co. E-mail: bob@hois.com

E-mail: bob@hois.com
Scope: Firm specializes in strategic planning; feasibility studies; profit enhancement; organizational studies; start-up businesses; turnarounds; business process re-engineering; industrial engineering; marketing; ecommerce.

47888 ■ Market Focus
12 Maryland Rd.
PO Box 402
Maplewood, NJ 07040
Ph:(973)378-2470
Fax: (973)378-2470
Co. E-mail: mcss66@marketfocus.com

E-mail: mcss66@marketfocus.com
Scope: Offers advisory services to executives of corporate business units and mid-sized companies in the development and implementation of corporate and market strategies. Studies relate to business planning, new market/product entry, acquisitions and industry/competitive profiles for firms in advanced technology, business and financial services and basic industry. Projects focus on practical, effective approaches to maximizing the potential of existing operations and exploiting future growth opportunities. Practice philosophy emphasizes close client relationships, active management participation and senior consultant involvement. **Publications:** "Are Your Customers Buying What You're Selling", Constructive Strategy Newsletter; "Improving Productivity: Now More Than Ever", Constructive Strategy Newsletter; "Surviving in Hard Times", NJ Contractor. **Seminars:** Charting a Course for Future Company Growth; Marketing Planning; Construction Marketing in the 90's; Marketing and The CFO.

47889 ■ Market Ways International Corp.
656 E Golf Rd.
Arlington Heights, IL 60005
Ph:(847)593-2040
Fax: (775)888-9258
Scope: Franchise development and marketing consultancy offering services in personnel, management, and advertising media strategies. Industries served: retail, wholesale, distributor, and manufacturer. **Publications:** P. Finamore, A Debt to Society, documentary about the Driving Under the Influence offender from arrest to sentencing to jail to mandatory work release program, Sheriff of Cook County, IL (14 minutes); co-writer of WLS'/ABC's The Mourning After documenting the pain and punishment of the effects of drunk driving; Silver microphones award, Telly Award.

47890 ■ Marketing Leverage Inc.
180 Glastonbury Blvd.
Glastonbury, CT 06033
Ph:(860)633-1422
Free: 800-633-1422
Fax: (860)659-8664
Co. E-mail: office@marketingleverage.com
URL: http://www.marketingleverage.com

E-mail: office@marketingleverage.com
Scope: Consults with senior management at leading corporations to improve performance by maximizing customer value. We specialize in the targeting, retention and satisfaction of customers for companies in services industries with particular expertise in insurance, financial services, health care and technology services. Most clients belong to the Fortune 1000 group. Specific services include customer research,

analysis of lifetime value, development of customer retention strategies, evaluation of web strategies, working with client teams.

47891 ■ Marketing Plus
10 Townview Ln.
Petaluma, CA 94952
Ph:(707)763-2162
Fax: (707)765-2162
Scope: Provides marketing and management consulting for small to medium sized businesses. The firm's services include market determination and goal setting, development of marketing plans and strategies, and sales training and management. A focus of the consultant's expertise is the management of concurrent growth. Industries served: predominately service industries. **Seminars:** Goal Setting; Niche Marketing; 10 Most Frequent Marketing Mistakes; Hiring Winners.

47892 ■ Marketing Resource Group
31 Valley Forge Way
Foxborough, MA 02035
Ph:(508)543-8452
Fax: (508)842-7252
Scope: Customized sales skills and field training systems for sales people, sales managers, executives, and non-selling staff. Curriculums can be developed and branded for in-house program to be used with future trainees and new hires. Pre-screening of sales candidates and strategic consulting also available. **Seminars:** Basic Sales Skills, Consultative Selling, Relationship Selling, Networking to Maximize Your Business, Six Critical Steps for Every Sales Call, Selling Skills for the Non-Sales Professional, Effective Sales Management, Maximizing Revenue.

47893 ■ A. Marks & Associates
436 W Frontage Rd., Ste. 2D
Northfield, IL 60093
Ph:(847)784-9950
Fax: (847)784-9875
Co. E-mail: info@grow-business.com

E-mail: info@grow-business.com
Scope: Provides marketing, sales and customer service expertise to small and medium size manufacturing, distribution and service businesses wishing to reach their full growth potential. Assists ISO and QS certified companies in measuring customer satisfaction. Develops lower cost marketing and sales strategic alternatives for companies wishing to improve their marketing productivity.

47894 ■ Maximum Response Marketing
PO Box 505 Sta. Central
Halifax, NS, Canada B3J 2R7
Ph:(902)444-9457
Fax: (902)444-9457
Co. E-mail: maxresponse@hotmail.com
URL: http://www.maximumresponse.ca

E-mail: maxresponse@hotmail.com
Scope: Specialists in designing effective, results-driven, direct marketing programs that generate inquiries, orders or donations for business, consumer and not-for-profit. **Publications:** Interviewed for feature article on Marketing in "Business Voice" magazine March 2001 & March 200 issues. FAQ's about Direct Marketing featured in the "Atlantic Black Book" 1995-1996. **Seminars:** 2004 - Mount Saint Vincent University - Direct Mail Fundarising Communications & Fundraising; 2003- Atlantic Regional Meeting - United Way of Canada - Federal Privacy Legislation; 2002 - United Way of Canada National Conference - DM Campaign Basics; 2002 - Bayers Lake Business Seminar Service; Using DM to group your business. 2001 - Atlantic Regional Meeting - United Way of Canada - Presentation on Bill C G Federal Privacy Legislation. 1999-Atlantic Philanthropy Conference-Tips, Tools & Techniques: DM Fundraising 101; Guest Lecturer-Dalhousie University-Direct Marketing Tips Tools & Techinques and A Strategic Approach to Direct Mail Creative; ACOA (Atlantic Canada Opportunities Agency)-Trade Outreach Sessions-How to Use Direct Marketing to Build Your Business in the Export Mar-

ketplace; NS Dept. of Agriculture-bi-annual conference-How to Cultivate Your Customers Using Direct Marketing Tools.

47895 ■ Scott McGarvey Associates
345 N Canal St., Ste. 905
Chicago, IL 60606-1360
Ph:(312)648-6275
Co. E-mail: smcg@gsbalum.uchicago.edu

E-mail: smcg@gsbalum.uchicago.edu
Scope: Build marketing knowledge base encompassing market assessment, customer needs analysis, business environment, competitive vulnerabilities, and industry benchmarking. Define marketing strategies and customer value proposition to enable clients to reach the customers that are most profitable for their business. Enable a more efficient sales pipeline with powerful suspecting/prospecting tools. Design, test and refine marketing approaches that integrate direct marketing, advertising, electronic marketing, and telephone canvassing. **Seminars:** The Customer Value Proposition: How to Create a Marketing Theme that Distinguishes Your Enterprise from Competition Improving customer satisfaction, loyalty and retention; How to Build a Direct Channel while keeping the Peace with Intermediaries.

47896 ■ Medical Imaging Consultants Inc.
1037 Rte. 46 E G-2
Clifton, NJ 07013-2445
Ph:(973)574-8000
Free: 800-589-5685
Fax: (973)574-8001
Co. E-mail: info@micinfo.com
URL: http://www.micinfo.com

E-mail: info@micinfo.com
Scope: Provides management consulting services to hospitals, imaging centers, health-care companies and insurance companies. Firm specializes in interim management; crisis management; turnarounds; market research; and new product development. **Seminars:** Sectional Anatomy & Imaging Strategies; CT Cross-Trainer; CT Registry Review Program; MR Cross-Trainer; Digital Mammography Essentials for Technologists; Radiology Trends for Technologists.

47897 ■ Mefford, Knutson & Associates Inc.
6437 Lyndale Ave. S
Richfield, MN 55423-1465
Ph:(612)869-8011
Free: 800-831-0228
Fax: (612)893-1806
Co. E-mail: don@mkaonline.net
URL: http://www.mkaonline.net

E-mail: don@mkaonline.net
Scope: Firm specializes in start-up businesses; strategic planning; mergers and acquisitions; joint ventures; divestitures; business process re-engineering; personnel policies and procedures; market research; new product development and cost controls.

47898 ■ James G. Patterson - The Cogent Communicator
9571 E Caldwell Dr.
Tucson, AZ 85747-9218
Ph:(520)574-9353
Fax: (520)574-0620
Co. E-mail: cogent@indirect.com
URL: http://home.flash.net/~cogent

E-mail: cogent@indirect.com
Scope: Trainer and consultant in quality and communication. Specialties include ISO 9000, TQM, quality audits, communication audits, effective writing, presentation skills and negotiating. Actively promotes speaking and consulting to association groups. Serves corporate and government audiences worldwide. **Publications:** "Benchmarking Basics Crisp", 1995; "Supervisory Communication AMI", 1995; "Negotiating AMACOM worksmart series" 1995; "Intro to ISO 9000", Crisp Publications, 1994; "Leadership Development", ASTD Info-line 1994. **Seminars:** Intro to ISO 9000; Implementing an Effective TQM Program;

Teambuilding; Leadership Development; Effective Writing; Presentation Skills for Executives; Negotiation Skills; Customer Service. **Special Services:** Maintains ISO 9000 "Nicodemus" software.

47899 ■ James J. Prihoda & Associates
400 Island Way, Ste. 707
Clearwater Beach, FL 33767
Ph:(727)446-4082
Scope: Specializes in marketing and sales.

47900 ■ The Richmark Group Inc.
39 S LaSalle, 5th Fl.
Chicago, IL 60603-1605
Ph:(312)368-0800
Free: 800-889-2128
Fax: (312)368-0832
Co. E-mail: mail@richmark.com
URL: http://www.richmark.com

E-mail: mail@richmark.com
Scope: Provides marketing services, specializing in solving channel marketing problems, such as using distributors, dealers, wholesalers, and representatives appropriately. Also skilled in unique end-user segmentation, launching new products, evaluating acquisitions, reducing marketing costs, entering international markets, and auditing customer satisfaction. Industries served: data processing, telecommunications, factory automation, electrical/electronic products, office supplies, furniture, and industrial supplies. **Seminars:** Channels Management for the Changing Market; Reengineering the Price Discount Structure; Customer Satisfaction Studies that Produce Actionable Results; Marketing for the Sales Force.

47901 ■ Douglas F. Roberts
555 Kirkland Way
Kirkland, WA 98033
Ph:(425)822-9718
Fax: (425)827-4473
Scope: Using a proactive approach to strategic planning, customer focus, effective sales and marketing plans, and technical training, we develop custom programs specifically fitting your requirements and schedule, providing a foundation for continued business success in the medical device industry. **Publications:** Effective Respiratory Specimen Collections, 1995 On-Air Productions. **Seminars:** Proactive Marketing in a Managed Care Environment.

47902 ■ Gary Ruben Inc., Marketing Communications Consultants
931 E 86th St., Ste. 206
Indianapolis, IN 46240-1860
Ph:(317)251-5330
Scope: A communications and marketing consulting firm whose services include: advertising agency selection, advertising agency performance review; advertising program structuring, creative assistance, advertising program measurement, public relations program structuring, advertising department personnel development, in-house agency structuring, and executive counseling. Industries served include supermarket chains, franchise systems, and retail products and services.

47903 ■ Sales Systems Specialists
3051 N Course Dr., Ste. 401
Pompano Beach, FL 33069-3347
Ph:(954)978-6665
Scope: Provides advertising, marketing research, marketing and sales strategies for technical firms. Industries served: manufacturers of technical products. **Seminars:** Offers the following programs: seminar training for new concepts and new products; new business seminars for personnel on direct mail and tele-marketing programs. Other workshops and seminars can be custom tailored to enhance sales, marketing and public relations goals.

47904 ■ The Sanderson Group Inc.
219 Manahan Ct.
East Brunswick, NJ 08816
Ph:(732)254-8440
Fax: (732)254-8450
Co. E-mail: tsgrobin@aol.com

URL: http://thesandersongroup.com

E-mail: tsgrobin@aol.com
Scope: Provides innovative marketing and sales solutions tailored to each client's individual business needs. Helps clients grow and manage their businesses. Services provided include strategic and marketing planning, target marketing with expertise in college/teen markets, integrated marketing programs, sampling, event marketing, new product development, corporate communications, strategic alliance formation, web site strategic partnerships, Web site development and marketing, new business development, market research, sales and field force creation and management, and customer acquisition.

47905 ■ SCG Promotions Ltd.
124 E 40th St., Ste. 1102
New York, NY 10016-1723
Ph:(212)867-2210
Fax: (212)867-2539
Co. E-mail: enzer@scgpromotions.com
URL: http://www.scg-promotion-media.com

E-mail: enzer@scgpromotions.com
Scope: Marketing promotion/communications and research consulting firm that offers a total service marketing program. Clients include consumer product and services with a database of over 4000 brands. Industries served: food, beverage, health and beauty aids. **Seminars:** Strategic Trends in Sales Promotion; Selling-By-Seminar.

47906 ■ The Shannon Management Group.
415 Walnut St.
PO Box 702
Coshocton, OH 43812
Ph:(740)622-2600
Fax: (740)622-9638
Co. E-mail: info@shannonmanagementgroup.com
URL: http://www.shannonmanagementgroup.com

E-mail: info@shannonmanagementgroup.com
Scope: Serving broad range of industries and public sector organizations and foundations. Specializing in human resources recruiting and outplacement counseling on international scale for businesses of all sizes. Offers expertise in human resources policies and procedures, supervisor development, manager leadership style development, interview training, etc. Provides consulting to small business in human resources, advertising, marketing, sales, public relations and community relations. **Seminars:** Time Management workshop.

47907 ■ Tom Shillock Consulting
5545 SW Windsor Ct.
Portland, OR 97221-2150
Ph:(503)291-7928
Fax: (503)221-2052
Co. E-mail: shillock@ee.pdx.edu

E-mail: shillock@ee.pdx.edu
Scope: Offers consulting services in marketing and communications including public relations and advertising. Industries served: high technology.

47908 ■ Harvey C. Skoog
3737 N Robert Rd., No. A
Prescott Valley, AZ 86314
Ph:(928)772-1448
Scope: Firm has expertise in taxes, payroll, financial planning, budgeting, buy/sell planning, business start-up, fraud detection, troubled business consulting, acquisition, and marketing. Serves the manufacturing, construction, and retailing industries in Arizona.

47909 ■ Kenneth E. Stone
460 Heady Hall
Ames, IA 50011-1070
Ph:(515)294-6269
Fax: (515)294-1700
Co. E-mail: kstone@iastate.edu

E-mail: kstone@iastate.edu
Scope: Conducts seminars on competing with the mass merchandisers and "Big Box" stores. Helps re-

tailers develop strategies at the firm level and community level. **Publications:** "Encyclopedia of Rural America, the Land and People", ABC-CLIO Inc., 1998.

47910 ■ Stratamar Inc.
5661 Seapine Rd.
Hilliard, OH 43026
Ph:(614)529-2945
Fax: (614)529-2945
Co. E-mail: info@stratamar.com
URL: http://www.stratamar.com

E-mail: info@stratamar.com
Scope: A full-spectrum strategic marketing consulting company. Areas of concentration include product development, product management, strategic planning, development and implementation of tactical marketing plans, and internet marketing. The primary focus is upon maximizing the benefit/cost ratio of promotions through the use of direct marketing, low cost media, and the like. **Publications:** Newsletter:"Business Plans", February, 2006. **Special Services:** Includes web page designing and hosting services via an affiliate, Designing Web.

47911 ■ Syed Hussayn TMCI
95 October Ln.
Aurora, ON, Canada L4G 7A1
Ph:(905)949-4555
Fax: (905)949-9116
Co. E-mail: syedn.hussain@sympatico.ca

E-mail: syedn.hussain@sympatico.ca
Scope: Business process re-engineering, change management, financial restructuring & insolvency, consumer & corporate bankruptcy, financial/debt management, investments & insurance advisory services, management/executive development, marketing management, organizational development, needs assessment, financial counselling, succession planning, performance management/measurement, program evaluation, project management, strategic planning and import/export advisory. **Publications:** "Innovative Management"; "Team Building and Leadership"; "Financial Planning"; "Estate Planning"; "Risk Management"; "Export/Import Trade Finance Mechanics"; "Marketing and Sales Management"; "What Your Banker Needs to Know"; "Building A Successful Financial Plan". **Seminars:** Workplace Solutions Seminars; Export Development; Executive Education & Leadership Development; Financial Planning; Estate Planning; Succession Planning; Wealth Accumulation and Management; Strategic Planning/Competitive Positioning.

47912 ■ The Tactix Group
1619 N 102 St.
Omaha, NE 68114
Ph:(402)393-3800
Fax: (402)393-5151
Co. E-mail: info@thetactixgroup.com
URL: http://www.thetactixgroup.com

E-mail: info@thetactixgroup.com
Scope: Offers integrated marketing system design and implementation, for customer relationship management. Serves manufacturing, distributing, high-tech, banking, and executive benefit industries. **Special Services:** Saleslogix (Client Server) Sales Automation Software; Automated Customer Loyalty Systems.

47913 ■ Ultimate Wealth Inc.
2533 N Carson St.
Carson City, NV 89706
Ph:(702)953-0264
Fax: (702)932-8670
Co. E-mail: robert@ultimatewealth.com
URL: http://www.ultimatewealth.com

E-mail: robert@ultimatewealth.com
Scope: Specializes in consulting and training services in the area of Internet marketing. Hosts regular seminars, teleclasses, and offers training products as well as full consulting services to businesses worldwide. **Seminars:** How to Create Your Own Product in 1 Day, Apr, 2006.

47914 ■ Viewtech Market Research & Analysis
2004 Glendora Dr.
District Heights, MD 20747
Ph:(301)350-1111
Fax: (301)350-1428
Scope: Independent market or research firm offers management, administrative, and data processing support services. Additional services include: conference planning, program evaluation, direct mailings, feasibility studies, advertising specialties, and workshops and seminars. Also conducts in-store and in-school testing. Industries served: retail trade, transportation operations, and management, as well as government agencies. **Publications:** "The Marketing Guide for the Non-Marketing Manager". **Seminars:** The Art of Marketing; Building on New Opportunities; Surviving and Training As Entrepreneurs in the 21st Century; Imagination, Courage and Integrity in Marketing Research; Marketing & Selling Your Day Care Center; New 2003 Venture.

47915 ■ WestWayne/Tampa
401 E Jackson St., Ste. 3600
Tampa, FL 33602-5525
Ph:(813)202-1200
Fax: (813)202-1264
Co. E-mail: info@westwayne.com
URL: http://www.westwayne.com

E-mail: info@westwayne.com
Scope: Advertising agency and marketing consultant.

47916 ■ WMB and Associates
2182 Bent Oak Dr., Ste. 100
Apopka, FL 32712-3925
Ph:(407)889-5632
Fax: (407)889-5632
Co. E-mail: Statmanz@earthlink.net
URL: http://home.earthlink.net/~statmanz

E-mail: Statmanz@earthlink.net
Scope: Consulting statistician and market analyst providing adjunct services that enhance a product portfolio. Fifteen plus years in primary and secondary consumer research ranging from the design and analysis of mail, intercept, telephone, Web and E-mail based surveys to focus group moderating. Analytical support involves statistical analysis support for market research that include quality of service, travel intentions, attraction ridership, competitive analysis and market projections, product concept design and testing, magazine design/content and readership, advertising awareness/effectiveness, acquisition and retention studies, demographic and psychographic segmentation and market tracking programs.

47917 ■ Women's Global Business Alliance L.L.C.
501 Westport Ave., Ste. 205
Norwalk, CT 06851
Ph:(203)454-1540
Fax: (203)938-7475
Co. E-mail: administration@wgba-business.com
URL: http://www.wgba-business.com

E-mail: administration@wgba-business.com
Scope: Provides information regarding advanced information to impact business operations. Builds high-level business connections and alliances among senior-executive corporate women worldwide to improve the performance of the companies they lead. Direct and personal dialogues with influential business and world leaders. Private Peer Counsel™ groups. Access to resources, experts and insights to promote direct, positive and responsible impact on the bottom-line. **Special Services:** Peer Counsel™.

47918 ■ Alan J. Zell- Ambassador of Selling
PO Box 69
Portland, OR 97207-0069
Ph:(503)241-1988
Fax: (503)241-1989
Co. E-mail: azell@aol.com
URL: http://www.sellingselling.com

E-mail: azell@aol.com

Scope: An advisory service for those who sell their services, products or their organization's ideas, information, and skills through face-to-face and telephone conversations, printed materials, the media, electronic communications, schools, guilds, trade shows, and display presentations. Industries served: minority and woman-owned businesses; government and education; medicine, law, accounting, technology, manufacturers, distributors, and retailers; professional and trade associations; and nonprofit organizations. **Publications:** Selling Situations; What Customers need to know; Turnover & Return on Investment; The Ultimate Business Oxymoron; Walkin The Aisles, Looking at the Booths, etc. **Seminars:** Ambassador Of Selling. **Special Services:** Web-site critique from sales/selling point of view.

47919 ■ Zogby International
901 Broad St.
Utica, NY 13501
Ph:(315)624-0200
Free: 877-462-7655
Fax: (315)624-0210
Co. E-mail: marketing@zogby.com
URL: http://www.zogby.com

E-mail: marketing@zogby.com
Scope: Firm specializes in providing market research and analysis services. **Publications:** "Just who are you calling anyway?". **Seminars:** The Research Authority, Oct, 2006; Christian Science Monitor Breakfast, Oct, 2006.

FRANCHISES AND BUSINESS OPPORTUNITIES

47920 ■ Carlson Wagonlit Travel Associates, Inc.
Carlson Companies, Inc
7915 FM 1960 W, Ste. 110
Houston, TX 77070
Ph:(281)955-1569
Free: 800-678-8241
URL: http://www.carlsontravel.com
No. of Franchise Units: 1,100. **No. of Company-Owned Units:** 21. **Founded:** 1888. **Franchised:** 1984. **Description:** Offers discount travel services, including airfare and hotel accommodations. **Equity Capital Needed:** $79,985-$164,000 start-up. **Franchise Fee:** $29,900. **Financial Assistance:** No. **Training:** Yes.

47921 ■ Discovery Map International LLC
Starr Map Co. LLC
PO Box 1278
Anacortes, WA 98221-6278
Ph:(360)588-0144
Free: 877-820-7827
Fax: (360)588-8344
No. of Franchise Units: 14. **No. of Company-Owned Units:** 6. **Founded:** 1987. **Franchised:** 1999. **Description:** Advertising, sales, distribution of maps. **Equity Capital Needed:** Estimated initial investment $14,300-$18,250. **Franchise Fee:** $18,000. **Financial Assistance:** No. **Training:** Yes.

47922 ■ Homestart
HomeStart Direct LLC
PO Box 1185
Fuquay-Varina, NC 27526
Fax: (919)567-9676
No. of Company-Owned Units: 2. **Founded:** 1997. **Franchised:** 1999. **Description:** A direct mail marketing program that targets the homebuyer market. **Equity Capital Needed:** Approximately $3,500, not including franchise fee. **Franchise Fee:** $9,700-$12,950. **Financial Assistance:** No. **Training:** Yes.

47923 ■ United Marketing Solutions
Next Generation Media
7644 Dynatech Ct.
Springfield, VA 22153
Ph:(703)644-0200
Free: 800-368-3501

Fax: (703)455-8519
Co. E-mail: tim.church@unitedol.com
URL: http://www.unitedol.com
No. of Franchise Units: 32. **Founded:** 1981. **Franchised:** 1982. **Description:** Home based direct mail advertising, direct sales, business-to-business. **Equity Capital Needed:** $75,000-$100,000, including 6-9 months living expenses. **Franchise Fee:** $39,500. **Financial Assistance:** SBA and Third party financing. **Training:** Offers 1 week at corporate headquarters, two subsequent follow up visits in franchise territory. Continuous toll-free support plus national annual conference, and annual sales conference.

COMPUTERIZED DATABASES

47924 ■ *AdAgeGlobal*
Crain Communications Inc.
1155 Gratiot Ave.
Detroit, MI 48207
Ph:(313)446-6000
Free: 800-678-2427
Fax: (313)446-0361
Co. E-mail: info@crain.com
URL: http://www.crain.com
Description: Contains news, feature articles, and inside information on international advertising and marketing issues. Includes daily news and advertising market reports. Includes material from the print version of *Advertising Age* magazine. Covers such issues as how products and brands cross borders and become established in other countries; worldwide advertiser rankings; marketing strategies of international companies; and more. Includes special reports, daily conference listings, international advertising agency reports, information on world products and brands, and other up-to-date material. **Type:** Full text.

47925 ■ *BtoB*
Crain Communications Inc.
1155 Gratiot Ave.
Detroit, MI 48207
Ph:(313)446-6000
Free: 800-678-2427
Fax: (313)446-0361
Co. E-mail: info@crain.com
URL: http://www.crain.com
Description: Contains news, articles, and features from the monthly print version of *BtoB*, as well as content exclusive to the online version. Contains daily news reports, analysis, and articles on business-to-business marketing and related issues. Includes coverage of e-commerce and current business events. Includes editorials and feature articles from the monthly magazine. **Availability:** Online: Crain Communications Inc. **Type:** Full text.

47926 ■ *ExecutiveSelect - Sales & Marketing Executives Edition*
Hunt-Scanlon Publishing
700 Fairfield Ave.
Stamford, CT 06902
Ph:(203)352-2920
Free: 800-477-1199
Fax: (203)352-2930
Co. E-mail: info@hunt-scanlon.com
URL: http://www.hunt-scanlon.com
Price: $495, individuals annual unlimited use subscription. **Entries Include:** Company name, phone number, individual name, phone number, industry specialization, SIC codes. **Database Covers:** More than 13,000 sales and marketing professionals in over 9,500 companies in the U.S.

LIBRARIES

47927 ■ Boston Public Library–Kirstein Business Branch
20 City Hall Ave.
Boston, MA 02108
Ph:(617)523-0860

Co. E-mail: info@bpl.org
URL: http://www.bpl.org/research/kbb/kbbhome.htm
Contact: Dolores Schueler, Bus.Br.Libn.
Scope: Business administration, retailing, advertising, finance, marketing, real estate, insurance, banking, taxation, accounting, investments, economics, business law, small business. **Services:** Copying is available through the library's interlibrary loan department; reference faxing up to 3 pages. **Holdings:** Moody's Manuals (1935 to present in print; 1909-1997 in microfiche); Commercial and Financial Chronicle, 1957-1987; Bank and Quotation Record, 1928-1987; Standard and Poor's Daily Stock Price Record: New York and American Stock Exchanges, 1962 to present; over-the-counter stocks, 1968 to present; domestic and foreign trade directories; city directories; telephone directories for New England and U.S. cities with populations over 100,000 for New England cities and towns; Standard Stock Market Service, 1921-1922; Standard Stock Offerings, 1925-1939; National Stock Summary, 1927 to present; Standard & Poor's Stock Guide, 1943 to present; New York and American Stock Exchange companies Annual and 10K reports on microfiche (1987-1996); Wall Street Journal on microfilm (latest 10 years); Wall Street Transcript on microfilm (latest 5 years); D-U-N-S Business Identification Service (November 1973 -1995). **Subscriptions:** 700 journals and other serials; 13 newspapers.

47928 ■ Carnegie Library of Pittsburgh–Library Center
Business Dept.
612 Smithfield St.
Pittsburgh, PA 15222
Ph:(412)281-7141
Fax: (412)471-1724
Co. E-mail: wernerr@carnegielibrary.org
URL: http://www.clpgh.org/locations/business/
Contact: Roye Werner, Dept.Hd.
Scope: Investments, small business, entrepreneurship, management, marketing, insurance, advertising, personal finance, accounting, real estate, job and career, international business. **Services:** Interlibrary loan; Library open to the public. **Holdings:** 14,000 business volumes; VF materials; microfilm; looseleaf services; AV cassettes. **Subscriptions:** 350 business journals, serials, and newspapers.

47929 ■ Chicago Public Library Central Library–Business/Science/Technology Division
Harold Washington Library Center
400 S. State St., 4th Fl.
Chicago, IL 60605
Ph:(312)747-4450
Fax: (312)747-4975
URL: http://www.chipublib.org/001hwlc/hwbst.html
Contact: Marcia Dellenbach, BST Div.Chf.
Scope: Small business, marketing, technology, corporate reports, investments, management, personnel, patents, physical and biological sciences, medicine, health, computer science, careers, environmental information, gardening, cookbooks. **Services:** Interlibrary loan; copying; division open to the public. **Holdings:** 415,000 books; 52,100 bound periodical volumes; 33,000 reels of microfilm; Securities and Exchange Commission (SEC) reports; federal specifications and standards; American National Standards Institute standards; corporate Annual reports. **Subscriptions:** 4000 journals and other serials; 8 newspapers.

47930 ■ Enterprise Newfoundland and Labrador–Business Resource Centre
Viking Bldg.
136 Crosbie Rd.
St. John's, NL, Canada A1B 3K3
Ph:(709)772-6022
Fax: (709)772-6090
Co. E-mail: info@cbsc.ic.gc.ca
URL: http://www.cbsc.org/af
Contact: Beulah Bouzane, Dir.
Scope: Marketing, small business, economic and regional development. **Services:** Copying; SDI; center open to the public. **Holdings:** 10,000 books; 20 VF drawers of subject files; Standard Industrial Classification (SIC) files. **Subscriptions:** 300 journals and other serials.

47931 ■ Philip Morris–Corporate Library
100 Park Ave., 17th Fl.
New York, NY 10017
Ph:(917)663-3863
Fax: (917)663-5317
Co. E-mail: david.deschenes@us.pm.com
Contact: David Deschenes, Dir./Sr.Res.Libn.
Scope: Business, marketing, finance, tobacco. **Services:** Library not open to the public. **Holdings:** 2000 books; microfiche; tobacco trade literature. **Subscriptions:** 160 journals and other serials; 20 newspapers.

47932 ■ University of Kentucky–Business & Economics Information Center
B&E Info. Ctr., Rm. 116
100 W. Gatton College of Business
Lexington, KY 40406-0093
Ph:(859)257-5868
Fax: (859)323-9496
Co. E-mail: mrazeeq@pop.uk.edu
URL: http://www.uky.edu/~BEIC
Contact: Michael A. Razeeq, Bus.Ref.Libn.
Scope: Business, economics, business management, marketing, finance, accounting. **Services:** Library open to the public for reference use only.

RESEARCH CENTERS

47933 ■ Cleveland Public Library–Cleveland Research Center
Louis Stokes Wing, Rm. 219
325 Superior Ave.
Cleveland, OH 44114-1271
Ph:(216)623-2999
Fax: (216)623-6987
Co. E-mail: crc@cpl.org
URL: http://www.cpl.org
Contact: Robert Murnan, Res.Libn.
E-mail: crc@cpl.org
Scope: Marketing, business and industry, competitive intelligence, management, genealogy, and history.

47934 ■ Marketing Research Association
110 National Dr., 2nd Fl.
Glastonbury, CT 06033
Ph:(860)682-1000
Fax: (860)682-1010
Co. E-mail: larry.brownell@mra-net.org
URL: http://www.mra-net.org
Contact: Larry Brownell, Exec.Dir.
E-mail: larry.brownell@mra-net.org
Scope: Market research, including data collection, research, and end-user needs. **Publications:** Blue Book Research Services Directory (annually); Newsletter (monthly). **Educational Activities:** Conferences.

47935 ■ Northwestern University–Center for Retail Management
Kellogg School of Management
2001 Sheridan Rd.
Evanston, IL 60208
Ph:(847)467-3600
Fax: (847)467-3620
Co. E-mail: r-blattberg@kellogg.northwestern.edu
URL: http://www.kellogg.northwestern.edu/research/retail/
Contact: Prof. Robert C. Blattberg PhD, Exec.Dir.
E-mail: r-blattberg@kellogg.northwestern.edu
Scope: Improvement of marketing and retailing practices by retailers and manufacturers, including developing new methods to help retailers provide greater value to their customers, increasing manufacturers understanding of retailers goals and objectives, and developing marketing programs that deliver greater value to customers.

47936 ■ Wayne State College–Nebraska Business Development Center
Gardner Hall 101
Wayne, NE 68787
Ph:(402)375-7575
Fax: (402)375-7574
Co. E-mail: nbdc@wsc.edu
URL: http://www.wsc.edu/academic/business/nbdc.htm

Contact: Loren Kucera, Dir.
E-mail: nbdc@wsc.edu
Scope: Management education, market research, marketing plans, strategic planning, financial planning, cash flow budgeting, capital budgeting, loan packaging, and rural development. **Services:** Consulting. **Publications:** NBDC Business Calendar (annually). **Educational Activities:** Continuing education program.

START-UP INFORMATION

47937 ■ **"10 Hottest Deals in Franchising"** in *Black Enterprise* (Vol. 35, September 2004, No. 2, pp. 77)
Pub: Earl G. Graves Publishing Co. Inc.
Ed: Wendy Harris. **Description:** According to industry experts, a new franchise business opens in the U.S. every eight minutes. A listing of the best ten franchising opportunities for African Americans is presented.

47938 ■ **"An agent for change"** in *BlackEnterprise* (Vol. 31, No. 6, January 2001, pp. 99)
Pub: Earl Graves Publishing Co.
Ed: Robyn D. Clarke. **Description:** Profile of Sanyu Barnicoat, owner of the consulting firm, The Change Agents Group in West Orange, New Jersey. Ms. Barnicoat trains and coaches individuals, small groups, and major corporations on ways to make changes in an organization, and how to cope with those changes in the workplace.

47939 ■ **"Beating the odds: remembering the basics of business can help"** in *Black Enterprise* (Vol. 32, No. 6, January 2002, pp. 35)
Pub: Earl Graves Publishing Co.
Ed: Glenn Townes. **Description:** The key to starting and sustaining a small business is to have a strong, basic understanding of business practices. Advice is given to manage small businesses.

47940 ■ **"Big Bucks in Big Mouth"** in *Small Business Opportunities* (Vol. 14, No. 1, January 2002, pp. 96, 103)
Pub: Harris Publications, Inc.
Description: Profile of Reggie Smith and Ed Hughes, co-owners of Bocaza Mexican Grille, launched in 1996. As an opening promotion, they handed out free samples of food to passing motorists and pedestrians.

47941 ■ **"Black Dotcom Shake-Up"** in *Black Enterprise* (Vol. 31, No. 5, December 2000, pp. 134)
Pub: Earl Graves Publishing Co.
Ed: Sonya A. Donaldson. **Description:** Many Internet start-ups that gambled on a big payoff are now rolling snake-eyes.

47942 ■ *The Black Enterprise Guide to Starting Your Own Business*
Pub: John Wiley & Sons, Inc.
Ed: Wendy Beech. **Released:** 1999. **Price:** $19.95.

47943 ■ **"Breaking Into the Chains"** in *Hispanic Business* (October 2004, pp. 108, 110, 112)
Pub: Hispanic Business
Ed: Julie Bennett. **Description:** Several Hispanic leaders are among the owners of franchises across the nation. Information regarding general franchising opportunities is included.

47944 ■ **"Bringing home the dough"** in *BlackEnterprise* (Vol. 32, No. 3, October 2001, pp. 68)
Pub: Earl Graves Publishing Co.
Ed: Brandi Forte. **Description:** Profile of Paul Chisholm, personal chef, who consults with contracted clients to prepare fine cuisine to their specifications.

47945 ■ **"Building for the future"** in *Black Enterprise* (Vol. 32, No. 7, February 2002, pp.)
Pub: Earl Graves Publishing Co.
Ed: Glenn Townes. **Description:** Profile of Anthony Thompson's Kwame Building Group Inc., a St. Louis-based provider of construction management, contract-claims management, estimating, scheduling and engineering services.

47946 ■ **"Building on success"** in *Black Enterprise* (Vol. 32, No. 9, April 2002, pp. 70)
Pub: Earl Graves Publishing Co.
Ed: Carolyn M. Brown. **Description:** Profile of Freedie Lee and Yolanda Sherman and their business and Website, Illustrationsnetwork.com, that will showcase the artwork of minority artists and photographers to big corporations. Financial advice is offered to help the couple sustain their new business in the future and through their retirement by investing wisely.

47947 ■ **"Building vs. buying"** in *BlackEnterprise* (Vol. 31, No. 6, January 2001, pp. 39)
Pub: Earl Graves Publishing Co.
Ed: Glenn Townes. **Description:** Ideas are presented to would-be entrepreneurs on the advantages and disadvantages to buying an existing business or building one from scratch.

47948 ■ **"Capital Ventures"** in *Black Enterprise* (Vol. 30, No. 11, July 2000, pp. 235)
Pub: Earl Graves Publishing Co.
Ed: Eric L. Smith. **Description:** Gaining access to existing sources of financing remains a priority for black-owned firms.

47949 ■ **"Careful planning"** in *BlackEnterprise* (Vol. 32, No. 2, September 2001, pp. 50)
Pub: Earl Graves Publishing Co.
Ed: Paul McCoy-Pinderhughes. **Description:** Information offered to start a travel/meeting and event planning business.

47950 ■ *The Complete Startup Guide for the Black Entrepreneur*
Pub: Career Press
Ed: Bill Bourdreaux. **Price:** $15.99.

47951 ■ **"Destined for success"** in *Hispanic Business* (Vol. 22, No. 6, June 2000, pp. 20)
Pub: Hispanic Business
Ed: Vivienne Heines. **Description:** Profile of Mary Rodas, who began her business career when she was four years old. Ms. Rodas, now 24 years old, is president of Catalyst Toys. Daughter of Salvadoran immigrants, Ms. Rodas says the greatest obstacle to her success is her age, not her ethnicity.

47952 ■ **"Dialtone's Unlikely Arc"** in *Hispanic Business* (Vol. 24, No. 5, May 2002, pp. 36, 38)
Pub: Hispanic Business Inc.
Ed: Jonathan J. Higuera. **Description:** Profile of Alvaro Albarracin and his successful Internet startup, Dialtone Internet Inc.

47953 ■ **"The e-changes are just beginning"** in *Hispanic Business* (Vol. 22, No. 6, June 2000, pp. 30)
Pub: Hispanic Business
Ed: Jorge Chapa. **Description:** Hispanic businesses are part of the Internet revolution, with most of them maintaining their own Web sites. Two areas where Hispanic entrepreneurs may have a competitive advantage are in the provision of services to the Hispanic population in the U.S. and connecting Hispanic Americans to their families and home countries.

47954 ■ **"Entrepreneurial Web Hub Debuts"** in *Hispanic Business* (September 2004, pp. 20)
Pub: Hispanic Business
Description: America Online Latino and Ford Motor Company have teamed to launch a Spanish-language Web hub that will assist Hispanics to start or grow small businesses.

47955 ■ **"Finding financing"** in *Black Enterprise* (Vol. 32, No. 6, January 2002, pp. 8)
Pub: Earl Graves Publishing Co.
Ed: Bevolyn Williams-Harold. **Description:** Minority entrepreneurs may need to look for more innovative capital resources, such as minority-focused venture capital funds or community-based securitization programs, to maintain cash flow.

47956 ■ **"Finding Funding"** in *Black Enterprise* (Vol. 34, No. 7, February 2004, pp. 48)
Pub: Earl Graves Publishing Co.
Ed: Alan Hughes. **Description:** An overview of government grants offered to minority startup businesses is presented, along with information about the U.S. Small Business Association's resources.

47957 ■ **"Food resources"** in *Black Enterprise* (Vol. 32, No. 5, December 2001, pp. 46)
Pub: Earl Graves Publishing Co.
Ed: Paula McCoy-Pinderhughes. **Description:** Resources are given for starting an African-American owned retail grocery store.

47958 ■ **"Franchising"** in *Black Enterprise* (Vol. 32, No. 10, May 2002, pp. 101)
Pub: Earl Graves Publishing Co.
Ed: Carolyn M. Brown. **Description:** Franchising is one of the fastest growing segments of American business and is seen as an ideal partnership for an independent entrepreneur. More minorities are discovering franchising opportunities by increased recruiting by companies like Wendy's, Merry Maids, Jan Pro, Subway, Church's Chicken (TM), and Interim Healthcare. Profile of aforementioned franchise opportunities are included.

47959 ■ "Going legit" in *BlackEnterprise*
(Vol. 31, No. 12, July 2001, pp. 53)
Pub: Earl Graves Publishing Co.
Ed: Jason P. McKay. **Description:** Gregory D. Evans, the founder and CEO of the Cyber Group Network Corporation, has created E-Snitch, an electronic snitching device that uses wireless networks and satellites to locate missing or stolen computers anywhere in the world within a five-foot radius of the stolen PC.

47960 ■ "Hanging tough: Wilhelmina Bell-Taylor overcame cancer to launch a successful business" in *Black Enterprise*
(Oct. 2002, pp. 55)
Pub: Earl Graves Publishing Co.
Ed: Phaedra Brotherton. **Description:** Profile of Wilhelmina Bell-Taylor, who was diagnosed with Hodgkin's disease when she was only 19 years old. At age 54, Bell-Taylor is the founder and president of BETAH Associates Inc., a management counseling, communications, information, and administrative services firm located in Bethesda, Maryland. The company started as a home-based operation, incorporated in 1994.

47961 ■ "Harnessing Rhino Power" in *Hispanic Business* **(July/August 2002, pp. 73)**
Pub: Hispanic Business
Description: Profile of Humberto Barrera, owner of Rhino Computer Systems. Barrera's computer consulting company is expected to gross more than $100,000 in its first fiscal year. The entrepreneur answers questions about his company, philosophy, employees, and marketing.

47962 ■ "An Inspirational Launch" in *Hispanic Business* **(June 2002, pp. 20)**
Pub: Hispanic Business
Description: Inspiration Networks, a producer and distributor of religious television programming, will help launch a cable network for Hispanics in the United States. The network will feature religious and family-oriented programming 24 hours a day.

47963 ■ "It's in the card" in *BlackEnterprise*
(Vol. 31, No. 12, July 2001, pp. 50)
Pub: Earl Graves Publishing Co.
Ed: Paula McCoy-Pinderhughes. **Description:** American Express launches the Community Business Card, a new source of funding for entrepreneurs and small business owners who want to start and grow their companies. The program, called AmEx Community Business Credit Card, is designed for microenterprises with less than five employees and a capital need of less than $35,000 a year. Each time the business owner uses the card, AmEx will contribute one percent of that purchase to one of three select Microenterprise Development Organizations (MDO), which in turn provide loans and technical assistance to the microenterprise requesting the capital.

47964 ■ "Keep them flying" in *BlackEnterprise* **(Vol. 31, No. 11, June 2001, pp. 74)**
Pub: Earl Graves Publishing Co.
Ed: Paula McCoy-Pinderhughes. **Description:** Advice is given to an airplane mechanic who is interested in becoming a minority business supplier of aircraft components and parts. Sources such as the Small Business Development Council, under the auspices of the SBA; the Boeing Company's Supplier Diversity Program; the National Minority Supplier Development Council; and the National Black Chamber of Commerce are all profiled.

47965 ■ "Learning the Game of Hard Knocks" in *Hispanic Business* **(October 2003, pp. 36, 38)**
Pub: Hispanic Business
Ed: Scott Williams. **Description:** A pair of aspiring marketers find out that unexpected problems are often part and parcel of starting new business ventures.

47966 ■ "Mentor Wanted" in *Black Enterprise* **(Vol. 35, January 2005, No. 6, pp. 97)**
Pub: Earl G. Graves Publishing Co. Inc.

Ed: Tanisha A. Sykes. **Description:** Young African American man is looking for a mentor to help him start his own clothing business. The entrepreneur has placed some shirts in an area store, but is unsure of marketing and manufacturing of his clothing.

47967 ■ "Miami Upstart Goes National" in *Hispanic Business* **(October 2002, pp. 86)**
Pub: Hispanic Business
Ed: Roger Harris. **Description:** Profile of Nextrox, an Internet service provider based in Miami, Florida, has grown into a national information technology company in less than seven years.

47968 ■ "Minority-certified paper company sets up shop in Canton Twp." in *Crain's Detroit Business* **(Vol. 19, No. 16, April 21, 2003, pp. 6)**
Pub: Crain Communications Inc., Detroit
Ed: Michael Strong. **Description:** Twin Pines Paper LLC, paper manufacturer, has opened in Canton, Michigan. Twin Pines is the first and only minority-certified paper manufacturer in the Midwest. The startup company produces tissues, toilet paper, and paper towels.

47969 ■ "More Immigrant Women Begin Opening Own Businesses" in *San Jose Mercury News* **(February 23, 2005)**
Pub: Knight-Ridder/Tribune Business News
Ed: Steve Johnson. **Description:** San Francisco's Bay Area has become a popular site for immigrant women entrepreneurs.

47970 ■ "More than a green thumb" in *Black Enterprise* **(Vol. 32, No. 5, December 2001, pp. 46)**
Pub: Earl Graves Publishing Co.
Ed: Bridget McCrea. **Description:** Profile of Roderick Gay, founder and president of Preferred Landscape in College Park, Georgia.

47971 ■ "Moving Pictures" in *Hispanic Business* **(Vol. 23, No. 5, May 2001, pp. 66, 68)**
Pub: Hispanic Business
Ed: Andrea Siedsma. **Description:** Profile of Hispanic entrepreneurs Javier Jimenez and Matthew Cullen, co-founders of Motion Theory, a graphic design and production studio that combines motion graphics computer animation, Web-site design and programming, film and digital video shooting and, editing and post-production work.

47972 ■ "On the fast track" in *Black Enterprise* **(Vol. 32, No. 9, Ap)**
Pub: Earl Graves Publishing Co.
Ed: Alan Hughes. **Description:** Profile of Shawn D. Baldwin, president and CEO of Capital Management Group Securities in Chicago who launched an asset management firm with eight employees in March 2002.

47973 ■ "A Plan for Today's Money Market" in *Hispanic Business* **(March 2003, pp. 42, 44)**
Pub: Hispanic Business
Ed: Andrea Siedsma. **Description:** A well-crafted business plan is essential for an entrepreneur to obtain capital. The plan must emphasize honesty, credibility, and the details of marketing. Sandra Delarosa, a California female entrepreneur, outlines the details of her business plan for procuring capital. Web sites to assist in writing a business plan are included.

47974 ■ "Powerful forces" in *Black Enterprise* **(Vol. 32, No. 6, January 2002, pp. 69)**
Pub: Earl Graves Publishing Co.
Ed: Bridget McCrea. **Description:** Profile of three women entrepreneurs who took on the high tech industry and succeeded with their startup companies. The articles discusses the fact that African American women are forging ahead in this male-dominated field.

47975 ■ "Roberts' Internet venture to set up shop in Detroit" in *Crain's Detroit Business* **(Vol. 16, No. 16, April 17, 2000, pp. 34)**
Pub: Crain Communications, Inc.
Ed: Matt Roush. **Description:** Profile of Roy Roberts telling how he will move his new minority-vendor Internet trade exchange to downtown Detroit.

47976 ■ "Small Business Spotlight" in *Small Business Opportunities* **(Vol. 14, No. 1, January 2002, pp. 110)**
Pub: Harris Publications, Inc.
Description: Profiles of three franchise startups, including a Sign-A-Rama that opened in a Puerto Rican neighborhood in Chicago's north side through the Latino Economic Development Assistance Corporation (LEDAC); Hi Frequency Marketing, a Carrboro, North Carolina-based company focusing on the youth marked; and Buffalo Lube Associates, operator of 15 Valvoline Instant Oil Change centers in New York.

47977 ■ "Small Businesses Fuel Growth" in *Success* **(Vol. 47, No. 3, July 2000, pp. 16)**
Pub: Success Publishing, Inc.
Description: A study showing that small businesses are getting a boost from ever-cheaper information technology and easier access to financial assistance, and are helping to fuel the U.S. economy's record expansion. The study also predicts that this segment of the American economy will see a shift in management as well as the labor force over the next 15 years. Entrepreneurs will no longer be predominately young, white men. They will be older women, many of whom will also be Hispanic and African-American, reflecting the same shift in the U.S. population as a whole.

47978 ■ "Success line" in *Success* **(Vol. 47, No. 3, July 2000, pp. 78)**
Pub: Success Publishing, Inc.
Description: Questions are answered on starting a business, including loans and grants, patents, and federal certification for minority- or woman-owned business.

47979 ■ "Taking care of business" in *BlackEnterprise* **(Vol. 31, No. 12, July 2001, pp. 46)**
Pub: Earl Graves Publishing Co.
Ed: Bridget McCrea. **Description:** Brothers, Fred and Richard Calloway, have founded a company that caters to a decidedly male customer base with its barber, dry cleaning, and car wash services. In 1998, with approximately $30,000 of combined personal savings, the brothers created Male Care.

47980 ■ "Taking the 'dis' out of disability" in *Black Enterprise* **(Vol. 32, No. 9, March 2002, pp. 102)**
Pub: Earl Graves Publishing Co.
Ed: Alan Hughes. **Description:** Profile of Carmen Jones who triumphed over a crippling car accident and built a marketing firm that serves disabled consumers.

47981 ■ "Technology makes a comeback: fizzling dotcoms were last year's news" in *Black Enterprise* **(Vol. 32, No. 8, March 2002, pp. 87)**
Pub: Earl Graves Publishing Co.
Ed: Sonya A. Donaldson. **Description:** How African Americans fit into the discussion of venture capitalists, startups, and the technology industry is discussed. Interviews with various experts tell how African Americans can find the capital needed to fund a business venture.

47982 ■ "Third time's the charm" in *BlackEnterprise* **(Vol. 32, No. 2, September 2001, pp. 53)**
Pub: Earl Graves Publishing Co.
Ed: Bridget McCrea. **Description:** Profile of Reggie P. Best of Netilla Networks Inc. Founded in 1999, the 30-employee networking service firm supplies secure Web access to office applications, or simply put, it lets small- to medium-size businesses use the Web as an extension to the office network.

47983 ■ "Touched by an Angel" in
BlackEnterprise **(Vol. 31, No. 11, June 2001, pp. 242)**
Pub: Earl Graves Publishing Co.
Ed: Roger Barnes. **Description:** In-depth coverage of venture capital funding programs for African American businesses.

47984 ■ "Uncle Sam, Paralegal" in *Hispanic Business* **(June 2002, pp. 22)**
Pub: Hispanic Business
Ed: Teresa Talerico. **Description:** The Small Business Administration has launched a new Web site that assists entrepreneurs with legal requests. Since Hispanic entrepreneurs are eligible for a number of federal and state programs that are subject to changing regulations, the site will be very beneficial.

47985 ■ "Valor on the Front Lines" in *Hispanic Business* **(Vol. 23, No. 10, October, 2001, pp. 12)**
Pub: Hispanic Business
Ed: Jonathan J. Higuera. **Description:** Profile of Valor Telecom, the first Hispanic-owned telephone carrier that targets customers in remote regions of the Southwest. Valor has opened call centers in Texarkana, Texas; Carlsbad, New Mexico; and Espanola, New Mexico, with headquarters in Irving, Texas.

47986 ■ "Wanted" in *Black Enterprise* **(Vol. 32, No. 6, January 2002, pp. 3)**
Pub: Earl Graves Publishing Co.
Ed: Bridget McCrea. **Description:** Profile of David Vinson's company, Optate Inc, a Michigan-based online employee-relationship management firm. Vinson explains how his approach to staffing paid off when it came time to seek financing.

47987 ■ "Yes, you can" in *Black Enterprise* **(Vol. 31, No. 5, December 2000, pp. 64)**
Pub: Earl Graves Publishing Co.
Ed: Feona Huff. **Description:** How to start, operate and grow a business while developing yourself and pursuing your personal goals.

ASSOCIATIONS AND OTHER ORGANIZATIONS

47988 ■ Alliance of Minority Women for Business and Political Development
1316 Fenwick, Ste. 908
Silver Spring, MD 20910
Ph:(301)585-8051
Fax: (301)681-3681
Contact: Brenda Alford, Pres.
Membership: Organizations in support of minority women in business and politics. **Purpose:** Seeks to increase number of minority women business owners as elected officials, especially on the state level. Political action committee supports candidates through fundraising, endorsements, and training. **Publications:** *Power in Color and Gender* (quarterly).

47989 ■ American Association of Minority Businesses
PO Box 35432
Charlotte, NC 28235
Ph:(704)596-1870
Fax: (704)599-6146
Co. E-mail: ckelly@aambnet.com
URL: http://www.aambnet.com
Contact: Charles L. Kelly, Pres./CEO
Membership: Businesses in the United States that are owned or operated by individuals belonging to a racial or ethnic minority. **Purpose:** Promotes effective, ethical, and profitable operation of minority-owned businesses. Conducts educational programs for members and their staff; makes available management, personnel, operational, technical, customer service, and financial support to members. **Publications:** *Business Partner* (quarterly).

47990 ■ American Islamic Chamber of Commerce
PO Box 93033
Albuquerque, NM 87199-3033

Co. E-mail: islam@americanislam.org
URL: http://americanislam.org
Membership: Individuals and organizations. **Purpose:** Seeks to advance the interests of Islamic-owned businesses in the United States. Conducts business education programs; provides technical and management assistance to Islamic-owned businesses.

47991 ■ Asian American Hotel Owners Association
66 Lenox Pointe NE
Atlanta, GA 30324-3170
Ph:(404)816-5759
Fax: (404)816-6260
Co. E-mail: info@aahoa.com
URL: http://www.aahoa.com
Contact: Fred Schwartz, Pres.
Description: Serves as advocacy, educational, and professional development group for Asian-American hotel owners. **Publications:** *AAHOA Lodging Business Magazine* (monthly).

47992 ■ Asian Women in Business
358 5th Ave., Ste. 504
New York, NY 10001
Ph:(212)868-1368
Fax: (212)868-1373
Co. E-mail: info@awib.org
URL: http://www.awib.org
Contact: Bonnie Wong, Pres.
Membership: Asian-American women in business. **Purpose:** Seeks to enable Asian-American women to achieve their entrepreneurial potential. Serves as a clearinghouse on issues affecting small business owners; provides technical assistance and other support to members; sponsors business and entrepreneurial education courses. **Publications:** Newsletter (quarterly).

47993 ■ Caribbean American Chamber of Commerce and Industry
63 Flushing Ave.
Brooklyn Navy Yard, Bldg. No. 5, Mezzanine A
Brooklyn, NY 11205
Ph:(718)834-4544
Fax: (718)834-9774
Co. E-mail: rahastick@msn.com
URL: http://www.caribbeantradecenter.com
Contact: Roy A. Hastick Sr., Pres./CEO
Description: Promotes economic development among Caribbean American, African American, Hispanic and other minority entrepreneurs.

47994 ■ Center for Economic Options
910 Quarrier St., Ste. 206
Charleston, WV 25301
Ph:(304)345-1298
Fax: (304)342-0641
Co. E-mail: info@economicoptions.org
URL: http://www.centerforeconomicoptions.org
Contact: Pam Curry, Exec.Dir.
Description: Seeks to improve the economic position and quality of life for women, especially low-income and minority women. Works to provide access to job training and employment options to women. Supports self-employed women and small business owners by offering training and technical assistance and information. Advocates women's legal right to employment, training, education, and credit. Seeks to inform the public on economic issues related to women; while activities are conducted on local and state levels, group cooperates with national and international organizations on issues relating to employment and economic justice for women. Maintains speakers' bureau and library. Compiles statistics; conducts research. **Publications:** *Women and Employment News* (quarterly).

47995 ■ Cuban American National Council
1223 SW 4th St.
Miami, FL 33135
Ph:(305)642-3484
Fax: (305)642-9122
Co. E-mail: csantana@cnc.org
URL: http://www.cnc.org
Contact: Maria Cristina Santana, Sec.
Description: Aims to identify the socioeconomic needs of the Cuban population in the U.S. and to pro-

mote needed human services. Services the needy through research and human services while advocating on behalf of Hispanics and other minority groups. **Publications:** *The Council Letter* (quarterly); *The Cubanization and Hispanicization of Metropolitan Miami*; *Ethnic Block Voting and Polarization in Miami*; *Ethnic Segregation in Greater Miami: 1980-1990*; *Freedom of Speech in Miami*; *Housing Needs of the Hispanic Elderly in Greater Miami*; *Laws and Politics in Florida's Redistricting*; *Miami Mosaic: Ethnic Relations in Dade County*; *Miami's Latin Businesses*; *Recommendations for the United States Government Measurements of Race and Ethnicity*. **Telecommunication Services:** electronic mail, gmd@cnc.org.

47996 ■ Disabled Businesspersons Association
San Diego State University Interwork Industry
3590 Camino del Rio N
San Diego, CA 92108-1716
Ph:(619)594-8805
Fax: (619)594-4208
Co. E-mail: info@disabledbusiness.com
URL: http://www.ChallengedAmerica.org
Contact: Mr. Urban Miyares, Pres.
Description: Assists active and enterprising individuals with disabilities maximize their rehabilitation and potential in the workplace and business, and work with vocational rehabilitation, government, education and business. Encourages the participation and enhances the performance of the disabled in the work force. Membership is not a prerequisite for services or assistance. **Publications:** *Challenged America Newsletter* (quarterly); *dba Advisor* (quarterly).

47997 ■ Diversity Information Resources
2105 Central Ave. NE
Minneapolis, MN 55418
Ph:(612)781-6819
Fax: (612)781-0109
Co. E-mail: info@diversityinforesources.com
URL: http://www.diversityinforesources.com
Contact: Leslie Bonds, Exec.Dir.
Description: Promotes businesses with minority, women, veteran, service-disabled veteran and HUB-Zone ownership. Compiles and publishes minority and women-owned business directories to acquaint major corporations and government purchasing agents with the products and services of minority and women-owned firms. Sponsors national supplier diversity seminars. **Publications:** *National Minority and Women-Owned Business Directory* (annual); *Purchasing People in Major Corporations* (annual); *Supplier Diversity Information Resource Guide* (annual).

47998 ■ Grand Council of Hispanic Societies in Public Service
PO Box 636, Stuyvesant Sta.
New York, NY 10009
Ph:(212)615-6625
Contact: Debra Martinez, Pres.
Membership: Umbrella organization for 22 Hispanic societies. **Purpose:** Advocates affirmative action, equal employment, and economic opportunities for Hispanics.

47999 ■ Latin Business Association
120 S San Pedro St., Ste. 530
Los Angeles, CA 90012
Ph:(213)628-8510
Fax: (323)722-5050
Co. E-mail: rsarmiento@ultpartnership.com
URL: http://www.lbausa.com
Contact: Rick Sarmiento, Chm./CEO
Membership: Latino business owners and corporations. **Purpose:** Assists Latino business owners to develop their businesses. **Publications:** *Latin Business Association Business Directory* (periodic); *Latin Business Association Business Journal* (monthly); *Latin Business Association Business Newsletter* (monthly).

48000 ■ Latino American Management Association
419 New Jersey Ave. SE
Washington, DC 20003
Ph:(202)546-3803
Fax: (202)546-3807

URL: http://www.lamausa.com
Contact: Stephen Denlinger, Pres./CEO
Membership: Corporations. **Purpose:** Promotes the interests of Hispanic and other minority-owned business firms through marketing and procurement information, education and training activities, publications, public policy advocacy initiatives, and outreach programs. **Publications:** *Business Owner's Guide to the Business Opportunity Development Reform Act of 1988*; *Handbook for Self-Marketing Under the SBA Section 8(A) Program*; *Watch on Washington* (quarterly); *Watch on Washington Update* (biweekly).

48001 ■ Milton S. Eisenhower Foundation
1875 Connecticut Ave. NW, Ste. 410
Washington, DC 20009-5737
Ph:(202)234-8104
Fax: (202)234-8484
Co. E-mail: info@eisenhowerfoundation.org
URL: http://www.eisenhowerfoundation.org
Contact: Allan Curtis PhD, Pres./CEO
Description: Dedicated to youth investment and economic development in the inner city by reducing the school dropout rate, crime, welfare dependency, drug abuse, unemployment, and family instability. Works as a "mediating institution" to finance, technically assist, and evaluate minority nonprofit organizations. Assists more than 30 local programs based on the themes of: organizing neighborhoods; early intervention for at-risk youth; creating extended families; facilitating employment and remedial education. Also integrates community-oriented policing to assist minority nonprofit-led ventures. Operates international exchanges with Eastern Europe, France, Great Britain, Japan, and other countries. Founded as the private sector continuation of the National Violence Commission and the Kenner Riot Commission, established by former President Johnson. **Publications:** *Patriotism, Democracy, and Common Sense: Restoring America's Promise at Home and Abroad.* Publishes commission updates and policy papers.

48002 ■ National Association of Hispanic Publications
Natl. Press Bldg.
529 14th St. NW, Ste. 1085
Washington, DC 20045
Ph:(202)662-7250
Fax: (202)662-7251
Co. E-mail: tomoliver@nahp.org
URL: http://www.nahp.org
Contact: Thomas Oliver, Exec. Dir./CEO
Membership: Newspapers, magazines, and other periodicals published in Spanish (or bilingually in English and Spanish) in the United States. **Purpose:** Promotes adherence to high standards of ethical and professional standards by members; advocates continuing professional development of Hispanic journalists and publishers. Provides technical assistance to members in areas including writing and editing skills, circulation and distribution methods, attracting advertisers, obtaining financing, design and layout, and graphic arts. Conducts public service programs including voter registration drives. **Publications:** *The Hispanic Press* (quarterly).

48003 ■ National Association of Investment Companies
1300 Pennsylvania Ave. NW, Ste. 700
Washington, DC 20004
Ph:(202)204-3001
Fax: (202)204-3022
Co. E-mail: rgreene@naicvc.com
URL: http://www.naicvc.com
Contact: Robert L. Greene, Pres./CEO
Description: Aims to: represent the minority small business investment company industry in the public sector; provide industry education; develop research material on the activities of the industry; promote the growth of minority-owned small businesses by informing the public of their contribution to the vitality of the nation's economy; collect and disseminate relevant business and trade information to members; facilitate the exchange of new ideas and financing strategies; assist organizing groups attempting to form or acquire minority enterprise small business investment compa-

nies; provide management and technical assistance to members; monitor regulatory agency actions. Conducts three professional seminars; sponsors research; compiles statistics. **Publications:** *NAIC Membership Directory* (annual); *National Association of Investment Companies—Perspective* (monthly).

48004 ■ National Association of Minority Automobile Dealers
8201 Corporate Dr., Ste. 190
Lanham, MD 20785
Ph:(301)306-1614
Fax: (301)306-1493
Co. E-mail: nationaloffice@namad.org
URL: http://www.namad.org
Contact: Sheila Vaden-Williams Esq., Pres.
Description: Automobile dealers. Acts as liaison between membership, the federal government, the community, and industry representatives; seeks to better the business conditions of its members on an ongoing basis. Serves as a confidential spokesperson for dealers. Offers business analysis, financial counseling, and short- and long-term management planning. Conducts research programs; compiles statistics. **Publications:** *NAMAD Newsletter* (bimonthly); *Resource Guide* (annual).

48005 ■ National Black MBA Association
180 N Michigan Ave., Ste. 1400
Chicago, IL 60601
Ph:(312)236-2622
Fax: (312)236-0390
Co. E-mail: mail@nbmbaa.org
URL: http://www.nbmbaa.org
Contact: Ms. Barbara L. Thomas, Pres./CEO
Description: Business professionals, lawyers, accountants, and engineers concerned with the role of blacks who hold advanced management degrees. Works to create economic and intellectual wealth for the black community. Encourages blacks to pursue continuing business education; assists students preparing to enter the business world. Provides programs for minority youths, students, and professionals, and entrepreneurs including workshops, panel discussions, and Destination MBA seminar. Sponsors job fairs. Works with graduate schools. Operates job placement service. **Publications:** *Black MBA Magazine*; *National Black MBA Association—Newsletter* (monthly); *NBMBAA Program Book* (annual).

48006 ■ National Federation of Hispanic Owned Newspapers
20 W 22nd St., Ste. 808
New York, NY 10010-5804
Ph:(708)652-6397
Co. E-mail: eldinews@eldinews.com
Contact: Carlos Carrilio, Pres.
Description: Publishers and editors representing 70 Hispanic newspapers printed in the U.S. and Puerto Rico. Promotes the Hispanic print media as a valuable means of communication; encourages recruitment and training of Hispanics as print journalists. Serves as clearinghouse providing information on current Hispanic newspapers and those out of print. Works to ensure that member newspapers are listed in national media directories. Seeks to increase advertiser awareness and use of Hispanic print media. Conducts research and compiles statistics on the Hispanic reading market. Sponsors speakers' bureau. Conducts educational and research programs; operates placement service. **Publications:** *National Hispanic Media Directory* (annual); *National Rate Book* (annual); *Ultima Hora* (quarterly).

48007 ■ National Hispanic Corporate Council
1530 Wilson Blvd., Ste. 110
Arlington, VA 22209
Ph:(703)807-5137
Fax: (703)807-0567
Co. E-mail: csoto@nhcc-hq.org
URL: http://www.nhcc-hq.org
Contact: Carlos Soto, Pres./CEO
Description: Corporate think tank serving Fortune 1000 companies and their representatives as a principal resource for information, expertise and counsel about Hispanic issues affecting corporate objectives,

and to advocate for increased employment, leadership and business opportunities for Hispanics in corporate America. **Publications:** *NHCC News* (quarterly).

48008 ■ National Minority Business Council
25 W 45th St., Ste. 301
New York, NY 10036
Ph:(212)997-4753
Fax: (212)997-5102
Co. E-mail: nmbc@msn.com
URL: http://www.nmbc.org
Contact: John F. Robinson, Pres./CEO
Description: Represents minority businesses in all areas of industry and commerce. Seeks to increase profitability by developing marketing, sales, and management skills in minority businesses. Acts as an informational source for the national minority business community. Includes program such as: legal services plan that provides free legal services to members in such areas as sales contracts, copyrights, estate planning, and investment agreement; business referral service that develops potential customer leads; international trade assistance program that provides technical assistance in developing foreign markets; executive banking program that teaches members how to package a business loan for bank approval; procurement outreach program for minority and women business owners. Conducts continuing management education and provides assistance in teaching youth the free enterprise system. **Publications:** *Corporate Minority Vendor Directory* (annual); *Corporate Purchasing Directory* (annual) ; *NMBC Business Report* (biennial).

48009 ■ National Minority Supplier Development Council
1040 Ave. of the Americas, 2nd Fl.
New York, NY 10018
Ph:(212)944-2430
Fax: (212)719-9611
Co. E-mail: nmsdc1@aol.com
URL: http://www.nmsdcus.org
Contact: Harriet R. Michel, Pres.
Description: Provides a direct link between its 3,500 corporate members and minority-owned businesses (Black, Hispanic, Asian and Native American) and increases procurement and business opportunities for minority businesses of all sizes. **Publications:** *Minority Supplier News*; *National Minority Supplier Development Council—Annual Report* (annual).

48010 ■ National Society of Hispanic MBAs
1303 Walnut Hill Ln., Ste. 100
Irving, TX 75038
Ph:(214)596-9338
Free: 877-467-4622
Fax: (214)596-9325
Co. E-mail: lhassler@nshmba.org
URL: http://www.nshmba.org
Contact: Lourdes M. Hassler, CEO
Description: Hispanic MBA professional business network dedicated to economic and philanthropic advancement. **Publications:** *The Bottom Line* (monthly).

48011 ■ PUSH Commerical Division
930 E 50th St.
Chicago, IL 60615-2702
Ph:(773)373-3366
Fax: (773)373-3571
Co. E-mail: info@rainbowpush.org
URL: http://www.rainbowpush.org
Contact: Rev. Willie T. Barrow, Co-Chm.
Description: A bureau of Operation PUSH. Minority-owned franchises and small businesses; minority individuals who are self-employed. Seeks the creation of a black common market in the U.S. Works to facilitate the opening of new markets for black-owned businesses. Provides technical assistance to members, including market research and analysis, financial counseling, and packaging and marketing services. Negotiates with major U.S. corporations to help create business opportunities for blacks. Conducts workshops on job hunting and business management. Bestows Black Diamond Award to businesses and

individuals who have done the most to improve the economic status of blacks in the U.S. Maintains archive. **Publications:** *Membership List* (quarterly); Newsletter (monthly). Also publishes brochure.

48012 ■ United States Hispanic Chamber of Commerce
2175 K St. NW, Ste. 100
Washington, DC 20037
Ph:(202)842-1212
Free: 800-874-2286
Fax: (202)842-3221
Co. E-mail: ushcc@ushcc.com
URL: http://www.ushcc.com
Contact: Michael L. Barrera, Pres./CEO
Description: Hispanic and other business firms interested in the development of Hispanic business and promotion of business leadership and economic interests in the Hispanic community. Promotes positive image of Hispanics and encourages corporate involvement with Hispanic firms. Conducts business-related workshops, conferences, and management training; reports on business achievements and vendor programs of major corporations; compiles statistics. **Publications:** *Chamber Weekly* (weekly); *Hispanic Trends* (quarterly); *Networking* (quarterly).

REFERENCE WORKS

48013 ■ "$1 Billion Outreach" in *Hispanic Business* (April 2005, pp. 14)
Pub: Hispanic Business
Description: Marriott International Inc. plans to spend $1 billion with minority- and women-owned suppliers over the next five years.

48014 ■ "The 75 Most Powerful African Americans in Corporate America" in *Black Enterprise* (Vol. 35, February 2005, No. 7, pp. 104)
Pub: Earl G. Graves Publishing Co. Inc.
Ed: Kenneth Meeks. **Description:** The 75 most powerful African American corporate leaders are highlighted, including 18 who hold CEO positions.

48015 ■ "88-Year-Old Printing Company in Ch. 11, Hopes to Rebound" in *Crain's Detroit Business* (Vol. 21, January 3, 2005, No. 1, pp. 20)
Pub: Crain Communications Inc. - Detroit
Ed: Robert Ankeny. **Description:** Waterman and Sons Printing Co., one of Detroit's oldest black-owned businesses, founded in 1916, has filed for Chapter 11 protection from creditors during company reorganization.

48016 ■ "2004 Corporate Elite Directory" in *Hispanic Business* (January/February 2004, pp. 36, 38, 40, 42, 44, 46)
Pub: Hispanic Business
Description: A listing of the Hispanic Business 2004 Corporate Elite Directory, with a brief profile of each winner.

48017 ■ "2005 Corporate Elite Directory" in *Hispanic Business* (January/February 2005, pp. 22)
Pub: Hispanic Business
Description: Profile of George Reyes, CFO at Google. Reyes helped to stage Google's $1.67 billion IPO. The trend for Hispanic men and women to hold high level positions continues to grow.

48018 ■ "2005 National Minority Supplier Development Council Conference and Business Opportunity Fair" in *Entrepreneur* (Vol. 33, Aug. 2005)
Pub: Entrepreneur Media Inc.
Ed: Steve Cooper. **Description:** The National Minority Supplier Development Council conference and business opportunity fair is held annually. The event hosts CEOs, purchasing executives, minority entrepreneurs and government decision-makers.

48019 ■ "2006 Hispanic Business Diversity Report: Employment" in *Hispanic Business* (September 2006, pp. 40, 42, 44, 48, 50)
Pub: Hispanic Business
Description: Fifty businesses promoting business with the Hispanic community are profiled.

48020 ■ "The "A" team" in *WorkingWoman* (Vol. 25, No. 5, May 2000, pp. 24)
Pub: Lang Communications Inc.
Ed: Adele M. Stan. **Description:** The work of the President's Interagency Council on Women covers both international and domestic issues, including universal equality for females in education, health care and economic opportunity. It also provides a forum for career-minded women to be publicly noticed.

48021 ■ "Access to Capital: Closing the 'Gap'" in *Hispanic Business* (September 2004, pp. 46)
Pub: Hispanic Business
Description: Increasing access to capital for Hispanic companies will require a broad infrastructure along with policy changes. A number of Hispanic organizations are eager to help define strategies.

48022 ■ "Access to Capital: Government Financiers" in *Hispanic Business* (September 2004, pp. 44)
Pub: Hispanic Business
Description: Growing affluence has created opportunities for Hispanics to participate in public policy issues affecting the finance industry. Brief profiles of 16 leaders are highlighted.

48023 ■ "Access to Capital: Money to Grow" in *Hispanic Business* (October 2004, pp. 98-100)
Pub: Hispanic Business
Ed: Joel Russell. **Description:** Commercial bank loans are a popular choice for Hispanic entrepreneurs. Most Hispanic-owned firms use commercial bank loans and personal savings to start or expand their businesses. Statistical data included.

48024 ■ "Accessing Minority Markets" in *Hispanic Business* (Vol. 24, No. 5, May 2002, pp. 14)
Pub: Hispanic Business Inc.
Ed: Holly Ocasio Rizzo. **Description:** The U.S. Chamber of Commerce has launched a new program called, Access America, in order to gain a foothold with Hispanics and other minorities.

48025 ■ "Action Yet in Need of Affirming" in *Hispanic Business* (Vol. 23, No. 7/8, July/August 2001, pp. 29)
Pub: Hispanic Business
Ed: Harry P. Pachon. **Description:** An overview of data that supports the continued use of affirmative action programs.

48026 ■ "Adapt or die: surviving the government's digital push" in *Black Enterprise* (Vol. 33, No. 6, January 2003, pp. 42)
Pub: Earl Graves Publishing Co.
Ed: Rebecca Rohan. **Description:** The economic survival of black-owned businesses depends on their knowledge of using technology. In the government's move towards a paperless operation, African American businesses must learn how to take advantage of the new opportunities that technology brings.

48027 ■ "Advocate or Competitor?" in *Hispanic Business* (Vol. 24, No. 1/2, January/February 2002, pp. 18-20, 22)
Pub: Hispanic Business Inc.
Description: A summary of the United States Hispanic Chamber of Commerce (USHCC) making a business decision to publish a new magazine called Hispanic Trends and the controversy arising from this publication.

48028 ■ "Aegis of Success" in *Hispanic Business* (June 2002, pp. 16)
Pub: Hispanic Business
Ed: Rick Laezman. **Description:** New York manufacturer, Aegis Electronic Systems, has procured federal contracts for aerospace and military programs.

48029 ■ "Affirmative Action Front and Center" in *Hispanic Business* (March 2003, pp. 20, 22, 24)
Pub: Hispanic Business
Ed: Tim Dougherty. **Description:** The Supreme Court will consider two related cases with implications for college-bound Hispanic students.

48030 ■ *African Entrepreneurship: Theory & Reality*
Pub: University Press of Florida
Ed: Anita Spring and Barbara E. McDade. **Released:** 1998. **Price:** $49.95.

48031 ■ "Alarcon Backs McCain Bill" in *Hispanic Business* (March 2003, pp. 18)
Pub: Hispanic Business
Description: The president and CEO of Spanish Broadcasting System, Raul Alercon, is in favor of the Telecommunications Ownership Diversification Act of 2003, introduced by Senator John McCain (R-AZ). The bill would provide a tax deferral for companies that sell broadcast properties to minority-owned broadcasters and new entrants into the industry.

48032 ■ "Alchemist Among the Vines" in *Hispanic Business* (Vol. 24, No. 4, April 2002, pp. 20-21)
Pub: Hispanic Business Inc.
Ed: Scott Williams. **Description:** Profile of Reynaldo Robledo, a Mexican immigrant who rose to become owner of his own vineyard, winery, and vineyard management company.

48033 ■ "An Attractive Site" in *Black Enterprise* (Vol. 36, November 2005, No. 4, pp. 74)
Pub: Earl G. Graves Publishing Co. Inc.
Ed: James C. Johnson. **Description:** Tips to help a Website network with African American professionals and manage the costs associated with advertising on the site are listed.

48034 ■ "Answering the call: security firm is expanding as demand increases" in *Black Enterprise* (Vol. 32, No. 8, March 2002, pp. 52)
Pub: Earl Graves Publishing Co.
Ed: Alan Hughes. **Description:** Profile of Protection Corporations of America, a security company that hopes to answer the nation's call for increased security for business.

48035 ■ "Any Room on the Board?" in *Hispanic Business* (Vol. 24, No. 1/2, January/February 2002, pp. 24, 26)
Pub: Hispanic Business Inc.
Ed: Jonathan Higuera. **Description:** Closing the diversity gap on Fortune 1000 boards means understanding the job description for the position and developing the skills required to perform the duties. It is estimated that 82 Hispanics currently hold 114 board seats among the Fortune 1000, a 52 percent increase over 2001, but still a short parity with the Hispanic population.

48036 ■ "Arlington the Site of HD Career Expo" in *Hispanic Business* (Vol. 23, No. 10, October, 2001, pp. 104)
Pub: Hispanic Business
Description: The diversity recruitment division of Hispanic Business, HireDiversity.com, will host a national Diversity Career Expo November 13, 2001, at the Hyatt Regency Crystal City in Arlington, Virginia.

48037 ■ "Art Noir" in *Black Enterprise* (Vol. 35, December 2004, No. 5, pp. 62)
Pub: Earl G. Graves Publishing Co. Inc.
Ed: Glenn Townes. **Description:** Profile of two entrepreneurs committed to bringing upscale black art and custom frame design to Philadelphia, Pennsylvania.

48038 ■ "The art of Web selling: company finds a smart way to boost sales" in *Black Enterprise* (Vol. 33, No. 6, January 2003, pp. 41)
Pub: Earl Graves Publishing Co.
Ed: Rebecca Rohan. **Description:** Business owner, Glenn King, Exotica Art & Fashion, has found a unique way to sell imported art and artifacts using online auctions.

48039 ■ **"At Top Speed"** in *Hispanic Business* (July/August 2004, pp. 26)
Pub: Hispanic Business
Description: Hispanic-owned companies grew at the same rate as the U.S. economy in 2004; statistical composites of the top 100 Hispanic companies picked by Hispanic Business, along with company performance by industry are highlighted.

48040 ■ **"Atlanta Life to manage investments"** in *BlackEnterprise* (Vol. 32, No. 2, September 2001, pp. 22)
Pub: Earl Graves Publishing Co.
Ed: Matthew S. Scott. **Description:** Recognizing the need for progressive growth and expansion, Atlanta Life Insurance Company has formed the Atlanta Life Financial Group Inc., a new holding company that allows the nation's second largest black-owned life insurance company to become a full-service financial services organization. The firm will begin operation by the end of 2001.

48041 ■ **"Atlanta Life to Manage MetLife Assets"** in *Black Enterprise* (Vol. 35, November 2004, No. 4, pp. 32)
Pub: Earl G. Graves Publishing Co. Inc.
Ed: Aisha Jefferson. **Description:** Atlanta Life Investment Advisors, the nation's largest African-American owned, privately held stock insurance company, agreed with MetLife to manage $50 million of MetLife's assets.

48042 ■ **"Atlanta ranked No. 1 in business owner diversity"** in *Atlanta Business Chronicle* (Vol. 24, No. 10, August 10, 2001, pp. 45A)
Pub: American City Business Journals Inc.
Ed: G. Scott Thomas. **Description:** Compared to 180 other cities, Atlanta has the most diverse mix of entrepreneurs, according to a study by the Demographics Daily; Miami was second. The index has three components, which are divided along gender and racial lines: women in business, blacks in business, and Hispanics in business.

48043 ■ **"Automotive Dealers Move Wheels"** in *Hispanic Business* (Vol. 22, No. 6, June 2000, pp. 100)
Pub: Hispanic Business
Ed: Christopher D. Lancette, Scott Williams, Joel Russell. **Description:** Paul Young Auto Mall in Laredo, Texas, is one of the top ten Hispanic-owned auto dealerships in the United States, with revenues of $95.97 million. Paul Young, Jr., owner of the company, says that the firm's growth is partially due to the town's population increase.

48044 ■ **"B-School Gets Stamp of Approval"** in *Black Enterprise* (Vol. 34, July 2004, No. 12, pp. 26)
Pub: Earl G. Graves Publishing Co. Inc.
Ed: Tamara E. Holmes. **Description:** Medgar Evers College School of Business has achieved accreditation. The historically black college plans to contact alumni within a few years of graduation to track the success of its graduates in the business world.

48045 ■ **"B-to-b goes online: e-commerce among companies is rapidly changing the nature of procurement"** in *Hispanic Business* (May 2000, pp. 50)
Pub: Hispanic Business
Ed: Jennifer Riley. **Description:** Online business deals by small- and medium-sized U.S. firms will reach a total of $1.3 trillion by 2003, according to Forrester Research. The Internet has become a key forum for firms seeking to purchase goods and services.

48046 ■ **"B2G Supplies Revenue Gains"** in *Hispanic Business* (July/August 2002, pp. 32, 34)
Pub: Hispanic Business
Ed: U. S. defense spending boosts revenues for the Hispanic Business High-Tech 50, the nation's largest Hispanic-owned high-tech businesses. A list of the 2002 High-Tech 50 is included, featuring ranking for 2002 and 2001, company/location, CEO, product/service, number of employees, and revenue for 2001.

48047 ■ **"Back from the Brink"** in *BlackEnterprise* (Vol. 31, No. 8, March 2001, pp. 47)
Pub: Earl Graves Publishing Co.
Ed: Glenn Townes. **Description:** Profiles of minority small business owners who were able to rebuild their businesses after facing major setbacks.

48048 ■ **"Back to the Root"** in *Entrepreneur* (Vol. 33, September 2005, No. 9, pp. 116)
Pub: Entrepreneur Media Inc.
Ed: Lori Kozlowski. **Description:** Profile of Dr. Rick Kitties and Gina Paige co-founders of African Ancestry Inc. The firm allows African Americans to obtain genealogical information confidentially.

48049 ■ **"Back Talk with Chris Gardner"** in *Black Enterprise* (Vol. 37, January 2007, No. 6, pp. 112)
Pub: Earl G. Graves Publishing Co. Inc.
Ed: Kenneth Meeks. **Description:** Profile of with Chris Gardner and his Chicago company, Gardner Rich L.L.C., a multimillion-dollar investment firm. During an interview, Gardner discusses his rise from homelessness. His story became a book, The Pursuit of Happyness and was recently released as a film starring Will Smith.

48050 ■ **"Back Talk: With Billionaire & BET CEO Robert L. Johnson"** in *Black Enterprise* (Vol. 35, January 2005, No. 6, pp. 112)
Pub: Earl G. Graves Publishing Co. Inc.
Ed: Kenneth Meeks. **Description:** In 1991, Robert L. Johnson became the first African American to take his company public on the New York Stock Exchange. Along with Black Entertainment Television, Johnson is also the first principle black owner of a major sports franchise, the NBA Charlotte Bobcats. Interview with Johnson explores his views on his accomplishments.

48051 ■ **"Banking on Culture"** in *Boston Business Journal* (Vol. 23, No. 31, September 5, 2003, pp. 3)
Pub: American City Business Journals
Ed: Edward Mason. **Description:** Raymond K. Tung, president and CEO of Asian American Bank, reports the firm is targeting Asian Americans as a first phase of expansion strategy. Asian American, located in Boston, Massachusetts' Chinatown neighborhood, is celebrating its tenth anniversary.

48052 ■ **"B.E. teams up with CNNfn"** in *Black Enterprise* (Vol. 33, No. 6, January 2003, pp. 10)
Pub: Earl Graves Publishing Co.
Description: Blackenterprise.com and CNNfn have partnered to bring "The Economic Divide in America" online. The series reports on race, gender, education, and housing, as well as factors affecting an individual's ability to build wealth.

48053 ■ **"B.E. Wall St. All-Stars"** in *Black Enterprise* (Vol. 33, No. 3, October 2002, pp. 88)
Pub: Earl Graves Publishing Co.
Ed: Matthew S. Scott, Alan Hughes, Laura Egodigwe, Sonia Alleyne, Sonya A. Donaldson, Latif Lewis, Sophia Rose, Reginald Hart, Daniel Brown. **Description:** The Top 50 African Americans on Wall Street are profiled. Black Enterprise chose these professionals and entrepreneurs as proven power hitters who consistently succeed despite market conditions.

48054 ■ **"Beauty and the Beast"** in *Hispanic Business* (Vol. 23, No. 11, November 2001, pp. 62-64)
Pub: Hispanic Business Inc.
Ed: Ralph Gray. **Description:** Results of the 2001 Hispanic Business Buyer Satisfaction Index is divided nearly evenly between pick up trucks and SUVs on one hand, and road-hugging sedans on the other. Profiles of vehicle choices are included.

48055 ■ **"Behind the Curve"** in *Hispanic Business* (Vol. 24, No. 5, May 2002, pp. 40-41)
Pub: Hispanic Business Inc.
Ed: Teresa Talerico. **Description:** Hispanic small business owners are slow to accept technology. The importance of keeping up with technology for a small business is discussed.

48056 ■ **"Best of the Best"** in *Hispanic Business* (June 2002, pp. 32, 34, 36)
Pub: Hispanic Business
Ed: Holly Ocasio Rizzo. **Description:** The Hispanic Business 500 listing of the 500 largest Hispanic firms in the U.S. shows how managers have achieved success, despite the social barriers facing minority entrepreneurs.

48057 ■ **"Beyond Big Macs"** in *Hispanic Business* (December 2002, pp. 50-52)
Pub: Hispanic Business
Ed: Janet Perez. **Description:** Profile of John Lopez, who was named Entrepreneur of the Year by Hispanic Business Magazine. Lopez is president and CEO of Lopez Foods, a meat processing company that supplies products to McDonald's, Wal-Mart Supercenters, and Sam's Clubs.

48058 ■ **"A Bicultural Bias"** in *Hispanic Business* (December 2003, pp. 24, 26)
Pub: Hispanic Business
Ed: Abel Ramirez Magana. **Description:** Research shows Hispanics succeed in mainstream U.S. society on their own terms. According to a study conducted by the PEW Hispanic Center, second generation Hispanic births will outpace the rate of Hispanic immigration. Statistical data included.

48059 ■ **"Big Clients Push Construction Boom"** in *Hispanic Business* (Vol. 22, No. 6, June 2000, pp. 102)
Pub: Hispanic Business
Ed: Christopher D. Lancette, Scott Williams, Joel Russell. **Description:** Hispanic-owned construction and steel company, Ideal Group, is ranked 52nd in the Hispanic Business 500 with revenues of $73.26 million in 1999. CEO, Frank Venegas, Jr., says that the company's growth has been encouraged by clients such as Chrysler and Ford who support the development.

48060 ■ **"Big Goals, Small Steps"** in *Hispanic Business* (January/February 2003, pp. 46, 48)
Pub: Hispanic Business
Ed: Frank McCoy. **Description:** Since the Minority Business Development Agency (MBDA) no longer documents contracts awarded to minority-owned companies, minority business owners feel they are not getting their share of contracts.

48061 ■ **"BizWare"** in *Hispanic Business* (Vol. 23, No. 11, November 2001, pp. 70)
Pub: Hispanic Business Inc.
Ed: Roger Harris. **Description:** Hispanic programmers offer a software package for the mom-and-pop entrepreneur to develop a Web site for their business.

48062 ■ **"Black Board Directors Form Network"** in *Black Enterprise* (Vol. 35, December 2004, No. 5, pp. 38)
Pub: Earl G. Graves Publishing Co. Inc.
Ed: K. Terrell Reed. **Description:** According to the Investor Research Center, nearly 185 blacks sit on corporate boards, sharing 321 board seats out of 3,447. A recent gathering brought top black executives together to address a diversity agenda in board rooms.

48063 ■ **"Black Enterprise.com"** in *Black Enterprise* (Vol. 31, No. 5, December 2000, pp. 12)
Pub: Earl Graves Publishing Co.
Description: Web features in the December 2000 virtual desktop for African Americans, including Black filmmakers, financial planning, and career choices, are reviewed.

48064 ■ **"Black Enterprise's 2000 Business Entertaining Guide"** in *Black Enterprise* (Vol. 31, No. 5, December 2000, pp. 153)
Pub: Earl Graves Publishing Co.
Ed: Ray Isle. **Description:** How you handle a business dinner can make the difference between success or failure.

48065 ■ "Black Farmers Sue USDA for $20.5 Billion" in *Black Enterprise* (Vol. 35, December 2004, No. 5, pp. 36)
Pub: Earl G. Graves Publishing Co. Inc.
Ed: Tamara E. Holmes. Description: A class action lawsuit charging the U.S. Department of Agriculture with denying fair loans and farm programs to 25,000 black farmers is discussed. The Black Farmers and Agriculturist Association and 11 other plaintiffs have filed the suit.

48066 ■ "Black Firm Sues SBA, Alleges Funding Bias" in *Boston Business Journal* (Vol. 23, No. 30, August 29, 2003, pp. 18)
Pub: American City Business Journals
Ed: Kent Hoover. Description: The racial discrimination lawsuit filed by minority-owned Small Business Investment Corporation against the U.S. Small Business Administration is addressed. Topics include management teams, funding of minority business, and business start-up loans.

48067 ■ "Black Technology Pioneers Credit Family Support for Success" in *San Jose Mercury News* (February 26, 2005)
Pub: Knight-Ridder/Tribune Business News
Ed: Jon Fortt. Description: IBM sponsored Black Family Technology Week at East Side Union High School; Mark Dean, one of the early inventors of the IBM PC, was a keynote speaker at the event.

48068 ■ "Blazing New Trails" in *Black Enterprise* (Vol. 35, October 2004, No. 3, pp. 145)
Pub: Earl G. Graves Publishing Co. Inc.
Ed: Nkechi I. Olisemeka. Description: Winners of the 2004 Black Enterprise Small Business Awards are profiled. These entrepreneurs help redefine small business excellence for black companies.

48069 ■ "Blown Away By Katrina" in *Black Enterprise* (Vol. 36, November 2005, No. 4, pp. 148)
Pub: Earl G. Graves Publishing Co. Inc.
Ed: Alan Hughes. Description: More than 60,000 African American businesses were destroyed by Hurricane Katrina. Rebuilding costs are estimated to reach at least $100 billion and jobs could be created and Black entrepreneurs in construction and other sectors could benefit.

48070 ■ "Bob Johnson Makes Hotel History" in *Black Enterprise* (Vol. 36, February 2006, No. 7, pp. 40)
Pub: Earl G. Graves Publishing Co. Inc.
Ed: Wendy Isom. Description: Robert L. Johnson, CEO of RLJ Development LLC, is the primary developer of the $100 million plan to build a Hilton Hotel and condominium community in Norfolk, Virginia. The project should create about 350 new jobs in the area.

48071 ■ "Brainy Is As Brainy Does" in *BlackEnterprise* (Vol. 31, No. 7, February 2001, pp. 134)
Pub: Earl Graves Publishing Co.
Ed: Mary H. McCormack. Description: The article suggests that sometimes putting too much thought in a business plan can actually undermine the company. Tips to keep small business on track are presented.

48072 ■ "Breakthroughs for black-owned agencies" in *BlackEnterprise* (Vol. 32, No. 2, September 2001, pp. 21)
Pub: Earl Graves Publishing Co.
Ed: Lloyd Gite. Description: Don Coleman and Burrell, two of the nation's largest black-owned advertising agencies made breakthroughs in the advertising industry by scoring major contracts with Kmart and General Mills, respectively.

48073 ■ "Bridgewater Interiors Closes $400 Million Deal" in *Black Enterprise* (Vol. 35, January 2005, No. 6, pp. 28)
Pub: Earl G. Graves Publishing Co. Inc.
Ed: Tamara E. Holmes. Description: Bridgewater Interiors LLC has secured a $400 million contract from the Chrysler Group, a division of DaimlerChrysler, making it the largest deal ever awarded to a minority business by the automaker. Bridgewater also won a $500 million annual contract with Ford Motor Company in 2004. Details of the contract are outlined.

48074 ■ "Broadcast News: B.E. Breaks Ground With New TV Program" in *Black Enterprise* (Vol. 34, No. 5, December 2003, pp. 159)
Pub: Earl Graves Publishing Co.
Description: Black Enterprise has teamed with Central City Productions Inc. to create a new program called, "The Black Enterprise Report", devoted to covering trends and accomplishments of minority business and professional executives.

48075 ■ "Building the Minority High-Tech Work Force" in *Hispanic Business* (Vol. 23, No. 7/8, July/August 2001, pp. 116)
Pub: Hispanic Business
Description: The Council on Competitiveness has received a $23 million grant to establish a non-profit organization to address the critical shortage of women and minorities in the high-tech industries sector in the U.S.

48076 ■ "Building the Perfect Tech CEO" in *Hispanic Business* (Vol. 23, No. 5, May 2001, pp. 28, 30)
Pub: Hispanic Business
Ed: Jonathan J. Higuera. Description: Profile of Grey Reyes, president and CEO of the Silicon-based Brocade Communications Systems. Mr. Reyes has vowed to make the storage area network infrastructure provider an industry leader.

48077 ■ "Bullish on minority business: MBDA director sees better days ahead" in *Black Enterprise* (Vol. 32, No. 8, March 2002, pp. 28)
Pub: Earl Graves Publishing Co.
Description: Despite the slow economy, Ronald N. Langston, national director of the Minority Business Development Agency, states that minority businesses across the board have been expanding and growing.

48078 ■ "Burrell CEO Steps Down" in *Black Enterprise* (Vol. 35, August 2004, No. 1, pp. 23)
Pub: Earl G. Graves Publishing Co. Inc.
Ed: Dahna M. Chandler. Description: Thomas J. Burrell, founder of a black-owned advertising firm, is stepping down as chairman and CEO of his Chicago, Illinois-based company. Burrell is credited with redefining the advertising industry.

48079 ■ "Burying the Hatchet" in *Hispanic Business* (March 2003, pp. 18)
Pub: Hispanic Business
Description: After years of contention, the National Association of Minority Automobile Dealers and the National Association of Hispanic Automobile Dealers have united to promote diversity in the automobile industry.

48080 ■ "Bush Backs Contracting Program" in *Hispanic Business* (Vol. 23, No. 10, October, 2001, pp. 22)
Pub: Hispanic Business
Ed: Patricia Guadalupe. Description: The Bush Administration will defend before the U.S. Supreme Court a federal program that uses race as a factor in determining contract awards. The Republican Party, in conjunction with the Republican National Hispanic Assembly, is offering training sessions for Spanish-speaking political activists and would-be GOP candidates. Ida Castro has been named director of the DNC's Women's Vote Center.

48081 ■ "Can't Save the Farm" in *Black Enterprise* (Vol. 31, No. 5, December 2000, pp. 34)
Pub: Earl Graves Publishing Co.
Ed: Hamil R. Harris. Description: Legal relief arrives too late to harvest benefits for black farmers.

48082 ■ "Capital Access" in *Hispanic Business* (July/August 2004, pp. 68, 70, 72, 74)
Pub: Hispanic Business
Description: Top financial leaders discuss the challenges in mid-size company expansion. The growth of the U.S. Hispanic economy is paving the way for these businesses.

48083 ■ "Capital City Bank & Trust Co. expands to Albany" in *Atlanta Business Chronicle* (Vol. 24, No. 8, July 27, 2001, pp. 16A)
Pub: American City Business Journals Inc.
Ed: Meredith Jordan. Description: Capitol City Bank and Trust Co., an African American bank that promotes small business, will open a branch in Albany. The new Capital City branch, the fifth, will provide jobs for about ten people.

48084 ■ "Capital expansion" in *Black Enterprise* (Vol. 31, No. 5, December 2000, pp. 66)
Pub: Earl Graves Publishing Co.
Ed: Paula McCoy-Pinderhughes. Description: The owner of a 2-1/2 year old women's sportswear and gift company asks where to find angel investors or venture capitalists.

48085 ■ "Captains of Capital" in *Hispanic Business* (March 2003, pp. 30-34, 36-38)
Pub: Hispanic Business
Description: Ways in which the Hispanic Business 500 are finding growth capital are presented. Three Hispanic entrepreneurs are featured, showing how they met this investment challenge. Statistical data included.

48086 ■ "Cardenas' Star on the Rise" in *Hispanic Business* (Vol. 23, No. 5, May 2001, pp. 12)
Pub: Hispanic Business
Ed: Rick Laezman. Description: Profile of successful businessman, Tony Cardenas, and California Assemblyman (D-Sylmar, California), is the first Hispanic elected to represent the San Fernando Valley. Mr. Cardenas states that the number one issue for his district is healthcare.

48087 ■ "Caribbean Connection: This Shipping Professional is Taking His Company Overseas" in *Black Enterprise* (Vol. 34, July 2004, No. 12)
Pub: Earl G. Graves Publishing Co. Inc.
Ed: Arlene McKanic. Description: Franklin Vieira, CEO of minority owned Caribbean Cargo & Package Services, a shipping firm headquartered at John F. Kennedy International Airport in New York City, is expanding his company overseas. The company's Brooklyn, New York branch also helps individuals and small businesses shipping merchandise to the Caribbean.

48088 ■ "Cartel Creativo wins army contract" in *Hispanic Business* (Vol. 22, No. 10, October 2000, pp. 24)
Pub: Hispanic Business
Ed: Teresa Talerico. Description: An advertising contract aimed at recruiting more Hispanics into the U.S. Army has been won by Hispanic-owned Cartel Creativo. The Army plans to recruit 80,000 new soldiers in 2000 and to increase the proportion from ethnic minorities.

48089 ■ "Carver vs. OneUnited" in *Black Enterprise* (Vol. 35, December 2004, No. 5, pp. 96)
Pub: Earl G. Graves Publishing Co. Inc.
Ed: Sakina P. Spruell. Description: Profile of Deborah Wright, who has set her sights on making her firm a billion dollar giant. Carver was involved in a failed attempt in a takeover bid for Independence Federal Savings Bank.

48090 ■ "Caucus Decries Bush Plan" in *Hispanic Business* (Vol. 23, No. 5, May 2001, pp. 20)
Pub: Hispanic Business
Ed: Patricia Guadalupe. Description: The Congressional Hispanic Caucus states that the Bush tax plan will not benefit Hispanics.

48091 ■ "Caviar Dreams" in *Black Enterprise* (Vol. 36, November 2005, No. 4, pp. 180)
Pub: Earl G. Graves Publishing Co. Inc.
Ed: Tennille M. Robinson. Description: Profile of David E. Mills, the 36-year-old owner of Emperor's

Roe, the only black-owned caviar company in the U.S. Mills offers a breakdown of the four basic types of caviar, including Beluga, Oscetra, Sevruga, and American Sturgeon, along with tips for serving.

48092 ■ "Celebrate Success. Embrace Innovation" in *Black Enterprise* **(Vol. 37, February 2007, No. 7, pp. 145)**
Pub: Earl G. Graves Publishing Co. Inc.
Description: 2007 Women of Power Summit provides networking opportunities, empowerment sessions, and nightly entertainment. More than 500 executive women of color are expected to attend this inspiring summit in Phoenix, February 7-10.

48093 ■ "Celebrating Business Heroes" in *Hispanic Business* **(December 2002, pp. 58-60)**
Pub: Hispanic Business
Ed: Scott Williams. **Description:** Hispanic CEO's share their challenges while seeing a successful market niche, including an artist who designs pools, waterfalls, and water sculptures; founders of BLVD magazine, a doctor who treats varicose veins, and a magazine offering branding advice.

48094 ■ "Celebration of Culture and Commerce" in *Hispanic Business* **(September 2003, pp. 34, 36, 38)**
Pub: Hispanic Business
Ed: Janet Perez. **Description:** Ethnic event marketing works throughout the year, but hits a high season during Hispanic Heritage Month. Calendar of Hispanic cultural events is included.

48095 ■ "Chain Lightening" in *Hispanic Business* **(May 2005, pp. 72, 74)**
Pub: Hispanic Business
Ed: Dale Buss. **Description:** Hispanics are fueling the growth in franchise ownership. Franchising tips are shared by Detroit's Ruben Acosta, franchising expert and lawyer, and founder of Pizza Patron.

48096 ■ "The Challenges of Equal Access" in *Atlanta Business Chronicle* **(Vol. 23, No. 51, May 25, 2001, pp. 1B)**
Pub: American City Business Journals Inc.
Ed: Edward Davis. **Description:** Edward Davis, dean of the School of Business at Clark Atlanta University, moderated a roundtable discussion with leaders of Atlanta's African-American business community. The group discussed capital issues, equal access as well as other key factors for entrepreneurship.

48097 ■ "Chamber trouble: organizations in California and Texas suffer high-profile resignations" in *Hispanic Business* **(Vol.22, July-Aug. 2000)**
Pub: Hispanic Business
Ed: Peter Brennan. **Description:** Hispanic business groups in California and Texas have suffered a series of high-profile resignations during 2000, including the departure of Alex Torres as chair and president of the California Hispanic Chamber of Commerce, and Ray Leal, president of the Texas Association of Mexican American Chambers of Commerce.

48098 ■ "The changing face of technology" in *Hispanic Business* **(Vol. 22, No. 10, October 2000, pp. 26)**
Pub: Hispanic Business
Ed: Scott Williams. **Description:** The representation of Hispanic professionals in U.S. business is discussed. Barriers to Hispanics achieving their full potential at school or university and the growing number of Hispanics graduating in math, science and engineering are analyzed.

48099 ■ "Changing of the Guard" in *Hispanic Business* **(Vol. 24, No. 1/2, January/February 2002, pp. 57)**
Pub: Hispanic Business Inc.
Description: The 2002 Hispanic Business Federal Elite Directory, listing 20 members of Congress, 51 judges, 13 military leaders, and 93 government executives, including officers in all three branches of government.

48100 ■ "Changing hats" in *Black Enterprise* **(Vol. 31, No. 5, December 2000, pp. 71)**
Pub: Earl Graves Publishing Co.
Ed: Carolyn M. Brown. **Description:** Profile of Tim Cobb, founder of RelevantKnowledge, discussing his many business ventures.

48101 ■ "The chemistry of super-growth" in *Hispanic Business* **(Vol. 21, No. 12, December 1999, pp. 26)**
Pub: Hispanic Business
Ed: Scott Williams. **Description:** It is becoming increasingly common for firms to focus on what they do best, according to Plaza Group Inc.'s CEO, Randy Velerde. He won the 1999 Hispanic Business Magazine Entrepreneur of the Year Award.

48102 ■ *Chinese Ethnic Business*
Pub: Routledge Inc.
Ed: Eric Fong; Chiu Ming Luk. **Released:** October 2006. **Description:** Impact of globalization on Chinese ethnic small businesses is covered, focusing on U.S., Australia, and Canada.

48103 ■ "Chocolate Maker Plans New Plant in Pauls Valley, Okla" in *Knight-Ridder/Tribune Business News* **(April 11, 2002, pp. ITEM02101008)**
Pub: Knight-Ridder Inc.
Ed: Ed Godfrey. **Description:** Jerry Couch, general manager of Ada-based Bedre Chocolates, owned by the Chickasaw Nation, hopes to make Pauls valley a tourist stop for his candy store.

48104 ■ "Citizens expands through tough times" in *Black Enterprise* **(Vol. 32, No. 5, December 2001, pp. 21)**
Pub: Earl Graves Publishing Co.
Ed: Ann Brown. **Description:** America's fourth largest black-owned bank, Atlanta-based Citizens Trust Bank, plans to expand despite its parent company reporting second quarter losses.

48105 ■ "Clicking online: mergers, consolidations predicted for Hispanic targeted Web sites in 2000" in *Hispanic Business* **(Dec. 1999, pp. 60)**
Pub: Hispanic Business
Ed: Vaughn Hagerty. **Description:** The emergence of Hispanic-targeted sites on the Internet is discussed. Developments of StarMedia Networks Inc. and quepasa.com are highlighted.

48106 ■ "Coca-Cola Bottler Up for Sale: CEO J. Bruce Llewellyn Seeks Retirement" in *Black Enterprise* **(Vol. 37, December 2006, No. 5, pp. 31)**
Pub: Earl G. Graves Publishing Co. Inc.
Ed: Marcia A. Wade. **Description:** J. Bruce Llewellyn of Brucephil Inc., the parent company of the Philadelphia Coca-Cola Bottling Co. has agreed to sell its remaining shares to Coca-Cola Co., which previously owned 31 percent of Philly Coke. Analysts believe that Coca-Cola will eventually sell its shares to another bottler.

48107 ■ "Connecting businesses through technology's window" in *BlackEnterprise* **(Vol. 32, No. 3, October 2001, pp. 52)**
Pub: Earl Graves Publishing Co.
Ed: Patrice Banks. **Description:** Profile of Div200.com, the Internet procurement service portal for supplier diversity. Its national database gives minority business owners the opportunity to build successful business relationships with larger corporations.

48108 ■ "Connections for Business" in *Black Enterprise* **(Vol. 35, November 2004, No. 4, pp. 81)**
Pub: Earl G. Graves Publishing Co. Inc.
Ed: Matthew S. Scott. **Description:** Profile of Hamet Watt, former partner in a North Carolina venture capital firm called New Africa Opportunity Fund, that helps black and minority-owned companies secure funding. Four years later Watt joined NextMedium Inc., but is also committed to mentoring minority entrepreneurs.

48109 ■ "Construction in the Fast Mode" in *Hispanic Business* **(Vol. 23, No. 7/8, July/August 2001, pp. 44, 46, 48, 50, 52, 54, 56)**
Pub: Hispanic Business
Ed: Joel Russell. **Description:** Aggressive builders gain momentum during good times and keep it going when the economy slows. Statistical data included.

48110 ■ "Contacts for Contracts" in *Hispanic Business* **(Vol. 23, No. 7/8, July/August 2001, pp. 98)**
Pub: Hispanic Business
Description: As the energy sector heats up, opportunities for minority vendors should also increase. Contacts for minority vendors seeking contracts are listed, including Web sites for the Small Business Administration (SBA) and the National Minority Supplier Development Council are included.

48111 ■ "Convention Calendar" in *Black Enterprise* **(Vol. 34, No. 5, December 2003, pp. 68)**
Pub: Earl Graves Publishing Co.
Description: Calendar of upcoming conventions of interest to African American businesses.

48112 ■ "Corporate Elite" in *Hispanic Business* **(January/February 2005, pp. 30, 32, 34, 38, 40, 42)**
Pub: Hispanic Business
Description: Profiles of leading Hispanic corporate leaders include Richard A. Gonzalez, Abbott Laboratories; Carolos M. Morales, Merrill Lynch; James J. Padilla, Ford Motor Co.; William D. Perez, Nike; Marie Quintana Cummiskey, PepsiCo; and Felicia D. Thornton, Albertsons Inc., as well as others.

48113 ■ "Courting Trouble" in *Inc.* **(October 1, 2003)**
Pub: Gruner & Jahr USA Publishing
Ed: Nadine Heintz. **Description:** Profile of an entrepreneur facing mail fraud charges engaged in a fraudulent scheme to obtain certification as a disadvantaged small business in 2000, in order to procure government road-construction contracts set aside for minorities and women.

48114 ■ "Crain's List; Largest black-owned businesses" in *Crain's Detroit Business* **(Vol. 19, No. 15, April 14, 2003, pp. 22)**
Pub: Crain Communications Inc., Detroit
Description: A list of the twenty largest black-owned businesses in the Detroit area are listed.

48115 ■ "Cream of the crop" in *BlackEnterprise* **(Vol. 31, No. 10, May 2001, pp. 47)**
Pub: Earl Graves Publishing Co.
Ed: Paula McCoy-Pinderhughes, Roger Barnes. **Description:** The theme of the sixth annual Black Enterprise/Bank of America Entrepreneurs Conference is "Leading in a Changing Economy: Innovation, Transformation, Growth". The Black Enterprise Small Business Awards categories include Emerging Company of the Year, Business Innovator of the Year, the Rising Star Award, and the Kidpreneurs Award. Statistical data included.

48116 ■ "Creating human links" in *Black Enterprise* **(Vol. 33, No. 3, October 2002, pp. 66)**
Pub: Earl Graves Publishing Co.
Ed: Shani Smothers. **Description:** Founder of Youth LINKS USA, Alicia R. Jones, helps to eradicate technical literacy for youth in the Detroit, Michigan area. Jones offers training in software programs and A certification for computer repair up to the Microsoft Certified Engineer Training.

48117 ■ "Cropping Up" in *Hispanic Business* **(May 2005, pp. 14)**
Pub: Hispanic Business
Description: Pennsylvania State University established the new Latino Agricultural Center that will work to develop agricultural educational resources and offer a Spanish class for agricultural professionals.

48118 ■ "Cruise Control: Yacht Captain Charts Luxury Liners" in *Black Enterprise* **(Vol. 35, August 2004, No. 1, pp. 63)**
Pub: Earl G. Graves Publishing Co. Inc.
Ed: Maureen Jenkins. Description: Profile of David Linnear, yacht captain for an upscale yacht charter company which sails from Lake Michigan harbors. Linnear is just one of 13 African American Coast Guard licensed merchant marine captains in the U.S. The firm owns a fleet of four vessels and prices start at $500, depending on vessel's size, cruise destination, and type of amenities chosen.

48119 ■ "Cultural Access Moves into Medical Research" in *Hispanic Business* **(Vol. 23, No. 5, May 2001, pp. 6)**
Pub: Hispanic Business
Description: Cultural Access Group, a multicultural marketing firm, hired Raul Lopez to manage its new Miami office.

48120 ■ "Culture Cash" in *Hispanic Business* **(June 2005, pp. 86)**
Pub: Hispanic Business
Ed: Keith Rosenblum. Description: Distributors are using ethnicity as a means to grow their businesses.

48121 ■ "Cutting the layoff line" in *Black Enterprise* **(Vol. 32, No. 5, December 2001, pp. 22)**
Pub: Earl Graves Publishing Co.
Ed: K. Terrell Reed. Description: An overview of black-owned broadcasting companies and how they have avoided the mass layoffs and hiring freezes plaguing other media companies.

48122 ■ "DaimlerChrysler AG wants to double minority purchases" in *Crain's Detroit Business* **(Vol. 16, No. 21, May 22, 2000, pp. 45)**
Pub: Crain Communications, Inc.
Ed: Michael Woodyard. Description: The automaker is joining with Comerica Inc. and ASG Renaissance to develop business plans for 52 minority suppliers, 30 of which will be from the metropolitan Detroit area.

48123 ■ "The Dangers of a Lack of Accountability" in *Automotive News* **(Vol. 20, October 4, 2004, No. 40, pp. 8)**
Pub: Crain Communications Inc.
Ed: Keith Crain. Description: Plans for developing a downtown district, called African Town, in Detroit that would fund money to black-owned businesses is discussed. Many individuals claim the plan is both discriminatory and illegal.

48124 ■ "De la Torre Named to Hall of Fame" in *Hispanic Business* **(Vol. 23, No. 5, May 2001, pp. 20)**
Pub: Hispanic Business
Description: Profile of Martha C. de la Torre, publisher of the Southern California Spanish language weekly El Clasificado. Ms. de la Torre was inducted into the National Association of Women Business Owners Hall of Fame in March 2001.

48125 ■ "Dealt a double blow" in *Hispanic Business* **(Vol. 22, No. 10, October 2000, pp. 20)**
Pub: Hispanic Business
Ed: Patricia Guadalupe. Description: The alleged misuse of the Small Business Administration's (SBA) funds and the lack of contracts awarded to minority firms are examined. An audit of the SBA criticizes its spending of $22 million on certification of only 3,000 firms.

48126 ■ "Dear white boss; What it's really like to be a black manager" in *Harvard Business Review* **(Vol. 80, No. 11, November 2002, pp. 76)**
Pub: Harvard Business School Press
Description: This fictional letter describes what it is like to be different in the workplace and sheds light on the sometimes subtle and often systemic racial biases in the corporate world.

48127 ■ "Demand surges in manufacturing" in *Hispanic Business* **(Vol. 22, No. 6, June 2000, pp. 106)**
Pub: Hispanic Business
Ed: Christopher D. Lancette, Scott Williams, Joel Russell. Description: Hispanic-owned automotive powertrain maker UniBoring Company Inc. ranks 33rd in the Hispanic Business 500 table with revenues totaling $110 million in 1999. The company's growth is due to the strong economic climate in the U.S., says CEO Facundo Bravo.

48128 ■ "Destination" in *Hispanic Business* **(June 2005, pp. 92)**
Pub: Hispanic Business
Ed: Joel Russell. Description: According to the National Automobile Dealers Association, car dealers reported an average of 2.2 percent in revenue gains for 2004. Hispanic car dealers are using the superstore concept to promote growth.

48129 ■ "Detroit Public Schools Pick IT Firms" in *Crain's Detroit Business* **(Vol. 22, December 18, 2006, No. 51, pp. 18)**
Pub: Crain Communications Inc. - Detroit
Ed: Tom Henderson. Description: Vision IT was retained by the City of Detroit for a five year contract at $9.8M per year. Vision IT was one of five minority owned firms picked to share five year, $58M contracts previously held by Comcast and Strategic Staffing. Three of the contracts were rescinded after a protest over the bidding process and results was filed by the previous contractors.

48130 ■ "Detroit schools bond program sets standard for minority work" in *Crain's Detroit Business* **(Vol. 19, No. 13, March 31, 2003, pp. 20)**
Pub: Crain Communications Inc., Detroit
Ed: Laura Bailey. Description: Forty-six percent of the work completed on the Detroit Public School's $1.5 billion building program has gone to minority-owned businesses, higher than the traditional 30 percent goal for construction projects.

48131 ■ "A different kind of service" in *BlackEnterprise* **(Vol. 32, No. 3, October 2001, pp. 54)**
Pub: Earl Graves Publishing Co.
Ed: Quincy L. Lewis. Description: Profile of Reginald Ball, who served as a Secret Service agent for the U.S. Treasury Department. Ball has created RB Industries, a general-line industrial products distribution company based in Sterling Heights, Michigan.

48132 ■ "Discrimination's new name" in *Hispanic Business* **(Vol. 22, No. 9, September 2000, pp. 12)**
Pub: Hispanic Business
Ed: Christopher Lancette. Description: Issues concerning the exclusion of Hispanic contractors from the minority-contracting program of the Memphis School Board, Tennessee, is discussed.

48133 ■ "Diversity Defined" in *Hispanic Business* **(January/February 2003, pp. 64, 66)**
Pub: Hispanic Business
Description: Results of the Hispanic Business Corporate Diversity Survey show that diversity is defined in different terms from company to company. In a recent online poll, IBM was named the country's number one company for providing opportunity to minority-owned firms. A listing of corporations seeking multicultural and bilingual workers is included.

48134 ■ "The Diversity Game" in *Forbes* **(Vol. 170, No. 12, December 9, 2002, pp. 140)**
Pub: Forbes Magazine
Ed: Tomas Kellner. Description: Information about the Small Business Administration's Section 8(a) program and its reform are examined. The program was created by President Nixon to foster black capitalism and sets aside up to $6 billion a year worth of government contracts for small companies owned by minorities or women.

48135 ■ "A Diversity Plan Turns 100" in *Hispanic Business* **(September 2003, pp. 30, 32)**
Pub: Hispanic Business
Ed: Gina Binole. Description: Ford Motor Company has prospered for 100 years by marketing to the Hispanic market. James Padilla, president of Ford's North American production, discusses the fact that Ford Motor Company understands the power of the Hispanic consumer and the importance of the Hispanic business owner.

48136 ■ "Dollars for Scholars" in *Hispanic Business* **(September 2003, pp. 64, 66, 68)**
Pub: Hispanic Business
Description: A select guide to scholarships for the study of business or law is presented.

48137 ■ "Driving Change on the Car Lot" in *Hispanic Business* **(Vol. 24, No. 4, April 2002, pp. 24)**
Pub: Hispanic Business Inc.
Ed: Tim Dougherty. Description: Ford hopes to increase its ranks of Hispanic auto dealers through a new, innovative partnership. Statistical data is presented showing the number of dealers per manufacturer, with GM leading the way with 122 auto dealers.

48138 ■ "E-Ticket in the Caribbean" in *Hispanic Business* **(Vol. 23, No. 7/8, July/August 2001, pp. 68)**
Pub: Hispanic Business
Ed: Abel Magana. Description: Overview of 'The Leadership Forum for Hispanics in the New Economy', held in San Juan, Puerto Rico in April 2001. The event was the first Hispanic Internet Summit.

48139 ■ "Eateries team up for clout" in *Black Enterprise* **(Vol. 31, No. 5, December 2000, pp. 170)**
Pub: Earl Graves Publishing Co.
Ed: Ann Brown. Description: Black restaurant association wants to help owners grow their businesses.

48140 ■ "Eight Black Physicians Partnered to Open an International House of Pancakes in Harlem..." in *Black Enterprise* **(Vol. 35, Dec. 2004)**
Pub: Earl G. Graves Publishing Co. Inc.
Ed: Nkechi Olisemeka. Description: In its first month of operation, a restaurant opened by eight African American doctors is ranked 14th in sales among the International House of Pancakes franchises. The franchise has 1,167 franchises located throughout 48 states and Canada.

48141 ■ "8(a) Advantage or Disadvantage?" in *Hispanic Business* **(March 2003, pp. 60)**
Pub: Hispanic Business
Description: The advantages and disadvantages of participating in the Small Business Administration's program are discussed by a few Hispanic small business owners currently contracting with the U.S. government.

48142 ■ "80 Elite Hispanic Women Directory" in *Hispanic Business* **(Vol. 24, No. 4, Apr. 2002, pp. 32)**
Pub: Hispanic Business Inc.
Description: A listing the 80 successful Hispanic women listed on the Hispanic Women Directory. A brief profile of each is included.

48143 ■ "Elite Company" in *Hispanic Business* **(December 2002, pp. 54)**
Pub: Hispanic Business
Description: The four finalists in the Hispanic Business magazine's Entrepreneur of the Year award are profiled. The finalists hail from the aerospace, auto retailing, and telecommunications industries.

48144 ■ "Entravision Acquires Three L.A. Stations" in *Hispanic Business* **(March 2003, pp. 20)**
Pub: Hispanic Business
Description: Entravision, upon regulatory approval, will acquire three radio stations in the greater Los Angeles area serving the Hispanic market. Statistical data included.

48145 ■ "Entrepreneurial Enthusiasm" in *Black Enterprise* **(Vol. 34, No. 7, February 2004, pp. 32)**
Pub: Earl Graves Publishing Co.
Ed: Carolyn M. Brown. Description: Approximately 41 percent of American youth feel that owning a business will provide more security than working for a company, and 81 percent believe there is more job satisfaction owning your own company rather working for someone else.

48146 ■ *The Entrepreneurial Process: Economic Growth, Men, Women & Minorities*
Pub: Greenwood Publishing Group, Inc.
Ed: Paul D. Reynolds and Sammis B. White. Released: 1997. Price: $59.95 (cloth).

48147 ■ "Entrepreneurs Have Accepted the Challenge" in *Hispanic Business* **(Vol. 23, No. 11, November 2001, pp. 30, 32)**
Pub: Hispanic Business Inc.
Description: Highlights from the Eleventh Annual Hispanic Business Magazine Entrepreneur of the Year Award ceremony are presented.

48148 ■ "Entrepreneurs Under Siege" in *Hispanic Business* **(Vol. 23, No. 11, November 2001, pp. 36-37)**
Pub: Hispanic Business Inc.
Ed: Tim Dougherty. Description: The terrorist attacks in Washington and New York have cast a pall over small business community nationwide. Experts are divided on long-term forecasts and what the federal government's response should be to small business.

48149 ■ "Entrepreneurship on the Rise" in *Home Business* **(Vol. 12, March/April 2005, No. 2, pp. 44)**
Pub: Home Business Magazine
Description: According to a study by the Office of Advocacy of the U.S. Small Business Administration, entrepreneurship for women, blacks, and Latinos has risen from 1979 to 2003.

48150 ■ "Ethnic Enterprises and their Clientele" in *Journal of Small Business Management* **(Vol. 38, No. 2, April 2000, pp. 48)**
Pub: West Virginia University
Ed: Linda M. Dyer, Christopher A. Ross. Description: An examination of the relationships between ethnic-minority businesses and their co-ethnic customers is given.

48151 ■ "An Evening with the Brain Trust" in *Hispanic Business* **(October 2003, pp. 40)**
Pub: Hispanic Business
Description: Academics, diplomats, investors, and CEOs come together to discuss public policy at the U.S. Hispanic Economic Summit, hosted at the Organization of American States in the Hall of the Americas.

48152 ■ "Ex-Tiger adds trucking company to his lineup" in *Crain's Detroit Business* **(Vol. 16, No. 9, February 28, 2000, pp. 1)**
Pub: Crain Communications, Inc.
Ed: Terry Kosdrosky. Description: Former Detroit Tiger Cecil Fielder is moving back to Detroit. Cecil will be in charge of developing new business for minority trucking firm, Betz Trucking.

48153 ■ "Experienced players in the new economy" in *Hispanic Business* **(Vol. 22, No. 7-8, July-August 2000, pp. 40)**
Pub: Hispanic Business
Ed: Joel Russell. Description: A directory of the top 50 Hispanic American technology businesses is presented, ranked by revenue.

48154 ■ "Fade to Black" in *Black Enterprise* **(Vol. 31, No. 5, December 2000, pp. 107)**
Pub: Earl Graves Publishing Co.
Ed: George Alexander. Description: Black filmmakers make the most profitable movies, but still fight for dollars and respect.

48155 ■ "Fast Change for Lopez Foods" in *Hispanic Business* **(January/February 2004, pp. 58, 60)**
Pub: Hispanic Business
Description: Profile of John Lopez, owner of the 13th largest Hispanic-owned company in the U.S. Lopez Foods produces meat products for McDonald's and Wal-Mart.

48156 ■ "Feature Filmdom" in *Hispanic Business* **(March 2004, pp. 16)**
Pub: Hispanic Business
Description: Profile of Fernando Espuelas, who is launching a feature-film division called VOY Pictures LLC. Espuelas hopes to establish the firm as a hub for Latino film in Hollywood and tap into the growing English-language Hispanic film market.

48157 ■ "FedBizOpps Opens for Biz" in *Hispanic Business* **(Vol. 23, No. 10, October, 2001, pp. 24)**
Pub: Hispanic Business
Ed: Derek Reveron. Description: The Federal Acquisition Regulation Council (FARC), has set up a Web site providing information on all government contracts worth $25,000 or more. The FARC oversees government procurement. As of October 1, 2001, all government agencies will post procurement notices on the site, and several links to other helpful sites are included.

48158 ■ "Federal File: News & Developments in the Business of Government" in *Hispanic Business* **(December 2001, pp. FG4, FG6, FG14, FG16)**
Pub: Hispanic Business
Description: The Department of Agriculture has an Outreach Office that helps socially disadvantaged farmers and farm workers gain access to federal programs. Federal government employment opportunities for minorities are presented with a listing of internship opportunities. Hispanic entrepreneurs owning 8(a) firms secured 14.4 percent of federal contracts for fiscal year 2000.

48159 ■ "Federated Department Stores Inc." in *Black Enterprise* **(Vol. 34, No. 4, November 2003, pp. 62)**
Pub: Earl Graves Publishing Co.
Description: Profile of William L. Hawthorne III, newly elected vice president/diversity and deputy general counsel of Federated Department Stores Inc., located in Cincinnati, Ohio.

48160 ■ "The 51 percent rule fallout" in *Hispanic Business* **(Vol. 22, No. 3, March 2000, pp. 40)**
Pub: Hispanic Business
Ed: Derek Reveron. Description: The decision of the National Minority Supplier Development Council to alter the minority status of businesses is examined. Minority status will now be given to companies with 30 percent of their non-voting stock owned by minorities compared with 51 percent previously.

48161 ■ "The 51 Percent Solution" in *Hispanic Business* **(Vol. 21, No. 12, December 1999, pp. 74)**
Pub: Hispanic Business
Ed: Joel Russell. Description: The National Minority Supplier Development Council board has postponed a vote on whether to alter the definition of a minority-owned firm. This change has been opposed by the U.S. Hispanic Chamber of Commerce and other groups.

48162 ■ "Film Producer Has Activist's Heart" in *Hispanic Business* **(Vol. 24, No. 5, May 2002, pp. 16)**
Pub: Hispanic Business Inc.
Ed: Rick Laezman. Description: Profile of David Valdes who says he wants to concentrate on Hispanic-themed films.

48163 ■ "Financial services welcome the good times" in *Hispanic Business* **(Vol. 22, No. 6, June 2000, pp. 104)**
Pub: Hispanic Business

48164 ■ "Focus on Fundraising" in *Black Enterprise* **(Vol. 35, September 2004, No. 2, pp. 63)**
Pub: Earl G. Graves Publishing Co. Inc.
Ed: Sonia Alleyne. Description: Advice is given to a black woman pursuing a business management career organizing fundraising events.

48165 ■ "Focus on emerging markets" in *Black Enterprise* **(Vol. 32, No. April 2002, 9, pp. 30)**
Pub: Earl Graves Publishing Co.
Ed: Matthew S. Scott. Description: Presentation of trends in the minority community, focusing on publicly traded companies pursuing the minority marketplace, are minority-owned, and are southeast-based large- and mid-cap companies.

48166 ■ "Food For Thought" in *Black Enterprise* **(Vol. 34, No. 3, October 2003, pp. 20)**
Pub: Earl Graves Publishing Co.
Ed: Latif Lewis. Description: Profile of Charles "Chuck" James III, owner of the 120-year-old family business, C.H. James & Company. James has partnered with Goldman Sachs Urban Investment Group to assess potential acquisitions in the food processing industry. James hopes to increase the presence of minority firms in the area of supplier diversity.

48167 ■ "Food Industry Veteran Has It His Way" in *Black Enterprise* **(Vol. 35, February 2005, No. 7, pp. 36)**
Pub: Earl G. Graves Publishing Co. Inc.
Ed: Latif Lewis. Description: Charles H. James III became Burger King's largest African American franchise. James now owns 37 stores in the Chicago area. Profile of James is included.

48168 ■ "Franchise to go: despite a recession some of these businesses are hot" in *Black Enterprise* **(Vol. 32, No. 9, April 2002, pp. 46)**
Pub: Earl Graves Publishing Co.
Ed: Alan Hughes. Description: The advantages of buying a franchise business are examined. Recommendations for choosing a franchise are also discussed.

48169 ■ "The Franchising Formula" in *Hispanic Business* **(Vol. 22, No. 5, May 2000, pp. 60)**
Pub: Hispanic Business
Ed: Vivienne Heins, Scott Williams. Description: It has become increasingly common for Hispanic Americans to become involved in franchising ventures. Successful franchise operations are profiled, including Kentucky Fried Chicken, Minuteman Press, and U-Save Auto Rental.

48170 ■ "Franchising" in *Hispanic Business* **(Vol. 23, No. 5, May 2001, pp. 50)**
Pub: Hispanic Business
Description: The International Franchise Association reports the need to educate emerging entrepreneurs about the 75 various industries offering franchise opportunities to Hispanics.

48171 ■ "Franchising: Model of Success" in *Hispanic Business* **(September 2004, pp. 90)**
Pub: Hispanic Business
Ed: Monica Valencia. Description: Hispanics are a growing force for the franchise industry. Many Hispanics choose franchising because of the business model already provided.

48172 ■ "Friends in High Places" in *Hispanic Business* **(Vol. 23, No. 7/8, July/August 2001, pp. 62, 64)**
Pub: Hispanic Business
Ed: Scott Williams. Description: Profile of the newly formed Hispanic Network of Entrepreneurs. The

Ed: Christopher Lancette, Scott Williams, Joel Russell. Description: Hispanic-owned equipment leasing company, Somerset Capital Group, is 89th in the Hispanic Business 500 table and had revenues totaling $48 million in 1999.

group hopes to ease the way for a new generation of Hispanic entrepreneurs in the high-tech industry, business development, venture capital financing, recruiting and exchange of ideas.

48173 ■ "From Barracks to Boardroom" in *Hispanic Business* **(Vol. 24, No. 1/2, January/February 2002, pp. 59-60)**
Pub: Hispanic Business Inc.
Ed: Vivienne Heines. **Description:** Because of the technical training and education received during military service, many recruits are developing a work ethic proven to improve employment prospects.

48174 ■ "From Real Estate to Retirement Plan" in *Black Enterprise* **(Vol. 34, No. 3, October 2003, pp. 29)**
Pub: Earl Graves Publishing Co.
Ed: Carmen Brown. **Description:** Profile of Bradley Simmons, the 40-year-old English teacher, who was encouraged by his brother, a real estate entrepreneur to switch careers and open Bestrow Realty in Harlem, New York. Simmons offers financial planning advice.

48175 ■ "Frontier Online" in *Business Week* **(No. 3694, August 14, 2000, pp. F8)**
Pub: McGraw-Hill, Inc.
Description: The number of federal contracts awarded to small businesses dropped by 23 percent from 1997 to 1999, from 6.4 million to 4.9 million, with minority- and women-owned companies hardest hit.

48176 ■ "Full-Court Press" in *Hispanic Business* **(May 2005, pp. 20, 22)**
Pub: Hispanic Business
Ed: Kevin Brass. **Description:** Business publishers are aggressively targeting the Hispanic executive market to grow circulation of their business magazines. These publications include Hispanic Business, Latin Trade, Latino Leaders, Poder, and Hispanic Trends.

48177 ■ "Future brightens for the inner city" in *Hispanic Business* **(Vol. 22, No. 6, June 2000, pp. 32)**
Pub: Hispanic Business
Ed: Andrea Siedsma. **Description:** Latino Initiatives for the Next Century is a non-profit organization aimed at helping Hispanic communities and businesses to join in the redevelopment of inner-city neighborhoods. The agency will invest $300 million in such projects.

48178 ■ "The Future of Franchising: Taking Advantage of the Changing Complexion of the American Economy" in *Black Enterprise* **(Vol. 32, No. 2)**
Pub: Earl Graves Publishing Co.
Ed: C. Everett Wallace. **Description:** Franchising remains one of the fastest growing segments of the American business economy. The article addresses the potential business franchise opportunity in minority communities with information for the following franchises: Jan-Pro Cleaning Systems, AAMCO Transmissions, SIGN-A-RAMA, Chick-fil-A, Sunoco Inc., Kumon Math and Reading Centers, Choice Hotels, Liberty Tax Service, Dunhill Staffing Systems Inc., The Athlete's Foot, KFC, Meineke, Denny's, Subway, Coverall Cleaning Concepts, Church's Chicken, and Wendy's.

48179 ■ "Getting the Corner Office" in *Black Enterprise* **(Vol. 35, August 2004, No. 1, pp. 78)**
Pub: Earl G. Graves Publishing Co. Inc.
Ed: Maureen Jenkins. **Description:** Profiles of African American women who have been successful in various businesses.

48180 ■ "Getting a Leg up: Montemayor y Asociados Partners with Web-Hed Technologies" in *Hispanic Business* **(Vol. 22, No. 5, May 2000, pp. 18)**
Pub: Hispanic Business
Ed: Teresa Talerico. **Description:** Web development and hosting venture Web-Hed Technologies Inc. has formed a joint venture with advertising firm Montemayor y Asociados. Through this arrangement, Montemayor will be able to offer clients an extensive range of Web-Hed's interactive services.

48181 ■ "Getting a Piece of the Federal Pie" in *Hispanic Business* **(Vol. 23, No. 7/8, July/August 2001, pp. 38)**
Pub: Hispanic Business
Ed: Joel Russell. **Description:** The number of large Hispanic high-tech firms that sell to the federal government has dropped by half in the last five years.

48182 ■ "Giving Where It Counts: Blackgiving.com Lets Consumers Choose Their Charities" in *Black Enterprise* **(Vol. 34, July 2004, No. 12)**
Pub: Earl G. Graves Publishing Co. Inc.
Ed: Anthony S. Calypso. **Description:** Profile of Blackgiving.com, developed by Vince Martin. The site is designed to reach African Americans and helps fund charitable causes that already exist.

48183 ■ "Global financing options" in *BlackEnterprise* **(Vol. 31, No. 8, March 2001, pp. 48)**
Pub: Earl Graves Publishing Co.
Ed: Paula McCoy-Pinderhughes. **Description:** Small business services provided by the Export-Import Banks of the United States, are profiled. The Export-Import (Ex-Im) Bank of the U.S. is an independent government agency that offers a number of financing options to minority- and women-owned export companies, including credit insurance and working capital guarantees on commercial loans.

48184 ■ "Going digital for dollars" in *Black Enterprise* **(Vol. 33, No. 3, October 2002, pp. 145)**
Pub: Earl Graves Publishing Co.
Ed: Bernadette Williams. **Description:** The future of electronic commerce is discussed, including ways information technology can be used in the vision, creativity, and long-term planning for small business entrepreneurs. Security issues to protect small businesses, joint marketing between firms selling a similar product or service, and ways for African American small business owners can target their markets.

48185 ■ "Going Private: How VCs Can Get in the Game" in *Venture Capital Journal* **(Vol. 42, No. 10, October 2002, pp. 49)**
Pub: Thomas Venture Economics
Ed: Jonathan Bell. **Description:** A trend towards venture capital firms to reverse course and help companies go private is examined. To minimize the risk that the transaction may be questionable as being unfair to minority shareholders, an independent and disinterested committee of the company's board should handle negotiations.

48186 ■ "Gonzales and Lizarraga Speak Out" in *Hispanic Business* **(January/February 2003, pp. 20, 22)**
Pub: Hispanic Business
Ed: Joel Russell. **Description:** A new coalition of 130 local chambers have created the Coalition of Hispanic Chambers of Commerce for Fairness and Inclusion, in the hopes of changing the U.S. Hispanic Chamber of Commerce.

48187 ■ "Gonzales Names PepsiCo VP" in *Hispanic Business* **(Vol. 23, No. 11, November 2001, pp. 20)**
Pub: Hispanic Business Inc.
Ed: Teresa Talerico. **Description:** Profile of David Gonzales, vice president of community affairs at PepsiCo. Throughout his career, Gonzales has worked to ensure that minority-owned businesses have contract and vending opportunities with PepsiCo.

48188 ■ *Greater Phoenix Chamber Membership List—Minority-Owned or Operated Businesses*
Pub: Greater Phoenix Chamber of Commerce
Price: $25, members; $30, nonmembers. **Covers:** 295 minority-owned or operated businesses in the greater Phoenix, Arizona area. **Entries Include:** Contact details.

48189 ■ "Growing From the Middle" in *Hispanic Business* **(July/August 2004, pp. 20, 22, 24)**
Pub: Hispanic Business
Ed: Joel Russell. **Description:** Medium-sized companies have become a powerful force in economic development. These companies have balanced expansion strategies and financial stability, and many are Hispanic-owned.

48190 ■ "Growing Influence" in *Hispanic Business* **(January/February 2005, pp. 18, 20)**
Pub: Hispanic Business
Ed: Craig Mauro. **Description:** Increasing political clout and attention will help Hispanic small business and lead to immigration reform.

48191 ■ "A Growing Market for Talk" in *Hispanic Business* **(Vol. 24, No. 4, April 2002, pp. 22)**
Pub: Hispanic Business Inc.
Ed: Rick Laezman. **Description:** The Hispanic public-speaking industry has entered a growth mode, and Hispanic motivational speakers are finding corporations, associations and schools eager to hire them.

48192 ■ "Growing Representation?" in *Hispanic Business* **(Vol. 24, No. 1/2, January/February 2002, pp. 28, 30)**
Pub: Hispanic Business Inc.
Description: Corporate boards have more Hispanic members in 2002, but the article questions whether the increase is reflective of a trend or just better survey data used. A listing of the 2002 Hispanic Business Boardroom Elite is presented. Statistical data included.

48193 ■ "Growth Amid Uncertainty" in *Hispanic Business* **(Vol. 23, No. 11, November 2001, pp. 12)**
Pub: Hispanic Business Inc.
Ed: Patricia Guadalupe. **Description:** The theme for the annual MED Week gathering of minority entrepreneurs was: Strategies for Growth in the American Economy. Federal officials discussed ways for minority entrepreneurs to expand their businesses in the aftermath of September 11. Forecasts for various industries were presented.

48194 ■ "The Growth of Minority Car Dealerships" in *Minority Business Journal* **(Vol. 17, No. 5, September/October 2001, pp. 3, 6-7)**
Pub: Minority Business Journal
Ed: Nicholas R. Hunter. **Description:** Today auto manufacturers work to draw not only minority buyers for their vehicles, but also for minorities to buy their dealerships to sell automobiles. Small profiles are given on successful minority dealers throughout the country, as well as information about Ford's Minority Retailer Development Program and the Ford Dealership Office Management Training Program.

48195 ■ "Guarded About the Hispanic Economy" in *Hispanic Business* **(Vol. 24, No. 5, May 2002, pp. 18, 20, 22, 25)**
Pub: Hispanic Business Inc.
Description: Although the U.S. economy is expected to continue its slow recovery, some forecast worsening Hispanic joblessness, declining revenues for Hispanic-owned firms, and a drop-off in U.S.-Latin American trade.

48196 ■ "The 'Guerrilla' Approach" in *Hispanic Business* **(July/August 2004, pp. 28)**
Pub: Hispanic Business
Ed: Anthony Limon. **Description:** Profile of Jorge Granados, owner of the Miami-based telecommunications provider Latin Node Inc. The firm listed revenue growth of 107,993 percent from 1999 to 2003.

48197 ■ "Guzman to Head CHCC" in *Hispanic Business* **(December 2001, pp. 14)**
Pub: Hispanic Business
Description: Profile of Melinda Guzman, the first woman elected president of the California Hispanic Chambers of Commerce. Ms. Guzman recently won the Luminary Award for business leadership from the National Association of Women Business Owners.

48198 ■ "A Hand Up: Urban, Minority Entrepreneurs are Hotter Than Ever-So Where is Their Funding?" in *Entrepreneur* **(Vol. 31, Sept. 2003)**
Pub: Entrepreneur Media, Inc.
Ed: Joshua Kurlantzick. **Description:** Venture capitalists and large financial institutions are investing in minority-owned companies, although smaller banks are cutting commitments to African-American owned firms.

48199 ■ "Handicapping the Hispanic Economy" in *Hispanic Business* **(November 2002, pp. 18-20)**
Pub: Hispanic Business
Description: The future trends in elections, labor, international trade, technology education and banking access to loans are discussed by experts.

48200 ■ "Handing it over: businesses need a plan for passing the torch" in *Black Enterprise* **(Vol. 32, No. 8, March 2002, pp. 50)**
Pub: Earl Graves Publishing Co.
Ed: Alan Hughes. **Description:** A listing of things a sole proprietor should consider before having a succession plan drawn up for a business is presented. According to the U.S. Census Bureau, nearly 90 percent of the 823,500 African American-owned businesses in 1997, were sole proprietorships.

48201 ■ "Have a Talent for Sales?" in *Black Enterprise* **(Vol. 36, November 2005, No. 4, pp. 60)**
Pub: Earl G. Graves Publishing Co. Inc.
Ed: Eve Tahmincioglu. **Description:** African American women are looking towards direct-selling as a means of empowerment and selling products targeted to African Americans. Our Own Image is a firm that sells Afrocentric products ranging from decor items to cosmetics.

48202 ■ "HB Diversity Stock Index" in *Hispanic Business* **(December 2006, pp. 10)**
Pub: Hispanic Business
Description: Listing of top 45 Hispanic businesses shows stock symbol and values from January 3 to November 6, 2006, along with percent of change.

48203 ■ "Head of the class" in *Black Enterprise* **(Vol. 32, No. 10, May 2002)**
Pub: Earl Graves Publishing Co.
Ed: Sonja D. Brown. **Description:** The editors have identified 12 companies that rank among the top guns of small business.

48204 ■ "Headed for the Web" in *Hispanic Business* **(Vol. 22, No. 6, June 2000, pp. 158)**
Pub: Hispanic Business
Description: The Association of Hispanic Advertising Agencies, meeting in Puerto Rico, has been told that Hispanics are enthusiastically embracing the Internet as an advertising medium.

48205 ■ "Heading Up in a Down Year" in *Hispanic Business* **(June 2002, pp. 38, 40, 42)**
Pub: Hispanic Business
Description: Revenue for the Hispanic Business 500 grew 10.9 percent in 2001, despite an economic slowdown in the U.S. Statistical data included.

48206 ■ "Health service heats ups" in *Hispanic Business* **(Vol. 22, No. 6, June 2000, pp. 108)**
Pub: Hispanic Business
Ed: Christopher D. Lancette, Scott Williams, Joel Russell. **Description:** Hispanic-owned hospital company Pan American Hospital/Pan American Medical Centers ranks sixth in the Hispanic Business 500 tables, with revenues of $339.28 million in 1999. The company owes most of its growth to a deal with United Health Care.

48207 ■ "Healthy prospects" in *Black Enterprise* **(Vol. 32, No. 9, April 2002, pp.)**
Pub: Earl Graves Publishing Co.
Ed: Wendy Pelle-Beer. **Description:** Profile of Juanita Simmons, owner of an exercise studio, who

worked through the StoreWorks program to purchase a new building for her studio. StoreWorks is a collaborative partnership between the Neighborhood Housing Services Community Development Corp., the City of New York's Department of Housing Preservation and Development, the Department of Housing and Urban Development, and participating private lenders; available only in New York City.

48208 ■ "Hedging Its Bets" in *Hispanic Business* **(October 2003, pp. 44, 46, 48)**
Pub: Hispanic Business
Ed: Derek Reveron. **Description:** Global Partners Group (GPG) launches an innovated program to create the next generation of hedge fund managers. GPG is based in Fort Lauderdale, Florida and is Hispanic-owned.

48209 ■ "A heritage of success" in *Hispanic Business* **(Vol. 22, No. 3, March 2000, pp. 18)**
Pub: Hispanic Business
Ed: Patricia Guadalupe. **Description:** The forward planning and management information techniques put in place by Ed Fernandez, founder of Sherikon Inc., enabled the company to continue trading successfully following his sudden death in a plane crash. The importance of management information systems are discussed.

48210 ■ "Herman J. Russell Passes Torch" in *Black Enterprise* **(Vol. 34, No. 6, January 2004, pp. 19)**
Pub: Earl Graves Publishing Co.
Ed: Tamara E. Holmes. **Description:** Herman J. Russell, founder and CEO of H.J. Russell & Company, one of the nation's largest black-owned firms, has stepped down. Russell's youngest son, Michael, will take over day-to-day operations while the elder Russell remains chairman.

48211 ■ "Hey, you can't do that!" in *BlackEnterprise* **(Vol. 31, No. 7, February 2001, pp. 57)**
Pub: Earl Graves Publishing Co.
Ed: Bridget McCrea. **Description:** Profile of Edward Russell and Nicholas Stracick, partners in the company All Pro Sports Camps, Inc. After two years of presentations to the Walt Disney Company, Disney rejected the partners plans for a multi-use sports complex to be built in Orlando, Florida. The article shows how this small business went up against Disney and won.

48212 ■ "High designs: the architect's career is taking flight" in *Black Enterprise* **(Vol. 33, No. 3, October 2002, pp. 74)**
Pub: Earl Graves Publishing Co.
Ed: Christina Morgan. **Description:** Profile of Chauncey Tucker, architectural consultant in charge of the design, development and maintenance of new and existing plans for LaGuardia, Newark, and Teterboro airports for the Port Authority of New York and New Jersey.

48213 ■ "Hire Diversity: Diversity Leaders" in *Hispanic Business* **(October 2004, pp. 130)**
Pub: Hispanic Business
Description: A listing of top corporations dedicated to workplace diversity and seeking multicultural and bilingual employees is presented.

48214 ■ "His stand on football: Reginald Rutledge creates a stadium rush" in *Black Enterprise* **(Vol. 33, No. 6, January 2003, pp. 89)**
Pub: Earl Graves Publishing Co.
Ed: Sonia Alleyne. **Description:** Profile of Reginald Rutledge, telecommunications engineer in Texas. Rutledge has been building miniature football stadiums for years, and now sells his creations to clients that include the NFL Players Association, the NCAA, as well as private collectors.

48215 ■ "Hispanic Auto Dealers Form Group" in *Hispanic Business* **(Vol. 24, No. 4, April 2002, pp. 14)**
Pub: Hispanic Business Inc.
Description: The National Hispanic Automobile Dealers Association was formed to address long-standing industry inequalities and lack of access to capital.

48216 ■ "Hispanic Banking Initiatives" in *Hispanic Business* **(October 2002, pp. 14)**
Pub: Hispanic Business
Description: Harris Bank, in the Chicago, Illinois area, is piloting a new program to assist Hispanic customers who are seeking loans, but have no credit history.

48217 ■ "Hispanic Business 100 Influentials" in *Hispanic Business* **(October 2003)**
Pub: Hispanic Business
Description: Members of the Hispanic Business 100 Most Influential Hispanics for 2003 are profiled. As Hispanic leaders reach new levels of success and status, they dispel stereotypes and set the precedent for further progress.

48218 ■ "Hispanic Business 500 Directory" in *Hispanic Business* **(June 2005)**
Pub: Hispanic Business
Description: Directory of the Hispanic 500 Business is presented. The directory includes company name and location, CEO, type of business, number of employees, year started, and 2004 revenue. Statistical data included.

48219 ■ "The Hispanic Business 500" in *Hispanic Business* **(June 2002, pp. 44, 46, 48, 50, 52, 54, 56, 58, 60, 62, 64)**
Pub: Hispanic Business
Description: A listing of the Hispanic Business 500 is presented. Burt Automotive became the largest Hispanic company in the U.S. for 2002, with revenues of almost $1.5 billion.

48220 ■ "The Hispanic Business 2002 Top 50 Exporters" in *Hispanic Business* **(November 2002, pp. 38-39)**
Pub: Hispanic Business
Description: A listing of the top 50 Hispanic companies exporting goods includes ranking, company name and location, CEO, number of employees, number of Hispanic employees, 2001 revenues, revenue from exports, 2001 export sales, 2000 export sales, 2000-2001 export sales growth percentages, products or services, and destination.

48221 ■ "Hispanic Business Fastest-Growing 100" in *Hispanic Business* **(July/August 2004, pp. 30, 32, 34)**
Pub: Hispanic Business
Description: A listing of Hispanic Business' top 100 Hispanic-owned companies. These companies highlight niche-market success in a moderate-growth economy. Statistical data includes sales growth 1999-2003, gross sales, profit range, number of employees, and year founded.

48222 ■ "Hispanic Business Stock Index Debuts" in *Hispanic Business* **(March 2003, pp. 12, 14)**
Pub: Hispanic Business
Ed: Juan Solana, Joel Russell. **Description:** Hispan-Telligence, a research unit of Hispanic Business Inc. has developed the Hispanic Business Stock Index (HBSI) to track countries or industries to provide a barometer of conditions for firms in the U.S. Hispanic market. Statistical data included.

48223 ■ "Hispanic Business Top 50 Companies for Diversity" in *Hispanic Business* **(September 2006, pp. 32-34)**
Pub: Hispanic Business
Ed: Jenn Holmes. **Description:** Hispanic influence on the American corporate world is explored. Statistical data included.

48224 ■ "Hispanic Business - Woman of the Year: Making the Case for Small Business" in *Hispanic Business* **(March 2003, pp. 26-28)**
Pub: Hispanic Business
Ed: Patricia Guadalupe. **Description:** Profile of Congresswoman Nydia Velazquez, Hispanic Business magazine's first Woman of the Year. Velazquez is known for her uncompromising advocacy on behalf of small businesses.

48225 ■ "Hispanic Chamber of Commerce creates venture fund" in *Wall Street Journal* (February 22, 2000, pp. B2)
Pub: Dow Jones & Co., Inc.
Ed: Paulette Thomas. Description: Statistical information regarding the venture fund created by the Hispanic Chamber of Commerce is cited.

48226 ■ "Hispanic women taking the reins" in *Hispanic Business* (Vol. 22, No. 6, June 2000, pp. 118)
Pub: Hispanic Business
Ed: Jim Medina. Description: The number of U.S.-based, Hispanic women-owned companies grew by 205.6 percent between 1987 and 1996, according to the National Foundation for Women Business Owners. Their annual sales for the period reached $67.3 billion.

48227 ■ "HispanicBusiness.com, AOL Team Up" in *Hispanic Business* (Vol. 23, No. 7/8, July/August 2001, pp. 72)
Pub: Hispanic Business
Ed: Jeanette Jaramillo. Description: The Hispanic Business magazine Web site will supply content for the new Latino channel on AOL. The Web site will feature a national online directory of Hispanic-owned businesses, a searchable database for visitors to access business service providers from a range of industries or location, daily news, magazine articles, stock recommendations, a career center, and research on the Hispanic market.

48228 ■ "HispanicBusiness.com Expands" in *Hispanic Business* (Vol. 23, No. 5, May 2001, pp. 18)
Pub: Hispanic Business
Description: HispanicBusiness.com, the official Web site of Hispanic Business magazine, has launched a series of online and offline initiatives designed to reposition the site as a full-service resource center.

48229 ■ "Hispanics who write the checks" in *Hispanic Business* (Vol. 22, No. 11, November 2000, pp. 74)
Pub: Hispanic Business
Ed: James E. Garcia. Description: A discussion concerning the donations made to political parties by Hispanic American businessmen. The growing importance of minorities in politics and the interest of political parties in the Hispanic vote are discussed.

48230 ■ "Hispanics Gravitating Toward the 'Net" in *Hispanic Business* (March 2003, pp. 24)
Pub: Hispanic Business
Description: According to a recent study called the America Online/Roper ASW U.S. Hispanic Cyberstudy, 48 percent of Hispanic Internet users have gone online in the last two years. Statistical data included.

48231 ■ "Hispanics Now Top Minority" in *Hispanic Business* (March 2003, pp. 16)
Pub: Hispanic Business
Description: According to the 2000 U.S. Census, Hispanics are now the nation's largest minority group, surpassing African Americans.

48232 ■ "Hispanics on Wall Street" in *Hispanic Business* (Vol. 23, No. 10, October, 2001, pp. 14)
Pub: Hispanic Business
Ed: Vivienne Heines. Description: The New America Alliance held an October 2001 Wall Street Summit in New York City. The primary goal of the summit is to bridge the gap between Wall Street and the Hispanic community. The New America Alliance is dedicated to promoting the well-being of the U.S. Hispanic community, with an emphasis on education, economic and political empowerment, strategic philanthropy, and public-policy advocacy.

48233 ■ "Hispantelligence quarterly" in *Hispanic Business* (March 2003, pp. 10)
Pub: Hispanic Business
Description: The Hispanic Business Stock Index and Stock Market Indexes are compared, as well as a presentation of trade statistics and macroeconomic statistics.

48234 ■ "Hispantelligence Report" in *Hispanic Business* (January/February 2004, pp. 8)
Pub: Hispanic Business
Description: Stock market indexes compared to Hispanic companies, changes in Hispanic occupations and Hispanic employment by the numbers is presented. Statistical data included.

48235 ■ "Hispantelligence Reports" in *Hispanic Business* (June 2005, pp. 12)
Pub: Hispanic Business
Description: Presentation of the Hispanic Business Stock Index shows the current value of thirteen Hispanic companies from January 3 through April 21, 2005. Growth for Hispanic-owned businesses is reflected in a graph showing numbers from years 1987 through 2010.

48236 ■ "Hit Discriminators Where it Hurts" in *Black Enterprise* (Vol. 34, No. 4, November 2003, pp. 28)
Pub: Earl Graves Publishing Co.
Ed: Darrell Williams. Description: African American consumers account for 5 percent of all U.S. consumer spending and 4 percent of Gross Domestic Product, making them a powerful force in the U.S. economy. However, black consumers believe they are still greeted with suspicion about intentions and skepticism about ability to pay.

48237 ■ "A Home Court Advantage" in *Hispanic Business* (Vol. 23, No. 11, November 2001, pp. 38, 40)
Pub: Hispanic Business Inc.
Ed: Vivienne Heines. Description: The new American Airlines Center in Dallas, Texas will set a new standard for minority participation in construction and operations. American Airlines has been recognized as a model for its commitment to minority- and women-owned businesses, which won contracts totaling more than $94 million during the sports center's construction.

48238 ■ "Home Sweet Equity" in *Hispanic Business* (October 2004, pp. 102, 104, 106)
Pub: Hispanic Business
Ed: John Cox. Description: Increasing homeownership rates are becoming a new source of capital for Hispanic entrepreneurs. Home equity loans in the Hispanic community have grown to 5.3 percent in 2001, up from 4 percent in 1993. Statistical data included.

48239 ■ "The Honored Few" in *Hispanic Business* (January/February 2004, pp. 48-50)
Pub: Hispanic Business
Description: Hispanics hold 69 board seats at Fortune 500 corporations, totaling about 1.6 percent of the available seats.

48240 ■ *How to Be an Entrepreneur and Keep Your Sanity: The African-American Guide to Owning, Building and Maintaining Successfully Your Own Small Business*
Pub: Amber Books
Ed: Paula McCoy Pinderhughes. Released: May 2004. Price: $14.95. Description: Ten easy steps to becoming a successful African-American entrepreneur.

48241 ■ "How to beat the big-box retailers" in *Hispanic Business* (Vol. 22, No. 6, June 2000, pp. 110)
Pub: Hispanic Business
Ed: Christopher D. Lancette, Scott Williams, Joel Russell. Description: Hispanic-owned hardware reseller Analytical Computer Services ranks 114th in the Hispanic Business 500 table with revenues totaling $33.6 million in 1999.

48242 ■ "How They Did It" in *Crain's Detroit Business* (Vol. 19, No. 13, March 31, 2003, pp. 20)
Pub: Crain Communications Inc., Detroit
Ed: Laura Bailey. Description: The Detroit Public School system was able to get minority-owned and Detroit-based businesses to invest in its $1.5 billion building program.

48243 ■ "Howard University's School of Communications has Been Named After John H. Johnson" in *Black Enterprise* (Vol. 34, No. 6, January 2004)
Pub: Earl Graves Publishing Co.
Ed: Carolyn M. Brown. Description: John H. Johnson, publisher and chairman of Johnson Publishing Company has been honored by Howard University, with the university's School of Communication being named after him. Johnson Publishing is the largest black-owned publishing company in America.

48244 ■ "Hungry for Success" in *Black Enterprise* (Vol. 34, No. 7, February 2004, pp. 137)
Pub: Earl Graves Publishing Co.
Ed: Alfred A. Edmond, Jr. Description: Advice is given to a young African American man who wants to own a food distribution company.

48245 ■ "IBOC Grows in Oklahoma" in *Hispanic Business* (September 2004, pp. 20)
Pub: Hispanic Business
Description: International Bancshares Corporation (IBOC), Hispanic-owned, acquired Local Financial Corporation. The deal sets IBOC's assets at nearly $9.5 billion on a pro forma basis.

48246 ■ "Immigration Reform, Latin American Trade Issues Piled on Congress's Plate" in *Hispanic Business* (November 2006, pp. 24)
Pub: Hispanic Business
Ed: Patricia Guadalupe. Description: Immigration and trade issues with Latin American countries and Mexico are discussed.

48247 ■ "The Impact of Immigrant Entrepreneurs" in *Business Week* (February 7, 2007)
Pub: McGraw-Hill Companies
Ed: Kerry Miller. Description: Overview of immigrant entrepreneur's impact on economic development and their status as a driving force for the U.S. economy.

48248 ■ "In the Black" in *Hispanic Business* (May 2005, pp. 18)
Pub: Hispanic Business
Ed: Joel Russell. Description: Projected surpluses brighten the future outlook for the U.S. Hispanic Chamber of Commerce. Statistical data included.

48249 ■ "Ink turns crimson at Clover" in *Crain's Detroit Business* (Vol. 19, No. 4, January 27, 2003, pp. 3)
Pub: Crain Communications Inc., Detroit
Ed: Andrew Dietderich. Description: Minority-owned Clover Technologies Inc., located in Wixom, Michigan has ceased operations. The firm is liquidating assets in order to pay secured lenders.

48250 ■ "The inn crowd" in *Black Enterprise* (Vol. 32, No. 5, December 2001, pp. 126)
Pub: Earl Graves Publishing Co.
Ed: Lee Anna Jackson. Description: An overview of black-owned bed and breakfast establishments in America. Information is provided for joining the African American Association of Innkeepers International.

48251 ■ "Inspiring Black Investors" in *Black Enterprise* (Vol. 35, January 2005, No. 6, pp. 58)
Pub: Earl G. Graves Publishing Co. Inc.
Ed: Derek T. Dingle. Description: Profile of John W. Rogers Jr., owner of Airel Capital Management, one of the most powerful firms on Wall Street. In 1983, Rogers launched his first family of equity mutual funds managed by African Americans.

48252 ■ "Investors Buy Michigan Chronicle Parent Firm" in *Crain's Detroit Business* (Vol. 19, No. 4, January 27, 2003, pp. 18)
Pub: Crain Communications Inc., Detroit
Ed: Jennette Smith. Description: Real Times LLC has acquired the Michigan Chronicle, the Chicago Defender, New Pittsburgh Courier and the Memphis Tri-State Defender, all African-American newspapers.

48253 ■ "Jackson CEO: company growing from within" in *Atlanta Business Chronicle* (Vol. 25, No. 20, October 25, 2002, pp. 26A)
Pub: American City Business Publications, Inc.
Ed: Meredith Jordan. Description: Profile of Jackson Securities Inc. Reuben McDaniel III, president and CEO of Jackson Securities, an investment banking concern and is owned by former Atlanta, Georgia mayor, Maynard Jackson, is the only company that covers all publicly traded minority companies.

48254 ■ "Java anyone?" in *Black Enterprise* (Vol. 31, No. 5, December 2000, pp. 178)
Pub: Earl Graves Publishing Co.
Ed: Ann Brown. Description: A comprehensive list of coffeehouses owned by African Americans.

48255 ■ "J.C. Watts First Black John Deere Dealer" in *Black Enterprise* (Vol. 37, November 2006, No. 4, pp. 36)
Pub: Earl G. Graves Publishing Co. Inc.
Ed: Kiara Ashanti. Description: Profile of former Congressman J.C. Watts Jr., a man who grew up in rural America and is the first African American to own a John Deere Dealership.

48256 ■ "J.D. Power Study: Hispanics Prefer Imports" in *Hispanic Business* (March 2003, pp. 18)
Pub: Hispanic Business
Description: Hispanics, the largest minority group in America, prefer purchasing imported vehicles, according to a study performed by J.D. Power and Associates. The study also showed Hispanics rate fuel economy, price, and resale values much higher than non-Hispanic buyers.

48257 ■ "John Deere Named In Discrimination Suit" in *Black Enterprise* (Vol. 35, August 2004, No. 1, pp. 30)
Pub: Earl G. Graves Publishing Co. Inc.
Ed: Aisha Jefferson. Description: After working for John Deere for 30 years, Kenny Edwards wanted to become an entrepreneur by purchasing his own John Deere agricultural dealership. Edwards has sued the company for discrimination when it turned down his bid for ownership. Of the 1,400 John Deere agricultural dealerships in the U.S. non are African-American owned, and only 5 percent of owners include women, Hispanics, and Asians.

48258 ■ "John Ladaga" in *Hispanic Business* (January/February 2005, pp. 56)
Pub: Hispanic Business
Description: Profile of John Ladaga, vice president and general manager service delivery for EDS America discusses his company's diversity program in detail.

48259 ■ "Keep on Truckin'" in *Hispanic Business* (Vol. 23, No. 11, November 2001, pp. 56-58)
Pub: Hispanic Business Inc.
Ed: Ralph Gray. Description: Today's Hispanic CEOs prefer sports utility vehicles. A profile of trucks, particularly upscale sport utility vehicles from brands like Cadillac, Lexus, BMW, and Lincoln are profiled. Statistical data included.

48260 ■ "Keeping America safe" in *Black Enterprise* (Vol. 32, No. 5, Decembe)
Pub: Earl Graves Publishing Co.
Ed: Michelle Buckley. Description: Profile of Reginald Daniel and his 1996 startup, Scientific & Engineering Solutions Information Technology consulting firm. Daniel was designated this year's Ernst & Young's IT Consulting Entrepreneur of the Year from Maryland, and National Black Chamber of Commerce name him Entrepreneur of the Year.

48261 ■ "Keeping it all in the family" in *BlackEnterprise* (Vol. 31, No. 6, January 2001, pp. 40)
Pub: Earl Graves Publishing Co.
Ed: Glenn Townes. Description: The importance of having a succession plan for a business is stressed and advice is given to develop such a plan.

48262 ■ "Keeping It All in the Family" in *Black Enterprise* (Vol. 31, No. 5, December 2000, pp. 66)
Pub: Earl Graves Publishing Co.
Ed: Glenn Townes. Description: Profile of James Olan Hutcheson, founder and president of ReGeneration Partners, offers advice in handling the future of family-owned businesses.

48263 ■ "KeyCorp Named Top SBA Lender" in *Hispanic Business* (January/February 2003, pp. 14)
Pub: Hispanic Business
Description: KeyCorp was named top minority business lender by the Cleveland District Office of the U.S. Small Business Administration for fiscal year ending September 30, 2002.

48264 ■ "Kid-Friendly Business Sources" in *Black Enterprise* (Vol. 37, January 2007, No. 6, pp. 40)
Pub: Earl G. Graves Publishing Co. Inc.
Ed: Carolyn M. Brown. Description: Financial or business camps are a great way to encourage a child who interested in starting his or her own business. A number of these camps are available each year including Kidpreneurs Conference and Bull and Bear Investment Camp. Other resources are available online. Resources included.

48265 ■ "Kid from the capital makes good" in *Hispanic Business* (Vol. 22, No. 11, November 2000, pp. 20)
Pub: Hispanic Business
Ed: Derek Reveron. Description: The lifestyle, political career and entrepreneurship of Raul Fernandez is profiled. His founding of the Internet based company Proxicom Inc. in 1991 is discussed.

48266 ■ "Latinas' Businesses and Earnings are Seeing Major Growth" in *Marketing to Women* (Vol. 19, October 2006, No. 10, pp. 2)
Pub: EPM Communications, Inc.
Description: According to Hispanic Business Inc., Hispanic woman-owned businesses grew 64 percent between 1997 and 2004. Latinas' median incomes also grew. Statistical data included.

48267 ■ "Latinocare Goes Public" in *Hispanic Business* (June 2002, pp. 28)
Pub: Hispanic Business
Description: LatinoCare Management Corporation, a medical manager network, has become a publicly traded company. The Hispanic firm is located in Southern California.

48268 ■ "A launching point to the next step" in *Hispanic Business* (Vol. 22, No. 6, June 2000, pp. 42)
Pub: Hispanic Business
Ed: Derek Reveron. Description: Potomac Management Group Inc., founded as a part-time information technology and logistics consultancy by Dennis Garcia in 1992, has won a $22 million, 5-year contract from the U.S. Coast Guard. The company expects revenues to reach over $8 million in 2000.

48269 ■ "LBA event draws a crowd" in *Hispanic Business* (Vol. 22, No. 11, November 2000, pp. 14)
Pub: Hispanic Business
Ed: Andrea Siedsma. Description: A presentation of events at the Latino Business Expo in September 2000, organized by the Latin Business Association, showing the growth of Hispanic American businesses.

48270 ■ "Leaders Prepare for Lean Times" in *Hispanic Business* (Vol. 23, No. 11, November 2001, pp. 14)
Pub: Hispanic Business Inc.
Ed: Mark Hagland. Description: Terrorism and business development were the topics at the 19th Annual United States Hispanic Leadership Institute (USHLI) conference, held September 27-30 in Chicago, Illinois. Juan Andrade, President of the USHLI, feels that the focus on terrorism will interfere with effective business development growth.

48271 ■ "Leading the Way" in *Black Enterprise* (Vol. 35, February 2005, No. 7, pp. 57)
Pub: Earl G. Graves Publishing Co. Inc.
Ed: Bridget McCrea. Description: Profile of Lisa Williams, one of a few African American women leaders in the high-tech logistics and supply management field. Williams' firm conducts original research and offers technology services to help clients move information, goods, and capital within and between organizations.

48272 ■ "Lessons from the 8(A) Leaders" in *Hispanic Business* (March 2005, pp. 54, 56)
Pub: Hispanic Business
Ed: Jonathan J. Higuera. Description: Hispanic contractors are finding more opportunity in the U.S. government's 8(a) minority business development program. Top Hispanic 8(a) companies are listed.

48273 ■ "Listening for opportunity" in *Hispanic Business* (Vol. 22, No. 9, September 2000, pp. 16)
Pub: Hispanic Business
Ed: Peter Brennan. Description: Internet-based firm, Globe-1, assists minority companies to compete for government agency contracts by offering help in the procurement of contracts.

48274 ■ "Living the Lifestyle of the Successful Businessperson" in *Hispanic Business* (March 2005, pp. 62)
Pub: Hispanic Business
Ed: Leslie A. Westbrook. Description: Profile of Watsonville Mayor, Ana Ventura Phares. Her father is the former vice-president of harvesting at Dole.

48275 ■ "Loan Stars" in *Hispanic Business* (March 2004, pp. 38, 40)
Pub: Hispanic Business
Ed: Johanna Knapschaefer. Description: From micro-loans to Small Business Administration (SBA) programs, banks are slowly waking up to the possibilities of the Hispanic market.

48276 ■ "Looking ahead" in *Black Enterprise* (Vol. 32, No. , , pp.)
Pub: Earl Graves Publishing Co.
Description: A discussion exploring the future of Glory Foods Inc. since the death of its co-founder and president, William F. Williams. Glory Foods is a distributor of prepackaged soul food.

48277 ■ "Looking for a bull market" in *BlackEnterprise* (Vol. 32, No. 3, October 2001, pp. 38)
Pub: Earl Graves Publishing Co.
Ed: Nicole Halsey. Description: African American mutual funds are growing as the slow market recovery continues. A brief overview of the Ariel Appreciation (CAAPX) and Ariel (ARGFX) Funds, Brown Capital Management Small Co. Fund (BCSIX), as well as the DEM Equity Investor Fund (DEMEX) is presented. The DEM fund invests in companies owned or controlled by women, African, Hispanic, Asian, and Native Americans, and is managed by Nathan A. Chapman Jr., president of Chapman Capital Management in Baltimore, Maryland.

48278 ■ "A Macro View at Microsoft" in *Hispanic Business* (January/February 2005, pp. 24, 26, 28)
Pub: Hispanic Business
Ed: Judi Erickson. Description: Orlando Ayala is targeting small and mid-size companies around the world to increase the global reach of technology firm Microsoft. Orlando discusses marketing strategies for selling Microsoft Business Solutions worldwide.

48279 ■ "Maintaining Momentum" in *Hispanic Business* (October 2003, pp. 86)
Pub: Hispanic Business
Description: Profile of Jamie Gutierrez Vela, president of Midwest Maintenance Company, reporting sales that have more than tripled in the last five years. Ms. Gutierrez was named entrepreneur of the year by the University of Nebraska's Center for Entrepreneurship.

48280 ■ "Major League Baseball Signs Partnership Pacts" in *Hispanic Business* (March 2002, pp. 12)
Pub: Hispanic Business
Description: Major League Baseball has signed an agreement with the National Minority Supplier Development Council and Women's Business Enterprise National Council, as part of its Diverse Business Partners Program. The program is intended to cultivate partnerships with minority- and women-owned companies.

48281 ■ "The Major Leagues: Have Front-Office Positions Opened Up for Blacks?" in *Black Enterprise* (Vol. 37, February 2007, No. 7, pp.)
Pub: Earl G. Graves Publishing Co. Inc.
Ed: Alexis McCombs. **Description:** Major leave sports teams are hiring more African Americans to manage and coach teams. Statistical data included.

48282 ■ *Major Studies of Minority Business: A Bibliographic Review*
Pub: Joint Center for Political and Economic Studies, Inc.
Ed: Timothy Bates. **Released:** 1992. **Price:** $42.50.

48283 ■ "Making Entrepreneurship Job One" in *Black Enterprise* (Vol. 32, No. 10, May 2002, pp. 12)
Pub: Earl Graves Publishing Co.
Ed: Earl G. Graves Sr. **Description:** The state of minority-owned businesses is discussed. Statistical data included.

48284 ■ "Making strides, but losing ground?" in *Black Enterprise* (Vol. 32, No. April 2002, 9, pp. 30)
Pub: Earl Graves Publishing Co.
Ed: Alan Hughes. **Description:** Female minority-owned businesses are growing at a greater rate than all women-owned firms with Hispanics leading the way, and African American next, then Asian and lastly Native American.

48285 ■ "The Man Who Started It All" in *Hispanic Business* (January/February 2003, pp. 24, 26)
Pub: Hispanic Business
Description: In an interview, David Lizarraga, answers questions about his role as new leader of the Coalition of Hispanic Chambers for Fairness and Inclusion.

48286 ■ "Mazda's Minority Dealers" in *Minority Business Journal* (Vol. 17, No. 5, September/October 2001, pp. 2)
Pub: Minority Business Journal
Description: Mazda hosts the Second Minority Dealer Symposium at Dillard University, a privately held, historically black liberal arts institution. An overview of the current state of Mazda was presented to the minority dealers.

48287 ■ "MBDA's new horizons" in *Hispanic Business* (Vol. 22, No. 11, November 2000, pp. 18)
Pub: Hispanic Business
Ed: Patricia Guadalupe. **Description:** Issues are presented concerning the report by the Minority Business Development Agency in 2000, which revealed rapid growth in the expansion of Hispanic American businesses to $1-trillion in 1998 from $700-billion in 1990.

48288 ■ "Medical Emergency" in *Hispanic Business* (May 2005, pp. 76, 78)
Pub: Hispanic Business
Ed: Susan Kreimer. **Description:** The U. S. healthcare industry is struggling to meet the needs of hiring enough qualified Hispanic professionals including nurses, doctors, administrative staff, executives, and emergency personnel. Statistical data included.

48289 ■ "A Melting Pot with Flavor" in *Hispanic Business* (December 2003, pp. 20-21)
Pub: Hispanic Business

Description: Convergence of the Hispanic population with mainstream American culture has created a unique market for the future. To understand the cultural dynamics of the market, researchers have divided the population using a quadrant system; an example of the cultural matrix is provided.

48290 ■ "Merger Fever" in *Hispanic Business* (Vol. 23, No. 10, October, 2001, pp. 42, 44)
Pub: Hispanic Business
Ed: Derek Reveron. **Description:** Hispanic advertising agencies are becoming increasingly attractive takeover targets for international conglomerates, because of the growing confidence in the market. It is predicted that the Spanish-speaking population will become a more powerful force in industry growth.

48291 ■ "Mexican Industries Goes Under" in *Hispanic Business* (Vol. 23, No. 10, October, 2001, pp. 28, 30)
Pub: Hispanic Business
Ed: Jonathan J. Higuera.. **Description:** Profile of the Hispanic-owned automotive supplier Mexican Industries, which filed for bankruptcy in early 2001. The Detroit-based company was founded by former Major Leaguer Hank Aguirre, and was being run by his three daughters and one son when it filed for Chapter 11. According to Yolanda Gomez-Stupka, president of the Michigan Hispanic Chamber of Commerce, portions of Mexican Industries may survive, but the company will not be the same.

48292 ■ "Mexican grocery gets wired" in *Hispanic Business* (Vol. 22, No. 5, May 2000, pp. 14)
Pub: Hispanic Business
Ed: Andrea Siedsma. **Description:** Mexgrocer.com, due to launch on May 5, 2000, will be the first online grocery to focus exclusively on Mexican food. It will target middle- to upper-income Hispanics, mainly Mexican Americans.

48293 ■ "Miami's Royal Palm Sells for $127.5 M" in *Black Enterprise* (Vol. 35, February 2005, No. 7, pp. 38)
Pub: Earl G. Graves Publishing Co. Inc.
Ed: Tamara Holmes. **Description:** Royal Palm Crowne Plaza Resort, the black-owned luxury hotel in Miami, Florida, was sold to The Falor Company for $127.5 million. Details of the transaction are included.

48294 ■ "Microsoft Sees 'Untapped Territory'" in *Hispanic Business* (Vol. 23, No. 5, May 2001, pp. 46)
Pub: Hispanic Business
Ed: Jim Medina. **Description:** Small minority-owned businesses are being offered free technology workshops by Microsoft Corporation, through October 2001.

48295 ■ "Might of the roundtable" in *Hispanic Business* (Vol. 22, No. 6, June 2000, pp. 22)
Pub: Hispanic Business
Ed: Janet Perez. **Description:** The Minority Business Roundtable is a newly formed advocacy group aimed at providing a unified public voice for minority-controlled and owned corporations across the U.S.

48296 ■ "Milwaukee Businesswoman Opens Plus-Size Clothing Store to Fill Need" in *Milwaukee Journal Sentinel* (November 16, 2003)
Pub: Journal Sentinel
Ed: Tannette Johnson-Elie. **Description:** Profile of Cynthia Simpson, a plus-size African American woman who opened a store to meet the shopping needs of larger women, focusing on African American women who prefer trendy clothing with an Afrocentric flair.

48297 ■ "Minorities meet opportunities" in *Hispanic Business* (Vol. 22, No. 9, September 2000, pp. 14)
Pub: Hispanic Business
Ed: Scott Williams. **Description:** The marketing expertise of the National Minority Supplier Development Council and the purchasing power of the Latin Business Association have been combined at the Latino Business Expo, held in Los Angeles, California.

48298 ■ "Minorities Push to Keep Supplier Program" in *Plastics News* (Vol. 16, July 12, 2004, No. 19, pp. 10)
Pub: Crain Communications Inc.
Ed: Terry Kosdrosky. **Description:** Minority suppliers are interviewed, discussing the U.S. automakers' purchasing program. These suppliers are urging automakers to develop more rigorous auditing policies for minority purchasing and to establish consequences for Tier 1 suppliers that fall short of goals.

48299 ■ "Minority Architects Say Reaching Out to Youth Will Help Add Diversity" in *Crain's Detroit Business* (Vol.16, No.31,July 31,2000, pp.35)
Pub: Crain Communications, Inc.
Ed: Jennette Smith. **Description:** Detroit-area minority architects are reaching out to raise awareness to women, youth, and minorities in this white-male dominated profession.

48300 ■ "Minority Banks are Called to Account" in *Inc.* (October 1, 2003)
Pub: Gruner & Jahr USA Publishing
Ed: Patrick J. Sauer. **Description:** California's Chinese banks come under fire for discrimination. These banks help immigrants to become entrepreneurs, but do not lend enough to African Americans or Latinos.

48301 ■ "Minority Banks are Thriving: Deposits Jumped 213 percent in Five Years" in *Atlanta Business Chronicle* (Vol. 25, Jan. 10, 2003, pp.1A)
Pub: American City Business Publications, Inc.
Ed: Meredith Jordan. **Description:** According to the Federal Reserve Bank, Georgia's minority-owned banks have experienced robust growth in the past five years, outpacing even state and national banks. For example, Capitol City Bank and Trust deposits have grown 218 percent since 1997.

48302 ■ "Minority Biz of the Year" in *Hispanic Business* (March 2002, pp. 10)
Pub: Hispanic Business
Description: A. Anthony Corp. was honored by the Upstate New York Regional Minority Purchasing Council as the Minority Supplier of the Year.

48303 ■ *Minority Business Development Agency—Directory of Regional & District Offices and Funded Organizations*
Pub: U.S. Minority Business Development Agency
Covers: about 9 regional and district offices of the Minority Business Development Agency; approximately 73 agency-funded minority business development centers which offer business services for a nominal fee to current and prospective minority business operators. **Entries Include:** For regional offices—Office name, address, phone, states served, director name. For district offices—Office address and phone, names of district officers. For development centers—Center name, address, phone, project director name. **Arrangement:** Separate geographical lists for regional offices, district offices, and development centers.

48304 ■ "Minority Business Group Looks to Cement Ties with Foreign Automakers" in *Crain's Detroit Business* (Vol. 19, No. 40, October 13, 2003)
Pub: Crain Communications Inc., Detroit
Ed: Terry Kosdrosky. **Description:** The Michigan Minority Business Development Council has changed its by-laws to include foreign-owned automakers as board members. The change is hoped to forge closer ties between member auto suppliers and foreign-owned automakers.

48305 ■ "Minority Businesses Look For a Boost From Super Bowl and Beyond" in *Crain's Detroit Business* (Vol. 21, October 10, 2005, No. 43)
Pub: Crain Communications Inc. - Detroit
Ed: Sheena Harrison. **Description:** Minority and women business owners are capitalizing on the opportunities presented by the Super Bowl XL coming to Detroit, Michigan. More than 1,100 of these companies have applied or are participating in the Super

Bowl's Emerging Business Program open to any certified minority- or woman-owned firm in the state. It also provides training and networking to help compete in contracts.

48306 ■ "Minority Certification Needs Examination" in *Crain's Detroit Business* **(Vol. 18, No. 20, May 20, 2002, pp. 8)**
Pub: Crain Communications Inc. - Detroit
Description: Commitments by automakers and large suppliers from minority-owned firms has helped them to grow and to get some of that business, the smaller minority-owned businesses have often formed partnerships or joint ventures with larger, non-minority firms, thus helping the smaller to grow.

48307 ■ *Minority Enterprise in the Nineties: A Questionable Future?*
Pub: Babson College
Ed: Rudy Winston, editor. **Released:** 1992.

48308 ■ "Minority-Owned Businesses Up" in *Inc.* **(April 2000, pp. 145)**
Pub: The Goldhirsh Group
Ed: Christopher Caggiano. **Description:** The rising economic tide of the 1990s helped minority-owned business in America. The U.S. Small Business Administration estimates that the number of minority-owned businesses more than doubled from 1987 to 1997, from a quarter million to a half million businesses, and that the revenues they collectively generated grew more than fourfold.

48309 ■ "Minority Report" in *Entrepreneur* **(Vol. 32, October 2004, No. 10, pp. 59)**
Pub: Entrepreneur Media Inc.
Ed: C.J. Prince. **Description:** Historically, women and minority-owned businesses have received less venture capital, with only 4.2 percent of all venture capital in 2003 going to women-led companies. The Kauffman Fellows Program educates and trains future venture capitalists and is led by 14 fellows, eight of which are from minority groups (two are black, five are Asian, and one is Middle Eastern, three are women).

48310 ■ "A Minority Role in the Homeland" in *Hispanic Business* **(November 2002, pp. 22-23)**
Pub: Hispanic Business
Ed: Patricia Guadalupe. **Description:** The role of small minority-owned businesses was discussed at the annual Minority Enterprise Development Week conference. Some fear that the current homeland security proposals will erode opportunity for federal contracting for small minority-owned firms.

48311 ■ "Missing Part of the Equation" in *Hispanic Business* **(July/August 2002, pp. 50, 52, 54)**
Pub: Hispanic Business
Ed: Dora Elia, Gonzalez y Musielak. **Description:** Hispanic women continue to be underrepresented in the sciences and engineering fields. Statistical data included.

48312 ■ "Mixed Fate for Black Law Firms" in *Black Enterprise* **(Vol. 34, No. 4, November 2003, pp. 27)**
Pub: Earl Graves Publishing Co.
Ed: Cliff Hocker. **Description:** Of the 12 original law firms highlighted in an August 1993 issue of Black Enterprise, only one-fourth are still operating. Profiles of the existing firms are included.

48313 ■ "A Model Chamber Tackles Complex Issues" in *Hispanic Business* **(July/August 2002, pp. 64-66)**
Pub: Hispanic Business
Ed: Joel Russell. **Description:** The Mexican American Network of Odessa (MANO), Texas shows how local leadership can make a difference for constituent businesses. Profile of Iris Correa, executive director of the model Hispanic chamber is also highlighted.

48314 ■ "Money Rules" in *Hispanic Business* **(September 2004, pp. 34-36, 38, 40, 42)**
Pub: Hispanic Business

Ed: Joel Russell. **Description:** Profile of Roel Campos, the first Hispanic to serve on the Securities and Exchange Commission. Campos wants major investment banks to provide more business loans to minority-owned small businesses in the U.S.

48315 ■ "More steady growth: Hispanic ad expenditures increase 11 percent to reach nearly $1.9 billion" in *Hispanic Business* **(Dec. 1999, pp.56)**
Pub: Hispanic Business
Ed: Tim Dougherty. **Description:** Expansion in Hispanic advertising expenditures slowed to 11 percent in 1999, from 21 percent in 1998. However, the Top 50 Advertiser total rose 30 percent to $545.97 million. The impact of the Internet on Hispanic advertising is discussed.

48316 ■ "Mrs., Mom, and CEO" in *Black Enterprise* **(Vol. 32, No. 9, April 2)**
Pub: Earl Graves Publishing Co.
Ed: Monique R. Brown. **Description:** Profile of Vickie Clark, owner and founder of a family owned, home-based business that transports kids back and forth to various activities.

48317 ■ "Multiculturalism Grows Up" in *Hispanic Business* **(Vol. 24, No. 4, April 2002, pp. 58, 60)**
Pub: Hispanic Business Inc.
Description: An interview with Gustavo De La Torre, manager of Worldwide Diversity & Multiculture at Intel Corporation, about diversity in the workplace.

48318 ■ "The Myth of Benign 'Resistance'" in *Hispanic Business* **(Vol. 23, No. 7/8, July/August 2001, pp. 28)**
Pub: Hispanic Business
Ed: Todd Gaziano. **Description:** Government contract procurement preferences are inherently discriminatory. The U.S. government must follow the same laws that apply to everyone else. The article suggests, that programs to help the disadvantaged without regard to ethnicity are fine; those that use racial or ethnic stereotypes are not.

48319 ■ "NASA Training Program" in *Black Enterprise* **(Vol. 30, No. 10, May 2000, pp. 52)**
Pub: Earl Graves Publishing Co.
Ed: Gerda Gallop-Goodman. **Description:** Small, disadvantaged businesses learn how to vie for contracts.

48320 ■ "National Association of Black Accountants" in *Black Enterprise* **(Vol. 35, December 2004, No. 5, pp. 86)**
Pub: Earl G. Graves Publishing Co. Inc.
Description: Norman Jenkins, vice president of Marriott International Inc., was inducted as present and CEO of the National Association of Black Accounts.

48321 ■ "Netting a bigger piece of the action" in *Hispanic Business* **(Vol. 22, No. 5, May 2000, pp. 38)**
Pub: Hispanic Business
Ed: Jonathan J. Higuera. **Description:** Ways in which Hispanic businesses can use the Internet are discussed. Tejas Office Products Inc., Burt Automotive Network and Gonzalez Plumbing are profiled.

48322 ■ "Networking is a Click Away" in *Black Enterprise* **(Vol. 34, No. 6, January 2004, pp. 101)**
Pub: Earl Graves Publishing Co.
Description: Information is given for the 2004 B.E. Entrepreneurs Conference to be held May 12-16, 2004 in Dallas, Texas. Nominations are also being accepted for BE Small Business Awards.

48323 ■ "Networking for Success" in *Hispanic Business* **(Vol. 24, No. 4, April 2002, pp. 26)**
Pub: Hispanic Business Inc.
Ed: Scott Williams. **Description:** Advanced interpersonal communication skills enable women executives to climb the career ladder. Interviews with successful Hispanic women include Patricia Romero Cronin, VP at IBM; Cari Dominguez, EEOC Chair; and Rebeca Johnson, VP of ethnic and urban marketing at Frito-Lay Inc.

48324 ■ "A New Breed of Entrepreneurs" in *Black Enterprise* **(Vol. 37, November 2006, No. 4, pp. 16)**
Pub: Earl G. Graves Publishing Co. Inc.
Description: Black entrepreneurs are an important part of the chain for providing economic opportunities within the community. Many black business owners are more likely to hire black employees and apply innovative strategies in building their businesses rather than taking the traditional route.

48325 ■ "The New Chairman" in *Hispanic Business* **(January/February 2003, pp. 22, 24)**
Pub: Hispanic Business
Description: J.R. Gonzales will assume leadership of the U.S. Hispanic Chamber of Commerce. In an interview Gonzales answers questions regarding his platform as new chairman.

48326 ■ "New Detroit survey targets metro area minority business" in *Crain's Detroit Business* **(Vol. 16, No. 7, February 14, 2000, pp. 37)**
Pub: Crain Communications, Inc.
Ed: Robert Ankeny. **Description:** New Detroit Inc. has commissioned Wayne State University's Center for Urban Studies to conduct a three-year survey of how minority businesses are faring in the metro Detroit area.

48327 ■ "New Dynamic for Nonprofits" in *Hispanic Business* **(Vol. 23, No. 7/8, July/August 2001, pp. 104, 106)**
Pub: Hispanic Business
Ed: James E. Garcia. **Description:** A recent survey by Independent Sector, a national umbrella group of 700 non-profit agencies and foundations, found that Hispanic contributions have increased due to the growth of Hispanic middle class and wealthy entrepreneurs.

48328 ■ "New Face at the SBA" in *Hispanic Business* **(Vol. 23, No. 10, October, 2001, pp. 32, 34)**
Pub: Hispanic Business
Ed: Scott Williams. **Description:** Profile of Hector V. Barreto, the new administrator of the U.S. Small Business Administration (SBA), hopes to make the agency more responsive to the small-business community. Statistical data included.

48329 ■ "The new fact of HACR" in *Hispanic Business* **(Vol. 21, No. 12, December 1999, pp. 22)**
Pub: Hispanic Business
Ed: Patricia Guadalupe. **Description:** The role of the Hispanic Association on Corporate Responsibility (HACR), will collaborate with U.S. firms to identify opportunities which will allow Hispanic business activity to expand, according to Anna Escobeda Cabral, the association's new leader.

48330 ■ "New Foundation" in *Hispanic Business* **(June 2005, pp. 20)**
Pub: Hispanic Business
Description: Hispanic Advertising Agencies Foundation was created by the Association of Hispanic Advertising Agencies in an effort to fund and distribute market research related to Hispanic consumers. The foundation will also offer educational opportunities and scholarships to individuals pursuing a career in Hispanic advertising.

48331 ■ "The New Frontier" in *Hispanic Business* **(July/August 2004, pp. 36, 38)**
Pub: Hispanic Business
Ed: Joel Russell. **Description:** Television networks are offering Hispanics more option in programming. Jeff Valdez, chairman of SiTV, discusses the six years he spent convincing local cable systems there was a need for English-speaking channels to reach out to the Hispanic community.

48332 ■ "A New Game for Johnson: BET Founder Looking to Acquire Baseball Franchise" in *Black Enterprise* **(Vol. 33, No. 7, Feb. 2003, pp. 19)**
Pub: Earl Graves Publishing Co.

Ed: Cliff Hocker. **Description:** Profile of BET found and CEO Robert L. Johnson, the first African American majority owner of a Major League Baseball franchise.

48333 ■ **"New Political Players on the Scene"** in *Hispanic Business* **(January/ February 2005, pp. 14)**
Pub: Hispanic Business
Ed: Patricia Guadalupe. **Description:** Henry Cuellar, John Salazar and Luis Fortuno are the new Hispanic member of the U.S. Senate. Issues involving the Central American Free Trade Agreement (CAFTA) and visa concerns are addressed.

48334 ■ **"New TV Network on the Launch Pad"** in *Hispanic Business* **(March 2003, pp. 14)**
Pub: Hispanic Business
Description: Expresion Media Group, based in Chicago, has started sales for a new Hispanic cable television network that will launch nationally in May 2003. The network will offer both Spanish and bilingual original programming, independent films, and music features geared toward successful Hispanics between the ages of 18-49.

48335 ■ **"New Urban Entertainment shuts doors"** in *Black Enterprise* **(Vol. 33, No. 7, February 2003, pp. 20)**
Pub: Earl Graves Publishing Co.
Ed: Aisha I. Jefferson. **Description:** Profile of New Urban Entertainment TV (NUE-TV), an African American-focused cable network and how it failed to acquire much-needed financing.

48336 ■ **"A new venue for seeking capital"** in *BlackEnterprise* **(Vol. 32, No. 3, October 2001, pp. 56)**
Pub: Earl Graves Publishing Co.
Ed: Paula McCoy-Pinderhughes. **Description:** The first-ever three-day conference aimed at helping African American and other minority technology-based businesses was held in Chantilly, Fairfax County, Virginia, from July 11-13, 2001. The Emerging Business Forum (EBF) will host its second conference next fall.

48337 ■ **"New World Border"** in *Hispanic Business* **(Vol. 23, No. 7/8, July/August 2001, pp. 14)**
Pub: Hispanic Business
Ed: Scott Williams. **Description:** A group of business representatives from California, Arizona, New Mexico, and Texas have formed the non-profit Southwest Hispanic Economic Alliance (SHEA) to address Mexico/U.S. border and other issues of concern to the region's large Hispanic population.

48338 ■ **"New Wright Museum CEO: Increase Role in Schools"** in *Crain's Detroit Business* **(Vol. 22, December 11, 2006, No. 50, pp. 13)**
Pub: Crain Communications Inc. - Detroit
Ed: Sherri Begin. **Description:** African American History Museum wants to form more partnerships with schools and businesses to increase the value and quality of education in Detroit history. CEO hopes the museum will become a model for national identity.

48339 ■ **"NFL Reaches Out"** in *Crain's Detroit Business* **(Vol. 21, January 3, 2005, No. 1, pp. 12)**
Pub: Crain Communications Inc. - Detroit
Ed: Jennette Smith. **Description:** Super Bowl XL Host Committee and the National Football League have partnered to create an emerging-business program that encourages minority- and women-owned business to participate in the Super Bowl. The committee will also announce plans for a $2 million youth center to be located in Detroit.

48340 ■ **"Night of Stars"** in *Hispanic Business* **(January/February 2004, pp. 20, 22, 24)**
Pub: Hispanic Business
Ed: Joel Russell. **Description:** CEO's put on the glitz for Hispanic Business magazine's Entrepreneur of the Year Awards. The ceremony was held at the Century Plaza Hotel, located on the Avenue of the Stars, Los Angeles, California. Headline sponsors of the event included Ford Motor Company and Office Depot.

48341 ■ **"NMSDC Confab"** in *Hispanic Business* **(Vol. 23, No. 10, October, 2001, pp. 22)**
Pub: Hispanic Business
Description: The 2001 National Minority Supplier Development Council Conference and Business Opportunity Fair was held October 28-31 at the Georgia World Congress Center in Atlanta.

48342 ■ **"NMSDC Honors PepsiCo, Toyota"** in *Hispanic Business* **(January/February 2005, pp. 16)**
Pub: Hispanic Business
Description: National Minority Supplier Development Council honored PepsiCo and Toyota Motor Manufacturing North America for their increased use of minority suppliers. PepsiCo increased it's partnerships with minority suppliers by 11 percent in 2003.

48343 ■ **"No Small Change"** in *Black Enterprise* **(Vol. 32, No. 8, March 2002, pp. 64)**
Pub: Earl Graves Publishing Co.
Ed: Lee Anna Jackson. **Description:** Profile of Joyce Harris, Web page designer.

48344 ■ **"The 100 most influential Hispanics"** in *Hispanic Business* **(Vol. 22, No. 10, October 2000, pp. 30)**
Pub: Hispanic Business
Description: A list of the 100 most influential and innovative Hispanic citizens chosen by Hispanic Business magazine is presented. Their achievements, ideas and plans for their companies or sphere of influence are described.

48345 ■ **"100 Most Influential Hispanics"** in *Hispanic Business* **(October 2002, pp. 40)**
Pub: Hispanic Business
Description: The 100 most influential Hispanics chosen by Hispanic Business magazine for recent achievements having national impact are profiled. Forty-four winners are officials in federal agencies, with the rest working in state government, corporate America, nonprofits, and the entertainment or sports professions.

48346 ■ **"Open Your Books To Grow Your Business"** in *My Business* **(November/ December 2001, pp. 42)**
Pub: My Business Magazine
Ed: Shannon Scully. **Description:** Open book management (OBM), is described by its originator, Victor Ornelas owner of a Latino marketing firm in Dallas, Texas. Open book management is a company policy that requires the business owner to share the company's financial information with its employees.

48347 ■ **"The Opportunity is Knocking"** in *Black Enterprise* **(Vol. 34, No. 7, February 2004)**
Pub: Earl Graves Publishing Co.
Description: The 2004 "Black Enterprise/General Motors Entrepreneurs Conference" will be held in Dallas, Texas. This year's theme will be, "Taking Business Beyond Boundaries", and will present industry experts, venture capitalists, and entrepreneurs. The event is geared to provide information and inspiration for African American executives, professionals, entrepreneurs, and wealth-accumulators.

48348 ■ **"Opposition to Auto Group Grows"** in *Hispanic Business* **(Vol. 24, No. 5, May 2002, pp. 17)**
Pub: Hispanic Business Inc.
Ed: Tim Dougherty. **Description:** A group of Hispanic auto dealers is voicing opposition to the U.S. Hispanic Chamber of Commerce's efforts to form a national Hispanic automobile dealers association.

48349 ■ **"OSDBU Directory"** in *Hispanic Business* **(December 2002, pp. FRG12-FRG14)**
Pub: Hispanic Business
Description: Minority entrepreneurs use the Office of Small and Disadvantaged Business Utilization (OSDBU) as their first point of contact for selling products or services to the federal government. A directory of OSDBU agencies is presented. Statistical data included.

48350 ■ **"Out of the box and onto the Web"** in *Hispanic Business* **(Vol. 22, No. 6, June 2000, pp. 48)**
Pub: Hispanic Business
Ed: Vaughn Hagerty. **Description:** More than 70 percent of the largest Hispanic-owned businesses in the U.S. have an Internet presence in 2000, up from just 13.2 percent in 1996.

48351 ■ **"Paint Hustle: New Orleans Artist Went from the Streets to Mainstream"** in *Black Enterprise* **(Vol. 35, December 2004, No. 5, pp. 77)**
Pub: Earl G. Graves Publishing Co. Inc.
Ed: Sean Drakes. **Description:** Profile of Lionel Milton, artist who went from painting graffiti on public sites in New Orleans, Louisiana, to creating sets for MTVs Real World and P.Diddy's show, Making the Band. Milton relates his path to finding a niche for his artwork as an African American artist.

48352 ■ **"Panasonic Tunes In Hispanic Market"** in *Hispanic Business* **(March 2003, pp. 24)**
Pub: Hispanic Business
Description: Panasonic has started a series of print ads and television commercials featuring Spanish-language spots for their PV-DC252 Palmcorder and high-definition 42-inch plasma monitor. The article sites examples of other companies following the same trend, marketing to the Hispanic population in the U.S.

48353 ■ **"Panel to Monitor Minority Contracts"** in *Hispanic Business* **(March 2004, pp. 12)**
Pub: Hispanic Business
Ed: Patricia Guadalupe. **Description:** The National Minority Compliance Board in Washington DC will monitor corporate and governmental minority purchasing activities.

48354 ■ **"Partners in Style"** in *Hispanic Business* **(May 2005, pp. 64, 66)**
Pub: Hispanic Business
Ed: Jaime Adame. **Description:** Luis Delgado, co-founder and CEO of Samy Salon Collections, the top-selling hair care brand on the Home Shopping Network, discusses his plan to fund his company's expansion.

48355 ■ **"A Passion for the Work"** in *Hispanic Business* **(January/February 2004, pp. 30, 34)**
Pub: Hispanic Business
Ed: Scott Williams. **Description:** Members of the Corporate Elite directory credit their cultural work ethic and enthusiasm for their success.

48356 ■ *The Peebles Principles: Insights from an Entrepreneur's Life of Business Success, Making Deals, and Creating a Fortune from Scratch*
Pub: John Wiley and Sons Inc.
Ed: R. Donahue Peebles. **Released:** April 2007. **Price:** $29.99. **Description:** Successful entrepreneur shares his business experience. Peebles went from CEO of the nation's largest Black-owned real estate development firm to founding his own firm.

48357 ■ **"Penny wise, pound foolish"** in *Black Enterprise* **(Vol. 32, No. 10, May 2002, pp. 44)**
Pub: Earl Graves Publishing Co.
Ed: Alan Hughes. **Description:** The importance of maintaining separate personal and business accounts is discussed.

48358 ■ **"Perfect Storm Strikes CEOs"** in *Hispanic Business* **(Vol. 24, No. 4, April 2002, pp. 16, 18)**
Pub: Hispanic Business Inc.
Ed: Derek Reveron. **Description:** A new study shows that insurance premiums will rise during the next few years, squeezing profits and swelling the ranks of the uninsured, and small Hispanic-owned businesses and their employees are said to be among those hardest hit.

48359 ■ "Perfecting the Growth Spurt" in *Hispanic Business* (Vol. 23, No. 11, November 2001, pp. 24-25, 28)
Pub: Hispanic Business Inc.
Ed: James E. Garcia. **Description:** Profile of Juan Mencia, CEO of The Cube Corporation. The Cube Corporation provides facility management services to the federal government. Mencia was the winner of the Hispanic Business Entrepreneur of the Year 2001 Award. Brief profiles of runners up are included.

48360 ■ "Pharmed Wins for Innovation" in *Hispanic Business* (Vol. 23, No. 7/8, July/August 2001, pp. 6)
Pub: Hispanic Business
Description: The Pharmed Group, ranked 24th on the Hispanic Business 500, won the 2001 Cutting Edge Award from the Greater Miami Chamber of Commerce, for exceptional innovative business techniques.

48361 ■ "Pick a niche and fill it" in *Hispanic Business* (Vol. 22, No. 7-8, July-August 2000, pp. 44)
Pub: Hispanic Business
Description: An analysis is presented showing how Hispanic American chief executive officers have achieved fast-growing companies in slow growing industries.

48362 ■ "Picking Up the Pieces" in *Black Enterprise* (Vol. 32, No. 9, April 2002, pp. 44)
Pub: Earl Graves Publishing Co.
Ed: Bridget McCrea. **Description:** Patrick Duroseau, founder and president of Marnic Technologies, tell how he and his firm and employees are carrying on after the terrorist attacks of September 11, 2001.

48363 ■ "Pioneering Black Ad Agency Closes Doors Forever" in *Black Enterprise* (Vol. 35, August 2004, No. 1, pp. 28)
Pub: Earl G. Graves Publishing Co. Inc.
Ed: Carolyn M. Brown. **Description:** After 27 years of operation as a leading African-American owned advertising agency, the Chisholm-Mingo Group Inc. is closing its doors. Economic setbacks contributing to the 9-11 terrorist attacks contributed to the company's demise.

48364 ■ "Pioneers in a Wider World" in *Hispanic Business* (March 2003, pp. 30-31, 34, 36, 38, 40-42, 44, 46, 48, 50, 52, 54, 56-57)
Pub: Hispanic Business
Description: The list of Elite Hispanic Women documents the broadening range of female achievement and leadership, and includes a short profile of the 80 women making the list. Statistical data included.

48365 ■ "Power and Influence on the Hill" in *Hispanic Business* (March 2005, pp. 12)
Pub: Hispanic Business
Ed: Patricia Guadalupe. **Description:** Lobby groups are helping Hispanics to enjoy greater representation in Washington, D.C.

48366 ■ "Power PACs" in *Hispanic Business* (March 2005, pp. 16, 18)
Pub: Hispanic Business
Ed: Joel Russell. **Description:** Hispanic political action committees almost tripled campaign contributions to political parties during the 2003-2004 election cycle. Statistical data included.

48367 ■ "Procurement: Federal File" in *Hispanic Business* (December 2002, pp. FRG10)
Pub: Hispanic Business
Description: An overview of the Small Business Administration new PRO-Net Contractor Registration Merge program. This program will streamline contracting by helping create a single, user-friendly acquisition system.

48368 ■ "Productive Lessons from a Tech Meltdown" in *Hispanic Business* (Vol. 23, No. 7/8, July/August 2001, pp. 6)
Pub: Hispanic Business
Ed: Jesus Chavarria. **Description:** A brief look at the long-term effects of technology on the Hispanic economy, and the need to deal with Hispanics as consumers as well as entrepreneurial innovators.

48369 ■ "A Profile in Success" in *Hispanic Business* (Vol. 23, No. 5, May 2001, pp. 56)
Pub: Hispanic Business
Ed: Vivienne Heines. **Description:** A beneficiary of early career encouragement, Frank Montano inspires others to realize their potential. Mr. Montano, president and CEO of Moto Photo Inc., uses goal-setting and planning in employee training sessions.

48370 ■ "Program Boosts Minority Supplier Chain" in *Hispanic Business* (March 2003, pp. 20)
Pub: Hispanic Business
Description: Chrysler Group, Comerica Bank, and ASG Renaissance launched a new program in 2000 that increased the quality performance, productivity, and ability of minority suppliers to the automotive industry. Statistical data included.

48371 ■ "Programs" in *Black Enterprise* (Vol. 34, No. 5, December 2003, pp. S8)
Pub: Earl Graves Publishing Co.
Description: Profile of Finding Leaders Among Minorities Everywhere (FLAME) program. The program is designed to build confidence and encourage professional growth.

48372 ■ "The promise of solidarity" in *BlackEnterprise* (Vol. 32, No. 2, September 2001, pp. 14)
Pub: Earl Graves Publishing Co.
Ed: Earl G. Graves, Sr. **Description:** An overview of the political activism of minority-owned businesses in the U.S.

48373 ■ "Public companies push the envelope" in *Hispanic Business* (Vol. 22, No. 6, June 2000, pp. 116)
Pub: Hispanic Business
Ed: Christopher D. Lancette, Scott Williams, Joel Russell. **Description:** Seven of the 100 largest companies on the Hispanic Business 500 list trade as public companies. Five are from Florida, with one each from Texas and California. Most of these public companies are the result of mergers or are conglomerates.

48374 ■ "Putting the 'E' in Your Business" in *Hispanic Business* (Vol. 22, No. 5, May 2000, pp. 36)
Pub: Hispanic Business
Ed: Vaughn Hagerty. **Description:** It is important for Hispanic business enterprises to consider how electronic commerce will affect their business. It must be recognized that the Internet is now a permanent feature of the business environment.

48375 ■ "Putting Pension Funds to Work" in *Hispanic Business* (November 2003, pp. 38, 40)
Pub: Hispanic Business
Ed: Holly Ocasio Rizzo. **Description:** New America Alliance has launched an initiative to channel state pension fund money into Hispanic investment firms.

48376 ■ "Putting the brakes on transportation" in *Hispanic Business* (Vol. 22, No. 6, June 2000, pp. 112)
Pub: Hispanic Business
Ed: Christopher D. Lancette, Scott Williams, Joel Russell. **Description:** Hispanic-owned trucking company Pan American Express Inc. ranks 173rd in the Hispanic Business 500 table with 1999 revenues of almost $22.3 million. Most of the firm's growth has come from the acquisition of refrigerated trucking company Zero Motor Freight.

48377 ■ "QA: Shopping for Capital" in *Black Enterprise* (Vol. 35, January 2005, No. 6, pp. 44)
Pub: Earl G. Graves Publishing Co. Inc.
Ed: James C. Johnson. **Description:** Finding capital for a small, black-owned media company might be attained from private equity firms. Equity financing allows a business to obtain funds without incurring debt or repaying a specific amount of money at a particular time.

48378 ■ "Quicker SBA Loans" in *Business Week* (No. 3698, September 11, 2000, pp. F6)
Pub: McGraw-Hill, Inc.
Description: The Small Business Administration plans to enlarge its Community Express pilot program, which aims to streamline loan reviews for companies in low-income areas or those owned by minorities, women, or veterans.

48379 ■ "Race-Conscious Agenda: Poll Shows Most African Americans Want Affirmative Action Reform" in *Black Enterprise* (Vol. 34, Nov. 2003)
Pub: Earl Graves Publishing Co.
Ed: Marcia A. Wade. **Description:** A poll conducted in June 2003 by Black America's Political Action Committee suggests that African Americans believe affirmative action is good in principle but needs to be reformed.

48380 ■ "Raising the Bar" in *Hispanic Business* (June 2005, pp. 104, 106)
Pub: Hispanic Business
Ed: Anthony Limon. **Description:** Hispanics benefit as law firms bid to reflect a more diversified clientele. Profile of Salomon Chiquiar-Rabinovich is included.

48381 ■ "Reaching the silver screen" in *Black Enterprise* (Vol. 32, No. 5, December 20)
Pub: Earl Graves Publishing Co.
Ed: George Alexander. **Description:** Problems encountered by black filmmakers trying to distribute their films are discussed.

48382 ■ "Read the fine print" in *Black Enterprise* (Vol. 33, No. 7, February 2003, pp. 6)
Pub: Earl Graves Publishing Co.
Ed: Alan Hughes. **Description:** Information regarding the black business community and the progress of the BE 100s, as well as insight into issues affecting African Americans on Capitol Hill is provided by Alan Hughes at blackenterprise.com.

48383 ■ "Ready for Progress" in *Hispanic Business* (January/February 2005, pp. 44, 46, 48)
Pub: Hispanic Business
Description: With corporate board diversity in a holding pattern, new regulations may work as a vehicle for change. Hispanics hold 95 seats on boards of directors at Fortune 500 companies, down by one from 2004.

48384 ■ "Recognizing Gifted Entrepreneurs" in *Black Enterprise* (Vol. 34, No. 3, October 2003, pp. 150)
Pub: Earl Graves Publishing Co.
Description: Black Enterprise is accepting nominations for the 2004 Black Enterprise Small Business Awards; the public is encouraged to nominate African-Americans from their communities.

48385 ■ "Recruitment: Hispanic Employment Program Managers" in *Hispanic Business* (December 2002, pp. FRG6-FRG8)
Pub: Hispanic Business
Description: Contact information is provided from the Hispanic Employment Program Manager's Directory (HEPM); these managers are responsible with improving the representation of Hispanics in the work force.

48386 ■ "Representation for hire" in *Black Enterprise* (Vol. 32, No. 10, May 2002, pp. 24)
Pub: Earl Graves Publishing Co.
Ed: Joyce Jones. **Description:** Ways in which small businesses can lobby politicians are presented.

48387 ■ "Retiring Minds" in *Hispanic Business* (March 2005, pp. 50)
Pub: Hispanic Business
Ed: Joel Russell. **Description:** The large number of federal managers retiring is creating new opportunities for Hispanics. Federal agencies and mid-career outreach agencies are listed.

48388 ■ "The Return of the Black Entrepreneur" in *Business Week Online* (Oct. 8, 2002)
Pub: McGraw-Hill Inc.
Ed: Kimberly Weisul. **Description:** A recent study conducted by the Ewing Marion Kauffman Foundation shows that the number of African American entrepreneurs in the U.S. is on the rise. A second phase of the study will be published sometime in 2003.

48389 ■ "The Rich Get Richer" in *Hispanic Business* (June 2005, pp. 26, 28, 30)
Pub: Hispanic Business
Description: Although the 500 largest Hispanic-owned U.S. businesses reported strong growth in 2004, only a few of the companies accounted for most of the new revenues. Statistical data included.

48390 ■ "Riding Out the Crash" in *Hispanic Business* (Vol. 23, No. 5, May 2001, pp. 42, 44-45)
Pub: Hispanic Business
Ed: Derek Reveron. **Description:** Hispanic-themed Web sites that focus on niche markets stand the best chance of long-term survival. An interview with Fernando Espuelas, CEO of StarMedia is presented.

48391 ■ "Riding the Telecom-Computer Convergence" in *Hispanic Business* (Vol. 23, No. 7/8, July/August 2001, pp. 60)
Pub: Hispanic Business
Ed: Joel Russell. **Description:** An overview of the fast-growth, high-tech Hispanic firms specializing in networking and system integration. Statistical data included.

48392 ■ "Riding the tech wave" in *Hispanic Business* (Vol. 22, No. 7-8, July-August 2000, pp. 30)
Pub: Hispanic Business
Ed: Jennifer Riley. **Description:** Ralph G. Moore, president of consulting firm RGMA believes that e-commerce and the Internet hold many opportunities for small, minority-owned businesses to take part in procurement.

48393 ■ "The right stuff" in *BlackEnterprise* (Vol. 32, No. 3, October 2001, pp. 51)
Pub: Earl Graves Publishing Co.
Ed: Paula McCoy-Pinderhughes. **Description:** Advice is offered to entrepreneurs wishing to bid on NASA contracts, including information on the Small and Disadvantaged Business Utilization at NASA headquarters in Washington DC, and the Training and Development for Small Businesses in Advanced Technologies (TADSBAT) program. Five African American-owned businesses are on NASA's FY 2000 Top 100 List of Prime Contractors.

48394 ■ "Roll On: Davin Enjoys Just Spinning Your Wheels" in *Black Enterprise* (Vol. 34, No. 4, November 2003, pp. 180)
Pub: Earl Graves Publishing Co.
Ed: Linda S. Lawson. **Description:** Profile of Ian Hardman, CEO of Davin Wheels in Rhode Island. The company's patented chrome rims adorn the cars of executives and celebrities alike, ranging in price from $12,000-$14,000, with custom rims costing more.

48395 ■ "Romar Group Newest NASCAR Licensee" in *Black Enterprise* (Vol. 35, November 2004, No. 4, pp. 32)
Pub: Earl G. Graves Publishing Co. Inc.
Ed: Nicole M. Richardson. **Description:** Romar Group Inc., one of the nation's largest black-owned apparel companies, received a promotional licensee deal from NASCAR.

48396 ■ "Room for Growth in the Big Apple" in *Black Enterprise* (Vol. 31, No. 5, December 2000, pp. 64)
Pub: Earl Graves Publishing Co.
Ed: Robyn D. Clarke. **Description:** The qualities that set Esystems Inc apart from the competition are discussed with owner Glenwood Elam Jr.

48397 ■ "Rough Ride to Recovery: Black-Owned Mutual Funds Brace for a Bumpy Bull Ride" in *Black Enterprise* (Vol. 34, No. 5, December 2003)
Pub: Earl Graves Publishing Co.
Ed: Tanisha A. Sykes. **Description:** Profile of black-owned mutual funds and the problems faced by these funds in a weak economy.

48398 ■ "Safe Seats Don't Make Sound Politics" in *Hispanic Business* (Vol. 24, No. 5, May 2002, pp. 26, 28)
Pub: Hispanic Business Inc.
Ed: Joel Russell. **Description:** Hispanic representation in Congress is increasing, but not at the same rate as the population increases in the United States.

48399 ■ "Same Markets, New Marketplaces" in *Black Enterprise* (Vol. 35, September 2004, No. 2, pp. 34)
Pub: Earl G. Graves Publishing Co. Inc.
Ed: Malik Singleton. **Description:** According to a study performed by the Center for Women's Business Research, African American women entrepreneurs in nontraditional sectors rose between 1997 and 2002. Wisconsin, Delaware, and Oregon were among the top states experiencing the rise, with Wisconsin reporting 453 percent growth in the number of African American women-owned businesses. Statistical data included.

48400 ■ "Sanchez Gets Texas Nomination" in *Hispanic Business* (Vol. 24, No. 4, April 2002, pp. 12)
Pub: Hispanic Business Inc.
Ed: Tim Dougherty. **Description:** Tony Sanchez is the first Hispanic to win the nomination for Governor of the State of Texas.

48401 ■ "SBA Government Procurement Office Directory" in *Hispanic Business* (December 2002, pp. FRG16)
Pub: Hispanic Business
Description: A listing of the Small Business Administration's Government Procurement Offices is presented. These offices assist small businesses obtain federal contracts.

48402 ■ "SBA Head Opposes Relaxing 'Minority' Terms" in *Wall Street Journal* (December 13, 1999, pp. A2)
Pub: Dow Jones & Co., Inc.
Ed: Paulette Thomas. **Description:** An interview with the Small Business Administration head, Aida Alvarez.

48403 ■ "SBA Increases Bond Maximum" in *Hispanic Business* (Vol. 23, No. 5, May 2001, pp. 24)
Pub: Hispanic Business
Description: The U.S. Small Business Administration (SBA) has increased the size of surety bonds to increase contracting opportunities for small, minority, and women contractors. In fiscal year 2000, the Surety Bond Guarantee Program backed more than 1,795 final bonds on contracts valued at nearly $328.9 million.

48404 ■ "SBA Spared Budget Blues" in *Hispanic Business* (Vol. 22, No. 1/2, January/February, pp. 16)
Pub: Hispanic Business
Ed: Patricia Guadalupe. **Description:** Congress gives the agency a boost in its fiscal 2000 budget. Various programs of the SBA are highlighted, including The New Market Venture Capital Program, an initiative aimed at increasing the number of minority businesses.

48405 ■ "Searching for a city" in *BlackEnterprise* (Vol. 32, No. 3, October 2001, pp. 32)
Pub: Earl Graves Publishing Co.
Ed: Sakina P. Spruell. **Description:** Web sites offering information about Philadelphia, Atlanta, and Charlotte are presented, focusing on the fact these three cities are preferred by African Americans in which to live and work.

48406 ■ "Setting aside a reliance on set-asides" in *Washington Business Journal* (Vol. 22, No. 3, May 23, 2003, pp. 35)
Pub: Washington Business Journal
Ed: Tania Anderson. **Description:** An examination of the management and development of Native Technologies, an American Indian-owned company is presented.

48407 ■ "Sharing the Wealth" in *Hispanic Business* (March 2003, pp. 46, 48, 50)
Pub: Hispanic Business
Ed: Maryann Hammers. **Description:** The Rockefeller Foundation and Hispanics in Philanthropy have partnered to help Hispanics make wise decisions when making contributions to charities and organizations.

48408 ■ "Shop Shifting" in *Hispanic Business* (April 2005, pp. 18, 20)
Pub: Hispanic Business
Ed: Joel Russell. **Description:** Hispanic advertising agencies are faced with identity issues that involve integration and specialization. As more mainstream agencies become more multicultural, Hispanic agencies will become more mainstream.

48409 ■ *Small Business Loan Program Kit*
Pub: International Wealth Success, Incorporated
Ed: Tyler G. Hicks. Released: 2006. Price: $100.00.
Description: Guide to the Small Business Loan Program that offers loans to small and minority-owned companies doing work for government agencies, large corporations, hospitals, universities, and similar organizations.

48410 ■ "Small Businesses Are Engine to American Economy" in *Atlanta Business Chronicle* (Vol. 24, No. 9, August 3, 2001, pp. 10B)
Pub: American City Business Journals Inc.
Ed: Paige Bowers. **Description:** Senator Max Cleland discusses what he has done in support of small business in America. The Senator's support includes reducing taxes on small businesses, broadening health care options and boosting the opportunities for minority and women-owned enterprises.

48411 ■ "Small Exporters in a Big World" in *Hispanic Business* (November 2003, pp. 42-43, 46, 48, 50)
Pub: Hispanic Business
Ed: Jennifer Riley. **Description:** Hispanic firms that have succeeded abroad show they can compete in the large and profitable markets of the global economy. Statistical data included.

48412 ■ "Small businesses dissatisfied with SBA" in *Black Enterprise* (Vol. 31, No. 5, December 2000, pp. 29)
Pub: Earl Graves Publishing Co.
Ed: Joyce Jones. **Description:** A report issued by the General Accounting Office (GAO) shows that the Small Business Administration is not effective in securing contracts for 8(a) program participants.

48413 ■ "Snatching Victory from Defeat" in *Hispanic Business* (September 2006, pp. 58, 60, 62)
Pub: Hispanic Business
Ed: Holly Ocasio-Rizzo. **Description:** Impacts felt by setbacks in affirmative action for Hispanics are discussed.

48414 ■ "The Social Security Conundrum" in *Hispanic Business* (Vol. 23, No. 10, October, 2001, pp. 36, 38)
Pub: Hispanic Business
Ed: Patricia Guadalupe. **Description:** As debate over proposals to privatize portions of Social Security, one thing is beyond dispute, the status quo is not an option. Social Security rates of return for average-income Hispanic Americans are discussed. Statistical data included.

48415 ■ **"Specialty Shops"** in *Hispanic Business* (June 2005, pp. 96)
Pub: Hispanic Business
Ed: Keith Rosenblum. **Description:** Hispanics selling to other Hispanics has created the largest retailers listed on the magazine's top 500 companies. Statistical data included.

48416 ■ **"Spending Spree"** in *Hispanic Business* (December 2001, pp. 38, 40, 56)
Pub: Hispanic Business
Description: Overall growth in the Hispanic ad market slowed in 2001, yet Hispanic purchasing power continued to rise. A list of the top 60 advertisers in the Hispanic Market for 2001 is spotlighted. Statistical data included.

48417 ■ **"Spirited leadership: Carl Horton named President & CEO of Absolut"** in *Black Enterprise* (Vol. 32, No. 9, April 2002, pp. 28)
Pub: Earl Graves Publishing Co.
Ed: Derek T. Dingle. **Description:** Profile of Carol Horton, new president and CEO of The Absolut Spirits Company. Horton has become the industry's top-ranking African American as well as one of the most powerful black executives in corporate America. Horton views his new role as a transition from corporate execute to an entrepreneur of a start-up.

48418 ■ **"Starting From Zero: Entrepreneur Reaps Success During Rocky Tech Times"** in *Black Enterprise* (Vol. 34, July 2004, No. 12, pp. 53)
Pub: Earl G. Graves Publishing Co. Inc.
Ed: Bridget McCrea. **Description:** Profile of Glenn Davis, owner of Virginia-based BranCore Technologies. Working from home, Davis borrowed $15,000 from his 401(k) to launch his minority-owned firm that provides project management and e-commerce consulting.

48419 ■ **"Status Symbols, Bargain Prices"** in *Hispanic Business* (June 2002, pp. 84)
Pub: Hispanic Business
Ed: Ralph Gray. **Description:** Hispanic Business Automotive Survey of Hispanic CEOs resulted in a list of several entry-level luxury sedans offering prestige for less than $38,000.

48420 ■ **"Sticking to what she knows"** in *BlackEnterprise* (Vol. 32, No. 2, September 2001, pp. 46)
Pub: Earl Graves Publishing Co.
Ed: Quincy Lewis. **Description:** Profile of Sheri Huguely, president of entertainment consulting firm Glue Inc. In 2000, the company had revenues of $252,000 with a goal of $350,000 for 2001.

48421 ■ **"Stock Index Changes with the Times"** in *Hispanic Business* (March 2004, pp. 10)
Pub: Hispanic Business
Ed: Juan Solana, Michael Caplinger. **Description:** Barometer of conditions for companies in the U.S. Hispanic market is presented. Statistical data included.

48422 ■ **"The Strategic Planning Payoff"** in *Hispanic Business* (June 2002, pp. 66)
Pub: Hispanic Business
Ed: Scott Williams. **Description:** The importance of writing a good business plan is stressed. Eighty-two percent of Hispanic Business 500 companies have all written successful business plans.

48423 ■ **"Strength in diversity"** in *Hispanic Business* (Vol. 22, No. 7-8, July-August 2000, pp. CA4)
Pub: Hispanic Business
Ed: Joel Russell. **Description:** California's biggest Hispanic businesses are active in a wide range of sectors, including auto detailing, manufacturing and health care. The combined revenue of the state's top 100 Hispanic companies amounted to $2.98 billion in 1999, with the service sector being the largest.

48424 ■ **"Striving for 'Critical Mass'"** in *Hispanic Business* (Vol. 23, No. 10, October, 2001, pp. 16)
Pub: Hispanic Business
Ed: Rick Laezman. **Description:** The LaRaza Lawyers Association of California is working to strengthen Hispanic legal influence. Despite the fact that Hispanics account for more than 30 percent of California's population, only 4 percent are attorneys.

48425 ■ **"The Struggle for Sales Overseas"** in *Hispanic Business* (November 2002, pp. 36)
Pub: Hispanic Business
Ed: Joel Russell. **Description:** Statistics are shared regarding Hispanic companies exporting products are featured. Overall exports for the first seven months of 2002 were down 8 percent from same period in 2001.

48426 ■ **"Study shows businesses are slow to embrace e-commerce"** in *Black Enterprise* (Vol. 32)
Pub: Earl Graves Publishing Co.
Ed: Bevolyn Williams-Harold. **Description:** The Minority Business Development Agency is urging minority-owned businesses to use e-commerce to help grow their companies. Statistical data included.

48427 ■ **"Sunshine State Summit"** in *Hispanic Business* (March 2003, pp. 26, 28)
Pub: Hispanic Business
Ed: Abel Magana. **Description:** The Florida State Hispanic Chamber of Commerce Conference is highlighted. The event, held January 22-23, 2003, announced a series of 15 regional seminars organized through the cooperation of the U.S. Chamber of Commerce, the Small Business Administration, and the newly formed National Coalition of Hispanic Chambers of Commerce.

48428 ■ **"Supplier Diversity"** in *Hispanic Business* (September 2004, pp. 18)
Pub: Hispanic Business
Description: The National Minority Supplier Development Council held its annual conference and Business Opportunity Fair in Washington, DC. The council reports more than 15,000 minority-owned businesses it has certified supply nearly $80 billion annually in goods and services to the council's 3,500 corporation members.

48429 ■ **"Suppliers Called On To Boost Minority Deals"** in *Crain's Detroit Business* (Vol. 21, October 3, 2005, No. 43)
Pub: Crain Communications Inc. - Detroit
Ed: Terry Kosdrosky. **Description:** According to Tony Brown, chairman Michigan's minority business association, many of the top auto suppliers are not purchasing from minority-owned companies.

48430 ■ **"Surviving a corporate marriage"** in *Black Enterprise* (Vol. 32, No. 7, February 2002, pp. 66)
Pub: Earl Graves Publishing Co.
Ed: Valerie Gay Francois. **Description:** Information is offered to help employees learn to reposition themselves for advancement when the company they work for is considering a merger or acquisition. One such tip, suggests buying the company.

48431 ■ **"The sweet smell of success"** in *BlackEnterprise* (Vol. 32, No. 3, October 2001, pp. 52)
Pub: Earl Graves Publishing Co.
Ed: Glenn Townes. **Description:** Profile of Bo-Dacious Baskets!!, the company that won the Minority Business Plan Competition in Philadelphia, Pennsylvania. Entrepreneur Cassandra Hayes is the owner of Bo-Dacious Baskets!!, the three year old, five-employee gift-service business.

48432 ■ **"Symbolism with a Bottom Line"** in *Hispanic Business* (Vol. 23, No. 7/8, July/August 2001, pp. 16)
Pub: Hispanic Business
Ed: Leigh Miller. **Description:** In April 2001, Georgia Governor Roy Barnes signed a state law designating Hispanics as an official minority group. Hispanic businesses will now qualify as minority-owned firms.

48433 ■ **"Taking the Leap. Minority Staffing Services Owner Proves He Can Make It in MA"** in *Boston Business Journal* (Vol. 23, Aug. 22, 2003)
Pub: American City Business Journals
Ed: Mark Micheli. **Description:** Profile of Kelvin Bernard, president of Total Technical Services Inc.; Bernard was born in Costa Rica and runs his profitable business in the Boston, Massachusetts area.

48434 ■ **"Tangled Web"** in *Hispanic Business* (December 2001, pp. 58)
Pub: Hispanic Business
Ed: Derek Reveron. **Description:** Estimated 2001 Internet revenues for Hispanic dot-coms are discussed, including StarMedia, one of the first Hispanic dot-coms. StarMedia is also facing an uncertain future.

48435 ■ **"Tapping the Talent Pool of Hispanic Affluence"** in *Hispanic Business* (Vol. 24, No. 1/2, January/February 2002, pp. 6)
Pub: Hispanic Business Inc.
Ed: Jesus Chavarria. **Description:** A brief overview of the growth of Hispanic affluence in America and the important role that plays for Hispanic entrepreneurs and marketers. Hispanic Business magazine plans to organize training and educational events with sessions on Latin American trade, B2B e-commerce strategies, Hispanic online consumers, and cross-border banking.

48436 ■ **"The 100 Influentials"** in *Hispanic Business* (October 2004, pp. 38)
Pub: Hispanic Business
Description: Hispanic Business Directory of the 100 most influential Hispanics is presented. The list focuses on politics, the financial industry, and non-profit organizations, and the growing power and influence of these leaders. Profiles of these leaders are included.

48437 ■ **"This Just In"** in *Crain's Detroit Business* (Vol. 19, No. 40, October 13, 2003, pp. 1)
Pub: Crain Communications Inc., Detroit
Description: Bridgewater Interiors has taken over a Johnson Controls Inc. operation, creating 600 new jobs in Warren, Michigan. The new operation is a joint-venture between Johnson Controls and Detroit-based Epsilon LLC, a minority-owned firm.

48438 ■ **"Thumbs Up"** in *Hispanic Business* (July/August 2002, pp. 16)
Pub: Hispanic Business
Ed: Patricia Guadalupe. **Description:** Hector Barreto wins praise for his stewardship of the Small Business Administration, but the Bush administration receives criticism.

48439 ■ **"A time of lower returns"** in *Hispanic Business* (Vol. 22, No. 11, November 2000, pp. 36)
Pub: Hispanic Business
Ed: Joel Russell. **Description:** The performance of the top 50 Hispanic American businesses whose export trade was worth $592.11-million in 1999, a drop of 38 percent on the previous year is examined. The effect of globalization on exports is discussed.

48440 ■ **"A Time to Shine: Awards Celebration Spotlights Today's Successful Entrepreneurs"** in *Black Enterprise* (Vol. 34, No. 4, November 2003)
Pub: Earl Graves Publishing Co.
Description: Black Enterprise recognizes outstanding African American entrepreneurs, including small business owners and top-level executives who appear on the BE 100s lists.

48441 ■ **"Titans Tune In"** in *Hispanic Business* (May 2005, pp. 46, 48)
Pub: Hispanic Business
Ed: Kevin Brass. **Description:** The ever-expanding Hispanic technology market is increasing sales for computers and helping to equip the small to mid-size Hispanic firms who spent $14.8 billion on IT in 2004. Statistical data included.

48442 ■ "To Fill A Widening Niche" in *Hispanic Business* **(July/August 2002, pp. 36, 38, 42, 44, 46, 48)**
Pub: Hispanic Business
Ed: Description: The companies listed on the Hispanic Business Fastest-Growing 100 all rely on core competencies and specific niche markets to create growth, resulting in 62.6 percent per year. Statistics data included.

48443 ■ "A Toast to Success" in *Hispanic Business* **(July/August 2004, pp. 52, 54, 56, 58, 62, 66)**
Pub: Hispanic Business
Description: Hispanic Business Magazine celebrated 25 years of progress. Six hundred of the most successful and influential members of the U.S. Hispanic community were represented.

48444 ■ "Too Much Information?" in *Black Enterprise* **(Vol. 37, December 2006, No. 5, pp. 59)**
Pub: Earl G. Graves Publishing Co. Inc.
Ed: James C. Johnson. Description: African American business owners often face the dilemma of whether or not to divulge their minority status when soliciting new customers and financial institutions. The quality of the products or services is always the key factor and race should never define one's business; however, it is appropriate to market oneself as a minority or women-owned business, especially if the company is in an industry where those clients are offered top-tier contracts.

48445 ■ "Top 10 Business Schools for Hispanics" in *Hispanic Business* **(September 2004, pp. 78, 80, 82, 84)**
Pub: Hispanic Business
Description: The top ten business schools for Hispanics are profiled. Stanford University, Yale University, and New York University were listed as the top three, respectively.

48446 ■ "Top 10 Law Schools for Hispanics" in *Hispanic Business* **(September 2003, pp. 56, 58, 60, 62)**
Pub: Hispanic Business
Description: Top 10 law schools for Hispanic students to consider are listed, with University of Texas at Austin's School of Law rated number one, followed by University of Miami's School of Law.

48447 ■ "Top 25 Hispanic Ad Agencies" in *Hispanic Business* **(December 2003, pp. 42, 44, 46, 48, 50)**
Pub: Hispanic Business
Description: A listing of the top 25 Hispanic advertising agencies is presented, with 23 of the 25 agencies reporting increased billings since 2002. Statistical data included.

48448 ■ "Top Cities For African Americans: The Results Are In." in *Black Enterprise* **(Vol. 34, July 2004, No. 12, pp. 78)**
Pub: Earl G. Graves Publishing Co. Inc.
Ed: Carolyn M. Brown, David A. Padgett. Description: Top ten cities for African Americans to live and work are listed, seven of the ten are in the South, five of the ten have a Black mayor, and half have a black city population that is over 50 percent.

48449 ■ "Top Ten Schools for Hispanics: Engineering" in *Hispanic Business* **(September 2006, pp. 76, 78, 80)**
Pub: Hispanic Business
Description: Top ten universities offering engineering degrees targeted to Hispanic students include, University Texas at El Paso, Purdue University, Georgia Institute of Technology, Massachusetts Institute of Technology, University of California Irvine, Michigan State University, University of Central Florida, Stanford University, University of Texas at Austin, and University of New Mexico.

48450 ■ "Top Ten Schools for Hispanics MBA" in *Hispanic Business* **(September 2006, pp. 70, 72, 74)**
Pub: Hispanic Business

Description: Top ten universities offering MBA programs targeted to Hispanic students include, Stanford University; University of California, Berkley; Dartmouth College; University of Texas at Austin; New York University; Yale University; University of Miami; Duke University; Columbia University; and Florida International University.

48451 ■ "Top Ten Schools for Hispanics: Medical" in *Hispanic Business* **(September 2006, pp. 82, 84, 86)**
Pub: Hispanic Business
Description: Top ten universities offering medical degrees geared towards Hispanic students include, Stanford University, University of Texas Health Science Center, University of Texas Medical Branch, University of New Mexico, University of Miami, University of Texas Southwestern Medical Center at Dallas, University of Illinois, University of Texas at Houston, University of Arizona, and Texas A&M.

48452 ■ "A Tough Row to Hoe" in *Hispanic Business* **(October 2002, pp. 26, 28)**
Pub: Hispanic Business
Ed: Lou Gallegos. Description: An increasing number of Hispanics in the U.S. are taking up farming. Lou Gallegos, a U.S. Department of Agriculture official, discusses current trends and offers policy recommendations to promote Hispanic farming owner and prosperity.

48453 ■ "Toyota's Opportunity Exchange" in *Hispanic Business* **(September 2002, pp. 8)**
Pub: Hispanic Business
Description: Toyota Motor Manufacturing America will hold its annual trade fair and conference for Tier I suppliers in November. Toyota's Opportunity Exchange was created to build business relationships between direct, or Tier I, suppliers and MBEs.

48454 ■ "Transform Your Life" in *Black Enterprise* **(Vol. 37, January 2007, No. 6, pp. 14)**
Pub: Earl G. Graves Publishing Co. Inc.
Description: Through the magazine, television and radio programs, events, and the website, the various platforms of Black Enterprise will provide the tools necessary to achieve success in business ventures, career aspirations, and personal goals.

48455 ■ "Trouble in Little Cuba" in *Hispanic Business* **(Vol. 23, No. 10, October, 2001, pp. 20)**
Pub: Hispanic Business
Ed: Scott Williams. Description: An overview of the problems facing the Cuban American National Foundation (CANF) under its current leadership. The CANF was formed to oppose the revolutionary government of Cuban dictator Fidel Castro.

48456 ■ "Trouble in Tennessee" in *Hispanic Business* **(October 2002, pp. 18)**
Pub: Hispanic Business
Ed: Jonathan J. Higuera. Description: Hispanic small business owners charge they are being blocked from local government contract work, officials deny the charge.

48457 ■ TRY US National Minority Business Directory
Pub: Diversity Information Resources Inc.
Ed: Leslie Bonds, Editor. Released: Annual, January. Covers: over 7,000 minority-owned companies capable of supplying their goods and services on national or regional levels. Entries Include: Company name, address, phone, fax, name of principal executive, number of employees, date established, trade and brand names, financial keys, products or services, names of three customers, certification status, minority identification, gross sales. Arrangement: Classified by product or service, then geographical and alphabetical. Indexes: Company, product/service, keyword.

48458 ■ "Tuned In" in *Hispanic Business* **(December 2006, pp. 52)**
Pub: Hispanic Business

Ed: Hildy Medina. Description: Hispanic radio stations are profiled. A listing of the top 10 stations for 2006 is included.

48459 ■ "Turning the Silver Screen Gold" in *Hispanic Business* **(March 2004, pp. 24-26, 28-29)**
Pub: Hispanic Business
Ed: Joel Russell. Description: Santiago Pozo, CEO of Arenas Entertainment hopes to transform the firm into a movie studio with a Hispanic focus to tap into the growing market. The company has secured the first half of a $24 million mezzanine financing strategy.

48460 ■ "The 2000 Hispanic Business 500 Directory" in *Hispanic Business* **(Vol.22, No.6, June 2000, pp. 66)**
Pub: Hispanic Business
Description: Directories of the largest Hispanic-owned business enterprises in the U.S. are presented.

48461 ■ "The 2001 Hispanic Business High-Tech 50 Directory" in *Hispanic Business* **(Vol. 23, No. 7/8, July/Aug. 2001, pp. 40)**
Pub: Hispanic Business
Description: Presentation of the top 50 high-tech Hispanic businesses in the U.S. for 2001. The directory includes each company's location, CEO, product or service, number of employees, and year 2000 revenue.

48462 ■ *United States Commission on Minority Business Development, Final Report*
Pub: Superintendent of Documents
Released: 1995. Price: $40.00. Description: Provides information on minority business programs established by the government, including the Small Business Administration (SBA), Federal Procurement Program, and Capital Ownership Development Program. Prepared by the U.S. Commission on Minority Business Development.

48463 ■ "U.S. Hispanic Market Has Special Character" in *Hispanic Business* **(January/February 2005, pp. 8)**
Pub: Hispanic Business
Ed: Jesus Chavarria. Description: Latin American and U.S. Hispanics have become one in the eyes of corporations, investors and executives, and the same holds true with global economies. Statistical data included.

48464 ■ "U.S.-Mexico Relations Remain on Front Burner" in *Hispanic Business* **(Vol. 23, No. 11, November 2001, pp. 20)**
Pub: Hispanic Business Inc.
Ed: Patricia Guadalupe. Description: Despite the September 11 attacks, the U.S.-Mexico agenda will continue to work on issues of trade, immigration, and other issues of interest to both countries.

48465 ■ "Unrealized Potential" in *Hispanic Business* **(July/August 2002, pp. 58, 60, 62)**
Pub: Hispanic Business
Ed: Jonathan J. Higuera. Description: Reasons for the U.S.-Mexico border trade has failed to live up to some expectations of the North American Free Trade Agreement (NAFTA). Statistical data included.

48466 ■ "Upfront: Be Flexible or Fold" in *My Business* **(June/July 2002, pp. 13-14)**
Pub: My Business Magazine
Ed: Karen E. Klein. Description: Sometimes a small firm needs to steer away from original business plans in order to grow. Martha C. de al Torre, Hispanic Business Woman of the Year 2000, tells how she learned to be flexible and creative with her business plan.

48467 ■ "The VC Process" in *Hispanic Business* **(March 2004, pp. 36-37)**
Pub: Hispanic Business
Ed: Joel Russell. Description: Hispanics have lagged behind in the private-equity market, but experts offer ways for them to improve acquiring venture financing.

48468 ■ **"Venerable Financial Firms to Join"** in *Altanta Journal-Constitution* (February 7, 2007)

Pub: Cox Newspapers, Inc.

Ed: Tom Walker. **Description:** Atlanta Life Financial Group acquired Jackson Securities LLC, merging the two largest black-owned enterprises in Atlanta, Georgia.

48469 ■ **"Venus's Designs"** in *Inc.* (September 1, 2003)

Pub: Gruner & Jahr USA Publishing

Ed: Nicole Gull. **Description:** Profile of Venus Williams' interior design firm V Star Interiors. V Starr has six active accounts and projects gross sales of about $1 million for 2003.

48470 ■ **"Verizon Breaks New Ads"** in *Hispanic Business* (March 2003, pp. 16)

Pub: Hispanic Business

Description: Firms promoting the use of Spanish language ad campaigns, Web sites and media campaigns are profiled.

48471 ■ **"A Vision for Recycling"** in *Business Journal-Milwaukee* (Vol. 20, No. 51, September 5, 2003, pp. A14)

Pub: American City Business Journals, Inc.

Ed: David Schuyler. **Description:** Profile of Elia Lemke and Joe Tate, who formed Sauceda Sanitation LLC, a small woman-owned business. Lemke has limited business background and Tate is the retired chairman and founder of Superior Services Inc.

48472 ■ **"Voice of Experience"** in *Hispanic Business* (Vol. 23, No. 7/8, July/August 2001, pp. 32-33)

Pub: Hispanic Business

Ed: Janet Perez. **Description:** Federico Pena brings a lot to the table as the featured speaker at the 2001 Hispanic Business Entrepreneur of the Year Award gala. An interview with Mr. Pena is included, discussing his perspective on the challenges facing Hispanic entrepreneurs.

48473 ■ **"Volvo Opens Supplier Diversity Office"** in *Hispanic Business* (July/August 2002, pp. 10)

Pub: Hispanic Business

Description: Volvo Truck North America Inc. announced the development of a supplier diversity office to help diversity suppliers conduct business with the company.

48474 ■ **"Wall Street Rogues: Fast Cars, Women, and Cash. These Financial Whizzes Had It All"** in *Black Enterprise* (Vol. 35, August 2004, No. 1)

Pub: Earl G. Graves Publishing Co. Inc.

Ed: Alan Hughes. **Description:** Alan Brian Bond, one time Wall Street all-star, conspired with a broker to inflate client fees from 1993 to 1998. Bonds clients, mostly African Americans, lost nearly $57 million.

48475 ■ **"Washington Insider: Hispanics Crash House Small-Biz Groups"** in *Hispanic Business* (March 2003, pp. 12)

Pub: Hispanic Business

Ed: Patricia Guadalupe. **Description:** Profiles of Hispanic government officials and the offering of bonds in Mexico are highlighted.

48476 ■ **"Washington Insider: Issues Count More Than Affiliation"** in *Hispanic Business* (July/August 2004, pp. 12)

Pub: Hispanic Business

Ed: Patricial Guadalupe. **Description:** Political issues affecting Hispanic business are examined.

48477 ■ **"Washington Insider: Small Business Overlooked?"** in *Hispanic Business* (March 2003, pp. 16)

Pub: Hispanic Business

Ed: Patricia Guadalupe. **Description:** Initiatives to address the current economic slowdown and its effect on minority entrepreneurs is addressed. Also discussed is the Small Business Administration's Internet site designed to assist small business owners with employees serving in the military reserves.

48478 ■ **"Web features"** in *Black Enterprise* (Vol. 32, No. 6, January 2002, pp. 8)

Pub: Earl Graves Publishing Co.

Description: Websites featuring online employment services and the best cities for African Americans are highlighted.

48479 ■ **"What Gives?"** in *Entrepreneur* (Vol. 28, No. 9, September 2000, pp. 20)

Pub: Entrepreneur Media Inc.

Ed: Julie Monahan. **Description:** An audit finds problems with the Small Disadvantaged Business Certification program.

48480 ■ **"Where Do You Go From Here"** in *Black Enterprise* (Vol. 31, No. 5, December 2000, pp. 87)

Pub: Earl Graves Publishing Co.

Ed: Carolyn M. Brown. **Description:** The Black Wealth Initiative is used to review financial goals and adjust strategy to ensure a brighter future.

48481 ■ **"Who Are We?"** in *Hispanic Business* (July/August 2004, pp. 16)

Pub: Hispanic Business

Description: Excerpts of Henry Cisneros rebuttal to a Harvard professor's contention that Hispanics are challenging America's identity. However, evidence from successful cities across the nation, population diversity is a driving force in the new economy.

48482 ■ **"A Whole New Chamber"** in *Hispanic Business* (November 2003, pp. 32, 34)

Pub: Hispanic Business

Ed: Joel Russell. **Description:** Leadership plots a new course for the U.S. Hispanic Chamber of Commerce. A listing of the newly elected U.S. Hispanic Chamber of Commerce Board is presented.

48483 ■ **"Why Bright Star Shines"** in *Hispanic Business* (January/February 2004, pp. 14-16, 18)

Pub: Hispanic Business

Ed: Joel Russell. **Description:** Profile of Marcelo Claure, CEO of Brightstar and winner of the Hispanic Business Entrepreneur of the Year Award. Brightstar Corporation, a cellular phone distributor, reported double-digit growth for six years. Claure attributes the firm's success to smart use of technology and an aggressive approach to training.

48484 ■ **Women Entrepreneurs**

Pub: Edward Elgar Publishing, Incorporated

Ed: Andrea Smith-Hunter. **Released:** October 2006. **Price:** $120.00. **Description:** Focus is on women entrepreneurs; information includes human capital, network structures and financial capital, with comparative analysis across racial lines.

48485 ■ **"Working virtually works for her"** in *Black Enterprise* (Vol. 32, No. 7, February 2002, pp. 51)

Pub: Earl Graves Publishing Co.

Ed: Bridget McCrea. **Description:** Profile of Victoria Parham, owner and president of Virtual Support Services LLC. Parham's firm provides administrative support, such as email and database management, travel arrangements, scheduling, and customer-relationship management and support to a national client base, all done virtually.

48486 ■ **"Wrestling with the bear"** in *Black Enterprise* (Vol. 33, No. 3, Oct. 2002, pp. 46)

Pub: Earl Graves Publishing Co.

Ed: Nicole Halsey. **Description:** An overview of black-owned mutual fund companies is presented, including Ariel, Brown Cap, DEM Equity, Edgar Lomax, Kenwood Growth, Lou Holland Growth, MDL Broad Market, and Profit Value. Statistical data included.

48487 ■ **"You Can Build It, But They Might Not Come"** in *Inc.* (July 1, 2004)

Pub: Inc. Magazine

Ed: Patrick J. Sauer. **Description:** Broadway Cinemas, a black-owned movie theater that opened in 1999 in the West end of downtown Louisville, Kentucky is profiled.

48488 ■ **"You've got the power!"** in *Black Enterprise* (Vol. 31, No. 5, December 2000, pp. 166)

Pub: Earl Graves Publishing Co.

Ed: Robyn D. Clarke. **Description:** The value of communicating with confidence and power through your body language is examined.

TRADE PERIODICALS

48489 ■ **Black Enterprise**

Pub: Earl Graves Publishing Co.

Contact: Earl G. Graves, Editor & Publisher

Released: Monthly. **Price:** $15.95 U.S.; $29.95 other countries. **Description:** Black-oriented business magazine.

48490 ■ **The Columbus Times**

Pub: Columbus Times

Contact: Ophelia Devore Mitchell, CEO

Released: Weekly (Wed.). **Description:** Black community newspaper.

48491 ■ **Hispanic Business**

Pub: Hispanic Business Inc.

Released: Monthly, 10/year. **Description:** English-language business magazine catering to Hispanic professionals.

48492 ■ **Minority Business Entrepreneur**

Pub: Minority Business Entrepreneur

Contact: Ginger Conrad, Publisher

E-mail: gconrad@mbemag.com

Ed: Emilia Richwine, Editor, erichwine@mbemag.com. **Released:** Bimonthly. **Price:** $18; $30 two years. **Description:** Business magazine for ethnic minority and women business owners.

48493 ■ **Multicultural Marketing News**

Pub: Multicultural Marketing Resources Inc.

Contact: Lisa Skriloff, Editor-in-Chief

Released: Bimonthly. **Price:** $700 for Multicultural Marketing News only; $250 for MMN Online only. **Description:** Covers minority- and women-owned businesses and corporations that sell to them. Provides story ideas, diverse resources for journalists, and contacts for marketing executives. Recurring features include a calendar of events, business profiles, and a feature on a trend in multicultural marketing.

48494 ■ **NMBC Business Report**

Pub: National Minority Business Council Inc.

Contact: John Robinson, Publisher

Ed: Julian Reynolds, Editor. **Released:** Semiannual. **Price:** Free. **Description:** Focuses on business issues relevant to the minority business community.

48495 ■ **Securities Pro**

Pub: Securities Pro

Contact: Tony Chapelle, Editor & Publisher

E-mail: tonychapelle@hotmail.com

Released: Monthly. **Price:** $207. **Description:** Reports on African-American firms and individuals involved in the investments industry. Covers hirings, firings, job promotions, new accounts, and trends. Also ranks black investment banks, money management firms, and black stocks. Recurring features include a calendar of events, job listings, and interviews. Publishes annual listing of the 100 Wealthiest African American entreprenuers, heirs, and executives.

VIDEOCASSETTES/ AUDIOCASSETTES

48496 ■ **Ebony/Jet Guide to Black Excellence: The Entrepreneurs**

Home Vision Cinema

c/o Image Entertainment

20525 Nordhoff St., Ste. 200

Chatsworth, CA 91311

URL: http://www.homevision.com

Released: 1992. **Price:** $24.95. **Description:** A look at three African-Americans who have built their own businesses: John H. Johnson of Johnson Publishing Company, Joshua I. Smith of the Maxima Corporation, and Oprah Winfrey, talk show host and CEO of Harpo Productions. **Availability:** VHS.

TRADE SHOWS AND CONVENTIONS

48497 ■ DesigNation
DesigNation, Inc.
300 M St., SW, Ste. N110
Washington, DC 20024
Ph:(202)488-1530
Fax: (202)488-3838
Co. E-mail: info@designation.net
URL: http://www.designation.net
Released: Annual. **Audience:** Designers from around the world, their companies, clients, and suppliers. **Principal Exhibits:** Exhibits of interest to designers holding college degrees who are practicing graphic, industrial, fashion, textile, and interior design.

CONSULTANTS

48498 ■ Custom Consulting Inc.
6315 Bayside Dr.
New Port Richey, FL 34652-2040
Ph:(727)844-5065
Fax: (727)844-5064
Co. E-mail: diwago@customconsulting.com
URL: http://www.customconsulting.com

E-mail: diwago@customconsulting.com
Scope: Provides systems development personnel on a temporary basis. Specializes in mainframe, mini and Client/server development environments.

48499 ■ Joel Greenstein & Associates
6212 Nethercombe Ct.
McLean, VA 22101

Ph:(703)893-1888
Co. E-mail: jgreenstein@contractmasters.com

E-mail: jgreenstein@contractmasters.com
Scope: Provides services to minority and women-owned businesses and government agencies. Experienced in interpreting federal and agency-specific acquisition regulations and contract terms and conditions. Offers assistance with preparing technical and cost proposals and sealed bids.

COMPUTERIZED DATABASES

48500 ■ HispanTelligence
Hispanic Business
425 Pine Ave.
Santa Barbara, CA 93117-3709
Ph:(805)964-4554
Fax: (805)964-5539
Description: Contains information on thousands of Hispanic-owned companies in the United States. For each company, provides name, executive officers, address, telephone number, fax number, year established, number of employees, number of Hispanic employees, Hispanic ownership data, subsidiaries, minority certification status, U.S. Standard Industrial Classification (SIC) codes, line of business, import and export activities, and financial data. **Availability:** Batch: Hispanic Business. **Type:** Directory.

48501 ■ National Directory of Minority-Owned Business Firms
Business Research Services Inc.
4701 Sangamore Rd., Ste. S-155
Bethesda, MD 20816

Ph:(301)229-5561
Free: 800-845-8420
Fax: (301)229-6133
Co. E-mail: brspubs@sba8a.com
URL: http://www.sba8a.com
Description: Contains information on approximately 30,000 minority-owned businesses in the United States. Provides name, address, telephone number, name and title of contact, minority group, certification status, date founded, number of employees, description of products or services, U.S. Standard Industrial Classification (SIC) codes, sales volume, government contracting experience, and references. Corresponds to the *National Directory of Minority-Owned Business Firms.* **Availability:** CD-ROM: Business Research Services Inc; Diskette: Business Research Services Inc;Batch: Business Research Services Inc. **Type:** Directory.

48502 ■ Small Business Innovative Research Current Solicitations
Wheeling Jesuit University
316 Washington Ave.
Wheeling, WV 26003
Ph:(304)243-4341
Free: 800-678-6882
Fax: (304)243-4388
Co. E-mail: technology@nttc.edu
URL: http://www.nttc.edu
Description: Contains solicitations for the Small Business Innovation Research (SBIR) Program and the Small Business Technology Transfer (STTR) Pilot Program. Programs seek to stimulate U.S. technological innovation by funding small business research projects. The database assists users in exploring topics for which funding is available. **Type:** Full text.

Mobile Business

ASSOCIATIONS AND OTHER ORGANIZATIONS

48503 ■ Modular Building Institute
944 Glenwood Station Ln., Ste. 204
Charlottesville, VA 22901-1480
Ph:(434)296-3288
Free: 888-811-3288
Fax: (434)296-3361
Co. E-mail: info@mbinet.org
URL: http://www.mbinet.org
Contact: Tom Hardiman CAE, Exec.Dir.
Membership: Manufacturers and dealers of mobile and modular commercial units. Serves as a national structure for dealing with regulations. **Purpose:** Enhances the future growth and capabilities of the industry by encouraging innovation and quality among its members. Conducts surveys of the industry. Compiles statistics from industry and government surveys. Operates educational programs. **Publications:** *Annual Industry Survey* (annual); *Commercial Modular Construction* (bimonthly); Membership Directory (annual).

TRADE PERIODICALS

48504 ■ *Mobile Radio Technology*
Pub: Prism Business Media
Contact: Mercy Contreras, Publisher
E-mail: mercy_contreras@intertec.com
Ed: Donny Jackson, Editor, djackson@primediabusiness.com. **Released:** Monthly. **Price:** $3 single issue; $2 single issue. **Description:** Technical magazine for the mobile communications industry.

TRADE SHOWS AND CONVENTIONS

48505 ■ Mobile Air Conditioning Society Worldwide Convention and Trade Show
Mobile Air Conditioning Society Worldwide
PO Box 88
225 S. Broad St.
Lansdale, PA 19446
Ph:(215)631-7020
Fax: (215)631-7017
Co. E-mail: info@macsw.org
URL: http://www.macsw.org
Released: Annual. **Audience:** Mobile air-conditioning distributors, installers, service personnel, manufacturers, and suppliers to the industry. **Principal Exhibits:** Parts and products for the air-conditioning trade. **Dates and Locations:** 2007 Feb 01-03, Phoenix, AZ.

FRANCHISES AND BUSINESS OPPORTUNITIES

48506 ■ Altracolor Systems
111 Phlox Ave.
Metairie, LA 70001
Free: 800-727-6567
Fax: (504)471-0144
No. of Franchise Units: 60. **Founded:** 1989. **Franchised:** 1991. **Description:** Mobile auto painting and plastic repair. **Equity Capital Needed:** $37,500-$53,950 total investment; $11,700 cash liquidity. **Franchise Fee:** $8,000-$19,950. **Royalty Fee:** $95/week. **Financial Assistance:** In-house financing available. **Training:**

48507 ■ Fast-teks On-site Computer Serviced
15310 Amberly Dr., No. 185
Tampa, FL 33647

Free: 800-262-1671
Fax: (813)932-2485
No. of Franchise Units: 57. **Founded:** 2003. **Franchised:** 2004. **Description:** On-site computer repair services. **Equity Capital Needed:** $34,500-$57,950. **Franchise Fee:** $19,500-$39,500. **Royalty Fee:** 7%. **Financial Assistance:** No. **Training:** Offers 2 days training at headquarters and 2 days on-site with ongoing support provided.

48508 ■ Knifex
208-1810 Alberni St.
Vancouver, BC, Canada V6G 1B3
Ph:(604)647-0133
Free: 877-956-4229
Fax: (604)647-0120
Co. E-mail: c.cooper@knifex.com
URL: http://www.knifex.com
No. of Franchise Units: 10. **Founded:** 1999. **Description:** A mobile business company offering commercial and residential kitchens with the ability to shop for different products at their door. **Franchise Fee:** $10,000-$15,000. **Financial Assistance:** Yes. **Training:** Yes.

48509 ■ Par-T-Zone
2353 N 970 W
Clinton, UT 84015
Ph:(801)825-7278
Free: 800-506-7278
Fax: (801)732-6511
No. of Company-Owned Units: 3. **Founded:** 2004. **Franchised:** 2005. **Description:** Mobile childrens party set-ups. **Equity Capital Needed:** $15,000-$25,000. **Franchise Fee:** $18,900. **Financial Assistance:** No. **Training:** Provides training and ongoing support.

ASSOCIATIONS AND OTHER ORGANIZATIONS

48510 ■ Association for Multicultural Counseling and Development
1285 Cheyenne Blvd.
Madison, TN 37115
Ph:(615)876-5117
URL: http://www.bgsu.edu/colleges/edhd/programs/AMCD/HomePage.html
Contact: Dr. Canary Hogan, Membership Chair
Description: Represents professionals involved in counseling careers in educational settings, social services, and community agencies; interested individuals and students. Seeks to develop programs aimed at improving ethnic and racial empathy and understanding; foster personal growth and improve educational opportunities for all minorities in the U.S.; defend human and civil rights; provide in-service and pre-service training for members and others in the profession. Works to enhance members' ability to serve as behavioral change agents. Offers placement service. **Publications:** *Journal of Multicultural Counseling and Development* (quarterly); Newsletter (3/year).

48511 ■ Common Destiny Alliance
CODA EDPL Benjamin Bldg.
University of Maryland
College Park, MD 20742
Ph:(301)405-0639
Fax: (301)405-3573
Co. E-mail: mh267@umail.umd.edu
URL: http://www.education.umd.edu/CODA/index.html
Contact: Walter Allen, Scholar
Membership: Organizations and scholars interested in working to end prejudice. **Purpose:** Fosters the viewpoint that cultural diversity is "a resource that can help the nation attain goals such as improving economic productivity and the academic achievement of all children." Seeks to end racial isolation in schools, neighborhoods, and the work force. Promotes social policies, especially those related to education, that encourage racial and ethnic understanding and cooperation. Conducts research to identify the causes of racism and means to overcome racism. **Publications:** *Toward a Common Destiny: Improving Race and Ethnic Relations in America*; *Tracking, Diversity, and Educational Equity: What's New in the Research?*.

48512 ■ Ethnic and Multicultural Information Exchange Roundtable
Office for Library Outreach Services
50 E Huron
Chicago, IL 60611
Ph:(312)280-4295
Free: 800-545-2433
Fax: (312)280-3256
Co. E-mail: sorange@ala.org
URL: http://www.ala.org/ala/emiert/aboutemiert/aboutemiert.htm
Contact: Dr. Plummer Alston Jones Jr., Chm.
Membership: A round table of the ALA. **Purpose:** Exchanges information about minority materials and li-

brary services for minority groups in the U.S. Conducts educational programs with a focus on multicultural librarianship. **Publications:** *Directory of Ethnic & Multicultural Publishers, Distributors and Resource Organizations, 5th Ed.* (periodic); *EMIE Bulletin* (quarterly) ; *Ventures Into Culture: A Resource Book of Multicultural Materials and Programs, 2nd Edition (2001)* (periodic).

48513 ■ Institute of HeartMath
14700 W Park Ave.
Boulder Creek, CA 95006
Ph:(831)338-8500
Fax: (831)338-8504
Co. E-mail: info@heartmath.org
URL: http://www.heartmath.org
Contact: Sara Paddison, Pres./CEO
Purpose: Works to create a cultural shift in how organizations view people, and how people view each other and themselves. Seeks to scientifically validate the intelligence of the heart. Conducts biomedical research programs on the sources of stress, including work with post-cardiac patients, people interested in emotional management, educators serving child populations of at risk, learning disabled, at risk for violence, and in all sectors of society. **Publications:** *Heartmath Solution*; *Research Overview* (annual).

48514 ■ International Federation for the Protection of the Rights of Ethnic, Religious, Linguistic and Other Minorities
11-25 30th Ave.
Long Island City, NY 11102
Ph:(718)728-3330
Fax: (718)956-9583
Contact: Mr. Menelaos G. Tzelios, Sec.Gen.
Membership: Individuals united in protecting the human rights of ethnic, religious, and linguistic minorities. Reports human rights violations. **Publications:** Newsletter (quarterly).

48515 ■ Multicultural Education, Training, and Advocacy
240A Elm St., Ste. 22
Somerville, MA 02144
Ph:(617)628-2226
Fax: (617)628-0322
Co. E-mail: rlr@shore.net
Contact: Roger Rice, Exec. Dir.
Membership: Attorneys, parents, organizers, and trainers. **Purpose:** Serves as an educational defense body for minority children and children from low-income families. Conducts research and educational programs. **Publications:** *A Handbook for Immigrant Parents to Protect the Rights of Your Children* (monthly); *Educational Equity*.

48516 ■ National Association of Public Sector Equal Opportunity Officers
City of Tallahassee Equal Opportunity Department
300 S Adams St.
Tallahassee, FL 32301
Ph:(850)891-8290
Fax: (850)891-8733
Co. E-mail: ofuanis@talgov.com
URL: http://www.talgov.com

Contact: Sharon Ofuani
Membership: Equal employment opportunity officers and coordinators, human resources managers, employee relations directors, attorneys, lawmakers, consultants, community relations specialists, and other associated professionals in the public sector. **Purpose:** Promotes the professionalism of equal opportunity workers and an understanding of diversity as means for improving the quality of life for all citizens. Serves as a resource for the public and private sectors through education and training. Provides recruitment assistance for professional, technical, and executive/managerial positions. Acts as a clearinghouse for members on effective problem solving and decision making.

48517 ■ National MultiCultural Institute
3000 Connecticut Ave. NW, Ste. 438
Washington, DC 20008-2556
Ph:(202)483-0700
Fax: (202)483-5233
Co. E-mail: nmci@nmci.org
URL: http://www.nmci.org
Contact: Elizabeth Pathy Salett MSW, Pres.
Description: Seeks to work with individuals, organizations, and communities in creating a society that is strengthened and empowered by its diversity. Leads efforts to increase communication, understanding, and respect among diverse groups and addresses important issues of multiculturalism facing society today. Provides organizational training and consulting on diversity issues and develops leading edge projects in the field. Cross-cultural conflict resolution, and initiating cross-cultural dialogues. Programs serve professionals in such fields as management, human resource development, education, health and mental health, social services, refugee resettlement, mediation, and law enforcement. **Publications:** *Crossing Cultures in Mental Health*; *Developing Diversity Training for the Workplace: A Guide for Trainers*; *Multicultural Case Studies for Diversity Training*; *Race, Ethnicity and Self: Identity in Multicultural Perspective*; *Teaching Skills and Cultural Competency: A Guide for Trainers*.

REFERENCE WORKS

48518 ■ "$1 Billion Outreach" in *Hispanic Business* (April 2005, pp. 14)
Pub: Hispanic Business
Description: Marriott International Inc. plans to spend $1 billion with minority- and women-owned suppliers over the next five years.

48519 ■ "Adapting to a multicultural workforce" in *Safety & Health* (Vol. 163, No. 3, March 2001, pp. 282)
Pub: National Safety Council
Description: Issues concerning the effectiveness of health and safety measures presented to company employees are discussed, by way of answering the concerns of a safety professional. It is emphasized that all employees' communication needs should be addressed to ensure effectiveness of safety regulations.

48520 ■ "Affirmative Action on Trial" in *Hispanic Business* **(September 2003, pp. 40-42, 44)**
Pub: Hispanic Business
Ed: Holly Ocasio Rizzo. **Description:** The nation's law and business schools are struggling to raise minority enrollment, and the new U.S. Supreme Court ruling struck down a plan giving Hispanics and other minorities extra points toward undergraduate admission.

48521 ■ "Any Room on the Board?" in *Hispanic Business* **(Vol. 24, No. 1/2, January/February 2002, pp. 24, 26)**
Pub: Hispanic Business Inc.
Ed: Jonathan Higuera. **Description:** Closing the diversity gap on Fortune 1000 boards means understanding the job description for the position and developing the skills required to perform the duties. It is estimated that 82 Hispanics currently hold 114 board seats among the Fortune 1000, a 52 percent increase over 2001, but still a short parity with the Hispanic population.

48522 ■ "Back to Basics: Ex-Dotcommers Create New Beginnings through Low-Tech Businesses" in *Entrepreneur* **(Vol. 31, No. 9, September 2003)**
Pub: Entrepreneur Media, Inc.
Ed: Mark Henricks. **Description:** A growing number of ex-dotcommers are starting new businesses in low-technology fields associated with immigrant Americans.

48523 ■ "Banking on Diversity" in *Hispanic Business* **(November 2006, pp. 74, 76)**
Pub: Hispanic Business
Ed: Leanndra Martinez. **Description:** Analysis and advice for recruiting and hiring a multicultural workforce is presented.

48524 ■ "A Bicultural Bias" in *Hispanic Business* **(December 2003, pp. 24, 26)**
Pub: Hispanic Business
Ed: Abel Ramirez Magana. **Description:** Research shows Hispanics succeed in mainstream U.S. society on their own terms. According to a study conducted by the PEW Hispanic Center, second generation Hispanic births will outpace the rate of Hispanic immigration. Statistical data included.

48525 ■ "Blockbuster Stores Get Hispanic Theme" in *Hispanic Business* **(January/February 2003, pp. 17)**
Pub: Hispanic Business
Description: Blockbuster stores are incorporating bilingual and Spanish language signage in nearly 1,000 retail stores across the country.

48526 ■ "Boosting Corporate Diversity" in *Hispanic Business* **(April 2005, pp. 14)**
Pub: Hispanic Business
Description: Many corporate managers believe that diversity programs provide a competitive edge because they improve a company's performance and leadership. The University of Texas, Austin started a program to expand the number of diverse students for their MBA program.

48527 ■ *Catching the Wave of Workforce Diversity: Powerful New Skills for Managers*
Pub: BookPartners, Inc.
Ed: Joy Boszioch. **Released:** 1995. **Price:** $14.95.

48528 ■ *Chinese Ethnic Business*
Pub: Routledge Inc.
Ed: Eric Fong; Chiu Ming Luk. **Released:** October 2006. **Description:** Impact of globalization on Chinese ethnic small businesses is covered, focusing on U.S., Australia, and Canada.

48529 ■ "The clumsy multinational" in *Harvard Business Review* **(Vol. 80, No. 9, September 2002, pp. 128)**
Pub: Harvard Business School Press
Ed: John Kenneth Galbraith. **Description:** Reprints of material from "The defense of the multinational company", printed in Harvard Business Review, April 1978, in which the author criticizes many existing business attitudes.

48530 ■ "Corporate Diversity" in *Hispanic Business* **(January/February 2005, pp. 50, 52, 54)**
Pub: Hispanic Business
Description: In response to the ever-changing consumer and workforce demographics, corporate diversity means creating programs that integrate with core company values and accountability measures. Ways to measure the return on investment for these practices are presented.

48531 ■ "Cracks in the Melting Pot" in *Inc.* **(Volume 27, December 2005, No. 12, pp. 27-29)**
Pub: Inc. Magazine
Ed: Stephanie Clifford. **Description:** Because of stiff Visa restrictions, entrepreneurial immigrants are finding opportunities overseas. Statistical data included.

48532 ■ "Cropping Up" in *Hispanic Business* **(May 2005, pp. 14)**
Pub: Hispanic Business
Description: Pennsylvania State University established the new Latino Agricultural Center that will work to develop agricultural educational resources and offer a Spanish class for agricultural professionals.

48533 ■ "Crossing the clothesline" in *Hispanic Business* **(Vol. 22, No. 3, March 2000, pp. 14)**
Pub: Hispanic Business
Ed: Graham Witherall. **Description:** Issues concerning the influence of Hispanics in California's garment industry are presented. The majority of the 150,000 cutting and sewing workers in the garment industry are Hispanic, but none have reached management status. This discrepancy is discussed.

48534 ■ *Cultural Diversity: Challenges and Opportunities*
Pub: Pfeiffer & Co.
Ed: Catherine D. Fyock. **Price:** $75.00 (leader's guide, looseleaf); $9.95 (participant's workbook, paper). **Description:** Part of the Managing Diversity Workshop Series.

48535 ■ "Despite Push for Diversity, Hotels Struggle to Find Qualified Applicants" in *San Diego Business Journal* **(Vol. pp.)**
Pub: San Diego Business Journal Associates
Ed: Connie Lewis. **Description:** Hotels and resorts are trying to attract more qualified minorities and women to the industry, but are finding a shortage of applicants.

48536 ■ *Diversity Activities and Training Designs*
Pub: Pfeiffer & Co.
Ed: Julie O'Mara. **Price:** $159.00 (looseleaf). **Description:** Contains 25 workshop and meeting designs for addressing diversity in the workplace.

48537 ■ *Diversity Awareness Profile*
Pub: Pfeiffer & Co.
Ed: Karen Grote. **Price:** $3.95. **Description:** Manager's Version also available, same price. The *Profile* can be administered and processed in 1 hours, and can be used alone or as part of a larger diversity program. Use it to help employees become aware of their unintentional biases and overcome them.

48538 ■ "Diversity in the Big City" in *Hispanic Business* **(June 2002, pp. 80)**
Pub: Hispanic Business
Ed: Vivienne Heines. **Description:** The New York Times conducted a study that reveals that both hiring managers and job seekers in the New York metropolitan area equate diversity with equal opportunity and fairness, thus seeing diversity as a contribution to a good work environment. Statistical data included.

48539 ■ *Diversity Bingo: An Experiential Learning Event*
Pub: Pfeiffer & Co.
Price: $99.95 (trainer's package, looseleaf); $49.95 (diversity bingo cards, 50-card pack). **Description:** Trainer's package includes 50 bingo cards; additional cards may be purchased separately. Based on bingo, game helps participants overcome their biases and communicate.

48540 ■ "Diversity Defined" in *Hispanic Business* **(January/February 2003, pp. 64, 66)**
Pub: Hispanic Business
Description: Results of the Hispanic Business Corporate Diversity Survey show that diversity is defined in different terms from company to company. In a recent online poll, IBM was named the country's number one company for providing opportunity to minority-owned firms. A listing of corporations seeking multicultural and bilingual workers is included.

48541 ■ "Diversity in the Workplace" in *My Business* **(February/March 2004, pp. 15)**
Pub: My Business Magazine
Ed: Dennis McCafferty. **Description:** Legal experts offer advice on workplace practices involving ethnic diversity.

48542 ■ "Driving Force" in *Hispanic Business* **(April 2005, pp. 56, 58)**
Pub: Hispanic Business
Ed: Anthony Limon. **Description:** Analysis and advice relating to recruitment and career development in the auto industry is given. Due to the high volume of car sales in 2005, new sales and service professionals will be recruited by dealerships.

48543 ■ *Dynamics of Diversity: Strategic Programs for Your Organization*
Pub: Crisp Publications, Inc.
Ed: Odette Pollar and Rafael Gonzalez. **Price:** $9.95.

48544 ■ "Embracing Diversity, Not Division" in *Black Enterprise* **(Vol. 34, No. 7, February 2004, pp. 14)**
Pub: Earl Graves Publishing Co.
Ed: Earl G. Graves, Sr. **Description:** Diversity, whether corporate or otherwise, is not only respecting and honoring the differences between cultures, it also means recognizing the cultural variety that exists within and among minority groups, including language, heritage, or skin color.

48545 ■ "Emerging Threat: Human Rights Claims" in *Harvard Business Review* **(Vol. 81, No. 8, August 2003, pp. 16)**
Pub: Harvard Business School Press
Ed: Elliot Schrage. **Description:** In this historical overview, U.S. courts are accepting an increasing number of human rights cases against companies involving the Alien Tort Statute (ATS) enacted in 1789. This act grants original jurisdiction to the U.S. federal courts for civil actions brought by an alien for a tort committed in violation of international law. In 1980, the first significant civil rights case was brought using ATS.

48546 ■ "Federal File: News & Developments in the Business of Government" in *Hispanic Business* **(December 2001, pp. FG4, FG6, FG14, FG16)**
Pub: Hispanic Business
Description: The Department of Agriculture has an Outreach Office that helps socially disadvantaged farmers and farm workers gain access to federal programs. Federal government employment opportunities for minorities are presented with a listing of internship opportunities. Hispanic entrepreneurs owning 8(a) firms secured 14.4 percent of federal contracts for fiscal year 2000.

48547 ■ "Fire fight" in *Entrepreneur* **(Vol. 30, No. 2, February)**
Pub: Entrepreneur Media Inc.
Ed: Michelle Prather. **Description:** Employers of H-1B workers are coming under fire, facing accusations that they are laying off American workers in order to hire applicants from other countries who are willing to work for lower wages.

48548 ■ "Fixing Diversity-Challenged Companies" in *Black Enterprise* **(Vol. 36, February 2006, No. 7, pp. 74)**
Pub: Earl G. Graves Publishing Co. Inc.
Ed: Lee Anna Jackson. **Description:** R. Roosevelt Thomas, Jr., founder of The American Institute for Managing Diversity, believes most corporations have replaced the term "affirmative action" with "diversity" but has not changed its mindset of employees or modified company culture.

48549 ■ "Found in Translation" in *Inc.* (Oct, 2006, pp. 41-42)

Pub: Gruner & Jahr USA Publishing

Ed: Joshua Hyatt. Description: Two-thirds of the population growth by 2050 will comprise of immigrants. Adapting your business climate to the changing ethnicity has latent benefits in customer identification with your company.

48550 ■ "Fox News Program Grooms Minority Apprentices for Top Jobs" in *Hispanic Business* (December 2006, pp. 50-51)

Pub: Hispanic Business

Ed: Hildy Medina. Description: Victor Garcia is an example of the minority workers Fox News is grooming for top level jobs in the corporation.

48551 ■ *Gendered Processes: Korean Small Business Ownership*

Pub: LFB Scholarly Publishing LLC

Ed: Eunju Lee. Released: November 2005. Price: $60.00. Description: Examination of the gender processes among Korean immigrants becoming small business owners in the New York City metropolitan area.

48552 ■ "Get Hired Now! A 28-Day Program for Landing the Job You Want" in *Black Enterprise* (Vol. 37, October 2006, No. 3, pp. 119)

Pub: Earl G. Graves Publishing Co. Inc.

Ed: C.J. Hayden; Frank Traditi. Description: Finding a job can be a challenge. Surveys estimate that 74 to 85 percent of those available are never advertised. Tips for searching out employment opportunities and landing the job you desire are explored.

48553 ■ "Growing Influence" in *Hispanic Business* (January/February 2005, pp. 18, 20)

Pub: Hispanic Business

Ed: Craig Mauro. Description: Increasing political clout and attention will help Hispanic small business and lead to immigration reform.

48554 ■ "Having a Black Woman In Charge Shows the Construction Field is Changing" in *Sacramento Bee* (November 27, 2005)

Pub: The Sacramento Bee

Ed: Blair Anthony Robertson. Description: Profile of Lydia Gartrell, who speaks to being underestimated by others in the construction industry. Gartrell is an African American woman who runs construction projects for Ikea's new sites.

48555 ■ "The hidden challenge of cross-border negotiations" in *Harvard Business Review* (Vol. 80, No. 3, March 2002, pp. 76)

Pub: Harvard Business School Press

Ed: James K. Sebenius. Description: A discussion of how national culture can influence decision-making and governance in business. Strategies for how businesses can conduct themselves are examined.

48556 ■ "Hire Diversity: Diversity Leaders" in *Hispanic Business* (October 2004, pp. 130)

Pub: Hispanic Business

Description: A listing of top corporations dedicated to workplace diversity and seeking multicultural and bilingual employees is presented.

48557 ■ "Hispanic Employment Program Managers Directory" in *Hispanic Business* (December 2001, pp. FG8, FG10 FG12)

Pub: Hispanic Business

Description: The Hispanic Employment Program Manager program assists in increasing the number of Hispanics employed in the U.S. workforce. A list of participating agencies is included.

48558 ■ "Hispantelligence Report" in *Hispanic Business* (September 2003, pp. 12-13)

Pub: Hispanic Business

Description: Comparison of stock market indexes and Hispanic companies, Hispanic occupational structure, education, Hispanic purchasing power, and investment traits of Hispanic Americans are featured. Statistical data included.

48559 ■ "Housing, Immigration Called Keys to the Future" in *Boston Globe* (January 31, 2005)

Pub: New York Times Company

Ed: Diane E. Lewis. Description: In order to compete in the global economy, Boston will need more affordable housing and immigrants. Richard Florida, an urban theorist, ranked Boston number three in the U.S. after measuring cities' abilities to attract the hip, educated people who encompass the creative class.

48560 ■ "Immigration Reform" in *Hispanic Business* (March 2004, pp. 14)

Pub: Hispanic Business

Description: Issues regarding U.S. immigration policies are examined.

48561 ■ "Immigration Reform, Latin American Trade Issues Piled on Congress's Plate" in *Hispanic Business* (November 2006, pp. 24)

Pub: Hispanic Business

Ed: Patricia Guadalupe. Description: Immigration and trade issues with Latin American countries and Mexico are discussed.

48562 ■ "The importance of being multilingual" in *Business Week Online* (Sept. 5, 2002)

Pub: McGraw-Hill Inc.

Ed: Thane Peterson. Description: The importance of bilingualism to small business as an opening to globalization is examined.

48563 ■ "In Pursuit of a Bias-Free Workplace" in *Hispanic Business* (January/February 2003, pp. 44, 48)

Pub: Hispanic Business

Ed: Patricia Guadalupe. Description: A survey conducted by PricewaterhouseCoopers, called The Diversity Survey: A Nationwide Survey on the State of Workplace Diversity, shows that most respondents to the survey felt employers saw diversity as important in the workplace and that working in a diverse environment important, however most felt that during a recession, diversity programs would not be a key in employment decisions.

48564 ■ "In a World of Pay" in *Harvard Business Review* (Vol. 81, No. 11, November 2003, pp. 31)

Pub: Harvard Business School Press

Ed: Bronwyn Fryer. Description: Compensation for expatriate staff and executives is analyzed.

48565 ■ "The Internship Edge" in *Hispanic Business* (Vol. 23, No. 10, October, 2001, pp. 90, 92)

Pub: Hispanic Business

Ed: Janet Perez. Description: For young Hispanics entering the work force, internships can provide an advantage. A profile of Belinda Stubblefield, vice president of global diversity at Delta Airlines, has developed initiatives that enable Delta to attract and leverage a highly skilled, diverse work force.

48566 ■ "IRS Agrees to Pursue Legislative Changes to Section 6103" in *Tax Notes* (Vol. 102, No. 3, January 19, 2004, pp. 295-298)

Pub: Tax Notes International

Ed: Heather Bennett, Timothy Catts. Description: The issue of using taxpayer identification numbers in conflict with immigrations laws is examined.

48567 ■ *The Jewish Century*

Pub: Princeton University Press

Ed: Yuri Slezkins. Released: August 2006. Price: $18.95. Description: Success and vulnerability of individuals of Jewish descent is discussed, uncovering the 'Jewish Revolution' within the Russian Revolution.

48568 ■ "John Ladaga" in *Hispanic Business* (January/February 2005, pp. 56)

Pub: Hispanic Business

Description: Profile of John Ladaga, vice president and general manager service delivery for EDS America discusses his company's diversity program in detail.

48569 ■ "The language of safety" in *Rough Notes* (Vol. 146, No. 4, April 2003, pp. 24)

Pub: Rough Notes

Ed: Elisabeth Boone. Description: Accidents and injuries sustained by non-English speaking workers can be reduced or avoided when they learn by doing. Training industrial workers has been a success with Best Institute Inc., headed by Joseph E. Harcarz, Sr., CEO.

48570 ■ "Latinas' Businesses and Earnings are Seeing Major Growth" in *Marketing to Women* (Vol. 19, October 2006, No. 10, pp. 2)

Pub: EPM Communications, Inc.

Description: According to Hispanic Business Inc., Hispanic woman-owned businesses grew 64 percent between 1997 and 2004. Latinas' median incomes also grew. Statistical data included.

48571 ■ "Locker Room Tactics" in *Hispanic Business* (October 2002, pp. 76)

Pub: Hispanic Business

Ed: Teresa Talerico. Description: Professional coaching is used to help individuals and companies obtain results and reach goals. Corporate diversity training can work to combat workplace discrimination.

48572 ■ "Lonely at the Top: Blacks Are a Fraction of Top Editors at Mainstream Magazines" in *Black Enterprise* (Vol. 35, September 2004, No. 2)

Pub: Earl G. Graves Publishing Co. Inc.

Ed: Carolyn M. Brown. Description: According to an Equal Employment Opportunity Commission report, the magazine industry is less diverse than other media. A study commissioned by the Magazine Publishers of America discovered management in the industry approaches diversity not in race, gender, or ethnicity, but rather in a diversity of perspectives, knowledge, and styles.

48573 ■ "Madame chairman" in *WorkingWoman* (Vol. 25, No. 5, May 2000, pp. 30)

Pub: Lang Communications Inc.

Ed: Karen Bennett. Description: Christine Lagarde holds the top position of one of the world's biggest law firms, Baker and McKenzie. Issues concerning her attitudes towards the firm, law, cultural differences and balancing family needs with the demands of work, are presented.

48574 ■ "Maine Tribes Express Interest in Naval Base Redevelopment Project" in *Portland Press Herald* (December 17, 2005)

Pub: Blethen Maine Newspapers, Inc.

Ed: Kevin Wack. Description: The Penobscot Indian Nation and the Passamaquoddy Tribe are interested in redeveloping the Brunswick Naval Air Station. Plans include the manufacture of environmentally friendly wood-based products, aviation maintenance and manufacturing of airplane parts, and production of renewable energy.

48575 ■ "Man Behind the News" in *Hispanic Business* (July/August 2002, pp. 22, 24, 26)

Pub: Hispanic Business

Ed: Tim Dougherty. Description: Profile of Rolando Santos, broadcaster now executive vice president and general manager of CNN Headline News.

48576 ■ *Managing Diversity in Organizations*

Pub: University of Alabama Press

Ed: Robert T. Golembiewski. Released: 1995. Price: $25.95.

48577 ■ *Managing Diversity: The Complete Desk Reference*

Pub: Pfeiffer & Co.

Ed: Lee Gardenswartz and Anita Rowe. Price: $95.00.

48578 ■ "Managing a Multicultural Workforce" in *BlackEnterprise* (Vol. 31, No. 12, July 2001, pp. 120)

Pub: Earl Graves Publishing Co.

Description: In order to maintain a competitive edge, it has become critical that company's use appropriate management of their multicultural workforce in order to remain competitive in the marketplace.

48579 ■ **"Master of Her Retail Space"** in *Crain's New York Business* (Vol. 23, January 29, 2007, No. 5, pp. F11)
Pub: Crain Communications, Inc.
Ed: Elisabeth Butler. **Description:** Profile of Amira Yunis and her position as executive vice president of Newmark Knight Frank Retail. Ms. Yunis won the Real Estate Board of New York's Retail Deal of the Year award for putting Trader Joe's into Union Square. She brokered $10 million in business last year as well.

48580 ■ *Mastering Diversity*
Pub: Merritt Co.
Ed: James Walsh. **Released:** 1995. **Price:** $29.95.

48581 ■ **"Match Made in Heaven"** in *Hispanic Business* (June 2002, pp. 82)
Pub: Hispanic Business
Description: The Web site HireDiversity.com links professionals with corporations seeking multicultural and bilingual job candidates from entry- to senior-management-level positions. A listing of 24 such companies and contacts are included.

48582 ■ **"More Area Employers Seeking Spanish-Speaking Workers"** in *Ledger* (February 27, 2005)
Pub: Knight-Ridder/Tribune Business News
Ed: Kyle Kennedy. **Description:** Employers in the Lakeland area are looking to hire multilingual employees able to communicate in both English and Spanish.

48583 ■ **"More Minority Portfolio Managers Sought"** in *Sacramento Bee* (November 13, 2005)
Pub: The Sacramento Bee
Ed: Gilbert Chan. **Description:** Most private equity senior staff are white males from Ivy League schools; women and minorities continue to be ignored by money management companies. Many of the major money manager firms have paid millions in damages to settle sex-discrimination cases.

48584 ■ **"Multiculturalism Grows Up"** in *Hispanic Business* (Vol. 24, No. 4, April 2002, pp. 58, 60)
Pub: Hispanic Business Inc.
Description: An interview with Gustavo De La Torre, manager of Worldwide Diversity & Multiculture at Intel Corporation, about diversity in the workplace.

48585 ■ **"Multilingual Execs in Demand"** in *Hispanic Business* (March 2005, pp. 15)
Pub: Hispanic Business
Description: According to Korn/Ferry International, the need for multilingual executives is growing in the U.S. Statistical data included.

48586 ■ **"A New Breed of Entrepreneurs"** in *Black Enterprise* (Vol. 37, November 2006, No. 4, pp. 16)
Pub: Earl G. Graves Publishing Co. Inc.
Description: Black entrepreneurs are an important part of the chain for providing economic opportunities within the community. Many black business owners are more likely to hire black employees and apply innovative strategies in building their businesses rather than taking the traditional route.

48587 ■ **"New Political Players on the Scene"** in *Hispanic Business* (January/February 2005, pp. 14)
Pub: Hispanic Business
Ed: Patricia Guadalupe. **Description:** Henry Cuellar, John Salazar and Luis Fortuno are the new Hispanic member of the U.S. Senate. Issues involving the Central American Free Trade Agreement (CAFTA) and visa concerns are addressed.

48588 ■ **"Not Just Telenovelas"** in *The Record* (November 12, 2005)
Pub: New Jersey Media Group
Ed: Hugh R. Morley. **Description:** Teaneck, New Jersey's Univision 41, WXTV, is the first Spanish-language news program to get more viewers in a single New York area newscast than any other English-speaking channel. With the growth of new Spanish language immigrants, advertisers are seeking their attention.

48589 ■ **"Numbers Game"** in *Entrepreneur* (Vol. 32, No. 1, January 2004, pp. 30)
Pub: Entrepreneur Media, Inc.
Ed: Stephen Barlas. **Description:** High technology firms relying on the H-1B Visa to fill engineering and technical jobs with foreign workers face a drop in the number of visas available in 2004.

48590 ■ **"One Man's Alien is Another's Employee"** in *Inc.* (October 2005, pp. 32)
Pub: Inc. Magazine
Ed: Darren Dahl. **Description:** Iowa reports a 26 percent hike in Hispanics living in the state and reports that these foreign-born workers are vital to its growing economy.

48591 ■ **"A Place for More Hispanics?"** in *Hispanic Business* (March 2002, pp. 56)
Pub: Hispanic Business
Ed: Patricia Guadalupe. **Description:** Currently there is a push to get more Hispanics on the federal payroll, to help diversity government agencies.

48592 ■ **"Race-Conscious Agenda: Poll Shows Most African Americans Want Affirmative Action Reform"** in *Black Enterprise* (Vol. 34, Nov. 2003)
Pub: Earl Graves Publishing Co.
Ed: Marcia A. Wade. **Description:** A poll conducted in June 2003 by Black America's Political Action Committee suggests that African Americans believe affirmative action is good in principle but needs to be reformed.

48593 ■ **"Racial divisions still hang over efforts to foster cooperation"** in *Crain's Detroit Business* (Vol. 19, No. 17, April 28, 2003)
Pub: Crain Communications Inc., Detroit
Ed: Terry Kosdrosky. **Description:** Issues of segregation and racism in the Detroit metropolitan and surrounding areas are discussed. Business leaders are hoping to attract new residents to Detroit and to change the tone of political discourse.

48594 ■ **"Reaching Out to Low-Wage Countries"** in *Washington Business Journal* (Vol. 22, September 26, 2003)
Pub: Washington Business Journal
Ed: Tania Anderson. **Description:** Outsourcing of work overseas by engineering and computer firms has increased during the economic recession.

48595 ■ **"Recruitment Contacts"** in *Hispanic Business* (Vol. 24, No. 1/2, January/February 2002, pp. 62)
Pub: Hispanic Business Inc.
Description: A listing of corporations seeking multicultural and bilingual candidates is presented.

48596 ■ **"Recruitment: Hispanic Employment Program Managers"** in *Hispanic Business* (December 2002, pp. FRG6-FRG8)
Pub: Hispanic Business
Description: Contact information is provided from the Hispanic Employment Program Manager's Directory (HEPM); these managers are responsible with improving the representation of Hispanics in the work force.

48597 ■ **"Setting aside a reliance on set-asides"** in *Washington Business Journal* (Vol. 22, No. 3, May 23, 2003, pp. 35)
Pub: Washington Business Journal
Ed: Tania Anderson. **Description:** An examination of the management and development of Native Technologies, an American Indian-owned company is presented.

48598 ■ **"Speak employees' language to build their loyalty"** in *Atlanta Business Chronicle* (Vol. 24, No. 3, June 22, 2001, pp. 62A)
Pub: American City Business Journals Inc.
Ed: Eileen Brill Wagner. **Description:** Due to the multicultural workplace, businesses in Phoenix, Arizona are contracting to more foreign language firms.

48599 ■ **"State Investigates 'Tribal Coverage"** in *San Francisco Business Times* (Vol. 18, No. 6, September 19, 2003, pp. 1)
Pub: American City Business Journals
Ed: Daniel S. Levine. **Description:** Native Americans are being hired and leased back to avoid workers compensation costs to employers, which may be against California law.

48600 ■ **"Status Woe: Contractors' Illegal Workers Could Put You in a Legal Pickle"** in *Entrepreneur* (Vol. 32, No. 4, April 2004, pp. 23)
Pub: Entrepreneur Media, Inc.
Ed: Chris Penttila. **Description:** Small businesses can face lawsuits and fines up to $10,000 per illegal alien employee for every day worked on-site. It is important for small firms, when outsourcing, to review contracts with vendors supplying contract workers.

48601 ■ **"Sun Sets on H-1B Visa Provision"** in *Hispanic Business* (December 2003, pp. 12)
Pub: Hispanic Business
Description: The economic downturn, especially in the high-tech sector, has caused the number of H-1B visas in America to fall.

48602 ■ **"Tapping the Ethnic Marketplace Without Getting Lost in Translation"** in *Sacramento Bee* (November 20, 2005)
Pub: The Sacramento Bee
Ed: Thuy-Doan Le. **Description:** Potential pitfalls for successful dealing in a multicultural marketplace include mistranslation, mixed messages, and unintended slights due to ignorance of a culture.

48603 ■ *Team-Building for Diverse Work Groups: A Practical Guide to High-Performance and Diverse Teams*
Pub: Richard Chang Associates
Ed: Selma Myers. **Released:** 1995. **Price:** $12.95.

48604 ■ **"VC & Visas: Foreign Workers After the Fall"** in *Venture Capital Journal* (Vol. 41, No. 8, August 2000, pp. 6, 8, 10)
Pub: Venture Economics
Description: The failure of the dot-com industry has not hurt foreign workers with H-1B visas and venture-backed companies because of the critical need for those worker's expertise. Statistical data included.

48605 ■ **"Viewpoint: Rule on Race, Gender Data Has Outlived Its Intent"** in *American Banker* (Vol. 171, December 15, 2006, No. 240, pp. 11)
Pub: SourceMedia, Inc.
Ed: David Lizarraga; Fred Jordan. **Description:** Information regarding the Federaladopted Regulation B is presented. The regulation bars regulated financial institutions from targeting minorities in marketing or advertising campaigns or tracking or recording lending data by race, ethnicity, or gender.

48606 ■ **"Virtual Money Chain: Company Changes the Rules of Wire Transfers Through the Internet"** in *Black Enterprise* (Vol.34, No.4, Nov. 2003)
Pub: Earl Graves Publishing Co.
Ed: Tamara E. Holmes. **Description:** Profile of the technology firm, iKobo Inc., located in Atlanta, Georgia. The company offers electronic money transfer services and merchant payments, targeting foreign service sector workers and small- to medium-size businesses.

48607 ■ **"Wanted: African American Professional for Hire"** in *Black Enterprise* (Vol. 37, November 2006, No. 4, pp. 93)
Pub: Earl G. Graves Publishing Co. Inc.
Ed: Joe Watson. **Description:** Excerpt from the book, Without Excuses: Unleash the Power of Diversity to Build Your Business, speaks to the lack of diversity in the corporate arena and why executives, recruiters, and HR professionals claim they are unable to find qualified individuals of different races when hiring.

48608 ■ "Workforce Diversity in Small Business" in *Journal of Small Business Management* (Vol. 38, No. 3, July 2000, pp. 27)
Pub: West Virginia University
Ed: Don Gudmundson, Linda S. Hartenian. **Description:** While it would seem that hiring a diverse workforce would be advantageous to any firm that wants to compete globally, such diversity in fact entails costs as well as benefits for the small firm. This study explores the relationship between workforce diversity in small businesses and the small business owner/manager's motivation to diversify, the owner/manager's personal characteristics (ethnicity, age, education, and gender), and the number of family members employed in the small business.

48609 ■ "Working Hard for the Money" in *Black Enterprise* (Vol. 36, February 2006, No. 7, pp. 44)
Pub: Earl G. Graves Publishing Co. Inc.
Ed: Brenda Porter. **Description:** Black women with bachelor's degrees are securing more positions than Hispanic and white women with the same education level. The trend may be a result of black women working more hours and/or working more than job.

48610 ■ *Working Together: Succeeding in a Multicultural Organization*
Pub: Crisp Publications, Inc.
Ed: George Simons with Amy J. Zuckerman. **Released:** Revised edition. **Price:** $10.95.

48611 ■ *Workplace Diversity: A Manager's Guide to Solving Problems & Turning Diversity into a Competitive Advantage*
Pub: Adams Publishing
Ed: Katherine Esty. **Released:** 1995. **Price:** $10.95.

48612 ■ *A Workshop for Managing Diversity in the Workplace*
Pub: Pfeiffer & Co.
Ed: Sandra Kanu Kogod. **Price:** $79.95 (looseleaf). **Description:** Includes 18 workshop activities, background information on diversity, instructions on preparing for the workshop, and over one dozen handouts.

48613 ■ "The world in your backyard" in *WorkingWoman* (Vol. 25, No. 2, February 2000, pp. 72)
Pub: Lang Communications Inc.
Ed: Caitlin Kelly. **Description:** There are 617 consulates in the U.S., offering services in international marketing, labor and culture.

TRADE PERIODICALS

48614 ■ *Affirmative Action Register*
Pub: Affirmative Action Register
Ed: Joyce R. Green, Editor. **Released:** Monthly. **Price:** Free to qualified subscribers; $15 by mail. **Description:** Journal for business, academia, non-profit organizations and the government to use in recruiting females, Native Americans, minorities, veterans, and persons with disabilities.

48615 ■ *The Columbus Times*
Pub: Columbus Times
Contact: Ophelia Devore Mitchell, CEO
Released: Weekly (Wed.). **Description:** Black community newspaper.

48616 ■ *HR Reporter*
Pub: LRP Publications
Ed: Andrea Gold, Editor, agold@lrp.com. **Released:** Monthly, 12/year. **Price:** $325, U.S., Canada, and Mexico plus shipping/handling. **Description:** Covers issues in human relations, corporate policies and programs, and new concepts, theories, and trends. Recurring features include a two-page Update with notes on new reports and publications, tips, and a calendar of events. Remarks: Includes quarterly special issue.

VIDEOCASSETTES/ AUDIOCASSETTES

48617 ■ *Bridges: Skills to Manage a Diverse Workforce*
LearnCom HR Consulting and Training
38 Discovery, Ste. 250
Irvine, CA 92618
Ph:(515)440-0890
Free: 800-698-8263
Fax: (515)221-3149
Co. E-mail: nhartline@learncom.com
URL: http://www.learncomhr.com
Released: 1990. **Price:** $175.00. **Description:** An eight-part series designed to train supervisors and managers to deal with a culturally diverse workforce. The tapes are available individually or as a set. Trainer's manuals and participants manuals are included. **Availability:** VHS; 3/4U.

48618 ■ *Choices*
LearnCom HR Consulting and Training
38 Discovery, Ste. 250
Irvine, CA 92618
Ph:(515)440-0890
Free: 800-698-8263
Fax: (515)221-3149
Co. E-mail: nhartline@learncom.com
URL: http://www.learncomhr.com
Released: 1990. **Price:** $175.00. **Description:** A 12-part training course, designed to help train managers in EEO and affirmative action. Tapes are available as a set or individually. Trainer and participant manuals are included. **Availability:** VHS; 3/4U.

48619 ■ *Combating Racism*
Chinese for Affirmative Action
The Kuo Bldg.
17 Walter U. Lum Pl.
San Francisco, CA 94108
Ph:(415)274-6750
Fax: (415)397-8770
Co. E-mail: caa@caasf.org
URL: http://www.caasf.org
Released: 1973. **Description:** In this program various community representatives from San Francisco are interviewed as to what can be done to combat racism. Among those interviewed were Leonard Carter, George Tamsak, Mack Hall, Shone Martinez, John Chinn, and Margaret Cruz. **Availability:** EJ.

48620 ■ *Equal Opportunity*
Mercedes Maharis Productions
3066 El Camino Ave.
Las Vegas, NV 89102
Ph:(702)221-9337
Fax: (702)221-9079
Co. E-mail: cruiser@skylink.net
URL: http://www.seaspirit.com
Released: 1983. **Description:** This program explores the meaning of equal opportunity within the context of affirmative action, racial discrimination, past discrimination, union contracts, seniority, fairness and the Bill of Rights. **Availability:** VHS; 3/4U.

48621 ■ *Making Diversity Work*
American Management Association
9 Galen St.
PO Box 9119
Watertown, MA 02472
Ph:(617)926-4600
Free: 800-225-3215
Fax: (617)923-1875
URL: http://www.amanet.org
Released: 1993. **Price:** $215.00. **Description:** Contains information on today's growing diversity in the work force and offers three basic guidelines that can help make diversity work. **Availability:** VHS.

48622 ■ *Managing Cultural Differences*
Gulf Publishing Co.
PO Box 2608
Houston, TX 77252-2608
Ph:(713)520-4448
Free: 800-231-6275

Fax: (713)204-4433
Co. E-mail: csv@gulfpub.com
URL: http://www.gulfpub.com
Released: 1984. **Price:** $95.00. **Description:** This program gives an in-depth look at how cultural differences can affect business and management practices. **Availability:** VHS; 3/4U.

48623 ■ *Managing Diversity*
Excellence in Training Corp.
1303 Marsh Ln.
Carrollton, TX 75006
Free: 800-747-6569
Released: 1991. **Price:** $725.00. **Description:** A look at how to go beyond dealing with diversity to gaining from it. **Availability:** VHS; 3/4U; Special order formats.

48624 ■ *Meeting the Diversity Challenge*
American Management Association
9 Galen St.
PO Box 9119
Watertown, MA 02472
Ph:(617)926-4600
Free: 800-225-3215
Fax: (617)923-1875
URL: http://www.amanet.org
Price: $395.00. **Description:** Points out six major challenges that are faced by management and offers specific guidelines to promote a diverse work force. **Availability:** VHS.

48625 ■ *Prejudice: A Lesson to Forget*
Capital Communications
2357-3 S. Tamiami Tr.
Venice, FL 34296
Ph:(941)492-4688
Free: 800-822-5678
Fax: (941)492-4923
Released: 1973. **Description:** An interview with people who exhibit unconscious prejudices against minorities. **Availability:** VHS; 3/4U.

48626 ■ *Understanding EEOC, Part 1-3*
RMI Media
1365 N. Winchester
Olathe, KS 66061
Ph:(913)768-1696
Fax: (913)768-0184
Co. E-mail: actmedia@act.org
URL: http://www.rmimedia.com
Released: 1987. **Price:** $80.00. **Description:** In this three-part series, equal employment opportunity laws are explained and followed by suggestions for companies seeking to develop practices, policies, and procedures in this area. **Availability:** VHS; 3/4U.

48627 ■ *Vegetable Soup 1*
GPN Educational Media
Box 80669
Lincoln, NE 68501-0669
Ph:(402)472-2007
Free: 800-228-4630
Fax: 800-306-2330
URL: http://gpn.unl.edu
Released: 1975. **Description:** By dramatizing the positive value of human diversity, this series counters the negative, destructive effects of racial prejudice and isolation. Also available in 78 15-minute programs. All programs are available individually. **Availability:** VHS; 3/4U; CC.

48628 ■ *Vegetable Soup 2*
GPN Educational Media
Box 80669
Lincoln, NE 68501-0669
Ph:(402)472-2007
Free: 800-228-4630
Fax: 800-306-2330
URL: http://gpn.unl.edu
Released: 1978. **Description:** The second season of a series that promotes racial and ethnic harmony. Also available in 60 15-minute programs. All programs are available individually. **Availability:** VHS; 3/4U; CC.

48629 ■ *Why Value Diversity?*
American Management Association
9 Galen St.
PO Box 9119
Watertown, MA 02472

Ph:(617)926-4600
Free: 800-225-3215
Fax: (617)923-1875
URL: http://www.amanet.org
Price: $395.00. **Description:** Provides insights for managers to deal with the growing diversity of today's work force. **Availability:** VHS.

48630 ■ *The Work Prejudice Film*
Phoenix Learning Group
2349 Chaffee Dr.
St. Louis, MO 63146
Ph:(314)569-0211
Free: 800-221-1274
Fax: (314)569-2834
URL: http://www.phoenixlearninggroup.com
Released: 1974. **Description:** Investigates stereotypes and the world of work, encouraging the viewer to explore choices and educational opportunities. Part of the six-program "Work and You" series. **Availability:** VHS; 3/4U.

48631 ■ *Working Together: Managing Cultural Diversity*
Excellence in Training Corp.
1303 Marsh Ln.
Carrollton, TX 75006
Free: 800-747-6569
Released: 1991. **Description:** A video training program designed to teach viewers how to develop sensitivity to other cultures and be more effective in a multicultural environment. A leader's guide and workbooks are included. **Availability:** VHS; 3/4U; Special order formats.

TRADE SHOWS AND CONVENTIONS

48632 ■ National Black Masters of Business Administration Annual Conference and Exposition
National Black MBA Association, Inc.
180 N. Michigan Ave., Ste. 1400
Chicago, IL 60601
Ph:(312)236-2622
Fax: (312)236-0390
URL: http://www.nbmbaa.org
Released: Annual. **Audience:** Minority professionals and minority graduate students. **Principal Exhibits:** Fortune 500 corporations information and job recruitment services, and entrepreneurs for the Merchants Career Fair.

CONSULTANTS

48633 ■ Center for Managing Diversity Inc.
806 Twin Oaks Dr.
Potomac, MD 20854-2922
Ph:(301)762-1427
Scope: The firm provides comprehensive seminars on diversity management and general management. These seminars provide a step-by-step approach to managing diversity in the workplace. In addition, the firm conducts these seminars for individual organizations to suit theirs and their diverse work force's specific needs. **Publications:** "Ten Steps for Managing a Diverse Workforce". **Seminars:** Developing, Implementing and Maintaining a Diversity Management Program.

48634 ■ D.C.W. Research Associates International
2606 Parkdale Dr.
PO Box 5469
Kingwood, TX 77339-2476
Ph:(832)689-0923
Fax: (281)359-4238
Co. E-mail: dcwigg@earthlink.net

E-mail: dcwigg@earthlink.net
Scope: Provides consulting and training services in human resources professional management and or-

ganizational development with particular emphasis on: organizational analysis; human resource strategic planning; executive education; training program design and delivery; multicultural interventions such as the economic benefits of management of diversity in the workforce and the cultural determinants of international/global management; and program monitoring, evaluation, and analysis. Industries served: private industries, start-ups, energy, education and computer organizations, nonprofits, as well as government agencies (both U.S. and foreign). **Publications:** D. Wigglesworth, "Meeting the Needs of the Multicultural Workforce," in J. Kummerow (editor), New Directions in Career Planning and the Workplace, Consulting Psychologists Press, Inc. (1992); "International/Intercultural O.D." in W. Rothwell (editor), Organization Development Competencies, Pfeiffer Associates Publishers (1993); and "Diversity and Team Building" in M. Berger (editor) Cross-Cultural Team Building, McGraw-Hill Ltd., London, England (1995). **Seminars:** Managing the Multicultural Workforce; Negotiating With Integrity; Conflict Resolution; The Cultural Determinants of Business; Intercultural/International Project Management; The Challenge of Tomorrow's Workforce Today; Identity and Culture.

48635 ■ Ethnicity & Mental Health Associates
81 Pondfield Rd., Ste. 5
Bronxville, NY 10708-3907
Ph:(914)961-1940
Fax: (914)961-1940
Scope: Managing cultural diversity in the workplace and in the delivery of services to multi ethnic/racial groups (consumers). Also offers on-site workshops, consultations, and training. Industries served: corporations; nonprofit organizations including schools, colleges, health, mental health and human service organizations; and government agencies. **Publications:** Consultants have produced publications which explore the psychological nature of ethnic identity and how it influences behavior; also videos Proud To Be Me and Ethnic Sharing-Valuing Diversity. **Seminars:** Managing Cultural Diversity in the Workplace; Roots and Wings: Raising Children in a Multi-ethnic Society; Prejudice Reduction.

48636 ■ Lee Grossman Associates
9030 Forestview Rd.
Evanston, IL 60203-1913
Ph:(847)679-6796
Scope: Offers counsel in managing change, personnel issues and organization development. **Publications:** The Change Agent, American Management Association, Fat Paper, Diets for Trimming Paperwork, McGraw Hill. **Seminars:** Making Affirmative Action Work.

48637 ■ H & A International
13815 Ella Lee Ln., Ste. 100
Houston, TX 77077
Ph:(281)496-9044
Fax: (281)496-3671
Co. E-mail: dhuiras@huirasassoc.com
URL: http://www.huirasassoc.com

E-mail: dhuiras@huirasassoc.com
Scope: Executive, business, and team coaching. Accredited in Insights Learning and Development an International Psychometric Assessment tool for personal, business, sales, management, team effectiveness and learning styles. **Publications:** Contributes articles monthly to DBA Magazine, (Houston's business magazine); also wrote and facilitates seven continuing education programs for University of Houston. **Seminars:** Management Leadership/Development Certification workshop. City Slickers for Corporate America Leadership workshop. Additional workshops in communication and teambuilding. **Special Services:** Consulting with e-learning to develop on-line programs that incorporate the different learning styles.

48638 ■ Human Resource Solutions Inc.
244 5th Ave.
New York, NY 10001-7604
Ph:(212)316-2800

Fax: (212)316-6994
Co. E-mail: golivero@nyc.rr.com

E-mail: golivero@nyc.rr.com
Scope: Organizational performance improvement firm provides consulting services in executive coaching, process consulting, team building, organization development, management training, strategic planning retreats, quality and productivity enhancement, and conflict resolution. Industries served: manufacturing, retail, communications, computers, and government.

48639 ■ ITEC Inc.
Summit Twr.
5835 Callaghan, Ste. 360
San Antonio, TX 78228
Free: 800-681-4832
Fax: (210)523-6880
Co. E-mail: itecinc@ix.netcom.com

E-mail: itecinc@ix.netcom.com
Scope: Designs materials and conducts workshops for companies and agencies with culturally diverse workforces. Sees diversity as a positive factor in creativity and high productivity; specializes in supervisory/managerial development, as well as maintenance, mechanic, and support staff empowerment. Assists organizations to develop "in-house capacity" by training and developing their own employees to perform task analysis, curriculum development, job aid design, and "train the trainer" sessions. Develops surveys and assessments for all stages of strategic planning; facilitates all phases of processes, including the team building and implementation/coaching phase, for profit, non-profit, and government offices. Industries served: private and government offices. **Publications:** Distributors for INSCAPE (DiSC, Time, Diversity, etc), CRM Learning (Films and MultiMedia, CRISP Learning Books, & AV Materials). **Seminars:** The Challenge of Leadership; Managing Diversity via Empowerment; Basic Leadership Skills for Women; The Challenge of Team Building; Conflict Management; Controlling and Eliminating Employee Absenteeism; Managing Stress and Preventing Burnout; Managing Performance; Making Meetings Work; Taming and Training the Pen; No-Limit Secretary; Managing Organizational Change; Effective Problem Solving and Decision Making. **Special Services:** Some assessment instruments, AV materials are on-line.

48640 ■ Kochman Mavrelis Associates Inc.
845 N Ridgeland Ave.
Oak Park, IL 60302
Ph:(708)383-9235
Free: 800-723-7640
Fax: (708)383-9084
Co. E-mail: tomkma@aol.com
URL: http://www.kmadiversity.com

E-mail: tomkma@aol.com
Scope: Offers guidance through the various stages of growth and understanding that lead to effective management of cultural differences. Specifically, managers can learn to identify patterns of cultural difference, social experiences, issues and concerns of a socially and culturally diverse workforce; develop effective interventionist strategies; and adopt a group or organizational philosophy that recognizes the value of cultural diversity. Serves private industries as well as government agencies.

48641 ■ McClure Associates Inc.
PO Box 40637
Mesa, AZ 85274-0637
Ph:(480)829-6801
Fax: (480)968-5897
Co. E-mail: lmcclure@mcclureassociates.com
URL: http://www.mcclureassociates.com

E-mail: lmcclure@mcclureassociates.com
Scope: Nationally recognized expert in preventing employee violence. Also train in managing anger, conflict, stress and change. Provide expert witness analysis and testimony. **Publications:** "Angry Women: Stop Letting Anger Control Your Life!," Impact Publi-

cations, 2003; " Managing High-Risk Behaviors," Impact Publications, 2003; "Angry Men: Managing Anger In UnForgiving World," 2004. **Seminars:** The Risky Business: Managing Violence in the Workplace™program.

48642 ■ Navarro, Kim & Associates
529 N Charles St., Ste. 202
Baltimore, MD 21201-5043
Ph:(410)837-6317
Fax: (410)837-6294
Co. E-mail: bnavarro@sprynet.com

E-mail: bnavarro@sprynet.com
Scope: Firm specializes in bridging the gap between firms and non-traditional ethnic communities, especially in community development and institutional building.

48643 ■ New Dynamics Associates
72 Shore Dr.
PO Box 595
Laconia, NH 03247-0595
Ph:(603)524-1115
Free: 800-580-4651
Fax: (603)528-7912
Co. E-mail: newdynam@aol.com
URL: http://www.newdynamicsconsulting.com

E-mail: newdynam@aol.com
Scope: Provides organization development consulting to a variety of organizations, specializing in the management of diversity and working in flat inclusive structures. **Publications:** A Male/Female Continuum: Paths to Colleagueship Pierce, Wagner, and Page; Sexual Orientation and Identity H. Wishik and C. Pierce; The Power Equity Group Pierce. Definitions for Multicultural Dialogue: What's Best for What I'm Trying to Say? David Wagner. **Seminars:** Sexual Orientation and Identity; Journeys of Race and Culture.

48644 ■ Pope & Associates Inc.
11800 Conrey Rd., Ste. 240
Cincinnati, OH 45249
Ph:(513)671-1277
Fax: (513)671-1815
Co. E-mail: info@popeandassociates.com
URL: http://www.popeandassociates.com

E-mail: info@popeandassociates.com
Scope: Personnel Diversity consultants and trainers who have developed an approach to Workforce Diversity designed to improve working relationships and reduce interpersonal barriers by focusing on the needs of all employees. Consulting services include organizational diagnosis, program design and evaluation, conflict management, personnel counseling, and organizational change interventions. Industries served: agri-business, banking/insurance/finance, chemicals/pharmaceuticals, communications/publishing, education, energy, entertainment, food and beverages, government, health services, manufacturing, research and development, transportation, and wholesale/retail. **Publications:** "Relationship Mapping". **Seminars:** Managing Personnel Diversity; Diversity SOS: Skills for Ongoing Success; Diversity Learning Lab; Understanding Gender Dynamics; Consulting Pairs®.

48645 ■ ProActive English
1001 Pine St., Ste. 1004
San Francisco, CA 94109
Ph:(415)752-2270
Co. E-mail: infopae@proactive-english.com
URL: http://www.proactive-english.com

E-mail: infopae@proactive-english.com
Scope: Offers on-site individual and small group language and communication training. Sets up learning plans tailored to the needs and schedules of managers and executives who are non-native English speakers. Serves all industries. **Seminars:** Communicating in Business Situations; Presentations and Pronunciation.

48646 ■ Professional Psychological Services
4130 Linden Ave., Ste. 309
Dayton, OH 45432

Ph:(513)254-7301
Fax: (513)254-2117
Co. E-mail: ppsdocs@aol.com

E-mail: ppsdocs@aol.com
Scope: Offers clinical services, human relations training, multicultural and pluralistic training, and staff development and training.

48647 ■ PROGroup Inc.
1 Main St. SE, Ste. 200, Riverplace
Minneapolis, MN 55414
Ph:(612)379-7223
Free: 800-651-4093
Fax: (612)379-7048
Co. E-mail: progroup@progroupinc.com
URL: http://www.progroupinc.com

E-mail: progroup@progroupinc.com
Scope: Improves work cultures by liberating the potential of every employee. Services result in healthier, more productive work environments that directly impact the bottom line. It has formed national and international alliances that make it even more effective in helping organizations with the challenges and opportunities of expanding national and international marketplaces and a more diverse workforce. Services include organizational assessment, strategic diversity planning, executive coaching, diversity task forces, diversity initiative roll-outs, facilitation of diversity training programs, and Train-the-Trainer sessions. **Seminars:** Women Change makers; Linkage, Apr, 2006.

48648 ■ Simmons Associates Inc.
31 N Sugan Rd.
PO Box 712
New Hope, PA 18938
Ph:(215)862-3020
Fax: (215)862-3077
Co. E-mail: info@simassoc.com
URL: http://www.simmonsassoc.com

E-mail: info@simassoc.com
Scope: Human resource consultants active in managing diversity, eliminating sexual harassment management, development, executive training, leadership, cross cultural communications, career strategies for minorities and professional women. **Seminars:** Leadership 2020 ®: Managing Diversity for Increased Productivity; Eliminating and Responding to Sexual harassment; Effective Interviewing Selection; Diversity 2020 ®; Selfhelp Career Strategies for Professional Women and Minorities; Vectors ®.

48649 ■ Horace Williams
1466 San Pasqual St.
Pasadena, CA 91106
Ph:(626)793-3524
Scope: Management consultant specializing in multiculturalism and program evaluation.

RESEARCH CENTERS

48650 ■ Intercultural Communication Institute
8835 SW Canyon Ln.,Ste 238
Portland, OR 97225
Ph:(503)297-4622
Fax: (503)297-4695
Co. E-mail: ici@intercultural.org
URL: http://www.intercultural.org
Contact: Milton Bennett PhD, Dir.
E-mail: ici@intercultural.org
Scope: Intercultural communication, international education; diversity; counseling; conflict, negotiation and mediation.

48651 ■ Medical College of Wisconsin–Center for the Study of Bioethics
8701 Watertown Plank Rd.
Milwaukee, WI 53226
Ph:(414)456-8498
Fax: (414)456-6511

Co. E-mail: rshapiro@mcw.edu
Contact: Robyn Shapiro JD, Dir.
E-mail: rshapiro@mcw.edu
Scope: Ethics studies, with special emphasis on AIDS, abortion, drug testing, euthanasia, fetal rights, genetics, technology assessment and allocation of resources, and multicultural approaches to bioethics. **Services:** Bioethics online service. **Publications:** Bioethics Bullentin (biennially). **Educational Activities:** Master of Arts in Bioethics.

48652 ■ National MultiCultural Institute
3000 Connecticut Ave. NW, Ste. 438
Washington, DC 20008-2556
Ph:(202)483-0700
Fax: (202)483-5233
Co. E-mail: nmci@nmci.org
URL: http://www.nmci.org
Contact: Elizabeth Pathy Salett, Pres.
E-mail: nmci@nmci.org
Scope: Race and racism, preventing prejudice and bias, workforce diversity, multicultural education, cross-cultural mental health, and cross-cultural conflict resolution. **Publications:** Abstracts (annually). **Educational Activities:** Training in cultural awareness, cultural competency, and prejudice and bias prevention.

48653 ■ University of Houston–African American Studies Program
629 Agnes Arnold Hall
Houston, TX 77024-3047
Ph:(713)743-2811
Fax: (713)743-2818
Co. E-mail: jconyers@uh.edu
URL: http://www.hfac.uh.edu/aas
Contact: Dr. James L. Conyers Jr., Dir.
E-mail: jconyers@uh.edu
Scope: Public policy-related issues and topics focused on African Americans in Houston, Texas, and throughout the U.S. **Services:** Food and clothing drives. **Publications:** Ujima (biennially). **Educational Activities:** Conferences, forums, and workshops; Cultural programs, for the community; Graduate Fellowship Initiative; Instruction emphasizing cultural and historical heritage of Africans and black Americans, analyzing and critically examining sociological, psychological, economic, and political aspects of the black community, as it exists in the U.S. and Africa.

48654 ■ University of Texas at Arlington–Women and Minorities Research and Resource Center
Box 19599
Arlington, TX 76019
Ph:(817)272-3131
Fax: (817)272-3117
Co. E-mail: womensstudies@uta.edu
URL: http://www.uta.edu/womens_studies/
Contact: Beth Anne Shelton, Dir.
E-mail: womensstudies@uta.edu
Scope: Women and work, particularly the interrelationships between work and family, women entrepreneurs and owners of small businesses, and the effect of on-site child care facilities on employee, family, company, and child. Activities encompass studies of demographic trends and projections, education, reentry of mature women to higher education, and sex equity.

48655 ■ University of Wisconsin— Milwaukee–Institute on Race and Ethnicity
PO Box 413
Milwaukee, WI 53201
Ph:(414)229-6701
Fax: (414)229-4581
Co. E-mail: jfk2@uwm.edu
URL: http://www.uwm.edu/Dept/IRE
Contact: Dr. Joyce F. Kirk, Exec.Dir.
E-mail: jfk2@uwm.edu
Scope: Race and ethnicity. **Publications:** Ethnicity and Public Policy Series; Kaleidoscope II Newsletter (annually). **Educational Activities:** Conferences, seminars, and colloquia; Symposia on pedagogical and research issues. **Awards:** Minority faculty research awards (annually).

START-UP INFORMATION

48656 ■ "Hot 100" in *Entrepreneur* (Vol. 31, No. 6, June 2003, pp. 64)
Pub: Entrepreneur Media Inc.
Ed: Amanda C. Kooser. **Description:** Twenty-five of the 100 companies hitting the year's hottest industry for 2003 come from the business services sector, nine providing logistics services (such as freight-handling, trucking and transportation) and six providing marketing and advertising services.

48657 ■ *Learn by Doing: A Step-by-Step How-To Guide about Multi-Level Marketing*
Pub: Gary's Ideas
Ed: Gary Molatore. **Released:** 1998. **Price:** $30.00.

48658 ■ "A One-Stop Marketing Shop" in *Entrepreneur* (Vol. 31, No. 10, October 2003, pp. 112)
Pub: Entrepreneur Media, Inc.
Description: Profile of PRstore LLC, offering franchises to former corporate marketing executives wishing to own a retail business. The firm has created more than 50 standard customizable products that franchisees use to help clients develop marketing campaigns.

ASSOCIATIONS AND OTHER ORGANIZATIONS

48659 ■ **Multi-Level Marketing International Association**
119 Stanford Ct.
Irvine, CA 92612
Ph:(949)854-0484
Fax: (949)854-7687
Co. E-mail: info@mlmia.com
URL: http://www.mlmia.com
Contact: Doris Wood, Chair
Membership: Companies, support groups, and distributors. **Purpose:** Seeks to strengthen and improve the Multi-Level Marketing (also known as Network Marketing) industry in the U.S. and abroad. (Multi-Level Marketing is a method of selling products directly, independently, and usually out of the home, without the medium of a retail outlet.) Provides educational services to consumers and law enforcement agencies. Serves as an information source for the industry. Offers recommendations for start-up companies; maintains speakers' bureau; conducts training programs. **Publications:** *Connecting Point*; *Corporate Directory - Support Directory* (quarterly). **Telecommunication Services:** electronic bulletin board; electronic mail, doriswood@mlmia.com; teleconference.

REFERENCE WORKS

48660 ■ "Being Small, Looking Big" in *Boston Business Journal* (Vol. 23, No. 21, June 27, 2003, pp. 24)
Pub: American City Business Journals
Ed: Chelsea Lowe. **Description:** Nancy Michaels of Impression Impact, Inc. discusses ways small companies can market themselves in a way that makes them look large, without spending large amounts of money to do so.

48661 ■ "Business Integrator Entrepreneur Marries Technology and Advertising to Grow Business" in *Black Enterprise* (Vol. 35, Jan. 2005, No. 6)
Pub: Earl G. Graves Publishing Co. Inc.
Ed: Nichole Lewis. **Description:** Interactive marketing strategies have helped POWERi to grow in the travel and tourism industry despite a slowdown since the terrorist attacks of 9-11. The firm operates three lines of business: technology within an advertising agency that could also provide marketing strategy and graphic design services. The firm reported revenues of $1 million in 2003.

48662 ■ "Cross-Training" in *Entrepreneur* (Vol. 31, No. 9, July 2003, pp. 83)
Pub: Entrepreneur Media, Inc.
Ed: Kim T. Gordon. **Description:** Multichannel marketing, using broadcast, direct mail, email and print campaigns, are being used to attract customers and increase sales.

48663 ■ "Done Deal: How One Sales Pro Closed a Big Customer" in *Sales and Marketing.com* (Vol. 156, No. 3, March 2004, pp. 9)
Pub: VNU eMedia, Inc.
Description: Tanya Spaulding, principal with Shea Inc., a marketing design firm in Minnesota, recalls a situation where she had to help a client in a highly desirable retail space to either rebrand the business, create a new business, or to sell the property.

48664 ■ "East End PR Firm Helps Give Webshots One More Shot" in *Long Island Business News* (February 27, 2004)
Pub: Dolan Media Newswires
Ed: Claude Solnik. **Description:** Profile of Webshots, a company providing online digital photo services. The firm hired Vineberg Communications to provide market research and to handle media and analyst relations.

48665 ■ *A Great Way to Get Wealth: How to Start & Build a Network Marketing Business from Your Home*
Pub: Colonial Press
Released: 1993. **Price:** $19.95.

48666 ■ "Listening Begins at Home" in *Harvard Business Review* (Vol. 81, No. 11, November 2003, pp. 106)
Pub: Harvard Business School Press

Ed: James R. Stengel, Andrea L. Dixon, Chris T. Allen. **Description:** The utilization of market research techniques to identify and address employee concerns is analyzed in an examination of Proctor and Gamble.

48667 ■ "A Matter of Opinion" in *Entrepreneur* (Vol. 31, No. 8, August 2003, pp. 72)
Pub: Entrepreneur Media, Inc.
Ed: Elizabeth Goodgold. **Description:** According to Jeffrey G. Jordan, market researcher for 1-on-One Marketing Associates, mystery shopping, customer comment cards, on-site intercepting, Web site evaluation and toll-free telephone numbers are great ways to get customer feedback.

48668 ■ *Multi-Level Money: The Complete Guide to Generating, Closing & Working with All the Prospects You Need to Make Real Money Every Month in Network*
Pub: JLA Publications
Ed: Jeffrey Lant. **Released:** 1995. **Price:** $19.95.

48669 ■ "A One-Stop Marketing Shop" in *Entrepreneur* (Vol. 31, No. 10, October 2003, pp. 112)
Pub: Entrepreneur Media, Inc.
Description: Profile of PRstore LLC, offering franchises to former corporate marketing executives wishing to own a retail business. The firm has created more than 50 standard customizable products that franchisees use to help clients develop marketing campaigns.

48670 ■ *Power Multi-Level Marketing*
Pub: Quantum Leap
Ed: Mark Yarnell. **Released:** 1993. **Price:** $10.00.

48671 ■ "Speak Up! The Ins and Outs of Hiring a Spokesperson" in *Entrepreneur* (Vol. 32, No. 2, February 2004, pp. 75)
Pub: Entrepreneur Media, Inc.
Ed: Nancy Michaels. **Description:** Pros and cons to hiring a spokesperson to represent a small company are discussed. Resources are included.

48672 ■ *Successful Network Marketing for the Twenty-First Century*
Pub: Oasis Press
Ed: Rod Nichols. **Released:** 1995. **Price:** $15.95.

48673 ■ "Vector Marketing" in *Mississippi Business Journal* (Vol. 29, January 2007, No. 2, pp. 6)
Pub: Venture Publications, Inc.
Description: Profile of Rebecca Huckeby, of Vector Marketing. Huckeby placed in the Top 25 sales reps from more than 40,000 sales representatives nationwide.

48674 ■ "Worth a Try" in *Entrepreneur* (Vol. 31, No. 8, August 2003, pp. 71)
Pub: Entrepreneur Media, Inc.
Ed: Elizabeth Goodgold. **Description:** Maureen Murphy, president of Direct Effectz, a direct-marketing

consulting firm in San Diego, California recommends offering free samples, even in the service area. Direct Effectz offers a free marketing audit to interested companies.

VIDEOCASSETTES/ AUDIOCASSETTES

48675 ■ *Beware the Naked Man Who Offers You His Shirt*
PBS Home Video
Catalog Fulfillment Center
PO Box 751089
Charlotte, NC 28275-1089
Ph:800-531-4727
Free: 800-645-4PBS
Co. E-mail: info@pbs.org
URL: http://www.pbs.org
Released: 1990. **Price:** $395.00. **Description:** The author of "Swim With the Sharks Without Being Eaten Alive" offers insights and advice on increasing sales productivity. **Availability:** VHS; 3/4U.

48676 ■ *Creating a Winner: The Real Secrets of Successful Marketing*
Warner Home Video, Inc.
5775 Linder Canyon Rd.
Westlake Village, CA 91362
URL: http://whv.warnerbros.com
Released: 1989. **Price:** $59.95. **Description:** A video sponsored by Inc. Magazine and AT&T, outlining the best procedures for marketing a product. **Availability:** VHS.

48677 ■ *How to Win Marketing Wars in the 1990s*
Excellence in Training Corp.
1303 Marsh Ln.
Carrollton, TX 75006
Free: 800-747-6569
Released: 1991. **Price:** $395.00. **Description:** A three-part discussion of principles of global marketing strategies. **Availability:** VHS; 3/4U; Special order formats.

48678 ■ *Marketing*
Coast Telecourses
11460 Warner Ave.
Fountain Valley, CA 92708-2597
Ph:(714)241-6109
Free: 800-547-4748
Fax: (714)241-6286
Co. E-mail: coastlearning@cccd.edu
URL: http://www.coastlearning.org
Released: 1992. **Description:** A video course in marketing. **Availability:** VHS; 3/4U; Q.

48679 ■ *Marketing Research*
GPN Educational Media
Box 80669
Lincoln, NE 68501-0669
Ph:(402)472-2007
Free: 800-228-4630
Fax: 800-306-2330
URL: http://gpn.unl.edu
Released: 1988. **Price:** $69.95. **Description:** Looks at the format, systematic approach and the informal, casual methods of marketing research, and how companies make their marketing decisions. **Availability:** VHS.

48680 ■ *Marketing Strategy*
Kantola Productions, LLC
55 Sunnyside Ave.
Mill Valley, CA 94941-1935
Ph:(415)381-9363
Free: 800-989-8273
Fax: (415)381-9801
Co. E-mail: info@kantola.com
URL: http://kantola.com
Released: 1988. **Price:** $189.00. **Description:** Part one of two part program introduces the fundamentals of a solid marketing plan. In part two, Professors Thomas S. Robertson and David J. Reibstein present a marketing strategy audit that identifies the key points of a good plan. Originally presented at the Aresty Institute for Executive Education at the Wharton School. Comes with audiocassette and study guide. **Availability:** VHS.

48681 ■ *Philip Kotler on Competitive Marketing*
Video Arts, Inc.
c/o Aim Learning Group
8238-40 Lehigh
Morton Grove, IL 60053-2615
Free: 877-444-2230
Fax: (416)252-2155
Co. E-mail: service@aimlearninggroup.com
URL: http://www.aimlearninggroup.com
Price: $995.00. **Description:** Kotler, a professor at the Kellogg Business School at Northwestern University, provides the fundamentals of successful marketing in the contemporary business environment through panel discussions with business leaders and other experts. **Availability:** VHS.

CONSULTANTS

48682 ■ Eastern Point Consulting Group Inc.
75 Oak St.
Newton, MA 02464
Ph:(617)965-4141
Fax: (617)965-4172
Co. E-mail: info@eastpt.com
URL: http://www.eastpt.com

E-mail: info@eastpt.com
Scope: Specializes in bringing practical solutions to complex challenges. Provides consultation and training in managing diversity; comprehensive sexual-harassment policies and programs; organizational development; benchmarks 360 skills assessment; executive coaching; strategic human resource planning; team building; leadership development for women; mentoring programs; and gender issues in the workplace. **Seminars:** Leadership Development for Women.

FRANCHISES AND BUSINESS OPPORTUNITIES

48683 ■ Halstrom High School
Halsrom Education Company
2204 El Camino Real, 310
Oceanside, CA 92054
Ph:(760)721-0121
Free: 888-HAL-STRO
Fax: (760)721-6127
Co. E-mail: mhalasz@halstrom.org
URL: http://www.halstrom.org
No. of Franchise Units: 3. **No. of Company-Owned Units:** 3. **Founded:** 1985. **Franchised:** 2005. **Description:** This franchise opportunity is for people who value education, are highly ethical, independent, energized, respectful, responsible, possess strong communication skills, and appreciate the meaning of the word, 'alternative.' Franchisees must demonstrate that they have a strong background in sales, management, marketing, and education. Successful franchisees must also have a strong desire to build a successful business that serves a vital role in their communities. **Equity Capital Needed:** $118,213-$228,371. **Franchise Fee:** $40,000 license fee. **Training:** Offers 10 days franchise and staff training, both locally and nationally with ongoing support.

LIBRARIES

48684 ■ Alticor Inc.–Corporate Library
7575 E. Fulton St.
Ada, MI 49355
Ph:(616)787-7400
Fax: (616)787-7142
Co. E-mail: corporate_library@accessbusinessgroup.com
Contact: Gary Stevens, Corp.Libn.
Scope: Chemistry, direct selling, business. **Services:** Interlibrary loan; copying; SDI; Library not open to the public. **Holdings:** 10,000 books; 10,000 archival items. **Subscriptions:** 1400 journals and other serials; 7 newspapers.

New Product Development

START-UP INFORMATION

48685 ■ "American Megatrends vets start a new company" in *Atlanta Business Chronicle* (Vol. 24, No. 11, August 17, 2001, pp. 2A)
Pub: American City Business Journals Inc.
Ed: Mary Jane Credeur. **Description:** Two former engineers of American Megatrends Inc. have formed iVivity Inc., which has received over $11 million in venture capital backup. Sukha Ghosh and Sanjay Sehgal are now designing a data storage management storage product they hope will revolutionize the market. Their iDISX (Distributed Intelligent Storage exchange) product will operate, diagnose and repair data storage networks.

48686 ■ "Join the club: launching your first product" in *Entrepreneur* (Vol. 31, No. 5, May 2003, pp. 132)
Pub: Entrepreneur Media Inc.
Ed: Don Debelak. **Description:** An inexperienced inventor can gain valuable knowledge and insight by joining an inventor's club. Steps to help find the right group and make the most of a membership are listed.

48687 ■ "Less Is More: Believe It Or Not" in *Entrepreneur* (Vol. 31, No. 8, August 2003, pp. 114)
Pub: Entrepreneur Media, Inc.
Ed: Don Debelak. **Description:** Melody Ross, founder of Chatterbox Inc. in Eagle, Idaho, tells how she was able to successfully market her line of products for scrapbooking. Ross projects $4 million in sales for 2003.

48688 ■ "A matter of safety" in *Black Enterprise* (Vol. 32, No. 9, April 2002)
Pub: Earl Graves Publishing Co.
Ed: Alan Hughes. **Description:** Orlando Robinson tells how a tragic event in his life prompted him to launch his own company, D&D Innovations Inc. His first product is the Seatbelt Shifter Lock, which requires the seatbelt to be locked before the car can be taken out of the park position.

48689 ■ "Ready For Launch" in *My Business* (June/July 2002, pp. 16)
Pub: My Business Magazine
Ed: Vicki Gerson. **Description:** Creativity is the key in successfully introducing a new product to the market.

48690 ■ "We'll drink to that! " in *Entrepreneur* (Vol. 31, No. 4, April 2003, pp. 112)
Pub: Entrepreneur Media Inc.
Ed: Nichole L. Torres. **Description:** Profile of Christopher J. Miller, Craig Cook, Robert Pfeiffer, Heike Pfeiffer and Kerri Bryant, co-founders of Low Carb Living Inc. Inspired by the renewed popularity of the Atkins diet, the entrepreneurs produce low carbohydrate alternatives to traditional margarita mixes, including Baja Bob's Sugar Free and Low Garb Bar and Party Mixes.

48691 ■ "You're the Inspiration" in *Entrepreneur* (Vol. 33, September 2005, No. 9, pp. 96)
Pub: Entrepreneur Media Inc.
Ed: Nichole L. Torres. **Description:** Ways to patent and market a new product are shared by StartupNation.com. A business-advice Website that is run by small business experts, Jeff and Rich Sloan is highlighted.

REFERENCE WORKS

48692 ■ "A Market for Ideas" in *The Economist* (Vol. 377, October 22-28, 2005, No. 8449, pp. 3-6, 8-10, 12-18)
Pub: The Economist Newspaper Ltd.
Description: The magazine presents information collected from a survey conducted on issues of patents and technology. Protection of intellectual property can be good for both the technology industry and its customers. The patent system, companies preparing for intellectual-property battles, a new intellectual-property business model, sharing intellectual property, Indian and Chinese competition in innovation, and new markets for intellectual property are among issues investigated.

48693 ■ *Achieving Planned Innovation: A Proven System for Success with New Products & Services*
Pub: The Free Press
Ed: Frank R. Bacon and Thomas W. Butler. **Released:** 1998. **Price:** $29.50; $30.00.

48694 ■ "American Axle hopes new 4WD unit can shift it into high gear" in *Crain's Detroit Business* (Vol. 18, No. 51, Dec. 23, 2002, pp. 17)
Pub: Crain Communications Inc., Detroit
Ed: Terry Kosdrosky. **Description:** Profile of the new power-transfer units, called PTUs. PTUs are manufactured by American Axle & Manufacturing Holdings Inc., BorgWarner Inc, and Magna International Inc.'s Magna Steyr. The products are used on smaller power-utility vehicles.

48695 ■ "Amgen Looking to Develop Medicines with Competitors" in *Providence Business News* (Vol. 18, No. 20, September 1, 2003, pp. 2)
Pub: Providence Business News, Inc.
Ed: Marni Leff Kottle. **Description:** Efforts by Amgen to find competitor with promising drug for joint venture scheme are discussed. Topics include testing of new drugs, possible profits from new drugs, and Amgen's falling market share.

48696 ■ "Avalanche Gear Alert!" in *Fortune* (Vol. 151, February 21, 2005, No. 4, pp. 36)
Pub: Time Inc.
Ed: Paul Tolme. **Description:** With the increase in avalanche deaths, the ski industry is developing new equipment for the backcountry skier. Profile of Salt

Lake City's Black Diamond, the company that developed AvaLung2, that extracts air through a breathing tube and vents deadly CO2 away from a victim's face. The company's CEO has survived two avalanches.

48697 ■ "Aven Hopes Portable Microscope Drives Growth" in *Crain's Detroit Business* (Vol. 22, December 18, 2006, No. pp. 16)
Pub: Crain Communications Inc. - Detroit
Ed: Tom Henderson. **Description:** New portable microscope and digital camera to be marketed by Ann Arbor firm. This product combines a high resolution camera, with a series of in-house developed lenses. Target markets are crime scene investigations and quality control in manufacturing.

48698 ■ "Avoiding Invention Scams" in *Black Enterprise* (Vol. 37, January 2007, No. 6, pp. 46)
Pub: Earl G. Graves Publishing Co. Inc.
Ed: James C. Johnson. **Description:** Invention promotion firms provide inventors assistance in developing a prototype for product development. It is important to research these companies before making a commitment to work with them because there are a number of these firms that are not legitimate and have caused independent inventors to lose thousands of dollars by making false claims as to the market potential of the inventions.

48699 ■ "Battenberg is riding along with Segway" in *Crain's Detroit Business* (Vol. 18, No. 24, June 17, 2002, pp. 8)
Pub: Crain Communications Inc. - Detroit
Ed: Mary Kramer. **Description:** Profile of the Segway Human Transporter, a two-wheel scooter designed to help overweight Americans.

48700 ■ "Better Way for Better Made?" in *Crain's Detroit Business* (Vol. 21, October 3, 2005, No. 43, pp. 3)
Pub: Crain Communications Inc. - Detroit
Ed: Brent Snavely. **Description:** Better Made Snack Foods Inc. is hoping its new products will boost sales for the firm. The company has put together a new executive team and signed a new union contract.

48701 ■ "Beyond the Big Idea: You've Got a Million-Dollar Idea; Now All You Need is a Strategy To Make It Marketable" in *Entrepreneur* (Vol. 32)
Pub: Entrepreneur Media Inc.
Ed: Karen E. Spaeder. **Description:** Inventors who were able to bring their ideas to life share their successes.

48702 ■ "Bio Solutions Acquisition" in *Mississippi Business Journal* (Vol. 29, January 2007, No. 2, pp. 9)
Pub: Venture Publications, Inc.
Ed: Wally Northway **Description:** Bio Solutions Manufacturing Inc. acquired an oil and grease extraction technology for the removal of fat, oil and grease from organic waste effluent.

48703 ■ "Boston Scientific Looks To Expand Its Products Beyond Stents" in *Boston Globe* **(February 2, 2005)**
Pub: New York Times Company
Ed: Ross Kerber. **Description:** Boston Scientific executives are looking to expand beyond stents into technology areas such as implantable cardiac defibrillators, and small spinal implants for pain management. The company has also developed an endoscopy system that includes a digital camera which could replace other instruments currently used for colonoscopies.

48704 ■ "Breakfast Yogurt" in *Dairy Foods* **(Vol. 103, No. 10, October 2002, pp. 12)**
Pub: Business News Publishing Co.
Description: Profile of Dean Foods Company, Dallas, Texas, and their new yogurt sticks for breakfast and snacks.

48705 ■ "Breaking the Ice: Want Skeptical Customers to Warm Up to Your Product?" in *Entrepreneur* **(Vol. 33, February 2005, No. 2, pp. 120)**
Pub: Entrepreneur Media Inc.
Ed: Don Debelak. **Description:** Peter Lerman, inventor, and marketer, Lou Matinale have partnered to license and market Lerman's invention, the Sno-Easy. The Sno-Easy is an ergonomic shovel that allows users to shovel snow without bending or twisting.

48706 ■ "Breath of Fresh Air: How Do You Sell Buyers On an Invention That Creates a New Product Category?" in *Entrepreneur* **(October 2004)**
Pub: Entrepreneur Media Inc.
Ed: Don Debelak. **Description:** Profile of Dr. Robert Pincus and Dr. Scott Gold, founders of SaltAire, a drug-free, pH-balanced saline nasal rinse. The spray is used to moisturize nasal passages and flush out irritants. The doctors share how they started with $150,000 in 1997 and 1998 and project sales of $1.1 million for 2004.

48707 ■ "Bringing Back a Classic" in *Inc.* **(August 1, 2003)**
Pub: Gruner & Jahr USA Publishing
Ed: Leigh Buchanan. **Description:** Profile of Betty Morris, the woman who founded Shrinky Dinks in 1973 and by the 1980s the products were seen everywhere.

48708 ■ "Bucking the Odds at Amylin" in *Business Week* **(January 9, 2006, No. 3966, pp. 64, 66)**
Pub: McGraw-Hill Companies
Ed: Arlene Weintraub. **Description:** Profile of Ginger Graham, chief executive at Amylin Pharmaceuticals Inc., who was considering retirement before taking the reins at Amylin. Graham, who is a diabetic, has helped the company attain government approval on two diabetes drugs.

48709 ■ "Bulk chocolate" in *Prepared Foods* **(Vol. 171, No. 5, May 2002, pp. 83)**
Pub: Business News Publishing Co.
Description: Cocoa powder, chocolate liquor, press cake and bean nibs, as well as bulk finished chocolate items, are offered by one of only a handful of U.S. companies manufacturing chocolate from cocoa bean to finished products.

48710 ■ "Burning Cash, MannKind is Raising More Money" in *San Fernando Valley Business Journal* **(Vol. 11, December 2006, No. 25, pp. 11)**
Pub: San Fernando Valley Business Journal Associates
Ed: Chris Coates. **Description:** MannKind Corp., the biopharmaceutical developer, plans to raise $400 million to help fund Technosphere, a cornerstone product for diabetes that has been in research and development for over a decade.

48711 ■ "The Change Up: Find New Uses for Your Products" in *My Business* **(February/March 2003, pp. 15)**
Pub: My Business Magazine

Ed: Evelyn Beck. **Description:** Diversification of a product can be a good tool for increasing sales, but it is imperative to do research.

48712 ■ "Chatom Offers Wines With Cause Tie-Ins" in *Marketing to Women* **(Vol. 19, November 2006, No. 11, pp. 5)**
Pub: EPM Communications, Inc.
Description: She Wines, a line of wines created to benefit heart disease and breast cancer research, was introduced by women-owned and run Chatom Vineyards. The winery is based in Calaveras County, California.

48713 ■ "Chocolate temperers" in *Candy Industry* **(Vol. 167, No. 4, April 2002, pp. 88)**
Pub: Stagnito Communications Inc.
Description: Preview of the new Chocovision chocolate temperer. The Revolution Series, produced by Chocovision Corp., Poughkeepsie, NY, represents the most efficient tabletop chocolate processing equipment that allows for the highest degree of accuracy along with ease of operation, replacing the Sinsation Series temperers.

48714 ■ "Cigar Company Promoting Hand-Rolled Products, Delta Blues" in *Mississippi Business Journal* **(Vol. 29, January 2007, No. 2, pp. 3)**
Pub: Venture Publications, Inc.
Ed: Lynn Lofton **Description:** Profile of Avalon Cigars, a boutique cigar manufacturer that uses a proprietary pecan-aging process in their cigars.

48715 ■ "Cobasys Powers Up for Possible IPO; New Deal, HQ Spur Optimism" in *Crain's Detroit Business* **(Vol. 20, December 20, 2004, No. 51)**
Pub: Crain Communications Inc. - Detroit
Ed: Andrew Dietderich. **Description:** Cobasys LLC is planning an initial public offering in 2006 or 2007. Meanwhile, the firm plans to consolidate its executive, engineering and product development under one roof in Orion Township, Michigan.

48716 ■ "Commercialization gets attention in life-science funding" in *Crain's Detroit Business* **(Vol. 19, No. 1, January 6, 2003, pp. 16)**
Pub: Crain Communications Inc., Detroit
Ed: Laura Bailey. **Description:** The Michigan Economic Development Corporation created the Life Sciences Corridor that will distribute up to $1 billion in settlement money from tobacco companies over 20 years to develop the life-science industry. Startup firms feel that the funding guideline proposals favor funds for research over those for commercialization.

48717 ■ "Crazy Drivers: The Clubs About To Shake Up Golf" in *Wall Street Journal* **(Vol. 249, January 2007, No. 5, pp. P1-P4)**
Pub: Dow Jones & Co. Inc.
Ed: Wall Street Journal **Description:** New top-of-the-line unconventional clubs by makers such as Nike and Calaway have been introduced to the marketplace. Golf traditionalists are concerned the clubs will take the challenge away.

48718 ■ "Customers as Innovators" in *Harvard Business Review* **(Vol. 80, No. 4, April 2002, pp. 74)**
Pub: Harvard Business School Press
Ed: Eric Stefan, von Hippel Thomke. **Description:** A radically new approach to research and development is described. Companies are now encouraging customers to design and develop their own products and advice is given on how this can be achieved.

48719 ■ "Cyberkinetics Plans for Clinical Trials" in *Providence Business News* **(Vol. 18, No. 20, September 1, 2003, pp. 1)**
Pub: Providence Business News, Inc.
Ed: Mike Colias. **Description:** Product development taking place at Providence-based Cyberkinetics Inc. is discussed. Topics include drug testing, strategic planning, and company funding.

48720 ■ "Delphi engineers hoping carbon dioxide puts a chill in the air" in *Business First of Buffalo* **(Vol. 18, No. 46, Aug. 12, 2002, pp. 1)**
Pub: Knight-Ridder/Tribune Business News
Ed: Tom Hartley. **Description:** Delphi Harrison Thermal Systems of Lockport, New York, is exploring the use of carbon dioxide to replace ozone-damaging fluorocarbons in car air conditioners.

48721 ■ "Detroit Free Press Macomb Small Business Column" in *Detroit Free Press* **(September 29, 2005)**
Pub: Knight-Ridder/Tribune Business News
Ed: Carol Cain. **Description:** Former police officer, Steve Russ, describes his new product invention, Flak Vest Hangars. The hangars are designed to hold bulletproof vests.

48722 ■ "Detroit Free Press Oakland Small Business Column" in *Detroit Free Press* **(May 26, 2005)**
Pub: Knight-Ridder/Tribune Business News
Ed: Carol Cain. **Description:** Stephen Wiesman worked as a firefighter until being injured in 2002. Wiesman plans to introduce a new product he developed that will make stoves safer to use. Also featured: David Moncur's marketing, creative and technology consulting company.

48723 ■ "Detroit Free Press Wayne Small Business Column" in *Detroit Free Press* **(June 23, 2005)**
Pub: Knight-Ridder/Tribune Business News
Ed: Carol Cain. **Description:** Robert Mazur invented a handheld tool for opening medicine bottles, soup cans and plastic packaging after watching his grandmother struggle to open her medicine bottles.

48724 ■ "Diesel Gets Cleaner and Greener" in *Business Week* **(February 20, 2006, No. 3972, pp. 49)**
Pub: McGraw-Hill Companies
Ed: Gail Edmondson. **Description:** DaimlerChrysler has engineered a new emissions technology that promises to burn diesel fuels cleanly as gasoline. The automobile manufacturer has also unveiled its clean-diesel exhaust system in its Mercedes E-class sedans.

48725 ■ "Energy: Coming soon to a roof over you: solar shingles" in *Red Herring* **(No. 105, October 1, 2001, pp. 28)**
Pub: Herring Communications
Ed: Bridget Eklund. **Description:** Profile of the new construction material for roofing, solar shingles, and its growth into mainstream construction.

48726 ■ "Entrepreneur Column" in *Entrepreneur.com* **(February 16, 2006)**
Pub: Entrepreneur Media Inc.
Ed: Tamara Monosoff. **Description:** Five steps to help license a new product or invention are outlined.

48727 ■ *The Entrepreneur and Small Business Problem Solver*
Pub: John Wiley & Sons, Incorporated
Ed: William A. Cohen. **Released:** December 2005. **Price:** $24.95 (US); $31.99 (Canadian). **Description:** Revised edition of the resource for entrepreneurs and small business owners that covers everything from start-up financing and loans to new product promotion and more.

48728 ■ "Farmingdale-based THM Scientific Introduces Product Line Based on Sustainable Agriculture" in *Long Island Business News* **(Feb.6, 2004)**
Pub: Dolan Media Newswires
Ed: Adina Genn. **Description:** Profile of Peter Felix and James Sottilo, two arborists who have partnered to develop and produce Rootgrow, a line of organic-compost tea, brewers and related products and services that will preserve the soil. The partners are targeting homeowners, corporate parks, golf courses, and municipalities.

48729 ■ "Filmmakers Face Some Big Challenges On Tiny Cellphones" in *Wall Street Journal* (Vol. 248, December 2006, No. 145, pp. B1)
Pub: Dow Jones & Co. Inc.
Ed: Peter Grant **Description:** American entertainment industry and wireless companies invest billions of dollars into bringing movie and TV content to the video-capable small screen cellphones now flooding the market. Hollywood hopes this new market will become their "third screen".

48730 ■ "Finding your innovation sweet spot" in *Harvard Business Review* (Vol. 81, No. 3, March 2003, pp. 120)
Pub: Harvard Business School Press
Ed: Jacob Goldenberg, Roni Horowitz, Amnon Levav, David Mazursky. **Description:** Five innovative patterns that can be used for product innovation are presented. These patterns manipulate existing components of a product to come up with something ingenious and viable. The patterns include multiplication, subtraction, division, task unification, and attribute dependency.

48731 ■ "Five Ideas to Watch" in *Inc.* (August 1, 2004)
Pub: Inc. Magazine
Ed: Nicole Gull. **Description:** Five new ideas for products are presented, including a new window-mounted device that can detect brush fires; a new dog tag for the armed forces containing a wireless chip that carries medical and other key information for medics; pumps and motors that respond to electrical impulses; shopping carts that double as exercise equipment; and Steak n Shake's eight new milk shake flavors.

48732 ■ "Flight of Fancy? Launching a High-Tech Product Can be a Technical and Financial Challenge" in *Entrepreneur* (Vol. 32, August 2004)
Pub: Entrepreneur Media Inc.
Ed: Don Debelak. **Description:** Profile of William J. Boyer Jr. and partner and co-founder Ray Henson, who helped Boyer with the technical aspects of their digEplayer, a portable battery-operated in-flight entertainment system used on passenger tray tables. The company saw $1 millions in sales, first quarter 2004.

48733 ■ "Food for Thought" in *Black Enterprise* (Vol. 36, February 2006, No. 7, pp. 60)
Pub: Earl G. Graves Publishing Co. Inc.
Ed: James C. Johnson. **Description:** Advice is offered to would-be entrepreneur wishing to introduce a new snack food product to Frito-Lay Corporation.

48734 ■ "From Concept to Customer" in *Black Enterprise* (Vol. 36, November 2005, No. 4, pp. 124)
Pub: Earl G. Graves Publishing Co. Inc.
Ed: Sakina P. Spruell, James C. Johnson. **Description:** Six steps to bring a new product to market are outlined.

48735 ■ "From Idea to Marketplace" in *Small Business Opportunities* (Vol. 17, May 2005, No. 3, pp. 62, 64, 130)
Pub: Harris Publications Inc.
Ed: Kurt Kirckof. **Description:** Ideas to help inventors decide what to do with a newly developed product are shared.

48736 ■ "From idea to inspiration" in *Entrepreneur* (Vol. 30, No. 3, March 2002, pp. 29)
Pub: Entrepreneur Media Inc.
Ed: Mark Henricks. **Description:** Book review of 'The Big Idea', written by attorney Steven D. Strauss. The books tells how many products came to exist.

48737 ■ "GeoPhoenix is ready for its close-up" in *Red Herring* (January 2003, pp. 23)
Pub: Herring Communications Inc.
Ed: Nisha Ramachandran. **Description:** Profile of the Zoominator, a tiny new device promising users a new way to access information.

48738 ■ "Group Sees Window of Opportunity" in *Pittsburgh Business Times* (Vol. 23, No. 3, August 8, 2003, pp. 1)
Pub: Pittsburgh Business Times
Ed: Christopher Davis. **Description:** A new company, jointly owned by GE Plastics and Bayer Polymers, will sell a new polycarbonate glazing technology; the new company, called Exatec, will be led by CEO Clemens Kaiser.

48739 ■ "Growth Outside the Core" in *Harvard Business Review* (Vol. 81, No. 12, December 2003, pp. 66)
Pub: Harvard Business School Press
Ed: Chris Zook, James Allen. **Description:** Six methods to launch corporate growth into adjacent businesses, using Nike Inc.'s diversification from athletic shoes to golf equipment and apparel is explored. The methods include entering new geographies, using new distribution channels, developing new services and products, and targeting new customer segments.

48740 ■ "Hand In Hand" in *Entrepreneur* (Vol. 31, No. 8, August 2003, pp. 68)
Pub: Entrepreneur Media Inc.
Ed: Jane Easter Bahls. **Description:** If you negotiate well, joining forces with a big firm can be the smart way to get a new product to the marketplace. The product may be just what a big company needs to boost slumping sales.

48741 ■ "Hard Cell" in *Fast Company* (May 2001, pp. 108)
Pub: Fast Company
Ed: George Anders. **Description:** Is there anything more routine than making a call (or even surfing the Web) on a wireless phone? The process of making a stylish phone is anything but routine, and the story of the Kyocera Smartphone is a case study in creativity, design and engineering. The article addresses the obstacles to launching a new product in a crowded market.

48742 ■ "Have It Your Way" in *Forbes* (Vol. 175, February 14, 2005, No. 3, pp. 78)
Pub: Forbes Magazine Inc.
Ed: Melanie Wells. **Description:** Companies are tapping consumers to create new products with appeal. When General Motors announces its new Hummer He3, it will feature equipment inspired by customers.

48743 ■ "He Came. He Saw. He Took On the Whole Power-Tool Industry" in *Inc.* (Volume 27, July 2005, No. 7, pp. 86-91)
Pub: Inc. Magazine
Ed: Melba Newsome. **Description:** Profile of Stephen Gass, inventor of the new SawStop, a power saw whose blade stops immediately when it comes into contact with the user's body.

48744 ■ "Hot Kicks, Cool Price" in *Black Enterprise* (Vol. 37, December 2006, No. 5, pp. 34)
Pub: Earl G. Graves Publishing Co. Inc.
Ed: Topher Sanders. **Description:** Stephon Marbury of the New York Nicks introduced a new basketball shoe, the Starbury One, costing $14.98. The shoes are an addition to the Starbury clothing line and although the privately owned company would not disclose figures; stores sold out of a month's worth of inventory in merely three days.

48745 ■ "Hot Product" in *Pittsburgh Business Times* (Vol. 22, No. 52, July 11, 2003, pp. 3)
Pub: Pittsburgh Business Times
Ed: Christopher Davis. **Description:** Profile of a new product from Pittsburgh, Pennsylvania-based Menasha Packaging Company.

48746 ■ "How to build a blockbuster" in *Harvard Business Review* (Vol. 80, No. 10, October 2002, pp. 18)
Pub: Harvard Business School Press
Ed: Gary Lynn, Richard Reilly. **Description:** Colgate-Palmolive's debut of a new toothpaste is used as a case study to understand why the product achieved only a one percent market share.

48747 ■ "How do you narrow your product options?" in *Wall Street Journal* (March 17, 2003, pp. R3)
Pub: Dow Jones & Co. Inc.
Ed: Carl Bialik. **Description:** Profile of DNA-testing device developers Kalyan Handique and Sundaresh Brahmasandra and the founders of HandyLab Inc.

48748 ■ "How to Pitch a Brilliant Idea" in *Harvard Business Review* (Vol. 81, No. 9, September 2003, pp. 117)
Pub: Harvard Business School Press
Ed: Kimberly D. Elsbach. **Description:** Ways screenwriters propose ideas to producers can be applied to business marketing are highlighted. An ongoing study of how products are presented to the U.S. film and television industry (Hollywood) from screenwriters is presented; from this research various self-destructive and effective personality types emerged and are described.

48749 ■ "Hydrogen: The Next Fuel for Laptops?" in *San Jose Mercury News* (March 2, 2005)
Pub: Knight-Ridder/Tribune Business News
Ed: Therese Poletti. **Description:** Millennium Cell, a small firm in New Jersey is working on a hydrogen-fueled battery that may eventually provide eight hours of power for laptop computers.

48750 ■ "In the Mood" in *Entrepreneur* (Vol. 33, October 2005, No. 10, pp. 130)
Pub: Entrepreneur Media Inc.
Ed: Don Debelak. **Description:** Overcoming retailer resistance when introducing a new product is discussed using the story of an entrepreneur who was trying to sell her interior home lighting products to retailers.

48751 ■ "In With the New: Get Your Customers to Get Rid of Your Products-So They Can Buy More" in *Entrepreneur* (Vol. 31, No. 5, May 2003)
Pub: Entrepreneur Media Inc.
Ed: Kimberly L. McCall. **Description:** Strategies being used by entrepreneurs to embrace disposable products in order to boost income are discussed.

48752 ■ "Innovating for Cash" in *Harvard Business Review* (Vol. 81, No. 9, September 2003, pp. 76)
Pub: Harvard Business School Press
Ed: James P. Andrew, Harold L. Sirkin. **Description:** The majority of new products are financially disappointing and sometimes failures. Models for companies looking to develop a profitable new products include: integrator, orchestrator, and licensor.

48753 ■ "Innovating a Classic at Airstream" in *Harvard Business Review* (Vol. 81, No. 10, October 2003, pp. 18)
Pub: Harvard Business School Press
Ed: Gardiner Morse. **Description:** Airstream trailers are once again trendy; Dicy Riegel discusses Thor Industries and how it transformed the aluminum-clad trailer into a new, trendy item. Sales have increased since Thor acquired Airstream in 1980.

48754 ■ "Innovation at the speed of information" in *Harvard Business Review* (Vol. 79, No. 1, January 2001, pp. 149)
Pub: Harvard Business School Publishing Corp.
Ed: Steven D. Eppinger. **Description:** Effective exchange of information during the early stages of product development can reduce redesign time in the later stages. Use of the Design Structure Matrix can help accomplish this.

48755 ■ "The Innovator's Next Bestseller?" in *Inc.* (September 1, 2004)
Pub: Inc. Magazine
Ed: Mike Hofman. **Description:** Clayton M. Christensen, Harvard Business School professor and author, explains how to spot industry-changing innovations.

48756 ■ "It's a Woman's World" in *Black Enterprise* (Vol. 36, November 2005, No. 4, pp. 80)
Pub: Earl G. Graves Publishing Co. Inc.
Ed: Tennille M. Robinson. Description: Miriam Muley named her company 85% Niche after the percentage of sales directly and indirectly influenced by women. The firm offers brand marketing and new product development services. Statistical data included.

48757 ■ "Jewelry Mixes Fashion and Healing Energies" in *Marketing to Women* (Vol. 19, November 2006, No. 11, pp. 5)
Pub: EPM Communications, Inc.
Description: Body Rocks combines fashion and spirituality in their new line of jewelry and accessories that harness the healing properties of specific stones.

48758 ■ "Join Hands" in *Entrepreneur* (Vol. 33, September 2005, No. 9, pp. 138)
Pub: Entrepreneur Media Inc.
Ed: Don Debelak. Description: Profile of Shawn Donegan, founder of Trac Tool Inc., Cleveland, Ohio. Donegan signed a licensing deal with inventor Mike Puczkowski to sell the Speed Rollers paint applicator system to professional painting contractors. Steps for entrepreneurs to market inventions are examined.

48759 ■ "Just the Tiqit" in *Red Herring* (January 2003, pp. 26)
Pub: Herring Communications Inc.
Ed: Dean Takahashi. Description: Profile of Tiqit Computers, a Silicon Valley startup, developing a PC into a device that could fit into a pants pocket.

48760 ■ "Katrina Cottages At Lowe's" in *Mississippi Business Journal* (Vol. 28, September 2006, No. 36, pp. 23)
Pub: Venture Publications, Inc.
Description: Lowe's Companies Inc. is now selling several designs of Katrina Cottages, designed to withstand heavy rain and winds up to 140 miles per hour. Katrina Cottages meet new hurricane codes and International Building Code and range from 544 square feet to 1,340 square feet.

48761 ■ "Kill a Brand, Keep a Customer" in *Harvard Business Review* (Vol. 81, No. 12, December 2003, pp. 86)
Pub: Harvard Business School Press
Ed: Nirmalya Kumar. Description: An examination of the process of brand discontinuation and how this process can be used to improve customer loyalty. Methods include the portfolio approach, the segment approach, merging brands, and selling brands.

48762 ■ "License to Thrive" in *Entrepreneur* (Vol. 33, October 2005, No. 10, pp. 22)
Pub: Entrepreneur Media Inc.
Ed: Mark Henricks. Description: Today large companies are willing to license their patents, trademarks and other intellectual property to small companies that can profitably bring them to market.

48763 ■ "Luxury for the Little People" in *Inc.* (August 1, 2003)
Pub: Gruner & Jahr USA Publishing
Ed: Mike Hofman. Description: A look at America's passion for new luxury goods.

48764 ■ "MacroChem Advances Relaunch of Viagra Rival" in *Boston Business Journal* (Vol. 23, No. 31, September 5, 2003, pp. 1)
Pub: American City Business Journals
Ed: Mark Hollmer. Description: Lexington, Massachusetts-based MacroChem Corporation, led by president and CEO Bob DeLuccia, is expanding Phase II clinical trials for a new topical hormone drug that will rival Viagra.

48765 ■ "Marketing: Use 2003 As a Building Year" in *Atlanta Business Chronicle* (Vol. 25, No. 20, October 25, 2002, pp. 10B)
Pub: American City Business Publications, Inc.
Ed: Alf Nucifora. Description: Several suggestions are given for using the year 2003 to build marketing endeavors, including the pushing of innovation and experimentation with new products.

48766 ■ "A Matter of Taste" in *Fast Company* (March 2005, No. 92, pp. 35)
Pub: Gruner & Jahr USA Publishing
Ed: Lucas Conley. Description: Senomyx Inc., a biotechnology firm in La Jolla, California, is developing chemical compounds known as flavor enhancers that could be used in commercial products. Research is being funded by such corporations as Nestle SA, Coca-Cola, Kraft, and Campbell Soup Company.

48767 ■ "Milwaukee, Wis., to Host Biotech Finance Gathering in 2007" in *Milwaukee Journal Sentinel* (December 14, 2005)
Pub: Journal Sentinel, Inc.
Ed: Kathleen Gallagher. Description: Venture capitalists representing more than $7 billion and biotechnology and medical device startups will meet in Milwaukee in September 2007 for the largest industry event in the Midwest. The BIO Med-America Venture-Forum expects 75 to 100 VCs to attend.

48768 ■ "Needed on the Frontline" in *Pittsburgh Business Times* (Vol. 23, No. 8, September 12, 2003, pp. 19)
Pub: Pittsburgh Business Times
Ed: Lynne Glover. Description: Profile of Frontline Healthcare LLC, founded by three local women, provides healthcare products designed by nurses. The firm, founded in 2002, introduced its new Personal Products Caddy Pack for hospital patients.

48769 ■ "New Products Hit Showfloor: Expo! Expo!" in *Tradeshow Week* (Vol. 34, November 29, 2004, No. 48, pp. 47)
Pub: Reed Business Information
Ed: Margo McCall. Description: New technology products and services were unveiled at the Expo! Expo! Show. The show's highlights include Accumanage, a new software program that provides an exhibitor management system that can be used by show management or exhibitors to complete company profiles for a directory listing.

48770 ■ "News and Reviews" in *Home Business* (Vol. 13, January/February 2006, No. 1, pp. 98)
Pub: Home Business Magazine
Description: Information for closing business deals online, Web-based human resources small business software, noise canceling audio headphones, and tips for launching and marketing new products is given.

48771 ■ "The next best thing to being there?" in *E-business Advisor* (Vol. 18, No. 10, October 2000, pp. 11)
Pub: Advisor Media, Inc.
Description: A profile of PictureTel, who has developed the next generation of videoconferencing systems, called the Picture Tel900 Series. The systems are based on the iPower architecture, jointly developed by PictureTel and Intel Corporation.

48772 ■ "Nike Develops Brand for Women" in *Marketing to Women* (Vol. 20, January 2007, No. 1, pp. 8)
Pub: EPM Communications, Inc.
Description: A new brand of tennis shoes for women will hit shelves in spring 2007. The brand Tailwind will combine contemporary fashion with athletic performance and is a result of marketing partnership between Payless Shoe Source and Exeter Brands Group, a subsidiary of Nike.

48773 ■ "One of a kind? Make your product conform to break away from the norm" in *Entrepreneur* (Vol. 30, No. 12, December 2002, pp. 144)
Pub: Entrepreneur Media Inc.
Ed: Don Debelak. Description: One of the challenges facing entrepreneurs when developing a new invention is making sure it is a product consumers will accept.

48774 ■ "Orthodontist turns inventor of breast prothesis" in *Atlanta Business Chronicle* (Vol. 25, November 29, 2002, No. 25, pp. 4C)
Pub: American City Business Publications, Inc.

Ed: Leslie Williams Johnson. Description: Terry Ferguson created Radiant Impressions, a breast prosthesis, when his wife struggled to find comfortable prosthetic options after her mastectomy. The new breast prosthesis, which features a silicon foam core, is 40-50 percent lighter than the typical prosthesis.

48775 ■ "PL chocolates" in *Private Label Buyer* (Vol. 16, No. 4, April 2002, pp. 47)
Pub: Stagnito Communications Inc.
Description: World's Finest Chocolate, a longtime provider of chocolates for fundraising ventures, is offering private label products, including chocolate bars, panned confections and twist-wrapped items.

48776 ■ "Pontiac-GMC Dealers are Excited About New Products" in *Automotive News* (Vol. 9, January 31, 2005, No. 3, pp. 24)
Pub: Crain Communications Inc.
Ed: K.C. Crain. Description: General Motors is banking on new products that include the G6 and Torrent SUV models to help dealers increase sales and market share in 2005 and 2006.

48777 ■ "The Power of Spin" in *The Economist* (Vol. 377, October 1-7, 2005, No. 8446, pp. 76-77)
Pub: The Economist Newspaper Ltd.
Description: Canadian engineer, Louis Michaud, has developed a way to create artificial whirlwinds like a tornado, these whirlwinds can be controlled and harnessed in order to generate power. Michaud calls his invention the 'atmospheric vortex engine'.

48778 ■ "Prepaid Card Benefits Breast Cancer Research" in *Marketing to Women* (Vol. 19, November 2006, No. 11, pp. 5)
Pub: EPM Communications, Inc.
Description: NetSpend prepaid card marketer and financial services company, ACE Cash Express partner to launch a reloadable prepaid debit card for breast cancer research. A portion of all purchases made with the pink All-Access Visa Card through October 2007 will be donated to breast cancer research and educational charities.

48779 ■ "Radiant heat company markets hotproduct" in *Business First of Buffalo* (Vol. 18, No. 46, August 12, 2002, pp. 15)
Pub: Knight-Ridder/Tribune Business News
Ed: Joe Iannarelli. Description: Profile of Radiant Heat Inc., the company that promotes the use of floor heating by means of hot water using tubing under floors carrying hot water.

48780 ■ "Rapiscan Opens Plant" in *Mississippi Business Journal* (Vol. 28, September 2006, No. 36, pp. 22)
Pub: Venture Publications, Inc.
Description: Profile of Rapiscan Systems, a division of OSI Systems Inc., Rapiscan has opened a new factory in Ocean Springs to manufacture Rapiscan Gamma Radiographic Detection Systems for deployment around the world. Statistical data included.

48781 ■ "Research's reward" in *Crain's Detroit Business* (Vol. 18, No. 51, Dec. 23, 2002, pp. 1)
Pub: Crain Communications Inc., Detroit
Ed: Laura Bailey. Description: Since starting their firm in 1991, James Downward and Judith Erb, have developed six patents and have 6 patents pending. Their company IA Inc, and its subsidiary Threefold Sensors, has developed the Endotect biosensor for widespread detection of compounds that mimic estrogen and appear to cause birth defects.

48782 ■ "Ring It Up. Way Systems Helps Convert Cell Phones into Portable Cash Registers" in *Boston Business Journal* (Vol. 23, Aug. 22, 2003)
Pub: American City Business Journals
Ed: Mark Hollmer. Description: Way Systems Inc., Medford, Massachusetts, expects to manufacture a device that can be attached to a cell phone and would convert it into a portable point of sale terminal.

48783 ■ *Risk-Free Entrepreneur*
Pub: Adams Media Corporation
Ed: Don Debelak. **Released:** June 2006. **Price:** $14.95. **Description:** Information is offered to help entrepreneurs to develop an idea for a product or service and have other companies provide the marketing, manufacturing and staff.

48784 ■ "Rivaling a Giant" in *Boston Business Journal* (Vol. 23, No. 30, August 29, 2003, pp. 3)
Pub: American City Business Journals
Ed: Tom Witkowski. **Description:** Profile of Enterasys Networks efforts to capture market share away from rival giant Cisco Systems Inc. Topics include market development, product development, and competition.

48785 ■ "Run for the border" in *Entrepreneur* (Vol. 30, No. 3, March 2002, pp. 123)
Pub: Entrepreneur Media Inc.
Ed: Don Debelak. **Description:** Some inventors are setting up deals with U.S. manufacturers to produce a new product, but when that fails, they are turning to foreign manufacturers to save money; risks involved in doing so are also discussed.

48786 ■ "Sage unveils big plans for small business" in *Accounting Today* (Vol. 14, No. 13, July 24, 2000, pp. 29)
Pub: Faulkner & Gray, Inc.
Description: Accounting software development group Sage, announced plans to make several e-commerce innovations this year tied to its new accounting software product, BusinessWorks Gold. Sage said that the product, designed for companies of 50 or fewer employees, will be "the foundation for delivering e-commerce and e-management capabilities to the small business marketplace."

48787 ■ "S&P Top 10: Covance In, Amgen Out" in *Business Week Online* (January 31, 2005)
Pub: McGraw-Hill Companies
Ed: Kenneth Shea, Robert Gold, Steve Biggar. **Description:** A listing of the Standard & Poor's Top Ten Portfolio is presented. A drug development services firm has replaced Amgen for Top Investment Ranking. Statistical data included.

48788 ■ "A Sea Change for Artificial Bones" in *Business Week* (February 20, 2006, No. 3972, pp. 65)
Pub: McGraw-Hill Companies
Ed: Helena Oh. **Description:** Researchers at the U.S. Energy Department's Lawrence Berkeley National Laboratory are working on the development of artificial bones from oysters, abalone, and other hard-shelled ocean dwellers.

48789 ■ "Seeing the light" in *Boston Business Journal* (Vol. 22, No. 15, May 17, 2002)
Pub: MCP, Inc.
Ed: Sean McFadden. **Description:** Profile of Rhonda Kallman, founder of New Century Brewing Co. Kallman introduced Edison Light Beer in September 2001 locally, and it will enter the national market by late 2003.

48790 ■ "Silent treatment: Want big buzz? keep your mouth shut" in *Entrepreneur* (Vol. 30, No. 3, March 2002, pp. 97)
Pub: Entrepreneur Media Inc.
Ed: April Pennington. **Description:** Profile of Interactive Imagination, the multimedia entertainment company that introduced the fantasy world of Magi-nation collectible cards into the game industry one piece at a time.

48791 ■ "Silverado's Clean Coal Technology Coming To Choctaw County" in *Mississippi Business Journal* (Vol. 29, January 2007, No. 2, pp. 22)
Pub: Venture Publications, Inc.
Ed: Lynn Lofton **Description:** Silverado Green Fuel Inc. will build a new $26 million clean coal technology project in Choctaw County which promises to help decrease the country's dependence on foreign oil and make Mississippi the center of alternative fuel production.

48792 ■ *Six SIGMA for Small Business*
Pub: Entrepreneur Press
Ed: Greg Brue. **Released:** October 2005. **Price:** $19.95 (US), $26.95 (Canadian). **Description:** Jack Welch's Six SIGMA approach to business covers accounting, finance, sales and marketing, buying a business, human resource development, and new product development.

48793 ■ "Smoother Ice Cream From Winter Wheat" in *Business Week* (No. 3772, March 4, 2002, pp.73)
Pub: McGraw-Hill Inc.
Description: Scientists who study ice cream say they have a way to improve its texture using winter wheat proteins.

48794 ■ "Success Products" in *Black Enterprise* (Vol. 37, February 2007, No. 7, pp. 135)
Pub: Earl G. Graves Publishing Co. Inc.
Ed: Tanisha A. Sykes. **Description:** Using innovative resources that are already at your fingertips instead of trying to reach out to companies first is a great way to discover whether you have a viable idea or product. Be motivated to start an e-newsletter letting people know about your products and attend conferences like The Motivation Show, the world's largest exhibition of motivational products and services related to performance in business.

48795 ■ "Suppliers Picked for Pilot Program" in *Crain's Detroit Business* (Vol. 21, January 24, 2005, No. 4, pp. 18)
Pub: Crain Communications Inc. - Detroit
Ed: Mary Connelly, Robert Sherefkin. **Description:** Johnson Controls Automotive Group has been selected by the Chrysler Group pilot program that gets suppliers involved in early product development.

48796 ■ "Take It For Granted" in *Entrepreneur* (Vol. 33, January 2005, No. 1, pp. 50)
Pub: Entrepreneur Media Inc.
Ed: David Worrell. **Description:** U.S. Small Business Innovative Research grants and contracts provide funding for small companies to develop high tech products. The programs are divided into two phases: one is to study the feasibility of a new technology or idea, the second to encourage commercialization of a particular technology.

48797 ■ "Takes the cake" in *Black Enterprise* (Vol. 32, No. 10, May 2002, pp. 58)
Pub: Earl Graves Publishing Co.
Ed: Ron Childs. **Description:** Profile of Amy Hilliard, senior vice president of integrated marketing at Burrell Communications Groups Inc. Hilliard thrives on creating and launching products.

48798 ■ "Talented work force credited for right ideas" in *Crain's Detroit Business* (Vol. 19, No. 13, March 31, 2003, pp. 14)
Pub: Crain Communications Inc., Detroit
Description: Profile of Menlo Institute LLC, the software development services company. Rick Sheridan, co-founder and instructor believes the success of the firm lies in having the right product at the right time developed by the right people.

48799 ■ "Taste, Bud" in *Fast Company* (July 2001, pp. 62)
Pub: Fast Company
Ed: Cheryl Dahle. **Description:** Profile of John Harrison, the official taster for Edy's Grand Ice Cream, in Oakland, California. Harrison also makes regular visits to supermarkets around the country for random taste tests.

48800 ■ "Technically correct" in *Pittsburgh Business Times* (Vol. 22, No. 46, May 30, 2003, pp. 19)
Pub: Pittsburgh Business Times
Ed: Maria Guzzo. **Description:** Profiles of product lines and new product development at the Michael Baker Corporation, including business creativity, market share, and business strategy.

48801 ■ "This little drug went to the market" in *Ingram's* (Vol. 28, No. 6, June 2002, pp. 27)
Pub: Show Me Publishing, Inc.
Description: Information regarding the funding activity of VasoGenix Pharmaceuticals and the ongoing development of their calitonin gene-related peptide is presented. The company is seeking $5 million in second-round venture capital funding to develop the peptide which has three possible uses, one of which increases blood flow stimulation in balloon angioplasties to decrease strokes and heart attacks.

48802 ■ "3G Wireless Networks: Worth the Wait?" in *E-business Advisor* (Vol. 18, No. 7, July 2000, pp. 12)
Pub: Advisor Media, Inc.
Ed: Phillip Redman. **Description:** Third-generation wireless networks (3G) are about to be implemented in Asia and Europe, but North American users will have to wait a few years before the technology becomes available for them.

48803 ■ "TomTom GO910: On the Road Again" in *Black Enterprise* (Vol. 37, January 2007, No. 6, pp. 52)
Pub: Earl G. Graves Publishing Co. Inc.
Ed: Stephanie Young. **Description:** TomTom GO 910 is a GPS navigator that offers detailed maps of the U.S., Canada, and Europe. Consumers view their routes by a customizable LCD screen showing everything from the quickest to the shortest routes available or how to avoid toll roads. Business travelers may find this product invaluable as it also functions as a cell phone and connects to a variety of other multi-media devices.

48804 ■ "Toying with new ideas" in *Entrepreneur* (Vol. 31, No. 4, April 2003, pp. 81)
Pub: Entrepreneur Media Inc.
Ed: Elizabeth J. Goodgold. **Description:** Profile of Edward Roberts, co-founder and CEO of Zoinks!, a 7,700-square-foot toy store located in Boston, Massachusetts. Roberts and partner Thomas Brown have geared the store to singles.

48805 ■ "Trend Central: What's new with candy?" in *American Demographics* (October 1, 2001, pp. 24)
Pub: Business Magazines & Media
Description: Candy makers are using demographics and health trends to develop new products, including the Mar's company's Dulce de Leche targeted at the Hispanic community; Cream-savers by Lifesaver; Harry Potter candy; and healthy candy filled with vitamins that actually promise dental benefits.

48806 ■ "Trial By Fire" in *Entrepreneur* (Vol. 33, October 2005, No. 10, pp. 112)
Pub: Entrepreneur Media Inc.
Ed: Sara Wilson. **Description:** Profile of Bruce Black and Matt Ferris, co-founders of a company that develops home-safety devices, including the Vocal Smoke Detector. The detector plays a personally recorded voice message in an emergency. The two entrepreneurs developed the idea while competing in an MBA program at the University of Georgia.

48807 ■ "Viking Adds Rangetops" in *Mississippi Business Journal* (Vol. 28, September 2006, No. 36, pp. 24)
Pub: Venture Publications, Inc.
Description: Viking Range Corp. has added a continuous grate gas rangetop and electric rangetop stove to its Designer Series products line.

48808 ■ "Vonage V-Phone: Use Your Laptop to Make Calls Via the Internet" in *Black Enterprise* (Vol. 37, January 2007, No. 6, pp. 52)
Pub: Earl G. Graves Publishing Co. Inc.
Ed: James C. Johnson. **Description:** Overview of the Vonage V-Phone, which is small flash drive device that lets you make phone calls through a high-speed Internet connection and plugs into any computer's USB port. Business travels may find this product to be a wonderful solution as it includes 250MB of memory and can store files, digital photos, MP3s, and more.

48809 ■ **"Wanted: Something New Under the Sun" in** *Inc.* **(July 1, 2003)**
Pub: Gruner & Jahr USA Publishing
Ed: Adam Hanft. **Description:** Consumers are lacking interest in new products because so few exciting new items are cropping up in most industries today.

48810 ■ **"Wendy's beefs up its salad offerings" in** *Business First Columbus* **(Vol. 18, No. 25, February 8, 2002, pp. A12)**
Pub: Business First Columbus, Inc.
Ed: Laura Newpoff. **Description:** A preview of Wendy's International Inc.'s new 'designer greens'.

48811 ■ **"Where Segway Finds Traction" in** *Inc.* **(September 1, 2003)**
Pub: Gruner & Jahr USA Publishing
Ed: Rod Kurtz. **Description:** Profile of Segway LLC, maker of the human transporter, a self-balancing personal transportation device designed to go anywhere people do. It gives people everywhere the ability to move faster and carry more, allowing them to commute, shop, and run errands more efficiently while also having fun.

48812 ■ **"The World Bank's Innovation Market" in** *Harvard Business Review* **(Vol. 80, No. 11, November 2002, pp. 104)**
Pub: Harvard Business School Press
Ed: Gary Robert Chapman, Hamel Wood. **Description:** A description of ways a new-products team at the World Bank created an Innovation Marketplace, a forum that allowed people to present ideas for alleviating poverty to potential funding sources.

48813 ■ **"The Write Stuff: What Does it Take to Launch a Brand-New Product?" in** *Entrepreneur* **(Vol. 32, December 2004, No. 12, pp. 104)**
Pub: Entrepreneur Media Inc.
Ed: Amanda C. Kooser. **Description:** Barry Farber, entrepreneur, shares tips for successfully bringing a new product to the marketplace.

TRADE PERIODICALS

48814 ■ *Product Alert*
Pub: Marketing Intelligence Service Ltd.
Contact: Kathy Siefferman, Publications Director
Ed: Diane Beach, Editor. **Released:** Biennial, 2/month. **Price:** $700. **Description:** Reports on new consumer goods launched in American retailing, including foods and beverages, non-prescription drugs, cosmetics and toiletries, and miscellaneous household items. Lists products that are an extension of an existing product line, package changes, and marketing plans. Recurring features include pictures as well as descriptions of the products.

48815 ■ *Product Design and Development*
Pub: Reed Business Information
Contact: Jim Colford, Assoc. Publisher
E-mail: jcolford@reedbusiness.com
Released: Monthly. **Description:** Features product solutions and new technologies for the design engineering market.

48816 ■ *Product Safety & Liability Reporter*
Pub: Bureau of National Affairs Inc.
Ed: Gary A. Weinstein, Editor, gweinstein@bna.com.
Released: Weekly. **Description:** Provides coverage of current administrative, legislative, judicial, and industry developments relating to product safety and product liability. Covers significant advances under the Consumer Product Safety Act, the National Highway Traffic Administration, and other consumer safety protection statutes and agencies.

CONSULTANTS

48817 ■ *2010 Fund 5*
24351 Spartan St., Ste. 120
Mission Viejo, CA 92691

Ph:(949)583-1992
Scope: Funds in formation that will invest in technologies licensed from 30 universities. **Seminars:** Chair, Corporate Investment and Strategic Alliance Conferences.

48818 ■ **Aurora Management Partners Inc.**
4485 Tench Rd., Ste. 340A
Suwanee, GA 30024
Ph:(770)904-5207
Co. E-mail: rturcotte@auroramp.com
URL: http://www.auroramp.com

E-mail: rturcotte@auroramp.com
Scope: Firm specializes in turnaround management and reorganization consulting. **Publications:** Back From The Brink - Bland Farms; New Breed of Turnaround Managers; Key Performance Drivers - Bland Farms; The Missing Element in Corporate Governance Ratings.

48819 ■ **C. Clint Bolte & Associates**
809 Philadelphia Ave.
Chambersburg, PA 17201
Ph:(717)263-5768
Fax: (717)263-8945
Co. E-mail: clint@clintbolte.com
URL: http://www.clintbolte.com

E-mail: clint@clintbolte.com
Scope: Provides management consulting services to firms involved with the printing industry. Services include outsourcing studies, graphics supply chain management studies, company and equipment valuations, plant layout services, litigation support, fulfillment warehouse consulting and product development services. **Publications:** "Time to Break Through the Glass Ceiling," The Seybold Report, May, 2006; "Challenges & Opportunities Presented by Postal Rate Increases," The Seybold Report, May, 2006; "Packaging Roll Sheeting Comes of Age," The Seybold Report, May, 2006; "Diversifying With Mailing & Fulfillment Services," The Seybold Report, Jan, 2006.

48820 ■ **Bran Management Services Inc.**
7116 Lupton Dr., Ste. 100
Dallas, TX 75225-1735
Ph:(214)739-2340
Fax: (214)739-2360
Scope: Offers management consulting services to companies in manufacturing, distribution and services to help them cope with growth and change. Helps small businesses create and identify product strategies. Services include developing international business opportunities; turnaround management; sales and marketing development; business planning; acquisitions and mergers.

48821 ■ **ByrneMRG**
22 Isle of Pines Dr.
Hilton Head Island, SC 29928
Ph:(215)630-7411
Free: 888-816-8080
Co. E-mail: info@byrnemrg.com
URL: http://www.byrnemrg.com

E-mail: info@byrnemrg.com
Scope: Firm specializes in management consulting, including department management, equipment evaluation and selection, project management, R and D planning, and database design and management. **Publications:** "Implementing Solutions to Everyday Issues".

48822 ■ **Casino, Hotel & Resort Consultants L.L.C.**
8100 Via Del Cerro Ct.
Las Vegas, NV 89117
Ph:(702)646-7200
Fax: (702)646-6680
Co. E-mail: info@hraba.com
URL: http://www.hraba.com

E-mail: info@hraba.com
Scope: Casino and hospitality industry consultants. Firm specializes in developing and implementing cus-

tomized forecast and labor management control systems that deliver immediate, positive impact to the company's bottom line. We are involved in production planning, emply surveys and communication, inventory management, business process reviews, audits, development and implementation of key management reports. **Seminars:** Payroll Cost Control and Effective Staff Scheduling

48823 ■ **Comer & Associates L.L.C.**
5255 Holmes Pl.
Boulder, CO 80303
Ph:(303)786-7986
Free: 888-950-3190
Fax: (303)473-9830
URL: http://www.comerassociates.com
Scope: Specialize in developing markets & businesses. Marketing support includes: developing & writing strategic & tactical business plans; developing & writing focused, effective market plans; researching market potential & competition; implementing targeted marketing tactics to achieve company objectives; conducting customer surveys to determine satisfaction & attitudes toward client. Maintains a network of database research specialists, market communications providers, public relations firms, internet resources, focus group facilitators, technical writers & executive recruiters to assist with any project. Organization development support includes: executive/management training programs; executive coaching; team building; developing effective organization structures & processes; management of change in dynamic & competitive environments; individual coaching for management & leadership effectiveness. **Seminars:** Developing a strategic market plan; market research: defining your opportunity; management & leadership effectiveness; team building; developing a business plan.

48824 ■ **Federer Resources Inc.**
106 E 6th St.
Austin, TX 78701-3659
Ph:(512)476-8800
Scope: Firm specializes in feasibility studies; start-up businesses; small business management; mergers and acquisitions; joint ventures; divestitures; interim management; crisis management; turnarounds; production planning; team building; appraisals and valuations.

48825 ■ **Flor & Associates**
179 Schan Dr.
Churchville, PA 18966
Ph:(215)355-7466
Fax: (215)355-7464
Co. E-mail: fredflor@msn.com

E-mail: fredflor@msn.com
Scope: Business Development Consulting helping companies increase the value of their businesses. Services include: market development for technologies and products; product positioning strategies; technology assessment; competitive intelligence and analysis; team augmentation and facilitation; business growth strategies including acquisitions, licensing, and partnerships.

48826 ■ **Global Technology Transfer**
1500 Dixie Hwy.
Covington, KY 41011
Ph:(859)431-1262
Fax: (859)431-5148
Co. E-mail: arzembrodt@worldnet.att.net

E-mail: arzembrodt@worldnet.att.net
Scope: Firm specializes in product development; quality assurance; new product development; and total quality management focusing on household chemical specialties, especially air fresheners. Utilizes latest technology from global resources. Specializes in enhancement products for home and automobile.

48827 ■ **Gordian Concepts & Solutions**
16 Blueberry Ln.
Lincoln, MA 01773
Ph:(617)259-8341

Co. E-mail: gordian@usa1.com

E-mail: gordian@usa1.com
Scope: An engineering and management consultancy, the firm offers a broad range of general, financial, and valuation services, civil and tax litigation support, helps clients to enter new businesses, to plan new products and services, to evaluate feasibility, and assists with their due diligence efforts. Targets industrial concerns engaged in manufacturing, assembly, warehousing, energy production, process systems and biotechnology, steel, paper, and electronics. Also services businesses such as retailing, financial services, health-care, satellite broadcasting and cable television, outdoor advertising, and professional practices.

48828 ■ Health Strategy Group Inc.
46 River Rd.
Chatham, NY 12037
Ph:(518)392-6770
Scope: Provides consulting services in the areas of strategic planning, feasibility studies, start-up businesses, organizational development, market research, customer service audits, new product development, marketing, public relations.

48829 ■ Hewitt Development Enterprises
1717 N Bayshore Dr., Ste. 2154
Miami, FL 33132
Ph:(305)372-0941
Free: 800-631-3098
Fax: (305)372-0941
Co. E-mail: info@hewittdevelopment.com
URL: http://www.hewittdevelopment.com

E-mail: info@hewittdevelopment.com
Scope: A manufacturing management consulting firm. Specializes in strategic planning; profit enhancement; start-up businesses; interim management; crisis management; turnarounds; production planning; Just-in-Time inventory management; and project management.

48830 ■ Hills Consulting Group Inc.
6 Partridge Ct.
Novato, CA 94945
Ph:(415)898-3944
Scope: Strategic marketing consulting and training firm. Specializes in strategic planning; marketing surveys; market research; customer service audits; new product development; competitive analysis; and sales forecasting.

48831 ■ Hornberger & Associates
1966 Lombard St., Ste. 200
San Francisco, CA 94123
Ph:(415)346-2106
Fax: (415)346-9993
Co. E-mail: info@hornbergerassociates.com
URL: http://www.hornbergerassociates.com

E-mail: info@hornbergerassociates.com
Scope: Firm specializes in Internet marketing, strategic planning; new product development; client acquisition and retention; helping banks and brokerage firms do more business with affluent clients. **Seminars:** Building a Marketing Plan Directed at Emerging Wealth Baby Boomers.

48832 ■ Intuition Design Inc.
508 2nd St.
PO Box 696
Chesapeake City, MD 21915
Ph:(410)885-2513
Fax: (410)885-3094
Co. E-mail: rob@intuitiondesign.com
URL: http://www.intuitiondesign.com

E-mail: rob@intuitiondesign.com
Scope: Provides cost-effective product development services. Intuition excels in identifying problems, evaluating concepts, and providing practical product solutions.

48833 ■ Key Communications Group Inc.
5617 Warwick Pl.
Chevy Chase, MD 20815-5503

Ph:(301)656-0450
Free: 800-705-5353
Fax: (301)656-4554
Co. E-mail: mr.dm@verizon.net

E-mail: mr.dm@verizon.net
Scope: Direct marketing and publishing consultants specializing in subscriber and member acquisition for newsletters and other niche B2B publications, organizations and associations. Specialties: small and start-up businesses; mergers and acquisitions; joint ventures; divestitures; product development; employee surveys and communication; market research; customer service audits; new product development; direct marketing; and competitive intelligence.

48834 ■ Kubba Consultants Inc.
801 Glendale Rd.
Glenview, IL 60025
Ph:(847)729-0051
Fax: (847)729-8765
Co. E-mail: edkubba@aol.com
URL: http://www.kubbainc.com

E-mail: edkubba@aol.com
Scope: Industrial and business-to-business marketing research and consulting. Services include new product research, new market evaluation, competitor analysis and customer value analysis.

48835 ■ Marketing Leverage Inc.
180 Glastonbury Blvd.
Glastonbury, CT 06033
Ph:(860)633-1422
Free: 800-633-1422
Fax: (860)659-8664
Co. E-mail: office@marketingleverage.com
URL: http://www.marketingleverage.com

E-mail: office@marketingleverage.com
Scope: Consults with senior management at leading corporations to improve performance by maximizing customer value. We specialize in the targeting, retention and satisfaction of customers for companies in services industries with particular expertise in insurance, financial services, health care and technology services. Most clients belong to the Fortune 1000 group. Specific services include customer research, analysis of lifetime value, development of customer retention strategies, evaluation of web strategies, working with client teams.

48836 ■ Medical Imaging Consultants Inc.
1037 Rte. 46 E G-2
Clifton, NJ 07013-2445
Ph:(973)574-8000
Free: 800-589-5685
Fax: (973)574-8001
Co. E-mail: info@micinfo.com
URL: http://www.micinfo.com

E-mail: info@micinfo.com
Scope: Provides management consulting services to hospitals, imaging centers, health-care companies and insurance companies. Firm specializes in interim management; crisis management; turnarounds; market research; and new product development. **Seminars:** Sectional Anatomy & Imaging Strategies; CT Cross-Trainer; CT Registry Review Program; MR Cross-Trainer; Digital Mammography Essentials for Technologists; Radiology Trends for Technologists.

48837 ■ Mefford, Knutson & Associates Inc.
6437 Lyndale Ave. S
Richfield, MN 55423-1465
Ph:(612)869-8011
Free: 800-831-0228
Fax: (612)893-1806
Co. E-mail: don@mkaonline.net
URL: http://www.mkaonline.net

E-mail: don@mkaonline.net
Scope: Firm specializes in start-up businesses; strategic planning; mergers and acquisitions; joint ventures; divestitures; business process re-engineering; personnel policies and procedures; market research; new product development and cost controls.

48838 ■ The New Marketing Network Inc.
405 N Wabash Ave., Fl. 48
Chicago, IL 60611
Ph:(312)670-0096
Fax: (312)670-0126
Co. E-mail: info@newmarketingnetwork.com
URL: http://www.newmarketingnetwork.com

E-mail: info@newmarketingnetwork.com
Scope: Firm specializes in new product development; business and brand franchise expansion; Strategic planning and positioning; qualitative and quantitative Research; value added focus group moderating.

48839 ■ Partners for Market Leadership Inc.
400 Galleria Pky., Ste. 1500
Atlanta, GA 30339
Ph:(770)850-1409
Free: 800-984-1110
Co. E-mail: dcarpenter@market-leadership.com
URL: http://www.market-leadership.com

E-mail: dcarpenter@market-leadership.com
Scope: Change management firm. Provides consulting services in the areas of strategic planning, start-up businesses, mergers and acquisitions, joint ventures, divestitures, interim management, crisis management, turnarounds, new product development, sales management and competitive analysis.

48840 ■ Stratamar Inc.
5661 Seapine Rd.
Hilliard, OH 43026
Ph:(614)529-2945
Fax: (614)529-2945
Co. E-mail: info@stratamar.com
URL: http://www.stratamar.com

E-mail: info@stratamar.com
Scope: A full-spectrum strategic marketing consulting company. Areas of concentration include product development, product management, strategic planning, development and implementation of tactical marketing plans, and internet marketing. The primary focus is upon maximizing the benefit/cost ratio of promotions through the use of direct marketing, low cost media, and the like. **Publications:** Newsletter:"Business Plans", February, 2006. **Special Services:** Includes web page designing and hosting services via an affiliate, Designing Web.

48841 ■ Strategic MindShare Consulting
1401 Brickell Ave., Ste. 640
Miami, FL 33131
Ph:(305)377-2220
Fax: (305)377-2280
Co. E-mail: dee@strategicmindshare.com
URL: http://www.strategicmindshare.com

E-mail: dee@strategicmindshare.com
Scope: Firm specializes in strategic planning; feasibility studies; profit enhancement; organizational development; start-up businesses; mergers and acquisitions; joint ventures; divestitures; interim management; crisis management; turnarounds; new product development and competitive analysis. **Publications:** "Top Ten CEO Burning Issues for 2005"; "Top Ten Consumer Behavioral Trends for 2005"; "The Influence Factors".

48842 ■ Via Nova Consulting
1228 Winburn Dr.
Atlanta, GA 30344
Ph:(404)761-7484
Fax: (404)762-7123
Scope: Consulting services in the areas of strategic planning; privatization; executive searches; market research; customer service audits; new product development; competitive intelligence; and Total Quality Management (TQM).

COMPUTERIZED DATABASES

48843 ■ PRODUCTSCAN

Marketing Intelligence Service Ltd.
6473 D Rte. 64
Naples, NY 14512-9726
Ph:(585)374-6326
Free: 800-836-5710
Fax: (585)374-5217
Co. E-mail: mi@productscan.com
URL: http://www.productscan.com
Contact: Tom Vierhile, Gen. Mgr.
Released: Weekly. **Database Covers:** More than 200,000 new consumer goods (foods, beverages, HBA, household, pet and tobacco products) launched around the world. Compiled from the newsletters " Product Alert" and " International Product Alert. " **Database Includes:** Brand and product name; manufacturer name; distributor name, corporate affiliates, distribution market, industry; product category name and code, flavors, ingredients, sample availability, package type, package material, shelving, package tags, innovation, Universal Product Code (UPC), description, stock keeping units; date and title of publication in which cited, previous reports.

RESEARCH CENTERS

48844 ■ Ball State University–Center for Organizational Resources

Carmichael Hall, Rm. 201
Muncie, IN 47306-0365
Ph:(765)285-2770
Free: 800—541-9313
Fax: (765)285-1284
Co. E-mail: dboyd@bsu.edu
URL: http://www.bsu.edu/cor
Contact: Delaina Boyd, Dir.
E-mail: dboyd@bsu.edu
Scope: Development of existing businesses, including corporate training, executive development, adult literacy, technology transfer, strategic planning, human resource development, needs assessment, creativity, program evaluation, consultant selection, computer software, new product development, sales training, marketing strategy development, hospitality training, and customer service strategy development. **Services:** Contract Consulting. **Educational Activities:** Customized training and open-enrollment seminars (monthly).

48845 ■ Canadian Innovation Centre

490 Dutton Dr., Unit 1A
Waterloo, ON, Canada N2L 6H7
Ph:(519)885-5870
Free: 800—265-4559
Fax: (519)885-5729
Co. E-mail: lhendry@innovationcentre.ca
URL: http://www.innovationcentre.ca
Contact: Linda Hendry, Gen.Mgr.
E-mail: lhendry@innovationcentre.ca
Scope: Processes involved in invention, innovation, and entrepreneurship. Projects include an evaluation and implementation model for new product innovations, completion of research and development strategies in high technology companies, innovation in smalland medium-sized firms. **Services:** Invention Assistance Program, which assesses all aspects of an invention and aids in its development; Marketing Services, which provides market research assistance to small, medium, and large companies.

48846 ■ Center for Innovation

Ina Mae Rude Entrepreneur Ctr.
4200 James Ray Dr.
Grand Forks, ND 58203
Ph:(701)777-3132
Fax: (701)777-2339
Co. E-mail: bruce@innovators.net
URL: http://www.innovators.net
Contact: Bruce Gjovig, CEO/Entrepreneur Coach
E-mail: bruce@innovators.net

Scope: Works with applied research personnel at the University and other institutions to facilitate the commercialization of new technologies by providing support services to entrepreneurs, inventors, and small manufacturers in the areas of invention evaluation, technology commercialization, SBIR applications, technical development, licensing, and business development, including market feasibility studies and marketing and business plans. **Services:** Commercial Evaluations for Emerging Technologies (11/year). **Publications:** Annual Report; Business Plan: Step-by-Step (occasionally); Entrepreneur Kit (occasionally); Marketing Plan: Step by Step (occasionally). **Educational Activities:** Conferences and workshops (monthly), Seed and Angel Capital, Entrepreneur Startups, Business Planning, Market Feasibility.

48847 ■ IIT Research Institute

10 W 35th St.
Chicago, IL 60616
Ph:(312)567-4972
Fax: (312)567-4021
Co. E-mail: dmccormick@iitri.org
URL: http://www.iitri.org
Contact: David L. McCormick PhD, Sr.VP/Dir.
E-mail: dmccormick@iitri.org
Scope: Preclinical toxicology, inhalation toxicology, genetic toxicology, immunotoxicology, neurotoxicology, cancer chemoprevention, cancer chemotherapy, carcinogenesis, cancer research, inhalation technology, aerosol science, preclinical drug development, microbiology, molecular biology, virology, biodefense, analytical chemistry, biochemistry, pharmacology, and pharmacokinetics.

48848 ■ Institute for the Future

124 University Ave., 2nd Fl.
Palo Alto, CA 94301
Ph:(650)854-6322
Fax: (650)854-7850
Co. E-mail: info@iftf.org
URL: http://www.iftf.org
Contact: Marina Gorbis, Exec.Dir.
E-mail: info@iftf.org
Scope: Forecasting and planning techniques, development and assessment of new information technology, strategic planning assistance, policy analysis, and market outlooks for new products and next-generation technologies. Areas of special interest include long-range planning and forecasting, emerging technologies, health care, domestic and global development, and education and training. The Institute assists organizations in planning their long-term future, with staff expertise in business, communications, economics, engineering, health care, history, law, mathematics, physics, psychology, sociology, statistics, and systems analysis. **Publications:** Ten-Year Forecast. **Educational Activities:** Annual Conference; Summer Institute.

48849 ■ Iowa State University of Science and Technology–Center for Industrial Research and Service

2272 Howe Hall, Ste. 2620
Ames, IA 50011-2272
Ph:(515)294-3420
Fax: (515)294-4925
Co. E-mail: rcox@iastate.edu
URL: http://www.ciras.iastate.edu
Contact: Ronald A. Cox, Dir.
E-mail: rcox@iastate.edu
Scope: Problem areas of business, manufacturing, technology transfer, productivity, new product design, manufacturing processes, marketing, and related topics. Acts as a problem-handling facility and a clearinghouse for efforts to help Iowa's industry grow through studies highlighting not only production and management problems but also markets and profit potential of possible new developments. **Services:** Consults with industry on special problems; Information retrieval, available to industry and professional groups within the state; Statewide University Center Program for Iowa Businesses. **Publications:** CIRASNews (quarterly). **Educational Activities:** Workshops, briefings, and specialized extension courses for various phases of industry in the state.

48850 ■ National Research Council Canada–Industrial Materials Institute

75 E Mortagne Blvd.
Boucherville, QC, Canada J4B 6Y4
Ph:(450)641-5050
Fax: (450)641-5101
Co. E-mail: imi-info@cncr-nrc.gc.ca
URL: http://www.imi.nrc.ca/
Contact: Dr. Blaise Champagne, Dir.Gen.
E-mail: imi-info@cncr-nrc.gc.ca
Scope: Engineering materials, emphasizing process modeling and optimization, process development, and process instrumentation. **Publications:** Annual Report. **Educational Activities:** Polyblends and Composites Seminar (annually).

48851 ■ Pennsylvania State University–Institute for the Study of Business Markets

484 Business Bldg.
University Park, PA 16802-3603
Ph:(814)863-2782
Fax: (814)863-0413
Co. E-mail: isbm@psu.edu
URL: http://www.isbm.org
Contact: Dr. Gary L. Lilien, Res.Dir.
E-mail: isbm@psu.edu
Scope: Business-to-business marketing and sales, including studies on new products, market structure and operations, eBusiness, market communications, channels relationships, buying strategies and operations, public policy, and customer value. Acts as the United States partner of the International Marketing and Purchasing Group, which is studying relationships between members of international distribution channels. Collaborates with marketing professionals nationally and internationally. **Services:** Business marketing research support; Doctoral dissertation support. **Publications:** ISBM Insights; Marketplace: The ISBM Review Newsletter (semiannually); Working papers. **Educational Activities:** Joint educational programs, with Pennsylvania State Executive Programs; Seminars and special courses, for industry and academicians; Short courses and conferences; Special-interest consortia. **Awards:** ISBM Business Marketing Doctoral Award Support Competition (annually), that provides research funding to doctoral students in business-to-business marketing.

48852 ■ Sela, Inc.

545 West End Ave.
New York, NY 10024
Ph:(212)787-7925
Fax: (212)580-2731
Co. E-mail: selausa@aol.com
Contact: Jon Speller, Dir.
E-mail: selausa@aol.com
Scope: Metals extraction and medical electronics.

48853 ■ University of Missouri—Columbia–Power Electronics Research Center

349 Engineering Bldg. West
Electrical & Computer Engineering Department
Columbia, MO 65211
Ph:(573)882-8373
Fax: (573)882-0397
Co. E-mail: oconnellr@missouri.edu
Contact: Dr. Robert M. O'Connell, Dir.
E-mail: oconnellr@missouri.edu
Scope: Collaborates with industry, integrating the fields of power electronics in new products to establish a world leadership position for U.S. industry in power electronic equipment and systems markets. Focuses on adjustable speed AC drives, automotive power electronics, finite element analysis of electrical machines, harmonics in electric utility systems, harmonic compensators and power line conditioners, and modern control strategies using ASIC, smart power chips, microprocessors, and digital signal processors. **Educational Activities:** Academic programs and research experiences to educate engineers in power electronics.

48854 ■ University of Missouri—St. Louis–Center for Business and Industrial Studies
College of Business Administration
1 University Dr.
St. Louis, MO 63121
Ph:(314)516-6108
Fax: (314)516-6827
Co. E-mail: ldsmith@umsl.edu
URL: http://www.umsl.edu/~cbis/cbis.html
Contact: Dr. L. Douglas Smith, Dir.
E-mail: ldsmith@umsl.edu
Scope: Managerial problems, including risk management, planning, business development, job analysis/job evaluation, design and evaluation of incentive systems, inventory management and control, competition, market concentration, market demographics, market penetration, market segmentation, buyer behavior, marketing research designs for new product development and product positioning, measurement of promotional effectiveness, and design and administration of surveys. Specific projects include development of computer software for operations in public transit systems and forecasting models for losses on loan portfolios of financial institutions.

48855 ■ University of Pennsylvania–SEI Center for Advanced Studies in Management
700 Jon M. Hunstman Hall
Wharton School
3730 Walnut St.
Philadelphia, PA 19104-6340
Ph:(215)898-2349
Fax: (215)898-1703
Co. E-mail: windj@wharton.upenn.edu
URL: http://www-marketing.wharton.upenn.edu/SEI/
Contact: Prof. Jerry Wind, Dir.
E-mail: windj@wharton.upenn.edu
Scope: The future of management education, focusing on the unfolding global business environment and the education demanded to meet its challenges.

48856 ■ Virginia Polytechnic Institute and State University–Center for High Performance Manufacturing
102 Durham Hall, 0118
Blacksburg, VA 24061
Ph:(540)231-6201
Fax: (540)231-3322
Co. E-mail: ret@vt.edu
URL: http://www.chpm.ise.vt.edu
Contact: Prof. Robert E. Taylor PhD, Dir.
E-mail: ret@vt.edu
Scope: Flexible automation and lean manufacturing, production and information technologies, rapid prototyping and rapid tooling, manufacturing logistics and supply chain management, low-cost composite manufacturing. **Educational Activities:** Short courses.

REFERENCE WORKS

48857 ■ **"3Q a good one for local firms, if you ignore auto industry" in** *Crain's Detroit Business* **(Vol. 22, November 13, 2006, No. 46, pp. 3)**
Pub: Crain Communications Inc. - Detroit
Ed: Tom Henderson **Description:** Although the difficulties of the auto industry dominate the news, non-automotive businesses are doing very well with double digit growth. Michigan still lags the S & P because of the size of the auto industry and the depth of the associated troubles.

48858 ■ **Adoption Resource Book**
Pub: HarperCollins
Contact: Lois Gilman, Author
Released: Irregular, latest edition 4. **Price:** $16.95, individuals paper. **Publication Includes:** List of public and private adoption agencies, support groups, and services. **Entries Include:** Agency name, address, phone, special requirements. Principal content of the publication is a discussion of adoption procedures and requirements, including adoption of foreign children and open adoption. **Arrangement:** Geographical.

48859 ■ **"Borders of Life" in** *Crain's Detroit Business* **(Vol.22, December 18, 2006, No. 51, pp. 1)**
Pub: Crain Communications Inc. - Detroit
Ed: Andrew Dieterich. **Description:** Southeast Michigan offers faster serious health care options to Canadian residents in nearby Windsor and southwest Ontario. Statistics on available facilities are included in this article.

48860 ■ **Directory of Community Care Facilities**
Pub: California Department of Social Services
Contact: Tanya De La Cruz
Ed: Tanya De La Cruz, Editor. **Released:** Quarterly. **Price:** $75. **Covers:** adoption and home finding agencies, residential care facilities for adults and children, preschool care centers, and day care centers located in California and licensed by the California Department of Social Services. Health facilities are not listed. **Entries Include:** Facility name, address, phone; name of director or administrator; capacity; license limitations (age, sex, hours of care, etc.) **Arrangement:** Geographical.

48861 ■ **"A Gambling Man: Career Transitions that Put a Vegas Hotshot on Top" in** *Black Enterprise* **(Vol. 37, October 2006, No. 3, pp. 89)**
Pub: Earl G. Graves Publishing Co. Inc.
Ed: Laura Egodigwe. **Description:** Interview with Lorenzo Creighton, president and chief operating officer of MGM Mirage's New York-New York Hotel and Casino. Creighton talks about his history and the challenges he faced since he didn't come from the casino industry.

48862 ■ **"Indiana Electric Utility for Sale" in** *Crain's Chicago Business* **(Vol. 30, January 2007, No. 5, pp. 12)**
Pub: Crain Communications, Inc.
Description: Northern Indiana's electric utility is for sale and is expected to fetch between $3.4 and $4 billion.

48863 ■ **"Local Daily Papers Hit Hard by Declining Circulation" in** *Crain's Detroit Business* **(Vol. 22, December 4, 2006, No. 49, pp. 3)**
Pub: Crain Communications Inc. - Detroit
Ed: Tom Henderson. **Description:** Subscription cancellations continue exceed lead national trend of declining reliance for information from printed sources. National and local statistics are included in this summary.

48864 ■ **National Agricultural Aviation Association—Membership Directory**
Pub: National Agricultural Aviation Association
Contact: Peggy Knizner, Astt. Exec. Dir.
Ed: Andrew Moore, Editor. **Released:** Annual. **Covers:** nearly 1300 executives, pilots, and supplier companies engaged primarily in aerial application. **Entries Include:** For chapter and supplier company members—Name, spouse's name, company name, address, phone. **Arrangement:** Classified by type of membership; chapter members are then geographical; supplier company members are then by product.

48865 ■ **National Association for Drama Therapy—Membership List**
Pub: National Association for Drama Therapy
Released: Annual, August. **Covers:** about 400 registered drama therapists and NADT members. **Entries Include:** Name, address, membership category. **Arrangement:** Separate alphabetical sections for registered drama therapists and regular members. **Indexes:** Geographical.

48866 ■ **National Council of Acoustical Consultants—Directory**
Pub: National Council of Acoustical Consultants
Released: Annual. **Covers:** 125 acoustical consulting firms, primarily in the United States. **Entries Include:** Company name, address, phone, name of principal executive, list of services. **Arrangement:** Alphabetical.

48867 ■ **The Theatre Listing**
Pub: Professional Association of Canadian Theatres
Contact: Kirsten Kamper
Ed: Kristen Kamper, Editor. **Released:** Annual, January; latest edition 2005. **Price:** $34. **Covers:** over 300 English-language professional theatres in Canada. **Entries Include:** Theatre name, address, phone, fax, e-mail, internet sites, contacts, key personnel;, budget, mandates, facilities, submissions, repertoire, play development and other programs, affiliations. **Arrangement:** Regional. **Indexes:** Companies and Rental Spaces; Governments and Organizations; Advertisers; Last names; Festivals.

48868 ■ **"Venture Michigan Makes First Investment Commitments" in** *Crain's Detroit Business* **(Vol. 23, January 29, 2007, No. 5, pp. 17)**
Pub: Crain Communications Inc. - Detroit
Ed: Amy Lane. **Description:** First investment commitments to smaller venture capital fund providers is made by state venture group. Investments are in capital funds that support start-up firms with a Michigan presence that engage in new product development, research, and technology in non-manufacturing sectors.

SOURCES OF SUPPLY

48869 ■ **IAAM Guide to Members and Services**
Pub: International Association of Assembly Managers
Contact: J. D. Wilson, CON
Released: Annual, January. **Covers:** over 3,000 auditorium, arena, stadium, exhibit hall, and theatre managers and their facilities and suppliers. **Entries Include:** Member name, title, name of facility, address, phone, initial year of membership, services, e-mail. **Arrangement:** Alphabetical. **Indexes:** Geographical (with facility seating capacity, square feet of exhibit space), product and services.

TRADE PERIODICALS

48870 ■ **Operations and Fulfillment**
Pub: Primedia Business
Contact: Heather Retzlaff, Special Projects Mgr.
E-mail: hretzlaff@primediabusiness.com
Released: Monthly. **Description:** Trade publication focusing on operations issues faced by catalog and direct response companies. Includes articles on order processing, warehousing, materials handling, and facilities management.

TRADE SHOWS AND CONVENTIONS

48871 ■ **Great Lakes Industrial Show**
North American Exposition Co.
33 Rutherford Ave.
Boston, MA 02129
Ph:(617)242-6092
Free: 800-225-1577
Fax: (617)242-1817
Co. E-mail: naexpo@hotmail.com
URL: http://www.naexpo.com
Released: Annual. **Audience:** Buyers and officers from maintenance, material handling, engineering, production, purchasing, management, shipping and related professionals. **Principal Exhibits:** Industrial products, machine tools, hand tools, pneumatics, hydraulics, plant engineering, and maintenance, paper and packaging, plastics, rubber products, material handling equipment, and dies and stampings.

START-UP INFORMATION

48872 ■ "Angel on you Side" in *Entrepreneur* (Vol. 28, No. 10, October 2000, pp. 171)
Pub: Entrepreneur Media Inc.
Ed: Pamela Rohland. **Description:** The best place to find angel investors for funding is within your current circle of contacts: family members, friends and professional associates, as well as, chamber of commerce, banks, accounting firms, universities, business incubators, regional or state economic development agencies, editors of business publications and even potential customers.

48873 ■ "Building on experience" in *Black Enterprise* (Vol. 33, No. 6, Jan. 2003, pp. 39)
Pub: Earl Graves Publishing Co.
Ed: Bridget McCrea. **Description:** Profile of Angelo R. Perryman, who used his 22 years of experience in the construction industry to launch his own firm. Perryman used personal savings and loans from family members for his startup.

48874 ■ "Can I Use My Retirement Savings To Start a Business?" in *Fortune* (Vol. 151, February 21, 2005, No. 4, pp. 134)
Pub: Time Inc.
Ed: Janice Revell. **Description:** According to Martin Nissenbaum, the national director of personal income tax planning at Ernst & Young, a 401(k) savings plan could be used to start a new business, but the funds would first need to be rolled into an IRA, since the 401 (k) does not allow this kind of investment; IRS rules dictating 'prohibited transactions' are described to help entrepreneurs avoid legal issues when using retirement investments for startup money.

48875 ■ "Charging Ahead" in *Inc.* (January 1, 2004)
Pub: Gruner & Jahr USA Publishing
Ed: Bobbie Gossage. **Description:** Nearly 50 percent of all small business startups are financed with credit cards.

48876 ■ "Credit card financing: Tempting but risky for small businesses" in *Crain's Detroit Business* (Vol. 16, No. 33, August 14, 2000, pp. 13)
Pub: Crain Communications, Inc.
Ed: Brent Snavely. **Description:** Counselors from the Service Corps of Retired Executives believe that entrepreneurs should never use credit cards to finance a business. A variety of resources for advice and funding are investigated.

48877 ■ "Does cutting costs sound like a good start-up idea?" in *Entrepreneur* (Vol. 30, No. 10, October 2002, pp. 134)
Pub: Entrepreneur Media Inc.
Description: Bob Meyer, publisher of BarterNews Magazine offers five tips for entrepreneurs to use the practice of bartering to reduce startup costs.

48878 ■ "Entrepreneurs test start-ups-on the side" in *Wall Street Journal* (May 7, 2002, pp. B6)
Pub: Wall Street Journal
Ed: Jeff Bailey. **Description:** Many entrepreneurs are working fulltime jobs in order to finance their start-ups since venture capital and start-up funding has become more difficult to acquire.

48879 ■ "Financial Roulette" in *Entrepreneur* (Vol. 28, No. 6, June 2000, pp. 68)
Pub: Entrepreneur Media Inc.
Ed: David R. Evanson. **Description:** Is borrowing from your IRA to fund a business startup a healthy risk or a tragic mistake?

48880 ■ "Financing" in *Crain's Detroit Business* (Vol. 19, No. 49, December 8, 2003, pp. 13)
Pub: Crain Communications Inc., Detroit
Description: Sources of money for startup firms are listed.

48881 ■ "Finding Cash for Your Business" in *Black Enterprise* (Vol. 35, February 2005, No. 7, pp. 82)
Pub: Earl G. Graves Publishing Co. Inc.
Ed: Donald Jay Korn. **Description:** Financing alternatives to banks and venture capitalists are available to small businesses in the form of a micro-loan from a lender, family or friends.

48882 ■ "Finding financing" in *Black Enterprise* (Vol. 32, No. 6, January 2002, pp. 8)
Pub: Earl Graves Publishing Co.
Ed: Bevolyn Williams-Harold. **Description:** Minority entrepreneurs may need to look for more innovative capital resources, such as minority-focused venture capital funds or community-based securitization programs, to maintain cash flow.

48883 ■ "Fostering Urban Entrepreneurship" in *Black Enterprise* (Vol. 34, No. 4, November 2003, pp. 46)
Pub: Earl Graves Publishing Co.
Ed: Charlene Carter. **Description:** The winners of the third annual Miller Urban Entrepreneurs Business Grant Competition are highlighted. Each winner was awarded $20,000 to fund a business venture or expansion.

48884 ■ "Funding a Franchise Startup" in *Hispanic Business* (Vol. 23, No. 5, May 2001, pp. 52, 54)
Pub: Hispanic Business
Ed: Barbara Beckley. **Description:** Funding sources available for franchise start-ups are presented. The Certified Development Company, a private, non-profit organization licensed by the SBA; the Small Business Investment Companies (SBICs), which provide equity capital and long-term debt financing; and the Community Development Corporations (CDCs) are among the resources profiled.

48885 ■ "Learning business was key" in *Crain's Detroit Business* (Vol. 19, No. 13, March 31, 2003, pp. 13)
Pub: Crain Communications Inc., Detroit
Description: Profile of David Fry, president and CEO of Fry Inc. Fry, a former Harvard University professor, started his firm with financing from family members. The company tripled in size in a short period of time, and Fry shares his experiences of learning about his business as it grew.

48886 ■ "The Million-Dollar Post-it Note" in *Inc.* (February 1, 2002)
Pub: Inc. Magazine
Ed: George Gendron. **Description:** Ways to make money stretch for a business startup, sometimes called entrepreneurial bootstrapping, are discussed.

48887 ■ "New Stratford, Conn., Needlework Quickly Gains Fans" in *Connecticut Post* (January 31, 2003)
Pub: Knight-Ridder/Tribune Business News
Ed: Stephania H. Davis. **Description:** Profile of Janet Kemp Fine Yarns and Needlework. Kemp tells how she and her husband obtained a second mortgage on their home in order to start her business. The store features high quality yarns, patterns, and accessories for the crafts of knitting, embroidering and needlepoint.

48888 ■ "Pilot program to assist young entrepreneurs" in *Black Enterprise* (Vol. 32, No. 6, January 2002, pp. 37)
Pub: Earl Graves Publishing Co.
Ed: Paula McCoy-Pinderhughes. **Description:** Profile of the Prudential Young Entrepreneur Program, a three-year pilot entrepreneurial development project funded by the Prudential Foundation, a nonprofit, grant-making organization of the Newark, New Jersey-based Prudential Insurance Company of America. The program is designed to offer young adults in urban areas opportunity to train to become a small business owner.

48889 ■ "Rising money" in *Entrepreneur* (Vol. 30, No. 1, January 2002, pp. 36)
Pub: Entrepreneur Media Inc.
Ed: Steve Cooper. **Description:** A listing of financial sources used by entrepreneurs in 2001, information about customer trust, and other areas of interest to small business is presented. Statistical data included.

48890 ■ "Sister, can you share five bucks" in *WorkingWoman* (Vol. 25, No. 7, August 2000, pp. 20)
Pub: Lang Communications Inc.
Ed: Kathleen Jacobs. **Description:** Women will be the main beneficiaries of a new organization set up to ensure business women have easier access to enterprise loans by asking every female in America to donate $5.

48891 ■ "Start-Up Funding Options" in *Home Business* (Vol. 12, October 2005, No. 5, pp. 28, 30-31, 78-79)
Pub: Home Business Magazine

Ed: Jim R. Sapp. **Description:** Alternatives for funding a start-up home-based business include using your savings account, credit cards, 401(k) or Keogh retirement plans, life insurance, second mortgage line of credit, pawn shop, or selling accumulated items no longer needed.

48892 ■ **"A stealthier way to raise money"** in *Harvard Business Review* (Vol. 78, No. 5, September-October 2000, pp. 18)
Pub: Harvard Business School Publishing Corp.
Ed: David Champion. **Description:** Many entrepreneurs are seeking funding from private investors and corporations rather than from venture capital companies. The dangers from venture capitalists are that they demand control, and because of their networking, they may inadvertently reveal company secrets.

48893 ■ **"Touched by an Angel"** in *BlackEnterprise* (Vol. 31, No. 11, June 2001, pp. 242)
Pub: Earl Graves Publishing Co.
Ed: Roger Barnes. **Description:** In-depth coverage of venture capital funding programs for African American businesses.

48894 ■ **"What's Up Doc?"** in *Entrepreneur* (Vol. 28, No. 10, October 2000, pp. 132)
Pub: Entrepreneur Media Inc.
Ed: Geoff Williams. **Description:** A profile of Health4her.com. The founders of this successful Internet-based business tell how they started with their own money.

48895 ■ **"What's Your Problem?"** in *Entrepreneur.com* (Vol. 34, February 2006, No. 2, pp. 102)
Pub: Entrepreneur Media Inc.
Ed: Sarah Edwards, Paul Edwards. **Description:** Entrepreneur asks whether he should us zero percent credit cards to finance his home-based business.

48896 ■ **"Where Seed Money Really Comes From"** in *Inc.* (August 1, 2003)
Pub: Gruner & Jahr USA Publishing
Ed: Cara Cannella. **Description:** The four "F's" for small business financing are explored: founders, family, friends and foolhardy investors.

REFERENCE WORKS

48897 ■ **"An Acquired Taste"** in *Entrepreneur* (Vol. 32, October 2004, No. 10, pp. 62)
Pub: Entrepreneur Media Inc.
Ed: Crystal Detamore-Rodman. **Description:** Tim Johnstone is a former division manager for a large bank working on the due-diligence team that analyzed companies the bank wanted to buy. Johnstone's experience helped him when he decided to purchase the Anywear Shoe Company in Seattle, Washington. The firm manufactures and distributes professional footwear.

48898 ■ **"Alternative Capital Sourcing"** in *My Business* (September/October 2001, pp. 42)
Pub: My Business Magazine
Ed: Al Hattal. **Description:** Profile of the Small Business Administration (SBA) program, Small Business Investment Company (SBIC). The SBIC assists both high-risk small businesses and start-ups that might not otherwise receive funding.

48899 ■ **"Behind the Deals"** in *Entrepreneur* (Vol. 28, No. 6, June 2000, pp. 38)
Pub: Entrepreneur Media Inc.
Ed: Cynthia E. Griffin. **Description:** Small Business Investment Companies (SBIC) are the private investors who quietly serve the capital interests of business are discussed.

48900 ■ **"Bowling for drug research: families take entrepreneurial tack in signing up biotech firms"** in *Wall Street Journal* (Feb. 27, 2003)
Pub: Dow Jones & Co. Inc.
Ed: Vanessa Fuhrmans. **Description:** Families of Spinal Muscular Atrophy signed a contract with Decode Genetics Inc. to fund their research programs.

48901 ■ **"Corporate Collateral"** in *Entrepreneur* (Vol. 28, No. 7, July 2000, pp. 38)
Pub: Entrepreneur Media Inc.
Ed: Cynthia E. Griffin. **Description:** Where to get money to grow your company, including big companies as resources.

48902 ■ **"Finance with Plastic?"** in *My Business* (September/October 2001, pp. 41)
Pub: My Business Magazine
Ed: Shannon Scully. **Description:** Nearly one-half of all small business owners with ten or less employees used credit cards to finance their business in 1998. The pros and cons of such practice are presented.

48903 ■ **"Financing"** in *Entrepreneur* (Vol. 28, No. 8, August 2000, pp. 134)
Pub: Entrepreneur Media Inc.
Ed: Cynthia E. Griffin. **Description:** Nonprofit organizations are testing finance programs to help low-income individuals start and sustain businesses.

48904 ■ *Financing Your Business*
Pub: Prentice Hall
Ed: Iris Lorenz-Fife. **Released:** 1997. **Price:** $13.95. **Description:**

48905 ■ **"First Base: Finding Ways to Finance Your Venture"** in *Crain's Detroit Business* (Vol. 19, No. 49, December 8, 2003, pp. 13)
Pub: Crain Communications Inc., Detroit
Ed: Laura Bailey. **Description:** Most entrepreneur's use their own money, or borrow from family and friends when starting a new business, others might use a more risky method of using a home-equity loan on their home.

48906 ■ **"Give 'Em Credit"** in *Entrepreneur* (Vol. 31, No. 8, August 2003, pp. 55)
Pub: Entrepreneur Media, Inc.
Ed: Crystal Detamore-Rodman. **Description:** Credit unions now offering loans to small businesses. Many entrepreneurs suggest that credit unions offer better rates, as well as better service than dealing with banks.

48907 ■ *Guerrilla Financing: Alternative Techniques to Finance Any Small Business*
Pub: Houghton Mifflin Co.
Ed: Bruce J. Blechman and Jay C. Levinson. **Released:** 1992. PR $10.75. **Description:** Describes innovative approaches to evaluating assets, unearthing alternative finance sources, and marketing yourself and your business.

48908 ■ **"Helping the Economy, One Snip at a Time"** in *New York Times* (November 2, 2003, pp. 1)
Pub: The New York Times
Ed: Joseph P. Fried. **Description:** Profile of a hair salon owner who has grown her business by borrowing from people close to her, as well as loans from the Small Business Administration and the Women's Venture Fund, a nonprofit group.

48909 ■ **"Hidden treasure"** in *Entrepreneur* (Vol. 30, No. 2, February 2002, pp. 56)
Pub: Entrepreneur Media Inc.
Ed: Sean P. Melvin. **Description:** In a tightened economy, entrepreneurs can look for capital in the nooks, crannies, equipment and real estate the business already owns.

48910 ■ **"The Home Stretch"** in *Entrepreneur* (Vol. 33, January 2005, No. 1, pp. 52)
Pub: Entrepreneur Media Inc.

Ed: Scott Bernard Nelson. **Description:** If a down payment is the only thing keeping you from a home mortgage, borrowing from an Individual Retirement Account (IRA) is allowable for first time home buyers ($10,000 each or $20,000 for a couple).

48911 ■ **"Invoice-buying deals thrive on one thing: The cash factor"** in *Crain's Detroit Business* (Vol. 17, No. 44, October 22, 2001, pp. 22)
Pub: Crain Communications, Inc.
Ed: Katie Merx. **Description:** Often called last-resort financing, factoring will become increasingly popular as more traditional forms of financing become difficult obtain. Factoring is the practice of selling invoices in order to get money quickly. A list of firms with factoring programs is listed.

48912 ■ **"A Little Bit Goes a Long Way"** in *My Business* (September/October 2001, pp. 46)
Pub: My Business Magazine
Ed: Shannon Scully. **Description:** Profile of microloan programs, which provide funding to small companies that don't qualify for conventional bank loans. The article includes sources to learn more about microloans, and lists Web sites of lenders.

48913 ■ **"Loans, grants, and more"** in *BlackEnterprise* (Vol. 32, No. 2, September 2001, pp. 46)
Pub: Earl Graves Publishing Co.
Ed: Paul McCoy-Pinderhughes. **Description:** A list of government-sponsored programs, small business loans, and grants for small business are highlighted, including the Commerce Business Daily lists of government-awarded contracts; the Federal Procurement Data System; the U.S. Department of Housing and Urban Development; the 7(a) loan program; and the Small Business Innovation Research program.

48914 ■ **"The Master Negotiator: How To Use the Power of Persuasion to Raise Dollars"** in *Black Enterprise* (Vol. 34, No. 2, September 2003)
Pub: Earl Graves Publishing Co.
Ed: Sonya Kimble-Ellis. **Description:** Profile of 17-year-old Amelia Landreth, who negotiated funds to pay for varsity and junior high basketball teams. Landreths power of persuasion can help all entrepreneurs to raise money.

48915 ■ **"Microlending - Arizona Style"** in *Hispanic Business* (March 2002, pp. 16)
Pub: Hispanic Business
Ed: Jonathan J. Higuera. **Description:** Profile of Frank Ballesteros, who borrows from the U.S. Small Business Administration and other financial institutions and lends to the working poor.

48916 ■ **"Military Now One of the Big Guns in Tech Financing"** in *Washington Business Journal* (Vol. 22, No. 16, August 22, 2003, pp. 30)
Pub: Washington Business Journal
Ed: Roger Hughlett. **Description:** Sentel, Alexandria, Virginia, is one of a growing number of small high-tech companies foregoing traditional efforts at raising funds by, instead, contacting the U.S. Military and other U.S. government agencies.

48917 ■ **"Money Is Out There, But Where?"** in *Crain's Chicago Business* (Vol. 30, January 2007, No. 1, pp. 12)
Pub: Crain Communications, Inc.
Ed: Dee Gill. **Description:** Chicago is a great place to start a business and entrepreneurs have a wealth of free help, resources, and information available to them. Unfortunately, most have no idea these services even exist and as a result money set aside for small businesses never gets spent. SourceLink is one such service that can help entrepreneurs find those resources.

48918 ■ **"More than friends"** in *Entrepreneur* (Vol. 30, No. 3, March 2002, pp. 66)
Pub: Entrepreneur Media Inc.
Ed: Jennifer Pellet. **Description:** Profile of Circle Lending, an online service that enables would-be borrowers to create and administer business loans with family and friends.

48919 ■ "Networking Provides Partnership's Funding" in *Wall Street Journal* **(October 14, 2003, pp. B4)**
Pub: Dow Jones & Co. Inc.
Ed: Paulette Thomas. **Description:** Case study of William G. Nelson showing ways to move from a career in finance to an entrepreneurial life on a shoestring budget through networking.

48920 ■ "Nonprofit Consolidation to Increase" in *Crain's Detroit Business* **(Vol. 22, November 27, 2006, No. 48, pp. 20)**
Pub: Crain Communications Inc. - Detroit
Ed: Sherri Begin. **Description:** Reduced funding from foundations and pension shortfalls have resulted in consolidation of the nonprofit industry in Michigan. Efficiencies are to be gained by eliminating duplication of services.

48921 ■ *Raising Capital*
Pub: Raising Capital
Ed: Andrew J. Sherman. **Price:** $34.95.

48922 ■ "Reaching for the Stars" in *Black Enterprise* **(Vol. 34, No. 2, September 2003, pp. 48)**
Pub: Earl Graves Publishing Co.
Ed: Demetria Lucas. **Description:** Profile of Gerard Dure, self-proclaimed "King of Hair" and specialist at hair weaving. Dure is stylist to top models and Hollywood stars. He needed $200,000 to renovate a former warehouse into his salon and negotiated a deal for someone to clean out the warehouse in exchange for six months fee rent in the salon.

48923 ■ "Richmond Times-Dispatch, Va., Business Briefs Column" in *Knight-Ridder/Tribune Business News* **(October 23, 2001, pp. ITEM01296031)**
Pub: Knight-Ridder/Tribune Business News
Description: The Richmond Economic Development Corporation in Virginia, has been awarded $450,000 by the U.S. Treasury Department to create a loan source for small businesses lacking access to traditional financing.

48924 ■ *Risk-Free Entrepreneur*
Pub: Adams Media Corporation

Ed: Don Debelak. **Released:** June 2006. **Price:** $14.95. **Description:** Information is offered to help entrepreneurs to develop an idea for a product or service and have other companies provide the marketing, manufacturing and staff.

48925 ■ "Tapping Into Your Warm Market" in *Home Business* **(Vol. 13, January/February 2006, No. 1, pp. 72, 74-75)**
Pub: Home Business Magazine
Ed: Nora Caley. **Description:** According to Circle Lending, family and friends account for more than half of investment dollars for start-up companies, this funding is called a warm market. Websites offering start-up funding are included.

48926 ■ "They're Certifiable" in *Entrepreneur* **(Vol. 28, No. 10, October 2000, pp. 36)**
Pub: Entrepreneur Media Inc.
Ed: Cynthia E. Griffin. **Description:** The importance of "accredited investors" when looking for money is reviewed.

48927 ■ "Women Business Owners Seek Financing" in *Marketing to Women* **(Vol. 19, December 2006, No. 2, pp. 8)**
Pub: EPM Communications, Inc.
Description: A study by the Center for Women's Business Research shows that women business owners have become more savvy when seeking financial support for their business ventures. Statistical data included.

SOURCES OF SUPPLY

48928 ■ *Government Giveaways for Entrepreneurs III*
Pub: Information USA Inc.
Contact: Matthew Lesko, Author
Released: Biennial, 5th edition, October 1996. **Covers:** about 300 government programs and 9,000 sources of free help for persons wanting to start or expand a business. **Arrangement:** Geographical.

VIDEOCASSETTES/ AUDIOCASSETTES

48929 ■ *ESOPS: The Ultimate Way to Finance a Company*
Chesney Communications
2302 Martin St., Ste. 125
Irvine, CA 92612
Ph:(949)263-5500
Free: 800-223-8878
Fax: (949)263-5506
Released: 1989. **Price:** $49.95. **Description:** A way of selling stock tax free and still controlling the company is demonstrated. **Availability:** VHS; 3/4U.

48930 ■ *Flexing Your Creative Muscle in the Financial Marketplace*
1st Financial Training Services
1515 E. Woodfield Rd., Ste. 345
Schaumburg, IL 60173
Ph:(847)969-0900
Free: 800-442-8662
Fax: (847)969-0521
Co. E-mail: sales@1stfinancialtraining.com
URL: http://www.1stfinancialtraining.com
Released: 1987. **Price:** $299.00. **Description:** Dr. Berry shows the diverse array of areas that a financial institution can get involved in. **Availability:** VHS; 3/4U.

48931 ■ *Raising Capital in Turbulent Times*
Chesney Communications
2302 Martin St., Ste. 125
Irvine, CA 92612
Ph:(949)263-5500
Free: 800-223-8878
Fax: (949)263-5506
Released: 1989. **Price:** $49.95. **Description:** Shows that, even when the economy is looking bad, there are still places for people to get capital. **Availability:** VHS; 3/4U.

START-UP INFORMATION

48932 ■ **"My Best Practices: Sell smarter. Streamline your office. Work better. Crush competition"** in *FSB* (Vol. 10, No. 9, Dec. 1, 2000, pp. 54)
Pub: Time Inc.
Description: If you really want to outdistance competitors, the author recommends using today's new technology as powerfully as possible to run your business.

48933 ■ **"Setting Up a Productive Home Office"** in *Home Business* (Vol. 12, October 2005, No. 5, pp. 82, 84)
Pub: Home Business Magazine
Ed: Aliza Pilar, Sherman Risdahl. **Description:** Things to consider when purchasing furniture, hardware, software and electronics for a small home-based business are examined.

48934 ■ *Working for Yourself: An Entrepreneur's Guide to the Basics*
Pub: Kogan Page, Limited
Ed: Jonathan Reuvid. **Released:** September 2006.
Description: Guide for starting a new business venture, focusing on raising financing, legal and tax issues, marketing, information technology, and site location.

REFERENCE WORKS

48935 ■ **"4Smartphone's Mobility Solution for Small and Medium Size Businesses"** in *Small Business Opportunities* (Vol. 17, May 2005, No. 3)
Pub: Harris Publications Inc.
Description: 4SmartPhone provides mobility solutions that enable small companies to share information across any device from a central platform from anywhere.

48936 ■ **"5 Moves to Make Before the New Year"** in *My Business* (December/January 2004, pp. 14)
Pub: My Business Magazine
Ed: Barbara Weltman. **Description:** Small business tax planning is essential for a company to be successful. Financial tips to help small firms are listed, focusing on general strategy, equipment, cars, retirement plans, and gift giving.

48937 ■ **"A Little Lost? Get Directions at Your Fingertips"** in *Entrepreneur* (Vol. 31, No. 10, October 2003, pp. 46)
Pub: Entrepreneur Media, Inc.
Ed: Mike Hogan. **Description:** Profile of Mapopolis. com's ClearRoute service, offering traffic flow and other real-time street data, is presented.

48938 ■ **"Achieving High Reliability"** in *PC Magazine* (March 7, 2000, pp. 142)
Pub: Ziff-Davis Publishing Company
Ed: Frank J. Derfler, Jr., Gary Gunnerson. **Description:** A guide to shopping for reliable wideband con-

nection services is presented. Local and regional broadband providers such as telcos often charge much less than nationwide ISPs. Reliability is important because a growing E-business can put great strain on a network. Key technologies include server clustering, load balancing and physically separate LANs for storage and servers. E-business companies should purchase as much 'high availability' technology as they can afford.

48939 ■ **"Adapt or die: surviving the government's digital push"** in *Black Enterprise* (Vol. 33, No. 6, January 2003, pp. 42)
Pub: Earl Graves Publishing Co.
Ed: Rebecca Rohan. **Description:** The economic survival of black-owned businesses depends on their knowledge of using technology. In the government's move towards a paperless operation, African American businesses must learn how to take advantage of the new opportunities that technology brings.

48940 ■ **"Advisor Tips"** in *E-business Advisor* (Vol. 18, No. 7, July 2000, pp. 52)
Pub: Advisor Media, Inc.
Ed: Larry C. Whipple. **Description:** Tips on architecting Web applications are presented. A good architecture can solve problems before they happen, provide for growth of the site, and make the development and AQ run smoother.

48941 ■ **"Age of the iPod-icame, isaw, I conquered"** in *Entrepreneur.com* (Vol. 34, January 2006, No. 1, pp. 17)
Pub: Entrepreneur Media Inc.
Ed: Steve Cooper. **Description:** Apple Computer's iPod has sold over 20 million units since 2001. This portable audio player has created an entire economy of accessories and imitators.

48942 ■ **"All in One"** in *Entrepreneur* (Vol. 32, No. 2, February 2004, pp. 44)
Pub: Entrepreneur Media, Inc.
Ed: Gisela M. Pedroza. **Description:** Profile of Samsung's new SPH-i700 Windows-powered Pocket PC. The device allows the user to manage work with desktop applications and to communicate through voice, email and photo images.

48943 ■ **"Almost office"** in *Entrepreneur* (Vol. 30, No. 12, December 2002, pp. 64)
Pub: Entrepreneur Media Inc.
Description: Profile of software that allows the use of Linux, while retaining use of Microsoft office, including CrossOver Office 1.2, Sun StarOffice Suite 6.0, and Ximian Desktop Professional Edition.

48944 ■ **"And Now, the Handheld Trainer"** in *Business Week* (January 9, 2006, No. 3966, pp. 92)
Pub: McGraw-Hill Companies
Ed: Toddi Gutner, Lourdes Lee Valeriano. **Description:** Profile of the PumpPod, Companion World's Progio programs, iAmplify, and Alive Yoga; these programs offer fitness training on handheld devices.

48945 ■ **"Answer the Call"** in *Entrepreneur* (Vol. 33, September 2005, No. 9, pp. 32)
Pub: Entrepreneur Media Inc.
Ed: Amanda C. Kooser. **Description:** Many small companies are switching from land phone lines to cellular phones for office use and employees on the road.

48946 ■ **"AOL's new service for small businesses"** in *PC Magazine* (Vol. 9, No. 12, December 2000, pp. 30)
Pub: Ziff-Davis Publishing Company
Ed: Mary Gillen. **Description:** AOL has launched its Netscape NetBusiness service, located on the AOL WorkPlace Channel, Netscape NetCenter CompuServe, ICQ, MapQuest and Digital City. The service is designed to help small businesses use the Web to increase productivity.

48947 ■ **"Apple of Your Eye?"** in *Entrepreneur* (Vol. 31, No. 8, August 2003, pp. 40)
Pub: Entrepreneur Media, Inc.
Description: Profile of Apple's Keynote 1.1 presentation software. The software is compatible with PowerPoint files and will compete with Microsoft.

48948 ■ **"Aside from taking M-commerce requests, Quixi wouldn't do anything on the Web"** in *Inc.* (November 15, 2000, pp. 33)
Pub: The Goldhirsh Group
Description: Information about the virtual assistant Quixi and other helper systems being installed in vehicles.

48949 ■ **"At a Laptop Near You..."** in *Entrepreneur* (Vol. 32, December 2004, No. 12, pp. 56)
Pub: Entrepreneur Media Inc.
Ed: Amanda C. Kooser. **Description:** EmperorLinux sells laptops from manufacturers like Dell, IBM and Sharp loaded and tested with Linux. Hewlett-Packard offers its own Linux laptop, the HP Compaq Business Notebook nx5000.

48950 ■ **"At Last, Stirrings in the PC Market"** in *Barron's* (August 25, 2003, pp. T3)
Pub: Barron's
Ed: Mark Veverka. **Description:** Personal computer sales, long expected to benefit from the need for consumers to replace aging systems, have finally begun to increase, according to reports from market leaders at Hewlett-Packard and Dell.

48951 ■ **"The Automated Agent"** in *Rough Notes* (Vol. 146, No. 9, September 2003, pp. 92)
Pub: Rough Notes
Ed: Michael J. Weinberg. **Description:** An examination of newer technology making work easier and more efficient for insurance agents. Topics include laptops, cell phones, and email accounts.

48952 ■ **"Automation Accountability"** in *Rough Notes* (Vol. 145, No. 1, January 2003, pp. 82)
Pub: Rough Notes

Ed: Nancy Doucette. **Description:** Mary Eisenhart and Cherly Koch are business consultants who advise that agencies that shift to automation should not only fully utilize the new system, but ought to also change the procedure to obtain the return on investment.

48953 ■ "Back It Up" in *Black Enterprise* **(Vol. 35, October 2004, No. 3, pp. 72)**
Pub: Earl G. Graves Publishing Co. Inc.
Ed: Sonya A. Donaldson. **Description:** A small business owner is looking for an online storage or backup company to store the company's data.

48954 ■ "Bandleader" in *Entrepreneur* **(Vol. 30, No. 2, February 2002, pp. 31)**
Pub: Entrepreneur Media Inc.
Ed: Mike Hogan. **Description:** Profile of the new network wireless technology that can achieve speeds of up to 108Mbps.

48955 ■ "Bar None" in *Entrepreneur* **(Vol. 32, December 2004, No. 12, pp. 24)**
Pub: Entrepreneur Media Inc.
Ed: Amanda C. Kooser. **Description:** New bar code regulations affecting retailers and suppliers, called Sunrise 2005, go into effect January 1, 2005. This process allows businesses to scan different types of codes used worldwide, and ultimately, the 14-digit Global Trade Item Number.

48956 ■ "Battery Tests" in *Entrepreneur* **(Vol. 33, September 2005, No. 9, pp. 46)**
Pub: Entrepreneur Media Inc.
Ed: Amanda C. Kooser. **Description:** American Power Conversion and Compact Power Systems make battery products that keep cell phones up and running, costing $10-$15.

48957 ■ "The Best of 2000: PCs" in *PC Magazine* **(January 2, 2001, pp. 145)**
Pub: Ziff-Davis Publishing Company
Description: A listing and description of the best PC products of 2000 are presented. Among the notable products are the HP Vectra line, IBM Small Business Solutions, Sun Microsystems' Sun Ray 1, Micron Millennia MAX XP, Dell Dimension 4100, the IBM ThinkPad line, and the Dell Precision Workstation 420 Mini Tower.

48958 ■ "Better Searching with Win 2000 Indexing-A valuable feature enables fast, detailed content searches" in *PC Magazine* **(Dec. 5, 2000)**
Pub: Ziff-Davis Publishing Company
Ed: Craig Stinson. **Description:** The indexing service in Microsoft Windows 2000 was originally built as a search engine for Internet Information Servers. Then it was realized that the technology could be applied to regular office documents. The result is a service that locates documents in mass storage devices. Testing has proved a dramatic increase in the speed of searches.

48959 ■ "Big Box vs. Online" in *Hispanic Business* **(March 2003, pp. 25)**
Pub: Hispanic Business
Ed: Roger Harris. **Description:** Internet shoppers are finding very competitive pricing between purchasing online versus going to a brick and mortar store. An online shopping checklist is provided to assist consumers when making purchases online.

48960 ■ "BlackBerry Harvest" in *Entrepreneur* **(Vol. 32, September 2004, No. 9, pp. 40)**
Pub: Entrepreneur Media Inc.
Description: Research in Motion (RIM) is expanding the BlackBerry to include other devices which will be available late 2004.

48961 ■ "Bluetooth: Get Wired Without the Wires" in *E-business Advisor* **(Vol. 18, No. 10, October 2000, pp. 14)**
Pub: Advisor Media, Inc.
Ed: Brent A. Miller, Chatschik Bisbikian. **Description:** Bluetooth is an emerging open specification that could

revolutionize wireless communications in everything from desktop computers to telephone headsets. The basic idea is short-range communications that don't have to operate in licensed spectrum and a replacement for cables. This article takes a look at the uses of Bluetooth, and the origins and founders of the Bluetooth Special Users Group.

48962 ■ "Book It!" in *Entrepreneur* **(Vol. 31, No. 7, July 2003, pp. 42)**
Pub: Entrepreneur Media, Inc.
Ed: Gisela M. Pedroza. **Description:** Profile of Compaq's Evo Computer Notebook N620C that allows users to work more than five hours before recharging. The notebook offers 802.11b and Bluetooth wireless options.

48963 ■ "Box Office" in *Entrepreneur* **(Vol. 32, December 2004, No. 12, pp. 54)**
Pub: Entrepreneur Media Inc.
Ed: Steve Cooper. **Description:** Profile of NetSapiens' V-Box, a portable plug 'n' play PBX that delivers multi-person voice over Internet Protocol (VoIP) with a set of built-in controls. Growing businesses will enjoy features like auto-attendant, interactive voice response, local extensions, multi-way conferencing, voice mail notification via email or SMS, and call-forwarding options.

48964 ■ "Bright ideas" in *Entrepreneur* **(Vol. 31, No. 6, June 2003, pp. 48)**
Pub: Entrepreneur Media Inc.
Ed: Marc Spiwak. **Description:** Five ultra-portable projectors for making presentations are profiled, including the InFocus LP70, Toshiba TDP-P5, Philips LC5241, Hewlett-Packard MP3800, and ViewSonic's PJ551. Most of these projectors include direct VGA, composite and S-Video inputs, remote controls, and built-in speakers.

48965 ■ "Bright lights" in *Entrepreneur* **(Vol. 30, No. 2, Feb)**
Pub: Entrepreneur Media Inc.
Ed: Amanda C. Kooser. **Description:** Information about various portable projectors to help with presentations is offered, including a shopping list for Epson PowerLite 600p, Hitachi CP-X270W, InFocus LP280, Optoma ExPro750, and Sharp PG-C20XU.

48966 ■ "Build a Better Business" in *Black Enterprise* **(Vol. 35, October 2004, No. 3, pp. 136)**
Pub: Earl G. Graves Publishing Co. Inc.
Ed: Robert Anthony, Sonya A. Donaldson. **Description:** Emerging new technologies can help small businesses seem larger than they really are. Co-founder of Krazy Kickz, Sam Robinson, tells how upgrading the company's phone system led to a better customer service system.

48967 ■ *Building Your Own High-Tech Small Office*
Pub: I D G Books Worldwide
Ed: Robert Richardson. **Released:** 1998. **Price:** $39.99.

48968 ■ "Buried Alive-There's no such thing as a paperless office" in *PC Computing* **(March 2000, pp. 104)**
Pub: Ziff-Davis Inc.
Ed: Nora Isaacs. **Description:** Electronic document management can reduce the paper clutter in an office and make information easier to store and retrieve. A brief description of new document management hardware and software are presented, including Visioineer's OneTouch 8600 scanner, Caere's OmniPage Pro 10 OCR and PageKeeper Pro 3.0 software, Corex's CardScan Office Solution, Ricoh's e-Cabinet, Xerox's DocuShare 2.1, and Lotus's Domino.Doc software.

48969 ■ "Business Integrator Entrepreneur Marries Technology and Advertising to Grow Business" in *Black Enterprise* **(Vol. 35, Jan. 2005, No. 6)**
Pub: Earl G. Graves Publishing Co. Inc.
Ed: Nichole Lewis. **Description:** Interactive marketing strategies have helped POWERi to grow in the

travel and tourism industry despite a slowdown since the terrorist attacks of 9-11. The firm operates three lines of business: technology within an advertising agency that could also provide marketing strategy and graphic design services. The firm reported revenues of $1 million in 2003.

48970 ■ "Business Intelligence" in *E-business Advisor* **(Vol. 18, No. 8, August 2000, pp. 22)**
Pub: Advisor Media, Inc.
Ed: Claudia Imhoff. **Description:** A description of the concept of Corporate Information Factory (CIF), which provides a high-level guide to developing an e-business plan.

48971 ■ "Businesses Must Now Notify of Possible ID Theft" in *Crain's Detroit Business* **(Vol. 23, January 8, 2007, No. 2, pp. 6)**
Pub: Crain Communications Inc. - Detroit
Ed: Amy Lane. **Description:** New bill requires businesses, state agencies, and local government to notify individuals of a security breech that is likely to cause individual loss, injury or identity theft.

48972 ■ "Buying Guide" in *My Business* **(April/May 2004, pp. 18-19)**
Pub: My Business Magazine
Description: Profiles of five new computer notebooks, including Apple's PowerBook G4, IBM ThinkPad R50, HP Pavillion zd7000, Dell Inspiron XPS, and Toshiba Portege M100. Tips for purchasing the right notebook computer are also offered.

48973 ■ "B.Y.O. GPS" in *Business 2.0* **(Vol. 6, September 2005, No. 8, pp. 132)**
Pub: Time, Inc.
Ed: Matthew Maier. **Description:** Owning your own portable GPS system is a wiser choice than the renting the costly units offered by car rental companies. Reviews of the Magellan RoadMate 760, Palm GPS Navigator, Microsoft Streets & Trips 2005 are included.

48974 ■ "Cable-Free USB" in *Entrepreneur* **(Vol. 33, October 2005, No. 10, pp. 41)**
Pub: Entrepreneur Media Inc.
Description: An overview of the wireless Universal serial bus, expected to reach the market by the end of 2005, is presented.

48975 ■ "Cable cuts out slice of the broadband pie" in *InfoWorld* **(Vol. 23, No. 5, January 29, 2001, pp. 40)**
Pub: InfoWorld
Ed: Jennifer Jones. **Description:** Cable modem service continues to hold a lead over DSL in the broadband sector. Industry leaders, such as AT&T and Media One, and America Online and Time Warner, are banking on that lead as part of their merger plans. These mergers are expected to bring high-speed Internet access to home users and focus on telecommuting.

48976 ■ "Call Forward: No Question About It" in *Entrepreneur* **(Vol. 32, November 2004, No. 11, pp. 17)**
Pub: Entrepreneur Media Inc.
Ed: Amanda C. Kooser. **Description:** Battery technology is having difficulty keeping pace with the fast-paced communications industry.

48977 ■ "Call Waiting?" in *Entrepreneur* **(Vol. 31, No. 7, July 2003, pp. 37)**
Pub: Entrepreneur Media, Inc.
Ed: Mike Hogan. **Description:** IP telephony entrepreneurs and users now have the Internet as an alternative to public-switched telephone networks, offering cost savings and services and productivity enhancements, as well as future new devices.

48978 ■ "Calling All VoIP Adopters: Tech Shows" in *Tradeshow Week* **(Vol. 34, November 29, 2004, No. 48, pp. 54)**
Pub: Reed Business Information
Ed: Margo McCall. **Description:** Ways Voice over Internet protocol can improve small business are discussed, including information about established companies and startups providing the service.

48979 ■ **"Calling the Shots: Is a VoIP Telephone System in Your Company's Future?"** in *Entrepreneur* (Vol. 32, October 2004, No. 10, pp. 57)

Pub: Entrepreneur Media Inc.

Ed: Mike Hogan. **Description:** Voice over Internet Protocol (VoIP) systems can be used by small companies using IP Centrex systems. Like other all-digital systems, IP Centrex benefits from the cost-effectiveness of an Internet transmission foundation and requires no on-site telephone equipment to purchase other than desk sets. System management, security, upgrades and redeployment are all handled by the service provider.

48980 ■ **"Can You Hear Me Yet?"** in *Black Enterprise* (Vol. 35, August 2004, No. 1, pp. 61)

Pub: Earl G. Graves Publishing Co. Inc.

Ed: Sonya A. Donaldson. **Description:** Small businesses have many choices when it comes to voice over Internet protocol. A listing of several providers and their Websites are given. It is important to remember that whether using landline-based wireless or Web-based services could cost more than traditional phone services.

48981 ■ **"Carry a Tune"** in *Fast Company* (August 2001, pp. 38)

Pub: Fast Company

Ed: Alison Overholt. **Description:** Profile of the DUO-64 Digital E-Cassette from Digisette, that comes with software to access a library of more than 17,000 titles of audiobooks and periodicals.

48982 ■ **"Carry Your Memory"** in *Tampa Tribune* (November 28, 2005)

Pub: Media General, Inc.

Ed: Richard Mullins. **Description:** Flash drives, or jump drives, are small devices that enable users to store digital memory and carry it with them on a keychain. Makers are dressing them up with metal studs, fluorescent rubber, faux leather, even silver buckles.

48983 ■ **"CEO Buyer's Guide: Computers"** in *Hispanic Business* (November 2002, pp. BG4)

Pub: Hispanic Business

Description: Profile of IBM's ThinkPad X30 notebook; IBM's eServer BladeCenter, and Microsoft's Works Suite 2003.

48984 ■ **"CEO Buyer's Guide: Office"** in *Hispanic Business* (November 2002, pp. BG18-BG19)

Pub: Hispanic Business

Description: Short profiles of the Brother HL-2460N laser printer; the CanoScan 8000F high-speed flatbed scanner; Pitney Bowes DM1000 Mailing System; Brother PT-1500PC computer label printer; Canon i550 color bubble jet printer; and Brother HL-1870N network-ready monochrome laser printer, are presented.

48985 ■ **"Chilling Out"** in *Forbes* (Vol. 174, December 27, 2004, No. 13, pp. 64)

Pub: Forbes Magazine Inc.

Ed: Bruce Upbin. **Description:** Cooligy, a startup company in Mountain View, California, has developed a fluid-and-pip concept that cools laptop computers.

48986 ■ **"Cisco rolls out small business DSL router"** in *InfoWorld* (Vol. 22, No. 17, April 24, 2000, pp. 65)

Pub: InfoWorld

Ed: Rebecca Sykes. **Description:** Cisco Systems introduced a DSL (Digital Subscriber Line) router designed to help service providers and resellers provide fast Internet access for small businesses and home offices. The Cisco 827 ADSL (Asymmetrical Digital Subscriber Line) router can deliver features ranging from differentiated class of service to voice over DSL. For example, with differentiated class of service, customers can prioritize bandwidth by signing on for premium, standard, or best-effort service, classed by specific application or user.

48987 ■ *Cisco Network Design Solutions for Small-Medium Businesses*

Pub: Pearson Technology Group Canada

Ed: Peter Rybaczyk. **Released:** August 2004. **Price:** $73.00. **Description:** Solutions for computer networking professionals using computer networks within a small to medium-sized business. Topics cover not only core networking issues and solutions, but security, IP telephony, unified communications, customer relations management, wireless LANs, and more.

48988 ■ **"A clearer view"** in *Black Enterprise* (Vol. 33, No. 6, January 2003, pp. 43)

Pub: Earl Graves Publishing Co.

Description: Review of KDS' XF-7b DynaFlat LCD computer monitor, which features a 1,024 at a 60Hz refresh rate, with little or no blurring.

48989 ■ **"A Close Call: Cell Phone Offers Good Mix of Price and Performance"** in *Black Enterprise* (Vol. 35, January 2005, No. 6, pp. 50)

Pub: Earl G. Graves Publishing Co. Inc.

Ed: Sonya A. Donaldson. **Description:** Profile of Siemens' cell phone, CF62T. The phone offers a combination of price and performance and provides up to 220 hours of standby time and 300 minutes of talk time using a lithium-ion battery.

48990 ■ **"Color-Blind?"** in *Entrepreneur* (Vol. 32, December 2004, No. 12, pp. 49)

Pub: Entrepreneur Media Inc.

Ed: Mike Hogan. **Description:** The cost of owning a color laser printer has dropped significantly, making them more affordable for small companies.

48991 ■ **"Color Scheme"** in *Entrepreneur* (Vol. 32, No. 1, January 2004, pp. 39)

Pub: Entrepreneur Media, Inc.

Ed: Steve Cooper. **Description:** Profile of Minolta's DiALTA CF2002 printer/copier. The printer offer full-color documents at the rate of 20 ppm and black-and-white at 31 ppm. It also includes workgroup publishing options like stapling and folding.

48992 ■ **"Combo Magic"** in *My Business* (April/May 2003, pp. 24)

Pub: My Business Magazine

Description: Options for choosing mobile phone/personal digital assistant combinations are explored.

48993 ■ **"Come Together. Is It Time to Combine Your Voice and Data Networks?"** in *Entrepreneur* (Vol. 33, January 2005, No. 1, pp. 44)

Pub: Entrepreneur Media Inc.

Ed: Amanda C. Kooser. **Description:** Information that enables a small business to network voice and data over the same network is presented.

48994 ■ **"Companies struggle to define technology ROI"** in *Atlanta Business Chronicle* (Vol. 25, November 15, 2002, No. 23 pp. 5C)

Pub: American City Business Publications, Inc.

Ed: Don Reichardt. **Description:** Defining the return on investment (ROI) for technology projects is difficult for most companies. Companies currently want to see a definite financial benefit before agreeing to additional investments. Projects are no longer justifiable by claiming they will permit better management.

48995 ■ *The Computer Glossary: The Complete Illustrated Desk Reference*

Pub: AMACOM

Ed: Alan Freedman. **Released:** 1994, seventh edition. **Price:** $36.95 (paper). **Description:** Provides over 4300 definitions of computer terms, including the proper names of specific products and companies.

48996 ■ **"Control Freak"** in *Fast Company* (May 2001, pp. 62)

Pub: Fast Company

Ed: Amy Wilson Sheldon. **Description:** Profile of the Proton SRC-2000 Smart Remote Control device that will custom-program commands to suit the specs of electronic devices with an optional docking station that allows to connect to a computer.

48997 ■ **"Cool Pics"** in *Entrepreneur.com* (Vol. 34, February 2006, No. 2, pp. 47)

Pub: Entrepreneur Media Inc.

Ed: Mike Hogan. **Description:** Profile of Nikon's Coolpix P1, the first Wi-Fi-capable digital camera.

48998 ■ **"Cool Tools"** in *My Business* (April/May 2002, pp. 19)

Pub: My Business Magazine

Description: Profile of a portable charging cartridge for mobile phones and PDA's, a fingerprint security system for computers, pocket email composer, and an electrical surge protector for notebook computers.

48999 ■ **"Copy Talk"** in *Entrepreneur* (Vol. 32, October 2004, No. 10, pp. 54)

Pub: Entrepreneur Media Inc.

Ed: Amanda C. Kooser. **Description:** Entrepreneurs who need to capture magazine articles, book pages, notes, contracts and other documents when away from the office could benefit from the Planon System Solutions DocuPen, a handheld pen-style scanner; other models are offered by SolutionWorx's C-Pens line, WizCom Technologies' InfoScan and QuickLink scanners; prices for all range from $110 to $200.

49000 ■ **"Copy That"** in *Entrepreneur* (Vol. 31, Oct. 2003)

Pub: Entrepreneur Media, Inc.

Ed: Amanda C. Kooser. **Description:** Profiles of various copy machines suited for growing businesses are highlighted.

49001 ■ **"Covert Operations"** in *Entrepreneur* (Vol. 31, No. 8, August 2003, pp. 51)

Pub: Entrepreneur Media, Inc.

Ed: Amanda C. Kooser. **Description:** The importance of using spyware and a good firewall to protect company information is stressed. Free spyware detection products can be downloaded free of charge, but a more complete solution offered by Lavasoft or Pest-Patrol may be a better choice. Anti-spyware should become an overall part of a company's security plan and should be reviewed periodically.

49002 ■ **"Cut the Cord: Presentations Don't Have to Be a Hassle"** in *Entrepreneur* (Vol. 32, December 2004, No. 12, pp. 50)

Pub: Entrepreneur Media Inc.

Ed: Amanda C. Kooser. **Description:** Wireless technology enables entrepreneurs to give presentations using the D-Link Wireless Presentation Gate that allows users to connect to VGA-compatible machines like projectors, LCD panels or monitors wirelessly.

49003 ■ **"Cutting Edge"** in *Entrepreneur* (Vol. 33, March 2005, No. 3, pp. 48)

Pub: Entrepreneur Media Inc.

Description: Profile of Motorola's Razr V3 cellular phone, offering email support, Bluetooth, speaker phone and world phone capabilities.

49004 ■ **"Cutting Lines: Giving New Meaning to the Term 'Mobile Phone'"** in *Entrepreneur* (Vol. 31, No. 10, October 2003, pp. 45)

Pub: Entrepreneur Media, Inc.

Ed: Mike Hogan. **Description:** Mobility Communications Systems (MCS), an Internet Protocol (IP) telephony server that broadcasts voice calls anywhere a wireless LAN can broadcast data, is examined.

49005 ■ **"Data to Go: When You're on the Move, Stay Connected for Less"** in *Entrepreneur* (Vol. 33, February 2005, No. 2, pp. 38)

Pub: Entrepreneur Media Inc.

Ed: Amanda C. Kooser. **Description:** Profile of Phoenix, 4SmartPhone, which offers mobile access to email, calendars, contracts and shared files, making it attractive for small business use.

49006 ■ **"Dell and NetObjects make small business play"** in *Network World* (October 24, 2000, pp. NA)

Pub: Network World Inc.

Ed: Ashlee Vance. **Description:** Dell plans to pre-install NetObject's software for building Web sites on some Dell desktops and notebooks. The software helps users build, publish and promote their own Web sites under the co-branded product title NetObjects Fusion Dell Edition.

49007 ■ "Dell Rolls Out New Models, Upgrade Program" in *eWeek* (February 1, 2005)
Pub: Ziff Davis Media Inc.
Description: Dell introduced several new computer notebooks, mobile workstations and services for small business users, including the new Latitude notebooks, Precision mobile work stations.

49008 ■ "Dell's High-End Home Run" in *Business Week Online* (February 17, 2006)
Pub: McGraw-Hill Companies
Description: Review of Dell's new XPS 400 computer, a high-end computer equipped with an Intel Pentium D930, a dual-core processor that divides the labor of one core in order to get more work done more efficiently.

49009 ■ "Desktop Roundup: Here's How To Find the Perfect PC For Your Small Business Buck" in *Black Enterprise* (Vol. 34, No. 3, October 2003)
Pub: Earl Graves Publishing Co.
Ed: Cristina Gair. **Description:** Profiles of computer desktops from eMachines, Dell, Sony and Hewlett-Packard are presented, using a price point of $700, excluding monitor. Technical support from each manufacturer, as well as hardware and software packages, was also investigated.

49010 ■ "Dial again" in *Black Enterprise* (Vol. 32, No. 10, May 2002, pp. 109)
Pub: Earl Graves Publishing Co.
Ed: Ann Brown. **Description:** Every day more businesses are becoming wireless and cell phone companies are vying for small business accounts. Questions are presented to help small business choose a service.

49011 ■ "Digital Defenses: A Business's Network Is its Castle" in *Red Herring* (January 2003, pp. 52)
Pub: Herring Communications Inc.
Ed: Lee Bruno. **Description:** The challenge for most small companies is to be able to keep the line of communication and commerce open, while securing and protecting critical business information.

49012 ■ "Digital Fingerprints" in *Forbes* (Vol. 174, December 13, 2004, No. 12, pp. 110)
Pub: Forbes Magazine Inc.
Ed: Daniel Lyons. **Description:** Profiles of data storage products designed to store information such as emails, electronic checks, x-rays and other items. Digital data is growing at the rate of 90 percent per year.

49013 ■ "Do You Copy?" in *Entrepreneur* (Vol. 32, November 2004, No. 11, pp. 64)
Pub: Entrepreneur Media Inc.
Ed: Amanda C. Kooser. **Description:** Profiles of copy machines useful to a growing business are highlighted. Multi-function devices can handle printing and copying needs without having to invest in multiple machines.

49014 ■ "Domino's says new system saves dough" in *Crain's Detroit Business* (Vol. 19, No. 8, February 24, 2003, pp. 13)
Pub: Crain Communications Inc., Detroit
Ed: Michael Strong. **Description:** Domino's Pizza LLC has begun a new computerized system, called Pulse that will save the company and franchisees both time and money.

49015 ■ "Double Down" in *Entrepreneur* (Vol. 33, September 2005, No. 9, pp. 50)
Pub: Entrepreneur Media Inc.
Ed: Amanda C. Kooser. **Description:** The next-generation of DVD burners is profiled. A listing of manufacturers, models, contact information and DL write speed is included.

49016 ■ "DSL Users Brace for Bumpy Ride" in *Home Office Computing* (Vol. 18, No. 11, November 2000, pp. 19)
Pub: Scholastic Inc.
Ed: Bonny L. Georgia. **Description:** Tips for protecting yourself when dealing with DSL providers are given.

49017 ■ "Easy Router" in *Entrepreneur* (Vol. 32, No. 2, February 2004, pp. 45)
Pub: Entrepreneur Media, Inc.
Ed: Steve Cooper. **Description:** Profile of the new wireless gear by Netgear; its new WGT624 108Mbps Wireless Firewall Router offers twice the data throughput of 54Mbps 802.11 wireless routers and is as much as 10 times faster than 802.11b devices, yet maintains backward compatibility with both.

49018 ■ "The end of the PC world as we know it" in *Red Herring* (No. 106, October 15, 2001, pp. 16)
Pub: Herring Communications
Ed: Anthony B. Perkins. **Description:** A discussion of reasons for the slowing market in PC sales, including Internet-enabled cell phones, handheld organizers, and email devices. The result of price wars has forced the larger makers to not only merge, but also diversify their companies.

49019 ■ "English-Spanish Made Easy" in *Hispanic Business* (June 2002, pp. 94)
Pub: Hispanic Business
Ed: Alexandra Salas Rojas. **Description:** Profile of Word Magic's English-Spanish translation software is presented. Word Magic software will help increase the rate at which business can be conducted over language boundaries.

49020 ■ "The Essential Tech Toolbox" in *Hispanic Business* (Vol. 23, No. 5, May 2001, pp. 38, 40)
Pub: Hispanic Business
Ed: Gina Binole. **Description:** A list of tech must-haves for the competitive business owner, including profiles of the Palm Pilot, cellular phones, Application Service Providers (ASP), firewall protection, anti-virus software, wireless local area network, wireless broadband, Web services, and P3P (privacy enhancing technology).

49021 ■ "Ethentica Ethenticator MS 3000 PC Card" in *PC Magazine* (February 6, 2001, pp. 26)
Pub: Ziff-Davis Publishing Company
Ed: Sally Wiener Grotta. **Description:** Review of Ethentica Ethenticator MS 3000 PC Card, the fingerprint verification scanner used for mobile security. In addition to protecting the data on a laptop, the device replaces passwords on favorite Web sites and applications and even fills out personal information on user-selected Internet forms.

49022 ■ "ety8 Bluetooth Earphones: Music to Your Ears" in *Sales & Marketing Management* (Vol. 159, January-February 2007, No. 1, pp. 40)
Pub: VNU Business Media
Ed: Julia Chang. **Description:** Profile of Etymotic Research's new Bluetooth earphones with an iPod adapter, starting at $199.

49023 ■ "Face-Off: Online Postage" in *FSB* (Vol. 10, No. 9, December 1, 2000, pp. 116)
Pub: Time Inc.
Ed: Julie Sloane. **Description:** The article examines two new online postage sites, stamps.com and pitney-bowes.com.

49024 ■ "A Fair Case: These Pretty Laptop Cases Are Pretty Functional, Too" in *Entrepreneur* (Vol. 32, July 2004, No. 7, pp. 34)
Pub: Entrepreneur Media Inc.
Ed: Nichole L. Torres. **Description:** Nicole Arslanian and Julie Lazarus, founders of Talene Reilly Inc., and sisters Emily and Helena McHugh, founders of Casauri, have both designed laptop cases that look like fashionable handbags.

49025 ■ "Fair Share" in *Entrepreneur* (Vol. 33, January 2005, No. 1, pp. 44)
Pub: Entrepreneur Media Inc.
Description: Profile of 3Com OfficeConnect wireless cable/DSL gateway that provides Internet-sharing solutions for small business or home users.

49026 ■ "Fair Share" in *Entrepreneur.com* (Vol. 34, January 2006, No. 1, pp. 36)
Pub: Entrepreneur Media, Inc.
Ed: Amanda C. Kooser. **Description:** Actiontec offers a wireless network that allows users on up to three computers to share one computer, allowing the printer to be placed anywhere because it does not need to be connected to a computer with wires.

49027 ■ "Falling for a Scan" in *Entrepreneur* (Vol. 31, No. 8, August 2003, pp. 50)
Pub: Entrepreneur Media, Inc.
Ed: Amanda C. Kooser. **Description:** Scanners are gaining in popularity with entrepreneurs to create promotional materials or to upload images to a small business' Website. Statistical data included.

49028 ■ "Farming IT Out" in *Home Office Computing* (Vol. 18, No. 10, October 2000, pp. 16)
Pub: Scholastic Inc.
Ed: Mark Kakkuri. **Description:** Information Technology (IT) outsourcing services are ready to help home office workers with everything from setting up a computer to building a broadband LAN.

49029 ■ "Feel the Burn" in *Entrepreneur* (Vol. 32, August 2004, No. 8, pp. 40)
Pub: Entrepreneur Media Inc.
Ed: Amanda C. Kooser. **Description:** DVD-burner technology has become popular for small business with double-layer (DL) DVD technology being the best in terms of storage space for companies looking for a new data backup method.

49030 ■ "Feeling Loaded Down? Use Partnerships to Bag New Customers" in *My Business* (October/November 2003, pp. 44)
Pub: My Business Magazine
Ed: Paige Orr. **Description:** Michael Hess, president and chief executive of Road Wired, a technology travel accessory firm, partnered with Travelpro International, a luggage manufacturer and distributor. This partnership has helped Hess to grow his business.

49031 ■ "Firms Will Spend Less on Buildings and Equipment This Year" in *Kiplinger Letter* (Vol. 78, January 19, 2007, No. 2)
Pub: Kiplinger
Description: Small business will spend about 2 percent less in building and equipment purchases in 2007. Industrial equipment, telecommunications and diesel engines will be the hardest hit.

49032 ■ "Flash: our outlook on what's new, what's hot and what's happening" in *Entrepreneur* (Vol. 31, No. 5, May 2003, pp. 6)
Pub: Entrepreneur Media Inc.
Description: Floppy disks are becoming obsolete and analog wireless service is being phased out over the next five years; Supermarkets are partnering with toy retailers; and hot dogs and fondue are going gourmet.

49033 ■ "Flowfinity Wireless and Partners Extend Microsoft Business Solutions to BlackBerry" in *Internet Wire* (February 14, 2005)
Pub: COMTEX News Network Inc.
Description: Flowfinity Wireless, a provider of wireless application products and platforms, is committed to helping enterprises capitalize on the benefits of connecting Microsoft systems to BlackBerry.

49034 ■ "Form finder" in *Entrepreneur* (Vol. 30, No. 3, March 2002, pp. 40)
Pub: Entrepreneur Media Inc.
Ed: Liane Gouthro. **Description:** Profile of Cosmi Swift Ware Personal and Business Legal Forms to Go software; this software will create more than 200 legal documents including bankruptcies, wills and leases; basic legal help is also included.

49035 ■ "Forward Thinking" in *PC Magazine* (February 20, 2001, pp. 7)
Pub: Ziff-Davis Publishing Company
Ed: Michael J. Miller. **Description:** There are a variety of wireless devices on the market. A top rated wireless

home gateway is the D-Link D1713. Network services can also be difficult to set up, so a recommended solution is HomeRF. A suggested service package is Metricom Ricochet. A preferred device comes from IBM.

49036 ■ "Found in Cyberspace" in *Entrepreneur* **(Vol. 28, No. 10, October 2000, pp. 60)**
Pub: Entrepreneur Media Inc.
Ed: Mike Hogan. **Description:** The benefits of online data storage are discussed.

49037 ■ "Free At Last!" in *Entrepreneur* **(Vol. 33, October 2005, No. 10, pp. 49)**
Pub: Entrepreneur Media Inc.
Ed: Mike Hogan. **Description:** Review of Uniden's new UIP1868P phone system is presented. The new cordless phone offers office features and low-cost Internet calling through Packet8.

49038 ■ "Free to Roam" in *Entrepreneur* **(Vol. 32, September 2004, No. 9, pp. 42)**
Pub: Entrepreneur Media Inc.
Ed: Steve Cooper. **Description:** Profile of Sharp's Linux-based Zaurus SL-6000, a PDA for mobile workers. The device supports desktop applications like IBM's WebSphere, Microsoft Outlook, and some Word and Excel.

49039 ■ "Fujitsu Biometric Notebook PC" in *Black Enterprise* **(Vol. 35, December 2004, No. 5, pp. 70)**
Pub: Earl G. Graves Publishing Co. Inc.
Description: Profile of LifeBook P7000, an ultra-portable PC featuring a fingerprint sensor for increased mobile security.

49040 ■ "G Whiz!" in *Entrepreneur* **(Vol. 33, January 2005, No. 1, pp. 46)**
Pub: Entrepreneur Media Inc.
Ed: Amanda C. Kooser. **Description:** Profile of the new all-in-one iMac Computer, the iMac G5.

49041 ■ "Gadget: Danger Hiptop" in *Red Herring* **(No. 106, October 15, 2001, pp. 18)**
Pub: Herring Communications
Ed: Rafe Needleman. **Description:** Profile of Danger's new integrated cell phone/data service; in addition to a browser and phone, the product comes with email, instant messaging, calendar, phone book, and games.

49042 ■ "Gadgets" in *Business Week* **(January 9, 2006, No. 3966, pp. 30)**
Pub: McGraw-Hill Companies
Ed: Burt Helm. **Description:** Profile of Sony's new portable e-reader device that allows users to store and view digital books. The device will sell for $300 to $500.

49043 ■ "Get Hooked on an Intranet" in *Success* **(Vol. 47, No. 3, July 2000, pp. 55)**
Pub: Success Publishing, Inc.
Ed: Michael S. Foley. **Description:** This "keeper" can profit and organize your business. Two top picks that allow your small business to collaborate online for free.

49044 ■ "Get Organized" in *Entrepreneur* **(Vol. 32, November 2004, No. 11, pp. 62)**
Pub: Entrepreneur Media Inc.
Ed: Liane Cassavoy. **Description:** FileAmigo LE from Sierra Software allows users to custom design databases and reports and its Pro version allows for sharing content over a network.

49045 ■ "Get with the program!" in *Entrepreneur* **(Vol. 31, No. 5, May 2003, pp. 58)**
Pub: Entrepreneur Media Inc.
Ed: Mie-Yun Lee. **Description:** The 2003 Complete Guide to Software is presented. The guide covers various software tools that help to make small businesses more productive.

49046 ■ "Get it together" in *Entrepreneur* **(Vol. 30, No. 3, March 2002, pp. 40)**
Pub: Entrepreneur Media Inc.
Ed: Liane Gouthro. **Description:** Profile of Drag Strip 3.8 from Aladdin systems; this application provides shortcuts to commonly used files, folders, applications and sites.

49047 ■ "GigaTrans hopes to get share of wireless market" in *Crain's Detroit Business* **(Vol. 19, No. 16, April 21, 2003, pp. 12)**
Pub: Crain Communications Inc., Detroit
Ed: Andrew Dietderich. **Description:** Profile of James Rose, CEO and his two-year-old firm GigaTrans, a wireless Internet service provider. The company hopes to serve small and medium-size business customers.

49048 ■ "Giving Small Biz Short Shrift" in *Business Week* **(No. 3660, December 20, 1999, pp. 32)**
Pub: McGraw-Hill, Inc.
Description: The failure of Apple Computer to encourage having a small business customer base is reviewed.

49049 ■ *Glossbrenner's Guide to Shareware for Small Businesses*
Pub: TAB Books, Inc.
Ed: Alfred Glossbrenner. **Released:** 1992. **Price:** $37.95; $27.95 (paper).

49050 ■ "Go Pro 2.4 GHZ Gyrotransport Air Mouse Presenter" in *Sales & Marketing Management* **(Vol. 159, January-February 2007, No. 1, pp. 42)**
Pub: VNU Business Media
Description: Profile of Gyrotransport mouse that comes equipped with software for Windows and eight programmable functions.

49051 ■ "Go retro! Budget tight?" in *Entrepreneur* **(Vol. 31, No. 4, April 2003, pp. 41)**
Pub: Entrepreneur Media Inc.
Ed: Mike Hogan. **Description:** Many small businesses are purchasing used computers for office use in order to save costs; a listing of companies offering used PCs or replacement parts is included.

49052 ■ "Going solo" in *Entrepreneur* **(Vol. 28, No. 11, November 2000, pp. 34)**
Pub: Entrepreneur Media Inc.
Ed: Gisela M. Pedroza. **Description:** Profile of the Solo 9300 Portable PC from Gateway.

49053 ■ "Going Somewhere?" in *Entrepreneur* **(Vol. 31, No. 9, September 2003, pp. 50)**
Pub: Entrepreneur Media, Inc.
Ed: Michael Gross. **Description:** Profiles of the Brother Mprint Microprinter, the Canon i70 Color Bubble Jet Printer, and the HP DeskJet 450e small printers that are very portable.

49054 ■ "Great Expectations: Think Your Business Technology Is All That and a Bag of Microchips? Well, It's Not" in *Entrepreneur*
Pub: Entrepreneur Media Inc.
Ed: Amanda C. Kooser. **Description:** Upgrading technologies like radio frequency identification (RFID), computers to tablet PCs, ultrawideband (UWB), VoIP and Wi-Fi are new technologies designed to have an impact of the way business is conducted.

49055 ■ "Grist: More Power Than Point" in *Inc.* **(August 1, 2003)**
Pub: Gruner & Jahr USA Publishing
Ed: Adam Hanft. **Description:** Although there is an estimated 400 million computers using Microsoft's computer software program PowerPoint, many believe it radically oversimplifies issues.

49056 ■ "Group sees beauty in an attempt to revive BeOS operating system" in *Wall Street Journal* **(February 5, 2003, pp. B4A)**
Pub: Dow Jones & Co. Inc.
Ed: Nick Baker. **Description:** OpenBeOS project wants to revive the operating system first introduced in 1995, but now defunct by Be Inc.

49057 ■ "Group Effort" in *Entrepreneur* **(Vol. 32, November 2004, No. 11, pp. 64)**
Pub: Entrepreneur Media Inc.
Ed: Gisela M. Pedroza. **Description:** Dell's monochrome laser printer 1700n can lower the cost of printing because it uses a high-capacity toner cartridge. The machine prints 25 ppm.

49058 ■ "Grow Your Technology" in *Home Office Computing* **(Vol. 18, No. 10, October 2000, pp. 52)**
Pub: Scholastic Inc.
Ed: David Haskin. **Description:** Strategies for supporting a home business with best tech resources and support while staying within the budget are presented. The first step is to evaluate the existing tech set up, using a consultant, if necessary. Other tech strategies include developing a professional Web presence, providing adequate customer support and handling remote workers. Products and services for home office administration are listed.

49059 ■ "The Growing Opportunity in Server Consolidation" in *Venture Capital Journal* **(Vol. 42, No. 9, September 2002, pp. 36-37)**
Pub: Thomas Venture Economics
Ed: Roger Lee. **Description:** Reducing the number of servers to a manageable number allows corporations to save money on real estate, power consumption, security, and IT administration.

49060 ■ "Guerrilla Marketing via Wi-Fi" in *Business 2.0* **(Vol. 6, July 2005, No. 6, pp. 112)**
Pub: Time, Inc.
Description: Apple's AirPort Express allows users to listen to music and print off site using an Ethernet cable as well as other business essentials.

49061 ■ "Guiding Light" in *Entrepreneur* **(Vol. 31, No. 11, November 2003, pp. 56)**
Pub: Entrepreneur Media, Inc.
Ed: Gisela M. Pedroza. **Description:** Profile of Forever Flashlights designed to help keep offices safe in the event of a power outage.

49062 ■ "gWHIZ!: swimming through the alphabet soup of today's wireless standards" in *Entrepreneur* **(Vol. 31, No. 6, June 2003, pp. 39)**
Pub: Entrepreneur Media Inc.
Ed: Daniel Tynan. **Description:** By the end of 2003, products supporting combinations of wireless devices will be available. The Institute of Electrical and Electronics Engineers will finalize specification this summer enabling the Wi-Fi Alliance to begin testing and certifying the interoperability of various "g" devices.

49063 ■ "Half Pints: Wireless Routers Have the Size Advantage" in *Entrepreneur* **(Vol. 33, January 2005, No. 1, pp. 42)**
Pub: Entrepreneur Media Inc.
Ed: Amanda C. Kooser. **Description:** Business travelers can now access the Internet in hotel rooms via a wireless travel router. These devices are manufactured by D-Link, Netgear, SMC and 3Com.

49064 ■ "Hands Down" in *Entrepreneur* **(Vol. 32, No. 4, April 2004, pp. 38)**
Pub: Entrepreneur Media, Inc.
Ed: Amanda C. Kooser. **Description:** Profile of the new USB fingerprint identifier being used in place of passwords for computer security.

49065 ■ "Hard copy" in *Entrepreneur* **(Vol. 28, No. 11, November 2000, pp. 34)**
Pub: Entrepreneur Media Inc.
Ed: Gisela M. Pedroza. **Description:** Profile of the Xerox WorkCentre XD125f copier/printer.

49066 ■ "Have Ricochet, Will Travel" in *PC Magazine* **(February 20, 2001, pp. 35)**
Pub: Ziff-Davis Publishing Company
Ed: Matthew D. Sarrel. **Description:** A profile of the recently launched Ricochet, a second-generation wireless data service now available in 22 major U.S. cities, including Atlanta, Baltimore, New York, San Diego and Washington, D.C., with plans to add 35 more cities this year.

49067 ■ "Head of the Class: Multitasking Made Easy" in *Black Enterprise* **(Vol. 35, November 2004, No. 4, pp. 68)**
Pub: Earl G. Graves Publishing Co. Inc.
Ed: Sonya A. Donaldson. **Description:** Profile of the all-in-one desktop MultiPass MP390 color inkjet from Carton. The printer also copies, faxes, and scans.

49068 ■ "Help for Your Small Business: Office 2000's Small Business Tools can help you manage and run a small business more effectively" in *PCMagazine*
Pub: Ziff-Davis Publishing Company
Ed: Neil Randall. **Description:** Microsoft Office 2000 Small Business Tools suite is a useful package that comes standard with any Office 2000 version except the Standard Edition. While it is not a full-featured financial package, it has some notable features. The suite comes with four components: Business Planner (BP), Small Business Customer Manager (SBCM), Direct Mail Manager (DMM), and Small Business Financial Manager (SBFM). Particularly useful are the quick financial summaries available through SBFM and the wealth of information and assistance covered in the Business Planner module.

49069 ■ "Here Comes the Sun" in *Entrepreneur* **(Vol. 32, December 2004, No. 12, pp. 16)**
Pub: Entrepreneur Media Inc.
Ed: Gisela M. Pedroza. **Description:** Profile of the Luxury Atomic Solar G-Shock Watch, geared to the international business traveler. The watch features local time for 30 cities around the world.

49070 ■ "Hide and Click: Optio S4 is Small but Powerful" in *Black Enterprise* **(Vol. 34, No. 7, February 2004, pp. 54)**
Pub: Earl Graves Publishing Co.
Ed: Sonya A. Donaldson. **Description:** Profile of Pentax Optio S4 camera with crisp 4-megapixel digital images, whether using wide angle or telephoto modes.

49071 ■ "High-Speed Web Access" in *Black Enterprise* **(Vol. 35, February 2005, No. 7, pp. 162)**
Pub: Earl G. Graves Publishing Co. Inc.
Ed: Leslie Guess Royal. **Description:** It is important for small businesses be equipped with high-speed Internet services to run a timely, efficient company. Statistical data, as well as pricing, is included.

49072 ■ "The Hispanic Market Goes Wireless" in *Hispanic Business* **(March 2003, pp. 50-52)**
Pub: Hispanic Business
Ed: Cindy Waxer. **Description:** Of the top 60 advertisers in the Hispanic market, four are telecommunications carriers, demonstrating the Hispanic community's interest in wireless communication. Statistical data included.

49073 ■ "Hit the Mark" in *My Business* **(August/September 2002, pp. 28-35)**
Pub: My Business Magazine
Description: Seven small business trends that will position a company for success are profiled. These trends include mentoring programs, e-mail marketing, customer service, personalized products and services, employee stock ownership plans, targeting markets, and automation.

49074 ■ "The HOC 100" in *Home Office Computing* **(Vol. 18, No. 12, December 2000, pp. 52)**
Pub: Scholastic Inc.
Description: Award-winning products for 2000 are discussed, including the Apple Power Mac G4 Cube, which earned the Product of the Year rating for its slick design, superb features and high-end performance, although it lacks bundled software and is overpriced.

49075 ■ "Hogan's Inferno" in *Entrepreneur* **(Vol. 28, No. 8, August 2000, pp. 48)**
Pub: Entrepreneur Media Inc.
Ed: Mike Hogan. **Description:** The poor quality of technical support for PC users is discussed.

49076 ■ "Holding pattern: It's not time to go 3G quite yet" in *Entrepreneur* **(Vol. 30, No. 2, February 2002, pp. 31)**
Pub: Entrepreneur Media Inc.
Ed: Mike Hogan. **Description:** Plans for a 30-enabling bandwidth auction can be expected sometime in 2004 and network rollouts in 2006 when applications will be compelling enough to get customers to buy.

49077 ■ "Hook up" in *Entrepreneur* **(Vol. 30, No. 1, January 2002, pp. 43)**
Pub: Entrepreneur Media Inc.
Ed: Mike Hogan. **Description:** Profile of the Belkin USB 10/100 Ethernet Adapter that provides instant network access for any desktop or laptop with a USB port.

49078 ■ "Hot Disks" in *Entrepreneur* **(Vol. 32, August 2004, No. 8, pp. 44)**
Pub: Entrepreneur Media Inc.
Ed: Liane Cassavoy. **Description:** Profiles of small business tools include Avanquest's Design & Print Business Edition for creating marketing materials; Mozilla's Firefox 0.8 browser; Avidian Technologies' all-in-one Prophet 2004 that lets a business manage sales opportunities via email without switching applications; and Symantec's pcAnywhere, allows helpdesk staff access the company's PCs without leaving the help desk.

49079 ■ "How to identify your enemies before they destroy you" in *Harvard Business Review* **(Vol. 80, No. 10, October 2002, pp. 115)**
Pub: Harvard Business School Press
Ed: Paul J. Farshad. **Description:** Genuine threats to an established business are discussed, including the tools necessary to determine what emerging technologies constitute disruptive innovations and must be addressed and which technologies can be ignored.

49080 ■ "HP iPAQ h6315 Pocket PC Phone Edition" in *Black Enterprise* **(Vol. 35, December 2004, No. 5, pp. 71)**
Pub: Earl G. Graves Publishing Co. Inc.
Description: Profile of HPs iPAQ h6315 pocket personal computer, phone, and camera.

49081 ■ "Hybrid Phones Hold Promise of Cellular, VoIP" in *Boston Globe* **(March 7, 2005)**
Pub: New York Times Company
Ed: Peter J. Howe. **Description:** Experts discuss hybrid phone technology.

49082 ■ "I Want My Cell TV" in *Entrepreneur.com* **(Vol. 34, February 2006, No. 2, pp. 42)**
Pub: Entrepreneur Media Inc.
Ed: Mike Hogan. **Description:** Vodcasts can be made with any videocam or even some cellular phones. Open Media Network offers free distribution and MPEG Nation charges $5 to host a video for six months. FilmLoop and Pic2Vid allow users to build a video using digital pictures and a voice-over.

49083 ■ "I Want my WTV" in *Entrepreneur* **(Vol. 32, No. 1, January 2004, pp. 22)**
Pub: Entrepreneur Media, Inc.
Ed: Gisela M. Pedroza. **Description:** Profile of Sharp Electronics Corporation new wireless 15-inch television, perfect for any office; the TV also allows the user to play a videocassette or DVD.

49084 ■ "IBM Corp." in *PC Magazine* **(March 7, 2000, pp. 158)**
Pub: Ziff-Davis Publishing Company
Ed: Bruce Brown, Cade Metz, Carol Venezia. **Description:** IBM's Netfinity 5000 server, priced at

$3,960 with a 600MHz Pentium III CPU and dual 9GB hard disks, works well with its $2,259 PC 300PL desktop client and bundled software to create an excellent E-business solution. The company backs up its E-services solution with top-notch service and high-quality hardware. IBM offers customers the Home Page Creator and Small Business WebConnections products through its IBM Global Small Business organization. Both tools are very well designed; Home Page Creator is a Java tool that lets users build and publish a storefront from within the browser, while the higher-end WebConnections service package includes Internet access, E-mail and file sharing for five to 100 clients. IBM earns the Editors' Choice rating for the best E-business hardware, software and service solutions.

49085 ■ *IBM on Demand Technology for the Growing Business: How to Optimize Your Computing Environment for Today and Tomorrow*
Pub: Maximum Press
Ed: Jim Hoskins. **Released:** June 2005. **Price:** $29.95. **Description:** IBM is offering computer solutions to small companies entering the On Demand trend in business.

49086 ■ "IBM Readies Linux Suite for Small Biz" in *Network World* **(November 6, 2000, pp. NA)**
Pub: Network World Inc.
Ed: Ed Scannell. **Description:** A profile of IBM's Linux suite for small businesses.

49087 ■ "If BlackBerry Gets Smushed..." in *Business Week* **(January 9, 2006, No. 3966, pp. 16)**
Pub: McGraw-Hill Companies
Ed: Stephen H. Wildstrom. **Description:** Alternatives to using BlackBerry email services are discussed in the event of the service being shut down by patent infringement charges. GoodLink from Good Technology offers similar services as does Microsoft with its Exchange email system which is being upgraded.

49088 ■ "IM: When Time Matters" in *Hispanic Business* **(November 2002, pp. 34)**
Pub: Hispanic Business
Ed: Roger Harris. **Description:** Instant Messaging software is the perfect solution to emergencies and conferencing for small businesses; more than 20 million people worldwide use Instant Messaging in business, and it is predicted by International Data Corp. that more than 300 million will be using the method by 2005.

49089 ■ "Imaging: Changing the Way We Do Business" in *Rough Notes* **(Vol. 146, No. 3, March 2003, pp. 56)**
Pub: Rough Notes
Ed: Robert E. Dunn. **Description:** Hotchkiss Insurance Agency Inc. reduced paper workload by using imaging or digital scanning of documents. This process enables the firm to focus on customer services and communications.

49090 ■ "In this corner" in *Entrepreneur* **(Vol. 31, No. 5, May 2003, pp. 39)**
Pub: Entrepreneur Media Inc.
Ed: Amanda C. Kooser. **Description:** Profiles of the newest lightweight computer notebooks are presented, including information on the Fujitsu LifeBook P-2000, Dell's Latitude X200, IBM ThinkPad X30, Hewlett-Packard Compaq Evo N410C, and the Toshiba Portege 4010 are among those profiled.

49091 ■ "In-Depth View" in *Entrepreneur* **(Vol. 33, September 2005, No. 9, pp. 18)**
Pub: Entrepreneur Media Inc.
Ed: Gisela M. Pedroza. **Description:** E-D 3-D Wireless Glasses, costing under $100, allow users to view 3-D imaging and also work for graphic applications such as CAD and charting in wide spreadsheets, as well as gaming.

49092 ■ "In Search Of The Pay Off: What's more confusing than buying tech products?" in *FSB* (Vol. 10, No. 9, December 1, 2000, pp. 48)
Pub: Time Inc.
Ed: Jim Seymour. **Description:** The article recommends being selective in the technologies purchased for small companies. It is important that decisions be based on the return of your investment.

49093 ■ "In a Snap! Fuji Offers New Photo Options" in *Black Enterprise* (Vol. 35, November 2004, No. 4, pp. 64)
Pub: Earl G. Graves Publishing Co. Inc.
Ed: Sonya A. Donaldson. **Description:** Profile of Fuji's new ScanSnap scanner that is able to scan anything from legal documents to business cards, as well as handwritten notes, at a fast speed.

49094 ■ "The Inc. Life" in *Inc.* (September 2005, pp. 82)
Pub: Inc. Magazine
Description: Five technology tools for small business are profiled, including the VAIO T350 notebook with built-in cellular modem; Jabra JX10, a min headset that can be used with Bluetooth phones; Samsung's SCH-i730, a Windows Mobile smart phone; Nintendo's Game Boy Micro; and Casio's Exilim EX-S500 camera.

49095 ■ "Incremental upgrades boosts smaller firms" in *Atlanta Business Chronicle* (Vol. 25, November 15, 2002, No. 23 pp. 4C)
Pub: American City Business Publications, Inc.
Ed: Tom Barry. **Description:** Currently, many companies are approaching technology upgrades from a "less is more" perspective. Influenced by fear of being sued or losing information, many firms are increasing spending on security upgrades. In general, big technology projects are being approached with small steps. Information on services provided by a few technology companies is included.

49096 ■ "Inking Up: Now Coming to a Printer Near You-Files From a Cell Phone or PDA" in *Entrepreneur* (Vol. 31, No. 7, July 2003, pp. 37)
Pub: Entrepreneur Media, Inc.
Ed: Mike Hogan. **Description:** Nokia and other cell phone and handset makers are equipping models to read email, contact lists and photos to network printers or to infrared- or Bluetooth-enabled printers.

49097 ■ "Inside the box: Buyer's guide: New software slowing you down?" in *Entrepreneur* (Vol. 30, No. 1, January 2002, pp. 44)
Pub: Entrepreneur Media Inc.
Ed: Amanda C. Kooser. **Description:** Comparisons of the AMD Athlon and Intel Pentium 4 processors to use when making performance upgrades to office PCs.

49098 ■ "Intel Inside: The Chips Get Hot" in *Barron's* (August 25, 2003, pp. T1)
Pub: Barron's
Ed: Bill Alpert. **Description:** Growing demand for Intel's market-leading Pentium microprocessors has moved the company to project an 11-percent increase for third quarter sales. Investors welcomed the news by bidding Intel's share price up a dollar, or nearly 4 percent, to more than $27/share.

49099 ■ "The iPod Squad" in *Entrepreneur* (Vol. 33, February 2005, No. 2, pp. 40)
Pub: Entrepreneur Media Inc.
Ed: Amanda C. Kooser. **Description:** Software applications are making iPods more practical for small business use. Profile of the ProVue Panorama iPod Organizer, which can handle data from any program that exports into text files.

49100 ■ "Is My Partnership Fair?" in *Inc.* (July 1, 2004)
Pub: Inc. Magazine
Description: A small business entrepreneur of a 50-50 partnership talks about protecting ideas and the pros and cons of leasing versus purchasing new technology.

49101 ■ "Is Your Phone System Moving You Forward Or Chaining You Down?" in *Ingram's* (Vol. 29, No. 8, August 2003, pp. 15)
Pub: Show Me Publishing, Inc.
Ed: Kevin Tubbesing. **Description:** Benefits of Ethernet systems to companies looking to upgrade telephone systems are explored.

49102 ■ *ISO 9000 for Small Businesses*
Pub: Butterworth-Heinemann
Ed: Ray L. Tricker. **Released:** 1997. **Price:** $28.95.

49103 ■ "It Even Makes Calls!" in *Fortune* (Vol. 151, January 10, 2005, No. 1, pp. 55)
Pub: Time Inc.
Ed: Stephanie N. Mehta. **Description:** Advances in technology have brought about cellular phones that can take pictures, browse the Internet, send email messages, play MP3 music files, record short videos, as well as making telephone calls.

49104 ■ "IT Risk Assessment: Who Needs It?" in *Ingram's* (Vol. 29, No. 7, July 2003, pp. 23)
Pub: Show Me Publishing, Inc.
Ed: Scott Brouillette. **Description:** Businesses that fail to embrace technology put themselves at a disadvantage. However, companies that fail to plan for implementing information technology and related government regulations could suffer financially.

49105 ■ "It's All Talk" in *Entrepreneur* (Vol. 33, September 2005, No. 9, pp. 44)
Pub: Entrepreneur Media Inc.
Ed: Amanda C. Kooser. **Description:** Samsung has introduced a new way to decrease the amount of typing required to send a text message via cell phones using VoiceMode voice-to-text technology.

49106 ■ "It's Fall, And The Shopping Is Easy" in *Fortune* (Vol. 142, No. 10, October 30, 2000, pp. 208)
Pub: Time Inc.
Ed: Joel Dreyfuss. **Description:** When the office computers are more than three years old, it's probably time to consider some new hardware. And now is a great opportunity.

49107 ■ "It's got wings!" in *Entrepreneur* (Vol. 30, No. 12, December 2002, pp. 61)
Pub: Entrepreneur Media Inc.
Ed: Mike Hogan. **Description:** A growing number of small businesses are using the Linux servers and are now trying the operating system out on knowledge worker PCs.

49108 ■ "Keep Hand Injuries at Arm's Length" in *San Jose Mercury News* (February 28, 2005)
Pub: Knight-Ridder/Tribune Business News
Ed: Nicole C. Wong. **Description:** Facts to avoid carpal tunnel syndrome, trigger thumb, and Dequervain's tenosynovitis while using a keyboard are listed.

49109 ■ "Keep it Simple" in *Entrepreneur. com* (Vol. 34, February 2006, No. 2, pp. 60)
Pub: Entrepreneur Media Inc.
Ed: Chris Penttila. **Description:** Twenty-five tips for fine tuning a small business are outlined, focusing on technology, money, banking, taxes, credit and collection, accounting systems, mergers, management, and marketing ideas.

49110 ■ "Keeping your computer safe" in *Women in Business* (Vol. 53, No. 7, January-February 2002, pp. 21)
Pub: The ABWA Co Inc.
Ed: Rachel Warbington. **Description:** Businesses can keep their computer hardware safe in several ways. Purchasing a surge protector, utilizing a firewall and maintaining backup files are necessary.

49111 ■ "Keeping pace with technology" in *Women in Business* (Vol. 54, No. 2, March-April 2002, pp. 22)
Pub: The ABWA Co Inc.
Ed: Mary-Lane Kamberg. **Description:** Businesswomen must take information technology courses to remain computer literate in the 21st century workplace. Online education sites and information technology courses are listed.

49112 ■ "Key Bored? Innovative Alternatives to the Old QWERTY Keyboard" in *Entrepreneur* (Vol. 33, January 2005, No. 1, pp. 27)
Pub: Entrepreneur Media Inc.
Ed: Amanda C. Kooser. **Description:** One-handed keyboards, split keyboards, and folding keyboards are only three of many alternatives to the traditional qwerty keyboard.

49113 ■ "Kick the Habit" in *Home Office Computing* (Vol. 17, No. 1, January 1999, pp. 67)
Pub: Line56 Media
Ed: Joanne Cleaver. **Description:** A guide to using technology for more efficient time management in home offices is presented. A good filing system can make a difference when organizing an office. A service called Paper Tiger combines the assistance of a professional organizer with maintenance software.

49114 ■ "A Knack for Macs" in *Entrepreneur* (Vol. 31, No. 10, October 2003, pp. 56)
Pub: Entrepreneur Media, Inc.
Ed: Amanda C. Kooser. **Description:** Profile of Mac's new desktop G5 processor and the MAC OX X version 10.3 upgrade called Panther.

49115 ■ "Know Your Way Around?" in *Entrepreneur.com* (Vol. 34, January 2006, No. 1, pp. 22)
Pub: Entrepreneur Media Inc.
Ed: Jill Amadio. **Description:** GPS navigation is being seen in more new cars and trucks. These systems help employees save time and gas finding business destinations.

49116 ■ "A La Modem" in *Entrepreneur* (Vol. 31, No. 8, August 2003, pp. 46)
Pub: Entrepreneur Media, Inc.
Ed: Gisela M. Pedroza. **Description:** Profile of Belkin's F5D5530-W High Speed Cable Modem which provides fast broadband Internet connection to users beyond the reach of DSL or T1.

49117 ■ "Lapping It Up" in *Entrepreneur* (Vol. 33, September 2005, No. 9, pp. 48)
Pub: Entrepreneur Media Inc.
Description: Profile of Toshiba Qosmio G25-AV513 laptop, equipped to do any computing task including gaming, recording, watching television and DVDs.

49118 ■ "Laser pointers" in *Entrepreneur* (Vol. 30, No. 2, February 2002, pp. 36)
Pub: Entrepreneur Media Inc.
Ed: Amanda C. Kooser. **Description:** A comparison of inkjet and laser printers is presented, along with features and pricing.

49119 ■ "The Latest and Greatest Disease" in *Fortune* (Vol. 142, No. 9, October 16, 2000, pp. 312X)
Pub: Time Inc.
Ed: Joel Dreyfuss. **Description:** Is it time to upgrade your hardware and software products?

49120 ■ "Lead the Way: New Gadgets Blaze Trails for Mobile Workers" in *Entrepreneur* (Vol. 31, No. 9, September 2003, pp. 39)
Pub: Entrepreneur Media, Inc.
Ed: Mike Hogan. **Description:** Profile of DIAD IV, a downsized PC with GPS to pinpoint a driver's location, and a cell phone and keypad for messaging, is presented.

49121 ■ "Leasingsecrets.com" in *Entrepreneur* (Vol. 31, No. 8, August 2003, pp. 6)
Pub: Entrepreneur Media, Inc.
Ed: Steve Cooper. **Description:** Cost saving tips and other secrets of equipment leasing and financing are offered through leasingsecrets.com.

49122 ■ "Let Your Fingers Do the Locking: Forgotten That Password?" in *Fortune* (Vol. 151, January 24, 2005, No. 2, pp. 42)
Pub: Time Inc.
Ed: Peter Lewis. **Description:** Profile of the new technology that allows users to access computers with fin-

gerprint-reading devices. American Power Conversion, Sony, IBM, and other firms have developed password-management devices that can act as a lock and key for encrypting specific files and folders on a computer.

49123 ■ **"Let's Move" in** *Black Enterprise* **(Vol. 34, No. 6, January 2004, pp. 46)**
Pub: Earl Graves Publishing Co.
Ed: Sonya A. Donaldson. **Description:** Ways to transfer data from one PC to another include such tools as Eisenworld's Alohabob PC Relocator or Alohabob PC Relocator Ultra Control, but it is recommended to back data up routinely.

49124 ■ **"Letters count at keypadding design firm Digit Wireless" in** *Boston Business Journal* **(Vol. 22, No. 14, May 10, 2002, pp. 19)**
Pub: MCP, Inc.
Ed: Phil Sweeney. **Description:** Founder David Levy and CEO, John Facella of Digit Wireless LLC, are promoting the use of their patented keyboard that has letters alongside numbers on mobile phones.

49125 ■ **"Lifestyle: Innovated accoutrements for discerning executives" in** *Hispanic Business* **(March 2003, pp. 45)**
Pub: Hispanic Business
Description: Profiles of the Compaq Presario 2800 wireless-ready notebook computer, the Gateway Profile 4 all-in-one PC, the new Audi TT Coupe, and the Leica Duovid 812x42 binoculars are among the items listed.

49126 ■ **"A Light Touch" in** *Entrepreneur* **(Vol. 32, July 2004, No. 7, pp. 46)**
Pub: Entrepreneur Media Inc.
Ed: Steve Cooper. **Description:** Profile of IBM's ThinkPad X40, weighing in at only 2.1 pounds.

49127 ■ **"Lighten Up! Weighed Down By Your Portable PC?" in** *Entrepreneur* **(Vol. 31, October. 2003)**
Pub: Entrepreneur Media, Inc.
Ed: Mike Hogan. **Description:** The latest portable computers from Dell, Fujitsu, Hewlett-Packard, IBM and Toshiba include combinations of heavyweight computing in ultra-light forms.

49128 ■ **"Listen Up! Get the Scoop on Bluetooth Headsets With This Guide" in** *Entrepreneur.com* **(Vol. 34, February 2006, No. 2, pp. 34)**
Pub: Entrepreneur Media Inc.
Ed: Amanda C. Kooser. **Description:** Profile of the new Bluetooth m9obile phone headset. The Essentials Network features a guide that helps individuals choose the headset suited to them.

49129 ■ **"Living the Lifestyle of the Successful Businessperson" in** *Hispanic Business* **(January/February 2005, pp. 63, 64)**
Pub: Hispanic Business
Ed: Leslie A. Westbrook. **Description:** Victor Lopez, senior vice president at Hyatt Hotels Corporation believes balance is the key to a successful executive lifestyle. Profile of X9 GPS that allows users to map a route and upload the information onto a watch is included.

49130 ■ **"Living with Linux" in** *PC Magazine* **(February 6, 2001, pp. 63)**
Pub: Ziff-Davis Publishing Company
Ed: Oliver Rist. **Description:** The initial furor over Linux is cooling and the open-source operating system is now assuming a role as a viable alternative to NT and Unix. Linux has established a reputation as a reliable server OS that will stand up under the most strenuous testing. It is a plug-and-forget OS that runs quickly over older hardware and will automatically scale to large numbers of users. Linux is a good choice for Web servers and Internet and E-mail gateways as well as file and print server chores. A new automated installation routine reflects the open-source community's efforts to improve ease of use.

49131 ■ **"Logitech MX Revolution Cordless Laser Mouse" in** *Sales & Marketing Management* **(Vol. 159, January-February 2007, No. 1, pp. 42)**
Pub: VNU Business Media
Description: Profile of MX Revolution's ergonomic mouse that allows scrolling through 100 pages of text, priced at $99.99.

49132 ■ **"Low-Cost Teleconferencing" in** *My Business* **(February/March 2004, pp. 17)**
Pub: My Business Magazine
Description: Profile of Apple's new iSight, a cylindrical camera and microphone that connects to a Macintosh computer via high-speed firewire and Apple's proprietary multimedia Internet messaging software iCath-AV, providing always-on videoconferencing.

49133 ■ **"The mac pack: some entrepreneurs would rather switch than fight" in** *Entrepreneur* **(Vol. 31, No. 5, May 2003, pp. 23)**
Pub: Entrepreneur Media Inc.
Ed: Amanda C. Kooser. **Description:** Because of security issues and licensing agreements, more entrepreneurs are switching to Macintosh computers, including the Apple iMac (Power PC-based system) with the Mac OS X Operating system.

49134 ■ **"Make 'Em an Offer: Entrepreneurs Can Save Big Bucks Bidding for Equipment on eBay. Learn Which Strategies Work Best" in** *Entrepreneur*
Pub: Entrepreneur Media Inc.
Ed: Melissa Campanelli. **Description:** Small businesses are saving money purchasing equipment on eBay's online auction site. Some of eBay's loyal small business customers offer insight into this practice.

49135 ■ **"Make That To Go" in** *Entrepreneur* **(Vol. 31, No. 8, August 2003, pp. 34)**
Pub: Entrepreneur Media, Inc.
Description: Profile of IBM's ThinkPad T40, available in a variety of applications, including Intel's new Centrino technology and Wi-Fi networking capability.

49136 ■ **"Makeover Magic: The Experts Work Their Mojo on Our 'Biz 101' Tech Makeover Winners Outdated Web Site" in** *Entrepreneur* **(July 2004)**
Pub: Entrepreneur Media Inc.
Ed: Amanda C. Kooser. **Description:** Interland Web designers offer ways to help small businesses update a Web site in order to attract new business and retain customer base.

49137 ■ **"Making the Call" in** *Hispanic Business* **(May 2005, pp. 42)**
Pub: Hispanic Business
Ed: Scott Williams. **Description:** Internet phone systems are helping small companies cut costs, however it is important to have the necessary resources to support Voice over Internet Protocol (VoIP) systems. Presently, AT&T, Latin Node, Verizon, Vonage, and 8x8 Inc. offer services that use standard phone lines rather than requiring new data network equipment.

49138 ■ **"Making Contact" in** *Entrepreneur* **(Vol. 33, August 2005, No. 8, pp. 42)**
Pub: Entrepreneur Media Inc.
Ed: Amanda C. Kooser. **Description:** Entrepreneurs can now hire services for their mobile devices that automatically back up a phone's address book, as well as synchronizing the phone with contacts, calendar and tasks with a computer via the Internet.

49139 ■ **"Martindale's Calculators On-Line Center" in** *Entrepreneur* **(Vol. 33, September 2005, No. 9, pp. 6)**
Pub: Entrepreneur Media Inc.
Ed: Steve Cooper. **Description:** Martindale's offers more than 20,000 calculators on its Website which can compute data for any type of business.

49140 ■ **"Maximize Your Resources" in** *Small Business Opportunities* **(Vol. 13, No. 6, November 2001, pp. 12, 133)**
Pub: Harris Publications, Inc.

Ed: Mike Foster. **Description:** Ideas and suggestions are offered to use more of the software programs on a computer besides word processing, with emphasis on training.

49141 ■ **"Meet Your New Executives" in** *Inc.* **(Volume 28, January 2006, No. 1, pp. 57-58)**
Pub: Inc. Magazine
Ed: David H. Freedman. **Description:** Are computers replacing executives in the business place? New, powerful software is capable of understanding data.

49142 ■ **"Memory gap" in** *Entrepreneur* **(Vol. 30, No. 3, March 2002, pp. 42)**
Pub: Entrepreneur Media Inc.
Ed: Mike Hogan. **Description:** Profile of Evergreen's CPU/memory upgrade bundles.

49143 ■ **"Merrill Lynch Phones Ahead" in** *Fast Company* **(November 2001, pp. 156)**
Pub: Fast Company
Ed: Paul C. Judge. **Description:** Merrill Lynch has determined that the telephone is the most important tool for the investment industry; the company is using voice over Internet protocol (VOIP) to conduct business.

49144 ■ **"Micron Technology Inc." in** *PC Magazine* **(March 7, 2000, pp. 158)**
Pub: Ziff-Davis Publishing Company
Ed: Bruce Brown, Cade Metz, Carol Venezia. **Description:** Client and server machines from Micron Technology are reviewed as part of an E-services solution that includes software and services. The NetFrame 3400 server is a 600MHz Pentium II machine with dual 9.1GB Wide Ultra3 SCSI hard drives and 256MB of RAM, while the ClientPro CS desktop PC has a similar CPU with an S3 graphics card, 40x CD-ROM, 13GB hard disk and 17-inch monitor. Micron does not offer its own small business portal and has fewer online applications than some competitors, but it does provide extensive Web-site development and hosting services as well as basic Internet access through its recently acquired HostPro ISP. Users can also obtain higher-speed access through Micron Internet Services (MIS) with a variety of access plans geared to different business types. The server is expensive but works well and has hot-swappable drives. The desktop PC is very expandable, but suffers from annoying design glitches.

49145 ■ **"Microsoft Launches Small Business Web Services" in** *Network World* **(September 25, 2000, pp. NA)**
Pub: Network World Inc.
Ed: George A. Chidi, Jr. **Description:** A profile of Microsoft's new program that brings small businesses into cyberspace. Microsoft's Business Web Services are designed for non-technical small business customers, providing domain registration, business e-mail, site creation and hosting, e-commerce and Web-based marketing services.

49146 ■ **"Microsoft Windows Millennium Edition" in** *Home Office Computing* **(Vol. 18, No. 10, October 2000, pp. 26)**
Pub: Scholastic Inc.
Ed: Eric Grevstad. **Description:** Microsoft Windows Millenium Edition (Windows ME) is a better and more useful product for home users than Windows 2000, which needs faster, newer hardware for full performance. WindowsME comes with multimedia enhancements including Windows Movie Maker and Windows Image Acquisition programming interface. Also, users can download, free of cost, Internet Explorer 5.5 and Windows Media Player 7.

49147 ■ *Microsoft Windows Small Business Server 2003 R2 Administrator's Companion*
Pub: Microsoft Press
Ed: Charlie Russel; Sharon Crawford. **Released:** July 2006. **Price:** $80.99. **Description:** Profile of Microsoft's Small Business Server R2.

49148 ■ **"Mirra, Mirra" in** *Entrepreneur* **(Vol. 32, No. 1, January 2004, pp. 38)**
Pub: Entrepreneur Media, Inc.

Ed: Mike Hogan. **Description:** A recent study conducted by the University of California, Berkeley, found that nearly 800MB of new information is generated by each person per year. Much is in multimedia files, such as digital photos, music, movies, and Microsoft Office output.

49149 ■ "Mobile Moguls" in *Small Business Opportunities* **(Vol. 12, No. 3, May 2000, pp. 120)**
Pub: Harris Publications, Inc.
Description: A profile of Sharp's new portable PCs that offer flexibility and productivity in one device with three operating positions.

49150 ■ "MoGo Mouse BT" in *Sales & Marketing Management* **(Vol. 159, January-February 2007, No. 1, pp. 42)**
Pub: VNU Business Media
Description: Profile of the palm-sized MoGo Mouse that connects to any Bluetooth-enabled computer.

49151 ■ "Movin' On Up" in *Entrepreneur* **(Vol. 31, No. 9, September 2003, pp. 68)**
Pub: Entrepreneur Media, Inc.
Ed: Mike Hogan. **Description:** Five ways to upgrade technology and boost a small company's productivity are presented.

49152 ■ "Moving Out: When to Outsource Your Server Operations" in *My Business* **(December/January 2004, pp. 42)**
Pub: My Business Magazine
Ed: Paige Orr. **Description:** Tips for small companies wishing to outsource server operations are presented. These firms manage critical business and network applications.

49153 ■ "My Best Practices: Do you want to sell smarter and don't know how?" in *Fortune* **(Vol. 142, No. 14, December 18, 2000, pp. 292B)**
Pub: Time Inc.
Ed: Adam Dell. **Description:** In-depth article explains how to use the technology available to work smarter and beat the competition.

49154 ■ "My Gadget" in *My Business* **(February/March 2004, pp. 17)**
Pub: My Business Magazine
Ed: Lena Basha. **Description:** Profile of AccuCard, a self-updating address book designed for use with Microsoft Outlook. The service will send personalized quarterly emails to every small business contact, requesting updated or confirmation of correct contact information and automatically updates information every three months.

49155 ■ "Naked at Work: Psst! The Boss is Watching" in *Black Enterprise* **(Vol. 34, No. 5, December 2003, pp. 55)**
Pub: Earl Graves Publishing Co.
Ed: Sonja D. Brown. **Description:** Review of the book, "The Naked Employee: How Technology is Compromising Workplace Privacy". The book argues that technology is robbing employees their right to privacy at work.

49156 ■ "Network It" in *Entrepreneur* **(Vol. 33, March 2005, No. 3, pp. 48)**
Pub: Entrepreneur Media Inc.
Description: Profile of Belkin's Wireless Pre-N router that includes software for both Mac and Windows applications.

49157 ■ "The Networked Home" in *Home Office Computing* **(Vol. 18, No. 12, December 2000, pp. 89)**
Pub: Scholastic Inc.
Ed: Bonny L. Georgia. **Description:** This article tells what the home-based worker can do to automate their house and how to set up security systems. One such product mentioned is home automation software that helps to automate different functions such as turning on lights and appliances.

49158 ■ "Networking Made Easy; Three Quick Tips for Setting Up a Wired Connection" in *Black Enterprise* **(Vol. 34, No. 2, September 2003)**
Pub: Earl Graves Publishing Co.
Ed: Rebecca Rohan. **Description:** Small businesses using more than one PC are able to network their computers by using a home LAN, allowing users to share files among all PCs by dragging and dropping them in Windows Explorer, a broadband connection can also be shared.

49159 ■ "New Computer Sellers Bite Into Market..." in *Crain's Chicago Business* **(Vol. 26, No. 50, December 15, 2003)**
Pub: Crain Communications, Inc.
Ed: H. Lee Murphy. **Description:** MDG Computers Canada Inc., CompUSA, and Fry's Electronics are three new computer retailers to open in the Chicago, Illinois area. Experts are concerned the market will become overcrowded with computer specialists.

49160 ■ "New Computer Sellers Bite Into Market; MDG, Fry's Set to Debut, While CompUSA Grows Again" in *Crains Chicago Business* **(Vol. 26)**
Pub: Crain Communications, Inc.
Ed: H. Lee Murphy. **Description:** MDG Computers Canada Inc., CompUSA, and Fry's Electronics are three new computer retailers to open in the Chicago, Illinois area. Experts are concerned the market will become overcrowded with computer specialists.

49161 ■ *New Employment Issues in the Electronic Workplace*
Pub: M. Lee Smith Publishers & Printers
Ed: Susan E. Culbreath. **Released:** 1998. **Price:** $47.00.

49162 ■ "The New Hispanic Information Economy" in *Hispanic Business* **(November 2003, pp. 26, 28, 30)**
Pub: Hispanic Business
Ed: Scott Williams. **Description:** A convergence of market demand and capable researchers has created a viable market for numbers on U.S. Hispanics. Within the realm of public policy, Hispanics are gaining attention.

49163 ■ "The New Kid: Another Wireless Technology is Moving into the Neighborhood" in *Entrepreneur* **(Vol. 32, July 2004, No. 7, pp. 25)**
Pub: Entrepreneur Media Inc.
Ed: Steve Cooper. **Description:** Ultra Wide Band (UWB) wireless communication technology transmits data in short, low-powered pulses over a wide range of frequency spectrums. The new technology could help entrepreneurs to use UWB as wireless backup drives, transferring data from a scanner or connecting with a camera for videoconferencing wirelessly.

49164 ■ "New Money in Old Goods" in *Small Business Opportunities* **(Vol. 17, May 2005, No. 3, pp. 50, 52)**
Pub: Harris Publications Inc.
Ed: Chuck Green. **Description:** Profile of John Lee and Edward McKinley, partners selling refurbished computer equipment. The two men share ideas for running their successful business.

49165 ■ "A New Tone" in *Hispanic Business* **(September 2004, pp. 86, 88)**
Pub: Hispanic Business
Ed: Sam Diaz. **Description:** Profiles of the new wireless phones are presented, including the Motorola MPX, Handspring Treo 600, Nokia 6820, Samsung VM-A680, Nokia N0Gage, and Mobitv.

49166 ■ "The Newest Cell Phones" in *Hispanic Business* **(January/February 2003, pp. 62)**
Pub: Hispanic Business
Ed: Roger Harris. **Description:** Profiles of the latest cell phones reaching the market; some come equipped with a global positioning system chip, others are Internet-able phones, and are smaller and more light-weight.

49167 ■ "News and Reviews" in *Home Business* **(Vol. 13, January/February 2006, No. 1, pp. 98)**
Pub: Home Business Magazine
Description: Information for closing business deals online, Web-based human resources small business software, noise canceling audio headphones, and tips for launching and marketing new products is given.

49168 ■ "News from the Small Business Front" in *My Business* **(June/July 2002, pp. 14)**
Pub: My Business Magazine
Description: Plans for using wireless technology for small businesses to develop a global wireless Internet network are discussed. Information on the Family and Medical Leave Act is presented.

49169 ■ "NEXIS Finally Goes Dot-Com" in *Information Today* **(Vol. 17, No. 10, November 2000, pp. 32)**
Pub: Information Today, Inc.
Ed: Mick O'Leary. **Description:** New nexis.com service blends old-style depth with new-style ease, with their news database and additional business and legislative data from LEXIS on the Web.

49170 ■ "Nikon's Newly Created Long Island Unit to Scout Tech Trends for the Home Office" in *Long Island Business News* **(March 12, 2004)**
Pub: Dolan Media Newswires
Ed: Ken Schachter. **Description:** Nikon is developing a new division to scout technology, products and market trends for the home office.

49171 ■ "No Brainer: Simple Ways to Solve Your Own Tech Problems" in *My Business* **(October/November 2002, pp. 44)**
Pub: My Business Magazine
Ed: Melany Klinck. **Description:** Prevention is the key to keeping computers up and working for small home-based businesses; a listing of free tech Web sites offering repair, support and other services, is included.

49172 ■ "Nokia 9300 SmartPhone" in *Black Enterprise* **(Vol. 35, December 2004, No. 5, pp. 70)**
Pub: Earl G. Graves Publishing Co. Inc.
Description: Profile of Nokia's 9300 SmartPhone with 80 MB of storage and Bluetooth. The phone offers basic office tools such as documents, spreadsheets, presentations, calendar and contacts.

49173 ■ "Nortel Net-telephony package aims at small businesses" in *InfoWorld* **(Vol. 22, No. 27, July 3, 2000, pp. 46)**
Pub: InfoWorld
Ed: Peter Sayer. **Description:** Nortel Networks will add a quality of service management tool to its range of enterprise IP telephony products. The Business Policy Switch, part of the Business Series range of products, formerly known as Enterprise Edge, is designed to enable small businesses to manage the quality of service for IP telephony, messaging, and call center services delivered over the LAN and WAN.

49174 ■ "Not Every Small Business will be able to (or should) Jump on Linux Immediately" in *Inc.* **(June 2000, pp. 100)**
Pub: The Goldhirsh Group
Ed: Dan Orzech. **Description:** The Linux Operating System is hot. It's inexpensive. And it works. But can you run your company on it?

49175 ■ "Not In My Inbox: Moving Large Files Is As Easy AS FTP" in *Black Enterprise* **(Vol. 34, No. 3, October 2003, pp. 51)**
Pub: Earl Graves Publishing Co.
Ed: Rebecca Rohan. **Description:** Moving large files is easy using an FTP site. File Transfer Protocol (FTP) is the protocol that allows users to leave files in one or more unattended directories for others to pick up. Instruction for using this procedure is listed.

49176 ■ "Not Your Father's Business Card" in *Success* **(Vol. 47, No. 2, June 2000, pp. 12)**
Pub: Success Publishing, Inc.

Description: The latest business cards are palm-sized CD's, rounded, oval, rectangular, square, even custom shapes, that carry video, audio, and/or data in a format small enough to clip into a shirt pocket.

49177 ■ "Now Presenting" in *Entrepreneur* **(Vol. 31, No. 8, August 2003, pp. 36)**
Pub: Entrepreneur Media, Inc.
Description: Profile of the Margi Presenter-to-Go, an expansion card slot adaptor that allows the user to hook a PDA up to a projector or display. The device features PowerPoint integration and also works with Microsoft Office programs.

49178 ■ "Now, ear this" in *Black Enterprise* **(Vol. 33, No. 6, January 2003, pp. 43)**
Pub: Earl Graves Publishing Co.
Ed: Sonya A. Donaldson. **Description:** Review of Plantronics' MX100 cellular headset, which is compatible with most cell phones, including Samsung, Motorola, Audiovox and Kyocera.

49179 ■ "Ode to a Server" in *Entrepreneur. com* **(Vol. 34, February 2006, No. 2, pp. 38)**
Pub: Entrepreneur Media Inc.
Ed: Amanda C. Kooser. **Description:** Computer servers are the most important piece of hardware to a small business. It is important to choose the one best-suited to a company's needs. Profiles of various servers are included.

49180 ■ Office Automation: A Systems Approach
Pub: South-Western Publishing Co.
Ed: Ray Charles. **Released:** 1995. **Price:** $56.95.

49181 ■ "Office Offers" in *Entrepreneur* **(Vol. 31, No. 11, November 2003, pp. 60)**
Pub: Entrepreneur Media, Inc.
Ed: Amanda C. Kooser. **Description:** Profile of Microsoft's new Office 2003 Small Business Edition. The software includes Excel, Outlook, PowerPoint, Publisher and Works, and updates like junk mail handling, XML file support in Word and Excel, and OneNote that lets users capture and organize notes.

49182 ■ Office Systems: People, Procedures, and Technology
Pub: Paradigm Publishing, Inc.
Ed: Rosemary T. Fruehling. **Released:** Second edition, 1992. **Price:** $29.95.

49183 ■ "On Display" in *Entrepreneur* **(Vol. 31, No. 9, September 2003, pp. 46)**
Pub: Entrepreneur Media, Inc.
Ed: Gisela M. Pedroza. **Description:** Profile of the Viewsonic VP171b flat-panel computer display, featuring a high-definition screen with an ultra-slim bezel making it a great desktop or wall-hanging display.

49184 ■ "On the Edge" in *Entrepreneur* **(Vol. 33, October 2005, No. 10, pp. 40)**
Pub: Entrepreneur Media Inc.
Ed: Amanda C. Kooser. **Description:** Sony's new VAIO T-Series computer notebooks come equipped with built-in SmartWi wireless WAN for easy access to the Internet over Cingular's high-speed EDGE network.

49185 ■ "On the Fast Track: How Technology Is Speeding Incentive Delivery" in *Sales & Marketing Management* **(Vol. 157, February 2005)**
Pub: VNU Business Media
Ed: Alan Horowitz. **Description:** Profile of the software company Synygy Inc. and its enterprise incentive management product. The software and services help to manage incentive compensation for sales staff, or any employee of a company, which promotes sales growth and employee motivation.

49186 ■ "On a Roll" in *Entrepreneur* **(Vol. 28, No. 8, August 2000, pp. 23)**
Pub: Entrepreneur Media Inc.
Ed: Gisela M. Pedroza. **Description:** A review of Label Writer Turbo, which aids with mailing efforts for small businesses.

49187 ■ "One-Button Backups: Creating a Batch File is as Easy as...(Tech 1-2-3)" in *Black Enterprise* **(Vol. 34, No. 4, November 2003, pp. 55)**
Pub: Earl Graves Publishing Co.
Ed: Rebecca Rohan. **Description:** Ways to create batch files for backing up key files in their latest state, using a simple Windows format are presented.

49188 ■ "One Company's Junk" in *Success* **(Vol. 47, No. 5, October 2000, pp. 12)**
Pub: Success Publishing, Inc.
Description: Sites that market used, surplus, or outdated IT equipment are examined.

49189 ■ "One Iota" in *Business Week* **(No. 3761, December 10, 2001, pp. SB4)**
Pub: McGraw-Hill Inc.
Description: Seventy-six percent of entrepreneurs surveyed say switching to DSL for their Internet connection improved productivity.

49190 ■ "The Online Office" in *Success* **(Vol. 47, No. 3, July 2000, pp. 18)**
Pub: Success Publishing, Inc.
Description: A new company aims to help small businesses compete in today's market with free business services via the Internet. TeamOn.com is offering integrated business-class email, customer management, and office applications such as expense reports, customer service, calendars, and up to 50 MB in shared file storage.

49191 ■ "Only Time Will Tell" in *My Business* **(June/July 2004, pp. 22)**
Pub: My Business Magazine
Description: Profile of new software and broadcast technology developed by Microsoft that enables wrist watches to provide information updated via FM radio signals, weather reports, personal instant messages, personal calendars, and other consumer and business reviews and resources.

49192 ■ "Open Source Solutions: Good Enough for E-Business?" in *E-business Advisor* **(Vol. 18, No. 6, June 2000, pp. 10)**
Pub: Advisor Media, Inc.
Ed: Dan Sullivan. **Description:** The most widely supported Open Source solutions, including Linux, Apache, and Perl, can be used to create a stable, reliable e-business architecture. Linux, while not as scalable or reliable as UNIX, works well for small- and mid-sized Web sites. Apache and Perl both have strong developer support in key areas, such as a database access and performance.

49193 ■ "Out With the Old?" in *Entrepreneur* **(Vol. 31, No. 8, August 2003, pp. 43)**
Pub: Entrepreneur Media, Inc.
Ed: Mike Hogan. **Description:** Profiles of computer servers for small businesses to consider when upgrading systems, with information on Intel's new Itanium 26M processor and the 64-bit computing of AMD's 32/64-bit Opteron chips compared.

49194 ■ "Own or Rent? Revisiting the Pros and Cons of Leasing vs. Purchasing" in *Black Enterprise* **(Vol. 34, No. 6, January 2004, pp. 44)**
Pub: Earl Graves Publishing Co.
Ed: Rebecca Rohan. **Description:** Information for small-to-medium-sized companies to consider regarding the purchase or rental of PCs, printers, fax machines, and copiers for their offices is examined.

49195 ■ "Pack a Punch" in *Entrepreneur* **(Vol. 31, No. 8, August 2003, pp. 34)**
Pub: Entrepreneur Media, Inc.
Description: Profile of Toshiba's XGA resolution TDP-D1 projector, used for large meeting rooms where lights cannot be dimmed.

49196 ■ "Panasonic Tunes In Hispanic Market" in *Hispanic Business* **(March 2003, pp. 24)**
Pub: Hispanic Business
Description: Panasonic has started a series of print ads and television commercials featuring Spanish-

language spots for their PV-DC252 Palmcorder and high-definition 42-inch plasma monitor. The article sites examples of other companies following the same trend, marketing to the Hispanic population in the U.S.

49197 ■ "Passing the Buck" in *Entrepreneur* **(Vol. 32)**
Pub: Entrepreneur Media Inc.
Ed: Mike Hogan. **Description:** Voice over Internet Protocol (VoIP) can save long distance phone charges for small companies. Telecom International has a new device that transfers cellular calls to its VoIP network.

49198 ■ "The Path of Lease Resistance" in *Home Office Computing* **(Vol. 19, No. 1, January 2001, pp. 85)**
Pub: Scholastic Inc.
Ed: Todd W. Carter. **Description:** Some small business owners have turned to leasing instead of purchasing new computer equipment in order to keep offices up to date and minimize problems with obsolescence. Leasing allows faster upgrades than conventional purpose, frees up money for other investments and makes sense for property with a relatively short useful life span. The IRS distinguishes between a true or 'operating' lease, which may be tax-deductible, and a 'finance' lease, which it does not recognize as a business expense.

49199 ■ "PDA price plunge" in *WorkingWoman* **(Vol. 25, No. 2, February 2000, pp. 74)**
Pub: Lang Communications Inc.
Ed: Steve Morgenstern. **Description:** More moderately priced personal digital assistants have been introduced. New special-purpose search engines such as ditto.com, and search engines for hard-to-find information are now available.

49200 ■ "Peaks & Silicon Valleys" in *Entrepreneur* **(Vol. 30, No. 2, February 2002, pp. 28)**
Pub: Entrepreneur Media Inc.
Description: Despite the over-inflated market of Silicon Valley, the cost of outfitting the office has dropped since the heyday of dotcoms, and salaries have increased. Statistical data included.

49201 ■ "A perfect pair" in *Entrepreneur* **(Vol. 30, No. 3, March 2002, pp. 37)**
Pub: Entrepreneur Media Inc.
Ed: Mike Hogan. **Description:** An overview of the new wireless communications and wireless personal digital assistants. Resources for information as well as pricing about the Compaq Computer IPAQ PC Wireless Pack, Handspring Treo 180, Motient Mobile Modem for Palm VI, Motorola Accompit 009, Palm palm 1705, and Research in Motion BlackBerry 957, is included.

49202 ■ "Perific Wireless Dual Mouse" in *Sales & Marketing Management* **(Vol. 159, January-February 2007, No. 1, pp. 42)**
Pub: VNU Business Media
Description: Profile of Perific's wireless mouse that eliminates repetitive motion injuries for users.

49203 ■ "Peripherals Vision" in *Entrepreneur* **(Vol. 32, No. 1, January 2004, pp. 42)**
Pub: Entrepreneur Media, Inc.
Ed: Amanda C. Kooser. **Description:** Profiles of Microsoft's Wireless Optical Desktop Elite package and Logitech's Cordless Click! Optical Mouse.

49204 ■ "Personal Business" in *Business Week* **(December 19, 2005, No. 3964, pp. 95)**
Pub: McGraw-Hill Companies
Ed: Gene G. Marcial. **Description:** Profile of Expeditors International of Seattle, Washington, a freight forwarder and customs broker; licensing and patents for intellectual property; and biotech firm Sonus Pharaceuticals.

49205 ■ "Personal Decision" in *Entrepreneur* **(Vol. 31, No. 8, August 2003, pp. 51)**
Pub: Entrepreneur Media, Inc.
Ed: Frank Ohlhorst, Michael Gros. **Description:** Things to consider when purchasing a combination

personal digital assistant (PDA) are discussed. The CRN Test Center evaluated five products that combine cell phone service, wireless email, instant messaging and Web accessibility.

49206 ■ "Phone, Camera, Action!(Wireless)" in *Entrepreneur* (Vol. 31, No. 8, August 2003, pp. 43)
Pub: Entrepreneur Media, Inc.
Ed: Mike Hogan. Description: Profile of Nokia's new 3650 color phone is presented. The phone will produce 10-second video clips or photos that can be sent over GSM/GPRS cell networks to a customer or coworker.

49207 ■ "Phone on the Range" in *Entrepreneur* (Vol. 33, October 2005, No. 10, pp. 40)
Pub: Entrepreneur Media Inc.
Ed: Mike Hogan. Description: Midwest Wireless in Minnesota offers a VoIP/cellular combination for home, office and mobile calls, and fixed and mobile broadband served by one voicemail/email inbox with all the special calling features of traditional telecoms.

49208 ■ "Picture Perfect " in *Entrepreneur* (Vol. 32)
Pub: Entrepreneur Media Inc.
Ed: Amanda C. Kooser. Description: Inexpensive cameras can be used to create brochures and other materials necessary for a small business.

49209 ■ "Picture This" in *Entrepreneur* (Vol. 32, July 2004, No. 7, pp. 46)
Pub: Entrepreneur Media Inc.
Ed: Gisela M. Pedroza. Description: Profile of Epson's Stylus Photo RX600 that allows pictures to be printed from digital media without connecting to a computer.

49210 ■ "Pipe Dreams" in *Business Week* (No. 3670, February 28, 2000, pp. f32)
Pub: McGraw-Hill, Inc.
Description: Affordable alternatives to T1 Internet service for small companies are discussed.

49211 ■ "Pocket protector" in *Entrepreneur* (Vol. 30, No. 1, January 2002, pp. 44)
Pub: Entrepreneur Media Inc.
Ed: Amanda C. Kooser. Description: Profile of Microsoft's Pocket PC 2002, which includes enterprise-oriented features designed to prompt security-conscious network professionals to standardize company-wide on the operating system.

49212 ■ "Portable lite" in *Entrepreneur* (Vol. 31, No. 5, May 2003, pp. 35)
Pub: Entrepreneur Media Inc.
Ed: Mike Hogan. Description: Intel's new Centrino chip package is allowing for lighter weight computer notebooks. Information about Intel's Pentium M is included.

49213 ■ "Power Play" in *Entrepreneur* (Vol. 32, August 2004, No. 8, pp. 42)
Pub: Entrepreneur Media Inc.
Ed: Gisela M. Pedroza. Description: Belkin's Universal Power Adapter can recharge all electronic devices in a car, plane or from any standard AC wall outlet, making it a good choice for business travel.

49214 ■ *Power Up Your Small-Medium Business: A Guide to Enabling Network Technologies*
Pub: Cisco Press
Ed: Robyn Aber. Released: March 2004. Price: $39.95 (US), $57.95 (Canadian). Description: Network technologies geared to small and medium-size business, focusing on access, IP telephony, wireless technologies, security, and computer network management.

49215 ■ "Pretty Picture" in *Entrepreneur.com* (Vol. 34, January 2006, No. 1, pp. 40)
Pub: Entrepreneur Media Inc.
Description: Profile of Canon's Pixma iP8500 photo printer the provides high-quality collateral material and proofing for small-format publications for small business; the printer is also compatible with Mac computers.

49216 ■ *Pro Windows Small Business Server 2003*
Pub: Apress L.P.
Ed: Tony Campbell. Released: July 2006. Price: $39.99. Description: Profile of Microsoft's Windows Small Business Server, designed for companies with 50 or fewer employees.

49217 ■ *Procedures for the Automated Office*
Pub: Prentice Hall
Ed: Sharon Burton, Nelda Shelton and Lucy M. Jennings. Released: 1998. Price: $45.00; $32.00.

49218 ■ "The Promised Bandwidth" in *Black Enterprise* (Vol. 31, No. 5, December 2000, pp. 74)
Pub: Earl Graves Publishing Co.
Ed: Manuel A. Brown. Description: For consumers and small businesses, there is still hope for broadband technology.

49219 ■ "Proper Care and Feeding: Think Your CDs and DVDs are Indestructible? Guess Again" in *Entrepreneur* (Vol. 32, September 2004)
Pub: Entrepreneur Media Inc.
Description: Proper care of computer CDs and DVDs is shared. It is best to label disks with non-solvent-based felt tip markers rather than adhesive labels and to keep disks out of direct sunlight.

49220 ■ "The Pulse" in *Sales & Marketing Management* (Vol. 159, January-February 2007, No. 1, pp. 9)
Pub: VNU Business Media
Description: According to a survey conducted by Extraprise, 63 percent of all business-to-business companies will implement marketing automation technology in 2007.

49221 ■ "Put Your Finger On It" in *Entrepreneur* (Vol. 33, January 2005, No. 1, pp. 20)
Pub: Entrepreneur Media Inc.
Ed: Gisela M. Pedroza. Description: Profile of Microsoft's Optical Desktop with Fingerprint Reader. The keyboard allows users to log on to PC files and favorite Websites with the touch of a finger.

49222 ■ "Put Your Web Applications to the Test" in *E-business Advisor* (Vol. 18, No. 7, July 2000, pp. 44)
Pub: Advisor Media, Inc.
Ed: Guy Tal. Description: Testing Web applications has become more complex because the applications themselves have become increasingly sophisticated and interactive. The process of testing Web applications using Mercury Interactive's Astra Quick Test and Astra LoadTest is discussed.

49223 ■ "Quick and lightening" in *WorkingWoman* (Vol. 25, No. 6, June 2000, pp. 120)
Pub: Lang Communications Inc.
Ed: Steve Morgenstern. Description: Advice is provided on purchasing extra lightweight portable laptop computers, with focus on maintaining a wide variety of functions. An evaluation of six ultra-portable computers is presented.

49224 ■ "Reality TV for Business" in *Hispanic Business* (September 2003, pp. 74)
Pub: Hispanic Business
Ed: Roger Harris. Description: Profile of the new lower priced and higher quality videoconferencing devices affordable for all small companies.

49225 ■ "Recognize this Voice? Speech Recognition Reduces Keyboard Tedium" in *Black Enterprise* (Vol. 36, February 2006, No. 7, pp. 68)
Pub: Earl G. Graves Publishing Co. Inc.
Description: Profile of Dragon Naturally Speaking 8, the Windows software that allows users to store voice profiles on a central server and transcribe from digital recorders or any handheld device that supports the Microsoft Pocket PC operating system. The professional system sells for $799.

49226 ■ "Recycled Fortune" in *Small Business Opportunities* (March 2005)
Pub: Harris Publications Inc.
Description: Profile of Rapid Refill Ink; Dan P. White started his ink cartridge remanufacturing firm in 2002. The company uses state-of-the-art technology and equipment to refill 1,100 various inkjet cartridges and 200 models of laser toner cartridges.

49227 ■ "Remote Control" in *Home Office Computing* (Vol. 18, No. 10, October 2000, pp. 46)
Pub: Scholastic Inc.
Ed: Jeffrey D. Zbar. Description: Organization strategies for telemanagers who work remotely, while the staff remains on-site at the corporate campus are outlined. Views of three telemanagers on such strategies, including keeping the office working seamlessly, tackling staff problems and maintaining morale are presented.

49228 ■ "The Replacements" in *Entrepreneur* (Vol. 31, No. 7, July 2003, pp. 46)
Pub: Entrepreneur Media, Inc.
Ed: Marc Spiwak. Description: Profiles of new high-end portable notebook computers are presented. The CRN Test Center examined five high-end notebooks from Acer, Fujitsu, Hewlett-Packard, Sharp and Toshiba.

49229 ■ "Reproduction Right" in *Fast Company* (July 2001, pp. 52)
Pub: Fast Company
Ed: Alison Overholt. Description: Profile of the SiPix Pocket Printer A6, from SiPix Inc. The SiPix Pocket Printer A6 is a handheld peripheral that is as light as a Discman and is small enough to slip into a briefcase.

49230 ■ "Rich in Fiber" in *Entrepreneur* (Vol. 33, October 2005, No. 10, pp. 48)
Pub: Entrepreneur Media Inc.
Ed: Amanda C. Kooser. Description: Verizon's new FiOS Internet Service for Business is currently available in California, Florida and Texas with expansion to 14 other states slated for late 2005. The fiber-to-the-premises services uses fiber optics instead of copper wire, and is geared to small businesses with 50 or less employees.

49231 ■ "Right off the Shelf or Made-to-Order?" in *Fortune* (Vol. 141, No. 12, June 12, 2000, pp. F274Z)
Pub: Time Inc.
Ed: Joel Dreyfuss. Description: The critical decisions for purchasing office technology, such as buying or building yourself, are covered.

49232 ■ "The Right Tool for the Job" in *Inc.* (Volume 27, December 2005, No. 12, pp. 136)
Pub: Inc. Magazine
Description: Profile of new office products, including audio- and video-conferencing and a color laser printer.

49233 ■ "Road Warrior" in *Inc.* (November 15, 2000, pp. 33)
Pub: The Goldhirsh Group
Description: An information article covering the latest in digital personal assistants.

49234 ■ "Road Warriors" in *BlackEnterprise* (Vol. 32, No. 2, September 2001, pp. 106)
Pub: Earl Graves Publishing Co.
Ed: Marilyn Zelinsky Syarto. Description: Telecommunications equipment and use of technology during business travel are explained.

49235 ■ "Room to Grow" in *Entrepreneur* (Vol. 32, November 2004, No. 11, pp. 64)
Pub: Entrepreneur Media Inc.
Ed: Steve Cooper. Description: Profile of Hewlett-Packard's HP StorageWorks NAS 200s. The system provides a flexible network-attached storage solution for small businesses.

49236 ■ **"Rout and About"** in *Entrepreneur* (Vol. 32, December 2004, No. 12, pp. 54)
Pub: Entrepreneur Media Inc.
Ed: Gisela M. Pedroza. **Description:** Profile of Netgear's WGR101 wireless travel router that allows users to deploy a wireless network and share a single, fast Internet connection in any conference room, hotel room or other Wi-Fi sport with Internet Access, making it a good choice for the business traveler.

49237 ■ *Running Your Small Business on a Mac*
Pub: Pearson Technology Group Canada
Ed: Doug Hanley. **Released:** November 2006. **Price:** $39.99. **Description:** Tips for using a Mac computer for small business is presented. The book offers shortcuts to iWork and email.

49238 ■ **"A Safe Bet"** in *Entrepreneur* (Vol. 31, No. 7, July 2003, pp. 42)
Pub: Entrepreneur Media, Inc.
Ed: Steve Cooper. **Description:** Profile of SonicWALL's TELE3 TZX combination firewall and VPN, allowing users to access office networks safely over a broadband connection while allowing Web browsing by other networked family members.

49239 ■ **"Safety First"** in *Entrepreneur* (Vol. 31, No. 11, November 2003, pp. 60)
Pub: Entrepreneur Media, Inc.
Ed: Marc Spiwak, Michael Gross. **Description:** The National Cyber Security Alliance report that only 60 percent of broadband users have a firewall installed on their computers. Two new firewalls designed for small networks were reviewed by the CRN Test Center: the WatchGuard Firebox SOHO 6 and the SonicWall SOHO TZW (Trusted Zone for Wireless). Both firewalls include wireless and VPN capabilities.

49240 ■ **"Save the Date"** in *Entrepreneur* (Vol. 31, No. 10, October 2003, pp. 57)
Pub: Entrepreneur Media, Inc.
Ed: Liane Cassavoy. **Description:** Profile of Now Up-to-Date & Contact from Power On Software; the software allows users to share schedules, create appointments and coordinates tasks without server software.

49241 ■ **"Savings in the Mall"** in *Home Office Computing* (Vol. 19, No. 1, January 2001, pp. 22)
Pub: Scholastic Inc.
Ed: Dan Costa. **Description:** The U.S. Postal Service (USPS) approved PC-based postage services in August 1999, giving birth to a slew of Internet postage start-ups and adding new life to old-school postage-meter providers like Pitney Bowes and the postal service itself.

49242 ■ **"Say Cheese!"** in *Entrepreneur* (Vol. 33, March 2005, No. 3, pp. 48)
Pub: Entrepreneur Media, Inc.
Ed: Amanda C. Kooser. **Description:** Digital cameras can help small companies create brochures to market their business. Profiles of various digital cameras include Kodak's EasyShare DX7590, Canon Power-Shot and Epson L-500V.

49243 ■ **"Scan Artists"** in *Entrepreneur* (Vol. 33, March 2005, No. 3, pp. 50)
Pub: Entrepreneur Media, Inc.
Ed: Amanda C. Kooser. **Description:** Canon, Epson and Microtek have developed scanners geared to home offices and small businesses.

49244 ■ **"Screen Dream"** in *Entrepreneur* (Vol. 33, February 2005, No. 2, pp. 42)
Pub: Entrepreneur Media, Inc.
Description: Profile of Samsung's SyncMaster 711t LCD computer monitor offering high contrast ratio, high adjustability, and good image quality.

49245 ■ **"Screen Test: Time for a Monitor Upgrade?"** in *Entrepreneur* (Vol. 32, October 2004, No. 10, pp. 54)
Pub: Entrepreneur Media, Inc.
Ed: Amanda C. Kooser. **Description:** Profiles of the latest flat-panel computer monitors are showcased, including Sony's SDM-S94, ViewSonic's VIH9xs, Hewlett-Packard's L1902, Samsung's SyncMaster 193P, NEC-Mitsubishi MultiSync LCD 1960NXi, BenQ's FP992, and more.

49246 ■ **"Second Chances"** in *Black Enterprise* (Vol. 34, No. 2, September 2003, pp. 58)
Pub: Earl Graves Publishing Co.
Ed: Sonya A. Donaldson. **Description:** Refurbished or remanufactured office equipment is becoming more popular to small companies during tough economic times. Many top vendors are now offering refurbished equipment and technology, as well as trade in programs, rental and leasing programs, and financing options.

49247 ■ **"Second wind"** in *Entrepreneur* (Vol. 31, No. 4, April 2003, pp. 18)
Pub: Entrepreneur Media, Inc.
Ed: Amanda C. Kooser. **Description:** The latest trend is for small businesses to add new peripherals to computer systems rather than upgrade PCs as often. A few examples of the latest add-ons to improve the performance and extend the lifespan of computers are external hard drives, personal storage, CD-RW drives, and new flat-panel display monitors.

49248 ■ **"Secure your network"** in *PC Magazine* (June 27, 2000, pp. 183)
Pub: Ziff-Davis Publishing Company
Ed: Frank J. Derfler, Jr. **Description:** Several turnkey hardware/software firewall products are reviewed, including Check Points VPN-1 Appliance 330 and Cisco's Secure PIX Firewall 515, as well as, similar tools from Progressive Systems, WatchGuard and e-Soft. The products use NAT and other powerful techniques such as packet and address filtering to ensure Internet security. Each can be used as a combined router/firewall, but such a solution results in a single point of failure and leaves the entire network vulnerable if it is penetrated. Effectiveness and availability of high-end features such as VPN support are key elements to look for when choosing a firewall.

49249 ■ **"Secure Your Wireless"** in *My Business* (August/September 2002, pp. 24)
Pub: My Business Magazine
Ed: Michael Grebb. **Description:** Information on wireless technology that is affordable and helpful to small business is discussed, along with security issues.

49250 ■ **"Server it Right"** in *Entrepreneur* (Vol. 31, No. 11, November 2003, pp. 57)
Pub: Entrepreneur Media, Inc.
Ed: Steve Cooper. **Description:** Profile of D-Link's DP-311P Wireless Print Server that allows users to use printers wirelessly.

49251 ■ **"Set Up a Voice Mail and Fax System-Give your company the appearance of corporate professionalism"** in *PC Magazine* (Mar.21,2000, pp.115)
Pub: Ziff-Davis Publishing Company
Ed: M. David Stone. **Description:** A good alternative for providing reliable voice mail services for a small business is to dedicate a computer outfitted with voice modems and a voice mail software package to the task. The same system can be used to handle fax traffic in a professional manner. Products that are reliable for such a dedicated usage include Fax Works from Thought Communications, SuperVoice from Pacific Image Communications, and TalkWorks Pro from Symantec.

49252 ■ **"Shady Business"** in *Entrepreneur* (Vol. 30, No. 2, February 2002, pp. 22)
Pub: Entrepreneur Media, Inc.
Ed: Gisela M. Pedroza. **Description:** Profile of eShades, made by Inviso Inc., are glasses that project an image the size of a desktop monitor at a comfortable distance.

49253 ■ **"Share Safely"** in *Entrepreneur* (Vol. 32, November 2004, No. 11, pp. 62)
Pub: Entrepreneur Media, Inc.
Ed: Liane Cassavoy. **Description:** Ipswitch's WS_FTP Professional 9.0 allows for secure file transfers, and adds PGP (Pretty Good Privacy) encryption for increased security.

49254 ■ **"Sharing Digital Shots Snap with Picasa 2.0"** in *Tampa Tribune* (January 24, 2005)
Pub: Knight-Ridder/Tribune Business News
Ed: Doug Stanley. **Description:** Profile of Picasa 2.0, free photo-management program from Google; the software allows users to find, organize, edit, share and preserve digital pictures.

49255 ■ **"Shock Treatment"** in *My Business* (April/May 2002, pp. 46)
Pub: My Business Magazine
Ed: Joel Ostroff. **Description:** Ways to protect home business equipment from temporary power surges are explored, including surge protectors or protecting an entire house with a meter socket surge arrestor at the electric meter, and indoor and outdoor panel-mounted next to the circuit breaker panel.

49256 ■ **"Shopping List"** in *Entrepreneur* (Vol. 32, No. 2, February 2004, pp. 43)
Pub: Entrepreneur Media, Inc.
Description: A listing of the various manufacturers and models of computer switches. Contact information, number of ports, and type are also included.

49257 ■ **"Shopping List: Thin is When It Comes to Monitors. Try These Models for Size"** in *Entrepreneur* (Vol. 32, October 2004, No. 10, pp. 56)
Pub: Entrepreneur Media Inc.
Description: Profiles of thin computer monitors are presented, offering manufacturer and model, contact, features, input, and pricing.

49258 ■ **"Singin' the Blues: Is It the End for Bluetooth?"** in *Entrepreneur* (Vol. 33, March 2005, No. 3, pp. 44)
Pub: Entrepreneur Media Inc.
Ed: Mike Hogan. **Description:** In order to increase use in the U.S., Bluetooth will triple data rates to 3Mbps with a simultaneous decrease in power consumption. Other improvements will be in security, power consumption and the ability to send signals to multiple devices at the same time.

49259 ■ **"The Skinny"** in *Entrepreneur* (Vol. 32, September 2004, No. 9, pp. 42)
Pub: Entrepreneur Media Inc.
Ed: Steve Cooper. **Description:** Profile of Sony's VAIO X505 ultra-thin computer notebook, retailing at $3,000.

49260 ■ **"Slim Down: Sick of Your Bulky PC? A Desktop Replacement Notebook Could Be the Answer"** in *Entrepreneur* (Vol. 32, July 2004, No. 7)
Pub: Entrepreneur Media Inc.
Ed: Amanda C. Kooser. **Description:** Desktop replacement notebooks are fast replacing larger desktop computers. Things to consider when choosing a new computer are discussed.

49261 ■ **"Slow Down and Back Up"** in *My Business* (October/November 2003, pp. 12)
Pub: My Business Magazine
Ed: Julie Bawden Davis. **Description:** Small businesses need to back up work daily to avoid losses. Solutions to data backup issues for the small business owner are listed.

49262 ■ *The Small Business Computer Book: A Guide in Plain English*
Pub: Upstart Publishing Co., Inc.
Ed: Robert K. Moskowitz. **Released:** 1993. **Price:** $19.95 (paper). **Description:** Guide to office automation, covering identifying where computers are needed, how to use computer information resources, and available computer products, hardware, and software.

49263 ■ **"The Small-Business Network"** in *PC Magazine* (August 1, 2000, pp. 101)
Pub: Ziff-Davis Publishing Company
Ed: Jim Seymour. **Description:** Small business owners are interested in putting together networks for just a small group of users. This article suggests a Windows 95 or Windows 98 network and how to put it together.

49264 ■ *The Small Business Owner's Manual: Everything You Need to Know to Start Up and Run Your Business*
Pub: Career Press, Incorporated
Ed: Joe Kennedy. **Released:** June 2005. **Price:** $19.99 (US), $26.95 (Canadian). **Description:** Comprehensive guide for starting a small business, focusing on twelve ways to obtain financing, business plans, selling and advertising products and services, hiring and firing employees, setting up a Web site, business law, accounting issues, insurance, equipment, computers, banks, financing, customer credit and collection, leasing, and more.

49265 ■ "Small-Business Printing" in *PC Magazine* (August 8, 2000, pp. 101)
Pub: Ziff-Davis Publishing Company
Ed: Jim Seymour. **Description:** An overview is provided of three different ways for small businesses to use a printer with their network. First, is to attach it to the network directly by using a vendor-supplied network connection. Secondly, is to use an external point server box. And thirdly, by using a printer that is connected to a different PC on the network.

49266 ■ "Small Fry" in *Entrepreneur* (Vol. 33, January 2005, No. 1, pp. 44)
Pub: Entrepreneur Media Inc.
Description: Profile of the OQO Model 01 notebook computer, a full Windows XP PC that's only a bit larger than a PDA. The small computer runs Windows XP OS, Bluetooth and Wi-Fi.

49267 ■ "Small-Office Firewalls" in *PC Magazine* (June 27, 2000, pp. 198)
Pub: Ziff-Davis Publishing Company
Description: Hardware and software products for small offices are reviewed. All offer a WAN port for connecting to an Internet router and a LAN port for connecting to the network as well as built-in DHCP servers and clients. WatchGuard Technologies' WatchGuard SOHO earns a very good rating, while several other products, including the SonicWall SOHO, Linksys EtherFast and NetGear Rt311, earn a good rating. Features to look for include reporting capabilities, content filtering and VPN options.

49268 ■ "Small Office/Home Office" in *Hispanic Business* (Vol. 22, No. 1/2, January/February, pp. 92)
Pub: Hispanic Business
Description: The feature is designed to provide emerging entrepreneurs with practical tips for operating a small or home office. Home-based business insurance, business licensing, and next-generation scanners are discussed.

49269 ■ "Smart Answers" in *Business Week* (June 12, 2000, pp. F14)
Pub: McGraw-Hill, Inc.
Description: The Better Business Bureau can help small businesses having problems with credit-card processors.

49270 ■ "Smart Tech Solutions For Small Businesses" in *Black Enterprise* (Vol. 35, August 2004, No. 1, pp. 61)
Pub: Earl G. Publishing Co. Inc.
Ed: Schuyler K. Esprit. **Description:** Ramon Ray's Technology Solutions for Growing Businesses is reviewed. Finding the right products for a small business can maximize productivity while minimizing costs.

49271 ■ "Smarty pants" in *Entrepreneur* (Vol. 30, No. 3, March 2002, pp. 42)
Pub: Entrepreneur Media Inc.
Ed: Gisela M. Pedroza. **Description:** Profile of the ready-made SmartStep 100D computer, priced lower than other brands.

49272 ■ "Snap n' Print" in *Entrepreneur* (Vol. 32, November 2004, No. 11, pp. 18)
Pub: Entrepreneur Media Inc.
Ed: Gisela M. Pedroza. **Description:** Profile of Epson's portable PictureMate that prints photographs immediately and supports CompactFlash, Memory Stick, Microdrive, MMC, Secure Digital, SmartMedia and xD and printing can be done with or without a computer.

49273 ■ "Snare and Share Alike: Here's a Quick and Easy Way to Capture Video" in *Black Enterprise* (Vol. 34, No. 6, January 2004, pp. 46)
Pub: Earl Graves Publishing Co.
Ed: Rebecca Rohan. **Description:** Ways to move old movies to archive or new video for Internet use to a PC are explained, along with capture device and software.

49274 ■ "Soft Touch" in *Entrepreneur* (Vol. 31, No. 7, July 2003, pp. 22)
Pub: Entrepreneur Media, Inc.
Ed: Gisela M. Pedroza. **Description:** Profile of Man & Machine Inc.'s FX100, a flexible roll-up keyboard that is water-resistant and is compatible with every handheld device on the market, pocket PCs, smart phones, and palm OS devices.

49275 ■ "Software, computer leasing providers jockey to survive" in *Crain's Detroit Business* (Vol. 16, No. 46, November 13, 2000, pp. 16)
Pub: Crain Communications, Inc.
Ed: Katie Merx. **Description:** Several Detroit-area technology companies are asking small businesses to rent software and computer equipment rather than purchasing the equipment.

49276 ■ "SoniqCast Element" in *Black Enterprise* (Vol. 35, December 2004, No. 5, pp. 70)
Pub: Earl G. Graves Publishing Co. Inc.
Description: Profile of SoniqCast Aireo MP3 player, offering wireless capability, an FM stereo receiver, dual headphones, and an FM transmitter.

49277 ■ "Sony Ericsson's T310/T316 Mobile Phone" in *Black Enterprise* (Vol. 34, No. 5, December 2003, pp. S6)
Pub: Earl Graves Publishing Co.
Ed: Donalson A. Sonya. **Description:** Profile of Sony Ericsson's T310/T316 mobile phone, equipped with many features that will appeal to small business owners.

49278 ■ "Speak and Slide: Siemens' Small Phone Packs in Big Features" in *Black Enterprise* (Vol. 34, No. 7, February 2004, pp. 54)
Pub: Earl Graves Publishing Co.
Ed: Schuyler Esprit. **Description:** Profile of Siemens SL56, a full-color cellular phone with features such as voice command, Internet access, extended electronic organizer, and multi-language capability.

49279 ■ "Speak and spell" in *Entrepreneur* (Vol. 30, No. 1, January 2002, pp. 31)
Pub: Entrepreneur Media Inc.
Ed: Mike Hogan. **Description:** Profile of the new Cybiko Extreme from Cybiko Inc. Although marketed as a teen PDA/game machine, it can be used as a walkie-talkie or to send voice notes, email and instant messages up to 300 feet away.

49280 ■ "Sprinkling Data Dust" in *Entrepreneur* (Vol. 28, No. 11, November 2000, pp. 28)
Pub: Entrepreneur Media, Inc.
Ed: Amanda C. Kooser. **Description:** The importance of defragmenting PC hard drives to speed up your computer is discussed.

49281 ■ "Storage on the Go" in *Black Enterprise* (Vol. 35, September 2004, No. 2, pp. 58)
Pub: Earl G. Graves Publishing Co. Inc.
Ed: Sonya A. Donaldson. **Description:** USB flash drives store large amounts of data and other media in a small keychain type of device.

49282 ■ "Store More" in *Entrepreneur* (Vol. 31, No. 10, October 2003, pp. 50)
Pub: Entrepreneur Media, Inc.
Ed: Steve Cooper. **Description:** Profile of Iomega's NAS A205m network-attached storage server, which requires a 10-minute configuration to install.

49283 ■ "Stretching Room" in *Home Office Computing* (Vol. 18, No. 10, October 2000, pp. 42)
Pub: Scholastic Inc.
Ed: Lisa Kanarek. **Description:** A description of how Georgia's Creations' principal, Georgia Cox, used her design skills to create a two-story home office in the middle of her three-level house. Unique features of the home office, analysis of her business and computer hardware and software used in the business are presented.

49284 ■ "Study shows businesses are slow to embrace e-commerce" in *Black Enterprise* (Vol. 32)
Pub: Earl Graves Publishing Co.
Ed: Bevolyn Williams-Harold. **Description:** The Minority Business Development Agency is urging minority-owned businesses to use e-commerce to help grow their companies. Statistical data included.

49285 ■ "The Super-Cheap Supercomputer" in *Business 2.0* (Vol. 6, May 2005, No. 4, pp. 30)
Pub: Time, Inc.
Ed: Om Malik. **Description:** Estimated costs for creating high-performance computers used for supercomputing are given.

49286 ■ "Surge Sentinel" in *Hispanic Business* (Vol. 23, No. 10, October, 2001, pp. 102)
Pub: Hispanic Business
Ed: Roger Harris. **Description:** Profile of the Pulsar Espirit, which is designed to protect two network servers from blackouts and power surges, and it is the first UPS to use XML tags that enable remote control via the Internet.

49287 ■ "The Tablet PC" in *Rough Notes* (Vol. 145, No. 1, January 2003, pp. 90)
Pub: Rough Notes
Ed: John Ashenhurst. **Description:** Microsoft Corporation introduces the Table PC, which comes as a notebook computer or as a slate. Insurance companies will find it relevant to operations.

49288 ■ "Tablet Tools" in *Entrepreneur* (Vol. 31, No. 10, October 2003, pp. 57)
Pub: Entrepreneur Media, Inc.
Ed: Liane Cassavoy. **Description:** Profile of MindManager 2002 from Mindjet Software, to capture, organize and share information.

49289 ■ "Take a virtual drive" in *Hispanic Business* (Vol. 22, No. 3, March 2000, pp. 58)
Pub: Hispanic Business
Ed: Abel Magana. **Description:** Apple Computer's iMac was the first computer to be produced without a floppy drive. Following iMac's launch in 1998, several companies began offering digital information storage on the Internet. The services offered by such companies are discussed.

49290 ■ "Take One Tablet" in *Black Enterprise* (Vol. 34, No. 4, November 2003, pp. 55)
Pub: Earl Graves Publishing Co.
Ed: Sonya A. Donaldson. **Description:** New Tablet PC technology is explained comparing functions as compared to laptops and portable computers.

49291 ■ "Take a SIP" in *Entrepreneur* (Vol. 33, October 2005, No. 10, pp. 46)
Pub: Entrepreneur Media Inc.
Ed: Amanda C. Kooser. **Description:** Session Initiation Protocol (SIP) is a signaling protocol that establishes sessions with an IP network, and is fast becoming the top choice for VoIP systems.

49292 ■ "Take Your Pick: Palm OS or Pocket PC?" in *Entrepreneur* (Vol. 31, No. 11, November 2003, pp. 58)
Pub: Entrepreneur Media, Inc.
Ed: Amanda C. Kooser. **Description:** Profiles of new personal digital assistants (PDAs) on the market, including Palm OS and Pocket PC devices.

49293 ■ "Taking Care of Business: Downloadable Programs For Your Enterprise" in *Black Enterprise* (Vol. 34, July 2004, No. 12, pp. 145)
Pub: Earl G. Graves Publishing Co. Inc.
Ed: Jennifer L. Smith. Description: Websites offering free, downloadable small business software are presented. Everything from accounting, computer security, as well as investment programs is available from these sites.

49294 ■ "Taking the fear out of buying a personal computer" in *Women in Business* (Vol. 53, No. 3, May-June, 2001, pp. 22)
Pub: The ABWA Co. Inc.
Ed: Melissa Will. Description: When buying a computer for the first time, the most important thing is to research products before the purchase. Factors to consider include price, the computer's use, and warranties.

49295 ■ "Tall Order" in *Entrepreneur* (Vol. 32, December 2004, No. 12, pp. 58)
Pub: Entrepreneur Media Inc.
Ed: Mike Hogan. Description: Quality of service and coverage, option plans, prices and customer service have all improved in the cell phone industry.

49296 ■ "Taming the Techno Beast" in *Business Week* (May 22, 2000, pp. F30)
Pub: McGraw-Hill, Inc.
Description: The critical issue of changing technology boils down to one impossibly complex question: how to manage it coherently.

49297 ■ "Tap Into the Corporate LAN" in *Home Office Computing* (Vol. 18, No. 9, September 2000, pp. 79)
Pub: Scholastic Inc.
Ed: Wayne Kawamoto. Description: Technologies for accessing office LANs from home are discussed.

49298 ■ "Tape Backup isn't the sexiest technology on the network, but it is one of the most essential" in *PC Magazine* (April 4, 2000, pp. 155)
Pub: Ziff-Davis Publishing Company
Ed: Steve Rigney. Description: Six tape drives are evaluated, and test results illustrate that a purchase decision depends on specific circumstances and type of business. In these tests, the $4,000 Exabyte Mammoth-2 was fastest. For a small business, the $1,000 Ecrix VXA-1 and the $1,500 Benchmark Tape Systems DLT1 are recommended. Customers are reminded that software typically does not come with a tape drive, and in most cases, even a driver will have to be purchased separately.

49299 ■ "Tech firms uncertain about tech forecast" in *Atlanta Business Chronicle* (Vol. 25, November 15, 2002, No. 23 pp. 2C)
Pub: American City Business Publications, Inc.
Ed: Charles Davidson. Description: Many technology executives in Atlanta expect customers to buy more business products or services during the first or second quarter of 2003, and IDC expects the global information technology market to grow 9 percent to $1 trillion during 2003. Details on technology spending for various companies are included.

49300 ■ "Tech, Please: 'Next-Generation CIOs' Offer More Than Just Tech Advice" in *Entrepreneur* (Vol. 33, January 2005, No. 1, pp. 22)
Pub: Entrepreneur Media Inc.
Ed: Mark Henricks. Description: Successful chief information officers understand the business in which they work. They should continually examine new technologies and competitors' IT practices, and bring in new products, services and process improvements.

49301 ■ "Tech Toy" in *Entrepreneur* (Vol. 31, No. 10, October 2003, pp. 26)
Pub: Entrepreneur Media, Inc.
Ed: Gisela M. Pedroza. Description: Profile of Sony's robot dog called AIBO Cyber-Blue, when connected with AIBO EYES software, the robot dog connects to Internet-enabled PC or mobile devices and can take digital snapshots and email them to another location.

49302 ■ "Tech Watch: BlackBerry 7100t" in *Sales & Marketing Management* (Vol. 157, January 2005, No. 1, pp. 23)
Pub: VNU Business Media
Description: Profile of the new BlackBerry 7100t, the phone that allows users to directly access their customer relationship management systems.

49303 ■ "Technically correct" in *Pittsburgh Business Times* (Vol. 22, No. 46, May 30, 2003, pp. 19)
Pub: Pittsburgh Business Times
Ed: Maria Guzzo. Description: Profiles of product lines and new product development at the Michael Baker Corporation, including business creativity, market share, and business strategy.

49304 ■ "Techniques: Microcases" in *Inc.* (November 15, 2000, pp. 128-129)
Pub: The Goldhirsh Group
Description: Solutions for two problems are addressed: customers and staff out of sync with the home office; and stalled Web sites and crashing e-mail.

49305 ■ "Technology Can't Replace Your Best Asset: People" in *My Business* (June/July 2002, pp. 24)
Pub: My Business Magazine
Ed: Michael Grebb. Description: The pros and cons of replacing people with technology for small business are examined.

49306 ■ "Technology Column" in *Tampa Tribune* (March 7, 2005)
Pub: Knight-Ridder/Tribune Business News
Ed: Doug Stanley. Description: Accessing computers wirelessly can be setup to an existing network router by using a wireless access point and running an auto-setup program.

49307 ■ "The Technology Discrepancy" in *Sales & Marketing Management* (Vol. 157, January 2005, No. 1, pp. 9)
Pub: VNU Business Media
Ed: Jennifer Gilbert. Description: Sales teams equipped with cutting-edge technology are believed to be more successful than counterparts not well-equipped. Results of a survey of managers performed by S&MM/Equation Research are discussed. Statistical data included.

49308 ■ "Technophobe Help Desk" in *Sales & Marketing Management* (Vol. 157, January 2005, No. 1, pp. 23)
Pub: VNU Business Media
Description: A listing of the best ways to back up important data is provided.

49309 ■ *The Telecommuter's Advisor: Working in the Fast Lane*
Pub: Aegis Publishing Group, Ltd.
Ed: June Langhoff. Released: 1996. Price: $14.95. Description: Provides valuable insights and strategies for working effectively from any remote location. Includes tips and suggestions for setting up a home office; improving productivity by utilizing the latest communications equipment; and handling e-mail accounts.

49310 ■ "That's Handy" in *Entrepreneur* (Vol. 31, No. 9, September 2003, pp. 46)
Pub: Entrepreneur Media, Inc.
Ed: Steve Cooper. Description: Profile of BlackBerry 6210 wireless handheld that provides email, phone, Internet, short messaging service and organizer applications in one tiny gadget.

49311 ■ "That's the Spot" in *Entrepreneur. com* (Vol. 34, February 2006, No. 2, pp. 35)
Pub: Entrepreneur Media Inc.
Description: JiWire and Wi Finder help locate hot spots for Internet access before you hit the roads. The software can be downloaded at no charge and includes a directory of more than 70,000 hot spots in 103 countries.

49312 ■ "They're all round, but..." in *Crain's Detroit Business* (Vol. 19, No. 10, March 10, 2003, pp. 33)
Pub: Crain Communications Inc., Detroit
Description: Information for using computer CD-Roms, including DVD-R, DVD-RW, DVDRW, and DVD-RAM, is presented.

49313 ■ "Think Small" in *Entrepreneur* (Vol. 31, No. 10, October 2003, pp. 50)
Pub: Entrepreneur Media, Inc.
Ed: Gisela M. Pedroza. Description: Profile of IBM's ThinkCentre S50, a smaller and quieter, but very powerful, desktop computer.

49314 ■ "Think Small" in *PC Magazine* (November 21, 2000, pp. 5a)
Pub: Ziff-Davis Publishing Company
Ed: Sarah L. Roberts-Witt. Description: E-commerce enablers are offering e-procurement and B2B e-commerce geared to small businesses.

49315 ■ "Thinking About Security" in *PC Magazine* (January 4, 2000, pp. 191)
Pub: Ziff-Davis Publishing Company
Ed: Steve Rigney. Description: Companies must deal with data security, but first must determine what their security needs and risks are. Once that is established the company can look to firewalls, data security devices, network security software, virtual private networks and network address transmittal devices. Costs of these different solutions must also be considered.

49316 ■ "This Phone Connects" in *Fast Company* (September 2001, pp. 70)
Pub: Fast Company
Ed: Alison Overholt. Description: Profile of Samsung's 1300 Wireless Digital Assistant phone.

49317 ■ *301 Great Ideas for Using Technology to Grow Your Business*
Pub: Inc. Publishing
Ed: Phaedra Hise. Released: 1998. Price: $14.95.

49318 ■ "Throwing Money at Technology Isn't the Solution" in *My Business* (April/May 2002, pp. 18)
Pub: My Business Magazine
Ed: Michael Grebb. Description: Not all business problems can be solved by technology. Small firms must first identify and analyze an issue then break the problem down into three components: process, people, and technology.

49319 ■ "Time to Change" in *Entrepreneur. com* (Vol. 34, January 2006, No. 1, pp. 27)
Pub: Entrepreneur Media Inc.
Ed: Eric Bender. Description: March 11, 2007 begins the newly extended daylight-saving time that will always begin on the second Sunday of March and end on the first Sunday of November each year. If your system is no longer supported by your software, you must manually change your computer's clocks.

49320 ■ "Time for an Upgrade" in *Hispanic Business* (June 2002, pp. 78)
Pub: Hispanic Business
Ed: Derek Reveron. Description: Mid-size companies can now purchase the same high-powered computer equipment once only affordable to large corporations.

49321 ■ "Tips & Trends" in *Small Business Opportunities* (Vol. 17, November 2005, No. 6, pp. 14)
Pub: Harris Publications Inc.
Description: A roundup of new products and services to run a small business include profiles of Xerox's color multifunction system; holiday signs; the new Consumer Action Handbook; technology accessories for CD/DVDs, cellular phones, and iPods; and a new tape dispenser.

49322 ■ "To-Dos and Tunes: PDA and MP3 Phones Arrive" in *PC Magazine* (February 6, 2001, pp. 34)
Pub: Ziff-Davis Publishing Company

Ed: Bruce Brown, Marge Brown. **Description:** The Sprint PCS TP 3000, a combination single-band mobile phone and personal digital assistant (PDA) with an integrated MP3 music player, is reviewed.

49323 ■ **"To the swift"** in *Entrepreneur* (Vol. 30, No. 1, January 2002, pp. 39)
Pub: Entrepreneur Media Inc.
Ed: Mike Hogan. **Description:** An overview of the new high speed computers, offering up to 3.5GHz processors.

49324 ■ **"Toshiba Qosmio E15-AV Notebook PC"** in *Black Enterprise* (Vol. 35, December 2004, No. 5, pp. 71)
Pub: Earl G. Graves Publishing Co. Inc.
Description: Profile of Toshiba's Notebook PC computer, Qosmio E15-AV, featuring one-touch CD/TV/DVD player capability.

49325 ■ **"Total Tote (Tech Toy)"** in *Entrepreneur* (Vol. 31, No. 8, August, 2003, pp. 18)
Pub: Entrepreneur Media, Inc.
Ed: Gisela M. Pedroza. **Description:** Profile of APC's Travel Power Case, a notebook carrying case with a built-in charging station allowing user to keep all gadgets charged without having to carry power adapters for every device.

49326 ■ **"Tray chic"** in *Entrepreneur* (Vol. 31, No. 5, May 2003, pp. 18)
Pub: Entrepreneur Media Inc.
Ed: Gisela M. Pedroza. **Description:** PC Tables LLC has created a collapsible, lightweight table for laptop computers. The table is portable and can be used anywhere, including the airport, a hotel lobby or other public space.

49327 ■ **"Treo"** in *Business Week* (January 16, 2006, No. 3967, pp. 18)
Pub: McGraw-Hill Companies
Ed: Stephen H. Wildstrom. **Description:** Profile of the new Treo 700w which runs on Microsoft software. The new device is the first Pocket PC that offers home screen features such as speed-dial buttons and two boxes for entering text.

49328 ■ **"Trouble In PDA Paradise"** in *Entrepreneur* (Vol. 31, No. 7, July 2003, pp. 44)
Pub: Entrepreneur Media, Inc.
Ed: Amanda C. Kooser. **Description:** An overview of information for entrepreneurs when choosing personal digital assistant devices is provided. Many entrepreneurs will find built-in Wi-Fi or Bluetooth, flash memory and wireless communication capabilities attractive.

49329 ■ **"True Blue"** in *Entrepreneur* (Vol. 31, No. 8, August 2003, pp. 46)
Pub: Entrepreneur Media, Inc.
Ed: Amanda C. Kooser. **Description:** A sampling of Bluetooth computer hardware add-ons is presented. Information is provided to help small business owners decide which devices are right for their company.

49330 ■ **"Turn Back the Hands of Time: Travel to the Past with Windows' System Restore"** in *Black Enterprise* (Vol. 34, No. 7, February 2004)
Pub: Earl Graves Publishing Co.
Ed: Rebecca Rohan. **Description:** Information for using the System Restore option on computers equipped with Windows ME or XP is offered. This system will return a computer back to a time when Windows was running fine by creating restore points, specific dated information and data that lets it recreate the essentials of the operating environment to the last check point before a problem occurred.

49331 ■ **"Twice as Nice"** in *Home Office Computing* (Vol. 18, No. 8, August 2000, pp. 40)
Pub: Scholastic Inc.
Ed: Dan Costa. **Description:** Reasons are listed for adding a second line to a home office.

49332 ■ **"2001 : A Home Office Odyssey"** in *Home Office Computing* (Vol. 18, No. 9, September 2000, pp. 44)
Pub: Scholastic Inc.
Ed: David Haskin. **Description:** A guide to upcoming products and technologies of interest to home office users is presented.

49333 ■ **"Tying the Knot"** in *Entrepreneur* (Vol. 33, February 2005, No. 2, pp. 46)
Pub: Entrepreneur Media Inc.
Ed: Mike Hogan. **Description:** Wi-Fi and Voice over Internet Protocol (VoIP) providers have teamed to work on a new generation of Wi-Fi routers used for Internet calling and wireless networking at the same time.

49334 ■ **Uniplex: A Guide to Integrated Office Automation**
Pub: Prentice Hall
Ed: Nigel Girling. **Released:** 1991. **Price:** $32.00 (paper).

49335 ■ **"United Front"** in *Entrepreneur* (Vol. 33, January 2005, No. 1, pp. 47)
Pub: Entrepreneur Media Inc.
Ed: Mike Hogan. **Description:** Unified messaging (UM) or unified communications (UC) will allow voice mail, email, and instant messaging to be delivered to the same inbox.

49336 ■ **"Universal connectivity"** in *Entrepreneur* (Vol. 30, No. 1, January 2002, pp. 43)
Pub: Entrepreneur Media Inc.
Ed: Mike Hogan. **Description:** Profile of the Toshiba Portege 4000 portable computer, that adds Wi-Fi and Bluetooth wireless technologies to its motherboard, along with an Ethernet adapter and a 56Kbps modem.

49337 ■ **"Unleash the Wireless Future"** in *Microsoft Executive Circle* (Vol. 1, No. 2, Q2 2001, pp. 28-29, 31)
Pub: Putman Media
Ed: Rex Davenport. **Description:** The benefits for using wireless networks in business are highlighted, including the listing of benefits from the Wireless LAN Association; a wireless checklist according to the Meta Group's Peter Firstbrook; and a listing of terms used when communicating about wireless networks.

49338 ■ **"Urban Media CTO pushes broadband envelope"** in *InfoWorld* (Vol. 22, No. 23, June 5, 2000, pp. 32)
Pub: InfoWorld
Ed: Susan E. Fisher. **Description:** Paul Mockapetris, the CTO of Urban Media, is currently dedicating his time to the development of the technical means to deliver broadband to small and mid-sized businesses for free. Urban Media is taking the classic loss leader approach to business. The idea is that, once customers have whet their Internet appetite on the free 200Kbps access Urban Media serves to each desktop, they will be hungry for additional goodies from the on-site service provider. The Palo Alto, California company's menu of pay services includes local and long-distance voice, managed e-mail, videoconferencing, and VPNs.

49339 ■ **"Video To Go"** in *Entrepreneur* (Vol. 31, No. 9, September 2003, pp. 32)
Pub: Entrepreneur Media, Inc.
Ed: Gisela M. Pedroza. **Description:** Profile of the Blue Thunder Mini Cam from Digital Integrated Systems; the system can be used for video mail and videoconferencing while traveling.

49340 ■ **"Viewer's Choice"** in *Entrepreneur* (Vol. 30, No. 3, March 2002, pp. 44)
Pub: Entrepreneur Media Inc.
Ed: Amanda C. Kooser. **Description:** Videoconferencing is offering entrepreneurs, as well as established small businesses, a safe, timesaving and economical choice to decrease the amount of business travel the would otherwise have to do. A resource guide for choosing the proper Web cam is included.

49341 ■ **"Virtual Camcorder"** in *PC Magazine* (April 4, 2000, pp. 61)
Pub: Ziff-Davis Publishing Company
Ed: Luisa Simone. **Description:** Producing training videos, software demos, and step-by-step tutorials just got a lot easier thanks to Camtasia 1.0.2, from TechSmith Corporation. This utility captures screen images in sequence to create AVI movies of any Windows program.

49342 ■ **"Virtual Private Networks: Editors' Hot Links"** in *PC Magazine* (January 4, 2000, pp. 146)
Pub: Ziff-Davis Publishing Company
Ed: Frank J. Derfler, Jr. **Description:** A directory of Internet infrastructure products for small business are listed and reviewed.

49343 ■ **"Virtual Private Networks"** in *PC Magazine* (January 4, 2000, pp. 146)
Pub: Ziff-Davis Publishing Company
Ed: Frank J. Derfler, Jr. **Description:** Test procedures of VPN products from six vendors are presented. The companies are TimeStep, Intel, Altiga Networks, Lucent Technologies and Check Point. The first five vendors supplied hardware and software packaged VPN gateways for the test, while Check Point's product was software that came installed in a Pentium III PC server.

49344 ■ **"A Virtual Wallet"** in *PC Magazine* (December 14, 1999, pp. 12)
Pub: Ziff-Davis Publishing Company
Ed: Gary Gunnerson. **Description:** Micropayments technology, or 'electronic wallets', make it possible to purchase items over the Internet without using a credit card. Because online merchants have been slow to adopt e-wallet technologies, e-wallet products are beginning to support a standard way of filling out purchase forms, often via Electronic Commerce Markup Language (ECML) standardized tags.

49345 ■ **"Voices Carry"** in *Entrepreneur* (Vol. 28, No. 11, November 2000, pp. 36)
Pub: Entrepreneur Media Inc.
Ed: Eric Brown. **Description:** Profile of EnGenius SN-900 Ultra cordless phone system, which boasts the most extensive range of any cordless phone on the market.

49346 ■ **"VoIP Lessons: Learn How to Get Around Potential Problems"** in *Entrepreneur* (Vol. 33, January 2005, No. 1, pp. 26)
Pub: Entrepreneur Media Inc.
Ed: Amanda C. Kooser. **Description:** Cost savings, convenience and features make voice over Internet protocol (VoIP) attractive to growing businesses.

49347 ■ **"VPNs Go Mainstream"** in *Home Office Computing* (Vol. 18, No. 12, December 2000, pp. 16)
Pub: Scholastic Inc.
Ed: Mark Kakkuri. **Description:** As more firms tire of costly dial-in equipment and toll-free lines, or even costlier leased-line wide area networks, virtual private networks (VPNs) are becoming the hottest trends in telework technology.

49348 ■ **"VPNs and Windows 2000: With Windows 2000, standards-based virtual private networking is integrated into the operating system"** in *PC Magazine*
Pub: Ziff-Davis Publishing Company
Ed: Eric Greenberg. **Description:** Microsoft Windows 2000 offers powerful standards-based dial-up VPN capabilities that should ease the complexity of deploying VPN functionality to the desktop. VPNs provide a path toward lower networking costs, power security capabilities, enhanced productivity for remote users and rapidly deployable e-business services. VPN security, digital certificates, and PKI are discussed.

49349 ■ **"Walk 'N' Talk"** in *Entrepreneur* (Vol. 30, No. 2, February 2002, pp. 35)
Pub: Entrepreneur Media Inc.
Ed: Mike Hogan. **Description:** Profile of EnGenius SN-920 handsets that allow users to get calls from the base unit across 250,000 square feet of space, 12 floors of an office building, or 3,000 acres of land.

49350 ■ "Wall-To-Wall: Wireless Jacks are the 'In' Thing for Networking" in *Entrepreneur* (Vol. 33, January 2005, No. 1, pp. 41)
Pub: Entrepreneur Media Inc.
Ed: Amanda C. Kooser. **Description:** Wi-Fi jacks are the newest hardware offering to make Wi-Fi easier and less expensive for small businesses.

49351 ■ "Walled In" in *Entrepreneur* (Vol. 32, No. 4, April 2004, pp. 34)
Pub: Entrepreneur Media, Inc.
Ed: Amanda C. Kooser. **Description:** Profile of Firebox 700 from WatchGuard Technologies, offering security to a network with broadband Internet access.

49352 ■ "Wants vs. Needs: How to Shop Wisely for Technology" in *My Business* (December/January 2004, pp. 40)
Pub: My Business Magazine
Ed: Tamara E. Holmes. **Description:** Regardless of industry, there are certain technology needs important to all small businesses, including workstations, handheld devices, cellular phones, wireless networks, and teleconferencing equipment.

49353 ■ "Weighing Wireless Options" in *My Business* (December/January 2003, pp. 24)
Pub: My Business Magazine
Ed: Michael Grebb. **Description:** Wireless computer networks are profiled.

49354 ■ "What a Lightweight!" in *Entrepreneur* (Vol. 31, No. 8, August 2003, pp. 36)
Pub: Entrepreneur Media, Inc.
Description: Profile of the ViewSonic PJ250 lightweight projector used by sales teams in the field, as well as for meetings and presentations.

49355 ■ "What a Relief!" in *Entrepreneur* (Vol. 31, No. 8, August 2003, pp. 57)
Pub: Entrepreneur Media, Inc.
Ed: Joan Szabo. **Description:** Under the new Jobs and Growth Tax Reconciliation Act of 2003, companies can deduct 100 percent of equipment costs. Under prior law, the limit was $25,000, now under Section 179 allowance for taxable years beginning in 2003, 2004, and 2005 quadruples to $100,000. The 2003 act also improves the temporary bonus depreciation.

49356 ■ "What's Next? Hardware that Can Straddle Wireless LANs and Cellular Networks" in *Entrepreneur* (Vol. 32, December 2004, No. 12, pp. 49)
Pub: Entrepreneur Media Inc.
Ed: Amanda C. Kooser. **Description:** Integration of services like voice over Internet Protocol (VoIP) can create more flexible work environments between cellular phones, software and computers.

49357 ■ "What's That Ringing in iPod's Ears?" in *Business Week* (January 16, 2006, No. 3967, pp. 70-71)
Pub: McGraw-Hill Companies
Ed: Spencer E. Ante. **Description:** Verizon's new V Cast is set to put songs on cellular phones, challenging Apple's position in the digital music sector. V Cast Music will offer more than 500,000 songs when first launched with 1 million by spring 2006.

49358 ■ "What's Your 'ROI?" in *My Business* (February/March 2003, pp. 24)
Pub: My Business Magazine
Ed: Michael Grebb. **Description:** The importance of analyzing a small business's risk-of-investment is discussed, particularly the technology needed for a particular business. New software is profiled.

49359 ■ "When a BlackBerry Is Overkill: The Phones Are Fine for Reading, But Not Writing e-Mails" in *Business Week* (January 31, 2005, pp. 20)
Pub: McGraw-Hill Companies
Ed: Stephen H. Wildstrom. **Description:** Profile of Microsoft's Windows Mobile Smartphone software, Motorola MPx220 flip phone, and the Audiovox SMT5600 bar-type phone.

49360 ■ "When BlackBerry Use Causes Pain" in *San Jose Mercury News* (February 28, 2005)
Pub: Knight-Ridder/Tribune Business News
Ed: Nicole C. Wong. **Description:** Repetitive stress injuries are common among desktop and laptop computer users.

49361 ■ "When your computer goes bye, make sure data stays put" in *Crain's Detroit Business* (Vol. 18, No. 22, June 3, 2002, pp. 57)
Pub: Crain Communications Inc. - Detroit
Ed: Andrew Dietderich. **Description:** Tips for erasing data from a computer hard drive before disposing of the PC are offered.

49362 ■ "When in Doubt, Outsource" in *PC Magazine* (January 4, 2000, pp. 146)
Pub: Ziff-Davis Publishing Company
Ed: Frank J. Derfler, Jr. **Description:** Carriers that will set up and maintain a VPN server, provide technical support for employees, and meet security threats are described.

49363 ■ "Which Switch? Speed Up Your Network's Performance With a Fast Ethernet Switch" in *Entrepreneur* (Vol. 33, August 2005, No. 8, pp. 46)
Pub: Entrepreneur Media Inc.
Ed: Amanda C. Kooser. **Description:** Faster, more efficient Ethernets for a growing small business are profiled. Manufacturers, models, contact and type are listed.

49364 ■ "Why Bad Projects Are So Hard to Kill" in *Harvard Business Review* (Vol. 81, No. 2, February 2003, pp. 48)
Pub: Harvard Business School Press
Ed: Isabelle Royer. **Description:** Research into ways a company might continue to invest money in a technology that will never be marketable, and points out businesses don't often appreciate the need for those individuals who are willing to terminate a bad project.

49365 ■ "Wi-Fi is a Must for New Office Space on Long Island" in *Long Island Business News* (February 13, 2004)
Pub: Dolan Media Newswires
Ed: Nick Anastasi. **Description:** Small businesses are looking for office space offering high-speed wireless technology in the form of Wi-Fi connectivity.

49366 ■ "Will disruptive innovations cure health care?" in *Harvard Business Review* (Vol. 78, No. 5, September-October 2000, pp. 102)
Pub: Harvard Business School Publishing Corp.
Ed: John Richard, Clayton M. Kenagy, Christensen Bohmer. **Description:** This article discusses the need for "disruptive" technological innovations in the health care industry. The authors argue that technology that ultimately improves an industry will at first be disruptive and appear to threaten the profits of companies in the industry. Graphs are included.

49367 ■ "A Wireless Decision" in *Hispanic Business* (Vol. 23, No. 5, May 2001, pp. 78)
Pub: Hispanic Business
Ed: Roger Harris. **Description:** Wireless networking equipment and services are examined for small business.

49368 ■ "Wireless Freedom: Installing an AirPort Network Can Be a Breeze" in *Black Enterprise* (Vol. 34, July 2004, No. 12, pp. 54)
Pub: Earl G. Graves Publishing Co. Inc.
Ed: Kenneth Meeks. **Description:** AirPort cards and an AirPort Base Station can network computers wirelessly thorough a home or small business.

49369 ■ "Wireless Phones Get Organized" in *Home Office Computing* (Vol. 19, No. 1, January 2001, pp. 20)
Pub: Scholastic Inc.
Ed: Dan Costa. **Description:** If your pockets are over-packed with cell phones, electronic organizers, digital voice recorders, and other gadgets, help is on the way. A new breed of smart phones will combine voice, e-mail, and Web data capability with appointment, phone book, and other personal information management in a single, stylish mobile handset.

49370 ■ "Wise Up! When It Comes to Inventing a Successful Product, Experience May Be Your Best Asset" in *Entrepreneur* (Vol. 31, October 2003)
Pub: Entrepreneur Media, Inc.
Ed: Don Debelak. **Description:** Profile of Bob Olodort, founder of Think Outside Inc. in Santa Clara, California. The company offers the Stowaway Keyboard, a full-size portable keyboard designed for use with small handheld devices.

49371 ■ "Wish List: What Do People Want Most in a Cell Phone" in *Entrepreneur* (Vol. 32, No. 1, January 2004, pp. 37)
Pub: Entrepreneur Media, Inc.
Ed: Mike Hogan. **Description:** Most people purchasing cellular phones are looking for features that include digital cameras and push-to-talk services.

49372 ■ "WNET discovers 'virtual' solution to storage needs" in *InfoWorld* (Vol. 23, No. 5, January 29, 2001, pp. 56)
Pub: InfoWorld
Ed: Dan Neel. **Description:** New York TV station WNET found a way to expand storage without drastically expanding costs. After viewing several hardware-based storage area network solutions, it decided on a storage virtualization software solution from DataCore Software. Storage virtualization allowed the placement of multiple storage devices into one virtual storage disk. The benefits were rapid storage growth and reconfiguration, simple management, and much lower costs.

49373 ■ "Work Gear" in *St. Louis Post-Dispatch* (November 5, 2004)
Pub: Knight-Ridder/Tribune Business News
Ed: Jo Krummrich. **Description:** Perfect Solutions Digital Map Distance Finder calculates the miles and travel times between destinations, making it a good device for field reps.

49374 ■ "Work and Play" in *Fast Company* (November 2001, pp. 48)
Pub: Fast Company
Ed: Alison Overholt. **Description:** Profile of the Shark MX personal digital assistant, which allows the user to move from game playing to sending and receiving email, schedule appointments, or to use the calculator and address book.

49375 ■ "Working IT: Have You Been Putting Off Tech Spending?" in *Entrepreneur* (Vol. 32, October 2004, No. 10, pp. 95)
Pub: Entrepreneur Media Inc.
Ed: Mark Henricks. **Description:** Ways to negotiate existing contracts to lower technology costs by 10 to 20 percent are presented.

49376 ■ "Working on Thin Air" in *Hispanic Business* (October 2004, pp. 116, 118)
Pub: Hispanic Business
Ed: Scott Williams. **Description:** Wireless electronic devices are being used increasingly by business travelers. Profiles of Sandisk Cruzer Titanium high-speed flash drive, Garmin iQue 3200 Global Positioning System, Sony's TR3A computer notebook, Mirra personal computer server, Kensington WiFi Detector, and HP iPAQ H6315 Pocket PC are included.

49377 ■ "Workplace Wellness" in *Small Business Opportunities* (March 2005)
Pub: Harris Publications Inc.
Description: Ergonomics is the applied science of design, particularly in the workplace. Ten steps to assure a better and healthier workplace that is ergonomically sound are listed.

49378 ■ "World of Wi-Fi" in *Entrepreneur* (Vol. 31, No. 8, August 2003, pp. 30)
Pub: Entrepreneur Media, Inc.
Ed: Steve Cooper. **Description:** The top ten cities offering the best wireless Internet accessibility are listed by Bert Sperling of Fast Forward Inc.

49379 ■ "XML for All" in *Entrepreneur* (Vol. 28, No. 11, November 2000, pp. 28)

Pub: Entrepreneur Media Inc.

Ed: Amanda C. Kooser. **Description:** XML is the leading contender to replace HyperText Markup Language (HTML). Extensible Markup Language is more versatile than HTML, and allows for more advanced e-business applications on the Web.

49380 ■ "XML: What's Still Needed for B2B?" in *E-business Advisor* (Vol. 18, No. 5, May 2000, pp. 44)

Pub: Advisor Media, Inc.

Ed: Rik Drummond. **Description:** Order fulfillment is an important component of B2B e-commerce and involved integration of many underlying applications. IT and business managers are finding XML to be a preferred means of integrating applications together into processes. The issues of security, semantics, and the choreography of how the applications interact with each other are discussed.

49381 ■ "You Can Run" in *Entrepreneur* (Vol. 31, No. 6, June 2003, pp. 39)

Pub: Entrepreneur Media Inc.

Ed: Mike Hogan. **Description:** The importance of wireless technology and its impact for small businesses and workers is discussed.

49382 ■ "You hire them to do the tough work, but how easy is it to work with them?" in *E-business Advisor* (Vol. 18, No. 10, Oct. 2000, pp. 12)

Pub: Advisor Media, Inc.

Description: Market researcher and consulting firm the Aberdeen Group predicts that IT firms' spending on professional service automation will grow from $100 million to $1.3 billion by 2003.

49383 ■ "Your Kind of News: Free Personalized Information for the Public" in *Black Enterprise* (Vol. 34, No. 7, February 2004, pp. 140)

Pub: Earl Graves Publishing Co.

Ed: Jennifer L. Smith. **Description:** Profile of a free Website offering articles and press releases from more than 70 major sources on topics relevant to business, including finance and computing.

49384 ■ "Your PC Post Office" in *Hispanic Business* (Vol. 22, No. 1/2, January/February, pp. 88)

Pub: Hispanic Business

Ed: Lamont Wood. **Description:** To print your own postage, all you need is a PC with Internet connection and a printer.

49385 ■ "Zone of Defense" in *Entrepreneur* (Vol. 32, No. 4, April 2004, pp. 42)

Pub: Entrepreneur Media Inc.

Ed: Amanda C. Kooser. **Description:** Profile of ZoneAlarm Pro, a firewall to protect computers from everything from worms to spyware, as well as ad-blockers and cookie controls.

TRADE PERIODICALS

49386 ■ *PC WORLD*

Pub: 101 Communications

Contact: Phil Lemmons, Editorial Dir.

Released: Quarterly. **Price:** $19.97 for 12 issues; $30.97 Canada for 12 issues. **Description:** Technology or business magazine meeting the informational needs of tech-savvy managers, both at work and at home.

49387 ■ *Small Business Systems*

Pub: Charles Moore Associates Inc.

49388 ■ *Software*

Pub: John Wiley & Sons Inc.

Ed: Prof. D.E. Comer, Editor. **Released:** 15/yr. **Price:** $2,510 other countries print; $3,345 institutions, other countries print; $3,680 institutions, other countries print and online combined. **Description:** Journal for those who design, implement, or maintain computer software.

49389 ■ *Telecom Asia*

Pub: Advanstar Communications

Ed: Robert Poe, Editor. **Released:** Monthly. **Price:** $480 Hong Kong only; $86 U.S. (within Asia); $96 U.S. (outside Asia). **Description:** Trade magazine for planning, engineering, and operational managers responsible for the design, installation, marketing, and maintenance of public and private telecom systems and networks in Asia and the Pacific Rim.

VIDEOCASSETTES/ AUDIOCASSETTES

49390 ■ *The Art of Telecommunication*

Bennu Productions, Inc.

350 5th Ave.

New York, NY 10118-0110

Ph:(212)563-8020

Fax: (212)563-8006

Price: $49.95. **Description:** Describes the telephone skills that are an integral part of the business world today. Also discusses office protocol, basic telecommunications equipment, and the facsimile machine. **Availability:** VHS.

49391 ■ *Business World's Guide to Computers*

MPI Home Video

16101 S. 108th Ave.

Orland Park, IL 60467

Ph:(708)460-0555

Free: 800-323-0442

Fax: (708)873-3177

URL: http://www.mpihomevideo.com

Released: 1990. **Price:** $19.98. **Description:** Constant change in the computer industry makes choosing the right computer for your long-term business needs difficult. Top business leaders provide reliable information on what may be the most important purchasing decision a company can make. **Availability:** VHS.

49392 ■ *Micro Video Learning System*

Cambridge Educational

c/o Films Media Group

PO Box 2053

Princeton, NJ 08843-2053

Free: 800-257-5126

Fax: (609)671-0266

Co. E-mail: custserve@filmsmediagroup.com

URL: http://www.cambridgeol.com

Released: 1985. **Description:** A series of instructional tapes about various brands of computer software. **Availability:** VHS.

49393 ■ *WordPerfect 5.0*

American Media, Inc.

4621 121st St.

Urbandale, IA 50323-2311

Ph:(515)224-0919

Free: 888-776-8268

Fax: (515)327-2555

Co. E-mail: custsvc@ammedia.com

URL: http://www.ammedia.com

Released: 1990. **Price:** $39.95. **Description:** No computer experience is necessary to become competent in this word proessing system after watching this course. **Availability:** VHS; 3/4U.

TRADE SHOWS AND CONVENTIONS

49394 ■ Cincinnati Business Expo/Fall

Industry Week

The Penton Media Bldg.

1300 E 9th St., Ste. 316

Cleveland, OH 44114-1503

Ph:(216)696-7000

Fax: (513)528-1131

Co. E-mail: iwinfo@industryweek.com

URL: http://www.industryweek.com

Released: Annual. **Audience:** Business professionals. **Principal Exhibits:** Business services, office equipment, computers, mailing equipment, and office furniture and supplies.

49395 ■ Utah Computer & Business Show/ Tech 20/20

Trade Shows West

2880 S. Main, Ste. 110

Salt Lake City, UT 84115

Ph:(801)485-0176

Free: 800-794-3706

Fax: (801)485-0241

Released: Annual. **Audience:** Infomation management, system integrators, software development, net working, internet, computer aided drafting, computers, word processing, data processing. **Principal Exhibits:** Automated office and business products and related equipment, supplies, and services.

CONSULTANTS

49396 ■ AA Antivirus

1608 W Campbell Ave., Ste. 370

Campbell, CA 95008

Ph:(408)374-8000

Free: 800-478-1828

Fax: (408)374-2045

Co. E-mail: info@aaantivirus.com

URL: http://www.aaantivirus.com

E-mail: info@aaantivirus.com

Scope: A full-service Internet and networking company. Offers a range of local area networking and wide area networking solutions to small and medium sized businesses. Assists business owners and administrators in planning, purchasing and installing networks.

49397 ■ Warren Acuff

4133 Ponca Rd.

Omaha, NE 68112-1123

Ph:(402)451-2805

Fax: (402)451-8303

Scope: Specialists in all phases of computers: micros, minis, and mainframes.

49398 ■ Advanced Network Consulting

475 Park Ave. S Ste. 9

New York, NY 10016

Ph:(212)378-4109

Fax: (212)376-6782

Scope: A provider of LAN consulting as well as hardware and software services. Server-based solutions include backup, antivirus LAN/WAN design, implementation and support, system administration and hardware warrantee contracts, and office automation for small businesses.

49399 ■ Agility Computer Network Services L.L.C.

1332 N Halsted St., Ste. 400

Chicago, IL 60622

Ph:(312)587-9894

Free: 877-244-5484

Fax: (312)587-9948

Co. E-mail: support@agilitynetworks.com

URL: http://www.agilitynetworks.com

E-mail: support@agilitynetworks.com

Scope: Firm provides networking and other related computer consulting services.

49400 ■ Alexander Associates

230 Cotuit Rd.

PO Box 400

Marstons Mills, MA 02648

Ph:(508)428-3000

Fax: (508)428-0935

Co. E-mail: info@alexsoft.com

URL: http://www.alexsoft.com

E-mail: info@alexsoft.com

Scope: Provides computer technology expertise for industrial operations worldwide. Offers outsourced development and application support for a broad spectrum of commercial and not-for-profit entities in Insurance, Health-care, Bio-tech, Communications, Government.

49401 ■ Analytical Solutions
20426 Blythe St.
Winnetka, CA 91306
Ph:(818)998-4774
Free: 800-859-4774
Fax: (818)718-7239
Scope: Enterprise document management and retention system consulting. Data processing system consultant offering local area network expertise and providing feasibility studies, user surveys and system evaluations, systems analyses and design, system development and implementation, project management, disaster planning, corporate strategic planning and sales and marketing group optimization. Serves private industries as well as government agencies.

49402 ■ Bell Industries Tech.logix Group
1960 E Grand Ave., Ste. 560
El Segundo, CA 90245
Ph:(310)563-2355
Free: (866)782-2355
Fax: (310)648-7280
Co. E-mail: information@bellind.com
URL: http://www.belltechlogix.com

E-mail: information@bellind.com
Scope: Experienced in network topologies. Installs, configures, maintains and supports the local and wide area network technologies. Offers connectivity services that includes secure Internet/Intranet communication solutions, virus scanning, and firewall protections.

49403 ■ David L. Boslaugh
44148 Bristow Cir.
Ashburn, VA 20147
Ph:(703)729-2526
Scope: Consultant provides advice on computer systems engineering and integration and software engineering.

49404 ■ Branchline Income Tax Services
5901 Westmnstr Blvd.
Garden Grove, CA 92845
Ph:(714)892-4801
Fax: (714)892-4807
Scope: Offers business financial system design and programming. Specializes in complete system design from concept to final delivery. Provides knowledge of IBM mainframes and PC. Strategic planning utilizes CASE methodology and system development LIFR cycle. Additional expertise in networking and telecommunications and in database system design for business application with very strong user interface. Industries served: aerospace, finance, retail, nonprofit, and automotive.

49405 ■ W.A. Buie Consulting Services
2355 Sumter Dr.
PO Box 857
Garner, NC 27529-0857
Ph:(919)550-3747
Co. E-mail: adrian@hakpenguin.com
URL: http://www.hakpenguin.com

E-mail: adrian@hakpenguin.com
Scope: An Internet service provider for individuals, organizations, or companies. Services include Web site rental, Web page creation, URL submission to search engines and domain name set up.

49406 ■ Business Logic Inc.
220 E 23rd St., Ste. 809
New York, NY 10010
Ph:(212)505-9555
Fax: (212)725-4808
Co. E-mail: blogic@blogicnyc.com
URL: http://www.blogicnyc.com

E-mail: blogic@blogicnyc.com
Scope: Specializes in information systems and technology. Provides a high level of information technology support and development services to companies and governmental organizations of all sizes. Specializes in understanding the business and information needs of organizations and in finding, designing, de-

veloping and implementing solutions to these needs. A large percentage of current projects involve the integration of oracle and sql server databases with web sites, intranet sites, and client server applications. Business Logic is also involved in data warehousing and datamining applications.

49407 ■ Champion Networks L.L.C.
1081 Mere Point Rd.
Brunswick, ME 04011
Ph:(207)725-8903
Fax: (207)721-0186
Co. E-mail: salesrequest@championnetworks.com
URL: http://www.championnetworks.com

E-mail: salesrequest@championnetworks.com
Scope: Firm specializes in network integration, total wide area network solutions, and network services.

49408 ■ Cohn Consulting Corp.
2627 Sandy Plains Rd., Ste. 204
Marietta, GA 30066-4289
Ph:(770)321-5532
Fax: (770)321-4497
Co. E-mail: info@cohnconsultingcorp.com
URL: http://www.cohnconsultingcorp.com

E-mail: info@cohnconsultingcorp.com
Scope: Firm provides a wide range of PC and LAN services.

49409 ■ Colonial Heritage Consultants Ltd.
11808-123 Rancho Bernardo Rd., Ste. 413
PO Box 28744
San Diego, CA 92128
Ph:(858)254-2425
Fax: (858)451-0338
Co. E-mail: bill@colonialheritage.com
URL: http://www.colonialheritage.com

E-mail: bill@colonialheritage.com
Scope: Active in all phases of data processing consulting including scoping company requirements, organizing internal data processing organizations, education, equipment selection, and software consulting/creation. Primary industries of applications in real estate, financial planning, medical, accounting, and legal fields. Serves private industries as well as government agencies. AllPac/SBT Dealer. **Seminars:** Telemagic Users Group; SBT Users Group; Novell Users Group.

49410 ■ Computer Connections Inc.
1241-2 E Dixon Blvd., Ste. 2
PO Box 321
Shelby, NC 28150
Ph:(704)482-0057
Fax: (704)482-0950
Co. E-mail: timwease@carolina.rr.com
URL: http://www.painlesspc.net

E-mail: timwease@carolina.rr.com
Scope: A full service computer company specializing in client/server networking environments. Services, upgrades, and repairs most IBM compatible computers. Networking services include network design, implementation, and administration of Novell and Windows NT networks.

49411 ■ Crawley & Associates Inc.
121 Lincoln Ave.
Fair Lawn, NJ 07410
Ph:(973)636-7350
Free: 877-427-2953
Fax: (973)636-7360
Co. E-mail: sales@crawleyinc.com
URL: http://www.crawleyinc.com

E-mail: sales@crawleyinc.com
Scope: A full-service consulting firm specializing in computer network design, installation and support. Assists with strategic planning, implementation and on-going support of computer information systems.

49412 ■ Creative Associates International Inc.
5301 Wisconsin Ave. NW, Ste. 700
Washington, DC 20015-2015

Ph:(202)966-5804
Fax: (202)363-4771
Co. E-mail: creative@caii.com
URL: http://www.caii-dc.com

E-mail: creative@caii.com
Scope: Supports public, private and non-governmental institutions that are makers and managers of change and transition. Builds the individual and organizational means to join forces for progress through education, information and communication.

49413 ■ Data Concepts
984 S Reading Rd.
Bloomfield Hills, MI 48304
Ph:(248)258-5964
Fax: (248)258-5866
Co. E-mail: sales@rdataconcepts.com

E-mail: sales@rdataconcepts.com
Scope: Data processing consultant offering expertise in the following areas: office automation, feasibility and needs assessment, system design, hardware and software selection, custom program development, database design, networks, spreadsheet templates, computer modeling, sales, training, computer service and upgrades, accounting software and installation of hardware and software. Focus is to offer many professional computer services to small and medium-sized businesses of all types, and government agencies for short and long-term projects. Maintains a network of specialists to assist in multi-dimensional projects.

49414 ■ Del Technology Inc.
7407 E Via Estrella Ave., Ste. 10
Scottsdale, AZ 85258
Ph:(480)483-7588
Fax: (480)483-7533
Scope: Provides services in three areas: management consulting, information technology, and micro business. Focuses on organizational assessment, business process reengineering, quality assurance program development, hardware/software evaluation and acquisition, applications software development, systems integration, LAN support, and new technology training. Industries served: all. **Publications:** "Standards for Information Systems Development and Project Administration". **Seminars:** Organization for Future Technology; Business Reengineering; Managing Successful Projects; Planning and Implementing the Information Systems Architecture; and Successfully Managing the Information Resource.

49415 ■ Dennis M. Dengel
17 Peckham Rd.
Poughkeepsie, NY 12603
Ph:(845)452-2126
Scope: Offers data processing and custom programming in RPG and COBOL for IBM computers. Provides applications for accounts payable/receivable, payroll, general ledger, and inventory. Also repairs and upgrades PCs.

49416 ■ Dimension Data
12120 Sunset Hills Rd., Ste. 550
Reston, VA 20190
Ph:(571)203-4000
Fax: (571)203-4001
URL: http://www.didata.com
Scope: A global technology company. Provides solutions and services that optimize and manage the performance of IT infrastructure to enable businesses to build competitive advantage.

49417 ■ DLM Consultants Inc.
566 Croyden Ct., Ste. 200
Sunnyvale, CA 94087
Ph:(408)736-5650
Fax: (408)733-2384
Scope: Offers contract programming, software and systems development, and seminars and training. Network management, database development, and project management. **Seminars:** How to Be a Computer Consultant; Introduction to Small Business Systems; Use of Spreadsheets in a Small Business Environment; Database Applications in a Small Business Environment.

49418 ■ E-netegrations Inc.
111 Broadway Ave., Ste. 133
PO Box 109
Boise, ID 83705
Ph:(208)343-2541
Free: 877-593-3638
Fax: (208)343-2612
Co. E-mail: support@e-netegrations.com

E-mail: support@e-netegrations.com
Scope: Telecommunications systems installation consultant. Experience ranges from cable splicing to (LAN) Local Area Network, (WAN) Wide Area Network design, engineering, consulting, and communications distributions installation and desktop videoconferencing. **Special Services:** e-access™; e-workplace™.

49419 ■ TRECI/Thomas R. Egan Consulting Inc.
1012 Ronda Ln.
Birmingham, AL 35214
Ph:(205)796-9541
Fax: (205)744-9404
Co. E-mail: tegan@treci.com
URL: http://www.treci.com

E-mail: tegan@treci.com
Scope: Provides consultation and design services, installation, and service/maintenance for several network platforms.

49420 ■ Electronic Solutions Co.
1414 Broadwood Ave.
PO Box 2501
Cinnaminson, NJ 08077
Ph:(856)786-3700
Fax: (856)829-1823
Co. E-mail: info.homeowner@electronicsolutionsco.com
URL: http://www.electronicsolutionsco.com

E-mail: info.homeowner@electronicsolutionsco.com
Scope: Provides services in home automation, home management systems, process control and data communications. **Seminars:** Lighting Control System Design; Advanced Custom System Controllers; Technical Aspects of Whole House Systems; Communication Protocols: The Good, The Bad & The Ugly.

49421 ■ EM Microelectronic-US Inc.
5475 Mark Dabling Blvd., Ste. 200
Colorado Springs, CO 80918-3848
Ph:(719)598-9224
Fax: (719)593-2864
Co. E-mail: info@emmicro-us.com
URL: http://www.emmicroelectronic.com

E-mail: info@emmicro-us.com
Scope: An engineering and computer consultancy serving businesses in the U.S. The firm provides top-quality design, development and technical support.

49422 ■ Enact Expert Systems
59 Dow Ave.
Arlington, MA 02476
Ph:(617)646-7676
Fax: (617)643-1646
Scope: Develops PC & clients/server applications using Visual C, Visual Basic, Access SQL Server, and other tools. Specializes in knowledge-based and decision automation software.

49423 ■ ePartners Inc.
800 5th Ave., Ste. 4100
Seattle, WA 98104
Ph:(425)748-5177
Free: 888-883-9797
Fax: (425)748-5178
Co. E-mail: info@epartnersolutions.com
URL: http://www.epartnersolutions.com

E-mail: info@epartnersolutions.com
Scope: A total solutions provider that designs, develops, implements, integrates, hosts, manages and supports comprehensive eBusiness solutions.

49424 ■ William J. Fejes
7 Renda St.
New Fairfield, CT 06812
Ph:(203)522-2614
Fax: (203)467-0457
Co. E-mail: bill_fejes@timeinc.com

E-mail: bill_fejes@timeinc.com
Scope: Company specializes in information and records management, retention scheduling, information systems, integrating imaging technology with optical disk, space planning, off-site record storage, and disaster planning systems.

49425 ■ Frankel and Topche P.C.
1700 Galloping Hill Rd.
Kenilworth, NJ 07033
Ph:(908)298-7700
Fax: (908)298-7701
Co. E-mail: info@frankelandtopche.com
URL: http://www.frankelandtopche.com

E-mail: info@frankelandtopche.com
Scope: Offers financial consulting for closely held businesses. Assists in mergers and acquisitions, tax planning, strategic business planning, family succession planning, accounting, auditing, and obtaining financing. The firm serves small businesses in the service, retail, wholesale, and manufacturing industries. Specializes in real estate, lumber and building materials, and service businesses.

49426 ■ Frazier Consulting Service Inc.
207 N Main St.
PO Box 957
Leland, MS 38756
Ph:(662)686-7324
Fax: (662)686-4446
Co. E-mail: alf@tecinfo.com

E-mail: alf@tecinfo.com
Scope: Agricultural consultants interested in investigation of special agricultural problems-crop damage, chemical drift, products liability, disease, insects, weeds and other problems. Industries served: insurance companies, farmers, attorneys, and chemical companies.

49427 ■ Gimbel Associates
71 Longview Dr.
Churchville, PA 18966-1636
Ph:(215)357-8830
Fax: (781)723-8941
Co. E-mail: bigjgimbel@aol.com
URL: http://www.gimbelassociates.com

E-mail: bigjgimbel@aol.com
Scope: Help organizations create, utilize, analyze and manage information. Specializes in helping small businesses select and install microcomputers and integrate microcomputer-based applications into their organizations. **Seminars:** How to Become a Successful Consultant in Your Own Field; How to Computerize Your Small Business. **Special Services:** Is Microrim Rbase consultant. Offers LANtastic network support.

49428 ■ Glades Crop Care Inc.
949 Turner Quay
Jupiter, FL 33458
Ph:(561)746-3740
Fax: (561)746-3775
Co. E-mail: cmellinger@gladescropcare.com
URL: http://www.gladescropcare.com

E-mail: cmellinger@gladescropcare.com
Scope: Offers customized crop health management programs, development and implementation of vegetable IPM programs, professional custom field research of age chemicals and biotechnology products for residue, efficacy performance studies and breeding. Crops: vegetables, citrus, sugarcane, turf, rice and ornaments. Food safety consultation and certified 3rd party audits. **Seminars:** Getting the Most for Your Money: An Effective Weed Control Program.

49429 ■ GlobalNET Corp.
12845 Capricorn St.
Stafford, TX 77477

Ph:(281)240-4321
Fax: (281)240-4003
Scope: Specializes in the installation, configuration, and technical support of local (LAN) and wide (WAN) Area Networks. Installs Multi-User and Multi-Platform systems (i.e. DOS, OS2, Windows NT, UNIX, NextStep, and Macintosh) which perform Accounting, client/server Database, Word Processing, Spreadsheet, and Computer Aide Design (CAD) tasks in a variety of industries. **Seminars:** Networking training services.

49430 ■ Gnossos Software Inc.
1720 I St. NW, Ste. 510
Washington, DC 20006
Ph:(202)463-1200
Free: (866)676-2525
Fax: (202)785-9562
Co. E-mail: support@gnossos.com
URL: http://www.gnossos.com

E-mail: support@gnossos.com
Scope: Provides productivity solutions for clients who automate with personal computers (PCs). Offers a full range of micro-software training, consulting, and applications development nationally and internationally. Assists with gaining competitive advantage through the strategic use of PCs. Industries served: trade associations, large corporations, venture start-ups, and law firms.

49431 ■ GSC Associates Inc.
2727 Xanthia Ct.
Denver, CO 80238-2611
Ph:(303)388-6355
Co. E-mail: info@gscassociates.com
URL: http://www.gscassociates.com

E-mail: info@gscassociates.com
Scope: Computer design consultants and systems integrators. **Publications:** "A Measurement and Monitoring System for Tracking and Visualizing Collaboration Metrics in Real-time and for Later Analysis", Jun. 2005; "UML and Human Performance Modeling", Mar. 2005;

49432 ■ High-Tech Enterprise Solutions Inc.
13 East A St.
Brunswick, MD 21716-1406
Ph:(301)834-5778
Fax: (301)834-5587
Co. E-mail: info@high-techus.com
URL: http://www.high-techus.com

E-mail: info@high-techus.com
Scope: Data processing consultancy specializing in total computer systems integration and support. Provides the technical support that you expect to handle repairs, installations, and other issues after the sale.

49433 ■ IMC Internet
355 Sackett Point Rd., Ste. 13
North Haven, CT 06473
Ph:(203)949-1688
Free: 800-840-9989
Fax: (203)269-9963
Co. E-mail: info@imcinternet.net
URL: http://www.imcinternet.net

E-mail: info@imcinternet.net
Scope: Specializes in the development of total office solutions for business, which includes office networking, client/ server technologies, internet access and computer sales.

49434 ■ InteleNet Communications Inc.
17222 Von Karman Ave.
Irvine, CA 92614
Ph:(949)784-4000
Free: (866)211-4436
Fax: (949)851-1088
Co. E-mail: support@intelenet.com
URL: http://www.intelenet.net

E-mail: support@intelenet.com
Scope: Offers expert consulting services in the following areas: connectivity, support and maintenance;

LAN/WAN design, installation, support and maintenance; systems administration; software development and design, installation, support and maintenance of ISDN-based telecommuting applications.

49435 ■ Interface Computer Associates
PO Box 70023
Reno, NV 89502
Ph:(775)857-8777
Free: 800-379-3839
Fax: (775)857-2567
Co. E-mail: icanv@icanv.com
URL: http://www.icanv.com

E-mail: icanv@icanv.com
Scope: Data processing consultants offering complete system design, implementation and training for end-users, particularly in small businesses. Operates on the concept of providing systems to meet individual needs and then actually interfacing new computer users and their systems together: with the goal of the computer doing business the way the client does business, not the other way around. **Seminars:** Develops specialized training applications to instruct clients how to not only exist within their computer environments, but how to change them as well.

49436 ■ KCS Computer Technology Inc.
9524 Franklin Ave.
Franklin Park, IL 60131
Ph:(847)288-9820
Fax: (847)288-9822
Co. E-mail: sales@kcstech.com
URL: http://www.kcstech.com

E-mail: sales@kcstech.com
Scope: Computer consulting firm specializing in software and computer reselling, Windows NT, Lantastic and Novell network installation and maintenance, custom programming, network communications fax/modem server installation and maintenance, Internet setup and training, custom html programming services, network and phone cabling, computer leasing, data conversion and data recovery and maintenance contracts.

49437 ■ KeyLAN Consulting Inc.
PO Box 333
North Gower, ON, Canada K0A 2T0
Ph:(613)489-2336
Fax: (613)489-4190
Co. E-mail: keylan@keylan.ca
URL: http://www.keylan.ca

E-mail: keylan@keylan.ca
Scope: Specializes in all facets of local area networking, including purchasing, installation, administration, training, automation, disaster planning, high security databases, and security consulting.

49438 ■ LAN Solutions
449 Hillway Dr.
Emerald Hills, CA 94062-3313
Ph:(650)261-1300
Fax: (650)361-8012
Co. E-mail: info@lansol.com
URL: http://www.lansol.com

E-mail: info@lansol.com
Scope: Microsoft Windows 98, NT, 2000, XP, ME, 2003, network PC desktop integrator consultant offering Microsoft MCSE certified installation, service and consulting. Services include network design and needs analysis, CD-Rom and FAX design and installation, network and Internet e-mail design and installation, network troubleshooting and diagnostics, network performance optimization, system manager and user training and network cabling installation.

49439 ■ LBC Networks
675 King St. W, Ste. 210
Toronto, ON, Canada M5V 1M9
Ph:(416)727-9200
Fax: (416)929-1173
URL: http://www.lbcnetworks.com
Scope: Services include Novell to NT migration, firewall and Internet security, support, Linux, email solutions, virtual private networks, data wiring, network management, and web design.

49440 ■ Liberty Net
3624 Market St.
Philadelphia, PA 19104
Ph:(215)387-6440
Free: 888-865-7624
Fax: (215)387-2333
Co. E-mail: info@libertynet.org

E-mail: info@libertynet.org
Scope: Firm specializes in Internet programming and web development. programs include UNIX, Perl, CGI, and GIS.

49441 ■ Jerome W. McGee & Associates
7826 Eastern Ave. NW, Ste. 30
Washington, DC 20012-1324
Ph:(202)726-7272
Fax: (202)726-2946
Scope: Business consultants experienced in office automation, small business management, invention and patent counseling, technology commercialization, loan packaging and business plan development. **Seminars:** Marketing Research for the High-Technology Business; Introduction to Microcomputers; Marketing Technological Products to Industry; How to Evaluate Your Technical Idea; Patenting Your Own Invention.

49442 ■ MindLabs.net
317 N Broad St., Ste. 402
Philadelphia, PA 19107
Ph:(215)923-4447
Co. E-mail: email@mindlabs.net
URL: http://www.mindlabs.net

E-mail: email@mindlabs.net
Scope: Provides Solutions include website design and development, website makeovers, ongoing maintenance and support, website hosting, and Internet marketing.

49443 ■ Morgan Parker & Johnson Inc.
45 Wall St., Ste. 2201
New York, NY 10005-1918
Ph:(212)968-1100
Fax: (212)308-1565
Co. E-mail: info@mpj.com
URL: http://www.mpj.com

E-mail: info@mpj.com
Scope: A New York-based corporation which serves the needs of banks, brokerage firms and other financial concerns by providing consultants and consultant teams to solve challenges in "computer and people systems" technology. Assists in the design and use of technology which serves users. Specializes in the areas of Enterprise Computing (both data driven and process control driver), Methodologies/Tools and Object and Neural Technology. Expertise also includes object-oriented program development and client server systems. **Seminars:** Firm conducts seminars including Objects Made Easy, Client/Server Object Oriented Development, and others. **Special Services:** Offers a mentoring program which provides Immersion Training for existing employees in VisualWorks SmallTalk.

49444 ■ Mountain Realty Inc.
590 Main St.
PO Box 349
Young Harris, GA 30582
Ph:(706)379-3115
Free: 800-201-5526
Fax: (706)379-2575
Co. E-mail: chuck@ssg-i.com
URL: http://www.ssg-i.com

E-mail: chuck@ssg-i.com
Scope: Specializes in custom applications and systems development for micro and mid-range business systems. Industries served: manufacturing, retail, construction, and general office automation.

49445 ■ P. Murphy & Associates Inc.
4405 Riverside Dr., Ste. 105
Burbank, CA 91505-4050
Ph:(818)841-2002

Fax: (818)841-2122
Co. E-mail: jody@pmurphy.com
URL: http://www.pmurphy.com

E-mail: jody@pmurphy.com
Scope: Computer consultant firm. Provides staff on a contract, contract-to-hire or direct placement basis.

49446 ■ Richard D. Murphy
5212 Spring Ave.
Kansas City, MO 64133
Ph:(816)356-5827
Fax: (816)358-3076
Scope: Offers scientific and engineering services and computer consulting. Services include: general technical advice (engineering and scientific industries), accident reconstruction (legal profession), scientific computations (advice, algorithms, program development), and small business computer assistance (software development and hardware advice). Serves private industries as well as government agencies.

49447 ■ Net Transforms Inc.
520 Herndon Pky., Ste. B
Herndon, VA 20170
Ph:(703)464-0042
Free: 888-291-0120
Fax: (703)464-5825
Co. E-mail: info@nettransforms.com; sales@ nettransforms.com
URL: http://www.ntllc.com

E-mail: info@nettransforms.com; sales@ nettransforms.com
Scope: Principal focus is the application of information technologies to enhance the effectiveness of the business environment, including collecting, organizing and storing information; and designing, building and maintaining the appropriate architecture to make information available.

49448 ■ NetKnowledge Technologies L.L.C.
300 Pistachio Cir.
Irving, TX 75063
Ph:(214)213-6226
Fax: (972)910-0059
Co. E-mail: info@dassnagar.com
URL: http://www.nktllc.com

E-mail: info@dassnagar.com
Scope: Works with executives worldwide to solve pressing business problems through the integration of business strategy and operations; information technology; and change management. **Special Services:** An application that allows users to receive and pay all utility bills online using the web, corporate Intranets, or Extranets as well as broadcast the bills using push technology.

49449 ■ Networked Solutions Inc.
4280 Caparosa Cir.
Melbourne, FL 32940
Ph:(321)259-3242
Fax: (321)259-3846
Co. E-mail: info@ensusa.com
URL: http://www.ensusa.com

E-mail: info@ensusa.com
Scope: Company capabilities include requirements analysis, computer system setup, network design and installation, software development, and training and support. Specializes in simultaneous Internet web and email access via LAN.

49450 ■ Paladin Consultants L.L.C.
11 Beech Ct.
Chatham, NJ 07928
Ph:(973)635-0080
Fax: (973)701-8151
Co. E-mail: info@atpaladn.com
URL: http://www.paladn.com

E-mail: info@atpaladn.com
Scope: Versatile designer of business systems and custom software for small and medium-sized businesses. Database and scientific applications is a specialty. Industries served: all.

49451 ■ Parachute Computer Services Inc.
3500 Oakmont Ste. 101
Austin, TX 78765
Ph:(512)374-1898
Fax: (512)374-9753
Scope: LAN/WAN services, on-site consultation, remote administration, and training. **Seminars:** Offers on-site training for clients of all ages and skill levels, in Microsoft Office and GoldMine 4.0.

49452 ■ Perceptive Technology Corp.
11309 Park Central Pl.
Dallas, TX 75230
Ph:(214)368-0900
URL: http://www.perceptive.net
Scope: Services include, business web site design and hosting, Internet connectivity, web server co-location, Intranet design, LAN/WAN design and consulting.

49453 ■ Priority Process Associates Inc.
1236 E Horseshoe Bend Ct.
Rochester Hills, MI 48306
Ph:(248)608-8966
Fax: (248)608-8966
Scope: A management consulting firm with expertise in computer technology, telecommunications, and information services. Provides the following specific services: business process re-engineering-establishes correctly implemented, computer technologies that empower and accelerate work groups to act autonomously but in concert with corporate goals, document work-flow analysis-models and simulates the flow of documents through selected organizational processes, enterprise metrics-identifies unique metrics for enterprises to evaluate their continuous improvement of business processes, cost justification-identifies value using Activity Based Costing and innovative approaches to quantify time-to-market reductions, project profitability, and reduce and manage costs, proposal development-generates Requests for Proposals to solicit competitive quotations for cost effective off-the-shelf software, computer hardware, and communication products, implementation planning-negotiates implementation plans for clients through qualified software vendors, custom software integrators, and hardware, communication, and outsource suppliers, project auditing-audits the integration, installation and use of on-time, quality enterprise multi-vendor software, hardware and communications systems on computer networks, training-expands clients knowledge through information sources, and client-specific management seminars and skill building workshops. Serves manufacturing industries in the United States.

49454 ■ R&S Design Computer Services Inc.
10 W Fron St.
Media, PA 19063
Ph:(610)565-5523
Fax: (610)892-3983
Co. E-mail: info@rsdesign.com
URL: http://www.rsdesign.com

E-mail: info@rsdesign.com
Scope: Offers the sale, installation and configuration of PC software for business and home use. Also offers training for a wide variety of software applications, and maintenance and repair of hardware and network systems.

49455 ■ Research Applications Inc.
414 Hungerford Dr., Ste. 220
Rockville, MD 20850-4125
Ph:(301)251-6717
Free: 888-311-6221
Fax: (301)251-6719
Co. E-mail: dfriedman@researchapps.com
URL: http://www.researchapps.com

E-mail: dfriedman@researchapps.com
Scope: Offers counsel on the development and administration of job performance evaluation and assessment, cognitive ability tests, large scale survey administration, management training, logistical support for meetings and conferences, computer pro-

gramming support for survey and test and measurement projects, and development of financial, auditing and training software for small business. International experts and specialists in the development of mail test decks to test United States and foreign-made postal handling equipment. Specialists in computer generated and computer adaptive achievement test design and administration. Serves private industries as well as government agencies. **Seminars:** Gender Awareness in the Workplace; Humor in the Workplace; Understanding and Using Assessments (Validity/Reliability); Diversity in the Workplace; Structured Interviews.

49456 ■ S & S Office Solutions Inc.
3480 Johnson Ferry Rd.
Roswell, GA 30075
Ph:(770)518-0868
Fax: (770)518-4483
Co. E-mail: info@ssos.com
URL: http://www.ssos.com

E-mail: info@ssos.com
Scope: Specialists in designing, installing, and consulting for LANs (Local Area Networks) and wiring systems for professional offices (MCSE). **Special Services:** Microsoft certified partner.

49457 ■ SBA Computers Inc.
922 Talon Dr.
O'Fallon, IL 62269
Ph:(618)628-9590
Fax: (618)622-3717
Co. E-mail: info@sbacomputers.com
URL: http://www.sbacomputers.com

E-mail: info@sbacomputers.com
Scope: Provides web site and domain hosting. Also offers domain registration services.

49458 ■ Schneider Associates
1485 Chain Bridge Rd., Ste. 201
McLean, VA 22101
Ph:(703)442-8927
Fax: (703)442-8929
Co. E-mail: schnassoc@aol.com

E-mail: schnassoc@aol.com
Scope: Information consultants specializing in the design and implementation of data and information processing systems for litigation support. Specializes in the development of software packages for the storage and retrieval of information describing documents, exhibits, transcripts, and events of legal cases. **Seminars:** Provides inhouse seminars on modern litigation methods ranging from general overviews to specific topics such as document control, various methods of document processing, selecting litigation support vendors, etc. **Special Services:** Developed FIND-IT and FINDLAW litigation support software.

49459 ■ Simplified Technology Co.
PO Box 8281
Fremont, CA 94537
Ph:(510)794-5520
Free: 800-782-4435
Co. E-mail: sales200521@simplifiedtechnology.com
URL: http://www.simplifiedtechnology.com

E-mail: sales200521@simplifiedtechnology.com
Scope: Firm specializes in providing system security, networking, custom software development and data availability.

49460 ■ Michael Slavitch Consulting
62 Renfrew Ave.
Ottawa, ON, Canada K1S 1Z4
Ph:(613)234-5149
Co. E-mail: slavitch@loran.com
URL: http://www.slavitch.com/cv.html

E-mail: slavitch@loran.com

49461 ■ SON Systems International Inc.
PO Box 517
Chadds Ford, PA 19317
Free: 800-525-8211

Fax: (484)631-0513
Co. E-mail: bisolutions@sonsystems.com
URL: http://www.sonsystems.com

E-mail: bisolutions@sonsystems.com
Scope: Computer consultant and software provider.

49462 ■ Systems Alternatives International L. L.C.
1705 Indian Wood Cir., Ste. 100
Maumee, OH 43537
Ph:(419)891-1100
Fax: (419)891-1045
Co. E-mail: sales@sysalt.com
URL: http://www.sysalt.com

E-mail: sales@sysalt.com
Scope: Firm specializes in selling hardware and software. Provides innovative software and quality information technology services to the unique needs of the recycling and metals industries.

49463 ■ Taranto & Associates Inc.
144 Duran Dr.
PO Box 6216
San Rafael, CA 94903
Ph:(415)472-2670
Free: 800-522-8649
Fax: (415)472-2673
Co. E-mail: irwin@taranto.com
URL: http://www.taranto.com

E-mail: irwin@taranto.com
Scope: Provides computer systems and programming services with emphasis on helping the small business operate more efficiently. Recent experience with retail pet shops and apparel merchants, but has served all types of retail stores, and with auction processing for professional auctioneers and nonprofit organizations. Can set up complete turn-key systems anywhere in the U.S. **Special Services:** The AUCTIONEER; ProAUCTIONEER.

49464 ■ Verbit & Co.
19 Bala Ave.
Bala Cynwyd, PA 19004
Ph:(610)668-9840
Scope: The management consulting services of Verbit & Company apply to practically every facet of a business, from operations and administration to financial and information systems management. These services include: general management - to assist executives and managers fulfill their mission and to assure that adequate planning of day-to-day operations occurs; that controls are sufficient to safeguard valuable resources; and that results of decisions are reviewed in sufficient time to effect continuing action. Financial planning and control - to develop accounting, budgeting, forecasting, and other information systems for the management of resources and evaluation of strategies. Information systems and electronic data processing - to promote efficient and effective use of computers in company operations; operations planning and control - to design systems to promote effective management of production facilities; cost accounting and management - to design systems to record and report costs of operations; and human resources - to review organizational structures, personnel planning and compensation programs. Other services include: evaluation of desk-top computer systems for small firms; CAD/CAM implementation plan and orderly introduction of CAD/CAM to client company; and public sector services to assist with evaluation and implementation of governmental accounting systems and law enforcement information systems. Industries served: manufacturing, distribution, metals casting, equipment and components, professional services, healthcare, retail, nonprofit, and government. **Seminars:** Presents seminars on Integrating Manufacturing Management Systems with Business Systems; Negotiating Information Systems Agreements with Suppliers. **Special Services:** Low volume document/image scanning; low volume document scanning -OCR editing.

49465 ■ Waters Instruments Inc.
13705 26th Ave. N, Ste. 102
Plymouth, MN 55441

Ph:(763)551-1125
Fax: (763)509-7450
URL: http://www.wtrs.com

49466 ■ WNF Consulting Inc.
PO Box 42118
Phoenix, AZ 85080
Ph:(480)940-4808
Co. E-mail: info@wnf.com
URL: http://www.wnf.com

E-mail: info@wnf.com
Scope: Firm specializes in network analysis and design. Consulting engineers assist in understanding the characteristics of each network resource and segment, optimization of network hierarchy based on usage requirements, system performance and effective resource utilization, optimization of pooled server and application configurations, storage management methodology for day-to-day storage management, and storage management methodology for automated storage management. **Special Services:** Identity Management Service.

49467 ■ Zentek Computer Consulting
5222 Woodlawn St.
Bellaire, TX 77401
Ph:(713)667-8228
Co. E-mail: zentek@acm.org
URL: http://www.zentekconsulting.com

E-mail: zentek@acm.org
Scope: Provides computer management and support for small business. Specializes in supporting and training physicians, attorneys, and executives.

COMPUTERIZED DATABASES

49468 ■ *SOFTBASE: Reviews, Companies, and Products*
Guide IT LLC
1173 Colusa Ave.
PO Box 8120
Berkeley, CA 94707
Ph:(510)525-6220
Fax: (510)525-1568
Co. E-mail: softbase@searchsoftbase.com
URL: http://www.searchsoftbase.com
Description: Contains information on the Information Technology industry, with detailed descriptions on more than 12,000 information technology products.

Includes company information, including personnel names, addresses, telephone numbers, URLs, e-mails, and a description of the company. Product information includes system requirements, availability, vendor support, and a product description. These product and company descriptions are linked to independent third-party reviews abstracted from more than 200 trade journals and industry magazines. **Availability:** Online: Guide IT LLC, Thomson Dialog, Thomson Dialog, CSA. **Type:** Bibliographic; Directory.

LIBRARIES

49469 ■ Chicago Public Library Central Library–Business/Science/Technology Division
Harold Washington Library Center
400 S. State St., 4th Fl.
Chicago, IL 60605
Ph:(312)747-4450
Fax: (312)747-4975
URL: http://www.chipublib.org/001hwlc/hwbst.html
Contact: Marcia Dellenbach, BST Div.Chf.
Scope: Small business, marketing, technology, corporate reports, investments, management, personnel, patents, physical and biological sciences, medicine, health, computer science, careers, environmental information, gardening, cookbooks. **Services:** Interlibrary loan; copying; division open to the public. **Holdings:** 415,000 books; 52,100 bound periodical volumes; 33,000 reels of microfilm; Securities and Exchange Commission (SEC) reports; federal specifications and standards; American National Standards Institute standards; corporate Annual reports. **Subscriptions:** 4000 journals and other serials; 8 newspapers.

49470 ■ IBM Canada, Ltd.–Research Information Centre
3600 Steeles Ave., E.
F2/270
Markham, ON, Canada L3R 9Z7
Ph:(905)316-5000
Fax: (905)316-2535
Co. E-mail: awharton@ca.ibm.com
URL: http://www.ibm.com/ca/en/
Contact: Anne Wharton, Res.Coord.
Scope: Market intelligence, information technology. **Services:** Center not open to the public. **Holdings:** Books; magazines. **Subscriptions:** 80 journals and other serials; 5 newspapers.

49471 ■ Lexington Community College–Learning Resource Center
221 Oswald Bldg.
Cooper Dr.
Lexington, KY 40506-0235
Ph:(859)246-6380
Fax: (859)246-4675
Co. E-mail: charles.james@kctcs.edu
URL: http://www.bluegrass.kctcs.edu/LCC/LIB/
Contact: Charles James, Lib.Dir.
Scope: Associated health technologies, computer information systems, business technology, undergraduate general education. **Services:** Interlibrary loan; copying; Library open to the public. **Holdings:** 37,000 volumes. **Subscriptions:** 218 journals and other serials.

49472 ■ York Technical College–Anne Springs Close Library
452 S. Anderson Rd.
Rock Hill, SC 29732
Ph:(803)327-8025
Fax: (803)327-4535
Co. E-mail: kjones@yorktech.com
URL: http://www.yorktech.com/library
Contact: Kristine Jones, Hd.Libn.
Scope: Industrial engineering technology, health and human services, business and office systems technology, liberal arts, computer science. **Services:** Interlibrary loan; Library open to the public. **Holdings:** 27,000 books; 50,574 microforms; 1813 videocassettes. **Subscriptions:** 475 journals and other serials; 13 newspapers; 40 databases.

RESEARCH CENTERS

49473 ■ Organizational Systems Research Association
UPO 2478
Department of Information Systems
Morehead State University
Morehead, KY 40351-1689
Ph:(606)783-2718
Fax: (606)783-5025
Co. E-mail: d.everett@morehead-st.edu
URL: http://www.osra.org
Contact: Dr. Donna R. Everett, Exec.Dir.
E-mail: d.everett@morehead-st.edu
Scope: End-user systems as an academic discipline, focusing on analysis, design, and administration of interrlated end-user information support systems. **Publications:** Information Technology, Learning, and Performance Journal. **Educational Activities:** Research conference (annually).

START-UP INFORMATION

49474 ■ "Office Search Engine" in *Success* **(Vol. 47, No. 1, January 2000, pp. 23)**
Pub: Success Publishing, Inc.
Ed: David Carnoy. **Description:** Offices2share.com finds corporate space for start-ups.

49475 ■ "Setting Up a Productive Home Office" in *Home Business* **(Vol. 12, October 2005, No. 5, pp. 82, 84)**
Pub: Home Business Magazine
Ed: Aliza Pilar, Sherman Risdahl. **Description:** Things to consider when purchasing furniture, hardware, software and electronics for a small home-based business are examined.

49476 ■ "Yours, Mine, Ours" in *My Business* **(October/November 2002, pp. 35-37)**
Pub: My Business Magazine
Ed: Kathleen Landis. **Description:** The benefits of sharing office space by small businesses are discussed. This method works especially well for startups and home offices that are expanding. Various firms successfully using this concept are profiled.

ASSOCIATIONS AND OTHER ORGANIZATIONS

49477 ■ Independent Office Products and Furniture Dealers Association
301 N Fairfax St.
Alexandria, VA 22314
Ph:(703)549-9040
Free: 800-542-6672
Fax: (703)683-7552
Co. E-mail: info@iopfda.org
URL: http://www.iopfda.org
Contact: Chris Bates, Pres.
Description: Distributors of new and recycled office furniture and office accessories. Explores the effect of the office environment on productivity and quality of life; encourages effective utilization of contract sales staff in an attempt to anticipate the changing nature of the office furnishings market. Serves independent dealers and works with their trading partners to develop programs and opportunities that help strengthen the dealer position in the marketplace. Sponsors specialized forums to offer members targeted networking, educational programming and industry promotional opportunities. **Publications:** Membership Directory (annual).

49478 ■ International Association of Lighting Designers
Merchandise Mart, Ste. 9-104
200 World Trade Ctr.
Chicago, IL 60654
Ph:(312)527-3677
Fax: (312)527-3680
Co. E-mail: marsha@iald.org
URL: http://www.iald.org

Contact: Marsha L. Turner CAE, Exec.VP
Membership: Represents professionals, educators, students, and others working in the field of lighting design worldwide. **Purpose:** Promotes the benefits of quality lighting design and emphasizes the potential impact of lighting on architectural design and environmental quality. Furthers professional standards of lighting designers and seeks to increase their function in the interior design industry. Sponsors national awards program, summer intern program for qualified college students interested in lighting design as a profession, and career development lectures and seminars. **Publications:** *e-Reflections* (monthly) ; *International Association of Lighting Designers— Membership Directory* (annual); *Why Hire an IALD Lighting Designer?*.

49479 ■ National Association of Display Industries
3595 Sheridan St., Ste. 200
Hollywood, FL 33021
Ph:(954)893-7225
Fax: (954)893-8375
Co. E-mail: nadi@nadi-global.com
URL: http://www.nadi-global.com
Contact: Klein Merriman, Exec.Dir.
Description: Represents and promotes the visual merchandising profession. **Publications:** *NADIrect to You* (bimonthly); *NADI's Visual Merchandising/Store Planning Design Directory* (periodic).

49480 ■ Planning and Visual Education Partnership
3595 Sheridan St., Ste. 200
Hollywood, FL 33021
Ph:(954)893-7300
Fax: (954)893-8375
Co. E-mail: pave@p-a-v-e.info
URL: http://p-a-v-e.info
Contact: Greg M. Gorman, Chm.
Membership: Retail executives, visual merchandisers, store planners, architects, specifiers, students. **Purpose:** Seeks to educate and motivate members and encourage interaction among their related fields. Holds annual design competition; offers an internship program; donates proceeds of shows toward financial aid for students.

REFERENCE WORKS

49481 ■ "The ABCs of setting up a home office" in *Women in Business* **(Vol. 54, No. 5, September-October 2002, pp. 23)**
Pub: The ABWA Company, Inc.
Ed: Kathleen Isaacson. **Description:** Necessary equipment, possible financing and requisite legislation for home offices are discussed.

49482 ■ "Answer the Call" in *Entrepreneur* **(Vol. 33, September 2005, No. 9, pp. 32)**
Pub: Entrepreneur Media Inc.
Ed: Amanda C. Kooser. **Description:** Many small companies are switching from land phone lines to cellular phones for office use and employees on the road.

49483 ■ "Atlanta's Top 25 Commercial Interior Design Firms" in *Atlanta Business Chronicle* **(Vol. 25, No. 21, November 1, 2002, pp. 28C)**
Pub: American City Business Publications, Inc.
Description: The top 25 commercial interior design companies in the Atlanta, Georgia area are ranked by design fees in 2001. Among other data listed are the number of Atlanta area employees including designers, and services focused upon and kinds of facilities.

49484 ■ "The Automated Agent" in *Rough Notes* **(Vol. 146, No. 9, September 2003, pp. 92)**
Pub: Rough Notes
Ed: Michael J. Weinberg. **Description:** An examination of newer technology making work easier and more efficient for insurance agents. Topics include laptops, cell phones, and email accounts.

49485 ■ "Automatic Turn-Off" in *My Business* **(April/May 2002, pp. 47)**
Pub: My Business Magazine
Description: According to Energize America Education, installing occupancy sensors can reduce office lighting energy use by 25-50 percent and up to 75 percent in warehouses and restrooms.

49486 ■ "Automation Accountability" in *Rough Notes* **(Vol. 145, No. 1, January 2003, pp. 82)**
Pub: Rough Notes
Ed: Nancy Doucette. **Description:** Mary Eisenhart and Cherly Koch are business consultants who advise that agencies that shift to automation should not only fully utilize the new system, but ought to also change the procedure to obtain the return on investment.

49487 ■ "Boxing Match" in *Entrepreneur* **(Vol. 33, September 2005, No. 9, pp. 32)**
Pub: Entrepreneur Media Inc.
Ed: Jill Amadio. **Description:** Due to their spacious rear cargo compartments, low lift-over and soaring ceiling heights, the new boxy styled vehicles may be well-suited to small businesses.

49488 ■ "Build a Better Business" in *Black Enterprise* **(Vol. 35, October 2004, No. 3, pp. 136)**
Pub: Earl G. Graves Publishing Co. Inc.
Ed: Robert Anthony, Sonya A. Donaldson. **Description:** Emerging new technologies can help small businesses seem larger than they really are. Co-founder of Krazy Kickz, Sam Robinson, tells how upgrading the company's phone system led to a better customer service system.

49489 ■ "B.Y.O. GPS" in *Business 2.0* **(Vol. 6, September 2005, No. 8, pp. 132)**
Pub: Time, Inc.
Ed: Matthew Maier. **Description:** Owning your own portable GPS system is a wiser choice than the renting the costly units offered by car rental companies. Reviews of the Magellan RoadMate 760, Palm GPS Navigator, Microsoft Streets & Trips 2005 are included.

49490 ■ "Changing Spaces" in *My Business* (June/July 2004, pp. 12-13)
Pub: My Business Magazine
Ed: Lee Gimpel. Description: Companies are discovering they don't have to be in the creative industry to benefit from inspired office design.

49491 ■ "Checking Inn at the Office" in *Home Office Computing* (Vol. 18, No. 10, October 2000, pp. 92)
Pub: Scholastic Inc.
Ed: William Van Winkle. Description: While sending workers home lets a company move to smaller quarters, thus saving money, the firm still needs to accommodate telecommuters and mobile workers when they do come in, whether its for two days, a week, or only one day per month. Firms are looking to a practical solution: hoteling. Most hoteling spaces are designed by architectural and planning firms to make the workplace comfortable and inviting for transient workers.

49492 ■ "A Clean Sweep: Take Your Work Environment from Cluttered to Clear with these Steps" in *Entrepreneur* (Vol. 32, July 2004, No. 7)
Pub: Entrepreneur Media Inc.
Ed: Romanus Wolter. Description: Ways to create a work environment conducive to accomplishing multiple tasks are listed.

49493 ■ *Complete Guide to Building & Outfitting an Office in Your Home*
Pub: Betterway Books
Ed: Jerry Germer. Released: 1994. Price: $18.99.

49494 ■ "Cruising in the Corner Office" in *Business Week* (January 16, 2006, No. 3967, pp. 62, 64)
Pub: McGraw-Hill Companies
Ed: Larry Armstrong. Description: Howard Becker's van conversions offer all the conveniences of a corner office for the busy executive. Custom features can include satellite TV antenna and telephone systems, PC with high-speed Internet, toilet and tanks, aviation-style LED lighting, independent rear suspension, and electric window shades.

49495 ■ "Data Disposal Questions" in *Hispanic Business* (Vol. 23, No. 7/8, July/August 2001, pp. 112, 114)
Pub: Hispanic Business
Ed: Roger Harris. Description: The legal, technical, and financial issues involved in disposing office equipment are discussed.

49496 ■ "Ergonomics & Economics" in *Crain's Detroit Business* (Vol. 21, November 7, 2005, No. 45, pp. 1)
Pub: Crain Communications Inc. - Detroit
Ed: Amy Lane. Description: A Michigan advisory committee is meeting to devise rules to govern how employers must identify and address workplace conditions that put workers at risk for job-related injuries caused by repetitive motion, force and other factors. Business lobbyists charge the committee's work violates a provision of the Department of Labor and Economic Growth budget that prohibits the use of state funds to develop mandates stronger than federal voluntary ergonomics guidelines.

49497 ■ "Everything in its Place: Can the Art of Feng Shui Help You Optimize Your Business?" in *Entrepreneur* (Vol. 32, August 2004, No. 8)
Pub: Entrepreneur Media Inc.
Ed: Gwen Moran. Description: According to Jami Lin, consultant at Feng-Shui-Interior-Design.com, feng shui, the Chinese art of placement can dramatically increase a store's appeal.

49498 ■ "Firms Will Spend Less on Buildings and Equipment This Year" in *Kiplinger Letter* (Vol. 78, January 19, 2007, No. 2)
Pub: Kiplinger
Description: Small business will spend about 2 percent less in building and equipment purchases in 2007. Industrial equipment, telecommunications and diesel engines will be the hardest hit.

49499 ■ "Fitting Home Offices Into Small Spaces" in *Home Business* (Vol. 12, March/April 2005, No. 2, pp. 82, 84-87)
Pub: Home Business Magazine
Ed: Aliza Sherman. Description: Efficient furniture and equipment is the key to outfitting a small home-based office.

49500 ■ "Form Follows Function" in *Small Business Opportunities* (Vol. 12, No. 3, May 2000, pp. 52-53)
Pub: Harris Publications, Inc.
Description: According to a survey conducted by the American Society of Interior Designers (ASID), business owners stress function over image and look for office design. Comfort and privacy were key elements in design.

49501 ■ "Furnishing an Alternative for Tenants" in *Washington Business Journal* (Vol. 22, No. 14, August 8, 2003, pp. 33)
Pub: Washington Business Journal
Ed: Tania Anderson. Description: HQ Global Workplaces provides full service office suites that are equipped with office furniture, telecommunications equipment and technical support. California-based Borland Software is one of many companies that have used services provided by HQ Global Workplaces.

49502 ■ "Getting Started" in *Inc.* (Volume 27, March 2005, No. 3, pp. 48, 51)
Pub: Inc. Magazine
Ed: Nicole Gull. Description: All-in-one office suites are making a comeback with entrepreneurs; some are finding shared suites to be less time-consuming and more economical.

49503 ■ "Give 'Em Space: A Well-Designed Work Space, that is" in *Entrepreneur* (Vol. 32, No. 1, January 2004, pp. 77)
Pub: Entrepreneur Media, Inc.
Ed: Kimberly L. McCall. Description: By providing optimal work space to a sales team can improve their performance and increase sales.

49504 ■ "Go retro! Budget tight?" in *Entrepreneur* (Vol. 31, No. 4, April 2003, pp. 41)
Pub: Entrepreneur Media Inc.
Ed: Mike Hogan. Description: Many small businesses are purchasing used computers for office use in order to save costs; a listing of companies offering used PCs or replacement parts is included.

49505 ■ "Hello, can we take photos of your home office today?" in *Business First Columbus* (Vol. 18, No. 26, February 15, 2002, pp. 48)
Pub: Business First Columbus, Inc.
Ed: Robin Hepler. Description: Presentations of home office design are presented.

49506 ■ "Here's How To Purchase Used Goods Wisely" in *My Business* (October/November 2003, pp. 14)
Pub: My Business Magazine
Description: Ways to purchase used office equipment are evaluated, suggesting buying certified used equipment directly from manufacturers, or from companies that refurbish equipment and sell with warranties.

49507 ■ "Home Office, Simplified" in *Home Office Computing* (Vol. 18, No. 7, July 2000, pp. 54)
Pub: Scholastic Inc.
Ed: Jeffery D. Zbar. Description: Home-based workers often develop bad habits that lead to disorganization and reduce productivity. It is important to take control of a home office and manage the workspace effectively. Three home workers teamed with organizational experts to discuss their own weaknesses.

49508 ■ *Home Office - Small Office Quick Planner*
Pub: Gardeners' Guide
Released: 1995. Price: $18.95.

49509 ■ "Homework 2001" in *Small Business Opportunities* (Vol. 13, No. 5, September 2001, pp. 72-73)
Pub: Harris Publications, Inc.
Description: It is estimated that every week 8,000 people decide to work at home, equating to nearly 55 million people with home-based offices. This increase is making a positive impact on home design, floor plans and building materials.

49510 ■ "Hot Tip: Limo as Mobile Office" in *Inc.* (November 15, 2000, pp. 26)
Pub: The Goldhirsh Group
Description: The owner of a janitorial services company has outfitted a limousine and three vans with an inverter, a device that lets him and his workers use laptops, printers and fax machines to save time and money for his company.

49511 ■ *Increasing Productivity and Profit in the Workplace: A Guide to Office Planning and Design*
Pub: John Wiley & Sons, Inc.
Ed: M. Glynn Shumake. Released: 1992. Price: $64.95. Description: Describes how to design workspaces to increase productivity and efficiency and reduce costs.

49512 ■ "It's Never E-nough" in *Business Week* (No. 3689, July 10, 2000, pp. F14)
Pub: McGraw-Hill, Inc.
Description: Highlights of surveys of companies with 20-49 employees regarding the future of small business, including information about the Internet, Palmtops, networks, e-backlash, the bottom line, cost cutting, outsourcing, leasing, and Internet Telephony.

49513 ■ "Keep It Professional" in *Home Office Computing* (Vol. 18, No. 10, October 2000, pp. 89)
Pub: Scholastic Inc.
Ed: Joanne Cleaver. Description: Operating a business from home raises many thorny issues of how to separate work and personal life in order to keep the business professional in appearance. Defining the office involves examining traffic patterns employees, customers and delivery people must take to reach the home office. Once the office is clearly defined protecting the home is important, as is investing in top-notch technology to make the home office look professional.

49514 ■ "Keeping pace with technology" in *Women in Business* (Vol. 54, No. 2, March-April 2002, pp. 22)
Pub: The ABWA Co Inc.
Ed: Mary-Lane Kamberg. Description: Businesswomen must take information technology courses to remain computer literate in the 21st century workplace. Online education sites and information technology courses are listed.

49515 ■ "Leasing 101: need a new fleet but low on dough? Leasing may be the key" in *Entrepreneur* (Vol. 30, No. 12, December 2002, pp. 43)
Pub: Entrepreneur Media Inc.
Ed: Jill Amadio. Description: Whether handling commercial vehicle leasing in-house or outsourcing to a fleet management company or through the car supplier, fleet leasing makes economic sense because of the 5-7 percent discount off the vehicles' total price.

49516 ■ "Let The Buyer Beware" in *Small Business Opportunities* (Vol. 13, No. 6, November 2001, pp. 20)
Pub: Harris Publications, Inc.
Description: The Imaging Supplies Coalition (ISC), offers information on Telemarketing Fraud and Piracy, including the principal ways to spot a phone scam.

49517 ■ "Make Your Office Fun Place to Be in 2007" in *San Diego Business Journal* (Vol. 28, January 1, 2007, No. 1, pp. 12)
Pub: San Diego Business Journal Associates
Ed: Ted Owen. Description: Matt Weinstein, author of the book entitled, Managing to Have Fun at Work, outlines 52 fun things to do while working.

49518 ■ "A Modest Defense of the Cubicle" in *Inc.* (September 1, 2004)
Pub: Inc. Magazine
Ed: Patrick J. Sauer. Description: Mixtures of open and closed spaces will replace cubicles and enable laptop-toting employees to work in large, sunny idea centers.

49519 ■ "My Gadget" in *My Business* (June/July 2004, pp. 22)
Pub: My Business Magazine
Description: Jason Knief, owner of a beer, wine and spirits store, uses the gadget called, Whispering Windows. The device attaches to a window or other flat surface and produces smooth and steady musical sounds that attract customers.

49520 ■ "Nature's Way" in *Crain's Detroit Business* (Vol. 18, No. 19, May 13, 2002, pp)
Pub: Crain Communications Inc. - Detroit
Ed: Jennette Smith. Description: Materials such as wood and stone, as well as a return to nature and more flexibility, are some of the more popular trends in office design.

49521 ■ "Newsstand" in *Home Business* (Vol. 13, January/February 2006, No. 1, pp. 38-39)
Pub: Home Business Magazine
Description: Topics include marketing of office supplies and equipment, rising gas prices, toxic office environments, entrepreneurship, and online retailing.

49522 ■ "Not Every Small Business will be able to (or should) Jump on Linux Immediately" in *Inc.* (June 2000, pp. 100)
Pub: The Goldhirsh Group
Ed: Dan Orzech. Description: The Linux Operating System is hot. It's inexpensive. And it works. But can you run your company on it?

49523 ■ *Office Design*
Pub: Watson-Guptill Publications, Inc.
Ed: Peter B. Brandt. Released: 1992. Price: $35.00.

49524 ■ *Office Design That Really Works! Design for the 90s*
Pub: Affinity Publishing
Ed: Kathleen R. Allen. Released: 1995. Price: $13.95.

49525 ■ "Office Down Below" in *Home Office Computing* (Vol. 18, No. 8, August 2000, pp. 42)
Pub: Scholastic Inc.
Ed: Marilyn Zelinsky Syarto. Description: Ideas for converting a basement into a home office are offered.

49526 ■ "The Office" in *Entrepreneur* (Vol. 33, October 2005, No. 10, pp. 76)
Pub: Entrepreneur Media Inc.
Ed: April Y. Pennington. Description: A neat and organized work space can inspire and increase productivity. Tips to organize an office are offered.

49527 ■ "Office Furniture Dealers" in *San Diego Business Journal* (Vol. 28, January 8, 2007, No. 2, pp. 13)
Pub: San Diego Business Journal Associates
Ed: Liz Wiedemann. Description: Listing of office furniture dealers ranked by number of local full-time employees as of December 1, 2006. Company contact information is also included.

49528 ■ "Office Makeover Contest Winner" in *My Business* (December/January 2003, pp. 32)
Pub: My Business Magazine
Description: Tom Withers, owner of Josephson's Men's Clothing store in downtown Red Wing, Minnesota, tells how he updated his office in order to be more organized and productive.

49529 ■ "An Office of One's Own" in *Entrepreneur* (Vol. 31, No. 9, September 2003, pp. 105)
Pub: Entrepreneur Media, Inc.

Description: Advice for setting up a home office without an actual office area is given by Susan Silver, president of Positively Organized, a firm located in Los Angeles, California. Location, space saving ideas, file cabinets, and storage is discussed.

49530 ■ "Office Optional" in *Inc.* (Volume 27, December 2005, No. 12, pp. 42, 44)
Pub: Inc. Magazine
Ed: Darren Dahl. Description: Profile of Point B, a consulting firm employee 223 workers. Co-founders Tim Jenkins and Darran Littlefield run their firm virtually with employees in Seattle, Denver, Phoenix, and Portland, Oregon, and each consultant works with clients locally. Three tips for running a virtual office are outlined.

49531 ■ "An Office With Ambiance" in *Home Office Computing* (Vol. 18, No. 10, October 2000, pp. 64)
Pub: Scholastic Inc.
Ed: Marilyn Zelinsky Syarto. Description: Two steps to transform a dreary home office into a comfortable retreat that is conducive to creativity are, replacing junk with objects that bring joy, and adding lighting, color, sound, and air circulation to the area. Products for creating such an environment are showcased.

49532 ■ "Out of This World" in *My Business* (April/May 2002, pp. 46)
Pub: My Business Magazine
Description: Profile of Details, the Grand Rapids, Michigan company that is changing the way companies outfit the workplace with innovated ideas to fit the employee.

49533 ■ "Own or Rent? Revisiting the Pros and Cons of Leasing vs. Purchasing" in *Black Enterprise* (Vol. 34, No. 6, January 2004, pp. 44)
Pub: Earl Graves Publishing Co.
Ed: Rebecca Rohan. Description: Information for small-to-medium-sized companies to consider regarding the purchase or rental of PCs, printers, fax machines, and copiers for their offices is examined.

49534 ■ "Peaks & Silicon Valleys" in *Entrepreneur* (Vol. 30, No. 2, February 2002, pp. 28)
Pub: Entrepreneur Media Inc.
Description: Despite the over-inflated market of Silicon Valley, the cost of outfitting the office has dropped since the heyday of dotcoms, and salaries have increased. Statistical data included.

49535 ■ "Personal Style" in *Hispanic Business* (May 2005, pp. 80)
Pub: Hispanic Business
Ed: Leslie A. Westbrook. Description: Carmen Melian, vice-president at Sotheby's, recommends that executives should buy a little better than they can afford when outfitting business space with art collections.

49536 ■ "Pipe Dreams" in *Business Week* (No. 3670, February 28, 2000, pp. f32)
Pub: McGraw-Hill, Inc.
Description: Affordable alternatives to T1 Internet service for small companies are discussed.

49537 ■ "Printing in the Privacy of Your Hotel Room" in *Law Firm Inc.* (October 2004)
Pub: American Lawyer Media LP
Ed: John Bringardner. Description: Small, lightweight computer printers that fit into a business traveler's carry-on luggage are profiled, including HP DeskJet 450wbt, Canon i80, and the Brother MW-140BT.

49538 ■ "Professional Organizer Sets Up Shop" in *Bellingham Business Journal* (January 2007, pp. 4)
Pub: Sun News Inc.
Description: Profile of Cathy Gersich, a professional organizer and owner of PriOrganize. PriOrganize provides an invaluable organizational service to help individuals simplify their homes and offices.

49539 ■ "Purchasing Power" in *Small Business Opportunities* (Spring 2005)
Pub: Harris Publications Inc.
Description: Profile of Save It Now!, the franchised group purchasing organization. The firm negotiated for Fortune 500 volume discounted prices for up to 40 percent and service guarantees with national vendors. Currently the service boasts membership of 4,000 small to medium-sized businesses.

49540 ■ "Put It In Drive" in *Entrepreneur.com* (Vol. 34, February 2006, No. 2, pp. 34)
Pub: Entrepreneur Media Inc.
Ed: Mike Hogan. Description: According to a study conducted by The Dieringer Research Group, 21 million Americans work in their automobiles; mobile workers are taking care of business in planes, trains and automobiles. Requirements to equip your automobile for teleworking are outlined.

49541 ■ "Quick and lightening" in *WorkingWoman* (Vol. 25, No. 6, June 2000, pp. 120)
Pub: Lang Communications Inc.
Ed: Steve Morgenstern. Description: Advice is provided on purchasing extra lightweight portable laptop computers, with focus on maintaining a wide variety of functions. An evaluation of six ultra-portable computers is presented.

49542 ■ "Quiet Riot" in *Fast Company* (May 2001, pp. 50)
Pub: Fast Company
Ed: Ian Wylie. Description: Information is offered for designing call centers to reduce office noise and glare.

49543 ■ "Restored 1948 warehouse home to studio, architects" in *Business First Columbus* (Vol. 18, No. 26, Febr)
Pub: Business First Columbus, Inc.
Ed: Lori Murray. Description: Architects show how they designed a business and home to fit a perfect balance.

49544 ■ "The Right Tool for the Job" in *Inc.* (Volume 27, December 2005, No. 12, pp. 136)
Pub: Inc. Magazine
Description: Profile of new office products, including audio- and video-conferencing and a color laser printer.

49545 ■ "Saving Those Whiteboard Moments" in *Success* (Vol. 47, No. 5, October 2000, pp. 14)
Pub: Success Publishing, Inc.
Description: Overview of Mimio, a completely portable Digital Meeting Assistant, created by Virtual Ink, a Boston-based technology company. Mimio allows the user to instantly export anything written on a whiteboard to a personal computer.

49546 ■ "Shed Some Light on Your Work" in *My Business* (April/May 2002, pp. 47)
Pub: My Business Magazine
Ed: Dave Donelson. Description: When the workplace is improperly lit, employees can suffer from eyestrain, headache, muscle strain, fatigue, stress and poor morale. Many times efforts to save energy increase safety risks.

49547 ■ "Site Watch for Home Workers" in *Home Office Computing* (Vol. 18, No. 11, November 2000, pp. 20)
Pub: Scholastic Inc.
Ed: Sonya Donaldson. Description: Profiles of Web sites designed to help the home worker, including vistaprint.com, dotphoto.com, pitneybowes.com, and egreetings.com.

49548 ■ *The Small Business Owner's Manual: Everything You Need to Know to Start Up and Run Your Business*
Pub: Career Press, Incorporated
Ed: Joe Kennedy. Released: June 2005. Price: $19.99 (US), $26.95 (Canadian). Description: Comprehensive guide for starting a small business, focusing

on twelve ways to obtain financing, business plans, selling and advertising products and services, hiring and firing employees, setting up a Web site, business law, accounting issues, insurance, equipment, computers, banks, financing, customer credit and collection, leasing, and more.

49549 ■ "Small Office Space: Tear Down Those Walls" in *My Business* **(April/May 2002, pp. 43)**
Pub: My Business Magazine
Ed: Shannon Skully. **Description:** A Philadelphia law firm shows how it tore down its office walls to create an open environment to allow teams to work together more efficiently on projects.

49550 ■ "Space Centered" in *Inc.* **(September 1, 2003)**
Pub: Gruner & Jahr USA Publishing
Ed: Brett Martin. **Description:** The use of feng shui for the office to restore balance is investigated.

49551 ■ "Start your engines" in *Entrepreneur* **(Vol. 30, No. 12, December 2002, pp. 41)**
Pub: Entrepreneur Media Inc.
Ed: Jill Amadio. **Description:** A special guide to commercial vehicles is presented which includes information on vehicle leasing, an industry overview, and a product/service evaluation.

49552 ■ "Stretching Room" in *Home Office Computing* **(Vol. 18, No. 10, October 2000, pp. 42)**
Pub: Scholastic Inc.
Ed: Lisa Kanarek. **Description:** A description of how Georgia's Creations' principal, Georgia Cox, used her design skills to create a two-story home office in the middle of her three-level house. Unique features of the home office, analysis of her business and computer hardware and software used in the business are presented.

49553 ■ "Take a Seat" in *Inc.* **(August 1, 2003)**
Pub: Gruner & Jahr USA Publishing
Ed: Stacy Perman. **Description:** Office furniture designed to help an office look good, but also make an employee feel good, are profiled.

49554 ■ "Taking the fear out of buying a personal computer" in *Women in Business* **(Vol. 53, No. 3, May-June, 2001, pp. 22)**
Pub: The ABWA Co. Inc.
Ed: Melissa Will. **Description:** When buying a computer for the first time, the most important thing is to research products before the purchase. Factors to consider include price, the computer's use, and warranties.

49555 ■ "Taxing matters" in *Entrepreneur* **(Vol. 30, No. 12, December 2002, pp. 43)**
Pub: Entrepreneur Media Inc.
Ed: Jill Amadio. **Description:** There is a significant tax advantage for small business owners to lease rather than purchase vehicles.

49556 ■ "TCHI Consulting: www.tchiconsulting.com" in *Entrepreneur* **(Vol. 31, No. 12, December 2003, pp. 8)**
Pub: Entrepreneur Media Inc.
Ed: Steve Cooper. **Description:** Profile of a Web site offering tips and resources for setting up a business office.

49557 ■ "Tips & Trends" in *Small Business Opportunities* **(Vol. 12, No. 3, May 2000, pp. 14)**
Pub: Harris Publications, Inc.
Ed: **Description:** A roundup of hot happenings, events and products for a small business, including an overview of cordless phones, Dymo lettering labelers, Clean Power System's surge protectors, and a portable LCD projector.

49558 ■ "Trading Office Spaces" in *Inc.* **(October 2005, pp. 102-111)**
Pub: Inc. Magazine

Ed: Patrick J. Sauer. **Description:** Five companies who designed their offices on a reasonable budget are featured. A well-designed workspace contributes to efficiency.

49559 ■ "Tray chic" in *Entrepreneur* **(Vol. 31, No. 5, May 2003, pp. 18)**
Pub: Entrepreneur Media Inc.
Ed: Gisela M. Pedroza. **Description:** PC Tables LLC has created a collapsible, lightweight table for laptop computers. The table is portable and can be used anywhere, including the airport, a hotel lobby or other public space.

49560 ■ "Virtual reality, chief whatiffer...this is EDS?" in *Crain's Detroit Business* **(Vol. 18, No. 22, June 3, 2002, pp. 22)**
Pub: Crain Communications Inc. - Detroit
Ed: Michelle Franzen Martin. **Description:** Moveable furniture, wireless laptops, picnic tables help describe the unusual workspace developed at Electronic Data Systems Corporation (EDS), located in Troy, MI.

49561 ■ "Wants vs. Needs: How to Shop Wisely for Technology" in *My Business* **(December/January 2004, pp. 40)**
Pub: My Business Magazine
Ed: Tamara E. Holmes. **Description:** Regardless of industry, there are certain technology needs important to all small businesses, including workstations, hand-held devices, cellular phones, wireless networks, and teleconferencing equipment.

49562 ■ "Wearing Her Work on Her Sleeve" in *Home Business* **(Vol. 13, January/February 2006, No. 1, pp. 80)**
Pub: Home Business Magazine
Ed: Sandy Larson. **Description:** Profile of Eileen Parzek who sells work-at-home related merchandise including t-shirts, caps, mugs, mouse pads, and clocks.

49563 ■ "Whatever it takes" in *BlackEnterprise* **(Vol. 32, No. 3, October 2001, pp. 54)**
Pub: Earl Graves Publishing Co.
Ed: Mark Richard Moss. **Description:** Review of the publication, 'Off-the-Wall Marketing Ideas.' The book offers advice on such diverse topics as business card design, generating publicity and "Pro Bono: Civic Marketing."

49564 ■ "What's the word? (Extra: Commercial Vehicle Guide)" in *Entrepreneur* **(Vol. 30, No. 12, December 2002, pp. 43)**
Pub: Entrepreneur Media Inc.
Ed: Jill Amadio. **Description:** Terms and phrases used when negotiation lease terms on company commercial vehicles are defined.

49565 ■ "Winter has Me Down. What Can I Do at Work" in *Crain's New York Business* **(Vol. 23, January 29, 2007, No. 5, pp. 47)**
Pub: Crain Communications, Inc.
Description: Getting enough sunlight is important to a person's health. If you are not getting enough sunlight due to long days at the office, a good remedy is light therapy, products can be purchased as inexpensive as $89.

49566 ■ "Work Area Clutter is Not a Problem Unless It's a Problem" in *St. Louis Post-Dispatch* **(January 30, 2005)**
Pub: Knight-Ridder/Tribune Business News
Ed: Repps Hudson. **Description:** David Munz, a professor of organizational psychology at St. Louis University and also a business consultant, discusses workplace clutter issues.

49567 ■ "Work Gear" in *St. Louis Post-Dispatch* **(January 14, 2005)**
Pub: Knight-Ridder/Tribune Business News
Ed: Jo Krummrich. **Description:** Profile of Fiskars 12-inch paper trimmer and three-hole punch that saves desktop and drawer space by combining two tools into one device.

49568 ■ "Workers Simply Want to Be Organized" in *Home Office Computing* **(Vol. 18, No. 12, December 2000, pp. 23)**
Pub: Scholastic Inc.
Ed: Marilyn Zelinsky Syarto. **Description:** File-Maker's database software is helping home-based workers get organized with digital file cabinets.

49569 ■ "Workspace Wonders" in *Small Business Opportunities* **(Vol. 16, No. 2, March 2004, pp. 80)**
Pub: Harris Publications, Inc.
Description: Affordable and stylish products to equip a home office are presented by TOPDEQ (Tomorrow's Office Products Delivered Extremely Quickly), whose U.S. office is located in Cranbury, New Jersey. TOPDEQ offers a 120-page catalog of European designed office and home furnishings now available in the U.S.

49570 ■ "Your PC Post Office" in *Hispanic Business* **(Vol. 22, No. 1/2, January/February, pp. 88)**
Pub: Hispanic Business
Ed: Lamont Wood. **Description:** To print your own postage, all you need is a PC with Internet connection and a printer.

SOURCES OF SUPPLY

49571 ■ *Independent Cash Register Dealers Association—Membership Directory*
Pub: Independent Cash Register Dealers Association (ICRDA)
Contact: Denise Haygood
Ed: Casey A. Neel, Editor. **Released:** Annual, January. **Price:** $100. **Covers:** about 545 member manufacturers, dealers, and suppliers of cash register and point-of-sale systems. **Entries Include:** Company name, name of owner, name of spouse, address, and phone; code indicating franchises held. **Arrangement:** Alphabetical. **Indexes:** Geographical, personal name.

VIDEOCASSETTES/ AUDIOCASSETTES

49572 ■ *Automating the Office*
Time-Life Video and Television
1450 Palmyra Ave.
Richmond, VA 23227-4420
Ph:(804)266-6330
Free: 800-950-7887
Fax: (757)427-7905
Released: 1985. **Description:** A series of programs that clarify modern methods of automating workplaces for maximum efficency and productivity. **Availability:** VHS; 3/4U; Special order formats.

CONSULTANTS

49573 ■ AA Antivirus
1608 W Campbell Ave., Ste. 370
Campbell, CA 95008
Ph:(408)374-8000
Free: 800-478-1828
Fax: (408)374-2045
Co. E-mail: info@aaantivirus.com
URL: http://www.aaantivirus.com

E-mail: info@aaantivirus.com
Scope: A full-service Internet and networking company. Offers a range of local area networking and wide area networking solutions to small and medium sized businesses. Assists business owners and administrators in planning, purchasing and installing networks.

49574 ■ ABI Designs Inc.
8555 SW Apple Way, Ste. 120
Portland, OR 97225-1775

Ph:(503)292-0151
Fax: (503)292-0685
Co. E-mail: walkinthelight@hotmail.com

E-mail: walkinthelight@hotmail.com
Scope: Provides interior design services to architectural firms and individuals.

49575 ■ Advanced Network Consulting
475 Park Ave. S Ste. 9
New York, NY 10016
Ph:(212)378-4109
Fax: (212)376-6782
Scope: A provider of LAN consulting as well as hardware and software services. Server-based solutions include backup, antivirus LAN/WAN design, implementation and support, system administration and hardware warrantee contracts, and office automation for small businesses.

49576 ■ Agility Computer Network Services L.L.C.
1332 N Halsted St., Ste. 400
Chicago, IL 60622
Ph:(312)587-9894
Free: 877-244-5484
Fax: (312)587-9948
Co. E-mail: support@agilitynetworks.com
URL: http://www.agilitynetworks.com

E-mail: support@agilitynetworks.com
Scope: Firm provides networking and other related computer consulting services.

49577 ■ Lino J. Agosti & Associates
1901 W Tudor Rd.
Anchorage, AK 99517-3184
Ph:(907)243-3556
Fax: (907)243-6709
Co. E-mail: tim.agosti@alaska.com

E-mail: tim.agosti@alaska.com
Scope: Offers food facility design, interior design and feasibility planning. Service offered: concept development, design, feasibility.

49578 ■ AIM Associates
100 Fair St.
Petaluma, CA 94952-2515
Ph:(707)763-3300
Co. E-mail: info@aimgreen.com
URL: http://www.aimgreen.com

E-mail: info@aimgreen.com
Scope: AIM Associates has been providing Green and High Performance building consulting, integrated design team management, and full architectural and engineering services. provides consulting to cities, school districts, A/E firms, R&D facilities, other businesses, and individuals. Architectural and project management firm. Peer review, integrated design team management, performance based design **Special Services:** 3D computer design imaging and photo montages using form*Z and Photoshop; computer drafting using MiniCad and AutoCad; energy use simulation and optimization using Energy 10.

49579 ■ Anshen Allen
901 Market St., Ste. 600
San Francisco, CA 94103
Ph:(415)882-9500
Fax: (415)882-9523
Co. E-mail: inquire@anshen.com
URL: http://www.anshen.com

E-mail: inquire@anshen.com
Scope: Offers full architectural consulting services from feasibility studies through construction administration. Also provides space planning and interior design services and facilities management utilizing CAD and data base management.

49580 ■ A.P. Designs
33 Merrall Dr.
Lawrence, NY 11559
Ph:(516)239-2931
Fax: (516)239-2932

Scope: Interior design business. Industries served: all industries and individuals requiring interior design services. **Seminars:** Ann Pollack gives seminars to various organizations regarding the proper use of home design.

49581 ■ Apple Electrical Services Inc.
11237 Somerset Ave.
Beltsville, MD 20705
Ph:(301)345-9409
Fax: (301)345-9530
Co. E-mail: cissel2@aol.com

E-mail: cissel2@aol.com
Scope: Electrical lighting and design consultants specializing in interior and exterior lighting systems. Industries served: residential, commercial and industrial, as well as government agencies.

49582 ■ Architectural Alliance
400 Clifton Ave. S
Minneapolis, MN 55403-3299
Ph:(612)871-5703
Fax: (612)871-7212
URL: http://www.archalliance.com
Scope: Offers architectural design, interior design, facility studies, programming, space planning, facilities master planning and renovation design services. Project types have included corporate offices, computer/data centers, retail facilities, college and university buildings, other educational facilities, airport facilities and public facilities (parks, city halls, police facilities, etc.). Industries served: public and private corporations/companies, school districts, public colleges and universities, public (state and federal) agencies, commercial developers, municipalities and other institutions. **Special Services:** AutoCAD; Archibus facilities management software.

49583 ■ Array Healthcare Facilities Solutions
2520 Renaissance Blvd., Ste. 110
King of Prussia, PA 19406
Ph:(610)270-0599
Free: 800-828-8199
Fax: (610)270-0995
Co. E-mail: pmoffson@arrayhfs.com
URL: http://www.arrayhfs.com

E-mail: pmoffson@arrayhfs.com
Scope: Provides comprehensive architectural, facility master planning, interior design, project management, design/building and computer-aided facilities management services. Clients include nonprofit healthcare corporations, academic health centers, investor-owned enterprises, start-up entrepreneurs, management companies for long-term care units, physician groups and developers serving medical niche markets. Also serves government agencies.

49584 ■ ASAI Architecture
1200 Grand Blvd.
Kansas City, MO 64106
Ph:(816)221-5011
Fax: (816)221-5014
Co. E-mail: asai@asaiarch.com
URL: http://www.asaiarch.com

E-mail: asai@asaiarch.com
Scope: Provides programming, planning and urban design, architecture, engineering, interior design, space planning, graphics, landscape architecture, energy engineering, construction documents, feasibility studies, zoning and codes analysis, development analysis, computer aided design, computer based specifications, cost estimating, construction management and value engineering. Projects include the design of civic, criminal justice, educational, library, recreational, governmental/public, healthcare facilities and multi-family housing. Also experienced in historic preservation and restoration. Industries served: governmental organizations, criminal justice, public administration, corporate administration, education and recreation. **Seminars:** Consensus Building in the Planning of Public Facilities; Juvenile Detention and Adult Detention Facilities.

49585 ■ BBLM Architects
924 Cherry St., Fl. 1
Philadelphia, PA 19107-2411
Ph:(215)625-2500
Fax: (215)625-0275
Scope: Offers architecture, planning, and interior design consulting services, including color, furnishings, and lighting. Recent experience in healthcare design. Serves private institutions as well as government agencies.

49586 ■ Beck Powell & Parsons Inc.
29 W Susquehanna Ave., Ste. 300
Towson, MD 21204
Ph:(410)828-9220
Fax: (410)828-9661
Co. E-mail: main@beckpowell.com
URL: http://www.beckpowell.com

E-mail: main@beckpowell.com
Scope: Architecture and interior design firm. Provides design services to governmental, corporate and institutional clients. **Publications:** Active Solar Energy System Design Practice; Better Homes and Gardens; Solar Energy Analysis Guide.

49587 ■ Bell Industries Tech.logix Group
1960 E Grand Ave., Ste. 560
El Segundo, CA 90245
Ph:(310)563-2355
Free: (866)782-2355
Fax: (310)648-7280
Co. E-mail: information@bellind.com
URL: http://www.belltechlogix.com

E-mail: information@bellind.com
Scope: Experienced in network topologies. Installs, configures, maintains and supports the local and wide area network technologies. Offers connectivity services that includes secure Internet/Intranet communication solutions, virus scanning, and firewall protections.

49588 ■ Burt Hill
400 Morgan Ctr.
101 E Diamond St.
Butler, PA 16001-5977
Ph:(724)285-4761
Fax: (724)285-6815
Co. E-mail: dianne.sinz@burthill.com
URL: http://www.burthill.com

E-mail: dianne.sinz@burthill.com
Scope: Offers architecture and engineering consulting services including space planning, facility management, building evaluation, and interior design, feasibility studies, facility evaluation surveys, energy management, solar engineering, telecommunications engineering and real estate development. Industries served: healthcare, medical research, high-tech, education, corporate, housing, and manufacturing worldwide, with emphasis on the Eastern U.S. **Publications:** Contributing author of the "Laboratory Design Construction and Renovation.Participants, Process, and Product," which was published by the Board on Chemical Sciences and Technology, National Research Council, 1999; Guidelines for planning and designing Biomedical Research Facilities, 1999; Advances Technology Facilities Design: 1996 Review; Improving Collaboration: Architects and Engineers, Design and Construction; published by American Institute of Architects (1996); Fundamentals of Building Energy Dynamics; Energy Conservation and Management Strategies, published by The MIT Press (1996); Teaching Space Utilization, Managing one of Higher Education's Most Significant Assests (1996). **Seminars:** Advanced Technology Facilities Design and the Technology Intensive Workspace; Energy Conservation in Commercial Buildings — Current Practice; Healthcare in the Baltics: Meeting the 21st Century; Architectural and Engineering Practice in the 21st Century; Classrooms of the Future; Classrooms of the Future; Campus-Wide Information Networks; Risk Allocation and Dispute Avoidance in Construction; Achieving Architectural and Engineering Collaboration in Building Design; Designing for Improved

Occupant Comfort and Productivity; Construction Procurement; International Health Care; Campus-Wide Information Network.

49589 ■ Cambridge Seven Associates Inc.
1050 Massachusetts Ave.
Cambridge, MA 02138
Ph:(617)492-7000
Fax: (617)492-7007
Co. E-mail: marketing@c7a.com
URL: http://www.c7a.com

E-mail: marketing@c7a.com
Scope: Offers consulting in architecture, planning graphic, exhibit, habitat, and interior design. Industries served: colleges and universities, retail, corporations, museums, aquariums, and government agencies. **Publications:** "How Green is Your City?," Metropolis, Sep, 2006; "Designing and Building for the Class of 2020," Sep, 2006; "Dumping Steel, " The Boston Globe, Jun, 2006; "Healing Architecture," Architectural Record, Jun, 2005. **Seminars:** Where We Learn seminar; 2002 North Atlantic SCUP's.

49590 ■ Carmichael/Associates
3963 N Woodlawn Ct., Ste. 3
Wichita, KS 67220-1991
Ph:(316)681-1535
Fax: (316)681-1548
Scope: Architectural consultant active in legal assistance, library design, church design, healthcare projects, nursing homes, clinics, apartments, governmental buildings, renovations and remodeling work, residential/commercial, heavy truck maintenance and operations design, and small college buildings and planning.

49591 ■ Cassway/Albert Ltd.
1528 Walnut St., Ste. 1100
Philadelphia, PA 19102
Ph:(215)545-4900
Fax: (215)545-8222
Co. E-mail: cal@icdc.com

E-mail: cal@icdc.com
Scope: Consultants in architecture, landscape architecture, urban planning, interior design, and space planning.

49592 ■ Champion Networks L.L.C.
1081 Mere Point Rd.
Brunswick, ME 04011
Ph:(207)725-8903
Fax: (207)721-0186
Co. E-mail: salesrequest@championnetworks.com
URL: http://www.championnetworks.com

E-mail: salesrequest@championnetworks.com
Scope: Firm specializes in network integration, total wide area network solutions, and network services.

49593 ■ Chicago-Edison Electrical & Lighting
189 Poplar Pl., Ste. 3
North Aurora, IL 60542
Ph:(630)264-6940
Fax: (630)264-6942
Co. E-mail: larry@chicago-edison.com
URL: http://www.chicago-edison.com

E-mail: larry@chicago-edison.com
Scope: Lighting systems consultants. **Publications:** "An Efficient Solution: The right energy investments could pay big dividends", Barron's Magazine, Feb, 2002; The Benefits of High Efficiency Lighting.

49594 ■ Cohn Consulting Corp.
2627 Sandy Plains Rd., Ste. 204
Marietta, GA 30066-4289
Ph:(770)321-5532
Fax: (770)321-4497
Co. E-mail: info@cohnconsultingcorp.com
URL: http://www.cohnconsultingcorp.com

E-mail: info@cohnconsultingcorp.com
Scope: Firm provides a wide range of PC and LAN services.

49595 ■ Cole & Goyette Architects & Planners Inc.
955 Massachusetts Ave.
Cambridge, MA 02139
Ph:(617)491-5662
Fax: (617)492-0856
Co. E-mail: colegoyette@earthlink.net
URL: http://www.colegoyette.com

E-mail: colegoyette@earthlink.net
Scope: Offers services in architecture & planning, interior design & design review for educational, commercial, residential & governmental clients.

49596 ■ Computer Connections Inc.
1241-2 E Dixon Blvd., Ste. 2
PO Box 321
Shelby, NC 28150
Ph:(704)482-0057
Fax: (704)482-0950
Co. E-mail: timwease@carolina.rr.com
URL: http://www.painlesspc.net

E-mail: timwease@carolina.rr.com
Scope: A full service computer company specializing in client/server networking environments. Services, upgrades, and repairs most IBM compatible computers. Networking services include network design, implementation, and administration of Novell and Windows NT networks.

49597 ■ Crawley & Associates Inc.
121 Lincoln Ave.
Fair Lawn, NJ 07410
Ph:(973)636-7350
Free: 877-427-2953
Fax: (973)636-7360
Co. E-mail: sales@crawleyinc.com
URL: http://www.crawleyinc.com

E-mail: sales@crawleyinc.com
Scope: A full-service consulting firm specializing in computer network design, installation and support. Assists with strategic planning, implementation and on-going support of computer information systems.

49598 ■ Cutten Associates/Lighting Design
PO Box 6926
Tahoe City, CA 96145-6926
Ph:(530)583-5002
Fax: (530)583-5525
Scope: Design consultant, offer expertise in lighting design and electrical engineering. Industries served: construction: residential, commercial, and industrial; also government agencies. **Seminars:** Have taught Illuminating Engineering Society of North America (IESNA) lighting fundamentals course. **Special Services:** Auto CAD LT capability.

49599 ■ dEpagnier Furniture
14201 Notley Rd.
Silver Spring, MD 20904
Ph:(301)384-1663
Fax: (301)384-3201
Scope: Specializes in custom design and fabrication of furniture for corporate, residential or professional spaces. Performs architectural exterior and interior design consulting work with extensive knowledge in traditional cabinet making skills, solid woods and joinery. Design expertise in Greene and Greene genre of the American Arts and Crafts Movement. Offers advice on use, location and types of domestic woods in place of foreign exotic woods. Offers artistic high end functional quality built furniture. **Seminars:** Marquetry.

49600 ■ Design Collective Inc.
151 E Nationwide Blvd.
Columbus, OH 43215
Ph:(614)464-2880
Fax: (614)464-1180
Co. E-mail: dcitn@aol.com

E-mail: dcitn@aol.com
Scope: Firm offers expertise in interior design to clients in the commercial trade industry in the United States.

49601 ■ Dimension Data
12120 Sunset Hills Rd., Ste. 550
Reston, VA 20190
Ph:(571)203-4000
Fax: (571)203-4001
URL: http://www.didata.com
Scope: A global technology company. Provides solutions and services that optimize and manage the performance of IT infrastructure to enable businesses to build competitive advantage.

49602 ■ E-netegrations Inc.
111 Broadway Ave., Ste. 133
PO Box 109
Boise, ID 83705
Ph:(208)343-2541
Free: 877-593-3638
Fax: (208)343-2612
Co. E-mail: support@e-netegrations.com

E-mail: support@e-netegrations.com
Scope: Telecommunications systems installation consultant. Experience ranges from cable splicing to (LAN) Local Area Network, (WAN) Wide Area Network design, engineering, consulting, and communications distributions installation and desktop videoconferencing. **Special Services:** e-access™; e-workplace™.

49603 ■ Eaton Design Group Inc.
8115 Old Dominion Dr., Ste. 100
McLean, VA 22102
Ph:(703)790-8444
Free: 800-291-8444
Fax: (703)893-3256
Co. E-mail: eatondesgn@aol.com

E-mail: eatondesgn@aol.com
Scope: Nationally recognized McLean-based space planning and interior design firm.

49604 ■ TRECI/Thomas R. Egan Consulting Inc.
1012 Ronda Ln.
Birmingham, AL 35214
Ph:(205)796-9541
Fax: (205)744-9404
Co. E-mail: tegan@treci.com
URL: http://www.treci.com

E-mail: tegan@treci.com
Scope: Provides consultation and design services, installation, and service/maintenance for several network platforms.

49605 ■ Engineered Lighting Products
10768 Lower Azusa Rd.
El Monte, CA 91731
Ph:(626)579-0943
Fax: (626)579-6803
Co. E-mail: elp2@aol.com
URL: http://www.elplighting.com

E-mail: elp2@aol.com
Scope: Firm offers lighting consulting for commercial, residential, and industrial projects. Provides design, specifications, and illumination calculations. Maintains a studio for mock-up design.

49606 ■ ePartners Inc.
800 5th Ave., Ste. 4100
Seattle, WA 98104
Ph:(425)748-5177
Free: 888-883-9797
Fax: (425)748-5178
Co. E-mail: info@epartnersolutions.com
URL: http://www.epartnersolutions.com

E-mail: info@epartnersolutions.com
Scope: A total solutions provider that designs, develops, implements, integrates, hosts, manages and supports comprehensive eBusiness solutions.

49607 ■ Ergometrics Inc.
192 Monroe Ct.
Holland, PA 18966-2722
Ph:(215)968-6943
Fax: (215)968-4250

Co. E-mail: ergodave@aol.com

E-mail: ergodave@aol.com
Scope: Occupational and forensic ergonomic services addressing work-site evaluations accident investigations, office ergonomics, tool, product and equipment evaluations, product liability, workplace accidents and occupational injuries. Experience in heavy industrial, light industrial, service and office environments.

49608 ■ Error Analysis Inc.
5811 Amaya Dr., Ste. 205
La Mesa, CA 91942-4156
Ph:(619)464-4427
Fax: (619)464-4992
Co. E-mail: info@erroranalysis.com
URL: http://www.erroranalysis.com

E-mail: info@erroranalysis.com
Scope: Firm dedicated to research and consulting in the fields of human factors, safety and accident reconstruction. Provides consulting and expert witness services to attorneys, the insurance industry and businesses throughout the world. **Publications:** Safety Handbook and numerous articles and papers related to safety. **Seminars:** Safety; Risk Management; Premises and Product Liability.

49609 ■ Fowlie & Associates
630 Skyline Dr.
Ventura, CA 93003-1143
Ph:(805)644-0201
Fax: (805)644-0201
Scope: Offers environmentally conscious architectural services, including interior design, urban planning, building program development, and site analysis. Industries served: educational, industrial, residential, commercial, and municipal facilities in southern California.

49610 ■ FRCH Design Worldwide
311 Elm St., Ste. 600
Cincinnati, OH 45202
Ph:(513)241-3000
Fax: (513)241-5015
Co. E-mail: info@frch.com
URL: http://www.frch.com

E-mail: info@frch.com
Scope: Offers interior design, architectural, and construction expertise. Also offers extensive lighting design services.

49611 ■ Glaser Associates Inc.
304 E 8th St.
Cincinnati, OH 45202-2231
Ph:(513)665-9555
Fax: (513)665-9857
Co. E-mail: shaber@glaserworks.com
URL: http://www.glaserworks.com

E-mail: shaber@glaserworks.com
Scope: Architectural consulting firm offers master planning, site and feasibility analysis, architectural and interior design, space planning, renovation, and adaptive reuse. Industries served: museums, higher education and mixed-use developments.

49612 ■ GlobalNET Corp.
12845 Capricorn St.
Stafford, TX 77477
Ph:(281)240-4321
Fax: (281)240-4003
Scope: Specializes in the installation, configuration, and technical support of local (LAN) and wide (WAN) Area Networks. Installs Multi-User and Multi-Platform systems (i.e. DOS, OS2, Windows NT, UNIX, NextStep, and Macintosh) which perform Accounting, client/server Database, Word Processing, Spreadsheet, and Computer Aide Design (CAD) tasks in a variety of industries. **Seminars:** Networking training services.

49613 ■ Hillier Architecture
500 Alexander Pk.
Princeton, NJ 08543-6395
Ph:(609)452-8888

Free: 888-445-5437
Fax: (609)452-8332
Co. E-mail: info@hillier.com
URL: http://www.hillier.com

E-mail: info@hillier.com
Scope: Provides services in architecture, planning, interior design, engineering, construction management, strategic facilities planning, real estate evaluation and graphic design. Industries served: public and private sector.

49614 ■ Humanics ErgoSystems Inc.
PO Box 17388
Encino, CA 91416-7388
Ph:(818)345-3746
Fax: (818)705-3903
Co. E-mail: questions@humanics-es.com
URL: http://www.humanics-es.com

E-mail: questions@humanics-es.com
Scope: Specializes in occupational ergonomics; ergonomic workplace evaluations; ergonomics research; ergonomic seminars and training; psychological and biomechanics testing (EMG, dynamic lumbar motion, strength assessment, nerve conduction); product evaluations; compliance with ergonomic standards; and expert witnessing. Serves all industries in the U.S. and worldwide. **Publications:** "Hard Facts About Soft Machines: The Science of Seated Posture," edited by Lueder, R. and Noro, K., London and Philadelphia: Taylor & Francis, Ltd., 1994; "Work Postures and Ergonomics," R. Lueder, Chiropractic Family Practice. J. Sweere, ed. Aspen Pub., 1992; "The ERgonomics Payoff," Holt Rhinehart and Winston of Canada, (1987). **Seminars:** Presents a variety of seminars, including How to Conduct a Workplace Assessment; How to Reduce Cumulative Trauma in Your Workplace; and How to Evaluate Ergonomic Seats, Workstations, Keyboards, and Other Products. **Special Services:** Accesses variety of online commercial, academic, and government databases. Skilled in the areas of technical ergonomics research and analysis.

49615 ■ Illuminated Concepts Inc.
23422 Peralta Dr., Ste. B
Laguna Hills, CA 92653
Ph:(949)455-9914
Fax: (949)951-3603
Co. E-mail: oclights@yahoo.com
URL: http://www.oclights.com

E-mail: oclights@yahoo.com
Scope: Provides extensive design and installation services for both interiors and exteriors lighting. Specialist in low voltage lighting and fiber optic systems. Installation services are also offered.

49616 ■ IMC Internet
355 Sackett Point Rd., Ste. 13
North Haven, CT 06473
Ph:(203)949-1688
Free: 800-840-9989
Fax: (203)269-9963
Co. E-mail: info@imcinternet.net
URL: http://www.imcinternet.net

E-mail: info@imcinternet.net
Scope: Specializes in the development of total office solutions for business, which includes office networking, client/ server technologies, internet access and computer sales.

49617 ■ IRI Design Associates Inc.
1650 Broadway front, Ste. 306
New York, NY 10019-6833
Ph:(212)582-1882
Fax: (212)481-1856
Scope: Full service interior architectural and design firm. Industries served: all.

49618 ■ Jacobs-Schneider Interior Design Inc.
1012 E 75th St.
Indianapolis, IN 46240-2843
Ph:(317)251-0312

Fax: (317)251-0339
Scope: Interior design consulting firm.

49619 ■ Kajioka Design Associates
2614 Ross Rd.
Chevy Chase, MD 20815-3835
Ph:(301)565-3535
Fax: (301)565-3535
Scope: Interior design consultant (licensed and certified in Maryland and Virginia) provides expertise in space planning, complete furnishings and installation of window treatments, floor and wall coverings, and in other areas.

49620 ■ KCS Computer Technology Inc.
9524 Franklin Ave.
Franklin Park, IL 60131
Ph:(847)288-9820
Fax: (847)288-9822
Co. E-mail: sales@kcstech.com
URL: http://www.kcstech.com

E-mail: sales@kcstech.com
Scope: Computer consulting firm specializing in software and computer reselling, Windows NT, Lantastic and Novell network installation and maintenance, custom programming, network communications fax/modem server installation and maintenance, Internet setup and training, custom html programming services, network and phone cabling, computer leasing, data conversion and data recovery and maintenance contracts.

49621 ■ Keon Mitchell B Architectural Lighting Consultants
2256 Linden Ave.
Highland Park, IL 60035-2006
Ph:(847)433-0840
Fax: (847)433-0839
Co. E-mail: mitchkohn@aol.com

E-mail: mitchkohn@aol.com
Scope: Full service architectural lighting design firm provides interior lighting design for commercial projects.

49622 ■ KeyLAN Consulting Inc.
PO Box 333
North Gower, ON, Canada K0A 2T0
Ph:(613)489-2336
Fax: (613)489-4190
Co. E-mail: keylan@keylan.ca
URL: http://www.keylan.ca

E-mail: keylan@keylan.ca
Scope: Specializes in all facets of local area networking, including purchasing, installation, administration, training, automation, disaster planning, high security databases, and security consulting.

49623 ■ T. Kondos Associates
333 W 39th St., Ste. 202
New York, NY 10018-1429
Ph:(212)736-5510
Fax: (212)594-6332
Co. E-mail: info@tkondos.com
URL: http://www.tkondos.com

E-mail: info@tkondos.com
Scope: Full service architectural lighting design firm. Expertise with product development, budgeting, production, and equipment specification.

49624 ■ Lam Partners Inc.
84 Sherman St.
Cambridge, MA 02140
Ph:(617)354-4502
Fax: (617)497-5038
Co. E-mail: info@lampartners.com
URL: http://www.lampartners.com

E-mail: info@lampartners.com
Scope: Architectural lighting consultants experienced in all phases of lighting design including artificial lighting, daylighting, lighting for urban design, and custom fixture design.

49625 ■ LAN Solutions
449 Hillway Dr.
Emerald Hills, CA 94062-3313
Ph:(650)261-1300
Fax: (650)361-8012
Co. E-mail: info@lansol.com
URL: http://www.lansol.com

E-mail: info@lansol.com
Scope: Microsoft Windows 98, NT, 2000, XP, ME, 2003, network PC desktop integrator consultant offering Microsoft MCSE certified installation, service and consulting. Services include network design and needs analysis, CD-Rom and FAX design and installation, network and Internet e-mail design and installation, network troubleshooting and diagnostics, network performance optimization, system manager and user training and network cabling installation.

49626 ■ Robert J. Laughlin & Associates
180 Park Ave. N, Ste. 4H
Winter Park, FL 32789
Ph:(407)740-0160
Fax: (407)629-0411
Scope: Full service architectural lighting design firm.

49627 ■ LBC Networks
675 King St. W, Ste. 210
Toronto, ON, Canada M5V 1M9
Ph:(416)727-9200
Fax: (416)929-1173
URL: http://www.lbcnetworks.com
Scope: Services include Novell to NT migration, firewall and Internet security, support, Linux, email solutions, virtual private networks, data wiring, network management, and web design.

49628 ■ Lighting Design Collaborative
1216 Arch St., Ste. 3A
Philadelphia, PA 19107-2835
Ph:(215)569-2115
Fax: (215)569-2580
Co. E-mail: lcohen@ldc-pa.com

E-mail: lcohen@ldc-pa.com
Scope: Architectural lighting design firm offering expertise with commercial, interior and exterior, hotel/hospitality, retail, mixed-use, museum, healthcare, transportation, and educational projects. Serves private industries as well as government agencies.

49629 ■ Luminations Inc.
5506 Goodland Ave.
Valley Village, CA 91607
Ph:(818)769-0076
Scope: Lighting consultants experienced with commercial, retail, institutional and residential projects.
Special Services: Autocad V.2000

49630 ■ Major Electric Supply Inc.
123 High St.
Pawtucket, RI 02860
Ph:(401)724-7100
Free: 800-444-1660
Fax: (401)727-7563
Co. E-mail: showroom@majorelectricsupply.com
URL: http://www.majorelectricsupply.com

E-mail: showroom@majorelectricsupply.com
Scope: Firm provides extensive lighting design services for commercial, residential, theatrical, and landscape projects.

49631 ■ E.F. Marburger and Son Inc.
9999 Allisonville Rd.
Fishers, IN 46038
Ph:(317)841-7250
Fax: (317)841-7260
Co. E-mail: kmarburger@efmarburger.com
URL: http://www.efmarburger.com

E-mail: kmarburger@efmarburger.com
Scope: Offers counsel to architects, designers, interior decorators and institutions, on the proper type of carpeting to be used in commercial applications. Furnishes sound absorbing and sound loss transmission data on carpet wall coverings. Also offers counsel on acoustical absorption and sound transmission factors on other types of acoustical products.

49632 ■ Marconi Designs
12370 S Saratoga-Sunnyvale Rd.
Saratoga, CA 95070
Ph:(408)973-8330
Fax: (408)446-2607
Co. E-mail: patricia@marconidesigns.com
URL: http://ww.wahlichusa.com/design

E-mail: patricia@marconidesigns.com
Scope: Provides interior design, space planning and facility design for commercial office buildings of any size. Renovation, remodel and reconfiguration of personnel workspaces and existing buildings are the firm's specialties. Tenant improvements for new & existing office space are also handled. Serves: electronics, medical, banking industries & government agencies in California, statewide, with emphasis on San Francisco Bay Area.

49633 ■ C.E. Marquardt Lighting Design
13498 SE Wiese Rd.
Boring, OR 97009-9323
Ph:(503)658-5505
Scope: Architectural lighting design firm offering expertise in both interior and exterior lighting. Services include custom control design, ceiling and skylight design, computer mockups, scale models, and lighting art.

49634 ■ Marshall Craft Associates Inc.
6112 York Rd.
Baltimore, MD 21212-2611
Ph:(410)532-3131
Fax: (410)532-9206
Co. E-mail: contact@marshallcraft.com
URL: http://www.marshallcraft.com

E-mail: contact@marshallcraft.com
Scope: Firm specializes in architecture, interior design, and planning. Offers professional services to health-care, academic, corporate and government clients.

49635 ■ Maxdeco Interior Design Inc.
160 Fresh Ponds Rd.
East Brunswick, NJ 08816-2408
Ph:(732)821-7850
Co. E-mail: maxdeco@att.net

E-mail: maxdeco@att.net
Scope: Interior design and decoration consultation and planning for commercial, institutional and residential clients. Serves private industries as well as government agencies in New Jersey, New York City and Philadelphia.

49636 ■ Michaels Associates Design Consultants Inc.
14809 N 73rd St., Ste. 100
Scottsdale, AZ 85260-3113
Ph:(480)998-7476
Fax: (480)998-9390
Co. E-mail: info@madeline.com
URL: http://www.madcinc.com

E-mail: info@madeline.com
Scope: Twenty year specialization in all areas of library (public, academic, corporate & national) programming & planning, including needs assessments & interior & graphic design. Michaels Associates expertise also includes ADA audits, furniture & product design for offices, lighting & graphic design. **Publications:** Library Planning; Library Interior Design and Furniture; Technology and Library Design and Planning; Library Tours. **Seminars:** Creative Learning Seminars; Library Interior Planning & Design; Accessible, Healthy, Imaginative Spaces: Old & New; Fresh Looks for Library Interiors; The Future is Now: Library Planning & Design for the 21st Century; ADA Furnishings Response for Today's Libraries; Lighting & Libraries; Library Planning Based on New Functional Space Guidelines; Crime Prevention through Environmental Design.

49637 ■ MindLabs.net
317 N Broad St., Ste. 402
Philadelphia, PA 19107

Ph:(215)923-4447
Co. E-mail: email@mindlabs.net
URL: http://www.mindlabs.net

E-mail: email@mindlabs.net
Scope: Provides Solutions include website design and development, website makeovers, ongoing maintenance and support, website hosting, and Internet marketing.

49638 ■ Net Transforms Inc.
520 Herndon Pky., Ste. B
Herndon, VA 20170
Ph:(703)464-0042
Free: 888-291-0120
Fax: (703)464-5825
Co. E-mail: info@nettransforms.com; sales@nettransforms.com
URL: http://www.ntllc.com

E-mail: info@nettransforms.com; sales@nettransforms.com
Scope: Principal focus is the application of information technologies to enhance the effectiveness of the business environment, including collecting, organizing and storing information; and designing, building and maintaining the appropriate architecture to make information available.

49639 ■ Networked Solutions Inc.
4280 Caparosa Cir.
Melbourne, FL 32940
Ph:(321)259-3242
Fax: (321)259-3846
Co. E-mail: info@ensusa.com
URL: http://www.ensusa.com

E-mail: info@ensusa.com
Scope: Company capabilities include requirements analysis, computer system setup, network design and installation, software development, and training and support. Specializes in simultaneous Internet web and email access via LAN.

49640 ■ Robert Newell Lighting Design
654 N Ave. W
Westfield, NJ 07090-1432
Ph:(908)654-9304
Fax: (908)654-9302
Scope: Full service architectural lighting design firm offers experience with commercial, corporate, educational, religious and residential environments.

49641 ■ Notari Associates
175 W Ostend St., Ste. 100
Baltimore, MD 21230-3731
Ph:(410)752-0330
Fax: (410)685-6364
Co. E-mail: info@notariassociates.com
URL: http://www.notariassociates.com

E-mail: info@notariassociates.com
Scope: Architectural firm offering project management and interior design services.

49642 ■ Parachute Computer Services Inc.
3500 Oakmont Ste. 101
Austin, TX 78765
Ph:(512)374-1898
Fax: (512)374-9753
Scope: LAN/WAN services, on-site consultation, remote administration, and training. **Seminars:** Offers on-site training for clients of all ages and skill levels, in Microsoft Office and GoldMine 4.0.

49643 ■ Perceptive Technology Corp.
11309 Park Central Pl.
Dallas, TX 75230
Ph:(214)368-0900
URL: http://www.perceptive.net
Scope: Services include, business web site design and hosting, Internet connectivity, web server colocation, Intranet design, LAN/WAN design and consulting.

49644 ■ Pinnix Design Inc.
2507 Goldcup Ln.
PO Box 8004
Reston, VA 20191-4219

Ph:(703)620-1167
Fax: (703)715-0811
Scope: Architecture, bio-remediation, provides services in commercial interior design, space planning, architectural interior design, construction, specifications, procurement and installation management for commercial, institutional and industrial spaces. Serves private industries, particularly construction, as well as government agencies in the mid-Atlantic, northern and southeastern United States.

49645 ■ The Plant Works
3930 Graphic Ctr. Dr.
Las Vegas, NV 89118
Ph:(702)795-3600
Fax: (702)795-4643
Co. E-mail: info@plantworksnow.com
URL: http://www.plantworksnow.com

E-mail: info@plantworksnow.com
Scope: Specializes in the use of live and silk interior plants in interior design. Work includes design stage consulting for light, HVAC systems; plant varieties and design location - specimen foliage selection and location from Florida to California nurseries. Also provides custom-built silk specimen trees, flowers and accessories, including design and installation in Nevada and around the world.

49646 ■ Plantkeeper Inc.
2211 N Beckley Ave.
PO Box 226142
Dallas, TX 75208
Ph:(214)752-5750
Free: 800-340-4488
Fax: (214)651-0540
Co. E-mail: plants@plantkeeperinc.com
URL: http://www.plantkeeperinc.com

E-mail: plants@plantkeeperinc.com
Scope: Interior design consultants specializing in plants and containers. Serving architects, developing companies and other commercial accounts. Provides interior design and maintenance for bank, office buildings, hotels, malls and restaurants.

49647 ■ Patrick B Quigley & Associates Inc.
2340 Plz., Del Amo, Ste. 125
Torrance, CA 90501
Ph:(310)533-6064
Fax: (310)320-3482
Co. E-mail: lightning@pbqa.com
URL: http://www.pbqa.com

E-mail: lightning@pbqa.com
Scope: Firm offers full service architectural and landscape lighting design. Experienced with cruise vessels, hotels, theme parks, civic centers, libraries, office interiors, and residences.

49648 ■ R&S Design Computer Services Inc.
10 W Fron St.
Media, PA 19063
Ph:(610)565-5523
Fax: (610)892-3983
Co. E-mail: info@rsdesign.com
URL: http://www.rsdesign.com

E-mail: info@rsdesign.com
Scope: Offers the sale, installation and configuration of PC software for business and home use. Also offers training for a wide variety of software applications, and maintenance and repair of hardware and network systems.

49649 ■ M. Richler and Associates Ltd.
85 Skymark Dr., Ste. 2603
North York, ON, Canada M2H 3P2
Ph:(416)491-5264
Fax: (416)491-4557
Scope: A general management consulting firm specializing in acquisitions and mergers, costing and pricing, office layout design and management, production management and taxation, particularly for small businesses. Industries served: manufacturing, retail, wholesale, import/export, design services, and gov-

ernment agencies. **Publications:** "Contact" 1995 Budget Release. Also, 1996-2000 Budget Releases. **Seminars:** Keeping the Cottage in the Family; Maximizing Capital Gains Exemption; Minimizing Probate Fees; Plant Reorganization; Departmental Scheduling.

49650 ■ Roeder Design
3878 Oak Lawn Ave., Ste. 220
Dallas, TX 75219
Ph:(214)528-2300
Fax: (214)521-2300
Co. E-mail: robert@roederdesign.com

E-mail: robert@roederdesign.com
Scope: Lighting design consulting firm experienced with cruise ships, residences, hotels, casinos, office buildings, retail showrooms, and health-care facilities.

49651 ■ Rowland Design Inc.
701 E New York St.
Indianapolis, IN 46202
Ph:(317)636-3980
Fax: (317)263-2065
Co. E-mail: info@rowlanddesign.com
URL: http://www.rowlanddesign.com

E-mail: info@rowlanddesign.com
Scope: Architecture, interior design, environmental graphic design, club consulting, alternative workplace strategies, space planning, thematic entertainment, hospitality design, and museum/exhibit design.

49652 ■ RTKL Associates Inc.
901 S Bond St.
Baltimore, MD 21231
Ph:(410)537-6000
Fax: (410)276-2136
Co. E-mail: baltimore-info@rtkl.com
URL: http://www.rtkl.com

E-mail: baltimore-info@rtkl.com
Scope: Provides architecture, engineering, planning and urban design, interior architecture and design, landscape architecture, and environmental graphic design services for clients in public and private sector. Engaged in office, retail, hospitality, mixed-use, health sciences, entertainment, transportation, residential, and planning projects worldwide.

49653 ■ S & S Office Solutions Inc.
3480 Johnson Ferry Rd.
Roswell, GA 30075
Ph:(770)518-0868
Fax: (770)518-4483
Co. E-mail: info@ssos.com
URL: http://www.ssos.com

E-mail: info@ssos.com
Scope: Specialists in designing, installing, and consulting for LANs (Local Area Networks) and wiring systems for professional offices (MCSE). **Special Services:** Microsoft certified partner.

49654 ■ SBA Computers Inc.
922 Talon Dr.
O'Fallon, IL 62269
Ph:(618)628-9590
Fax: (618)622-3717
Co. E-mail: info@sbacomputers.com
URL: http://www.sbacomputers.com

E-mail: info@sbacomputers.com
Scope: Provides web site and domain hosting. Also offers domain registration services.

49655 ■ Warfel Schrager Architectural Lighting L.L.C.
412 Main St., Ste. H
Ridgefield, CT 06877
Ph:(203)438-1188
Fax: (203)438-2299
Co. E-mail: sschrager@wsal-llc.com
URL: http://www.warfelschrager.com

E-mail: sschrager@wsal-llc.com
Scope: Experienced with architectural lighting design, including projects in historic preservation, public atri-

ums, commercial lobbies, corporate reception areas, exterior lighting, offices, art collections, and restaurants.

49656 ■ Chris Shaff Consulting
8641 Dasher Ave. NW
North Canton, OH 44720-4611
Ph:(330)494-1921
Scope: Specializes in business forms manufacturing and administration.

49657 ■ Simplified Technology Co.
PO Box 8281
Fremont, CA 94537
Ph:(510)794-5520
Free: 800-782-4435
Co. E-mail: sales200521@simplifiedtechnology.com
URL: http://www.simplifiedtechnology.com

E-mail: sales200521@simplifiedtechnology.com
Scope: Firm specializes in providing system security, networking, custom software development and data availability.

49658 ■ Michael John Smith
3118 Richmond Ave., Ste. 100
Houston, TX 77098
Ph:(713)850-1488
Fax: (713)850-7525
Co. E-mail: michael@mjslight.com
URL: http://www.mjslight.com

E-mail: michael@mjslight.com
Scope: Full service architectural lighting design firm provides expertise with interior, exterior, landscape, facade, roadway, and industrial illumination.

49659 ■ Spacial Design
524 San Anselmo Ave., Ste. 146
San Anselmo, CA 94960
Ph:(415)457-3195
Fax: (415)457-1876
Co. E-mail: contactus@spacialdesign.com
URL: http://www.spacialdesign.com

E-mail: contactus@spacialdesign.com
Scope: Specializes in space planning for kitchens, closets and office. Works with individual homeowners and small businesses. Also advises clients on setting up systems and then designing spaces to accommodate those systems. **Seminars:** Kitchen Planning Seminar, Sonoma Valley Adult School, Oct, 2006.

49660 ■ Gary Steffy Lighting Design
2900 S State St., Ste. 12
Ann Arbor, MI 48104
Ph:(734)747-6630
Free: 800-537-1230
Fax: (734)747-6629
Co. E-mail: grs@gsld.net
URL: http://www.gsld.net

E-mail: grs@gsld.net
Scope: Lighting design consultants for interior and exterior lighting needs. Additional area of expertise is landscape lighting. Serves private industries as well as government agencies. **Seminars:** Office Lighting; Lighting for Electronic Offices; Lighting Design; Historic Lighting.

49661 ■ Symmes Maini & McKee Associates
1000 Massachusetts Ave.
Cambridge, MA 02138
Ph:(617)547-5400
Fax: (617)354-5758
Co. E-mail: info@smma.com
URL: http://www.smma.com

E-mail: info@smma.com
Scope: A full service architecture, master planning, urban design, and interior design firm serving healthcare, educational, financial, and commercial institutions with particular emphasis on hospitals, research laboratories, office buildings, and educational structures including athletic facilities.

49662 ■ Systems Alternatives International L. L.C.
1705 Indian Wood Cir., Ste. 100
Maumee, OH 43537
Ph:(419)891-1100
Fax: (419)891-1045
Co. E-mail: sales@sysalt.com
URL: http://www.sysalt.com

E-mail: sales@sysalt.com
Scope: Firm specializes in selling hardware and software. Provides innovative software and quality information technology services to the unique needs of the recycling and metals industries.

49663 ■ TLA-Lighting Consultants Inc.
7 Pond St.
Salem, MA 01970
Ph:(978)745-6870
Fax: (978)741-4420
Co. E-mail: tmlattla@aol.com

E-mail: tmlattla@aol.com
Scope: Offers counsel on lighting installation design, lighting product design, lighting energy conservation studies and daylighting, optical systems design, system evaluation and testing, and product and market planning. Serves private industries as well as government agencies. **Seminars:** Reflector Design - Theory and Practice.

49664 ■ Waters Instruments Inc.
13705 26th Ave. N, Ste. 102
Plymouth, MN 55441
Ph:(763)551-1125
Fax: (763)509-7450
URL: http://www.wtrs.com

49665 ■ Scott M. Watson Inc.
15200 Shady Grove Rd., Ste. 350
Rockville, MD 20850
Ph:(301)869-8800
Fax: (301)869-8802
Co. E-mail: smwiald@aol.com

E-mail: smwiald@aol.com
Scope: Lighting design consultant for new and renovated commercial, institutional, and high-end residential projects. Particular expertise provided in lighting layouts, fixture specifications, control groupings, dimmer specifications, shop drawing review, punch-out and focus of installations. Custom fixtures and applications designed as needed. Serves architects, interior designers, and owners, as well as government agencies. **Seminars:** Lectures on lighting design, including commercial lighting design and applications. Member of visiting faculty, Environmental Design Dept., Baltimore from 1993-2000, Sections of ED-100 and Ed-150 bi-annually. **Special Services:** AutoCad R2000, Lumen Micro, Visual.

49666 ■ WNF Consulting Inc.
PO Box 42118
Phoenix, AZ 85080
Ph:(480)940-4808
Co. E-mail: info@wnf.com
URL: http://www.wnf.com

E-mail: info@wnf.com
Scope: Firm specializes in network analysis and design. Consulting engineers assist in understanding the

characteristics of each network resource and segment, optimization of network hierarchy based on usage requirements, system performance and effective resource utilization, optimization of pooled server and application configurations, storage management methodology for day-to-day storage management, and storage management methodology for automated storage management. **Special Services:** Identity Management Service.

FRANCHISES AND BUSINESS OPPORTUNITIES

49667 ■ California Closet Company
1000 Fourth St., Ste. 800
San Rafael, CA 94901
Ph:(415)256-8500
Free: 800-241-3222
Fax: (415)256-8501
No. of Franchise Units: 104. **No. of Company-Owned Units:** 4. **Founded:** 1978. **Franchised:** 1982. **Description:** Custom closet design, manufacture, and installation. **Equity Capital Needed:** $200,400-$433,800 total investment; $150,000 net worth, $75,000-$150,000 cash liquidity. **Franchise Fee:** $45,900. **Royalty Fee:** 6%. **Financial Assistance:** No. **Training:** Provides 1 week at headquarters, 2 weeks at franchisees location, 2 weeks mentor training with ongoing support.

49668 ■ Stratis Business Centers
Regus Business Centres, plc
555 N Point Center E, 4th Fl.
Alpharetta, GA 30022
Ph:(678)366-5215
Free: 888-778-7284
Fax: (678)366-4661
No. of Franchise Units: 50. **Founded:** 1996. **Franchised:** 1997. **Description:** provider of office space and business telecom services. **Equity Capital Needed:** $110,000-$280,000. **Franchise Fee:** $50,000. **Financial Assistance:** No. **Training:** Yes.

LIBRARIES

49669 ■ Tech-U-Fit Corporation–Library
400 Madison St., No. 210
Alexandria, VA 22314
Ph:(703)549-0512
Fax: (703)548-0780
Contact: John Molino
Scope: Engineering, psychology, human factors engineering, ergonomics. **Holdings:** 200 volumes.

RESEARCH CENTERS

49670 ■ Lighting Research Institute, Inc.
PO Box 1550
Hendersonville, NC 28793-1550
Ph:(828)692-1904
Fax: (828)692-6820
Contact: Alfred B. Gough, Pres.
Scope: Photobiology, vision, lighting system applications, human performance and psychology. **Publications:** Annual Report. **Educational Activities:** Illumination Roundtable with the National Bureau of Standards.

49671 ■ New Jersey Institute of Technology–Center for Architecture and Building Science Research
335 Campbell Hall
323 Martin Luther King Blvd.
Newark, NJ 07102-1982
Ph:(973)596-3097
Fax: (973)596-8443
Co. E-mail: deane.evans@njit.edu
URL: http://www.njit.edu/Directory/Centers/cabsr
Contact: Deane M. Evans, Exec.Dir.
E-mail: deane.evans@njit.edu
Scope: The relationship between the built environment and the institutions, policies and trends that shape it, emphasizing building types and environments related to housing, education, health and aging, and developmental disabilities planning. The center also studies ways to optimize the use of available resources to create more effective and efficient environments to better serve users' needs, cost effective methods and approaches to translate research concepts into practice through programs, policies and actions devoted to improving new and existing facilities and related social conditions. programs, policies and actions devoted to improving new and existing facilities and related social conditions.

49672 ■ Rensselaer Polytechnic Institute–Lighting Research Center
21 Union St.
Troy, NY 12180
Ph:(518)687-7100
Fax: (518)687-7120
Co. E-mail: ream@rpi.edu
URL: http://www.lrc.rpi.edu
Contact: Prof. Mark S. Rea PhD, Dir.
E-mail: ream@rpi.edu
Scope: Lighting systems, including studies in vision, visibility, daylighting, efficient lighting technologies, architecture, building systems interactions, control systems, design tools, glass science, lighting economics, technology transfer, vision, transportation lighting, light and health, and human responses to lighting, including productivity, mood, and perception of brightness and spaciousness. **Publications:** Delta Portfolios (periodically); Design books, evaluations; NLPIP Lighting Answers (periodically); NLPIP Specifier Reports (periodically). **Educational Activities:** Colloquia (biweekly); Industrial partners program; Roundtables, workshops, teleconferences, symposia, tours, demonstrations, and presentations; Utility Personnel Training Seminars.

49673 ■ University of Quebec at Montreal–Centre for Study of Biological Interactions Between Environment and Health–Centre de recherche interdisciplinaire sur la biologie, la santé, la société et l'environnement
PO Box 8888
Montreal, QC, Canada H3C 3P8
Ph:(514)987-3915
Fax: (514)987-6183
Co. E-mail: vandalec.louise@uqam.ca
URL: http://www.unites.uqam.ca/cinbiose/
Contact: Louise Vandelac, Dir.
E-mail: vandalec.louise@uqam.ca
Scope: Occupational health, ergonomics.

START-UP INFORMATION

49674 ■ "Inside or Out?" in *Black Enterprise* (Vol. 35, October 2004, No. 3, pp. 60)
Pub: Earl G. Graves Publishing Co. Inc.
Ed: Alan Hughes. **Description:** The pros and cons of outsourcing for a newly formed company are addressed.

EDUCATIONAL PROGRAMS

49675 ■ **Best Practices in Strategic Outsourcing: It's Not Just for manufacturing Anymore**
American Management Association
1601 Broadway
New York, NY 10019
Ph:(212)586-8100
Free: 800-262-9699
Fax: (212)903-8168
Co. E-mail: customerservice@amanet.org
URL: http://www.amanet.org
Price: $1,995 for non-members; $1,795 for AMA members. **Description:** Covers the pros and cons of outsourcing, be able to recognize the cost reduction areas to increase value, and implementation of outsourcing program. **Locations:** New York, NY; Atlanta, GA; Chicago, IL; Washington, DC; and San Francisco, CA.

REFERENCE WORKS

49676 ■ "Asia Rising" in *Black Enterprise* (Vol. 35, October 2004, No. 3, pp. 46)
Pub: Earl G. Graves Publishing Co. Inc.
Ed: Donald Jay Korn. **Description:** China and India are two emerging global economies making them attractive for investing. Manufacturing and high tech jobs are being outsourced to both countries. It is important to research before investing in China and India, as well as any international funds.

49677 ■ "Bring the New Economy Home" in *Home Office Computing* (Vol. 18, No. 12, December 2000, pp. 66)
Pub: Scholastic Inc.
Ed: William Van Winkle. **Description:** A guide to so-called New Economy concepts that can benefit a small business is presented. Small and home-based firms can seldom afford in-house expert help, and outsourcing is a viable option for a variety of business processors. Experts recommend that companies outsource to providers with other clients in the same line of business.

49678 ■ "Business-to-Consumer E-Commerce: What is(n't) the Problem?" in *E-business Advisor* (Vol. 18, No. 8, August 2000, pp. 6)
Pub: Advisor Media, Inc.

Ed: Jane M. Falla. **Description:** Customers are grumbling, investors are threatening, and start-ups are sweating since the downturn of dot-coms. Despite the apparent dire straits, consumer online buying marches on and B2C e-commerce sights will need to outsource or find the correct packaged technology to keep pace with all of the changes occurring.

49679 ■ "Call Centers In the Rec Room" in *Business Week* (January 23, 2006, No. 3968, pp. 76-77)
Pub: McGraw-Hill Companies
Ed: Michelle Conlin. **Description:** Homeshoring provides an alternative to offshoring, whereby American companies are finding a cheap alternative to overseas call centers in the form of stay-at-home moms, the disabled, retirees, and others. Statistical data included.

49680 ■ "Case Study" in *Inc.* (July 1, 2004)
Pub: Inc. Magazine
Ed: Rod Kurtz. **Description:** Profile of Everdream, a software provider in California who outsourced its North Carolina call center to a firm in San Jose, Costa Rica. The move cut 25 percent in operating expenses, but might not have been the best decision for the company.

49681 ■ "Chunk of Change: Navigating Employment Taxes" in *My Business* (June/July 2004, pp. 14)
Pub: My Business Magazine
Description: Many companies are outsourcing company payrolls to payroll service firms because they believe it is more efficient to let the service handle the payroll and tax withholding issues involved.

49682 ■ "Clients breathe easy thanks to outsourced tech support" in *Colorado Springs Business Journal* (March 7, 2003)
Pub: Dolan Media Newswires
Ed: Becky Huley. **Description:** Profile of Jeff Harrell, president and owner of Advanced Business Solutions, offering secure information technology services, Internet access filtered email and custom software services to companies.

49683 ■ "Close the Loop" in *Entrepreneur* (Vol. 31, No. 10, October 2003, pp. 82)
Pub: Entrepreneur Media, Inc.
Ed: Chris Penttila. **Description:** Today companies can outsource most types of work, a trend entrepreneurs are using to grow their business.

49684 ■ "Commentary: Departure of Jobs Hurts National Security" in *Long Island Business News* (February 6, 2004)
Pub: Dolan Media Newswires
Ed: John Kiernan. **Description:** The trend to send jobs overseas not only hurts America's economy, but also jeopardizes national security in the long term. National policy must be created to encourage and keep manufacturing jobs and capacity in the U.S.

49685 ■ "Commentary: Is America III Positioned for Global Economy?" in *Long Island Business News* (February 6, 2004)
Pub: Dolan Media Newswires
Ed: Jerry Kremer. **Description:** Two million jobs have been lost to overseas workers since 2000. Many of these positions went overseas to countries such as China, India, Japan, as well as others. Major American corporations are able to save money by outsourcing to these countries.

49686 ■ "Companies Team to Help Small Law Firms" in *Crain's Detroit Business* (Vol. 19, No. 45, November 10, 2003, pp. 41)
Pub: Crain Communications Inc., Detroit
Ed: Robert Ankeny. **Description:** Professional Human Capital LLC offers administrative and human-resource services to small law firms and solo practitioners in the Metropolitan Detroit area. The new company will handle tasks specific to law firms, including payroll, taxes and health insurance.

49687 ■ "Continuing to Shine" in *Hispanic Business* (December 2001, pp. 10)
Pub: Hispanic Business
Ed: Holly Ocasio Rizzo. **Description:** The demand for temporary industrial and clerical workers has increased since mid-September 2001. Companies that lay people off still need work done, so they hire temporary workers.

49688 ■ "Contractors Market" in *Rough Notes* (Vol. 145, No. 1, January 2003, pp. 64)
Pub: Rough Notes
Ed: Larry G. France. **Description:** Specialty lines markets deal with the tightening market on insurance needed by contractors and subcontractors on contractors' risks. A directory of insurance agents providing contractors insurance is included.

49689 ■ "Data Centers: Infrastructure upgrades ahead" in *Red Herring* (No. 102, August 15, 2001, pp. 74-75)
Pub: Herring Communications
Ed: Om Malik. **Description:** For corporations to outsource their information technology infrastructures to data centers, those data centers need to upgrade to carrier-class equipment.

49690 ■ "E-Mail the Way it Should Be" in *PC Computing* (April 2000, pp. 117)
Pub: Ziff-Davis Inc.
Ed: Bonny L. Georgia. **Description:** It is possible for a company to save a substantial amount of money if they outsource their e-mail. This article focuses in on some of the companies that offer these services and give brief evaluations.

49691 ■ "The Economics" in *Law Firm Inc.* (August 2004)
Pub: American Lawyer Media LP
Ed: Sam Collier. **Description:** Law firms should compare costs when planning to outsource technology services based on combination of capacity (the number of users and workstations), complexity and features, and service level.

49692 ■ "Efulfillment Service" in *Entrepreneur.com* **(Vol. 34, February 2006, No. 2, pp. 6)**
Pub: Entrepreneur Media Inc.
Description: Efulfillment Service helps companies outsource fulfillment needs for fees starting at $68.50 per month.

49693 ■ "Eliminate Fulfillment Problems" in *E-business Advisor* **(Vol. 18, No. 3, March 2000, pp. 28)**
Pub: Advisor Media, Inc.
Ed: Patrick Rigney. **Description:** The best ways to integrate an online system with an existing business is to establish a separate order fulfillment center, or to outsource order processing. Orders are then sent directly to the company's warehouse.

49694 ■ "Farming IT Out" in *Home Office Computing* **(Vol. 18, No. 10, October 2000, pp. 16)**
Pub: Scholastic Inc.
Ed: Mark Kakkuri. **Description:** Information Technology (IT) outsourcing services are ready to help home office workers with everything from setting up a computer to building a broadband LAN.

49695 ■ "First-Class Delivery" in *Small Business Opportunities* **(Vol. 13, No. 5, September 2001, pp. 66, 80)**
Pub: Harris Publications, Inc.
Ed: Diana Singer. **Description:** By outsourcing mail, a company can increase productivity and achieve numerous economies. A step-by-step approach to mail center management is outlined.

49696 ■ "For the People" in *Entrepreneur. com* **(Vol. 34, February 2006, No. 2, pp. 68)**
Pub: Entrepreneur Media Inc.
Ed: Joshua Kurlantzick. **Description:** The U.S. government's contract budget has grown to $300 billion and is growing due to more outsourcing to contractors. Entrepreneurs share secrets to procuring government contracts.

49697 ■ "Forget India, Outsource to Oregon!" in *Venture Capital Journal* **(December 1, 2004)**
Pub: Thomason Financial Inc.
Description: Reasons for venture capitals to target investments in Oregon and the Pacific Northwest rather than India or China are presented. Experienced angel investors and venture capitalists are taking the lead in building Oregon's high-tech entrepreneurial community.

49698 ■ "The Freeland Conundrum" in *Inc.* **(December 1, 2004)**
Pub: Inc. Magazine
Ed: Mike Brewster. **Description:** Contract workers can save small business money, but there could be hidden costs in an office full of temporary workers.

49699 ■ "GM's Way Or the Highway" in *Business Week* **(December 19, 2005, No. 3964, pp. 48-49)**
Pub: McGraw-Hill Companies
Ed: Steve Hamm. **Description:** With $15 billion in deals to discourse, General Motors is changing technology outsourcing business.

49700 ■ "Hearing Them Out" in *Sales & Marketing Management*
Pub: VNU Business Media
Ed: Betsy Cummings. **Description:** Administaff, the human resources outsourcing company located in Kingwood, Texas, credits its sales team's input for its success.

49701 ■ "Help Wanted" in *Entrepreneur.com* **(Vol. 34, February 2006, No. 2, pp. 80)**
Pub: Entrepreneur Media Inc.
Ed: Chris Penttila. **Description:** Globalization, outsourcing and competition for capital are putting pressure on small companies to operate more like large businesses. Ideas for hiring CEOs for a small firm are included.

49702 ■ "Help Wanted: Net Profits: Want to Hand a Project to a Freelancer But Don't Know Where to Start?" in *Entrepreneur* **(Vol. 31, Sept.2003)**
Pub: Entrepreneur Media, Inc.
Ed: Melissa Campanelli. **Description:** Outsourcing can save small businesses time, money and frustration by outsourcing work and the Internet is a good way to find talent.

49703 ■ "Help Wanted" in *Small Business Opportunities* **(Vol. 12, No. 5, September 2000, pp. 10, 130)**
Pub: Harris Publications, Inc.
Ed: John Orth. **Description:** Outsourcing human resources functions to a Professional Employer Organization (PEO) allows entrepreneurs to focus on their core competencies, knowing that trained professionals are handling the administrative and HR activities of the business. The article offers a questionnaire to determine if it is time to outsource and a guideline for choosing the right PEO.

49704 ■ "Here Comes Trouble: Avoid Independent Contractor Snags" in *Entrepreneur* **(Vol. 33, February 2005, No. 2, pp. 50)**
Pub: Entrepreneur Media Inc.
Ed: Joan Szabo. **Description:** Internal Revenue Service inspects worker classification searching for entrepreneurs who misclassify workers as independent contractors instead of actual employees of the company. It is simpler for the IRS to collect taxes from business owners rather than independent contractors. Employers must deduct for income taxes, Social Security and Medicare taxes, and pay unemployment taxes on wages paid to employees.

49705 ■ *How to Start a Bankruptcy Forms Processing Service*
Pub: Graphico Publishing Company
Ed: Victoria Ring. **Released:** September 2004. **Price:** $59.99. **Description:** Due to the increase in bankruptcy filings, attorneys are outsourcing related jobs in order to reduce overhead.

49706 ■ "The Importance of Well-Crafted Terms" in *Law Firm Inc.* **(August 2004)**
Pub: American Lawyer Media LP
Ed: Mark Hanchet, Edward Hansen. **Description:** Agreements involving complex technology relationships should be negotiated and drafted with the idea of avoiding future litigation because of the long-term partnerships they create. These contracts cover such issues as outsourcing and enterprise resources planning (ERP) licensing and implementation agreements; risk avoidance, scope of services, service levels and cost need to be agreed upon before the contract is signed.

49707 ■ "It's 2006! Whatcha Gonna Do About It?" in *Inc.* **(Volume 28, January 2006, No. 1, pp. 78-85, 113)**
Pub: Inc. Magazine
Ed: Stephanie Clifford. **Description:** Various entrepreneurs give advice to help small businesses face new challenges in 2006. Topics include investments, the economy, small business trends, logistics, business communication such as blogs, energy issues, consumer products, real estate, interest rates and outsourcing.

49708 ■ "It's Never E-nough" in *Business Week* **(No. 3689, July 10, 2000, pp. F14)**
Pub: McGraw-Hill, Inc.
Description: Highlights of surveys of companies with 20-49 employees regarding the future of small business, including information about the Internet, Palmtops, networks, e-backlash, the bottom line, cost cutting, outsourcing, leasing, and Internet Telephony.

49709 ■ "Job Inside" in *Fast Company* **(September 2001, pp. 177)**
Pub: Fast Company
Ed: George Anders. **Description:** The intranet is intended for internal use, but for small and mid-size companies outsourcing may be the best option for this technology.

49710 ■ "Leasing 101: need a new fleet but low on dough? Leasing may be the key" in *Entrepreneur* **(Vol. 30, No. 12, December 2002, pp. 43)**
Pub: Entrepreneur Media Inc.
Ed: Jill Amadio. **Description:** Whether handling commercial vehicle leasing in-house or outsourcing to a fleet management company or through the car supplier, fleet leasing makes economic sense because of the 5-7 percent discount off the vehicles' total price.

49711 ■ "Life Sciences Span The Globe: U.S. VCs Like to Spend Money in their Backyards" in *Venture Capital Journal* **(October 1, 2004)**
Pub: Thomason Financial Inc.
Ed: Matthew Sheahan. **Description:** U.S. life science companies took about $3.6 billion in venture capital funding in 2004, more than 70 percent of the worldwide total, but Europe and Canada are working to attract these same companies. The cost advantages in both Canada and Europe are discussed.

49712 ■ "Lowest bid is not always best for hiring contractor" in *Business First Columbus* **(Vol. 18, No. 25, February 8, 2002, pp.)**
Pub: Business First Columbus, Inc.
Ed: Susanna Barton. **Description:** Tips for choosing the correct contractor for the job are offered.

49713 ■ "Maine Says Flooring Companies Need to Pay Subcontractor Taxes" in *Portland Press Herald* **(April 8, 2005)**
Pub: Blethen Maine Newspapers, Inc.
Ed: Matt Wickenheiser. **Description:** Maine has determined that floor covering firms using subcontractors should be required to pay unemployment taxes on their wages. Guidelines for the state's ABC Test for unemployment taxes are covered.

49714 ■ *Make it Big in the $100 Billion Outsource Contracting Industry: Turn Your Knowledge Experience & Commitment into Lifetime Strategic Partnerships*
Pub: Westfield Press
Ed: Robert W. Jennings edited by John Passaro. **Released:** 1997. **Price:** $49.95 (cloth). **Description:** Turn your knowledge, experience & commitment into your own successful business. Teaches you how to use your career experiences & strengths to tap into this huge & expanding market. All specialties are needed from operating entire corporate copy centers to data processing centers.

49715 ■ "Management to Go" in *Success* **(Vol. 47, No. 6, November 2000, pp. 54)**
Pub: Success Publishing, Inc.
Ed: Eddy Goldberg, Paul Gallagher. **Description:** Virtual CEO's can be your key to succeeding in the new economy. Thanks to the Internet, outsourcing business operations that used to be considered essential, even confidential, makes good business sense today.

49716 ■ "Medfone Expanding Its Wantagh Headquarters" in *Long Island Business News* **(March 5, 2004)**
Pub: Dolan Media Newswires
Ed: Nick Anastasi. **Description:** Medfone National Inc. is expanding and renovating its corporate headquarters in New York. The firm acts as a call center serving all fields of the health industry, specializing in outsourced calling and Web-based solutions for the electronic retailing, direct marketing, pharmaceuticals, hospital, medical practice and managed care segments.

49717 ■ "Moving Out: When to Outsource Your Server Operations" in *My Business* **(December/January 2004, pp. 42)**
Pub: My Business Magazine
Ed: Paige Orr. **Description:** Tips for small companies wishing to outsource server operations are presented. These firms manage critical business and network applications.

49718 ■ "New War Means New Contracts" in *Hispanic Business* **(March 2002, pp. 58)**
Pub: Hispanic Business
Ed: Patricia Guadalupe, Frank McCoy. **Description:** Outsourcing and a security buildup will impact procurement for minority firms in the U.S. Statistics for the Department of Defense, the Department of Transportation, and the Department of Justice, all concerned with terrorist threats, are presented.

49719 ■ "Northern Trust Close To an Outsourcing Foothold in Britain" in *American Banker* **(Vol. 170, February 3, 2005, No. 23, pp. 2)**
Pub: Thomson Financial Media Inc.
Ed: Laurie Kulikowski. **Description:** Northern Trust, headquartered in Chicago, Illinois, is close to closing an outsourcing deal with Insight Investment Management Ltd of London, England. Northern Trust would provide back- and middle-office services, including record keeping and trade matching, confirmation, and settlement to the firm. Insight Investment manages $140.5 billion of assets.

49720 ■ "Offshoring Could Boost Your Career" in *Fortune* **(Vol. 151, January 24, 2005, No. 2, pp. 36)**
Pub: Time Inc.
Ed: Anne Fisher. **Description:** According to a study conducted by Duke University's Fuqua School of Business and Archstone Consulting, American businesses with offshore operations will ship 81 percent more research jobs, 55 percent more engineering, and 75 percent more human resources overseas (69 percent of which are already in India). American managers will be needed to oversee these operations.

49721 ■ "Offshoring Isn't Such a Sure Thing" in *Inc.* **(September 2005, pp. 32, 34)**
Pub: Inc. Magazine
Ed: Lora Koldony. **Description:** According to a new survey conducted by DiamondCluster International, a Chicago, Illinois management consulting firm, U.S. companies are finding that sending work overseas can be more difficult than it is worth.

49722 ■ "Outsource the Outsourcing" in *Inc.* **(Volume 27, December 2005, No. 12, pp. 55-56)**
Pub: Inc. Magazine
Ed: Darren Dahl. **Description:** Offshore contractors are helping entrepreneurs connect with offshore firms in order to outsource work overseas.

49723 ■ "Outsourced e-mail" in *PC Computing* **(April 2000, pp. 117)**
Pub: Ziff-Davis Inc.
Ed: Bonny L. Georgia. **Description:** Ferris Research predicts that within one year, e-mail traffic will increase three to five times, and storage requirements could more than double. The article shows how to outsource e-mail in order to increase business.

49724 ■ "Outsourcers go big" in *InfoWorld* **(Vol. 23, No. 5, January 29, 2001, pp. 48)**
Pub: InfoWorld
Ed: Brian Fonseca, Jennifer Jones. **Description:** Outsourcers and application service providers (ASP), feeling the pressure of the dot-com collapse and finding fewer companies on which to simply ride alongside, are beginning to focus on the needs of large enterprises and tailor their services for complex environments.

49725 ■ "Outsourcing" in *PC Computing* **(April 2000, pp. 185)**
Pub: Ziff-Davis Inc.
Ed: Christine Grech Wendin. **Description:** Small and medium-size companies are increasingly turning to the Web to get the business of running their businesses done. According to a recent Hambrecht and Quist study, the Internet business services market will grow to $6.6 billion in three years.

49726 ■ "Passing the Baton" in *Sales & Marketing Management* **(Vol. 157, January 2005, No. 1, pp. 34)**
Pub: VNU Business Media
Ed: Sara Calabro. **Description:** Outsourcing sales staff is becoming widely accepted in the industry. Outsourcing works best for products with short sales cycles.

49727 ■ "Pinstriped Populist" in *New York Times* **(November 12, 2006, pp. 15)**
Pub: New York Times Company
Ed: David Sirota. **Description:** Profile of Lou Dobbs, author of How the Government, Big Business, and Special Interest Groups Are Waging War on the American Dream and How to Fight Back. Dobbs, a financial journalist, examines wages, corruption, trade, outsourcing, immigration and health care.

49728 ■ "The portable CEO" in *WorkingWoman* **(Vol. 25, No. 2, February 2000, pp. 54)**
Pub: Lang Communications Inc.
Ed: Betsy Wiesendanger. **Description:** Bettina Whyte, temporary CEO of APS Holding, discusses the new trend of outsourcing being used by companies.

49729 ■ "The Problem of Perceptions: Reasons for Outsourcing the Sexual Harassment Investigation" in *Employment Relations Today* **(Vol.27, No.1)**
Pub: John Wiley & Sons, Inc.
Ed: Jonathan Day. **Description:** Management of sexual harassment allegations by human resource departments are explored. Topics addressed include employee perceptions of harassment cases, and the outsourcing of an investigation to an independent third party.

49730 ■ "PSI Uses Technology to Keep Call-Center Biz in U.S." in *Crain's Detroit Business* **(Vol. 21, December 19, 2005, No. 51, pp. 10)**
Pub: Crain Communications Inc. - Detroit
Ed: Anjali Fluker. **Description:** Larry Evans, president and owner of PSI based in West Bloomfield Township, Michigan, has invested nearly $500,000 into expanding his business. The move includes new technology and the addition of about 50 workers. Evans discusses the advantages to keeping his operations here rather than offshore outsourcing the work.

49731 ■ "Rising Drug Costs" in *Venture Capital Journal* **(October 1, 2204)**
Pub: Thomason Financial Inc.
Ed: Alastair Goldfisher. **Description:** With the rising costs of conducting clinical trials of new drugs, technology companies may choose offshore outsourcing of research and development to save money. However, the cost of new drug development is rising worldwide. Statistical data included.

49732 ■ "Scorecard & Blueprint" in *Hispanic Business* **(Vol. 24, No. 5, May 2002, pp. 48)**
Pub: Hispanic Business Inc.
Ed: Joel Russell. **Description:** The 2003 Federal budget rates agencies on five different management criteria. Under the plan, nearly one-quarter of all federal workers will have their jobs outsourced.

49733 ■ "Seeking outside help" in *Crain's Detroit Business* **(Vol. 19, No. 8, February 24, 2003, pp. 11)**
Pub: Crain Communications Inc., Detroit
Ed: Katie Merx. **Description:** Area hospitals have begun outsourcing essential medical services as well as the traditionally outsourced non-medical services.

49734 ■ "Singh-ing His Praises" in *Inc.* **(September 1, 2004)**
Pub: Inc. Magazine
Ed: Rod Kurtz. **Description:** Profile of Manmohan Singh, one of India's top economists and newly elected to the prime minister's chair. According to Amit Maheswari, CEO of i-Vantage, a Cambridge, Massachusetts outsourcing firm employing 300 employees in India, credits Singh with making outsourcing to Indian companies popular in the U.S. and elsewhere.

49735 ■ "Some outplacement firms benefit in down economy" in *Boston Business Journal* **(Vol. 22, No. 14, May 10, 2002, pp. 38)**
Pub: MCP, Inc.
Ed: Pam Derringer. **Description:** Corporate spending for outplacement has declined so there is more competition, but those who have size, reputation and niche have a chance of surviving in the down economy.

49736 ■ "Squeezed out? Is there any room left for small businesses in federal contracting?" in *Entrepreneur* **(Vol. 31, No. 4, April 2003)**
Pub: Entrepreneur Media Inc.
Ed: Chris Penttila. **Description:** In 2001, contract bundling cost small businesses an estimated $13 billion. Technology, engineering and outsourcing companies are expected to benefit from new Homeland Security projects, but the question is, will that include small companies.

49737 ■ "States Target Outsourcing" in *Inc.* **(July 1, 2004)**
Pub: Inc. Magazine
Ed: Darren Dahl. **Description:** Several states hope legislation efforts will help curb the trend toward outsourcing to companies overseas.

49738 ■ "Straight to the Outsource: Sales Force: Feeling the Crunch?" in *Entrepreneur* **(Vol. 31, No. 9, September 2003, pp. 83)**
Pub: Entrepreneur Media, Inc.
Ed: Kimberly L. McCall. **Description:** Outsourcing sales functions allows a small business to eliminate many of the costs associated with an in-house sales division.

49739 ■ "Subcontractors on the hook in fight over stadium overruns" in *Crain's Detroit Business* **(Vol. 19, No. 5, February 3, 2003, pp. 1)**
Pub: Crain Communications Inc., Detroit
Ed: Robert Ankeny. **Description:** Subcontracts say they are caught in the middle of a battle over cost overruns in the construction of the new Ford Field's structural-steel contracts.

49740 ■ "Sweat rewards" in *Entrepreneur* **(Vol. 30, No. 3, Marc)**
Pub: Entrepreneur Media Inc.
Ed: Amanda C. Kooser, Geoff Williams. **Description:** Predictions for hot business trends in 2002 are presented, including online learning, kiosks, online games, bartering, alternative health for pets, managing outsourcing, maternity clothing, life coaches, alternative energy, e-books, plus-size clothing, ethnic foods, personalization themes, boomer menopause, luxury products and services for middle income consumers, technology, marketing, money and management.

49741 ■ "Taking It Outside: Outsourcing Can Be a Great Time Saver-But Mind the Costs" in *Black Enterprise* **(Vol. 34, No. 5, December 2003)**
Pub: Earl Graves Publishing Co.
Ed: Bridget McCrea. **Description:** Profile of C. Michael Greer, owner of The Little Coupon Book, and ways he is marketing his franchise venture in the Atlanta, Georgia area.

49742 ■ "Taking It Outside: Outsourcing Can Be a Great Time Saver-But Mind the Costs" in *Black Enterprise* **(Vol. 34, No. 5, December 2003)**
Pub: Earl Graves Publishing Co.
Ed: Bridget McCrea. **Description:** Profile of C. Michael Greer, owner of The Little Coupon Book, and ways he is marketing his franchise venture in the Atlanta, Georgia area.

49743 ■ "Tech Takeout" in *Entrepreneur* **(Vol. 31, No. 9, September 2003, pp. 48)**
Pub: Entrepreneur Media, Inc.
Description: Entrepreneurs are outsourcing information technology support services to save money; outsourcing is the fastest-growing area of the technology services market, including technical support to online CRM applications.

49744 ■ **"The Telework Puzzle"** in *Home Office Computing* (Vol. 19, No. 1, January 2001, pp. 90)
Pub: Scholastic Inc.
Ed: Lisa Roberts. **Description:** TManage Inc founder and CEO, Glenn Lovelace, discusses the factors that make telecommuting programs succeed or fail. Lovelace was director of telecommuting for Nortel Networks before starting his own consulting firm to outsource telework programs.

49745 ■ **"Texas considers outsourcing real estate needs"** in *Atlanta Business Chronicle* (Vol. 25, December 6, 2002, No. 26, pp. 30C)
Pub: American City Business Publications, Inc.
Ed: Matt Hudgins. **Description:** The Texas Building and Procurement Commission is considering outsourcing the administration of over 1,100 state-government leases. The outsourcing deal could be worth $4-$6 million per year in landlord commissions. The article discusses competing firms for the contract.

49746 ■ **"Thanks to the Xerox, the company reduced its outsourcing by 77.6 percent for the first six months of the year"** in *Inc.* (Nov. 15, 2000)
Pub: The Goldhirsh Group
Description: The CEO of a company tells how a new copier is helping the company grow.

49747 ■ **"They're not employees, they're people"** in *Harvard Business Review* (Vol. 80, No. 2, February 2002, pp. 70)
Pub: Harvard Business School Press
Ed: Peter F. Drucker. **Description:** Two fast-moving trends that are changing the way companies manage talent, the number of employees who are not longer traditional employees, and the growing number of companies that have outsourced employee relations is featured.

49748 ■ **"Timothy Askew: 54, Founder and CEO of Corporate Rain Inc (CRI)..."** in *Entrepreneur* (Vol. 32, No. 1, January 2004, pp. 23)
Pub: Entrepreneur Media, Inc.
Ed: April Y. Pennington. **Description:** Profile of Timothy Askew, founder and CEO of Corporate Rain Inc., an executive sales outsourcing boutique. Askew invested $10,000 in his startup in 1996 and sales are estimated at $1.9 million for 2003. CRIs sales force is made up of entrepreneurs and former executives with PhDs or higher and use the peer-to-peer approach to selling.

49749 ■ **"Tulsa-Based Dollar Thrifty Automotive Group Inc. to Outsource Call Center"** in *Journal Record (Oklahoma City, OK)* (February 8, 2007)
Pub: Journal Record
Description: Dollar Thrifty Automotive Group Inc. shares plans to outsource its call center services, including reservations and customer support services, to PRC in Plantation, Florida.

49750 ■ **"The Upside and Downside of Outsourcing"** in *Business Week* (February 20, 2006, No. 3972, pp. 18)
Pub: McGraw-Hill Companies
Description: Foreign companies are outsourcing jobs to the U.S. at record rates. Eight percent of U.S. workers are employed in the service industry, 19 percent in manufacturing, and only 1 percent in farming.

49751 ■ **"Users inch to security outsourcers"** in *InfoWorld* (Vol. 23, No. 5, January 29, 2001, pp. 10)
Pub: InfoWorld
Ed: Brian Fonseca, Heather Harreld. **Description:** Distributed denial of service (DDoS) attacks by hackers on the Web sites of major U.S. companies are a continuing threat. Despite these attacks, many companies maintain a low-key attitude toward network security and are not allotting the necessary funds to stave off problems. Smaller companies may feel safe, but smaller to medium-size businesses are being used as launching sites for attacks on major organizations.

49752 ■ **"Using a Reverse RFP Process to Assess Your Outsourcing Options"** in *Employment Relations Today* (Vol. 27, No. 2, Summer 2000, pp. 7)
Pub: John Wiley & Sons, Inc.
Ed: Jay F. Stright and Frank J. Candio. **Description:** Outsourcing is becoming a general principle of the knowledge economy as people focus on their competencies and engage specialists in other fields. The Reverse Request for Proposals approach to assessing outsourcing possibilities is presented.

49753 ■ **"Vendors tweak strategies to help clients buy"** in *Atlanta Business Chronicle* (Vol. 25, November 15, 2002, No. 23 pp. 3C)
Pub: American City Business Publications, Inc.
Ed: Don Reichardt. **Description:** As companies need to re-engineer costly legacy system, some are seeking less expensive alternatives. Leasing and outsourcing are becoming more popular alternatives. Details on alternatives being offered by vendors are included.

49754 ■ **"Virtual Assistants A Reality: Now You Can Outsource an Assistant's Job to A Remote Provider"** in *Broker Magazine* (Vol. 7)
Pub: Thomson Media Inc.
Ed: Brad Finkelstein. **Description:** A virtual assistant is an independent entrepreneur providing administrative, creative and/or technical services on a contractual basis. Profile of Jackie Kiadii, who runs a virtual assistance company specializing in the mortgage industry, is included.

49755 ■ **"We Must Lose the Entitlement Mentality"** in *Crain's Detroit Business* (Vol. 21, October 17, 2005, No. 43, pp. 9)
Pub: Crain Communications Inc. - Detroit

Ed: Mary Kramer. **Description:** Thomas Friedman, New York Times columnist, has written a book that identifies ten trends that are making the global economic playing field more level. Friedman offers advice, although not specifically focused on Michigan manufacturing, in the areas of outsourcing, offshoring and new supply-chain systems.

49756 ■ **"When in Doubt, Outsource"** in *PC Magazine* (January 4, 2000, pp. 146)
Pub: Ziff-Davis Publishing Company
Ed: Frank J. Derfler, Jr. **Description:** Carriers that will set up and maintain a VPN server, provide technical support for employees, and meet security threats are described.

49757 ■ **"Where the Jobs Are"** in *Business Week* (January 16, 2006, No. 3967, pp. 42-43)
Pub: McGraw-Hill Companies
Ed: Nandini Lakshman. **Description:** The number of foreign workers at Indian information technology and outsourcing companies has tripled to 30,000 in two years. Foreign workers earn about $350 per month.

49758 ■ **"Workload S.O.S."** in *Women In Business* (Vol. 52, No. 5, September-October 2000, pp. 30)
Pub: The ABWA Co., Inc.
Ed: Mary-Lane Kamberg. **Description:** Issues are presented concerning the solutions to staff shortages which occur as a result of workload fluctuations. The use of temporary staff, outside consultants, and the outsourcing of work are discussed.

CONSULTANTS

49759 ■ **C. Clint Bolte & Associates**
809 Philadelphia Ave.
Chambersburg, PA 17201
Ph:(717)263-5768
Fax: (717)263-8945
Co. E-mail: clint@clintbolte.com
URL: http://www.clintbolte.com

E-mail: clint@clintbolte.com
Scope: Provides management consulting services to firms involved with the printing industry. Services include outsourcing studies, graphics supply chain management studies, company and equipment valuations, plant layout services, litigation support, fulfillment warehouse consulting and product development services. **Publications:** "Time to Break Through the Glass Ceiling," The Seybold Report, May, 2006; "Challenges & Opportunities Presented by Postal Rate Increases," The Seybold Report, May, 2006; "Packaging Roll Sheeting Comes of Age," The Seybold Report, May, 2006; "Diversifying With Mailing & Fulfillment Services," The Seybold Report, Jan, 2006.

START-UP INFORMATION

49760 ■ "Green Acres" in *Small Business Opportunities* (Vol. 13, No. 5, September 2001, pp. 60, 64)
Pub: Harris Publications, Inc.
Description: Profile of United Landscape, Inc., specializing in landscape construction and full-service grounds maintenance. Jack Wernis and Sam LaGrasso tell how they turned their part-time, after-school venture into a multi-million dollar landscape service.

ASSOCIATIONS AND OTHER ORGANIZATIONS

49761 ■ National Association of Part-Time and Temporary Employees
5800 Barton, Ste. 201
PO Box 3805
Shawnee, KS 66203
Ph:(913)962-7740
Fax: (913)631-0489
Co. E-mail: napte-champion@worldnet.att.net
URL: http://www.members.tripod.com/~napte
Contact: Preston L. Conner, Pres.
Purpose: Promotes the economic and social interests of persons working on a part-time, contingent, or temporary basis through research, advocacy, and member services. Offers short-term portable health insurance. **Publications:** *NAPTE Tempo* (bimonthly). Also publishes career development materials.

REFERENCE WORKS

49762 ■ *How to Become a Successful Weekend Entrepreneur: Secrets of Making an Extra $100 or More Each Week Using Your Spare Time*
Pub: Prima Publishing & Communications
Ed: Basye. **Released:** 1993. **Price:** $10.95, (paper).
Description: Covers more than 100 part-time, weekend entrepreneurial opportunities. Includes sections for mothers working at home, teens, computer geniuses, and retirees.

RESEARCH CENTERS

49763 ■ New Ways to Work
103 Morris St., Ste. A
Sebastopol, CA 95472
Ph:(707)824-4000
Fax: (707)824-4410
Co. E-mail: sgtrippe@nww.org
URL: http://www.nww.org
Contact: Steve Trippe, Pres.
E-mail: sgtrippe@nww.org
Scope: Flexible scheduling and staffing arrangements, including job sharing, flexible hours, telecommuting, extended leaves, and part-time temps and contract workers. Research on these issues focuses on youths, contingent workers, the legal profession, and other particular groups. **Publications:** Work Times (quarterly). **Educational Activities:** Programs, to educate employers and employees in work time options and policy issues; Workshops, to educate employers and employees in work time options and policy issues.

START-UP INFORMATION

49764 ■ **"The Beginning of a Whole New Friendship"** in *Black Enterprise* **(Vol. 34, No. 5, December 2003, pp. S5)**
Pub: Earl Graves Publishing Co.
Ed: Jennifer L. Smith. **Description:** Financial Literacy for Teens group teaches young entrepreneurs how to start a new company, including tips for employing a startup.

49765 ■ **"Buddy System"** in *Entrepreneur* **(Vol. 33, October 2005, No. 10, pp. 118)**
Pub: Entrepreneur Media Inc.
Ed: Nichole L. Torres. **Description:** Choosing a friend as a business partner is not always a good business decision, it is important to evaluate a person's knowledge and business skills before partnering a startup company.

49766 ■ **"Finding Investors"** in *Home Business* **(Vol. 12, March/April 2005, No. 2, pp. 74)**
Pub: Home Business Magazine
Ed: Nora Caley. **Description:** Home business startups need partners, rather than investors, to help with startup costs. And these partners expect to play a role in the business.

49767 ■ **"Howdy, Partner"** in *Entrepreneur* **(Vol. 32, October 2004, No. 10, pp. 104)**
Pub: Entrepreneur Media Inc.
Ed: Nichole L. Torres. **Description:** When considering a virtual partnership with an entrepreneur met over the Internet, one must communicate, check references and histories, and establish set duties in writing.

49768 ■ **"Howle turns to new tech start-up"** in *Atlanta Business Chronicle* **(Vol. 24, No. 14, September 7, 2001, pp. 3A)**
Pub: American City Business Journals Inc.
Ed: Mary Jane Credeur. **Description:** C. Tycho Howle, co-founder of Harbinger Corporation, recently formed a venture with a dozen other entrepreneurs called nuMethods LLC. The venture is currently in the process of developing a program that would allow businesses to electronically trade enormous amounts of information. Atlanta's Deloitte & Touche partner Joseph L. Morettini says the way the product is presented to potential buyers will determine if it will succeed.

49769 ■ **"If at First You Don't Succeed..."** in *Black Enterprise* **(Vol. 34, No. 4, Nov. 2003, pp. 48)**
Pub: Earl Graves Publishing Co.
Ed: Zakiyyah El-Amin. **Description:** Profile of Linda A. Banks and Terri Michele, who, together, attempted various business ventures, but found their true calling when starting a childcare center in Pittsburgh, Pennsylvania.

49770 ■ **"Is My Partnership Fair?"** in *Inc.* **(July 1, 2004)**
Pub: Inc. Magazine

Description: A small business entrepreneur of a 50-50 partnership talks about protecting ideas and the pros and cons of leasing versus purchasing new technology.

49771 ■ **"Market Planning 101"** in *Home Business* **(Vol. 12, October 2005, No. 5, pp. 42, 44-45)**
Pub: Home Business Magazine
Ed: Christopher J. Bachler. **Description:** A quick marketing plan for any small business is presented and includes all the basic information required to attract loans, partners, business services and even Small Business Administration assistance.

49772 ■ **"Merger to Join Cambridge, Mass., Rivals in Anti-Aging Work"** in *Boston Globe* **(January 14, 2003)**
Pub: Knight Ridder/Tribune Business News
Ed: Jeffrey Krasner. **Description:** Two Cambridge, Massachusetts start-ups with technologies to discover the genetic factors behind aging, have announced a merger to create one single company in order to become a leader in the emerging field that will treat diseases of aging. A second round of venture funding is expected from the firms' original backers, which includes MPM Capital LP, Arch Venture Partners, and Oxford Bioscience Partners.

49773 ■ **"On the fast track"** in *Black Enterprise* **(Vol. 32, No. 9, Ap)**
Pub: Earl Graves Publishing Co.
Ed: Alan Hughes. **Description:** Profile of Shawn D. Baldwin, president and CEO of Capital Management Group Securities in Chicago who launched an asset management firm with eight employees in March 2002.

49774 ■ *Partnership: Small Business Start-Up Kit*
Pub: Nova Publishing Company
Ed: Daniel Sitarz. **Released:** November 2005. **Price:** $29.95. **Description:** Guidebook detailing partnership law by state covering the formation and use of partnerships as a business form. Information on filing requirements, property laws, legal liability, standards, and the new Revised Uniform Partnership Act is covered.

49775 ■ **"Strong Structure"** in *Black Enterprise* **(Vol. 34, July 2004, No. 12, pp. 48)**
Pub: Earl G. Graves Publishing Co. Inc.
Ed: Alan Hughes. **Description:** Advice is given for launching a small business. The entrepreneur needs information for choosing the business structure that is right for his new firm. Guidelines for choosing a sole proprietorship, partnership, limited liability company, C corporation, and S corporation are outlined.

EDUCATIONAL PROGRAMS

49776 ■ **AMA's Course on Mergers and Acquisitions**
American Management Association
1601 Broadway
New York, NY 10019

Ph:(212)586-8100
Free: 800-262-9699
Fax: (212)903-8168
Co. E-mail: customerservice@amanet.org
URL: http://www.amanet.org
Price: $4,395.00 for non-members; $3,995.00 for AMA members. **Description:** Four day seminar for executive managers; covers organizational, financial, planning, tax, and risk aspects of mergers and acquisitions. **Locations:** San Francisco, CA; Boca Raton, FL; Chicago, IL; and Boston, MA.

REFERENCE WORKS

49777 ■ **"3rd Annual LP Survey & Report Card"** in *Venture Capital Journal* **(October 1, 2005)**
Pub: Thomason Financial Inc.
Description: The difference between general partners and limited partners is examined. An overview of the Third Annual LP Survey & Report Card is presented.

49778 ■ **"The $7B Question"** in *Venture Capital Journal* **(October 1, 2005)**
Pub: Thomason Financial Inc.
Description: Speculations are made regarding Google's next venture-backed company it will buy. Information is outlined on past Google acquisitions.

49779 ■ **"Acquisitions Likely to Pick Up, But Pressure Remains"** in *Crain's Detroit Business* **(Vol. 19, No. 45, November 10, 2003, pp. 14)**
Pub: Crain Communications Inc., Detroit
Ed: Terry Kosdrosky. **Description:** Automotive suppliers see good opportunities in 2004, with nearly 15 percent reporting earnings in double-digit percentages of sales, while about 65 percent will break even or report single-digit earnings.

49780 ■ **"Acquisitions helped increase offerings"** in *Crain's Detroit Business* **(Vol. 19, No. 13, March 31, 2003, pp. 12)**
Pub: Crain Communications Inc., Detroit
Description: Special report on Integration Projects Inc., now called Dewpoint Inc. after acquisition the company modified service offerings in order to cope with the market.

49781 ■ **"Advanced Accessory looks to acquire with new owner"** in *Crain's Detroit Business* **(Vol. 19, No. 16, April 21, 2003, pp. 1)**
Pub: Crain Communications Inc., Detroit
Ed: Terry Kosdrosky. **Description:** A private-equity company bought majority control of Advanced Accessory Systems LLC in Sterling Heights, Michigan, the firm makes roof racks and towing hitches with reported sales of $329.8 million in 2002 sales, and employs 2,300 people.

49782 ■ "Adventures in the Paper Trade: Boise Buys OfficeMax" in *Barron's* **(July 21, 2003, pp. 15)**
Pub: Barron's
Ed: Michael Santoli. Description: Boise Cascade's $9/share offer for office products retailer OfficeMax, an also-ran in its market, totals $1.2 billion. Forest products manufacturer Boise Cascade is taking the risk in the belief that diversification is key to survival.

49783 ■ "Aetna" in *Business Week* **(January 16, 2006, No. 3967, pp. 47-48)**
Pub: McGraw-Hill Companies
Ed: Jessi Hempel. Description: Profile of incoming CEO at Aetna, Ron Williams, responsible for the firm's growth. Williams plans to cut operating costs, increase offerings, target baby boomers, and build the company's merger and acquisitions.

49784 ■ "AK Steel Goes Ahead with Bid for National" in *Pittsburgh Post-Gazette* **(April 11, 2003)**
Pub: Knight-Ridder/Tribune Business News
Ed: Jim McKay. Description: An overview of AK Steel's attempt to acquire the assets of National Steel Corporation is presented.

49785 ■ "Amgen Looking to Develop Medicines with Competitors" in *Providence Business News* **(Vol. 18, No. 20, September 1, 2003, pp. 2)**
Pub: Providence Business News, Inc.
Ed: Marni Leff Kottle. Description: Efforts by Amgen to find competitor with promising drug for joint venture scheme are discussed. Topics include testing of new drugs, possible profits from new drugs, and Amgen's falling market share.

49786 ■ "Anadarko Seeks Bidders for Possible Buyout" in *Houston Business Journal* **(Vol. 34, No. 14, August 15, 2003, pp. 3)**
Pub: American City Business Journals
Description: Anadarko Petroleum to pursue opportunities to be acquired by a larger company. Topics include business losses, economic conditions and the implementation of cost control measures.

49787 ■ "Analysts: Pricing, Material Costs to Spur Supplier Mergers" in *Crain's Detroit Business* **(Vol. 21, January 10, 2005, No. 2, pp. 19)**
Pub: Crain Communications Inc. - Detroit
Ed: Julie Armstrong. Description: Consolidation of automotive suppliers will rise in 2005 because of high raw-material prices and pricing pressures from automakers.

49788 ■ "Anatomy of a Merger" in *Rough Notes* **(Vol. 145, No. 2, February 2003, pp. 66)**
Pub: Rough Notes
Ed: Paul J. DiStefano. Description: When insurance agencies merge, the principals should address the issues of equity allocation, compensations, and the assumption of roles and responsibilities.

49789 ■ *Anatomy of a Merger: The Causes & Effects of Mergers & Acquisitions*
Pub: Prentice Hall General Reference & Travel
Ed: Alexandra Post. Released: 1993. Price: $72.00.

49790 ■ "Ann Arbor's QuatRx Pharmaceuticals Files for Stock Offering" in *Crain's Detroit Business* **(Vol. 22, February 13, 2006, No. 7, pp. 25)**
Pub: Crain Communications Inc. - Detroit
Ed: Andrew Dieterich. Description: QuatRx Pharmaceuticals Company, based in Ann Arbor, Michigan, filed an initial public offering in the hopes of raising $86 million. The firm develops and commercializes products in the endocrine, metabolic, and cardiovascular therapeutic areas.

49791 ■ "Apple Wanted Cornice To Supply Tiny Hard Drives for a New Device, the iPod Mini" in *Inc.* **(October 2005, pp. 59-60)**
Pub: Inc. Magazine
Ed: Michael Fitzgerald. Description: Carmillo Martino, CEO of Cornice, maker of tiny hard drives with one-inch planters for storing music or digital files, offers insight into his decision to turn down Apple's offer to supply these hard drives for the iPod Mini.

49792 ■ "Application Integration for Real-Time B2B" in *E-business Advisor* **(Vol. 18, No. 9, September 2000, pp. 20)**
Pub: Advisor Media, Inc.
Ed: David S. Linthicum. Description: Business-to-business (B2B) application integration, an extension of enterprise application integration, is the unrestricted sharing of data and business processes among any connected applications and data sources, inside or outside the company. B2B application integration enables outside trading partners to access accurate information on demand.

49793 ■ "Arranged Marriages: We present our media-merger dream team" in *Red Herring* **(No. 102, August 15, 2001, pp. 90-91, 93)**
Pub: Herring Communications
Ed: Paul R. LaMonica. Description: The article presents three hypothetical digital entertainment partnerships, including a marriage of AOL Time Warner and RealNetworks, a deal between Sony and TiVo, and lastly a merger between Paul Allen's Charter Communications and Metro-Goldwyn-Mayer Studios.

49794 ■ "ASC Specialty Cars to Get Sony Multimedia Products Under Deal" in *Crain's Detroit Business* **(Vol. 21, January 17, 2005, No. 3, pp. 29)**
Pub: Crain Communications Inc. - Detroit
Ed: Terry Kosdrosky. Description: ASC specialty cars will be equipped with Sony sound and multimedia products through a partnership between ASC Inc. and Sony. The deal will help Sony bring new consumer electronics to the auto industry sooner.

49795 ■ "Ask Inc: Dividing the Corporate Pie" in *Inc.* **(July 1, 2003)**
Pub: Gruner & Jahr USA Publishing
Description: Two business partners grapple over who's entitled to what; plus ways to update a business plan.

49796 ■ "Ask Inc." in *Inc.* **(September 1, 2004)**
Pub: Inc. Magazine
Description: A small stationery shop in Kansas is looking for new investors and the vice president of a residential mortgage brokerage wants to hire a coach or trainer to work with the firm's CEO.

49797 ■ "Ask Inc. Partnerships" in *Inc.* **(November 2006, pp. 57)**
Pub: Gruner & Jahr USA Publishing
Description: Buyouts of partners that leave the company require accurate assessment of the current value of the stock. That may require hiring a consultant to put a current value on the business to arrive at an amicable settlement.

49798 ■ "AT&T Set for Expensive Branding Campaign" in *Sacramento Bee* **(December 29, 2005)**
Pub: The Sacramento Bee
Ed: Clint Swett. Description: Former SBC Communications' acquisition of AT&T Corporation has the firm setting a new national identity in an expensive branding campaign. The advertising will begin New Year's Eve and run for a year.

49799 ■ "AT&T Set To Take On Cable As Purchase is Cleared" in *Wall Street Journal* **(Vol. 248, December 2006, No. 153, pp. A3)**
Pub: Dow Jones & Co. Inc.
Ed: Amol Sharma, Corey Boles Description: FCC approved the largest deal in the U.S. telecommunications industry between AT&T and BellSouth Corp. The merger places new pressure on its considerably smaller competitors like Verizon and Vonage.

49800 ■ "Atlanta Life to Manage MetLife Assets" in *Black Enterprise* **(Vol. 35, November 2004, No. 4, pp. 32)**
Pub: Earl G. Graves Publishing Co. Inc.
Ed: Aisha Jefferson. Description: Atlanta Life Investment Advisors, the nation's largest African-American owned, privately held stock insurance company, agreed with MetLife to manage $50 million of MetLife's assets.

49801 ■ "Auto insurer files for $350 million initial public offering" in *Atlanta Business Chronicle* **(Vol. 25, No. 19, Oct. 18, 2002, pp. 3A)**
Pub: American City Business Publications, Inc.
Ed: Lisa R. Schoolcraft. Description: Infinity Property and Casualty Corporation, located in Alpharetta, Georgia, will be the second company in the metropolitan Atlanta, Georgia area to file for an initial public offering in the previous two months. An insurer of high-risk drivers and a unit of the American Financial Group Inc., Infinity is looking to raise $350 million from the move, according to a filing with the U.S. Securities and Exchange Commission.

49802 ■ "Auto Consolidation Likely to Speed Up" in *Crain's Detroit Business* **(Vol. 23, January 8, 2007, No. 2, pp. 15)**
Pub: Crain Communications Inc. - Detroit
Ed: Brent Snaveley. Description: Further consolidations and bankruptcies in the auto supply business are increasing. Industry is in the midst of a major restructuring.

49803 ■ "Bank merger aims for 2002 wrap" in *Crain's Detroit Business* **(Vol. 16, No. 49, December 4, 2000, pp. 7)**
Pub: Crain Communications, Inc.
Ed: Katie Merx. Description: ABN Amro North America will acquire two Michigan banks, making it a formidable power in both mortgage and commercial banking.

49804 ■ "Bank acquisitions likely to pick up in 2003" in *Atlanta Business Chronicle* **(Vol. 25, January 10, 2003, No. 31, pp. 9A)**
Pub: American City Business Publications, Inc.
Ed: Meredith Jordan. Description: Atlanta banking insiders predict that there will be a rush to acquire small banks in Atlanta in 2003. Main Street Banks Inc. has acquired First National Bank of Johns Creek for $26.2 million.

49805 ■ "Bank Stock Binge" in *Black Enterprise* **(Vol. 35, January 2005, No. 6, pp. 34)**
Pub: Earl G. Graves Publishing Co. Inc.
Ed: Nicole Lewis. Description: Bank analyst, Fred Cummings, discusses which banks are likely to survive the current economic conditions affecting the industry. Recent economic and business trends have created an environment for bank mergers and acquisitions in the Midwest, according to Cummings.

49806 ■ "Banking on California" in *San Francisco Business Times* **(Vol. 18, No. 6, September 19, 2003, pp. 19)**
Pub: American City Business Journals
Ed: Mark Calvey. Description: Citibank's purchase of California Federal Bank last year has gone smoothly, the next task is to attract customers from other large competitors.

49807 ■ "Barter systems put the 'trade' in trade group" in *Crain's Detroit Business* **(Vol. 19, No. 16, April 21, 2003, pp. 16)**
Pub: Crain Communications Inc., Detroit
Ed: Laura Bailey. Description: Barter exchanges, trade association and Chambers of Commerce help small businesses enjoy bulk-buying discounts and to buy and sell goods and services.

49808 ■ "BBoC and FSB to merge: more deals within banking community are possible" in *Black Enterprise* **(Vol. 33, No. 3, October 2002, pp. 31)**
Pub: Earl Graves Publishing Co.
Ed: Cliff Hocker. Description: The merger between Boston Bank of Commerce and Los-Angeles-based Family Savings Bank is discussed, as well as Atlanta's Citizens Trust Bank is seeking to acquire Birmingham's CFS Bancshares Inc.

49809 ■ **"B.E. teams up with CNNfn"** in *Black Enterprise* (Vol. 33, No. 6, January 2003, pp. 10)
Pub: Earl Graves Publishing Co.
Description: Blackenterprise.com and CNNfn have partnered to bring "The Economic Divide in America" online. The series reports on race, gender, education, and housing, as well as factors affecting an individual's ability to build wealth.

49810 ■ **"Before You Try To Sell, Make Sure You Know What Buyers Want"** in *Inc.* (April 1, 2005)
Pub: Inc. Magazine
Ed: Norm Brodsky. **Description:** Most small business owners have an inflated idea of their company's value. When purchasing a new business, it is important to look at a firm's sales free cash flow, a function of profit, not sales.

49811 ■ **"Behind the Scenes"** in *Washington Business Journal* (Vol. 22, No. 12, July 25, 2003, pp. 18)
Pub: Washington Business Journal
Ed: Tim Mazzucca. **Description:** Shane Chalke, CEO of Herndon, Virginia-based AnnuityNet, markets software products to investment and insurance firms. AnnuityNet acquired a subsidiary of Wachovia Bank for an undisclosed price.

49812 ■ **"The Best CEO in Silicon Valley"** in *Black Enterprise* (Vol. 35, September 2004, No. 2, pp. 108)
Pub: Earl G. Graves Publishing Co. Inc.
Ed: Alan Hughes. **Description:** Profile of John W. Thompson, chairman and CEO of Symantic Corporation, leader in the network security software industry. Thompson is responsible for identifying potential acquisition targets, including the recent $370 million acquisition of Brightmail in June 2004.

49813 ■ **"A Better Way to Innovate"** in *Harvard Business Review* (Vol. 81, No. 7, July 2003, pp. 12)
Pub: Harvard Business School Press
Ed: Henry W. Chesbrough. **Description:** Companies can profit not only from accepting innovations from other firms, but also from sharing innovations with other firms.

49814 ■ **"Biddeford, Maine, Partners Highlight Weirdest eBay 'Auctions on New Web Site"** in *Portland Press Herald* (July 8, 2005)
Pub: Blethen Maine Newspapers, Inc.
Ed: Matt Wickenheiser. **Description:** Mark Greenlaw and partner Chaz Kraynak have created a new Website that collects the weirdest items from online auction house eBay.

49815 ■ **"Big Deal"** in *Entrepreneur* (Vol. 33, January 2005, No. 1, pp. 63)
Pub: Entrepreneur Media Inc.
Ed: Gwen Moran. **Description:** Tips for growing companies to consider when partnering with a competitor.

49816 ■ **"Big Generic Pharma"** in *The Economist* (Vol. 376, July 30-August 5, 2005, No. 8437, pp. 58)
Pub: The Economist Newspaper Ltd.
Description: The merger between Teva, Israel's largest pharmaceutical company with American Ivax makes Teva the world leader in generic pharmaceuticals.

49817 ■ **"The Big Guns"** in *Entrepreneur* (Vol. 31, No. 11, November 2003, pp. 68)
Pub: Entrepreneur Media, Inc.
Ed: David Worrell. **Description:** Ways to secure venture capital for a small business are explored, including raising money from a venture capitalist who is also an important business partner and potential customer.

49818 ■ **"The Big Squeeze"** in *Venture Capital Journal* (Vol. 42, No. 5, May 2002, pp. 20-26)
Pub: Thomas Venture Economics
Ed: Dan Primack. **Description:** Market pressures have forced most banks, venture firms, technology companies to scale back and slow growth.

49819 ■ **"Bio Solutions Acquisition"** in *Mississippi Business Journal* (Vol. 29, January 2007, No. 2, pp. 9)
Pub: Venture Publications, Inc.
Ed: Wally Northway **Description:** Bio Solutions Manufacturing Inc. acquired an oil and grease extraction technology for the removal of fat, oil and grease from organic waste effluent.

49820 ■ **"Biz By the Book"** in *Small Business Opportunities* (Vol. 17, September 2005, No. 5, pp. 58, 60)
Pub: Harris Publications Inc.
Ed: Vicki Gerson. **Description:** Partners, Ann Christophersen and Linda Bubon sell books for women and children. Women & Children First hosts events and book signings to promote the shop. Steps to open and market a book store are included.

49821 ■ **"Blattner Brunner Buys Into D.C."** in *Pittsburgh Business Times* (Vol. 23, No. 8, September 12, 2003, pp. 1)
Pub: Pittsburgh Business Times
Ed: Patty Tascarella, Greg Lohr. **Description:** Blattner Brunner Inc., a leading advertising agency, has acquired MHI Communications; the firm is led by CEO Michael Brunner.

49822 ■ **"Bloopers & Blunders"** in *Small Business Opportunities* (Vol. 16, November 2004, No. 6, pp. 72)
Pub: Harris Publications Inc.
Ed: Joanne G. Sujansky. **Description:** Seven mistakes made by company leaders and ways to avoid them are explained: lack of trust, failure to shape and share vision, unclear expectations, insufficient modeling of desire behaviors, too little partnering, failure to retain top talent, and too little celebration of success.

49823 ■ **"Bridgewater Interiors Closes $400 Million Deal"** in *Black Enterprise* (Vol. 35, January 2005, No. 6, pp. 28)
Pub: Earl G. Graves Publishing Co. Inc.
Ed: Tamara E. Holmes. **Description:** Bridgewater Interiors LLC has secured a $400 million contract from the Chrysler Group, a division of DaimlerChrysler, making it the largest deal ever awarded to a minority business by the automaker. Bridgewater also won a $500 million annual contract with Ford Motor Company in 2004. Details of the contract are outlined.

49824 ■ **"Bridging the Gap"** in *Sales & Marketing Management*
Pub: VNU Business Media
Ed: David Macey. **Description:** Retail-specific marketing solutions are becoming more important as effective ways to influence buying behavior in today's consumer market.

49825 ■ **"Brokerage to be acquired by Phoenix Company"** in *Crain's Detroit Business* (Vol. 18, No. 51, December 23, 2002, pp. 3)
Pub: Crain Communications Inc., Detroit
Ed: Jennette Smith. **Description:** The Dietz Organization, a boutique real estate brokerage is being bought by Hendricks and Partners Inc. The combined company is expected to handle over $4 billion annually in transactions.

49826 ■ **"Bryson Buys Two Agencies"** in *Mississippi Business Journal* (Vol. 29, January 2007, No. 2, pp. 8)
Pub: Venture Publications, Inc.
Ed: Wally Northway **Description:** Bryson Insurance acquires Banks Insurance and Shackleford Brothers & Fortenberry.

49827 ■ **"The Buddy System: These Longtime Friends Formed a Growing CPA Firm"** in *Black Enterprise* (Vol. 35, August 2004, No. 1, pp. 47)
Pub: Earl G. Graves Publishing Co. Inc.
Ed: Robert Janis. **Description:** Profile of three friends who formed a full-service certified public accounting firm in 1996. Benford Brown & Associates performs audits, accounting services, tax services, and business consulting.

49828 ■ **"Build a Successful Business Partner Network"** in *E-business Advisor* (Vol. 18, No. 5, May 2000, pp. 36)
Pub: Advisor Media, Inc.
Ed: Tim Claxton. **Description:** Business-to-business initiatives require online collaborative partnerships via a business partner network (BPN), also known as extranet. BPNs come with many benefits including speeding up joint projects, reducing costs and cycle times, supplies delivery on time and providing 24x7 customer service. Strategies for building an extranet, managing extranets and the future of BPNs are presented.

49829 ■ **"Building the Mommy Track"** in *Inc.* (September 1, 2003)
Pub: Gruner & Jahr USA Publishing
Description: Ways for small companies to handle maternity leave, small business acquisitions, and commercial leases are discussed.

49830 ■ **"Burying the Hatchet"** in *Hispanic Business* (March 2003, pp. 18)
Pub: Hispanic Business
Description: After years of contention, the National Association of Minority Automobile Dealers and the National Association of Hispanic Automobile Dealers have united to promote diversity in the automobile industry.

49831 ■ **"Business Diary"** in *Crain's Detroit Business* (Vol. 19, No. 15, April 14, 2003, pp. 20)
Pub: Crain Communications Inc., Detroit
Description: Recent acquisitions, nominations for the United Way Volunteer Center of Oakland County's Home Town Business Champion Award, and area contracts are topics covered.

49832 ■ **"Business and the Internet"** in *Ingram's* (Vol. 27, No. 4, April 2001, pp. 22)
Pub: Show Me Publishing, Inc.
Ed: Carol Rudder. **Description:** Online businesses have moved to online networks working together to provide solutions to complex business problems.

49833 ■ **"Cable cuts out slice of the broadband pie"** in *InfoWorld* (Vol. 23, No. 5, January 29, 2001, pp. 40)
Pub: InfoWorld
Ed: Jennifer Jones. **Description:** Cable modem service continues to hold a lead over DSL in the broadband sector. Industry leaders, such as AT&T and Media One, and America Online and Time Warner, are banking on that lead as part of their merger plans. These mergers are expected to bring high-speed Internet access to home users and focus on telecommuting.

49834 ■ **"Cablevision in Talks to Sell Fox Sports Stake to Comcast"** in *Long Island Business News* (February 27, 2004)
Pub: Dolan Media Newswires
Description: Cablevision Systems is negotiating a sale in its stake in many Fox regional sports networks to Comcast Corporation. These sports channels would be used as the foundation for a new nationwide sports network.

49835 ■ **"Calif. Company snaps up Texas Winn-Dixie center"** in *Atlanta Business Chronicle* (Vol. 25, December 6, 2002, No. 26, pp. 32C)
Pub: American City Business Publications, Inc.
Ed: Michael Whiteley. **Description:** Industrial Realty Group (IRG), Torrance, California, has acquired the South Fort Worth, Texas distribution center of Winn-Dixie Stores Inc. The grocer had pulled out of the Texas and Oklahoma markets five months earlier. The deal closed on 11/15/02; the purchase is part of IRG's strategy of acquiring buildings at low costs in order to offer low lease rates.

49836 ■ **"California Regulators Approve SBC, AT&T Merger"** in *Sacramento Bee* (November 19, 2005)
Pub: The Sacramento Bee
Description: Details of the $16 billion merger of telephone companies SBC Communications Inc. and

AT&T Corporation are discussed. The merger will create the largest telecommunications company in the U.S.

49837 ■ **"California takes a tumble"** in *Red Herring* (March 2003, pp. 65)
Pub: Herring Communications Inc.
Ed: Sarah Fallon. **Description:** Statistical data covering initial public offerings in the State of California, as well as Illinois, Nevada, Alabama and Rhode Island.

49838 ■ **"Callon Adds Inventory"** in *Mississippi Business Journal* (Vol. 28, September 2006, No. 36, pp. 24)
Pub: Venture Publications, Inc.
Description: Callon Petroleum Co. has acquired 12 offshore oil drilling tracts at the Outer Continental Shelf.

49839 ■ **"Capital City Beverage To Distribute Energy Drink"** in *Mississippi Business Journal* (Vol. 29, January 2007, No. 2, pp. 30)
Pub: Venture Publications, Inc.
Description: Capital City Beverage Company has created a distribution deal with Who's Your Daddy Inc. CCBC will distribute the entire line of Who's Your Daddy "King of Energy" drinks in 18 counties of Central Mississippi.

49840 ■ **"Carlyle looking for more acquisitions after buying Breed"** in *Crain's Detroit Business* (Vol. 19, No. 11, March 17, 2003, pp. 20)
Pub: Crain Communications Inc., Detroit
Ed: Rhoda Miel. **Description:** The Carlyle Management Group looks at slow economic conditions as an opportunity to buy other automotive parts-makers, including plastics processors.

49841 ■ *Cases in Corporate Acquisitions, Buyouts, Mergers & Takeovers*
Pub: Thomson Gale
Released: Published December, 1999. **Price:** $415, individuals. **Covers:** Approximately 300 significant acquisitions, mergers, and takeovers that involved at least one U.S. -based corporation during the 20th century. **Entries Include:** Company name, background information, financial data, transaction details, evaluation of outcome.

49842 ■ **"Cashflow: July 1-15, 2001"** in *Red Herring* (No. 102, August 15, 2001, pp. 28)
Pub: Herring Communications
Ed: Elizabeth Lamb. **Description:** Presentation using graphs and charts showing the seven companies that went public during the first two weeks of July 2001. Only one of the firms was a technology company.

49843 ■ **"Cashflow: July 15-31, 2001"** in *Red Herring* (No. 103, September 1, 2001, pp. 30)
Pub: Herring Communications
Ed: Elizabeth Lamb. **Description:** During the weeks of July 15-31, 2001 there were five tech and 12 non-tech Initial Public Offerings (IPOs), and nearly 1,600 mergers and acquisitions.

49844 ■ **"Cashflow: September 1-15, 2001"** in *Red Herring* (No. 106, October 15, 2001, pp. 32)
Pub: Herring Communications
Ed: Mark A. Mowrey. **Description:** With U.S. markets closed in the wake of the September 11 terrorist attacks, public equity-related activity slowed to a standstill, as well as venture investment announcements and IPOs. Statistical data included, with graphs showing global IPOs, venture capital investments by U.S. firms, and global M&A announcements.

49845 ■ **"Caution: Merger Ahead"** in *Ingram's* (Vol. 28, No. 9, September 2002, pp. 20)
Pub: Show Me Publishing, Inc.
Ed: James M. Selle. **Description:** A guide for considerations when small businesses consider a merger are presented, including issues such as expansion, additional products and/or services, new markets, and a competitor's customers base.

49846 ■ **"CB Acquisition"** in *San Fernando Valley Business Journal* (Vol. 11, December 2006, No. 25, pp. 23)
Pub: San Fernando Valley Business Journal Associates
Ed: Barbara Sheppard. **Description:** CB Richard Ellis Group Inc. acquired Trammell Crow, the Dallas-based real estate company, for $1.8 billion.

49847 ■ **"CBC and Chrysler Strike Deal"** in *Black Enterprise* (Vol. 37, December 2006, No. 5, pp. 36)
Pub: Earl G. Graves Publishing Co. Inc.
Ed: Kiara Ashanti. **Description:** Congressional Black Foundation and Chrysler Financial have partnered to provide financial education to students at historically black colleges and universities. The prime objective of the program is to reduce the number of college students that graduate with poor credit scores and high debt.

49848 ■ **"CEO sells IT company to help it grow"** in *Crain's Detroit Business* (Vol. 18, No.)
Pub: Crain Communications Inc. - Detroit
Ed: Andrew Dietderich. **Description:** Ciber Inc. has purchased Southfield, Michigan's Decision Consultants Inc., an information technology services company.

49849 ■ **"Changing hands"** in *WorkingWoman* (Vol. 25, No. 2, February 2000, pp. 38)
Pub: Lang Communications Inc.
Ed: Carol Leonetti Dannhauser. **Description:** Several corporate leaders offer advice for employees to maintain a flexible job description in order to be a viable through a company merger.

49850 ■ **"Chart-Toppers; Largest M&A Deals in U.S. History"** in *Crain's Chicago Business* (Vol. 30, January 2007, No. 4, pp.30)
Pub: Crain Communications, Inc.
Ed: Michelle Evans; Christina Galoozis. **Description:** Profiles of the largest mergers and acquisitions of 2006, which rose to $1.6 trillion. This is close to the record year of 2000 during the peak of the dot-com boom.

49851 ■ **"Chase Reshapes PE Investments"** in *Venture Capital Journal* (Vol. 40, No. 10, November 2000, pp. 28)
Pub: Venture Economics
Description: Chase Capital Partners is reorganizing a $5 billion portfolio. In order to free more capital for future investments, Chase will be trimming down its commitments in some leveraged buyout funds.

49852 ■ **"Checkers to Grow After Eliminating Rally's Name Locally"** in *Crain's Detroit Business* (Vol. 23, January 22-28, 2007, No. 4, pp. 10)
Pub: Crain Communications Inc. - Detroit
Ed: Brent Snaveley. **Description:** Fast food restaurant chain, Checkers, is planning expansion in Michigan after buyout and elimination of Rally's company name.

49853 ■ **"The Chinese Are Coming"** in *Inc.* (Volume 27, July 2005, No. 7, pp. 32)
Pub: Inc. Magazine
Ed: Darren Dahl. **Description:** Chinese companies acquired 649 U.S. firms in 2004, focusing on textile, appliance, electronics, and auto parts manufacturing sectors.

49854 ■ **"Cingular Increases Bid for AT&T Wireless"** in *Atlanta Journal-Constitution* (February 17, 2004)
Pub: Knight-Ridder/Tribune Business News
Ed: Robert Luke. **Description:** Information on the bidding war for AT&T Wireless between Cingular Wireless and Britain's Vodafone Group.

49855 ■ **"Citigroup Names President Of GDB"** in *Wall Street Journal* (Vol. 248, December 2006, No. 145, pp. B10)
Pub: Dow Jones & Co. Inc.

Ed: Rick Carew **Description:** Profile of Michael Zink, new president of GDB of Citigroup. Zink played a top in the integration of South Korea's KorAm Bank, which Citigroup acquired in April 2004

49856 ■ **"Citigroup, NCLR Announce $105 million Revitalization Pact"** in *Hispanic Business* (March 2003, pp. 16)
Pub: Hispanic Business
Description: Citigroup and the National Council of La Raza have entered into a $105 million strategic partnership to provide up to $100 million to finance affordable housing and community facilities serving the Hispanic community.

49857 ■ **"Citizens expands through tough times"** in *Black Enterprise* (Vol. 32, No. 5, December 2001, pp. 21)
Pub: Earl Graves Publishing Co.
Ed: Ann Brown. **Description:** America's fourth largest black-owned bank, Atlanta-based Citizens Trust Bank, plans to expand despite its parent company reporting second quarter losses.

49858 ■ **"City Bank Expands as Merger Bid Threatens Branches"** in *Pacific Business News* (Vol. 41, No. 16, June 27, 2003, pp. 12)
Pub: American City Business Journals
Ed: Eddy Conway. **Description:** City Bank is fighting a hostile takeover by Central Pacific Bank by opening new branches on Oahu and the big island. If Central Pacific Bank's offer of an exchange of stocks and $70 per share is a success, it plans to shut many of City Banks' branches.

49859 ■ **"Clean-Water Company Begins a Growth Spurt"** in *Portland Press Herald* (April 22, 2005)
Pub: Blethen Maine Newspapers, Inc.
Ed: Matt Wickenheiser. **Description:** Vortechnics acquired Stormwater Management Inc. a competitor located in Portland, Oregon. Vortechnics makes systems that clean storm water runoff from parking lots, roads and other surfaces. Vortechnics CEO, David Miley, believes the company is a good example of how small businesses can grow.

49860 ■ **"Clicking online: mergers, consolidations predicted for Hispanic targeted Web sites in 2000"** in *Hispanic Business* (Dec. 1999, pp. 60)
Pub: Hispanic Business
Ed: Vaughn Hagerty. **Description:** The emergence of Hispanic-targeted sites on the Internet is discussed. Developments of StarMedia Networks Inc. and quepasa.com are highlighted.

49861 ■ **"Close-Knit"** in *Forbes* (December 25, 2000, pp. 134)
Pub: Forbes Magazine
Ed: Brigid McMenamin. **Description:** A look at two large, privately held firms that have come up with different solutions to keeping their family-owned, private companies family-owned and private. Cited are Milliken & Company, a big textile firm that remains in the hands of the family, and Hearst Corporation, a diversified media giant, that is still privately held.

49862 ■ **"Clubs merge"** in *Des Moines Business Record* (Vol. 18, No. 41, October 14, 2002, pp. 16)
Pub: Business Publication Corporation
Description: The Embassy Club and the Des Moines Club have completed a merger. The present management of the Embassy Club will manage the combined group, named the Des Moines Embassy Club.

49863 ■ **"Co-Ed Management"** in *Entrepreneur* (Vol. 28, No. 2, February 2000, pp. 34)
Pub: Entrepreneur Media Inc.
Ed: Cynthia E. Griffin. **Description:** Diversity in your management team can help your Initial Public Offering (IPO) soar.

49864 ■ **"CO-OP Network Makes Deal With 7-Eleven"** in *The Record* (November 18, 2005)
Pub: New Jersey Media Group

Ed: Richard Newman. **Description:** Credit union members in New Jersey will be able to access automated teller machines in 7-Eleven convenience stores. Nine credit unions have joined with 7-Eleven in a deal that will allow members to use debit cards for free withdrawals.

49865 ■ "Cobasys Powers Up for Possible IPO; New Deal, HQ Spur Optimism" in Crain's Detroit Business (Vol. 20, December 20, 2004, No. 51)
Pub: Crain Communications Inc. - Detroit
Ed: Andrew Dietderich. **Description:** Cobasys LLC is planning an initial public offering in 2006 or 2007. Meanwhile, the firm plans to consolidate its executive, engineering and product development under one roof in Orion Township, Michigan.

49866 ■ "Coke Dives Into 'Enhanced' Beverage Market with Fuze Beverage Purchase" in Altanta Journal-Constitution (February 2, 2007)
Pub: Cox Newspapers, Inc.
Ed: Duane Stanford. **Description:** Coca-Cola purchased Fuze Beverage, a company that sells ready-to-drink juices and teas in funky bottles. Details of the transaction are included.

49867 ■ "Commentary: Mergers: A Meeting of the Minds" in Long Island Business News (February 13, 2004)
Pub: Dolan Media Newswires
Ed: Claude Solnik. **Description:** The merger of New York Community Bancorp and Roslyn Bancorp is used to demonstrate the importance of good relationships for mergers and acquisitions to be successful.

49868 ■ "Company Catalyst" in Boston Business Journal (Vol. 23, No. 25, July 25, 2003, pp. 3)
Pub: American City Business Journals
Ed: Allison Connolly. **Description:** Christoph Westphal of Waltham, Massachusetts Polaris Venture Partners, had no experience in the venture capital sector before being hired as a general partner. Polaris Venture Partners has signed three deals since hiring Mr. Westphal.

49869 ■ "Compass Group PLC" in Crain's Chicago Business (Vol. 30, January 2007, No. 4, pp. 36)
Pub: Crain Communications, Inc.
Ed: Gregory Meyer. **Description:** Larry Levy, Chicago entrepreneur, sold his remaining 51 percent stake in Levy Restaurants for $250 million to the United Kingdom's Compass Group PLC.

49870 ■ "Conflicts and Conflict Resolution in International Anti-trust: Do We Need International Competition Rules?" in World Economy (Vol. 24)
Pub: Blackwell Publishers, Inc.
Ed: Henning Klodt. **Description:** The wave of company mergers and acquisitions in the world which are driven by globalization and deregulation could lead to oligopolies in national markets and the world. This paper looks into solutions such as national anti-trust laws applying internationally, or establishing an international competition policy.

49871 ■ "Connecticut's Biggest Bank Heading to Long Island" in Long Island Business News (March 12, 2004)
Pub: Dolan Media Newswires
Ed: David Reich-Hale. **Description:** Webster Financial Corporation of Waterbury, Connecticut, will open branches in Long Island, New York. Webster also branched out into Massachusetts and Rhode Island in 2003 when it acquired Firstfed America Bancorp.

49872 ■ "Consolidation can mean a lot to small business" in Atlanta Business Chronicle (Vol. 24, No. 8, July 27, 2001, pp. 3B)
Pub: American City Business Journals Inc.
Ed: Miquiel Banks. **Description:** Consolidation can affect small businesses in positive or negative ways.

For example, the merger of Wachovia and First Union banks may mean more opportunities for small banks, because small banks have excellent customer service and consumers know that. On the other hand, small businesses benefit when they merge with larger ones because cost management issues become less problematic.

49873 ■ "Consorting with Competitors" in Harvard Business Review (Vol. 80, No. 1, January 2002, pp. 21)
Pub: Harvard Business School Press
Ed: Christopher Kurt. **Description:** Personal insight is given into forming industry consortia, using specifications called Universal Description, Discover, and Integration (UDDI). UDDI allows for integrations of ideas electronically via a directory, and keeps the consortia on track.

49874 ■ "Contacts for Contracts" in Hispanic Business (Vol. 22, No. 1/2, January/February, pp. 84)
Pub: Hispanic Business
Ed: Aimee R. Haeussler. **Description:** Despite industry mergers, some financial institutions are taking pains to reach out to minority vendors. Many of the procurement programs aimed at minority and women-owned businesses offer more than just a chance to compete for corporate contracts.

49875 ■ "A Conversation With Michael Beauregard, Huron Capital Partners" in Crain's Detroit Business (Vol. 21, January 31, 2005, No. 5)
Pub: Crain Communications Inc. - Detroit
Ed: Michelle Martinez. **Description:** The outlook for non-automotive mergers and acquisitions are discussed with Michael Beauregard, a partner with Huron Capital Partners. Beauregard predicts a strong economic climate for 2005.

49876 ■ "Coronado: Program Looks to Empower Restaurateurs" in San Diego Business Journal (Vol. 28, January 15, 2007, No. 3, pp. 17)
Pub: San Diego Business Journal Associates
Ed: Brad Graves. **Description:** Coronado restaurant owners have created the Empower Partnership in order to promote energy efficiency by distributing special hardware to the area.

49877 ■ Corporate Growth Report Weekly
Pub: NVST.Inc.
Ed: Walter Jurek, Editor. **Released:** Weekly, fifty times per year. **Publication Includes:** Current acquisition and merger transactions. **Entries Include:** Buyer and seller names and locations, annual sales and net income for each, seller's net worth and price-earnings ratio, and purchase price, including terms and various ratios. **Arrangement:** Classified by Standard Industrial Classification (SIC) code.

49878 ■ "Counterpoint: Why So Many Mergers & Acquisitions Fail" in Success from Failure (August 2000)
Pub: Vision Quest Publishing, Inc.
Ed: K.LW. Stephen Cheung. **Description:** A report by ACG Network shows that nearly half of all prospective deals never close and that even among mergers that are consummated, as many as 70 percent fail to meet expectations, in fact a very high percentage failed completely after the merger.

49879 ■ "Coupon mailer raises banner with an Innovative acquisition" in Crain's Detroit Business (Vol. 19, No. 9, March 3, 2003, pp. 24)
Pub: Crain Communications Inc., Detroit
Ed: Jennette Smith. **Description:** Marketshare Inc., a direct-mail coupon book marketing firm has purchased Innovative Media LLC, maker of large vinyl banners.

49880 ■ "Cross Atlantic Capital Partners" in Venture Capital Journal (Vol. 40, No. 10, November 2000, pp. 56-57)
Pub: Venture Economics
Description: Gerry McCrory, an Irish entrepreneur came to America in 1998 to visit venture capitalists in

Silicon Valley, California and Boston, Massachusetts. Mr. McCrory presented his plans for a strategic partnership between a seed-stage fund based in Ireland and a U.S. venture capital firm. The results of that visit are explored, along with a listing of some of the Cross Atlantic Partners portfolio companies.

49881 ■ "Crucial triad" in Daily Business Review (Vol. 77, No. 198, March 24, 2003, pp. AA4)
Pub: American Lawyer Media LP
Ed: David Geyer, Elizabeth Lampert. **Description:** Ways in which law firm partners can use the triad of business development, marketing and media relations to better serve clients is explained.

49882 ■ "CSFB to Acquire DLJ in Buyout" in Venture Capital Journal (Vol. 40, No. 10, October 2000, pp. 12, 14)
Pub: Venture Economics
Description: Profile of the proposed acquisition of investment bank Donaldson, Lufkin & Jenrette Inc. by Credit Suisse Group AG's Credit Suisse First Boston for $11.5 billion.

49883 ■ "Culture Shock" in Entrepreneur (Vol. 31, No. 9, July 2003, pp. 77)
Pub: Entrepreneur Media, Inc.
Ed: Marc Diener. **Description:** With increasing numbers of international, multinational and transnational corporations, culture is playing a major role in negotiations.

49884 ■ "Cutting-Edge Accountant" in Crain's New York Business (Vol. 23, January 29, 2007, No. 5, pp. F22)
Pub: Crain Communications, Inc.
Ed: Barbara Benson. **Description:** Profile of Vice President of Corporate Development for Health Insurance Plan of Greater New York, Steve Zeng. HIP plans to go public after a merger with Group Health Incorporated.

49885 ■ "CyberStaking: Why Partnerships Matter" in E-business Advisor (Vol. 18, No. 9, September 2000, pp. 10)
Pub: Advisor Media, Inc.
Ed: Wendy Lea, Scott Creighton. **Description:** Partnerships, a start-up's key to success in the new economy, act to secure future markets, ease multi-channel strategies and lock out potential rivals. Electronic commerce partnerships often include the launching of joint ventures, formations of a third company, exclusivity agreements, and shared revenues and equity.

49886 ■ "Dan Case's Next Great IPO" in Fast Company (May 2001, pp. 175)
Pub: Fast Company
Ed: Paul C. Judge. **Description:** Profile of Dan Case, who is helping IPO-starved Silicon Valley adjust to the new realities of competition, finance, and innovation.

49887 ■ "Dana Has Cash, Looks for Ways to Spend It" in Crain's Detroit Business (Vol. 21, January 31, 2005, No. 5, pp. 12)
Pub: Crain Communications Inc. - Detroit
Description: Dana Corporation is considering various mergers and acquisitions of companies working in the vehicle and engine compartment sector of the industry.

49888 ■ "David Nicklaus Column" in St. Louis Post-Dispatch (March 2, 2005)
Pub: Knight-Ridder/Tribune Business News
Ed: David Nicklaus. **Description:** Details of the acquisition of May Department Stores Company by Federated Department Stores Inc. is examined.

49889 ■ "Deal Jitters?" in Inc. (October 2005, pp. 48)
Pub: Inc. Magazine
Ed: Dalia Fahmy. **Description:** Many firms are now purchasing insurance when acquiring a company. Purchase protection cover financial losses if a seller makes false claims in a sale contract, and should be used in deals valued at least $10 million.

49890 ■ **"Deal would double Pilot Industries' price"** in *Crain's Detroit Business* (Vol. 18, No. 49, December 9, 2002, pp. 25)
Pub: Crain Communications Inc., Detroit
Description: Less than one year after purchasing, Cerberus Institutional Buyers LP will sell Pilot Industries Inc. to Martinrea International Inc.

49891 ■ **"Delivering At Domino's Pizza"** in *Fortune* (Vol. 151, February 7, 2005, No. 3, pp. 28)
Pub: Time Inc.
Ed: Julia Boorstin. **Description:** Domino's Pizza has seen its stock climb 26 percent since going public in July 2004. In an interview with Domino's CEO, David Brandon, he tells how he helped overhaul the company's training program and dropped the employee turnover rate by 60 percent. The franchiser has also opened 1,200 new stores in the past five years, two-thirds of them overseas.

49892 ■ **"Denbury Selects Digital Oilfield"** in *Mississippi Business Journal* (Vol. 29, January 2007, No. 2, pp. 13)
Pub: Venture Publications, Inc.
Ed: Wally Northway **Description:** Independent oil and gas company Denbury Resources Inc. has signed a multi-year license agreement with Digital Oilfield Inc. 's OpenInvoice Image and OpenContract PriceBook solutions to automate and streamline its invoicing processes.

49893 ■ **"Department of Justice grounds DC air"** in *BlackEnterprise* (Vol. 32, No. 3, October 2001, pp. 32)
Pub: Earl Graves Publishing Co.
Ed: Cliff Hocker. **Description:** The U.S. Department of Justice denied the merger of United Airlines and US Airways. The proposed merger would have created the spring-off company, DC Air, making it the largest minority-owned airline in the United States.

49894 ■ **"Detroit Free Press Wayne Small Business Column"** in *Detroit Free Press* (September 8, 2005)
Pub: Knight-Ridder/Tribune Business News
Ed: Carol Cain. **Description:** Two downtown Northville, Michigan bicycle shops have partnered to increase sales. The two stores carry different product lines.

49895 ■ **"'Devil in the Details' of Chase/J.P. Morgan Merger"** in *Venture Capital Journal* (Vol. 40, No. 10, October 2000, pp. 26)
Pub: Venture Economics
Description: An overview of the proposed merger between J.P. Morgan Capital Corporation and Chase Capital Partners, is presented.

49896 ■ **"Disney Collaboration"** in *San Fernando Valley Business Journal* (Vol. 11, December 2006, No. 25, pp. 23)
Pub: San Fernando Valley Business Journal Associates
Ed: Barbara Sheppard. **Description:** The Walt Disney Co. will develop footwear exclusively for sale at Payless ShoeSource stores. The first products will be in stores in spring 2007.

49897 ■ **"Dr. Warren's Lonely Hearts Club"** in *Business Week* (February 20, 2006, No. 3972, pp. 82)
Pub: McGraw-Hill Companies
Ed: Christopher Palmeri. **Description:** EHarmony and Dr. Warren's Lonely Hearts Club are profiled. EHarmony is offering a new service for married couples over the age of 21. The service is touted as a marriage wellness program whereby each spouses answers 310 questions to determine the couple's strengths and weaknesses.

49898 ■ **"Domains of the Day: A New Domain Could Mean the Dawn of a New Mobile Age"** in *Entrepreneur* (Vol. 32, August 2004, No. 8, pp. 31)
Pub: Entrepreneur Media Inc.
Ed: Amanda C. Kooser. **Description:** .mTLD, which stands for mobile Top Level Domain is a new domain

suffix like .com, expressly for mobile use. Leaders like Hewlett-Packard, Microsoft, Nokia, Samsung Electronics, Sun Microsystems, T-Mobile International and Vodafone have partnered to set up a registry company to manage the new mTLD once the Internet Corporation for Assigned Names and Numbers grants approval.

49899 ■ **"Dot-Com for Sale"** in *E-business Advisor* (Vol. 18, No. 10, October 2000, pp. 48)
Pub: Advisor Media, Inc.
Ed: Ben Chen. **Description:** Gaining customers, skilled employees, knowledge, and strategic alliances are some of the reasons for the flurry of acquisitions and mergers in the dot.com world. This article examines reasons, and discusses the things to look for when contemplating a business move, including goal compatibility, cost for acquiring a new customer base, and whether the new company would have what the existing company does not have and needs.

49900 ■ **"Dream Team or Nightmare Relationship"** in *My Business* (April/May 2003, pp. 34-37)
Pub: My Business Magazine
Ed: Nancy Mann Jackson. **Description:** The trials and tribulations of business partnerships are discussed by various business owners. Tips for making a partnership work successfully include communication, legal advice, and shared responsibilities.

49901 ■ **"Drugmaker Ups Dosage; Acquisition Expected to Double Revenue"** in *Crain's New York Business* (Vol. 23, January 22, 2007, No. 4, pp. 4)
Pub: Crain Communications, Inc.
Description: Barr Pharmaceuticals Inc. won a bidding war to acquire Pliva for $2.5 billion. The acquisition is expected to double Barr's revenue which had been falling over the last two years.

49902 ■ **"Dry Powder Dilemma"** in *Venture Capital Journal* (Vol. 42, No. 5, May 2002, pp. 32-35)
Pub: Thomas Venture Economics
Ed: Jesse Reyes. **Description:** A critical look at the issue that is high priority for both general partners and limited partners, un-invested capital. Statistical data included.

49903 ■ **"The Dubious Logic of Global Megamergers"** in *Harvard Business Review* (Vol. 78, No. 4, July 2000, pp. 65)
Pub: Harvard Business School Publishing Corp.
Ed: Pankaj Ghemawat, Fariborz Ghadar. **Description:** Economic theorists discuss the emerging global economy and strategies for dealing with globalization. Theorists provide empirical research that shows global industries are decreasing in concentration since World War Two.

49904 ■ **"Dumars company diversifies with deal for Troy tech firm"** in *Crain's Detroit Business* (Vol. 19, No. 4, January 27, 2003, pp. 26)
Pub: Crain Communications Inc., Detroit
Ed: Terry Kosdrosky. **Description:** Profile of Joe Dumars who heads up companies in the automotive supply industry and telecommunications, has just acquired the Troy-based Technical Solutions Inc., giving Detroit Technologies Inc. the capability to install telecommunications and computer software, hardware and infrastructure.

49905 ■ **"Dura buys German maker of steering column parts"** in *Crain's Detroit Business* (Vol. 16, No. 49, December 4, 2000, pp. 5)
Pub: Crain Communications, Inc.
Ed: Michael Strong. **Description:** Rochester Hills, Michigan-based Dura Automotive Systems Inc., has acquired Reiche Automotive for approximately $20 million, including the assumption of $4 million in debt.

49906 ■ **"E-Cognita founders to lead group at Miller, Canfield"** in *Crain's Detroit Business* (Vol. 19, No. 15, April 14, 2003, pp. 25)
Pub: Crain Communications Inc., Detroit
Ed: Jennette Smith. **Description:** Founders of the technology company E-Cognita, will be working with the newly formed capital-markets lending group at the Detroit law firm Miller, Canfield, Paddock and Stone PLC. E-Cognita Technologies Inc. developed software called StreamLoaner and Lexicon to manage transactions and automate documents and is used by lenders, lawyers, and other parties involved in loan closings.

49907 ■ **"E-mail Marketer Looks for More Clout"** in *Atlanta Business Chronicle* (Vol. 25, December 13, 2002, No. 27, pp. A3)
Pub: American City Business Publications, Inc.
Ed: Mary Jane Credeur. **Description:** Silverpop Systems Inc. has acquired Epigraphx LLC, Redwood, California. The acquisition took place in December 2002, as part of Silverpop's initiative to grow in the e-mail marketing industry. The deal will increase staff to 55 and will triple Silverpop's revenues, which remain undisclosed. The deal also expands Silverpop's client roster and increased profits are discussed by Silverpop CEO, Bill Nussey.

49908 ■ **"E-Marketplaces: Opportunity or Threat?"** in *E-business Advisor* (Vol. 18, No. 7, July 2000, pp. 32)
Pub: Advisor Media, Inc.
Ed: Elizabeth Sara. **Description:** Businesses in the e-marketplace arena are obliged, not only to adapt their existing business processes to take advantage of the Web's inherent benefits, but also to keep their relatively new e-commerce solutions functionally current and flexible to keep in step with the market. Participating in private business-to-business (B2B) sales channels offer the advantage of enhanced contractual relationships with business partners. Price structures for products are included.

49909 ■ **"EarthLink Inc. to purchase customers of Orlando ISP"** in *Atlanta Business Chronicle* (Vol. 25, No. 19, October 18, 2002, pp. 31A)
Pub: American City Business Publications, Inc.
Ed: Chad Eric Watt. **Description:** Volaris Online, located in Orlando, Florida, will sell its base of dial-up Internet service customers to EarthLink Inc., Atlanta, Georgia. A total of 250,000 Volaris subscribers will be affected by the sale, and will likely result in Volaris trimming a large number of its 300-person staff. EarthLink has made a practice of building its subscriber base through the acquisition of smaller Internet service providers.

49910 ■ **"EastGroup Buys Buildings"** in *Mississippi Business Journal* (Vol. 29, January 2007, No. 4, pp. 9)
Pub: Venture Publications, Inc.
Ed: Wally Northway **Description:** EastGroup Properties acquired three business distribution buildings in Charlotte, NC, for $9.3 million. This increases EastGroup's total portfolio to almost 24 million square feet of properties in the Charlotte area under development.

49911 ■ **"Ebank gains altitude after midflight change"** in *Atlanta Business Chronicle* (Vol. 24, No. 9, August 3, 2001, pp. 19A)
Pub: American City Business Journals Inc.
Ed: Meredith Jordan. **Description:** Ebank.com Inc., based in Atlanta, Georgia, was headed for certain disaster as a dot-com bank. According to Jim Box, the new president and CEO, has turned the company around 100 percent, and the company is growing financially and considering acquisitions and still enjoys a presence on the Web.

49912 ■ **"eBay"** in *DSN Retail Fax* (Vol. 10, No. 26, June 30, 2003)
Pub: Lebhar-Friedman Inc.
Description: UPS and eBay have extended their partnership and introduced a new line of shipping tools for eBay customers.

49913 ■ **"ebrary Snags Key Investors for Pay-Per-Use Service"** in *Information Today* (Vol. 17, No. 11, December 2000, pp. 41)
Pub: Information Today, Inc.
Ed: Paula J. Hane. Description: ebrary, an online research library, announced a joint investment by three leading publishing and information service companies: Random House, Inc., Pearson, and The McGraw-Hill Companies.

49914 ■ **"ECD short of cash at critical time as partners pull out of ventures"** in *Crain's Detroit Business* (Vol. 19, No. 8, Feb. 24, 2003)
Pub: Crain Communications Inc., Detroit
Ed: Andrew Dietderich. Description: Energy Conversion Devices Inc. has lost funding from three companies for joint ventures in fuel-cell development.

49915 ■ **"Eight Black Physicians Partnered to Open an International House of Pancakes in Harlem..."** in *Black Enterprise* (Vol. 35, Dec. 2004)
Pub: Earl G. Graves Publishing Co. Inc.
Ed: Nkechi Olisemeka. Description: In its first month of operation, a restaurant opened by eight African American doctors is ranked 14th in sales among the International House of Pancakes franchises. The franchise has 1,167 franchises located throughout 48 states and Canada.

49916 ■ **"The Endangered Department Store"** in *Boston Globe* (February 13, 2005)
Pub: New York Times Company
Ed: Keith Reed. Description: The merger between Macy's and Filene's is causing experts to question whether mass-market department stores are on the decline. Many department stores are reinventing themselves in order to stay competitive with the luxury high-end and low-cost discount stores.

49917 ■ **"Engaging Before Merger"** in *Rough Notes* (Vol. 146, No. 9, September 2003, pp. 68)
Pub: Rough Notes
Ed: G. Edward Kalbaugh. Description: Ways to improve an agency's chance of being acquired by a larger firm, including cost control, market development, and profitability, are discussed.

49918 ■ **"Enterprising Union Creates $100M Bank"** in *Houston Business Journal* (Vol. 34, No. 15, August 22, 2003, pp. 1A)
Pub: American City Business Journals
Ed: Jim Greer. Description: Houston Commercial Bank and Enterprise Bank will merge, retaining the Enterprise Bank name and offer four locations.

49919 ■ **"Environmental firm EQ bulks up with 2 acquisitions"** in *Crain's Detroit Business* (Vol. 19, No. 6, February 10, 2003, pp. 21)
Pub: Crain Communications Inc., Detroit
Ed: Brent Snavely. Description: EQ-The Environmental Company, has purchased bankrupt Franklin Environmental Services Inc., the firm's second acquisition in two months. EQ is located in Wayne, Michigan.

49920 ■ **"Even as the M&A Market Heats Up, Unloading a Company Gets Trickier"** in *Inc.* (May 1, 2005)
Pub: Inc. Magazine
Ed: Description: According to a recent survey conducted by PricewaterhouseCoopers, one of every two business owners plan to sell their company in the next ten years, resulting in a glut of companies on the market, forcing down valuations and giving new leverage to buyers.

49921 ■ **"Ex-burger king teams with Hawkins; Group may be pursuing KFC deal"** in *Crain's Detroit Business* (Vol. 18, No.51, Dec. 23, 2002, pp. 1)
Pub: Crain Communications Inc., Detroit
Ed: Michael Strong. Description: Profile of La-Van Hawkins, owner of 117 Pizza Hut restaurants in Michigan. Hawkins has hired Jerome Lowes, a former CEO of Burger King Inc., and is hoping to acquire KFC Inc., the chicken fast food chain.

49922 ■ **"Ex-Publisher Wants to Stop Gannett's Purchase of HomeTown"** in *Crain's Detroit Business* (Vol. 21, January 31, 2005, No. 5, pp. 34)
Pub: Crain Communications Inc. - Detroit
Ed: Jennette Smith. Description: U.S. Department of Justice is investigating a proposed joint-operating agreement between Gannett Co. Inc. and HomeTown Communications Network. Details of the proposed merger are presented.

49923 ■ **"Extract, Transform and Load"** in *Barron's* (August 11, 2003, pp. T2)
Pub: Barron's
Ed: Mark Veverka. Description: Extract, Transform and Load (ETL), a model of middleware enterprise software, is ousting Enterprise Application Integration (EAI) as the standard of choice. EAI is more elegant and robust, but ETL gets the job done for less. Netgear's initial public offering is discussed, and San Francisco, California-based Pacific Growth Equities efforts to expand are examined.

49924 ■ **"A Fair Trade"** in *Entrepreneur* (Vol. 31, October 2003)
Pub: Entrepreneur Media, Inc.
Ed: C.J. Prince. Description: The ongoing battle between Qwest Communications International Inc. and the SEC about the firm's reportedly recognizing $2 billion in revenue from "swap" sales dating back to 1999.

49925 ■ **"False Start"** in *Venture Capital Journal* (October 1, 2005)
Pub: Thomason Financial Inc.
Ed: Lawrence Aragon. Description: A recap of the venture-backed IPO market for 2005 is presented. So far, seven VC-backed companies have gone public and raised $550 million by the end of August 2005. There were 33 IPOs for the first seven months of 2005. Statistical data included.

49926 ■ **"Family Partnerships Under Scrutiny"** in *Inc.* (Volume 27, July 2005, No. 7, pp. 26)
Pub: Inc. Magazine
Ed: Allen P. Roberts Jr. Description: The Internal Revenue Service is taking steps to investigate the way business owners avoid paying estate taxes.

49927 ■ **"Farmingdale-based THM Scientific Introduces Product Line Based on Sustainable Agriculture"** in *Long Island Business News* (Feb.6, 2004)
Pub: Dolan Media Newswires
Ed: Adina Genn. Description: Profile of Peter Felix and James Sottilo, two arborists who have partnered to develop and produce Rootgrow, a line of organic-compost tea, brewers and related products and services that will preserve the soil. The partners are targeting homeowners, corporate parks, golf courses, and municipalities.

49928 ■ **"Faurecia May Buy to Grow, but Only If It Fits Plan"** in *Crain's Detroit Business* (Vol.23, January 15, 2007, No.3, pp. 1)
Pub: Crain Communications Inc. - Detroit
Ed: Brent Snaveley. Description: European interiors supplier may enter domestic supply market by purchasing acquisitions in U.S. market if they match their business plan. A global giant, but currently not in the U.S. domestic market, Faurecia was invited in by General Motors since nearly 40 percent of domestic competition is bankrupt or struggling financially.

49929 ■ **"FedEx Moves to Expand With Purchase of Kinko's"** in *New York Times* (December 31, 2003, pp. C1)
Pub: The New York Times
Ed: Claudia H. Deutsch. Description: FedEx Corporation plans to expand its business with small- to mid-size companies by acquiring Kinko's, a company that serves small- to mid-size businesses.

49930 ■ **"Fee Bargain: Law Firm Mergers May Give You More Room to Negotiate Legal Fees"** in *Entrepreneur* (Vol. 31, No. 7, July 2003, pp. 27)
Pub: Entrepreneur Media, Inc.
Ed: Chris Penttila. Description: In the soft economy, law firms are struggling to stay afloat with fewer clients and increasing operational costs, therefore some firms are merging offering lower fees and more services.

49931 ■ **"Feeling Loaded Down? Use Partnerships to Bag New Customers"** in *My Business* (October/November 2003, pp. 44)
Pub: My Business Magazine
Ed: Paige Orr. Description: Michael Hess, president and chief executive of Road Wired, a technology travel accessory firm, partnered with Travelpro International, a luggage manufacturer and distributor. This partnership has helped Hess to grow his business.

49932 ■ **"Financial Industry Expects Growth Amid Radical Changes"** in *Crain's Detroit Business* (Vol. 19, No. 45, November 10, 2003, pp. 24)
Pub: Crain Communications Inc., Detroit
Ed: Katie Merx. Description: Southeast Michigan banks are expecting increases across the board in commercial lines of business, credit unions are expected to expand, and mortgage companies and brokers are offering new services to keep business brisk when interest rates rise. Venture capital and mergers-and-acquisition are also projected to do well.

49933 ■ **"Financial Services Market Changing"** in *Rough Notes* (Vol. 146, No. 3, March 2003, pp. 68)
Pub: Rough Notes
Ed: Phil Zinkewicz. Description: The feared consequences of the Financial Services Modernization Act of 1999 were of ensuing mergers and acquisitions among banks and insurers, never occurred. What followed was more competition and business among insurers and banks and more choices for consumers.

49934 ■ *Financing Your Small Business*
Pub: Barron's Educational Series, Incorporated
Ed: Robert Walter. Released: March 2004. Price: $18.95 (US), $27.50 (Canadian). Description: Tips for raising venture capital, dealing with bank officials, and initiating public offerings of stock shares for small business.

49935 ■ **"The fine art of friendly acquisition"** in *Harvard Business Review* (Vol. 78, No. 6, November-December 2000, pp. 100)
Pub: Harvard Business School Publishing Corp.
Description: An overview of mergers and acquisitions (M&A) and how LBO companies regularly create more value through M&A than most corporate officials do.

49936 ■ **"Firms shape students into future workers"** in *Atlanta Business Chronicle* (Vol. 24, No. 11, August 17, 2001, pp. 3B)
Pub: American City Business Journals Inc.
Ed: Paige Boweres. Description: Companies, such as Zcorum Inc., are working with Atlanta-area colleges and universities through the Intellectual Capital Partnership Program, a statewide economic development initiative that teams universities with companies so that companies can meet their immediate information technology staff needs. The initiative and its impact are discussed.

49937 ■ **"First Data: New Terminal POS Lift for Small Outfits"** in *American Banker* (Vol. 172, January 17, 2006, No. 11, pp. 17)
Pub: SourceMedia, Inc.
Ed: David Breitkopf. Description: First Data Corporation has partnered with Microsoft Corporation and Hewlett Packard Company to devise a more complete point of sale terminal for small retailers. The terminal will accept most transactions and will track account information, track inventory, and work with customer relationship software.

49938 ■ *FirstList*
Pub: Vision Quest Publishing Inc.
Contact: Robert Weicherding, CNT
Released: 8 editions per year. Price: $250, individuals per year. Covers: companies that are candidates for merger or acquisition; potential buyers seeking acquisitions; sources of financing, companies seeking financing; joint venture and licensing opportunities. Recent issue listed over 1,000 acquisition opportunities. Entries Include: Company name, location, sales, type of business, profits, and price. Arrangement: Classified by Standard Industrial Classification (SIC) code.

49939 ■ "Fitness 24 Buys DAC Club" in *Mississippi Business Journal* (Vol. 29, January 2007, No. 2, pp. 8)
Pub: Venture Publications, Inc.
Ed: Wally Northway Description: Regional fitness management company DAC sold its fitness club in Olive Branch to Fitness 24. DAC sold this facility in order to increase overall profitability of its existing clubs.

49940 ■ "Flight of Fancy? Launching a High-Tech Product Can be a Technical and Financial Challenge" in *Entrepreneur* (Vol. 32, August 2004)
Pub: Entrepreneur Media Inc.
Ed: Don Debelak. Description: Profile of William J. Boyer Jr. and partner and co-founder Ray Henson, who helped Boyer with the technical aspects of their digEplayer, a portable battery-operated in-flight entertainment system used on passenger tray tables. The company saw $1 millions in sales, first quarter 2004.

49941 ■ "FNC, HomeSafe Team Up" in *Mississippi Business Journal* (Vol. 29, January 2007, No. 2, pp. 19)
Pub: Venture Publications, Inc.
Description: Mississippi technology companies FNC Inc., and HomeSafe Inspection Inc. are teaming up to help provide lenders with easy access to advanced home inspection technologies.

49942 ■ "For Better or Worse" in *Entrepreneur* (Vol. 33, October 2005, No. 10, pp. 104)
Pub: Entrepreneur Media Inc.
Ed: Nichole L. Torres. Description: Three couples share their experience of running their companies together.

49943 ■ "For Biggest, No Brakes On This Trend" in *American Banker* (Vol. 170, February 4, 2005, No. 24, pp. 1)
Pub: Thomson Financial Media Inc.
Ed: David Boraks. Description: Retail banking is opening new branches at the rate of one every three hours and expected to continue through 2005. Since the population and growth is not keeping pace, competition and price cutting could lead to more closing and mergers in the industry.

49944 ■ "Forecast for IPOs? Wait Till Next Year" in *Venture Capital Journal* (Vol. 41, No. 8, August 2000, pp. 16-17)
Pub: Venture Economics
Description: It is predicted that the IPO market will not improve until the economy recovers, but it is a good time to be a venture capitalist.

49945 ■ "Foreclosures: Troubled Owners Offered Free Help" in *Altanta Journal-Constitution* (February 1, 2007)
Pub: Cox Newspapers, Inc.
Ed: Julie B. Hairston. Description: Georgia Department of Labor and Federal Reserve Bank have partnered to offer assistance to homeowners facing mortgage foreclosure, information can be ascertained by calling 1-888-995-HOPE.

49946 ■ "Forget the Series; St. Louis has Bragging Rights for Job Growth" in *St. Louis Post-Dispatch* (December 19, 2004)
Pub: Knight-Ridder/Tribune Business News
Ed: David Nicklaus. Description: St. Louis area reported 42,000 new jobs for the period October 2003

to October 2004, and if the trend continues could be the most jobs added to the region since 1988. St. Louis also saw three initial public offerings in 2004. Las Vegas, Nevada is also reporting high growth for the same time period.

49947 ■ "Former Wrestling Star Body Slams Private Equity" in *Venture Capital Journal* (Vol. 42, No. 9, September 2002, pp. 15-16)
Pub: Thomas Venture Economics
Ed: Michael V. Copeland. Description: Profile of Ira Lubert, co-founder/principal of Lubert-Alder Management Inc. of Philadelphia, Pennsylvania; Lubert targets his market to mid- to late-stage companies that can't go public and don't want to be sold right away.

49948 ■ "Forward: Startups: Network-chip makers may be in danger of extinction" in *Red Herring* (No. 102, August 15, 2001, pp. 22-23)
Pub: Herring Communications
Ed: Dean Takahaski. Description: Theoretically, network-processor startups could be saved by large company acquisitions, but several large firms have already purchased their favorites.

49949 ■ "Founders Face Off" in *Forbes* (Vol. 175, February 14, 2005, No. 3, pp. 46)
Pub: Forbes Magazine Inc.
Ed: Dorothy Pomerantz. Description: Bill Gates and Paul Allen are in a head-to-head battle for the purchase of cable company Comcast.

49950 ■ "Fraction action: can't afford an entire jet? Try winging it with a piece of one" in *Entrepreneur* (Vol. 31, No. 4, April 2003)
Pub: Entrepreneur Media Inc.
Ed: Christopher Elliott. Description: Fractional-ownership options, or the equivalent of owning a timeshare in a plane, are a unique strategy for small businesses with smaller travel budgets.

49951 ■ "French Fried: GE Wins in Vivendi Deal" in *Barron's* (September 8, 2003, pp. 18)
Pub: Barron's
Ed: Jonathan R. Laing. Description: Vivendi Universal's entertainment division, encompassing movie and television production, cable broadcasting, and theme parks, was finally sold to GE subsidiary NBC after a seemingly endless courtship.

49952 ■ "Friends forever?" in *Entrepreneur* (Vol. 31, No. 6, June 2003, pp. 77)
Pub: Entrepreneur Media Inc.
Ed: Marc Diener. Description: In the real world friendship is better for business than business in for friendship. When business deals get rocky, valued relationships often fall apart.

49953 ■ "Fruit of the Vine" in *Business First Buffalo* (Vol. 19, No. 40, June 27, 2003, pp. 1)
Pub: American City Business Journals, Inc.
Ed: Tom Hartley. Description: Robert Wilmers, a top banking industry executive in Buffalo, New York, acquired the French winery Chateau Haut-Bailly in 1998 and currently sold the 400-year old winery to the chairman and president of M and T Bank.

49954 ■ "Fund-Raising Falters, VCs Keep Cutting Back" in *Venture Capital Journal* (Vol. 42, No. 10, October 2002, pp. 18-20)
Pub: Thomas Venture Economics
Description: Venture capital firms refunded more money to limited partners than they raised in the second quarter 2002, the first time that has happened.

49955 ■ "Furniture.com stages revival, forges ties with non-com allies" in *Boston Business Journal* (Vol. 22, No. 11, April 19, 2002, pp. 1)
Pub: MCP, Inc.
Description: Furniture.com Inc., which went into bankruptcy, is making a comeback by partnering with brick-and-mortar retailers like Levitz Furniture Corporation and Seaman Furniture Company Inc.; Furniture.com is being backed by Resurgence Asset Management LLC.

49956 ■ "Genzyme Battles An Old Adversary" in *Boston Globe* (January 25, 2005)
Pub: New York Times Company
Ed: Jeffrey Krasner. Description: A new battle over intellectual property has erupted between Genzyme Corporation and Transkaryotic Therapies Inc. (TKT) of Cambridge, Massachusetts. Genzyme has sued TKT claiming that the firm's method of purifying a treatment for a particular disease infringed on Genzyme's proprietary technology.

49957 ■ "Gerald Greenwald: This Time, He's Taking the Train" in *Business Week* (January 31, 2005, pp. 14)
Pub: McGraw-Hill Companies
Ed: Michael Arndt. Description: Greenbriar Equity Group has partnered with Berkshire Partners to purchase North America's largest builder of locomotives, General Motors' Electro-Motive Division, making it the fourth purchase in the transportation sector for Greenbriar.

49958 ■ "Getting a Leg up: Montemayor y Asociados Partners with Web-Hed Technologies" in *Hispanic Business* (Vol. 22, No. 5, May 2000, pp. 18)
Pub: Hispanic Business
Ed: Teresa Talerico. Description: Web development and hosting venture Web-Hed Technologies Inc. has formed a joint venture with advertising firm Montemayor y Asociados. Through this arrangement, Montemayor will be able to offer clients an extensive range of Web-Hed's interactive services.

49959 ■ "Giving mergers a head start" in *Harvard Business Review* (Vol. 80, No. 10, October 2002, pp. 20)
Pub: Harvard Business School Press
Ed: Randy Croyle, Patrick Kager. Description: Advice is given for managing the process of merging two companies. Relying on former company employees can help ameliorate difficulties to antitrust laws, and smooth the merger process.

49960 ■ "GM Set To Unleash $3B In IT Deals" in *Crain's Detroit Business* (Vol. 21, December 19, 2005, No. 51, pp. 1)
Pub: Crain Communications Inc. - Detroit
Ed: Andrew Dietderich. Description: General Motors Corporation announced plans for $3 Billion worth of information technology contracts to be awarded to more than 40 technology contractors and subcontracts from the Detroit area.

49961 ■ "Going Private: How VCs Can Get in the Game" in *Venture Capital Journal* (Vol. 42, No. 10, October 2002, pp. 49)
Pub: Thomas Venture Economics
Ed: Jonathan Bell. Description: A trend towards venture capital firms to reverse course and help companies go private is examined. To minimize the risk that the transaction may be questionable as being unfair to minority shareholders, an independent and disinterested committee of the company's board should handle negotiations.

49962 ■ "Going Public" in *Entrepreneur* (Vol. 31, No. 11, November 2003, pp. 65)
Pub: Entrepreneur Media, Inc.
Ed: C.J. Prince. Description: Reverse mergers are investigated. A reverse merger allows private companies to become public by acquiring or merging with a public 'shell' company.

49963 ■ "Good Sports" in *Entrepreneur* (Vol. 32, September 2004, No. 9, pp. 104)
Pub: Entrepreneur Media Inc.
Ed: Nichole Torres. Description: Profile of Deirdre and Phil Barrows and Faith and Rob Schroeder, partners in a business venture that sells penalty flags to sports fans. Deirdre came up with the idea while watching her husband throw things at the television when football officials made bad calls. The firm, Call Your Own! expects to gross around $40,000 in their first year.

49964 ■ **"A Good Time for an IPO Gold Mine?"** in *Entrepreneur* (Vol. 33, March 2005, No. 3, pp. 62)
Pub: Entrepreneur Media Inc.
Ed: Jennifer Pellet. Description: The best time to buy initial public offering stocks is when markets are flagging, because companies have an easier time going public at that time.

49965 ■ **"Google's Banker"** in *Fortune* (Vol. 149, No. 9, May 3, 2004, pp. 105)
Pub: Time, Inc.
Ed: Adam Lashinsky. Description: Venture capital information is discussed, including the impact of Google going public; Michael Moritz and his partners will likely reap hundreds of millions of dollars.

49966 ■ **"Got Leverage? Dollar Signs: If You're Ready to Sell, You've Got the Upper Hand"** in *Entrepreneur* (Vol. 31, No. 9, September 2003)
Pub: Entrepreneur Media, Inc.
Ed: C.J. Prince. Description: With increased private equity activity, large buyout firms will be looking towards entrepreneurs. Statistical data included.

49967 ■ **"GPs Say Valuation Standard Is 'Important' But Can't Agree on One"** in *Venture Capital Journal* (Vol. 42, No. 10, Oct. 2002, pp. 47-48)
Pub: Thomas Venture Economics
Ed: Colin Blaydon, Michael Horvath. Description: Results from a survey conducted by Foster Center for Private Equity at the Tuck School of Business are presented. The survey was sent to 550 venture capital general partnerships.

49968 ■ **"Grice, Lund & Tarkington Merges with Oregon Firm"** in *San Diego Business Journal* (Vol. 28, January 15, 2007, No. 3, pp. 19)
Pub: San Diego Business Journal Associates
Ed: Andy Killion. Description: Accounting firm, Grice, Lund & Tarkington has merged with Aldrich Kilbride & Tatone. The two firms will operate under the Aldrich Kilbride & Tatone name. The merger will improve the company's ability to address client needs in the changing world of accounting and financial services.

49969 ■ **"Group thinking"** in *Crain's Detroit Business* (Vol. 19, No. 16, April 21, 2003, pp. 16)
Pub: Crain Communications Inc., Detroit
Description: Information about bartering and exchanges for small businesses is presented.

49970 ■ **"Growing for broke"** in *Harvard Business Review* (Vol. 80, No. 9, September 2002, pp. 27)
Pub: Harvard Business School Press
Ed: Paul Hemp. Description: Experts discuss a hypothetical situation whereby a small firm desires to grow and expand by acquiring another company.

49971 ■ *Growing Local Value: How to Build Business Partnerships That Strengthen Your Community*
Pub: Berrett-Koehler Publishers, Incorporated
Ed: Laury Hammel; Gun Denhart. Released: December 2006. Price: $15.00. Description: Advice and examples are provided for building socially responsible entrepreneurship.

49972 ■ **"Hand In Hand"** in *Entrepreneur* (Vol. 31, No. 8, August 2003, pp. 68)
Pub: Entrepreneur Media, Inc.
Ed: Jane Easter Bahls. Description: If you negotiate well, joining forces with a big firm can be the smart way to get a new product to the marketplace. The product may be just what a big company needs to boost slumping sales.

49973 ■ *Happy About Joint Venturing: The 8 Critical Factors of Success*
Pub: Happy About
Ed: Valerie Orsoni-Vauthey. Released: June 2006. Price: $23.95. Description: An overview of joint venturing is presented.

49974 ■ **"Harvard Pilgrim Purchases Medical Benefits Company"** in *Boston Globe* (March 8, 2005)
Pub: New York Times Company
Ed: Liz Kowalczyk. Description: Health Plans Inc. has been purchased by Harvard Pilgrim Health Care. The move will help position Harvard Pilgrim, the second-largest health insurer in Massachusetts, to compete with Blue Cross and Blue Shield of Massachusetts. Harvard Pilgrim is also considering a move into the self-insured market.

49975 ■ **"Hawkins says Pizza Hut sold to parent firm"** in *Crain's Detroit Business* (Vol. 19, No. 11, March 17, 2003, pp. 3)
Pub: Crain Communications Inc., Detroit
Ed: Michelle Strong. Description: LaVan Hawkins, owner of Wolverine Pizza LLC, plans to sell its 89 Pizza Hut restaurants in Michigan. The deal is scheduled to close in March.

49976 ■ **"Heartland completes $2B purchase of Masco Tech"** in *Crain's Detroit Business* (Vol. 16, No. 49, December 4, 2000, pp. 5)
Pub: Crain Communications, Inc.
Ed: Michael Strong. Description: Heartland Industrial Partners L.P., last week completed its acquisition of Taylor, Michigan-based Masco Tech Inc. The $2 billion deal includes the assumption of Masco Tech's debt of $500 million.

49977 ■ **"Heritage Networks Wins Showdown"** in *Black Enterprise* (Vol. 34, No. 3, October 2003, pp. 19)
Pub: Earl Graves Publishing Co.
Ed: Jeffrey McKinney. Description: Heritage Networks has teamed with Warner Brothers Domestic Television to win syndication rights for Showtime at the Apollo, beginning with the 2003-2004 season. Statistical data included.

49978 ■ **"His Rock Club Was In Ruins. His Partnership Was Crumbling"** in *Inc.* (May 1, 2006)
Pub: Inc. Magazine
Ed: Lora Kolodny. Description: Allan Fingerhut's Minneapolis nightclub owed $170,000 in overdue real estate taxes on a business he had a childhood friend running for him. Fingerhut discusses the problems involved in mixing business and friendship.

49979 ■ **"Hispanic Business Teams With World-Class Designer"** in *Hispanic Business* (June 2002, pp. 14)
Pub: Hispanic Business
Ed: Derek Reveron. Description: Hispanic Business magazine has teamed with design firm Garcia Media to give the periodical a more contemporary look.

49980 ■ **"Holliday Fenoglio Begins Buyout of Lend Lease"** in *South Florida Business Journal* (Vol. 23, No. 48, July 4, 2003, pp. 4)
Pub: American City Business Journals
Ed: Jim Freer. Description: Lend Lease Corporation announced it would take a $300 million write down and close U.S. operations. As part of this plan, it is expected to sell U.S. assets, with Morgan Stanley probably buying the real estate contracts. The sale of Lend Lease's brokerage division Holliday Fenoglio Fowler, is also proceeding thus returning Holliday Fenoglio to independent status.

49981 ■ **"Hollinger Contacts VC Giant"** in *Crain's Chicago Business* (Vol. 26, No. 50, December 15, 2003, pp. 1)
Pub: Crain Communications, Inc.
Ed: Jeremy Mullman. Description: Hicks Muse & Furst Inc., an investment firm located in Texas, is hoping to acquire Conrad Black's controlling interest in Hollinger International Inc., owner of the Chicago Sun-Times. Details of the negotiations are presented. Statistical data included.

49982 ■ **"Hollinger Contacts VC Giant; Hicks Muse Could See Synergies with Radio Here"** in *Crains Chicago Business* (Vol. 26, No. 50)
Pub: Crain Communications, Inc.
Ed: Jeremy Mullman. Description: Hicks Muse & Furst Inc., an investment firm located in Texas, is hop-ing to acquire Conrad Black's controlling interest in Hollinger International Inc., owner of the Chicago Sun-Times. Details of the negotiations are presented. Statistical data included.

49983 ■ **"Hollinger VC Unit has Family Ties; Black's Nephew has Few Hits, Many Misses With Fund"** in *Crains Chicago Business* (Vol. 26, No. 51)
Pub: Crain Communications, Inc.
Ed: Jeremy Mullman. Description: Matthew Doullo is the nephew of Conrad Black, chairman of Hollinger International Inc. Doullo runs the venture investment unit of Hollinger International. A profile of Doullo is provided.

49984 ■ **"Hollinger VC Unit has Family Ties"** in *Crain's Chicago Business* (Vol. 26, No. 51, December 22, 2003, pp. 3)
Pub: Crain Communications, Inc.
Ed: Jeremy Mullman. Description: Matthew Doullo is the nephew of Conrad Black, chairman of Hollinger International Inc. Doullo runs the venture investment unit of Hollinger International. A profile of Doullo is provided.

49985 ■ **"Home Builder Falls Under SEC Scrutiny"** in *Orlando Business Journal* (Vol. 20, No. 10, August 22, 2003, pp. 1)
Pub: American City Business Journals, Inc.
Ed: Jill Krueger. Description: The merger with a Colorado petroleum company gave Whitemark Homes Inc. an entry to the stock exchange. Whitemark also purchased a consulting firm, which collapsed and was brought under investigation.

49986 ■ **"Hoping for a Bad Winter"** in *Forbes* (Vol. 175, January 10, 2005, No. 1, No. 13, pp. 153)
Pub: Forbes Magazine Inc.
Ed: Tatiana Serafin. Description: Recent mergers and expansions have Advance Auto Parts looking to surpass AutoZone by becoming the nation's top automotive parts and accessories retailer. Statistical data included.

49987 ■ *How to Form Your Own Partnership*
Pub: Sphinx Publishing
Ed: Edward A. Haman. Released: 1995. Price: $19.95.

49988 ■ **"How Partnerships Can Avoid Tax Surprises"** in *Venture Capital Journal* (July 1, 2003)
Pub: Thomson Financial Inc.
Description: Tax planning ideas helpful to the venture capital industry are examined. Issues discussed include establishing a partnership status, contribution requirements, capital account allocation, tax basis allocation, distributions, and state filing requirements.

49989 ■ **"How Rupert Plans to Counterpunch Cable"** in *Business Week* (February 20, 2006, No. 3972, pp. 42)
Pub: McGraw-Hill Companies
Ed: Ronald Grover, Cliff Edwards. Description: Rupert Murdoch, CEO of DirecTV Group Inc. and Charles W. Ergen, CEO of EchoStar Communications Corporation, are discussing a $1 billion wireless data and voice network plan that would bundle the same services cable companies and phone companies offer customers.

49990 ■ **"How Snapple Got Its Juice Back"** in *Harvard Business Review* (Vol. 80, No. 1, January 2002, pp. 47)
Pub: Harvard Business School Press
Ed: John Deighton. Description: Quaker Oats bought Snapple for $1.4 million, only to sell it four years later for $300 million to Triarc. Triarc then reorganized the brand and sold it to Cadbury Schweppes for about $1 billion. Returning the company required changes in management, packaging, and products.

49991 ■ **"How To Conduct Due Diligence"** in *Inc.* (October 1, 2004)
Pub: Inc. Magazine
Ed: Darren Dahl. Description: It is imperative to be sure there is nothing amiss when acquiring a new business. Things to keep in mind when conducting due diligence are listed.

49992 ■ **"How To Work (If You Must) With Your Spouse"** in *Inc.* (October 1, 2004)
Pub: Inc. Magazine
Ed: Michael S. Hopkins. **Description:** The challenges of partnering with a spouse in a business venture are observed. Recommendations to overcome these challenges are offered.

49993 ■ **"How To Work With a Partner (Year After Year After Year)"** in *Inc.* (October 1, 2004)
Pub: Inc. Magazine
Ed: Patrick J. Sauer. **Description:** Ways to create a lasting business partnership are examined.

49994 ■ **"Howdy Partner!"** in *Home Business* (Vol. 12, March/April 2005, No. 2, pp. 44)
Pub: Home Business Magazine
Description: Strategic alliances, agreements that establish exchange relationships between two cooperating companies, can help small businesses grow.

49995 ■ **"IBM, Microsoft, others plan alliance to help conduct business online"** in *Wall Street Journal* (February 6, 2002, pp. B4)
Pub: Wall Street Journal
Description: The plans being made to form alliances for conducting business transactions online by such companies as IBM, Microsoft and others, are discussed.

49996 ■ **"IBOC Grows in Oklahoma"** in *Hispanic Business* (September 2004, pp. 20)
Pub: Hispanic Business
Description: International Bancshares Corporation (IBOC), Hispanic-owned, acquired Local Financial Corporation. The deal sets IBOC's assets at nearly $9.5 billion on a pro forma basis.

49997 ■ **"If Not the Word, What? Leaders Speak"** in *Tradeshow Week* (Vol. 34, November 29, 2004, No. 48, pp. 20)
Pub: Reed Business Information
Ed: Heidi Genoist. **Description:** The merger between the International Association for Exhibition Management (IAEM) and the Society of Independent Show Organizers is discussed. The merger is expected to give a greater voice to the tradeshow industry as well as attract more high-level executives to the association.

49998 ■ **"The Importance of Well-Crafted Terms"** in *Law Firm Inc.* (August 2004)
Pub: American Lawyer Media LP
Ed: Mark Hanchet, Edward Hansen. **Description:** Agreements involving complex technology relationships should be negotiated and drafted with the idea of avoiding future litigation because of the long-term partnerships they create. These contracts cover such issues as outsourcing and enterprise resources planning (ERP) licensing and implementation agreements; risk avoidance, scope of services, service levels and cost need to be agreed upon before the contract is signed.

49999 ■ **"In Texas a 'transformative' merger"** in *Barron's* (August 18, 2003, pp. T3)
Pub: Barron's
Ed: Mark Veverka. **Description:** The merger of Pervasive Software and Data Junction Corporation, signals a major shift in the market for application integration middleware. The two companies will combine efforts in extract, transform, and load (ETL) technology, which is poised to replace the pricier enterprise application integration (EAI) model.

50000 ■ **"Industry Experts Expect Mergers to Remain Strong Among Banks"** in *Long Island Business News* (February 13, 2004)
Pub: Dolan Media Newswires
Ed: Claude Solnik. **Description:** The banking industry is expecting a rise in mergers and acquisitions in the near future. Analysts believe midsize banks could be attractive takeover targets.

50001 ■ **"Informal Partnership gives Agents Clout"** in *Rough Notes* (Vol. 145, No. 1, January 2003, pp. 34)
Pub: Rough Notes
Ed: Dave Willis. **Description:** Bill Russell and Tom McCorkle are president and chairman of Combined Agents of America LLC. The organization enables small regional brokers to become partners without having to buy a franchise or share income.

50002 ■ **"Information Technology Software"** in *Business Week* (January 23, 2006, No. 3968, pp. 65-66)
Pub: McGraw-Hill Companies
Ed: Sarah Lacy. **Description:** Profile of Oracle's John Wookey and his boss, Larry Ellison. The two are working to meld together the company's latest string of acquisitions.

50003 ■ **"Inheriting business as challenging as starting one"** in *Atlanta Business Chronicle* (Vol. 24, No. 13, August 24, 2001, pp. 5B)
Pub: American City Business Journals Inc.
Ed: Tara Milligan. **Description:** Taking over a business that is already operating has unique challenges. In the article is a case study of Carl Greenway's takeover of the Molly Maid franchise in Memphis five years ago, when it had six employees and eight dilapidated cars. It now has 24 employees, and competes against the national leader Merry Maids, which is also headquartered in Memphis.

50004 ■ **"Initial Public Optimism"** in *Business Week* (No. 3670, February 28, 2000, pp. f6)
Pub: McGraw-Hill, Inc.
Description: A survey of the number of companies planning to go public.

50005 ■ *Instant Income*
Pub: McGraw-Hill Inc.
Ed: Janet Switzer. **Released:** February 2007. **Price:** $30.95 (CND). **Description:** Book covers small business advertising techniques, marketing, joint ventures, and sales.

50006 ■ **"Integration managers: special leaders for special times"** in *Harvard Business Review* (Vol. 78, No. 6, November-December 2000, pp. 108)
Pub: Harvard Business School Publishing Corp.
Description: In order to figure out the best way to merge with other businesses, companies are appointing a new and unique kind of manager. This is important, since last year companies globally invested $3.3 trillion on mergers and acquisitions, 32 percent more than was spent in 1998.

50007 ■ **"Investment Firms Forge Partnerships"** in *Venture Capital Journal* (Vol. 41, No. 8, August 2000, pp. 14, 16)
Pub: Venture Economics
Description: Report of investment firm mergers which includes information about the merger between European incubator inVentures with New York-based search firm Redwood Partners; and the merger between Washington-based Core Capital Parners and GCI Venture Partners.

50008 ■ **"Investor: Advance Notification"** in *Red Herring* (No. 102, August 15, 2001, pp. 82-83)
Pub: Herring Communications
Ed: Eric Moskowitz. **Description:** An overview of the U.S. Securities and Exchange Commission's Rule 10b5, which allows insiders to sell shares 365 days a year, as long as they have a prearranged, written sales plan with their broker.

50009 ■ **"Investors Buy Michigan Chronicle Parent Firm"** in *Crain's Detroit Business* (Vol. 19, No. 4, January 27, 2003, pp. 18)
Pub: Crain Communications Inc., Detroit
Ed: Jennette Smith. **Description:** Real Times LLC has acquired the Michigan Chronicle, the Chicago Defender, New Pittsburgh Courier and the Memphis Tri-State Defender, all African-American newspapers.

50010 ■ **"IPO Aftermarket: I'm a Bull! No, I'm a Bear! Wait, I'm a ... Blear!"** in *Venture Capital Journal* (Vol. 42, No. 9, Sept. 2002, pp. 46)
Pub: Thomas Venture Economics
Description: Information on the confused "blear" market is presented, including a list of Initial Public Offerings with offering price, bid price, percent change, business description, and date of IPO.

50011 ■ **"IPO Aftermarket: New Issues Could Start to Gather Momentum in Spring"** in *Venture Capital Journal* (Vol. 42, No. 5, May 2002, pp. 59)
Pub: Thomas Venture Economics
Description: A list of Initial Public Offerings with offering price, bid price, percent change, business description, and date of IPO is presented. Of the 35 venture-backed companies that went public between April 2001 and March 2002, 54 percent were trading at or above their IPO prices.

50012 ■ **"IPO Aftermarket: New Issues Struggle to Overcome the Enron Effect"** in *Venture Capital Journal* (Vol. 42, No. 8, August 2002, pp. 50)
Pub: Thomas Venture Economics
Description: A list of Initial Public Offerings with offering price, bid price, percent change, business description, and date of IPO is presented.

50013 ■ **"IPO Aftermarket"** in *Venture Capital Journal* (Vol. 41, No. 8, August 2000, pp. 46-47)
Pub: Venture Economics
Description: Between July 2000 and June 2001, 136 venture-backed companies went public with 39 trading at or above their initial public offering. Listing of the 136 IPOs is displayed. Statistical data included.

50014 ■ **"IPO illusions"** in *WorkingWoman* (Vol. 25, No. 6, June 2000, pp. 36)
Pub: Lang Communications Inc.
Ed: James M. Pethokoukis. **Description:** The investment potential of new issues, initial public offerings, is discussed, from the perspective of the individual investor, with focus on the difficulty in obtaining such investments and the risks involved.

50015 ■ **"IPO an Inner City 100 First"** in *Inc.* (October 1, 2003)
Pub: Gruner & Jahr USA Publishing
Ed: Jess McCuan. **Description:** Molina Healthcare becomes the first Inc. Inner City company to go public.

50016 ■ **"IPO Monitor"** in *Venture Capital Journal* (Vol. 40, No. 10, November 2000, pp. 64)
Pub: Venture Economics
Description: A listing of the 12 venture-backed companies that went public during the month of September 2000, raising a total of $1.154 billion.

50017 ■ **"IPO Review"** in *Red Herring* (No. 99, June 15 & July 1, 2001, pp. 61)
Pub: Herring Communications
Ed: Debbie Gravitz. **Description:** A look at last year's top Initial Public Offerings (IPOs), venture capital firms, and banks, before and after the fall of the economy.

50018 ■ **"IPO Revival Not a Sure Thing"** in *Business Journal-Milwaukee* (Vol. 20, No. 52, September 12, 2003, pp. A1)
Pub: American City Business Journals, Inc.
Ed: Michael Muckian. **Description:** Brookfield, Wisconsin-based HomeMed, a manufacturer of medical technology, is planning an initial public offering. HomeMed, led by president and CEO, Herschel Peddicord, has annual sales of $30 million.

50019 ■ **"IPO Scandal Means Venture Capitalists Need To Be More Vigilant"** in *Venture Capital Journal* (Vol. 42, No. 10, October 2002, pp. 50)
Pub: Thomas Venture Economics
Ed: Thomas C. McConnell. **Description:** Initial Public Offering practices are the latest business practices to come under regulatory, Congressional and media scrutiny.

50020 ■ **"IPOs/Recent Issues"** in *Venture Capital Journal* (Vol. 42, No. 9, September 2002, pp. 44-45)
Pub: Thomas Venture Economics
Description: Information on recent IPOs for BioDelivery Sciences International Inc., and Healthetech Inc. is provided.

50021 ■ **"IPOs: Things of the Past"** in *Crain's New York Business* (Vol. 23, January 1, 2007, No. 1, pp. 14)
Pub: Crain Communications, Inc.
Description: Relegence Corp., a Manhattan-based company that gathers business information from around the globe and allows people to personalize the news delivered to their desktops, was acquired by AOL. The new trend in the business realm is to slowly grow then be acquired by a larger company instead of going public.

50022 ■ **"Irby Buys Two Companies"** in *Mississippi Business Journal* (Vol. 29, January 2007, No. 4, pp. 8)
Pub: Venture Publications, Inc.
Ed: Wally Northway **Description:** Stuart C. Irby Co., a subsidiary of Sonepar USA acquires Burmeister Electric Co. and High Voltage Testing Laboratories. Profiles of both acquired companies included.

50023 ■ **"Is Excite@Home The AOL of Broadband?"** in *Fortune* (Vol. , No. 11, December 6, 1999, pp. 156+)
Pub: Time Inc.
Ed: Eric Nee. **Description:** Excite@Home has become the leading supplier of broadband access to the Internet, with almost 1 million subscribers. It gained this position through the merger of @Home and Excite. Company strategy is to combine content and distribution.

50024 ■ **"It's Not Easy Being Green"** in *Inc.* (November 1, 2004)
Pub: Inc. Magazine
Ed: Jess McCuan. **Description:** Jeffrey Hollender and Alan Newman disagreed about strategy, fought bitterly-and created two successful companies. They'd set out to change the world, but really changed each other in the end.

50025 ■ **"IXL Enterprises to merge with Scient Corp."** in *Atlanta Business Chronicle* (Vol. 24, No. 9, August 3, 2001, pp. 12A)
Pub: American City Business Journals Inc.
Description: Scient Corp. based in New York and iXL Enterprises Inc of Atlanta, Georgia have agreed to merge. The two companies will then become subsidiaries of the New York-based parent, called Scient Management, the new company will be headed by veteran leaders of both companies.

50026 ■ **"Jackmont Hospitality Acquires Four T.G.I. Friday's Restaurants"** in *Black Enterprise* (Vol. 35, September 2004, No. 2, pp. 32)
Pub: Earl G. Graves Publishing Co. Inc.
Ed: Aisha Jefferson. **Description:** Jackmont Hospitality Inc. recently acquired four T.G.I. Friday urban-based restaurants in Maryland, Washington DC, and Philadelphia. Details of the merger are presented.

50027 ■ **"Jadi's Journey; Move to OU Incubator Could Lead to Funding"** in *Crain's Detroit Business* (Vol. 22, January 9, 2006, No. 2, pp. 3)
Pub: Crain Communications Inc. - Detroit
Ed: Sheena Harrison. **Description:** Jadi Inc. should receive $3 million in grants and federal funding for its new navigation systems for military robots. The firm has moved into the SmartZone Business Incubator at Oakland University in Michigan.

50028 ■ **"Jewelry Lines Picked Up"** in *Mississippi Business Journal* (Vol. 29, January 2007, No. 4, pp. 12)
Pub: Venture Publications, Inc.
Ed: Wally Northway **Description:** Lil McKinnon-Hicks, a jewelry artist producing work under the name of McKinnon HeartCraft has recently had two lines of her jewelry picked up by national entities.

50029 ■ **"Joining Forces"** in *Home Business* (Vol. 12, October 2005, No. 5, pp. 64, 66)
Pub: Home Business Magazine
Ed: Priscilla Y. Huff. **Description:** Through the use of the Internet and affordable technology, home-based business owners are forming virtual alliances to help one another grow their businesses.

50030 ■ **"Joining Forces"** in *Sales & Marketing Management*
Pub: VNU Business Media
Ed: Dale Buss. **Description:** Special-ingredient manufacturers are lending value to some food and beverage brands to attract the attention of grocery store shoppers.

50031 ■ **"Jubilee! JAM Returning June 2007"** in *Mississippi Business Journal* (Vol. 29, January 2007, No. 1, pp. 3)
Pub: Venture Publications, Inc.
Description: TCB Entertainment, The Jackson Arts And Music Foundation (JAM Foundation) has formed a partnership to bring back Jubilee!JAM to the Capital City. Festival slated for June 15-16.

50032 ■ **"Katrina Cottages At Lowe's"** in *Mississippi Business Journal* (Vol. 28, September 2006, No. 36, pp. 23)
Pub: Venture Publications, Inc.
Description: Lowe's Companies Inc. is now selling several designs of Katrina Cottages, designed to withstand heavy rain and winds up to 140 miles per hour. Katrina Cottages meet new hurricane codes and International Building Code and range from 544 square feet to 1,340 square feet.

50033 ■ **"Keep it Simple"** in *Entrepreneur. com* (Vol. 34, February 2006, No. 2, pp. 60)
Pub: Entrepreneur Media Inc.
Ed: Chris Penttila. **Description:** Twenty-five tips for fine tuning a small business are outlined, focusing on technology, money, banking, taxes, credit and collection, accounting systems, mergers, management, and marketing ideas.

50034 ■ **"Knight Ridder's Happy Ending?"** in *Business Week* (February 20, 2006, No. 3972, pp. 26)
Pub: McGraw-Hill Companies
Ed: Jon Fine. **Description:** Rumors suggest that The McClatchy Company partnered with The Times Company, may bid to purchase Knight Ridder Inc.

50035 ■ **"Lake Success Based Astoria Financial Finds Fewer Acquisition Opportunities..."** in *Long Island Business News* (Mar. 5, 2004)
Pub: Dolan Media Newswires
Description: Astoria Financial Corporation, with $22.5 billion in assets from bank acquisitions, expects to see fewer mergers in the industry.

50036 ■ **"Large industrial gas companies setting sights on Detroit"** in *Crain's Detroit Business* (Vol. 19, No. 4, January 27, 2003, pp. 21)
Pub: Crain Communications Inc., Detroit
Ed: Michael Strong. **Description:** Welding equipment suppliers and independent industrial gas suppliers in the metro Detroit, Michigan area are consolidating to improve product offerings and tap into new customer bases.

50037 ■ **"Largest Shareholder Urges Knight Ridder to Sell Itself"** in *Sacramento Bee* (November 2, 2005)
Pub: The Sacramento Bee
Ed: Dale Kasler. **Description:** Shareholders urged Knight Ridder to put the company up for sale. Knight Ridder owns 32 daily papers. The move represents issues facing the newspaper industry's decline in circulation.

50038 ■ **"Las Vegas Sands Sets IPO Strike Price"** in *Tradeshow Week* (Vol. 34, December 13, 2004, No. 50, pp. 3)
Pub: Reed Business Information
Description: The owner of the Sands Expo and Convention Center and Venetian Resort Casino Hotel estimates it will generate more than a half billion dollars in its upcoming initial public offering.

50039 ■ **"Laterals keep coming"** in *Daily Business Review* (Vol. 77, No. 198, March 24, 2003, pp. AA2)
Pub: American Lawyer Media LP
Ed: Matthew Haggman. **Description:** Law firms are becoming increasingly dependent upon hiring laterals for growing their business rather than promoting from within.

50040 ■ **"Laterals? Pass"** in *Daily Business Review* (Vol. 77, No. 146, Jan. 7, 2003, pp. A8)
Pub: American Lawyer Media LP
Ed: Anthony Lin. **Description:** Many of the nation's top law firms poach partners from each other in order to provide more services.

50041 ■ **"Latinocare Goes Public"** in *Hispanic Business* (June 2002, pp. 28)
Pub: Hispanic Business
Description: LatinoCare Management Corporation, a medical manager network, has become a publicly traded company. The Hispanic firm is located in Southern California.

50042 ■ **"LDM Technologies makes play for bankrupt Soo Plastics"** in *Crain's Detroit Business* (Vol. 18, No. 50, December 16, 2002, pp. 5)
Pub: Crain Communications Inc., Detroit
Ed: Terry Kosdrosky. **Description:** LDM Technologies Inc., automotive plastics supplier, has offered to purchase the bankrupt Soo Plastics Inc. for $8.5 million, plus inventories.

50043 ■ **"Leadership Training"** in *Black Enterprise* (Vol. 37, January 2007, No. 6, pp. 56)
Pub: Earl G. Graves Publishing Co. Inc.
Ed: Sonia Alleyne. **Description:** Profile of Theopolis Holman, Group Vice-President of Duke Energy, who discusses how he prepared for the merger between Duke Energy and Cinergy. Holman oversees a division of 9,000 service contractors and employees.

50044 ■ **"Leap of Faith"** in *Entrepreneur* (Vol. 32, October 2004, No. 10, pp. 21)
Pub: Entrepreneur Media Inc.
Ed: Crystal Detamore-Rodman. **Description:** Businesses moving from being a privately-owned business to a publicly held company are faced with many concerns. New standards aimed at placing more stringent controls on corporate accounting practices coupled with pressure for short-term performance are two such examples.

50045 ■ **"Leap Wireless Talks Merger with MetroPCS"** in *San Diego Business Journal* (Vol. 28, January 15, 2007, No. 3, pp. 10)
Pub: San Diego Business Journal Associates
Ed: Mike Allen. **Description:** Merger plans between Leap Wireless International Inc. and MetroPCS Communications are discussed.

50046 ■ **"Legal News Publisher Sells His Interest in Company"** in *Crain's Detroit Business* (Vol. 22, February 13, 2006, No. 7, pp. 26)
Pub: Crain Communications Inc. - Detroit
Ed: Tom Henderson. **Description:** John Parks sold his minority interest in Detroit Legal News Publishing LLC to the Minneapolis-based Dolan Media Company. The move came after Parks retired from the firm. Parks will continue to serve as a consultant through 2006.

50047 ■ *Let's Buy a Company: How to Accelerate Growth Through Acquisitions*
Pub: Career Press, Incorporated
Ed: H. Lee Rust. **Released:** December 2005. **Price:** $18.99 (US), $25.95 (Canadian). **Description:** Advice for negotiating terms and pricing as well as other aspects of mergers and acquisitions in small companies.

50048 ■ **"Let's Make a Deal"** in *Business Journal-Milwaukee* (Vol. 20, No. 47, August 8, 2003, pp. A23)
Pub: American City Business Journals, Inc.

Ed: Becca Mader. Description: A growing trend among Milwaukee-based manufacturers is to acquire German companies. Topics include strategic planning, market development, and foreign operations.

50049 ■ "Let's Make a Dual" in *Entrepreneur* (Vol. 32, November 2004, No. 11, pp. 70)
Pub: Entrepreneur Media Inc.
Ed: Jennifer Pellet. Description: Dual-class ownership may be a good choice for companies fearful of an initial public offering.

50050 ■ "Leveraged growth. Expanding sales without sacrificing profits" in *Harvard Business Review* (Vol. 80, No. 10, October 2002, pp. 68)
Pub: Harvard Business School Press
Ed: John Hagel. Description: The concept of leveraged growth, where growth does not occur by acquisitions, rather relying upon skills and assets that a firm already has available.

50051 ■ "License To Thrive" in *Inc.* (August 2005, pp. 38)
Pub: Inc. Magazine
Ed: Erik Sherman. Description: The right partnership can drive sales, while it also reduces workload. The art of the alliance is outlined.

50052 ■ "LifeSecure Goes National" in *Crain's Detroit Business* (Vol. 23, January 29, 2007, No. 5, pp. 17)
Pub: Crain Communications Inc. - Detroit
Ed: Tom Henderson. Description: Small Brighton firm that specializes in long term insurance care Purchased a Dallas company to get licenses to sell in 41 states. Acquisition was the key to success in growing nationally and rapidly.

50053 ■ "Liz Clairborne Acquires Urban Sportswear Brand Enyce" in *Black Enterprise* (Vol. 34, No. 7, February 2004, pp. 29)
Pub: Earl Graves Publishing Co.
Ed: Tamara E. Holmes. Description: Liz Claiborne Inc. acquired Enyce from Sport Brands International for $114 million. The sportswear is expected to have net sales of $95 million in 2003. Liz Claiborne will use the clothing to gain exposure to urban consumers.

50054 ■ "Local ISPs NAS, Open Access Join Forces" in *Bellingham Business Journal* (January 2007, pp. A6)
Pub: Sun News Inc.
Description: Local Internet service providers, OpenAccess ad Network Access Services, Inc., have recently joined forces.

50055 ■ "Local execs buy ad agency from parent" in *Crain's Detroit Business* (Vol. 19, No. 15, April 14, 2003, pp. 25)
Pub: Crain Communications Inc., Detroit
Ed: Jennette Smith. Description: Profile of the ad agency called re:group. The firm was purchased by a group of local executives at the Ann Arbor office of Fitch:Worldwide from London-based Cordiant Communications Group PLC and they've taken the business private.

50056 ■ "Lockport, N.Y.-Based First Niagara Financial to Open More Branches, Buy Bank" in *The Buffalo News* (April 11, 2203)
Pub: Knight-Ridder/Tribune Business News
Ed: Chet Bridger. Description: First Niagara Financial Groups intends to open new branches in Buffalo, Rochester and Syracuse, New York markets and is looking for a bank acquisition in Pennsylvania.

50057 ■ "Long Island's East End to Get a New TV Station" in *Long Island Business News* (March 5, 2004)
Pub: Dolan Media Newswires
Description: Frazer Dougherty, East Hampton Studios and Tom Scott, Nantucket Nectars are partnering to launch an East End television station called Plum TV. The station would carry community events and local news.

50058 ■ "Long-Time Music Publisher Sings" in *San Fernando Valley Business Journal* (Vol. 11, November 2006, No. 24, pp. 26)
Pub: San Fernando Valley Business Journal Associates
Ed: Description: Profile of Alfred Publishing Co., a successful company that publishes music-related material and its acquisition of Daisy Rock Guitars, makers of acoustic and electrical guitars for women and girls.

50059 ■ "The Lookout: It's time to play some war games" in *Red Herring* (No. 103, September 1, 2001, pp. 94)
Pub: Herring Communications
Ed: Paul R. LaMonica. Description: Profile of CACI International, an information technology company whose number one customer was the U.S. Department of Defense. The article discusses the firm's successful initiatives to diversify.

50060 ■ "Loving the IPO Comeback" in *Inc.* (July 1, 2004)
Pub: Inc. Magazine
Ed: Gossagem Bobbie. Description: The IPO market has rebounded with a tenfold increase by April 2004 over the same period in 2003; 118 companies filed with the Securities and Exchange Commission to go public.

50061 ■ "L.P. Confidential" in *Venture Capital Journal* (Vol. 42, No. 8, August 2002, pp. 18-29)
Pub: Thomas Venture Economics
Description: Four anonymous Limited Partners discuss current hot issues in the venture capital sector.

50062 ■ "The LP Report Card" in *Venture Capital Journal* (October 1, 2005)
Pub: Thomason Financial Inc.
Ed: Jerry Borrell. Description: Important issues confronting the private equity industry are addressed. Topics include deployments and exits; management fees; carry; valuations and write-downs; succession; and terms and agreements.

50063 ■ "LPs Reconsider the Value of IRRs" in *Venture Capital Journal* (Vol. 42, No. 5, May 2002, pp. 5-6)
Pub: Thomas Venture Economics
Ed: Carolina Braunschweig. Description: The Institutional Limited Partners Association (ILPA) wants to do away with the traditional method of using internal rates of return (IRRs), saying they are meaningless. Instead, the ILPA wants venture capital firms to adopt a "cash-in and cash-out" policy.

50064 ■ "The Lure of Bay State Technology" in *Boston Globe* (February 7, 2005)
Pub: New York Times Company
Ed: Robert Weisman. Description: Overseas investors are seeking acquisitions in Massachusetts, focusing on the state's high-technology and life sciences start-ups. Two deals are presented.

50065 ■ "Mail-Order Medical Suppliers Combined" in *Tampa Tribune* (November 23, 2005)
Pub: Media General, Inc.
Ed: Carol Gentry. Description: Warburg Pincus, a global investment group has bought Chronic Care Solutions Inc. and MP TotalCare Inc. The merger called CCS Medical Inc., will become the second-largest mail-order supplier in the U.S.

50066 ■ "Major League Baseball Signs Partnership Pacts" in *Hispanic Business* (March 2002, pp. 12)
Pub: Hispanic Business
Description: Major League Baseball has signed an agreement with the National Minority Supplier Development Council and Women's Business Enterprise National Council, as part of its Diverse Business Partners Program. The program is intended to cultivate partnerships with minority- and women-owned companies.

50067 ■ "Making B2B Better" in *E-business Advisor* (Vol. 18, No. 5, May 2000, pp. 10)
Pub: Advisor Media, Inc.
Description: The next generation of business-to-business models is what Giga Research Fellow, Gig Graham, calls electronic partner networks (EPNs), where business partners share a common network, establish a trustworthy means of collaboration, and conduct business through the use of structured electronic contracts and agreements.

50068 ■ "Making a Clean Break" in *Atlanta Business Chronicle* (Vol. 25, December 6, 2002, No. 26, pp. 1B)
Pub: American City Business Publications, Inc.
Ed: Lee Hall. Description: When a business determines that it must terminate a client, being honest and sharing blame are important elements of the process. Business relationships can become strained to the point that they no longer work.

50069 ■ "Manhattan-based Terra Holdings Acquires Dunemere Associates" in *Long Island Business News* (February 6, 2004)
Pub: Dolan Media Newswires
Description: Manhattan-based Terra Holdings, has acquired a majority interest in East Hampton-based Dunemere Associates Real Estate. Terra operates as the holding company for several real estate firms across the U.S.

50070 ■ "Manufacturer AmerTac Buys Night Light Maker" in *The Record* (November 8, 2005)
Pub: New Jersey Media Group
Ed: Kathleen Lynn. Description: AmerTac, manufacturer of lighting products, has acquired Elumina Lighting Technologies Inc., a Canadian company. The move will give AmerTack ownership of Elumina's patented safety technology for night lights and other lighting products.

50071 ■ "Masco Installs Two Subsidiaries in Deals Worth $719M" in *Crain's Detroit Business* (Vol. 16, No. 49, December 4, 2000, pp. 3)
Pub: Crain Communications, Inc.
Ed: Leslie Green. Description: Masco Corporation announced it is acquiring two installation companies in transactions valued at $719 million.

50072 ■ "McClatchy Among Possible Suitors for Knight Ridder" in *Sacramento Bee* (December 9, 2005)
Pub: The Sacramento Bee
Ed: Dale Kasler. Description: American newspapers are reporting a drop in revenues, profits and stock prices due to lower circulation. Shareholders for Knight Ridder Inc. are putting pressure on the newspaper chain.

50073 ■ "Medstat Acquisition May Bring More Jobs" in *Crain's Detroit Business* (Vol. 22, September 25-October 1, 2006, No. 39, pp. 1, 38-39)
Pub: Crain Communications Inc. - Detroit
Ed: Michelle Martinez. Description: Health care cost data and analysis company purchases competitor for expansion in local market. Consolidation in Ann Arbor may bring more jobs to this area.

50074 ■ "Merger with Advo May Mean Shift in Business for Valassis" in *Crain's Detroit Business* (Vol. 232, January 8, 2007, No. 2, pp. 4)
Pub: Crain Communications Inc. - Detroit
Ed: Bill Shea. Description: The merger of Valassis and Advo is a long term strategy to grow the business into direct mailing. Valassis has been limited solely to the insert mailings in periodicals.

50075 ■ "Merger Fever" in *Hispanic Business* (Vol. 23, No. 10, October, 2001, pp. 42, 44)
Pub: Hispanic Business
Ed: Derek Reveron. Description: Hispanic advertising agencies are becoming increasingly attractive takeover targets for international conglomerates, because of the growing confidence in the market. It is predicted that the Spanish-speaking population will become a more powerful force in industry growth.

50076 ■ "Merger Finally Gets Green Light" in *Hispanic Business* **(November 2003, pp. 72)**
Pub: Hispanic Business
Ed: Tim Dougherty. **Description:** Federal Communications Commission votes along party lines to sanction Univision's merger with Hispanic Broadcasting Corporation, positioning the firm as the nation's leading Spanish language broadcaster.

50077 ■ "Merger to Form Nation's Largest Freight Consolidator" in *Chicago Tribune* **(March 1, 2005)**
Pub: Knight-Ridder/Tribune Business News
Ed: John Schmeltzer. **Description:** Yellow Roadway Corporation announces plans to acquire USF Corporation for about $1.4 billion. The merger will create revenues of around $9 billion for Yellow Roadway, and employ more than 70,000 workers in 1,000 locations.

50078 ■ *Mergers and Acquisitions from A to Z*
Pub: Amacom
Ed: Andrew J. Sherman, Milledge A. Hart. **Released:** December 2005. **Price:** $47.00. **Description:** Guide for the entire process of mergers and acquisitions, including taxes, accounting, laws, and projected financial gain.

50079 ■ "Michigan Bank Finally Gets Georgia Toehold" in *American Banker* **(Vol. 170, February 3, 2005, No. 23, pp. 1)**
Pub: Thomson Financial Media Inc.
Ed: John Reosti. **Description:** Capitol Bancorp Ltd. of Michigan has acquired Peoples State Bank in Jeffersonville, Georgia. The acquisition will qualify Capitol as a Georgia holding company, enabling them to charter banks and open branches in the state.

50080 ■ "Michigan Firm Buys Signs Now" in *Bradenton Herald* **(February 11, 2005)**
Pub: Bradenton Herald
Ed: Matt Griswold. **Description:** Allegra Network LLC, a Michigan-based sign company has purchased Signs Now Corporation's assets and franchise agreements. The sale will have little impact on local stores. Allegra is the franchisor for six various printing brands in the U.S., Canada and Japan; leading brands include Allegra Print & Imaging, American Speedy Printing Centers, and Insty-Prints.

50081 ■ "Microsoft Buys Enterprise Anti-Virus Firm" in *eWeek* **(February 8, 2005)**
Pub: Ziff Davis Media Inc.
Description: Microsoft's acquisition of Sybari Software Inc., the maker of enterprise-ready anti-virus software, is examined.

50082 ■ "Microsoft's Bulging Security Portfolio" in *Business Week Online* **(February 9, 2005)**
Pub: McGraw-Hill Companies
Ed: Jay Greene. **Description:** Microsoft intends to be a leader in software security. After buying the privately held Sybari, Microsoft will increase its protection for email servers by scanning email for attached viruses before they reach business networks.

50083 ■ "Midsize suppliers will buy others or be bought" in *Crain's Detroit Business* **(Vol. 19, No. 4, January 27, 2003, pp. 20)**
Pub: Crain Communications Inc., Detroit
Ed: Rhoda Miel. **Description:** Midsize suppliers to the automotive industry are having to either buy or sell businesses in order to survive in the marketplace.

50084 ■ "Milwaukee Harley Shifts Gears" in *Business Journal-Milwaukee* **(Vol. 20, No. 46, August 1, 2003, pp. A3)**
Pub: American City Business Journals, Inc.
Ed: Rich Rovito. **Description:** Milwaukee, Wisconsin's Harley-Davidson and Buell, operated by owner Bob Michel, is housed in a 36,000-square foot motorcycle dealership. Michel has acquired the business from his partner Paul Kegel, for $4 million with a financing package from Associated Bank.

50085 ■ "Minority Certification Needs Examination" in *Crain's Detroit Business* **(Vol. 18, No. 22, May 20, 2002, pp. 8)**
Pub: Crain Communications Inc. - Detroit
Description: Commitments by automakers and large suppliers from minority-owned firms has helped them to grow and to get some of that business, the smaller minority-owned businesses have often formed partnerships or joint ventures with larger, non-minority firms, thus helping the smaller to grow.

50086 ■ "Mississippi-Corporate Partnership Boosts Shipyards" in *Sun Herald* **(April 11, 2003)**
Pub: Knight-Ridder/Tribune Business News
Ed: David Tortorano. **Description:** The planned three-year expansion at two Mississippi shipyards will add 2,000 new jobs to the area.

50087 ■ "The Month in Review: Who Made News?" in *Venture Capital Journal* **(Vol. 42, No. 5, May 2002, pp. 15, 16-17)**
Pub: Thomson Venture Economics
Description: Abstracts of stories from the pages of the VCJ's sister publication, Private Equity Week, are presented. A Web address is provided to see entire stories.

50088 ■ "More deals, smaller portions" in *Crain's Detroit Business* **(Vol. 19, No. 4, January 27, 2003, pp. 1)**
Pub: Crain Communications Inc., Detroit
Ed: Terry Kosdrosky. **Description:** A comparison of merger and acquisition activity between years 2001 and 2002 is highlighted. Statistical data included.

50089 ■ "MSN Signs DIY Expert With Female Focus" in *Marketing to Women* **(Vol. 20, January 2007, No. 1, pp. 8)**
Pub: EPM Communications, Inc.
Description: MSN and the online community devoted to women, Be Jane, team up to bring the subject of women's home improvement to a broader audience via the Internet. Video clips, animated tutorials, articles, message boards, and blogs will address such varied topics as repairing holes in dry wall to painting a garage door.

50090 ■ "Murdoch's Bid for DirecTV Parent May Lead to Launch of New Networks" in *Boston Globe* **(April 11, 2003)**
Pub: Knight-Ridder/Tribune Business News
Ed: Peter J. Howe. **Description:** Rupert Murdoch has made a bid for the parent company of satellite television provider DirecTV, which could provide some of the popular British interactive television systems currently available in Murdoch's British satellite unit.

50091 ■ "Navteq Corp." in *Crain's Chicago Business* **(Vol. 30, January 2007, No. 4, pp. 36)**
Pub: Crain Communications, Inc.
Description: Traffic.com, a company that gathers data that allows drivers to get real-time traffic updates, was acquired by Navteq Corp., creator of digital maps for GPS and search engines.

50092 ■ "NCR Spinoff Hits Home" in *San Diego Business Journal* **(Vol. 28, January 15, 2007, No. 3, pp. 38)**
Pub: San Diego Business Journal Associates
Ed: Brad Graves. **Description:** NCR Corporation will spin off its Teradata Data Warehousing business to shareholders to help both companies focus on customer base, business strategy and operational needs.

50093 ■ "Nemes Allen Merges with Wisconsin Firm; Accountants to Pursue Middle-Market Clients" in *Crain's Detroit Business* **(Vol. 19, No. 44)**
Pub: Crain Communications Inc., Detroit
Ed: Katie Merx. **Description:** Bingham Farms, Michigan accounting firm Nemes Allen & Company plans to merge with Virchow Krause & Company LLP, located in Madison, Wisconsin. The deal is described as a pure merger, with no cash exchanged.

50094 ■ "Nemes Allen Merges with Wisconsin Firm" in *Crain's Detroit Business* **(Vol. 19, No. 44, November 3, 2003, pp. 1)**
Pub: Crain Communications Inc., Detroit
Ed: Katie Merx. **Description:** Bingham Farms, Michigan accounting firm Nemes Allen & Company plans to merge with Virchow Krause & Company LLP, located in Madison, Wisconsin. The deal is described as a pure merger, with no cash exchanged.

50095 ■ "Networking Provides Partnership's Funding" in *Wall Street Journal* **(October 14, 2003, pp. B4)**
Pub: Dow Jones & Co. Inc.
Ed: Paulette Thomas. **Description:** Case study of William G. Nelson showing ways to move from a career in finance to an entrepreneurial life on a shoestring budget through networking.

50096 ■ "New Issues: There's a Side Door into the Public Markets" in *Red Herring* **(No. 99, June 15 & July 1, 2001, pp. 138)**
Pub: Herring Communications
Ed: Stephen Lacey. **Description:** The alternative to an Initial Public Offering (IPO), is coming back into style: Divestiture. Divestiture is when a company simply distributes shares of a subsidiary to its own stockholders, in a one-step spin-off.

50097 ■ "New Jersey Builder Hovnanian Enters Chicago Home Market" in *Chicago Tribune* **(March 3, 2005)**
Pub: Knight-Ridder/Tribune Business News
Ed: Sharon Stangenes. **Description:** Details of New Jersey developer Hovnanian Enterprises Inc.'s purchase of Town & Country Homes; the deal will position Hovnanian to begin development in the Chicago area. Statistical data included.

50098 ■ "New Laws Take On Delaware Subsidiaries" in *Inc.* **(January 1, 2005)**
Pub: Inc. Magazine
Ed: Lora Kolodny. **Description:** New York Tax Courts have imposed taxes on revenue derived from intellectual property.

50099 ■ "New Team Joins Raymond James Investment Office" in *Crain's Detroit Business* **(Vol. 16, No. 50, December 11, 2000, pp. 21)**
Pub: Crain Communications, Inc.
Ed: Katie Merx. **Description:** Raymond James & Associates Inc. restocked its automotive investment banking office this week with a team from Pricewaterhouse Coopers L.L.P.

50100 ■ "New Wright Museum CEO: Increase Role in Schools" in *Crain's Detroit Business* **(Vol. 22, December 11, 2006, No. 50, pp. 13)**
Pub: Crain Communications Inc. - Detroit
Ed: Sherri Begin. **Description:** African American History Museum wants to form more partnerships with schools and businesses to increase the value and quality of education in Detroit history. CEO hopes the museum will become a model for national identity.

50101 ■ "Newsstand" in *Home Business* **(Vol. 12, October 2005, No. 5, pp. 38-39)**
Pub: Home Business Magazine
Description: Various topics are covered, including information about home-based business tax deductions, the link between home computers and entrepreneurship, income gaps, demographics of home-based business owners, creation of more home-based businesses due to merger-related job cuts, and frivolous lawsuits against home-based entrepreneurs.

50102 ■ "Next step: Bricks and mortar" in *Crain's Detroit Business* **(Vol. 19, No. 10, March 10, 2003, pp. 11)**
Pub: Crain Communications Inc., Detroit
Ed: Laura Bailey. **Description:** Howard Bell, the newly appointed head of Wayne State University's Research and Technology Park is working towards a 10-20 year project that will result in a mix of emerging companies with satellite offices of Wayne State's largest industry partners.

50103 ■ "NextWave to Buy Go Networks, Lists on Nasdaq" in *San Diego Business Journal* **(Vol. 28, January 8, 2007, No. 2, pp. 5)**
Pub: San Diego Business Journal Associates
Ed: Brad Graves. **Description:** NextWave Wireless Inc. will pay $13.3 million and assume $7.46 million in debt purchasing Go Networks Inc. Details of the agreement are shared.

50104 ■ "Nike Develops Brand for Women" in *Marketing to Women* **(Vol. 20, January 2007, No. 1, pp. 8)**
Pub: EPM Communications, Inc.
Description: A new brand of tennis shoes for women will hit shelves in spring 2007. The brand Tailwind will combine contemporary fashion with athletic performance and is a result of marketing partnership between Payless Shoe Source and Exeter Brands Group, a subsidiary of Nike.

50105 ■ "No IPO market? No problem. Call Ravisent" in *Red Herring* **(No. 106, October 15, 2001, pp. 94)**
Pub: Herring Communications
Ed: Christopher Byron. **Description:** Shares of Ravisent Technologies have fallen on hard times since 1999, but amidst the turmoil, the company has announced plans for an acquisition. Ravisent makes multimedia software and hardware devices for PCs and the Internet.

50106 ■ "No, They Can't Do It Themselves" in *Inc.* **(July 1, 2004)**
Pub: Inc. Magazine
Ed: Jess McCuan. **Description:** Founders of the do-it-yourself journal, ReadyMade magazine, partnered with a small Colorado publisher in order to compete with rival Budget Living.

50107 ■ "Nonprofit Consolidation to Increase" in *Crain's Detroit Business* **(Vol. 22, November 27, 2006, No. 48, pp. 20)**
Pub: Crain Communications Inc. - Detroit
Ed: Sherri Begin. **Description:** Reduced funding from foundations and pension shortfalls have resulted in consolidation of the nonprofit industry in Michigan. Efficiencies are to be gained by eliminating duplication of services.

50108 ■ "North Fork Bancorp Acquires GreenPoint Financial" in *Long Island Business News* **(February 20, 2004)**
Pub: Dolan Media Newswires
Ed: Claude Solnik. **Description:** North Fork Bancorp has acquired GreenPoint Financial, increasing North Fork's assets over $50 billion. John Adams Kansas, CEO of North Fork Bancorp is interviewed.

50109 ■ "North Fork Bancorp to Trim Employees of Two Acquisitions" in *Long Island Business News* **(March 12, 2004)**
Pub: Dolan Media Newswires
Description: North Fork Bankcorp Inc. plans to layoff nearly 300 workers at Trust Company of New Jersey as well as some workers at GreenPoint Financial Corporation as a result of its acquisition of the two banks.

50110 ■ "Northwest Accord To Allow Flying For Other Carriers" in *Wall Street Journal* **(Vol. 248, December 2006, No. 149, pp. B2)**
Pub: Dow Jones & Co. Inc.
Ed: Associated Press **Description:** Regional Pinnacle Airlines Corporation struck a 10-year agreement with Northwest Airlines Corp. to expand Pinnacle's flying to other carriers in exchange for an unsecured claim in Northwest's bankruptcy proceedings.

50111 ■ "Now, on to the Really Big Time" in *Inc.* **(October 17, 2000, pp. 88)**
Pub: The Goldhirsh Group
Description: No sooner had some Inc. 500 companies made this year's list than their founders sold the business or took it public.

50112 ■ "Now Showing: Win Partners by Letting Them See You're Made Of" in *Entrepreneur* **(Vol. 31, No. 9, September 2003)**
Pub: Entrepreneur Media, Inc.
Ed: David Newton. **Description:** Ways to expand a business beyond current markets, using alliances with larger businesses, licensing of technology to others or spending resources for more internal development, are explored.

50113 ■ "Nuance Gains Voice in Noisy Speech Market" in *San Francisco Business Times* **(Vol. 18, No. 2, August 22, 2003, pp. 3)**
Pub: American City Business Journals
Ed: Lizette Wilson. **Description:** Examination of ScanSoft's acquisition of rival SpeechWorks International Inc., maker of speech recognition products. Topics include market development plans, market share, and strategic planning.

50114 ■ "NW Miss. Firms Merge To Meet Growing Needs Of Region" in *Mississippi Business Journal* **(Vol. 28, September 2006, No. 37, pp. 20)**
Pub: Venture Publications, Inc.
Ed: Wally Northway **Description:** Law firm Smith Phillips Mitchell & Scott has merged with law firm Nowak & Neyman to create Smith Phillips Mitchell Scott & Nowak, LLP. The firm now covers most of the Northwest Mississippi region.

50115 ■ "Oil Slicks" in *Inc.* **(October 1, 2003)**
Pub: Gruner & Jahr USA Publishing
Ed: Tahl Raz. **Description:** Tim Marquez and Rod Eson were on their way to revolutionizing the oil industry until they ran into legal issues that tore them apart.

50116 ■ "Okla. City-based BancFirst Plans $25M Public Offering" in *Journal Record* **(February 5, 2004)**
Pub: Dolan Media Company
Description: A $25 million public offering by BancFirst Corporation will be underwritten by Advest and Howe Barnes Investments. BancFirst has more than $2.9 billion in assets.

50117 ■ "Older firm gets venture funds" in *Wall Street Journal* **(March 25, 2003, pp. B4)**
Pub: Dow Jones & Co. Inc.
Ed: Raymond Hennessey. **Description:** Because of the low number of initial public offerings, older firms are receiving venture capital.

50118 ■ "On the Merge" in *Entrepreneur* **(Vol. 33, October 2005, No. 10, pp. 87)**
Pub: Entrepreneur Media Inc.
Ed: Sara Wilson. **Description:** Scott D'Entremont, co-founder of a conferencing services provider, shares insight into helping employees feel a sense of unity when merging two companies.

50119 ■ "On the Same Page" in *Crain's Detroit Business* **( )**
Pub: Crain Communications Inc. - Detroit
Ed: Terry Kosdrosky. **Description:** Automakers, suppliers, and tooling companies are trying to standardize standard parts used by all facets of the industry, using a standard e-catalog, called e-tooling.

50120 ■ "Once is Not Enough" in *Forbes* **(October 30, 2000, pp. 280)**
Pub: Forbes Magazine
Ed: Daniel Kruger. **Description:** The ways small companies should select a securities underwriter for additional offerings is discussed.

50121 ■ "Oregon Food Producer Hitches Wagon to Big Brand-Name Star" in *Business Journal-Portland* **(Vol. 18, No. 33, October 12, 2001, pp. 16)**
Pub: American City Business Journals, Inc. (Portland)
Ed: Shelly Strom. **Description:** Family-owned YoCream has announced a partnership with Dannon Yogurt to produce frozen yogurt products.

50122 ■ "Out of stock" in *Entrepreneur* **(Vol. 30, No. 3, March 2002, pp. 65)**
Pub: Entrepreneur Media Inc.
Ed: Jennifer Pellet. **Description:** In the right circumstances, going private might be the best solution for a company. The special circumstances involved in going private are discussed.

50123 ■ "Partnering for Success" in *Rough Notes* **(Vol. 146, No. 4, April 2003, pp. 32)**
Pub: Rough Notes
Description: Robyn Holt is the manager of Fraser, Yamor, Jacob and Young, the firm that has entered into a partnership with Western Valley Insurance Associates Inc.

50124 ■ "Partners in Branding" in *Sales and Marketing.com* **(Vol. 156, No. 3, March 2004, pp. 10)**
Pub: VNU eMedia, Inc.
Ed: Jennifer Gilbert. **Description:** Marketing partnerships should be formed for brand-building as much as they are formed for increasing sales. The three main reasons for companies to partner is to bring new customers to current target markets, to extend a brand to a new product or service, and to preempt competition.

50125 ■ "Partnership Terminations" in *Journal of Accountancy* **(Vol. 199, January 2005, No. 1, pp. 73)**
Pub: American Institute of Certified Public Accountants
Ed: Edward J. Schnee. **Description:** The Internal Revenue Code as it pertains to partnership terminations is discussed.

50126 ■ "Patriarch Adds $7 Million Auto Supplier to its Holdings" in *Crain's Detroit Business* **(Vol. 22, February 6, 2006, No. 6, pp. 3)**
Pub: Crain Communications Inc. - Detroit
Ed: Brent Snavely. **Description:** Patriarch Partners LLC (New York City) bought Jacobs Industries Inc. of Fraser, Michigan for $7 million, the firm's third automotive acquisition since December 2005. Jacobs had filed for Chapter 11 bankruptcy in September 2005.

50127 ■ "PayPal Pushes For Business Use; A Hit With Consumers" in *Investor's Business Daily* **(October 24, 2003, pp. A04)**
Pub: Investor's Business Daily, Inc.
Ed: Pete Barlas. **Description:** Online payment firms are betting on Internet retail credit card sales to continue growth. Profile of the partnership created by PayPal and Cybersource Corporation is included.

50128 ■ "Penske Eyes Russia, China" in *Crain's Detroit Business* **(Vol. 23, January 22-28, 2007, No. 4, pp. 3, 20)**
Pub: Crain Communications Inc. - Detroit
Ed: Robert Sherefkin. **Description:** UnitedAuto Group is exploring opportunities in China and Russia with Mitsui & Co. Ltd. Roger Penske, Chairman and CEO of UnitedAuto Group is looking to diversify outside the United States for growth possibly through joint ventures and local partnership.

50129 ■ "Personal Business" in *Business Week* **(January 9, 2006, No. 3966, pp. 94)**
Pub: McGraw-Hill Companies
Ed: Mara der Hovanesian. **Description:** Topics include a takeover of auto lender Americredit, overseas shipping, and retail shopping in China.

50130 ■ "Personalized Profits" in *Small Business Opportunities* **(Vol. 13, No. 5, September 2001, pp. 82)**
Pub: Harris Publications, Inc.
Description: Profile of franchise embroidery shops, EmbroidMe, the newest franchise venture from SIGN*A*RAMA, and owner and president Ray Titus. EmbroidMe has partnered with Brother, the leading manufacturer of embroidery equipment and accessories, in order to provide lettering on everything from baby blankets to corporate logos. Facts and figures for investing are included.

50131 ■ "Playskool Makes Product for Moms" in *Marketing to Women* (Vol. 20, January 2007, No. 1, pp. 3)
Pub: EPM Communications, Inc.
Description: Playskool has linked with Sourcebooks Inc. to produce a line of parenting books designed for both new and experienced mothers.

50132 ■ "Plugging In: Networking Skills That Promise Success" in *Black Enterprise* (Vol. 34, No. 7, February 2004, pp. 61)
Pub: Earl Graves Publishing Co.
Ed: Lee Anna Jackson. **Description:** Reviews are presented of two books that teach business networking skills.

50133 ■ "Post founder trying to buy bankrupt energy company" in *Atlanta Business Chronicle* (Vol. 25, January 10, 2003, No. 31, pp. 3A)
Pub: American City Business Publications, Inc.
Ed: Jarred Schenke. **Description:** Future Energy Resources Corporation has petitioned a federal court for approval to sell the company to Post Properties founder John Williams for $1.5 million. Williams was part of the original group that put nearly $10 million into Future Energy before it filed for Chapter 11 in November 2002.

50134 ■ "Power Lunch" in *St. Louis Post-Dispatch* (February 25, 2005)
Pub: Knight-Ridder/Tribune Business News
Ed: Jerri Stroud. **Description:** An overview of the merger between Nextel Communications Inc. and Sprint. The merger is expected to blend the consumer-oriented strength of Sprint with Nextel's power in business communications.

50135 ■ "Powerhouse Tech Companies Merge" in *Black Enterprise* (Vol. 35, November 2004, No. 4, pp. 28)
Pub: Earl G. Graves Publishing Co. Inc.
Ed: Cliff Hocker. **Description:** Two high-tech firms in Alexandria, Virginia have merged to better compete for homeland defense contracts.

50136 ■ "Prepaid Card Benefits Breast Cancer Research" in *Marketing to Women* (Vol. 19, November 2006, No. 11, pp. 5)
Pub: EPM Communications, Inc.
Description: NetSpend prepaid card marketer and financial services company, ACE Cash Express partner to launch a reloadable prepaid debit card for breast cancer research. A portion of all purchases made with the pink All-Access Visa Card through October 2007 will be donated to breast cancer research and educational charities.

50137 ■ "Prewitt With Prudential" in *Mississippi Business Journal* (Vol. 29, January 2007, No.4, pp. 9)
Pub: Venture Publications, Inc.
Ed: Wally Northway **Description:** Prudential Real Estate Affiliates Inc., awarded its' newest franchise to Ann Prewitt & Associates. Aligning with Prudential Real Estate Network will enable Prudential Ann Prewitt Realty to enhance the quality of their service.

50138 ■ "Price Equals Value Plus Terms" in *Journal of Accountancy*
Pub: American Institute of Certified Public Accountants
Ed: Joel Sinkin. **Description:** Business valuations, succession planning, and buy-sell agreements are discussed, focusing on the certified public accountants role in reviewing the interrelationship of five key variables: the down payment at closing, the length of the payout period on the balance due, the profitability of the deal, the duration of the post-closing retention period with adjustments for lost clients, and the multiple (preferred price based on a multiple of the gross billings).

50139 ■ "Price for News Was $25 Million" in *Crain's Detroit Business* (Vol. 21, October 10, 2005, No. 43, pp. 20)
Pub: Crain Communications Inc. - Detroit
Ed: Jennette Smith. **Description:** MediaNews Group disclosed the amount of $25 million to purchase The Detroit News in August 2005. The deal will give the Denver-based group editorial assets of the newspaper and a limited-partnership interest in the Detroit joint operating agreement.

50140 ■ "Private Investors Purchase a Controlling Stake at Ecoboard Holdings" in *Long Island Business News* (February 13, 2004)
Pub: Dolan Media Newswires
Ed: Ben Abelson. **Description:** Ecoboard Holdings Inc., manufacturer of plastic lumber, has raised nearly $750,000 from Long Island Capital Alliance's annual venture capital forum. The company's products are used mainly for outdoor applications such as decks, bridges, and piers.

50141 ■ "Private Matters" in *Red Herring* (No. 87, December 18, 2000, pp. 228-233)
Pub: Herring Communications, Inc.
Ed: J.P. Vicente. **Description:** With public markets in tumult, private buyouts are coming back into vogue.

50142 ■ "Profile: Local Web Developer Plays a Starring Role in NASA's Mission to Mars" in *Crains Chicago Business* (Vol. 26, No. 51)
Pub: Crain Communications, Inc.
Ed: Paul Merrion. **Description:** Profile of Web site developer Critical Mass Inc., the firm that designed a Web site for the National Aeronautics and Space Administration, one of the highest traffic Web sites in history. Critical Mass partnered with eTouch Systems Corporation, whose software updates the NASA site continuously. Web site visitors can access information on humans in space or exploration of the universe with links to specialized sites for children, students, educators and journalists.

50143 ■ "Profitable Finish-Knock on Wood" in *Small Business Opportunities* (January 2006)
Pub: Harris Publications Inc.
Description: Veneer One sells its custom-made wood veneer panels and doors to designers and architects.

50144 ■ "Promised Land" in *Entrepreneur* (Vol. 33, August 2005, No. 8, pp. 26)
Pub: Entrepreneur Media Inc.
Ed: Mark Henricks. **Description:** As the Israeli-Palestinian conflict abates American entrepreneurs, particularly in technology areas, are looking to Israel as a new business opportunity.

50145 ■ "Proquest's Slimdown Has Little Effect on Local Jobs" in *Crain's Detroit Business* (Vol. 23, January 29, 2007, No. 5, pp. 13)
Pub: Crain Communications Inc. - Detroit
Ed: Bill Shea. **Description:** Proquest's realignment of business objectives will shift the emphasis of its operations to Dallas, but will not result in significant local job losses. A merger between the spun-off Information and Learning unit and Cambridge Information Group has been formed to continue that business and lease the current Ann Arbor facilities.

50146 ■ "PS Cleaning Products, Lightning Join to Promote Line" in *Tampa Tribune* (December 23, 2005)
Pub: Media General, Inc.
Ed: Alan Snel. **Description:** American HomeHealth, a startup from St. Petersburg, Florida, has partnered with the St. Pete Times Forum and Tampa Bay Lightning local games to promote its PS brand of home cleaners, soaps and disinfectants. The $2 million deal will feature PS advertisements on the Forum's Zamboni ice machines, trash cans and electronic signs and PS soap will be used in the bathrooms.

50147 ■ "Public companies push the envelope" in *Hispanic Business* (Vol. 22, No. 6, June 2000, pp. 116)
Pub: Hispanic Business
Ed: Christopher D. Lancette, Scott Williams, Joel Russell. **Description:** Seven of the 100 largest companies on the Hispanic Business 500 list trade as public companies. Five are from Florida, with one each from Texas and California. Most of these public companies are the result of mergers or are conglomerates.

50148 ■ "Public opinion" in *Entrepreneur* (Vol. 30, No. 10, October 2002, pp. 76)
Pub: Entrepreneur Media Inc.
Ed: Jennifer Pellet. **Description:** Issues currently facing companies that wish to file an Initial Public Offering are discussed. The first quarter 2002 saw only 15 firms go from private to public.

50149 ■ "Publix chief leads quietly" in *Atlanta Business Chronicle* (Vol. 24, No. 13, August 31, 2001, pp. 3A)
Pub: American City Business Journals Inc.
Ed: Jarred Schenke. **Description:** Bob Moore is the president of Publix Super Markets Inc., an Atlanta company that has opened 97 stores after entering the market a decade ago. Moore, who started at Publix as a stock boy, has moved up the ranks, and has seen Publix grab 27.4 percent of the metro grocery market share. Publix has future plans of launching an online site and acquiring a grocery chain to promote further growth.

50150 ■ "The Pump-and-Dump Economy" in *Wall Street Journal* (Vol. 248, January 2007, No. 146, pp. A16)
Pub: Dow Jones & Co. Inc.
Ed: Michael S. Malone **Description:** Start-ups are not aiming for an IPo in their business plan these days. Instead most newly-formed private companies set goals to be acquired by an established company which could lead to a radical shift in the U.S. economy.

50151 ■ "Putting Focus on 4 Famed Firms" in *Crain's New York Business* (Vol. 22, November 27, 2006, No. 48, pp. 17)
Pub: Crain Communications, Inc.
Ed: Aaron Elstein. **Description:** Crain's spotlight on key statistics of four well-known businesses in the New York area includes information on Eileen Fisher Inc., Key Food Stores Co-Operative Inc., Ziff Davis Holdings Inc., and Publishers Clearing House.

50152 ■ "Putting the brakes on transportation" in *Hispanic Business* (Vol. 22, No. 6, June 2000, pp. 112)
Pub: Hispanic Business
Ed: Christopher D. Lancette, Scott Williams, Joel Russell. **Description:** Hispanic-owned trucking company Pan American Express Inc. ranks 173rd in the Hispanic Business 500 table with 1999 revenues of almost $22.3 million. Most of the firm's growth has come from the acquisition of refrigerated trucking company Zero Motor Freight.

50153 ■ "PVC Index" in *Venture Capital Journal* (Vol. 40, No. 10, November 2000, pp. 68-72)
Pub: Venture Economics
Description: Presentation of the Warburg Pincus/ Venture Economics Post-Venture Capital Index. The Post-Venture Capital Index (PVCI) defines "venture-backed" companies as public companies that have received financing from a U.S. venture capital firm or buyouts limited partnership prior to going public.

50154 ■ "Pyrotechnics fire up the crowd at meetings" in *Atlanta Business Chronicle* (Vol. 24, No. 14, September 7, 2001, pp. S15)
Pub: American City Business Journals Inc.
Ed: Lucy Pritchett. **Description:** Pyrotechnics, the use of indoor lighting shows, has increased in popularity in recent years. Dawna VanHook, Axxis Inc.'s production manager discusses the use of pyrotechnics and how they appeal to company employees. This technology can be used for events such as product introductions, company peak sales announcements, and company mergers.

50155 ■ "R&G: Growing Branches Through New Acquisitions" in *Orlando Business Journal* (Vol. 20, No. 6, July 25, 2003, pp. 31)
Pub: American City Business Journals, Inc.
Ed: Chad Eric Watt. **Description:** In an interview with Jack Koegel, president of R-G Crown Bank, he discusses the firm changing its name and partnering with R&G Financial of Puerto Rico.

50156 ■ "RBS Takes Stake in Home Developer" in *Crain's Detroit Business* (Vol. 21, January 10, 2005, No. 2, pp. 5)
Pub: Crain Communications Inc. - Detroit
Ed: Shena Harrison. **Description:** In order to gain market share in the resident home development sector, Harris Homes Development Corporation and Bayberry Construction have merged. The firm will build homes in Washtenaw County, Michigan.

50157 ■ "Redleaf, UPenn Launch PenNetWorks" in *Venture Capital Journal* (Vol. 40, No. 10, October 2000, pp. 6, 8)
Pub: Venture Economics
Description: The technology operating company, Redleaf Group Inc., partnered with the University of Pennsylvania in August to form PenNetWorks, an on-campus Internet accelerator. The accelerator is owned by the University and managed by Redleaf.

50158 ■ "Reed Acquires Manufacturing Shows" in *Tradeshow Week* (Vol. 34, December 13, 2004, No. 50, pp. 3)
Pub: Reed Business Information
Description: Reed Exhibitions has acquired a series of regional manufacturing tradeshows with the purchase of Advanced Manufacturing and Productivity Exposition series from the Technical Exhibitions and Conferences. The shows focus on automated manufacturing, assembly systems and information technology.

50159 ■ "Relief Is Finally Coming with A Rise in M&A" in *Venture Capital Journal* (July 1, 2003)
Pub: Thomson Financial Inc.
Description: According to experts, mergers and acquisitions are expected to rise over the next year and a half, thus reinforcing the role of the venture capitalist by promoting the growth of promising new technology companies, and also making money for entrepreneurs, employees and limited partners. Statistical data included.

50160 ■ "RenaLab Acquired" in *Mississippi Business Journal* (Vol. 29, January 2007, No. 3, pp. A10)
Pub: Venture Publications, Inc.
Description: Renal Advantage Inc. has completed it's previously announced acquisition of RenaLab from Fresenius Medical Care North America.

50161 ■ "Resistance is Futile: EDS has been on a buying binge" in *Red Herring* (No. 102, August 15, 2001, pp. 84-85)
Pub: Herring Communications
Ed: J.P. Vicente. **Description:** Electronics Data Systems' (EDS) acquired Sabre's airline outsourcing unit, Systematics, and Structural Dynamics Research Corporation in 2001, despite the slowing of mergers and acquisitions.

50162 ■ "Resolving Owner Conflicts" in *Rough Notes* (Vol. 145, No. 9, September 2002, pp. 26)
Pub: Rough Notes
Ed: Paul J. DiStefano. **Description:** Lack of communications between owners of the insurance agency often results in disagreements. Unresolved conflict among owners can impede the future of an agency, whether the issue relates to money or operating philosophy.

50163 ■ "Restaurant King, Hotel Developer to Hook Up" in *Altanta Journal-Constitution* (January 31, 2007)
Pub: Cox Newspapers, Inc.
Ed: Leon Stafford. **Description:** Bob Amic and Novare Group are partnering to develop all restaurants for Twelve Hotels. Profiles of both companies are included.

50164 ■ "Retail Rut: Sears Holders Might Get a $10 Payout. But Don't Expect Much More from the Stock" in *Barron's* (July 21, 2003, pp. 15)
Pub: Barron's
Ed: Robin Goldwyn Blumenthal. **Description:** Sears Roebuck's credit-loan subsidiary went to Citigroup for

$6 billion, considerably less than the expected $7 billion, but was still enough to give $10/share in cash to stockholders.

50165 ■ "Retirement-Plan Administer To Be Bought For $115 Million" in *Wall Street Journal* (Vol. 248, December 2006, No. 149, pp. C5)
Pub: Dow Jones & Co. Inc.
Ed: Wall Street Journal News **Description:** Charles Schwab Corp. acquires 401(K) Co. for $115 million. 401(K) overseas $22 billion in retirement assets.

50166 ■ "Roseville, Calif., Gourmet Gift Firm Puts Buyout on Hold" in *Sacramento Bee* (October 21, 2005)
Pub: The Sacramento Bee
Ed: Clint Swett. **Description:** Shari's Berries International, famous for its chocolate-dipped strawberries, has put its management-led buyout on hold in order to concentrate on the holiday season. Unforgettable Gifts Inc. had offered $1.69 million in cash along with $1.26 million in promissory notes as well as assumption of the firm's $2.35 million debt.

50167 ■ "Rouge Industries' Russian Suitor Promises New Furnace" in *Crain's Detroit Business* (Vol. 19, No. 43, October 27, 2003, pp. 17)
Pub: Crain Communications Inc., Detroit
Ed: Terry Kosdrosky. **Description:** Severstal, the Russian steel manufacturer vying to purchase Dearborn, Michigan steelmaker Rouge Industries Inc., plans to build an electric arc furnace. Rouge Industries employs about 2,600 employees.

50168 ■ "Rumblings" in *Crain's Detroit Business* (Vol. 19, No. 1, January 6, 2003, pp. 22)
Pub: Crain Communications Inc., Detroit
Description: Crain's Detroit Business and WJR AM 760 radio station along with the Rehabilitation Institute of Michigan have launched a competition to find the '50 Fittest CEOs' in metropolitan Detroit. According to an investment banker, Compuware Corporation is being targeted for acquisition. A listing of the top six law firms in the Detroit area making The National Law Journal 250 for 2002 is presented.

50169 ■ "San Diego to Host Tech Summit" in *Hispanic Business* (Vol. 24, No. 5, May 2002, pp. 42)
Pub: Hispanic Business Inc.
Description: Technology and cross-border trade were among the issues of focus at the Hispanic Business Tech Summit held in November, 2001. Specific seminars included, B2B E-Commerce, E-Business Expansion, Strategic Online Alliances, Cross-Border Trends, and NAFTA.

50170 ■ "Scientific Industries Acquires New Assets from Spectrum Labs" in *Long Island Business News* (March 12, 2004)
Pub: Dolan Media Newswires
Description: Scientific Industries Inc. is set to acquire certain assets from Spectrum Laboratories Inc. for nearly $300,000. The chromatography and peristaltic pump-systems products and related items would increase Scientific Industries' current laboratory equipment product line.

50171 ■ "Screen Test" in *Success* (Vol. 47, No. 1, January 2000, pp. 18)
Pub: Success Publishing, Inc.
Ed: Jeffrey Adduci. **Description:** Four questions to determine if a business should go public.

50172 ■ "Secondaries Ready For The Big Leagues" in *Venture Capital Journal* (July 1, 2003)
Pub: Thomson Financial Inc.
Description: The lack of corporate buying and a weak IPO market are leaving funds with little or no opportunity to improve returns. Statistical data included.

50173 ■ *The Secret of Exiting Your Business Under Your Terms!*
Pub: Outskirts Press, Incorporated

Ed: Gene H. Irwin. **Released:** August 2005. **Price:** $29.95. **Description:** Topics include how to sell a business for the highest value, tax laws governing the sale of a business, finding the right buyer, mergers and acquisitions, negotiating the sale, and using a limited auction to increase future value of a business.

50174 ■ "SEE Change" in *Crain's Detroit Business* (Vol. 22, February 6, 2006, No. 6, pp. 3)
Pub: Crain Communications Inc. - Detroit
Ed: Brent Snavely. **Description:** Richard Golden has added his SEE (Selective Eyewear Elements) line to his D.O.C stores in order to boost sales. SEE offers high-fashion frames priced between $179 and $279, compared to the designer styles at $250 to $700.

50175 ■ "Sharing Marketing Expenses" in *Rough Notes* (Vol. 145, No. 9, September 2002, pp. 80)
Pub: Rough Notes
Ed: Michael J. Weinberg. **Description:** Information about marketing expenses related to sales which insurance agents and agencies can share, include business meals, contributions to community organizations, direct mail, and telemarketing.

50176 ■ "Shell Shock?" in *Entrepreneur* (Vol. 32, December 2004, No. 12, pp. 15)
Pub: Entrepreneur Media Inc.
Ed: David Worrell. **Description:** Lawmakers and regulators are working to implement tougher rules for public companies, which will impact future initial public offerings and mergers.

50177 ■ "Shopping Spree; Ramco-Gershenson Rings Up $500M in Acquisitions in 2004" in *Crain's Detroit Business* (Vol. 21, January 31, 2005)
Pub: Crain Communications Inc. - Detroit
Ed: Jennette Smith. **Description:** Retailer Ramco-Gershenson Properties Trust, a Farmington Hills, Michigan real estate investment trust, has purchased or placed under contract nine shopping centers and property in Florida and two retail centers in Farmington Hills and Rochester Hills, as well as shopping centers in Indiana and Georgia.

50178 ■ "Simon Group Offers Cobranded Giftcard" in *Marketing to Women* (Vol. 19, October 2006, No. 10, pp. 9)
Pub: EPM Communications, Inc.
Description: Komen Foundation partners with Simon Property Group to produce a cobranded Simon Pink Ribbon Giftcard. This Visa debit card issued by MetaBank are sold at Simon malls nationwide and online at Simon.com. One dollar from every card purchased will be donated to the Komen Foundation.

50179 ■ "A Singular Hookup" in *Kiplinger's Personal Finance Magazine* (Vol. 58, No. 5, May 2004, pp. 21)
Pub: Kiplinger Washington Editors, Inc.
Description: Cingular's merger with AT&T Wireless is good news for customers. The merger will bring better service and products, without higher prices. With AT&T Wireless' spectrum, Cingular can reduce coverage gaps, guarantee fewer dropped calls and provide better voice quality on cell phones, as well as high-speed wireless data networks. More telecommunications mergers are discussed.

50180 ■ "Small banks may draw buyers' interest" in *Atlanta Business Chronicle* (Vol. 24, No. 13, August 24, 2001, pp. 3A)
Pub: American City Business Journals Inc.
Ed: Meredith Jordan. **Description:** Some 34 banks in Georgia will complete five years of independent existence over the next few years, meaning that, under Georgia law, they will become vulnerable to takeover by bank holding companies. There were five new banks established in 1996, twelve in 1997, seventeen in 1998, fourteen in 1999, and seventeen in 2000. Article discusses what makes some banks attractive takeover targets.

50181 ■ "SoBran Partners with U.S. Navy" in *Black Enterprise* (Vol. 37, October 2006, No. 3, pp. 38)
Pub: Earl G. Graves Publishing Co. Inc.
Ed: Glenn Townes. Description: SoBran Inc., partnered with Lockheed Martin and signed a three-Tear production service contract with the Naval Aviation Depot in Jacksonville, Florida. The $44 million contract will allow SoBran to transport and warehouse materials for Navy facilities.

50182 ■ "Software firms end duel with an acquisition" in *Atlanta Business Chronicle* (Vol. 25, January 10, 2003, No. 31, pp. 3A)
Pub: American City Business Publications, Inc.
Ed: Mary Jane Credeur. Description: Call center software company Knowlagent Inc. has acquired the assets of its main competitor, Simtrex Corporation.

50183 ■ "Software Firms Predict M&A Increase for 2003" in *Atlanta Business Chronicle* (Vol. 25, November 15, 2002, No. 23 pp. 8C)
Pub: American City Business Publications, Inc.
Ed: Robert Mullins, Sarah Lacy. Description: According to a survey by RBC Capital Markets, most software companies expect merger and acquisition activity in the industry to increase in 2003, as acquiring firms are adjusting to lower valuations now associated with the industry.

50184 ■ "Some Relief Over End of Pixelworks Merger" in *Business Journal-Portland* (Vol. 20, No. 23, August 8, 2003, pp. 8)
Pub: American City Business Journals, Inc.
Ed: Aliza Earnshaw. Description: The proposed merger between Pixelworks Inc. and Genesis Microchip Inc. has been scrapped. Genesis Microchip, led by CEO Eric Erdman, reported lower than expected revenues for the second quarter 2003.

50185 ■ "South Florida Developers Combine Capitalism, Charity in Bottled-Water Company" in *Miami Herald* (June 28, 2004)
Pub: Knight-Ridder/Tribune Business News
Ed: Gillian Wee. Description: Bernard Werner, real estate developer, and partner David Garfinkle, have invested $2 million in Euphoria Water, founded by Zalman Lipskar and Dovy Ainsforth. Euphoria donates at least 20 percent of profits to charity.

50186 ■ "Space Trade" in *Crain's New York Business* (Vol. 22, November 27, 2006, No. 48, pp. 33)
Pub: Crain Communications, Inc.
Description: US Airways' $8 million bid for a hostile takeover of Delta Air Lines would form a merger that would free up 10 percent of the airport slots on the East Coast and create the nation's largest airline.

50187 ■ "Starbucks Gets A New Look" in *Frozen Food Age* (Vol. 50, No. 3, October 2001, pp. 12)
Pub: VNU Business Media
Description: Enterprise IG, located in San Francisco, California, has partnered with Starbucks Ice Cream Partnership (a joint venture with Dreyer's Grand Ice Cream) in order to provide brand identity and help its product stand out on store shelves.

50188 ■ "Start Your Blogs" in *Venture Capital Journal* (January 1, 2005)
Pub: Thomason Financial Inc.
Ed: Lawrence Aragon. Description: It is predicted that venture capital firms will use Internet blogs as a means for building business relationships. One by-product of blogs will be that brands will move away from venture firms to individual partners.

50189 ■ "Still Percolating" in *Hispanic Business* (December 2002, pp. 42)
Pub: Hispanic Business
Ed: Tim Dougherty. Description: The proposed merger between Univision and Hispanic Broadcasting Corporation are expected to win regulatory approval. Information regarding the merger is discussed.

50190 ■ "Stillwater-Based Southwest Bancorp Inc. to Buy Bank of Kansas" in *Journal Record (Oklahoma City, OK)* (February 6, 2007)
Pub: Journal Record
Description: Details concerning the recent agreement for Southwest Bancorp Inc. to purchase Bank of Kansas are presented. Statistical data included.

50191 ■ "Stock Basics Offer Insights on Value of Local Bank Merger" in *Pacific Business News* (Vol. 41, No. 17, July 4, 2003, pp. 9)
Pub: American City Business Journals
Ed: Eddy Conway. Description: The value of the merger of Central Pacific Bank and City Bank is discussed.

50192 ■ "Straining Under Sarbanes-Oxley" in *Business Journal-Milwaukee* (Vol. 20, No. 48, August 15, 2003, pp. A1)
Pub: American City Business Journals, Inc.
Ed: Michael Muckian. Description: Small businesses that are publicly traded may suffer under the new Sarbanes-Oxley Act of 2002. The new law was passed in an effort to protect public shareholders from corporate scandals.

50193 ■ *Strategic Partnerships: An Entrepreneur's Guide to Joint Ventures and Alliances*
Pub: Kaplan Publishing
Ed: Robert Wallace. Released: September 2004.
Price: $22.00. Description: Ways to develop and execute joint venture relationships with larger business entities for small company owners.

50194 ■ "Strength in Numbers" in *Home Office Computing* (Vol. 18, No. 11, November 2000, pp. 58)
Pub: Scholastic Inc.
Ed: Jeffrey D. Zbar. Description: When competing with bigger companies, small businesses need to develop partnerships to help snag the big projects.

50195 ■ "Supply Chain Challenges: Building Relationships" in *Harvard Business Review* (Vol. 81, No. 7, July 2003, pp. 64)
Pub: Harvard Business School Press
Ed: Julia Kirby. Description: The development of business logistics systems is discussed.

50196 ■ "Support the Advocate!" in *Bellingham Business Journal* (December 2006, pp. 3)
Pub: Sun News Inc.
Ed: Drew Graham. Description: The Whatcom Business Advocate is now a pull-out section of the Business Journal. One of the premier news publications the newsletter reaches more than 30,000 individual readers each month. The newsletter and journal are excellent sources for advertisers.

50197 ■ "Surviving a corporate marriage" in *Black Enterprise* (Vol. 32, No. 7, February 2002, pp. 66)
Pub: Earl Graves Publishing Co.
Ed: Valerie Gay Francois. Description: Information is offered to help employees learn to reposition themselves for advancement when the company they work for is considering a merger or acquisition. One such tip, suggests buying the company.

50198 ■ "Take Our Outfit - Please! How do you start a small business?" in *Business Week Online* (December 23, 2002)
Pub: McGraw-Hill Inc.
Ed: Gabor Garai. Description: Entrepreneurs are finding that one way to start up a new company is to purchase a division of a larger firm, thus allowing mid-size companies to be rid of unprofitable divisions rather than shutting them down.

50199 ■ "Takeover Offer Is Accepted By Parent Of Argo-Tech" in *Wall Street Journal* (Vol. 248, December 2006, No. 152, pp. A7)
Pub: Dow Jones & Co. Inc.
Ed: Reuters News Service Description: Eaton Corp., is to acquire AT Holdings Corp., parent of Argo-Tech Corp. Argo-Tech makers of military and aerospace fuel pumps as well as numerous non-aerospace businesses provides 60% of all commercial airliner fuel pumps, yet these non-aerospace businesses won't be included in the transaction, leaving this vital area of commercial airliner manufacture with an uncertain future.

50200 ■ "Taking Flight: Angel Investors are Flocking Together to Your Advantage" in *Entrepreneur* (Vol. 32, October 2004, No. 10, pp. 34)
Pub: Entrepreneur Media Inc.
Ed: David Worrell. Description: Angel investors are partnering to help screen deals and mentor entrepreneurs. Thirty member groups of the Angel Capital Association have put an average of $1.85 million into an average of 5.3 investments annually, with each group averaging about 50 individual angels. Deal terms vary, but many report purchasing 20 to 30 percent of a company's stock when investing.

50201 ■ "Taking it to the Street" in *Hispanic Business* (March 2004, pp. 30, 32, 34)
Pub: Hispanic Business
Ed: Scott Williams. Description: An IPO provided the fuel to help propel Molina Healthcare from a midsize care provider to a major company. Profile of CEO, J. Mario Molina is included.

50202 ■ "Taubman-Simon battle employs an army of high-priced advisers" in *Crain's Detroit Business* (Vol. 19, No. 17, April 28, 2003, pp. 4)
Pub: Crain Communications Inc., Detroit
Ed: Brent Snavely. Description: An overview of information regarding Taubman Centers Inc.'s battle to defeat a hostile takeover by rival mall developer Simon Property Group Inc. Today lawyers, accountants and lobbyists tend to be the weapons of choice on the corporate-takeover battlefield.

50203 ■ "Team players" in *Crain's Detroit Business* (Vol. 18, No. 17, April 29,)
Pub: Crain Communications Inc. - Detroit
Ed: Michael Strong. Description: Profile of Hawkins Food Group LLC, whose co-owners, Van Hawkins and Conrad Mallet, hope to prepare for an initial public offering.

50204 ■ "A Team Sport" in *Entrepreneur* (Vol. 31, No. 9, September 2003, pp. 27)
Pub: Entrepreneur Media, Inc.
Ed: Mark Henricks. Description: Review of the book, "How Breakthroughs Happen", describing technology brokering, the processes that occurs when inventors borrow existing ideas from one or more fields and gather the people, funding and other assets needed to assemble and apply those ideas elsewhere.

50205 ■ "Telecom: As companies go bankrupt, buyout firms lick their chops" in *Red Herring* (No. 105, October 1, 2001, pp. 24-25)
Pub: Herring Communications
Ed: Om Malik. Description: Interview with Arun Sarin, who sees the current problems faced by the telecom industry as an opportunity to make money.

50206 ■ "The 10 Least Wired Industries" in *PC Computing* (April 2000, pp. 64)
Pub: Ziff-Davis Inc.
Ed: Naomi Graychase. Description: As of August 1999, 158 Internet companies went public, raising more than $12.9 billion and have a total market cap of $278 billion. While it has become tougher to enter the online world, there are ten industries that are still up for grabs. These ten are dry cleaners, home and building supplies, funeral services, gas companies/stations, microbreweries, pawnbrokers, piano tuners/movers, plumbers, seamstresses/tailors, and taxis.

50207 ■ "The Pantry Expands Presence" in *Mississippi Business Journal* (Vol. 29, January 2007, No. 2, pp. 8)
Pub: Venture Publications, Inc.
Ed: Wally Northway Description: Eight convenience stores in Mississippi and Florida have been acquired by The Pantry Inc. Statistical data included.

50208 ■ "There's Something About Harry" in *Venture Capital Journal* **(Vol. 42, No. 5, May 2002, pp. 18-19)**
Pub: Thomas Venture Economics
Ed: Charles R. Feller. **Description:** Profile of Harry Turner, Director of Park Street Capital. Turner believes he has an inside track on reviewing some of the really good partnerships that have established track records and are rather small.

50209 ■ "This Detective has Rediscovered a Lost Art" in *Fortune* **(Vol. 149, No. 9, May 3, 2004, pp. 58)**
Pub: Time, Inc.
Ed: Andy Serwer. **Description:** Profile of James Mintz, owner of corporate investigation firm, who has partnered with TRACE, a British database firm to form a joint venture called Art Recovery. Art Recovery compares TRACE's two databases, and recovers the work for museums, galleries, auction houses, and more.

50210 ■ "This just in" in *Crain's Detroit Business* **(Vol. 19, No. 17, April 28, 2003, pp. 1)**
Pub: Crain Communications Inc., Detroit
Ed: Brett Snavely, Laura Bailey, Robert Ankeny. **Description:** AlixPartners LLC, based in Southfield, Michigan has landed the high-profile bankrupt Fleming Cos. Inc., Dallas, Texas. Quadrants Inc. of Wixom, Michigan plans to develop a $55 million, 68-acre industrial park in Green Oak Township, Michigan.

50211 ■ "This Just In" in *Crain's Detroit Business* **(Vol. 19, No. 1, January 6, 2003, pp. 1)**
Pub: Crain Communications Inc., Detroit
Description: The possible acquisition of Rootlevel Inc. by Carriersnet Group Inc. is covered. Rootlevel is a Web application and database development company while Carriersnet, is an electronic-logistics company in international shipping. The deal was triggered by the need to develop a system that connects the shipping industry via the Internet.

50212 ■ "Three's Company: American Carriers Are Finally Bringing 3G Cellular Service to a Phone Near You" in *Entrepreneur* **(September 2004)**
Pub: Entrepreneur Media Inc.
Ed: Mike Hogan. **Description:** Third generation phone service will not only improve voice call quality, but also provide tools such as email downloads, text messages, and retrieval of corporate files over a cellular network quicker, more graphics for Web browsing, streaming audio, video and transfer of high-resolution color photos.

50213 ■ "Tight buyout financing may boost use of employee stock plans" in *Wall Street Journal* **(April 30, 2002, pp. B6)**
Pub: Wall Street Journal
Ed: Jeff Bailey. **Description:** Employee stock ownership plans are helping small businesses to resolve succession issues while winning more backing from banks. Statistical data included.

50214 ■ "Tips for cutting costs" in *Crain's Detroit Business* **(Vol. 18, No. 32, August 12, 2002, pp. 12)**
Pub: Crain Communications Inc., Detroit
Description: The Small Business Administration offers advice to small businesses for cutting business expenses, including inventory, payments, overhead, management compensation, equipment costs, expansion, joint ventures, risk management, and the use of buying groups.

50215 ■ "Titan May Build Plant" in *Mississippi Business Journal* **(Vol. 28, September 2006, No. 36, pp. 24)**
Pub: Venture Publications, Inc.
Description: Titan Technologies Inc. of Albuquerque N.M. has received $100,000 and an exclusive license agreement from Ally Investment LLE to build recycling facilities in Texas, Oklahoma, Mississippi and Louisiana.

50216 ■ "To Do: Determine the Value of My Failed Startup's IP" in *Venture Capital Journal* **(Vol. 42, No. 10, October 2002, pp. 43-44)**
Pub: Thomas Venture Economics
Ed: Thomas D. Halket. **Description:** Investors who have representatives on a company's board have a legal duty to maximize the value of a company's assets.

50217 ■ "To Sell or Not to Sell? Here's How to Decide" in *American Banker* **(Vol. 170, February 4, 2005, No. 24, pp. 11)**
Pub: Thomson Financial Media Inc.
Ed: Steinar Ryen, Oliver Sommer. **Description:** Directors of regional banks are questioning whether it is in shareholder's interest to remain independent or to sell the bank. The top five FDIC-insured banks and savings institutions in the U.S. control only 41 percent of the assets in FDIC-insured institutions, in Canada the top six control 87 percent of assets, and in Australia the top five control 75 percent.

50218 ■ "TodaysMama.com Relaunches Website" in *Marketing to Women* **(Vol. 20, January 2007, No. 1, pp. 3)**
Pub: EPM Communications, Inc.
Description: TodaysMama.com, an online resource for mothers, debuted its enhanced Website. They have partnered with Kiva, a charitable organization, to fund microloans to entrepreneurs in developing nations.

50219 ■ "Tomboy Tools Ties in With Pink Hammer" in *Marketing to Women* **(Vol. 19, October 2006, No. 10, pp. 9)**
Pub: EPM Communications, Inc.
Description: The Komen Foundation partners with Tomboy Tools, manufacturer of ergonomically designed tools for women, for an exception to its "no pink tools" slogan. The "Pink for a Purpose" special-edition hammer is available through the company's website or their home-party distribution network.

50220 ■ "The Top 25 IPOs of 2000" in *Red Herring* **(No 99, June 15 & July 1, 2001, pp. 62, 64)**
Pub: Herring Communications
Ed: Lorraine Fry. **Description:** After a wild ride, the IPO market gets back to basics. The number of tech IPOs fell in the fourth quarter. The article includes a listing of the top 25 IPOs of 2000, including rank, issuer, ticker, issue month, IPO size, and percent change since December.

50221 ■ "Tough Mama" in *Forbes* **(December 25, 2000, pp. 232)**
Pub: Forbes Magazine
Ed: Kelly Barron. **Description:** Profile of Gertrude Boyle, 76, and her son, who took their Portland, Oregon business, Columbia Sportswear public.

50222 ■ "Toward Transparency" in *Venture Capital Journal* **(October 1, 2005)**
Pub: Thomason Financial Inc.
Description: Transparency in the venture capital market is defined. Venture firms need to respond to their investors' demands for more openness.

50223 ■ "Trade Group Endorsements For Every Specialty" in *Rough Notes* **(Vol. 145, No. 9, September 2002, pp. 88)**
Pub: Rough Notes
Ed: Dennis Pillsbury. **Description:** The Lighthouse Underwriters LLC was founded by Arthur Seifert and underwrites insurance only after developing a relationship with the association or trade group it will be insuring.

50224 ■ "Trading Private Equity Publicly May not fly" in *Red Herring* **(No. 105, October 1, 2001, pp. 36)**
Pub: Herring Communications
Ed: Julie Landry. **Description:** For venture capital to obtain liquidity, venture capitalists will have to open their long-closed books. Laurence Allen, CEO of NYPPE hopes to change private equity by taking the private out of private equity, thus making it easier to trade restricted securities in private companies and limited partnerships, using his firm's electronic communications network (ECN).

50225 ■ "Traveling Right" in *Small Business Opportunities* **(Vol. 12, No. 5, September 2000, pp. 17)**
Pub: Harris Publications, Inc.
Description: Merger creates full-service travel company to help small businesses get where they are going. Biztravel@myCompany is the first travel management offering to provide smaller businesses with the full service and travel options that larger businesses usually receive.

50226 ■ "Tulsa-based Dollar Thrifty Automotive Group Buys Franchise" in *Journal Record (Oklahoma City, OK)* **(February 5, 2007)**
Pub: Journal Record
Description: Details of Dollar Thrifty Automotive Groups purchase of Thrifty Car Rental franchise are presented.

50227 ■ "Tulsa-based Dollar Thrifty Buys Franchises" in *Journal Record* **(February 4, 2004)**
Pub: Dolan Media Company
Description: Growth strategy to acquire Dollar and Thrifty franchisees in key U.S. and Canadian operations by Dollar Thrifty Automotive Group is discussed.

50228 ■ "Tuning in to the stock market: Two Hispanic radio firms launch IPOs" in *Hispanic Business* **(Vol. 21, No. 12, December 1999, pp. 52)**
Pub: Hispanic Business
Ed: Joel Russell. **Description:** Spanish Broadcasting System and Radio Unica have both gone public. This means that most of the Hispanic market's leading broadcasters now sell their equity on public exchanges.

50229 ■ "Turf wars" in *Crain's Detroit Business* **(Vol. 19, No. 15, April 14, 2003, pp. 3)**
Pub: Crain Communications Inc., Detroit
Ed: Andrew Dietderich. **Description:** General Sports and Entertainment LLC acquired U.S. Synthetic Grass, called General Sports Turf.

50230 ■ "Turning Corn Into Clothing" in *Forbes* **(Vol. 175, January 31, 2005, No. 2, pp. 98)**
Pub: Forbes Magazine Inc.
Ed: Michael Freedman. **Description:** Tate & Lyle has joined DuPont to create an ingredient for a new synthetic fabric called Sorona. The product uses 50 percent less petroleum because of the use of a corn-based sugar, resulting in cost savings. The new fabric will be used in woven or knitted materials for carpets and apparel. A new plant is under construction in Loudon, Tennessee.

50231 ■ "Turning Vendors Into Partners" in *Inc.* **(August 2005, pp. 94-98, 100)**
Pub: Inc. Magazine
Ed: Michael Fitzgerald. **Description:** Five questions to ask before committing to a supplier are answered.

50232 ■ "Two Growing Hispanic Radio Companies Broadcast Expansion Plans" in *Hispanic Business* **(October 2006, pp. 16)**
Pub: Hispanic Business
Description: Border Media Partners purchased two CBS-owned radio stations in San Antonio, Texas. Details of the transaction are included.

50233 ■ "2002 BE Banks" in *Black Enterprise* **(Vol. 33, No. 6, January 2003, pp. 24)**
Pub: Earl Graves Publishing Co.
Ed: Alan Hughes. **Description:** Harbor Bankshares Corporation, parent company of The Harbor Bank of Maryland, had formed two new subsidiaries designed to spur economic development in the greater Baltimore-Washington DC metropolitan area.

50234 ■ "UM Licenses System to Cigna" in *Crain's Detroit Business* **(Vol. 22, December 18, 2006, No. 51, pp. 18)**
Pub: Crain Communications Inc. - Detroit

Ed: Andrew Dietderich. **Description:** University of Michigan and Cigna HealthCare have entered an agreement to license a system to identify and address health risks for individuals. Health Risks and wellness programs at the worksite are also available to employers.

50235 ■ "Unions Buying Amalgamated; CFL, Other Groups Take Stake in Bank Long Tied to Labor" in *Crains Chicago Business* (Vol. 26, No. 51)
Pub: Crain Communications, Inc.
Ed: Steven R. Strahler. **Description:** Amalgamated Bank of Chicago is being sold to a group of unions. Details of the transaction are investigated. Statistical data included.

50236 ■ "Unions Buying Amalgamated" in *Crain's Chicago Business* (Vol. 26, No. 51, December 22, 2003, pp. 3)
Pub: Crain Communications, Inc.
Ed: Steven R. Strahler. **Description:** Amalgamated Bank of Chicago is being sold to a group of unions. Details of the transaction are investigated. Statistical data included.

50237 ■ "The U.S. Postal Service and eBay Are Offering a Delivery Tracking Service" in *Traffic World* (Vol. 267, Oct. 27, 2003)
Pub: Traffic World
Description: The U.S. Postal service and eBay have partnered to offer shipment tracking and other postal-related services.

50238 ■ "The Urge to Merge" in *Black Enterprise* (Vol. 35, August 2004, No. 1, pp. 50)
Pub: Earl G. Graves Publishing Co. Inc.
Ed: Bridget McCrea. **Description:** According to a recent survey, 20 percent of more than 400 CEOs of high-growth small businesses plan to use mergers and acquisitions to generate new business growth.

50239 ■ "The Urge to Merge" in *Fortune* (Vol. 151, February 21, 2005, No. 4, pp. 21)
Pub: Time Inc.
Ed: Shawn Tully. **Description:** Corporate American has launched new mergers after three years of avoiding new deals. Forty-eight new deals equaling $1 billion or more were announced between November 2004 and January 2005. Experts warn that historically, big deals produce twice as many failures as winners.

50240 ■ "US Airways Stock Up 5 Percent on Day Merger Try Ends" in *Charlotte Observer* (February 1, 2007)
Pub: Knight-Ridder/Tribune Business News
Ed: Steve Harrison. **Description:** US Airways stock rose 5 percent on the day Doug Parker, CEO, cancelled his offer to purchase Delta Air Lines.

50241 ■ "VC-backed IPOs Roared In Q2, But Whither the Enron Effect?" in *Venture Capital Journal* (Vol. 42, No. 8, August 2002, pp. 11-14)
Pub: Thomas Venture Economics
Ed: Colleen Marie O'Connor, Lawrence Aragon. **Description:** Accounting scandals, CEO misdeeds and a bear market have put a major crunch on the IPO market, and the near future doesn't look promising. Statistical data included.

50242 ■ "VCs Feel the Love from Wall Street" in *Venture Capital Journal* (February 1, 2005)
Pub: Thomason Financial Inc.
Description: Despite a slow beginning, 2004 ended a strong year for initial public offerings (IPOs), marking the strongest year since the Internet bubble. Two-hundred sixteen companies went public last year, three times more than 2002.

50243 ■ "VCs Try Partnering for Successful Incubation" in *Venture Capital Journal* (February 1, 2005)
Pub: Thomason Financial Inc.
Description: Today, incubator companies comprise small operations sponsored by individual investors, to

entrepreneurial clusters housed by venture capitalists, to groups evolving into stand-alone venture funds themselves. An incubator backed by multiple venture firms has become a popular model.

50244 ■ "Venerable Financial Firms to Join" in *Altanta Journal-Constitution* (February 7, 2007)
Pub: Cox Newspapers, Inc.
Ed: Tom Walker. **Description:** Atlanta Life Financial Group acquired Jackson Securities LLC, merging the two largest black-owned enterprises in Atlanta, Georgia.

50245 ■ "Venture-backed IPOs Rebound from Q2 Slump" in *Venture Capital Journal* (Vol. 40, No. 10, November 2000, pp. 10, 12, 14)
Pub: Venture Economics
Description: Venture-backed companies raised more than $7.57 billion in the third quarter of 2000. Statistical data included.

50246 ■ "A Vision for Recycling" in *Business Journal-Milwaukee* (Vol. 20, No. 51, September 5, 2003, pp. A14)
Pub: American City Business Journals, Inc.
Ed: David Schuyler. **Description:** Profile of Elia Lemke and Joe Tate, who formed Sauceda Sanitation LLC, a small woman-owned business. Lemke has limited business background and Tate is the retired chairman and founder of Superior Services Inc.

50247 ■ "Vivid Buys Amerigos, Char" in *Mississippi Business Journal* (Vol. 29, January 2007, No. 3, pp. A8)
Pub: Venture Publications, Inc.
Description: Amerigo Restaurant Corp. have transferred ownership of their five restaurants to Vivid Restaurant Concepts. Vivid will continue to operate the Jackson's Char and Amerigo restaurants as well as Tennessee's three Amerigo restaurants.

50248 ■ "Waiting in the Wings" in *Entrepreneur* (Vol. 32, No. 1, January 2004, pp. 21)
Pub: Entrepreneur Media, Inc.
Ed: David Worrell. **Description:** Market experts are predicting a rise in the number of Initial Public Offerings (IPOs) in 2004, although there is still strength in biotech and pharmaceutical companies, other sectors such as real estate, business services, healthcare and manufacturing are growing.

50249 ■ "Wal-Mart Said to Be Weighing Bid for Massachusetts-Based BJ's Wholesale Club" in *Boston Globe* (April 11, 2003)
Pub: Knight-Ridder/Tribune Business News
Ed: Chris Reidy. **Description:** Wal-Mart Stores Inc. is considering a bid to purchase BJ's Wholesale Club Inc., located in Natick, Massachusetts. The chain operates about 140 club stores with sales of nearly $5.9 billion in 2002.

50250 ■ "The Walking Time Bomb" in *Inc.* (December 1, 2003)
Pub: Gruner & Jahr USA Publishing
Description: How to defuse an abusive partner, intellectual property issues, and renting property rather than buying are topics discussed.

50251 ■ "Waning Risk Tolerance Haunts Tech IPOs" in *Venture Capital Journal* (Vol. 42, No. 5, May 2002, pp. 6, 8, 10-11)
Pub: Thomas Venture Economics
Ed: Colleen Marie O'Connor, Robyn Kurdek. **Description:** The level of risk the Initial Public Offering investors are willing to take continues to fall, causing problems for venture-backed technology startups.

50252 ■ "Watch your step" in *Entrepreneur* (Vol. 31, No. 6, June 2003, pp. 55)
Pub: Entrepreneur Media Inc.
Ed: Joan Szabo. **Description:** The IRS is promising to crack down on small business owners not reporting business income, focusing on abusive tax shelters, offshore credit card abuse, high-income nonfilers, and high-income taxpayers engaged in partnerships, trusts or S corporations, as well as selecting 50,000 random returns from 2001.

50253 ■ "Web.Preneuring" in *Small Business Opportunities* (Vol. 17, November 2005, No. 6, pp. 90, 94)
Pub: Harris Publications Inc.
Ed: Chuck Green. **Description:** Profile of Scott Kolbe and Mike Stout, entrepreneurs who started Icon Digital Design in a basement. The partners base their success on being graphic designers with strong work ethics.

50254 ■ "Week In Review" in *Crain's Detroit Business* (Vol. 16, No. 49, December 4, 2000, pp. 46)
Pub: Crain Communications, Inc.
Description: An undisclosed company is interested in buying the City of Detroit's Power and Lighting Department. Mayor Dennis Archer said he would entertain any offer. Also covered in the article is information regarding the Mechanical Dynamics Inc. company, based in Ann Arbor, Michigan.

50255 ■ "Weiss, Peck & Greer Venture Partners Vanishes in Lightspeed" in *Venture Capital Journal* (Vol. 40, No. 10, November 2000, pp. 16, 18)
Pub: Venture Economics
Description: The executives with Weiss, Peck & Greer Venture Partners have left the firm in order to start a new company named Lightspeed Venture Partners. The new company has also formed a charitable initiative named Lightspeed Bright Futures, an ongoing partnership with Plugged In and OpNet, a pair of non-profit organizations working to bridge the digital divide.

50256 ■ "Wells Fargo to Buy Southwest Community Bank Parent" in *San Diego Business Journal* (Vol. 28, January 15, 2007, No. 3, pp. 5)
Pub: San Diego Business Journal Associates
Ed: Mike Allen. **Description:** Details of Wells Fargo Bank's purchase of Placer Sierra Bancshares are profiled.

50257 ■ "Wells, Maine, Duo Start Custom Electronics Business" in *Portland Press Herald* (August 26, 2005)
Pub: Blethen Maine Newspapers, Inc.
Ed: Edward D. Murphy. **Description:** Profile of Jeff Binette and Jason Robie, friends who started the company, SmartHome Solutions. The firm outfits homes with home theaters, whole-house audio systems, and multiple Internet and phone connections.

50258 ■ "What's a Company Worth? It Depends on Which GP You Ask" in *Venture Capital Journal* (Vol. 42, No. 5, May 2002, pp. 40-41)
Pub: Thomas Venture Economics
Ed: Colin Blaydon, Michael Horvath. **Description:** Now, GPs are spending nearly as much time managing LP relationships as their portfolio companies, with valuation reporting being one of the most difficult issues being faced. Venture capitalists may not really understand the value of some portfolio companies.

50259 ■ "When a partner doesn't work out" in *My Business* (November/December 2001, pp. 48)
Pub: My Business Magazine
Ed: Denise O'Berry. **Description:** Issues to consider before starting a business with a partner are examined.

50260 ■ "When Taking Candy From Babies Makes Sense" in *Fortune* (Vol. 141, No. 17, April 3, 2000, pp. 304)
Pub: Time Inc.
Ed: Carolyn T. Geer. **Description:** Advice is given regarding partnership agreements, including information about the Uniform Transfers to Minors Act.

50261 ■ "When You Speak, Lawmakers Listen" in *My Business* (June/July 2004, pp. 41)
Pub: My Business Magazine
Description: Lawmakers are interested in small business. The National Federation of Independent Busi-

ness (NFIB) advocates for small business through its Member Ballot, the largest opinion-gathering effort of its type. Results are given to lawmakers. Currently issues revolved around employer retirement savings accounts, postal rates, debit cards, project labor agreements, and OSHA regulations.

50262 ■ "Why Do They Keep Leaving" in *Harvard Business Review* **(Vol. 81, No. 2, February 2003, pp. 14)**
Pub: Harvard Business School Press
Ed: Jeffrey A. King. **Description:** Statistical analysis of companies that have not gone through a merger show that attrition rates are about 10 percent, while companies that merge have attrition rates nearly double for as long as nine years after the merger. Reasons include stress and perceived lack of advancement opportunities. Research shows that even executives hired after a merger, leave at these elevated rates.

50263 ■ "Why Online Exchanges Died" in *Inc.* **(August 1, 2003)**
Pub: Gruner & Jahr USA Publishing
Ed: Cara Cannella. **Description:** According to a report by the Winter 2003 edition of the California Management Review, of the 1,500 business-to-business exchanges started, only 43 percent remain in operation, citing the fact that most buyers placed a premium on long-term relationships with vendors.

50264 ■ "Why SPACs Are Luring VCs Into Public Market" in *Venture Capital Journal* **(October 1, 2005)**
Pub: Thomason Financial Inc.
Description: Private non-control investors are increasingly playing a role in public control acquisition equities in order to give the private equity firm a low-risk and low-cost method to leverage the public markets while backing entire management teams.

50265 ■ *Wikinomics: How Mass Collaboration Changes Everything*
Pub: Penguin Group
Ed: Don Tapscott. **Released:** November 2006. **Price:** $25.95. **Description:** Guide to collaborate plans change beliefs about business hierarchies.

50266 ■ "Wingate Inn, the Preferred Hotel of the Company of Friends" in *Fast Company* **(March 2005, No. 92, pp. 94)**
Description: Profile of Wingate Inn, with 150 hotels nationwide, and its partnership with the Company of Friends; membership in the Company of Friends guarantees the best available rate when staying at a Wingate Inn. The hotel chain offers business travelers free high speed wired and wireless Internet access.

50267 ■ "Winning with the big box retailers" in *Harvard Business Review* **(Vol. 78, No. 5, September-October 2000, pp. 26)**
Pub: Harvard Business School Publishing Corp.
Ed: David Eric, Harding Schwalm. **Description:** The relationship of window maker Pella Corporation to the Wall-Mart chain is discussed. The manufacturer offered the big-box store a focused, branded product line.

50268 ■ "Witness Systems adopts anti-takeover plan" in *Atlanta Business Chronicle* **(Vol. 25, November 15, 2002, No. 23 pp. 3A)**
Pub: American City Business Publications, Inc.
Ed: Mary Jane Credeur. **Description:** Witness Systems Inc. has adopted a "shareholder rights" plan in 2002 to prevent hostile takeovers. The company believes its stock is currently undervalued. Other area technology companies have recently adopted similar plans.

50269 ■ "Words of Wisdom Reap Huge Rewards" in *Success* **(Vol. 47, No. 6, November 2000, pp. 50)**
Pub: Success Publishing, Inc.
Ed: Sharon Nelton. **Description:** Jonathan Carson was growing accustomed to being a fish that gobbled up smaller fish. Last fall his Boston-based company,

FamilyEducation Network, acquired Information Please LLC. In March, it snapped up three other dot.coms in the K-12 education field: FunBrain.com LLC, SchoolCash.com, and MyGradeBook.com. In late June, Carson and his company were themselves swallowed up by one of the biggest education fishes of all, a London-based media giant.

50270 ■ "Work with me" in *WorkingWoman* **(Vol. 25, No. 6, June 2000, pp. 40)**
Pub: Lang Communications Inc.
Ed: Eilene Zimmerman. **Description:** Georgina Curran and Petra Vester founded Lbdtogo.com in 1999 selling little black dresses. They wish to increase turnover by forming partnerships with other electronic retailers and are seeking advice on the best way of doing this.

50271 ■ "Wrestling for Web dominance" in *Hispanic Business* **(Vol. 22, No. 7-8, July-August 2000, pp. 106)**
Pub: Hispanic Business
Ed: Vaughn Hagerty. **Description:** Global consolidation is taking place among the Internet's Hispanic-targeted Web sites. Among the companies set to gain a dominant position in the sector is Spanish telecom provider Terra Networks with its proposed $12.5 billion acquisition of Web service provider Lycos.

50272 ■ "Yes, You Still Can Go Public" in *Inc.* **(Volume 27, July 2005, No. 7, pp. 38)**
Pub: Inc. Magazine
Ed: David Ian Miller. **Description:** London, England investors are clamoring for American IPOs. Profile of Alternative Investment Market (AIM) in London is included.

50273 ■ "You Can Count on Me: A Friend Can Make the Best Kind of Business Partner" in *Entrepreneur* **(Vol. 32, November 2004, No. 11, pp. 36)**
Pub: Entrepreneur Media Inc.
Ed: Aliza Pilar Sherman. **Description:** Profiles of friends who ventured into businesses together. Lynn Harris Medcalf and Susan Apgood teamed to launch News Generation, a public relations firm in Atlanta, Georgia. Sarah Eck and Brook Jay, partnered to create All Terrain Productions, an events-marketing firm in Chicago, Illinois.

50274 ■ "Your Best M&A Strategy" in *Harvard Business Review* **(Vol. 81, No. 3, March 2003, pp. 16)**
Pub: Harvard Business School Press
Ed: Sam Rovit. **Description:** A director with Bain and Company argues that companies that make frequent acquisitions perform best when they buy throughout the economic cycle. Companies that buy during specific parts of the cycle lag behind the constant buyers.

50275 ■ "Zalenko and Virchow Krause Join; Firm Wants 'Critical Mass' Locally" in *Crain's Detroit Business* **(Vol. 21, January 3, 2005, No. 1)**
Pub: Crain Communications Inc. - Detroit
Ed: Katie Merx. **Description:** Zalenko & Associates PC has merged with Virchow Krause & Company LLP, making it a leader in the accounting sector in Michigan. The merge will place the firm as eighth-largest in the state with 105 employees.

50276 ■ "Zander's Chip Shot; New CEO Faces Tough Call on Semiconductor Unit" in *Crain's Chicago Business* **(Vol. 26, No. 51, December 22, 2003)**
Pub: Crain Communications, Inc.
Ed: Julie Johnsson. **Description:** Edward Zander, new CEO of Motorola Inc., is faced with the dilemma to sell or spin off the company's struggling semiconductor unit. The company is making plans for an initial public offering of its chip business, which saw $5 billion in revenue, but is also considering interest from rivals and private-equity firms.

50277 ■ "Zen and the Art of Acquisition" in *Success* **(Vol. 47, No. 2, June 2000, pp. 64)**
Pub: Success Publishing, Inc.
Ed: Eddy Goldberg. **Description:** Selling you company might be a good strategy, but the article explores other options.

50278 ■ "Zurich Canada Alliance with ING Brings Efficiencies" in *Rough Notes* **(Vol. 145, No. 12, December 2002, pp. 114)**
Pub: Rough Notes
Ed: Phil Zinkewicz. **Description:** ING Canada acquired Zurich's Canadian personal and small business Property Casualty business and Zurich will renew large accounts of both companies. Robert Landry is the president and CEO of Zurich North American Canada.

VIDEOCASSETTES/
AUDIOCASSETTES

50279 ■ *Fergi Builds a Business*
Phoenix Learning Group
2349 Chaffee Dr.
St. Louis, MO 63146
Ph:(314)569-0211
Free: 800-221-1274
Fax: (314)569-2834
URL: http://www.phoenixlearninggroup.com
Released: 1990. **Price:** $400.00. **Description:** The process of forming and building a business is demonstrated. Included are dealing with success, failure, partnerships, corporations, capital and profits. **Availability:** VHS; EJ; 3/4U; Special order formats.

50280 ■ *Partnership Series*
Excellence in Training Corp.
1303 Marsh Ln.
Carrollton, TX 75006
Free: 800-747-6569
Released: 1990. **Price:** $895.00. **Description:** A four-part program designed to build more effective management. **Availability:** VHS; 3/4U; Special order formats.

50281 ■ *The Price: Update*
Commonwealth Films, Inc.
223 Commonwealth Ave.
Boston, MA 02116
Ph:(617)262-5634
Fax: (617)262-6948
Co. E-mail: info@commonwealthfilms.com
URL: http://www.commonwealthfilms.com
Released: 1989. **Price:** $395.00. **Description:** An updated version of the film on mergers, antitrust violations, and other big business dealings. **Availability:** VHS; 3/4U.

CONSULTANTS

50282 ■ AB Associates
7380 Sherman Rd.
Chesterland, OH 44026-2050
Ph:(330)672-1219
Fax: (330)672-9806
Co. E-mail: raggarwa@bsa3.kent.edu

E-mail: raggarwa@bsa3.kent.edu
Scope: Offers expertise in the areas of banking, capital budgeting, investing in emerging markets, international risk analysis, strategic planning, international accounting, management of foreign exchange and other accounting and financial policies. Additional services include acquisition and merger analysis, the valuation of a proposed purchase and development of appropriate post-merger managerial policies, and the implementation of computer-based receivable and inventory management policies.

50283 ■ Access Management Corp.
6135 Park S Dr.
PO Box 12059
Charlotte, NC 28220-2059
Ph:(704)554-9000
Fax: (704)552-9768
Scope: Provides international management services specializing in trade financing (Worldwide Factoring) market development, licensing/technology transfer,

and marketing. Experienced in merger/acquisition brokering, trade financing, letter of credit discounting and forfeiting, factoring, equipment financing, and debt recovery. **Seminars:** Frequent public speaker and seminar leader on marketing strategies, international technology transfer, licensing and career planning.

50284 ■ Agri-Personnel
5120 Old Bill Cook Rd.
Atlanta, GA 30349-0319
Ph:(404)768-5701
Fax: (404)768-5705
Scope: Agribusiness consultants active in executive/professional/technical recruitment and placement, and in mergers, acquisitions, and divestitures in various industries including dairy, feed, food, fertilizer, farm chemicals, poultry and egg, animal health, and pulp and paper.

50285 ■ AgriCapital Corp.
1410 Broadway, Ste. 1802
New York, NY 10018
Ph:(212)944-9500
Fax: (212)944-9525
Co. E-mail: info@agricapital.com
URL: http://www.agricapital.com

E-mail: info@agricapital.com
Scope: Provides investment banking services for agribusiness clients in the United States and abroad, including financial consulting, debt and equity placements and joint ventures, and mergers and acquisitions. Industries served: agribusiness and food companies. **Publications:** "Seedworld".

50286 ■ Air Communication Corp.
3300 Airport Rd.
Boulder, CO 80301
Ph:(303)440-4075
Free: 877-572-6800
Fax: (303)440-6355
Co. E-mail: info@aircommcorp.com
URL: http://www.aircommcorp.com

E-mail: info@aircommcorp.com
Scope: Aviation engineering consultants offering to clients design and FAA approval of aircraft accessories and aircraft modifications, as well as general business planning services, including acquisitions and mergers.

50287 ■ ALCO Capital Group Inc.
745 5th Ave., Ste. 1506
New York, NY 10151-1504
Ph:(212)751-9150
Free: 800-233-2526
Fax: (212)371-2768
Co. E-mail: alco745@aol.com
URL: http://www.alcocapital.com

E-mail: alco745@aol.com
Scope: Consultants in financially troubled situations, specializing in Chapter 11 rehabilitations; Chapter 7 liquidation; interface with the creditors' committee; arrange for and provide funding for company rehabilitation; evaluation of company operations and procedures. Expertise includes: investments, acquisitions, auctions, and liquidations.

50288 ■ AMC International Inc.
PO Box 11292
Beverly Hills, CA 90213-4292
Ph:(310)652-5620
Fax: (310)652-6709
Co. E-mail: inquiry@amcusa.com
URL: http://www.amcusa.com

E-mail: inquiry@amcusa.com
Scope: Offers day-to-day business management, business turnaround, marketing strategies, development/refinement of corporate mission, and merger and acquisition evaluations. Industries served: all.

50289 ■ American Appraisal Associates Inc.
411 E Wisconsin Ave., Ste. 1900
Milwaukee, WI 53202

Free: 800-558-8650
Fax: (414)221-7065
Co. E-mail: moreinfo@american-appraisal.com
URL: http://www.american-appraisal.com

E-mail: moreinfo@american-appraisal.com
Scope: Performs valuations of business enterprises and their securities for tax-related purposes, estate, gift and income taxes, mergers and acquisitions including fairness opinions, and ESOPs. **Publications:** "Estimation of Hospital Real Property Values for Ad Valorem Tax Purposes"; "Developing Discount Rates in a global Environment"; "Discount Rates for Foreign Investments"; "Getting a Grip on Foreign Discount Rates".

50290 ■ Aquinas Group
1733 Green Valley Rd.
Havertown, PA 19083
Ph:(610)449-2290
Fax: (610)482-9157
Co. E-mail: rhrabner@theaquinasgroup.com
URL: http://www.theaquinasgroup.com

E-mail: rhrabner@theaquinasgroup.com
Scope: Offers business, financial and management consulting services. Activities include corporate planning and finance, production and marketing, management systems, organization development, merger and acquisition, start-up and venture capital. Serves private industries as well as government agencies. Investment banking services. **Seminars:** Productivity and Profit Improvement; Business Planning and Financing; Operational Auditing.

50291 ■ ARDITO Information & Research Inc.
1019 Sedwick Dr., Ste. G
Wilmington, DE 19803
Ph:(302)479-5373
Free: 800-836-9068
Fax: (302)479-5375
Co. E-mail: sardito@ardito.com
URL: http://www.ardito.com

E-mail: sardito@ardito.com
Scope: A full-service information and research firm. Provides information in area of financial data, published research, demographic data, industry-specific publications, competitor data, marketing and sales trends, new product developments, government relations, bibliographies. Industries served are pharmaceutical, health, publishing, and environment, and business.

50292 ■ The Argus Group
16633 Ventura Blvd., Ste. 1330
Encino, CA 91436-2403
Ph:(818)990-7200
Fax: (818)990-7909
Co. E-mail: cbercy@aol.com

E-mail: cbercy@aol.com
Scope: Provides services in all aspects of business planning, organization, startup, expansion, diversification, acquisition, marketing, product development, finance, general management, and exporting. Also offers special consulting facilities and assistance for smaller companies and new ventures. Industries served: manufacturing, distribution, government agencies, marketing, mail order, retail, service and international trades. **Seminars:** Offers special workshops for small business owners and managers, covering marketing, advertising, finance and other topics of current interest.

50293 ■ Associated Management Systems Inc.
999 Commercial St.
Palo Alto, CA 94303-4925
Ph:(650)852-9041
Fax: (650)967-9992
Co. E-mail: amsn@rcn.com

E-mail: amsn@rcn.com
Scope: The firm's entrepreneurial and professional expertise includes corporate management, invest-

ment banking, finance, strategic planning, risk evaluation, due diligence studies and management audits. Also assists with mergers and acquisitions, and provides management for turnaround situations. Undertakes project packaging, plant relocations, capital restructuring and funding. Industries served: agriculture, real estate, insurance, computers, communications, retail/wholesale, electronics/instruments, paper/printing, food processing, furniture/home products, travel, transportation, recreation, heavy industry, pharmaceuticals, and government agencies.

50294 ■ Associated Marketers
10 E Hartshorn Dr.
Short Hills, NJ 07078-1630
Ph:(973)376-3835
Scope: Consulting services limited to area of mergers and acquisitions through a network of associates. Active in serving manufacturing, distributing and service businesses seeking new corporate homes, acquiring additional businesses, or divesting divisions or subsidiaries. Fields served include appliances, housewares, advertising, industrial, publishing, building materials, printing and graphic arts, banking, insurance, apparel and textiles, automotive, transportation, home furnishings, food and confectionery products, leisure products, mail order, natural resources, plastics, packaging, and service businesses and retailing.

50295 ■ Atlantic Management Company Inc.
875 Greenland Rd., Orchard Pk., Ste. A12
Portsmouth, NH 03801
Ph:(603)436-8009
Fax: (603)427-0146
Co. E-mail: amc@atlantic-mgmt.com
URL: http://www.atlantic-mgmt.com

E-mail: amc@atlantic-mgmt.com
Scope: Offers business valuation services in connection with employee stock ownership plans, fairness opinions, management buyouts, mergers and acquisitions, divorce, stockholder disputes, estate planning and estate and gift tax. Additional ESOP advisory services include feasibility studies, equity allocations, and financing proposals. Serves private industries as well as government agencies. **Publications:** "Lock, stock, and barrel; A well connected hedge firm buys Bushmaster Firearms," Mainebiz, May, 2006; "Tips for lawyers when working with appraisers," New Hampshire Bar Review, Oct, 2005; "A win all around," Worcester Telegram & Gazette, Mar, 2005. **Seminars:** Valuing the Closely Held Company; Employee Stock Ownership Plans: An Overview; Employee Stock Ownership Plans: Corporate Planning Tool.

50296 ■ Bain & Company Inc.
131 Dartmouth St.
Boston, MA 02116
Ph:(617)572-2000
Fax: (617)572-2427
Co. E-mail: corporate.inquiries@bain.com
URL: http://www.bain.com

E-mail: corporate.inquiries@bain.com
Scope: Management consulting firm which focuses on helping clients improve their financial performance. Specifically, the firm operates in these areas: corporate and business unit strategy, manufacturing, mergers and acquisitions, value managed relationships, information technology, retailing, customer base management and retention, distribution and logistics, high technology, cost reduction, consumer marketing, change management, and healthcare. Client base represents virtually all economic sectors manufacturing, wholesaling, retailing, transportation, and services.

50297 ■ Samuel D. Begola Associates Inc.
37264 Agar
Sterling Heights, MI 48310
Ph:(586)977-3335
Fax: (586)977-3335
Scope: A full service business valuation and financial management consulting firm. Part of the firm's function is to provide both manufacturing and service organizations with the kind of talent they need to get the job

done. Provides business valuation for Employee Stock Option Plans (ESOPs), buy/sell agreements, solvency opinions in leveraged buyouts, loan procurement and government loan assistance, merger and acquisitions, reorganizations, government sales contracts, minority business expertise, machine rate and quote systems, business plans, marketing, and administrative and turnaround management talent.

50298 ■ Bennett and Co.
45 Water St.
Newburyport, MA 01950
Ph:(978)462-1966
Fax: (978)463-2062
Co. E-mail: sales@bennettcompany.com
URL: http://www.bennettcompany.com

E-mail: sales@bennettcompany.com
Scope: Offers services in the following fields: mergers and acquisitions, acquisition financing, acquisition searches, refinancing, and financial restructuring. Also specializes in business turnaround consulting. Industries served: manufacturing, distribution, and service.

50299 ■ Biomedical Management Resources
PO Box 521125
Salt Lake City, UT 84152-1125
Ph:(801)272-4668
Fax: (801)277-3290
Co. E-mail: SeniorManagement@
    BiomedicalManagement.com
URL: http://www.biomedicalmanagement.com

E-mail: SeniorManagement@
    BiomedicalManagement.com
Scope: Provides business development, interim management, and executive search services. Assists companies in strategic alliances, corporate partnering, business acquisition. Demonstrated success in identifying recruiting, and placing key managers in difficult to hire positions.

50300 ■ Broadview International
520 Madison Ave., 10th Fl.
New York, NY 10022
Ph:(212)284-8100
Fax: (212)284-8101
URL: http://www.broadview.com
Scope: An investment banking firm specializing in mergers and acquisitions within the information technology, media, healthcare technology and communications industries. Also private equity investor in these industries.

50301 ■ Business Brokers Hawaii L.L.C.
PO Box 1810
Kihei, HI 96753
Ph:(808)879-8833
Free: (866)239-1567
Fax: (808)879-5966
Co. E-mail: md@BusinessBrokersHawaii.com
URL: http://www.business-brokers.com

E-mail: md@BusinessBrokersHawaii.com
Scope: Offers buying or selling existing businesses, creation of new businesses, business evaluation and appraisal, assistance to clients on expansion and mergers, consultation with owners of businesses in trouble, and consultation on Unites States, Japan and Chinese commerce. **Seminars:** How to Start Your Own Business; How to Make a Sick Business Well Again; How to do Fiscal Forecasting and Cash Flow Projections.

50302 ■ Business Team
1901 S Bascom Ave., Ste. 400
Campbell, CA 95008
Ph:(408)246-1102
Fax: (408)246-2219
Co. E-mail: sanjose@business-team.com
URL: http://www.business-team.com

E-mail: sanjose@business-team.com
Scope: Business consulting services offered to companies looking for buyers. Specializes in mergers and acquisitions, business brokerage, and valuations. **Seminars:** Business Valuation - Enhancing the Value of Your Company.

50303 ■ Carl M. Caplan, D.D.S., M.B.A.
2910 Lightfoot Dr.
Baltimore, MD 21209
Ph:(410)484-3658
Scope: Firm provides business services in the area of employment/partnership/new doctor agreements, practice management and mergers/acquisitions/sales and/or liquidation, practice valuation, and staff development and training.

50304 ■ The Change Agents
2557 Via Verde, Ste. 400
Walnut Creek, CA 94595-3451
Ph:(925)939-6236
Fax: (925)934-4674
Co. E-mail: thechangeagents@sbcglobal.net

E-mail: thechangeagents@sbcglobal.net
Scope: Provides consulting services related to mergers, acquisitions and divestitures. Services offered include: assisting acquiring companies in establishing and managing effective acquisition programs; representing sellers in the sale of their companies, and bringing buyers and sellers together. Additional consulting services include: advising on the structure of leveraged buy-outs; mediating sales between partners or in family succession; business valuations; due diligence examination of the marketing function; post-acquisition integration advice; and corporate strategy and planning. **Seminars:** Everything You Always Wanted to Know About Selling or Buying Your Building Service Company.

50305 ■ Diego Chevere & Co.
Metro Parque 7, Ste. 204
Metro Office
Caparra, PR 00922
Ph:(787)774-9595
Fax: (787)774-9566
Co. E-mail: dcco@coqui.net

E-mail: dcco@coqui.net
Scope: Business consultants offering assistance with financial projections, strategic business planning, mergers, reorganizations, EDP system design, and cash management. Serves private industries as well as government agencies. **Seminars:** EDP System Development; Loan Package Preparation.

50306 ■ Cole, Warren and Long Inc.
2 Penn Ctr. Plz., Ste. 312
Philadelphia, PA 19102
Ph:(215)563-0701
Free: 800-394-8517
Fax: (215)563-2907
Co. E-mail: cwlserch@cwl-inc.com
URL: http://www.cwl-inc.com

E-mail: cwlserch@cwl-inc.com
Scope: Offers management guidance to commercial, industrial, and government organizations specializing in the areas of organization studies, executive searches, acquisitions and mergers, compensation programs, audits, and improvement seminars. Conducts marketing, economic, and systems studies; counsels on profit improvement, manpower control, operations, and systems integration.

50307 ■ Consortium House
15 Bostan Rd.
PO Box 177
Malden on Hudson, NY 12453
Ph:(845)246-2336
Fax: (845)246-2338
Co. E-mail: eugenegs@aol.com

E-mail: eugenegs@aol.com
Scope: Offers its services to book, perodical, multimedia, and electronic publishers. Specializes in web strategies and in education, training, professional and general trade markets. Advises in financial and business development, marketing, new product development, fulfillment and distribution, venture investment, mergers and acquisitions, literary and publishing properties, project management, and operating systems troubleshooting. **Publications:** Setting Industry-

Wide Distribution Standards, Small Press, Jan-Feb, (1997); Rules of Thumb in Pricing and Profitability, PMA Newsletter, Sept., (1996). From Eyeballs to i Balls: Reaching the Reader, Foreward Magazine Jan. 2001; Need to Know Guide to Books on Demand, Foreward Mag. June 2000; The Transformation of Book Manufacturing, DMA Newsletter, 12/00. **Seminars:** Has presented Electronic Publishing; Print on Demand; Money and Publishing; Managing Profitability; and Strategic and Business Plan Development.

50308 ■ The Consulting Firm Inc.
64 Sierra Ct., Ste. 1200
Old Bridge, NJ 08857
Ph:(732)679-5520
Fax: (732)679-9451
Co. E-mail: efields128@aol.com
URL: http://www.edfields.com

E-mail: efields128@aol.com
Scope: Offers acquisition and venture investment services including search, evaluation, negotiation, and financing. Also advises on product, profit center evaluation, and personnel benefits. Firm assists companies with serious business problems and those whose performance should be much better. Serves all industries. **Publications:** "The Essentials of Finance and Accounting for Nonfinancial Managers". **Seminars:** Presents seminars on strategic planning; competitive marketing strategy; human resource development; and financial management.

50309 ■ CorDev Financial Inc.
Stanford Financial Sq., 2600 El Camino Real, Ste. 400
Palo Alto, CA 94306
Ph:(650)493-9111
Fax: (650)493-9115
Co. E-mail: robert@cordevfinancial.com
URL: http://www.cordevfinancial.com

E-mail: robert@cordevfinancial.com
Scope: Specializes in corporate mergers and acquisitions for small to mid-sized companies and CEO consulting.

50310 ■ Corporate Business Services of America Inc.
PO Box 1352
Conway, AR 72032
Ph:(501)329-2592
Co. E-mail: fghorton@yahoo.com

E-mail: fghorton@yahoo.com
Scope: Business management consulting firm specializes in profit engineering, management consulting, and business coaching. Industries served: businesses with sales in the $500,000 to $25,000,000 range. **Special Services:** Confidential data file of private buyers for business and financial instruments; business planning and coaching.

50311 ■ Corporate Growth Assistance Ltd.
1 Benvenuto Pl., Ste. 420
Toronto, ON, Canada M4V 2L1
Ph:(416)222-7772
Fax: (416)222-6091
Co. E-mail: cgal19yr@netcom.ca

E-mail: cgal19yr@netcom.ca
Scope: Represents extensive experience in facilitating profitable growth and liquidity and will deliver: A broad network of contacts providing access to investment options, funding, and business development opportunities, the talent necessary to provide solid strategic and operating guidance, the experience to generate high rates of return while effectively managing challenging situations, hands on professionalism; A commitment to execution so as to maximize profit, market share and team building. Client involvement has included: computerized car valuation database management for the insurance industry; dimensional art reproduction; dining and bedroom furniture manufacturing; employee and family assistance programs.

50312 ■ James W. Davidson Company Inc.
23 Forest View Rd.
Wallingford, PA 19086

Co. E-mail: jwdmsd@comcast.net

E-mail: jwdmsd@comcast.net
Scope: Offers counsel to clients to improve business strategy, organization, controls, management effectiveness and profits. Provides planning, problem-analysis and implementation assistance. Also performs thorough, in-depth executive recruiting and acquisition and divestment search and analysis. Experienced with large and small manufacturing and service companies, including new ventures.

50313 ■ DeVries & Company Inc.
800 W 47th St.
Kansas City, MO 64112
Ph:(816)756-0055
Fax: (816)756-0061
Scope: Investment banking/financial consulting firm which helps companies solve financial problems and achieve growth and diversification goals. Helps established companies raise capital, and assists new and developing companies secure venture capital and create public markets for their stocks. Provides confidential services to companies who want to sell or merge, aids companies in acquiring other companies, helps individuals and companies structure and negotiate leveraged buyouts, provides financial guidance, shapes business strategy and develops operating and financial strategies. Also performs business valuations for estate and gift tax and ESOPS. Renders fairness opinions and expert witness services.

50314 ■ Dorn & Associates Inc.
8506 Bass Lake Rd., Ste. 140
New Hope, MN 55428
Ph:(763)533-7689
Fax: (763)533-1143
Scope: Services include accounting, marketing, employment/partnership, new doctor agreements, personnel issues and human resources assessment, practice management, practice merger/acquisition/sale and/or liquidation, practice surveys and valuation, staff development and training.

50315 ■ Duff & Phelps L.L.C.
311 S Wacker Dr., Ste. 4200
Chicago, IL 60606
Ph:(312)697-4600
Fax: (312)697-0115
URL: http://www.duffllc.com
Scope: Financial business consultancy that provides going-concern business valuations of closely held companies and their securities, fairness and solvency opinions, and expert witness testimony, middle market investment banking services and private placement of debt and equity securities.

50316 ■ Executive Consultants Inc.
78 Carlton Dr. NE
Atlanta, GA 30342
Ph:(404)255-4801
Fax: (404)255-4801
Co. E-mail: spider42000@yahoo.com

E-mail: spider42000@yahoo.com
Scope: Offers mergers and acquisition consulting, estate planning, pension planning, profit sharing advice, and insurance planning.

50317 ■ Fowler, Anthony & Co.
20 Walnut St., 3rd Fl.
Wellesley Hills, MA 02481
Ph:(781)237-4201
Fax: (781)237-7718
Scope: Offers consulting services and direct investment into small businesses in mergers and acquisitions, capital financing and venture capital. Active with the following industries: communications, computer related, consumer, distribution, electronic components and instrumentation, multimedia, on-line database/publishing, industrial products and equipment, food processing, multimedia, healthcare services, medical/health related and publishing.

50318 ■ Frankel and Topche P.C.
1700 Galloping Hill Rd.
Kenilworth, NJ 07033

Ph:(908)298-7700
Fax: (908)298-7701
Co. E-mail: info@frankelandtopche.com
URL: http://www.frankelandtopche.com

E-mail: info@frankelandtopche.com
Scope: Offers financial consulting for closely held businesses. Assists in mergers and acquisitions, tax planning, strategic business planning, family succession planning, accounting, auditing, and obtaining financing. The firm serves small businesses in the service, retail, wholesale, and manufacturing industries. Specializes in real estate, lumber and building materials, and service businesses.

50319 ■ Haas Wheat & Partners L.P.
300 Crescent Ct., Ste. 1700
Dallas, TX 75201-1876
Ph:(214)871-8300
Fax: (214)871-8317
Scope: Business consulting firm offering expertise with mergers and acquisitions and financial investment in United States.

50320 ■ Jenam Securities Inc.
10 Kingsbridge Garden Cir., Ste. 506
Mississauga, ON, Canada L5R 3K6
Ph:(905)890-9245
Fax: (905)890-3229
URL: http://www.thebusinessplace.com
Scope: Assists in the buying and selling of businesses, arranging bank financing, venture capital loans/investments, mergers, and acquisitions.

50321 ■ Johnson, Butler & Co.
2600 Mission St., Ste. 206
San Marino, CA 91108
Ph:(626)799-5200
Fax: (626)799-5274
Co. E-mail: info@johnsonbutler.com
URL: http://www.johnsonbutler.com

E-mail: info@johnsonbutler.com
Scope: Serves as a consultant and intermediary in merger-acquisition work, representing either buyer or seller. Performs acquisition searches for corporate buyers. Arranges corporate divestitures, management buyouts, joint ventures and financing. Other services include business valuations and strategic planning. Experienced in numerous industries including industrial product manufacturing, consumer goods manufacturing, distribution in all fields, hospitality industry services and life sciences.

50322 ■ KFA Services
6710 128th St. SW
Edmonds, WA 98026
Ph:(425)745-6860
Fax: (425)745-6860
Scope: Offers consulting services in financial, accounting, and economic analysis including business valuations, financial projections and feasibility analysis, cost accounting, economic loss determination, mergers and acquisitions, and business policy and planning assistance. Also provides litigation support and construction claims analysis. Serves private industries as well as government agencies. **Seminars:** Economic Feasibility Analysis; The Use of Current Value Accounting for Measuring Port Profitability; Damages for Construction Delays: Analyzing Contractor Claims for Home Office Overhead Costs.

50323 ■ Kibel Green Inc.
2001 Wilshire Blvd., Ste. 420
Santa Monica, CA 90403
Ph:(310)829-0255
Free: (866)875-0255
Fax: (310)453-6324
Co. E-mail: info@kginc.com
URL: http://www.kginc.com

E-mail: info@kginc.com
Scope: Business consultants top middle market companies providing the following services: Turnaround/Crisis management, Value Creation and Investment Banking. Industries served include: manufacturing,

service, technology, retail, distribution and real estate. **Publications:** "How to Turn Around a Financially Troubled Company"; "The Value Creation Bible for the Mid-Market"; "How to Turn Around a Financially Troubled Real Estate".

50324 ■ L.G. Kranick & Associates
1517 W Pierce St.
Milwaukee, WI 53204-1236
Ph:(414)671-3636
Fax: (414)671-4264
Scope: consulting services includes economic analysis of industry trends and long-range planning; market and product surveys and analysis; mergers and acquisitions; manufacturing methods and systems; organization structure and development; and interim management.

50325 ■ Lyons Hollis Associates Inc.
15R Hartford Ave., Ste. 2A-D
PO Box 809
Granby, CT 06035-0809
Ph:(860)653-4770
Fax: (860)653-4263
Co. E-mail: jlyons@lyonshollis.com
URL: http://www.lyonshollis.com

E-mail: jlyons@lyonshollis.com
Scope: Strategic financial advisers to owners of health-care, management consulting, marketing/communications, technology and professional services firms.

50326 ■ Management Resource Center Inc.
3020 Old Ranch Pky., 3rd Fl.
Seal Beach, CA 90740
Ph:(562)799-5510
Fax: (562)799-5594
Co. E-mail: info@mrcworldwide.com
URL: http://www.mrcworldwide.com

E-mail: info@mrcworldwide.com
Scope: Business consultants experienced in mergers and acquisitions, divestitures, strategic planning, executive leadership, product strategy, valuation, ESOPs, venture capital, and management development. Industries served: graphic arts, printing, manufacturing, distribution, electronics, service, and high-technology and investment banking advisory services. **Seminars:** Executive Leadership; Integration; Strategic Planning; Valuation; Mergers and Acquisitions.

50327 ■ James V. McTevia & Associates
30300 Telegraph Rd., Ste. 185
Bingham Farms, MI 48025
Ph:(248)646-2711
Fax: (248)646-2714
Co. E-mail: mctevia@mctevia.com
URL: http://www.mctevia.com

E-mail: mctevia@mctevia.com
Scope: Firm specializes in reorganization programs for businesses with serious financial problems. Services include debt restructuring, bankruptcy trustees, liquidations, management reorganization and acquisitions and mergers. Serves private industries as well as government agencies. **Publications:** "Survival in The Face of Change"; "Tips for Picking An Outside Adviser"; "Out-of Court Problem Solving and Restructuring: Guide to a Successful Outcome"; "Business Problem Solving". **Seminars:** Preventing or Structuring a Reorganization without Court Supervision, Michigan Association of Certified Public Accountants, Jun, 2006.

50328 ■ Mertz Associates Inc.
1 Riverwood Pl., N17W24222 Riverwood Dr., Ste. 305
Waukesha, WI 53188
Ph:(262)523-4200
Fax: (262)523-4202
Co. E-mail: mertz@mertz.com
URL: http://www.mertz.com

E-mail: mertz@mertz.com
Scope: A merger and acquisition consulting firm representing either dedicated buyers or sellers of compa-

nies across the U.S. Clients range from small privately held companies to large public companies in all industries.

50329 ■ New Century Consultants
1600 2nd St.
Gulfport, MS 39501-2135
Ph:(228)864-3999
Fax: (228)868-4960
Co. E-mail: new-century@cwix.com

E-mail: new-century@cwix.com
Scope: Provides management consulting and strategies in public relations, communications, marketing, and advertising. Specializes in consulting services to the music, entertainment and casino industries. Recent experience with new business start-ups and new business acquisitions. Serves private industries as well as government agencies. Training, Executive Search. **Seminars:** Communicating With Power; Writing With Power; Communicating With Employees; Communicating With the Customer; Customer Service Communications; Creativity and Communications.

50330 ■ Nimark Group Inc.
238 Osborne Rd.
Harrison, NY 10528-3732
Ph:(914)967-7600
Scope: Specialists in merger, acquisition, divestiture analysis and negotiation for middle market companies. Services include business valuations. Also provides expertise in crisis management. **Seminars:** How to Sell Your Business for the Most Profit.

50331 ■ The Rehmann Group
5800 Gratiot Rd., Ste. 201
PO Box 2025
Saginaw, MI 48605-2025
Ph:(989)799-9580
Free: (866)799-9580
Fax: (989)799-0227
URL: http://www.rehmann.com
Scope: Offers general business services that include profit enhancement consulting, investigative services (Kerby Bailey), assistance in preparation of a business plan, aid in obtaining financing, employee benefit plan analysis, systems counseling, incentive plans, cash management, marketing plans and research, as well as business valuations (litigation support) and mergers and acquisitions. Specializing in services for health care, manufacturing and governmental units. **Publications:** "BWG Magazine".

50332 ■ M. Richler and Associates Ltd.
85 Skymark Dr., Ste. 2603
North York, ON, Canada M2H 3P2
Ph:(416)491-5264
Fax: (416)491-4557
Scope: A general management consulting firm specializing in acquisitions and mergers, costing and pricing, office layout design and management, production management and taxation, particularly for small businesses. Industries served: manufacturing, retail, wholesale, import/export, design services, and government agencies. **Publications:** "Contact" 1995 Budget Release. Also, 1996-2000 Budget Releases. **Seminars:** Keeping the Cottage in the Family; Maximizing Capital Gains Exemption; Minimizing Probate Fees; Plant Reorganization; Departmental Scheduling.

50333 ■ Robbinex Inc.
41 Stuart St.
Hamilton, ON, Canada L8L 1B5
Ph:(905)523-7510
Free: 888-762-2463
Fax: (905)523-4998
Co. E-mail: robbinex@robbinex.com
URL: http://www.robbinex.com

E-mail: robbinex@robbinex.com
Scope: Business consultants specializing in the merger and acquisition area and financial planning for small to medium size companies. Other services include business financing, crisis management, acquisition search, business valuations, joint ventures and venture capital, resolution of partnership problems, implementation of franchise programs, and general assistance in site selection. **Seminars:** How to Start a Small Business; How to Buy a Business; How to Successfully Manage Medium to Small Businesses; Expansion Through Acquisition; Growth Through Franchising; How to Borrow Money from a Bank; Syndicating Equity. **Special Services:** Robbinex®.

50334 ■ Sam Rosenbaum & Co.
419 Northfield Ave.
West Orange, NJ 07052-3091
Ph:(973)736-2323
Fax: (973)325-9080
Scope: Specialist in mergers, acquisitions, and divestitures. Also has expertise in marketing.

50335 ■ Siebrand-Wilton Associates Inc.
PO Box 337
Marlboro, NJ 07746-0337
Ph:(732)972-1456
Fax: (732)972-0214
Co. E-mail: clientsvcs@s-wa.com
URL: http://www.swausa.com

E-mail: clientsvcs@s-wa.com
Scope: Firm assesses, plans and implements human resources aspects of mergers/acquisitions. Offers human resources consulting in compensation and benefit plan design, mergers and acquisitions (HR aspects), business ethics assessment and development, editing, writing and association management services, and contract professionals and interim executives. **Publications:** "Should Government or Business Try to Save Medicare?," HR News; "Executive Temping," HR Horizons; "When is an Employee Truly an Employee?," HR Magazine; "Examining Your Insurance Carrier," HR Magazine.

50336 ■ Stalley Associates Inc.
10635 James Cir. S
Minneapolis, MN 55431-4157
Ph:(952)888-0617
Fax: (952)888-5403
Co. E-mail: info@stalley.com
URL: http://www.stalley.com

E-mail: info@stalley.com
Scope: Advises management of companies in the areas of finance, administrative and general management, corporate objectives, policies and procedures, and management and organization audits. Firm has developed a particular expertise in advising management of young and growing companies. Advises in strategic planning, capital planning and financing strategies, securing private and public investment capital, establishing strategic alliances, management and staff organizational restructuring, working with board of directors, shareholders and serving as chief financial officer and chief operations officer on a contract basis.

50337 ■ Stockton Bates L.L.P.
42 S 15th St., Ste. 600
Philadelphia, PA 19102
Ph:(215)241-7500
Fax: (215)567-3813
URL: http://www.stocktonbates.com
Scope: Business consultants whose wide-ranging services include operational audits, mergers and acquisitions expertise, litigation support, and computer hardware and software consulting. Industries served: manufacturing, construction, services, banking, retail and wholesale, and government agencies.

50338 ■ Throne & Co.
49 N Main St.
Stewartstown, PA 17363-4030
Ph:(717)993-3201
Fax: (717)993-2627
Co. E-mail: jthrone@throneco.com

E-mail: jthrone@throneco.com
Scope: Business consultants, specializing in mergers and acquisitions with service specialization in leveraged buyouts, foreign investors, joint ventures, divestitures, marketing, and licensing. Consulting also in negotiations, evaluations and structuring. **Seminars:** How to maximize the value of your business and exit on your own terms. **Special Services:** Buyer Searches using various proprietary and commercial data bases.

50339 ■ Value Creation Group Inc.
7820 Scotia Dr., Ste. 2000
Dallas, TX 75248-3115
Ph:(972)980-7407
Fax: (972)980-4619
Co. E-mail: john.antos@valuecreationgroup.com
URL: http://www.valuecreationgroup.com

E-mail: john.antos@valuecreationgroup.com
Scope: General business experts offering predictive strategic planning, Activity-Based Costing (ABC), Activity-Based Management (ABM), mergers and acquisitions, outsourcing, re-engineering, process management, web-enabling technology, bench marking, installation of financial systems, executive search, training, teams, activity based budgeting, operational auditing, feature costing. Industries served: financial services, food, health-care, insurance, manufacturing, electronics, real estate, consumer products, nonprofit, telecommunication, oil, service, data processing, hotel and resort and government agencies. **Publications:** Handbook of process management based (predictive accounting), ALCPA 2002; Activity Based Management for Service Environments, Government Entities, & Nonprofit Organizations; Driving Value Using Activity Based Budgeting; Process Based Accounting leveraging Processes to Predict Results; Handbook of Supply Chain Management; Economic Value Management Applications and Techniques; The Change Handbook: Group Methods for Creating the Future. **Seminars:** Predictive Accounting; Performance measures; ABM for Manufacturing; ABM for Service Organizations; Finance and Accounting for Non-Financial Executives; Return on Investment/Capital Expenditure Evaluation; Planning and Cost Control; The Next Step Intermediate Finance and Accounting for Non-financial Managers; Activity-Based Budgeting; Friendly Finance for Fund Raisers; Strategic Outsourcing.

50340 ■ Mark Vanderstelt
9831 Gulfstream Ct.
Fishers, IN 46038
Ph:(317)576-9328
Fax: (317)576-9328
Scope: Consulting services include financial planning and analysis, inventory control, cash management, return on investment, budgeting, pricing, system design and analysis, mergers and acquisitions, feasibility studies, data processing, cost systems and controls, and performance measurement. Also performs operational and financial reviews.

50341 ■ Vencon Management Inc.
301 W 53rd St.
New York, NY 10019
Ph:(212)581-8787
Fax: (208)955-5165
Co. E-mail: vencon@worldnet.att.net
URL: http://www.venconinc.com

E-mail: vencon@worldnet.att.net
Scope: Venture capital firm and management consultants to corporations and entrepreneurs. Specializes in the areas of mergers and acquisitions evaluation and negotiation, and the preparation of marketing and business plans. Assists small or new businesses in expansion plans and financing. Also involved in new enterprise planning with industry and communities for rural economic analysis. Industries served: nanotechnology, photonics, optics, environment, semiconductor, electronics, chemicals, alternative energy, and health. **Seminars:** Holds venture capital forums.

50342 ■ Wabash Equity Group
5460 W 84th St.
Indianapolis, IN 46268-1523
Ph:(317)579-6698
Fax: (317)228-1142

Co. E-mail: jjaquajr@msn.com

E-mail: jjaquajr@msn.com
Scope: Business and financial consultants specializing in mergers and acquisitions for small companies and investments in small companies in central Indiana. Industries served: low tech manufacturing firms.

50343 ■ Wellbrock Inc.
27 Tall Timbers Rd.
Watchung, NJ 07069
Ph:(908)753-0590
Fax: (908)753-7197
Scope: Business consultant for small businesses regarding mergers, acquisitions, real estate, and venture capital.

50344 ■ White, Nelson & Company L.L.P.
2400 E Katella Ave., Ste. 900
Anaheim, CA 92806
Ph:(714)978-1300
Fax: (714)978-7893
Co. E-mail: info@whitenelson.com
URL: http://www.whitenelson.com

E-mail: info@whitenelson.com
Scope: Computer technologies and international tax consultants. Mergers and acquisitions consultants for manufacturing and distribution organizations. **Publications:** Financial Planning Guide; Small Business Guide.

50345 ■ Robert E. Wright Tax and Accounting
3533 Moncure Ave.
Falls Church, VA 22041-2017
Ph:(703)379-0592
Scope: Business consultants specializing in tax and accounting services, including preparation of business and personal tax returns, quarterly reports, amended returns and special forms (1040s, 1120s, 990s, 941s, 1040Xs, 1099s, etc.). Additional services include the setup and maintenance of bookkeeping systems and the preparation of financial statements, articles of incorporation, corporate minutes and resolutions, articles of partnership, employment agreements, contracts, leases, deeds, promissory notes, etc.; assistance with documentation and accounting services required for business licenses and permits, certificates of authority, and tax-exempt status.

RESEARCH CENTERS

50346 ■ Babson College–Arthur M. Blank Center for Entrepreneurship
Babson Park, MA 02459
Ph:(781)239-4420
Fax: (781)239-4178
Co. E-mail: jmckellar@babson.edu
URL: http://www.babson.edu/eship
Contact: Jim McKellar, Asst.Dir.

E-mail: jmckellar@babson.edu
Scope: Entrepreneurship and new and growing businesses, including studies in venture capital, starting and financing new value-creating ventures, family businesses, franchises, and harvesting enterprises through IPO's, merger or sale, and family succession. **Publications:** Babson Entreprenuerial Review; Frontiers of Entrepreneurship Research (annually). **Educational Activities:** Babson Entrepreneurship Research Conference (annually). **Awards:** Sponsors Global Academy of Distinguished Entrepreneuers, for outstanding entrepreneuership.

50347 ■ Drexel University–Center for Research in Technology and Strategy
Academic Bldg.
Management Department
3141 Chestnut
Philadelphia, PA 19104
Ph:(215)895-1797
Fax: (215)895-2891
Co. E-mail: weinerj@drexel.edu
Contact: Dr. Joan Weiner
E-mail: weinerj@drexel.edu
Scope: Interdisciplinary studies in technology and innovation, including mergers and acquisitions, productivity, corporate strategies, national security, and human resource management. **Educational Activities:** Doctoral program in strategic management.

ASSOCIATIONS AND OTHER ORGANIZATIONS

50348 ■ American Society for Public Administration
1301 Pennsylvania Ave. NW, Ste. 840
Washington, DC 20004
Ph:(202)393-7878
Fax: (202)638-4952
Co. E-mail: info@aspanet.org
URL: http://www.aspanet.org
Contact: Antoinette Samuel CAE, Exec.Dir.
Description: Promotes excellence in public service, including government, nonprofit and private sectors, and academic community. **Publications:** *PA Times* (monthly); *Public Administration Review* (bimonthly). National Conference Program book.

50349 ■ Institute of Public Administration - USA
411 Lafayette St., Ste. 303
New York, NY 10003-7032
Ph:(212)992-9898
Fax: (212)995-4876
Co. E-mail: info@theipa.org
Contact: David Mammen, Pres.
Description: Private research, educational, and consulting agency consisting of research staff, associates, and board of trustees. Conducts domestic and international research and education in public administration, public finance, citizenship and ethics, management, urban development and government organization and policy problems. Makes available consultation and technical services specializing in urban and metropolitan studies, governmental management, charter and code revision and reorganization, personnel and training for governmental service, public enterprise, financing and organization, urban transportation, contracting, ethics, and private-public sector cooperation in the United States and abroad. **Publications:** Reports (periodic). **Telecommunication Services:** phone referral service, (212)730-5480.

50350 ■ National Academy of Public Administration
1100 New York Ave. NW, Ste. 1090E
Washington, DC 20005-3934
Ph:(202)347-3190
Fax: (202)393-0993
Co. E-mail: academy@napawash.org
URL: http://www.napawash.org
Contact: William Shields, VP for Administration
Description: Works to respond to specific requests from public agencies and non-governmental organizations. Promotes discourse on emerging trends in governance through standing panels and external funding. Assists federal agencies, congressional committees, state and local governments, civic organizations, and institutions overseas through problem solving, objective research, rigorous analysis, information sharing, development strategies for change, and connecting people and ideas. Promotes forward-looking ideas and of analyzing successes and failures

of government reform. **Publications:** Annual Report (annual); Papers (periodic). Also publishes study results in panel reports.

50351 ■ National Forum for Black Public Administrators
777 N Capitol St. NE, Ste. 807
Washington, DC 20002
Ph:(202)408-9300
Free: 888-766-9951
Fax: (202)408-8558
Co. E-mail: jsaunders@nfbpa.org
URL: http://www.nfbpa.org
Contact: John E. Saunders III, Exec. Dir.
Description: Black city and county managers and assistant managers; chief administrative officers; agency directors; bureau and division heads; corporate executives; students. Works to promote, strengthen, and expand the role of blacks in public administration. Seeks to focus the influence of black administrators toward building and maintaining viable communities. Develops specialized training programs for managers and executives. Provides national public administrative leadership resource and skills bank. Works to further communication among black public, private, and academic institutions. Addresses issues that affect the administrative capacity of black managers. **Publications:** *The Forum* (quarterly); *Resource Guide* (annual); Membership Directory (semiannual).

50352 ■ Section for Women in Public Administration
1120 G St. NW, Ste. 700
Washington, DC 20005-3885
Ph:(202)393-7878
Fax: (202)638-4952
Co. E-mail: jhutch@vcu.edu
URL: http://carbon.cudenver.edu/public/gspa/swpa
Contact: Janet Hutchinson, Managing Ed.
Description: Established by the American Society for Public Administration to initiate action programs appropriate to the needs and concerns of women in public administration. Promotes equal educational and employment opportunities for women in public service, and full participation and recognition of women in all areas of government. Develops strategies for implementation of ASPA policies of interest to women in public administration; recommends qualified women to elective and appointive ASPA governmental leadership positions; acts as forum for communication among professional and laypeople interested in the professional development of women in public administration. **Publications:** *Bridging the Gap* (semiannual); Membership Directory (periodic).

50353 ■ Southern Public Administration Education Foundation
2103 Fairway Ln.
Harrisburg, PA 17112
Ph:(717)540-5477
Fax: (215)893-1763
Co. E-mail: spaef@spaef.com
URL: http://spaef.com
Contact: Dr. Jack Rabin, Pres.
Description: Represents researchers and scholars. Produces publications to educate scholars and practi-

tioners. Publishes electronic journals. **Publications:** *Journal of Health and Human Resources Administration* (quarterly); *Public Administration Quarterly* (quarterly).

REFERENCE WORKS

50354 ■ "Detroit Public Schools Pick IT Firms" in *Crain's Detroit Business* **(Vol. 22, December 18, 2006, No. 51, pp. 18)**
Pub: Crain Communications Inc. - Detroit
Ed: Tom Henderson. **Description:** Vision IT was retained by the City of Detroit for a five year contract at $9.8M per year. Vision IT was one of five minority owned firms picked to share five year, $58M contracts previously held by Comcast and Strategic Staffing. Three of the contracts were rescinded after a protest over the bidding process and results was filed by the previous contractors.

50355 ■ "A New View of Downtown. Perceptions Improve; Concerns Remain" in *Business Journal-Milwaukee* **(Vol. 20, No. 51, September 5, 2003)**
Pub: American City Business Journals, Inc.
Ed: Pete Millard. **Description:** Monica Dignam, president of Monalco Inc., stated recently that because of efforts to improve the image of Milwaukee, Wisconsin, people are more willing to visit, shop and live in the city.

50356 ■ "Share the Health: When Encouraging Healthy Living, You've Got to Walk the Walk" in *Entrepreneur* **(Vol. 33, January 2005, No. 1)**
Pub: Entrepreneur Media Inc.
Ed: Kimberly Olson. **Description:** Small companies are promoting healthy lifestyles by offering lunchtime walks, nutrition seminars, and subscriptions to health information Websites. They could also offer prizes for participation.

50357 ■ "Smart Businesses See Value, and Profit, in Promoting Women" in *Crain's Chicago Business* **(Vol. 30, February 2007, No. 6, pp. 30)**
Pub: Crain Communications, Inc.
Ed: Marc J. Lane. **Description:** Despite U.S. corporations making little progress in advancing women to leadership positions over the past ten years, enlightened corporate decision makers understand that gender diversity is good business as the highest percentages of women officers yielded, on average, a 34 percent higher total return to shareholders and a 35.1 percent higher return on equity than those firms with the lowest percentages of women officers, according to a 2004 Catalyst study of Fortune 500 companies.

TRADE PERIODICALS

50358 ■ American City and County
Pub: Primedia Business
Contact: Bill Wolpin, Editorial Director
E-mail: bwolpin@primediabusiness.com
Released: Monthly. **Price:** $67. **Description:** Municipal and county administration magazine.

50359 ■ American Review of Public Administration
Pub: Sage Publications Inc.
Ed: Guy B. Adams, Editor, adams@missouri.edu. **Released:** Quarterly. **Price:** $84; $434 institutions. **Description:** Academic journal covering public administration.

50360 ■ Canadian Public Administration (Administration publique du Canada)
Pub: Institute of Public Administration of Canada
Ed: Prof. Barbara Wake Carroll, Editor. **Released:** Quarterly. **Price:** $125 institutions; $140 other countries USA institutions; $140 USA individuals; $140 institutions, other countries; $32 single issue; $35 other countries. **Description:** Journal printing refereed articles by administrative practitioners and academics for university teachers and public servants in federal, provincial, and municipal government (English and French).

50361 ■ CQ Monitor
Pub: Congressional Quarterly
Contact: David Hawkings, Managing Editor
Released: Daily. **Price:** $1,549, U.S. **Description:** Reports on current legislative news and information of the U.S. Congress. Recurring features include columns titled The Pulse of Congress, People on the Move, Laws Enacted, Meetings, Today, and Future Listings.

50362 ■ Demokratizatsiya
Pub: Heldref Publications
Contact: Vladimir Brovkin, Exec. Ed.
E-mail: brovkinv@yahoo.com
Released: Quarterly. **Price:** $119 plus postage charges for outside U.S.; $52 institutions plus postage charges for outside U.S. **Description:** Journal covering past and current political, economical, social, and legal changes and developments in the Soviet Union and its successor states.

50363 ■ Governing Magazine
Pub: Times Publishing Co.
Contact: Peter Harkness, Ed. & Pub.
E-mail: pharkness@governing.com
Released: Monthly, Web Offset. **Price:** $19.95 special introductory rate 1yr.; $59.95 foreign. **Description:** Magazine serving the public sector of federal, state and local government.

50364 ■ Illinois Issues
Pub: University of Illinois
Released: Monthly. **Price:** $39.95. **Description:** Magazine focusing on public affairs and state and local government.

50365 ■ Journal of Policy Analysis and Management
Pub: John Wiley & Sons Inc.
Ed: Maureen Pirog, Editor, jpam@indiana.edu. **Released:** 4/year. **Price:** $365; $365 Canada and Mexico In Canada, add 7% GST; $389 other countries; $830 institutions print & online; $870 institutions, Canada and Mexico print only, in Canada, add 7% GST; $904 institutions, other countries print only; $913 institutions print & online; $953 institutions, Canada and Mexico print & online, in Canada, add 7% GST; $987 institutions, other countries print & online. **Description:** Journal publishing articles on issues in public policy and public management.

50366 ■ Missouri Municipal Review
Pub: Missouri Municipal League
Ed: Katie Bradley, Editor. **Released:** Monthly, (Feb/March and Oct/Nov issues combined). **Description:** Magazine for local officials actively engaged in the procurement of products and services, policy-making, and local government administration.

50367 ■ Municipal Leader
Pub: Association of Manitoba Municipalities
Contact: Terry Ross
Released: Quarterly. **Description:** Magazine covering news affecting the administration of municipalities in Manitoba, Canada. Includes calendar of events, policy updates and municipal profiles.

50368 ■ Municipal World
Pub: Municipal World Inc.
Contact: Susan Gardner, Advertising Dir
E-mail: sgardner@municipalworld.com
Released: Monthly. **Price:** $55 plus GST; $99 two years plus GST / HST; $80 international cdn. per year; $140 3 years plus GST / HST. **Description:** Magazine published monthly in the interest of good local government, covering municipal law, planning, techonology, economic development and administration.

50369 ■ PA Times
Pub: American Society for Public Administration
Contact: Patricia Yearwood, Sen. Dir. for Member Svcs.
Released: Monthly. **Price:** $50 first class mail; $75 out of country. **Description:** Public administration newspaper (tabloid).

50370 ■ Public Administration Review
Pub: American Society for Public Administration
Contact: Larry D. Terry, Editor-in-Chief
E-mail: par@utdallas.edu
Released: Bimonthly. **Price:** $90; $130 foreign. **Description:** Public administration journal.

50371 ■ Public Affairs Report
Pub: Institute of Governmental Studies
Ed: Gerald C. Lubenow, Editor. **Released:** Bimonthly, 6/year. **Price:** Free. **Description:** Publishes essays on emerging governmental and public policy issues of significance to public officials and citizens in both California and the nation. Covers such subjects as pollution, politics, finance, transportation, health and housing policy, and California-Mexico trade relations. Recurring features include bibliographies.

50372 ■ Public Management (PM)
Pub: International City/County Management Association
Ed: Beth Payne, Editor. **Released:** Monthly. **Price:** $36 domestic, one year; $52 other countries. **Description:** Magazine for local government administrators.

50373 ■ Sage Public Administration Abstracts
Pub: Sage Publications Inc.
Released: Quarterly. **Price:** $863.04 institutions print only; $209 print only; $237 single issue institutions; $68 single issue. **Description:** Journal containing abstracts on public administration.

50374 ■ Tennessee Town & City
Pub: Tennessee Municipal League
Contact: Margaret Mahery, Exec. Dir.
E-mail: mmahery@tml1.org
Ed: Gael Stahl, Editor, gstahl@tml1.org. **Released:** Semimonthly. **Price:** $6 members; $15 nonmembers; $1 single issue. **Description:** Newspaper on politics and public management.

TRADE SHOWS AND CONVENTIONS

50375 ■ Maryland Municipal League Convention
Maryland Municipal League
1212 W St.
Annapolis, MD 21401
Ph:(410)268-5514
Free: 800-492-7121
Fax: (410)268-7004
Co. E-mail: mml@mdmunicipal.org
URL: http://www.mdmunicipal.org
Released: Annual. **Audience:** Municipal officials and other county and state officials. **Principal Exhibits:** Office equipment, public works equipment, insurance companies, consulting firms, recreation equipment, computers, engineering firms, police equipment, and code publishers. **Dates and Locations:** 2007 Jun.

50376 ■ NCSL - National Conference of State Legislatures Annual Meeting and Exhibition
National Conference of State Legislatures
7700 E 1st Pl.
Denver, CO 80230
Ph:(303)364-7700
Fax: (303)364-7800
Co. E-mail: info@ncsl.org
URL: http://www.ncsl.org
Released: Annual. **Audience:** Key legislators, senior staff, state and federal agency personnel, government relations managers, and business and associations executives. **Principal Exhibits:** Products and technology that have impact on the states. **Dates and Locations:** 2007 Aug 05-09, Boston, MA; 2008 Jul 22-26, New Orleans, LA.

50377 ■ New Jersey League of Municipalities
New Jersey League of Municipalities
407 W State St.
Trenton, NJ 08618
Ph:(609)695-3481
Fax: (609)695-0151
Co. E-mail: league@njslom.com
URL: http://www.njslom.com
Released: Annual. **Audience:** Municipal officials. **Principal Exhibits:** Municipal products and services.

CONSULTANTS

50378 ■ Institute of Public Administration
411 Lafayette St., Ste. 303
New York, NY 10003
Ph:(212)992-9899
Free: 800-258-1102
Fax: (212)995-4876
Co. E-mail: info@theipa.org
URL: http://www.theipa.org

E-mail: info@theipa.org
Scope: A private nonprofit consulting, research and education organization experienced in management of governments and public enterprises. Firm's activities are directed toward the solution of emerging problems of government, organization, financial management and policies, and public enterprises in the United States and abroad. Emphasizes innovation, demonstration of new techniques, and communication among governments and between the public and private sectors. Programs are financed chiefly by contracts with local, state and federal governments, international aid agencies and foreign governments, public enterprises, and by foundation grants. Areas of concentration include personnel administration, structures and resources of local legislative bodies, training, structure and financing of public enterprises, public finance, financial management and anticorruption systems, urban and regional planning, organization and management, city/county charter revision, urban transportation, public sector ethics and citizenship, and management of government procurement systems. **Seminars:** Offers a range of seminars and training workshops tailored to the needs of participants.

50379 ■ National Center for Public Policy Research
501 Capitol Ct. NE
Washington, DC 20002
Ph:(202)543-4110
Fax: (202)543-5975
Co. E-mail: info@nationalcenter.org
URL: http://www.nationalcenter.org

E-mail: info@nationalcenter.org
Scope: Nonprofit organization offers advice and information on international affairs and United States domestic affairs. Sponsors Project 21. Has a special emphasis an environmental and regulatory issues and civil rights issues. **Publications:** National Policy Analysis; Legal Briefs; White Paper, National Policy Analysis 523.

50380 ■ North Carolina Fair Share
530 N Person St.
PO Box 12543
Raleigh, NC 27605

Ph:(919)832-7130
Fax: (919)832-4635
Co. E-mail: ncfslrw@aol.com

E-mail: ncfslrw@aol.com
Scope: Social services firm consults on community organizing and lobbying for health issues.

50381 ■ Practice Development Counsel
60 Sutton Pl. S
New York, NY 10022
Ph:(212)593-1549
Fax: (212)980-7940
Co. E-mail: pwhaserot@pdcounsel.com
URL: http://www.pdcounsel.com

E-mail: pwhaserot@pdcounsel.com
Scope: Specializes in business development, service quality, retention, organizational development work/ life excellence, and conflict resolution for professional firms. Provides coaching, client relationship management and quality service programs; strategic marketing planning/implementation; ancillary businesses/ diversification; market research, trend watching, benchmarking; facilitation and planning for retreats and creative decision making; new business proposals and presentations; marketing communications and public relations; and business development training, coaching, and materials. Also offers speaker's services - engagements, publicity, etc. Industries served: law, accounting, and financial services, executive search, design, architecture, real estate, and management consultants worldwide. **Publications:** "The Rainmaking Machine: Marketing Planning, Strategy and Management For Law Firms"; "The Marketer's Handbook of Tips & Checklists"; "Venturesome Questions: The Law Firms Guide to Developing a New Business Venture". **Seminars:** Managing Work Expectations; Effective Coaching Skills; Service Quality; End-Running the Resistance Professionals Have to Getting Client Input; Ancillary Business Activities; Marketing for Professional Firms; Marketing Ethics; Business Development Training; Trends in Professional Services Marketing; Client Relationship Management; Collaborative Culture; Reaching Consensus; Conflict Resolution; Worklife Balance; Generaltional Issues; Preparing New Partners; Becoming the Employer of Choice; A Marketing Approach to Recruiting; Implementing Workplace Flexibility; The Business Case for Flexible Work Arrangements. **Special Services:** The Flexible Firm™; AuthenticWorks™; Coach-for-the-Coach™.

50382 ■ Praxis Media Inc.
48 Harbourview Ave.
South Norwalk, CT 06854-4822
Ph:(203)866-6666
Fax: (203)853-8299
Co. E-mail: aldo@praxismediainc.com

E-mail: aldo@praxismediainc.com
Scope: Media needs analysis and project planning specialists provide services in product introductions, communications planning, technology application, promotion and marketing communications. Also assists with focus groups, research, concept development, creative development, scripting and executive speech coaching/training. Industries served: financial services, high-tech, travel and leisure, health and pharmaceutical and telecommunications.

50383 ■ Public Administration Service
7927 Jones Branch Dr., Ste. 100 S
McLean, VA 22102-3322
Ph:(703)734-8970
Fax: (703)734-4965
Co. E-mail: postmaster@pashq.org
URL: http://www.pashq.org

E-mail: postmaster@pashq.org
Scope: Performs a variety of consulting and research work in serving the special needs of governments and other public service institutions. Services range from technical studies of central management problems to analyses of public policy issues, and in development administration water sewerage management and sys-

tems, rural development, and small farmer organization privatization, and management. Devoted exclusively to improving the conduct of public activities. Consulting services in the United States include organization and management, data processing and automation plans, position classification and compensation plans, police and fire service studies, public works and utilities studies, and parks management studies.

50384 ■ Public Policy Communications
4163 Dingman Dr.
Sanibel, FL 33957
Ph:(941)395-6773
Fax: (941)395-6779
Scope: Provides strategic communications for progressive causes, candidates, and socially-responsible businesses. These include public relations strategies, political campaign planning, organizational development, and training. Substantial work in report writing, editing and design as well as production of a full range of media materials. Industries served: nonprofit, social change organizations, foundations, political campaigns, environmentally and consumer-oriented businesses, and government agencies. **Publications:** "Winning Local and State Elections," Free Press Mac-Millan; "Giving the Media Your Message, and The News Media and the Big Lie". **Seminars:** Giving the Media Your Message; Effective Public Relations Practices; Winning Your Election; Understanding the Government Budget Process; How to Be an Effective Advocate; Strategic Planning for Non-Profits.

50385 ■ Public Sector Consultants Inc.
600 W St. Joseph St., Ste. 10
Lansing, MI 48933-2267
Ph:(517)484-4954
Fax: (517)484-6549
Co. E-mail: psc@pscinc.com
URL: http://www.pscinc.com

E-mail: psc@pscinc.com
Scope: Offers policy research expertise, specializing in opinion polling, public relations, conference planning, and legislative and economic analysis. Industries served: associations, education, environment, health-care, and public finance in Michigan.

50386 ■ Reed Royalty Public Affairs Inc.
30205 Hillside Ter.
San Juan Capistrano, CA 92675-1542
Ph:(949)240-2022
Fax: (949)240-0304
Scope: A governmental relations consultant who provides lobbying for changes in laws and government regulations, helps in obtaining licenses and permits, provides corporate training in governmental relations and assistance in winning government contracts. Services includ crisis management, business association management and issue-specific community and media relations.

RESEARCH CENTERS

50387 ■ Boston College–Center on Wealth and Philanthropy
McGuinn Hall 515
140 Commonwealth Ave.
Chestnut Hill, MA 02467
Ph:(617)552-4070
Fax: (617)552-3903
Co. E-mail: paul.schervish@bc.edu
URL: http://www.bc.edu/research/swri
Contact: Prof. Paul G. Schervish PhD, Dir.
E-mail: paul.schervish@bc.edu
Scope: Spirituality, wealth, philanthropy and other aspects of cultural life in an age of affluence. Projects explore the association among philanthropy, income, and wealth; the organizational and moral determinants of giving and volunteering; and the implications for fundraising and philanthropy. **Services:** Consulting. **Publications:** Research reports. **Educational Activities:** Presentations; Research seminars.

50388 ■ California State University, Long Beach–Graduate Center for Public Policy and Administration
ET-235
College of Health & Human Services
1250 Bellflower Blvd.
Long Beach, CA 90840-4602
Ph:(562)985-4178
Fax: (562)985-4672
Co. E-mail: mdede@csulb.edu
URL: http://www.csulb.edu/~beachmpa
Contact: Martha Deed, Dir.
E-mail: mdede@csulb.edu
Scope: Public policy and administrative problems, including transportation, port development, fiscal controls, contracting for services, management, organizational behavior, and productivity. Collects, compiles, and analyzes municipal data. Seeks to develop increased competency and perspective of administrative process of government. **Educational Activities:** Graduate education program, in public policy and administration; Graduate certificate programs, in public management analysis, public sector financial management, employer-employee relations and personnel management, transportation policy and planning, and urban executive management.

50389 ■ California State University, Long Beach–Graduate Center for Public Policy and Administration–Bureau of Governmental Research and Services
1250 Bellflower Blvd.
Long Beach, CA 90840
Ph:(562)985-4194
Fax: (562)985-4672
Co. E-mail: govserv@csulb.edu
URL: http://www.csulb.edu/~govserv/index.htm
Contact: Martha J. DeDe PhD, Dir.
E-mail: govserv@csulb.edu
Scope: Assists faculty members in the development of research grant proposals and in the financial management of grants received for investigations in urban government, public transportation policy, public personnel management, financial management, and general management skills. **Services:** Research services, for local public policy and administration community. **Educational Activities:** Professional and career training institutes; Public service workshops; Training in research models, for graduate students.

50390 ■ Carleton University–Carleton Research Unit on Innovation, Science, and Environment
Dunton Tower, Rm. 1005
School of Public Policy & Administration
1125 Colonel By Dr.
Ottawa, ON, Canada K1S 5B6
Ph:(613)520-2547
Fax: (613)520-2551
Co. E-mail: bruce_doern@carleton.ca
URL: http://www.carleton.ca/spa/Research/cruise.htm
Contact: Bruce Doern, Dir.
E-mail: bruce_doern@carleton.ca
Scope: Program evaluation and scientific and technical activities; science and technical indicators, technology diffusion and standards; local level industrial agglomeration or "clustering"; energy/environment policies; and information technologies. **Services:** Consulting. **Publications:** Journal (annually). **Educational Activities:** Conference (annually).

50391 ■ Carleton University–Centre for Policy and Program Assessment
School of Public Policy & Administration
1125 Colonel By Dr.
Ottawa, ON, Canada K1S 5B6
Ph:(613)520-2547
Fax: (613)520-2551
Co. E-mail: susan_phillips@carleton.ca
URL: http://www.carleton.ca/sppa
Contact: Dr. Susan Phillips, Dir.
E-mail: susan_phillips@carleton.ca
Scope: Canadian and provincial government policies, urban policy, economic policy, and law. **Publications:** How Ottawa Spends. **Educational Activities:** Conferences, short courses.

50392 ■ Citizens Budget Commission
11 Penn Plz., Ste. 640
New York, NY 10119
Ph:(212)279-2605
Fax: (212)868-4745
Co. E-mail: dfortuna@cbcny.org
URL: http://www.cbcny.org
Contact: Diana Fortuna, Pres.
E-mail: dfortuna@cbcny.org
Scope: Management of New York City and New York State's fiscal affairs and service delivery. Specific studies include reviews of city and state expense budgets, tax policy, public services, capital budget, and state-city financial relationships. **Publications:** Research Reports. **Awards:** Award for High Civic Service to New York (annually); Prize for Public Service Innovation (annually).

50393 ■ Citizens League Research Institute
1331 Euclid Ave.
Cleveland, OH 44113
Ph:(216)241-5340
Fax: (216)736-7626
Co. E-mail: staff@citizensleague.org
URL: http://www.citizensleague.org
Contact: Michael J. Thomas, Exec.Dir.
E-mail: staff@citizensleague.org
Scope: Local government structure, performance, and financing focusing on the Greater Cleveland (7-county) region. Cooperates with public officials and civic organizations on improvement of local governmental procedures in order to obtain greater economy and efficiency in administration of public affairs. **Publications:** Special Reports (semiannually). **Educational Activities:** Citizen study committee meetings and breakfast forums (periodically). **Awards:** Civic Service Award (annually); Rawson Public Service Internship.

50394 ■ Claremont McKenna College–Reed Institute for Applied Statistics
Bauer N 320
500 E 9th St.
Claremont, CA 91711
Ph:(909)621-8876
Co. E-mail: janet.myhre@claremontmckenna.edu
URL: http://reed.claremontmckenna.edu
Contact: Dr. Janet M. Myhre, Dir.
E-mail: janet.myhre@claremontmckenna.edu
Scope: Public and private management decisions, including model building and forecasting research. Involves mathematics and economics students in the research program. **Educational Activities:** Seminars and math clinics; Conferences.

50395 ■ Cleveland State University–Research and Public Service Initiative
Maxine Goodman Levin College of Urban Affairs
2121 Euclid Ave., UR 364
Cleveland, OH 44115
Ph:(216)687-2134
Fax: (216)687-9277
Co. E-mail: ziona@urban.csuohio.edu
Contact: Ziona Austrian PhD, Dir.
E-mail: ziona@urban.csuohio.edu
Scope: Urban policy, including neighborhood development and housing, economic development, public finance, public works management, sacred landmarks, and leadership development. Programs focus on applied research, training, technical assistance, and database development. Coordinates the Northeast Ohio Research Consortium. Part of the Ohio Urban University Program. **Services:** Community service projects; Data and policy analysis; Database development; Technical assistance and training. **Publications:** Data Reports; Policy Reports; Refereed journals; Research Reports. **Educational Activities:** Conferences (periodically), on issues of local, state, federal, and international importance; Neighborhood Leadership Cleveland.

50396 ■ Cornell University–Department of City Regional Planning–Program in International Studies in Planning
106 W Sibley Hall
Ithaca, NY 14853-3901
Ph:(607)255-4331
Fax: (607)255-1971
Co. E-mail: lb21@cornell.edu
URL: http://www.dcrp.cornell.edu/programs/isp.mgi
Contact: Prof. Lourdes Beneria, Dir.
E-mail: lb21@cornell.edu
Scope: Analysis of the regional and spatial dimensions of development issues with a focus—although by no means exclusive—on the Third World, including political economy of regional and national development; planning and the global economy; critical development theory; project planning and administration; political ecology and international environmental planning; community economic development; gender and development; infrastructure; and NGOs and social movements. Areas of research include Latin America, Caribbean, Africa, Europe, and Southeast Asia. **Educational Activities:** Annual one-semester lecture series; Courses abroad; Seminars; Seminars, held Fridays with visiting lecturers in the spring; Student travel grants.

50397 ■ Council on Foreign Relations
The Harold Pratt House
58 E 68th St.
New York, NY 10021
Ph:(212)434-9400
Fax: (212)434-9800
Co. E-mail: dkellogg@cfr.org
URL: http://www.cfr.org/
Contact: David Kellogg, Sr.VP
E-mail: dkellogg@cfr.org
Scope: Long-range foreign policy problems, including area, political, economic, and strategic studies. Administers International Affairs, Military, State Department, and Murrow press fellowship programs. **Publications:** Annual Report; Foreign Affairs (bimonthly). **Educational Activities:** Seminars.

50398 ■ Florida State University–Florida Center for Public Management
102 Herb Morgan Bldg.
2035 E Paul Dirac Dr.
Tallahassee, FL 32306-2821
Ph:(850)644-6460
Fax: (850)644-0152
Co. E-mail: sbaldwin@admin.fsu.edu
URL: http://www.fcpm.fsu.edu
Contact: Shawn Baldwin, Dir.
E-mail: sbaldwin@admin.fsu.edu
Scope: Studies state, county, and city government management, planning, and budgeting. **Services:** Conference planning. **Educational Activities:** Florida Certified Public Manager Program; Florida Government Technology Conference; Management consulting and training.

50399 ■ George Washington University–Center for International Science and Technology Policy
1957 E St. NW, Ste. 403
Washington, DC 20052
Ph:(202)994-7292
Fax: (202)994-1639
Co. E-mail: vonortas@gwu.edu
URL: http://www.gwu.edu/~cistp
Contact: Dr. Nicholas S. Vonortas, Dir.
E-mail: vonortas@gwu.edu
Scope: Interdisciplinary research and policy analysis. Program includes such disciplines as public administration, political science, economics, international affairs, and environmental resources for application to science and technology policy, international science policy, technology transfer, research and development policy, risk analysis and management, regulatory process, institutional analysis, public perception assessment, space policy, environmental quality, economics of technology, networks and information and telecommunications policy. **Educational Activities:** Seminar series, in science and technology policy; Symposia.

50400 ■ Harvard University–A. Alfred Taubman Center for State and Local Government
John F. Kennedy School of Government
79 John F. Kennedy St.
Cambridge, MA 02138
Ph:(617)495-2199
Fax: (617)496-1722
Co. E-mail: eglaeser@harvard.edu
URL: http://www.ksg.harvard.edu/taubmancenter/
Contact: Edward L. Glaeser, Dir.
E-mail: eglaeser@harvard.edu
Scope: Politics, public management, and public finance in state and local government, land use policy, transportation, community development and growth management, strategic uses of new technology, education, and governance. **Publications:** Annual Report. **Educational Activities:** Forums and conferences (periodically).

50401 ■ Institute of Public Administration
411 Lafayette St., Ste. 303
New York, NY 10003-7032
Ph:(212)992-9898
Fax: (212)995-4876
Co. E-mail: info@theipa.org
URL: http://www.theipa.org
Contact: David Mammen, Pres.
E-mail: info@theipa.org
Scope: Governmental policy and management problems, especially with respect to governmental management, financial management, budgeting, accounting, policy analysis, ethics in government, regional planning, public finance, public-private sector relations, and problems arising out of urbanization, both in the United States and abroad, including studies on local government transition and reorganization, legislative organization, civil service reform, modernizing human resource management, contract and procurement management, public authorities, public enterprises, charter and administrative code revision, urban government decision making and policy directions, revision of legislative codes, and city/county reorganization and consolidation studies. **Services:** Local and overseas training, for civil service personnel and public managers; Short- and long-term consultation services; Technical assistance, for national and international governments, and national and local government reorgainzation and improvement, financial management, anti-corruption, tax administration, and reform. **Educational Activities:** Seminars, at home and abroad; Workshops.

50402 ■ Institute for Tax Administration
900 Wilshire Blvd., Ste. 624
Los Angeles, CA 90017-4707
Ph:(213)623-1103
Fax: (818)842-3930
Contact: James B. Horn, Dir.
Scope: Tax administration for developing countries and state and local governmental agencies in the U.S., especially those which want to improve effectiveness of their organizations, systems, and methods and to increase their public revenues. Conducts studies on tax models; techniques for measuring compliance levels by tax, by industry, by occupation, and by size; techniques for estimating effect on revenue collections; means of determining administrative cost versus tax yield in various tax areas as a guide to planning; and tax burden on economic and geographic segments of the population. **Services:** Consulting services; Tax education programs, for the public; Technical assistance. **Educational Activities:** Seminars, in Spanish, Chinese, Korean, and Japanese (nationally and internationally); Seminars, in Spanish, Chinese, Korean; Short summer tax courses, in customs, sales, income, ans excise, property, and value-added tax, and tax fraud administration; Three month customs course and tax administration course (semiannually), at the Academy; Trains key staff members, in mechanisms and techniques of modern tax administration.

50403 ■ Massachusetts Administration and Finance Executive Office–Human Resources Division–Research/Survey Office
1 Ashburton Pl., Rm. 301
Boston, MA 02108-1515
Ph:(617)727-3555
Co. E-mail: ffahey@hrd.state.ma.us
Contact: Fran Fahey, Dir., Policy
E-mail: ffahey@hrd.state.ma.us
Scope: Human resources.

50404 ■ Murray State University–Bureau of Business and Economic Research
307 Business Bldg.
College of Business & Public Affairs
Murray, KY 42071
Ph:(270)809-4433
Fax: (270)809-3788
Co. E-mail: david.shideler@murraystate.edu
URL: http://www.murraystate.edu/qacd/cbpa/bber
Contact: David Shideler, Dir.
E-mail: david.shideler@murraystate.edu
Scope: Business development, economic planning, economic impact analysis, socio-economic issues for Western Kentucky and neighboring states. **Publications:** State of the Economy in Western Kentucky (semiannually); Business and Public Affairs Journal (periodically); Research reports; Western Kentucky Quarterly Economic Report (quarterly). **Educational Activities:** Seminars (semiannually), for local civic and educational organizations.

50405 ■ Ohio University–Institute for Local Government Administration and Rural Development
The Ridges Bldg., 22
Athens, OH 45701
Ph:(740)593-4388
Fax: (740)593-4398
Co. E-mail: info@ilgard.ohiou.edu
URL: http://www.ilgard.ohiou.edu
Contact: Mark L. Weinberg, Dir.
E-mail: info@ilgard.ohiou.edu
Scope: Provides state and local officials in Ohio (with primary focus in Southeast Ohio) with research and technical assistance in economic development, public policy and administration, and survey research and geographic information systems, including aid in linking local and regional officials with state and national resource persons. **Services:** Provides expertise, in geographic information systems and computer mapping; Rural microwave network, for state and local officials. **Publications:** Educational Access; Employment and Business Opportunities for Low Income Populations in SE Ohio; Environmental Risk; WK Kellogg Training Manuals. **Educational Activities:** Policy forums; Training programs, for local government; Workshops, on computer applications, dispute resolution, environmental bargaining, and financial management.

50406 ■ Oklahoma State University–Center for Local Government Technology
200 Cordell N
Stillwater, OK 74078-8088
Ph:(405)744-6049
Fax: (405)744-7268
Co. E-mail: michael.hughes@okstate.edu
URL: http://clgt.okstate.edu/
Contact: Dr. Michael Hughes, Dir.
E-mail: michael.hughes@okstate.edu
Scope: Provides technical assistance and educational programs at state, county, and municipal government levels relating to engineering, management technology, and accounting, including county officer training, computer applications in small city and county government, vehicle fleet management, tax procedures, productivity in local government, and street, road, and bridge maintenance. **Publications:** Manuals; Newsletters (quarterly); Project Journals; Technical Fact Sheets; Workbooks. **Educational Activities:** Certification program, for county assissors and deputies; Seminars; Workshops.

50407 ■ Public/Private Ventures
2000 Market St., Ste. 600
Philadelphia, PA 19103
Ph:(215)557-4400
Fax: (215)557-4469
Co. E-mail: publications@ppv.org
URL: http://www.ppv.org
Contact: Gary Walker, Pres. Emeritus
E-mail: publications@ppv.org
Scope: Youth (after-school programs, mentoring, high-risk networks, job training, sectoral employment and other workforce development efforts), community and faith-based initiatives, prison re-entry, literacy,
program replication and expansion. **Services:** Faith-Based Intiative; Provides technical assistance, to businesses, states, cities, and organizations; Three national demonstration projects, Community Change for Youth Development, Faith-Based Initiatives, and Workforce Development. **Publications:** Annual report; Newsletter; Policy briefs; Reports. **Educational Activities:** Conferences; Workshops (periodically).

50408 ■ Queen's University at Kingston–Institute of Intergovernmental Relations
Rm. 301
School of Policy Studies
Queen's University
Kingston, ON, Canada K7L 3N6
Ph:(613)533-2080
Fax: (613)533-6868
Co. E-mail: iigr@iigr.ca
URL: http://www.iigr.ca
Contact: Sean Conway, Dir.
E-mail: iigr@iigr.ca
Scope: Political, financial, and administrative intergovernmental relations and policymaking in federal systems, with particular emphasis on Canada, including self-generated projects and contract research. Specific research themes and projects include an examination of the Canadian federation, constitutional reform, the relationship between Quebec and its Confederation partners, the relationship between the structure of the Canadian federal system and the design and implementation of public policy (especially in the economic sphere), impact of the global economy on Canadian federalism, federalism and political theory, the structure of central institutions, the conduct of intergovernmental relations, and fiscal federalism and federal-provincial financial relations. **Publications:** Annual Reports; Bibliographies on Federalism; Canada: The State of the Federation (annually); Monographs; Reflections Series; Research Paper Series. **Educational Activities:** Institute's Advisory Council; Kenneth R. MacGregor Lectureship in Intergovernmental Relations; Seminars, on regionalism, economic policy, fiscal relations, interest groups, and other topics pertinent to Canadian federalism.

50409 ■ Rutgers University–National Center for Public Productivity
Hill Hall 701
360 King Blvd.
Newark, NJ 07102
Ph:(973)353-5093
Fax: (973)353-5907
Co. E-mail: mholzen@pipeline.com
URL: http://newark.rutgers.edu/~ncpp/ncpp.html
Contact: Dr. Marc Holzer, Exec.Dir.
E-mail: mholzen@pipeline.com
Scope: Applications of productivity improvement concepts and theoretical research in all functional areas focusing on productivity measurement, productivity dissemination, curriculum development, and labor-management relations. Seeks to improve productivity in the public sector. **Services:** Technical training and assistance. **Publications:** Newsletter (quarterly); Public Productivity and Management Review (quarterly).

50410 ■ Tennessee State University–Institute of Government
CB 140
330 10th Ave. N
Nashville, TN 37203
Ph:(615)963-7241
Fax: (615)963-7245
Co. E-mail: arizzo@tnstate.edu
URL: http://www.tnstate.edu/IOG/instgov.html
Contact: Dr. Ann-Marie Rizzo, Dir.
E-mail: arizzo@tnstate.edu
Scope: Public administration and public services. **Services:** Training and consultation programs for government and nonprofit organizations. **Publications:** The Public Servant (3/year).

50411 ■ University of California at Berkeley–Institute of Governmental Studies
109 Moses Hall, No. 2370
Berkeley, CA 94720-2370
Ph:(510)642-1474
Fax: (510)642-3020
Co. E-mail: bruce@cain.berkeley.edu
URL: http://www.igs.berkeley.edu
Contact: Prof. Bruce E. Cain, Dir.
E-mail: bruce@cain.berkeley.edu
Scope: American national, state, and local government and politics, public policy, public organization and administration, urban-metropolitan problems, federalism and intergovernmental relations, comparative methodology, and technology and government. **Publications:** Monographs; Public Affairs Report (quarterly); Research Reports. **Educational Activities:** Conferences; Lectures; Seminars, on government policies and social issues; Workshops.

50412 ■ University of Delaware–Institute for Public Administration
180 Graham Hall
College of Human Services, Education & Public Policy
Newark, DE 19716-7380
Ph:(302)831-8971
Fax: (302)831-3488
Co. E-mail: jlewis@udel.edu
URL: http://www.ipa.udel.edu
Contact: Jerome R. Lewis, Dir.
E-mail: jlewis@udel.edu
Scope: Integral unit of University of Delaware. Research, education, and public service program areas include civic education, conflict resolution, health care policy, land use planning, organizational development, school leadership, state and local management, water resources management, and women's leadership. **Publications:** Reports. **Educational Activities:** Policy forums; Training workshops, certificate programs.

50413 ■ University of Georgia–Carl Vinson Institute of Government
Lucy Cobb Complex
201 N Milledge Ave.
Athens, GA 30602-5482
Ph:(706)542-2736
Fax: (706)542-9301
Co. E-mail: wrigley@cviog.uga.edu
URL: http://www.cviog.uga.edu
Contact: Steve Wrigley, Dir.
E-mail: wrigley@cviog.uga.edu
Scope: Government, public administration, public finance, public personnel administration, science and technology policy, public law, and organizational development. **Services:** Technical and consultative advice and assistance, to state and local government officials. **Publications:** Monographs (7/year); Project Reports; State and Local Government Review (3/year); Teaching Georgia Government Newsletter (quarterly). **Educational Activities:** Citizen education services, to schools and citizens; Short courses, for state and local government officials; Workshops.

50414 ■ University of Maryland at College Park–Institute for Governmental Service
4511 Knox Rd., Ste. 205
College Park, MD 20742
Ph:(301)403-4610
Fax: (301)403-4222
Co. E-mail: igs@umd.edu
URL: http://www.vprgs.umd.edu/igs
Contact: Dr. Robin Parker Cox, Dir.
E-mail: igs@umd.edu
Scope: Strategic planning, fiscal issues, land use and annexation, program evaluation, personnel management, and other related governmental areas. **Publications:** Compensation Survey of Maryland Local Governments (occasionally); Did You Know (occasionally); Handbook for Maryland Municipal Officials (annually); Home Rule Options in Maryland (5/year); Maryland Government Report (annually); Outreach Newsletter (5/year).

50415 ■ University of Minnesota, Duluth–Center for Community and Regional Research
329 Cina Hall
Duluth, MN 55812
Ph:(218)726-6300

Fax: (218)726-6386
Co. E-mail: lknopp@d.umn.edu
URL: http://www.d.umn.edu/ccrr/
Contact: Lawrence M. Knopp Jr., Director
E-mail: lknopp@d.umn.edu
Scope: Public agencies in northeastern Minnesota, including survey research; human services; environmental issues; and business concerns. **Educational Activities:** Conferences.

50416 ■ University of North Carolina at Chapel Hill–Institute of Government
Knapp-Sanders Bldg., CB 3330
Chapel Hill, NC 27599-3330
Ph:(919)966-5381
Fax: (919)962-0654
Co. E-mail: thornburg@sog.unc.edu
URL: http://www.sog.unc.edu
Contact: Thomas Thornburg
E-mail: thornburg@sog.unc.edu
Scope: Legal, administrative, and financial aspects of state and local government, with emphasis on North Carolina governments. **Services:** Consulting services, for state and local officials. **Publications:** Popular Government (quarterly); School Law Bulletin (quarterly). **Educational Activities:** Conferences; Recurring seminars; Schools, on governmental problems and procedures; Short courses and training, for elected and appointed officials and citizens groups.

50417 ■ University of North Florida–Center for Community Initiatives
Department of Sociology & Anthropology, Bldg. 51/2219
4567 St. Johns Bluff Rd. S
Jacksonville, FL 32224
Ph:(904)620-2463
Fax: (904)620-4415
Co. E-mail: jwill@unf.edu
URL: http://www.unf.edu/coas/cci/
Contact: Jeffry A. Will PhD, Dir.
E-mail: jwill@unf.edu
Scope: Community, local, state and federal programs affecting community life in Northeast Florida.

50418 ■ University of South Dakota–Government Research Bureau
Dakota Hall 233
414 E Clark St.
Vermillion, SD 57069
Ph:(605)677-5708
Fax: (605)677-8808
Co. E-mail: william.anderson@usd.edu
URL: http://www.usd.edu/grb/
Contact: William D. Anderson, Dir.
E-mail: william.anderson@usd.edu
Scope: Governmental problems, including studies of state and local government, public administration, political party organization, political behavior, governmental finance, and miscellaneous governmental problems connected with South Dakota. Provides research training for students of the University. **Services:** Clearinghouse, for information on governmental administration; Consultation services, for governmental officials. **Publications:** Public Affairs (quarterly).

50419 ■ University of Utah–Center for Public Policy and Administration
260 S Central Campus Dr., Rm. 214
Salt Lake City, UT 84112-9154
Ph:(801)581-6781

Fax: (801)587-7861
Co. E-mail: david.patton@cppa.utah.edu
URL: http://www.cppa.utah.edu
Contact: W. David Patton PhD, Dir.
E-mail: david.patton@cppa.utah.edu
Scope: Local and state government finance, organization, and administration; environment, resources, and energy; welfare reform; health research and policy; education; and regional governance. **Services:** Consultation, to local, county, and state governments; Technical assistance; Training. **Publications:** Local Government Finance Survey; Planning and Zoning Manual; Policy briefing papers; Policy Perspectives. **Educational Activities:** Master Public Administration Alumni Conference; Policy Conference; Public administration educational programs; Utah Leadership Education and Development Program; Women's Conference. **Awards:** Dalmas Nelson Lectureship; Dalmas Nelson Student Award.

50420 ■ Virginia Commonwealth University–Center for Public Policy
919 W Franklin St.
PO Box 843061
Richmond, VA 23284-3061
Ph:(804)828-6837
Fax: (804)828-6838
Co. E-mail: rholswor@vcu.edu
URL: http://www.vcu.edu/cppweb/cpphome.html
Contact: Dr. Robert Holsworth, Exec.Dir.
E-mail: rholswor@vcu.edu
Scope: Public policy matters, with special attention to health policy, urban and metropolitan development, and state and local government and politics.

START-UP INFORMATION

50421 ■ "Stars of PR" in *Entrepreneur* (Vol. 30, No. 10, October 2002, pp. 91)
Pub: Entrepreneur Media Inc.
Ed: Nichole L. Torres. **Description:** Media stories imply credibility for a new business starting up. Strategies used for public relations by Starbucks, Red Bull, and Amazon.com are discussed.

ASSOCIATIONS AND OTHER ORGANIZATIONS

50422 ■ Public Relations Society of America
33 Maiden Ln., 11th Fl.
New York, NY 10038-5150
Ph:(212)460-1400
Fax: (212)995-0757
Co. E-mail: exec@prsa.org
URL: http://www.prsa.org
Contact: Catherine A. Bolton, Exec.Dir./COO
Description: Professional society of public relations practitioners in business and industry, counseling firms, government, associations, hospitals, schools, and nonprofit organizations. Conducts professional development programs. Maintains a Professional Resource Center. Offers accreditation program. **Publications:** *The Public Relations Strategist* (quarterly); *Public Relations Tactics* (monthly); Directories (annual); Newsletter (monthly). Also publishes research studies, and abstracts. **Telecommunication Services:** electronic mail, catherine.bolton@prsa.org; TDD, (212)254-3464.

EDUCATIONAL PROGRAMS

50423 ■ Public Relations-More Than Publicity
EEI Communications
66 Canal Ctr. Plz., Ste. 200
Alexandria, VA 22314-5507
Ph:(703)683-7453
Free: 888-253-2762
Fax: (703)683-7310
Co. E-mail: train@eeicommunications.com
URL: http://www.eeicommunications.com/training
Price: $895. **Description:** Seminar for middle managers, project directors, and mid-level communications professionals, that covers writing a plan and how to create productive relationships with any organization's range of constituencies, from employees to community decision makers, including defining public relations and its components, public relations tools and effective writing, identifying audiences, special public relations functions, and public relations and management. **Locations:** Alexandria, VA; Silver Spring, MD; and Washington, DC.

50424 ■ Public Relations: Strategies for Success
American Management Association
1601 Broadway
New York, NY 10019
Ph:(212)586-8100
Free: 800-262-9699
Fax: (212)903-8168
Co. E-mail: customerservice@amanet.org
URL: http://www.amanet.org
Price: $1,595.00 for non-members; $1,495.00 for AMA members. **Description:** For marketing and communications professionals with no PR experience; covers working with the media, successful PR techniques, and benefits of PR efforts. **Locations:** Washington, DC; and Chicago, IL.

50425 ■ Public Relations: Strategies for Success (Canada)
Canadian Management Centre
150 York St., 5th Fl.
Toronto, ON, Canada M5H 3S5
Ph:(416)214-5678
Free: 800-262-9699
Fax: (416)313-4985
Co. E-mail: cmcinfo@cmctraining.org
URL: http://cmcamai.org
Price: $1,795.00 Canadian. **Description:** For professionals with little or no PR experience; covers working with the media, successful PR techniques, and benefits of PR efforts. **Locations:** Toronto, ON.

REFERENCE WORKS

50426 ■ "American Dreamers Nominations Due Thursday" in *Crain's Detroit Business* (Vol. 22, December 11, 2006, No. 50, pp. 9)
Pub: Crain Communications Inc. - Detroit
Description: Detroit was built on the hopes and dreams of many immigrants from other countries. Nominations of business successes of first-generation immigrants are ending soon and will be listed in March, 2007.

50427 ■ "Bad Rap: Has Your Industry Got an Image Problem? Here's How to Cope" in *Entrepreneur* (Vol. 32, No. 1, January 2004, pp. 28)
Pub: Entrepreneur Media, Inc.
Ed: Geoff Williams. **Description:** Entrepreneurs working in industry sectors with bad reputations can do several things to overcome those obstacles.

50428 ■ "Ballooning Riches" in *Small Business Opportunities* (Vol. 16, No. 3, May 2004, pp. 46, 48)
Pub: Harris Publications, Inc.
Description: Profile of Landmark Creations of Burnsville, Minnesota. The firm offers fun and affordable inflatables to attract clients, and build a company's product image or brand.

50429 ■ "The Brand of Success" in *Small Business Opportunities* (Vol. 16, No. 2, March 2004, pp. 118, 120)
Pub: Harris Publications, Inc.
Ed: James Feldman. **Description:** Brand image is critical to a small business' success. Marketing materials serve two purposes. Guidelines to create or design promotions materials are presented.

50430 ■ "Bureau begins PR campaign to change images of Detroit" in *Crain's Detroit Business* (Vol. 19, No. 6, February 10, 2003, pp. 16)
Pub: Crain Communications Inc., Detroit
Ed: Jennette Smith. **Description:** The Detroit Metro Convention and Visitors Bureau is committed to promoting a good image for the city of Detroit for vacation and business travel and events.

50431 ■ "Case Study" in *Inc.* (August 1, 2004)
Pub: Inc. Magazine
Ed: Lora Kolodny. **Description:** Kuma Reality Games talks about the controversy of its new video game based on the Iraq war. Keith Halper, CEO of the firm, believes that publicity can work as free advertising.

50432 ■ "Chamber Kicks Off Weekly Member-Appreciation Program" in *Bellingham Business Journal* (December 2006, pp. 4)
Pub: Sun News Inc.
Description: Bellingham Women Chamber of Commerce and Industry celebrates various businesses within its membership with a member appreciation program.

50433 ■ "Chicago's Top Brands" in *Crain's Chicago Business* (Vol. 30, January 2007, No. 3, pp. 15)
Pub: Crain Communications, Inc.
Description: Profiles of five Chicago companies which made the list of Interbrand Corp., a global marketing firm, most powerful brands in the world.

50434 ■ "Corporate Image-Maker Sees Hope for Symbol, Pain for Computer Associates" in *Long Island Business News* (March 5, 2004)
Pub: Dolan Media Newswires
Ed: Ken Schachter. **Description:** Ann Stephenson, chief executive of Stephenson Group, a corporate image-maker specializing in technology companies, discusses ways she would rehabilitate the images of Symbol Technologies and Computer Associates. Both firms are facing government investigations into accounting procedures and the sudden departure of high-ranking executives.

50435 ■ "Cracking Jones Soda's Secret Formula" in *Fast Company* (March 2005, No. 92, pp. 74)
Pub: Gruner & Jahr USA Publishing
Ed: Ryan Underwood. **Description:** Peter van Stolk, founder and CEO of Jones Soda Company, believes his secret ingredient to his product's success is the customer.

50436 ■ **"Declaring War On Wal-Mart"** in *Business Week* (February 7, 2005, No. 3919, pp. 31)
Pub: McGraw-Hill Companies
Ed: Aaron Bernstein. **Description:** Wal-Mart has launched an ad campaign in January with the message: Wal-Mart is working for everyone. The retailer is fighting back against allegations of sex discrimination, poverty-level wages, and non-union workforce.

50437 ■ **"Detroit: No vacancy; New hotels may not bring enough rooms"** in *Crain's Detroit Business* (Vol. 19, No. 6, February 10, 2003, pp. 15)
Pub: Crain Communications Inc., Detroit
Ed: Robert Ankeny. **Description:** The Book Cadillac Hotel is planning a $150 million renovation, creating 500 new rooms for Detroit visitors, but it still may not be enough new rooms for the city.

50438 ■ *Do-it-Yourself Advertising, Direct Mail, & Publicity: Ready-to-Use Templates, Worksheets, & Samples for Creating Ads, Direct Mail Pieces*
Pub: Adams Publishing
Ed: Sarah White. **Released:** 1995. **Price:** $17.95.

50439 ■ **"Ex-BBDO Exec Forms New Agency"** in *Crain's Detroit Business* (Vol. 21, January 24, 2005, No. 4, pp. 18)
Pub: Crain Communications Inc. - Detroit
Ed: Jean Halliday. **Description:** Profile of Mike Vogel, former CEO of Omnicom Group's BBDO Detroit has left that firm in order to form RTV Communications Group. Vogel's new firm will consist of RTV Consulting, Consolidated Purchasing Partners and Vineyard Group, all located in Auburn Hills, Michigan. RTV offers marketing, strategy, consulting, creative, public relations, advertising, media, events and printing services.

50440 ■ **"Five Questions"** in *Sales & Marketing Management* (Vol. 157, January 2005, No. 1, pp. 15)
Pub: VNU Business Media
Description: Kim Olson, director of Brand Public Relations, answers five questions regarding marketing strategies for small, growing companies.

50441 ■ **"For the Love of the Game: How One Woman Scores in the Sports Entertainment Industry"** in *Black Enterprise* (Vol. 35, August 2004)
Pub: Earl G. Graves Publishing Co. Inc.
Ed: Zakiyyah El-Amin. **Description:** Profile of Cydni Bickerstaff, founder of Bickerstaff Sports & Entertainment. Bickerstaff is a full-service sports marketing, managing, and event production company, specializing in marketing and promotions, sporting events, athlete appearances, and sponsorships.

50442 ■ **"Ford to Mark 100th Anniversary This Year"** in *San Jose Mercury News* (April 11, 2003)
Pub: Knight-Ridder/Tribune Business News
Ed: Matt Nauman. **Description:** Ford Motor Company will use its 100th Anniversary as a tool to market its vehicles, through reminders of Ford's impact over the past century.

50443 ■ **"Gadget Gurus"** in *Entrepreneur* (Vol. 33, September 2005, No. 9, pp. 22)
Pub: Entrepreneur Media Inc.
Ed: Steve Cooper. **Description:** According to a study conducted by Burson-Marsteller, a global public relations agency, 86 percent of technology-driven leaders who try products and technologies first then relay their experiences online via blogs and/or discussion forums, are consulted by family and friends for advice before purchasing tech equipment.

50444 ■ **"Getting Ink: Need Exposure?"** in *Entrepreneur* (Vol. 33, February 2005, No. 2)
Pub: Entrepreneur Media Inc.
Ed: Kim T. Gordon. **Description:** Hiring a publicist or a public relations firm can help establish media contacts. Six practical tips to get media coverage for a small firm are listed.

50445 ■ **"Gilded and Gelded. Hard-Won Lessons From the PR Wars"** in *Harvard Business Review* (Vol. 81, No. 10, October 2003, pp. 44)
Pub: Harvard Business School Press
Ed: Dick Martin. **Description:** The ways in which AT&T mismanaged itself into a public relations problem are evaluated.

50446 ■ **"Goodbye, Retainers"** in *Inc.* (November 2006, pp. 35,38)
Pub: Gruner & Jahr USA Publishing
Ed: Stefanie Clifford. **Description:** Pay-as-you-go, results based public relations are replaced the traditional retainer system. Significant costs are realized on a timely basis.

50447 ■ **"Gridlock Alert; Who is Driving"** in *Crain's New York Business* (Vol. 22, December 11, 2006, No. 50, pp. 14)
Pub: Crain Communications, Inc.
Description: Traffic jams in Manhattan impose enormous costs on the economy, argued The Partnership for New York City. The Business Advocacy Group called for greater study of the issue before establishing congestion pricing fees for cars that enter the most crowded sections of Manhattan.

50448 ■ **"Hoover's Introduces Competitive Intelligence and Media Monitoring Service"** in *Information Today* (Vol. 17, No. 11, Dec. 2000, pp. 31)
Pub: Information Today, Inc.
Description: Hoover's announces its Intelligence Monitor, a Web service for businesses that need timely market and competitive intelligence information.

50449 ■ *Improving Your Company Image*
Pub: Crisp Publications, Inc.
Ed: Sylvia Blishak. **Price:** $9.95.

50450 ■ **"Keeping Mums"** in *Entrepreneur* (Vol. 33, February 2005, No. 2, pp. 71)
Pub: Entrepreneur Media Inc.
Ed: Mark Henricks. **Description:** Owner of an advertising agency in San Antonio, Texas tells how he hired a pregnant woman in 1995. The two worked out a plan whereby she could telecommute two days a week in order for her to be with her new baby. She has since become a partner in the ad, marketing and public relations agency that reports $30 million in annual billings.

50451 ■ **"King Kullen Freshening Up Image"** in *Long Island Business News* (May 7, 2004)
Pub: Dolan Media Newswires
Ed: David Reich-Hale. **Description:** Profile of King Kullen, America's first supermarket. The company is revamping stores as it faces competition from Stop & Shop and Waldbaum's.

50452 ■ **"Kraft Not Alone"** in *Crain's Chicago Business* (Vol. 30, February 2007, No. 6, pp. 8)
Pub: Crain Communications, Inc.
Description: Consumer watchdog group, The Center for Science in the Public Interest, has been putting pressure on food companies to be more truthful on their product labels. Listing of companies who have had misleading claims on their products is included.

50453 ■ **"Living High on the Blog"** in *Entrepreneur* (Vol. 33, February 2005, No. 2, pp. 65)
Pub: Entrepreneur Media Inc.
Ed: Gwen Moran. **Description:** Reach Communications Consulting founder, William Arruda, discovered an 800 percent hike in traffic on his firm's Website after being mentioned on an Internet blog; ways to add blogs to a public relations campaign are investigated.

50454 ■ **"Logos That Turn Heads"** in *Inc.* (December 1, 2003)
Pub: Gruner & Jahr USA Publishing
Ed: Nicole Gull. **Description:** Many companies are now using people as walking, talking advertisements by displaying or tattooing their logos on them.

50455 ■ *Media Relations in Your Spare Time: A Step-by-Step Guide for Anyone in Business*
Pub: National Association of Manufacturers
Ed: Laura Brown. **Released:** 1995. **Price:** $37.50.

50456 ■ **"Moms Want Ads to Address Them as Women"** in *Marketing to Women* (Vol. 19, October 2006, No. 10, pp. 3)
Pub: EPM Communications, Inc.
Description: A study by Draft Chicago found that in advertising mothers want to be spoken to as a well rounded individual instead of as only a mom. Statistical data included.

50457 ■ **"The Mother of Stunt Marketers"** in *Business 2.0* (Vol. 6, July 2005, No. 6, pp. 60-61)
Pub: Time, Inc.
Ed: Elizabeth Esfahani. **Description:** The Publicity Stunts Hall of Fame highlights the crazy things people have done as marketing tricks that generated publicity and increased sales for products.

50458 ■ **"A New View of Downtown. Perceptions Improve; Concerns Remain"** in *Business Journal-Milwaukee* (Vol. 20, No. 51, September 5, 2003)
Pub: American City Business Journals, Inc.
Ed: Pete Millard. **Description:** Monica Dignam, president of Monalco Inc., stated recently that because of efforts to improve the image of Milwaukee, Wisconsin, people are more willing to visit, shop and live in the city.

50459 ■ *O'Dwyer's Directory of Public Relations Firms*
Pub: J.R. O'Dwyer Company Inc.
Contact: Fraser P. Seitel, Sen. Ed.
E-mail: yusake@aol.com
Released: Annual, latest edition January, 2005. **Price:** $150, individuals. **Covers:** over 2,900 public relations firms; international coverage. **Entries Include:** Firm name, address, phone, principal executives, branch and overseas offices, billings, date founded, and 19,000 clients are cross-indexed. **Arrangement:** Geographical by country. **Indexes:** Specialty (beauty and fashions, finance/investor, etc.), geographical, client.

50460 ■ **"PR Leads www.prleads.com"** in *Entrepreneur* (Vol. 32, No. 1, January 2004, pp. 10)
Pub: Entrepreneur Media, Inc.
Ed: Steve Cooper. **Description:** Website that directs journalists to clients based on the client's expertise. Membership can be purchased on a three-month trial basis, or annually.

50461 ■ **"PR Power"** in *Entrepreneur* (Vol. 31, No. 11, November 2003, pp. 97)
Pub: Entrepreneur Media, Inc.
Ed: Gwen Moran. **Description:** Services designed to help promote media relations for small companies are listed.

50462 ■ *Public Relations Cases*
Pub: Wadsworth Publishing Co.
Ed: Jerry A. Hendrix. **Released:** Second edition, 1992. **Price:** $30.95.

50463 ■ *Public Relations Tactics—Member Services Directory—The Blue Book*
Pub: Public Relations Society of America (PRSA)
Released: Annual, January; latest edition 2004. **Covers:** PRSA members—headquaters, staff contacts, and chapter, section, and district information. **Entries Include:** Name, professional affiliation and title, address, phone, membership rank. **Arrangement:** Alphabetical. **Indexes:** Geographical, organizational.

50464 ■ *The Public Relations Writer's Handbook*
Pub: The Free Press
Ed: Merry Aronson and Donald E. Spetner. **Released:** 1993. **Price:** $19.95.

50465 ■ "Pump Up with PR" in *Small Business Opportunities* (Vol. 16, No. 2, March 2004, pp. 10)
Pub: Harris Publications, Inc.
Ed: Patricia Faulhaber. **Description:** Fourteen proven tips in public relations and publicity for small businesses. Public relations technically revolve around media relations, press releases, trade shows, brand creation, marketing communications, internal messaging, special event planning, networking and more.

50466 ■ "A Rap for Manners: Angelo Ellerbee Refines the Rough on Urban Artist" in *Black Enterprise* (Vol. 34, No. 5, December 2003, pp. 66)
Pub: Earl Graves Publishing Co.
Ed: Christina Morgan. **Description:** Profile of Angelo Ellerbee, an image consultant heading Double Xxposure, a public relations and management company. The firm specializes in total imaging and teaches young rap and R & B acts everything from diction to travel.

50467 ■ "Relationship builder" in *Pittsburgh Business Times* (Vol. 22, No. 46, May 30, 2003, pp. 15)
Pub: Pittsburgh Business Times
Ed: Christopher Davis. **Description:** Profile of Selena Schmidt, owner of Pittsburgh-based Grounds for Appeal, providing corporate image building, public relations management, and stresses the importance of professional associations.

50468 ■ "Smart Businesses See Value, and Profit, in Promoting Women" in *Crain's Chicago Business* (Vol. 30, February 2007, No. 6, pp. 30)
Pub: Crain Communications, Inc.
Ed: Marc J. Lane. **Description:** Despite U.S. corporations making little progress in advancing women to leadership positions over the past ten years, enlightened corporate decision makers understand that gender diversity is good business as the highest percentages of women officers yielded, on average, a 34 percent higher total return to shareholders and a 35.1 percent higher return on equity than those firms with the lowest percentages of women officers, according to a 2004 Catalyst study of Fortune 500 companies.

50469 ■ "Somebody's Watching You" in *Inc.* (September 2005, pp. 75-76)
Pub: Inc. Magazine
Ed: David H. Freedman. **Description:** Search engines such as Google are having an impact on business in two ways. First, the ability to find information on the Web is critical to any business success; and companies are now freely examined by anyone, making it necessary to adapt a firm to public scrutiny.

50470 ■ "Speak Up! The Ins and Outs of Hiring a Spokesperson" in *Entrepreneur* (Vol. 32, No. 2, February 2004, pp. 75)
Pub: Entrepreneur Media, Inc.
Ed: Nancy Michaels. **Description:** Pros and cons to hiring a spokesperson to represent a small company are discussed. Resources are included.

50471 ■ "SteelSalvor Chooses Lois Paul & Partners to Kick Start Public Relations, Strategic Communications Initiative" in *PR Newswire*
Pub: PR Newswire Association LLC
Description: SteelSalvor, the only marketing company that maintains an online auction serving the steel industry, has appointed Lois Paul & Partners LLC as its marketing and public relations partner.

50472 ■ "Sweet Reward: Reaching Out to the Media Really Does Pay Off" in *Entrepreneur* (Vol. 31, No. 9, July 2003, pp. 81)
Pub: Entrepreneur Media, Inc.
Ed: April Y. Pennington. **Description:** Profile of Fran Bigelow, owner of Fran's Chocolates Ltd., opened in 1982. Bigelow sent letters to food editors educating them on the fine chocolates she uses and included samples. The editors published articles that gave her store more exposures and Bigelow was named The Best Chocolatier in America by The Book of Chocolate.

50473 ■ "Taking the Hospitality Test" in *Crain's Detroit Business* (Vol. 21, October 10, 2005, No. 43, pp. 11)
Pub: Crain Communications Inc. - Detroit
Ed: Robert Ankeny. **Description:** According to Service Advantage International, limo drivers, hotel help, waitresses and store clerks are friendly, courteous, neat and professional, but few service workers were able to recommend any Detroit attractions to visitors.

50474 ■ "To the Extreme: Watch Sales Grow by Making a Positive Lasting Impression" in *Sales & Marketing Management* (Vol. 157, January 2005)
Pub: VNU Business Media
Ed: Sara Calabro. **Description:** Positive Response, a marketing consulting firm in Ohio, developed an extreme marketing plan to help CSi Complete gain the competitive edge to win approval to sell its customer satisfaction measurement services for collision repair companies. Positive Response created a three-step mail campaign targeted to collision repair services over six weeks.

50475 ■ *The Unabashed Self-Promoter's Guide: What Every Man, Woman, Child and Organization in America Needs to Know about...Exploiting the Media*
Pub: JLA Publications
Ed: Jeffrey Lant. **Released:** Second edition, 1992. **Price:** $35.00 (paper).

50476 ■ "Unhappy LPs Pass on New Mayfield Fund" in *Venture Capital Journal* (September 1, 2005)
Pub: Thomason Financial Inc.
Description: Mayfield, the venture capital firm founded in 1969, has suffered a blow to its reputation in the VC industry because a departing limited partner has reported Mayfield's arrogant manner used in the handling of a management fee issue.

50477 ■ "Wal-Mart's Clean Bill of Health?" in *Business Week Online* (February 9, 2005)
Pub: McGraw-Hill Companies
Ed: Wendy Zellner. **Description:** In order to improve its image, Wal-Mart has reported the results of a new survey it conducted about employees' healthcare coverage. The nationwide survey, commissioned from Segmentation Company, found the percentage of workers with healthcare coverage at Wal-Mart is about the same as employees working for other retailers.

50478 ■ "Warming Up to Cold Calls" in *Inc.* (November 1, 2004)
Pub: Inc. Magazine
Ed: Nicole Gull. **Description:** Samantha Ettus, CEO of Ettus Media Management, a New York City public relations and branding agency spends much of her time making cold calls in order to land new accounts.

50479 ■ "What's In a Name?" in *Inc.* (July 1, 2004)
Pub: Inc. Magazine
Ed: Bobbie Gossage. **Description:** Choosing a company or brand name is critical to success. Ways to get the name your small company deserves are outlined.

50480 ■ "Why There's No Escaping the Blog" in *Fortune* (Vol. 151, January 10, 2005, No. 1, pp. 44)
Pub: Time Inc.
Ed: David Kirkpatrick, Daniel Roth, Oliver Ryan. **Description:** Microsoft has unveiled a plan to develop a new service called MSN Spaces, an online software that allows users to easily create and maintain blogs on the Internet. The power of blogs and bloggers to make or break a product or service is examined.

50481 ■ "A World of Difference" in *Entrepreneur* (Vol. 32, October 2004, No. 10, pp. 78)
Pub: Entrepreneur Media Inc.
Ed: April Y. Pennington. **Description:** Entrepreneurs are committed to civic responsibility. They are actively working in communities for positive change through not only donations and in-house recycling programs, but also through a hands-on approach to social issues.

50482 ■ *Writing Effective News Releases: How to Get Free Publicity for Yourself, Your Business, or Your Organization*
Pub: Piccadilly Books
Ed: Catherine V. McIntyre. **Released:** 1992. **Price:** $17.00 (paper).

50483 ■ "You Can Count on Me: A Friend Can Make the Best Kind of Business Partner" in *Entrepreneur* (Vol. 32, November 2004, No. 11, pp. 36)
Pub: Entrepreneur Media Inc.
Ed: Aliza Pilar Sherman. **Description:** Profiles of friends who ventured into businesses together. Lynn Harris Medcalf and Susan Apgood teamed to launch News Generation, a public relations firm in Atlanta, Georgia. Sarah Eck and Brook Jay, partnered to create All Terrain Productions, an events-marketing firm in Chicago, Illinois.

50484 ■ "Your Story Here" in *Black Enterprise* (Vol. 36, February 2006, No. 7, pp. 57)
Pub: Earl G. Graves Publishing Co. Inc.
Ed: Kenneth Meeks. **Description:** BlackNews.com will feature a press release on its Website, an email and fax to every African American newspaper, magazine, radio station and TV station for only $150. Diversity City Media Inc., the multicultural marketing and public relations firm not only runs the Website, but also Black PR.com a press release distribution service.

TRADE PERIODICALS

50485 ■ *The Levison Letter*
Pub: Ivan Levison & Associates
Ed: Ivan Levison, Editor, ivan@levison.com. **Released:** Monthly. **Price:** Free. **Description:** Offers tips for improving marketing.

50486 ■ *Public Relations Strategist*
Pub: Public Relations Strategist
Released: Quarterly. **Price:** $150; $160 Canada; $170 out of country; $34 students. **Description:** Public relations magazine containing articles on crisis management and establishing corporate reputation.

VIDEOCASSETTES/ AUDIOCASSETTES

50487 ■ *The Crisis Interview: A Media Relations Guide for Field Personnel*
Gulf Publishing Co.
PO Box 2608
Houston, TX 77252-2608
Ph:(713)520-4448
Free: 800-231-6275
Fax: (713)204-4433
Co. E-mail: csv@gulfpub.com
URL: http://www.gulfpub.com
Price: $495.00. **Description:** Offers media relations training for managers, supervisors, and field personnel. Dramatization shows a chemical company supervisor who is in the unaccustomed role of spokesperson as he arrives to oversee a cleanup of a chemical spill. Illustrates issues such as the community's right to know, how to take control of a situation, what is expected from a spokesperson, and how to end an interview on your own terms. Includes reference guide. **Availability:** VHS.

CONSULTANTS

50488 ■ **Sol Abrams Public Relations Counsel & Marketing Consultants**
331 Webster Dr.
New Milford, NJ 07646
Ph:(201)262-4111
Fax: (201)262-7669

Scope: Independent consulting provides publicity, public relations and marketing counsel and services to management of private and public enterprises. Also serves as public relations consultants to other public relations consulting firms, advertising agencies and marketing companies. Provides expert witness services involving public relations. Also lectures, trains, teaches, and conducts seminars in public relations and marketing. Industries served: corporate management, businesses large and small including real estate, construction, entertainment, food, fashion, fundraising, automotive, aviation, franchising, government agencies, and nonprofit organizations. **Seminars:** How to Select a Public Relations Firm; Publicity and Promotion for Small Business Owner; Expose Yourself - Don't Be a Secret Agent -Increase Your Sales, Incomes, Images, Publicity, Profits and Prestige via Professional Public Relations.

50489 ■ Bitner Goodman
5310 NW 33rd Ave., Ste. 218
Fort Lauderdale, FL 33309-6300
Ph:(954)730-7730
Fax: (954)730-7130
Co. E-mail: info@bitner.com
URL: http://www.bitner.com

E-mail: info@bitner.com
Scope: A public relations, advertising and marketing consultancy. Serves industries including: travel, technology, telecommunications, financial services, consumer products, health-care, government, automotive, real estate and retail.

50490 ■ Burns Public Relations Services Inc.
1660 W 2nd St., Ste. 410
Cleveland, OH 44113
Ph:(216)621-5950
Scope: Full service public communicators and consultants. Specializations: marketing strategies, urban affairs, minority business enterprise; and Affirmative Action programming.

50491 ■ Kelley Chunn & Associates
184 Dudley St., Ste. 106
PO Box 2348
Boston, MA 02119
Ph:(617)427-0997
Fax: (617)427-3997
Co. E-mail: kc4info@aol.com
URL: http://www.kelleychunn.com

E-mail: kc4info@aol.com
Scope: Helps businesses, nonprofits and individuals develop multicultural, cause-related marketing and public relations strategies. Strategic planning, media relations, event planning and management. **Seminars:** Crisis communications; Guerrilla marketing; Ethnic marketing.

50492 ■ Donna Cornell Enterprises Inc.
68 N Plank Rd., Ste. 204
Newburgh, NY 12550-2122
Ph:(845)565-0088
Fax: (845)565-0084
Co. E-mail: rc@cornellcareercenter.com
URL: http://www.dce.com

E-mail: rc@cornellcareercenter.com
Scope: Offers services in career consultant, professional search, job placement, and national professional search. **Publications:** "The Power of the Woman Within".

50493 ■ Coyne Associates
4010 E Lake St.
Minneapolis, MN 55406
Ph:(612)724-1188
Fax: (612)722-1379
Scope: A marketing and public relations consulting firm specializing in assisting architectural, engineering, and contractor/developer firms. Services include marketing plains and audits, strategic planning, corporate identity, turnarounds, and sales training.

50494 ■ Wayne Dean Public Relations
1064 Palmetto St.
Mobile, AL 36604-3041

Scope: Provides complete public relations consulting services to all industries, including government agencies, but particularly small businesses and organizations unable to justify hiring a large agency. A speciality is religious organizations and churches as the Firm's principal is a full-time pastor as well as consultant. Services include programming and budgeting, publicity (news releases, electronic spots, features), advertising, promotions, writing and editing, staff training, speeches, and internal communication. Also does publicist work for entertainment industry. Operates Internet Vending of Collectible and other items-goods and services. **Publications:** Advisor on Share the Experience video on Mobile Mardi Gras.

50495 ■ Devillier Communications Inc.
5335 Wisconsin Ave. NW, Ste. 440
Washington, DC 20015
Ph:(202)885-5544
Fax: (202)885-5541
Co. E-mail: info@devillier.com
URL: http://www.devillier.com

E-mail: info@devillier.com
Scope: A public relations firm and marketing consultancy. Firm develops innovative solutions for a wide range of extraordinary clients.

50496 ■ Steve Emerine Strategic Public Relations
PO Box 41824
Tucson, AZ 85717-1824
Ph:(520)323-1441
Fax: (520)881-4043
Co. E-mail: steveemerine@webtv.net

E-mail: steveemerine@webtv.net
Scope: Services offered in crisis management, environmental problems, litigation public relations, government relations, publicity, writing, editing, and public information planning. **Seminars:** Crisis Public Relations, Media Relations, Environmental and Neighborhood Relations.

50497 ■ Russ Fons Public Relations
7509 Turtle Dove Ct.
Las Vegas, NV 89129-6032
Ph:(702)658-7654
Free: 888-658-7654
Fax: (702)658-1349
Co. E-mail: russfons@cox.net
URL: http://www.russfons.com

E-mail: russfons@cox.net
Scope: Offers corporate counseling and image development; media relations; marketing communications and product publicity; event management and special promotions; and graphic design and production. Industries served: all worldwide. Licensing and merchandising, literary services, Hispanic communications. Revenue Sharing/PI Advertising. **Publications:** The Executive Crisis Manager, a planning guide to surviving corporate crisis.

50498 ■ Health Strategy Group Inc.
46 River Rd.
Chatham, NY 12037
Ph:(518)392-6770
Scope: Provides consulting services in the areas of strategic planning, feasibility studies, start-up businesses, organizational development, market research, customer service audits, new product development, marketing, public relations.

50499 ■ hightechbiz.com
4209 Santa Monica Blvd., Ste. 201
Los Angeles, CA 90029-3027
Ph:(818)216-9356
Free: 877-648-4753
Fax: (323)913-3355
Co. E-mail: info@hightechbiz.com
URL: http://www.hightechbiz.com

E-mail: info@hightechbiz.com
Scope: Business development, strategic planning and investing in high tech companies. Turnaround

consulting and financial sort our of distressed business and start up companies with strong emphasis on technology. A full service marketing agency specializing in integrated marketing solutions. Products and services include marketing surveys; positioning surveys; strategic & tactical plans; implementation plans; management consulting; product brochures; product catalogs; product packaging; product data sheets; direct mail programs; media research; competitive research; complete creative; production and film; media placement; corporate identity; in-house creative; public relations; logos & stationary; annual reports; publications; corporate brochures; corporate videos; trade show booth graphics; concept & design; copywriting; computerized production; illustration/cartoons; computer graphics; Internet home page design; media relations; financial relations; news releases; feature length stories; new product releases; and tracking and clipping.

50500 ■ C. W. Hines and Associates Inc.
344 Churchill Cir., Sanctuary Bay
White Stone, VA 22578
Ph:(804)435-8844
Fax: (804)435-8855
Co. E-mail: turtlecwh@aol.com
URL: http://www.cwhinesassociates.org

E-mail: turtlecwh@aol.com
Scope: Management consultants with expertise in the following categories: advertising and public relations, health and human resources, management sciences, organizational development, computer sciences, financial management, behavioral sciences, environmental design, technology transfer, project management, facility management, program evaluation, and business therapy. Also included are complementary areas such as sampling procedures, job training, managerial effectiveness, corporate seminars, gender harassment, training for trainers, and leadership and management skills development. **Publications:** Money Muscle, 120 Exercises To Build Spiritual And Financial Strength, 2004; Inside Track: Executives Coaching Executives. **Seminars:** Career Development; Coaching and Counseling for Work Success; Communicating More Effectively in a Diverse Work Environment; Communications 600: Advanced Skills for Relationship Building; Customer Service: Building a Caring Culture.

50501 ■ Jeffrey Lant Associates Inc.
50 Follen St., Ste. 507
Cambridge, MA 02238
Ph:(617)547-6372
Fax: (617)547-0061
Co. E-mail: drjlant@worldprofit.com
URL: http://www.jeffreylant.com

E-mail: drjlant@worldprofit.com
Scope: Firm sets up businesses online, design websites and assist with marketing. **Publications:** Web Wealth: How to Turn the World Wide Web Into a Cash Hose for Your Business.Whatever Youre Selling!, 1997; The Consultants Kit: Establishing and Operating Your Successful Consulting Business. **Seminars:** Business and personal development, including Establishing and Operating Your Successful Consulting Business; Successfully Promoting Your Small Business and Professional Practice; Succeeding in Your Mail Order Business; Successfully Raising Money for Your Nonprofit Organization from Foundations, Corporations and Individuals; Money Making Marketing: Finding the People Who Need What Youre Selling and Making Sure They Buy It; Getting Corporations, Foundations, and Individuals to Give You the Money Your Nonprofit Organization Needs.

50502 ■ Marenghi Public Relations Inc.
690 Canton St., Ste. 240
Westwood, MA 02090-2324
Ph:(781)915-5000
Fax: (781)326-9370
Co. E-mail: info@marenghi.com
URL: http://www.marenghi.com

E-mail: info@marenghi.com
Scope: Full-service marketing and sales support agency serving high-tech and information businesses.

Strategic counsel, value proposition analysis, positioning and messaging, sales tools, media and analyst relations, speaker placement, editorial services, media coaching, etc.

50503 ■ Gary Ruben Inc., Marketing Communications Consultants
931 E 86th St., Ste. 206
Indianapolis, IN 46240-1860
Ph:(317)251-5330
Scope: A communications and marketing consulting firm whose services include: advertising agency selection, advertising agency performance review, advertising program structuring, creative assistance, advertising program measurement, public relations program structuring, advertising department personnel development, in-house agency structuring, and executive counseling. Industries served include supermarket chains, franchise systems, and retail products and services.

50504 ■ S&S Public Relations Inc.
100 Village Green, Ste. 220
Lincolnshire, IL 60069
Ph:(847)955-0700
Free: 800-287-2279
Fax: (847)955-7720
Co. E-mail: ssimon@sspr.com
URL: http://www.sspr.com

E-mail: ssimon@sspr.com
Scope: Offers a wide range of public relations consulting services particularly for franchisers, authors, consultants, and various products.

50505 ■ The Shannon Management Group.
415 Walnut St.
PO Box 702
Coshocton, OH 43812
Ph:(740)622-2600
Fax: (740)622-9638
Co. E-mail: info@shannonmanagementgroup.com
URL: http://www.shannonmanagementgroup.com

E-mail: info@shannonmanagementgroup.com
Scope: Serving broad range of industries and public sector organizations and foundations. Specializing in human resources recruiting and outplacement counseling on international scale for businesses of all sizes. Offers expertise in human resources policies and procedures, supervisor development, manager leadership style development, interview training, etc. Provides consulting to small business in human resources, advertising, marketing, sales, public relations and community relations. **Seminars:** Time Management workshop.

50506 ■ Tom Shillock Consulting
5545 SW Windsor Ct.
Portland, OR 97221-2150
Ph:(503)291-7928
Fax: (503)221-2052
Co. E-mail: shillock@ee.pdx.edu

E-mail: shillock@ee.pdx.edu
Scope: Offers consulting services in marketing and communications including public relations and advertising. Industries served: high technology.

50507 ■ Sparkworks Media
325 W Republican St.
Seattle, WA 98119
Ph:(206)284-5500
Fax: (206)284-6611
Co. E-mail: info@sparkworksmedia.com
URL: http://www.sparkworksmedia.com

E-mail: info@sparkworksmedia.com
Scope: Offers counsel on media and video production for medium and small businesses, governmental and educational institutions. Editing and other post production work as required. Distribution and marketing for products produced. Full Service Production firm for video and new media. **Special Services:** Motion Graphics and non-linear editing.

50508 ■ Alan J. Zell- Ambassador of Selling
PO Box 69
Portland, OR 97207-0069
Ph:(503)241-1988
Fax: (503)241-1989
Co. E-mail: azell@aol.com
URL: http://www.sellingselling.com

E-mail: azell@aol.com
Scope: An advisory service for those who sell their services, products or their organization's ideas, information, and skills through face-to-face and telephone conversations, printed materials, the media, electronic communications, schools, guilds, trade shows, and display presentations. Industries served: minority and woman-owned businesses; government and education; medicine, law, accounting, technology, manufacturers, distributors, and retailers; professional and trade associations; and nonprofit organizations. **Publications:** Selling Situations; What Customers need to know; Turnover & Return on Investment; The Ultimate Business Oxymoron; Walkin The Aisles, Looking at the Booths, etc. **Seminars:** Ambassador Of Selling. **Special Services:** Web-site critique from sales/selling point of view.

Publicity/Advertising

START-UP INFORMATION

50509 ■ **"Big Bucks in Big Mouth"** in *Small Business Opportunities* (Vol. 14, No. 1, January 2002, pp. 96, 103)
Pub: Harris Publications, Inc.
Description: Profile of Reggie Smith and Ed Hughes, co-owners of Bocaza Mexican Grille, launched in 1996. As an opening promotion, they handed out free samples of food to passing motorists and pedestrians.

50510 ■ **"Food fair: how one caterer's soiree made her the talk of the town"** in *Entrepreneur* (Vol. 31, No. 5, May 2003, pp. 77)
Pub: Entrepreneur Media Inc.
Ed: April Y. Pennington. **Description:** Profile of Connie Chantilis and her catering firm, Two Sisters, located in Dallas, Texas. Chantilis expects 2003 sales to approach the $3 million mark.

50511 ■ **"Ready For Launch"** in *My Business* (June/July 2002, pp. 16)
Pub: My Business Magazine
Ed: Vicki Gerson. **Description:** Creativity is the key in successfully introducing a new product to the market.

50512 ■ **"Stars of PR"** in *Entrepreneur* (Vol. 30, No. 10, October 2002, pp. 91)
Pub: Entrepreneur Media Inc.
Ed: Nichole L. Torres. **Description:** Media stories imply credibility for a new business starting up. Strategies used for public relations by Starbucks, Red Bull, and Amazon.com are discussed.

50513 ■ **"To get product on shelves, knock on a lot of doors"** in *Crain's Detroit Business* (Dec. 16, 2002, pp. 18)
Pub: Crain Communications Inc., Detroit
Ed: Laura Bailey. **Description:** Various entrepreneurs share tips for successfully marketing new products.

ASSOCIATIONS AND OTHER ORGANIZATIONS

50514 ■ **Advertising Club of New York**
235 Park Ave. S, 6th Fl.
New York, NY 10003-1405
Ph:(212)533-8080
Fax: (212)533-1929
Co. E-mail: gina@theadvertisingclub.org
URL: http://www.theadvertisingclub.org
Contact: Gina Grillo, Exec. Dir.
Membership: Professionals in advertising, publishing, marketing, and business. **Purpose:** Sponsors educational and public service activities, promotional and public relations projects, and talks by celebrities and advertising persons. Conducts annual advertising and marketing course, which offers classes in copywriting, special graphics, verbal communication, advertising production, sale promotion, marketing and management. Sponsors competitions and charitable programs. **Publications:** *ACNY Membership Roster* (annual); *The Advertising Club Insider* (quarterly); *ANDY Souvenir Journal* (annual); *Auction Catalogue and Program* (annual).

50515 ■ **Advertising Council**
261 Madison Ave., 11th Fl.
New York, NY 10016-2303
Ph:(212)922-1500
Free: 800-933-7727
Fax: (212)922-1676
Co. E-mail: info@adcouncil.org
URL: http://www.adcouncil.org
Contact: Peggy Conlon, Pres./CEO
Membership: Founded and supported by American business, media, and advertising sectors to conduct public service advertising campaigns. **Purpose:** Encourages advertising media to contribute time and space and advertising agencies to supply creative talent and facilities to further timely national causes. Specific campaigns include: Drug Abuse Prevention; AIDS Prevention; Teen-Alcoholism; Child Abuse; Crime Prevention; Forest Fire Prevention. **Publications:** *PSA Bulletin* (bimonthly); *Report to the American People* (annual).

50516 ■ **Advertising and Marketing International Network**
12323 Nantucket
Wichita, KS 67235
Ph:(316)531-2342
Fax: (316)722-8353
Co. E-mail: vaughn.sink@shscom.com
URL: http://www.aminworldwide.com
Contact: B. Vaughn Sink, Exec. Dir.
Membership: Comprised of cooperative worldwide network of non-competing independent advertising agencies organized to provide facilities and branch office services for affiliated agencies. **Publications:** *AMIN Directory* (annual).

50517 ■ **Advertising Women of New York**
25 W 45th St., Ste. 403
New York, NY 10036
Ph:(212)221-7969
Fax: (212)221-8296
Co. E-mail: awny@awny.org
URL: http://www.awny.org
Contact: Liz Schroeder, Exec. Dir.
Description: Women in advertising and related industries that provides a forum for professional growth, serves as catalyst for enhancement and advancement of women; promotes philanthropic endeavors. Conducts events of interest and benefit to members and non-members involved in the industry. Membership concentrated in the metropolitan New York area. **Publications:** *Advertising Women of New York—Annual Roster* (annual).

50518 ■ **American Academy of Advertising**
Coll. of Mass Communications
Texas Tech University
Box 43082
Lubbock, TX 79409-3082
Ph:(806)742-3385
Fax: (806)742-1085
Co. E-mail: donald.jugenheimer@ttu.edu
URL: http://www.americanacademyofadvertising.org
Contact: Donald W. Jugenheimer, Exec.Sec.
Description: Serves as professional organization of college and university teachers of advertising. **Publications:** *AAA Newsletter* (quarterly); *Journal of Advertising* (quarterly); *Proceedings of the Conference of the American Academy of Advertising* (annual); *Roster of Members* (annual).

50519 ■ **American Advertising Federation**
1101 Vermont Ave. NW, Ste. 500
Washington, DC 20005-6306
Ph:(202)898-0089
Fax: (202)898-0159
Co. E-mail: aaf@aaf.org
URL: http://www.aaf.org
Contact: Wally S. Snyder, Pres./CEO
Purpose: Works to advance the business of advertising as a vital and essential part of the American economy and culture through government and public relations; professional development and recognition; community service, social responsibility and high standards; and benefits and services to members. Operates Advertising Hall of Fame, Hall of Achievement, and National Student Advertising Competition. Maintains Speaker's Bureau. **Publications:** *American Advertising Federation—Government Report* (monthly); *American Advertising Magazine* (quarterly); *Communicator* (monthly); *Newsline* (monthly).

50520 ■ **American Association of Advertising Agencies**
405 Lexington Ave., 18th Fl.
New York, NY 10174-1801
Ph:(212)682-2500
Fax: (212)682-8391
Co. E-mail: barbara@aaaa.org
URL: http://www.aaaa.org
Contact: O. Burtch Drake, Pres./CEO
Purpose: Fosters development of the advertising industry; assists member agencies to operate more efficiently and profitably. Sponsors member information and international services. Maintains 47 committees. Conducts government relations. **Publications:** *AAAA Publications Catalog* (periodic); *The Reporter* (bimonthly); *Roster of Members* (annual).

50521 ■ **American Lutheran Publicity Bureau**
PO Box 327
Delhi, NY 13753-0327
Ph:(607)746-7511
Fax: (607)746-7511
Co. E-mail: fred@theschumachers.org
URL: http://www.alpb.org
Contact: Pr. Frederick J. Schumacher, Exec.Dir.
Purpose: Organized by laymen and pastors of the Lutheran church to publicize its teachings, work, and activities in a movement towards Lutheran unity. Helps Lutherans to explain their faith to non-Lutherans and the unchurched and to discuss important issues in church and society. **Publications:** *For All the Saints: Prayer Book*; *Forum Letter* (monthly); *Heaven on*

Earth: A Lutheran-Orthodox Odyssey; *Lutheran Forum* (quarterly); *O'Lord, Teach Me to Pray*; *Pro Ecclesia* (quarterly).

50522 ■ ARF - Advertising Research Foundation
432 Park Ave. S
New York, NY 10016
Ph:(212)751-5656
Fax: (212)319-5265
Co. E-mail: info@thearf.org
URL: http://www.thearf.org
Contact: Robert L. Barocci, Pres./CEO
Membership: Advertisers, advertising agencies, research organizations, associations, and the media are regular members of the foundation; colleges and universities are associate members. **Purpose:** Objectives are to: further scientific practices and promote greater effectiveness of advertising and marketing by means of objective and impartial research; develop new research methods and techniques; analyze and evaluate existing methods and techniques, and define proper applications; establish research standards, criteria, and reporting methods. Compiles statistics and conducts research programs. **Publications:** *ARF Transcript Proceedings* (periodic); *Journal of Advertising Research* (bimonthly).

50523 ■ Association of Free Community Papers
PO Box 1989
Idaho Springs, CO 80452
Free: 877-203-2327
Fax: (781)459-7770
Co. E-mail: afcp@afcp.org
URL: http://www.afcp.org
Contact: Craig S. McMullin, Exec. Dir.
Description: Represents publishers of nearly 3,000 free circulation papers and shopping/advertising guides. Offers national classified advertising placement service and national marketing for industry recognition. Conducts charitable programs. Sponsors competitions and compiles industry statistics. **Publications:** *Free Paper Ink* (monthly).

50524 ■ Association of Independent Commercial Producers
3 W 18th St., 15th Fl.
New York, NY 10011
Ph:(212)929-3000
Fax: (212)929-3359
Co. E-mail: info@aicp.com
URL: http://www.aicp.com
Contact: Matthew Miller, Pres./CEO
Description: Represents the interests of companies that specialize in producing television commercials for advertisers and agencies, and the businesses that furnish supplies and services to this industry. Serves as a collective voice for the industry before government and business councils, and in union negotiations; disseminates information; works to develop industry standards and tools; provides professional development; and markets American production. **Publications:** *AICP Membership Directory* (annual); *AICP National Newsletter.* **Telecommunication Services:** electronic mail, mattm@aicp.com.

50525 ■ Association of National Advertisers
708 Third Ave.
New York, NY 10017-4270
Ph:(212)697-5950
Fax: (212)661-8057
Co. E-mail: rliodice@ana.net
URL: http://www.ana.net
Contact: Robert D. Liodice, Pres./CEO
Description: Serves the needs of members by providing marketing and advertising industry leadership in traditional and e-marketing, legislative leadership, information resources, professional development and industry-wide networking. Maintains offices in New York City and Washington, DC. **Publications:** *The Advertiser* (bimonthly).

50526 ■ Children's Advertising Review Unit
70 W 36th St.
New York, NY 10018
Ph:(212)705-0111

Fax: (212)705-0132
Co. E-mail: elascoutx@caru.bbb.org
URL: http://www.caru.org
Contact: Elizabeth Lascoutx, Dir.
Description: Participants include advertisers and advertising agencies. Monitors and evaluates child-directed advertising in all media; reviews advertising prior to its release upon request. Seeks voluntary change when advertising is found to be inaccurate, misleading, or otherwise inconsistent with the association's Self-Regulatory Guidelines for Children's Advertising. Acts as arbitrator in cases where the truthfulness of advertising claims comes under question by a competitor and entertains consumer complaints. Maintains Advisory Board to gather and disseminate information on the ways in which children perceive and understand advertising, and to revisit guidelines to ensure they remain current. Provides a Safe Harbor program under COPPA for the association's supporters. **Publications:** *A Parent's Guide: Advertising and Your Child*; *Self-Regulatory Guidelines for Children's Advertising.*

50527 ■ Eight Sheet Outdoor Advertising Association
PO Box 2680
Bremerton, WA 98310-0344
Ph:(360)377-9867
Free: 800-874-3387
Fax: (360)377-9870
Co. E-mail: davidjacobs@esoaa.com
URL: http://www.esoaa.com
Contact: David D. Jacobs, Exec. Dir.
Purpose: Promotes the use of 8-sheet poster panels in outdoor advertising. (8-sheet signs are smaller than the usual 24-sheet ones, and are most commonly composed of 1 or 3 sheets covering an area of 6 x 12 feet). **Publications:** *Display* (monthly); *Eight Sheet Outdoor Advertising Association-Sources: A Guide to Suppliers of Outdoor Materials and Services* (annual); *Rates and Allotments: 8 Sheet Poster Panels in the Top Population Ranked Markets* (annual).

50528 ■ Intermarket Agency Network
5307 S 92nd St.
Hales Corners, WI 53130
Ph:(414)425-8800
Fax: (414)425-0021
Co. E-mail: bille@nonbox.com
URL: http://www.intermarketnetwork.com
Contact: Bill Eisner, Exec. Dir.
Description: An active network of high-powered marketing/communications agencies in the United States, Canada, Central and South America, and Europe.

50529 ■ International Advertising Association
521 5th Ave., Ste. 1807
New York, NY 10175
Ph:(212)557-1133
Fax: (212)983-0455
Co. E-mail: iaa@iaaglobal.org
URL: http://www.iaaglobal.org
Contact: Nubia Martinez, Exec. Asst.
Membership: Global network of advertisers, advertising agencies, the media and related services, spanning 99 countries. **Purpose:** Demonstrates to governments and consumers the benefits of advertising as the foundation of diverse, independent media. Protects and advances freedom of commercial speech and consumer choice, encourages greater practice and acceptance of advertising self-regulation, provides a forum to debate emerging professional marketing communications issues and their consequences in the fast-changing world environment, and takes the lead in state-of-the-art professional development through education and training for the marketing communications industry of tomorrow. Conducts research on such topics as restrictions and taxes on advertising, advertising trade practices and related information, and advertising expenditures around the world. Sponsors IAA Education Program. Has compiled recommendations for international advertising standards and practices. **Publications:** *The Case for Advertising Self-Regulation*; *IAA Annual Report* (annual); *IAA Membership Directory* (annual); *IAA Week-*

ly (weekly); *Monographs on Severely Restricted or Forbidden Advertising Practices.* **Telecommunication Services:** electronic mail, nubia@iaaglobal.org.

50530 ■ International Communications Agency Network
PO Box 490
Rollinsville, CO 80474-0490
Ph:(303)258-9511
Fax: (303)484-4087
Co. E-mail: info@icomagencies.com
URL: http://www.icomagencies.com
Contact: Mr. Gary Burandt, Exec. Dir.
Description: Network of non-competing advertising agencies. Provides an interchange of management information, international facilities, and branch office service for partner agencies. Provides discounts on syndicated services and access to 1000 computer databases. **Publications:** *Agency Client Lists* (monthly); *Best Practices*; *Facts About Membership* (semiannual); *The Globe* (monthly); *Member Surveys*; *Membership Roster* (annual). **Telecommunication Services:** electronic mail, burandt@icomagencies. com.

50531 ■ Los Angeles Advertising Agencies Association
4223 Glencoe Ave., Ste. C-100
Marina del Rey, CA 90292
Ph:(310)823-7320
Fax: (310)823-7325
Co. E-mail: submissions@laaaa.com
URL: http://www.laaaa.com
Contact: Susan Franceschini, Exec.Dir.
Purpose: Assists heads of advertising agencies in the Western U.S. to operate their agencies more effectively and profitably. Offers assistance to agency management and staff. Provides a forum for discussion and exchange of information. Promotes members' interests. **Publications:** *Newsletter* (quarterly).

50532 ■ Mailing and Fulfillment Service Association
1421 Prince St., Ste. 410
Alexandria, VA 22314-2806
Ph:(703)836-9200
Free: 800-333-6272
Fax: (703)548-8204
Co. E-mail: mfsa-mail@mfsanet.org
URL: http://www.mfsanet.org
Contact: David A. Weaver, Pres./CEO
Membership: Commercial direct mail producers, letter shops, mailing list houses, fulfillment operations, and advertising agencies. Conducts special interest group meetings. Offers specialized education; conducts research programs. **Publications:** *MFSA Wage Salary, and Fringe Benefit Survey* (semiannual); *Performance Profiles: The Financial Ratios for the Mailing Service Industry* (annual); *Postscripts* (monthly); *Who's Who: MASA's Buyers' Guide to Blue Ribbon Mailing Services* (annual). **Telecommunication Services:** electronic mail, daweaver@mfsanet.org.

50533 ■ Marketing and Advertising Global Network
PO Box 38653
Pittsburgh, PA 15238
Ph:(412)968-5755
Fax: (412)968-5763
Co. E-mail: mxdirector@verizon.net
URL: http://www.magnetglobal.org
Contact: Cheri D. Gmiter, Exec.Dir./Controller
Membership: Cooperative network of non-competing advertising, marketing, merchandising, and public relations agencies. **Purpose:** Aims to bring about, through mutual cooperation, greater accomplishment and efficiency in the management of member advertising agencies. Other goals are: to raise standards of the advertising agency business through the exchange of information relative to agency management and all phases of advertising; to exchange information on all common problems, such as management, sales development, market studies, agency functions, and operations. Aims to inform the general public of current global marketing trends. **Publications:** *MAGNET Matters* (3/year); *This Week at MAGNET* (weekly).

50534 ■ National Advertising Review Board

70 W 36th St., 13th Fl.
New York, NY 10018
Free: (866)334-6272
Co. E-mail: jguthrie@narc.bbb.org
Contact: Howard Bell, Chm.
Membership: Individuals from industry and the public. **Purpose:** Sponsored by the National Advertising Review Council for the purpose of sustaining high standards of truth and accuracy in national advertising. Aims to maintain a self-regulatory mechanism that responds constructively to public complaints about national advertising and which significantly improves advertising performance and credibility. **Publications:** *NARB Panel Reports.*

50535 ■ National Association of Publishers' Representatives

54 Cove Rd.
Huntington, NY 11743
Ph:(631)223-2200
Fax: (631)351-0526
Co. E-mail: napr@naprassoc.com
URL: http://www.naprassoc.com
Contact: Armand Villiger, Exec. Dir.
Membership: Independent publishers' representatives selling advertising space for more than one publisher of consumer, industrial, direct response, and trade publications. **Publications:** *NAPR Newsletter* (monthly); Membership Directory (annual).

50536 ■ Outdoor Advertising Association of America

1850 M St. NW, Ste. 1040
Washington, DC 20036
Ph:(202)833-5566
Fax: (202)833-1522
Co. E-mail: kklein@oaaa.org
URL: http://www.oaaa.org
Contact: Ken Klein, Exec. VP for Government Relations
Membership: Firms owning, erecting, and maintaining standardized poster panels and painted display advertising facilities. Aims to provide leadership, services, and standards to promote, protect and advance the outdoor advertising industry.

50537 ■ Point-of-Purchase Advertising International

1600 Duke St., Ste. 400
Alexandria, VA 22314
Ph:(703)373-8800
Fax: (703)373-8801
Co. E-mail: info@popai.com
URL: http://www.popai.com
Contact: Richard K. Blatt, Pres./CEO
Membership: Producers and suppliers of point-of-purchase advertising signs and displays and national and regional advertisers and retailers interested in use and effectiveness of signs, displays, and other point-of-purchase media. Conducts student education programs; maintains speakers' bureau. **Publications:** *Better Marketing at the Point-of-Purchase; Exhibit Directory* (periodic); *Harvard Business School Case History: L'Eggs Products Incorporated; Industry Magazine* (periodic); *Merchandising Yearbook Awards* (annual); *Point of Purchase Advertising: A Marketing In-Store Arsenal; POPAI News* (bimonthly). **Telecommunication Services:** electronic mail, dblatt@popai.com.

50538 ■ Promotional Products Association International

3125 Skyway Cir. N
Irving, TX 75038-3526
Ph:(972)252-0404
Free: 888-IAM-PPAI
Fax: (972)258-3007
Co. E-mail: steves@ppa.org
URL: http://www.ppa.org
Contact: Steve Slagle CAE, Pres.
Membership: Suppliers and distributors of promotional products including incentives, imprinted ad specialties, premiums, and executive gifts. **Purpose:** Promotes industry contacts in 60 countries. Holds executive development and sales training seminars.

Conducts research and compiles statistics. Administers industry advertising and public relations program. Maintains speakers' bureau. Conducts trade shows, regional training, publishes educational resources. **Publications:** *Distributor Update* (monthly); *PPB Newslink; Promotional Products Association International—Membership Directory and Reference Guide* (annual); *Promotional Products Business* (monthly); *Supplier Update* (biweekly). Also produces educational and promotional publications and audiovisual resources.

50539 ■ Radio Advertising Bureau

1320 Greenway Dr., Ste. 500
Irving, TX 75038-2587
Ph:(212)681-7214
Free: 800-232-3131
Fax: (212)681-7217
Co. E-mail: jhaley@rab.com
URL: http://www.rab.com
Contact: Jeffrey M. Haley, Pres./CEO
Membership: Includes radio stations, radio networks, station sales representatives, and allied industry services, such as producers, research firms, schools, and consultants. **Purpose:** Calls on advertisers and agencies to promote the sale of radio time as an advertising medium. Sponsors program to increase professionalism of radio salespeople, awarding Certified Radio Marketing Consultant designation to those who pass examination. Sponsors regional marketing conferences. Conducts extensive research program into all phases of radio sales. Issues reports on use of radio by national, regional, and local advertisers. Speaks before conventions and groups to explain benefits of radio advertising. Sponsors Radio Creative Fund. Compiles statistics. **Publications:** *Guide to Competitive Media* (biennial); *RAB Instant Background: Profiles of 100 Businesses* (annual); *RAB Media Fact Book* (annual); *Radio Co-op Sources* (annual); *Radio Sales Today* (semiweekly); *Retail Marketing Kit* (monthly). **Telecommunication Services:** electronic mail, member_response@rab.com.

50540 ■ Scenic America

1634 I St. NW, Ste. 510
Washington, DC 20006
Ph:(202)638-0550
Fax: (202)638-3171
Co. E-mail: scenic@scenic.org
URL: http://www.scenic.org
Contact: Kevin Fry, Pres.
Description: Safeguards natural beauty and community character through billboard and sign control, appropriate siting of cellular towers and other utilities, promotion of scenic byways, context-sensitive highway design, and protection of scenic landscapes and cityscapes. Advocates for the preservation of scenic beauty, open space, and quality of life. Fights billboard proliferation and other forms of visual pollution; works for the conservation of scenic byways and for context-sensitive highway design. **Publications:** *Aesthetics, Community Character, and the Law; Fighting Billboard Blight: An Action for Citizens and Public Officials; Getting It Right In the Right-of-Way: Citizen Participation in Context-Sensitive Highway Design; Gift of the Journey: America's Scenic Roadways; The Highway Beautification Act: A Broken Law; Looking at Change Before it Occurs; Power to the People: Strategies for Reducing the Visual Impact of Overhead Utilities; Signs, Signs: The Economic and Environment Benefits of Community Sign Control; Taming Wireless Telecommunications Towers; Tree Conservation Ordinances: Land Use Regulations Go Green; Trees Are Treasure: Sustaining the Community Forest; Viewpoints* (quarterly). **Telecommunication Services:** electronic mail, fry@scenic.org.

50541 ■ Television Bureau of Advertising

3 E 54th St., 10th Fl.
New York, NY 10022-3108
Ph:(212)486-1111
Fax: (212)935-5631
Co. E-mail: info@tvb.org
URL: http://www.tvb.org
Contact: Christopher J. Rohrs, Pres.
Membership: Television stations, station sales representatives, and program producers/syndicates. **Pur-**

pose: Strives to increase advertiser dollars to U.S. spot television. Represents television stations to the advertising community. **Telecommunication Services:** electronic mail, crohrs@tvb.org.

50542 ■ Traffic Audit Bureau for Media Measurement

212 Madison Ave., Ste. 1504
New York, NY 10016
Ph:(212)972-8075
Fax: (212)972-8928
Co. E-mail: inquiry@tabonline.com
URL: http://www.tabonline.com
Contact: Joseph C. Philport, Pres./CEO
Membership: Advertisers, advertising agencies, operators of outdoor advertising plants, bus shelter advertising companies, and backlighted display and painted bulletin companies. **Purpose:** Sets standard practices for the evaluation of circulation and visibility of outdoor advertising; issues statements on the circulation values of outdoor advertising plants. Encourages standardization of terminology and practices in the industry. Seeks to educate those involved in out-of-home media on ways of developing circulation data for advertising sites. Compiles statistics. **Publications:** *Building Accountability for Out of Home Media; Calculating Daily Effective Circulation (DEC); Planning for Out-of-Home Media; Standard Procedures for the Evaluation of Outdoor Advertising; TABBriefs; Tabulations* (quarterly); *What You Should Know About the New TAB Audit.* **Telecommunication Services:** electronic mail, joephilport@tabonline.com.

50543 ■ Transworld Advertising Agency Network

7920 Summer Lake Ct.
Fort Myers, FL 33907
Ph:(239)433-0669
Fax: (239)433-1366
Co. E-mail: info@taan.org
URL: http://www.taan.org
Contact: Gary Lessner, Pres.
Membership: Independently owned advertising agencies that cooperate for exchange of management education and information, reciprocal service, and personal local contact. **Purpose:** Allows members to seek aid of other members in campaign planning, creative services, merchandising, public relations, publicity, media, research, and test facilities. Conducts annual expertise audit. **Publications:** *TAAN Newsletter* (quarterly); *Transcript* (semiannual). **Telecommunication Services:** electronic mail, gary@taan.org.

DIRECTORIES OF EDUCATIONAL PROGRAMS

50544 ■ *O'Dwyer's New York Public Relations Directory*

Pub: J.R. O'Dwyer Company Inc.
Contact: Eileen Kelly, Sales Mgr.
Released: Annual, latest edition 2000, new edition expected 2003. **Price:** $50, individuals plus $4.00 for postage. **Covers:** Approximately 600 public relations firms, 840 corporations, 225 trade associations, and 500 public relations service firms; over 50 executive recruiters and employment agencies. **Entries Include:** Contact information.

50545 ■ *Red Book—A Directory of the PRSA Counselors Academy*

Pub: Public Relations Society of America (PRSA)
Contact: Gale Spreter
E-mail: gale.spreter@prsa.org
Released: latest edition 2004 edition. **Covers:** Public relations firms and academy members. **Entries Include:** Name and contact information.

REFERENCE WORKS

50546 ■ *Advertising—Agencies & Counselors Directory*

Pub: infoUSA Inc.
Released: Annual. **Entries Include:** Name, address, phone, size of advertisement, name of owner or man-

ager, number of employees, year first in "Yellow Pages." Compiled from telephone company "Yellow Pages," nationwide. **Arrangement:** Geographical.

50547 ■ *The Advertising Handbook for Small Business*
Pub: Self-Counsel Press, Inc.
Ed: Dell Dennison. **Released:** 1994, second edition. **Price:** $10.95 (paper). **Description:** Formerly *The Advertising Handbook*.

50548 ■ "Almost Famous: Market Yourself as an Expert" in *My Business* (October/November 2003, pp. 45)
Pub: My Business Magazine
Ed: Nancy Mann Jackson. **Description:** The importance of establishing one's self as an expert in the particular field in which you are selling will help a salesperson stand out from competitors. Tips includes speaking at conferences, creating informational products, the use of newspapers and magazines or business publications, writing articles, or doing guest spots on television or radio shows.

50549 ■ "Association Listing" in *Black Enterprise* (Vol. 34, No. 5, December 2003, pp. 6)
Pub: Earl Graves Publishing Co.
Description: Black Enterprise offers a Directory of Associations on its Web site to help startup businesses, research or networking.

50550 ■ "Bad image may keep patent board away" in *Crain's Detroit Business* (Vol. 16, No. 12, March 20, 2000, pp. 53)
Pub: Crain Communications, Inc.
Ed: Matt Roush. **Description:** Birmingham, Michigan attorney, Eric Dobrusin, has been instrumental in establishing the year-old National Patent Board, a nonprofit alternative dispute mechanism for intellectual property cases.

50551 ■ "Bald Ambition: Hell-Bent on Getting Attention? Try a Zany Marketing Stunt" in *Entrepreneur* (Vol. 32, December 2004, No. 12, pp. 28)
Pub: Entrepreneur Media Inc.
Ed: Geoff Williams. **Description:** Gary Arnold, owner of Gary's Uptown Restaurant and Bar, offered discounts to balding customers every Wednesday and received national press.

50552 ■ "Ballooning Riches" in *Small Business Opportunities* (Vol. 16, No. 3, May 2004, pp. 46, 48)
Pub: Harris Publications, Inc.
Description: Profile of Landmark Creations of Burnsville, Minnesota. The firm offers fun and affordable inflatables to attract clients, and build a company's product image or brand.

50553 ■ "Banners Tout Development" in *Mississippi Business Journal* (Vol. 29, January 2007, No. 4, pp. 11)
Pub: Venture Publications, Inc.
Ed: Wally Northway **Description:** Flashy banners have been erected all over downtown Jackson's business district. The banner idea, originated by a local restaurateur, is designed to bring visual attention to many unnoticed development projects and businesses in the area.

50554 ■ "Beau Rivage Resort And Casino" in *Mississippi Business Journal* (Vol. 29, January 2007, No. 2, pp. 6)
Pub: Venture Publications, Inc.
Description: Profile of Brian J. Bork, Executive Director of Advertising for the Beau Rivage Resort and Casino in Biloxi. Bork manages a team of graphic artists, production assistants and account coordinators.

50555 ■ "Being Small, Looking Big" in *Boston Business Journal* (Vol. 23, No. 21, June 27, 2003, pp. 24)
Pub: American City Business Journals
Ed: Chelsea Lowe. **Description:** Nancy Michaels of Impression Impact, Inc. discusses ways small companies can market themselves in a way that makes them look large, without spending large amounts of money to do so.

50556 ■ "A Bonding Experience" in *Ingram's* (Vol. 28, No. 9, September 2002, pp. 23)
Pub: Show Me Publishing, Inc.
Ed: Mike Glynn. **Description:** Scouting for an ad agency, Maris Brenner from The Lodge of Four Seasons, regards track record as important and so chose Kupper Parker Communications, while Bob Sullivan of Boulevard Brewing Company says that an agency should have a clear understanding of what the business is and chose CHRW Advertising. Kansas Lottery chose Barkley Evergreen and Partners because of the firm's imagination.

50557 ■ "Bovine Blues?" in *Entrepreneur* (Vol. 31, No. 8, August 2003, pp. 25)
Pub: Entrepreneur Media, Inc.
Ed: Mark Henricks. **Description:** Review of the book, "Purple Cow: Transform Your Business by Being Remarkable", written by Seth Godin. Godin believes every company needs something phenomenal, counterintuitive and exciting in order to take attention away from competitors.

50558 ■ "BP Amoco wants to sell much more than gas at its new stations" in *The New York Times* (July 25, 2000, pp. C6)
Pub: The New York Times Company
Ed: Kruti Trivedi. **Description:** BP Amoco is spending $7 billion to present a fresh brand image through BP Connect, a new round of service stations with cafilatte, solar panels, imaginatively-lit markets and e-commerce kiosks. Thus far, 20 percent of gas stations revenues come from the convenience markets. The bright green and yellow stations will be featured in ads, created by Ogilvy & Mather Worldwide promoting BP as a green company. The campaign will cost $100 million a year.

50559 ■ "Brand Me: Marketing Techniques to Make You Stand Out" in *Black Enterprise* (Vol. 35, December 2004, No. 5, pp. 78)
Pub: Earl G. Graves Publishing Co. Inc.
Ed: Lee Anna Jackson. **Description:** Branding is important when marketing a product or service. Proper branding can make a product stand out from competitors.

50560 ■ "The Brand Report Card" in *Harvard Business Review* (Vol. 78, No. 1, January 2000, pp. 147)
Pub: Harvard Business School Publishing Corp.
Ed: Kevin Lane Keller. **Description:** The importance of brand management transcends all industry types and companies. Brand image and consumer perception should be continually analyzed to help maintain a product's foothold in the market.

50561 ■ "The Brand of Success" in *Small Business Opportunities* (Vol. 16, No. 2, March 2004, pp. 118, 120)
Pub: Harris Publications, Inc.
Ed: James Feldman. **Description:** Brand image is critical to a small business' success. Marketing materials serve two purposes. Guidelines to create or design promotions materials are presented.

50562 ■ "Branding: Not Just for Big-Budget Businesses" in *Ingram's* (Vol. 29, No. 8, August 2003, pp. 16)
Pub: Show Me Publishing, Inc.
Ed: T. DeWayne Ables. **Description:** Basic information regarding the importance of properly branding products in order to increase sales is examined.

50563 ■ "Brave New World" in *Home Office Computing* (Vol. 18, No. 9, September 2000, pp. 92)
Pub: Scholastic Inc.
Ed: Jeffery D. Zbar. **Description:** Horror author Stephen King stirred the publishing world with his Riding the Bullet, an e-book that sold for $2.50 a copy online. Resources for creative professionals range from file-sharing sites that let artists post and sell content while retaining their own copyrights. Experts warn that some sites charge fees ranging from 20 to 50 percent of sales. Authors should aggressively market their works at other Web sites and e-zines. Publicity and power are much the same in the E-publishing world.

50564 ■ "Break Through Ads" in *My Business* (February/March 2003, pp. 13-14)
Pub: My Business Magazine
Ed: Kathleen Landis. **Description:** The use of vehicles with signs for advertising is investigated. Various options are explored, including hand-painted signs, vinyl signs, decals, magnetic signs, and adhesive vinyl wraps.

50565 ■ "Build Your Web Identity" in *E-business Advisor* (Vol. 18, No. 5, May 2000, pp. 30)
Pub: Advisor Media, Inc.
Ed: Maria Szalay, James J. Datovech. **Description:** With about 800 million Web pages deployed over eight million Web sites, e-commerce companies have to follow certain fundamental design and marketing principles in their Web strategy. Key tips for such strategy are provided.

50566 ■ *Burrelle's Media Directory*
Pub: BurrellesLuce
Contact: Kay Guindon
Price: $1895 Single user per annum; $275 Additional per user, 2nd-5th user; $250 Additional per user, 6th-12th user. **Covers:** Approximately 300,000 media contacts and 60,000 media outlets, print and electronic media in North America. **Entries Include:** Name, address, phone, fax, names and titles of key personnel, geographical area served, subsidiary and branch names and locations, description. **Arrangement:** Geographical; magazines are arranged by subject. **Indexes:** Name, subject, geographical.

50567 ■ "Business Development through Philanthropy" in *Ingram's* (Vol. 27, No. 12, December 2001, pp. 23)
Pub: Show Me Publishing, Inc.
Description: The use of philanthropy for business development is discussed. As a business owner, this activity will improve company image and expand networking opportunities.

50568 ■ "Buzz Skill" in *Entrepreneur* (Vol. 33, October 2005, No. 10, pp. 81)
Pub: Entrepreneur Media Inc.
Ed: Gwen Moran. **Description:** Profile of Dave Balter, known as the Buzzmaster. Balter founded the Boston, Massachusetts marketing agency, BzzAgent Inc. Balter promotes word-of-mouth marketing through a network of 92,000 volunteers he calls BzzAgents.

50569 ■ "C&S Marketing to be CoreLogic" in *Sacramento Bee* (October 25, 2005)
Pub: The Sacramento Bee
Ed: Dale Kasler. **Description:** C&S Marketing recently changed its name to CoreLogic. The software maker, located in Sacramento, California, helps mortgage lenders detect fraud and estimate property values and was recently named one of the nation's 500 fastest growing private companies by Inc. magazine.

50570 ■ "Celeb-Savvy Publisher" in *Crain's New York Business* (Vol. 23, January 29, 2007, No. 5, pp. F24)
Pub: Crain Communications, Inc.
Ed: Matthew Flamm. **Description:** Profile of Jason Binn who is the founder and chief executive of Niche Media Holdings, a publisher of glossy magazines such as Gotham and Los Angeles Confidential. His innovative techniques led to a successful company which reports $40 million in annual revenues.

50571 ■ "Change of Face: Tactics: Is Your Logo Losing Its Luster?" in *Entrepreneur* (Vol. 31, No. 9, September 2003, pp. 87)
Pub: Entrepreneur Media, Inc.
Ed: Kim T. Gordon. **Description:** The importance of a company logo is stressed, including facts on the three types of logos used. Ways to determine if a company's logo has become dated and needs to be updated are explored.

50572 ■ "The Change Up: Find New Uses for Your Products" in *My Business* (February/March 2003, pp. 15)
Pub: My Business Magazine

Ed: Evelyn Beck. Description: Diversification of a product can be a good tool for increasing sales, but it is imperative to do research.

50573 ■ "Chart-toppers" in *Entrepreneur* **(Vol. 30, No. 3, March 2002, pp. 88)**
Pub: Entrepreneur Media Inc.
Ed: Nichole L. Torres. Description: The use of charts in getting business publicity is explored.

50574 ■ "Clicks to Bricks" in *Entrepreneur* **(Vol. 33, August 2005, No. 8, pp. 44)**
Pub: Entrepreneur Media Inc.
Ed: Melissa Campanelli. Description: Following a current trend, more e-tailers are opening brick-and-mortar stores. This move will strengthen brand-name recognition, give local customers a place to shop or return merchandise, lower promotional fees, and expand a customer base.

50575 ■ "Clueing in customers." in *Harvard Business Review* **(Vol. 81, No. 2, February 2003, pp. 100)**
Pub: Harvard Business School Press
Ed: Leonard L. Berry, Neeli Bendapudi. Description: Evidence management is discussed by examining how the Mayo Clinic has continually worked to provide as positive an experience as possible to its patients. As a result, word of mouth about the hospital is quite positive, along with strong customer loyalty.

50576 ■ "Cold gold" in *Entrepreneur* **(Vol. 30, No. 3, March 2002, pp. 92)**
Pub: Entrepreneur Media Inc.
Ed: Jerry Fisher. Description: Advice is given on using true originality in advertising, spotlighting Amana Appliances in Amana, Iowa.

50577 ■ "Commentary: Testimonials-Let Your Customers Do the Talking" in *Long Island Business News* **(March 12, 2004)**
Pub: Dolan Media Newswires
Ed: Adina Genn. Description: Long Island businesses are cultivating customer testimonials on the Web, in brochures and on site. Tips for using customer praise to promote a business are included.

50578 ■ "Commentary: Testimonials-Let Your Customers Do the Talking" in *Long Island Business News* **(March 12, 2004)**
Pub: Dolan Media Newswires
Ed: Adina Genn. Description: Long Island businesses are cultivating customer testimonials on the Web, in brochures and on site. Tips for using customer praise to promote a business are included.

50579 ■ *The Complete Guide to Publicity: Maximize Visibility for Your Products, Services & Organizations*
Pub: N T C Contemporary Publishing Co.
Ed: Joe Marconi. Released: 1999. Price: $39.95.

50580 ■ "Council Promotes Banners, Tours to Publicize Super Bowl" in *Crain's Detroit Business* **(Vol. 21, October 10, 2005, No. 43, pp. 33)**
Pub: Crain Communications Inc. - Detroit
Ed: Jennette Smith. Description: Detroit's Tourism Economic Development Councils is recommending the use of banners on businesses and downtown tours as a means to publicize and market Super Bowl XL. The move is expected to help businesses after the game has departed.

50581 ■ "Crucial triad" in *Daily Business Review* **(Vol. 77, No. 198, March 24, 2003, pp. AA4)**
Pub: American Lawyer Media LP
Ed: David Geyer, Elizabeth Lampert. Description: Ways in which law firm partners can use the triad of business development, marketing and media relations to better serve clients is explained.

50582 ■ "Cybersearch Specialist" in *Crain's New York Business* **(Vol. 23, January 29, 2007, No. 5 ,pp. F16)**
Pub: Crain Communications, Inc.
Ed: Amanda Fung. Description: Profile of Matthew Greitzer, director of search engine marketing for Ave-

nue A/Razorfish. The firm has garnered more than twenty search marketing campaigns from clients such as Schering-Plough and Verizon and is the largest buyer of search advertising.

50583 ■ "Doctored Image" in *Entrepreneur* **(Vol. 30, No. 3, March 2002, pp. 25)**
Pub: Entrepreneur Media Inc.
Ed: Elizabeth J. Goodgold. Description: Often, tuning up a brand on a product, is just what the doctor ordered to increase sales.

50584 ■ "Dot your eyes" in *Entrepreneur* **(Vol. 30, No. 2, February 2002, pp. 25)**
Pub: Entrepreneur Media Inc.
Ed: Elizabeth J. Goodgold. Description: Innovated shuttle bus painting is helping off-airport parking companies increase business.

50585 ■ "E-mail Marketer Looks for More Clout" in *Atlanta Business Chronicle* **(Vol. 25, December 13, 2002, No. 27, pp. A3)**
Pub: American City Business Publications, Inc.
Ed: Mary Jane Credeur. Description: Silverpop Systems Inc. has acquired Epigraphx LLC, Redwood, California. The acquisition took place in December 2002, as part of Silverpop's initiative to grow in the e-mail marketing industry. The deal will increase staff to 55 and will triple Silverpop's revenues, which remain undisclosed. The deal also expands Silverpop's client roster and increased profits are discussed by Silverpop CEO, Bill Nussey.

50586 ■ "Entrepreneur Column" in *Entrepreneur.com* **(September 15, 2005)**
Pub: Entrepreneur Media Inc.
Ed: Kim Gordon. Description: In order to develop a marketing campaign to develop referrals for a small business, you must determine whether you are marketing to the influencers or the influential. Steps for winning referrals from both groups are outlined.

50587 ■ "Exec has Firm Grip on Software Sales" in *Crain's New York Business* **(Vol. 23, January 29, 2007, No. 5, pp. F13)**
Pub: Crain Communications, Inc.
Ed: Amanda Fung. Description: Profile of Amanda Fung and her position as business and marketing officer for Microsoft Corp's New York/New Jersey district. Her precision helped bring in revenues of more than $492 million for her region in 2006 and her team expects this year's revenues to exceed $600 million.

50588 ■ "A Family Affair-In Advertising" in *Business Week* **(No. 3762, December 17, 2001, pp. 10)**
Pub: McGraw-Hill Inc.
Description: More companies are using family settings to promote products.

50589 ■ "The Fiberglass Menagerie" in *Inc.* **(February 1, 2002)**
Pub: Inc. Magazine
Ed: Ed Engel. Description: Profile of FAST Corporation, the manufacturer of fiberglass roadside figures used for business advertising.

50590 ■ "Filmmakers Face Some Big Challenges On Tiny Cellphones" in *Wall Street Journal* **(Vol. 248, December 2006, No. 145, pp. B1)**
Pub: Dow Jones & Co. Inc.
Ed: Peter Grant. Description: American entertainment industry and wireless companies invest billions of dollars into bringing movie and TV content to the video-capable small screen cellphones now flooding the market. Hollywood hopes this new market will become their "third screen."

50591 ■ "Ford to Mark 100th Anniversary This Year" in *San Jose Mercury News* **(April 11, 2003)**
Pub: Knight-Ridder/Tribune Business News
Ed: Matt Nauman. Description: Ford Motor Company will use its 100th Anniversary as a tool to market its vehicles, through reminders of Ford's impact over the past century.

50592 ■ "Freedom of Speech: The legacy you leave yourself" in *Atlanta Business Chronicle* **(Vol. 24, No. 10, August 10, 2001, pp. 39A)**
Pub: American City Business Journals Inc.
Ed: Jeffrey Gitomer. Description: The best way to gain new leads and market yourself is to give a free speech. That is, make a speech for free, but do not give a sales pitch, at a civic organization, for example. The advantages of providing a speaking engagement for gratis are listed. Six tactics of free speech are listed.

50593 ■ "Fresh Ideas" in *Entrepreneur* **(Vol. 32, December 2004, No. 12, pp. 91)**
Pub: Entrepreneur Media Inc.
Ed: Gwen Moran. Description: Anthony Shurman, president of Yosha! Enterprises was inspired by a movie to give his Momints breath mints to department store and mall Santas during the holiday. Radio stations started mentioning the promotion on their stations, giving Shurman more impact than a typical marketing campaign.

50594 ■ "Getting the Dish; Blogs Allow Everyone to be a Critic" in *Crain's New York Business* **(Vol. 23, January 29, 2007, No. 5, pp. 48)**
Pub: Crain Communications, Inc.
Description: Blogs are changing the landscape of the dining scene. Everyone can be a critic on such blogs as Chowmaster.com, Mouthfulsfood.com, or Thestrongbuzz.com among hosts of others.

50595 ■ "Getting Ink: Need Exposure?" in *Entrepreneur* **(Vol. 33, February 2005, No. 2)**
Pub: Entrepreneur Media Inc.
Ed: Kim T. Gordon. Description: Hiring a publicist or a public relations firm can help establish media contacts. Six practical tips to get media coverage for a small firm are listed.

50596 ■ *Getting Publicity: A Do-It-Yourself Guide for Small Business and Non-Profit Groups*
Pub: Self-Counsel Press, Inc.
Ed: Tana Fletcher and Julia Rockler. Released: 1990. Price: $12.95 (paper).

50597 ■ *Getting Publicity: The Very Best Book for Your Small Business*
Pub: Self-Counsel Press, Inc.
Ed: Tana Fletcher. Released: 1995. Price: $14.95.

50598 ■ "Getting Stars to Shine: Dawn To Dusk Image Agency has an A-List Clientele" in *Black Enterprise* **(Vol. 34, No. 4, Nov. 2003, pp. 43)**
Pub: Earl Graves Publishing Co.
Ed: Bridget McCrea. Description: Profile of Dawn To Dusk Image Agency based in Los Angeles and New York is presented. The 10-employee firm represents independent artists who create hairstyles, makeup, wardrobes, and overall images of stars.

50599 ■ "Gilded and Gelded. Hard-Won Lessons From the PR Wars" in *Harvard Business Review* **(Vol. 81, No. 10, October 2003, pp. 44)**
Pub: Harvard Business School Press
Ed: Dick Martin. Description: The ways in which AT&T mismanaged itself into a public relations problem are evaluated.

50600 ■ "Good Timing" in *Entrepreneur* **(Vol. 32, August 2004, No. 8, pp. 65)**
Pub: Entrepreneur Media Inc.
Ed: Gwen Moran. Description: Scott Tests, COO and co-founder of Mindbridge Software Inc. in Pennsylvania, takes advantage of slow news periods to announce the release of his company's new products.

50601 ■ "Guerrilla Tactic Targets Golfers" in *Inc.* **(October 1, 2004)**
Pub: Inc. Magazine
Ed: Jess McCuan. Description: Profile of CPRi, a staffing firm based in Chicago, Illinois, affixes its logo to golf carts at charity tournaments for publicity.

50602 ■ "Guerrillas in our Midst" in *Crain's Chicago Business* (Vol. 30, January 2007, No. 3, pp. 16)
Pub: Crain Communications, Inc.
Ed: Steve Hendershot. Description: Guerrilla Marketing is an innovative way of getting a company's products name to consumers by attention-grabbing antics.

50603 ■ "Has Your Company Found Its Voice?" in *Fast Company* (August 2001, pp. 40)
Pub: Fast Company
Ed: Paul C. Judge. Description: Some brands really talk the talk, and sophisticated technology has the power to turn a customer's interaction with an automated call center into a virtual marketing conversation.

50604 ■ "Helping Hand" in *Crain's New York Business* (Vol. 23, January 15, 2007, No. 3, pp. 24)
Pub: Crain Communications, Inc.
Description: Bronx officials created a $6.75 million fund providing no-interest loans to businesses that make energy-saving renovations. Companies are also eligible for state and federal subsidies through the three Empire Zones and the Empowerment Zone. Bronx Overall Economic Development Corp. is also reaching out to businesses across the country trying to lure them to the region.

50605 ■ "Hey, Got a Qpass Rookie Card?" in *Fast Company* (November 2001, pp. 44)
Pub: Fast Company
Ed: Alison Overholt. Description: Profile of Seattle-based Qpass, and vice president of marketing Norman Guadagno, who launched a campaign to bring employees up to speed on the firm's restructured business model and newly designed logo using trading cards.

50606 ■ "Highland Park, Budco are happy together" in *Crain's Detroit Business* (Vol. 19, No. 6, Feb. 10, 2003, pp. 16)
Pub: Crain Communications Inc., Detroit
Ed: Robert Ankeny. Description: Profile of Budco, the growing marketing and communications company, will settle in the city of Highland Park, Michigan.

50607 ■ "Hit the Road" in *Entrepreneur* (Vol. 31, No. 10, October 2003, pp. 87)
Pub: Entrepreneur Media, Inc.
Ed: Elizabeth Goodgold. Description: The Adopt-a-Highway program also provides a means for a small business to gain visibility while doing good.

50608 ■ "Home In on Your Image" in *My Business* (June/July 2002, pp. 15)
Pub: My Business Magazine
Ed: Lisa Waddle. Description: Artist, Jean Steinhardt, helps small businesses set themselves apart from large competitors by drawing owner's homes or small office buildings used for mailing and marketing materials.

50609 ■ "How to build a blockbuster" in *Harvard Business Review* (Vol. 80, No. 10, October 2002, pp. 18)
Pub: Harvard Business School Press
Ed: Gary Lynn, Richard Reilly. Description: Colgate-Palmolive's debut of a new toothpaste is used as a case study to understand why the product achieved only a one percent market share.

50610 ■ "Image is Everything" in *Entrepreneur* (Vol. 32, September 2004, No. 9, pp. 106)
Pub: Entrepreneur Media Inc.
Description: Profile of Sandy Meyers, marketer of materials that incorporate fine art. Meyers uses the process of securing fine art prints and displaying them on items such as luggage tags, postcards, mouse pads, and coffee mugs, instead of a company's logo for marketing purposes. She also runs Visual Promotions, a firm that creates point-of-purchase and trade show banners and displays.

50611 ■ "In-Your-Face-Selling" in *Inc.* (November 2006, pp. 33)
Pub: Gruner & Jahr USA Publishing
Ed: Adam Bluestein. Description: A strong approach to closing business to business deals is to take a small group to the customer to meet with the client and show the support that's available if you're chosen. While an expensive approach due to travel expenses, the pay-offs are very lucrative in the long term. The client identifies more with your company after a face to face meeting.

50612 ■ "It's All About the Image" in *Crain's New York Business* (Vol. 22, December 11, 2006, No. 50, pp. 26)
Pub: Crain Communications, Inc.
Description: Advantage Consulting Services, a Los Angeles-based Internet marketing consultancy, offers businesses the service of creating and maintaining their MySpace pages.

50613 ■ "Job Titles of the Future" in *Fast Company* (August 2001, pp. 36)
Pub: Fast Company
Ed: Christine Canabou. Description: Profile of Kimberly Kay Railsback, designer who helps build corporate image for businesses, working for InteQ Corporation, a management-service provider in Massachusetts.

50614 ■ "King Kullen Freshening Up Image" in *Long Island Business News* (May 7, 2004)
Pub: Dolan Media Newswires
Ed: David Reich-Hale. Description: Profile of King Kullen, America's first supermarket. The company is revamping stores as it faces competition from Stop & Shop and Waldbaum's.

50615 ■ "Kmart Makes Branding Pro Its New Chief" in *Black Enterprise* (Vol. 35, December 2004, No. 5, pp. 33)
Pub: Earl G. Graves Publishing Co. Inc.
Ed: Sonia Alleyne. Description: Kmart's appointment of Aylwin Lewis makes him the sixth African American to head a Fortune 500 company at this time, eighth to ever hold the position. Kmart believes Lewis' strong reputation for branding and team building will increase the retailer's profits. Statistical data included.

50616 ■ "Knowledge Networks: Making the Brand" in *Venture Capital Journal* (Vol. 41, No. 8, August 2000, pp. 18)
Pub: Venture Economics
Ed: Alistair Christopher. Description: Profile of Knowledge Networks, a marketing intelligence system firm, claims they offer an exclusive service to businesses that shows a concise view of consumers and their behavior toward advertising, brands, and buying.

50617 ■ "Kraft Not Alone" in *Crain's Chicago Business* (Vol. 30, February 2007, No. 6, pp. 8)
Pub: Crain Communications, Inc.
Description: Consumer watchdog group, The Center for Science in the Public Interest, has been putting pressure on food companies to be more truthful on their product labels. Listing of companies who have had misleading claims on their products is included.

50618 ■ "Lights, Camera, Action! Do You Dream of Promoting Your Business On Oprah Or the Today Show, But Don't Know Where To Start?" in *Entrepreneur*
Pub: Entrepreneur Media Inc.
Ed: Eileen Figure Sandlin. Description: Lee Snijders, founder of Lee Snijders Designs, explains how, after appearing on HGTV's decorating show, Designers' Challenge, he was shocked at the response. By the next morning he had received 225 emails requesting his interior design service. Four steps to promote a business on a television show are presented.

50619 ■ "Lights, camera, action" in *Entrepreneur* (Vol. 31, No. 4, April 2003, pp. 126)
Pub: Entrepreneur Media Inc.
Ed: Don Debelak. Description: Steps to take in order to get a new product featured on a home shopping network are presented.

50620 ■ "Lights, Camera, Trauma!" in *Crain's Chicago Business* (Vol. 26, No. 50, December 15, 2003, pp. 1)
Pub: Crain Communications, Inc.
Ed: Sarah A. Klein. Description: Chicago-area hospitals are enjoying the publicity they are gaining through reality television shows featuring births, women's specials, and documentaries about children's hospitals. Despite the costs incurred to accommodate camera crews, the hospitals are seeing a rise in donations.

50621 ■ "Living High on the Blog" in *Entrepreneur* (Vol. 33, February 2005, No. 2, pp. 65)
Pub: Entrepreneur Media Inc.
Ed: Gwen Moran. Description: Reach Communications Consulting founder, William Arruda, discovered an 800 percent hike in traffic on his firm's Website after being mentioned on an Internet blog; ways to add blogs to a public relations campaign are investigated.

50622 ■ "Logo design reflects on your business; so take it seriously" in *San Antonio Business Journal* (Vol. 15, No. 4, Feb. 16, 2001, pp. 18)
Pub: American City Business Journals, Inc.
Ed: Lara August. Description: The importance of a business logo are discussed, focusing on designer choice and guidelines for development.

50623 ■ "Looking For Winning Small Businesses" in *Crain's Detroit Business* (Vol. 23, February 5, 2007, No. 6, pp. 27)
Pub: Crain Communications Inc. - Detroit
Description: Award recognizes small companies who are exceptionally innovative or who have grown through difficult problems to be stronger. It is open to all firms over three years old with one hundred fifty employees or less in Wayne, Oakland, Macomb, Livingston and Washtenaw counties.

50624 ■ "Making New Memories at Little Cheese Shop" in *Business Journal-Milwaukee* (Vol. 20, No. 45, July 25, 2003, pp. A15)
Pub: American City Business Journals, Inc.
Ed: Becca Mader. Description: Profile of Linda Lutz and brother-in-law Howard Lutz, who reopened West Allis Cheese & Sausage Shop after it closed in 2001. They have rebranded the company, expanded the line of foods it makes, began marketing the foods to local shopping malls, as well as changing the labels to make the small company profitable.

50625 ■ "Making a scene: your special event won't be so special if nobody hears about it." in *Entrepreneur* (Vol. 31, No. 5, May 2003, pp. 79)
Pub: Entrepreneur Media Inc.
Ed: Kim T. Gordon. Description: Various methods to promote a special event for a small business are covered, including the use of magazines and newspapers or television and radio.

50626 ■ "Man With the Golden Touch" in *Black Enterprise* (Vol. 35, October 2004, No. 3, pp. 53)
Pub: Earl G. Graves Publishing Co. Inc.
Ed: Demetria Lucas. Description: Profile of Darrick Lee Warfield, owner of the Atlanta-based Goldfinger C.S., with revenues of $300,000 reported in 2003. Warfield and his three employees design album covers, Websites, logos, and advertisements. While in high school, Warfield won a national design competition for the American Can Company.

50627 ■ "Marketing: How to Get Some Attention" in *Business Week Online* (October 18, 2002)
Pub: McGraw-Hill Inc.
Ed: Karen E. Klein. Description: Small businesses can be at a disadvantage when it comes to publicity. Tips for getting press coverage and attracting business partners for a small Midwest cabinet shop are offered.

50628 ■ "Marketing" in *Inc.* (Volume 27, March 2005, No. 3, pp. 36)
Pub: Inc. Magazine
Ed: Lora Kolodny. **Description:** The art of writing a press release is investigated.

50629 ■ *Marketing Myths*
Pub: Bell Springs Publishing
Ed: K. J. Clancy and R. S. Shulman. **Price:** $19.95.
Description: Marketing, promotion, and spreading the word about your product or service is essential to every business, big or small. Here is the help you need to cut through the theories and myths, and deal with the real world of finding and keeping customers and clients.

50630 ■ *Marketing in the Not-for-Profit Sectors*
Pub: Butterworth-Heinemann
Ed: Margaret Kinnell-Evans and Jennifer MacDougall. **Released:** 1997. **Price:** $32.95; $34.95.

50631 ■ "Marketing Quandary: VCs See a Growing Need for Differentiation" in *Venture Capital Journal* (Vol. 41, No. 8, August 2000, pp. 31-33)
Pub: Venture Economics
Ed: Charles Fellers. **Description:** Marketing partners become a new addition to several venture capital firms by focusing on mentoring and promoting portfolio companies.

50632 ■ *Marketing Without Advertising*
Pub: Bell Springs Publishing
Ed: Michael Phillips and Salli Rasberry. **Price:** 18.95.
Description: Argues with documented proof that almost all advertising is totally ineffective and an utter waste of money and that most business owners have been successfully duped into believing that advertising is both necessary and productive in spite of obvious evidence to the contrary. Includes more than a hundred tried and tested marketing strategies that have worked for all kinds of small businesses.

50633 ■ "Media Planning: The Seven 'Undeniable Truths'" in *Ingram's* (Vol. 28, No. 9, September 2002, pp. 27)
Pub: Show Me Publishing, Inc.
Ed: John McGuigan. **Description:** A guide for planning and executing integrated marketing programs for clients is provided.

50634 ■ "The Mother of Stunt Marketers" in *Business 2.0* (Vol. 6, July 2005, No. 6, pp. 60-61)
Pub: Time, Inc.
Ed: Elizabeth Esfahani. **Description:** The Publicity Stunts Hall of Fame highlights the crazy things people have done as marketing tricks that generated publicity and increased sales for products.

50635 ■ "My Business Manual: Due Diligence" in *My Business* (December/January 2003, pp. 44)
Pub: My Business Magazine
Ed: Julie Bawden Davis. **Description:** A good customer service program ensures repeat business. Five easy ways to gain new customers are also listed.

50636 ■ "My Business Manual: One Step Ahead" in *My Business* (December/January 2003, pp. 43)
Pub: My Business Magazine
Ed: Alan S. Horowitz. **Description:** Customer loyalty programs are discussed, including tips on starting a frequent buyer program.

50637 ■ "My Business Manual: Open Up" in *My Business* (December/January 2003, pp. 41-42)
Pub: My Business Magazine
Ed: John Rubino. **Description:** Five ways to grow a business by targeting new customers are highlighted, including identification of the new target market, becoming part of the community, know the limitations of a business, getting clients interested in a product, and ways to market a new product.

50638 ■ "Nab your Niche" in *Entrepreneur* (Vol. 31, No. 6, June 2003, pp. 100)
Pub: Entrepreneur Media Inc.
Ed: Nichole L. Torres. **Description:** Finding a niche in the home-remodeling market is important; according to the National Association of Home Builders, 1.35 million new single-family homes will be built in the U.S. in 2003, and remodeling is at all time highs.

50639 ■ "The Name Game" in *Entrepreneur* (Vol. 33, January 2005, No. 1, pp. 72)
Pub: Entrepreneur Media Inc.
Ed: Jane Easter Bahls. **Description:** Under the legal doctrine, reverse confusion, small companies can file lawsuits against large corporations over trademark infringement.

50640 ■ "Net Company: Don't Shout, Listen" in *Fast Company* (August 2001, pp. 129)
Pub: Fast Company
Ed: Fara Warner. **Description:** The article shows how the Proctor & Gamble company has turned the Internet into a device for listening to customers, and also experiment with their brands.

50641 ■ "New CEO: So What is Moto, Anyway?" in *Crain's Chicago Business* (Vol. 26, No. 51, December 22, 2003, pp. 20)
Pub: Crain Communications, Inc.
Ed: Julie Johnsson. **Description:** Newly appointed CEO of Motorola, Edward Zander, wants to fashion a distinctive corporate image for the electronics giant. The firm reports $27 billion in revenues and Zander feels the firm needs to better define itself.

50642 ■ "The new culture of criticism is hurting you and your company" in *Fast Company* (May 2001, pp. 102)
Pub: Fast Company
Ed: Seth Godin. **Description:** The five ways to be an unfair critic, and in turn hurt your business, are listed.

50643 ■ *The New Direct Marketing: How to Implement a Profit-Driven Database Marketing Strategy*
Pub: McGraw-Hill Professional Book Group
Released: 3rd ed. 1998. **Price:** $114.95; $79.95.

50644 ■ "New Office Created to Market Michigan for Films" in *Crain's Detroit Business* (Vol. 22, December 18, 2006, No. 51, pp. 19)
Pub: Crain Communications Inc. - Detroit
Ed: Bill Shea. **Description:** Michigan to organize marketing for film making in the region. New office will concentrate on luring movie companies to film in Michigan

50645 ■ *The New Publicity Kit*
Pub: John Wiley & Sons, Inc.
Ed: Jeanette Smith. **Released:** 1995. **Price:** $42.50.

50646 ■ "New York Community Bancorp Renames All of Its Branches..." in *Long Island Business News* (February 6, 2004)
Pub: Dolan Media Newswires
Ed: Claude Solnik. **Description:** New York Community Bancorp has rebranded its bank branches in Nassau and Suffolk in order to create a more clearly defined network of regional banks. Information regarding the bank's reorganization efforts is explained.

50647 ■ "Newsletter company to nearly double in size" in *Atlanta Business Chronicle* (Vol. 25, January 10, 2003, No. 31, pp. 5A)
Pub: American City Business Publications, Inc.
Ed: Jim Lovel. **Description:** NewRx which presently publishes 24 health and medicine-related newsletters, will double its size with the addition of 20 more publications. The Georgia International Convention Center has hired four marketing consultants to promote the grand opening of the College Park Center.

50648 ■ *1,001 Ways to Market Yourself & Your Small Business*
Pub: Berkley Publishing Group
Ed: Lisa Shaw. **Released:** 1997. **Price:** $12.95.

50649 ■ "Organizers Say Houston Will Be Ready for XXXVIII" in *Houston Chronicle* (April 11, 2003)
Pub: Knight-Ridder/Tribune Business News
Ed: Bill Murphy. **Description:** Organizers of Super Bowl 38 contend the city of Houston will be ready for the event. A checklist of things the city needs to complete before the game is included.

50650 ■ "The Power of Your Reputation Equals Profits Can Be a Tangible Business Strategy" in *Black Enterprise* (Vol. 35, August 2004, No. 1)
Pub: Earl G. Graves Publishing Co. Inc.
Ed: Description: Ways a woman used her reputation to promote her graphic design business are outlined.

50651 ■ "PR Leads www.prleads.com" in *Entrepreneur* (Vol. 32, No. 1, January 2004, pp. 10)
Pub: Entrepreneur Media, Inc.
Ed: Steve Cooper. **Description:** Website that directs journalists to clients based on the client's expertise. Membership can be purchased on a three-month trial basis, or annually.

50652 ■ "PR Power" in *Entrepreneur* (Vol. 31, No. 11, November 2003, pp. 97)
Pub: Entrepreneur Media, Inc.
Ed: Gwen Moran. **Description:** Services designed to help promote media relations for small companies are listed.

50653 ■ "Press Conference: You've Worked Hard to Land That Media Interview-So Don't Blow Your Opportunity" in *Entrepreneur*
Pub: Entrepreneur Media Inc.
Ed: Kim T. Gordon. **Description:** Techniques for handling print, radio and television interviews are offered. Preparation is stressed as a key to a successful interview.

50654 ■ "Promotions for Pennies; You don't need a Madison Avenue budget to turn heads" in *Business Week Online* (November 1, 2002)
Pub: McGraw-Hill Inc.
Description: Debbie Patt, owner of Clarendon Cheesecakes, explains how, despite a limited advertising budget, finds creative, low-cost marketing strategies that draw attention to her products, including the use of her products for nonprofit fundraisers.

50655 ■ *Proven Promotions for Kitchen & Bathroom Businesses*
Pub: National Kitchen & Bath Association.
Ed: Jim Krengel and Lori J. Krengel. **Released:** 1997.
Price: $50.00.

50656 ■ *Publicity Power: A Practical Guide to Effective Promotion*
Pub: Crisp Publications, Inc.
Ed: Charles Mallory. **Price:** $9.95.

50657 ■ "Pump Up with PR" in *Small Business Opportunities* (Vol. 16, No. 2, March 2004, pp. 10)
Pub: Harris Publications, Inc.
Ed: Patricia Faulhaber. **Description:** Fourteen proven tips in public relations and publicity for small businesses. Public relations technically revolve around media relations, press releases, trade shows, brand creation, marketing communications, internal messaging, special event planning, networking and more.

50658 ■ "Puzzleman to the Rescue" in *My Business* (December/January 2003, pp. 12-13)
Pub: My Business Magazine
Ed: Melany Klinck. **Description:** Profile of Cypriana Porter, owner of the educational toy store called The Gingerbread House. Porter invented the superhero Puzzleman to increase sales.

50659 ■ "Quick pick" in *Entrepreneur* (Vol. 31, No. 6, June 2003, pp. 81)
Pub: Entrepreneur Media Inc.
Ed: Elizabeth J. Goodgold. **Description:** A new service just launched, Major Newswire, will send press releases to more than 85,000 journalists, editors and newswire services for a fee of $349.

50660 ■ "A Rap for Manners: Angelo Ellerbee Refines the Rough on Urban Artist" in *Black Enterprise* (Vol. 34, No. 5, December 2003, pp. 66)
Pub: Earl Graves Publishing Co.
Ed: Christina Morgan. Description: Profile of Angelo Ellerbee, an image consultant heading Double Xxposure, a public relations and management company. The firm specializes in total imaging and teaches young rap and R & B acts everything from diction to travel.

50661 ■ "Relationship builder" in *Pittsburgh Business Times* (Vol. 22, No. 46, May 30, 2003, pp. 15)
Pub: Pittsburgh Business Times
Ed: Christopher Davis. Description: Profile of Selena Schmidt, owner of Pittsburgh-based Grounds for Appeal, providing corporate image building, public relations management, and stresses the importance of professional associations.

50662 ■ "Riding the Airwaves" in *Entrepreneur.com* (Vol. 34, February 2006, No. 2, pp. 75)
Pub: Entrepreneur Media Inc.
Ed: Kim T. Gordon. Description: Six steps to promote a small business is to conduct a public relations radio tour are outlined. It is important to target the right media for a product or service.

50663 ■ "Risky Business: Wacky Marketing Moves Put These Businesses on the Map" in *Entrepreneur* (Vol. 32, August 2004, No. 8, pp. 26)
Pub: Entrepreneur Media Inc.
Ed: April Y. Pennington. Description: Creating controversy is a good way to build a brand.

50664 ■ *The Royal Guide to Direct Mail for Small Businesses*
Pub: Butterworth-Heinemann
Ed: Thomas. Released: 1997. Price: $28.95.

50665 ■ "Sales & Marketing: The Power of Brand" in *Ingram's* (Vol. 27, No. 6, June 2001, pp. 23)
Pub: Show Me Publishing, Inc.
Ed: Jean Hughes. Description: The answer to increasing product usage is to leverage the company's brand and to strengthen account relationships.

50666 ■ "Sales & Marketing: Why Advertise Anyway?" in *Ingram's* (Vol. 27, No. 5, May 2001, pp. 28)
Pub: Show Me Publishing, Inc.
Ed: Rob Pearcy. Description: Business plans need to include a marketing budget for advertising in order to be successful.

50667 ■ "Sales Secrets: Persistence is key to building your brand" in *Atlanta Business Chronicle* (Vol. 25, No. 21, November 1, 2002, pp. 2B)
Pub: American City Business Publications, Inc.
Ed: Jeffrey Gitomer. Description: A suggested formula for building a brand is discussed, along with branding step recommendations.

50668 ■ "Saving the Day: Does Your Brand Need Triage? Here's Something to Help" in *Entrepreneur* (Vol. 31, No. 9, September 2003, pp. 27)
Pub: Entrepreneur Media, Inc.
Ed: Mark Henricks. Description: Review of the book, "Brand Aid", to help entrepreneurs make the most out of their brand using limited resources.

50669 ■ "The science behind six degrees." in *Harvard Business Review* (Vol. 81, No. 2, Feb. 2003, pp. 16)
Pub: Harvard Business School Press
Ed: Gardiner Morse. Description: Duncan Watts answers questions about his research into network science and how it can help explain why products sell, and how companies effectively manage themselves. Critical elements of this field of study are human behavior, group dynamics, and perception.

50670 ■ "The Science of Status" in *Inc.* (September 1, 2003)
Pub: Gruner & Jahr USA Publishing
Ed: Nadine Heintz. Description: The roles that perceptions play in the marketplace are observed.

50671 ■ "Sea Change" in *Inc.* (January 1, 2002)
Pub: Inc. Magazine
Ed: John Grossmann. Description: Profile of Henry Lovejoy, wholesaler of ecologically acceptable fish and shellfish; Lovejoy shares ways he was able to brand his product.

50672 ■ "Seeking Up-and-Comers Under 30." in *Crain's Detroit Business* (Vol. 23, February 5, 2007, No. 6, pp. 26)
Pub: Crain Communications Inc. - Detroit
Description: Crain's is looking for the best twenty in their 20's feature. Unlike their forty in their 40's, which honors proven business successes, this feature emphasizes imaginative, out of the box, creative thinkers that are shaking things up.

50673 ■ "A Sign of the Times" in *Small Business Opportunities* (Vol. 14, No. 1, January 2002, pp. 82, 84)
Pub: Harris Publications, Inc.
Ed: Mark Agost. Description: Insights into engineering a safe, durable and effective business sign are covered. The importance to have a sign designed to fit aesthetically to enhance the environment along with maintenance and inspection of the sign is stressed.

50674 ■ *The Small Business Bible: Everything You Need to Know to Succeed in Your Small Business*
Pub: John Wiley & Sons, Incorporated
Ed: Steven D. Strauss. Released: December 2004. Price: $19.95 (US), $28.99 (Canadian). Description: Comprehensive guide to starting and running a successful small business. Topics include bookkeeping and financial management, marketing, publicity, and advertising.

50675 ■ "Small Firms Emphasize Trade-Show Marketing" in *Crain's Detroit Business* (Vol. 21, February 7, 2005, No. 6, pp. 24)
Pub: Crain Communications Inc. - Detroit
Ed: DeAnna Belger. Description: According to a recent survey, more small companies in Michigan rely on trade shows than their larger competitors. Most respondents reported attending trade shows to generate sales leads, increase visibility, and to network.

50676 ■ "Smile: Your Company's Under Attack" in *PC Computing* (March 2000, pp. 42)
Pub: Ziff-Davis Inc.
Ed: Jamais Cascio. Description: Online consumer complaint sites, which are increasing in popularity, result in bad publicity for companies, and, the means by which the company chooses to handle the sites can be detrimental for company public relations. Companies have launched high-profile lawsuits and directly threatened the owner of the complaint domain. The reaction by the companies to the sites brings much more attention to the complaints than the original site. The best way to handle complaints is to respond to customers and work to resolve issues rather than ignoring them. Customer support sites are very easy to establish, and it is an easy way to keep in contact with customers.

50677 ■ "Somebody's Watching You" in *Inc.* (September 2005, pp. 75-76)
Pub: Inc. Magazine
Ed: David H. Freedman. Description: Search engines such as Google are having an impact on business in two ways. First, the ability to find information on the Web is critical to any business success; and companies are now freely examined by anyone, making it necessary to adapt a firm to public scrutiny.

50678 ■ "Speak Up! The Ins and Outs of Hiring a Spokesperson" in *Entrepreneur* (Vol. 32, No. 2, February 2004, pp. 75)
Pub: Entrepreneur Media, Inc.
Ed: Nancy Michaels. Description: Pros and cons to hiring a spokesperson to represent a small company are discussed. Resources are included.

50679 ■ "Spread the Word" in *BlackEnterprise* (Vol. 31, No. 10, May 2001, pp. 110)
Pub: Earl Graves Publishing Co.
Ed: Holly Aguirre. Description: Successful ways to build a Web site for advertising a small business are shown, including search engines, links on other sites, and offline sources that include word-of-mouth and traditional advertising and marketing.

50680 ■ "Spreading Viruses Can be a Good Thing" in *Crain's Chicago Business* (Vol. 30, January 2007, No. 3, pp. 18)
Pub: Crain Communications, Inc.
Ed: Steve Hendershot. Description: Viral Marketing, spreading a company's message by email which directs consumers to the company's website, is another of the creative new marketing techniques finding success online. Downsides of this powerful tool are explored.

50681 ■ "Starbucks Gets A New Look" in *Frozen Food Age* (Vol. 50, No. 3, October 2001, pp. 12)
Pub: VNU Business Media
Description: Enterprise IG, located in San Francisco, California, has partnered with Starbucks Ice Cream Partnership (a joint venture with Dreyer's Grand Ice Cream) in order to provide brand identity and help its product stand out on store shelves.

50682 ■ "Striking Up the Brand Band" in *Houston Business Journal* (Vol. 34, No. 19, September 19, 2003, pp. 17A)
Pub: American City Business Journals
Ed: Judy Rider. Description: Easterly and Company, Houston, Texas, is a marketing company led by Gary D. Easterly, president; the marketing firm has received new branding contract from several Enron subsidiaries.

50683 ■ "Success Off the Shelf" in *Hispanic Business* (October 2003, pp. 88)
Pub: Hispanic Business
Ed: Joel Russell. Description: Two Hispanic authors share expertise on branding and on managing money.

50684 ■ "Summer Could Help Lick Tourism Slump" in *Pacific Business News* (Vol. 41, No. 16, June 27, 2003, pp. 1)
Pub: American City Business Journals
Ed: Prabha Natarajan. Description: Hawaii experienced a poor showing in the tourism industry the first two quarters of 2003. State and private tourism marketers are marketing to Japan and airline flights have increased between Japan and Hawaii.

50685 ■ "Sweetwoods' a man with a brand" in *Atlanta Business Chronicle* (Vol. 24, No. 14, September 7, 2001, pp. 26A)
Pub: American City Business Journals Inc.
Ed: Walter Woods. Description: John Sweetwood, part of the management committee of Bass Hotels & Resorts, has been behind advertisements such as the Energizer bunny and Purina Dog Chow. Having been hired in 1997 as president of Holiday Inn Express, he now enjoys working for the parent company. Despite the recent cutbacks in the hotel industry, Sweetwood says his company is going strong.

50686 ■ "Switching Tracks" in *Black Enterprise* (Vol. 34, July 2004, No. 12, pp. 124)
Pub: Earl G. Graves Publishing Co. Inc.
Ed: Sonya A. Donaldson. Description: Profile of BITco USA Inc., the Florida-based firm that installs equipment such as radios, surveillance cameras, and automatic fare boxes on buses and rail cars. The family owned business won the bid for a Website makeover that would help the build company's image.

50687 ■ "Take the Plunge" in *Entrepreneur* (Vol. 32, November 2004, No. 11, pp. 93)
Pub: Entrepreneur Media Inc.
Ed: Jerry Fisher. **Description:** Advertising promotions that use 'bad news' as an opener can be unusual enough to generate interest.

50688 ■ "Takes the cake" in *Black Enterprise* (Vol. 32, No. 10, May 2002, pp. 58)
Pub: Earl Graves Publishing Co.
Ed: Ron Childs. **Description:** Profile of Amy Hilliard, senior vice president of integrated marketing at Burrell Communications Groups Inc. Hilliard thrives on creating and launching products.

50689 ■ *Target Smart: Database Marketing for the Small Business*
Pub: PSI Research
Ed: Jay Newberg and Claudio Marcus. **Released:** 1997. **Price:** $19.95.

50690 ■ "Tastes Differ" in *Crain's New York Business* (Vol. 22, December 11, 2006, No. 50, pp. 24)
Pub: Crain Communications, Inc.
Description: Executives for reality shows say that the key to getting one's products on air is to be available on short notice, be patient, and have a great product. Many shows not only mention vendors by name but they also feature them on their websites.

50691 ■ "Tell-A-Friend Wizard" in *Entrepreneur* (Vol. 33, September 2005, No. 9, pp. 6)
Pub: Entrepreneur Media Inc.
Ed: Steve Cooper. **Description:** Tell-a-Friend Wizard helps to add customized buttons to any Website that allow visitors to recommend a product or service. The service starts at $5.95 per month.

50692 ■ "Third Degree Advertising Names VP for Solomon Inc." in *Journal Record* (June 25, 2003)
Pub: Dolan Media Company
Description: Profile of Randy Nichols, newly named vice president for Solomon Inc., a research and branding division of Third Degree Advertising and Communications.

50693 ■ "Three questions you need to ask about your brand" in *Harvard Business Review* (Vol. 80, No. 9, September 2002, pp. 80)
Pub: Harvard Business School Press
Ed: Kevin Lane Keller, Brian Sternthal, Alice Tybout. **Description:** Successful brand positioning is not so much about differentiating a product from competitors as it is in understanding the frame of reference in which the product must compete for attention. Various companies' efforts are explored.

50694 ■ "Thumbs Up! Rave Reviews Could be All the Advertising You Need" in *Entrepreneur* (Vol. 32, July 2004, No. 7, pp. 71)
Pub: Entrepreneur Media Inc.
Ed: Nancy Michaels. **Description:** Owner of a software/Web site design business is offered advice for word-of-mouth marketing after having little success with radio and newspaper ads.

50695 ■ "Too Much Information?" in *Black Enterprise* (Vol. 37, December 2006, No. 5, pp. 59)
Pub: Earl G. Graves Publishing Co. Inc.
Ed: James C. Johnson. **Description:** African American business owners often face the dilemma of whether or not to divulge their minority status when soliciting new customers and financial institutions. The quality of the products or services is always the key factor and race should never define one's business; however, it is appropriate to market oneself as a minority or women-owned business, especially if the company is in an industry where those clients are offered top-tier contracts.

50696 ■ "Top Area Advertising Agencies" in *Ingram's* (Vol. 28, No. 9, September 2002, pp. 29)
Pub: Show Me Publishing, Inc.
Description: A listing of the top Kansas area advertising agencies ranked in 2001, according to capitalized billings. The top three are Bernstein-Rein Advertising Inc., Barkley Evergreen and Partners Inc., and Valentine Radford Inc.

50697 ■ "Turn classmates into customers" in *Black Enterprise* (Vol. 33, No. 3, October 2002, pp. S2)
Pub: Earl Graves Publishing Co.
Ed: LaToya S. Foye. **Description:** Suggestions are offered for successfully marketing a business, including targeting classmates as customers. The nonprofit organization BUILD (Businesses United in Investing, Lending and Development) encourages young people to develop businesses is highlighted.

50698 ■ "Up Front: Broad Brand" in *My Business* (April/May 2004, pp. 12-13)
Pub: My Business Magazine
Ed: Gary M. Stern. **Description:** Ways a business can increase business by creating a fresh brand are explored. Tips for successful branding include naming a brand appropriately, generating publicity, remaining focused, creating a slogan, and integrating graphics with your mission.

50699 ■ "Up Front: Thinking Outside the Box" in *My Business* (April/May 2003, pp. 8-9)
Pub: My Business Magazine
Ed: Kathleen Landis. **Description:** One of the best ways to build a business is to ask clients for referrals; author Maribeth Kuzmeski, business consultant and author refers to client referrals as "strategic alliances", which allow two companies to create an advantage over competitors.

50700 ■ "Upfront: Don't Say That" in *My Business* (April/May 2002, pp. 13-14)
Pub: My Business Magazine
Ed: Ivan Sylvester. **Description:** Market consultant and trainer, Merrie Spaeth, believes that public communication is all about the power of negatives. Spaeth sends out a monthly e-mail known as "The Bimbo Award", that recognizes public comments that cause the listener to believe exactly the opposite of what is said. Spaeth and her employees teach big and small firms how to communicate effectively.

50701 ■ "What Becomes an Icon Most" in *Harvard Business Review* (Vol. 81, No. 3, March 2003, pp. 43)
Pub: Harvard Business School Press
Ed: Douglas B. Holt. **Description:** Brands become icons by providing myths for the society. Ways some brands become icons and maintain the power to hold its market place for years is examined. The most successful brands create myths, most often in the U.S., by creating an intimate and credible relationship with the desire of Americans to be rebels.

50702 ■ "What Do Your Customers See?" in *Inc.* (February 1, 2002)
Pub: Inc. Magazine
Ed: Bo Burlingame. **Description:** Ways to market a product, inventory, finding a niche for the product, and responding to the loss of a key supplier are the issues addressed.

50703 ■ "What I've Learned About Women" in *Marketing to Women* (Vol. 19, November 2006, No. 1, pp. 2)
Pub: EPM Communications, Inc.
Ed: Lisa Finn. **Description:** Over the years the women's marketing landscape has changed a great deal. Companies are more open to testing their ideas and doing research and women are helping marketers do their job better by expressing their opinions to companies.

50704 ■ "What Not To Do in a Press Release" in *Inc.* (January 1, 2004)
Pub: Gruner & Jahr USA Publishing
Ed: Nicole Gull. **Description:** Entrepreneurs should double-check all information before allowing a press release to be printed.

50705 ■ "What You Look Like Online" in *Black Enterprise* (Vol. 37, January 2007, No. 6, pp. 56)
Pub: Earl G. Graves Publishing Co. Inc.
Ed: Marcia A. Reed-Woodard. **Description:** Of 100 executive recruiters 77 percent stated that they use search engines to check the backgrounds of potential job candidates, according to a survey conducted by ExecuNet. Of those surveyed 35 percent stated that they eliminate potential candidates based on information they find online so it is important to create a positive Web presence which highlights professional image qualities.

50706 ■ "Whatever it takes" in *BlackEnterprise* (Vol. 32, No. 3, October 2001, pp. 54)
Pub: Earl Graves Publishing Co.
Ed: Mark Richard Moss. **Description:** Review of the publication, 'Off-the-Wall Marketing Ideas.' The book offers advice on such diverse topics as business card design, generating publicity and "Pro Bono: Civic Marketing."

50707 ■ "Who's Talking Behind Your Back?" in *Crain's Chicago Business* (Vol. 30, January 2007, No. 3, pp. 18)
Pub: Crain Communications, Inc.
Ed: Steve Hendershot. **Description:** Chicago's Word of Mouth Marketing Association, Womma, cultivates, studies, and celebrates consumers telling others about a company or its products or services. Success stories included.

50708 ■ "Why Image Matters" in *My Business* (December/January 2003, pp. 28-31)
Pub: My Business Magazine
Ed: Shannon Scully. **Description:** Solutions for building a small business' image are explored, using various companies as examples, including a home remodeling company, garage door/window sales company, retail bicycle shop, candy and snack food manufacturer and retailer, and a public relations firm.

50709 ■ "Young Professional Share Ideas" in *San Fernando Valley Business Journal* (Vol. 12, January 2007, No. 2, pp. 1)
Pub: San Fernando Valley Business Journal Associates
Ed: Chris Coates. **Description:** Interview with four young business professionals from various fields who talk about gaining creditability in the workplace, image, and marketing.

50710 ■ "Your Story Here" in *Black Enterprise* (Vol. 36, February 2006, No. 7, pp. 57)
Pub: Earl G. Graves Publishing Co. Inc.
Ed: Kenneth Meeks. **Description:** BlackNews.com will feature a press release on its Website, an email and fax to every African American newspaper, magazine, radio station and TV station for only $150. Diversity City Media Inc., the multicultural marketing and public relations firm not only runs the Website, but also Black PR.com a press release distribution service.

SOURCES OF SUPPLY

50711 ■ *Promotion Industry Sourcebook*
Pub: Primedia Business
Contact: Kerry J. Smith
Ed: Betsy Spethmann, Editor, bspethmann@charter.net. **Released:** Annual, October. **Price:** $49.95. **Covers:** Approximately 350 promotion agencies and marketing services/supplier companies. **Entries Include:** Company name, address, phone, name and title of contact, description of service. **Arrangement:** Classified by product or service.

TRADE PERIODICALS

50712 ■ *Accutips*
Pub: Accudata America
Released: Monthly. **Price:** Free. **Description:** Discusses promotion and marketing issues relevant to businesses.

50713 ■ *Creative Marketing*
Pub: Association of Retail Marketing Services Inc.
Contact: Gerri Hopkins
Ed: Gerri Hopkins, Editor. **Released:** Quarterly. **Price:** Free. **Description:** Provides information on the Association's activities in the retail incentive marketing field and developments within the industry. Contains announcements of premium incentive trade shows, retail promotion shows, and general industry news. Carries items of interest such as continuity programs, tape plans, trading stamps, self-liquidators, traffic builders, advertising specialties, and controlled markdown. Recurring features include interviews, news of research, reports of meetings, news of educational opportunities, and a calendar of events.

50714 ■ *E-Tactics Letter*
Pub: E-Tactics Inc.
Ed: Sarah Stambler, Editor. **Released:** Monthly. **Price:** $149, U.S. and Canada email delivery; $249, elsewhere fax delivery. **Description:** Covers marketing information and techniques for businesses to increase profits and sales by using electronic delivery channels such as email, faxes, websites, and cable television. Recurring features include interviews and news of research.

50715 ■ *The Gauge*
Pub: Delahaye Medialink
Contact: Katharine Delahaye Paine, Publisher
E-mail: kpaine@delahaye.com
Ed: William Teunis Paarlberg, Editor, wpaarlberg@aol.com. **Released:** Bimonthly. **Price:** $75. **Description:** Provides information on and evaluates marketing communications activities of companies. Recurring features include interviews, news of research, and a calendar of events.

50716 ■ *The Publicity Hound*
Pub: Joan Stewart
Contact: Joan Stewart, Publisher
E-mail: jstewart@publicityhound.com
Released: Bimonthly. **Price:** $49.95. **Description:** Provides techniques and strategies on self-promotion and inexpensive publicity. Recurring features include letters to the editor, interviews, news of research, book reviews, news of educational opportunities, notices of publications available, and columns titled Advice From Media People, Seasonal Story Ideas, Resource Page, Success Stories, and Media Insider Secrets. Does not report public relations agency staff changes.

VIDEOCASSETTES/ AUDIOCASSETTES

50717 ■ *Ad Campaigns That Work*
Instructional Video
2219 C St.
Lincoln, NE 68502
Ph:(402)475-6570
Free: 800-228-0164
Fax: (402)475-6500
Co. E-mail: feedback@insvideo.com
URL: http://www.insvideo.com
Price: $89.95. **Description:** Three successful ad agency executives furnish information on successful ad campaigns and why they were successful. Covers principles of successful advertising. **Availability:** VHS.

50718 ■ *Advertising the Small Business*
NETCHE (Nebraska Educational Television Council for Higher Education)
1800 N. 33rd St.
Lincoln, NE 68583

Ph:(402)472-3611
Fax: (402)472-1785
Co. E-mail: netche@unl.edu
URL: http://www.netche.org/
Released: 1981. **Price:** $100.00. **Description:** These two tapes, provide a step-by-step instructional course on how to best publicize a small business, from research/planning to managing/implementation. **Availability:** VHS; 3/4U.

50719 ■ *Advertising: The Hidden Language*
First Light Video Publishing
2321 Abbot Kinney Blvd., Top Fl.
Venice, CA 90291
Free: 800-262-8862
Fax: (310)574-0886
Co. E-mail: sales@firstlightvideo.com
URL: http://www.firstlightvideo.com
Description: Features Dr. Phillip Bell as he demostrates how successful ads grab the consumer and make them want to purchase the product. **Availability:** VHS.

50720 ■ *Advertising Tricks Without the Gimmicks*
Instructional Video
2219 C St.
Lincoln, NE 68502
Ph:(402)475-6570
Free: 800-228-0164
Fax: (402)475-6500
Co. E-mail: feedback@insvideo.com
URL: http://www.insvideo.com
Price: $79.00. **Description:** Offers an overview and practical hints on the basics of advertising. **Availability:** VHS.

50721 ■ *Promotion: Polishing the Apple*
RMI Media
1365 N. Winchester
Olathe, KS 66061
Ph:(913)768-1696
Fax: (913)768-0184
Co. E-mail: actmedia@act.org
URL: http://www.rmimedia.com
Released: 1991. **Price:** $89.95. **Description:** Presents promotional mixes developed by Apple Computers for the Apple IIc, the Macintosh, and the Macintosh Office to demonstrate successful uses of print and television advertising. **Availability:** VHS.

CONSULTANTS

50722 ■ **Sol Abrams Public Relations Counsel & Marketing Consultants**
331 Webster Dr.
New Milford, NJ 07646
Ph:(201)262-4111
Fax: (201)262-7669
Scope: Independent consulting provides publicity, public relations and marketing counsel and services to management of private and public enterprises. Also serves as public relations consultants to other public relations consulting firms, advertising agencies and marketing companies. Provides expert witness services involving public relations. Also lectures, trains, teaches, and conducts seminars in public relations and marketing. Industries served: corporate management, businesses large and small including real estate, construction, entertainment, food, fashion, fundraising, automotive, aviation, franchising, government agencies, and nonprofit organizations. **Seminars:** How to Select a Public Relations Firm; Publicity and Promotion for Small Business Owner; Expose Yourself - Don't Be a Secret Agent -Increase Your Sales, Incomes, Images, Publicity, Profits and Prestige via Professional Public Relations.

50723 ■ **COMsciences Inc.**
6210 Wilshire Blvd., Ste. 200
Los Angeles, CA 90048
Ph:(323)937-7607
Fax: (323)937-0160
Co. E-mail: info@comsciences.com
URL: http://www.comsciences.com

E-mail: info@comsciences.com
Scope: Firm offers research services to support public relations, corporate advertising, impact of new communications media, communication entertainment, and iternet/web development. Also provides strategic management consulting on communications, marketing, opinion surveys, and organizational development and assessment. The company specializes in media campaigns and evaluation tools. Also conducts government sponsored and media sponsored surveys. Serves all industry sectors, especially .com, wireless telecommunications, interactive media, and consumer electronics. **Publications:** "Wanted: Radical Thinking," PMG World Magazine, Mar, 2003. **Special Services:** Spin™; Event™; NewsMaker Polling™; TradeShow™; mPoll™; mVote™; iMAP™; wForum; mCRM™.

50724 ■ **Steve Emerine Strategic Public Relations**
PO Box 41824
Tucson, AZ 85717-1824
Ph:(520)323-1441
Fax: (520)881-4043
Co. E-mail: steveemerine@webtv.net

E-mail: steveemerine@webtv.net
Scope: Services offered in crisis management, environmental problems, litigation public relations, government relations, publicity, writing, editing, and public information planning. **Seminars:** Crisis Public Relations, Media Relations, Environmental and Neighborhood Relations.

50725 ■ **Russ Fons Public Relations**
7509 Turtle Dove Ct.
Las Vegas, NV 89129-6032
Ph:(702)658-7654
Free: 888-658-7654
Fax: (702)658-1349
Co. E-mail: russfons@cox.net
URL: http://www.russfons.com

E-mail: russfons@cox.net
Scope: Offers corporate counseling and image development; media relations; marketing communications and product publicity; event management and special promotions; and graphic design and production. Industries served: all worldwide. Licensing and merchandising, literary services, Hispanic communications. Revenue Sharing/PI Advertising. **Publications:** The Executive Crisis Manager, a planning guide to surviving corporate crisis.

50726 ■ **Holcomb Gallagher Adams Advertising Inc.**
300 Marconi Blvd., 3rd Fl., Ste. 303
Columbus, OH 43215
Ph:(614)221-3343
Fax: (614)221-3367
URL: http://www.hgainc.com
Scope: Consults in strategic marketing planning, and new business, brand equity, creative strategy, and media strategy development. Industries served: consumer goods and services, manufacturing, retail, business-to-business products and services, education, travel, and tourism.

50727 ■ **Syed Hussayn TMCI**
95 October Ln.
Aurora, ON, Canada L4G 7A1
Ph:(905)949-4555
Fax: (905)949-9116
Co. E-mail: syedn.hussain@sympatico.ca

E-mail: syedn.hussain@sympatico.ca
Scope: Business process re-engineering, change management, financial restructuring & insolvency, consumer & corporate bankruptcy, financial/debt management, investments & insurance advisory services, management/executive development, marketing management, organizational development, needs assessment, financial counselling, succession planning, performance management/measurement, program evaluation, project management, strategic planning and import/export advisory. **Publications:**

"Innovative Management"; "Team Building and Leadership"; "Financial Planning"; "Estate Planning"; "Risk Management"; "Export/Import Trade Finance Mechanics"; "Marketing and Sales Management"; "What Your Banker Needs to Know"; "Building A Successful Financial Plan". **Seminars:** Workplace Solutions Seminars; Export Development; Executive Education & Leadership Development; Financial Planning; Estate Planning; Succession Planning; Wealth Accumulation and Management; Strategic Planning/Competitive Positioning.

50728 ■ Alan J. Zell- Ambassador of Selling

PO Box 69
Portland, OR 97207-0069
Ph:(503)241-1988
Fax: (503)241-1989
Co. E-mail: azell@aol.com
URL: http://www.sellingselling.com

E-mail: azell@aol.com

Scope: An advisory service for those who sell their services, products or their organization's ideas, information, and skills through face-to-face and telephone conversations, printed materials, the media, electronic communications, schools, guilds, trade shows, and display presentations. Industries served: minority and woman-owned businesses; government and education; medicine, law, accounting, technology, manufacturers, distributors, and retailers; professional and trade associations; and nonprofit organizations. **Publications:** Selling Situations; What Customers need to know; Turnover & Return on Investment; The Ultimate Business Oxymoron; Walkin The Aisles, Looking at the Booths, etc. **Seminars:** Ambassador Of Selling. **Special Services:** Web-site critique from sales/selling point of view.

COMPUTERIZED DATABASES

50729 ■ ABI/INFORM

ProQuest
300 N Zeeb Rd.
PO Box 1346
Ann Arbor, MI 48106
Ph:(734)761-4700
Free: 800-521-0600
Fax: (734)761-6450
Co. E-mail: info@il.proquest.com
URL: http://www.proquest.com
Description: Provides full text access or bibliographic citations to articles in publications in business and management information worldwide. Includes 2.7 million indexes and abstracts. Comprised of three editions on CD-ROM:; ABI/INFORM Global covers more than 1600 sources, including more than 350 titles from outside the United States.; ABI/INFORM Research covers more than 700 sources.; ABI/INFORM Select covers about 350 sources with coverage beginning in 1991. **Availability:** Online: Ovid Technologies Inc., ProQuest, Thomson Dialog, Questel; Orbit, Gesellschaft fur Betriebswirtschaftliche Information mbH, STN International, Colorado Alliance of Research Libraries, Financial Times, Online Computer Library Center Inc. (OCLC), LexisNexis, EINS - European Information Network Services, Thomson Dialog; Batch: Nerac Inc. **Type:** Full text; Bibliographic; Image.

50730 ■ Advertiser & Agency Red Books Plus

LexisNexis Group
121 Chanlon Rd.
New Providence, NJ 07974
Ph:(908)464-6800
Free: 800-526-4902
Fax: (908)771-7704
Co. E-mail: customer.support@lexisnexis.com
URL: http://www.redbooks.com
Released: Quarterly. **Description:** CD-ROM. Covers 15,750 of the world's top advertisers, their products and what media they use, as well as 13,900 U.S. and international ad agencies and nearly 100,000 key executives worldwide in management, creative, and

media positions. **Entries Include:** For advertisers—Company name, job function/title, product/brand name, advertising expenditures by media. For personnel—Name and title.

50731 ■ PR Newswire

PR Newswire Inc.
810 7th Ave., 32nd Fl.
New York, NY 10019
Ph:(212)596-1500
Free: 800-832-5522
Fax: 800-793-9313
Co. E-mail: information@prnewswire.com
URL: http://www.prnewswire.com
Description: Contains the complete text of more than 1,000 news releases issued by a variety of organizations and transmitted to the press by PR Newswire each day. Covers primarily business and financial news as well as sports, labor, entertainment, medicine, science, and general interest news. News releases include name and telephone number of issuing organization. Source organizations include some 20,000 corporations, public relations agencies, trade associations, labor unions, civic and cultural organizations, political parties, and government agencies. Note: on DIALOG, the database is contained in two separate files, one with current news May 1999 to date; the other with archive news from 1987 to April 1999. **Availability:** Online: Thomson Dialog, Thomson Dialog, Dow Jones & Co. Inc., LexisNexis, LexisNexis, Track Data Corp., Bloomberg LP, Prospero Technologies LLC. **Type:** Directory; Full text.

LIBRARIES

50732 ■ Burson-Marsteller–Knowledge Center

230 Park Ave., S.
New York, NY 10003
Ph:(212)614-4257
Fax: (212)598-5581
URL: http://www.bm.com
Contact: Robert Schrott, Mgr.
Scope: Advertising, public relations, marketing research. **Services:** Interlibrary loan; Library open to clients and librarians. **Holdings:** 1000 books. **Subscriptions:** 100 journals and other serials.

50733 ■ Campbell Mithun–Library & Information Services

222 S. 9th St.
Minneapolis, MN 55402
Ph:(612)347-1509
Fax: (612)347-1041
Co. E-mail: virginia_ferestad@campbell-mithun.com
URL: http://www.campbellmithun.com
Contact: Virginia Ferestad, VP, Dir.
Scope: Advertising, marketing. **Services:** Interlibrary loan; copying; permission to use Library may be requested. **Holdings:** 1000 books; 1000 volumes of client records; 500 files of pamphlets and clippings; 500 competitive advertising files; 1200 picture files. **Subscriptions:** 1000 journals and other serials.

50734 ■ D'Arcy Masius Benton & Bowles–Information Center

1 Memorial Dr.
St. Louis, MO 63102
Ph:(314)342-3925
Fax: (314)342-3584
URL: http://www.scriptorium.lib.duke.edu/hartman/dmbb/
Contact: Rosanne Hadjri, Libn.
Scope: Advertising. **Services:** Library not open to the public. **Holdings:** 750 volumes; 375 VF drawers of pamphlets and clippings. **Subscriptions:** 750 journals and other serials.

50735 ■ Earle Palmer Brown–Information Center

6400 Goldsboro Rd.
Bethesda, MD 20817
Ph:(301)263-2200
Fax: (301)263-2254
URL: http://www.epb.com

Scope: Advertising, marketing, business. **Services:** Center not open to the public. **Holdings:** 250 books. **Subscriptions:** 40 journals and other serials; 7 newspapers.

50736 ■ Foote Cone & Belding–Information Center - SF

1600 Battery St.
San Francisco, CA 94111-1802
Ph:(415)820-8000
URL: http://www.fcb.com/index_main.html
Contact: Angela Moore-Evans
Scope: Advertising. **Services:** Interlibrary loan; center not open to the public. **Holdings:** Figures not available.

50737 ■ Grey Worldwide–Information Center

777 3rd Ave., 6th Fl.
New York, NY 10017
Ph:(212)546-2000
Co. E-mail: espross@grey.com
URL: http://www.grey.com/
Contact: Ellen Spross, Mgr.
Scope: Advertising, marketing, business, new business development. **Services:** Interlibrary loan. **Holdings:** 500 books; 200 directories. **Subscriptions:** 200 journals and other serials; 5 newspapers.

50738 ■ Information Resources Center–Library

800 Hennepin Ave.
Minneapolis, MN 55403
Ph:(612)334-6031
Fax: (612)334-1421
Co. E-mail: kspanier@clynch.com
Contact: Kristine Spanier, Know.Mgr.
Scope: Advertising. **Services:** Library not open to the public. **Holdings:** 250 books. **Subscriptions:** 1400 journals and other serials; 7 newspapers.

50739 ■ Ketchum Advertising–Library Services

Six PPG Place
Pittsburgh, PA 15222
Ph:(412)456-3977
Fax: (412)456-3834
Scope: Advertising, marketing, general reference. **Services:** Interlibrary loan. **Holdings:** 1100 books; 40 VF drawers of marketing material; reference collection; annual reports. **Subscriptions:** 450 journals and other serials.

50740 ■ Martin/Williams Advertising Inc. –Library

60 S. 6th St., Ste. 2800
Minneapolis, MN 55402
Ph:(612)340-0800
URL: http://www.martinwilliams.com
Scope: Advertising, marketing, business. **Services:** Library open to agency employees and clients; open to the public with special permission. **Holdings:** Figures not available.

50741 ■ McCann-Erickson Advertising of Canada Ltd.–Information Centre

10 Bay St., Ste. 1012
Toronto, ON, Canada M5J 2S3
Ph:(416)594-6400
Fax: (416)594-6272
Co. E-mail: contact@mccann.com
URL: http://www.mccann.com/
Contact: Valerie Walton, Info.Ctr.Mgr.
Scope: Advertising, marketing, business, industry. **Services:** Center not open to the public. **Holdings:** 1000 books. **Subscriptions:** 90 journals and other serials.

50742 ■ Reader's Digest–Marketing Information Center

260 Madison Ave.
New York, NY 10016
Ph:(212)850-7034
Fax: (212)683-8142
URL: http://www.readersdigest.com
Contact: Helen Fledderus, Cons.
Scope: Advertising, marketing, and media research. **Services:** Interlibrary loan. **Holdings:** 800 volumes; 23 lateral file drawers of commodity and industry data. **Subscriptions:** 74 journals and other serials.

RESEARCH CENTERS

50743 ■ Boston College–Center for Corporate Citizenship
Wallace E. Carroll School of Management
55 Lee Rd.
Chestnut Hill, MA 02467-3942
Ph:(617)552-4545
Fax: (617)552-8499
Co. E-mail: bradley.googins.1@bc.edu
URL: http://www.bcccc.net/
Contact: Bradley G. Googins PhD, Exec.Dir.
E-mail: bradley.googins.1@bc.edu
Scope: Corporate community relations, public-private partnerships, corporate voluntarism, corporate citizenship, and corporate philanthropy. Projects include designing corporate social vision, best practice research, analyses of corporate images within local communities, impact of corporation's external affairs

on employee behavior, and profiles of community relations professionals. **Services:** Contract research and consulting. **Publications:** Annual report; Research reports (periodically). **Educational Activities:** Administers certificates in corporate community involvement; Conferences; Seminars and institutes. **Awards:** $5,000 to a MBA student, for a paper on corporate citizenship.

50744 ■ Massachusetts College of Art–Design Research Unit
Tower Bldg., 6th Fl., Rm. 611
621 Huntington Ave.
Boston, MA 02115
Ph:(617)879-7793
Fax: (617)566-4034
Co. E-mail: rstreit@massart.edu
URL: http://babel.massart.edu/dru
Contact: Dan Wallis, Pres.
E-mail: rstreit@massart.edu

Scope: Design research and services, focusing on printed matter, including posters, letterheads, annual reports, brochures, identity systems, exhibition design, industrial design, illustration, and photography. **Services:** Provides design services to educational, research, charitable, and non-profit organizations. **Educational Activities:** Educational training in design, printing, and business.

50745 ■ Radio and Television Research Council
234 5th Ave., Ste. 417
New York, NY 10001
Ph:(212)481-3038
Fax: (212)481-3071
Co. E-mail: rtrcnyc@aol.com
Contact: Stacey Lynn Koerner, Pres.
E-mail: rtrcnyc@aol.com
Scope: Radio and televison focusing on the problems and techniques used to study each as an advertising medium and as a means of social communication.

Purchasing

ASSOCIATIONS AND OTHER ORGANIZATIONS

50746 ■ American Purchasing Society
8 E Galena Blvd., Ste. 203
Aurora, IL 60506
Ph:(630)859-0250
Fax: (630)859-0270
Co. E-mail: support@american-purchasing.com
URL: http://www.american-purchasing.com
Contact: Dr. Harry E. Hough, Pres.
Description: Seeks to certify qualified purchasing personnel. Maintains speakers' bureau and placement service. Conducts research programs; compiles statistics including salary surveys. Provides consulting service for purchasing, materials management, and marketing. Conducts seminars and online courses. **Publications:** *Annual Report of Purchasing Salaries and Employment Trends* (annual) ; *Benchmarking Purchasing* (annual); *Contemporary Management*; *50 Tips for Outstanding Purchasing*; *Handbook of Buying and Purchasing Management*; *How to Become a Smart MRO Buyer*, *How To Get the Best Results from your Purchasing Department* (biennial); *Policies and Procedures Manual for Purchasing with Job Descriptions*; *Professional Purchasing* (monthly); *Purchasing Fundamentals for Today's Buyer*, *The Resume Handbook*; *The Search of How to Get a Higher Salary*; *10 Checklists for Buyers and Purchasing Managers*; *25 Cost Saving Tips for Businesses*; *What a Salesperson Should Know about the Law.*

50747 ■ National Purchasing Institute
65 Enterprise
Aliso Viejo, CA 92656
Ph:(949)715-7857
Free: 800-246-7143
Fax: (949)715-6931
Co. E-mail: executivedirector@
    nationalpurchasinginstitute.com
URL: http://www.nationalpurchasinginstitute.com
Contact: Diane Palmer CPPB, Pres.
Description: Purchasing agents, directors of purchasing and procurement, buyers, and others employed by governmental, educational, or other tax-supported agencies. Seeks to improve the field through development of simplified standards of specifications, improved communication, and promotion of uniform purchasing laws. Compiles statistics. **Publications:** *Annual Conference Program* (annual); *Membership Roster* (annual); *Public Purchasing Review* (bimonthly).

EDUCATIONAL PROGRAMS

50748 ■ CMC's Course in Purchasing Management (Canada)
Canadian Management Centre
150 York St., 5th Fl.
Toronto, ON, Canada M5H 3S5
Ph:(416)214-5678

Free: 800-262-9699
Fax: (416)313-4985
Co. E-mail: cmcinfo@cmctraining.org
URL: http://cmcamai.org
Price: $1,695.00 Canadian. **Description:** Covers the impact purchasing has on a company's budget, ISO 9000, purchasing laws, and future trends. **Locations:** Toronto, ON.

50749 ■ Fundamentals of Purchasing for the New Buyer
American Management Association
1601 Broadway
New York, NY 10019
Ph:(212)586-8100
Free: 800-262-9699
Fax: (212)903-8168
Co. E-mail: customerservice@amanet.org
URL: http://www.amanet.org
Price: $1,795.00 for non-members; $1,695.00 for AMA members. **Description:** Covers the steps involved in purchasing, negotiating, working with vendors and suppliers, using e-procurement, and the materials management process. **Locations:** Anaheim, CA; Fort Lauderdale, FL; Atlanta, GA; Chicago, IL; New York, NY; Philadelphia, PA; and Dallas, TX.

50750 ■ Fundamentals of Purchasing for the New Buyer (Canada)
Canadian Management Centre
150 York St., 5th Fl.
Toronto, ON, Canada M5H 3S5
Ph:(416)214-5678
Free: 800-262-9699
Fax: (416)313-4985
Co. E-mail: cmcinfo@cmctraining.org
URL: http://cmcamai.org
Price: $1,595.00 Canadian. **Description:** Covers the steps involved in purchasing, negotiating, working with vendors and suppliers, cost and price analysis, and types of purchase contracts. **Locations:** Calgary, AB; Mississauga, ON; and Toronto, ON.

50751 ■ The Legal Aspects of Purchasing and Supply Chain Management
American Management Association
1601 Broadway
New York, NY 10019
Ph:(212)586-8100
Free: 800-262-9699
Fax: (212)903-8168
Co. E-mail: customerservice@amanet.org
URL: http://www.amanet.org
Price: $1,795.00 for non-members; $1,695.00 for AMA members. **Description:** Covers purchasing agreements and contracts, governmental regulations and codes, product and service specifications, creating relationships with suppliers, and dispute and problem solving. **Locations:** New York, NY.

50752 ■ Purchasing and Supply Management
American Management Association
1601 Broadway
New York, NY 10019
Ph:(212)586-8100
Free: 800-262-9699

Fax: (212)903-8168
Co. E-mail: customerservice@amanet.org
URL: http://www.amanet.org
Price: $2,095 for non-members; $1,895 for AMA members. **Description:** Covers effectively communicating with suppliers, including forming partnerships while meeting the operations financial goals, price and cost analysis, recognize the economic indicators, and evaluation of contracts, and supply agreements. **Locations:** New York, NY; Chicago, IL; and Myrtle Beach, SC.

REFERENCE WORKS

50753 ■ Basics of Budgeting, Purchasing & Financial Statements
Pub: Amacom New Media, Inc.
Ed: Robert G. Finney. **Released:** 1999. **Price:** $39.95.

50754 ■ "Better Ways to Buy: Educate Yourself with a Consumer Handbook" in Black Enterprise (Vol. 35, December 2004, No. 5, pp. 160)
Pub: Earl G. Graves Publishing Co. Inc.
Ed: Stephanie Young. **Description:** Profile of the Consumer Action Handbook published by the U.S. General Services Administration. Along with consumer tips, the book lists contacts for corporations, federal agencies, better business bureaus, and local governments, as well as car manufacturers and dispute resolution programs and national consumer organizations.

50755 ■ Common Sense Purchasing: Hard Knock Lessons Learned from a Purchasing Pro
Pub: Booksurge, LLC
Ed: Tom DePaoli. **Released:** September 2004. **Price:** $10.95. **Description:** Guide to purchasing and negotiating deals.

50756 ■ "End of Some Tariffs a Boon to Suppliers" in Crain's Detroit Business (Vol. 22, December 18, 2006, No. 51, pp. 6)
Pub: Crain Communications Inc. - Detroit
Ed: Brent Snavely. **Description:** Relaxation of tariffs on corrosion resistant steels will reduce supply costs for automotive suppliers. Tariffs were removed for imports from France, Canada, Australia, and Japan but remain in effect for Korea and Germany.

50757 ■ "New Beginnings for VIBE" in Black Enterprise (Vol. 37, November 2006, No. 4, pp. 34)
Pub: Earl G. Graves Publishing Co. Inc.
Ed: Mashaun D. Simon. **Description:** Danyel Smith replaced Mimi Valdes as editor-in-chief of VIBE magazine after the Wicks Group, private equity firm focused on selected segments of the media, communications, and information industries, purchased the magazine.

50758 ■ "The Power of the Group" in *Black Enterprise* (Vol. 34, No. 4, November 2003, pp. 165)

Pub: Earl Graves Publishing Co.
Ed: Shayna T. Bayard. **Description:** The advantages of membership privileges are overviewed, profiling the benefits of AAA membership.

50759 ■ "Suiting Up; Yes, You're Smart, But Can You Look the Part" in *Crain's Chicago Business* (Vol. 30, February 2007, No. 6, pp. 39)

Pub: Crain Communications, Inc.
Ed: Kate Ryan. **Description:** For investment bankers, fashion is a must. Advice for men and women included.

50760 ■ "The thrifty boss" in *Forbes* (Vol. 6, No. 5, March 2003, pp. 46)

Pub: Forbes Magazine
Ed: Victoria Murphy. **Description:** Profile of purchasing software from Ariba. Statistical data included.

TRADE PERIODICALS

50761 ■ *Business Consumer's Advisor*

Pub: Buyers Laboratory Inc.
Contact: Jane Lyons
Ed: Daria Hoffman, Editor. **Released:** Monthly. **Price:** $175 plus $10 s/h. **Description:** Focuses on office equipment and supplies, offering purchasing advice and exploring methods of increasing office productivity through appropriate management of the equipment and its operators. Offers readers a chance to share their experiences, evaluate products and equipment, and gives results of Buyers Laboratory's testing.

50762 ■ *Caveat Emptor*

Pub: Ontario Public Buyers Association
Ed: C.B. Bott, Editor. **Released:** 4/year. **Price:** $99, individuals $99/year. **Description:** Contains information of interest to anyone who spends public funds. Recurring features include updates on OPBA's Internet Bid Document Advertising System and internal databank and articles dealing with new technology, management issues, and methodology related to the expenditure of public funds.

50763 ■ *Inside Supply Management*

Pub: Institute for Supply Management
Contact: Holly Johnson, Sr. VP
E-mail: hjohnson@ism.ws
Ed: Roberta Duffy, Editor, rduffy@ism.ws. **Released:** Monthly. **Description:** Trade magazine for purchasing and supply managers.

50764 ■ *The Journal of Supply Chain Management*

Pub: Institute for Supply Management
Contact: Julia Ogden, Vice President
E-mail: jogden@napm.org
Ed: Alvin Williams, Editor. **Released:** Quarterly. **Price:** $89 domestic print online; $55 international print online; $193 institutions print premium online; $175 institutions print standard online; $166 institutions premium online only; $119 institutions, other countries print premium online; $108 institutions, other countries print standard online; $103 institutions, other countries premium online only; $83 print online Europe; $119 institutions, other countries print premium online Europe. **Description:** Academic journal covering purchasing and supply management.

50765 ■ *Modern Purchasing*

Pub: Rogers Media Publishing
Contact: Tim Dimopoulos, Publisher
Ed: J. Terrett, Editor, terrett@cycor.ca. **Released:** 10/ year. **Price:** $41. **Description:** Magazine for purchasing professionals.

50766 ■ *NAEB Bulletin*

Pub: National Association of Educational Buyers Inc.
Ed: Doreen Murner, Editor, dmurner@naeb.org. **Released:** Monthly, except May and April. **Price:** Included in membership. **Description:** Features information on institutional purchasing and news of the Association. Recurring features include a calendar of events, reports of meetings, news of educational opportunities, job listings, book reviews, notices of publications available, and columns titled Professional Perspective, Market Index, and Roamin' With Yeoman.

50767 ■ *NASPO Newsletter*

Pub: National Association of State Purchasing Officials
Ed: Leslie Scott, Editor, lflynn@iglov.rom. **Released:** Quarterly, 2/year. **Price:** Included in membership. **Description:** Covers Association activities and purchasing innovations in state governments. Reports on developments in energy efficiency and recycling. Recurring features include news from the states, resources available, a calendar of events, and reports of state and federal legislation.

50768 ■ *Professional Purchasing*

Pub: American Purchasing Society
Contact: Harry E. Hough Ph.D.
Ed: Harry E. Hough, Ph.D., Editor, hehough@mgci. com. **Released:** Monthly. **Description:** Provides information on policies, procedures, methods, and prices of purchasing. Features price indexes. Recurring features include letters to the editor, news of research, reports of meetings, news of educational opportunities, job listings, book reviews, and notices of publications available.

50769 ■ *Progressive Purchasing*

Pub: Purchasing Management Association of Canada (PMAC)
Ed: A. Marshall, Editor, amarshall@pmac.ca. **Released:** Bimonthly. **Price:** Included in membership. **Description:** Presents news on the association's C. P.P. Accreditation program, new developments in purchasing, industry trends, and profiles of membership. Recurring features include a calendar of events, summary of national activities, and a column titled the National President's Message. **Remarks:** Also available in French.

50770 ■ *Purchasing Magazine*

Pub: Reed Business Information
Contact: Kathy Doyle, Publisher
E-mail: k.doyle@reedbusiness.com
Ed: Kevin Fitzgerald, Editor, kevinf@cahners.com. **Released:** Semimonthly, (monthly Jan., Aug., July and Dec.). **Description:** Magazine for buying professionals.

50771 ■ *Supplier Selection and Management Report*

Pub: IOMA Inc.
Contact: Perry Patterson, Publisher
E-mail: ppatterson@ioma.com
Ed: Joe Mazel, Editor, jmazel@ioma.com. **Released:** Monthly, 12/year. **Price:** $269, U.S.; $319, elsewhere.

Description: Provides information for supply managers. **Remarks:** Also available via e-mail in Adobe Acrobat.

TRADE SHOWS AND CONVENTIONS

50772 ■ **ISM Annual International Supply Management Conference**

Institute for Supply Management
2055 E. Centennial Cir.
PO Box 22160
Tempe, AZ 85285-2160
Ph:(480)752-6276
Free: 800-888-6276
Fax: (480)752-7890
URL: http://www.ism.ws
Released: Annual. **Audience:** Purchasing professionals and general public. **Principal Exhibits:** Auctions, business service, capital equipment, computer hardware/software, consulting services, e-business services/software, logistics and transportation, MRO, office supply, procurement card services. **Dates and Locations:** 2007 May 06-09, Las Vegas, NV.

CONSULTANTS

50773 ■ **Mark Vanderstelt**

9831 Gulfstream Ct.
Fishers, IN 46038
Ph:(317)576-9328
Fax: (317)576-9328
Scope: Consulting services include financial planning and analysis, inventory control, cash management, return on investment, budgeting, pricing, system design and analysis, mergers and acquisitions, feasibility studies, data processing, cost systems and controls, and performance measurement. Also performs operational and financial reviews.

RESEARCH CENTERS

50774 ■ **Arizona State University–CAPS Research**

ASU Research Pk.
2055 E Centennial Cir.
PO Box 22160
Tempe, AZ 85285-2160
Ph:(480)752-2277
Fax: (480)491-7885
Co. E-mail: pcarter@capsresearch.org
URL: http://www.capsresearch.org
Contact: Phillip Carter, Exec.Dir.
E-mail: pcarter@capsresearch.org
Scope: World-class purchasing, performance benchmarks, supplier partnerships, total quality management, purchasing measurement, non-traditional purchasing, cycle-time reduction, total cost models, futures study, and minority business enterprise best practices. **Publications:** Research reports (quarterly); Practix (quarterly); Critical Issue reports (quarterly). **Educational Activities:** Best Practices Forums/ Workshops (10/year), for senior purchasing and supply management practitioners; Critical Issue Partnership Eevents.

ASSOCIATIONS AND OTHER ORGANIZATIONS

50775 ■ National Conference on Peacemaking and Conflict Resolution
1718 E Speedway Blvd., No. 305
Tucson, AZ 85719
Ph:(520)670-1541
Fax: (520)884-9676
Co. E-mail: peaceweb@apeacemaker.net
URL: http://www.apeacemaker.net
Contact: Ann Yellott, Admin./Network Coor.
Purpose: Promotes the use and acceptance of nonviolent solutions to conflict resolution and peacemaking. Works as a liaison between national and international groups with similar goals. Sponsors educational programs and training in methods of nonviolent conflict resolution. **Publications:** *The Peacemaker* (annual). **Telecommunication Services:** electronic mail, ncpcr@apeacemaker.net.

TRADE SHOWS AND CONVENTIONS

50776 ■ Society for Human Resource Management (SHRM) The HRM Marketplace Exposition
Society for Human Resource Management
1800 Duke St.
Alexandria, VA 22314
Ph:(703)548-3440
Free: 800-283-SHRM
Fax: (703)535-6490
Co. E-mail: shrm@shrm.org
URL: http://www.shrm.org
Released: Annual. **Audience:** Human resource management and related professionals. **Principal Exhibits:** Human resource management products and services; including relocation human resource information systems, recruitment, executive search, temporary/contact personnel employee compensation and benefits, incentive program information, childcare/eldercare, and drug testing information.

CONSULTANTS

50777 ■ Ambler Growth Strategy Consultants Inc.
3432 Reading Ave.
Hammonton, NJ 08037-8008
Ph:(609)567-9669
Free: 888-253-6662
Fax: (609)567-3810
Co. E-mail: ambler@ambler.com
URL: http://www.aldonna.com

E-mail: ambler@ambler.com
Scope: Growth strategies, strategic assessments, CEO coaching. **Publications:** "Celebrate Selling: The

Consultative-Relationship Way". **Seminars:** Strategic Leadership; Managing Innovation; Breaking Through Classic Barriers to Growth; Energize Your Enterprise; Capture Your Competitive Advantage; Four Entrepreneurial Styles; Perservance and Resilience; Real-Time Strategic Planning/RO1. **Special Services:** The Growth Strategist™.

50778 ■ Effectiveness Resource Group Inc.
PO Box 7149
Bellevue, WA 98008-1149
Ph:(206)949-4171
Fax: (425)957-9186
Co. E-mail: don@consultdon.com
URL: http://www.consultdon.com

E-mail: don@consultdon.com
Scope: Provides problem-solving help to client organizations in public and private sectors so they can release and mobilize the full potential of their personnel to achieve productive and satisfying results. Emphasis is on technical/human productivity improvement projects and systems, total human resource systems design and implementation, and a whole systems approach to organizational change design and implementation. Serves private industries as well as government agencies. Consults with both internal and external consultants via e-mail and phone. Also offers executive coaching. **Seminars:** Life/Work Goals Exploration; Influencing Change Thru Consultation; Designing and Leading Participative Meetings; Designing, Leading and Managing Change; Project Management and Leadership; Performance Management; Productive Management of Differences; Performance Correction.

50779 ■ Focus Performance Systems Inc.
13911 Ridgedale Dr., Ste. 430
Minnetonka, MN 55305
Ph:(952)595-8000
Fax: (952)595-0679
Co. E-mail: info@focustools.com
URL: http://www.focustools.com

E-mail: info@focustools.com
Scope: Consultants specializing in the development and implementation of problem-solving, decision-making, and team processes for managers/supervisors and key people in a variety of organizations. Industries served: manufacturing, industrial, insurance/banking, healthcare and government. **Seminars:** How To Create Innovative Solutions On Demand, Jul, 2006; Essential tools to solve problems, make decisions and execute plans, faster and more effectively, Jul, 2006. **Special Services:** Decision Focus®; Team Focus™.

50780 ■ Goldore Consulting Inc.
120-5 St. NW
PO Box 590
Linden, AB, Canada T0M 1J0
Ph:(403)546-4208
Fax: (403)546-4208
Co. E-mail: goldore@leadershipessentials.com

E-mail: goldore@leadershipessentials.com

Scope: Provides consulting service in Leadership and management skills. Industries served: primarily charities, non-profits; some businesses. **Seminars:** O Desafio de Lideranca; The Challenge Of Leadership; Le Challenge du Leadership; El Desafio de Liderazgo; Tantangan Kipeminpinan.

50781 ■ Harris Advertising
4162 Fenton Rd.
Flint, MI 48507-2473
Ph:(810)232-4120
Scope: Conducts leadership training seminars for businesses and organizations. Participants learn problem solving techniques, communications skills, conflict resolution, leadership styles, dynamics of group development and participation, time management, and successful meeting management. Serves private industries as well as government agencies.

50782 ■ Organizational Improvement Associates
15 Princeton Ln.
New Fairfield, CT 06812
Ph:(203)746-8687
Fax: (203)746-8687
Co. E-mail: daveknibbe@earthlink.net

E-mail: daveknibbe@earthlink.net
Scope: Specializes in high-performance team development, executive coaching, employee development programs, performance management and reward systems, and dispute mediation. Industries served: consumer products, telecommunications, finance, healthcare, amusement/leisure, hospitality/lodging, retail, and pharmaceuticals worldwide.

50783 ■ The Performance Builders Publishing
PO Box 160150
Nashville, TN 37216
Free: (866)222-2606
Fax: (931)526-8376
Co. E-mail: customersfirst@pbbooks.org
URL: http://www.pbbooks.org

E-mail: customersfirst@pbbooks.org

50784 ■ Performance Dynamics Group
1400 N Sam Houston Pky. E, Ste. 130
Houston, TX 77032
Ph:(281)987-8875
Fax: (281)987-2153
Co. E-mail: ingram@pdq.net

E-mail: ingram@pdq.net
Scope: An organizational consulting group whose approach to learning and employee empowerment is designed to be both effective and efficient in achieving the specific knowledge and skill goals of a given program, and also to foster and develop initiative, self confidence, creative problem-solving ability and interpersonal effectiveness of all participants. **Seminars:** Programs for organizations include: Accelerated Approach to Change (2 days); Commitment to Quality (1 day); Managing Cultural Diversity (2 days); The Cor-

porate Energizer (1/2 day); The Power Pole Experience (1/2 day); Team Assessment (1/2 day); and Self-Directed Work Teams (2 days).

50785 ■ Sanford Consulting

52 Perry Corners Rd.
Amenia, NY 12501
Ph:(845)373-8960
Fax: (845)373-8961
Co. E-mail: sanford@mohawk.com

E-mail: sanford@mohawk.com
Scope: Helps businesses find, sell, (to), and keep customers. Provides management and marketing services, including problem analysis and solution design for new business development, market analysis and segmentation, departmental organization, and administrative policies and procedures. Industries served: small business, telecommunications, professional services, healthcare, and nonprofits in the continental United States. **Seminars:** Trade show succes; Finding customers; Business attitudes at not for profit and others.

50786 ■ The Walk The Talk Co.

2925 LBJ Fwy., Ste. 201
Dallas, TX 75234
Ph:(972)243-8863
Free: 800-888-2811
Fax: (972)243-0815
Co. E-mail: info@walkthetalk.com
URL: http://www.walkthetalk.com

E-mail: info@walkthetalk.com
Scope: Assists a wide variety of organizations in implementing POSITIVE DISCIPLINE®, the proprietary performance management system developed by the firm which concentrates on individual responsibility and decision making instead of disciplinary penalties.

Helps organizations develop and implement PEER REVIEW, a proven system that helps solve employee problems in a remarkable way-through employees; and MULTISOURCE360®, an evaluation process whereby feedback is compiled from a full-range of sources, including a self-evaluation, leadership development workshops and keynote presentations and publications. **Publications:** "Positive Discipline"; "Leadership Secrets of Santa Claus"; "Start Right-Stay Right"; "Walk Awhile In MY Shoes"; "Listen Up, Leader!"; "Five Star Teamwork"; "Ethics4Everyone"; "Leadership Courage"; "The Manager's Communication Handbook"; "180 Ways To Walk The Recognition Talk"; "The Manager's Coaching Handbook". **Seminars:** Walk the Talk; Coaching for Continuous Improvement; Managing Employee Performance; Customized Management Development Forums; Keynote presentations; Leadership Development Workshops; Consulting Services and Publications; Customer service training; Ethics & Values training.

RESEARCH CENTERS

50787 ■ Institute for the Development of Emotional and Life Skills

4400 East West Hwy.
Bethesda, MD 20814
Ph:(301)986-1479
Fax: (301)680-3756
Co. E-mail: bguerney@nire.org
URL: http://www.nire.org
Contact: Dr. Bernard Guerney Jr., Pres.
E-mail: bguerney@nire.org
Scope: Applied studies of marriage and family intervention, parenting and parent education programs, filial therapy, therapeutic programs for parent and children, relationship enhancement programs, inter-

personal relationships, communication and problem-solving skills, and premarital, marital, and family enrichment programs. **Educational Activities:** Training programs for professionals and the public.

50788 ■ Manchester College–Peace Studies Institute–Program in Conflict Resolution

Box 105
604 E College Ave.
North Manchester, IN 46962
Ph:(260)982-4151
Fax: (260)982-5043
Co. E-mail: tamcelwee@manchester.edu
URL: http://www.manchester.edu/Academics/
    departments/Peace_Studies/index.htm
Contact: Tim McElwee, Dir.
E-mail: tamcelwee@manchester.edu
Scope: Peace, societal violence, social responsibility, socially-responsible investing. **Publications:** Bulletin of the Peace Studies Institute (annually); Connections Newsletter (quarterly). **Educational Activities:** Church as Peacemaker and the Ropchan Lecture series (5/year).

50789 ■ National Institute of Relationship Enhancement

4400 East-West Hwy., Ste. 28
Bethesda, MD 20814-4501
Ph:(301)986-1479
Fax: (301)680-3756
Co. E-mail: info@nire.org
URL: http://www.nire.org
Contact: Dr. Bernard Guerney Jr., Dir.
E-mail: info@nire.org
Scope: Interpersonal and conflict resolution skills for individuals and organization personnel, new methods for enhancing family and personnel relationships, and mental health education and interpersonal skills. **Educational Activities:** Practicum training; Workshops for training professionals, organizational personnel, and families.

Research and Development

START-UP INFORMATION

50790 ■ "The Amazing, Real-Life Adventures of Microfly" in *Venture Capital Journal* (Vol. 42, No. 8, August 2002, pp. 30-31)
Pub: Thomas Venture Economics
Ed: Michael V. Copeland. Description: Profile of a robotic fly that weighs less than a paper clip and its promising technological value is discussed.

50791 ■ "EISC partners start-up with unique technology" in *Toledo Business Journal* (Vol. 19, No. 2, February 2003, pp. 23)
Pub: Telex Communications, Inc.
Ed: Susan Ford. Description: Profile of Energystics Technologies, Ltd. and Tom Sheperak, president and CEO, who is working on three applications for his unique Energy Beam(TM) technology that has the capability to move electricity through the air without a wire to heat, melt, or vaporize materials. EISC, the Small Business Development Center for technology and manufacturing, has established an on-site lab where Sheperak is developing and testing prototypes.

50792 ■ *Entrepreneurship: Frameworks and Empirical Investigations from Forthcoming Leaders of European Research*
Pub: Elsevier Science and Technology Books
Ed: Johan Wiklund; Dimo Dimov; Jerome A. Katz; Dean Shepherd. Released: July 2006. Price: $99.95.
Description: Entrepreneurial research and theory cover the early growth of research-based startups and the role of learning in international entrepreneurship, focusing on Europe.

50793 ■ "Image is Everything" in *Red Herring* (No. 99, June 15 & July 1, 2001, pp. 114, 116)
Pub: Herring Communications
Ed: Dean Takahashi. Description: Profile of Bob Weinschenk, CEO of Pixim, producer of image-sensor chips for digital cameras and other imaging devices. Statistical data included.

50794 ■ "Madison, Wis., University Research Park Expands Again" in *Milwaukee Journal Sentinel* (December 1, 2005)
Pub: Journal Sentinel, Inc.
Ed: Kathleen Gallagher. Description: University Research Park in Madison is expanding in order to accommodate 20 incubator suites for young companies being spun out of research findings at the University of Wisconsin-Madison.

50795 ■ "Montreal: A Fertile Ground For VC Exploration" in *Venture Capital Journal* (Vol. 42, No. 5, May 2002, pp. 54)
Pub: Thomas Venture Economics
Description: Montreal, Quebec is becoming the hot spot for technological development, and is supported by a strong investment community and world-class local venture capital environment.

50796 ■ "The Quebec Story: Low Cost, Low Risk, Tremendous Opportunity" in *Venture Capital Journal* (Vol. 42, No. 5, May 2002, pp. 48, 50)
Pub: Thomas Venture Economics
Ed: Peter Diekmeyer. Description: Canada's venture capital center has become a hotbed of technology startups because of the unique incentives, including tax incentives, low business costs, Montreal's close ties to Europe, and an educated workforce focused on technology.

50797 ■ "Revenge of the neurons" in *Red Herring* (No. 105, October 1, 2001, pp. 58-63)
Pub: Herring Communications
Ed: Stephan Herrera. Description: Rival startups blaze divergent trails to develop drug treatments for brain disorders. Information regarding stem cell research, as well as new drug discoveries, is discussed. Statistical data included.

50798 ■ "Soothe operator: word-of-mouth was the cure for discouragement" in *Entrepreneur* (Vol. 30, No. 12, December 2002, pp. 112)
Pub: Entrepreneur Media Inc.
Ed: April Y. Pennington. Description: Profile of Resheda Hagen, breast-feeding counselor and mother; Hagen began selling lanolin to new mothers for its healing power.

50799 ■ "There's Life In Life Science" in *Venture Capital Journal* (Vol. 42, No. 8, August 2002, pp. 32-35)
Pub: Thomas Venture Economics
Ed: Adam Reinebach. Description: Venture capitalists are taking a real interest in life sciences. Profiles of four venture-backed startups are presented, including PTC Therapeutics Inc., working in small molecule drug discovery; Sensors for Medical Solutions Inc., medical sensors; Medical Scientists Inc., predictive modeling software; and Message Pharmaceuticals, drug discovery focusing on messenger RNA. Statistical data included.

REFERENCE WORKS

50800 ■ "$1 Million Grant Program Aims to Boost Renewable Energy" in *Milwaukee Journal Sentinel* (December 13, 2005)
Pub: Journal Sentinel, Inc.
Ed: Thomas Content. Description: Wisconsin's Governor Jim Doyle has proposed a $1 million grant to invest in renewable energy technologies for the state, including ethanol, biodiesel and waste-to-energy power.

50801 ■ "60 Seconds On Doing the Impossible" in *Fast Company* (March 2005, No. 92, pp. 32)
Pub: Gruner & Jahr USA Publishing
Ed: Ryan Underwood. Description: Interview with Peter Diamandis, who created the competition that awarded the $10 million Ansari X Prize to SpaceShipOne for shuttling into suborbital space twice in two weeks. Diamandis is expanding his focus to include prizes for nanotechnology.

50802 ■ "Aastrom Gets $22M Financing Boost; Stem-Cell Trials Pique Wall Street's Interest" in *Crain's Detroit Business* (January 17, 2005)
Pub: Crain Communications Inc. - Detroit
Ed: Andrew Dietderich. Description: Aastrom Biosciences Inc. is committed to obtaining approval by the U.S. Food and Drug Administration for approval of stem-cell-based products for general medical use. The firm has secured $22 million capital to conduct clinical stem-cell trial tests at William Beaumont Hospital.

50803 ■ "Addressing the Inhibitors" in *Washington Business Journal* (Vol. 21, No. 50, April 11, 2003, pp. 28)
Pub: Washington Business Journal
Ed: Chris Silva. Description: Drugs designed to bolster viral fusion inhibitors are being developed by Panacos Pharmaceuticals Inc. An anti-HIV drug was approved by the U.S. Food and Drug Administration in March, which offers opportunities for a new type of drug.

50804 ■ "Against the Grain" in *Red Herring* (No. 105, October 1, 2001, pp. 54-57)
Pub: Herring Communications
Ed: Stephan Herrera. Description: Agricultural biotechnology's third wave, producing therapeutic proteins from plants, should help the beleaguered field improve its public image. An interview with Mich Hein, president and founder of Epicyte, which produces drugs with molecular farming is included. Statistical data included.

50805 ■ "AgraQuest Fumigant OK'd" in *Sacramento Bee* (November 18, 2005)
Pub: The Sacramento Bee
Ed: Jim Wasserman. Description: AgraQuest Inc. announced approval by both federal and state agencies for its natural soil fumigant that could help replace methyl bromide, the chemical soil sterilizer. AgraQuest is based in Davis, California and reports revenues at $4.2 million for 2005. The firm's products are based on naturally occurring fungus.

50806 ■ "Albany's High-Tech Park Already Creating Jobs" in *Tampa Tribune* (November 28, 2005)
Pub: Media General, Inc.
Ed: Gary Haber. Description: Albany NanoTech, located 150 miles north of New York City, is a $3 billion research and development complex for researchers from industry, as well as professors and students from the University at Albany who are working on next-generation miniature computer chips.

50807 ■ "Alternative Energy Attracts Big Money" in *Atlanta Journal-Constitution* (January 24, 2007)
Pub: Cox Newspapers, Inc.

Ed: Dan Chapman. **Description:** Major corporations, venture capitalists, investment banks, hedge funds and farmers spent $71 billion globally on renewable energy research.

50808 ■ "Alternative Energy Powers Up In Michigan - Part 1 of 2" in *Crain's Detroit Business* **(Vol. 22, February 6, 2006, No. 6, pp. 10)**
Pub: Crain Communications Inc. - Detroit
Ed: Amy Lane. **Description:** McKenzie Bay International Ltd. Located in Farmington Hills, Michigan is launching a commercial wind-energy system that generates and distributes electricity at customer locations, and supplements power from a conventional utility.

50809 ■ "Alternative Energy Powers Up In Michigan - Part 2 of 2" in *Crain's Detroit Business* **(Vol. 22, February 6, 2006, No. 6, pp. 10)**
Pub: Crain Communications Inc. - Detroit
Ed: Amy Lane. **Description:** Michigan is pushing to become the nations' epicenter for research and development into new technology for biodiesel fuels made from renewable resources such as vegetable oil recycled from restaurants or produced from sunflowers, soybeans and canola plants.

50810 ■ "Amgen Looking to Develop Medicines with Competitors" in *Providence Business News* **(Vol. 18, No. 20, September 1, 2003, pp. 2)**
Pub: Providence Business News, Inc.
Ed: Marni Leff Kottle. **Description:** Efforts by Amgen to find competitor with promising drug for joint venture scheme are discussed. Topics include testing of new drugs, possible profits from new drugs, and Amgen's falling market share.

50811 ■ "'Angels' Seek to Expand Territory; Investors Begin to Target Waukesha County" in *Milwaukee Journal Sentinel* **(December 12, 2005)**
Pub: Journal Sentinel, Inc.
Ed: Kathleen Gallagher. **Description:** IQ Corridor Angel Network is targeting Waukesha County to help develop a series of high-tech companies from Chicago through Milwaukee and Madison onto Minneapolis. The firm is seeking ideas related to manufacturing equipment needed by biotech and other high-tech companies, especially those in Madison, Wisconsin.

50812 ■ "Ann Arbor's QuatRx Pharmaceuticals Files for Stock Offering" in *Crain's Detroit Business* **(Vol. 22, February 13, 2006, No. 7, pp. 25)**
Pub: Crain Communications Inc. - Detroit
Ed: Andrew Dieterich. **Description:** QuatRx Pharmaceuticals Company, based in Ann Arbor, Michigan, filed an initial public offering in the hopes of raising $86 million. The firm develops and commercializes products in the endocrine, metabolic, and cardiovascular therapeutic areas.

50813 ■ "Aquaculture Becoming Big Business in Rhode Island" in *Providence Business News* **(Vol. 18, No. 16, August 4, 2003, pp. 3)**
Pub: Providence Business News, Inc.
Ed: Laura Rickstson. **Description:** The growing aquaculture industry in Rhode Island is examined, including market share of fish industry, market development, and industry forecasts.

50814 ■ "Ask the attorney" in *Red Herring* **(March 2003, pp. 73)**
Pub: Herring Communications Inc.
Description: Legal issues are addressed that include the following topics, pharmaceutical patents, government support for research and development, global commerce, intellectual property rights, the transfer of customer lists from European subsidiary to its U.S. parent company, trademark dilution, venture financing, selling a business, stock options, corporate tax deductions, small business patent methods, and employee use of Instant Messaging with clients.

50815 ■ "Assist.com www.assist.com/assist. htm" in *Entrepreneur* **(Vol. 32, No. 1, January 2004, pp. 10)**
Pub: Entrepreneur Media, Inc.
Ed: Steve Cooper. **Description:** When a small business is searching for a white paper or any research, Assist.com's search engine indexes PDF files that are downloadable free.

50816 ■ "Avoiding Invention Scams" in *Black Enterprise* **(Vol. 37, January 2007, No. 6, pp. 46)**
Pub: Earl G. Graves Publishing Co. Inc.
Ed: James C. Johnson. **Description:** Invention promotion firms provide inventors assistance in developing a prototype for product development. It is important to research these companies before making a commitment to work with them because there are a number of these firms that are not legitimate and have caused independent inventors to lose thousands of dollars by making false claims as to the market potential of the inventions.

50817 ■ "Beaumont Aims to Commercialize Research" in *Crain's Detroit Business* **(Vol. 22, January 16, 2006, No. 3, pp. 3)**
Pub: Crain Communications Inc. - Detroit
Ed: Michelle Martinez. **Description:** William Beaumont Hospital is planning to commercialize its clinical trials and medical research. The move will help Beaumont supplement the hospital's research unit budget to $22.6 million in 2006.

50818 ■ "Before You Do That 'Amazing' Biotech Deal, Read This Story" in *Venture Capital Journal* **(Vol. 42, No. 8, August 2002, pp. 36-37)**
Pub: Thomas Venture Economics
Ed: Ravi Chiruvolu. **Description:** Biotechnology startups always require a longer incubation period. The author shares his experiences with biotechnology deals.

50819 ■ "Behind the looking glass" in *Red Herring* **(March 2003, pp. 58)**
Pub: Herring Communications Inc.
Ed: Celeste Biever. **Description:** A listing of everyday products manufactured through nanotechnology is presented, including antibacterial products, self-cleaning glass, sunscreens, tennis balls and more.

50820 ■ "Belt-Tightening at Pfizer?" in *Business Week Online* **(February 9, 2005)**
Pub: McGraw-Hill Companies
Ed: Amy Barrett. **Description:** Pfizer is expected to announce a major restructuring of the company in order to cut costs, but its sales force is believed to be safe from cuts.

50821 ■ "Berridge Confident of Evolving Work Force" in *Ledger* **(March 6, 2005)**
Pub: Knight-Ridder/Tribune Business News
Ed: Kyle Kennedy. **Description:** Florida High Tech Corridor Council's president, Randy Berridge is committed to bringing more high tech business and jobs to Central Florida.

50822 ■ "Betting the Farm" in *Business 2.0* **(Vol. 6, September 2005, No. 8, pp. 108)**
Pub: Time, Inc.
Ed: Erick Schonfeld. **Description:** The continual advancement of genetically modified crops is paying off for Monsanto after the company took the big risk on biotechnology.

50823 ■ "Big-League R&D Gets Its Own eBay" in *Fortune* **(Vol. 149, No. 9, May 3, 2004, pp. 74)**
Pub: Time, Inc.
Ed: David Kirkpatrick. **Description:** Start of the new Internet-driven revolution in Research and Development is discussed. Experts predict research will be judged on scientific merits, not where researchers attended school or live.

50824 ■ "Big Pharm's Favorite Gadfly" in *Business Week* **(December 19, 2005, No. 3964, pp. 50-51)**
Pub: McGraw-Hill Companies
Ed: Amy Barrett. **Description:** Dr. Steven E. Nissen, leader of clinical trials, works to ascertain drug safety.

50825 ■ "Bio-Pharmaceutical Emphasis" in *San Diego Business Journal* **(Vol. 28, January 15, 2007, No. 3, pp. 11)**
Pub: San Diego Business Journal Associates
Ed: Katie Weeks. **Description:** Huya Bioscience International LLC, with offices in both San Diego, California and Shanghai, China, is partnering with Organon in order to discover new biopharmaceuticals.

50826 ■ "BioGift Goes After Cancer Tissue Niche" in *Business Journal-Portland* **(Vol. 20, No. 25, August 22, 2003, pp. 1)**
Pub: American City Business Journals, Inc.
Ed: Robin J. Moody. **Description:** BioGift Anatomical Inc., located in Tigard, Oregon, is seeking body donations from individuals with cancer in order to extend its cancer research and education programs.

50827 ■ "Biographies" in *Venture Capital Journal* **(February 1, 2006)**
Pub: Thomason Financial Inc.
Description: Profiles of leading venture capital firms including Canaan Partners, BA Venture Partners, Orrick, Alta Partners, Inter West Partners, New Enterprise Associates, and Frazier Healthcare Ventures.

50828 ■ "Biomedical, Marine Research Funds Could Grow If Voters Approve Seed Money" in *Portland Press Herald* **(November 2, 2005)**
Pub: Blethen Maine Newspapers, Inc.
Ed: Edward D. Murphy. **Description:** Maine's Department of Economic and Community Development says the $20 million on the state's election ballot would not be enough to fund projects designed to help biomedical and marine research programs.

50829 ■ "Biotech Balance: Mutual Fund Diversification Lets Investors Temper Biotech's Risk" in *Black Enterprise* **(Vol. 34, No. 4, Nov. 2003)**
Pub: Earl Graves Publishing Co.
Ed: James A. Anderson. **Description:** Information for investing in Biotechnology is examined.

50830 ■ "Biotech" in *Business Week* **(January 23, 2006, No. 3968, pp. 38, 40)**
Pub: McGraw-Hill Companies
Ed: Arlene Weintraub. **Description:** Biotechnology funding was always difficult to find in the U.S., but even more so since the Korean scandal made the headlines. South Korean scientist Hwang Woo Suk faked 11 lines of embryonic stem cells he claimed to have created through cloning in May 2005.

50831 ■ "Biotech: Frankenforests cropping up" in *Red Herring* **(No. 105, October 1, 2001, pp. 25-26)**
Pub: Herring Communications
Ed: Stasia Bochnowski. **Description:** An overview of genetic tree engineering is presented, with research focused on developing trees with faster growth rates, lower levels of lignin (a polymer that must be removed to make paper and pulp), and resistance to pests and diseases.

50832 ■ "Biotech Takes Heart in Potential New Drug" in *Pacific Business News* **(Vol. 41, No. 23, August 15, 2003, pp. 1)**
Pub: American City Business Journals
Ed: Terrance Sing. **Description:** Hawaii-based Hawaii Biotech Inc. has developed a new drug that is expected to reduce heart tissue damage. The new drug, called Cardax, has achieved positive results in clinical tests at the Medical College of Wisconsin.

50833 ■ "Blues offer grant to study nurse shortage" in *Crain's Detroit Business* **(Vol. 19, No. 15, April 14, 2003, pp. 14)**
Pub: Crain Communications Inc., Detroit

Ed: Ian McClure. **Description:** Blue Cross Blue Shield of Michigan Foundation, located in Detroit, Michigan, is providing grant opportunities for new programs and research to help ease the nursing shortage facing the state.

50834 ■ "Born in an infertility clinic, nursed in a dish" in *Atlanta Business Chronicle* **(Vol. 25, No. 22, November 8, 2002, pp. 20A)**
Pub: American City Business Publications, Inc.
Ed: Julie Bryant. **Description:** BresaGen Inc. has four stem cell lines for use in research on finding new treatments for various debilitating illnesses. The firm has not revealed the name of the Atlanta, Georgia infertility clinic from which it received the needed human embryos to obtain the stem cell lines. The stem cell process is examined.

50835 ■ "Bowling for drug research: families take entrepreneurial tack in signing up biotech firms" in *Wall Street Journal* **(Feb. 27, 2003)**
Pub: Dow Jones & Co. Inc.
Ed: Vanessa Fuhrmans. **Description:** Families of Spinal Muscular Atrophy signed a contract with Decode Genetics Inc. to fund their research programs.

50836 ■ "BresaGen moves slowly to grow stem cell work" in *Atlanta Business Chronicle* **(Vol. 25, November 8, 2002, No. 22 pp. 1A)**
Pub: American City Business Publications, Inc.
Ed: Julie Bryant. **Description:** BresaGen Inc., located in Athens, Georgia, is working with stem cells to find treatments for various human conditions. BresaGen has received $1.6 million in U.S. government grants and has entered into various licensing and distribution accords with the National Institutes of Health.

50837 ■ "Briefing: Semiconductors" in *Red Herring* **(No. 99, June 15 & July 1, 2001, pp. 100-101)**
Pub: Herring Communications
Ed: Dean Takahashi. **Description:** An overview of the downturn in the high tech sector.

50838 ■ "Bright Lights" in *Red Herring* **(No. 99, June 15 & July 1, 2001, pp. 55-56, 58)**
Pub: Herring Communications
Ed: Lee Bruno. **Description:** With nanotechnology lighting the way, a new class of optical switches are vying to usher in more efficient communications networks.

50839 ■ "Bucking the Odds at Amylin" in *Business Week* **(January 9, 2006, No. 3966, pp. 64, 66)**
Pub: McGraw-Hill Companies
Ed: Arlene Weintraub. **Description:** Profile of Ginger Graham, chief executive at Amylin Pharmaceuticals Inc., who was considering retirement before taking the reins at Amylin. Graham, who is a diabetic, has helped the company attain government approval on two diabetes drugs.

50840 ■ "Buoyed by Biotech" in *Venture Capital Journal* **(February 1, 2006)**
Pub: Thomason Financial Inc.
Description: Life science venture capitalists gathered in San Francisco, California recently to discuss backing life sciences startups that are developing drugs and creating innovated medical devices.

50841 ■ "Business Briefs" in *St. Louis Post-Dispatch* **(December 8, 2004)**
Pub: Knight-Ridder/Tribune Business News
Description: Orion Genomics LLC, based at the Center for Emerging Technologies incubator, received a federal grant to research the genetic code of the agricultural pest roundworm. Research is directed at finding alternative ways to destroy or ward off the pest that are more effective than chemical pesticides now used. The company and researchers at North Carolina State University will share the $1.59 million grant.

50842 ■ *Business Research: An Informal Guide*
Pub: Crisp Publications, Inc.
Ed: Paul R. Timm and Rick Farr. **Price:** $9.95.

50843 ■ "Cancer Scans a Lifesaver for Crystal Maker" in *Orlando Business Journal* **(Vol. 20, No. 8, August 8, 2003, pp. 2)**
Pub: American City Business Journals, Inc.
Ed: Chad Eric Watt. **Description:** Profile of Crystal Photonics, founded by physicist Bruce Chai to produce artificial crystals. The firm has become one of the top crystal makers in the world.

50844 ■ "Caritas Seeking Cambridge Lab Space" in *Boston Globe* **(February 4, 2005)**
Pub: New York Times Company
Ed: Jeffrey Krasner. **Description:** Caritas Christi Health Care is planning to lease 100,000 square feet of laboratory space in Cambridge to increase its healthcare and biotechnology research. The move is expected to give the firm a higher profile and better access to scientists and local companies.

50845 ■ "Cashflow: August 1-15, 2001" in *Red Herring* **(No. 105, October 1, 2001, pp. 32)**
Pub: Herring Communications
Ed: Mark A. Mowrey. **Description:** Although venture investment in the technology-related sectors remained low, activity in the biotechnology sector was increasing during the period of August 1-15, 2001. Statistical data included.

50846 ■ "The Change Up: Find New Uses for Your Products" in *My Business* **(February/March 2003, pp. 15)**
Pub: My Business Magazine
Ed: Evelyn Beck. **Description:** Diversification of a product can be a good tool for increasing sales, but it is imperative to do research.

50847 ■ "Chaos, Inc." in *Red Herring* **(January 2003, pp. 38)**
Pub: Herring Communications Inc.
Ed: Mitchell M. Waldrop. **Description:** Profile of Santa Fe-based BiosGroup, a 20 year old startup, that recently ran a simulation to help Procter & Gamble achieve an inventory reduction of 25 percent.

50848 ■ "Chinese Supplier Plans R&D Center in Canton Twp." in *Crain's Detroit Business* **(Vol. 21, October 31, 2005, No. 44, pp. 15)**
Pub: Crain Communications Inc. - Detroit
Ed: Terry Kosdrosky. **Description:** Chinese auto supplier, Tempo Group, is planning to locate its research and development center in Canton Township, Michigan. The center will employ up to 200 people.

50849 ■ "A clarion call: the tech and telecom sectors are finally on the mend" in *Barron's* **(Vol. 82, No. 58, February 17, 2003, pp. 28)**
Pub: Barron's
Ed: Sandra Wood. **Description:** Tech and telecom research specialists, Scott Cleland and William Whyman, are optimistic about the end of the bear market in those sectors, including software, cable TV, and the Baby Bells.

50850 ■ "Clearwater Man Puts Technology To Work" in *Tampa Tribune* **(November 27, 2005)**
Pub: Media General, Inc.
Ed: Will Rodgers. **Description:** Denny Klein of Airport Business Center has developed a gas that speeds welding and fusing times and also improves automobile fuel efficiency by at least 30 percent.

50851 ■ "Cottage industry pays off for Eskimo women" in *Alaska Business Monthly* **(Vol. 18, No. 10, Oct. 2002, pp. 82)**
Pub: Alaska Business Publishing Company, Inc.
Ed: Gerry Watkins. **Description:** Profile of explorer/anthropologist, John J. Teal, Jr. Teal, a Harvard/Yale anthropologist, has established the Institute of Northern Agricultural Research. Through the domestication of the musk ox, Teal not only conducts research on the animal, his work has enabled Alaskan women to use the wool to make hand knitted items that are sold to a co-op, thus providing income for their families.

50852 ■ "Crossing the Gene Barrier" in *Business Week* **(January 16, 2006, No. 3967, pp. 72-77, 80)**
Pub: McGraw-Hill Companies
Ed: Arlene Weintraub. **Description:** Biotechnology scientists Harry M. Meade and Nils Lonberg are mixing the genetic materials of man and beats in new ways in order to develop treatments of life threatening diseases such as cancer and arthritis. Medical ethics of genetic research are also discussed.

50853 ■ "Customers as Innovators" in *Harvard Business Review* **(Vol. 80, No. 4, April 2002, pp. 74)**
Pub: Harvard Business School Press
Ed: Eric Stefan, von Hippel Thomke. **Description:** A radically new approach to research and development is described. Companies are now encouraging customers to design and develop their own products and advice is given on how this can be achieved.

50854 ■ "Cyberkinetics Plans for Clinical Trials" in *Providence Business News* **(Vol. 18, No. 20, September 1, 2003, pp. 1)**
Pub: Providence Business News, Inc.
Ed: Mike Colias. **Description:** Product development taking place at Providence-based Cyberkinetics Inc. is discussed. Topics include drug testing, strategic planning, and company funding.

50855 ■ "Dealing with Reality" in *Pittsburgh Business Times* **(Vol. 23, No. 6, August 29, 2003, pp. 15)**
Pub: Pittsburgh Business Times
Ed: Christopher Davis. **Description:** Robotics Foundry president, William Thomasmeyer, hopes to develop robotics research into viable business opportunities in the Pittsburgh, Pennsylvania area.

50856 ■ "Design Principal" in *Fast Company* **(September 2001, pp. 48)**
Pub: Fast Company
Description: Profile of Chris Bangle, design chief for BMW. Bangle explains the importance of providing time for reflection on what's important to the customer, when designing new automobiles.

50857 ■ "Detection Redirection" in *Washington Business Journal* **(Vol. 22, No. 9, July 4, 2003, pp. 13)**
Pub: Washington Business Journal
Ed: Chris Silva. **Description:** Marketing of cancer detection technology by Washington, DC-based biotechnology firm Protiveris Inc. is examined.

50858 ■ "Dialogue Picks Up on St. Louis' Status in IT and Biotech" in *St. Louis Post-Dispatch* **(November 3, 2004)**
Pub: Knight-Ridder/Tribune Business News
Ed: David Nicklaus. **Description:** St. Louis reports dozens of startup biotechnology companies and venture capital funds to back them. According to a study conducted by the Battelle Institute, St. Louis has become competitive in both life sciences and information technology sectors.

50859 ■ "Digital Defenses Sector Analysis" in *Red Herring* **(January 2003, pp. 64)**
Pub: Herring Communications Inc.
Description: An analysis of the digital defense sector in the U.S. is presented. Statistical data includes a listing of private companies, date founded, number of employees, funding, and number of funding rounds. Industry sectors include biological security, digital identity, managed security services, and network security.

50860 ■ "Doctor's Little Helpers" in *Red Herring* **(No. 99, June 15 & July 1, 2001, pp. 50-52, 54)**
Pub: Herring Communications
Ed: Stephan Herrera. **Description:** Nanotechnology doesn't look so far out and flimsy for medical applications anymore. Quantum Dot, in Hayward, California and C Sixty, in Toronto, Canada are profiled.

50861 ■ "A Dose of News: Neurocrine Biosciences Inc." in *San Diego Business Journal* **(Vol. 28, January 15, 2007, No. 3, pp. 11)**
Pub: San Diego Business Journal Associates
Ed: Katie Weeks. **Description:** Neurocrine Biosciences Inc. reported positive preliminary results from part two of a study for its drug candidates to treat endometriosis.

50862 ■ "Down to a Science" in *Entrepreneur* **(Vol. 31, No. 8, August 2003, pp. 54)**
Pub: Entrepreneur Media, Inc.
Ed: Dian Vujovich. **Description:** Profile of the Eaton Vance Worldwide Health Sciences Fund (ETHSX), which has a five-year average total return of 12.67 percent. The fund invests in health, sciences and biotechnology firms worldwide.

50863 ■ "ECD short of cash at critical time as partners pull out of ventures" in *Crain's Detroit Business* **(Vol. 19, No. 8, Feb. 24, 2003)**
Pub: Crain Communications Inc., Detroit
Ed: Andrew Dietderich. **Description:** Energy Conversion Devices Inc. has lost funding from three companies for joint ventures in fuel-cell development.

50864 ■ "Ed Otto, Director of Biotechnology at RCCC" in *Charlotte Observer* **(February 8, 2007)**
Pub: Knight-Ridder/Tribune Business News
Ed: Gail Smith-Arrants. **Description:** Profile of Ed Otto, director of biotechnology at Rowan-Cabarrus Community College. Before taking the position at RCCC, Otto directed the Food and Drug Administration office responsible for regulating cellular, tissue and gene therapies products.

50865 ■ "Emergency services gets a breath of fresh air" in *Red Herring* **(January 2003, pp. 56)**
Pub: Herring Communications Inc.
Ed: Alan Zeichick. **Description:** Profile of the new emergency-response system, developed by Airwave System, and currently being used in six counties of the United Kingdom. The system involves a common terrestrial radio service for emergency workers. After September 11, 2001, the U.S. is working to develop such a system to replace the antiquated radio equipment unsuitable for data transmission.

50866 ■ "End of the Road" in *Entrepreneur* **(Vol. 31, No. 8, August 2003, pp. 24)**
Pub: Entrepreneur Media, Inc.
Ed: Joshua Kurlantzick. **Description:** Two Department of Commerce programs, the Advanced Technology Program (ATP) and the Manufacturing Extension Partnership (MEP) may be discontinued as part of the 2004 federal budget. The ATP program assists small firms by supporting research and development, while the MEP aids manufacturers in upgrading technology and human resources.

50867 ■ "Engine of Progress" in *Fast Company* **(November 2001, pp. 144)**
Pub: Fast Company
Ed: Fara Warner. **Description:** General Motors is developing vehicles that will use a hybrid gasoline-electric engine that can be used in the traditionally styled vehicles that consumers love.

50868 ■ "Extreme hunter scores big with tiny funds" in *Red Herring* **(March 2003, pp. 52)**
Pub: Herring Communications Inc.
Ed: Niall McKay. **Description:** Profile of Jonathan Trent, an astrobiologist at NASA. Trent discovered a breakthrough in 1991 that may revolutionize a segment of nanotechnology known as molecular manufacturing.

50869 ■ "An eye for a dye" in *Red Herring* **(March 2003, pp. 60)**
Pub: Herring Communications Inc.
Ed: Michael V. Copeland. **Description:** Optiva's nanotechnology has attracted JP Morgan Partners investment.

50870 ■ "The fabric of consumer reality" in *Red Herring* **(March 2003, pp. 54)**
Pub: Herring Communications Inc.
Ed: Alan Zeichick. **Description:** The economics of nanotechnology are discussed. In order for a particular consumer good to be priced competitively, the nano-scale components required must be manufactured in bulk, using techniques similar to those used in making larger-scale products.

50871 ■ "Fabricating Photons" in *Red Herring* **(No. 99, June 15 & July 1, 2001, pp. 110, 112-113)**
Pub: Herring Communications
Ed: Om Malik. **Description:** Optical chips will revolutionize computer networks, but it will remain on the fringe of networks until many obstacles to its commercialization are overcome.

50872 ■ "Farmingdale-based THM Scientific Introduces Product Line Based on Sustainable Agriculture" in *Long Island Business News* **(Feb.6, 2004)**
Pub: Dolan Media Newswires
Ed: Adina Genn. **Description:** Profile of Peter Felix and James Sottilo, two arborists who have partnered to develop and produce Rootgrow, a line of organic-compost tea, brewers and related products and services that will preserve the soil. The partners are targeting homeowners, corporate parks, golf courses, and municipalities.

50873 ■ "Firm Wins Grant for Robotic Vehicle" in *Pittsburgh Business Times* **(Vol. 23, No. 4, August 15, 2003, pp. 3)**
Pub: Pittsburgh Business Times
Ed: Maria Guzzo. **Description:** A U.S. Army research grant will be used at Applied Perception Inc. to develop a robotic vehicle; topics include military research, robotic vehicles, and battlefield applications of the vehicle.

50874 ■ "Flight of Fancy? Launching a High-Tech Product Can be a Technical and Financial Challenge" in *Entrepreneur* **(Vol. 32, August 2004)**
Pub: Entrepreneur Media Inc.
Ed: Don Debelak. **Description:** Profile of William J. Boyer Jr. and partner and co-founder Ray Henson, who helped Boyer with the technical aspects of their digEplayer, a portable battery-operated in-flight entertainment system used on passenger tray tables. The company saw $1 millions in sales, first quarter 2004.

50875 ■ "From Cow Pies to Clean Power" in *Business 2.0* **(Vol. 7, January/February 2006, No. 1, pp. 24)**
Pub: Time, Inc.
Ed: Elizabeth Esfahani. **Description:** Panda Energy is developing a method that converts cow dung into bio-gas fuel which would in turn power the production of ethanol.

50876 ■ "Fund Profile" in *Venture Capital Journal* **(February 1, 2006)**
Pub: Thomason Financial Inc.
Description: Profile of Aisling Capital, founded in 2002 as Perseus-Soros BioPharmaceutical Fund. The VC invests in biopharmaceutical companies that require $15M to $30M of new capital.

50877 ■ "Gad Zeus!" in *Atlanta Business Chronicle* **(Vol. 24, No. 10, August 10, 2001, pp. 1B)**
Pub: American City Business Journals Inc.
Description: The Zeus Robotic Surgical System, a prototype robotic computer, is one of six undergoing a national trial of robotic surgery. Atlanta Medical Center is one of six undertaking the experiment of the systems, which are made by California-based Computer Motion.

50878 ■ "Genetic Medicine's Next Big Step" in *Fortune* **(Vol. 151, January 10, 2005, No. 1, pp. 54)**
Pub: Time Inc.
Ed: John Simons. **Description:** RNA interference (RNAi) is a process that is able to block threatening

genetic signals in diseased cells, such as those that can proliferate a virus. This process could lead to the breakthrough needed for the struggling drug industry. Profile of Alnylam Pharmaceutical in Cambridge, Massachusetts is included.

50879 ■ "Genzyme Battles An Old Adversary" in *Boston Globe* **(January 25, 2005)**
Pub: New York Times Company
Ed: Jeffrey Krasner. **Description:** A new battle over intellectual property has erupted between Genzyme Corporation and Transkaryotic Therapies Inc. (TKT) of Cambridge, Massachusetts. Genzyme has sued TKT claiming that the firm's method of purifying a treatment for a particular disease infringed on Genzyme's proprietary technology.

50880 ■ "Georgia medical device business growing" in *Atlanta Business Chronicle* **(Vol. 25, No. 19, October 18, 2002, pp. 3A)**
Pub: American City Business Publications, Inc.
Ed: Julie Bryant. **Description:** The number of medical device companies operating in the state of Georgia currently totals more than 225, with growth centered in the small- to medium-size category. However, industry leaders in the state contend that the medical device industry has yet to take-off in the state. Many of these firms are divisions of much larger companies.

50881 ■ "Getting the truth into workplace surveys" in *Harvard Business Review* **(Vol. 80, No. 1, January 2002, pp. 111)**
Pub: Harvard Business School Press
Ed: Palmer Morrel-Samuels. **Description:** Workplace surveys and the differences between good ones and bad ones, which seems to be informed design, are discussed.

50882 ■ *Global Electronic Business Research: Opportunities and Directions*
Pub: Idea Group Publishing
Ed: Nabeel A.Y. Al-Qirim. **Released:** October 2005.
Description: Importance electronic commerce research plays in small to medium-sized enterprises in various countries.

50883 ■ "Going Private: How VCs Can Get in the Game" in *Venture Capital Journal* **(Vol. 42, No. 10, October 2002, pp. 49)**
Pub: Thomson Venture Economics
Ed: Jonathan Bell. **Description:** A trend towards venture capital firms to reverse course and help companies go private is examined. To minimize the risk that the transaction may be questionable as being unfair to minority shareholders, an independent and disinterested committee of the company's board should handle negotiations.

50884 ■ "Grants for Rural Biz" in *Inc.* **(September 1, 2003)**
Pub: Gruner & Jahr USA Publishing
Ed: Amy Gunderson. **Description:** States with a number of farms and fields are making more grants available to small businesses. The program, EPSCor, is funded mostly by the National Science Foundation and fosters scientific research in rural areas.

50885 ■ "Guilford Pharmaceuticals gets dose of health news" in *Washington Business Journal* **(Vol. 22, No. 3, May 23, 2003, pp. 25)**
Pub: Washington Business Journal
Ed: Robert J. Terry. **Description:** An examination into the growing success of Guilford Pharmaceuticals Inc., including new contracts with Pfizer Inc., U.S. Food and Drug Administration approval of new products and research and development efforts.

50886 ■ *Handbook of Quality Research in Entrepreneurship*
Pub: Edward Elgar Publishing, Incorporated
Ed: Neergaard. **Released:** March 2007. **Price:** $215.00. **Description:** Advice for researchers to make informed choices and to design more stringent and sophisticated studies in the field of entrepreneurship.

50887 ■ "The Holy Wafer" in *Red Herring* **(No. 99, June 15 & July 1, 2001, pp. 106-107)**
Pub: Herring Communications
Ed: Alan Zeichick. **Description:** Alan Zeichick, principal technology analysts with Camden Associates, explains how a single silicon water is transformed into the hundreds of microchips that make up an integrated circuit, including step-by-step illustrations.

50888 ■ "Hot Bets in the Cold North" in *Business Week* **(December 19, 2005, No. 3964, pp. 24)**
Pub: McGraw-Hill Companies
Ed: Robert Barker. **Description:** Companies drilling for coalbed methane in Canada include Apache, EnCana, Nexen, and Quicksilver Resources.

50889 ■ "Houston Leads Research in Superconducting Wire" in *Houston Business Journal* **(Vol. 34, No. 7, June 27, 2003, pp. 27A)**
Pub: American City Business Journals
Ed: Andrew P. Coleman. **Description:** The University of Houston has brought in $300 million in 15 years in grants for technology research.

50890 ■ *How to Find Information about Companies*
Pub: Washington Researchers, Ltd.
Ed: Washington Researchers. **Released:** 1994. **Price:** $395.00 (each volume); $885.00 (three-volume set). **Description:** Volume 1 lists 9,000 information resources. Volume 2 and Volume 3 provide guidance for researching companies.

50891 ■ "How Surveys Influence Customers" in *Harvard Business Review* **(Vol. 80, No. 5, May 2002, pp. 18)**
Pub: Harvard Business School Press
Ed: Vicki G. Morwitz, Paul M. Dholakia. **Description:** New research indicates that a customer survey can enhance the loyalty and profitability of already satisfied customers. Surveys seem to crystallize existing opinions and focus attention on them.

50892 ■ "Hydrogen: The Next Fuel for Laptops?" in *San Jose Mercury News* **(March 2, 2005)**
Pub: Knight-Ridder/Tribune Business News
Ed: Therese Poletti. **Description:** Millennium Cell, a small firm in New Jersey is working on a hydrogen-fueled battery that may eventually provide eight hours of power for laptop computers.

50893 ■ "If the Gene Fits" in *Fast Company* **(November 2001, pp. 140)**
Pub: Fast Company
Ed: George Anders. **Description:** Overview of information regarding the technology used in genetics, including the Nichols Institute and Quest Diagnostics.

50894 ■ "In the Chips; Handheld Lab Gets HandyLab $6M" in *Crain's Detroit Business* **(Vol. 22, January 23, 2006, No. 4, pp. 1)**
Pub: Crain Communications Inc. - Detroit
Ed: Tom Henderson. **Description:** HandyLab Inc., Ann Arbor, Michigan, will use $6 million of venture capital to hire sales and marketing teams to bring its first medical diagnostic device to market. The firm was founded in 2000 by a group of engineering graduates from University of Michigan.

50895 ■ "The Incredible Shrinking Man" in *Fast Company* **(November 2001, pp. 62)**
Pub: Fast Company
Ed: Alison Overholt. **Description:** Profile of the research being done at International Business Machines Corporation's Almaden Research Center.

50896 ■ "Ingenta, Inc. Announces 19 New Publisher Portal Partnerships" in *Information Today* **(Vol. 17, No. 11, December 2000, pp. 23)**
Pub: Information Today, Inc.
Description: Ingenta, Inc. announces new partnerships to expand its research offerings.

50897 ■ "Innovation and Incentives: VCs Find Partner in Quebec" in *Venture Capital Journal* **(Vol. 42, No. 5, May 2002, pp. 47)**
Pub: Thomas Venture Economics
Ed: Alistair Christopher. **Description:** The Quebec government offers a research and development tax credit to local businesses, which is attracting the attention of U.S. venture capitalists.

50898 ■ *Innovation Methodologies in Enterprise Research*
Pub: Edward Elgar Publishing, Incorporated
Ed: Hine. **Released:** December 2006. **Price:** $75.00. **Description:** The importance of qualitative, interpretist research in the field of enterprise research is discussed. The book stresses how enterprise research is a new method and permits a wide scope for new and innovative research studies.

50899 ■ *International Entrepreneurship*
Pub: Edward Elgar Publishing, Incorporated
Ed: Oviatt. **Released:** March 2007. **Price:** $295.00. **Description:** Universities are focusing research efforts on international entrepreneurship. The book features critical articles on the topic.

50900 ■ "Invention: Scientist puts circuits on paper" in *Red Herring* **(No. 102, August 15, 2001, pp. 25)**
Pub: Herring Communications
Ed: Avi Machlis. **Description:** Profile of Andrew Shipway, the scientist who invented the patent-pending process which allows electrical circuits to be created using a standard laser printer.

50901 ■ "Investing To Fight Disease; It May Be Better For Your Soul Than For Your Bottom Line" in *Business Week* **(February 7, 2005, No. 3919)**
Pub: McGraw-Hill Companies
Ed: Carol Marie Cropper. **Description:** Investment trusts that target diseases such as Alzheimer's, breast and ovarian cancer, diabetes, prostate cancer and rheumatoid arthritis are discussed. Developed by WellSpring BioCapital Partners in 2004, VIOLTs, short for Vertical Investments of Life Sciences Trusts, hold shares of companies developing or marketing treatments for these diseases.

50902 ■ "The Investment Trap" in *Inc.* **(Volume 27, December 2005, No. 12, pp. 144)**
Pub: Inc. Magazine
Ed: Adam Hanft. **Description:** Companies that invest more money into research and development don't always report better results in terms of growth and profitability, however research and development spending continues to swell.

50903 ■ "IPOs/Recent Issues" in *Venture Capital Journal* **(Vol. 42, No. 9, September 2002, pp. 44-45)**
Pub: Thomas Venture Economics
Description: Information on recent IPOs for BioDelivery Sciences International Inc., and Healthetech Inc. is provided.

50904 ■ "Jazzin' Up the Chips" in *Red Herring* **(No. 99, June 15 & July 1, 2001, pp. 118)**
Pub: Herring Communications
Ed: Scott Tyler Shafer. **Description:** Profile of Jazio, developer of technology that allows faster chip-to-chip communications.

50905 ■ "Kaiser Getting a Transplant" in *San Francisco Business Times* **(Vol. 18, No. 1, August 15, 2003, pp. 1)**
Pub: American City Business Journals
Ed: Meg Walker. **Description:** Dr. Sharon Inokuchi is leading a team that is launching a new kidney transplant program at San Francisco's Kaiser Permanent. The new transplant program may help the health maintenance organization build a reputation as a leading medical research facility.

50906 ■ "Kansas City Cardiology Works Towards Advancements" in *Ingram's* **(Vol. 29, No. 9, September 2003, pp. 24)**
Pub: Show Me Publishing, Inc.
Description: Medical research being conducted in the Greater Kansas City, Missouri area is examined. Topics include cardiology, electrophysiology, and cardiovascular implants.

50907 ■ "Laser 'Breakthrough': Changing the Silicon Game" in *San Jose Mercury News* **(March 7, 2005)**
Pub: Knight-Ridder/Tribune Business News
Ed: Dean Takahashi. **Description:** Mario Paniccia discusses the continuous wave silicon laser being developed by him and his team of researchers at Intel. The laser could launch a new stage in electronics.

50908 ■ "Laurel Touby" in *Entrepreneur* **(Vol. 30, No. 2, February 2002, pp. 18)**
Pub: Entrepreneur Media Inc.
Ed: Michelle Prather. **Description:** Profile of Laurel Touby, founder of Mediabistro.com in New York City. Mediabistro.com is an online and offline community for media and creative professionals.

50909 ■ "The Life Sciences Building Boom" in *Boston Globe* **(January 31, 2005)**
Pub: New York Times Company
Ed: Jeffrey Krasner. **Description:** Boston, Massachusetts has experienced growth in the life sciences sector since 2003 and this growth is expected to continue through 2007. More than 24 life-sciences projects are underway, including laboratories, hospital expansions, academic centers and housing for scientists.

50910 ■ "Life Sciences Span The Globe: U.S. VCs Like to Spend Money in their Backyards" in *Venture Capital Journal* **(October 1, 2004)**
Pub: Thomason Financial Inc.
Ed: Matthew Sheahan. **Description:** U.S. life science companies took about $3.6 billion in venture capital funding in 2004, more than 70 percent of the worldwide total, but Europe and Canada are working to attract these same companies. The cost advantages in both Canada and Europe are discussed.

50911 ■ "Local Investors Eye Chip Plant" in *Orlando Business Journal* **(Vol. 20, No. 11, August 29, 2003, pp. 1)**
Pub: American City Business Journals, Inc.
Ed: Chad Eric Watt. **Description:** Profile of Bill Cochrane, a former research and development vice president at Agere Systems Inc., has joined with others in an effort to buy and reopen Agere Systems Inc, a microchip factory in Orlando, Florida.

50912 ■ "Local Labs are Working to Perfect DNA Probes" in *Kansas City Star* **(March 8, 2005)**
Pub: Knight-Ridder/Tribune Business News
Ed: Julius A. Karash. **Description:** Children's Mercy Hospital and Phylogenetix Laboratories Inc. have partnered to complete the development of patented DNA probes for detecting diseases; when completed the probes will be brought to market.

50913 ■ "Long Island's Patent Production Falls Nearly 20 Percent Since 1988" in *Long Island Business News* **(March 5, 2004)**
Pub: Dolan Media Newswires
Ed: Ken Schachter. **Description:** Long Island's future economic health is tied to industries such as life sciences, software development and defense-industry prototyping and design rather than large-scale manufacturing. Patent growth is used to gauge the economic progress of the area.

50914 ■ "Long-Term Technology" in *Black Enterprise* **(Vol. 34, No. 4, November 2003, pp. 34)**
Pub: Earl Graves Publishing Co.
Ed: Nicole Lewis. **Description:** Financial managers for the Philadelphia Public Employee Retirement System has used a long-term approach to investing and maintains the fund's allocation in technology without changes.

50915 ■ *Look Before You Leap: Market Research Made Easy*
Pub: Self-Counsel Press, Inc.
Ed: Dell Dennison, Don Doman, and Margaret Doman. **Released:** 1993, first edition. **Price:** $12.95 (paper).

50916 ■ "MacroChem Advances Relaunch of Viagra Rival" in *Boston Business Journal* (Vol. 23, No. 31, September 5, 2003, pp. 1)
Pub: American City Business Journals
Ed: Mark Hollmer. **Description:** Lexington, Massachusetts-based MacroChem Corporation, led by president and CEO Bob DeLuccia, is expanding Phase II clinical trials for a new topical hormone drug that will rival Viagra.

50917 ■ "Maine Office of Innovation Releases Plan for Research Development" in *Portland Press Herald* (November 4, 2005)
Pub: Blethen Maine Newspapers, Inc.
Ed: Matt Wickenheiser. **Description:** Maine's Office of Innovation is proposing a plan that would double the amount of money spent on research and development statewide. The plan proposes $1 billion in annual spending for 2010, with increases from both private and public organizations.

50918 ■ "The Malaria Fighter" in *Business 2.0* (Vol. 7, January/February 2006, No. 1, pp. 116-118, 120, 122, 124)
Pub: Time, Inc.
Ed: Michael Myser. **Description:** Profile of scientist, Stephen Hoffman, entrepreneur who's research is aimed at attacking global diseases.

50919 ■ "Marriage of Expedience" in *Red Herring* (No. 99, June 15 & July 1, 2001, pp. 108)
Pub: Herring Communications
Ed: Bridget Eklund. **Description:** University of California Berkeley Professor Dave Patterson, is developing a chip called intelligent random access memory (IRAM), which will connect a microprocessor and a memory chip to improve speed and efficiency.

50920 ■ "A Matter of Taste" in *Fast Company* (March 2005, No. 92, pp. 35)
Pub: Gruner & Jahr USA Publishing
Ed: Lucas Conley. **Description:** Senomyx Inc., a biotechnology firm in La Jolla, California, is developing chemical compounds known as flavor enhancers that could be used in commercial products. Research is being funded by such corporations as Nestle SA, Coca-Cola, Kraft, and Campbell Soup Company.

50921 ■ "Mechanical Minds" in *Red Herring* (No. 105, October 1, 2001, pp. 64-69)
Pub: Herring Communications
Ed: Thomas Maeder. **Description:** New surgical methods, devices, and research efforts could revolutionize the treatment of brain disorders. The article offers insight into current approaches, including brain salad surgery, shock therapy, neural networks, sound effects, eyes, and thought into action, which are all yielding new devices to improve quality of life for patients.

50922 ■ "Mechanically inclined" in *Entrepreneur* (Vol. 31, No. 4, April 2003, pp. 168)
Pub: Entrepreneur Media Inc.
Ed: April Y. Pennington. **Description:** Profile of Colin Angle, Helen Greiner, and Rod Brooks, co-founders of iRobot, a firm started with technology but no product.

50923 ■ "Med Tech Carl Goldfischer" in *Venture Capital Journal* (January 1, 2005)
Pub: Thomason Financial Inc.
Description: According to Carl Goldfischer, managing director at Bay City Capital, the best thing that could happen to the medical device market in 2005 is that large and small companies continue creating new products that improve disease management.

50924 ■ "The Merry Go-Round" in *The Economist* (Vol. 377, October 1-7, 2005, No. 8446, pp. 60)
Pub: The Economist Newspaper Ltd.
Description: In the global drug industry, no regulation is more important than that of the U.S. Food and Drug Administration. The industry boasts $550 billion in annual sales.

50925 ■ "The microbe warrior. (Bioterrorism)" in *Red Herring* (January 2003, pp. 58)
Pub: Herring Communications Inc.
Ed: Suzanne McGee. **Description:** Profile AgION Technologies, the company developing products financed from the Homeland Security Fund. The firm's products show great promise in the areas of national security, intelligence, or military applications.

50926 ■ "Milwaukee, Wis., to Host Biotech Finance Gathering in 2007" in *Milwaukee Journal Sentinel* (December 14, 2005)
Pub: Journal Sentinel, Inc.
Ed: Kathleen Gallagher. **Description:** Venture capitalists representing more than $7 billion and biotechnology and medical device startups will meet in Milwaukee in September 2007 for the largest industry event in the Midwest. The BIO Med-America Venture-Forum expects 75 to 100 VCs to attend.

50927 ■ "Money-Preneuring" in *Small Business Opportunities* (Vol. 16, No. 3, May 2004, pp. 62, 64)
Pub: Harris Publications, Inc.
Ed: Norman Brown. **Description:** International stocks might be one way to invest in overseas markets.

50928 ■ "MSU Enlists Biz Help On $1B Isotope Project Bid" in *Crain's Detroit Business* (Vol. 21, January 24, 2005, No. 4, pp. 1)
Pub: Crain Communications Inc. - Detroit
Ed: Sherri Begin. **Description:** Michigan State University is calling in help from the Michigan Business Group to bring the Rare Isotope Accelerator to its campus. The project is a $1 billion project of the U.S. Department of Energy.

50929 ■ "Nanomaterials: The Road to Lilliput" in *Red Herring* (No. 99, June 15 & July 1, 2001, pp. 48-50)
Pub: Herring Communications
Ed: Philip E. Ross. **Description:** A pot of gold awaits those who can manufacture materials atom by atom, if they can actually pull it off. Statistical data included.

50930 ■ "Nanotech Grows" in *Red Herring* (No. 99, June 15 & July 1, 2001, pp. 46-47)
Pub: Herring Communications
Description: A brief chronology of nanotechnology. Nanotechnology is the science of the extremely small, nano meaning one-billionth.

50931 ■ "Nanotechnology sector analysis" in *Red Herring* (March 2003, pp. 62)
Pub: Herring Communications Inc.
Description: An overview of the nanotechnology industry is presented, including information nano-based devices that can change electronics one atom at a time.

50932 ■ "NASA Logs on for Team Encounter in Space" in *Houston Business Journal* (Vol. 34, No. 18, September 12, 2003, pp. 1)
Pub: American City Business Journals
Ed: Jenna Colley. **Description:** Team Encounter LLC, Houston, Texas, a private space vehicles company, is preparing to send a spacecraft into orbit in 2005. Team Encounter has obtained a contract from NASA to send the Inertial Stellar Compass into orbit aboard its spacecraft.

50933 ■ "The New Hispanic Information Economy" in *Hispanic Business* (November 2003, pp. 26, 28, 30)
Pub: Hispanic Business
Ed: Scott Williams. **Description:** A convergence of market demand and capable researchers has created a viable market for numbers on U.S. Hispanics. Within the realm of public policy, Hispanics are gaining attention.

50934 ■ *The New Products Workshop*
Pub: The McGraw-Hill Companies
Ed: Barry Feig. **Price:** $24.95. **Description:** Guide for developing and marketing new and existing products for small businesses. Includes case histories of successful products/businesses.

50935 ■ "The New Way to Make Babies" in *Business 2.0* (Vol. 7, January/February 2006, No. 1, pp. 22)
Pub: Time, Inc.
Ed: Theodore Kinn. **Description:** Review of the book by a Harvard Business School professor. The book discusses the business of making babies.

50936 ■ "NextEnergy gets $2M from feds" in *Crain's Detroit Business* (Vol. 19, No. 10, March 10, 2003, pp. 29)
Pub: Crain Communications Inc., Detroit
Ed: Laura Bailey. **Description:** The state of Michigan's alternative-fuel research center, NextEnergy, received $2 million from an appropriations bill signed by President George W. Bush.

50937 ■ "The Nonprofit Motive" in *Fortune* (Vol. 148, No. 8, October 13, 2003, pp. 214)
Pub: Time Inc.
Ed: David Whitford. **Description:** Profile of entrepreneur Art Mellor who co-founded three companies, including Midnight Networks, a computer network testing firm. Mellor was CTO of the computer network configuration management startup, Gold Wire Technology, when he was diagnosed with multiple sclerosis. Meller, with his neurologist, Dr. Tim Vartania, founded the Boston Cure Project.

50938 ■ "NY State Senator Introduces Bill to Obtain Federal Funding for Genetic Research" in *Long Island Business News* (February 13, 2004)
Pub: Dolan Media Newswires
Ed: Rosmaria Mancini. **Description:** A bill introduced by Senator Ken LaValle, R-New York, would create an 'institute' that would work to obtain federal grant money for genetics research at institutions throughout New York State.

50939 ■ "Opportunities emerge in a new age of miracle materials. (Nanotechnology)" in *Red Herring* (March 2003, pp. 50)
Pub: Herring Communications Inc.
Ed: Lee Bruno. **Description:** An overview of nanotechnology, the study of materials smaller than 100 nanometers, or approximately 1/100th the width of a human hair. Nanotechnology involves two main areas of research.

50940 ■ "OSI Pharmaceuticals Hopes to Get FDA Approval for Its Cancer Drug" in *Long Island Business News* (February 13, 2004)
Pub: Dolan Media Newswires
Ed: Ken Schachter. **Description:** OSI Pharmaceuticals Inc., a Long Island biotechnology firm, are awaiting FDA approval of its cancer drug, Tarceva. The drug is an Epidermal Growth Factor Receptor tyrosine kinase inhibitor.

50941 ■ "Pain Medicine May Keep Jobs in Ann Arbor, Pfizer CEO Says" in *Crain's Detroit Business* (Vol. 22, February 13, 2006, No. 7, pp. 1)
Pub: Crain Communications Inc. - Detroit
Ed: Andrew Dietderich. **Description:** The development of the drug Lyrica is responsible for saving some 14,000 jobs in Michigan, according to Hank McKinnell, Pfizer CEO and chairman. The new pain medication is expected to reach sales of $900 million in 2006.

50942 ■ "Pall Corp. Plans to Sell New Bacteria-Detection System to Blood Banks" in *Long Island Business News* (February 20, 2004)
Pub: Dolan Media Newswires
Description: The U.S. Food and Drug Administration (FDA) has approved Pall Corporation's system for detecting bacteria in blood platelets. The new system will cut testing time by about 20 percent, increasing the supply of blood available for transfusion.

50943 ■ "Patent expiration to hit MSU" in *Crain's Detroit Business* (Vol. 19, No. 14, April 7, 2003, pp. 3)
Pub: Crain Communications Inc., Detroit
Ed: Laura Bailey. **Description:** Michigan State University Foundation will lose $25 million annually when patents on two cancer drugs the university holds expire.

50944 ■ "Peanut Growers to Ramp Up Research Work" in *Kiplinger Letter* (Vol. 78, January 19, 2007, No. 2)
Pub: Kiplinger
Description: Peanut Foundation will fund $9.5 million in USDA and industry for research to improve the flavor and nutrient content of peanuts, while boosting their oil content.

50945 ■ "Portland Seeks Biotech Park to Stimulate New Business" in *Portland Press Herald* (December 13, 2005)
Pub: Blethen Maine Newspapers, Inc.
Ed: Kelley Bouchard. **Description:** Portland, Maine officials are proposing the development of a biotechnology park in order to compete for tenants seeking similar locations in the Boston, Massachusetts area.

50946 ■ "The Power of Spin" in *The Economist* (Vol. 377, October 1-7, 2005, No. 8446, pp. 76-77)
Pub: The Economist Newspaper Ltd.
Description: Canadian engineer, Louis Michaud, has developed a way to create artificial whirlwinds like a tornado, these whirlwinds can be controlled and harnessed in order to generate power. Michaud calls his invention the 'atmospheric vortex engine'.

50947 ■ "Private Company Profiles" in *Red Herring* (No. 99, June 15 & July 1, 2001, pp. 124, 126)
Pub: Herring Communications
Ed: Mark Chediak. **Description:** Cross-section profiles of nine privately held semiconductor companies is presented.

50948 ■ "Putting Research on the Map" in *Hispanic Business* (July/August 2004, pp. 14)
Pub: Hispanic Business
Description: A strategic partnership has been formed between the research division of Hispanic Business Inc. and Geoscape International Inc. to produce and commercialize value-added market research products, as well as the provision of license information for research, analysis and editorial publication.

50949 ■ "QuatRx uses $10M in venture capital for psoriasis drug" in *Crain's Detroit Business* (Vol. 19, No. 12, March 24, 2003, pp. 12)
Pub: Crain Communications Inc., Detroit
Ed: Renee Saunders. **Description:** QuatRx, a biopharmaceutical company located in Ann Arbor, Michigan, hopes that the recent $10 million venture capital financing received will help find a cure for psoriasis and other ailments.

50950 ■ "R and D Spending Jumps as Firms Foresee Recovery" in *Atlanta Business Chronicle* (Vol. 26, No. 10, August 15, 2003, pp. 1)
Pub: American City Business Publications, Inc.
Ed: Mary Jane Credeur. **Description:** The first signs of economic recovery for the greater Atlanta, Georgia area are in the form of higher research and development spending by local technology firms.

50951 ■ "R&D comes to services: Bank of America's pathbreaking experiments" in *Harvard Business Review* (Vol. 81, No. 4, April 2003, pp. 70)
Pub: Harvard Business School Press
Ed: Stefan Thomke. **Description:** A description of the process that Bank of America has used to create new service concepts for retail banking is presented. A group of the company's branches have become a laboratory where a research team conducts service experiments with actual customers. The program shows what a true Research and Development operation might look like in a service business.

50952 ■ "Real Estate Ambitions" in *Black Enterprise* (Vol. 37, January 2007, No. 6, pp. 101)
Pub: Earl G. Graves Publishing Co. Inc.
Ed: Description: National Real Estate Investors Association is a nonprofit trade association for both advanced as well as novice real estate investors that offers information on builders to contractors to banks. When looking to become a real estate investor utilize this organization, talk to various investors like the president of your local chapter, let people know your aspirations, and see if you can find a partner who has experience in the field. Resources included.

50953 ■ "Renal Solutions" in *Pittsburgh Business Times* (Vol. 22, No. 51, July 4, 2003, pp. 1)
Pub: Pittsburgh Business Times
Ed: Patty Tascarella. **Description:** Renal Solutions Inc., led by CEO Peter DeComo, has received $2 million in venture capital funding. The firm raised nearly $16.7 million in first round venture capital funding.

50954 ■ "Renewed Biotech Interest Boosts BioCryst" in *Birmingham Business Journal* (Vol. 20, No. 35, August 29, 2003, pp. 1)
Pub: American City Business Journals, Inc.
Ed: Tom Bassing. **Description:** Difficult financial times facing BioCryst Pharmaceuticals Inc. are discussed, especially falling stock prices, cash flow problems, and financial management.

50955 ■ *Research Centers Directory*
Pub: Thomson Gale
Released: Annual, latest edition 32nd, Published September, 2004; new edition expected 33rd, Sept. 2005. **Price:** $760, individuals base edition. **Covers:** About 13,600 university, government, and other nonprofit research organizations established on a permanent basis to carry on continuing research programs in all areas of study; includes research institutes, laboratories, experiment stations, research parks, technology transfer centers, and other facilities and activities; coverage includes Canada. **Entries Include:** Unit name, name of parent institution, address, phone, fax, name of director, e-mail addresses, urls, year founded, governance, staff, educational activities, public services, sources of support, annual volume of research, principal fields of research, publications, special library facilities, special research facilities. **Arrangement:** Classified by broad subjects, then alphabetical by unit name. **Indexes:** Alphabetical (includes centers, institutions, and keywords), subject, geographical, personal name.

50956 ■ "Research Funding New Uses for Eggs, Prune Juice" in *Kiplinger Letter* (Vol. 78, January 19, 2007, No. 2)
Pub: Kiplinger
Description: Researchers are placing genes that can produce therapeutic proteins into the genes of hens that create human interferon b-1a, an antiviral drug as well as an antibody that fights melanoma. The oxidants in prune juice are proving to retard oxidation of fatty acids in meat, thus keeping meat fresher for longer periods of time.

50957 ■ *Research Services Directory*
Pub: Grey House Publishing
Contact: Leslie MacKenzie, Publisher
E-mail: lmackenzie@greyhouse.com
Released: Annual, latest edition 9, 2003/04. **Price:** $495, individuals softcover. **Covers:** more than 8,000 commercial laboratories, consultants, firms, data collection and analysis centers, individuals, and facilities in the private sector that conduct contractual or proprietary research in all areas of business, government, humanities, social science, and science and technology. **Entries Include:** Firm name, address, phone, fax, toll-free number, e-mail name of chief executive, name and title of contact, date founded, staff size and composition, rates charged, annual revenues, professional memberships, parent and/or affiliate organizations, description of research services and principal clients, affiliates, patents, licenses, special equipment. **Arrangement:** Alphabetical. **Indexes:** Research firm name, geographical, personal name, subject.

50958 ■ "Researchers Test Bioterrorism Sensors in Greenwich Village and on Long Island" in *Long Island Business News* (March 5, 2004)
Pub: Dolan Media Newswires
Ed: Ken Schachter. **Description:** Researchers are testing bioterrorism sensors for the Long Island Partnership for Homeland Security. The project includes area defense contractors, technology companies and research institutions.

50959 ■ "Rising Drug Costs" in *Venture Capital Journal* (October 1, 2204)
Pub: Thomason Financial Inc.
Ed: Alastair Goldfisher. **Description:** With the rising costs of conducting clinical trials of new drugs, technology companies may choose offshore outsourcing of research and development to save money. However, the cost of new drug development is rising worldwide. Statistical data included.

50960 ■ "Running a Biotech Operation Here is Reasonably Cheap, Study Finds" in *Pittsburgh Business Times* (Vol. 23, No. 2, August 1, 2003)
Pub: Pittsburgh Business Times
Ed: Maria Guzzo. **Description:** Industry analysts report that the Pittsburgh, Pennsylvania region offers a wide range of benefits to biotechnology firms. A new report from Boyd Company has found that the region offers economic advantages for biomedical research firms.

50961 ■ "Scanning For Dollars" in *Fortune* (Vol. 151, January 10, 2005, No. 1, pp. 60)
Pub: Time Inc.
Ed: Julie Schlosser. **Description:** New technology is being used by marketers to study consumer emotions and motivations. Functional magnetic resonance imaging (fMRI) detects the flow of blood to the brain's centers of pleasure, thought or memory. Researchers suggest that blood flow increases in areas of the prefrontal cortex when an individual likes what he or she is seeing.

50962 ■ "Sci-Finance" in *Entrepreneur* (Vol. 30, No. 2, February 2002)
Pub: Entrepreneur Media Inc.
Ed: Joshua Kurlantzick. **Description:** Because the National Science Foundation (NSF) has fallen behind the National Institutes of Health (NIH) in funding, there is less money to finance business innovations. The NIH focuses their research into biomedical sciences.

50963 ■ "SciTech Developments to Watch" in *Business Week* (January 16, 2006, No. 3967, pp. 87)
Pub: McGraw-Hill Companies
Description: Scientific and technological developments discussed include a pain-free alternative to pricking fingers for blood sugar readings for diabetics through the use of infrared light bounced off the white of an individual's eye; carbon nanotubes for electronic components; and information about tree farms.

50964 ■ "A Sea Change for Artificial Bones" in *Business Week* (February 20, 2006, No. 3972, pp. 65)
Pub: McGraw-Hill Companies
Ed: Helena Oh. **Description:** Researchers at the U.S. Energy Department's Lawrence Berkeley National Laboratory are working on the development of artificial bones from oysters, abalone, and other hard-shelled ocean dwellers.

50965 ■ "Seeing Face Value: Cosmetic Medical Spa Captures Ethnic Skin Care Market" in *Black Enterprise* (Vol. 35, February 2005, No. 7, pp. 51)
Pub: Earl G. Graves Publishing Co. Inc.
Ed: Bridget McCrea. **Description:** When owners opened their cosmetic medical spa, they chose to avoid advertising for reputation, media exposure and physician referrals to grow their business. Drs. Eliot F. Battle and Monte O. Harris, noted academic physicians and researchers, have developed a customized approach to ethnic skin care.

50966 ■ "Series A, For Arthritis: Proprius Pharmaceuticals Inc." in *San Diego Business Journal* (Vol. 28, January 15, 2007, No. 3, pp. 38)
Pub: San Diego Business Journal Associates
Ed: Brad Graves. **Description:** Atlas Venture of Waltham, Massachusetts and Forward Ventures of San Diego provided venture capital to Proprius Pharmaceuticals Inc. in order to develop a drug to treat osteoarthritis. Series A funding equaled $11 million and may grow to $17 million.

50967 ■ "Shake 'Em Up" in *Forbes* (Vol. 175, February 14, 2005, No. 3, pp. 58)
Pub: Forbes Magazine Inc.
Ed: Andy Stone. **Description:** Profile of Kevin Goodwin, founder of SonoSite and creator of a handheld ultrasound device, a laptop-size machine that scans patients immediately.

50968 ■ "The Silicon Killer" in *Red Herring* (No. 99, June 15 & July 1, 2001, pp. 102, 104-105)
Pub: Herring Communications
Ed: Glenn Zorpette. **Description:** The discovery of gallium nitride (GaN) could lead researchers to a supertransistor; if the transistors could be fabricated economically, GaN could be the cornerstone of several communication technologies.

50969 ■ "Silverado's Clean Coal Technology Coming To Choctaw County" in *Mississippi Business Journal* (Vol. 29, January 2007, No. 2, pp. 22)
Pub: Venture Publications, Inc.
Ed: Lynn Lofton **Description:** Silverado Green Fuel Inc. will build a new $26 million clean coal technology project in Choctaw County which promises to help decrease the country's dependence on foreign oil and make Mississippi the center of alternative fuel production.

50970 ■ "Slick Trick" in *Tampa Tribune* (December 2, 2005)
Pub: Media General, Inc.
Ed: Angela Delgado. **Description:** Profile of Lee Briante, of Greasecar Vegetable Fuel Systems located in Massachusetts. The company has converted nearly 2,000 automobiles in the U.S. with engines running on vegetable oil.

50971 ■ "Solar Cells: The New Light Fantastic" in *Business Week Online* (January 31, 2005)
Pub: McGraw-Hill Companies
Ed: Olga Kharif. **Description:** Solar cell prices have fallen 5 to 6 percent a year, but that trend is expected to change since they will be manufactured through complex processes similar to those used for making computer processors and memory cards.

50972 ■ "Stand by NASA research" in *Red Herring* (March 2003, pp. 17)
Pub: Herring Communications Inc.
Description: NASA research and development has resulted in growth in technology sectors such as communications, energy and the robotics industry.

50973 ■ *Start-ups That Work: Surprise Research on What Makes or Breaks a New Company*
Pub: Penguin Group
Ed: Joel Kurtzman; Glenn Rifkin. **Released:** October 2005. **Price:** $25.95.

50974 ■ "Studying Molecules to Build a Better Grape" in *Business Week* (February 20, 2006, No. 3972, pp. 65)
Pub: McGraw-Hill Companies
Description: Canadian researchers at the University of British Columbia in Vancouver are studying molecules in order to make finer wines.

50975 ■ "SV Life Sciences Sets Sights on Fourth Fund" in *Venture Capital Journal* (October 1, 2005)
Pub: Thomason Financial Inc.
Description: SV Life Sciences, of Boston, Massachusetts, is looking to raise $400 million for its fourth round of venture funding; it already has 27 portfolio companies.

50976 ■ "Take It For Granted" in *Entrepreneur* (Vol. 33, January 2005, No. 1, pp. 50)
Pub: Entrepreneur Media Inc.
Ed: David Worrell. **Description:** U.S. Small Business Innovative Research grants and contracts provide funding for small companies to develop high tech products. The programs are divided into two phases: one is to study the feasibility of a new technology or idea, the second to encourage commercialization of a particular technology.

50977 ■ *Technological Entrepreneurship*
Pub: Edward Elgar Publishing, Incorporated
Ed: Donald Siegel. **Released:** October 2006. **Price:** $230.00. **Description:** Technological entrepreneurship at universities is discussed. The book covers four related topics: university licensing and patenting; science parks and incubators; university-based startups; and the role of academic science in entrepreneurship.

50978 ■ "Technology is Biggest Export" in *Hispanic Business* (November 2002, pp. 25-26, 30)
Pub: Hispanic Business
Ed: Jonathan J. Higuera. **Description:** Predications are made concerning future exports; the list of winners included information technology, auto parts, medical devices, services, processed foods, and chemicals. Statistical data includes largest U.S. export products, top purchasers of U.S. exports. Government Web sites providing foreign market research to small companies are listed.

50979 ■ *Technology Opportunities: Researching Emerging & Critical Technologies*
Pub: Washington Researchers, Ltd.
Released: First edition, 1994. **Price:** $275.00. **Description:** Provides descriptions and full contact information for organizations that monitor technology development, licensing, and commercial applications for existing and emerging technologies.

50980 ■ "Technorati www.technorati.com" in *Entrepreneur* (Vol. 32, No. 1, January 2004, pp. 10)
Pub: Entrepreneur Media, Inc.
Ed: Steve Cooper. **Description:** Profile of Technorati, a blog research that tracks 1 million blogs, and also offers a tool called Watchlists that monitors changes in Google rankings.

50981 ■ "This Week: McD's Tests Trans-Free Oil in 1,200 Locations" in *Crain's Chicago Business* (Vol. 29, December 2006, No. 50, pp. 1)
Pub: Crain Communications, Inc.
Ed: Julie Jargon. **Description:** Just under ten percent of McDonald's U.S. outlets are performing initial tests with trans fat-free oil in their foods. Pressure is high as rival fast food restaurants have already introduced these trans fat-free foods and New York passed the ban which takes place in July.

50982 ■ "The true believer" in *Red Herring* (March 2003, pp. 56)
Pub: Herring Communications Inc.
Ed: Lee Bruno. **Description:** Scientific developments that are transforming nanotechnology from science fiction to reality are explored, including challenges facing the nanotechnology industry and the talents and skills needed for newcomers to the industry.

50983 ■ "Truth or Consequences" in *Red Herring* (No. 99, June 15 & July 1, 2001, pp. 120)
Pub: Herring Communications
Ed: Dean Takahashi **Description:** The worldwide market for chip-verification software is expected to grow nearly 16 percent annually.

50984 ■ *Unique 3-in-1 Research & Development Directory*
Pub: Government Data Publications Inc.
Released: Annual. **Covers:** firms that received research and development contracts from the federal

government during preceding fiscal year. **Entries Include:** Awardee name, address, agency, description of work, dollar amount of contract, and other pertinent data. Additional contracts are listed in 'M R&D Contracts Monthly,' published in the same arrangement; $96.00 per year. **Arrangement:** First section alphabetical by name of firm; second section geographical by awarding agency; third section classified by nature of work. Similar information in each section.

50985 ■ *U.S. Source Book of R & D Spenders*
Pub: Schonfeld & Associates Inc.
Contact: Carol Greenhut
Released: Annual. **Price:** $395, individuals book; $495, individuals book and disk. **Covers:** 5,700 public companies in the U.S. That spend money on research and development. **Entries Include:** Company name, address, phone, names and titles of key personnel, financial data, research and development budgets, fiscal year close, Standard Industrial Classification (SIC) code. **Arrangement:** Geographical by state, then classified by ZIP code. **Indexes:** Company name.

50986 ■ "USDA Plans to Charge Farm Commodity Groups a Fee for Research" in *Kiplinger Letter* (Vol. 78, January 5, 2007, No. 1)
Pub: Kiplinger
Description: Farm commodity groups can expect to pay fees for research. The Agricultural Department's research services already charges 10 percent for companies and other agencies while farm commodity groups and other nonprofits were exempt.

50987 ■ "Use It or Lose It: Is Your Business Usable-or Disposable? Figure It Out Before Your Competitors Gain an Edge" in *Entrepreneur* (Vol.32)
Pub: Entrepreneur Media Inc.
Ed: Mark Henricks. **Description:** Geoffrey Hart explains his concerns of usability when setting out to develop a medical device for soothing and entertaining children during the process of anesthetizing them for medial or dental procedures.

50988 ■ "VCs See Bottom, Expect To Do More Deals" in *Venture Capital Journal* (July 1, 2003)
Pub: Thomson Financial Inc.
Description: According to a survey conducted by Venture Capital Journal, VCs are feeling more optimistic, yet cautious, about the industry and are predicting a slow recovery. More startups are experiencing funding, particularly seed- and early-stage rounds, focusing both by industry and region. Life sciences and nanotechnology are receiving the most interest.

50989 ■ "Voices of Innovation" in *Business Week* (January 23, 2006, No. 3968, pp. 20)
Pub: McGraw-Hill Companies
Ed: Jay Greene. **Description:** Rick Rashid, Microsoft Corporation's senior vice president, pushes his 700 research and development scientists to go after big challenges.

50990 ■ "When the Chips are Down" in *Red Herring* (No. 99, June 15 & July 1, 2001, pp. 122)
Pub: Herring Communications
Ed: Tom Stein. **Description:** As the semiconductor sector cools off, venture capitalists seek companies with staying power.

50991 ■ *Where to Get the Money & Management Help for New Business Start-Ups & Small-Business Growth: East-South Central Region, AL, KY, MS, TN*
Pub: Special Reports, Inc.
Ed: Richard S. Guyer and Frank J. Domeracki. **Released:** 1998. **Price:** $197.00.

50992 ■ "Where is the new frontier of innovation?" in *Fast Company* (September 2001, pp. 128)
Pub: Fast Company
Ed: Fara Warner. **Description:** Fast-paced experimentation, distributed intelligence, total teamwork: the

scientific formulation behind the new economy is still disrupting the status quo. In this case, 20,000 leagues under the sea; to appreciate the world-changing impact of digital technology, explore the world of the Monterey Bay Aquarium Research Institute.

50993 ■ "Whose drug is it, anyway?" in *Washington Business Journal* **(Vol. 21, No. 44, Feb. 28, 2003, pp. 2,6)**
Pub: Washington Business Journal
Ed: Jennifer Taylor. Description: Alleged legal loopholes abound keeping generic drug companies from getting their products to market faster. President Bush has proposed new rules that might fix one of those loopholes. Large companies with costly employee benefit plans are getting involved also. Drug companies with blockbuster drugs try to keep patents in effect as long as possible, claiming that research and development costs are astronomical.

50994 ■ "Wisconsin Biotech Aims to Create Artificial Heart Tissue" in *Milwaukee Journal Sentinel* **(December 8, 2005)**
Pub: Journal Sentinel, Inc.
Ed: Kathleen Gallagher. Description: InvivoSciences LLC plans to make artificial heart tissue. The firm has chosen Wisconsin for its location because of the Medical College of Wisconsin's support for entrepreneurs along with several state programs that support young companies.

TRADE PERIODICALS

50995 ■ *Chemical Process Alert*
Pub: Technical Insights/M John Wiley & Sons Inc.
Contact: Kenneth Kovaly, President
Released: Weekly. Price: $890, U.S. and Canada; $990, elsewhere. Description: Reports on the latest cutting-edge technology available in the chemical process.

50996 ■ *Defense Environment Alert*
Pub: Inside Washington Publishers
Contact: Suzanne Yohannan, Managing Editor
Released: Biweekly, every other Wednesday. Price: $615, U.S. and Canada; $665, elsewhere. Description: Reports on defense policies for cleanup, compliance, and pollution prevention.

50997 ■ *Dentaletter*
Pub: MPL Communications Inc.
Contact: John Hobez, Managing Editor
Ed: Dr. Brian Waters, Editor. Released: 11/year. Price: $119. Description: Publishes news of dental research. Also covers related web sites.

50998 ■ *Technology Access Report*
Pub: UVentures
Released: Monthly. Price: $497, individuals; $497, elsewhere plus $90. Description: Contains news, analysis, and notices of opportunities in research and development, resources, contracts and funding, joint ventures, licensing, and other information regarding technology transfer and commercialization processes, and management of technology, especially from universities and government labs, across all industries.

CONSULTANTS

50999 ■ Consultants International and Consulting Industries International
Worldway Ctr., No. 91435
Los Angeles, CA 90009
Ph:(310)670-1177
Fax:(310)670-1177
Scope: Offers management consulting toward the goals of profit, productivity, quality, and morale improvements; new products research and development and marketing; office and factory automation; and research and development of concepts-to-systems of virtually anything from concept-to-completion. Publications: Piece of the action- How to make greatly increased profits, Productivity & Quality at NO Cost & 1000: 1 ROI. Fortunes From Ideas- How-To Protect License &/or Sell Intellectual Properties at Lowest Cost, Time, Money.

51000 ■ Health Strategy Group Inc.
46 River Rd.
Chatham, NY 12037
Ph:(518)392-6770
Scope: Provides consulting services in the areas of strategic planning, feasibility studies, start-up businesses, organizational development, market research, customer service audits, new product development, marketing, public relations.

51001 ■ Hills Consulting Group Inc.
6 Partridge Ct.
Novato, CA 94945
Ph:(415)898-3944
Scope: Strategic marketing consulting and training firm. Specializes in strategic planning; marketing surveys; market research; customer service audits; new product development; competitive analysis; and sales forecasting.

51002 ■ Kubba Consultants Inc.
801 Glendale Rd.
Glenview, IL 60025
Ph:(847)729-0051
Fax: (847)729-8765
Co. E-mail: edkubba@aol.com
URL: http://www.kubbainc.com

E-mail: edkubba@aol.com
Scope: Industrial and business-to-business marketing research and consulting. Services include new product research, new market evaluation, competitor analysis and customer value analysis.

51003 ■ Margiloff & Associates
621 Royalview St.
Duarte, CA 91010-1346
Ph:(626)303-1266
Fax: (626)303-0127
Co. E-mail: margiloff@compuserve.com

E-mail: margiloff@compuserve.com
Scope: Energy and water conservation studies, analysis of research and development, licensing, economics and project management. Projects involve development, training, utility review, cost analysis, manufacturing system improvement, process modeling and expert witness services. Clients are in the food, chemical, fermentation, energy, financial and legal services, government and general manufacturing fields.

51004 ■ Medical Imaging Consultants Inc.
1037 Rte. 46 E G-2
Clifton, NJ 07013-2445
Ph:(973)574-8000
Free: 800-589-5685
Fax: (973)574-8001
Co. E-mail: info@micinfo.com
URL: http://www.micinfo.com

E-mail: info@micinfo.com
Scope: Provides management consulting services to hospitals, imaging centers, health-care companies and insurance companies. Firm specializes in interim management; crisis management; turnarounds; market research; and new product development. Seminars: Sectional Anatomy & Imaging Strategies; CT Cross-Trainer; CT Registry Review Program; MR Cross-Trainer; Digital Mammography Essentials for Technologists; Radiology Trends for Technologists.

51005 ■ Miller, Hellwig Associates
150 W End Ave.
New York, NY 10023-5713
Ph:(212)799-0471
Fax: (212)877-0186
Co. E-mail: millerhelwig@earthlink.net

E-mail: millerhelwig@earthlink.net
Scope: Consulting services in the areas of start-up businesses; small business management; employee surveys and communication; performance appraisals; executive searches; team building; personnel policies and procedures; market research. Also involved in improving cross-cultural and multi-cultural relationships, particularly with Japanese clients. Seminars: Objectives and standards/recruiting for boards of directors.

51006 ■ Organizational Futures
56 Pine St., Ste. 2b
Providence, RI 02903
Ph:(401)351-7110
Fax: (401)351-7158
Scope: Builder of agile human networks to champion innovation and mobilize change; to pursue business opportunities; to custom design agile organizations and communities, to foster civic engagement. Seminars: Facilitating for Results.

51007 ■ Plans and Solutions Inc.
PO Box 8905
Gaithersburg, MD 20898-8905
Ph:(301)947-8150
Fax: (240)525-5601
Co. E-mail: info@plansandsolutions.com
URL: http://www.plansandsolutions.com

E-mail: info@plansandsolutions.com
Scope: Business and strategic planning, market research and development. Most clients are minority-owned businesses in the USA and companies overseas that want to begin or increase exports to the United States and Canada. Publications: "Building an Import/Export Business," John Wiley & Sons, 2002.

51008 ■ Via Nova Consulting
1228 Winburn Dr.
Atlanta, GA 30344
Ph:(404)761-7484
Fax: (404)762-7123
Scope: Consulting services in the areas of strategic planning; privatization; executive searches; market research; customer service audits; new product development; competitive intelligence; and Total Quality Management (TQM).

COMPUTERIZED DATABASES

51009 ■ *Directory of Federal Laboratory and Technology Resources*
Wheeling Jesuit University
316 Washington Ave.
Wheeling, WV 26003
Ph:(304)243-4341
Free: 800-678-6882
Fax: (304)243-4388
Co. E-mail: technology@nttc.edu
URL: http://www.nttc.edu
Description: Provides and overview of more than 700 federal R&D facilities, with more than 100,000 scientists and engineers active in virtually every field of science and technology. Includes abstracts describing the expertise, facilities, equipment, and research thrusts at federal laboratories run by such agencies as NASA and the departments of Energy, Defense, and Health & Human Services. Availability: Online: Wheeling Jesuit University. Type: Directory.

51010 ■ *Federal Laboratory Research and Technology*
Wheeling Jesuit University
316 Washington Ave.
Wheeling, WV 26003
Ph:(304)243-4341
Free: 800-678-6882
Fax: (304)243-4388
Co. E-mail: technology@nttc.edu
URL: http://www.nttc.edu
Description: Provides information about ongoing federal research that has not yet resulted in a patent or licensable technology and gives details on facilities, equipment, and areas of Technology expertise in federal laboratories. Includes examples of technologies successfully commercialized and collaborations between companies and laboratories to develop commercially promising research. Type: Full text.

51011 ■ *Federal and University Research and Technology*
Wheeling Jesuit University
316 Washington Ave.
Wheeling, WV 26003

Ph:(304)243-4341
Free: 800-678-6882
Fax: (304)243-4388
Co. E-mail: technology@nttc.edu
URL: http://www.nttc.edu
Description: Provides information about research projects, expertise, and facilities at federal, university, and some industrial laboratories. Combines the Federal Laboratory Research and Technology (described in a separate entry), Directory of Federal Laboratory and Technology Resources (described in a separate entry), and other databases. **Type:** Full text; Directory.

51012 ■ *Small Business Innovative Research Awards*
Wheeling Jesuit University
316 Washington Ave.
Wheeling, WV 26003
Ph:(304)243-4341
Free: 800-678-6882
Fax: (304)243-4388
Co. E-mail: technology@nttc.edu
URL: http://www.nttc.edu
Description: Lists Small Business Innovation Research (SBIR) Program award winners and abstracts of their winning projects. Provides information on potentially useful technology under development and products emerging with the aid of SBIR funding. **Type:** Directory; Bibliographic.

51013 ■ *Small Business Innovative Research Current Solicitations*
Wheeling Jesuit University
316 Washington Ave.
Wheeling, WV 26003
Ph:(304)243-4341
Free: 800-678-6882
Fax: (304)243-4388
Co. E-mail: technology@nttc.edu
URL: http://www.nttc.edu
Description: Contains solicitations for the Small Business Innovation Research (SBIR) Program and the Small Business Technology Transfer (STTR) Pilot Program. Programs seek to stimulate U.S. technological innovation by funding small business research projects. The database assists users in exploring topics for which funding is available. **Type:** Full text.

51014 ■ *Small Business Innovative Research Past Solicitations*
Wheeling Jesuit University
316 Washington Ave.
Wheeling, WV 26003
Ph:(304)243-4341
Free: 800-678-6882
Fax: (304)243-4388
Co. E-mail: technology@nttc.edu
URL: http://www.nttc.edu
Description: Contains past solicitations for the Small Business Innovation Research (SBIR) Program and the Small Business Technology Transfer (STTR) Pilot Program. **Availability:** Online: Wheeling Jesuit University. **Type:** Full text.

51015 ■ *Small Business Innovative Research Solicitations and Awards*
Wheeling Jesuit University
316 Washington Ave.
Wheeling, WV 26003
Ph:(304)243-4341
Free: 800-678-6882
Fax: (304)243-4388
Co. E-mail: technology@nttc.edu
URL: http://www.nttc.edu
Description: Combines Small Business Innovation Research (SBIR) Program and the Small Business

Technology Transfer (STTR) Pilot Program solicitations, and Small Business Innovative Research (SBIR) awards databases. Provides an overview of all SBIR/STTR activity. **Availability:** Online: Wheeling Jesuit University. **Type:** Full text.

51016 ■ *University Resources*
Wheeling Jesuit University
316 Washington Ave.
Wheeling, WV 26003
Ph:(304)243-4341
Free: 800-678-6882
Fax: (304)243-4388
Co. E-mail: technology@nttc.edu
URL: http://www.nttc.edu
Description: Provides information about ongoing university research that has not yet resulted in a patent or licensable technology and gives details on facilities, equipment, and areas of Technology expertise in university laboratories. **Availability:** Online: Wheeling Jesuit University. **Type:** Full text.

LIBRARIES

51017 ■ Allen County Public Library–Business and Technology Department
200 E. Berry St., 1st Fl.
PO Box 2270
Fort Wayne, IN 46801-2270
Ph:(260)421-1200
Fax: (260)421-1386
URL: http://www.acpl.lib.in.us
Contact: Mark Wendt, Mgr.
Scope: Business, economics, investments, sciences, medicine, agriculture, automobiles, home economics, management, manufacturing, engineering, law. **Services:** Interlibrary loan; copying. **Holdings:** 80,000 books; 22,000 bound periodical volumes. **Subscriptions:** 1500 journals and other serials; 45 newspapers.

51018 ■ Honeywell–Federal Manufacturing Technologies–Technical Information Center (Box 4)
Box 419159
Kansas City, MO 64141-6159
Ph:(816)997-2694
Fax: (816)997-3686
Contact: Martha Conley, Libn.
Scope: Materials, processing, computers, manufacturing. **Services:** Interlibrary loan; center not open to the public. **Holdings:** 6000 books; military and federal specifications and standards; technical reports; vendor catalogs. **Subscriptions:** 300 journals and other serials.

RESEARCH CENTERS

51019 ■ Midwest Research Institute
425 Volker Blvd.
Kansas City, MO 64110-2299
Ph:(816)753-7600
Fax: (816)753-8420
Co. E-mail: info@mriresearch.org
URL: http://www.mriresearch.org
Contact: James L. Spigarelli, Pres./CEO
E-mail: info@mriresearch.org
Scope: Conducts research, development, and engineering activities in the major areas of health, chemis-

try, the environment, national security and defense, agriculture and food safety, and technology. Specific interests in the health area are pharmaceutical development and regulatory support, vaccine development, preclinical toxicology, metabolism studies, integrated clinical and preclinical drug development support, phytochemicals and designer foods, pesticide product registration support, chemistry support for toxicology, biotechnology, immunoassay development, DNA assay development, proteomics, high through-put automated assay systems, nanotechnology, food safety, seed technology, antibody production, biosensor development, electromagnetic field effects, neurobehavioral toxicology, reversal theory, and health risk behavior. In the field of chemistry, MRI focuses on analytical chemistry methods, including method development, improvement, validation, and application for programs involving immunoanalytical chemistry, exposure assessment, biological monitoring, industrial hygiene, environmental monitoring, chemical surety, site remediation, demilitarization, atmospheric chemistry, and product analysis of foods, consumer and commercial products, drinking water, and other materials. Environmental programs address environmental measurements, emission inventory development, emission factor development, modeling, water quality, waste minimization, pollution prevention, environmental control strategy development, process analysis and industry profiling, nonpoint source pollution, ambient air toxics, indoor air quality, industrial hygiene, multimedia environmental sampling and analysis, environmental impact assessment, facility assessment, environmental audits, waste processing and characterization, waste combustion, solar soil detoxification, risk analysis, regulatory support, policy analysis, cooling tower performance testing, permitting assistance, and tank and pipeline management. Technology areas include thermoelectrics, microclimate conditioning systems, industrial systems evaluation, safety engineering, engineering design, prototype development, bench-scale testing, technology testing, dental biomaterial formulation, dental polymer development, pipeline coating technology, deicing chemical evaluation, traffic engineering, economic impact assessment, financial and business analysis, economic development, strategic planning, international programs, instructional material development, training program design and presentation, technology transfer, etc. **Services:** Science Pioneers program, that provides science related activities, written materials, and services to students and teachers in the 36 school districts of Greater Kansas City. **Publications:** Innovations; Midwest Research Institute Annual Report. **Educational Activities:** Science Pioneers; Workshops, seminars.

51020 ■ National Conference on the Advancement of Research
108 Johnston St.
Savannah, GA 31405
Ph:(912)355-2259
Fax: (912)355-2251
Co. E-mail: ncargalin@aol.com
URL: http://www.ncar.org
Contact: Dr. Melvyn P. Galin, Exec.Sec.
E-mail: ncargalin@aol.com
Scope: Advancement of research and development at every level of society. **Educational Activities:** Annual conference, to discuss policy issues relating to research; Forums, for members on problems in the field; International conferences and seminars, for academic, industry, governement and research associated organizations.

Retailing

START-UP INFORMATION

51021 ■ "Bird Biz Takes Off" in *Small Business Opportunities* (Vol. 12, No. 2, March 2000, pp. 64, 66)
Pub: Harris Publications, Inc.
Ed: Marie Sherlock. **Description:** Shop owners, Brian and Janet Shelton, opened their bird biz emporium, Wild Bird Shop in 1993, and are now earning $500,000 a year.

51022 ■ "Cart Blanche: Think Retailing is Strictly Brick-and-Mortar Opportunity? Not So." in *Entrepreneur* (Vol. 31, No. 8, Aug. 2003, pp. 78)
Pub: Entrepreneur Media Inc.
Ed: Nichole L. Torres. **Description:** From hair products to cooking utensils to candy and cookies, entrepreneurs are making big money selling from kiosks in local malls. Examples of successful kiosks businesses are presented.

51023 ■ "Cracking the Code" in *My Business* (October/November 2003, pp. 49)
Pub: My Business Magazine
Description: The top ten franchising industries are listed in the following order: fast food, retail, service, automotive, restaurants, maintenance, building and construction, retail-food, business services, and lodging. It is advised to seek legal advice before purchasing a franchise business.

51024 ■ *Cute Little Store: Between the Entrepreneurial Dream and Business Reality*
Pub: Outskirts Press, Incorporated
Ed: Adeena Mignogna. **Released:** May 2006. **Price:** $11.95. **Description:** Challenges of starting and growing a retail business are profiled.

51025 ■ "Entrepreneur plans 31 strip malls for underserved areas" in *Crain's Detroit Business* (Vol. 16, No. 23, June 5, 2000, pp. 54)
Pub: Crain Communications, Inc.
Ed: Jennette Smith. **Description:** Djelosh "George" Juncaj plans to bring convenience retail to some of the most economically depressed areas of Detroit.

51026 ■ "Eye Candy: Life is Sweet for Two Visionaries Who Mix Sugary Treats with Style" in *Entrepreneur* (Vol. 32, No. 4, April 2004, pp. 168)
Pub: Entrepreneur Media, Inc.
Ed: April Y. Pennington. **Description:** Profile of Dylan Lauren and Jeff Rubin, co-founders of Dylan's Candy Bar. The New York City-based candy retailers project sales of more than $10 million for 2004.

51027 ■ "Food resources" in *Black Enterprise* (Vol. 32, No. 5, December 2001, pp. 46)
Pub: Earl Graves Publishing Co.
Ed: Paula McCoy-Pinderhughes. **Description:** Resources are given for starting an African-American owned retail grocery store.

51028 ■ "Football Fever" in *Small Business Opportunities* (Vol. 13, No. 6, November 2001, pp. 54-55)
Pub: Harris Publications, Inc.
Ed: Stan Roberts. **Description:** Profile of Charlotte Begley, retailer who earns $500,000 a year selling licensed football products. Ms. Begley attends three trade shows a year to find the latest designs, colors and styles.

51029 ■ "Franchise Finds" in *Small Business Opportunities* (Vol. 16, No. 2, March 2004, pp. 146)
Pub: Harris Publications, Inc.
Description: Profile of three franchises, including Window Butler, offering residential and commercial window cleaning; More Space Place, a specialty retail company featuring Murphy Beds, space saving furniture, custom closets, garage and home products; and Wild Noodles, a quick-serve restaurant offer ethnic noodle dishes.

51030 ■ "Get Rich in 2004" in *Small Business Opportunities* (Vol. 16, No. 1, January 2004, pp. 22)
Pub: Harris Publications, Inc.
Description: Profiles of the best twenty franchise businesses to startup in 2004 are listed, including profiles and contact information for each. The companies features are Contours Express, Blind Butler, Best Personalized Books, Bark Busters, Home Helpers, Blind Brokers Network, Hometeam Inspections Service Inc., Lazylawn, Handyman Service, Lantis Fireworks, retail shops from Liberty Opportunities (Dollar Store), advanced window tinting systems, Green Concepts, Christmas Concepts, window washing, Badge-A-Minit, LeGourmet Gift Basket, Homeowner Referral Network, and Ding King.

51031 ■ *How to Start a Home-Based Online Retail Business*
Pub: Globe Pequot Press
Ed: Jeremy Shepherd. **Released:** February 2007. **Price:** $18.95. **Description:** Information for starting an online retail, home-based business is shared.

51032 ■ "The Merchant of Bay Ridge" in *Forbes* (Vol. 174, December 27, 2004, No. 13, pp. 80)
Pub: Forbes Magazine Inc.
Ed: Phyllis Berman. **Description:** Profile of Joseph Cohen, the 17-year-old entrepreneur who developed a thriving online retail business called Bay Ridge.

51033 ■ "A One-Stop Marketing Shop" in *Entrepreneur* (Vol. 31, No. 10, October 2003, pp. 112)
Pub: Entrepreneur Media, Inc.
Description: Profile of PRstore LLC, offering franchises to former corporate marketing executives wishing to own a retail business. The firm has created more than 50 standard customizable products that franchisees use to help clients develop marketing campaigns.

51034 ■ *Scrapbooking for Profit: Cashing in on Retail, Home-Based and Internet Opportunities*
Pub: Allworth Press
Ed: Rebecca Pittman. **Released:** June 2005. **Price:** $19.95 (US), $22.95 (Canadian). **Description:** Eleven strategies for starting a scrapbooking business, including brick-and-mortar stores, home-based businesses, and online retail and wholesale outlets.

51035 ■ "Selling Serenity" in *Small Business Opportunities* (Vol. 13, No. 5, September 2001, pp. 74, 130)
Pub: Harris Publications, Inc.
Ed: Marie Sherlock. **Description:** Profile of Judy Wallace, who runs a store called Serenity Shop, that sells inspirational products for those struggling with or recovering from addictions.

51036 ■ "Service Franchises Hold Advantages Over Retail Operations" in *Long Island Business News* (May 7, 2004)
Pub: Dolan Media Newswires
Ed: Adina Genn. **Description:** The advantages service franchises have over owning a retail franchise are discussed. Discussions with various franchise owners are included.

51037 ■ "Shoestring Start-Ups" in *Small Business Opportunities* (Vol. 16, November 2004, No. 6, pp. 22, 24, 26, 28, 30-32, 34, 36, 38, 40)
Pub: Harris Publications Inc.
Description: Fifty businesses that can be started for less than $500 are presented, including selling personalized products, event planning, flea markets, advertising, watches, Web site designer, home delivery service, mail order, lawn and landscape services, windshield repair, meal delivery, handmade bunk beds, party lawn signs, computer repair, cruise travel, window washing, lingerie, online discount stores, pet sitting, ramps, security products, sunglasses, moving services, holiday decorating, birthday packages, errand service, online auctions, information broker, personal trainer, mortgage programs, and more.

51038 ■ *Small Business Desk Reference*
Pub: Penguin Books (USA) Incorporated
Ed: Gene Marks. **Released:** December 2004. **Price:** $29.95 (US), $44.00 (Canadian). **Description:** Comprehensive guide for starting or running a successful small business, focusing on buying a business or franchise, writing a business plan, financial management, accounting, legal issues, human resources management, operations, marketing, sales, customer service, taxes, insurance, and ethics. Information for launching a restaurant, property management firm, retail outlet, consulting firm, and service business is included.

51039 ■ "Standing on Their Own: Couple Decides to Go It Alone With Their Own Woody's Hot Dogs Kiosk" in *Entrepreneur* (Vol. 31, July 2003)
Pub: Entrepreneur Media Inc.
Ed: Devlin Smith, Jodie Carter. **Description:** Profile of David and Chris Lycan, who operate a hot dog kiosk at the Lowe's Home Improvement Warehouse in Colorado, Springs, Colorado.

51040 ■ *Starting a Yahoo! Business for Dummies*
Pub: John Wiley & Sons, Incorporated
Ed: Rob Snell. **Released:** June 2006. **Price:** $24.99.
Description: Rob Snell offers advice for turning online browsers into buyers, increase online traffic, and build an online store from scratch.

51041 ■ "Strong Future Brewing" in *Small Business Opportunities* (Spring 2005)
Pub: Harris Publications Inc.
Description: Profile of The Coffee Beanery, Ltd. The franchise supports upscale cafes, retail stores, carts and kiosks specializing in Arabica coffee. Franchise facts included.

51042 ■ "Your Retail Riches" in *Small Business Opportunities* (Winter 2005)
Pub: Harris Publications Inc.
Description: Pricester.com offers affordable, easily implemented solutions for those wishing to start an online retail Website. Pricester acts as a complete online trading community and will facilitate barter transactions, auctions, and reverse auctions.

ASSOCIATIONS AND OTHER ORGANIZATIONS

51043 ■ Electronic Retailing Association
2000 N 14th St., Ste. 300
Arlington, VA 22201
Ph:(703)841-1751
Free: 800-987-6462
Fax: (703)841-1860
Co. E-mail: contact@retailing.org
URL: http://www.retailing.org
Contact: Ms. Barbara Tulipane CAE, Pres./CEO
Description: Serves companies that use the power of electronic media to sell goods and services to the public. Its global membership includes television, radio and Internet retailers, along with expert back-end suppliers. **Publications:** *E-News Weekly* (weekly); *Electronic Retailer* (monthly); *Marketing, Meetings and Membership* (monthly); *Retailing.org* (bimonthly); *Retailing.org Daily* (daily).

51044 ■ National Association for Retail Marketing Services
PO Box 906
Plover, WI 54467-0906
Ph:(715)342-0948
Free: 888-52N-ARMS
Fax: (715)342-1943
Co. E-mail: admin@narms.com
URL: http://www.narms.com
Contact: Daniel C. Borschke CAE, Pres./CEO
Membership: Individuals and businesses providing retail merchandising services. **Purpose:** Seeks to advance the retail merchandising industries. Represents members' collective interests; facilitates communication and cooperation among members. **Publications:** *The Retail Merchandiser* (quarterly).

51045 ■ National Retail Federation
325 7th St. NW, Ste. 1100
Washington, DC 20004
Ph:(202)783-7971
Free: 800-NRF-HOW2
Fax: (202)737-2849
Co. E-mail: mullint@nrf.com
URL: http://www.nrf.com
Contact: Tracy Mullin, Pres./CEO
Purpose: Represents state retail associations, several dozen national retail associations, as well as large and small corporate members representing the breadth and diversity of the retail industry's establishment and employees. Conducts informational and educational conferences related to all phases of retailing including financial planning and cash management, taxation, economic forecasting, expense planning, shortage control, credit, electronic data processing, telecommunications, merchandise management, buying, traffic, security, supply, materials handling, store planning and construction, personnel administration,

recruitment and training, and advertising and display. **Publications:** *NRF Foundation Focus* (quarterly); *NRF Update* ; *STORES Magazine* (monthly); *Washington Retail Report* (weekly).

51046 ■ Planning and Visual Education Partnership
3595 Sheridan St., Ste. 200
Hollywood, FL 33021
Ph:(954)893-7300
Fax: (954)893-8375
Co. E-mail: pave@p-a-v-e.info
URL: http://p-a-v-e.info
Contact: Greg M. Gorman, Chm.
Membership: Retail executives, visual merchandisers, store planners, architects, specifiers, students. **Purpose:** Seeks to educate and motivate members and encourage interaction among their related fields. Holds annual design competition; offers an internship program; donates proceeds of shows toward financial aid for students.

DIRECTORIES OF EDUCATIONAL PROGRAMS

51047 ■ *Directory of Private Accredited Career Schools and Colleges of Technology*
Pub: Accrediting Commission of Career Schools and Colleges of Technology
Released: On web page. **Price:** Free. **Description:** Covers 3900 accredited post-secondary programs that provide training programs in business, trade, and technical fields, including various small business endeavors. Entries offer school name, address, phone, description of courses, job placement assistance, and requirements for admission. Arrangement is alphabetical.

REFERENCE WORKS

51048 ■ "All Systems Go" in *Entrepreneur* (Vol. 32, December 2004, No. 12, pp. 52)
Pub: Entrepreneur Media Inc.
Ed: Melissa Campanelli. **Description:** Importance for e-tailers to integrate accounting, inventory and customer management back-end systems is stressed. This setup will enable your Website to become a focal point of contact with customers from tracking packages, reviewing past orders, and viewing sales quotes, answering FAQs and logging support calls.

51049 ■ "Another Wave of HQ Job Cuts at Sears" in *Crain's Chicago Business* (Vol. 26, No. 50, December 15, 2003, pp. 1)
Pub: Crain Communications, Inc.
Ed: Sandra Jones. **Description:** Sears, Roebuck and Company employed 5,300 workers at its Hoffman Estates headquarters in Illinois at the first of 2003, and the staff was cut to 4,800 by December, with further cuts predicted. After Sears sold its 94-year-old credit card division, the company's stores could not generate enough income to make up for the loss of credit card profits. Statistical data included.

51050 ■ "Apple Squares Off Against Resellers" in *Inc.* (September 1, 2004)
Pub: Inc. Magazine
Ed: Cara Cannella. **Description:** The legal battle between Apple and its resellers that began four years ago is examined. The battle started when resellers concluded that Apple was mistreating them by opening outlets near their businesses.

51051 ■ "Appleseed's distribution center expands" in *Boston Business Journal* (Vol. 22, No. 12, April 26, 2002, pp. 5)
Pub: MCP, Inc.
Ed: Donna L. Goodison. **Description:** Appleseed's Inc. is expanding its distribution center due to growth.

51052 ■ "Arbor Realty Provides $35M in Financing" in *Long Island Business News* (February 27, 2004)
Pub: Dolan Media Newswires
Ed: Nick Anastasi. **Description:** Arbor Realty Limited Partnership has provided $35 million in financing to assist Prime Outlets Acquisition Company for the acquisition of 36 major outlet centers in the U.S. and Puerto Rico from Prime Retail Inc.

51053 ■ "Are the Tax-Free Net's Days Numbered?" in *Home Office Computing* (Vol. 18, No. 7, July 2000, pp. 16)
Pub: Scholastic Inc.
Ed: Jeffery D. Zbar. **Description:** With the three-year moratorium on Web taxes set to expire in October 2001, the federally appointed Advisory Commission on Electronic Commerce (ACEC) has submitted recommendations designed to kill or slow adoption of new taxes. That means dot-coms would be exempt from charging sales taxes, while traditional retailers would still be required to charge sales taxes.

51054 ■ *ARMS Supermarket Promotion Show*
Pub: Association of Retail Marketing Services Inc.
Contact: Gerri Hopkins, Exec. Dir.
Released: Annual. **Price:** Free. **Covers:** Approximately 66 retailers involved in the ARMS supermarket promotion show, held annually. **Entries Include:** Organization name, address, phone, fax, booth number and location, exhibit description, names and titles of key personnel. **Arrangement:** Alphabetical by company name.

51055 ■ "The Art of the Sale" in *Entrepreneur* (Vol. 31, No. 8, August 2003, pp. 58)
Pub: Entrepreneur Media, Inc.
Ed: Chris Penttila. **Description:** Selling has become more difficult in the slumping economy, and salespersons face greater demands in a more competitive environment and require better sales skills.

51056 ■ "At Their Service" in *Entrepreneur* (Vol. 31, No. 7, July 2003, pp. 40)
Pub: Entrepreneur Media, Inc.
Ed: Melissa Campanelli. **Description:** Online retailers should never abandoned good customer services, even during a slower economy. Online shoppers have grown to expect excellent customer service from the Web sites in which they purchase.

51057 ■ "Atlanta Slips a Notch as Retailers Shop Elsewhere" in *Atlanta Business Chronicle* (Vol. 26, No. 14, September 12, 2003, pp. 5A)
Pub: American City Business Publications, Inc.
Ed: Lisa R. Schoolcraft. **Description:** The Atlanta, Georgia area has declined as a location for new retail development projects. Industry analysts at North American Properties state that shopping center developers are concerned about the region's lagging economic conditions.

51058 ■ "Atlanta's Top 25 Shopping Centers" in *Atlanta Business Chronicle* (Vol. 25, No. 21, November 1, 2002, pp. 30C)
Pub: American City Business Publications, Inc.
Description: The top 25 shopping centers in the Atlanta area are ranked by square feet. Among other data listed are number of stores, parking space amount, management firms, owners, and anchor tenants.

51059 ■ "Attention, Online Shoppers, Be Wary" in *Sacramento Bee* (November 28, 2005)
Pub: The Sacramento Bee
Ed: Clint Swett. **Description:** Internet safety for consumers is discussed. According to a survey conducted by the Business Software Alliance and Forrester Research, 61 percent of respondents are concerned about Internet security when making purchases. It is important to always use a secured Web page when entering personal information.

51060 ■ "August, Ga., Lacks Demographics to Draw Upscale Retailers" in *Augusta Chronicle* (February 17, 2004)
Pub: Knight-Ridder/Tribune Business News
Ed: James Gallagher. Description: Profile of HiFi Buys, a high-end electronics retailer expanding in the Atlanta, Georgia area.

51061 ■ *Avon: Building the World's Premier Company for Women*
Pub: John Wiley & Sons, Incorporated
Ed: Laura Klepacki. Released: May 2006. Price: $21.99. Description: Profile of Avon, the world's largest direct sales company. Avon representatives number four million in over 140 countries.

51062 ■ "Back to business with Staples: new chief works to reclaim the chain's roots" in *Barron's* (Vol. 82, No. 59, Feb. 24, 2003, pp. T8)
Pub: Barron's
Ed: Lawrence Strauss. Description: Profile of Ronald L. Sargent, newly appointed CEO of Staples. Sargent is refocusing the retailer on its original vision, the small business customer, and is committed to raising earnings as the best way to raising share prices.

51063 ■ "Bagging the Right Customers" in *Business 2.0* (Vol. 6, May 2005, No. 4, pp. 56-57)
Pub: Time, Inc.
Ed: Andrew Tilin. Description: Bagmaker Timbuk2 is prospering through the use of exploiting the areas between niche obscurity and mass-market dullness. Big-box retailers offer a large selection within a broadly defined product category while smaller specialty stores serve a finely defined market segment with brand more important than price.

51064 ■ "Bar None" in *Entrepreneur* (Vol. 32, December 2004, No. 12, pp. 24)
Pub: Entrepreneur Media Inc.
Ed: Amanda C. Kooser. Description: New bar code regulations affecting retailers and suppliers, called Sunrise 2005, go into effect January 1, 2005. This process allows businesses to scan different types of codes used worldwide, and ultimately, the 14-digit Global Trade Item Number.

51065 ■ "Bar None" in *My Business* (December/January 2004, pp. 11)
Pub: My Business Magazine
Ed: Tamara E. Holmes. Description: The 2005 Sunrise mandate, instituted by the Uniform Code Council Inc., will require all retailers to have systems able to read 13-digit bar codes in addition to the 12-digit bar code numbers already standard in the U.S. The change is required EAN International, the global body that issues product codes overseas, currently uses an 8-digit and 13-digit system.

51066 ■ "Barnes & Noble unit is dropped by 2 big chains" in *Wall Street Journal* (February 5, 2003, pp. B4)
Pub: Dow Jones & Co. Inc.
Ed: Jeffrey A. Trachtenberg. Description: Sterling Publishing, owned by Barnes & Noble, lost contracts with both Borders Group Inc. and Costco Wholesale Corporation.

51067 ■ "Beall's Push to Expand Existing Florida Stores Reaps Dividends On Grand Scale" in *Bradenton Herald* (January 20, 2005)
Pub: Bradenton Herald
Ed: Dana Sanchez. Description: Beall's Inc. plans to expand all of its Florida outlet stores that are smaller than 20,000 square feet in size. The firm has 258 outlet stores in the state. With the increases space, the stores will begin selling books, multimedia and children's items along with more clothing.

51068 ■ "Bean Counter" in *Forbes* (Vol. 175, February 14, 2005, No. 3, pp. 78)
Pub: Forbes Magazine Inc.
Ed: Peter Kafka. Description: Profile of James Donald, CEO of Starbucks, who's responsible for growth of the coffee company. Statistical data included.

51069 ■ "Better Off Red" in *Entrepreneur.com* (Vol. 34, February 2006, No. 2, pp. 74)
Pub: Entrepreneur Media Inc.
Ed: Gwen Moran. Description: People are moving away from traditional Valentine's gifts and buying more meaningful gifts for their loved ones. Marketing experts suggest retailers use red to merchandise products, suggest products as perfect gifts for the holiday, and use heart shaped items.

51070 ■ "Better Ways to Buy: Educate Yourself with a Consumer Handbook" in *Black Enterprise* (Vol. 35, December 2004, No. 5, pp. 160)
Pub: Earl G. Graves Publishing Co. Inc.
Ed: Stephanie Young. Description: Profile of the Consumer Action Handbook published by the U.S. General Services Administration. Along with consumer tips, the book lists contacts for corporations, federal agencies, better business bureaus, and local governments, as well as car manufacturers and dispute resolution programs and national consumer organizations.

51071 ■ "Big Box vs. Online" in *Hispanic Business* (March 2003, pp. 25)
Pub: Hispanic Business
Ed: Roger Harris. Description: Internet shoppers are finding very competitive pricing between purchasing online versus going to a brick and mortar store. An online shopping checklist is provided to assist consumers when making purchases online.

51072 ■ "Big Retailers Discover Metro Milwaukee" in *Business Journal-Milwaukee* (Vol. 20, No. 46, August 1, 2003, pp. A27)
Pub: American City Business Journals, Inc.
Ed: Mark Kass. Description: Chicago, Illinois-based Crate and Barrel, a home products retailer, is planning to open a new store in Wauwatosa, Wisconsin. The Milwaukee region is attracting many national retail chains to its urban and suburban areas.

51073 ■ "Bill Would Ease Rules on Store Price Tags" in *Crain's Detroit Business* (Vol. 22, December 4, 2006, No. 49, pp. 6)
Pub: Crain Communications Inc. - Detroit
Ed: Amy Lane. Description: New bill will aid attraction of new members of the retailing industry to come to Michigan. Video scanning is now permissible to replace individual pricing tags or labels if certain conditions are met.

51074 ■ "Blow-Ho-Ho! Inflatables Sales On Rise" in *Crain's Chicago Business* (Vol. 26, No. 51, December 22, 2003, pp. 22)
Pub: Crain Communications, Inc.
Ed: Brian McCormick. Description: The latest trend in neighborhood decorating comes in the form of inflatable snowmen, Santas, and toy soldiers. These decorations were commonly seen at malls and car lots, but have been scaled down to appeal to the residential homeowner for holidays.

51075 ■ "BP Amoco wants to sell much more than gas at its new stations" in *The New York Times* (July 25, 2000, pp. C6)
Pub: The New York Times Company
Ed: Kruti Trivedi. Description: BP Amoco is spending $7 billion to present a fresh brand image through BP Connect, a new round of service stations with cafilatte, solar panels, imaginatively-lit markets and e-commerce kiosks. Thus far, 20 percent of gas stations revenues come from the convenience markets. The bright green and yellow stations will be featured in ads, created by Ogilvy & Mather Worldwide promoting BP as a green company. The campaign will cost $100 million a year.

51076 ■ "Brentwood's Blue Light Special" in *Washington Business Journal* (Vol. 22, No. 15, August 15, 2003, pp. 1)
Pub: Washington Business Journal
Ed: Eleni Kretikos. Description: The move by Kmart Corporation to put one of its Washington, DC's stores up for sale is discussed. Topics include business losses, business relocation, and corporation reorganizations.

51077 ■ "Bricks & Clicks" in *Entrepreneur* (Vol. 33, October 2005, No. 10, pp. 64)
Pub: Entrepreneur Media Inc.
Ed: Gwen Moran. Description: Retailers are using eBay as a way to retail slow-moving merchandise from stores. Information for setting up a proper store on eBay is shared.

51078 ■ "Bridging the Gap" in *Sales & Marketing Management*
Pub: VNU Business Media
Ed: David Macey. Description: Retail-specific marketing solutions are becoming more important as effective ways to influence buying behavior in today's consumer market.

51079 ■ "Brighton, Howell Hope Plans Boost Retail" in *Crain's Detroit Business* (Vol. 21, January 17, 2005, No. 3, pp. 28)
Pub: Crain Communications Inc. - Detroit
Ed: Sheena Harrison. Description: Plans by Livingston County Communities, Brighton and Howell, are underway to attract new businesses. Road construction, new signs, and beautification projects are some of the improvements planned for retail growth in the area.

51080 ■ "Budget Sportswear Store Coming to Tampa, Fla." in *Tampa Tribune* (November 22, 2005)
Pub: Media General, Inc.
Ed: Michael Sasso. Description: Steve & Barry's University Sportswear is expanding to Tampa, Florida. The retailer offers t-shirts, college-branded sweatshirts and varsity jackets, all for $9.98 or less.

51081 ■ "Bulking up; Dollar Castle's ruler plans retailing, distribution kingdom" in *Crain's Detroit Business* (Dec. 9, 2002, pp. 3)
Pub: Crain Communications Inc., Detroit
Ed: Laura Bailey. Description: Profile of Dollar Castle's owner Eddie Denha and his successful management style.

51082 ■ "Bull in a China Shop? If That's How Parents Feel Bringing Kids Into Your Store, They'll Pass You By" in *Entrepreneur* (Vol. 32)
Pub: Entrepreneur Media Inc.
Description: Many retail operations are setting up an area for children to play while parents shop.

51083 ■ "Bunny Money" in *Entrepreneur* (Vol. 30, No. 3, March 2002)
Pub: Entrepreneur Media Inc.
Ed: Michelle Prather. Description: Gift basket retailers, as well as gift shops, are expecting higher profits on Easter sales this year.

51084 ■ "The Business Week News You Need to Know" in *Business Week* (January 23, 2006, No. 3968, pp. 30-31)
Pub: McGraw-Hill Companies
Ed: Harry Maurer. Description: News about the Detroit Auto Show, job growth, Home Depot's expansion plans, Internet search engines, new executive pay rules, the stock market, and more.

51085 ■ "The Business Week News You Need To Know" in *Business Week* (January 9, 2006, No. 3966, pp. 24-25)
Pub: McGraw-Hill Companies
Ed: Harry Maurer. Description: Information of 2005 holiday sales, interest rates, a medical device lawsuit, television cable news programming, the retailer Wal-Mart, Albertson's grocery stores, Alaska drilling, Microsoft's European business, and other issues is offered.

51086 ■ "But Wait, There's More" in *Entrepreneur* (Vol. 31, No. 11, November 2003, pp. 98)
Pub: Entrepreneur Media, Inc.
Ed: Gwen Moran. Description: Gift-with-purchase promotions can increase sales, build a brand and make customers feel good about shopping in your store.

51087 ■ "California Dreamin'" in *Entrepreneur* (Vol. 31, No. 9, September 2003, pp. 22)
Pub: Entrepreneur Media, Inc.
Description: A listing of the best areas for retail in America is presented, with California having six of the best metropolitan areas.

51088 ■ "Capture the Tag: Are RFID Tags in Danger of Being Hacked?" in *Entrepreneur* (Vol. 33, February 2005, No. 2, pp. 66)
Pub: Entrepreneur Media Inc.
Ed: Gwen Moran. **Description:** Retail cashiers should be alerted to look for radio frequency identification (RFID) tags that look unusual, if so, check the product information manual.

51089 ■ "Card-Carrying Kids" in *Sacramento Bee* (November 12, 2005)
Pub: The Sacramento Bee
Ed: Jon Ortiz. **Description:** Marketing Workshop Inc. conducted a survey that showed one in five adults purchased gift cards for their children ages 5-8 years old. Kay Palna, a professor at Iowa State University, is concerned the practice will encourage materialism by teaching children to worry about money at too young an age.

51090 ■ "Case Study" in *Inc.* (December 1, 2004)
Pub: Inc. Magazine
Ed: Lora Kolodny. **Description:** Intellinitiative's board games were selling fast until a giant brand took over and pushed them out of the store.

51091 ■ "Catch-22: Are Small Companies that Buy from Giant Retailers Sleeping with the Enemy" in *Entrepreneur* (Vol. 31, No. 9, September 2003)
Pub: Entrepreneur Media, Inc.
Ed: Joshua Kurlantzick. **Description:** Small retailers have to compete with megastores such as Sam's Club, Target, Wal-Mart and others, with main suppliers, putting more stress on small businesses.

51092 ■ "Champion Sells Five Retail Centers, Closes 12 Others" in *Crain's Detroit Business* (Vol. 21, January 10, 2005, No. 2, pp. 22)
Pub: Crain Communications Inc. - Detroit
Ed: Jennette Smith. **Description:** Champion Enterprises Inc., a manufactured home producer, sold four retail centers in Kentucky and Texas and will sell one center in South Carolina. The company will also close 12 retail centers in seven states.

51093 ■ "Checking Out" in *Harvard Business Review* (Vol. 78, No. 2, March 2000, pp. 22)
Pub: Harvard Business School Publishing Corp.
Description: Online shoppers routinely abandon their shopping carts without buying anything—and that's bad news for e-tailers.

51094 ■ "Choose Your Path" in *Entrepreneur* (Vol. 33, March 2005, No. 3, pp. 114)
Pub: Entrepreneur Media Inc.
Ed: Nichole L. Torres. **Description:** Three various retail paths for entrepreneurs to choose when starting a new retail venture are discussed.

51095 ■ "Churn Plagues Wal-Mart Labor Effort" in *Tampa Tribune* (December 23, 2005)
Pub: Media General, Inc.
Ed: Michael Sasso. **Description:** Wal-Mark Workers Association is having difficulty organizing the retailer's workforce due to the high rate of members quitting their jobs with the retailer. The association is backed by two unions, the United Food and Commercial Workers Union and the Service Employees International Union along with the advocacy group, the Association of Community Organizations for Reform Now.

51096 ■ "Claire's Baubles, Bangles, and Profits" in *Business Week Online* (February 8, 2005)
Pub: McGraw-Hill Companies

Ed: Michael Souers. **Description:** Profile of Claire's Stores, retailer catering to girls and young women. The chain is expanding its global reach overseas because the market is saturated in the U.S. Claire's stocks are expected to climb in the next year.

51097 ■ "Clicks to Bricks" in *Entrepreneur* (Vol. 33, August 2005, No. 8, pp. 44)
Pub: Entrepreneur Media Inc.
Ed: Melissa Campanelli. **Description:** Following a current trend, more e-tailers are opening brick-and-mortar stores. This move will strengthen brand-name recognition, give local customers a place to shop or return merchandise, lower promotional fees, and expand a customer base.

51098 ■ "Closing Raises Loan Questions" in *Pittsburgh Business Times* (Vol. 23, No. 3, August 8, 2003, pp. 1)
Pub: Pittsburgh Business Times
Ed: Tim Schooley, Suzanne Elliott. **Description:** May Department Stores Company announced the closing of its Lord and Taylor store in downtown Pittsburgh, Pennsylvania. The city council has accepted that it will not be repaid the $11.75 million loan it made to the May Company upon the store's opening three years ago.

51099 ■ "Coke Out to Woo Mall Rats Here With Lounge" in *Crain's Chicago Business* (Vol. 26, No. 51, December 22, 2003, pp. 9)
Pub: Crain Communications, Inc.
Ed: Kate MacArthur. **Description:** Coca-Cola has created the Coca-Cola Red Lounge for teenagers shopping at the north suburban Vernon Hills, Westfield Shoppingtown Hawthorn Center, as well as another site in Los Angeles, California. Coke is trying to build a brand with young people, separating it from being a brand for older folks. Statistical data included.

51100 ■ "Cold Remedy Control has Pharmacies on Hot Seat" in *Milwaukee Journal Sentinel* (December 6, 2005)
Pub: Journal Sentinel, Inc.
Ed: Doris Hajewski. **Description:** A new Wisconsin law classifies cold remedies with pseudoephedrine a controlled substance. A controlled substance can be sold only by a licensed pharmacist in the state. Grocers, convenience stores and other retail outlets can no longer sell any cold remedies containing pseudoephedrine.

51101 ■ "Collectibles Cash-In" in *Small Business Opportunities* (Vol. 17, November 2005, No. 6, pp. 100, 104)
Pub: Harris Publications Inc.
Description: Profile of Vintage Stock, a leader in buying and selling new and pre-owned entertainment products. The company is the only retailer specializing in new and vintage merchandise.

51102 ■ "Coming of age" in *Boston Business Journal* (Vol. 22,)
Pub: MCP, Inc.
Ed: Phil Sweeney. **Description:** Online retailers are learning ways to survive in a slowing economy.

51103 ■ "Coming Full Circle" in *Washington Business Journal* (Vol. 22, No. 16, August 22, 2003, pp. 1)
Pub: Washington Business Journal
Ed: Eleni Kretikos. **Description:** Because of its Bohemian atmosphere, access to the Metro subway system and a dense concentration of high-income earners, Dupont Circle development is once again a hot real estate market for retailers.

51104 ■ "Commentary: Fresh-Air Shopping" in *Journal Record (Oklahoma City, OK)* (February 2, 2007)
Pub: Journal Record
Ed: Darren Currin. **Description:** RCL Mortgage Group discusses plans to build an open-air shopping mall in Oklahoma City, Oklahoma. Statistical details included.

51105 ■ "Commentary: Good customer service-a ghost of retail's past?" in *Colorado Springs Business Journal* (March 7, 2003)
Pub: Dolan Media Newswires
Ed: Marylou Doehrman. **Description:** The importance of a good customer service policy for retail stores is stressed, citing that a good policy will keep customers coming back.

51106 ■ "Company Tracks Shoppers, Issues Coupons on Tendencies" in *Tampa Tribune* (November 16, 2005)
Pub: Media General, Inc.
Ed: Richard Mullins. **Description:** Catalina Marketing, based in St. Petersburg, Florida, tracks purchases for stores like Kash n' Karry, Meijer and Safeway. The firm records the purchases through customer loyalty cards, credit cards and debit cards and offers targeted coupons to specific customers.

51107 ■ "Company Unveils Program to Evaluate Car Dealerships" in *Westchester County Business Journal* (Vol. 44, January 31, 2005, No. 5, pp. 3)
Pub: Westfair Communications Inc.
Description: TUV Rheinland North America Inc. has developed a program to certify automobile dealerships to insure they meet certain business practice standards. The automotive retail management program consists of eight factors, including the use of a mystery shopper to evaluate customer service performance.

51108 ■ "Competition Forces Malls to Redefine Marketing" in *Atlanta Business Chronicle* (Vol. 26, No. 11, August 22, 2003, pp. 3A)
Pub: American City Business Publications, Inc.
Ed: Jim Lovel. **Description:** Small shopping centers have a larger customer base than larger regional malls in the Atlanta, Georgia area.

51109 ■ "Condos Coming To U.S. 301 Property" in *Bradenton Herald* (January 22, 2005)
Pub: Bradenton Herald
Description: Upscale residential condominiums and retail space is planned for about 211 acres of land in Palmetto, Florida on U.S. 301. Sanctuary Development Partners, an alliance between Corvus International and Svenson Enterprises, paid $15 million for the property.

51110 ■ "Consumer Finance" in *Business Week* (January 16, 2006, No. 3967, pp. 38)
Pub: McGraw-Hill Companies
Ed: Peter Burrows. **Description:** A new trend shows online brands offering shoppers Bill Me later payment options in order to spur sales growth and offer a billing method to consumers uneasy about using their credit cards on the Internet. So far 230 e-commerce sites offer this service.

51111 ■ "Consumers Look for Post-Holiday Sales" in *Sacramento Bee* (December 27, 2005)
Pub: The Sacramento Bee
Ed: Jon Ortiz. **Description:** Retailers are becoming increasingly dependent on post-holiday sales. Shoppers tend to purchase new items seen in sales and promotions while returning unwanted items.

51112 ■ "Contacts for Contracts" in *Hispanic Business* (January/February 2003, pp. 60)
Pub: Hispanic Business
Description: A list of procurement contacts to large retailers is presented for minority vendors. Contracting opportunities with large retailers is not limited to large and medium-sized firms. A Web address is given for the RedWire Diversity E-Business Network, a purchasing collective and database of information for more than 2,500 Hispanic-owned businesses is also included.

51113 ■ "Control your inventory in a world of lean retailing" in *Harvard Business Review* **(Vol. 78, No. 6, November-December 2000, pp. 169)**
Pub: Harvard Business School Publishing Corp.
Description: The production schedules and sourcing strategies of manufacturers is probed, offering a new approach as to how companies can predict their inventory requirements more accurately.

51114 ■ "Cost Transparency: The Net's Real Threat to Prices and Brands" in *Harvard Business Review* **(Vol. 78, No. 2, March 2000, pp. 43)**
Pub: Harvard Business School Publishing Corp.
Ed: Indrajit Sinha. **Description:** The vast sea of information about prices, competitors, and features that is readily available on the Internet helps buyers "see through" the costs of products and services. That's bad news for manufacturers and retailers, and there are ways to fight back.

51115 ■ "Coupons Go Cellular" in *Sacramento Bee* **(December 16, 2005)**
Pub: The Sacramento Bee
Ed: Jim Wasserman. **Description:** Phone coupons are expected to become effective marketing tools for retailers. Users are able to download free software into cellular phones and forward the offers to friends.

51116 ■ "Court Expands Accommodation Obligations in Retail Stores" in *Employment Relations Today* **(Vol. 26, No. 4, Winter 2000, pp. 119)**
Pub: John Wiley & Sons, Inc.
Ed: Arthur F. Silbergeld. **Description:** A discussion about the interpretation of the Americans with Disabilities Act of 1990 with regard to space planning by retail stores. A court case, Lieber v. Macy's West Inc., will determine whether or not retail stores must accommodate the space requirements of disabled individuals.

51117 ■ "Crain's List; Largest Multitenant Retail Properties" in *Crain's Detroit Business* **(Vol. 19, No. 14, April 7, 2003, pp. 45)**
Pub: Crain Communications Inc., Detroit
Description: A listing of the 20 largest multi-tenant retail properties in the Detroit, Michigan area is presented.

51118 ■ "Crossroads of Growth" in *Crain's Detroit Business*
Pub: Crain Communications Inc. - Detroit
Ed: Brent Snavely. **Description:** Ray Township officials are working with developers on the township's first proposed shopping center. Officials have made it clear they will not approve anything resembling big-box retail, like Wal-Mart or Meijer at the site.

51119 ■ "Customs Expansion Would Hurt Riverfront" in *Crain's Detroit Business* **(Vol. 21, October 24, 2005, No. 43, pp. 8)**
Pub: Crain Communications Inc. - Detroit
Ed: Description: Plans for a new customs inspection area in Detroit would improve international crossings for both freight and vehicle traffic. The plan might also include major retail shops. Some experts fear the plan, which calls for a new road in the middle of downtown, would hurt the new pedestrian-friendly promenade which is bringing visitors to the area.

51120 ■ "Cuts in Retail, Manufacturing Hurt Northern New Jersey's Job Growth" in *The Record* **(November 9, 2005)**
Pub: New Jersey Media Group
Ed: Kathleen Lynn. **Description:** According to the federal Bureau of Labor Statistics, northern New Jersey firms are not hiring new employees. Statistical data included.

51121 ■ "Damariscotta, Maine, Merchants Worry About Wal-Mart" in *Portland Press Herald* **(December 1, 2005)**
Pub: Blethen Maine Newspapers, Inc.
Ed: Dennis Hoey. **Description:** Plans for a new Wal-Mart in Damariscotta, Maine has small business retailers concerned about competition. Many downtown merchants believe a Wal-Mart store will detract from the downtown area and force many out of business.

51122 ■ "Dare to Compare." in *Entrepreneur* **(Vol. 33, January 2005, No. 1, pp. 43)**
Pub: Entrepreneur Media Inc.
Ed: Melissa Campanelli. **Description:** Online merchants wishing to grow their business might consider placing products on comparison shopping Websites. These sites display product information in a simple format and lets buyers compare and choose the best product from a list of different retailers.

51123 ■ "David Nicklaus Column" in *St. Louis Post-Dispatch* **(March 2, 2005)**
Pub: Knight-Ridder/Tribune Business News
Ed: David Nicklaus. **Description:** Details of the acquisition of May Department Stores Company by Federated Department Stores Inc. is examined.

51124 ■ "The Death and Life of Buy.com" in *Forbes* **(January 21, 2002, p. 86)**
Pub: Forbes Magazine
Ed: Quentin Hardy. **Description:** Profile of Scott Blum who hopes to rebuild the online retailer Buy.com. Blum founded the dot.com in 1997 and bought back control of the Internet retailer in November 2001.

51125 ■ "Declaring War On Wal-Mart" in *Business Week* **(February 7, 2005, No. 3919, pp. 31)**
Pub: McGraw-Hill Companies
Ed: Aaron Bernstein. **Description:** Wal-Mart has launched an ad campaign in January with the message: Wal-Mart is working for everyone. The retailer is fighting back against allegations of sex discrimination, poverty-level wages, and non-union workforce.

51126 ■ "Delta Apparel Earnings Drop" in *Altanta Journal-Constitution* **(February 3, 2007)**
Pub: Cox Newspapers, Inc.
Ed: Tammy Joyner. **Description:** Delta Apparel reported a drop in second-quarter profits, citing a weak retail market. The clothing distributor operates Fun-Tees. Statistical data included.

51127 ■ "Department-Store Chain Boosts N.J. Index" in *The Record* **(November 13, 2005)**
Pub: New Jersey Media Group
Ed: William Conroy. **Description:** Federated Department Stores Inc. pushed the Asbury Park Press/Bloomberg 75 index to a 2.48 percent gain in November 2005. Statistical data included for the index, which is made up of 75 companies.

51128 ■ "Detroit Free Press Macomb Small Business Column" in *Detroit Free Press* **(June 30, 2005)**
Pub: Knight-Ridder/Tribune Business News
Ed: Carol Cain. **Description:** Retailers along Mack Avenue in Grosse Pointe Woods are offering employees of all St. John Health System discounts in order to increase customer activity.

51129 ■ "Detroit looks for retail to follow housing growth" in *Crain's Detroit Business* **(Vol. 18, No. 45, November 11, 2002, pp. 16)**
Pub: Crain Communications Inc., Detroit
Ed: Robert Ankeny. **Description:** Officials from the City of Detroit, along with private-sector leaders, predict a growth in retail in 2003, following the growth trend in new housing development. Statistical data included.

51130 ■ "Developer Plans Open-Air Mall Anchored by Wal-Mart" in *Sacramento Bee* **(November 5, 2005)**
Pub: The Sacramento Bee
Ed: Jon Ortiz. **Description:** South Sac LLC located in San Francisco, California, purchased property from developer Buzz Oates to highlight a Wal-Mart Supercenter store.

51131 ■ "Developers Jockey for Retail at Trade Center" in *Crain's New York Business* **(Vol. 20, No. 12, March 22, 2004, pp. 1)**
Pub: Crain Communications, Inc.
Ed: Christine Haughney. **Description:** The Port Authority of New York and New Jersey is making plans for retail space to be built on the World Trade Center site. Developers are lobbying to manage the projects, with The Related Companies the leading contender.

51132 ■ "Devoted Shopper Resurrects Jacobson's Department Store in Central Florida" in *Orlando Sentinel* **(October 11, 2004)**
Pub: Orlando Sentinel
Ed: Chris Cobbs. **Description:** Profile of Tammy Giaimo, who purchased Jacobson's when it closed. Giaimo liked the clothing and shopping experience at Jacobson's and hopes to lure customers to the personal-shopper services the store provides. The store will sell women's fashions, men's clothing, and household furnishings.

51133 ■ *Dictionary of Retailing & Merchandising*
Pub: John Wiley & Sons, Inc.
Ed: Jerry M. Rosenberg. **Price:** $27.95.

51134 ■ *Directory of Department Stores*
Pub: Chain Store Guide
Released: Annual, 2005. **Price:** $335, individuals Directory. **Covers:** 214 department store companies, 1,500 shoe store companies, 200 jewelry store companies, 95 optical store companies, and 70 leather and luggage store companies in the United States and Canada, with annual sales of at least $250,000. **Entries Include:** Company name; physical and mailing addresses; phone and fax numbers, company e-mail and web addresses; listing type; total sales; industry sales; total selling square footage; store prototype sizes; total units; units by trade name; trading areas; projected openings and remodelings; self-distributing indicator; distribution center locations; resident buyers' name and location; leased departments area, name, and location; mail order catalog indicator; Internet order processing indicator; private label softlines, hardlines, and credit card indicators; furniture styles and price lines; average number of checkouts; year founded; public company indicator; parent company name and loction; subsidiaries' names and locations; regional and divisional office locations; key personnel with titles; store locations, with address, phone number, and manager name (department stores only). **Arrangement:** Geographical. **Indexes:** Alphabetical, product lines, exclusions.

51135 ■ "Dot-com Seeks Firm Footing" in *Boston Business Journal* **(Vol. 22, No. 11, April 19, 2002, pp. 11)**
Pub: MCP, Inc.
Ed: Scott Savitz. **Description:** Shoebuy.com Inc. has 10,000 products with 220 brands and increasing numbers of customers. By sticking to a disciplined marketing style, this dot.com online retailer has been able to grow steadily.

51136 ■ "Double Play: Could Sending a Paper Catalog to Customers Boost Your E-Commerce Business?" in *Entrepreneur* **(Vol. 32, September 2004)**
Pub: Entrepreneur Media Inc.
Ed: Melissa Campanelli. **Description:** Many e-tailers are using catalogs to increase Internet sales. Statistical data included.

51137 ■ "Dutch fund pays nearly $14M for Sunrise retail center" in *Black Enterprise* **(Vol. 33, No. 198, March 24, 2003, pp. A1)**
Pub: Earl Graves Publishing Co.
Ed: Terry Sheridan. **Description:** The Dutch fund DIM Vastgoed NV paid $13.97 million for the Sunrise Town Center in Sunrise, in an effort to continue its investment interest in Main Street and Main Street commercial properties.

51138 ■ "E-Brand Lessons" in *Small Business Opportunities* **(Vol. 12, No. 5, September 2000, pp. 18)**
Pub: Harris Publications, Inc.
Description: The results of a comprehensive study of Internet users' opinions and perceptions of 250 technology brands, ranking them on overall performance and key brand attributes are examined. These results can help small businesses improve their presence on the Web.

51139 ■ "E-retailers turn to the printed page to put their wares before consumers" in *The New York Times* (July 10, 2000, pp. C12)
Pub: The New York Times Company
Ed: Bob Tedeschi. Description: Online retailers have started using or developing programs that will mail catalogs to consumers.

51140 ■ "E-Tail Therapy" in *Entrepreneur* (Vol. 33, January 2005, No. 1, pp. 35)
Pub: Entrepreneur Media Inc.
Ed: Heather Clancy. Description: Accessing marketing products via the Internet is growing in popularity.

51141 ■ "Eastland Future Unclear: Local Merchants Say They're OK Amid Closings of 4 More Stores" in *Charlotte Observer* (February 8, 2007)
Pub: Knight-Ridder/Tribune Business News
Ed: Nichole Monroe Bell. Description: Retailers in the Eastland Mall that market goods to shoppers looking for the urban, hip-hop look are most successful.

51142 ■ "Eight Tips to Spot Bad Checks" in *My Business* (February/March 2003, pp. 15)
Pub: My Business Magazine
Description: According to the Nilson Report, nearly 1.2 million bad checks are written daily in the U.S., equating to approximately $55.8 million in losses to retailers. Eight tips to spot a bad check are listed.

51143 ■ "El Cajon: Bookseller Still Shining From the Sunbelt" in *San Diego Business Journal* (Vol. 28, January 15, 2007, No. 3, pp. 16)
Pub: San Diego Business Journal Associates
Ed: Katie Weeks. Description: Discount bookseller and publisher, Sunbelt Publications Inc., celebrated its 22nd anniversary. Sunbelt serves more than 1,000 customers in the Southern California and Baja area with 2,500 regional books and maps from 150 publishers.

51144 ■ "Employees Sue Best Buy for Race, Gender Discrimination" in *Sacramento Bee* (December 9, 2005)
Pub: The Sacramento Bee
Ed: Rachel Osterman. Description: Retailer, Best Buy is being sued for race and gender discrimination for alleged lower wages than those paid to white males and for steering women employees away from high-paying sales jobs.

51145 ■ "The Endangered Department Store" in *Boston Globe* (February 13, 2005)
Pub: New York Times Company
Ed: Keith Reed. Description: The merger between Macy's and Filene's is causing experts to question whether mass-market department stores are on the decline. Many department stores are reinventing themselves in order to stay competitive with the luxury high-end and low-cost discount stores.

51146 ■ *The Essential Online Solution: The 5-Step Formula for Small Business Success*
Pub: John Wiley & Sons, Incorporated
Ed: Rick Segel; Barbara Callan-Bogia. Released: October 2006. Price: $22.95. Description: Strategies to help any small business increase its online presence and compete with big retail chains. Tips for success Web design are included.

51147 ■ "Everything in its Place: Can the Art of Feng Shui Help You Optimize Your Business?" in *Entrepreneur* (Vol. 32, August 2004, No. 8)
Pub: Entrepreneur Media Inc.
Ed: Gwen Moran. Description: According to Jami Lin, consultant at Feng-Shui-Interior-Design.com, feng shui, the Chinese art of placement can dramatically increase a store's appeal.

51148 ■ "Factory Card Gets Back in Party Mood" in *Crain's Chicago Business* (Vol. 26, No. 50, December 15, 2003, pp. 6)
Pub: Crain Communications, Inc.
Ed: H. Lee Murphy. Description: Profile of Factory Card & Party Outlet Corporation is presented. The firm

filed Chapter 11 reorganization in April 2002, and investors have seen the stock rise from less than $2 to more than $20 in 2003. The company plans to open ten more stores in 2004.

51149 ■ "Factory Card Gets Back in Party Mood; Judicious Growth, Curtailed Costs Restore Firms Health" in *Crains Chicago Business* (Vol. 26)
Pub: Crain Communications, Inc.
Ed: H. Lee Murphy. Description: Profile of Factory Card & Party Outlet Corporation is presented. The firm filed Chapter 11 reorganization in April 2002, and investors have seen the stock rise from less than $2 to more than $20 in 2003. The company plans to open ten more stores in 2004.

51150 ■ "Failure is Glorious" in *Fast Company* (November 2001, pp. 35)
Pub: Fast Company
Ed: Ian Wylie. Description: Alberto Alessi transformed his family's ho-hum housewares business into a trend setting design giant. His secret: walking the borderline between genius and failure.

51151 ■ "Fantastic Plastic" in *Entrepreneur* (Vol. 31, No. 9, September 2003, pp. 84)
Pub: Entrepreneur Media, Inc.
Description: The trend towards giving gift cards is growing. Retailers sold more than $36 billion worth of gift cards in 2002. A Website selling cards for less than $1 each is featured.

51152 ■ "The Fast Lane: A New Concept in Retail is Popping Up All Over" in *Entrepreneur* (Vol. 33, January 2005, No. 1, pp. 64)
Pub: Entrepreneur Media Inc.
Ed: Gwen Moran. Description: Profile of Russell Miller, founder of Vacant, a company that sets up here today, gone tomorrow pop-up retail locations for hard-to-find items. These stores stay open two weeks to a month. Another option for short term sales would be a kiosk at a local mall.

51153 ■ "February sales at Claire's jump 6 percent" in *Daily Business Review* (Vol. 77, No. 187, March 7, 2003)
Pub: American Lawyer Media LP
Ed: AnaMaria Colmenares. Description: Claire's Stores sales rose 6 percent despite a plunge in consumer confidence and a drop in national retail sales. The company currently operates 2,900 stores worldwide and is looking to expand into Spain. Statistical data included.

51154 ■ "Federated Department Stores Inc." in *Black Enterprise* (Vol. 34, No. 4, November 2003, pp. 62)
Pub: Earl Graves Publishing Co.
Description: Profile of William L. Hawthorne III, newly elected vice president/diversity and deputy general counsel of Federated Department Stores Inc., located in Cincinnati, Ohio.

51155 ■ "$55M in redevelopment planned for Livonia sites" in *Detroit Business* (Vol. 19, No. 14, April 7, 2003, pp. 6)
Pub: Crain Communications Inc., Detroit
Ed: Laura Bailey. Description: Phoenix Land Development has plans for 94 ranch condominiums and 45,000 square feet of retail space in the City of Livonia, Michigan. Phoenix will also develop on the site of the former George Burns Theatre with a drug store and a bank.

51156 ■ "Fighting the Borg" in *Forbes* (Vol. 174, December 27, 2004, No. 13, pp. 186)
Pub: Forbes Magazine Inc.
Ed: Christopher Steiner. Description: Wal-Mart's expansion into the food market has hurt Kroger by taking a third of its market. Kroger has been able to maintain its standing as the largest pure grocery company in the U.S.

51157 ■ "Finishing Touches: the Fashion Statement is in the Detail" in *Black Enterprise* (Vol. 37, January 2007, No. 6, pp. 106)
Pub: Earl G. Graves Publishing Co. Inc.
Ed: Sonia Alleyne. Description: Men are discovering the importance of dressing for success. Paying attention to the details such as shoes, socks, cuffs, and collars are just as important as finding the right suit.

51158 ■ "First Data: New Terminal POS Lift for Small Outfits" in *American Banker* (Vol. 172, January 17, 2006, No. 11, pp. 17)
Pub: SourceMedia, Inc.
Ed: David Breitkopf. Description: First Data Corporation has partnered with Microsoft Corporation and Hewlett Packard Company to devise a more complete point of sale terminal for small retailers. The terminal will accept most transactions and will track account information, track inventory, and work with customer relationship software.

51159 ■ "Fit For a Waif" in *Business Week* (February 20, 2006, No. 3972, pp. 14)
Pub: McGraw-Hill Companies
Ed: Louise Lee. Description: Banana Republic has introduced a size "00" to its line of women's pants, skirts, and dresses. The small size is expected to attract teen girls to the store.

51160 ■ "Flea-market bill would ban sales of certain items" in *Crain's Detroit Business* (Vol. 16, No. 49, December 4, 2000, pp. 44)
Pub: Crain Communications, Inc.
Ed: Amy Lane. Description: At the urging of Michigan retailers, legislators have introduced a bill that targets products that retailers claim thieves are prone to steal from stores then turn over to flea markets, swap meets and other "unused property markets".

51161 ■ "Flower Power" in *My Business* (February/March 2004, pp. 45-46)
Pub: My Business Magazine
Ed: Jamie Roberts. Description: Profile of John Halaris, who owns three floral KaBloom retail chains in Rhode Island. KaBloom is presently the fastest growing floral retail chain in the U.S.

51162 ■ "Food Porn" in *Forbes* (Vol. 175, February 14, 2005, No. 3, pp. 102)
Pub: Forbes Magazine Inc.
Ed: Seth Lubove. Description: Profile of John Mackey, founder of Whole Foods, who markets his food as sensual, preaching organic virtue. This strategy has helped Whole Foods to become the nation's largest natural and organic food retailer.

51163 ■ "Food/Retail Sales" in *Entrepreneur* (Vol. 32, No. 1, January 2004, pp. 206)
Pub: Entrepreneur Media, Inc.
Description: Profiles of food and retail franchises available to entrepreneurs, including candy shops.

51164 ■ "For Beall's, Bigger Is Always Better" in *Bradenton Herald* (February 14, 2005)
Pub: Bradenton Herald
Ed: Dana Sanchez. Description: The growth of Beall's Inc. from a dry-goods store to a national chain, with sales approaching $1 billion, is profiled. Retail experts analyze the key factors to explain the retailer's growth.

51165 ■ "For Big-Box Retailers, It's Market, Market, Market" in *Long Island Business News* (March 12, 2004)
Pub: Dolan Media Newswires
Ed: Claude Solnik. Description: Large retailers are scaling down plans for building stores in Long Island in order to grow in the Long Island, New York area, due to shortage of large parcels of land as well as tougher zoning restrictions.

51166 ■ "For the small retailer, life on the Internet is one big bazaar" in *The New York Times* (March 27, 2000, pp. D9)
Pub: The New York Times Company
Ed: Barbara Whitaker. Description: Profiles of GeniusBabies.com, YarnXpress.com, Pacific Cookie and others. Statistical data included.

51167 ■ "Franchisees of Huntington Station-based Relax the Back Find Success on Long Island" in *Long Island Business News* (February 6, 2004)
Pub: Dolan Media Newswires
Ed: Adina Genn. Description: Profile of Carey and CiCi Goldberg, husband and wife franchisees of Relax the Back, offering products to help find the right chair, mattress and pillow for customers in order to keep their spine aligned. The Goldbergs looked for a franchise that would allow them to target the baby boomers and senior citizens who drive the nation's economy.

51168 ■ "The franchising industry continues to heighten" in *Atlanta Business Chronicle* (Vol. 24, No. 11, August 17, 2001, pp. 48A)
Pub: American City Business Journals Inc.
Ed: Alf Nucifora. Description: Franchising generates an estimated $1 trillion annually in the U.S., with the top franchise industries including fast food, retail, service, automotive, restaurants, maintenance, building and construction, retail-food, business services, and lodging. The service sector is creating the news.

51169 ■ "A Fresh Look for Northeast Brookfield" in *Business Journal-Milwaukee* (Vol. 20, No. 51, September 5, 2003, pp. A1)
Pub: American City Business Journals, Inc.
Ed: Mark Kass. Description: As part of urban redevelopment, the city of Brookfield, Wisconsin, is considering finding a major retail or office development for the area. One company that was named as a possible candidate is Costco Wholesale Corporation.

51170 ■ "Furniture.com stages revival, forges ties with non-com allies" in *Boston Business Journal* (Vol. 22, No. 11, April 19, 2002, pp. 1)
Pub: MCP, Inc.
Description: Furniture.com Inc., which went into bankruptcy, is making a comeback by partnering with brick-and-mortar retailers like Levitz Furniture Corporation and Seaman Furniture Company Inc.; Furniture.com is being backed by Resurgence Asset Management LLC.

51171 ■ "Goodwill Gets Back Into Retail Game" in *Crain's Detroit Business* (Vol. 21, January 17, 2005, No. 3, pp. 22)
Pub: Crain Communications Inc. - Detroit
Ed: Sherri Begin. Description: Goodwill Industries of Greater Detroit will launch a retail business using the Internet. Items donated will be sold on the Website at a fixed price rather auction format. Goodwill provides employee and training services to individuals with disabilities and other special needs.

51172 ■ "Graphiti: Eking out e-commerce" in *Red Herring* (No. 103, September 1, 2001, pp. 28)
Pub: Herring Communications
Ed: Elizabeth Lamb. Description: Online retail continues with steady growth; the number of online shoppers has risen by 50 percent worldwide, from 2000. Statistical data included.

51173 ■ "Greensboro firm buys Sembler retail center" in *Atlanta Business Chronicle* (Vol. 25, January 10, 2003, No. 31, pp. 10A)
Pub: American City Business Publications, Inc.
Ed: Jarred Schenke. Description: Steven D. Bell and Company has purchased the Henry Towne Center from The Sembler Company. The 720,700-square foot center was sold for around $50 million. Bassett Furniture Industries Inc. will open a store near the Mall of Georgia.

51174 ■ "Group Buys Bradenton, Fla.-Area Retail Center" in *Bradenton Herald* (January 5, 2005)
Pub: Bradenton Herald
Ed: Matt Griswold. Description: Kash n' Karry was purchased by New York real estate firm Gemini Real Estate Advisors LLC and 10 other investors, for the sum of $15.2 million. The store is located in the Ranch Lake Plaza in Bradenton, Florida. Gemini Real Estate

Advisors LLC is one of many nationwide companies focusing on tenant-in-common, 1031 exchanges. This process allows individuals to invest with a large firm in tax-free pieces of commercial real estate.

51175 ■ "Guaranteed Results" in *Entrepreneur* (Vol. 33, March 2005, No. 3, pp. 87)
Pub: Entrepreneur Media Inc.
Ed: Gwen Moran. Description: Tips for offering money-back guarantees are offered, stressing the importance of spelling out terms, use guarantees selectively, and promise only what you can control.

51176 ■ "Handleman's reliance on Kmart, Wal-Mart troubles some" in *Crain's Detroit Business* (Vol. 18, No. 23, June 10, 2002, pp. 17)
Pub: Crain Communications Inc. - Detroit
Ed: Brent Snavely. Description: Music distributor, Handleman Co., reported sales of $1.34 billion for 2001, but the company remains vulnerable because more than 70 percent of its sales come from Kmart Corporation and Wal-Mart Stores Inc.

51177 ■ "Happy Returns" in *Entrepreneur* (Vol. 32, No. 1, January 2004, pp. 39)
Pub: Entrepreneur Media, Inc.
Ed: Melissa Campanelli. Description: The importance of repeat business from customers, for both online retailers and brick-and-mortar businesses is discussed.

51178 ■ "Happy Returns" in *Entrepreneur. com* (Vol. 34, January 2006, No. 1, pp. 40)
Pub: Entrepreneur Media Inc.
Ed: Melissa Campanelli. Description: Online retailers should make the return process as easy as possible for customers by using a prepaid return label or box, give a longer time for returns, and to look at returns as an opportunity by providing good customer service.

51179 ■ "The Hidden Value of Slow Sellers" in *Inc.* (October 2005, pp. 36)
Pub: Inc. Magazine
Description: According to a recent study that tracked sales at an online grocery store, a reduced choice of products led to a drop in sales, and fewer customers.

51180 ■ "Hiring True Believers" in *Sacramento Bee* (November 14, 2005)
Pub: The Sacramento Bee
Ed: Rachel Osterman. Description: Many retailers hire loyal customers during the holiday season because they understand that shoppers who know and love their store can be the best possible sales staff.

51181 ■ "Hispantelligence Report" in *Hispanic Business* (October 2006, pp. 10)
Pub: Hispanic Business
Description: Presentation of the Hispanic Business Stock Index shows the current value of thirteen Hispanic companies from January 3 through July 7, 2006. Hispanic-owned businesses by sales and receipts are presented.

51182 ■ "History Lesson" in *Entrepreneur* (Vol. 33, September 2005, No. 9, pp. 19)
Pub: Entrepreneur Media Inc.
Ed: Sara Wilson. Description: Melissa and Randy Rolston, founders of the Victorian Trading Company in Kansas, wholesale and retail Victorian-themed artifacts and antiques. The couple started with a $200 investment in 1986 and project 2005 sales to hit $15 million.

51183 ■ "Hollywood, Fla., Men's Shop is Tailor-Made for Success" in *South Florida Sun-Sentinel* (January 3, 2005)
Pub: South Florida Sun-Sentinel
Ed: Karen-Janine Cohen. Description: Profile of Berlin, one of the oldest stores in Hollywood, Florida. The store is run by co-founder Lewis Cohen and his daughter Ronnie Cohen Coaches, who also serves as the stores personal shopper assisting customers in their purchases.

51184 ■ "Home Depot Swings into Spring Hiring Season" in *Atlanta Journal-Constitution* (January 30, 2007)
Pub: Cox Newspapers, Inc.
Ed: Matt Kempner. Description: Home Depot shares its plan to create 15,000 new jobs nationwide. The retailer added the same number in 2006.

51185 ■ "Hot Kicks, Cool Price" in *Black Enterprise* (Vol. 37, December 2006, No. 5, pp. 34)
Pub: Earl G. Graves Publishing Co. Inc.
Ed: Topher Sanders. Description: Stephon Marbury of the New York Nicks introduced a new basketball shoe, the Starbury One, costing $14.98. The shoes are an addition to the Starbury clothing line and although the privately owned company would not disclose figures; stores sold out of a month's worth of inventory in merely three days.

51186 ■ "Hot Stuff" in *Entrepreneur* (Vol. 32, No. 2, February 2004, pp. 43)
Pub: Entrepreneur Media, Inc.
Description: E-commerce analysts are researching the best online retail areas, predicting growth in food and beverage sales, used sporting goods, home products such as hardware, flowers and health and beauty products. Statistical data included.

51187 ■ "Houston-Based Restaurant Chain Uses Mystery Shoppers to Ensure Quality" in *Beaumont Enterprise* (January 24, 2005)
Pub: Beaumont Enterprise
Ed: Rachel Stone. Description: Restaurants, department stores, movie theaters, hotels, apartment complexes, banks, law firms, and many other businesses are using mystery shoppers to evaluate their businesses.

51188 ■ "How to beat the big-box retailers" in *Hispanic Business* (Vol. 22, No. 6, June 2000, pp. 110)
Pub: Hispanic Business
Ed: Christopher D. Lancette, Scott Williams, Joel Russell. Description: Hispanic-owned hardware reseller Analytical Computer Services ranks 114th in the Hispanic Business 500 table with revenues totaling $33.6 million in 1999.

51189 ■ "How Blue Will Christmas Be? As sales keep plunging, retailers are panicking" in *Fortuneit* (Vol. 146, No. 9, Nov. 11, 2002, pp. 127)
Pub: Time Inc.
Ed: Cora Daniels. Description: Predictions regarding the retail conditions for Christmas 2002 are discussed. Since retail accounts for 23 percent of the U.S. gross domestic product, the holiday season is crucial.

51190 ■ "How I Did It" in *Inc.* (Volume 28, January 2006, No. 1, pp. 86-88)
Pub: Inc. Magazine
Ed: Sasha Issenberg. Description: In an interview, Joe Sitt, explains how he has lured the nation's top retail chains into inner cities and yuppie downtown communities.

51191 ■ "How To Beat WalMart" in *Business 2.0* (Vol. 6, May 2005, No. 4, pp. 108-114)
Pub: Time, Inc.
Ed: Matthew Maier. Description: Four rules to help companies to compete with a nearby WalMart store, along with ways to not compete.

51192 ■ "How To Crack Big-Box Retail" in *Inc.* (October 1, 2004)
Pub: Inc. Magazine
Ed: Rod Kurtz. Description: Ways to land a small business' product on the shelves of big-box retailers are explored.

**51193 ■ *How Walmart is Destroying America (And the World): And What You Can Do About It*
Pub: Ten Speed Press
Ed: Bill Quinn. Released: April 2005. Price: $10.95. Description: Wal-Mart employs 1.5 million employees and operates more than 3,500 stores, making it the largest private employer globally. Wal-Mart's impact on mom-and-pop business is discussed.

51194 ■ "Hypermediation: Commerce as Clickstream" in *Harvard Business Review* (Vol. 78, No. 1, January 2000, pp. 46)
Pub: Harvard Business School Publishing Corp.
Ed: Nicholas G. Carr. Description: On the Web, profits will be made a penny at a time.

51195 ■ "If You Build It" in *Entrepreneur* (Vol. 31, No. 8, August 2003, pp. 30)
Pub: Entrepreneur Media, Inc.
Ed: Steve Cooper. Description: eBrain Market Research/Consumer Electronics Association present a survey asking consumers what features in a Web site make them more apt to purchase a product. Statistical data included.

51196 ■ "If You Market, They Will Come" in *Success* (Vol. 47, No. 1, January 2000, pp. 50)
Pub: Success Publishing, Inc.
Ed: Rivka Tadjer. Description: Three easy steps to draw customers to your online store.

51197 ■ "In the Mood" in *Entrepreneur* (Vol. 33, October 2005, No. 10, pp. 130)
Pub: Entrepreneur Media Inc.
Ed: Don Debelak. Description: Overcoming retailer resistance when introducing a new product is discussed using the story of an entrepreneur who was trying to sell her interior home lighting products to retailers.

51198 ■ "In-Rel May Grow Further in Memphis" in *Memphis Business Journal* (Vol. 25, No. 16, August 15, 2003, pp. 3)
Pub: American City Business Journals
Ed: Kate Miller Morton. Description: Lake Worth, Florida-based In-Rel Management Inc. has acquired the Clark Tower in Memphis, Tennessee for $40.1 million. The firm buys and manages commercial and retail properties.

51199 ■ "In Retail Fashion" in *Black Enterprise* (Vol. 35, December 2004, No. 5, pp. 84)
Pub: Earl G. Graves Publishing Co. Inc.
Ed: Sonia Alleyne. Description: A college student seeking a retail management position is also interested in retail marketing and fabric designs.

51200 ■ "In retail, discounters beat out high-end stores" in *Atlanta Business Chronicle* (Vol. 25, January 10, 2003, No. 31, pp. 23A)
Pub: American City Business Publications, Inc.
Ed: Tom Barry. Description: The Georgia Economic Outlook 2003 survey indicates that in the coming months, inexpensive goods will fare better than luxury items in the retail sector.

51201 ■ "In Search of...Can Customers Search Your Website-And Actually Find What They Need?" in *Entrepreneur* (Vol. 32, November 2004, No. 11)
Pub: Entrepreneur Media Inc.
Ed: Melissa Campanelli. Description: Netpreneurs are improving search functions in order to compete with the success of Google. Options for upgrading Web sites are offered.

51202 ■ "Indian Retail Reform" in *The Economist* (Vol. 376, July 16-22, 2005, No. 8435, pp. 39-40)
Pub: The Economist Newspaper Ltd.
Description: Wal-Mart and other American companies are working to break into India's retail sector, which has been closed to outsiders for a long time. Many large retailers are using India as a significant source of supplies to support their efforts.

51203 ■ "Industry Fights Law on Violent Video Games" in *Crain's Detroit Business* (Vol. 21, October 24, 2005, No. 43, pp. 1)
Pub: Crain Communications Inc. - Detroit
Ed: Andrew Dietderich. Description: If passed, a new law would limit the sale or rental of certain violent video games to individuals under the age of 17. Retailers could be fined up to $5,000 for each offense.

51204 ■ "Inking the Deal" in *Kiplinger's Personal Finance Magazine* (Vol. 54, No. 12, December 2000, pp. 26)
Pub: The Kiplinger Washington Editors, Inc.
Ed: Catherine Siskos. Description: This holiday season, online retailers are publishing print catalogs to attract customers.

51205 ■ "Inside Job" in *Entrepreneur* (Vol. 33, March 2005, No. 3, pp. 132)
Pub: Entrepreneur Media Inc.
Ed: Nichole L. Torres. Description: According to a survey financed by the National Retail Federation, students and parents are spending $2.6 billion on dorm room and apartment furnishings for college living spaces.

51206 ■ "The Inside Scoop: One Expert's Take on Today's Retail Scene" in *Entrepreneur* (Vol. 32, July 2004, No. 7, pp. 70)
Pub: Entrepreneur Media Inc.
Ed: Gwen Moran. Description: An interview with Paco Underhill, consumer behavior specialist, discusses retail trends to help increase sales.

51207 ■ "Inspirational Notes" in *Black Enterprise* (Vol. 36, December 2005, No. 5, pp. 138)
Pub: Earl G. Graves Publishing Co. Inc.
Description: Profile of Sheraun Britton-Parris, who launched an inspirational t-shirt company. According to Marketdata Enterprises Inc., Americans are seeking psychological sustenance and motivational products made up 55 percent of retail sales in 2003.

51208 ■ "Internet Opens World of Sales" in *Roanoke Times* (January 21, 2005)
Pub: Roanoke Times
Ed: Jenny Kincaid. Description: Retailers are selling items that don't sell in their shops on eBay and other online auction sites. Libby Snider-Chittum, an eBay Internet specialist with Business Seed Capital in Roanoke, Virginia, works with small businesses that are expanding or in need of business loans. Snider-Chittum offers seminars for small companies in rural communities and individuals to teach them how to sell items, personal or business, on eBay.

51209 ■ "Internet Tax Won't Be Collected Anytime Soon" in *Crain's Detroit Business* (Vol. 17, No. 44, October 22, 2001, pp. 3)
Pub: Crain Communications, Inc.
Ed: Amy Lane, Brent Snavely. Description: The State of Michigan joins a multistate table to collect more taxes from Internet and mail-order companies, but it could be 2003 before collection begins.

51210 ■ "It's Down to a Waiting Game" in *Tampa Tribune* (December 24, 2005)
Pub: Media General, Inc.
Description: Procrastinators had retailers frustrated over holiday sales in December 2005. According to a survey conducted by the International Council of Shopping Centers, many consumers wait until after December 18 to do their Christmas shopping.

51211 ■ "It's an investment: Events require funds, planning" in *Atlanta Business Chronicle* (Vol. 24, No. 14, September 7, 2001, pp. S17)
Pub: American City Business Journals Inc.
Ed: Mary Kirkman. Description: Kristy Trenaman, Humana Inc.'s corporate communications manager, Eddie Kraft, Nanz & Kraft Florists part-owner, and Robin Hall, Dant Clayton Corporation's bid administrator, talk about budgeting for anniversary events planning. Anniversary celebrations are ways to gain employee loyalty and increase sales, having proven to be successful in these areas.

51212 ■ "It's OK If You Shop Til You Drop" in *Tampa Tribune* (November 19, 2005)
Pub: Media General, Inc.
Ed: Ted Jackovics. Description: Quick Quality Care is opening mini-clinics in retail stores offering non-emergency medical treatment to shoppers. Shoppers check in and are given a beeper to carry enabling them to shop until they can be seen by a medical professional.

51213 ■ "It's That Time of Season" in *Entrepreneur* (Vol. 31, No. 8, August 2003, pp. 75)
Pub: Entrepreneur Media, Inc.
Ed: Catherine Seda. Description: Summer provides the perfect environment to increase online shopping for the holiday season by using perks such as free shipping, clearances, featured sale items, suggested items, and gift idea centers or personal shoppers.

51214 ■ "January Retail Sales Will Exaggerate Consumer Spending Strength" in *Kiplinger Letter* (Vol. 78, January 19, 2007, No. 2)
Pub: Kiplinger
Description: Gift cards sold during the holidays are likely to spur retail sales for January 2007. Retail sales are expected to hit 3.5 percent for 2007, lower than last year's 4 percent.

51215 ■ "Java Enabled" in *Entrepreneur* (Vol. 32, December 2004, No. 12, pp. 164)
Pub: Entrepreneur Media Inc.
Ed: April Y. Pennington. Description: Profile of Jeremy Gursey, founder of Mocha Kiss Coffee. Gursey runs catered coffee bars, retail stores on movie lots that serve hot and ice-blended coffee beverages, and sells gourmet coffee beans to wholesalers.

51216 ■ "Join the club?" in *Black Enterprise* (Vol. 33, No. 6, January 2003, pp. 87)
Pub: Earl Graves Publishing Co.
Description: The use of purchasing a card club for shopping is discussed, stressing the importance of comparison shopping to save money.

51217 ■ "Jolting Joe" in *Washington Business Journal* (Vol. 22, No. 12, July 25, 2003, pp. 23)
Pub: Washington Business Journal
Ed: Eleni Kretikos. Description: Dwayne Walker, operational chief of M.E. Swing Coffee Roasters, has been working at the 87-year-old coffee company since 1989. The coffee company's retail operations expanded after new city regulations forced it to halt wholesaling roasting.

51218 ■ "Katrina Cottages At Lowe's" in *Mississippi Business Journal* (Vol. 28, September 2006, No. 36, pp. 23)
Pub: Venture Publications, Inc.
Description: Lowe's Companies Inc. is now selling several designs of Katrina Cottages, designed to withstand heavy rain and winds up to 140 miles per hour. Katrina Cottages meet new hurricane codes and International Building Code and range from 544 square feet to 1,340 square feet.

51219 ■ "Kirkland's, Gap Will Close At Leases' End" in *Bradenton Herald* (January 22, 2005)
Pub: Bradenton Herald
Ed: Kurt D. Schultheis. Description: Both Kirkland's and the Gap plan to close stores in the DeSoto Square Mall when their leases expire; a spokesperson for the Gap declined comment; Wendy Scott, district manager for Kirkland's reports that the company is in no danger.

51220 ■ "Kmart cuts 46 jobs at Troy HQ" in *Crain's Detroit Business* (Vol. 16, No. 49, December 4, 2000, pp. 4)
Pub: Crain Communications, Inc.
Ed: Brent Snavely. Description: Kmart Corporation's restructuring effort has claimed 46 jobs, and could result in more cuts. The positions were eliminated in early November from a department that manages merchandise buying. The employees did receive severance packages based on length of service.

51221 ■ "Kmart scurries to tie loose ends as approval of Ch. 11 plan nears" in *Crain's Detroit Business* (Vol. 19, No. 15, April 14, 2003)
Pub: Crain Communications Inc., Detroit
Ed: Brent Snavely. Description: Information regarding Kmart Corporation's bankruptcy is discussed, including bids for 64 leases from retailers including Lowe's Companies Inc., J.C. Penney Company Inc. and Target Corporation.

51222 ■ "Kmart closings to take another slice from Little Caesar" in *Crain's Detroit Business* (Vol. 19, No. 4, January 27, 2003, pp. 7)
Pub: Crain Communications Inc., Detroit
Ed: Brent Snavely. Description: The proposed closing of 326 Kmart stores will also close 101 Little Caesar Pizza Stations located inside the retail stores. Contracts between the two companies lapsed in August 2002 and the two companies have been in negotiations for at least six months.

51223 ■ "Kmart Makes Branding Pro Its New Chief" in *Black Enterprise* (Vol. 35, December 2004, No. 5, pp. 33)
Pub: Earl G. Graves Publishing Co. Inc.
Ed: Sonia Alleyne. Description: Kmart's appointment of Aylwin Lewis makes him the sixth African American to head a Fortune 500 company at this time, eighth to ever hold the position. Kmart believes Lewis' strong reputation for branding and team building will increase the retailer's profits. Statistical data included.

51224 ■ "Kohl's Announces Plans to Open Its First Baltimore County, Md. Store" in *Baltimore Sun* (April 11, 2003)
Pub: Knight-Ridder/Tribune Business News
Ed: Lorraine Mirabella. Description: Kohl's Corporation plans to open its first store in Baltimore Country, Maryland to anchor the redeveloped Yorkridge Shopping Center in Lutherville.

51225 ■ "Kohl's, Lowe's Set to Move into WNY" in *Business First Buffalo* (Vol. 19, No. 47, August 15, 2003, pp. 1)
Pub: American City Business Journals, Inc.
Ed: James Fink. Description: Plans by Kohl's Department Stores and Lowe's Companies to open stores in the greater Buffalo, New York area are discussed.

51226 ■ "La Habra, Calif., Entrepreneur Starts Errand-Running Service for Busy Workers" in *San Gabriel Valley Tribune* (July 8, 2004)
Pub: San Gabriel Valley Tribune
Ed: Andrew Blazier. Description: Profile of Sherri Durbin, owner of Consider It Done!, a new errand service. Durbin charges $32 per hour for services performed by her team of six independent contractors. Durban also founded an international mystery shopping and staffing company that she continues to manage.

51227 ■ "Last-Minute Shoppers Boost Holiday Retail Sales" in *Sacramento Bee* (December 29, 2005)
Pub: The Sacramento Bee
Ed: Jon Ortiz. Description: Last minute shoppers increased sales for many retailers in the Sacramento area, setting a strong finish to the 2005 shopping season. Chain store sales were reported up by 2.8 percent for the week before Christmas Day.

51228 ■ "Later Easter, War Crimp March Retail Sales" in *Atlanta Journal-Constitution* (April 11, 2003)
Pub: Knight-Ridder/Tribune Business News
Ed: Renee DeGross. Description: Cooler weather concerns, the Iraqi War, and a late Easter all contributed to lower retail sales for March 2003. Statistical data included.

51229 ■ "Legislation aims to tax Internet sales" in *Crain's Detroit Business* (Vol. 19, No. 1, January 6, 2003, pp. 20)
Pub: Crain Communications Inc., Detroit
Ed: Amy Lane. Description: The State of Michigan is considering imposing a multi-state agreement that would streamline processes for collecting sales tax on Internet purchases. The Michigan Department of Treasury estimates tax losses of $273 in the current fiscal year.

51230 ■ "Letting A Store's Expert Do Shopping Can Make Choices Easier, Quicker" in *Orange County Register* (December 23, 2004)
Pub: Freedom Communications Inc.
Ed: Jit Fong Chin. Description: Profile of Sascha Cewe, a personal shopper at Saks Fifth Avenue in Orange County, Florida.

51231 ■ "Lights, camera, action" in *Entrepreneur* (Vol. 31, No. 4, April 2003, pp. 126)
Pub: Entrepreneur Media Inc.
Ed: Don Debelak. Description: Steps to take in order to get a new product featured on a home shopping network are presented.

51232 ■ "Loehmann's New Owner Keeps the Faith" in *Fortune* (Vol. 151, February 7, 2005, No. 3, pp. 26)
Pub: Time Inc.
Ed: Barney Gimbel. Description: Profile of Bahrain's First Islamic Investment Bank, a Middle East-based investment firm located in the U.S. Through its American subsidiary, Crescent Capital Investment, the company has invested $2 billion into the U.S. market, particularly businesses that don't sell alcohol, charge interest, or allow gambling, produce tobacco, make unwholesome entertainment, or deal with pork.

51233 ■ "Lord and Taylor Exit Leave Hole" in *Pittsburgh Business Times* (Vol. 23, No. 2, August 1, 2003, pp. 1)
Pub: Pittsburgh Business Times
Ed: Tim Schooley. Description: Lord and Taylor, owned by May Department Stores Company, will close its store in downtown Pittsburgh, Pennsylvania; the 125,000 square foot store opened only three years ago.

51234 ■ "Luring MP3ers Back to the Mall" in *Business 2.0* (Vol. 7, January/February 2006, No. 1, pp. 32)
Pub: Time, Inc.
Ed: Rob Levine. Description: Sam Goody hopes hip9 new listening lounges will lure MP3 fans back to the mall. Retail experts give their opinions.

51235 ■ "Lyon Twp. apple orchard eyed for $70M development" in *Crain's Detroit Business* (Vol. 19, No. 13, March 31, 2003, pp. 6)
Pub: Crain Communications Inc., Detroit
Ed: Andrew Dietderich. Description: Plans to clear a popular 191-acre apple orchard in Lyon Township, Michigan are underway. The plans call for single-family homes and attached condominiums and nearly 120,000 square feet of retail space.

51236 ■ "Macy's Adds a Restaurant" in *Sacramento Bee* (December 20, 2005)
Pub: The Sacramento Bee
Ed: Jon Ortiz. Description: Sacramento's Macy's store opened a Cosi restaurant that will employee 30 people. The casual restaurant will offer salads, sandwiches, pizza, soups, bagels, gourmet coffees and desserts. Cosi Inc. runs more than 90 restaurants in 17 states across the nation and plans to open about 500 between 2005 and 2009.

51237 ■ "Mail Carriers Bring Home the Goods for Holiday Online Shoppers" in *Portland Press Herald* (December 22, 2005)
Pub: Blethen Maine Newspapers, Inc.
Ed: Elbert Aull. Description: U.S. Postal Service officials in Maine reported mail volume two to three times greater than normal on Wednesday, December 21, 2005, due in part to online holiday shopping.

51238 ■ "Making Sense of Scanner Data" in *Harvard Business Review* (Vol. 78, No. 2, March 2000, pp. 24)
Pub: Harvard Business School Publishing Corp.
Ed: Peter Rossi, Phil DeLurgio, David Kantor. Description: A new statistical technique, called Bayesian shrinkage, can help manufacturers target their retail promotions.

51239 ■ "Mall Makeover" in *South Florida Business Journal* (Vol. 23, No. 52, August 1, 2003, pp. 35)
Pub: American City Business Journals
Ed: Chad Heiges. Description: The Galleria mall in Fort Lauderdale, Florida plans to add new upscale stores, offer new signs and reorganize parking after renovations are completed in February 2004.

51240 ■ "Man Power: Tips To Get Male Shoppers Spending in Your Store" in *Entrepreneur* (Vol. 32, October 2004, No. 10, pp. 91)
Pub: Entrepreneur Media Inc.
Ed: Nancy Michaels. Description: Tips for marketing to men are presented.

51241 ■ "Manny, Moe, & Jack Are In the Driver's Seat" in *License!* (Vol. 6, No. 6, July 2003, pp. 22)
Pub: Advantstar Communications, Inc.
Ed: Teresa Andreoli. Description: Pep Boys, the auto aftermarket retail and service chain, will begin licensing property for apparel, accessories, and toys for kids, as well as novelty collectibles and how-to books for car maintenance and repair for adults.

51242 ■ "Many unhappy returns" in *Entrepreneur* (Vol. 31, No. 6, June 2003, pp. 74)
Pub: Entrepreneur Media Inc.
Ed: Joanne Cleaver. Description: Jim Dion, retail consultant, advises his clients to add a complaint and returns section to a customer database in order to track customer services.

51243 ■ "Marketers Hang Their Hopes on Holiday Promotions" in *Sacramento Bee* (December 21, 2005)
Pub: The Sacramento Bee
Ed: Jon Ortiz. Description: Companies depend on holiday marketing promotions in order to increase sales. Seasonal packaging plans begin during the summer before each Christmas holiday, can boost a company's sales, and increase brand recognition while making a statement about a company's self-image.

51244 ■ "A Matter of Opinion" in *Entrepreneur* (Vol. 31, No. 8, August 2003, pp. 72)
Pub: Entrepreneur Media, Inc.
Ed: Elizabeth Goodgold. Description: According to Jeffrey G. Jordan, market researcher for 1-on-One Marketing Associates, mystery shopping, customer comment cards, on-site intercepting, Web site evaluation and toll-free telephone numbers are great ways to get customer feedback.

51245 ■ "Mega Wal-Marts Crush Business Diversity" in *Bellingham Business Journal* (January 2007, pp. C14)
Pub: Sun News Inc.
Description: Small businesses are the backbone of the Bellingham economy. Wal-Mart threatens the economic diversity by flattening competition and erasing longtime family-owned businesses.

51246 ■ "Milwaukee Businesswoman Opens Plus-Size Clothing Store to Fill Need" in *Milwaukee Journal Sentinel* (November 16, 2003)
Pub: Journal Sentinel
Ed: Tannette Johnson-Elie. Description: Profile of Cynthia Simpson, a plus-size African American woman who opened a store to meet the shopping needs of larger women, focusing on African American women who prefer trendy clothing with an Afrocentric flair.

51247 ■ "Mind Your Pricing Cues" in *Harvard Business Review* (Vol. 81, No. 9, September 2003, pp. 96)
Pub: Harvard Business School Press
Ed: Eric Anderson, Duncan Simester. Description: Research on buying habits are documented here. Some aspects of the research includes: pricing goods that end in 9 increased sales ($34 versus $39.99), sales signs can have a positive or negative effect, and the fact that too many signs results in lower sales.

51248 ■ "Mitch Siegler: 41 President of Sovietski collection in San Diego" in *Entrepreneur* (Vol. 30, No. 1, January 2002, pp. 19)
Pub: Entrepreneur Media Inc.
Ed: April Pennington. Description: Profile of the catalog marketer of gear, gifts and collectibles from Russia and Eastern Europe, Mitch Siegler.

51249 ■ "Money Corner" in *Home Business* (Vol. 13, January/February 2006, No. 1, pp. 78)
Pub: Home Business Magazine
Description: Small Business Administration loans, retirement information, small business taxes, and Valentine's Day gift-buying tips are included.

51250 ■ "Mood Music" in *Entrepreneur* (Vol. 31, No. 9, July 2003, pp. 79)
Pub: Entrepreneur Media, Inc.
Ed: Elizabeth Goodgold. Description: A marketing consultant addresses ways that music can be used to increase sales. Some retailers are actually defined by the style of music used in their shops.

51251 ■ "More Bang for Your Buck" in *Entrepreneur* (Vol. 32)
Pub: Entrepreneur Media Inc.
Ed: Nichole L. Torres. Description: Associated Surplus Dealers/Associated Merchandise Dealers (ASD/MD) Trade Show Las Vegas, produced by VNU Expositions, offers small business entrepreneurs and eBay resellers a cost-effective venue for selling products. The show includes 3,500 exhibitors with products ranging from dollar-store merchandise to general merchandise such as toys, gifts, electronics, health and beauty, and fashion accessories.

51252 ■ "More Retail Chains Heading this Way" in *Crain's Chicago Business* (Vol. 26, No. 51, December 22, 2003, pp. 6)
Pub: Crain Communications, Inc.
Ed: H. Lee Murphy. Description: Staples Inc., Dick's Sporting Goods, Ross Stores Inc. (apparel), National Wholesale Liquidators Inc., Home Now Furniture LLC, and Anna's Linens Inc., are among the retailers looking to enter the Chicago, Illinois retail market. The new trend is prompted by the upswing in the economy, along with the closing of Montgomery Ward & Company and Service Merchandise.

51253 ■ "More Retail Chains Heading this Way; Drawn by Vacant Sites, Competitive Considerations" in *Crains Chicago Business* (Vol. 26, No. 51)
Pub: Crain Communications, Inc.
Ed: H. Lee Murphy. Description: Staples Inc., Dick's Sporting Goods, Ross Stores Inc. (apparel), National Wholesale Liquidators Inc., Home Now Furniture LLC, and Anna's Linens Inc., are among the retailers looking to enter the Chicago, Illinois retail market. The new trend is prompted by the upswing in the economy, along with the closing of Montgomery Ward & Company and Service Merchandise.

51254 ■ "More than a store: independent specialty stores are adding art installations, yoga classes" in *WWD* (Oct. 17, 2002, pp. S60)
Pub: Fairchild Publications, Inc.
Ed: Kavita Daswani. Description: Various retailers explain how they have increased profits by diversifying their inventory. Ways for retailers to expand a boutique beyond its apparel roots are presented.

51255 ■ "Murdock Carrousel Sold" in *Charlotte Observer* (January 31, 2007)
Pub: Knight-Ridder/Tribune Business News
Ed: Bob Fliss. Description: Details on the sale of the Murdock Carrousel shopping center are highlighted. The deal was reported at $281 million.

51256 ■ "My Favorite Fiascos" in *Fast Company* (November 2001, pp. 38)
Pub: Fast Company
Description: Alberto Alessi discusses his favorite business disasters, customer savvy, and customer loyalty.

51257 ■ "My Gadget" in *My Business* (June/July 2004, pp. 22)
Pub: My Business Magazine
Description: Jason Knief, owner of a beer, wine and spirits store, uses the gadget called, Whispering Windows. The device attaches to a window or other flat surface and produces smooth and steady musical sounds that attract customers.

51258 ■ "Mystery Shoppers Enjoy Being Spies" in *Atlanta Journal-Constitution* (January 29, 2005)
Pub: Atlanta Journal-Constitution
Ed: Renee DeGross. Description: Department stores and other retailers are using mystery shoppers to see their stores the way their customers see them; hotels and restaurants chains have begun using mystery shoppers also.

51259 ■ "Mystery Shoppers Help Provide Certainty for Several Major Companies" in *Chicago Tribune* (July 4, 2004)
Pub: Chicago Tribune
Ed: Becky Yerak. Description: Mystery shoppers assist businesses to improve customer service. Profile of Barb Bullock, a certified mystery shopper, is included.

51260 ■ "Mystery Shoppers Keep Eye on Customer Service" in *Washington Times* (July 8, 2004)
Pub: Washington Times
Ed: Donna DeMarco. Description: Profile of Max Jakeman, mystery shopper in Alexandria, Virginia. According to the National Center for Professional Mystery Shoppers and Merchandisers, $400-$600 million is spent annually in this field. Statistical data included.

51261 ■ "Mystery Shoppers Take a Second Glance at Customer Service" in *Business Record* (Vol. 22, August 30, 2004, No. 35, pp. 1)
Pub: Business Publication Corporation
Ed: Erin Morain. Description: Prairie Life Health & Fitness center in West Des Moines, Iowa uses mystery shoppers to conduct market research.

51262 ■ "National Shopping Service Announces 150,000th Mystery Shopper" in *Internet Wire* (October 26, 2004)
Pub: COMTEX News Network Inc.
Description: National Shopping Service provides evaluation and feedback to its customers through a mystery shopper program. The firm has more than 150,000 registered mystery shoppers performing over 30,000 client visits per month.

51263 ■ "Neuburger Outgrows Pajamas" in *San Francisco Business Times* (Vol. 17, No. 51, July 25, 2003, pp. 1)
Pub: American City Business Journals
Ed: Ryan Tate. Description: Profile of retail clothing store, Neuburger; topics include market share, market development and profits.

51264 ■ "New Chain 'Drug Stores' in Long Island Fill the Gap..." in *Long Island Business News* (January 30, 2004)
Pub: Dolan Media Newswires
Ed: Claude Solnik. Description: Profile of the new drug stores opening up in the Long Island, New York area, as well as across the country. These stores carry everything from clothing to electronics and are open extended hours, in order to fill the gap between independent grocery stores and large, big-box retailers.

51265 ■ "New Computer Sellers Bite Into Market..." in *Crain's Chicago Business* (Vol. 26, No. 50, December 15, 2003)
Pub: Crain Communications, Inc.
Ed: H. Lee Murphy. Description: MDG Computers Canada Inc., CompUSA, and Fry's Electronics are three new computer retailers to open in the Chicago, Illinois area. Experts are concerned the market will become overcrowded with computer specialists.

51266 ■ "New Computer Sellers Bite Into Market; MDG, Fry's Set to Debut, While CompUSA Grows Again" in *Crains Chicago Business* (Vol. 26)
Pub: Crain Communications, Inc.
Ed: H. Lee Murphy. Description: MDG Computers Canada Inc., CompUSA, and Fry's Electronics are three new computer retailers to open in the Chicago, Illinois area. Experts are concerned the market will become overcrowded with computer specialists.

51267 ■ "New Lease on Life" in *Small Business Opportunities* (Vol. 16, No. 1, January 2004, pp. 102-103)
Pub: Harris Publications, Inc.
Description: Profile of Charles Loudermilk, founder of Aaron's Sales Lease Ownership and Aaron's Rents Inc., providing rental, sales and lease ownership and the specialty retailing of residential and office furniture, consumer electronics, and home appliances. Aaron's operates 468 corporate stores and 232 franchises in 43 states and Puerto Rico.

51268 ■ "New Lenox Drawing Up Plans for a Big Mall" in *Chicago Tribune* (February 25, 2005)
Pub: Knight-Ridder/Tribune Business News
Ed: Stanley Ziemba. Description: Plans for a new outdoor shopping mall in New Lenox, Illinois are discussed. The development would include six or more major retailers and dozens of smaller retailers, restaurants, theaters and other amenities and attractions.

51269 ■ "New Rules Cut Health Risks from Lead in Children's Jewelry" in *Kansas City Star* (February 9, 2005)
Pub: Knight-Ridder/Tribune Business News
Ed: Paul Wenske. Description: In a move to reduce health risks for children, the U.S. Consumer Product Safety Commission has established guidelines for children's metal jewelry. New procedures for manufacturers, importers and retailers for testing lead in the jewelry have also been developed.

51270 ■ "New Shopping Centers on Tap in Fast-Growing Livingston County" in *Crain's Detroit Business* (Vol. 22, January 2, 2006, No. 1)
Pub: Crain Communications Inc. - Detroit
Ed: Sheena Harrison. Description: Construction on a new shopping center is underway in Green Oaks of Livingston County, Michigan and is expected to be one of the state's top shopping destinations. Another retail center is being planned in Hartland, Township.

51271 ■ "The New Sounds of Selling" in *Business 2.0* (Vol. 6, May 2005, No. 4, pp. 58, 60)
Pub: Time, Inc.
Ed: Thomas Mucha. Description: Smart marketers are using music clips, beeps and other sound bites to attract consumer attention quickly.

51272 ■ "Newsstand" in *Home Business* (Vol. 13, January/February 2006, No. 1, pp. 38-39)
Pub: Home Business Magazine
Description: Topics include marketing of office supplies and equipment, rising gas prices, toxic office environments, entrepreneurship, and online retailing.

51273 ■ "No Line At 6 a.m. Black Friday" in *Tampa Tribune* (December 7, 2005)
Pub: Media General, Inc.
Ed: Michael Sasso. Description: A group of independent retailers share marketing ideas they use to increase sales during the holidays, especially on Black Friday, the day after Thanksgiving.

51274 ■ "Northwest Herbs & Extracts opens in Vancouver's Uptown Village" in *Vancouver, WA Business Journal* (February 28, 2003)
Pub: Dolan Media Newswires
Ed: Charlie Devereux. Description: Profile of Northwest Herbs & Extracts, and storeowner and herbalist Julia Mercer. Mercer stocks her store with over 200 varieties of dried herbs, as well as a wide selection of essential oils, tinctures and custom tea blends.

51275 ■ **"Novel Ideas: Two Entrepreneurs Write Books About Their Experiences-And Learn Something in the Process"** in *Entrepreneur* (Vol. 32)
Pub: Entrepreneur Media Inc.
Ed: Aliza Pilar Sherman. Description: Profiles of Lisa Price, president of a manufacturing and retail company that specializes in homemade body care products and Lisa Hammons, founder and CEO of Femail Creations, a handcrafted-gift catalog and Website featuring female-focused products created by women. Both entrepreneurs wrote books about their business and personal lives and offer advice for publishing a book.

51276 ■ **"Old becomes new; Wave of practicality poses challenge to retailers this holiday season"** in *Crain's Detroit Business* (Vol. 16, No. 49)
Pub: Crain Communications, Inc.
Ed: Joseph Serwach. Description: Kmart Corporation CEO, Chuck Conaway, and other retailers said they expect a more challenging retail market this Christmas compared with the record spending experienced last year.

51277 ■ **"On the Lookout"** in *Entrepreneur* (Vol. 33, October 2005, No. 10, pp. 82)
Pub: Entrepreneur Media Inc.
Ed: Gwen Moran. Description: Watching current events and celebrity styles help retailers predict trends.

51278 ■ **"$160M plan pushed for NE Ann Arbor"** in *Crain's Detroit Business* (Vol. 19, No. 1, Jan. 6, 2003, pp. 1)
Pub: Crain Communications Inc., Detroit
Ed: Laura Bailey. Description: A proposed new development in Ann Arbor, Michigan is facing expensive environmental clean up on the site before development can begin. Neighbors in the area are concerned about the plans for development, as are existing businesses. The $160 million project would include offices, a health center, housing and retail space.

51279 ■ **"Online Sales Booming; Retailers Rethink Web Biz as Sales Increase"** in *Crain's Detroit Business* (Vol. 19, No. 1, Jan. 6, 2003, pp. 3)
Pub: Crain Communications Inc., Detroit
Ed: Brent Snavely. Description: Total consumer online sales were up 29 percent during the period November 1 and December 20, 2002. This increase has many retailers rethinking their online sales potential. Tips for developing successful Web sites are presented.

51280 ■ **"Online Sales Continue To Climb at L.L. Bean, Other Retailers"** in *Portland Press Herald* (December 13, 2005)
Pub: Blethen Maine Newspapers, Inc.
Ed: Edward D. Murphy. Description: L.L. Bean reports a 47 percent rise in sales over 2004. Other online retailers are also experiencing increased sales in 2004.

51281 ■ **"Online Shoppers Begin Their Quest in Earnest"** in *Sacramento Bee* (November 28, 2005)
Pub: The Sacramento Bee
Ed: Jim Wasserman. Description: Cyber Monday is the Monday after Thanksgiving. It is expected to be the largest online shopping day of the year, with spending reaching more than $400 million for the day.

51282 ■ **"Online Sites are Registering with Couples"** in *HFN* (January 26, 2004, pp. 22)
Pub: Fairchild Publications
Ed: Faye Musselman. Description: Only 16 percent of bridal couples register on Internet registries, the numbers are growing. A listing of Web sites offering bridal registries and their specialties is presented.

51283 ■ **"Panorama Place"** in *San Fernando Valley Business Journal* (Vol. 12, January 2007, No. 1, pp. 13)
Pub: San Fernando Valley Business Journal Associates
Description: Maefield Development will break ground on a retail center and 500-unit condominium complex in a central Panorama City community that has been suffering since the closing of Montgomery Ward.

51284 ■ **"Patterns of Disruption in Retailing"** in *Harvard Business Review* (Vol. 78, No. 1, January 2000, pp. 42)
Pub: Harvard Business School Publishing Corp.
Ed: Clayton M. Christensen, Richard S. Tedlow. Description: The past may not tell us everything about the future of electronic commerce, but it reveals more than we might expect.

51285 ■ **"PayPal Pushes For Business Use; A Hit With Consumers"** in *Investor's Business Daily* (October 24, 2003, pp. A04)
Pub: Investor's Business Daily, Inc.
Ed: Pete Barlas. Description: Online payment firms are betting on Internet retail credit card sales to continue growth. Profile of the partnership created by PayPal and Cybersource Corporation is included.

51286 ■ **"Penney"** in *Business Week* (January 9, 2006, No. 3966, pp. 82, 84)
Pub: McGraw-Hill Companies
Ed: Robert Berner. Description: Profile of Myron "Mike" Ullman III, chief executive for J.C. Penney's, who has launched new brand management techniques to boost the retailer's sales and earnings.

51287 ■ **"Personal Business"** in *Business Week* (January 9, 2006, No. 3966, pp. 94)
Pub: McGraw-Hill Companies
Ed: Mara der Hovanesian. Description: Topics include a takeover of auto lender Americredit, overseas shipping, and retail shopping in China.

51288 ■ **"Personal Shoppers Give Clients a Stress-Free Alternative to Shopping"** in *Colorado Springs Business Journal* (December 10, 2004)
Pub: Dolan Media Newswires
Ed: Stephanie Cline. Description: Many department stores offer personal shopping services to their customers. Profile of Mary Smith, a personal shopper, is included.

51289 ■ **"Pines Tract Plans Unveiled"** in *Miami Herald* (March 9, 2005)
Pub: Knight-Ridder/Tribune Business News
Ed: Patrick Danner. Description: Real estate investment trust, Duke Realty Corporation, announced plans to develop 40 acres in Pembroke Pines. The retail development will include 400,000 square feet of space, and eight office buildings may also be built.

51290 ■ **"Plantation, Fla., Mayor Blasts Aggressive Mall Kiosk Sales Tactics"** in *South Sun-Sentinel* (October 10, 2003)
Pub: Knight Ridder/Tribune Business News
Ed: Jeremy Milarsky. Description: Mayor Rae Carole Armstrong, Plantation, Florida, is unhappy with the aggressive sales tactics used by kiosks at an area mall. Armstrong met mall management about its policy regarding hawking by workers at the kiosks.

51291 ■ **"Plato's Closet, a Retail Outlet, Sells Teenagers Brand-Name Labels for Less"** in *Long Island Business News* (March 5, 2004)
Pub: Dolan Media Newswires
Ed: Adina Genn. Description: Profile of Plato's Closet, a retail outlet offering used, current teen fashions with designer labels from Abercrombie & Fitch, Bebe, South Pole and Tommy Hilfiger, with an average price of $10. Plato's Closet offers franchise opportunities.

51292 ■ **"Portland, Maine, Surplus Store Sells Clothes From Flooded Mississippi Mall"** in *Portland Press Herald* (September 20, 2005)
Pub: Blethen Maine Newspapers, Inc.
Ed: Tux Turkel. Description: Marden's Surplus & Salvage is a salvage company that does business after major disasters. The company is selling items from Gulf Coast stores impacted by the hurricanes last summer.

51293 ■ **"Portland's Small Retailers Launch 'Independents' Day' Campaign to Buy Locally"** in *Portland Press Herald* (December 23, 2005)
Pub: Blethen Maine Newspapers, Inc.

Ed: Edward D. Murphy. Description: Nearly two dozen Portland, Maine retailers are planning a campaign to encourage consumers and businesses to buy from local stores and suppliers.

51294 ■ **"The Power of the Group"** in *Black Enterprise* (Vol. 34, No. 4, November 2003, pp. 165)
Pub: Earl Graves Publishing Co.
Ed: Shayna T. Bayard. Description: The advantages of membership privileges are overviewed, profiling the benefits of AAA membership.

51295 ■ **"Power Shopping"** in *Entrepreneur* (Vol. 28, No. 4, April 2000, pp. 62)
Pub: Entrepreneur Media Inc.
Ed: Cynthia E. Griffin. Description: When it comes to shopping for clothing, household items and cars, studies have shown women wield a tremendous amount of influence.

51296 ■ **"Price Fix"** in *Entrepreneur* (Vol. 33, September 2005, No. 9, pp. 56)
Pub: Entrepreneur Media Inc.
Ed: C.J. Prince. Description: Small business owners are watching their industries larger retailers and manufacturers for insight into pricing goods.

51297 ■ **"PriceSmart Doubles Profits: PriceSmart Inc."** in *San Diego Business Journal* (Vol. 28, January 15, 2007, No. 3, pp. 10)
Pub: San Diego Business Journal Associates
Ed: Mike Allen. Description: PriceSmart Inc., San Diego-based operator of warehouse retail stores located mainly in the Caribbean, reported $202.5 million in revenue for 2006.

51298 ■ **"Primal Need"** in *Entrepreneur.com* (Vol. 34, February 2006, No. 2, pp. 20)
Pub: Entrepreneur Media Inc.
Ed: April Y. Pennington. Description: According to Patrick Hanlon, founder and CEO of Thinktopia, customers need to feel a bond with a particular brand in order to make purchases.

51299 ■ **"Private Matters: Retail Alert: Keep an Eye on New RFID Privacy Legislation"** in *Entrepreneur* (Vol. 32, October 2004, No. 10, pp. 38)
Pub: Entrepreneur Media Inc.
Ed: Amanda C. Kooser. Description: Wireless capabilities that track products as they move through the supply chain, known as radio frequency identification (RFID) are growing in popularity with retailers. Several states are considering privacy legislation to regulate RFID so companies could not collect and use data collected regarding customers.

51300 ■ **"Protect Your Profits"** in *Small Business Opportunities* (Vol. 12, No. 2, March 2000, pp. 20)
Pub: Harris Publications, Inc.
Ed: Marie Sherlock. Description: Criminal sociologist, Rosemary Erickson, provides tips for small business owners to protect their enterprise against robberies.

51301 ■ **"Q&A"** in *Home Office Computing* (Vol. 18, No. 7, July 2000, pp. 13)
Pub: Scholastic Inc.
Ed: Cristina Gair. Description: Jay Westermeier, attorney at Piper, Maybury, Rudnick & Wolfe, in Washington, D.C., discusses ways to avoid legal problems when selling goods and services online.

51302 ■ **"Quick Fix: Do SBA Express Loans Really Shortchange Entrepreneurs?"** in *Entrepreneur* (Vol. 32, No. 4, April 2004, pp. 27)
Pub: Entrepreneur Media, Inc.
Ed: Julie Monahan. Description: Profile of the U.S. Small Business Administration's Express program that guaranteed loans to thousands of entrepreneurs. Retailers with gross sales of $6 million or less, wholesalers with 100 employees or less, and manufacturers with 500 employees or less, are eligible for Express Loans.

51303 ■ *QuickBooks X for Dummies*
Pub: John Wiley & Sons, Incorporated
Ed: Stephen L. Nelson. **Released:** November 2006.
Price: $21.99. **Description:** Key features of Quick-
Books software for small business are introduced. Invoicing and credit memos, recoding sales receipts,
accounting, budgeting, taxes, payroll, financial reports, job estimating, billing, tracking, data backup,
are among the features.

51304 ■ "The Ratings Game" in
Entrepreneur (Vol. 31, No. 8, August 2003,
pp. 45)
Pub: Entrepreneur Media, Inc.
Ed: Melissa Campanelli. **Description:** Many small
business e-entrepreneurs are following the lead of
Amazon.com and Drugstore.com by posting uncensored reviews and ratings of products sold on the
firm's Website. The pros and cons of this practice are
examined.

51305 ■ "Reality check: threat of lawsuit
changes discriminatory payment practices"
in *Black Enterprise* (Vol. 33, No. 3, Oct. 2002,
pp. 178)
Pub: Earl Graves Publishing Co.
Ed: Lee Anna Jackson. **Description:** Lawyers in
Washington, DC have filed a lawsuit against retailers
that are refusing to accept out-of-state checks from African American customers. Patterns of discrimination
are surfacing through the use of testers from The
Equal Rights Center (TERC) attempting to purchase
items with checks at various retail establishments.

51306 ■ "The relationship between quality,
time and cost" in *Women in B usiness* (Vol.
53, No. 2, March-April, 2001, pp. 34)
Pub: The ABWA Co. Inc.
Description: Advice on factors to consider when buying goods or services is presented. The opportunity of
costs of quality, speed and savings are considered;
and ways of assessing one against the other are discussed.

51307 ■ "Relief on Wheels? Mall Strollers
Play DVDs" in *Tampa Tribune* (November 23,
2005)
Pub: Media General, Inc.
Ed: Marla Marino. **Description:** A new trend at shopping malls is to install DVD players showing G-rated
movies on all strollers. The move is expected to keep
parents in stores longer, and ultimately spend more
money.

51308 ■ "Research methods" in
Entrepreneur (Vol. 31, No. 5, May 2003, pp.
40)
Pub: Entrepreneur Media Inc.
Ed: Amanda C. Kooser. **Description:** Forty-six of all
Americans are more likely to shop at a physical store
than purchase a product over the Internet.

51309 ■ "Resources: Web Sites,
Organizations, Events and More to Grow
Your Business" in *Entrepreneur* (Vol. 32,
July 2004, No. 7, pp. 8)
Pub: Entrepreneur Media Inc.
Ed: Steve Cooper. **Description:** Online printing and
mailing services are offered by Mailersclub; Auction-
Bytes is a free email newsletter that covers online auctions; Microsoft's Software Asset Management
programs alerts companies when licenses are expiring and standardizes and centralizes the licensing
process; U.S. Census Bureau's American Community
Survey provides statistical data for small business
marketing; Retailwire, provides news to retail professionals; Daypop is a specialized search engine; StumbleUpon is a free browser toolbar; and
CoolSiteoftheDay spotlights good Web sites.

51310 ■ "Retail" in *Business 2.0* (Vol. 6, July
2005, No. 6, pp. 30)
Pub: Time, Inc.
Description: In a move to attract customers, retailer
store the Gap is reorganizing its stores by creating
separate entrances for men and women. The stores
will display women's items in a boutique-like environment while stressing the basics to male consumers.

51311 ■ "Retail" in *Entrepreneur* (Vol. 32,
No. 1, January 2004, pp. 238)
Pub: Entrepreneur Media, Inc.
Description: Profiles of an art and custom framing
franchise and franchise opportunities for owning a
UPS Store.

51312 ■ "Retail Experts Laud Costco's
Shopping Strategy" in *Business Journal-
Portland* (Vol. 20, No. 22, August 1, 2003, pp.
11)
Pub: American City Business Journals, Inc.
Ed: Carol Tice. **Description:** Marketing strategy used
by Costco Companies is examined, including management styles, U.S. economic conditions, and business planning.

51313 ■ "Retail Holdouts - But at What
Price" in *Inc.* (March 2000, pp. 88)
Pub: The Goldhirsh Group
Description: According to the United States Small
Business Administration, 70 percent of small busi-
nesses have no Web sales capabilities whatsoever.
The article looks at small businesses with no Web
sales.

51314 ■ "Retail Kiosk" in *Black Enterprise*
(Vol. 36, November 2005, No. 4, pp. 64)
Pub: Earl G. Graves Publishing Co. Inc.
Ed: Marcia Layton Turner. **Description:** According to
Specialty Retail Report, more than $10 billion is spent
at carts and kiosks in malls, subway stations, and ups-
cale resorts. Advice for starting a kiosk for under
$10,000 is offered.

51315 ■ "Retail Rut: Sears Holders Might Get
a $10 Payout. But Don't Expect Much More
from the Stock" in *Barron's* (July 21, 2003,
pp. 15)
Pub: Barron's
Ed: Robin Goldwyn Blumenthal. **Description:** Sears
Roebuck's credit-loan subsidiary went to Citigroup for
$6 billion, considerably less than the expected $7 billion, but was still enough to give $10/share in cash to
stockholders.

51316 ■ "Retail Stores Taking Health Care
Debit Cards Must Upgrade Systems" in
Kiplinger Letter (Vol. 82, January 12, 2007,
No. 1)
Pub: Kiplinger
Description: Internal Revenue Services is requiring
retailers accepting health care debit cards to install
electronic systems that restrict debit card purchases
to qualified medical expenses. The system upgrades
must be in place by 2009.

51317 ■ "Retailer Torrid Looks to Tap into
Plus-Size Apparel Market for Teenagers" in
Tampa Tribune (August 8, 2003)
Pub: Knight Ridder/Tribune Business News
Ed: Cherie Jacobs. **Description:** Torrid, a retailer
specializing in fashions for young women sizes 12-26
is profiled.

51318 ■ "Retailers Beginning to Get Holiday
Spirit" in *Crain's Detroit Business* (Vol. 19,
No. 42, October 20, 2003, pp. 1)
Pub: Crain Communications Inc., Detroit
Ed: Brent Snavely. **Description:** Metropolitan Detroit
retailers expect sales increases for the holidays in
2003, and have ordered more inventory than 2002.

51319 ■ "Retailers Beginning to Get Holiday
Spirit; Many Boost Inventory in Hopes of
Strong Sales" in *Crain's Detroit Business*
(Vol. 19)
Pub: Crain Communications Inc., Detroit
Ed: Brent Snavely. **Description:** Metropolitan Detroit
retailers expect sales increases for the holidays in
2003, and have ordered more inventory than 2002.

51320 ■ "Retailers, Beware" in *Entrepreneur*
(Vol. 28, No. 4, April 2000, pp. 58)
Pub: Entrepreneur Media Inc.
Description: A recent study by Harte-Hanks Market
Research found that 69 percent of consumers are dis-
satisfied with the service they receive and, therefore,
don't feel a need to be loyal to the stores in which they
shop.

51321 ■ "Retailers Draw Link Between
Halloween, Christmas Sales" in *Sacramento
Bee* (October 30, 2005)
Pub: The Sacramento Bee
Ed: Jon Ortiz. **Description:** Experts suggest a strong
link between Halloween and winter holiday sales. Hal-
loween is becoming a strong indicator of consumer
spending for the months of November and December.

51322 ■ "Retailers Have Disappointing
March" in *Baltimore Sun* (April 11, 2003)
Pub: Knight-Ridder/Tribune Business News
Ed: Lorraine Mirabella. **Description:** March 2003 saw
disappointing retail sales for both outlet as well as upscale chains. The war and a weakened economy continue to put a crimp on consumer spending.

51323 ■ "Retailers Helped by Chill, Gas Price
Dip" in *The Record* (November 4, 2005)
Pub: New Jersey Media Group
Ed: Joan Verdon. **Description:** Falling gas prices and
warmer temperatures boosted New Jersey's retail
sales in October 2005. A recent survey shows that
consumers are more price-driven in 2005.

51324 ■ "Retailers Optimistic They Can
Compete for Slice of Macomb" in *Crain's
Detroit Business* (Vol. 21, October 31, 2005,
No. 44, pp. 3)
Pub: Crain Communications Inc. - Detroit
Ed: Brent Snavely. **Description:** Retail development,
housing growth and the shopping mall in Clinton
Township are among the factors for Parisian building
a store that will anchor the new mall called Partridge
Creek.

51325 ■ "Retailers' Outlook 'Rosy'" in
Milwaukee Journal Sentinel (December 14,
2005)
Pub: Journal Sentinel, Inc.
Ed: Doris Hajewski. **Description:** Retail experts are
predicting a profitable holiday season. The International Council of Shopping Centers' retail chain index
reported this week a 0.9 percent rise over the previous
week.

51326 ■ "Retailers' Siren Song" in
Kiplinger's Personal Finance Magazine (Vol.
54, No. 11, November 2000, pp. 130)
Pub: The Kiplinger Washington Editors, Inc.
Ed: Elizabeth Razzi. **Description:** Merchants use
psychology to entice you into spending more. Knowing what they know will make you a smarter shopper.

51327 ■ "Retailers Welcome Valentine's Day
Gift Binge" in *Bradenton Herald* (February 5,
2005)
Pub: Bradenton Herald
Ed: Dana Sanchez. **Description:** Valentine's Day
helps retailers show off creativity with unique gift items
in order to maximize sales. The Valentine holiday
ranks third in sales after Christmas and Easter for
many retailers of candies and chocolates.

51328 ■ "Retailing Experts See Rise in
Label-Conscious Male Shoppers" in *Atlanta
Journal-Constitution* (February 17, 2004)
Pub: Knight-Ridder/Tribune Business News
Ed: Renee DeGross. **Description:** Male consumers
are becoming an important force in retail sales.

51329 ■ *Retailing Management*
Pub: Richard D. Irwin, Inc.
Ed: Michael Levy and Barton A. Weitz. **Released:**
1991. **Price:** $64.95.

51330 ■ "Rewarding Rebates" in *Black
Enterprise* (Vol. 36, November 2005, No. 4,
pp. 166)
Pub: Earl G. Graves Publishing Co. Inc.
Ed: Stephanie Young. **Description:** The National Retail Federation reports that online rebate offers from
stores provide ease in use while avoiding the hassle
of finding serial numbers and product codes, filling out
paperwork, and mailing in paperwork.

51331 ■ "RFID: Plenty of Mixed Signals" in Business Week Online (January 31, 2005)
Pub: McGraw-Hill Companies
Ed: Sarah Lacy. **Description:** Suppliers remain skeptical of radio-frequency identification technology to manage inventories.

51332 ■ "Riding the Rebates; Wixom Company Grows by Hitching Itself to National Retail Trend" in Crain's Detroit Business (Vol. 20)
Pub: Crain Communications Inc. - Detroit
Ed: Andrew Dietderich. **Description:** Profile of Al Goldberg, founder of The Express Group, a rebate fulfillment company. Goldberg attributes his business plan to a meeting with Kmart executives 23 years ago.

51333 ■ "Right of Fashion" in Entrepreneur. com (Vol. 34, February 2006, No. 2, pp. 30)
Pub: Entrepreneur Media Inc.
Ed: Sara Wilson. **Description:** Profile of Stacey Pecor of Olive and Bette's Co. Inc., a New York City-based women's retail clothing store.

51334 ■ "Rocket Science Retailing Is Almost Here Are You Ready?" in Harvard Business Review (Vol. 78, No. 4, July 2000, pp. 115)
Pub: Harvard Business School Publishing Corp.
Ed: Marshall L. Fisher, Ananth Raman, Anna Sheen McClelland. **Description:** Research shows that e-commerce firms are having problems delivering the products that customers order online while department stores increasingly rely on markdowns to attract customers.

51335 ■ "A rose by any other name" in Harvard Business Review (Vol. 81, No. 3, March 2003, pp. 29)
Pub: Harvard Business School Press
Ed: Daniel Stone. **Description:** Five experts give opinions on the choices facing a fictional paper goods manufacturer. Should the fictional company become a supplier for a retailer that has decided to create its own line of party goods, or should it put its efforts behind its own brand?

51336 ■ "A rosy sales picture" in Crain's Detroit Business (Vol. 19, No. 7, February 17, 2003, pp. 25)
Pub: Crain Communications Inc., Detroit
Ed: Brent Snavely. **Description:** May is the best month for florists, followed by February. It is estimated that Valentines Day 2003 saw more flowers sold in the Detroit metropolitan area than during any week of the year.

51337 ■ "Running Hot-and Cold-on the Web" in Business Week Online (Nov. 15, 2002)
Pub: McGraw-Hill Inc.
Ed: Karen E. Klein. **Description:** With the inception of annual search engine fees and a drop in Internet sales, a small retail business selling heating pads and ice packs online and wholesale to gift shops, is questioning the value of selling online.

51338 ■ "Saco's Downtown Merchants Say Big-Box Retailers Are Hurting Businesses" in Portland Press Herald (April 19, 2005)
Pub: Blethen Maine Newspapers, Inc.
Ed: Seth Harkness. **Description:** Slow growth in downtown districts can be attributed to big-box stores and supermarkets. A recent study showed that Saco, Maine businesses reported 5.9 percent annual increase in sales since 1996, however some merchants refuse to work together effectively to compete with large retailers.

51339 ■ "Safeway gets in shape for food fight" in San Francisco Business Times (Vol. 16, No. 42, May 24, 2002, pp. 1)
Pub: San Francisco Business Times Inc.
Ed: Mark Calvey. **Description:** Safeway Inc. is preparing for increased competition in the grocery industry since Wal-Mart plans to sell groceries at 40 California stores in the next few years. Safeway's consolidated purchasing and other efforts to reduce expenses are discussed along with forecasts about pricing.

51340 ■ "Saks Offers Complimentary 'Personal Shopper' Service in Long Island Store" in Newsday (August 22, 2004)
Pub: Newsday
Ed: Jacqueline Rivkin. **Description:** Long Island Saks Fifth Avenue store is offering personal shopping service to its customers in order to build customer relations.

51341 ■ "A Sales Channel They Can't Resist" in Business 2.0 (Vol. 6, September 2005, No. 8, pp. 90)
Pub: Time, Inc.
Ed: Elizabeth Esfahani. **Description:** The secret to cable television's QVC network is discussed. QVC has the ability to capitalize on the art and science of television retailing through real-time lighting, camera angles, and dialogue to maximize sales and profits.

51342 ■ "Sales Report: Once Tainted by Get-Rich-Quick Schemes, the Direct-Sales Industry is Changing its Image" in Entrepreneur (July 2004)
Pub: Entrepreneur Media Inc.
Ed: Nichole L. Torres. **Description:** Direct selling has become an industry whereby an independent consultant bringing a portable kit of wares to homes to share in a demonstration. According to the Direct Selling Association, the direct-selling industry accounted for more than $28 billion in 2002, with an estimated 13 million independent direct salespersons in the U.S. The five elements creating the evolution in direct selling are outlined.

51343 ■ "San Jose, Calif., Woman is Secret Shopper Evaluating Quality of Business" in San Jose Mercury News (August 10, 2004)
Pub: San Jose Mercury News
Ed: Michele Chandler. **Description:** Mystery shoppers routinely snoop around stores and restaurants at the request of business owners in order to survey the quality of their products, pricing, and services.

51344 ■ "Scare Tactics: Creative Ways to Profit from Halloween" in Entrepreneur (Vol. 32, October 2004, No. 10, pp. 90)
Pub: Entrepreneur Media Inc.
Description: Retailers thinking Halloween does not fit their brand, can apply three listed methods that will draw customers in during the holiday.

51345 ■ "Search Engines Help Shoppers To Buy Locally" in Wall Street Journal (Vol. 248, January 2007, No. 148, pp. B1-B3)
Pub: Dow Jones & Co. Inc.
Ed: James Covert **Description:** Several new search engines help customers compare prices and find out whether items are in stock at local stores.

51346 ■ "Season's Ho! Ho! Turns No! No! No!" in Atlanta Business Chronicle (Vol. 25, January 3, 2003, No. 30, pp. 3B)
Pub: American City Business Publications, Inc.
Ed: Alf Nucifora. **Description:** Retailing over the holidays was not impressive. Internet sales were positive, posting double-digit, year-to-year, seasonal increases around 30-70 percent for various categories. Statistical data included.

51347 ■ "Secrets of the Great White North-The world's hush-hush 3-commerce powerhouse is just a few miles away" in PC Computing (April 2000)
Pub: Ziff-Davis Inc.
Ed: Jim Conley. **Description:** Canadian retailers saw a banner year in 1999, with record sales both online and offline. Exchange rates, shipping costs, and support concerns have kept many U.S. companies from expanding to the Canadian market, but the article suggests the savvy retailer will realize the opportunity.

51348 ■ "Seeing the Light" in Entrepreneur (Vol. 33, September 2005, No. 9, pp. 92)
Pub: Entrepreneur Media Inc.
Ed: Chris Penttila. **Description:** It is predicted that a move to extend daylight savings time would be an economic boom to small businesses. Consumers would spend the extra daylight time shopping, dining at restaurants, working out at fitness centers, etc.

51349 ■ "Seen & Noted: Fitness-Minded Bare Motivations in Stores" in Crain's Chicago Business (Vol. 30, January 2007, No. 2, pp. 19)
Pub: Crain Communications, Inc.
Ed: Kevin Davis. **Description:** Motivated by New Year's resolutions and the film release of Rocky Balboa, consumers are purchasing fitness equipment on a large scale.

51350 ■ "Selling Innovation" in Sales and Marketing.com (Vol. 156, No. 3, March 2004, pp. 56)
Pub: VNU eMedia, Inc.
Ed: Scott Owens. **Description:** Profile of Mike Curran, owner of U.S. Interactive. Curran created Take-Home Defensive Driving, the nation's first state-certified driving course on video. The firm has trained more than 2 million Americans to drive more safely.

51351 ■ "Seniority Rules" in Entrepreneur (Vol. 31, No. 10, October 2003, pp. 88)
Pub: Entrepreneur Media, Inc.
Ed: Elizabeth Goodgold. **Description:** Individuals aged 65 and older make up 12 percent of the population but account for more than 48 percent of discretionary purchases. The director of Marketing Directions Service suggests that entrepreneurs should market to this age group as the way they wish to be seen: full of vitality and reflecting realistic aspirations.

51352 ■ "Shelby Supervisor Hopes Township Plan Can Spur More Growth" in Crain's Detroit Business (Vol. 21, January 31, 2005, No. 5, pp. 35)
Pub: Crain Communications Inc. - Detroit
Ed: Anjali Fluker. **Description:** Plans for new buildings and upgrades to older buildings along Shelby Township, Michigan's Van Dyke corridor are highlighted. The master plan would create a center of activity for shopping, entertainment, recreation and municipal buildings.

51353 ■ "Shipping out" in Entrepreneur (Vol. 31, No. 6, June 2003, pp. 42)
Pub: Entrepreneur Media Inc.
Ed: Melissa Campanelli. **Description:** Many online retailers have followed Amazon.com and have begun offering free shipping with purchases. The advantages and downside to providing this service are discussed.

51354 ■ "Shopping Centers That Sizzle: Entertainment Elements Enliven Malls" in Tourist Attractions and Parks (Vol. 35, January 2005, No. 1)
Pub: Kane Communications Inc.
Description: In order to boost revenues, shopping centers and malls are adding miniature golf courses, rock climbing, restaurants, live entertainment and more.

51355 ■ "Shopping Magazines Gain Popularity by Telling Readers Exactly Where to Buy" in San Diego Union-Tribune (October 14, 2004)
Pub: San Diego Union-Tribune
Ed: Jennifer Davies. **Description:** Shopping magazines, sometimes referred to as magalogs, are growing in popularity. The publications offer advice on fashion, beauty products and home decor. Most of the magazines offer a Web site as a critical part of the business, with direct links to retailers featured in the magazine.

51356 ■ "Shopping Spies Help Retail Businesses Keep Eye on Service" in Charlotte Observer (October 10, 2004)
Pub: Charlotte Observer
Ed: Leigh Dyer. **Description:** Charlotte, North Carolina-based Belk Department Stores is using mystery shoppers in order to enforce store policies. The store managers' annual bonus is based on this program.

51357 ■ **"Showing Products In a Better Light"** in *Business 2.0* (Vol. 6, September 2005, No. 8, pp. 62)
Pub: Time, Inc.
Ed: Jennifer Alsever. **Description:** Retailers are crediting improved lighting to increased sales; skylights, shelf lights, and pendant lighting are being used to highlight products.

51358 ■ **"Simmons' Dream: Sell Off Mattress Retailers"** in *Atlanta Business Chronicle* (Vol. 26, No. 10, August 10, 2003, pp. 3)
Pub: American City Business Publications, Inc.
Ed: Lisa R. Schoolcraft. **Description:** Plans by Simmons Company to sell off its retail mattress stores are presented. Topics include poor economic conditions, business losses, and dwindling market share.

51359 ■ **"Site Pursued for Residential, Retail Project"** in *Sarasota Herald Tribune* (January 29, 2005, pp. D1)
Pub: Sarasota Herald-Tribune
Ed: Kevin McQuaid. **Description:** Ram Development Company is nearing a deal to purchase the Herald-Tribune building on South Tamiami Trail for possible redevelopment as a retail and residential project.

51360 ■ **"SKG Motorsports Races to Open New Poway Site"** in *San Diego Business Journal* (Vol. 28, January 15, 2007, No. 3, pp. 12)
Pub: San Diego Business Journal Associates
Ed: Jessica Long. **Description:** Auto customization shop, SKG Motorsports, reported $3 million in sales for 2006.

51361 ■ **"The Skinflint Goes Shopping"** in *Forbes* (December 24, 2001, p. 100)
Pub: Forbes Magazine
Ed: Stephen Manes. **Description:** The article explores shopping bargains online. Price-comparison Web sites are great places to gather information, but many often miss the best deals.

51362 ■ **"Smooth Operator"** in *Home Business* (Vol. 12, October 2005, No. 5, pp. 93)
Pub: Home Business Magazine
Ed: Sandy Larson. **Description:** Profile of Mark Williams, a California online retailer specializing in men's and women's grooming products.

51363 ■ **"The Soft Sell; Few Soft-Goods Vendors Have Developed Formal Programs to Tap Into the Bridal Market"** in *HFN* (January 26, 2004)
Pub: Fairchild Publications
Description: Soft goods suppliers have not tapped into the bridal market in the same way china, crystal and silver goods suppliers have. WestPoint Stevens has a formal registry program, but most home textile vendors ignore the bridal market, instead relying on retailers and Web sites to sell goods.

51364 ■ **"Spanish Firm Hopes U.S. Is In the Bag"** in *Crain's Chicago Business* (Vol. 26, No. 51, December 22, 2003, pp. 14)
Pub: Crain Communications, Inc.
Ed: Sandra Jones. **Description:** Profile of Frag Comercio Internacional, one of Spain's biggest handbag makers. The firm has opened a store in Chicago, Illinois and hopes to expand retail operations to 100 stores across the nation. The store offers an ever-changing choice of purses and totes, all priced at $32. The handbags will be displayed museum-style, using a minimalist concept.

51365 ■ **"Specialty Shops"** in *Hispanic Business* (June 2005, pp. 96)
Pub: Hispanic Business
Ed: Keith Rosenblum. **Description:** Hispanics selling to other Hispanics has created the largest retailers listed on the magazine's top 500 companies. Statistical data included.

51366 ■ **"Spotlight on Retailing"** in *The Record* (November 12, 2005)
Pub: New Jersey Media Group

Ed: Joan Verdon. **Description:** Profile of Lee Long and Linda Rogers, owners of The Children's Exchange stores in Bergen County, New Jersey. The partners started their children's used clothing and furniture stores in 1988 and have watched customers grow from buying for their children to buying for their grandchildren.

51367 ■ **Start and Run a Profitable Retail Business: A Step-by-Step Business Plan**
Pub: Self-Counsel Press, Inc.
Ed: Michael M. Coltman. **Released:** Third edition, 1993. **Price:** $14.95 (paper).

51368 ■ **"Steal This Customer"** in *Internet World* (Vol. 7, No. 1, January 15, 2001, pp. 32)
Pub: Mecklermedia Corporation
Ed: Jason Black. **Description:** Acquiring and retaining customers is a major problem for online retailers, but need not be insurmountable. Many consumers use the Web for the online equivalent of window-shopping and price comparison; competing retailers have the opportunity to lure buyers with better offers, and Internet technology can greatly speed the process. Advertisements can be sent directly to the screen of a user browsing a competitor's site with the aid of Dash.com, Gator.com and other browser add-ons.

51369 ■ **"Stock Watch: Aeropostale Flies Past Competitors"** in *Crain's New York Business* (Vol. 20, No. 12, March 22, 2004, pp. 3)
Pub: Crain Communications, Inc.
Ed: Tommy Fernandez. **Description:** Stock prices for Aeropostale, Inc., the teen clothing retailer, have tripled in one year. Statistical data included.

51370 ■ **"Stop payment"** in *Crain's Detroit Business* (Vol. 19, No. 16, April 21, 2003, pp. 1)
Pub: Crain Communications Inc., Detroit
Ed: Brent Snavely. **Description:** Information is given on a ruling in the Kmart Corporation bankruptcy case on the $327 million in payments by Kmart to suppliers, the ruling could impact bankruptcy cases in the future.

51371 ■ **"Storefront Column"** in *Daily Press* (April 11, 2003)
Pub: Knight-Ridder/Tribune Business News
Ed: Audra Barlow. **Description:** Profile of John Robert Curtis, Jr., owner of a one-of-a-kind bookstore located in the heart of historic Williamsburg, Virginia. The Bookpress Ltd. prides itself on finding and selling rare books.

51372 ■ **"Straight talking: to tell or not to tell?"** in *Entrepreneur* (Vol. 30, No. 10, October 2002, pp. 47)
Pub: Entrepreneur Media Inc.
Ed: Melissa Campanelli. **Description:** A study conducted by the Consumer Web Watch shows that less than 30 percent of respondents trust information on Web sites that sell products and services.

51373 ■ **"Strike Up the Brand"** in *Small Business Opportunities* (Vol. 16, November 2004, No. 6, pp. 92, 94)
Pub: Harris Publications Inc.
Ed: Stan Roberts. **Description:** Profile of Michael Perlman, president of BrandsMartUSA. The retailer has earned awards and offers a Website of promotions ranging from art galleries for children to lunchtime specials. The discount house earns $580 million a year.

51374 ■ **Successful Retailing: Your Step-by-Step Guide to Avoiding Pitfalls and Finding Profit as an Independent Retailer**
Pub: Upstart Publishing Co., Inc.
Ed: Paula Wardell. **Released:** Second edition, 1993. **Price:** $24.95 (paper). **Description:** Topics covered include the merchandise plan, the purchase order, inventory management, financial control, merchandising techniques, and buying strategies. Includes a bibliography, a glossary, an index, statistical data, and blank forms.

51375 ■ **"Sweet Rewards"** in *Entrepreneur* (Vol. 31, No. 8, August 2003, pp. 75)
Pub: Entrepreneur Media, Inc.
Ed: Kim T. Gordon. **Description:** Win over existing customers with a customer loyalty program and increase sales at the same time.

51376 ■ **"Swezey's Department Store Sites Sought By a Diversity of Businesses"** in *Long Island Business News* (January 30, 2004)
Pub: Dolan Media Newswires
Ed: Nick Anastasi. **Description:** Grocers and bookstores are looking to purchase real estate once used by Swezey's Department Stores. The article carries information on the many plans underway.

51377 ■ **"SwiftCD Taps PayPal as On-Demand Payment Engine"** in *DVD Report* (Vol. 8, No. 16, August 18, 2003)
Pub: PBI Media LLC
Description: SwiftCD signs a deal to have the PayPal e-commerce system handle transactions.

51378 ■ **"Symbol Technologies Inc. Hires Former IBM Executive"** in *Long Island Business News* (March 5, 2004)
Pub: Dolan Media Newswires
Description: Profiles of Verlin P. Youd, vice president of retail systems for Symbol Technologies Inc., and Anthony Bartolo, vice president and general manager of wireless infrastructure division.

51379 ■ **"Symbol Technologies Wins Landmark Lawsuit in Nevada Federal Court"** in *Long Island Business News* (January 30, 2004)
Pub: Dolan Media Newswires
Description: A federal judge in Nevada has ruled that a coalition of bar code companies did not infringe on patents of the Lemelson Foundation, saving retail chains hundreds of millions in royalties.

51380 ■ **"Talking Shop: Wonder What Makes Shoppers Tick?"** in *Entrepreneur* (Vol. 31, No. 9, September 2003, pp. 62)
Pub: Entrepreneur Media, Inc.
Ed: Elizabeth Goodgold. **Description:** ESPN Zone, Hot Topic, Starbucks, Anthropologie and Build-A-Bear Workshop share tips to target customers, develop an enduring brand, create a destination, sell a lifestyle and build a relationship with customers.

51381 ■ **"Target plans superstores"** in *Crain's Detroit Business* (Vol. 19, No. 14, April 7, 2003, pp. 48)
Pub: Crain Communications Inc., Detroit
Ed: Brent Snavely. **Description:** Target Corporation has announced plans to build 30-35 grocery and merchandise stores per year, calling them SuperTarget.

51382 ■ **"Taubman Plans Spur Optimism"** in *Crain's Detroit Business* (Vol. 22, November 27, 2006, No. 48, pp. 20)
Pub: Crain Communications Inc. - Detroit
Ed: Sheena Harrison. **Description:** Expansion at Twelve Oaks and Partridge Creek will rejuvenate retail business in those areas. People think positively when they see new businesses and expansions rather than the skepticism that inhibits retail sales levels.

51383 ■ **"Taubman-Simon battle employs an army of high-priced advisers"** in *Crain's Detroit Business* (Vol. 19, No. 17, April 28, 2003, pp. 4)
Pub: Crain Communications Inc., Detroit
Ed: Brent Snavely. **Description:** An overview of information regarding Taubman Centers Inc.'s battle to defeat a hostile takeover by rival mall developer Simon Property Group Inc. Today lawyers, accountants and lobbyists tend to be the weapons of choice on the corporate-takeover battlefield.

51384 ■ **"Tech Talk"** in *St. Louis Post-Dispatch* (December 11, 2004)
Pub: Knight-Ridder/Tribune Business News
Ed: David Sheets. **Description:** In November, several mall kiosks were found to be selling counterfeit Nintendo video games and game players in the St. Louis, Missouri area. Among the games are Donkey Kong and Mario Bros. titles.

51385 ■ "Technology Evolving At Beall's" in *Bradenton Herald* **(February 14, 2005)**
Pub: Bradenton Herald
Ed: Dana Sanchez. **Description:** Profile of Don Keller, production manager of one of Beall's Inc.'s two large distribution centers. Keller is phasing in voice recognition technology in its warehouses to increase efficiency in handling inventories.

51386 ■ "The Problem" in *Inc.* **(April 1, 2005)**
Pub: Inc. Magazine
Ed: Lora Kolodny. **Description:** Lance Fried, CEO of Freestyle Audio and inventor of a waterproof MP3 player for surfers, swimmers, water skiers, and snowboard enthusiasts, planned to market his device to small surf shops. Fried discusses the issues involved in selling to big-box retailers.

51387 ■ "Thinking outside the big box" in *Ingram's* **(Vol. 28, No. 3, March 2002, pp. 74)**
Pub: Show Me Publishing, Inc.
Ed: Carl A. LaSala. **Description:** Replacement tenancy is the best solution for an empty building after a major retailer has closed. Cooperation from local officials and the property owner may be required if the new business is not the same type as the previous one.

51388 ■ "Thinking Out of the Clamshell" in *Business 2.0* **(Vol. 6, July 2005, No. 6, pp. 58)**
Pub: Time, Inc.
Ed: Siri Schubert. **Description:** Thomas Perlmutter invented a tool designed to open clamshell packages. The OpenX tool opens the plastic packaging used to hold products and offer theft protection to retailers while displaying the item inside.

51389 ■ "Time to Collect? Tacking Taxes Onto Internet Sales Could Soon Become Mandatory" in *Entrepreneur.com* **(Vol. 34, February 2006, No. 2)**
Pub: Entrepreneur Media Inc.
Ed: Melissa Campanelli. **Description:** Online retailers can voluntarily add sales taxes to bills originating in the 19 states that have signed onto the Streamlined Sales and Use Tax Agreement, that makes it easier for retailers doing business in multiple states to calculate, collect and remit existing use taxes.

51390 ■ "Tips & Trends" in *Small Business Opportunities* **(Vol. 17, September 2005, No. 5, pp. 14)**
Pub: Harris Publications Inc.
Description: Tips and trends important to small business include the addition of a coffeemaker that also makes soup, tea or cocoa; paper shredders; headsets; a sales resource guide for retailers; information for the Federal Citizen Information Center; and Creative Colors, the franchise offering mobile equipment to home-based businesses.

51391 ■ "'Tis the Season" in *Entrepreneur* **(Vol. 32, October 2004, No. 10, pp. 52)**
Pub: Entrepreneur Media Inc.
Ed: Melissa Campanelli. **Description:** It's never too early for online retailers to prepare for the holiday season. Fulfillment and inventory operations need to be assessed.

51392 ■ "Too High a Price for Black Ink" in *Business Week* **(January 23, 2006, No. 3968, pp. 25)**
Pub: McGraw-Hill Companies
Ed: Robert Barker. **Description:** Although Office Depot is on a roll, its stock is overvalued. Statistical data included on both Office Depot and Staples stock.

51393 ■ "Top Dollar" in *Entrepreneur* **(Vol. 32, No. 1, January 2004, pp. 78)**
Pub: Entrepreneur Media, Inc.
Ed: Gwen Moran. **Description:** Sales at dollar stores across the nation were up nearly 7 percent in 2002. Sales strategies for dollar stores are given by Sue Goldstein, retail industry consultant.

51394 ■ "Toward the Development of Measures of Distinctive Competencies among Small Independent Retailers" in *Journal of Small Business Management*
Pub: West Virginia University
Ed: Jeffrey E. McGee, Mark Peterson. **Description:** To remain competitive in markets increasingly dominated by large discount chains, "category killers", and other mass-merchandisers, small independent retailers need to develop distinctive competencies. A study providing insight into the multidimensional character of distinctive competencies by measuring the resources and capabilities possessed by 255 independent drug stores is presented.

51395 ■ "Training Wheels" in *Inc.* **(October 2005, pp. 51-52)**
Pub: Inc. Magazine
Ed: Nadine Heintz. **Description:** Ben Serotta developed a plan to teach retailers how to sell the bicycles he manufactures. Serotta's plan helps retailers custom-fit the bike to its buyer.

51396 ■ "Turning South; Sterling Heights Pushes Redevelopment of Older Areas as Vacant Land Dries Up" in *Crain's Detroit Business* **(Vol. 21)**
Pub: Crain Communications Inc. - Detroit
Ed: Anjali Fluker. **Description:** Many areas in the city of Sterling Heights, Michigan are zoned for mixed-use projects. The city is seeking developers to renovate vacant sites to bring a lifestyle center that combines retail, commercial and residential space.

51397 ■ "Up Front" in *Business Week* **(January 16, 2006, No. 3967, pp. 11-12, 14)**
Pub: McGraw-Hill Companies
Ed: Dan Beucke. **Description:** Information regarding construction wages in the U.S., Chrysler's new Baby Bentley sedan, teen trends, online sales taxes, and airline competition are among the topics discussed.

51398 ■ "Urban Pioneers" in *Hispanic Business* **(September 2006, pp. 18, 20)**
Pub: Hispanic Business
Ed: Michael Todd. **Description:** Profile of Primestor, the Los Angeles, California-based developer, is bringing first-class retailers to forgotten Hispanic neighborhoods.

51399 ■ "Vacancies up but investors still high on retail" in *Atlanta Business Chronicle* **(Vol. 25, December 13, 2002, No. 27, pp. A5)**
Pub: American City Business Publications, Inc.
Ed: Lisa R. Schoolcraft. **Description:** Despite lower retail rents and more empty stores in 2002 than 2001, real estate investors continue to buy Atlanta, Georgia area retail properties, largely due to the fact that investment funds are available. The market for small investors who pool funds continues to drive this trend. A report by Marcus and Millichap provides some hope that rents will recover some of the losses as 2003 progresses.

51400 ■ *Visual Merchandising & Store Design—Buyers' Guide Issue*
Pub: ST Media Group International Inc.
Released: Annual, January 2005. **Publication Includes:** Over 1,300 manufacturers and distributors of retail display equipment and products; nearly 600 store design, lighting, and visual merchandising firms; related trade and professional associations. **Entries Include:** For manufacturers and service firms—Company name, address, phone, name and title of contact, number of employees, sales volume, products. Similar data given for associations. **Arrangement:** Alphabetical. **Indexes:** Product, fax number.

51401 ■ "W. Alabama a Sweet Home - and Office - for Retailers" in *Houston Business Journal* **(Vol. 34, No. 16, August 29, 2003, pp. 2)**
Pub: American City Business Journals
Ed: Nancy Sarnoff. **Description:** Several retailers on West Alabama in Houston, Texas are establishing their shops on the ground floor, or next door to, their homes.

51402 ■ "Wal-Mart Expansion Plans Feed Grocery Competition" in *Crain's Detroit Business* **(Vol. 19, No. 45, November 10, 2003, pp. 26)**
Pub: Crain Communications Inc., Detroit
Ed: Brent Snavely. **Description:** Wal-Mart Stores Inc. plans to expand operations, putting pressure on profits and market share of the top grocery chains.

51403 ■ "Wal-Mart Said to Be Weighing Bid for Massachusetts-Based BJ's Wholesale Club" in *Boston Globe* **(April 11, 2003)**
Pub: Knight-Ridder/Tribune Business News
Ed: Chris Reidy. **Description:** Wal-Mart Stores Inc. is considering a bid to purchase BJ's Wholesale Club Inc., located in Natick, Massachusetts. The chain operates about 140 club stores with sales of nearly $5.9 billion in 2002.

51404 ■ "Wal-Mart's Clean Bill of Health?" in *Business Week Online* **(February 9, 2005)**
Pub: McGraw-Hill Companies
Ed: Wendy Zellner. **Description:** In order to improve its image, Wal-Mart has reported the results of a new survey it conducted about employees' healthcare coverage. The nationwide survey, commissioned from Segmentation Company, found the percentage of workers with healthcare coverage at Wal-Mart is about the same as employees working for other retailers.

51405 ■ "Wearing Her Work on Her Sleeve" in *Home Business* **(Vol. 13, January/February 2006, No. 1, pp. 80)**
Pub: Home Business Magazine
Ed: Sandy Larson. **Description:** Profile of Eileen Parzek who sells work-at-home related merchandise including t-shirts, caps, mugs, mouse pads, and clocks.

51406 ■ "Web Retailing: The prodigal e-commerce sites return" in *Red Herring* **(No. 105, October 1, 2001, pp. 96-97)**
Pub: Herring Communications
Ed: Dan Briody. **Description:** Both Wal-Mart and Kmart announced the buy-back of their independent Web sites, Walmart.com and BlueLight.com, and are reintegrating them back into their core businesses. Statistical data included.

51407 ■ "Welcome Back, Mom and Pop" in *Harvard Business Review* **(Vol. 78, No. 3, May 2000, pp. 24)**
Pub: Harvard Business School Publishing Corp.
Ed: Richard Metters, Michael Ketzenberg, George Gillen. **Description:** Big retailers are starting to think small again.

51408 ■ "What's In Store? Get Ahead of the Game with the Latest Retail Trends" in *Entrepreneur* **(Vol. 33, September 2005, No. 9, pp. 84)**
Pub: Entrepreneur Media Inc.
Ed: Gwen Moran. **Description:** Technology integration, solution-oriented merchandising, colors and graphics, and fewer SKUs are the latest trends in retailing.

51409 ■ "What's It Worth? Get Your Prices Right, Or It'll Cost You" in *Entrepreneur* **(Vol. 32, December 2004, No. 12, pp. 92)**
Pub: Entrepreneur Media Inc.
Ed: Gwen Moran. **Description:** Retail experts advise independent retailers to know their margins in order to master higher sales volumes. Buy one get one free offers can backfire, and it might be wiser to use longer-term loyalty programs.

51410 ■ "What's Your Problem? Your Store May Not Be a Big, City-Slicker Business" in *Entrepreneur* **(Vol. 31, No. 9, July 2003, pp. 104)**
Pub: Entrepreneur Media, Inc.
Description: Ways a small clothing store and hair salon business in a small town can increase sales are discussed.

51411 ■ "When It Comes to Shopping, Safety Comes First" in *Home Business* (Vol. 13, January/February 2006, No. 1, pp. 56)
Pub: Home Business Magazine
Ed: Sandy Larson. Description: Profile of Tracy Richter, inventor of a safety strap that secures infant car seats to shopping carts. Mother of three is dedicated to promoting awareness of the safety issues when using infant seats in shopping carts.

51412 ■ "Whistle Shop: Turn Your Store Into a Destination by Making Shopping an Event" in *Entrepreneur* (Vol. 33, March 2005, No. 3, pp. 86)
Pub: Entrepreneur Media Inc.
Ed: Gwen Moran. Description: Ways to create more entertaining shopping experiences are offered by Debbie Allen, a retail consultant and author of Confessions of Shameless Self Promoters.

51413 ■ "Who benefits from price promotions?" in *Harvard Business Review* (Vol. 80, No. 9, September 2002, pp. 22)
Pub: Harvard Business School Press
Ed: Shuba Srinivasan. Description: Research has shown that reducing prices temporarily as part of a marketing campaign can adversely affect a retail company.

51414 ■ "Wholesale changes: Mom-and-Pop stores are so passe" in *Entrepreneur* (Vol. 30, No. 2, February 2002, pp. 19)
Pub: Entrepreneur Media Inc.
Ed: Nichole L. Torres. Description: Some retailers are revamping the layout of stores to give the look of a warehouse in order to attract more customers.

51415 ■ "Why 'Buy' Buttons Are Booming" in *Business 2.0* (Vol. 6, July 2005, No. 6, pp. 36)
Pub: Time, Inc.
Ed: Elizabeth Esfahani. Description: Three technologies to help online e-tailers to close sales include customization, online catalogs, and dynamic imaging of products.

51416 ■ "Williams-Sonoma Tries a New Recipe: Pottery Barn Kids is a hit" in *Business Week* (May 6, 2002, pp. 36)
Pub: McGraw-Hill Inc.
Ed: Louise Lee. Description: Profile of the San Francisco-based specialty retailer that is aggressively pushing into new retail sectors including the kids market and a furniture catalog.

51417 ■ "With the Big Dogs" in *Crain's Detroit Business* (Vol. 21, December 19, 2005, No. 51, pp. 3)
Pub: Crain Communications Inc. - Detroit
Ed: Brent Snavely. Description: Profile of Pet Supplies 'Plus' franchises. The pet food retailer's expansion makes it the third-largest pet food retailers in the nation. Statistical data included.

51418 ■ "World Savings Bank Opens First LI Location" in *Long Island Business News* (February 6, 2004)
Pub: Dolan Media Newswires
Ed: Ben Abelson. Description: World Savings Bank, a retail-oriented bank, is expanding from Oakland, California into Long Island, New York. Another branch is expected to open in the summer of 2004. Other banks in the area are welcoming the new competition.

51419 ■ "A Year of Advice is Prize in Woman-Owned Program" in *Crain's Detroit Business* (Vol. 21, December 12, 2005, No. 50, pp. 2)
Pub: Crain Communications Inc. - Detroit
Description: Three Detroit-area woman-owned businesses will receive professional assistance from the Athena PowerLink program. The winners must be companies that are majority-owned by a woman, operating for at least two years, have a minimum of two employees, annual revenue of $250,000 or more in manufacturing or retail, or $100,000 in service business, and have clearly defined goals.

51420 ■ "Your New Neighborhood" in *Small Business Opportunities* (May 2005)
Pub: Harris Publications Inc.
Ed: Hector Ocri. Description: Key tips for retailers to succeed in diverse ethnic communities are shared.

51421 ■ *Your Own Shop: How to Open and Operate a Successful Retail Business*
Pub: The McGraw-Hill Companies
Ed: Ruth Jacobson. Released: 1991. Price: $12.95 (paper).

51422 ■ "Yule be Sorry" in *Entrepreneur* (Vol. 28, No. 10, October 2000, pp. 56)
Pub: Entrepreneur Media Inc.
Ed: Melissa Campanelli. Description: Planning for Internet business for Christmas operations is explored. LeapFrog, a California company, shares problems they encountered during the 1999 holiday season.

SOURCES OF SUPPLY

51423 ■ *Linux Buyer's Guide*
Pub: Specialized Systems Consultants Inc.
Ed: Richard Vernon, Editor, ljeditor@ssc.com. Released: Annual. Price: $6, single issue. Covers: Lists more than 2,000 products for Linux, services, and Linux software and hardware vendors. Entries Include: Vendor name, address, phone, products, applications.

STATISTICAL SOURCES

51424 ■ *RMA Annual Statement Studies*
Pub: Robert Morris Associates (RMA)
Released: Annual. Price: $175.00 2004-05 edition, $105.00. Description: Contains composite balance sheets and income statements for more than 360 industries, including the accounting, auditing, and bookkeeping industries. Also contains five years of comparative historical data for discerning trends. Includes 16 commonly used ratios, computed for most of the size groupings for nearly every industry.

51425 ■ *Value Retailing in the 1990s: Off-Pricers, Factory Outlets, and Closeout Stores*
Pub: John Wiley & Sons, Inc.
Released: 1994. Price: $345.00 (Print on Demand). Description: Published by Packaged Closeout Stores Facts. Examines off-price stores and manufacturers' outlets, covering market size and growth, competition, industry trends, and consumers. Also includes profiles of value retailers and regional outlet mall developers.

TRADE PERIODICALS

51426 ■ *Barnard's Retail Trend Report*
Pub: Barnard Enterprises Inc.
Contact: Kurt Barnard, Publisher & Chief Editor
E-mail: kbarnard@retailtrends.com
Released: Bimonthly. Price: $179; $199, other countries; $45, single issue. Description: Forecasts predictions, analyzes, explains, and identifies trends and events affecting retail operations. Recurring features include market statistics and news of research.

51427 ■ *Catalog Success Magazine*
Pub: North American Publishing Co.
Contact: Matt Griffin, Assoc. Ed.
Released: Monthly. Description: Professional journal covering information for executives involved in the business-to-business and consumer catalog industry.

51428 ■ *Inside Retailing*
Pub: Lebhar-Friedman Inc.
Ed: Ken Schept, Editor, kschept@lf.com. Released: Biweekly. Price: $229, U.S.; $350, elsewhere. Description: Provides up-to-date information on what is happening in the retail industry and how current economic conditions affect retailing. Summarizes actions, acquisitions, and policies of major retail chains across the U.S. Discusses problems facing retail operations, i.e., shoplifting and retaining customer loyalty.

51429 ■ *Loeb Retail Letter*
Pub: Loeb Associates Inc.
Contact: Phyllis Loeb
Ed: Walter F. Loeb, Editor, loeb@idt.net. Released: 11/year. Price: $300, U.S.; $325, Canada; $350, elsewhere. Description: Publishes articles on the retail industry. Recurring features include news of research.

51430 ■ *NSSRA Newsletter*
Pub: National Ski & Snowboard Retailers Association
Contact: Thomas B. Doyle, President
E-mail: tdoyle@nssra.com
Released: Quarterly. Price: Included in membership. Description: Informs ski and snowboard retail stores on critical industry issues such as guidelines and litigation exposure and marketing.

51431 ■ *The Retail Challenge*
Pub: International Council of Shopping Centers
Released: Quarterly. Price: $195, members; $295, nonmembers. Description: Covers "the nuts and bolts of retailing and provides the industry know-how to boost your merchant's productivity." Features how-to information on selling techniques, customer service, motivation, operations, advertising, promotion, and marketing.

51432 ■ *Retail Info Systems News*
Pub: Edgell Communications Inc.
Contact: Andrew Gaffney, Group Publisher
Released: Monthly, 12/yr. Description: RIS News serves the retail market targeting the technology buying team.

51433 ■ *Western-English Industry Report*
Pub: Western English Retailers Association
Contact: Susan Leach, Exec. Editor
Released: Bimonthly. Price: $29. Description: Disseminates information on trends, markets, business techniques, and issues on the nation's retailers of Western and English apparel, tack, and equipment.

VIDEOCASSETTES/ AUDIOCASSETTES

51434 ■ *Beware the Naked Man Who Offers You His Shirt*
PBS Home Video
Catalog Fulfillment Center
PO Box 751089
Charlotte, NC 28275-1089
Ph:800-531-4727
Free: 800-645-4PBS
Co. E-mail: info@pbs.org
URL: http://www.pbs.org
Released: 1990. Price: $395.00. Description: The author of "Swim With the Sharks Without Being Eaten Alive" offers insights and advice on increasing sales productivity. Availability: VHS; 3/4U.

51435 ■ *Shoplifting Prevented*
American Media, Inc.
4621 121st St.
Urbandale, IA 50323-2311
Ph:(515)224-0919
Free: 888-776-8268
Fax: (515)327-2555
Co. E-mail: custsvc@ammedia.com
URL: http://www.ammedia.com
Released: 1988. Price: $450.00. Description: Employees are shown some simple things they can do to keep their store from getting ripped off. Availability: VHS; 3/4U.

TRADE SHOWS AND CONVENTIONS

51436 ■ Celebrating 25 Years in the Canadian Craft Industry
Canadian Craft and Hobby Association
24 - 1410 40th Ave. NE, Ste. 24
Calgary, AB, Canada T2E 6L1

Ph:(403)291-0559
Free: 888-991-0559
Fax: (403)291-0675
Co. E-mail: ccha@cdncraft.org
URL: http://www.cdncraft.org
Released: 3/yr. **Audience:** Retail store owners, distributors, and manufacturers (bonafide businesses only). **Principal Exhibits:** Products from the fabric, hobby, craft, sewing, art, floral, games, needlecraft, ceramics, collector's items, and yarn industries.

51437 ■ NAMA National Expo - National Automatic Merchandising Association
National Automatic Merchandising Association
20 N Wacker Dr., Ste. 3500
Chicago, IL 60606-3102
Ph:(312)346-0370
Fax: (312)704-4140
Co. E-mail: expo@vending.org
URL: http://www.vending.org
Released: Annual. **Audience:** Vending, coffee service and foodservice management companies. **Principal Exhibits:** Vending, coffee service and foodservice equipment, products, and services. **Dates and Locations:** 2007 Oct 11-13, Chicago, IL; 2008 Oct 16-18, St. Louis, MO.

51438 ■ NAMA Spring Expo
National Automatic Merchandising Association
20 N Wacker Dr., Ste. 3500
Chicago, IL 60606-3102
Ph:(312)346-0370
Fax: (312)704-4140
Co. E-mail: expo@vending.org
URL: http://www.vending.org
Released: Annual. **Audience:** Vending & office coffee service companies. **Principal Exhibits:** Vending and office coffee service equipment, supplies & services. **Dates and Locations:** 2007 Mar 22-23, Las Vegas, NV.

51439 ■ Retail Technology
Messe Dusseldorf North America - MDNA
150 N. Michigan Ave., Ste. 2920
Chicago, IL 60601
Ph:(312)781-5180
Fax: (312)781-5188
Co. E-mail: info@mdna.com
URL: http://www.mdna.com
Released: Triennial. **Principal Exhibits:** International trade fair for retail information, communications and security technology.

CONSULTANTS

51440 ■ G.G.W. and Associates
1213 Hampton Dr.
Jackson, MI 49203
Ph:(517)782-2255
Fax: (517)784-1256
Scope: Consultants to retail businesses with services that include profit and loss strategy, business planning (short or long term), marketing strategies, market survey analysis, advertising budget, merchandise control systems and effective internal security and employee communications programs. Serves private industries as well as government agencies. **Seminars:** Retraining for the 90's; How to Start and Manage a Small Business.

51441 ■ Gordian Concepts & Solutions
16 Blueberry Ln.
Lincoln, MA 01773
Ph:(617)259-8341
Co. E-mail: gordian@usa1.com

E-mail: gordian@usa1.com
Scope: An engineering and management consultancy, the firm offers a broad range of general, financial, and valuation services, civil and tax litigation support, helps clients to enter new businesses, to plan new products and services, to evaluate feasibility, and assists with their due diligence efforts. Targets industrial concerns engaged in manufacturing, assembly, ware-

housing, energy production, process systems and bio-technology, steel, paper, and electronics. Also services businesses such as retailing, financial services, health-care, satellite broadcasting and cable television, outdoor advertising, and professional practices.

51442 ■ Stan Knipe & Associates
3176 Silver Sands Cir.
Virginia Beach, VA 23451-1185
Ph:(757)496-5475
Fax: (757)560-7631
Co. E-mail: sknipe3566@aol.com

E-mail: sknipe3566@aol.com
Scope: Specializes in retail management, strategic and organizational planning and operations, and consumer repair service. Groupware facilitator. **Seminars:** Leadership and management development.

51443 ■ Lougheed Resource Group Inc.
17608 Deer Isle Cir.
Winter Garden, FL 34787
Ph:(407)654-1212
Fax: (407)654-5419
Co. E-mail: Info@lrgmanagement.com
URL: http://www.lrgconstruction.com

E-mail: Info@lrgmanagement.com
Scope: Construction consultants specializing in project strategies, scope preparation, contract negotiation, project management, document and code evaluation, peer reviews, scheduling/estimates, dispute resolution, and forensic analysis expert testimony.

51444 ■ Kurt Salmon Associates
1355 Peachtree St. NE, Ste. 900
Atlanta, GA 30309
Ph:(404)892-0321
Fax: (404)898-9590
Co. E-mail: atlanta.office@kurtsalmon.com
URL: http://www.kurtsalmon.com

E-mail: atlanta.office@kurtsalmon.com
Scope: A global management consulting firm committed exclusively to the retail, consumer products and health care industries.

FRANCHISES AND BUSINESS OPPORTUNITIES

51445 ■ Aarons Sales & Leasing
Aaron Rents, Inc.
309 E Paces Ferry Rd.
Atlanta, GA 30305
Ph:(678)402-3445
Free: 800-551-6015
Fax: (678)402-3540
No. of Franchise Units: 379. **No. of Company-Owned Units:** 761. **Founded:** 1955. **Franchised:** 1992. **Description:** Franchises retailing business. **Equity Capital Needed:** $450,000 net worth; $300,000 liquid. **Franchise Fee:** $50,000. **Financial Assistance:** Yes. **Training:** Yes. .

51446 ■ Adam & Eve Stores
PHE, Inc. - AEFC, Inc.
302 Meadowland Dr.
Hillsborough, NC 27278
Ph:(919)644-8100
Fax: (919)644-8150
URL: http://www.adameve.com
No. of Company-Owned Units: 5. **Founded:** 1970. **Franchised:** 2004. **Description:** The adult industry is now offering retail store franchise opportunities. With over 30 years experience and over 4,000,000 customers nationwide, you benefit from the Adam & Eve brand name recognized around the country. **Equity Capital Needed:** $100,000-$196,500; cash $30,000. **Franchise Fee:** $30,000. **Financial Assistance:** No. **Training:** Training and support program will show you everything from planning 'open buys' to buying, working with vendors, merchandise inventory control, and the merchandising and display products in your store. On-site training prior to opening.

51447 ■ Beachcomber Body & Soul
3245 Comber Way
Surrey, BC, Canada V3W 5V8
Ph:(604)591-8611
Fax: (604)597-2853
Co. E-mail: info@beachcomberbodyandsoul.com
URL: http://www.beachcomberbodyandsoul.com
Founded: 1978. **Franchised:** 2004. **Description:** Manufacturer of hot tubs since 1978, has long recognized that the hot tub is the ultimate health and wellness product. Over the years, we have seen that the benefits of hydrotherapy have created a growing interest in health and wellness by our customers. In response to this interest, Beachcomber's commitment is to provide our customers with the finest quality products and broadest selection of unique and innovative health and wellness products. **Equity Capital Needed:** $240,000-$280,000, dependant on tenant improvement requirement. **Franchise Fee:** $29,900. **Training:** Extensive training and support provided by franchisor.

51448 ■ BEI Polar Clips
BEI Franchising Inc.
2525 Miller Rd.
Kalamazoo, MI 49001
Ph:(269)388-4425
Free: (866)765-2740
No. of Franchise Units: 18. **Founded:** 2002. **Franchised:** 2003. **Description:** Custom made polarized clip-on sunglasses. **Equity Capital Needed:** $25,000-$30,000, total investment. **Franchise Fee:** $20,000. **Financial Assistance:** No. **Training:** Yes.

51449 ■ Bell World
5055 Satellite Dr.
Mississauga, ON, Canada L4W 5K7
Ph:(514)420-8228
Free: 800-361-9119
Fax: (514)893-8015
Co. E-mail: franchise@bellworld.ca
URL: http://www.bell.ca
No. of Franchise Units: 255. **No. of Company-Owned Units:** 115. **Founded:** 1999. **Franchised:** 1999. **Description:** Bell Distribution Inc. is North America's first retail chain to provide complete and integrated communications solution, featuring the leading wire line, wireless, internet, and satellite technologies. The Bell World/Espace Bell stores provide a one-stop shopping experience which better serves consumers. **Training:** Yes, excluding Saskatchewan and Manitoba.

51450 ■ Ben Franklin & Ben Franklin Crafts
Franklin Franchising, Inc.
PO Box 744
Sturtevant, WI 53177-0744
Ph:(269)445-1928
Free: 800-992-9307
Fax: (262)681-6743
URL: http://www.benfranklinstores.com
No. of Franchise Units: 460. **Founded:** 1879. **Franchised:** 1936. **Description:** Chain of independently owned craft and variety stores. Franchising craft, dollar, and general merchandise stores to serve the needs of your community. **Equity Capital Needed:** From $70,000. **Franchise Fee:** $4,000-$18,000. **Financial Assistance:** Third party financing available. **Training:** Full support provided; training, merchandise, advertising, operational, and real estate.

51451 ■ Buck or Two
Denninghouse Inc.
8200 Jane St.
Concord, ON, Canada L4K SA7
Ph:(905)738-3180
Free: 800-890-8633
Fax: (905)738-3176
No. of Franchise Units: 260. **No. of Company-Owned Units:** 40. **Founded:** 1987. **Franchised:** 1990. **Description:** Retailing business. **Equity Capital Needed:** $100,000 Canadian funds. **Franchise Fee:** $50,000 Canadian funds. **Financial Assistance:** Yes. **Training:** Yes.

51452 ■ Buck or Two Extreme Retail Inc.
8200 Jane St.
Concord, ON, Canada L4K 5A7

Ph:(905)738-3180
Fax: (905)738-0680
URL: http://www.buckortwo.com
Founded: 1990. **Description:** Buck or Two Extreme Retails is a unique retail store outlet across Canada specializing in the sale of retail consumerables with price points of $1.00, $1.50 and $2.00.

51453 ■ DirectBuy
8450 Broadway
Merrillville, IN 46410
Ph:(219)648-7357
Free: 800-827-6400
Fax: (219)755-6208
Co. E-mail: dbowen@ucctotalhome.com
URL: http://www.directbuyfranchising.com
No. of Franchise Units: 128. **No. of Company-Owned Units:** 1. **Founded:** 1971. **Franchised:** 1972. **Description:** DirectBuy is an international leader in providing the best alternative to conventional retail buying. Members of DirectBuy are able to avoid traditional markups and purchase from an unprecedented selection of quality merchandise, direct from manufacturers, at unparalleled prices. **Equity Capital Needed:** $225,000-$706,000. **Franchise Fee:** $55,000. **Training:** Provides 6 weeks training, field sales and service support.

51454 ■ Discount Sport Nutrition
Discount Sport Nutrition Franchising, L.P.
1920 Abrams Pky., Ste. 422
Dallas, TX 75214
Ph:(972)489-7925
Fax: (214)292-8619
Co. E-mail: franchising@sportsupplements.com
URL: http://www.sportsupplements.com
No. of Franchise Units: 5. **Founded:** 1996. **Franchised:** 2000. **Description:** Nutritional sport supplements retail store. **Equity Capital Needed:** $80,000-$170,000. **Franchise Fee:** $25,000. **Financial Assistance:** No. **Training:** 3 phase initial hands on training program located at current stores, as well as your location. Provides assistance with site location, leases, layout design, suppliers, advertising, marketing, and ongoing assistance.

51455 ■ The Forzani Group
4855 Louis B. Mayer St.
Laval, QC, Canada H7P 6C8
Ph:(450)687-5200
Fax: (450)687-1079
Co. E-mail: glachapelle@forzani.com
URL: http://www.forzanigroup.com
Description: The Forzani Group Ltd. ("FGL") is one of Canada's largest retailer of sporting goods, offering a comprehensive assortment of brand-name and private-label products, operating stores from coast to coast, under five corporate banners: Sport Chek, Forzani's, Sports Experts, Coast Mountain Sports and Sport Mart and also on-line at Sportchek.ca and www.sportmart.ca. The Forzani Group is also a franchisor under the banners: Sports Experts, Intersport, RnR, Econosports and Atmosphere.

51456 ■ Furla
Furla Licensing (USA), Inc.
389 Fifth Ave., Ste. 700
New York, NY 10016
Ph:(212)213-1177
Fax: (212)685-5910
Co. E-mail: bruce@furlausa.com
URL: http://www.furlausa.com
No. of Franchise Units: 18. **No. of Company-Owned Units:** 15. **Founded:** 1927. **Franchised:** 1998. **Description:** Furla sells women's handbags, shoes, belts, small leather goods, watches, jewelry and accessories. All products are exclusively designed by our own cadre of designers and primarily manufactured in Italy. Furla products are updated classic in styling and targeted towards the upscale modern woman with prices ranging between $180-$350 for handbags and shoes. Our brand is known worldwide through over 200 exclusive shops. **Equity Capital Needed:** $284,000-$480,000. **Franchise Fee:** $25,000. **Financial Assistance:** No direct financing, but very competitive invoice terms, generous

product buyback program and a merchandise credit rebate for qualifying new stores. **Training:** 1 week training program at New York City office and in our corporate stores. Provides initial store set-up and opening training and ongoing training as requested.

51457 ■ Giant Tiger/Tigre Geant
Giant Tiger Stores Limited
2480 Walkley Rd.
Ottawa, ON, Canada K1G 6A9
Ph:(613)521-8222
Fax: (613)521-2523
Co. E-mail: careers@gianttiger.com
URL: http://www.gianttiger.com
No. of Franchise Units: 128. **No. of Company-Owned Units:** 46. **Founded:** 1961. **Franchised:** 1964. **Description:** Franchise involves retailing services. **Financial Assistance:** Yes. **Training:** Training, site selection, lease negotiations and advisory council are provided.

51458 ■ Great Canadian Dollar Store (1993) Ltd.
2957 Jutland Rd., Ste. 101
Victoria, BC, Canada V8T 5J9
Ph:(250)388-0123
Free: 877-388-0123
Fax: (250)388-9763
Co. E-mail: www.dollarstores.com
URL: http://www.dollarstores.com
No. of Franchise Units: 120. **Founded:** 1993. **Franchised:** 1993. **Description:** Offers an excellent opportunity to market a wide range of exciting merchandise. **Equity Capital Needed:** $150,000-$400,000. **Franchise Fee:** $19,880. **Training:** Offers training and ongoing support.

51459 ■ Hometown Hearth & Grill
Suburban Franchising, Inc.
240 Rte. 10 West
Whippany, NJ 07981
Free: 888-298-0031
Co. E-mail: dlefevere@suburbanenergy.com
URL: http://www.suburbanfranchising.com
No. of Franchise Units: 1. **No. of Company-Owned Units:** 10. **Founded:** 1993. **Franchised:** 2004. **Description:** HomeTown Hearth & Grill franchise is an upscale unique retail hearth and outdoor living specialty store. The franchise offers gas grills, outdoor products, fireplaces, hearth stoves, replacement parts and accessories that transform indoor and outdoor spaces with elegance and warmth. The franchises utilize specialized retail software for POS tracking and ordering. **Equity Capital Needed:** $300,000+ for startup and 1 year operating capital. **Franchise Fee:** $39,500. **Financial Assistance:** SBA and conventional small business loans. **Training:** We offer 2+ weeks of initial start-up training site selection, build out, and inventory assistance. Ongoing assistance in retail sales, marketing an management.

51460 ■ Imagine This Sold
7050 Weston Rd., Ste. 225
Woodbridge, ON, Canada L4L 8G7
Free: (866)571-2941
Fax: (905)264-2996
Co. E-mail: peter@imaginethissold.com
Description: Imagine This Sold is the new retail marketplace! Bringing together both buyers and sells in a mutually beneficial way that allows goods to be marketed and sold effectively in this new global economy via a bricks and mortar store environment.

51461 ■ Java Dave's Coffee
Java Dave's Executive Coffee Service
6239 E 15th St.
Tulsa, OK 74112
Ph:(918)836-5570
Free: 800-725-7315
Fax: (918)835-4348
No. of Franchise Units: 13. **No. of Company-Owned Units:** 2. **Founded:** 1988. **Franchised:** 1993. **Description:** Retail store. **Equity Capital Needed:** $150,000. **Franchise Fee:** $17,500. **Financial Assistance:** Yes. **Training:** Yes.

51462 ■ Let's Make Wine
2424 N Federal Hwy., Ste. 455
Boca Raton, FL 33431
Ph:(561)416-9096
Free: 888-416-9755
Fax: (561)416-9098
Co. E-mail: franchiseinfo@letsmakewine.com
URL: http://www.letsmakewine.com
No. of Company-Owned Units: 4. **Founded:** 2003. **Franchised:** 2004. **Description:** Upscale retail stores where franchisees offer customers the opportunity to make their own great tasting wine. Perfect for corporate events, parties or private reserves. The process is simple and fun to do! Customers select bottles, corks and custom design their own labels. Wine related giftware provides multiple revenue streams. Immediate opportunities in FL, CO, TX, WY, OH, AR, DC, KS, NE and IN. **Equity Capital Needed:** $226,500-$405,000. **Franchise Fee:** $35,000. **Training:** Comprehensive orientation, training, support, and wine-making operations will be provided at the Let's Make Wine Orientation University at our facility in Thompson, GA or at one of our owned locations in FL. Training will address POS and accounting software programs, marketing, merchandising, winemaking, and administration.

51463 ■ Love Boutique
17551-108 Ave. NW
Edmonton, AB, Canada T5S 1G2
Ph:(780)486-0433
Fax: (780)486-5714
No. of Franchise Units: 2. **No. of Company-Owned Units:** 19. **Founded:** 1978. **Franchised:** 1999. **Description:** Retailing business. **Equity Capital Needed:** $165,000+ Canadian. **Franchise Fee:** $30,000 Canadian. **Financial Assistance:** No. **Training:** Yes.

51464 ■ Max Muscle
1641 S Sinclair St.
Anaheim, CA 92806
Ph:(480)664-0851
Free: (866)MAX-MUSC
Fax: (775)822-0164
No. of Franchise Units: 86. **No. of Company-Owned Units:** 1. **Founded:** 1991. **Franchised:** 2001. **Description:** The franchise deals mainly with retailing. **Equity Capital Needed:** $50,000. **Franchise Fee:** 25,000. **Financial Assistance:** Yes. **Training:** Yes.

51465 ■ Nicholby's Franchise Systems Inc.
3671 Victoria Park Ave., Unit 6
Toronto, ON, Canada M1W 3K6
Ph:(416)492-6424
Fax: (416)492-4852
Co. E-mail: rob@nicholbys.com
No. of Franchise Units: 22. **No. of Company-Owned Units:** 4. **Founded:** 1980. **Description:** Retail stores operating in hospitals, hotels, highways and office buildings. **Equity Capital Needed:** $27,000-$66,000; $27,000-$66,000. **Franchise Fee:** $9,900. **Training:** Offers 3-4 weeks training and ongoing support.

51466 ■ Peaberry Coffee
Peaberry Coffee Franchise, Inc.
1299 E 58th Ave.
Denver, CO 80216
Ph:(303)292-9324
Free: 888-740-4200
Fax: (303)292-5179
No. of Franchise Units: 7. **No. of Company-Owned Units:** 5. **Founded:** 1990. **Franchised:** 2003. **Description:** Colorado roaster & coffee retail stores. **Equity Capital Needed:** $197,000-$479,000. **Franchise Fee:** $35,000. **Financial Assistance:** No. **Training:** Yes.

51467 ■ Personal Edge
Centre Du Rasoir
10200 Cote de Liesse
Montreal (Lachine), QC, Canada H8T 1A3
Ph:(514)636-4512
Fax: (514)636-8356
Co. E-mail: jean-claude@cdrem.com
URL: http://www.personaledge.com

No. of Franchise Units: 70. **Founded:** 1959. **Franchised:** 1980. **Description:** Our stores, located in major shopping malls, feature one of Canada's largest selection of electric shavers and other personal grooming products, as well as small household appliances and specialty gifts from leading manufacturers. We have a unique mix of quality brand name products and on-site repair services. **Equity Capital Needed:** $50,000-$80,000. **Franchise Fee:** $30,000. **Training:** Yes.

51468 ■ Port City Java
PCJ Franchising Co., LLC
2101 Market St.
Wilmington, NC 28403
Ph:(910)796-6646
Fax: (910)796-6611
No. of Franchise Units: 24. **No. of Company-Owned Units:** 10. **Founded:** 1995. **Franchised:** 2003. **Description:** Gourmet coffee cafe with wireless web. **Equity Capital Needed:** $100,000 liquid capital; $350,000 net worth. **Franchise Fee:** $27,500. **Financial Assistance:** Yes. **Training:** Yes.

51469 ■ Preplayed
9 West Aylesbury Rd., Ste. F-G
Timonium, MD 21093
Ph:(410)560-0551
Free: (866)640-7529
Fax: (410)560-6355
No. of Franchise Units: 5. **Founded:** 2003. **Franchised:** 2003. **Description:** Buy/sell CDs, movies, video games, etc. **Equity Capital Needed:** $265,000-$322,000. **Franchise Fee:** $25,000. **Financial Assistance:** No. **Training:** Yes.

51470 ■ Save-A-Deck
201 - 17834 106 Ave.
Edmonton, AB, Canada T5S 1V4
Free: (866)313-3325
Fax: (780)470-3227
Co. E-mail: marcusc@telusplanet.net
Description: Save-A-Deck specializes in franchising and the sale of products to franchisees including vinyl decking and aluminum railings for sundecks, stairways, and related applications for both the residential, as well as commercial client base.

51471 ■ Saxbys Coffee
Proven Record, Inc.
101 Convention Ctr. Dr., Ste. 701
Las Vegas, NV 89109
Ph:(702)380-7826
Fax: (702)447-9122
Co. E-mail: john@saxbyscoffee.com
URL: http://www.saxbyscoffee.com
No. of Franchise Units: 8. **Founded:** 2002. **Franchised:** 2003. **Description:** Coffee retail store, specializing in gourmet espresso drinks, smoothies, and tea. An affordable initial investment, a rewarding career, a simple business to own and operate, and an easy restaurant to staff. **Equity Capital Needed:** $50,000 cash, $200,000 equity. **Franchise Fee:** $30,000. **Financial Assistance:** No. **Training:** 5 day owner training before opening the store and a 5 day owner and employee training upon opening the store.

51472 ■ Smart Cartridge Canada
493 Roumefort
Montreal, QC, Canada H9C 2S6
Free: 888-962-7822
Fax: (514)620-3628
Co. E-mail: enquiries@smart-cartridge.ca
URL: http://www.smart-cartridge.ca
No. of Franchise Units: 30. **No. of Company-Owned Units:** 1. **Founded:** 2000. **Franchised:** 2002. **Description:** refilling & remanufacturing of inkjet and laser cartridges within a retail environment. A unique, affordable and outstanding business concept with endless opportunities - 5 fantastic revenue streams: inkjet refilling, laser remanufacturing, digital photo processing (instant prints), reconditioned brand name printers, media products and accessories - we truly are a one stop print solutions store! **Equity Capital Needed:** $150,000, includes working capital. **Franchise Fee:** $30,000. **Training:** Full training and ongoing support provided.

51473 ■ Sports Experts 2000 Inc.–The Forzani Group
The Forzani Group, Ltd.
4855 Louis-B Mayer St.
Laval, QC, Canada H7P 6C8
Ph:(450)687-5200
Fax: (450)687-1079
Co. E-mail: mstcharles@forzanigroup.com
URL: http://www.forzanigroup.com
No. of Franchise Units: 225. **No. of Company-Owned Units:** 275. **Founded:** 1967. **Franchised:** 1967. **Description:** Retailer and wholesaler of sporting goods clothing, footwear and equipment. **Equity Capital Needed:** Varies. **Franchise Fee:** Banner specific. **Training:** Yes.

51474 ■ Theater Xtreme
250 Corporate Blvd., No. E
Newark, DE 19702
Ph:(302)455-1334
Fax: (302)455-1612
No. of Franchise Units: 6. **No. of Company-Owned Units:** 5. **Founded:** 2003. **Franchised:** 2004. **Description:** Home theaters and furnishings. **Equity Capital Needed:** $400,000-$700,000. **Franchise Fee:** $40,000. **Royalty Fee:** 4%. **Financial Assistance:** Third party financing available. **Training:** Offers 2 weeks at headquarters, on-site and ongoing electronic training. ning.

51475 ■ Vintage Stock
202 E 32nd St.
Joplin, MO 64804
Ph:(417)623-1550
Fax: (417)782-0024
No. of Company-Owned Units: 13. **Founded:** 1980. **Franchised:** 2005. **Description:** DVDs, videogames, music and sports cards. **Equity Capital Needed:** $337,700-$585,400. **Franchise Fee:** $30,000. **Royalty Fee:** 5%. **Financial Assistance:** No. **Training:** Offers 1 week of training at headquarters, 2-3 weeks on-site and ongoing support.

51476 ■ Watch It! Inc.
10544B-82 Ave.
Edmonton, AB, Canada T6E 2A4
Ph:(780)435-2824

Fax: (780)434-5039
Co. E-mail: franchise@canadawatches.com
URL: http://www.watchit.ca
No. of Franchise Units: 7. **No. of Company-Owned Units:** 4. **Founded:** 1999. **Franchised:** 2004. **Description:** Watch It! Is a cool and funky retail boutique that offers a wide selection of premium brand name watches, sunglasses and accessories. With its trademarked names, a consistent look and feel across stores, low start-up costs and operating procedures that are polished and efficient, purchasing a Watch It franchise is a sensible investment. **Equity Capital Needed:** $200,000-$250,000. **Franchise Fee:** $25,000. **Training:** Yes.

51477 ■ Wild Bird Centers of America
130 Fifth Ave., 10th Fl.
New York, NY 10011-4399
Ph:(212)242-4399
Description: Retail store that offers more than just bird feeders and seed. The store offers a wide selection of products including exclusive seed blends that are field-tested and proven to attract a wide variety of wild birds. In addition to an extensive selection of feeders, birdbaths, nest boxes and other bird feeding products, the stores offer a variety of backyard and nature-oriented gifts and books, plus a wide range of binoculars and spotting scopes. **Equity Capital Needed:** $94,900-$152,300 total investment; $30,000-$50,000 cash required. **Training:** You receive a turn-key, proven business system, comprehensive training and support.

51478 ■ Your Dollar Store With More Inc.
1626 Richter St., Ste. 102
Kelowna, BC, Canada V1Y 2M3
Ph:(250)860-4225
Fax: (250)860-4215
Co. E-mail: ydswm@dollarstore.ca
URL: http://www.dollarstore.ca
No. of Franchise Units: 181. **No. of Company-Owned Units:** 3. **Founded:** 1998. **Franchised:** 1998. **Description:** The franchise is a family owned dollar store franchise with 100 years of franchising and retail business experience. **Equity Capital Needed:** $40,000. **Franchise Fee:** $20,000. **Training:** Yes.

COMPUTER SYSTEMS/ SOFTWARE

51479 ■ Business Controller
MicroBiz
1 Park Way
Upper Saddle River, NJ 7458
Ph:800-385-0072
Fax: (201)785-1568
Co. E-mail: info@microbiz.com
URL: http://www.microbiz.com
Price: Contact MicroBiz for pricing. **Description:** This new version of the Business Controller Plus for Windows is a true 32 bit program that runs in Windows or NT. The software does inventory, invoicing, customer tracking, accounts receivable, reordering, purchasing and much more. It also includes a Query module that allows you to design your own reports and it's Internet Ready!

START-UP INFORMATION

51480 ■ **"Strong Structure"** in *Black Enterprise* (Vol. 34, July 2004, No. 12, pp. 48)
Pub: Earl G. Graves Publishing Co. Inc.
Ed: Alan Hughes. **Description:** Advice is given for launching a small business. The entrepreneur needs information for choosing the business structure that is right for his new firm. Guidelines for choosing a sole proprietorship, partnership, limited liability company, C corporation, and S corporation are outlined.

REFERENCE WORKS

51481 ■ **"Backing Mike's Pro-Biz Tax Plan"** in *Crain's New York Business* (Vol. 23, January 22, 2007, No. 4, pp. 12)
Pub: Crain Communications, Inc.
Ed: Description: New York's Mayor Bloomberg wants to revamp the unincorporated business tax which would help S corporations, since these companies must report profits as income on their personal tax forms, they are effectively taxed twice. Small Companies would benefit from a new credit which would partially offset that burden. He also wants to eliminate the city's 4 percent sales tax on footwear and clothing purchases to boost the city's economy and would help compete with New Jersey.

51482 ■ *Entrepreneurial Finance*
Pub: Pearson Education, Limited
Ed: Philip J. Adelman; Alan M. Marks. **Released:** July 2006. **Price:** $87.35. **Description:** Financial aspects of running a small business are covered; topics include sole proprietorships, partnerships, limited liability companies, and private corporations.

51483 ■ *Fast-Track Business Start-Up Kit: California*
Pub: DP Group, Incorporated
Ed: Carolyn Usinger. **Released:** September 2006. **Price:** $29.00. **Description:** Step-by-step guide for starting and running a business in California, including information on sole proprietors, partnerships, limited liability companies, S and C corporations, as well as details concerning business entities, sales taxes, environmental issues, human resources, and more.

51484 ■ **"For some companies, it pays to be private"** in *Red Herring* (March 2003, pp. 66)
Pub: Herring Communications Inc.
Ed: Michael V. Copeland. **Description:** Currently, an increasing number of private companies are being valued at a higher multiple than public counterparts.

51485 ■ *Forming Corporations and Partnerships*
Pub: TAB Books, Inc.
Ed: John Cotton Howell. **Released:** 1991. **Price:** $14.95. **Description:** Provides information on corporations and partnerships, covering special corporate tax and insurance, pros and cons of various business entities, duties and responsibilities of corporate officers, and rights, duties, and obligations of parties in joint ventures.

51486 ■ *How to Form Your Own Corporation without a Lawyer for Under $75.00*
Pub: Dearborn Trade Publishing Inc.
Ed: Ted Nicholas; Sean P. Melvin. **Price:** $19.95.

51487 ■ *Incorporate Your Business: A 50 State Legal Guide to Forming a Corporation*
Pub: Nolo
Ed: Anthony Mancuso. **Released:** August 2001. **Price:** $50.00. **Description:** Legal guide to incorporating a business in the U.S., covering all 50 states.

51488 ■ *Incorporating Form Samples or Information for the Fifty States*
Pub: Data Notes Publishing Co.
Contact: A. C. Doyle
Ed: A. C. Doyle, Editor. **Released:** Irregular, Latest edition 1999. **Price:** $49.95. **Description:** Microfiche. Includes a list of state agencies that handle incorporation applications and actual forms. **Entries Include:** Agency name, address. **Arrangement:** Geographical.

51489 ■ **"IRS Will Remove Tax Trap for One-Person S Corporations"** in *Kiplinger Letter* (Vol. 82, January 12, 2007, No. 1)
Pub: Kiplinger
Description: Internal Revenue Service is developing a new system that will clarify S corporation owners in states that are not allowed to deduct one-participant group health insurance plans, however, to get the deduction, the S firm must pay the medical premium.

51490 ■ *The Law of Corporations, Partnerships, & Sole Proprietorships Instructor's Guide*
Pub: Delmar Publishers
Ed: Angela Schneeman. **Released:** 1993. **Price:** $12.50.

51491 ■ **"A Road Less Taxed"** in *My Business* (February/March 2004, pp. 40)
Pub: My Business Magazine
Ed: Karen M. Kroll. **Description:** An explanation of the most common business structures and the ways taxes are generated for each is presented, including sole proprietorship, partnership, Limited Liability Corporation, S corporation, and C corporation.

51492 ■ *Simplified Incorporation Kit*
Pub: Nova Publishing Company
Ed: Daniel Sitarz. **Released:** March 2007. **Price:** $19.95. **Description:** Kit includes all the forms, instructions, and information necessary for incorporating any small business in any state (CD-ROM included).

51493 ■ **"Tax plan could prompt corporations to move to C"** in *Crain's Detroit Business* (Vol. 19, No. 5, Feb. 3, 2003, pp. 13)
Pub: Crain Communications Inc., Detroit
Ed: Katie Merx. **Description:** Under President Bush's tax plan, S-type corporations and limited liability companies could lose many benefits.

51494 ■ **"Watch your step"** in *Entrepreneur* (Vol. 31, No. 6, June 2003, pp. 55)
Pub: Entrepreneur Media Inc.
Ed: Joan Szabo. **Description:** The IRS is promising to crack down on small business owners not reporting business income, focusing on abusive tax shelters, offshore credit card abuse, high-income nonfilers, and high-income taxpayers engaged in partnerships, trusts or S corporations, as well as selecting 50,000 random returns from 2001.

51495 ■ **"Your Loss Is Your Gain"** in *Entrepreneur* (Vol. 31, No. 5, May 2003, pp. 50)
Pub: Entrepreneur Media Inc.
Ed: Joan Szabo. **Description:** One of the advantages of an S corporation is the firm's annual income or losses are passed to shareholder; gains are reflected on individual shareholder's tax returns, and losses are deductible. If a small business suffered losses due to a slow economy, it may be able to save taxes from those losses if the firm has Section 1244 stock.

TRADE PERIODICALS

51496 ■ *Taxes—The Tax Magazine*
Pub: CCH Inc.
Contact: Kurt Diefenbach, Managing Editor
Released: Monthly. **Price:** $245; $270 internet; $365 print & internet. **Description:** Magazine on tax laws and regulations.

COMPUTERIZED DATABASES

51497 ■ *Federal Income Taxation of S Corporations*
Thomson RIA
395 Hudson St., 4th Fl.
New York, NY 10014
Ph:(212)367-6300
Free: 800-431-9025
Co. E-mail: ria@thomson.com
URL: http://ria.thomson.com
Description: Contains the full text of the fourth edition of Federal Income Taxation of S Corporations. Covers income tax issues spanning the entire life of an S corporation, from election to operation to termination. Provides authoritative interpretations and insights into rules and regulations controlling S corporations. Includes guidance on daily operation and long-term maintenance of the S corporation. **Availability:** Online: Thomson RIA, Thomson West; CD-ROM: Thomson RIA. **Type:** Full text.

LIBRARIES

51498 ■ **Cornell University–Johnson Graduate School of Management–Library (101 S)**
101 Sage Hall
Ithaca, NY 14853

Ph:(607)255-3389
Fax: (607)255-8633
Co. E-mail: mgtref@cornell.edu
URL: http://www.library.cornell.edu/johnson
Contact: Donald Schnedeker, Dir.
Scope: Business administration and management science, finance, investment, accounting, marketing, managerial economics, operations management and quantitative analysis. **Services:** Interlibrary loan. **Holdings:** 160,000 volumes; 1096 non-book materials; 813,000 microfiche; 3200 microfilm; 300 CD-ROMs. **Subscriptions:** 1300 journals and other serials; 23 newspapers.

RESEARCH CENTERS

51499 ■ Jackson State University–Bureau of Business and Economic Research
1230 Raymond Rd., Box 500
Jackson, MS 39204
Ph:(601)979-2795
Fax: (601)914-0833
Co. E-mail: cathy.d.turner@jsums.edu
URL: http://www.jsums.edu/business/bber/
Contact: Cathy D. Turner, Asst. to the Dir.

E-mail: cathy.d.turner@jsums.edu
Scope: Small business, including applied and theoretical studies which contribute to the development of Mississippi business economy. **Services:** Consulting for local business. **Publications:** Annual Demographic Databook (annually); Economic Indicators (monthly); Reports. **Educational Activities:** School of Business Annual Research Symposiums; Seminars in areas of finance, marketing, management, accounting, and secretarial education, for business personnel and entrepreneurs in the Jackson area. **Awards:** Research Awards, for faculty.

51500 ■ St. Francis Xavier University–Coady International Institute
PO Box 5000
Antigonish, NS, Canada B2G 2W5
Ph:(902)867-3960
Free: (866)-820-7835
Fax: (902)867-3907
Co. E-mail: coady@stfx.ca
URL: http://www.coady.stfx.ca
Contact: Mary Coyle, Dir.
E-mail: coady@stfx.ca
Scope: International development, community development, adult education, health education, gender

and development, advocacy, microenterprise, microcredit, peacebuilding, evaluation. **Publications:** Coady Connection (biennially).

51501 ■ University of Maryland at College Park–Dingman Center for Entrepreneurship
3570 Van Munching Hall
Robert H. Smith School of Business
College Park, MD 20742
Ph:(301)405-9510
Fax: (301)314-7973
Co. E-mail: aepstein@rhsmith.umd.edu
URL: http://www.rhsmith.umd.edu/dingman/
Contact: Asher Epstein, Mng.Dir.
E-mail: aepstein@rhsmith.umd.edu
Scope: Entrepreneurship, new venture creation, technology commercialization, and venture capital. **Services:** Assistance, to emerging growth firms through mentor program; Business Plan Reviews. **Publications:** Newsletters for the entrepreneurial community and for volunteers (monthly). **Educational Activities:** Dingman Day Lunches; Industry forums; Networking breakfasts; Seminars; Speaker events, in entrepreneurship and entrepreneurship concentration in MBA curriculum; Venture Capital Forums.

START-UP INFORMATION

51502 ■ "Digital Rules" in *Forbes* **(February 19, 2001, pp. 51)**
Pub: Forbes Magazine
Ed: Rich Karlgaard. **Description:** The article proves that, despite the New Economy, it still takes brains, salesmanship, guts and a whole lot of persistence to launch and run a startup.

51503 ■ "Reeling in the Big Ones" in *Entrepreneur* **(Vol. 28, No. 1, January 2000, pp. 138)**
Pub: Entrepreneur Media Inc.
Ed: Bill Kelley. **Description:** Most entrepreneurs would love to land large corporate accounts, but they often don't try for one simple reason: they're afraid.

51504 ■ "Reeling In the Big One" in *Inc.* **(August 1, 2004)**
Pub: Inc. Magazine
Ed: Jess McCuan. **Description:** Ways a startup business can land a large, brand name client are examined.

51505 ■ "Start with Nothing" in *Inc.* **(February 1, 2002)**
Pub: Inc. Magazine
Ed: Emily Barker. **Description:** Greg Gianforte, founder of the software company Brightwork Development Inc., shares his secrets for launching a successful new company, with a focus on sales.

ASSOCIATIONS AND OTHER ORGANIZATIONS

51506 ■ Association of Retail Marketing Services
10 Drs. James Parker Blvd., Ste. 103
Red Bank, NJ 07701-1500
Ph:(732)842-5070
Fax: (732)219-1938
Co. E-mail: info@goarms.com
Contact: Gerri Hopkins, Exec.Dir.
Description: Devoted to the promotional needs of the retail industry. Recommends incentive promotion at the retail level. Offers legal and legislative services and public relations programs. Conducts research programs; compiles statistics. Publishes newsletter and sponsors a tradeshow. **Publications:** *Creative Marketing* (quarterly); Membership Directory (annual). Also publishes mailing lists and case studies.

51507 ■ Association of Sales Administration Managers
Box 1356
Laurence Harbor, NJ 08879
Ph:(732)264-7722
Co. E-mail: asamnet@aol.com
Contact: Bill Martin, Sec.-Treas.
Description: Independent consultants providing sales and marketing services, including establishing broker and rep sales networks, field sales management, and marketing and branch office administrative services. Primary expertise is in the consumer packaged goods field, both private label and branded. Offers consulting services.

51508 ■ Canadian Professional Sales Association–L'association Canadienne des Professionnels de la Vente
310 Front St. W, Ste. 800
Toronto, ON, Canada M5V 3B5
Ph:(416)408-2685
Free: 888-267-CPSA
Fax: (416)408-2684
URL: http://www.cpsa.com
Contact: Harvey Copeman, Pres./CEO
Membership: Professional salespeople. **Purpose:** Promotes professional advancement of members. Represents members' interests before government agencies, industrial organizations, and the public. Conducts continuing professional education programs. **Publications:** *Contact* (bimonthly).

51509 ■ Direct Selling Association
1667 K St. NW, Ste. 1100
Washington, DC 20006
Ph:(202)452-8866
Fax: (202)452-9010
Co. E-mail: info@dsa.org
URL: http://www.dsa.org
Contact: Mr. Neil H. Offen, Pres.
Membership: Manufacturers and distributors selling consumer products through person-to-person sales, by appointment, and through home-party plans. Products include food, gifts, house wares, dietary supplements, cosmetics, apparel, jewelry, decorative accessories, reference books, and telecommunications products and services. **Purpose:** Offers specialized education; conducts research programs; compiles statistics. Maintains hall of fame. Sponsors Direct Selling Education Foundation. **Publications:** *Data Tracker* (quarterly); *News from Neil* (monthly); *State Status Sheet* (weekly); Annual Report (annual).

51510 ■ Direct Selling Education Foundation
1667 K St. NW, Ste. 1100
Washington, DC 20006-1660
Ph:(202)452-8866
Fax: (202)452-9015
Co. E-mail: info@dsef.org
URL: http://www.dsef.org
Contact: Mr. Jeremy B. Taylor, Exec.Dir.
Description: Serves the public interest with education, information, and research, thereby enhancing acceptance and public awareness of direct selling in the global marketplace. **Publications:** *DSEF: A Foundation That Works*; *Moral Suasion*.

51511 ■ Marketing Agencies Association Worldwide
460 Summer St., 4th Fl.
Stamford, CT 06901
Ph:(203)978-1590
Fax: (203)969-1499
Co. E-mail: keith.mccracken@maaw.org
URL: http://www.maaw.org
Contact: Mr. Keith McCracken, Acting Exec.Dir.
Description: Represents the interests of CEOs, presidents, managing directors and principals of top marketing services agencies. Provides opportunity for marketing professionals to meet with peers, raise company profile on both a national and a global platform, and influence the future of industry. Fosters networking through conferences.

51512 ■ Professional Society for Sales and Marketing Training
5905 NW 54th Cir.
Coral Springs, FL 33067
Free: 800-219-0096
Fax: 800-219-0096
URL: http://www.smt.org
Contact: Steve Bistritz, Pres.
Membership: Directors of training. **Purpose:** Seeks to improve sales, marketing, and customer relations through training. Conducts educational conferences and sales training clinics. **Publications:** *Trainer Talk* (bimonthly).

51513 ■ Sales Professionals USA
PO Box 149
Arvada, CO 80001
Ph:(303)534-4937
Free: 888-763-7767
Co. E-mail: salespro@salesprofessionals-usa.com
URL: http://www.salesprofessionals-usa.com
Contact: Sharon Herbert, Natl.Pres.
Membership: Salespersons, owners of small businesses, and those interested in free enterprise from Australia, Singapore, New Zealand, and the United States. **Purpose:** Endeavors to increase an individual's effectiveness and earning power in any field of salesmanship, in particular creative salesmanship. Fosters the interchange of ideas, techniques, philosophies, and concepts relative to salesmanship; encourages high standards and ethical behavior for those in selling; maintains a good relation between business and the buying public; educates and increases the abilities of those currently engaged in selling; promotes the profession to youth. Conducts in-class sales training for high school and college students; sponsors symposia and workshops. Maintains speakers' bureau. **Publications:** *Wired for Sales* (quarterly).

51514 ■ World Federation of Direct Selling Associations
1667 K St. NW
Washington, DC 20006
Ph:(202)452-8866
Fax: (202)452-9010
Co. E-mail: info@wfdsa.org
URL: http://www.wfdsa.org
Contact: Neil H. Offen, Sec.
Purpose: Organized for the purpose of promoting the common business interests of its members. Exchanges information among members. Fosters highest standards of direct selling practices, consumer protection and ethics in the marketplace, by adoption and promotion of the Codes of Conduct for Direct Selling. Improves communications through sponsorship

of World Congress of direct selling. Encourages personal relationships and cooperation among people in direct selling. Promotes education internationally through programs and funding, relying on the United States Direct Selling Education Foundation (USDSEF) to help it towards this objective. **Publications:** *WFDSA Directory of Members* (annual); *World Federation News* (bimonthly).

EDUCATIONAL PROGRAMS

51515 ■ Advanced Sales Management Level 2
American Management Association
1601 Broadway
New York, NY 10019
Ph:(212)586-8100
Free: 800-262-9699
Fax: (212)903-8168
Co. E-mail: customerservice@amanet.org
URL: http://www.amanet.org
Price: $1,995 for non-members; $1,795 for AMA members. **Description:** Covers increasing productivity and efficiency through team building, adapting to a changing environment, and decision, and problem solving techniques. **Locations:** Cities throughout the United States.

51516 ■ Advanced Sales Management—Level 2 (Canada)
Canadian Management Centre
150 York St., 5th Fl.
Toronto, ON, Canada M5H 3S5
Ph:(866)400-4941 ext. 2252
Free: 877-CMC-2500
Fax: (416)313-4985
Co. E-mail: cmcinfo@cmctraining.org
URL: http://www.cmcamai.org
Price: $1,850 Canadian. **Description:** Covers an overview of the sales environment today, organizing a productive sales force, planning and forecasting, and techniques for motivational team building. **Locations:** Toronto, ON.

51517 ■ Coaching Your Sales Team
American Management Association
1601 Broadway
New York, NY 10019
Ph:(212)586-8100
Free: 800-262-9699
Fax: (212)903-8168
Co. E-mail: customerservice@amanet.org
URL: http://www.amanet.org
Price: $1,795 for non-members; $1,595 for AMA members. **Description:** Covers effective training and coaching techniques while building a confident and positive sales team. **Locations:** New York, NY; Washington, DC; Chicago, IL; Atlanta, GA; and San Francisco, CA.

51518 ■ Cross Selling Successfully: Maximizing Customer Relationships (Canada)
Canadian Management Centre
150 York St., 5th Fl.
Toronto, ON, Canada M5H 3S5
Ph:(866)400-4941 ext. 2252
Free: 877-CMC-2500
Fax: (416)313-4985
Co. E-mail: cmcinfo@cmctraining.org
URL: http://www.cmcamai.org
Price: $995 Canadian. **Description:** Covers capitalizing on your profitability through your existing customer base, improve your methods on screening the positive and negative effects of cross selling, and take control of the obstacles the effect cross selling. **Locations:** Toronto, ON.

51519 ■ Enhancing Your Presentation Skills: A Seminar for Sales Professionals
American Management Association
1601 Broadway
New York, NY 10019
Ph:(212)586-8100
Free: 800-262-9699

Fax: (212)903-8168
Co. E-mail: customerservice@amanet.org
URL: http://www.amanet.org
Price: $1,795.00; $1,595.00 for AMA members. **Description:** Three-day seminar covers creating a professional image, understanding your product and your competition, utilizing emotion, organizational skills, and handling questions. **Locations:** Chicago, IL; and New York, NY.

51520 ■ Fundamental Selling Techniques for the New or Prospective Salesperson—Level 1 (Canada)
Canadian Management Centre
150 York St., 5th Fl.
Toronto, ON, Canada M5H 3S5
Ph:(866)400-4941 ext. 2252
Free: 877-CMC-2500
Fax: (416)313-4985
Co. E-mail: cmcinfo@cmctraining.org
URL: http://www.cmcamai.org
Price: $1,595 Canadian. **Description:** For sales people with less than one year of experience; covers a five-step process of prospecting, building relationships, sales presentations, and the various types of closes. **Locations:** Toronto, ON.

51521 ■ Fundamentals of Sales Management (Canada)
Canadian Management Centre
150 York St., 5th Fl.
Toronto, ON, Canada M5H 3S5
Ph:(416)214-5678
Free: 800-262-9699
Fax: (416)313-4985
Co. E-mail: cmcinfo@cmctraining.org
URL: http://www.cmcamai.org
Price: $1,795.00 Canadian. **Description:** Covers transitioning from sales person to manager, recruiting and interviewing, proven management techniques, establishing training, and coaching skills. **Locations:** Vancouver, BC; Mississauga, ON; and Toronto, ON.

51522 ■ Fundamentals of Sales Management—Level 1 (Canada)
Canadian Management Centre
150 York St., 5th Fl.
Toronto, ON, Canada M5H 3S5
Ph:(866)400-4941 ext. 2252
Free: 877-CMC-2500
Fax: (416)313-4985
Co. E-mail: cmcinfo@cmctraining.org
URL: http://www.cmcamai.org
Price: $1,795 Canadian. **Description:** Covers the differences between selling and managing, and discover how sales managers influence organizations. **Locations:** Toronto, ON.

51523 ■ Fundamentals of Sales Management for the Newly Appointed Sales Manager
American Management Association
1601 Broadway
New York, NY 10019
Ph:(212)586-8100
Free: 800-262-9699
Fax: (212)903-8168
Co. E-mail: customerservice@amanet.org
URL: http://www.amanet.org
Price: $1,795.00 for non-members; $1,695.00 for AMA members. **Description:** Covers transitioning from sales person to manager, proven management techniques, establishing training, and coaching skills. **Locations:** Scottsdale, AZ; Anaheim, CA; San Francisco, CA; Washington, DC; Atlanta, GA; Chicago, IL; and New York, NY.

51524 ■ Fundamentals of Selling Techniques for the New or Prospective Salesperson (Canada)
Canadian Management Centre
150 York St., 5th Fl.
Toronto, ON, Canada M5H 3S5
Ph:(416)214-5678
Free: 800-262-9699
Fax: (416)313-4985
Co. E-mail: cmcinfo@cmctraining.org
URL: http://cmcamai.org

Price: $1,595.00 Canadian. **Description:** Covers prospecting, building client relationships, handling objections, and closing methods. **Locations:** Toronto, ON.

51525 ■ Managing the Distributor Sales Network
American Management Association
1601 Broadway
New York, NY 10019
Ph:(212)586-8100
Free: 800-262-9699
Fax: (212)903-8168
Co. E-mail: customerservice@amanet.org
URL: http://www.amanet.org
Price: $1,895 for non-members; $1,695 for AMA members. **Description:** Covers building a distributor network. **Locations:** New York, NY; Washington, DC; Chicago, IL; and San Francisco, CA.

51526 ■ National Accounts Management
American Management Association
1601 Broadway
New York, NY 10019
Ph:(212)586-8100
Free: 800-262-9699
Fax: (212)903-8168
Co. E-mail: customerservice@amanet.org
URL: http://www.amanet.org
Price: $1,895.00.00 for non-members; $1,695.00 for AMA members. **Description:** Covers the benefits of developing a major national accounts program, and techniques and strategies for success. **Locations:** Chicago, IL; and New York, NY.

51527 ■ Principles of Professional Selling
American Management Association
1601 Broadway
New York, NY 10019
Ph:(212)586-8100
Free: 800-262-9699
Fax: (212)903-8168
Co. E-mail: customerservice@amanet.org
URL: http://www.amanet.org
Price: $1,745.00 for non-members; $1,695.00 for AMA members. **Description:** Three-day seminar for seasoned sales professionals; covers consultative selling, planning the sales process, building relationships with customers, the sales process, utilizing technology, listening skills, telephone techniques, and time management. **Locations:** San Francisco, CA; Washington, DC; Chicago, IL; and New York, NY.

51528 ■ Principles of Professional Selling Level 2
American Management Association
1601 Broadway
New York, NY 10019
Ph:(212)586-8100
Free: 800-262-9699
Fax: (212)903-8168
Co. E-mail: customerservice@amanet.org
URL: http://www.amanet.org
Price: $1,895 for non-members; $1,695 for AMA members. **Description:** Covers selling techniques in order to close the deal, including building partnerships, creating new business, time management, prioritizing, and an understanding of your customers needs. **Locations:** Cities throughout the United States.

51529 ■ Principles of Professional Selling—Level 2 (Canada)
Canadian Management Centre
150 York St., 5th Fl.
Toronto, ON, Canada M5H 3S5
Ph:(866)400-4941 ext. 2252
Free: 877-CMC-2500
Fax: (416)313-4985
Co. E-mail: cmcinfo@cmctraining.org
URL: http://www.cmcamai.org
Price: $1,795 Canadian. **Description:** Covers keys to professionalism, business development, techniques for selling, telephone skills, and closing the sale. **Locations:** Toronto, ON.

51530 ■ Selling to Major Accounts: A Strategic Approach
American Management Association
1601 Broadway
New York, NY 10019
Ph:(212)586-8100
Free: 800-262-9699
Fax: (212)903-8168
Co. E-mail: customerservice@amanet.org
URL: http://www.amanet.org
Price: $1,895.00 for non-members; $1,695.00 for AMA members. **Description:** Covers strategies for developing successful relationships with major accounts. **Locations:** San Francisco, CA.

51531 ■ Selling to Senior Executives
American Management Association
1601 Broadway
New York, NY 10019
Ph:(212)586-8100
Free: 800-262-9699
Fax: (212)903-8168
Co. E-mail: customerservice@amanet.org
URL: http://www.amanet.org
Price: $1,695.00 for non-members; $1,495.00 for AMA members. **Description:** Covers the business benefits of selling to senior executives, and strategies and techniques for building successful sales relationships with them. **Locations:** Atlanta, GA; and New York, NY.

51532 ■ Selling to Senior Executives Level 3
American Management Association
1601 Broadway
New York, NY 10019
Ph:(212)586-8100
Free: 800-262-9699
Fax: (212)903-8168
Co. E-mail: customerservice@amanet.org
URL: http://www.amanet.org
Price: $1,695 for non-members; $1,495 for AMA members. **Description:** Covers selling techniques that will get you through the channels to the principal decision makers, how to convey an effective presentation to close deals faster. **Locations:** New York, NY; Washington, DC; Chicago, IL; and San Francisco, CA.

51533 ■ Selling to Senior Executives—Level 3 (Canada)
Canadian Management Centre
150 York St., 5th Fl.
Toronto, ON, Canada M5H 3S5
Ph:(866)400-4941 ext. 2252
Free: 877-CMC-2500
Fax: (416)313-4985
Co. E-mail: cmcinfo@cmctraining.org
URL: http://www.cmcamai.org
Price: $1,395 Canadian. **Description:** Covers the function of the executive buyer, implement an effective sales presentation to senior executives, and build upon relationships. **Locations:** Toronto, ON.

51534 ■ Strategic Sales Negotiations
American Management Association
1601 Broadway
New York, NY 10019
Ph:(212)586-8100
Free: 800-262-9699
Fax: (212)903-8168
Co. E-mail: customerservice@amanet.org
URL: http://www.amanet.org
Price: $1,695.00 for non-members; $1,495.00 for AMA members. **Description:** Covers the tools, techniques, and negotiation tactics for effectively influencing a buyer's perception of cost, benefits, and value. **Locations:** Chicago, IL.

51535 ■ Strategic Sales Negotiations (Canada)
Canadian Management Centre
150 York St., 5th Fl.
Toronto, ON, Canada M5H 3S5
Ph:(866)400-4941 ext. 2252
Free: 877-CMC-2500
Fax: (416)313-4985
Co. E-mail: cmcinfo@cmctraining.org
URL: http://www.cmcamai.org

Price: $1,595 Canadian. **Description:** Covers improving your closing ratios and higher profit margins, including negotiation tools, client relationships, and be able to counteract competitive offers. **Locations:** Toronto, ON.

51536 ■ Strategies for Selling Technical/ Industrial Products
American Management Association
1601 Broadway
New York, NY 10019
Ph:(212)586-8100
Free: 800-262-9699
Fax: (212)903-8168
Co. E-mail: customerservice@amanet.org
URL: http://www.amanet.org
Price: $1,695.00 for non-members; $1,595.00 for AMA members. **Description:** Covers strategies for successful selling of technical products. **Locations:** Anaheim, CA; and Atlanta, GA.

51537 ■ Time and Territory Management for Salespeople
American Management Association
1601 Broadway
New York, NY 10019
Ph:(212)586-8100
Free: 800-262-9699
Fax: (212)903-8168
Co. E-mail: customerservice@amanet.org
URL: http://www.amanet.org
Price: $1,695.00 for non-members; $1,495.00 for AMA members. **Description:** Two-day seminar covers setting goals, attitude, organizational skills, developing a territory strategy, and increasing productivity. **Locations:** Chicago, IL; and New York, NY.

51538 ■ Time and Territory Management for Salespeople (Canada)
Canadian Management Centre
150 York St., 5th Fl.
Toronto, ON, Canada M5H 3S5
Ph:(416)214-5678
Free: 800-262-9699
Fax: (416)313-4985
Co. E-mail: cmcinfo@cmctraining.org
URL: http://cmcamai.org
Price: $1,595.00 Canadian. **Description:** Covers sales techniques that focus on value instead of price, the difference between selling and negotiating, and developing strong client relationships. **Locations:** Toronto, ON.

51539 ■ Value-added Selling
American Management Association
1601 Broadway
New York, NY 10019
Ph:(212)586-8100
Free: 800-262-9699
Fax: (212)903-8168
Co. E-mail: customerservice@amanet.org
URL: http://www.amanet.org
Price: $1,595.00 for non-members; $1,495.00 for AMA members. **Description:** Covers various selling techniques, providing business solutions to clients, partnering with clients, and measuring results. **Locations:** Chicago, IL.

REFERENCE WORKS

51540 ■ "6 Secrets of eBay Sales Success" in *My Business* (December/January 2004, pp. 46)
Pub: My Business Magazine
Ed: Kate Westbrook. **Description:** Small business owners are finding success selling products and services using eBay. Six tips to help a small business use eBay are provided.

51541 ■ "20 Words That Sell" in *Small Business Opportunities* (Vol. 16, November 2004, No. 6, pp. 12, 20)
Pub: Harris Publications Inc.
Ed: Dawn Josephson. **Description:** Communication expert shares insight into the twenty words that can increase sales and profits.

51542 ■ "Actioncoaching.com" in *Entrepreneur.com* (Vol. 34, January 2006, No. 1, pp. 6)
Pub: Entrepreneur Media Inc.
Ed: Steve Cooper. **Description:** The Business Coaching Franchise has launched its new Action-Coaching.com, a franchise offering small business owners topics for growing a business, marketing, and selling products and services.

51543 ■ "Ada Liquor Store Growing Through a Lighthearted Approach to Sales" in *Journal Record* (June 24, 2003)
Pub: Dolan Media Company
Ed: Janice Francis-Smith. **Description:** Profile of Townsend's Bottle Shop, Ada, Oklahoma. Townsend's wife, a former English teacher, writes the catchy sales ads for the store, which have increased sales.

51544 ■ "Agents Urged to Answer the Call" in *Rough Notes* (Vol. 145, No. 12, December 2002, pp. 127)
Pub: Rough Notes
Ed: John Chivvis. **Description:** During the conference of the Independent Insurance Agents and Brokers of America, a call to action for interface improvements was made. These improvements will streamline the insurance buying and selling process.

51545 ■ "All Fired Up: With the Right Marketing Plan, Your Product Will Blaze Trails Across the Globe" in *Entrepreneur* (Vol. 32, July 2004)
Pub: Entrepreneur Media Inc.
Ed: Don Debelak. **Description:** Entrepreneurs share steps to successfully market products and services. Profile of Robustion Products Inc., maker of the Java-Log for fireplaces is included.

51546 ■ "Almost Famous: Market Yourself as an Expert" in *My Business* (October/November 2003, pp. 45)
Pub: My Business Magazine
Ed: Nancy Mann Jackson. **Description:** The importance of establishing one's self as an expert in the particular field in which you are selling will help a salesperson stand out from competitors. Tips includes speaking at conferences, creating informational products, the use of newspapers and magazines or business publications, writing articles, or doing guest spots on television or radio shows.

51547 ■ "Along For the Ride: Losing Touch With Your Reps?" in *Entrepreneur* (Vol. 31, No. 10, October 2003, pp. 87)
Pub: Entrepreneur Media, Inc.
Ed: Kimberly L. McCall. **Description:** Managers should occasionally go on field visits with reps in order to keep a sales staff at its best.

51548 ■ *Alpha Dogs: How Your Small Business Can Become a Leader of the Pack*
Pub: HarperInformation
Ed: Donna Fenn. **Released:** December 2005. **Price:** $24.95. **Description:** Ways for an entrepreneur to outsmart competitors in the marketplace, to generate higher sales, and earn lasting customer and employee loyalty.

51549 ■ "Another Act" in *Entrepreneur* (Vol. 31, No. 7, July 2003, pp. 40)
Pub: Entrepreneur Media, Inc.
Ed: Liane Cassavoy. **Description:** Profile of ACT!, the contact management and sales-force automation application. The software is now available in a Web version.

51550 ■ "Appearances Count" in *Small Business Opportunities* (Vol. 12, No. 2, March 2000, pp. 12)
Pub: Harris Publications, Inc.
Ed: Lin Grensing-Pophal. **Description:** Ways to produce revenue-generating sales letters from a home computer are explored.

51551 ■ "Are Customers Selling For You?" in *Sales and Marketing.com* (Vol. 156, No. 3, March 2004, pp. 22)
Pub: VNU eMedia, Inc.
Ed: Michael Schrage. **Description:** Although there are three types of clients, those that willingly and effectively serve as sales references are the most valuable to a small business.

51552 ■ "The art of Web selling: company finds a smart way to boost sales" in *Black Enterprise* (Vol. 33, No. 6, January 2003, pp. 41)
Pub: Earl Graves Publishing Co.
Ed: Rebecca Rohan. **Description:** Business owner, Glenn King, Exotica Art & Fashion, has found a unique way to sell imported art and artifacts using online auctions.

51553 ■ "The Art of the Sale" in *Entrepreneur* (Vol. 31, No. 8, August 2003, pp. 58)
Pub: Entrepreneur Media, Inc.
Ed: Chris Penttila. **Description:** Selling has become more difficult in the slumping economy, and salespersons face greater demands in a more competitive environment and require better sales skills.

51554 ■ "As seen on TV" in *Entrepreneur* (Vol. 30, No. 2, Fe)
Pub: Entrepreneur Media Inc.
Ed: Kim T. Gordon. **Description:** A winning formula for direct response TV advertising is presented. Entrepreneurs can create TV spots and keep costs down.

51555 ■ "Ask the Etiquette Doctor" in *Sales and Marketing.com* (Vol. 153, No. 3, March 2004, pp. 52)
Pub: VNU eMedia, Inc.
Description: When giving a presentation at a client's office it is best to arrive ten minutes earlier than the scheduled appointment.

51556 ■ "Ask Inc.: Do I Have to Go to School?" in *Inc.* (October 1, 2003)
Pub: Gruner & Jahr USA Publishing
Description: Advice is given to individuals considering entrepreneurship, focusing on sales strategies for individuals who hate to sell and the whether an entrepreneur needs a college degree.

51557 ■ "Ask Inc." in *Inc.* (August 1, 2004)
Pub: Inc. Magazine
Description: Examples to jump-start sales are offered for a managed-care consulting firm and a small skin care business.

51558 ■ "Assembling a Crack Sales Team" in *Hispanic Business* (October 2003, pp. 92, 94, 96)
Pub: Hispanic Business
Ed: Teresa Talerico. **Description:** Doing it well and then training and retaining new recruits can make all the difference to a sales operation.

51559 ■ "Attract Stragglers" in *Sales & Marketing Management* (Vol. 159, January-February 2007, No. 1, pp. 14)
Pub: VNU Business Media
Ed: Leo Jakobson. **Description:** Employee sales incentive programs are profiled.

51560 ■ "Back to Basics: Want to Create a Strong Sales Foundation?" in *Entrepreneur* (Vol. 32, No. 1, January 2004, pp. 78)
Pub: Entrepreneur Media, Inc.
Ed: Barry Farber. **Description:** Six ways to build a strong sales foundation are presented, beginning with the assertion to never make assumptions about prospects.

51561 ■ "Balancing Act" in *Sales and Marketing.com* (Vol. 147, No. 2, February 2004, pp. 16)
Pub: VNU eMedia, Inc.
Ed: Julia Chang. **Description:** Many small businesses are learning that work/life balances, as well as financial rewards, for sales and marketing employees have become increasingly important.

51562 ■ "Bargaining Power" in *Sales & Marketing Management* (Vol. 157, February 2005, No. 2, pp. 20)
Pub: VNU Business Media
Description: According to a recent survey, nearly 48 percent of managers have to coach sales reps on negotiation skills because many are afraid to risk ruining a client relationship they worked hard to build.

51563 ■ "The Bargaining Table" in *Small Business Opportunities* (Vol. 17, November 2005, No. 6, pp. 12, 20)
Pub: Harris Publications Inc.
Ed: John Patrick Dolan. **Description:** Ways for salespersons to prepare when negotiating a deal are presented. An inventory of three items to help establish your position is outlined along with a list of a counterpart's position.

51564 ■ "Belt-Tightening at Pfizer?" in *Business Week Online* (February 9, 2005)
Pub: McGraw-Hill Companies
Ed: Amy Barrett. **Description:** Pfizer is expected to announce a major restructuring of the company in order to cut costs, but its sales force is believed to be safe from cuts.

51565 ■ "Big Deal: Landing a Large Account Doesn't Have to Be Out of Your Reach" in *Entrepreneur*
Pub: Entrepreneur Media Inc.
Ed: Barry Farber. **Description:** Five strategies to increase sales, and land large accounts, are examined.

51566 ■ "The Bill's In the Mail"Bill Me Later" Payment Option" in *Entrepreneur.com* (Vol. 34, February 2006, No. 2, pp. 36)
Pub: Entrepreneur Media Inc.
Ed: Melissa Campanelli. **Description:** I4 Commerce's Bill Me Later Service provides payment options for Web customers, eliminating the need for clients to post their credit card numbers on the Internet.

51567 ■ "Blogs Can Provide Testimonials" in *Sales & Marketing Management* (Vol. 159, January-February 2007, No. 1, pp. 8)
Pub: VNU Business Media
Ed: Betsy Cummings. **Description:** Third party blogs are helping small companies market and promote products and services.

51568 ■ "Boosting sales through in-store sampling programs" in *Incentive* (Vol. 174, No. 8, August 2000, pp. 85)
Pub: Bill Communications
Ed: Joan M. Steinauer. **Description:** This article tells how businesses can fill their consumers' stomachs and empty their wallets at the same time.

51569 ■ "Branding: Not Just for Big-Budget Businesses" in *Ingram's* (Vol. 29, No. 8, August 2003, pp. 16)
Pub: Show Me Publishing, Inc.
Ed: T. DeWayne Ables. **Description:** Basic information regarding the importance of properly branding products in order to increase sales is examined.

51570 ■ "Breakthrough Performance: Sales Success" in *Entrepreneur* (Vol. 31, No. 9, September 2003, pp. 84)
Pub: Entrepreneur Media, Inc.
Ed: Barry Farber. **Description:** Five proven strategies to excel at breakthrough selling are examined. A breakthrough is defined as any significant advance or development that removes a barrier to progress.

51571 ■ "Bridging the Gap: Networking Can Be Key to Creating Sales Opportunities." in *Entrepreneur* (Vol. 32, November 2004, No. 11, pp. 89)
Pub: Entrepreneur Media Inc.
Ed: Barry Farber. **Description:** Steps for successful business networking are listed to help entrepreneurs bridge the gap, a strategy that helps build a foundation of contacts that will provide sales opportunities.

51572 ■ "Bright ideas" in *Entrepreneur* (Vol. 31, No. 6, June 2003, pp. 48)
Pub: Entrepreneur Media Inc.
Ed: Marc Spiwak. **Description:** Five ultra-portable projectors for making presentations are profiled, including the InFocus LP70, Toshiba TDP-P5, Philips LC5241, Hewlett-Packard MP3800, and ViewSonic's PJ551. Most of these projectors include direct VGA, composite and S-Video inputs, remote controls, and built-in speakers.

51573 ■ "Bring Back Old Territories" in *Sales & Marketing Management* (Vol. 158, November-December 2006, No. 11, pp. 13)
Pub: VNU Business Media
Description: Dave Lakhani, president of Bold Approach, offers tips to generate new business leads.

51574 ■ "Build a Strong Customer-Brand Relationship" in *E-business Advisor* (Vol. 18, No. 4, April 2000, pp. 34)
Pub: Advisor Media, Inc.
Ed: Doug Barton. **Description:** The article shows how the Internet is changing marketing practices as companies focus on developing customer loyalty instead of building brand images through advertising and traditional distribution channels. The two main factors driving sales are now customer loyalty and price.

51575 ■ *Business Warrior: Strategy for Entrepreneurs*
Pub: Clearbridge Publishing
Ed: Sun Tzu. **Released:** September 2006. **Price:** $19.95. **Description:** Advice to help entrepreneurs understand competitive strategies in order to succeed, focusing on sales, marketing, and personnel management.

51576 ■ "But Wait, There's More" in *Entrepreneur* (Vol. 31, No. 11, November 2003, pp. 98)
Pub: Entrepreneur Media, Inc.
Ed: Gwen Moran. **Description:** Gift-with-purchase promotions can increase sales, build a brand and make customers feel good about shopping in your store.

51577 ■ "By the Book" in *Entrepreneur.com* (Vol. 34, February 2006, No. 2, pp. 77)
Pub: Entrepreneur Media Inc.
Ed: Kimberly L. McCall. **Description:** Reviews of three new books to help managers motivate sales teams include, In Selling To Big Companies, by Jill Konrath; Jack, You're Fired! The Top 66 Reasons for Firing Sales Professionals...and How You Can Avoid Every Single One of Them, by Jack Perry; and Leading Leaders: How to Manage Smart, Talented, Rich and Powerful People, by Jeswald Salacuse.

51578 ■ "California Job Growth Slows" in *Sacramento Bee* (November 19, 2005)
Pub: The Sacramento Bee
Ed: Rachel Osterman. **Description:** Job growth in California is slowing down. As of July 2005, employer payrolls were up by an average of 20,900 positions per month, but have slowed to around 10,000.

51579 ■ "Campaign Close-Up: Cargill" in *Sales & Marketing Management* (Vol. 158, November-December 2006, No. 11, pp. 15)
Pub: VNU Business Media
Ed: Jackie Hunzinger. **Description:** Profile of Cargill whose current advertising campaign shows how the company delivers its food from the processing plant to the dinner table.

51580 ■ "Cash in Your Attic: Is Your Junk Someone Else's Treasure?" in *Black Enterprise* (Vol. 37, November 2006, No. 4, pp. 156)
Pub: Earl G. Graves Publishing Co. Inc.
Ed: Angela P. Moore-Thorpe. **Description:** Selling items accumulated over the years or purchased at auctions or garage sales can be a lucrative way to make extra cash. Advice and resources on auctions, collecting, and consignment shops included.

51581 ■ "Catalog companies show the upstarts that they know a thing or two about Internet retailing" in *The New York Times* (May 15,2000, pp.C16)
Pub: The New York Times Company
Ed: Bob Tedeschi. **Description:** Well-established catalog firms see profits from e-commerce grow sharply, and have a high rate of success in converting online browsers into buyers.

51582 ■ "Catch the Carrot" in *Entrepreneur. com* (Vol. 34, February 2006, No. 2, pp. 74)
Pub: Entrepreneur Media Inc.
Ed: Barry Farber. **Description:** Being true to one's self, honesty and integrity, along with a bit of humor are the true secrets to successful salesmanship.

51583 ■ "Caterpillar" in *Sales & Marketing Management* (Vol. 158, October 2006, No. 10, pp. 17)
Pub: VNU Business Media
Ed: Tali Arbel. **Description:** VSA Partners located in Chicago and Saint Louis offer marketing strategies they use to promote Caterpillar, the global leader of earth-moving equipment.

51584 ■ "Caveats to Selling Financial Services" in *Journal of Accountancy* (Vol. 199, January 2005, No. 1, pp. 29)
Pub: American Institute of Certified Public Accountants
Ed: Bart H. Siegel. **Description:** Certified Public Accounts will face new challenges when offering separately managed accounts, customized bond portfolio services, mutual funds, insurance or other investment products and services.

51585 ■ "The Change Up: Find New Uses for Your Products" in *My Business* (February/March 2003, pp. 15)
Pub: My Business Magazine
Ed: Evelyn Beck. **Description:** Diversification of a product can be a good tool for increasing sales, but it is imperative to do research.

51586 ■ "Channel Surfing" in *Sales and Marketing.com* (Vol. 156, No. 3, March 2004, pp. 7)
Pub: VNU eMedia, Inc.
Ed: Jennifer Gilbert. **Description:** According to a report from Mercer Management Consulting, called "Do You Know Who Your Profitable Channel Partners Are?", smaller channels can provide higher growth potential, leading to higher profit margins, despite the common belief that larger channels such as retailers and distributors are the most profitable.

51587 ■ "Check It Out" in *Entrepreneur* (Vol. 32, November 2004, No. 11, pp. 14)
Pub: Entrepreneur Media Inc.
Description: Nancy Michaels latest offering, Perfecting Your Pitch: 10 Proven Strategies/or Winning the Clients Everyone Wants, shows how entrepreneurs can generate new clients or customers and close deals.

51588 ■ "Chicago Mercantile Exchange" in *Sales & Marketing Management* (Vol. 159, January-February 2007, No. 1, pp. 10)
Pub: VNU Business Media
Ed: Jackie Hunzinger. **Description:** Chicago Mercantile Exchange (CME) is focusing their 2007 advertising campaign on reaching customers from various sectors. The campaign will run in various financial journals and magazines.

51589 ■ "Chick magnet: How can you attract women to your business?" in *Entrepreneur* (Vol. 30, No. 3, March 2002, pp. 93)
Pub: Entrepreneur Media Inc.
Ed: Kim T. Gordon. **Description:** Nine out of ten households identify women as the primary shopper and in the past five years, women-owned businesses have increased at twice the rate of firms overall, therefore whether targeting businesses or consumers, it is important to improve ways of marketing to women in order to be successful.

51590 ■ "Closer Call" in *Entrepreneur* (Vol. 33, October 2005, No. 10, pp. 85)
Pub: Entrepreneur Media Inc.
Ed: Kimberly L. McCall. **Description:** Five traits to look for when hiring a sales staff are investigated.

51591 ■ *Closing the Sale: A Process Not a Problem*
Pub: Crisp Publications, Inc.
Ed: Virden J. Thornton. **Price:** $9.95. **Description:** Shows how to correctly demonstrate products and services to ensure a sale.

51592 ■ "Commentary: 'Opportunity Calls': Networking With an Agenda" in *Long Island Business News* (February 20, 2004)
Pub: Dolan Media Newswires
Description: All sales leads tend to come from a close network of long-term business associates.

51593 ■ "Compulsory ethics education and the cognitive moral development of salespeople" in *Journal of Business Ethics* (Vol. 28, No. 3)
Pub: Kluwer Academic Publishers
Ed: George Izzo. **Description:** The results of research conducted on the effect of compulsory ethics education on the moral development of real estate salespeople using comparative statistical measures of ethical reasoning ability.

51594 ■ "Computer-Assisted Consulting" in *Hispanic Business* (Vol. 24, No. 5, May 2002, pp. 50)
Pub: Hispanic Business Inc.
Ed: Roger Harris. **Description:** BRS software products will help business consultants to become more successful. The software packages offer solid advice on everything from writing business and marketing plans to development of pricing and sales strategies.

51595 ■ "A Confidence Boost" in *Sales & Marketing Management* (Vol. 158, October 2006, No. 10, pp. 19)
Pub: VNU Business Media
Ed: Bill Raymond. **Description:** Accountability is a key component of developing an effective sales staff.

51596 ■ *Consultative Sales Power*
Pub: Crisp Publications, Inc.
Ed: Karen Mantyla. **Released:** 1995. **Price:** $9.95.

51597 ■ "Consumer Finance" in *Business Week* (January 16, 2006, No. 3967, pp. 38)
Pub: McGraw-Hill Companies
Ed: Peter Burrows. **Description:** A new trend shows online brands offering shoppers Bill Me later payment options in order to spur sales growth and offer a billing method to consumers uneasy about using their credit cards on the Internet. So far 230 e-commerce sites offer this service.

51598 ■ "Cooperation vs. conflict" in *Incentive* (Vol. 174, No. 7, July 2000, pp. 78)
Pub: Bill Communications
Ed: John Farrell. **Description:** Selling should never be viewed as a winner-take-all game. Collaboration between channel relationships is necessary to solve customer-business issues.

51599 ■ "Crain's Co-Sponsoring Sales-Training Seminar" in *Crain's Detroit Business* (Vol. 22, January 2, 2006, No. 1, pp. 17)
Pub: Crain Communications Inc. - Detroit
Ed: Joanne Scharich. **Description:** Crain's Detroit Business will sponsor a sales-training seminar at Schoolcraft College in Livonia, Michigan. Contact information included.

51600 ■ *Crank 'em Up!: Brilliant Sales Contests and Bright Ideas to Turn on Your Team and Turn Up Results*
Pub: Self-Counsel Press, Inc.
Ed: Bruce Fuller. **Released:** 1994. **Price:** $10.95 (paper).

51601 ■ "Crashing Past the Gatekeepers-Part Two" in *Business Week Online* (April 24, 2002)
Pub: McGraw-Hill, Inc.
Ed: Michelle Nichols. **Description:** Various approaches are discussed to get passed the barriers, such as secretaries and switchboards, preventing salespersons from reaching potential clients.

51602 ■ *Crossing the Chasm: Marketing and Selling Disruptive Products to Mainstream Customers*
Pub: HarperInformation
Ed: Geoffrey A. Moore. **Released:** September 2002. **Price:** $17.95. **Description:** A guide for marketing in high-technology industries, focusing on the Internet.

51603 ■ "Customer-Centric CRM Requires Perspective in 360 degrees" in *Microsoft Executive Circle* (Vol. 1, No. 2, Q2 2001, pp. 22-24, 27)
Pub: Putman Media
Ed: Ronni T. Marshak. **Description:** Customer Relationship Management tools must monitor sales processes, marketing campaigns, customer service, and customer behavior in order to be successful.

51604 ■ "Customer Loyalty" in *Small Business Opportunities* (Vol. 16, No. 3, May 2004, pp. 18, 20)
Pub: Harris Publications, Inc.
Ed: Jill Griffin. **Description:** Twelve laws of loyalty in order to develop non-customers into loyal advocates are explained.

51605 ■ "Customerretention.com: www. customerretention.com" in *Entrepreneur* (Vol. 31, No. 10, October 2003, pp. 6)
Pub: Entrepreneur Media, Inc.
Ed: Steve Cooper. **Description:** Website that provides consulting services to small and large companies on customer retention strategies.

51606 ■ "The Daily Ground" in *Entrepreneur* (Vol. 28, No. 2, February 2000, pp. 147)
Pub: Entrepreneur Media Inc.
Ed: Michelle Prather. **Description:** In an industry of high-visibility brand names, they don't have one. So how does this family's coffee company stay in business?

51607 ■ "Dangle Carrots: How To Keep Your Sales Force Hopping" in *My Business* (October/November 2003, pp. 45)
Pub: My Business Magazine
Ed: Lena Basha. **Description:** Four tips to help motive a sales team are listed, including sales strategies that involve team efforts, providing the necessary tools to a sales force, setting realistic goals, and the use of rewards to motivate.

51608 ■ "Dealing With Bonus Backlash" in *Sales and Marketing.com* (Vol. 147, No. 2, February 2004, pp. 7)
Pub: VNU eMedia, Inc.
Ed: Melinda Ligos. **Description:** Three steps to help motivate a sales staff in a year of lower commissions and bonuses are listed, including short term rewards, holding a compensation seminar, and convincing the staff that management is committed to helping them increase their income.

51609 ■ "Dealing With a Slumping Rep" in *Sales and Marketing.com* (Vol. 156, No. 3, March 2004, pp. 12)
Pub: VNU eMedia, Inc.
Description: David MacDonald, senior sales director at SAS, a software firm in Cary, North Carolina, prefers to work with a sales rep in a slump, rather than giving up on him or her.

51610 ■ "Deals on Wheels" in *Kiplinger's Personal Finance Magazine* (Vol. 54, No. 12, December 2000, pp. 30)
Pub: The Kiplinger Washington Editors, Inc.
Ed: Erin Burt. **Description:** To drive home sales pitches, enterprising advertisers will pay to turn cars into billboards.

51611 ■ "Desperately Seeking Sales Stars" in *Sales & Marketing Management* (Vol. 158, October 2006, No. 10, pp. 44)
Pub: VNU Business Media
Ed: Julia Chang. Description: Competition to hire sales personnel is growing; companies strategic plans for recruiting successful sales teams are presented.

51612 ■ "Devil's advocate" in *Entrepreneur* (Vol. 31, No. 5, May 2003, pp. 75)
Pub: Entrepreneur Media Inc.
Ed: Kimberly L. McCall. Description: Ethics in sales is the topic covered. Good conscience sales make for good business sense.

51613 ■ "Dialing up devotion" in *Incentive* (Vol. 174, No. 9, September 2000, pp. 72)
Pub: Bill Communications
Ed: Libby Estell. Description: Telemarketing is a tough business, but computer seller Insight Enterprises calls upon incentives to boost both sales and spirits while putting turnover on hold. A brief overview of their program is discussed, including goals, strategies, and results.

51614 ■ "Digging Deeper" in *Sales and Marketing.com* (Vol. 147, No. 2, February 2004, pp. 8)
Pub: VNU eMedia, Inc.
Ed: Betsy Cummings. Description: In a slowing economy, sales staff should try to sell more to existing customers. In order to achieve this goal, sales people could focus on developing a network of contacts in positions both above and below the salesperson's initial connection.

51615 ■ "Do You Work for Free?" in *My Business* (February/March 2004, pp. 50)
Pub: My Business Magazine
Ed: Susan Palmquist. Description: When negotiating with potential clients, it is important to let a client have only a sampling of your expertise and to remain professional.

51616 ■ "Does Your Sales Management Stink?" in *Sales & Marketing Management* (Vol. 159, January-February 2007, No. 1, pp. 12)
Pub: VNU Business Media
Description: Tips for build and assess a successful sales team are explored.

51617 ■ "Done Deal: How One Sales Pro Closed a Big Customer" in *Sales & Marketing Management* (Vol. 158, October 2006, No. 10, pp. 15)
Pub: VNU Business Media
Ed: Betsy Cummings. Description: Sam Braunstein convinced area stores that athletic sports-support equipment is a necessary product to be sold in sporting goods stores.

51618 ■ "Double header" in *WorkingWoman* (Vol. 25, No. 5, May 2000, pp. 38)
Pub: Lang Communications Inc.
Ed: Eilene Zimmerman. Description: The Female Athlete company has 70 percent of its sales generated by catlogs and 30 percent from Web sites sales. Issues concerning marketing strategies to direct customers away from traditional catalog buying to purchasing on-line are presented.

51619 ■ "Double Play: Could Sending a Paper Catalog to Customers Boost Your E-Commerce Business?" in *Entrepreneur* (Vol. 32, September 2004)
Pub: Entrepreneur Media Inc.
Ed: Melissa Campanelli. Description: Many e-tailers are using catalogs to increase Internet sales. Statistical data included.

51620 ■ "Drawing the Line: The Right Way To Do Business With Friends" in *Sales & Marketing Management* (Vol. 157, February 2005, No. 2, pp. 18)
Pub: VNU Business Media
Ed: Sara Calabro. Description: The best way to handle business relationships with friends is to use the same client-customer principles of other deals, including putting everything in writing.

51621 ■ "Driving Force" in *Hispanic Business* (April 2005, pp. 56, 58)
Pub: Hispanic Business
Ed: Anthony Limon. Description: Analysis and advice relating to recruitment and career development in the auto industry is given. Due to the high volume of car sales in 2005, new sales and service professionals will be recruited by dealerships.

51622 ■ "E-Marketplaces: Opportunity or Threat?" in *E-business Advisor* (Vol. 18, No. 7, July 2000, pp. 32)
Pub: Advisor Media, Inc.
Ed: Elizabeth Sara. Description: Businesses in the e-marketplace arena are obliged, not only to adapt their existing business processes to take advantage of the Web's inherent benefits, but also to keep their relatively new e-commerce solutions functionally current and flexible to keep in step with the market. Participating in private business-to-business (B2B) sales channels offer the advantage of enhanced contractual relationships with business partners. Price structures for products are included.

51623 ■ "E-Train" in *Sales & Marketing Management* (Vol. 157, February 2005, No. 2, pp. 20)
Pub: VNU Business Media
Description: Arcadian Software offers software designed to guide users through negotiations by analyzing human interactions and negotiation theory. The program contains four tools: Quick Plan, Full Plan, Problem Solver, and Profiler.

51624 ■ "EBay's Bid To Go Beyond Auctions Isn't Selling Well" in *Wall Street Journal* (Vol. 248, December 2006, No. 145, pp. B1)
Pub: Dow Jones & Co. Inc.
Ed: Vauhine Vara. Description: While trying to entice online shoppers with it's new eBay Express Website, the outlook seems bleak. Many of the early users report disappointment with the lack of increased exposure. In-Depth stock figures and projections included.

51625 ■ "Employees Sue Best Buy for Race, Gender Discrimination" in *Sacramento Bee* (December 9, 2005)
Pub: The Sacramento Bee
Ed: Rachel Osterman. Description: Retailer, Best Buy is being sued for race and gender discrimination for alleged lower wages than those paid to white males and for steering women employees away from high-paying sales jobs.

51626 ■ "Employers important in shaping health care" in *Atlanta Business Chronicle* (Vol. 25, November 15, 2002, No. 23 pp. 37A)
Pub: American City Business Publications, Inc.
Ed: Julie Bryant. Description: According to the National Business Coalition on Health, employers are in a unique position to influence health care's direction by acting as an advocate for high-quality health care and as a prudent purchaser. Steps taken by the Coca Cola Company and American Greetings Corporation are discussed.

51627 ■ "Engineering the Engineer" in *Sales & Marketing Management* (Vol. 157, January 2005, No. 1, pp. 11)
Pub: VNU Business Media
Description: Sales presentations by an engineer to a prospective customer can help seal the deal. Three steps to accomplish this strategy are presented.

51628 ■ "Entrepreneur Column" in *Entrepreneur* (August 4, 2005)
Pub: Entrepreneur Media Inc.
Ed: Tom Hopkins. Description: The meaning behind a customer's desire to shop around before purchasing a product or service is examined. It is important for small business owners to research their competition.

51629 ■ "Entrepreneur Column" in *Entrepreneur.com* (September 29, 2005)
Pub: Entrepreneur Media Inc.
Ed: Al Lautenslager. Description: Activities designed to develop a sound marketing routine are listed. It is suggested to incorporate at least three to five of the activities as daily practice.

51630 ■ "Explore the Art of Consultative Selling" in *Journal of Accountancy* (Vol. 199, January 2005)
Pub: American Institute of Certified Public Accountants
Ed: John E. Graziano, Patrick J. Flanagan. Description: Traditional selling vs. consultative selling techniques when integrating financial planning into an accounting practice are explored.

51631 ■ "The Exporting Advantage" in *Inc.* (August 2005, pp. 40, 42)
Pub: Inc. Magazine
Ed: Jeff Bailey. Description: Brothers Jon, Keith and Mark Pavlansky sell rubber dirt to Mexican growers. Their company, Hibco Plastics transformed their company while increasing sales by marketing their products in Mexico.

51632 ■ "The Extra Mile: Customer Service That's a Step Beyond" in *Sales & Marketing Management* (Vol. 158, October 2006, No. 10, pp. 14)
Pub: VNU Business Media
Description: An independent knife distributor shares the story of gifting a hunting knife to a client, resulting in increased orders.

51633 ■ "Face to face" in *Incentive* (Vol. 174, No. 9, September 2000, pp. 102)
Pub: Bill Communications
Ed: Andrea Nierenberg. Description: Tips for sales communication in the electronic age where less face-to-face meetings occur.

51634 ■ "Feeling Loaded Down? Use Partnerships to Bag New Customers" in *My Business* (October/November 2003, pp. 44)
Pub: My Business Magazine
Ed: Paige Orr. Description: Michael Hess, president and chief executive of Road Wired, a technology travel accessory firm, partnered with Travelpro International, a luggage manufacturer and distributor. This partnership has helped Hess to grow his business.

51635 ■ "Finding Prospects By Using The Internet" in *Rough Notes* (Vol. 145, No. 9, September 2002, pp. 46)
Pub: Rough Notes
Ed: Steve Anderson. Description: Marketing for agencies has been helped by access to the Internet. There are business databases like Dun and Bradstreet and R.H. Donnelley from which lists of prospects are available.

51636 ■ "The First Task" in *Business Week Online* (February 17, 2006)
Pub: McGraw-Hill Companies
Description: Building a partner-based relationship with customers, coupled with self-respect, is a great way for salespersons to increase sales.

51637 ■ *The First-Time Sales Manager: A Survival Guide*
Pub: Self-Counsel Press, Inc.
Ed: Theodore G. Tyssen. Released: 1994. Price: $8.95 (paper).

51638 ■ "Fishing for trouble" in *Entrepreneur* (Vol. 30, No. 12, December 2002, pp. 112)
Pub: Entrepreneur Media Inc.
Ed: Barry Farber. Description: The fine line between being persistent and being obnoxious when trying to close sales is defined, with tips showing how to be persistent without annoying prospects.

51639 ■ "Five Questions: Diane Primo, Vice President, Chief Marketing Office, CDW" in *Sales & Marketing Management* (Vol. 157, February 2005)
Pub: VNU Business Media
Description: Dian Primo, vice president and chief marketing officer for CDW answers questions regarding brand loyalty, marketing and sales functions, innovation, and more.

51640 ■ "Five Questions" in *Sales & Marketing Management* (Vol. 158, October 2006, No. 10, pp. 17)
Pub: VNU Business Media
Description: Warren Church, marketer, discusses branding for business-to-business firms.

51641 ■ "5 Steps to Bigger Sales" in *Incentive* (Vol. 174, No. 10, October 2000, pp. 117)
Pub: Bill Communications
Ed: Vincent Alonzo. **Description:** Advice is given to correct the five most common problems facing sales staff: poor leadership, lack of desire to excel, not listening, an inability to adapt to the client, and transactional vs. consultative.

51642 ■ "The Flaw of averages" in *Harvard Business Review* (Vol. 80, No. 11, November 2002, pp. 20)
Pub: Harvard Business School Press
Ed: Sam Savage. **Description:** The use of an average figure to represent an uncertain quantity can lead to a wrong answer in accounting, investment and sales. Software exists that can fix this flaw.

51643 ■ "Focus on fundamentals to get back in sales groove" in *Atlanta Business Chronicle* (Vol. 24, No. 11, August 17, 2001, pp. 49A)
Pub: American City Business Journals Inc.
Ed: Jeffrey Gitomer. **Description:** Tips for getting back on the sales track after a slump include studying the basics, revisit plans for success, five things that can be done to work smarter and harder are listed.

51644 ■ "Follow Your Leader" in *Entrepreneur* (Vol. 32, No. 4, April 2004, pp. 124)
Pub: Entrepreneur Media, Inc.
Ed: Romanus Wolter. **Description:** Ways an entrepreneur can find someone to mentor them with business issues are listed. Mentors can help aspiring entrepreneurs to increase sales, create a business plan, as well as handling other challenges.

51645 ■ "Free Tuition: Win New Customers With Educational Programs" in *Sales & Marketing Management* (Vol. 157, February 2005, No. 2, pp. 20)
Pub: VNU Business Media
Ed: Julia Chang. **Description:** Many companies have begun offering free sales and marketing seminars in their stores to attract small business owners. Office Depot held a series of seminars that incorporated some product pitches, but the real goal was to build a relationship with its small business customers.

51646 ■ "Freedom of Speech: The legacy you leave yourself" in *Atlanta Business Chronicle* (Vol. 24, No. 10, August 10, 2001, pp. 39A)
Pub: American City Business Journals Inc.
Ed: Jeffrey Gitomer. **Description:** The best way to gain new leads and market yourself is to give a free speech. That is, make a speech for free, but do not give a sales pitch, at a civic organization, for example. The advantages of providing a speaking engagement for gratis are listed. Six tactics of free speech are listed.

51647 ■ "From Digital Image to Document" in *Sales & Marketing Management* (Vol. 158, November-December 2006, No. 11, pp. 62)
Pub: VNU Business Media
Ed: Tali Arbel. **Description:** Free Web-based application, scanR.com, allows users to convert camera phone snapshots into files that can be sent to email or faxed to other locations.

51648 ■ "Get Over It!" in *Entrepreneur* (Vol. 31, No. 10, October 2003, pp. 88)
Pub: Entrepreneur Media, Inc.
Ed: Barry Farber. **Description:** Three effective ways to succeed at selling are listed.

51649 ■ "Get in tune: keep your site visitors dialed in and buying" in *Entrepreneur* (Vol. 31, No. 5, May 2003, pp. 79)
Pub: Entrepreneur Media Inc.
Ed: Catherine Seda. **Description:** Opt-in offers can provide a coupon, a free report, or a newsletter to customers.

51650 ■ "Getting past 'No': how do you turn that 'no' into a 'yes'?" in *Entrepreneur* (Vol. 31, No. 6, June 2003)
Pub: Entrepreneur Media Inc.
Ed: Barry Farber. **Description:** Four qualities to close sales are listed, including the belief in ones self and product or service, the value brought to the customer, unique factors that make you different, and persistence.

51651 ■ "Getting Organized" in *Small Business Opportunities* (Vol. 16, No. 2, March 2004, pp. 60)
Pub: Harris Publications, Inc.
Ed: Barbara Hemphill. **Description:** Six simple steps for increasing sales and relieving stress are presented.

51652 ■ "Getting To No" in *Inc.* (October 1, 2003)
Pub: Gruner & Jahr USA Publishing
Ed: Nicole Gull. **Description:** Sales strategy of Y2 Marketing, the firm that is selective about its customers, is profiled.

51653 ■ "Give 'Em Space: A Well-Designed Work Space, that is" in *Entrepreneur* (Vol. 32, No. 1, January 2004, pp. 77)
Pub: Entrepreneur Media, Inc.
Ed: Kimberly L. McCall. **Description:** By providing optimal work space to a sales team can improve their performance and increase sales.

51654 ■ "GM Hopes Boosting Mileage Will Slow Big Models' Sales Drain" in *Milwaukee Journal Sentinel* (December 10, 2005)
Pub: Journal Sentinel, Inc.
Ed: Thomas Content. **Description:** General Motors Corporation is promoting mileage ratings of its SUV models in the hopes of increasing sales for these vehicles.

51655 ■ "Go major league" in *Entrepreneur* (Vol. 31, No. 4, April 2003, pp. 81)
Pub: Entrepreneur Media Inc.
Ed: Kimberly L. McCall. **Description:** The benefits of team selling are good for the salesperson, team and the company overall. The team concept will help to close sales, maintain the client, create a happier customer environment, and provide unity within the firm.

51656 ■ "Go Live: They've Got Questions, You've Got Answers." in *Entrepreneur* (Vol. 33, March 2005, No. 3, pp. 90)
Pub: Entrepreneur Media Inc.
Ed: Catherine Seda. **Description:** When designing a Website, consider offering a live chat that helps customers with any frustrations navigating the site, while taking customer service to a higher level.

51657 ■ "Good Company" in *Entrepreneur* (Vol. 33, September 2005, No. 9, pp. 84)
Pub: Entrepreneur Media Inc.
Ed: Barry Farber. **Description:** Simple strategies to use when selling to a client who is smarter and is more experienced are listed.

51658 ■ "Good References, Easy to Find" in *Sales and Marketing.com* (Vol. 156, No. 3, March 2004, pp. 20)
Pub: VNU eMedia, Inc.
Ed: Daniel Tynan. **Description:** Profile of co-founders David Sroka and Darren Smith of Point of Reference, a Web site that manages customer testimonials. These testimonials can be used as a tool for closing sales.

51659 ■ "Grow Your Market" in *PC Computing* (April 2000, pp. 100)
Pub: Ziff-Davis Inc.

Ed: Jason Compton. **Description:** Maps of all kinds can add value to a Web site and even increase customer usage. This article gives brief evaluations of map databases that can be used.

51660 ■ "Hands On" in *Inc.* (August 2005, pp. 29-30)
Pub: Inc. Magazine
Ed: Adam L. Penenberg. **Description:** Up to 35 percent of all pay-per-click Internet advertising transactions may be fraudulent. Statistical data included.

51661 ■ "Have a Talent for Sales?" in *Black Enterprise* (Vol. 36, November 2005, No. 4, pp. 60)
Pub: Earl G. Graves Publishing Co. Inc.
Ed: Eve Tahmincioglu. **Description:** African American women are looking towards direct-selling as a means of empowerment and selling products targeted to African Americans. Our Own Image is a firm that sells Afrocentric products ranging from decor items to cosmetics.

51662 ■ "Healthy, Wealthy and Wise" in *Home Business* (Vol. 13, January/February 2006, No. 1, pp. 40)
Pub: Home Business Magazine
Ed: Sandy Larson. **Description:** Brian Reinhardt, marketer of weight loss, fitness and personal development products shares his secret to staying physically and financially fit.

51663 ■ "Hearing Them Out" in *Sales & Marketing Management*
Pub: VNU Business Media
Ed: Betsy Cummings. **Description:** Administaff, the human resources outsourcing company located in Kingwood, Texas, credits its sales team's input for its success.

51664 ■ "HelpStar" in *Sales & Marketing Management* (Vol. 157, February 2005, No. 2, pp. 22)
Pub: VNU Business Media
Description: Profile of HelpStar, the help-desk request-tracking and request management system. The system supports sales calls, follows up on customer problems, creates a history of customer contacts, and prioritizes customer requests for businesses.

51665 ■ "Hewlett-Packard Was Far From First To Try 'PreTexting'" in *Wall Street Journal* (Vol. 248, December 2006, No. 149, pp. A1)
Pub: Dow Jones & Co. Inc.
Ed: John A. Emshwiller **Description:** Hewlett-Packard Co. as well as all the major lenders can no longer use 'Pretexting'- the practice of impersonating people in order to receive phone or financial records, as it is now being federally prohibited.

51666 ■ "Hidden Assets" in *Hispanic Business* (June 2002, pp. 68)
Pub: Hispanic Business
Ed: Derek Reveron. **Description:** Cutting sales and marketing departments are usually the first departments to be downsized in an economic downturn. Experts advise an opposite strategy.

51667 ■ "The Hidden Value of Slow Sellers" in *Inc.* (October 2005, pp. 36)
Pub: Inc. Magazine
Description: According to a recent study that tracked sales at an online grocery store, a reduced choice of products led to a drop in sales, and fewer customers.

51668 ■ *High Performance Selling*
Pub: Streamline Press
Ed: Ken Greenwood. **Released:** 1995. **Price:** $24.95.

51669 ■ "A High ROI Weapon" in *Ingram's* (Vol. 28, No. 5, May 2002, pp. 29)
Pub: Show Me Publishing, Inc.
Ed: Richard Delaney. **Description:** A sales development training program can give a high return-on-investment for small businesses. The gains in sales quickly pays for the expenses incurred in training.

51670 ■ *High Trust Selling: Make More Money, in Less Time, with Less Stress*
Pub: Nelson Business
Ed: Todd Duncan. **Released:** January 2003. **Price:** $22.99. **Description:** Laws governing salesmanship are divided into two sections. The first deals with attitudes, aptitudes, and abilities required for successful selling; the second with communication, courtship, camaraderie and commitments between salespeople and their clients.

51671 ■ "Hiring the Right People to Rep Your Products" in *Black Enterprise* (Vol. 35, November 2004, No. 4, pp. 54)
Pub: Earl G. Graves Publishing Co. Inc.
Ed: Robert Janis. **Description:** Tips for finding the right salesperson for a new product are presented.

51672 ■ "Hiring True Believers" in *Sacramento Bee* (November 14, 2005)
Pub: The Sacramento Bee
Ed: Rachel Osterman. **Description:** Many retailers hire loyal customers during the holiday season because they understand that shoppers who know and love their store can be the best possible sales staff.

51673 ■ *A History of Small Business in America*
Pub: University of North Carolina Press
Ed: Mansel G. Blackford. **Released:** January 2003. **Price:** $18.95. **Description:** History of American small business from the colonial era to present, showing how it has played a role in the nation's economic, political, and cultural development across manufacturing, sales, services and farming.

51674 ■ "Holiday Bonus" in *Entrepreneur* (Vol. 33, September 2005, No. 9, pp. 48)
Pub: Entrepreneur Media Inc.
Ed: Melissa Campanelli. **Description:** According to a recent study, Websites offering a gift-idea center during the 2004 holidays were the most successful. Four ideas for adding special features to a Website for holiday 2005 are included.

51675 ■ "Home Depot" in *Sales & Marketing Management* (Vol. 159, January-February 2007, No. 1, pp. 15)
Pub: VNU Business Media
Ed: Sarah Boehle. **Description:** Home Depot's Web-based training program is being used as a successful case study for other firms.

51676 ■ "Home Office vs. the Field" in *Sales & Marketing Management*
Pub: VNU Business Media
Ed: Robin Freedman, Andy Watt. **Description:** The issue whether a sales manager should address one rep's mistake in front of the entire sales team is examined by a salesperson and a sales manager.

51677 ■ "Home Office vs. the Field" in *Sales and Marketing.com* (Vol. 156, No. 3, March 2004, pp. 13)
Pub: VNU eMedia, Inc.
Description: A salesperson and manager debate who should be responsible for handling an angry client.

51678 ■ "How About a Little Browser Branding?" in *Sales & Marketing Management* (Vol. 159, January-February 2007, No. 1, pp. 45)
Pub: VNU Business Media
Description: Toolbars with built-in search engines can be customized to particular target markets.

51679 ■ "How can you find the elusive prospect hot button" in *Atlanta Business Chronicle* (Vol. 24, No. 14, September 7, 2001, pp. 6B)
Pub: American City Business Journals Inc.
Ed: Jeffrey Gitomer. **Description:** Jeffrey Gitomer, president of BuyGitomer, talks about finding the hot button on a customer when pitching sales; the hot button that needs to be pushed in order to achieve a common ground a customer and move the sale. Several examples are given for ways in which to find a customer's hot button and further the success of the sale.

51680 ■ "How David Steinberg Wins Friends, Influences People, and Moves a Whole Lot of Cell Phones" in *Inc.* (Volume 27, March 2005, No. 3)
Pub: Inc. Magazine
Ed: Ian Mount. **Description:** Profile of David Steinberg, CEO of InPhonic, maker of mobile phone handsets and Web services. Steinberg has grown his firm to nearly $200 million annual revenue in five years.

51681 ■ "How to Lose Customers" in *Inc.* (Volume 27, July 2005, No. 7, pp. 49, 51)
Pub: Inc. Magazine
Ed: Norm Brodsky. **Description:** A commitment to customer service can help a small business attract customers away from competitors.

51682 ■ "How to Make Tough Sales Without Pressure" in *Home Business* (Vol. 13, January/February 2006, No. 1, pp. 52)
Pub: Home Business Magazine
Ed: Bill Brooks. **Description:** Fourteen tips for striking a balance to increase sales are outlined. It is important for salespeople to be aggressive without being abrasive, persistent or pushy.

51683 ■ "How to Win a Marquee Account" in *Sales and Marketing.com* (Vol. 156, No. 3, March 2004, pp. 72)
Pub: VNU eMedia, Inc.
Ed: John Zimmer. **Description:** Profile of Toshiba America Medical Systems, which sells medical imaging products for the diagnosis and treatment of heart disease, cancer and stroke. Toshiba's marketing strategy has helped them achieve double-digit growth in an otherwise sluggish market.

51684 ■ "In the Chips; Handheld Lab Gets HandyLab $6M" in *Crain's Detroit Business* (Vol. 22, January 23, 2006, No. 4, pp. 1)
Pub: Crain Communications Inc. - Detroit
Ed: Tom Henderson. **Description:** HandyLab Inc., Ann Arbor, Michigan, will use $6 million of venture capital to hire sales and marketing teams to bring its first medical diagnostic device to market. The firm was founded in 2000 by a group of engineering graduates from University of Michigan.

51685 ■ "In their corner" in *Entrepreneur* (Vol. 31, No. 6, June 2003, pp. 79)
Pub: Entrepreneur Media Inc.
Ed: Kimberly L. McCall. **Description:** Reasons to devote coaching time to the elite sales performers are listed.

51686 ■ "In High Spirits: How to Get Yourself and Your Business Fired up from the Inside out" in *Entrepreneur* (Vol. 31, No. 4, April 2003)
Pub: Entrepreneur Media Inc.
Ed: Barry Farber. **Description:** Four keys to help increase and maintain enthusiasm in a company include the following: learn something new everyday, revel in the smallest steps toward success, set goals and stick to them, and protect the environment around you.

51687 ■ "In Marketing and Sales, Know When to Back Away" in *Folio: the Magazine for Magazine Management* (Vol. 30, No. 1, January 2001, pp. 10)
Pub: Intertec Publishing Corp.
Description: Ad sales people should address these four areas with advertisers: (1) What are their concerns about ad clutter? What are their frustrations about consumer indifference? (2) What are their fears about retailer clout? (3) There is mounting pressure on margin. How can you help? (4) Discuss the pressure to maintain a real point of difference. Follow this formula to have a good start to leveraging relationships into business.

51688 ■ "In with the New" in *Entrepreneur* (Vol. 28, No. 10, October 2000, pp. 102)
Pub: Entrepreneur Media Inc.
Ed: Mark Henricks. **Description:** The key to fast growth lies is not only treating your existing customers well, but also in seeking new customers.

51689 ■ "In Praise of the 'Thank You' Note: Want to make an impression?" in *Business Week Online* (March 7, 2002)
Pub: McGraw-Hill, Inc.
Description: Handwritten thank you notes can be used as a sales and marketing tool for small businesses. A thank you note displays an attitude of gratitude no ad slogan or coffee mug can match.

51690 ■ "In Times of Crisis" in *Entrepreneur* (Vol. 31, No. 9, September 2003, pp. 83)
Pub: Entrepreneur Media, Inc.
Ed: Elizabeth Goodgold. **Description:** Four tips for selling security products to prospective customers are outlined.

51691 ■ "In With the New: Get Your Customers to Get Rid of Your Products-So They Can Buy More" in *Entrepreneur* (Vol. 31, No. 5, May 2003)
Pub: Entrepreneur Media Inc.
Ed: Kimberly L. McCall. **Description:** Strategies being used by entrepreneurs to embrace disposable products in order to boost income are discussed.

51692 ■ "In-Your-Face-Selling" in *Inc.* (November 2006, pp. 33)
Pub: Gruner & Jahr USA Publishing
Ed: Adam Bluestein. **Description:** A strong approach to closing business to business deals is to take a small group to the customer to meet with the client and show the support that's available if you're chosen. While an expensive approach due to travel expenses, the payoffs are very lucrative in the long term. The client identifies more with your company after a face to face meeting.

51693 ■ *Increasing Sales with Better Selling Techniques*
Pub: Retail Strategies & Publishing, Inc.
Ed: Paula Wardell. **Price:** $8.95.

51694 ■ "An Industry Resource: Thee Direct Selling Association Membership List" in *Success* (Vol. 47, No. 6, November 2000, pp. 74)
Pub: Success Publishing, Inc.
Description: The Direct Selling Association (DSA), the Washington, D.C.-based trade organization that promotes, protects, and polices the industry, reports that 55 percent of Americans have purchased goods or services through direct sales, a number that tops television and online computer services combined. Research results are presented.

51695 ■ "The ins and outs: Sales Force: Answering the eternal question" in *Entrepreneur* (Vol. 30, No. 3, March 2002, pp. 87)
Pub: Entrepreneur Media Inc.
Ed: Kimberly L. McCall. **Description:** Three myths regarding inside and outside sales teams are explored. In general, inside teams that do all their selling over the phone are generally less expensive to run and easier to manage, while outside teams working in the field establish the crucial personal link that allows a real glimpse into sales prospects.

51696 ■ "The Inside Scoop: One Expert's Take on Today's Retail Scene" in *Entrepreneur* (Vol. 32, July 2004, No. 7, pp. 70)
Pub: Entrepreneur Media Inc.
Ed: Gwen Moran. **Description:** An interview with Paco Underhill, consumer behavior specialist, discusses retail trends to help increase sales.

51697 ■ *Instant Cashflow: Hundreds of Proven Strategies to Win Customers, Boost Margins and Take More Money Home*
Pub: McGraw-Hill Companies
Ed: Bradley J. Sugars. **Released:** December 2005. **Price:** $16.95 (US), $22.95 (Canadian). **Description:** Nearly 300 proven marketing and sales strategies are shared by the author, a self-made millionaire. Advice on creating the proper mindset, generating new leads, boosting the conversion rate of leads to sales, maximizing the value of the average sale, and measuring results is included.

51698 ■ *Instant Income*
Pub: McGraw-Hill Inc.
Ed: Janet Switzer. **Released:** February 2007. **Price:** $30.95 (CND). **Description:** Book covers small business advertising techniques, marketing, joint ventures, and sales.

51699 ■ "Internet Companies Learn How to Personalize Service" in *The New York Times* (August 28, 2000, pp. C8(L))
Pub: The New York Times Company
Ed: Susan Stellin. **Description:** Technologies for delivering customized, individually-oriented 'one to one marketing' or 'targeted merchandising' are still in the early stages of development, but are already in use by Amazon.com.

51700 ■ "The isolation process: a powerful path to more sales" in *Atlanta Business Chronicle* (Vol. 25, November 15, 2002, No. 23 pp. 4B)
Pub: American City Business Publications, Inc.
Ed: Jeffrey Gitomer. **Description:** The isolation process is described as a method for overcoming stalls in prospective sales and getting to the truth. Isolate the stall, consider it as the only objection, and present the situation as if the stall did not exist. Often, a stall turns out to be a buy signal.

51701 ■ "It's an investment: Events require funds, planning" in *Atlanta Business Chronicle* (Vol. 24, No. 14, September 7, 2001, pp. S17)
Pub: American City Business Journals Inc.
Ed: Mary Kirkman. **Description:** Kristy Trenaman, Humana Inc.'s corporate communications manager, Eddie Kraft, Nanz & Kraft Florists part-owner, and Robin Hall, Dant Clayton Corporation's bid administrator, talk about budgeting for anniversary events planning. Anniversary celebrations are ways to gain employee loyalty and increase sales, having proven to be successful in these areas.

51702 ■ "It's the Service, Stupid! Want Repeat Business?" in *Sales and Marketing. com* (Vol. 156, No. 3, March 2004, pp. 8)
Pub: VNU eMedia, Inc.
Ed: Betsy Cummings. **Description:** Customer service is critical to saving existing clients.

51703 ■ "It's That Time of Season" in *Entrepreneur* (Vol. 31, No. 8, August 2003, pp. 75)
Pub: Entrepreneur Media, Inc.
Ed: Catherine Seda. **Description:** Summer provides the perfect environment to increase online shopping for the holiday season by using perks such as free shipping, clearances, featured sale items, suggested items, and gift idea centers or personal shoppers.

51704 ■ "Job Market Thaw" in *Sales and Marketing.com* (Vol. 156, No. 3, March 2004, pp. 24)
Pub: VNU eMedia, Inc.
Description: Future job market trends for ten different industries are examined. The ten featured industries include construction, energy, financial services, healthcare/pharmaceutical, hospitality/travel, real estate, services, technology, telecommunications, and transportation.

51705 ■ "Keep The Ball Rolling" in *Rough Notes* (Vol. 145, No. 2, February 2002, pp. 79)
Pub: Rough Notes
Ed: Roger Sitkins. **Description:** For an agency to keep moving forward, agents should have an attitude of looking for improvement in themselves and their agency, have a prospect pipeline, a proactive sales management, training and education program.

51706 ■ "Kill the Commissions" in *Inc.* (August 1, 2004)
Pub: Inc. Magazine
Ed: Cara Cannella. **Description:** The case for dropping individual commission for sales teams is explored.

51707 ■ *Knock Your Socks Off Selling*
Pub: Amacom
Ed: Jeffrey Gitomer. **Released:** May 1999. **Price:** $17.95. **Description:** Tips for salespeople to succeed in a competitive sales environment.

51708 ■ "Landing the big fish" in *Crain's Detroit Business* (Vol. 19, No. 6, February 10, 2003, pp. 3)
Pub: Crain Communications Inc., Detroit
Ed: Laura Bailey. **Description:** Networking and persistence are the two most important factors needed for small companies to win sales with major corporations.

51709 ■ "Last But Not Least" in *Entrepreneur* (Vol. 27, No. 12, December 1999, pp. 144)
Pub: Entrepreneur Media Inc.
Ed: Marc Diener. **Description:** Whether in desperation or by design, the final offer is one of the strongest, and trickiest, plays in deal making.

51710 ■ "Lead Generator: Quick Ideas for Better Sales Leads" in *Sales and Marketing. com* (Vol. 156, No. 3, March 2004, pp. 9)
Pub: VNU eMedia, Inc.
Description: Three tips to promote successful lead generation by a sales staff are listed, including the creation of an internal chat room to make it easier for field offices to communicate.

51711 ■ "Lead Generator: Quick Ideas For Better Sales Leads" in *Sales & Marketing Management* (Vol. 157, January 2005, No. 1, pp. 11)
Pub: VNU Business Media
Description: Three techniques that general leads for a sales team are listed.

51712 ■ "Learn Your Lines" in *Entrepreneur*
Pub: Entrepreneur Media Inc.
Ed: Kimberly L. McCall. **Description:** Eight steps to help sales reps improve selling techniques over the phone.

51713 ■ "Leveraged growth. Expanding sales without sacrificing profits" in *Harvard Business Review* (Vol. 80, No. 10, October 2002, pp. 68)
Pub: Harvard Business School Press
Ed: John Hagel. **Description:** The concept of leveraged growth, where growth does not occur by acquisitions, rather relying upon skills and assets that a firm already has available.

51714 ■ "License To Thrive" in *Inc.* (August 2005, pp. 38)
Pub: Inc. Magazine
Ed: Erik Sherman. **Description:** The right partnership can drive sales, while it also reduces workload. The art of the alliance is outlined.

51715 ■ "Life is just a bowl of jelly beans and so is sales" in *Atlanta Business Chronicle* (Vol. 24, No. 13, August 31, 2001, pp. 36A)
Pub: American City Business Journals Inc.
Ed: Jeffrey Gitomer. **Description:** Jeffrey Gitomer, president of BuyGitomer, talks about the positive effects of incorporating humor into sales. When humor is added, it adds fun to the sale, and the person purchasing also has more fun. Gitomer provides ways to add that humor into everyday sales experiences.

51716 ■ "Lights, camera, action" in *Entrepreneur* (Vol. 31, No. 4, April 2003, pp. 126)
Pub: Entrepreneur Media Inc.
Ed: Don Debelak. **Description:** Steps to take in order to get a new product featured on a home shopping network are presented.

51717 ■ "Location, Location, Location" in *Sales & Marketing Management* (Vol. 159, January-February 2007, No. 1, pp. 28)
Pub: VNU Business Media
Ed: Rebecca Aronauer. **Description:** Five best cities for marketers include, Atlanta, Las Vegas, Miami, Phoenix and San Diego.

51718 ■ "Lou Fusz Cultivates Returns on Car-Selling Business" in *St. Louis Post-Dispatch* (July 23, 2004)
Pub: Knight-Ridder/Tribune Business News
Ed: Linda Tucci. **Description:** Louis F. Fusz Jr., owner of auto dealerships in the St. Louis area, discusses his sales philosophy. Fusz's five children are all interested in being a part of the business.

51719 ■ *Low Profile Selling*
Pub: NAPL
Ed: Tom Hopkins. **Price:** $24.95 (non-members); $24.95 (members). **Description:** Covers the "low profile" approach to selling, including tips and advice on how to give better service, win customers over from your competition, and recognize the personality types of your customers.

51720 ■ "Lucky Charms" in *Small Business Opportunities* (Vol. 14, No. 1, January 2002, pp. 12)
Pub: Harris Publications, Inc.
Ed: Paul Hanlon. **Description:** Selling strategies to build a larger client base for small business, including prospecting, customer confidence, and learning from past mistakes are covered.

51721 ■ *Lucrative List Building*
Pub: Morgan James Publishing, LLC
Ed: Glen Hopkins. **Released:** July 2006. **Price:** $13.95. **Description:** List building guaranteed to double profits is outlined.

51722 ■ "Making the Grade: Want to Create a Team of 'A' Players?" in *Sales and Marketing.com* (Vol. 156, No. 3, March 2004, pp. 24)
Pub: VNU eMedia, Inc.
Ed: Julia Chang. **Description:** During poor economic conditions, good managers focus on the "nearly there" team members, they are the players that show the potential to become good salespersons. Strategies for turning sales reps with potential into "A" players are outlined.

51723 ■ "Making the Most Of It" in *Sales & Marketing Management*
Pub: VNU Business Media
Ed: Robin Kocina. **Description:** Mid-America Events & Expos Inc. specializes in bringing businesses and potential customers together in the same room. The firm is committed to teaching exhibitors how to best benefit from these face-to-face interactions.

51724 ■ "Making Your Case: Think Client Testimonials are Just Icing on the Cake?" in *Entrepreneur* (Vol. 33, January 2005, No. 1, pp. 64)
Pub: Entrepreneur Media Inc.
Ed: Kimberly L. McCall. **Description:** Customer testimonials can act as a case study for increasing sales.

51725 ■ "Maponics: www.maponics.com" in *Entrepreneur* (Vol. 32, November 2004, No. 11, pp. 6)
Pub: Entrepreneur Media Inc.
Ed: Steve Cooper. **Description:** A Website featuring custom mapping, geographic targeting and sales territory analysis is profiled.

51726 ■ "Marketing E-Coaches" in *Entrepreneur* (Vol. 28, No. 10, October 2000, pp. 30)
Pub: Entrepreneur Media Inc.
Ed: Robert McGarvey. **Description:** A listing of Web sites to help improve your marketing savvy.

51727 ■ "Marketing and sales" in *Boston Business Journal* (Vol. 22, No. 14, May 10, 2002, pp. 22)
Pub: MCP, Inc.
Ed: Ken Cook. **Description:** The difference between marketing and sales, and how each is important and supports the other for sustainable growth, is discussed.

51728 ■ *Marketing Without Money for Small and Midsize Businesses: 300 FREE and Cheap Ways to Increase Your Sales*
Pub: Halle House Publishing
Ed: Nicholas E. Bade. **Released:** July 2005. **Price:** $16.95. **Description:** Three hundred practical low-cost or no-cost strategies to increase sales, focusing on free advertising, free marketing assistance, and free referrals to the Internet.

51729 ■ *Mastering the Complex Sales: How to Compete and Win When the Stakes Are High!*
Pub: John Wiley & Sons, Incorporated
Ed: Jeff Thull. **Released:** May 2003. **Price:** $24.95. **Description:** Guide to compete for and win in complex selling, the business-to-business transactions involving multiple decisions by multiple people from multiple perspectives.

51730 ■ *Maximum Marketing, Minimum Dollars: The Top 50 Ways to Grow Your Small Business*
Pub: Kaplan Books
Ed: Kim Gordon. **Released:** April 2006. **Price:** $24.00. **Description:** Marketing tips to increase sales are presented. Small business owners will learn to maximize marketing with 50 innovative and affordable methods, including online marketing.

51731 ■ *"Meet & Potatoes"* in *Entrepreneur* (Vol. 30, No. 3, March 2002, pp. 89)
Pub: Entrepreneur Media Inc.
Ed: Barry Farber. **Description:** Ideas to help entrepreneurs to network outside of a safe, familiar circle of contracts are presented.

51732 ■ *"Mind Your Manners"* in *Sales & Marketing Management*
Pub: VNU Business Media
Ed: Kathryn Droullard. **Description:** With new technologies, business communications are becoming less personal as a result of email messages and high-tech devices. A guide to help sales reps avoid 25 common mistakes when corresponding with clients is presented.

51733 ■ *"The Missing Link?"* in *Entrepreneur* (Vol. 33, September 2005, No. 9, pp. 88)
Pub: Entrepreneur Media Inc.
Ed: Catherine Seda. **Description:** The much-overlooked marketing strategy of getting links from other Websites to yours is examined. This tool will bring more visitors to a site while helping to achieve higher search engine rankings.

51734 ■ *"Money & Manners"* in *Small Business Opportunities* (Vol. 17, September 2005, No. 5, pp. 12)
Pub: Harris Publications Inc.
Ed: Lydia Ramsey. **Description:** Rudeness can cost a small business sales and revenue. A true/false quiz is offered to judge a company's business etiquette.

51735 ■ *"Mood Music"* in *Entrepreneur* (Vol. 31, No. 9, July 2003, pp. 79)
Pub: Entrepreneur Media, Inc.
Ed: Elizabeth Goodgold. **Description:** A marketing consultant addresses ways that music can be used to increase sales. Some retailers are actually defined by the style of music used in their shops.

51736 ■ *"More bang"* in *Entrepreneur* (Vol. 30, No. 2, February)
Pub: Entrepreneur Media Inc.
Ed: Chris Penttila. **Description:** Presentation of twenty-five tips for under $1,000 that will make a business better, from marketing to sales, and employees to equipment.

51737 ■ *"A More Profitable Harvest"* in *Business 2.0* (Vol. 6, May 2005, No. 4, pp. 66)
Pub: Time, Inc.
Ed: Bridget Finn. **Description:** Blue Mountain Arts makes money by giving away free greeting cards online and selling flowers to go with the greetings. ProFlowers has grown to third-largest flower retailer in the nation.

51738 ■ *"The Mother of Stunt Marketers"* in *Business 2.0* (Vol. 6, July 2005, No. 6, pp. 60-61)
Pub: Time, Inc.
Ed: Elizabeth Esfahani. **Description:** The Publicity Stunts Hall of Fame highlights the crazy things people have done as marketing tricks that generated publicity and increased sales for products.

51739 ■ *"Musical sales? You better, you better, you bet"* in *Atlanta Business Chronicle* (Vol. 25, November 29, 2002, No. 25, pp. 2B)
Pub: American City Business Publications, Inc.
Ed: Jeffrey Gitomer. **Description:** Music's long-lasting effect on people is relative to successful sales techniques. Effective selling relies on changes in approach, the creation of a memorable pitch, rehearsing, and passion. Tips for effective selling are presented.

51740 ■ *"MySpace for Business: Are You Connected?"* in *Sales & Marketing Management* (Vol. 158, November-December 2006, No. 11, pp. 20)
Pub: VNU Business Media
Ed: Rebecca Aronauer. **Description:** Joining an online community can prove profitable to any salesperson.

51741 ■ *"Nail the Sale: Need Some Surefire Ways to Seal the Deal with Customers?"* in *Entrepreneur* (Vol. 33, March 2005, No. 3, pp. 86)
Pub: Entrepreneur Media Inc.
Ed: Barry Farber. **Description:** Five tips to help master closing sales are presented.

51742 ■ *"Needful things?"* in *Entrepreneur* (Vol. 30, No. 12, December 2002, pp. 109)
Pub: Entrepreneur Media Inc.
Ed: Nichole L. Torres. **Description:** Ways to sell non-essential items are examined.

51743 ■ *"Negotiate from Strength"* in *Success* (Vol. 47, No. 3, July 2000, pp. 74)
Pub: Success Publishing, Inc.
Ed: Scott Smith. **Description:** Successful deal-making depends largely on preparation.

51744 ■ *"New Tacks for Tough Times"* in *Business Week Online* (Oct. 17, 2002)
Pub: McGraw-Hill Inc.
Ed: Roger Franklin. **Description:** According to a small business survey, 75 percent of the 5,000 firms responding, have a positive attitude about the future, and predict bottom-line growth. One-third of the companies expect significant expansion.

51745 ■ *"No experience necessary"* in *Entrepreneur* (Vol. 30, No. 12, December 2002, pp. 109)
Pub: Entrepreneur Media Inc.
Ed: Kimberly L. McCall. **Description:** Entrepreneurs are finding that untrained, fresh sales talent can be a powerful means to build a sales force. Tips for hiring novice sales personnel are presented.

51746 ■ *"No Surrender"* in *Entrepreneur* (Vol. 33, January 2005, No. 1, pp. 63)
Pub: Entrepreneur Media Inc.
Ed: Barry Farber. **Description:** Obstacles, rejections and refusals can be used as a tool to take a sales program to the next level.

51747 ■ *"The Not-So-Talented Tenth"* in *Sales & Marketing Management* (Vol. 158, November-December 2006, No. 11, pp. 16)
Pub: VNU Business Media
Ed: Michelle Marchetti. **Description:** New sales staff at Financial Resources of America must complete the company's five-day training program before selling to customers.

51748 ■ *"Nothing but Net"* in *Success* (Vol. 47, No. 4, September 2000, pp. 80)
Pub: Success Publishing, Inc.
Ed: Debbie Selinsky. **Description:** Quixtar combines the best in relationship sales and the Internet's unlimited potential.

51749 ■ *"Now that they've come, what can we sell them?"* in *The New York Times* (March 27, 2000, pp. D9, H9)
Pub: The New York Times Company
Ed: Bob Tedeschi. **Description:** How companies are converting free common interest sites to commercial ends is examined.

51750 ■ *"October Recap"* in *Sales & Marketing Management* (Vol. 159, January-February 2007, No. 1, pp. 48)
Pub: VNU Business Media
Description: Problems among older and younger sales representatives are discussed.

51751 ■ *"October Winner"* in *Sales & Marketing Management* (Vol. 159, January-February 2007, No. 1, pp. 48)
Pub: VNU Business Media
Description: Profile of Andrew M. Podner, product specialist at Southwest Region Sigma Corporation located in Houston, Texas.

51752 ■ *"Ok, let's review"* in *Entrepreneur* (Vol. 30, No. 10, October 2002, pp. 91)
Pub: Entrepreneur Media Inc.
Ed: Kimberly L. McCall. **Description:** Guidelines for use during performance reviews of sales staff that praise performers and weed out low producers are given.

51753 ■ *"On the Cheap: Creative Ways to Stretch Your Marketing Dollar"* in *Sales and Marketing.com* (Vol. 156, No. 3, March 2004, pp. 10)
Pub: VNU eMedia, Inc.
Description: Customer testimonials are a powerful way to enhance a sales rep's credibility with new clients.

51754 ■ *"On the Cheap"* in *Sales & Marketing Management* (Vol. 158, November-December 2006, No. 11, pp. 14)
Pub: VNU Business Media
Description: Clear Channel offers five-second commercial spots to help small firms afford advertising.

51755 ■ *"On the Fast Track: How Technology Is Speeding Incentive Delivery"* in *Sales & Marketing Management* (Vol. 157, February 2005)
Pub: VNU Business Media
Ed: Alan Horowitz. **Description:** Profile of the software company Synygy Inc. and its enterprise incentive management product. The software and services help to manage incentive compensation for sales staff, or any employee of a company, which promotes sales growth and employee motivation.

51756 ■ *"On the Same Page: Gain Competitive Edge With a Company-Wide Focus on Customers"* in *Sales & Marketing Management* (Vol. 157, Jan. 2005)
Pub: VNU Business Media
Ed: Sara Calabro. **Description:** Customer touchpoint management (CTM) is the understanding that a company's relationship with customers is not just about sales, but is the responsibility of the entire business.

51757 ■ *"On Target: Get the Specifics on Potential Customers"* in *Entrepreneur* (Vol. 31, No. 11, November 2003, pp. 99)
Pub: Entrepreneur Media, Inc.
Ed: April Y. Pennington. **Description:** A client support/sales department can help a small business target specific customers.

51758 ■ *"One More For the Road"* in *Sales & Marketing Management* (January 2005)
Pub: VNU Business Media
Ed: Denis Jensen. **Description:** Sales executives, as well as management, should avoid the pitfalls of drinking when entertaining business clients. One accident involving an employee under the influence will cause insurance rates to go up.

51759 ■ **"...Or Your Money Back" in** *Inc.* **(September 2005, pp. 46)**
Pub: Inc. Magazine
Ed: Dee Gill. **Description:** Money-back guaranties will entice customers, thus increase sales.

51760 ■ **"A pain in the supply chain" in** *Harvard Business Review* **(Vol. 80, No. 5, May 2002, pp. 31)**
Pub: Harvard Business School Press
Ed: John Butman. **Description:** Four experts offer their opinions on the aggressive promotion strategy of a fictional manufacturer that is trying to meet the wildly ambitious sales goals set by its CEO.

51761 ■ **"Passing the Baton" in** *Sales & Marketing Management* **(Vol. 157, January 2005, No. 1, pp. 34)**
Pub: VNU Business Media
Ed: Sara Calabro. **Description:** Outsourcing sales staff is becoming widely accepted in the industry. Outsourcing works best for products with short sales cycles.

51762 ■ **"Passing the Torch" in** *Entrepreneur* **(Vol. 31, No. 11, November 2003, pp. 97)**
Pub: Entrepreneur Media, Inc.
Ed: Kimberly L. McCall. **Description:** Ways to hire and introduce a replacement managing a sales team are examined.

51763 ■ **"People who need people" in** *Entrepreneur* **(Vol. 31, No. 5, May 2003, pp. 76)**
Pub: Entrepreneur Media Inc.
Ed: Barry Farber. **Description:** Six ways to make a connection with a customer in order to close sales are listed.

51764 ■ **"Perfect Proposals" in** *Sales & Marketing Management* **(Vol. 159, January-February 2007, No. 1, pp. 9)**
Pub: VNU Business Media
Description: Michael McLaughlin, principal at Mind-Share Consulting LLC, offers tips for developing sales proposals, and stresses keeping it simple.

51765 ■ **"Playing games with customers" in** *Harvard Business Review* **(Vol. 81, No. 4, April 2003, pp. 21)**
Pub: Harvard Business School Press
Ed: Keith Ferrazzi, Jane Chen, Zhan Li. **Description:** Many U.S. companies and the U.S. Army are using computer games to sell products and recruit soldiers.

51766 ■ **"Politics as Usual?" in** *Sales and Marketing.com* **(Vol. 156, No. 3, March 2004, pp. 14)**
Pub: VNU eMedia, Inc.
Ed: Amy Moerke. **Description:** Guidelines for discussing politics with clients are presented. The course of conversation will be determined by the relationship between salesperson and client.

51767 ■ **"Pop Quiz: A Quick Test Of Your Managerial Skills" in** *Sales & Marketing Management* **(Vol. 157, January 2005, No. 1, pp. 17)**
Pub: VNU Business Media
Description: Ways to determine whether a small business is capitalizing on its return on sales investment are presented.

51768 ■ **"Pop Quiz: A Quick Test of Your Managerial Skills" in** *Sales & Marketing Management* **(Vol. 157, February 2005, No. 2, pp. 17)**
Pub: VNU Business Media
Description: Three questions to determine whether you are an approachable or intimidating sales manager to your sales teams are asked.

51769 ■ **"Pop Quiz: A Quick Test of Your Managerial Skills" in** *Sales and Marketing. com* **(Vol. 147, No. 2, February 2004, pp. 15)**
Pub: VNU eMedia, Inc.
Description: A quiz to determine whether a sales commission plan needs updating is provided. Answers are provided by Peter Gundy, principal and sales compensation practice leader; and Andrew De-Lannoy, principal, both of Mellon Human Resources and Investor Solutions.

51770 ■ **"The Power of Permission-Based Prospecting" in** *Home Business* **(Vol. 12, October 2005, No. 5, pp. 46)**
Pub: Home Business Magazine
Ed: Bill Brooks. **Description:** Permission-based prospecting is founded on the principle that prospects are more interested in receiving a sales presentation when it is their idea to do so.

51771 ■ **The Power of Personal Sales: 501 Ways to Turn Self-Promotion into Profit**
Pub: Select Press
Ed: Fred Berns. **Released:** 1997. **Price:** $26.50.

51772 ■ **"Pre-Showtime class on the art of selling space" in** *Atlanta Business Chronicle* **(Vol. 25, No. 21, November 1, 2002, pp. 9C)**
Pub: American City Business Publications, Inc.
Ed: Leslie Williams Johnson. **Description:** "Marketing Commercial Real Estate 101-The Experts Talk" is being offered as a class to real estate professionals before they attend the annual Showtime tradeshow. The class, focusing on selling commercial real estate space, is available at no charge for the 1,600 members of the Atlanta Commercial Board of Realtors.

51773 ■ **"Predicting the outcome of a sale is easy. Sort of" in** *Atlanta Business Chronicle* **(Vol. 25, January 10, 2003, No. 31, pp. 8B)**
Pub: American City Business Publications, Inc.
Ed: Jeffrey Gitomer. **Description:** A crystal ball for business is not a thing of fantasy. You can predict the future with three things: information about your sales prospect and the business in which they are involved, the right questions, and an idea that may help the prospect. How these three things can come together to give a clear view of the future of a sale is discussed.

51774 ■ **Professional Selling**
Pub: Crisp Publications, Inc.
Ed: Rebecca Morgan. **Price:** $10.95.

51775 ■ **"Profiting - Adding an affiliate program links site content to product sales" in** *PC Magazine* **(February 20, 2001, pp. 133)**
Pub: Ziff-Davis Publishing Company
Ed: Neil Randall. **Description:** Banner ads are a way for Web site developers to make a profit. Placing a banner ad on the page directs interested site visitors to the advertiser's site. The affiliate network tracks the origin of the visit and pays the host of the originating site a percentage of all sales. Some pay a fee just for directing a visitor to a site. Commission Junction offers commissions from more than 1,600 companies in a wide variety of industries. LinkShare offers commissions from just over 500 companies, but they are major organizations.

51776 ■ **"Promoting Praise: Incorporating Client Feedback Into Your Motivation Efforts" in** *Sales & Marketing Management* **(Vol. 157, Jan. 2005)**
Pub: VNU Business Media
Ed: Kathryn Droullard. **Description:** Positive customer feedback can be used as a tool to motivate sales teams.

51777 ■ **Prospecting: The Key to Sales Success**
Pub: Crisp Publications, Inc.
Ed: Virden J. Thornton. **Price:** $10.95. **Description:** Explains the concepts of prospecting and networking, and how they can be used in a successful marketing strategy.

51778 ■ **"The Pulse" in** *Sales & Marketing Management* **(Vol. 159, January-February 2007, No. 1, pp. 9)**
Pub: VNU Business Media
Description: According to a survey conducted by Extraprise, 63 percent of all business-to-business companies will implement marketing automation technology in 2007.

51779 ■ **"Pump 'em up at the office" in** *Incentive* **(Vol. 174, No. 10, October 2000, pp. 149)**
Pub: Bill Communications

Description: The principal cause of friction between independent sales representatives and their manufacturer is lack of understanding of each others' functions. Seven ways to motivate sales representatives and useful tips are discussed.

51780 ■ **"Pump it Up" in** *Entrepreneur* **(Vol. 32, No. 2, February 2004, pp. 73)**
Pub: Entrepreneur Media, Inc.
Ed: Barry Farber. **Description:** Three things to build, maintain and project confidence when making a sale are explained.

51781 ■ **"Put sales last to succeed" in** *Rough Notes* **(Vol. 146, No. 3, March 2003, pp. 124)**
Pub: Rough Notes
Ed: Michael Jans. **Description:** The secret of agents experiencing explosive growth is through creative Unique Selling Proposition. The proposition has a hook so unique or gripping it makes the customer ask for more information.

51782 ■ **"Quality Time: Not Getting What You Want Out of Your Sales Meeting? Here are 5 Tips to Point You in the Right Direction" in** *Entrepreneur*
Pub: Entrepreneur Media Inc.
Ed: Kimberly L. McCall. **Description:** Besides confidence building, information dissemination, and company strategies, sales meetings can also be used to inspire a sales team to produce. Steps to changing dull sales meetings into creative sales meetings are listed.

51783 ■ **"A Quick Test of Your Managerial Skills" in** *Sales & Marketing Management* **(Vol. 158, October 2006, No. 10, pp. 19)**
Pub: VNU Business Media
Description: Al Siebert, director of the Resiliency Center located in Portland, Oregon discusses the need for resiliency in salespeople.

51784 ■ **"Radical Rendezvous: Bye-Bye Boring" in** *Entrepreneur* **(Vol. 31, No. 9, July 2003, pp. 79)**
Pub: Entrepreneur Media, Inc.
Ed: Kimberly L. McCall. **Description:** Sales conferences offer excellent opportunities for reps to discuss a new product launch, and to regroup and re-energize. Chris Lytle, author of The Accidental Salesperson, offers ideas for a lively sales conference on a low budget.

51785 ■ **"Reaching Out: Finding Good Leads Takes More Than Just Making a Few Phone Calls." in** *Entrepreneur* **(Vol. 32, December 2004, No. 12)**
Pub: Entrepreneur Media Inc.
Ed: Barry Farber. **Description:** Prospecting for leads is more than making a phone call. Three methods for creating a successful sales prospecting program are investigated.

51786 ■ **"Ready? Set? Search! Rev Up Your Sales With Comparison-Shopping Engines" in** *Entrepreneur* **(Vol. 31, No. 9, September 2003, pp. 87)**
Pub: Entrepreneur Media, Inc.
Ed: Catherine Seda. **Description:** According to a survey conducted in January 2003, more than 50 percent of shoppers believe comparison-shopping search engines save time and money. The sites offer product descriptions, prices, and customer testimonials.

51787 ■ **"Ready To Go: How An Online Tool Helped One Company Speed Distribution of Marketing Materials To Reps" in** *Sales & Marketing Management*
Pub: VNU Business Media
Ed: Alan Horowitz. **Description:** Allstate Insurance, is providing its sales reps access to thousands of sales and marketing materials via a Web-hosted service that automates order fulfillment and inventory management of sales and marketing materials. Research indicates that without this type of service, sales reps spend 25 percent of their time searching for and assembling information for sales calls.

51788 ■ "Recruit From Another Industry" in *Sales & Marketing Management* **(Vol. 157, February 2005, No. 2, pp. 16)**
Pub: VNU Business Media
Description: Recruiting a top salesperson from another industry does not guarantee the same results when selling in a new sector.

51789 ■ "Reducing Turnover" in *Automotive News* **(Vol. 79, January 24, 2005, No. 6131, pp. 38)**
Pub: Crain Communications Inc.
Ed: Donna Harris, K.C. Crain. **Description:** Car dealers are moving away from paying sales staff conventional commission on gross profits of vehicles sold. Many dealers are offering both salary and commission, along with bonuses for volume and repeat business.

51790 ■ "Refer madness" in *Entrepreneur* **(Vol. 30, No. 3, March 2002, pp. 87)**
Pub: Entrepreneur Media Inc.
Ed: Nichole L. Torres. **Description:** The impact of word-of-mouth advertising by online customers is discussed.

51791 ■ "Reining In Office Rumors" in *Inc.* **(November 1, 2004)**
Pub: Inc. Magazine
Description: Finding sales talent and controlling office gossip are key topics discussed.

51792 ■ "Relationship Advice" in *Entrepreneur* **(Vol. 32, No. 1, January 2004, pp. 47)**
Pub: Entrepreneur Media, Inc.
Ed: Liane Cassavoy. **Description:** Profile of Salesnet's online Customer Relation Management application that includes tools for managing accounts and contacts.

51793 ■ *Relationship Selling: Building Trust to Sell Your Service*
Pub: Self-Counsel Press, Inc.
Ed: Karen Johnston and Jean Withers. **Released:** 1992, second edition. **Price:** $12.95 (paper).

51794 ■ "Relax Your Grip" in *Black Enterprise* **(Vol. 36, February 2006, No. 7, pp. 71)**
Pub: Earl G. Graves Publishing Co. Inc.
Ed: Lee Anna Jackson. **Description:** Profile of Cassandra Hayes, director of U.S. External Communications for Avon. Hayes offers insight to managers on ways to delegate responsibility in the organization, which in turn, frees her from worry when she is not at the workplace.

51795 ■ "Remote Control" in *Entrepreneur* **(Vol. 32, December 2004, No. 12, pp. 92)**
Pub: Entrepreneur Media Inc.
Ed: Kimberly L. McCall. **Description:** Pros and cons when considering a program that allows sales reps to telecommute are examined.

51796 ■ "Resources: Web Sites, Organizations, Events and More To Grow Your Business" in *Entrepreneur* **(Vol. 32, September 2004, No. 9, pp. 8)**
Pub: Entrepreneur Media Inc.
Ed: Steve Cooper. **Description:** Resources to help small business are featured including the Small Business Administration's effort to help teen entrepreneurs launch a business; KnockNow an online community of entrepreneurs, executives, venture capitalists, angel investors, service sector companies, and government; the SBA's business Website offering information on small business development, financial assistance, taxes, laws and regulations, international trade, workplace issues, buying and selling and federal forms.

51797 ■ "Retailers Draw Link Between Halloween, Christmas Sales" in *Sacramento Bee* **(October 30, 2005)**
Pub: The Sacramento Bee
Ed: Jon Ortiz. **Description:** Experts suggest a strong link between Halloween and winter holiday sales. Halloween is becoming a strong indicator of consumer spending for the months of November and December.

51798 ■ "Retailers' Siren Song" in *Kiplinger's Personal Finance Magazine* **(Vol. 54, No. 11, November 2000, pp. 130)**
Pub: The Kiplinger Washington Editors, Inc.
Ed: Elizabeth Razzi. **Description:** Merchants use psychology to entice you into spending more. Knowing what they know will make you a smarter shopper.

51799 ■ "Retailers Welcome Valentine's Day Gift Binge" in *Bradenton Herald* **(February 5, 2005)**
Pub: Bradenton Herald
Ed: Dana Sanchez. **Description:** Valentine's Day helps retailers show off creativity with unique gift items in order to maximize sales. The Valentine holiday ranks third in sales after Christmas and Easter for many retailers of candies and chocolates.

51800 ■ "Retailing Your Personal Lines Accounts" in *Rough Notes* **(Vol. 146, No. 9, September 2003, pp. 56)**
Pub: Rough Notes
Ed: Troy Korsgaden. **Description:** Ways for insurance agents to increase personal insurance lines; topics include strategic marketing, techniques in selling, and tips on improving customer service.

51801 ■ "Reward Me: Rebates and Incentives Make Buying all the More Appealing" in *Entrepreneur* **(Vol. 32, December 2004, No. 12, pp. 39)**
Pub: Entrepreneur Media Inc.
Ed: Jill Amadio. **Description:** Rebates and incentives can help clear inventory. New car dealers use this approach often near the end of a model year.

51802 ■ "A rewarding experience" in *Incentive* **(Vol. 174, No. 8, August 2000, pp. 12)**
Pub: Bill Communications
Ed: Don Mogelefsky. **Description:** Inspiring a sales force, rewarding a customer, or recognizing an employee can all be done easily and efficiently online.

51803 ■ "Rewarding Rebates" in *Black Enterprise* **(Vol. 36, November 2005, No. 4, pp. 166)**
Pub: Earl G. Graves Publishing Co. Inc.
Ed: Stephanie Young. **Description:** The National Retail Federation reports that online rebate offers from stores provide ease in use while avoiding the hassle of finding serial numbers and product codes, filling out paperwork, and mailing in paperwork.

51804 ■ "Rewards For Recruiting: Incentivize Your Reps For Bringing In New Hires" in *Sales & Marketing Management* **(Vol. 157, February 2005)**
Pub: VNU Business Media
Ed: Julia Chang. **Description:** Referrals from current sales staff help attract top sales people. Some companies are using incentives to encourage salespeople to bring qualified candidates on board.

51805 ■ "The right carrot" in *Entrepreneur* **(Vol. 30, No. 2, February 20)**
Pub: Entrepreneur Media Inc.
Ed: Kimberly L. McCall. **Description:** Ways to motivate and retain sales professionals are explored, including a discussion on the importance of a good compensation plan.

51806 ■ "Right at Home with Telecommuting" in *Business Week* **(No. 3761, December 10, 2001, pp. SB4)**
Pub: McGraw-Hill Inc.
Description: According to a survey of small business executives, conducted by Sales & Marketing Management, 86 percent believe that a sales staff can work as productively from home as in the office.

51807 ■ "Right on Target" in *Entrepreneur* **(Vol. 33, February 2005, No. 2, pp. 65)**
Pub: Entrepreneur Media Inc.
Ed: Barry Farber. **Description:** Hot button issues to recruit and maintain customers are discussed. A hot button is anything that is of major importance to a prospective client.

51808 ■ "Ringing Up Sales" in *Small Business Opportunities* **(Vol. 12, No. 2, March 2000, pp. 52)**
Pub: Harris Publications, Inc.
Ed: Stan Roberts. **Description:** Investigation into the use of a toll-free phone number for small business sales.

51809 ■ "The Road to Healthy Sales " in *Sales & Marketing Management*
Pub: VNU Business Media
Ed: Michael Schrage. **Description:** The importance of using sales-support software geared to a particular small business is stressed.

51810 ■ "Said The Spider" in *Entrepreneur* **(Vol. 28, No. 4, April 2000, pp. 149)**
Pub: Entrepreneur Media Inc.
Ed: Barry Farber. **Description:** Learn to win sales from our eight-legged friend's greatest architectural accomplishment, the spider web. It can help you to allocate at a glance, make connections, think on the road, and look into the future.

51811 ■ "The Sales Auction: Is Bidding for Leads the Sales Trend of the Future" in *Sales and Marketing.com* **(Vol. 156, No. 3, March 2004)**
Pub: VNU eMedia, Inc.
Ed: Michael Schrage. **Description:** Would a more rigorous and impartial mechanism for allocating sales leads, prospects, and territories lead to a better sales force by forming an auction lot? Salespeople would be allowed to bid on prospects they feel they could turn into clients. Bids could be percentages of anticipated commissions, and a portion could come from existing clients' proceeds, or even the company's Bid4Prospects program.

51812 ■ "The Sales Force that Rocks" in *Business 2.0* **(Vol. 6, July 2005, No. 6, pp. 102-107)**
Pub: Time, Inc.
Ed: Paul Sloan. **Description:** Guitar Center store in Jacksonville, Florida accredits its success to the use of ex-rockers to sell their merchandise. The store boasts its status as the nation's largest guitar center. Statistical data included.

51813 ■ *Sales Forecasting Management: Understanding the Techniques, Systems & Management of the Sales Forecasting Process*
Pub: Sage Publications, Inc.
Ed: John T. Mentzer and Carol C. Bienstock. **Released:** 1998. **Price:** $67.00.

51814 ■ "Sales" in *Inc.* **(Volume 27, March 2005, No. 3, pp. 38)**
Pub: Inc. Magazine
Ed: Mike Brewster. **Description:** Large corporations require a request for proposal when purchasing products or services in order to comply with corporate governance standards.

51815 ■ *Sales Magic: Revolutionary New Techniques that Will Double Your Sales Volume in 21 Days*
Pub: William Morrow & Co., Inc.
Ed: Kerry Johnson. **Released:** 1995. **Price:** $12.00.

51816 ■ "" in *Sales & Marketing Management* **(Vol. 158, October 2006, No. 10, pp. 11)**
Pub: VNU Business Media
Description: Ideas for creating a business blog are presented. Blogs can feature ideas, criticisms, and insights.

51817 ■ "Sales & Marketing: The Power of Brand" in *Ingram's* **(Vol. 27, No. 6, June 2001, pp. 23)**
Pub: Show Me Publishing, Inc.
Ed: Jean Hughes. **Description:** The answer to increasing product usage is to leverage the company's brand and to strengthen account relationships.

51818 ■ **"Sales & Marketing: Why Advertise Anyway?"** in *Ingram's* (Vol. 27, No. 5, May 2001, pp. 28)
Pub: Show Me Publishing, Inc.
Ed: Rob Pearcy. **Description:** Business plans need to include a marketing budget for advertising in order to be successful.

51819 ■ *Sales Promotion Essentials: The 10 Basic Sales Promotion Techniques...& How to Use Them*
Pub: N T C Contemporary Publishing Co.
Ed: Don E. Schultz, William A. Robinson and Lisa A. Petrison. **Released:** 3rd ed. 1997. **Price:** $19.95.

51820 ■ **"Sales Report: Once Tainted by Get-Rich-Quick Schemes, the Direct-Sales Industry is Changing its Image"** in *Entrepreneur* (July 2004)
Pub: Entrepreneur Media Inc.
Ed: Nichole L. Torres. **Description:** Direct selling has become an industry whereby an independent consultant bringing a portable kit of wares to homes to share in a demonstration. According to the Direct Selling Association, the direct-selling industry accounted for more than $28 billion in 2002, with an estimated 13 million independent direct salespersons in the U.S. The five elements creating the evolution in direct selling are outlined.

51821 ■ **"Sales Secrets"** in *Atlanta Business Chronicle* (Vol. 25, Nov. 8, 2002, No. 22 pp. 2B)
Pub: American City Business Publications, Inc.
Ed: Jeffrey Gitomer. **Description:** A list of elements that businesses may need in order to maintain a stellar sales team is given. Businesses are urged to focus on the sales cycle, not the salesperson.

51822 ■ **"Sales Secrets: Persistence is key to building your brand"** in *Atlanta Business Chronicle* (Vol. 25, No. 21, November 1, 2002, pp. 2B)
Pub: American City Business Publications, Inc.
Ed: Jeffrey Gitomer. **Description:** A suggested formula for building a brand is discussed, along with branding step recommendations.

51823 ■ **"Sales Strategies"** in *Small Business Opportunities* (Vol. 17, November 2005, No. 6, pp. 64)
Pub: Harris Publications Inc.
Ed: Steve Bookbinder. **Description:** Seven things every business owner must do in order to prepare for a first meeting with a client.

51824 ■ **"S&MM Pulse"** in *Sales & Marketing Management* (Vol. 158, October 2006, No. 10, pp. 16)
Pub: VNU Business Media
Description: Information to help small companies embrace the Intered for IT and marketing is presented.

51825 ■ **"Say It and Sell It"** in *Sales & Marketing Management* (Vol. 158, November-December 2006, No. 11, pp. 13)
Pub: VNU Business Media
Description: Ways to renew a contract with a price increase are defined.

51826 ■ **"Search Engines Help Shoppers To Buy Locally"** in *Wall Street Journal* (Vol. 248, January 2007, No. 148, pp. B1-B3)
Pub: Dow Jones & Co. Inc.
Ed: James Covert **Description:** Several new search engines help customers compare prices and find out whether items are in stock at local stores.

51827 ■ *Secrets of Successful Selling*
Pub: Contemporary Books, Inc.
Ed: Charles R. Whitlock. **Released:** 1993. **Price:** $8.95 (paper).

51828 ■ **"Seen & Noted: Fitness-Minded Bare Motivations in Stores"** in *Crain's Chicago Business* (Vol. 30, January 2007, No. 2, pp. 19)
Pub: Crain Communications, Inc.
Ed: Kevin Davis. **Description:** Motivated by New Year's resolutions and the film release of Rocky Balboa, consumers are purchasing fitness equipment on a large scale.

51829 ■ **"Seller's Market: Selling on eBay Can Help You Grow Your Business, But is This Site the Right Marketplace For You?"** in *Entrepreneur*
Pub: Entrepreneur Media Inc.
Ed: Melissa Campanelli. **Description:** Nearly 430,000 entrepreneurs are selling products on eBay on either a part-time or full-time basis. eBay can be used as a vehicle to grow a small business.

51830 ■ **"Serving Your Client-And Yourself"** in *Sales and Marketing.com* (Vol. 156, No. 3, March 2004, pp. 20)
Pub: VNU eMedia, Inc.
Ed: Daniel Tynan. **Description:** Profile of Craig Elias, founder of InnerSell, a firm through which salespeople can locate services for their customers, make referrals, and earn a percentage of the deal.

51831 ■ **"Share the Wealth"** in *Entrepreneur* (Vol. 32, November 2004, No. 11, pp. 90)
Pub: Entrepreneur Media Inc.
Ed: Kimberly L. McCall. **Description:** One person on a sales staff should not be the only rep responsible for a company's biggest and best accounts. Steps to ensure well-distributed accounts are presented.

51832 ■ **"Shift in business strategy helps Littlearth turn around financials"** in *Pittsburgh Business Times* (Vol. 22, No. 42, May 2, 2003)
Pub: Pittsburgh Business Times
Ed: Tim Schooley. **Description:** Littlearth increased the prices of recycled handbags and belts by 30 percent and increased sales by 20 percent.

51833 ■ **"Shifting Into Growth Mode"** in *Sales and Marketing.com* (Vol. 156, No. 3, March 2004, pp. 12)
Pub: VNU eMedia, Inc.
Ed: Michele Marchetti. **Description:** Managers will be required to makes changes to maximize productivity of sales teams as firms shift from survival mode to growth mode. Several management tactics are outlined.

51834 ■ **"Shopping in palm of the hand is making its holiday debut"** in *The New York Times* (November 11, 2000, pp. A1)
Pub: The New York Times Company
Ed: Leslie Kaufman. **Description:** We are all used to making purchases online, particularly during the holiday season. But, this year, the new thing is wireless or mobile shopping. More people are making purchases over the Internet this year using their wireless digital assistants or their cellular telephones.

51835 ■ **"Short and Sweet"** in *Entrepreneur* (Vol. 32, No. 2, February 2004, pp. 74)
Pub: Entrepreneur Media, Inc.
Ed: Kimberly L. McCall. **Description:** Tactics that can be used to shorten a sales cycle in order to increase profits are explained.

51836 ■ **"Show Me the Money"** in *Sales and Marketing.com* (Vol. 156, No. 3, March 2004, pp. 16)
Pub: VNU eMedia, Inc.
Ed: Julia Chang. **Description:** As companies transfer from cost cutting to growth strategies, sales commission plans will also change. Salespersons will have higher quotas and underperformers will most likely receive lower commissions than top performers.

51837 ■ **"Site Matters"** in *Sales and Marketing.com* (Vol. 156, No. 3, March 2004, pp. 40)
Pub: VNU eMedia, Inc.

Ed: Julie Barker. **Description:** It is imperative to match a sales meeting's goals with the right site in order to achieve success.

51838 ■ **"Six Degrees: Can Who Your Employees Know Make a Difference in Your Sales?"** in *Entrepreneur* (Vol. 32, No. 1, January 2004, pp. 27)
Pub: Entrepreneur Media, Inc.
Ed: Amanda C. Kooser. **Description:** New computer software is making it easier to increase sales through relationship mining or relationship capital management. Three startup software companies, Spoke Software Inc., Visible Path Corporation, and ZeroDegrees Inc., all offer versions of this software.

51839 ■ *Six SIGMA for Small Business*
Pub: Entrepreneur Press
Ed: Greg Brue. **Released:** October 2005. **Price:** $19.95 (US), $26.95 (Canadian). **Description:** Jack Welch's Six SIGMA approach to business covers accounting, finance, sales and marketing, buying a business, human resource development, and new product development.

51840 ■ **"Size Matters: Does Your Product Jam a Lot of Benefits Into a Small Package? Here's How to Sell It"** in *Entrepreneur* (August 2004)
Pub: Entrepreneur Media Inc.
Ed: Jerry Fisher. **Description:** Expert advertising advice is given to help sell a product. If a product offers many benefits, using a headline to set the consumer up and a footline to give the payoff, can be a key to a great sales campaign.

51841 ■ *Small Business Desk Reference*
Pub: Penguin Books (USA) Incorporated
Ed: Gene Marks. **Released:** December 2004. **Price:** $29.95 (US), $44.00 (Canadian). **Description:** Comprehensive guide for starting or running a successful small business, focusing on buying a business or franchise, writing a business plan, financial management, accounting, legal issues, human resources management, operations, marketing, sales, customer service, taxes, insurance, and ethics. Information for launching a restaurant, property management firm, retail outlet, consulting firm, and service business is included.

51842 ■ *The Small Business Owner's Manual: Everything You Need to Know to Start Up and Run Your Business*
Pub: Career Press, Incorporated
Ed: Joe Kennedy. **Released:** June 2005. **Price:** $19.99 (US), $26.95 (Canadian). **Description:** Comprehensive guide for starting a small business, focusing on twelve ways to obtain financing, business plans, selling and advertising products and services, hiring and firing employees, setting up a Web site, business law, accounting issues, insurance, equipment, computers, banks, financing, customer credit and collection, leasing, and more.

51843 ■ **"Small Firms Emphasize Trade-Show Marketing"** in *Crain's Detroit Business* (Vol. 21, February 7, 2005, No. 6, pp. 24)
Pub: Crain Communications Inc. - Detroit
Ed: DeAnna Belger. **Description:** According to a recent survey, more small companies in Michigan rely on trade shows than their larger competitors. Most respondents reported attending trade shows to generate sales leads, increase visibility, and to network.

51844 ■ **"Smart Money: Where to Spend Your Marketing Dollars When a Product Isn't Selling"** in *Entrepreneur* (Vol. 33, January 2005, No. 1)
Pub: Entrepreneur Media Inc.
Ed: Nancy Michaels. **Description:** Marketing tips for selling under-performing products are provided.

51845 ■ **"A smarter way to sell commodities"** in *Harvard Business Review* (Vol. 80, No. 4, April 2002, pp. 24)
Pub: Harvard Business School Press
Ed: Ajay Kohli, Robert S. Lurie. **Description:** Commodities sellers can differentiate their products from those of the competition by reducing risk for their customers according to marketing experts, Robert Lurie and Ajay Kohli.

51846 ■ "Software, Hard Profit" in *Small Business Opportunities* (Vol. 16, No. 1, January 2004, pp. 80, 84)
Pub: Harris Publications, Inc.
Ed: Chuck Green. **Description:** Profile of Mike Hennel, owner of Silvon Software. The software company makes $12 million annually helping customers analyze sales trends in order to minimize costs.

51847 ■ "Spring cleaning" in *Entrepreneur* (Vol. 31, No. 4, April 2003, pp. 44)
Pub: Entrepreneur Media Inc.
Ed: Melissa Campanelli. **Description:** There are a variety of software tools available to make sure a Web site is in good working order. Keynote NetMechanic spots and fixes common HTML code errors and generates a repaired file to upload to the Web host.

51848 ■ "Straight to the Outsource: Sales Force: Feeling the Crunch?" in *Entrepreneur* (Vol. 31, No. 9, September 2003, pp. 83)
Pub: Entrepreneur Media, Inc.
Ed: Kimberly L. McCall. **Description:** Outsourcing sales functions allows a small business to eliminate many of the costs associated with an in-house sales division.

51849 ■ *Streetwise Small Business Book of Lists: Hundreds of Lists to Help You Reduce Costs, Increase Revenues, and Boost Your Profits!*
Pub: Adams Media Corporation
Ed: Gene Marks. **Released:** September 2006. **Price:** $25.95. **Description:** Strategies to help small business owners locate services, increase sales, and lower expenses.

51850 ■ "Stress Case? Is the Pressure to 'Get the Sale' Getting to You? Keep Your Cool With These Stress-Busters" in *Entrepreneur* (Vol. 32)
Pub: Entrepreneur Media Inc.
Ed: Barry Farber. **Description:** Effective remedies to alleviate stress for sales reps are presented, including the use of a 20-minute power nap.

51851 ■ "The Struggle for Sales Overseas" in *Hispanic Business* (November 2002, pp. 36)
Pub: Hispanic Business
Ed: Joel Russell. **Description:** Statistics are shared regarding Hispanic companies exporting products are featured. Overall exports for the first seven months of 2002 were down 8 percent from same period in 2001.

51852 ■ "Substitute Presenter" in *Sales & Marketing Management* (Vol. 157, February 2005, No. 2, pp. 11)
Pub: VNU Business Media
Description: Ideas for better sales leads are discussed.

51853 ■ *Successful Enjoyable Selling: How to Get the Best Out of Your Career*
Pub: Rainier Publishing
Ed: Paul W. Richards. **Released:** 1996. **Price:** $9.95.

51854 ■ *The Successful Exhibitor's Handbook: Trade Show Techniques for Beginners and Pros*
Pub: Self-Counsel Press, Inc.
Ed: Barry Siskind. **Released:** 1993, second edition. **Price:** $14.95 (paper).

51855 ■ "Successful firms keep sales teams highly motivated" in *Atlanta Business Chronicle* (Vol. 24, No. 13, August 24, 2001, pp. 7B)
Pub: American City Business Journals Inc.
Ed: Jim Triandiflou. **Description:** An interview with Jim Triandiflou, CEO of Ockham Technologies Inc. Triandiflou points out that the top sales executive of a firm is responsible for 100 percent of a company's revenues but only 15-20 percent of its expenses, so such executives must hire the right people and set goals for them that are aligned with the company's best interests. The sales executive must retain control so that the company and its investors are not hit with surprises like missed sales targets.

51856 ■ "Sun Microsystems Remakes Its Sales Force" in *Wall Street Journal* (Vol. 248, December 2006, No. 149, pp. B3)
Pub: Dow Jones & Co. Inc.
Ed: Christopher Lawton **Description:** Sun Microsystems makes a dramatic change in the retraining of its' sales force to focus on customers' needs in growing their businesses.

51857 ■ "Sure, it would be easier on the Web - but let's haggle" in *The New York Times* (December 13, 2000, pp. D13, H13)
Pub: The New York Times Company
Ed: Bernard Stamler. **Description:** Media buying is still done in an old-fashioned way, despite the availability of the Internet.

51858 ■ "Table Talk" in *Sales & Marketing Management* (Vol. 159, January-February 2007, No. 1, pp. 33)
Pub: VNU Business Media
Description: Marketing leaders focus on the impacts of globalization of business, customers and products.

51859 ■ "Take-Aways" in *Sales & Marketing Management* (Vol. 158, October 2006, No. 10, pp. 16)
Pub: VNU Business Media
Description: Tips for using music for branding products or services are presented by Paul Anthony, CEO of Rumblefish.

51860 ■ "Tapping local markets can pay off" in *Wall Street Journal* (May 14, 2002, pp. B4)
Pub: Wall Street Journal
Ed: Jeff Bailey. **Description:** Harvey Saltzman of Triangle Printers Inc does business locally as well as nationally, but states that his local customers often boost his firms sales at a lower operating cost.

51861 ■ "Target Practice" in *Entrepreneur* (Vol. 31, No. 8, August 2003, pp. 72)
Pub: Entrepreneur Media, Inc.
Ed: Barry Farber. **Description:** The key to landing a sale can sometimes lie in clearing away the obstacles that can make a salesperson miss the mark. Five practical and effective strategies to apply to sales are investigated.

51862 ■ "Team Players" in *Entrepreneur* (Vol. 33, October 2005, No. 10, pp. 85)
Pub: Entrepreneur Media, Inc.
Ed: Catherine Seda. **Description:** Questions for planning an affiliate program for marketing a business are presented, focusing on hiring Internet marketers to promote your business with no up-front costs.

51863 ■ "Team Up for Riches" in *Small Business Opportunities* (Vol. 16, No. 2, March 2004, pp. 154, 170)
Pub: Harris Publications, Inc.
Ed: Brian Tracy. **Description:** Review of Brain Tracy's book, Goals: New Book Shows How! The book offers 21 ways to set and achieve goals in every area of life. Tracy suggests putting the customer on your team to build sales and increase your bottom line.

51864 ■ "The Technology Discrepancy" in *Sales & Marketing Management* (Vol. 157, January 2005, No. 1, pp. 9)
Pub: VNU Business Media
Ed: Jennifer Gilbert. **Description:** Sales teams equipped with cutting-edge technology are believed to be more successful than counterparts not well-equipped. Results of a survey of managers performed by S&MM/Equation Research are discussed. Statistical data included.

51865 ■ "Technophobe Help Desk" in *Sales & Marketing Management* (Vol. 158, October 2006, No. 10, pp. 22)
Pub: VNU Business Media
Description: Traditional marketing channels are based on self-reported surveys, circulation audits and promotional code tracking, however, Web analytics provide actual site traffic, including page hits, number of visits, browser usage and visitors' regional origin.

51866 ■ "That's the Spirit" in *Entrepreneur* (Vol. 33, October 2005, No. 10, pp. 83)
Pub: Entrepreneur Media Inc.
Ed: Kim T. Gordon. **Description:** Four steps to increase sales and promote customer loyalty for the 2005 holiday season are outlined, including customer rewards, holiday promotions, donations to charities, and holding a holiday party.

51867 ■ "The ROI Treatment: Get Better Results by Creating an ROI Model" in *Entrepreneur* (Vol. 31, No. 11, November 2003, pp. 100)
Pub: Entrepreneur Media, Inc.
Ed: Catherine Seda. **Description:** Developing a return on investment (ROI) model for a business can be done in five simple steps, starting with researching market demand.

51868 ■ "They've Got Mail - From You" in *My Business* (June/July 2004, pp. 45)
Pub: My Business Magazine
Ed: Nancy Mann Jackson. **Description:** A customer newsletter can help build strong relationships with clients and attract new customers.

51869 ■ "A Thorough Assessment: Want to Evaluate Your Management Skills?" in *Sales and Marketing.com* (Vol. 156, No. 3, March 2004)
Pub: VNU eMedia, Inc.
Ed: Julia Chang. **Description:** Profile of the Hay Group's multirater tests for technology executives. The firm rated 276 technology executives and found the most accurate performance ratings came from direct reports, followed by managers. Self and peer assessments were the poorest, citing executives tend to overrate their performance and that of colleagues.

51870 ■ "Timothy Askew: 54, Founder and CEO of Corporate Rain Inc (CRI)..." in *Entrepreneur* (Vol. 32, No. 1, January 2004, pp. 23)
Pub: Entrepreneur Media, Inc.
Ed: April Y. Pennington. **Description:** Profile of Timothy Askew, founder and CEO of Corporate Rain Inc., an executive sales outsourcing boutique. Askew invested $10,000 in his startup in 1996 and sales are estimated at $1.9 million for 2003. CRIs sales force is made up of entrepreneurs and former executives with PhDs or higher and use the peer-to-peer approach to selling.

51871 ■ "Tips & Trends" in *Small Business Opportunities* (Vol. 17, September 2005, No. 5, pp. 14)
Pub: Harris Publications Inc.
Description: Tips and trends important to small business include the addition of a coffeemaker that also makes soup, tea or cocoa; paper shredders; headsets; a sales resource guide for retailers; information for the Federal Citizen Information Center; and Creative Colors, the franchise offering mobile equipment to home-based businesses.

51872 ■ *Titanium EBay: A Tactical Guide to Becoming a Millionaire PowerSeller*
Pub: Penguin Group Incorporated
Ed: Skip McGrath. **Released:** June 2006. **Price:** $24.95. **Description:** Advice is given to help anyone selling items on eBay to become a Power Seller, an award presented based on monthly gross merchandise sales.

51873 ■ "To the Extreme: Watch Sales Grow by Making a Positive Lasting Impression" in *Sales & Marketing Management* (Vol. 157, January 2005)
Pub: VNU Business Media
Ed: Sara Calabro. **Description:** Positive Response, a marketing consulting firm in Ohio, developed an extreme marketing plan to help CSi Complete gain the competitive edge to win approval to sell its customer satisfaction measurement services for collision repair companies. Positive Response created a three-step mail campaign targeted to collision repair services over six weeks.

51874 ■ "To Haggle or Nor to Haggle? Tips On Negotiating at the Car Dealership" in *Black Enterprise* (Vol. 35, November 2004, No. 4, pp. 192)
Pub: Earl G. Graves Publishing Co. Inc.
Ed: Lee Anna Jackson. **Description:** Tips to use when negotiating a new vehicle sale are addressed.

51875 ■ "Top 10 characteristics of Cintas' top salesperson" in *Atlanta Business Chronicle* (Vol. 24, No. 8, July 27, 2001, pp. 2B)
Pub: American City Business Journals Inc.
Ed: Jeffrey Gitomer. **Description:** Cintas has over 100 salespeople on staff, and Terri Norris is number one in sales. Norris claims her success is due to her positive attitude, her willingness to help others, self-assurance and common sense.

51876 ■ "Top Secrets: Psst! Think You Know Everything About Sales?" in *Entrepreneur* (Vol. 31, No. 8, August 2003, pp. 62)
Pub: Entrepreneur Media, Inc.
Ed: Brian Tracy. **Description:** Three steps to greater sales success are cited: prospecting, presenting, and closing, better known as the "iron triangle" of selling. Tips to achieve sales success using the "iron triangle" are presented.

51877 ■ "Touchdown!" in *Rough Notes* (Vol. 145, No. 2, February 2002, pp. 92)
Pub: Rough Notes
Ed: Troy Korsgaden. **Description:** Like a good quarterback, running a successful insurance agency has to have the qualities of persistence which will overcome people's distrust of sales people and commitment which is backed up by assessment of a situation, visualization of the goals to be achieved and an action plan to accomplish the agency's goals.

51878 ■ "Trading Spaces" in *Entrepreneur* (Vol. 31, No. 11, November 2003, pp. 98)
Pub: Entrepreneur Media, Inc.
Ed: Barry Farber. **Description:** Feedback from customers can help sales teams succeed. The five universal factors for selling success are listed.

51879 ■ "Training Day: Need a Sales Trainer to Whip Your Staff Into Shape?" in *Entrepreneur* (Vol. 32, October 2004, No. 10, pp. 90)
Pub: Entrepreneur Media Inc.
Ed: Kimberly L. McCall. **Description:** Sales trainers can rev up a sales team by teaching closing skills. Tips for finding the right sales coach are presented.

51880 ■ "Training Wheels" in *Inc.* (October 2005, pp. 51-52)
Pub: Inc. Magazine
Ed: Nadine Heintz. **Description:** Ben Serotta developed a plan to teach retailers how to sell the bicycles he manufactures. Serotta's plan helps retailers custom-fit the bike to its buyer.

51881 ■ "The Trust Factor" in *Small Business Opportunities* (Vol. 16, No. 2, March 2004, pp. 18, 20)
Pub: Harris Publications, Inc.
Ed: Sam Christensen. **Description:** Three steps to discover the missing link to sales success, all center around trust, involve the discovery process, organizing and analyzing descriptive material, and making your words matter.

51882 ■ "Trying to Reach a Senior Level Executive?" in *Sales & Marketing Management* (Vol. 159, January-February 2007, No. 1, pp. 9)
Pub: VNU Business Media
Description: Ernest Nicastro, principal of Positive Response LLC, offers advice for reaching the attention of top level executives when trying to sell products or services.

51883 ■ "Trying Times: Every Once in a While, You'll Meet Difficult Customers" in *Entrepreneur* (Vol. 31, No. 9, July 2003, pp. 80)
Pub: Entrepreneur Media, Inc.
Ed: Barry Farber. **Description:** Ways to deal with difficult customers for salespeople are discussed, including the know-it-all customer, the silent type, and the indecisive prospect.

51884 ■ "A Typology of Situational Factors" in *Journal of Business Ethics* (Vol. 46, No. 3, Sept. 2003, pp. 213)
Pub: Kluwer Academic Publishers Group
Ed: William T. Ross, Diana C. Robertson. **Description:** Two dimensions of situational factors expected to influence decision-making about ethical issues among sales representatives: universal vs. particular and direct vs. indirect, are explored.

51885 ■ *The Ultimate Guide to Electronic Marketing for Small Business: Low-Cost/High Return Tools and Techniques That Really Work*
Pub: John Wiley & Sons, Incorporated
Ed: Tom Antion. **Released:** June 2005. **Price:** $19.95 (US), $25.99 (Canadian). **Description:** Online marketing techniques for small business to grow and increase sales.

51886 ■ "Unforgettable as Usual" in *Home Business* (Vol. 12, October 2005, No. 5, pp. 36, 100)
Pub: Home Business Magazine
Ed: Sandy Larson. **Description:** Patricia Fripp, an award-winning keynote speaker and sales trainer, explains ways to make each sales presentation unforgettable. The twelve biggest mistakes made by salespeople when making presentations are included.

51887 ■ "Up and Running: Energize Salespeople To Get Out Of a First-Quarter Slump" in *Sales & Marketing Management* (Vol. 157, February 2005)
Pub: VNU Business Media
Ed: Betsy Cummings. **Description:** It is critical to jump-start sales early in a new year. The importance of choosing incentives that work is addressed.

51888 ■ "Use Webcasting to Grow Your Home Business" in *Home Business* (Vol. 12, March/April 2005, No. 2, pp. 36, 38, 60-61)
Pub: Home Business Magazine
Ed: Dr. Jeffrey Lant. **Description:** Online marketing is a good way for a home business to increase sales. Webcasting allows entrepreneurs to speak live to people through a computer.

51889 ■ "Using the right bait" in *Crain's Detroit Business* (Vol. 19, No. 6, February 10, 2003, pp. 3)
Pub: Crain Communications Inc., Detroit
Description: Seven tips to successfully close deals are presented.

51890 ■ "The Value of Networking" in *Home Business* (Vol. 13, January/February 2006, No. 1, pp. 42, 44-45)
Pub: Home Business Magazine
Ed: Christopher J. Bachler. **Description:** Networking skills to market and grow a business, including a list of prospects, are discussed.

51891 ■ "Vector Marketing" in *Mississippi Business Journal* (Vol. 29, January 2007, No. 2, pp. 6)
Pub: Venture Publications, Inc.
Description: Profile of Rebecca Huckeby, of Vector Marketing. Huckeby placed in the Top 25 sales reps from more than 40,000 sales representatives nationwide.

51892 ■ "Vendors tweak strategies to help clients buy" in *Atlanta Business Chronicle* (Vol. 25, November 15, 2002, No. 23 pp. 3C)
Pub: American City Business Publications, Inc.
Ed: Don Reichardt. **Description:** As companies need to re-engineer costly legacy system, some are seeking less expensive alternatives. Leasing and outsourcing are becoming more popular alternatives. Details on alternatives being offered by vendors are included.

51893 ■ "A View From the Top" in *Sales and Marketing.com* (Vol. 156, No. 3, March 2004, pp. 19)
Pub: VNU eMedia, Inc.
Ed: Julia Chang. **Description:** The importance of management team building is stressed; weekly meetings are one way to discuss each department's issues.

51894 ■ "Wanted: Brainy in Business" in *Sales & Marketing Management* (Vol. 158, October 2006, No. 10, pp. 18)
Pub: VNU Business Media
Ed: Michel Marchetti. **Description:** Eric McMath, SerachLogix Group, offers tips and techniques for hiring a successful sales team for any business.

51895 ■ "Warm Up to Cold Calls" in *Sales & Marketing Management* (Vol. 158, October 2006, No. 10, pp. 15)
Pub: VNU Business Media
Description: Shawn Greene, owner of Savage and Green, a sales training company in California, provides tips for effective telemarketing.

51896 ■ "Warp Speed" in *Sales & Marketing Management* (Vol. 157, Jan. 20, 2005)
Pub: VNU Business Media
Ed: Michele Marchetti. **Description:** According to Patricia Gardner, founder of Maximum Sales, sales and management consulting firm in Sparks, Maryland, the most important thing small companies neglect during a high-growth period, is to write job descriptions for its sales staff and other employees.

51897 ■ "What Customer Relationship?" in *Sales & Marketing Management* (Vol. 159, January-February 2007, No. 1, pp. 11)
Pub: VNU Business Media
Ed: Scott Horstein. **Description:** Customer relationship management is explained; marketing strategies using this concept are included.

51898 ■ "What is Del.icio.us and How Is It Used?" in *Sales & Marketing Management* (Vol. 159, January-February 2007, No. 1, pp. 17)
Pub: VNU Business Media
Description: Profile of the social book-marking Web service that allows users to see saved sites of other members of the service.

51899 ■ "What a Lightweight!" in *Entrepreneur* (Vol. 31, No. 8, August 2003, pp. 36)
Pub: Entrepreneur Media, Inc.
Description: Profile of the ViewSonic PJ250 lightweight projector used by sales teams in the field, as well as for meetings and presentations.

51900 ■ "What Makes You Great? Close Deals by Selling Value" in *My Business* (October/November 2003, pp. 43)
Pub: My Business Magazine
Ed: Melany Klinck. **Description:** Author and trainer, Tom Reilly, advocates value-added selling to small businesses, arguing that price is not the primary driver of most buying decisions.

51901 ■ "What Should I Do? Last Year's Poor Performance Can Push This Year's Quotas Higher" in *Sales & Marketing Management*
Pub: VNU Business Media
Description: Strategies to pacify a sales team faced with higher quotas are presented.

51902 ■ "What Should You Do" in *Sales and Marketing.com* (Vol. 156, No. 3, March 2004, pp. 8)
Pub: VNU eMedia, Inc.
Description: Reorganizing sales territories can sometimes help reenergize sales reps. Solutions to this reorganization are offered to help avoid angering salespeople or disrupting client/seller relationships.

51903 ■ "What Women Want" in *Entrepreneur* **(Vol. 32, No. 2, February 2004, pp. 54)**
Pub: Entrepreneur Media, Inc.
Ed: Joanne Cleaver. **Description:** Small business owners are targeting market strategies toward women consumers, a market once ignored. Women pay attention to detail in product design and service and require a longer selling process because they wish to understand what they are purchasing.

51904 ■ "What's your problem? People don't open junk mail, so send a postcard" in *Entrepreneur* **(Vol. 30, No. 3, March 2002, pp. 142)**
Pub: Entrepreneur Media Inc.
Description: Information for using postcards as a sales and marketing tool is discussed.

51905 ■ "When your good sales go bad: Ask, don't whine" in *Atlanta Business Chronicle* **(Vol. 24, No. 13, August 24, 2001, pp. 3B)**
Pub: American City Business Journals Inc.
Ed: Jeffrey Gitomer. **Description:** Salespeople need to know how to respond to disappointments, and to turn setbacks into new opportunities. Several possible scenarios and appropriate responses are discussed.

51906 ■ "Where Everyone's a Winner: Sure, the Annual Trip to Hawaii Is a Great Reward For Your Top Performers" in *Sales & Marketing Management*
Pub: VNU Business Media
Ed: Julia Chang. **Description:** Motivational strategies that benefit an entire sales team, rather than rewarding only the top few salespeople, can provide greater success. In a recent survey, 68 percent of workers stated that more award opportunities would further motivate them in their jobs.

51907 ■ "Whistle Blowers" in *Sales and Marketing.com* **(Vol. 156, No. 3, March 2004, pp. 30)**
Pub: VNU eMedia, Inc.
Ed: Julie Barker. **Description:** Profile of CIBA Vision's self-coaching model for sales executives is presented. Dow Jones Business News reported CIBA's fourth-quarter sales increased more than 20 percent after implementing the new program. In order for the program to be successful, sales reps must commit to their own learning, and must strategize and critique immediately before and after a sales call.

51908 ■ "Who benefits from price promotions?" in *Harvard Business Review* **(Vol. 80, No. 9, September 2002, pp. 22)**
Pub: Harvard Business School Press
Ed: Shuba Srinivasan. **Description:** Research has shown that reducing prices temporarily as part of a marketing campaign can adversely affect a retail company.

51909 ■ "Who pays to get it there? Net Profits" in *Entrepreneur* **(Vol. 3)**
Pub: Entrepreneur Media Inc.
Ed: Melissa Campanelli. **Description:** The issue of shipping and handling charges is one of the most critical facing online merchants today.

51910 ■ "Wholesale changes: Mom-and-Pop stores are so passe" in *Entrepreneur* **(Vol. 30, No. 2, February 2002, pp. 19)**
Pub: Entrepreneur Media Inc.
Ed: Nichole L. Torres. **Description:** Some retailers are revamping the layout of stores to give the look of a warehouse in order to attract more customers.

51911 ■ "Why 'Buy' Buttons Are Booming" in *Business 2.0* **(Vol. 6, July 2005, No. 6, pp. 36)**
Pub: Time, Inc.
Ed: Elizabeth Esfahani. **Description:** Three technologies to help online e-tailers to close sales include customization, online catalogs, and dynamic imaging of products.

51912 ■ "Why Do So Many Salespeople Fail to Get It?" in *Home Business* **(Vol. 12, March/April 2005, No. 2, pp. 54)**
Pub: Home Business Magazine
Ed: Bill Brooks. **Description:** The importance for home-based business owners to understand the keys to successful selling is stressed.

51913 ■ "Why Haven't You Called" in *Atlanta Business Chronicle* **(Vol. 25, November 29, 2002, No. 25, pp. 1B)**
Pub: American City Business Publications, Inc.
Ed: Don Reichardt. **Description:** Business leaders have the tendency to blame slumping sales on the economy, but many factors contribute to lower sales. A company's future and success depends partly on the ability to confront other possible causes of declining sales, such as altered consumer behavior, pricing changes, sales force difficulties, and new competitive pressure.

51914 ■ "Why Johnny Can't Sell...And What to Do About it" in *Sales & Marketing Management* **(Vol. 158, October 2006, No. 10, pp. 54)**
Pub: VNU Business Media
Ed: Tali Arbel. **Description:** Review of the book, Why Johnny Can't Sell...And What to Do About It is presented. Authors Michael J. Nick and Robert F. Kantin, sales marketing experts, share insight into tools to help salespeople to reach leads and increase sales.

51915 ■ "Winds of Change" in *Entrepreneur* **(Vol. 33, October 2005, No. 10, pp. 82)**
Pub: Entrepreneur Media Inc.
Ed: Barry Farber. **Description:** Ten ways to help customers adjust to changes in your firm's products or services are outlined, focusing on how the changes will help them.

51916 ■ "Winning the paper chase" in *Incentive* **(Vol. 174, No. 10, October 2000, pp. 123)**
Pub: Bill Communications
Ed: Libby Estell. **Description:** Profile of the Kelly Paper Company, that has locked in its customer base and boosted sales by using a points-based loyalty program that allows customers to choose from among a variety of rewards.

51917 ■ "Works Great! Sales success" in *Entrepreneur* **(Vol. 30, No. 2, February 2002,)**
Pub: Entrepreneur Media Inc.
Ed: Barry Farber. **Description:** The use of customer testimonials to increase sales is examined.

51918 ■ "Writing the big ones" in *Rough Notes* **(Vol. 146, No. 3, March 2003, pp. 126)**
Pub: Rough Notes
Ed: Michael J. Weinberg. **Description:** Big sales goals can be achieved by visualization and customer relationship management, as well as knowledge and expertise of the product or service to the prospective target market.

51919 ■ "Your Business needs to be E-Commerce - so what now?" in *Ingram's* **(Vol. 27, No. 7, July 2001, pp. 19)**
Pub: Show Me Publishing, Inc.
Description: Management techniques and theory are outlined for e-commerce management. Some techniques include treating online and offline sales the same way, organize and prioritize what the Website needs to accomplish, and consider market potential.

51920 ■ "Your Secret Weapon" in *Small Business Opportunities* **(Vol. 16, No. 3, May 2004, pp. 10, 120)**
Pub: Harris Publications, Inc.
Ed: Lynn A. Robinson. **Description:** Intuition can be the secret weapon used to make successful sales.

51921 ■ "Yourshop@Black Enterprise.com" in *Black Enterprise* **(Vol. 31, No. 2, September 2000, pp. 215)**
Pub: Earl Graves Publishing Co.
Ed: Dorett Smith. **Description:** Small business can join the e-commerce revolution. If you are considering

a Web presence to sell your company's products online, you'll need to weigh a number of factors related to e-business planning, such as productivity and functionality, advertising, sales, and service.

51922 ■ "You've Got to DISTURB 'EM" in *Rough Notes* **(Vol. 145, No. 2, February 2003, pp. 96)**
Pub: Rough Notes
Ed: Francis W. Potter. **Description:** Ways to sell insurance by using vivid illustrations are presented.

TRADE PERIODICALS

51923 ■ *Counterman*
Pub: Babcox
Contact: Jon Owens, Publisher
E-mail: jowens@babcox.com
Ed: Brian Cruickshank, Editor, bcruickshank@babcox.com. **Released:** Monthly. **Price:** Free to qualified subscribers. **Description:** Magazine devoted to improving the effectiveness of professional automotive parts counter-sales personnel.

51924 ■ *Issues & Answers in Sales Management*
Pub: Clement Communications Inc.
Contact: Robert J. Smith, Sr.Art.Ed.
Released: Biweekly. **Price:** $195, individuals. **Description:** Provides sales managers and supervisors with techniques and strategies to improve customer service and profits. Includes topics such as the Internet, tradeshow tips, and cold-calling hints.

51925 ■ *The Journal of Personal Selling and Sales Management*
Pub: Pi Sigma Epsilon
Ed: Kenneth R. Evans, Editor, jpssm@missouri.edu. **Released:** Quarterly. **Price:** $219 institutions includes free online access; $65 print only; $251 institutions other countries includes free online access; $81 other countries print only. **Description:** Academic journal devoted to issues in personal selling and sales management.

51926 ■ *New Account Selling*
Pub: The Dartnell Corp.
Contact: Annie Chesney
Ed: Terry Breen, Editor. **Released:** Biweekly. **Price:** $58.50. **Description:** Offers ideas and inspiration related to selling to new accounts. Covers "cold calling," prospecting, and techniques for maintaining new customers. Features quizzes on sales skills. Recurring features include interviews, news of research, news of educational opportunities, book reviews, and a column titled Inspiration.

51927 ■ *Retailer and Marketing News*
Pub: Retailer and Marketing News
Contact: Michael J. Anderson, Editor & Publisher
Released: Monthly. **Price:** $18. **Description:** Trade journal (tabloid) for retail dealers.

51928 ■ *Sales and Marketing Executive Report*
Pub: The Dartnell Corp.
Ed: Prudy Taylor, Editor. **Released:** Biweekly. **Price:** $168. **Description:** Discusses topics of interest to managers, including motivating and training sales personnel, executive self-improvement, and advertising and public relations strategies. Recurring features include news of research, letters to the editor, book reviews, a calendar of events, and columns titled Sales/Marketing Briefs and Special Report.

51929 ■ *Sales & Marketing Report*
Pub: Lawrence Ragan Communications Inc.
Contact: Lisa Ban
Ed: John Cowan, Editor. **Released:** Monthly. **Price:** $149; $159, Canada. **Description:** Provides information about strategic sales coaching, building a high performance sales team, boosting morale and productivity, and managing time more effectively.

51930 ■ *The Selling Advantage*
Pub: Progressive Business Publications
Ed: Phil Ahr, Editor. **Released:** Semimonthly. **Price:** $94.56, individuals. **Description:** Explores new strategies and proven techniques to improve sales performance. Recurring features include book reviews and a column titled Tale of the Sale.

51931 ■ *Selling Power*
Pub: Personal Selling Power
Contact: Gerhard Gschwandtner, Publisher
Released: Monthly, 10 times a year. **Price:** $33 U.S. 1-year only; $56 Canada 1-year (includes GST); $76 international 1-year only; $155 U.S. 3-year only; $50 Canada 3-year (includes GST); $19 digital edition - 1 yr only. **Description:** Magazine presenting motivational and sales skills and techniques for sales and marketing executives.

51932 ■ *Selling to Seniors*
Pub: CD Publications
Ed: Jean Van Ryzin, Editor. **Released:** Monthly. **Price:** $294, individuals. **Description:** Suggests effective ways to reach the "over 50" market by emphasizing successful marketing strategies. Recurring features include interviews, case studies, and demographic data. Remarks: Incorporates the former Maturity Market Perspectives and Mature Market Report. Editor: Allison Patterson

51933 ■ *Targets*
Pub: Salesforce Training & Consulting Inc.
Ed: Lorraine Jeffrey, Editor, lorraine@salesforcetraining.com. **Released:** Quarterly. **Price:** $20, Free. **Description:** Provides sales professionals with information on developments and improvements within the marketing, sales, and advertising industries. Recurring features include columns titled Publishers Podium, Guest Column, Hints-Tips-Ideas, and Sales Manager's Corner.

51934 ■ *What's Working for American Companies in International Sales & Marketing*
Pub: Progressive Business Publications
Ed: Julie Power, Editor, power@pbb.com. **Released:** Semimonthly. **Price:** $391, individuals. **Description:** Offers real world examples and the latest news from around the world to supply sales and marketing professionals an edge in international business. Recurring features include interviews, news of research, a calendar of events, news of educational opportunities, and a column titled Sharpen Your Judgment.

51935 ■ *What's Working in Sales Management*
Pub: Progressive Business Publications
Ed: Steve Trimble, Editor. **Released:** Semimonthly. **Price:** $264, individuals. **Description:** Acts as a time-saving resource for busy sales managers. Recurring features include interviews, news of research, a calendar of events, and news of educational opportunities.

VIDEOCASSETTES/ AUDIOCASSETTES

51936 ■ *Achieve Success by Prospecting with Phillip Wexler*
Instructional Video
2219 C St.
Lincoln, NE 68502
Ph:(402)475-6570
Free: 800-228-0164
Fax: (402)475-6500
Co. E-mail: feedback@insvideo.com
URL: http://www.insvideo.com
Price: $95.00. **Description:** Phillip Wexler offers prospecting training program for sales people. Only available in the U.S. **Availability:** VHS.

51937 ■ *American Business Sales Series*
Instructional Video
2219 C St.
Lincoln, NE 68502

Ph:(402)475-6570
Free: 800-228-0164
Fax: (402)475-6500
Co. E-mail: feedback@insvideo.com
URL: http://www.insvideo.com
Description: Business education series aimed at improving phone-selling skills. **Availability:** VHS.

51938 ■ *Ask for the Order. . .and Get It!*
Dartnell Corp.
360 Hiatt Dr.
Palm Beach Gardens, FL 33418
Ph:(561)622-6520
Free: 800-341-7874
Fax: (561)622-2423
Co. E-mail: custserve@lrp.com
URL: http://www.dartnellcorp.com
Released: 1972. **Description:** Hammers home a key principle of salesmanship—to get an order you must ask for it; from the "Tough-Minded Salesmanship" series. **Availability:** VHS; 3/4U; Special order formats.

51939 ■ *Ask for the Order...and Get It! (Revised)*
Excellence in Training Corp.
1303 Marsh Ln.
Carrollton, TX 75006
Free: 800-747-6569
Released: 1991. **Price:** $469.00. **Description:** An updated look at the timeless issues of selling. **Availability:** VHS; 3/4U; Special order formats.

51940 ■ *Bakery Merchandising 101*
International Dairy-Deli-Bakery Association (IDDBA)
313 Price Pl., Ste. 202
PO Box 5528
Madison, WI 53705-0528
Ph:(608)238-7908
Fax: (608)238-6330
Co. E-mail: iddba@iddba.org
Price: $50.00. **Description:** Discusses ways for successful promotion and product appeal to help increase bakery sales. **Availability:** VHS.

51941 ■ *Bakery Merchandising Certificate Program*
International Dairy-Deli-Bakery Association (IDDBA)
313 Price Pl., Ste. 202
PO Box 5528
Madison, WI 53705-0528
Ph:(608)238-7908
Fax: (608)238-6330
Co. E-mail: iddba@iddba.org
Price: $160.00. **Description:** Examines the benefits of suggestive selling, sampling, displays, and event merchandising. **Availability:** VHS.

51942 ■ *Beware the Naked Man Who Offers You His Shirt*
PBS Home Video
Catalog Fulfillment Center
PO Box 751089
Charlotte, NC 28275-1089
Ph:800-531-4727
Free: 800-645-4PBS
Co. E-mail: info@pbs.org
URL: http://www.pbs.org
Released: 1990. **Price:** $395.00. **Description:** The author of "Swim With the Sharks Without Being Eaten Alive" offers insights and advice on increasing sales productivity. **Availability:** VHS; 3/4U.

51943 ■ *Business Library Series: Sales and Motivation*
Instructional Video
2219 C St.
Lincoln, NE 68502
Ph:(402)475-6570
Free: 800-228-0164
Fax: (402)475-6500
Co. E-mail: feedback@insvideo.com
URL: http://www.insvideo.com
Price: $19.95. **Description:** Offers humorous look at the fundamental elements of executing a sale. Emphasizes planning and determination as the essence of everyday success. **Availability:** VHS.

51944 ■ *Clean, Fresh & Friendly*
International Dairy-Deli-Bakery Association (IDDBA)
313 Price Pl., Ste. 202
PO Box 5528
Madison, WI 53705-0528
Ph:(608)238-7908
Fax: (608)238-6330
Co. E-mail: iddba@iddba.org
Price: $160.00. **Description:** Deli customer service training video. **Availability:** VHS.

51945 ■ *The Cold Call*
Video Arts, Inc.
c/o Aim Learning Group
8238-40 Lehigh
Morton Grove, IL 60053-2615
Free: 877-444-2230
Fax: (416)252-2155
Co. E-mail: service@aimlearninggroup.com
URL: http://www.aimlearninggroup.com
Released: 1976. **Price:** $695.00. **Description:** This program demonstrates the specific skills and disciplines of telephone selling, and the dangers of ignoring them. **Availability:** VHS; 8mm; 3/4U; Special order formats.

51946 ■ *The Competitive Edge*
Film Library/Greater Los Angeles Safety Council
600 Wilshire Blvd., No. 1263
Los Angeles, CA 90017
Ph:(213)385-6461
Free: 800-421-9585
Fax: (213)385-8405
URL: http://www.lasafety.org
Released: 1989. **Description:** This program emphasizes finding out your customer's most immediate concern, and selling to that concern. **Availability:** VHS; 3/4U.

51947 ■ *Customer-Responsive Selling*
Excellence in Training Corp.
1303 Marsh Ln.
Carrollton, TX 75006
Free: 800-747-6569
Price: $995.00. **Description:** A comprehensive program for increasing sales, customer satisfaction, and the corporate image. Workshop materials are available. **Availability:** VHS; 3/4U; Special order formats.

51948 ■ *Customer Service 101*
International Dairy-Deli-Bakery Association (IDDBA)
313 Price Pl., Ste. 202
PO Box 5528
Madison, WI 53705-0528
Ph:(608)238-7908
Fax: (608)238-6330
Co. E-mail: iddba@iddba.org
Price: $50.00. **Description:** Teaches how to build repeat business, increase sales, and maximize productivity. **Availability:** VHS.

51949 ■ *Dealing with Difficult Prospects*
American Management Association
9 Galen St.
PO Box 9119
Watertown, MA 02472
Ph:(617)926-4600
Free: 800-225-3215
Fax: (617)923-1875
URL: http://www.amanet.org
Price: $495.00. **Description:** Contains information and techniques on how to sell successfully, even to the most difficult prospect. **Availability:** VHS.

51950 ■ *The Effective Manager*
Nightingale-Conant Corp.
6245 W. Howard St.
Niles, IL 60714
Ph:(847)647-0300
Free: 800-560-6081
URL: http://www.nightingale.com
Price: $95.00. **Description:** A series of award-winning programs designed to promote effective management and help increase sales. Audio tapes and booklets are included, and the series can be purchased individually or as a set. **Availability:** VHS.

51951 ■ *Explode Those Sales Myths*
Dartnell Corp.
360 Hiatt Dr.
Palm Beach Gardens, FL 33418
Ph:(561)622-6520
Free: 800-341-7874
Fax: (561)622-2423
Co. E-mail: custserve@lrp.com
URL: http://www.dartnellcorp.com
Released: 1976. **Description:** Designed to explode misleading old tales and beliefs that negatively affect salesmanship. **Availability:** VHS; 3/4U; Special order formats.

51952 ■ *Five Steps to Successful Selling*
Cambridge Educational
c/o Films Media Group
PO Box 2053
Princeton, NJ 08843-2053
Free: 800-257-5126
Fax: (609)671-0266
Co. E-mail: custserve@filmsmediagroup.com
URL: http://www.cambridgeol.com
Released: 1990. **Price:** $54.95. **Description:** Zig Ziglar condenses his years of selling experience down to this presentation on sales techniques. **Availability:** VHS.

51953 ■ *Follow-Up: Proven Methods & Strategies That Will Covert Your Contacts into Closings*
Tapeworm Video Distributors
27833 Hopkins Ave., Unit 6
Valencia, CA 91355
Ph:(661)257-4904
Fax: (661)257-4820
Co. E-mail: sales@tapeworm.com
URL: http://www.tapeworm.com
Price: $29.95. **Description:** Sales education training program that offers tips on how to become a successful multiple call salesperson, including skills that will help with follow through and follow-up until the sale is final. **Availability:** VHS.

51954 ■ *Friendly Persuasion: The Art of Converting Objections into Sales*
American Media, Inc.
4621 121st St.
Urbandale, IA 50323-2311
Ph:(515)224-0919
Free: 888-776-8268
Fax: (515)327-2555
Co. E-mail: custsvc@ammedia.com
URL: http://www.ammedia.com
Released: 1985. **Description:** Salesman Joe Batten outlines the objection-into-sales theories that profit salesman best in any area. **Availability:** VHS; 3/4U.

51955 ■ *Handling Objections*
American Management Association
9 Galen St.
PO Box 9119
Watertown, MA 02472
Ph:(617)926-4600
Free: 800-225-3215
Fax: (617)923-1875
URL: http://www.amanet.org
Price: $695.00. **Description:** Presents a three step process on the secrets of successful selling. **Availability:** VHS.

51956 ■ *A Happy Beginning*
Resources for Education & Management, Inc.
1804 Montreal Ct., Ste. A
Tucker, GA 30084
Released: 1971. **Description:** An examination of closing the sale, asking for the order, and answering the customer's objections. How to become a confident sale closer. **Availability:** VHS; 3/4U.

51957 ■ *How to Close the Sale*
Dartnell Corp.
360 Hiatt Dr.
Palm Beach Gardens, FL 33418
Ph:(561)622-6520
Free: 800-341-7874
Fax: (561)622-2423

Co. E-mail: custserve@lrp.com
URL: http://www.dartnellcorp.com
Released: 1981. **Description:** This program shows salespeople how to ask for the order, and how to get it. **Availability:** VHS; 3/4U; Special order formats.

51958 ■ *How to Find New Customers*
Instructional Video
2219 C St.
Lincoln, NE 68502
Ph:(402)475-6570
Free: 800-228-0164
Fax: (402)475-6500
Co. E-mail: feedback@insvideo.com
URL: http://www.insvideo.com
Price: $39.95. **Description:** Top sales professionals furnish advice on how to be successful in sales. Includes Leroy Leale, sales rep. from Shearson Lehman Bros.; Jim Kilcoyne, account executive for SARNS/3M; and Elaine Bailey, sales rep. for Connect Software. **Availability:** VHS.

51959 ■ *How to Raise Your Batting Average in Selling*
Dartnell Corp.
360 Hiatt Dr.
Palm Beach Gardens, FL 33418
Ph:(561)622-6520
Free: 800-341-7874
Fax: (561)622-2423
Co. E-mail: custserve@lrp.com
URL: http://www.dartnellcorp.com
Released: 1968. **Description:** Dr. Peale shows how any salesman can operate at peak efficiency that will eventually help improve sales average. **Availability:** VHS; 3/4U; Special order formats.

51960 ■ *How to Take the Butt Out of a Sales Rebuttal*
Dartnell Corp.
360 Hiatt Dr.
Palm Beach Gardens, FL 33418
Ph:(561)622-6520
Free: 800-341-7874
Fax: (561)622-2423
Co. E-mail: custserve@lrp.com
URL: http://www.dartnellcorp.com
Released: 1967. **Description:** A look at how to cope with the difficult problem of rebutting a customer's objection-without being objectionable. **Availability:** VHS; 3/4U; Special order formats.

51961 ■ *Knowing the Prospect*
Resources for Education & Management, Inc.
1804 Montreal Ct., Ste. A
Tucker, GA 30084
Released: 1971. **Description:** Shows the relationship of product or service benefits to the sales prospect's personal goals, and illustrates the value of knowing a prospect's needs. Ignores the fast-talking sales pitch. **Availability:** VHS; 3/4U.

51962 ■ *Making It Live*
Resources for Education & Management, Inc.
1804 Montreal Ct., Ste. A
Tucker, GA 30084
Released: 1971. **Description:** This tape demonstrates a key to sales success-knowing your product or service and telling your story with enthusiasm and conviction. **Availability:** VHS; 3/4U.

51963 ■ *The Making of a Salesman*
Professional Development, Inc.
27955 Clemens Rd.
Westlake, OH 44145
Ph:(216)892-0770
Fax: (216)892-0105
Released: 1984. **Description:** Provides basic material to enhance a sales training program. All programs are available individually. **Availability:** VHS; 3/4U; Special order formats.

51964 ■ *Manage Your Time to Build Your Territory*
Dartnell Corp.
360 Hiatt Dr.
Palm Beach Gardens, FL 33418

Ph:(561)622-6520
Free: 800-341-7874
Fax: (561)622-2423
Co. E-mail: custserve@lrp.com
URL: http://www.dartnellcorp.com
Released: 1974. **Description:** An examination of time thieves that rob salespeople of both hours and sales volume. From the "Tough-Minded Salesmanship" series. **Availability:** VHS; 3/4U; Special order formats.

51965 ■ *Managing Sales Stress*
American Management Association
9 Galen St.
PO Box 9119
Watertown, MA 02472
Ph:(617)926-4600
Free: 800-225-3215
Fax: (617)923-1875
URL: http://www.amanet.org
Price: $495.00. **Description:** Outlines techniques on handling stress from day-to-day sales. **Availability:** VHS.

51966 ■ *Million Dollar Sales Strategy*
Nightingale-Conant Corp.
6245 W. Howard St.
Niles, IL 60714
Ph:(847)647-0300
Free: 800-560-6081
URL: http://www.nightingale.com
Price: $39.95. **Description:** Jim Cathcart and Dr. Tony Alessandra share tips on time management, prospecting, closing, and successful customer relations. **Availability:** VHS.

51967 ■ *Negotiating Profitable Sales*
Video Arts, Inc.
c/o Aim Learning Group
8238-40 Lehigh
Morton Grove, IL 60053-2615
Free: 877-444-2230
Fax: (416)252-2155
Co. E-mail: service@aimlearninggroup.com
URL: http://www.aimlearninggroup.com
Released: 197?. **Price:** $695.00. **Description:** The first program in this two-part series exposes and analyzes the most-frequent and costly errors of untrained negotiators and shows a salesman being briefed by his superiors. The second program shows the prepared salesman actually negotiating with the buyer. The programs are available individually. Also available as a seminar kit. **Availability:** VHS; 8mm; 3/4U; Special order formats.

51968 ■ *The New Selling with Service*
RMI Media
1365 N. Winchester
Olathe, KS 66061
Ph:(913)768-1696
Fax: (913)768-0184
Co. E-mail: actmedia@act.org
URL: http://www.rmimedia.com
Released: 1993. **Price:** $89.95. **Description:** Philip Wexler explains how to implement a marketing philosophy to maintain and increase customers. **Availability:** VHS.

51969 ■ *Non-Verbal Communication*
Salenger Films, Inc.
1635 12th St.
Santa Monica, CA 90404-9988
Ph:(310)450-1300
Free: 800-775-5025
Fax: (310)450-1010
Co. E-mail: salenger@aol.com
URL: http://salengerfilms.visualnet.com
Released: 1979. **Description:** Helps the sales trainee become more aware of the non-verbal messages others send and become more conscious of his own. **Availability:** 3/4U; Special order formats.

51970 ■ *Overcoming Objections*
Film Library/Greater Los Angeles Safety Council
600 Wilshire Blvd., No. 1263
Los Angeles, CA 90017
Ph:(213)385-6461

Free: 800-421-9585
Fax: (213)385-8405
URL: http://www.lasafety.org
Released: 198?. **Description:** This film emphasizes the importance of understanding the customer's point of view. **Availability:** VHS; 3/4U.

51971 ■ *Path to Profit*
International Dairy-Deli-Bakery Association (IDDBA)
313 Price Pl., Ste. 202
PO Box 5528
Madison, WI 53705-0528
Ph:(608)238-7908
Fax: (608)238-6330
Co. E-mail: iddba@iddba.org
Price: $160.00. **Description:** Analyzes strategies for increasing bakery impulse sales and bottom-line profitability. Discusses how to control shrink and effectively schedule labor. **Availability:** VHS.

51972 ■ *The Perfect Sale*
Thomson National Education Training Group (NETg)
14624 N. Scottsdale Rd., Ste. 300
Phoenix, AZ 85254
Ph:(480)315-4000
Free: 800-265-1900
Fax: (480)315-4001
Co. E-mail: info@netg.com
URL: http://www.netg.com
Released: 1984. **Description:** This program emphasizes the art of selling from approach to close. **Availability:** VHS; 3/4U.

51973 ■ *Prescription for Complaints*
Video Arts, Inc.
c/o Aim Learning Group
8238-40 Lehigh
Morton Grove, IL 60053-2615
Free: 877-444-2230
Fax: (416)252-2155
Co. E-mail: service@aimlearninggroup.com
URL: http://www.aimlearninggroup.com
Released: 1975. **Price:** $695.00. **Description:** This program shows a six-step, objective method for dealing with customer complaints. **Availability:** VHS; 8mm; 3/4U; Special order formats.

51974 ■ *Presenting the Story*
Resources for Education & Management, Inc.
1804 Montreal Ct., Ste. A
Tucker, GA 30084
Released: 1971. **Description:** How a salesman can best communicate benefits to a customer. Emphasis is on preparation of the story and practice. **Availability:** VHS; 3/4U.

51975 ■ *The Real Estate Success Series*
Council of Real Estate Brokerage Managers
430 N. Michigan Ave.
Chicago, IL 60611
Free: 800-621-8738
Fax: (312)329-8882
Co. E-mail: infro@crb.com
URL: http://www.crb.com
Released: 1981. **Description:** This training series, designed to increase skills and profitability through proven training techniques, concentrates on building sales skills step-by-step. **Availability:** VHS; 3/4U.

51976 ■ *Real Selling: How to Increase Sales in Growing Companies*
Excellence in Training Corp.
1303 Marsh Ln.
Carrollton, TX 75006
Free: 800-747-6569
Released: 1990. **Price:** $495.00. **Description:** A five-part sales training program that shows how to make more sales, more effectively. Workbooks are included. **Availability:** VHS; 3/4U; Special order formats.

51977 ■ *The Sales Film*
American Media, Inc.
4621 121st St.
Urbandale, IA 50323-2311
Ph:(515)224-0919
Free: 888-776-8268
Fax: (515)327-2555

Co. E-mail: custsvc@ammedia.com
URL: http://www.ammedia.com
Released: 1982. **Description:** Fundamental sales techniques are covered for new, as well as seasoned salespeople. This program includes in-field and industrial sales practices, with methods that bring results. **Availability:** VHS; 3/4U.

51978 ■ *The Sales Professionals: Building Your Clients' Confidence*
Video Arts, Inc.
c/o Aim Learning Group
8238-40 Lehigh
Morton Grove, IL 60053-2615
Free: 877-444-2230
Fax: (416)252-2155
Co. E-mail: service@aimlearninggroup.com
URL: http://www.aimlearninggroup.com
Released: 1991. **Price:** $790.00. **Description:** The need for long-term client trust is emphasized in this video, which focuses on how to be a consultant, problem solver, and partner. **Availability:** VHS; 8mm; 3/4U; Special order formats.

51979 ■ *Self-Motivation in Selling*
LearnCom HR Consulting and Training
38 Discovery, Ste. 250
Irvine, CA 92618
Ph:(515)440-0890
Free: 800-698-8263
Fax: (515)221-3149
Co. E-mail: nhartline@learncom.com
URL: http://www.learncomhr.com
Released: 1979. **Description:** A look at how to avoid sales slumps and maintain peak performances. Four untitled programs cover frustrations and turndowns, seeking feedback, how to keep personal problems from affecting performance, and how sales managers can keep their people motivated. **Availability:** VHS; 3/4U.

51980 ■ *Sell It to Me!*
Government VideoSource, Inc.
461 Miller Dr.
Elgin, IL 60123-7232
Ph:(847)931-1955
Released: 1994. **Price:** $870.00. **Description:** Presents foundation skills in a series of situations will help sales people improve their salesmanship. Includes a leader's guide and briefcase book let. **Availability:** VHS.

51981 ■ *Selling in the '90s*
Nightingale-Conant Corp.
6245 W. Howard St.
Niles, IL 60714
Ph:(847)647-0300
Free: 800-560-6081
URL: http://www.nightingale.com
Released: 1990. **Price:** $95.00. **Description:** Sales guru Larry Wilson offers this guide to maintaining a competitive edge in sales. Included is a look at what consumers really want, the keys to partnership selling, and how to deliver a product through dreams and solutions. Two audio cassettes and two workbooks are included. **Availability:** VHS.

51982 ■ *Selling Skills: Have I Got a Deal for You!*
Cambridge Educational
c/o Films Media Group
PO Box 2053
Princeton, NJ 08843-2053
Free: 800-257-5126
Fax: (609)671-0266
Co. E-mail: custserve@filmsmediagroup.com
URL: http://www.cambridgeol.com
Released: 1991. **Price:** $79.00. **Description:** For maximum effectiveness, learn to match sales style with the product being sold. Real-life dramatic skits bring different sales techniques to life. **Availability:** VHS.

51983 ■ *Selling: The Power of Confidence*
Film Library/Greater Los Angeles Safety Council
600 Wilshire Blvd., No. 1263
Los Angeles, CA 90017

Ph:(213)385-6461
Free: 800-421-9585
Fax: (213)385-8405
URL: http://www.lasafety.org
Released: 1989. **Description:** Pride makes for the most successful sales staff, and this program explains how to achieve it. **Availability:** VHS; 3/4U.

51984 ■ *Service That Sells*
International Dairy-Deli-Bakery Association (IDDBA)
313 Price Pl., Ste. 202
PO Box 5528
Madison, WI 53705-0528
Ph:(608)238-7908
Fax: (608)238-6330
Co. E-mail: iddba@iddba.org
Price: $160.00. **Description:** Bakery customer service training video. **Availability:** VHS.

51985 ■ *Sharpen Your Sales Presentation: Make It a Winner*
Dartnell Corp.
360 Hiatt Dr.
Palm Beach Gardens, FL 33418
Ph:(561)622-6520
Free: 800-341-7874
Fax: (561)622-2423
Co. E-mail: custserve@lrp.com
URL: http://www.dartnellcorp.com
Released: 1981. **Description:** Gaining attention, arousing interest, key benefit selling, the demonstration, and closing on cue are among the sales techniques outlined and defined by Joe Batten. **Availability:** VHS; 3/4U; Special order formats.

51986 ■ *So You Want to Be a Success at Selling?*
Video Arts, Inc.
c/o Aim Learning Group
8238-40 Lehigh
Morton Grove, IL 60053-2615
Free: 877-444-2230
Fax: (416)252-2155
Co. E-mail: service@aimlearninggroup.com
URL: http://www.aimlearninggroup.com
Released: 1982. **Price:** $790.00. **Description:** Four videos that describe the fundamental skills of selling, from the initial research to the close. Part 1 focuses on the preparation, including client research and product knowledge. Part 2 looks at the skills and techniques of sales presentation. Part 3 shows how to deal with problem clients. Part 4 demonstrates the tactics for successfully closing a sale. Also available as a complete seminar kit. **Availability:** VHS; 8mm; 3/4U; Special order formats.

51987 ■ *Suggestive Selling 101*
International Dairy-Deli-Bakery Association (IDDBA)
313 Price Pl., Ste. 202
PO Box 5528
Madison, WI 53705-0528
Ph:(608)238-7908
Fax: (608)238-6330
Co. E-mail: iddba@iddba.org
Price: $50.00. **Description:** Teaches how to understand and encourage impulse sales, increase sales, and close sales using product samples. **Availability:** VHS.

51988 ■ *Time Is Money!*
Aspen Publishers
7201 McKinney Circ.
Frederick, MD 21704
Ph:(301)644-3599
Free: 800-638-8437
Fax: (301)644-3550
URL: http://www.aspenpublishers.com
Released: 197?. **Description:** Helps solve salespeople's time problems by teaching them good habits, and provides them with timesaving techniques so they'll spend their time more profitably. **Availability:** VHS; 3/4U.

51989 ■ *Time and Territory Management*
American Management Association
9 Galen St.
PO Box 9119
Watertown, MA 02472

Ph:(617)926-4600
Free: 800-225-3215
Fax: (617)923-1875
URL: http://www.amanet.org
Price: $495.00. **Description:** Instructs salespeople to take full advantage of prime selling time and how to turn downtime into productive time. **Availability:** VHS.

51990 ■ *Tony Alessandra, Ph.D.: On Collaborative Selling*
Instructional Video
2219 C St.
Lincoln, NE 68502
Ph:(402)475-6570
Free: 800-228-0164
Fax: (402)475-6500
Co. E-mail: feedback@insvideo.com
URL: http://www.insvideo.com
Price: $95.00. **Description:** Part of the Tony Alessandra, Ph.D. Series. Offers advice on how to change from persuading, telling, and selling to problem-solving, asking, and helping. Also discusses how to develop your competitive advantage statement, explore customer needs, assure customer satisfaction, and how to question, listen, create, and select options. **Availability:** VHS.

51991 ■ *The Unorganized Salesperson*
Video Arts, Inc.
c/o Aim Learning Group
8238-40 Lehigh
Morton Grove, IL 60053-2615
Free: 877-444-2230
Fax: (416)252-2155
Co. E-mail: service@aimlearninggroup.com
URL: http://www.aimlearninggroup.com
Released: 199?. **Price:** $790.00. **Description:** These two videos show how to organize one's time and skills to be more effective in selling. **Availability:** VHS; 8mm; 3/4U; Special order formats.

51992 ■ *What Is Salesmanship?*
Resources for Education & Management, Inc.
1804 Montreal Ct., Ste. A
Tucker, GA 30084
Released: 1971. **Description:** This tape introduces the idea that selling can be broken down into identifiable steps, each of which can improve selling success. **Availability:** VHS; 3/4U.

51993 ■ *When You're Turned Down—Turn On!*
Dartnell Corp.
360 Hiatt Dr.
Palm Beach Gardens, FL 33418
Ph:(561)622-6520
Free: 800-341-7874
Fax: (561)622-2423
Co. E-mail: custserve@lrp.com
URL: http://www.dartnellcorp.com
Released: 1977. **Description:** Examines the question: When is a turndown a true rejection and when is it just a disguised objection?; from the "Tough—Minded Salesmanship" series. **Availability:** VHS; 3/4U; Special order formats.

51994 ■ *Zig Ziglar: 5 Steps to Successful Selling*
Nightingale-Conant Corp.
6245 W. Howard St.
Niles, IL 60714
Ph:(847)647-0300
Free: 800-560-6081
URL: http://www.nightingale.com
Price: $54.95. **Description:** Ziglar examines the personality traits that are shared by the nation's top salespersons, and offers a program to develop these traits. **Availability:** VHS.

51995 ■ *Zig Ziglar: Selling, a Great Way to Reach the Top*
Nightingale-Conant Corp.
6245 W. Howard St.
Niles, IL 60714
Ph:(847)647-0300
Free: 800-560-6081

URL: http://www.nightingale.com
Released: 1987. **Price:** $49.95. **Description:** Ziglar offers this guide to developing winning sales skills, including relating to the client, presenting a product and closing the deal. **Availability:** VHS.

CONSULTANTS

51996 ■ The Beveridge Consulting Group Inc.
113 N Grant St.
Barrington, IL 60010
Ph:(847)381-7797
Free: 800-227-4332
Fax: (847)381-7301
Co. E-mail: info@beveridgeinc.com
URL: http://www.beveridgeinc.com

E-mail: info@beveridgeinc.com
Scope: Sales, marketing and management consultants. Special emphasis on the development of professional, sophisticated selling skills as well as modern sales management systems. **Seminars:** BOSS - The Mandatory Business Operating System Standards; Sales Management - Why The Best Are Better; Proactive Customer Focused Sales; Marketing In The Age Of Technology.

51997 ■ William Blades L.L.C.
9814 E Hidden Green Dr.
Scottsdale, AZ 85262
Ph:(480)563-5355
Fax: (480)563-0515
Co. E-mail: bill@williamblades.com
URL: http://www.williamblades.com

E-mail: bill@williamblades.com
Scope: A business consulting firm with expertise in marketing and sales. Presents seminars, workshops, and keynotes on the following topics: Re-energizing the Organization; Professional Selling/Marketing; Corporate Culture; Proactive Leadership; World-Class Customer Service; Creativity; Great Teamwork. List of publications, audios, and videos is available from firm. **Publications:** "Selling-The Mother of All Enterprise"; "Leadership Defined"; "Why Do We Make Change So Hard?"; "10 Crucial Steps for Sales Management Success". **Seminars:** Sales Leadership Culture Creativity; Sales and Management.

51998 ■ Bran Management Services Inc.
7116 Lupton Dr., Ste. 100
Dallas, TX 75225-1735
Ph:(214)739-2340
Fax: (214)739-2360
Scope: Offers management consulting services to companies in manufacturing, distribution and services to help them cope with growth and change. Helps small businesses create and identify product strategies. Services include developing international business opportunities; turnaround management; sales and marketing development; business planning; acquisitions and mergers.

51999 ■ Coyne Associates
4010 E Lake St.
Minneapolis, MN 55406
Ph:(612)724-1188
Fax: (612)722-1379
Scope: A marketing and public relations consulting firm specializing in assisting architectural, engineering, and contractor/developer firms. Services include marketing plains and audits; strategic planning; corporate identity; turnarounds; and sales training.

52000 ■ Harding & Co.
9 Sommer Ave.
Maplewood, NJ 07040
Ph:(973)763-9284
Fax: (973)763-9347
Co. E-mail: fharding@hardingco.com
URL: http://www.hardingco.com

E-mail: fharding@hardingco.com
Scope: Firm specializes in sales management, client development, and employee training. **Publications:**

"Rain Making: The Professional's Guide to Attracting New Clients"; "Creating Rainmakers: The Managers Guide to Training Professionals to Attract New Clients"; "Cross-Selling Success: A Rainmakers Guide to Professional Account Development".

52001 ■ High Probability Selling
103 Chesley Dr., Ste. 200
Media, PA 19063
Ph:(610)566-1535
Free: 800-394-7762
Fax: (610)891-2711
Co. E-mail: contact_us@highprobsell.com
URL: http://www.highprobsell.com

E-mail: contact_us@highprobsell.com
Scope: Consultancy transforms sales training into a model of integrity which eliminates sales resistance and establishes relationships of trust and respect, sales management and target marketing. Industries served: all. **Publications:** "Turning the Numbers-Game Upside-Down". **Seminars:** High Probability Selling and High Probability Prospecting.

52002 ■ Keiei Senryaku Corp.
19191 S Vermont Ave., Ste. 530
Torrance, CA 90502
Ph:(310)366-3331
Free: 800-951-8780
Fax: (310)366-3330
Co. E-mail: takenakaes@earthlink.net

E-mail: takenakaes@earthlink.net
Scope: Consulting services in the areas of strategic planning; feasibility studies; profit enhancement; organizational development; start-up businesses; mergers and acquisitions; joint ventures; divestitures; executive searches; sales management; competitive analysis. Entering Japanese market.

52003 ■ William E. Kuhn & Associates
234 Cook St.
Denver, CO 80206-5305
Ph:(303)322-8233
Fax: (303)322-9032
Co. E-mail: billkuhn1@cs.com

E-mail: billkuhn1@cs.com
Scope: Firm specializes in strategic planning; profit enhancement; small business management; mergers and acquisitions; joint ventures; divestitures; human resources management; performance appraisals; team building; sales management; appraisals and valuations.

52004 ■ Marketing Resource Group
31 Valley Forge Way
Foxborough, MA 02035
Ph:(508)543-8452
Fax: (508)842-7252
Scope: Customized sales skills and field training systems for sales people, sales managers, executives, and non-selling staff. Curriculums can be developed and branded for in-house program to be used with future trainees and new hires. Pre-screening of sales candidates and strategic consulting also available. **Seminars:** Basic Sales Skills, Consultative Selling, Relationship Selling, Networking to Maximize Your Business, Six Critical Steps for Every Sales Call, Selling Skills for the Non-Sales Professional, Effective Sales Management, Maximizing Revenue.

52005 ■ Max Sacks International
2442 NW Market St., Ste. 409
Seattle, WA 98107
Ph:(206)706-4119
Free: 800-488-4629
Fax: (206)706-5359
Co. E-mail: contact@maxsacks.com
URL: http://www.maxsacks.com

E-mail: contact@maxsacks.com
Scope: Offers sales and sales management training and consulting. Industries served: all. **Seminars:** Track Selling System, 2006; The Guaranteed Close; World Class Selling; Sales Management Coaching; Telemarketing; World Class Customer Service.

52006 ■ Porter Henry & Co.

353 Lexington Ave., 15th Fl.
New York, NY 10016
Ph:(212)953-5544
Fax: (212)953-5899
Co. E-mail: sales@porterhenry.com
URL: http://www.porterhenry.com

E-mail: sales@porterhenry.com
Scope: Consulting and custom-designed training in sales and sales management. Work includes salesforce studies and needs analyses, systems design, and visual sales presentations. Have 25 validated sales and sales management training programs. **Publications:** McGraw Hill Book: The Sales Strategist-6 Breakthrough Strategies to Win New Business. **Seminars:** AccountAbility; ManageAbility; SalesAbility: All three are series of workshops (1-2 day each) totaling 25 off-the-shelf programs. Moblie sales/motivation, 1999. Infield reinforcement selling skills and motivational program for sales people. **Special Services:** Introduced (1998) "SalesAbility Coach" (CD-ROM), unique selling skills tool that (1) Training and (2) Measures. 10 Sales Skills.

52007 ■ James J. Prihoda & Associates

400 Island Way, Ste. 707
Clearwater Beach, FL 33767
Ph:(727)446-4082
Scope: Specializes in marketing and sales.

52008 ■ Syed Hussayn TMCI

95 October Ln.
Aurora, ON, Canada L4G 7A1
Ph:(905)949-4555
Fax: (905)949-9116
Co. E-mail: syedn.hussain@sympatico.ca

E-mail: syedn.hussain@sympatico.ca
Scope: Business process re-engineering, change management, financial restructuring & insolvency, consumer & corporate bankruptcy, financial/debt management, investments & insurance advisory services, management/executive development, marketing management, organizational development, needs assessment, financial counselling, succession planning, performance management/measurement, program evaluation, project management, strategic planning and import/export advisory. **Publications:** "Innovative Management"; "Team Building and Leadership"; "Financial Planning"; "Estate Planning"; "Risk Management"; "Export/Import Trade Finance Mechanics"; "Marketing and Sales Management"; "What Your Banker Needs to Know"; "Building A Successful Financial Plan". **Seminars:** Workplace Solutions Seminars; Export Development; Executive Education & Leadership Development; Financial Planning; Estate Planning; Succession Planning; Wealth Accumulation and Management; Strategic Planning/Competitive Positioning.

52009 ■ The Tactix Group

1619 N 102 St.
Omaha, NE 68114
Ph:(402)393-3800
Fax: (402)393-5151
Co. E-mail: info@thetactixgroup.com
URL: http://www.thetactixgroup.com

E-mail: info@thetactixgroup.com
Scope: Offers integrated marketing system design and implementation, for customer relationship management. Serves manufacturing, distributing, high-tech, banking, and executive benefit industries. **Special Services:** Saleslogix (Client Server) Sales Automation Software; Automated Customer Loyalty Systems.

FRANCHISES AND BUSINESS OPPORTUNITIES

52010 ■ DEI Franchising Systems

888 7th Ave., 9th Fl.
New York, NY 101006
Ph:(212)581-7390
Free: 800-224-2140
Co. E-mail: franchise@dei-sales.com
URL: http://www.dei-sales.com
No. of Franchise Units: 31. **No. of Company-Owned Units:** 1. **Founded:** 1979. **Franchised:** 2003. **Description:** Sales training industry. **Equity Capital Needed:** $60,000-$75,000. **Franchise Fee:** $50,000. **Royalty Fee:** 7%. **Financial Assistance:** No. **Training:** Offers 2 weeks home-based training and 2 weeks at headquarters with ongoing support.

52011 ■ D.E.I. Sales Training Systems, Inc.

D.E.I. Management Group, Inc.
888 7th Ave., 9th Fl.
New York, NY 10106
Free: 800-224-2140
Fax: (212)245-7897
No. of Franchise Units: 30. **No. of Company-Owned Units:** 1. **Founded:** 1979. **Franchised:** 2003. **Description:** Selling and delivering of sales training programs. **Equity Capital Needed:** $65,000. **Franchise Fee:** $50,000. **Financial Assistance:** No. **Training:** Yes.

52012 ■ Sandler Sales Institute (Canada) Ltd.

3625 McGill St.
Vancouver, BC, Canada V5K 1J3
Ph:(604)254-4341
Free: 800-669-3537
Fax: (604)251-8060
Co. E-mail: rtaylor@sandler.com
URL: http://www.sandler.com
No. of Franchise Units: 216. **Founded:** 1967. **Franchised:** 1983. **Description:** Sales and sales management training. Provides ongoing incremental reinforced sales and management training for individuals and companies. **Equity Capital Needed:** $80,000. **Franchise Fee:** $65,000. **Training:** Provides personal coaching, ongoing reinforced training and coaching support with excellent products and programs.

LIBRARIES

52013 ■ Canadian Professional Sales Association–Sales Resource Centre

310 Front St. W., Ste. 800
Toronto, ON, Canada M5J 3B5
Ph:(416)408-2685
Free: 888-267-2772
Fax: (416)408-2684
Co. E-mail: afredericks@cpsa.com
URL: http://www.cpsa.com
Contact: Anna Fredericks, Mgr.
Scope: Sales - management, negotiation, selling skills, training, marketing, presentations, meetings, conventions, industry directories, speakers bureau. **Services:** Interlibrary loan; copying; Library open to the public by permission only. **Holdings:** 4000 books; 400 audiocassettes; 400 videotapes. **Subscriptions:** 10 journals and other serials.

52014 ■ Point-of-Purchase Advertising International–Information Center

1660 L. St., NW, 10th Fl.
Washington, DC 20036
Ph:(202)530-3000
Fax: (202)530-3030
Co. E-mail: info@popai.com
URL: http://www.popai.com
Contact: Richard K. Blatt, Pres.
Scope: Point-of-purchase research information, slide and videotape presentation. **Holdings:** 162 volumes; reports; surveys; 10 research publications; 10 reference guides; 200 audio seminars. **Subscriptions:** 90 journals and other serials; 10 newspapers.

RESEARCH CENTERS

52015 ■ University of Akron–Fisher Institute for Professional Selling

302 Buchtel Mall
Akron, OH 44325
Ph:(330)972-6303
Fax: (330)972-6588
Co. E-mail: jhawes@uakron.edu
URL: http://www3.uakron.edu/cba/fisherin/index.html
Contact: Jon Hawes, Dir.
E-mail: jhawes@uakron.edu
Scope: Professional selling techniques and sales management. **Services:** Consulting; Corportate training. **Educational Activities:** Continuing education courses, and management development courses for sales executives; Seminars.

Scientific and Technical Research/Development

START-UP INFORMATION

52016 ■ "The Amazing, Real-Life Adventures of Microfly" in *Venture Capital Journal* (Vol. 42, No. 8, August 2002, pp. 30-31)
Pub: Thomas Venture Economics
Ed: Michael V. Copeland. **Description:** Profile of a robotic fly that weighs less than a paper clip and its promising technological value is discussed.

52017 ■ "Commercialization gets attention in life-science funding" in *Crain's Detroit Business* (Vol. 19, No. 1, January 6, 2003, pp. 16)
Pub: Crain Communications Inc., Detroit
Ed: Laura Bailey. **Description:** The Michigan Economic Development Corporation created the Life Sciences Corridor that will distribute up to $1 billion in settlement money from tobacco companies over 20 years to develop the life-science industry. Startup firms feel that the funding guideline proposals favor funds for research over those for commercialization.

52018 ■ "EISC partners start-up with unique technology" in *Toledo Business Journal* (Vol. 19, No. 2, February 2003, pp. 23)
Pub: Telex Communications, Inc.
Ed: Susan Ford. **Description:** Profile of Energystics Technologies, Ltd. and Tom Sheperak, president and CEO, who is working on three applications for his unique Energy Beam(TM) technology that has the capability to move electricity through the air without a wire to heat, melt, or vaporize materials. EISC, the Small Business Development Center for technology and manufacturing, has established an on-site lab where Sheperak is developing and testing prototypes.

52019 ■ *Entrepreneurship: Frameworks and Empirical Investigations from Forthcoming Leaders of European Research*
Pub: Elsevier Science and Technology Books
Ed: Johan Wiklund; Dimo Dimov; Jerome A. Katz; Dean Shepherd. **Released:** July 2006. **Price:** $99.95.
Description: Entrepreneurial research and theory cover the early growth of research-based startups and the role of learning in international entrepreneurship, focusing on Europe.

52020 ■ "Madison, Wis., University Research Park Expands Again" in *Milwaukee Journal Sentinel* (December 1, 2005)
Pub: Journal Sentinel, Inc.
Ed: Kathleen Gallagher. **Description:** University Research Park in Madison is expanding in order to accommodate 20 incubator suites for young companies being spun out of research findings at the University of Wisconsin-Madison.

52021 ■ "Montreal: A Fertile Ground For VC Exploration" in *Venture Capital Journal* (Vol. 42, No. 5, May 2002, pp. 54)
Pub: Thomas Venture Economics
Description: Montreal, Quebec is becoming the hot spot for technological development, and is supported by a strong investment community and world-class local venture capital environment.

52022 ■ "NASA Offers Free Rocket Scientists" in *Inc.* (August 1, 2004)
Pub: Inc. Magazine
Ed: Jess McCuan. **Description:** NASA has created a new outreach program that offers small businesses up to 40 hours of free high-tech and engineering advice under the Space Alliance Technology Outreach Program, which began as a state-run project in 1995 in the State of Florida and went national in 2001.

52023 ■ "A private space race" in *Wall Street Journal* (Feb. 5, 2003, pp. B1)
Pub: Dow Jones & Co. Inc.
Ed: J. Lynn Lunsford. **Description:** Entrepreneur Peter Diamandis has founded and helped to fund the St. Louis, Missouri, based X Prize Foundation, which will award a $10 million prize to the first private venture to fund, design and launch a manned space vehicle. Twenty-four entrepreneur-led teams are vying for the prize and the recent accident aboard the Space Shuttle Columbia has not deterred any in that quest. The foundation's rules for the spacecraft say only that it must be able to hold three passengers and must be able to fly 62 miles up and return safely two times in the course of two weeks.

52024 ■ "The Quebec Story: Low Cost, Low Risk, Tremendous Opportunity" in *Venture Capital Journal* (Vol. 42, No. 5, May 2002, pp. 48, 50)
Pub: Thomas Venture Economics
Ed: Peter Diekmeyer. **Description:** Canada's venture capital center has become a hotbed of technology startups because of the unique incentives, including tax incentives, low business costs, Montreal's close ties to Europe, and an educated workforce focused on technology.

52025 ■ "TechTalk: Big Bargain: 'Chipless' Semiconductor Startups" in *Venture Capital Journal* (Vol. 42, No. 10, October 2002, pp. 38-39)
Pub: Thomas Venture Economics
Ed: Ravi Chiruvolu. **Description:** The 'soft silicon' approach to manufacturing chips give customers absolute control over intellectual property, allowing for a faster time to market, and if there is an error in the chip, it can be corrected quickly and inexpensively.

52026 ■ "There's Life In Life Science" in *Venture Capital Journal* (Vol. 42, No. 8, August 2002, pp. 32-35)
Pub: Thomas Venture Economics
Ed: Adam Reinebach. **Description:** Venture capitalists are taking a real interest in life sciences. Profiles of four venture-backed startups are presented, including PTC Therapeutics Inc., working in small molecule drug discovery; Sensors for Medical Solutions Inc., medical sensors; Medical Scientists Inc., predictive modeling software; and Message Pharmaceuticals, drug discovery focusing on messenger RNA. Statistical data included.

ASSOCIATIONS AND OTHER ORGANIZATIONS

52027 ■ **Federation of American Scientists**
1717 K St. NW, Ste. 209
Washington, DC 20036
Ph:(202)546-3300
Fax: (202)675-1010
Co. E-mail: fas@fas.org
URL: http://www.fas.org
Contact: Henry C. Kelly, Pres.
Description: Natural and social scientists, engineers, and individuals concerned with problems of science and society. Aims to "act on public issues where the opinions of scientists are relevant, those which affect science or in which the experience or perspective of scientists is a needed guide." Functions through testimony to Congress and government agencies, public statements, and articles. Maintains the Federation of American Scientists Fund, a research and education arm of the association. **Publications:** *FAS Public Interest Report* (bimonthly).

REFERENCE WORKS

52028 ■ "$1 Million Grant Program Aims to Boost Renewable Energy" in *Milwaukee Journal Sentinel* (December 13, 2005)
Pub: Journal Sentinel, Inc.
Ed: Thomas Content. **Description:** Wisconsin's Governor Jim Doyle has proposed a $1 million grant to invest in renewable energy technologies for the state, including ethanol, biodiesel and waste-to-energy power.

52029 ■ "60 Seconds On Doing the Impossible" in *Fast Company* (March 2005, No. 92, pp. 32)
Pub: Gruner & Jahr USA Publishing
Ed: Ryan Underwood. **Description:** Interview with Peter Diamandis, who created the competition that awarded the $10 million Ansari X Prize to SpaceShipOne for shuttling into suborbital space twice in two weeks. Diamandis is expanding his focus to include prizes for nanotechnology.

52030 ■ "A Market for Ideas" in *The Economist* (Vol. 377, October 22-28, 2005, No. 8449, pp. 3-6, 8-10, 12-18)
Pub: The Economist Newspaper Ltd.
Description: The magazine presents information collected from a survey conducted on issues of patents and technology. Protection of intellectual property can be good for both the technology industry and its customers. The patent system, companies preparing for intellectual-property battles, a new intellectual-property business model, sharing intellectual property, Indian and Chinese competition in innovation, and new markets for intellectual property are among issues investigated.

52031 ■ "Aastrom Gets $22M Financing Boost; Stem-Cell Trials Pique Wall Street's Interest" in *Crain's Detroit Business* **(January 17, 2005)**
Pub: Crain Communications Inc. - Detroit
Ed: Andrew Dietderich. Description: Aastrom Biosciences Inc. is committed to obtaining approval by the U.S. Food and Drug Administration for approval of stem-cell-based products for general medical use. The firm has secured $22 million capital to conduct clinical stem-cell trial tests at William Beaumont Hospital.

52032 ■ "Addressing the Inhibitors" in *Washington Business Journal* **(Vol. 21, No. 50, April 11, 2003, pp. 28)**
Pub: Washington Business Journal
Ed: Chris Silva. Description: Drugs designed to bolster viral fusion inhibitors are being developed by Panacos Pharmaceuticals Inc. An anti-HIV drug was approved by the U.S. Food and Drug Administration in March, which offers opportunities for a new type of drug.

52033 ■ "AgraQuest Fumigant OK'd" in *Sacramento Bee* **(November 18, 2005)**
Pub: The Sacramento Bee
Ed: Jim Wasserman. Description: AgraQuest Inc. announced approval by both federal and state agencies for its natural soil fumigant that could help replace methyl bromide, the chemical soil sterilizer. AgraQuest is based in Davis, California and reports revenues at $4.2 million for 2005. The firm's products are based on naturally occurring fungus.

52034 ■ "Albany's High-Tech Park Already Creating Jobs" in *Tampa Tribune* **(November 28, 2005)**
Pub: Media General, Inc.
Ed: Gary Haber. Description: Albany NanoTech, located 150 miles north of New York City, is a $3 billion research and development complex for researchers from industry, as well as professors and students from the University at Albany who are working on next-generation miniature computer chips.

52035 ■ "Alternative Energy Attracts Big Money" in *Altanta Journal-Constitution* **(January 24, 2007)**
Pub: Cox Newspapers, Inc.
Ed: Dan Chapman. Description: Major corporations, venture capitalists, investment banks, hedge funds and farmers spent $71 billion globally on renewable energy research.

52036 ■ "Alternative Energy Powers Up In Michigan - Part 1 of 2" in *Crain's Detroit Business* **(Vol. 22, February 6, 2006, No. 6, pp. 10)**
Pub: Crain Communications Inc. - Detroit
Ed: Amy Lane. Description: McKenzie Bay International Ltd. Located in Farmington Hills, Michigan is launching a commercial wind-energy system that generates and distributes electricity at customer locations, and supplements power from a conventional utility.

52037 ■ "Alternative Energy Powers Up In Michigan - Part 2 of 2" in *Crain's Detroit Business* **(Vol. 22, February 6, 2006, No. 6, pp. 10)**
Pub: Crain Communications Inc. - Detroit
Ed: Amy Lane. Description: Michigan is pushing to become the nations' epicenter for research and development into new technology for biodiesel fuels made from renewable resources such as vegetable oil recycled from restaurants or produced from sunflowers, soybeans and canola plants.

52038 ■ "Amgen Looking to Develop Medicines with Competitors" in *Providence Business News* **(Vol. 18, No. 20, September 1, 2003, pp. 2)**
Pub: Providence Business News, Inc.
Ed: Marni Leff Kottle. Description: Efforts by Amgen to find competitor with promising drug for joint venture scheme are discussed. Topics include testing of new drugs, possible profits from new drugs, and Amgen's falling market share.

52039 ■ "'Angels' Seek to Expand Territory; Investors Begin to Target Waukesha County" in *Milwaukee Journal Sentinel* **(December 12, 2005)**
Pub: Journal Sentinel, Inc.
Ed: Kathleen Gallagher. Description: IQ Corridor Angel Network is targeting Waukesha County to help develop a series of high-tech companies from Chicago through Milwaukee and Madison onto Minneapolis. The firm is seeking ideas related to manufacturing equipment needed by biotech and other high-tech companies, especially those in Madison, Wisconsin.

52040 ■ "Ann Arbor's QuatRx Pharmaceuticals Files for Stock Offering" in *Crain's Detroit Business* **(Vol. 22, February 13, 2006, No. 7, pp. 25)**
Pub: Crain Communications Inc. - Detroit
Ed: Andrew Dieterich. Description: QuatRx Pharmaceuticals Company, based in Ann Arbor, Michigan, filed an initial public offering in the hopes of raising $86 million. The firm develops and commercializes products in the endocrine, metabolic, and cardiovascular therapeutic areas.

52041 ■ "Aquaculture Becoming Big Business in Rhode Island" in *Providence Business News* **(Vol. 18, No. 16, August 4, 2003, pp. 3)**
Pub: Providence Business News, Inc.
Ed: Laura Rickstson. Description: The growing aquaculture industry in Rhode Island is examined, including market share of fish industry, market development, and industry forecasts.

52042 ■ "Beaumont Aims to Commercialize Research" in *Crain's Detroit Business* **(Vol. 22, January 16, 2006, No. 3, pp. 3)**
Pub: Crain Communications Inc. - Detroit
Ed: Michelle Martinez. Description: William Beaumont Hospital is planning to commercialize its clinical trials and medical research. The move will help Beaumont supplement the hospital's research unit budget to $22.6 million in 2006.

52043 ■ "Before You Do That 'Amazing' Biotech Deal, Read This Story" in *Venture Capital Journal* **(Vol. 42, No. 8, August 2002, pp. 36-37)**
Pub: Thomas Venture Economics
Ed: Ravi Chiruvolu. Description: Biotechnology startups always require a longer incubation period. The author shares his experiences with biotechnology deals.

52044 ■ "Behind the looking glass" in *Red Herring* **(March 2003, pp. 58)**
Pub: Herring Communications Inc.
Ed: Celeste Biever. Description: A listing of everyday products manufactured through nanotechnology is presented, including antibacterial products, self-cleaning glass, sunscreens, tennis balls and more.

52045 ■ "Berridge Confident of Evolving Work Force" in *Ledger* **(March 6, 2005)**
Pub: Knight-Ridder/Tribune Business News
Ed: Kyle Kennedy. Description: Florida High Tech Corridor Council's president, Randy Berridge is committed to bringing more high tech business and jobs to Central Florida.

52046 ■ "Betting the Farm" in *Business 2.0* **(Vol. 6, September 2005, No. 8, pp. 108)**
Pub: Time, Inc.
Ed: Erick Schonfeld. Description: The continual advancement of genetically modified crops is paying off for Monsanto after the company took the big risk on biotechnology.

52047 ■ "Big Generic Pharma" in *The Economist* **(Vol. 376, July 30-August 5, 2005, No. 8437, pp. 58)**
Pub: The Economist Newspaper Ltd.
Description: The merger between Teva, Israel's largest pharmaceutical company with American Ivax makes Teva the world leader in generic pharmaceuticals.

52048 ■ "Big-League R&D Gets Its Own eBay" in *Fortune* **(Vol. 149, No. 9, May 3, 2004, pp. 74)**
Pub: Time, Inc.
Ed: David Kirkpatrick. Description: Start of the new Internet-driven revolution in Research and Development is discussed. Experts predict research will be judged on scientific merits, not where researchers attended school or live.

52049 ■ "Big Pharma Eyeing Startups" in *Venture Capital Journal* **(October 1, 2204)**
Pub: Thomason Financial Inc.
Ed: Tom York. Description: Larger pharmaceutical companies are seeking more investment deals and partnerships with emerging companies due to patent expirations and new drugs going to market.

52050 ■ "Big Pharm's Favorite Gadfly" in *Business Week* **(December 19, 2005, No. 3964, pp. 50-51)**
Pub: McGraw-Hill Companies
Ed: Amy Barrett. Description: Dr. Steven E. Nissen, leader of clinical trials, works to ascertain drug safety.

52051 ■ "Bio-Pharmaceutical Emphasis" in *San Diego Business Journal* **(Vol. 28, January 15, 2007, No. 3, pp. 11)**
Pub: San Diego Business Journal Associates
Ed: Katie Weeks. Description: Huya Bioscience International LLC, with offices in both San Diego, California and Shanghai, China, is partnering with Organon in order to discover new bio-pharmaceuticals.

52052 ■ "BioGift Goes After Cancer Tissue Niche" in *Business Journal-Portland* **(Vol. 20, No. 25, August 22, 2003, pp. 1)**
Pub: American City Business Journals, Inc.
Ed: Robin J. Moody. Description: BioGift Anatomical Inc., located in Tigard, Oregon, is seeking body donations from individuals with cancer in order to extend its cancer research and education programs.

52053 ■ "Biographies" in *Venture Capital Journal* **(February 1, 2006)**
Pub: Thomason Financial Inc.
Description: Profiles of leading venture capital firms including Canaan Partners, BA Venture Partners, Orrick, Alta Partners, Inter West Partners, New Enterprise Associates, and Frazier Healthcare Ventures.

52054 ■ "Biomedical, Marine Research Funds Could Grow If Voters Approve Seed Money" in *Portland Press Herald* **(November 2, 2005)**
Pub: Blethen Maine Newspapers, Inc.
Ed: Edward D. Murphy. Description: Maine's Department of Economic and Community Development says the $20 million on the state's election ballot would not be enough to fund projects designed to help biomedical and marine research programs.

52055 ■ "Biometric conversion" in *Red Herring* **(January 2003, pp. 63)**
Pub: Herring Communications Inc.
Ed: Andrew P. Madden. Description: Biometrics is the use of technology to verify a person's identity based on physical or behavioral characteristics, such as fingerprints and facial recognition. Profile of Identix, the market leader in the use of biometrics is included.

52056 ■ *BioScan: The Worldwide Biotech Industry Reporting Service*
Pub: Oryx Press
Contact: Julie Simonson
Ed: Janet Woolum, Editor. Released: Annual, bimonthly supplements. Price: $975 per year, including supplements. Covers: Over 1,800 companies currently doing product research and development in food processing, agriculture, medicine, and other fields in the biotechnology industry. Entries Include: Company name, address, phone, names and titles of key personnel, number of employees (including number of Ph.Ds), date founded, names and description of subsidiaries, names of principal investors and per-

centage of investment, name and description of agreements or contracts, description of research and development, products available, products in development, list of subject terms. **Arrangement:** Alphabetical. **Indexes:** Subject, company/subsidiary name, investor, geographical.

52057 ■ "Biotech" in Business Week (January 23, 2006, No. 3968, pp. 38, 40)
Pub: McGraw-Hill Companies
Ed: Arlene Weintraub. **Description:** Biotechnology funding was always difficult to find in the U.S., but even more so since the Korean scandal made the headlines. South Korean scientist Hwang Woo Suk faked 11 lines of embryonic stem cells he claimed to have created through cloning in May 2005.

52058 ■ "Biotech Hotbeds: Where Are They, and How Do You Get One?" in Venture Capital Journal (October 1, 2004)
Pub: Thomason Financial Inc.
Ed: Dan Primack. **Description:** Boston, San Diego, San Francisco, and Research Triangle Park are earning the reputation in the life sciences sector as biotech hotbeds, clusters or hubs. These centers rely on four things: there is at least one large, nonprofit research institution strong in the field of biomedicine, close proximity to venture capital firms investing in biotech companies, local government officials have an interest in enhancing business environment for biotech companies, and there are a few publicly-traded biotech companies in the area.

52059 ■ "Biotech II Alan Frazier" in Venture Capital Journal (January 1, 2005)
Pub: Thomason Financial Inc.
Description: In an interview with Alan Frazier, founder of Frazier Healthcare Ventures in Seattle, Washington, he discusses the best and worst things that could happen in biotechnology in 2005. Frazier sites a continued IPO market that prices good companies appropriately along with mergers and acquisitions would be positive for the sector.

52060 ■ "Biotech Takes Heart in Potential New Drug" in Pacific Business News (Vol. 41, No. 23, August 15, 2003, pp. 1)
Pub: American City Business Journals
Ed: Terrance Sing. **Description:** Hawaii-based Hawaii Biotech Inc. has developed a new drug that is expected to reduce heart tissue damage. The new drug, called Cardax, has achieved positive results in clinical tests at the Medical College of Wisconsin.

52061 ■ "Born in an infertility clinic, nursed in a dish" in Atlanta Business Chronicle (Vol. 25, No. 22, November 8, 2002, pp. 20A)
Pub: American City Business Publications, Inc.
Ed: Julie Bryant. **Description:** BresaGen Inc. has four stem cell lines for use in research on finding new treatments for various debilitating illnesses. The firm has not revealed the name of the Atlanta, Georgia infertility clinic from which it received the needed human embryos to obtain the stem cell lines. The stem cell process is examined.

52062 ■ "Boston Scientific Looks To Expand Its Products Beyond Stents" in Boston Globe (February 2, 2005)
Pub: New York Times Company
Ed: Ross Kerber. **Description:** Boston Scientific executives are looking to expand beyond stents into technology areas such as implantable cardiac defibrillators, and small spinal implants for pain management. The company has also developed an endoscopy system that includes a digital camera which could replace other instruments currently used for colonoscopies.

52063 ■ "Bowling for drug research: families take entrepreneurial tack in signing up biotech firms" in Wall Street Journal (Feb. 27, 2003)
Pub: Dow Jones & Co. Inc.
Ed: Vanessa Fuhrmans. **Description:** Families of Spinal Muscular Atrophy signed a contract with Decode Genetics Inc. to fund their research programs.

52064 ■ "BresaGen moves slowly to grow stem cell work" in Atlanta Business Chronicle (Vol. 25, November 8, 2002, No. 22 pp. 1A)
Pub: American City Business Publications, Inc.
Ed: Julie Bryant. **Description:** BresaGen Inc., located in Athens, Georgia, is working with stem cells to find treatments for various human conditions. BresaGen has received $1.6 million in U.S. government grants and has entered into various licensing and distribution accords with the National Institutes of Health.

52065 ■ "Bucking the Odds at Amylin" in Business Week (January 9, 2006, No. 3966, pp. 64, 66)
Pub: McGraw-Hill Companies
Ed: Arlene Weintraub. **Description:** Profile of Ginger Graham, chief executive at Amylin Pharmaceuticals Inc., who was considering retirement before taking the reins at Amylin. Graham, who is a diabetic, has helped the company attain government approval on two diabetes drugs.

52066 ■ "Buoyed by Biotech" in Venture Capital Journal (February 1, 2006)
Pub: Thomason Financial Inc.
Description: Life science venture capitalists gathered in San Francisco, California recently to discuss backing life sciences startups that are developing drugs and creating innovated medical devices.

52067 ■ "Burning Cash, MannKind is Raising More Money" in San Fernando Valley Business Journal (Vol. 11, December 2006, No. 25, pp. 11)
Pub: San Fernando Valley Business Journal Associates
Ed: Chris Coates. **Description:** MannKind Corp., the biopharmaceutical developer, plans to raise $400 million to help fund Technosphere, a cornerstone product for diabetes that has been in research and development for over a decade.

52068 ■ "Business Briefs" in St. Louis Post-Dispatch (December 8, 2004)
Pub: Knight-Ridder/Tribune Business News
Description: Orion Genomics LLC, based at the Center for Emerging Technologies incubator, received a federal grant to research the genetic code of the agricultural pest roundworm. Research is directed at finding alternative ways to destroy or ward off the pest that are more effective than chemical pesticides now used. The company and researchers at North Carolina State University will share the $1.59 million grant.

52069 ■ "The Business of Nanotech" in Business Week (February 14, 2005, No. 3920, pp. 64)
Pub: McGraw-Hill Companies
Ed: Stephen Baker, Adam Aston. **Description:** Soon cars, chips and even golf balls will be produced using new materials engineered down to the level of individual atoms. Some 1,200 nano startups have emerged globally.

52070 ■ "Cancer Scans a Lifesaver for Crystal Maker" in Orlando Business Journal (Vol. 20, No. 8, August 8, 2003, pp. 2)
Pub: American City Business Journals, Inc.
Ed: Chad Eric Watt. **Description:** Profile of Crystal Photonics, founded by physicist Bruce Chai to produce artificial crystals. The firm has become one of the top crystal makers in the world.

52071 ■ "Caritas Seeking Cambridge Lab Space" in Boston Globe (February 4, 2005)
Pub: New York Times Company
Ed: Jeffrey Krasner. **Description:** Caritas Christi Health Care is planning to lease 100,000 square feet of laboratory space in Cambridge to increase its healthcare and biotechnology research. The move is expected to give the firm a higher profile and better access to scientists and local companies.

52072 ■ "A case for clinical informatics" in Ingram's (Vol. 28, No. 6, June 2002, pp. 61)
Pub: Show Me Publishing, Inc.
Description: Ideas and forecasting of future genetic and clinical trends in the health care industry are examined. Analysts believe genomics and medical informatics will combine to form clinical informatics, which will be a hybrid of laboratory testing and genetic analysis.

52073 ■ "Centerpoint is sidelined" in Red Herring (March 2003, pp. 67)
Pub: Herring Communications Inc.
Ed: Om Malik. **Description:** The demise of Centerpoint Broadband Technologies, a high-profile startup, developing wireless technologies and a new optical-transport mechanism, is chronicled.

52074 ■ "Central Indiana's High-Tech Incubator Lands First Tenant" in Indianapolis Star (September 24, 2002)
Pub: Knight Ridder/Tribune Business News
Ed: Jack Naudi. **Description:** Profile of central Indiana's newest high-tech incubator, the Haelan Group, a small company with a big high-tech vision to improve health care. The startup firm is geared toward life sciences, and will be run by Indiana University's Advanced Research and Technology Institute.

52075 ■ "Chaos, Inc." in Red Herring (January 2003, pp. 38)
Pub: Herring Communications Inc.
Ed: Mitchell M. Waldrop. **Description:** Profile of Santa Fe-based BiosGroup, a 20 year old startup, that recently ran a simulation to help Procter & Gamble achieve an inventory reduction of 25 percent.

52076 ■ The China List
Pub: Asia Marketing & Management
Contact: James W. Chan PhD, Pres.
E-mail: jameschan@comcast.net
Released: Updated regularly. **Database Covers:** More than 5,500 scientific, technical, engineering, medical, research and development, educational, and professional companies and libraries in the People's Republic of China that buy Western information products and services. **Database Includes:** Organization or company name and address, name, gender, title of decision-maker.

52077 ■ "Chinese Supplier Plans R&D Center in Canton Twp." in Crain's Detroit Business (Vol. 21, October 31, 2005, No. 44, pp. 15)
Pub: Crain Communications Inc. - Detroit
Ed: Terry Kosdrosky. **Description:** Chinese auto supplier, Tempo Group, is planning to locate its research and development center in Canton Township, Michigan. The center will employ up to 200 people.

52078 ■ "Clearwater Man Puts Technology To Work" in Tampa Tribune (November 27, 2005)
Pub: Media General, Inc.
Ed: Will Rodgers. **Description:** Denny Klein of Airport Business Center has developed a gas that speeds welding and fusing times and also improves automobile fuel efficiency by at least 30 percent.

52079 ■ "Crossing the Gene Barrier" in Business Week (January 16, 2006, No. 3967, pp. 72-77, 80)
Pub: McGraw-Hill Companies
Ed: Arlene Weintraub. **Description:** Biotechnology scientists Harry M. Meade and Nils Lonberg are mixing the genetic materials of man and beats in new ways in order to develop treatments of life threatening diseases such as cancer and arthritis. Medical ethics of genetic research are also discussed.

52080 ■ "Cyberkinetics Plans for Clinical Trials" in Providence Business News (Vol. 18, No. 20, September 1, 2003, pp. 1)
Pub: Providence Business News, Inc.
Ed: Mike Colias. **Description:** Product development taking place at Providence-based Cyberkinetics Inc. is discussed. Topics include drug testing, strategic planning, and company funding.

52081 ■ "Dealing with Reality" in Pittsburgh Business Times (Vol. 23, No. 6, August 29, 2003, pp. 15)
Pub: Pittsburgh Business Times

Ed: Christopher Davis. **Description:** Robotics Foundry president, William Thomasmeyer, hopes to develop robotics research into viable business opportunities in the Pittsburgh, Pennsylvania area.

52082 ■ "Detection Redirection" in *Washington Business Journal* **(Vol. 22, No. 9, July 4, 2003, pp. 13)**
Pub: Washington Business Journal
Ed: Chris Silva. **Description:** Marketing of cancer detection technology by Washington, DC-based biotechnology firm Protiveris Inc. is examined.

52083 ■ "Dialogue Picks Up on St. Louis' Status in IT and Biotech" in *St. Louis Post-Dispatch* **(November 3, 2004)**
Pub: Knight-Ridder/Tribune Business News
Ed: David Nicklaus. **Description:** St. Louis reports dozens of startup biotechnology companies and venture capital funds to back them. According to a study conducted by the Battelle Institute, St. Louis has become competitive in both life sciences and information technology sectors.

52084 ■ "Digital Defenses Sector Analysis" in *Red Herring* **(January 2003, pp. 64)**
Pub: Herring Communications Inc.
Description: An analysis of the digital defense sector in the U.S. is presented. Statistical data includes a listing of private companies, date founded, number of employees, funding, and number of funding rounds. Industry sectors include biological security, digital identity, managed security services, and network security.

52085 ■ "Distributed Generation: Breaking the grid lock" in *Red Herring* **(No. 103, September 1, 2001, pp. 76-77)**
Pub: Herring Communications
Ed: Linda Rastelli. **Description:** In-depth article discussing legislation across the United States, that is working to restructure state electricity industries.

52086 ■ "A Dose of News: Neurocrine Biosciences Inc." in *San Diego Business Journal* **(Vol. 28, January 15, 2007, No. 3, pp. 11)**
Pub: San Diego Business Journal Associates
Ed: Katie Weeks. **Description:** Neurocrine Biosciences Inc. reported positive preliminary results from part two of a study for its drug candidates to treat endometriosis.

52087 ■ "Down to a Science" in *Entrepreneur* **(Vol. 31, No. 8, August 2003, pp. 54)**
Pub: Entrepreneur Media, Inc.
Ed: Dian Vujovich. **Description:** Profile of the Eaton Vance Worldwide Health Sciences Fund (ETHSX), which has a five-year average total return of 12.67 percent. The fund invests in health, sciences and biotechnology firms worldwide.

52088 ■ "Early Stage Deals Could Come Back" in *Venture Capital Journal* **(October 1, 2204)**
Pub: Thomason Financial Inc.
Ed: Tom York. **Description:** Life sciences sector is expected to see a surge in investment opportunities in 2005, which will result in turning promising technologies into new companies.

52089 ■ "Ed Otto, Director of Biotechnology at RCCC" in *Charlotte Observer* **(February 8, 2007)**
Pub: Knight-Ridder/Tribune Business News
Ed: Gail Smith-Arrants. **Description:** Profile of Ed Otto, director of biotechnology at Rowan-Cabarrus Community College. Before taking the position at RCCC, Otto directed the Food and Drug Administration office responsible for regulating cellular, tissue and gene therapies products.

52090 ■ "Electric Shoes and 'Breadcrumbs' for the Troops" in *Venture Capital Journal* **(Vol. 42, No. 9, September 2002, pp. 26-27)**
Pub: Thomas Venture Economics
Ed: Michael V. Copeland. **Description:** New defense technologies being developed to protect U.S. troops during wartime are presented.

52091 ■ "Elite Company" in *Hispanic Business* **(December 2002, pp. 54)**
Pub: Hispanic Business
Description: The four finalists in the Hispanic Business magazine's Entrepreneur of the Year award are profiled. The finalists hail from the aerospace, auto retailing, and telecommunications industries.

52092 ■ "Emergency services gets a breath of fresh air" in *Red Herring* **(January 2003, pp. 56)**
Pub: Herring Communications Inc.
Ed: Alan Zeichick. **Description:** Profile of the new emergency-response system, developed by Airwave System, and currently being used in six counties of the United Kingdom. The system involves a common terrestrial radio service for emergency workers. After September 11, 2001, the U.S. is working to develop such a system to replace the antiquated radio equipment unsuitable for data transmission.

52093 ■ "Environmental technology firm files bankruptcy" in *Atlanta Business Chronicle* **(Vol. 25, December 20, 2002, No. 28, pp. 8A)**
Pub: American City Business Publications, Inc.
Ed: Mary Jane Credeur. **Description:** Apyron Technologies Inc., a manufacturer of commercial water, air and emissions purification and detoxification products, has filed for Chapter 7 bankruptcy in the U.S. Bankruptcy Court, Atlanta, Georgia. The eight-year-old firm has raised nearly $17 million over that same period, and lists for around $2 million in claims.

52094 ■ "Extreme hunter scores big with tiny funds" in *Red Herring* **(March 2003, pp. 52)**
Pub: Herring Communications Inc.
Ed: Niall McKay. **Description:** Profile of Jonathan Trent, an astrobiologist at NASA. Trent discovered a breakthrough in 1991 that may revolutionize a segment of nanotechnology known as molecular manufacturing.

52095 ■ "An eye for a dye" in *Red Herring* **(March 2003, pp. 60)**
Pub: Herring Communications Inc.
Ed: Michael V. Copeland. **Description:** Optiva's nanotechnology has attracted JP Morgan Partners investment.

52096 ■ "The fabric of consumer reality" in *Red Herring* **(March 2003, pp. 54)**
Pub: Herring Communications Inc.
Ed: Alan Zeichick. **Description:** The economics of nanotechnology are discussed. In order for a particular consumer good to be priced competitively, the nano-scale components required must be manufactured in bulk, using techniques similar to those used in making larger-scale products.

52097 ■ "Farmingdale-based THM Scientific Introduces Product Line Based on Sustainable Agriculture" in *Long Island Business News* **(Feb.6, 2004)**
Pub: Dolan Media Newswires
Ed: Adina Genn. **Description:** Profile of Peter Felix and James Sottilo, two arborists who have partnered to develop and produce Rootgrow, a line of organic-compost tea, brewers and related products and services that will preserve the soil. The partners are targeting homeowners, corporate parks, golf courses, and municipalities.

52098 ■ *Federal Research in Progress (FEDRIP)*
Pub: Office of Product Management
Released: Monthly. **Database Covers:** more than 150,000 federally-funded research projects currently in progress in the physical sciences, engineering, health, agriculture, and life sciences areas. **Database Includes:** Project title, starting date, principal investigator, performing and sponsoring organization, detailed abstract, description of the research, objective, and findings (when available).

52099 ■ *Federal Research Report*
Pub: CD Publications

Contact: Leonard Eiserer, CON
Ed: Leonard Eiserer, Editor, eiserer@aol.com. **Released:** Weekly. **Price:** $284 per year. **Covers:** Government and foundation grants and contracts for research, development, and education. **Entries Include:** Grant title; name, address, and phone of contact; deadline; amount. **Arrangement:** Classified by discipline or field of interest.

52100 ■ "Firm Suiting Up for New Space Flights" in *San Fernando Valley Business Journal* **(Vol. 12, January 2007, No. 1, pp. 12)**
Pub: San Fernando Valley Business Journal Associates
Ed: Mark R. Madler. **Description:** Profile on Orbital Outfitters, a company that wants to revolutionize the space industry by designing the next generation of space suits targeting crew and passengers for space travel through commercial and privately funded space flight. The firm also has an administrative office in Washington, D.C. to better deal with the regulations which oversee the New Space industry.

52101 ■ "Firm Wins Grant for Robotic Vehicle" in *Pittsburgh Business Times* **(Vol. 23, No. 4, August 15, 2003, pp. 3)**
Pub: Pittsburgh Business Times
Ed: Maria Guzzo. **Description:** A U.S. Army research grant will be used at Applied Perception Inc. to develop a robotic vehicle; topics include military research, robotic vehicles, and battlefield applications of the vehicle.

52102 ■ "Flight of Fancy? Launching a High-Tech Product Can be a Technical and Financial Challenge" in *Entrepreneur* **(Vol. 32, August 2004)**
Pub: Entrepreneur Media Inc.
Ed: Don Debelak. **Description:** Profile of William J. Boyer Jr. and partner and co-founder Ray Henson, who helped Boyer with the technical aspects of their digEplayer, a portable battery-operated in-flight entertainment system used on passenger tray tables. The company saw $1 millions in sales, first quarter 2004.

52103 ■ "Frank Otto Named EDO's COO" in *Long Island Business News* **(February 27, 2004)**
Pub: Dolan Media Newswires
Description: Profile of Frank Otto, newly appointed COO of defense contractor, Long Island Forum for Technology.

52104 ■ "From Cow Pies to Clean Power" in *Business 2.0* **(Vol. 7, January/February 2006, No. 1, pp. 24)**
Pub: Time, Inc.
Ed: Elizabeth Esfahani. **Description:** Panda Energy is developing a method that converts cow dung into bio-gas fuel which would in turn power the production of ethanol.

52105 ■ "Fueling tomorrow's growth" in *Harvard Business Review* **(Vol. 80, No. 9, September 2002, pp. 51)**
Pub: Harvard Business School Press
Ed: Robert McGarvey. **Description:** New sources of oil, new fuels, and conservation are discussed in an overview of future products.

52106 ■ "Fund Profile" in *Venture Capital Journal* **(February 1, 2006)**
Pub: Thomason Financial Inc.
Description: Profile of Aisling Capital, founded in 2002 as Perseus-Soros BioPharmaceutical Fund. The VC invests in biopharmaceutical companies that require $15M to $30M of new capital.

52107 ■ *Futuretech*
Pub: John Wiley & Sons Inc. Scientific/Technical/Medical Publishing
Ed: Harry Goldstein, Editor, hgoldste@wiley.com. **Released:** 18x/yr. **Publication Includes:** List of companies, laboratories, and researchers involved in advanced technology projects that will have broad applications in various industries, including high temper-

ature resistant ceramic parts, plastic structural materials, and low cost dewater processes for solid-liquid systems (coal slurry, paper pulp, etc.); international coverage. **Entries Include:** Company, laboratory, or researcher name, address, phone, background information, financial and technical data, analysis of market potential and investment opportunities. Principal content is articles and analyses of advanced technologies; focus is on one technology per issue.

52108 ■ "Genetic Medicine's Next Big Step" in Fortune (Vol. 151, January 10, 2005, No. 1, pp. 54)
Pub: Time Inc.
Ed: John Simons. **Description:** RNA interference (RNAi) is a process that is able to block threatening genetic signals in diseased cells, such as those that can proliferate a virus. This process could lead to the breakthrough needed for the struggling drug industry. Profile of Alnylam Pharmaceutical in Cambridge, Massachusetts is included.

52109 ■ "Genzyme Battles An Old Adversary" in Boston Globe (January 25, 2005)
Pub: New York Times Company
Ed: Jeffrey Krasner. **Description:** A new battle over intellectual property has erupted between Genzyme Corporation and Transkaryotic Therapies Inc. (TKT) of Cambridge, Massachusetts. Genzyme has sued TKT claiming that the firm's method of purifying a treatment for a particular disease infringed on Genzyme's proprietary technology.

52110 ■ "Georgia medical device business growing" in Atlanta Business Chronicle (Vol. 25, No. 19, October 18, 2002, pp. 3A)
Pub: American City Business Publications, Inc.
Ed: Julie Bryant. **Description:** The number of medical device companies operating in the state of Georgia currently totals more than 225, with growth centered in the small- to medium-size category. However, industry leaders in the state contend that the medical device industry has yet to take-off in the state. Many of these firms are divisions of much larger companies.

52111 ■ "Getting Girls to the Lab Bench" in Business Week (February 7, 2005, No. 3919, pp. 42)
Pub: McGraw-Hill Companies
Ed: Catherine Arnst. **Description:** In order to remain competitive in the engineering and science sectors, women must be encouraged to enter these fields.

52112 ■ "Good for Business: Houston is a Hot Spot for Economic Growth" in Black Enterprise (Vol. 37, October 2006, No. 3, pp. 216)
Pub: Earl G. Graves Publishing Co. Inc.
Ed: Jeanette Valentine. **Description:** Fast-growing sectors in the biotechnology and healthcare industries are among the driving forces of Houston's economic growth. More than 76,000 small businesses in the area employ about one in four area workers, according to the Small Business Administration. Housing and business costs are 26 and 11 percent below the national average, respectively, garnering the attention of corporate giants.

52113 ■ "Good Health is Just a Costly Way to Die" in Red Herring (No. 103, September 1, 2001, pp. 54-58, 60)
Pub: Herring Communications
Ed: Thomas Maeder. **Description:** The war against disease is never won, and successful cures merely delay the inevitable. The article questions the goals of medicine while fighting premature death.

52114 ■ "Grants for Rural Biz" in Inc. (September 1, 2003)
Pub: Gruner & Jahr USA Publishing
Ed: Amy Gunderson. **Description:** States with a number of farms and fields are making more grants available to small businesses. The program, EPSCor, is funded mostly by the National Science Foundation and fosters scientific research in rural areas.

52115 ■ "Guilford Pharmaceuticals gets dose of health news" in Washington Business Journal (Vol. 22, No. 3, May 23, 2003, pp. 25)
Pub: Washington Business Journal
Ed: Robert J. Terry. **Description:** An examination into the growing success of Guilford Pharmaceuticals Inc., including new contracts with Pfizer Inc., U.S. Food and Drug Administration approval of new products and research and development efforts.

52116 ■ "Handicapping the Hispanic Economy" in Hispanic Business (November 2002, pp. 18-20)
Pub: Hispanic Business
Description: The future trends in elections, labor, international trade, technology education and banking access to loans are discussed by experts.

52117 ■ "Health-care foundation awards its first grants" in Atlanta Business Chronicle (Vol. 25, January 10, 2003, No. 31, pp. 7A)
Pub: American City Business Publications, Inc.
Ed: Julie Bryant. **Description:** The Healthcare Georgia Foundation has finalized its first round of grants. The foundation, its genesis brought about as part of a judgment against Blue Cross and Blue Shield of Georgia, awarded grants totaling $4.3 million. Serologicals Corporation's CEO, David Dodd, assumes the duties of Georgia Biomedical Partnership chairman.

52118 ■ "A Hidden Gem? Quebec Looks To Flex Muscle" in Venture Capital Journal (Vol. 42, No. 5, May 2002, pp. 44-45)
Pub: Thomas Venture Economics
Ed: Danielle Fugazy. **Description:** American venture capitalists have not invested much in Quebec's industry in the past, but the continuous growth Quebec is seeing in the fields of engineering, transportation, telecommunications, aeronautics and aerospace technology, medical research, computer science and biotechnology, has American VCs taking a second look.

52119 ■ "Hot Bets in the Cold North" in Business Week (December 19, 2005, No. 3964, pp. 24)
Pub: McGraw-Hill Companies
Ed: Robert Barker. **Description:** Companies drilling for coalbed methane in Canada include Apache, EnCana, Nexen, and Quicksilver Resources.

52120 ■ "House Wants Bigger Business-Tax Cut" in Crain's Detroit Business (Vol. 21, October 31, 2005, No. 44, pp. 6)
Pub: Crain Communications Inc. - Detroit
Ed: Amy Lane. **Description:** A new plan that would heighten and accelerate business tax-cuts was passed by the Senate in October 2005. The plan would use $700 million to support growth and technology-oriented businesses while $300 million would go to programs that support life-sciences, emerging technology and related sectors.

52121 ■ "Houston Leads Research in Superconducting Wire" in Houston Business Journal (Vol. 34, No. 7, June 27, 2003, pp. 27A)
Pub: American City Business Journals
Ed: Andrew P. Coleman. **Description:** The University of Houston has brought in $300 million in 15 years in grants for technology research.

52122 ■ "How do you narrow your product options?" in Wall Street Journal (March 17, 2003, pp. R3)
Pub: Dow Jones & Co. Inc.
Ed: Carl Bialik. **Description:** Profile of DNA-testing device developers Kalyan Handique and Sundaresh Brahmasandra and the founders of HandyLab Inc.

52123 ■ "How to Win a Marquee Account" in Sales and Marketing.com (Vol. 156, No. 3, March 2004, pp. 72)
Pub: VNU eMedia, Inc.
Ed: John Zimmer. **Description:** Profile of Toshiba America Medical Systems, which sells medical imag-

ing products for the diagnosis and treatment of heart disease, cancer and stroke. Toshiba's marketing strategy has helped them achieve double-digit growth in an otherwise sluggish market.

52124 ■ "Hydrogen: The Next Fuel for Laptops?" in San Jose Mercury News (March 2, 2005)
Pub: Knight-Ridder/Tribune Business News
Ed: Therese Poletti. **Description:** Millennium Cell, a small firm in New Jersey is working on a hydrogen-fueled battery that may eventually provide eight hours of power for laptop computers.

52125 ■ "In the Chips; Handheld Lab Gets HandyLab $6M" in Crain's Detroit Business (Vol. 22, January 23, 2006, No. 4, pp. 1)
Pub: Crain Communications Inc. - Detroit
Ed: Tom Henderson. **Description:** HandyLab Inc., Ann Arbor, Michigan, will use $6 million of venture capital to hire sales and marketing teams to bring its first medical diagnostic device to market. The firm was founded in 2000 by a group of engineering graduates from University of Michigan.

52126 ■ "In Your Face: Cross Your Fingers, Hold Your Breath...And Put Out Ads With No Holds Barred" in Entrepreneur (Vol. 31, October 2003)
Pub: Entrepreneur Media, Inc.
Ed: Jerry Fisher. **Description:** An examination of the advertising used for TheraSeed treatment, an alternative to surgery to treat prostate cancer is presented.

52127 ■ "The Incredible Shrinking Man" in Fast Company (November 2001, pp. 62)
Pub: Fast Company
Ed: Alison Overholt. **Description:** Profile of the research being done at International Business Machines Corporation's Almaden Research Center.

52128 ■ Inside R&D
Pub: John Wiley & Sons Inc. Scientific/Technical/ Medical Publishing
Contact: Lyn Schmidt
Ed: Harry Goldstein, Editor, hgoldste@wiley.com. **Released:** Weekly. **Publication Includes:** Lists of companies and researchers developing new advanced technology products or processes, including metal glass film depositors, cell immobilization systems, and squeeze casting techniques. **Entries Include:** Company or researcher name, address, phone, name of contact, description of product or process. Principal content is articles introducing or explaining new technologies.

52129 ■ International Research Centers Directory
Pub: Thomson Gale
Released: Annual, latest edition 18th, Published Nov. 2006. **Price:** $665, individuals. **Covers:** over 9,500 research and development facilities maintained outside the United States by governments, universities, or independent organizations, and concerned with all areas of physical, social, and life sciences, technology, business, military science, public policy, and the humanities. **Entries Include:** Facility name, address, phone, fax, telex, e-mail, urls, name of parent agency or other affiliation, date established, number of staff, type of activity and fields of research, special research facilities, publications, educational activities, services, and library holdings. **Arrangement:** Subject. **Indexes:** Name/keyword, subject, geographical, personal name.

52130 ■ "Investing To Fight Disease; It May Be Better For Your Soul Than For Your Bottom Line" in Business Week (February 7, 2005, No. 3919)
Pub: McGraw-Hill Companies
Ed: Carol Marie Cropper. **Description:** Investment trusts that target diseases such as Alzheimer's, breast and ovarian cancer, diabetes, prostate cancer and rheumatoid arthritis are discussed. Developed by WellSpring BioCapital Partners in 2004, VIOLTs, short for Vertical Investments of Life Sciences Trusts, hold shares of companies developing or marketing treatments for these diseases.

52131 ■ "The Investment Trap" in *Inc.* (Volume 27, December 2005, No. 12, pp. 144)
Pub: Inc. Magazine
Ed: Adam Hanft. **Description:** Companies that invest more money into research and development don't always report better results in terms of growth and profitability, however research and development spending continues to swell.

52132 ■ "IPOs/Recent Issues" in *Venture Capital Journal* (Vol. 42, No. 9, September 2002, pp. 44-45)
Pub: Thomas Venture Economics
Description: Information on recent IPOs for BioDelivery Sciences International Inc., and Healthetech Inc. is provided.

52133 ■ "It's Alive! New Software You Play Dr. Frankenstein" in *Black Enterprise* (Vol. 35, November 2004, No. 4, pp. 64)
Pub: Earl G. Graves Publishing Co. Inc.
Ed: Schuyler K. Esprit. **Description:** Review of Peter Plantec's book, Virtual Humans: Creating the Illusion Personality. The book is a resource for graphic designers, scientific researchers, students, technophobes and is accompanied by a CD-ROM that allows the user to build a virtual character.

52134 ■ "It's a Stretch" in *Entrepreneur* (Vol. 30, No. 1, January 2002, pp. 48)
Pub: Entrepreneur Media Inc.
Ed: Mark Henricks. **Description:** The difficulty for small businesses to bridge the gap between a good product and enough capacity to fulfill the needs of big customers who can help grow a business. Expansion loans are difficult to procure for small businesses, especially in new technologies areas.

52135 ■ "JSU Receives Record Funding" in *Mississippi Business Journal* (Vol. 28, September 2006, No. 36, pp. 23)
Pub: Venture Publications, Inc.
Description: Jackson State University has been granted a record $56 million in research and other sponsored programs awards for the external funding of 175 projects from federal and state agencies.

52136 ■ "Just the Tiqit" in *Red Herring* (January 2003, pp. 26)
Pub: Herring Communications Inc.
Ed: Dean Takahashi. **Description:** Profile of Tiqit Computers, a Silicon Valley startup, developing a PC into a device that could fit into a pants pocket.

52137 ■ "Kansas City Cardiology Works Towards Advancements" in *Ingram's* (Vol. 29, No. 9, September 2003, pp. 24)
Pub: Show Me Publishing, Inc.
Description: Medical research being conducted in the Greater Kansas City, Missouri area is examined. Topics include cardiology, electrophysiology, and cardiovascular implants.

52138 ■ "Laser 'Breakthrough': Changing the Silicon Game" in *San Jose Mercury News* (March 7, 2005)
Pub: Knight-Ridder/Tribune Business News
Ed: Dean Takahashi. **Description:** Mario Paniccia discusses the continuous wave silicon laser being developed by him and his team of researchers at Intel. The laser could launch a new stage in electronics.

52139 ■ "The Life Sciences Building Boom" in *Boston Globe* (January 31, 2005)
Pub: New York Times Company
Ed: Jeffrey Krasner. **Description:** Boston, Massachusetts has experienced growth in the life sciences sector since 2003 and this growth is expected to continue through 2007. More than 24 life-sciences projects are underway, including laboratories, hospital expansions, academic centers and housing for scientists.

52140 ■ "Life Sciences Industry Outlook" in *Ingram's* (Vol. 28, No. 6, June 2002, pp. 65)
Pub: Show Me Publishing, Inc.
Description: The life sciences industry in Kansas City, Missouri is profiled. Topics covered include media aspects, industry funding, workforce issues, collaboration, and commercialization.

52141 ■ "Life Sciences Span The Globe: U.S. VCs Like to Spend Money in their Backyards" in *Venture Capital Journal* (October 1, 2004)
Pub: Thomason Financial Inc.
Ed: Matthew Sheahan. **Description:** U.S. life science companies took about $3.6 billion in venture capital funding in 2004, more than 70 percent of the worldwide total, but Europe and Canada are working to attract these same companies. The cost advantages in both Canada and Europe are discussed.

52142 ■ "Little Things Make a Big Difference at NanoOpto" in *Venture Capital Journal* (Vol. 42, No. 10, October 2002, pp. 33-34)
Pub: Thomas Venture Economics
Ed: Ken Ryan. **Description:** The growing field of nanotechnology is examined.

52143 ■ "Local Labs are Working to Perfect DNA Probes" in *Kansas City Star* (March 8, 2005)
Pub: Knight-Ridder/Tribune Business News
Ed: Julius A. Karash. **Description:** Children's Mercy Hospital and Phylogenetix Laboratories Inc. have partnered to complete the development of patented DNA probes for detecting diseases; when completed the probes will be brought to market.

52144 ■ "Long Island's Patent Production Falls Nearly 20 Percent Since 1988" in *Long Island Business News* (March 5, 2004)
Pub: Dolan Media Newswires
Ed: Ken Schachter. **Description:** Long Island's future economic health is tied to industries such as life sciences, software development and defense-industry prototyping and design rather than large-scale manufacturing. Patent growth is used to gauge the economic progress of the area.

52145 ■ "The Lure of Bay State Technology" in *Boston Globe* (February 7, 2005)
Pub: New York Times Company
Ed: Robert Weisman. **Description:** Overseas investors are seeking acquisitions in Massachusetts, focusing on the state's high-technology and life sciences start-ups. Two deals are presented.

52146 ■ "Maine Office of Innovation Releases Plan for Research Development" in *Portland Press Herald* (November 4, 2005)
Pub: Blethen Maine Newspapers, Inc.
Ed: Matt Wickenheiser. **Description:** Maine's Office of Innovation is proposing a plan that would double the amount of money spent on research and development statewide. The plan proposes $1 billion in annual spending for 2010, with increases from both private and public organizations.

52147 ■ "The Malaria Fighter" in *Business 2.0* (Vol. 7, January/February 2006, No. 1, pp. 116-118, 120, 122, 124)
Pub: Time, Inc.
Ed: Michael Myser. **Description:** Profile of scientist, Stephen Hoffman, entrepreneur who's research is aimed at attacking global diseases.

52148 ■ "A Matter of Taste" in *Fast Company* (March 2005, No. 92, pp. 35)
Pub: Gruner & Jahr USA Publishing
Ed: Lucas Conley. **Description:** Senomyx Inc., a biotechnology firm in La Jolla, California, is developing chemical compounds known as flavor enhancers that could be used in commercial products. Research is being funded by such corporations as Nestle SA, Coca-Cola, Kraft, and Campbell Soup Company.

52149 ■ "Med Tech Carl Goldfischer" in *Venture Capital Journal* (January 1, 2005)
Pub: Thomason Financial Inc.
Description: According to Carl Goldfischer, managing director at Bay City Capital, the best thing that could happen to the medical device market in 2005 is that large and small companies continue creating new products that improve disease management.

52150 ■ "The Merry Go-Round" in *The Economist* (Vol. 377, October 1-7, 2005, No. 8446, pp. 60)
Pub: The Economist Newspaper Ltd.
Description: In the global drug industry, no regulation is more important than that of the U.S. Food and Drug Administration. The industry boasts $550 billion in annual sales.

52151 ■ "The microbe warrior. (Bioterrorism)" in *Red Herring* (January 2003, pp. 58)
Pub: Herring Communications Inc.
Ed: Suzanne McGee. **Description:** Profile AgION Technologies, the company developing products financed from the Homeland Security Fund. The firm's products show great promise in the areas of national security, intelligence, or military applications.

52152 ■ "Milwaukee, Wis., to Host Biotech Finance Gathering in 2007" in *Milwaukee Journal Sentinel* (December 14, 2005)
Pub: Journal Sentinel, Inc.
Ed: Kathleen Gallagher. **Description:** Venture capitalists representing more than $7 billion and biotechnology and medical device startups will meet in Milwaukee in September 2007 for the largest industry event in the Midwest. The BIO Med-America Venture-Forum expects 75 to 100 VCs to attend.

52153 ■ "Missing Part of the Equation" in *Hispanic Business* (July/August 2002, pp. 50, 52, 54)
Pub: Hispanic Business
Ed: Dora Elia, Gonzalez y Musielak. **Description:** Hispanic women continue to be underrepresented in the sciences and engineering fields. Statistical data included.

52154 ■ "MRI and the national defense" in *Ingram's* (Vol. 28, No. 6, June 2002, pp. 73)
Pub: Show Me Publishing, Inc.
Description: A review of the increased role in biological terrorism research given to the Midwest Research Institute is offered. The organization receives 75 percent of its funding from the national government, and has seen an increased need for biological terrorism research after the terrorist mailings of anthrax.

52155 ■ "MSU Enlists Biz Help On $1B Isotope Project Bid" in *Crain's Detroit Business* (Vol. 21, January 24, 2005, No. 4, pp. 1)
Pub: Crain Communications Inc. - Detroit
Ed: Sherri Begin. **Description:** Michigan State University is calling in help from the Michigan Business Group to bring the Rare Isotope Accelerator to its campus. The project is a $1 billion project of the U.S. Department of Energy.

52156 ■ "Nanotech Steve Jurvetson" in *Venture Capital Journal* (January 1, 2005)
Pub: Thomason Financial Inc.
Description: Steve Jurvetson's firm Draper Fisher Jurvetson, has invested in more than 20 nanotech, MEMS and novel materials startups. Jurvetson suggests the best thing to happen to the nanotechnology sector in 2005 would be major restructuring of immigration and education policy to prioritize science and engineering, the worst, more federal restrictions on immigration or freedom of scientific research like stem cell policy.

52157 ■ "Nanotechnology sector analysis" in *Red Herring* (March 2003, pp. 62)
Pub: Herring Communications Inc.
Description: An overview of the nanotechnology industry is presented, including information nano-based devices that can change electronics one atom at a time.

52158 ■ "NASA Logs on for Team Encounter in Space" in *Houston Business Journal* (Vol. 34, No. 18, September 12, 2003, pp. 1)
Pub: American City Business Journals
Ed: Jenna Colley. **Description:** Team Encounter LLC, Houston, Texas, a private space vehicles company, is preparing to send a spacecraft into orbit in 2005. Team Encounter has obtained a contract from NASA to send the Inertial Stellar Compass into orbit aboard its spacecraft.

52159 ■ "The New Way to Make Babies" in *Business 2.0* **(Vol. 7, January/February 2006, No. 1, pp. 22)**
Pub: Time, Inc.
Ed: Theodore Kinn. Description: Review of the book by a Harvard Business School professor. The book discusses the business of making babies.

52160 ■ "Next step: Bricks and mortar" in *Crain's Detroit Business* **(Vol. 19, No. 10, March 10, 2003, pp. 11)**
Pub: Crain Communications Inc., Detroit
Ed: Laura Bailey. Description: Howard Bell, the newly appointed head of Wayne State University's Research and Technology Park is working towards a 10-20 year project that will result in a mix of emerging companies with satellite offices of Wayne State's largest industry partners.

52161 ■ "NextEnergy gets $2M from feds" in *Crain's Detroit Business* **(Vol. 19, No. 10, March 10, 2003, pp. 29)**
Pub: Crain Communications Inc., Detroit
Ed: Laura Bailey. Description: The state of Michigan's alternative-fuel research center, NextEnergy, received $2 million from an appropriations bill signed by President George W. Bush.

52162 ■ "Northfield Hits Blood-Test Hurdle" in *Wall Street Journal* **(Vol. 248, December 2006, No. 145, pp. A10)**
Pub: Dow Jones & Co. Inc.
Ed: Thomas M Burton Description: Northfield Laboratories Inc., is expected to be first to market with a blood-substitute. Stock plummets after reports of numerous deaths hint to FDA approval setback.

52163 ■ "Northrop Grumman in Bethpage Celebrates National Engineers Week..." in *Long Island Business News* **(March 5, 2004)**
Pub: Dolan Media Newswires
Description: Northrop Grumman holds an annual paper airplane contest in Bethpage, as well as the company's three other sites in St. Augustine, Florida, Hollywood, Maryland, and Niceville, Florida. Categories include distance, accuracy, and longest flight time.

52164 ■ "Northrop Grumman in Bethpage Celebrates National Engineers Week with Paper Airplane Contest" in *Long Island Business News* **(Mar. 5, 04)**
Pub: Dolan Media Newswires
Description: Northrop Grumman holds an annual paper airplane contest in Bethpage, as well as the company's three other sites in St. Augustine, Florida, Hollywood, Maryland, and Niceville, Florida. Categories include distance, accuracy, and longest flight time.

52165 ■ "NY State Senator Introduces Bill to Obtain Federal Funding for Genetic Research" in *Long Island Business News* **(February 13, 2004)**
Pub: Dolan Media Newswires
Ed: Rosmaria Mancini. Description: A bill introduced by Senator Ken LaValle, R-New York, would create an 'institute' that would work to obtain federal grant money for genetics research at institutions throughout New York State.

52166 ■ "Opportunities emerge in a new age of miracle materials. (Nanotechnology)" in *Red Herring* **(March 2003, pp. 50)**
Pub: Herring Communications Inc.
Ed: Lee Bruno. Description: An overview of nanotechnology, the study of materials smaller than 100 nanometers, or approximately 1/100th the width of a human hair. Nanotechnology involves two main areas of research.

52167 ■ "OSI Pharmaceuticals Hopes to Get FDA Approval for Its Cancer Drug" in *Long Island Business News* **(February 13, 2004)**
Pub: Dolan Media Newswires
Ed: Ken Schachter. Description: OSI Pharmaceuticals Inc., a Long Island biotechnology firm, are awaiting FDA approval of its cancer drug, Tarceva. The drug is an Epidermal Growth Factor Receptor tyrosine kinase inhibitor.

52168 ■ "Pain Medicine May Keep Jobs in Ann Arbor, Pfizer CEO Says" in *Crain's Detroit Business* **(Vol. 22, February 13, 2006, No. 7, pp. 1)**
Pub: Crain Communications Inc. - Detroit
Ed: Andrew Dietderich. Description: The development of the drug Lyrica is responsible for saving some 14,000 jobs in Michigan, according to Hank McKinnell, Pfizer CEO and chairman. The new pain medication is expected to reach sales of $900 million in 2006.

52169 ■ "Pall Corp. Plans to Sell New Bacteria-Detection System to Blood Banks" in *Long Island Business News* **(February 20, 2004)**
Pub: Dolan Media Newswires
Description: The U.S. Food and Drug Administration (FDA) has approved Pall Corporation's system for detecting bacteria in blood platelets. The new system will cut testing time by about 20 percent, increasing the supply of blood available for transfusion.

52170 ■ "Patent expiration to hit MSU" in *Crain's Detroit Business* **(Vol. 19, No. 14, April 7, 2003, pp. 3)**
Pub: Crain Communications Inc., Detroit
Ed: Laura Bailey. Description: Michigan State University Foundation will lose $25 million annually when patents on two cancer drugs the university holds expire.

52171 ■ "Patient Capital: How Life Sciences Investments Touch Us All" in *Venture Capital Journal* **(December 1, 2004)**
Pub: Thomason Financial Inc.
Description: National Venture Capital Association's report explains the role venture capital plays in the expansion and enhancement of health and medical systems. The venture capital industry has invested almost $41 billion in more than 6,600 biotechnology and medical device companies in the last 20 years. Statistical data included.

52172 ■ "Peanut Growers to Ramp Up Research Work" in *Kiplinger Letter* **(Vol. 78, January 19, 2007, No. 2)**
Pub: Kiplinger
Description: Peanut Foundation will fund $9.5 million in USDA and industry for research to improve the flavor and nutrient content of peanuts, while boosting their oil content.

52173 ■ "A Perfect Brainstorm" in *Inc.* **(October 1, 2003)**
Pub: Gruner & Jahr USA Publishing
Ed: Alison Stein Wellner. Description: New scientific research suggests that brainstorming can help an entrepreneur attain business visions and goals.

52174 ■ "Personal Business" in *Business Week* **(December 19, 2005, No. 3964, pp. 95)**
Pub: McGraw-Hill Companies
Ed: Gene G. Marcial. Description: Profile of Expeditors International of Seattle, Washington, a freight forwarder and customs broker; licensing and patents for intellectual property; and biotech firm Sonus Pharaceuticals.

52175 ■ "Plan Would Share Wealth From $1B Fund" in *Crain's Detroit Business* **(Vol. 21, October 24, 2005, No. 43, pp. 26)**
Pub: Crain Communications Inc. - Detroit
Ed: Amy Lane. Description: Life-sciences, technology, tourism, manufacturing, agriculture, film-production, and defense companies will all benefit from $101 million in government funds to support growing or technology-oriented businesses.

52176 ■ "Portland Seeks Biotech Park to Stimulate New Business" in *Portland Press Herald* **(December 13, 2005)**
Pub: Blethen Maine Newspapers, Inc.
Ed: Kelley Bouchard. Description: Portland, Maine officials are proposing the development of a biotechnology park in order to compete for tenants seeking similar locations in the Boston, Massachusetts area.

52177 ■ "Positive defense for networks" in *Red Herring* **(January 2003, pp. 60)**
Pub: Herring Communications Inc.
Ed: Sarah Fallon. Description: An overview of intrusion detection systems is presented.

52178 ■ "The Power of Spin" in *The Economist* **(Vol. 377, October 1-7, 2005, No. 8446, pp. 76-77)**
Pub: The Economist Newspaper Ltd.
Description: Canadian engineer, Louis Michaud, has developed a way to create artificial whirlwinds like a tornado, these whirlwinds can be controlled and harnessed in order to generate power. Michaud calls his invention the 'atmospheric vortex engine'.

52179 ■ "Powering the imagination" in *Red Herring* **(No. 103, September 1, 2001, pp. 74)**
Pub: Herring Communications
Ed: Bridget Eklund. Description: Information explaining the way fuels cells produce electricity is presented using illustrations.

52180 ■ "Private Company Profiles" in *Red Herring* **(No. 103, September 1, 2001, pp. 80)**
Pub: Herring Communications
Ed: Stasia Bochnowski. Description: A cross section of five privately held companies in the energy market, including Metallic Power, NxtPhase, RealEnergy, Serveon, and USPowerSolutions.

52181 ■ "Public Company Profiles" in *Red Herring* **(No. 103, September 1, 2001, pp. 81)**
Pub: Herring Communications
Ed: Mark Chediak. Description: A cross section of four publicly held companies in the energy market, including Capstone Turbine, Catalytica Energy Systems, FuelCell Energy, and Vestas Wind Systems.

52182 ■ "QuatRx uses $10M in venture capital for psoriasis drug" in *Crain's Detroit Business* **(Vol. 19, No. 12, March 24, 2003, pp. 12)**
Pub: Crain Communications Inc., Detroit
Ed: Renee Saunders. Description: QuatRx, a biopharmaceutical company located in Ann Arbor, Michigan, hopes that the recent $10 million venture capital financing received will help find a cure for psoriasis and other ailments.

52183 ■ "R and D Spending Jumps as Firms Foresee Recovery" in *Atlanta Business Chronicle* **(Vol. 26, No. 10, August 15, 2003, pp. 1)**
Pub: American City Business Publications, Inc.
Ed: Mary Jane Credeur. Description: The first signs of economic recovery for the greater Atlanta, Georgia area are in the form of higher research and development spending by local technology firms.

52184 ■ "Renal Solutions" in *Pittsburgh Business Times* **(Vol. 22, No. 51, July 4, 2003, pp. 1)**
Pub: Pittsburgh Business Times
Ed: Patty Tascarella. Description: Renal Solutions Inc., led by CEO Peter DeComo, has received $2 million in venture capital funding. The firm raised nearly $16.7 million in first round venture capital funding.

52185 ■ "Renewed Biotech Interest Boosts BioCryst" in *Birmingham Business Journal* **(Vol. 20, No. 35, August 29, 2003, pp. 1)**
Pub: American City Business Journals, Inc.
Ed: Tom Bassing. Description: Difficult financial times facing BioCryst Pharmaceuticals Inc. are discussed, especially falling stock prices, cash flow problems, and financial management.

52186 ■ "Renowned Scientist's Research on Aging Delivers Anti-Aging Supplement; Juvenon Energy Formula" in *PR Newswire* **(January 13, 2003)**
Pub: PR Newswire Association, Inc.
Description: Profile of Dr. Bruce Ames, professor of molecular and cell biology and researcher, and Tory Hagen and their Juvenon Energy Formula. The Juvenon supplement consists of two mitochondrial-activating components that improve energy levels, reduce signs of aging in revitalized cells and increase burning of fat for energy.

52187 ■ *Research Centers Directory*
Pub: Thomson Gale
Released: Annual, latest edition 32nd, Published September, 2004; new edition expected 33rd, Sept. 2005. **Price:** $760, individuals base edition. **Covers:** About 13,600 university, government, and other nonprofit research organizations established on a permanent basis to carry on continuing research programs in all areas of study; includes research institutes, laboratories, experiment stations, research parks, technology transfer centers, and other facilities and activities; coverage includes Canada. **Entries Include:** Unit name, name of parent institution, address, phone, fax, name of director, e-mail addresses, urls, year founded, governance, staff, educational activities, public services, sources of support, annual volume of research, principal fields of research, publications, special library facilities, special research facilities. **Arrangement:** Classified by broad subjects, then alphabetical by unit name. **Indexes:** Alphabetical (includes centers, institutions, and keywords), subject, geographical, personal name.

52188 ■ "Research Funding New Uses for Eggs, Prune Juice" in *Kiplinger Letter* (Vol. 78, January 19, 2007, No. 2)
Pub: Kiplinger
Description: Researchers are placing genes that can produce therapeutic proteins into the genes of hens that create human interferon b-1a, an antiviral drug as well as an antibody that fights melanoma. The oxidants in prune juice are proving to retard oxidation of fatty acids in meat, thus keeping meat fresher for longer periods of time.

52189 ■ *Research Services Directory*
Pub: Grey House Publishing
Contact: Leslie MacKenzie, Publisher
E-mail: lmackenzie@greyhouse.com
Released: Annual, latest edition 9, 2003/04. **Price:** $495, individuals softcover. **Covers:** more than 8,000 commercial laboratories, consultants, firms, data collection and analysis centers, individuals, and facilities in the private sector that conduct contractual or proprietary research in all areas of business, government, humanities, social science, and science and technology. **Entries Include:** Firm name, address, phone, fax, toll-free number, e-mail name of chief executive, name and title of contact, date founded, staff size and composition, rates charged, annual revenues, professional memberships, parent and/or affiliate organizations, description of research services and principal clients, affiliates, patents, licenses, special equipment. **Arrangement:** Alphabetical. **Indexes:** Research firm name, geographical, personal name, subject.

52190 ■ "Researchers Test Bioterrorism Sensors in Greenwich Village and on Long Island" in *Long Island Business News* (March 5, 2004)
Pub: Dolan Media Newswires
Ed: Ken Schachter. **Description:** Researchers are testing bioterrorism sensors for the Long Island Partnership for Homeland Security. The project includes area defense contractors, technology companies and research institutions.

52191 ■ "Research's reward" in *Crain's Detroit Business* (Vol. 18, No. 51, Dec. 23, 2002, pp. 1)
Pub: Crain Communications Inc., Detroit
Ed: Laura Bailey. **Description:** Since starting their firm in 1991, James Downward and Judith Erb, have developed six patents and have 6 patents pending. Their company IA Inc, and its subsidiary Threefold Sensors, has developed the Endotect biosensor for widespread detection of compounds that mimic estrogen and appear to cause birth defects.

52192 ■ "Rising Drug Costs" in *Venture Capital Journal* (October 1, 2204)
Pub: Thomason Financial Inc.
Ed: Alastair Goldfisher. **Description:** With the rising costs of conducting clinical trials of new drugs, technology companies may choose offshore outsourcing of research and development to save money. However, the cost of new drug development is rising worldwide. Statistical data included.

52193 ■ "Running a Biotech Operation Here is Reasonably Cheap, Study Finds" in *Pittsburgh Business Times* (Vol. 23, No. 2, August 1, 2003)
Pub: Pittsburgh Business Times
Ed: Maria Guzzo. **Description:** Industry analysts report that the Pittsburgh, Pennsylvania region offers a wide range of benefits to biotechnology firms. A new report from Boyd Company has found that the region offers economic advantages for biomedical research firms.

52194 ■ "Safe and Secure" in *Business First Columbus* (Vol. 18, No. 26, February 15, 2002, pp. A21)
Pub: Business First Columbus, Inc.
Ed: Drew Bracken. **Description:** Columbus, Ohio scientist develops a method for password security by typing bar-code.

52195 ■ "Scanning For Dollars" in *Fortune* (Vol. 151, January 10, 2005, No. 1, pp. 60)
Pub: Time Inc.
Ed: Julie Schlosser. **Description:** New technology is being used by marketers to study consumer emotions and motivations. Functional magnetic resonance imaging (fMRI) detects the flow of blood to the brain's centers of pleasure, thought or memory. Researchers suggest that blood flow increases in areas of the prefrontal cortex when an individual likes what he or she is seeing.

52196 ■ "Sci-Finance" in *Entrepreneur* (Vol. 30, No. 2, February 2002)
Pub: Entrepreneur Media Inc.
Ed: Joshua Kurlantzick. **Description:** Because the National Science Foundation (NSF) has fallen behind the National Institutes of Health (NIH) in funding, there is less money to finance business innovations. The NIH focuses their research into biomedical sciences.

52197 ■ *Science et Technologie au Quebec*
Pub: Quebec Dans Le Monde
Released: Biennial, latest edition 6; 2006-2007 edition. **Price:** $49.95, individuals. **Covers:** over 1,250 scientific associations, periodicals, research and development facilities, and research centers in Quebec. **Entries Include:** Organization name, address, phone, fax, toll-free phone, description of services. **Arrangement:** Alphabetical. **Indexes:** Subject.

52198 ■ "Scientific Industries Acquires New Assets from Spectrum Labs" in *Long Island Business News* (March 12, 2004)
Pub: Dolan Media Newswires
Description: Scientific Industries Inc. is set to acquire certain assets from Spectrum Laboratories Inc. for nearly $300,000. The chromatography and peristaltic pump-systems products and related items would increase Scientific Industries' current laboratory equipment product line.

52199 ■ "SciTech Developments to Watch" in *Business Week* (January 16, 2006, No. 3967, pp. 87)
Pub: McGraw-Hill Companies
Description: Scientific and technological developments discussed include a pain-free alternative to pricking fingers for blood sugar readings for diabetics through the use of infrared light bounced off the white of an individual's eye; carbon nanotubes for electronic components; and information about tree farms.

52200 ■ "A Sea Change for Artificial Bones" in *Business Week* (February 20, 2006, No. 3972, pp. 65)
Pub: McGraw-Hill Companies
Ed: Helena Oh. **Description:** Researchers at the U.S. Energy Department's Lawrence Berkeley National Laboratory are working on the development of artificial bones from oysters, abalone, and other hard-shelled ocean dwellers.

52201 ■ "Seeing Face Value: Cosmetic Medical Spa Captures Ethnic Skin Care Market" in *Black Enterprise* (Vol. 35, February 2005, No. 7, pp. 51)
Pub: Earl G. Graves Publishing Co. Inc.

Ed: Bridget McCrea. **Description:** When owners opened their cosmetic medical spa, they chose to avoid advertising for reputation, media exposure and physician referrals to grow their business. Drs. Eliot F. Battle and Monte O. Harris, noted academic physicians and researchers, have developed a customized approach to ethnic skin care.

52202 ■ "Series A, For Arthritis: Proprius Pharmaceuticals Inc." in *San Diego Business Journal* (Vol. 28, January 15, 2007, No. 3, pp. 38)
Pub: San Diego Business Journal Associates
Ed: Brad Graves. **Description:** Atlas Venture of Waltham, Massachusetts and Forward Ventures of San Diego provided venture capital to Proprius Pharmaceuticals Inc. in order to develop a drug to treat osteoarthritis. Series A funding equaled $11 million and may grow to $17 million.

52203 ■ "Shake 'Em Up" in *Forbes* (Vol. 175, February 14, 2005, No. 3, pp. 58)
Pub: Forbes Magazine Inc.
Ed: Andy Stone. **Description:** Profile of Kevin Goodwin, founder of SonoSite and creator of a handheld ultrasound device, a laptop-size machine that scans patients immediately.

52204 ■ "Slick Trick" in *Tampa Tribune* (December 2, 2005)
Pub: Media General, Inc.
Ed: Angela Delgado. **Description:** Profile of Lee Briante, of Greasecar Vegetable Fuel Systems located in Massachusetts. The company has converted nearly 2,000 automobiles in the U.S. with engines running on vegetable oil.

52205 ■ "Software Tops List of Industries Projected to Grow" in *Hispanic Business* (March 2003, pp. 59)
Pub: Hispanic Business
Description: Software, healthcare, and nanotechnology are predicted to be the fastest growing business opportunities for entrepreneurs, according to the U.S. Department of Labor. Statistical data included.

52206 ■ "Solar Cells: The New Light Fantastic" in *Business Week Online* (January 31, 2005)
Pub: McGraw-Hill Companies
Ed: Olga Kharif. **Description:** Solar cell prices have fallen 5 to 6 percent a year, but that trend is expected to change since they will be manufactured through complex processes similar to those used for making computer processors and memory cards.

52207 ■ "Space and Technology" in *The Economist* (Vol. 376, July 16-22, 2005, No. 8435, pp. 75-76)
Pub: The Economist Newspaper Ltd.
Description: NASA's new administrator, Dr. Mike Griffin, wants to capitalize on existing technical and workforce assets as a cost-effective and efficient means for building a new space vehicle; good news for Texas and Florida where many workers live.

52208 ■ "Spy tech" in *Crain's Detroit Business* (Vol. 19, No. 11, March 17, 2003, pp. 11)
Pub: Crain Communications Inc., Detroit
Ed: Jennette Smith. **Description:** Ann Arbor-based research and development firm, Veridian, is a specialist in national security work. The firm reported 2002 revenue of nearly $79 million, and has increased sales by 10 percent a year for the past few years.

52209 ■ "Stand by NASA research" in *Red Herring* (March 2003, pp. 17)
Pub: Herring Communications Inc.
Description: NASA research and development has resulted in growth in technology sectors such as communications, energy and the robotics industry.

52210 ■ "State to seek VC to ease biotech cuts" in *Crain's Detroit Business* (Vol. 19, No. 8, February 24, 2003, pp. 1)
Pub: Crain Communications Inc., Detroit

Ed: Amy Lane. **Description:** Governor Jennifer Granholm, in an attempt to cut the state's budget, has cut $12.5 million from Michigan life sciences funding and is seeking venture capitalists to pick up the slack.

52211 ■ "Studying Molecules to Build a Better Grape" in *Business Week* **(February 20, 2006, No. 3972, pp. 65)**
Pub: McGraw-Hill Companies
Description: Canadian researchers at the University of British Columbia in Vancouver are studying molecules in order to make finer wines.

52212 ■ "SV Life Sciences Sets Sights on Fourth Fund" in *Venture Capital Journal* **(October 1, 2005)**
Pub: Thomason Financial Inc.
Description: SV Life Sciences, of Boston, Massachusetts, is looking to raise $400 million for its fourth round of venture funding; it already has 27 portfolio companies.

52213 ■ "Take It For Granted" in *Entrepreneur* **(Vol. 33, January 2005, No. 1, pp. 50)**
Pub: Entrepreneur Media Inc.
Ed: David Worrell. **Description:** U.S. Small Business Innovative Research grants and contracts provide funding for small companies to develop high tech products. The programs are divided into two phases: one is to study the feasibility of a new technology or idea, the second to encourage commercialization of a particular technology.

52214 ■ "Tech Detective: Lasers at PARC" in *Venture Capital Journal* **(Vol. 42, No. 10, October 2002, pp. 31-32)**
Pub: Thomas Venture Economics
Ed: Michael V. Copeland. **Description:** Profile of PARC laboratory located at the Palo Alto Research Center in California. PARC is an expert in laser technology.

52215 ■ *Technological Entrepreneurship*
Pub: Edward Elgar Publishing, Incorporated
Ed: Donald Siegel. **Released:** October 2006. **Price:** $230.00. **Description:** Technological entrepreneurship at universities is discussed. The book covers four related topics: university licensing and patenting; science parks and incubators; university-based startups; and the role of academic science in entrepreneurship.

52216 ■ "Technology is Biggest Export" in *Hispanic Business* **(November 2002, pp. 25-26, 30)**
Pub: Hispanic Business
Ed: Jonathan J. Higuera. **Description:** Predications are made concerning future exports; the list of winners included information technology, auto parts, medical devices, services, processed foods, and chemicals. Statistical data includes largest U.S. export products, top purchasers of U.S. exports. Government Web sites providing foreign market research to small companies are listed.

52217 ■ "Tenet Healthcare Ends Fight over Heart Program at Stuart, Fla. Medical Center" in *Palm Beach Post* **(April 11, 2003)**
Pub: Knight-Ridder/Tribune Business News
Ed: Phil Galewitz. **Description:** Tenet Healthcare Corporation has dropped its long-standing opposition to a new open-heart surgery program at Martin Memorial Medical Center, located in Stuart, Florida. There are four hospitals in the area now performing open-heart surgery and are among the most profitable hospitals in the region.

52218 ■ "Think Tech; Automation Alley" in *Crain's Detroit Business* **(Vol. 21, October 3, 2005, No. 43, pp. 1)**
Pub: Crain Communications Inc. - Detroit
Ed: Andrew Dietderich, Sheena Harrison. **Description:** Two technology companies are working to keep and attract technology companies and jobs to Southeastern Michigan. The state lost 17,600 tech jobs between 2002 and 2003. Automation Alley of Troy and Sparks of Ann Arbor hope to double the number of tech companies and triple the number of tech workers by 2010.

52219 ■ "This little drug went to the market" in *Ingram's* **(Vol. 28, No. 6, June 2002, pp. 27)**
Pub: Show Me Publishing, Inc.
Description: Information regarding the funding activity of VasoGenix Pharmaceuticals and the ongoing development of their calitonin gene-related peptide is presented. The company is seeking $5 million in second-round venture capital funding to develop the peptide which has three possible uses, one of which increases blood flow stimulation in balloon angioplasties to decrease strokes and heart attacks.

52220 ■ "The true believer" in *Red Herring* **(March 2003, pp. 56)**
Pub: Herring Communications Inc.
Ed: Lee Bruno. **Description:** Scientific developments that are transforming nanotechnology from science fiction to reality are explored, including challenges facing the nanotechnology industry and the talents and skills needed for newcomers to the industry.

52221 ■ "U.S. Needs Help from the Private Sector to Combat Terrorism" in *Venture Capital Journal* **(Vol. 42, No. 9, September 2002, pp. 40)**
Pub: Thomas Venture Economics
Ed: Leighton Read. **Description:** The private sector will play a major role in homeland security by developing and producing antiterrorism countermeasures.

52222 ■ *U.S. Source Book of R & D Spenders*
Pub: Schonfeld & Associates Inc.
Contact: Carol Greenhut
Released: Annual. **Price:** $395, individuals book; $495, individuals book and disk. **Covers:** 5,700 public companies in the U.S. That spend money on research and development. **Entries Include:** Company name, address, phone, names and titles of key personnel, financial data, research and development budgets, fiscal year close, Standard Industrial Classification (SIC) code. **Arrangement:** Geographical by state, then classified by ZIP code. **Indexes:** Company name.

52223 ■ "USDA Plans to Charge Farm Commodity Groups a Fee for Research" in *Kiplinger Letter* **(Vol. 78, January 5, 2007, No. 1)**
Pub: Kiplinger
Description: Farm commodity groups can expect to pay fees for research. The Agricultural Department's research services already charges 10 percent for companies and other agencies while farm commodity groups and other nonprofits were exempt.

52224 ■ "VCs raid biotechs, nab talent" in *San Francisco Business Times* **(Vol. 16, No. 42, May 24, 2002, pp. 1)**
Pub: San Francisco Business Times Inc.
Ed: Brendan Doherty. **Description:** Venture capital companies are hiring scientists and other experts from the biotechnology industry, making it harder for research firms to get good talent.

52225 ■ "VCs See Bottom, Expect To Do More Deals" in *Venture Capital Journal* **(July 1, 2003)**
Pub: Thomson Financial Inc.
Description: According to a survey conducted by Venture Capital Journal, VCs are feeling more optimistic, yet cautious, about the industry and are predicting a slow recovery. More startups are experiencing funding, particularly seed- and early-stage rounds, focusing both by industry and region. Life sciences and nanotechnology are receiving the most interest.

52226 ■ "Voices of Innovation" in *Business Week* **(January 23, 2006, No. 3968, pp. 20)**
Pub: McGraw-Hill Companies
Ed: Jay Greene. **Description:** Rick Rashid, Microsoft Corporation's senior vice president, pushes his 700 research and development scientists to go after big challenges.

52227 ■ "Waiting in the Wings" in *Entrepreneur* **(Vol. 32, No. 1, January 2004, pp. 21)**
Pub: Entrepreneur Media, Inc.
Ed: David Worrell. **Description:** Market experts are predicting a rise in the number of Initial Public Offerings (IPOs) in 2004, although there is still strength in biotech and pharmaceutical companies, other sectors such as real estate, business services, healthcare and manufacturing are growing.

52228 ■ "Whose drug is it, anyway?" in *Washington Business Journal* **(Vol. 21, No. 44, Feb. 28, 2003, pp. 2,6)**
Pub: Washington Business Journal
Ed: Jennifer Taylor. **Description:** Alleged legal loopholes abound keeping generic drug companies from getting their products to market faster. President Bush has proposed new rules that might fix one of those loopholes. Large companies with costly employee benefit plans are getting involved also. Drug companies with blockbuster drugs try to keep patents in effect as long as possible, claiming that research and development costs are astronomical.

52229 ■ "Why the Old Rules Don't Apply" in *Business Week* **(February 14, 2005, No. 3920, pp. 68)**
Pub: McGraw-Hill Companies
Ed: Stephen Baker, Adam Aston. **Description:** An overview of nanotechnology. Venture capital firm Draper Fisher Jurvetson has invested $95 million in eleven nanotechnology startup companies.

52230 ■ "Wisconsin Biotech Aims to Create Artificial Heart Tissue" in *Milwaukee Journal Sentinel* **(December 8, 2005)**
Pub: Journal Sentinel, Inc.
Ed: Kathleen Gallagher. **Description:** InvivoSciences LLC plans to make artificial heart tissue. The firm has chosen Wisconsin for its location because of the Medical College of Wisconsin's support for entrepreneurs along with several state programs that support young companies.

52231 ■ "York, Pa.-Based Company Plans to Build Ethanol Plant in Northeast" in *Patriot-News* **(April 11, 2003)**
Pub: Knight-Ridder/Tribune Business News
Ed: Mary Klaus. **Description:** Penn-Mar Ethanol LLC plans to build the first ethanol plant in the Northeast and use corn to make ethanol for fuel, dry distillers grain for cattle and carbon dioxide for soft drinks.

TRADE PERIODICALS

52232 ■ *Advanced Manufacturing Technology*
Pub: Technical Insights/M John Wiley & Sons Inc.
Ed: Leo O'Connor, Editor. **Released:** Monthly. **Price:** $660, U.S. and Canada; $720, elsewhere. **Description:** Reports on technological advances that are contributing to robotics, computer graphics, flexible automation, computer-integrated manufacturing, and new techniques for machining. Covers techniques for cutting costs, improving product quality, and increasing productivity. Includes supplements titled Test and Measurement Alert and Assembly Technologies.

52233 ■ *Advanced Materials & Composites News*
Pub: Composites Worldwide Inc.
Contact: Susan Loud, Managing Editor
Ed: Steve Loud, Editor, steve@compositesnews.com. **Released:** 23/year. **Price:** $598, U.S. and Canada; $628, elsewhere. **Description:** Reviews recent developments in composites, ceramics, high-performance plastics, adhesives, metals, and coatings. Concentrates on materials specifically designed for demanding conditions. Informs readers of pertinent international news on composites in the broad infrastructure and building fields and primary structural systems, including highways, roads, ports, harbors, bridges, buildings, and other construction. Also covers

transportation, marine, offshore oil/gas, industrial, sports and other market sectors and applications. Recurring features include news of research and product development and technology, reports of meetings, book reviews, notices of publications available, and patent reviews. **Remarks:** E-mail supplement available titled Composites eNews.

52234 ■ *AICHE Journal*
Pub: American Institute of Chemical Engineers
Contact: Haeja Han, Publisher & Executive Editor
E-mail: haejh@aiche.org
Ed: Stanley Sandler, Editor, sandler@che.udel.edu. **Released:** Monthly. **Price:** $145 members in North America; $270 members International; $1,250 nonmembers in North America; $1,472 nonmembers International; $195 members online only; $245 members with online; North America; $395 members with online; International. **Description:** Magazine on chemical engineering research.

52235 ■ *Alloy Digest*
Pub: ASM International
Ed: Dennis Rahoi, Editor, drahoi@charterMI.net. **Released:** Bimonthly. **Price:** $557 nonmembers; $307 members. **Description:** Engineering research journal.

52236 ■ *The Anatomical Record*
Pub: John Wiley & Sons Inc.
Contact: David H. Bernanke, Managing Editor
E-mail: dbernanke@anatomy.umsmed.edu
Ed: Roger R. Markwald, Ph.D., Editor, markwald@musc.edu. **Released:** 18 issues. **Price:** $5,295 institutions print; $5,475 institutions, Canada and Mexico print, in Canada add 7% GST; $5,628 institutions, other countries print; $5,825 institutions print & online; $6,005 institutions, Canada and Mexico print & online, in Canada add 7% GST; $6,158 institutions, other countries print & online. **Description:** Research journal.

52237 ■ *Applied Engineering in Agriculture*
Pub: American Society of Agricultural Engineers
Released: Bimonthly. **Price:** $65 members; $127 nonmembers plus foreign postage. **Description:** Peer-reviewed journal focused on practical applications of current research related to engineering for agricultural, food and biological systems.

52238 ■ *Artificial Cells, Blood Substitutes and Immobilization Biotechnology*
Pub: Marcel Dekker Inc.
Contact: Thomas M.S. Chang PhD, Editor-in-Chief
Released: Bimonthly, 6/yr. **Price:** $500 print and online; $1,868 institutions print version. **Description:** Research journal integrating biotechnology, polymer chemistry, and engineering and also covers research on molecules, cells, and artificial cells.

52239 ■ *Biochemistry and Cell Biology (Biochimie et Biologie Cellulaire)*
Pub: National Research Council Canada, NRC Research Press
Contact: Bruce P. Dancik, Editor-in-Chief
Ed: James R. Davie, PhD, Editor, davie@cc.umanitoba.ca. **Released:** Bimonthly. **Price:** $171; $520 institutions. **Description:** Scholarly journal on biochemistry research (English and French).

52240 ■ *Biomedical Products*
Pub: Reed Business Information
Contact: Don Ransdell, VP, Publishing Dir.
E-mail: dransdell@reedbusiness.com
Released: Monthly. **Description:** Journal covering life science research and biotechnology products.

52241 ■ *Biopolymers*
Pub: John Wiley & Sons Inc.
Contact: Dora Castiblanco, Advertising Mgr
Ed: Alexander Steinbuchel, Editor. **Released:** 24/year. **Price:** $835 U.S. print; $835 Canada and Mexico print, in Canada add 7% GST; $1,015 other countries print; $6,995 institutions print, U.S.; $7,235 institutions, Canada and Mexico print, in Canada add 7% GST; $7,439 institutions, other countries print;

$7,695 institutions print & online, U.S.; $7,935 institutions, Canada and Mexico print & online, in Canada add 7% GST; $8,139 institutions, other countries print & online. **Description:** Journal containing original research papers on the structure, properties, interactions and assemblies of biomolecules. Deals with organic and physical chemistry; experimental and theoretical research. Subjects include broad aspects of biospectroscopy. Also covers static and dynamic aspects of structure.

52242 ■ *BioTechniques*
Pub: Eaton Publishing
Contact: Mary McCarthy PhD, Editor-in-Chief
E-mail: mccarthy@biotechniques.com
Released: Monthly. **Description:** Research journal.

52243 ■ *Biotechnology Advances*
Pub: Elsevier Science B.V.
Contact: M. Moo-Young, Exec. Ed.
Ed: E.A. Bayer, Editor. **Released:** 8/yr. **Price:** $1,595 institutions except Europe and Japan; $1,427 institutions European countries; $189,300 institutions Japan. **Description:** Journal covering research, reviews and patent abstracts on biotechnology.

52244 ■ *Biotechnology & Bioengineering*
Pub: John Wiley & Sons Inc.
Contact: Elmer L. Gaden Jr., Founding Editor
Ed: Douglas C. Clark, Editor, clark@cchem.berkeley.edu. **Released:** 28/year. **Price:** $695; $695 Canada and Mexico In Canada, add 7% GST; $863 other countries; $4,995 institutions; $5,275 institutions, Canada and Mexico In Canada, add 7% GST; $5,513 institutions, other countries. **Description:** Journal providing an international forum for original research on all aspects of biochemical and microbial technology, including products, process development and design, and equipment.

52245 ■ *Brain, Behavior, and Immunity*
Pub: Elsevier Science B.V.
Ed: K.W. Kelley, Editor. **Released:** Bimonthly, 6/yr. **Price:** $774 institutions for all countries except Europe and Japan; $336 for all countries except Europe and Japan; $136 students for all countries except Europe and Japan. **Description:** Journal publishing research data on the interactions between the nervous system and the immune system at the molecular, cellular, and organismic levels.

52246 ■ *Canadian Journal of Chemistry (Revue Canadienne de Chimie)*
Pub: National Research Council Canada, NRC Research Press
Released: Monthly. **Price:** $1,099 institutions print only; $345 print ed. **Description:** Journal on research in chemistry (English and French).

52247 ■ *Cell Motility and the Cytoskeleton*
Pub: John Wiley & Sons Inc.
Contact: B.R. Brinkley, Editor-in-Chief
E-mail: brinkley@bcm.tmc.edu
Released: 12/year. **Price:** $475 print, U.S.; $475 Canada and Mexico print, in Canada add 7% GST; $547 other countries print; $3,995 institutions print, U.S.; $4,115 institutions, Canada and Mexico print, in Canada add 7% GST; $4,217 institutions, other countries print; $4,395 institutions print & online, U.S.; $4,515 institutions, Canada and Mexico print & online, in Canada add 7% GST; $4,617 institutions, other countries print & online. **Description:** Science research journal.

52248 ■ *Cellular Immunology*
Pub: Elsevier Science B.V.
Contact: E.M. Shevach, Editor-in-Chief
Ed: J. Braun, Editor. **Released:** 12/year. **Price:** $517,200 institutions Japan; $4,951 institutions European countries; $3,858 institutions for all countries except Europe and Japan. **Description:** International journal publishing original investigations of the immunological activities of cells in experimental or clinical situations.

52249 ■ *Cereal Chemistry*
Pub: American Association of Cereal Chemists

Contact: Steven C. Nelson, Publisher
E-mail: snelson@scisoc.org
Released: Bimonthly, 6/year. **Price:** $79 single issue; $89 single issue other countries; $450 U.S.; $480 other countries. **Description:** Journal focusing on cereal chemistry and research on raw materials, processes and products in the cereals area.

52250 ■ *Chemical Engineering Research and Design (ChERD)*
Pub: Taylor & Francis
Contact: Prof. John Garside, Honorary Ed.
E-mail: john.garside@umist.ac.uk
Released: Monthly, 12/yr. **Price:** $721 nonmembers print; $847.18 nonmembers online; $862.39 nonmembers print and online; $887.40 nonmembers other countries for print and online combined; $742 nonmembers other countries for print only; $847.18 nonmembers other countries for online only. **Description:** Journal publishing papers on all aspects of experimental work, development and theory in chemical engineering.

52251 ■ *Chemical Monographs Review*
Pub: The Chemists' Club Library
Ed: Mildred Hunt, Editor. **Released:** Quarterly. **Description:** Publishes current chemical and related technical and scientific book reviews, along with publisher source, page count, ISBN, and price. Recurring features include book reviews.

52252 ■ *Chemical and Petroleum Engineering*
Pub: Kluwer Academic/Plenum Publishing Corp.
Contact: John Hwang, Translations Editor
Ed: B.V. Gusev, Editor. **Released:** 12/year. **Price:** $3,096 institutions print or online. **Description:** Research journal. A translation of Khimicheskoe: Neftyanoe Mashinostroenie.

52253 ■ *Clinical Immunology*
Pub: Elsevier Science B.V.
Contact: A. Saxon, Editor-in-Chief
E-mail: ASAxon@mednet.ucla.edu
Released: 12/year. **Price:** $291,800 institutions Japan; $2,207 institutions for all countries except Europe and Japan; $2,655 institutions European countries. **Description:** Journal publishing original research, in the molecular and cellular bases of immunological disease.

52254 ■ *Communication Outlook*
Pub: Artificial Language Laboratory
Released: Quarterly. **Price:** $18 North and South America; $24 other countries; $5 single copy. **Description:** Magazine reporting on the newest developments in the application of technology for neurologically impaired persons.

52255 ■ *Corrosion*
Pub: NACE International
Contact: Angela Jarrell, Managing Editor
E-mail: angela.jarrell@mail.nace.org
Released: Monthly. **Price:** $170 nonmembers print & online access; $220 nonmembers print & online access; international; $320 libraries print & online access; $340 libraries print & online access; international; $95 members print & online access; $85 members online access; $150 nonmembers online access; $280 libraries online access. **Description:** Journal on corrosion science and engineering research.

52256 ■ *Diesel & Gas Turbine Worldwide*
Pub: Diesel & Gas Turbine Publications
Contact: Mark McNeely, Editor & Publisher
E-mail: mmcneely@dieselpub.com
Released: Monthly, (Jan./Feb., July/Aug. issues combined). **Price:** $65; Free to qualified subscribers. **Description:** International magazine covering the design, application, and operation of diesel, natural gas, and gas turbine engine systems.

52257 ■ *DISCOVERY*
Pub: Office of Research and Creative Activity
Ed: Annette Trinity-Stevens, Editor, annettet@montana.edu. **Released:** Monthly, during the academic year. **Price:** Free. **Description:** Features news of University research in agriculture, engineering, life sciences, and the humanities.

52258 ■ DNA and Cell Biology
Pub: Mary Ann Liebert Incorporated Publishers
Contact: Mark I. Greene M.D., Editor-in-Chief
Released: Monthly. **Price:** $459 online ed.; $483 print ed.; $568 print and online eds.; $747 other countries print ed.; $840 other countries print and online eds.; $1,690 institutions online ed.; $1,771 institutions print ed.; $2,115 institutions print and online eds.; $1,945 institutions, other countries print ed.; $2,287 institutions, other countries print and online eds. **Description:** Medical journal providing research findings in cell biology.

52259 ■ Earth and Mineral Sciences
Pub: Pennsylvania State University
Contact: Colleen Swetland, Editorial Assistant
E-mail: swetland@ems.psu.edu
Ed: June Heywood, Editor, heywood@ems.psu.edu. **Released:** 2/year. **Description:** Magazine covering research on mineral engineering, earth sciences, and materials science and engineering.

52260 ■ Electric Machines Components and Systems
Pub: Taylor & Francis
Ed: S.A. Nasar, Editor, snasar@engr.uky.edu. **Released:** Monthly. **Price:** $1,746 institutions; $773. **Description:** Journal publishing original theoretical and applied research in electromechanics, electric machines, and power systems.

52261 ■ Electrical Engineering in Japan
Pub: John Wiley & Sons Inc.
Ed: Koki Matsuse, Editor. **Released:** 16/yr. **Price:** $7,550 institutions print, U.S.; $7,742 institutions, Canada and Mexico print, in Canada add 7% GST; $7,854 institutions, other countries print; $8,305 institutions online and print, U.S.; $8,497 institutions, Canada and Mexico online and print, in Canada add 7% GST; $8,609 institutions, other countries online and print. **Description:** Journal publishing original research results in power generation, transmission and conversion, electrical machinery, and related subjects. Translated from Japanese.

52262 ■ Engineering Design and Automation
Pub: John Wiley & Sons Inc.
Released: Quarterly. **Description:** Journal of new research on the design and analysis of production systems, artificial intelligence, and neural networks.

52263 ■ Environmental Toxicology and Chemistry
Pub: Society of Environmental Toxicology & Chemistry
Contact: Dr. C.H. Ward, Editor-in-Chief
Released: Monthly. **Description:** Official journal of the Society of Environmental Toxicology and Chemistry; contains research in environmental chemistry and toxicology and hazard/risk assessment.

52264 ■ Experimental Heat Transfer
Pub: Taylor & Francis
Contact: Prof. Dimos Poulikakos, Editor-in-Chief
E-mail: dimos.poulikakos@ethz.ch
Released: Quarterly. **Price:** $271; $568 institutions. **Description:** Forum for original research on heat and mass transfer and in related fluid flows.

52265 ■ Gear Technology
Pub: Randall Publishing Inc.
Contact: Michael Goldstein, Pres., Publisher, Ed.-in-Ch.
Released: Bimonthly. **Description:** Magazine featuring design, testing, processing, and new technology for gears and gear manufacturing products, and equipment.

52266 ■ Geomicrobiology Journal
Pub: Taylor & Francis
Ed: Henry Ehrlich, Editor, ehrlich@rpi.edu. **Released:** 8/year. **Price:** $316; $1,022 institutions. **Description:** Journal publishing research and review articles on microbial transformations of materials that comprise the earth's crust.

52267 ■ Human Mutation
Pub: John Wiley & Sons Inc.
Contact: Dr. Mark H. Paalman Jr., Managing Editor
E-mail: humu@wiley.com
Ed: Dr. Haig H. Kazazian, Jr., Editor. **Released:** Monthly, 12/yr. **Price:** $1,185 institutions print, U.S.; $1,329 institutions, Canada and Mexico print, in Canada add 7% GST; $1,413 institutions, other countries print; $1,304 institutions print and online, U.S.; $1,448 institutions, Canada and Mexico print and online, in Canada add 7% GST; $1,532 institutions, other countries print and online. **Description:** Journal containing information about mutation research and genetic disorders.

52268 ■ IBM Journal of Research and Development
Pub: IBM Corp.
Contact: John J. Ritsko Jr., Editor-in-Chief
E-mail: ritsko@us.ibm.com
Released: Bimonthly. **Price:** $299 North America; $316 other countries. **Description:** Technical journal focusing on professional scientific research and engineering developments.

52269 ■ IEEE Computational Science and Engineering
Pub: Institute of Electrical and Electronics Engineers Inc.
Contact: Norman Chonacky, Editor-in-Chief
E-mail: norman.chonacky@yale.edu
Released: Bimonthly. **Description:** Journal providing information or developments in computational biology, chemistry, and physics.

52270 ■ Inside R&D
Pub: Technical Insights/M John Wiley & Sons Inc.
Ed: Charles Joslin, Editor. **Released:** Weekly. **Description:** Describes research and development breakthroughs in industry, government, and academic labs, with an emphasis on technology transfer. Emphasizes how the results of the research covered can be applied practically by industry. Recurring features include news of research and columns titled Managing Innovation, Trends, and Forecasts and Analyses.

52271 ■ International Journal of Adaptive Control and Signal Processing
Pub: John Wiley & Sons Inc.
Contact: Mike J. Grimble, Managing Editor
Released: Monthly, 10/yr. **Price:** $1,505 print, other countries; $2,005 institutions, other countries combined print with online, in Canada add 7% GST; $2,206 institutions, other countries combined print with online, in Canada add 7% GST. **Description:** Journal covering research in industrial control systems. Also features numerical aspects of algorithms and expert systems.

52272 ■ International Journal on Artificial Intelligence Tools
Pub: World Scientific Publishing Company Inc.
Contact: Dr. J.J.P. Tsai, Editor-in-Chief
E-mail: bourbaki@binghanton.edu
Ed: Dr. Nikolaos G. Bourbakis, Editor. **Released:** Bimonthly, 6/yr. **Price:** $564 institutions print & electronic; U.S.; $536 institutions electronic only; U.S.; $205 print only; U.S.; $355 institutions, other countries print & electronic, for developing countries; $337 institutions, other countries electronic only, for developing countries. **Description:** Journal covering design, development, and testing of AI tools.

52273 ■ International Journal of Computer Integrated Manufacturing
Pub: Taylor & Francis
Contact: Prof. Stephen Newman, Editor-in-Chief
Released: 8/yr. **Price:** $1,681 institutions online only; $1,017 institutions online only; $1,769 institutions print & online; $1,071 institutions print & online; $886 print only; $535 print only. **Description:** Journal containing information of new knowledge, research and applications used in specific manufacturing situations.

52274 ■ International Journal of Computer Simulation
Pub: University of Wisconsin-Eau Claire

Contact: George W. Zobrist, Editor-in-Chief
Released: Quarterly. **Description:** Journal covering research and development, product development, and tutorials in computer simulation.

52275 ■ International Journal of Energy Research
Pub: John Wiley & Sons Inc.
Ed: Prof. J.T. McMullan, Editor. **Released:** Monthly, 15/yr. **Price:** $3,440 print only; $4,585 institutions, other countries print only; $5,044 institutions, other countries combined print with online. **Description:** Journal providing information on energy research and development.

52276 ■ International Journal of Expert Systems
Pub: University of California Press
Ed: Mehdi Harandi, Editor. **Released:** Quarterly. **Description:** Computer Science Journal.

52277 ■ International Journal of Hyperthermia
Pub: Taylor & Francis
Contact: Nancy J. Dewhirst, Managing Editor
E-mail: nancy@radonc.duke.edu
Ed: Y. Tanaka, Editor, ijh-ju@mail.taisuitsu.or.jp. **Released:** 8/yr. **Price:** $1,923 institutions print & online; $1,827 institutions print & online; $1,163 institutions print & online; $1,105 institutions print & online. **Description:** Journal containing information on research and clinical papers on hyperthermia.

52278 ■ International Journal of Intelligent Systems
Pub: John Wiley & Sons Inc.
Ed: Ronald R. Yager, Editor. **Released:** Monthly, 12/yr. **Price:** $190 print only; $190 Canada and Mexico in Canada, add 7% GST; $262 other countries print only; $2,299 institutions print only; $2,419 institutions, Canada and Mexico in Canada, add 7% GST; $2,521 institutions, other countries print only; $2,529 institutions combined print with online access rates; $2,649 institutions, Canada and Mexico add 7% GSTt in Canada; $2,751 institutions, other countries combined print with online access rates. **Description:** Journal featuring peer-reviewed work on the systematic development of theory used in the construction of intelligent systems. Covers areas such as man-computer interactions and the use of language, neural networks, and machine learning; includes book reviews.

52279 ■ Journal of the American Oil Chemists' Society
Pub: AOCS Press
Contact: John P. Cherry
Released: Monthly. **Description:** Technical journal devoted to fundamental and practical research in the field of fats, oils, oleochemicals, proteins, surfactants, and detergents.

52280 ■ Journal of Andrology
Pub: American Society of Andrology
Contact: Peter Schlegel, Co-Ed.-in-Ch.
Released: Bimonthly. **Description:** Journal covering clinical and laboratory research in the structure and function of the male reproductive system and male gametes.

52281 ■ Journal of Biochemical and Molecular Toxicology
Pub: John Wiley & Sons Inc.
Ed: Ernest Hodgson, PhD, Editor, ernest_hodgson@ncsu.edu. **Released:** Bimonthly, 6/yr. **Price:** $140; $140 Canada and Mexico in canada, add 7% gst; $176 other countries. **Description:** Journal featuring reseach papers, rapid communications, and mini-reviews focusing on the molecular mechanisms of action and detoxication of exogenous and endogenous chemical toxic agents. The scope includes effects on organisms at all stages of development.

52282 ■ Journal of Bioenergetics and Biomembranes
Pub: Kluwer Academic/Plenum Publishing Corp.
Contact: Dr. Peter L. Pederson, Editor-in-Chief

Released: 6/year. Price: $142 print or online; $728 institutions print or online; $142 print or online; $727 institutions, other countries print or online. Description: Journal focusing on biological membranes research.

52283 ■ Journal of Biological Rhythms
Pub: Sage Publications Inc.
Contact: Marin Zatz, Editor-in-Chief
E-mail: edjbr@earthlink.net
Released: Bimonthly. Price: $748 institutions print & e-access; $710.60 institutions e-access only; $718.08 institutions print only; $164 print only; $132 single issue institutions; $36 single issue. Description: Journal focusing on experimental biological research.

52284 ■ Journal of Catalysis
Pub: Elsevier Science B.V.
Contact: E. Iglesia, Editor-in-Chief
Released: 16/year. Price: $554,200 institutions Japan; $77,500 Japan. Description: Journal reporting original research data on heterogeneous and homogeneous catalysis, studies relating catalytic properties with chemical processes at surfaces, studies of the chemistry of surfaces, and engineering studies related to catalysis.

52285 ■ Journal of Cellular Biochemistry
Pub: John Wiley & Sons Inc.
Contact: C. Fred Fox, Exec. Editor
E-mail: fredfox@microbio.ucla.edu
Released: 18/year. Price: $6,510 institutions print, U.S.; $6,690 institutions, Canada and Mexico print, in Canada, add 7% GST; $6,843 institutions, other countries print; $600 print, U.S.; $600 Canada and Mexico print, in Canada add 7% GST; $696 other countries print; $7,161 institutions print & online, U.S.; $7,341 institutions, Canada and Mexico print & online, in Canada, add 7% GST; $7,494 institutions, other countries print & online. Description: Research journal.

52286 ■ Journal of Chemical Ecology
Pub: Kluwer Academic/Plenum Publishing Corp.
Contact: John T. Romeo, Editor-in-Chief
Released: 12/year. Price: $1,556 institutions print or online; $245 print or online; $1,552 institutions, other countries print or online; $244 print or online. Description: Scientific Research Journal

52287 ■ Journal of Chemical Technology and Biotechnology
Pub: John Wiley & Sons Inc.
Contact: J. Melling, Editor-in-Chief
E-mail: jmelling@ptdprolog.net
Released: Monthly, 12/yr. Price: $810 print, U.K.; $1,425 other countries print; $1,900 institutions, other countries print; $2,090 institutions, other countries print and online combined. Description: Journal on scientific discoveries and inventions in the disciplines of biotechnology and chemical technology.

52288 ■ Journal of Clinical Microbiology
Pub: ASM Journals
Contact: Andrew B. O'derdonk, Editor-in-Chief
Released: Monthly. Price: $345 online; $540 institutions print; $607.76 Canada institutions, print; $610 institutions, other countries in Europe, print; $635 institutions, other countries in Latin America, print; $639 institutions, other countries rest of the world, print. Description: Journal publishing primary research in microbiological aspects of human and animal infections and infestations, with particular emphasis on their etiologic agents, diagnosis, and epidemiology.

52289 ■ Journal of Communications Technology and Electronics
Pub: John Wiley & Sons Inc.
Released: Monthly, 12/yr. Price: $4,012 U.S. and Canada; $4,613 other countries. Description: Journal of research in communications and electronics engineering from the Russian Academy of Sciences.

52290 ■ Journal of Environmental Engineering
Pub: American Society of Civil Engineers
Ed: Katherine M. Banks, Editor. Released: Monthly. Price: $234 members domestic; $585 domestic; $936 institutions domestic; $211 members print only; $527 print only; $843 institutions print only; $282 members print only; $633 print only; $984 institutions print only; $259 print & online. Description: Journal on the practice and status of research in environmental engineering science, systems engineering, and sanitation.

52291 ■ Journal of Investigative Surgery
Pub: Taylor & Francis
Released: Bimonthly, 6/yr. Price: $912 institutions online only; $551 institutions online only; $960 institutions print & online; $580 institutions print & online; $415 print only; $251 print only. Description: Biomedical research journal dealing with scientific articles for the advancement of surgery, to the ultimate benefit of patient care and rehabilitation.

52292 ■ Journal of Labelled Compounds and Radiopharmaceuticals
Pub: John Wiley & Sons Inc.
Ed: Prof. J.R. Jones, Editor, j.r.jones@surrey.ac.uk. Released: Monthly, 14/yr. Price: $3,050 worldwide, in Canada, add 7% GST; $4,070 institutions, other countries in Canada, add 7% GST; $4,477 institutions, other countries combined print with online access rates. Description: Journal providing original scientific manuscripts on recent research and development in labelled compound preparation, analytical control, self radiolysis, quality control handling and storage.

52293 ■ Journal of Materials in Civil Engineering
Pub: American Society of Civil Engineers
Ed: Antonio Nanni, Editor. Released: Bimonthly. Price: $510 institutions domestic; $534 institutions international; $255 domestic; $279 international; $128 members domestic; $152 members international. Description: Journal on current topics of materials in civil engineering.

52294 ■ Journal of Molecular Recognition (JMR)
Pub: John Wiley & Sons Inc.
Contact: Dr. Irwin M. Chaiken, Founding Ed.
Released: Bimonthly, 6/yr. Price: $700 print only rates; $1,395 institutions worldwide, in Canada, add 7% GST; $1,535 institutions, other countries combined print with online access rates. Description: Journal containing articles and research papers on the study of molecular interactions in various fields, such as biology, chemistry, and medicine.

52295 ■ Journal of Morphology
Pub: John Wiley & Sons Inc.
Contact: Carl Gans, Editor Emeritus
E-mail: carolus@uts.cc.utexas.edu
Ed: Frederick W. Harrison, Editor. Released: 12/year. Price: $4,395 institutions; $4,515 institutions, Canada and Mexico In Canada, add 7% GST; $4,617 institutions, other countries; $4,835 institutions print & online; $4,955 institutions, Canada and Mexico print & online; $5,057 institutions, other countries print & online. Description: Medical research journal.

52296 ■ Journal of Natural History
Pub: Taylor & Francis
Ed: A. Polaszek, Editor. Released: Semimonthly, 24/yr.(double print issues per yr.). Price: $7,341 institutions print & online; $6,974 institutions print & online; $4,449 institutions print & online; $4,227 institutions print & online. Description: Journal publishing papers on research, reviews, opinions and correspondence in systematics and evolutionary and interactive biology, taxonomic works in entomology and zoology, cladistics, experimental taxonomy, parasitology, ecology, behaviour and the interaction of organisms with their environment.

52297 ■ Journal of Neurochemistry
Pub: Blackwell Publishing Inc.
Ed: Anthony J. Turner, Editor. Released: Bimonthly, Fortnightly. Price: $845 U.S. personal print online; $802 U.S. personal: online only; $3,888 U.S. institutional: premium print online; $3,533 U.S. institutional: print standard online; $3,358 U.S. institutional: premium online only; $231 U.S. American Society for Euro chemistry online only. Description: Journal providing coverage of significant advances in neurochemistry and molecular and cellular biology.

52298 ■ Journal of Pharmaceutical Sciences
Pub: American Pharmaceutical Association
Ed: Dr. Ronald T. Borchardt, Editor. Released: Monthly. Price: $325 print; $385 other countries print; $1,125 institutions print or online; $1,182 institutions, other countries print; $1,238 institutions print and online; $1,295 institutions, other countries print and online. Description: Professional journal publishing research articles in the pharmaceutical sciences.

52299 ■ Journal of Polymer Science
Pub: John Wiley & Sons Inc.
Ed: Mitsuo Sawamoto, Editor, jps.sawamoto@living.polym.kyoto-u.ac.jp. Released: 48/year. Price: $365 print only; $365 Canada and Mexico print only, in Canada add 7% GST; $389 out of country print only; $830 institutions print only; $870 institutions, Canada and Mexico print only; $904 institutions, other countries print only; $913 institutions print & online; $953 institutions, Canada and Mexico print & online, in Canada add 7% GST; $987 institutions, other countries print & online. Description: Journal publishing results of fundamental research in all areas of high polymer chemistry and physics. Three monthly editions: Polymer Chemistry, Polymer Physics, and Polymer Letters.

52300 ■ Journal of Pressure Vessel Technology
Pub: American Society of Mechanical Engineers
Ed: S.Y. Zamrik, Editor. Released: Quarterly. Price: $50 members USA, print & online; $75 members international, print & online; $43 members internet only; $265 nonmembers USA & Canada, print & online; $290 nonmembers international, print & online. Description: Journal focusing on pressure vessel research.

52301 ■ Journal of Turbomachinery
Pub: American Society of Mechanical Engineers
Contact: David C. Wisler, Vice President
Released: Quarterly. Price: $50 members U.S.; $85 members print & online; $43 members international; $328 nonmembers print & online; $363 nonmembers internet only. Description: Technical magazine featuring scholarly research on turbomachinery technology.

52302 ■ Journal of Visualization and Computer Animation
Pub: John Wiley & Sons Inc.
Contact: Nadia Magnenat Thalmann, Editor-in-Chief
E-mail: thalmann@miralab.unige.ch
Released: Quarterly, 5/yr. Description: Journal featuring research papers, film case studies, and critiques of the latest uses of computer animation.

52303 ■ Journal of Waterway, Port, Coastal, and Ocean Engineering
Pub: American Society of Civil Engineers
Ed: Vijay Panchang, Editor. Released: Bimonthly. Description: Journal on engineering research and practice concerned with dredging, floods, ice, pollution, sediment transport, and tidal wave action that affect shorelines, waterways, and harbors.

52304 ■ Machine Design
Pub: Penton Media Inc.
Contact: Paul Dvorak, Senior Editor
E-mail: jdifranco@penton.com
Ed: Ronald Khol, Editor, rkhol@penton.com. Released: 22/year. Price: $139.50 Canada; $211.50 two years Canada; $153 other countries; $261 two years International. Description: Magazine on design engineering function.

52305 ■ Microbiology Abstracts Section A
Pub: Cambridge Scientific Abstracts
Released: Monthly, except December. Description: Scientific journal covering research and applications in agricultural, chemical, pharmaceutical industries.

52306 ■ Microscopy Research and Technique
Pub: John Wiley & Sons Inc.
Contact: George Ruben, Editor-in-Chief
Released: Monthly, 18/yr. Price: $625 print, U.S.; $625 Canada and Mexico print, in Canada add 7%

GST; $769 other countries print; $6,295 institutions print, U.S.; $6,439 institutions, Canada and Mexico print, in Canada add 7% GST; $6,523 institutions, other countries print; $6,925 institutions print and online, U.S.; $7,069 institutions, Canada and Mexico print and online, in Canada add 7% GST; $7,153 institutions, other countries print and online. **Description:** Journal covering the application of and research on advanced microscopy.

52307 ■ Molecular Physics
Pub: Taylor & Francis
Contact: Prof. H.F. Schaefer III, Advisory Board
E-mail: hfs@arches.uga.edu
Ed: Prof. Jean-Pierre Hansen, Editor, molphys@ch. cam.ac.uk. **Released:** Semimonthly, 24/yr. **Price:** $6,575 institutions online; $1,101 print; $6,246 institutions print & online. **Description:** Journal containing information on research papers on chemical physics.

52308 ■ Neurobiology of Learning and Memory
Pub: Elsevier Science B.V.
Ed: W. Greenough, Editor, pgold@uiuc.edu. **Released:** Bimonthly, 6/yr. **Price:** $1,142 institutions for all countries except Europe and Japan; $541 for all countries except Europe and Japan; $271 students for all countries except Europe and Japan. **Description:** Journal publishing information on current neural-oriented behavioral research. Emphasizes the areas of neural plasticity and the mechanisms of learning and memory.

52309 ■ Numerical Heat Transfer, Part A: Applications
Pub: Taylor & Francis
Contact: W.J. Minkowycz, Editor-in-Chief
E-mail: wjm@uic.edu
Released: 20/year. **Price:** $4,072 institutions; $1,514. **Description:** Journal publishing research in the field of heat and mass transfer, and fluid flow.

52310 ■ Particulate Science and Technology
Pub: Taylor & Francis
Contact: Dr. Malay K. Majumder, Editor-in-Chief
E-mail: mazumder@ualr.edu
Released: Quarterly. **Price:** $220; $555 institutions. **Description:** Journal publishing original research and review material dealing with particulate science and technology.

52311 ■ The Plant Cell
Pub: American Society of Plant Biologists
Contact: John Long, Managing Editor
E-mail: jlong@aspb.org
Released: Monthly. **Price:** $75 single issue; $160 members print; $325 nonmembers online and print; $1,860 institutions online only; $110 students student member-print. **Description:** Academic research journal reporting major advances in plant cellular and molecular biology.

52312 ■ Progress in Photovoltaics
Pub: John Wiley & Sons Inc.
Contact: Dr. Paul A. Lynn, Managing Editor
Released: Monthly, 8/yr. **Price:** $495 worldwide, in Canada, add 7% GST; $1,440 institutions worldwide, in Canada, add 7% GST; $1,584 institutions, other countries combined print with online access rates. **Description:** Journal focusing on pratical implementation and research in the field of photovoltaics.

52313 ■ The Quarterly Review of Biology
Pub: University of Chicago Press
Ed: Albert D. Carlson, Editor. **Released:** Quarterly. **Price:** $255 institutions; $29 students and retirees; $44; $68.75 single issue institutions; $16 single issue individuals; $230 institutions electronic only, all over the world; $277.85 institutions Canada; $263 institutions rest of world; $52.08 Canada; $52 rest of world. **Description:** Journal reviewing recent research and newly published books and software dealing with the life sciences.

52314 ■ R & D Magazine
Pub: Reed Business Information
Contact: Tim Studt, Editor-in-Chief

E-mail: tstudt@reedbusiness.com
Released: Monthly. **Description:** Magazine serving research scientists, engineers, and technical managers. Reports significant advances, problems, and trends that affect the performance, funding, and adminstration of applied research and development.

52315 ■ Random Structures & Algorithms
Pub: John Wiley & Sons Inc.
Contact: Joel Spencer, Editor-in-Chief
E-mail: spencer@cims.nyu.edu
Released: 8/yr. **Price:** $1,130 institutions print; $1,226 institutions, Canada and Mexico print Canada, add 7% GST; $1,282 institutions, other countries print; $1,243 institutions print with online; $1,339 institutions, Canada and Mexico Canada, add 7% GST; $1,395 institutions, other countries. **Description:** Journal describing research on random structures and applications of probabilistic techniques to problem solving in mathematics, computer science and operations research.

52316 ■ Rapid Communications in Mass Spectrometry
Pub: John Wiley & Sons Inc.
Ed: Dr. David Goodlett, Editor, goodlett@u. washington.edu. **Released:** Semimonthly, 24/yr. **Price:** $2,150 print, U.K.; $3,865 print, worldwide, in Canada add 7% GST; $5,150 institutions print, in Canada add 7% GST; $5,665 institutions print and online, in Canada add 7% GST. **Description:** Journal containing information on research ideas and results on all aspects of the science of gas-phase ions.

52317 ■ Reviews in Medical Virology
Pub: John Wiley & Sons Inc.
Contact: Dr. Brian W.J. Mahy, Editor-in-Chief
E-mail: virology@bellsouth.net
Released: Bimonthly, 6/yr. **Price:** $405 print, U.K.; $725 print, worldwide, in Canada add 7% GST; $965 institutions print, worldwide, in Canada add 7% GST; $1,062 institutions print and online in Canada add 7% GST. **Description:** Journal focusing on current research and new information on all viruses of medical importance.

52318 ■ Rubber Chemistry and Technology
Pub: Rubber Division
Contact: Linda Corcoran, Managing Editor
Ed: Dr. Krishna C. Baranwal, Editor. **Released:** Periodic, 5/year. **Price:** $425 U.S. and Canada institutions, companies and libraries; $390 nonmembers print only; $531.25 other countries institutions, companies and libraries; $487.50 nonmembers other countries, print only; $797.50 other countries print & online. **Description:** Journal on developments in the technology of rubber.

52319 ■ Sensor Technology
Pub: Technical Insights/M John Wiley & Sons Inc.
Ed: Leo O'Connor, Editor. **Released:** Monthly. **Price:** $650, U.S. and Canada year; $710, elsewhere year. **Description:** Informs readers of the latest scientific and technological developments in the field of sensors. Focuses on process and machine control, including robotics; also covers environmental and medical uses. Recurring features include a calendar of events, news of research, book reviews, and columns titled Key Patents and Keep an Eye On.

52320 ■ SIAM Journal on Optimization
Pub: Society for Industrial & Applied Mathematics
Contact: N.I.M. Gould, Editor-in-Chief
E-mail: n.gould@rl.ac.uk
Released: Quarterly. **Price:** $90 members; $461 nonmembers; $94 members other countries; $521 nonmembers other countries; $65 electronic member; $437.95 electronic nonmember. **Description:** Journal featuring research and expository articles on the theory and practice of optimization.

52321 ■ SIAM Journal on Scientific Computing
Pub: Society for Industrial & Applied Mathematics
Contact: Howard Elman, Editor-in-Chief
E-mail: elman@cs.umd.edu
Released: Bimonthly. **Price:** $96 members; $608 nonmembers; $102 members other countries; $708

nonmembers other countries; $60 electronic members; $577.60 electronic nonmembers. **Description:** Journal containing research articles on solving scientific problems through the use of computers.

52322 ■ Software Process
Pub: John Wiley & Sons Inc.
Contact: Prof. Darren Dalcher, Editor-in-Chief
E-mail: d.dalcher@mdx.ac.uk
Released: 4/yr. **Price:** $150 print, U.K.; $270 other countries print; $540 institutions, other countries print; $594 institutions, other countries print and online combined. **Description:** Journal for those involved in the software development process. Features experience reports, research papers, and critical discussion.

52323 ■ Somatic Cell and Molecular Genetics
Pub: Kluwer Academic/Plenum Publishing Corp.
Contact: Sophia Conyers, Media Coordinator
Ed: Richard Davidson, Editor. **Released:** 4/year. **Price:** $914 institutions print or online ed.; $129 print ed. **Description:** Journal presenting genetics research.

52324 ■ Strategic S&T
Pub: EPRI
Ed: Gail McCarthy, Editor. **Released:** 3/year. **Description:** Profiles research projects, results, and activities of the SS&T program. Recurring features include news of research, reports of meetings, and listing of SS&T reports with ordering information.

52325 ■ Supramolecular Science
Pub: Butterworth-Heinemann
Contact: Wolfgang Knoll, Editor-in-Chief
Released: Quarterly. **Price:** $170 annual British pounds; $160 other countries British pounds. **Description:** Journal providing a forum uniting supramolecular research from a wide range of disciplines, including materials science chemistry, physics, and polymer science.

52326 ■ Systems and Computers in Japan
Pub: John Wiley & Sons Inc.
Ed: Michiyuki Venohara, Editor. **Released:** 14/year. **Price:** $5,900 institutions print only; $6,040 institutions, Canada and Mexico print only. In Canada, add 7% GST; $6,159 institutions, other countries print only; $6,490 institutions print & online; $6,630 institutions, Canada and Mexico print & online. In Canada, add 7% GST; $6,749 institutions, other countries print & online. **Description:** Translation journal reports on Japanese developments in computer architecture, large system design, advanced digital circuitry, data transmission, interface devices, data processing, programming techniques, automata, formal languages, and biomedical applications of computers.

52327 ■ Teratogenesis, Carcinogenesis and Mutagenesis
Pub: John Wiley & Sons Inc.
Contact: Philippe Shubick, Editor-in-Chief
Released: Bimonthly. **Description:** Journal publishing research on the detection, classification, and evaluation of risk associated with exposure to environmental agents which may induce teratogenesis, carcinogenesis, or mutagenesis.

52328 ■ Teratology
Pub: John Wiley & Sons Inc.
Ed: Lewis B. Holmes, Editor. **Released:** Monthly. **Description:** Journal publishing reports on the investigation of abnormal fetal development in humans and in experimetnal animal models.

52329 ■ Transactions of the ASAE
Pub: American Society of Agricultural Engineers
Contact: Donna M. Hull
E-mail: hull@asabe.org
Released: Bimonthly. **Price:** $35 members; $74 nonmembers; $63 members; $125 nonmembers; $70 members; $21 nonmembers; $126 members; $386 nonmembers. **Description:** Agricultural engineering peer-reviewed research journal.

52330 ■ Virology
Pub: Elsevier Science B.V.

Contact: R.A. Lamb, Editor-in-Chief
E-mail: ralamb@northwestern.edu
Released: 26/year. **Price:** $615 for all countries except Europe and Japan; $5,006 institutions for all countries except Europe and Japan; $123 students for all countries except Europe and Japan. **Description:** Scientific journal publishing research results in all branches of virology.

52331 ■ *Yeast*
Pub: John Wiley & Sons Inc.
Contact: R.B. Wickner, Editor-in-Chief
Released: 16/yr. **Price:** $1,895 elsewhere print, in Canada add 7% GST; $2,525 institutions print, in Canada add 7% GST; $2,778 institutions print and online, worldwide, in Canada add 7% GST. **Description:** Journal containing information on current yeast research and pertinent reviews.

52332 ■ *Zoo Biology*
Pub: John Wiley & Sons Inc.
Contact: Dan Wharton, Exec. Editor
Released: 6/year. **Price:** $1,565 institutions Print; $1,625 institutions, Canada and Mexico Print - for Canada, add 7% GST; $1,676 institutions, other countries Print; $275 Print; $275 Canada and Mexico Print - for Canada, add 7% GST; $311 other countries Print; $1,722 institutions print & online; $1,782 institutions, Canada and Mexico print & online, for Canada, add 7% GST; $1,833 institutions, other countries print & online. **Description:** Journal featuring research on wild animals in captive settings.

VIDEOCASSETTES/ AUDIOCASSETTES

52333 ■ *The Science of Energy*
Human Relations Media
41 Kensico Dr.
Mount Kisco, NY 10549
Ph:(914)244-0486
Free: 800-833-2004
Fax: (914)244-0485
Co. E-mail: orders@hrmvideo.com
URL: http://www.hrmvideo.com
Released: 1994. **Price:** $189. **Description:** Introduces students to biology and physics, touching on the scientific history of energy from Galileo to Einstein, thermodynamics, the sun as the Earth's energy source, photosynthesis and respiration. Complete with teacher's resource book. **Availability:** VHS.

52334 ■ *Science on Ice: Research in Antarctica*
Encyclopedia Britannica
331 N. LaSalle St.
Chicago, IL 60610
Ph:(312)347-7159
Free: 800-323-1229
Fax: (312)294-2104
URL: http://www.britannica.com
Released: 1988. **Price:** $59.00. **Description:** Illustrates the advantages of researching in the Antarctica and provides information on some of the current research taking place in the region. **Availability:** VHS; 3/4U; SVS.

52335 ■ *Technical Studies*
Home Vision Cinema
c/o Image Entertainment
20525 Nordhoff St., Ste. 200
Chatsworth, CA 91311
URL: http://www.homevision.com
Released: 1981. **Description:** This series is designed to illustrate the practical application of concepts in materials and engineering science. **Availability:** VHS; 3/4U.

TRADE SHOWS AND CONVENTIONS

52336 ■ American Technical Education Association National Conference on Technical Education
American Technical Education Association
c/o North Dakota State College of Science
800 N. 6th St.
Wahpeton, ND 58076-0002
Ph:(701)671-2301
Fax: (701)671-2260
URL: http://www.ateaonline.org
Released: Annual. **Audience:** Technical educators and administrators of post-secondary technical education. **Principal Exhibits:** Supplies and services related to post secondary technical education.

52337 ■ Estuarine Research Federation Conference
Estuarine Research Federation
PO Box 510
University of Southwest Louisiana
Dept. of Biology
Port Republic, MD 20676
Ph:(410)586-0997
Fax: (410)586-9226
Co. E-mail: webmaster@erf.org
URL: http://www.erf.org
Released: Biennial. **Principal Exhibits:** Exhibits for persons actively engaged in biological, hydrographic, or related investigations of estuarine problems.

CONSULTANTS

52338 ■ Bio-Technical Resources
1035 S 7th St.
Manitowoc, WI 54220
Ph:(920)684-5518
Fax: (920)684-5519
Co. E-mail: info@biotechresources.com
URL: http://www.biotechresources.com

E-mail: info@biotechresources.com
Scope: Provides innovative solutions for the development of biotechnology products and processes through contract services in research and development, bioprocess scale-up, pilot scale manufacturing, technology and economic assessments. **Publications:** "Reduction of Background Interference in the Spectrophotometric Assay of Mevalonate Kinase," 2006; "A Soluble Form of Phosphatase in Saccharomyces cerevisiae Capable of Converting Farnesyl Diphosphate to E, E-Farnesol," 2006; "Ascorbate Biosynthesis: A Diversity of Pathways," BIOS Scientific Publishers, 2004; "The Biotechnology of Ascorbic Acid Manufacture," BIOS Scientific Publishers, 2004; "Detection of Farnesyl Diphosphate Accumulation in Yeast ERG9 Mutants," 2003; "Reverse Two-Hybrid System: Detecting Critical Interaction Domains and Screening for Inhibitors," Eaton Publishing, 2000. **Seminars:** Metabolic Engineering for Industrial Production of Glucosamine and N-Acetylglucosamine, Soc. Ind. Micro. Annual Meeting, Aug, 2003; Metabolic Engineering of E. coli for the Industrial Production of Glucosamine, Seventh Annual Symposium on Industrial and Fermentation Microbiology, Apr, 2003.

52339 ■ BioChem Technology Inc.
100 Ross Rd., Ste. 201
King of Prussia, PA 19406
Ph:(610)768-9360
Fax: (610)768-9363
Co. E-mail: sales@biochemtech.com
URL: http://www.biochemtech.com

E-mail: sales@biochemtech.com
Scope: Consultants in wastewater treatment processes specializing in evaluation and optimization of biological nutrient removal facilities. On-line process monitoring and control of wastewater treatment processes as well as yeast, bacterial or fungal fermenta-

tion. Experience in biochemical process development, wastewater treatment process design, fermentation system design, process and plant design, biochemical engineering research and a variety of engineering specialties. Undertakes a wide variety of projects which range from preliminary feasibility studies to the development and optimization of a biological process. **Special Services:** BioGuide®; BioChem®.

52340 ■ Education Development Center
55 Chapel St.
Newton, MA 02458-1060
Ph:(617)969-7100
Free: 800-225-4276
Fax: (617)969-5979
Co. E-mail: comment@edc.org
URL: http://www.edc.org

E-mail: comment@edc.org
Scope: Non-profit organization; Health and Human Development Programs division specializes in promoting health and justice across the life cycle in many settings. HHD conducts research, evaluation, program development and professional development activities.

52341 ■ Flett Research Ltd.
440 DeSalaberry Ave.
Winnipeg, MB, Canada R2L 0Y7
Ph:(204)667-2505
Fax: (204)667-2505
Co. E-mail: flett@flettresearch.ca
URL: http://www.flettresearch.ca

E-mail: flett@flettresearch.ca
Scope: Provides environmental audits and assessments. Offers contract research and consultation on environmental topics, specializing in limnology, with emphasis in microbiology, bio-geochemistry and radio-chemistry. Performs dating of sediments via Pb-210 and CS-137 methods, to determine sediment accumulation rates in lakes. One of a handful of labs in the world able to carry out total mercury and methyl mercury analyses at the sub-nanogram and L concentration in water.

52342 ■ Innovative Scientific Analysis & Computing
Flagstaff Rd.
PO Box 1636
Boulder, CO 80306-1636
Ph:(303)440-7673
Fax: (303)545-6674
Co. E-mail: ros5e@isaac.com
URL: http://www.isaac.com

E-mail: ros5e@isaac.com
Scope: Engineering services includes mathematical analysis (specializing in optimal estimation), scientific programming, and database design and development, data encryption and security.

52343 ■ Mankind Research Foundation
1315 Apple Ave.
Silver Spring, MD 20910-3614
Ph:(301)587-8686
Fax: (301)585-8959
Scope: Firm provide an organization for scientific development and application of technology that could have positive impact on the health, education, and welfare of mankind. Provide solution to seek and apply futuristic solutions to current problems. Provides services in the areas of advanced sciences, biotechnical, bionic, biocybernetic, biomedical, holistic health, bioimmunology, solar energy, accelerated learning, and sensory aids for handicapped. Current specific activities involve research in AIDS, drug abuse, affordable housing, food for the hungry, and literacy and remedial education.

52344 ■ Midwest Research Institute
425 Volker Blvd.
Kansas City, MO 64110
Ph:(816)753-7600
Fax: (816)753-8420
Co. E-mail: info@mriresearch.org
URL: http://www.mriresearch.org

E-mail: info@mriresearch.org
Scope: An independent, not-for-profit organization that performs research and development under contract with industry, government, and other private and public groups. Areas of current research and development include: chemistry, biological sciences, toxicology, health research, management sciences, environmental sciences, hazardous waste, renewable energy, materials sciences, pharmaceutical product development, and national security and defense. Has operated and managed the National Renewable Energy Laboratory (NREL) in Golden, Colorado for the U.S. Department of Energy since its inception in 1977. **Publications:** Annual Report (May).

52345 ■ Technology Management Group
3 Penny Ln.
PO Box 3260
Woodbridge, CT 06525-1531
Ph:(203)387-1430
Fax: (203)387-1470
Co. E-mail: info@commtechsoftware.com

E-mail: info@commtechsoftware.com
Scope: Consulting services include analysis of market opportunities; product introductions; new ventures; acquisitions analysis; licensing, joint ventures, and OEM arrangements. Emphasis on polymers, medical devices, biotechnology, pharmaceuticals, and chemicals.

COMPUTERIZED DATABASES

52346 ■ *BooksInPrint.com Professional*
R.R. Bowker LLC
630 Central Ave.
New Providence, NJ 07974
Ph:(908)268-1090
Free: 800-526-9537
Fax: (908)665-3528
Co. E-mail: info@bowker.com
URL: http://www.bowker.com
Description: Contains bibliographic descriptions and ordering information for more than ¾ million books currently in print or declared out of print (from July 1979 to date), active and inactive audios and videos, and soon-to-be-published titles from some 50,000 publishers. Also contains more than 700,000 full-text reviews, more than 200,000 book jacket images, and author biographies. Coverage includes scholarly, popular, adult, juvenile, reprint, and other books on all subjects published by U.S. publishers or exclusively distributed in the United States and available to the trade or general public for single- or multiple-copy purchases. Such items as government publications, Bibles, free books, and subscription-only titles are excluded. Also provides the complete text of reviews from *Library Journal*, *Publisher's Weekly*, and *School Library Journal*. Corresponds to *Books in Print*, *Books Out of Print*, *Forthcoming Books*, *Books in Print Supplement*, *Scientific and Technical Books in Print*, *Medical and Health Care Books in Print*, *Children's Books in Print*, *Paperbound Books in Print*, and *Law Books in Print*. Subject classification scheme utilizes more than 72,000 Library of Congress subject headings as well as Sears headings. **Availability:** Online: Thomson Gale, Colorado Alliance of Research Libraries, Thomson Dialog; CD-ROM: R.R. Bowker LLC. **Type:** Bibliographic.

RESEARCH CENTERS

52347 ■ American Defense Institute
1055 N Fairfax St., Ste. 200
Alexandria, VA 22314
Ph:(703)519-7000
Fax: (703)519-8627

Co. E-mail: ebm1@americandefinst.org
URL: http://www.ojc.org/adi/
Contact: Capt. Eugene (Red) McDaniel, Pres.
E-mail: ebm1@americandefinst.org
Scope: Defense and national security policy issues, focusing on the privileges and obligations of citizenship in a free society and America's strength and freedom in the 21st century. Special projects include a military voter program which encourages service personnel to register and vote. **Services:** National speakers bureau. **Publications:** ADI Briefs; ADI Newsletter; ADI Security Review. **Educational Activities:** National Security Leadership Seminar (annually), in Washington; POW awareness campaign. **Awards:** Outstanding Leadership Award, for individual citizens committed to America's national defense.

52348 ■ New Mexico State University–Arts and Sciences Research Center
Department RC
Breland Hall 163
CB MSC 3335
Las Cruces, NM 88003-8001
Ph:(505)646-7441
Fax: (505)646-6096
Co. E-mail: rczernia@nmsu.edu
URL: http://www.nmsu.edu/~artsci/Research/center.html
Contact: Dr. Robert J. Czerniak, Dir./Assoc. Dean
E-mail: rczernia@nmsu.edu
Scope: Administers research activities in the arts and physical, natural, and behavioral sciences. Also serves as coordinating center for faculty research in the College. **Publications:** Newsletter (annually).

52349 ■ Polytechnic University–Institute for Technology and Enterprise
New York Information Technology Center
55 Broad St., Ste. 13B
New York, NY 10004
Ph:(212)547-7030
Fax: (212)547-7029
Co. E-mail: horwitch@poly.edu
URL: http://www.ite.poly.edu
Contact: Prof. Mel Horwitch, Dir.
E-mail: horwitch@poly.edu
Scope: High-level education, including the integration of new technologies, particularly the Internet and intranets, and multimedia, with business strategy as they affect management. **Educational Activities:** Round Tables (periodically); Workshops (periodically).

52350 ■ San Diego State University–Mount Laguna Observatory
Department of Astronomy
5500 Campanile Dr.
San Diego, CA 92182-1221
Ph:(619)594-6182
Fax: (619)594-1413
Co. E-mail: etzel@sciences.sdsu.edu
URL: http://mintaka.sdsu.edu
Contact: Dr. Paul B. Etzel, Dir.
E-mail: etzel@sciences.sdsu.edu
Scope: Astronomy. **Publications:** MLOA Newsletter (3/year). **Educational Activities:** Planetarium shows, lectures, and telescope viewing; Summer Star Party, for the public viewing Friday and Saturday nights in the summer.

52351 ■ State University of New York at Binghamton–Institute for Materials Research
Vestal Pky. E
Binghamton, NY 13902-6000
Ph:(607)777-4623
Fax: (607)777-4623
Co. E-mail: stanwhit@binghamton.edu
URL: http://materials.binghamton.edu
Contact: Prof. M. Stanley Whittingham, Dir.
E-mail: stanwhit@binghamton.edu
Scope: Preparation and physical and chemical properties of novel inorganic oxide materials using, in particular, soft chemistry approaches. Current research focuses on finding new synthetic routes to prepare

metastable compounds that cannot be prepared by traditional techniques and the understanding and exploitation of ionic motion in solids and its use in electrochromic devices and batteries. **Publications:** Papers, books, and reviews.

52352 ■ Syracuse University–Center for Technology and Information Policy
Maxwell Sch. of Citizenship & Public Affairs
400 Eggers Hall
Syracuse, NY 13244-1090
Ph:(315)443-1890
Fax: (315)443-1075
Co. E-mail: sibretsc@maxwell.syr.edu
URL: http://www.maxwell.syr.edu/ctip/ctip.htm
Contact: Stuart Bretschneider PhD, Dir.
E-mail: sibretsc@maxwell.syr.edu
Scope: Nexus of technology, information, and public policy, particularly computer-based technological forecasting and assessment, management of scientific and technical information flows in organizations, technological innovation studies, and Pacific Rim science policy. **Publications:** TIPP Working Paper series.

52353 ■ University of Delaware–Center for Molecular and Engineering Thermodynamics
233 Colburn Lab
Department of Chemical Engineering
Newark, DE 19716
Ph:(302)831-4500
Fax: (302)831-4466
Co. E-mail: cmet@che.udel.edu
URL: http://www.che.udel.edu/cmet
Contact: Prof. Stanley I. Sandler, Dir.
E-mail: cmet@che.udel.edu
Scope: Chemical engineering, including molecular thermodynamics and its applications in environmental problems, purification of pharmaceuticals and biological materials, and new separations technologies. Theoretical research areas also include ab-initio quantum mechanics calculations, Monte Carlo and molecular dynamics simulation and statistical mechanics, development of new applied thermodynamics methods for equations of state and activity coefficients models, and the description of surfactant and micellar solutions.

52354 ■ University of Toronto–Institute for the History and Philosophy of Science and Technology
Victoria College, Rm. 316
91 Charles St. W
Toronto, ON, Canada M5S 1K7
Ph:(416)978-5397
Fax: (416)978-3003
Co. E-mail: ihpst.info@utoronto.ca
URL: http://www.chass.utoronto.ca/ihpst/
Contact: Prof. R. Paul Thompson, Dir.
E-mail: ihpst.info@utoronto.ca
Scope: History and philosophy of science and technology, particularly the history of biology, including classification, invertebrate morphology, Darwinism, and ecology; history of chemistry, including the eighteenth and nineteenth centuries; history of mathematics, including foundation of analysis, eighteenth and nineteenth century mechanics, Joseph Lagrange, Nicolas Sadi Carnot, and Jean Le Rond d'Alembert; history of medicine, including history of social medicine/public health,; medicine and national socialism; history of microbiology; history of physics, including Kepler, Descartes, seventeenth through nineteenth century electromagnetism; history of technology, including medieval and Renaissance, eighteenth century French technology and war; medieval and Renaissance science; Science Revolution; the Enlightenment; Victorian science; Romanticism; Canadian science, including Arctic exploration; and philosophy of science, including probability, statistics, experimental science, language, early modern natural philosophy, and foundations of Newtonian dynamics; exact sciences in antiquity. **Educational Activities:** Colloquia and public lectures (biweekly).

REFERENCE WORKS

52355 ■ "Consumers Look for Post-Holiday Sales" in *Sacramento Bee* **(December 27, 2005)**
Pub: The Sacramento Bee
Ed: Jon Ortiz. **Description:** Retailers are becoming increasingly dependent on post-holiday sales. Shoppers tend to purchase new items seen in sales and promotions while returning unwanted items.

52356 ■ "Crowds Form Early at Sacramento, Calif.-Area Retailers to Get Microsoft Xbox" in *Sacramento Bee* **(November 22, 2005)**
Pub: The Sacramento Bee
Description: Microsoft's Xbox 360, selling for $399 sold at record rates for holiday 2005. Microsoft is one of three major console makers selling next-generation gaming boxes. Sony and Nintendo versions will not be available until spring 2006.

52357 ■ "Hiring True Believers" in *Sacramento Bee* **(November 14, 2005)**
Pub: The Sacramento Bee
Ed: Rachel Osterman. **Description:** Many retailers hire loyal customers during the holiday season because they understand that shoppers who know and love their store can be the best possible sales staff.

52358 ■ "Holiday Week Can Be Extra-Productive for Some Sacramento, Calif.-Area Workers" in *Sacramento Bee* **(December 28, 2005)**
Pub: The Sacramento Bee
Ed: Rachel Osterman. **Description:** Many Sacramento, California executives use the week between Christmas and New Year's as a time to clean, file, and plan for the upcoming year.

52359 ■ "Last-Minute Shoppers Boost Holiday Retail Sales" in *Sacramento Bee* **(December 29, 2005)**
Pub: The Sacramento Bee
Ed: Jon Ortiz. **Description:** Last minute shoppers increased sales for many retailers in the Sacramento area, setting a strong finish to the 2005 shopping season. Chain store sales were reported up by 2.8 percent for the week before Christmas Day.

52360 ■ "A Life Experience is Part of the Package" in *Sacramento Bee* **(November 21, 2005)**
Pub: The Sacramento Bee
Ed: Jon Ortiz. **Description:** Holiday marketing of Carnival Corporation's cruise ships is outlined. The Miami, Florida cruise line partnered with Cooper DDB to advertise its ships with images of shoppers carrying large foil-wrapped replicas of Carnival ships.

52361 ■ "Marketers Hang Their Hopes on Holiday Promotions" in *Sacramento Bee* **(December 21, 2005)**
Pub: The Sacramento Bee
Ed: Jon Ortiz. **Description:** Companies depend on holiday marketing promotions in order to increase sales. Seasonal packaging plans begin during the summer before each Christmas holiday, can boost a company's sales, and increase brand recognition while making a statement about a company's self-image.

52362 ■ "Mingling at Business Holiday Parties Made Easier for Some" in *Sacramento Bee* **(November 29, 2005)**
Pub: The Sacramento Bee
Ed: Gilbert Chan. **Description:** Tips to ease anxiety over attending holiday business parties are shared, including the use of networking for career building.

52363 ■ "Retailers Draw Link Between Halloween, Christmas Sales" in *Sacramento Bee* **(October 30, 2005)**
Pub: The Sacramento Bee
Ed: Jon Ortiz. **Description:** Experts suggest a strong link between Halloween and winter holiday sales. Halloween is becoming a strong indicator of consumer spending for the months of November and December.

52364 ■ "Roseville, Calif., Gourmet Gift Firm Puts Buyout on Hold" in *Sacramento Bee* **(October 21, 2005)**
Pub: The Sacramento Bee
Ed: Clint Swett. **Description:** Shari's Berries International, famous for its chocolate-dipped strawberries, has put its management-led buyout on hold in order to concentrate on the holiday season. Unforgettable Gifts Inc. had offered $1.69 million in cash along with $1.26 million in promissory notes as well as assumption of the firm's $2.35 million debt.

52365 ■ "Sacramento, Calif.-Area Train Shop Continues to Grow" in *Sacramento Bee* **(December 19, 2005)**
Pub: The Sacramento Bee
Ed: Jon Ortiz. **Description:** Profile of Bruce Eldredge, owner of Bruce's Train Shop in Sacramento, California; Eldredge credits more than 30 percent of his sales to holiday shopping.

START-UP INFORMATION

52366 ■ *The Complete Small Business Start-up Guide*
Pub: John Wiley & Sons, Incorporated
Ed: Lisa Rogak. **Released:** November 2004. **Price:** $14.95. **Description:** Guide to starting a small company, focusing on development of a business plan, organizational structure, advertising, hiring, selection of suppliers, and using the Internet to market your firm.

52367 ■ "Market Planning 101" in *Home Business* (Vol. 12, October 2005, No. 5, pp. 42, 44-45)
Pub: Home Business Magazine
Ed: Christopher J. Bachler. **Description:** A quick marketing plan for any small business is presented and includes all the basic information required to attract loans, partners, business services and even Small Business Administration assistance.

REFERENCE WORKS

52368 ■ "Avoiding Invention Scams" in *Black Enterprise* (Vol. 37, January 2007, No. 6, pp. 46)
Pub: Earl G. Graves Publishing Co. Inc.
Ed: James C. Johnson. **Description:** Invention promotion firms provide inventors assistance in developing a prototype for product development. It is important to research these companies before making a commitment to work with them because there are a number of these firms that are not legitimate and have caused independent inventors to lose thousands of dollars by making false claims as to the market potential of the inventions.

52369 ■ "Business Services" in *Ingram's* (Vol. 29, No. 8, August 2003, pp. 33)
Pub: Show Me Publishing, Inc.
Description: Listing of service oriented businesses in the Kansas City, Missouri area is presented.

52370 ■ "City Guide for Moms Launched" in *Marketing to Women* (Vol. 20, January 2007, No. 1, pp. 3)
Pub: EPM Communications, Inc.
Description: ModernMom.com has launched a series of city guides on the Internet designed to highlight local businesses that offer goods and services a mother may need. Los Angeles, San Francisco, Chicago, New York City, Seattle, Austin Minneapolis, Atlanta, San Diego, Boston, Philadelphia and Washington D.C. are cities included so far in Modern Mom City Guides.

52371 ■ "Do ask. Do Tell" in *Folio: the Magazine for Magazine Management* (Vol. 30, No. 1, January 2001, pp. 2)
Pub: Intertec Publishing Corp.
Description: The things to ask when looking for a new supplier are outlined.

52372 ■ "Get a second opinion" in *Entrepreneur* (Vol. 30, No. 2, February 2002, pp. 56)
Pub: Entrepreneur Media Inc.
Ed: Jennifer Pellet. **Description:** The importance of checking out potential clients, partners and suppliers for small business is discussed.

52373 ■ "Host With the Most" in *Small Business Opportunities* (Vol. 13, No. 5, September 2001, pp. 58)
Pub: Harris Publications, Inc.
Ed: Carla Vincent. **Description:** Seven-steps to guide small businesses in finding the right Web host, with the right size, a reasonable price, and competent technical support staff.

52374 ■ "In Search of the Operator" in *Wall Street Journal* (May 8, 2002, pp. D1)
Pub: Wall Street Journal
Ed: Jane Spencer. **Description:** An overview of automated customer service systems. Statistical data included.

52375 ■ "Know Thy Worth" in *Entrepreneur.com* (Vol. 34, February 2006, No. 2, pp. 50)
Pub: Entrepreneur Media Inc.
Ed: C.J. Prince. **Description:** A business valuation can help an owner put a precise number on the company's present and future value. It will help when choosing to sell the business, gifting the business to heirs, recruiting new investors, or bringing employees into ownership.

52376 ■ "Legal Aid: Sample Legal Documents can Lower Your Attorney Fees" in *Black Enterprise* (Vol. 37, October 2006, No. 3, pp. 210)
Pub: Earl G. Graves Publishing Co. Inc.
Ed: Tamara E. Holmes. **Description:** FreeLegalForms.net provides thousands of free legal forms. These forms are not a substitute for consultation with an attorney but the sample documents can help save you time and money.

52377 ■ "Lowest bid is not always best for hiring contractor" in *Business First Columbus* (Vol. 18, No. 25, February 8, 2002, pp.)
Pub: Business First Columbus, Inc.
Ed: Susanna Barton. **Description:** Tips for choosing the correct contractor for the job are offered.

52378 ■ "Moving Out: When to Outsource Your Server Operations" in *My Business* (December/January 2004, pp. 42)
Pub: My Business Magazine
Ed: Paige Orr. **Description:** Tips for small companies wishing to outsource server operations are presented. These firms manage critical business and network applications.

52379 ■ "Nina Zagat: My Biggest Mistake" in *Inc.* (April 2000, pp. 145)
Pub: The Goldhirsh Group
Ed: Mike Hofman. **Description:** Nina Zagat, publisher of restaurant and travel guides offers important information as a guide before putting your business online.

52380 ■ "On the Freight Train" in *Small Business Opportunities* (Vol. 12, No. 5, September 2000, pp. 20)
Pub: Harris Publications, Inc.
Description: Ten tips when considering a transportation agent are listed, including information on travel and transport associations to contact for assistance.

52381 ■ "On the paper trail" in *Boston Business Journal* (Vol. 22, No. 3, February 22, 2002, pp. S7)
Pub: MCP, Inc.
Ed: Susan Shinn Poe. **Description:** Tips for finding a company to store business documents are offered, along with electronic versus paper methods of storage.

52382 ■ "Online Self-Publishing Services" in *Black Enterprise* (Vol. 37, November 2006, No. 4, pp. 90)
Pub: Earl G. Graves Publishing Co. Inc.
Description: Profiles of five online self-publishing services.

52383 ■ "Orchestrating Assistance; Chambers of Commerce" in *Crain's New York Business* (Vol. 22, November 13, 2006, No. 46, pp. 38)
Pub: Crain Communications, Inc.
Description: Listing of local chapters of New York's chambers of commerce. These organizations serve as sources of information and representation for local business interest provide a number of services and a wide variety of programs for small businesses.

52384 ■ "Penny-Wise, Site-Foolish" in *Inc.* (February 1, 2002)
Pub: Inc. Magazine
Ed: Jill Hecht Maxwell. **Description:** There are thousands of Web-hosting providers, information is provided to choose the right one, including a list of resources.

52385 ■ "The relationship between quality, time and cost" in *Women in B usiness* (Vol. 53, No. 2, March-April, 2001, pp. 34)
Pub: The ABWA Co. Inc.
Description: Advice on factors to consider when buying goods or services is presented. The opportunity of costs of quality, speed and savings are considered; and ways of assessing one against the other is discussed.

52386 ■ "Remote Control" in *My Business* (February/March 2004, pp. 14)
Pub: My Business Magazine
Ed: Lee Gimpel. **Description:** Five questions to ask a mobile solution vendor before hiring their services are listed.

52387 ■ "Revving in the Motor City: Michelle Sherman Chauffeurs Us through Detroit" in *Black Enterprise* (Vol. 34, No. 4, Nov. 2003, pp. 176)
Pub: Earl Graves Publishing Co.
Ed: Sonia Alleyne. **Description:** Empowerment Zone funding has attributed to new construction for both

business and entertainment in Detroit, Michigan; new jobs have grown at the rate of 1.77 percent since 1998 and are forecasted to grow to an annual rate of 9.1 percent through 2010.

52388 ■ "Searching for Relief" in *My Business* **(April/May 2003, pp. 49)**
Pub: My Business Magazine
Ed: Charlotte Franck. **Description:** The importance of defining goals when choosing a business consultant is stressed. One small business owner tells how she used bartering as a strategy for acquiring consulting services.

52389 ■ "Shop Around: Getting Estimates Can Save You a Bundle" in *Black Enterprise* **(Vol. 34, No. 4, November 2003, pp. 166)**
Pub: Earl Graves Publishing Co.
Ed: Siobhan Benet. **Description:** The importance of shopping around for any business service or purchase is discussed, whether searching for a contractor, car purchase, or appliances.

52390 ■ "Shopping for the Right Database" in *Business Week Online* **(December 13, 2001)**
Pub: McGraw-Hill, Inc.
Description: Questions are answered regarding the development of a marketing database for a small business that retails and distributes environmental safety products, but all information applies to any small business.

52391 ■ "Some small biz markets underserved by CPAs" in *Journal of Accountancy* **(Vol. 190, No. 6, December 2000, pp. 30)**
Pub: Harborside Financial Center
Description: A recent survey of nearly 700 small businesses in the manufacturing, professional services, government, non-profit and other sectors revealed they generally get advice and services relating to health care, HR management and legal and compliance issues from lawyers, insurance brokers, government agencies, the Internet and reference books rather than from their accountants.

52392 ■ "TodaysMama.com Relaunches Website" in *Marketing to Women* **(Vol. 20, January 2007, No. 1, pp. 3)**
Pub: EPM Communications, Inc.
Description: TodaysMama.com, an online resource for mothers, debuted its enhanced Website. They

have partnered with Kiva, a charitable organization, to fund microloans to entrepreneurs in developing nations.

52393 ■ "Toyota Center Bypasses Ticketmaster" in *Houston Business Journal* **(Vol. 34, No. 14, August 15, 2003, pp. 2A)**
Pub: American City Business Journals
Ed: Jennifer Dawson. **Description:** Houston, Texas entertainment venues are offering alternative ticket sales options besides Ticketmaster.

52394 ■ "The Turning of Atlanta" in *Harvard Business Review* **(Vol. 81, No. 12, December 2003, pp. 18)**
Pub: Harvard Business School Press
Description: Atlanta, Georgia Mayor Shirley Franklin addresses questions regarding layoffs and work performance, prioritization, maintaining communication with the public, measurement of achievement, and remaining challenges for the city.

52395 ■ "What Do Your Customers See?" in *Inc.* **(February 1, 2002)**
Pub: Inc. Magazine
Ed: Bo Burlingame. **Description:** Ways to market a product, inventory, finding a niche for the product, and responding to the loss of a key supplier are the issues addressed.

52396 ■ "When is using a property manager appropriate?" in *Wall Street Journal* **(April 10, 2002, pp. B10)**
Pub: Wall Street Journal
Ed: Ray A. Smith. **Description:** The difference between hiring a third party property manager and dealing with tenants yourself is presented.

52397 ■ *Which Business?: Help in Selecting Your New Venture*
Pub: PSI Research
Ed: Nancy Drescher. **Released:** 1997. **Price:** $18.95.

CONSULTANTS

52398 ■ Expense Control Systems Inc.
117 E Butler Ave.
Ambler, PA 19002
Ph:(215)643-4610
Fax: (215)643-4614
Scope: Telecommunications consulting service specializing in voice and data network analyses, equipment evaluations, and accounting services. It serves all industries nationwide.

52399 ■ Service 800
PO Box 634
Deerfield, IL 60015-0634
Ph:(847)940-9333
Fax: (847)940-9808
Co. E-mail: sales@telephoneservice.com
URL: http://www.telephoneservice.com

E-mail: sales@telephoneservice.com
Scope: Telecommunications consultants and brokers of broadband and local telecom services.

RESEARCH CENTERS

52400 ■ Indiana Small Business Development Center
1 N Capitol Ave., Ste. 900
Indianapolis, IN 46204
Ph:(317)234-2082
Free: 888—472-3244
Fax: (317)232-8872
Co. E-mail: leadcenter@isbdc.org
URL: http://www.isbdc.org
Contact: Bruce Kidd, Interim State Dir.
E-mail: leadcenter@isbdc.org
Scope: Small business development. **Services:** Management consulting, business evaluation, and assistance with identification, of business and management problems. **Educational Activities:** Conferences and workshops, for small business owners and those starting new businesses; co-sponsors are universities, professionals, I.E., attorneys, and CPAs; Specialized training and individual consultation, in business management, marketing, and finance; Workshops and forums.

52401 ■ Murray State University–Small Business Development Center
Business Bldg., Rm. 253
Murray, KY 42071-0009
Ph:(270)762-2856
Fax: (270)762-3049
Co. E-mail: rosemary.miller@murraystate.edu
Contact: Rosemary Miller, Dir.
E-mail: rosemary.miller@murraystate.edu
Scope: Provides consulting for new small businesses in the state of Kentucky, including startup procedures, business plan development, marketing techniques, financial planning, cash flow analysis, taxes, management techniques, and computer applications. **Services:** Workshops.

Selling a Business

START-UP INFORMATION

52402 ■ *Legal Guide for Starting and Running a Small Business*
Pub: NOLO
Ed: Fred Steingold, Lisa Guerin. **Released:** March 2005. **Price:** $34.99. **Description:** Information for starting a new business focusing on choosing a business structure, taxes, employees and independent contractors, trademark and service marks, licensing and permits, leasing and improvement of commercial space, buying and selling of a business, and more.

REFERENCE WORKS

52403 ■ "The ABSc of ESOPs" in *My Business* (February/March 2003, pp. 36-38)
Pub: My Business Magazine
Ed: Nancy Mann Jackson. **Description:** Employee Stock Ownership Programs (ESOPs), established by Congress in 1974, are examined. Five myths regarding ESOPs are also listed.

52404 ■ "An Acquired Taste" in *Entrepreneur* (Vol. 32, October 2004, No. 10, pp. 62)
Pub: Entrepreneur Media Inc.
Ed: Crystal Detamore-Rodman. **Description:** Tim Johnstone is a former division manager for a large bank working on the due-diligence team that analyzed companies the bank wanted to buy. Johnstone's experience helped him when he decided to purchase the Anywear Shoe Company in Seattle, Washington. The firm manufactures and distributes professional footwear.

52405 ■ "The Anatomy of a Sale" in *Inc.* (September 2005, pp. 116-123, 160, 162, 164, 168)
Pub: Inc. Magazine
Ed: Bo Burlingham. **Description:** This magazine was recently the focus of a business drama, the valuable lessons learned are explored when the company went up for sale.

52406 ■ "Arvin Meritor Says It's Done Selling" in *Crain's Detroit Business* (Vol. 23, February 5, 2007, No. 6, pp. 29)
Pub: Crain Communications Inc. - Detroit
Ed: Brent Snaveley. **Description:** Auto Supplier Arvin Meritor, Inc. has completed selling off its non-core businesses and will now concentrate on growing those globally. $200M capital was raised in the sale of its last non core businesses in 2006.

52407 ■ "Ask the attorney" in *Red Herring* (March 2003, pp. 73)
Pub: Herring Communications Inc.
Description: Legal issues are addressed that include the following topics, pharmaceutical patents, government support for research and development, global commerce, intellectual property rights, the transfer of customer lists from European subsidiary to its U.S. parent company, trademark dilution, venture financing, selling a business, stock options, corporate tax deductions, small business patent methods, and employee use of Instant Messaging with clients.

52408 ■ "Bidding war" in *Entrepreneur* (Vol. 30, No. 12, December 2002, pp. 32)
Pub: Entrepreneur Media Inc.
Ed: Chris Sandlund. **Description:** EBay reports that nearly 12,000 businesses are posted for sale each month, up 35 percent from 2001. While eBay lists the businesses for sale, the Web site plays no role in working out details for the transaction.

52409 ■ "Bottle Shoppe Owner Looking to Sell" in *Bellingham Business Journal* (December 2006, pp. A6)
Pub: Sun News Inc.
Description: Profile of The Bottle Shop, a specialty beer store owned by Dave Morales. Morales is ready to sell The Bottle Shop which has a steady, loyal customer base.

52410 ■ "Brentwood's Blue Light Special" in *Washington Business Journal* (Vol. 22, No. 15, August 15, 2003, pp. 1)
Pub: Washington Business Journal
Ed: Eleni Kretikos. **Description:** The move by Kmart Corporation to put one of its Washington, DC's stores up for sale is discussed. Topics include business losses, business relocation, and corporation reorganizations.

52411 ■ "Business for Sale Update" in *Inc.* (September 2000, pp. 82)
Pub: The Goldhirsh Group
Ed: Jill Andresky Fraser. **Description:** Buyers have an unusually high number of solid companies to choose from. It is recommended to have your business in tip-top shape before taking it to market.

52412 ■ *Buying & Selling Small Business*
Pub: Self-Counsel Press, Inc.
Ed: Michael M. Coltman. **Released:** 1994. **Price:** $9.95 (paper).

52413 ■ "CEO Runs a Site with Bite" in *Crain's New York Business* (Vol. 23, January 29, 2007, No. 5, pp. F17)
Pub: Crain Communications, Inc.
Ed: Julie Satow. **Description:** Profile of chief executive, Ryan Slack of PropertyShark.com, a Brookly-based website that has a membership of over 200,000. The site offers users access to property information such as sales prices, code violatiohs, appraisal values and previous owners.

52414 ■ "Coca-Cola Bottler Up for Sale: CEO J. Bruce Llewellyn Seeks Retirement" in *Black Enterprise* (Vol. 37, December 2006, No. 5, pp. 31)
Pub: Earl G. Graves Publishing Co. Inc.
Ed: Marcia A. Wade. **Description:** J. Bruce Llewellyn of Brucephil Inc., the parent company of the Philadel-phia Coca-Cola Bottling Co. has agreed to sell its remaining shares to Coca-Cola Co., which previously owned 31 percent of Philly Coke. Analysts believe that Coca-Cola will eventually sell its shares to another bottler.

52415 ■ *The Complete Guide to Selling Your Business*
Pub: Upstart Publishing Co., Inc.
Ed: Paul S. Sperry and Beatrice H. Mitchell. **Price:** $21.95 (paper). **Description:** Step-by-step guide for business owners on determining how and when to sell the business. Contains examples and sample documents.

52416 ■ *Complete Idiot's Guide to Buying & Selling a Business*
Pub: Macmillan Publishing Co. Inc.
Ed: Gottlieb. **Released:** 1998. **Price:** $18.95.

52417 ■ "Consider Your Options" in *Forbes* (December 25, 2000, pp. 278)
Pub: Forbes Magazine
Ed: Chana R. Schoenberger. **Description:** The unknowns in valuing a business are explored. The classic way is to compute the discounted present value of future cash payouts, but one expert suggests you should also add in the firm's 'real options'.

52418 ■ "Consulting the Homeland" in *Crain's New York Business* (Vol. 23, January 29, 2007, No. 5, pp. F9)
Pub: Crain Communications, Inc.
Ed: Samantha Marshall. **Description:** Profile of Wendy Cai, director of Chinese Services Group, Deloitte & Touche USA, and one-time owner of e-commerce company Hagglers.com. She is one of the youngest directors in Deloitte's history and advises Fortune 500 companies on China investments ranging from $10 to $50 million.

52419 ■ "Curtain Call?" in *Entrepreneur* (Vol. 32, October 2004, No. 10, pp. 72)
Pub: Entrepreneur Media Inc.
Ed: David Worrell. **Description:** Profile of Chuck Hawkes, executive coach with DreamsFulfilled in Charlotte, North Carolina. Hawkes helps executives and entrepreneurs discover what they want to do after selling a business or retiring.

52420 ■ "Deciding to Sell Your Business" in *Small Business Opportunities* (Vol. 17, May 2005, No. 3, pp. 126)
Pub: Harris Publications Inc.
Description: Book review of Ned Minor's, Deciding to Sell Your Business: The Key to Wealth and Freedom. Minor asks the reader questions to determine whether selling a business is the right move.

52421 ■ "Deciding Which Shares to Share" in *Inc.* (May 2000, pp. 171)
Pub: The Goldhirsh Group
Description: An overview for small businesses thinking of selling shares of their company.

52422 ■ "For Cash-Strapped Cloudveil, It Was a Very Hard Offer to Refuse" in *Inc.* **(August 2005, pp. 44-45)**
Pub: Inc. Magazine
Ed: Dimitra Kessenides. **Description:** Founders, Stephen Sullivan and Brian Cousins were faced with the prospect of selling their six-year-old company after failing to raise enough capital to fuel production. The sportswear firm offers clothing and gear targeted to hard-core skiers and mountain climbers.

52423 ■ "Go For the Gold" in *Entrepreneur* **(Vol. 32, October 2004, No. 10, pp. 68)**
Pub: Entrepreneur Media Inc.
Ed: David Worrell. **Description:** Planning for the day an entrepreneur will sell their business is critical. Growth potential is key when determining a company's worth.

52424 ■ "Got Leverage? Dollar Signs: If You're Ready to Sell, You've Got the Upper Hand" in *Entrepreneur* **(Vol. 31, No. 9, September 2003)**
Pub: Entrepreneur Media, Inc.
Ed: C.J. Prince. **Description:** With increased private equity activity, large buyout firms will be looking towards entrepreneurs. Statistical data included.

52425 ■ *Guide to Buying & Selling a Business, Vol. 2*
Pub: Practitioners Publishing Co.
Ed: William R. Bischoff. **Released:** 1995.

52426 ■ *Guide to Selling Your Business*
Pub: John Wiley & Sons, Inc.
Ed: Rexford E. Umbenhaur. **Released:** 1999. **Price:** $24.95 (paper).

52427 ■ "Hank Aaron Moves Closer to Benching Himself with Sale of Dealerships" in *Atlanta Journal-Constitution* **(January 20, 2007)**
Pub: Cox Newspapers, Inc.
Ed: Mike Tierney. **Description:** Hank Aaron, retired Braves baseball player, plans to sell all but one of his Atlanta areas automobile dealerships.

52428 ■ *How to Buy and/or Sell a Small Business for Maximum Profit: A Step-by-Step Guide*
Pub: Atlantic Publishing Company
Ed: Rene V. Richards. **Released:** August 2005. **Price:** $24.95. **Description:** Suggestions, insights and techniques for buying and selling small businesses, includes advice on when to buy or sell, how to market the business, explanation of legal and financial documents involved in the sale and closing of a deal.

52429 ■ *How to Create a Buy-Sell Agreement & Control the Destiny of Your Small Business*
Pub: Nolo Press
Ed: Anthony Mancuso and Bethany K. Laurence. **Released:** 1998. **Price:** $49.95 (diskette). **Description:** Show business owners how to draft a buy-sell agreement, which ensures a smooth transition following the departure of a business partner.

52430 ■ "How Do I Value a Small Business?" in *Fortune* **(Vol. 142, No. 9, October 16, 2000, pp. 312T)**
Pub: Time Inc.
Description: Whether selling, buying, or settling a dispute, the article suggests hiring a broker or investment banker to establish a price.

52431 ■ "Indiana Electric Utility for Sale" in *Crain's Chicago Business* **(Vol. 30, January 2007, No. 5, pp. 12)**
Pub: Crain Communications, Inc.
Description: Northern Indiana's electric utility is for sale and is expected to fetch between $3.4 and $4 billion.

52432 ■ "Investor: Advance Notification" in *Red Herring* **(No. 102, August 15, 2001, pp. 82-83)**
Pub: Herring Communications

Ed: Eric Moskowitz. **Description:** An overview of the U.S. Securities and Exchange Commission's Rule 10b5, which allows insiders to sell shares 365 days a year, as long as they have a prearranged, written sales plan with their broker.

52433 ■ "Itching to Make Your Mark?" in *Inc.* **(February 1, 2002)**
Pub: Inc. Magazine
Ed: Jill Andresky Fraser. **Description:** Profile of a rubber-stamp and marking-device manufacturing business on the market for $575,000. The pros and cons to buying such a business are discussed.

52434 ■ "Keeping Employees" in *Success* **(Vol. 47, No. 5, October 2000, pp. 12)**
Pub: Success Publishing, Inc.
Description: Equity compensation and employee stock ownership programs (ESOPs) as options for family-owned businesses to use as an exit strategy are discussed.

52435 ■ "Knight Ridder's Happy Ending?" in *Business Week* **(February 20, 2006, No. 3972, pp. 26)**
Pub: McGraw-Hill Companies
Ed: Jon Fine. **Description:** Rumors suggest that The McClatchy Company partnered with The Times Company, may bid to purchase Knight Ridder Inc.

52436 ■ "Largest Shareholder Urges Knight Ridder to Sell Itself" in *Sacramento Bee* **(November 2, 2005)**
Pub: The Sacramento Bee
Ed: Dale Kasler. **Description:** Shareholders urged Knight Ridder to put the company up for sale. Knight Ridder owns 32 daily papers. The move represents issues facing the newspaper industry's decline in circulation.

52437 ■ "Masco to Reduce Jobs, Businesses" in *Crain's Detroit Business* **(Vol. 21, November 7, 2005, No. 45, pp. 41)**
Pub: Crain Communications Inc. - Detroit
Ed: Sheena Harrison. **Description:** Masco Corporation plans to consolidate or sell many of its businesses, the move is expected to save the company $200 million by the end of 2007.

52438 ■ *Mergers and Acquisitions from A to Z*
Pub: Amacom
Ed: Andrew J. Sherman, Milledge A. Hart. **Released:** December 2005. **Price:** $47.00. **Description:** Guide for the entire process of mergers and acquisitions, including taxes, accounting, laws, and projected financial gain.

52439 ■ "MGM Taking Bids for Two Casinos in Detroit" in *Crain's Detroit Business* **(Vol. 21, February 7, 2005, No. 6, pp. 3)**
Pub: Crain Communications Inc. - Detroit
Ed: Robert Ankeny. **Description:** MGM Mirage Inc. announced plans for a buyout in spring 2004, but under Michigan law, no casino owner can have more than 10 percent interest in more than one casino.

52440 ■ "Murdock Carrousel Sold" in *Charlotte Observer* **(January 31, 2007)**
Pub: Knight-Ridder/Tribune Business News
Ed: Bob Fliss. **Description:** Details on the sale of the Murdock Carrousel shopping center are highlighted. The deal was reported at $281 million.

52441 ■ *Negotiating the Purchase or Sale of a Business*
Pub: Bell Springs Publishing
Ed: James C. Comiskey. **Price:** $18.95. **Description:** This guide will help the seller determine a fair asking price, prepare for the sale, and deal with prospective buyers. Includes legal and tax aspects of a sale, the contract, and common financing agreements.

52442 ■ "New Jersey Firm Busy Westbrook, Maine, Online Classified Company" in *Portland Press Herald* **(December 7, 2005)**
Pub: Blethen Maine Newspapers, Inc.

Ed: Matt Wickensheiser. **Description:** The Journal Register has purchased JobsInTheUS, an online employment classifieds company. The Journal Register owns papers in Connecticut, Pennsylvania, Ohio, Rhode Island, New York, and Michigan.

52443 ■ "Now, on to the Really Big Time" in *Inc.* **(October 17, 2000, pp. 88)**
Pub: The Goldhirsh Group
Description: No sooner had some Inc. 500 companies made this year's list than their founders sold the business or took it public.

52444 ■ "One of Portland, Maine's Fastest Growing Tech Companies is Sold" in *Portland Press Herald* **(December 20, 2005)**
Pub: Blethen Maine Newspapers, Inc.
Ed: Matt Wickenheiser. **Description:** IntelliCare Inc., one of Portland, Maine's largest technology companies was recently acquired by PolyMedica Corporation. The firm is a telemedicine company offering telephone-based nursing services and technology.

52445 ■ "Out of Control" in *Inc.* **(September 1, 2003)**
Pub: Gruner & Jahr USA Publishing
Ed: Susan Hansen. **Description:** Profile of Travis Parsons, founder of Elogex, an Internet-based software application that would enable clients to coordinate shipping and delivery services across multiple warehouses and destinations. When Parsons sold the firm he also lost his decision-making power.

52446 ■ *Preparing Your Business for Sale: Sell Your Business for the Most Money!*
Pub: RDS Associates, Inc.
Ed: Russell L. Brown. **Released:** 1998. **Price:** $29.95; $49.95.

52447 ■ *Purchase and Sale of Small Businesses: Tax and Legal Aspects*
Pub: John Wiley & Sons, Inc.
Ed: Marc J. Lane. **Released:** Second edition, 1991. **Price:** $137.50.

52448 ■ "Rollups Redux" in *Business Week* **(No. 3666, January 31,, 2000 pp. 6)**
Pub: McGraw-Hill, Inc.
Description: Informative report on small companies selling out to big business.

52449 ■ "Roseville, Calif., Gourmet Gift Firm Puts Buyout on Hold" in *Sacramento Bee* **(October 21, 2005)**
Pub: The Sacramento Bee
Ed: Clint Swett. **Description:** Shari's Berries International, famous for its chocolate-dipped strawberries, has put its management-led buyout on hold in order to concentrate on the holiday season. Unforgettable Gifts Inc. had offered $1.69 million in cash along with $1.26 million in promissory notes as well as assumption of the firm's $2.35 million debt.

52450 ■ "A Run of Luck" in *Entrepreneur* **(Vol. 33, March 2005, No. 3, pp. 55)**
Pub: Entrepreneur Media Inc.
Ed: David Worrell. **Description:** Profile of Client Profiles Inc., a legal software company. CEO White McIsaac, tells how he wanted to sell his business, while maintaining control of the company's direction.

52451 ■ *The Secret of Exiting Your Business Under Your Terms!*
Pub: Outskirts Press, Incorporated
Ed: Gene H. Irwin. **Released:** August 2005. **Price:** $29.95. **Description:** Topics include how to sell a business for the highest value, tax laws governing the sale of a business, finding the right buyer, mergers and acquisitions, negotiating the sale, and using a limited auction to increase future value of a business.

52452 ■ *Sell Your Business Your Way: Getting Out, Getting Rich, and Getting on with Your Life*
Pub: American Management Association
Ed: Rick Rickertsen; Robert Gunther. **Released:** 2006. **Price:** $27.95.

52453 ■ "Selling into the Middle Market on the Downswing Can Be Costly" in *Success from Failure* **(August 2000)**
Pub: Vision Quest Publishing, Inc.
Ed: Mitchell L. Frankel. Description: An examination of ways in which to maximize the sale of a business when profitability is low.

52454 ■ "Small businesses fret over delays in eliminating an unpopular 1999 law" in *Wall Street Journal* **(July 19, 2000, pp. A1)**
Pub: Dow Jones & Co., Inc.
Ed: Tom Herman. Description: A discussion regarding the law that governs small businesses selling part or whole on an installment plan.

52455 ■ "Small Business Adviser: Aim resources at biggest accounts" in *Crain's Chicago Business* **(Vol. 23, October 9, 2000, pp. 23)**
Pub: Crain Communications, Inc. Crain Communications, Inc.
Ed: Michael Silverman. Description: A salable company has three basic ingredients: a sustainable sales base, profitability and the people necessary to perpetuate growth. LR Printing is in that position right now.

52456 ■ "Small businesses fight to repeal tax-law change" in *Crain's Detroit Business* **(Vol. 16, No. 16, April 17, 2000, pp. 32)**
Pub: Crain Communications, Inc.
Ed: Amy Lane. Description: Small business officials in Michigan, and elsewhere, are lobbying Washington to repeal a tax-law change that could kill sales of businesses or affect the transactions' price.

52457 ■ "Smooth Selling" in *My Business* **(September/October 2001, pp. 34-37)**
Pub: My Business Magazine
Ed: Jamie Clary. Description: Insights from former small business owners are offered to help sell a business. In addition to attorneys and brokers, various books and Web sites are given; information for investing the income received from the sale, and the six most costly selling mistakes are summarized.

52458 ■ "Sold for $20 Million" in *Black Enterprise* **(Vol. 31, No. 5, December 2000, pp. 30)**
Pub: Earl Graves Publishing Co.
Description: A profile of Charles "Chuck" H. James III, who sold his ProduceOnline.com, an online venture looking to streamline transactions between wholesale buyers and sellers of fresh produce.

52459 ■ *Stop Working: Start a Business, Globalize It, and Generate Enough Cash Flow to Get Out of the Rat Race*
Pub: Eye Contact Media
Ed: Rohan Hall. Released: November 2004. Price: $19.99. Description: Advice is given to small companies to compete in the global marketplace by entrepreneur using the same strategy for his own business.

52460 ■ "Surviving the New Economy" in *Inc.* **(October 1, 2003)**
Pub: Gruner & Jahr USA Publishing
Ed: Nadine Heintz. Description: Profile of Data Return and its management. Data Return is a Web-hosting firm sold by Sunny Vanderbeck, who is considering buying his company back.

52461 ■ "Timing the Sale" in *Success* **(Vol. 47, No. 4, September 2000, pp. 74)**
Pub: Success Publishing, Inc.
Ed: Margaret Crane. Description: Selling a family business can be the right move. This article investigates the 10 reasons the owner of a family business made the sale.

52462 ■ "To Sell or Not to Sell? Here's How to Decide" in *American Banker* **(Vol. 170, February 4, 2005, No. 24, pp. 11)**
Pub: Thomson Financial Media Inc.
Ed: Steinar Ryen, Oliver Sommer. Description: Directors of regional banks are questioning whether it is in shareholder's interest to remain independent or to sell the bank. The top five FDIC-insured banks and savings institutions in the U.S. control only 41 percent of the assets in FDIC-insured institutions, in Canada the top six control 87 percent of assets, and in Australia the top five control 75 percent.

52463 ■ "The Ultimate Employee Buy-In" in *Inc.* **(Volume 27, December 2005, No. 12, pp. 107-111, 114-116)**
Pub: Inc. Magazine
Ed: John Case. Description: Employee stock ownership plans, or ESOPs, are becoming a trend among small companies, an alternative to entrepreneurs rather than selling their firm.

52464 ■ *Ultimate Guide to Buying or Selling Your Business*
Pub: Entrepreneur Press
Ed: Ira N. Nottonson. Released: September 2004. Price: $24.95 (US), $35.95 (Canadian). Description: Proven strategies to evaluate, negotiate, and buy or sell a small business. Franchise and family business succession planning is included.

52465 ■ *Unlocking the Value of Your Business: How to Increase It, Measure It & Negotiate a Sale Price - In Easy, Step-by-Step Terms*
Pub: Charter Oak Press
Ed: Thomas W. Horn. Released: 1998. Price: $29.95.

52466 ■ "Workaholic Cooks Up Site" in *Crain's New York Business* **(Vol. 23, January 29, 2007, No. 5, pp. F3)**
Pub: Crain Communications, Inc.
Ed: Lisa Fickenscher. Description: Profile of Jason R. Finger and his Internet company, SeamlessWeb.com, a service that allows consumers and corporate employees to order food from member restaurants. Food giant, Aramark bought the firm last year.

52467 ■ "Zen and the Art of Acquisition" in *Success* **(Vol. 47, No. 2, June 2000, pp. 64)**
Pub: Success Publishing, Inc.
Ed: Eddy Goldberg. Description: Selling you company might be a good strategy, but the article explores other options.

VIDEOCASSETTES/ AUDIOCASSETTES

52468 ■ *Selling a Business*
TomKat Productions
2537 S. Gessner, Ste. 114
Houston, TX 77063
Fax: (713)975-0532
Co. E-mail: tom@tomkatpro.com
URL: http://www.tomkatpro.com/index.html
Released: 1994. Price: $59.95. Description: Includes interviews with consultants and attorneys. Availability: VHS.

CONSULTANTS

52469 ■ The Blaine Group Inc.
8665 Wilshire Blvd., Ste. 301
Beverly Hills, CA 90211
Ph:(310)360-1499
Fax: (310)360-1498
Co. E-mail: blaine@pacificnet.net
URL: http://www.blainegroupinc.com

E-mail: blaine@pacificnet.net
Scope: The firm provides a variety of special communications services to its clients. These include managing crisis situations; conceiving and coordinating seminars and press conferences; event and party planning; developing master plans and collateral materials; proposal, article, letter and speech writing; conducting surveys; and publishing newsletters and brochures. We both create and implement.

52470 ■ Business Brokers Hawaii L.L.C.
PO Box 1810
Kihei, HI 96753
Ph:(808)879-8833
Free: (866)239-1567
Fax: (808)879-5966
Co. E-mail: md@BusinessBrokersHawaii.com
URL: http://www.business-brokers.com

E-mail: md@BusinessBrokersHawaii.com
Scope: Offers buying or selling existing businesses, creation of new businesses, business evaluation and appraisal, assistance to clients on expansion and mergers, consultation with owners of businesses in trouble, and consultation on Unites States, Japan and Chinese commerce. Seminars: How to Start Your Own Business; How to Make a Sick Business Well Again; How to do Fiscal Forecasting and Cash Flow Projections.

52471 ■ Business Team
1901 S Bascom Ave., Ste. 400
Campbell, CA 95008
Ph:(408)246-1102
Fax: (408)246-2219
Co. E-mail: sanjose@business-team.com
URL: http://www.business-team.com

E-mail: sanjose@business-team.com
Scope: Business consulting services offered to companies looking for buyers. Specializes in mergers and acquisitions, business brokerage, and valuations. Seminars: Business Valuation - Enhancing the Value of Your Company.

52472 ■ The Change Agents
2557 Via Verde, Ste. 400
Walnut Creek, CA 94595-3451
Ph:(925)939-6236
Fax: (925)934-4674
Co. E-mail: thechangeagents@sbcglobal.net

E-mail: thechangeagents@sbcglobal.net
Scope: Provides consulting services related to mergers, acquisitions and divestitures. Services offered include: assisting acquiring companies in establishing and managing effective acquisition programs; representing sellers in the sale of their companies, and bringing buyers and sellers together. Additional consulting services include: advising on the structure of leveraged buy-outs; mediating sales between partners or in family succession; business valuations; due diligence examination of the marketing function; post-acquisition integration advice; and corporate strategy and planning. Seminars: Everything You Always Wanted to Know About Selling or Buying Your Building Service Company.

52473 ■ Corporate Business Services of America Inc.
PO Box 1352
Conway, AR 72032
Ph:(501)329-2592
Co. E-mail: fghorton@yahoo.com

E-mail: fghorton@yahoo.com
Scope: Business management consulting firm specializes in profit engineering, management consulting, and business coaching. Industries served: businesses with sales in the $500,000 to $25,000,000 range. Special Services: Confidential data file of private buyers for business and financial instruments; business planning and coaching.

52474 ■ James W. Davidson Company Inc.
23 Forest View Rd.
Wallingford, PA 19086
Co. E-mail: jwdmsd@comcast.net

E-mail: jwdmsd@comcast.net
Scope: Offers counsel to clients to improve business strategy, organization, controls, management effectiveness and profits. Provides planning, problem-analysis and implementation assistance. Also performs thorough, in-depth executive recruiting and acquisition and divestment search and analysis. Experienced with large and small manufacturing and service companies, including new ventures.

52475 ■ DeVries & Company Inc.
800 W 47th St.
Kansas City, MO 64112
Ph:(816)756-0055
Fax: (816)756-0061
Scope: Investment banking/financial consulting firm which helps companies solve financial problems and achieve growth and diversification goals. Helps established companies raise capital, and assists new and developing companies secure venture capital and create public markets for their stocks. Provides confidential services to companies who want to sell or merge, aids companies in acquiring other companies, helps individuals and companies structure and negotiate leveraged buyouts, provides financial guidance, shapes business strategy and develops operating and financial strategies. Also performs business valuations for estate and gift tax and ESOPS. Renders fairness opinions and expert witness services.

52476 ■ Duff & Phelps L.L.C.
311 S Wacker Dr., Ste. 4200
Chicago, IL 60606
Ph:(312)697-4600
Fax: (312)697-0115
URL: http://www.duffllc.com
Scope: Financial business consultancy that provides going-concern business valuations of closely held companies and their securities, fairness and solvency opinions, and expert witness testimony, middle market investment banking services and private placement of debt and equity securities.

52477 ■ Equity Partners Of America Ltd.
1450 W Long Lake Rd., Ste. 340
Troy, MI 48098

Ph:(248)952-0300
Fax: (248)952-0314
Co. E-mail: equitypartners@email.msn.com

E-mail: equitypartners@email.msn.com
Scope: Private investment bank specializes in debt and equity capital procurement; buying and selling businesses; shareholder value enhancement strategies; and litigation and alternative dispute resolution assistance; including expert witness assistance. Serves manufacturing, distribution and service industries. **Seminars:** Preparation of a business plan; Use of financial statements in damage claims; Determining the value of a business; When to sell a family business.

52478 ■ Hampton Group
9110-B Alcosta Blvd., Ste. 238
San Ramon, CA 94583
Ph:(925)830-3447
Free: 800-820-6424
Fax: (925)831-8194
Co. E-mail: dataforpeter@hotmail.com

E-mail: dataforpeter@hotmail.com
Scope: Consults on the buying and selling of small and medium-sized businesses.

52479 ■ Management Services & Development Ltd.
103 Carmalt Ave.
Punxsutawney, PA 15767
Ph:(814)938-8170
Free: 800-633-0688
Fax: (814)938-8177
Co. E-mail: rdm@MergerMentor.com

URL: http://www.mergermentor.com

E-mail: rdm@MergerMentor.com
Scope: Specializes in valuation and financial services for acquisition or sale of businesses. Performs appraisals and facilitates the actual transfer of business ownership. Also specializes in the sale of privately owned manufacturing businesses. Professional intermediaries who handle all phases of the project including initial analysis, planning, valuating, qualifying of prospective buyers, negotiations and execution of the transaction. Industries served: businesses, manufacturing firms and government agencies. States and Canada. **Seminars:** Exit Planning; How to Determine the Value of Your Business; How to Maximize the Value of Your Business; Success without Stress.

52480 ■ Mertz Associates Inc.
1 Riverwood Pl., N17W24222 Riverwood Dr., Ste. 305
Waukesha, WI 53188
Ph:(262)523-4200
Fax: (262)523-4202
Co. E-mail: mertz@mertz.com
URL: http://www.mertz.com

E-mail: mertz@mertz.com
Scope: A merger and acquisition consulting firm representing either dedicated buyers or sellers of companies across the U.S. Clients range from small privately held companies to large public companies in all industries.

EDUCATIONAL PROGRAMS

52481 ■ AMA's Course for President's and CEO's
American Management Association
1601 Broadway
New York, NY 10019
Ph:(212)586-8100
Free: 800-262-9699
Fax: (212)903-8168
Co. E-mail: customerservice@amanet.org
URL: http://www.amanet.org
Price: $5,000 for non-members; $4,595 for AMA members. **Description:** Covers recognizing new growth opportunities, both inside and outside your company, risk taking to advance, create positive relations with your employees' and taking the initial steps towards a merger or acquisition, **Locations:** Phoenix, AZ; Hilton Head Island, SC; New York, NY; and San Francisco, CA.

52482 ■ AMA's Course for Senior Executives
American Management Association
1601 Broadway
New York, NY 10019
Ph:(212)586-8100
Free: 800-262-9699
Fax: (212)903-8168
Co. E-mail: customerservice@amanet.org
URL: http://www.amanet.org
Price: $3,300 for non-members; $3,000 for AMA members. **Description:** Covers how the decisions you make shape the end result, including leadership skills, strategy and performance, align and motivate a positive workforce. **Locations:** San Francisco, CA; New York, NY; and Hilton Head Is., SC.

52483 ■ Executive Effectiveness Unit 2
American Management Association
1601 Broadway
New York, NY 10019
Ph:(212)586-8100
Free: 800-262-9699
Fax: (212)903-8168
Co. E-mail: customerservice@amanet.org
URL: http://www.amanet.org
Price: $2,122 for non-members; $1,997 for AMA members. **Description:** Covers influencing, coaching skills, teamwork through mentoring, effective negotiating, and presentation skills. **Locations:** San Francisco, CA; New York, NY; and Washington, DC.

REFERENCE WORKS

52484 ■ *Retiring to Your Own Business: How You Can Launch a Satisfying, Productive and Prosperous Second Career*
Pub: The New Career Centers, Inc.
Ed: Gustav Berle. **Released:** 1993. **Price:** $14.95. **Description:** Provides information for retirees on starting a business. Lists various retirement opportunities.

52485 ■ *Start Your Own Business After 50—or 60—or 70!*
Pub: Bristol Publishing Enterprises, Inc.
Ed: Lauraine Snelling. **Released:** 1990. **Price:** $8.95, plus $2.50 shipping. **Description:** Profiles 64 business owners who started their first businesses after age 50.

52486 ■ "Tucson, Ariz., Senior Citizen Keeps Moving with Dance Studio" in *Arizona Daily Star* (October 7, 2002)
Pub: Knight Ridder/Tribune Business News
Ed: Edward L. Cook. **Description:** Profile of Zircon Zelda, a dance studio catering to senor citizens, located in Tucson, Arizona. Helen Hart, owner, has 60 years of experience as a professional dancer, singer, choreographer and comedian.

LIBRARIES

52487 ■ Virginia Commonwealth University–Virginia Center on Aging–Information Resources Center (PO Bo)
PO Box 980229
Richmond, VA 23298-0229
Ph:(804)828-1525
Fax: (804)828-7905
URL: http://views.vcu.edu/vcoa
Contact: Dr. Ed Ansello, Dir.
Scope: Gerontology, mental health, sociology and the politics of aging, geriatrics, family relationships, long-term care. **Services:** Library open to the public with restrictions. **Holdings:** 1500 books; 100 reports; 4 archives; 100 AV items.

START-UP INFORMATION

52488 ■ **"At Your Service"** in *Small Business Opportunities* (Vol. 12, No. 3, May 2000, pp. 70, 72, 74, 76, 78, 80-82, 84)
Pub: Harris Publications, Inc.
Description: Service businesses sell the commodities of time and convenience. The article presents the 15 best businesses to start and run from the home, including landscape/gardening, computer/internet tutor, e-commerce specialist, elder care, window washing, reunion planner, bookkeeper, children's party planner, personalized products, errand service, food delivery service, children's taxi service, personal chef, and repair/restoration services.

52489 ■ **"Cash From Trash: 1-800-Got-Junk?"** in *Fortune* (Vol. 148, No. 9, October 27, 2003, pp. 196)
Pub: Time Inc.
Ed: Justin Martin. **Description:** Profile of Brian Scudamore's startup franchise called Got-Junk. The firm is one of the fastest growing franchises in North America with $12.6 million in revenue in 2003.

52490 ■ **"Got Fit?"** in *Success* (Vol. 47, No. 6, November 2000, pp. 18)
Pub: Success Publishing, Inc.
Ed: Debbie Selinsky. **Description:** Jennifer Floren, a graduate of Dartmouth College, helps new college grads find their way into the work world. Three years into the business, experince.com has 100 employees across the country.

52491 ■ **"Homebased Moneymakers"** in *Small Business Opportunities* (Vol. 12, No. 5, September 2000, pp. 74, 76)
Pub: Harris Publications, Inc.
Description: Ten quick and easy businesses that can be started from home for less than $100, including an inventory service, apartment preparation service, summer snack shop, plant watering service, messenger/fast errand service, bartender for private parties, framing service, online auction business, gardening consultant, and making scrapbooks for clients.

52492 ■ **"Hot 100"** in *Entrepreneur* (Vol. 31, No. 6, June 2003, pp. 64)
Pub: Entrepreneur Media Inc.
Ed: Amanda C. Kooser. **Description:** Twenty-five of the 100 companies hitting the year's hottest industry for 2003 come from the business services sector, nine providing logistics services (such as freight-handling, trucking and transportation) and six providing marketing and advertising services.

52493 ■ *How to Make Money While You Look for a Job*
Pub: Booklocker.com, Incorporated
Ed: Donna Boyette. **Released:** March 2005. **Price:** $11.95. **Description:** Six steps to make money while searching for employment are outlined, from setting up a home-based office to selling a service.

52494 ■ **"Keep them flying"** in *BlackEnterprise* (Vol. 31, No. 11, June 2001, pp. 74)
Pub: Earl Graves Publishing Co.
Ed: Paula McCoy-Pinderhughes. **Description:** Advice is given to an airplane mechanic who is interested in becoming a minority business supplier of aircraft components and parts. Sources such as the Small Business Development Council, under the auspices of the SBA; the Boeing Company's Supplier Diversity Program; the National Minority Supplier Development Council; and the National Black Chamber of Commerce are all profiled.

52495 ■ **"The perils of starting a service firm"** in *Wall Street Journal* (May 28, 2002, pp. B5)
Pub: Wall Street Journal
Ed: Jeff Bailey. **Description:** Must-know advice is offered for would-be entrepreneurs wishing to start a service firm, is presented. Statistical data included.

52496 ■ **"Seasonal Wonder"** in *Small Business Opportunities* (Vol. 12, No. 2, March 2000, pp. 68)
Pub: Harris Publications, Inc.
Ed: Bill Watson. **Description:** The article shows how to make up to $500,000 a season with a snow removal business.

52497 ■ **"Service Franchises Hold Advantages Over Retail Operations"** in *Long Island Business News* (May 7, 2004)
Pub: Dolan Media Newswires
Ed: Adina Genn. **Description:** The advantages service franchises have over owning a retail franchise are discussed. Discussions with various franchise owners are included.

52498 ■ **"Sharing the wealth: never mind the dismal economy."** in *Entrepreneur* (Vol. 31, No. 5, May 2003, pp. 88)
Pub: Entrepreneur Media Inc.
Ed: Chris Penttila. **Description:** Opportunities for starting a luxury business are explored.

52499 ■ **"Silver (and Gold) in Senior Services"** in *Home Business* (Vol. 13, January/February 2006, No. 1, pp. 32, 34, 66, 68)
Pub: Home Business Magazine
Ed: Priscilla Y. Huff. **Description:** Fifteen home-based businesses targeting senior citizens include medical claims assistance, senior care consulting, nutrition, in-home care, money managers, seamstress/tailoring, handyman services, financial planning, home business consulting, home delivery, exercise, computer consulting, antique appraisals, lawn and garden services, and transcription and/or video services.

52500 ■ *Small Business Desk Reference*
Pub: Penguin Books (USA) Incorporated
Ed: Gene Marks. **Released:** December 2004. **Price:** $29.95 (US), $44.00 (Canadian). **Description:** Com-prehensive guide for starting or running a successful small business, focusing on buying a business or franchise, writing a business plan, financial management, accounting, legal issues, human resources management, operations, marketing, sales, customer service, taxes, insurance, and ethics. Information for launching a restaurant, property management firm, retail outlet, consulting firm, and service business is included.

52501 ■ **"Strike it Rich!"** in *Small Business Opportunities* (Vol. 16, No. 3, May 2004, pp. 22-24, 26, 28, 30, 32, 34, 36, 38, 40-42, 44, 98)
Pub: Harris Publications, Inc.
Description: Profiles of fifteen service business to consider, including electrical services, windshield repair, waste management, automotive repair, wedding photography, dryer vent cleaning, home helpers, supermarket services, garage makeovers, window blinds cleaning, concrete coating, carpet and upholstering cleaning, slip and fall prevention, and home cleaning.

52502 ■ **"Taking care of business"** in *BlackEnterprise* (Vol. 31, No. 12, July 2001, pp. 46)
Pub: Earl Graves Publishing Co.
Ed: Bridget McCrea. **Description:** Brothers, Fred and Richard Calloway, have founded a company that caters to a decidedly male customer base with its barber, dry cleaning, and car wash services. In 1998, with approximately $30,000 of combined personal savings, the brothers created Male Care.

52503 ■ **"20 Top Biz for 2002"** in *Small Business Opportunities* (V. 14, No. 1, 1/2002, pp. 22-24, 26, 28, 30, 32, 34, 36, 38, 40, 130)
Pub: Harris Publications, Inc.
Description: Twenty recession-proof businesses for potential entrepreneurs to startup are profiled, including health food store, cleaning service, handyman service agency, cart vendors, window cleaning, dance studio, information broker, landscaping, sign shop, auto paint repair service, computer maintenance, closet/storage organizer, childproofing safety business, hair salon, specialty cake bakery, pet chauffer business, senior services, and delivery services.

ASSOCIATIONS AND OTHER ORGANIZATIONS

52504 ■ **Coalition of Service Industries**
1090 Vermont Ave. NW, Ste. 420
Washington, DC 20005
Ph:(202)289-7460
Fax: (202)775-1726
URL: http://www.uscsi.org
Contact: J. Robert Vastine, Pres.
Description: Increases attention to measurement of productivity in services and revises national economic indicators to account for services. Represents US service sector in multilateral trade negotiations. Works with interested groups internationally. **Publications:** *CSI Reports* (quarterly); *The Service Economy* (quarterly).

REFERENCE WORKS

52505 ■ **"Aerobatic Ace: Young Pilot Flies Plane That's Smaller Than a Car" in** *Black Enterprise* **(Vol. 34, No. 2, September 2003, pp. S9)**
Pub: Earl Graves Publishing Co.
Ed: Raelyn C. Johnson. Description: Profile of Jamail Larkins, 19-year-old owner of Larkins Enterprises Inc. Larkins' aviation and advertising company has gone from selling flight training books to selling satellite navigation systems. He flies himself to speaking engagements and air shows where he advertises for Delta, AeroShell, and Power Serve International.

52506 ■ **"Affordable Franchises" in** *BlackEnterprise* **(Vol. 32, No. 2, September 2001, pp. 88)**
Pub: Earl Graves Publishing Co.
Ed: Bridget McCrea. Description: A list of 15 franchises that offer opportunities for African American business owners, based on a national survey franchisors that are members of the the of the International Franchise Association (IFA), the existing number of African American franchise units, and companies that have franchises within three price ranges: $10,000-$50,000, $50,000-$150,000, and $150,000-$350,000 (inclusive of total start-up costs and franchise fee). Franchises listed include Coverall Cleaning Concepts, Molly Maid Inc., Liberty Tax Service, Kumon North America, ECW Corp., Crown Trophy, SIGN-A-RAMA, Ace Cash Express Inc., MGW Group Inc., Express Personnel Services, Meineke Discount Muffler Shops Inc., Cinnabon Inc., Jiffy Lube International Inc., Denny's Inc., Church's Chicken.

52507 ■ **"Appetite for Destruction" in** *Washington Business Journal* **(Vol. 22, No. 14, August 8, 2003, pp. 29)**
Pub: Washington Business Journal
Ed: Tim Pappa. Description: Brad Schofield, president of Safeguard Shredding, said that the mobile document shredding company is planning a major expansion program. The firm's business is increasing since medical companies are required to destroy patient records under the 2003 Health Insurance Portability Accountability Act.

52508 ■ **"Bankruptcy Could Cost Firm $310M" in** *Atlanta Business Chronicle* **(Vol. 26, No. 9, August 8, 2003, pp. 1A)**
Pub: American City Business Publications, Inc.
Ed: Mary Jane Credeur. Description: Atlanta, George-based Global Payments Inc., a transaction processing company, may lose about $310 million if financially-troubled Air Canada does not pay its debts. Global Payments is the primary processor of the airline's tickets that are purchased with credit cards and debit cards.

52509 ■ **"Bits and Bytes" in** *Kansas City Star* **(February 1, 2005)**
Pub: Knight-Ridder/Tribune Business News
Ed: David Hayes. Description: Weathernews offers current weather reports, forecasts, color radar, airport weather, travel forecasts and local photos on its mobile phone service.

52510 ■ **"Bridging the On-the-Road Blues" in** *Business Journal-Milwaukee* **(Vol. 20, No. 50, August 29, 2003, pp. A30)**
Pub: American City Business Journals, Inc.
Ed: Becca Mader. Description: An examination of services offered by Milwaukee, Wisconsin-based BridgeStreet Accommodations Inc. Topics covered include employee housing, cost control advantages, and area competition.

52511 ■ **"Business Services" in** *Entrepreneur* **(Vol. 31, No. 5, May 2003, pp. 8)**
Pub: Entrepreneur Media Inc.
Description: A directory of business services is presented, listing such services as franchise consultation, attorneys, entrepreneurial information radio shows, sales and marketing plans, business startup information, home-based businesses, raising business capital, e-businesses, B2B sales leads, and software.

52512 ■ **"Catering to Fickle Customers" in** *Hispanic Business* **(June 2005, pp. 90)**
Pub: Hispanic Business
Ed: Kevin Savetz. Description: Despite heavy demand, service companies reported slow revenue growth in 2004. Statistical data included.

52513 ■ **"Changing gears: Gregory Blache pilots against the tide on the Mississippi River" in** *Black Enterprise* **(Vol. 33, No. 6, Jan. 2003)**
Pub: Earl Graves Publishing Co.
Ed: Shani Smothers. Description: Profile of Gregory J. Blache, 33-year-old entrepreneur riverboat pilot, who guides over 95 percent of ship traffic on the Mississippi River.

52514 ■ **"Charlotte, N.C., Jeweler Offers to Sell Stuff for You on eBay" in** *Charlotte Observer* **(April 2, 2004)**
Pub: Knight-Ridder/Tribune Business News
Ed: Leigh Dyer. Description: Profile of Ernest Perry, owner of Perry's at SouthPark, a drop-off store where sellers can leave jewelry items to be sold on eBay. Drop-off stores appeal to those who lack Internet skills or have the time to maintain online auctions. Other drop-off operations include AuctionDrop, QuikDrop International, Snappy Auctions, iSold It and PicureIt-Sold.

52515 ■ **"Cheap frills" in** *Boston Business Journal* **(Vol. 22, No. 22, May 10, 2002, pp. 36)**
Pub: MCP, Inc.
Ed: Linda Goodspeed. Description: The Concierge of Boston Inc. and Tillenger's Concierge both see that, while the slowing economy has caused layoffs and cutbacks on concierge services, clients' employees who remain create more demand for concierge services.

52516 ■ **"Check Provider Says It Plans to Close Call Center in Charlotte" in** *Charlotte Observer* **(February 6, 2007)**
Pub: Knight-Ridder/Tribune Business News
Ed: Rick Rothacker. Description: Clarke American Checks Inc. is closing its call center located in Charlotte, North Carolina. Clarke provides checks and other services to financial institutions and customers.

52517 ■ **"Check's in the Mail" in** *Small Business Opportunities* **(Vol. 12, No. 5, September 2000, pp. 58-59)**
Pub: Harris Publications, Inc.
Ed: Annette Wood. Description: A profile of Contemporary Communications Incorporated, a direct mail service that sorts, folds, and inserts items, then delivers the mail to the post office for clients across the nation.

52518 ■ **"Clean Sweep" in** *Entrepreneur* **(Vol. 24, No. 7, July 1996, pp. 59)**
Pub: Entrepreneur Media, Inc.
Ed: Cynthia E. Griffin. Description: Many home offices are plagued by disorganization, and often can be helped with the services of a professional organizer. One woman's home is used to illustrate how the aid of a member of the National Association of Professional Organizers can make a home office run more efficiently.

52519 ■ **"Click on a Fortune" in** *Small Business Opportunities* **(Vol. 17, May 2005, No. 3, pp. 22-24, 26-28, 30, 32, 34, 36, 38, 40, 42, 44)**
Pub: Harris Publications Inc.
Description: Fifteen growing service franchises are highlighted. Profiles of the following franchise and independent startup opportunities include Island Ink-Jet, Wireless Toyz, homemade foods, Children's Orchard, carpet cleaning, concierge services, family books, Putt-Putt golf centers, glass replacement, online auction sales, mystery shoppers, Earl of Sandwich, Instant FX, senior care, and real estate investing.

52520 ■ **"Concierge: At Your Service" in** *Ventura County Star* **(February 11, 2005)**
Pub: Ventura County Star
Ed: Allison Bruce. Description: Profile of Cynthia Adkins, owner of the San Diego-based Concierge At Large Inc. The company is often kept on retainer by firms offering its services as a marketing device.

52521 ■ **"Conquering Clutter" in** *American Medical News* **(Vol. 41, No. 4, January 26, 1998, pp. 11)**
Pub: American Medical News
Ed: Maureen Glabman. Description: A professional organizer can assist physicians with the paperwork that sometimes threatens to disrupt the orderly course of business in a medical practice. The organizer will create a system for filing papers that are needed and discarding others. The doctor will profit from the time saved by having information readily at hand.

52522 ■ **"Damage Control" in** *Black Enterprise* **(Vol. 36, December 2005, No. 5, pp. 54)**
Pub: Earl G. Graves Publishing Co. Inc.
Ed: Michelle K. Massie. Description: International Catastrophe Solutions specializes in fire and water restoration, dehumidification, mold remediation, and soot and asbestos removal. The company sent workers to help victims of Hurricane Katrina.

52523 ■ *Delivering Knock Your Socks Off Service, 4th Edition*
Pub: American Management Association
Ed: Performance Research Associates. Released: 2006.

52524 ■ **"Demolition Man: This Entrepreneur Builds His Business by Tearing Things Down" in** *Black Enterprise* **(Vol. 34, No. 5, December 2003)**
Pub: Earl Graves Publishing Co.
Ed: Glenn Townes. Description: Profile of Jamie Potter and his small business, Cut Core Demolition Company. The Los Angeles, California-based firm specializes in demolition and site cleaning.

52525 ■ **"Detroit Free Press Wayne Small Business Column" in** *Detroit Free Press* **(July 21, 2005)**
Pub: Knight-Ridder/Tribune Business News
Ed: Carol Cain. Description: Mark Slagle, owner of Mr. Handyman of Southeastern Wayne County franchise, discusses growing a small business in a tough economy. Mr. Handyman offers full-service repair and maintenance for homeowners.

52526 ■ **"Easy Does It" in** *Entrepreneur* **(Vol. 28, No. 6, June 2000, pp. 22)**
Pub: Entrepreneur Media Inc.
Ed: Mark Henricks. Description: Michelle Paster's education business has no debt, more customers than it can handle, and a hands-on owner whose concern for quality requires her to do virtually everything herself.

52527 ■ **"Everything In Its Place" in** *San Fernando Valley Business Journal* **(Vol. 8, No. 12, June 9, 2003, pp. 23)**
Pub: San Fernando Business Journal
Ed: Rosanna Mah. Description: Profile of Dorothy Breininger, owner of Canoga Park, California-based Center for Organization and Goal Planning. Breininger provides professional organization services to large and small companies.

52528 ■ **"Eye on the Storm" in** *Entrepreneur* **(Vol. 33, September 2005, No. 9, pp. 43)**
Pub: Entrepreneur Media Inc.
Ed: Heather Clancy. Description: Profile of Marc Patti, founder of Paul Consulting in Tallahassee, Florida. Along with software programmer, Wes Holden, Patti has developed software called Debris Information Management System that tracks loads of debris moved to collection sites after hurricanes, floods, and earthquakes.

52529 ■ **"Fear of Filing"** in *Working Woman* **(Vol. 25, No. 2, February 2000, pp. 84)**
Pub: MacDonald Communications Corp.
Ed: Tamar Schreibman. **Description:** A professional e-organizer was hired to classify and manage the hundreds of documents on a company's PC to help the business run more smoothly.

52530 ■ **"Finding the potential in down and dirty jobs"** in *Wall Street Journal* **(April 23, 2002, pp. B5)**
Pub: Wall Street Journal
Ed: Paulette Thomas. **Description:** Profile of a woman who runs a service that cleans up dog wastes for pet owners.

52531 ■ **"FIOS TV"** in *Crain's New York Business* **(Vol. 22, November 27, 2006, No. 48, pp. 33)**
Pub: Crain Communications, Inc.
Description: FiOs TV is a television service offered by Verizon and is currently available in small cities and suburban areas in seven states. The company won a statewide TV franchise in New Jersey and is doing business in forty Long Island communities.

52532 ■ **"Five Ideas To Watch"** in *Inc.* **(October 1, 2004)**
Pub: Inc. Magazine
Ed: Lora Kolodny. **Description:** Five new products and services are highlighted, including an online dating service, mobile television, global positioning systems for golfers, and a new pooper scooper for pets.

52533 ■ **"For Centre Region Concierge, It's All in the Details"** in *Centre Daily Times* **(January 30, 2005)**
Pub: Centre Daily Times
Ed: Anne Danahy. **Description:** Profile of Thom Brewster, founder of Nittany Valley Concierge in the Centre Region of Pennsylvania; Brewster is only one of the many new concierge services across the U.S., an industry which has been growing by nearly 60 percent annually.

52534 ■ **"Former Teacher in Munster, Ind., Makes Transition to Professional Organizer"** in *The Times* **(November 16, 2002)**
Pub: Knight Ridder/Tribune Business News
Ed: Sharon Porta. **Description:** Profile of Elaine Kokai, founder and president of Better Organized. Kokai made the move from school teacher to professional organizer, and describes her new career like being in a different classroom everyday.

52535 ■ **"The franchising industry continues to heighten"** in *Atlanta Business Chronicle* **(Vol. 24, No. 11, August 17, 2001, pp. 48A)**
Pub: American City Business Journals Inc.
Ed: Alf Nucifora. **Description:** Franchising generates an estimated $1 trillion annually in the U.S., with the top franchise industries including fast food, retail, service, automotive, restaurants, maintenance, building and construction, retail-food, business services, and lodging. The service sector is creating the news.

52536 ■ **"GE Whiz!"** in *Entrepreneur* **(Vol. 28, No. 1, January 2000, pp. 32)**
Pub: Entrepreneur Media Inc.
Ed: Cynthia E. Griffin. **Description:** GE Capital to offer services for small businesses.

52537 ■ **"Get the Picture?"** in *Entrepreneur* **(Vol. 31, No. 11, November 2003, pp. 91)**
Pub: Entrepreneur Media, Inc.
Ed: Mark Henricks. **Description:** Geographic information systems (GIS) software can help dispatchers route vehicles to needed service areas quickly, and might trim a logistical outlay by as much as 5-10 percent.

52538 ■ **"Goose Busters"** in *Pittsburgh Business Times* **(Vol. 23, No. 5, August 5, 2003, pp. 19)**
Pub: Pittsburgh Business Times
Ed: Tim Schooley. **Description:** A Wild Goose Chase, founded by Gretta McIntyre, provides goose clearing services to a broad range of clients in western Pennsylvania. The company uses dogs, such as collies, to chase away geese from housing neighborhoods and commercial sites.

52539 ■ **"Government Hooks Man for Phishing"** in *Cardline* **(Vol. 4, No. 13, March 26, 2004, pp. 1)**
Pub: Thomson Media Inc.
Description: An identity-theft scam has been shut down. Zachary Keith Hill used the logos of Internet service provider America Online (AOL) and the online payment service, PayPal to scam consumers into revealing credit card numbers and other confidential information.

52540 ■ **"Groom to Grow: Animal Grooming is More Than a Pet Project for a Former HR Executive"** in *Entrepreneur* **(Vol. 32, December 2004, No. 12)**
Pub: Entrepreneur Media Inc.
Ed: Jeri Yoshida. **Description:** Profile of Kerri Evans who left her corporate job to run her Aussie Pet Mobile. The franchise provides pet-grooming services.

52541 ■ **"Guaranteed Results"** in *Entrepreneur* **(Vol. 33, March 2005, No. 3, pp. 87)**
Pub: Entrepreneur Media Inc.
Ed: Gwen Moran. **Description:** Tips for offering money-back guarantees are offered, stressing the importance of spelling out terms, use guarantees selectively, and promise only what you can control.

52542 ■ **"HelpStar"** in *Sales & Marketing Management* **(Vol. 157, February 2005, No. 2, pp. 22)**
Pub: VNU Business Media
Description: Profile of HelpStar, the help-desk request-tracking and request management system. The system supports sales calls, follows up on customer problems, creates a history of customer contacts, and prioritizes customer requests for businesses.

52543 ■ **"A High-Flying Time: Ronald Mays Zips Through the Air with Jets of His Own"** in *Black Enterprise* **(Vol. 34, No. 2, September 2003)**
Pub: Earl Graves Publishing Co.
Ed: Raelyn C. Johnson. **Description:** Profile of Ronald Mays, owner of Montgomery Jet Center in Montgomery, Alabama. Mays was the 2002 winner of CLACK ENTERPRISE's Emerging Company of the Year. The center offers services ranging from chartering to pilot staffing.

52544 ■ *A History of Small Business in America*
Pub: University of North Carolina Press
Ed: Mansel G. Blackford. **Released:** January 2003. **Price:** $18.95. **Description:** History of American small business from the colonial era to present, showing how it has played a role in the nation's economic, political, and cultural development across manufacturing, sales, services and farming.

52545 ■ **"Hooked Up to Profit"** in *Small Business Opportunities* **(Vol. 17, May 2005, No. 3, pp. 92)**
Pub: Harris Publications Inc.
Ed: Stan Roberts. **Description:** Profile of Rob Wheeles, former salesman, who decided to start Mr. Hook-It-Up home theater solutions with his wife Donna. The firm now reports sales at $1.4 million annually.

52546 ■ **"Houston-Based ChaseCom L.P."** in *Black Enterprise* **(Vol. 35, December 2004, No. 5, pp. 38)**
Pub: Earl G. Graves Publishing Co. Inc.
Ed: Malik Singleton. **Description:** ChaseCom LP in Houston, Texas has opened a new call center in Fort Smith, Arkansas creating 140 jobs paying $8 to $12 per hour. The firm provides telecom services and customer support.

52547 ■ **"I'm with the Band"** in *Entrepreneur* **(Vol. 31, No. 11, November 2003, pp. 132)**
Pub: Entrepreneur Media, Inc.
Ed: Nichole L. Torres. **Description:** Profile of Luke Eddins of Luke Hits LLC. Eddins helps match band's music to the musical needs of film and television producers.

52548 ■ **"In the Black"** in *My Business* **(August/September 2002, pp. 45)**
Pub: My Business Magazine
Ed: Ivan Sylvester. **Description:** Profile of brothers, Andy and Doug Hoiland, who own a Jet-Black franchise that does driveway repair.

52549 ■ *International Handbook of Women and Small Business Entrepreneurship*
Pub: Edward Elgar Publishing, Incorporated
Ed: Sandra L. Fielden. **Released:** June 2005. **Price:** $165.00. **Description:** The number of women entrepreneurs is growing at a faster rate than male counterparts worldwide. Insight into the phenomenon is targeted to scholars and students of women in management and entrepreneurship as well as policymakers and small business service providers.

52550 ■ **"It's All About Convenience"** in *Success* **(Vol. 47, No. 6, November 2000, pp. 88)**
Pub: Success Publishing, Inc.
Ed: Jane Shealy. **Description:** Consumers are spending big bucks on time saving services. If you can save time for consumers, they will shell out millions for the convenience. The field is diverse, but the common thread is simple: these businesses make life a little easier.

52551 ■ **"Job Market Thaw"** in *Sales and Marketing.com* **(Vol. 156, No. 3, March 2004, pp. 24)**
Pub: VNU eMedia, Inc.
Description: Future job market trends for ten different industries are examined. The ten featured industries include construction, energy, financial services, healthcare/pharmaceutical, hospitality/travel, real estate, services, technology, telecommunications, and transportation.

52552 ■ **"JPMorgan Chase Regional Economist Forecasts Long Island Growth for 2004"** in *Long Island Business News* **(January 30, 2004)**
Pub: Dolan Media Newswires
Description: Marc Goloven, an economist for JPMorgan Chase predicts economic growth of about 4 percent nationwide and in the Long Island, New York region. Goloven attributes this in part to the fact that many small businesses suffered less economic damage in the last few years. Long Island has shifted away from the manufacturing sector to the services industry, helping the area.

52553 ■ **"Keeping it all in the family"** in *BlackEnterprise* **(Vol. 31, No. 6, January 2001, pp. 40)**
Pub: Earl Graves Publishing Co.
Ed: Glenn Townes. **Description:** The importance of having a succession plan for a business is stressed and advice is given to develop such a plan.

52554 ■ **"The Lean Service Machine"** in *Harvard Business Review* **(Vol. 81, No. 10, October 2003, pp. 123)**
Pub: Harvard Business School Press
Ed: Cynthia Karen Swank. **Description:** Jefferson Pilot Financial is featured as a service company that has taken a page from management used by the manufacturing industry to cut costs.

52555 ■ **"Libraries Turn Page on Subscription Disruption"** in *Houston Business Journal* **(Vol. 34, No. 9, July 11, pp. 1)**
Pub: American City Business Journals
Ed: Jenna Colley. **Description:** The Houston Public Library System in Texas, had its periodical subscriptions interrupted due to the bankruptcy of its third party subscription service, RoweCom. Approval of a new third party subscription contract is not expected before August 2003.

52556 ■ **"Lightning Speed"** in *Entrepreneur* **(Vol. 28, No. 3, March 2000, pp. 26)**
Pub: Entrepreneur Media Inc.
Ed: Gene Koprowski. **Description:** DSL's are quickly growing in popularity among cost-conscious businesses, according to a report by Cahners h-Stat Group, a leading industry research firm.

52557 ■ "Loehmann's New Owner Keeps the Faith" in *Fortune* (Vol. 151, February 7, 2005, No. 3, pp. 26)

Pub: Time Inc.

Ed: Barney Gimbel. **Description:** Profile of Bahrain's First Islamic Investment Bank, a Middle East-based investment firm located in the U.S. Through its American subsidiary, Crescent Capital Investment, the company has invested $2 billion into the U.S. market, particularly businesses that don't sell alcohol, charge interest, or allow gambling, produce tobacco, make unwholesome entertainment, or deal with pork.

52558 ■ *Low-Budget Online Marketing for Small Business*

Pub: Self-Counsel Press, Incorporated

Ed: Holley Berkley. **Released:** July 2005. **Price:** $14.95, CD-Rom. **Description:** Low-cost, effective online marketing tips for small companies selling products or services over the Internet.

52559 ■ "Making Contact" in *Entrepreneur* (Vol. 33, August 2005, No. 8, pp. 42)

Pub: Entrepreneur Media Inc.

Ed: Amanda C. Kooser. **Description:** Entrepreneurs can now hire services for their mobile devices that automatically back up a phone's address book, as well as synchronizing the phone with contacts, calendar and tasks with a computer via the Internet.

52560 ■ "A Man's World?" in *Entrepreneur* (Vol. 31, No. 8, August 2003, pp. 26)

Pub: Entrepreneur Media, Inc.

Ed: Aliza Pilar Sherman. **Description:** Interview with three women entrepreneurs examining the challenges women entrepreneurs face in today's marketplace. The panel consisted of Cristi Cristich, CEO and founder of Cristek Interconnects Inc., maker of connectors and cabling for medical and military applications; Sheri L. Parrack, president and CEO of Texas Motor Transportation Consultants, a professional registration, tax and title service company; and Terrie Jones, owner of AGSI, a provider of information technology resource solutions.

52561 ■ *Marketing Your Service Business: Plan a Winning Strategy*

Pub: Self-Counsel Press, Inc.

Ed: Jean Withers. **Released:** Second edition, 1992. **Price:** $12.95 (paper).

52562 ■ "Medfone Expanding Its Wantagh Headquarters" in *Long Island Business News* (March 5, 2004)

Pub: Dolan Media Newswires

Ed: Nick Anastasi. **Description:** Medfone National Inc. is expanding and renovating its corporate headquarters in New York. The firm acts as a call center serving all fields of the health industry, specializing in outsourced calling and Web-based solutions for the electronic retailing, direct marketing, pharmaceuticals, hospital, medical practice and managed care segments.

52563 ■ "Miami-Area Professional Organizer Rescues Clients Drowning in Paper" in *Miami Herald* (November 3, 2001)

Pub: Knight Ridder/Business Tribune News

Ed: Cara Buckley. **Description:** Profile of Marsha Sims, owner of Sort-It-Out Inc. Sims helps small businesses in the Miami, Florida area to organize offices.

52564 ■ "Money Is Out There, But Where?" in *Crain's Chicago Business* (Vol. 30, January 2007, No. 1, pp. 12)

Pub: Crain Communications, Inc.

Ed: Dee Gill. **Description:** Chicago is a great place to start a business and entrepreneurs have a wealth of free help, resources, and information available to them. Unfortunately, most have no idea these services even exist and as a result money set aside for small businesses never gets spent. SourceLink is one such service that can help entrepreneurs find those resources.

52565 ■ "Mrs., Mom, and CEO" in *Black Enterprise* (Vol. 32, No. 9, April 2)

Pub: Earl Graves Publishing Co.

Ed: Monique R. Brown. **Description:** Profile of Vickie Clark, owner and founder of a family owned, home-based business that transports kids back and forth to various activities.

52566 ■ "New St. Peters-based Company Helps Customers Take Care of Day-to-Day Errands" in *St. Charles County Business Record* (February 2, 2005)

Pub: Dolan Media Newswires

Ed: Rachel Brown. **Description:** Profile of Barb Krug, founder of Errands on the Run. The company offers services such as grocery shopping, picking up prescription drugs and dry cleaning, gift shopping and returns, vacation planning, addressing invitations and cards, paying bills, delivering meals, renewing licenses, and provides a pet taxi service.

52567 ■ "New Shop in Tulsa, Okla., Helps Customers Sell Merchandise on eBay" in *Tulsa World* (March 12, 2004)

Pub: Knight-Ridder/Tribune Business News

Ed: Nicole Nascenzi. **Description:** Profile of Brian Barlow, owner of a new eBay drop-off store called Esell. Barlow will assist customers to sell items collecting dust in attics, garages, shops or warehouses.

52568 ■ *No More Cold Calls*

Pub: JLA Publications

Ed: Jeffrey Lant. **Released:** 1993. **Price:** $39.95 (paper). **Description:** Step-by-step guide focusing on making more profits in the service industry.

52569 ■ "No Place Like Home" in *Entrepreneur* (Vol. 32, December 2004, No. 12, pp. 108)

Pub: Entrepreneur Media Inc.

Ed: Rebecca Villaneda. **Description:** Husband and wife, Mike and Kerri Little, founders of Home Helpers, providing 24-hour-a-day home care to about 400 senior clients. Services include companionship, grocery shopping, personal care, transportation and laundry.

52570 ■ "Northeast Ohio Cottage Industry of eBay Drop-Off Stores Emerges" in *News-Herald, Willoughby* (April 3, 2004)

Pub: Knight-Ridder, Tribune Business News

Ed: Dave Truman. **Description:** Online eBay trading assistants, called Drop Off stores, not affiliated with eBay, work like consignment shops for customers. California has the most drop off stores, but the trend is spreading across the nation.

52571 ■ "Omniplex on the Case" in *Black Enterprise* (Vol. 37, December 2006, No. 5, pp. 38)

Pub: Earl G. Graves Publishing Co. Inc.

Ed: Glenn Townes. **Description:** Office of Personnel Management in Washington D.C. recently awarded a service contract to Omniplex World Services Corp. Virginia-based, The Chantilly, will perform security investigations and background checks on current and prospective federal employees and military personnel and contractors.

52572 ■ *Opportunities in Your Own Service Business*

Pub: N T C Contemporary Publishing Co.

Ed: Robert McKay. **Released:** 1999. **Price:** $11.95 (paper).

52573 ■ "Outsourcing" in *PC Computing* (April 2000, pp. 185)

Pub: Ziff-Davis Inc.

Ed: Christine Grech Wendin. **Description:** Small and medium-size companies are increasingly turning to the Web to get the business of running their business done. According to a recent Hambrecht and Quist study, the Internet business services market will grow to $6.6 billion in three years.

52574 ■ "PayPal" in *Cardline* (Vol. 4, No. 13, March 26, 2004, pp. 1)

Pub: Thomson Media Inc.

Description: PayPal's payment service expansion into the online market provides opportunities into the international market. Statistical data included.

52575 ■ "People Growers Deals With Personal Growing Pains" in *Business Journal-Portland* (Vol. 20, No. 22, August 1, 2003, pp. 3)

Pub: American City Business Journals, Inc.

Ed: Robin J. Moody. **Description:** Profile of Windy Baty, owner of People Growers. The home-based firm helps companies organize on-site health fairs and promotes wellness among employees.

52576 ■ "Professional Organizer Gives Tips on Cleaning Up Messy Desks" in *The Record* (January 13, 2003)

Pub: Stockton Newspapers Inc.

Ed: Joe Goldeen. **Description:** Tips for keeping work areas organized are offered by professional organizer, Barbara Hemphill. One of Hemphill's trademark tools is the FAT system - File, Act, or Toss.

52577 ■ "PSI Uses Technology to Keep Call-Center Biz in U.S." in *Crain's Detroit Business* (Vol. 21, December 19, 2005, No. 51, pp. 10)

Pub: Crain Communications Inc. - Detroit

Ed: Anjali Fluker. **Description:** Larry Evans, president and owner of PSI based in West Bloomfield Township, Michigan, has invested nearly $500,000 into expanding his business. The move includes new technology and the addition of about 50 workers. Evans discusses the advantages to keeping his operations here rather than offshore outsourcing the work.

52578 ■ "Q&A" in *Home Office Computing* (Vol. 18, No. 7, July 2000, pp. 13)

Pub: Scholastic Inc.

Ed: Cristina Gair. **Description:** Jay Westermeier, attorney at Piper, Maybury, Rudnick & Wolfe, in Washington, D.C., discusses ways to avoid legal problems when selling goods and services online.

52579 ■ *Quality of Service: Making It Really Work*

Pub: The McGraw-Hill Companies

Ed: Bo Edvardsson, John Ouvreveit and Bertil Thomasson. **Released:** 1995. **Price:** $34.95. **Description:** Provides instruction and examples on how to apply Total Quality Service Management to a service business.

52580 ■ "Quick Drop Franchise Opens in Virginia Beach, Va., for Storefront eBay Sales" in *Virginian-Pilot* (March 16, 2004)

Pub: Knight-Ridder, Tribune Business News

Ed: Carolyn Shapiro. **Description:** Quik Drop has opened its seventh franchise. The new store is located in Virginia Beach, Virginia and is owned by Ned Griffith.

52581 ■ "QuikDrop Authorized by State of Illinois and State of MI to Offer eBay Drop-Off Store Franchises" in *PR Newswire* (Mar. 29, 2004)

Pub: PR Newswire Association, Inc.

Description: QuikDrop International has obtained the rights by both Michigan and Illinois to franchise eBay drop-off stores, and approval is pending in Maryland and Virginia. QuickDrop is now approved in 41 states.

52582 ■ "R&D comes to services: Bank of America's pathbreaking experiments" in *Harvard Business Review* (Vol. 81, No. 4, April 2003, pp. 70)

Pub: Harvard Business School Press

Ed: Stefan Thomke. **Description:** A description of the process that Bank of America has used to create new service concepts for retail banking is presented. A group of the company's branches have become a laboratory where a research team conducts service experiments with actual customers. The program shows what a true Research and Development operation might look like in a service business.

52583 ■ **"Remote Control"** in *My Business* (February/March 2004, pp. 14)
Pub: My Business Magazine
Ed: Lee Gimpel. **Description:** Five questions to ask a mobile solution vendor before hiring their services are listed.

52584 ■ **"Sell2All Launches DropShop Services for Selling on eBay"** in *Comtex* (April 1, 2004)
Pub: Market Wire
Description: Profile of Sell2All, and the opening of its first location in Lincoln, Nebraska, as well as its DropShop services. The service will assist customers take their items into a DropShop location, utilize Sell2All's professional expertise and operations to place them on eBay and sell for the highest return possible.

52585 ■ **"Services"** in *Entrepreneur* (Vol. 32, No. 1, January 2004, pp. 242)
Pub: Entrepreneur Media, Inc.
Description: Profiles of service industry franchises available, including FiltaFry, a mobile cooking oil filtration management service; Music Go Round, a used musical instrument dealer; AmeriSpec, home inspection service.

52586 ■ **"Services finalists"** in *Crain's Detroit Business* (Vol. 16, No. 26, June 26, 2000, pp. E-15)
Pub: Crain Communications, Inc.
Description: Profiles of service industry executives, including Edward Christian, Chairman, president and CEO of Saga Communications Inc., Grosse Pointe Farms, Michigan; Kerry Brian Budry, CEO and president, QEK Global Solutions, Bloomfield Hills, Michigan; Pam Hassevoort, CEO of Foreway Transportation Inc., Coopersville, Michigan; and William Rauwerdink, former executive vice president, CFO Lason Inc., Troy, Michigan.

52587 ■ **"Serving Your Client-And Yourself"** in *Sales and Marketing.com* (Vol. 156, No. 3, March 2004, pp. 20)
Pub: VNU eMedia, Inc.
Ed: Daniel Tynan. **Description:** Profile of Craig Elias, founder of InnerSell, a firm through which salespeople can locate services for their customers, make referrals, and earn a percentage of the deal.

52588 ■ **"Setting Up Shop"** in *Home Office Computing* (Vol. 18, No. 10, October 2000, pp. 90)
Pub: Scholastic Inc.
Ed: William Van Winkle. **Description:** Online hosting companies have gone far beyond building Web storefronts and are evolving into E-business service providers (eBSPs) with wide assortments of front-end and back-end office tools. They often provide basics such as Web site setup and hosting free and generate revenue with premium value-added services such as marketing, site traffic monitoring, credit-card processing and inventory management. Tips for choosing a service provider are included.

52589 ■ **"SGS Automotive Services Offering Vehicle Inspections on eBay"** in *PR Newswire* (April 1, 2004)
Pub: PR Newswire Association, Inc.
Description: SGS Automotive Services will begin offering its comprehensive vehicle inspections services on eBay, providing the convenience of professional inspections done at individual's homes and offices. SGS is the nation's largest vehicle inspection firm.

52590 ■ **"SoBran Partners with U.S. Navy"** in *Black Enterprise* (Vol. 37, October 2006, No. 3, pp. 38)
Pub: Earl G. Graves Publishing Co. Inc.
Ed: Glenn Townes. **Description:** SoBran Inc., partnered with Lockheed Martin and signed a three-Tear production service contract with the Naval Aviation Depot in Jacksonville, Florida. The $44 million contract will allow SoBran to transport and warehouse materials for Navy facilities.

52591 ■ **"Soft Landing: James Garrett Took a Leap of Faith and Found Security"** in *Black Enterprise* (Vol. 34, No. 2, September 2003, pp. 51)
Pub: Earl Graves Publishing Co.
Ed: Cristina Gair. **Description:** Profile of James Garrett, founder of Sentel Corporation, an engineering and software services company providing homeland security devices and other services. Garrett left a government position to become an entrepreneur and tried various businesses before finding his niche.

52592 ■ **"Some Service-Related Businesses Surge Ahead"** in *Atlanta Business Chronicle* (Vol. 25, January 10, 2003, No. 31, pp. 21A)
Pub: American City Business Publications, Inc.
Ed: Leslie Williams Johnson. **Description:** According to the Georgia Economic Outlook 2003 report, the service business sector will grow despite the fact that some areas will face difficult times. The forecasts for specific types of services are discussed.

52593 ■ *Start & Run Your Own Profitable Service Business*
Pub: Prentice Hall
Ed: Irving Burstiner. **Released:** 1992. **Price:** $19.95 (paper). **Description:** Provides step-by-step information on how to start and operate a service business, covering writing a business plan, choosing a location, marketing, and financial advice. Includes model business plan, sample income tax returns, and list of franchises. Part of Landscape Management series.

52594 ■ **"State, Utilities to Debate How to Meet Power Needs"** in *Crain's Detroit Business* (Vol. 22, November 27, 2006, No. 48, pp. 14)
Pub: Crain Communications Inc. - Detroit
Ed: Amy Lane. **Description:** Michigan Public Service Commission will chair discussions with state power companies on meeting the energy needs for 2007. New policies are on the agenda from building new power plants to purchasing required amounts of energy from renewable sources.

52595 ■ **"Strength in diversity"** in *Hispanic Business* (Vol. 22, No. 7-8, July-August 2000, pp. CA4)
Pub: Hispanic Business
Ed: Joel Russell. **Description:** California's biggest Hispanic businesses are active in a wide range of sectors, including auto detailing, manufacturing and health care. The combined revenue of the state's top 100 Hispanic companies amounted to $2.98 billion in 1999, with the service sector being the largest.

52596 ■ *Sustaining Knock Your Socks Off Service*
Pub: AMACOM
Ed: Ron Zemke and Thomas K. Connellan. **Released:** 1993. **Price:** $17.95 (paper); ($16.15 for AMA members).

52597 ■ **"Taking the Hospitality Test"** in *Crain's Detroit Business* (Vol. 21, October 10, 2005, No. 43, pp. 11)
Pub: Crain Communications Inc. - Detroit
Ed: Robert Ankeny. **Description:** According to Service Advantage International, limo drivers, hotel help, waitresses and store clerks are friendly, courteous, neat and professional, but few service workers were able to recommend any Detroit attractions to visitors.

52598 ■ **"The Tech Track"** in *Hispanic Business* (January/February 2005, pp. 56, 58)
Pub: Hispanic Business
Ed: Anthony Limon. **Description:** The Information Technology Association of America reports a 2 percent increase in employment for first quarter periods of 2003 and 2004. The technology sector is slowly reabsorbing displaced workers, however banking, finance, manufacturing, food service and transportation accounted for 89 percent of new IT jobs. Statistical data included.

52599 ■ **"Technology is Biggest Export"** in *Hispanic Business* (November 2002, pp. 25-26, 30)
Pub: Hispanic Business
Ed: Jonathan J. Higuera. **Description:** Predications are made concerning future exports; the list of winners included information technology, auto parts, medical devices, services, processed foods, and chemicals. Statistical data includes largest U.S. export products, top purchasers of U.S. exports. Government Web sites providing foreign market research to small companies are listed.

52600 ■ **"Trash to Treasure"** in *Small Business Opportunities* (Summer 2005)
Pub: Harris Publications Inc.
Description: Brian Scudamore started his junk removal service while attending college and was awarded a Young Entrepreneur of the Year Award. His firm will remove any non-hazardous items from a home, business, or worksite.

52601 ■ **"Uncommon Enterprise: Chasing Business"** in *My Business* (April/May 2003, pp. 54)
Pub: My Business Magazine
Description: Profile of David Marcks and his Border collies; Marcks has established two Geese Police Academies for Border collie training. Marcks, founder and president of New Jersey-based Geese Police, Inc. offers franchises in fives states to round up unwanted geese on corporate sites.

52602 ■ **"Uncommon Enterprise: Rain Man"** in *My Business* (December/January 2004, pp. 58)
Pub: My Business Magazine
Ed: Shannon Skully. **Description:** Profile of Richard Heinichen, bottler of rain water. Heinichen uses reverse osmosis to rid the rainwater of impurities making it safe for drinking; he also holds the first patent issued for bottling rainwater in the U.S.

52603 ■ **"The Upside and Downside of Outsourcing"** in *Business Week* (February 20, 2006, No. 3972, pp. 18)
Pub: McGraw-Hill Companies
Description: Foreign companies are outsourcing jobs to the U.S. at record rates. Eight percent of U.S. workers are employed in the service industry, 19 percent in manufacturing, and only 1 percent in farming.

52604 ■ **"Virtual Assistants A Reality: Now You Can Outsource an Assistant's Job to A Remote Provider"** in *Broker Magazine* (Vol. 7)
Pub: Thomson Media Inc.
Ed: Brad Finkelstein. **Description:** A virtual assistant is an independent entrepreneur providing administrative, creative and/or technical services on a contractual basis. Profile of Jackie Kiadii, who runs a virtual assistance company specializing in the mortgage industry, is included.

52605 ■ **"Virtually Yours"** in *Black Enterprise* (Vol. 36, November 2005, No. 4, pp. 116)
Pub: Earl G. Graves Publishing Co. Inc.
Ed: Bridget McCrea. **Description:** The virtual assistant industry is creating opportunities for aspiring entrepreneurs as well as small business owners.

52606 ■ **"Waiting in the Wings"** in *Entrepreneur* (Vol. 32, No. 1, January 2004, pp. 21)
Pub: Entrepreneur Media, Inc.
Ed: David Worrell. **Description:** Market experts are predicting a rise in the number of Initial Public Offerings (IPOs) in 2004, although there is still strength in biotech and pharmaceutical companies, other sectors such as real estate, business services, healthcare and manufacturing are growing.

52607 ■ **"Web Wise"** in *Inc.* (November 15, 2000, pp. 130)
Pub: The Goldhirsh Group
Description: The four basic categories to address in order to make the Web work for businesses are addressed.

52608 ■ "What Price Time?" in *Home Office Computing* (Vol. 18, No. 10, October 2000, pp. 14)
Pub: Scholastic Inc.
Ed: William Van Winkle. **Description:** A list of new companies bringing service providers and users together to help save time is provided.

52609 ■ "When in Doubt Grab a Mouse, or a Phone" in *Crain's Chicago Business* (Vol. 30, January 2007, No. 1, pp. 12)
Pub: Crain Communications, Inc.
Ed: Dee Gill. **Description:** Interview with Maria Meyers, network coordinator for U.S.SourceLink, a nonprofit designed to give entrepreneurs and small business owners easy access to resources. Meyers talks about the program, its history and impact on the community, the website itself, and the grass-roots marketing needed to inform consumers of the services available.

52610 ■ "Winning Recipe-Superhot & Sizzling" in *Small Business Opportunities* (January 2006)
Pub: Harris Publications Inc.
Description: Profile of FiltaFry franchise that cleans deep fryers and recycles oil for restaurants.

52611 ■ "Wired Right: Ian Kery Is Ready To Take Freeman's New Electrical Division To the West Coast and Beyond" in *Tradeshow Week* (Vol. 34)
Pub: Reed Business Information
Ed: Heidi Genoist. **Description:** An interview with Ian Kery, owner of Toronto, Canada's largest electrical firm. Kery is selling that firm and moving to Anaheim, California to launch its West Coast Electrical Division. Kery provides tradeshow electrical services.

52612 ■ "Work Space" in *Tribune* (February 8, 2005)
Pub: Knight-Ridder/Tribune Business News
Ed: AnnMarie Cornejo. **Description:** Profile of Barbara Mitchell, owner of Guaranteed Green. She leases plants to banks, restaurants, grocery stores, hotels and offices in the area.

52613 ■ "Working virtually works for her" in *Black Enterprise* (Vol. 32, No. 7, February 2002, pp. 51)
Pub: Earl Graves Publishing Co.
Ed: Bridget McCrea. **Description:** Profile of Victoria Parham, owner and president of Virtual Support Services LLC. Parham's firm provides administrative support, such as email and database management, travel arrangements, scheduling, and customer-relationship management and support to a national client base, all done virtually.

52614 ■ "www.circles.com" in *Entrepreneur* (Vol. 28, No. 9, September 2000, pp. 145)
Pub: Entrepreneur Media Inc.
Ed: Robert McGarvey. **Description:** Information about the concierge service Circles offers to busy businesses. Their concierges will do anything to help out, from walking dogs, babysitting, ticket purchases to sold-out events, or overseeing household projects. Their belief is that an employee will be more productive if issues at home are running smoothly.

52615 ■ "A Year of Advice is Prize in Woman-Owned Program" in *Crain's Detroit Business* (Vol. 21, December 12, 2005, No. 50, pp. 2)
Pub: Crain Communications Inc. - Detroit
Description: Three Detroit-area woman-owned businesses will receive professional assistance from the Athena PowerLink program. The winners must be companies that are majority-owned by a woman, operating for at least two years, have a minimum of two employees, annual revenue of $250,000 or more in manufacturing or retail, or $100,000 in service business, and have clearly defined goals.

FRANCHISES AND BUSINESS OPPORTUNITIES

52616 ■ ACFN - The ATM Franchise Business
ACFN Franchised, Inc.
96 N 3rd St., Ste. 600
San Jose, CA 95112
Ph:888-794-2236
Fax: 888-708-8600
Co. E-mail: franchising@acfn.info.com
URL: http://www.acfnfranchised.com
No. of Franchise Units: 59. **No. of Company-Owned Units:** 2. **Founded:** 1986. **Franchised:** 2003. **Description:** The ATM FRANCHISE business. Develop & operate your own private network of ATM machines in hotels and Other travel & entertainment based businesses. Potential to earn significant long term residual income. Proven business plan with impressive list of corporate clients. Prior experience not necessary. **Equity Capital Needed:** Varies. **Franchise Fee:** $29,000. **Financial Assistance:** Yes. **Training:** 1 week at corporate office in California and ongoing support in all aspects of operating your ATM network.

52617 ■ Black Diamond Golf
10914 Wye Dr.
San Antonio, TX 78217
Ph:(210)590-2384
Fax: (210)590-2385
No. of Franchise Units: 55. **No. of Company-Owned Units:** 1. **Founded:** 2001. **Franchised:** 2003. **Description:** Golf club cleaning system. **Equity Capital Needed:** $25,000-$100,000 total investment; $100,000-$500,000 net worth, $50,000 cash liquidity. **Franchise Fee:** $3,000-$50,000. **Royalty Fee:** None. **Financial Assistance:** No. **Training:** Provides 2 days at headquarters with ongoing support including grand opening.

52618 ■ Choose Home
9324 E Raintree Dr., No. 100
Scottsdale, AZ 85260
Free: (866)370-4227
Fax: (480)451-4915
No. of Company-Owned Units: 1. **Founded:** 1998. **Franchised:** 2004. **Description:** Senior-care services. **Equity Capital Needed:** $49,900-$90,900. **Franchise Fee:** $21,500. **Royalty Fee:** 3-5%. **Financial Assistance:** No. **Training:** Offers 1 week at headquarters with ongoing support including grand opening assistance.

52619 ■ Coyote Enterprises Inc.
3151 Airway Ave., Ste. A1
Costa Mesa, CA 92626-4620
Ph:(714)963-0700
Free: 888-806-7944
Fax: (714)963-7799
No. of Franchise Units: 7. **Founded:** 2000. **Franchised:** 2001. **Description:** Tire and wheel installation supplies, etc. **Equity Capital Needed:** $50,000. **Franchise Fee:** $25,000. **Financial Assistance:** YES. **Training:** Yes.

52620 ■ DoctorDisc CD Swap Shops
DoctorDisc Franchising, LLC.
PO Box 1954
Morristown, TN 37816
Ph:(423)581-1004
Fax: (423)581-1004
No. of Company-Owned Units: 1. **Founded:** 1993. **Franchised:** 1997. **Description:** Cassettes, CDs, movies and video games. **Equity Capital Needed:** $60,550-$175,500, total investment. **Franchise Fee:** $18,500. **Financial Assistance:** No. **Training:** Yes.

52621 ■ DoodyCalls
5 Burke Ct.
Palmyra, VA 22963
Free: 800-366-3922
Fax: (703)995-0601
No. of Franchise Units: 13. **No. of Company-Owned Units:** 3. **Founded:** 2000. **Franchised:** 2004.

Description: Pet waste removal service. **Equity Capital Needed:** $42,400-$66,700. **Franchise Fee:** $20,000. **Royalty Fee:** 6%. **Financial Assistance:** No. **Training:** Offers 30 hours training at headquarters and ongoing training as needed.

52622 ■ The Drug Test Consultant
130 Fifth Ave., 10th Fl.
New York, NY 10011-4399
Ph:(212)242-4399
Description: Home drug testing. **Equity Capital Needed:** $2,995 total investment; $2,995 cash required. **Training:** Provides all the training, mentoring and written materials.

52623 ■ Energy Wise, Inc.
215 Dutton Ave.
Sebastopol, CA 95472
Ph:(707)824-8775
Fax: (707)824-6967
No. of Franchise Units: 8. **Founded:** 1990. **Franchised:** 1996. **Description:** Major appliance maintenance and services. **Equity Capital Needed:** $30,000. **Franchise Fee:** $12,500. **Financial Assistance:** No. **Training:** Yes.

52624 ■ Flamingo A Friend
FAF Franchising Inc.
110 Crosscut Rd.
Alabaster, AL 35007
Ph:(205)621-7400
No. of Franchise Units: 8. **Founded:** 1994. **Franchised:** 1998. **Description:** Special occasion yard decorations. **Equity Capital Needed:** $5,000 down; balance paid end of 12 months. **Franchise Fee:** $2,500 and up. **Financial Assistance:** Yes. **Training:** YES.

52625 ■ The Franchise Co., Inc.
5397 Eglinton Ave. W, Ste. 108
Etobicoke, ON, Canada M9C 5K6
Ph:(416)620-4700
Fax: (416)620-9955
Co. E-mail: info@thefranchisecompany.com
URL: http://www.thefranchisecompany.com
No. of Franchise Units: 1,800. **Founded:** 1992. **Description:** Focus is on home and business services with six distinct systems as California Closets, Certa ProPainters, Stained Glass Overlay, Paul Davis Restoration (US), College Pro Painters, Action Window Cleaners and Nutri-Lawn. **Equity Capital Needed:** Varies.

52626 ■ The Ident-A-Kid Program
Ident-A-Kid Services of America, Inc.
2810 Scherer Dr., Ste. 100
St. Petersburg, FL 33716
Free: 800-890-1000
Fax: (727)576-8258
Co. E-mail: franchise@ident-a-kid.com
URL: http://www.Ident-A-Kid.com
No. of Franchise Units: 230. **Founded:** 1986. **Franchised:** 2000. **Description:** Provides laminated child ID cards that contain photograph, fingerprints, and physical description. Program is marketed through public and private schools. **Equity Capital Needed:** $24,900 total investment, including equipment, software, supplies, marketing, materials, etc. **Franchise Fee:** $24,400. **Financial Assistance:** Financial guidance possible. **Training:** Provides 2day training session at the distributor's residence. Training includes: The identification process, equipment operation, computer and marketing techniques.

52627 ■ Mr. Appliance
1010 N University Parks Dr.
Waco, TX 76707
Free: 800-490-7501
Fax: (254)745-2590
Co. E-mail: international@dwyergroup.com
URL: http://www.mrappliance.com
No. of Franchise Units: 91. **Founded:** 1996. **Franchised:** 1996. **Description:** Home and commercial appliance repair and maintenance. **Equity Capital Needed:** $35,000-$72,000. **Franchise Fee:** $19,950, per 100,000 pop. **Training:** Initial, on-site, intranet and ongoing support.

52628 ■ Mr. Handyman of Canada
5190 Shuttle Dr.
Mississauga, ON, Canada L4W 4J8
Ph:(905)629-7755
Free: (866)338-7755
Fax: (905)629-3070
Co. E-mail: canada@mrhandyman.com
URL: http://www.mrhandyman.ca
No. of Franchise Units: 230. **Founded:** 2001. **Franchised:** 2002. **Description:** Mr. Handyman is mainly a cash business with low inventory, high-repeat customers, daytime business hours, and a protected territory with minimal space requirements. A Right Start program will assist you in launching your business. **Equity Capital Needed:** $35,000-$60,000. **Franchise Fee:** $9,900. **Training:** Continued ongoing support consists of marketing/advertising programs; meetings and conventions for networking and comprehensive training manuals.

52629 ■ Party America
P.A. Acquisitions
980 Atlantic Ave., Ste. 103
Alameda, CA 94501
Ph:(510)747-1800
Fax: (510)747-1810
Co. E-mail: franchising@partyamerica.com
URL: http://www.partyamerica.com
No. of Franchise Units: 65. **No. of Company-Owned Units:** 205. **Founded:** 1980. **Franchised:** 1987. **Description:** Party America, 2004 Party Retailer of the Year, is the party specialty retailer that captures the "Party Experience" by offering the most comprehensive everyday and seasonal merchandise needed to throw a great party. **Equity Capital Needed:** $150,000 liquid capital; $348,000-$532,000 total capital investment. **Franchise Fee:** $25,000. **Financial Assistance:** Listed with the SBA Registry whose franchisees enjoy the benefits of a streamlined review process for SBA loan applications. **Training:** Training program is provided on the operation, merchandising

and management of a Party America store. Manuals are included.

52630 ■ Pirtek USA
501 Haverty Ct.
Rockledge, FL 32955
Ph:(321)504-4422
Fax: (321)504-4433
No. of Franchise Units: 280. **Founded:** 1980. **Description:** Offers industrial services. **Equity Capital Needed:** $100,000 minimum. **Franchise Fee:** $42,000. **Financial Assistance:** No. **Training:** Yes.

52631 ■ Play N Trade Franchise Inc.
3400 Irvine Ave., Bldg. 118
Newport Beach, CA 92660
Ph:(949)486-6000
Fax:(949)486-6001
No. of Franchise Units: 20. **Founded:** 2001. **Franchised:** 2003. **Description:** New & used video games. **Equity Capital Needed:** $120,000. **Franchise Fee:** $20,000. **Royalty Fee:** 3%. **Financial Assistance:** No. **Training:** Training available at headquarters and ongoing support.

52632 ■ Precision Door Service
Precision Holdings of Brevard, Inc.
2395 S Washington Ave., Ste. 5
Titusville, FL 32780
Ph:(321)225-3500
Free: 888-833-3494
Fax: (321)225-3511
Co. E-mail: info@precisiondoor.net
URL: http://www.precisiondoor.net
No. of Franchise Units: 72. **No. of Company-Owned Units:** 1. **Founded:** 1997. **Franchised:** 1999. **Description:** Garage door repair and installation service. **Equity Capital Needed:** $200,000. **Franchise Fee:** $10,000-$800,000. **Royalty Fee:** $250.00+ per week. **Financial Assistance:** Up to 65% of the initial fee if over $100,000. **Training:** Complete training and ongoing support.

52633 ■ Receil it Professional Ceiling Restoration
175-B Liberty St.
Copiague, NY 11726
Ph:(631)842-0099
Free: 800-CEI-LING
Fax: (631)980-7668
No. of Franchise Units: 3. **No. of Company-Owned Units:** 1. **Founded:** 1992. **Franchised:** 2002. **Description:** Restoration or cleaning of drop ceilings. **Equity Capital Needed:** $55,000. **Franchise Fee:** $17,500. **Financial Assistance:** No. **Training:** Yes.

52634 ■ Servicemaster of Canada Limited
5462 Timberlea Blvd.
Mississauga, ON, Canada L4W 2T7
Ph:(905)670-0000
Free: 800-263-5928
Fax: (905)670-0077
Co. E-mail: thould@smclean.com
URL: http://www.servicemaster.com
No. of Franchise Units: 1,500. **Founded:** 1948. **Franchised:** 1950. **Description:** Offers a variety of services including disaster restoration, commercial carpet and upholstery cleaning, residential carpet and upholstery cleaning, contract janitorial services. **Equity Capital Needed:** Franchise fee + working capital. **Franchise Fee:** $23,000-$48,000. **Financial Assistance:** Financing available OAC. **Training:** Offers 2 weeks at ServiceMaster Academy then ongoing support out of Canadian Head Office.

52635 ■ Window Master
23704-5 No. 154 El Toro Rd.
Lake Forest, CA 92630
Ph:(270)897-4567
No. of Franchise Units: 5. **No. of Company-Owned Units:** 1. **Founded:** 1981. **Description:** Window cleaning. **Equity Capital Needed:** $500-$1,495. **Financial Assistance:** Yes. **Training:** Yes.

Site Selection

START-UP INFORMATION

52636 ■ "Business Incubator Has a Fish Wriggling Off of the Hook" in *St. Louis Post-Dispatch* (August 27, 2004)
Pub: Knight-Ridder/Tribune Business News
Ed: David Nicklaus. Description: Marcia Mellitz, founder of Symbiontics Inc., is considering a move to Wisconsin because of lack of funding. The firm is developing treatments for genetic disorders known as lysosomal storage diseases. It was launched with $3.5 million.

52637 ■ *The Canadian Small Business Survival Guide: How to Start and Operate Your Own Successful Business*
Pub: Dundurn Group
Ed: Benjamin Gallander. FRQ September 2004. Price: $18.99. Description: Ideas for starting and running a successful small business. Topics include selecting a business, financing, government assistance, locations, franchises, and marketing ideas.

52638 ■ "Former Airline Workers Navigate Into Florida Liquor Business" in *Bradenton Herald* ()
Pub: Bradenton Herald
Ed: Tilde Herrera. Description: Profile of Lori Clay and Herb Rice who left the airline industry to open a Florida liquor business. The store sells more than 300 kinds of wine, 75 brands of liquor, and seven various beers. The new entrepreneurs chose Florida because Florida has no state income tax and enjoys a large population of seniors.

52639 ■ "Gray Might be a Geek, thought DeVeau, but he was a Geek with Vision" in *Inc.* (May 2000, pp. 94)
Pub: The Goldhirsh Group
Ed: David H. Freedman. Description: An internet company finds its niche in an unlikely place, a depressed factory town in Lynn, Massachusetts. The article tells of its success.

52640 ■ "Money Talks to New Economy Firms: More Startups Choose Chicago for Home Base" in *Crain's Chicago Business* (Vol. 23, Nov. 27, 2000)
Pub: Crain Communications, Inc. Crain Communications, Inc.
Ed: Judith Nemes. Description: More new economy startups are choosing Chicago to headquarter their new businesses, partly because of the huge influx of venture capital targeting that sector.

52641 ■ "Roberts' Internet venture to set up shop in Detroit" in *Crain's Detroit Business* (Vol. 16, No. 16, April 17, 2000, pp. 34)
Pub: Crain Communications, Inc.
Ed: Matt Roush. Description: Profile of Roy Roberts telling how he will move his new minority-vendor Internet trade exchange to downtown Detroit.

52642 ■ "Ventura County Star, Calif., Business Briefs Column" in *Ventura County Star* (December 27, 2002)
Pub: Knight Ridder/Tribune Business News
Description: A listing of new businesses scheduled to open in Ventura, California at the end of 2002, including Body Circuit for Women, a fitness center for women.

52643 ■ *Working for Yourself: An Entrepreneur's Guide to the Basics*
Pub: Kogan Page, Limited
Ed: Jonathan Reuvid. Released: September 2006. Description: Guide for starting a new business venture, focusing on raising financing, legal and tax issues, marketing, information technology, and site location.

REFERENCE WORKS

52644 ■ "An African American in Paris: Ricki Stevenson's Entree to the City of Light" in *Black Enterprise* (Vol. 35, January 2005, No. 6)
Pub: Earl G. Graves Publishing Co. Inc.
Ed: Maureen Jenkins. Description: Profile of Paris as a city that attracts African Americans for business and pleasure. Many black entrepreneurs are enjoying Paris as a great place to grow their business.

52645 ■ "Allen Tate Expanding to Research Triangle Park: Firm Expects Raleigh Market to Grow Faster" in *Charlotte Observer* (January 31, 2007)
Pub: Knight-Ridder/Tribune Business News
Ed: Doug Smith; Dudley Price. Description: Allen Tate Realtors expanded its operations to the Research Triangle area. The firm is predicting a strong market and growth in Charlotte, North Carolina.

52646 ■ "Atlanta's Top 10 Condo Office Parks" in *Atlanta Business Chronicle* (Vol. 25, December 6, 2002, No. 26, pp. 28C)
Pub: American City Business Publications, Inc.
Description: The Gates at Laurel Springs is the top ranked condo office park in Atlanta, with 311,590 square feet of space. A full ranking, including total square feet, number of buildings, developer, amenities, and more, is listed.

52647 ■ "Brighton, Howell Hope Plans Boost Retail" in *Crain's Detroit Business* (Vol. 21, January 17, 2005, No. 3, pp. 28)
Pub: Crain Communications Inc. - Detroit
Ed: Sheena Harrison. Description: Plans by Livingston County Communities, Brighton and Howell, are underway to attract new businesses. Road construction, new signs, and beautification projects are some of the improvements planned for retail growth in the area.

52648 ■ "Calculate This" in *My Business* (April/May 2002, pp. 45)
Pub: My Business Magazine

Description: Short article with important information when choosing how large office space for a company should be, including a Web site offering a free online office and meeting space calculator.

52649 ■ "California Dreamin'" in *Entrepreneur* (Vol. 31, No. 9, September 2003, pp. 22)
Pub: Entrepreneur Media, Inc.
Description: A listing of the best areas for retail in America is presented, with California having six of the best metropolitan areas.

52650 ■ "Casting Wider Net in Realty Rehab Market" in *American Banker* (Vol. 169, December 28, 2004, No. 247, pp. 1)
Pub: Thomson Financial Media
Ed: Laura Thompson Osuri. Description: K Bank of Owings Mills, Maryland makes loans to borrowers with little or no real estate development experience. K Bank's $489 million-asset purchase-and-rehabilitation fund has brought about a reemergence to Baltimore, Maryland as a place to own a business.

52651 ■ "CB Richard Ellis Nabs Leasing Contract of 175 Fulton Ave. in Hempstead" in *Long Island Business News* (February 27, 2004)
Pub: Dolan Media Newswires
Ed: Nick Anastasi. Description: Stratford Business Corporation will oversee the leasing of CB Richard Ellis' office building in Hempstead, New York. The seven-story building currently has 40,000 square feet of available office space, with suites ranging in size from 500 to 25,000 square feet.

52652 ■ "Checking In: Chicago: Cheryl Burton Whirls Through the Windy City" in *Black Enterprise* (Vol. 34, July 2004, No. 12, pp. 150)
Pub: Earl G. Graves Publishing Co. Inc.
Ed: Description: Chicago, Illinois is presented as a city that welcomes entrepreneurial spirit. A tour of the city is also offered showcasing hotels and restaurants of interest to the business or vacationing traveler.

52653 ■ "Choosy tenants are finding bargains, flexibility" in *Atlanta Business Chronicle* (Vol. 24, No. 9, August 3, 2001, pp. 4C)
Pub: American City Business Journals Inc.
Description: According to a worldwide survey, the high-technology company of today wants office space with Internet access, which ranks highest on the list of priorities. Additional options include flexible lease arrangements and closeness to public transportation.

52654 ■ "Chrysler Deal Has SET Looking at Opening New Plant In Ohio" in *Crain's Detroit Business* (Vol. 21, October 10, 2005, No. 43, pp. 42)
Pub: Crain Communications Inc. - Detroit
Ed: Terry Kosdrosky. Description: After winning a big contract from the Chrysler Group, SET Enterprises Inc. is planning to open a new plant in Cleveland,

Ohio. SET is a Warren, Michigan metal processor. The deal will supply steel blanks for the Dodge Durango SUV and Dodge Caravan and Chrysler Town & Country minivans.

52655 ■ "Church Case May Impact Land Use" in *Crain's Detroit Business* **(Vol. 23, January 8, 2007, No. 2, pp. 18)**
Pub: Crain Communications Inc. - Detroit
Ed: Jennette Smith. **Description:** Southfield legal battle to be precedent setting for the issue of conversion of business property to church and other nonprofit use. Loss of tax revenue is the central issue. This is a universal problem nationally and may end up at the U.S. Supreme Court.

52656 ■ "Citizens Bank To Lend Low-Interest Loans to Firms Relocating to Massachusetts" in *Boston Globe* **(February 4, 2005)**
Pub: New York Times Company
Ed: Sasha Talcott. **Description:** A partnership between Citizens Bank and the State of Massachusetts will offer loans to companies expanding or relocating to the state. The loans will be set at a fixed rate of 3.5 percent and for every $400,000 borrowed, the company will be required to create one new job.

52657 ■ "Coagulating-Powder Firm Seeks Site To Build New Factory In Florida" in *Bradenton Herald* **(January 6, 2005)**
Pub: Bradenton Herald
Ed: Dana Sanchez. **Description:** Biolife LLC has plans to expand its coagulating-powder plant. The firm is looking to purchase land in the airport area where its existing manufacturing plan is located. The company reports annual sales of $1.7 million and employs 39 individuals.

52658 ■ "The Companies" in *Inc.* **(October 17, 1999, pp. 57)**
Pub: The Goldhirsh Group
Description: A listing of the top employers in the United States, with statistics including the number of full-time employees, company benchmarks for the year, HR policies, customer information, and global trends. Also listed are the number of companies that made the Inc. 500 last year, those that broke $100 million in sales, and which ones are only five years old.

52659 ■ "Connecting Firms with Needed Funds; Financial Assistance" in *Crain's New York Business* **(Vol. 22, November 13, 2006, No. 46, pp. 32)**
Pub: Crain Communications, Inc.
Description: Listing of organizations that provide incentives or financial assistance to firms that are based in New York or are relocating to the area.

52660 ■ "A Conversation With Steve Cassin, Macomb County Director of Planning and Economic Development" in *Crain's Detroit Business* **(Vol. 21)**
Pub: Crain Communications Inc. - Detroit
Ed: Anjali Fluker. **Description:** In an interview with Steve Cassin, director of planning and economic development for Macomb County, Michigan, he talks about the challenges and initiatives his county is taking on in a move to attract new business to the area.

52661 ■ "Crashing Past the Gatekeepers-Part Two" in *Business Week Online* **(April 24, 2002)**
Pub: McGraw-Hill, Inc.
Ed: Michelle Nichols. **Description:** Various approaches are discussed to get passed the barriers, such as secretaries and switchboards, preventing salespersons from reaching potential clients.

52662 ■ "Daimler deal: You can see state's offer - for $11,538" in *Atlanta Business Chronicle* **(Vol. 25, November 15, 2002, No. 23 pp. 3A)**
Pub: American City Business Publications, Inc.
Ed: Walter Woods. **Description:** According to the Department of Industry, Trade and Tourism, seeing the economic incentive package offered by the state to DaimlerChrysler AG, to bring a truck plant to Georgia, will cost $11,538 in administrative costs. The deal has not been finalized.

52663 ■ "Detroit falls on list of best places for biz" in *Crain's Detroit Business* **(Vol. 18, No. 24, June 17, 2002, pp. 29)**
Pub: Crain Communications Inc. - Detroit
Ed: Eric Morath. **Description:** According to Forbes magazine and the Milken Institute, Detroit fell further on the list of best places to do business and advance a career in 2001, falling 29 spots to 91. The ranking was based on three factors: job creation, growth in average wages, and growth in technology industries.

52664 ■ "Developer Sees a Bright Future for Downtown St. Louis" in *St. Louis Post-Dispatch* **(November 19, 2004)**
Pub: Knight-Ridder/Tribune Business News
Ed: Mary Jo Feldstein. **Description:** Richard Baron has been committed to rebuilding and enriching parts of St. Louis for more than 25 years. Baron co-founded the Center of Creative Arts, and along with his business, McCormack Baron Salazar Inc, he is able to merge business interests with philanthropy and civic work.

52665 ■ "Downsizing Smarts: When you should move to a smaller office" in *My Business* **(April/May 2002, pp. 45)**
Pub: My Business Magazine
Ed: Dan Rafter. **Description:** Profile of Charlotte Addington Weikel, owner of B-Fit Pilates Center in Tampa, Florida. Weikel is considering downsizing her studio from 2,300 square feet to a more affordable space. Cynthia McKay, president and CEO of Le Gourmet Gift Basket chose a small space when moving her business from her home.

52666 ■ "Drawn to York County: Less-Expensive Homes, Good Schools Attract Charlotteans" in *Charlotte Observer* **(February 4, 2007)**
Pub: Knight-Ridder/Tribune Business News
Ed: Taylor Bright. **Description:** York County, North Carolina offers low-priced homes and good schools, making it attractive to workers and small business.

52667 ■ "Economic Developers Expect a Busier Year in '03" in *Atlanta Business Chronicle* **(Vol. 25, December 6, 2002, No. 26, pp. 8A)**
Pub: American City Business Publications, Inc.
Ed: Jarred Schenke. **Description:** The Georgia Department of Industry, Trade and Tourism and Georgia Power Company, Georgia's largest economic development organizations, are working to attract more companies to the state. This trend could generate business for industrial real estate planners.

52668 ■ *The Emerging Digital Economy: Entrepreneurship, Clusters, and Policy*
Pub: Springer
Ed: Borje Johansson; Charlie Karlsson; Roger Stough. **Released:** August 2006. **Price:** $119.00. **Description:** The new economy, or digital economy, and its impact on the way industries and firms choose to locate and cluster geographically.

52669 ■ "Entrepreneur Column" in *Entrepreneur.com* **(December 28, 2006)**
Pub: Entrepreneur Media Inc.
Ed: Paige Arnof-Fenn. **Description:** Reflections and insight into setting practical business goals of a home-based business, including office relocation and organization.

52670 ■ *Facility Layout and Location: An Analytical Approach*
Pub: Prentice Hall
Ed: Richard L. Francis, Jr. **Released:** Second edition, 1991. **Price:** $89.33.

52671 ■ "Fantastic Sams To Open Manatee County, Fla. Hair Salon" in *Bradenton Herald* **(January 5, 2005)**
Pub: Bradenton Herald
Ed: Kurt D. Schultheis. **Description:** Lee Kline, owner of the new Fantastic Sams hair salon explains reasons for his site selection in the Cortez Commons Plaza in Manatee County, Florida.

52672 ■ "Florida is Fastest-Growing State in U.S." in *Tampa Tribune* **(December 22, 2005)**
Pub: Media General, Inc.
Ed: Chris Echegaray. **Description:** Florida was ranked as the fastest growing state in the U.S., followed by Texas and California.

52673 ■ "For Big-Box Retailers, It's Market, Market, Market" in *Long Island Business News* **(March 12, 2004)**
Pub: Dolan Media Newswires
Ed: Claude Solnik. **Description:** Large retailers are scaling down plans for building stores in Long Island in order to grow in the Long Island, New York area, due to shortage of large parcels of land as well as tougher zoning restrictions.

52674 ■ "Franklin pitches Atlanta to free-trade delegates" in *Atlanta Business Chronicle* **(Vol. 25, November 8, 2002, No. 22 pp. 1A)**
Pub: American City Business Publications, Inc.
Ed: Walter Woods. **Description:** Atlanta Mayor, Shirley Franklin, is trying to persuade the Free Trade Area of the Americas (FTAA) to locate its headquarters in Atlanta, Georgia. FTAA is a trade federation of 34 Western democracies that is slated to take effect by 2005.

52675 ■ "Fresh Sets of Eyes on Detroit" in *Crain's Detroit Business* **(Vol. 22, January 30, 2006, No. 5, pp. 1)**
Pub: Crain Communications Inc. - Detroit
Ed: Andrew Dietderich. **Description:** Out-of-town investors and developers are seeing the City of Detroit in a new light after Super Bowl XL. Downtown Detroit is overcoming its negative image.

52676 ■ "Georgia ranks so-so in business 'survival index'" in *Atlanta Business Chronicle* **(Vol. 24, No. 14, September 7, 2001, pp. 5B)**
Pub: American City Business Journals Inc.
Ed: Chaundra Frierson. **Description:** According to the Small Business Survival Committee's latest survey, Georgia ranks at 23 out of the District of Columbia and 50 states regarding friendliness to small businesses. The study focused on areas such as estate tax, unemployment taxes, health insurance taxes, personal income taxes, capital gains taxes, corporate income taxes, property taxes, and sales taxes.

52677 ■ "Good for Business: Houston is a Hot Spot for Economic Growth" in *Black Enterprise* **(Vol. 37, October 2006, No. 3, pp. 216)**
Pub: Earl G. Graves Publishing Co. Inc.
Ed: Jeanette Valentine. **Description:** Fast-growing sectors in the biotechnology and healthcare industries are among the driving forces of Houston's economic growth. More than 76,000 small businesses in the area employ about one in four area workers, according to the Small Business Administration. Housing and business costs are 26 and 11 percent below the national average, respectively, garnering the attention of corporate giants.

52678 ■ "Group Buys Bradenton, Fla.-Area Retail Center" in *Bradenton Herald* **(January 5, 2005)**
Pub: Bradenton Herald
Ed: Matt Griswold. **Description:** Kash n' Karry was purchased by New York real estate firm Gemini Real Estate Advisors LLC and 10 other investors, for the sum of $15.2 million. The store is located in the Ranch Lake Plaza in Bradenton, Florida. Gemini Real Estate Advisors LLC is one of many nationwide companies focusing on tenant-in-common, 1031 exchanges. This process allows individuals to invest with a large firm in tax-free pieces of commercial real estate.

52679 ■ *A Guide to Site Planning & Landscape Construction*
Pub: John Wiley & Sons, Inc.
Ed: Harvey M. Rubenstein. **Released:** 1996. **Price:** $75.00.

52680 ■ "Helping Hand" in *Crain's New York Business* (Vol. 23, January 15, 2007, No. 3, pp. 24)
Pub: Crain Communications, Inc.
Description: Bronx officials created a $6.75 million fund providing no-interest loans to businesses that make energy-saving renovations. Companies are also eligible for state and federal subsidies through the three Empire Zones and the Empowerment Zone. Bronx Overall Economic Development Corp. is also reaching out to businesses across the country trying to lure them to the region.

52681 ■ "Historic Redevelopment Pushes Kirtland, Ohio Ice Cream Shop to Relocate" in *Willoughby News-Herald* (September 13, 2002)
Pub: Knight-Ridder/Tribune Business News
Ed: Dave Truman. **Description:** Historic redevelopment has forced the owners of the family run Quirke's Carriage House ice cream shop to relocate. The historic development closed the street in front of the shop. Patty Quirke has run the business with her five children since the death of her husband Patrick in 1999.

52682 ■ "Hot Spots" in *Entrepreneur* (Vol. 33, October 2005, No. 10, pp. 68)
Pub: Entrepreneur Media Inc.
Ed: Mark Henricks. **Description:** Top twenty large cities, ten med-size cities, and the top ten states for starting or relocating an existing business are listed. Also included is the Entrepreneurial Activity Index to help measure the best spots to start or expand a business.

52683 ■ "How Do Producers Select Host Cities?" in *Tradeshow Week* (Vol. 34, November 29, 2004, No. 48, pp. 38)
Pub: Reed Business Information
Ed: Michael Hughes. **Description:** Hotel capacity plays a major role in choosing a site for a tradeshow, followed by total available exhibit space. Statistical data included.

52684 ■ "Image-Building Needs to Include Problem-Solving" in *St. Louis Post-Dispatch* (February 18, 2005)
Pub: Knight-Ridder/Tribune Business News
Ed: David Nicklaus. **Description:** The Council on Competitiveness is assisting the City of St. Louis in building a culture of innovation and encourages the city to promote a branding campaign to attract new business.

52685 ■ "It looks as if they got it right this time" in *Crain's Detroit Business* (Vol. 18, No. 50, December 16, 2002, pp. 8)
Pub: Crain Communications Inc., Detroit
Ed: Keith Crane. **Description:** The redevelopment of Detroit's riverfront property is discussed.

52686 ■ "Jeepers, Creepers" in *Entrepreneur* (Vol. 32, July 2004, No. 7, pp. 75)
Pub: Entrepreneur Media Inc.
Ed: Joanne Cleaver. **Description:** Anthony Crews, founder of startup Leading Edge Recovery Solutions, a debt-collections agency, shares his concern for security when choosing his office space.

52687 ■ "Kar Nut Products Gets New HQ; Snack-Maker Cites Growth for Need for Space" in *Crain's Detroit Business* (Vol. 21, January 10, 2005)
Pub: Crain Communications Inc. - Detroit
Ed: Anjali Fluker. **Description:** Kar Nut Products Company moved its headquarters from Ferndale to Madison Heights, Michigan. The relocation is the result of company growth for the maker of snacks and trail mixes. Details of the new facility and statistical data is included.

52688 ■ "Kohl's, Lowe's Set to Move into WNY" in *Business First Buffalo* (Vol. 19, No. 47, August 15, 2003, pp. 1)
Pub: American City Business Journals, Inc.
Ed: James Fink. **Description:** Plans by Kohl's Department Stores and Lowe's Companies to open stores in the greater Buffalo, New York area are discussed.

52689 ■ "Lease Lessons" in *Entrepreneur* (Vol. 32, December 2004, No. 12, pp. 106)
Pub: Entrepreneur Media Inc.
Ed: Nichole L. Torres. **Description:** Tips for securing the first commercial real estate for a small business is shared.

52690 ■ "The least lease" in *Entrepreneur* (Vol. 30, No. 3, March 2002, pp. 65)
Pub: Entrepreneur Media Inc.
Ed: Jennifer Pellet. **Description:** Because of the economic downturn, commercial real estate has become more affordable and companies are able to bargain for lower priced leases.

52691 ■ "Let's make a deal" in *Atlanta Business Chronicle* (Vol. 24, No. 9, August 3, 2001, pp. B1)
Pub: American City Business Journals Inc.
Ed: Chaundra Frierson. **Description:** Small businesses have a wide array of location options to choose from in the commercial real estate market. In Atlanta, Georgia, there are 200 million square feet of office space available. The article provides additional information on various small businesses and commercial real estate in Atlanta.

52692 ■ "Let's roll up our sleeves" in *Crain's Detroit Business* (Vol. 18, No. 50, December 16, 2002, pp. 8)
Pub: Crain Communications Inc., Detroit
Description: Two hundred million dollars worth of redevelopment projects for Detroit's riverfront are discussed.

52693 ■ "Local Businesses Discover There's No Place Like Home" in *Bradenton Herald* (February 7, 2005)
Pub: Bradenton Herald
Ed: Kurt D. Schultheis. **Description:** Profile of individuals who leave their hometowns, but return to raise their families and develop successful small businesses.

52694 ■ "Location, Location, Location" in *Black Enterprise* (Vol. 36, November 2005, No. 4, pp. 64)
Pub: Earl G. Graves Publishing Co. Inc.
Ed: James C. Johnson. **Description:** Advice is given to would-be entrepreneur wishing to open a plus-size clothing boutique, with a focus on site selection.

52695 ■ "Location, Location, Location" in *Inc.* (October 17, 2000, pp. 57)
Pub: The Goldhirsh Group
Description: Small business statistics covering the state with the biggest gain in companies since 1999, the biggest drop in companies since 1999, the top five metro areas by number of companies, and the top five states by number of companies per million residents.

52696 ■ "Lockport Tops Eastern Niagara List" in *Business First Buffalo* (Vol. 19, No. 44, July 25, 2003, pp. 1)
Pub: American City Business Journals, Inc.
Ed: G. Scott Thomas. **Description:** A ranking of neighborhoods in Erie and Niagara Counties, New York revealed Lockport, located in Eastern Niagara County, has a good reputation among residents and was rated the seventh fastest-growing town in western New York.

52697 ■ "Long Island's Industrial Agencies Spend $733 Million in 2003 on Economic Incentives" in *Long Island Business News* (February 20, 2004)
Pub: Dolan Media Newswires
Ed: Nick Anastasi. **Description:** Eight industrial development agencies in Long Island spent more than $733 million in economic incentives to draw and retain companies in the area.

52698 ■ "Map your Next Location" in *PC Computing* (April 2000, pp. 91)
Pub: Ziff-Davis Inc.
Ed: Jason Compton. **Description:** Five easy steps are given to help pick a new business location using AnySite.com.

52699 ■ "Marysville, Calif., Downtown Building Gets New Look, New Name" in *Marysville Appeal-Democrat* (January 26, 2003)
Pub: Knight Ridder/Tribune Business News
Ed: Scott Bransford. **Description:** The Library Square building, renamed Downtown Plaza in Marysville, California, has been renovated to attract new businesses. Shops at the building now include a Pizza Guys franchise, and Curves women's fitness and weight loss center. Rental prices are included.

52700 ■ "Michael Witt Hired as Long Island Partnership 'Concierge'" in *Long Island Business News* (February 20, 2004)
Pub: Dolan Media Newswires
Ed: Ken Schachter. **Description:** Plans to attract and retain companies in the Long Island, New York region are discussed with newly appointed executive director of the Long Island Partnership, Michael Watt. Watt describes his position as being a corporate concierge.

52701 ■ "Moving Daze" in *Law Firm Inc.* (October 2004)
Pub: American Lawyer Media LP
Ed: Kristin Eliasberg. **Description:** Things to consider when a law firm is relocating the business. Many firms consult a real estate professional to help with planning the move, as well as finding the right space and negotiating the deal.

52702 ■ "My Kind of Town" in *Entrepreneur* (Vol. 33, January 2005, No. 1, pp. 27)
Pub: Entrepreneur Media Inc.
Description: According to the Visa Entrepreneurial Index, Austin, Texas scored 95 points out of 100 as the most entrepreneurial city in the U.S. The study was based on the following two main criteria: average number of new business licenses and DBA registrations, and the number of utility patents issued.

52703 ■ "Nassau County Executive Tom Suozzi Proposes Empire Zone" in *Long Island Business News* (March 5, 2004)
Pub: Dolan Media Newswires
Ed: Rosmaria Mancini. **Description:** Tom Suozzi, Nassau County Executive, would like to see the County included in the currently established 72 empire zones in the state of New York. These zones offer incentives, such as property tax abatements and utility rate reductions for companies within its boundaries, and encourages other businesses outside of New York to relocate or current firms to remain in the area.

52704 ■ "NextEnergy May Get HQ" in *Crain's Detroit Business* (Vol. 22, February 6, 2006, No. 6, pp. 11)
Pub: Crain Communications Inc. - Detroit
Ed: Amy Lane. **Description:** Nextek Power Systems Inc. is considering a move to the Detroit area in order to be a major player in the state's NextEnergy Center. NextEnergy is a nonprofit corporation charged with advancing Michigan's alternative-energy industry.

52705 ■ "North Cobb office market healthier than most" in *Atlanta Business Chronicle* (Vol. 25, December 6, 2002, No. 26, pp. 20C)
Pub: American City Business Publications, Inc.
Ed: Martin Sinderman. **Description:** The office submarket at Atlanta's I-75 North/Marietta/Johnson Ferry Road has seen some increased tenant activity, particularly in the Town Center area. Statistical data included.

52706 ■ "Now Showing: Hard At Work" in *My Business* (April/May 2002, pp. 44)
Pub: My Business Magazine
Ed: Roseanne Hooper. **Description:** Profile of The Propel Group, a graphic design firm in Dallas, Texas. The firm purchased a 55-year-old movie theatre as a marketing tool for designing advertising, Web pages, catalogs and logos for clients.

52707 ■ "Office Down Below" in *Home Office Computing* (Vol. 18, No. 8, August 2000, pp. 42)
Pub: Scholastic Inc.
Ed: Marilyn Zelinsky Syarto. **Description:** Ideas for converting a basement into a home office are offered.

52708 ■ "Office Space: It's better to rent than own" in *Red Herring* (No. 103, September 1, 2001, pp. 85)
Pub: Herring Communications
Ed: Duff McDonald. **Description:** More technology firms are using the sale-leaseback transaction as an alternative to monetizing real estate assets.

52709 ■ "OKC Chamber of Commerce Finds Many Firms Interested in City" in *Journal Record* (February 4, 2004)
Pub: Dolan Media Company
Ed: Darren Currin. **Description:** The Greater Oklahoma City Chamber of Commerce is seeing increased interest from companies looking to relocate to the area, as well as existing local firms looking to expand.

52710 ■ "On the Waterfront" in *Inc.* (August 1, 2003)
Pub: Gruner & Jahr USA Publishing
Ed: David J. Dent. **Description:** Ways Portland, Maine encourages entrepreneurs to choose their city to start new companies are discussed.

52711 ■ "$160M plan pushed for NE Ann Arbor" in *Crain's Detroit Business* (Vol. 19, No. 1, Jan. 6, 2003, pp. 1)
Pub: Crain Communications Inc., Detroit
Ed: Laura Bailey. **Description:** A proposed new development in Ann Arbor, Michigan is facing expensive environmental clean up on the site before development can begin. Neighbors in the area are concerned about the plans for development, as are existing businesses. The $160 million project would include offices, a health center, housing and retail space.

52712 ■ "The outside advantage" in *My Business* (April/May 2002, pp. 48)
Pub: My Business Magazine
Ed: Marcia Jablonski. **Description:** Things to consider when moving a home business to a space away from the house are presented, including trying to control additional costs for the move.

52713 ■ "Owning Up" in *Entrepreneur* (Vol. 31, No. 8, August 2003, pp. 65)
Pub: Entrepreneur Media, Inc.
Ed: Mark Henricks. **Description:** Is a business better off renting or buying its location? This question is answered by looking at the benefits of purchasing property to build equity and control costs.

52714 ■ "Phoenix" in *Sales & Marketing Management* (Vol. 159, January-February 2007, No. 1, pp. 41)
Pub: VNU Business Media
Description: Phoenix, Arizona is the nation's fastest growing city, making it a top choice for conventions and seminars.

52715 ■ "Portland Considered for Maine Hydrogen Development Site" in *Portland Press Herald* (November 10, 2005)
Pub: Blethen Maine Newspapers, Inc.
Ed: Tux Turkel. **Description:** South Portland and Auburn, Maine are being considered as the site for commercial hydrogen production plants. Hydrogen would be made from renewable resources such as solar electric panels. Potential customers include United Parcel Services fleets.

52716 ■ "Priority. Fast, Cheap, and Ready To Move-in." in *Inc.* (November 2006, pp. 23-24)
Pub: Gruner & Jahr USA Publishing
Ed: Amy Feldman **Description:** Web-based real estate services are transforming the commercial real estate industry. Site selection need not be limited to a local area with the nationwide data banks on line.

52717 ■ "Reimagining Union Station" in *Ingram's* (Vol. 29, No. 1, January 2003, pp. 13)
Pub: Show Me Publishing, Inc.
Ed: Jack Cashill. **Description:** A presentation of the history of Union Station, Kansas City, Missouri is given, along with the names of those linked to that history. The author suggests the dramatization of the stories would make the building embraceable by the public.

52718 ■ "Retailers Optimistic They Can Compete for Slice of Macomb" in *Crain's Detroit Business* (Vol. 21, October 31, 2005, No. 44, pp. 3)
Pub: Crain Communications Inc. - Detroit
Ed: Brent Snavely. **Description:** Retail development, housing growth and the shopping mall in Clinton Township are among the factors for Parisian building a store that will anchor the new mall called Partridge Creek.

52719 ■ "Running a Biotech Operation Here is Reasonably Cheap, Study Finds" in *Pittsburgh Business Times* (Vol. 23, No. 2, August 1, 2003)
Pub: Pittsburgh Business Times
Ed: Maria Guzzo. **Description:** Industry analysts report that the Pittsburgh, Pennsylvania region offers a wide range of benefits to biotechnology firms. A new report from Boyd Company has found that the region offers economic advantages for biomedical research firms.

52720 ■ "Salvation Army Picks Center Site" in *Crain's Detroit Business* (Vol. 21, October 24, 2005, No. 43, pp. 24)
Pub: Crain Communications Inc. - Detroit
Ed: Sherri Begin. **Description:** Salvation Army of Metropolitan Detroit has chosen 27 acres at Conner and Frankfort for its new community center. The center would include an events hall library, computer center, pool, gymnasium, dance studio, fitness equipment, a track, a classroom and childcare and senior citizen areas.

52721 ■ "San Diego: Baja a Prudent Choice for Realty Company" in *San Diego Business Journal* (Vol. 28, January 8, 2007, No. 2, pp. 29)
Pub: San Diego Business Journal Associates
Ed: Pat Broderick. **Description:** Prudential California Realty is opening its newest office in Baja, California. The new division will employ 25 agents.

52722 ■ "A San Francisco Chronicle: George Dewey's View of the Bay" in *Black Enterprise* (Vol. 34, No. 3, October 2003, pp. 142)
Pub: Earl Graves Publishing Co.
Ed: Sonia Alleyne. **Description:** George Dewey, an investment banking director for Citigroup Global Markets Inc., relocated to the San Francisco Bay area two years ago, and recommends the city as one of the best cities because it is a thriving business center.

52723 ■ "Scouting a Perfect Site" in *My Business* (October/November 2003, pp. 49)
Pub: My Business Magazine
Description: The art and science of selecting a site to start a franchise is discussed, including the use of costly global positioning systems.

52724 ■ "Searching for a city" in *BlackEnterprise* (Vol. 32, No. 3, October 2001, pp. 32)
Pub: Earl Graves Publishing Co.
Ed: Sakina P. Spruell. **Description:** Web sites offering information about Philadelphia, Atlanta, and Charlotte are presented, focusing on the fact these three cities are preferred by African Americans in which to live and work.

52725 ■ "Setting Sail" in *Crain's New York Business* (Vol. 23, January 15, 2007, No. 3, pp. 25)
Pub: Crain Communications, Inc.
Description: Small business tenants are finding that they are able to move their firms a short distance away and avoid renewing leases that are demanding up to double the rent for the next lease cycle.

52726 ■ "Several buildings may change hands in coming months" in *Crain's Detroit Business* (Dec. 16, 2002, pp. 17)
Pub: Crain Communications Inc., Detroit
Ed: Jennette Smith. **Description:** A number of metropolitan Detroit office buildings are for sale. Negotiations are underway for some high-profile properties, such as Motorola Inc. in Farmington Hills and Compuware Corporation's headquarters, also located in Farmington Hills.

52727 ■ "Show me the money" in *Entrepreneur* (Vol. 31, No. 6, June 2003, pp. 108)
Pub: Entrepreneur Media Inc.
Ed: Todd D. Maddocks. **Description:** A couple have found the ideal property for their franchise business and need to secure financing for the deal.

52728 ■ "Sleepy Little Towns Turn High Tech" in *Home Office Computing* (Vol. 19, No. 1, January 2001, pp. 17)
Pub: Scholastic Inc.
Ed: Lisa Roberts. **Description:** The agricultural town of Petaluma, California suddenly found itself a high-tech center when local firm Ceret Corp was acquired by networking giant Cisco Systems and 40 other telecom firms established facilities in the area. Petaluma has become a model for many other rural areas whose economies are disappearing. Tazwell County, Virginia has adopted a similar strategy in an effort to attract high-technology companies to an area where population has been declining.

52729 ■ "Smart Set" in *Inc.* (November 1, 2003)
Pub: Gruner & Jahr USA Publishing
Ed: Bobbie Gossage. **Description:** Hiring incentives and tax abatements are attracting new business to the Lawrence, Kansas area, especially in the area of biotechnology.

52730 ■ "South Okla. City Chamber Seeks to Attract Large Bookstore" in *Journal Record* (February 5, 2004)
Pub: Dolan Media Company
Ed: Darren Currin. **Description:** South Oklahoma City Chamber of Commerce is attempting to lure Borders Books to the southwest portion of the city. Ann Arbor, Michigan-based Borders already operates two locations in the Oklahoma City area.

52731 ■ "Spatial Concerns" in *Small Business Opportunities* (Vol. 16, No. 2, March 2004, pp. 68)
Pub: Harris Publications, Inc.
Ed: Stephen Roulac. **Description:** Warehouses are now being used as prime office space.

52732 ■ "Study" in *Crain's Detroit Business* (Vol. 18, No. 18, May 6, 2002, pp. 6)
Pub: Crain Communications Inc. - Detroit
Ed: Amy Lane. **Description:** Michigan ranks well against competitor states on many business factors, but remains bogged down by high business costs, according to a study performed by SRI International, formerly known as the Stanford Research Institute. The study compared Michigan with 17 other states.

52733 ■ "Study: State 12th-best for small biz" in *Crain's Detroit Business* (Vol. 17, No. 44, October 22, 2001, pp. 20)
Pub: Crain Communications, Inc.
Ed: Laura Bailey. **Description:** The state of Michigan was rated the 12th-most friendly state for entrepreneurs by a recent study conducted by the Small Business Survival Committee. The most business-friendly state is Nevada, followed by South Dakota and Washington; lowest were Maine, Hawaii, Rhode Island, and the District of Columbia.

52734 ■ "Sublease steals kick-starting leasing in Portland" in *Atlanta Business Chronicle* (Vol. 25, December 6, 2002, No. 26, pp. 31C)
Pub: American City Business Publications, Inc.
Ed: Heidi J. Stout. **Description:** In the western suburbs of Portland, Oregon, an oversupply in office and flex space has led to leases being offered at 50 cents on the dollar from original lease rates. Tenants are finally starting to take advantage of these lease deals. The amount of sublease space has decreased, much to the relief of landlords.

52735 ■ "Sweet Victory" in *My Business* (December/January 2004, pp. 12)
Pub: My Business Magazine
Ed: Jamie Roberts. **Description:** Profile of Mike and Carol Hamilton, owners of Carol Hamilton's Chutters

General Store, offering 650 glass jars filled with candy, making the store the home of the largest candy counter in the world. The Littleton, New Hampshire store is one in a trend of small companies restoring and maintaining the main streets of towns in America. These small firms believe they can compete against large chains by offering unique customer service and products.

52736 ■ "Swezey's Department Store Sites Sought By a Diversity of Businesses" in *Long Island Business News* **(January 30, 2004)**
Pub: Dolan Media Newswires
Ed: Nick Anastasi. **Description:** Grocers and bookstores are looking to purchase real estate once used by Swezey's Department Stores. The article carries information on the many plans underway.

52737 ■ "A Tale of Two Cities" in *Fast Company* **(May 2001, pp. 143)**
Pub: Fast Company
Ed: Scott Kirsner. **Description:** Seattle Mayor Paul Schell, says that his job is to turn the city into a 'platform for the creative experience', and the city is creating a place where telecommunications, biotech, software, and the Web are all coming together with music, architecture, and art.

52738 ■ "A Tale of Two Cities: Livin' La Vida Boca" in *Fast Company* **(May 2001, pp. 155)**
Pub: Fast Company
Ed: David Dorsey. **Description:** If you think of Boca Raton, Florida as a retirement village for New York snowbirds, you're wrong. It is the future of the Internet, and Boca-technos are convinced that they live at the epicenter of a new age in computing, a major global center for wireless technology, software development, and Internet traffic.

52739 ■ "Taubman Plans Spur Optimism" in *Crain's Detroit Business* **(Vol. 22, November 27, 2006, No. 48, pp. 20)**
Pub: Crain Communications Inc. - Detroit
Ed: Sheena Harrison. **Description:** Expansion at Twelve Oaks and Partridge Creek will rejuvenate retail business in those areas. People think positively when they see new businesses and expansions rather than the skepticism that inhibits retail sales levels.

52740 ■ "Tech and the City: What Cities Are Rising Fast on the High-Tech Horizon?" in *Entrepreneur* **(Vol. 32, October 2004, No. 10, pp. 36)**
Pub: Entrepreneur Media Inc.
Ed: Melissa Campanelli. **Description:** U.S. cities offering opportunity for high-tech companies include Camden, New Jersey where the New Jersey Economic Development Authority is developing the Camden Waterfront Technology Center; Madison, Wisconsin's economic development initiative, Technology Zone Program; Tucson, Arizona, with area companies working with the SBA SBIR and SBTT federal grant programs to attract high tech companies; and South Lafayette, Louisiana's Acadiana Technology Immersion Center.

52741 ■ "Tech towns: which U.S. cities are today's hotbeds of technology?" in *Entrepreneur* **(Vol. 31, No. 6, June 2003, pp. 24)**
Pub: Entrepreneur Media Inc.
Ed: Amanda C. Kooser. **Description:** Atlanta, Georgia; Austin, Texas, and Boise, Idaho are becoming the largest growing cities for the technology industries.

52742 ■ "The Top 25" in *Entrepreneur* **(Vol. 31, No. 10, October 2003, pp. 22)**
Pub: Entrepreneur Media, Inc.
Description: The top 25 cities for entrepreneurs are ranked, with Las Vegas, Nevada leading the way for entrepreneurial activity and job growth.

52743 ■ "Top Cities For African Americans: The Results Are In." in *Black Enterprise* **(Vol. 34, July 2004, No. 12, pp. 78)**
Pub: Earl G. Graves Publishing Co. Inc.
Ed: Carolyn M. Brown, David A. Padgett. **Description:** Top ten cities for African Americans to live and

work are listed, seven of the ten are in the South, five of the ten have a Black mayor, and half have a black city population that is over 50 percent.

52744 ■ "Top 25 Cities" in *Entrepreneur* **(Vol. 30, No, 10, October 2002, pp. 30)**
Pub: Entrepreneur Media Inc.
Description: The top 25 cities to start or move an existing business to are listed, with Washington, DC ranking first with highest small-business growth.

52745 ■ "Trading Places" in *Small Business Opportunities* **(Vol. 12, No. 3, May 2000, pp. 12, 58)**
Pub: Harris Publications, Inc.
Description: To secure good office space at favorable lease terms, the small business owner needs to be savvy and ask the right questions. Tips from a pro are offered.

52746 ■ "TV One Auditions District for HQ" in *Washington Business Journal* **(Vol. 22, No. 9, July 4, 2003, pp. 1)**
Pub: Washington Business Journal
Ed: Greg A. Lohr. **Description:** Marketing efforts and attempts to find larger office facilities for TV One are presented.

52747 ■ "Utilities Boost Companies; Utility Services" in *Crain's New York Business* **(Vol. 22, November 13, 2006, No. 46, pp. 36)**
Pub: Crain Communications, Inc.
Description: Listing of companies that provide utility programs, incentives and benefits to small businesses looking to relocate within the five boroughs of New York City or expand their businesses in the area.

52748 ■ "Vacancies up but investors still high on retail" in *Atlanta Business Chronicle* **(Vol. 25, December 13, 2002, No. 27, pp. A5)**
Pub: American City Business Publications, Inc.
Ed: Lisa R. Schoolcraft. **Description:** Despite lower retail rents and more empty stores in 2002 than 2001, real estate investors continue to buy Atlanta, Georgia area retail properties, largely due to the fact that investment funds are available. The market for small investors who pool funds continues to drive this trend. A report by Marcus and Millichap provides some hope that rents will recover some of the losses as 2003 progresses.

52749 ■ "W. Alabama a Sweet Home - and Office - for Retailers" in *Houston Business Journal* **(Vol. 34, No. 16, August 29, 2003, pp. 2)**
Pub: American City Business Journals
Ed: Nancy Sarnoff. **Description:** Several retailers on West Alabama in Houston, Texas are establishing their shops on the ground floor, or next door to, their homes.

52750 ■ "What Makes Topeka Unique" in *Ingram's* **(Vol. 29, No. 8, August 2003, pp. S6)**
Pub: Show Me Publishing, Inc.
Ed: Dale Garrison. **Description:** An overview of the services, cultural attractions and more that Topeka, Kansas offers to those interested in starting or relocating a small business.

52751 ■ "When small firms work from big-name locations" in *Boston Business Journal* **(Vol. 22, No. 3, February 22, 2002, pp. S6)**
Pub: MCP, Inc.
Ed: Mark Micheli. **Description:** Profile of HQ Global Workplaces, Massachusetts' largest management company of executive office suites.

52752 ■ "Who's No. 1?" in *Entrepreneur* **(Vol. 32, December 2004, No. 12, pp. 26)**
Pub: Entrepreneur Media Inc.
Ed: Judith Potwora. **Description:** According to experts, city rankings are targeted to large corporations, small business owners should choose location based on how well-suited an area is to a particular product or service.

52753 ■ "Why Kansas City Needs a New Downtown Arena" in *Ingram's* **(Vol. 29, No. 1, January 2003, pp. 15)**
Pub: Show Me Publishing, Inc.
Ed: William R. Worley. **Description:** Bill Worley, chairman of Kingston Environmental, explains why Kansas City, Missouri needs a new downtown area, despite objections from others.

52754 ■ "Wi-Fi is a Must for New Office Space on Long Island" in *Long Island Business News* **(February 13, 2004)**
Pub: Dolan Media Newswires
Ed: Nick Anastasi. **Description:** Small businesses are looking for office space offering high-speed wireless technology in the form of Wi-Fi connectivity.

52755 ■ "Wisconsin Biotech Aims to Create Artificial Heart Tissue" in *Milwaukee Journal Sentinel* **(December 8, 2005)**
Pub: Journal Sentinel, Inc.
Ed: Kathleen Gallagher. **Description:** InvivoSciences LLC plans to make artificial heart tissue. The firm has chosen Wisconsin for its location because of the Medical College of Wisconsin's support for entrepreneurs along with several state programs that support young companies.

52756 ■ "Workforce Board Seeks To Improve Jobs" in *Bradenton Herald* **(January 28, 2005)**
Pub: Bradenton Herald
Ed: Matt Griswold. **Description:** The Suncoast Workforce Board is working to improve the Manatee-Sarasota business climate through education of employees. After a study of the region's economy, the area benefits from its desirable geography and is among the nation's top performing regions, but has issues with its workforce.

52757 ■ "Year's biggest industrial deal months in making" in *Atlanta Business Chronicle* **(Vol. 25, December 13, 2002, No. 27, pp. A3)**
Pub: American City Business Publications, Inc.
Ed: Jarred Schenko. **Description:** APL Logistics Inc., will build a 992,000 square foot warehouse distribution complex in Douglas County, Georgia. The complex will be developed by Catellus Development Corporation and is expected to be completed in 2004. The Douglas County site was chosen over one in Cobb County because of access to Hartsfield Atlanta International Airport and a highway.

52758 ■ "Your space is the place" in *Fast Company* **(May 2001, pp. 60)**
Pub: Fast Company
Ed: Alison Wellner. **Description:** According to Stephen Roulac, founder and CEO of the Roulac Group Inc., a consulting firm based in San Rafael, California that specializes in real estate, states that people are now selecting where they want to live, then seeking employment, whereas in the past it was the opposite.

TRADE PERIODICALS

52759 ■ *Business Facilities*
Pub: Group C Communications Inc.
Contact: Ted Coene, Publisher
E-mail: dgoldstein@groupc.com
Ed: Jennifer Staats, Editor, jstaats@groupc.com. **Released:** Monthly. **Description:** Professional magazine focusing on corporate expansion, commercial/industrial real estate, and economic development.

52760 ■ *Expansion Management*
Pub: Penton Media Inc.
Contact: Michael Keating, Publisher
E-mail: mkeating@penton.com
Released: Monthly, 7 issues. **Price:** $49.50 Canada; $67.50 international. **Description:** Magazine assisting executives and managers worldwide in planning and overseeing their companies' facilities development and other expansion and relocation activities.

52761 ■ *Site Selection Magazine*
Pub: Conway Data Inc.
Contact: Julie Clarke, Circulation Mgr
Released: Bimonthly, 6/year. **Price:** $90; $130 out of country; $155 two years; $241 two years other countries. **Description:** Magazine on real estate and site selectors.

52762 ■ *Urban Land Magazine*
Pub: Urban Land Institute
Contact: Karen Schaar, Managing Editor
E-mail: kschaar@uli.org
Released: Monthly, 11/yr. **Price:** $15 single issue. **Description:** Professional magazine for land use and development practitioners.

CONSULTANTS

52763 ■ Architectural Research Consultants Inc.
220 Gold Ave. SW, Ste. A
PO Box 1158
Albuquerque, NM 87102
Ph:(505)842-1254
Fax: (505)766-9269
Co. E-mail: jppetronis@arcplanning.com
URL: http://www.arcplanning.com/

E-mail: jppetronis@arcplanning.com
Scope: Performs feasibility studies, site selection, site development plans, zoning and utilization studies, geographic information management, community planning, preservation planning, cultural resource management; determination of the demand for services and establishing operating parameters for service delivery systems. Develops comprehensive statement of facility and organization requirements based on functional and environmental needs; assessment of the physical and functional suitability of existing facilities; and plans and development of guidelines for future endeavors and master planning. Special expertise in education facilities, hospitals, and recreational facilities. Other services include identification and documentation of information resources, preparation and assistance in preparation of proposals and specialized management consulting. Serves private industries as well as government agencies.

52764 ■ LSA Associates Inc.
20 Executive Pk., Ste. 200
Irvine, CA 92614-5981
Ph:(949)553-0666
Fax: (949)553-8076
Co. E-mail: irvine@lsa-assoc.com
URL: http://www.lsa-assoc.com

E-mail: irvine@lsa-assoc.com
Scope: Provides environmental planning and assessment services to public and private clients. Offers professional services in the following areas: environmental assessment, community planning, natural resources analysis, transportation, cultural resources, noise and air quality analysis and GIS.

52765 ■ Pomeroy Appraisal Associates Inc.
Pomeroy Pl., 225 W Jefferson St.
Syracuse, NY 13202-2334
Ph:(315)422-7106
Fax: (315)476-1011
Co. E-mail: info@pomeroyappraisal.com
URL: http://www.pomeroyappraisal.com

E-mail: info@pomeroyappraisal.com
Scope: Advises clients on commercial and industrial properties, site analysis, real estate tax problems, land development, and all types of real estate valuation problems and projects.

52766 ■ Project Advantage Inc.
24 Frank Lloyd Write Dr., Lobby M
PO Box 325
Ann Arbor, MI 48106
Ph:(734)930-4300
Free: 800-320-3328
Fax: (734)930-4299
Co. E-mail: info@projectadvantage.com

E-mail: info@projectadvantage.com
Scope: A relocation services consultancy that helps corporations and organizations plan and implement major facility re-locations. The firm assists its clients in four areas: strategic relocation planning, master planning, relocation implementation planning, and specialized relocation training programs for the relocation teams. Serves large corporations in all industries, as well as organizations and government entities. **Publications:** "Systematic Management of Government Re-locations"; "Systematic Management of Business Re-locations".

52767 ■ Space Management Programs Inc.
55 W Wacker Dr., 6th Fl.
Chicago, IL 60601
Ph:(312)263-0700
Fax: (312)263-1228
Co. E-mail: info@smp.ghk.net
URL: http://smp.ghk.net

E-mail: info@smp.ghk.net
Scope: A facilities and technology consulting firm consisting of an interdisciplinary team of architects, industrial designers and interior designers experienced in all aspects of design and corporate relocation. Available for site evaluation, strategic planning through the writing of briefs, or architectural programs through space planning, design and construction documents.

Small Business Development

START-UP INFORMATION

52768 ■ **"The art of making a plan and making it happen"** in *The New York Times* (December 18, 2000, pp. C16)
Pub: The New York Times Company
Ed: Lisa Belkin. **Description:** Business plans for the self-employed are discussed.

52769 ■ **"Beating the odds: remembering the basics of business can help"** in *Black Enterprise* (Vol. 32, No. 6, January 2002, pp. 35)
Pub: Earl Graves Publishing Co.
Ed: Glenn Townes. **Description:** The key to starting and sustaining a small business is to have a strong, basic understanding of business practices. Advice is given to manage small businesses.

52770 ■ **"Business information centers"** in *BlackEnterprise* (Vol. 31, No. 12, July 2001, pp. 48)
Pub: Earl Graves Publishing Co.
Ed: Roger Barnes. **Description:** Profile of the Small Business Administration's (SBA) Business Information Center (BIC), the government-funded business resource with more than 65 BIC offices in more than 35 states. BICs provide a one-stop location for information, education, workshops, and training designed to address a broad variety of business start-up and development issues.

52771 ■ **"Can I Use My Retirement Savings To Start a Business?"** in *Fortune* (Vol. 151, February 21, 2005, No. 4, pp. 134)
Pub: Time Inc.
Ed: Janice Revell. **Description:** According to Martin Nissenbaum, the national director of personal income tax planning at Ernst & Young, a 401(k) savings plan could be used to start a new business, but the funds would first need to be rolled into an IRA, since the 401(k) does not allow this kind of investment; IRS rules dictating 'prohibited transactions' are described to help entrepreneurs avoid legal issues when using retirement investments for startup money.

52772 ■ **"Coming to America"** in *Inc.* (November 1, 2004)
Pub: Inc. Magazine
Ed: David J. Dent. **Description:** Profile of StartSmart a program designed to help immigrants become entrepreneurs. The program is run by the not-for-profit economic development agency called Coastal Enterprises, and offers classes in entrepreneurship, one-on-one coaching, and start-up loans to immigrants and refugees. Five people helped by the program are highlighted.

52773 ■ **"A Fistful of Hours"** in *Inc.* (October 2000, pp. 58)
Pub: The Goldhirsh Group
Description: Start-up barter exchanges hope to make the world their oyster.

52774 ■ **"Franchising"** in *Black Enterprise* (Vol. 32, No. 10, May 2002, pp. 101)
Pub: Earl Graves Publishing Co.
Ed: Carolyn M. Brown. **Description:** Franchising is one of the fastest growing segments of American business and is seen as an ideal partnership for an independent entrepreneur. More minorities are discovering franchising opportunities by increased recruiting by companies like Wendy's, Merry Maids, Jan Pro, Subway, Church's Chicken (TM), and Interim Healthcare. Profile of aforementioned franchise opportunities are included.

52775 ■ **"Home Work"** in *Black Enterprise* (Vol. 37, October 2006, No. 3, pp. 78)
Pub: Earl G. Graves Publishing Co. Inc.
Ed: James C. Johnson. **Description:** Information on starting a resume-writing service is profiled.

52776 ■ **"Inside the Customer-Focused Company"** in *Harvard Business Review* (Vol. 78, No. 3, May 2000, pp. S20)
Pub: Harvard Business School Publishing Corp.
Ed: Cary Jehl Broussard. **Description:** The article shows how a change agent, or type of business consultant, and vocal consumers help structure an entire organization.

52777 ■ **"It's in the card"** in *BlackEnterprise* (Vol. 31, No. 12, July 2001, pp. 50)
Pub: Earl Graves Publishing Co.
Ed: Paula McCoy-Pinderhughes. **Description:** American Express launches the Community Business Card, a new source of funding for entrepreneurs and small business owners who want to start and grow their companies. The program, called AmEx Community Business Credit Card, is designed for microenterprises with less than five employees and a capital need of less than $35,000 a year. Each time the business owner uses the card, AmEx will contribute one percent of that purchase to one of three select Microenterprise Development Organizations (MDO), which in turn provide loans and technical assistance to the microenterprise requesting the capital.

52778 ■ **"License to Bill?"** in *Black Enterprise* (Vol. 34, No. 4, November 2003, pp. 48)
Pub: Earl Graves Publishing Co.
Ed: Alan Hughes. **Description:** Information for starting a home-based business and licensing processes are discussed.

52779 ■ *Make It Your Business: The Definitive Guide to Launching, Managing, & Succeeding in Your Own Business*
Pub: Pocket Books
Ed: Stephen Schiffman. **Released:** 1999. **Price:** $14.00.

52780 ■ **"Marketing Know-How"** in *Black Enterprise* (Vol. 30, No. 5, December 1999, pp. 42)
Pub: Earl Graves Publishing Co.
Ed: Gerda Gallop-Goodman. **Description:** Advice is given to an entrepreneur who wants to expand a small African American ceramic statues business.

52781 ■ **"Peer to peer"** in *Harvard Business Review* (Vol. 78, No. 5, September-October 2000, pp. 32)
Pub: Harvard Business School Publishing Corp.
Ed: Roberta Fusaro. **Description:** Two peer groups for CEOs, offered in the Boston area, and conducted by the Catlin Group and the Commonwealth Institute, help CEOs of start-up high tech companies deal with the challenges of their new position.

52782 ■ **"Pilot program to assist young entrepreneurs"** in *Black Enterprise* (Vol. 32, No. 6, January 2002, pp. 37)
Pub: Earl Graves Publishing Co.
Ed: Paula McCoy-Pinderhughes. **Description:** Profile of the Prudential Young Entrepreneur Program, a three-year pilot entrepreneurial development project funded by the Prudential Foundation, a nonprofit, grant-making organization of the Newark, New Jersey-based Prudential Insurance Company of America. The program is designed to offer young adults in urban areas opportunity to train to become a small business owner.

52783 ■ **"Reeling In the Big One"** in *Inc.* (August 1, 2004)
Pub: Inc. Magazine
Ed: Jess McCuan. **Description:** Ways a startup business can land a large, brand name client are examined.

52784 ■ **"The Root of the Business: Drawing on one's ethnicity leads to a passionate niche"** in *My Business* (April/May 2002, pp. 36-39)
Pub: My Business Magazine
Ed: Kathleen Landis. **Description:** Ways in which creative entrepreneurs have taken their heritage and turned it into a profitable business are examined. Information to contact the Minority Business Development Agency, National Association of Asian American Professionals, Africa-American Business Link, AllSmallBiz.com, Shopping for Identity: The Marketing of Ethnicity, and Hispanic Business Magazine is provided.

52785 ■ **"Shoestring Start-Ups"** in *Small Business Opportunities* (Vol. 13, No. 6, November 2001, pp. 22-24, 26, 28, 30, 32, 34, 36, 116)
Pub: Harris Publications, Inc.
Description: The top 50 small business that can be started with little or no capital are previewed, some as little as $100 or less, including the ten steps to follow when starting a new business.

52786 ■ **"Small-Business Wonder:SmartOnline.com provides the tools and experti se to take the trepidation out of launching a new business"**in*PCMagazine*
Pub: Ziff-Davis Publishing Company
Ed: Greg Alwang. **Description:** SmartOnline.com provides Web-hosted business tools aimed at small businesses and entrepreneurs. SmartOnline.com assists with everything from starting, financing, and ex-

panding a small business to corresponding with customers. More than just a resource for small-business owners, SmartOnline.com conveys the look and feel of a polished CD-based application in an up-to-date online form.

52787 ■ "Starts Slow, Jobs Grow" in *Business Week* (No. 3689, July 10, 2000, pp. F8)
Pub: McGraw-Hill, Inc.
Description: Many banks are tightening credit requirements for small business loans, venture capitalists are growing more demanding, and angel investors may not be feeling so generous in an uncertain stock market.

52788 ■ "Street Smarts: Don't Sign Anything Yet" in *Inc.* (January 1, 2005)
Pub: Inc. Magazine
Ed: Norm Brodsky. **Description:** When starting a new business, it is important for entrepreneurs to beware of commitments made in the process.

52789 ■ "Street Smarts: The Myths About Niches" in *Inc.* (August 1, 2004)
Pub: Inc. Magazine
Ed: Norm Brodsky. **Description:** For a small business starting out, finding its niche is key, being prepared for it to change and keep on changing is essential.

52790 ■ "Strong Structure" in *Black Enterprise* (Vol. 34, July 2004, No. 12, pp. 48)
Pub: Earl G. Graves Publishing Co. Inc.
Ed: Alan Hughes. **Description:** Advice is given for launching a small business. The entrepreneur needs information for choosing the business structure that is right for his new firm. Guidelines for choosing a sole proprietorship, partnership, limited liability company, C corporation, and S corporation are outlined.

52791 ■ "Yes, you can" in *Black Enterprise* (Vol. 31, No. 5, December 2000, pp. 64)
Pub: Earl Graves Publishing Co.
Ed: Feona Huff. **Description:** How to start, operate and grow a business while developing yourself and pursuing your personal goals.

ASSOCIATIONS AND OTHER ORGANIZATIONS

52792 ■ Action for Enterprise
2009 N 14th St., Ste. 301
Arlington, VA 22201
Ph:(703)243-9172
Fax: (703)243-9123
Co. E-mail: info@actionforenterprise.org
URL: http://www.actionforenterprise.org
Contact: Frank Lusby, Exec. Dir./Founder
Description: Seeks to design and implement small enterprise development programs, based on a comprehensive analysis of business sectors and the interrelationships of enterprises that function within them. Initiates efforts to develop sustainable business development service providers at the local level.

52793 ■ American Businesspersons Association
Hillsboro Executive Ctr. N
350 Fairway Dr., Ste. 200
Deerfield Beach, FL 33441-1834
Ph:(954)571-1877
Free: 800-221-2168
Fax: (954)571-8582
Co. E-mail: membership@assnservices.com
URL: http://www.aba-assn.com
Contact: Jack Furnari, Exec. Dir.
Description: Owners of businesses and individuals in executive, managerial, and sales capacities. Provides substantial discounts, affordable insurance, products and other special services to members. **Publications:** *Forum* (quarterly).

52794 ■ Association of Small Business Development Centers
8990 Burke Lake Rd.
Burke, VA 22015

Ph:(703)764-9850
Fax: (703)764-1234
Co. E-mail: info@asbdc-us.org
URL: http://www.asbdc-us.org
Contact: Donald T. Wilson, Pres./CEO
Description: Local centers providing advice for those planning to establish a small business. Aims to facilitate information exchange among members and to represent their interests before the federal government. Informs the Small Business Administration on issues of interest to the small business community. **Publications:** *Business Plan for Special Use Permits Training Manual*; *Business Plan Workbook for Special Use Permits*.

52795 ■ BEST Employers Association
2505 McCabe Way
Irvine, CA 92614
Ph:(949)253-4080
Free: 800-433-0088
Fax: (949)222-1004
Co. E-mail: info@bestlife.com
URL: http://www.bestlife.com
Contact: Donald R. Lawrenz, Owner/Chm./Pres./ CEO
Purpose: Provides small independent businesses with managerial, economic, financial, and sales information helpful for business improvement. Organizes and sponsors healthcare alliances for small employers. (The acronym BEST stands for Beneficial Employees Security Trust). **Publications:** *Newsbeat* (quarterly).

52796 ■ British-American Business Council
52 Vanderbilt Ave., 20th Fl.
New York, NY 10017
Ph:(212)661-5660
Fax: (212)661-1886
Co. E-mail: info@babinc.org
URL: http://www.babc.org
Contact: Ian Stopps CBE, Chm.
Description: British and American businesses. Strives to provide a forum in which members can exchange information and ideas. Hosts various programs and activities. **Publications:** *UK & USA* (biennial); Newsletter (quarterly).

52797 ■ Canadian Association of Family Enterprise–Association Canadienne des Entreprises Familiales
1388 C Cornwall Rd.
Oakville, ON, Canada L6J 7W5
Ph:(416)538-9992
Free: (866)849-0099
Fax: (416)538-9556
Co. E-mail: office@cafenational.org
URL: http://www.cafemembers.org/cafenational
Contact: Lawrence Barns, Natl. CEO
Membership: Family-owned businesses. **Purpose:** Seeks to "encourage, educate, and inform members in disciplines unique to the family business." Fosters increased understanding of the importance of family-owned enterprises in the national economy among government agencies and the public. Gathers and disseminates information of interest to members. Conducts educational and lobbying activities. Provides technical support and advisory services to small businesses in areas including succession planning, taxation, family law, and arbitration and mediation. Maintains network of Family Councils, which serve as a forum for discussion of family and business matters. **Publications:** *Family Business Magazine* (quarterly); *Family Enterpriser* (quarterly); *International Magazine for Family Businesses* (bimonthly); Membership Directory (annual). **Telecommunication Services:** electronic mail, lbarns@cafenational.org.

52798 ■ Canadian Federation of Independent Business–Federation Canadienne de l'Entreprise Independante
4141 Yonge St., Ste. 401
Willowdale, ON, Canada M2P 2A6
Ph:(416)222-8022
Fax: (416)222-7593
Co. E-mail: cfib@cfib.ca
URL: http://www.cfib.ca
Contact: Catherine Swift, Pres./CEO

Membership: Independent businesses. **Purpose:** Promotes economic well-being of members and seeks to maintain a healthy domestic business climate. Represents members' interests before government agencies, labor and industrial organizations, and the public.

52799 ■ Employers of America
PO Box 1874
Mason City, IA 50402-1874
Ph:(641)424-3187
Co. E-mail: employer@employerhelp.org
URL: http://www.employerhelp.org
Contact: Mr. Jim Collison, Pres.
Description: Assists employers, managers, and supervisors in keeping their businesses profitable by maintaining the best possible workplace policies and practices, and to deal safely, effectively, and profitably with employees. Publishes weekly "HRmadeEasy" eLetter to help members achieve more with their employees. **Publications:** *HRmadeEasy* (weekly).

52800 ■ Entrepreneurs' Organization
500 Montgomery St., Ste. 500
Alexandria, VA 22314
Ph:(703)519-6700
Fax: (703)519-1864
Co. E-mail: info@eonetwork.org
URL: http://www.eonetwork.org
Contact: Troy Hazard, Pres.
Membership: Entrepreneurs under the age of 40 who have either founded, co-founded, are a controlling shareholders of, or own a firm with annual gross revenues exceeding $1000000. **Purpose:** Serves as a focal point for communication among members; provides educational programs; facilitates small group meetings with leading entrepreneurs. Conducts charitable and educational programs; operates speakers' bureau; compiles statistics. Membership is by invitation only. **Publications:** *Axis* (monthly); *Octane* (quarterly); *Overdrive* (monthly).

52801 ■ The Entrepreneurship Institute
3592 Corporate Dr., Ste. 101
Columbus, OH 43231
Ph:(614)895-1153
Free: 800-736-3592
Fax: (614)895-1473
Co. E-mail: tei@tei.net
URL: http://www.tei.net
Contact: Dr. Jan W. Zupnick, Pres.
Description: Provides encouragement and assistance to entrepreneurs who operate companies with revenue in excess of $1 million. Unites financial, legal, and community resources to help foster the success of companies. Promotes sharing of information and interaction between members. Operates President's forums and projects which are designed to improve communication between businesses, develop one-to-one business relationships between small and mid-size businesses and local resources, provide networking, and stimulate the growth of existing companies. **Publications:** *The President's Forum* (monthly).

52802 ■ International Small Business Consortium
3309 Windjammer St.
Norman, OK 73072
Co. E-mail: sb@isbc.com
URL: http://www.isbc.com
Description: Works to assist small businesses in maximizing the Internet in the most cost-efficient manner. Aims to improve the image and credibility of the SME community, to help promote SMEs in general and to provide a means for SMEs to be better known internationally. Helps small businesses apply the Internet to further their business goals and to help them find support and answers in dealing with all business aspects.

52803 ■ National Association for Business Organizations
3 Woodthorne Ct., No. 12
Owings Mills, MD 21117
Ph:(410)363-3698
Co. E-mail: nahbb@msn.com
Contact: Rudolph Lewis, Pres.

Purpose: Business organizations that develop and support small businesses that have the capability to provide their products or services on a national level. Promotes small business in a free market system; represents the interests of small businesses to government and community organizations on small business affairs; monitors and reviews laws that affect small businesses; promotes a business code of ethics. Supplies members with marketing and management assistance; encourages joint marketing services between members. Operates a Home Based Business Television Network that provides an affordable audio/visual media for small and home based businesses. **Publications:** Newsletter (periodic).

52804 ■ **National Association of Private Enterprise**
PO Box 15550
Long Beach, CA 90815
Free: 888-244-0953
Fax: (714)844-4942
Contact: Laura Squiers, Exec.Dir.
Description: Employers and employees of small businesses; self-employed individuals. Seeks to ensure the continued growth of private enterprise through education, benefits programs such as health insurance, and legislation. Promotes the common interest of members. Convention/Meeting: none. **Publications:** NAPE News (quarterly).

52805 ■ **National Association for the Self-Employed**
PO Box 612067
DFW Airport
Dallas, TX 75261-2067
Free: 800-232-6273
Fax: 800-551-4446
Co. E-mail: mpetron@nase.org
URL: http://www.nase.org
Contact: Robert Hughes, Pres.
Membership: Self-employed and small independent businesspersons. **Purpose:** Acts as an advocate at the state and federal levels for self-employed people. Provides discounts on products and services important to self-employed and small business owners. **Publications:** Get Connected (biweekly); NASE Annual Report (annual); Self-Employed America (bimonthly); Washington Watch (weekly).

52806 ■ **National Business Association**
PO Box 700728
Dallas, TX 75370
Ph:(972)458-0900
Free: 800-456-0440
Fax: (972)960-9149
Co. E-mail: info@nationalbusiness.org
URL: http://www.nationalbusiness.org
Contact: Raj Nisankarao, Pres.
Membership: Employed owners of small businesses. **Purpose:** Promotes and assists the growth and development of small businesses. Aids members in obtaining government small business and education loans; makes available insurance policies and software in conjunction with the U.S. Small Business Administration. Maintains career, educational institution, and scholarship information program for members and their dependents. Offers over 100 benefits, services and programs in the areas of Business, Health, Lifestyle and Education. **Publications:** Biz Corner (weekly) ; NBA boss (bimonthly).

52807 ■ **National Business Incubation Association**
20 E Circle Dr., No. 37198
Athens, OH 45701-3571
Ph:(740)593-4331
Fax: (740)593-1996
Co. E-mail: info@nbia.org
URL: http://www.NBIA.org
Contact: Dinah Adkins, Pres./CEO
Description: Incubator developers and managers; corporate joint venture partners, venture capital investors; economic development professionals. (Incubators are business assistance programs providing business consulting services and financing assistance to start-up and fledgling companies.) Helps newly

formed businesses to succeed. Educates businesses and investors on incubator benefits; offers specialized training in incubator formation and management. Conducts research and referral services; compiles statistics; maintains speakers' bureau; publishes information relevant to business incubation and growing companies. **Publications:** A Comprehensive Guide to Business Incubation; The Art and Craft of Technology Business Incubation; Business Incubation: Building Companies, Jobs, and Wealth; Forging the Incubator: How to Design and Implement a Feasibility Study for Business Incubation Programs; NBIA Business Incubation Industry Directory (annual); NBIA Memberabilia (biweekly); NBIA Review (bimonthly); NBIA UPdates (bimonthly).

52808 ■ **National Small Business Association**
1156 15th St. NW, Ste. 1100
Washington, DC 20005
Ph:(202)293-8830
Free: 800-345-6728
Fax: (202)872-8543
Co. E-mail: press@nsba.biz
URL: http://www.nsba.biz
Contact: Paul Hense, Chm.
Membership: Small businesses including manufacturing, wholesale, retail, service, and other firms. **Purpose:** Works to advocate at the federal level on behalf of smaller businesses. **Publications:** Advocate (bimonthly).

52809 ■ **SOHO America**
PO Box 941
Hurst, TX 76053-0941
Free: 800-495-SOHO
Fax: 800-841-4445
Co. E-mail: soho@1sas.com
URL: http://www.soho.org
Description: Provides virtual community for small business and home office professionals with information pertaining to small and home-based businesses.

52810 ■ **Support Services Alliance**
107 Prospect St.
Schoharie, NY 12157
Free: 800-836-4772
Co. E-mail: info@ssamembers.com
URL: http://smallbizgrowth.com
Contact: Steve Cole, Pres.
Description: Small businesses (less than 50 employees), the self-employed, and associations of such individuals. Provides services and programs such as group purchasing discounts, health coverage, legislative advocacy, and business and financial support services. **Publications:** Capital Crier; Small-Biz Growth (monthly). **Telecommunication Services:** electronic mail, membershipservices@ssamembers.com; additional toll-free number, (800)909-2772.

REFERENCE WORKS

52811 ■ **"The 100 Best Companies To Work For"** in Fortune (Vol. 151, January 24, 2005, No. 2, p. 72)
Pub: Time Inc.
Ed: Robert Levering, Milton Moskowitz, Ann Harrington, Nadira A. Hira, Christopher Tkaczyk. **Description:** Complete listing of the best 100 companies to work for in the U.S. is presented. Businesses are categorized by large company, 10,000-plus employees; midsize, 2,500 to 10,000 employees; and small, 1,000 to 2,500 employees. Republic Bancorp topped out as number one small company, followed by Xilinx and Griffin Hospital.

52812 ■ **"A Sobering Vacation"** in Wall Street Journal (Vol. 248, December 2006, No. 142, pp. P1-P5)
Pub: Dow Jones & Co. Inc.
Ed: Christina Binkley **Description:** Profiles of new high-end addiction treatment centers opening in the Malibu area.

52813 ■ *Advice from the Lemonade Stand: A Back to Basics Book for Business*
Pub: Lafayette Publishing Co.
Ed: Carroll Cobb; edited by Joanna Bremer. **Released:** 1998. **Price:** $22.00.

52814 ■ **"All-star performance"** in Incentive (Vol. 174, No. 10, October 2000, pp. 126)
Pub: Bill Communications
Ed: Nancy K. Austin. **Description:** Placing only the brightest stars at the center of your business universe will eventually bring your company crashing down to earth.

52815 ■ **"Ask Inc. Education"** in Inc. (November 2006, pp. 51-52)
Pub: Gruner & Jahr USA Publishing
Ed: John Corsault **Description:** While there are many successful entrepreneurs who didn't attend or finish college, odds for successful businesses still favor those who complete their education seven to one.

52816 ■ **"Avoid litigation"** in *Black Enterprise* (Vol. 32, No. 8, March 2002, pp. 49)
Pub: Earl Graves Publishing Co.
Ed: Bridget McCrea. **Description:** Entrepreneurs cannot afford the financial and emotional stress that comes with legal litigation. Key areas to help small business avoid lawsuits are examined.

52817 ■ *Avoiding Mistakes in Your Small Business*
Pub: Crisp Publications, Inc.
Ed: David Karlson. **Price:** $15.95. **Description:** Part of the Small Business & Entrepreneurship Series.

52818 ■ **"Back from the Brink"** in *BlackEnterprise* (Vol. 31, No. 8, March 2001, pp. 47)
Pub: Earl Graves Publishing Co.
Ed: Glenn Townes. **Description:** Profiles of minority small business owners who were able to rebuild their businesses after facing major setbacks.

52819 ■ *Bare-Bones Guide to Starting a Successful Small Business*
Pub: Pilot Books
Price: $9.95.

52820 ■ *Beating the Odds in Small Business*
Pub: Small Business Matters, Inc.
Ed: Tom Culley. **Released:** 1998. **Price:** $29.95; $20.00.

52821 ■ *Beyond Entrepreneurship: Turning Your Business into an Enduring Great Company*
Pub: Prentice Hall
Ed: James C. Collins and William C. Lazier. **Released:** 1992. **Price:** $19.95.

52822 ■ *The Big Instruction Book of Small Business (New Mexico Edition)*
Pub: Gallopade Publishing Group
Ed: Carole Marsh. **Released:** 1997. **Price:** $39.95 (library binding).

52823 ■ **"A Brand to Unify the Region"** in *Milwaukee Journal Sentinel* (December 15, 2005)
Pub: Journal Sentinel, Inc.
Ed: Rick Romell. **Description:** Newly formed Milwaukee Regional Economic Development Council has designated the seven area counties as "Milwaukee 7" in order to unite the communities into an economic unit that will attract and retain business growth in the region.

52824 ■ *Break the Curve: The Entrepreneur's Small Business Blueprint*
Pub: International Thomson Publishing
Ed: Tim Burns. **Released:** 1998. **Price:** $19.95.

52825 ■ "Build a Better Business" in *Black Enterprise* (Vol. 35, October 2004, No. 3, pp. 136)
Pub: Earl G. Graves Publishing Co. Inc.
Ed: Robert Anthony, Sonya A. Donaldson. **Description:** Emerging new technologies can help small businesses seem larger than they really are. Co-founder of Krazy Kickz, Sam Robinson, tells how upgrading the company's phone system led to a better customer service system.

52826 ■ *Building a Profitable Business: A Proven Step-by-Step Guide to Starting and Running Your Own Business*
Pub: Bob Adams, Inc.
Ed: Charles Chickadel and Greg Straughn. **Released:** Second edition, 1994. **Price:** $15.95 (paper).

52827 ■ *Building a Successful Business: What Every New Business Must Know Before Even Thinking about Making That Million Bucks!*
Pub: C D S, Inc.
Ed: Jack Funderburk. **Released:** 1997. **Price:** $24.95.

52828 ■ *Business Basics: A Microbusiness Start-Up Guide*
Pub: PSI Research
Ed: Gerald Dodd; illustrated by Tim Sample. **Released:** 1998. **Price:** $16.95.

52829 ■ *The Business Forms on File Collection*
Pub: Facts on File, Inc.
Released: 1995. **Price:** $125.00 (paper). **Description:** Contains 125 forms used in business, including legal and expense forms, security analysis forms, and personnel record forms.

52830 ■ *Business Opportunities in the United States: The Complete Reference Guide to Practices and Procedures*
Pub: Irwin Professional Publishing
Ed: Robert F. Cushman and R. Lawrence Soares, editors. **Released:** 1992. **Price:** $90.00.

52831 ■ *Business Start-Up Guide: How to Create, Grow & Manage Your Own Successful Enterprise*
Pub: Tycoon Publishing
Ed: Tom Severance; edited by Becky Colgan. **Released:** 1998. **Price:** $19.95.

52832 ■ "A Catalyst for Innovation" in *Fortune* (Vol. 142, No. 6, September 18, 2000, pp. 248)
Pub: Time Inc.
Ed: Daniel Kadlec. **Description:** Both presidential candidates have found common ground on at least one tax initiative. Both would like to make permanent a tax credit for companies engaging in costly research and development.

52833 ■ "Celebrate Success. Embrace Innovation" in *Black Enterprise* (Vol. 37, February 2007, No. 7, pp. 145)
Pub: Earl G. Graves Publishing Co. Inc.
Description: 2007 Women of Power Summit provides networking opportunities, empowerment sessions, and nightly entertainment. More than 500 executive women of color are expected to attend this inspiring summit in Phoenix, February 7-10.

52834 ■ *Complete Idiot's Guide to Starting Your Own Business*
Pub: Macmillan Publishing Co.
Ed: Ed Paulson and Marcia Layton. **Released:** 2nd ed. 1998. **Price:** $18.95.

52835 ■ *The Complete Information Bank for Entrepreneurs & Small Business Managers*
Pub: Center for Entrepreneurship & Small Business Management
Ed: Ron Christy and Billy M. Jones. **Released:** 2nd ed. 1998. **Price:** $29.95.

52836 ■ "Contacts for Contracts" in *Hispanic Business* (Vol. 22, No. 1/2, January/February, pp. 84)
Pub: Hispanic Business
Ed: Aimee R. Haeussler. **Description:** Despite industry mergers, some financial institutions are taking pains to reach out to minority vendors. Many of the procurement programs aimed at minority and women-owned businesses offer more than just a chance to compete for corporate contracts.

52837 ■ *The Couple's Business Guide: How to Start & Grow a Small Business Together*
Pub: Berkley Publishing Group
Ed: Amy Lyon. **Released:** 1997. **Price:** $12.00.

52838 ■ *Creating the Successful 21st Century Enterpise*
Pub: The Free Press
Ed: Main. **Released:** 1997. **Price:** $25.00.

52839 ■ *Creating Your Own Business, Vol. 1: A Guide to Success*
Pub: MidAmerica Leadership Foundation
Ed: Harold P. Welsch and Joseph S. Roberts. **Released:** 1997. **Price:** $29.95.

52840 ■ "CultureScape and the Redemption of Kansas City" in *Ingram's* (Vol. 29, No. 8, August 2003, pp. 13)
Pub: Show Me Publishing, Inc.
Ed: Jack Cashill. **Description:** An unidentified architect is planning to redevelop an area of Kansas City, Missouri. The plan is called, The Bush Creek CultureScape, and will include the Irish Museum and Cultural Center and parks.

52841 ■ "Database Dollars" in *Small Business Opportunities* (Vol. 12, No. 5, September 2000, pp. 44)
Pub: Harris Publications, Inc.
Ed: Carla Vincent. **Description:** A customer database can help find new customers, increase sales, and build clientele. Ways to develop a database are outlined.

52842 ■ "Despite Smaller Loans, SBA Breaks Records" in *Inc.* (November 1, 2004)
Pub: Inc. Magazine
Ed: Darren Dahl. **Description:** The U. S. Small Business Administration backed a record number of loans in 2004, providing $15 billion in loans to businesses. These loans have helped small and family-owned small business to create 1.5 million jobs.

52843 ■ "Differentiating Legal Issues by Business Type" in *Journal of Small Business Management* (Vol. 44, October 2006, No. 4, pp. 563)
Pub: Blackwell Publishing, Inc.
Ed: Sandra Malach; Peter Robinson; Tannis Radcliffe. **Description:** A fundamental issue when forming a business and its strategic operation is developing legal strategies to better protect the assets of the business and entrepreneur. An analysis of data indicated that certain legal issues are relevant to specific types of new ventures while certain legal issues are important to all new ventures. Depending on the category of business, the relevancy of individual legal issues will vary. Statistical data included.

52844 ■ *Directory of Venture Capital and Private Equity Firms*
Pub: Grey House Publishing
Released: latest edition 9th; Published 2006. **Price:** $450, individuals Softcover; $889, individuals online database with free directory. **Covers:** 3,000 domestic and international venture capital and private equity firms. **Entries Include:** Firm name, address, phone, fax, e-mail, URL, description of services, names and titles of key personnel.

52845 ■ "Do it already!" in *Entrepreneur* (Vol. 30, No. 1, January 2002, pp. 43)
Pub: Entrepreneur Media Inc.
Ed: Amanda C. Kooser. **Description:** iBizResources.com encourages brick-and-mortar businesses to get online and use the new technologies available to small businesses. The site offers technical services, e-commerce tools, marketing, promotion and business products and services.

52846 ■ "The Early Bird Gets the Worm" in *Black Enterprise* (Vol. 37, January 2007, No. 6, pp. 111)
Pub: Earl G. Graves Publishing Co. Inc.
Ed: Tykisha N. Lundy. **Description:** General Motors hosts the Black Enterprise Conference And Expo: Where Deals Are Made at Walt Disney World's Swan and Dolphin Resort, May 9-12. The conference will offer great information to entrepreneurs.

52847 ■ *Entrepreneurially Yours: A Compilation of Articles about Starting and Managing a Small Business*
Pub: Business of Your Own
Ed: Millicent G. Lownes. **Released:** 1990. **Price:** $5.95 (paper).

52848 ■ *The Entrepreneur's Guide to Growing Up: Taking Your Small Company to the Next Level*
Pub: Self-Counsel Press, Inc.
Ed: Edna Sheedy. **Released:** 1993. **Price:** $8.95. **Description:** Guide to managing small business growth after start-up.

52849 ■ "Entrepreneurs Learn to Implement Ideas" in *San Fernando Valley Business Journal* (Vol. 11, November 2006, No. 23, pp. 1)
Pub: San Fernando Valley Business Journal Associates
Ed: Chris Coates. **Description:** Overview of the Dream and Discover 2006 Entrepreneurs Conference at College of the Canyons. The conference included four seminars ranging from small business practices, growth strategies and the various challenges of starting a business.

52850 ■ *Entrepreneurship for the Nineties*
Pub: Prentice Hall
Ed: Gordon B. Baty. **Released:** 1990. **Price:** $32.95 (paper). A guide written for the potential entrepreneur by an author who is an entrepreneur.

52851 ■ *The Essence of Small Business*
Pub: Prentice Hall
Ed: Colin Barrow. **Released:** 2nd ed. 1998. **Price:** contact suppl. for price info. (cloth).

52852 ■ "Forward Thinking" in *PC Magazine* (March 7, 2000, pp. 7)
Pub: Ziff-Davis Publishing Company
Ed: Michael J. Miller. **Description:** The Y2K crisis has passed and companies are now focusing on the task of moving their IT infrastructures into the 21st century. Hardware and software integration should be a great part of this effort as companies move to centralized administration, single log-ons, and a greater reliance on certificates and directories. Microsoft's Windows 2000 has arrived and should be a part of this movement. New applications and Web services will facilitate this integration for smaller organizations. New network infrastructures will provide high-speed connections for both local and remote users, wireless access to data and virtual private networks.

52853 ■ "Four Starrs Moves, Doubles Size" in *Bellingham Business Journal* (January 2007, pp. A6)
Pub: Sun News Inc.
Description: Danielle Starr, owner of Four Starrs Boutique is moving to a location double the size of the original. The women's boutique sells cosmetics and clothing lines not readily available to the area.

52854 ■ *From Executive to Entrepreneur: Making the Transition*
Pub: AMACOM
Ed: Gilbert G. Zoghlin. **Released:** 1991. **Price:** $24.95 ($22.45 for AMA members). **Description:** Guide to the risks and rewards of entrepreneuring. Details the skills needed to make the transition.

52855 ■ "Future brightens for the inner city" in *Hispanic Business* (Vol. 22, No. 6, June 2000, pp. 32)
Pub: Hispanic Business

Ed: Andrea Siedsma. **Description:** Latino Initiatives for the Next Century is a non-profit organization aimed at helping Hispanic communities and businesses to join in the redevelopment of inner-city neighborhoods. The agency will invest $300 million in such projects.

52856 ■ *George Washington's First Business: A Guide to Starting New Ventures*
Pub: Career Advancement Center, Inc.
Ed: Eric Gelb. **Released:** 1998. **Price:** $19.95.

52857 ■ "Getting Ahead Of the Weather" in *Fortune* (Vol. 151, February 7, 2005, No. 3, pp. 87)
Pub: Time Inc.
Ed: Abraham Lustgarten. **Description:** The National Oceanic and Atmospheric Administration estimates a third of the U.S. gross domestic product is affected by weather in the form of slowed transportation, inflated energy costs, and interrupted sales. Steps some businesses are taking to protect their firms against the elements are profiled.

52858 ■ *Getting Started*
Pub: Self-Counsel Press, Inc.
Ed: Dan Kennedy. **Released:** 1991. **Price:** $7.95 (paper). **Description:** Provides guidance on the practical aspects of starting a business, finding the best location and choosing a memorable company name.

52859 ■ "Going Global: Lessons from Late Movers" in *Harvard Business Review* (Vol. 78, No. 2, March 2000, pp. 132)
Pub: Harvard Business School Publishing Corp.
Ed: Christopher A. Bartlett, Sumantra Ghoshal. **Description:** Contrary to popular wisdom, companies from the fringes of the world economy can become global players. What they need is organizational confidence, a clear strategy, a passion for learning, and the leadership to bring these factors together.

52860 ■ "Grist: A Passport to America" in *Inc.* (October 1, 2004)
Pub: Inc. Magazine
Ed: Adam Hanft. **Description:** Ways blue states and red states are learning to communicate and do business are highlighted.

52861 ■ "Guerrilla Marketing via Wi-Fi" in *Business 2.0* (Vol. 6, July 2005, No. 6, pp. 112)
Pub: Time, Inc.
Description: Apple's AirPort Express allows users to listen to music and print off site using an Ethernet cable as well as other business essentials.

52862 ■ *Have You Got What It Takes?*
Pub: Self-Counsel Press, Inc.
Ed: Douglas A. Gray. **Released:** 1993, third edition. **Price:** $12.95 (paper). **Description:** Provides checklists, quizzes and worksheets for entrepreneurs to assess their small business skills.

52863 ■ *The Home Office and Small Business Answer Book: Solutions to the Most Frequently Asked Questions about Starting and Running Home Offices*
Pub: Henry Holt & Co., Inc.
Ed: Janet Attard. **Released:** 1993. **Price:** $40.00; $19.95 (paper).

52864 ■ "Home Sweet Office: Giving to Charity" in *Sales & Marketing Management* (Vol. 157, January 2005, No. 1, pp. 52)
Pub: VNU Business Media
Ed: Kathryn Droullard. **Description:** Small business owners may find giving time and services to charities can have more impact than writing a check. Many times volunteering can be a great networking tool.

52865 ■ *Honey, I Want to Start My Own Business: A Planning Guide for Couples*
Pub: Harper Business
Ed: Azriela Jaffe; foreword by John Gray. **Released:** 1997. **Price:** $13.00.

52866 ■ "Hot Shots: 200 Up And Coming Companies" in *Forbes* (Vol. 172, No. 9, October 27, 2003, pp. 139)
Pub: Forbes Magazine
Ed: Cecily J. Fluke, Lesley Kump. **Description:** Share prices of 200 entrepreneurial firms are up an average of 58 percent over the last years, earnings per share increased 19 percent and return on equity rose 15 percent. Statistical data showing the companies recent performance is included.

52867 ■ "Hot Shots: U.S. Top 15" in *Forbes* (Vol. 6, No. 20, October 27, 2003, pp. 53)
Pub: Forbes Magazine
Description: A ranking of America's top small companies (under $500 million in revenues, but otherwise according to criteria similar to those ranked under $1 billion).

52868 ■ *How to Form Your Own Indiana Corporation Before the Inc. Dries!*
Pub: P. Gaines Co.
Ed: Phillip G. Williams. **Released:** 2nd ed. 1997. **Price:** $31.95 (diskette; paper) Vol. 4.

52869 ■ *How to Incorporate & Start a Business in Colorado*
Pub: Adams Media Corp.
Ed: J. W. Dicks. **Released:** 1998. **Price:** $16.95.

52870 ■ *How to Incorporate & Start a Business in Georgia*
Pub: Adams Media Corp.
Ed: J. W. Dicks. **Released:** 1997. **Price:** $16.95.

52871 ■ *How to Incorporate & Start a Business in Indiana*
Pub: Adams Media Corp.
Ed: J. W. Dicks. **Released:** 1997. **Price:** $16.95.

52872 ■ *How to Incorporate & Start a Business in Minnesota*
Pub: Adams Media Corp.
Ed: J. W. Dicks. **Released:** 1997. **Price:** $16.95.

52873 ■ *How to Incorporate & Start a Business in Nevada*
Pub: Adams Media Corp.
Ed: J. W. Dicks. **Released:** 1997. **Price:** $16.95.

52874 ■ *How to Incorporate & Start a Business in Oregon*
Pub: Adams Media Corp.
Ed: J. W. Dicks. **Released:** 1997. **Price:** $16.95.

52875 ■ *How to Incorporate & Start a Business in Tennessee*
Pub: Adams Media Corp.
Ed: J. W. Dicks. **Released:** 1997. **Price:** $16.95.

52876 ■ *How to Incorporate & Start a Business in Virginia*
Pub: Adams Media Corp.
Ed: J. W. Dicks. **Released:** 1997. **Price:** $16.95.

52877 ■ *How to Incorporate & Start a Business in Washington*
Pub: Adams Media Corp.
Ed: J. W. Dicks. **Released:** 1997. **Price:** $16.95.

52878 ■ *How to Really Start Your Own Business*
Pub: Inc. Publishing
Price: $73.25 (spiral).

52879 ■ *How to Run Your Business So It Doesn't Run You*
Pub: Borah Press
Ed: Linda L. Francis. **Released:** 1998. **Price:** $24.50.

52880 ■ *How to Set up Your Own Small Business Student Study Guide*
Pub: American Institute of Small Business
Ed: Max Fellek. **Released:** 1997. **Price:** $19.95.

52881 ■ *How to Start A Business*
Pub: Prima Publishing

Ed: Hicks. **Price:** $17.95.

52882 ■ *How to Start a Business in California*
Pub: Sourcebooks, Inc.
Ed: Mark P. Eissman and Mark Warda. **Released:** 1998. **Price:** $16.95.

52883 ■ *How to Start a Business in Illinois*
Pub: Sourcebooks, Inc.
Ed: Edwin T. Gania and Mark Warda. **Released:** 2nd ed. 1998. **Price:** $16.95.

52884 ■ *How to Start a Business in Michigan*
Pub: Sourcebooks, Inc.
Ed: Edward A. Haman and Mark Warda. **Released:** 2nd ed. 1998. **Price:** $16.95.

52885 ■ *How to Start a Business in New York*
Pub: Sourcebooks, Inc.
Ed: Paul W. Barnard and Mark Warda. **Released:** 1997. **Price:** $16.95.

52886 ■ *How to Start a Business in Pennsylvania*
Pub: Sourcebooks, Inc.
Ed: Desiree A. Petrus and Mark Warda. **Released:** 1997. **Price:** $16.95.

52887 ■ *How to Start a Business without Quitting Your Job: The Moonlight Entrepreneur's Guide*
Pub: Ten Speed Press
Ed: Philip Holland. **Released:** 1992. **Price:** $9.95 (paper).

52888 ■ *How to Start a Business in Texas*
Pub: Sourcebooks, Inc.
Ed: William R. Brown and Mark Warda. **Released:** 2nd ed. 1998. **Price:** $16.95.

52889 ■ *How to Start & Finance a Business That Works for You*
Pub: International Wealth Success, Inc.
Ed: Tyler G. Hicks; edited by S. David Hicks. **Released:** 1999. **Price:** $24.75.

52890 ■ *How to Start Your Own Business— and Succeed*
Pub: The McGraw-Hill Companies
Ed: Arthur H. Kuriloff. **Released:** Second edition, 1992. **Price:** $29.95.

52891 ■ "How to Survive When You've Lost Your Monopoly" in *Success from Failure* (August 2000)
Pub: Vision Quest Publishing, Inc.
Ed: Terry Brock. **Description:** At some point in time a small business will suffer a setback. Doug Wolford, general manager at Network Solutions, shares important lessons that will help a company thrive from any setback encountered.

52892 ■ "How To Assemble a Board of Directors" in *Inc.* (October 1, 2004)
Pub: Inc. Magazine
Ed: Nicole Gull. **Description:** Advice for putting together a Board of Directors that will best serve a small business is given.

52893 ■ "How resilience works" in *Harvard Business Review* (Vol. 80, No. 5, May 2002, pp. 46)
Pub: Harvard Business School Press
Ed: Diane L. Coutu. **Description:** The three characteristics of companies and individuals that enable them to bounce back from adversity are highlighted; each has the capacity to accept reality, find meaning in some aspect of life, and improvise.

52894 ■ "Huron to Announce $25M Deal, Eyes New $250M Fund" in *Crain's Detroit Business* (Vol. 23, No. 3, January 15, 2007, pp. 26)
Pub: Crain Communications Inc. - Detroit
Ed: Tom Henderson. **Description:** Huron Capital Partners L.L.C. is coming off a record year for deal volume. A new $25M deal was announced, two more under letters of intent, and has begun raising funds for large $250M fund by the end of 2007.

52895 ■ *If You're Clueless about Starting Your Own Business & Want to Know More*
Pub: Dearborn Financial Publishing, Inc.
Ed: Seth Godin. **Released:** 1997. **Price:** $15.95.

52896 ■ "Imagining a Web Beyond the Browser: a new kind of dot" in *Fortune* (Vol. 141, No. 4, February 21, 2000, pp. 274+)
Pub: Time Inc.
Ed: Mark Gimein. **Description:** DoDots has developed a platform for producing Internet applications that could make the browser obsolete. Free applications called 'dots' would replace Web pages and be displayed on just part of a computer screen while other applications are running.

52897 ■ "Incubators that actually work? You won't find them only in Internet space" in *Inc.* (November 2000, pp. 64)
Pub: The Goldhirsh Group
Description: In an Inc. survey of more than 30 incubator-savvy CEOs and experts in the field, eight non-profit incubators throughout the nation stood out.

52898 ■ "The Internationalization of new and small firms" in *Journal of Business Venturing* (Vol. 16, No. 4, July 2001, pp. 333)
Pub: Elsevier Science, Inc.
Ed: Paul Westhead, Mike Wright, Deniz Ucbasaran. **Description:** A comparative study of the parameters affecting the success or failure of small exporting and non-exporting firms is presented. In particular, the assumption that positive benefits will accrue from exporting is investigated.

52899 ■ "It's The Business Model, Stupid!" in *Fortune* (Vol. 143, No. 1, January 8, 2001, pp. 54)
Pub: Time Inc.
Ed: Geoffrey Colvin. **Description:** An investigation into the reasons businesses fail. Fortune's Dot-Com Deathwatch is up to 135 failed companies in the past year, mostly startups with bad business models.

52900 ■ *Jane Applegate's Strategies for Small Business Success*
Pub: NAL Dutton
Ed: Jane Applegate. **Released:** 1995. **Price:** $12.95.

52901 ■ "The Joy of Quitting" in *Fortune* (Vol. 141, No. 3, February 7, 2000, pp. 199+)
Pub: Time Inc.
Description: The new economy is changing the way people look at their jobs. The article suggests that leaving a job you are unhappy doing is the right thing to do.

52902 ■ "Kid-Friendly Business Sources" in *Black Enterprise* (Vol. 37, January 2007, No. 6, pp. 40)
Pub: Earl G. Graves Publishing Co. Inc.
Ed: Carolyn M. Brown. **Description:** Financial or business camps are a great way to encourage a child who interested in starting his or her own business. A number of these camps are available each year including Kidpreneurs Conference and Bull and Bear Investment Camp. Other resources are available online. Resources included.

52903 ■ *Last Best Hope: How to Start & Grow Your Own Business*
Pub: McClelland & Stewart Tundra Books
Ed: Rod McQueen. **Released:** 1997. **Price:** $29.99 (cloth); $16.95; $19.99 (paper).

52904 ■ "The Launch" in *Inc.* (October 17, 2000, pp. 57)
Pub: The Goldhirsh Group
Description: This article sites statistics including the Inc. 500 by sector, initial start-up capital, how CEOs raised that start-up capital, and the Top 10 fastest growing companies that were formed in 1995.

52905 ■ *Launching Your First Small Business: Make the Right Decisions During Your First 90 Days*
Pub: C C H, Inc.

Ed: Joel Handelsman. **Released:** 1998. **Price:** $14.95.

52906 ■ "Leading Lenders Shift as 2006 Activity Slows" in *Crain's New York Business* (Vol. 22, December 11, 2006, No. 50, pp. 28)
Pub: Crain Communications, Inc.
Description: HSBC, leader of last year's SBA loans, recorded steep declines in both the value and number of its SBA loans. Bank of America took first place in the number of SBA loans for 2006, while J.P. Morgan Chase captured second place.

52907 ■ "Loan guarantees: costs of default and benefits to small firms" in *Journal of Business Venturing* (Vol. 16, No. 6, Nov. 2001, pp. 595)
Pub: Elsevier Science, Inc.
Ed: Allan L. Riding, George Haines, Jr. **Description:** Research examining types of loan guarantees for the development of small firms is presented. Particular attention is given to international variations in default rates and cost benefits, with focus on the Canadian policy of loan guarantees.

52908 ■ "Local Gelato King is Getting Ready to Expand His Empire" in *Bellingham Business Journal* (January 2007, pp. A4)
Pub: Sun News Inc.
Description: Profile Sirena Gelato, owned by Fahri Ugurlu, who has decided to expand the business by adding a wholesale component.

52909 ■ "Looking For Winning Small Businesses" in *Crain's Detroit Business* (Vol. 23, February 5, 2007, No. 6, pp. 27)
Pub: Crain Communications Inc. - Detroit
Description: Award recognizes small companies who are exceptionally innovative or who have grown through difficult problems to be stronger. It is open to all firms over three years old with one hundred fifty employees or less in Wayne, Oakland, Macomb, Livingston and Washtenaw counties.

52910 ■ "Looking for The Prevailing Wind The bulls and bears are both blowing plenty of hot air these days" in *Fortune* (May 15, 2000, p. 441)
Pub: Time Inc.
Ed: Jim Griffin. **Description:** The two sides do agree on one thing, though: the economy is so good, it hurts. A discussion of the ways the good economy is impacting the stock market.

52911 ■ *Make Money with Your PC!*
Pub: Ten Speed Press
Ed: Lynn Waldorf. **Released:** 1994. **Price:** $7.95. **Description:** Describes how to start a PC-based business; topics covered include buying hardware and software; marketing tools; pricing, billing, and collection; taxes; management and brainstorming techniques; and resource guides to associations, software programs, publications, and other services.

52912 ■ "Mapping the World of Customer Satisfaction" in *Harvard Business Review* (Vol. 78, No. 3, May 2000, pp. 30)
Pub: Harvard Business School Publishing Corp.
Ed: Regina Fazio Maruca. **Description:** Traditional satisfaction surveys often obscure the differences among customers in different regions of the country and different areas of the world.

52913 ■ *McGraw-Hill Guide to Starting Your Own Business: A Step-by-Step Blueprint*
Pub: The McGraw-Hill Companies
Ed: Stephen C. Harper. **Released:** 1992. **Price:** $12.95 (paper). **Description:** The first part of this book discusses the entrepreneurial character types and allows the reader to examine his/her own traits and qualities. Short self-analysis tests are included. The second part discusses how to put together an effective business plan.

52914 ■ "Meeting the Challenge of Disruptive Change" in *Harvard Business Review* (Vol. 78, No. 2, March 2000, pp. 66)
Pub: Harvard Business School Publishing Corp.
Ed: Clayton M. Christensen, Michael Overdorf. **Description:** It's no wonder that innovation is so difficult for established firms. They employ highly capable workers, only to set them to work within processes and business models that doom them to failure. This article shows ways out of this dilemma.

52915 ■ *The Mid-Career Entrepreneur: How to Start a Business and Be Your Own Boss*
Pub: Dearborn Financial Publishing, Inc.
Ed: Joseph R. Mancuso. **Released:** 1993. **Price:** $17.95 (paper), plus $5.00 shipping. **Description:** Provides information on making the transition from executive to entrepreneur when in mid-career (30 to 50 years old). Covers buying a business, franchising option, analyzing a business plan, and obtaining a business loan.

52916 ■ "Mississippi Children's Home Services" in *Mississippi Business Journal* (Vol. 29, January 2007, No. 4, pp. 6)
Pub: Venture Publications, Inc.
Description: Profile of Kelly Shannon, Development Coordinator of Mississippi Children's Home Services. She was previously Special Projects Officer of the Mississippi Department of Health's Communications Office.

52917 ■ "Mixed-use development deserves a good look" in *Crain's Detroit Business* (Vol. 16, No. 49, December 4, 2000, pp. 8)
Pub: Crain Communications, Inc.
Description: Ugly strip developments, traffic congestion and sprawl are being avoided by the proposed 80-acre, mixed-use development Bloomfield Park, in Bloomfield Township, Michigan.

52918 ■ "Money Is Out There, But Where?" in *Crain's Chicago Business* (Vol. 30, January 2007, No. 1, pp. 12)
Pub: Crain Communications, Inc.
Ed: Dee Gill. **Description:** Chicago is a great place to start a business and entrepreneurs have a wealth of free help, resources, and information available to them. Unfortunately, most have no idea these services even exist and as a result money set aside for small businesses never gets spent. SourceLink is one such service that can help entrepreneurs find those resources.

52919 ■ "The network of relationships between the economic environment and the entrepreneurial culture firms" in *Journal of Business Venturing*
Pub: Elsevier Science, Inc.
Ed: Antonio Minguzzi, Renato Passaro. **Description:** A new study theorizes that the entrepreneurial culture in small companies is influenced by their relationships with the economic environment.

52920 ■ "New Business on Champion Street Uncorks a New Trend" in *Bellingham Business Journal* (January 2007, pp. A4)
Pub: Sun News Inc.
Description: Overview of Whatcom Winemakers which has developed a fresh new concept for the wine industry, do-it-yourself winemaking. The winemaking shop is slated to open in February.

52921 ■ "New Deli Destination Coming to Town" in *Bellingham Business Journal* (December 2006, pp. A3)
Pub: Sun News Inc.
Description: Heidi Rosebush, a former Trader Joe's manager, will be opening Destination Deli, a sandwich cart serving sandwiches using local ingredients from bakeries and farms. Heidi will also develop a Web site that allows customers to place and pay for orders online.

52922 ■ "New Detroit survey targets metro area minority business" in *Crain's Detroit Business* (Vol. 16, No. 7, February 14, 2000, pp. 37)
Pub: Crain Communications, Inc.
Ed: Robert Ankeny. Description: New Detroit Inc. has commissioned Wayne State University's Center for Urban Studies to conduct a three-year survey of how minority businesses are faring in the metro Detroit area.

52923 ■ "1999 McKinsey Awards" in *Harvard Business* (Vol. 78, No. 1, January 2000, pp. 137)
Pub: Harvard Business School Publishing Corp.
Description: This article defines the three types of businesses companies are engaged in: customer service, operations, and product development.

52924 ■ *Nobody Gets Rich Working for Somebody Else: An Entrepreneur's Guide*
Pub: Crisp Publications, Inc.
Ed: Roger Fritz. Released: 1993. Price: $15.95 (paper). Description: Provides start-up business information. Includes case studies, worksheets, checklists, and examples.

52925 ■ "The Numbers" in *Fortune* (Vol. 142, No. 9, October 16, 2000, pp. 64)
Pub: Time Inc.
Description: Executive's opinions regarding the future of the U.S. economic conditions. Statistics are shown.

52926 ■ "Old King Coal Comes Back: Actually, It Never Really Left" in *Fortune* (Vol. 151, February 21, 2005, No. 4, pp. 114)
Pub: Time Inc.
Ed: Jeremy Main. Description: Profile of Peabody Energy, owner of the largest coalmine in the world, the North Antelope-Rochelle Mine. The coal industry is working to improve the mining, transporting, and burning of coal in order to increase production.

52927 ■ *Open Your California Business in 24 Hours: It's Not As Hard As You Think*
Pub: Nolo Press
Ed: Peri H. Pakroo. Released: 1998. Price: $24.95.

52928 ■ *Operating a Really Small Business*
Pub: Crisp Publications, Inc.
Ed: Betty Bivins. Price: $15.95. Description: Part of the Small Business & Entrepreneurship Series.

52929 ■ "Orchestrating Assistance; Chambers of Commerce" in *Crain's New York Business* (Vol. 22, November 13, 2006, No. 46, pp. 38)
Pub: Crain Communications, Inc.
Description: Listing of local chapters of New York's chambers of commerce. These organizations serve as sources of information and representation for local business interest provide a number of services and a wide variety of programs for small businesses.

52930 ■ *Out of Work? Get into Business!: Shifting Gears and Turning Job Loss into Success*
Pub: Self-Counsel Press, Inc.
Ed: Don Doman. Released: 1994, first edition. Price: $9.95 (paper).

52931 ■ "Overcome Your B2B Challenge" in *E-business Advisor* (Vol. 18, No. 4, April 2000, pp. 22)
Pub: Advisor Media, Inc.
Ed: Tom Hennings. Description: Developing a business-to-business (B2B) Web portal is more difficult than constructing a business-to-consumer (B2C0) e-commerce site. The article sites the differences and offers advice.

52932 ■ "Panorama Place" in *San Fernando Valley Business Journal* (Vol. 12, January 2007, No. 1, pp. 13)
Pub: San Fernando Valley Business Journal Associates
Description: Maefield Development will break ground on a retail center and 500-unit condominium complex in a central Panorama City community that has been suffering since the closing of Montgomery Ward.

52933 ■ *The Prentice Hall Small Business Survival Guide: A Blueprint for Success*
Pub: Prentice Hall
Ed: Compiled by Prentice Hall editorial staff. Released: 1993. Price: $16.95.

52934 ■ *Principles of Small Business*
Pub: International Thomson Publishing
Ed: Robert Brown and Barrow. Released: 1997. Price: $23.95.

52935 ■ *Quality Business: Quality Issues & Smaller Firms*
Pub: Routledge
Ed: Julian North and Robert Blackburn. Released: 1998. Price: $90.00 (cloth).

52936 ■ "The Quest for Resilience" in *Harvard Business Review* (Vol. 81, No. 9, September 2003, pp. 52)
Pub: Harvard Business School Press
Ed: Gary Hamel, Lisa Valikangas. Description: Once-successful billion dollar companies are now finding it increasingly difficult to return the same level of profits as in the past. Companies that continue to perform well are able to quickly adapt to changes often by introducing new and/or unconventional ideas.

52937 ■ "Quicker SBA Loans" in *Business Week* (No. 3698, September 11, 2000, pp. F6)
Pub: McGraw-Hill, Inc.
Description: The Small Business Administration plans to enlarge its Community Express pilot program, which aims to streamline loan reviews for companies in low-income areas or those owned by minorities, women, or veterans.

52938 ■ "Real Estate Niches Continue as Bright Spots" in *Crain's Detroit Business* (Vol. 22, November 27, 2006, No. 48, pp. 18)
Pub: Crain Communications Inc. - Detroit
Ed: Jennette Smith. Description: Five year downward trend and transition period has driven real estate professionals into niche marketing in redevelopment and mixed use projects. Smaller projects are very successful in downtown areas with assistance of the local communities.

52939 ■ "Resource Line" in *Black Enterprise* (Vol. 37, January 2007, No. 6, pp. 6)
Pub: Earl G. Graves Publishing Co. Inc.
Description: Interactive Media Editor, Philana Patterson, writes a column for blackenterprise.com that offers advice and provides resources for entrepreneurs, corporate executives, business owners, and budding investors.

52940 ■ "Riverview, Trenton try to salvage riverfront dreams" in *Crain's Detroit Business* (Vol. 16, No. 49, December 4, 2000, pp. 41)
Pub: Crain Communications, Inc.
Ed: Terry Kosdrosky. Description: Plans to develop a shipping yard via truck and rail in the Riverview and Trenton areas in suburban Detroit.

52941 ■ *The Road to Self-Employment: A Practical Guide to Microbusiness Development*
Pub: Women's Business Training Center
Ed: Gerri P. Norington; edited by Linda C. Pulg; illustrated by J. Bird Design staff; photographed by Doreen Clough. Released: 1997. Price: $24.95; 5 vols. Vol. 1.

52942 ■ *SBA Hotline Answer Book*
Pub: John Wiley & Sons, Inc.
Ed: Gustav Berle. Released: 1991. Price: $14.95 (paper). Description: Compilation of the 200 queries most often received through the Small Business Administration's (SBA) telephone hotline service. Includes an appendix of SBA field offices, SCORE major offices, small business investment companies, minority business development centers, and other institutions.

52943 ■ "SBA Includes Area Banks in Community Investment" in *Bradenton Herald* (November 5, 2006)
Pub: Bradenton Herald
Ed: Tilde Herrera. Description: Small Business Administration loans have changed in the last decade allowing local banks to tap a market of businesses not able to receive conventional financing because they do not have the collateral or are too new.

52944 ■ "SBA Spared Budget Blues" in *Hispanic Business* (Vol. 22, No. 1/2, January/February, pp. 16)
Pub: Hispanic Business
Ed: Patricia Guadalupe. Description: Congress gives the agency a boost in its fiscal 2000 budget. Various programs of the SBA are highlighted, including The New Market Venture Capital Program, an initiative aimed at increasing the number of minority businesses.

52945 ■ *Secrets to Running a Successful Business*
Ed: Jeanette L. Rosenberg. Released: 1994. Price: $19.95. Description: This book contains information on building a successful small business or home-based business. It covers all facets of business development, including the creation of a business plan, customer satisfaction, communication skills, goal setting, and time management. The information is based on interviews with CEOs and other successful business owners, as well as the author's own experience in the field of business advertising.

52946 ■ *Send 'Em One White Sock: 67 Outrageously Simple Ideas from Around the World for Building Your Business*
Pub: The McGraw-Hill Companies
Ed: Stan Rapp and Thomas L. Collins. Released: 1998. Price: $18.00.

52947 ■ "Small Business Advisor: A pressing matter" in *Crain's Chicago Businesss*
Pub: Crain Communications, Inc. Crain Communications, Inc.
Ed: Barbara B. Buchholz. Description: Twenty years ago, when Robert and Lynne Pascal were seeking a challenge, they started a printing company and are now moving their business to the Internet.

52948 ■ "Small Business Advisor: Choose kids' or collectors' market" in *Crain's Chicago Business* (Vol. 23, November 13, 2000, pp. SB17)
Pub: Crain Communications, Inc. Crain Communications, Inc.
Ed: Warren Denniston. Description: Checkerboard Toys Inc. faces numerous challenges, including business focus and capital funding.

52949 ■ "Small Business Advisor: Identify and protect your niches" in *Crain's Chicago Business* (Vol. 23, October 9, 2000, pp. SB15)
Pub: Crain Communications, Inc. Crain Communications, Inc.
Ed: Lisa Kieres. Description: Unlike most printers, Robert and Lynne Pascal are in an enviable position, with great growth trends and outlook.

52950 ■ *The Small Business Directory*
Pub: U.S. Government Printing Office
Released: 1992. Price: $79.95. Description: Lists booklets and videocassettes to help start and manage a small business. Compiled by the Small Business Administration (SBA).

52951 ■ *The Small Business Handbook*
Pub: Simon & Schuster Trade
Ed: Irving Burstiner. Released: 3rd ed. 1997. Price: $20.00. Description:

52952 ■ "Small Business: Just When Hopes Were High" in *Business Week* (January 8, 2007)
Pub: McGraw-Hill Companies
Ed: James Mehring. Description: Overview of the reasons for a fall in confidence concerning the economy among small businesses and the affect this could have in the coming year.

52953 ■ Small Business Kit for Dummies
Pub: I D G Worldwide
Ed: Richard D. Harroch. **Released:** 1998. **Price:** $24.99 (CD-ROM). **Description:** Ties in to all...For Dummies small business titles. Book CD-ROM package contains all the forms and documents needed and step-by-step walk-throughs to start and run a small business successfully.

52954 ■ The Small Business Start-Up Guide: A Surefire Blueprint to Successfully Launch Your Own Business
Pub: Sourcebooks, Inc.
Ed: Hal Root and Steve Koenig. **Released:** 2nd ed. 1997. **Price:** $12.95.

52955 ■ "Small Firm Bankruptcy" in Journal of Small Business Management (Vol. 44, October 2006, No. 4, pp. 493)
Pub: Blackwell Publishing, Inc.
Ed: Richard Carter; Howard Van Auken. **Description:** Results of a survey attempt to identify the root causes of bankruptcy in firms. Statistical data included.

52956 ■ Small Firms and Economic Growth
Pub: Ashgate Publishing Co., Inc.
Ed: Zoltan J. Acs. **Released:** 1995. **Price:** $420.00.

52957 ■ Small Firms, Large Concerns: The Development of Small Business in Comparative Perspective
Pub: Oxford University Press, Inc.
Ed: Konosuke Odaka and Minoru Sawai. **Released:** 1999. **Price:** $70.00.

52958 ■ Small Time Operator: How to Start Your Own Small Business, Keep Your Books, Pay Your Taxes, & Stay out of Trouble!
Pub: Bell Springs Publishing
Ed: Bernard Kamoroff. **Released:** 22nd ed. 1998. **Price:** $16.95.

52959 ■ Small Time Operator: The Software
Pub: Bell Springs Publishing
Ed: Bernard Kamoroff CPA, Steve Steinke and Emil Krause. **Price:** $29.95 (diskette). **Description:** For people with a spreadsheet program, here is the same bookkeeping system as the one in Small Time Operator, on a ready-to-use spreadsheet file (template). The disk contains 23 spreadsheets: income and expenditure ledgers; profit and loss statement; balance sheet; payroll; cash flow; net worth; petty cash; partner's capital; credit ledger; inventory control; business plan. invoice form; mailing list; loan amortization; and telephone-address file. Includes 184-page manual.

52960 ■ Smart Start Your Arizona Business
Pub: PSI Research
Released: 1997. **Price:** $19.95.

52961 ■ Smart Start Your Arkansas Business
Pub: PSI Research
Released: 1998. **Price:** $19.95.

52962 ■ Smart Start Your California Business
Pub: PSI Research
Released: 1997. **Price:** $19.95.

52963 ■ Smart Start Your Colorado Business
Pub: PSI Research
Released: 1997. **Price:** $19.95.

52964 ■ Smart Start Your Connecticut Business
Pub: PSI Research
Released: 1998. **Price:** $19.95.

52965 ■ Smart Start Your Florida Business
Pub: PSI Research
Released: 1997. **Price:** $19.95.

52966 ■ Smart Start Your Georgia Business
Pub: PSI Research
Released: 1997. **Price:** $19.95.

52967 ■ Smart Start Your Hawaii Business
Pub: PSI Research
Released: 1998. **Price:** $19.95.

52968 ■ Smart Start Your Illinois Business
Pub: PSI Research
Released: 1998. **Price:** $19.95.

52969 ■ Smart Start Your Indiana Business
Pub: PSI Research
Released: 1998. **Price:** $19.95.

52970 ■ Smart Start Your Kentucky Business
Pub: PSI Research
Released: 1997. **Price:** $19.95.

52971 ■ Smart Start Your Maryland Business
Pub: PSI Research
Released: 1997. **Price:** $19.95.

52972 ■ Smart Start Your Massachusetts Business
Pub: PSI Research
Released: 1997. **Price:** $19.95.

52973 ■ Smart Start Your Michigan Business
Pub: PSI Research
Released: 1998. **Price:** $19.95.

52974 ■ Smart Start Your New Jersey Business
Pub: PSI Research
Released: 1997. **Price:** $19.95.

52975 ■ Smart Start Your New York Business
Pub: PSI Research
Released: 1997. **Price:** $19.95.

52976 ■ Smart Start Your North Carolina Business
Pub: PSI Research
Released: 1997. **Price:** $19.95.

52977 ■ Smart Start Your Ohio Business
Pub: PSI Research
Released: 1998. **Price:** $19.95.

52978 ■ Smart Start Your Oregon Business
Pub: PSI Research
Released: 1997. **Price:** $19.95.

52979 ■ Smart Start Your Pennsylvania Business
Pub: PSI Research
Released: 1997. **Price:** $19.95.

52980 ■ Smart Start Your Tennessee Business
Pub: PSI Research
Released: 1998. **Price:** $19.95.

52981 ■ Smart Start Your Texas Business
Pub: PSI Research
Released: 1997. **Price:** $19.95.

52982 ■ Smart Start Your Virginia Business
Pub: PSI Research
Released: 1997. **Price:** $19.95.

52983 ■ Smart Start Your Washington Business
Pub: PSI Research
Released: 1997. **Price:** $19.95.

52984 ■ Smart Start Your Washington, D.C. Business
Pub: PSI Research
Released: 1998. **Price:** $19.95.

52985 ■ Smart Start Your Wisconsin Business
Pub: PSI Research
Released: 1998. **Price:** $19.95.

52986 ■ So You Want to Own Your Own Business: A Guide for Beginning Entrepreuners
Pub: Star Mountain, Inc.
Released: 1997. **Price:** $16.95.

52987 ■ "Springboard to Success" in Black Enterprise (Vol. 35, December 2004, No. 5, pp. 84)
Pub: Earl G. Graves Publishing Co. Inc.
Ed: Nkechi Olisemeka. **Description:** Profile of Pamela G. Carlton, co-founder and president of Springboard, committed to assisting underrepresented groups neglected early in their career.

52988 ■ Start, Run & Grow a Successful Small Business
Pub: C C H, Inc.
Ed: Susan Jacksach; designed by Tim Kaage; contribution by Martin Bush. **Released:** 2nd ed. 1998. **Price:** $24.95.

52989 ■ The Start-Up Guide: A One-Year Plan for Entrepreneurs
Pub: Upstart Publishing Co., Inc.
Ed: David H. Bangs, Jr. **Released:** 1994. **Price:** $39.95. **Description:** Contains information on starting a business, including sources of credit, risks, rules for dealing with investors and vendors, maintaining enthusiasm, and financing. Comes with forms, worksheets, and additional information sources.

52990 ■ Start Your New Business Now!
Pub: Visions Communications
Ed: Arlene Appelbaum. **Released:** 1997. **Price:** $48.00.

52991 ■ Start Your Own Business
Pub: Dimension Four Enterprises, Inc.
Ed: Caleb McAfee. **Released:** 1998. **Price:** $24.95.

52992 ■ Start Your Own Business: A Beginner's Guide
Pub: PSI Research
Released: 2nd ed. 1997. **Price:** $24.95 (diskette).

52993 ■ Start Your Own Business: A Smart & Simple Guide
Pub: Entrepreneur Media
Released: 1998. **Price:** $19.95; $24.95.

52994 ■ Start Your Own Business After 50—or 60—or 70!
Pub: Bristol Publishing Enterprises, Inc.
Ed: Lauraine Snelling. **Released:** 1990. **Price:** $8.95, plus $2.50 shipping. **Description:** Profiles 64 business owners who started their first businesses after age 50.

52995 ■ Start Your Own Business in Thirty Days
Pub: Berkley Publishing Group
Ed: Gary J. Grappo. **Released:** 1998. **Price:** $12.00. **Description:** Grappo offers thirty key concepts that will help readers launch their own successful venture.

52996 ■ Starting and Operating a Business
Pub: Oasis Press
Ed: Michael D. Jenkins. **Released:** 1992. **Price:** $295.00 (3-ring binder).

52997 ■ Starting a Successful Business on the West Coast
Pub: Self-Counsel Press, Inc.
Ed: Douglas L. Clark. **Released:** Third edition, 1992. **Price:** $14.95 (paper).

52998 ■ Starting Your Own Business & Making It a Success
Pub: T F S Publishing
Ed: John O. Alaba. **Released:** 1998. **Price:** $20.00. **Description:** Written for entrepreneurs and people interested in a start-up business.

52999 ■ "Stats of the Month" in *Business Week* (No. 3761, December 10, 2001, pp. SB9)
Pub: McGraw-Hill Inc.
Description: Statistical data regarding issues facing small business growth is presented.

53000 ■ *Steps to Small Business Start-Up: Everything You Need to Know to Turn Your Idea into a Successful Business*
Pub: Upstart Publishing Co., Inc.
Ed: Linda Pinson and Jerry Hinnett. **Released:** 1993. **Price:** $22.95 (paper). **Description:** Step-by-step guide to starting a small business, covering record-keeping, marketing, and business planning. Also provides information on choosing a business and a name, choosing a legal structure, obtaining business licenses and permits, and copyrights, trademarks, and patents. Contains forms, examples, and worksheets.

53001 ■ *Succeeding in Small Business: The 101 Toughest Problems and How to Solve Them*
Pub: NAL Dutton
Ed: Jane Applegate. **Released:** 1992. **Price:** $13.95 (paper).

53002 ■ "Success Products" in *Black Enterprise* (Vol. 37, February 2007, No. 7, pp. 135)
Pub: Earl G. Graves Publishing Co. Inc.
Ed: Tanisha A. Sykes. **Description:** Using innovative resources that are already at your fingertips instead of trying to reach out to companies first is a great way to discover whether you have a viable idea or product. Be motivated to start an e-newsletter letting people know about your products and attend conferences like The Motivation Show, the world's largest exhibition of motivational products and services related to performance in business.

53003 ■ "Supply Chain Challenges: Building Relationships" in *Harvard Business Review* (Vol. 81, No. 7, July 2003, pp. 64)
Pub: Harvard Business School Press
Ed: Julia Kirby. **Description:** The development of business logistics systems is discussed.

53004 ■ *Surviving the Start-up Years in Your Own Business*
Pub: F & W Publishing, Inc.
Ed: Joyce S. Marder. **Released:** 1991. **Price:** $7.95 (paper). **Description:** Topics covered include money management; marketing; employee issues; obtaining capital; expansion; pricing; sales techniques; and other subjects. Includes forms, charts, and references.

53005 ■ "Taking On the Energy Crunch" in *Fortune* (Vol. 151, February 7, 2005, No. 3, pp. 97)
Pub: Time Inc.
Ed: Marc Gunther. **Description:** The appeal of wind power, because of zero fuel costs, is discussed along with other alternatives to oil and gas. General Motors, BMW, and S.C. Johnson are buying landfill gas to save money and to help clean the air; the aluminum industry spends $750 for recycled cans; environmentally designed 'green' buildings are another alternative.

53006 ■ "Taking Sides" in *Entrepreneur* (Vol. 33, September 2005, No. 9, pp. 26)
Pub: Entrepreneur Media Inc.
Ed: April Y. Pennington. **Description:** Three forces are changing the way to grow a business: an abundance of consumer goods; outsourcing to Asia; and automation of routine work. Six key abilities for the Conceptual Age are design, story, symphony, empathy, play and meaning.

53007 ■ "Tastes Differ" in *Crain's New York Business* (Vol. 22, December 11, 2006, No. 50, pp. 24)
Pub: Crain Communications, Inc.
Description: Executives for reality shows say that the key to getting one's products on air is to be available on short notice, be patient, and have a great product. Many shows not only mention vendors by name but they also feature them on their websites.

53008 ■ "Tee Off Online" in *Black Enterprise* (Vol. 37, January 2007, No. 6, pp. 52)
Pub: Earl G. Graves Publishing Co. Inc.
Ed: James C. Johnson. **Description:** The E-Com Resource Center is one of many resources that are available for those interested in starting an e-commerce business. One of the first steps is to create a business plan, of which there are free samples available at BPlans.com.

53009 ■ "Thanks to the Xerox, the company reduced its outsourcing by 77.6 percent for the first six months of the year" in *Inc.* (Nov. 15, 2000)
Pub: The Goldhirsh Group
Description: The CEO of a company tells how a new copier is helping the company grow.

53010 ■ "The Champagne Group Launches 'Manager Makeover' Program" in *Bellingham Business Journal* (January 2007, pp. 4)
Pub: Sun News Inc.
Description: Twelve-year-old business and leadership coaching company, The Champagne Group, is launching their new Manager Makeover Program. The five-step, customized program equips managers with techniques on becoming leaders who can resolve conflicts and increase performance.

53011 ■ "The Eco-Advantage. The Green 50" in *Inc.* (November 2006, pp. 79-103)
Pub: Gruner & Jahr USA Publishing
Ed: Larry Kanters **Description:** Fifty entrepreneurs are highlighted who have found a different way to do business that is more friendly to the environment. Some range from being directed at finding renewable sources of energy while others just wanted to find an eco-friendly business model.

53012 ■ "The Pantry Expands Presence" in *Mississippi Business Journal* (Vol. 29, January 2007, No. 2, pp. 8)
Pub: Venture Publications, Inc.
Ed: Wally Northway **Description:** Eight convenience stores in Mississippi and Florida have been acquired by The Pantry Inc. Statistical data included.

53013 ■ "Time Right For Tech Upgrade? That Depends" in *Mississippi Business Journal* (Vol. 29, January 2007, No. 2, pp. 1)
Pub: Venture Publications, Inc.
Ed: Becky Gillette **Description:** Most people wait until their computer or office equipment breaks down before replacing it. Advice on when and how to upgrade equipment for the least business downtime is covered.

53014 ■ "Toward the Development of Measures of Distinctive Competencies among Small Independent Retailers" in *Journal of Small Business Management*
Pub: West Virginia University
Ed: Jeffrey E. McGee, Mark Peterson. **Description:** To remain competitive in markets increasingly dominated by large discount chains, "category killers," and other mass-merchandisers, small independent retailers need to develop distinctive competencies. A study providing insight into the multidimensional character of distinctive competencies by measuring the resources and capabilities possessed by 255 independent drug stores is presented.

53015 ■ "Transform Your Life" in *Black Enterprise* (Vol. 37, January 2007, No. 6, pp. 14)
Pub: Earl G. Graves Publishing Co. Inc.
Description: Through the magazine, television and radio programs, events, and the website, the various platforms of Black Enterprise will provide the tools necessary to achieve success in business ventures, career aspirations, and personal goals.

53016 ■ *201 Great Ideas for Your Small Business*
Pub: Bloomberg Press
Ed: Jane Applegate. **Released:** 1998. **Price:** $14.95.

53017 ■ *The Ultimate No B.S., No Holds Barred, Kick Butt, Take No Prisoners, and Make Tons of Money Business Success Book*
Pub: Self-Counsel Press, Inc.
Ed: Dan Kennedy. **Released:** 1993. **Price:** $16.95 (business package); $8.95 (paper); $14.95 (two audiocassettes). **Description:** Business package includes book plus audiocassettes.

53018 ■ "Unleashing The Millennium" in *Fortune* (Vol. 141, No. 5, March 6, 2000, pp. 16+)
Pub: Time Inc.
Ed: Paul Krugman. **Description:** An inquiry into what went right with the free market system at the turn of the century, and whether this trend will continue.

53019 ■ *The Unofficial Guide to Starting a Business*
Pub: MacMillan Publishing Co., Inc.
Released: 1998. **Price:** $16.00.

53020 ■ "Utilities Boost Companies; Utility Services" in *Crain's New York Business* (Vol. 22, November 13, 2006, No. 46, pp. 36)
Pub: Crain Communications, Inc.
Description: Listing of companies that provide utility programs, incentives and benefits to small businesses looking to relocate within the five boroughs of New York City or expand their businesses in the area.

53021 ■ *Vault Reports: A Guide to Starting Your Own Business*
Pub: Houghton Mifflin Co.
Released: 1998. **Price:** $14.00. **Description:** Insider advice on starting your own business.

53022 ■ "VC Company to Double One Fund, Add $40M Fund." in *Crain's Detroit Business* (Vol. 23, January 15,2007, No. 3, pp. 26)
Pub: Crain Communications Inc. - Detroit
Ed: Tom Henderson. **Description:** Local Venture Capital firm adds personnel and expands funds to increase business. First fund is doubled to $20M and began raising money for a second fund of $40M.

53023 ■ *VentureTrac: Complete Business Development Program*
Pub: Tangent Publishing
Ed: Andrew J. Batchelor, Jr. and Timothy E, Nesmith. **Released:** 1997. **Price:** $129.00 (diskette). **Description:** A step-by-step guide assisting the entrepreneur in the development of a comprehensive business plan that can be used to obtain financing for start-up venture or expanding an existing company.

53024 ■ "Waking Up IBM: How a Gang of Unlikely Rebels Transformed Big Blue" in *Harvard Business Review* (Vol. 78, No. 4, July 2000, pp. 137)
Pub: Harvard Business School Publishing Corp.
Ed: Gary Hamel. **Description:** The article reviews how IBM avoided insolvency by introducing new ideas for business development.

53025 ■ "Waterfront, Airport on Top of List For Port" in *Bellingham Business Journal* (January 2007, pp. B5)
Pub: Sun News Inc.
Ed: Dan Hiestand. **Description:** New Whatcom redevelopment for the former Georgia-Pacific waterfront property is in the works. The city and port have been working to create a cohesive plan for the site. Sixty-eight percent of the property leaves ownership in the public's hands.

53026 ■ *We Own It: Starting & Managing Cooperatives & Employee-Owned Businesses*
Pub: Bell Springs Publishing Co.
Ed: Peter Honigsberg, Bernard Kamoroff and Jim Beatty. **Released:** Revised edition, 1991. **Price:** $14.00 (paper).

53027 ■ "What Really Works" in *Harvard Business Review* (Vol. 81, No. 7, July 2003, pp. 42)
Pub: Harvard Business School Press
Ed: Nitin Nohria, William Joyce, Bruce Roberson. Description: Management practices that result in business success are examined.

53028 ■ When in Doubt Grab a Mouse, or a Phone" in *Crain's Chicago Business* (Vol. 30, January 2007, No. 1, pp. 12)
Pub: Crain Communications, Inc.
Ed: Dee Gill. Description: Interview with Maria Meyers, network coordinator for U.S.SourceLink, a non-profit designed to give entrepreneurs and small business owners easy access to resources. Meyers talks about the program, its history and impact on the community, the website itself, and the grass-roots marketing needed to inform consumers of the services available.

53029 ■ "Where to Find Business Answers; Advice and Education" in *Crain's New York Business* (Vol. 22, November 13, 2006, No. 46, pp. 24)
Pub: Crain Communications, Inc.
Description: Listing of organizations and agencies that provide training, financial and managerial advice, and technical expertise to current or would-be business owners.

53030 ■ "Why Good Projects Fail Anyway" in *Harvard Business Review* (Vol. 81, No. 9, September 2003, pp. 109)
Pub: Harvard Business School Press
Ed: Nadim F. Matta, Ronald N. Ashkenas. Description: Suggestions for designing projects, including business plans that have a greater chance of success than most are provided.

53031 ■ "Why the Valley Way is Here to Stay" in *Fortune* (Vol. 141, No. 11, May 29, 2000, pp. 36+)
Pub: Time Inc.
Ed: J. Bradford DeLong. Description: Despite the bluster about the new economy, not much is actually new. Productivity is at the same rate experienced in the 1960s.

53032 ■ *Working Knowledge: What You Need to Know Before Opening a Business*
Pub: Echelon Publishing
Ed: William A. Walls. Released: 1994. Price: $29.95 (3-ring binder).

53033 ■ *World Class: Thriving Locally in the Global Economy*
Pub: Simon & Schuster, Inc.
Ed: Rosabeth M. Kanter. Released: 1995. Price: $25.00.

53034 ■ "XML offers flexibility, ebXML sorts it out" in *Crain's Detroit Business* (Vol. 16, No. 47, November 13, 2000, pp. 18)
Pub: Crain Communications, Inc.
Ed: Jeffrey Kosseff. Description: Computer language that allows flexibility in communicating data is explored.

53035 ■ "XML: The Only Chance for a Worldwide Standard" in *E-business Advisor* (Vol. 18, No. 4, April 2000, pp. 10)
Pub: Advisor Media, Inc.
Ed: Rik Drummond. Description: The second meeting of the Electronic Business XML (ebXML) Initiative to produce a global standard for e-commerce was held in February 2000. There are eight project teams in ebXML. Activities of the project teams, are presented with special emphasis on the Transport/Routing and Packaging team, aimed at developing technical specifications for the e-commerce server intercommunications architecture are presented.

53036 ■ "Your Business needs to be E-Commerce - so what now?" in *Ingram's* (Vol. 27, No. 7, July 2001, pp. 19)
Pub: Show Me Publishing, Inc.
Description: Management techniques and theory are outlined for e-commerce management. Some tech-

niques include treating online and offline sales the same way, organize and prioritize what the Website needs to accomplish, and consider market potential.

53037 ■ "Your Man On The Hill" in *Fortune* (Vol. 142, No. 9, October 16, 2000, pp. 312B)
Pub: Time Inc.
Ed: Julie Rose. Description: Senator Kit Bond, who runs the Committee on Small Business, has become an unrelenting advocate for small business interests, and agencies like the SBA and OSHA pay attention.

53038 ■ *Your New Business: A Personal Plan for Success*
Pub: Crisp Publications, Inc.
Ed: Charles Martin. Released: 1993. Price: $15.95 (paper).

53039 ■ *Your Way: Starting Your Own Business in Rural South Dakota*
Pub: Pine Hill Press, Inc.
Ed: Tom Kilian. Released: 1997.

TRADE PERIODICALS

53040 ■ *Business Ideas & Shortcuts*
Pub: Editorial Board
Ed: Peter Joseph, Editor. Released: Monthly. Price: $99 year. Description: Contains special reports, practical ideas, tips, and guidelines on current business opportunities and shortcuts to profits. Covers specific topics, such as how to be a manufacturer without investing; how to get free national advertising; how to protect your business; and how to tap overlooked sources of financing. Recurring features include columns titled Business Shortcut of the Month and Unique Ideas for Entrepreneurs.

53041 ■ *Business Opportunities Journal(online)*
Pub: Business Service Corp.
Contact: Carl Rawlins, Advertising Mgr
E-mail: carlrawlins@cox.net
Released: Monthly. Description: Newspaper covering businesses for sale.

53042 ■ *Entrepreneur Magazine*
Pub: Entrepreneur Media Inc.
Contact: Rieva Lesonsky, Editorial Dir.
E-mail: rlesonsky@entrepreneur.com
Released: Monthly. Price: $19.97; $4.99 single issue. Description: Magazine covering small business management and operation.

53043 ■ *Entrepreneur's Bizstartups.com*
Pub: Entrepreneur Media Inc.
Contact: Jim Kahn, Publisher
E-mail: kspaeder@entrepreneur.com
Released: Monthly. Price: $15.97; $31.97 other countries; $13.97 special online. Description: Magazine for Generation X entrepreneurs (age 35 and under). Articles cover hot businesses to start; ideas for running and growing a business; cutting-edge technology; management; motivation and more.

53044 ■ *Entrepreneurship Theory and Practice*
Pub: Baylor University
Contact: Sharon Johnson Bracken, Managing Editor
E-mail: sharon.k.johnson@baylor.edu
Released: Quarterly. Price: $106 print & online; $365 institutions print & premium online. Description: Academic journal on entrepreneurship, family-owned businesses, and small business management.

53045 ■ *Journal of Entrepreneurial and Small Firm Finance*
Pub: University of California Press
Released: 3/yr. Description: Journal that focuses on small business and financial issues.

53046 ■ *SBANE Enterprise*
Pub: Smaller Business Association of New England
Ed: Julie Scofield, Editor. Released: 8-9/year. Price: Included in membership; $49, nonmembers. Descrip-

tion: Reports on matters of concern to those who are engaged in small businesses in the New England area. Includes news of government actions and legislation and economic trends. Recurring features include items on business education opportunities, members, and Association activities.

53047 ■ *The Small Business Advisor*
Pub: Small Business Advisors Inc.
Contact: Joseph Gelb, Publisher
Ed: Ann Liss, Editor. Released: Monthly. Price: $45, U.S.; $90, Canada. Description: Seeks to help emerging growth companies increase profits. Considers small business issues, including marketing sales, finance, taxes, organizing, competition, management, and human resources. Recurring features include letters to the editor, interviews, and columns titled Info Bank, In the Mail Box, Taxes, Human Resources, Marketing, Insurance, and Law. Remarks: Publication suspended in 1980; resumed publication Fall 1993.

53048 ■ *Small Business Opportunities*
Pub: Harris Publications Inc.
Contact: Stanley Harris, Publisher
Ed: Susan Rakowski, Editor. Released: Bimonthly, (plus 4 special editions). Price: $9.97. Description: How-to magazine for small business owners.

VIDEOCASSETTES/AUDIOCASSETTES

53049 ■ *American Institute of Small Business: Setting Up a Home-Based Business*
American Institute of Small Business (AISB)
7515 Wayzata Blvd., Ste. 126
Minneapolis, MN 55426
Ph:(612)545-7001
Free: 800-328-2906
Fax: (612)545-7020
Co. E-mail: AISBOFMN@AOL.COM
URL: http://www.accessil.com/aisb
Released: 199?. Price: $69.95. Description: Step-by-step guide to operating a business out of your home. Availability: VHS.

53050 ■ *American Institute of Small Business: Starting a Business—Advice from Experts*
American Institute of Small Business (AISB)
7515 Wayzata Blvd., Ste. 126
Minneapolis, MN 55426
Ph:(612)545-7001
Free: 800-328-2906
Fax: (612)545-7020
Co. E-mail: AISBOFMN@AOL.COM
URL: http://www.accessil.com
Released: 199?. Price: $69.95. Description: Business commentators from Money, Fortune, and Newsweek magazines give tips on taxes, obtaining financing, and other issues. Availability: VHS.

53051 ■ *Beyond Start-Up: Management Lessons for Growing Companies*
Video Arts, Inc.
c/o Aim Learning Group
8238-40 Lehigh
Morton Grove, IL 60053-2615
Free: 877-444-2230
Fax: (416)252-2155
Co. E-mail: service@aimlearninggroup.com
URL: http://www.aimlearninggroup.com
Released: 1989. Price: $395.00. Description: Don't settle for being a small company—find out what it takes to expand your business. Availability: VHS; 3/4U.

53052 ■ *Changing Values: Moving Toward the Future - Trends That Will Affect Your Business*
Government VideoSource, Inc.
461 Miller Dr.
Elgin, IL 60123-7232
Ph:(847)931-1955
Price: $595. Description: Explains the importance of identifying change in an everchanging culture. Introduces new values emerging in the workplace. Availability: VHS.

53053 ■ The Entrepreneurs: Risk Takers
RMI Media
1365 N. Winchester
Olathe, KS 66061
Ph:(913)768-1696
Fax: (913)768-0184
Co. E-mail: actmedia@act.org
URL: http://www.rmimedia.com
Released: 1989. **Price:** $70.00. **Description:** College and high school students gain a special understanding of small business from this series. **Availability:** VHS; 3/4U.

53054 ■ Finding a Niche: Determining Business Potential
Instructional Video
2219 C St.
Lincoln, NE 68502
Ph:(402)475-6570
Free: 800-228-0164
Fax: (402)475-6500
Co. E-mail: feedback@insvideo.com
URL: http://www.insvideo.com
Price: $99.00. **Description:** Outlines the process of selecting an appropriate market for your product, including profile development of potential customers and planning and implementing a feasability study. **Availability:** VHS.

53055 ■ Growing a Business
Ambrose Video Publishing, Inc.
145 W. 45th St., Ste. 1115
New York, NY 10036
Ph:(212)768-7373
Free: 800-526-4663
Fax: (212)768-9292
Co. E-mail: customerservice@ambrosevideo.com
URL: http://www.ambrosevideo.com
Released: 1989. **Price:** $1295.00. **Description:** This video shows the steps taken by different people to start up a business. **Availability:** VHS.

53056 ■ How to Start Your Own Successful Business
Instructional Video
2219 C St.
Lincoln, NE 68502
Ph:(402)475-6570
Free: 800-228-0164
Fax: (402)475-6500
Co. E-mail: feedback@insvideo.com
URL: http://www.insvideo.com
Price: $29.95. **Description:** Illustrates correct procedures for establishing and maintaining an effective business. Covers marketing, managing, financing, business insurance, buying an existing business, franchising, home-based business, youth entrepreneurial business, negotiating deals, and projecting your ideas. **Availability:** VHS.

53057 ■ I Can Do It! Stew Leonard
Direct Cinema Ltd.
PO Box 10003
Santa Monica, CA 90410-1003
Ph:(310)636-8200
Free: 800-525-0000
Fax: (310)636-8228
Co. E-mail: orders@directcinemalimited.com
URL: http://www.directcinema.com
Released: 1985. **Description:** The dairy king explains the details and knowledge he used to devise a phenomenonally successful business. **Availability:** VHS; 3/4U; Special order formats.

53058 ■ Inc. Magazine Business Success Programs
Cambridge Educational
c/o Films Media Group
PO Box 2053
Princeton, NJ 08843-2053
Free: 800-257-5126
Fax: (609)671-0266
Co. E-mail: custserve@filmsmediagroup.com
URL: http://www.cambridgeol.com
Released: 1987. **Price:** $99.95. **Description:** These four programs contain a step-by-step explanation of what must be done to succeed in business. **Availability:** VHS; CC.

53059 ■ Inc. Magazine's How to (Really) Start Your Own Business
Cambridge Educational
c/o Films Media Group
PO Box 2053
Princeton, NJ 08843-2053
Free: 800-257-5126
Fax: (609)671-0266
Co. E-mail: custserve@filmsmediagroup.com
URL: http://www.cambridgeol.com
Released: 1986. **Price:** $29.95. **Description:** An authoritative guide to starting a small business, including tips on investment acquisition, business planning, financing and more. **Availability:** VHS.

53060 ■ Inside Business Today
GPN Educational Media
Box 80669
Lincoln, NE 68501-0669
Ph:(402)472-2007
Free: 800-228-4630
Fax: 800-306-2330
URL: http://gpn.unl.edu
Released: 1989. **Description:** Leaders in business and industry tell their success stories in this extensive series. **Availability:** VHS; 3/4U.

53061 ■ Inside Business Today...The '90s
GPN Educational Media
Box 80669
Lincoln, NE 68501-0669
Ph:(402)472-2007
Free: 800-228-4630
Fax: 800-306-2330
URL: http://gpn.unl.edu
Released: 1990. **Price:** $2765.00. **Description:** Second part of the Inside Business series. Contains 30 sections which discusses various areas of business concerns in the 1990s. **Availability:** VHS.

53062 ■ New or Used? Buying a Firm or Starting Your Own
Instructional Video
2219 C St.
Lincoln, NE 68502
Ph:(402)475-6570
Free: 800-228-0164
Fax: (402)475-6500
Co. E-mail: feedback@insvideo.com
URL: http://www.insvideo.com
Price: $99.00. **Description:** Details the different options open to anyone wanting to start or obtain their own business. Discusses the various factors to be considered when putting a value on a company, negotiating price and terms, and closing the deal. **Availability:** VHS.

53063 ■ Small Business in a Big World
Instructional Video
2219 C St.
Lincoln, NE 68502
Ph:(402)475-6570
Free: 800-228-0164
Fax: (402)475-6500
Co. E-mail: feedback@insvideo.com
URL: http://www.insvideo.com
Price: $99.00. **Description:** Demonstrates how small business has contributed to the overall economy. Includes profiles of small retail, service, manufacturing, professional, high tech, wholesale, and warehousing operations at work. **Availability:** VHS.

53064 ■ The Ten Commandments of Networking
TomKat Productions
2537 S. Gessner, Ste. 114
Houston, TX 77063
Fax: (713)975-0532
Co. E-mail: tom@tomkatpro.com
URL: http://www.tomkatpro.com/index.html
Released: 1994. **Price:** $39.95. **Description:** One-part seminar and one-part live demonstration of various networking situations, geared toward the entrepreneur who wants to expand and cultivate personal and business relationships. **Availability:** VHS.

53065 ■ Understanding Business Valuation
Chesney Communications
2302 Martin St., Ste. 125
Irvine, CA 92612
Ph:(949)263-5500
Free: 800-223-8878
Fax: (949)263-5506
Released: 1987. **Description:** A look for the small businessman at how to plan the future of his company-growth, reinvestment and possible sale. **Availability:** VHS; 3/4U.

TRADE SHOWS AND CONVENTIONS

53066 ■ Business World Exhibition/Quebec City
Martin International
500 Place d'Armes, Ste. 2910
Montreal, QC, Canada H2Y 2W2
Ph:(514)288-3931
Fax: (514)288-0641
Co. E-mail: smartin@martin-intl.com
URL: http://www.martin-intl.com
Released: Annual. **Audience:** Trade professionals and members. **Principal Exhibits:** International showcase, regional markets show, technology show, finance and accounting, advertising/home office/computers, travel and convention show, procurement show, small business summit.

53067 ■ Cincinnati Business Expo/Fall
Industry Week
The Penton Media Bldg.
1300 E 9th St., Ste. 316
Cleveland, OH 44114-1503
Ph:(216)696-7000
Fax: (513)528-1131
Co. E-mail: iwinfo@industryweek.com
URL: http://www.industryweek.com
Released: Annual. **Audience:** Business professionals. **Principal Exhibits:** Business services, office equipment, computers, mailing equipment, and office furniture and supplies.

CONSULTANTS

53068 ■ 2010 Fund 5
24351 Spartan St., Ste. 120
Mission Viejo, CA 92691
Ph:(949)583-1992
Scope: Funds in formation that will invest in technologies licensed from 30 universities. **Seminars:** Chair, Corporate Investment and Strategic Alliance Conferences.

53069 ■ Aurora Management Partners Inc.
4485 Tench Rd., Ste. 340A
Suwanee, GA 30024
Ph:(770)904-5207
Co. E-mail: rturcotte@auroramp.com
URL: http://www.auroramp.com

E-mail: rturcotte@auroramp.com
Scope: Firm specializes in turnaround management and reorganization consulting. **Publications:** Back From The Brink - Bland Farms; New Breed of Turnaround Managers; Key Performance Drivers - Bland Farms; The Missing Element in Corporate Governance Ratings.

53070 ■ Biomedical Management Resources
PO Box 521125
Salt Lake City, UT 84152-1125
Ph:(801)272-4668
Fax: (801)277-3290
Co. E-mail: SeniorManagement@
  BiomedicalManagement.com
URL: http://www.biomedicalmanagement.com

E-mail: SeniorManagement@
  BiomedicalManagement.com

Scope: Provides business development, interim management, and executive search services. Assists companies in strategic alliances, corporate partnering, business acquisition. Demonstrated success in identifying recruiting, and placing key managers in difficult to hire positions.

53071 ■ BPT Consulting Associates Ltd.
12 Parmenter Rd., Ste. B6
Londonderry, NH 03053
Ph:(603)437-8484
Co. E-mail: bptcons@tiac.net
URL: http://www.bptconsulting.com

E-mail: bptcons@tiac.net
Scope: Provides management consulting expertise and resources to cross-industry clients with services for: Business Management consulting, People/Human Resources Transition and Training programs, and a full cadre of multi-disciplined Technology Computer experts. Virtual consultants with expertise in e-commerce, supply chain management, organizational development, and business application development consulting. **Seminars:** Business: MRPII, DRPII, JIT/TQC. Business Requirements Analysis, Small Business Start-Up, Strategic Planning. People: Team Building, Performance Evaluation, Career Transition and Counseling Seminars. Technology: User Training for Customized Software, Internet, Full array of application development, i.e., C, Java, website development. **Special Services:** Provides a full array of computer and related user training services. Resources include application developers, database developers and managers, project management experts for a full array of industries (manufacturing, software, defense, healthcare, pharmaceutical, and small business).

53072 ■ CEO Advisors
848 Brickell Ave., Ste. 603
Miami, FL 33131
Ph:(305)371-8560
Fax: (305)371-8563
Co. E-mail: info@ceoadvisors.us
URL: http://www.ceoadvisors.us

E-mail: info@ceoadvisors.us
Scope: Specializes in strategic planning; profit enhancement; start-up businesses; venture capital; appraisals and valuations. **Seminars:** Innovation and High Performance Organizations.

53073 ■ Chamberlain & Cansler Inc.
2251 Perimeter Park Dr.
Atlanta, GA 30341
Ph:(770)457-5699
Scope: Firm specializes in strategic planning; profit enhancement; small business management; interim management; crisis management; turnarounds.

53074 ■ Chartered Management Co.
125 S Wacker Dr., Ste. 300
Chicago, IL 60606-4402
Ph:(312)214-2575
Scope: Operations improvement consultants. Specializes in strategic planning; feasibility studies; management audits and reports; profit enhancement; start-up businesses; mergers and acquisitions; joint ventures; divestitures; interim management; crisis management; turnarounds; business process re-engineering; venture capital; and due diligence.

53075 ■ Clayton/Curtis/Cottrell
1722 Madison Ct.
Louisville, CO 80027
Ph:(303)665-2005
Fax: (303)665-2276
Scope: Firm specializes packaged goods, telecommunications, direct marketing & printing, & packaging industries. Services include strategic planning; profit enhancement; start-up businesses; mergers and acquisitions; joint ventures; divestitures; interim management; crisis management; turnarounds; market size, segmentation and rates of growth; competitor intelligence; image & reputation, & competitive analysis.

53076 ■ Comer & Associates L.L.C.
5255 Holmes Pl.
Boulder, CO 80303
Ph:(303)786-7986
Free: 888-950-3190
Fax: (303)473-9830
URL: http://www.comerassociates.com
Scope: Specialize in developing markets & businesses. Marketing support includes: developing & writing strategic & tactical business plans; developing & writing focused, effective market plans; researching market potential & competition; implementing targeted marketing tactics to achieve company objectives; conducting customer surveys to determine satisfaction & attitudes toward client. Maintains a network of database research specialists, market communications providers, public relations firms, internet resources, focus group facilitators, technical writers & executive recruiters to assist with any project. Organization development support includes: executive/management training programs; executive coaching; team building; developing effective organization structures & processes; management of change in dynamic & competitive environments; individual coaching for management & leadership effectiveness. **Seminars:** Developing a strategic market plan; market research: defining your opportunity; management & leadership effectiveness; team building; developing a business plan.

53077 ■ The Corlund Group L.L.C.
101 Federal St., Ste. 310
Boston, MA 02110
Ph:(617)423-9364
Fax: (617)423-9371
Co. E-mail: info@corlundgroup.com
URL: http://www.corlundgroup.com

E-mail: info@corlundgroup.com
Scope: Boutique firms offers services in the areas of leadership, governance, and change, with a particular focus on CEO and senior executive succession planning, including assessment, development, and orchestrating succession processes with management and Boards of Directors. Also Board governance effectiveness. **Publications:** "Leadership Due Diligence: The Neglected Governance Frontier," Directorship, Sep, 2001; "Leadership Due Diligence: Managing the Risks," The Corporate Board, Aug, 2001; "Succession: The need for detailed insight," Directors and Boards, 2001; "CEO Succession: Who's Doing Due Diligence?," 2001.

53078 ■ Corporate Consulting Inc.
3333 Belcaro Dr.
Denver, CO 80209
Ph:(303)698-9292
Fax: (303)698-9292
Co. E-mail: corpcons@compuserve.com

E-mail: corpcons@compuserve.com
Scope: Specializes in feasibility studies; organizational development; small business management; mergers and acquisitions; joint ventures; divestitures; interim management; crisis management; turnarounds; financing; appraisals and valuations; and due diligence studies.

53079 ■ Crystal Clear Communications Inc.
8989 N Port Washington Rd., Ste. 210
Milwaukee, WI 53217-1667
Ph:(414)228-8799
Scope: Specializes in strategic planning; organizational development; small business management; mergers and acquisitions; joint ventures; divestitures; strategy implementation; executive coaching.

53080 ■ Development Resource Consultants
PO Box 118
Rancho Cucamonga, CA 91729
Ph:(909)902-7655
Fax: (909)476-6942
Co. E-mail: info@gotodrc.com

E-mail: info@gotodrc.com
Scope: A small business advisory service specializing in office re-organization, employee training in office organization, communication skills, sales training and career counseling.

53081 ■ Dimond Hospitality Consulting Group Inc.
5710 Stoneway Trl.
Nashville, TN 37209
Ph:(615)353-0033
Fax: (615)352-5290
Co. E-mail: dimond@dimondconsultinggroup.com
URL: http://www.dimondconsultinggroup.com

E-mail: dimond@dimondconsultinggroup.com
Scope: Specializes in strategic planning; start-up businesses; business process re-engineering; team building; competitive analysis; venture capital; competitive intelligence; and due diligence. Offers litigation support. Comprehensive hospitality consulting firm that serves as an adviser to leading hotel companies, independent hotels, lending institutions, trustees, law firms, investment companies and municipalities in the areas of:Asset management, Acquisition due diligence, Arbitration ,Disposition advisory services, Exit strategies, Financial review and analysis, Impact studies, Mediation.

53082 ■ donphin.com Inc.
5713 Corporate Way, Ste. 101
West Palm Beach, FL 33407
Ph:(561)688-1000
Free: 800-234-3304
Fax: (561)688-1142
Co. E-mail: inquiry@donphin.com
URL: http://www.donphin.com

E-mail: inquiry@donphin.com
Scope: Offers a comprehensive approach to understanding and applying a broad range of business principles: legal compliance issues, management concerns, health and safety, customer service, marketing, information management. Industries served: all developing small businesses. **Publications:** "Doing Business Right!". **Seminars:** Doing Business Right!; HR That Works!.

53083 ■ Dropkin & Co.
390 George St.
New Brunswick, NJ 08901
Ph:(732)828-3211
Fax: (732)828-4118
Co. E-mail: murray@dropkin.com
URL: http://www.dropkin.com

E-mail: murray@dropkin.com
Scope: Firm specializes in feasibility studies; business management; business process re-engineering; and team building, healthcare and housing. **Publications:** "Guide to Auditing Nonprofit Organizations"; "The Cash Flow Management Book for Nonprofits"

53084 ■ Dubuc Lucke & Co.
414 Walnut St., Ste607
Cincinnati, OH 45202
Ph:(513)579-8330
Fax: (513)241-6669
Scope: Consulting services in the areas of profit enhancement; small business management; mergers and acquisitions; joint ventures; divestitures; interim management; crisis management; turnarounds; appraisals; valuations; due diligence; and international trade.

53085 ■ The DuMond Group
5282 Princeton Ave.
Westminster, CA 92683-2753
Ph:(714)373-0610
Scope: Firm specializes in organizational development; small business management; employee surveys and communication; performance appraisals; and team building.

53086 ■ Dunelm International
14 S Bryn Mawr Ave., Ste. 206
Bryn Mawr, PA 19010-3216
Ph:(610)520-4491
Fax: (610)520-4492
Scope: Firm specializes in feasibility studies; start-up businesses; interim management; crisis manage-

ment; turnarounds; business process re-engineering; sales forecasting; supply chain solution and project management.

53087 ■ Facility Directions Inc.
PO Box 761
Manchester, MO 63011
Ph:(636)256-4400
Free: 800-536-0044
Fax: (636)227-2868
Co. E-mail: walty@facilitydirections.com
URL: http://www.facilitydirections.com

E-mail: walty@facilitydirections.com
Scope: Firm specializes in service to financial institutions; strategic planning; feasibility studies; facility and space planning; attitude surveys; site selection. **Publications:** Newsletter — "Directions".

53088 ■ Federer Resources Inc.
106 E 6th St.
Austin, TX 78701-3659
Ph:(512)476-8800
Scope: Firm specializes in feasibility studies; start-up businesses; small business management; mergers and acquisitions; joint ventures; divestitures; interim management; crisis management; turnarounds; production planning; team building; appraisals and valuations.

53089 ■ First Strike Management Consulting Inc.
401 Loblolly Ave.
PO Box 1188
Little River, SC 29566-1188
Ph:(843)385-6338
Fax: (843)390-1004
Co. E-mail: fsmc.hq@fsmc.com
URL: http://www.fsmc.com

E-mail: fsmc.hq@fsmc.com
Scope: A management consulting firm that provides services such as proposals, enterprise systems, management systems, and staff augmentation. Specializes in new business proposals, project management support and training. **Publications:** Project Management for Executives, Project Risk Management, Project Communications Management, Winning Proposals, Four Computer Based Training (CBT) courses. **Seminars:** Preparing Winning Proposals in Response to Government RFPs.

53090 ■ Global Technology Transfer
1500 Dixie Hwy.
Covington, KY 41011
Ph:(859)431-1262
Fax: (859)431-5148
Co. E-mail: arzembrodt@worldnet.att.net

E-mail: arzembrodt@worldnet.att.net
Scope: Firm specializes in product development; quality assurance; new product development; and total quality management focusing on household chemical specialties, especially air fresheners. Utilizes latest technology from global resources. Specializes in enhancement products for home and automobile.

53091 ■ Great Lakes Consulting Group Inc.
1217 S Walnut St.
South Bend, IN 46619-4305
Ph:(574)287-4500
Fax: (574)234-8207
Scope: Provides consulting services in the areas of strategic planning; feasibility studies; start-up businesses; small business management; mergers and acquisitions; joint ventures; divestitures; interim management; crisis management; turnarounds; business process re-engineering; venture capital; and international trade.

53092 ■ Grimmick Consulting Services
455 Donner Way
San Ramon, CA 94583
Ph:(925)735-9090
Fax: (925)735-1100
Co. E-mail: grimmick@pacbell.net

E-mail: grimmick@pacbell.net
Scope: Provides consulting services in the areas of strategic planning; organizational assessment; organizational development; leadership development and Baldrige Criteria.

53093 ■ Health Strategy Group Inc.
46 River Rd.
Chatham, NY 12037
Ph:(518)392-6770
Scope: Provides consulting services in the areas of strategic planning, feasibility studies, start-up businesses, organizational development, market research, customer service audits, new product development, marketing, public relations.

53094 ■ Hewitt Development Enterprises
1717 N Bayshore Dr., Ste. 2154
Miami, FL 33132
Ph:(305)372-0941
Free: 800-631-3098
Fax: (305)372-0941
Co. E-mail: info@hewittdevelopment.com
URL: http://www.hewittdevelopment.com

E-mail: info@hewittdevelopment.com
Scope: A manufacturing management consulting firm. Specializes in strategic planning; profit enhancement; start-up businesses; interim management; crisis management; turnarounds; production planning; Just-in-Time inventory management; and project management.

53095 ■ Holt Capital
1100 Dexter Ave. N
Seattle, WA 98109
Ph:(206)676-3822
Fax: (206)789-8034
Co. E-mail: info@holtcapital.com
URL: http://www.holtcapital.com

E-mail: info@holtcapital.com
Scope: Connects companies with capital. Mergers and acquisitions, finance through debt and leasing, private equity and venture capital. Is a registered Investment Advisor. **Publications:** "Is Your First Paragraph a Turn-off?"; "Bubble Rubble: Bridging the Price Gap for an Early-Stage Business"; "Are You Ready For The New New Economy?"; "Could I Get Money or Jail Time With That? The Sarbanes-Oxley Act Of 2002 gives early-stage companies More Risks". **Seminars:** Attracting Private Investors; Five Proven Ways to Finance Your Company.

53096 ■ Idi-Supply Inc.
3866 N Fratney St.
PO Box 12050
Milwaukee, WI 53212
Ph:(414)961-2365
Fax: (414)961-1582
Scope: Firm specializes in start-up businesses; small business management; mergers and acquisitions; joint ventures; divestitures; venture capital; appraisals; valuations; and international trade.

53097 ■ Institute for Management Excellence
PO Box 5459
Lacey, WA 98509-5459
Ph:(360)412-0404
URL: http://www.itstime.com
Scope: Management consulting and training focuses on improving productivity, using "best practices" and creative techniques. Practices based on company's theme, "It's time for new ways of doing business." Industries Served: Public Sector, Law Enforcement, Finance/Banking, Non-Profit, Computers/High Technology, Education, Human Resources, Utilities. **Publications:** "The Other Side of Midnight, 2000: An Executive Guide to the Year 2000 Problem" ISBN: 0-9643853-9-2, Authors: Barbara Taylor and Martha Daniel. **Seminars:** The Personality Game, Team Building and Communication Skills, Sexual Harassment and Discrimination Prevention. **Special Services:** Project management for computer systems implementations, including web/internet consulting.

53098 ■ International Management Consulting Group Inc.
1309 Harlan Dr., Ste. 205
Bellevue, NE 68005-6604
Ph:(402)291-4545
Free: 800-665-4624
Fax: (402)291-4343
Co. E-mail: imcg@neonramp.com

E-mail: imcg@neonramp.com
Scope: Offers the following operational effectiveness programs: productivity improvement programs directed toward any sized business; business and strategic planning for executives; executive and employee seminars; work measurement and performance accounting; relocation planning and management services; job design, job analysis and human resources selection consulting; executive out placement services; and total quality management business processes re-engineering, procurement and purchasing practices. Also provides analysis of business problems faced by entrepreneurs and small business owners. Consultants seek cost savings for clients while expanding into new markets and managed growth opportunities for any sized businesses. Industries served: nearly all; but specialize in the following: insurance, transportation (passenger), family-owned businesses, and light manufacturing heavy production environment and wholesale/retail. **Publications:** "Why Every Executive Needs a Coach™," 1997; "The Professional Job Finding System™," 1997; "Why Small Business Is Where It's AT in the 1990's"; "It's All in the Plan," Small Business Reports, Jun, 1994; "Six Tips for Picking a Consultant," Small Business Reports, Jan, 1994. **Seminars:** Why Every Executive Needs a Coach; Strategic Planning for the 21st Century Executive; Mistakes Managers Make: And How to Avoid Them; Entrepreneurship in the 1990's; How to Start a Small Business and Survive; Time Management for Business Owners; Stress Management: How to Live With Stress; How to Select a Consultant in the 1990's; Total Quality Management: What's It All About; Business Process Reengineering; Activity-Based Learning™. **Special Services:** Activity-based learning™.

53099 ■ Johnston Co.
1646 Massachusetts Ave., Ste. 22
Lexington, MA 02420
Ph:(781)862-7595
Fax: (781)862-9066
Co. E-mail: info@johnstoncompany.com
URL: http://www.johnstoncompany.com

E-mail: info@johnstoncompany.com
Scope: Firm specializes in management audits and reports; start-up businesses; small business management; mergers and acquisitions; joint ventures; divestitures; interim management; crisis management; turnarounds; cost controls; financing; venture capital.

53100 ■ Keiei Senryaku Corp.
19191 S Vermont Ave., Ste. 530
Torrance, CA 90502
Ph:(310)366-3331
Free: 800-951-8780
Fax: (310)366-3330
Co. E-mail: takenakaes@earthlink.net

E-mail: takenakaes@earthlink.net
Scope: Consulting services in the areas of strategic planning; feasibility studies; profit enhancement; organizational development; start-up businesses; mergers and acquisitions; joint ventures; divestitures; executive searches; sales management; competitive analysis. Entering Japanese market.

53101 ■ Key Communications Group Inc.
5617 Warwick Pl.
Chevy Chase, MD 20815-5503
Ph:(301)656-0450
Free: 800-705-5353
Fax: (301)656-4554
Co. E-mail: mr.dm@verizon.net

E-mail: mr.dm@verizon.net
Scope: Direct marketing and publishing consultants specializing in subscriber and member acquisition for

newsletters and other niche B2B publications, organizations and associations. Specialties: small and start-up businesses; mergers and acquisitions; joint ventures; divestitures; product development; employee surveys and communication; market research; customer service audits; new product development; direct marketing; and competitive intelligence.

53102 ■ M-Squared Inc.
7101 Creedmoor Rd., Ste. 130
Raleigh, NC 27613-1684
Ph:(919)848-4300
Fax: (919)848-1125
Co. E-mail: msquared@m2i.com

E-mail: msquared@m2i.com
Scope: Consultants will develop business plans and critiques, business goals and objectives, and strategic and operational planning, and assist with new business start-ups. Business negotiation including buy/sell businesses, contract negotiation, debt negotiation, mediation, and arbitration. Expertise with loan packaging and counseling, management training seminars and coaching, motivational training and team-building, and design and implementation of financial and operational controls. Industries served: all small businesses (under 50 employees), as well as government agencies. Seminars: Exploring Entrepreneurship; Strategic Planning for Small Business; Financial Analysis and Projections; Company Team Building.

53103 ■ Management Resource Partners
181 2nd Ave., Ste. 542
San Mateo, CA 94401-3813
Ph:(650)401-5850
Fax: (650)401-5850
Scope: Firm specializes in strategic planning; small business management; mergers and acquisitions; joint ventures; divestitures; interim management; crisis management; turnarounds; venture capital; appraisals and valuations.

53104 ■ Mefford, Knutson & Associates Inc.
6437 Lyndale Ave. S
Richfield, MN 55423-1465
Ph:(612)869-8011
Free: 800-831-0228
Fax: (612)893-1806
Co. E-mail: don@mkaonline.net
URL: http://www.mkaonline.net

E-mail: don@mkaonline.net
Scope: Firm specializes in start-up businesses; strategic planning; mergers and acquisitions; joint ventures; divestitures; business process re-engineering; personnel policies and procedures; market research; new product development and cost controls.

53105 ■ Colmen Menard Company Inc.
The Woods, 994 Old Eagle School Rd., Ste. 1000
Wayne, PA 19087
Ph:(484)367-0300
Fax: (484)367-0305
Co. E-mail: cmci@colmenmenard.com
URL: http://www.colmenmenard.com

E-mail: cmci@colmenmenard.com
Scope: Merger and acquisition corporate finance and business advisory services for public and private companies located in North America.

53106 ■ Miller, Hellwig Associates
150 W End Ave.
New York, NY 10023-5713
Ph:(212)799-0471
Fax: (212)877-0186
Co. E-mail: millerhelwig@earthlink.net

E-mail: millerhelwig@earthlink.net
Scope: Consulting services in the areas of start-up businesses; small business management; employee surveys and communication; performance appraisals; executive searches; team building; personnel policies and procedures; market research. Also involved in improving cross-cultural and multi-cultural relationships, particularly with Japanese clients. Seminars: Objectives and standards/recruiting for boards of directors.

53107 ■ The Nelson Group Ltd.
5 Milk St., Ste. 4
Portland, ME 04101
Ph:(207)775-1199
Fax: (207)775-0141
URL: http://www.nelsonltd.com
Scope: Consulting services in the areas of strategic planning; organizational development; small business management; mergers and acquisitions; joint ventures; divestitures; interim management; crisis management; turnarounds; performance appraisals; executive searches; outplacement; and team building.

53108 ■ Organization Counselors Inc.
44 W Broadway, Ste. 1102
PO Box 987
Salt Lake City, UT 84101
Ph:(801)363-2900
Fax: (801)363-0861
Co. E-mail: jpanos@xmission.com

E-mail: jpanos@xmission.com
Scope: Firm specializes in organizational development; employee surveys and communication; outplacement; team building; total quality management (TQM) and continuous improvement. Seminars: Correcting Performance Problems; Total Quality Management; Employee Selection; Performance Management.

53109 ■ Parker Consultants Inc.
67 Mason St.
Greenwich, CT 06830
Ph:(203)869-9400
Scope: Firm specializes in strategic planning; organizational development; small business management; performance appraisals; executive searches; team building; and customer service audits.

53110 ■ Partners for Market Leadership Inc.
400 Galleria Pky., Ste. 1500
Atlanta, GA 30339
Ph:(770)850-1409
Free: 800-984-1110
Co. E-mail: dcarpenter@market-leadership.com
URL: http://www.market-leadership.com

E-mail: dcarpenter@market-leadership.com
Scope: Change management firm. Provides consulting services in the areas of strategic planning, start-up businesses, mergers and acquisitions, joint ventures, divestitures, interim management, crisis management, turnarounds, new product development, sales management and competitive analysis.

53111 ■ Performance Consulting Group
8535 Baymeadows Rd., Ste. 143-3
Jacksonville, FL 32202
Ph:(904)448-4473
Fax: (904)287-1244
Scope: Consulting services in the areas of strategic planning; profit enhancement; product development; production planning.

53112 ■ Rose & Crangle Ltd.
117 N 4th St.
PO Box 285
Lincoln, KS 67455-0285
Ph:(785)524-5050
Fax: (785)524-3130
Co. E-mail: rcltd@nckcn.com

E-mail: rcltd@nckcn.com
Scope: Firm provides evaluation, planning and policy analyses for universities, associations, foundations, governmental agencies and private companies engaged in scientific, technological or educational activities. Special expertise in the development of new institutions. Special skills in providing planning and related group facilitation workshops.

53113 ■ Rothschild Strategies Unlimited L.L.C.
PO Box 7568
Wilton, CT 06897-7568
Ph:(203)846-6898
Fax: (203)847-1426

Co. E-mail: bill@strategyleader.com
URL: http://www.strategyleader.com

E-mail: bill@strategyleader.com
Scope: Consults with senior management and business level strategy teams to develop overall strategic direction, set priorities and creates sustainable competitive advantages and differentiators. Enables organizations to enhance their own strategic thinking and leadership skills so that they can continue to develop and implement profitable growth strategies. Publications: "Putting It All Together-a guide to strategic thinking"; "Competitive Advantage"; "Ristaker, Caretaker, Surgeon & Undertaker-four faces of strategic leadership". Special Services: StrategyLeader®.

53114 ■ Sklar & Associates
1101 S Arlington Ridge Rd. Ste. 511
Arlington, VA 22202-1925
Ph:(202)257-5061
Fax: (202)828-4130
Co. E-mail: sklarincdc@aol.com
URL: http://www.sklarinc.com

E-mail: sklarincdc@aol.com
Scope: Provides Audit Oversight services to listed corporations on Sarbanes-Oxley compliance. Seminars: Financial Analysis in MBA; Emerging Company Finance; Due Diligence in Business Acquisition; Business Valuation. Special Services: Financial Modeling. Course titled Understanding and Detecting Deceptive Creative Accounting Practices.

53115 ■ Harvey C. Skoog
3737 N Robert Rd., No. A
Prescott Valley, AZ 86314
Ph:(928)772-1448
Scope: Firm has expertise in taxes, payroll, financial planning, budgeting, buy/sell planning, business start-up, fraud detection, troubled business consulting, acquisition, and marketing. Serves the manufacturing, construction, and retailing industries in Arizona.

53116 ■ Strategic Mangement Services
3126 Duval St.
Austin, TX 78705
Ph:(512)477-4094
Fax: (512)478-8301
Scope: Devlops business and strategic plans for beginning or established companies. Provides management and leadership consulting and training. Industries served: insurance, health care, restaurant, small manufacturing.

53117 ■ Strategic MindShare Consulting
1401 Brickell Ave., Ste. 640
Miami, FL 33131
Ph:(305)377-2220
Fax: (305)377-2280
Co. E-mail: dee@strategicmindshare.com
URL: http://www.strategicmindshare.com

E-mail: dee@strategicmindshare.com
Scope: Firm specializes in strategic planning; feasibility studies; profit enhancement; organizational development; start-up businesses; mergers and acquisitions; joint ventures; divestitures; interim management; crisis management; turnarounds; new product development and competitive analysis. Publications: "Top Ten CEO Burning Issues for 2005"; "Top Ten Consumer Behavioral Trends for 2005"; "The Influence Factors".

53118 ■ Turnaround Inc.
3415 A St. NW
Gig Harbor, WA 98335
Ph:(253)857-6730
Fax: (253)857-6344
Co. E-mail: info@turnround-inc.com
URL: http://www.turnaround-inc.com

E-mail: info@turnround-inc.com
Scope: Firm provides interim executive management assistance and management advisory to small, medium and family-owned businesses that are not meeting their goals. Services include acting as an interim exec-

utive or on-site manager. Extensive practices in arena of bankruptcy management. **Publications:** "How to Identify Problem and Promising Management"; "How to Tell if Your Company is a Bankruptcy Candidate"; "Signs that Your Company is in Trouble"; "The Turnaround Specialist: How to File a Petition Under 11 USC 11". **Seminars:** Competitive Intelligence Gathering.

53119 ■ **ValueNomics Value Specialists**
10 Almaden Blvd., Ste. 1450
San Jose, CA 95113-2226
Ph:(408)257-8521
Fax: (408)257-1146
Co. E-mail: value@valuenomics.com
URL: http://www.valuenomics.com

E-mail: value@valuenomics.com
Scope: Specializes in valuations; appraisals; strategic planning; feasibility studies; mergers and acquisitions; joint ventures; divestitures; competitive intelligence; and due diligence. Acts as an expert witness. Offers litigation support. **Publications:** "The Business of Business Valuation and the CPA as an expert witness". **Special Services:** ValueNomics®.

53120 ■ **Venture Marketing Association, Business Development Services**
800 Palisade Ave., Ste. 907
Fort Lee, NJ 07024
Ph:(201)924-7435
Fax: (201)224-8757
Co. E-mail: venturemkt@aol.com
URL: http://www.myventure.biz

E-mail: venturemkt@aol.com
Scope: Specializes in franchise program development and small businesses. Provides hands-on assistance in planning and implementing strategic marketing/management plans. Clients include franchisors, small business owners and individuals. Cost-effective fees for those in transition, facing unemployment, researching a franchise or starting a business. Industries served: service, retail, and distribution. **Seminars:** Franchise Your Business; How to Research a Franchise Services.

53121 ■ **Young & Associates Inc.**
121 E Main St.
PO Box 711
Kent, OH 44240
Ph:(330)678-0524
Free: 800-525-9775
Fax: (330)678-6219
Co. E-mail: online@younginc.com
URL: http://www.younginc.com

E-mail: online@younginc.com
Scope: Provides a variety of consulting, educational, and research services, including strategic planning, marketing, market research, human resources planning and management, site/location feasibility studies, development of business plans, and organizational analysis and development. Specialists in small and mid-size companies. Have served over 1000 clients in a variety of industries, ranging from small, local businesses with revenues under 200000 dollars to large, multinational companies with revenues in excess of 1.5 billion dollars. Industries served: manufacturers (business-to-business and consumer), banking, healthcare (hospitals and practitioners), retailers, and services. **Special Services:** The Compliance Monitoring System™; Compliance Monitoring Update Service™; The Compliance Review Program™; Compliance Review Program Update Service™.

COMPUTERIZED DATABASES

53122 ■ *SBA Online*
U.S. Small Business Administration (SBA)
409 3rd St. SW
Washington, DC 20416
Ph:(202)205-6400
Free: 800-U-ASK-SBA

Fax: (202)205-7064
URL: http://www.sba.gov
Description: Contains information of use to owners of small businesses, including an overview of U.S. Small Business Adminstration (SBA) programs, business development programs, financial services/loans, government contracting opportunities, legislation and regulations, small business facts, small business minority programs, and a listing of SBA offices. Includes a calendar of events, information files on special targeted SBA programs, and message areas for networking with the small business community. Enables the user to obtain gateway access to other U.S. federal agency bulletin board services. **Availability:** Online: U.S. Small Business Administration (SBA). **Type:** Bulletin board; Full text; Directory.

53123 ■ *Small Business Innovative Research Current Solicitations*
Wheeling Jesuit University
316 Washington Ave.
Wheeling, WV 26003
Ph:(304)243-4341
Free: 800-678-6882
Fax: (304)243-4388
Co. E-mail: technology@nttc.edu
URL: http://www.nttc.edu
Description: Contains solicitations for the Small Business Innovation Research (SBIR) Program and the Small Business Technology Transfer (STTR) Pilot Program. Programs seek to stimulate U.S. technological innovation by funding small business research projects. The database assists users in exploring topics for which funding is available. **Type:** Full text.

COMPUTER SYSTEMS/ SOFTWARE

53124 ■ **Business Simulator**
Strategic Management Group, Inc.
3624 Market St., 3rd Fl.
Philadelphia, PA 19104
Ph:(215)387-4000
Free: 800-445-7089
Fax: (215)387-3653
Co. E-mail: rachael.ellis@smginc.com
URL: http://www.smginc.com
Price: $69.95. **Description:** Software program allowing the user to simulate running a start-up company through the various phases of development.

LIBRARIES

53125 ■ **Boston Public Library–Kirstein Business Branch**
20 City Hall Ave.
Boston, MA 02108
Ph:(617)523-0860
Co. E-mail: info@bpl.org
URL: http://www.bpl.org/research/kbb/kbbhome.htm
Contact: Dolores Schueler, Bus.Br.Libn.
Scope: Business administration, retailing, advertising, finance, marketing, real estate, insurance, banking, taxation, accounting, investments, economics, business law, small business. **Services:** Copying is available through the library's interlibrary loan department; reference faxing up to 3 pages. **Holdings:** Moody's Manuals (1935 to present in print; 1909-1997 in microfiche); Commercial and Financial Chronicle, 1957-1987; Bank and Quotation Record, 1928-1987; Standard and Poor's Daily Stock Price Record: New York and American Stock Exchanges, 1962 to present; over-the-counter stocks, 1968 to present; domestic and foreign trade directories; city directories; telephone directories for New England and U.S. cities with populations over 100,000 for New England cities and towns; Standard Stock Market Service, 1921-1922; Standard Stock Offerings, 1925-1939; National Stock Summary, 1927 to present; Standard & Poor's Stock Guide, 1943 to present; New York and American Stock Exchange companies Annual and 10K re-

ports on microfiche (1987-1996); Wall Street Journal on microfiche (latest 10 years); Wall Street Transcript on microfilm (latest 5 years); D-U-N-S Business Identification Service (November 1973 -1995). **Subscriptions:** 700 journals and other serials; 13 newspapers.

53126 ■ **Business Development Bank of Canada–Research & Information Centre**
5 Place Ville Marie, Ste. 300
Montreal, QC, Canada H3B 5E7
Ph:(514)283-7632
Fax: (514)283-0439
Co. E-mail: odette.lavoie@bdc.ca
Contact: Odette Lavoie, Sr.Info.Spec.
Scope: Small business, management, Canadian business and industry, banking and finance, development banking. **Services:** Interlibrary loan; Library not open to the public. **Holdings:** 5000 books; CD-ROMs. **Subscriptions:** 100 journals and other serials; 7 newspapers.

53127 ■ **Carnegie Library of Pittsburgh–Library Center**
Business Dept.
612 Smithfield St.
Pittsburgh, PA 15222
Ph:(412)281-7141
Fax: (412)471-1724
Co. E-mail: wernerr@carnegielibrary.org
URL: http://www.clpgh.org/locations/business/
Contact: Roye Werner, Dept.Hd.
Scope: Investments, small business, entrepreneurship, management, marketing, insurance, advertising, personal finance, accounting, real estate, job and career, international business. **Services:** Interlibrary loan; Library open to the public. **Holdings:** 14,000 business volumes; VF materials; microfilm; looseleaf services; AV cassettes. **Subscriptions:** 350 business journals, serials, and newspapers.

53128 ■ **Chicago Public Library Central Library–Business/Science/Technology Division**
Harold Washington Library Center
400 S. State St., 4th Fl.
Chicago, IL 60605
Ph:(312)747-4450
Fax: (312)747-4975
URL: http://www.chipublib.org/001hwlc/hwbst.html
Contact: Marcia Dellenbach, BST Div.Chf.
Scope: Small business, marketing, technology, corporate reports, investments, management, personnel, patents, physical and biological sciences, medicine, health, computer science, careers, environmental information, gardening, cookbooks. **Services:** Interlibrary loan; copying; division open to the public. **Holdings:** 415,000 books; 52,100 bound periodical volumes; 33,000 reels of microfilm; Securities and Exchange Commission (SEC) reports; federal specifications and standards; American National Standards Institute standards; corporate Annual reports. **Subscriptions:** 4000 journals and other serials; 8 newspapers.

53129 ■ **Employment Support Center–Library**
1556 Wisconsin Ave., NW
Washington, DC 20001-3747
Ph:(202)628-2919
Fax: (703)790-1469
Co. E-mail: jobclubs@hotmail.com
URL: http://www.angelfire.com/biz/jobclubs
Scope: Employment networking, self-esteem, starting your own business, setting up job clubs, training facilitators, maintaining a large job bank, providing job-searching skills. **Services:** Library open to the public. **Holdings:** 150 articles; books; periodicals; videos on job search; interviews; reports; manuscripts. **Subscriptions:** 4 journals and other serials; 2 newspapers.

53130 ■ **Enterprise Newfoundland and Labrador–Business Resource Centre**
Viking Bldg.
136 Crosbie Rd.
St. John's, NL, Canada A1B 3K3
Ph:(709)772-6022
Fax: (709)772-6090

Co. E-mail: info@cbsc.ic.gc.ca
URL: http://www.cbsc.org/af
Contact: Beulah Bouzane, Dir.
Scope: Marketing, small business, economic and regional development. **Services:** Copying; SDI; center open to the public. **Holdings:** 10,000 books; 20 VF drawers of subject files; Standard Industrial Classification (SIC) files. **Subscriptions:** 300 journals and other serials.

53131 ■ Greater Oviedo Chamber of Commerce–Business Library
PO Box 621236
Oviedo, FL 32762-1236
Ph:(407)365-6500
Fax: (407)365-6587
Co. E-mail: fay@oviedochamber.org
URL: http://www.oviedochamber.org
Contact: Fay I. Stoner, Off.Mgr.
Scope: Small business; central Florida business. **Services:** Copying; Library open to the public. **Holdings:** 3 books; 10 reports; periodicals. **Subscriptions:** 3 newspapers.

53132 ■ Indian River Area Library
PO Box 160
Indian River, MI 49749
Ph:(231)238-8581
Fax: (231)238-9494
Co. E-mail: indrivl@northland.lib.mi.us
URL: http://www.libnet.org/iriver/
Contact: Cindy Lou Poquette, Dir.
Scope: Small business, careers, fine arts, music, dance. **Services:** Interlibrary loan; copying; Library open to the public (fee for non-residents to check out materials). **Holdings:** 45,000 books; 2500 videocassettes; 2000 microfiche; videocassettes; sound cassettes; DVDs; CDs; periodicals; large print books. **Subscriptions:** 78 journals and other serials; 3 newspapers.

53133 ■ Knoxville Business College–Library
720 N. 5th Ave.
Knoxville, TN 37917
Ph:(865)524-3043
Fax: (865)637-0127
Co. E-mail: library@kbcollege.edu
Contact: Mary A. McHugh, Dir., Lib.Svc.
Scope: Business, physical therapy, occupational therapy, administration, medical administration, legal administration, small business, secretarial science, paralegal, hotel and restaurant management. **Services:** Interlibrary loan; copying; SDI. **Holdings:** 6700 books; 10 VF drawers; 214 volumes on microfilm; 1 cabinet of microfiche. **Subscriptions:** 106 journals and other serials.

53134 ■ National Small Business Benefits Association–Library
2244 N. Grand Ave., E.
Springfield, IL 62702
Ph:(217)544-0881
Fax: (217)544-5816
Co. E-mail: t-shirtz@t-shirtz.com
URL: http://www.t-shirtz.com
Scope: Small businesses. **Services:** Library open to the public with restrictions. **Holdings:** 300 volumes.

53135 ■ Nations Bank–Business Resource Center
3401 Westend Ave., Ste. 110
Nashville, TN 37203
Ph:(615)749-4088
Fax: (615)749-3685
Co. E-mail: Lillie.Taylor@NationsBank.com
Contact: Lillie Taylor, Libn.
Scope: Small business. **Services:** Copying; Library open to the public with restrictions. **Holdings:** 2000

books; 6 VF drawers of archives. **Subscriptions:** 160 journals and other serials.

53136 ■ New York State Small Business Development Center–Research Network
State University of New York Plaza, 41 State St.
Albany, NY 12246
Ph:(518)443-5265
Fax: (518)443-5275
URL: http://www.nyssbdc.org
Contact: Darrin Conroy, Dir.
Scope: Small business. **Services:** Copying; faxing; document delivery. **Holdings:** 1000 books; 20 CD-ROMs. **Subscriptions:** 40 journals and other serials; 10 newspapers.

53137 ■ Newfoundland Department of Industry, Trade and Technology–Registry
PO Box 8700
St. John's, NL, Canada A1B 4J6
Ph:(709)729-5982
Fax: (709)729-5936
Scope: Economics, energy, small business, oil and gas. **Holdings:** Figures not available.

53138 ■ Piedmont Technical College–Library
PO Box 1467
Greenwood, SC 29648-1467
Ph:(864)941-8440
Fax: (864)941-8558
Co. E-mail: librarian@ptc.edu
URL: http://www.ptc.edu/library/
Contact: Cindy Davies, Lib.Dir.
Scope: Economics, technology, allied health, nursing, small business, computer science, criminal justice. **Services:** Interlibrary loan; copying; Library open to the public. **Holdings:** 28,000 books; 400 bound periodical volumes; 3500 reels of microfilm; 2000 AV programs. **Subscriptions:** 325 journals and other serials; 10 newspapers.

53139 ■ Saskatchewan Research Council–Information Services
125-15 Innovation Blvd.
Saskatoon, SK, Canada S7N 2X8
Ph:(306)933-5454
Fax: (306)933-7446
Co. E-mail: library@src.sk.ca
URL: http://www.src.sk.ca
Contact: Colleen Marshall, Rec. & Info.Mgt.Coord.
Scope: Chemistry, geology, air quality, toxicology and environmental health, forest management and research, water resources and management, environmental research and engineering, chemistry and chemical engineering, geography, remote sensing, agriculture and biotechnology, energy and business. **Services:** Interlibrary loan; copying; Center open to the public with restrictions. **Holdings:** 22,500 monographs; 2900 SRC-authored publications. **Subscriptions:** 280 periodicals.

53140 ■ U.S.D.A.–National Agricultural Library–Rural Information Center (10301)
10301 Baltimore Ave., Rm. 304
Beltsville, MD 20705
Ph:(301)504-5372
Free: 800-633-7701
Fax: (301)504-5181
Co. E-mail: ric@nal.usda.gov
URL: http://www.nal.usda.gov/ric/
Contact: Patricia LaCaille John, Coord.
Scope: Economic development; small business development; city and county government services; government and private grants and funding sources; rural communities; community leadership; natural resources. **Services:** Reference; center open to the public. **Holdings:** Figures not available.

53141 ■ University of Colorado—Boulder–William M. White Business Library
Leeds School of Business
Campus Box 184
Boulder, CO 80309-0184
Ph:(303)492-8367
Fax: (303)735-0333
Co. E-mail: buslib@colorado.edu
URL: http://ucblibraries.colorado.edu/business
Contact: Carol Krismann, Dept.Hd., Bus.Bibliog.
Scope: Ethics, information systems, business policy, economics and law, small business, management and organization, finance and accounting, marketing, transportation, management science, real estate, insurance, taxation. **Services:** Interlibrary loan; copying; Library open to the public. **Holdings:** 90,000 volumes; 201,565 microforms. **Subscriptions:** 690 journals; 15 newspapers.

53142 ■ Warren County Community College–Library–Special Collections (475 R)
475 Rte. 57 W.
Washington, NJ 07882-4343
Ph:(908)689-7614
Fax: (908)835-1283
Co. E-mail: dorenstein@warren.edu
URL: http://www.warren.cc.nj.us
Contact: David Orenstein, Lib.Dir.
Scope: Business, humanities, American history, law. **Services:** Interlibrary loan; copying; Library open to the public. Provides services for the deaf; closed-captioned videos are available. **Holdings:** 33,600 books; 18 lin.ft. of archival materials; 1630 videocassettes; 325 audiocassettes; 45 compact discs. **Subscriptions:** 332 journals and other serials.

RESEARCH CENTERS

53143 ■ Laval University–Centre for Entrepreneurship and Small Business
Rm. 1663
School of Business
Ste. Foy, QC, Canada G1K 7P4
Ph:(418)656-2490
Fax: (418)656-2624
Co. E-mail: yvon.gasse@mng.ulaval.ca
URL: http://www.fsa.ulaval.ca/cepme
Contact: Yvon Gasse PhD, Dir.
E-mail: yvon.gasse@mng.ulaval.ca
Scope: Small and medium-sized businesses and entrepreneurship, including growth strategies and technological innovations to promote development. **Educational Activities:** Training sessions and seminars.

53144 ■ University of Quebec at Trois-Rivieres–Research Institute on Small and Medium Sized Businesses
Pavillon Desjardins-Hydro-Quebec
3351, Blvd. des Forges
PO Box 500
Trois-Rivieres, QC, Canada G9A 5H7
Ph:(819)376-5235
Fax: (819)376-5138
Co. E-mail: inrpme@uqtr.ca
URL: http://www.uqtr.ca/inrpme/
Contact: Claire de la Durantaye, Dir.
E-mail: inrpme@uqtr.ca
Scope: Small business and entrepreneurship, including management, strategy, finance, operation, marketing, information systems innovation, regional sciences, and economics. **Publications:** Revue Internationale PME Scientific Magazine (3/year). **Educational Activities:** Postgraduate assistance; Weekly research seminars, in fall and winter terms.

START-UP INFORMATION

53145 ■ "Do This, Get Rich" in *Business 2.0* **(Vol. 6, May 2005, No. 4, pp. 78-86)**
Pub: Time, Inc.
Ed: Michael V. Copeland, Om Malik, Erick Schonfeld. **Description:** Profiles of the eleven hottest business opportunities are presented, including computer upgrades, advertising on the Web, specialty baby furniture, professional medical employment services, interior design for hotels, Web-enabled subscription and service monitoring, search engines for podcasts, RFID tags to track drugs and supplies in hospitals, software to save energy in homes and businesses, software and hardware to monitor and control a boat's onboard systems.

53146 ■ "Halsey Minor's Virtual Train Station" in *Business Week Online* **(February 9, 2005)**
Pub: McGraw-Hill Companies
Description: Harry Minor, tech entrepreneur, talks about his latest venture, called Grand Central, that helps companies interconnect their software via the Internet. Minor has been working on Grand Central for five years.

53147 ■ "A Hearing Aid for Cell Phones" in *Business 2.0* **(Vol. 6, July 2005, No. 6, pp. 34)**
Pub: Time, Inc.
Ed: Matthew Maier. **Description:** Sound ID, the new Palo Alto, California startup has developed wireless headsets with software to help hearing impaired users. The system uses sound-processing algorithms to analyze acoustic environments and separates background noise from the voice signal.

53148 ■ "Setting Up a Productive Home Office" in *Home Business* **(Vol. 12, October 2005, No. 5, pp. 82, 84)**
Pub: Home Business Magazine
Ed: Aliza Pilar, Sherman Risdahl. **Description:** Things to consider when purchasing furniture, hardware, software and electronics for a small home-based business are examined.

53149 ■ "Site-isfaction" in *Entrepreneur* **(Vol. 28, No. 10, October 2000, pp. 146)**
Pub: Entrepreneur Media Inc.
Ed: Amanda C. Kooser. **Description:** The article suggests that, with the new "no-HTML-required" Web editors, small companies can design their own Web sites.

53150 ■ "Solo Mission: Paul Stannard used to make software for other companies" in *Entrepreneur* **(Vol. 30, No. 3, March 2002, pp. 160)**
Pub: Entrepreneur Media Inc.
Ed: Michelle Prather. **Description:** Profile of Paul Stannard, founder and CEO of SmartDraw.com, located in San Diego, California. Stannard has been manufacturing diagramming software since 1994.

53151 ■ "Start with Nothing" in *Inc.* **(February 1, 2002)**
Pub: Inc. Magazine
Ed: Emily Barker. **Description:** Greg Gianforte, founder of the software company Brightwork Development Inc., shares his secrets for launching a successful new company, with a focus on sales.

ASSOCIATIONS AND OTHER ORGANIZATIONS

53152 ■ Business Software Alliance
1150 18th St. NW, Ste. 700
Washington, DC 20036
Ph:(202)872-5500
Fax: (202)872-5501
Co. E-mail: software@bsa.org
URL: http://www.bsa.org
Contact: Robert Holleyman, Pres./CEO
Description: Computer software publishers. Promotes the free world trade of business software by combating international software piracy, advancing intellectual property protection, and increasing market access. **Publications:** *Guide to Software Management* (annual); *Software Review* (quarterly). **Telecommunication Services:** electronic mail, webmaster@bsa.org.

53153 ■ Information Technology Association of America
1401 Wilson Blvd., Ste. 1100
Arlington, VA 22209
Ph:(703)522-5055
Fax: (703)525-2279
Co. E-mail: rlaurence@itaa.org
URL: http://www.itaa.org
Contact: Robert Laurence, Pres.
Description: A division of the Information Technology Association of America; software companies involved in the development or marketing of software for personal, midrange, and mainframe computers. Promotes the software industry and addresses specific problems of the industry. Represents the industry before various governmental units; provides educational programs to members; conducts research and makes available legal services. Develops standards. **Publications:** *The Criteria of Quality: A Strategic Approach to ISO 9,000 Compliance for Information Technology Companies; Financial Operating Ratios for Software Companies; ITAA Software Industry Briefing Book; Quality Goes Global: An ITAA Guide to ISO 9,000 Standard Series for Information Technology Companies; Software Industry Executive Newsletter* (bimonthly).

EDUCATIONAL PROGRAMS

53154 ■ Accessible Web Design: Complying with Section 508
EEI Communications
66 Canal Ctr. Plz., Ste. 200
Alexandria, VA 22314-5507
Ph:(703)683-7453
Free: 888-253-2762
Fax: (703)683-7310
Co. E-mail: train@eeicommunications.com
URL: http://www.eeicommunications.com/training
Price: $395. **Description:** Covers what the law is and whom it applies, using HTML and CSS coding techniques to meet the guidelines, creating fluid design that adapts to user needs, using free validation to check site for accessibility, and putting the compliance icon on completed site. **Locations:** Alexandria, VA; Silver Spring, MD; and Washington, DC.

53155 ■ Adobe Acrobat Capture
EEI Communications
66 Canal Ctr. Plz., Ste. 200
Alexandria, VA 22314-5507
Ph:(703)683-7453
Free: 888-253-2762
Fax: (703)683-7310
Co. E-mail: train@eeicommunications.com
URL: http://www.eeicommunications.com/training
Price: $395. **Description:** Covers the converting of large volumes of paper documentation to searchable Adobe PDF documents, including project planning, setting up scanner, optimizing PDF file size and quality, building a PDF database, and tackle the common OCR problems and tips. **Locations:** Alexandria, VA; Silver Spring, MD; and Washington, DC.

53156 ■ Adobe Acrobat II
EEI Communications
66 Canal Ctr. Plz., Ste. 200
Alexandria, VA 22314-5507
Ph:(703)683-7453
Free: 888-253-2762
Fax: (703)683-7310
Co. E-mail: train@eeicommunications.com
URL: http://www.eeicommunications.com/training
Price: $695. **Description:** Seminar that covers the advanced features of Adobe Acrobat, focusing on making documents accessible and flexible, incorporating digital signatures and security settings, creating and modifying PDF forms and multimedia presentations, using the engineering and technical features, and using Adobe Acrobat for professional publishing. **Locations:** Alexandria, VA; Silver Spring, MD; and Washington, DC.

53157 ■ Adobe Acrobat Section 508 Accessibility
EEI Communications
66 Canal Ctr. Plz., Ste. 200
Alexandria, VA 22314-5507
Ph:(703)683-7453
Free: 888-253-2762
Fax: (703)683-7310
Co. E-mail: train@eeicommunications.com
URL: http://www.eeicommunications.com/training
Price: $395. **Description:** Covers the regulations by the Federal Government's Section 508 accessibility and the features of Adobe Acrobat software designed to meet the regulations, including definition of accessibility, authoring for accessibility, working with existing PDF files, forms, and scanned documents, using the

accessibility checker, and tags palette, and testing your PDF files for accessibility. **Locations:** Alexandria, VA; Silver Spring, MD; and Washington, DC.

53158 ■ Adobe After Effects II
EEI Communications
66 Canal Ctr. Plz., Ste. 200
Alexandria, VA 22314-5507
Ph:(703)683-7453
Free: 888-253-2762
Fax: (703)683-7310
Co. E-mail: train@eeicommunications.com
URL: http://www.eeicommunications.com/training
Price: $695. **Description:** Seminar that builds on the foundation of After Effects I that covers the techniques that production environments use and learn to reverse-engineer popular effects seen on TV, including working with Rotoscoping techniques, keying and mattes, motion matching and video stabilization, 3D layers, cameras, and lights, titling effects and filters, altering time and displacement, and rendering the movies and batching. **Locations:** Alexandria, VA; Silver Spring, MD; and Washington, DC.

53159 ■ Adobe FrameMaker III: Structured
EEI Communications
66 Canal Ctr. Plz., Ste. 200
Alexandria, VA 22314-5507
Ph:(703)683-7453
Free: 888-253-2762
Fax: (703)683-7310
Co. E-mail: train@eeicommunications.com
URL: http://www.eeicommunications.com/training
Price: $695. **Description:** Seminar using Adobe FrameMaker as an authoring tool for creating XML documents, including structured interface and add and edit elements and attributes, documents with structured content EDD (Element Definition Document) and DTD (Document Type Definitions), converting unstructured documents, and the latest tools availible for cross-media publishing. **Locations:** Alexandria, VA; Silver Spring, MD; and Washington, DC.

53160 ■ Adobe InDesign III
EEI Communications
66 Canal Ctr. Plz., Ste. 200
Alexandria, VA 22314-5507
Ph:(703)683-7453
Free: 888-253-2762
Fax: (703)683-7310
Co. E-mail: train@eeicommunications.com
URL: http://www.eeicommunications.com/training
Price: $695. **Description:** 2-day seminar that explores the advanced features within Adobe InDesign, including transparency features, feathering, and drop shadows, hyperlinks for PDF or DHTML, create a book list, formatting an index, generate a table of contents, advanced frame techniques and color management, and XML and other cross-media publishing support. **Locations:** Alexandria, VA; Silver Spring, MD; and Washington, DC.

53161 ■ Adobe Photoshop Camera Raw
EEI Communications
66 Canal Ctr. Plz., Ste. 200
Alexandria, VA 22314-5507
Ph:(703)683-7453
Free: 888-253-2762
Fax: (703)683-7310
Co. E-mail: train@eeicommunications.com
URL: http://www.eeicommunications.com/training
Price: $395. **Description:** Covers digital photography, including the raw file format, conversion from raw files to other formats, DNG and metadata, streamline image editing, and batch processing. **Locations:** Alexandria, VA; Silver Spring, MD; and Washington, DC.

53162 ■ Adobe Photoshop Digital Mastery
EEI Communications
66 Canal Ctr. Plz., Ste. 200
Alexandria, VA 22314-5507
Ph:(703)683-7453
Free: 888-253-2762
Fax: (703)683-7310
Co. E-mail: train@eeicommunications.com
URL: http://www.eeicommunications.com/training

Price: $695. **Description:** Covers techniques for photo recovery, image enhancements, and professional portrait work. **Locations:** Alexandria, VA; Silver Spring, MD; and Washington, DC.

53163 ■ Apple DVD Studio Pro I
EEI Communications
66 Canal Ctr. Plz., Ste. 200
Alexandria, VA 22314-5507
Ph:(703)683-7453
Free: 888-253-2762
Fax: (703)683-7310
Co. E-mail: train@eeicommunications.com
URL: http://www.eeicommunications.com/training
Price: $695. **Description:** Seminar that covers creating menus within DVD Studio Pro, creating slide shows, adding subtitles and closed captioning, multiple language/audio streams, DVD-ROM content and Internet access, options to encode high quality video, creating and working with buttons, overlays, markers, and stories, basic scripting, advanced menu design, working with and creating transitions, using alternate and mixed angles, and Dolby, surround, and PCM audio encoding. **Locations:** Alexandria, VA; Silver Spring, MD; and Washington, DC.

53164 ■ Apple Final Cut Pro I
EEI Communications
66 Canal Ctr. Plz., Ste. 200
Alexandria, VA 22314-5507
Ph:(703)683-7453
Free: 888-253-2762
Fax: (703)683-7310
Co. E-mail: train@eeicommunications.com
URL: http://www.eeicommunications.com/training
Price: $695. **Description:** Seminar that covers editing using Apple, including working with interface, video standard and HD basics, marking and editing, timeline control, single- and double-sided trimming, master clips, subclips and working with markers, capturing video, importing and exporting assets, working with audio and mixing audio tracks, applying transitions, adding and working with filters, build a composite image, change clip speeds, create motion effects, adding text and graphics, working with and creating animated titles, and finishing and outputting. **Locations:** Alexandria, VA; Silver Spring, MD; and Washington, DC.

53165 ■ Apple Motion I
EEI Communications
66 Canal Ctr. Plz., Ste. 200
Alexandria, VA 22314-5507
Ph:(703)683-7453
Free: 888-253-2762
Fax: (703)683-7310
Co. E-mail: train@eeicommunications.com
URL: http://www.eeicommunications.com/training
Price: $695. **Description:** Covers real-time motion graphics, including using generators, working with layers and objects, use and create customized templates, particles and parameter behaviors, blend modes, nonlinear editing and motion, key-framing, audio and setting markers, and create text effects. **Locations:** Alexandria, VA; Silver Spring, MD; and Washington, DC.

53166 ■ ASP.NET with VB.NET and C I
EEI Communications
66 Canal Ctr. Plz., Ste. 200
Alexandria, VA 22314-5507
Ph:(703)683-7453
Free: 888-253-2762
Fax: (703)683-7310
Co. E-mail: train@eeicommunications.com
URL: http://www.eeicommunications.com/training
Price: $995. **Description:** Seminar that covers the introduction to Web forms, including controls HTML, server, and Web, ASP.NET application, state management, and error handling. **Locations:** Alexandria, VA; Silver Spring, MD; and Washington, DC.

53167 ■ ASP.NET with VB.NET and C II
EEI Communications
66 Canal Ctr. Plz., Ste. 200
Alexandria, VA 22314-5507
Ph:(703)683-7453

Free: 888-253-2762
Fax: (703)683-7310
Co. E-mail: train@eeicommunications.com
URL: http://www.eeicommunications.com/training
Price: $995. **Description:** Seminar that goes in detail on Web applications and Microsoft's ASP.NET, including data binding, data controls and templates, consuming and manipulating data, and create and manage .NET components and assemblies. **Locations:** Alexandria, VA; Silver Spring, MD; and Washington, DC.

53168 ■ ASP.NET with VB.NET and C III
EEI Communications
66 Canal Ctr. Plz., Ste. 200
Alexandria, VA 22314-5507
Ph:(703)683-7453
Free: 888-253-2762
Fax: (703)683-7310
Co. E-mail: train@eeicommunications.com
URL: http://www.eeicommunications.com/training
Price: $995. **Description:** Seminar that builds on the learned skills of Web applications and Microsoft's ASP.NET with VB.NET and C I, and II, including web services, localization and globalization, Web accessibility **Locations:** Alexandria, VA; Silver Spring, MD; and Washington, DC.

53169 ■ Cascading Style Sheets II
EEI Communications
66 Canal Ctr. Plz., Ste. 200
Alexandria, VA 22314-5507
Ph:(703)683-7453
Free: 888-253-2762
Fax: (703)683-7310
Co. E-mail: train@eeicommunications.com
URL: http://www.eeicommunications.com/training
Price: $395. **Description:** Covers the conversion of an HTML Web site to a site that uses Cascading Style Sheets, including text enhancements, link color control, table conversion to precise positioning, layering with text and graphics, DHTML effects, a watermark background image, and validation CSS code. **Locations:** Alexandria, VA; Silver Spring, MD; and Washington, DC.

53170 ■ Color Management for Digital Publishing
EEI Communications
66 Canal Ctr. Plz., Ste. 200
Alexandria, VA 22314-5507
Ph:(703)683-7453
Free: 888-253-2762
Fax: (703)683-7310
Co. E-mail: train@eeicommunications.com
URL: http://www.eeicommunications.com/training
Price: $695. **Description:** Covers color theory and color models, build and edit ICC profiles, color management at the OS level, and setup. **Locations:** Alexandria, VA; Silver Spring, MD; and Washington, DC.

53171 ■ Digital Scanning for Production
EEI Communications
66 Canal Ctr. Plz., Ste. 200
Alexandria, VA 22314-5507
Ph:(703)683-7453
Free: 888-253-2762
Fax: (703)683-7310
Co. E-mail: train@eeicommunications.com
URL: http://www.eeicommunications.com/training
Price: $695. **Description:** Seminar designed for those using any digital purpose, including direct reproduction or inclusion in page layout programs. **Locations:** Alexandria, VA; Silver Spring, MD; and Washington, DC.

53172 ■ Digital Video Production for Streaming and DVD
EEI Communications
66 Canal Ctr. Plz., Ste. 200
Alexandria, VA 22314-5507
Ph:(703)683-7453
Free: 888-253-2762
Fax: (703)683-7310
Co. E-mail: train@eeicommunications.com
URL: http://www.eeicommunications.com/training
Price: $995. **Description:** Seminar the teaches the process of producing video for distribution via the

Web, CD, DVD and computer-based presentations, including writing, directing, shooting, recording, capture, edit, and encode/compress effective digital video for training, marketing, internal communications, public information, and other uses. Also, communicate effectively with internal clients/staff, video crews, and editing facilities. **Locations:** Alexandria, VA; Silver Spring, MD; and Washington, DC.

53173 ■ Introduction to ASP.NET 2.0 Applications
EEI Communications
66 Canal Ctr. Plz., Ste. 200
Alexandria, VA 22314-5507
Ph:(703)683-7453
Free: 888-253-2762
Fax: (703)683-7310
Co. E-mail: train@eeicommunications.com
URL: http://www.eeicommunications.com/training
Price: $695. **Description:** Seminar designed for ASP.NET programmers, includes ASP.NET 2.0 applications, master pages, Web parts and personalized API, ADO.NET 2.0 and data-bound controls, membership and role management API, and Web form wizards. **Locations:** Alexandria, VA; Silver Spring, MD; and Washington, DC.

53174 ■ Introduction to Net and ASP.NET
EEI Communications
66 Canal Ctr. Plz., Ste. 200
Alexandria, VA 22314-5507
Ph:(703)683-7453
Free: 888-253-2762
Fax: (703)683-7310
Co. E-mail: train@eeicommunications.com
URL: http://www.eeicommunications.com/training
Price: $695. **Description:** Covers Microsoft.NET and ASP.NET Web pages in both Visual Basic.NET and C (pronounced C-sharp), including Microsoft.Net framework, common language run-time, base framework classes, ADO.NET, ASP.NET, .NET compact framework, XML Web services, and .NET languages **Locations:** Alexandria, VA; Silver Spring, MD; and Washington, DC.

53175 ■ Introduction to PHP
EEI Communications
66 Canal Ctr. Plz., Ste. 200
Alexandria, VA 22314-5507
Ph:(703)683-7453
Free: 888-253-2762
Fax: (703)683-7310
Co. E-mail: train@eeicommunications.com
URL: http://www.eeicommunications.com/training
Price: $695. **Description:** Seminar that covers an open-source scripting language for developing database-driven Web sites, including how to download and install PHP on Web server, using PHP to respond to HTML form submissions, sending e-mail messages with PHP, SQL and querying databases with PHP, and managing state information with cookies and sessions. **Locations:** Alexandria, VA; Silver Spring, MD; and Washington, DC.

53176 ■ JavaServer Pages for Nonprogrammers
EEI Communications
66 Canal Ctr. Plz., Ste. 200
Alexandria, VA 22314-5507
Ph:(703)683-7453
Free: 888-253-2762
Fax: (703)683-7310
Co. E-mail: train@eeicommunications.com
URL: http://www.eeicommunications.com/training
Price: $995. **Description:** Seminar that covers JavaServer Pages (JSP) to create interactive Web sites based on the Java programming language, including setting up the JSP development environment, JSP syntax summary, Java objects and JavaBeans, JSP tag libraries, and create and use Java servlets. **Locations:** Alexandria, VA; Silver Spring, MD; and Washington, DC.

53177 ■ Layout Software Basics
EEI Communications
66 Canal Ctr. Plz., Ste. 200
Alexandria, VA 22314-5507

Ph:(703)683-7453
Free: 888-253-2762
Fax: (703)683-7310
Co. E-mail: train@eeicommunications.com
URL: http://www.eeicommunications.com/training
Price: $395. **Description:** Seminar that provides an introduction to publishing and graphics software, including a step-by-step introduction through the terms and tools of applications used by graphic designers, illustrators, photographers, and editors. **Locations:** Alexandria, VA; Silver Spring, MD; and Washington, DC.

53178 ■ Macromedia Authorware II
EEI Communications
66 Canal Ctr. Plz., Ste. 200
Alexandria, VA 22314-5507
Ph:(703)683-7453
Free: 888-253-2762
Fax: (703)683-7310
Co. E-mail: train@eeicommunications.com
URL: http://www.eeicommunications.com/training
Price: $1,095. **Description:** Seminar covers the functions and variables, decision loops, judging, and use of the new LMS and Accessibility tools, including using the Calculation icon, create sequential branching using the Decision icon, reading and writing external files, and adding basic 508 compliancy by using the Knowledge Object. **Locations:** Alexandria, VA; Silver Spring, MD; and Washington, DC.

53179 ■ Macromedia Captivate
EEI Communications
66 Canal Ctr. Plz., Ste. 200
Alexandria, VA 22314-5507
Ph:(703)683-7453
Free: 888-253-2762
Fax: (703)683-7310
Co. E-mail: train@eeicommunications.com
URL: http://www.eeicommunications.com/training
Price: $695. **Description:** Seminar that teaches how to create professional quality, interactive simulations and software demonstrations without any programming or multimedia knowledge, including basics, captions and timelines, images, pointer paths, buttons, and highlight boxes, movies, rollover captions and rollover images, slide labels and notes, audio, animation, and question slides. **Locations:** Alexandria, VA; Silver Spring, MD; and Washington, DC.

53180 ■ Macromedia ColdFusion II
EEI Communications
66 Canal Ctr. Plz., Ste. 200
Alexandria, VA 22314-5507
Ph:(703)683-7453
Free: 888-253-2762
Fax: (703)683-7310
Co. E-mail: train@eeicommunications.com
URL: http://www.eeicommunications.com/training
Price: $995. **Description:** Seminar that covers advanced programming techniques, including complex programming concepts such as arrays and loops, deploy application-level security, read information from and write information to text files on server, use the Verify search engine, schedule templates to run on a recurring basis, perform multiple queries as a transaction, and build intelligent "agents" for the Web. **Locations:** Alexandria, VA; Silver Spring, MD; and Washington, DC.

53181 ■ Macromedia Fireworks II
EEI Communications
66 Canal Ctr. Plz., Ste. 200
Alexandria, VA 22314-5507
Ph:(703)683-7453
Free: 888-253-2762
Fax: (703)683-7310
Co. E-mail: train@eeicommunications.com
URL: http://www.eeicommunications.com/training
Price: $695. **Description:** Covers Web page designs, including masks to create photomontages, create vector graphics, slicing advanced page designs, generate HTML and JavaScript code, swap images, and create pop-up images. **Locations:** Alexandria, VA; Silver Spring, MD; and Washington, DC.

53182 ■ Macromedia Flash III
EEI Communications
66 Canal Ctr. Plz., Ste. 200
Alexandria, VA 22314-5507
Ph:(703)683-7453
Free: 888-253-2762
Fax: (703)683-7310
Co. E-mail: train@eeicommunications.com
URL: http://www.eeicommunications.com/training
Price: $695. **Description:** Covers project creation from planning and development, working with XML, advanced animation and interaction concepts and sound applications, and integrating video with Flash. **Locations:** Alexandria, VA; Silver Spring, MD; and Washington, DC.

53183 ■ Microsoft Excel II
EEI Communications
66 Canal Ctr. Plz., Ste. 200
Alexandria, VA 22314-5507
Ph:(703)683-7453
Free: 888-253-2762
Fax: (703)683-7310
Co. E-mail: train@eeicommunications.com
URL: http://www.eeicommunications.com/training
Price: $695. **Description:** Seminar covering the advanced features of Excel, including advanced formulas, PivotTables, and analysis tools, including customizing workbook and toolbars, working with multiple data sources, edit macros, test data, and protect worksheets. **Locations:** Alexandria, VA; Silver Spring, MD; and Washington, DC.

53184 ■ Microsoft Project II
EEI Communications
66 Canal Ctr. Plz., Ste. 200
Alexandria, VA 22314-5507
Ph:(703)683-7453
Free: 888-253-2762
Fax: (703)683-7310
Co. E-mail: train@eeicommunications.com
URL: http://www.eeicommunications.com/training
Price: $695. **Description:** Seminar that covers workload adjustments and developing tracking skills to ensure a successful project completion, including fine-tuning task, resource, and assignment information, reorganizing phases and tasks, analyzing the critical path, leveling over-allocated resources, documenting resource details with reports, create consumption rates, track project progress, create an interim plan, and documenting the project's progress with reports. **Locations:** Alexandria, VA; Silver Spring, MD; and Washington, DC.

53185 ■ Object-Oriented Programming (OOP) Boot Camp
EEI Communications
66 Canal Ctr. Plz., Ste. 200
Alexandria, VA 22314-5507
Ph:(703)683-7453
Free: 888-253-2762
Fax: (703)683-7310
Co. E-mail: train@eeicommunications.com
URL: http://www.eeicommunications.com/training
Price: $395. **Description:** Seminar that teaches what it means to give objects characteristics that can be transferred to, added to, and combined with other objects to make a complete program, including classes and objects, fields, properties, methods, and events, encapsulating, inheritance and polymorphisms, overloading, overriding, and shadowing. **Locations:** Alexandria, VA; Silver Spring, MD; and Washington, DC.

53186 ■ Structured Query Language (SQL) I
EEI Communications
66 Canal Ctr. Plz., Ste. 200
Alexandria, VA 22314-5507
Ph:(703)683-7453
Free: 888-253-2762
Fax: (703)683-7310
Co. E-mail: train@eeicommunications.com
URL: http://www.eeicommunications.com/training
Price: $695. **Description:** Seminar that covers how to organize and extract information from relational databases, including design relational databases, proper syntax for SQL statements, analyze and orga-

nize data, retrieve, insert, update, and delete data, use aggregate functions, write queries from multiple tables, and normalize data. **Locations:** Alexandria, VA; Silver Spring, MD; and Washington, DC.

53187 ■ Structured Query Language (SQL) II

EEI Communications
66 Canal Ctr. Plz., Ste. 200
Alexandria, VA 22314-5507
Ph:(703)683-7453
Free: 888-253-2762
Fax: (703)683-7310
Co. E-mail: train@eeicommunications.com
URL: http://www.eeicommunications.com/training
Price: $695. **Description:** Seminar that provides critical information for writing advanced database queries using complex databases, including design subqueries, data dictionaries, establish database security, create and manage sequences and indexes, and create stored procedures. **Locations:** Alexandria, VA; Silver Spring, MD; and Washington, DC.

53188 ■ Typography and Font Management

EEI Communications
66 Canal Ctr. Plz., Ste. 200
Alexandria, VA 22314-5507
Ph:(703)683-7453
Free: 888-253-2762
Fax: (703)683-7310
Co. E-mail: train@eeicommunications.com
URL: http://www.eeicommunications.com/training
Price: $395. **Description:** Covers the various electronic typefaces used in desktop publishing applications, including installing, managing, and troubleshooting fonts. **Locations:** Alexandria, VA; Silver Spring, MD; and Washington, DC.

53189 ■ Web Design Hands-on

EEI Communications
66 Canal Ctr. Plz., Ste. 200
Alexandria, VA 22314-5507
Ph:(703)683-7453
Free: 888-253-2762
Fax: (703)683-7310
Co. E-mail: train@eeicommunications.com
URL: http://www.eeicommunications.com/training
Price: $1,595. **Description:** 5-day seminar that covers designing a Web site using Macromedia Dreamweaver and Fireworks. Specifics include, planning, budgeting and estimating, mapping navigation, sketching on paper, breaking down a site into image tables, establishing links and creating rollover graphics, and publishing a site on the World Wide Web. **Locations:** Alexandria, VA; Silver Spring, MD; and Washington, DC.

53190 ■ Web Graphics with Adobe Photoshop and ImageReady

EEI Communications
66 Canal Ctr. Plz., Ste. 200
Alexandria, VA 22314-5507
Ph:(703)683-7453
Free: 888-253-2762
Fax: (703)683-7310
Co. E-mail: train@eeicommunications.com
URL: http://www.eeicommunications.com/training
Price: $695. **Description:** Covers creating high-quality, low-bandwidth graphics for the Web, including optimizing GIFs and JPEGs, creating transparent GIF graphics and animated GIFs and rollovers, create background tiles and sliced graphics, create navigation bars and buttons, image maps, and correct photographs for the Web. **Locations:** Alexandria, VA; Silver Spring, MD; and Washington, DC.

53191 ■ Web Usability and Design Techniques

EEI Communications
66 Canal Ctr. Plz., Ste. 200
Alexandria, VA 22314-5507
Ph:(703)683-7453
Free: 888-253-2762
Fax: (703)683-7310
Co. E-mail: train@eeicommunications.com
URL: http://www.eeicommunications.com/training
Price: $695. **Description:** Seminar Web design and development, including design guidelines, effective use of images and color, writing good code, safe Cascading Style Sheets (CSS), creating usable sites, accessibility, and browser incompatibilities. **Locations:** Alexandria, VA; Silver Spring, MD; and Washington, DC.

53192 ■ Writing for the Web II

EEI Communications
66 Canal Ctr. Plz., Ste. 200
Alexandria, VA 22314-5507
Ph:(703)683-7453
Free: 888-253-2762
Fax: (703)683-7310
Co. E-mail: train@eeicommunications.com
URL: http://www.eeicommunications.com/training
Price: $695. **Description:** Seminar for persons with 3-5 years' experience as a Web writer or editor, or have completed Writing for the Web I, covering how to define your genre and audience, develop a structure for your Web content, working with subject matter experts who aren't writers, making the most of your writing project, giving and getting feedback, writing links that work for your client, how to write menus so clients can use them, and recasting a print article for the Web. **Locations:** Alexandria, VA; Silver Spring, MD; and Washington, DC.

53193 ■ XML Development I

EEI Communications
66 Canal Ctr. Plz., Ste. 200
Alexandria, VA 22314-5507
Ph:(703)683-7453
Free: 888-253-2762
Fax: (703)683-7310
Co. E-mail: train@eeicommunications.com
URL: http://www.eeicommunications.com/training
Price: $695. **Description:** Covers Extensible Markup Language (XML) that enables the Web designer to create information that is evolvable, including XML structure and syntax, create well-formed XML documents and document type definitions (DTDs) and schemas, valid XML documents, using entities, display using Cascading Style Sheets, data binding, and object model scripts. **Locations:** Alexandria, VA; Silver Spring, MD; and Washington, DC.

53194 ■ XML Development II

EEI Communications
66 Canal Ctr. Plz., Ste. 200
Alexandria, VA 22314-5507
Ph:(703)683-7453
Free: 888-253-2762
Fax: (703)683-7310
Co. E-mail: train@eeicommunications.com
URL: http://www.eeicommunications.com/training
Price: $695. **Description:** Covers XSLT and how it is used to convert XML data for presentational purposes, modify data structure, and to create non-XML files, including building XSLT applications, transforming XML to HTML, PDF, and Word. **Locations:** Alexandria, VA; Silver Spring, MD; and Washington, DC.

53195 ■ XML Development III

EEI Communications
66 Canal Ctr. Plz., Ste. 200
Alexandria, VA 22314-5507
Ph:(703)683-7453
Free: 888-253-2762
Fax: (703)683-7310
Co. E-mail: train@eeicommunications.com
URL: http://www.eeicommunications.com/training
Price: $995. **Description:** Seminar that covers the integration of XML into Web applications using ASP, Cold Fusion, PHP and Java, including the guidelines for translating XML structure to a relational database model, rules for modeling, techniques for storing, transmitting, and displaying content, data access mechanisms that expose relational data as XML, and how to use related technologies when processing XML data. **Locations:** Alexandria, VA; Silver Spring, MD; and Washington, DC.

REFERENCE WORKS

53196 ■ "10 Local Companies Make Inc. List of Fastest-Growing" in *Crain's Detroit Business* (Vol. 21, October 31, 2005, No. 44, pp. 32)

Pub: Crain Communications Inc. - Detroit
Ed: Laura Bommarito. **Description:** Ten local companies made the Inc. magazine's annual list of the 500 fastest-growing businesses in the U.S. The three top rankings include, Arbor Networks, seller of network security and software equipment, ranked No. 9; Commodity Sourcing Group, No. 22, buys and distributes goods and services for health care organizations; and BullsEye Telecom, provider of telephone and Internet services to businesses ranked No. 82.

53197 ■ "Accounting Moves to the Web" in *Home Office Computing* (Vol. 18, No. 8, August 2000, pp. 36)

Pub: Scholastic Inc.
Ed: Victoria Hall Smith. **Description:** Profiles of the online versions of both Peachtree and NetLedger's accounting suites software.

53198 ■ "Added Security" in *Entrepreneur* (Vol. 33, January 2005, No. 1, pp. 43)

Pub: Entrepreneur Media Inc.
Ed: Liane Cassavoy. **Description:** Profile of Safe-Guard Easy 4.0 from Utimaco Safeware. The software encrypts the entire contents of a computer hard drive.

53199 ■ "Advisor Answers" in *E-business Advisor* (Vol. 18, No. 4, April 2000, pp. 42)

Pub: Advisor Media, Inc.
Ed: Michael Cobb. **Description:** Information regarding denial-of-service (DOS) attacks, a major concern as much-publicized events are creating major headlines, is covered. These attacks involve overloading a Web site with bogus requests, making it impossible to process legitimate requests.

53200 ■ "Advisor Tips" in *E-business Advisor* (Vol. 18, No. 7, July 2000, pp. 52)

Pub: Advisor Media, Inc.
Ed: Larry C. Whipple. **Description:** Tips on architecting Web applications are presented. A good architecture can solve problems before they happen, provide for growth of the site, and make the development and AQ run smoother.

53201 ■ "Aftermarket Hits Its Stride" in *Venture Capital Journal* (November 1, 2004)

Pub: Thomason Financial Inc.
Ed: Lawrence Aragon. **Description:** Of the six venture-backed companies listed in September 2004, most posted strong aftermarket performances. Thereavance Inc., a drug company in San Francisco; IntraLase Corporation, maker of software for lasers used in eye surgery; and PlanetOut Inc., which operates gay and lesbian-themed Websites, went public as of October 15, 2004.

53202 ■ "Almost office" in *Entrepreneur* (Vol. 30, No. 12, December 2002, pp. 64)

Pub: Entrepreneur Media Inc.
Description: Profile of software that allows the use of Linux, while retaining use of Microsoft office, including CrossOver Office 1.2, Sun StarOffice Suite 6.0, and Ximian Desktop Professional Edition.

53203 ■ "Analyze This" in *Black Enterprise* (Vol. 34, No. 6, January 2004, pp. 41)

Pub: Earl Graves Publishing Co.
Ed: Ashley Gibson. **Description:** Profile of Charles Phillips, technology expert and rated America's best software analyst, has been appointed new executive vice president of Oracle Corporation.

53204 ■ "Analyze This: Charles Phillips Makes Bold Career Move to Oracle as Executive Vice President" in *Black Enterprise* (Vol. 34, No. 6)

Pub: Earl Graves Publishing Co.
Ed: Ashley Gibson. **Description:** Profile of Charles Phillips, technology expert and rated America's best software analyst, has been appointed new executive vice president of Oracle Corporation.

53205 ■ "Analyze This" in *Forbes* **(April 1, 2002, p. 96)**
Pub: Forbes Magazine
Ed: Erika Brown. **Description:** Sales for business intelligence software are booming. Business intelligence software is designed to make all company data from all divisions compatible with each other.

53206 ■ "Anatomy of a Startup" in *Black Enterprise* **(Vol. 35, November 2004, No. 4, pp. 112)**
Pub: Earl G. Graves Publishing Co. Inc.
Ed: Sonya A. Donaldson. **Description:** Profile of Ken Coleman, founder of the technology startup ITM Software in Silicon Valley, California. Coleman started his new firm after retiring from Silicon Graphics Inc.

53207 ■ "And Now, the Handheld Trainer" in *Business Week* **(January 9, 2006, No. 3966, pp. 92)**
Pub: McGraw-Hill Companies
Ed: Toddi Gutner, Lourdes Lee Valeriano. **Description:** Profile of the PumpPod, Companion World's Progio programs, iAmplify, and Alive Yoga; these programs offer fitness training on handheld devices.

53208 ■ "Antivirus Extras" in *Entrepreneur* **(Vol. 31, No. 10, October 2003, pp. 57)**
Pub: Entrepreneur Media, Inc.
Ed: Liane Cassavoy. **Description:** Profile of Global HAURI's ViRobot Expert that fights more than computer viruses, it will also treat spyware as a virus.

53209 ■ "AOL woos small businesses with e-comm plan " in *Network World* **(September 18, 2000, pp. 12)**
Pub: Network World Inc.
Ed: Ellen Messmer. **Description:** A profile of AOL's new Netbusiness that helps small businesses start e-commerce sites.

53210 ■ "Apple of Your Eye?" in *Entrepreneur* **(Vol. 31, No. 8, August 2003, pp. 40)**
Pub: Entrepreneur Media, Inc.
Description: Profile of Apple's Keynote 1.1 presentation software. The software is compatible with Power-Point files and will compete with Microsoft.

53211 ■ "Arbortext's bread and butter" in *Crain's Detroit Business* **(Vol. 19, No. 11, March 17, 2003, pp. 25)**
Pub: Crain Communications Inc., Detroit
Ed: Andrew Dietderich. **Description:** Arbortext Inc.'s software is based on extensible markup language, also called XML, the programming language that allows developers to describe and deliver structured data from any application.

53212 ■ "Arbortext's windfall" in *Crain's Detroit Business* **(Vol. 19, No. 11, March 17, 2003, pp. 3)**
Pub: Crain Communications Inc., Detroit
Ed: Andrew Dietderich. **Description:** Arbortext, a company making editing and publishing software for business-related content, has landed an $8.75 round of financing from venture capital firms.

53213 ■ "BEA's Next Act" in *Barron's* **(July 28, 2003, pp. T2)**
Pub: Barron's
Ed: Mark Veverka. **Description:** Software firm, BEA Systems, is under competitive stress for market share in applications servers sector, an arcane but highly lucrative back-end technology of great usefulness in e-commerce and Internet applications.

53214 ■ "Behind the Curve" in *Hispanic Business* **(Vol. 24, No. 5, May 2002, pp. 40-41)**
Pub: Hispanic Business Inc.
Ed: Teresa Talerico. **Description:** Hispanic small business owners are slow to accept technology. The importance of keeping up with technology for a small business is discussed.

53215 ■ "Behind the Scenes" in *Washington Business Journal* **(Vol. 22, No. 12, July 25, 2003, pp. 18)**
Pub: Washington Business Journal
Ed: Tim Mazzucca. **Description:** Shane Chalke, CEO of Herndon, Virginia-based AnnuityNet, markets software products to investment and insurance firms. AnnuityNet acquired a subsidiary of Wachovia Bank for an undisclosed price.

53216 ■ "Being Big Brother: Shh...Spy Tool Helps You Snoop Undetected" in *Black Enterprise* **(Vol. 35, October 2004, No. 3, pp. 72)**
Pub: Earl G. Graves Publishing Co. Inc.
Ed: Schuyler K. Esprit. **Description:** Profile of Spector Spyware for Macintosh computers. The software tracks the computer use of employees, family members, and even unwanted users of a computer. The package is easy to install.

53217 ■ "The Best CEO in Silicon Valley" in *Black Enterprise* **(Vol. 35, September 2004, No. 2, pp. 108)**
Pub: Earl G. Graves Publishing Co. Inc.
Ed: Alan Hughes. **Description:** Profile of John W. Thompson, chairman and CEO of Symantic Corporation, leader in the network security software industry. Thompson is responsible for identifying potential acquisition targets, including the recent $370 million acquisition of Brightmail in June 2004.

53218 ■ "The Best of Technology Q&A: Answers to Readers' Most-Asked Questions" in *Journal of Accountancy* **(Vol. 198, December 2004, No. 6)**
Pub: American Institute of Certified Public Accountants
Ed: Stanley Zarowin. **Description:** In depth analysis of various accounting software programs are presented, including Microsoft's Excel 2000.

53219 ■ "BizWare" in *Hispanic Business* **(Vol. 23, No. 11, November 2001, pp. 70)**
Pub: Hispanic Business Inc.
Ed: Roger Harris. **Description:** Hispanic programmers offer a software package for the mom-and-pop entrepreneur to develop a Web site for their business.

53220 ■ "Bookless Bookkeeping" in *PC Magazine*
Pub: Ziff-Davis Publishing Company
Ed: Richard Morochove. **Description:** An overview of seven inexpensive accounting programs for small businesses.

53221 ■ "BorderWare to ship e-commerce gateways for small business use" in *Network World* **(December 6, 1999, pp. NA)**
Pub: Network World Inc.
Ed: Ellen Messmer. **Description:** A profile of BorderWare Technologies line of three firewall-based gateway products for use in small business e-commerce sites that require a minimum of technical expertise. The BorderWare Office Gateway is intended for use by organizations with ten or less employees.

53222 ■ "Brent Bannerman" in *Entrepreneur* **(Vol. 31, No. 6, June 2003, pp. 23)**
Pub: Entrepreneur Media Inc.
Ed: April Y. Pennington. **Description:** Profile of Brent Bannerman, founder of IE-Engine, the Waltham, Massachusetts business insurance and benefits software developer; Bannerman has projected 2003 sales of $10 million for his company that was founded in 2000.

53223 ■ "Bronto Email Marketing Toolkit" in *Entrepreneur.com* **(Vol. 34, February 2006, No. 2, pp. 6)**
Pub: Entrepreneur Media Inc.
Description: Free guide offered by Bronto software focuses on email marketing for small business.

53224 ■ "Bug Control" in *Entrepreneur* **(Vol. 32, No. 4, April 2004, pp. 34)**
Pub: Entrepreneur Media, Inc.
Ed: Eric Bender. **Description:** Small companies have become a target for cyber attacks. Antivirus makers have started initiatives to respond more quickly and predictably to hackers by the use of antivirus software used along with a properly configured firewall.

53225 ■ "Build a Better Virus" in *Inc.* **(September 1, 2003)**
Pub: Gruner & Jahr USA Publishing
Ed: Bobbie Gossage. **Description:** University of Calgary teaches students about computer viruses by having them create their own virus. This course has become very controversial because of security concerns.

53226 ■ "Bulk Mail Through the Internet" in *PC Magazine* **(April 4, 2000, pp. 115)**
Pub: Ziff-Davis Publishing Company
Ed: Marge Brown. **Description:** With services like DirectNet and Internet direct mail service offered from Pitney Bowes, businesses can have mass mailings sent within three business days without having to leave their offices.

53227 ■ "Buried Alive-There's no such thing as a paperless office" in *PC Computing* **(March 2000, pp. 104)**
Pub: Ziff-Davis Inc.
Ed: Nora Isaacs. **Description:** Electronic document management can reduce the paper clutter in an office and make information easier to store and retrieve. A brief description of new document management hardware and software are presented, including Visioineer's OneTouch 8600 scanner, Caere's OmniPage Pro 10 OCR and PageKeeper Pro 3.0 software, Corex's CardScan Office Solution, Ricoh's e-Cabinet, Xerox's DocuShare 2.1, and Lotus's Domino.Doc software.

53228 ■ *Business Feasibility Analysis Pro*
Pub: Prentice Hall PTR
Ed: Palo Alto Software. **Released:** August 2006. **Price:** $28.40. **Description:** Profile of software developed to support small business management and/or entrepreneurship text. Step-by-step instructions are provided.

53229 ■ "Business-to-Consumer E-Commerce: What is(n't) the Problem?" in *E-business Advisor* **(Vol. 18, No. 8, August 2000, pp. 6)**
Pub: Advisor Media, Inc.
Ed: Jane M. Falla. **Description:** Customers are grumbling, investors are threatening, and start-ups are sweating since the downturn of dot-coms. Despite the apparent dire straits, consumer online buying marches on and B2C e-commerce sights will need to outsource or find the correct packaged technology to keep pace with all of the changes occurring.

53230 ■ "Buying Guide: Software" in *My Business* **(June/July 2004, pp. 18-19)**
Pub: My Business Magazine
Description: Information about Norton's Antivirus 2004, Trend Micro's PC-cillin Internet Security 2004, eXtendia Antivirus, Panda Titanium Antivirus 2004, and McAfee Internet Security Suite is provided.

53231 ■ "Buzzwords: Plog" in *Inc.* **(September 1, 2004)**
Pub: Inc. Magazine
Ed: Ian Ybarra. **Description:** Plogs are Web-based tools where co-workers can create an archive of observations and data for projects. So far, companies using plogs have created the software in-house.

53232 ■ "Can Gates Remember Being Small?" in *Fortune* **(Vol. 148, No. 12, December 8, 2003, pp. 204H)**
Pub: Time Inc.
Ed: David Lidsky, David Whitford. **Description:** In an interview with Bill Gates, he answers questions about his days of being a small businessman and the things that attributed to his success with Microsoft.

53233 ■ "C&S Marketing to be CoreLogic" in *Sacramento Bee* **(October 25, 2005)**
Pub: The Sacramento Bee
Ed: Dale Kasler. **Description:** C&S Marketing recently changed its name to CoreLogic. The software maker, located in Sacramento, California, helps mortgage lenders detect fraud and estimate property values and was recently named one of the nation's 500 fastest growing private companies by Inc. magazine.

53234 ■ "Capture the Tag: Are RFID Tags in Danger of Being Hacked?" in *Entrepreneur* (Vol. 33, February 2005, No. 2, pp. 66)
Pub: Entrepreneur Media Inc.
Ed: Gwen Moran. Description: Retail cashiers should be alerted to look for radio frequency identification (RFID) tags that look unusual, if so, check the product information manual.

53235 ■ "Case Study" in *Inc.* (July 1, 2004)
Pub: Inc. Magazine
Ed: Rod Kurtz. Description: Profile of Everdream, a software provider in California who outsourced its North Carolina call center to a firm in San Jose, Costa Rica. The move cut 25 percent in operating expenses, but might not have been the best decision for the company.

53236 ■ "Catuity starts reaping loyalty-card rewards" in *Crain's Detroit Business* (Vol. 19, No. 10, March 10, 2003, pp. 32)
Pub: Crain Communications Inc., Detroit
Ed: Andrew Dietderich. Description: Catuity Inc., a Detroit-based firm working with Visa USA Inc. provides software for the credit-card company's new smart cards.

53237 ■ "Caught In the Crossfire" in *Inc.* (August 1, 2003)
Pub: Gruner & Jahr USA Publishing
Ed: Ellen Neubone. Description: New spam filters are making it difficult for small companies relying on email for marketing strategies.

53238 ■ "Click Here For Credit Info" in *Business Week* (No. 3761, December 10, 2001, pp.SB4)
Pub: McGraw-Hill Inc.
Description: Profile of QuickBooks Pro, the software that gives direct access to credit reports from Dun & Bradstreet for a mere $10 per report.

53239 ■ "Commercial Fraud Insight" in *Entrepreneur.com* (Vol. 34, January 2006, No. 1, pp. 6)
Pub: Entrepreneur Media Inc.
Ed: Steve Cooper. Description: Experian offers commercial fraud and authentication software to help small businesses verify addresses, tax ID numbers, phone numbers, DBA names and more. The database represents more than 16 million U.S. businesses.

53240 ■ "Computer-Assisted Consulting" in *Hispanic Business* (Vol. 24, No. 5, May 2002, pp. 50)
Pub: Hispanic Business Inc.
Ed: Roger Harris. Description: BRS software products will help business consultants to become more successful. The software packages offer solid advice on everything from writing business and marketing plans to development of pricing and sales strategies.

53241 ■ "Consumer Research" in *Business 2.0* (Vol. 6, September 2005, No. 8, pp. 36)
Pub: Time Inc.
Ed: Bridget Finn. Description: Umbria Communications in Boulder, Colorado is turning the Internet into a marketing bonanza. The firm's software called Buzz Report searches 13 million blogs to uncover consumer's feelings about new products and trends.

53242 ■ "Cool New Software, Free of Charge" in *Inc.* (November 2006, pp. 42-43)
Pub: Gruner & Jahr USA Publishing
Ed: Michael Fitzgerald. Description: Free of charge software is available to help you run your business. From project management to managing email and customer relations, programs are available on line or free o charge to assist you. Six examples are highlighted in this article.

53243 ■ "Cool Tools: Take Adobe Acrobat to the next level with Compose 4.1" in *Entrepreneur* (Vol. 30, No. 2, February 2002, pp. 34)
Pub: Entrepreneur Media Inc.
Ed: Liane Gouthro. Description: Profile of Compose 4.1 from Infodata, which offers publishing tools to add features to documents.

53244 ■ "Coordinating Staff With IT Technology" in *Ingram's* (Vol. 27, No. 8, August 2001, pp. 23)
Pub: Show Me Publishing, Inc.
Ed: Michael May. Description: The management of employees use of information technology is discussed. Advice is given on software training and Internet usage monitoring.

53245 ■ "Cover Your Assets" in *Success* (Vol. 47, No. 6, November 2000, pp. 62)
Pub: Success Publishing, Inc.
Ed: Paul Gallagher. Description: If you're connected to the Internet, you need a firewall. This article offers information on easy-to-install solutions, including ZoneAlarm by Zone Labs, McAfee Personal Firewall by McAfee.com, and Norton Personal Firewall by Symantec.

53246 ■ "Covert Operations" in *Entrepreneur* (Vol. 31, No. 8, August 2003, pp. 51)
Pub: Entrepreneur Media, Inc.
Ed: Amanda C. Kooser. Description: The importance of using spyware and a good firewall to protect company information is stressed. Free spyware detection products can be downloaded free of charge, but a more complete solution offered by Lavasoft or Pest-Patrol may be a better choice. Anti-spyware should become an overall part of a company's security plan and should be reviewed periodically.

53247 ■ "CRM: Buy or Rent?" in *Sales and Marketing.com* (Vol. 156, No. 3, March 2004, pp. 40)
Pub: VNU eMedia, Inc.
Ed: Daniel Tynan. Description: An analyst with Aberdeen Group in Boston, Massachusetts, discusses issues facing small companies when choosing a customer relation management system (CRM). There are two types of systems available: traditional CRM software that can be purchased, or renting off-the-shelf CRM applications at Web sites like Salesforce.com or Salesnet.

53248 ■ "Data key to Centerstone's resource-tracking software" in *Boston Business Journal* (Vol. 22, No. 11, April 19, 2002, pp. 19)
Pub: MCP, Inc.
Ed: Tom Witrowski. Description: Mathew Meyer, CEO and founder of Centerstone Software Inc., sells workplace management software used by architects, interior designers, security firms, and real estate management companies.

53249 ■ "Data Discovery" in *Entrepreneur* (Vol. 31, No. 7, July 2003, pp. 40)
Pub: Entrepreneur Media, Inc.
Ed: Liane Cassavoy. Description: Profile of EasyRecovery Lite 6.0 from Ontrack Data Recovery, software that allows computer users to recover data from up to 25 files lost from computer viruses, computer crashes, or human error.

53250 ■ "Database Dollars" in *Small Business Opportunities* (Vol. 12, No. 5, September 2000, pp. 44)
Pub: Harris Publications, Inc.
Ed: Carla Vincent. Description: A customer database can help find new customers, increase sales, and build clientele. Ways to develop a database are outlined.

53251 ■ "Delayed Obsolescence" in *Hispanic Business* (March 2005, pp. 64)
Pub: Hispanic Business
Ed: Kevin Savetz. Description: Advance planning by small companies can help make technology investments last over the years. Small business software purchases should be made with future use in mind.

53252 ■ "Delivering the Right Technology at the Right Time" in *Rough Notes* (Vol. 146, No. 9, September 2003, pp. 62)
Pub: Rough Notes
Ed: Nancy Doucette. Description: Applied Systems' services and products for the insurance industry are discussed. Business management software, sales management software, and product support are profiled.

53253 ■ "Dell and NetObjects make small business play" in *Network World* (October 24, 2000, pp. NA)
Pub: Network World Inc.
Ed: Ashlee Vance. Description: Dell plans to pre-install NetObject's software for building Web sites on some Dell desktops and notebooks. The software helps users build, publish and promote their own Web sites under the co-branded product title NetObjects Fusion Dell Edition.

53254 ■ "Desktop Publishing" in *Home Office Computing* (Vol. 18, No. 9, September 2000, pp. 73)
Pub: Scholastic Inc.
Ed: Susan Glinert. Description: A profile of the latest desktop publishing software is provided.

53255 ■ "Detroit Free Press Wayne Small Business Column" in *Detroit Free Press* (June 9, 2005)
Pub: Knight-Ridder/Tribune Business News
Ed: Carol Cain. Description: Brian Kruger, owner of the Dutch software firm specializing in publishing products, has chosen the Ford Building in Downtown Detroit to locate WoodWing USA Inc. The firm has grown to eight employees since opening in 2003.

53256 ■ "Digital Video Editing" in *Home Office Computing* (Vol. 19, No. 1, January 2001, pp. 77)
Pub: Scholastic Inc.
Ed: Dave Johnson. Description: Five digital video (DV) editing packages aimed at a variety of users are reviewed.

53257 ■ "The Dimensions of Ping Fu" in *Inc.* (Volume 27, December 2005, No. 12, pp. 90-97, 132, 134-135)
Pub: Inc. Magazine
Ed: John Brant. Description: Profile of Ping Fu, owner of a software firm called Geomagic in Research Triangle Park, North Carolina. Geomagic has defined and dominated the high-tech field of digital shape sampling and processing or DSSP, which entails scanning an object with optical beams, rendering it on a computer screen three-dimensionally for manufacturing, testing, and inspection purposes.

53258 ■ "Do It Yourself" in *Entrepreneur* (Vol. 32, September 2004, No. 9, pp. 71)
Pub: Entrepreneur Media Inc.
Ed: Gwen Moran. Description: Many companies are offering preformatted design templates that allow users to customize and print business cards, stationery, menus, newsletters, postcards, brochures, tickets, as well as providing printing services.

53259 ■ "Double Down" in *Entrepreneur* (Vol. 33, September 2005, No. 9, pp. 50)
Pub: Entrepreneur Media Inc.
Ed: Amanda C. Kooser. Description: The next-generation of DVD burners is profiled. A listing of manufacturers, models, contact information and DL write speed is included.

53260 ■ "Dumars company diversifies with deal for Troy tech firm" in *Crain's Detroit Business* (Vol. 19, No. 4, January 27, 2003, pp. 26)
Pub: Crain Communications Inc., Detroit
Ed: Terry Kosdrosky. Description: Profile of Joe Dumars who heads up companies in the automotive supply industry and telecommunications, has just acquired the Troy-based Technical Solutions Inc., giving Detroit Technologies Inc. the capability to install telecommunications and computer software, hardware and infrastructure.

53261 ■ "E-Business Cards" in *Hispanic Business* (Vol. 23, No. 10, October, 2001, pp. 100)
Pub: Hispanic Business
Ed: Roger Harris. Description: Profile of the Web-based Scout service, a software system that automatically updates contact information in a user's computer address book. Scout is a service from Ants.com, a start-up backed by venture capital from such firms as Bertelsmann Venture Capital.

53262 ■ "E-Cognita plots Web software for commercial real estate loans" in *Crain's Detroit Business* (Vol. 16, No. 46, Nov. 13, 2000, pp. 32)
Pub: Crain Communications, Inc.
Ed: Jennette Smith. Description: The Birmingham, Michigan-based E-Cognita Technologies Inc. has developed software and services to automate commercial real estate lending.

53263 ■ "E-Mail Alternative" in *Entrepreneur* (Vol. 32, No. 1, January 2004, pp. 47)
Pub: Entrepreneur Media, Inc.
Ed: Liane Cassavoy. Description: Eudora 6.0s new SpamWatch feature sends spam to a junk mail folder, making it an alternative to Outlook Express for email.

53264 ■ "E-Mail Secrets Revealed" in *Home Office Computing* (Vol. 18, No. 12, December 2000, pp. 48)
Pub: Scholastic Inc.
Ed: Helen Bradley. Description: Tips for making effective use of E-mail software and services are presented.

53265 ■ "E-Train" in *Sales & Marketing Management* (Vol. 157, February 2005, No. 2, pp. 20)
Pub: VNU Business Media
Description: Arcadian Software offers software designed to guide users through negotiations by analyzing human interactions and negotiation theory. The program contains four tools: Quick Plan, Full Plan, Problem Solver, and Profiler.

53266 ■ "E-Train" in *Sales and Marketing. com* (Vol. 156, No. 3, March 2004, pp. 18)
Pub: VNU eMedia, Inc.
Description: Profile of Qarbon's ViewletBuilder4, software that enables training managers to create presentations for software demonstrations or product features. The software works like a digital camera, and text, images, quizzes and interactive zones can be added to the slides.

53267 ■ "Easy Math" in *Entrepreneur* (Vol. 31, No. 5, May 2003, pp. 38)
Pub: Entrepreneur Media Inc.
Ed: Liane Cassavoy. Description: Profile of Simply Accounting 2003 software from ACCPAC International, offering a complete accounting system including payroll and departmental accounting for $169 for the basic version.

53268 ■ "eBay Auction Integration Will Be a Major Player with Irun's Website Builder Tools" in *PR Newswire* (December 2, 2003)
Pub: PR Newswire Association, Inc.
Description: Irun Corporation announced that its Website builder now includes auction integration as part of its service. This service will allow businesses a single point for managing their e-commerce Website and eBay auctions.

53269 ■ "EC Outlook returns from Ohio." in *Houston Business Journal* (Vol. 33, No. 51, May 2, 2003, pp. 1A)
Pub: Houston Business Journal
Ed: Jennifer Dawson. Description: EC Outlook moved from Houston to Ohio in 2002, now the company has moved back to Houston and expects to hire about 30 new employees.

53270 ■ "Emageon Vies With Big Guns" in *Birmingham Business Journal* (Vol. 20, No. 39, September 26, 2003, pp. 1)
Pub: American City Business Journals, Inc.
Ed: Tom Bassing. Description: Profile of Emageon Inc., maker of inter-connectable software for hospital diagnostic equipment.

53271 ■ "En Garde! Herby Raynaud's Fencing Fancy" in *Black Enterprise* (Vol. 34, No. 3, October 2003, pp. 139)
Pub: Earl Graves Publishing Co.
Ed: Ashley Gibson. Description: Profile of Herby Raynaud, 32-year-old software developer for the Union Bank of Switzerland, located in Weehawken, New Jersey. Raynaud is an avid fencer and is currently training for the U.S. Olympic team.

53272 ■ "Enterprise Solutions" in *Hispanic Business* (October 2004, pp. 120, 122)
Pub: Hispanic Business
Ed: Kevin Savetz. Description: Software makers are targeting mid-size companies with new applications that boost business efficiency.

53273 ■ *The Entrepreneurial Culture Network Advantage Within Chinese and Irish Software Firms*
Pub: Edward Elgar Publishing, Incorporated
Ed: Tsang. Released: October 2006. Price: $95.00.
Description: Ways national cultural heritage influences entrepreneurial ventures are discussed.

53274 ■ "The Evolution of XML Schemes" in *E-business Advisor* (Vol. 18, No. 5, May 2000, pp. 26)
Pub: Advisor Media, Inc.
Ed: James Tauber. Description: The idea behind the extensible markup language (XML) is to provide a standard way of attaching labels to unfamiliar objects, thus establishing a meaning for the objects. However, XML defines neither the meaning nor the set of familiar labels, which is a key part of its extensibility.

53275 ■ "Extract, Transform and Load" in *Barron's* (August 11, 2003, pp. T2)
Pub: Barron's
Ed: Mark Veverka. Description: Extract, Transform and Load (ETL), a model of middleware enterprise software, is ousting Enterprise Application Integration (EAI) as the standard of choice. EAI is more elegant and robust, but ETL gets the job done for less. Netgear's initial public offering is discussed, and San Francisco, California-based Pacific Growth Equities efforts to expand are examined.

53276 ■ "Eye on the Storm" in *Entrepreneur* (Vol. 33, September 2005, No. 9, pp. 43)
Pub: Entrepreneur Media Inc.
Ed: Heather Clancy. Description: Profile of Marc Patti, founder of Paul Consulting in Tallahassee, Florida. Along with software programmer, Wes Holden, Patti has developed software called Debris Information Management System that tracks loads of debris moved to collection sites after hurricanes, floods, and earthquakes.

53277 ■ "Ezsupport Life" in *Entrepreneur. com* (Vol. 34, February 2006, No. 2, pp. 6)
Pub: Entrepreneur Media Inc.
Description: Profile of EzSupport Life, a free, automated online customer-support solution for small businesses.

53278 ■ "Facing the Cyber Threat" in *Hispanic Business* (Vol. 24, No. 5, May 2002, pp. 30, 32, 34)
Pub: Hispanic Business Inc.
Ed: Derek Reveron. Description: Computer security is now at the forefront of every small business; the risks are real requiring serious defense measures.

53279 ■ "Fantastic Forum" in *Entrepreneur* (Vol. 33, September 2005, No. 9, pp. 92)
Pub: Entrepreneur Media Inc.
Ed: Chris Penttila. Description: Video on Location Inc., a full-service video production firm located in Rockville, Maryland uses virtual collaboration software among its 16 employees to create commercials, Webcasts, instructional videos and more. The software allows workers to collaborate online from various locations.

53280 ■ "Fighting Spyware: Microsoft to the Rescue?" in *Business Week* (February 7, 2005, No. 3919, pp. 22)
Pub: McGraw-Hill Companies
Ed: Stephen H. Wildstrom. Description: Spyware has become the biggest threat to the security of Windows computer users. The software can be installed on a computer without your knowledge or consent. A visit to the wrong Website can place software on your PC that changes your browser homepage, steals passwords, or bombards you with ads.

53281 ■ "Find Online Training That Pays Off" in *Fortune* (Vol. 151, February 7, 2005, No. 3, pp. 34)
Pub: Time Inc.
Ed: Anne Fisher. Description: Online courses that help employees obtain needed knowledge are discussed. According to Pathlore Software, a firm that designs online curriculums for various companies, suggests a three-stage approach to online employee learning.

53282 ■ "Finding the office suite that's perfect for you" in *Women In Business* (Vol. 52, No. 4, July 2000, pp. 38)
Pub: The ABWA Co., Inc.
Ed: Rachel Warbington. Description: The selection of suitable office software suites are presented. The Microsoft Office 2000 suite and other complimentary Microsoft packages such as PhotoDraw, Publisher or FrontPage are reviewed.

53283 ■ "Firefox Is Hot; Thunderbird's Not" in *St. Louis Post-Dispatch* (December 17, 2004)
Pub: Knight-Ridder/Tribune Business News
Ed: David Sheets. Description: Web browsers, Firefox and Thunderbird are profiled.

53284 ■ "Firewalls first line of system defenses" in *Business First Columbus* (Vol. 18, No. 38, May 10, 2002, pp. A21)
Pub: Business First Columbus, Inc.
Ed: Diana Barnum. Description: Charles Isaacs, owner of CRI Business Solutions and president of the Columbus Computer Society, recommends that business computers should have firewalls and antivirus protection. Road Runner, a Columbus, Ohio company, has introduced Road Runner Guardian, a firewall service and virtual private network.

53285 ■ "First Data: New Terminal POS Lift for Small Outfits" in *American Banker* (Vol. 172, January 17, 2006, No. 11, pp. 17)
Pub: SourceMedia, Inc.
Ed: David Breitkopf. Description: First Data Corporation has partnered with Microsoft Corporation and Hewlett Packard Company to devise a more complete point of sale terminal for small retailers. The terminal will accept most transactions and will track account information, track inventory, and work with customer relationship software.

53286 ■ "Focus remained on primary customers" in *Crain's Detroit Business* (Vol. 19, No. 13, March 31, 2003, pp. 14)
Pub: Crain Communications, Inc.
Description: Profile of Troy, Michigan-based New World Systems Corporation, developer of software for public safety and public administration organizations.

53287 ■ "For-Your-Own-Good Innovation" in *Inc.* (September 1, 2003)
Pub: Gruner & Jahr USA Publishing
Ed: Rod Kurtz. Description: The California firm, Payment Protection Systems, sells a dashboard device called On Time to used car dealers. The device disables a vehicle if the owner does not make a scheduled payment. Flexplay Technologies in New York has invented a disc to curb software and copyright piracy.

53288 ■ "Forget VC: Successful Entrepreneur Says Good Riddance" in *Venture Capital Journal* (October 1, 2004)
Pub: Thomason Financial Inc.
Description: In an interview, Harry Gruber, founder and CEO of Kintera Inc., a company providing software and services to help nonprofits conduct fundraising via the Internet. Gruber discusses the advantages, as well as the disadvantages of using venture capital to grow a business, particularly the control venture capitalists gain over a firm.

53289 ■ "Form finder" in *Entrepreneur* (Vol. 30, No. 3, March 2002, pp. 40)
Pub: Entrepreneur Media Inc.
Ed: Liane Gouthro. Description: Profile of Cosmi Swift Ware Personal and Business Legal Forms to Go software; this software create more than 200 legal documents including bankruptcies, wills and leases; basic legal help is also included.

53290 ■ "Former Information Warrior D'Amico Now Fighting Cyberwarfare" in *Long Island Business News* **(March 12, 2004)**
Pub: Dolan Media Newswires
Ed: Ken Schachter. Description: Profile of Anita D'Amico, director of the 18-person company, Secure Decisions. The firm developed software used by the Navy Command and Control ship USS Blue Ridge for war games. A new initiative calls for the sale of the system to new markets, including epidemiology to track disease and outbreaks, and law enforcement to track crime patterns.

53291 ■ "Forward Thinking" in *PC Magazine* **(March 7, 2000, pp. 7)**
Pub: Ziff-Davis Publishing Company
Ed: Michael J. Miller. Description: The Y2K crisis has passed and companies are now focusing on the task of moving their IT infrastructures into the 21st century. Hardware and software integration should be a great part of this effort as companies move to centralized administration, single log-ons, and a greater reliance on certificates and directories. Microsoft's Windows 2000 has arrived and should be a part of this movement. New applications and Web services will facilitate this integration for smaller organizations. New network infrastructures will provide high-speed connections for both local and remote users, wireless access to data and virtual private networks.

53292 ■ "Free for All: How Linus and the Free Software Movement Undercut the High-Tech Titans" in *Harvard Business Review* **(Vol. 78, July 2000)**
Pub: Harvard Business School Publishing Corp.
Ed: John T. Landry. Description: Peter Wayner, a journalist and former programmer, discusses the history of open-source software such as Linux.

53293 ■ "Free! (With Purchase)" in *Business 2.0* **(Vol. 7, January/February 2006, No. 1, pp. 113-115)**
Pub: Time, Inc.
Ed: John Battelle. Description: Profile of Scott McNealy, CEO of Sun Microsystems. McNealy is giving away software in order to sell the company's hardware.

53294 ■ "Get the Picture?" in *Entrepreneur* **(Vol. 31, No. 11, November 2003, pp. 91)**
Pub: Entrepreneur Media, Inc.
Ed: Mark Henricks. Description: Geographic information systems (GIS) software can help dispatchers route vehicles to needed service areas quickly, and might trim a logistical outlay by as much as 5-10 percent.

53295 ■ "Get with the program!" in *Entrepreneur* **(Vol. 31, No. 5, May 2003, pp. 58)**
Pub: Entrepreneur Media Inc.
Ed: Mie-Yun Lee. Description: The 2003 Complete Guide to Software is presented. The guide covers various software tools that help to make small businesses more productive.

53296 ■ "Get it together" in *Entrepreneur* **(Vol. 30, No. 3, March 2002, pp. 40)**
Pub: Entrepreneur Media Inc.
Ed: Liane Gouthro. Description: Profile of Drag Strip 3.8 from Aladdin systems; this application provides shortcuts to commonly used files, folders, applications and sites.

53297 ■ "Getting Around" in *PC Magazine* **(February 20, 2001, pp. 67)**
Pub: Ziff-Davis Publishing Company
Ed: Walaika Haskins. Description: New Web services and software are attempting to make life easier for business travelers. Offerings from companies such as i-tinerary Travel Solutions and SideStep seek to provide hassle-free travel.

53298 ■ "Getting started on the Web" in *Hispanic Business* **(Vol. 22, No. 5, May 2000, pp. 98)**
Pub: Hispanic Business

Ed: Roger Harris. Description: Small businesses wishing to establish a Web site must ensure that they find a site developer who really understands their requirements. It is also worth considering using pre-packaged site-builder software.

53299 ■ "Give Me a Break" in *Entrepreneur. com* **(Vol. 34, January 2006, No. 1, pp. 36)**
Pub: Entrepreneur Media Inc.
Ed: Mike Hogan. Description: New tax preparation software can help small companies file federal and state taxes. H&R Block and Intuit have versions for every type of business entity and provide all necessary forms and instructions in an easy-to-follow format. Cost of the software is also tax deductible.

53300 ■ "Go Pro 2.4 GHZ Gyrotransport Air Mouse Presenter" in *Sales & Marketing Management* **(Vol. 159, January-February 2007, No. 1, pp. 42)**
Pub: VNU Business Media
Description: Profile of Gyrotransport mouse that comes equipped with software for Windows and eight programmable functions.

53301 ■ "Good-bye Doesn't Mean Forever" in *Inc.* **(January 1, 2002)**
Pub: Inc. Magazine
Ed: Emily Barker. Description: Profile of SelectMinds maintains a database of former employees for employers.

53302 ■ "Good News for News Overload" in *My Business* **(October/November 2003, pp. 24)**
Pub: My Business Magazine
Description: News aggregators are free or low-cost solutions for small businesses to save time when searching for information on the Internet. NewsGator also offers users the ability to integrate the found information into Outlook software.

53303 ■ "Good Timing" in *Entrepreneur* **(Vol. 32, August 2004, No. 8, pp. 65)**
Pub: Entrepreneur Media Inc.
Ed: Gwen Moran. Description: Scott Tests, COO and co-founder of Mindbridge Software Inc. in Pennsylvania, takes advantage of slow news periods to announce the release of his company's new products.

53304 ■ "The Great Software Equalizer" in *Hispanic Business* **(Vol. 24, No. 4, April 2002, pp. 64)**
Pub: Hispanic Business Inc.
Ed: Roger Harris. Description: With Oracle Small Business Suite 7.5, small companies will have use of a suite of office applications costing only $99 per month.

53305 ■ "The Great Wall" in *Entrepreneur* **(Vol. 32, No. 4, April 2004, pp. 38)**
Pub: Entrepreneur Media, Inc.
Ed: Eric Bender. Description: For Internet security, it is essential for all small businesses to use a firewall to protect software and hardware. Information about Windows XP, Zone Labs' free ZoneAlarm and ZoneAlarm Pro is given.

53306 ■ "Grist: More Power Than Point" in *Inc.* **(August 1, 2003)**
Pub: Gruner & Jahr USA Publishing
Ed: Adam Hanft. Description: Although there is an estimated 400 million computers using Microsoft's computer software program PowerPoint, many believe it radically oversimplifies issues.

53307 ■ "Groove makes it possible to light up the edge" in *Fast Company* **(May 2001, pp. 96)**
Pub: Fast Company
Ed: John Ellis. Description: Profile of Groove Networks Inc., and the software that makes it possible to share text, to share files, to communicate by voice, and to work with other computers in a secure environment.

53308 ■ "Grow Your Market" in *PC Computing* **(April 2000, pp. 100)**
Pub: Ziff-Davis Inc.
Ed: Jason Compton. Description: Maps of all kinds can add value to a Web site and even increase customer usage. This article gives brief evaluations of map databases that can be used.

53309 ■ *Growing Your Business Using QuickBooks 6.0*
Pub: Accelerated Learning Systems, Inc.
Ed: Released: 1998. Price: $149.00 (VHS) 4 cassettes. Description: Designated for small business owners & bookkeepers, covers QuickBooks software version 6.01 Vol. 1 covers Getting Started; Vol. 2 - Sales & Accounts Receivable; Vol. 3 Purchases & Accounts Payable; Vol. 4 - Payroll, Time Tracking & Networking. Basic & intermediate topics.

53310 ■ "Hand-to-hand combat" in *Black Enterprise* **(Vol. 31, No. 5, December 2000, pp. 72)**
Pub: Earl Graves Publishing Co.
Description: Information about the new software applications that take aim at viruses attacking Palm OS devices is covered.

53311 ■ "Handle Web Transactions with the BEA WebLogic Server" in *E-business Advisor* **(Vol. 18, No. 2, February 2000, pp. 30)**
Pub: Advisor Media, Inc.
Ed: Brian Benz. Description: A profile of BEA Systems' WebLogic Application Server, which offers excellent servlet development, deployment and management tools as well as outstanding class file selection and documentation.

53312 ■ "Handy Databases" in *PC Magazine* **(February 6, 2001, pp. 38)**
Pub: Ziff-Davis Publishing Company
Ed: Marge Brown. Description: A review of DDH Software's HanDBase Desktop databases, and other software, for Palm personal digital assistants (PDAs). The application offers 300 databases or users can create their own.

53313 ■ "Has the Free Software Paradox Been Solved?" in *Venture Capital Journal* **(September 1, 2005)**
Pub: Thomason Financial Inc.
Ed: Tom Stein. Description: Open source software is a popular investment for VCs in 2005. Open source is changing the way software is developed and used by corporations.

53314 ■ "Help for Your Small Business: Office 2000's Small Business Tools can help you manage and run a small business more effectively" in *PCMagazine*
Pub: Ziff-Davis Publishing Company
Ed: Neil Randall. Description: Microsoft Office 2000 Small Business Tools suite is a useful package that comes standard with any Office 2000 version except the Standard Edition. While it is not a full-featured financial package, it has some notable features. The suite comes with four components: Business Planner (BP), Small Business Customer Manager (SBCM), Direct Mail Manager (DMM), and Small Business Financial Manager (SBFM). Particularly useful are the quick financial summaries available through SBFM and the wealth of information and assistance covered in the Business Planner module.

53315 ■ "He's Still Standing" in *Black Enterprise* **(Vol. 34, No. 2, September 2003, pp. 43)**
Pub: Earl Graves Publishing Co.
Ed: Nicole Lewis. Description: Profile of William Burton, owner of Professional Systems Inc., a firm that consults, implements, and customizes computer software and hardware for clients in the Chicago, Illinois area. Burton has been successful despite rejections for loans.

53316 ■ "Hidden messages" in *Black Enterprise* (Vol. 32, No. 7, February 2002, pp. 56)
Pub: Earl Graves Publishing Co.
Ed: Cristina Gair. **Description:** Numerous developers and programmers have created software to detect steganography and to hide information. Steganography is a method of hiding encrypted messages within files or pictures. Profiles of some of the products available for small businesses are highlighted.

53317 ■ "Hot disks" in *Entrepreneur* (Vol. 30, No. 1, January 2002, pp. 41)
Pub: Entrepreneur Media Inc.
Ed: Liane Gouthro. **Description:** Profile of new software products available to small business, including Norton Internet Security 2002, network security software; Connectix's Virtual PC for Windows, terminal emulation software; and Microsoft's Great Plains Small Business Manager, integrated accounting software.

53318 ■ "How Adobe is Pushing Quark Off the Page" in *Business 2.0* (Vol. 6, September 2005, No. 8, pp. 56)
Pub: Time, Inc.
Ed: Mark Borden. **Description:** According to a market research firm, Adobe's InDesign has taken market share from Quark's XPress. Customers in publishing, advertising, and architecture are choosing Adobe because Quark's software has remained unchanged for four years.

53319 ■ "How ASPs Can Accelerate Your E-Business" in *E-business Advisor* (Vol. 18, No. 3, March 2000, pp. 20)
Pub: Advisor Media, Inc.
Ed: Lewis Ward. **Description:** E-commerce issues, including return policies, scalability and customer service are explored.

53320 ■ "How Good Are Google's Extras?" in *Business Week* (January 16, 2006, No. 3967, pp. 88-90)
Pub: McGraw-Hill Companies
Ed: **Description:** An overview of Froogle, Maps, Gmail, and Picasa 2, Google's added services is presented. These extras offer shopping information, satellite and road maps, photo editing software, and email at no charge to users.

53321 ■ "How MMetrics Is Making Mobile Content Count" in *Business 2.0* (Vol. 6, May 2005, No. 4, pp. 28)
Pub: Time, Inc.
Ed: Michael Myser. **Description:** MMetrics, the Seattle, Washington startup, is setting its course to do for mobile content what Nielsen Media Research did for television through the use of online interviews and monitoring of software installed on cellular phones.

53322 ■ "I Think We're Up to the Challenge" *Business Week Online* (March 16, 2002)
Pub: McGraw-Hill, Inc.
Description: An interview with Red Hat CEO, Matthew Szulik. Szulik talks about his strategy for turning free software into a profitable business.

53323 ■ "IBM Corp." in *PC Magazine* (March 7, 2000, pp. 158)
Pub: Ziff-Davis Publishing Company
Ed: Bruce Brown, Cade Metz, Carol Venezia. **Description:** IBM's Netfinity 5000 server, priced at $3,960 with a 600MHz Pentium III CPU and dual 9GB hard disks, works well with its $2,259 PC 300PL desktop client and bundled software to create an excellent E-business solution. The company backs up its E-services solution with top-notch service and high-quality hardware. IBM offers customers the Home Page Creator and Small Business WebConnections products through its IBM Global Small Business organization. Both tools are very well designed; Home Page Creator is a Java tool that lets users build and publish a storefront from within the browser, while the higher-end WebConnections service package includes Internet access, E-mail and file sharing for five to 100 clients. IBM earns the Editors' Choice rating for the best E-business hardware, software and service solutions.

53324 ■ "IBM readies Linux suite" in *InfoWorld* (Vol. 22, No. 45, November 6, 2000, pp. 5)
Pub: InfoWorld
Description: IBM Small Business Suite for Linux features applications and tools to make it easier for users, developers, and integrators to host and create messaging and collaboration systems, to build Web sites, and to manage data.

53325 ■ "IBM gives Lotus the muscle to punch above its weight" in *PC Magazine* (Vol. 9, No. 5, May 2000, pp. 34)
Pub: Ziff-Davis Publishing Company
Ed: Geoff Einon. **Description:** Profile of Raven, the new software that will be able to extend its searches beyond Notes databases to encompass company-wide data stores. Its information will be made available through a personalized Knowledge Portal that encapsulates any individual as a collection of contacts, tasks, interests and job focus.

53326 ■ "IBM Readies Linux Suite for Small Biz" in *Network World* (November 6, 2000, pp. NA)
Pub: Network World Inc.
Ed: Ed Scannell. **Description:** A profile of IBM's Linux suite for small businesses.

53327 ■ "In control: Organize your work-and your workers-with Wintility Pro" in *Entrepreneur* (Vol. 30, No. 2, February 2002, pp. 34)
Pub: Entrepreneur Media Inc.
Ed: Liane Gouthro. **Description:** Profile of the new software, Wintility Pro from PX Technologies, which catalogs important e-mail messages, documents everything from text files to presentations and also allows secure sharing within an organization.

53328 ■ "In the Groove" in *Entrepreneur* (Vol. 31, No. 7, July 2003, pp. 40)
Pub: Entrepreneur Media, Inc.
Ed: Liane Cassavoy. **Description:** Profile of Groove Workspace 2.5 from Groove Networks, providing tools that allow users to share and co-edit documents and chat; the software features enhanced integration with Microsoft Outlook, and the professional version with Microsoft's Sharepoint Team Services.

53329 ■ "In-Sync Web Authoring" in *PC Magazine* (February 20, 2001, pp. 38)
Pub: Ziff-Davis Publishing Company
Ed: Luisa Simone. **Description:** Macromedia has added to their hold on the Web authoring software market with recent releases of Dreamweaver and Fireworks. The three new products, Dreamweaver 4.0, Dreamweaver UltraDev 4.0, and Fireworks 4.0 have common interfaces and standardized keyboard shortcuts. New layouts and added features such as debugging, coding, and reference tools improve on the ease of use and capabilities of the products.

53330 ■ "In Texas a 'transformative' merger" in *Barron's* (August 18, 2003, pp. T3)
Pub: Barron's
Ed: Mark Veverka. **Description:** The merger of Pervasive Software and Data Junction Corporation, signals a major shift in the market for application integration middleware. The two companies will combine efforts in extract, transform, and load (ETL) technology, which is poised to replace the pricier enterprise application integration (EAI) model.

53331 ■ "Information Technology Software" in *Business Week* (January 23, 2006, No. 3968, pp. 65-66)
Pub: McGraw-Hill Companies
Ed: Sarah Lacy. **Description:** Profile of Oracle's John Wookey and his boss, Larry Ellison. The two are working to meld together the company's latest string of acquisitions.

53332 ■ "Inside the box: Buyer's guide: New software slowing you down?" in *Entrepreneur* (Vol. 30, No. 1, January 2002, pp. 44)
Pub: Entrepreneur Media Inc.

Ed: Amanda C. Kooser. **Description:** Comparisons of the AMD Athlon and Intel Pentium 4 processors to use when making performance upgrades to office PCs.

53333 ■ "Inspiring a Growth Industry. Inspiration Software Changes Heading and Reaps the Rewards" in *Business Journal-Portland* (Aug. 15, 2003)
Pub: American City Business Journals, Inc.
Ed: Aliza Earnshaw. **Description:** Profile of Inspiration Software Inc., located in Portland, Oregon. The small firm offers innovative educational software for elementary school students. The company's main clients are cash-strapped schools looking for ways to improve students' test scores.

53334 ■ "Integrate Enterprise Applications with XML" in *E-business Advisor* (Vol. 18, No. 5, May 2000, pp. 16)
Pub: Advisor Media, Inc.
Ed: David S. Linthicum. **Description:** The extensible markup language, or XML, can be used to develop enterprise application integration (EAI) software, as well as business-to-business (B2B) integration software. XML supports common metadata standards throughout the Internet to make B2B and internal enterprise application integration easier.

53335 ■ "Internet or Desktop" in *PC Magazine* (February 20, 2001, pp. 145)
Pub: Ziff-Davis Publishing Company
Ed: Wayne Kawamoto. **Description:** Reviews of accounting software packages that are available for the desktop or online.

53336 ■ "Internet Firewalls" in *Home Business* (Vol. 12, March/April 2005, No. 2, pp. 88)
Pub: Home Business Magazine
Ed: David P. Hunter. **Description:** Importance for a home-based business to use a good firewall to protect their computers is stressed. Information is offered to help choose the best firewall for a business.

53337 ■ "Intuit launches small business marketplace" in *Network World* (September 18, 2000, pp. NA)
Pub: Network World Inc.
Ed: Sam Costello. **Description:** A profile of QuickBooks Shopping Source, targeted at small businesses. The service will provide discounts on business supplies and services, ranging from computer to clothing, and even janitorial services.

53338 ■ "Intuitively clear: the king of personal-finance software sets sights on small business" in *Barron's* (Vol. 82, Feb. 24, 2003, pp.17)
Pub: Barron's
Ed: Jay Palmer. **Description:** Demand for software products by Intuit Inc. is likely to continue to increase, thereby positively affecting the company's stock price. One analyst predicts that the new company's earnings growth will exceed 50 percent in 2003, as more small businesses buy the new software packages.

53339 ■ "The iPod Squad" in *Entrepreneur* (Vol. 33, February 2005, No. 2, pp. 40)
Pub: Entrepreneur Media Inc.
Ed: Amanda C. Kooser. **Description:** Software applications are making iPods more practical for small business use. Profile of the ProVue Panorama iPod Organizer, which can handle data from any program that exports into text files.

53340 ■ "iRise: Real Promise in Simulations" in *Business Week Online* (February 2, 2005)
Pub: McGraw-Hill Companies
Ed: Olga Kharif. **Description:** Profile of iRise, the three year old software company that has created 300 custom-designed software packages.

53341 ■ "It's Alive! New Software You Play Dr. Frankenstein" in *Black Enterprise* (Vol. 35, November 2004, No. 4, pp. 64)
Pub: Earl G. Graves Publishing Co. Inc.

Ed: Schuyler K. Esprit. **Description:** Review of Peter Plantec's book, Virtual Humans: Creating the Illusion Personality. The book is a resource for graphic designers, scientific researchers, students, technophobes and is accompanied by a CD-ROM that allows the user to build a virtual character.

53342 ■ "It's a Team Thing" in *Black Enterprise* **(Vol. 35, December 2004, No. 5, pp. 67)**
Pub: Earl G. Graves Publishing Co. Inc.
Ed: Bridget McCrea. **Description:** Larry Sheffield's ability to build and motivate teams in NEC's Solutions Platform Group is examined. Sheffield oversees the company's 200 employees in the firm's mobile solutions, software, server, advanced optical, customer and high-performance computing divisions.

53343 ■ "Jazzed About Work" in *Fast Company* **(May 2001, pp. 193)**
Pub: Fast Company
Ed: Bill Breen. **Description:** Ray Ozzie, the creator of Lotus Notes and the founder of Groove Networks Inc., talks about the possibilities of software-enabled collaboration for businesses.

53344 ■ "Jeff Jonas" in *Entrepreneur* **(Vol. 32, September 2004, No. 9, pp. 24)**
Pub: Entrepreneur Media Inc.
Ed: Sara Wilson. **Description:** Profile of Jeff Jonas, founder of SRD, a company specializing in the large-scale identification of individuals and their relationships with others. SRD focuses on the production of patent-pending technologies and software products, particularly with the government to address issues of national concern while protecting individual's privacy.

53345 ■ "Just down the block" in *Entrepreneur* **(Vol. 30, No. 1, January 2002, pp. 18)**
Pub: Entrepreneur Media Inc.
Description: Adkey software has developed a program that denies access to users who used ad-filtering software that block a company's advertising.

53346 ■ "Keeping Their Options Open" in *Boston Business Journal* **(Vol. 23, No. 26, August 1, 2003, pp. 3)**
Pub: American City Business Journals
Description: Profile of Boston, Massachusetts-based Progressive Software Inc., including an examination of Boston-area technology companies as highlighted by the plight of Progressive Software Inc. Topics include economic conditions, competition, and financial management.

53347 ■ "Kick the Habit" in *Home Office Computing* **(Vol. 17, No. 1, January 1999, pp. 67)**
Pub: Line56 Media
Ed: Joanne Cleaver. **Description:** A guide to using technology for more efficient time management in home offices is presented. A good filing system can make a difference when organizing an office. A service called Paper Tiger combines the assistance of a professional organizer with maintenance software.

53348 ■ "Know Thy Customer: How CRM Software Helps One Company Deliver" in *My Business* **(October/November 2003, pp. 46)**
Pub: My Business Magazine
Ed: Karen J. Bannan. **Description:** The cost savings and benefits for small businesses using customer relationship management software to improve service, increase efficiency, reduce customer service calls, automate marketing, and retain existing customers are examined.

53349 ■ "Know Your Customers" in *PC Computing* **(April 2000, pp. 94)**
Pub: Ziff-Davis Inc.
Ed: Jason Compton. **Description:** Software and on-line solutions for digital mapping are reviewed. MapInfo's MapInfo Professional 5.5 offers almost unlimited options for both generating maps and analyzing information. ESRI's BusinessMap Pro, is a collection of

maps with solid graphing and charting features. The Corporate version adds extra business-to-business data. Microsoft's MapPoint 2000 is very easy to use, but has fewer features than BusinessMap Pro. DemographicsNow.com is a Web-based that includes interactive maps and helps users answer crucial questions about customers and works with the Autodesk Map Guide browser plug-in, which is easy to use.

53350 ■ "The Latest and Greatest Disease" in *Fortune* **(Vol. 142, No. 9, October 16, 2000, pp. 312X)**
Pub: Time Inc.
Ed: Joel Dreyfuss. **Description:** Is it time to upgrade your hardware and software products?

53351 ■ "Legal Eagle?" in *Entrepreneur* **(Vol. 32, October 2004, No. 10, pp. 89)**
Pub: Entrepreneur Media Inc.
Ed: Gwen Moran. **Description:** Important updates on marketing law are shared, including an amendment to telemarketing sales rules, Internet spam, and security software.

53352 ■ "Let Your Fingers Do the Locking: Forgotten That Password?" in *Fortune* **(Vol. 151, January 24, 2005, No. 2, pp. 42)**
Pub: Time Inc.
Ed: Peter Lewis. **Description:** Profile of the new technology that allows users to access computers with fingerprint-reading devices. American Power Conversion, Sony, IBM, and other firms have developed password-management devices that can act as a lock and key for encrypting specific files and folders on a computer.

53353 ■ "License to Upgrade" in *Entrepreneur* **(Vol. 32, September 2004, No. 9, pp. 44)**
Pub: Entrepreneur Media Inc.
Description: CDW offers a free Software License Tracker geared to a growing business.

53354 ■ "Life after business" in *Women In Business* **(Vol. 52, No. 2, March 2000, pp. 25)**
Pub: The ABWA Co., Inc.
Ed: Rachel Warbington. **Description:** Memories can be preserved either in computerized form or in a traditional scrapbook. Photographs will not deteriorate if they are retained in digital format, but products are also available to preserve traditional scrapbooks.

53355 ■ "Long Island's Patent Production Falls Nearly 20 Percent Since 1988" in *Long Island Business News* **(March 5, 2004)**
Pub: Dolan Media Newswires
Ed: Ken Schachter. **Description:** Long Island's future economic health is tied to industries such as life sciences, software development and defense-industry prototyping and design rather than large-scale manufacturing. Patent growth is used to gauge the economic progress of the area.

53356 ■ "Low-Cost Teleconferencing" in *My Business* **(February/March 2004, pp. 17)**
Pub: My Business Magazine
Description: Profile of Apple's new iSight, a cylindrical camera and microphone that connects to a Macintosh computer via high-speed firewire and Apple's proprietary multimedia Internet messaging software iCath-AV, providing always-on videoconferencing.

53357 ■ "A Macro View at Microsoft" in *Hispanic Business* **(January/February 2005, pp. 24, 26, 28)**
Pub: Hispanic Business
Ed: Judi Erickson. **Description:** Orlando Ayala is targeting small and mid-size companies around the world to increase the global reach of technology firm Microsoft. Orlando discusses marketing strategies for selling Microsoft Business Solutions worldwide.

53358 ■ "Macromedia Inc. Strikes Gold Worth $55M HQ Buy" in *San Francisco Business Times* **(Vol. 18, No. 2, August 22, 2003, pp. 1)**
Pub: American City Business Journals
Ed: James Temple. **Description:** Macromedia, provider of business Web and software applications, is moving its corporate headquarters to a group of San Francisco office buildings.

53359 ■ "Mail call" in *Entrepreneur* **(Vol. 31, No. 5, May 2003, pp. 38)**
Pub: Entrepreneur Media Inc.
Ed: Liane Cassavoy. **Description:** Profile of the Nelson Email Organizer from Caelo Software is presented. The software sorts email messaged by date and correspondent and sells for $39.95.

53360 ■ "Making Book" in *Entrepreneur* **(Vol. 33, February 2005, No. 2, pp. 37)**
Pub: Entrepreneur Media Inc.
Ed: Mike Hogan. **Description:** Microsoft Office 2003 has designed a new Office Small Business Accounting program that offers ease in connecting to other Office applications.

53361 ■ "Manage Projects in Real Time" in *PC Magazine* **(February 20, 2001, pp. 37)**
Pub: Ziff-Davis Publishing Company
Ed: Sheryl Canter. **Description:** A profile of the Internet-based, cross-platform project management solution software, TeamCenter 4.0, from Inovie Software.

53362 ■ "Manager in a box" in *Hispanic Business* **(Vol. 22, No. 10, October 2000, pp. 114)**
Pub: Hispanic Business
Ed: Roger Harris. **Description:** The Tenant Pro 5.0 property management software system is evaluated. The package is an easy to use product, combining an accounting program and a useful database management program, and is suitable for either small or very large numbers of properties.

53363 ■ "May I Help You?" in *Inc.* **(Volume 28, January 2006, No. 1, pp. 31-32)**
Pub: Inc. Magazine
Ed: Ellen Neuborne. **Description:** Life-chat software is helping online retailers attract buying customers. Life-chat vendors include LiveAdmins.com, LivePerson.com, and BoldChat.com.

53364 ■ "Meet Your New Executives" in *Inc.* **(Volume 28, January 2006, No. 1, pp. 57-58)**
Pub: Inc. Magazine
Ed: David H. Freedman. **Description:** Are computers replacing executives in the business place? New, powerful software is capable of understanding data.

53365 ■ "Microsoft Launches Small Business Web Services" in *Network World* **(September 25, 2000, pp. NA)**
Pub: Network World Inc.
Ed: George A. Chidi, Jr. **Description:** A profile of Microsoft's new program that brings small businesses into cyberspace. Microsoft's Business Web Services are designed for non-technical small business customers, providing domain registration, business e-mail, site creation and hosting, e-commerce and Web-based marketing services.

53366 ■ "Microsoft Lawyer Makes Living Hunting Down Pirates" in *Altanta Journal-Constitution* **(January 28, 2007)**
Pub: Cox Newspapers, Inc.
Ed: Bill Husted. **Description:** Mary Jo Schrade works to combat software piracy for Microsoft; Schrade uses leads from the public and secret shoppers buying computers and software that is then tested for legitimacy.

53367 ■ "Microsoft Makes Security Vow" in *Long Island Business News* **(February 6, 2004)**
Pub: Dolan Media Newswires
Description: Microsoft Corporation has offered $250,000 for the names of hackers responsible for the MyDoom computer worm targeting Windows operating systems. Microsoft has also redoubled its efforts to make its products more secure.

53368 ■ "Microsoft Money 2004 Small Business: www.microsoft.com/money/ business" in *Entrepreneur* **(Vol. 31, No. 12, December 2003, pp. 8)**
Pub: Entrepreneur Media Inc.
Ed: Steve Cooper. **Description:** Profile of Microsoft's latest money management software that allows businesses to download information for various financial institutions.

53369 ■ "Microsoft Project" in *Women In Business* **(Vol. 52, No. 5, September-October 2000, pp. 36)**
Pub: The ABWA Co., Inc.
Description: Issues concerning the benefits that can be gained from using office software packages such as Microsoft Project. The facilities offered by this computer program for the management of projects is reviewed.

53370 ■ "Microsoft spots" in *Entrepreneur* **(Vol. 30, No. 3, March 2002, pp. 44)**
Pub: Entrepreneur Media Inc.
Ed: Amanda C. Kooser. **Description:** Profile of Microsoft's Strategic Technology Protection Program that makes software safer for businesses.

53371 ■ "Microsoft to Unveil Product to Manage Net Communications" in *Boston Globe* **(March 7, 2005)**
Pub: New York Times Company
Ed: Hiawatha Bray. **Description:** Microsoft announced a new product that will allow businesses to manage telephones, instant messaging, email and video conferencing through a single system.

53372 ■ "Microsoft Windows Millennium Edition" in *Home Office Computing* **(Vol. 18, No. 10, October 2000, pp. 26)**
Pub: Scholastic Inc.
Ed: Eric Grevstad. **Description:** Microsoft Windows Millenium Edition (Windows ME) is a better and more useful product for home users than Windows 2000, which needs faster, newer hardware for full performance. WindowsME comes with multimedia enhancements including Windows Movie Maker and Windows Image Acquisition programming interface. Also, users can download, free of cost, Internet Explorer 5.5 and Windows Media Player 7.

53373 ■ *Microsoft Windows Small Business Server 2003 R2 Administrator's Companion*
Pub: Microsoft Press
Ed: Charlie Russel; Sharon Crawford. **Released:** July 2006. **Price:** $80.99. **Description:** Profile of Microsoft's Small Business Server R2.

53374 ■ "Microsoft's Bulging Security Portfolio" in *Business Week Online* **(February 9, 2005)**
Pub: McGraw-Hill Companies
Ed: Jay Greene. **Description:** Microsoft intends to be a leader in software security. After buying the privately held Sybari, Microsoft will increase its protection for email servers by scanning email for attached viruses before they reach business networks.

53375 ■ "Microsoft's Office-Come-Lately" in *Business Week Online* **(February 16, 2006)**
Pub: McGraw-Hill Companies
Description: Microsoft is releasing its newest version of Office suite products in 2006. The 2007 version will allow consumers to pick and choose the features they require.

53376 ■ "Mike and Wendy Sign, Seal and Deliver $450,000 a Year Sending Greeting Cards..." in *Small Business Opportunities* **(Vol. 17, May 2005)**
Pub: Harris Publications Inc.
Description: Profile of Mike and Wendy Zavilla who used customized software from Client Connection to create a greeting card mailing service. The couple shares insight into ways they are able to tap into each other's strengths.

53377 ■ "A "Milestone" for Web Services: Microsoft's Dan'l Lewin Talks About Indigo" in *Business Week Online* **(February 8, 2005)**
Pub: McGraw-Hill Companies
Description: In an interview with Daniel Lewin, vice president at Microsoft, he talks about the company's Web services strategy. Microsoft is planning to reveal the details of Indigo, the code name for a new way Microsoft is hoping software developers will embrace when creating software applications.

53378 ■ "Mix and Match" in *Internet World* **(Vol. 7, No. 1, January 15, 2001, pp. 60)**
Pub: Mecklermedia Corporation
Ed: David F. Carr. **Description:** The computer software industry is turning to component software, both as part of a company's offering or the total offering. As it stands now, many companies using these components look to more than one company when designing Web sites.

53379 ■ "Monitor and Manage Your Web Server" in *E-business Advisor* **(Vol. 18, No. 1, January 2000, pp. 38)**
Pub: Advisor Media, Inc.
Ed: Terrance A. Crow. **Description:** A profile of WebManage Technologies Enterprise Reporter 5.0 network management software, which monitors Web traffic and online files at an affordable price.

53380 ■ "Monitor Your E-Business Systems' Health" in *E-business Advisor* **(Vol. 17, No. 12, December 1999, pp. 22)**
Pub: Advisor Media, Inc.
Ed: Bill Jaeger. **Description:** E-businesses should implement a program of ongoing systems monitoring, which tracks and reports key metrics on business-critical systems, as well as occasional performance testing. Ongoing systems monitoring makes it possible to warn users about slowdowns in advance, thus building customer loyalty. A directory of systems-monitoring software and services companies is included.

53381 ■ "MyPayNet" in *Entrepreneur.com* **(Vol. 34, January 2006, No. 1, pp. 6)**
Pub: Entrepreneur Media Inc.
Ed: Steve Cooper. **Description:** MyPayNet is an electronic invoicing and payment service designed to help small companies send and receive payments electronically.

53382 ■ "The Myth of the Superstar CEO" in *Venture Capital Journal* **(November 1, 2004)**
Pub: Thomason Financial Inc.
Ed: Ravi Chiruvolu. **Description:** PeopleSoft, the enterprise software company, replaced its CEO Craig Conway with founder and chairman, Dave Duffield. Whether a superstar CEO is worth the time, effort and additional equity required to retain him or her is addressed.

53383 ■ "Navigate the Application Framework Terrain" in *E-business Advisor* **(Vol. 18, No. 1, January 2000, pp. 16)**
Pub: Advisor Media, Inc.
Ed: Dan Sullivan. **Description:** Software vendors are bringing various, differing e-business tools, suites, and vertical applications to the marketplace, all classified as e-business application frameworks. Meanwhile, certain e-business developers' requirements are emerging as centrally important, including scalability, security and reduced time to market. Product overviews are included.

53384 ■ "The New School" in *Entrepreneur.com* **(Vol. 34, February 2006, No. 2, pp. 28)**
Pub: Entrepreneur Media Inc.
Ed: Mark Henricks. **Description:** The School of the Future, backed by Microsoft Corporation, will give each pupil a PC and teachers will present lessons on interactive whiteboards that are connected to the Internet and equipped with speakers and capable of playing DVDs. Graduates will have digital literacy skills to meet employer demands.

53385 ■ "New World a Player in Public Safety" in *Crain's Detroit Business* **(Vol. 21, January 17, 2005, No. 3, pp. 28)**
Pub: Crain Communications Inc. - Detroit
Ed: Andrew Dietderich. **Description:** Profile of Larry Leinweber, owner of New World Systems Corporation based in Troy, Michigan. The firm sells and services software to help manage city, county and university public-safety departments. New World reported revenues of nearly $45 million in 2004 and expects it to climb to $50 million in 2005.

53386 ■ "News and Reviews" in *Home Business* **(Vol. 13, January/February 2006, No. 1, pp. 98)**
Pub: Home Business Magazine
Description: Information for closing business deals online, Web-based human resources small business software, noise canceling audio headphones, and tips for launching and marketing new products is given.

53387 ■ "Not On His Watch" in *Entrepreneur.com* **(Vol. 34, January 2006, No. 1, pp. 35)**
Pub: Entrepreneur Media Inc.
Ed: Sara Wilson. **Description:** Profile of Bryan Hammond, age 21, founder of ExploreAnywhere Software LLC. Hammond's computer-monitoring products cater to parents, employers and educators. The software company projects 2005 sales at more than $1 million.

53388 ■ "Novel microarray applications" in *Small Business Economic Trends* **(February 2002, pp. 1)**
Pub: National Federation of Independent Business Foundation
Ed: Neil McKenna. **Description:** Companies are exploring new applications and protocols in the areas of data-analysis software that is linked to microarrays obtained from gene expression and protein-drug interactions.

53389 ■ "Now Presenting..." in *Entrepreneur* **(Vol. 32, No. 1, January 2004, pp. 46)**
Pub: Entrepreneur Media, Inc.
Ed: Amanda C. Kooser. **Description:** Introductions to the new line of portable document cameras (PDCs) on the market. Most PDCs work through a projector or by hooking them up to a monitor.

53390 ■ "Nuance Gains Voice in Noisy Speech Market" in *San Francisco Business Times* **(Vol. 18, No. 2, August 22, 2003, pp. 3)**
Pub: American City Business Journals
Ed: Lizette Wilson. **Description:** Examination of ScanSoft's acquisition of rival SpeechWorks International Inc., maker of speech recognition products. Topics include market development plans, market share, and strategic planning.

53391 ■ "O2 Interactive Realizes Profits as it Builds Relationships" in *San Diego Business Journal* **(Vol. 28, January 8, 2007, No. 2, pp. 9)**
Pub: San Diego Business Journal Associates
Ed: Amy Yarnall. **Description:** O2 Interactive, seven-employee firm, that creates customer relation software for the homebuilding industry, doubled its sales in 2006.

53392 ■ "Office Offers" in *Entrepreneur* **(Vol. 31, No. 11, November 2003, pp. 60)**
Pub: Entrepreneur Media, Inc.
Ed: Amanda C. Kooser. **Description:** Profile of Microsoft's new Office 2003 Small Business Edition. The software includes Excel, Outlook, PowerPoint, Publisher and Works, and updates like junk mail handling, XML file support in Word and Excel, and OneNote that lets users capture and organize notes.

53393 ■ "On-Demand Software a Hot New Market" in *San Jose Mercury News* **(February 25, 2005)**
Pub: Knight-Ridder/Tribune Business News
Ed: John Boudreau. **Description:** On-demand software is being offered to new companies over the Internet. Small business owners discuss this software.

53394 ■ "On the Fast Track: How Technology Is Speeding Incentive Delivery" in *Sales & Marketing Management* **(Vol. 157, February 2005)**
Pub: VNU Business Media
Ed: Alan Horowitz. **Description:** Profile of the software company Synygy Inc. and its enterprise incentive management product. The software and services help to manage incentive compensation for sales staff, or any employee of a company, which promotes sales growth and employee motivation.

53395 ■ "On the Radar" in *E-business Advisor* (Vol. 18, No. 7, July 2000, pp. 8)
Pub: Advisor Media, Inc.
Description: E-marketplaces are still dogged by such problems as the inability to complete transactions and homegrown solutions that do not support improvements. Software vendors are faced with the need to supply packaged applications that offer four major functions: creating and sustaining markets, researching and building relationships, negotiating and closing deals, and fulfilling, settling, and servicing business.

53396 ■ "On a Roll" in *Entrepreneur* (Vol. 28, No. 8, August 2000, pp. 23)
Pub: Entrepreneur Media Inc.
Ed: Gisela M. Pedroza. **Description:** A review of Label Writer Turbo, which aids with mailing efforts for small businesses.

53397 ■ "One-Track Mind" in *Entrepreneur. com* (Vol. 34, February 2006, No. 2, pp. 33)
Pub: Entrepreneur Media Inc.
Ed: Heather Clancy. **Description:** Profile of Ananda Roberts, owner of nFocus Software, the maker of products that track data for the government, educational institutions, and nonprofit organizations. Roberts employs 35 workers at her Phoenix, Arizona company.

53398 ■ "Online Office" in *Entrepreneur* (Vol. 32, No. 1, January 2004, pp. 47)
Pub: Entrepreneur Media, Inc.
Ed: Liane Cassavoy. **Description:** Profile of Microsoft's Web conferencing with Office Live Meeting, which includes tools for application viewing and sharing, attendance reposing and recording.

53399 ■ "Only Time Will Tell" in *My Business* (June/July 2004, pp. 22)
Pub: My Business Magazine
Description: Profile of new software and broadcast technology developed by Microsoft that enables wrist watches to provide information updated via FM radio signals, weather reports, personal instant messages, personal calendars, and other consumer and business reviews and resources.

53400 ■ *Open Source Solutions for Small Business Problems*
Pub: Charles River Media
Ed: John Locke. **Released:** May 2004. **Price:** $39.95 (US), $55.95 (Canadian). **Description:** Open source software provides solutions to many small business problems such as tracking electronic documents, scheduling, accounting functions, managing contact lists, and reducing spam.

53401 ■ "Out of Control" in *Inc.* (September 1, 2003)
Pub: Gruner & Jahr USA Publishing
Ed: Susan Hansen. **Description:** Profile of Travis Parsons, founder of Elogex, an Internet-based software application that would enable clients to coordinate shipping and delivery services across multiple warehouses and destinations. When Parsons sold the firm he also lost his decision-making power.

53402 ■ "Out of Work from Offshoring, California Software Programmers Turn to eBay" in *San Jose Mercury News* (March 26, 2004)
Pub: Knight-Ridder/Tribune Business News
Ed: Matt Marshall. **Description:** Software programmers in California who have lost their jobs offshore, have listed themselves on eBay's auction site.

53403 ■ "Pain-Free Patching" in *Entrepreneur* (Vol. 32, November 2004, No. 11, pp. 62)
Pub: Entrepreneur Media Inc.
Ed: Liane Cassavoy. **Description:** Executive Software's Sitekeeper 3 allows information technology employees to determine hardware and software configuration throughout a company and lets you know if all products are licensed.

53404 ■ "Password Protection" in *Entrepreneur* (Vol. 32, December 2004, No. 12, pp. 52)
Pub: Entrepreneur Media Inc.
Ed: Liane Cassavoy. **Description:** Profile of Dekart's logon software. The $39 program allows users to store all Windows passwords on any portable storage device, much like a smart card, USB drive or hardware token.

53405 ■ "The Path of Lease Resistance" in *Home Office Computing* (Vol. 19, No. 1, January 2001, pp. 85)
Pub: Scholastic Inc.
Ed: Todd W. Carter. **Description:** Some small business owners have turned to leasing instead of purchasing new computer equipment in order to keep offices up to date and minimize problems with obsolescence. Leasing allows faster upgrades than conventional purpose, frees up money for other investments and makes sense for property with a relatively short useful life span. The IRS distinguishes between a true or 'operating' lease, which may be tax-deductible, and a 'finance' lease, which it does not recognize as a business expense.

53406 ■ "PC Maker Systemax Launches Software Unit" in *Long Island Business News* (January 30, 2004)
Pub: Dolan Media Newswires
Ed: Ken Schachter. **Description:** Profile of Systemax, Inc., the largest personal computer manufacturer in Long Island, New York. Systemax is now producing a business-software suite that will compete with companies such as Salesforce.com, PeopleSoft Inc., SAP AG and Siebel Systems Inc. The new unit, headed by Matthew Ehrlich, is called ProfitCenter Software, or PCS.

53407 ■ "A Penchant for Profits" in *Entrepreneur* (Vol. 33, August 2005, No. 8, pp. 53)
Pub: Entrepreneur Media Inc.
Ed: David Worrell. **Description:** Profile of co-founder and CEO of Avidian Technologies, Bellevue, Washington is presented. James Wong's firm has grown 400 percent annually since 2003, with more than 7,000 registers users of its software.

53408 ■ "A Perfect Visual PIM-for Some" in *PC Magazine* (February 20, 2001, pp. 52)
Pub: Ziff-Davis Publishing Company
Ed: Alfred Poor. **Description:** A profile of Info Select 6, a new personal information manager (PIM).

53409 ■ "Personal Business" in *Business Week* (January 23, 2006, No. 3968, pp. 87)
Pub: McGraw-Hill Companies
Ed: Gene G. Marcial. **Description:** Outback Steakhouse's chain of 1,298 restaurants is using a value menu to attract baby boomers to its restaurants across the country; Shamrock Capital Advisors has acquired a 6.2 percent stake in Intrado and an 11 percent share in iPass; Perficient's stocks have risen from 5.30 to 9.60 due to a surge in sales of its WebSphere software.

53410 ■ "Pick Your Startup Tool" in *Black Enterprise* (Vol. 36, November 2005, No. 4, pp. 74)
Pub: Earl G. Graves Publishing Co. Inc.
Ed: Sonya Donaldson. **Description:** Besides being a good business plan, financial management tools are an asset for planning a marketing strategy. Business Plan Pro Standard, QuickBooks, Peachtree, and Business Resource Software can help startups write business plans that include pricing strategy, advertising, and budgeting.

53411 ■ "Picture This" in *Entrepreneur* (Vol. 33, January 2005, No. 1, pp. 43)
Pub: Entrepreneur Media Inc.
Ed: Liane Cassavoy. **Description:** Profile of PhatPad 2.0 from PhatWare. The device allows users to draw pictures or write notes, as well as access artwork from a PC.

53412 ■ "Plexus Finds Success in Helping Manufacturers with Cost-Cutting Software" in *Crain's Detroit Business* (Vol. 22, January 16, 2006)
Pub: Crain Communications Inc. - Detroit
Ed: Andrew Dietderich. **Description:** Plexus Systems LLC offers software and services that help companies operate more efficiently from inventory to accounting. The software is used at 270 manufacturing locations.

53413 ■ "Plumbing Web Connection" in *Harvard Business Review* (Vol. 81, No. 9, September 2003, pp. 18)
Pub: Harvard Business School Press
Ed: Morse Gardiner. **Description:** Bob Sutor answers five questions about the future economic impact of the Internet on business, in particular Web service software.

53414 ■ "Point of Sale: Software Giants Focus on Selling to Small Businesses" in *Entrepreneur* (Vol. 32, November 2004, No. 11, pp. 26)
Pub: Entrepreneur Media Inc.
Ed: Liane Cassavoy. **Description:** Small companies spent $10.1 billion on off-the-shelf software and big-name software companies are targeting small businesses with more products.

53415 ■ "Power Agent Puts More Power in Agents' Hands" in *South Florida Business Journal* (Vol. 23, No. 48, July 4, 2003, pp. 31)
Pub: American City Business Journals
Ed: Stephen Van Drake. **Description:** Profile of Rexelex's Power Agent software, which debuted in 2002, and its success with travel agents. The software allows agents to take orders via the Internet even when the office is closed.

53416 ■ "Practical Ideas for Improving Your Business" in *Journal of Accountancy* (Vol. 199, February 2005, No. 2, pp. 108)
Pub: American Institute of Certified Public Accountants
Ed: Stanley Zarowin. **Description:** Computers are playing a vital role in business growth. Should business managers or information technology staff be in charge of choosing the technical products and services for a company?

53417 ■ "The Price is Right" in *Inc.* (July 1, 2003)
Pub: Gruner & Jahr USA Publishing
Description: Profiles of profit-analyzing software to help small businesses set pricing for products and services are investigated.

53418 ■ "Process Online Payments Quickly and Effectively" in *E-business Advisor* (Vol. 18, No. 6, June 2000, pp. 34)
Pub: Advisor Media, Inc.
Ed: Glenn T. Shesney. **Description:** Assessment Systems Inc. (ASI), a purveyor of electronically administered tests, has deployed Payment Plus' LiveProcessor electronic commerce software, greatly boosting the number of payments the company can transact per hour. LiveProcessor, a Linux-based system, can process hundreds of transactions per minute during periods of high volume, with per-transaction response time averaging less than three seconds.

53419 ■ "Profile: Local Web Developer Plays a Starring Role in NASA's Mission to Mars" in *Crain's Chicago Business* (December 22, 2003)
Pub: Crain Communications, Inc.
Ed: Paul Merrion. **Description:** Profile of Web site developer Critical Mass Inc., the firm that designed a Web site for the National Aeronautics and Space Administration, one of the highest traffic Web sites in history. Critical Mass partnered with eTouch Systems Corporation, whose software updates the NASA site continuously. Web site visitors can access information on humans in space or exploration of the universe with links to specialized sites for children, students, educators and journalists.

53420 ■ **"Profiting from open source"** in *Harvard Business Review* (Vol. 78, No. 5, September-October 2000, pp. 22)
Pub: Harvard Business School Publishing Corp.
Description: This article describes how Hewlett-Packard developed its e-speak software and plans to give it away. The company will relinquish all control of the code.

53421 ■ **"Protect the Source"** in *Entrepreneur* (Vol. 33, February 2005, No. 2, pp. 46)
Pub: Entrepreneur Media Inc.
Ed: Amanda C. Kooser. **Description:** The leading anti-virus option for Linux users is Central Command's Vexira AntiVirust. It is vital to check with IT personnel before purchasing security software, especially if mixing a Linux server with Windows.

53422 ■ **"Protect your computer from potential viruses"** in *Women In Business* (Vol. 52, No. 3, May 2000, pp. 39)
Pub: The ABWA Co., Inc.
Ed: Dale Garrison. **Description:** Computer experts point out with careful use of e-mail and the introduction of anti-virus software programs, many users can avoid damage to their computers from computer viruses.

53423 ■ **"Pursuits"** in *Inc.* (Volume 27, March 2005, No. 3, pp. 62-63)
Pub: Inc. Magazine
Ed: Jess McCuan. **Description:** Profile of Greg James, founder of Topics Entertainment, an educational software developer. After years of success, James is devoting time to environmental causes and is making changes in his personal life.

53424 ■ **"Put a Hacker to Work"** in *Inc.* (Volume 28, January 2006, No. 1, pp. 39, 42)
Pub: Inc. Magazine
Ed: Darren Dahl. **Description:** Profile of software developer, TopCoder, shares its strategy to find and register the world's best programmers through code-writing contests where they have hackers solve tricky math problems or algorithms. The Connecticut firm employs 65,000 coders globally.

53425 ■ **"Put Your Web Applications to the Test"** in *E-business Advisor* (Vol. 18, No. 7, July 2000, pp. 44)
Pub: Advisor Media, Inc.
Ed: Guy Tal. **Description:** Testing Web applications has become more complex because the applications themselves have become increasingly sophisticated and interactive. The process of testing Web applications using Mercury Interactive's Astra Quick Test and Astra LoadTest is discussed.

53426 ■ **"Quick Pick"** in *Entrepreneur* (Vol. 31, No. 10, October 2003, pp. 89)
Pub: Entrepreneur Media, Inc.
Ed: Elizabeth Goodgold. **Description:** Ways to build customer loyalty are discussed, including the use of software that helps create postcards and newsletters.

53427 ■ *QuickBooks All-in-One Desk Reference for Dummies*
Pub: John Wiley & Sons, Incorporated
Ed: Stephen L. Nelson. **Released:** January 2005. **Price:** $29.99 (US), $42.99 (Canadian). **Description:** Compilation of nine self-contained minibooks to get the most from QuickBooks accounting software. Companion Web site with sample business plan workbook and downloadable profit-volume cost analysis workbook included.

53428 ■ *QuickBooks for the New Bean Counter: Business Owner's Guide 2006*
Pub: Wheatmark
Ed: Joseph L. Catallini. **Released:** July 2006. **Price:** $21.95. **Description:** Profile of QuickBooks software, offering insight into using the software's accounting and bookkeeping functions.

53429 ■ *QuickBooks Simple Start for Dummies*
Pub: John Wiley & Sons, Incorporated
Ed: Stephen L. Nelson. **Released:** September 2004. **Price:** $28.99. **Description:** Profile of Intuits new accounting software geared to micro businesses. Advice is offered on daily, monthly, and yearly accounting activities covering records, sales tax, and reports.

53430 ■ *QuickBooks X on Demand*
Pub: Que
Ed: Gail Perry. **Released:** December 2006. **Price:** $34.99. **Description:** Step-by-step training for using various small business financial software programs; includes illustrated, full color explanations.

53431 ■ *QuickBooks X for Dummies*
Pub: John Wiley & Sons, Incorporated
Ed: Stephen L. Nelson. **Released:** November 2006. **Price:** $21.99. **Description:** Key features of Quick-Books software for small business are introduced. Invoicing and credit memos, recoding sales receipts, accounting, budgeting, taxes, payroll, financial reports, job estimating, billing, tracking, data backup, are among the features.

53432 ■ **"Reaching the Small Business Accounting Market"** in *Accounting Today* (Vol. 14, No. 12, July 10, 2000, pp. 41)
Pub: Faulkner & Gray, Inc.
Ed: Tracey Miller-Segarra. **Description:** There is a new crop of dot-coms seeking to stake their claims in the lucrative small business accounting software market by developing products designed exclusively for the Internet. A profile of three of these software products is presented.

53433 ■ **"Recognize this Voice? Speech Recognition Reduces Keyboard Tedium"** in *Black Enterprise* (Vol. 36, February 2006, No. 7, pp. 68)
Pub: Earl G. Graves Publishing Co. Inc.
Description: Profile of Dragon Naturally Speaking 8, the Windows software that allows users to store voice profiles on a central server and transcribe from digital recorders or any handheld device that supports the Microsoft Pocket PC operating system. The professional system sells for $799.

53434 ■ **"Recover Deleted E-Mail"** in *PC World* (Vol. 23, April 2005, No. 4, pp. 150)
Pub: PC World Communications, Inc.
Description: DTI Data Recovery's E-Recovery for Outlook Express allows users to recover email messages for a fee.

53435 ■ **"Renting software and the skills to go with it"** in *The New York Times* (May 22, 2000, pp. C4)
Pub: The New York Times Company
Ed: Laurie Flynn. **Description:** Many companies are taking a new path when acquiring software programs for their individual businesses. Instead of buying the software needed and hiring a technician to teach them how to use it, they have turned to renting the software. In this type of arrangement, the software company would handle this part of the business for them, saving money, time and manpower.

53436 ■ **"Repackage Your Words"** in *Sales & Marketing Management* (Vol. 159, January-February 2007, No. 1, pp. 45)
Pub: VNU Business Media
Description: Tips for presenting a PowerPoint slideshow are presented by Jerry Weissman, author of Presenting to Win: The Art of Telling Your Story.

53437 ■ **"Resources: Web Sites, Organizations, Events and More to Grow Your Business"** in *Entrepreneur* (Vol. 32, July 2004, No. 7, pp. 8)
Pub: Entrepreneur Media Inc.
Ed: Steve Cooper. **Description:** Online printing and mailing services are offered by Mailersclub; Auction-Bytes is a free email newsletter that covers online auctions; Microsoft's Software Asset Management programs alerts companies when licenses are expiring and standardizes and centralizes the licensing process; U.S. Census Bureau's American Community Survey provides statistical data for small business marketing; Retailwire, provides news to retail professionals; Daypop is a specialized search engine; StumbleUpon is a free browser toolbar; and CoolSiteoftheDay spotlights good Web sites.

53438 ■ **"The Road to Healthy Sales "** in *Sales & Marketing Management*
Pub: VNU Business Media
Ed: Michael Schrage. **Description:** The importance of using sales-support software geared to a particular small business is stressed.

53439 ■ **"RosettaNet: The Key to Supply Chain Efficiency?"** in *E-business Advisor* (Vol. 17, No. 12, December 1999, pp. 16)
Pub: Advisor Media, Inc.
Ed: Rik Drummond. **Description:** The RosettaNet consortium, established in 1998 by Fadi Chehade, aims to create a single software standard throughout the IT supply chain, thus standardizing e-business operations. RosettaNet is presently defining open interfaces among supply chain manufacturers, distributors, resellers, and customers. RosettaNet's goal is to help computer makers and distributors defend their business against Dell and other Web-based made-to-order computer sellers.

53440 ■ **"A Run of Luck"** in *Entrepreneur* (Vol. 33, March 2005, No. 3, pp. 55)
Pub: Entrepreneur Media Inc.
Ed: David Worrell. **Description:** Profile of Client Profiles Inc., a legal software company. CEO White McIsaac, tells how he wanted to sell his business, while maintaining control of the company's direction.

53441 ■ **"Safekeeping for Software"** in *Business 2.0* (Vol. 7, January/February 2006, No. 1, pp. 30)
Pub: Time, Inc.
Ed: Daniel Del Re. **Description:** Source codes should be kept in a safe place; an estimated 75 percent of licensing deals require putting source codes in escrow.

53442 ■ **"Safety First"** in *Entrepreneur* (Vol. 31, No. 11, November 2003, pp. 60)
Pub: Entrepreneur Media, Inc.
Ed: Marc Spiwak, Michael Gross. **Description:** The National Cyber Security Alliance report that only 60 percent of broadband users have a firewall installed on their computers. Two new firewalls designed for small networks were reviewed by the CRN Test Center: the WatchGuard Firebox SOHO 6 and the Sonic-Wall SOHO TZW (Trusted Zone for Wireless). Both firewalls include wireless and VPN capabilities.

53443 ■ **"Safety Measures"** in *Washington Business Journal* (Vol. 22, No. 16, August 22, 2003, pp. 18)
Pub: Washington Business Journal
Ed: Tim Pappa. **Description:** Gary Noesner, from Control Risks Groups, points out the importance of travel information. Control Risks offers software and services to make data acquisition easier. Such information can result in saving the lives of employees of international businesses or government officials in the field.

53444 ■ **"Sage unveils big plans for small business"** in *Accounting Today* (Vol. 14, No. 13, July 24, 2000, pp. 29)
Pub: Faulkner & Gray, Inc.
Description: Accounting software development group Sage, announced plans to make several e-commerce innovations this year tied to its new accounting software product, BusinessWorks Gold. Sage said that the product, designed for companies of 50 or fewer employees, will be "the foundation for delivering e-commerce and e-management capabilities to the small business marketplace."

53445 ■ "Sagent Technology Unveils New Enterprise Information Portal" in *Information Today* (Vol. 17, No. 10, November 2000, pp. 44)
Pub: Information Today, Inc.
Description: Sagent Technology, Inc., a provider of real-time, e-business intelligence solutions, has released a second-generation information portal that integrates a broad range of content and applications, and serves many types of businesses.

53446 ■ "SAP AG Starting Unit to Target Small, Medium-Sized Firms" in *Philadelphia Inquirer* (November 13, 2006)
Pub: Philadelphia Newspapers LLC
Ed: Akweli Parker. **Description:** SAP AG is launching a new office that will offer software to small and medium-sized businesses. The move will help to spur growth. Statistical data included.

53447 ■ "Save the Date" in *Entrepreneur* (Vol. 31, No. 10, October 2003, pp. 57)
Pub: Entrepreneur Media, Inc.
Ed: Liane Cassavoy. **Description:** Profile of Now Up-to-Date & Contact from Power On Software; the software allows users to share schedules, create appointments and coordinates tasks without server software.

53448 ■ "SBA Offers Free E-Commerce CD" in *Home Office Computing* (Vol. 19, No. 1, January 2001, pp. 22)
Pub: Scholastic Inc.
Ed: Lee Wertheimer. **Description:** The Small Business Administration (SBA) has teamed with a pair of small business Web sites to distribute a free CD-ROM with tools for creating an e-commerce site, plus advice on how to use it to make money. A profile of the disc, Build Your Own Business Web Site for Free, is included.

53449 ■ "Scammers Have Been Downloading Software From My Website Using Stolen PayPal Accounts. What Can I Do?" in *Inc.* (Vol. 27, July 2005)
Pub: Inc. Magazine
Description: PayPal accounts are being swiped with the identity-theft technique known as phishing. PayPal's seller-protection policy covers only physical goods, rendering dealers responsible for refunding any scammed customers.

53450 ■ "A Second Act for CRM" in *Inc.* (Volume 27, March 2005, No. 3, pp. 40, 42)
Pub: Inc. Magazine
Ed: Ellen Neuborne. **Description:** Customer relationship management software will manage customer databases. A recent study found that 60 percent of midsize companies will adopt or expand CRM usage over the next two years.

53451 ■ "Secret Weapon: Synopsys is Thriving Behind the Scenes in the Semiconductor Business" in *Barron's* (August 11, 2003, pp. 16)
Pub: Barron's
Ed: Mark Veverka. **Description:** CEO, Art de Geus's Synopsys, headquartered in Silicon Valley, California, is quietly making its case as a leading electronic-design automation firm, creating the software that semiconductor firms like Intel and AMD use to design microchips.

53452 ■ "Secure your network" in *PC Magazine* (June 27, 2000, pp. 183)
Pub: Ziff-Davis Publishing Company
Ed: Frank J. Derfler, Jr. **Description:** Several turnkey hardware/software firewall products are reviewed, including Check Points VPN-1 Appliance 330 and Cisco's Secure PIX Firewall 515, as well as, similar tools from Progressive Systems, WatchGuard and e-Soft. The products use NAT and other powerful techniques such as packet and address filtering to ensure Internet security. Each can be used as a combined router/firewall, but such a solution results in a single point of failure and leaves the entire network vulnerable if it is penetrated. Effectiveness and availability of high-end features such as VPN support are key elements to look for when choosing a firewall.

53453 ■ "Security Blanket" in *Entrepreneur* (Vol. 33, March 2005, No. 3, pp. 46)
Pub: Entrepreneur Media Inc.
Ed: Amanda C. Kooser. **Description:** AOL's 9.0 Security Edition offers McAfee VirusScan Online, anti-spyware controls, spyware protection, and anti-spim features and a firewall at no extra charge.

53454 ■ "Security Guide for Small Business" in *Entrepreneur.com* (Vol. 34, February 2006, No. 2, pp. 6)
Pub: Entrepreneur Media Inc.
Description: Microsoft and the U.S. Chamber of Commerce have developed a PDF guide to help small businesses secure computers and networks against viruses and hackers. A sample small business security plan is also included.

53455 ■ "Self-Service" in *Inc.* (October 2005, pp. 124-125, 128)
Pub: Inc. Magazine
Description: When choosing software to manage email it is important to consider four basic questions: what you want the email to do, an access point, security, and costs. Comparisons of Microsoft Outlook 2003, IBM Lotus Notes 7.0, Qualcomm Eudora 6.2, and Mozilla Thunderbird 1.0 software are shown.

53456 ■ "Send E-Mail Securely" in *Home Office Computing* (Vol. 18, No. 11, November 2000, pp. 28)
Pub: Scholastic Inc.
Ed: Victoria Hall Smith. **Description:** E-mail is not a sure way to send anything sensitive or confidential. Messages hop from server to server as they traverse the Internet, sometimes becoming garbled or lost, and unauthorized copies are often left along the way. A profile of a proprietary message- and file-delivery software solution is presented.

53457 ■ "Send Out the Search Party" in *Entrepreneur* (Vol. 33, January 2005, No. 1, pp. 47)
Pub: Entrepreneur Media Inc.
Ed: Amanda C. Kooser. **Description:** Blinkx and Copernic Desktop Search are two third-party desktop search tool programs.

53458 ■ "Services Offer Unlimited Music Rentals for a Monthly Fee" in *Kansas City Star* (February 4, 2005)
Pub: Knight-Ridder/Tribune Business News
Ed: Paul Wenske. **Description:** Microsoft's copy-protection software allows subscribers to move rented musical tracks from a computer to portable music players.

53459 ■ "Set up shop" in *Entrepreneur* (Vol. 30, No. 3, March 2002, pp. 40)
Pub: Entrepreneur Media Inc.
Ed: Liane Gouthro. **Description:** Profile of Peachtree's WebsiteCreatorpro software that makes it easy to point and click your way to a new Web site.

53460 ■ "Set Up a Voice Mail and Fax System-Give your company the appearance of corporate professionalism" in *PC Magazine* (Mar.21,2000, pp.115)
Pub: Ziff-Davis Publishing Company
Ed: M. David Stone. **Description:** A good alternative for providing reliable voice mail services for a small business is to dedicate a computer outfitted with voice modems and a voice mail software package to the task. The same system can be used to handle fax traffic in a professional manner. Products that are reliable for such a dedicated usage include Fax Works from Thought Communications, SuperVoice from Pacific Image Communications, and TalkWorks Pro from Symantec.

53461 ■ "Sharebuilder 401(k)" in *Entrepreneur.com* (Vol. 34, February 2006, No. 2, pp. 6)
Pub: Entrepreneur Media Inc.
Description: ShareBuilder 401(K) helps employers deliver retirement plans for a monthly fee of $15 per participant. The software merges with existing payroll and offers online payroll service.

53462 ■ "Sharing Digital Shots Snap with Picasa 2.0" in *Tampa Tribune* (January 24, 2005)
Pub: Knight-Ridder/Tribune Business News
Ed: Doug Stanley. **Description:** Profile of Picasa 2.0, free photo-management program from Google; the software allows users to find, organize, edit, share and preserve digital pictures.

53463 ■ "Shopping for the Right Database" in *Business Week Online* (December 13, 2001)
Pub: McGraw-Hill, Inc.
Description: Questions are answered regarding the development of a marketing database for a small business that retails and distributes environmental safety products, but all information applies to any small business.

53464 ■ "Simplify Web Development with Java Server Pages" in *E-business Advisor* (Vol. 17, No. 12, December 1999, pp. 38)
Pub: Advisor Media, Inc.
Ed: Tom Valesky. **Description:** The Java Server Pages (JSP) standard is fast becoming the architecture of choice for active Web page development. JSP, vendor-neutral and highly portable, simplifies Web page creation by giving developers full access to Java APIs and third-party libraries. JSP, built on top of the Java Servlet API, permits developers to use all Java capabilities as a scripting language.

53465 ■ "Six Degrees: Can Who Your Employees Know Make a Difference in Your Sales?" in *Entrepreneur* (Vol. 32, No. 1, January 2004, pp. 27)
Pub: Entrepreneur Media, Inc.
Ed: Amanda C. Kooser. **Description:** New computer software is making it easier to increase sales through relationship mining or relationship capital management. Three startup software companies, Spoke Software Inc., Visible Path Corporation, and ZeroDegrees Inc., all offer versions of this software.

53466 ■ "Smack Down! Show Those Numbers Who's Boss With a New Accounting Software Program" in *Entrepreneur* (Vol. 31, No. 10, October 2003)
Pub: Entrepreneur Media, Inc.
Ed: Michael Gros, Mario Morejon. **Description:** Profiles of new accounting software packages to help small firms manage business the way large corporations do, including MyBooks Pro and QuickBooks.

53467 ■ "Small Deals, Big Business" in *Washington Business Journal* (Vol. 22, No. 17, August 29, 2003, pp. 17)
Pub: Washington Business Journal
Description: The growing role of small business in the software industry is discussed. Topics include growing sales, marketing strategy, and market adaptability.

53468 ■ "Small Is Big" in *Forbes* (May 27, 2002, p. 88)
Pub: Forbes Magazine
Ed: Erika Brown. **Description:** Profile of Intuit's accounting software package QuickBooks Enterprise being marketed to small businesses.

53469 ■ "Small-Office Firewalls" in *PC Magazine* (June 27, 2000, pp. 198)
Pub: Ziff-Davis Publishing Company
Description: Hardware and software products for small offices are reviewed. All offer a WAN port for connecting to an Internet router and a LAN port for connecting to the network as well as built-in DHCP servers and clients. WatchGuard Technologies' WatchGuard SOHO earns a very good rating, while several other products, including the SonicWall SOHO, Linksys EtherFast and NetGear Rt311, earn a good rating. Features to look for include reporting capabilities, content filtering and VPN options.

53470 ■ "Small, Yes-But With A Big Back Office" in *Business Week* (No. 3853, October 13, 2003, pp. 86)
Pub: McGraw-Hill Inc.

Ed: Charles Haddad. Description: Information technology is helping small firms compete with large corporations. Web-based software allows small businesses to perform all functions electronically.

53471 ■ "Smart Design" in *Entrepreneur* (Vol. 30, No. 3, March 2002, pp. 40)
Pub: Entrepreneur Media Inc.
Ed: Liane Gouthro. Description: Profile of Adobe Illustrator software for vector-based graphics, now available in version 10.0; the application provides easier access to design tools, which include twist, bend and warp effects.

53472 ■ "Smart Tech Solutions For Small Businesses" in *Black Enterprise* (Vol. 35, August 2004, No. 1, pp. 61)
Pub: Earl G. Graves Publishing Co. Inc.
Ed: Schuyler K. Esprit. Description: Ramon Ray's Technology Solutions for Growing Businesses is reviewed. Finding the right products for a small business can maximize productivity while minimizing costs.

53473 ■ "Snare and Share Alike: Here's a Quick and Easy Way to Capture Video" in *Black Enterprise* (Vol. 34, No. 6, January 2004, pp. 46)
Pub: Earl Graves Publishing Co.
Ed: Rebecca Rohan. Description: Ways to move old movies to archive or new video for Internet use to a PC are explained, along with capture device and software.

53474 ■ "Soft Landing: James Garrett Took a Leap of Faith and Found Security" in *Black Enterprise* (Vol. 34, No. 2, September 2003, pp. 51)
Pub: Earl Graves Publishing Co.
Ed: Cristina Gair. Description: Profile of James Garrett, founder of Sentel Corporation, an engineering and software services company providing homeland security devices and other services. Garrett left a government position to become an entrepreneur and tried various businesses before finding his niche.

53475 ■ "Software that Asks Who Goes There?" in *Business Week Online* (February 26, 2002)
Pub: McGraw-Hill, Inc.
Description: The art and science of managing employee passwords is discussed, including the issues of tech support, legal requirements and the high costs involved for small business.

53476 ■ "Software Companies: Get Real with Revenue" in *Venture Capital Journal* (July 1, 2003)
Pub: Thomson Financial Inc.
Description: Analysts and accounts suggest that software companies should begin to record license fee revenue ratably over time, rather than up-front as they have traditionally done; Wall Street and venture capitalists do not agree.

53477 ■ "Software Company Makes List of Country's 500 Fastest-Growing Private Firms" in *Sacramento Bee* (October 19, 2005)
Pub: The Sacramento Bee
Ed: Dale Kasler. Description: C&S Marketing was listed as one of Inc. magazine's top 500 fastest growing companies. Firms were ranked according to percent sales growth from 2001 to 2004. The firm provides software to mortgage companies that help estimate property values and eliminate fraud.

53478 ■ *The Software Encyclopedia*
Pub: R.R. Bowker L.L.C.
Contact: Charlie Friscia, Dir.
E-mail: charlie.friscia@bowker.com
Released: Annual, latest edition May 2004; new edition expected May 2005. Price: $379, individuals for set of 2 volumes. Covers: over 40,100 software programs from over 3,845 publishers of software programs. Entries Include: For software—Title, version, release date, system requirements, price, ISBN, order number, description, publisher name. For publishers—Company name, address, phone, toll-free phone, fax, ISBN prefix, titles. Arrangement: Two alphabetical sections for software, one by title, the other by system/application; also, one alphabetical section for publishers. Indexes: Title, system/application.

53479 ■ "Software Gerry Langeler" in *Venture Capital Journal* (January 1, 2005)
Pub: Thomason Financial Inc.
Description: Gerry Langeler, co-founder of Mentor Graphics Corporation and general partner of OVP Venture Partners in Portland, Oregon, makes predictions for the software market in 2005 as well as what happened to the market in 2004.

53480 ■ "Software, Hard Profit" in *Small Business Opportunities* (Vol. 16, No. 1, January 2004, pp. 80, 84)
Pub: Harris Publications, Inc.
Ed: Chuck Green. Description: Profile of Mike Hennel, owner of Silvon Software. The software company makes $12 million annually helping customers analyze sales trends in order to minimize costs.

53481 ■ "Software Pacts Handed Off" in *Sacramento Bee* (November 3, 2005)
Pub: The Sacramento Bee
Ed: Andrew McIntosh. Description: California's Department of Technology Services awarded a $31.1 million contract to Computer Associates International Inc. for computer software maintenance. The company will help negotiate and consolidate the state's existing mainframe computer software maintenance contracts for security, data storage, and systems management software.

53482 ■ "The Software Patent Conundrum" in *eWeek* (February 3, 2005)
Pub: Ziff Davis Media Inc.
Description: According Greg Aharonian, patents are the best way to protect and support real innovation in the software industry. Software patent issues in both the U.S. and the European Union are discussed.

53483 ■ "Software for Rent" in *Hispanic Business* (Vol. 22, No. 6, June 2000, pp. 160)
Pub: Hispanic Business
Ed: Roger Harris. Description: The use of software leasing via the Internet is expected to show rapid growth as start-ups and small companies realize the cost-savings that can be achieved from a software vendor or an Application Service Provider.

53484 ■ "The Software to Secure Your Strategic Advantage" in *Journal of Business Strategies* (Vol. 21, No. 5, September 2000, pp. 33)
Pub: Center for Business and Economic Research
Ed: Sunny J. Baker. Description: Strategic planning is as important as ever, and now it must be done faster than ever before. The article examines software programs that can help.

53485 ■ "Software, computer leasing providers jockey to survive" in *Crain's Detroit Business* (Vol. 16, No. 46, November 13, 2000, pp. 16)
Pub: Crain Communications, Inc.
Ed: Katie Merx. Description: Several Detroit-area technology companies are asking small businesses to rent software and computer equipment rather than purchasing the equipment.

53486 ■ "Special Report" in *The Economist* (Vol. 376, July 16-22, 2005, No. 8435, pp. 65-67)
Pub: The Economist Newspaper Ltd.
Description: New, faster computer chips are impacting the business-software industry.

53487 ■ "Speech! Speech!" in *Forbes* (Vol. 175, February 14, 2005, No. 3, pp. 54)
Pub: Forbes Magazine Inc.
Ed: Stephen Manes. Description: Profile of ScanSoft Group Inc.'s new Dragon Naturally Speaking Software. The software allows the user to dictate text and see it appear on screen.

53488 ■ "SpeechWorks International" in *Boston Business Journal* (Vol. 22, No. 16, May 24, 2002, pp. 38)
Pub: MCP, Inc.
Description: Profile of Speechworks International software that assists in voice-activated telephone services. Statistical data included.

53489 ■ "Spring cleaning" in *Entrepreneur* (Vol. 31, No. 4, April 2003, pp. 44)
Pub: Entrepreneur Media Inc.
Ed: Melissa Campanelli. Description: There are a variety of software tools available to make sure a Web site is in good working order. Keynote NetMechanic spots and fixes common HTML code errors and generates a repaired file to upload to the Web host.

53490 ■ "Stacking the Digital Deck" in *Hispanic Business* (May 2005, pp. 32, 34, 36, 38)
Pub: Hispanic Business
Ed: Kevin Savetz. Description: The newest technology systems and business software can help small companies target new markets, increase productivity, and lower costs.

53491 ■ "Startup Hopes to Help Speed Payments to Vendors" in *Crain's Detroit Business* (Vol. 19, No. 42, October 20, 2003, pp. 18)
Pub: Crain Communications Inc., Detroit
Ed: Laura Bailey. Description: Profile of eFinNet Corporation, a startup financial services firm that speeds payments from large firms to small suppliers and eliminates direct banking, by linking the buyer, seller and lender through the Internet.

53492 ■ "Stay In Touch" in *Entrepreneur* (Vol. 33, September 2005, No. 9, pp. 44)
Pub: Entrepreneur Media Inc.
Ed: Description: Quickbooks, Peachtree, and Netsuite software offer complete accounting functions necessary for any growing small business.

53493 ■ "Stay in Touch" in *Entrepreneur* (Vol. 32, December 2004, No. 12, pp. 52)
Pub: Entrepreneur Media Inc.
Ed: Liane Cassavoy. Description: InTouch 3.6 from 01 Communique allows users to securely access a PC from any Web browser, including those on PDAs and cell phones. The software will run programs (including Outlook), and access and transfer files between PCs, as well as send a text message to a cell phone.

53494 ■ "A Step Beyond" in *Entrepreneur* (Vol. 32, July 2004, No. 7, pp. 44)
Pub: Entrepreneur Media Inc.
Ed: Steve Cooper. Description: Microsoft is sponsoring its Touch Point Series seminars to help small businesses capitalize on all of the features of its Office Suite software. The seminar content is refreshed on a quarterly basis.

53495 ■ "Stocks Go Up, Stocks Go Down, But Innovators Keep Innovating" in *San Jose Mercury News* (March 8, 2005)
Pub: Knight-Ridder/Tribune Business News
Ed: Chris O'Brien. Description: Profile of software developer, Paul Mercer. Mercer's self-financed startup, Iventor of Palo Alto, is creating a new generation of software for mobile devices.

53496 ■ "Superior Consultant Holdings sees demand for health care IT" in *Crain's Detroit Business* (Vol. 19, No. 13, March 31, 2003, pp. 4)
Pub: Crain Communications Inc., Detroit
Ed: Andrew Dietderich. Description: Compliance with the Health Insurance Portability and Accountability Act, quality mandates and physician connectivity are fueling demand for hardware and software and Southfield-based Superior Consultant Holdings Corporation is planning a new $5 million data-processing center.

53497 ■ "The Survey Says..." in *Inc.* (October 2005, pp. 44, 46)
Pub: Inc. Magazine
Ed: Ellen Neuborne. Description: New survey software helps companies know what consumers think about their products or services. SurveyMonkey, WebSurveyor, and Perseus Survey Solutions/EFM Workgroup are profiled.

53498 ■ "Tablet Tools" in *Entrepreneur* (Vol. 31, No. 10, October 2003, pp. 57)
Pub: Entrepreneur Media, Inc.
Ed: Liane Cassavoy. **Description:** Profile of Mind-Manager 2002 from Mindjet Software, to capture, organize and share information.

53499 ■ "Tackling the Competition" in *Home Business* (Vol. 12, March/April 2005, No. 2, pp. 80)
Pub: Home Business Magazine
Ed: Sandy Larson. **Description:** Profile of Stan Webber, creator of football coaching software.

53500 ■ "Taking Care of Business: Downloadable Programs For Your Enterprise" in *Black Enterprise* (Vol. 34, July 2004, No. 12, pp. 145)
Pub: Earl G. Graves Publishing Co. Inc.
Ed: Jennifer L. Smith. **Description:** Websites offering free, downloadable small business software are presented. Everything from accounting, computer security, as well as investment programs is available from these sites.

53501 ■ "Talented work force credited for right ideas" in *Crain's Detroit Business* (Vol. 19, No. 13, March 31, 2003, pp. 14)
Pub: Crain Communications Inc., Detroit
Description: Profile of Menlo Institute LLC, the software development services company. Rick Sheridan, co-founder and instructor believes the success of the firm lies in having the right product at the right time developed by the right people.

53502 ■ "Talk Direct" in *PC Magazine* (February 6, 2001, pp. 26)
Pub: Ziff-Davis Publishing Company
Ed: Sally Wiener Grotta. **Description:** Review of Veritel's Talk Direct, that allows dialing into your company's toll-free phone line and speaking your name to access all the telephony tools at the office. This software helps the company tighten control over costs while improving communication among employees.

53503 ■ "Tape Backup isn't the sexiest technology on the network, but it is one of the most essential" in *PC Magazine* (April 4, 2000, pp. 155)
Pub: Ziff-Davis Publishing Company
Ed: Steve Rigney. **Description:** Six tape drives are evaluated, and test results illustrate that a purchase decision depends on specific circumstances and type of business. In these tests, the $4,000 Exabyte Mammoth-2 was fastest. For a small business, the $1,000 Ecrix VXA-1 and the $1,500 Benchmark Tape Systems DLT1 are recommended. Customers are reminded that software typically does not come with a tape drive, and in most cases, even a driver will have to be purchased separately.

53504 ■ "Tax test" in *Wall Street Journal* (April 9, 2002, pp. D3)
Pub: Wall Street Journal
Ed: Charles Passy. **Description:** A comparison of the price and varying results of five different tax preparation software and services are presented, including Quicken TurboTax Home & Business. Statistical data included.

53505 ■ "Tax-Time Bytes" in *PC Magazine* (February 20, 2001, pp. 186)
Pub: Ziff-Davis Publishing Company
Ed: Kathy Yakal. **Description:** Reviews of tax preparation software is offered, including Kiplinger TaxCut Deluxe, Quicken Turbo Tax Deluxe, and Taxact 2000 Deluxe.

53506 ■ *Teach Yourself Microsoft Small Business Server in 21 Days*
Pub: Sams
Ed: Harry M. Brelsford. **Released:** 1999.

53507 ■ "Tech firms' juicy new prospect" in *Wall Street Journal* (April 22, 2002, pp. B1)
Pub: Wall Street Journal
Ed: Lee Gomes. **Description:** An overview of customer relationship management, including terrorism-tracking programs are presented.

53508 ■ "Tech Toy" in *Entrepreneur* (Vol. 31, No. 10, October 2003, pp. 26)
Pub: Entrepreneur Media, Inc.
Ed: Gisela M. Pedroza. **Description:** Profile of Sony's robot dog called AIBO Cyber-Blue, when connected with AIBO EYES software, the robot dog connects to Internet-enabled PC or mobile devices and can take digital snapshots and email them to another location.

53509 ■ "Techniques: Microcases" in *Inc.* (November 15, 2000, pp. 128-129)
Pub: The Goldhirsh Group
Description: Solutions for two problems are addressed: customers and staff out of sync with the home office; and stalled Web sites and crashing e-mail.

53510 ■ "The Telework Puzzle" in *Home Office Computing* (Vol. 19, No. 1, January 2001, pp. 90)
Pub: Scholastic Inc.
Ed: Lisa Roberts. **Description:** TManage Inc founder and CEO, Glenn Lovelace, discusses the factors that make telecommuting programs succeed or fail. Lovelace was director of telecommuting for Nortel Networks before starting his own consulting firm to outsource telework programs.

53511 ■ "That's the Spot" in *Entrepreneur. com* (Vol. 34, February 2006, No. 2, pp. 35)
Pub: Entrepreneur Media Inc.
Description: JiWire and Wi Finder help locate hot spots for Internet access before you hit the roads. The software can be downloaded at no charge and includes a directory of more than 70,000 hot spots in 103 countries.

53512 ■ "There's More Than One Way to Bust a Trust" in *Inc.* (Volume 27, December 2005, No. 12, pp. 24)
Pub: Inc. Magazine
Ed: Robert Litan. **Description:** The Federal Government failed to break Microsoft's monopoly; details of Microsoft's case are investigated.

53513 ■ "They Bought In. Now They Want to Bail Out" in *Harvard Business Review* (Vol. 81, No. 12, December 2003, pp. 28)
Pub: Harvard Business School Press
Ed: Eric McNulty. **Description:** A hypothetical case is presented in which a chief technology officer is required to justify a potential investment in customer relationship management software. Teaching highlights include evaluating whether the fictional company needs the software, techniques for selling an idea or project, and the importance of widespread support for the success of such ventures.

53514 ■ "Thinking About Security" in *PC Magazine* (January 4, 2000, pp. 191)
Pub: Ziff-Davis Publishing Company
Ed: Steve Rigney. **Description:** Companies must deal with data security, but first must determine what their security needs and risks are. Once that is established the company can look to firewalls, data security devices, network security software, virtual private networks and network address transmittal devices. Costs of these different solutions must also be considered.

53515 ■ "This Isn't Your Teenage Daughter's Diary: Web Logs Are a Big Hit With Everyone..." in *Black Enterprise* (Vol. 34, December 2003)
Pub: Earl Graves Publishing Co.
Ed: Rebecca Rohan. **Description:** Blogging, or Web logging, is journaling on the Web using special software that enables users to write directly in the blog, and is now being used by businesses.

53516 ■ "Thumbs Up! Rave Reviews Could be All the Advertising You Need" in *Entrepreneur* (Vol. 32, July 2004, No. 7, pp. 71)
Pub: Entrepreneur Media Inc.
Ed: Nancy Michaels. **Description:** Owner of a software/Web site design business is offered advice for word-of-mouth marketing after having little success with radio and newspaper ads.

53517 ■ "Time Right For Tech Upgrade? That Depends" in *Mississippi Business Journal* (Vol. 29, January 2007, No. 2, pp. 1)
Pub: Venture Publications, Inc.
Ed: Becky Gillette **Description:** Most people wait until their computer or office equipment breaks down before replacing it. Advice on when and how to upgrade equipment for the least business downtime is covered.

53518 ■ "Time for an upgrade? Adobe Photoshop's newest version" in *Black Enterprise* (Vol. 33, No. 3, October 2002, pp. 68)
Pub: Earl Graves Publishing Co.
Ed: Sonya A. Donaldson. **Description:** Profile of Adobe Photoshop 7.0 is given. Advice is offered on whether to upgrade to this new system or to wait for a more robust version.

53519 ■ "Today's Specialist" in *Entrepreneur* (Vol. 33, August 2005, No. 8, pp. 28)
Pub: Entrepreneur Media Inc.
Ed: Amanda C. Kooser. **Description:** The Microsoft Partner Program offers providers and resellers certification in specific disciplines and also gives access to Microsoft's support network.

53520 ■ "Top Cop" in *Forbes* (Vol. 175, January 10, 2005, No. 1, pp. 154)
Pub: Forbes Magazine Inc.
Ed: Victoria Murphy. **Description:** Profile of security software and services provided by Symantec and Thompson. Symantec's stock is up fivefold in the past five years, making it a good investment. Thompson buys new technology to keep pace with computer hackers.

53521 ■ "Treo" in *Business Week* (January 16, 2006, No. 3967, pp. 18)
Pub: McGraw-Hill Companies
Ed: Stephen H. Wildstrom. **Description:** Profile of the new Treo 700w which runs on Microsoft software. The new device is the first Pocket PC that offers home screen features such as speed-dial buttons and two boxes for entering text.

53522 ■ "UPS-Compliant Shipping Software" in *Modern Materials Handling* (Vol. 58, No. 7, July 2003, pp. 60)
Pub: Reed Business Information
Description: Shipping Manager Software Version 2.0 creates an all-in-one packing list and shipping labels from any printer and integrates with UPS Worldship.

53523 ■ "Users Size Up Tax Software: Product Ratings Gain, But Vendor Support Slips" in *Journal of Accountancy* (Vol. 198, October 2004)
Pub: American Institute of Certified Public Accountants
Ed: Stanley Zarowin. **Description:** Results of a survey covering tax-preparation software are discussed. Statistical data included.

53524 ■ "Vending Machines Get an Audit" in *South Florida Business Journal* (Vol. 24, No. 7, September 26, 2003, pp. 1)
Pub: American City Business Journals
Ed: Ed Duggan. **Description:** Jeff Stubins Vend Audit Controls Company offers a software product that will audit vending machines.

53525 ■ "A Virtual, Personal HR" in *PC Magazine* (December 19, 2000, pp. 7a)
Pub: Ziff-Davis Publishing Company
Ed: Sarah L. Roberts-Witt. **Description:** A preview of Authoria's software services that uses the Web to answer employees questions concerning their benefits. Authoria claims to save on average $1,700 annually per employee by cutting Human Resource time on benefits administration.

53526 ■ "Virtual Private Networks: Editors' Hot Links" in *PC Magazine* (January 4, 2000, pp. 146)
Pub: Ziff-Davis Publishing Company
Ed: Frank J. Derfler, Jr. **Description:** A directory of Internet infrastructure products for small business are listed and reviewed.

53527 ■ "Virtual Private Networks" in *PC Magazine* **(January 4, 2000, pp. 146)**
Pub: Ziff-Davis Publishing Company
Ed: Frank J. Derfler, Jr. **Description:** Test procedures of VPN products from six vendors are presented. The companies are TimeStep, Intel, Altiga Networks, Lucent Technologies and Check Point. The first five vendors supplied hardware and software packaged VPN gateways for the test, while Check Point's product was software that came installed in a Pentium III PC server.

53528 ■ "Virus Blockers" in *Entrepreneur* **(Vol. 31, No. 7, July 2003, pp. 40)**
Pub: Entrepreneur Media, Inc.
Ed: Liane Cassavoy. **Description:** Profile of Central Command's Vexira Antivirus computer software is available for multiple operating systems. The software monitors local and network drives, email attachments, and files for viruses and other threats.

53529 ■ "Voices of Innovation" in *Business Week* **(January 23, 2006, No. 3968, pp. 20)**
Pub: McGraw-Hill Companies
Ed: Jay Greene. **Description:** Rick Rashid, Microsoft Corporation's senior vice president, pushes his 700 research and development scientists to go after big challenges.

53530 ■ "VPNs and Windows 2000: With Windows 2000, standards-based virtual private networking is integrated into the operating system" in *PC Magazine*
Pub: Ziff-Davis Publishing Company
Ed: Eric Greenberg. **Description:** Microsoft Windows 2000 offers powerful standards-based dial-up VPN capabilities that should ease the complexity of deploying VPN functionality to the desktop. VPNs provide a path toward lower networking costs, power security capabilities, enhanced productivity for remote users and rapidly deployable e-business services. VPN security, digital certificates, and PKI are discussed.

53531 ■ "Ward off Competitors" in *PC Computing* **(April 2000, pp. 95)**
Pub: Ziff-Davis Inc.
Ed: Jason Compton. **Description:** Microsoft MapPoint 2000 will help a retail store use customer zip code and sales amount information to see how the proximity of a competitor will affect sales volumes.

53532 ■ "Web-based Accounting" in *Home Office Computing* **(Vol. 18, No. 11, November 2000, pp. 71)**
Pub: Scholastic Inc.
Ed: Wayne Kawamoto. **Description:** A software buyer's guide featuring integrated accounting software packages and Web-based services of value to the home office user. Among the featured products are BAport Accounting from BAport, the eLedger 2.0 application from Application Service Provider (ASP) eLedger, Peachtree Software's ePeachtree 2.0, Intacct, an online service that offers general ledger, accounts payable, accounts receivable, and human resources functions, NetLedger 4.0, and Bizfinity.

53533 ■ "Website Builder" in *Entrepreneur* **(Vol. 32, December 2004, No. 12, pp. 52)**
Pub: Entrepreneur Media Inc.
Ed: Liane Cassavoy. **Description:** Profile of Contribute 3.0, Macromedia's updated content Web creation tool, costing $149.

53534 ■ "Westinghouse software program finds a market" in *Pittsburgh Business Times* **(Vol. 22, No. 42, May 2, 2003, pp. 1)**
Pub: Pittsburgh Business Times
Ed: Maria Guzzo. **Description:** Westinghouse Electric Corporation's StatePointPlus Division markets software that manages computer networks, desktop computers and servers from a central operation.

53535 ■ "When a BlackBerry Is Overkill: The Phones Are Fine for Reading, But Not Writing e-Mails" in *Business Week* **(January 31, 2005, pp. 20)**
Pub: McGraw-Hill Companies

Ed: Stephen H. Wildstrom. **Description:** Profile of Microsoft's Windows Mobile Smartphone software, Motorola MPx220 flip phone, and the Audiovox SMT5600 bar-type phone.

53536 ■ "Why There's No Escaping the Blog" in *Fortune* **(Vol. 151, January 10, 2005, No. 1, pp. 44)**
Pub: Time Inc.
Ed: David Kirkpatrick, Daniel Roth, Oliver Ryan. **Description:** Microsoft has unveiled a plan to develop a new service called MSN Spaces, an online software that allows users to easily create and maintain blogs on the Internet. The power of blogs and bloggers to make or break a product or service is examined.

53537 ■ "Wi-Fi Reloaded: Maybe All Your 802.11B Network Needs is a Boost" in *Entrepreneur* **(Vol. 31, No. 7, July 2003, pp. 38)**
Pub: Entrepreneur Media, Inc.
Ed: Mike Hogan. **Description:** Various ways to boost existing 802.11b networks are examined, including the use of software and adaptors.

53538 ■ "Word Menu" in *Entrepreneur* **(Vol. 31, No. 8, August 2003, pp. 6)**
Pub: Entrepreneur Media, Inc.
Ed: Steve Cooper. **Description:** Profile of Write Brothers' reference software that helps entrepreneurs improve business communications. The software includes a reverse dictionary, an almanac and more.

53539 ■ "WTC mission is 'call to service' for Ann Arbor biotech firm" in *Crain's Detroit Business* **(Vol. 18, No. 18, May 6, 2002, pp. 1)**
Pub: Crain Communications Inc. - Detroit
Ed: Laura Bailey. **Description:** Software developed by the Ann Arbor biotech firm, Gene Codes Corporation, helped investigators in identifying victims from the attacks on the World Trade Center.

53540 ■ "Your Boss is Watching" in *PC Computing* **(March 2000, pp. 86)**
Pub: Ziff-Davis Inc.
Description: Web monitoring software is used by 45 percent of all companies and 17 percent of Fortune 1000 companies to make sure employees are not misusing the Web while at work. The WinWhatWhere Investigator software can record every keystroke an employee enters on a PC, while Elron Software's CommandView has the Message Inspector module that filters, stores and blocks emails at the network server. The article recommends that employees should minimize non-business-related web browsing on the company's computer.

53541 ■ "Your Own Style" in *Entrepreneur* **(Vol. 33, January 2005, No. 1, pp. 43)**
Pub: Entrepreneur Media Inc.
Ed: Liane Cassavoy. **Description:** Profile of High-Logic's Font Creator Program 4.5, users can select and edit any TrueType font and convert scanned images to TrueType fonts, including a font that looks like your own handwriting.

53542 ■ "Your Personal/Virtual Mentor" in *Small Business Opportunities* **(Vol. 12, No. 5, September 2000, pp. 68)**
Pub: Harris Publications, Inc.
Description: A description of the new software, Mentor, that provides just-in-time multimedia desktop training to computer users as an efficient alternative to traditional computer-based training.

53543 ■ "Zap It!" in *Entrepreneur* **(Vol. 28, No. 2, February 2000, pp. 28)**
Pub: Entrepreneur Media Inc.
Description: No more hassling with monstrous files, one click does the trick. To end the aggravation, try downloading Hermes.

TRADE PERIODICALS

53544 ■ *Business Computer Report*
Pub: Lawrence Oakly
Ed: Lawrence Oakly, Editor. **Released:** Monthly. **Description:** Reviews business applications software and hardware for IBM and compatible computers.

53545 ■ *PC Business Products*
Pub: Worldwide Videotex
Contact: Mark Wright
Released: Monthly. **Price:** $165, U.S. and Canada; $180, elsewhere outside North America. **Description:** Covers developments in software and hardware products and services. Includes list of performance ratings and prices.

53546 ■ *Technology Trends*
Pub: Enterprise Technology Corp.
Ed: Kevin J. Merz, Editor. **Released:** 6/year. **Description:** Discusses news on computer software technology and its perceived value to the business community.

CONSULTANTS

53547 ■ Business Resource Software Inc.
2013 Wells Branch Pky., Ste. 206
Austin, TX 78728
Ph:(512)251-7541
Free: 800-423-1228
Fax: (512)251-4401
Co. E-mail: sales@brs-inc.com
URL: http://www.brs-inc.com

E-mail: sales@brs-inc.com
Scope: Provides 'Expert System' software for strategy, planning and marketing in business planning and operation with the emerging personal computer technologies of spreadsheet and word processing to create a product which would assist in the development and evaluation of marketing strategies. **Special Services:** Insight for Sales Strategy applies expert system technology to analysis of complex sales. Plan Write Expert Edition is a business plan software.

53548 ■ Checkmark Software Inc.
724 Whalers Way, Bldg. H, Ste. 101
Fort Collins, CO 80525
Ph:(970)225-0522
Free: 800-444-9922
Fax: (970)225-0611
Co. E-mail: info@checkmark.com
URL: http://www.checkmark.com

E-mail: info@checkmark.com
Scope: Developer of accounting software tools for small businesses. **Special Services:** MultiLedger™

53549 ■ Claremont Consulting Group
4525 Castle Ln.
La Canada, CA 91011-1436
Ph:(818)249-0584
Fax: (818)249-5811
Scope: Consulting, coaching, training, & litigation support in project management, engineering management, system engineering & cost estimating. **Publications:** Over 85 publications, including, "What Every Engineer Should Know About Project Management." **Seminars:** Project Management, System Engineering & Cost Estimating.

53550 ■ Cogent Communications Inc.
1015 31st St. NW
Washington, DC 20007
Ph:(202)295-4200
Free: 877-875-4432
Fax: (202)295-9061
Co. E-mail: info@cogentco.com
URL: http://www.cogentco.com

E-mail: info@cogentco.com
Scope: Offers broadband data at speeds scalable from 100 Mbps to 1 Gbps.

53551 ■ DacEasy Inc.
17950 Preston Rd., Ste. 800
Dallas, TX 75252
Ph:(972)732-7500
Free: 800-322-3279
Fax: (972)713-6331
Co. E-mail: sales@daceasy.com
URL: http://www.daceasy.com

E-mail: sales@daceasy.com
Scope: Develops an accounting system for small businesses that integrates accounting, invoicing, payroll, communications, and management software into a single package. **Special Services:** DacEasy.

53552 ■ Global Business Consultants
120 Market Sq.
PO Box 776
Pinehurst, NC 28374-0776
Ph:(910)295-5991
Free: 800-991-4990
Fax: (910)295-5908
Co. E-mail: info@yourculturecoach.com

E-mail: info@yourculturecoach.com
Scope: Firm specializes in human resources management; project management; software development; and international trade. Offers litigation support.

53553 ■ Moneysoft Inc.
1 E Camelback Rd., Ste. 550
Phoenix, AZ 85012
Ph:(602)266-7710
Free: 800-966-7797
Co. E-mail: info@moneysoft.com
URL: http://www.moneysoft.com

E-mail: info@moneysoft.com
Scope: Specializes in the publication of software for the corporate acquisition and development community. Assists businesses develop acquisition goals and criteria that build shareholder value; determine whether an acquisition candidate meets their criteria, conduct analysis of the candidate's historic performance and position; estimate the candidate's future earnings capacity; prepare professional-quality valuations and appraisal reports for tax, business planning or litigation related matters; determine purchase price and optimal terms. Prepare a detailed plan to finance the acquisition; estimate the future earnings of the candidate after the acquisition; generate fact-filled acquisition proposals for presentation to management and funding sources; and manage and track fixed assets and depreciation. **Special Services:** Corporate Valuation Professional™; DealSense®; Buy-Out Plan®; Corporate Valuation™; Lightning Deal Reviewer®; Fixed Asset Pro™.

53554 ■ On-Q Software Inc.
13874 SW 11th St.
Miami, FL 33184
Ph:(305)553-2400
Free: 800-553-2862
Fax: (305)220-2666
Co. E-mail: info@on-qsoftware.com
URL: http://www.on-qsoftware.com

E-mail: info@on-qsoftware.com
Scope: Business software, including time and fixed fee billing, due date tracking, practice manager. **Special Services:** The Check Writing Partner.

53555 ■ Priority Process Associates Inc.
1236 E Horseshoe Bend Ct.
Rochester Hills, MI 48306
Ph:(248)608-8966
Fax: (248)608-8966
Scope: A management consulting firm with expertise in computer technology, telecommunications, and information services. Provides the following specific services: business process re-engineering-establishes correctly implemented, computer technologies that empower and accelerate work groups to act autonomously but in concert with corporate goals, document work-flow analysis-models and simulates the flow of documents through selected organizational processes, enterprise metrics-identifies unique metrics for enterprises to evaluate their continuous improvement of business processes, cost justification-identifies value using Activity Based Costing and innovative approaches to quantify time-to-market reductions, project profitability, and reduce and manage costs, proposal development-generates Requests for Proposals to solicit competitive quotations for cost effective off-the-shelf software, computer hardware, and communication products, implementation planning-negotiates implementation plans for clients through qualified software vendors, custom software integrators, and hardware, communication, and outsource suppliers, project auditing-audits the integration, installation and use of on-time, quality enterprise multivendor software, hardware and communications systems on computer networks, training-expands clients knowledge through information sources, and client-specific management seminars and skill building workshops. Serves manufacturing industries in the United States.

COMPUTERIZED DATABASES

53556 ■ *SOFTBASE: Reviews, Companies, and Products*
Guide IT LLC
1173 Colusa Ave.
PO Box 8120
Berkeley, CA 94707
Ph:(510)525-6220
Fax: (510)525-1568
Co. E-mail: softbase@searchsoftbase.com
URL: http://www.searchsoftbase.com
Description: Contains information on the Information Technology industry, with detailed descriptions on more than 12,000 information technology products. Includes company information, including personnel names, addresses, telephone numbers, URLs, e-mails, and a description of the company. Product information includes system requirements, availability, vendor support, and a product description. These product and company descriptions are linked to independent third-party reviews abstracted from more than 200 trade journals and industry magazines. **Availability:** Online: Guide IT LLC, Thomson Dialog, Thomson Dialog, CSA. **Type:** Bibliographic; Directory.

START-UP INFORMATION

53557 ■ **"All the Rage: Wondering What Everyone Will Be Crazy About in the Coming Year?"** in *Entrepreneur* (Vol. 33, January 2005, No. 1, pp. 84)
Pub: Entrepreneur Media Inc.
Ed: Sara Wilson. **Description:** Fitness and weight-loss, technical consulting, eBay drop-off stores, child tutoring/enrichment programs and senior care are among the top franchises for 2005.

53558 ■ **"Barter's latest comeback"** in *The Economist* (Vol. 357, No. 8, October 21, 2000, pp. 78)
Pub: Economist Newspaper Ltd.
Description: Most people know barter only from the playground, but a raft of American start-ups are trying to turn swapping into big business on the Internet.

53559 ■ **"Entrepreneurs test start-ups-on the side"** in *Wall Street Journal* (May 7, 2002, pp. B6)
Pub: Wall Street Journal
Ed: Jeff Bailey. **Description:** Many entrepreneurs are working fulltime jobs in order to finance their start-ups since venture capital and start-up funding has become more difficult to acquire.

53560 ■ **"Former Execs Go Franchising"** in *Boston Business Journal* (Vol. 23, No. 24, July 18, 2003, pp. 1)
Pub: American City Business Journals
Ed: Jill Lerner. **Description:** Several executives from the Boston, Massachusetts area that have been laid off by their firms, are starting their own franchises.

53561 ■ **"The Giant that would be King"** in *Red Herring* (No. 102, August 15, 2001, pp. 40-45)
Pub: Herring Communications
Ed: Robert LaFranco. **Description:** Microsoft transformed personal computing, is it about to reinvent entertainment? Streaming media is growing at a fast pace helping to promote new startup companies.

53562 ■ **"Hands On"** in *Inc.* (September 2000, pp. 107)
Pub: The Goldhirsh Group
Ed: Mike Hoffman. **Description:** Small-fry entrepreneurs who can't afford top legal or Human Resource advice may be confused by arcane federal rules. A thorough rundown on regulations covering small companies is included.

53563 ■ **"I'm Game: What Hot, New Pastime is Inspiring Entrepreneurs to Launch Businesses?"** in *Entrepreneur* (Vol. 32, September 2004)
Pub: Entrepreneur Media Inc.
Ed: Nichole L. Torres. **Description:** Cashflow 101 is the new business board game that teaches financial principles for accounting and investing. Profiles of entrepreneurs who launched a business after playing the game are included.

53564 ■ **"Kaleidoscope Yarns recently opened its doors at 15 Pearl Street"** in *Vermont Business Magazine* (Vol. 30, No. 9, Aug. 2002, pp. 18)
Pub: Vermont Business Magazine
Description: Profile of Kaleidoscope Yarns and its owners Marilyn and Bob Vincent. After 62 years, the shop continues to be a haven for knitters.

53565 ■ **"Military Service Equips Future Business Owners"** in *Home Business* (Vol. 12, March/April 2005, No. 2, pp. 44)
Pub: Home Business Magazine
Description: Twenty-two percent of American veterans are planning to purchase or start a small business, according to the Small Business Administration's Office of Advocacy.

53566 ■ **"Should You Get Incubated?"** in *E-business Advisor* (Vol. 18, No. 10, October 2000, pp. 18)
Pub: Advisor Media, Inc.
Ed: Kim M. Bayne. **Description:** Incubators, firms that take an idea and hatch it into a company, are on the increase. This article tells how to choose one and what to look for.

53567 ■ **"Small or Not, It's the Law"** in *Inc.* (September 2000, pp. 107)
Pub: The Goldhirsh Group
Ed: Ilan Mochari. **Description:** Frequent legal consultations add up, but many small business owners believe the cost is worth it for peace of mind and avoided litigation.

53568 ■ **"Take the Plunge! Teetering on the Edge of Unemployment?"** in *Entrepreneur* (Vol. 31, No. 11, November 2003, pp. 118)
Pub: Entrepreneur Media, Inc.
Ed: Nichole L. Torres. **Description:** Many individuals faced with losing their jobs are starting their own businesses, a trend seen across the nation.

53569 ■ **"Urban Legend: Do 90 Percent of Startups Really Fail to Make It Past Their First Year?"** in *Entrepreneur* (Vol. 31, No. 8, Aug., 2003)
Pub: Entrepreneur Media, Inc.
Ed: Karen E. Spaeder. **Description:** According to an economist with the Small Business Administration's Office of Advocacy, a business closure does not necessarily mean failure; exit strategies for businesses are discussed.

ASSOCIATIONS AND OTHER ORGANIZATIONS

53570 ■ **Academy of Legal Studies in Business**
120 Upham Hall - Dept. of Finance
Miami University
Oxford, OH 45056
Fax: (513)523-8180

Co. E-mail: herrondj@muohio.edu
URL: http://www.alsb.org
Contact: Prof. Daniel J. Herron, Exec. Sec.
Description: Teachers of business law and legal environment in colleges and universities. Promotes and encourages business law scholarship and teaching outside of the law school environment. **Publications:** *ALSB Newsletter* (3/year) ; *American Business Law Journal* (quarterly); *Journal of Legal Studies Education* (semiannual).

53571 ■ **Consumer Trends Forum International**
PO Box 2065
Lake Oswego, OR 97035
Ph:(503)620-6690
Fax: (503)620-6898
Co. E-mail: management@consumerexpert.org
URL: http://www.consumerexpert.org
Contact: Cathi McLain
Description: Provides global trend information and networking resources to assist members to identify and integrate trends into the design and marketing of consumer goods and services; educates businesses to interpret impact of trends on consumer needs and expectations. Hosts an annual Consumer Trends Forum with speakers addressing consumer trends. **Publications:** *Trendline* (biweekly).

53572 ■ **Small Business Legislative Council**
1100 H St. NW, Ste. 540
Washington, DC 20005
Ph:(202)639-8500
Fax: (202)296-5333
Co. E-mail: email@sblc.org
URL: http://www.sblc.org
Contact: John Satagaj, Pres./Gen. Counsel
Description: Serves as an independent coalition of trade and professional associations that share a common commitment to the future of small business. Represents the interests of small businesses in such diverse economic sectors as manufacturing, retailing, distribution, professional and technical services, construction, transportation, and agriculture. **Publications:** Newsletter (monthly).

REFERENCE WORKS

53573 ■ **"112 Million Handsets Can't Be Wrong"** in *Inc.* (July 1, 2004)
Pub: Inc. Magazine
Ed: Lora Kolodny. **Description:** Direct marketing via the cell phone is proving to be a success. Cell phone users are receiving, via text messages, promotions for area businesses.

53574 ■ **"2005 Corporate Elite Directory"** in *Hispanic Business* (January/February 2005, pp. 22)
Pub: Hispanic Business
Description: Profile of George Reyes, CFO at Google. Reyes helped to stage Google's $1.67 billion IPO. The trend for Hispanic men and women to hold high level positions continues to grow.

53575 ■ "A Sobering Vacation" in *Wall Street Journal* **(Vol. 248, December 2006, No. 142, pp. P1-P5)**
Pub: Dow Jones & Co. Inc.
Ed: Christina Binkley **Description:** Profiles of new high-end addiction treatment centers opening in the Malibu area.

53576 ■ "Abandoned by Your Accountants" in *Inc.* **(August 2005, pp. 19-21)**
Pub: Inc. Magazine
Ed: Amy Gunderson. **Description:** The Sarbanes-Oxley Act has overwhelmed accountants to the point that companies are finding it difficult to have their books audited. Statistical data included.

53577 ■ "Adapt or die: surviving the government's digital push" in *Black Enterprise* **(Vol. 33, No. 6, January 2003, pp. 42)**
Pub: Earl Graves Publishing Co.
Ed: Rebecca Rohan. **Description:** The economic survival of black-owned businesses depends on their knowledge of using technology. In the government's move towards a paperless operation, African American businesses must learn how to take advantage of the new opportunities that technology brings.

53578 ■ "Add An 'Inc' And Get Some Respect" in *Home Office Computing* **(Vol. 19, No. 1, January 2001, pp. 24)**
Pub: Scholastic Inc.
Ed: Jon Halpin. **Description:** The article discusses the fact that more small businesses are incorporating. Profiles of online incorporation services are provided.

53579 ■ "Advertising/Marketing" in *Hispanic Business* **(July/August 2002, pp. 14)**
Pub: Hispanic Business
Description: A discussion of corporations now using bilingual marketing campaigns that target the Hispanic community is presented.

53580 ■ "Almanac: Analysis" in *Inc.* **(October 17, 2000, pp. 67)**
Pub: The Goldhirsh Group
Ed: Martha E. Mangelsdorf. **Description:** What the characteristics of the Inc. 500 reveal about trends in the national economy are explored.

53581 ■ "Alternative Minimum Tax has Expanded Annually to Include More and More Taxpayers" in *Long Island Business News* **(March 5, 2004)**
Pub: Dolan Media Newswires
Ed: Ben Abelson. **Description:** An investigation into the alternative minimum tax (AMT) that began in the 1960s. In 1970 only 19,000 Americans owed the AMT growing to 2.5 million in 2003.

53582 ■ "Americans Have Grown Very Attached to Their Gadgets, Survey Finds" in *Portland Press Herald* **(December 23, 2005)**
Pub: Blethen Maine Newspapers, Inc.
Ed: Kelley Bouchard. **Description:** Americans are attached to high tech gadgets such as laptop computers, cellular phones, think pads, iPods, digital media receivers, etc. Demographics include every age group except seniors with annual incomes over $50,000.

53583 ■ "Analyze this: from "automation" to "effectiveness"" in *E-business Advisor* **(Vol. 18, No. 10, October 2000, pp. 10)**
Pub: Advisor Media, Inc.
Description: The market for analytics is rapidly expanding. The catch is that companies don't just need to identify who their customers are, they need to better figure out what customers do and why they do it.

53584 ■ *Anatomy of a Start-Up: Why Some New Businesses Succeed and Others Fail*
Pub: Inc. Publishing
Ed: Elizabeth K. Longsworth; introduction by Debbi Fields, Ranky Fields; foreword by George Gendron. **Released:** 1997. **Price:** $16.95; $14.50. **Description:** Provides information on start-ups, featuring 27 new business ventures and the business launch process.

53585 ■ "And Now a Syllable From Our Sponsor" in *Inc.* **(August 2005, pp. 22)**
Pub: Inc. Magazine
Description: New advertising campaigns are featuring one-second television commercials to promote products.

53586 ■ "The Anywhere Office" in *PC Computing* **(March 2000, pp. 146)**
Pub: Ziff-Davis Inc.
Ed: Jason Compton. **Description:** The article shows how to set up a virtual office.

53587 ■ "Are CIOs Obsolete?" in *Harvard Business Review* **(Vol. 78, No. 2, March 2000, pp. 55)**
Pub: Harvard Business School Publishing Corp.
Ed: Regina Fazio Maruca. **Description:** Are information technology and strategy now so much a part of each other that all senior managers are, or should be, obsolete?

53588 ■ "Are the Tax-Free Net's Days Numbered?" in *Home Office Computing* **(Vol. 18, No. 7, July 2000, pp. 16)**
Pub: Scholastic Inc.
Ed: Jeffery D. Zbar. **Description:** With the three-year moratorium on Web taxes set to expire in October 2001, the federally appointed Advisory Commission on Electronic Commerce (ACEC) has submitted recommendations designed to kill or slow adoption of new taxes. That means dot-coms would be exempt from charging sales taxes, while traditional retailers would still be required to charge sales taxes.

53589 ■ "Arm yourself for the coming battle over social security" in *Harvard Business Review* **(Vol. 80, No. 11, November 2002, pp. 52)**
Pub: Harvard Business School Press
Description: A visiting professor at Harvard Law School and a former member of the President's Committee to Strengthen Social Security describes the problems ahead for the Social Security system. He outlines three alternatives to reforming the system, including increasing contributions, decreasing growth of benefits for the affluent, and increasing returns on Social Security assets.

53590 ■ "ATMs Keep Evolving as Part of Customers' Everyday Life" in *Pacific Business News* **(Vol. 41, No. 24, August 22, 2003, pp. 10)**
Pub: American City Business Journals
Ed: Terri Inefuku. **Description:** Industry analysts state that the number of automated teller machines (ATMs) is rising in Hawaii. Bank of Hawaii has 475 ATMs, while First Hawaiian Bank has 184 ATMs in the state.

53591 ■ "Attract More Online Customers: Make Your Website Work Harder for You" in *Black Enterprise* **(Vol. 37, November 2006, No. 4, pp. 66)**
Pub: Earl G. Graves Publishing Co. Inc.
Ed: Description: Having an impressive presence on the Internet has become crucial. Detailed advice on making your website serve your business in the best way possible is included.

53592 ■ "Auto Review" in *Hispanic Business* **(March 2005, pp. 42, 44, 46, 48)**
Pub: Hispanic Business
Ed: Ralph Gray. **Description:** New car-based utility vehicles are offering consumers the best of owning an SUV and a sedan. Profiles of the Cadillac SRX, Lexus RX, Chevrolet Equinox, Chrysler Pacifica, Honda Pilot, Saturn Vue, Acura MDX, BMW X3, Infiniti FX45, Ford Freestyle, Nissan Murano, Range Rover, and other models are presented.

53593 ■ "Automaker pullback blamed for Detroit stamper's closing" in *Crain's Detroit Business* **(Vol. 19, No. 8, February 24, 2003, pp. 6)**
Pub: Crain Communications Inc., Detroit
Ed: Terry Kosdrosky. **Description:** Davis Tool & Engineering Company will close its doors after being

open for 65 years. The Detroit stamping plant is closing as the result of price competition and the automaker's recent trend to push component production back in-house.

53594 ■ "Automate Excel Functions: Easy-to-Create Macros Can Take Over Many Manual Processes" in *Journal of Accountancy* **(January 2005)**
Pub: American Institute of Certified Public Accountants
Ed: Jeff Lenning. **Description:** Macros can help accounts customize worksheets as well as export journal entries in Microsoft Excel into an accounting package and creating reports in Word.

53595 ■ "The Automotive Aftermarket Industry Association has Launched a New Online Feature for Its Members" in *Aftermarket Business* **(Jul. 03)**
Pub: Advanstar Communications, Inc.
Description: A new online service for members is being offered by the Automotive Aftermarket Industry Association. The service features easy access to legislators at its Legislative Action Center, including issues such as motor vehicle owners' right to repair, asbestos litigation reform, association health plans, class action reform and vehicle scrappage.

53596 ■ "Baby Bells must accept competition" in *Red Herring* **(January 2003, pp. 17)**
Pub: Herring Communications Inc.
Description: The four remaining Baby Bells must improve their businesses in order to remain competitive.

53597 ■ "Back to School" in *My Business* **(September/October 2001, pp. 24-25, 28-30)**
Pub: My Business Magazine
Ed: Shannon Scully, Lisa Waddle. **Description:** Small business owners are using boot camps, peer teaching, and e-learning to train their employees. Various small businesses share the unique ways they are training their work force.

53598 ■ "Balancing Act" in *Crain's Detroit Business* **(Vol. 22, January 30, 2006, No. 5, pp. 3)**
Pub: Crain Communications Inc. - Detroit
Ed: Sheena Harrison. **Description:** Small business leaders often take on more responsibilities than counterparts at large corporations. According to a recent study, high-level executives at successful small companies focus on teamwork, innovation, and strategic thinking.

53599 ■ "Balancing Act" in *Sales and Marketing.com* **(Vol. 147, No. 2, February 2004, pp. 16)**
Pub: VNU eMedia, Inc.
Ed: Julia Chang. **Description:** Many small businesses are learning that work/life balances, as well as financial rewards, for sales and marketing employees have become increasingly important.

53600 ■ "Ball of Yarn, Peace of Mind" in *Business Week* **(No. 3775, March 25, 2002, pp. 10)**
Pub: McGraw-Hill Inc.
Description: Knitting is becoming popular with younger women across America. The New York store, Gotta Knit, reports classes booked with women mainly in the age range of 20-30 years old.

53601 ■ "Banks Try to Make Tele-Touch Satisfy Small Businesses" in *American Banker* **(Vol. 171, November 27, 2006, No. 226, pp. 2)**
Pub: SourceMedia, Inc.
Ed: Jim Cole. **Description:** Banks serving small businesses continue to offer personalized services, while incorporating call centers and online service models to small business strategies. Statistical data included.

53602 ■ "Behind the Curve" in *Hispanic Business* **(Vol. 24, No. 5, May 2002, pp. 40-41)**
Pub: Hispanic Business Inc.

Ed: Teresa Talerico. **Description:** Hispanic small business owners are slow to accept technology. The importance of keeping up with technology for a small business is discussed.

53603 ■ "Better Off Red" in *Entrepreneur. com* **(Vol. 34, February 2006, No. 2, pp. 74)**
Pub: Entrepreneur Media Inc.
Ed: Gwen Moran. **Description:** People are moving away from traditional Valentine's gifts and buying more meaningful gifts for their loved ones. Marketing experts suggest retailers use red to merchandise products, suggest products as perfect gifts for the holiday, and use heart shaped items.

53604 ■ "Beyond the exchange: the future of B2B" in *Harvard Business Review* **(Vol. 78, No. 6, November-December 2000, pp. 86)**
Pub: Harvard Business School Publishing Corp.
Description: The evolution of business-to-business commerce on the Internet, and how it has been influenced by such revolutionary changes as an influx of specialists, a proliferation of creative business models, and new challenges for buyers and sellers. The article also forecasts the future of B2B on the Internet.

53605 ■ "The Big Bang: How Franchising Became an Economic Powerhouse the World Over" in *Entrepreneur* **(Vol. 32, No. 1, January 2004, pp. 86)**
Pub: Entrepreneur Media, Inc.
Ed: David J. Kaufmann. **Description:** David J. Kaufmann offers a perspective on the ways franchising has change the economy and opportunity for entrepreneurs during the last 25 years.

53606 ■ "Big Bonus" in *Entrepreneur* **(Vol. 30, No. 3, March 2002, pp. 77)**
Pub: Entrepreneur Media Inc.
Ed: Chris Sandlund. **Description:** Complying with government regulations costs small businesses with fewer than 20 employees 56 percent more per employee than those with 500 or more employees.

53607 ■ "The Big Picture" in *Fast Company* **(November 2001, pp. 134)**
Pub: Fast Company
Ed: George Anders. **Description:** The five technologies that are gaining universal acceptance and massive impact are profiled.

53608 ■ "Big five win little respect from small U.S. companies" in *Wall Street Journal* **(February 13, 2002, pp. A12)**
Pub: Wall Street Journal
Ed: Jeff Bailey. **Description:** A survey of nearly 400 small businesses by Cisco & Associates Inc, finds that 11.5 percent feel that the top five U.S. accounting firms, including Arthur Anderson and Deloitte & Touche, are unresponsive to small business.

53609 ■ "A Big Windfall for Small Biz" in *Business Week* **(No. 3843, July 28, 2003, pp. 14)**
Pub: McGraw-Hill Inc.
Ed: Kimberly Weisul. **Description:** President Bush's new tax, cuts which cut the capital gains tax from 20 percent to 15 percent, are encouraging entrepreneurs to sell their businesses.

53610 ■ "Bigfooting the Winter" in *Business Week* **(January 16, 2006, No. 3967, pp. 91)**
Pub: McGraw-Hill Companies
Ed: Lauren Young. **Description:** The latest in sports gear includes the Atlas 10 Series of snowshoes that are like all-terrain vehicles for your feet. They are constructed of light-weight plastic with high-end models offering ergonomically designed suspension systems for walking through snow with minimal effort.

53611 ■ "Bill Would Boost Small Businesses" in *Bradenton Herald* **(February 13, 2007)**
Pub: Bradenton Herald
Ed: Brian Neill. **Description:** U.S. Representative Vern Buchanan has introduced a bill in Congress that includes a provision that would enable small businesses to offer health insurance more readily through the formation of associations. The bill would also benefit small business owners by allowing them to deduct a larger portion of taxes for labor and capital expenditures.

53612 ■ "Black Enterprise's 2000 Business Entertaining Guide" in *Black Enterprise* **(Vol. 31, No. 5, December 2000, pp. 153)**
Pub: Earl Graves Publishing Co.
Ed: Ray Isle. **Description:** How you handle a business dinner can make the difference between success or failure.

53613 ■ "Blow-Ho-Ho! Inflatables Sales On Rise" in *Crain's Chicago Business* **(Vol. 26, No. 51, December 22, 2003, pp. 22)**
Pub: Crain Communications, Inc.
Ed: Brian McCormick. **Description:** The latest trend in neighborhood decorating comes in the form of inflatable snowmen, Santas, and toy soldiers. These decorations were commonly seen at malls and car lots, but have been scaled down to appeal to the residential homeowner for holidays.

53614 ■ "Boosting Corporate Diversity" in *Hispanic Business* **(April 2005, pp. 14)**
Pub: Hispanic Business
Description: Many corporate managers believe that diversity programs provide a competitive edge because they improve a company's performance and leadership. The University of Texas, Austin started a program to expand the number of diverse students for their MBA program.

53615 ■ "BorderWare to ship e-commerce gateways for small business use" in *Network World* **(December 6, 1999, pp. NA)**
Pub: Network World Inc.
Ed: Ellen Messmer. **Description:** A profile of Border-Ware Technologies line of three firewall-based gateway products for use in small business e-commerce sites that require a minimum of technical expertise. The BorderWare Office Gateway is intended for use by organizations with ten or less employees.

53616 ■ "Bradenton, Fla., Sees More Beach Weddings, Sells More Informal Bridal Wear" in *Bradenton Herald* **(March 22, 2004)**
Pub: Knight-Ridder/Tribune Business News
Ed: Dana Sanchez. **Description:** Economics and the trend towards smaller weddings, shows more couples saying their vows on beaches. This trend is reflected in the inventory, bookings and choice of venue for bridal-related businesses.

53617 ■ "Breaking Away" in *Inc.* **(October 1, 2004)**
Pub: Inc. Magazine
Ed: Nadine Heintz. **Description:** Companies are offering employees paid sabbaticals as a new benefit for long-term workers.

53618 ■ "Breaking Free from Budgets" in *Inc.* **(October 1, 2003)**
Pub: Gruner & Jahr USA Publishing
Ed: Suzanne McGee. **Description:** Exasperated by budgets that muzzle creativity, a growing number of small businesses are breaking free from financial constraints while conserving spending.

53619 ■ "Bridging the Gap" in *Sales & Marketing Management*
Pub: VNU Business Media
Ed: David Macey. **Description:** Retail-specific marketing solutions are becoming more important as effective ways to influence buying behavior in today's consumer market.

53620 ■ "Bring the New Economy Home" in *Home Office Computing* **(Vol. 18, No. 12, December 2000, pp. 66)**
Pub: Scholastic Inc.
Ed: William Van Winkle. **Description:** A guide to socalled New Economy concepts that can benefit a small business is presented. Small and home-based firms can seldom afford in-house expert help, and outsourcing is a viable option for a variety of business processors. Experts recommend that companies outsource to providers with other clients in the same line of business.

53621 ■ "Buck's Annual 401(k) Survey Shows Dramatic Growth In Web Administration" in *Employee Benefit Plan Review* **(Vol. 55, No. 7, Jan. 2001)**
Pub: Charles D. Spencer & Associates, Inc.
Description: Buck Consultant's 11th annual survey reports a dramatic increase in the number of employers who make use of Web technology to administer 401(k) plans.

53622 ■ "The Bucks Start Here" in *Business Week* **(No. 3658, December 6, 1999, pp. F10)**
Pub: McGraw-Hill, Inc.
Description: Small, fast growing companies are investing in their businesses without taking out new bank loans to do it. As bank rates rise and profit margins remain strong, these companies are choosing to finance growth from their own cash flow.

53623 ■ "Build a Successful Business Partner Network" in *E-business Advisor* **(Vol. 18, No. 5, May 2000, pp. 36)**
Pub: Advisor Media, Inc.
Ed: Tim Claxton. **Description:** Business-to-business initiatives require online collaborative partnerships via a business partner network (BPN), also known as extranet. BPNs come with many benefits including speeding up joint projects, reducing costs and cycle times, supplies delivery on time and providing 24x7 customer service. Strategies for building an extranet, managing extranets and the future of BPNs are presented.

53624 ■ "Building strength in New Mexico" in *New Mexico Business Journal* **(Vol. 26, No. 8, September 2002, pp. 30)**
Pub: New Mexico Business Journal
Ed: Janet Butler. **Description:** New Mexico health club membership is growing, following similar trends throughout the United States.

53625 ■ "A Bumper Crop of Worries" in *Tampa Tribune* **(November 30, 2005)**
Pub: Media General, Inc.
Ed: Will Rodgers. **Description:** Florida citrus growers face challenges of disease, development, hurricanes, and competition, hurting profits and land use.

53626 ■ "Burst of Energy" in *Entrepreneur. com* **(Vol. 34, February 2006, No. 2, pp. 46)**
Pub: Entrepreneur Media Inc.
Ed: Kristin Ohlson. **Description:** Renewable, clean energy is a growing sector. Liquid Resources produces nearly 3 million gallons of ethanol annually, with water as its only waste product.

53627 ■ "Business gurus talk about practicing basics" in *Atlanta Business Chronicle* **(Vol. 25, January 10, 2003, No. 31, pp. 4B)**
Pub: American City Business Publications, Inc.
Ed: Timothy S. Mescon, Michael H. Mescon. **Description:** In today's business environment, fad philosophies have been replaced by a new appreciation for the corny, basic, time-tested sage advice. Nine nuggets of corny business wisdom from a recent business event are discussed.

53628 ■ "Business and the Internet" in *Ingram's* **(Vol. 27, No. 4, April 2001, pp. 22)**
Pub: Show Me Publishing, Inc.
Ed: Carol Rudder. **Description:** Online businesses have moved to online networks working together to provide solutions to complex business problems.

53629 ■ "The Business of Nanotech" in *Business Week* **(February 14, 2005, No. 3920, pp. 64)**
Pub: McGraw-Hill Companies
Ed: Stephen Baker, Adam Aston. **Description:** Soon cars, chips and even golf balls will be produced using new materials engineered down to the level of individual atoms. Some 1,200 nano startups have emerged globally.

53630 ■ "California Job Growth Slows" in *Sacramento Bee* **(November 19, 2005)**
Pub: The Sacramento Bee
Ed: Rachel Osterman. **Description:** Job growth in California is slowing down. As of July 2005, employer payrolls were up by an average of 20,900 positions per month, but have slowed to around 10,000.

53631 ■ "California Teaming" in *Fast Company* **(November 2001, pp. 30)**
Pub: Fast Company
Ed: Heath Row. **Description:** Profile of Company of Friends, the organization whose mission is to bring southern California's multiple business communities closer and help other teams and organizations worldwide with collaboration.

53632 ■ "Call Centers In the Rec Room" in *Business Week* **(January 23, 2006, No. 3968, pp. 76-77)**
Pub: McGraw-Hill Companies
Ed: Michelle Conlin. **Description:** Homeshoring provides an alternative to offshoring, whereby American companies are finding a cheap alternative to overseas call centers in the form of stay-at-home moms, the disabled, retirees, and others. Statistical data included.

53633 ■ "Calling security" in *Entrepreneur* **(Vol. 30, No. 9, September 2002, pp. 23)**
Pub: Entrepreneur Media Inc.
Ed: Melissa Campanelli. **Description:** Both large and small businesses are implementing security-related technologies, including mailing services like PaperlessPOBox located in San Francisco, California.

53634 ■ "Card-Carrying Kids" in *Sacramento Bee* **(November 12, 2005)**
Pub: The Sacramento Bee
Ed: Jon Ortiz. **Description:** Marketing Workshop Inc. conducted a survey that showed one in five adults purchased gift cards for their children ages 5-8 years old. Kay Palna, a professor at Iowa State University, is concerned the practice will encourage materialism by teaching children to worry about money at too young an age.

53635 ■ "Case Study" in *Inc.* **(November 1, 2004)**
Pub: Inc. Magazine
Ed: Lora Kolodny. **Description:** PDAs are becoming extinct and being replaced by smart cell phones capable of both data and voice services.

53636 ■ "Cashless customers" in *WorkingWoman* **(Vol. 25, No. 2, February 2000, pp. 69)**
Pub: Lang Communications Inc.
Ed: Lisa Lee Freeman. **Description:** New business may be pulled in through barter networks. Business owners may establish reciprocal trading agreements.

53637 ■ "Casual rules" in *Incentive* **(Vol. 174, No. 9, September 2000, pp. 54)**
Pub: Bill Communications
Ed: Joan M. Steinauer. **Description:** When motivating with business casual apparel, keep in mind the functionality of casual business attire for your employees.

53638 ■ "Cataloging the web" in *Incentive* **(Vol. 174, No. 10, October 2000, pp. 99)**
Pub: Bill Communications
Ed: Emily Hodnett. **Description:** Online award catalogs have a lot to offer, but before you follow this trend, don't forget the benefits of print copy.

53639 ■ "Catch of the Day: Next up: distributed networks" in *Red Herring* **(No. 103, September 1, 2001, pp. 18)**
Pub: Herring Communications
Ed: Rafe Needleman. **Description:** The trend of distributed computing is covered. The distributed computing concept can be applied to scarce networking resources, particularly wireless bandwidth, in ways that could drive revenue by encouraging sales of devices for the end user.

53640 ■ "Chain Lightening" in *Hispanic Business* **(May 2005, pp. 72, 74)**
Pub: Hispanic Business
Ed: Dale Buss. **Description:** Hispanics are fueling the growth in franchise ownership. Franchising tips are shared by Detroit's Ruben Acosta, franchising expert and lawyer, and founder of Pizza Patron.

53641 ■ "Chamber trouble: organizations in California and Texas suffer high-profile resignations" in *Hispanic Business* **(Vol.22, July-Aug. 2000)**
Pub: Hispanic Business
Ed: Peter Brennan. **Description:** Hispanic business groups in California and Texas have suffered a series of high-profile resignations during 2000, including the departure of Alex Torres as chair and president of the California Hispanic Chamber of Commerce, and Ray Leal, president of the Texas Association of Mexican American Chambers of Commerce.

53642 ■ "Change Of Face" in *Entrepreneur* **(Vol. 28, No. 4, April 2000, pp. 125)**
Pub: Entrepreneur Media Inc.
Ed: Mark Henricks. **Description:** Entrepreneurial shapeshifters may be in one business today and something entirely different tomorrow. The key is knowing when it's time to change focus.

53643 ■ "Changes in Care" in *Pittsburgh Business Times* **(Vol. 23, No. 1, July 25, 2003, pp. 1s)**
Pub: Pittsburgh Business Times
Ed: Lynne Glover. **Description:** Lutheran Affiliated Services, led by CEO Greg Hughes, operates a chain of nursing homes and is the ninth-largest elder care firm in the Pittsburgh, Pennsylvania area. Hughes creates a more homelike atmosphere at the facilities.

53644 ■ "The Changing World of Crisis Management" in *Rough Notes* **(Vol. 145, No. 12, December 2002, pp. 74)**
Pub: Rough Notes
Ed: Deborah M. Hampton. **Description:** Crisis management, once used particularly for natural disaster management, has now expanded to market fluctuations, fuel prices, and terrorism.

53645 ■ "Chicago Tribune Business Agenda" in *Chicago Tribune* **(February 28, 2005)**
Pub: Knight-Ridder/Tribune Business News
Description: Economic predictions, unemployment rates, and manufacturing are issues discussed.

53646 ■ "CID businesses self-tax to fund improvements" in *Atlanta Business Chronicle* **(Vol. 24, No. 14, September 7, 2001, pp. 3C)**
Pub: American City Business Journals Inc.
Ed: Erica Stephens. **Description:** Atlanta has seen many Community Improvement Districts (CIDs) start up in recent years, with the popularity being that they let their own tax rates and regulations within the laws of the local government. Lynn Rainey of Jackel, Rainey, Busch, & Reed LLC, Tad Leithead of Urban One Associates, and George Berry of Cousins Properties Inc. share their views on CIDs.

53647 ■ "Class Reunion: Corporate Alumni Groups Keep Business Connections Going" in *Sales & Marketing Management* **(Vol. 157, January 2005)**
Pub: VNU Business Media
Ed: Julia Chang. **Description:** Alumni organizations are becoming a new source for hiring and business networking.

53648 ■ "Close the Loop" in *Entrepreneur* **(Vol. 31, No. 10, October 2003, pp. 82)**
Pub: Entrepreneur Media, Inc.
Ed: Chris Penttila. **Description:** Today companies can outsource most types of work, a trend entrepreneurs are using to grow their business.

53649 ■ "Close Shave" in *Portland Press Herald* **(September 28, 2005)**
Pub: Blethen Maine Newspapers, Inc.

Ed: Justin Ellis. **Description:** Lynden Pitt, owner of J & L Haircutters, is closing the shop he and his wife now run. Pitt's father opened the business nearly 60 years ago. Pitt plans to teach the art of barbering during his retirement.

53650 ■ "Club Meds: Could Drug-Buying Clubs Cure High Prescription Costs?" in *Entrepreneur* **(Vol. 32, November 2004, No. 11, pp. 24)**
Pub: Entrepreneur Media Inc.
Ed: Julie Monahan. **Description:** Fifty employers from the Fortune 500 are teaming to negotiate better prices with pharmaceutical companies to help ease the burden of high costs of prescription drugs for employees.

53651 ■ "Clutter Busters: From Closets to Cabinets to Garages, Americans' Clutter is Piling Up Like Never Before" in *Entrepreneur*
Pub: Entrepreneur Media Inc.
Ed: Nichole L. Torres. **Description:** According to the National Association of Professional Organizers, the increased public interest in organizing their lives, professional organizers have doubled in number in the last two years. Some of these entrepreneurs are manufacturing organizing products, while others are becoming professional consultants.

53652 ■ "Coke Out to Woo Mall Rats Here With Lounge" in *Crain's Chicago Business* **(Vol. 26, No. 51, December 22, 2003, pp. 9)**
Pub: Crain Communications, Inc.
Ed: Kate MacArthur. **Description:** Coca-Cola has created the Coca-Cola Red Lounge for teenagers shopping at the north suburban Vernon Hills, Westfield Shoppingtown Hawthorn Center, as well as another site in Los Angeles, California. Coke is trying to build a brand with young people, separating it from being a brand for older folks. Statistical data included.

53653 ■ "Commentary: 'About Us' Pages Spell Good Business, Consumer Confidence" in *Long Island Business News* **(February 27, 2004)**
Pub: Dolan Media Newswires
Ed: Adina Genn. **Description:** Small businesses are creating About Us pages on their Websites. These provide a site where a company can share information about its history, philosophies and mission. This information can be used as a marketing tool to attract new customers.

53654 ■ "Commentary: Research is Key To Getting Hired in 'Jobless Recovery'" in *Long Island Business News* **(January 30, 2004)**
Pub: Dolan Media Newswires
Description: In a slow job market, basic job search networking may not be enough to land a new position. Job seekers should focus on providing value and demonstration of skills and talents when contacting hiring managers, as well as doing research in finding good jobs that are available. Tips for doing this type of research are given.

53655 ■ "Commentary: Turning Job Losses to Indian Into Gains" in *Long Island Business News* **(January 30, 2004)**
Pub: Dolan Media Newswires
Description: An alternative strategy that might benefit the loss of jobs in the U.S. that are going to India, would be to utilize each nation's proven capabilities in homeland security by expanding defense co-production opportunities.

53656 ■ "Companies Adapt to Elder Care Needs" in *Orlando Sentinel* **(February 9, 2005)**
Pub: Orlando Sentinel
Ed: Harry Wessel. **Description:** Experts predict elder-care information and consultation will become common in the workplace, much like childcare for employees, in order to assist workers caring for elderly relatives.

53657 ■ *The Company We Keep: Reinventing Small Business for People, Community, and Place*
Pub: Chelsea Green Publishing
Ed: John Abrams. **Released:** May 2005. **Price:** $27.50 (US), $31.50 (Canadian). **Description:** The new business trend in social entrepreneurship as a business plan enables small business owners to meet the triple bottom line of profits for people (employees and owners), community, and the environment.

53658 ■ "The Competitiveness of Small and Medium Enterprises" in *Journal of Business Venturing* (Vol. 17, No. 2, March 2002, pp. 123)
Pub: Elsevier Science, Inc.
Ed: Thomas W.Y. Man, Theresa Lau, K.F. Chan. **Description:** The development of a conceptual model, patterned after the notion of competitiveness and the competency approach, is discussed. This conceptual model was developed to connect the performance of the traits small and medium-sized enterprises (SME), owner-managers and their companies have in common.

53659 ■ "Conflict of interest" in *Red Herring* (January 2003, pp. 23)
Pub: Herring Communications Inc.
Ed: Stacy Lawrence. **Description:** Most large U.S. firms still pay two-thirds of the money to auditors on non-audit services, however there is a shift toward spending their IT consulting budget elsewhere.

53660 ■ "Consumer Finance" in *Business Week* (January 16, 2006, No. 3967, pp. 38)
Pub: McGraw-Hill Companies
Ed: Peter Burrows. **Description:** A new trend shows online brands offering shoppers Bill Me later payment options in order to spur sales growth and offer a billing method to consumers uneasy about using their credit cards on the Internet. So far 230 e-commerce sites offer this service.

53661 ■ "Continuing to Shine" in *Hispanic Business* (December 2001, pp. 10)
Pub: Hispanic Business
Ed: Holly Ocasio Rizzo. **Description:** The demand for temporary industrial and clerical workers has increased since mid-September 2001. Companies that lay people off still need work done, so they hire temporary workers.

53662 ■ "Convenience pushes pendulum back to PPO coverage" in *Crain's Detroit Business* (Vol. 18, No. 16, April 22)
Pub: Crain Communications Inc. - Detroit
Ed: David Barkholz. **Description:** An interview with Kay Farnell, vice president of the family-owned Farnell Equipment Co. Farnell tells how her company's experiment with a health maintenance organization lasted only a year, only to return to a PPO.

53663 ■ "Convicts Stealing Small Business Jobs" in *My Business* (September/October 2001, pp. 19)
Pub: My Business Magazine
Description: Awarding federal contracts to Federal Prison Industries (FPI) is costing small businesses millions of dollars annually.

53664 ■ "COOs: Less Room At the Top" in *Business Week* (January 31, 2005, pp. 11)
Pub: McGraw-Hill Companies
Ed: Louis Lavelle, Ira Sager. **Description:** Since the dot.com demise, a number of companies are eliminating the position of Chief Operating Officer from their executive teams.

53665 ■ "A Corporate Peace Corps Catches On" in *Business Week* (January 31, 2005, pp. 14)
Pub: McGraw-Hill Companies
Ed: Jessi Hempel. **Description:** Corporate Peace Corps are created when a company lends top talent to charities. Nike will begin offering workers a five-week sabbatical to volunteer with aid groups, Pfizer and PricewaterhouseCoopers already send employees to developing countries to help nonprofit organizations. Nonprofit Building Blocks International helps to connect businesses to social causes.

53666 ■ "Corporate Present-Giving Looking Up After Slow Stretch" in *Milwaukee Journal Sentinel* (December 3, 2005)
Pub: Journal Sentinel, Inc.
Ed: Rick Romell. **Description:** According to a survey conducted by American Express, 71 percent of small businesses plan to give holiday gifts to clients and customers in 2005.

53667 ■ "Cracking the Code of Change" in *Harvard Business Review* (Vol. 78, No. 3, May 2000, pp. 133)
Pub: Harvard Business School Publishing Corp.
Ed: Michael Beer, Nitin Nohria. **Description:** New research indicates that combining "hard" and "soft" approaches to changing businesses can radically transform the way companies do change.

53668 ■ "Crafts Americana Group to Expand Presence in Vancouver, Wash." in *The Columbian* (February 22, 2003)
Pub: Knight-Ridder/Tribune Business News
Ed: Gretchen Fehrenbacher. **Description:** Profile of Crafts American Group, the company specializing in catalog and Web sales of craft supplies, is planning to expand with 40,000 square foot of new space, which includes retail space. The new building will offer a larger area for crafts classes and products, including quilting, tole painting, and knitting.

53669 ■ "A crafty Christmas: with people cutting spending, more gifts are homemade" in *Wall Street Journal* (Dec. 20, 2002, pp. W14)
Pub: Dow Jones & Co. Inc.
Ed: Danielle Reed. **Description:** The slow economy has turned people towards making homemade gifts for loved ones, particularly hand-knitted items.

53670 ■ "A Crash Diet for Dot-Coms" in *Kiplinger's Personal Finance Magazine* (Vol. 54, No. 8, August 2000, pp. 21)
Pub: The Kiplinger Washington Editors, Inc.
Ed: Melynda Dovel Wilcox. **Description:** With Web downsizing, the Internet superhighway is no longer the road to riches. But, high-tech employees still have a ticket to ride.

53671 ■ "A Crisis of Content: It's not just pop music." in *Time* (Vol. 156, No. 14, October 2, 2002, pp. 68)
Pub: Time Inc.
Description: Every industry that trades in intellectual property, from publishing to needlework patterns, could get Napsterized. Jim Hedgepath, president of Pegasus Originals, discusses problems encountered to protect his copyrighted cross-stitch needlework patterns.

53672 ■ "Cross-Border Property Deals" in *The Economist* (Vol. 376, July 30-August 5, 2005, No. 8437, pp. 67)
Pub: The Economist Newspaper Ltd.
Description: Property investors are ready to buy and to sell abroad. Property deals by region, including North America, Europe and Asia-Pacific are presented.

53673 ■ "Cross-Training" in *Entrepreneur* (Vol. 31, No. 9, July 2003, pp. 83)
Pub: Entrepreneur Media, Inc.
Ed: Kim T. Gordon. **Description:** Multichannel marketing, using broadcast, direct mail, email and print campaigns, are being used to attract customers and increase sales.

53674 ■ "Cultivating Teleworkers" in *Home Office Computing* (Vol. 18, No. 12, December 2000, pp. 102)
Pub: Scholastic Inc.
Ed: William Van Winkle. **Description:** Mutual fund company Putnam Investments used to be able to find qualified employees at job fairs. When that resource started to dry up they discovered that there is a ripe market for those workers that want to telecommute. This article takes a look at Putnam Investment's efforts and how well they have succeeded in their telecommuting program.

53675 ■ "Customs dictates" in *Entrepreneur* (Vol. 30, No. 3, March 2)
Pub: Entrepreneur Media Inc.
Ed: Michelle Prather. **Description:** Since September 11, 2001, importers and exporters can expect to experience greater unpredictability and harsher penalties for violating import/export regulations.

53676 ■ "Cyber Theft" in *Rough Notes* (Vol. 145, No. 2, February 2003, pp. 40)
Pub: Rough Notes
Ed: Phil Zinkwicz. **Description:** There has been a rise in cyber crimes involving breaches of computer systems, invasion by computer viruses, and loss of confidential information, intellectual property and financial losses. Insurance companies can provide appropriate coverage.

53677 ■ "Cybersecurity: Opportunities for Agents" in *Rough Notes* (Vol. 145, No. 1, January 2003, pp. 110)
Pub: Rough Notes
Ed: G. Edward Kalbaugh. **Description:** Any product or action to secure a wired or wireless work constitutes CyberSecurity, such as virus protection for computers, risk identification, insurance, risk assessment, and liability insurance. CyberSecurity promises to be one of the fastest growing businesses of the future, as more than $330 billion have been earmarked for the Department of Homeland Security.

53678 ■ "The Daily Paper of Tomorrow" in *Business Week* (January 9, 2006, No. 3966, pp. 20)
Pub: McGraw-Hill Companies
Ed: Jon Fine. **Description:** A six-point list of things for the future of daily newspapers include using Google to advertise, offer a news-digest daily, put more information online, increase local coverage, redesign products for more appeal, and build communities and businesses around community-created content.

53679 ■ "Damm Dotcoms!" in *Entrepreneur* (Vol. 28, No. 8, August 2000, pp. 78)
Pub: Entrepreneur Media Inc.
Ed: Brian O'Connell. **Description:** Online companies present problems for traditional businesses, but the real winners in traditional business are positioning themselves to ride the e-coattails.

53680 ■ "Deal Jitters?" in *Inc.* (October 2005, pp. 48)
Pub: Inc. Magazine
Ed: Dalia Fahmy. **Description:** Many firms are now purchasing insurance when acquiring a company. Purchase protection cover financial losses if a seller makes false claims in a sale contract, and should be used in deals valued at least $10 million.

53681 ■ "Debit Cards Ease FSA Administration Burden" in *Rough Notes* (Vol. 145, No. 9, September 2002, pp. 34)
Pub: Rough Notes
Ed: Len Strazewski. **Description:** Flexible spending accounts are not popular with employers nor employees owing to the heavy paperwork involved, but Congress may introduce legislation that will ease the administrative aspect so as to facilitate usage of the program.

53682 ■ "Delayed Obsolescence" in *Hispanic Business* (March 2005, pp. 64)
Pub: Hispanic Business
Ed: Kevin Savetz. **Description:** Advance planning by small companies can help make technology investments last over the years. Small business software purchases should be made with future use in mind.

53683 ■ "Dell and NetObjects make small business play" in *Network World* (October 24, 2000, pp. NA)
Pub: Network World Inc.
Ed: Ashlee Vance. **Description:** Dell plans to pre-install NetObject's software for building Web sites on some Dell desktops and notebooks. The software helps users build, publish and promote their own Web sites under the co-branded product title NetObjects Fusion Dell Edition.

53684 ■ "Dell, Other Corporations Shut Venture Units" in *Venture Capital Journal* **(February 1, 2005)**
Pub: Thomason Financial Inc.
Description: Nearly 166 corporate VCs spent $1.3 billion on 476 deals in 2004, compared to 2,155 deals totaling $16.9 billion in 2000. Investing venture capital by U.S. corporations continues to decline.

53685 ■ "Deloitte unit gets 1st woman" in *Crain's Detroit Business* **(Vol. 19, No. 17, April 28, 2003, pp. 3)**
Pub: Crain Communications Inc., Detroit
Ed: Katie Merx. **Description:** Deloitte & Touche LLP has named Sally Buckles, age 42, as the first woman to head its Detroit office and Great Lakes region. Buckles is the first woman to head one of the Big Four accounting firms.

53686 ■ "Design Innovation Brings Communications Challenges" in *Employee Benefit Plan Review* **(Vol. 55, No. 7, January 2001, pp. 27)**
Pub: Charles D. Spencer & Associates, Inc.
Ed: Sue Burzawa. **Description:** The 401(k) plan design evolved rapidly in the late 1990s, and that trend is continuing. Recent innovations, including automatic enrollment and Web access for information and transactions of plans, are expected to soon be common practice.

53687 ■ "Designs Changing as New Generation of Buyers Emerges" in *Chicago Tribune* **(March 6, 2005)**
Pub: Knight-Ridder/Tribune Business News
Ed: John Handley. **Description:** New generation home buyers desire streetscapes in their communities, larger homes, and more courtyards.

53688 ■ "Destination" in *Hispanic Business* **(June 2005, pp. 92)**
Pub: Hispanic Business
Ed: Joel Russell. **Description:** According to the National Automobile Dealers Association, car dealers reported an average of 2.2 percent in revenue gains for 2004. Hispanic car dealers are using the superstore concept to promote growth.

53689 ■ "Detroit Free Press Small Business Column" in *Detroit Free Press* **(June 6, 2005)**
Pub: Knight-Ridder/Tribune Business News
Ed: Carol Cain. **Description:** According to an American Express survey, a vast number of Michigan small business owners are planning summer vacations in 2005.

53690 ■ "Digging Deeper and Keeping Up" in *Employment Relations Today* **(Vol. 26, No. 4, Winter 2000, pp. 95)**
Pub: John Wiley & Sons, Inc.
Description: A bibliography of books that deal with the future of work and employment is presented. Topics include the Internet, unemployment, and employee relations.

53691 ■ "Distance Makes a Difference" in *Home Office Computing* **(Vol. 18, No. 8, August 2000, pp. 20)**
Pub: Scholastic Inc.
Ed: Cynthia Froggatt. **Description:** As increasing numbers of workers are working at home, bosses are discovering that traditional management practices may no longer apply. The three basic distinctions in telemanagment vs. traditional management methods are described.

53692 ■ "Diversity in the Big City" in *Hispanic Business* **(June 2002, pp. 80)**
Pub: Hispanic Business
Ed: Vivienne Heines. **Description:** The New York Times conducted a study that reveals that both hiring managers and job seekers in the New York metropolitan area equate diversity with equal opportunity and fairness, thus seeing diversity as a contribution to a good work environment. Statistical data included.

53693 ■ "Do-It-Yourself Insurance" in *Inc.* **(Volume 27, December 2005, No. 12, pp. 39-40, 42)**
Pub: Inc. Magazine
Ed: Alison Stein Wellner. **Description:** Individual insurance policies are becoming more popular, but premiums vary from state to state. The pros of cons of a small business replacing group health plans in favor for individual policies are discussed.

53694 ■ "Do You Need Web Services?" in *E-business Advisor* **(Vol. 18, No. 12, December 2000, pp. 16)**
Pub: Advisor Media, Inc.
Ed: Jeri Dube, David Sink. **Description:** Business to business (B2B) transactions are complicated, but new Web-based services will provide new ways for companies to integrate their systems and applications over the Internet. The services will enable companies to leverage their strengths and respond to events in real time. Standards for the new services are still under development and not all applications are suitable for use on the Web. The Universal Description, Discovery and Integrations (UDDI) initiative has developed a specification that will enable businesses to discover each other and conduct business with each other over the Internet.

53695 ■ "Dot-Com Distress" in *PC Magazine* **(February 20, 2001, pp. 67)**
Pub: Ziff-Davis Publishing Company
Ed: Sebastian Rupley. **Description:** A concise history of the dot-com industry is presented, including some optimism for the future of those e-tailers that survive.

53696 ■ "Down payment help" in *Black Enterprise* **(Vol. 33, No. 3, Oct. 2002, pp. 52)**
Pub: Earl Graves Publishing Co.
Ed: Nicole Graves. **Description:** Profile of the Nehemiah Corporation and its program that allows the seller or home builder to contribute from 1-6 percent of the contract sales price of the home to help facilitate the transaction, thus, the sellers gets the property's full market value and the buyer has little expense for the mortgage.

53697 ■ "Downtown Cafes Build on Lunchtime Basics" in *Crain's Chicago Business* **(Vol. 26, No. 51, December 22, 2003, pp. 16)**
Pub: Crain Communications, Inc.
Ed: Anne Spiselman. **Description:** Profiles of Earth Mothers and City Foods, two uniquely different cafes located in downtown Chicago, Illinois. Both restaurants offer soups, salads and sandwiches, either carryout or dine-in, but one relies almost entirely on organic products, some are sold in the front of the store; while City Foods is decorated with a few black tables, a couch with TV trays in front of it, food is served cafeteria style with Styrofoam, cardboard, and plastic containers and utensils.

53698 ■ "Drumming Up Business For the Democrats" in *Business Week* **(January 9, 2006, No. 3966, pp. 39)**
Pub: McGraw-Hill Companies
Ed: Richard S. Dunham. **Description:** Heath Shuler is among the new recruits running as candidates for Democratic seats; these new recruits are business executives offering financial experience that will make the party stronger.

53699 ■ "E-Biz Buzz" in *E-business Advisor* **(Vol. 18, No. 8, August 2000, pp. 58)**
Pub: Advisor Media, Inc.
Ed: Buzz Hunter. **Description:** Web users are becoming less receptive to traditional forms of marketing. E-commerce providers will find a lucrative market in small businesses by offering solid support, quick answers to questions, and easy access to other services and products.

53700 ■ "E-Commerce: When You Put Your 'John Hancock' on the Web Form!" in *Ingram's* **(Vol. 27, No. 5, May 2001, pp. 33)**
Pub: Show Me Publishing, Inc.
Ed: Arthur L. Smith. **Description:** Businesses are still finding ample opportunities from the electronic marketplace. Contracts made electronically are just as binding as the traditional paper contract.

53701 ■ "E-Procurement Catching On" in *Hispanic Business* **(October 2002, pp. 88)**
Pub: Hispanic Business
Ed: Tim Dougherty. **Description:** An increasing number of small businesses are turning to the Internet to fulfill purchasing needs, and happy with the results.

53702 ■ "Easy e-commerce" in *WorkingWoman* **(Vol. 25, No. 6, June 2000, pp. 107)**
Pub: Lang Communications Inc.
Ed: Nancy Henderson. **Description:** Intensive courses in the business use of the World Wide Web are described, with focus on choosing a course to fit your previous knowledge and your own requirements.

53703 ■ "Eat the upper crust" in *Entrepreneur* **(Vol. 30, No. 3, March 2002, pp. 28)**
Pub: Entrepreneur Media Inc.
Description: Whether at fine restaurants, or fast food chains, burgers are going gourmet.

53704 ■ "Eat, Drink and Be Merry, Trans Fats or No" in *San Diego Business Journal* **(Vol. 28, January 8, 2007, No. 2, pp. 31)**
Pub: San Diego Business Journal Associates
Ed: Thomas York. **Description:** Starbucks coffee shops will no longer use trans fats in any of its products. The announcement followed New York City's ban on trans fats in local eateries; San Francisco is considering the same move.

53705 ■ "Eco-Preneuring" in *Small Business Opportunities* **(Vol. 12, No. 3, May 2000, pp. 56, 58)**
Pub: Harris Publications, Inc.
Ed: Michael L. Eskew. **Description:** "Green" companies can find golden opportunities. The practice of eco-commerce, or environmentally responsible companies, can pay off in more efficient processes and products, and, therefore, reduce operating costs.

53706 ■ *The Emerging Digital Economy: Entrepreneurship, Clusters, and Policy*
Pub: Springer
Ed: Borje Johansson; Charlie Karlsson; Roger Stough. **Released:** August 2006. **Price:** $119.00. **Description:** The new economy, or digital economy, and its impact on the way industries and firms choose to locate and cluster geographically.

53707 ■ "The empire strikes back; Counterrevolutionary strategies for industry leaders" in *Harvard Business Review* **(Vol. 80, Nov. 2002, pp. 66)**
Pub: Harvard Business School Press
Ed: Richard D'Aveni. **Description:** Five ways that industry leaders can respond to revolutionary business models or disruptive technologies. The strategies are containment, shaping, absorption, neutralization and annulment.

53708 ■ "Employee Organizations: Tomorrow's Possibilities" in *Employment Relations Today* **(Vol. 26, No. 4, Winter 2000, pp. 53)**
Pub: John Wiley & Sons, Inc.
Ed: Arthur B. Shostak. **Description:** An investigation into the future of employees' organizations within corporations, focusing on the structure of corporate culture in the 21st century. The article identifies five factors that will influence employee groups in the future, which include economic expansion, communication systems, artificial intelligence, smart technology, and genetic engineering.

53709 ■ "The employee strikes back" in *Wall Street Journal* **(April 16, 2002, pp. B1)**
Pub: Wall Street Journal
Ed: Kemba J. Dunham. **Description:** The trend towards employees holding positions at two different firms in order to hedge their bets is growing increasingly popular among workers. Related information included.

53710 ■ "Employers Won't Give Big Pay Raises in 2006, Survey Finds" in *Sacramento Bee* **(December 3, 2005)**
Pub: The Sacramento Bee
Ed: Rachel Osterman. Description: According to a recent survey of more than 1,000 employers across the country, average salary increases will be 3.6 percent in 2006. Companies are expected to offer bonuses and incentive pay based on performance.

53711 ■ "The Endangered Department Store" in *Boston Globe* **(February 13, 2005)**
Pub: New York Times Company
Ed: Keith Reed. Description: The merger between Macy's and Filene's is causing experts to question whether mass-market department stores are on the decline. Many department stores are reinventing themselves in order to stay competitive with the luxury high-end and low-cost discount stores.

53712 ■ "Enterprising Moves" in *MEDIAWEEK* **(Vol. 11, No. 4, January 22, 2001, pp. 65)**
Pub: BPI Communications
Ed: Lori Lefevre. Description: Major publishers are building up their small-business books in a big way. Despite the large number of mergers in recent years, some 5.8 million small businesses continue to thrive, and several leading publishers hope to increase their coverage to win over new readers and ads.

53713 ■ "Entrepreneur Column" in *Entrepreneur.com* **(January 18, 2007)**
Pub: Entrepreneur Media Inc.
Ed: Tamara Monosoff. Description: Considerations of changing trends in inventors: who they are, how they operate, and how businesses are dealing with them both internally and externally.

53714 ■ "Evaluating and Managing a Potential Clawback Liability" in *Venture Capital Journal* **(Vol. 42, No. 9, September 2002, pp. 34-35)**
Pub: Thomas Venture Economics
Ed: Steven R. Franklin, Stig A. Colberg. Description: The trend towards venture capital fund management fee reductions is examined. Two steps for evaluating and managing potential clawback liabilities and ways to best determine who is responsible for the liability are included.

53715 ■ "Even "E-Active" Organizations Have a Lot to Learn" in *E-business Advisor* **(Vol. 18, No. 3, March 2000, pp. 8)**
Pub: Advisor Media, Inc.
Description: Most e-commerce companies understand the basic business concepts involved, such as Web portals, value chain and customer relations, but do not understand the issues of reintermediation, vortals and reverse markets. This article helps to bring meaning to these issues.

53716 ■ "Even as the M&A Market Heats Up, Unloading a Company Gets Trickier" in *Inc.* **(May 1, 2005)**
Pub: Inc. Magazine
Ed: Description: According to a recent survey conducted by PricewaterhouseCoopers, one of every two business owners plan to sell their company in the next ten years, resulting in a glut of companies on the market, forcing down valuations and giving new leverage to buyers.

53717 ■ "Exclusive Survey Reveals Diversity Trends" in *Hispanic Business* **(January/February 2003, pp. 34-35, 36, 38, 40-42)**
Pub: Hispanic Business
Description: According to the first Hispanic Business Corporate Diversity Survey, which focuses on public corporations among the top 60 advertisers in the Hispanic market, companies with Hispanic executives fare better in procurement and recruitment.

53718 ■ "Falling in Gov" in *Entrepreneur* **(Vol. 30, No. 3, March 200)**
Pub: Entrepreneur Media Inc.
Ed: Amanda C. Kooser. Description: E-government is the next fertile, immense market space on which young entrepreneurs should set their focus. E-government is businesses that provide technical services to state agencies.

53719 ■ "Family values: companies are catering to the needs of dad, mom and kids" in *Incentive* **(Vol. 174, No. 10, October 2000, pp. 9)**
Pub: Bill Communications
Ed: Libby Estell. Description: Family-friendly benefits continue to be a strong retention tool for employers. Workers are putting greater emphasis on family, expecting shorter work hours at the office, and thanks to a strong economy and tight labor market, employers have been accommodating.

53720 ■ "Fantastic Plastic" in *Entrepreneur* **(Vol. 31, No. 9, September 2003, pp. 84)**
Pub: Entrepreneur Media, Inc.
Description: The trend towards giving gift cards is growing. Retailers sold more than $36 billion worth of gift cards in 2002. A Website selling cards for less than $1 each is featured.

53721 ■ "Fast, Faster, and Fastest" in *Fortune* **(Vol. 142, No. 11, November 13, 2000, pp. F384FF)**
Pub: Time Inc.
Ed: Joel Dreyfuss. Description: The options for speedier Internet connections for small companies are explained to help decide the best service for your business.

53722 ■ "The Fast Lane: A New Concept in Retail is Popping Up All Over" in *Entrepreneur* **(Vol. 33, January 2005, No. 1, pp. 64)**
Pub: Entrepreneur Media Inc.
Ed: Gwen Moran. Description: Profile of Russell Miller, founder of Vacant, a company that sets up here today, gone tomorrow pop-up retail locations for hard-to-find items. These stores stay open two weeks to a month. Another option for short term sales would be a kiosk at a local mall.

53723 ■ "Fever Pitch: Pull Out Your Thermometers, 'Cause Things Are Heating Up!" in *Entrepreneur* **(Vol. 32, December 2004, No. 12, pp. 72)**
Pub: Entrepreneur Media Inc.
Ed: Karen Axelton, Steve Cooper, Amanda C. Kooser, April Y. Pennington, Karen E. Spaeder, Laura Tiffany, Nichole L. Torres, Sara Wilson, Natalia Olenicoff, Rebecca Villaneda, Jeri Yoshida. Description: Newest trends, hottest markets and business ideas for small companies in 2005 are presented, including the use of borrowing a business model.

53724 ■ "The 51 percent rule fallout" in *Hispanic Business* **(Vol. 22, No. 3, March 2000, pp. 40)**
Pub: Hispanic Business
Ed: Derek Reveron. Description: The decision of the National Minority Supplier Development Council to alter the minority status of businesses is examined. Minority status will now be given to companies with 30 percent of their non-voting stock owned by minorities compared with 51 percent previously.

53725 ■ "Filing for Bankruptcy" in *Black Enterprise* **(Vol. 34, No. 7, February 2004, pp. 12)**
Pub: Earl Graves Publishing Co.
Description: Personal bankruptcy filings have increased in 2003, however business bankruptcy filings decreased in the same year.

53726 ■ "The Film Biz Goes Filmless" in *Business 2.0* **(Vol. 6, July 2005, No. 6, pp. 30)**
Pub: Time, Inc.
Description: A move to distribute movies to theater houses digitally could save Hollywood up to $1 billion annually.

53727 ■ "Finding deals, small businesses buy more online" in *The New York Times* **(May 15, 2000, pp. C4)**
Pub: The New York Times Company
Ed: Laurie J. Flynn. Description: The findings of a survey conducted by Access Markets International Partners regarding e-commerce.

53728 ■ "Finding Your Way: Navigation Systems Move Beyond High-End Cars" in *Black Enterprise* **(Vol. 35, January 2005, No. 6, pp. 48)**
Pub: Earl G. Graves Publishing Co. Inc.
Ed: Anthony Calypso. Description: Positioning system-based navigation systems are being used in commercial, mass transit, and public safety applications. Companies are offering mounted or handheld personal navigation systems for cars, laptop computers, and even PDAs.

53729 ■ "Firms playing dot-name game" in *Atlanta Business Chronicle* **(Vol. 24, No. 9, August 3, 2001, pp. 3A)**
Pub: American City Business Journals Inc.
Ed: Mary Jane Credeur. Description: In an effort to protect corporate trademarks and combat unauthorized use of company names, businesses are beginning to register new domain names for upcoming Web addresses. Examples of these new names include .biz and .info.

53730 ■ "Firms Seek Tonic for Labor-Pool Headaches" in *Crain's Chicago Business* **(Vol. 23, September 11, 2000, pp. 4)**
Pub: Crain Communications, Inc.
Ed: Sarah A. Klein. Description: These days employees are looking for coverage for everything from acupuncture to chiropractic treatments to aromatherapy, and more insurers are offering those benefits to them.

53731 ■ "Firms Skid on Rising Oil and Gas Prices" in *Black Enterprise* **(Vol. 36, February 2006, No. 7, pp. 35)**
Pub: Earl G. Graves Publishing Co. Inc.
Ed: Wendy Isom. Description: Small businesses across the nation are facing economic difficulties incurred by rising oil and gas prices in the aftermath of Hurricane Katrina.

53732 ■ "Firms Turn to Perks in Lieu of Bonus Checks" in *Inc.* **(December 1, 2004)**
Pub: Inc. Magazine
Ed: Rod Kurtz. Description: According to a recent study, more employees are offering non-monetary awards rather than cash bonuses.

53733 ■ "Fixing Diversity-Challenged Companies" in *Black Enterprise* **(Vol. 36, February 2006, No. 7, pp. 74)**
Pub: Earl G. Graves Publishing Co. Inc.
Ed: Lee Anna Jackson. Description: R. Roosevelt Thomas, Jr., founder of The American Institute for Managing Diversity, believes most corporations have replaced the term "affirmative action" with "diversity" but has not changed its mindset of employees or modified company culture.

53734 ■ "Flash: our outlook on what's new, what's hot and what's happening" in *Entrepreneur* **(Vol. 31, No. 5, May 2003, pp. 6)**
Pub: Entrepreneur Media Inc.
Description: Floppy disks are becoming obsolete and analog wireless service is being phased out over the next five years; Supermarkets are partnering with toy retailers; and hot dogs and fondue are going gourmet.

53735 ■ "Flat Fee Delivers Flexibility" in *Detroit News* **(February 17, 2005)**
Pub: Detroit Newspapers
Ed: Elise Oberliesen. Description: Listing a home for sale with a flat fee or discount broker allows sellers more flexibility when pricing their home. Flat fee brokers list a home on a multiple listing service, a database of homes on the open market.

53736 ■ "Focus on emerging markets" in *Black Enterprise* **(Vol. 32, No. April 2002, 9, pp. 30)**
Pub: Earl Graves Publishing Co.
Ed: Matthew S. Scott. Description: Presentation of trends in the minority community, focusing on publicly traded companies pursuing the minority marketplace, are minority-owned, and are southeast-based large- and mid-cap companies.

53737 ■ "Follow the flight plan" in *Entrepreneur* **(Vol. 30, No. 1,)**
Pub: Entrepreneur Media Inc.
Ed: Geoff Williams. **Description:** The author suggests that learning to think like a fighter pilot will help entrepreneurs be successful. Many top managers from companies like Home Depot and FedEx have followed that trend.

53738 ■ "For Biggest, No Brakes On This Trend" in *American Banker* **(Vol. 170, February 4, 2005, No. 24, pp. 1)**
Pub: Thomson Financial Media Inc.
Ed: David Boraks. **Description:** Retail banking is opening new branches at the rate of one every three hours and expected to continue through 2005. Since the population and growth is not keeping pace, competition and price cutting could lead to more closing and mergers in the industry.

53739 ■ "For some companies, it pays to be private" in *Red Herring* **(March 2003, pp. 66)**
Pub: Herring Communications Inc.
Ed: Michael V. Copeland. **Description:** Currently, an increasing number of private companies are being valued at a higher multiple than public counterparts.

53740 ■ "For U.S. Small Biz, Fertile Soil in Europe" in *Business Week Online* **(April 3, 2002)**
Pub: McGraw-Hill, Inc.
Description: This year 2002 is turning out to be a great year for many small and midsize American companies selling to or operating in Europe, especially high-tech companies.

53741 ■ "The Forgotten Strategy" in *Harvard Business Review* **(Vol. 81, No. 11, November 2003, pp. 76)**
Pub: Harvard Business School Press
Ed: Pankaj Ghemawat. **Description:** Potential changes in business globalization strategies are examined.

53742 ■ "Friend or Faux? Why Big Businesses Want to Look Like You" in *My Business* **(February/March 2003, pp. 51)**
Pub: My Business Magazine
Ed: Harvey King. **Description:** To move away from the tarnished images of corporate executives, more big companies are spending money trying to appear small to the consumer.

53743 ■ "Furry Friends" in *Entrepreneur.com* **(Vol. 34, February 2006, No. 2, pp. 52)**
Pub: Entrepreneur Media Inc.
Ed: Jacquelyn Lynn. **Description:** With the cost of veterinary care rising, more insurance companies are offering health insurance coverage for pets and a growing number of firms are offering it in their voluntary insurance offerings to employees.

53744 ■ "The Future of Cyberwork" in *Employment Relations Today* **(Vol. 26, No. 4, pp. 61)**
Pub: John Wiley & Sons, Inc.
Description: Studies labor trends in Internet technology, focusing on how cyberwork will impact the decisions of managers and human resource departments by 2025. Topics addressed include the work and challenges of Internet-related professionals, as well as the changes the Internet will bring to the labor market.

53745 ■ "GE Whiz!" in *Entrepreneur* **(Vol. 28, No. 1, January 2000, pp. 32)**
Pub: Entrepreneur Media Inc.
Ed: Cynthia E. Griffin. **Description:** GE Capital to offer services for small businesses.

53746 ■ "Gearing Up For Expansion" in *Fast Company* **(March 2005, No. 92, pp. 90)**
Pub: Gruner & Jahr USA Publishing
Ed: Shonan Noronha. **Description:** Profile of Adobe's Acrobat 7 business software designed to allow users to take total control over the creation and distribution of important documents, as well as making them more accessible to clients, coworkers, and strategic partners.

53747 ■ "Get the Message? SMS Technology Could Bring Mobile Commerce Within Your Reach" in *Entrepreneur* **(Vol. 32, October 2004, No. 10)**
Pub: Entrepreneur Media Inc.
Ed: Amanda C. Kooser. **Description:** The international popularity of mobile-commerce is spreading to the U.S. Short Message Service (SMS) enables users to send queries as text messages over a mobile phone or device and receive answers to questions without links or web pages.

53748 ■ "Get Physical! Former Couch Potatoes are Jumping on a New Trend: Interactive Video Games" in *Entrepreneur* **(Vol. 32, August 2004)**
Pub: Entrepreneur Media Inc.
Ed: Steve Cooper. **Description:** New video games require players to physically interact with games. Sony Computer Entertainment American offers EyeToy, a motion-sensitive camera that plugs into a PlayStation 2 console and places the player's image into the game.

53749 ■ "Getting Ahead" in *Hispanic Business* **(June 2005, pp. 18)**
Pub: Hispanic Business
Description: According to a study from the Immigration Policy Center, immigrant women play an important role in the growth of women entrepreneurship in the U.S.

53750 ■ "Getting Ahead Of the Weather" in *Fortune* **(Vol. 151, February 7, 2005, No. 3, pp. 87)**
Pub: Time Inc.
Ed: Abraham Lustgarten. **Description:** The National Oceanic and Atmospheric Administration estimates a third of the U.S. gross domestic product is affected by weather in the form of slowed transportation, inflated energy costs, and interrupted sales. Steps some businesses are taking to protect their firms against the elements are profiled.

53751 ■ "Getting it together" in *Incentive* **(Vol. 174, No. 10, October 2000, pp. 138)**
Pub: Bill Communications
Description: To enhance recruitment and retention efforts, employer work/life programs are examined.

53752 ■ "Going Global" in *Home Office Computing* **(Vol. 18, No. 10, October 2000, pp. 87)**
Pub: Scholastic Inc.
Ed: David Harvey. **Description:** Small and home-based business are increasingly able to do business abroad by leveraging the power of the Internet and locating online tools and resources for tapping overseas markets. Steps to building an effective Web site are covered.

53753 ■ "Going Private: How VCs Can Get in the Game" in *Venture Capital Journal* **(Vol. 42, No. 10, October 2002, pp. 49)**
Pub: Thomas Venture Economics
Ed: Jonathan Bell. **Description:** A trend towards venture capital firms to reverse course and help companies go private is examined. To minimize the risk that the transaction may be questionable as being unfair to minority shareholders, an independent and disinterested committee of the company's board should handle negotiations.

53754 ■ "Gold's Buys Gym, Converts to Women's Facility in Tallahassee, Fla." in *Tallahassee Democratic* **(October 3, 2002)**
Pub: Knight Ridder/Tribune Business News
Ed: Juana Jordan. **Description:** Profile of Gold's Gym, and its expansion in the Tallahassee fitness market. The gym has renovated one of its centers to become a women's only gym.

53755 ■ "Gone Fishin'" in *Entrepreneur* **(Vol. 31, No. 10, October 2003, pp. 82)**
Pub: Entrepreneur Media, Inc.
Ed: Joanne Cleaver. **Description:** Advice for small firms that close the last week of the year, citing the fact that some companies actually profit from the shutdown.

53756 ■ "Good as Gold" in *Entrepreneur* **(Vol. 32, No. 1, January 2004, pp. 106)**
Pub: Entrepreneur Media, Inc.
Ed: Devlin Smith. **Description:** The hottest franchising trends for 2004 include senior care, child products and services, technology, home improvement, fitness, income tax preparation, business consulting, specialty ice cream and coffee.

53757 ■ "Got Game?" in *Entrepreneur* **(Vol. 32, October 2004, No. 10, pp. 95)**
Pub: Entrepreneur Media Inc.
Ed: Chris Penttila. **Description:** Entrepreneurial introspection is a growing trend in small business. Strategic plans implemented inside a company help give employees and managers a realistic look at the business and its goals.

53758 ■ "Got Leverage? Dollar Signs: If You're Ready to Sell, You've Got the Upper Hand" in *Entrepreneur* **(Vol. 31, No. 9, September 2003)**
Pub: Entrepreneur Media, Inc.
Ed: C.J. Prince. **Description:** With increased private equity activity, large buyout firms will be looking towards entrepreneurs. Statistical data included.

53759 ■ "Got anything smaller?" in *Entrepreneur* **(Vol. 30, No. 10, October 2002, pp. 83)**
Pub: Entrepreneur Media Inc.
Ed: Chris Sandlund. **Description:** A new trend shows that two out of three corporate executives prefer to work for smaller firms.

53760 ■ "Grading confusion: Computer makers balk at report card's methods" in *Waste News* **(Vol. 7, No. 16, December 10, 2001, pp. 1)**
Pub: Crain Communications Inc. - Akron
Ed: Joe Truini. **Description:** E-Waste is one of the fastest growing waste streams. The release of the Third Annual Computer Report Card that measures computer companies' effectiveness in clean production, protecting workers' health and making environmentally superior products was released. Results of the report are given.

53761 ■ "The Great Transition" in *Harvard Business Review* **(Vol. 81, No. 10, October 2003, pp. 70)**
Pub: Harvard Business School Press
Ed: Kenneth Kieberthal, Geoffrey Lieberthal. **Description:** Opportunities and perils faced by multinational corporations in the U.S. planning to set up operations in China are discussed. Specific suggestions are offered to help avoid or minimize problems.

53762 ■ "Green Business Push Blooms" in *Charlotte Observer* **(February 7, 2007)**
Pub: Knight-Ridder/Tribune Business News
Ed: Christopher D. Kirkpatrick. **Description:** Many energy companies are capitalizing on corporate guild about global warming. Companies offering environmental peace of mind are discussed.

53763 ■ "Grist: An Entrepreneurs Resolutions" in *Inc.* **(January 1, 2005)**
Pub: Inc. Magazine
Ed: Adam Hanft. **Description:** Small business New Year's resolutions are discussed, including recommendations to help grow a business.

53764 ■ "Grist: More Power Than Point" in *Inc.* **(August 1, 2003)**
Pub: Gruner & Jahr USA Publishing
Ed: Adam Hanft. **Description:** Although there is an estimated 400 million computers using Microsoft's computer software program PowerPoint, many believe it radically oversimplifies issues.

53765 ■ "Groom Your Workforce" in *PC Computing* **(March 2000, pp. 137)**
Pub: Ziff-Davis Inc.
Ed: Leslie Ayers. **Description:** Internet training will teach employees the best way to do their jobs more effectively, with the convenience of learning on their own time and at their own pace.

53766 ■ "Group Buys Bradenton, Fla.-Area Retail Center" in *Bradenton Herald* **(January 5, 2005)**
Pub: Bradenton Herald
Ed: Matt Griswold. Description: Kash n' Karry was purchased by New York real estate firm Gemini Real Estate Advisors LLC and 10 other investors, for the sum of $15.2 million. The store is located in the Ranch Lake Plaza in Bradenton, Florida. Gemini Real Estate Advisors LLC is one of many nationwide companies focusing on tenant-in-common, 1031 exchanges. This process allows individuals to invest with a large firm in tax-free pieces of commercial real estate.

53767 ■ "The Growing Opportunity in Server Consolidation" in *Venture Capital Journal* **(Vol. 42, No. 9, September 2002, pp. 36-37)**
Pub: Thomas Venture Economics
Ed: Roger Lee. Description: Reducing the number of servers to a manageable number allows corporations to save money on real estate, power consumption, security, and IT administration.

53768 ■ "Growth in a streamling sector" in *Hispanic Business* **(Vol. 22, No. 4, April 2000, pp. 24)**
Pub: Hispanic Business
Ed: Jonathan J. Higuera, Joel Russell. Description: Engineering services company, L&M Technologies, has improved personnel management, technical services and knowledge specialization in order to maintain its competitiveness in the federal contract market. The teaming of companies to improve expertise is discussed.

53769 ■ "Hack away" in *Entrepreneur* **(Vol. 30, No. 3, March)**
Pub: Entrepreneur Media Inc.
Ed: Amanda C. Kooser. Description: With cyberterrorism becoming a greater threat, more small businesses are hiring computer hackers as computer consultants.

53770 ■ "Hallandale Beach, Fla., City Leaders Criticize Dating Service Company" in *Miami Herald* **(December 2, 2003)**
Pub: Knight Ridder/Business Tribune News
Ed: Hector Florin. Description: Hallandale Beach, Florida city leaders are questioning the ethics of the dating service, Great Expectations.

53771 ■ "Hard Landing for Landlines" in *Crain's New York Business* **(Vol. 22, December 4, 2006, No. 49, pp. 3)**
Pub: Crain Communications, Inc.
Description: More than two million residential landline customers are choosing Internet telephone service and cell phones over their landlines. Verizon is suffering the greatest in this new trend.

53772 ■ "Heart of Gold: Nonprofits Are Reaping the Rewards of Starting For-Profit Ventures" in *Entrepreneur* **(Vol. 32, September 2004, No. 9)**
Pub: Entrepreneur Media Inc.
Ed: Chris Penttila. Description: Nonprofit organizations are looking to for-profit ventures in order to diversify revenue streams.

53773 ■ "Here to Stay: When You're Looking for New Hires, Temps May Not be as Temporary as You Might Think" in *Entrepreneur* **(Vol. 32, July 2004)**
Pub: Entrepreneur Media Inc.
Ed: Chris Penttila. Description: Temporary staffing agencies have filled at least 162,200 new temporary positions from April to July 2004, according to the U.S. Bureau of Labor Statistics. Companies are wary of hiring new full-time employees and are opting for temporary workers.

53774 ■ "High and Dry? A New Federal Contract Program May Not Be an Oasis After All" in *Entrepreneur* **(Vol. 32, No. 4, April 2004, pp. 20)**
Pub: Entrepreneur Media, Inc.
Ed: Stephen Barlas. Description: Other than defense and Homeland Security, federal contracts have been down. Procurement rules for Homeland Security contracts are being questioned by the U.S. Small Business Administration.

53775 ■ "Hit the Mark" in *My Business* **(August/September 2002, pp. 28-35)**
Pub: My Business Magazine
Description: Seven small business trends that will position a company for success are profiled. These trends include mentoring programs, e-mail marketing, customer service, personalized products and services, employee stock ownership plans, targeting markets, and automation.

53776 ■ "Holding a Job, Having a Life: The Next Level in Work" in *Employment Relations Today* **(Vol. 27, No. 2, Summer 2000, pp. 29)**
Pub: John Wiley & Sons, Inc.
Ed: Jill Casner-Lotto. Description: Many companies are employing new strategies that enhance business performance while helping employees experience a better balance between work and their personal lives. Research by the Work in America Institute is presented.

53777 ■ "Holding Pattern" in *Entrepreneur* **(Vol. 33, September 2005, No. 9, pp. 26)**
Pub: Entrepreneur Media Inc.
Ed: Mark Henricks. Description: Small business hiring has been at a standstill in 2005 and small business salaries fell 2.2 percent from January to June. Statistical data included.

53778 ■ "Home Office vs. the Field" in *Sales & Marketing Management*
Pub: VNU Business Media
Description: Incentives for sales teams are debated by a salesperson and sales manager.

53779 ■ "Home Offices as Status Symbol" in *Home Office Computing* **(Vol. 18, No. 12, December 2000, pp. 24)**
Pub: Scholastic Inc.
Ed: Lisa Roberts. Description: The article tells how people are spending large amounts of money on home offices.

53780 ■ "Home crafting stimulates togetherness" in *Retail Merchandiser* **(Vol. 42, No. 11, Nov. 2002, pp. 33)**
Pub: VNU Business Media
Description: The uncertain economic environment has more people spending time at home, which in turn promotes crafting; parents are spending time with children putting together easy craft kits. Chuck Waimon, COO of Fairfield Processing in Danbury, Connecticut shares his views on consumer trends in home crafts.

53781 ■ "Homework 2001" in *Small Business Opportunities* **(Vol. 13, No. 5, September 2001, pp. 72-73)**
Pub: Harris Publications, Inc.
Description: It is estimated that every week 8,000 people decide to work at home, equating to nearly 55 million people with home-based offices. This increase is making a positive impact on home design, floor plans and building materials.

53782 ■ "Honoring the Profit" in *PC Computing* **(April, 2000, pp. 58)**
Pub: Ziff-Davis Inc.
Ed: Jennifer Brandlon. Description: A Princeton University study of American attitudes towards materialism and faith reported that spiritual values still sway economic behavior.

53783 ■ "Host a Virtual Meeting: Collaborate with a Video Link and a Whiteboard" in *Journal of Accountancy* **(Vol. 199, February 2005, No. 2)**
Pub: American Institute of Certified Public Accountants
Ed: Nancy B. Nichols, Stephanie M. Bryant. Description: Microsoft offers software that lets a small business host a virtual meeting by computer, allowing participants to talk, share files, and see each other in real time.

53784 ■ "Hot Bets in the Cold North" in *Business Week* **(December 19, 2005, No. 3964, pp. 24)**
Pub: McGraw-Hill Companies
Ed: Robert Barker. Description: Companies drilling for coalbed methane in Canada include Apache, EnCana, Nexen, and Quicksilver Resources.

53785 ■ "Hotels skip surcharges, focus on conservation" in *Atlanta Business Chronicle* **(Vol. 24, No. 14, September 7, 2001, pp. S6)**
Pub: American City Business Journals Inc.
Ed: Erica Stephens. Description: Many hotels are eliminating surcharges, and instead focusing on ways to conserve energy. Matt Smith of the Ritz-Carlton Hotel Company has formed REACT, the Ritz-Carlton Energy Action and Conservation Teams. Hermann Gammeter has formed a committee to promote energy conservation. Due to the reactions from customers to surcharges, energy conservations are growing.

53786 ■ "How China Will Change Your Business" in *Inc.* **(Volume 27, March 2005, No. 3, pp. 70-80, 84)**
Pub: Inc. Magazine
Ed: Ted C. Fishman. Description: Fourteen important issues for entrepreneurs regarding China's economic expansion are covered.

53787 ■ "How to Ride the Fifth Wave" in *Business 2.0* **(Vol. 6, July 2005, No. 6, pp. 78-83, 85)**
Pub: Time, Inc.
Ed: Michael V. Copeland, Om Malik. Description: Affordable computing, infinite bandwidth, and open standards are driving an epic technological transformation expected to create new tech opportunities, as well as problems for those who are not able to adapt to the changes.

53788 ■ "HSAs-A Growing Trend In Health Benefits for Businesses and Individuals" in *Entrepreneur* **(Vol. 32, December 2004, No. 12, pp. 67)**
Pub: Entrepreneur Media Inc.
Description: Health savings accounts (HSAs) allow individuals with high-deductible health plans to put pre-tax money aside, spend it tax-free on qualified health expenses, earn interest tax-free and also save the money for health-care expenses in retirement. HSAs may be a way for small companies to manage health benefits costs by exchanging higher deductibles for lower premiums and tax advantages.

53789 ■ "Hyper business or just... hyperbusy?" in *Women in Business* **(Vol. 53, No. 3, May-June, 2001, pp. 12)**
Pub: The ABWA Co. Inc.
Ed: Sheryl Dawson. Description: The apparent trend for Americans to be working longer hours is due to factors including personnel cuts and an aging workforce. The rising cost of living and growing consumer demand for material goods also keeps Americans working longer hours.

53790 ■ "I Can't Seem to Hire the Right Bookkeeper. Should I Try Using a Personality Test?" in *Inc.* **(October 2005, pp. 62)**
Pub: Inc. Magazine
Description: Personality tests that screen job applicants for traits like reliability and dishonesty have become commonplace in most industries.

53791 ■ "I Feel Your Pain" in *Forbes* **(Vol. 174, December 27, 2004, No. 13, pp. 38)**
Pub: Forbes Magazine Inc.
Ed: Annie Murphy Paul. Description: Reasons corporate America continues to fall for workplace fads are addressed.

53792 ■ "I Spy...: Workplace Surveillance is Coming to Small and Midsize Businesses" in *Entrepreneur* **(Vol. 31, No. 8, August 2003, pp. 20)**
Pub: Entrepreneur Media, Inc.
Ed: Nichole L. Torres. Description: Nearly 20 percent of small companies actively monitor email and Internet

usage, and another 20 percent are considering the process, according to Mallary Tytel, president of Healthy Workplaces LLC. The consulting firm, located in Bolton, Connecticut, state that small to mid-size firms are more likely to use technological surveillance rather than pricier undercover detective agencies.

53793 ■ *IBM on Demand Technology for the Growing Business: How to Optimize Your Computing Environment for Today and Tomorrow*
Pub: Maximum Press
Ed: Jim Hoskins. **Released:** June 2005. **Price:** $29.95. **Description:** IBM is offering computer solutions to small companies entering the On Demand trend in business.

53794 ■ **"IBM, Microsoft, others plan alliance to help conduct business online" in** *Wall Street Journal* **(February 6, 2002, pp. B4)**
Pub: Wall Street Journal
Description: The plans being made to form alliances for conducting business transactions online by such companies as IBM, Microsoft and others, are discussed.

53795 ■ **"IBM Readies Linux Suite for Small Biz" in** *Network World* **(November 6, 2000, pp. NA)**
Pub: Network World Inc.
Ed: Ed Scannell. **Description:** A profile of IBM's Linux suite for small businesses.

53796 ■ **"I'd Rather Be Flying (Myself)" in** *Inc.* **(January 1, 2002)**
Pub: Inc. Magazine
Ed: Phaedra Hise. **Description:** Business owners have always been more likely than most people to be private pilots, and this practice is becoming more popular.

53797 ■ **"If Telemarketers Paid For Your Time" in** *Forbes* **(April 15, 2002, p. 225)**
Pub: Forbes Magazine
Ed: Ian Ayres, Barry Nalebuff. **Description:** Ideas are offered to help small businesses improve processes and services to help them prosper.

53798 ■ **"If the spirit moves you" in** *Fast Company* **(May 2001, pp. 54)**
Pub: Fast Company
Ed: Jill Rosenfield. **Description:** An overview of the executive retreats that have become a staple of corporate life.

53799 ■ **"I'll Trade You..." in** *Home Office Computing* **(Vol. 18, No. 9, September 2000, pp. 87)**
Pub: Scholastic Inc.
Ed: Steven Van Yoder. **Description:** An overview of Internet sites such as BarterTrust.com, Big-Vine and Ubarter have brought back the ancient concept of barter by linking members with trading networks to create mini-economies.

53800 ■ **"I'm O.K., You're Not" in** *Business Week* **(No. 3694, August 14, 2000, pp. F10)**
Pub: McGraw-Hill, Inc.
Description: Many entrepreneurs see the dot-com shakeout as an opportunity to recapture some lost business.

53801 ■ **"IM: When Time Matters" in** *Hispanic Business* **(November 2002, pp. 34)**
Pub: Hispanic Business
Ed: Roger Harris. **Description:** Instant Messaging software is the perfect solution to emergencies and conferencing for small businesses; more than 20 million people worldwide use Instant Messaging in business, and it is predicted by International Data Corp. that more than 300 million will be using the method by 2005.

53802 ■ **"The importance of being multilingual" in** *Business Week Online* **(Sept. 5, 2002)**
Pub: McGraw-Hill Inc.
Ed: Thane Peterson. **Description:** The importance of bilingualism to small business as an opening to globalization is examined.

53803 ■ **"In Accounting, Number of Registered Sole Practitioners Decreasing" in** *Long Island Business News* **(March 5, 2004)**
Pub: Dolan Media Newswires
Ed: David Reich-Hale. **Description:** The number of registered accounting sole practitioners in New York has decreased 25 percent since 2000, according to a public relations manager at the New York State Society of Certified Public Accountants.

53804 ■ **"In Brief: Discover Touting Gas Rewards" in** *American Banker* **(Vol. 172, January 31, 2007, No. 21, pp. 16)**
Pub: SourceMedia, Inc.
Ed: H. Michael Jalili. **Description:** Discover Financial Services LLC reported a direct correlation between energy prices and small business confidence. Discover's small business program that offers cash back on gasoline purchases has been successful. Statistical data included.

53805 ■ **"In office of the future, we'll all be scanned like a can of beans" in** *Wall Street Journal* **(April 10, 2002, pp. B1)**
Pub: Wall Street Journal
Ed: Suein L. Hwang. **Description:** It is predicted that barcodes on employees and cubicles will be used in the future in order to save space and money.

53806 ■ **"In-house corporate universities growing in popularity" in** *Crain's Detroit Business* **(Vol. 18, No. 24, June 17, 2002, pp. 15)**
Pub: Crain Communications Inc. - Detroit
Ed: Eric Morath. **Description:** A growing number of businesses are operating their own corporate university to train employees.

53807 ■ **"Indianapolis Indoor Day-Care Center Turns Dog's Life Into One of Fun" in** *Indianapolis Star* **(October 31, 2004)**
Pub: Indianapolis Star
Ed: Fred Kelly. **Description:** Pet owners are sending their dogs to daycare facilities while they are at work, a trend that's growing in popularity across the nation.

53808 ■ **"Industrial Metamorphosis" in** *The Economist* **(Vol. 377, October 1-7, 2005, No. 8446, pp. 69-70)**
Pub: The Economist Newspaper Ltd.
Description: Despite the drop in manufacturing jobs in America, manufacturing real output has been growing by nearly 4 percent annually since 1991, faster than overall GDP growth. Statistical data included.

53809 ■ **"Industry standards set a base for family pay range" in** *Business First Columbus* **(Vol. 18, No. 25, February 8, 2002, pp. B9)**
Pub: Business First Columbus, Inc.
Ed: Betsy Butler. **Description:** Industry standards are presented for the management of a family-owned business.

53810 ■ **"Internet Technologies-The constantly evolving Web is being driven by ever-growing human needs" in** *PC Magazine* **(Aug. 8, 2000, pp. 144)**
Pub: Ziff-Davis Publishing Company
Ed: John Clyman. **Description:** Emerging technologies will dramatically change the Internet in the next few years. Networking will become all-pervasive with the popularity of handheld devices and even household appliances that can be Web-enabled, although there is still no universal standard for interoperability. Instant messaging will become standardized despite the well-publicized war between AOL and Microsoft, partly as a result of government scrutiny. Virtually every application will exploit connectivity tools. Digital certificates and biometric user ID systems will enhance security by providing two-stage authentication. Content delivery will become more intelligent. Crucial trends include software agents for coordinating devices, the Portable Network Graphics (PNG) format, and even Net connections from space probes on other planets.

53811 ■ **"Investor: Boarding School" in** *Red Herring* **(No. 99, June 15 & July 1, 2001, pp. 130, 132)**
Pub: Herring Communications
Ed: Beverly Goodman. **Description:** An overview of the new audit committee rules adopted by the stock exchanges is presented. The volatility of today's market is discussed.

53812 ■ **"IPO Revival Not a Sure Thing" in** *Business Journal-Milwaukee* **(Vol. 20, No. 52, September 12, 2003, pp. A1)**
Pub: American City Business Journals, Inc.
Ed: Michael Muckian. **Description:** Brookfield, Wisconsin-based HomeMed, a manufacturer of medical technology, is planning an initial public offering. HomeMed, led by president and CEO, Herschel Peddicord, has annual sales of $30 million.

53813 ■ **"The IRS Wants You—Online" in** *Home Office Computing* **(Vol. 18, No. 12, December 2000, pp. 26)**
Pub: Scholastic Inc.
Ed: Jeffery D. Zbar. **Description:** Information is given regarding the Internal Revenue Service's effort to get small businesses to file tax returns online.

53814 ■ **"IT Risk Assessment: Who Needs It?" in** *Ingram's* **(Vol. 29, No. 7, July 2003, pp. 23)**
Pub: Show Me Publishing, Inc.
Ed: Scott Brouillette. **Description:** Businesses that fail to embrace technology put themselves at a disadvantage. However, companies that fail to plan for implementing information technology and related government regulations could suffer financially.

53815 ■ **"It's 2006! Whatcha Gonna Do About It?" in** *Inc.* **(Volume 28, January 2006, No. 1, pp. 78-85, 113)**
Pub: Inc. Magazine
Ed: Stephanie Clifford. **Description:** Various entrepreneurs give advice to help small businesses face new challenges in 2006. Topics include investments, the economy, small business trends, logistics, business communication such as blogs, energy issues, consumer products, real estate, interest rates and outsourcing.

53816 ■ **"It's Never E-nough" in** *Business Week* **(No. 3689, July 10, 2000, pp. F14)**
Pub: McGraw-Hill, Inc.
Description: Highlights of surveys of companies with 20-49 employees regarding the future of small business, including information about the Internet, Palmtops, networks, e-backlash, the bottom line, cost cutting, outsourcing, leasing, and Internet Telephony.

53817 ■ **"It's OK If You Shop Til You Drop" in** *Tampa Tribune* **(November 19, 2005)**
Pub: Media General, Inc.
Ed: Ted Jackovics. **Description:** Quick Quality Care is opening mini-clinics in retail stores offering non-emergency medical treatment to shoppers. Shoppers check in and are given a beeper to carry enabling them to shop until they can be seen by a medical professional.

53818 ■ **"J.D. Power Study: Hispanics Prefer Imports" in** *Hispanic Business* **(March 2003, pp. 18)**
Pub: Hispanic Business
Description: Hispanics, the largest minority group in America, prefer purchasing imported vehicles, according to a study performed by J.D. Power and Associates. The study also showed Hispanics rate fuel economy, price, and resale values much higher than non-Hispanic buyers.

53819 ■ **"Job Flight: Is it Real: Evidence is Scant, but a Shift Would be Welcome" in** *Barron's* **(August 11, 2003, pp. 26)**
Pub: Barron's
Ed: Gene Epstein. **Description:** Forecasts of a mass migration overseas of U.S. white collar jobs, representing nearly $150 billion in wages, may be fresh meat for a media frenzy, but are not supported by the data.

53820 ■ "Join the club?" in *Black Enterprise* (Vol. 33, No. 6, January 2003, pp. 87)
Pub: Earl Graves Publishing Co.
Description: The use of purchasing a card club for shopping is discussed, stressing the importance of comparison shopping to save money.

53821 ■ "The Joy of Quitting" in *Fortune* (Vol. 141, No. 3, February 7, 2000, pp. 199+)
Pub: Time Inc.
Description: The new economy is changing the way people look at their jobs. The article suggests that leaving a job you are unhappy doing is the right thing to do.

53822 ■ "Keep on Truckin'" in *Hispanic Business* (Vol. 23, No. 11, November 2001, pp. 56-58)
Pub: Hispanic Business Inc.
Ed: Ralph Gray. **Description:** Today's Hispanic CEOs prefer sports utility vehicles. A profile of trucks, particularly upscale sport utility vehicles from brands like Cadillac, Lexus, BMW, and Lincoln are profiled. Statistical data included.

53823 ■ "Keeping Customers Clueless?" in *Home Office Computing* (Vol. 18, No. 8, August 2000, pp. 22)
Pub: Scholastic Inc.
Ed: Laura Turley. **Description:** A recent report by Jupiter Communications states that as e-commerce continues to grow, so does customer dissatisfaction. Results of the report are examined.

53824 ■ "Know your limits" in *Entrepreneur* (Vol. 31, No. 6, June 2003, pp. 73)
Pub: Entrepreneur Media Inc.
Ed: Joanne Cleaver. **Description:** The U.S. Circuit Court of Appeals in California ruled that failure to fulfill a contract is just that and no more, fueling an emerging national precedent.

53825 ■ "Knowledge Management: Know What You Know" in *PC Magazine* (July 1, 2000, pp. 165)
Pub: Ziff-Davis Publishing Company
Ed: Sarah L. Roberts-Wilt. **Description:** Knowledge management encompasses an overarching business strategy to enable a company to make full use of the information, experience, and expertise resident in the company to serve customers better. Knowledge management needs data warehouses reporting engines, report-building software and ad-hoc query tools. In addition, tools are required to manage information from "soft" knowledge assets buried in text documents, spreadsheets, Web pages, and e-mail.

53826 ■ "Language and Markets in the U.S." in *Hispanic Business* (December 2002, pp. 16, 18, 20)
Pub: Hispanic Business
Description: Research shows that historically immigrants arriving to the U.S. have adopted the English language, and it is expected the same will hold true for new Hispanic individuals. However, there tend to be two Hispanic markets, one that is Spanish speaking, the other using English. Statistical data included.

53827 ■ "Laterals keep coming" in *Daily Business Review* (Vol. 77, No. 198, March 24, 2003, pp. AA2)
Pub: American Lawyer Media LP
Ed: Matthew Haggman. **Description:** Law firms are becoming increasingly dependent upon hiring laterals for growing their business rather than promoting from within.

53828 ■ "Laterals? Pass" in *Daily Business Review* (Vol. 77, No. 146, Jan. 7, 2003, pp. A8)
Pub: American Lawyer Media LP
Ed: Anthony Lin. **Description:** Many of the nation's top law firms poach partners from each other in order to provide more services.

53829 ■ "Latin Food Boom" in *Hispanic Business* (March 2005, pp. 15)
Pub: Hispanic Business
Description: Latin-themed restaurants are growing at a rate three times faster than any other food category.

53830 ■ *Legal Forms for Starting & Running a Small Business Vol. 2*
Pub: Nolo Press
Ed: Fred S. Steingold edited by Ralph Warner. **Released:** 1998. **Price:** $29.95.

53831 ■ "Legally bound" in *Crain's Detroit Business* (Vol. 19, No. 17, April 28, 2003, pp. 3)
Pub: Crain Communications Inc., Detroit
Ed: Laura Bailey. **Description:** Michigan law schools are reporting applications for enrollment up as much as 100 percent in the last two years, following a national trend.

53832 ■ "Let Your Fingers Do the Locking: Forgotten That Password?" in *Fortune* (Vol. 151, January 24, 2005, No. 2, pp. 42)
Pub: Time Inc.
Ed: Peter Lewis. **Description:** Profile of the new technology that allows users to access computers with fingerprint-reading devices. American Power Conversion, Sony, IBM, and other firms have developed password-management devices that can act as a lock and key for encrypting specific files and folders on a computer.

53833 ■ "License to Thrive" in *Entrepreneur* (Vol. 33, October 2005, No. 10, pp. 22)
Pub: Entrepreneur Media Inc.
Ed: Mark Henricks. **Description:** Today large companies are willing to license their patents, trademarks and other intellectual property to small companies that can profitably bring them to market.

53834 ■ "Life in the slow lane" in *Entrepreneur* (Vol. 30, No. 3, March 2002,)
Pub: Entrepreneur Media Inc.
Ed: Joshua Kurlantzick. **Description:** With Internet usage by businesses increasing, the United States Postal Service is seeing a decline in services. Several small private delivery courier services have developed in the past few years to compete with the USPS Priority Mail service. The new services the USPS now offers online are discussed.

53835 ■ "Like Hair, Barbers' Ranks Thinning" in *Chicago Tribune* (February 17, 2005)
Pub: Knight-Ridder/Tribune Business News
Ed: Tim Jones. **Description:** The number of barbers in the State of Iowa have dwindled 65 percent in the last thirty years, leaving the state with only 681 barbers. The entire nation has faced the same decline.

53836 ■ "Linking 'Em Up" in *Incentive* (Vol. 174, No. 10, October 2000, pp. 109)
Pub: Bill Communications
Ed: Joan M. Steinauer. **Description:** Golf professionals like Tiger Woods make the sport of golf a sought-after reward by employees, keeping the sport the top-requested award nationwide.

53837 ■ "The Little Guys Spy a Slowdown" in *Business Week* (No. 3691, July 24, 2000, pp. 26)
Pub: McGraw-Hill, Inc.
Description: Recent reports of sluggish hiring gains, flat vehicle sales and weak consumer spending confirm the findings from the National Federation of Independent Business' month survey of members, that small business optimism fell to 97.9 in June, its lowest level since the fall of 1993.

53838 ■ "Livin' la vida promo" in *Incentive* (Vol. 174, No. 10, October 2000, pp. 28)
Pub: Bill Communications
Ed: Libby Estell. **Description:** Marketers are targeting the growing Hispanic population in America.

53839 ■ "LMSB Deputy Commissioner stresses fairness for taxpayers" in *Journal of Accountancy* (Vol. 190, No. 4, October 2000, pp. 113)
Pub: Harborside Financial Center
Description: An interview with Deborah M. Nolan, IRS Deputy Commissioner of the Large and Mid-Size Business (LMSB) division. Ms. Nolan spoke of the service's strategic goals that would make filing tax returns easier and increase fairness of compliance enforcement.

53840 ■ "Local Entrepreneurs cash in on trend in women-only health clubs" in *Westchester County Business Journal* (Jan. 21, 2002, pp. 1)
Pub: Westfair Communications, Inc.
Ed: Elizabeth Hlotyak. **Description:** Recent statistics show that 52 percent of all health club members are women, according to the International Health, Racquet & Sportsclub Association, helping to lead to the creation of more women-only health clubs nationally and locally. Information about three centers, Simply Fit, Women for Fitness, Curves For Women and Curves For Women's Quickfit System is discussed.

53841 ■ "Locker Room Tactics" in *Hispanic Business* (October 2002, pp. 76)
Pub: Hispanic Business
Ed: Teresa Talerico. **Description:** Professional coaching is used to help individuals and companies obtain results and reach goals. Corporate diversity training can work to combat workplace discrimination.

53842 ■ "Lonely at the Top: Blacks Are a Fraction of Top Editors at Mainstream Magazines" in *Black Enterprise* (Vol. 35, September 2004, No. 2)
Pub: Earl G. Graves Publishing Co. Inc.
Ed: Carolyn M. Brown. **Description:** According to an Equal Employment Opportunity Commission report, the magazine industry is less diverse than other media. A study commissioned by the Magazine Publishers of America discovered management in the industry approaches diversity not in race, gender, or ethnicity, but rather in a diversity of perspectives, knowledge, and styles.

53843 ■ "The mac pack: some entrepreneurs would rather switch than fight" in *Entrepreneur* (Vol. 31, No. 5, May 2003, pp. 23)
Pub: Entrepreneur Media Inc.
Ed: Amanda C. Kooser. **Description:** Because of security issues and licensing agreements, more entrepreneurs are switching to Macintosh computers, including the Apple iMac (Power PC-based system) with the Mac OS X Operating system.

53844 ■ "Magna Carta for the Virtual Age" in *Home Office Computing* (Vol. 18, No. 12, December 2000, pp. 21)
Pub: Scholastic Inc.
Ed: Jeffrey D. Zbar. **Description:** Jennifer Johnson outlines 10 key practices a company needs in order to maintain "professionalism in the virtual workplace".

53845 ■ "The Major Leagues: Have Front-Office Positions Opened Up for Blacks?" in *Black Enterprise* (Vol. 37, February 2007, No. 7, pp.)
Pub: Earl G. Graves Publishing Co. Inc.
Ed: Alexis McCombs. **Description:** Major leave sports teams are hiring more African Americans to manage and coach teams. Statistical data included.

53846 ■ "Man in the Mirror" in *Incentive* (Vol. 174, No. 10, October 2000, pp. 93)
Pub: Bill Communications
Description: Once thought of as strictly a female domain, pampering products and services are increasingly popular among even the most macho of men.

53847 ■ "Manufacturing: Industrial Strength Integration" in *Microsoft Executive Circle* (Vol. 1, No. 2, Q2 2001, pp. 56-58)
Pub: Putman Media
Ed: Marty Weil. **Description:** The Internet has forced manufacturers to rethink business in order to stay

competitive. One global chemical maker handles 4.5 million transactions every month with a 2-3 second response time using the Internet to transact business.

53848 ■ "March Is National Craft Month" in *PR Newswire* **(March 7, 2003)**
Pub: PR Newswire Association, Inc.
Description: While other industries are experiencing a slowdown, the crafting industry is flourishing, due in large part, to its strong emotional appeal.

53849 ■ "Math Will Rock Your World" in *Business Week* **(January 23, 2006, No. 3968, pp. 54-58, 60, 62)**
Pub: McGraw-Hill Companies
Ed: Stephen Baker. **Description:** Businesses are using math experts in ways that were unthinkable years ago. They are changing personal data, trends, and online content into math, crunching the numbers, and discovering new ways to market products and services.

53850 ■ "Meet Your New Executives" in *Inc.* **(Volume 28, January 2006, No. 1, pp. 57-58)**
Pub: Inc. Magazine
Ed: David H. Freedman. **Description:** Are computers replacing executives in the business place? New, powerful software is capable of understanding data.

53851 ■ "Merrill Lynch Phones Ahead" in *Fast Company* **(November 2001, pp. 156)**
Pub: Fast Company
Ed: Paul C. Judge. **Description:** Merrill Lynch has determined that the telephone is the most important tool for the investment industry; the company is using voice over Internet protocol (VOIP) to conduct business.

53852 ■ "A Meta-Study of the Market" in *Hispanic Business* **(December 2002, pp. 22, 24, 26)**
Pub: Hispanic Business
Description: The results of a study on the subject of language usage among U.S. Hispanic consumers to track marketing trends are presented. The meta-study is a synthesis of earlier research and suggests that a significant number of individuals in the Hispanic market will conduct business in the English language.

53853 ■ "Metro firms maintain pay for called-up reservists" in *Crain's Detroit Business* **(Vol. 19, No. 14, April 7, 2003, pp. 1)**
Pub: Crain Communications Inc., Detroit
Ed: Robert Sherefkin, Robert Ankeny. **Description:** Major Detroit area firms, including auto suppliers and DTE Energy are paying salary differences for employees called up for active military duty. Many are also maintaining medical, dental and life insurance for several months, and some for years.

53854 ■ "Microsoft Buys Enterprise Anti-Virus Firm" in *eWeek* **(February 8, 2005)**
Pub: Ziff Davis Media Inc.
Description: Microsoft's acquisition of Sybari Software Inc., the maker of enterprise-ready anti-virus software, is examined.

53855 ■ "Mind over Matter" in *Entrepreneur* **(Vol. 28, No. 9, September 2000, pp. 42)**
Pub: Entrepreneur Media Inc.
Ed: Robert McGarvey. **Description:** Web-based intellectual property exchanges are explored. The editor emphasizes the importance of doing a thorough investigation before sacrificing the control over your idea.

53856 ■ "Mix and Match" in *Internet World* **(Vol. 7, No. 1, January 15, 2001, pp. 60)**
Pub: Mecklermedia Corporation
Ed: David F. Carr. **Description:** The computer software industry is turning to component software, both as part of a company's offering or the total offering. As it stands now, many companies using these components look to more than one company when designing Web sites.

53857 ■ "Mixed Grill: A Quarter's Menu: Good-and Some Bad—News" in *Barron's* **(July 7, 2003, pp. 22)**
Pub: Barron's
Ed: Shirley A. Lazo. **Description:** Nearly one hundred companies reported dividend increases in June 2003, up 10 percent from 2002, reflecting the influence of reduced taxes on certain corporate dividends. A corresponding and irregular increase in cutback is the negative counter to this trend.

53858 ■ "Mobilize! These Businesses Get Moving" in *My Business* **(August/September 2002, pp. 38-41)**
Pub: My Business Magazine
Ed: Kathleen Landis. **Description:** Many small business are now delivering services directly to the customer's front door as a means of better serving clients and setting themselves apart from competitors. Profiled in the article is a traveling dentist, veterinarian, car detailer, and a paper shredding firm.

53859 ■ "A Modest Defense of the Cubicle" in *Inc.* **(September 1, 2004)**
Pub: Inc. Magazine
Ed: Patrick J. Sauer. **Description:** Mixtures of open and closed spaces will replace cubicles and enable laptop-toting employees to work in large, sunny idea centers.

53860 ■ "A Modest Manifesto for Shattering the Glass Ceiling" in *Harvard Business Review* **(Vol. 78, No. 1, January 2000, pp. 127)**
Pub: Harvard Business School Publishing Corp.
Ed: Debra E. Meyerson, Joyce K. Fletcher. **Description:** Women, who were discriminated against in the past, are steadily making progress in the corporate world as they continually hold seats on corporate boards. The article suggests that even if that statement were the case, women at the highest levels of businesses are still rare.

53861 ■ "Mom and pop's retail secret: doggie in the window" in *Wall Street Journal* **(December 22, 1999, pp. B1)**
Pub: Dow Jones & Co., Inc.
Ed: Alexia Vargas. **Description:** The article tells how small businesses are using pets to attract customers into their shops.

53862 ■ "Monthly Report - December 1999" in *Small Business Economic Trends* **(December 1999, pp. COV)**
Pub: National Federation of Independent Business
Description: A survey of small and independent business owners shows some 20 percent of small businesses are having trouble recruiting qualified staff, while 28 percent reported higher labor costs for November 1999. The Small Business Optimism Index rose by 2 points in November 1999 to 103.2.

53863 ■ "Monthly Report - January 2000" in *Small Business Economic Trends* **(January 2000, pp. COV)**
Pub: National Federation of Independent Business
Description: The Index of Small Business Optimism dropped two points to 103.0 in December 1999. Some 22 percent of companies expect to increase their workforce in the next few months, and 23 percent cited finding skilled labor their main problem at the moment.

53864 ■ "Monthly Report - July 2000" in *Small Business Economic Trends* **(July 2000, pp. 1)**
Pub: National Federation of Independent Business
Ed: William C. Dunkelberg, Lara Chamberlain. **Description:** A survey of small business economic trends for the month of July 2000 is presented. Issues discussed include outlook, optimism index, earnings, prices, sales, employment, borrowings, worker compensation, capital outlays and inventories.

53865 ■ "Monthly Report - June 2000" in *Small Business Economic Trends* **(June 2000, pp. 1)**
Pub: National Federation of Independent Business

Description: Small firms' compensation for employees increased for 34 percent of the firms surveyed, while a definite skilled labor shortage was a problem for 24 percent of firms surveyed.

53866 ■ "Monthly Report - March 2000" in *Small Business Economic Trends* **(March 2000, pp. COV)**
Pub: National Federation of Independent Business
Description: A survey of small and independent business owners. The Index of Small Business Optimism fell three points to 100.6 in February 2000, compared to January 2000. Some 16 percent of companies expected to boost their workforce in the coming months.

53867 ■ "More Area Employers Seeking Spanish-Speaking Workers" in *Ledger* **(February 27, 2005)**
Pub: Knight-Ridder/Tribune Business News
Ed: Kyle Kennedy. **Description:** Employers in the Lakeland area are looking to hire multilingual employees able to communicate in both English and Spanish.

53868 ■ "More fly charter, wing it themselves" in *Crain's Detroit Business* **(Vol. 19, No. 9, March 3, 2003, pp. 18)**
Pub: Crain Communications Inc., Detroit
Ed: Michael Strong. **Description:** Many high-level executives are chartering or purchasing the own planes for business travel.

53869 ■ "More home-based businesses are leaving home" in *Atlanta Business Chronicle* **(Vol. 24, No. 8, July 27, 2001, pp. 9B)**
Pub: American City Business Journals Inc.
Ed: Eileen Brill Wagner. **Description:** Home-based businesses are no longer confined to home, as technology enables small business owners to do business anywhere and anytime. Home-based business owners have also formed support groups that meet in local coffee shops. Being mobile is an important way for home business owners to get an advantage over their traditional competition.

53870 ■ "Multiculturalism Grows Up" in *Hispanic Business* **(Vol. 24, No. 4, April 2002, pp. 58, 60)**
Pub: Hispanic Business Inc.
Description: An interview with Gustavo De La Torre, manager of Worldwide Diversity & Multiculture at Intel Corporation, about diversity in the workplace.

53871 ■ "Multilingual Execs in Demand" in *Hispanic Business* **(March 2005, pp. 15)**
Pub: Hispanic Business
Description: According to Korn/Ferry International, the need for multilingual executives is growing in the U.S. Statistical data included.

53872 ■ "My Life as a Blogger: A Growing Number of VCs Are Opening Themselves Up in Online Diaries" in *Venture Capital Journal* **(Jan. 1, 2005)**
Pub: Thomason Financial Inc.
Ed: Tom Stein. **Description:** Information about the new blog-related technologies and startup companies emerging is shared. Currently there are about twelve venture-related blogs on the Internet.

53873 ■ "National Survey Finds More Small-Business Owners Planning to Increase Their Staffs" in *Long Island Business News* **(January 30, 2004)**
Pub: Dolan Media Newswires
Ed: Ben Abelson. **Description:** According to a study done by the National Federation of Independent Business, 20 percent of U.S. small businesses plan to increase staff this year, a number higher than at any other point in the past 3-1/2 years. The financial services sector is leading the way in this trend.

53874 ■ "The need for privacy" in *Crain's Detroit Business* **(Vol. 18, No. 24, June)**
Pub: Crain Communications Inc. - Detroit
Ed: Michael Strong. **Description:** With long lines at airport security, local executives are purchasing small planes for business travel. Sales of small planes and fractional ownership of jets are rising.

53875 ■ **"The Need for Speed in New Millennium Leadership Styles" in** *Employment Relations Today* **(Vol. 27, No. 1, Spring 2000, pp. 61)**
Pub: John Wiley & Sons, Inc.
Ed: David Cottrell. Description: An overview of corporate management in an era of technological change, and the need for leadership styles that rely on quick decision-making and planning. Topics addressed include incorporating speed into company culture, streamlining processes, and implementing faster communication systems.

53876 ■ **"'Net Attacks to Plague Small and Midsize Firms" in** *Network World* **(October 16, 2000, pp. 108)**
Pub: Network World Inc.
Ed: David Legard. Description: Small and midsize companies are likely targets for Internet attacks, and many will suffer a successful attack between now and 2003, according to a report released by the market research firm Gartner Group.

53877 ■ **"New Face at the SBA" in** *Hispanic Business* **(Vol. 23, No. 10, October, 2001, pp. 32, 34)**
Pub: Hispanic Business
Ed: Scott Williams. Description: Profile of Hector V. Barreto, the new administrator of the U.S. Small Business Administration (SBA), hopes to make the agency more responsive to the small-business community. Statistical data included.

53878 ■ **"New Group Seeks Greater Hispanic Influence" in** *Hispanic Business* **(Vol. 23, No. 7/8, July/August 2001, pp. 24)**
Pub: Hispanic Business
Description: The newly formed National Advancement of Hispanic People (NAAHP) will pursue increased political and economic influence for U.S. Hispanics. The organization will rely on membership dues rather than corporate sponsorship.

53879 ■ **"New Muscle for Old Strip Malls" in** *Business 2.0* **(Vol. 6, July 2005, No. 6, pp. 50)**
Pub: Time, Inc.
Ed: Nicole Joseph. Description: 24 Hour Fitness chain is using abandoned grocery stores to startup new fitness centers. With big-box retailers taking over mid-size grocery stores, the $1 billion fitness chain sees an endless opportunity for expansion.

53880 ■ **"New NAPSLO President Helm" in** *Rough Notes* **(Vol. 145, No. 1, January 2003, pp. 40)**
Pub: Rough Notes
Ed: Phil Zinkewicz. Description: Nicholas D. Cortezi, president of the National Association of Professional Surplus Lines Offices, finds that risks that should not be in the standard insurance market are finding their way into the surplus lines market where they belong.

53881 ■ **"New Positions Emerging: How You Can Prepare for Them" in** *Women In Business* **(Vol. 52, No. 2, March 2000, pp. 30)**
Pub: The ABWA Co., Inc.
Ed: Diane Domeyer. Description: Women should plan for the new roles anticipated in the workplace as a result of technological advances.

53882 ■ **"The New Sounds of Selling" in** *Business 2.0* **(Vol. 6, May 2005, No. 4, pp. 58, 60)**
Pub: Time, Inc.
Ed: Thomas Mucha. Description: Smart marketers are using music clips, beeps and other sound bites to attract consumer attention quickly.

53883 ■ **"A new way of business" in** *Atlanta Business Chronicle* **(Vol. 24, No. 11, August 17, 2001, pp. 1A)**
Pub: American City Business Journals Inc.
Ed: Matt Gove. Description: The city of Atlanta, Georgia's business culture is being changed by the steady stream of new companies, giving an edge to the city's Southern gentility. The city was once run by a handful of powerful people. The city has been forced to accept other spheres of influences and some of the backlashes are discussed.

53884 ■ **"The Next Big Market" in** *Success* **(Vol. 47, No. 5, October 2000, pp. 36)**
Pub: Success Publishing, Inc.
Ed: Frank Solis. Description: According to the Census Bureau, Hispanics make up the nation's fastest-growing consumer segment, spending some $380 billion on products and services annually.

53885 ■ **"The Next Big Things: Nothing is more profitable than an investment idea whose time has come" in** *Fortune* **(Vol. 140, December 20, 1999)**
Pub: Time Inc.
Description: From bricks and mortar to biotech, seven themes for the next century and ten stocks to profit from are outlined.

53886 ■ **"The Next Big Trend: Cutting Mgmt. Fees" in** *Venture Capital Journal* **(Vol. 42, No. 9, September 2002, pp. 6, 8-9)**
Pub: Thomas Venture Economics
Ed: Lawrence Aragon. Description: Private equity firms are planning to cut fees or work out new fee arrangements with limited partners. VantagePoint Venture Partners' plans to defer fees for 18 months on its $1.6 billion Fund IV.

53887 ■ **"NFIB Education Foundation: small business economic survey" in** *Small Business Economic Trends* **(August 2000, pp. 1)**
Pub: National Federation of Independent Business
Description: The findings of the NFIB Education Foundation's small business quarterly economic survey conducted during July 2000 are discussed.

53888 ■ **"NFIB Report from the State Capitols" in** *My Business* **(September/October 2001, pp. 20-22)**
Pub: My Business Magazine
Description: Alphabetical listing of each state, including a brief description of small business issues facing that particular state.

53889 ■ **"Not Just Telenovelas" in** *The Record* **(November 12, 2005)**
Pub: New Jersey Media Group
Ed: Hugh R. Morley. Description: Teaneck, New Jersey's Univision 41, WXTV, is the first Spanish-language news program to get more viewers in a single New York area newscast than any other English-speaking channel. With the growth of new Spanish language immigrants, advertisers are seeking their attention.

53890 ■ **"Nothing but Net" in** *Fast Company* **(November 2001, pp. 36)**
Pub: Fast Company
Ed: Alison Overholt. Description: Profile of Wi-Fi networks, individual wireless network-access points and cards, which are growing in popularity.

53891 ■ **"Obesity Whets VC Appetites" in** *Inc.* **(Volume 27, June 2005, No. 6, pp. 26)**
Pub: Inc. Magazine
Ed: Michelle Leder. Description: Venture capitalists have invested millions in six anti-obesity companies in the past year.

53892 ■ **"Office Optional" in** *Inc.* **(Volume 27, December 2005, No. 12, pp. 42, 44)**
Pub: Inc. Magazine
Ed: Darren Dahl. Description: Profile of Point B, a consulting firm employee 223 workers. Co-founders Tim Jenkins and Darran Littlefield run their firm virtually with employees in Seattle, Denver, Phoenix, and Portland, Oregon, and each consultant works with clients locally. Three tips for running a virtual office are outlined.

53893 ■ **"Offshoring Could Boost Your Career" in** *Fortune* **(Vol. 151, January 24, 2005, No. 2, pp. 36)**
Pub: Time Inc.
Ed: Anne Fisher. Description: According to a study conducted by Duke University's Fuqua School of Business and Archstone Consulting, American businesses

with offshore operations will ship 81 percent more research jobs, 55 percent more engineering, and 75 percent more human resources overseas (69 percent of which are already in India). American managers will be needed to oversee these operations.

53894 ■ **"Old King Coal Comes Back: Actually, It Never Really Left" in** *Fortune* **(Vol. 151, February 21, 2005, No. 4, pp. 114)**
Pub: Time Inc.
Ed: Jeremy Main. Description: Profile of Peabody Energy, owner of the largest coalmine in the world, the North Antelope-Rochelle Mine. The coal industry is working to improve the mining, transporting, and burning of coal in order to increase production.

53895 ■ **"Old fashioned hobby returns to textile shop" in** *Los Angeles Business Journal* **(Vol. 25, No. 7, February 17, 2003, pp. 30)**
Pub: Los Angeles Business Journal
Ed: Koula Gianulias. Description: Profile of Lani's Needlepoint and Knit Works, a wholesale and retail shop located in Studio City, California. Owner, Lani Silver, has expanded her shop to include yarns and accessories to accommodate the new resurgence in knitting.

53896 ■ **"Older CEOs Plan to Work Past Age 65. They May Find That Harder Than They Expect" in** *Inc.* **(September 2005, pp. 27-29)**
Pub: Inc. Magazine
Ed: Stephanie Clifford. Description: The entrepreneurial revolution was part of the baby boomer phenomenon. The trend toward older CEOs planning to work past the age of 65 is growing.

53897 ■ **"On the Move?" in** *Entrepreneur* **(Vol. 31, No. 11, November 2003, pp. 65)**
Pub: Entrepreneur Media, Inc.
Ed: Jennifer Pellet. Description: E-Trade is offering a mortgage program that allows homeowners to move their current mortgages with the purchase of a new home.

53898 ■ **"On a role" in** *WorkingWoman* **(Vol. 25, No. 7, August 2000, pp. 79)**
Pub: Lang Communications Inc.
Ed: Russell Wild. Description: Acting classes can improve the performance of top executives who regularly have to make important speeches or give seminars to large groups of people.

53899 ■ **"On the Same Page: Newspaper Advertising is Generally Flat" in** *Hispanic Business* **(Vol. 21, No. 12, December 1999, pp. 70)**
Pub: Hispanic Business
Description: Trends in newspaper advertising aimed at Hispanic Americans are examined. The dominant market is Los Angeles, California, where advertising expenditure is anticipated to be $71.44 million in 1999.

53900 ■ **"Open Doors?" in** *Entrepreneur* **(Vol. 31, No. 9, September 2003, pp. 72)**
Pub: Entrepreneur Media, Inc.
Ed: Joshua Kurlantzick. Description: Government deregulation in the real estate industry is discussed.

53901 ■ **"Orchestrating Assistance; Chambers of Commerce" in** *Crain's New York Business* **(Vol. 22, November 13, 2006, No. 46, pp. 38)**
Pub: Crain Communications, Inc.
Description: Listing of local chapters of New York's chambers of commerce. These organizations serve as sources of information and representation for local business interest provide a number of services and a wide variety of programs for small businesses.

53902 ■ **"Other People's Money: A Pension Fund Learns About Soft Dollars-the Hard Way" in** *Barron's* **(July 7, 2003, pp. L7)**
Pub: Barron's
Ed: Erin E. Arvedlund. Description: The increasing influence wielded over pension funds by Wall Street, including which portfolio managers they hire and what companies they invest in, is a troubling trend, as evidenced in the case of the Nashville Municipal fund and consultant, William Keith Phillips.

53903 ■ "Outsource the Outsourcing" in *Inc.* (Volume 27, December 2005, No. 12, pp. 55-56)
Pub: Inc. Magazine
Ed: Darren Dahl. **Description:** Offshore contractors are helping entrepreneurs connect with offshore firms in order to outsource work overseas.

53904 ■ "Outsourced e-mail" in *PC Computing* (April 2000, pp. 117)
Pub: Ziff-Davis Inc.
Ed: Bonny L. Georgia. **Description:** Ferris Research predicts that within one year, e-mail traffic will increase three to five times, and storage requirements could more than double. The article shows how to outsource e-mail in order to increase business.

53905 ■ "Overview-small business optimism" in *Small Business Economic Trends* (April 2000, pp. 1)
Pub: National Federation of Independent Business
Description: The Index of Small Business Optimism rose slightly in March 2000 following a sharp drop in February 2000. Factors affecting small businesses, including prices and earnings, are discussed in detail.

53906 ■ "Overwhelmed nurses leaving medicine to help lawyers" in *Atlanta Business Chronicle* (Vol. 25, No. 20, October 25, 2002, pp. 3A)
Pub: American City Business Publications, Inc.
Ed: Julie Bryant. **Description:** There is currently a growing shortage of nurses because many of these professionals are tired of the low wages, demanding hours and minimal staff levels and are turning to the field of law to assist attorneys.

53907 ■ "Panasonic Tunes In Hispanic Market" in *Hispanic Business* (March 2003, pp. 24)
Pub: Hispanic Business
Description: Panasonic has started a series of print ads and television commercials featuring Spanish-language spots for their PV-DC252 Palmcorder and high-definition 42-inch plasma monitor. The article sites examples of other companies following the same trend, marketing to the Hispanic population in the U.S.

53908 ■ "Paper-Run Web Sites Prosper" in *Milwaukee Journal Sentinel* (December 18, 2005)
Pub: Journal Sentinel, Inc.
Ed: Paul Gores. **Description:** The trend towards Americans using online newspaper Websites is good news for the industry. Online newspaper sites saw an 11 percent increase in use over last year, prompting companies to develop new methods for delivery news in order to meet consumer demands.

53909 ■ "Part-Time Assignments" in *Black Enterprise* (Vol. 37, December 2006, No. 5, pp. 70)
Pub: Earl G. Graves Publishing Co. Inc.
Description: During critical change initiatives interim management, an employment model which uses senior-level executives to manage a special project or specific business function on a temporary basis, can have many benefits.

53910 ■ "Passing the Baton" in *Sales & Marketing Management* (Vol. 157, January 2005, No. 1, pp. 34)
Pub: VNU Business Media
Ed: Sara Calabro. **Description:** Outsourcing sales staff is becoming widely accepted in the industry. Outsourcing works best for products with short sales cycles.

53911 ■ "Paving the Cow Path" in *Rough Notes* (Vol. 146, No. 9, September 2003, pp. 40)
Pub: Rough Notes
Ed: John Ashenburst. **Description:** Overview of changes and future trends in the insurance industry. Topics covered include risk management services, Internet marketing of services, and insurance services offered through banks.

53912 ■ "Paying to lose" in *Sarasota Herald Tribune* (Nov. 11, 2002, pp. 10)
Pub: Sarasota Herald Tribune
Description: Franchises in Southwest Florida offering weight loss solutions are profiled, including Shapes Family Fitness, Gold's Gyms, Curves for Women, Weight Watchers, Jenny Craig, and LA Weight Loss. Health and medical statistics included.

53913 ■ "A Penny Not Saved" in *Entrepreneur* (Vol. 31, No. 8, August 2003, pp. 30)
Pub: Entrepreneur Media, Inc.
Ed: Steve Cooper. **Description:** According to a survey sponsored by the Employee Benefit Research Institute, the American Savings Education Council and Mathew Greenwald & Associates, more employees are planning to work more years before deciding to retire. Statistical data included.

53914 ■ "Perdue's home-work plan has failed past" in *Atlanta Business Chronicle* (Vol. 25, November 29, 2002, No. 25, pp. 1A)
Pub: American City Business Publications, Inc.
Ed: Sarah Rubenstein. **Description:** In an effort to reduce traffic congestion in Atlanta, Georgia, Governor-elect Sonny Perdue intends to persuade more companies to use telecommuting. Additionally, Perdue plans to identify 25,000 government employees who could telecommute at least part time.

53915 ■ "Perks for interns" in *Incentive* (Vol. 174, No. 10, October 2000, pp. 10)
Pub: Bill Communications
Ed: Jeanie Casison. **Description:** Forget about the guy in the next cube—companies are trying to make an impression on the workforce of the future.

53916 ■ "Pet Projects: Cats and Dogs and Babies, Oh My!" in *Entrepreneur* (Vol. 32, November 2004, No. 11, pp. 30)
Pub: Entrepreneur Media Inc.
Ed: Geoff Williams. **Description:** Small companies report on the success of allowing employees to bring pets to the office. Included are Hilary Kaye Associates, a public relations firm in California, with four adopted cats and allows employees to bring their cats to work with them. Small Dog Electronics, reseller of Macintosh computers, peripherals and software, believes dogs can be stress relievers in the workplace.

53917 ■ "Pet Sitting a Growing Business Nationwide" in *Journal Star* (August 24, 2004)
Pub: Journal Star
Ed: Anita Szoke. **Description:** Pet owners are choosing to hire sitters for their pets when away from home rather than boarding their animals. The number of pet walkers and pet sitters has grown 38 percent from 1990-2005, according to the U.S. Bureau of Labor Statistics.

53918 ■ "Pizza makers to add online orders" in *Crain's Detroit Business* (Vol. 16, No. 16, April 17, 2000, pp. 16)
Pub: Crain Communications, Inc.
Ed: Terry Kosdrosky. **Description:** Pizza chains will begin using the Internet for online ordering and a system to e-mail coupons to customers.

53919 ■ "Population Boom" in *Forbes* (Vol. 175, January 10, 2005, No. 1, pp. 152)
Pub: Forbes Magazine Inc.
Ed: Brett Pulley. **Description:** Univision broadcast network, a Spanish-language media entity in the U.S., is rated number one among Hispanics in every market. The network serves a market that is expected to grow to 48 million by 2010, up 113 percent since 1990.

53920 ■ "The portable CEO" in *WorkingWoman* (Vol. 25, No. 2, February 2000, pp. 54)
Pub: Lang Communications Inc.
Ed: Betsy Wiesendanger. **Description:** Bettina Whyte, temporary CEO of APS Holding, discusses the new trend of outsourcing being used by companies.

53921 ■ "Positive Peer Pressure" in *My Business* (December/January 2004, pp. 34-37)
Pub: My Business Magazine
Ed: Karen J. Bannan. **Description:** A new trend seen for small companies, has owners relying on peer groups for dealing with the pressures of running a business. Networking options can offer advice, education and camaraderie.

53922 ■ "Postage unpaid" in *Entrepreneur* (Vol. 30, No. 12, December 2002, pp. 77)
Pub: Entrepreneur Media Inc.
Description: The increasing use of electronic tax filing, known as the Electronic Federal Tax Payment System (EFTPS), is examined.

53923 ■ "Power to the Buyer With Group Buying Sites" in *E-business Advisor* (Vol. 18, No. 2, February 2000, pp. 10)
Pub: Advisor Media, Inc.
Ed: Erica Rugullies. **Description:** Group buying practices that enable customers to lower their acquisition costs and allow the vendor to reach new audiences, test new promotions and sell excess inventory are discussed.

53924 ■ "Profiting - Adding an affiliate program links site content to product sales" in *PC Magazine* (February 20, 2001, pp. 133)
Pub: Ziff-Davis Publishing Company
Ed: Neil Randall. **Description:** Banner ads are a way for Web site developers to make a profit. Placing a banner ad on the page directs interested site visitors to the advertiser's site. The affiliate network tracks the origin of the visit and pays the host of the originating site a percentage of all sales. Some pay a fee just for directing a visitor to a site. Commission Junction offers commissions from more than 1,600 companies in a wide variety of industries. LinkShare offers commissions from just over 500 companies, but they are major organizations.

53925 ■ "Protect Yourself" in *PC Computing* (April 2000, pp. 35)
Pub: Ziff-Davis Inc.
Ed: Paul Somerson. **Description:** The importance of network security for small businesses, home-based businesses, and teleworkers is the topic of this article.

53926 ■ "Pub grub grows up" in *Restaurant Business* (Vol. 101, No. 15, Sept. 15, 2002, pp. 76)
Pub: VNU Business Media
Ed: James Scarpa. **Description:** More and more beer pubs and microbreweries are upgrading their menus in the hopes of becoming more like Belgium, where a sophisticated beer cuisine is held in high regard.

53927 ■ "Publishing" in *Business Week* (January 9, 2006, No. 3966, pp. 29-30)
Pub: McGraw-Hill Companies
Ed: Louise Lee. **Description:** Web magazines are launching print versions of their publications in order to increase readership and advertising sales.

53928 ■ "Put It In Drive" in *Entrepreneur. com* (Vol. 34, February 2006, No. 2, pp. 34)
Pub: Entrepreneur Media Inc.
Ed: Mike Hogan. **Description:** According to a study conducted by The Dieringer Research Group, 21 million Americans work in their automobiles; mobile workers are taking care of business in planes, trains and automobiles. Requirements to equip your automobile for teleworking are outlined.

53929 ■ "Putting Hispanics Behind the Wheel" in *Hispanic Business* (September 2004, pp. 20)
Pub: Hispanic Business
Description: Ford, Toyota and Chevrolet have targeted the Hispanic market for new car sales. The top ten automobile brands are listed with number of Hispanic purchases and market share.

53930 ■ "Quarterly Report - February 2000" in *Small Business Economic Trends* (February 2000, pp. COV)
Pub: National Federation of Independent Business
Description: The Index of Small Business Optimism rose to 103.6 in January 2000, representing the highest reading since October 1997. Around one percent of companies expect to increase their workforce over the coming months, although 21 percent report that finding skilled labor is one of their main problems.

53931 ■ "Quarterly Report - May 2000" in *Small Business Economic Trends* (May 2000, pp. COV)
Pub: National Federation of Independent Business
Ed: William C. Dunkelberg, Elliot Steinberg. **Description:** The outlook for small businesses based on a number of economic indices is analyzed. The report was compiled from returns to a questionnaire from members of the National Federation of Independent Business.

53932 ■ "R-E-S-P-E-C-T: The Changing Attitudes Toward Home-Based Businesses" in *My Business* (October/November 2002, pp. 45)
Pub: My Business Magazine
Ed: Mardy Fornes. **Description:** The importance of developing a strong business plan is key to running a successful home business. Some of the obstacles faced by those operating a home-based company are discussed.

53933 ■ "Race-Conscious Agenda: Poll Shows Most African Americans Want Affirmative Action Reform" in *Black Enterprise* (Vol. 34, Nov. 2003)
Pub: Earl Graves Publishing Co.
Ed: Marcia A. Wade. **Description:** A poll conducted in June 2003 by Black America's Political Action Committee suggests that African Americans believe affirmative action is good in principle but needs to be reformed.

53934 ■ "Real Estate Niches Continue as Bright Spots" in *Crain's Detroit Business* (Vol. 22, November 27, 2006, No. 48, pp. 18)
Pub: Crain Communications Inc. - Detroit
Ed: Jennette Smith. **Description:** Five year downward trend and transition period has driven real estate professionals into niche marketing in redevelopment and mixed use projects. Smaller projects are very successful in downtown areas with assistance of the local communities.

53935 ■ "Redefining Sick Days" in *Sales & Marketing Management* (Vol. 157)
Pub: VNU Business Media
Ed: Kathryn Droullard. **Description:** Many companies are now offering flexible time-off policies whereby an employee can use sick time for reasons other than personal illness, such as family issues, personal needs, and stress. Allowing a workforce flexible time off not only motivates a staff, but can also lead to stronger management capabilities.

53936 ■ "Reducing Turnover" in *Automotive News* (Vol. 79, January 24, 2005, No. 6131, pp. 38)
Pub: Crain Communications Inc.
Ed: Donna Harris, K.C. Crain. **Description:** Car dealers are moving away from paying sales staff conventional commission on gross profits of vehicles sold. Many dealers are offering both salary and commission, along with bonuses for volume and repeat business.

53937 ■ "Relief on Wheels? Mall Strollers Play DVDs" in *Tampa Tribune* (November 23, 2005)
Pub: Media General, Inc.
Ed: Marla Marino. **Description:** A new trend at shopping malls is to install DVD players showing G-rated movies on all strollers. The move is expected to keep parents in stores longer, and ultimately spend more money.

53938 ■ "Renting software and the skills to go with it" in *The New York Times* (May 22, 2000, pp. C4)
Pub: The New York Times Company
Ed: Laurie Flynn. **Description:** Many companies are taking a new path when acquiring software programs for their individual businesses. Instead of buying the software needed and hiring a technician to teach them how to use it, they have turned to renting the software. In this type of arrangement, the software company would handle this part of the business for them, saving money, time and manpower.

53939 ■ "Research: Hispanics Love Their Internet" in *Hispanic Business* (July/August 2002, pp. 12)
Pub: Hispanic Business
Description: According to a study conducted by Roslow Research Group in spring 2002, 50 percent of U.S. Hispanics age 16 or older use the Internet.

53940 ■ "Resource Line" in *Black Enterprise* (Vol. 37, January 2007, No. 6, pp. 6)
Pub: Earl G. Graves Publishing Co. Inc.
Description: Interactive Media Editor, Philana Patterson, writes a column for blackenterprise.com that offers advice and provides resources for entrepreneurs, corporate executives, business owners, and budding investors.

53941 ■ "Respect Your Elders" in *Inc.* (September 1, 2003)
Pub: Gruner & Jahr USA Publishing
Ed: Donna Fenn. **Description:** Small companies are finding smart, reliable employees by hiring individuals over the age of 65.

53942 ■ "Retail" in *Business 2.0* (Vol. 6, July 2005, No. 6, pp. 30)
Pub: Time, Inc.
Description: In a move to attract customers, retailer store the Gap is reorganizing its stores by creating separate entrances for men and women. The stores will display women's items in a boutique-like environment while stressing the basics to male consumers.

53943 ■ "Retirement Communities Grow in Popularity in New Jersey" in *The Record* (November 3, 2005)
Pub: New Jersey Media Group
Ed: Dennis P. Carmody. **Description:** Retirees in New Jersey are seeking one floor homes with amenities such as social clubs and a gym, and are restricted to individuals age 55 and over.

53944 ■ "Retiring boomers to cut start-up launches, study says" in *Wall Street Journal* (March 14, 2000, pp. B4)
Pub: Dow Jones & Co., Inc.
Ed: Eleena De Lisser. **Description:** The impact of retiring boomers on small business startups is explored.

53945 ■ "The Right to Regulate Off-Duty Conduct" in *Employment Relations Today* (Vol. 27, No. 2, Summer 2000, pp. 101)
Pub: John Wiley & Sons, Inc.
Ed: Arthur F. Silbergeld and Stephanie T. Sasaki. **Description:** Many employers are attempting to exert control over off-duty conduct of employees that could be detrimental to profitability. The laws have not been well developed in most jurisdictions, but many companies have implemented policies restricting employees dating other employees and setting up or participating in competing businesses.

53946 ■ "Risky business: on the lookout for business insurance?" in *Entrepreneur* (Vol. 31, No. 6, June 2003, pp. 73)
Pub: Entrepreneur Media Inc.
Ed: Mark Henricks. **Description:** According to the Insurance Information Institute, fifteen percent of small businesses do not buy business insurance to cover their enterprises because it is harder to find, less affordable, and provides less protection.

53947 ■ "Role of Coach Critical to Success of New Producer" in *Rough Notes* (Vol. 145, No. 9, September 2002, pp. 30)
Pub: Rough Notes
Ed: Bud Antrim. **Description:** Trainees at insurance agencies like Rue Insurance, Trenton, New Jersey; JWF Companies, Indianapolis, Indiana; Johnson, Kendall and Johnson, Langhorne, Pennsylvania, who learn from coaches are able to produce earlier in their career. Mentors serve as models and training has become an important component in the company development program.

53948 ■ "A Rough Round: Why Golf's Prospects are Dimming" in *Barron's* (July 28, 2003, pp. 17)
Pub: Barron's
Ed: Jonathan R. Laing. **Description:** The U.S. was expecting to welcome an explosion in the popularity of golf, with stars like Tiger Woods attracting younger players to newly designed courses. Equipment makers were poised to profit, but not only were numbers flattened, fewer golfers were playing fewer rounds in 2000. Causes of the decrease are identified and solutions are offered.

53949 ■ "The Sales Auction: Is Bidding for Leads the Sales Trend of the Future" in *Sales and Marketing.com* (Vol. 156, No. 3, March 2004)
Pub: VNU eMedia, Inc.
Ed: Michael Schrage. **Description:** Would a more rigorous and impartial mechanism for allocating sales leads, prospects, and territories lead to a better sales force by forming an auction lot? Salespeople would be allowed to bid on prospects they feel they could turn into clients. Bids could be percentages of anticipated commissions, and a portion could come from existing clients' proceeds, or even the company's Bid4Prospects program.

53950 ■ "Sales Report: Once Tainted by Get-Rich-Quick Schemes, the Direct-Sales Industry is Changing its Image" in *Entrepreneur* (July 2004)
Pub: Entrepreneur Media Inc.
Ed: Nichole L. Torres. **Description:** Direct selling has become an industry whereby an independent consultant bringing a portable kit of wares to homes to share in a demonstration. According to the Direct Selling Association, the direct-selling industry accounted for more than $28 billion in 2002, with an estimated 13 million independent direct salespersons in the U.S. The five elements creating the evolution in direct selling are outlined.

53951 ■ "Sales of Scooters Get in the Fast Lane" in *Chicago Tribune* (February 21, 2005)
Pub: Knight-Ridder/Tribune Business News
Ed: John Schmeltzer. **Description:** Scooters have become the latest trend in two-wheeled vehicle sales in America. These vehicles are appealing to individuals mainly in urban areas.

53952 ■ "Save the Founder" in *Inc.* (October 2005, pp. 156)
Pub: Inc. Magazine
Ed: Adam Hanft. **Description:** No matter how large or successful a business becomes, it is necessary for its founder to remain its leader.

53953 ■ "Savings in the Mall" in *Home Office Computing* (Vol. 19, No. 1, January 2001, pp. 22)
Pub: Scholastic Inc.
Ed: Dan Costa. **Description:** The U.S. Postal Service (USPS) approved PC-based postage services in August 1999, giving birth to a slew of Internet postage start-ups and adding new life to old-school postage-meter providers like Pitney Bowes and the postal service itself.

53954 ■ "Scenes From the Talent Wars" in *Inc.* (Volume 28, January 2006, No. 1, pp. 29-31)
Pub: Inc. Magazine
Ed: Scott Westcott. **Description:** Employers are willing to go to extra lengths to recruit and retain talented

workers. A list of business jargon used in human resources is included.

53955 ■ **"Search Party" in** *Entrepreneur* **(Vol. 33, September 2005, No. 9, pp. 28)**
Pub: Entrepreneur Media Inc.
Ed: Heather Clancy. **Description:** The latest trend in team building at small companies is to send employees on scavenger hunts. Two firms offering such events, Teambonding in Massachusetts and New York City's Paint the Town Red expect sales to reach $2 million in 2005, a 30 percent rise from 2004 to 2005 respectively.

53956 ■ **"Second wind" in** *Entrepreneur* **(Vol. 31, No. 4, April 2003, pp. 18)**
Pub: Entrepreneur Media Inc.
Ed: Amanda C. Kooser. **Description:** The latest trend is for small businesses to add new peripherals to computer systems rather than upgrade PCs as often. A few examples of the latest add-ons to improve the performance and extend the lifespan of computers are external hard drives, personal storage, CD-RW drives, and new flat-panel display monitors.

53957 ■ **"Security Blanket: Terrorists changed your employees" in** *Entrepreneur* **(Vol. 30, No. 3, March 2002, pp. 19)**
Pub: Entrepreneur Media Inc.
Ed: Chris Penttila. **Description:** Since the terrorist attacks, employees want a sense of security combined with the opportunity to do good; work is no longer about making money. Employees also wish to find a better balance between work and home life. Advices is offered to management to help towards this trend.

53958 ■ **"Sedan Savvy" in** *Entrepreneur.com* **(Vol. 34, February 2006, No. 2, pp. 22)**
Pub: Entrepreneur Media Inc.
Ed: Jill Amadio. **Description:** Profile of three midsize passenger cars unveiled for 2006.

53959 ■ **"Send In the Robots!" in** *Fortune* **(Vol. 151, January 24, 2005, No. 2, pp. 140)**
Pub: Time Inc.
Ed: Stuart F. Brown. **Description:** New generation industrial robots can strip paint, inspect buried gas mains, traverse desserts, and even cut grass for golf courses. Computer and navigational technology costs have fallen making these robots affordable to most small businesses.

53960 ■ **"Sharper Image: Smartphones are the Brainier Mobile Choice" in** *Entrepreneur* **(Vol. 32, October 2004, No. 10, pp. 49)**
Pub: Entrepreneur Media Inc.
Ed: Amanda C. Kooser. **Description:** Sales of hybrid PDA/phone devices are rising, especially those geared towards entrepreneurs and mobile employees. Smart phone capabilities include global positioning systems, and are available from a range of suppliers. Information about Global Tracking Communications Inc., GPS Fleet Solutions, GPSnow.com, Pharos Science & Applications, TeleNavTrack, and Thales Navigation are a few companies listed with brief profiles.

53961 ■ **"Shopping Magazines Gain Popularity by Telling Readers Exactly Where to Buy" in** *San Diego Union-Tribune* **(October 14, 2004)**
Pub: San Diego Union-Tribune
Ed: Jennifer Davies. **Description:** Shopping magazines, sometimes referred to as magalogs, are growing in popularity. The publications offer advice on fashion, beauty products and home decor. Most of the magazines offer a Web site as a critical part of the business, with direct links to retailers featured in the magazine.

53962 ■ **"Should Doctors Own Hospitals?" in** *Business Week* **(February 20, 2006, No. 3972, pp. 63)**
Pub: McGraw-Hill Companies
Ed: Arlene Weintraub. **Description:** Controversy over the practice of doctors owning and running hospitals is discussed.

53963 ■ **"Signs of Life? You'll Need Plenty of Patience to Profit from M-Commerce" in** *Entrepreneur* **(Vol. 31, No. 10, October 2003, pp. 28)**
Pub: Entrepreneur Media, Inc.
Ed: Amanda C. Kooser. **Description:** M-Commerce, or mobile commerce, is discussed. The sector has seen disappointing early experiences, but many entrepreneurs are looking forward to a full-blown m-commerce future.

53964 ■ **"Singh-ing His Praises" in** *Inc.* **(September 1, 2004)**
Pub: Inc. Magazine
Ed: Rod Kurtz. **Description:** Profile of Manmohan Singh, one of India's top economists and newly elected to the prime minister's chair. According to Amit Maheswari, CEO of i-Vantage, a Cambridge, Massachusetts outsourcing firm employing 300 employees in India, credits Singh with making outsourcing to Indian companies popular in the U.S. and elsewhere.

53965 ■ **"Skinny Jeans Sticking Around for Fall" in** *Charlotte Observer* **(February 5, 2007)**
Pub: Knight-Ridder/Tribune Business News
Ed: Crystal Dempsey. **Description:** Clothing designers were showing skinny jeans in the fall/winter fashion shows for 2007.

53966 ■ **"Sleeping On the Job" in** *Incentive* **(Vol. 174, No. 10, October 2000, pp. 1S8)**
Pub: Bill Communications
Ed: Rachel L. Fox. **Description:** In the book Power Sleep (Harper Collins, 1999), author Dr. James B. Maas explores ways that employees can enjoy the benefits of taking naps at work, suggesting improved performance may be just a snooze away!

53967 ■ **"Sleepy Little Towns Turn High Tech" in** *Home Office Computing* **(Vol. 19, No. 1, January 2001, pp. 17)**
Pub: Scholastic Inc.
Ed: Lisa Roberts. **Description:** The agricultural town of Petaluma, California suddenly found itself a high-tech center when local firm Ceret Corp was acquired by networking giant Cisco Systems and 40 other telecom firms established facilities in the area. Petaluma has become a model for many other rural areas whose economies are disappearing. Tazwell County, Virginia has adopted a similar strategy in an effort to attract high-technology companies to an area where population has been declining.

53968 ■ **"Small businesses holding out on panic attack" in** *Atlanta Business Chronicle* **(Vol. 24, No. 13, August 31, 2001, pp. 2B)**
Pub: American City Business Journals Inc.
Ed: David Mildenberg. **Description:** Small business owners are keeping an eye on the slowing economy, but are not panicky about it, according to a Small Business InSight quarterly survey, which shows an overall score of 127, versus 130 in the previous quarter. Although the general economic slowdown is now the second-most pressing concern of small business owners, work force issues like finding qualified employees remains the top concern.

53969 ■ **"Small Biz Tentative about Testing Web Waters" in** *Crain's Detroit Business* **(Vol. 19, No. 9, March 3, 2003, pp. 29)**
Pub: Crain Communications Inc., Detroit
Ed: Laura Bailey. **Description:** Small businesses continue to shy away from electronic commerce.

53970 ■ ***Small Business or Entrepreneurial Related Newsletters and Periodicals***
Pub: Data Notes Publishing Co.
Ed: A.C. Doyle, Editor. **Released:** Irregular, latest edition July 1990; new edition expected 1996. **Covers:** about 100 listings of business newsletters and periodicals. **Entries Include:** Title of publication, description of content. **Arrangement:** Classified by line of business. **Indexes:** Subject.

53971 ■ **"Small-Business Exports Show Big Growth" in** *Hispanic Business* **(Vol. 22, No. 1/2, January/February, pp. 16)**
Pub: Hispanic Business
Description: Capsule of data from the Small Business Administration (SBA) showing small businesses with strong growth in exports. A Website with information on SBA positions and programs is also listed.

53972 ■ ***The Small Business Guide to HSAs***
Pub: Brick Tower Press
Ed: JoAnn Mills Laing. **Released:** September 2004. **Price:** $14.95. **Description:** Government-assisted Health Savings Accounts (HSAs) offer employees a tax-free way to accumulate savings to be used for qualified medical expenses, they can be rolled over without penalty for future spending, or invested to accumulate savings to pay for health needs after retirement. Employers offering HSAs can save up to two-thirds of business expenses on health insurance costs.

53973 ■ **"Small Businesses Are Raising Prices, in Latest Sign Inflation is Heating Up" in** *Wall Street Journal* **(May 2, 2000, pp. B2)**
Pub: Dow Jones & Co., Inc.
Ed: Rodney Ho. **Description:** A National Federation of Independent Business report is cited.

53974 ■ **"Small Deals, Big Business" in** *Washington Business Journal* **(Vol. 22, No. 17, August 29, 2003, pp. 17)**
Pub: Washington Business Journal
Description: The growing role of small business in the software industry is discussed. Topics include growing sales, marketing strategy, and market adaptability.

53975 ■ **"Small Firm Bankruptcy" in** *Journal of Small Business Management* **(Vol. 44, October 2006, No. 4, pp. 493)**
Pub: Blackwell Publishing, Inc.
Ed: Richard Carter; Howard Van Auken. **Description:** Results of a survey attempt to identify the root causes of bankruptcy in firms. Statistical data included.

53976 ■ **"Small Firms Slow to Board E-com Boat" in** *Accounting Today* **(Vol. 14, No. 14, August 7, 2000, pp. 27)**
Pub: Faulkner & Gray, Inc.
Description: The National Federation of Independent Business found in its survey of 1,055 small business owners that the Internet is not perceived for its potential. Most small businesses use Web sites simply because it's the thing to do.

53977 ■ **"Small Firms Still Strain for Space: Outlook Brighter for Companies in Need of More Room" in** *Crain's Chicago Business* **(Vol.23, Dec. 11)**
Pub: Crain Communications, Inc. Crain Communications, Inc.
Ed: H. Lee Murphy. **Description:** Small companies in the Chicago area are looking for larger offices because of business growth.

53978 ■ **"Small Firms Turn to Financial Futures for Fuel" in** *Wall Street Journal* **(November 3, 2003, pp. A2)**
Pub: Dow Jones & Co. Inc.
Ed: Russell Gold. **Description:** Many small- and medium-sized businesses are switching from utilities to deregulated energy markets for energy needs.

53979 ■ **"Smaller companies plan to build up inventories" in** *Wall Street Journal* **(February 15, 2002, pp. B6)**
Pub: Wall Street Journal
Description: According to a January survey conducted by the National Federation of Independent Businesses, small companies are planning to build their inventories.

53980 ■ **"Smaller, greener jobs dominate remodeling" in** *Atlanta Business Chronicle* **(Vol. 24, No. 13, August 31, 2001, pp. 5B)**
Pub: American City Business Journals Inc.

Ed: Matthew Slater. **Description:** The downturn in the economy has led to fewer large demands for remodeling, but it has also led to many demands for small remodeling jobs, such as kitchens and bathrooms.

53981 ■ **"Socialtext Update Knots Closer Enterprise Ties" in** *eWeek* **(February 7, 2005)**
Pub: Ziff Davis Media Inc.
Description: Profile of Socialtext Workspace 1.5, which integrates the wiki service with enterprise directories based on lightweight directory access protocol and Microsoft Active Directory. Socialtext develops enterprise social software that allows people and companies to use the Web to communicate more effectively.

53982 ■ **"Software Is Back - Sort of" in** *Red Herring* **(No. 102, August 15, 2001, pp. 18)**
Pub: Herring Communications
Ed: Rafe Needleman. **Description:** Vertical applications are discussed. Vertical applications take software applications, such as databases, spreadsheets, word processors, and customizes them for specific industries for Web-based applications.

53983 ■ **"Some small biz markets underserved by CPAs" in** *Journal of Accountancy* **(Vol. 190, No. 6, December 2000, pp. 30)**
Pub: Harborside Financial Center
Description: A recent survey of nearly 700 small businesses in the manufacturing, professional services, government, non-profit and other sectors revealed they generally get advice and services relating to health care, HR management and legal and compliance issues from lawyers, insurance brokers, government agencies, the Internet and reference books rather than from their accountants.

53984 ■ **"Some outplacement firms benefit in down economy" in** *Boston Business Journal* **(Vol. 22, No. 14, May 10, 2002, pp. 38)**
Pub: MCP, Inc.
Ed: Pam Derringer. **Description:** Corporate spending for outplacement has declined so there is more competition, but those who have size, reputation and niche have a chance of surviving in the down economy.

53985 ■ **"Some ideas to entertain: how to host a memorable party" in** *Utah Business* **(Vol. 16, No. 9, September 2002, pp. 50)**
Pub: American Diversified Publishing Co., Inc.
Ed: John Blodgett. **Description:** Current trends for planning business dinners and events are discussed. Many people and businesses are planning events centered on previous travel experiences or current events such as the Olympics.

53986 ■ **"Spatial Concerns" in** *Small Business Opportunities* **(Vol. 16, No. 2, March 2004, pp. 68)**
Pub: Harris Publications, Inc.
Ed: Stephen Roulac. **Description:** Warehouses are now being used as prime office space.

53987 ■ **"Speak employees' language to build their loyalty" in** *Atlanta Business Chronicle* **(Vol. 24, No. 3, June 22, 2001, pp. 62A)**
Pub: American City Business Journals Inc.
Ed: Eileen Brill Wagner. **Description:** Due to the multicultural workplace, businesses in Phoenix, Arizona are contracting to more foreign language firms.

53988 ■ **"Speaking up" in** *Entrepreneur* **(Vol. 31, No. 6, June 2003, pp. 46)**
Pub: Entrepreneur Media Inc.
Ed: Amanda C. Kooser. **Description:** According to a Yankee Group study, 25 percent of the 10-14 percent of small businesses that plan to upgrade or replace telephone systems in 2003, will move to Internet protocol telephony (IPT).

53989 ■ **"The Spies Have It" in** *Business Week* **(June 12, 2000, pp. F26)**
Pub: McGraw-Hill, Inc.
Description: Excerpts from an interview with CIA Officer Pamela J. Noe, who teaches the use of competitive intelligence at George Washington University and to small businesses.

53990 ■ **"Spies Like Us" in** *Business Week* **(June 12, 2000, pp. F24)**
Pub: McGraw-Hill, Inc.
Description: The growing importance of competitive intelligence for small business is investigated.

53991 ■ **"Spinoff Doctors" in** *Entrepreneur* **(Vol. 32, November 2004, No. 11, pp. 18)**
Pub: Entrepreneur Media Inc.
Ed: David Worrel. **Description:** Trends in the venture capital industry are spotlighted.

53992 ■ **"Spot of tea?" in** *Entrepreneur* **(Vol. 31, No. 4, April 2003, pp. 24)**
Pub: Entrepreneur Media Inc.
Description: As tea gains popularity, some restaurants are serving afternoon tea to increase sales during the slowest time of the day.

53993 ■ **"Spotting management fads." in** *Harvard Business Review* **(Vol. 80, No. 10, Oct. 2002, pp. 26)**
Pub: Harvard Business School Press
Ed: Danny Miller, Jon Hartwick. **Description:** Management fads for the past 40 years are used to make observations, concluding that fads are ultimately doomed because they tend to be overly simplistic and rarely change managerial techniques.

53994 ■ **"Spotting patterns on the fly" in** *Harvard Business Review* **(Vol. 80, No. 11, November 2002, pp. 45)**
Pub: Harvard Business School Press
Description: Two expert bird-watchers discuss the skills necessary to identify patterns in the field and how these skills can be applied to recognizing industry patterns and anticipating change.

53995 ■ **"Spy Games" in** *Entrepreneur* **(Vol. 32, August 2004, No. 8, pp. 26)**
Pub: Entrepreneur Media Inc.
Description: Security methods being used by companies include monitoring of Internet connections, background exams, email, computer files, video recording, recording phone conversations, voice mail, and polygraph exams.

53996 ■ **"Standing pat. Most employers not changing size of work force" in** *Crain's Detroit Business* **(Vol. 19, No. 9, March 3, 2003, pp. 1)**
Pub: Crain Communications Inc., Detroit
Description: Results of a survey conducted by Manpower Inc. regarding employers' expectations for April-June 2002 employment are presented.

53997 ■ **"Start Your Blogs" in** *Venture Capital Journal* **(January 1, 2005)**
Pub: Thomason Financial Inc.
Ed: Lawrence Aragon. **Description:** It is predicted that venture capital firms will use Internet blogs as a means for building business relationships. One by-product of blogs will be that brands will move away from venture firms to individual partners.

53998 ■ **"State biz bankruptcies rise despite national fall" in** *Crain's Detroit Business* **(Vol. 19, No. 10, March 10, 2003, pp. 18)**
Pub: Crain Communications Inc., Detroit
Ed: Michael Strong. **Description:** Nationally, business bankruptcies fell 3.9 percent, however they rose 20 percent in Southeast Michigan.

53999 ■ **"State Of The Unions" in** *Entrepreneur* **(Vol. 28, No. 10, October 2000, pp. 106)**
Pub: Entrepreneur Media Inc.
Ed: Jacquelyn Lynn. **Description:** Unions are eyeing workers in companies with as few as 30 employees.

54000 ■ **"The State of Small Business: Confident, yet cautious, in 2001" in** *Crain's Chicago Business* **(Vol. 23, December 11, 2000, pp. SB1)**
Pub: Crain Communications, Inc.
Ed: H. Lee Murphy. **Description:** Despite the slowing economy, small firms still look for growth.

54001 ■ **"States Target Outsourcing" in** *Inc.* **(July 1, 2004)**
Pub: Inc. Magazine
Ed: Darren Dahl. **Description:** Several states hope legislation efforts will help curb the trend toward outsourcing to companies overseas.

54002 ■ **"Staying Out of Court" in** *Business Week* **(No. 3702, October 9, 2000, pp. F16)**
Pub: McGraw-Hill, Inc.
Description: Alternatives to a courtroom battle are covered, including mediation, where a neutral party helps negotiate a settlement, and arbitration, where the neutral's decision is binding.

54003 ■ **"Stepping down" in** *Entrepreneur* **(Vol. 30, No. 2, February 2002, pp. 64)**
Pub: Entrepreneur Media Inc.
Ed: Chris Sandlund. **Description:** Some executives are taking lower positions during the economic slump.

54004 ■ **"Strength in Numbers" in** *Home Office Computing* **(Vol. 18, No. 9, September 2000, pp. 85)**
Pub: Scholastic Inc.
Ed: William Van Winkle. **Description:** Small business owners can join groups of their peers to leverage group and volume discounts on products and services. A profile of Demandline.com, a Web-based service that negotiates discounted long-distance telephone service contracts for small businesses is included.

54005 ■ **"Stresses of Elder Care Hitting the Workplace" in** *Boston Globe* **(July 11, 2004)**
Pub: Boston Globe
Ed: Tatsha Robertson. **Description:** According to elder care experts, more American working men and women are responsible for providing care for elderly relatives, making it the number one family matter faced by the employed. Some companies are beginning elder care programs as a recruitment tool.

54006 ■ **"Stretch Your Limits" in** *Entrepreneur* **(Vol. 32, December 2004, No. 12, pp. 108)**
Pub: Entrepreneur Media Inc.
Ed: Natalia Olenicoff. **Description:** IM=X Pilates franchises are now available. Pilates is one of the fastest growing fitness trends in the U.S.

54007 ■ **"Study: Detroit Second in Number of Cell-Phone Users" in** *Crain's Detroit Business* **(Vol. 19, No. 42, October 20, 2003, pp. 15)**
Pub: Crain Communications Inc., Detroit
Ed: Andrew Dietderich. **Description:** In a study conducted by New York City-based Scarborough Research, Metropolitan Detroit is second among major cities in the number of households using mobile-phone services. The study also showed that nationally, 66 percent of households own cell phones and spend about $60 monthly on services.

54008 ■ **"Succession Management for the Entire Organization" in** *Employment Relations Today* **(Vol. 27, No. 2, Summer 2000, pp. 53)**
Pub: John Wiley & Sons, Inc.
Ed: Scott T. Fleischmann. **Description:** Succession Management improves employee retention, protects critical positions within a company, provides a career path for employees, maintains competitive advantages in the marketplace, and maintains a high level of product and service quality. The process of succession management for all positions within an organization is described.

54009 ■ **"Sun CTO: New License Protects Developer Rights" in** *eWeek* **(February 7, 2005)**
Pub: Ziff Davis Media Inc.
Description: Profile of Greg Papadopoulos, chief technical officer of Sun Microsystems Inc. Papadopoulos explains the company's use of the newly created Common Development and Distribution License for its Open Solaris project.

54010 ■ **"Surveillance made easy"** in *Hispanic Business* (Vol. 22, No. 11, November 2000, pp. 80)
Pub: Hispanic Business
Ed: Vivienne Heines. **Description:** A profile of the services and products offered by surveillance company, SyTech, also known as Systems Engineering Tech Corp. The growth of the company and the popularity of its services are explored.

54011 ■ **"Survey"** in *Crain's Detroit Business* (Vol. 21, October 24, 2005, No. 43, pp. 1)
Pub: Crain Communications Inc. - Detroit
Ed: Tom Hdnderson. **Description:** According to the 2005 Michigan Women's Leadership Index, the number of top women executives has fallen by 20 percent over the last two years. The auto industry ranked lowest for upper-management opportunity for its female executives.

54012 ■ **"Survey Projects that Nation's Banks Will Spend More on Information Technology in 2004"** in *Long Island Business News* (Feb. 13, 2004)
Pub: Dolan Media Newswires
Ed: Claude Solnik. **Description:** According to a survey conducted by the American Bankers Association and Tower Group, U.S. banks will spend more money on information technology in 2004 than previous years. It is estimated that $21.2 billion will be spent on information technology this year.

54013 ■ **"Sweat rewards"** in *Entrepreneur* (Vol. 30, No. 3, Marc)
Pub: Entrepreneur Media Inc.
Ed: Amanda C. Kooser, Geoff Williams. **Description:** Predictions for hot business trends in 2002 are presented, including online learning, kiosks, online games, bartering, alternative health for pets, managing outsourcing, maternity clothing, life coaches, alternative energy, e-books, plus-size clothing, ethnic foods, personalization themes, boomer menopause, luxury products and services for middle income consumers, technology, marketing, money and management.

54014 ■ **"Sweater Set"** in *New Jersey Monthly* (Vol. 26, No. 10, October 2001, pp. 29)
Pub: Micro Media Affiliates
Description: The resurgence of the old craft of knitting is highlighted, spurring an increase in sales of yarn and knitting materials.

54015 ■ **"Sweet Victory"** in *My Business* (December/January 2004, pp. 12)
Pub: My Business Magazine
Ed: Jamie Roberts. **Description:** Profile of Mike and Carol Hamilton, owners of Carol Hamilton's Chutters General Store, offering 650 glass jars filled with candy, making the store the home of the largest candy counter in the world. The Littleton, New Hampshire store is one in a trend of small companies restoring and maintaining the main streets of towns in America. These small firms believe they can compete against large chains by offering unique customer service and products.

54016 ■ **"Syndication: The Emerging Model for Business in the Internet Era"** in *Harvard Business Review* (Vol. 78, No. 3, May 2000, pp. 85)
Pub: Harvard Business School Publishing Corp.
Ed: Kevin Werbach. **Description:** Many of the new rules about competition and strategy can be found in the concept of syndication, a way of doing business that has its origins in the entertainment world, but is now expanding to define the structure of e-business.

54017 ■ **"Take the Work Home"** in *Black Enterprise* (Vol. 36, December 2005, No. 5, pp. 72)
Pub: Earl G. Graves Publishing Co. Inc.
Ed: Marcia A. Reed-Woodard. **Description:** According to Jane Anderson, director of Midwest Institute of Telecommuting, there is a trend towards making jobs more mobile, which allows workers to access work from home. Statistical data included.

54018 ■ **"Taking Advantage of Technology"** in *Black Enterprise* (Vol. 31, No. 4, November 2000, pp. 57)
Pub: Earl Graves Publishing Co.
Ed: Paula McCoy-Pinderhughes. **Description:** Small business owners should "hire" the Internet to delegate and manage time-consuming activities such as accounting, marketing, office management, human resources, and administrative functions to cut operational costs and increase revenue.

54019 ■ **"Taking credit"** in *Entrepreneur* (Vol. 30, No)
Pub: Entrepreneur Media Inc.
Ed: Jennifer Pellet. **Description:** American Express, MasterCard and Visa are aggressively offering low introductory rates and perks like vendor discounts, reward programs and consulting services to small businesses.

54020 ■ **"Taking the Net by Storm"** in *Entrepreneur* (Vol. 28, No. 1, January 2000, pp. 50)
Pub: Entrepreneur Media Inc.
Ed: Melissa Campanelli. **Description:** According to a new study from high-tech market research firm, International Data Corporation, U.S. small businesses are accessing the Internet with a vengence.

54021 ■ **"Taking On the Energy Crunch"** in *Fortune* (Vol. 151, February 7, 2005, No. 3, pp. 97)
Pub: Time Inc.
Ed: Marc Gunther. **Description:** The appeal of wind power, because of zero fuel costs, is discussed along with other alternatives to oil and gas. General Motors, BMW, and S.C. Johnson are buying landfill gas to save money and to help clean the air; the aluminum industry spends $750 for recycled cans; environmentally designed 'green' buildings are another alternative.

54022 ■ **"Taking Sides"** in *Entrepreneur* (Vol. 33, September 2005, No. 9, pp. 26)
Pub: Entrepreneur Media Inc.
Ed: April Y. Pennington. **Description:** Three forces are changing the way to grow a business: an abundance of consumer goods; outsourcing to Asia; and automation of routine work. Six key abilities for the Conceptual Age are design, story, symphony, empathy, play and meaning.

54023 ■ **"A Tale of Two Cities"** in *Fast Company* (May 2001, pp. 143)
Pub: Fast Company
Ed: Scott Kirsner. **Description:** Seattle Mayor Paul Schell, says that his job is to turn the city into a 'platform for the creative experience', and the city is creating a place where telecommunications, biotech, software, and the Web are all coming together with music, architecture, and art.

54024 ■ **"Tap Into the Corporate LAN"** in *Home Office Computing* (Vol. 18, No. 9, September 2000, pp. 79)
Pub: Scholastic Inc.
Ed: Wayne Kawamoto. **Description:** Technologies for accessing office LANs from home are discussed.

54025 ■ **"Tapping Foreign Markets"** in *Home Office Computing* (Vol. 18, No. 10, October 2000, pp. 18)
Pub: Scholastic Inc.
Ed: Sonya Donaldson. **Description:** Small and home-based businesses are doing big business abroad. According to a recent study by the National Association for the Self-Employed, or NASE, more than 22 percent of its members have sold goods or services abroad, while one in 10 focuses solely on selling abroad. And of those who don't sell goods overseas, 20 percent said they would like to.

54026 ■ **"Tax Experts Are Standing By"** in *Business Week* (No. 3702, October 9, 2000, pp. F4)
Pub: McGraw-Hill, Inc.
Description: The IRS has opened a new unit for small business in order to strengthen education regarding the complex tax codes.

54027 ■ **"Tech and the City: What Cities Are Rising Fast on the High-Tech Horizon?"** in *Entrepreneur* (Vol. 32, October 2004, No. 10, pp. 36)
Pub: Entrepreneur Media Inc.
Ed: Melissa Campanelli. **Description:** U.S. cities offering opportunity for high-tech companies include Camden, New Jersey where the New Jersey Economic Development Authority is developing the Camden Waterfront Technology Center; Madison, Wisconsin's economic development initiative, Technology Zone Program; Tucson, Arizona, with area companies working with the SBA SBIR and SBTT federal grant programs to attract high tech companies; and South Lafayette, Louisiana's Acadiana Technology Immersion Center.

54028 ■ **"Tech Firms Prepare as Upgrade Cycle Set to Drive Growth"** in *Crain's Detroit Business* (Vol. 19, No. 45, November 10, 2003, pp. 20)
Pub: Crain Communications Inc., Detroit
Ed: Andrew Dietderich. **Description:** Computer networks and security will be the area small companies will need to upgrade during 2004, and Troy-based Data Management Inc. hopes to cash in on the trend.

54029 ■ **"Technology is Biggest Export"** in *Hispanic Business* (November 2002, pp. 25-26, 30)
Pub: Hispanic Business
Ed: Jonathan J. Higuera. **Description:** Predications are made concerning future exports; the list of winners included information technology, auto parts, medical devices, services, processed foods, and chemicals. Statistical data includes largest U.S. export products, top purchasers of U.S. exports. Government Web sites providing foreign market research to small companies are listed.

54030 ■ **"Telework Lowers Office Expense"** in *Home Office Computing* (Vol. 19, No. 1, January 2001, pp. 18)
Pub: Scholastic Inc.
Ed: Jeffery D. Zbar. **Description:** All the attention given to the human resources benefits of telework - increased employee satisfaction and enhanced recruitment, retention, and flexibility - ignores another significant upside of moving workers out of the corporate office: decreased real estate costs.

54031 ■ **"That Clicking Sound: Grandma's favorite hobby hooks a new generation of young, urban go-getters"** in *Time* (Vol. 155, Jan. 31, 2000)
Pub: Time Inc.
Description: Nearly four million women started knitting in 1999, and most were between the ages of 20 and 30. These women are seeing the craft as a means for relaxation and are boosting profits for the industry.

54032 ■ **"The Eco-Advantage. The Green 50"** in *Inc.* (November 2006, pp. 79-103)
Pub: Gruner & Jahr USA Publishing
Ed: Larry Kanters **Description:** Fifty entrepreneurs are highlighted who have found a different way to do business that is more friendly to the environment. Some range from being directed at finding renewable sources of energy while others just wanted to find an eco-friendly business model.

54033 ■ **"Theme Parks Go From One Extreme to Another to Scare Up Customers On Halloween"** in *Tampa Tribune* (October 27, 2005)
Pub: Media General, Inc.
Ed: Randy Diamond. **Description:** Central Florida's Busch Gardens and Universal Orlando's Island of Adventure are presenting Halloween events in order to draw guests. Exit surveys showed that Busch's Howlo-Scream was more intense than in the past.

54034 ■ **"There's No There There"** in *Red Herring* (No. 99, June 15 & July 1, 2001, pp. 134)
Pub: Herring Communications
Ed: David Lipschultz. **Description:** Distressed investors are those who assign value to companies that

other investors avoid. Distressed investors do not believe there is hidden value in the recent bankrupt technology firms.

54035 ■ "Think Ahead" in *Entrepreneur* **(Vol. 32, October 2004, No. 10, pp. 40)**
Pub: Entrepreneur Media Inc.
Ed: Mark Henricks. **Description:** Review of Seeing What's Next, written by Clayton M. Christensen, Scott D. Anthony, and Erik A. Roth. The book shows entrepreneurs ways to spot upcoming disruptive innovations that could threaten a company's success. A three-step process for predicting industry change is presented.

54036 ■ "This Call May Be Monitored" in *Inc.* **(Volume 27, June 2005, No. 6, pp. 29-30)**
Pub: Inc. Magazine
Ed: Jennifer Gill. **Description:** Companies are hiring professional snoops in order to improve customer satisfaction for their firm. Call center etiquette is examined.

54037 ■ "This Isn't Your Teenage Daughter's Diary: Web Logs Are a Big Hit With Everyone..." in *Black Enterprise* **(Vol. 34, December 2003)**
Pub: Earl Graves Publishing Co.
Ed: Rebecca Rohan. **Description:** Blogging, or Web logging, is journaling on the Web using special software that enables users to write directly in the blog, and is now being used by businesses.

54038 ■ "A Thousand to One" in *Entrepreneur* **(Vol. 28, No. 11, November 2000, pp. 22)**
Pub: Entrepreneur Media Inc.
Ed: Watts Wacker. **Description:** The possibility of using vending machines to sell high-priced items is discussed.

54039 ■ "Three Trends for 2005" in *Forbes* **(Vol. 175, January 31, 2005, No. 2, pp. 39)**
Pub: Forbes Magazine Inc.
Ed: Rich Karlgaard. **Description:** Video Weblogs (V-blogs) and inexpensive technology are performing business chores and offer rewards for entrepreneurs who understand how to knit these trends together.

54040 ■ "Tip Clubbing" in *Fortune* **(Vol. 142, No. 9, October 16, 2000, pp. 312)**
Pub: Time Inc.
Ed: Jennifer Pendleton. **Description:** Old-fashioned "leads" clubs are back in vogue where a firm handshake and a winning pitch can land you a few good business leads.

54041 ■ *The Tipping Point: How Little Things Can Make a Big Difference*
Pub: Little Brown & Company
Ed: Malcolm Gladwell. **Released:** January 2002. **Price:** $14.95. **Description:** Correlation between societal changes and marketing and business trends.

54042 ■ "Tips & Trends" in *Small Business Opportunities* **(Vol. 13, No. 6, November 2001, pp. 14)**
Pub: Harris Publications, Inc.
Description: The latest tips and trends for small business are presented, including information about the Motorola Timeport, a personal communicator; Jet-Set Management Group, Inc., an Internet modeling agency; contact information for those interested in franchise opportunities; and the notecard company Common Scents Cards, which offers greeting cards with scents.

54043 ■ "To DVD or not to DVD; Multimedia advertising comes in many shapes" in *Crain's Detroit Business* **(Vol. 19, No. 10, March 10, 2003)**
Pub: Crain Communications Inc., Detroit
Ed: Jennette Smith. **Description:** Companies are starting to use DVD's to promote products and services.

54044 ■ "To opt or not to opt" in *Working Woman* **(Vol. 25, No. 6, June 2000, pp. 22)**
Pub: Lang Communications Inc.
Ed: Ananda Chaudhuri. **Description:** Internet retailers are adopting a new approach to selling goods and services to consumers, known as permission-based marketing, by asking electronic mail users to agree to opt to receive advertisements.

54045 ■ "Transform Your Business Into a B2B Portal" in *E-business Advisor* **(Vol. 18, No. 4, April 2000, pp. 14)**
Pub: Advisor Media, Inc.
Ed: Nathaniel Palmer. **Description:** The concept of the corporate portal market evolved in less than a year to become one of the hottest sectors of the software industry as companies attempt to provide single access points for business transactions and the exchange of information.

54046 ■ "Transforming Life, Transforming Business: The Life-Science Revolution" in *Harvard Business Review* **(Vol. 78, No. 2, March 2000, pp. 96)**
Pub: Harvard Business School Publishing Corp.
Ed: Juan Enriquez, Ray A. Goldberg. **Description:** Advances in genetic research are setting off an industrial convergence that will have profound implications for the global economy. Farmers, computer companies, drug makers, chemical processors, and health care providers will all be drawn into the new life-science industry. This article will help show how companies can change the way they think about their businesses in order to make a successful transition.

54047 ■ "Travel...More and Less" in *Fast Company* **(September 2001, pp. 170)**
Pub: Fast Company
Ed: Ron Lieber. **Description:** In response to the economic downturn, small companies are cutting back on business travel.

54048 ■ "Trends" in *E-business Advisor* **(Vol. 17, No. 12, December 1999, pp. 8)**
Pub: Advisor Media, Inc.
Description: New business-to-business "e-market makers" are "reintermediaries" that enter supply chains and introduce new efficiencies and ways of buying and selling products and services. According to Dataquest, a unit of Gartner Group Inc., an e-market maker is an organization that develops a business-to-business, Internet Protocol (IP) network-based e-marketplace of buyers and sellers within a particular industry, geographic region, or affinity group.

54049 ■ "Tuning In to Telework" in *Home Office Computing* **(Vol. 18, No. 12, December 2000, pp. 107)**
Pub: Scholastic Inc.
Ed: Marilyn Zelinsky Syarto. **Description:** Telecommuting has reached even radio broadcasters. This article looks at one telecommuter who works for a New York radio station, but works out of his home in Connecticut. He maintains that it is important to still go into the office a few times a week and to have reliable technology.

54050 ■ "Turn It Off!" in *Entrepreneur* **(Vol. 31, No. 9, September 2003, pp. 77)**
Pub: Entrepreneur Media, Inc.
Ed: Joanne Cleaver. **Description:** According to managers at Traq-wireless, a telecommunications consulting firm, more than half of their corporate clients are enforcing strict no cell/no PDA/no BlackBerry policies during meetings.

54051 ■ "Unhelpful critique" in *Waste News* **(Vol. 7, No. 16, December 10, 2001, pp. 8)**
Pub: Crain Communications Inc. - Akron
Description: Problems associated with the computer report card recycling report are discussed.

54052 ■ "U.S. CFOs Bullish on Hiring" in *Long Island Business News* **(February 27, 2004)**
Pub: Dolan Media Newswires

Ed: Ben Abelson. **Description:** Second quarter 2004 saw chief financial officers of companies across the U.S. more optimistic about hiring new employees, but 90 percent were still reluctant to begin the process at present time.

54053 ■ "Unleash the Wireless Future" in *Microsoft Executive Circle* **(Vol. 1, No. 2, Q2 2001, pp. 28-29, 31)**
Pub: Putman Media
Ed: Rex Davenport. **Description:** The benefits for using wireless networks in business are highlighted, including the listing of benefits from the Wireless LAN Association; a wireless checklist according to the Meta Group's Peter Firstbrook; and a listing of terms used when communicating about wireless networks.

54054 ■ "Unlocking the Hidden Value in Organizations" in *Employment Relations Today* **(Vol. 27, No. 2, Summer 2000, pp. 63)**
Pub: John Wiley & Sons, Inc.
Ed: Charles O'Reilly III and Jeffrey Pfeffer. **Description:** Attracting and retaining qualified employees is one of the most important elements for success in today's business. A corporate culture that enables employees to utilize their talents and values the contributions of all workers is the key to this success.

54055 ■ "Up-to-date" in *Black Enterprise* **(Vol. 31, No. 5, December 2000, pp. 76)**
Pub: Earl Graves Publishing Co.
Ed: Sonya A. Donaldson. **Description:** How does a small business start a Website? That question is answered in this informative article.

54056 ■ "The Upside and Downside of Outsourcing" in *Business Week* **(February 20, 2006, No. 3972, pp. 18)**
Pub: McGraw-Hill Companies
Description: Foreign companies are outsourcing jobs to the U.S. at record rates. Eight percent of U.S. workers are employed in the service industry, 19 percent in manufacturing, and only 1 percent in farming.

54057 ■ "Vacancies up but investors still high on retail" in *Atlanta Business Chronicle* **(Vol. 25, December 13, 2002, No. 27, pp. A5)**
Pub: American City Business Publications, Inc.
Ed: Lisa R. Schoolcraft. **Description:** Despite lower retail rents and more empty stores in 2002 than 2001, real estate investors continue to buy Atlanta, Georgia area retail properties, largely due to the fact that investment funds are available. The market for small investors who pool funds continues to drive this trend. A report by Marcus and Millichap provides some hope that rents will recover some of the losses as 2003 progresses.

54058 ■ "VCs Investing Their Money in Nontech Firms" in *Atlanta Business Chronicle* **(Vol. 26, No. 14, September 12, 2003, pp. 3A)**
Pub: American City Business Publications, Inc.
Ed: Mary Jane Credeur. **Description:** Industry analysts state that venture capital companies are expanding into the non-tech sector. Noro-Moseley has invested $10 million in Cypress Communications Inc.

54059 ■ "Venture Capital: Its' hip to be old" in *Red Herring* **(No. 102, August 15, 2001, pp. 32)**
Pub: Herring Communications
Ed: Lawrence Aragon, Julie Landry. **Description:** Venture capitalists are growing more conservative since the downfall of dot-coms and are investing in older, self-funded companies.

54060 ■ "Venturing Forward?" in *Boston Business Journal* **(Vol. 23, No. 33, September 19, 2003, pp. 40)**
Pub: American City Business Journals
Ed: Edward Mason. **Description:** Business for venture capital companies is returning after a long dry spell since the stock market crash of 2000. Boston Millennia Partners has recently made four deals.

54061 ■ "Verifiers Try New Tactics To Counter Check Decline" in *American Banker* (Vol. 170, February 4, 2005, No. 24, pp. 12)
Pub: Thomson Financial Media Inc.
Ed: Will Wade. **Description:** In order to minimize revenue loss from declining check use, many companies that verify point-of-sale checks are offering new services.

54062 ■ "Viewer's Choice" in *Entrepreneur* (Vol. 30, No. 3, March 2002, pp. 44)
Pub: Entrepreneur Media Inc.
Ed: Amanda C. Kooser. **Description:** Videoconferencing is offering entrepreneurs, as well as established small businesses, a safe, timesaving and economical choice to decrease the amount of business travel the would otherwise have to do. A resource guide for choosing the proper Web cam is included.

54063 ■ "VPNs Go Mainstream" in *Home Office Computing* (Vol. 18, No. 12, December 2000, pp. 16)
Pub: Scholastic Inc.
Ed: Mark Kakkuri. **Description:** As more firms tire of costly dial-in equipment and toll-free lines, or even costlier leased-line wide area networks, virtual private networks (VPNs) are becoming the hottest trends in telework technology.

54064 ■ "Web Site Guides Activists" in *Motor Age* (Vol. 122, No. 11, November 2003, pp. 86)
Pub: Advanstar Communications, Inc.
Description: A new resource for auto aftermarket firms to communicate with legislative officials has been developed by the Automotive Aftermarket Industry Association (AAIA). Located in the Government section of the association's Web site, users can click on an area of interest and write to legislators.

54065 ■ "Welcome Back, Mom and Pop" in *Harvard Business Review* (Vol. 78, No. 3, May 2000, pp. 24)
Pub: Harvard Business School Publishing Corp.
Ed: Richard Metters, Michael Ketzenberg, George Gillen. **Description:** Big retailers are starting to think small again.

54066 ■ "We've Got To Get Our Hands on Some Workers" in *Business Week* (No. 3666, January 31, 2000, pp. 4)
Pub: McGraw-Hill, Inc.
Description: The impact of the labor market on small business in the year 2000 is investigated.

54067 ■ "What Comes Next" in *Business Week* (No. 3658, December 6, 1999, pp. F30)
Pub: McGraw-Hill, Inc.
Description: According to experts, small businesses will face similar problems over the next decade: low unemployment rates will continue, which means workers will be choosier; increasing health care costs; regulations; and work-family balancing. But the good news is that the trend seems to show these workers will still prefer working for small companies over large ones. Data from the U.S. Department of Labor is included.

54068 ■ "What Eliot Spitzer's Investigations Mean For You" in *Inc.* (May 1, 2005)
Pub: Inc. Magazine
Ed: Stephanie Clifford. **Description:** If a 401(k) provider or insurance company overcharges employees, a small business owner may be held liable. It is recommended that employers check fees, commission structures, and overrides with health care providers carefully.

54069 ■ "What It Takes to be a Successful Intrapreneur" in *Black Enterprise* (Vol. 36, December 2005, No. 5, pp.)
Pub: Earl G. Graves Publishing Co. Inc.
Ed: Nicole Marie Richardson. **Description:** Enterprising and innovative corporate professionals are being called intrapreneurs, or corporate entrepreneurship and corporate renewal professionals.

54070 ■ "What Venture Trends Can Tell You" in *Harvard Business Review* (Vol. 81, No. 7, July 2003, pp. 18)
Pub: Harvard Business School Press
Ed: William F. Meehan III, Ron Lemmens, Matthew R. Cohler. **Description:** The future of the U.S. venture capital industry and its investments are explored.

54071 ■ "What's In Store? Get Ahead of the Game with the Latest Retail Trends" in *Entrepreneur* (Vol. 33, September 2005, No. 9, pp. 84)
Pub: Entrepreneur Media Inc.
Ed: Gwen Moran. **Description:** Technology integration, solution-oriented merchandising, colors and graphics, and fewer SKUs are the latest trends in retailing.

54072 ■ "What's In Your Wallet? The Smartcard Is Emerging as a Major E-Commerce Tool" in *Black Enterprise* (Vol. 36, November 2005, No. 4)
Pub: Earl G. Graves Publishing Co. Inc.
Ed: Fiona Haley. **Description:** The trend towards the use of Smartcard technology could make cash transactions obsolete.

54073 ■ "What's Next: Power Surge" in *Inc.* (July 1, 2003)
Pub: Gruner & Jahr USA Publishing
Description: Thanks to new technology, your next Internet service provider might be the power company; electric utility companies are researching Internet service.

54074 ■ "When Taking Candy From Babies Makes Sense" in *Fortune* (Vol. 141, No. 17, April 3, 2000, pp. 304)
Pub: Time Inc.
Ed: Carolyn T. Geer. **Description:** Advice is given regarding partnership agreements, including information about the Uniform Transfers to Minors Act.

54075 ■ "Where the Jobs Are" in *Business Week* (January 16, 2006, No. 3967, pp. 42-43)
Pub: McGraw-Hill Companies
Ed: Nandini Lakshman. **Description:** The number of foreign workers at Indian information technology and outsourcing companies has tripled to 30,000 in two years. Foreign workers earn about $350 per month.

54076 ■ "Who has the next big idea?" in *Fast Company* (September 2001, pp. 108)
Pub: Fast Company
Ed: Daniel H. Pink. **Description:** Michael Hammer, consultant, author, evangelical business revolutionary, unleashed re-engineering on an unsuspecting public in the mid 1990s, now he's back with a new book, a new agenda, and a bunch of new ideas.

54077 ■ "Who Needs The Aggravation?" in *Forbes* (Vol. 170, No. 8, October 14, 2002, pp. 56)
Pub: Forbes Magazine
Ed: Carrie Coolidge. **Description:** With the new tough accounting rules, some small companies are deciding that it is better to not be a publicly traded firm.

54078 ■ "Wholesale changes: Mom-and-Pop stores are so passe" in *Entrepreneur* (Vol. 30, No. 2, February 2002, pp. 19)
Pub: Entrepreneur Media Inc.
Ed: Nichole L. Torres. **Description:** Some retailers are revamping the layout of stores to give the look of a warehouse in order to attract more customers.

54079 ■ "Why Do They Keep Leaving" in *Harvard Business Review* (Vol. 81, No. 2, February 2003, pp. 14)
Pub: Harvard Business School Press
Ed: Jeffrey A. King. **Description:** Statistical analysis of companies that have not gone through a merger show that attrition rates are about 10 percent, while companies that merge have attrition rates nearly double for as long as nine years after the merger. Reasons include stress and perceived lack of advancement opportunities. Research shows that even executives hired after a merger, leave at these elevated rates.

54080 ■ "Why Small Firms Can't Do Their Part" in *Hispanic Business* (Vol. 23, No. 11, November 2001, pp. 22)
Pub: Hispanic Business Inc.
Ed: Patricia Guadalupe. **Description:** As the government begins a buildup, a new report questions how much small business contractors will benefit. Statistics showing contracts to small disadvantaged businesses made by the SBA from 1997 to 2000 are presented.

54081 ■ "Why There's No Escaping the Blog" in *Fortune* (Vol. 151, January 10, 2005, No. 1, pp. 44)
Pub: Time Inc.
Ed: David Kirkpatrick, Daniel Roth, Oliver Ryan. **Description:** Microsoft has unveiled a plan to develop a new service called MSN Spaces, an online software that allows users to easily create and maintain blogs on the Internet. The power of blogs and bloggers to make or break a product or service is examined.

54082 ■ "Why Wi-Fi?" in *Hispanic Business* (November 2003, pp. 74)
Pub: Hispanic Business
Ed: Roger Harris. **Description:** According to one author, wireless Internet access has the potential to revolutionize operations at small companies.

54083 ■ "Winning the talent war for women: sometimes it takes a revolution" in *Harvard Business Review* (Vol. 78, No. 6, Nov.- Dec. 2000)
Pub: Harvard Business School Publishing Corp.
Description: The steps Deloitte and Touche is taking to retain women at its company.

54084 ■ "The Wisdom of Thoughtfulness: In Tight Labor Market, Bosses Find Value in Being Nice" in *The New York Times* (May 31, 2000, pp. C1)
Pub: The New York Times Company
Ed: Amy Zipkin. **Description:** A new survey finds employees value a caring boss more than they value money or fringe benefits.

54085 ■ "Women: dollars and sense" in *WorkingWoman* (Vol. 25, No. 2, February 2000, pp. S2)
Pub: Lang Communications Inc.
Ed: Kim A. Calero. **Description:** Women live longer than men by six years and 81 percent of the services and products are bought by women, yet women receive only 75 cents on the dollar that men are paid.

54086 ■ "Workers as Assets: A Good Start But..." in *Employment Relations Today* (Vol. 27, No. 1, Spring 2000, pp. 1)
Pub: John Wiley & Sons, Inc.
Ed: Thomas O. Davenport. **Description:** Issues discussed concern the management of human capital in corporations, focusing on the strategic benefits of employee development and loyalty. Topics addressed include how to invest in and gauge the benefits of human capital.

54087 ■ "Workers' Comp Rates to Fall" in *Sacramento Bee* (November 29, 2005)
Pub: The Sacramento Bee
Ed: Gilbert Chan. **Description:** California's State Compensation Insurance Fund announced a reduction in rates by an average 16 percent beginning January 1, 2006. Other carriers are reducing rates from 13 percent to 15 percent.

54088 ■ "Workers Simply Want to Be Organized" in *Home Office Computing* (Vol. 18, No. 12, December 2000, pp. 23)
Pub: Scholastic Inc.
Ed: Marilyn Zelinsky Syarto. **Description:** FileMaker's database software is helping home-based workers get organized with digital file cabinets.

54089 ■ "Working Hard for the Money" in *Black Enterprise* (Vol. 36, February 2006, No. 7, pp. 44)
Pub: Earl G. Graves Publishing Co. Inc.
Ed: Brenda Porter. **Description:** Black women with bachelor's degrees are securing more positions than

Hispanic and white women with the same education level. The trend may be a result of black women working more hours and/or working more than job.

54090 ■ "Working Wonders on the Web" in *Inc.* **(October 1, 2003)**
Pub: Gruner & Jahr USA Publishing
Ed: Leigh Buchanan. **Description:** The Internet isn't being used for decorative marketing sites only; small companies are using the Web to run some of their most strategic operations successfully.

54091 ■ "Workplace 2005: Telecommuting, Virtual Offices, Dispersed Staff..." in *Entrepreneur* **(Vol. 33, February 2005, No. 2, pp. 55)**
Pub: Entrepreneur Media Inc.
Ed: Amanda C. Kooser. **Description:** Overview of new trends and technologies to help a small business is presented. Several entrepreneurs offer insight into technologies that help them run their companies in an ever-changing business environment.

54092 ■ "XBRL Revisited: Grasp the Fundamentals to See How Businesses Use XBRL Today" in *Journal of Accountancy* **(Vol. 199, February 2005)**
Pub: American Institute of Certified Public
   Accountants
Ed: Neal J. Hannon, Robert J. Gold. **Description:** Extensible Business Reporting Language (XBRL) is increasing in popularity with investors, analysts, public companies and other securities market firms, including certified public accounting businesses. XBRL basics for use are presented.

54093 ■ "Y Stay Put? Generation Y Bounces From Job to Job" in *The Record* **(November 13, 2005)**
Pub: New Jersey Media Group
Ed: Catherine Holahan. **Description:** Americans born between 1977 and 1994 are known as Generation Y; these individuals do not consider long-term commitments in any one position. Generation Y saw too many of their baby boomer parents, who depended on job security, lose their jobs. Statistical data included.

54094 ■ "The Year 2000 Top Inc. 500" in *Inc.* **(October 17, 2000 pp. 57)**
Pub: The Goldhirsh Group
Description: The 2000 Inc. 500 Almanac, listing their top 500 pick companies by state.

54095 ■ "Young, Female, and Demanding" in *Inc.* **(Volume 28, January 2006, No. 1, pp. 27)**
Pub: Inc. Magazine
Description: Young Generation X women are burning out in the workplace at increasingly high numbers. Charlotte Shelton, a business professor at Rockhurst University in Missouri, believes changing attitudes placing high expectations on women are partly to blame.

54096 ■ "Your Boss is Watching" in *PC Computing* **(March 2000, pp. 86)**
Pub: Ziff-Davis Inc.
Description: Web monitoring software is used by 45 percent of all companies and 17 percent of Fortune 1000 companies to make sure employees are not misusing the Web while at work. The WinWhatWhere Investigator software can record every keystroke an employee enters on a PC, while Elron Software's CommandView has the Message Inspector module that filters, stores and blocks emails at the network server. The article recommends that employees should minimize non-business-related web browsing on the company's computer.

TRADE PERIODICALS

54097 ■ *Business Trends*
Pub: Bowes Publishers Ltd.
Contact: Kim Oliver, Publisher
Ed: Dave Paul, Editor. **Released:** Monthly. **Price:** $24 Canadian (GST included); $2 single issue; $48 elsewhere. **Description:** Magazine featuring local business-related articles for the Sarnia, Ontario area in Canada.

CONSULTANTS

54098 ■ Sklar & Associates
1101 S Arlington Ridge Rd. Ste. 511
Arlington, VA 22202-1925
Ph:(202)257-5061
Fax: (202)828-4130
Co. E-mail: sklarincdc@aol.com
URL: http://www.sklarinc.com

E-mail: sklarincdc@aol.com
Scope: Provides Audit Oversight services to listed corporations on Sarbanes-Oxley compliance. **Seminars:** Financial Analysis in MBA; Emerging Company Finance; Due Diligence in Business Acquisition; Business Valuation. **Special Services:** Financial Modeling. Course titled *Understanding and Detecting Deceptive Creative Accounting Practices.*

COMPUTERIZED DATABASES

54099 ■ *Stern's Management Review*
Stern and Associates
11260 Overland Ave., Ste. 16A
Culver City, CA 90230
Ph:(310)838-0551
Co. E-mail: info@hrconsultant.com
URL: http://www.hrconsultant.com/index.html
Description: Contains business management information and ideas from the print version of Stern's Management Review, a quarterly management newsletter. Includes the full text of editorials from the newsletter since 1992. Covers such issues as business trends, leadership, corporate downsizing, management, compensation, and much more. **Availability:** Online: Stern and Associates. **Type:** Full text.

LIBRARIES

54100 ■ Colorado Mountain College–Alpine Campus Library
PO Box 774688
Steamboat Springs, CO 80477
Ph:(970)870-4445
Fax: (970)870-4490
URL: http://www.coloradomtn.edu/library/
Contact: Larry Rouch, Lib.Dir.
Scope: Small business, hotel management, restaurant manangement, health and fitness, U.S. history and literature, American music, skiing. **Services:** Interlibrary loan; Library open to the public. **Holdings:** 30,000 books; 580 CDs; maps; state documents; CD-ROMs. **Subscriptions:** 225 journals and other serials; 15 newspapers.

54101 ■ Greater Oviedo Chamber of Commerce–Business Library
PO Box 621236
Oviedo, FL 32762-1236
Ph:(407)365-6500
Fax: (407)365-6587
Co. E-mail: fay@oviedochamber.org
URL: http://www.oviedochamber.org
Contact: Fay I. Stoner, Off.Mgr.
Scope: Small business; central Florida business. **Services:** Copying; Library open to the public. **Holdings:** 3 books; 10 reports; periodicals. **Subscriptions:** 3 newspapers.

54102 ■ Indian River Area Library
PO Box 160
Indian River, MI 49749
Ph:(231)238-8581
Fax: (231)238-9494
Co. E-mail: indrivl@northland.lib.mi.us
URL: http://www.libnet.org/iriver/
Contact: Cindy Lou Poquette, Dir.
Scope: Small business, careers, fine arts, music, dance. **Services:** Interlibrary loan; copying; Library

open to the public (fee for non-residents to check out materials). **Holdings:** 45,000 books; 2500 videocassettes; 2000 microfiche; videocassettes; sound cassettes; DVDs; CDs; periodicals; large print books. **Subscriptions:** 78 journals and other serials; 3 newspapers.

54103 ■ Small Business Administration–Reference Library
409 Third St., SW
Washington, DC 20416
Ph:(202)205-7033
Fax: (202)481-4302
URL: http://www.sba.gov
Contact: Margaret Hickey, Libn.
Scope: Small business, finance, management, venture capital. **Services:** Interlibrary loan; Library open to the public for reference use only. **Holdings:** 8000 volumes. **Subscriptions:** 72 journals and other serials.

RESEARCH CENTERS

54104 ■ Alabama Law Institute
PO Box 861425
Tuscaloosa, AL 35486-0013
Ph:(205)348-7411
Fax: (205)348-8411
Co. E-mail: rmccurley@ali.state.al.us
URL: http://www.ali.state.al.us/
Contact: Robert L. McCurley Jr., Dir.
E-mail: rmccurley@ali.state.al.us
Scope: Statutes of Alabama, including studies of existing laws with systematic revision of laws to be proposed to Alabama legislature. Conducts investigations into state tax structure, evidence, criminal law, business law, probate law, real property, and family law. Develops manuals for legislators, county commissioners, tax assessors and collectors, and other governmental offices. **Publications:** Annual Report. **Educational Activities:** Basic and advanced law courses, for probate judges; Capital Intern Program, allowing three students to work at the State Legislature.

54105 ■ Bradley University–Center for Business and Economic Research
1501 W Bradley Ave.
Peoria, IL 61625
Ph:(309)677-2262
Fax: (309)677-3257
Co. E-mail: bjg@bumail.bradley.edu
URL: http://www.bradley.edu/fcba/community/cber
Contact: Dr. Bernard Goitein, Dir.
E-mail: bjg@bumail.bradley.edu
Scope: Coordinates faculty research projects in program evaluation, consumer confidence, economic development, market research, needs assessment, impact analysis, modeling, forecasting, survey research, cost and price modeling, accounting and special purpose information systems, location analysis, financial planning, cost-benefit analysis, performance evaluation and productivity analysis. **Publications:** Peoria MSA Business Database Report (quarterly); Peoria MSA Consumer Sentiment (3/year).

54106 ■ East Tennessee State University–Tennessee Small Business Development Center
ETSU Innovation Laboratory
2109 W Market St.
Johnson City, TN 37614-0698
Ph:(423)439-8505
Fax: (423)439-8506
Co. E-mail: bjustice@mail.tsbdc.org
URL: http://www.tsbdc.org
Contact: Robert A. Justice, Dir.
E-mail: bjustice@mail.tsbdc.org
Scope: Small business assistance in the areas of business plans and strategies, financial forecasts, feasibility studies, financial statement analysis, credit establishment and collection policies, inventory control analysis, marketing plans, accounting and record-keeping systems, licenses, permits, tax authorities,

organizational structure, management succession, professional development, and buying and selling. **Services:** Provides free Internet access to clients (daily). **Educational Activities:** Consulting, technical assistance, and management assistance (daily); Workshops, seminars and conferences (weekly).

54107 ■ Indiana State University–Small Business Development Center
9th & Sycamore Sts.
Terre Haute, IN 47809-5402
Ph:(812)237-7676
Free: 800—227-7232
Fax: (812)237-7675
Co. E-mail: l-goodrich@indstate.edu
URL: http://www.indstate.edu/sbdc/
Contact: Laura E. Goodrich, Admin.Asst.
E-mail: l-goodrich@indstate.edu
Scope: Small business development and entrepreneurship. **Services:** Counseling; Training and referral services, to new and emerging small businesses.

54108 ■ Michigan State University–Institute for Public Policy and Social Research
321 Berkey Hall
East Lansing, MI 48824-1111
Ph:(517)355-6672
Fax: (517)432-1544
Co. E-mail: Douglas.Roberts@ssc.msu.edu
URL: http://www.ippsr.msu.edu
Contact: Douglas B. Roberts, Dir.
E-mail: Douglas.Roberts@ssc.msu.edu
Scope: Conducts social and policy research at the national, state, and local levels, focusing on improving the policy process to make governance more effective and developing better policies. **Services:** Public policy forums (quarterly). **Publications:** Policy briefs; SOSS Bulletins. **Educational Activities:** Conference, seminars, and special events; Political leadership program (monthly); Public Policy Seminars (monthly).

54109 ■ Pennsylvania Small Business Development Centers
423 Vance Hall
University of Pennsylvania
3733 Spruce St.
Philadelphia, PA 19104-6374
Ph:(215)898-1219
Fax: (215)573-2135
Co. E-mail: ghiggins@wharton.upenn.edu
URL: http://pasbdc.org
Contact: Greg Higgins, Dir.
E-mail: ghiggins@wharton.upenn.edu
Scope: Helps small businesses improve profitability and increase employment through programs of procurement, international trade, product development, and business law. **Services:** Free management consulting to entrepreneurs and prospective business

owners. **Educational Activities:** Training programs, workshops, and seminars.

54110 ■ University of Connecticut–Connecticut Small Business Development Center
2100 Hillside Rd., Unit 1094
Storrs, CT 06269-1094
Ph:(860)486-4135
Fax: (860)486-1576
Co. E-mail: csbdcinformation@sba.uconn.edu
URL: http://www.sbdc.uconn.edu
Contact: Richard S. Cheney, Interim State Dir.
E-mail: csbdcinformation@sba.uconn.edu
Scope: Provides business management research service to small and mid-size firms in Connecticut, including studies of pre-venture feasibility, the business plan, marketing, record-keeping, financial planning, production, loan packaging, general management, foreign developments with respect to national laws, product demands, available distribution channels, business customs and regulations, product export evaluation, and export sales strategies. **Services:** Consulting through the Marketing Technology Assistance Center and the Export Services Center; Professional, individual consulting through the Business Research Law Clinic and the Accounting Service Center. **Publications:** Reports (periodically). **Educational Activities:** Business management workshops, seminars, and conferences; Offers courses and group training programs.

54111 ■ University of Mississippi–Small Business Development Center
B19 Jeanette Phillips Dr.
PO Box 1848
University, MS 38677-1848
Ph:(662)915-1291
Fax: (662)915-5650
Co. E-mail: mvander@olemiss.edu
URL: http://www.olemissbusiness.com/sbdc/index. htm
Contact: Mike Vanderlip, Dir.
E-mail: mvander@olemiss.edu
Scope: Small business management, including feasibility studies, business law, venture capital, government contracting, and financial, production, and personnel management. **Services:** Management counseling and marketing assistance for entrepreneurs and small business owners and managers. **Educational Activities:** Seminars and training on small business development.

54112 ■ University of New Hampshire–New Hampshire Small Business Development Center
108 McConnell Hall
15 College Rd.
Durham, NH 03824

Ph:(603)862-2200
Fax: (603)862-4876
Co. E-mail: mary.collins@unh.edu
URL: http://www.nhsbdc.org
Contact: Mary E. Collins, Dir.
E-mail: mary.collins@unh.edu
Scope: Provides research support services to small businesses in New Hampshire. **Services:** Consulting and technical assistance. **Educational Activities:** Conferences, workshops and seminars.

54113 ■ Washington State University–Small Business Development Center
601 W First Ave.
Spokane, WA 99201-3899
Ph:(509)358-7765
Fax: (509)358-7764
Co. E-mail: clrk@wsu.edu
URL: http://www.wsbdc.org
Contact: Carolyn Clark, Dir.
E-mail: clrk@wsu.edu
Scope: Business and economic research designed to enhance the operation of small businesses, including feasibility studies; market research; computerized literature searches; new product evaluation and testing; community economic development searches; new product evaluation and testing; community economic development studies; economic impact analyses; consumer attitude studies; design, implementation, and analyses of surveys; and related contract research, specifically practical applied research at the individual company level. **Educational Activities:** Seminars and training programs, approximately 450 per year.

54114 ■ World Jurist Association
1000 Connecticut Ave. NW, Ste. 202
Washington, DC 20036
Ph:(202)466-5428
Fax: (202)452-8540
Co. E-mail: wja@worldjurist.org
URL: http://www.worldjurist.org
Contact: Margaret M. Henneberry, Exec.VP
E-mail: wja@worldjurist.org
Scope: International law and legal institutions, including studies on world peace through law, communications law, an international court system, international treaties and agreements, foreign investment disputes, real estate and business law, and legal education. Serves as a voluntary international association of the legal profession. **Publications:** Directory of law and judicial systems of nations; Law/Technology (quarterly); Pamphlets Series (occasionally); Report Series on Law-making Activities of International Organizations; Workpapers; The World Jurist (bimonthly). **Educational Activities:** World conferences (biennially), in odd years.

Socially Responsible Business Practices

START-UP INFORMATION

54115 ■ "Eco-Preneuring" in *Small Business Opportunities* (Vol. 12, No. 2, March 2000, pp. 54, 56)
Pub: Harris Publications, Inc.
Ed: Marie Sherlock. **Description:** Six-figure profits are only natural for avid recyclers who started an environmental home decor emporium.

54116 ■ "Focus on the Positive" in *Entrepreneur.com* (Vol. 34, February 2006, No. 2, pp. 110)
Pub: Entrepreneur Media Inc.
Ed: James Park. **Description:** Profile of Paul Graves and Brandon Koechlin, founders of PositivesDating.com. The partners stared their online dating/networking service for individuals with HIV/AIDS in 2005. The site has generated $60,000 in sales in 2005 and boasts nearly 2,500 members.

54117 ■ "How I Did It: Amber Chand" in *Inc.* (September 1, 2004)
Pub: Inc. Magazine
Ed: Hillary Johnson. **Description:** Profile of Amber Chand, a businesswoman who went from running a museum gift shop to co-founding Eziba with her brother-in-law. Chand's mission to foster social change was the idea behind the artisan handicrafts retailer which provides a market for entrepreneurs worldwide, especially those in war-torn nations.

54118 ■ "Inc. Case Study" in *Inc.* (November 2000, pp. 54)
Pub: The Goldhirsh Group
Description: Marian Cihacek chronicles the business she founded, Great Harvest Bread Company, that practically runs itself.

54119 ■ "Selling Serenity" in *Small Business Opportunities* (Vol. 13, No. 5, September 2001, pp. 74, 130)
Pub: Harris Publications, Inc.
Ed: Marie Sherlock. **Description:** Profile of Judy Wallace, who runs a store called Serenity Shop, that sells inspirational products for those struggling with or recovering from addictions.

54120 ■ "The Trading Post" in *Small Business Opportunities* (Vol. 12, No. 3, May 2000, pp. 94, 96, 98)
Pub: Harris Publications, Inc.
Ed: Marie Sherlock. **Description:** Sisters Paulette Wittwer and Tamara Patrick designed a business which specializes in folk art, clothing, and jewelry from around the world, while attempting to ensure that the sources for their merchandise are socially responsible.

ASSOCIATIONS AND OTHER ORGANIZATIONS

54121 ■ **As You Sow Foundation**
311 California St., Ste. 510
San Francisco, CA 94104
Ph:(415)391-3212
Fax: (415)391-3245
Co. E-mail: asyousow@asyousow.org
URL: http://www.asyousow.org
Contact: Michael Passoff, Associate Dir.
Description: Dedicated to promoting corporate social responsibility. **Publications:** *Proxy Season Preview*, *Unlocking the Power of the Proxy*.

54122 ■ **Business for Social Responsibility**
111 Sutter St., 12th Fl.
San Francisco, CA 94104
Ph:(415)984-3200
Fax: (415)984-3201
Co. E-mail: info@bsr.org
URL: http://www.bsr.org
Contact: Aron Cramer, CEO
Membership: Large, small, and medium-sized businesses. **Purpose:** Promotes responsible business behavior and serves as a resource to companies striving to make ethical business decisions.

54123 ■ **National Association of Public Sector Equal Opportunity Officers**
City of Tallahassee Equal Opportunity Department
300 S Adams St.
Tallahassee, FL 32301
Ph:(850)891-8290
Fax: (850)891-8733
Co. E-mail: ofuanis@talgov.com
URL: http://www.talgov.com
Contact: Sharon Ofuani
Membership: Equal employment opportunity officers and coordinators, human resources managers, employee relations directors, attorneys, lawmakers, consultants, community relations specialists, and other associated professionals in the public sector. **Purpose:** Promotes the professionalism of equal opportunity workers and an understanding of diversity as means for improving the quality of life for all citizens. Serves as a resource for the public and private sectors through education and training. Provides recruitment assistance for professional, technical, and executive/managerial positions. Acts as a clearinghouse for members on effective problem solving and decision making.

54124 ■ **National Partnership for Social Enterprise**
6 Brigade Hill Rd.
Morristown, NJ 07960-4901
Ph:(973)540-1900
Fax: (973)539-1661
Contact: Robert Corman, Pres.
Purpose: Works to develop and implement strategies for sustainable social change. Engages in market research, development, business planning and implementation. Works with grass roots groups, government, and businesses.

54125 ■ **Society for Corporate Environmental and Social Responsibility**
Dalhousie University
6100 University Ave.
Halifax, NS, Canada B3H3J5
Ph:(902)441-6756
Fax: (902)494-3728
Co. E-mail: cesr@dal.ca
URL: http://societyforcorporateenvironmentalandsocialresponsibility.dsu.c
Contact: Kable Frank, Chair
Description: Promotes sustainable development, social justice, peace, corporate responsibility, ethics, democracy, good governance, and human rights.

54126 ■ **Women's Healthy Environments Network**
24 Mercer St., Ste. 101
Toronto, ON, Canada M5V 1H3
Ph:(416)928-0880
Fax: (416)928-9640
Co. E-mail: when@web.ca
URL: http://www.whenvironments.ca
Contact: Kerri Brock, Co-Chair
Description: Women experts in environmental studies and issues. Works to implement community development projects to improve the environment. Provides a forum for discussion, information exchange, and the conducting of research related to women in the fields of planning, health, workplace, design, economy, urban and rural sociology, and community development. Initiates and organizes community projects. Advocates environmental protection, anti-discriminatory zoning practices, and the development of affordable housing. **Publications:** *Whitewash*; *Women and Environments* (quarterly).

REFERENCE WORKS

54127 ■ "5 Moves to Make Before the New Year" in *My Business* (December/January 2004, pp. 14)
Pub: My Business Magazine
Ed: Barbara Weltman. **Description:** Small business tax planning is essential for a company to be successful. Financial tips to help small firms are listed, focusing on general strategy, equipment, cars, retirement plans, and gift giving.

54128 ■ "Abuse-awareness initiative lets employers help parents" in *Business First Columbus* (Vol. 18, No. 26, February 15, 2002, pp. B7)
Pub: Business First Columbus, Inc.
Ed: Betsy Butler. **Description:** A new government initiative is allowing employers to assist employees in abuse cases.

54129 ■ "Acquire and Rewire" in *Memphis Business Journal* (Vol. 25, No. 16, August 15, 2003, pp. 31)
Pub: American City Business Journals
Ed: Rob Robertson. **Description:** First Tennessee Bank Memphis, led by president Charles Burkett, en-

courages managers to become involved in community affairs. The bank is the 31st largest bank in the U.S. and is expanding into Virginia.

54130 ■ "Ambitious business women search for mentors during challenging times" in *San Francisco Business Times* **(Vol. 16, No. 42, May 24, 2002)**
Pub: San Francisco Business Times Inc.
Ed: Kristen Bole. **Description:** Mentoring Circles, a San Francisco nonprofit, connects women business owners with established women in business. Mentoring programs at San Francisco area companies are also discussed.

54131 ■ "Angel Flight" in *Ingram's* **(Vol. 27, No. 12, December 2001, pp. 70)**
Pub: Show Me Publishing, Inc.
Description: Profile of Angel Flight, a nonprofit organization that provides free flights in the mid-west area to the needy, as well as terminally ill persons. Many of the pilots are retired businessmen.

54132 ■ "Are Green Funds True To Their Colors?" in *Fortune* **(Vol. 151, February 7, 2005, No. 3, pp. 106)**
Pub: Time Inc.
Ed: Marc Gunther. **Description:** Many social or environmental mutual funds do not own shares in any companies that promote alternative energy, organic farming, or other solutions to environmental problems. An example of such a practice is highlighted by the Sierra Club Stock Fund, that promises to 'invest for sustainable growth' but does not own shares in any environmental businesses.

54133 ■ "At the Service of Charity" in *Business Week Online* **(Oct. 23, 2002)**
Pub: McGraw-Hill Inc.
Description: An interview with Mari Saso, founder of Aki Designs, explains how he is trying out a new strategy for making philanthropy a priority, despite hard times. Saso recently launched a competition on the firm's Web site that allows nonprofits to apply for pro bono design and branding work from Aki Designs.

54134 ■ "At-work weight watchers programs gain popularity" in *Business First Columbus* **(Vol. 18, No. 26, February 15, 2002, pp. B5)**
Pub: Business First Columbus, Inc.
Ed: Jon E. Hale. **Description:** Profile of the new Weight Watchers' At Work Program.

54135 ■ "Author, Expert to Discuss Socially Responsible Business Methods" in *Portland Press Herald* **(April 20, 2005)**
Pub: Blethen Maine Newspapers, Inc.
Ed: Victoria Gannon. **Description:** Hunter Lovins, co-author of the book, Natural Capitalism-Creating the Next Industrial Revolution, spoke to a group of business owners regarding the three main tenets of natural capitalism.

54136 ■ "Banker Boosts Community" in *Crain's New York Business* **(Vol. 23, January 29, 2007, No. 5, pp. F14)**
Pub: Crain Communications, Inc.
Ed: Tom Fredrickson. **Description:** Profile of Maurice L. Coleman, New York Market Executive for Bank of America. Under his leadership, Bank of America is becoming a major player in community development in New York City, specifically targeting affordable housing and small businesses in low-income areas. Statistical data included.

54137 ■ "Be a complete lawyer" in *Daily Business Review* **(Vol. 77, No. 198, March 24, 2003, pp. A6)**
Pub: American Lawyer Media LP
Ed: Vance Salter. **Description:** The topic of pro bono work done by successful attorneys is discussed. The Supreme Court and the Florida Bar recognized the best performers with service awards at the Supreme Court of Florida.

54138 ■ "Book learnin'" in *Entrepreneur* **(Vol. 30, No. 10, October 2002, pp. 172)**
Pub: Entrepreneur Media Inc.

Ed: April Y. Pennington. **Description:** Profile of Sharon Anderson Wright, president and CEO of Half Price Books, Inc., the largest independently owned used bookstore in the U.S.

54139 ■ "Book Meets Girl" in *Entrepreneur. com* **(Vol. 34, February 2006, No. 2, pp. 112)**
Pub: Entrepreneur Media Inc.
Ed: Genevieve Jenkins. **Description:** Profile of Ellen Langas Campbell of Nou-Soma Communications, Inc. Campbell has written a series of inspirational books for girls between the ages of 8 and 12. The books encourage self-esteem and career focus.

54140 ■ "Broader Wheelchair Access Rules Proposed" in *Inc.* **(September 2005, pp. 32)**
Pub: Inc. Magazine
Ed: Allen P. Roberts Jr. **Description:** The Justice Department is considering changing the Americans With Disabilities Act to require companies to make all entryways wheelchair accessible, a move that would impact all small companies.

54141 ■ "Brown Delivers..." in *Ingram's* **(Vol. 29, No. 1, January 2003, pp. 31)**
Pub: Show Me Publishing, Inc.
Ed: Chris Becicka. **Description:** The United Parcel Service of America Inc., and its Chief Operating Officer Glenn Rice, are strong supporters of charitable causes, including women's issues. The company has donated land and a building site for a bronze statue honoring women. The firm has won awards for its hiring policies for women and minorities, given grants for poorly educated and illiterate women, and other philanthropic projects.

54142 ■ "Bucking Convention" in *Entrepreneur* **(Vol. 33, January 2005, No. 1, pp. 268)**
Pub: Entrepreneur Media Inc.
Ed: April Y. Pennington. **Description:** Profile of Scott Vincent Borba and Joey Shamah, founder of e.l.f. Cosmetics (Eyes. Lips. Face.) The cosmetic company sells every product for $1. During the month of October 2004, e.l.f. donated 20 percent of proceeds from its Shimmering Facial Whip to help fund Win Against Breast Cancer's research and services, and provided makeup in Color Therapy Care Packages to breast cancer patients in inner-city hospitals in Los Angeles.

54143 ■ "Building your own foundation" in *Ingram's* **(Vol. 27, No. 12, December 2001, pp. 28)**
Pub: Show Me Publishing, Inc.
Description: The benefits of creating a foundation or trust rather than donating to charitable organizations are examined. By creating a foundation, one can save money on taxes while retaining control of the funds being contributed to the community.

54144 ■ "Building Hope" in *Ingram's* **(Vol. 28, No. 6, June 2002, pp. 29)**
Pub: Show Me Publishing, Inc.
Description: Twenty volunteers joined their employer, Strickland Construction Company, and traveled to El Centro, Guatemala and Brazil to build dorms, homes, churches, community centers, and doctor's offices.

54145 ■ "Building a Portfolio" in *Crain's Detroit Business* **(Vol. 21, October 3, 2005, No. 43)**
Pub: Crain Communications Inc. - Detroit
Ed: Jennette Smith. **Description:** Profile of Fred Erb, who leased his Erb Lumber store locations to Carolina Holdings in 1993, however Erb did not sell the real estate. Erb has served the area as lumber baron, business mentor and philanthropist.

54146 ■ "Building Your Business" in *Small Business Opportunities* **(Vol. 17, May 2005, No. 3, pp. 12)**
Pub: Harris Publications Inc.
Ed: Carla Longley Vincent. **Description:** Seven ways for a small business to tap into customers and increase profits include the development of alliances, franchising, adding wholesale clients, sell to the government, work with nonprofits, market yourself, and create new goods or services.

54147 ■ "Business Buzz" in *Tribune* **(March 1, 2005)**
Pub: Knight-Ridder/Tribune Business News
Description: Three downtown San Luis Obispo bars are offering handicapped accessible access to persons with disabilities. Each tavern meets the Americans with Disabilities Act requirements.

54148 ■ "Business Development through Philanthropy" in *Ingram's* **(Vol. 27, No. 12, December 2001, pp. 23)**
Pub: Show Me Publishing, Inc.
Description: The use of philanthropy for business development is discussed. As a business owner, this activity will improve company image and expand networking opportunities.

54149 ■ "Canoga Park Purchase" in *San Fernando Valley Business Journal* **(Vol. 12, January 2007, No. 2, pp. 32)**
Pub: San Fernando Valley Business Journal Associates
Ed: Shelly Garcia. **Description:** Various recent real estate deals are profiled, including Planet Green, a company that provides recycling services to many non-profit agencies, which purchased a new 30,000-square-foot industrial property for $4.4 million.

54150 ■ "Causes and Effects" in *Harvard Business Review* **(Vol. 81, No. 7, July 2003, pp. 95)**
Pub: Harvard Business School Press
Ed: Carol L. Cone, Mark A. Feldman, Alison T. Da-Silva. **Description:** Companies must select the social causes they wish to become involved in and identified with carefully.

54151 ■ "CBC and Chrysler Strike Deal" in *Black Enterprise* **(Vol. 37, December 2006, No. 5, pp. 36)**
Pub: Earl G. Graves Publishing Co. Inc.
Ed: Kiara Ashanti. **Description:** Congressional Black Foundation and Chrysler Financial have partnered to provide financial education to students at historically black colleges and universities. The prime objective of the program is to reduce the number of college students that graduate with poor credit scores and high debt.

54152 ■ "CEO Incentives and Corporate Social Performance" in *Journal of Business Ethics* **(Vol. 45, No. 4, July 15, 2003, pp. 341)**
Pub: Kluwer Academic Publishers Group
Ed: Jean McGuire, Sandra Dow, Kamal Argheyd. **Description:** An examination of the relationship between CEO incentives and strong and weak corporate social performance is discussed.

54153 ■ "Charities find auto-show parties an ideal vehicle" in *Crain's Detroit Business* **(Vol. 19, No. 2, January 13, 2003, pp. 18)**
Pub: Crain Communications Inc., Detroit
Ed: Gary Anglebrandt. **Description:** The parties that follow the Charity Preview of the Detroit Auto Show raise funds for charities throughout the city. The Detroit Auto Dealers Association expected to raise $6.2 million for children's charities at the Preview, with an estimated additional $250,000 raised from the parties.

54154 ■ "Charity Pays" in *My Business* **(February/March 2004, pp. 41)**
Pub: My Business Magazine
Ed: Karen J. Bannan. **Description:** The welfare-to-work tax credit can benefit entrepreneurs in more ways than social responsibility, it allows new firms to hire more employees.

54155 ■ "Chatom Offers Wines With Cause Tie-Ins" in *Marketing to Women* **(Vol. 19, November 2006, No. 11, pp. 5)**
Pub: EPM Communications, Inc.
Description: She Wines, a line of wines created to benefit heart disease and breast cancer research, was introduced by women-owned and run Chatom Vineyards. The winery is based in Calaveras County, California.

54156 ■ "Cheap Tricks" in *The Economist* **(Vol. 377, October 1-7, 2005, No. 8446, pp. 62)**
Pub: The Economist Newspaper Ltd.
Description: Nicholas Negroponte, founder of MIT Media Lab, created an idea that would give a $100 laptop to every low-income child around the world. Negroponte unveiled his idea at the World Economic Forum. The program, One Laptop Per Child, could hurt the world's computer manufacturers.

54157 ■ "Chefs Show Off at Schoolcraft College Fundraiser" in *Crain's Detroit Business* **(Vol. 21, October 3, 2005, No. 43, pp. 20)**
Pub: Crain Communications Inc. - Detroit
Ed: Brent Snavely. **Description:** Schoolcraft College's annual Culinary Extravaganza allows forty-six metropolitan Detroit's best restaurants, wine distributors and wineries to offer sample offerings. The event, which also featured a silent auction, raised about $100,000 to be used for a scholarship fund.

54158 ■ "Clicking with Hispanics" in *Hispanic Business* **(March 2004, pp. 54, 56)**
Pub: Hispanic Business
Ed: Derek Reveron. **Description:** Michael Dell, CEO of Dell Inc., announces a new strategy to target the Hispanic computer buyer and the Tech Know program that gives at-risk children the opportunity to take home a Dell computer.

54159 ■ "CollectiveGood and eBay Team Up to Recycle Cell Phones for Charity" in *PR Newswire* **(March 25, 2004)**
Pub: PR Newswire Association, Inc.
Description: Profile of CollectiveGood, the mobile phone recycler; the firm has partnered with eBay to collect and resell cellular/mobile phones, pagers and PDA devices from eBay to help charities.

54160 ■ "Combined Health Agencies" in *San Diego Business Journal* **(Vol. 28, January 15, 2007, No. 3, pp. 33)**
Pub: San Diego Business Journal Associates
Ed: Stacey Bengtson. **Description:** Listing of combined health agencies includes agency leader, contact information, and the organization's mission.

54161 ■ *The Company We Keep: Reinventing Small Business for People, Community, and Place*
Pub: Chelsea Green Publishing
Ed: John Abrams. **Released:** May 2005. **Price:** $27.50 (US), $31.50 (Canadian). **Description:** The new business trend in social entrepreneurship as a business plan enables small business owners to meet the triple bottom line of profits for people (employees and owners), community, and the environment.

54162 ■ "A Corporate Peace Corps Catches On" in *Business Week* **(January 31, 2005, pp. 14)**
Pub: McGraw-Hill Companies
Ed: Jessi Hempel. **Description:** Corporate Peace Corps are created when a company lends top talent to charities. Nike will begin offering workers a five-week sabbatical to volunteer with aid groups, Pfizer and PricewaterhouseCoopers already send employees to developing countries to help nonprofit organizations. Nonprofit Building Blocks International helps to connect businesses to social causes.

54163 ■ "Cottage industry pays off for Eskimo women" in *Alaska Business Monthly* **(Vol. 18, No. 10, Oct. 2002, pp. 82)**
Pub: Alaska Business Publishing Company, Inc.
Ed: Gerry Watkins. **Description:** Profile of explorer/anthropologist, John J. Teal, Jr. Teal, a Harvard/Yale anthropologist, has established the Institute of Northern Agricultural Research. Through the domestication of the musk ox, Teal not only conducts research on the animal, his work has enabled Alaskan women to use the wool to make hand knitted items that are sold to a co-op, thus providing income for their families.

54164 ■ "Cover Story: The mean streets" in *Crain's Chicago Business* **(Vol.23, September 11, 2000)**
Pub: Crain Communications, Inc. Crain Communications, Inc.
Ed: Kevin Davis. **Description:** Patrick Macias has toughened it out in a neighborhood where many business owners have given up and fled. Not even an armed robbery ran him off.

54165 ■ "Creating a strong foundation" in *Black Enterprise* **(Vol. 33, No. 6, Jan. 2003, pp. 49)**
Pub: Earl Graves Publishing Co.
Ed: Curtis Simmons. **Description:** Members of the Theta Omega Chapter of Alpha Kappa Alpha Sorority Inc. are building assets in their community through grants, programs and scholarships. Tips for starting a foundation are included.

54166 ■ "A Decade Well Spent" in *Hispanic Business* **(October 2003, pp. 42)**
Pub: Hispanic Business
Ed: Janet Perez. **Description:** The Hispanic College Fund celebrates 10 years of helping the best and brightest get an education.

54167 ■ "Donations That Suit the Taxman" in *Business Week* **(February 20, 2006, No. 3972, pp. 92)**
Pub: McGraw-Hill Companies
Ed: Deborah L. Jacobs. **Description:** The IRS requires more than a standard receipt from a charity when claiming tax deductions; cash contributions over $250 require a canceled check or charity receipt.

54168 ■ "Eco-Preneuring" in *Small Business Opportunities* **(Vol. 12, No. 3, May 2000, pp. 56, 58)**
Pub: Harris Publications, Inc.
Ed: Michael L. Eskew. **Description:** "Green" companies can find golden opportunities. The practice of eco-commerce, or environmentally responsible companies, can pay off in more efficient processes and products, and, therefore, reduce operating costs.

54169 ■ *Entrepreneurship As Social Change: A Third New Movements in Entrepreneurship Book*
Pub: Edward Elgar Publishing, Incorporated
Ed: Steyaert. **Released:** February 2007. **Price:** $120.00. **Description:** Third book in a series, the edition examines entrepreneurship as a societal phenomenon.

54170 ■ "Entrepreneurship Center Receives Gift" in *Hispanic Business* **(March 2005, pp. 14)**
Pub: Hispanic Business
Description: Sergio Pino, chairman and CEO of Century Homebuilders, has given $2 million to Florida International University's Global Entrepreneurship Center.

54171 ■ *Entrepreneurship and Small Business*
Pub: Palgrave Macmillan
Ed: Paul Burns. **Released:** January 2007. **Price:** $74.95. **Description:** Entrepreneurial skills, focusing on good management practices are discussed. Topics include family businesses, corporate, international and social entrepreneurship.

54172 ■ "Equal access for all" in *BlackEnterprise* **(Vol. 32, No. 3, October 2001, pp. 62)**
Pub: Earl Graves Publishing Co.
Ed: Holly Aguirre. **Description:** Web tools that make the Internet accessible to the blind are presented, including programs like the free WeMedia Talking Browser and the National Institute of Standards and Technology's e-book reader for the blind that translates electronic text into Braille.

54173 ■ "Everyone's a Winner at the Chub Charity Challenge" in *Rough Notes* **(Vol. 145, No. 2, February 2003, pp. 68)**
Pub: Rough Notes
Ed: Edward O'Hare. **Description:** The Chubb Charity Challenge, an annual golf tournament, donated

$600,000 to hundreds of charities in the U.S. and Canada. Terry Cavanaugh of Chubb and Son spoke during the awards ceremony.

54174 ■ "The evolution of corporate diversity" in *Hispanic Business* **(Vol. 22, No. 9, September 2000, pp. 36)**
Pub: Hispanic Business
Ed: Janet Perez. **Description:** Issues concerning the positive benefits derived by American corporations through initiatives in the workplace to encourage diversity and employment of minority groups, such as Hispanics, are discussed.

54175 ■ "Facing new pressure" in *Atlanta Business Chronicle* **(Vol. 25, November 29, 2002, No. 25, pp. 1A)**
Pub: American City Business Publications, Inc.
Ed: Walter Woods. **Description:** Augusta National Golf Club is receiving pressure from several Georgia business leaders to alter its men-only membership policy. Business leaders fear the situation will become more controversial and add to Georgia's poor reputation for diversity.

54176 ■ "Families and Work: Some Future Probabilities" in *Employment Relations Today* **(Vol. 26, No. 4, Winter 2000, pp. 17)**
Pub: John Wiley & Sons, Inc.
Ed: David Macarov. **Description:** Issues discussed concern the relationship between family and work within the context of society, economics, and public policy. Topics addressed include the definition of family, government regulations regarding family rights and responsibilities, and the impact of stress and poverty on families.

54177 ■ "Feeling his oats" in *Entrepreneur* **(Vol. 30, No. 2, February 2002, p)**
Pub: Entrepreneur Media Inc.
Ed: April Pennington. **Description:** Profile of Lynn Rogers who started an oatmeal and oatmeal snacks company and donates a portion of profits to the athletic department at California State University, Fullerton.

54178 ■ "A Fight for Rights" in *Hispanic Business* **(October 2004, pp. 50, 52, 54)**
Pub: Hispanic Business
Ed: Jonathan J. Higuera. **Description:** Profile of Ann Marie Tallman, leader at the Mexican American Legal Defense and Educational Fund. Tallman is committed to adding economic rights to the group's agenda.

54179 ■ "Filling the Gap" in *My Business* **(April/May 2003, pp. 10)**
Pub: My Business Magazine
Ed: Tamara E. Holmes. **Description:** Information regarding the Uniformed Services Employment and Reemployment Rights Act is covered. The Act requires businesses to give employees leaves of absence for active duty, training, drills or other military operations.

54180 ■ "Firms maintain strong pro bono presence" in *Atlanta Business Chronicle* **(Vol. 25, November 15, 2002, No. 23 pp. SS10)**
Pub: American City Business Publications, Inc.
Ed: Tonya Layman. **Description:** Law firms, such as Kilpatrick Stockton LLP; Troutman Sanders LLP; Smith, Gambrell & Russell LLP; and Hunton & Williams are increasing pro bono activities. Often, pro bono work energizes lawyers at these firms and improves morale, and in some cases, months with the highest number of pro bono hours are also the months with the highest billable hours.

54181 ■ "First, Take a girl scout" in *Ingram's* **(Vol. 27, No. 12, December 2001, pp. 30)**
Pub: Show Me Publishing, Inc.
Description: Local community restaurants in Kansas City, Missouri have joined to use girl scout cookies as original deserts.

54182 ■ "Focus on Fundraising" in *Black Enterprise* **(Vol. 35, September 2004, No. 2, pp. 63)**
Pub: Earl G. Graves Publishing Co. Inc.
Ed: Sonia Alleyne. **Description:** Advice is given to a black woman pursuing a business management career organizing fundraising events.

54183 ■ "Food for the soul" in *Incentive* (Vol. 174, No. 7, July 2000, pp. 80)
Pub: Bill Communications
Ed: Jeanie Casison. Description: The employees at Morgan Stanley Dean Witter add a few artistic touches to a New York City intermediate school and boost their own morale in the process.

54184 ■ "Future brightens for the inner city" in *Hispanic Business* (Vol. 22, No. 6, June 2000, pp. 32)
Pub: Hispanic Business
Ed: Andrea Siedsma. Description: Latino Initiatives for the Next Century is a non-profit organization aimed at helping Hispanic communities and businesses to join in the redevelopment of inner-city neighborhoods. The agency will invest $300 million in such projects.

54185 ■ "Gift Management: The Business of Charitable Giving" in *My Business* (October/ November 2002, pp. 15)
Pub: My Business Magazine
Ed: Nancy Jackson. Description: Advice for charitable giving for small business owners is given, along with the listing of a Web site that rates hundreds of charities and soliciting organizations by financial and management practices.

54186 ■ "Girl power" in *Entrepreneur* (Vol. 31, No. 5, May 2003, pp. 28)
Pub: Entrepreneur Media Inc.
Ed: Aliza Pilar Sherman. Description: Social entrepreneurship looks at the way a business fits into a community; an interview with business owners who did that and also found ways to help women and girls using their companies in included.

54187 ■ "Giving Back" in *Inc.* (November 1, 2004)
Pub: Inc. Magazine
Ed: Jess McCuan. Description: Profile of Cynthia McKay, owner of a gift-basket business in Castle Rock, Colorado, which is stacked high with dog food and cat litter to be donated as part of her employee charitable giving program. Giving programs like McKay's are on the rise in America because entrepreneurs feel the need to give back.

54188 ■ "Giving Where It Counts: Blackgiving.com Lets Consumers Choose Their Charities" in *Black Enterprise* (Vol. 34, July 2004, No. 12)
Pub: Earl G. Graves Publishing Co. Inc.
Ed: Anthony S. Calypso. Description: Profile of Blackgiving.com, developed by Vince Martin. The site is designed to reach African Americans and helps fund charitable causes that already exist.

54189 ■ "Good Deeds and Watchful Eyes" in *Business Week Online* (March 8, 2002)
Pub: McGraw-Hill, Inc.
Description: According to a survey of owners and managers of small businesses, conducted by Princeton Survey Research Associates on behalf of the Better Business Bureau's Wise Giving Alliance, most small firms actively support charities and local community groups so they can keep a close watch on how the money is being used.

54190 ■ "Good Vibes: Socially Responsible Investing is Gaining Fans...and Clout" in *Barron's* (July 7, 2003, pp. L3)
Pub: Barron's
Ed: Robin Goldwyn Blumenthal. Description: High profile corporate corruption scandals, such as Enron and WorldCom, have helped strengthen the position of socially responsible investing advocates, even in the Wall Street community, where they were most widely derided. A review of the increasing influence of socially responsible investing is provided.

54191 ■ "Goodwill Gets Back Into Retail Game" in *Crain's Detroit Business* (Vol. 21, January 17, 2005, No. 3, pp. 22)
Pub: Crain Communications Inc. - Detroit
Ed: Sherri Begin. Description: Goodwill Industries of Greater Detroit will launch a retail business using the Internet. Items donated will be sold on the Website at a fixed price rather auction format. Goodwill provides employee and training services to individuals with disabilities and other special needs.

54192 ■ "Goodwill Hunting?" in *Entrepreneur* (Vol. 31, No. 9, September 2003, pp. 108)
Pub: Entrepreneur Media, Inc.
Ed: Devlin Smith. Description: Many new franchises are supporting charity and community causes as a primary mission, rather than the tradition side project of the organization.

54193 ■ *Grassroots NGOs by Women for Women: The Driving Force of Development in India*
Pub: SAGE Publications, Incorporated
Ed: Femida Handy; Meenaz Kassam; Suzanne Feeney; Bhagyashree Ranade. Released: July 2006. Price: $29.95. Description: Understanding the role of non-governmental organizations in women's development is offered through interviews with twenty women in India who have founded NGOs serving women.

54194 ■ "Green Grocer" in *Crain's New York Business* (Vol. 22, December 11, 2006, No. 50, pp. 33)
Pub: Crain Communications, Inc.
Ed: Tom Fredrickson. Description: Profile of Damian Mercado and his position as the manager of East New York Food Co-Op. The co-op sells organic produce in a low-income area which has a high rate of diabetes.

54195 ■ "Greyhound Racing" in *The Economist* (Vol. 376, July 16-22, 2005, No. 8435, pp. 29)
Pub: The Economist Newspaper Ltd.
Description: Greyhound racing is holding up in the poorer states, but tracks in more affluent regions are suffering. The American Greyhound Track Operators Association lists 46 greyhound courses in 2005, down from 50 in 2000. Animal cruelty is a continuing problem for the industry.

54196 ■ "Group connects out-of-towners, worthy cause" in *Atlanta Business Chronicle* (Vol. 24, No. 14, September 7, 2001, pp. S9)
Pub: American City Business Journals Inc.
Ed: Randy Southerland. Description: Hands on Atlanta is operating a community service program called Hospitality Helping Hands. This program has engaged the participation of over 25,000 visitors who have contributed over 75,000 hours of community service. Hands on Atlanta, organized in 1993 by Meeting Planners International, has had its program attract locals and visitors who are eager to contribute their services to the community.

54197 ■ *Growing Local Value: How to Build Business Partnerships That Strengthen Your Community*
Pub: Berrett-Koehler Publishers, Incorporated
Ed: Laury Hammel; Gun Denhart. Released: December 2006. Price: $15.00. Description: Advice and examples are provided for building socially responsible entrepreneurship.

54198 ■ "Gulfport, Miss., Business Club Considers Requesting Removal of Rebel Flag" in *Gulfport Sun Herald* (August 20, 2002)
Pub: Knight Ridder/Tribune Business News
Ed: Mike Cummings. Description: The Gulfport Business Club passed a resolution calling on the county to fly only eight American flags or to replace the Rebel flag with a historically accurate flag.

54199 ■ "The Handicapped Deserve More Help" in *Automotive News* (Vol. 79 February 14, 2005, No. 6134, pp. 12)
Pub: Crain Communications Inc.
Ed: Keith Crain. Description: Need for special-purpose vehicles to serve the disabled population is investigated.

54200 ■ "Helping HBO Discover Hispanics" in *Hispanic Business* (Vol. 23, No. 5, May 2001, pp. 16)
Pub: Hispanic Business
Ed: Rick Laezman. Description: Profile of Bernadette Aulestia, director of target marketing for movie network, HBO. Ms. Aulestia helped launch the HBO Latino channel.

54201 ■ "High-Tech Trash" in *Kiplinger's Personal Finance Magazine* (Vol. 55, No. 1, January, 2001, pp. 98)
Pub: The Kiplinger Washington Editors, Inc.
Ed: Christine Pulfrey. Description: Donating a computer or a phone to a charitable organization earns you a tax deduction for the value of the item, while helping your community.

54202 ■ "Hiring Employees With Disabilities" in *Inc.* (October 2005, pp. 29-32)
Pub: Inc. Magazine
Ed: Darren Dahl. Description: Habitat International, a carpet, turf and contract manufacturing firm in Chattanooga, Tennessee hires employees with disabilities. Three in four firms in the U.S. have no disabled workers employed. Statistical data included.

54203 ■ "Hit the Road" in *Entrepreneur* (Vol. 31, No. 10, October 2003, pp. 87)
Pub: Entrepreneur Media, Inc.
Ed: Elizabeth Goodgold. Description: The Adopt-a-Highway program also provides a means for a small business to gain visibility while doing good.

54204 ■ "Home Sweet Office: Giving to Charity" in *Sales & Marketing Management* (Vol. 157, January 2005, No. 1, pp. 52)
Pub: VNU Business Media
Ed: Kathryn Droullard. Description: Small business owners may find giving time and services to charities can have more impact than writing a check. Many times volunteering can be a great networking tool.

54205 ■ "Homeless Group Seeks to Buy Denver Hotel Property" in *Denver Post* (April 11, 2003)
Pub: Knight-Ridder/Tribune Business News
Ed: Mark P. Couch. Description: The Colorado Coalition for the Homeless is hoping to buy a 410-room hotel property to convert the building into a 200-unit apartment complex with an attached job-training center for the homeless in the area.

54206 ■ "Hometown Heroes: Doing Good by Doing Well" in *My Business* (November/ December 2001, pp. 26-30, 33-35)
Pub: My Business Magazine
Ed: Shannon Scully, Lisa Waddle. Description: Small business owners have long been in the forefront of giving back to their communities. The article takes a look at dozens of Main Street businesses that are making a difference since the terrorist attacks on 9-11.

54207 ■ "How I Did It" in *Inc.* (October 2005, pp. 132-134)
Pub: Inc. Magazine
Ed: Lora Kolodny. Description: In an interview, Paulette Cole tells how she wants to transform her New York City emporium ABC Home into a 100 percent socially responsible world market without jeopardizing the firm's $80 million in annual revenue.

54208 ■ "How They Did It" in *Crain's Detroit Business* (Vol. 19, No. 13, March 31, 2003, pp. 20)
Pub: Crain Communications Inc., Detroit
Ed: Laura Bailey. Description: The Detroit Public School system was able to get minority-owned and Detroit-based businesses to invest in its $1.5 billion building program.

54209 ■ "How To Give Your Money Away" in *Inc.* (October 1, 2004)
Pub: Inc. Magazine
Ed: Jess McCuan. Description: Entrepreneurs have difficulty finding a satisfying way to give back. Possibilities besides giving to a nonprofit include starting a family foundation or sponsoring educational programs.

54210 ■ *In Pursuit of Principle & Profit: Business Success through Social Responsibility*
Pub: The Putnam Publishing Group
Ed: Alan Reder. Released: 1995. Price: $22.95 (paper).

54211 ■ "Inner-City Light" in *Hispanic Business* **(September 2006, pp. 28, 30)**
Pub: Hispanic Business
Ed: Yolanda Perdomo Bindert. **Description:** Detroit Hispanic Development Corporation and local Detroit employers are helping young adults with educational and career opportunities.

54212 ■ "Investing in tomorrow" in *Success* **(Vol. 47, No. 3, July 2000, pp. 32)**
Pub: Success Publishing, Inc.
Ed: Eddy Goldberg. **Description:** Successful Internet entrepreneurs are changing the nature of giving.

54213 ■ "JPMorgan Chase Helps LI Crisis Center" in *Long Island Business News* **(February 20, 2004)**
Pub: Dolan Media Newswires
Ed: Ryan McCormick. **Description:** JPMorgan Chase operates a Community Builders Program that will provide $25,000 to the Long Island Crisis Center to help children who witness abuse in the home.

54214 ■ "Keeping to the fairway" in *Harvard Business Review* **(Vol. 81, No. 4, April 2003, pp. 29)**
Pub: Harvard Business School Press
Ed: Thomas J. Waite. **Description:** Four experts give opinions on the decision facing a fictional financial services company. Should the company continue to sponsor a golf tournament at a country club that has been attacked as sexist by a women's rights organization?

54215 ■ "KFC Forms Moms' Advisory Board" in *Marketing to Women* **(Vol. 19, October 2006, No. 10, pp. 3)**
Pub: EPM Communications, Inc.
Description: Kentucky Fried Chicken has formed an advisory board, KFC Moms Matter, to consul the company on how it can best meet mother's needs. The board consists of employees who are mothers as well as moms recruited from across the country.

54216 ■ "Leave a Legacy" in *Ingram's* **(Vol. 27, No. 12, December 2001, pp. 71)**
Pub: Show Me Publishing, Inc.
Description: Information about the nonprofit organization, Leave A Legacy, is given. The organization educates the public about opportunities for disposition of assets at death and leave a charitable legacy.

54217 ■ "Legendary Entrepreneur" in *Small Business Opportunities* **(Spring 2005)**
Pub: Harris Publications Inc.
Description: Profile of Jeno F. Paulucci, founder of Luigino's Inc. and creator of Michelina's brand. Paulucci was honored by Ernst & Young for his lifelong dedication to humanitarian efforts.

54218 ■ "Local Filmmaker Directs Smoking Ads" in *Milwaukee Journal Sentinel* **(December 13, 2005)**
Pub: Journal Sentinel, Inc.
Ed: Rick Romell. **Description:** Chris Smith, winner of a Sundance Film Festival's Award has directed production of four television anti-smoking commercials targeted to young people.

54219 ■ "Long Island Law Firm Takes Steps To Increase Pro Bono Work" in *Long Island Business News* **(February 6, 2004)**
Pub: Dolan Media Newswires
Ed: Claude Solnik. **Description:** Long Island law firms are stepping up efforts to offer pro bono services to those in need in the area.

54220 ■ "Lose weight for charity!" in *Bellingham Business Journal* **(January 2003, pp. C4)**
Pub: Wenatchee Business Journal
Description: Express Fitness for Women in Bellingham, Washington, is forming teams to compete to Get Fit to help raise money for local charities.

54221 ■ "Major Contributions to the Community" in *Home Business* **(Vol. 12, March/April 2005, No. 2, pp. 44)**
Pub: Home Business Magazine
Description: American small businesses donated nearly $40 billion to charities in 2004.

54222 ■ "Meredith Debuts Mag for Cancer Survivors" in *Marketing to Women* **(Vol. 19, October 2006, No. 10, pp. 5)**
Pub: EPM Communications, Inc.
Description: Meredith Corp.'s Special Interest Media Health Group debuts the first magazine geared specifically to women who have had breast cancer. Beyond: Live & Thrive After Breast Cancer includes personal stories, advice, resources, and up-to-date medical information.

54223 ■ "Metro firms maintain pay for called-up reservists" in *Crain's Detroit Business* **(Vol. 19, No. 14, April 7, 2003, pp. 1)**
Pub: Crain Communications Inc., Detroit
Ed: Robert Sherefkin, Robert Ankeny. **Description:** Major Detroit area firms, including auto suppliers and DTE Energy are paying salary differences for employees called up for active military duty. Many are also maintaining medical, dental and life insurance for several months, and some for years.

54224 ■ "Microlending - Arizona Style" in *Hispanic Business* **(March 2002, pp. 16)**
Pub: Hispanic Business
Ed: Jonathan J. Higuera. **Description:** Profile of Frank Ballesteros, who borrows from the U.S. Small Business Administration and other financial institutions and lends to the working poor.

54225 ■ "Minding Her Bees-Ness" in *Small Business Opportunities* **(Vol. 12, No. 5, September 2000, pp. 108)**
Pub: Harris Publications, Inc.
Description: A profile of Burt's Bees, famous for their earth-friendly, natural personal care products, and their commitment to giving back to nature by pledging $2 million to help preserve a remote forest in the state of Maine.

54226 ■ "Minority Architects Say Reaching Out to Youth Will Help Add Diversity" in *Crain's Detroit Business* **(Vol.16, No.31,July 31,2000, pp.35)**
Pub: Crain Communications, Inc.
Ed: Jennette Smith. **Description:** Detroit-area minority architects are reaching out to raise awareness to women, youth, and minorities in this white-male dominated profession.

54227 ■ "Money talks" in *Black Enterprise* **(Vol. 32, No. 9, April 2002, pp. 52)**
Pub: Earl Graves Publishing Co.
Ed: Holly Aguirre. **Description:** An introduction to the new talking automated teller machines, designed for the visually impaired.

54228 ■ "More Tales of the Inner City" in *Inc.* **(Volume 27, June 2005, No. 6, pp. 86-92, 94, 96-98, 100, 102-103)**
Pub: Inc. Magazine
Ed: Michael E. Porter. **Description:** Entrepreneurs across America are helping inner cities prosper economically and socially by growing their businesses in these areas. A listing of the top 100 street-smart companies is included.

54229 ■ "Motorola Foundation Funds 'Road Map' for Employers Who Hire People With Disabilities" in *Long Island Business News* **(February 6, 2004)**
Pub: Dolan Media Newswires
Ed: Ryan McCormick. **Description:** Motorola Foundation provides a grant for the National Center for Disability Services to develop and publish a 'road map' for employers who hire persons with disabilities.

54230 ■ "New Dynamic for Nonprofits" in *Hispanic Business* **(Vol. 23, No. 7/8, July/August 2001, pp. 104, 106)**
Pub: Hispanic Business
Ed: James E. Garcia. **Description:** A recent survey by Independent Sector, a national umbrella group of 700 non-profit agencies and foundations, found that Hispanic contributions have increased due to the growth of Hispanic middle class and wealthy entrepreneurs.

54231 ■ "New house, new food, new life" in *Ingram's* **(Vol. 28, No. 2, February 2002, pp. 38)**
Pub: Show Me Publishing, Inc.
Description: Profile of Newhouse treatment center and their new food culinary program; the center runs programs for battered women and their children, as well as the school for culinary arts.

54232 ■ *The New Social Entrepreneurship What Awaits Social Entrepreneurship Ventures?*
Pub: Edward Elgar Publishing, Incorporated
Ed: Perrini. **Released:** October 2006. **Price:** $120.00.
Description: Social entrepreneurship seeks to improve societal well-being within entrepreneurial organizations.

54233 ■ "No Small Plans" in *Inc.* **(December 1, 2004)**
Pub: Inc. Magazine
Ed: Patrick J. Sauer. **Description:** Profile of Harvey Robbins, small town entrepreneur, who sold his business and planned to retire with the $120 millions from the sale of his firm, National Floor Products. Robbins has made it his mission to revitalize his home town of Tuscumbia, Alabama.

54234 ■ "Nonprofits shift strategy to personal appeals" in *Atlanta Business Chronicle* **(Vol. 25, December 6, 2002, No. 26, pp. 5A)**
Pub: American City Business Publications, Inc.
Ed: Wendy Bowman-Litter. **Description:** In the Atlanta, Georgia area, non-profit organizations are using personal phone calls to longtime donors to thank them for past support. A simple thank-you call that doesn't include a request for additional financial support can be an effective way of keeping long-time donors.

54235 ■ "Oakdale Based Skills Unlimited Helps Long Island's Disabled Develop Skills and Find Work" in *Long Island Business News* **(Feb.20, 2004)**
Pub: Dolan Media Newswires
Ed: Ken Cerini. **Description:** Richard Kassnove, executive director of Skills Unlimited, helps disabled individuals find employment with Long Island, New York area businesses.

54236 ■ "On The Board" in *Inc.* **(October 1, 2004)**
Pub: Inc. Magazine
Ed: Patrick J. Sauer. **Description:** Profile of Benecard Services, the New Jersey company that processes and administers prescription drug and vision programs for health plans. The firm sponsors a New Jersey State Prison chess tournament by donating boards, pieces, clocks, and books.

54237 ■ "Philanthropy Award Winners" in *Crain's Detroit Business* **(Vol. 21, November 7, 2005, No. 45, pp. 25)**
Pub: Crain Communications Inc. - Detroit
Description: A list of individuals and organizations to be honored at the Association of Fundraising Professionals' 14th annual National Philanthropy Dinner is presented.

54238 ■ "Popular Lance Armstrong Wristbands Spawn Counterfits" in *Boston Globe* **(January 28, 2005)**
Pub: New York Times Company
Ed: Carolyn Shapiro. **Description:** The Lance Armstrong Foundation is taking steps to stop the sale of counterfit LiveStrong wristbands. The bracelets are sold for $1 each and raise money to support cancer survivors and cancer research. Nike has joined the Foundation with its Wear Yellow, Live Strong campaign to help support breast cancer survivors.

54239 ■ **"Portland, Maine, Surplus Store Sells Clothes From Flooded Mississippi Mall"** in *Portland Press Herald* (September 20, 2005)

Pub: Blethen Maine Newspapers, Inc.

Ed: Tux Turkel. **Description:** Marden's Surplus & Salvage is a salvage company that does business after major disasters. The company is selling items from Gulf Coast stores impacted by the hurricanes last summer.

54240 ■ **"Prepaid Card Benefits Breast Cancer Research"** in *Marketing to Women* (Vol. 19, November 2006, No. 11, pp. 5)

Pub: EPM Communications, Inc.

Description: NetSpend prepaid card marketer and financial services company, ACE Cash Express partner to launch a reloadable prepaid debit card for breast cancer research. A portion of all purchases made with the pink All-Access Visa Card through October 2007 will be donated to breast cancer research and educational charities.

54241 ■ **"Private Equity Firms Help Hurricane Victims"** in *Buyouts* (October 3, 2005)

Pub: Thomson Financial Inc.

Ed: Matthew Sheahan. **Description:** Private equity firms, along with their portfolio companies, reached out to help victims of Hurricanes Katrina and Rita through relief efforts.

54242 ■ **"Pursuits"** in *Inc.* (Volume 27, March 2005, No. 3, pp. 62-63)

Pub: Inc. Magazine

Ed: Jess McCuan. **Description:** Profile of Greg James, founder of Topics Entertainment, an educational software developer. After years of success, James is devoting time to environmental causes and is making changes in his personal life.

54243 ■ **"A Recipe for Success"** in *Black Enterprise* (Vol. 36, February 2006, No. 7, pp. 165)

Pub: Earl G. Graves Publishing Co. Inc.

Ed: Maya R. Payne. **Description:** Profile of Hecky Powell, founder of Hecky's Barbecue; Powell is dedicated to making youth job training the central focus of his restaurant. Since 1983, he has hired more than 200 young people.

54244 ■ **"Recovering from Tragedy - How Alta Has Coped with Losses"** in *Venture Capital Journal* (Vol. 42, No. 9, September 2002, pp. 24-25)

Pub: Thomas Venture Economics

Ed: Dan Primack. **Description:** Ways in which members of Alta Communications has coped in the aftermath of the terrorist attacks of 9/11 are discussed. Along with raising its new fund in a down market, each partner is very proud of their newly created foundation honoring two of their colleagues lost in the tragedy.

54245 ■ **"Rescue Mission"** in *Entrepreneur* (Vol. 33, August 2005, No. 8, pp. 15)

Pub: Entrepreneur Media Inc.

Ed: Joshua Kurlantzick. **Description:** Since 2000, U.S. entrepreneurs have focused on taking social enterprise overseas. Net Impact, the San Francisco clearinghouse for social enterprise has more than doubled membership in the last six years. Some foreign governments are seeking American small business owners to offer expertise and capital.

54246 ■ **"Restaurant Patrons Can Now Peruse the Menus and Prices of 110 Kansas City Area Restaurants..."** in *Kansas City Star* (March 11, 2005)

Pub: Knight-Ridder/Tribune Business News

Ed: Joyce Smith. **Description:** MaxImpact publishes and sells The Menu Guide for $6 to fundraisers who, in turn, sell them for $14.95. They donate 25 cents for each book sold to The Children's Place, an agency that helps young, neglected, abused or traumatized children. One restaurant owner reports doubling his business after listing in the directory.

54247 ■ **"The Right to Regulate Off-Duty Conduct"** in *Employment Relations Today* (Vol. 27, No. 2, Summer 2000, pp. 101)

Pub: John Wiley & Sons, Inc.

Ed: Arthur F. Silbergeld and Stephanie T. Sasaki. **Description:** Many employers are attempting to exert control over off-duty conduct of employees that could be detrimental to profitability. The laws have not been well developed in most jurisdictions, but many companies have implemented policies restricting employees dating other employees and setting up or participating in competing businesses.

54248 ■ **"Room for More"** in *Business First Columbus* (Vol. 18, No. 38, May)

Pub: Business First Columbus, Inc.

Ed: Lisa Hooker. **Description:** Owners of small businesses find that donating services can benefit charities. Greater Relocation Group, a Columbus, Ohio moving and storage company volunteers by storing items for the Komen Columbus Race for the Cure, which contributes funds for breast cancer treatment, services and education.

54249 ■ **"Rough Notes presents Community Service Award"** in *Rough Notes* (Vol. 146, No. 4, April 2003, pp. 98)

Pub: Rough Notes

Ed: Bob Bloss. **Description:** The Rough Notes publication awards the Giroux-Audet-Rua Insurance Agency the 2003 Community Service Award for volunteerism.

54250 ■ **"Salvation Army Picks Center Site"** in *Crain's Detroit Business* (Vol. 21, October 24, 2005, No. 43, pp. 24)

Pub: Crain Communications Inc. - Detroit

Ed: Sherri Begin. **Description:** Salvation Army of Metropolitan Detroit has chosen 27 acres at Conner and Frankfort for its new community center. The center would include an events hall library, computer center, pool, gymnasium, dance studio, fitness equipment, a track, a classroom and childcare and senior citizen areas.

54251 ■ **"Secure Fortune"** in *Small Business Opportunities* (Vol. 16, No. 3, May 2004, pp. 54, 56)

Pub: Harris Publications, Inc.

Ed: Vicki Gerson. **Description:** Profile of Dan Moceri and Greg Lernihan, who started their $43 million security systems and alarm enterprise with a laptop. The company closes one day a year to go into various communities to do work for the disadvantaged, working at food banks or other agencies.

54252 ■ **"September 11, 2001. A CEO's story"** in *Harvard Business Review* (Vol. 80, No. 10, October 2002, pp. 58)

Pub: Harvard Business School Press

Ed: Jeffrey W. Greenberg. **Description:** Marsh & McLennan Companies' offices in the World Trade Center were destroyed on September 11, 2001. Jeffrey W. Greenberg, chairman of Marsh & McLennan Companies Inc., recounts his immediate response to the airplane attack, efforts to save lives, locate people, recapture company data, help with the healing, inspire confidence, and generally insure that the company and its employees were able to continue.

54253 ■ **"Serving Fine Fare, Cafe Alters the Course of At-Risk Youth"** in *Chicago Tribune* (February 22, 2005)

Pub: Knight-Ridder/Tribune Business News

Ed: Dahleen Glanton. **Description:** Profile of Cafe Reconcile, a restaurant serving more than 150 customers daily. Cafe Reconcile began as an experiment in 2000 to help at-risk teens learn to make a living in the hotel and restaurant industry, and is now listed as one of the top 40 restaurants in New Orleans. Nearly 225 teens have graduated from the training program.

54254 ■ **"Serving the world's poor, profitably"** in *Harvard Business Review* (Vol. 80, No. 9, September 2002, pp. 48)

Pub: Harvard Business School Press

Ed: C.K. Prahalad, Allen Hammond. **Description:** Current belief's regarding the current challenges for doing business in underdeveloped regions of the world are investigated, using a hypothetical reference.

54255 ■ **"Sharing the Wealth"** in *Hispanic Business* (March 2003, pp. 46, 48, 50)

Pub: Hispanic Business

Ed: Maryann Hammers. **Description:** The Rockefeller Foundation and Hispanics in Philanthropy have partnered to help Hispanics make wise decisions when making contributions to charities and organizations.

54256 ■ **"Simon Group Offers Cobranded Giftcard"** in *Marketing to Women* (Vol. 19, October 2006, No. 10, pp. 9)

Pub: EPM Communications, Inc.

Description: Komen Foundation partners with Simon Property Group to produce a cobranded Simon Pink Ribbon Giftcard. This Visa debit card issued by Meta-Bank are sold at Simon malls nationwide and online at Simon.com. One dollar from every card purchased will be donated to the Komen Foundation.

54257 ■ **"Smoke screening"** in *Entrepreneur* (Vol. 30, No. 9, September 2002, pp. 30)

Pub: Entrepreneur Media Inc.

Ed: Chad Scheer. **Description:** Companies nationwide are considering imposing employee restrictions, not only on smoking, but also on cholesterol levels of employees in order to cut insurance costs and improve employee productivity. The American Civil Liberties Union wants the trend to stop with smoking.

54258 ■ *Social Entrepreneurship*

Pub: Palgrave Macmillan

Ed: Johanna Mair; Jeffrey Robinson; Kai Hockerts. **Released:** June 2006. **Price:** $80.00. **Description:** Social entrepreneurship is the process involving innovative approaches to solving social problems while creating economic value.

54259 ■ **"Social Grace"** in *Entrepreneur* (Vol. 33, September 2005, No. 9, pp. 91)

Pub: Entrepreneur Media Inc.

Ed: Sara Wilson. **Description:** Profile of Jeffrey Hollender, president of Burlington, Vermont's Seventh Generation. Hollender manufactures environmentally safe household and personal-care products. The firm offers employee incentives for community involvement.

54260 ■ **"South Florida Developers Combine Capitalism, Charity in Bottled-Water Company"** in *Miami Herald* (June 28, 2004)

Pub: Knight-Ridder/Tribune Business News

Ed: Gillian Wee. **Description:** Bernard Werner, real estate developer, and partner David Garfinkle, have invested $2 million in Euphoria Water, founded by Zalman Lipskar and Dovy Ainsforth. Euphoria donates at least 20 percent of profits to charity.

54261 ■ **"Southern Living Profiles Niceville, Fla.-Based Personal Chef Business"** in *Northwest Florida Daily News* (November 18, 2002)

Pub: Knight Ridder/Tribune Business News

Ed: Peggy May. **Description:** Profile of the catering business, Chef on the Go, and owner Mary Churillo of Niceville, Florida; each dish has a serving instruction label telling how long to reheat. Churillo also cooks for several elderly people to help them maintain their health.

54262 ■ **"Super Success in Spas"** in *Small Business Opportunities* (Vol. 16, No. 2, March 2004, pp. 92, 95)

Pub: Harris Publications, Inc.

Ed: Vicki Gerson. **Description:** Profile of Robert Hallam, founder of Dimension One Spas, designer and manufacturer of spas ranging in price from $4,000 to $30,000. Robert's wife handles the firm's customer service and is credited for its annual growth of 8-12 percent, reaching $48 million in 2002. Dimension Spas has partnered with Vision of Children Foundation by donating $100 for every spa sold to help end childhood blindness and vision disorders.

54263 ■ **"A Time to Donate" in** *Hispanic Business* **(Vol. 23, No. 11, November 2001, pp. 68)**
Pub: Hispanic Business Inc.
Description: Charitable deductions are discussed, with IRS resources listed.

54264 ■ **"Tomboy Tools Ties in With Pink Hammer" in** *Marketing to Women* **(Vol. 19, October 2006, No. 10, pp. 9)**
Pub: EPM Communications, Inc.
Description: The Komen Foundation partners with Tomboy Tools, manufacturer of ergonomically designed tools for women, for an exception to its "no pink tools" slogan. The "Pink for a Purpose" special-edition hammer is available through the company's website or their home-party distribution network.

54265 ■ **"Top-down diversity" in** *Hispanic Business* **(Vol. 22, No. 9, September 2000, pp. 42)**
Pub: Hispanic Business
Ed: Jonathan Higuera. **Description:** Research is presented showing corporate America is benefiting from the positive use of workplace diversity and a growing number of minority group employees in management positions.

54266 ■ **"Top-drawer advice: new software tells you how much your charitable contributions are worth" in** *Barron's* **(Vol.82, Feb.17, 2003, pp.T7)**
Pub: Barron's
Ed: Randall W. Forsyth, Theresa W. Carey. **Description:** Two programs that help value donations of used clothing and other goods and work well, include H & R Block Deduction Pro and Income Dynamics ItsDeductible tax preparation software.

54267 ■ **"The Tournament" in** *Inc.* **(January 1, 2002)**
Pub: Inc. Magazine
Ed: Norm Brodsky. **Description:** The story of how a storage company in Brooklyn, whose employees witnessed the terrible events of September 11, organized a basketball tournament for their employees to help build morale. The tournament was so successful they are planning the second annual competition.

54268 ■ **"Towering Goal" in** *Hispanic Business* **(April 2005, pp. 14)**
Pub: Hispanic Business
Description: Pedro Martin, CEO of Terra Group a financial real estate development firm in Miami, Florida is planning a foundation that will oversee the development and operation of a museum to be located in the Miami Freedom Tower. The museum will chronicle the history of the building.

54269 ■ **"Turn Public Problems into Private Account" in** *Harvard Business Review* **(Vol. 81, No. 8, August 2003, pp. 129)**
Pub: Harvard Business School Press
Ed: Rodman C. Rockefeller. **Description:** Four criteria are offered to guide companies looking to balance philanthropy and corporate earnings.

54270 ■ **"Value system" in** *Entrepreneur* **(Vol. 30, No. 3, March)**
Pub: Entrepreneur Media Inc.
Ed: Steven C. Bahls, Jane Easter Bahls. **Description:** Under Title VII of the Civil Rights Act of 1964, employers must make reasonable accommodations for employees' religious practices, unless doing so would impose an undue hardship on the company.

54271 ■ **"Venture Philanthropist" in** *Harvard Business Review* **(Vol. 78, No. 4, July 2000, pp. 26)**
Pub: Harvard Business School Publishing Corp.
Ed: Margaret Hanshaw. **Description:** Internet entrepreneur Martin Varsavsky is donating $11.2 million to help Argentina's Ministry of Education to provide Internet services to the country's 10 million grammar, high school, and university students.

54272 ■ **"Wal-Mart Helps Warm Up America At Crochet and Knit-Out Event" in** *Internet Wire* **(September 24, 2002)**
Pub: COMTEX
Description: Wal-Mart partnered with Warm Up America! Foundation and Craft Yarn Council of America, in order to donate afghans to battered women's shelters, hospitals, veterans' facilities and nursing homes. People are asked to knit or crochet a 7-inch by 9-inch rectangle to be joined with other rectangles to form an afghan.

54273 ■ **"Waltraud Prechter" in** *Crain's Detroit Business* **(Vol. 19, No. 1, January 6, 2003, pp. 12)**
Pub: Crain Communications Inc., Detroit
Ed: Terry Kosdrosky. **Description:** The widow of Heinz C. Prechter founded the Heinz C. Prechter Fund for Manic Depression after the death of her husband. Prechter was a German immigrant who became an industrialist in Michigan. The foundation will fund efforts to classify mental illness in the same way physical illnesses are classified.

54274 ■ **"Way to Give!" in** *Entrepreneur* **(Vol. 31, No. 9, September 2003, pp. 53)**
Pub: Entrepreneur Media, Inc.
Ed: Jennifer Pellet. **Description:** Because of high-profile cases of mismanagement by charitable programs, small businesses might consider online contribution systems for employees to contribute to worthy causes.

54275 ■ **"Weiss, Peck & Greer Venture Partners Vanishes in Lightspeed" in** *Venture Capital Journal* **(Vol. 40, No. 10, November 2000, pp. 16, 18)**
Pub: Venture Economics
Description: The executives with Weiss, Peck & Greer Venture Partners have left the firm in order to start a new company named Lightspeed Venture Partners. The new company has also formed a charitable initiative named Lightspeed Bright Futures, an ongoing partnership with Plugged In and OpNet, a pair of non-profit organizations working to bridge the digital divide.

54276 ■ **"What One Man Can Do" in** *Inc.* **(September 2005, pp. 144-153)**
Pub: Inc. Magazine
Ed: John Brant. **Description:** Profile of Bill Strickland who is in the business of changing lives. He is committed to ending poverty and uses beauty to help individuals compete in the marketplace. Strickland is looking to franchise his brand of hope.

54277 ■ **"What Taboo?" in** *Entrepreneur* **(Vol. 28, No. 10, October 2000, pp. 18)**
Pub: Entrepreneur Media Inc.
Ed: Alex Purugganan. **Description:** Office romance is on the rise and, believe it or not, most say there's nothing wrong with that.

54278 ■ **"Why Charities Don't Want Your Money" in** *Inc.* **(December 1, 2003)**
Pub: Gruner & Jahr USA Publishing
Ed: Jess McCuan. **Description:** Although circumstances may require a charitable organization to turn down particular contributions from businesses, entrepreneurs should still consider the idea of giving through their companies. In a 2002 Cone Communications study it was found that 53-percent of holiday shoppers surveyed planned to buy from retailers supporting social issues.

54279 ■ **"With the Right Guidance, Philanthropists Choose Best Way to Give" in** *Miami Herald* **(November 2003, 2003)**
Pub: Knight Ridder/Business Tribune News
Description: Accountability needs to considered when company's select organizations in which to make contributions.

54280 ■ **"Women of Courage International to hold second women's conference" in** *Pueblo Business Journal* **(February 28, 2003)**
Pub: Dolan Media Newswires

Ed: Lisa Seley. **Description:** The second women's conference in Pueblo, Colorado, hosted by the Women of Courage International, will be held in spring 2003. The conference is designed to give women and teen girls direction and hope in their lives.

54281 ■ **"Women mentoring women" in** *Women in Business* **(Vol. 53, No. 7, January-February 2002, pp. 28)**
Pub: The ABWA Co Inc.
Ed: Lisa Keating. **Description:** There are psychological and professional rewards for the mentor and the person who is mentored. Women mentors can assist new businesswomen to learn how to manage job stress and plan their careers or small business.

54282 ■ **"Words Fail Them" in** *Hispanic Business* **(May 2005, pp. 58)**
Pub: Hispanic Business
Ed: Joel Russell. **Description:** The lack of qualified bilingual counselors is making it difficult to manage the growing demand for Latino behavioral health programs.

54283 ■ **"Workers as Assets: A Good Start But..." in** *Employment Relations Today* **(Vol. 27, No. 1, Spring 2000, pp. 1)**
Pub: John Wiley & Sons, Inc.
Ed: Thomas O. Davenport. **Description:** Issues discussed concern the management of human capital in corporations, focusing on the strategic benefits of employee development and loyalty. Topics addressed include how to invest in and gauge the benefits of human capital.

54284 ■ **"The World Bank's Innovation Market" in** *Harvard Business Review* **(Vol. 80, No. 11, November 2002, pp. 104)**
Pub: Harvard Business School Press
Ed: Gary Robert Chapman, Hamel Wood. **Description:** A description of ways a new-products team at the World Bank created an Innovation Marketplace, a forum that allowed people to present ideas for alleviating poverty to potential funding sources.

54285 ■ **"A World of Difference" in** *Entrepreneur* **(Vol. 32, October 2004, No. 10, pp. 78)**
Pub: Entrepreneur Media Inc.
Ed: April Y. Pennington. **Description:** Entrepreneurs are committed to civic responsibility. They are actively working in communities for positive change through not only donations and in-house recycling programs, but also through a hands-on approach to social issues.

TRADE PERIODICALS

54286 ■ *Business Ethics*
Pub: Business Ethics
Contact: Jean Madson, Advertising Department
E-mail: jean.madson@business-ethics.com
Ed: Marjorie Kelly, Editor, marjorie.kelly@business-ethics.com. **Released:** Quarterly. **Description:** Business newsletter.

VIDEOCASSETTES/ AUDIOCASSETTES

54287 ■ *But I Don't Have Customers*
Government VideoSource, Inc.
461 Miller Dr.
Elgin, IL 60123-7232
Ph:(847)931-1955
Price: $595. **Description:** Explores the importance of treating internal customers with the respect they deserve by asking questions, keeping your work, and listening. **Availability:** VHS.

54288 ■ *10 Easy Ways to Keep Your Job*
Human Relations Media
41 Kensico Dr.
Mount Kisco, NY 10549

Ph:(914)244-0486
Free: 800-833-2004
Fax: (914)244-0485
Co. E-mail: orders@hrmvideo.com
URL: http://www.hrmvideo.com
Released: 1994. **Price:** $189. **Description:** David Letterman-style format introduces first-time employees to the common sense concepts of having and keeping a job, including taking initiative, leaving personal problems at home, problem solving, and more. Includes teacher's resource book. **Availability:** VHS.

RESEARCH CENTERS

54289 ■ Bentley College–Center for Business Ethics
175 Forest St., AAC 108
Waltham, MA 02452-4705
Ph:(781)891-2981
Fax: (781)891-2988
Co. E-mail: cbeinfo@bentley.edu
URL: http://www.bentley.edu/cbe
Contact: W. Michael Hoffman PhD, Exec.Dir.
E-mail: cbeinfo@bentley.edu
Scope: Business ethics in an industrial society, particularly in relationship to the activities of academe, corporations, labor, government, special interest groups, and various professions. Conducts surveys on topics such as business ethics curriculum and instilling ethical values in corporations. **Services:** Consulting. **Publications:** Bibliographies on business ethics topics; CBE News/Books and surveys; Conference proceedings. **Educational Activities:** Executive education and training programs. **Awards:** Executive Scholar and Research Fellow Programs; Hoffman Prize in Business Ethics.

54290 ■ Ethics Resource Center, Inc.
1747 Pennsylvania Ave. NW, Ste. 400
Washington, DC 20006
Ph:(202)737-2258

Free: 800—777-1285
Fax: (202)737-2227
Co. E-mail: pat@ethics.org
URL: http://www.ethics.org
Contact: Patricia J. Harned PhD, Pres.
E-mail: pat@ethics.org
Scope: Serves as a resource center for information, advice, and educational products and services intended to strengthen interest in organizational ethics and character education. Helps governments, companies, and associations establish standards of ethical conduct and design and implement educational programs that effectively communicate organizational values and personal responsibilities. **Publications:** Annual report; Ethics for Life Video Series; Ethics Today (10/ year); Ethics at Work Video Series; National Business Ethics survey reports; Survey reports. **Educational Activities:** Produces films and other instructional materials, for use in public schools to help teachers develop and reinforce positive values and character traits in students; Seminars, on business ethics and character education; Teacher training institutes; Workshops designed to assist in the development and implementation of corporate ethics programs. **Awards:** Stanley C. Pace Distinguished Award to Lecture on Leadership in Ethics.

54291 ■ Santa Clara University–Markkula Center for Applied Ethics
500 El Camino Real
Santa Clara, CA 95053-0633
Ph:(408)554-5319
Fax: (408)554-2373
Co. E-mail: ethics@scu.edu
URL: http://www.scu.edu/ethics
Contact: Kirk Hanson, Exec.Dir.
E-mail: ethics@scu.edu
Scope: Ethics in the areas of biotechnology and health care, education, business, government, global leadership, and emerging issues. Seeks to increase the understanding of the role of ethics in private and public decision-making processes. **Services:** Curriculum development; Consulting (weekly), for hospitals, businesses, schools, and nonprofit groups. **Publications:** At the Center (3/year); Ethics Outlook. **Educational Activities:** Business Ethics Conference (biennially); Lectures, on global leadership and ethics; Raising an Ethical Child (periodically), talks for parents; Symposia, workshops (weekly); Business and Organizational Ethics Partnership (quarterly), between businesses and ethics scholars.

54292 ■ University of Florida–Center for Applied Philosophy and Ethics in the Professions
332 Griffin-Floyd Hall
PO Box 118545
Gainesville, FL 32611-8545
Ph:(352)392-2084
Fax: (352)392-5577
Co. E-mail: rbaum@ufl.edu
Contact: Dr. Robert J. Baum, Dir.
E-mail: rbaum@ufl.edu
Scope: Professional and business ethics. **Publications:** Business and Professional Ethics Journal (quarterly); Professional Ethics (quarterly). **Educational Activities:** Conferences.

54293 ■ University of Virginia–Olsson Center for Applied Ethics
The Darden Sch.
PO Box 6550
Charlottesville, VA 22906
Ph:(434)924-0935
Fax: (434)924-6378
Co. E-mail: freemane@darden.virginia.edu
URL: http://www.darden.virginia.edu/olsson/index.
htm
Contact: R. Edward Freeman, Co-Dir.
E-mail: freemane@darden.virginia.edu
Scope: Socio/ethical issues relating to business, including standards of conduct. **Educational Activities:** Lectures and seminars, conducive to the exchange of ethical concepts among business executives, academia, and others.

START-UP INFORMATION

54294 ■ *Corporation: Small Business Start-Up Kit*
Pub: Nova Publishing Company
Ed: Daniel Sitarz. **Released:** February 2005. **Price:** $29.95. **Description:** Guidebook to help entrepreneurs start up and run a small business corporation. Book includes state and federal forms with instructions.

54295 ■ *How to Form Your Own California Corporation*
Pub: NOLO
Ed: Anthony Mancuso. **Released:** March 2005. **Price:** $59.99. **Description:** Instructions and forms required to incorporate any business in the State of California.

54296 ■ *The Small Business Start-Up Kit*
Pub: NOLO
Ed: Peri Pakroo. **Released:** April 2004. **Price:** $24.99. **Description:** Entrepreneurial advice for launching a new business. Topics include compliance with state regulations, sole proprietorships, partnerships, corporations, limited liability companies, as well as accounting and tax information.

ASSOCIATIONS AND OTHER ORGANIZATIONS

54297 ■ National Association for the Self-Employed
PO Box 612067
DFW Airport
Dallas, TX 75261-2067
Free: 800-232-6273
Fax: 800-551-4446
Co. E-mail: mpetron@nase.org
URL: http://www.nase.org
Contact: Robert Hughes, Pres.
Membership: Self-employed and small independent businesspersons. **Purpose:** Acts as an advocate at the state and federal levels for self-employed people. Provides discounts on products and services important to self-employed and small business owners. **Publications:** *Get Connected* (biweekly); *NASE Annual Report* (annual); *Self-Employed America* (bimonthly); *Washington Watch* (weekly).

REFERENCE WORKS

54298 ■ *Deduct It!: Lower Your Small Business Taxes*
Pub: NOLO
Ed: Stephen Fishman. **Released:** September 2005. **Price:** $34.99. **Description:** Ways to maximize business tax deductions for any type of small business owner (sole proprietor, partnership, LLC, corporation).

54299 ■ *Entrepreneurial Finance*
Pub: Pearson Education, Limited
Ed: Philip J. Adelman; Alan M. Marks. **Released:** July 2006. **Price:** $87.35. **Description:** Financial aspects of running a small business are covered; topics include sole proprietorships, partnerships, limited liability companies, and private corporations.

54300 ■ *Fast-Track Business Start-Up Kit: California*
Pub: DP Group, Incorporated
Ed: Carolyn Usinger. **Released:** September 2006. **Price:** $29.00. **Description:** Step-by-step guide for starting and running a business in California, including information on sole proprietors, partnerships, limited liability companies, S and C corporations, as well as details concerning business entities, sales taxes, environmental issues, human resources, and more.

54301 ■ "Focus on Finances" in *Entrepreneur.com* (Vol. 34, January 2006, No. 1, pp. 24)
Pub: Entrepreneur Media Inc.
Ed: Crystal Detamore-Rodman. **Description:** The Internal Revenue Service is starting to examine 5,000 random S corporation tax returns from the 2003 and 2004 tax years. The IRS is concerned that some S corporation owners are skimping on salaries in favor of a larger dividend distribution, which isn't subject to self-employment taxes.

54302 ■ "Handing it over: businesses need a plan for passing the torch" in *Black Enterprise* (Vol. 32, No. 8, March 2002, pp. 50)
Pub: Earl Graves Publishing Co.
Ed: Alan Hughes. **Description:** A listing of things a sole proprietor should consider before having a succession plan drawn up for a business is presented. According to the U.S. Census Bureau, nearly 90 percent of the 823,500 African American-owned businesses in 1997, were sole proprietorships.

54303 ■ *How to Form Your Own Corporation without a Lawyer for Under $75.00*
Pub: Dearborn Trade Publishing Inc.
Ed: Ted Nicholas; Sean P. Melvin. **Price:** $19.95.

54304 ■ "In Accounting, Number of Registered Sole Practitioners Decreasing" in *Long Island Business News* (March 5, 2004)
Pub: Dolan Media Newswires
Ed: David Reich-Hale. **Description:** The number of registered accounting sole practitioners in New York has decreased 25 percent since 2000, according to a public relations manager at the New York State Society of Certified Public Accountants.

54305 ■ "Island View Opening" in *Mississippi Business Journal* (Vol. 28, September 2006, No. 36, pp. 22)
Pub: Venture Publications, Inc.
Description: Profile of recently opened, privately held Island View Casino Resort and its two owners, Rick Carter and Terry Green. Carter and Green are the former owners of the Copa Casino.

54306 ■ *The Law of Corporations, Partnerships, & Sole Proprietorships Instructor's Guide*
Pub: Delmar Publishers
Ed: Angela Schneeman. **Released:** 1993. **Price:** $12.50.

54307 ■ "A Road Less Taxed" in *My Business* (February/March 2004, pp. 40)
Pub: My Business Magazine
Ed: Karen M. Kroll. **Description:** An explanation of the most common business structures and the ways taxes are generated for each is presented, including sole proprietorship, partnership, Limited Liability Corporation, S corporation, and C corporation.

54308 ■ *Small Business: An Entrepreneur's Plan*
Pub: Nelson Thomson Learning
Ed: Ronald A. Knowles. **Released:** December 2006. **Description:** Entrepreneur's guide to planning a small business.

54309 ■ "Small business could reap dividends" in *Wall Street Journal* (January 22, 2003, pp. B4C)
Pub: Dow Jones & Co. Inc.
Ed: Jane J. Kim. **Description:** An examination into the tax benefits for small business when changing classification from an S corporation to a C corporation is presented.

54310 ■ "Smart inventory: start electing superior filing options now" in *Barron's* (Vol. 82, No. 59, February 24, 2003, pp. 23)
Pub: Barron's
Ed: Joseph F. Gelband. **Description:** The use of laws from Section 475 of the tax code is one way in which investors can reduce capital gains tax on the sales of securities as long as an investor is considered a securities trader. Use of the provision allows losses to be fully deducted. An explanation of ways an S company can benefit on taxes by changing status to a C company is offered.

54311 ■ *Sole Proprietorship*
Pub: Nova Publishing Co.
Ed: Daniel Sitarz. **Released:** 2000.

54312 ■ "To L.L.C. or not to L.L.C.? That can be sticky question" in *Crain's Detroit Business* (Vol. 18, No. 49, December 9, 2002, pp. 14)
Pub: Crain Communications Inc., Detroit
Ed: Laura Bailey. **Description:** Important issues to be considered by all entrepreneurs regarding planning the structure of a new or existing small business are examined.

54313 ■ *Working Solo*
Pub: John Wiley & Sons Inc.
Contact: Terri Lonier, Author
Released: latest edition 2nd; Published April, 1998. **Price:** $14.95, individuals List price. **Covers:** over 1,000 solo business opportunities, as well as a resource section on publications, organizations, and other essential contacts for solo professionals.

54314 ■ *Working Solo Sourcebook*
Pub: John Wiley & Sons Inc.
Released: First edition 1995, latest edition 1998.
Covers: over 1,200 important business resources for entrepreneurs of all levels of experience and all types of businesses, including books, tapes, videos, training programs, associations, outlets, government agencies and programs.

VIDEOCASSETTES/ AUDIOCASSETTES

54315 ■ *Be Your Own Boss: Start a Business*
The Learning Seed
330 Telser Rd.
Lake Zurich, IL 60047
Free: 800-634-4941
Fax: (847)540-0854
Co. E-mail: info@learningseed.com
URL: http://www.learningseed.com
Released: 1992. **Price:** $89.00. **Description:** Four Chicago-area entrepreneurs offer advice on starting your own business and cover topics such as market research, location selection, promotion, financial planning, legal requirements and more. **Availability:** VHS.

54316 ■ *Doing Business*
The Cinema Guild
130 Madison Ave.
New York, NY 10016-7038

Ph:(212)685-6242
Free: 800-723-5522
Fax: (212)685-4717
Co. E-mail: info@cinemaguild.com
URL: http://www.cinemaguild.com
Released: 1981. **Description:** This documentary offers an insightful examination of self-managed businesses. The film is frank about the problems involved in going into business for oneself, including the delicacy of managing employees, arranging non-stressful working conditions, and balancing the desire for growth with a sense of family. **Availability:** 3/4U; Special order formats.

54317 ■ *How to Beat the Odds*
National Audiovisual Center
5285 Port Royal Rd.
Springfield, VA 22161
Ph:(703)605-4603
Free: 800-553-6847
Fax: (703)321-8547
Co. E-mail: orders@ntis.fedworld.gov
URL: http://www.ntis.gov/products/nac/index.asp
Released: 1980. **Price:** $95.00. **Description:** This video is designed to be an aid to small business owners trying to get ahead, and includes many strategies and tips from those entrepreneurs in the government bureaucracy. **Availability:** VHS; 3/4U.

54318 ■ *How to Start Your Own Successful Business*
Instructional Video
2219 C St.
Lincoln, NE 68502

Ph:(402)475-6570
Free: 800-228-0164
Fax: (402)475-6500
Co. E-mail: feedback@insvideo.com
URL: http://www.insvideo.com
Price: $29.95. **Description:** Illustrates correct procedures for establishing and maintaining an effective business. Covers marketing, managing, financing, business insurance, buying an existing business, franchising, home-based business, youth entrepreneurial business, negotiating deals, and projecting your ideas. **Availability:** VHS.

54319 ■ *New or Used? Buying a Firm or Starting Your Own*
Instructional Video
2219 C St.
Lincoln, NE 68502
Ph:(402)475-6570
Free: 800-228-0164
Fax: (402)475-6500
Co. E-mail: feedback@insvideo.com
URL: http://www.insvideo.com
Price: $99.00. **Description:** Details the different options open to anyone wanting to start or obtain their own business. Discusses the various factors to be considered when putting a value on a company, negotiating price and terms, and closing the deal. **Availability:** VHS.

ASSOCIATIONS AND OTHER ORGANIZATIONS

54320 ■ Alcoholics Anonymous World Services
PO Box 459
New York, NY 10163
Ph:(212)870-3400
Fax: (212)870-3003
URL: http://www.aa.org
Description: Individuals recovering from alcoholism. Maintains that members can solve their common problem and help others achieve sobriety through a twelve step program that includes sharing their experience, strength, and hope with each other. Self-supported through members' contributions, not an allied with any sect, denomination, political organization, or institution and does not endorse nor oppose any cause. **Publications:** *AA Comes of Age*; *Alcoholics Anonymous*; *As Bill Sees It*; *Dr. Bob and the Good Oldtimers*; *Pass it On*; *Twelve Steps and Twelve Traditions.* **Telecommunication Services:** teletype, (212)870-3199.

54321 ■ American Council on Alcoholism
1000 E Indian School Rd.
Phoenix, AZ 85014
Free: 800-527-5344
Fax: (602)264-7403
Co. E-mail: info@aca-usa.org
URL: http://www.aca-usa.org
Contact: Lloyd Vacovsky, Exec.Dir.
Description: Works to educate the public about the effects of alcohol, alcoholism, alcohol abuse, and the need for prompt, effective, affordable, and available treatment. **Publications:** *Frequently Asked Questions About Alcoholism*; *Recovery* (quarterly); *Teenage Drinking.*

54322 ■ American Outreach Association
5490 Delhart Rd., Ste. 205
Galax, VA 24333
Ph:(276)236-5934
Co. E-mail: info@americanoutreach.org
URL: http://www.americanoutreach.org
Contact: Charles Prusch, Pres.
Description: Collects and disseminates information on subjects such as alcoholism, drug abuse, inhalants, and smoking to the public. Organizes community awareness activities and presentations. Reviews drug policies, programs, and educational material. Assists business and industry in establishing drug-free work environments. Sponsors Project HOLD, a program that fosters a change of attitudes, values, and behaviors in the home away from drug abuse. Operates placement service; maintains speakers' bureau. **Publications:** *AOA Newsletter* (semiannual); *Health Watch* (quarterly); *Mommy, What are Drugs?*; *Mommy What are Inhalants?*; *Mommy, What is Alcohol?*; *Mommy, What is Smoking?*; *Mother Earth, What is Cultural Diversity?.*

54323 ■ Institute for a Drug-Free Workplace
8614 Westwood Center Dr., Ste. 950
Vienna, VA 22182

Ph:(703)288-4300
Fax: (703)506-0064
Co. E-mail: debernam@jacksonlewis.com
URL: http://www.drugfreeworkplace.org
Contact: Mark A. de Bernardo, Exec.Dir.
Description: Businesses, organizations, and individuals united to preserve the rights of employers and employees involved in corporate drug abuse prevention programs. Seeks to influence public policy pertaining to drug-abuse prevention in the workplace. Conducts surveys. **Publications:** *Avoiding Legal Liability: The 25 Most Common Employer Mistakes in Addressing Drug Abuse*; *Does Drug Testing Work?*; *Drug and Alcohol Abuse Prevention and the ADA: An Employer's Guide*; *Drug Testing in the Workplace: Basic Issues, Answers, and Options for Employees*; *Employee Assistance Programs: An Employer's Development and Implementation Guide*; *Employee Drug Education and Awareness and Supervisor Training: An Employer's Development and Implementation Guide*; *Guide to Dangerous Drugs*; *Guide to State and Federal Drug Testing Laws* (annual); *International Guide to Workplace Substance Abuse Prevention*; *Policy on Drug and Alcohol Abuse Prevention: An Employer's Development and Implementation Guide*; *What Every Employee Should Know About Alcohol Abuse: Answer to 25 Good Questions.*

54324 ■ Institute on Global Drug Policy
2600 9th St. N, Ste. 200
St. Petersburg, FL 33704-2744
Ph:(727)828-0211
Fax: (727)828-0212
Co. E-mail: evoth@storntvail.org
URL: http://www.dfaf.org/globaldrugpolicy.php
Contact: Eric A. Voth MD, Chm.
Purpose: Works to develop effective international policies and strategies to discourage drug use and legalization of illicit drugs. Disseminates accurate scientific information on drugs. Publications: none.
Convention/Meeting: none.

54325 ■ NAADAC The Association for Addiction Professionals
901 N Washington St., Ste. 600
Alexandria, VA 22314
Ph:(703)741-7686
Free: 800-548-0497
Fax: (703)741-7698
Co. E-mail: naadac@naadac.org
URL: http://www.naadac.org
Description: Promotes excellence in care by promoting the highest quality and most up-to-date, science-based services to clients, families and communities. Provides education, clinical training and certification. Among the organization's national certification programs are the National Certified Addiction Counselor, Tobacco Addiction Credential and the Masters Addiction Counselor designations. **Publications:** *Addiction Professional* (bimonthly); *The Basics of Addiction Counseling: A Desk Reference and Study Guide* (periodic); *Basics Of Addiction Counseling Independent Study Course* (periodic); *NAADAC News* (bimonthly). Also publishes annual conference papers.

54326 ■ Narcotics Anonymous
PO Box 9999
Van Nuys, CA 91409
Ph:(818)773-9999
Fax: (818)700-0700
Co. E-mail: fsmail@na.org
URL: http://www.na.org
Contact: Jeff Gershoff, Service Coor.
Purpose: Aims to recover addicts throughout the world, works to offer help to fellow addicts seeking recovery. Meets regularly to facilitate and stabilize their recovery. Uses 12-step program adapted from Alcoholics Anonymous to aid in the recovery process.
Publications: *A Guide to Public Information*; *Introductory Guide to NA*; *It Works: How and Why*; *Just For Today: Daily Meditations for Recovering Addicts*; *NA Update*; *The NA Way Magazine: The International Journal of the Fellowship of Narcotics Anonymous* (quarterly).

54327 ■ National Association of Addiction Treatment Providers
313 E Liberty St., Ste. 129
Lancaster, PA 17603-2748
Ph:(717)392-8480
Fax: (717)392-8481
Co. E-mail: rhunsicker@naatp.org
URL: http://www.naatp.org
Contact: Ronald J. Hunsicker, Pres./CEO
Membership: Corporate and private institutional alcohol and/or drug dependency treatment facilities. **Purpose:** Promotes awareness of chemical dependency as a treatable disease; advocates high standards of health care in substance abuse treatment facilities. Encourages member education. Maintains contact with U.S. Congress and state and local governments. Serves in an advisory capacity to the Joint Commission on Accreditation of Healthcare Organizations and to the Commission on Accreditation of Rehabilitation Facilities . Compiles statistics on chemical dependency treatment and recovery. **Publications:** *Benchmark Survey* (annual); *NAATP Visions* (10/year); *Annual Report* (annual).

54328 ■ National Association on Drug Abuse Problems
355 Lexington Ave.
New York, NY 10017
Ph:(212)986-1170
Fax: (212)697-2939
Co. E-mail: info@nadap.com
URL: http://www.nadap.org
Contact: John Darin, Pres.
Description: Serves as an information clearinghouse and referral bureau for corporations and local communities interested in prevention of substance abuse and treatment of substance abusers. Provides: resources to local communities seeking to combat drug and alcohol abuse; corporate services for employers interested in creating a drug-free workplace. Makes available vocational education services including training in job hunting, job interview workshops, training programs for substance abuse treatment professionals, and individual consultations for recovering substance abusers seeking to return to the job market. Provides

placement services; has conducted surveys on the employability of rehabilitated drug users and found that former addicts perform comparably with others hired for similar jobs. Operates Neighborhood Prevention Network, through which local communities develop parent support groups and youth peer leadership groups dedicated to combating drug and alcohol abuse. Maintains speakers' bureau. **Publications:** *Conference Proceedings* (biennial); *NADAP News/ Report* (quarterly).

54329 ■ Substance Abuse Librarians and Information Specialists
PO Box 9513
Berkeley, CA 94709-0513
Ph:(510)597-3440
Fax: (510)985-6459
Co. E-mail: salis@salis.org
URL: http://www.salis.org
Contact: Andrea Mitchell, Exec. Dir.
Membership: Individuals and organizations interested in the collection, organization, dissemination, exchange, and retrieval of materials concerning substance abuse, including alcohol, tobacco, and other drugs. **Purpose:** Provides professional development and exchange of information and concerns about access to and dissemination of information on substance abuse. Offers information on films, books, articles, pamphlets, reports, government publications, libraries, clearinghouses, and information centers. **Publications:** *SALIS News* (quarterly).

REFERENCE WORKS

54330 ■ "A Sobering Vacation" in *Wall Street Journal* **(Vol. 248, December 2006, No. 142, pp. P1-P5)**
Pub: Dow Jones & Co. Inc.
Ed: Christina Binkley **Description:** Profiles of new high-end addiction treatment centers opening in the Malibu area.

54331 ■ *Alcohol, Tobacco, & Other Drugs: Prevention in the Workplace: A Resource Guide*
Pub: Gordon Press Publishers
Released: 1995. **Price:** $251.95.

54332 ■ *Case Management Resource Guide*
Pub: Dorland Healthcare Information
Contact: V. Kelly
E-mail: vkelly@dorlandhealth.com
Released: Annual, latest edition 2005-2006. **Price:** $60, individuals for additional copy, per volume. **Entries Include:** Facility name, address, phone names and titles of key personnel; number of employees, geographical area served, type of service or programs provided branch office or parent organization name and phone, and credentials. **Database Covers:** in four regional volumes, lists 110,000 health care facilities and support services, including homecare, rehabilitation, psychiatric, and addiction treatment program; hospices, adult day care, and burn and cancer centers. **Arrangement:** Classified by service provided and location. **Indexes:** Company name, advertiser.

54333 ■ *Drugs for Abuse Digest: A Prevention Guide for the Family, School & Workplace*
Pub: Institute for Substance Abuse Research
Ed: Allan R. Pringle and Adrian Swain. **Released:** 1998. **Price:** $12.95.

54334 ■ *The Facts about Drug Use: Coping with Drugs and Alcohol in Your Family, at Work, in Your Community*
Pub: The Haworth Press, Inc.
Ed: Barry Stimmel. **Released:** 1992. **Price:** $24.95 (paper). **Description:** Guide for health professionals and the general public covering what drugs can do and how drug problems can be treated.

54335 ■ *Job Performance and Chemical Dependency*
Pub: Crisp Publications, Inc.
Ed: Robert B. Maddux and Lynda Voorhees. **Price:** $9.95.

54336 ■ *Management of Alcohol & Drug-Related Issues in the Workplace*
Pub: DIANE Publishing Co.
Released: 1997. **Price:** $35.00. **Description:** This report presents a variety of multidisciplinary approaches to the prevention, assistance, treatment and rehabilitation of alcohol- & drug-related problems in the workplace. Although experience has shown the difficulty of eliminating substance abuse, the policies presented are likely to yield constructive results for workers and employers alike.

54337 ■ *Narcotics and Drug Abuse*
Pub: Croner Publications Inc.
Contact: Rosa Padilla, Subscription Mgr.
Ed: Ruth Jordan, Editor. **Released:** Annual, quarterly updates. **Price:** $109.95, individuals plus $9.95 shipping per volume, includes updates. **Covers:** agencies, organizations, facilities, companies and persons actively opposed to the use and/or abuse of narcotics and drugs. In three volumes: volume 1, Connecticut, New Jersey, New York; volume 2, Alaska, Arizona, California, Colorado, Hawaii, Idaho, Montana, New Mexico, Nevada, Oregon, Utah, Washington, and Wyoming; volume 3, all others. **Entries Include:** For agencies, commissions, and facilities—Name, address, name of administrator, description of services. **Arrangement:** Alphabetical within organization types.

54338 ■ *National Prevention Network— Directory*
Pub: National Prevention Network
Contact: Stephanie McGencey, Dir./Prevention Svcs.
Released: Quarterly. **Covers:** state alcohol and drug abuse prevention agencies that serve as National Prevention Network state designees. **Entries Include:** Agency name, address, phone, name of director. **Arrangement:** Geographical.

54339 ■ *Substance Abuse in the Workplace*
Pub: Lewis Publishers
Ed: Reginald L. Campbell and R. Everett Langford. **Released:** 1995. **Price:** $59.95.

TRADE PERIODICALS

54340 ■ *Drug Detection Report*
Pub: Business Publishers Inc.
Ed: Nancy Dunham, Editor. **Released:** Bimonthly, 24/ year. **Price:** $337, individuals. **Description:** Reports on drug testing in the workplace, including regulations, legislation, and scientific developments. Discusses such topics as random testing, "reasonable suspicion" testing, and federal regulation of drug testing laboratories.

54341 ■ *Forensic Drug Abuse Advisor*
Pub: Forensic Drug Abuse Advisor Inc.
Ed: Steven B. Karch, M.D., Editor. **Released:** 10/ year. **Price:** $197, individuals. **Description:** Acts as a drug information source. Emphasizes the latest scientific discoveries in drug abuse, workplace drug testing, federal drug law, and forensic pathology. "An absolute necessity in drug related litigation." Recurring features include letters to the editor, news of research, a calendar of events, reports of meetings, news of educational opportunities, book reviews, and notices of publications available. Continuing medical education available.

54342 ■ *Hazelden Voice*
Pub: Hazelden Foundation
Ed: Marty Duda, Editor, mduda@hazelden.org. **Released:** 2/year. **Price:** Free. **Description:** Reports on Hazelden activities and programs, and discusses developments and issues in chemical dependency treatment and prevention.

54343 ■ *ICPA Reporter*
Pub: International Commission for the Prevention of Alcoholism and Drug Dependency
Contact: Gary B. Swanson, Managing Editor
Ed: Peter H. Landless, Editor, landlessp@gc. adventist.org. **Released:** Semiannual. **Price:** Free. **Description:** Reports on activities of the Commission worldwide, which seeks to prevent alcoholism and drug dependency. Recurring features include a calendar of events and notices of publications available.

54344 ■ *Journal of Drug Education*
Pub: Baywood Publishing Company Inc.
Ed: James Robinson, Editor. **Released:** Quarterly, 4/yr. **Price:** $300 institutions; $75. **Description:** Journal on the behavioral consequences of drug use and abuse for education professionals, health professionals, social service and Armed Forces personnel.

54345 ■ *The Prevention Researcher*
Pub: Integrated Research Services Inc.
Ed: Steven Ungerleider, Ph.D., Editor, suinteg@attglobal.net. **Released:** Quarterly, 4/year. **Price:** $36, individuals; $48 libraries. **Description:** Specializes in prevention topics for at-risk youth.

54346 ■ *Substance Abuse Funding Week*
Pub: CD Publications
Ed: Vladimire Herard, Editor. **Released:** Semimonthly. **Price:** $419, individuals. **Description:** Outlines detailed coverage of private and federal funding opportunities for alcohol, tobacco, and drug abuse programs.

VIDEOCASSETTES/ AUDIOCASSETTES

54347 ■ *Creating a Drug-Free Workplace*
Coastal Training Technologies Corp.
500 Studio Dr.
Virginia Beach, VA 23452
Ph:(757)498-9014
Free: 800-767-7703
Fax: (757)498-3657
Co. E-mail: sales@coastal.com
URL: http://www.coastal.com
Released: 1993. **Price:** $395. **Description:** Two acted stories illustrate workers having problems with drug and alcohol problems and who create problems for their companies. **Availability:** VHS.

54348 ■ *Disease Concept of Alcoholism/EAP*
New Dimension Media, Inc.
680 N Lake Shore Dr., Ste. 900
Chicago, IL 60611
Ph:(312)642-9400
Free: 800-288-4456
Fax: (312)642-9805
Co. E-mail: Info@NDMquestar.com
URL: http://www.ndmquestar.com
Released: 1986. **Price:** $50.00. **Description:** Information designed for supervisory training that stresses communication and motivation. **Availability:** VHS; 3/4U.

54349 ■ *The Drug-Free Workplace*
LearnCom HR Consulting and Training
38 Discovery, Ste. 250
Irvine, CA 92618
Ph:(515)440-0890
Free: 800-698-8263
Fax: (515)221-3149
Co. E-mail: nhartline@learncom.com
URL: http://www.learncomhr.com
Released: 1991. **Price:** $175.00. **Description:** A two-part program designed to make employees and managers aware of the provisions of the Drug-Free Workplace Act. Includes a Compliance and Implementation Guide, as well as participants manuals. **Availability:** VHS; 3/4U.

54350 ■ *Drug Testing in the Workplace*
American Bar Association
321 N. Clark St.
Chicago, IL 60610

Ph:(312)988-5000
Fax: (312)988-5528
Co. E-mail: abapubed@abanet.org
URL: http://www.abanet.org/publiced/
Released: 1987. **Price:** $295.00. **Description:** The story of what one company did about drug testing after a suspicious on-the-job accident. Urine and blood testing are demonstrated. **Availability:** VHS; 3/4U.

54351 ■ *Drugs in the Workplace*
Curtis, Inc.
2025 Reading Rd., Ste. 130
Cincinnati, OH 45202
Ph:(513)621-8895
Free: 800-733-2878
Fax: (513)621-0942
Co. E-mail: /curtisinc@fuse.net
URL: http://www.curtisinc.com
Description: A four-part series for supervisors demonstrating how to handle workers who engage in substance abuse. **Availability:** VHS.

54352 ■ *Drugs in the Workplace 2: What Every Manager and Supervisor Must Know*
Aspen Publishers
7201 McKinney Circ.
Frederick, MD 21704
Ph:(301)644-3599
Free: 800-638-8437
Fax: (301)644-3550
URL: http://www.aspenpublishers.com
Released: 1987. **Price:** $495.00. **Description:** Supervisors see what must be done to stop drug abuse in the workplace, and they also learn what, legally, they can and can't do about the problem. **Availability:** VHS; 3/4U.

54353 ■ *Managing a Drug-Free Work Environment*
Encyclopedia Britannica
331 N. LaSalle St.
Chicago, IL 60610
Ph:(312)347-7159
Free: 800-323-1229
Fax: (312)294-2104
URL: http://www.britannica.com
Released: 1989. **Price:** $495.00. **Description:** This film focuses on the role and responsibility of managers in counteracting drug abuse in the workplace. **Availability:** VHS; 3/4U.

54354 ■ *The Physiological Effects of Cocaine*
Phoenix Learning Group
2349 Chaffee Dr.
St. Louis, MO 63146
Ph:(314)569-0211
Free: 800-221-1274
Fax: (314)569-2834
URL: http://www.phoenixlearninggroup.com
Released: 198?. **Description:** Provides the professional with information on the physiological effects of cocaine. Also includes information on the history and physical properties of cocaine. **Availability:** VHS; 3/4U.

54355 ■ *Substance Abuse: Everyone's Problem*
AJN Video Library/Lippincott Williams & Wilkins
American Journal of Nursing
345 Hudson St., 16th Fl.
New York, NY 10014
Ph:(212)886-1200
Free: 800-256-4045
Fax: (212)886-1276
Co. E-mail: info@nursingcenter.com
URL: http://www.nursingcenter.com
Price: $250.00. **Description:** Describes the signs of drug and alcohol abuse and the steps to take if a staff member is suspected of having these problems. Also discusses how to plan and conduct a management conference, what to do when immediate action is needed, and how to motivate the staff member to seek help. Emphasis is placed on getting the employee to acknowledge that they have a problem and need help. **Availability:** VHS.

54356 ■ *Taking Action: Substance Abuse in the Workplace*
Phoenix Learning Group
2349 Chaffee Dr.
St. Louis, MO 63146
Ph:(314)569-0211
Free: 800-221-1274
Fax: (314)569-2834
URL: http://www.phoenixlearninggroup.com
Released: 1989. **Price:** $600.00. **Description:** This video will help managers implement an effective substance abuse prevention program for the workplace. **Availability:** VHS; 8mm; 3/4U.

54357 ■ *Taking Action 2: Frontline Against Drugs*
Aspen Publishers
7201 McKinney Circ.
Frederick, MD 21704
Ph:(301)644-3599
Free: 800-638-8437
Fax: (301)644-3550
URL: http://www.aspenpublishers.com
Released: 1991. **Price:** $600. **Description:** A follow-up video to "Taking Action," this program creates scenarios where workers at various levels are advised what to do when co-workers are abusing drugs or alcohol. **Availability:** VHS.

54358 ■ *Working Drug Free*
Altschul Group Corp.
Health Division
1560 Sherman Ave., Ste. 100
Evanston, IL 60201
Ph:(847)328-6700
Free: 800-323-9084
Fax: (847)328-6706
Price: $475.00. **Description:** The physiological effects of drugs on the brain are examined to illustrate the dangers involved and how this may hamper work performance. Produced in compliance with the Federal Drug-Free Workplace Act. **Availability:** VHS; 3/4U; Special order formats.

CONSULTANTS

54359 ■ **Bensinger, Du Pont & Associates**
20 N Wacker Dr., Ste. 920
Chicago, IL 60606-2901
Ph:(312)726-8620
Free: 800-227-8620
Fax: (312)726-1061
Co. E-mail: marie.apke@bensingerdupont.com
URL: http://www.bensingerdupont.com

E-mail: marie.apke@bensingerdupont.com
Scope: Employee Assistance Program (EAP) provider; gambling help line provider; consultant on substance abuse, drug testing and gambling addiction.

54360 ■ **Birenbaum & Associates**
917 Locust St., Ste. 1100
Saint Louis, MO 63101-1413
Ph:(314)241-1445
Fax: (314)241-1449
Co. E-mail: birenbaum@birenbaum.org

E-mail: birenbaum@birenbaum.org
Scope: Multi-association management firm and industrial relations specialists offering consultation to management in public and private sectors. Experienced also in meeting management. Clients in manufacturing, service industry, fire protection districts, and government throughout the U.S. **Seminars:** Alcohol/Drug Abuse Policies for Employers.

54361 ■ **Yale H. Caplan, PhD**
3411 Philips Dr.
Baltimore, MD 21208-1827
Ph:(410)486-7486
Fax: (410)653-4824
Co. E-mail: fortox@aol.com

E-mail: fortox@aol.com
Scope: Consultant in toxicology, drug and chemical analysis, workplace drug testing, and interpretation of toxicologic information. Serves as expert witness in drunk driving and drug testing cases.

54362 ■ **Cook International Inc.**
5659 Thicket Ln.
PO Box 2128
Columbia, MD 21044-2557
Ph:(301)596-0462
Scope: Offers both consultation and operational field services for both basic and complex security problems required by government and private industry. Services include security surveys and vulnerability studies, personnel background investigations, security guard training, preboard screening for airlines, internal/external investigations, building security planning and design, and drug abuse programs. Industries served: automobile dealers, retail stores, U.S. and local governments, and military installations. **Seminars:** Drug Abuse in Industry.

54363 ■ **Drug Testing Consultants Inc.**
10875 Main St., Ste. 107
PO Box 706
Fairfax, VA 22030-0706
Free: 800-944-8378
Fax: (703)352-7124
Scope: Conducts workplace drug testing programs for government and private sector in the United States.

54364 ■ **DW Smothers and Associates**
3137 Castro Valley Blvd., Ste. 215
PO Box 2804
Castro Valley, CA 94546
Ph:(510)728-9861
Free: 800-818-7654
Fax: (510)728-9802
Co. E-mail: staff@picoop.com
URL: http://www.picoop.com

E-mail: staff@picoop.com
Scope: Provides investigative consulting regarding loss prevention in areas of personnel safety and physical security. Active in systems and procedures design as well as development of same. Serves private industries as well as government agencies.

54365 ■ **Chris Frings & Associates**
633 Winwood Dr.
Birmingham, AL 35226-2837
Ph:(205)823-5044
Fax: (205)823-4283
Co. E-mail: chris@chrisfrings.com
URL: http://www.chrisfrings.com

E-mail: chris@chrisfrings.com
Scope: Provides expert testimony and consultation for court and arbitration regarding abused drug testing. Consultant to industry and labor relations attorneys with abused drug testing needs and problems. Also offers seminars and workshops and keynote speeches on management issues. **Publications:** "The Hitchhikers Guide to Effective Time Management: The only time management book you will ever need," AACC Press, 2004. **Seminars:** Workplace Drug Testing; Effective Time Management; Stress Management; Managing Change; Management and Leadership Strategies for Succeeding in the 21st Century.

54366 ■ **Richard Haynes & Associates L.L.C.**
1021 Temple St.
Charleston, WV 25312-2153
Ph:(304)346-6228
Fax: (304)346-9135
Co. E-mail: captrah@citynet.net

E-mail: captrah@citynet.net
Scope: Security management consultant. Offers the following services: security surveys and audits; security readiness for labor disputes; investigations; security training and awareness programs; special projects. Industries served: mining, petroleum, law enforcement, private security companies, and government agencies. **Publications:** Kanawha Valley Business Monthly - "Let's Talk Security," monthly series of articles on security topics. **Seminars:** Personal Protection Workshop: Workplace Violence.

54367 ■ Healy & Associates Inc.
3033 W Jefferson St.
Joliet, IL 60435-6449
Ph:(815)741-0102
Fax: (815)744-5412
Scope: Personal development consultant with experience in alcoholism and family treatment; employee assistance program consultation and implementation; health promotion programming on stress, smoking cessation, weight control; alcohol and drug related prevention and educational programming; and individual, group and family counseling. Serves private industries as well as government agencies. **Seminars:** Assertive Communication; Alcohol and Drug Problems in the Workplace; Chemical Dependency: Enabling vs. Intervention; Stress Management; Employee Assistance Programs; Smoking Cessation in the Workplace; Eating and Weight Issues; Cultural Diversity Training; Adapting to Change in the Workplace; Adapting to Shift Work.

54368 ■ Aantia Kersey Phd & Associates
17716 Oak Pk. Ave.
Tinley Park, IL 60477-3936
Ph:(708)460-6060
Fax: (708)460-6060
Co. E-mail: antia@juno.com

E-mail: antia@juno.com
Scope: Human resources development consultants offering employee assistance programs in alcohol and substance abuse for employees with problems, psychological services to industry and public and private organizations, and on-the-spot or by-mail psychological testing programs for selection, promotion, and transfer of employees. Serves private industries as well as government agencies. **Seminars:** Stress; Time Management; Smoking Cessation; Morale Improvement; Detection of Substance Abuse Among Employees.

54369 ■ Professional Alternatives Inc.
1 State St.
Boston, MA 02109
Ph:(617)722-6020
Fax: (617)722-6029
Co. E-mail: info@profalt.com
URL: http://www.profalt.com

E-mail: info@profalt.com
Scope: Human resources consulting firm specializes in substance and alcohol abuse programs.

54370 ■ Recovery Communications Inc.
PO Box 19910
Baltimore, MD 21211
Ph:(410)243-8352
Fax: (410)243-8558
Co. E-mail: tdrews3879@aol.com
URL: http://www.gettingthemsober.com

E-mail: tdrews3879@aol.com
Scope: Acts as expert witness and offers consultation in the field of substance abuse and addiction. Industries served: legal, health care, and government. **Seminars:** Attachments and Excited Miseries in the Workplace; Getting Past Stuck-Points in Recovery; Replacing the Excitement of Sickness.

54371 ■ Safety & Loss Control Associates
515 Arbor Ln.
PO Box 611
South Elgin, IL 60177
Ph:(847)622-1690
Fax: (847)622-1695
Co. E-mail: donneslund@aol.com
URL: http://www.safetyandlosscontrolassoc.com

E-mail: donneslund@aol.com
Scope: Assists contractors and industrial operators in reducing worker injuries and illnesses. Safety and training consulting includes employee training, supervisor and management seminars, OSHA compliance audits, pre-job inspections, expert witness work, accident investigation and reconstruction. Also provides expertise in ladders/scaffolds, fall protection, drugs/

alcohol in work place, confined space entry, blasting and man produced vibration, driving, trench safety, Hazcom and lockout/tagout. Serves the construction, insurance, legal profession and manufacturing industries. **Seminars:** Hazard Communication-Construction, Trench Safety, OSHA 30-hour Hazard Recognition Course; Communication and Interpersonal Skills Workshops; also designs and conducts specialized safety seminars.

54372 ■ VMC Consulting Service
12 S Division St.
Peekskill, NY 10566
Ph:(914)737-1977
Fax: (914)838-2331
Scope: Social issues counseling offered on family problems, dysfunctional disorders, and drug and alcohol abuse. Also provides expertise to companies including EAP consulting and assessment-referral services. Training extended to human resource management and staff on substance abuse problems. **Seminars:** Substance Abuse Problems: How to Deal With Them; Alcoholism in the Family and Workplace; Drug Addiction and the Consequences; Recognizing and Dealing With Substance Abuse Problems.

54373 ■ Richard C. Webber Associates L. L.C.
3760 S Highland Dr., Ste. 431, Highland Executive Plz.
Salt Lake City, UT 84106
Ph:(801)273-3322
Fax: (801)273-3321
Co. E-mail: rwebber@icscareers.com
URL: http://www.icscareers.com/regional-centers/utah.htm

E-mail: rwebber@icscareers.com
Scope: Human resources development consultant specializing in the development and presentation of drug and substance abuse programs, as well as executive and employee development programs. Areas of expertise include: instructor development (train-the-trainer), curriculum design/development, presentation skills/stage fright coping skills, and media relations. Leadership and motivation seminars are offered for both middle management and executives. Industries served: city, county, state, and federal law enforcement agencies; energy/oil; aerospace/aircraft; motion picture; and government agencies. **Publications:** "Drugs/Alcohol in the Workplace"; "Employment change and individual career marketing when looking to change career's". **Seminars:** Drugs/Alcohol in the Workplace; Instructor Development; Media Relations; Leadership; Stress Management; Time Management; Outplacement and Job Searching Skill Enhancement.

COMPUTERIZED DATABASES

54374 ■ ETOH Database
U.S. National Institute on Alcohol Abuse and Alcoholism
5635 Fishers Ln.
MSC 9304
Bethesda, MD 20892-9304
Ph:(301)443-3860
Fax: (301)443-6077
URL: http://www.niaaa.nih.gov
Description: Contains more than 100,000 citations, with abstracts, to worldwide literature on alcoholism research. Sources include periodicals, monographs, conference proceedings, reports, and dissertation abstracts. Also available on the Internet. **Availability:** Online: Ovid Technologies Inc. **Type:** Bibliographic.

LIBRARIES

54375 ■ Addictions Foundation of Manitoba–William Potoroka Memorial Library
1031 Portage Ave.
Winnipeg, MB, Canada R3G 0R8
Ph:(204)944-6277

Fax: (204)772-0225
Co. E-mail: library@afm.mb.ca
URL: http://www.afm.mb.ca
Contact: Pat Klimack
Scope: Alcohol and drug use and abuse, gambling, psychology, education, treatment, counseling, FASD. **Services:** Interlibrary loan; copying; Library open to the public. **Holdings:** 5500 books; 36 pamphlet titles; 916 videocassettes. **Subscriptions:** 30 journals and other serials.

54376 ■ Akeela Inc.–Library
4111 Minnesota Dr.
Anchorage, AK 99503
Ph:(907)565-1225
Fax: (907)276-5034
Co. E-mail: library@akeela.org
URL: http://www.akeela.org/
Contact: Anjana Roy, Libn.
Scope: Alcohol and other drugs. **Services:** Library open to the public. **Holdings:** 1500 curriculum and training materials; 4000 books; 1000 videotapes. **Subscriptions:** 160 journals and other serials.

54377 ■ Alcohol Research Group–Library
2000 Hearst Ave., Ste. 300
Berkeley, CA 94709-2176
Ph:(510)642-5208
Fax: (510)642-7175
Co. E-mail: amitchell@arg.org
URL: http://www.arg.org
Contact: Andrea L. Mitchell, Dir.
Scope: Alcohol use and abuse, epidemiology of alcohol use and allied problems, drug use and abuse, tobacco and use. **Services:** Copying; SDI; Library open to the public. **Holdings:** 6500 books; 54,000 reprints, reports, dissertations. **Subscriptions:** 300 journals and other serials.

54378 ■ Centers for Prevention and Intervention–Library
2000 Fordem Ave.
Madison, WI 53704
Ph:(608)246-7606
Fax: (608)246-7610
Co. E-mail: dmcenters@hotmail.com
URL: http://dir.civc.wisc.edu/view.
    asp?cat=5&cat1=65
Contact: Douglas McLain, Dir., AODA Prog./Int. Svcs.
Scope: Alcohol and drug abuse information; prevention and intervention curricula. **Services:** Videos for loan; Library open to the public. **Holdings:** 1500 books; 400 booklets; 2000 pamphlets; VF drawers. **Subscriptions:** 23 journals and other serials.

54379 ■ Centre for Addiction and Mental Health–Library
33 Russell St.
Toronto, ON, Canada M5S 2S1
Ph:(416)595-6144
Fax: (416)595-6601
Co. E-mail: library@camh.net
URL: http://www.camh.net
Scope: Alcoholism, substance abuse, psychiatric disorders, mental illness, mental health. **Services:** Interlibrary loan (in Canada only); AV loan (Ontario only); copying; SDI; Library open to the public. **Holdings:** 30,000 books; 11,000 reprints; 1250 audio/visual items. **Subscriptions:** 300 journals.

54380 ■ Drug & Alcohol Treatment Association of Rhode Island–In-Rhodes Resource Center–Library (102 D)
102 Dupont Dr.
Providence, RI 02907
Ph:(401)521-5759
Fax: (401)751-7850
Co. E-mail: jdipippo@dataofri.org
URL: http://www.dataofri.org/
Contact: Jean S. DiPippo, Rsrc.Coord.
Scope: Alcohol, tobacco, drugs, HIV, sexually transmitted diseases, domestic violence, mental health, parenting, mentoring, other isms and disorders, self-esteem gambling. **Services:** Library open to the public. **Holdings:** 1700 books; 1400 videocassettes; 375 audiocassettes; 4100 reference materials. **Subscriptions:** 2 journals and other serials.

54381 ■ Hazelden Foundation–Library and Information Resources
Box 11, CO-4
15245 Pleasant Valley Rd.
Center City, MN 55012
Ph:(651)213-4093
Free: 800-257-7810
Fax: (651)213-4411
Co. E-mail: bweiner@hazelden.org
URL: http://www.hazelden.org/library
Contact: Barbara S. Weiner, MLS, Libn.
Scope: Chemical dependency, treatment, chronic illness, spirituality, twelve steps, recovery, self-help, addictions. **Services:** Library open to the public with restrictions. **Holdings:** 13,000 books; 600 cassette tapes; 700 videos. **Subscriptions:** 90 journals and other serials.

54382 ■ Lakeview Center, Inc.–Library
1221 W. Lakeview Ave.
Pensacola, FL 32501
Ph:(850)432-1222
URL: http://www.ebaptisthealthcare.org/
      LakeviewCenter/
Scope: Psychiatry, psychology, alcoholism, drug addiction, children's and young adults' problems, management. **Services:** Interlibrary loan; copying; Library open to adult practitioners and interns. **Holdings:** 1921 books; 106 videocassettes; 75 kits; 227 government documents; 5 games. **Subscriptions:** 33 journals and other serials.

54383 ■ Maine State Office of Substance Abuse–Information and Resource Center
11 State House Sta.
AMHI Complex, Marquardt Bldg.
32 Blossom Ln.
Augusta, ME 04333-0011
Ph:(207)287-8900
Fax: (207)287-8910
Co. E-mail: osa.ircosa@maine.gov
URL: http://www.maine.gov/dhhs/osa/irc
Contact: Jo McCaslin, Coord.
Scope: Alcohol and drugs - use, abuse, dependency, education, prevention, and training. Youth suicide prevention. **Services:** Center open to school systems, community organizations, agencies, and professionals. **Holdings:** 1500 books; 1000 videotapes. **Subscriptions:** 20 journals and other serials.

54384 ■ National Clearinghouse for Alcohol and Drug Information–Library
Box 2345
Rockville, MD 20847-2345
Ph:(301)468-2600
Free: 800-729-6686
Fax: (301)468-6433
Co. E-mail: info@health.org
URL: ftp://ftp.health.org
Contact: Lizabeth J. Foster, Libn.
Scope: Alcohol, tobacco, and other drug abuse. **Services:** Interlibrary loan; copying; SDI; Library open to the public for reference use only. **Holdings:** 3721 books; 80,000 cataloged items; 80,000 accessioned items; digitized documents; reports; manuscripts. **Subscriptions:** 141 journals and other serials; 8 newspapers.

54385 ■ North Conway Institute–Resource Center - Alcohol and Drugs
168 Mt. Vernon St.
West Newton, MA 02165-2517
Ph:(617)742-0424
Contact: Rev. David A. Works, Pres.
Scope: Alcohol, drugs. **Services:** Center open to the public. **Holdings:** 800 books. **Subscriptions:** 50 journals and other serials.

54386 ■ Nova Scotia Department of Education–Drug Dependency Services Division–Library (Lord)
Lord Nelson Bldg.
5675 Spring Garden Rd.
Halifax, NS, Canada B3J 1H1
Ph:(902)424-7214
Fax: (902)425-0550
Contact: Ruth Vaughan

Scope: Health. **Services:** Interlibrary loan; copying. **Holdings:** 5000 books. **Subscriptions:** 50 journals and other serials; 3 newspapers.

54387 ■ Ohio Center for Prevention Studies–Ohio Safe Schools Center
Teachers Bldg., Rm. 439
PO Box 210109
Cincinnati, OH 45221-0109
Ph:800-788-7254
Fax: (513)556-3764
Co. E-mail: robert.canning@uc.edu
URL: http://www.uc.edu/
Contact: Bonnie Hedrick, Dir.
Scope: Drug abuse, alcohol, AIDS.

54388 ■ Prevention Research Center–Library
2150 Shattuck Ave., Ste. 900
Berkeley, CA 94704
Ph:(510)486-1111
Fax: (510)644-0594
Contact: Julie Murphy
Scope: Alcohol and drug abuse prevention research. **Services:** Library not open to the public. **Holdings:** 1500 books; 4000 reprints; 2000 reports. **Subscriptions:** 35 journals and other serials.

54389 ■ Rebok Memorial Library
12501 Old Columbia Pike
PO Box 4999
Silver Spring, MD 20904
Ph:(301)680-6495
Fax: (301)680-6090
Co. E-mail: ahecht@capaccess.org
URL: http://www.loc.gov/rr/main/religion/sevadv.html
Contact: Alan Hecht, Dir.
Scope: Social problems - alcohol, tobacco, narcotics; health and temperance general, history, religion, women's studies, family life. **Services:** Interlibrary loan; copying; SDI; Library open to the public with restrictions (appointment required for first visit). **Holdings:** 25,000 volumes. **Subscriptions:** 500 journals and other serials; 6 newspapers.

54390 ■ Research Institute on Addictions–Library
University at Buffalo
1021 Main St.
Buffalo, NY 14203-1016
Ph:(716)887-2511
Fax: (716)887-2490
URL: http://www.ria.buffalo.edu
Contact: Ann Mina Sawusch, MSW, MLS
Scope: Alcoholism, drug dependence, and alcohol and drug abuse physiological, psychological, sociological, biochemical, pharmacological aspects. **Services:** Copying; Library open to the public for reference use only. **Holdings:** 4000 books; 400 periodical titles. **Subscriptions:** 130 journals and other serials.

54391 ■ Rutgers University–Rutgers Center of Alcohol Studies–New Jersey Alcohol/Drug Resource Center and Clearinghouse (Smith)
Smithers Hall
607 Allison Rd.
Piscataway, NJ 08854-8001
Ph:(732)445-4442
Fax: (732)445-5944
Co. E-mail: ppage@rci.rutgers.edu
URL: http://alcoholstudies.rutgers.edu/
Contact: Penny B. Page, Dir.
Scope: Alcohol and drug use, alcohol and drug education, substance abuse prevention and treatment. **Services:** Interlibrary loan; copying; center and Library open to the public with restrictions. **Holdings:** 15,651 books and pamphlets; 130,000 reports; 250 microfiche; 1600 microfilms; 230 videos; 500 alcohol survey instruments. **Subscriptions:** 227 journals and other serials.

54392 ■ South Carolina (State) Department of Alcohol and Other Drug Abuse Services–The Drugstore Information Clearinghouse
101 Business Park Blvd.
Columbia, SC 29203-9498

Ph:800-942-3425
Fax: (803)896-5557
Co. E-mail: lfrederick@daodas.state.sc.us
URL: http://www.daodas.org/web/infosite
Contact: Lachelle Frederick, Admin.
Scope: Alcohol and other drug abuse - education, prevention, intervention, treatment. **Services:** Copying; clearinghouse open to the public with restrictions. **Holdings:** 3 VF drawers; 25 pamphlet titles.

54393 ■ South Carolina (State) Department of Mental Health–Earle E. Morris, Jr. Alcohol & Drug Addiction Treatment Center–Library (610 F)
610 Faison Dr.
Columbia, SC 29203
Ph:(803)935-7791
Fax: (803)935-6222
Contact: Michael Blanck, Lib.Hd.
Scope: Alcoholism, drug addiction, group and family therapy. **Services:** Interlibrary loan; Library not open to the public. **Holdings:** 2000 books. **Subscriptions:** 31 journals and other serials.

54394 ■ U.S. Drug Enforcement Administration–Library
700 Army Navy Dr.
Arlington, VA 22202
Ph:(202)307-8932
Fax: (202)307-8939
Contact: Rose Russo, Libn.
Scope: Narcotic addiction, dangerous drug abuse, law and legislation, law enforcement, drug abuse education, international control. **Services:** Interlibrary loan; Library not open to the public. **Holdings:** 10,000 books; 40 VF drawers. **Subscriptions:** 225 journals and other serials.

54395 ■ University of Washington–Alcohol & Drug Abuse Institute–Library (1107)
1107 N.E. 45th St., Ste. 120
Box 354805
Seattle, WA 98105-4631
Ph:(206)543-0937
Fax: (206)543-5473
Co. E-mail: adai@u.washington.edu
URL: http://lib.adai.washington.edu
Contact: Nancy Sutherland, Dir. of Lib.
Scope: Alcohol and drug abuse. **Services:** Interlibrary loan; SDI; Library open to the public. **Holdings:** 3500 books; 9000 reprints; 150 videos. **Subscriptions:** 100 journals and other serials.

54396 ■ West Central Georgia Regional Hospital–Library
PO Box 12435
Columbus, GA 31917-2435
Co. E-mail: wcgrh@dhr.state.ga.us
URL: http://www.wcgrh.org
Scope: Alcohol and drug abuse, bibliotherapy, brief and short-term therapy/counseling, consumer/patient education, forensic psychiatry, psychiatric nursing, psychiatric social work, psychology. **Holdings:** 4500 books; 246 bound periodical volumes; 325 AV programs.

54397 ■ Western State Psychiatric Center–Library
Box 1
Fort Supply, OK 73841
Ph:(580)766-2311
Fax: (580)766-2168
Contact: Karen Connell, Lib.Techn.
Scope: Substance abuse, psychiatry, psychology. **Services:** Interlibrary loan; copying; Library open to the public for reference use only. **Holdings:** 2778 books; 23 bound periodical volumes; 50 boxes of booklets, pamphlets, and reports; 59 audiotapes; 49 video recordings. **Subscriptions:** 20 journals and other serials; 10 newspapers.

RESEARCH CENTERS

54398 ■ Centre for Addiction and Mental Health–Social, Prevention, and Health Policy Research
33 Russell St.
Toronto, ON, Canada M5S 2S1
Ph:(416)535-8501
Fax: (416)595-6881
Contact: Dr. Louis Gliksman, Dir.
Scope: Health promotion and public education, development of treatment services, and employee assistance programs. Studies include alcohol management policy, needs assessment for intensive addiction treatment services, alcohol and violence, evaluation studies, and epidemiologic surveys. **Publications:** The Journal. **Educational Activities:** Consulting assistance; Courses, through the Centre's School for Addiction Studies.

54399 ■ Columbia University–Center for Social Policy and Practice in the Workplace
622 W 113th St.
New York, NY 10025
Ph:(212)854-5173
Fax: (212)854-2975
Co. E-mail: sa12@columbia.edu
URL: http://www.columbia.edu/cu/ssw/projects/
    workplace
Contact: Prof. Sheila H. Akabas PhD, Dir.
E-mail: sa12@columbia.edu
Scope: Policy and program issues in the area of work and social welfare policy, including job maintenance of the disabled in the workplace, analysis of Employee Assistance Programs, studies of gender integration, substance abuse in the workplace and programs. Provides a laboratory to test and evaluate service delivery patterns for occupational social workers and offers interdisciplinary training. **Services:** Counseling at the workplace on family and work related problems; Employment of people with disabilities; Regional Information Clearinghouses; Written training packages on new social service ideas. **Educational Activities:** Continuing education courses and workshops for social workers; Seminars on the organization and delivery of services to workers, open to human service, union, and personnel professionals; Training in the social management of employee benefits.

54400 ■ Indiana University Bloomington–Center for Studies of Law in Action
Sycamore Hall, Rm.302
Bloomington, IN 47405
Ph:(812)855-1783
Fax: (812)855-7542
Co. E-mail: dlindsay@indiana.edu
URL: http://www.indiana.edu/~rugs/ctrdir/csla.html
Contact: Darlena Lindsay, Prog.Coord.
E-mail: dlindsay@indiana.edu
Scope: Alcohol and transportation, the effects of drugs, pharmacology, and toxicology.

54401 ■ North Charles Mental Health Research and Training Foundation, Inc.
955 Massachusetts Ave., 5th Fl.
Cambridge, MA 02139
Ph:(617)864-0941
Fax: (617)876-9760
Co. E-mail: wmcauliffe@ntc.org
URL: http://www.northcharles.org
Contact: William McAuliffe PhD, Dir.
E-mail: wmcauliffe@ntc.org
Scope: Mental health and addictions/substance abuse, including behavioral studies and evaluations of substance abuse trends and treatments.

54402 ■ Oregon Research Institute
1715 Franklin Blvd.
Eugene, OR 97403
Ph:(541)484-2123
Fax: (541)484-1108
Co. E-mail: cynthia@ori.org
URL: http://www.ori.org
Contact: Cynthia Guinn, Exec.Dir.
E-mail: cynthia@ori.org
Scope: Behavioral sciences, including studies in tobacco prevention and cessation, compliance with diabetic regimens, children's social skills, personality structure, drug abuse prevention, depression and family interaction, special education technology, adolescent depression, and community child-rearing practices. Provides behavioral research and consultation services to other public and private agencies in fields of education, health, and mental health. **Educational Activities:** Colloquia; Professional seminars (monthly), open to the public; Research to Practice Annual Conference.

54403 ■ Rutgers University–Center of Alcohol Studies
607 Allison Rd.
Piscataway, NJ 08854-8001
Ph:(732)445-2190
Fax: (732)445-3500
URL: http://alcoholstudies.rutgers.edu
Contact: Robert J. Pandina PhD, Dir.
Scope: Causes and treatment of alcoholism and drug abuse, diverse actions of alcohol and other drugs on the body, means to prevent alcohol and other drug misuse, and the incidence and prevalence of normal and problem alcohol consumption in the U.S. and the world, including human enzyme systems important in alcohol metabolism, development of tolerance and physical dependence on alcohol, and hormonal changes. **Services:** Consulting; Outpatient clinical services. **Publications:** Journal of Studies on Alcohol (bimonthly); Monographs of the Rutgers Center of Alcohol Studies; National Institute of Alcohol Abuse and Alcoholism-Rutgers University Center of Alcohol Studies (NIAAA-RUCAS) Treatment Series. **Educational Activities:** Community and industrial workshops; Cooper Colloquium Series, during the academic year; Institute of Alcohol and Drug Studies (annually), in July; Summer School of Alcohol and Drug Studies, in August.

54404 ■ Stanford University–Stanford Prevention Research Center
Hoover Pavilion, Rm. N229, MC 5705
211 Quarry Rd.
Stanford, CA 94305-5705
Ph:(650)723-6254
Fax: (650)725-6906
Co. E-mail: fortmann@stanford.edu
URL: http://prevention.stanford.edu
Contact: Stephen P. Fortmann MD, Dir.
E-mail: fortmann@stanford.edu
Scope: Prevention and control of chronic disease. Stresses a public health or community approach to disease prevention and health promotion and seeks methods to improve the overall level of community health by favorably modifying the environmental and personal factors known to influence chronic disease incidence, including blood pressure, blood cholesterol, cigarette use, nutrition, obesity, physical activity, and stress. **Services:** Health Improvement Classes (daily), classes offered in exercise, smoking cessation, stress management, weight control, and nutrition for University faculty, staff, and families; Technical assistance, education, and training (daily), for the public, educators, health professionals, and communities; Worksite-based strategic planning and research (daily), in managed care. **Publications:** Catalogue available for health promotion materials (annually). **Educational Activities:** Postdoctoral research training program; Research seminars (weekly); Undergraduate and graduate level teaching activities at the University.

54405 ■ State University of New York at Buffalo–Research Institute on Addictions
1021 Main St.
Buffalo, NY 14203-1016
Ph:(716)887-2566
Co. E-mail: connors@ria.buffalo.edu
URL: http://www.ria.buffalo.edu
Contact: Gerard J. Connors PhD, Dir.
E-mail: connors@ria.buffalo.edu
Scope: Etiology, course, treatment, and prevention of alcoholism and substance abuse. Studies the following six aspects of substance abuse: normative patterns; biochemical, physiological, psychological, and social antecedents and consequences; biopsychosocial aspects of consumption in early and middle adulthood; family aspects; alcohol-drug interactions; and treatment and prevention strategies. **Services:** RIA Clinical Research Center, outpatient facilities. **Publications:** RIA Annual Report; RIA Report (quarterly). **Educational Activities:** Seminars (10/year), for researchers, treatment professionals, and interested persons; Substance Abuse Research Seminars.

54406 ■ University of Kentucky–Center on Drug and Alcohol Research
643 Maxwelton Ct.
Lexington, KY 40506-0350
Ph:(859)257-2355
Fax: (859)323-1193
Co. E-mail: cleukef@uky.edu
URL: http://cdar.uky.edu
Contact: Dr. Carl G. Leukefeld, Dir.
E-mail: cleukef@uky.edu
Scope: Biological, social, and psychological aspects of alcohol and drug abuse; and HIV/AIDS. Conducts household and other surveys. **Services:** Consulting and technical assistance for the community.

54407 ■ University of Washington–Addictive Behaviors Research Center
Box 351525
Department of Psychology
Seattle, WA 98195-1525
Ph:(206)685-1200
Fax: (206)685-1310
Co. E-mail: marlatt@u.washington.edu
URL: http://depts.washington.edu/abrc
Contact: Dr. G. Alan Marlatt, Dir.
E-mail: marlatt@u.washington.edu
Scope: Addictive behaviors, including alcohol abuse prevention, smoking, relapse prevention, harm reduction, and skills training. **Educational Activities:** Postdoctoral program in addictive behaviors.

Taxation

START-UP INFORMATION

54408 ■ *"Franchisor Contacts"* in *Hispanic Business* (October 2004, pp. 114)
Pub: Hispanic Business
Ed: Description: Contact information for franchising opportunities of interest to Hispanic entrepreneurs is presented. Opportunities in the following sectors is presented: automotive, business aids and services, education and training, cleaning and sanitation, employment services, grocery and specialty stores, tutoring and learning aids, packaging and mailing, rentals, restaurants, carry-outs and drive-ins.

54409 ■ *Legal Guide for Starting and Running a Small Business*
Pub: NOLO
Ed: Fred Steingold, Lisa Guerin. **Released:** March 2005. **Price:** $34.99. **Description:** Information for starting a new business focusing on choosing a business structure, taxes, employees and independent contractors, trademark and service marks, licensing and permits, leasing and improvement of commercial space, buying and selling a business, and more.

54410 ■ *"Pennsylvania"* in *Entrepreneur* (Vol. 28, No. 6, June 2000, pp. 155)
Pub: Entrepreneur Media Inc.
Ed: Cynthia E. Griffin. **Description:** Pennsylvania has designed a program to encourage entrepreneurial business ventures.

54411 ■ *The Small Business Start-Up Kit*
Pub: NOLO
Ed: Peri Pakroo. **Released:** April 2004. **Price:** $24.99. **Description:** Entrepreneurial advice for launching a new business. Topics include compliance with state regulations, sole proprietorships, partnerships, corporations, limited liability companies, as well as accounting and tax information.

54412 ■ *Working for Yourself: An Entrepreneur's Guide to the Basics*
Pub: Kogan Page, Limited
Ed: Jonathan Reuvid. **Released:** September 2006. **Description:** Guide for starting a new business venture, focusing on raising financing, legal and tax issues, marketing, information technology, and site location.

ASSOCIATIONS AND OTHER ORGANIZATIONS

54413 ■ **American Taxation Association**
5717 Bessie Dr.
Sarasota, FL 34233
Ph:(941)921-7747
Fax: (941)923-4093
Co. E-mail: fayres@ou.edu
Contact: Fran Ayres, Pres.
Description: Membership comprises primarily university professors teaching federal income tax, federal estate, and/or gift tax courses; other members are practitioners, including certified public accountants. Seeks to further taxation education. Researches the impact of the tax process, particularly tax code sections, on the social and economic structure of the U.S. Maintains speakers' bureau. **Publications:** *Journal of the American Taxation Association* (semiannual); Newsletter (3/year).

54414 ■ **Tax Executives Institute**
1200 G St. NW, Ste. 300
Washington, DC 20005-3814
Ph:(202)638-5601
Fax: (202)638-5607
Co. E-mail: asktei@tei.org
URL: http://www.tei.org
Contact: Michael P. Boyle, Intl.Pres.
Description: Professional society of executives administering and directing tax affairs for corporations and businesses. Maintains TEI Education Fund. **Publications:** *The Structure and Size of the Corporate Tax Department: An Empirical Analysis* ; *The Tax Executive* (bimonthly); *Value-Added Taxes - A Comparative Analysis.* **Telecommunication Services:** electronic mail, memberinfo@tei.org.

REFERENCE WORKS

54415 ■ *"5 Moves to Make Before the New Year"* in *My Business* (December/January 2004, pp. 14)
Pub: My Business Magazine
Ed: Barbara Weltman. **Description:** Small business tax planning is essential for a company to be successful. Financial tips to help small firms are listed, focusing on general strategy, equipment, cars, retirement plans, and gift giving.

54416 ■ *"5 Steps to Audit-Free Returns"* in *My Business* (February/March 2004, pp. 38)
Pub: My Business Magazine
Ed: Barbara Weltman. **Description:** Five ways to avoid listing questionable items on a small business tax return are discussed.

54417 ■ *"8 Detroit Projects Get More Than $170M in Tax Breaks"* in *Crain's Detroit Business* (Vol. 23, January 8, 2007, No. 2, pp. 10)
Pub: Crain Communications Inc. - Detroit
Ed: Robert Ankeny. **Description:** Brownfield state tax credits and state and local tax capture involve $839M in private investment and creation of 1,320 jobs.

54418 ■ *"33 Tool-and-Die Firms Get State Tax Breaks in 'Recovery' Zones"* in *Crain's Detroit Business* (Vol. 21, January 10, 2005, No. 2, pp. 10)
Pub: Crain Communications Inc. - Detroit
Ed: Amy Lane. **Description:** According to the Michigan Economic Development Corporation, 33 companies will benefit from Michigan's recovery zones that are located in eight tax-free zones for tool-and-die companies.

54419 ■ *"The 2003 Tax Relief Act: What Does It Mean for You?"* in *My Business* (October/November 2003, pp. 26)
Pub: My Business Magazine
Description: Three provisions of the 2003 Tax Relief Act are especially beneficial for small businesses, including the increase in spending, accelerated reduction in income-tax rates, and accelerating the reduction in the top marginal rate. Tax information is also provided for small businesses using trucks or SUVs, and the 50 percent bonus depreciation deduction.

54420 ■ *"2005 Standard Mileage Rates"* in *Home Business* (Vol. 12, March/April 2005, No. 2, pp. 78)
Pub: Home Business Magazine
Description: Starting January 1, 2005, standard mileage rates were increased by the Internal Revenue Service. The costs for operating an automobile for business, charitable, medical or moving expenses are: 40.5 cents a mile for all business miles driven, 15 cents a mile when figuring deductible medical or moving expenses, and 14 cents a mile when providing services to a charity.

54421 ■ *"Accumulated Earnings Tax: Deductibility of Paid But Contested Liabilities"* in *Journal of Accountancy* (January 2005)
Pub: American Institute of Certified Public
   Accountants
Ed: Ronald R. Hiner. **Description:** Under IRC Section 531, the accumulated earnings tax imposes a penalty tax on earnings accumulated beyond the reasonable needs of a business.

54422 ■ *"Adviser: Temporary tax act makes planning tough"* in *Crain's Cleveland Business* (Vol. 22, No. 43, October 22, 2001, pp. 11)
Pub: Crain Communications, Inc.
Ed: Scott Snow. **Description:** The Economic Growth and Tax Relief Act of 2001 provides the largest tax cut in more than 20 years. The new law will benefit small business owners and individuals rather and corporations.

54423 ■ *"Agreement on Internet taxes eludes deeply divided commission"* in *The New York Times* (March 21, 2000, pp. C1)
Pub: The New York Times Company
Ed: David Cay Johnston. **Description:** The U.S. commission appointed to advise Congress on Internet taxes may have no recommendations to report after a political split between committee factions. Eleven of the 19 Committee members, representing the business and anti-tax factions have sided with Chairman James S. Gilmore III, favoring a moratorium on Internet taxation until at least 2006. The Internet Tax Freedom Act, which brought the commission into being, calls for a majority vote of two-thirds, or 13 of the commission members.

54424 ■ "Ahead of the Curve" in *Ingram's* (Vol. 28, No. 9, September 2002, pp. 19)
Pub: Show Me Publishing, Inc.
Ed: Stephanie Guerin. **Description:** A guide for taking tax advantages before changes take place, such as knowing tax laws, offsetting capital gains with capital losses, setting up foundations, etc.

54425 ■ "Albany Eyes Real Estate Transfer Tax" in *Long Island Business News* (May 7, 2004)
Pub: Dolan Media Newswires
Ed: Rosmaria Mancini. **Description:** A proposal introduced by Senator Carl Marcellino and Assemblyman Tom DiNapoli would offer a two percent transfer tax on real property sales as a way to fund open space preservation.

54426 ■ "All About Me" in *My Business* (February/March 2004, pp. 41)
Pub: My Business Magazine
Ed: Melany Klinck. **Description:** The new 401(k), called the Solo 401(k) may be a tax-deferral tool for entrepreneurs, allowing them to defer more income.

54427 ■ "Alternative Minimum Tax has Expanded Annually to Include More and More Taxpayers" in *Long Island Business News* (March 5, 2004)
Pub: Dolan Media Newswires
Ed: Ben Abelson. **Description:** An investigation into the alternative minimum tax (AMT) that began in the 1960s. In 1970 only 19,000 Americans owed the AMT growing to 2.5 million in 2003.

54428 ■ "Amortization of Certain Intangible Assets" in *Journal of Accountacncy*
Pub: American Institute of Certified Public Accountants
Ed: Jennifer M. Mueller. **Description:** Intangible assets that are the result of contractual or legal rights are explained, including patents, licenses, trademarks, franchise and servicing rights.

54429 ■ "Are sec. 529 plans a better choice than education IRAs?" in *The Tax Adviser* (Vol. 32, No. 10, October 2001, pp. 668)
Pub: Harborside Financial Center
Ed: Philip E. Moore. **Description:** A comparison is made between Education IRAs and qualified tuition programs (Sec. 529 plans), to help parents identify the best way to save for their children's education.

54430 ■ "Are the Tax-Free Net's Days Numbered?" in *Home Office Computing* (Vol. 18, No. 7, July 2000, pp. 16)
Pub: Scholastic Inc.
Ed: Jeffery D. Zbar. **Description:** With the three-year moratorium on Web taxes set to expire in October 2001, the federally appointed Advisory Commission on Electronic Commerce (ACEC) has submitted recommendations designed to kill or slow adoption of new taxes. That means dot-coms would be exempt from charging sales taxes, while traditional retailers would still be required to charge sales taxes.

54431 ■ "As Clock Ticks on 2006, Tax Debate Continues" in *Crain's Detroit Business* (Vol. 22, December 11, 2006, No. 50, pp. 7)
Pub: Crain Communications Inc. - Detroit
Ed: Amy Lane. **Description:** State Legislature postpones action on state's business tax until 2007. Decision was made to wait until January due to the upcoming break for the Holidays and the complexity of the issues.

54432 ■ "Ask the attorney" in *Red Herring* (March 2003, pp. 73)
Pub: Herring Communications Inc.
Description: Legal issues are addressed that include the following topics, pharmaceutical patents, government support for research and development, global commerce, intellectual property rights, the transfer of customer lists from European subsidiary to its U.S. parent company, trademark dilution, venture financing, selling a business, stock options, corporate tax deductions, small business patent methods, and employee use of Instant Messaging with clients.

54433 ■ "At Senate Finance, membership has its privilege" in *Tax Notes* (Vol. 96, No. 14, September 30, 2002, pp. 1802-1806)
Pub: Tax Notes International
Ed: Martin A. Sullivan. **Description:** Members of the Senate Finance Committee are working on the draft Small Business and Farm Economic Recovery Act of 2002. The bill proposes tax breaks for economic sectors that already have a relatively light tax burden. It also contains many special provisions which would be politically beneficial to various members of the committee.

54434 ■ "Avoid Audits: Take Precautions to Prevent a Visit from the IRS" in *My Business* (February/March 2003, pp. 45)
Pub: My Business Magazine
Ed: Alan Breznick. **Description:** Ways to avoid an audit of a small business tax return are discussed.

54435 ■ "Avoid the Payroll Tax Trap: Using Withheld Payroll Taxes for Other Purposes Can be a Dangerous and Expensive Game" in *Journal of Accountancy*
Pub: American Institute of Certified Public Accountants
Ed: Howard Godfrey. **Description:** Penalties imposed on businesses using withheld payroll taxes for other purposes are discussed.

54436 ■ "Avoid the Tax Trap When Repaying Shareholder Loans" in *Journal of Accountancy*
Pub: American Institute of Certified Public Accountants
Ed: Brian K. Howell. **Description:** Certified public accountants can help clients avoid unnecessary taxes when repaying shareholder loans.

54437 ■ "Avoiding Year-End Tax Traps" in *Black Enterprise* (Vol. 34, No. 5, December 2003, pp. 85)
Pub: Earl Graves Publishing Co.
Ed: Laura Washington. **Description:** Information regarding the Alternative Minimum Tax (AMT) and an end-of-the-year tax strategy is given.

54438 ■ "Back to the Future" in *Inc.* (July 1, 2003)
Pub: Gruner & Jahr USA Publishing
Description: Analysis of President George W. Bush's tax cut and what it will mean to the economy.

54439 ■ "Backing Mike's Pro-Biz Tax Plan" in *Crain's New York Business* (Vol. 23, January 22, 2007, No. 4, pp. 12)
Pub: Crain Communications, Inc.
Ed: Description: New York's Mayor Bloomberg wants to revamp the unincorporated business tax which would help S corporations, since these companies must report profits as income on their personal tax forms, they are effectively taxed twice. Small Companies would benefit from a new credit which would partially offset that burden. He also wants to eliminate the city's 4 percent sales tax on footwear and clothing purchases to boost the city's economy and would help compete with New Jersey.

54440 ■ *Beat the Taxman 2006: Easy Ways to Save Tax in Your Small Business*
Pub: John Wiley & Sons, Incorporated
Ed: Stephen Thompson. **Released:** May 2006. **Price:** $21.95. **Description:** Tax advice is given to help small businesses maximize returns for 2006.

54441 ■ *Beat the Taxman 2007: Easy Ways to Save Tax in Your Small Business, 2007 Edition For the 2006 Tax Year*
Pub: John Wiley & Sons, Incorporated
Ed: Stephen Thompson. **Released:** December 2006. **Price:** $26.99. **Description:** Year-round tax planner for entrepreneurs; the book is written in a question and answer format to help small business owners save money on annual taxes.

54442 ■ *Beat the Taxman: Easy Ways to Tax Save in Your Small Business*
Pub: John Wiley & Sons, Incorporated

Ed: Stephen Thompson. **Released:** January 2005. **Price:** $26.99 (Canadian). **Description:** Concise tax planner to help entrepreneurs take advantage of current tax laws.

54443 ■ *Being Self-Employed: How to Run a Business Out of Your Home, Claim Travel and Depreciation and Earn a Good Income Well into Your 70s or 80s*
Pub: Allyear Tax Guides
Ed: Holmes F. Crouch, Irma Jean Crouch, Barbara J. MacRae. **Released:** September 2004. **Price:** $24.95 (US), $37.95 (Canadian). **Description:** Guide for small business to keep accurate tax records.

54444 ■ "Benefits of Old" in *My Business* (February/March 2004, pp. 39)
Pub: My Business Magazine
Ed: Mardy Fones. **Description:** Because of extension IRS reporting and administration requirements, many small businesses do not offer retirement benefits to employees.

54445 ■ "The Big Issues for Small Concerns: Listen up, candidates" in *Time Inc.* (Vol. 156, No. 3, July 17, 2000, pp. B7)
Pub: Time & Life Bldg., Rockefeller Center
Description: Small-business owners hate excessive regulations, taxes, red tape, and healthcare costs.

54446 ■ "Big Mistake: How to Avoid Common Tax Mistakes" in *My Business* (February/March 2003, pp. 46)
Pub: My Business Magazine
Ed: Tamara Holmes. **Description:** Small business owners should do tax planning before the end of the year in order to be prepared for April 15. Information is also provided for the IRS' free Electronic Federal Tax Payment System used for employee withholding taxes.

54447 ■ "Big Taxes Top Lansing Agenda, Will Granholm Proposal Shift?" in *Crain's Detroit Business* (Vol. 23, January 8, 2007, No. 2, pp. 1)
Pub: Crain Communications Inc. - Detroit
Ed: Amy Lane. **Description:** Legislators still unsure how to budget in wake of large deficits. Tax shifts likely, but original proposal from the Governor's office may have to be revised with new figures to be announced.

54448 ■ "A Big Windfall for Small Biz" in *Business Week* (No. 3843, July 28, 2003, pp. 14)
Pub: McGraw-Hill Inc.
Ed: Kimberly Weisul. **Description:** President Bush's new tax, cuts which cut the capital gains tax from 20 percent to 15 percent, are encouraging entrepreneurs to sell their businesses.

54449 ■ "Bigger Office, Bigger Breaks" in *Home Office Computing* (Vol. 18, No. 10, October 2000, pp. 19)
Pub: Scholastic Inc.
Ed: Jeffery D. Zbar. **Description:** Home-business tax deductions are covered.

54450 ■ "Bill Proposes Tax for Maine's Bottled Water Industry" in *Portland Press Herald* (October 14, 2005)
Pub: Blethen Maine Newspapers, Inc.
Ed: Seth Harkness. **Description:** Maine voters are considering a tax on water extracted from the state's land. Bryan Pullen draws water from a freshwater spring he purchased near his home in Harrison, Maine. A new tax would impose 20 cents on every gallon drawn, a move that Pullen believes will put him out of the bottled water business.

54451 ■ "Bill Requiring State Copy of Tax Form on Way to Granholm" in *Crain's Detroit Business* (Vol. 19, No. 45, November 10, 2003, pp. 6)
Pub: Crain Communications Inc., Detroit
Ed: Amy Lane. **Description:** Information on Michigan's Senate Bill 770, which requires employers to file

with the state a copy of the federal form that lists income paid to non-employees such as independent contractors, is provided. The bill is designed to help track income earned by independent contractors and the taxes owed to the State.

54452 ■ "Bill Would Boost Small Businesses" in *Bradenton Herald* (February 13, 2007)
Pub: Bradenton Herald
Ed: Brian Neill. Description: U.S. Representative Vern Buchanan has introduced a bill in Congress that includes a provision that would enable small businesses to offer health insurance more readily through the formation of associations. The bill would also benefit small business owners by allowing them to deduct a larger portion of taxes for labor and capital expenditures.

54453 ■ "Bills Would Restart SBT Rollback, Add New Tax Credits" in *Crain's Detroit Business* (Vol. 19, No. 40, October 13, 2003, pp. 6)
Pub: Crain Communications Inc., Detroit
Description: The State of Michigan is debating tax issues as a way to provide economic aid to companies in the state.

54454 ■ "Biz Leaders Want Quick Action on SBT replacement" in *Crain's Detroit Business* (Vol. 22, November 13, 2006, No. 46, pp. 1)
Pub: Crain Communications Inc. - Detroit
Ed: Amy Lane. Description: Business leaders are looking to Lansing for quick action to alleviate the business uncertainty quickly. Recent election results should clear the way for action between the governor and the House to act decisively to establish the new business tax structure to replace the single business tax.

54455 ■ "Biz has an interest in keeping Prop A" in *Crain's Detroit Business* (Vol. 18, No. 18, May 6, 2002, pp. 8)
Pub: Crain Communications Inc. - Detroit
Description: An examination of Michigan's Proposal A, that slashed taxes from an average of 34 mills to 6 mills for education.

54456 ■ "Booz Allen's Sweet Spot" in *Forbes* (Vol. 170, No. 12, December 9, 2002, pp. 190)
Pub: Forbes Magazine
Ed: Andrew T. Gillies. Description: Booz Allen Hamilton, the McLean, Virginia consulting firm that is helping the Internal Revenue Service to modernize and create an effective Web site for users, is profiled.

54457 ■ "Border Patrol" in *Entrepreneur* (Vol. 33, September 2005, No. 9, pp. 22)
Pub: Entrepreneur Media Inc.
Ed: Stephen Barlas. Description: Members of Congress are trying to reverse a decision handed down by the Sixth U.S. Circuit Court of Appeals, covering the states of Kentucky, Michigan, Ohio and Tennessee. The ruling states it is unconstitutional for the state of Ohio to offer tax incentives to existing Ohio companies to expand within the state.

54458 ■ "Botox Tax Could Throw Wrinkle Into Tax Code" in *Sacramento Bee* (December 19, 2005)
Pub: The Sacramento Bee
Ed: Andrew McIntosh. Description: California lawmakers are discussing plans whether to set a sales tax on botox wrinkle treatments. State residents are concerned, if passed, the law could impact taxing other drugs and medical procedures.

54459 ■ "Budget hole brings tax-hike whispers" in *Crain's Detroit Business* (Vol. 19, No. 4, January 27, 2003, pp. 6)
Pub: Crain Communications Inc., Detroit
Ed: Amy Lane. Description: The Michigan Chamber of Commerce is vehemently opposed to proposed state tax hikes, suggesting the state should cut spending before raising taxes.

54460 ■ "Building your own foundation" in *Ingram's* (Vol. 27, No. 12, December 2001, pp. 28)
Pub: Show Me Publishing, Inc.
Description: The benefits of creating a foundation or trust rather than donating to charitable organizations are examined. By creating a foundation, one can save money on taxes while retaining control of the funds being contributed to the community.

54461 ■ "Bush Growth Package Boost for Main Street" in *My Business* (April/May 2003, pp. 19)
Pub: My Business Magazine
Description: President Bush's recently unveiled growth package could offer tax relief to small business owners by increasing expensing limits and reducing individual income taxes.

54462 ■ "Bush talks up small business tax relief" in *Tax Notes* (Vol. 97, No. 9, December 2, 2002, pp. 1135-1136)
Pub: Tax Notes International
Ed: Patti Mohr. Description: President George W. Bush urged lawmakers to lessen the tax burden on small businesses and make the relevant regulations simpler. Bush said that tax cuts would boost the economy and add more jobs.

54463 ■ "Business dodges budget ax; But fee hikes, tax moves raise concerns" in *Crain's Detroit Business* (Vol. 19, No. 10, March 10, 2003)
Pub: Crain Communications Inc., Detroit
Ed: Amy Lane. Description: Michigan Governor Jennifer Granholm spared small business on some issues and programs in her proposed 2004 budget.

54464 ■ "Business Bookshelf" in *Small Business Opportunities* (Vol. 16, No. 2, March 2004, pp. 180)
Pub: Harris Publications, Inc.
Description: Reviews of the following books: Loopholes of the Rich, by Diane Kennedy, which tells how the rich legally make more money and pay less taxes; Real Estate Loopholes, by Diane Kennedy and Garrett Sutton, offering the secrets of successful real estate investing; and IRA Wealth, by Patrick W. Rice, addressing revolutionary IRA strategies for real estate investment.

54465 ■ "Business Groups Divided Over Cuts to MEDC Funding" in *Crain's Detroit Business* (Vol. 19, No. 17, April 28, 2003, pp. 6)
Pub: Crain Communications Inc., Detroit
Description: The Michigan Manufacturers Association, the Detroit Regional Chamber and eight other local chambers have formed a new coalition to urge lawmakers to not go beyond Governor Granholm's recommended reductions in the budget of the Michigan Economic Development Corporation because it would damage the state's ability to compete for business investments and jobs.

54466 ■ "The Business Week" in *Business Week* (December 19, 2005, No. 3964, pp. 28-29)
Pub: McGraw-Hill Companies
Ed: Harry Maurer. Description: Stocks, tax reform, a weak Japanese economy, wages, international investment, and airplane orders are among issues discussed.

54467 ■ "Businesses Assessing Granholm's Plans for SBT Overhaul" in *Crain's Detroit Business* (Vol. 21, January 31, 2005, No. 5, pp. 6)
Pub: Crain Communications Inc. - Detroit
Ed: Amy Lane. Description: Under a business-tax proposal, Michigan's single-business tax will not expire at the end of 2009. The pros and cons of this move are discussed with business experts from the state.

54468 ■ "Businesses Warn State: Don't Hurt Economy to Fix Budget" in *Crain's Detroit Business* (Vol. 19, No. 42, October 20, 2003, pp. 29)
Pub: Crain Communications Inc., Detroit
Ed: Amy Lane. Description: Business officials are warning Michigan's governor that any new or increased taxes or fees could increase job losses in the state.

54469 ■ "Bye-Bye, Tax Break" in *Business Week* (No. 3666, January 31, 2000, pp. 6)
Pub: McGraw-Hill, Inc.
Description: An explanation of the capital gains tax change for small business.

54470 ■ "California bill on Web sales tax" in *The New York Times* (September 1, 2000, pp. C2)
Pub: The New York Times Company
Ed: Lawrence M. Fisher. Description: The California State Assembly passes a bill to collect state sales tax from Internet sales.

54471 ■ "Can Spending A Day Stuck To A Velcro Wall Help Build A Team" in *Wall Street Journal* (Vol. 248, December 2006, No. 149, pp. B1)
Pub: Dow Jones & Co. Inc.
Ed: Jared Sandberg Description: Profiles of several companies offering office and corporate team-building exercise outings and events. Alternative methods of company employee bonding are covered.

54472 ■ *Canadian Small Business Kit for Dummies*
Pub: John Wiley & Sons, Incorporated
Ed: Margaret Kerr; JoAnn Kurtz. Released: May 2006. Price: $28.99. Description: Resources include information on changes to laws and taxes for small businesses in Canada.

54473 ■ "Can't Win For Losing: A Mutual Fund Tax Quirk Limits Your Capital Losses" in *Entrepreneur* (Vol. 31, No. 7, July 2003, pp. 52)
Pub: Entrepreneur Media, Inc.
Ed: Scott Bernard Nelson. Description: Investment losses stay within an investment fund even if the investment shows now gains.

54474 ■ "Capital Coverage" in *My Business* (October/November 2002, pp. 18-19)
Pub: My Business Magazine
Description: NFIB presents small business legislation, health care cost information, tax administration.

54475 ■ "Capital Gains Pains" in *Black Enterprise* (Vol. 34, No. 3, October 2003, pp. 34)
Pub: Earl Graves Publishing Co.
Ed: Matthew S. Scott. Description: Capital gains tax law is explained, stressing the Taxpayer Relief Act of 1997, allowing homeowners selling their home to exclude capital gains if they meet certain requirements.

54476 ■ "Capitol Coverage" in *My Business* (December/January 2004, pp. 16-17)
Pub: My Business Magazine
Ed: Description: The National Federation of Independent Business (NFIB) addresses current issues of importance to small businesses in the U.S., including unemployment insurance benefits, unfair trade regulation, health insurance, and taxes.

54477 ■ "Capitol hits brakes on tax plan" in *Crain's Detroit Business* (Vol. 19, No. 15, April 14, 2003, pp. 3)
Pub: Crain Communications Inc., Detroit
Ed: Amy Lane. Description: Michigan governor, Jennifer Granholm is seeking new business- and income-tax changes totaling nearly $100 million.

54478 ■ "Cash in: Tax talk: Cash accounting is about to get more use" in *Entrepreneur* (Vol. 30, No. 3, March 2002, pp. 74)
Pub: Entrepreneur Media Inc.
Ed: Joan Szabo. Description: A recently issued Internal Revenue Service procedure allows certain busi-

nesses with gross receipts of up to $10 million to use the cash method of accounting for income and expenses, rather than using the accrual method, making income taxable when received and expenses deductible when paid.

54479 ■ **"Cashing in Before You Join: Negotiating a Signing Bonus" in** *Black Enterprise* **(Vol. 37, October 2006, No. 3, pp. 90)**
Pub: Earl G. Graves Publishing Co. Inc.
Ed: Chauntelle Folds. Description: Information on how to research and negotiate a signing deal, including how to avoid a tax hit.

54480 ■ **"Cashing In on Bad Debts" in** *Hispanic Business* **(Vol. 24, No. 5, May 2002, pp. 52)**
Pub: Hispanic Business Inc.
Ed: Milton Zall. Description: Ways to claim bad debts as tax deductions are discussed.

54481 ■ **"A Catalyst for Innovation" in** *Fortune* **(Vol. 142, No. 6, September 18, 2000, pp. 248)**
Pub: Time Inc.
Ed: Daniel Kadlec. Description: Both presidential candidates have found common ground on at least one tax initiative. Both would like to make permanent a tax credit for companies engaging in costly research and development.

54482 ■ **"Caucus Decries Bush Plan" in** *Hispanic Business* **(Vol. 23, No. 5, May 2001, pp. 20)**
Pub: Hispanic Business
Ed: Patricia Guadalupe. Description: The Congressional Hispanic Caucus states that the Bush tax plan will not benefit Hispanics.

54483 ■ *CCH Business Owner's Toolkit Tax Guide*
Pub: C C H, Inc.
Ed: Susan M. Jacksack, Small Office Home Office Editorial Group Staff; illustrated by Tim Kaage; introduction by Martin Bush. Released: 1999. Price: $14.95; $17.95.

54484 ■ *CCH Toolkit Tax Guide 2007*
Pub: CCH, Inc.
Ed: Paul Gada. Released: January 2007. Price: $17.95. Description: Guide for filing 2007 tax forms for both personal and small businesses with expert line-by-line explanations.

54485 ■ **"Chamber prepares for fight over tax changes" in** *Crain's Detroit Business* **(Vol. 19, No. 13, March 31, 2003, pp. 5)**
Pub: Crain Communications Inc., Detroit
Ed: Amy Lane. Description: The Michigan Chamber of Commerce is opposed to the new budget measures planned by Governor Jennifer Granholm, saying they are disguised tax increases.

54486 ■ **"Chamber Revisits Business-Tax Proposal" in** *Crain's Detroit Business* **(Vol. 22, January 23, 2006, No. 4, pp. 19)**
Pub: Crain Communications Inc. - Detroit
Ed: Amy Lane. Description: Detroit's Regional Chamber of Commerce is seeking to replace the State's single-business tax set to expire in 2009. The new fee would start at $1,000 for businesses with Michigan sales over $350,000 and maximize at $1 million for those with sales over $100 million.

54487 ■ **"Changes at issue" in** *Crain's Detroit Business* **(Vol. 19, No. 15, April 14, 2003, pp. 33)**
Pub: Crain Communications Inc., Detroit
Description: Changes in Michigan tax laws opposed by the Michigan Chamber of Commerce are detailed. Statistical data included.

54488 ■ **"Changing times: tax relief for women business owners" in** *Women in Business* **(Vol. 54, No. 5, September-October 2002, pp. 12)**
Pub: The ABWA Company, Inc.

Ed: Edward Jones. Description: Wise retirement plan changes that could be implemented by women business owners as a result of the passage of the Economic Growth and Tax Relief Reconciliation Act of 2001 are discussed.

54489 ■ **"Charity Pays" in** *My Business* **(February/March 2004, pp. 41)**
Pub: My Business Magazine
Ed: Karen J. Bannan. Description: The welfare-to-work tax credit can benefit entrepreneurs in more ways than social responsibility, it allows new firms to hire more employees.

54490 ■ **"Chop, chop: Bush's plan changes all: tax planning" in** *Barron's* **(Vol. 82, No. 57, February 10, 2003, pp. 21)**
Pub: Barron's
Ed: Karen Hube. Description: A detailed analysis of the President's proposed new dividend tax cut, lifetime savings account, retirement savings accounts, and employer retirement savings accounts is provided, with an emphasis on the impacts on individuals.

54491 ■ **"Chunk of Change: Navigating Employment Taxes" in** *My Business* **(June/July 2004, pp. 14)**
Pub: My Business Magazine
Description: Many companies are outsourcing company payrolls to payroll service firms because they believe it is more efficient to let the service handle the payroll and tax withholding issues involved.

54492 ■ **"Church Case May Impact Land Use" in** *Crain's Detroit Business* **(Vol. 23, January 8, 2007, No. 2, pp. 18)**
Pub: Crain Communications Inc. - Detroit
Ed: Jennette Smith. Description: Southfield legal battle to be precedent setting for the issue of conversion of business property to church and other nonprofit use. Loss of tax revenue is the central issue. This is a universal problem nationally and may end up at the U.S. Supreme Court.

54493 ■ **"CID businesses self-tax to fund improvements" in** *Atlanta Business Chronicle* **(Vol. 24, No. 14, September 7, 2001, pp. 3C)**
Pub: American City Business Journals Inc.
Ed: Erica Stephens. Description: Atlanta has seen many Community Improvement Districts (CIDs) start up in recent years, with the popularity being that they let their own tax rates and regulations within the laws of the local government. Lynn Rainey of Jackel, Rainey, Busch, & Reed LLC, Tad Leithead of Urban One Associates, and George Berry of Cousins Properties Inc. share their views on CIDs.

54494 ■ **"Citgo Mulls Relocation to Houston" in** *Houston Business Journal* **(Vol. 34, No. 14, August 15, 2003, pp. 1)**
Pub: American City Business Journals
Ed: Monica Perin. Description: Citgo Petroleum Corporation announced plans to move corporate headquarters from Tulsa, Oklahoma to Houston, Texas. Topics include tax incentives, business incentives, and economic conditions.

54495 ■ **"Cities Talk Taxes; Mt. Clemens, Ann Arbor Look at Adding Income Levels to Help Fix Budgets" in** *Crain's Detroit Business* **(Vol. 21)**
Pub: Crain Communications Inc. - Detroit
Ed: Anjali Fluker, Sheena Harrison. Description: Mt. Clemons and Ann Arbor, Michigan are both considering an increase in city taxes. There are 22 cities in Michigan that levy an income tax, including Detroit, Pontiac, Hamtramck, Highland Park, Flint, Saginaw, and Grand Rapids.

54496 ■ **"Commuting Expenses: What is a 'Metropolitan Area'?" in** *Journal of Accountancy* **(Vol. 199, January 2005, No. 1, pp. 75)**
Pub: American Institute of Certified Public Accountants
Ed: Vinay S. Navani. Description: Under revenue ruling 1999-7, costs for traveling from one's residence to a fixed work location, costs can be deducted if they fall under certain criteria.

54497 ■ **"Companies don't have to be large to offer big benefits" in** *Business First Columbus* **(Vol. 18, No. 40, May 24, 2002, pp. B10)**
Pub: Business First Columbus, Inc.
Ed: Crystal Faulkner. Description: Tax advantages can help defray the cost of employee benefits, these benefits include health care, childcare, life insurance, etc.

54498 ■ **"A conceptual mistake in the calculation of social security taxes" in** *Tax Notes* **(Vol. 97, No. 2, October 14, 2002, pp. 283-285)**
Pub: Tax Notes International
Ed: M. Hayden Brown. Description: The Social Security Agency wants a self-employed person to pay the same amount of social security tax as paid by an employee of identical income combined with his employer. However, due to a mistake in Form 1040, a self-employed person actually has a lesser tax burden than an employed person and employer.

54499 ■ **"Congress Looking at Proposed Tax Deferral Program" in** *Atlanta Business Chronicle* **(Vol. 24, No. 10, August 10, 2001, pp. 40A)**
Pub: American City Business Journals Inc.
Ed: Andisheh Nouraee. Description: Tatum CFO Partners LLP is proposing the Bridge Act, a tax deferral program that will allow growing businesses (those with a growth rate of 10 percent during the previous two years, but under $10 million in gross annual revenue) to defer $250,000 in federal tax liability over two years. A coalition of small business groups and the House of Representatives Small Business Committee member Rep. Jim DeMint support Tatum.

54500 ■ **"Congress Moves to Repeal Business Sale Lump-Sum Rule" in** *Accounting Today* **(Vol. 14, No. 8, May 1, 2000, pp. 3)**
Pub: Faulkner & Gray, Inc.
Ed: David Cho. Description: Heeding the calls of the American Institute of CPAs and small business advocacy groups, the House of Representatives has fast-tracked a repeal of the law enacted last year that forces small business owners who are selling their businesses to immediately pay all taxes resulting from the sale in one lump sum.

54501 ■ **"Connecting Firms with Needed Funds; Financial Assistance" in** *Crain's New York Business* **(Vol. 22, November 13, 2006, No. 46, pp. 32)**
Pub: Crain Communications, Inc.
Description: Listing of organizations that provide incentives or financial assistance to firms that are based in New York or are relocating to the area.

54502 ■ **"A Conversation With Duane Tarnacki, Clark Hill PLC" in** *Crain's Detroit Business* **(Vol. 21, November 7, 2005, No. 45, pp. 25)**
Pub: Crain Communications Inc. - Detroit
Ed: Sherri Begin. Description: In an interview with Duane Tarnacki, partner at Clark Hill PLC located in Detroit, Michigan, he addresses the repeal of the estate tax and its meaning for nonprofit organizations.

54503 ■ *Corporations: Tax Choices for Business Planning—Explanation, Law & Regulations, Legislative History, Cases & Rulings, Indexes*
Pub: Prentice Hall
Ed: Compiled by Prentice Hall Editorial staff.

54504 ■ **"Court Review of IRS Abuse of Discretion" in** *Journal of Accountancy* **(Vol. 198, December 2004, No. 6, pp. 93)**
Pub: American Institute of Certified Public Accountants
Ed: Edward J. Schnee. Description: Under numerous code sections, the Internal Revenue Service is allowed to reduce or eliminate a tax liability for equity or hardship reasons at its discretion.

54505 ■ "Cracking the Code" in *Entrepreneur* (Vol. 32, August 2004, No. 8, pp. 48)
Pub: Entrepreneur Media Inc.
Ed: Jennifer Pellet. **Description:** Profile of the Taxpayer Education Communication Small Business/Self-Employed Operating Division provides information and resources to help small business owners understand tax codes.

54506 ■ "CRS reports on the so-call 'tax rebate'" in *Tax Notes* (Vol. 92, No. 4, July 23, 2001, pp. 567-570)
Pub: Tax Notes International
Ed: Gregg Esenwein, Steve Maguire. **Description:** Issues concerning the so-called tax rebate created by the Economic Growth and Tax Relief Reconciliation Act of 2001 are examined. Topics include a report by the Congressional Research Service that states the payment is not technically a tax rebate but is, instead, an advance on reduced tax liability for 2001 income, and that more than a quarter of all taxpayers, including low-income taxpayers, will not receive a payment.

54507 ■ *The Day Care Providers Tax Survival Manual:...A Complete Tax Guide & Recordkeeping System*
Pub: Cornerstone Publishing
Ed: Laurie Kerridge. **Released:** 2nd ed. 1997. **Price:** $21.50 (cloth).

54508 ■ "Death and Taxes" in *Atlanta Business Chronicle* (Vol. 23, No. 15, September 15, 2000, pp. 1B)
Pub: American City Business Journals, Inc.
Ed: Lauren Keating. **Description:** Opponents of the estate tax claim their assets are being taxed twice and that the time spent on financial planning, due to the tax, is detrimental to their businesses.

54509 ■ "Death and taxes" in *Crain's Chicago Business*
Pub: Crain Communications, Inc. Crain Communications, Inc.
Ed: Mary Ellen Podmolik. **Description:** Along with health care affordability, the federal death tax and President Clinton's recent veto of legislation passed by both the House and Senate to repeal it tops the list of hot-button issues facing small business owners as they head to the polls.

54510 ■ *Deduct It! Lower Your Small Business Taxes*
Pub: NOLO
Ed: Stephen Fishman. **Released:** November 2006. **Price:** $34.99. **Description:** Information is provided to help small companies maximize taxable deductions.

54511 ■ "Deduct Now, Pay Later: New Provisions Provide a Tax Break for Business Owners" in *Black Enterprise* (Vol. 34, No. 5, December 2003)
Pub: Earl Graves Publishing Co.
Ed: Donald Jay Korn. **Description:** New tax laws for 2003 are saving small business owners through equipment expensing and bonus depreciation.

54512 ■ "Deductible Gifts" in *Hispanic Business* (Vol. 23, No. 11, November 2001, pp. 68)
Pub: Hispanic Business Inc.
Ed: Milton Zall. **Description:** Tax rules for gift giving to employees, suppliers and customers are examined.

54513 ■ "Deducting the Cost of Laser Eye Surgery" in *Journal of Accountancy* (Vol. 198, December 2004, No. 6, pp. 92)
Pub: American Institute of Certified Public Accountants
Ed: W. Terry Dancer. **Description:** The Internal Revenue Service has issued a letter ruling that addresses whether surgical procedures to correct nearsightedness, farsightedness and astigmatism can be used as a tax deduction.

54514 ■ "Determination of a profit motive" in *Journal of Accountancy* (Vol. 190, No. 3, September 2000, pp. 94)
Pub: Harborside Financial Center
Ed: Cynthia Bolt Lee. **Description:** Information about the IRC section 183, "Activities Not Engaged in For Profit", which contains nine factors a taxpayer can use to determine whether an activity has a profit motive or is a hobby.

54515 ■ "Determining your deductions" in *Atlanta Business Chronicle* (Vol. 23, No. 26, December 1, 2000, pp. 1B)
Pub: American City Business Journals Inc.
Ed: Tony Heffernan. **Description:** Advice for properly timed tax actions for small business is given. Topics include using donations as tax deductions, making capital expenditures before the end of the year, and dismissing employees before December 31.

54516 ■ "Dividends Gushing from Tax Cut" in *Houston Business Journal* (Vol. 34, No. 13, August 8, 2003, pp. 1)
Pub: American City Business Journals
Ed: Jim Greer. **Description:** Changes in the federal tax laws have resulted in substantial profits for investors of Kinder Morgan Inc. Topics include value of company shares, tax laws, and dividend payments.

54517 ■ "DMC head may ask for drink tax" in *Crain's Detroit Business* (Vol. 19, No. 2, January 13, 2003, pp. 3)
Pub: Crain Communications Inc., Detroit
Ed: Katie Merx. **Description:** Hospitals and trauma centers in the Detroit area are banking on a proposed tax of 5 cents per alcoholic beverage served to provide revenue for their operations.

54518 ■ "Donations That Suit the Taxman" in *Business Week* (February 20, 2006, No. 3972, pp. 92)
Pub: McGraw-Hill Companies
Ed: Deborah L. Jacobs. **Description:** The IRS requires more than a standard receipt from a charity when claiming tax deductions; cash contributions over $250 require a canceled check or charity receipt.

54519 ■ "Don't Bet Your Life On It" in *Inc.* (August 2005, pp. 24-25)
Pub: Inc. Magazine
Description: The Internal Revenue Service is cracking down on split-dollar insurance, a common benefit given to company executives.

54520 ■ *Don't Let the IRS Destroy Your Small Business*
Pub: Addison Wesley Longman, Inc.
Ed: Michael Savage. **Released:** 1998. **Price:** $15.00; $7.95.

54521 ■ "Don't Take It Personally" in *My Business* (February/March 2004, pp. 42)
Pub: My Business Magazine
Ed: Karen J. Bannan. **Description:** Separating business from personal tax deductions is critical to all small businesses. Information to assist small businesses owners to decide what is deductible for business is examined.

54522 ■ "Don't Write Off That Tax Write-Off" in *Business Week* (February 14, 2005, No. 3920, pp. 91)
Pub: McGraw-Hill Companies
Description: According to June Walker, tax and financial consultant, many self-employed people cheat themselves out of legitimate tax deductions because the laws are not clear. Walker also authored a book offing small businesses tax solutions.

54523 ■ "Double taxation is double wrong" in *Atlanta Business Chronicle* (Vol. 25, January 10, 2003, No. 31, pp. 33A)
Pub: American City Business Publications, Inc.
Ed: Jeff Dickerson. **Description:** George W. Bush's plan to eliminate the tax on dividends is far from an attempt to help the rich, for nearly half of all tax-filers in 2000 who claimed dividend income earned less than $50,000. Bush's stimulus plan will help everyday Americans, and the class warfare crowd will have a difficult time finding fault with the plan.

54524 ■ "Dulling the Tax Bite" *Fortune* (Vol. 141, No. 9, May 1, 2000)
Pub: Time Inc.
Ed: Daniel Akst. **Description:** The IRS has cut small businesses some slack in three areas, but in doing so is conducting tougher audits.

54525 ■ "E-commerce: Too Valuable to Tax" in *Success* (Vol. 47, No. 2, June 2000, pp. 22)
Pub: Success Publishing, Inc.
Ed: Fred A. Gray. **Description:** E-commerce may be the greatest tool small businesses can employ. All small-business people need is to learn the technology and then put it to work. Taxing the Internet could destroy the success of e-commerce.

54526 ■ "An E-Mail from the IRS? Don't Believe It" in *Long Island Business News* (May 7, 2004)
Pub: Dolan Media Newswires
Ed: David Reich-Hale. **Description:** The U.S. Internal Revenue Service has posted a warning to taxpayers about an email scam that tries to trick taxpayers into giving personal information. The email appears to be an official memo from the IRS.

54527 ■ "The earned income tax credit and the child tax credit under the Tax Act of 2001" in *Tax Notes* (Vol. 92, No. 4, July 23, 2001)
Pub: Tax Notes International
Ed: Laurence S. Seidman, Saul D. Hoffman. **Description:** Issues concerning the interaction of the earned income tax credit (EITC), the child tax credit, the reduction of EITC marriage penalties, and the resulting structure of marginal tax rates, as they occur within the Economic Growth and Tax Relief Act of 2001, are examined. Topics include the introduction of a new 10 percent tax bracket, and the need for further marriage penalty tax reform and future marginal tax rate reduction. Statistical data included.

54528 ■ "Economic and Financial Indicators" in *The Economist* (Vol. 377, October 22-28, 2005, No. 8449, pp. 112-113)
Pub: The Economist Newspaper Ltd.
Description: Statistics involving fifteen developed economies as well as information on tax revenues and metal prices are presented.

54529 ■ "Economists Raise Concerns about South Carolina Governor's Tax Cut Proposal" in *The State* (February 17, 2004)
Pub: Knight-Ridder/Tribune Business News
Ed: Jennifer Talhelm. **Description:** Impact of the lower state income tax in South Carolina to schools, local governments and state-supported services. Economists address these issues.

54530 ■ "EGTRRA lowers rates and expands credits, education benefits" in *The Tax Adviser* (Vol. 32, No. 10, October 2001, pp. 677)
Pub: Harborside Financial Center
Ed: Ronald B. Hegt. **Description:** A summary of the Economic Growth and Tax Relief Reconciliation Act of 2001 is presented, including information on individual rate reductions, personal exemption phaseout repeal, itemized deduction phaseout repeal, AMT changes, child credit, adoption credit, dependent care credit, employer-provided childcare facilities, marriage penalty relief, education IRAs, student loan interest, QHEE deduction, and employer-provided education assistance.

54531 ■ "Electric Slide: Sign Up for Electric Filing, and You Could Get a Tax-Penalty Refund" in *Entrepreneur* (Vol. 32, November 2004, No. 11)
Pub: Entrepreneur Media Inc.
Ed: Joan Szabo. **Description:** The Internal Revenue Service will provide an automatic one-time penalty refund to some small business owners in order to encourage the use of the Electronic Federal Tax Payment System. Details of the program are included.

54532 ■ "Employer-Provided Education Benefits: Section 132(d) is Worth a Second Look" in *Journal of Accountancy* (Vol. 198, September 2004)
Pub: American Institute of Certified Public Accountants
Ed: Edmund D. Fenton, Jr. Description: An overview of the various ways employers are helping their employees with tax-free education benefits, including scholarships and grants under IRC Section 117 and education assistance programs under Section 127, as well as IRC Section 132(d).

54533 ■ "Employers Can Use State Programs to Help Employees Save for College Education" in *Employee Benefit Plan Review* (Vol. 55, No. 6)
Pub: Charles D. Spencer & Associates, Inc.
Ed: Sue Burzawa. Description: Most states offer either prepaid tuition programs or college savings plans, which allow workers to set aside tax deferred income to pay for college.

54534 ■ "Employers' extra credit" in *Hispanic Business* (Vol. 22, No. 6, June 2000, pp. 156)
Pub: Hispanic Business
Ed: Milton Zall. Description: A small business can earn between $1,500 and $8,500 per employee by hiring members of targeted group and qualifying for Work Opportunity Tax Credit and the Welfare to Work Tax Credit.

54535 ■ "End of Some Tariffs a Boon to Suppliers" in *Crain's Detroit Business* (Vol. 22, December 18, 2006, No. 51, pp. 6)
Pub: Crain Communications Inc. - Detroit
Ed: Brent Snavely. Description: Relaxation of tariffs on corrosion resistant steels will reduce supply costs for automotive suppliers. Tariffs were removed for imports from France, Canada, Australia, and Japan but remain in effect for Korea and Germany.

54536 ■ "Engler budget would cut small business taxes" in *Crain's Detroit Business* (Vol. 16, No. 5, January 31, 2000, pp. 7)
Pub: Crain Communications, Inc.
Ed: Amy Lane. Description: Buried in the back of Governor John Engler's new state budget is a $16.7 million tax cut for more than 32,300 small businesses.

54537 ■ "Engler's tax web" in *Wall Street Journal* (December 17, 2001, pp. A18)
Pub: Wall Street Journal
Description: An overview of Michigan's Governor John Engler's efforts to tax Internet Sales.

54538 ■ "Entrepreneur Column" in *Entrepreneur Column* (April 11, 2003)
Pub: Knight-Ridder/Tribune Business News
Ed: David Meier. Description: Tax information when using a car for business purposes is provided.

54539 ■ "The era of e-taxes" in *Hispanic Business* (Vol. 22, No. 3, March 2000, pp. 62)
Pub: Hispanic Business
Ed: Milton Zall. Description: The Internal Revenue Service has implemented the electronic filing and payment of taxes in 2000. Issues concerning the effect of the new method of filing and payment on small businesses are discussed.

54540 ■ "Estate of affairs" in *Entrepreneur* (Vol. 31, No. 4, April 2003, pp. 52)
Pub: Entrepreneur Media Inc.
Ed: Joshua Kurlantzick. Description: With the repealing of the federal estate tax in 2001, many entrepreneurs are taking advantage of the opportunity to inherit or pass on businesses without paying any tariff.

54541 ■ "Estate tax huge headache for small business owners" in *Indianapolis Business Journal* (Vol. 21, No. 15, June 26, 2000, pp. 33A)
Pub: IBJ Corp.
Ed: Scott Olson. Description: Opponents of the estate tax hope it will be phased out by 2010.

54542 ■ "Estate tax foes awaiting more shots at a repeal" in *Business First Columbus* (Vol. 18, No. 26, February 15, 2002, pp. A16)
Pub: Business First Columbus, Inc.
Ed: Kent Hoover. Description: A discussion regarding the issues facing estate tax reform is presented.

54543 ■ "Extra Credit" in *Entrepreneur* (Vol. 31, No. 5, May 2003, pp. 69)
Pub: Entrepreneur Media Inc.
Ed: Joanne Cleaver. Description: Information about the state income tax child-care credits offered by 25 states is given. Specifics of this credit vary from state to state, and most companies don't understand the specifics of the credit.

54544 ■ "EZ Does It" in *Entrepreneur* (Vol. 33, January 2005, No. 1, pp. 53)
Pub: Entrepreneur Media Inc.
Ed: Jennifer Pellet. Description: Recent changes in Internal Revenue Service regulations allow small business owners to double the dollar limit on expenses allowable on Schedule C-EZ, a simpler version of the Schedule C Form (Profit or Loss From Business).

54545 ■ "A family affair" in *Black Enterprise* (Vol. 33, No. 3, October 2002, pp. 154)
Pub: Earl Graves Publishing Co.
Ed: George Alexander. Description: The largest part of American wealth lies in the family-owned businesses that make up 80-90 percent of all business enterprises in North America. The importance of a succession plan for family-owned firms is discussed. A survey by the Family Firm Institute of 800 family-owned businesses showed that insufficient estate planning, failure to prepare for the inevitable transition, and lack of funds to pay estate taxes are the leading causes for most family-owned business failures.

54546 ■ "Family Partnerships Under Scrutiny" in *Inc.* (Volume 27, July 2005, No. 7, pp. 26)
Pub: Inc. Magazine
Ed: Allen P. Roberts Jr. Description: The Internal Revenue Service is taking steps to investigate the way business owners avoid paying estate taxes.

54547 ■ "Fancy-Sounding Tax Hurts S Corps" in *Inc.* (January 1, 2005)
Pub: Inc. Magazine
Ed: Darren Dahl. Description: A new tax, called the millionaires tax, may end up hurting small startups.

54548 ■ *Fast-Track Business Start-Up Kit: California*
Pub: DP Group, Incorporated
Ed: Carolyn Usinger. Released: September 2006. Price: $29.00. Description: Step-by-step guide for starting and running a business in California, including information on sole proprietors, partnerships, limited liability companies, S and C corporations, as well as details concerning business entities, sales taxes, environmental issues, human resources, and more.

54549 ■ "Federal stimulus can ensure recovery" in *Atlanta Business Chronicle* (Vol. 25, January 10, 2003, No. 31, pp. 32A)
Pub: American City Business Publications, Inc.
Ed: Jim Molis. Description: A stimulus package from the Federal Government will go a long way in helping the economy on its way to recovery. However, war with Iraq or North Korea would most certainly bring the economy back down.

54550 ■ "Federal Reserve Raises Key Interest Rate by Quarter Point" in *Boston Globe* (February 3, 2005)
Pub: New York Times Company
Ed: Robert Gavin. Description: The Federal Reserve raised key interest rates which will lead to higher charges on credit cards, home equity lines of credit, and other short-term loans. Savings and money market accounts are not expected to see a rise in interest rates.

54551 ■ "Feel the Burn" in *Entrepreneur* (Vol. 33, August 2005, No. 8, pp. 28)
Pub: Entrepreneur Media Inc.
Ed: Stephen Barlas. Description: The Workforce Health Improvement Program Act would allow small companies to deduct the costs for reimbursing employees' health club fees.

54552 ■ "Fifty States, a Thousand New Tax Laws" in *Inc.* (Volume 27, June 2005, No. 6, pp. 21-23)
Pub: Inc. Magazine
Ed: Amy Feldman. Description: States are decoupling tax codes from the federal government's tax code. Two key areas of divergence between state and federal tax codes are depreciation and estate taxes.

54553 ■ "Film-Industry Tax Break Backed" in *San Jose Mercury News* (February 17, 2005)
Pub: Knight-Ridder/Tribune Business News
Ed: Kate Folmar. Description: California's governor is backing a bill that would provide tax breaks to the entertainment industry in order to keep film productions in the state.

54554 ■ "Financial Advisors Give Last-Minute Tax Tips for Small Businesses" in *Long Island Business News* (February 13, 2004)
Pub: Dolan Media Newswires
Ed: Ben Abelson. Description: Last minute tax tips are offered to small businesses.

54555 ■ "Firm-and-Fixed-Plan Rule Reaffirmed" in *Journal of Accountancy* (Vol. 199, February 2005, No. 2, pp. 75)
Pub: American Institute of Certified Public Accountants
Ed: Edward J. Schnee. Description: Case of Merrill & Lynch Co. v. Commissioner is examined. The case involved the firm-and-fixed-plan rule.

54556 ■ "Fixing the Alternative Minimum Tax" in *Kiplinger Letter* (Vol. 82, January 12, 2007, No. 1)
Pub: Kiplinger
Description: Newly adopted rules demand that tax cuts must be offset by tax increases, spending reductions or both

54557 ■ "Focus on Finances" in *Entrepreneur.com* (Vol. 34, January 2006, No. 1, pp. 24)
Pub: Entrepreneur Media Inc.
Ed: Crystal Detamore-Rodman. Description: The Internal Revenue Service is starting to examine 5,000 random S corporation tax returns from the 2003 and 2004 tax years. The IRS is concerned that some S corporation owners are skimping on salaries in favor of a larger dividend distribution, which isn't subject to self-employment taxes.

54558 ■ "Food For Thought" in *Entrepreneur* (Vol. 32, September 2004, No. 9, pp. 50)
Pub: Entrepreneur Media Inc.
Ed: Jennifer Pellet. Description: Bills to return the meal and entertainment deduction to 80 percent are pending in both the House and Senate. This increase would help small businesses more than large corporations.

54559 ■ "For Small Businesses, Future of Biz Taxes Will be Crucial" in *Crain's Detroit Business* (Vol. 22, November 27, 2006, No. 48, pp. 15)
Pub: Crain Communications Inc. - Detroit
Ed: Sheena Harrison. Description: With the cancellation of the Single Business Tax, small businesses will be central in the talks and discussions on changes necessary to replace revenue losses. Also of concern is the difficulty of hiring qualified employees with affordable wages and benefits.

54560 ■ "Forgive Us Our Debts...The Creditor May, But the IRS Won't" in *Black Enterprise* (Vol. 34, July 2004, No. 12, pp. 143)
Pub: Earl G. Graves Publishing Co. Inc.

Ed: Leslie E. Royal. **Description:** While some mortgage lenders, car financiers, and credit card issuers may forgive debt when an individual agrees to pay a certain amount off the balance, the Internal Revenue Service will never write-off taxes owed.

54561 ■ "Former Airline Workers Navigate Into Florida Liquor Business" in *Bradenton Herald* **()**
Pub: Bradenton Herald
Ed: Tilde Herrera. **Description:** Profile of Lori Clay and Herb Rice who left the airline industry to open a Florida liquor business. The store sells more than 300 kinds of wine, 75 brands of liquor, and seven various beers. The new entrepreneurs chose Florida because Florida has no state income tax and enjoys a large population of seniors.

54562 ■ "Free yourself from taxes" in *Women in Business* **(Vol. 53, No. 7, January-February 2002, pp. 27)**
Pub: The ABWA Co Inc.
Description: Tax free investments are discussed, including municipal bonds and tax free unit investment trusts.

54563 ■ "Fun Money: Mixing Business and Pleasure Can Pay Off" in *Entrepreneur* **(Vol. 32, August 2004, No. 8, pp. 48)**
Pub: Entrepreneur Media Inc.
Ed: Joan Szabo. **Description:** Tax rules regarding business travel write-offs are examined.

54564 ■ "The Future is Here: The Modernizing of IRS e-File" in *Journal of Accountancy* **(Vol. 198, December 2004, No. 6, pp. 89)**
Pub: American Institute of Certified Public Accountants
Ed: Bert DuMars. **Description:** Ways the Internal Revenue Service is updating and modernizing electronic returns are listed.

54565 ■ "Gaining from a Loss" in *Hispanic Business* **(March 2004, pp. 50)**
Pub: Hispanic Business
Ed: Milton Zall. **Description:** Strategic use of net operating loss (NOL) from a business can help cut taxes and might even result in a tax refund.

54566 ■ "GAO blames IRS, Congress for small business tax woes" in *Accounting Today* **(Vol. 14, No. 16, September 4, 2000, pp. 3)**
Pub: Faulkner & Gray, Inc.
Ed: Ken Rankin. **Description:** The General Accounting Office found, in a study done for the Senate Small Business Committee, that Congress itself, creates problems by the complexity of the tax code and the IRS adds to them when it focuses attention on enforcement activities rather than efforts to prevent small business taxpayers from falling out of compliance in the first place.

54567 ■ "A Generally Beneficial Law" in *Hispanic Business* **(Vol. 23, No. 10, October, 2001, pp. 98)**
Pub: Hispanic Business
Ed: Milton Zall. **Description:** The effects of President Bush's tax cut package on individual small business owners may vary significantly. Small businesses operated as sole proprietorships, partnerships, or S corporations will directly benefit from the lowered tax rates.

54568 ■ "Georgia Legislature Passes Business Tax Break" in *Atlanta Journal-Constitution* **(March 4, 2005)**
Pub: Knight-Ridder/Tribune Business News
Ed: James Salzer. **Description:** Georgia Legislature approved a $1 billion tax break over the next ten years should create jobs.

54569 ■ "Georgia Small Businesses Welcome Proposed Tax-Write Off Bill" in *Atlanta Journal-Constitution* **(March 3, 2005)**
Pub: Knight-Ridder/Tribune Business News
Ed: Michael E. Kanell. **Description:** New legislation in Georgia, if passed, would allow small businesses to write off the cost of big purchases.

54570 ■ "Georgia ranks so-so in business 'survival index'" in *Atlanta Business Chronicle* **(Vol. 24, No. 14, September 7, 2001, pp. 5B)**
Pub: American City Business Journals Inc.
Ed: Chaundra Frierson. **Description:** According to the Small Business Survival Committee's latest survey, Georgia ranks at 23 out of the District of Columbia and 50 states regarding friendliness to small businesses. The study focused on areas such as estate tax, unemployment taxes, health insurance taxes, personal income taxes, capital gains taxes, corporate income taxes, property taxes, and sales taxes.

54571 ■ "Get outta here" in *Entrepreneur* **(Vol. 28, No. 7, July 2000, pp. 90)**
Pub: Entrepreneur Media Inc.
Ed: Terry L. Neal. **Description:** For tax breaks and investment opportunities, sometimes you just have to leave the country. The offshore industry has developed into a major business spanning the globe.

54572 ■ "Getting Out of an IRS Mess" in *Black Enterprise* **(Vol. 37, December 2006, No. 5, pp. 53)**
Pub: Earl G. Graves Publishing Co. Inc.
Ed: Carolyn M. Brown. **Description:** Owing back taxes to the IRS can lead to huge penalties and interest. Here are some tips on how to handle paying the IRS what you owe them.

54573 ■ "Getting Their Slice: Save Money, and Keep Employees Happy With Stock Ownership Plans" in *Entrepreneur* **(Vol. 32, September 2004)**
Pub: Entrepreneur Media Inc.
Ed: Joan Szabo. **Description:** Employee stock ownership plans and their tax-deferral benefits are examined.

54574 ■ "Gift Management: The Business of Charitable Giving" in *My Business* **(October/November 2002, pp. 15)**
Pub: My Business Magazine
Ed: Nancy Jackson. **Description:** Advice for charitable giving for small business owners is given, along with the listing of a Web site that rates hundreds of charities and soliciting organizations by financial and management practices.

54575 ■ "Give the BID Plan a Break" in *Crain's Detroit Business* **(Vol. 19, No. 45, November 10, 2003, pp. 8)**
Pub: Crain Communications Inc., Detroit
Description: A plan to raise $3 million a year in Detroit, through a self-imposed tax, was approved by property owners, based on a formula tied to property values. The Detroit City Council voted against creating the downtown business improvement district.

54576 ■ "Give Me a Break" in *Entrepreneur. com* **(Vol. 34, January 2006, No. 1, pp. 36)**
Pub: Entrepreneur Media Inc.
Ed: Mike Hogan. **Description:** New tax preparation software can help small companies file federal and state taxes. H&R Block and Intuit have versions for every type of business entity and provide all necessary forms and instructions in an easy-to-follow format. Cost of the software is also tax deductible.

54577 ■ "Give Me a Tax Break" in *Black Enterprise* **(Vol. 36, February 2006, No. 7, pp. 40)**
Pub: Earl G. Graves Publishing Co. Inc.
Ed: Joyce Jones. **Description:** If passed, the Mortgage Insurance Fairness Act would allow homeowners with a combined income under $100,000 to deduct the total amount of mortgage insurance payments on federal tax returns.

54578 ■ "Global Trade" in *Entrepreneur.com* **(Vol. 34, February 2006, No. 2, pp. 120)**
Pub: Entrepreneur Media Inc.
Ed: Nichole L. Torres. **Description:** Careful research and planning are required to start an international business. Many colleges are offering international business courses to help entrepreneurs understand issues concerning taxes, trade law, currency conversion, language translation and cultural understanding.

54579 ■ "Good Calls: Gains, Losses and Straddles" in *Barron's* **(July 7, 2003, pp. 19)**
Pub: Barron's
Ed: Joseph F. Gelband. **Description:** Techniques for negotiating the tax consequences of straddle investments, or plays both for and against a stock at the same time, are detailed. The Economic Recovery Tax Act of 1981 has made this process more difficult.

54580 ■ "Granholm to Propose New Revenue-Sharing Plan" in *Crain's Detroit Business* **(Vol. 23, January 29, 2007, No. 5, pp. 32)**
Pub: Crain Communications Inc. - Detroit
Ed: Amy Lane. **Description:** Revenue sharing to be a major part of Governor's fiscal 2008 budget proposal. This adds to the list of other legislative issues such as increased gas tax, replacing the single-business tax revenues, and changes to the broader tax structure.

54581 ■ "Green Machines" in *Entrepreneur. com* **(Vol. 34, February 2006, No. 2, pp. 51)**
Pub: Entrepreneur Media Inc.
Ed: Jennifer Pellet. **Description:** Under the Energy Tax Incentives Act of 2005, the government is offering tax incentives from $650 to $3,400 in tax credits for buying environmentally friendly vehicles.

54582 ■ "Greenspan Floats Sales Tax" in *Chicago Tribune* **(March 4, 2005)**
Pub: Knight-Ridder/Tribune Business News
Ed: William Neikirk. **Description:** Alan Greenspan, chairman of the U.S. Federal Reserve, is recommending consideration of a national sales tax as part of the restructuring of the federal tax system.

54583 ■ "A Gross Tax Proposal" in *Inc.* **(July 1, 2003)**
Pub: Gruner & Jahr USA Publishing
Description: A business activity tax stands to change the way taxes are calculated in the state of Kentucky.

54584 ■ "Group Buys Bradenton, Fla.-Area Retail Center" in *Bradenton Herald* **(January 5, 2005)**
Pub: Bradenton Herald
Ed: Matt Griswold. **Description:** Kash n' Karry was purchased by New York real estate firm Gemini Real Estate Advisors LLC and 10 other investors, for the sum of $15.2 million. The store is located in the Ranch Lake Plaza in Bradenton, Florida. Gemini Real Estate Advisors LLC is one of many nationwide companies focusing on tenant-in-common, 1031 exchanges. This process allows individuals to invest with a large firm in tax-free pieces of commercial real estate.

54585 ■ "Hands off small business!" in *My Business* **(September/October 2001, pp. 23)**
Pub: My Business Magazine
Description: The results of a recent survey by NFIB to its members is displayed. The survey included such issues as taxes, compensatory time off, pay disparities, ergonomics, competition with prisons, federal contract bundling, and Internet taxes.

54586 ■ "Haven't Filed Your Taxes Yet?" in *My Business* **(April/May 2002, pp. 15)**
Pub: My Business Magazine
Ed: John R. Halbrooks. **Description:** New tax legislation that applies to small business are listed, including deductions for mileage, equipment expense, social security, and cash accounting.

54587 ■ "Here Comes Trouble: Avoid Independent Contractor Snags" in *Entrepreneur* **(Vol. 33, February 2005, No. 2, pp. 50)**
Pub: Entrepreneur Media Inc.
Ed: Joan Szabo. **Description:** Internal Revenue Service inspects worker classification searching for entrepreneurs who misclassify workers as independent contractors instead of actual employees of the company. It is simpler for the IRS to collect taxes from business owners rather than independent contractors. Employers must deduct for income taxes, Social Security and Medicare taxes, and pay unemployment taxes on wages paid to employees.

54588 ■ "Here's a tip" in *Entrepreneur* (Vol. 30, No. 10, October 2002, pp. 58)
Pub: Entrepreneur Media Inc.
Ed: Joan Szabo. **Description:** In June, 2002, the Supreme Court ruled that the Internal Revenue Service has the right to charge restaurants additional Social Security taxes if it believes employees are underreporting tips.

54589 ■ "High-Tech Trash" in *Kiplinger's Personal Finance Magazine* (Vol. 55, No. 1, January, 2001, pp. 98)
Pub: The Kiplinger Washington Editors, Inc.
Ed: Christine Pulfrey. **Description:** Donating a computer or a phone to a charitable organization earns you a tax deduction for the value of the item, while helping your community.

54590 ■ "Higher Revenue Boosts Call for Tax Cut" in *Boston Globe* (February 2, 2005)
Pub: New York Times Company
Ed: Scott S. Greenberger. **Description:** Massachusetts Governor Mitt Romney is proposing an income tax cut that would cost the state $225 million in fiscal 2006. The state's tax total for January 2005 was 11.9 percent higher than January 2004, predicting projected revenue of $16.5 billion for fiscal 2005.

54591 ■ "Hire purpose" in *Entrepreneur* (Vol. 31, No. 4, April 2003, pp. 56)
Pub: Entrepreneur Media Inc.
Ed: Joan Szabo. **Description:** Tax credits from the Job Creation and Worker Assistance Act of 2002 have been extended through 2003, and could provide savings and help defray costs of maintaining employees on the payroll of small businesses.

54592 ■ *Home Business Tax Deductions: Keep What You Earn*
Pub: NOLO
Ed: Stephen Fishman. **Released:** November 2006. **Price:** $34.99. **Description:** Home business tax deductions are outlined. Basic information on the ways various business structures are taxed and how deductions work is included.

54593 ■ "The Home Office Deduction" in *My Business* (October/November 2002, pp. 46)
Pub: My Business Magazine
Ed: Milton Zall. **Description:** Requirements for using home office tax deductions are discussed.

54594 ■ "Home, Sweet Office" in *Entrepreneur* (Vol. 31, No. 11, November 2003, pp. 72)
Pub: Entrepreneur Media, Inc.
Ed: Jennifer Pellet. **Description:** Internal Revenue Service tax laws regarding the sale of a home that is also used as a home business are explained.

54595 ■ "Hooray for R. and D. It's time to make a popular and effective tax credit permanent" in *Time Inc.* (Vol. 156, No. 13, Sept. 25, 2000)
Pub: Time & Life Bldg., Rockefeller Center
Ed: Daniel Kadlec. **Description:** The tax credit is set to expire in 2004. Yet it is working so well that even presidential candidates can't disagree. Now is the time to make it permanent. Only then will anyone address how to make it better and less confusing, which is what we really should be talking about.

54596 ■ "House Wants Bigger Business-Tax Cut" in *Crain's Detroit Business* (Vol. 21, October 31, 2005, No. 44, pp. 6)
Pub: Crain Communications Inc. - Detroit
Ed: Amy Lane. **Description:** A new plan that would heighten and accelerate business tax-cuts was passed by the Senate in October 2005. The plan would use $700 million to support growth and technology-oriented businesses while $300 million would go to programs that support life-sciences, emerging technology and related sectors.

54597 ■ "How well is Appeals doing?" in *Tax Notes* (Vol. 96, No. 12, September 16, 2002, pp. 1564-1567)
Pub: Tax Notes International
Ed: George Guttman. **Description:** The effectiveness of the IRS Appeals Division is analyzed by measuring employee and taxpayer satisfaction and the length of time it takes the Appeals Division to process cases.

54598 ■ "How I Learned to Stop Worrying and Love the Death Tax" in *Inc.* (August 1, 2004)
Pub: Inc. Magazine
Ed: Nadine Heintz. **Description:** Ways to keep the death tax at bay are discussed by the owner of a plumbing business.

54599 ■ "How Not To Get Tripped Up by UBTI" in *Venture Capital Journal* (July 1, 2003)
Pub: Thomson Financial Inc.
Description: Business plans and projects for portfolio companies and venture capital funds have been weakened by the slow economy, resulting in devaluations, recapitalizations and fewer realizations, along with the need for funds to borrow in order to protect investments, thus raising the prospect of unrelated business taxable income (UBTI). Circumstances that would make borrowing a good option include dry funds, bridging calls, borrowing to pay expenses, or to accelerate realizations.

54600 ■ "How Partnerships Can Avoid Tax Surprises" in *Venture Capital Journal* (July 1, 2003)
Pub: Thomson Financial Inc.
Description: Tax planning ideas helpful to the venture capital industry are examined. Issues discussed include establishing a partnership status, contribution requirements, capital account allocation, tax basis allocation, distributions, and state filing requirements.

54601 ■ *How to Start an Internet Sales Business*
Pub: Lulu.com
Ed: Dan Davis. **Released:** August 2005. **Price:** $19.95. **Description:** Small business guide for launching an Internet sales company. Topics include business structure, licenses, and taxes.

54602 ■ "How Well is Appeals Doing?" in *Tax Notes* (Vol. 96, No. 12, September 16, 2002, pp. 1564-1567)
Pub: Tax Notes International
Ed: Warren Rojas. **Description:** Republicans in the U.S. House are developing a tax plan that would include provisions on unemployment benefits, corporate inversions, executive compensation and tax relief for small businesses. However, they may not have time to put it on the legislative calendar.

54603 ■ "HSAs-A Growing Trend In Health Benefits for Businesses and Individuals" in *Entrepreneur* (Vol. 32, December 2004, No. 12, pp. 67)
Pub: Entrepreneur Media Inc.
Description: Health savings accounts (HSAs) allow individuals with high-deductible health plans to put pre-tax money aside, spend it tax-free on qualified health expenses, earn interest tax-free and also save the money for health-care expenses in retirement. HSAs may be a way for small companies to manage health benefits costs by exchanging higher deductibles for lower premiums and tax advantages.

54604 ■ "Hunting Season: Feds Try to Protect the Little Guy From Payroll Tax Predators" in *Entrepreneur* (Vol. 32, September 2004, No. 9)
Pub: Entrepreneur Media Inc.
Ed: Stephen Barlas. **Description:** The Tax Administration Good Government Act gives the Internal Revenue Service tools to go after payroll/accounting firms that steal a client's employment tax payments, while protecting small businesses that hire the services.

54605 ■ "If You Built It" in *Entrepreneur* (Vol. 31, Oct. 2003)
Pub: Entrepreneur Media, Inc.
Ed: Joan Szabo. **Description:** A recent study conducted by PricewaterhouseCoopers, showed some fast-growth companies involved in new construction or remodels are missing out on significant tax deductions available by depreciating assets in new construction and major remodeling.

54606 ■ "Illinois Businesses Anxious about Governor's Plans on Fees, Taxes" in *Chicago Tribune* (April 11, 2003)
Pub: Knight-Ridder/Tribune Business News
Ed: John Schmeltzer. **Description:** Governor Rod Blagojevich plans to boost fees and taxes on Illinois businesses by as much as $600 million annually.

54607 ■ "Illinois Tax Scofflaws Land on New Internet List" in *Chicago Tribune* (March 2, 2005)
Pub: Knight-Ridder/Tribune Business News
Ed: Christi Parson, Ray Long. **Description:** The Illinois Department of Revenue posted delinquent taxpayers' names on the Internet hoping to embarrass the businesses and individuals into paying. Each of the 100 listed have owed more than $1,000 for the last six months or more.

54608 ■ "Impact of Personal and Situational Factors on Taxpayer Compliance" in *Journal of Business Ethics* (Vol. 47, No. 3, Oct. 15, 2003)
Pub: Kluwer Academic Publishers Group
Ed: Viswanath Umashanker Trivedi, Mohamed Shehata, Bernadette Lynn. **Description:** A study using a laboratory experiment with monetary incentives to test the impact of three personal factors (moral reasoning, value orientation and risk preference), and three situational factors (the presence/absence of audits, tax inequity, and peer reporting behavior), while controlling for the impact of other demographic characteristics, on tax compliance is presented.

54609 ■ "Income-tax cut could pause to help Detroit absorb state budget's hit" in *Crain's Detroit Business* (Dec. 9, 2002, pp. 3)
Pub: Crain Communications Inc., Detroit
Ed: Amy Lane. **Description:** The proposed rollback of Detroit city income tax is examined.

54610 ■ "Indiana Bill Would Multiply U.S. Development Tax Credit" in *American Banker* (Vol. 170, February 4, 2005, No. 24, pp. 4)
Pub: Thomson Financial Media Inc.
Ed: Ben Jackson. **Description:** Legislation is being considered for a bill that would give state tax breaks to small banks for investing in local development in Indiana. The bill is modeled after the Treasury Department's New Markets Tax Credit program. Indiana banks and thrifts whose investments qualify for the federal credit would also get state credit.

54611 ■ "Insiders' Tax Break" in *Forbes* (August 7, 2000, pp. 134)
Pub: Forbes Magazine
Ed: Ashlea Ebeling. **Description:** Reducing or eliminating capital gains taxes from stock investments using the three-year-old Section 1045 of the tax code is described.

54612 ■ "Interest Paid as an Administrative Expense" in *Journal of Accountancy* (Vol. 198, December 2004, No. 6, pp. 95)
Pub: American Institute of Certified Public Accountants
Ed: Michael H. Brown. **Description:** Tax laws regarding deductions used for interest paid by an estate are discussed.

54613 ■ "Internet Tax Won't Be Collected Anytime Soon" in *Crain's Detroit Business* (Vol. 17, No. 44, October 22, 2001, pp. 3)
Pub: Crain Communications, Inc.
Ed: Amy Lane, Brent Snavely. **Description:** The State of Michigan joins a multistate table to collect more taxes from Internet and mail-order companies, but it could be 2003 before collection begins.

54614 ■ **"IRS Agrees to Pursue Legislative Changes to Section 6103" in** *Tax Notes* **(Vol. 102, No. 3, January 19, 2004, pp. 295-298)**
Pub: Tax Notes International
Ed: Heather Bennett, Timothy Catts. **Description:** The issue of using taxpayer identification numbers in conflict with immigrations laws is examined.

54615 ■ **"IRS Boosts Enforcement Collections" in** *The Record* **(November 4, 2005)**
Pub: New Jersey Media Group
Ed: Kathleen Lynn. **Description:** The Internal Revenue Service has collected a record $47.3 billion in the last year in payments, penalties and interest payments through enforcement activities.

54616 ■ **"IRS to aid businesses, but tax code is a problem" in** *Birmingham Business Journal* **(Vol. 17, No. 22, June 2, 2000, pp. 10)**
Pub: American City Business Journals, Inc.
Ed: Ken Hoover. **Description:** The Internal Revenue Service has developed a new small business/self-employed division this year, but for many small business owners the problem is not within the agency, but within the tax code itself.

54617 ■ **"IRS Compliance Audits Will Affect 30,000 Small Businesses" in** *My Business* **(February/March 2003, pp. 19)**
Pub: My Business Magazine
Description: Tips from the Small Business Administration are listed to help small business owners when selected for National Research Program audits. The audits will help the IRS determine the level of tax compliance, ensure every taxpayer is paying a fair share, and determine new ways to catch tax cheaters.

54618 ■ **"IRS Cuts Mileage Rates for Deductions" in** *Milwaukee Journal Sentinel* **(December 6, 2005)**
Pub: Journal Sentinel, Inc.
Ed: Avrum D. Lank. **Description:** As of January 1, 2006, the Internal Revenue Service, will cut mileage rates from 48.5 cents to 44.5 cents per mile for standard mileage taxpayer rates.

54619 ■ **"IRS Errors Snag Entrepreneurs" in** *Inc.* **(October 1, 2003)**
Pub: Gruner & Jahr USA Publishing
Ed: Nadine Heintz. **Description:** Since 2001, thousands of small business owners were required to show proof of paid taxes because of an error in the Internal Revenues Service's Schedule K-1 program.

54620 ■ **"The IRS Goes Fishin'" in** *Inc.* **(July 1, 2003)**
Pub: Gruner & Jahr USA Publishing
Ed: Rod Kurtz. **Description:** Regulations governing small company's annual outings or party for employees are discussed.

54621 ■ **"IRS informants: everything you ever wanted to know about taxes" in** *Entrepreneur* **(Vol. 30, No. 12, December 2002, pp. 75)**
Pub: Entrepreneur Media Inc.
Description: Web sites offering tax information for small businesses are profiled, including the IRS site, CCH tax group site, Small Business Taxes & Management site, and Tax Planet.

54622 ■ **"IRS intent on stopping tax avoidance schemes, officials say" in** *Tax Notes* **(Vol. 96, No. 14, September 30, 2002, pp. 1833-1834)**
Pub: Tax Notes International
Ed: Fred Stokeld. **Description:** The IRS Small Business/Self-Employed Division plans to crack down on tax avoidance. The division will conduct more audits and look closely at offshore credit card accounts, tax shelters, and other methods commonly used to avoid taxes.

54623 ■ **"The IRS Wants You—Online" in** *Home Office Computing* **(Vol. 18, No. 12, December 2000, pp. 26)**
Pub: Scholastic Inc.

Ed: Jeffery D. Zbar. **Description:** Information is given regarding the Internal Revenue Service's effort to get small businesses to file tax returns online.

54624 ■ **"IRS Will Remove Tax Trap for One-Person S Corporations" in** *Kiplinger Letter* **(Vol. 82, January 12, 2007, No. 1)**
Pub: Kiplinger
Description: Internal Revenue Service is developing a new system that will clarify S corporation owners in states that are not allowed to deduct one-participant group health insurance plans, however, to get the deduction, the S firm must pay the medical premium.

54625 ■ **"Is Anyone Listening?" in** *Fortune* **(Vol. 142, No. 2, July 10, 2000, pp. 200B+)**
Pub: Time Inc.
Description: All small business owners agree that taxes are too high and complicated, health insurance is too expensive, and Washington has ignored these issues until this year. Washington seems to be learning the influence and power small businesses have in America.

54626 ■ **"Is Division of an IRA a Taxable Event?" in** *Journal of Accountancy* **(Vol. 199, February 2005, No. 2, pp. 78)**
Pub: American Institute of Certified Public Accountants
Ed: Charles J. Reichert. **Description:** Case of Cohen v. Commissioner involving the transfer of an individual retirement account (IRA) from one spouse to another due to a divorce is discussed.

54627 ■ **"Is Employer-Sponsored Health Insurance On Its Way Out?" in** *Kiplinger Letter* **(Vol. 84, January 26, 2007, No. 4)**
Pub: Kiplinger
Description: Congress is not expected to pass a bill that would count employer-provided health benefits as income, making them subject to taxes.

54628 ■ **"Is 'Equitable Remedy' Settlement Excludable from Gross Income?" in** *Journal of Accountancy* **(Vol. 198, December 2004, No. 6, pp. 94)**
Pub: American Institute of Certified Public Accountants
Description: A case testing the definition of personal physical injury or physical sickness in an equitable remedy is discussed.

54629 ■ **"It's Tax Time - Again" in** *Home Business* **(Vol. 12, March/April 2005, No. 2, pp. 76)**
Pub: Home Business Magazine
Description: A listing of tax benefits and deductions allowable for small, home-based businesses are explained.

54630 ■ *J. K. Lasser's Small Business Taxes: Your Complete Guide to a Better Bottom Line*
Pub: John Wiley & Sons, Incorporated
Ed: Barbara Weltman. **Released:** November 2004.
Price: $16.95. **Description:** Comprehensive guide providing tax strategies for any small business in the U.S. Sample forms and checklists included.

54631 ■ *JK Lasser's Small Business Taxes 2077: Your Complete Guide to a Better Bottom Line*
Pub: John Wiley & Sons, Incorporated
Ed: Barbara Weltman. **Released:** November 2006.
Price: $17.95. **Description:** J.K. Lasser's guide that offers tax facts and strategies for small businesses. The book helps to maximize deductions while learning tax planning strategies.

54632 ■ **"Just Call Him George W. Reagan" in** *Business Week Online* **(Jan. 8, 2003)**
Pub: McGraw-Hill Inc.
Ed: Joseph Weber. **Description:** President George W. Bush's new economic stimulus program is examined, focusing on the program's gains for small businesses.

54633 ■ **"Just the Tax" in** *Entrepreneur* **(Vol. 32, December 2004, No. 12, pp. 39)**
Pub: Entrepreneur Media Inc.
Ed: Jill Amadio. **Description:** Higher insurance deductibles required on leased company owned vehicles are usually allowable as tax deductions.

54634 ■ **"Keep it Simple" in** *Entrepreneur.com* **(Vol. 34, February 2006, No. 2, pp. 60)**
Pub: Entrepreneur Media Inc.
Ed: Chris Penttila. **Description:** Twenty-five tips for fine tuning a small business are outlined, focusing on technology, money, banking, taxes, credit and collection, accounting systems, mergers, management, and marketing ideas.

54635 ■ **"Kill The Estate Tax! World War I is over" in** *Time Inc.* **(Vol. 156, No. 7, August 14, 2000, pp. B20)**
Pub: Time & Life Bldg., Rockefeller Center
Ed: Daniel Kadlec. **Description:** The estate tax amounts to multiple taxation on enterprise and hard-earned savings. The estate tax was instituted, in part, to help fund World War I. The war is over.

54636 ■ **"Know the Rules" in** *Black Enterprise* **(Vol. 35, December 2004, No. 5, pp. 56)**
Pub: Earl G. Graves Publishing Co. Inc.
Ed: Arlene McKanic. **Description:** Rules and regulations governing home-based businesses have become more complex, especially tax laws. The Internal Revenue Service is unfair to home-based companies when it comes to deductions, while zoning codes create other barriers.

54637 ■ **"Lack o' tax: the return from these funds all yours" in** *Entrepreneur* **(Vol. 30, No. 3, March 2002, pp. 66)**
Pub: Entrepreneur Media Inc.
Ed: Dian Vujovich. **Description:** Profile of the Thomburg Limited Term Municipal National Bond Fund, a tax free municipal bond fund.

54638 ■ **"Lawsuit, Tax Lien Plague Post-Bankruptcy Orbcomm" in** *Washington Business Journal* **(Vol. 22, No. 9, July 4, 2003, pp. 5)**
Pub: Washington Business Journal
Ed: Roger Hughlett. **Description:** Orbcomm's post-bankruptcy battles to survive in light of the recent lawsuits and tax liens are discussed.

54639 ■ **"Layoffs, no tax hike in city's proposed budget" in** *Atlanta Business Chronicle* **(Vol. 25, No. 21, November 1, 2002, pp. 2A)**
Pub: American City Business Publications, Inc.
Ed: Sarah Rubenstein. **Description:** Atlanta Mayor, Shirley Frankin, will submit a 2003 budget to the Atlanta City Council seeking layoffs totaling a maximum of 300 employees, although tax increases will be excluded, according to Atlanta Chief Financial Officer, Rick Anderson.

54640 ■ **"Leaders Make Deal on Business Taxes" in** *Crain's Detroit Business* **(Vol. 21, November 7, 2005, No. 45, pp. 6)**
Pub: Crain Communications Inc. - Detroit
Ed: Amy Lane. **Description:** Michigan Governor Granholm, along with Republican legislators, agreed to a personal property tax relief plan for state manufacturers. The plan would provide any business moving workers or equipment into the state a single-business tax credit for 100 percent of personal-property taxes paid.

54641 ■ **"Leave It To Them: Make Sure Your Family Gets What It Needs by Including a Disclaimer Provision in Your Estate Plan" in** *Entrepreneur*
Pub: Entrepreneur Media Inc.
Ed: Scott Bernard Nelson. **Description:** With federal estate laws changing nearly every year, it is important to include a disclaimer provision when planning an estate, which would allow a couple to take advantage of the estate-tax exemption.

54642 ■ "Legislation aims to tax Internet sales" in *Crain's Detroit Business* (Vol. 19, No. 1, January 6, 2003, pp. 20)
Pub: Crain Communications Inc., Detroit
Ed: Amy Lane. Description: The State of Michigan is considering imposing a multi-state agreement that would streamline processes for collecting sales tax on Internet purchases. The Michigan Department of Treasury estimates tax losses of $273 in the current fiscal year.

54643 ■ "Legislature considers energy tax breaks" in *Crain's Detroit Business* (Vol. 18, No. 16, April 22, 2002, pp. 23)
Pub: Crain Communications Inc. - Detroit
Ed: Amy Lane. Description: New corporate tax breaks for alternative energy technologies could head for Michigan's State Legislature soon.

54644 ■ "A less taxing bite on small business" in *Black Enterprise* (Vol. 33, No. 6, January 2003, pp. 38)
Pub: Earl Graves Publishing Co.
Ed: Bridget McCrea. Description: Tax changes for 2002 and strategies for small businesses are outlined, including retirement accounts, depreciation allowances, company car write-off, and healthcare costs. Web sites offering tax resources are included.

54645 ■ "A Less Taxing Way to Invest" in *Black Enterprise* (Vol. 35, December 2004, No. 5, pp. 48)
Pub: Earl G. Graves Publishing Co. Inc.
Ed: Donald Jay Korn. Description: Long-term municipal bond funds are an attractive means for investors looking to increase their portfolio's yield. If these bonds are held in a taxable account rather than a tax-deferred retirement plan, taxes must be paid.

54646 ■ "Let It Roll: Reginald Bowser Bends Over Backward to Create Convenient 401(k) Transfers" in *Black Enterprise* (Vol. 34, December 2003)
Pub: Earl Graves Publishing Co.
Ed: Marcia A. Wade. Description: Profile of Rollover-Systems Inc., provides job changers a free and easy service to reallocate 401(k) investments to a tax-deferred IRA in less than 25 minutes.

54647 ■ "Let Them Eat Cake: When It Comes to Small Business, a New Tax-Cut Bill is Half-Baked" in *Entrepreneur* (Vol. 32, November 2004)
Pub: Entrepreneur Media Inc.
Ed: Stephen Barlas. Description: New tax incentives for U.S. manufacturers are discussed.

54648 ■ "LMSB Deputy Commissioner stresses fairness for taxpayers" in *Journal of Accountancy* (Vol. 190, No. 4, October 2000, pp. 113)
Pub: Harborside Financial Center
Description: An interview with Deborah M. Nolan, IRS Deputy Commissioner of the Large and Mid-Size Business (LMSB) division. Ms. Nolan spoke of the service's strategic goals that would make filing tax returns easier and increase fairness of compliance enforcement.

54649 ■ "Loss-Limit Repeal May be Tied to Tax Boost" in *Kansas City Star* (March 8, 2005)
Pub: Knight-Ridder/Tribune Business News
Ed: Rick Alm. Description: The repeal of Missouri's $500 loss limit for casino gamblers is debated.

54650 ■ "Maine Fishermen Welcome Amendment to Preserve Wharf Tax Rates" in *Portland Press Herald* (November 10, 2005)
Pub: Blethen Maine Newspapers, Inc.
Ed: Dennis Hoey. Description: Maine voters overwhelmingly approved a constitutional amendment that allows waterfront land use for commercial fishing activities to remain at its current tax rate.

54651 ■ "Maine Says Flooring Companies Need to Pay Subcontractor Taxes" in *Portland Press Herald* (April 8, 2005)
Pub: Blethen Maine Newspapers, Inc.
Ed: Matt Wickenheiser. Description: Maine has determined that floor covering firms using subcontractors should be required to pay unemployment taxes on their wages. Guidelines for the state's ABC Test for unemployment taxes are covered.

54652 ■ "Make Driving Less Taxing" in *My Business* (April/May 2003, pp. 10)
Pub: My Business Magazine
Ed: Alan Breznick. Description: Entrepreneurs can deduct up to $25,000 of a Sport Utility Vehicle's purchase price from income taxes if the SUV is heavy enough and as long as it is used mainly for business.

54653 ■ *Make Sure It's Deductible*
Pub: McGraw-Hill Inc.
Ed: Evelyn Jacks. Released: November 2006. Price: $22.95. Description: Tax planning, strategies are provided to help small businesses maximize deductions.

54654 ■ "Make Sure You Take Advantage of the Repatriation Tax Break Just Like the Big Boys" in *Inc.* (April 1, 2005)
Pub: Inc. Magazine
Ed: Stephanie Clifford. Description: Small companies are included in the American Job Creation Act of 2004. The Act drops the usual 35 percent rate to 5.25 percent to U.S. companies returning overseas profits to the U.S. and requires companies to invest the returned profit into their U.S. operations.

54655 ■ *Make Your Life Tax Deductible: Easy Techniques to Reduce Your Taxes and Start Building Wealth Immediately*
Pub: McGraw-Hill Companies
Ed: David Meier. Released: December 2005. Price: $16.95 (US), $22.95 (Canadian). Description: Over 150 tax deductions are listed to help small business owners lower taxes and boost profits.

54656 ■ "Making the Grade" in *Hispanic Business* (March 2004, pp. 51)
Pub: Hispanic Business
Ed: Milton Zall. Description: Tax codes can help save for college education, using Coverdell accounts, prepaid and state plans, Hope Scholarship Tax Credit, lifetime learning tax credit, or deductible interest.

54657 ■ "Many happy returns" in *WorkingWoman* (Vol. 25, No. 2, February 2000, pp. S8)
Pub: Lang Communications Inc.
Ed: Rebecca Reisner. Description: Questions regarding income tax return preparation, including personal income tax exemptions and home office expense deductions, are answered.

54658 ■ "Massachusetts House Plan Seeks More Excise Tax for Newer Cars" in *Boston Globe* (April 11, 2003)
Pub: Knight-Ridder/Tribune Business News
Ed: Rick Klein. Description: Issues regarding Massachusetts auto excise tax are reviewed.

54659 ■ *Mergers and Acquisitions from A to Z*
Pub: Amacom
Ed: Andrew J. Sherman, Milledge A. Hart. Released: December 2005. Price: $47.00. Description: Guide for the entire process of mergers and acquisitions, including taxes, accounting, laws, and projected financial gain.

54660 ■ "The Mini-K Advantage" in *Rough Notes* (Vol. 144, No. 12, December 2001, pp. 80)
Pub: Rough Notes
Description: Information about the new tax laws that benefit small business 401(k) retirement plans is given. Under the new tax laws, an individual making $100,000 per year can contribute $28,000 to a 401(k) plan.

54661 ■ "Mixed Grill: A Quarter's Menu: Good-and Some Bad—News" in *Barron's* (July 7, 2003, pp. 22)
Pub: Barron's
Ed: Shirley A. Lazo. Description: Nearly one hundred companies reported dividend increases in June 2003, up 10 percent from 2002, reflecting the influence of reduced taxes on certain corporate dividends. A corresponding and irregular increase in cutback is the negative counter to this trend.

54662 ■ "Money Corner" in *Home Business* (Vol. 13, January/February 2006, No. 1, pp. 78)
Pub: Home Business Magazine
Description: Small Business Administration loans, retirement information, small business taxes, and Valentine's Day gift-buying tips are included.

54663 ■ "Money-Preneuring" in *Small Business Opportunities* (Vol. 17, September 2005, No. 5, pp. 68, 128)
Pub: Harris Publications Inc.
Ed: Robert A. Adelson. Description: Three strategies to give non-family executives a share in the rewards of ownership without transferring any company stock are shared: offering a non-voting stock plan, a non-qualified deferred compensation plan, or a phantom stock plan.

54664 ■ "Money strategies: What to know about multi-state taxation" in *Atlanta Business Chronicle* (Vol. 25, No. 22, November 8, 2002, pp. 6B)
Pub: American City Business Publications, Inc.
Ed: Dan Kolber. Description: Businesses seeking efforts in other states are urged to be aware of taxation policies. A vast majority of states, including Georgia, place a variety of income taxes on firms conducting business in their state.

54665 ■ "More Tool-and-Die Firms to Get Tax Relief" in *Crain's Detroit Business* (Vol. 22, January 2, 2006, No. 1, pp. 20)
Pub: Crain Communications Inc. - Detroit
Ed: Amy Lane. Description: Under a new state law, Michigan tool-and-die firms will be able to take advantage of tax breaks.

54666 ■ "MSA Withdrawals: Rules on Tax Exclusion" in *Employee Benefit Plan Review* (Vol. 55, No. 12, June 2001, pp. 8)
Pub: Charles D. Spencer & Associates, Inc.
Description: Questions and answers focus on Cobra rules and tax rules for employee health plans. Employees are advised that they may pay medical bills by using an employer's medical savings account, which are known as Archer MSAs.

54667 ■ "National Association for the Exchange of Industrial Resources" in *Entrepreneur* (Vol. 33, August 2005, No. 8, pp. 4)
Pub: Entrepreneur Media Inc.
Ed: Steve Cooper. Description: The National Association for the Exchange of Industrial Resources assists U.S. businesses in the donation of excess inventory to the ill, needy or minors. These donations earn federal income tax deductions.

54668 ■ "The need for more, not less, quicker, not slower tax guidance" in *Tax Executive* (Vol. 52, No. 4, July 2000, pp. 323)
Pub: Tax Executives Institute, Inc.
Description: A copy of the letter the Tax Executives Institute sent to the U.S. House of Representatives regarding H.R. 1882, The Small Business Review Panel Technical Amendments Act, stating the reasons they oppose the application of the Regulatory Flexibility Act to the IRS.

54669 ■ "New Burdens on Home Builders Hurt Local Government" in *Atlanta Business Chronicle* (Vol. 25, December 6, 2002, No. 26, pp. 38A)
Pub: American City Business Publications, Inc.
Ed: Mark Fitzgerald. Description: Delays in permits for housing projects in Atlanta, Georgia, might add a substantial amount to the cost of a home; the problem also results in the delay of tax dollars being collected.

54670 ■ "New Congress may give business some gains" in *Atlanta Business Chronicle* (Vol. 25, November 15, 2002, No. 23 pp. 7A)
Pub: American City Business Publications, Inc.
Ed: Kent Hoover. **Description:** Various issues are being considered by Congress, including tax cuts and health care reform.

54671 ■ "New Law Offers Tax Relief for Individuals - But Only Temporarily" in *Practical Tax Strategies* (Vol. 67, No. 1, July 2001, pp. 30)
Pub: Warren, Gorham and Lamont
Ed: Robert E. Ward. **Description:** The author examines the Economic Growth and Tax Relief Reconciliation Act of 2001 and the tax benefits it offers individuals.

54672 ■ "New Law Significantly Alters Retirement Plan Landscape" in *Warren, Gorham and Lamont* (Vol. 67, No. 1, July 2001, pp. 36)
Pub: Warren, Gorham and Lamont
Ed: Barry Salkin. **Description:** The author examines the retirement planning effects, especially in regards to employee benefits and pension funds, of the Economic Growth and Tax Relief Reconciliation Act of 2001.

54673 ■ "New Laws Take On Delaware Subsidiaries" in *Inc.* (January 1, 2005)
Pub: Inc. Magazine
Ed: Lora Kolodny. **Description:** New York Tax Courts have imposed taxes on revenue derived from intellectual property.

54674 ■ "The New Roth 401(k)" in *Black Enterprise* (Vol. 36, December 2005, No. 5, pp. 50)
Pub: Earl G. Graves Publishing Co. Inc.
Ed: Rene Brinkley. **Description:** Both Roth IRA and the Roth 401(k) plans will allow workers to save money for retirement after taxes have been paid and pay no taxes on the money invested when withdrawn from the account in retirement. Suggestions are made for determining the use of a 401(k) versus a Roth 401(k).

54675 ■ "New Year, New Laws" in *Inc.* (Volume 28, January 2006, No. 1, pp. 24)
Pub: Inc. Magazine
Description: An entrepreneur's guide to new state policies taking effect in 2006, along with their positive, negative, mixed and uncertain impacts.

54676 ■ "Newsstand" in *Home Business* (Vol. 12, October 2005, No. 5, pp. 38-39)
Pub: Home Business Magazine
Description: Various topics are covered, including information about home-based business tax deductions, the link between home computers and entrepreneurship, income gaps, demographics of home-based business owners, creation of more home-based businesses due to merger-related job cuts, and frivolous lawsuits against home-based entrepreneurs.

54677 ■ "NFIB Building on Tax Cut Victory for Members" in *My Business* (September/October 2001, pp. 18)
Pub: My Business Magazine
Description: President Bush's tax refund will benefit small business in two ways: it returns money back to small business owners while giving the economy a needed boost.

54678 ■ "No Escape? Even the Internet May Not Be Able to Avoid Taxes" in *Entrepreneur* (Vol. 31, No. 4, April 2003, pp. 17)
Pub: Entrepreneur Media Inc.
Ed: Amanda C. Kooser. **Description:** The topic of taxation on the Internet is discussed.

54679 ■ "No Refuge" in *Entrepreneur* (Vol. 33, October 2005, No. 10, pp. 56)
Pub: Entrepreneur Media Inc.
Ed: Joan Szabo. **Description:** The American Jobs Creation Act of 2004 is examined. Under the new rules taxpayers must file annual informational returns (IRS Form 8886) to disclose every reportable transaction or tax shelter in which they are involved.

54680 ■ "Norquist Sees Antitax Crusade as Cornerstone of GOP Domination" in *Tax Notes* (Vol. 102, No. 3, January 19, 2004, pp. 307-317)
Pub: Tax Notes International
Ed: Warren Rojas. **Description:** In an interview with Americans for Tax Reform leader, Grover Glenn Norquist, he suggests that tax relief will be an asset for the Republican Party.

54681 ■ "A not-so-taxing CHANGE" in *Pittsburgh Business Times* (Vol. 20, No. 53, July 20, 2001, pp. 25)
Pub: Pittsburgh Business Times
Ed: Tracy Carbasho. **Description:** The Reconciliation Act features changes in four areas: updated 401(k) contribution schedule, increased employer contribution limits, shortened vesting schedule, and added 401(k) options.

54682 ■ "Now You See It: Payroll Tax is Likely the Tax You Most Want to Have Cut, But Will It Ever Happen?" in *Entrepreneur* (Vol. 31, Aug.2003)
Pub: Entrepreneur Media, Inc.
Ed: Chris Penttila. **Description:** Payroll taxes make up 34.9 percent of federal revenues and are expected to grow to 36.3 by 2004, thus making it the least-likely tax cut Americans will see take place.

54683 ■ "NYC Eyes Taxes on 'Luxury' Items" in *Long Island Business News* (February 20, 2004)
Pub: Dolan Media Newswires
Ed: Ben Abelson. **Description:** New York City's Independent Budget Office is proposing a new luxury tax of items such as cosmetic surgery, specialty coffee drinks, as well as reinstating fares on the Staten Island ferry.

54684 ■ "Officials discuss deferred comp, guidance and legislation for EOs" in *Tax Notes* (Vol. 96, No. 13, September 23, 2002, pp. 1693-1697)
Pub: Tax Notes International
Ed: Fred Stokeld, J. Christine Harris. **Description:** At an SBA conference, government officials discussed tax issues relating to employee benefits of nonprofit organizations and government entities.

54685 ■ "Ohio Investment Tax Credit Struck Down" in *Journal of Accountancy* (Vol. 199, January 2005, No. 1, pp. 76)
Pub: American Institute of Certified Public Accountants
Ed: Laura Lee Mannino. **Description:** It is important for small businesses to fully understand any tax credits offered by states designed to lure new business to their state.

54686 ■ "Oklahoma-Based Company to Renovate Rancho Cordova, Calif., Tax Board Buildings" in *Sacramento Bee* (December 28, 2005)
Pub: The Sacramento Bee
Ed: Andrew McIntosh. **Description:** The Franchise Tax Board is renovating two office buildings in the Rancho Cordova complex. The buildings will be used to store tax files.

54687 ■ "An old-fashioned fate: it takes the tax collector to really ruin somebody" in *Barron's* (Vol. 82, No. 58, February 17, 2003, pp. 31)
Pub: Barron's
Ed: Thomas G. Donlan. **Description:** Former Sprint CEO, William T. Esprey, was doubly unethical in formulating the tax evasion scam that ruined him; he also leaned on the company auditors, Ernst & Young, to form an illicit tax shelter.

54688 ■ "Operation no safe haven: there's $400 billion in unregulated money stashed in offshore hedge accounts" in *Red Herring* (Jan. 2003)
Pub: Herring Communications Inc.
Ed: Christopher Byron. **Description:** Offshore hedge funds provide an end run around the crackdown on U.S. companies. These accounts allow money to be moved anonymously in and out of the U.S. without going through a U.S. bank.

54689 ■ "Opinion" in *Crain's Detroit Business* (Vol. 21, February 7, 2005, No. 6, pp. 8)
Pub: Crain Communications Inc. - Detroit
Description: Information regarding the state of Michigan's legislation that would close a tax loophole for companies trying to beat the State Unemployment Tax Act is given. Detroit Tigers organization may have secretly help halt plans for an independent baseball team to move to Troy, Michigan.

54690 ■ "Out with the bad, in with the good" in *Entrepreneur* (Vol. 30, No. 12, December 2002, pp. 83)
Pub: Entrepreneur Media Inc.
Ed: Joan Szabo. **Description:** Investigation into the last-in, first-out method of inventory accounting and the first-in, first-out method are explained, along with their potential tax impact.

54691 ■ "Pa. comes in at No. 24 in small business study" in *Philadelphia Business Journal* (Vol. 19, No. 36, October 13, 2000, pp. 6)
Pub: Philadelphia Business Journal
Ed: Natalie Kostelni. **Description:** As a consequence of its high tax rates, Pennsylvania ranked 24th among the 50 states and the District of Columbia in the latest survey of the state's small business climate.

54692 ■ "Package deal" in *Entrepreneur* (Vol. 31, No. 4, April 2003, pp. 22)
Pub: Entrepreneur Media Inc.
Ed: Stephen Barlas. **Description:** The new economic stimulus package proposed by President George W. Bush would increase the annual allowance for expensing of capital investments from $25,000 to $75,000 for small businesses, and tie the ceiling in the future to inflation.

54693 ■ "Panel on taxing Internet sales ends its meetings in disagreement" in *The New York Times* (March 22, 2000, pp. D28, H28)
Pub: The New York Times Company
Ed: David Cay Johnston. **Description:** The meeting of the 19 member Advisory Commission on Electronic Commerce agreed on every issue but one for extending sales taxes to Internet businesses. The panel couldn't agree on whether businesses that have sales personnel in a state and sell over the Internet should pay sales tax. The commission members seemed to fall into three groups: five against taxation, six business representatives, and eight from various government offices. The panel's report moves to Congress without a recommendation.

54694 ■ "Papers Away: Tax Records Weighing You Down? Switch to Electronic Storage" in *Entrepreneur* (Vol. 32, October 2004, No. 10, pp. 60)
Pub: Entrepreneur Media Inc.
Ed: Joan Szabo. **Description:** Electronic tax records allow a small business to electronically store the documents involved in tax preparation. The method not only saves times, but also cuts expenses on paper and office space, improves security and access to documents.

54695 ■ "Passing Marks?" in *Entrepreneur* (Vol. 31, No. 11, November 2003, pp. 70)
Pub: Entrepreneur Media, Inc.
Ed: Joan Szabo. **Description:** Information on the Regulatory Flexibility Act (RFA) is presented. The RFA is a law designed to make sure federal agencies address the needs of small business when issuing rules and regulations.

54696 ■ "Paying the piper for Internet access" in *Red Herring* (No. 105, October 1, 2001, pp. 38)
Pub: Herring Communications
Ed: Tim Jackson. **Description:** Issues regarding Internet taxing are explored.

54697 ■ "Paying for Your Mistakes: Are You Overlooking Allowable Deductions in Your Business?" in *My Business* (February/March 2003, pp. 43)
Pub: My Business Magazine
Ed: Nancy Mann Jackson. **Description:** Most small business owners end up paying more in taxes because they overlook allowable deductions.

54698 ■ "Payroll Piggy Bank?" in *Entrepreneur* (Vol. 31, No. 9, September 2003, pp. 61)
Pub: Entrepreneur Media, Inc.
Ed: Joan Szabo. **Description:** Borrowing money withheld from employee paychecks to pay federal income, social security and Medicare taxes, as well as state and local taxes, is illegal and should never be considered.

54699 ■ "The PCAOB and the Future of Oversight" in *Journal Of Accountancy*
Pub: American Institute of Certified Public Accountants
Ed: Patrick J. McDonnell. **Description:** Review of the Sarbanes-Oxley Act of 2002 created by the Public Company Accounting Oversight Board (PCAOB) is presented. The role of the PCAOB is discussed.

54700 ■ "Pennsylvania Governor Says Business Taxes May Aid City of Pittsburgh Bailout" in *Pittsburgh Post-Gazette* (April 11, 2003)
Pub: Knight-Ridder/Tribune Business News
Ed: Johanna A. Pro. **Description:** According to Pennsylvania Governor Ed Rendell, a new plan to save the City of Pittsburgh from financial disaster could include a new tax on business.

54701 ■ "Pension Reform Enhances Sponsored Retirement Plans" in *San Diego Business Journal* (Vol. 22, No. 41, October 8, 2001, pp. 16)
Pub: San Diego Business Journal
Ed: Laura Just. **Description:** A listing of the new pension revisions effective in 2002 by the Economic Growth and Tax Relief Reconciliation Act of 2001 are presented.

54702 ■ "Pharmacies Fight Mail-Order Purchases, Medicaid Tax" in *Crain's Detroit Business* (Vol. 19, No. 43, October 27, 2003, pp. 6)
Pub: Crain Communications Inc., Detroit
Description: Michigan legislators are debating a bill that would restrict mail-order drug purchases for unions, businesses and health plans, as well as imposing a self-assessment tax in Medicaid reimbursement.

54703 ■ "Plan would gut MEDC to fund scholarships" in *Crain's Detroit Business* (Vol. 19, No. 14, April 7, 2003, pp. 1)
Pub: Crain Communications Inc., Detroit
Ed: Robert Ankeny. **Description:** The Michigan Economic Development Corporation could lose operating money if the House Republican proposal to cut $59 million from the business-attraction agency passes; the funds would be shifted to fully restore merit-scholarship funding in the 2004 state budget.

54704 ■ "Pocketbook Issues: The 2000 election brings some of small business's biggest issues to the forefront" in *Time Inc.* (Vol.155, May 2000)
Pub: Time & Life Bldg., Rockefeller Center
Ed: Edward Robinson. **Description:** For the first time in years, the nation's 25 million small business owners feel they have a stake in the election outcome.

54705 ■ "Port Adopts 2007 Strategic Budget" in *Bellingham Business Journal* (December 2006, pp. A3)
Pub: Sun News Inc.
Description: 2007 Strategic Budget adopted by the Port of Bellingham Board of Commissioners projects a 5 percent growth of operating revenues and no increase in the number of port employees. The entire Strategic Budget will be available on the Web at portofbellingham.com.

54706 ■ "Postage unpaid" in *Entrepreneur* (Vol. 30, No. 12, December 2002, pp. 77)
Pub: Entrepreneur Media Inc.
Description: The increasing use of electronic tax filing, known as the Electronic Federal Tax Payment System (EFTPS), is examined.

54707 ■ *PPC's Small Business Tax Guide*
Pub: Practitioners Publishing Company
Ed: Douglas L. Weinbrenner, Virginia R. Bergman, Toni M. Greenwall, James A. Keller, Scott Mayfield, Linda A. Markwood. **Released:** January 2005. **Price:** $135.00. **Description:** Business tax laws are covered in an easy to understand format.

54708 ■ *PPC's Small Business Tax Guide, Vol. 2*
Pub: Practitioners Publishing Company
Ed: Douglas L. Weinbrenner, Virginia R. Bergman, Toni M. Greenwall, James A. Keller, Scott Mayfield, Linda A. Markwood. **Released:** January 2005. **Price:** $135.00. **Description:** Second volume containing technical guide covering business tax laws.

54709 ■ "President signs tax cut bill with pension reform" in *Employee Benefit Plan Review* (Vol. 56, No. 1, July 2001, pp. 10)
Pub: Charles D. Spencer & Associates, Inc.
Description: President George W. Bush signed the Economic Growth and Tax Relief Reconciliation Act of 2001. Changes in the pension law were made in vesting provisions and compensation limits.

54710 ■ *Principles of Private Firm Valuation*
Pub: John Wiley & Sons, Incorporated
Ed: Stanley J. Feldman. **Released:** April 2005. **Price:** $79.95 (US), $115.99 (Canadian). **Description:** Tools and techniques to correctly perform private firm valuation, including value and how to measure it, valuing control, determining the size of the marketability discount, creating transparency and the implications for value, the value of tax pass-through entities versus a C corporation, etc.

54711 ■ "The Producers: Fixed Payouts Mimic Yield. But Will the Hit Keep Playing?" in *Barron's* (August 25, 2003, pp. F2)
Pub: Barron's
Ed: Erin E. Arvedlund. **Description:** New tax rules that punish investors in mutual funds with fixed payout schemes are prompting managers such as Martin E. Zweig to consider pulling out of the closed-end sector.

54712 ■ "Profit Globally, Give Globally" in *Harvard Business Review* (Vol. 81, No. 12, December 2003, pp. 16)
Pub: Harvard Business School Press
Ed: John Quelch, V. Kasturi Rangan. **Description:** An overview of ways corporations can and should increase non-domestic philanthropic aid is presented. Topics include sensitivity and diplomacy involved in international economic relations, and issues such as tax breaks and local law.

54713 ■ "Profit or Paycheck?" in *Hispanic Business* (June 2002, pp. 96)
Pub: Hispanic Business
Ed: Milton Zall. **Description:** There are two factors to consider when determining the salary of an owner-employee. The first is whether the corporation can accumulate earnings without a tax penalty and the second whether the IRS will disallow deductions on an owner's salary increase. A table showing owner taxes vs. corporate taxes is presented.

54714 ■ "Property Tax Woes Hit Indiana" in *Inc.* (October 1, 2004)
Pub: Inc. Magazine
Ed: Burt Helm. **Description:** Property tax hikes in Indiana have resulted in higher taxes for many entrepreneurs.

54715 ■ "Q&A" in *Home Office Computing* (Vol. 19, No. 1, January 2001, pp. 17)
Pub: Scholastic Inc.
Ed: Marilyn Zelinsky Syarto. **Description:** Are you excited or nervous about the new law that makes electronic signatures legal? Bill Brice, CEO of AlphaTrust, a Dallas-based electronic signature provider, discusses the nuts and bolts of using a digital ID.

54716 ■ "Qualified state tuition programs: EGTRRA update" in *The Tax Adviser* (Vol. 32, No. 10, October 2001, pp. 672)
Pub: Harborside Financial Center
Ed: Philip E. Moore. **Description:** The impact that the Economic Growth and Tax Relief Reconciliation Act (EGTRRA) will have on qualified state tuition programs (Sec. 529 plans) is discussed. The new law, will most likely, make Sec. 29 plans more popular.

54717 ■ *QuickBooks Simple Start for Dummies*
Pub: John Wiley & Sons, Incorporated
Ed: Stephen L. Nelson. **Released:** September 2004. **Price:** $28.99. **Description:** Profile of Intuits new accounting software geared to micro businesses. Advice is offered on daily, monthly, and yearly accounting activities covering records, sales tax, and reports.

54718 ■ *QuickBooks X for Dummies*
Pub: John Wiley & Sons, Incorporated
Ed: Stephen L. Nelson. **Released:** November 2006. **Price:** $21.99. **Description:** Key features of QuickBooks software for small business are introduced. Invoicing and credit memos, recoding sales receipts, accounting, budgeting, taxes, payroll, financial reports, job estimating, billing, tracking, data backup, are among the features.

54719 ■ "Remember The Nanny Tax? Now It's the Granny Tax" in *Fortune* (Vol. 141, No. 1, January 10, 2000, pp. 218)
Pub: Time Inc.
Ed: Carolyn T. Geer. **Description:** Determining when taxes are due for people who provide elder care are investigated. The tax that shook up the nanny world threatens those who employ home health-care workers.

54720 ■ "Renewed Effort for Reintroduced Rural Credit Bill" in *American Banker* (Vol. 170, February 2, 2005, No. 22, pp. 5)
Pub: Thomson Financial Media Inc.
Ed: Ben Jackson. **Description:** Rural Economic Invest Act was reintroduced at the end of January 2005. The bill gives banks and thrifts tax breaks for lending in rural areas.

54721 ■ "Republican Leaders Push More SBT Cuts" in *Crain's Detroit Business* (Vol. 21, December 19, 2005, No. 51, pp. 6)
Pub: Crain Communications Inc. - Detroit
Ed: Amy Lane. **Description:** Lawmakers are pushing for small business tax relief and a single-business tax rate cut.

54722 ■ "Resources: Web Sites, Organizations, Events and More To Grow Your Business" in *Entrepreneur* (Vol. 32, September 2004, No. 9, pp. 8)
Pub: Entrepreneur Media Inc.
Ed: Steve Cooper. **Description:** Resources to help small business are featured including the Small Business Administration's effort to help teen entrepreneurs launch a business; KnockNow an online community of entrepreneurs, executives, venture capitalists, angel investors, service sector companies, and government; the SBA's business Website offering information on small business development, financial assistance, taxes, laws and regulations, international trade, workplace issues, buying and selling and federal forms.

54723 ■ "Restaurants Watch Helplessly As Wait Staff Applications Dry Up" in *Bradenton Herald* (January 31, 2005)
Pub: Bradenton Herald
Ed: Tilde Herrera. **Description:** Restaurant owners in the Bradenton area are having difficulty hiring professional wait staff. Sean Murphy, owner of Beach Bistro and Mangrove Grill, believes waiting tables has become less attractive because of the tip reporting system used by the Internal Revenue Service.

54724 ■ "Revamped Retiring Plans" in *My Business* (April/May 2002, pp. 15)
Pub: My Business Magazine

Ed: Milt Zall. **Description:** Tax legislation signed into law by President Bush in 2001 made significant changes to retirement plans, including loans allowed, limit on annual additions raised, employer's tax deduction increase, increased limit for defined benefit plans, increased compensation limits, and small business tax credits.

54725 ■ "Revenue-Raising Ideas Could Hit Financial Services" in *American Banker* **(Vol. 170, February 2, 2005, No. 22, pp. 4)**
Pub: Thomson Financial Media Inc.
Ed: Hannah Bergman. **Description:** Proposed government tax regulations could affect the banking industry directly, including the elimination of deducting interest on home equity loans and requiring users of a tax shelter to prove that it has another economic benefit.

54726 ■ "Right Place, Right Time; Small Businesses Aren't Just Surviving." in *Business Week* **(No. 3853, Oct. 13, 2003, pp. 82)**
Pub: McGraw-Hill Inc.
Ed: Peter Coy. **Description:** Small business is becoming a strong force in the economy, especially since the Bush tax-cut program helps small companies.

54727 ■ "A Road Less Taxed" in *My Business* **(February/March 2004, pp. 40)**
Pub: My Business Magazine
Ed: Karen M. Kroll. **Description:** An explanation of the most common business structures and the ways taxes are generated for each is presented, including sole proprietorship, partnership, Limited Liability Corporation, S corporation, and C corporation.

54728 ■ "Robert Wagner Hosts The Litigation Explosion" in *Entrepreneur* **(Vol. 33, January 2005, No. 1, pp. 104)**
Pub: Entrepreneur Media Inc.
Description: The rewards of high income and owning your own business as a consultant providing asset protection, financial privacy and tax reduction are highlighted.

54729 ■ "Romney, Businesses Wrangle On 'Loopholes'" in *Boston Globe* **(January 31, 2005)**
Pub: New York Times Company
Description: Governor Mitt Romney is working to create business-friendly policies to create jobs in Massachusetts. So far, an estimated $210 million has been collected by closing corporate tax loopholes.

54730 ■ "The Roots of a Home" in *Crain's Detroit Business* **(Vol. 22, February 6, 2006, No. 6, pp. 19)**
Pub: Crain Communications Inc. - Detroit
Ed: Constance Crump. **Description:** Researching a home's history can add value as well as qualify the homeowner for tax credits when renovating.

54731 ■ "Ruling on Tax Incentives May Head to High Court" in *Crain's Detroit Business* **(Vol. 21, January 31, 2005, No. 5, pp. 33)**
Pub: Crain Communications Inc. - Detroit
Ed: Amy Lane. **Description:** A legal dispute in Ohio could have an impact of Michigan's main business-tax incentive, the Michigan Economic Growth Authority program whereby Michigan grants single-business-tax credits for incentives for corporate investment.

54732 ■ "Sarbanes-Oxley: A Guide for Venture Capitalists" in *Venture Capital Journal* **(November 1, 2004)**
Pub: Thomason Financial Inc.
Description: An overview of the Sarbanes Oxley Act (SOX) and how it relates to venture capitalists is presented. SOX is legislation passed by Congress in 2002 to deter and punish corporate accounting fraud and corruption.

54733 ■ *Sarbanes-Oxley for Small Businesses: Leveraging Compliance for Maximum Advantage*
Pub: John Wiley & Sons, Incorporated

Ed: Peggy M. Jackson. **Released:** November 2006. **Price:** $39.95. **Description:** Book lists five ways the Sarbane Oxley Act helps small businesses.

54734 ■ *Save $2000 to $8000 in Taxes with a Home-Based Business*
Pub: TKG Publishing
Ed: Greco Garcia. **Released:** February 2007. **Price:** $16.99. **Description:** Tax advice for a home-based business is given.

54735 ■ "Saving Will Get Sweeter" in *Kiplinger's Personal Finance Magazine* **(Vol. 54, No. 12, January, 2001, pp. 25)**
Pub: The Kiplinger Washington Editors, Inc.
Ed: Melynda Dovel Wilcox. **Description:** Watch for big changes to retirement plans that are aimed at attracting more employers and workers.

54736 ■ *Schaum's Outline Financial Management, Third Edition*
Pub: McGraw-Hill
Ed: Jae K. Shim; Joel G. Siegel. **Released:** May 2007. **Price:** $22.95 (CND). **Description:** Rules and regulations governing corporate finance, including the Sarbanes-Oxley Act are discussed.

54737 ■ "School Overcrowding Concerns Businesses" in *Bradenton Herald* **(February 11, 2005)**
Pub: Bradenton Herald
Ed: Description: Small businesses in the Lakewood Ranch district are worried that school overcrowding will discourage prospective employees from moving to the area. A Manatee County commissioner addressed the Lakewood Ranch Business Alliance discussing possible tax increases to help remedy the situation.

54738 ■ "Second Chance" in *Entrepreneur* **(Vol. 33, September 2005, No. 9, pp. 58)**
Pub: Entrepreneur Media Inc.
Ed: Joan Szabo. **Description:** The Streamlined Sales Tax Project (SSTP), if passed, would simplify and modernize sales and use tax collection and administration. An outline of the program is included.

54739 ■ "The Second-Home Tax Shelter" in *Hispanic Business* **(December 2002, pp. 56)**
Pub: Hispanic Business
Ed: Milton Zall. **Description:** Vacation homes rank as the number one status symbol in the U.S., according to American Demographics. The implications involved in owning a second home are discussed.

54740 ■ *The Secret of Exiting Your Business Under Your Terms!*
Pub: Outskirts Press, Incorporated
Ed: Gene H. Irwin. **Released:** August 2005. **Price:** $29.95. **Description:** Topics include how to sell a business for the highest value, tax laws governing the sale of a business, finding the right buyer, mergers and acquisitions, negotiating the sale, and using a limited auction to increase future value of a business.

54741 ■ "Section 404 Compliance in the Annual Report" in *Journal of Accountancy*
Pub: American Institute of Certified Public Accountants
Ed: Michael Ramos. **Description:** Most publicly traded companies in the U.S. will be required to comply with SEC rules by reporting the effectiveness of internal controls in the annual report. The content required in this report is covered.

54742 ■ "Senate Finance Committee tries to codify economic substance doctrine" in *Tax Notes* **(Vol. 96, No. 13, Sept. 23, 2002, pp. 1665-1667)**
Pub: Tax Notes International
Ed: Patti Mohr. **Description:** The Small Business and Farm Economic Recovery Act, a draft bill in the U.S. Senate Finance Committee, would provide tax breaks for small businesses and farms. It would be funded by a codification of the 'economic substance' doctrine governing business transactions resulting in tax savings.

54743 ■ "Senate votes to ease effect of high SBT bills" in *Crain's Detroit Business* **(Vol. 18, No. 49, December 9, 2002, pp. 6)**
Pub: Crain Communications Inc., Detroit
Ed: Amy Lane. **Description:** Information about the new single-business tax and certificate-of-need legislation is presented

54744 ■ "Senate Targets Payroll Tax Scam" in *Inc.* **(August 1, 2004)**
Pub: Inc. Magazine
Ed: Nadine Heintz. **Description:** Roger Cyr, owner of Lily Moon Cafe in Saco, Maine alleges that his payroll tax accountant stole tax payments from dozens of companies, including his own.

54745 ■ "Senators Call for Small-Biz Refunds" in *Inc.* **(August 1, 2003)**
Pub: Gruner & Jahr USA Publishing
Ed: Nadine Heintz. **Description:** Small businesses may be eligible for a refund of alternative minimum taxes paid. Statistical data included.

54746 ■ "Servicing Pitfalls: How To Avoid Having Your REMIC Disqualified" in *Banking & Financial Services Policy Report* **(Vol. 23, August 2004)**
Pub: Aspen Publishers Inc.
Ed: William M. O'Connor, Robert L. Bourguignon. **Description:** An overview of a real estate mortgage investment conduit (REMIC) is presented. The REMIC is part of the federal tax code that encourages investment in commercial real estate.

54747 ■ "Shrinking Surplus: George W. Bush, technology CEO?" in *Red Herring* **(No. 105, October 1, 2001, pp. 88-89)**
Pub: Herring Communications
Ed: J.P. Vicente. **Description:** Due to the deterioration in corporate profits, the U.S. is facing the largest quarterly drop in tax payments since 1992. Statistical data included.

54748 ■ *A Simplified Guide to Small Business Tax Deductions*
Pub: Frontline Publishers, Incorporated
Ed: Gladson I. Nwanna. **Released:** 2006. **Price:** $39.99. **Description:** An overview of federal tax deductions allowed for small businesses; also lists tax schedules and forms and the line to claim the deductions.

54749 ■ "Skokie Taxed by School-Business Rift" in *Chicago Tribune* **(March 9, 2005)**
Pub: Knight-Ridder/Tribune Business News
Ed: M. Daniel Gibbard. **Description:** School officials and Skokie business leaders are debating the end of a special tax that finances downtown redevelopment. The Skokie Village board is trying to negotiate a compromise acceptable to both sides.

54750 ■ *Small Business Desk Reference*
Pub: Penguin Books (USA) Incorporated
Ed: Gene Marks. **Released:** December 2004. **Price:** $29.95 (US), $44.00 (Canadian). **Description:** Comprehensive guide for starting or running a successful small business, focusing on buying a business or franchise, writing a business plan, financial management, accounting, legal issues, human resources management, operations, marketing, sales, customer service, taxes, insurance, and ethics. Information for launching a restaurant, property management firm, retail outlet, consulting firm, and service business is included.

54751 ■ *Small Business Legal Tool Kit*
Pub: Entrepreneur Press
Ed: Ira Nottonson; Theresa A. Pickner. **Released:** May 2007. **Price:** $36.95. **Description:** Legal expertise is provided by two leading entrepreneurial attorneys. Issues covered include forming and operating a business: taxes, contracts, leases, bylaws, trademarks, small claims court, etc.

54752 ■ *Small Business Management*
Pub: John Wiley & Sons, Incorporated
Ed: Margaret Burlingame. **Released:** March 2007. **Price:** $44.95. **Description:** Advice for starting and running a small business as well as information on the value and appeal of small businesses, is given. Topics include budgets, taxes, inventory, ethics, e-commerce, and current laws.

54753 ■ "Small Business Owners Want Tax Cuts, Less Regulation" in St. Louis Business Journal (Vol. 20, No. 40, June 12, 2000, pp. 23)
Pub: American City Business Journals, Inc.
Ed: Kent Hoover. Description: Small business owners surveyed by the National Federation of Independent Business list lower taxes as the main issue they want their state and federal elected officials to address.

54754 ■ Small Business Quickfinder Handbook
Pub: Practitioners Publishing Company
Released: January 2005. Price: $43.00. Description: Comprehensive coverage of tax information required for contractors, large and small, home builders, and other specialty trades.

54755 ■ The Small Business Start-Up Kit for California
Pub: NOLO
Ed: Peri Pakroo. Released: April 2004. Price: $24.99. Description: Handbook covering all aspects of starting a business in California, including information about necessary fees, forms, and taxes.

54756 ■ Small Business Survival Guide: Starting, Protecting, and Securing Your Business for Long-Term Success
Pub: Adams Media Corporation
Ed: Cliff Ennico. Released: October 2005. Price: $12.95 (US), $17.95 (Canadian). Description: Entrepreneurship in the new millennium. Topics include creditors, taxes, competition, business law, and accounting.

54757 ■ Small Business Tax Deductions 2006
Pub: Continuing Education of the Bar-California
Ed: Stephen Fishman. Released: June 2006. Price: $99.00. Description: Allowable tax deductions for small business in 2006 are explained.

54758 ■ Small Business Tax Guide: Guide to Small Business Tax
Pub: Data-Lynn Book Co.
Ed: Andrew J. Lynn. Released: 1992. Price: $24.95 (paper).

54759 ■ Small Business Taxation
Pub: CCH Incorporated
Ed: Gary Maydew. Released: February 2005. Price: $99.00. Description: Tax laws governing small business are outlined.

54760 ■ Small Business Taxes 2006: Your Complete Guide to a Better Bottom Line
Pub: John Wiley & Sons, Incorporated
Ed: Barbara Weltman. Released: November 2005. Price: $16.95 (US), $21.99 (Canadian). Description: Detailed information on new tax laws and IRS rules for small businesses.

54761 ■ Small Business Taxes Made Easy: How to Increase Your Deductions, Reduce What You Owe, and Boost Your Profits
Pub: McGraw-Hill Companies
Ed: Eva Rosenberg. Released: December 2004. Price: $16.95 (US), $24.95 (Canadian). Description: Tax expert gives advice to small business owners regarding tax issues. TaxMamma.com, run by Eva Rosenberg, is one of the top seven tax advice Websites on the Internet.

54762 ■ "Small Businesses Are Engine to American Economy" in Atlanta Business Chronicle (Vol. 24, No. 9, August 3, 2001, pp. 10B)
Pub: American City Business Journals Inc.
Ed: Paige Bowers. Description: Senator Max Cleland discusses what he has done in support of small business in America. The Senator's support includes reducing taxes on small businesses, broadening health care options and boosting the opportunities for minority and women-owned enterprises.

54763 ■ "Small Businesses Now Can Afford Big Benefits" in National Underwriter Life & Health-Financial Services Edition (Vol. 105, No. 42)
Pub: The National Underwriter Co.
Ed: Peter A. Welsh. Description: A review of the Economic Growth & Tax Relief Reconciliation Act of 2001 (EGTRBA) is presented, focusing on the impact this new law will have on small businesses. Statistical data included.

54764 ■ "Small business tax cuts 'complement' Bush plan" in Atlanta Business Chronicle (Vol. 23, No. 35, February 2, 2001, pp. 53A)
Pub: American City Business Journals Inc.
Ed: Kent Hoover. Description: Small businesses are expected to benefit from proposed tax cuts by the new Bush Administration, but they also want Congress to pass various other tax measures which would directly affect small businesses. The article outlines tax breaks being presented in a package by Senator Christopher S. Bond.

54765 ■ "Small business could reap dividends" in Wall Street Journal (January 22, 2003, pp. B4C)
Pub: Dow Jones & Co. Inc.
Ed: Jane J. Kim. Description: An examination into the tax benefits for small business when changing classification from an S corporation to a C corporation is presented.

54766 ■ "Small businesses fight to repeal tax-law change" in Crain's Detroit Business (Vol. 16, No. 16, April 17, 2000, pp. 32)
Pub: Crain Communications, Inc.
Ed: Amy Lane. Description: Small business officials in Michigan, and elsewhere, are lobbying Washington to repeal a tax-law change that could kill sales of businesses or affect the transactions' price.

54767 ■ Small Time Operator: How to Start Your Own Business, Keep Your Books, Pay Your Taxes, and Stay Out of Trouble
Pub: Bell Springs Publishing
Ed: Bernard B. Kamoroff. Released: February 2005. Price: $17.95. Description: Comprehensive guide for starting any kind of business.

54768 ■ Small Time Operator: How to Start Your Own Small Business, Keep Your Books, Pay Your Taxes, & Stay out of Trouble!
Pub: Bell Springs Publishing
Ed: Bernard Kamoroff. Released: 22nd ed. 1998. Price: $16.95.

54769 ■ "Smart inventory: start electing superior filing options now" in Barron's (Vol. 82, No. 59, February 24, 2003, pp. 23)
Pub: Barron's
Ed: Joseph F. Gelband. Description: The use of laws from Section 475 of the tax code is one way in which investors can reduce capital gains tax on the sales of securities as long as an investor is considered a securities trader. Use of the provision allows losses to be fully deducted. An explanation of ways an S company can benefit on taxes by changing status to a C company is offered.

54770 ■ "Soaring Angels" in Entrepreneur.com (Vol. 34, February 2006, No. 2, pp. 58)
Pub: Entrepreneur Media Inc.
Description: Tax incentives for individuals investing in young companies is increasing angel activity. Statistical data included.

54771 ■ "Spring cleaning: tips to get fiscal house in order" in Atlanta Business Chronicle (Vol. 23, No. 49, May 11, 2001, pp. 12B)
Pub: American City Business Journals Inc.
Ed: Paula Moore. Description: Businesses need to periodically re-evaluate their business plan and their current position. Spring is a good time to do this, once taxes have been filed. Various options should also be explored, dealing with items such as selling the company, allocating resources, managing succession plans, etc. Business tax planning is also needed.

54772 ■ "State Begins Hitting Biz for 'SUTA Dumping'" in Crain's Detroit Business (Vol. 21, February 7, 2005, No. 6, pp. 1)
Pub: Crain Communications Inc. - Detroit
Ed: Amy Lane. Description: According to the state of Michigan, employers try to lower their unemployment insurance tax rate by shifting payrolls to a new corporation or buying a firm with a lower tax rate, costing the state about $100 million in cumulative tax losses.

54773 ■ "State Budget Panel's Report Due this Week" in Crain's Detroit Business (Vol. 23, January 29, 2007, No. 5, pp. 6)
Pub: Crain Communications Inc. - Detroit
Ed: Amy Lane. Description: Advisory panel to issue recommendations to Governor for a way forward plan to address the chronic budget shortfalls and gloomy outlook; two ex-Michigan governors lead the panel.

54774 ■ "State looks to Indian casinos to add revenue" in Crain's Detroit Business (Vol. 19, No. 15, April 14, 2003, pp. 6)
Pub: Crain Communications Inc., Detroit
Ed: Amy Lane. Description: Michigan's governor, Jennifer Granholm and others, are looking to the state's American Indian tribes as a source of potential revenue by renegotiating state tribal gambling compacts that were signed by former Governor John Engler.

54775 ■ "State Senate Passes Bill To Cut $1B from SBT" in Crain's Detroit Business (Vol. 21, October 31, 2005, No. 44, pp. 28)
Pub: Crain Communications Inc. - Detroit
Ed: Amy Lane. Description: A new plan to cut Michigan's single-business tax by $1 billion over six years would start by instituting a $100 million single-business tax cut in 2006.

54776 ■ "Stimulus or Bust? Although Bush Touts Tax Cut, the B.E. 100s Have Mixed Feelings" in Black Enterprise (Vol. 34, September 2003)
Pub: Earl Graves Publishing Co.
Ed: Cliff Hocker. Description: Executives from the Black Enterprises 100 have mixed feeling as to the impact of President Bush's tax cuts on minority, small businesses.

54777 ■ "Stimulus plan offers some firms tax windfall" in Wall Street Journal (April 9, 2002, pp. B6)
Pub: Wall Street Journal
Ed: Jeff Bailey. Description: An overview of the Job Creation and Worker Assistance Act of 2002.

54778 ■ "A storm offshore" in Crain's Detroit Business (Vol. 19, No. 5, Feb. 3, 2003, pp. 11)
Pub: Crain Communications Inc., Detroit
Ed: Katie Merx. Description: The Internal Revenue Service will be scrutinizing offshore investments made by small businesses.

54779 ■ "Straining Under Sarbanes-Oxley" in Business Journal-Milwaukee (Vol. 20, No. 48, August 15, 2003, pp. A1)
Pub: American City Business Journals, Inc.
Ed: Michael Muckian. Description: Small businesses that are publicly traded may suffer under the new Sarbanes-Oxley Act of 2002. The new law was passed in an effort to protect public shareholders from corporate scandals.

54780 ■ "Study Says Change Tax Laws to Help Forest Products Industry Stay Competitive" in Portland Press Herald (March 25, 2005)
Pub: Blethen Maine Newspapers, Inc.
Ed: Tux Turkel. Description: A recent state-sponsored report, called Maine Future Forest Economy Project, showed a change in the state's tax laws would help the forest industry remain competitive, while encouraging private investment, increase cooperative among state government and industry, and increase the transfer of university sponsored research into next generation commercial products and applications.

54781 ■ **"Successful IT practices know their clients well"** in *Accounting Today* (Vol. 14, No. 7, April 17, 2000, pp. 26)
Pub: Faulkner & Gray, Inc.
Ed: James C. Metzler. Description: Small businesses make up the largest market in America and claim the client base of the majority of accounting firms. Recognizing key characteristics of the small business market is important to information technology (IT) firms and their professionals. This market choice has the potential to give an IT professional a tremendous sense of satisfaction because of the profound improvements that can take place in the business.

54782 ■ **"Surviving Sarbanes-Oxley"** in *Inc.* (September 2005, pp. 132-138)
Pub: Inc. Magazine
Ed: Amy Feldman. Description: The Sarbanes-Oxley Act was intended to crack down on large public companies, but the Act has created a burden for many smaller, private firms. Policymakers are looking into ways to undo damages. Five ways companies can comply to the Sarbanes-Oxley Act are listed.

54783 ■ **"SWARM Online services seek small biz through CPAs"** in *Accounting Today* (Vol. 14, No. 6, April 3, 2000, pp. 1)
Pub: Faulkner & Gray, Inc.
Ed: John M. Covaleski. Description: Internet entrepreneurs are seeking to leverage local tax and accounting firms to electronically deliver business products and services to small and mid-sized businesses.

54784 ■ **"Sweet Relief"** in *Entrepreneur.com* (Vol. 34, February 2006, No. 2, pp. 36)
Pub: Entrepreneur Media Inc.
Description: Small business technology tax laws include a $350 billion tax-relief packaged signed into law in 2003 and stayed in effect through 2005; Section 179 allows a small business to deduct up to $100,000 in equipment expenses.

54785 ■ **"The Switch from a SEP-IRA"** in *Business Week Online* (Dec. 24, 2002)
Pub: McGraw-Hill Inc.
Ed: Karen E. Klein. Description: Information is offered regarding the Economic Growth & Tax Relief Reconciliation Act of 2001, the tax relief bill signed by President Bush that makes changes in the estate-tax rates and amended pension-plan rules. The Act allows a rollover of a subchapter S company's SEP-IRA funds into a 401(k) and also allows for borrowing against the account.

54786 ■ **"Taking a Dive: A Federally Chartered Insurer of Pensions has Fallen on Hard Times. Taxpayers, Beware"** in *Barron's* (July 21, 2003)
Pub: Barron's
Ed: Jim McTague. Description: The government-run Pension Benefit Guaranty Corporation, which insures more than 30,000 defined-benefit plan payments comprising more than 40 million workers, could be bankrupt in ten years, according to Congress. A bailout would tax citizens in the tens of billions.

54787 ■ **"Tapping the Potential of Employee Ranks; Human Resources"** in *Crain's New York Business* (Vol. 22, November 13, 2006, No. 46, pp. 32)
Pub: Crain Communications, Inc.
Description: Listing of organizations that provide counseling and research on human resources issues, as well as offering employee recruitment and training, oftentimes with tax break incentives.

54788 ■ **"The Tax Act of 2001"** in *Hawaii Business* (Vol. 47, No. 2, August 2001, pp. 208)
Pub: Hawaii Business Publishing Co.
Ed: Scott Butera. Description: A review of the Economic Growth and Tax Relief Reconciliation Act of 2001 is presented. The law provides both tax-saving and financial-planning opportunities, the four areas of focus include personal taxation, education funding, retirement planning and estate planning.

54789 ■ **"A Tax Act"** in *Entrepreneur* (Vol. 31, No. 8, August 2003, pp. 55)
Pub: Entrepreneur Media, Inc.
Ed: Scott Bernard Nelson. Description: Latest tax cuts approved by Congress are investigated, citing investors and married couples with children being the winners of the new legislation.

54790 ■ **"Tax time is approaching"** in *Black Enterprise* (Vol. 33, No. 7, February 2003, pp. 6)
Pub: Earl Graves Publishing Co.
Description: Black Enterprise's Website provides a tax center offering tax advice for individuals and small businesses.

54791 ■ **"Tax Benefit is Worth Keeping"** in *Crain's New York Business* (Vol. 23, November 20, 2006, No. 47, pp. 10)
Pub: Crain Communications, Inc.
Description: New York City was desperate to spur housing construction in the 1970's so it created the 421-a program offering ten to twenty-five year reductions in property taxes. The Bloomberg administration wants to overhaul the tax break due to the strong housing market.

54792 ■ **"Tax Bill Doesn't Repeal Estate Tax Uncertainty"** in *Atlanta Business Chronicle* (Vol. 24, No. 1, June 8, 2001, pp. 5A)
Pub: American City Business Journals Inc.
Description: The federal estate law, which Congress repealed, can be reinstated in 2001 unless Congress passes a new law repealing it. Until then, the estate tax is phased out. The impact of estate tax on small business owners is discussed.

54793 ■ **"A tax break as big as a big SUV"** in *Wall Street Journal* (May 27, 2003, pp. D2)
Pub: Dow Jones & Co. Inc.
Ed: Stephen Power. Description: Small business owners are allowed to write off up to $100,000 for the purchase of a luxury SUV used for business.

54794 ■ **"Tax Breaks for Angels"** in *Inc.* (September 2005, pp. 30)
Pub: Inc. Magazine
Ed: Christina Galoozis. Description: In order to foster technology transfer, many states are rewarding early-stage investors. Statistical data included.

54795 ■ **"Tax Breaks: Don't Forget Your Home Office"** in *Business Week* (No. 3666, January 31, 2000, pp. 124E4)
Pub: McGraw-Hill, Inc.
Description: Home office deductions are probably the most overlooked federal income tax deduction. The article contains information to help home businesses take advantage of the much needed tax breaks they are entitled to.

54796 ■ **"Tax Breaks May Aid Dealers Pummeled by Katrina; Bush Official Also Touts 'Investment Opportunity'"** in *Automotive News* (September 2006)
Pub: Crain Communications, Inc.
Ed: Harry Stoffer. Description: Federal tax breaks will assist Gulf Coast auto dealers after the hurricanes that hit the area in 2005. Commerce Secretary, Carlos Gutierrez is encouraging those dealers to also reinvest in the area to help bring it back to its profit-making potential.

54797 ■ **"Tax plan could prompt corporations to move to C"** in *Crain's Detroit Business* (Vol. 19, No. 5, Feb. 3, 2003, pp. 13)
Pub: Crain Communications Inc., Detroit
Ed: Katie Merx. Description: Under President Bush's tax plan, S-type corporations and limited liability companies could lose many benefits.

54798 ■ **"Tax Cut Bill Includes Pension Reform, Other Provisions Affecting Employee Benefits"** in *Employee Benefit Plan Review* (Vol. 55, No. 12)
Pub: Charles D. Spencer & Associates, Inc.
Description: The Economic Growth and Tax Relief Reconciliation Act of 2001 represents a major advance in pension reform. The new law, which President George W. Bush expects to sign, includes an increase of the annual dollar limit for defined benefit plans.

54799 ■ **"Tax Cuts Unlikely, But Groups Push for Relief for Businesses"** in *Crain's Detroit Business* (Vol. 19, No. 45, November 10, 2003)
Pub: Crain Communications Inc., Detroit
Ed: Amy Lane. Description: An overview of Governor Jennifer Granholm's tax policy in the State of Michigan is presented, as well as ways it will affect small businesses in the state.

54800 ■ **"A Tax Deal Too Good to Be True?"** in *Business Week Online* (July 25, 2003)
Pub: McGraw-Hill Inc.
Ed: Anne Tergesen. Description: In May 2003, the U.S tax court declared tax breaks off-limits to a Texas partnership on the grounds that the donor had retained too much control over key decisions. The implications of this court order are discussed.

54801 ■ *Tax Deductions for Businesses & Self-Employed Individuals*
Pub: Bell Springs Publishing
Ed: Bernard B. Kamoroff, CPA. Price: $17.95. Description: Provides an encyclopedia of tax deductions.

54802 ■ **"Tax Experts Are Standing By"** in *Business Week* (No. 3702, October 9, 2000, pp. F4)
Pub: McGraw-Hill, Inc.
Description: The IRS has opened a new unit for small business in order to strengthen education regarding the complex tax codes.

54803 ■ **"Tax-Free Bill of Health: Health-Care Accounts with Tax Benefits"** in *Entrepreneur* (Vol. 33, January 2005, No. 1, pp. 50)
Pub: Entrepreneur Media Inc.
Ed: Joan Szabo. Description: Health Savings Accounts (HSAs), Health Reimbursement Arrangements (HRAs), Flexible Spending Accounts (FSAs), and Medical Savings Accounts (MSAs) are health-care spending accounts designed to help employees pay for health costs, while saving on taxes.

54804 ■ **"Tax-Free College Savings"** in *My Business* (August/September 2002, pp. 15)
Pub: My Business Magazine
Ed: Phillip L. Pennartz. Description: An overview of the 529 Plan that allows individuals to invest in mutual funds for a child's or grandchild's education with tax-free earnings.

54805 ■ **"Tax relief leads boomers to planned giving"** in *Crain's Detroit Business* (Vol. 16, No. 48, November 27, 2000, pp. 13)
Pub: Crain Communications, Inc.
Ed: Jeffrey Kosseff. Description: As baby boomers retire and investors reap the rewards of the strong stock market, estate planning has become more important than ever. Estate planning and tax breaks are covered.

54806 ■ **"Tax Law Changes Mean Money for Education and Retirement"** in *Ingram's* (Vol. 29, No. 1, January 2003, pp. 19)
Pub: Show Me Publishing, Inc.
Ed: Jackie Perlman. Description: The benefits granted under the Economic Growth and Tax Relief Reconciliation Act of 2001, allows incentives for education and retirement.

54807 ■ **"Tax Lien Sales: Money and Politics"** in *Atlanta Business Chronicle* (Vol. 25, January 10, 2003, No. 31, pp. 33A)
Pub: American City Business Publications, Inc.
Ed: Arthur E. Ferdinand. Description: Last year tax lien sales were a hot political topic, and were a way to raise tax revenue in the past. The politics surrounding tax lien sales in Atlanta, Georgia are discussed in detail.

54808 ■ *Tax Planning & Preparation Made Easy for the Self-Employed*
Pub: John Wiley & Sons, Inc.
Ed: Gregory L. Dent. **Released:** 1995. **Price:** $15.95.

54809 ■ **"Tax Possible for Anchorage, Alaska-Area Bed and Breakfast Businesses" in *Anchorage Daily News* (November 20, 2003)**
Pub: Knight Ridder/Tribune Business News
Ed: Sarana Schell. **Description:** Anchorage, Alaska bed and breakfasts may soon be required to collect hotel-motel taxes from guests, homes with one to three guests rooms would be exempt from the tax.

54810 ■ **"Tax 'Rebate' Notices Continue to Rankle Democrats" in *Tax Notes* (Vol. 92, No. 1, July 2, 2001, pp. 25-27)**
Pub: Tax Notes International
Ed: Amy Hamilton. **Description:** Issues concerning the political ramifications of an IRS notice sent to U.S. taxpayers announcing tax relief under the Economic Growth and Tax Relief Reconciliation Act of 2001 are examined, focusing on the political benefits Republicans and President George W. Bush may gain from the wording of the notice.

54811 ■ **"Tax Relief Act Is A Boon for VC" in *Venture Capital Journal* (July 1, 2003)**
Pub: Thomson Financial Inc.
Description: The impact of the Jobs and Growth Tax Relief Reconciliation Act of 2003 is discussed. The Act contains an estimated $330 billion in tax cuts, and implements many basic and revolutionary changes to the Internal Revenue Code which are good for investors.

54812 ■ **"Tax Rule Crimps Small Business Deals; Firms Get Creative in Seeking Remedy" in *Wall Street Journal* (January 26, 2000, pp. C1)**
Pub: Dow Jones & Co., Inc.
Ed: Karen Hube. **Description:** Innovative ways small businesses are using to avoid taxes when making deals are investigated.

54813 ■ *Tax Savvy for Small Business*
Pub: NOLO
Ed: Frederick W. Daily. **Released:** November 2006. **Price:** $36.99. **Description:** Strategies to help small business owners claim all legitimate deductions and keep accurate records.

54814 ■ *Tax Savvy for Small Business: Year-Round Tax Strategies to Save You Money*
Pub: NOLO
Ed: Frederick W. Daily, Bethany K. Laurence. **Released:** September 2005. **Price:** $36.99. **Description:** Tax strategies for small business. Includes the latest tax numbers and laws as well as current Internal Revenue Service forms and publications.

54815 ■ **"Tax Season Defanged" in *Journal of Accountancy* (Vol. 199)**
Pub: American Institute of Certified Public Accountants
Ed: Edward Mendlowitz. **Description:** Ways to help accounting firms create a successful tax season are examined, including fostering high morale among employees.

54816 ■ *Tax Smarts for Small Business*
Pub: Sourcebooks, Incorporated
Ed: James O. Parker. **Released:** December 2006. **Price:** $27.95. **Description:** Tax guide for small businesses.

54817 ■ **"Tax test" in *Wall Street Journal* (April 9, 2002, pp. D3)**
Pub: Wall Street Journal
Ed: Charles Passy. **Description:** A comparison of the price and varying results of five different tax preparation software and services are presented, including Quicken TurboTax Home & Business. Statistical data included.

54818 ■ **"Tax-Time Bytes" in *PC Magazine* (February 20, 2001, pp. 186)**
Pub: Ziff-Davis Publishing Company
Ed: Kathy Yakal. **Description:** Reviews of tax preparation software is offered, including Kiplinger TaxCut Deluxe, Quicken Turbo Tax Deluxe, and Taxact 2000 Deluxe.

54819 ■ **"Tax time: handling the mountain of work" in *Women In Business* (Vol. 52, No. 2, March 2000, pp. 12)**
Pub: The ABWA Co., Inc.
Ed: Jane Thomas. **Description:** Accountants involved in U.S. income tax find the period between late January and mid-April a very busy, exhausting time.

54820 ■ *Tax Tricks*
Pub: Concept Publishing
Ed: David Coleman. **Released:** 1995. **Price:** $20.00.

54821 ■ *Taxation & Small Businesses*
Pub: Organization for Economic Cooperation & Development
Ed: OECD staff. **Released:** 1994. **Price:** $20.00 (paper).

54822 ■ *The Taxation of Sole Proprietors*
Pub: Unicorn Research Corp.
Ed: James A. Fellows. **Released:** 1995. **Price:** $28.00.

54823 ■ *Taxes and Business Strategy: A Planning Approach*
Pub: Prentice Hall
Ed: Myron S. Scholes and M. Wolfson. **Released:** 1991. **Price:** $93.00.

54824 ■ **"Taxes on Roth IRAs" in *Black Enterprise* (Vol. 34, No. 7, February 2004, pp. 42)**
Pub: Earl Graves Publishing Co.
Ed: Matthew S. Scott. **Description:** Things to consider before converting a traditional IRA to a Roth IRA are discussed.

54825 ■ **"Taxes Set a Record in 2005" in *Milwaukee Journal Sentinel* (December 21, 2005)**
Pub: Journal Sentinel, Inc.
Ed: Mike Johnson. **Description:** According to a study done by a non-partisan taxpayers group, Wisconsin residents and businesses paid $56.5 billion in state, local and federal taxes, setting an all-time record. Statistical data included.

54826 ■ **"Taxing Concerns" in *Small Business Opportunities* (Vol. 12, No. 2, March 2000, pp. 98)**
Pub: Harris Publications, Inc.
Description: By being pro-active about taxes, small businesses can fine-tune outcomes, anticipate cash flow needs, and reduce accountant's fees.

54827 ■ **"Taxing matters" in *Entrepreneur* (Vol. 30, No. 12, December 2002, pp. 43)**
Pub: Entrepreneur Media Inc.
Ed: Jill Amadio. **Description:** There is a significant tax advantage for small business owners to lease rather than purchase vehicles.

54828 ■ **"Taxing Matters" in *Inc.* (December 1999, pp. 92)**
Pub: The Goldhirsh Group
Description: Tax deductions for home-based businesses are discussed.

54829 ■ **"Taxing News" in *Entrepreneur* (Vol. 28, No. 2, February 2000, pp. 28)**
Pub: Entrepreneur Media Inc.
Description: Government officials say they're losing sales tax revenues due to the tax-free Internet.

54830 ■ **"A Taxing Proposition" in *Black Enterprise* (Vol. 37, January 2007, No. 6, pp. 6)**
Pub: Earl G. Graves Publishing Co. Inc.
Description: Learn how to avoid tax problems on Black Enterprise's website, blackenterprise.com.

54831 ■ **"Taxing Unfairly...Brand Mascots... Slotting Wars...The Genetic Jerk" in *Fortune* (Vol. 141, No. 5, March 6, 2000, pp. 432L)**
Pub: Time Inc.
Description: Dozens of Asian-American entrepreneurs in Los Angeles say the IRS has unfairly targeted them for audits and has selectively charged an "ozone tax".

54832 ■ **"There are no magic words to alter tax law" in *Crain's Detroit Business* (Vol. 19, No. 11, March 17, 2003, pp. 9)**
Pub: Crain Communications Inc., Detroit
Ed: James Jenkins. **Description:** The double taxation of corporate profits is destructive to the American economy, according to Alan Greenspan, Federal Reserve Chairman, as well as leading academics.

54833 ■ **"Think Fast: Take Advantage of Faster Depreciation" in *Entrepreneur* (Vol. 32, December 2004, No. 12, pp. 62)**
Pub: Entrepreneur Media Inc.
Ed: Joan Szabo. **Description:** Entrepreneurs who own business real estate might want to perform a cost segregation study (CSS) on their property to review all costs associated with the purchase or construction of a building because of the Internal Revenue Service' willingness to allow business owners to accelerate depreciation on existing buildings or those being built.

54834 ■ **"Time to Collect? Tacking Taxes Onto Internet Sales Could Soon Become Mandatory" in *Entrepreneur.com* (Vol. 34, February 2006, No. 2)**
Pub: Entrepreneur Media Inc.
Ed: Melissa Campanelli. **Description:** Online retailers can voluntarily add sales taxes to bills originating in the 19 states that have signed onto the Streamlined Sales and Use Tax Agreement, that makes it easier for retailers doing business in multiple states to calculate, collect and remit existing use taxes.

54835 ■ **"A Time to Donate" in *Hispanic Business* (Vol. 23, No. 11, November 2001, pp. 68)**
Pub: Hispanic Business Inc.
Description: Charitable deductions are discussed, with IRS resources listed.

54836 ■ **"To the Rescue: Feel Like the IRS is Out to Get You? A Taxpayer Advocate Is On Your Side" in *Entrepreneur* (Vol. 32, July 2004)**
Pub: Entrepreneur Media Inc.
Ed: Joan Szabo. **Description:** The Internal Revenue Service's Taxpayer Advocate Service (TAS) offers assistance to small companies trying to resolve tax issues. TAS closed more than 205,000 open cases in 2003.

54837 ■ **"Too Sensible to Survive" in *The Economist* (Vol. 377, October 22-28, 2005, No. 8449, pp. 33-34)**
Pub: The Economist Newspaper Ltd.
Description: The tax reform panel has some good ideas, but they are not expected to be adopted because revenue-neutral tax reform will create both winners and losers.

54838 ■ **"Top 25 Overlooked Tax Deductions" in *Home Business* (Vol. 12, March/April 2005, No. 2, pp. 78)**
Pub: Home Business Magazine
Description: The top 25 most-overlooked tax deductions for small businesses are listed.

54839 ■ **"Top-drawer advice: new software tells you how much your charitable contributions are worth" in *Barron's* (Vol.82, Feb.17, 2003, pp.T7)**
Pub: Barron's
Ed: Randall W. Forsyth, Theresa W. Carey. **Description:** Two programs that help value donations of used clothing and other goods and work well, include H & R Block Deduction Pro and Income Dynamics ItsDeductible tax preparation software.

54840 ■ *Top Tax Saving Ideas for Today's Small Business: A Fresh Look after Tax Reform Legislation*
Pub: PSI Research
Ed: Thomas J. Stemmy. **Released:** 4th ed. 1998. **Price:** $16.95 (paper).

54841 ■ *Top Tax Savings Ideas: How to Survive in Today's Tough Tax Environment*
Pub: Entrepreneur Press
Ed: Thomas J. Stemmy. **Released:** March 2004. **Price:** $18.95 (US), $26.95 (Canadian). **Description:** Tax deductions, fringe benefits, and tax deferrals for small businesses.

54842 ■ **"Tracking T&E deductions"** in *Hispanic Business* (Vol. 22, No. 4, April 2000, pp. 77)
Pub: Hispanic Business
Ed: Milton Zall. **Description:** The Internal Revenue Service has revised its regulations concerning the claiming of travel and entertaining cost allowances. Documentary evidence is only required for individual bills or daily expenditure totals of over $75.

54843 ■ **"Traditional VS. Roth IRA"** in *Black Enterprise* (Vol. 37, October 2006, No. 3, pp. 58)
Pub: Earl G. Graves Publishing Co. Inc.
Ed: K. Parker; Carolyn M. Brown. **Description:** Government taxes the traditional IRAs different than it taxes Roth IRAs.

54844 ■ **"Treasury Officials Discuss Role of the OPR, Circular 230"** in *Tax Notes* (Vol. 102, No. 3, January 19, 2004, pp. 320-323)
Pub: Tax Notes International
Ed: Kenneth A. Gary. **Description:** Information is presented about the IRS Office of Professional Responsibility and Circular 230, regarding tax shelters.

54845 ■ **"The Trick is to Live"** in *Journal of Political Economy* (Vol. 111, No. 6, December 2003, pp. 18)
Pub: University of Chicago Press
Ed: Wojciech Kopczuk. **Description:** Because estate tax liability usually depends on how long one lives, it implicitly provides annuity income. In the absence of annuity markets, lump-sum estate taxation may be used to achieve the first-best solution for individuals with a sufficiently strong bequest motive. Calculations of the annuity embedded in the U.S. estate tax show that people with $10 million of assets may be effectively receiving $100,000 a year financed at actuarially fair rates by their tax payments. The insurance effect might reduce the marginal cost of funds (MCF) for the estate tax by as much as 30 percent, and the resulting MCF is within the range of estimates for the MCF for the income tax.

54846 ■ **"Two Detroit Riverfront Projects Win Tax Breaks"** in *Crain's Detroit Business* (Vol. 22, November 27, 2006, No. 48, pp. 25)
Pub: Crain Communications Inc. - Detroit
Ed: Amy Lane. **Description:** Tax credits and other assistance were approved by the Michigan Economic Growth Authority for two brownfield-redevelopment projects. Townhomes and retail space to be built just East of the Renaissance Center.

54847 ■ *Ultimate Small Business Advisor*
Pub: Entrepreneur Press
Ed: Andi Axman. **Released:** May 2007. **Price:** $30. 95. **Description:** Tip for starting and running a small business, including new tax rulings and laws affecting small business, are shared.

54848 ■ **"Uncle Sam says Turbo Charge your future"** in *Ingram's* (Vol. 28, No. 2, February 2002, pp. 23)
Pub: Show Me Publishing, Inc.
Description: A review of the new changes in tax laws for 2002 are given. Overall, Congress made 400 changes for this year.

54849 ■ **"Uncle Same Eases Up on Barter"** in *Business Week* (March 27, 2000, pp. F6)
Pub: McGraw-Hill, Inc.
Description: The IRS recently ruled that businesses are no longer required report barter transactions worth less than $1, which covers much of the free and low-cost banner-ad swaps popular among small companies.

54850 ■ **"Unfinished business: the disappearing Tax Act of 2001"** in *Tax Notes* (Vol. 91, No. 11, June 4, 2001, pp. 1652-1653)
Pub: Tax Notes International
Ed: Martin A. Sullivan. **Description:** The political implications of a sunset provision that would cause the entire Economic Growth and Tax Relief Reconciliation Act of 2001 to expire December 31, 2001, are examined, focusing on how the provision acts as a political defeat for Republicans who have supported President George W. Bush's tax cut proposals.

54851 ■ **"An Unsure Thing: Can't Pay Your Federal Tax Bill?"** in *Entrepreneur* (Vol. 31, No. 7, July 2003, pp. 55)
Pub: Entrepreneur Media, Inc.
Ed: Joan Szabo. **Description:** The U.S. Internal Revenue Service's Offer-In-Compromise (OIC) program, which allows taxpayers to settle tax bills for a lower amount than owed, needs a complete overhaul, according to the IRS Oversight Board.

54852 ■ **"Utilities Boost Companies; Utility Services"** in *Crain's New York Business* (Vol. 22, November 13, 2006, No. 46, pp. 36)
Pub: Crain Communications, Inc.
Description: Listing of companies that provide utility programs, incentives and benefits to small businesses looking to relocate within the five boroughs of New York City or expand their businesses in the area.

54853 ■ **"VAT Facts"** in *Entrepreneur* (Vol. 31, No. 10, October 2003, pp. 52)
Pub: Entrepreneur Media, Inc.
Ed: Amanda C. Kooser. **Description:** The Value Added Tax (VAT), required for purchases made in the European Union, now includes non-EU companies, and ranges from 15-25 percent.

54854 ■ **"VEBAs and 412(i)s: Maximize client deductions"** in *Accounting Today* (Vol. 14, No. 11, June 26, 2000, pp. 20)
Pub: Faulkner & Gray, Inc.
Ed: Lance Wallach. **Description:** There are two programs that, when properly constructed, can substantially reduce taxes for any type of business entity, including a sole proprietorship, partnership, S corporation, C corporation or limited liability partnership: The IRC Section 412(i) plan and the 501(c)(9) tax-exempt trust, which is commonly referred to as the voluntary employees beneficiary association (VEBA). Both programs are outlined.

54855 ■ **"Voters May Rule on Export Tax for Maine's Drinking Water"** in *Portland Press Herald* (September 24, 2005)
Pub: Blethen Maine Newspapers, Inc.
Ed: Seth Harkness. **Description:** Voters in Maine are voting on a measure that would tax nearly 20 cents of each gallon of bottled water taken from Maine wells. Supports believe the move is necessary to ensure bottled water companies do not extract too much water from the state's aquifiers.

54856 ■ **"Voters will be asked to expand industrial park"** in *Atlanta Business Chronicle* (Vol. 25, January 10, 2003, No. 31, pp. 4A)
Pub: American City Business Publications, Inc.
Ed: Charles E. Arnold. **Description:** Voters will be asked to vote on a 1-cent special local sales tax that will finance the preparation of a proposed $29.4 million, 842-acre industrial park expansion in Spalding County, Georgia. The expansion entails adding to an existing park ($21.7 million/652 acres) and creating another ($7.7. million/190 acres).

54857 ■ **"Voting With Their Pocketbooks"** in *Fortune* (Vol. 141, No. 10, May 15, 2000, pp. F372P)
Pub: Time Inc.
Ed: Edward Robinson. **Description:** A scorecard featuring the issues affecting small business owners in the 2000 election campaign.

54858 ■ **"Wanna trade? Tax Talk"** in *Entrepreneur* (Vol. 30, No. 2, February 2002, pp. 59)
Pub: Entrepreneur Media Inc.
Ed: Joan Szabo. **Description:** In a recent IRS ruling, reverse like-kind exchanges have become less perilous. The ruling became effective for exchanges taking place on or after September 15, 2000.

54859 ■ **"Warning Signs"** in *Entrepreneur. com* (Vol. 34, February 2006, No. 2, pp. 57)
Pub: Entrepreneur Media Inc.
Ed: Michael Rozbruch. **Description:** Three tax shelters entrepreneurs should avoid are outlined.

54860 ■ **"Washington gridlock worries small business groups"** in *Wall Street Journal* (November 1, 2000, pp. A1)
Pub: Dow Jones & Co., Inc.
Ed: Tom Herman. **Description:** Groups want repeal of 1999 law that says businesses that sell operations at a profit must pay a lump-sum capital gains tax.

54861 ■ **"Watch your step"** in *Entrepreneur* (Vol. 31, No. 6, June 2003, pp. 55)
Pub: Entrepreneur Media Inc.
Ed: Joan Szabo. **Description:** The IRS is promising to crack down on small business owners not reporting business income, focusing on abusive tax shelters, offshore credit card abuse, high-income nonfilers, and high-income taxpayers engaged in partnerships, trusts or S corporations, as well as selecting 50,000 random returns from 2001.

54862 ■ **"We won't drink to that (gulp!)"** in *Crain's Detroit Business* (Vol. 19, No. 3, January 20, 2003, pp. 8)
Pub: Crain Communications Inc., Detroit
Description: The State of California is considering taxing alcoholic beverages by a nickel a drink to help pay for the state's emergency rooms and trauma centers. The plan is expected to add $750 million to state coffers.

54863 ■ **"What About TIF?"** in *Ingram's* (Vol. 29, No. 1, January 2003, pp. 23)
Pub: Show Me Publishing, Inc.
Ed: Wesley Fields. **Description:** Answering critics of the Real Property Tax Increment Financing Allocation Act, the author states that private investors would not be stifled, but proper implementation of the statute has been. It is suggested that the statute would be beneficial to the city.

54864 ■ **"What Conservatives, Liberals, Stores and States Share"** in *The New York Times* (June 7, 2000, pp. D35, H35)
Pub: The New York Times Company
Ed: David Cay Johnston. **Description:** E-commerce tax policy is examined. Statistical data included.

54865 ■ **"What a Relief!"** in *Entrepreneur* (Vol. 31, No. 8, August 2003, pp. 57)
Pub: Entrepreneur Media, Inc.
Ed: Joan Szabo. **Description:** Under the new Jobs and Growth Tax Reconciliation Act of 2003, companies can deduct 100 percent of equipment costs. Under prior law, the limit was $25,000, now under Section 179 allowance for taxable years beginning in 2003, 2004, and 2005 quadruples to $100,000. The 2003 act also improves the temporary bonus depreciation.

54866 ■ **"What a relief! New tax laws mean more money stays in your business"** in *Entrepreneur* (Vol. 30, No. 12, December 2002, pp. 74)
Pub: Entrepreneur Media Inc.
Description: An overview of the Job Creation and Worker Assistance Act of 2002 and its impact on business taxes is presented.

54867 ■ "What's New for 2002 Returns?" in *My Business* (February/March 2003, pp. 42)
Pub: My Business Magazine
Ed: Barbara Weltman. **Description:** The changes for filing 2002 small business tax returns are presented.

54868 ■ "What's the Plan? How President Bush's Second-Term Agenda Will Affect You" in *Entrepreneur* (Vol. 33, January 2005, No. 1, pp. 24)
Pub: Entrepreneur Media Inc.
Ed: Crystal Detamore-Rodman. **Description:** President Bush is expected to carryover his first term agenda of making his income tax cuts permanent, a permanent repeal of estate tax, and an expansion of health savings accounts.

54869 ■ "What's Your Fiscal Year" in *My Business* (February/March 2003, pp. 44)
Pub: My Business Magazine
Ed: John Rubino. **Description:** Advice if given to small business owners for setting up a fiscal year, along with regulations for compliance.

54870 ■ "What's Your Problem?" in *Entrepreneur* (Vol. 31, No. 11, November 2003, pp. 124)
Pub: Entrepreneur Media, Inc.
Ed: Paul Edwards, Sarah Edwards. **Description:** Tax benefits of running a home-based business are investigated.

54871 ■ "Where Are the 529 Plans?" in *Black Enterprise* (Vol. 34, No. 5, December 2003, pp. 40)
Pub: Earl Graves Publishing Co.
Ed: Matthew S. Scott. **Description:** Information about the 529 state-sponsored college savings plan, giving individuals the ability to invest money in a pre-selected portfolio of stocks and bonds for future education expenses.

54872 ■ "Where Small Business Stands: Your Voice Sends A Clear Message to Lawmakers" in *My Business* (December/January 2003, pp. 47)
Pub: My Business Magazine
Description: Results of the National Federation of Independent Business (NFIB) Member Ballot are presented. This information is then relayed to government lawmakers to help them understand the issues important to small business in the U.S. Statistical data included on alternative minimum tax, English proficiency, generic drugs, medical malpractice, strict liability and health care tax credits.

54873 ■ "Will Power: Build Flexibility Into Your Estate Plan so Heirs Can Avoid the Pitfalls of Changing Tax Laws" in *Entrepreneur* (Vol. 32)
Pub: Entrepreneur Media Inc.
Ed: Scott Bernard Nelson. **Description:** Information about the ever-changing death tax law is cited. Currently the federal government allows heirs to inherit $1.5 million of an estate, the amount rises to $2 million in 2006 and $3-5 million in 2009, then disappears entirely for 2010, but reappears in 2011 with a $1 million exemption.

54874 ■ "Winning and Losing Lotteries: the Right to Future Income Isn't a Capital Gain" in *Barron's* (August 11, 2003, pp. 26)
Pub: Barron's
Ed: Joseph F. Gelband. **Description:** Two recent decisions in the U.S. Tax Court both involving lottery winners, illustrate the differences between how capital gains and ordinary income is levied.

54875 ■ "Wisconsin Economic Development Programs Could be Hurt by Tax Fight" in *Milwaukee Journal Sentinel* (December 8, 2005)
Pub: Journal Sentinel, Inc.
Ed: Rick Barrett. **Description:** Due to a court battle, state-sponsored tax incentive programs for businesses could actually undermine these programs designed to attract and retain businesses. Details of the lawsuit are discussed.

54876 ■ *Working for Yourself: Law and Taxes for Independent Contractors, Freelancers and Consultants*
Pub: NOLO
Ed: Stephen Fishman. **Released:** October 2004. **Price:** $39.99. **Description:** Laws and tax rules governing independent contractors, freelancers and consultants.

54877 ■ "Wrap It Up Right" in *Entrepreneur* (Vol. 32, December 2004, No. 12, pp. 68)
Pub: Entrepreneur Media Inc.
Ed: Scott Bernard Nelson. **Description:** Deferring income into next year and/or accelerating deductions can simplify year-end tax planning.

54878 ■ "Year-End Tax Tips" in *Black Enterprise* (Vol. 31, No. 5, December 2000, pp. 125)
Pub: Earl Graves Publishing Co.
Ed: Donald Jay Korn. **Description:** Don't wait until next year to plot your tax strategy. Tips to help slash your 2000 tax bill are provided.

54879 ■ "You Need a Break" in *Success* (Vol. 47, No. 1, January 2000, pp. 14)
Pub: Success Publishing, Inc.
Description: Ways to write off expenses for time spent working on your vacation are discussed. Jan Zobel, author of "Minding Her Own Business: The Self-Employed Woman's Guide to Taxes and Record-keeping" (Easthill Press, 1998), gives advice for deducting your family vacation as a business trip.

54880 ■ "Tastes great? Less taxing?" in *Barron's* (Vol. 82, No. 57, February 10, 2003, pp. T4)
Pub: Barron's
Ed: Randall W. Forsyth, Theresa W. Carey, Kathy Yakal. **Description:** Reviews of tax preparation software, including Intuit Turbo Tax Premier, TaxCut Platinum, and TaxACT Online.

TRADE PERIODICALS

54881 ■ *Corporate Directions*
Pub: CCH Inc.
Ed: Charles W. Edwards, Editor. **Released:** Biweekly. **Price:** $213. **Description:** Discusses coverage of SEC news and regulations affecting publicly-traded companies and their officers and directors. Follows trends in corporate goverance and investor relations. Recurring features include interviews, news of research, reports of meetings, news of educational opportunities, notices of publications available, analyses of SEC regulations and court opinions, industry surveys, and columns titled Litigation Update and News from the States.

54882 ■ *Executive's Tax and Management Report*
Pub: Aspen Publishers Inc.
Ed: Sara Vine, Editor, sara.vine@aspenpublishers.com. **Released:** 2/month. **Price:** $255. **Description:** Supplies information on how to obtain more tax-free cash from a company or business, cut a company's tax bill, increase personal deductions, and deal with new tax crackdowns.

54883 ■ *Intertax*
Pub: Kluwer Academic/Plenum Publishing Corp.
Ed: Dr. Barry Bracewell-Milnes, Editor. **Released:** Monthly. **Price:** $729 Euro; $861 U.S.D; $511 GBP. **Description:** Journal covering tax information worldwide.

54884 ■ *Small Business Council of America—Alert*
Pub: Small Business Council of America Inc.
Ed: Alan P. Cleveland, Editor. **Released:** Quarterly. **Price:** Included in membership. **Description:** Monitors federal tax legislation affecting small business. Reports on the Council's advocacy in support of legislation creating economic incentives for small businesses. Encourages members to participate in the legislative process. Recurring features include Council news and a calendar of events.

54885 ■ *Small Business Taxes and Management*
Pub: A/N Group Inc.
Contact: Steven A. Hopfenmuller, Publisher
Released: Semimonthly, Daily (Mon. thru Fri.). **Price:** $49.95. **Description:** Offers current tax news, reviews of recent cases, tax saving tips, and personal financial planning for small business owners. Includes articles on issues such as finance and management. Remarks: Available online only

VIDEOCASSETTES/ AUDIOCASSETTES

54886 ■ *CPE Network: Tax & Accounting Report*
Bisk Education
9417 Princess Palm Ave.
Tampa, FL 33619
Free: 800-874-7877
Co. E-mail: info@bisk.com
URL: http://www.bisk.com
Price: $1200.00. **Description:** Provides information on current tax regulations and current accounting and auditing changes. Video newsletter published 11 times per year. **Availability:** VHS.

54887 ■ *Tax Season Update: Small Businesses and Their Owners*
Bisk Education
9417 Princess Palm Ave.
Tampa, FL 33619
Free: 800-874-7877
Co. E-mail: info@bisk.com
URL: http://www.bisk.com
Price: $199.00. **Description:** Discusses year-end tax tips and the upcoming tax legislation affecting small businesses and their owners. Furnishes information on choice of entity, new tax rates, private pension plans, trusts, planning and strategies for small business, bankruptcy law, tax planning issues, and new penalty and compliance provisions. Includes workbook and quizzer. **Availability:** VHS.

CONSULTANTS

54888 ■ **General Business Services Corp.**
1020 N University Parks Dr.
PO Box 3146
Waco, TX 76707
Ph:(817)745-2525
Free: 800-583-6181
Fax: (817)745-2544
Scope: Firm provides financial management, business counseling, and tax-related products and services to business owners and professionals. Additional services include proper record-keeping systems, accurate tax return preparation, computer software services, and financial planning services. Initial and continuous training is available to franchisees in all areas: business and tax counseling, client acquisition and business operations. Training provided at headquarters in Waco, Texas and in the field. Ongoing managerial and technical support from field support managers and national office. Manuals, sales aids, advertising materials, tax services, product development and media relations training are also included. **Publications:** 1993 Tax Tips for the Small Business Owner and Professional. **Seminars:** National Office conducts local seminars across the nation and annual conventions for franchisees. Franchisees may conduct seminars for business owners and professionals.

54889 ■ **Gordian Concepts & Solutions**
16 Blueberry Ln.
Lincoln, MA 01773
Ph:(617)259-8341
Co. E-mail: gordian@usa1.com

E-mail: gordian@usa1.com
Scope: An engineering and management consultancy, the firm offers a broad range of general, financial,

and valuation services, civil and tax litigation support, helps clients to enter new businesses, to plan new products and services, to evaluate feasibility, and assists with their due diligence efforts. Targets industrial concerns engaged in manufacturing, assembly, warehousing, energy production, process systems and biotechnology, steel, paper, and electronics. Also services businesses such as retailing, financial services, health-care, satellite broadcasting and cable television, outdoor advertising, and professional practices.

54890 ■ Horwath International Association
420 Lexington Ave., Ste. 526
New York, NY 10170
Ph:(212)808-2000
Fax: (212)808-2020
Co. E-mail: contactus@horwath.com
URL: http://www.horwath.com

E-mail: contactus@horwath.com
Scope: Services include accounting, auditing, tax and management consulting. Provides innovative business solutions in the area of assurance, business services, consulting, corporate finance, risk management, tax and technology. **Seminars:** Demand Creation Training, Dec, 2006; Marketing, Dec, 2006.

54891 ■ Pioneer Business Consultants
9042 Garfield Ave., Ste. 312
Huntington Beach, CA 92646
Ph:(714)964-7600
Fax: (714)962-6585
Scope: Offers general management consulting specializing in business acquisitions, tax and business planning, cash flow analyses, business valuations and business sales and expert witness court testimony regarding business sales, valuations and accounting.

54892 ■ Marion S. Rice
5281 Pinnacle Rd.
Dayton, OH.45418
Ph:(937)847-1733
Fax: (937)847-0046
Scope: Provides consultation to individuals and small businesses on tax management and bookkeeping activities. **Special Services:** Tax preparation, electronic filing, and refund anticipation loans.

54893 ■ Harvey C. Skoog
3737 N Robert Rd., No. A
Prescott Valley, AZ 86314
Ph:(928)772-1448
Scope: Firm has expertise in taxes, payroll, financial planning, budgeting, buy/sell planning, business start-up, fraud detection, troubled business consulting, acquisition, and marketing. Serves the manufacturing, construction, and retailing industries in Arizona.

54894 ■ Donald C. Wright
3906 Lawndale Ln. N
Minneapolis, MN 55446-2940
Ph:(763)478-5595
Co. E-mail: donaldwright@compuserve.com

E-mail: donaldwright@compuserve.com
Scope: Consultant offers expertise in accounting and taxes, personal financial planning, strategic planning, pension/profit sharing planning and administration, professional practice management and surveys. Surveys and consultations performed worldwide. **Seminars:** Qualified pension plans and employee welfare benefit plans.

FRANCHISES AND BUSINESS OPPORTUNITIES

54895 ■ Cash Plus
Cash Plus, Inc.
3002 Dow Ave., Ste. 120
Tustin, CA 92780
Ph:(714)731-2274
Free: 888-707-2274

Fax: (714)731-2099
No. of Franchise Units: 85. **No. of Company-Owned Units:** 2. **Founded:** 1985. **Franchised:** 1987. **Description:** Check cashing service and related services, including money orders, wire transfers, cash advances, mailboxes, notary, UPS, fax, snacks, tax filing and other items. **Equity Capital Needed:** $160,200-$244,200. **Franchise Fee:** $35,000. **Financial Assistance:** Provides guidance on credit applications and business plans used by franchisees seeking third party financing. **Training:** Provides training including easy-to-run computerized operating system, promotions and check verification and payday advance process.

54896 ■ Taag International, Inc.
2420 Paliswood Rd. SW
Calgary, AB, Canada T2V 3P8
Ph:(403)238-5370
No. of Franchise Units: 6. **Founded:** 1987. **Description:** Offers business and property tax consulting. **Equity Capital Needed:** $35,000. **Franchise Fee:** $35,000. **Financial Assistance:** No. **Training:** Yes.

COMPUTERIZED DATABASES

54897 ■ *CCH PROTOS*
CCH Inc.
2700 Lake Cook Rd.
Riverwoods, IL 60015
Ph:(847)267-7000
Free: 800-525-3335
Fax: (773)866-3095
URL: http://www.cch.com
Description: Contains information on taxes in Canada. Includes interpretation bulletins, circulars, rulings, Department of Finance releases, Revenue Canada releases, court cases, Internal Revenue Canada documents, draft legislation and explanatory notes, CCH Tax newsletters, and more. **Type:** Bulletin board.

54898 ■ *e-JEP*
American Economic Association
2014 Broadway, Ste. 305
Nashville, TN 37203
Ph:(615)322-2595
Fax: (615)343-7590
Co. E-mail: aeainfo@vanderbilt.edu
URL: http://www.vanderbilt.edu/AEA
Description: Contains the full text of the *Journal of Economic Perspectives*. Includes articles, reports, and other material for economists and economics professionals. Features analysis and critiques of recent research findings and developments in public policy. Includes coverage of global economics issues and developments. Features articles on education in economics, employment issues for economists, and other issues of concern to professional economists. **Availability:** Online: American Economic Association, Thomson West; CD-ROM: American Economic Association. **Type:** Full text.

54899 ■ *Federal Income Taxation of Corporations and Shareholders*
Thomson RIA
395 Hudson St., 4th Fl.
New York, NY 10014
Ph:(212)367-6300
Free: 800-431-9025
Co. E-mail: ria@thomson.com
URL: http://ria.thomson.com
Description: Contains the full text of the seventh edition of Federal Income Taxation of Corporations and Shareholders, a treatise on the subject of corporate taxation. Covers all areas of corporate income taxation. Focuses on tax issues in the life-cycle of corporations. Includes details and analysis of how shareholders and corporations are affected by the Internal Revenue Code, the IRS, and tax-related court decisions. **Availability:** Online: Thomson RIA, Thomson West; CD-ROM: Thomson RIA. **Type:** Full text.

54900 ■ *Federal Income Taxation of S Corporations*
Thomson RIA
395 Hudson St., 4th Fl.
New York, NY 10014
Ph:(212)367-6300
Free: 800-431-9025
Co. E-mail: ria@thomson.com
URL: http://ria.thomson.com
Description: Contains the full text of the fourth edition of Federal Income Taxation of S Corporations. Covers income tax issues spanning the entire life of an S corporation, from election to operation to termination. Provides authoritative interpretations and insights into rules and regulations controlling S corporations. Includes guidance on daily operation and long-term maintenance of the S corporation. **Availability:** Online: Thomson RIA, Thomson West; CD-ROM: Thomson RIA. **Type:** Full text.

54901 ■ *Federal Taxation of Partnerships & Partners*
Thomson RIA
395 Hudson St., 4th Fl.
New York, NY 10014
Ph:(212)367-6300
Free: 800-431-9025
Co. E-mail: ria@thomson.com
URL: http://ria.thomson.com
Description: Contains the full text of the third edition of Federal Taxation of Partnerships and Partners, a treatise on the subject of partner and partnership taxation. Covers issues related to taxation throughout the life cycle of a partnership. Includes in-depth analysis and guidance on Internal Revenue Code provisions governing partnerships. Focuses on areas that may help reduce the amount of taxes levied on partner and partnership transactions. **Type:** Full text.

54902 ■ *Federal Taxes Weekly Alert*
Thomson RIA
395 Hudson St., 4th Fl.
New York, NY 10014
Ph:(212)367-6300
Free: 800-431-9025
Co. E-mail: ria@thomson.com
URL: http://ria.thomson.com
Description: Contains weekly updates, news, and time-critical information on U.S. federal taxes and taxation. Includes details on the latest actions and developments in Congress, as well as decisions and opinions from the courts, the federal treasury, the IRS, and other agencies. Includes updates on pending and current legislation. Includes comprehensive and authoritative analysis of federal tax laws, regulations, and issues, with specific attention given to their application and impact. **Availability:** Online: Thomson RIA, Thomson West. **Type:** Full text.

54903 ■ *IRS Practice and Procedure*
Thomson RIA
395 Hudson St., 4th Fl.
New York, NY 10014
Ph:(212)367-6300
Free: 800-431-9025
Co. E-mail: ria@thomson.com
URL: http://ria.thomson.com
Description: Contains the full text of the second edition of IRS Practice and Procedure, a treatise on the subject of IRS procedures. Clarifies IRS procedures and policies. Includes detailed procedural information on such activities as drafting a ruling request, preparing for an appeals conference, and dealing with an IRS revenue officer. Covers recent changes in tax laws, civil and criminal penalties, and IRS access to foreign-based records. **Availability:** Online: Thomson RIA, Thomson West; CD-ROM: Thomson RIA. **Type:** Full text.

54904 ■ *Limited Liability Companies: Tax & Business Law*
Thomson RIA
395 Hudson St., 4th Fl.
New York, NY 10014
Ph:(212)367-6300
Free: 800-431-9025
Co. E-mail: ria@thomson.com

URL: http://ria.thomson.com
Description: Contains the full text of Limited Liability Companies, a treatise on the subject. Includes in-depth and comprehensive analysis of tax rules and regulations for limited liability companies (LLCs) and limited liability partnerships (LLPs). Includes coverage of issues related to forming, operating, transferring, and dissolving LLCs and LLPs. Includes business and tax planning guidelines specifically designed to take advantage of the tax breaks available to LLCs and LLPs. Corresponds to the print volume of the same name. **Availability:** Online: Thomson RIA, Thomson West; CD-ROM: Thomson RIA. **Type:** Full text.

54905 ■ OneDisc
Tax Analysts
510 N Washington St., Ste. 400
Falls Church, VA 22046
Ph:(703)533-4400
Free: 800-955-2444
Co. E-mail: cservice@tax.org
URL: http://www.taxanalysts.com
Description: Contains many of the basic IRS documents including the Internal Revenue Code, the IRS Regulations, IRS Tax Information Publications, IRS Revenue Rulings, IRS Revenue Procedures, IRS Letter Rulings, and IRS Announcements. Features Tax Analysts' More Understandable Code and a Federal TaxGuide to make it easier to work with the Internal Revenue Code and related IRS regulations. **Availability:** CD-ROM: Tax Analysts. **Type:** Full text.

54906 ■ State and Local Taxes Weekly
Thomson RIA
395 Hudson St., 4th Fl.
New York, NY 10014
Ph:(212)367-6300
Free: 800-431-9025
Co. E-mail: ria@thomson.com
URL: http://ria.thomson.com
Description: Contains up-to-date information on state and local tax issues in all 50 states as well as the District of Columbia. Covers tax laws, legislation, rulings, and more. Includes expert tax analysis and commentary geared toward practicing tax attorneys. **Type:** Full text.

54907 ■ State Research Library
Tax Analysts
510 N Washington St., Ste. 400
Falls Church, VA 22046
Ph:(703)533-4400
Free: 800-955-2444
Co. E-mail: cservice@tax.org
URL: http://www.taxanalysts.com
Description: Provides a complete set of statutes and regulations from all 50 states, the District of Columbia, and U.S. possessions. Also includes a quick reference tax rate chart for each state for sales, use, income, estate, inheritance, gift, and gasoline taxes. **Availability:** Online: Thomson West. **Type:** Full text.

54908 ■ State Tax Notes
Tax Analysts
510 N Washington St., Ste. 400
Falls Church, VA 22046
Ph:(703)533-4400
Free: 800-955-2444
Co. E-mail: cservice@tax.org
URL: http://www.taxanalysts.com
Description: Follows tax developments in every state, and keeps track of interstate trends. Covers multi-state Organizations, state tax conferences, tax decisions from courts nationwide, rulings and regulations from revenue departments, and legislation in all 50 states each week. **Availability:** Online: Lexis-Nexis. **Type:** Full text.

54909 ■ The State Tax OneDisc
Tax Analysts
510 N Washington St., Ste. 400
Falls Church, VA 22046
Ph:(703)533-4400
Free: 800-955-2444
Co. E-mail: cservice@tax.org
URL: http://www.taxanalysts.com
Description: Contains tax statutes, regulations, and court cases for all 50 states and the District of Colum-

bia and governing territories.Includes directory information for all state revenue officials, state supreme court clerks, and state attorney generals. Also includes the U.S. tax code and pertinent regulations, State Supreme Court cases and U.S. Supreme Court cases dealing with taxes. **Availability:** CD-ROM: Tax Analysts. **Type:** Full text.

54910 ■ State Tax Today
Tax Analysts
510 N Washington St., Ste. 400
Falls Church, VA 22046
Ph:(703)533-4400
Free: 800-955-2444
URL: http://www.taxanalysts.com
Description: Covers tax news and documents from every state, the District of Columbia, and all U.S. possessions, complete with summaries and full text of legislation. Includes proposed and finalized regulations, *Revenue Rulings & Procedures*, supreme, appellate, and tax court opinions, and private letter rulings. **Availability:** Online: Tax Analysts. **Type:** Full text.

54911 ■ Tax Directory
Tax Analysts
510 N Washington St., Ste. 400
Falls Church, VA 22046
Ph:(703)533-4400
Free: 800-955-2444
Co. E-mail: cservice@tax.org
URL: http://www.taxanalysts.com
Description: Contains information on more than 20,00 tax professionals. Vol. One Government Officials Worldwide including state and federal officials, including taxwriting committees U.S. Department of Treasury and IRS, Tax Court Judges, International Financial Specialists, Tax and Business Journalists, Professional Associations, and Tax Groups and Coalitions. Vol. Two Corporate Tax Managers including names and contact information for tax managers in largest U.S corporations. Entries including industry description derived from the Securities and Exchange Commission's four-digit Standard Industry Classification code used by the listed companies for filing purposes. **Availability:** Online: LexisNexis; CD-ROM: Tax Analysts. **Type:** Directory.

54912 ■ Tax Notes
Tax Analysts
510 N Washington St., Ste. 400
Falls Church, VA 22046
Ph:(703)533-4400
Free: 800-955-2444
Co. E-mail: cservice@tax.org
URL: http://www.taxanalysts.com
Description: Contains the complete text of *Tax Notes Magazine*, covering all aspects of U.S. federal taxation. Includes news items and feature articles on tax developments, tax policy issues, and congressional developments. Also provides summaries of Internal Revenue Service (IRS) regulations, relevant court opinions, tax-related correspondence between the U.S. Treasury and the tax bar, IRS letter rulings and Technical Advice Memorandums, *Congressional Record* items, IRS manual changes, and IRS proposed and final regulations (with public comments). Also provides summaries of such documents as the IRS General Counsel Memorandums, Supreme Court tax-related opinions, and Actions on Decisions; IRS revenue rulings and revenue procedures; and tax-related reports from congressional tax-writing committees, the Joint Committee on Taxation, the IRS, U.S. Treasury, General Accounting Office, Congressional Budget Office, and other sources. **Availability:** Online: LexisNexis; CD-ROM: Tax Analysts. **Type:** Full text.

54913 ■ Tax Notes International
Tax Analysts
510 N Washington St., Ste. 400
Falls Church, VA 22046
Ph:(703)533-4400
Free: 800-955-2444
Co. E-mail: cservice@tax.org
URL: http://www.taxanalysts.com

Description: Covers tax news, digests, commentary, and documents at the International level. Provides updates on statutes, regulations, new court decisions, and a tax calendar covering important international tax events and conferences. **Availability:** Online: Tax Analysts, LexisNexis. **Type:** Full text.

54914 ■ TaxPractice
Tax Analysts
510 N Washington St., Ste. 400
Falls Church, VA 22046
Free: 800-955-2444
Co. E-mail: cservice@tax.org
URL: http://www.taxanalysts.com
Description: Covers all federal tax News related to tax practice and litigation. Reports on the most important new IRS rulings and regulations, and tax developments in Congress and the courts, and significant tax cases. Included with the Complete Federal Research Library. **Availability:** Online: LexisNexis. **Type:** Full text.

LIBRARIES

54915 ■ Arnold & Porter–Library
399 Park Ave.
New York, NY 10022-4690
Ph:(212)715-1382
Fax: (212)715-1399
Co. E-mail: kim.fenty@aporter.com
Contact: Kim R. Fenty, Lib.Mgr.
Scope: Litigation; law - tax, corporate, and environmental. **Services:** Interlibrary loan; Library not open to the public. **Holdings:** 20,000 books; 400 bound periodical volumes. **Subscriptions:** 205 journals and other serials; 15 newspapers.

54916 ■ Gardiner Roberts LLP–Library
Scotia Plaza, Ste. 3100
40 King St. W.
Toronto, ON, Canada M5H 3Y2
Ph:(416)865-6728
Fax: (416)865-6636
Co. E-mail: wroulston@gardiner-roberts.com
URL: http://www.gardiner-roberts.com
Contact: Wray Roulston, Hd.Libn.
Scope: Law - administrative, civil, commercial, insurance, municipal, real estate, tax; intellectual property; information technology. **Services:** Interlibrary loan; copying. **Holdings:** 2000 books; 300 bound periodical volumes; 500 reports; CD-ROMs. **Subscriptions:** 200 journals and other serials; 6 newspapers.

54917 ■ Greene Radovsky Maloney Share–Library
4 Embarcadero Ctr., Ste. 4000
San Francisco, CA 94111
Ph:(415)981-1400
Fax: (415)777-4961
Co. E-mail: info@grmslaw.com
URL: http://www.greeneradovsky.com
Contact: Mary Sigafoos, Libn.
Scope: Taxation. **Services:** Interlibrary loan; copying; Library not open to the public. **Holdings:** 1200 books; 75 bound periodical volumes. **Subscriptions:** 150 journals and other serials; 10 newspapers.

54918 ■ Ross & McBride–Library
PO Box 907
Hamilton, ON, Canada L8N 3P6
Ph:(905)526-9800
Fax: (905)526-0732
Co. E-mail: contact@rossmcbride.com
URL: http://www.rossmcbride.com/
Scope: Law, taxation. **Holdings:** Figures not available.

54919 ■ Southeastern University–Library
501 I St., SW
Washington, DC 20024
Ph:(202)478-8272
Fax: (202)488-8093
Co. E-mail: library@seu.edu
URL: http://www.seu.edu/gen/library/default.htm

Contact: O.D. Alexander, MLS, Dir.
Scope: Management, public administration, taxes, marketing, accounting, computer science, childhood development education, health services administration, business management, information systems, nonprofit management. **Services:** Interlibrary loan; copying; Library open to the public for reference use only. **Holdings:** 40,000 books; 53 bound periodical volumes. **Subscriptions:** 150 journals and other serials; 6 newspapers.

START-UP INFORMATION

54920 ■ "Kick Back and Relax" in *Entrepreneur*
Pub: Entrepreneur Media Inc.
Ed: Romanus Wolter. Description: Relaxation time is essential to entrepreneurial success. Four tips to help avoid burnout are listed, focusing on making relaxation an essential part of a regular routine.

ASSOCIATIONS AND OTHER ORGANIZATIONS

54921 ■ APQC
123 N Post Oak Ln., 3rd Fl.
Houston, TX 77024
Ph:(713)681-4020
Free: 800-776-9676
Fax: (713)681-8578
Co. E-mail: apqcinfo@apqc.org
URL: http://www.apqc.org
Contact: Carla O'Dell PhD, Pres.

54922 ■ Center for Creative Leadership
PO Box 26300
Greensboro, NC 27438-6300
Ph:(336)545-2810
Fax: (336)282-3284
Co. E-mail: info@leaders.ccl.org
URL: http://www.ccl.org
Contact: John Alexander, Pres.
Description: Promotes behavioral science research and leadership education. Publications: *Center for Creative Leadership Catalog* (annual); *Leadership in Action* (bimonthly); *Research Reports* (periodic).

54923 ■ Cost Management Group
10 Paragon Dr.
Montvale, NJ 07645-1773
Ph:(201)573-9000
Free: 800-638-4427
Fax: (201)474-1600
Co. E-mail: ima@imanet.org
URL: http://www.imanet.org/membership_communities_cost_management.asp
Description: A group within the Institute of Management Accountants. Seeks to improve the quality of corporate cost management systems. Educates business professionals about decision-making and productivity improvement. Provides a means of exchanging opinions and experiences about cost management systems. Conducts surveys; compiles statistics.

54924 ■ Employers Group
PO Box 15013
Los Angeles, CA 90015
Free: 800-748-8484
Fax: (213)742-0301
Co. E-mail: wmdahlman@employersgroup.com
URL: http://employersgroup.com
Contact: William A. Dahlman, Pres./CEO

Description: Provides human resources management services including wage, salary, and benefit surveys; personnel practices surveys; management counseling; management education programs; litigation surveillance; government relations; and research library service. Provides customized human resources services including employee opinion surveys and employee communications programs through its subsidiary, The Employers Group Service Corp. Offers unemployment insurance services, workers' compensation programs, and in-house management training programs. Conducts research and educational programs; maintains speakers' bureau. Publications: *California Employment Law* (annual); *California Wage and Hour GuideAL* (annual); Newsletter (monthly).

54925 ■ Human Resource Planning Society
317 Madison Ave., Ste. 1509
New York, NY 10017
Ph:(212)490-6387
Fax: (212)682-6851
Co. E-mail: info@hrps.org
URL: http://www.hrps.org
Contact: Walter J. Cleaver, Pres./CEO
Membership: Human resource planning professionals representing 160 corporations and 3000 individual members, including strategic human resources planning and development specialists, staffing analysts, business planners, line managers, and others who function as business partners in the application of strategic human resource management practices. Purpose: Seeks to increase the impact of human resource planning and management on business and organizational performance. Sponsors program of professional development in human resource planning concepts, techniques, and practices. Offers networking opportunities. Publications: *Human Resource Planning* (quarterly); *Human Resource Planning Society—Membership Directory* (annual). Also publishes educational materials on best practices.

54926 ■ Institute for Operations Research and the Management Sciences
7240 Parkway Dr., Ste. 310
Hanover, MD 21076
Ph:(443)757-3500
Free: 800-446-3676
Fax: (443)757-3515
Co. E-mail: informs@informs.org
URL: http://www.informs.org
Contact: Mark G. Doherty, Exec.Dir.
Description: International scientific society dedicated to improving operational processes, decision-making and management through the application of methods from science and mathematics. Represents operations researchers, management scientists, and those working in related fields within engineering and the information, decision, mathematical, and social sciences. Publications: *Information Systems Research* (quarterly); *INFORMS Journal on Computing* (quarterly); *Informs Transactions on Education* (periodic); *Interfaces* (bimonthly); *Management Science* (monthly); *Manufacturing and Service Operations Management*

(quarterly); *Marketing Science* (quarterly); *Mathematics of Operations Research* (quarterly); *Operations Research* (bimonthly); *OR/MS Today* (bimonthly); *Organization Science* (bimonthly) ; *PubsOnLine Suite*; *Transportation Science* (quarterly). Also publishes marketing management models.

54927 ■ International Production Planning and Scheduling Association
PO Box 5031
Incline Village, NV 89450
Ph:(775)833-3922
Co. E-mail: billk@ippsa.org
URL: http://www.ippsa.org
Description: Seeks to expand the knowledge of advanced planning and scheduling technology among manufacturing companies. Conducts educational planning and scheduling seminars and integrates Material and Capacity Management in its workshops. Publications: *Evaluating Scheduling Performance*; *FCS Book Description*; *Scheduling Methods that Work*; *Seminar Presenters Biography*.

54928 ■ International Society for the Study of Time
442 Brookhurst Ave.
Narberth, PA 19072
Co. E-mail: isst@studyoftime.org
URL: http://www.studyoftime.org
Contact: Dr. Thomas Weissert, Exec. Sec.
Membership: Scientists and humanists. Purpose: Explores the idea and experience of time and the role time plays in the physical, organic, intellectual, and social worlds. Encourages interdisciplinary study; provides a forum for exchange of ideas among members. Publications: *KronoScope* (semiannual); *The Study of Time*; *Time's News: An Aperiodic Newsletter* (annual).

54929 ■ Project Management Institute
4 Campus Blvd.
Newtown Square, PA 19073-3299
Ph:(610)356-4600
Fax: (610)356-4647
Co. E-mail: pmihq@pmi.org
URL: http://www.pmi.org
Contact: Gregory Balestrero, CEO
Membership: Corporations and individuals engaged in the practice of project management; project management students and educators. Purpose: Seeks to advance the study, teaching, and practice of project management. Establishes project management standards; conducts educational and professional certification courses; bestows Project Management Professional credential upon qualified individuals. Offers educational seminars and global congresses. Publications: *PM Network* (monthly); *PM Network's Career Track* (semiannual); *PMI Today* (monthly); *Project Management Institute—Annual Proceedings* (annual); *Project Management Journal* (quarterly). Also publishes abstracts, books, papers presented at past seminars, and special research reports.

54930 ■ Society for Advancement of Management
Texas A&M University - Corpus Christi
College of Business

6300 Ocean Dr. - FC 111
Corpus Christi, TX 78412
Ph:(361)825-6045
Free: 888-827-6077
Fax: (361)825-2725
Co. E-mail: moustafa@cob.tamucc.edu
URL: http://www.cob.tamucc.edu/sam
Contact: Dr. Moustafa H. Abdelsamad, Pres./CEO
Description: Represents management executives in industry commerce, government, and education. Fields of interest include management education, policy and strategy, MIS, international management, administration, budgeting, collective bargaining, distribution, incentives, materials handling, quality control, and training. **Publications:** *Management in Practice* (quarterly); *SAM Advanced Management Journal* (quarterly); *The SAM News International* (quarterly); *Society for Advancement of Management—International Management Conference Proceedings* (annual).

EDUCATIONAL PROGRAMS

54931 ■ Communicating, Negotiating, and Prioritizing Skills for Administrative Professionals (Canada)
Canadian Management Centre
150 York St., 5th Fl.
Toronto, ON, Canada M5H 3S5
Ph:(866)400-4941 ext. 2252
Free: 877-CMC-2500
Fax: (416)313-4985
Co. E-mail: cmcinfo@cmctraining.org
URL: http://www.cmcamai.org
Price: $1,395 Canadian. **Description:** Covers multitasking skills, effective prioritizing, teamwork and negotiation, time management, and increase morale for increased productivity. **Locations:** Toronto, ON

54932 ■ Managing Chaos: Dynamic Time Management, Recall, Reading, and Stress Management Skills for Administrative Professionals (Canada)
Canadian Management Centre
150 York St., 5th Fl.
Toronto, ON, Canada M5H 3S5
Ph:(866)400-4941 ext. 2252
Free: 877-CMC-2500
Fax: (416)313-4985
Co. E-mail: cmcinfo@cmctraining.org
URL: http://www.cmcamai.org
Price: $1,395 Canadian. **Description:** Covers uses for handling tremendous amounts of information, including better concentration and memorization, stress relievers, and effective multi-tasking. **Locations:** Toronto, ON.

54933 ■ Time Management (Canada)
Canadian Management Centre
150 York St., 5th Fl.
Toronto, ON, Canada M5H 3S5
Ph:(866)400-4941 ext. 2252
Free: 877-CMC-2500
Fax: (416)313-4985
Co. E-mail: cmcinfo@cmctraining.org
URL: http://www.cmcamai.org
Price: $1,395 Canadian. **Description:** Covers time management tools, including delegation, prioritizing, avoid unreasonable demands effectively, handle interruptions and tools for multi-tasking. **Locations:** Toronto, ON.

REFERENCE WORKS

54934 ■ "Alone in Your Time Zone: Are You Plagued by Chronic Lateness?" in *Black Enterprise* (Vol. 35, December 2004, No. 5, pp. 155)
Pub: Earl G. Graves Publishing Co. Inc.
Ed: Alfred A. Edmond Jr. **Description:** Issues involved with chronic lateness are discussed with tips to better manage time.

54935 ■ "The Balancing Act: How Busy Executives Make Their Lives Work" in *Black Enterprise* (Vol. 37, February 2007, No. 7, pp. 118)
Pub: Earl G. Graves Publishing Co. Inc.
Ed: Marcia A. Reed-Woodard. **Description:** More than 70 percent of women with children work outside the home, according to a 2005 survey conducted by the U.S. Department of Labor Bureau. One of the biggest struggles these women face is balancing family with career aspirations and climbing the corporate ranks.

54936 ■ "Balancing Act" in *My Business* (October/November 2002, pp. 42)
Pub: My Business Magazine
Ed: Tamara Holmes. **Description:** Candace Giles, owner of Candace Giles & Associates, a home-based real estate appraisal firm in Maryland, explains how she learned to balance her business and personal life.

54937 ■ "Beware the busy manager" in *Harvard Business Review* (Vol. 80, No. 2, February 2002, pp. 62)
Pub: Harvard Business School Press
Ed: Heike Bruch, Sumantra Ghoshal. **Description:** The business of executives and how the busiest ones may not necessarily be accomplishing that much work is discussed.

54938 ■ "The case against disorganization: how to arrest this time bandit" in *Black Enterprise* (Vol. 32, No. 8, March 2002, pp. 63)
Pub: Earl Graves Publishing Co.
Ed: Sonia Alleyne. **Description:** An interview with career consultant, Peggy Duncan. Duncan offers steps to become more organized, and as a result, more productive and time efficient.

54939 ■ "Cybersecretary" in *Women in Business* (Vol. 53, No. 5, September-October, 2001, pp. 34)
Pub: The ABWA Co. Inc.
Description: Personal information management systems can ensure that scheduling appointments and answering the phone are done correctly.

54940 ■ "Design Principal" in *Fast Company* (September 2001, pp. 48)
Pub: Fast Company
Description: Profile of Chris Bangle, design chief for BMW. Bangle explains the importance of providing time for reflection on what's important to the customer, when designing new automobiles.

54941 ■ "Easy Does It" in *Entrepreneur* (Vol. 33, October 2005, No. 10, pp. 122)
Pub: Entrepreneur Media Inc.
Ed: Romanus Wolter. **Description:** In order to be successful, entrepreneurs must learn to balance work time with their personal life as a small business grows. A good rule to follow: success is not about the number of hours worked, but the outcome of the efforts involved.

54942 ■ "Efficiency Creates Opportunity" in *Hispanic Business* (June 2002, pp. 74)
Pub: Hispanic Business
Ed: Scott Williams. **Description:** Efficiency experts agree that companies can become more efficient by fostering an environment of improvement.

54943 ■ *Enlightened Leadership: Best Practice Guidelines and Timesaving Tools for Easily Implementing Learning Organizations*
Pub: Learning House Publishing, Incorporated
Ed: Alan G. Thomas; Ralph L. LoVuolo; Jeanne C. Hillson. **Released:** September 2006, printable 3 times/year. **Price:** $21.00. **Description:** Book provides the tools required to create a learning organization management model along with a step-by-step guide for team planning and learning. The strategy works as a manager's self-help guide as well as offering continuous learning and improvement for company-wide success.

54944 ■ "5 Ways to Get Rid of Clutter: Spring Cleaning" in *My Business* (April/May 2003, pp. 12)
Pub: My Business Magazine
Ed: Julie Bawden Davis. **Description:** Experts offer five tips for eliminating clutter in work areas, thus increasing productivity.

54945 ■ "From office catnaps to lunchtime jogs" in *Wall Street Journal* (May 16, 2002, pp. D1)
Pub: Wall Street Journal
Ed: Sue Shellenbarger. **Description:** The art of balancing work and life is explored. Statistical data included.

54946 ■ "Get All Your Work Done in Half the Time, Be the Office Hero...and Go Home Early" in *PC Computing* (March 2000, pp. 128)
Pub: Ziff-Davis Inc.
Ed: Leslie Ayers. **Description:** Web-based courses that let people learn at their convenience are discussed. These courses are considered to be the best way to build technology and business skills.

54947 ■ "Get organized" in *Black Enterprise* (Vol. 33, No. 6, January 2003, pp. 10)
Pub: Earl Graves Publishing Co.
Description: Online advice is offered to get a career on track, tips for getting organized at work, and moving up the corporate ladder, are just a few of the issues addressed at this Web site.

54948 ■ "Getting Organized" in *Small Business Opportunities* (Vol. 16, No. 2, March 2004, pp. 60)
Pub: Harris Publications, Inc.
Ed: Barbara Hemphill. **Description:** Six simple steps for increasing sales and relieving stress are presented.

54949 ■ *Getting Things Done: The Art of Stress-Free Productivity*
Pub: Penguin Books (USA) Incorporated
Ed: David Allen. **Released:** December 2002. **Price:** $15.00. **Description:** Coach and management consultant recommends methods for stress-free performance under the premise that productivity is directly related to our ability to relax.

54950 ■ "Growing Pains" in *Inc.* (October 2000, pp. 20)
Pub: The Goldhirsh Group
Ed: Toby Toler. **Description:** The control of one's company and one's time are investigated, with comments from entrepreneurs about methods they have used in the past.

54951 ■ "Holiday Week Can Be Extra-Productive for Some Sacramento, Calif.-Area Workers" in *Sacramento Bee* (December 28, 2005)
Pub: The Sacramento Bee
Ed: Rachel Osterman. **Description:** Many Sacramento, California executives use the week between Christmas and New Year's as a time to clean, file, and plan for the upcoming year.

54952 ■ "Home Office, Simplified" in *Home Office Computing* (Vol. 18, No. 7, July 2000, pp. 54)
Pub: Scholastic Inc.
Ed: Jeffery D. Zbar. **Description:** Home-based workers often develop bad habits that lead to disorganization and reduce productivity. It is important to take control of a home office and manage the workspace effectively. Three home workers teamed with organizational experts to discuss their own weaknesses.

54953 ■ "Hot Disks" in *Entrepreneur* (Vol. 32, September 2004, No. 9, pp. 46)
Pub: Entrepreneur Media Inc.
Ed: Liane Cassavoy. **Description:** X1 Technologies produces an index of computer contents, including most popular file formats, email and attachments; Fonix has updated its speech interface application for

mobile phones; WorkPerfect Office 12 offers applications compatible with Microsoft and includes Presentations, Quattro Pro, WordPerfect and an address book; Project Insight's management software allows users to import and export projects.

54954 ■ "Hot Tip: Limo as Mobile Office" in *Inc.* **(November 15, 2000, pp. 26)**
Pub: The Goldhirsh Group
Description: The owner of a janitorial services company has outfitted a limousine and three vans with an inverter, a device that lets him and his workers use laptops, printers and fax machines to save time and money for his company.

54955 ■ *How to Get Things Done: Take Control of Your Time, Tasks, & Priorities, & Accomplish More Than You Ever Thought Possible*
Pub: Pryor Resources, Inc.
Released: 1997. **Price:** $199.95 (VHS) 3 cassettes.
Description: Presents a simple system of prioritizing that ensures important things always get done. Describes how to balance competing demands, use powerful delegating techniques to leverage time and effectiveness, and strengthen organization skills to streamline tasks.

54956 ■ "How to beat the Monday blues" in *Women in Business* **(Vol. 53, No. 3, May-June, 2001, pp. 16)**
Pub: The ABWA Co. Inc.
Ed: Liz Hubler. **Description:** Many people experience the 'Monday blues' feeling sometimes with regard to their work, but it can be overcome. Tips include suggestions for changing routines, asking for help, taking regular breaks and controlling time schedules.

54957 ■ "How To Love Your Layover" in *Business 2.0* **(Vol. 6, September 2005, No. 8, pp. 130)**
Pub: Time, Inc.
Ed: Georgia Flight. **Description:** Airports are offering business travelers creative ways to pass time while waiting for departures. Dallas/Fort Worth International Airport has opened a $1.2 billion Terminal D which highlights live music on the mezzanine level above the food court, as well as displaying artwork throughout the terminal.

54958 ■ "If you want something done right, delegate it" in *Women in Business* **(Vol. 53, No. 7, January-February 2002, pp. 13)**
Pub: The ABWA Co Inc.
Ed: Liz Hughes. **Description:** Delegation can provide a manager with an opportunity to trust their staff and evaluate their own communication skills. Delegation allows a manager additional time for strategic planning.

54959 ■ "It's All About Convenience" in *Success* **(Vol. 47, No. 6, November 2000, pp. 88)**
Pub: Success Publishing, Inc.
Ed: Jane Shealy. **Description:** Consumers are spending big bucks on time saving services. If you can save time for consumers, they will shell out millions for the convenience. The field is diverse, but the common thread is simple: these businesses make life a little easier.

54960 ■ "Just 'To-Do' It: Having Trouble Getting Organized? Start by Getting a Grip on Your To-Do List" in *Entrepreneur* **(August 2004)**
Pub: Entrepreneur Media Inc.
Ed: Mark Hendricks. **Description:** Successful entrepreneurs create a weekly to-do list in order to stay focused and organized.

54961 ■ "Kick the Habit" in *Home Office Computing* **(Vol. 17, No. 1, January 1999, pp. 67)**
Pub: Line56 Media
Ed: Joanne Cleaver. **Description:** A guide to using technology for more efficient time management in home offices is presented. A good filing system can make a difference when organizing an office. A service called Paper Tiger combines the assistance of a professional organizer with maintenance software.

54962 ■ "Kids @ Work" in *My Business* **(October/November 2002, pp. 42)**
Pub: My Business Magazine
Description: Multi-tasking is the key to running a successful business from home, while attending to a young family. Tips for working from home with young children are offered.

54963 ■ *Lean Six Sigmas That Works: A Powerful Action Plan for Dramatically Improving Quality, Increasing Speed, and Reducing Waste*
Pub: American Management Association
Ed: Bill Carreira; Bill Trudell. **Released:** 2006. **Price:** $21.95.

54964 ■ "Leave It at the Office" in *Home Office Computing* **(Vol. 19, No. 1, January 2001, pp. 104)**
Pub: Scholastic Inc.
Ed: Marshall F. Lager. **Description:** The importance of leaving work at the office is stressed in the article.

54965 ■ "Let Go" in *My Business* **(December/January 2003, pp. 35-37)**
Pub: My Business Magazine
Ed: Paul S. Howell. **Description:** A look at four small businesses that profited when their leaders learned to delegate work to employees. Owners of small companies tend to micromanage much more that managers in large corporations.

54966 ■ "A Little Equation that Creates Big Results" in *Home Business* **(Vol. 12, October 2005, No. 5, pp. 86)**
Pub: Home Business Magazine
Ed: Chris Widener. **Description:** Time management skills are essential to any successful business; entrepreneurs must learn to manage time properly.

54967 ■ "Manage Projects in Real Time" in *PC Magazine* **(February 20, 2001, pp. 37)**
Pub: Ziff-Davis Publishing Company
Ed: Sheryl Canter. **Description:** A profile of the Internet-based, cross-platform project management solution software, TeamCenter 4.0, from Inovie Software.

54968 ■ "A Message About Managing Email" in *Fast Company* **(August 2001, pp. 38)**
Pub: Fast Company
Ed: Christine Canabou. **Description:** Sabrina Horn, founder, president and CEO of the San Francisco-based Horn Group, a public relations firm, offers insight into managing email to avoid losing productive work time.

54969 ■ "Mission accomplish: manage multiple projects and meet deadlines" in *Women In Business* **(Vol. 52, No. 2, March 2000, pp. 38)**
Pub: The ABWA Co., Inc.
Ed: Jane Thomas. **Description:** Working women can manage their time more effectively if they look at their aims in the various sectors of life, and plan accordingly. They should ensure they do not waste time.

54970 ■ "Moms Say Missing Their Babies is Hardest Part of Returning to Work" in *Marketing to Women* **(Vol. 19, November 2006, No. 11, pp. 3)**
Pub: EPM Communications, Inc.
Description: According to a survey by Modern Mom, the hardest thing about going to work outside the home for mothers is the separation anxiety they experience with their children. This leads to problems like getting to the office on time and getting back to speed with projects.

54971 ■ "My 'Won't Do' List" in *My Business* **(February/March 2003, pp. 49)**
Pub: My Business Magazine
Ed: Terri Lonier. **Description:** Ways to streamline a small business owner's life are listed.

54972 ■ "The Office" in *Entrepreneur* **(Vol. 33, October 2005, No. 10, pp. 76)**
Pub: Entrepreneur Media Inc.
Ed: April Y. Pennington. **Description:** A neat and organized work space can inspire and increase productivity. Tips to organize an office are offered.

54973 ■ "Parent Trap?" in *Entrepreneur* **(Vol. 33, September 2005, No. 9, pp. 17)**
Pub: Entrepreneur Media Inc.
Ed: **Description:** Entrepreneurial parents have positive things to offer their children; however there are obstacles to overcome in meeting the challenges of parenting while running a successful company.

54974 ■ *Personal Time Management*
Pub: Crisp Publications, Inc.
Ed: Marion E. Haynes. **Released:** Revised edition. **Price:** $10.95.

54975 ■ "Plan Events that Will Fill Seats" in *Women In Business* **(Vol. 52, No. 2, March 2000, pp. 32)**
Pub: The ABWA Co., Inc.
Ed: Jane Thomas. **Description:** Kansas City Express Network is a network for professional women which helps them to make contacts, while also considering their lack of time. The group holds 1-1/2 hour monthly lunch meetings and plans meetings quarterly.

54976 ■ "Play Nice" in *Entrepreneur* **(Vol. 32, September 2004, No. 9, pp. 32)**
Pub: Entrepreneur Media Inc.
Ed: Mark Henricks. **Description:** Review of How Full Is Your Bucket? The book offers positive strategies for work and life management.

54977 ■ *Practical Time Management*
Pub: Crisp Publications, Inc.
Ed: Marion E. Haynes. **Released:** Revised edition. **Price:** $14.95.

54978 ■ *Practical Time Management: How to Get More Things Done in Less Time*
Pub: Self-Counsel Press, Inc.
Ed: Bradley C. McRae. **Released:** 1992, second edition. **Price:** $7.95 (paper).

54979 ■ "Prioritizing a Hectic Schedule" in *Sales & Marketing Management* **(Vol. 157, January 2005, No. 1, pp. 52)**
Pub: VNU Business Media
Ed: Kathryn Droullard. **Description:** Profile of Brian O'Neill, marketing and communications director at Circadian Technologies in Lexington, Massachusetts; O'Neill assists managers of extended-hour, shift-work operations to build time-management skills.

54980 ■ "Professional Organizer Sets Up Shop" in *Bellingham Business Journal* **(January 2007, pp. 4)**
Pub: Sun News Inc.
Description: Profile of Cathy Gersich, a professional organizer and owner of PriOrganize. PriOrganize provides an invaluable organizational service to help individuals simplify their homes and offices.

54981 ■ "Punching the Time Card" in *Incentive* **(Vol. 174, No. 8, August 2000, pp. 75)**
Pub: Bill Communications
Ed: Emily Hodnett. **Description:** Both busy consumers and hard-working employees like the time-saving nature of debit and stored value cards.

54982 ■ "Pushing the Right Buttons" in *Crain's Detroit Business* **(Vol. 23, January 15,2007, No. 3, pp. 11)**
Pub: Crain Communications Inc. - Detroit
Ed: Amy Lane. **Description:** Speed, flexibility, and time compression advantages are driving wireless companies to expand networks and facilities in Southeastern Michigan to further serve small business needs. Significant cost savings can be realized when converting from land-based fax and phone lines.

54983 ■ "Q&A" in *Home Office Computing* **(Vol. 18, No. 11, November 2000, pp. 15)**
Pub: Scholastic Inc.
Ed: Marilyn Zelinsky Syarto. **Description:** Are you drowning in e-mail? David Ferris, president of Ferris Research, a San Francisco-based consulting firm specializing in messaging and collaborative technology, discusses how to manage e-mail overload.

54984 ■ "Quitting time!" in *Incentive* **(Vol. 174, No. 10, October 2000, pp. 142)**
Pub: Bill Communications
Ed: Jennifer White. **Description:** Five strategies to enable workers to leave work early are explored.

54985 ■ "Ready To Go: How An Online Tool Helped One Company Speed Distribution of Marketing Materials To Reps" in *Sales & Marketing Management*
Pub: VNU Business Media
Ed: Alan Horowitz. **Description:** Allstate Insurance, is providing its sales reps access to thousands of sales and marketing materials via a Web-hosted service that automates order fulfillment and inventory management of sales and marketing materials. Research indicates that without this type of service, sales reps spend 25 percent of their time searching for and assembling information for sales calls.

54986 ■ "Running Into Profits" in *My Business* **(June/July 2004, pp. 16)**
Pub: My Business Magazine
Description: Jogging sessions fit into tight schedules may actually improve a company's profits.

54987 ■ "School's out; Working Moms are Worried" in *Marketing to Women* **(Vol. 20, January 2007, No. 1, pp. 5)**
Pub: EPM Communications, Inc.
Description: Catalyst, a non-profit research firm dedicated to expanding workplace opportunities to women, has discovered that work productivity tends to be drained by concern over their children's after-school time activities.

54988 ■ "Slack Off" in *Fast Company* **(August 2001, pp. 27)**
Pub: Fast Company
Ed: George Anders. **Description:** Who says being productive always means being busy? Not high-tech consultant Tom Demaro, who shares his reasons for being so up on downtime.

54989 ■ "The Sweet Spot: A Sugar-Coated Pitch Paid Off Big Time" in *Black Enterprise* **(Vol. 37, November 2006, No. 4, pp. 71)**
Pub: Earl G. Graves Publishing Co. Inc.
Ed: Laura Egodigwe. **Description:** In an interview with Debra Sandler, president of McNeil Nutritionals L. L.C., Sandler talks about the challenges of bringing a new product to the marketplace, how her personal experiences effect her business decisions, and the difficulties of re-entering the workforce.

54990 ■ *Take Back Your Time: How to Regain Control of Work, Information and Technology*
Pub: St. Martin's Press LLC
Ed: Jan Jasper. **Released:** November 1999. **Price:** $13.95. **Description:** Strategies to become more organized and productive.

54991 ■ "Taking Advantage of Technology" in *Black Enterprise* **(Vol. 31, No. 4, November 2000, pp. 57)**
Pub: Earl Graves Publishing Co.
Ed: Paula McCoy-Pinderhughes. **Description:** Small business owners should "hire" the Internet to delegate and manage time-consuming activities such as accounting, marketing, office management, human resources, and administrative functions to cut operational costs and increase revenue.

54992 ■ "The Easy Entree Expands Service to Accommodate Walk-In Customers" in *Bellingham Business Journal* **(December 2006, pp. 2)**
Pub: Sun News Inc.
Description: Evelyn Turner, owner of The Easy Entree, has expanded her business to now offer a walk-in service for customers. Patrons can create their own entrees or pick up pre-made entrees to take home and cook or freeze.

54993 ■ "There is no correlation at all between success and hours worked" in *Fast Company* **(June 2001, pp. 76)**
Pub: Fast Company
Ed: Seth Godin. **Description:** The article makes the suggestion to take the time to look at the future, and think about how decisions made now will matter in years to come.

54994 ■ "3 Ways to improve your business by getting a life" in *My Business* **(June/July 2002, pp. 26-32)**
Pub: My Business Magazine
Ed: Shannon Scully, Lisa Waddle. **Description:** Small business owners tell how they are able to make time for family, hobbies and relaxation, while running their successful firms. Although multitasking is essential for the small business owner, they must learn to delegate work, set limits, as well as separating personal identity from the company's identity.

54995 ■ *Time Management*
Pub: International Thomson Publishing
Ed: Chris Croft. **Released:** 1997. **Price:** $17.95.

54996 ■ *Time Management: Conquering the Clock*
Pub: Pfeiffer & Co.
Ed: Barrie Hopson and Mike Scally. **Price:** $7.95 (paper).

54997 ■ *To Do Doing Done*
Pub: Simon & Schuster Trade
Ed: G. Lynne Snead and Joyce Wycoff. **Released:** 1997. **Price:** $11.00.

54998 ■ "Transform Your Life" in *Black Enterprise* **(Vol. 37, January 2007, No. 6, pp. 14)**
Pub: Earl G. Graves Publishing Co. Inc.
Description: Through the magazine, television and radio programs, events, and the website, the various platforms of Black Enterprise will provide the tools necessary to achieve success in business ventures, career aspirations, and personal goals.

54999 ■ "Trucking firms hope bridge lanes cut shipping costs" in *Crain's Detroit Business* **(Vol. 18, No. 19, May 13, 2002, pp. 28)**
Pub: Crain Communications Inc. - Detroit
Ed: Michael Strong. **Description:** Transporters hope to see fewer delays and lower shipping costs associated with coming into the United States from Canada via the Ambassador Bridge with the creation of 'fast lanes' for regular bridge crossers.

55000 ■ "Turning Chaos Into Order" in *Sales and Marketing.com* **(Vol. 147, No. 2, February 2004, pp. 90)**
Pub: VNU eMedia, Inc.
Ed: Kristen Richards. **Description:** Getting organized will save an office worker time, money and stress. Time and effort is required up front, and the organization plan must be consistently followed, but it brings rewards in smoother workflow and less waste.

55001 ■ "What Price Time?" in *Home Office Computing* **(Vol. 18, No. 10, October 2000, pp. 14)**
Pub: Scholastic Inc.
Ed: William Van Winkle. **Description:** A list of new companies bringing service providers and users together to help save time is provided.

55002 ■ *What Self-Made Millionaires Really Think, Know and Do: A Straight-Talking Guide to Business Success and Personal Riches*
Pub: John Wiley & Sons, Incorporated
Ed: Richard Dobbins; Barrie Pettman. **Released:** September 2006. **Price:** $24.95. **Description:** Guide for understanding the concepts of entrepreneurial success; the book offers insight into bringing an idea into reality, marketing, time management, leadership skills, and setting clear goals.

55003 ■ "Where can you improve? Get the numbers" in *Crain's Detroit Business* **(Vol. 19, No. 3, January 20, 2003, pp. 14)**
Pub: Crain Communications Inc., Detroit
Ed: Laura Bailey. **Description:** First article to appear under Crain's Detroit Business's Small Business Solutions column. The column will offer advice from local small businesses for solving specific problems. This column address issues involved with time management.

55004 ■ "Women Want More Info on Wellness" in *Marketing to Women* **(Vol. 19, December 2006, No. 2, pp. 8)**
Pub: EPM Communications, Inc.
Description: IVilliage.com reports that although women consider wellness a top priority in their lives, studies show that two-thirds of women surveyed feel that their lives are out of balance. Statistical data included.

55005 ■ "Work, Interrupted: Think Work Distractions Are a Pain? Top CEOs Tend to Disagree" in *Entrepreneur* **(Vol. 32, September 2004, No. 9)**
Pub: Entrepreneur Media Inc.
Ed: Mark Henricks. **Description:** According to Stephanie Winston, an organization expert and author, top executives regard interruptions as a valuable tool for connecting with fellow workers.

55006 ■ "The workplace: learn to do more with less" in *Atlanta Business Chronicle* **(Vol. 25, No. 20, October 25, 2002, pp. 12B)**
Pub: American City Business Publications, Inc.
Ed: Emory Mulling. **Description:** Suggestions are given to improve workplace performance in these trying economic times. Training and matching the right person with the right skills for each job is important. Additionally, it is important to recognize that employees want to be developed and to increase their work skills base.

55007 ■ "Your own time" in *BlackEnterprise* **(Vol. 32, No. 3, October 2001, pp. 162)**
Pub: Earl Graves Publishing Co.
Description: Ways to relax away from business stress are explored.

TRADE PERIODICALS

55008 ■ *Working Together*
Pub: The Dartnell Corp.
Ed: Dionne Ellis, Editor, dellis@lrp.com. **Released:** Biweekly, 26/year. **Price:** $281.70, U.S.. **Description:** Provides non-management level employees motivational information to promote loyalty, cooperation, teamwork, and productivity. Contains articles with suggestions on work habits, customer relations, work safety, and similar topics. Recurring features include self-tests, cartoons, and columns titled Problem Clinic, Success Tips, In the Workplace, and Teamwork in Action.

VIDEOCASSETTES/ AUDIOCASSETTES

55009 ■ *Analyzing Our Time Usage*
Resources for Education & Management, Inc.
1804 Montreal Ct., Ste. A
Tucker, GA 30084
Released: 1972. **Description:** Two methods for managing time-breaking down the types of work we do and setting priorities-are discussed. **Availability:** VHS; 3/4U.

55010 ■ *Another Meeting*
Exec-U-Service Associates
4326 US Highway 1
Princeton, NJ 08540
Released: 1978. **Description:** Gives practical ideas on how to improve the results and time efficiency of meetings. A solid basis for analyzing the meeting process is explored. **Availability:** 3/4U.

55011 ■ *The Big Project: Not So Great Moments in Time Management*
Salenger Films, Inc.
1635 12th St.
Santa Monica, CA 90404-9988
Ph:(310)450-1300
Free: 800-775-5025
Fax: (310)450-1010
Co. E-mail: salenger@aol.com
URL: http://salengerfilms.visualnet.com
Released: 199?. **Price:** $395.00. **Description:** Time management session starter. **Availability:** VHS.

55012 ■ *Do It Now!*
Aspen Publishers
7201 McKinney Circ.
Frederick, MD 21704
Ph:(301)644-3599
Free: 800-638-8437
Fax: (301)644-3550
URL: http://www.aspenpublishers.com
Released: 197?. **Description:** This program examines what procrastination is, what causes it, and suggests techniques for breaking the habit. **Availability:** VHS; 3/4U.

55013 ■ *Don't Agonize—Organize Series with Dr. John Wayne Lee*
Instructional Video
2219 C St.
Lincoln, NE 68502
Ph:(402)475-6570
Free: 800-228-0164
Fax: (402)475-6500
Co. E-mail: feedback@insvideo.com
URL: http://www.insvideo.com
Price: $179.10. **Description:** Dr. John Wayne Lee teaches his techniques on time and self management. Only available in the U.S. **Availability:** VHS.

55014 ■ *The Effective Manager*
Nightingale-Conant Corp.
6245 W. Howard St.
Niles, IL 60714
Ph:(847)647-0300
Free: 800-560-6081
URL: http://www.nightingale.com
Price: $95.00. **Description:** A series of award-winning programs designed to promote effective management and help increase sales. Audio tapes and booklets are included, and the series can be purchased individually or as a set. **Availability:** VHS.

55015 ■ *Empowerment: Managing Your Time*
International Training Consultants, Inc.
1838 Park Oaks
Kemah, TX 77565
Free: 800-998-8764
Co. E-mail: itc@trainingitc.com
URL: http://www.trainingitc.com
Price: $495.00. **Description:** Part of the "Empowerment: The Employee Development Series." Teaches employees to become aware of how they manage their time and offers advice on how they can manage it better. Also discusses priority setting, daily planning, long-range planning, scheduling, and other time management functions. **Availability:** VHS.

55016 ■ *Empowerment: The Employee Development Series*
International Training Consultants, Inc.
1838 Park Oaks
Kemah, TX 77565
Free: 800-998-8764
Co. E-mail: itc@trainingitc.com
URL: http://www.trainingitc.com
Price: $10350.00. **Description:** Employee development series which prepares employees to meet the demands of today's workplace with skill and confidence. Covers such topics as time management, team work, communication, career advancement, working together, and problem solving. Comes with leader's guide, overhead transparencies, five participant booklets, and a complete participant's manual. **Availability:** VHS.

55017 ■ *Get the Edge with Time Management/Rick Barrera*
Instructional Video
2219 C St.
Lincoln, NE 68502
Ph:(402)475-6570
Free: 800-228-0164
Fax: (402)475-6500
Co. E-mail: feedback@insvideo.com
URL: http://www.insvideo.com
Price: $95.00. **Description:** Rick Barrera discusses time management skills. Points out how time management team affect success. Only available in the U.S. **Availability:** VHS.

55018 ■ *Getting Things Done: An Achiever's Guide to Better Time-Management*
Instructional Video
2219 C St.
Lincoln, NE 68502
Ph:(402)475-6570
Free: 800-228-0164
Fax: (402)475-6500
Co. E-mail: feedback@insvideo.com
URL: http://www.insvideo.com
Price: $79.95. **Description:** Offers a systematic approach to achieving goals through the use of time management, stressing the importance of proper prioritization. **Availability:** VHS.

55019 ■ *How to Get Control of Your Time and Your Job*
Aspen Publishers
7201 McKinney Circ.
Frederick, MD 21704
Ph:(301)644-3599
Free: 800-638-8437
Fax: (301)644-3550
URL: http://www.aspenpublishers.com
Released: 1983. **Description:** This is a complete program designed by time management expert Alan La Kein to help you learn to use your time effectively. **Availability:** VHS.

55020 ■ *How to Get Things Done*
Nightingale-Conant Corp.
6245 W. Howard St.
Niles, IL 60714
Ph:(847)647-0300
Free: 800-560-6081
URL: http://www.nightingale.com
Price: $95.00. **Description:** Time-management and time-allocation skills are presented, to help workers accomplish more in less time. Includes an audio cassette and book. **Availability:** VHS.

55021 ■ *Manage Your Time to Build Your Territory*
Dartnell Corp.
360 Hiatt Dr.
Palm Beach Gardens, FL 33418
Ph:(561)622-6520
Free: 800-341-7874
Fax: (561)622-2423
Co. E-mail: custserve@lrp.com
URL: http://www.dartnellcorp.com
Released: 1974. **Description:** An examination of time thieves that rob salespeople of both hours and sales volume. From the "Tough-Minded Salesmanship" series. **Availability:** VHS; 3/4U; Special order formats.

55022 ■ *Management of Time*
Resources for Education & Management, Inc.
1804 Montreal Ct., Ste. A
Tucker, GA 30084
Released: 1972. **Description:** Teaches supervisors how to manage time effectively. It consists of four modules: The Time of Our Lives; Analyzing Our Time Usage; Using Others to Save Time; and Our Time Is Our Time. **Availability:** VHS; 3/4U.

55023 ■ *Managing Time*
LearnCom HR Consulting and Training
38 Discovery, Ste. 250
Irvine, CA 92618
Ph:(515)440-0890

Free: 800-698-8263
Fax: (515)221-3149
Co. E-mail: nhartline@learncom.com
URL: http://www.learncomhr.com
Released: 1968. **Description:** Stimulates the day-to-day planning of work, use of personnel, staff, and use of time. **Availability:** VHS; 3/4U.

55024 ■ *Managing Your Time*
Resources for Education & Management, Inc.
1804 Montreal Ct., Ste. A
Tucker, GA 30084
Released: 1970. **Description:** Shows office workers more than 20 ways to manage their time more effectively. Time-saving suggestions are given for typing, filing, and dictation that pay off in increased productivity and efficiency. **Availability:** VHS; 3/4U.

55025 ■ *A Perfectly Normal Day*
Aspen Publishers
7201 McKinney Circ.
Frederick, MD 21704
Ph:(301)644-3599
Free: 800-638-8437
Fax: (301)644-3550
URL: http://www.aspenpublishers.com
Released: 197?. **Description:** Helps develop a new attitude toward interruptions and crises-and teaches us how to reduce and manage them. **Availability:** VHS; 3/4U.

55026 ■ *Personal Achievement Series—Time Management: How to Increase Your Productivity and Get the Results You Want*
Instructional Video
2219 C St.
Lincoln, NE 68502
Ph:(402)475-6570
Free: 800-228-0164
Fax: (402)475-6500
Co. E-mail: feedback@insvideo.com
URL: http://www.insvideo.com
Price: $69.95. **Description:** Outlines ways to eliminate time-wasting elements of daily life. Includes guidebook. **Availability:** VHS.

55027 ■ *Personal Time Management Video*
Instructional Video
2219 C St.
Lincoln, NE 68502
Ph:(402)475-6570
Free: 800-228-0164
Fax: (402)475-6500
Co. E-mail: feedback@insvideo.com
URL: http://www.insvideo.com
Price: $59.95. **Description:** Brian Tracy illustrates techniques to help put short-term goals in focus to gain long-term aspirations, overcome anxieties related to time restraints, and move on to complete any task. **Availability:** VHS.

55028 ■ *Time Is Money!*
Aspen Publishers
7201 McKinney Circ.
Frederick, MD 21704
Ph:(301)644-3599
Free: 800-638-8437
Fax: (301)644-3550
URL: http://www.aspenpublishers.com
Released: 197?. **Description:** Helps solve salespeople's time problems by teaching them good habits, and provides them with timesaving techniques so they'll spend their time more profitably. **Availability:** VHS; 3/4U.

55029 ■ *Time Management: Keeping the Monkey off Your Back*
Excellence in Training Corp.
1303 Marsh Ln.
Carrollton, TX 75006
Free: 800-747-6569
Released: 1991. **Price:** $595.00. **Description:** A discussion of ways to manage events, rather than being managed by events. **Availability:** VHS; 3/4U; Special order formats.

55030 ■ *Time Management for Managers*
Time-Life Video and Television
1450 Palmyra Ave.
Richmond, VA 23227-4420
Ph:(804)266-6330
Free: 800-950-7887
Fax: (757)427-7905
Released: 1980. **Description:** This six-part series of untitled programs covers the principles of time management, including decision-making, delegating, scheduling, and managing interruptions. It is designed to help managers become more productive in both personal and professional time. Available only as a set. **Availability:** VHS; 3/4U; Special order formats.

55031 ■ *Time Management for Managers and Professionals (41-1XX)*
Thomson National Education Training Group (NETg)
14624 N. Scottsdale Rd., Ste. 300
Phoenix, AZ 85254
Ph:(480)315-4000
Free: 800-265-1900
Fax: (480)315-4001
Co. E-mail: info@netg.com
URL: http://www.netg.com
Released: 1979. **Description:** Part of an integrated course aimed at teaching a strategy for time management which will enable participants to make better contributions to their organization. **Availability:** 3/4U.

55032 ■ *Time Management for Women*
Instructional Video
2219 C St.
Lincoln, NE 68502
Ph:(402)475-6570
Free: 800-228-0164
Fax: (402)475-6500
Co. E-mail: feedback@insvideo.com
URL: http://www.insvideo.com
Price: $79.95. **Description:** Kay Cronkite Waldo offers time management training for women, focusing on behavior patterns, energy cycles, efficiency vs. effectiveness, time wasters, decision-making factors, and the superwoman theory. **Availability:** VHS.

55033 ■ *The Time of Our Lives*
Resources for Education & Management, Inc.
1804 Montreal Ct., Ste. A
Tucker, GA 30084
Released: 1972. **Description:** Good planning is necessary if work is to fit into the time available. The keys of proper time management are introduced. **Availability:** VHS; 3/4U.

55034 ■ *The Time Trap*
American Media, Inc.
4621 121st St.
Urbandale, IA 50323-2311
Ph:(515)224-0919
Free: 888-776-8268
Fax: (515)327-2555
Co. E-mail: custsvc@ammedia.com
URL: http://www.ammedia.com
Released: 1982. **Description:** This program dramatically demonstrates techniques that can help individuals to manage their time better, avoiding those everyday time-wasting problems at the office. **Availability:** VHS; 3/4U.

55035 ■ *The Time of Your Life*
Aspen Publishers
7201 McKinney Circ.
Frederick, MD 21704
Ph:(301)644-3599
Free: 800-638-8437
Fax: (301)644-3550
URL: http://www.aspenpublishers.com
Released: 1985. **Price:** $570.00. **Description:** Based on Alan Lakein's bestseller, outlines 60 simple ideas on how to make more effective use of your time. A meeting guide and optional support materials are available. Revised and updated in 1991. **Availability:** VHS; 3/4U.

55036 ■ *The Two-Minute Drill*
Format International
2421 E. Washington St.
Indianapolis, IN 46201-4123
Released: 1979. **Description:** A program hosted by Fran Tarkenton, retired Minnesota Viking quarterback, that explores how to use time. Time is an ally—a positive approach to use the clock to your advantage. **Availability:** VHS; 3/4U.

55037 ■ *Using Others to Save Time*
Resources for Education & Management, Inc.
1804 Montreal Ct., Ste. A
Tucker, GA 30084
Released: 1972. **Description:** Delegation is defined as more than giving other people more work to do. It is shown to save time, and in the process, develop others' abilities. **Availability:** VHS; 3/4U.

CONSULTANTS

55038 ■ Associations Plus
13 Fountain Dr.
PO Box M
Valhalla, NY 10595-1922
Ph:(914)946-3802
Fax: (914)946-2674
Co. E-mail: mtrossi@aol.com

E-mail: mtrossi@aol.com
Scope: Human resource development experts specializing in sales training, support staff training, trade show selling, time management skills, and stress management training. **Seminars:** Non-verbal Communications; Time/Stress Management; Better Selling Techniques; Trade Show Sales Techniques.

55039 ■ Carson Research Center
2957 Flamingo Dr.
Miami Beach, FL 33140-3916
Ph:(305)534-8846
Free: 800-541-8846
Fax: (305)532-8826
Co. E-mail: gayle@gaylecarson.com
URL: http://www.gaylecarson.com

E-mail: gayle@gaylecarson.com
Scope: Human performance improvement consultants offering a wide variety of training opportunities for personnel of businesses of all kinds, state and national associations, and government agencies. General areas of training include: management training, assertiveness, time management, change management, sales training, supervisory skills, coping with difficult people, stress management, and strategic quality management and customer service, negotiation and shoe string marketing. Serves clients worldwide. Facilitation of board retreats, web-based programs available 24/7. **Publications:** Have over 20 books, audios and videos in the field of management, marketing, customer service and personal development. Dr. Carson has delivered programs in 49 states and over 50 countries. Has helped over 1000 clients in 50 different industries. **Seminars:** Dynamic Leadership; Business 2005; Negotiating to Win; How to Energize Your Life and Make the Difference You Want; Dealing with Difficult People; How to be A Great Coach; How To Turn Customer Service Into An Ongoing Profit Center. The Virtual Classroom. **Special Services:** Designing of websites for associations and developing of on-line CEU courses. On-line Certificate in Consulting program. Executive coaching and consulting.

55040 ■ Dr. Donald Kirkpatrick
1920 Hawthorne Dr.
Elm Grove, WI 53122
Ph:(262)784-8348
Fax: (262)784-7994
Co. E-mail: dleekirk@aol.com

E-mail: dleekirk@aol.com
Scope: Gives presentations for professional societies including ASTD, IQPC, Training and linkage, and conducts in-house seminars for all levels of management on various subjects including: leadership and motivation, communications, managing change, time management, supervisory/management selection, training and development, performance appraisal, coaching, managing conflict, decision making, how to conduct productive meetings, and Evaluating Training Programs: The Four Levels. Serves private industries as well as government agencies. **Publications:** Book Evaluating Training Programs; the Four Levels, Second Edition, Bennett-Koehler Publishers, San Francisco, CA 1998. Book: How to Improve Performance Through Appraisial and Coaching Amacon NY, NY 1983. New Books: Publishrs - Butterworth-Heinemann; 2001, Devleoping Supervisors and Team Leaders; Managing Change Effectively. Great Britain & USA. **Seminars:** Effective Communication; Leadership and Motivation; Teambuilding; Decision Making and Empowerment; Performance Appraisal and Coaching; How to Conduct Productive Meetings; How to Manage Change; Time Management; Orienting and Training Employees; Evaluating Training Programs; Training Tools/Supervisory; Management Inventories on Human Relations; Communications; Managing Change; Time Management; Performance Approval and Coaching; Modern Management; Leadership Motivation and Decision Making. Evaluating Training Programs: The Four Levels.

55041 ■ Leadership Training Associates
10022 Oak Tree Ct.
Lone Tree, CO 80124-9714
Ph:(303)706-9590
Scope: Provides training and consulting services to organizations across the country in the areas of: effective supervision, total quality management, leadership skills, managing time, coaching and counseling skills, stress management, effective communication, productivity improvement, and managing conflict. Serves private industries as well as government agencies. **Seminars:** Better Communication At Work; Skills for the Newly Appointed Manager; How to Beat Job Burnout; Dealing With Upset Customers and the Public; The Skill of Listening; Managing Conflict; Motivation and Positive Discipline; Time Management Strategies; Stress Management Techniques; Total Quality Management.

55042 ■ Organization Plus
14 Palmer Rd.
Beverly, MA 01915-2710
Ph:(978)922-6136
Fax: (978)922-0143
Co. E-mail: information@organizationplus.com
URL: http://www.organizationplus.com

E-mail: information@organizationplus.com
Scope: Organizing consultant specializing in time management, clutter control, office organization and as a business consultant. Serves individuals and small businesses (including home based). **Seminars:** Get Organized, Get Energized!; Triumph Over Time; The 3 Hour Transformation.

55043 ■ Quma Learning Systems Inc.
505 S Val vista Dr., Ste. 4
Mesa, AZ 85204
Ph:(480)545-8311
Free: 800-622-6463
Fax: (480)545-8233
Co. E-mail: info@quma.net
URL: http://www.quma.net

E-mail: info@quma.net
Scope: Works with corporate America in developing empowering cultures by laying the foundation of ownership spirit. Specializes in providing principles and tools for maximizing full potential in one's self by becoming more accountable, responsible and committed. **Publications:** "Money: An Owner's Manual"; "The Book on Mind Management "; "The Book On Mind Management Discussion Guide". **Seminars:** The Ownership Spirit; Visioneering; Life Management; Money: An Owner's Manual; Communicating For Success; Sustaining Peak Performance.

55044 ■ Smart Ways to Work
1441 Franklin St., Ste. 301
Oakland, CA 94612
Ph:(510)763-8482
Free: 800-599-8463

Fax: (510)763-0790
Co. E-mail: odette@smartwaystowork.com
URL: http://www.smartwaystowork.com

E-mail: odette@smartwaystowork.com
Scope: A management consulting firm specializing in the training of supervisors, managers and professional staff in the area of time management, problem solving, decision making and strategic planning. Assists businesses and corporations in developing and implementing programs for increased productivity, greater profit and improved employee morale. Serves private industries as well as government agencies. **Publications:** "Surviving Information Overload: How to Find, Filter, and Focus on What's Important"; "Take Back Your Life: Smart Ways to Simplify Daily Living"; "Organizing Your Workspace: A Guide to Personal Productivity"; "365 Ways to Simplify Your Work Life". **Seminars:** Managing Multiple Demands: Surviving Ground Zero; Defending Your Life: Balancing Work And Home; Desktop Sprawl: Conquer Your Paper Pile-Up.

55045 ■ SunCoach Inc.
6 Aberdeen Pl.
Fair Lawn, NJ 07410
Ph:(201)791-2396
Fax: (201)796-5490
Co. E-mail: sunny@suncoach.com
URL: http://www.suncoach.com

E-mail: sunny@suncoach.com
Scope: Consults with corporate and individual clients in the areas of time management and office space organization. Offers group seminars and personal coun-

seling in time management and related topics. **Publications:** "Organizing for the Spirit," Apr, 2004.

55046 ■ Harold Taylor Time Consultants Inc.
20 Wolverleigh Blvd.
Toronto, ON, Canada L3V 7V1
Ph:(905)853-9328
Free: 800-361-8463
Fax: (905)853-9390
Co. E-mail: Dafnis@taylorintime.com
URL: http://www.taylorontime.com

E-mail: Dafnis@taylorintime.com
Scope: Offers time management seminars or workshops for managers, salespeople, and support staff in all industries and organizations. Also available for keynote addresses. **Publications:** Shortcuts Through Life; Ten Principles of Scheduling; The Road to Success is Paved with Goals. **Seminars:** Making Time Work for You; Time management with the Palm; Managing Paperwork.

55047 ■ Time Masters - The Institute for Personal Excellence
776 South 980 East
Pleasant Grove, UT 84062-9531
Ph:(801)785-1105
Fax: (801)785-5035
Scope: Employs a telephone coaching approach to teaching personal productivity, one-on-one, to any location in the world. Focus is on implementation and application of success principles over four months. Gives guarantee on in the course. Training course focuses on motivation, personal leadership, time management, sales, and entrepreneurship. **Seminars:** The Time Masters Personal Productivity Seminars;

Personal Skills One-on-One Coaching (conducted by telephone).

55048 ■ TWD & Associates
431 S Patton Ave.
Arlington Heights, IL 60005-2253
Ph:(847)398-6410
Fax: (847)255-5095
Co. E-mail: tdoo@aol.com

E-mail: tdoo@aol.com
Scope: Consulting specialists in small business management particularly in the areas of personnel, training, marketing, franchising, sales, time management, budgeting, raising capital, and long-range planning. **Seminars:** Alternative Methods of Financing for Franchising; Effectiveness of Organizational Development Training Programs for Hourly-Hire Workers in Manufacturing Plants.

55049 ■ David L. Ward and Associates Inc.
360 Wellington Ave., Ste. 12-A
Chicago, IL 60657
Ph:(773)929-3993
Fax: (773)935-3779
Co. E-mail: dward@357.com
URL: http://www.wardmosaic.com

E-mail: dward@357.com
Scope: Specializes in mosaic glass art consulting. The firm provides various seminars on mosaic glass art. **Publications:** "Mosaic Glue Comparison Testing". **Seminars:** Provides more than forty different training programs that may be customized for different audiences; Mosaic Glass Art Workshop; Building Teamwork.

Trade Shows/Exhibiting

START-UP INFORMATION

55050 ■ **"Click on a Fortune"** in *Small Business Opportunities* (May 2005)
Pub: Harris Publications Inc.
Description: Franchise expo, Future Business Owners Spring Into Action, sponsored by the International Franchise Association, offers information to individuals interested in starting their own franchise business. Fifteen franchise opportunities are profiled in the article.

55051 ■ **"From Idea to Marketplace"** in *Small Business Opportunities* (May 2005)
Pub: Harris Publications Inc.
Description: Every inventor must learn information about patenting, manufacturing, packaging, marketing and shipping when planning to take an invention from idea to the marketplace.

ASSOCIATIONS AND OTHER ORGANIZATIONS

55052 ■ **Exhibit Designers and Producers Association**
1100 Johnson Ferry Rd., Ste. 300
Atlanta, GA 30342
Ph:(404)303-7310
Fax: (404)252-0774
Co. E-mail: pdicks@edpa.com
URL: http://www.edpa.com
Contact: Peter A. Dicks, Exec. Dir.
Membership: Firms designing and building exhibits for trade shows and museums. Conducts educational and research programs. **Publications:** *EDP Action News* (bimonthly); *EDPA.COMmunications* (monthly); *EDPA Today* (quarterly).

55053 ■ **Trade Show Exhibitors Association**
2301 S Lake Shore Dr., Ste. 1005
Chicago, IL 60616
Ph:(312)842-8732
Fax: (312)842-8744
Co. E-mail: tsea@tsea.org
URL: http://www.tsea.org
Contact: Stephen Schuldenfrei, Pres.
Description: Exhibitors working to improve the effectiveness of trade shows as a marketing tool. Purposes are to promote the progress and development of trade show exhibiting; to collect and disseminate trade show information; conduct studies, surveys, and student projects designed to improve trade shows; to foster good relations and communications with organizations representing others in the industry; to undertake other activities necessary to promote the welfare of member companies. Sponsors Exhibit Industry Education Foundation and professional exhibiting seminars; the forum series of educational programs on key issues affecting the industry. Maintains placement services; compiles statistics. **Publications:** *How to Develop a Successful Exhibit Marketing Plan* (periodic); *Trade Show Ideas Magazine* (monthly); Membership Directory (annual). Also publishes periodic special management reports, budget guide, salary survey, international exhibitors handbook and guide, and position statements.

REFERENCE WORKS

55054 ■ **"'04 Was Good Year for Show Managers"** in *Tradeshow Week* (Vol. 34)
Pub: Reed Business Information
Ed: Rachelle Crum. **Description:** According to Tradeshow Week's 2004 Show Management Salary Survey, salaries rose 3.6 percent more in 2004 over 2003 and are expected to increase by the same amount in 2005. Show managers averaged $58,822 in the U.S. and Canada for 2004, perks and bonuses were up 32 percent worth $14,159.

55055 ■ **"19th Annual Entrepreneurial Woman's Conference"** in *Entrepreneur* (Vol. 33, August 2005, No. 8, pp. 4)
Pub: Entrepreneur Media Inc.
Ed: Steve Cooper. **Description:** The Women's Business Development Center holds its annual Entrepreneurial Women's Conference for women business owners. The event presents a buyer's mart that allows the owners to market products and services to corporate and government buyers. There are also discussions and workshops addressing issues and trends affecting women-owned businesses.

55056 ■ **"2005-2006 Meetings, Conventions and Trade Shows"** in *Crain's Detroit Business* (Vol. 21, October 10, 2005, No. 43, pp. 17)
Pub: Crain Communications Inc. - Detroit
Description: A monthly breakdown of meetings, conventions and trade shows scheduled to be held in the Detroit, Michigan area is presented.

55057 ■ **"2005 National Minority Supplier Development Council Conference and Business Opportunity Fair"** in *Entrepreneur* (Vol. 33, Aug. 2005)
Pub: Entrepreneur Media Inc.
Ed: Steve Cooper. **Description:** The National Minority Supplier Development Council conference and business opportunity fair is held annually. The event hosts CEOs, purchasing executives, minority entrepreneurs and government decision-makers.

55058 ■ **"2005 Outlook: Low Growth Is OK"** in *Tradeshow Week* (Vol. 34, December 20, 2004, No. 51, pp. 8)
Pub: Reed Business Information
Ed: Michael Hughes. **Description:** The exhibition industry is predicting an increase in companies participating in shows. Fifty-six percent of show managers are predicting total gross revenue growth between 1 and 10 percent for 2005.

55059 ■ **"2007 Conference Calendar"** in *Journal of Business Communication* (Vol. 44, January 2007, No. 1, pp. 103)
Pub: Association for Business Communication
Description: Overview of 2007 Conference Calendar.

55060 ■ **"About His Life: Bob Dallmeyer"** in *Tradeshow Week* (Vol. 34, December 20, 2004, No. 51, pp. S4)
Pub: Reed Business Information
Ed: Gary Tufel. **Description:** Profile of Bob Dallmeyer, exhibitor, show manager, author, teacher, lecturer, and mentor in the exhibition industry. Tradeshow Week named him one of the industry's 100 Most Influential People and one of its Top Five Industry Entrepreneurs in 2003.

55061 ■ **"American Royal Center Kansas City, MO"** in *Tradeshow Week* (Vol. 34, November 29, 2004, No. 48, pp. S6)
Pub: Reed Business Information
Description: Profile of the American Royal Center in Kansas City, Missouri. The center is located next to the Kemper Arena, and home to the Annual American Royal Livestock and BBQ Contest and the American Royal Extravaganza. Amenities include on-site catering, parking, two loading docks, and drive-in capabilities.

55062 ■ **Annual Trade Show Directory**
Pub: Forum Publishing Co.
Released: Annual, September. **Price:** $39.95, individuals. **Covers:** over 1,800 merchandise trade shows throughout the United States and Canada. **Entries Include:** Company name, address, phone, estimated attendance and number of exhibitors, show description. **Arrangement:** Classified by product, then chronological. **Indexes:** Product, type of show.

55063 ■ **"The Answer Is Always Yes"** in *Forbes* (Vol. 175, February 14, 2005, No. 3, pp. 82)
Pub: Forbes Magazine Inc.
Ed: Victoria Murphy. **Description:** An overview of the tradeshow industry is presented. The Oregon Convention Center in Portland, Oregon has seen a $5.5 million loss in 2004.

55064 ■ **"Antiques Dealers Converge For Show in Portland, Maine"** in *Portland Press Herald* (September 17, 2005)
Pub: Blethen Maine Newspapers, Inc.
Ed: Beth Quimby. **Description:** Maine Antique Dealers Association celebrated its 76th annual show in September. The sixty-eight dealers attending reported a soft market with stable prices.

55065 ■ **"Art Lover Plays Fair Game"** in *Crain's New York Business* (Vol. 23, January 29, 2007, No. 5, pp. F19)
Pub: Crain Communications, Inc.
Ed: Miriam Kreinin Souccar. **Description:** Profile of Helen Allen and her art fairs, including Pulse, a contemporary art fair in Miami which took in more than

$10 million. Numerous dealers sold out their inventory on the first day of the fair. Her art fairs which in addition to Pulse include Ramsay and Art 212 are designed for a younger generation and feature more affordable pieces of work.

55066 ■ "Atlanta's Top Meeting and Exhibition Facilities" in *Atlanta Business Chronicle* (Vol. 24, No. 14, September 7, 2001, pp. S38)
Pub: American City Business Journals Inc.
Description: The top exhibition and meeting facilities in Atlanta are listed alphabetically. The first three facilities are 7 Stages, The 755 Club at Turner Field, and the 14th Street Playhouse.

55067 ■ "Away Game: Right Messages Will Help Exhibit Booth Bring in Business" in *Crain's Detroit Business* (Vol. 19, No. 49, December 8, 2003)
Pub: Crain Communications Inc., Detroit
Ed: Laura Bailey. **Description:** Ways to create an exhibit booth that will attract attention are discussed.

55068 ■ "Bandy Resigns As President of TSEA: Six-Year Head To Start Association Management Firm With Wife in April" in *Tradeshow Week* (Vol. 34)
Pub: Reed Business Information
Ed: Heidi Genoist. **Description:** Michael Bandy resigned as president of the Trade Show Exhibitors Association in order to launch an independent association management and consulting firm with his wife Dee Dee.

55069 ■ "Beyond ROI: Taking Advantage of PR" in *Tradeshow Week* (Vol. 34, November 29, 2004, No. 48, pp. 72)
Pub: Reed Business Information
Ed: David S. Cohen. **Description:** Tradeshows provide an opportunity for companies to implement a public relations campaign and provide a platform for marketing a produce, service, or company in a cost-effect manner.

55070 ■ "Big Religious Meetings Hold Promise of Big Payoffs for Local Economy" in *Crain's Detroit Business* (Vol. 22, February 13, 2006, No. 7)
Pub: Crain Communications Inc. - Detroit
Ed: Anjali Fluker. **Description:** Progressive National Baptist Convention and the National Baptist Convention USA Inc., are among the big events scheduled for the City of Detroit in the next few years. These religious conventions are expected to boost the economy of Southeast Michigan.

55071 ■ "Bromley, AHAA shine at Confab" in *Hispanic Business* (Vol. 22, No. 11, November 2000, pp. 12)
Pub: Hispanic Business
Ed: Peter Brennan. **Description:** A description is presented of events at the 'Advertising Age' Hispanic Creative Advertising Awards held in September 2000. Bromley Communications won eight medals, three of which were gold.

55072 ■ "Calling All VoIP Adopters: Tech Shows" in *Tradeshow Week* (Vol. 34, November 29, 2004, No. 48, pp. 54)
Pub: Reed Business Information
Ed: Margo McCall. **Description:** Ways Voice over Internet protocol can improve small business are discussed, including information about established companies and startups providing the service.

55073 ■ "CEA Makes Leaving Las Vegas Easier" in *Tradeshow Week* (Vol. 34, November 29, 2004, No. 48, pp. 6)
Pub: Reed Business Information
Description: The Consumer Electronics Association annually hosts the largest tradeshow in Las Vegas, Nevada. The association and the Transportation Security Administration have worked together to ease delays for attendees to get in and out of the Las Vegas airport by setting up seven checkpoint lanes for the 2005 show to be held in January.

55074 ■ "Celebrate Success. Embrace Innovation" in *Black Enterprise* (Vol. 37, February 2007, No. 7, pp. 145)
Pub: Earl G. Graves Publishing Co. Inc.
Description: 2007 Women of Power Summit provides networking opportunities, empowerment sessions, and nightly entertainment. More than 500 executive women of color are expected to attend this inspiring summit in Phoenix, February 7-10.

55075 ■ "Chris Brown Takes Helm: IAEM Chairman" in *Tradeshow Week* (Vol. 34, November 29, 2004, No. 48, pp. 22)
Pub: Reed Business Information
Description: An interview with Chris Brown, chairman-elect for the International Association for Exhibition Management (IAEM). Brown is committed to making the IAEM a major voice for the tradeshow industry.

55076 ■ "ComNet to showcase VOIP" in *InfoWorld* (Vol. 23, No. 5, January 29, 2001, pp. 8)
Pub: InfoWorld
Ed: Jennifer Jones, Heather Harreld. **Description:** WorldCom plans to migrate voice over IP (VoIP) technology at the ComNet 2001 trade show. Several other vendors, including hardware and network-management companies are expected to unveil new products at the show, but WorldCom is the first major carrier to pay serious attention to growing enterprise interest in VoIP.

55077 ■ "Composing a Conference; Motor City Music Festival Racing to Find Paying Sponsors" in *Crain's Detroit Business* (January 17, 2005)
Pub: Crain Communications Inc. - Detroit
Ed: Brent Snavely. **Description:** Local media and radio stations has offered in-kind sponsorship for the Motor City Music Conference Inc. (MC2), along with cooperation form clubs and concert venues and speaking commitments from various out-of-town music-industry executives. However, the event still needs monetary support.

55078 ■ "Conference Calendar" in *Marketing to Women* (Vol. 20, January 2007, No. 1, pp. 7)
Pub: EPM Communications, Inc.
Description: Calendar spotlighting women's business conferences through the month of June.

55079 ■ "Conference to Examine Doing Business in China" in *Crain's Detroit Business* (Vol. 21, October 31, 2005, No. 44, pp. 29)
Pub: Crain Communications Inc. - Detroit
Ed: Laura Bommarito. **Description:** Experts will meet at a conference set for December to discuss the risks and rewards of doing business with Chinese companies.

55080 ■ "Convention Calendar" in *Black Enterprise* (Vol. 36, November 2005, No. 4, pp. 82)
Pub: Earl G. Graves Publishing Co. Inc.
Description: The convention and trade show calendar for the month of November 2005, focusing on African American and women leadership issues, is presented.

55081 ■ "Crain's Family-Business Forum Set for Thursday" in *Crain's Detroit Business* (Vol. 21, October 3, 2005, No. 43, pp. 31)
Pub: Crain Communications Inc. - Detroit
Description: Stephen McClure of Gamily Business Consulting Group Inc. will speak at the first family-owned business forum sponsored by Crain's. Other sponsors include Derderian, Kann, Seyferth & Salucci PC; LaSalle Bank; Right Management Consultants; Michigan Business and Professional Association; and Andiamo Italia.

55082 ■ "D.C. Facility Plans Random Drug Testing" in *Tradeshow Week* (Vol. 34, December 13, 2004, No. 50, pp. 3)
Pub: Reed Business Information

Ed: Rachelle Crum. **Description:** For the first time, the Washington Convention Center is working with unions and contractors on a random drug testing program. The program will apply to both union and non-union workers. The program allows for 15 percent of any workers at the center to be tested on any given day.

55083 ■ "Demo 2002 Cuts the Fluff" in *Business Week Online* (Februa)
Pub: McGraw-Hill, Inc.
Description: An overview of the annual Demo conference held in Phoenix during February is presented.

55084 ■ "DigitalLife Tries New Approach: Reaching Consumers" in *Tradeshow Week* (Vol. 34, November 29, 2004, No. 48, pp. 56)
Pub: Reed Business Information
Ed: Margo McCall. **Description:** Profile of DigitalLife, a consumer tradeshow held in New York, October 2004. The show featured cell phones, digital cameras, music players, and handheld computers and the benefits they serve to small business.

55085 ■ "EAC Goes Beyond the Call of Duty" in *Tradeshow Week* (Vol. 34, December 6, 2004, No. 49, pp. S11)
Pub: Reed Business Information
Ed: Gary Tufel. **Description:** Profile of the Exhibitor Advisory Committee. The committee of 10-12 members assist exhibitors to produce successful tradeshows.

55086 ■ "The Early Bird Gets the Worm" in *Black Enterprise* (Vol. 37, January 2007, No. 6, pp. 111)
Pub: Earl G. Graves Publishing Co. Inc.
Ed: Tykisha N. Lundy. **Description:** General Motors hosts the Black Enterprise Conference And Expo: Where Deals Are Made at Walt Disney World's Swan and Dolphin Resort, May 9-12. The conference will offer great information to entrepreneurs.

55087 ■ "ECD short of cash at critical time as partners pull out of ventures" in *Crain's Detroit Business* (Vol. 19, No. 8, Feb. 24, 2003)
Pub: Crain Communications Inc., Detroit
Ed: Andrew Dietderich. **Description:** Energy Conversion Devices Inc. has lost funding from three companies for joint ventures in fuel-cell development.

55088 ■ "Energy Conference in Novi March 23" in *Crain's Detroit Business* (Vol. 22, February 6, 2006, No. 6, pp. 13)
Pub: Crain Communications Inc. - Detroit
Ed: Laura Bommarito. **Description:** The 2006 DTE Energy Conference and Exhibition in Partnership with The Engineering Society of Detroit will hold its one-day event on alternative energy sources and energy efficiency in Novi, Michigan at the Rock Financial Showplace March 23, 2006.

55089 ■ *Exhibiting at Tradeshows*
Pub: Crisp Publications, Inc.
Ed: Susan A. Friedmann. **Released:** 1992. **Price:** $10.95.

55090 ■ "Exhibitors Are Show Managers' Best Friends" in *Tradeshow Week* (Vol. 34, November 29, 2004, No. 48, pp. 40)
Pub: Reed Business Information
Ed: Rachelle Crum. **Description:** According to the Tradeshow Week's 14th Annual Survey of Exposition Managers, the average number of exhibiting companies in 2004 fell by 46 percent compared to 2003. However, three Tradeshow Weekly Quarterly Reports of Tradeshow Statistics show increases by as much as 5 percent. Statistical data included.

55091 ■ "Expanding Your Network of Contacts" in *Black Enterprise* (Vol. 35, January 2005, No. 6, pp. 111)
Pub: Earl G. Graves Publishing Co. Inc.
Ed: Lisa Downer. **Description:** Invitation to business owners, entrepreneurs and corporate executives is

extended for the 2005 Black Enterprise/General Motors Entrepreneurs Conference to be held in May 2005 in Dallas, Texas. The conference theme is, Seasons of Change, and explores the role that change management plays in gaining or retaining a competitive advantage.

55092 ■ "Expo Benefits as Big Names Go Natural" in Tradeshow Week (Vol. 34, November 29, 2004, No. 48, pp. 6)
Pub: Reed Business Information
Description: New Hope Natural Media reported a rise in attendance at its Natural Products Expo East in Washington, DC in 2004. The expo features natural food brands. The 2004 show added a seminar.

55093 ■ "Fandango Events Adds Show Division" in Tradeshow Week (Vol. 34, December 6, 2004, No. 49, pp. 2)
Pub: Reed Business Information
Description: Fandango Special Events, based in Baltimore, Maryland, has added a tradeshow division offering management services and custom booth design. The firm was founded in 1989 by Dawn and Erin Cermak and has grown to 120 employees.

55094 ■ "Football Fever" in Small Business Opportunities (Vol. 13, No. 6, November 2001, pp. 54-55)
Pub: Harris Publications, Inc.
Ed: Stan Roberts. Description: Profile of Charlotte Begley, retailer who earns $500,000 a year selling licensed football products. Ms. Begley attends three trade shows a year to find the latest designs, colors and styles.

55095 ■ "Futuristic Exhibit Designs Made From Tension Fabric" in Tradeshow Week (Vol. 34, December 6, 2004, No. 49, pp. S10)
Pub: Reed Business Information
Description: Profile of Transformit, creators of a new tension fabric structure used for exhibits and events. The system is made from aluminum extrusion frames and are freestanding for ease of use. The application of lighting can enhance designs.

55096 ■ "Global Spectrum: Making a Difference in the Convention Center Industry" in Tradeshow Week (Vol. 34, November 29, 2004, No. 48, pp. S2)
Pub: Reed Business Information
Description: Profile of Global Spectrum, a private management firm in the tradeshow sector. Global Spectrum is a subsidiary of Comcast-Spectator of Philadelphia, Pennsylvania. The company has increased management contracts for arenas, convention centers, stadiums and ice rinks by more than 500 percent since January 2000 when it was created.

55097 ■ "Greater Richmond Convention Center Richmond, VA" in Tradeshow Week (Vol. 34, November 29, 2004, No. 48, pp. S4)
Pub: Reed Business Information
Description: Profile of the Greater Richmond Convention Center in Richmond, Virginia, which opened in 2003. The center boasts 178,159 square feet of exhibit space, 80,000 square feet of meeting space, including a 30,550 square foot ballroom. The centers offers a 258 seat auditorium, full service business center, a cyber cafe with free Internet access, an 8,000 square foot banquet kitchen and a food court.

55098 ■ "Harborview Center Clearwater, FL" in Tradeshow Week (Vol. 34, November 29, 2004, No. 48, pp. S7)
Pub: Reed Business Information
Description: Profile of the Harborview Center in Clearwater, Florida. The facility hosts tradeshows, public consumer shows, meetings, banquets and weddings. The center can hold up to 1,600 guests and offers in-house catering, a decorator, drayage, and utilities services.

55099 ■ "Home-Buying Fair Appeals to First-Time Purchasers" in Sun Herald (February 10, 2005)
Pub: Knight-Ridder/Tribune Business News
Ed: Vivian Austin. Description: Homebuyers Fair held in Biloxi, Mississippi drew several residents look-

ing to purchase new homes. Realtors, homebuilders, banks, savings and loans, credit unions and government agencies distributed information and advice.

55100 ■ "How Do Producers Select Host Cities?" in Tradeshow Week (Vol. 34, November 29, 2004, No. 48, pp. 38)
Pub: Reed Business Information
Ed: Michael Hughes. Description: Hotel capacity plays a major role in choosing a site for a tradeshow, followed by total available exhibit space. Statistical data included.

55101 ■ "Hy-Vee Hall Des Moines, IA" in Tradeshow Week (Vol. 34, November 29, 2004, No. 48, pp. S6)
Pub: Reed Business Information
Description: Profile of Hy-Vee Hall, owned by Polk County in Des Moines, Iowa. The hall features on-site parking, catering services and telecommunications/Internet services and hosts tradeshows, exhibits, conventions, meetings, banquets, conferences, and consumer shows.

55102 ■ "IACVB Considers Changing Its Name" in Tradeshow Week (Vol. 34, December 20, 2004, No. 51, pp. 3)
Pub: Reed Business Information
Description: The Board of Directors of the International Association of Convention and Visitor Bureaus is considering changing the organization's name to the Destination Marketing Association. Members and non-members are encouraged to provide feedback at a published Website.

55103 ■ "IAEM Commission To Oversee Audits: Exhibitors To Constitute a Majority; Body Will Enforce Audit Standards" in Tradeshow Week (Vol. 34)
Pub: Reed Business Information
Ed: Margo McCall. Description: Event and Exhibition Audit Commission will begin certifying procedures used by tradeshow auditing firms in 2005. Auditors that successfully undergo a review by the commission will be entitled to use a seal of certification.

55104 ■ "If Not the Word, What? Leaders Speak" in Tradeshow Week (Vol. 34, November 29, 2004, No. 48, pp. 20)
Pub: Reed Business Information
Ed: Heidi Genoist. Description: The merger between the International Association for Exhibition Management (IAEM) and the Society of Independent Show Organizers is discussed. The merger is expected to give a greater voice to the tradeshow industry as well as attract more high-level executives to the association.

55105 ■ "Image is Everything" in Entrepreneur (Vol. 32, September 2004, No. 9, pp. 106)
Pub: Entrepreneur Media Inc.
Description: Profile of Sandy Meyers, marketer of materials that incorporate fine art. Meyers uses the process of securing fine art prints and displaying them on items such as luggage tags, postcards, mouse pads, and coffee mugs, instead of a company's logo for marketing purposes. She also runs Visual Promotions, a firm that creates point-of-purchase and trade show banners and displays.

55106 ■ "Internet World Fall 2000 Conference" in Information Today (Vol. 17, No. 11, December 2000, pp. 28)
Pub: Information Today, Inc.
Ed: Jane Dysart, Stephen Abram, Pete Stair. Description: A review of the Fall 2000 Penton Media's Internet World show, held at New York's Jacob Javits Convention Center.

55107 ■ "It's a Three-Ring Circus and Then Some" in Crain's Detroit Business (Vol. 22, January 16, 2006, No. 4, pp. 8)
Pub: Crain Communications Inc. - Detroit
Ed: Keith Crain. Description: Manufacturers at the 2006 North American International Auto Show continue to improve displays each year.

55108 ■ "James L. Knight International Center Miami, FL" in Tradeshow Week (Vol. 34, November 29, 2004, No. 48, pp. S7)
Pub: Reed Business Information
Description: Profile of the James L. Knight International Center, a sloped auditorium in downtown Miami, Florida that hosts international trade conferences, conventions, tradeshows, and civic events. The center is physically connected to the Hyatt Regency Miami which offers 612 guest rooms.

55109 ■ "Las Vegas Sands Sets IPO Strike Price" in Tradeshow Week (Vol. 34, December 13, 2004, No. 50, pp. 3)
Pub: Reed Business Information
Description: The owner of the Sands Expo and Convention Center and Venetian Resort Casino Hotel estimates it will generate more than a half billion dollars in its upcoming initial public offering.

55110 ■ "LBA event draws a crowd" in Hispanic Business (Vol. 22, No. 11, November 2000, pp. 14)
Pub: Hispanic Business
Ed: Andrea Siedsma. Description: A presentation of events at the Latino Business Expo in September 2000, organized by the Latin Business Association, showing the growth of Hispanic American businesses.

55111 ■ "A Little Friendly Advice: Exhibitor Advisory Committees Can Make a Difference" in Tradeshow Week (Vol. 34, December 6, 2004, No. 49)
Pub: Reed Business Information
Ed: Gary Tufel. Description: Exhibitor advisory committees, though rare, can be very useful in creating successful tradeshows if show managers are willing to act on their recommendations.

55112 ■ "Local Motion: For a Competitive Edge, Offer Items Made Locally" in Entrepreneur (Vol. 32, November 2004, No. 11, pp. 90)
Pub: Entrepreneur Media Inc.
Ed: Gwen Moran. Description: Trade shows, farmers markets, festivals, local events, as well as local business associations are good sources for locating manufacturers.

55113 ■ "Los Angeles Grabs Furniture Shows" in Tradeshow Week (Vol. 34, December 20, 2004, No. 51, pp. 3)
Pub: Reed Business Information
Ed: Rachelle Crum. Description: Karel Exposition Management is moving its semiannual Long Beach Furniture and Accessory Market from Long Beach to Los Angeles, California. The firm also intends to change the name to the Los Angeles Furniture and Accessory Market.

55114 ■ "Madler: Local Venues Replace Exotic Locales" in San Fernando Valley Business Journal (Vol. 12, January 2007, No. 2, pp. 43)
Pub: San Fernando Valley Business Journal Associates
Ed: Mark R. Madler. Description: Highlights of the Consumer Electronics Show in Las Vegas include high definition products such as broadband cell phones that allow downloading of video, ultra mobile PC's, and new equipment such as monitors that are capable of showing imagery in 3D without the need for special glasses.

55115 ■ "Maine Reweaves Thread of Former Textile Industry Into Artistry" in Portland Press Herald (September 6, 2005)
Pub: Blethen Maine Newspapers, Inc.
Ed: Edward D. Murphy. Description: Some of Maine's textile mills are returning to the state through craftspeople and artists who use the material to create art for companies wishing to stand out at trade shows, retailers to increase visibility, and architects creating a look that stands out in a crowd.

55116 ■ "Making the Most Of It" in Sales & Marketing Management
Pub: VNU Business Media

Ed: Robin Kocina. **Description:** Mid-America Events & Expos Inc. specializes in bringing businesses and potential customers together in the same room. The firm is committed to teaching exhibitors how to best benefit from these face-to-face interactions.

55117 ■ "MC, MMA Offering Manufacturing Management Program" in *Mississippi Business Journal* **(Vol. 29, January 2007, No. 3, pp. A15)**
Pub: Venture Publications, Inc.
Ed: M.R. Gorringe. **Description:** Mississippi Manufacturers Association and the School of Business at Mississippi College will offer a Certified Manager of Performance Excellence in Manufacturing Program. The program is built around the Baldridge Criteria for Performance Excellence.

55118 ■ "Medical Events' Popularity on the Rise" in *Tradeshow Week* **(Vol. 34, November 29, 2004, No. 48, pp. 6)**
Pub: Reed Business Information
Description: There are over 30 medical conferences held per business day in the U.S. according to the Biomedical Market Newsletter Group's Medical Industry Conference Calendar Newsletter.

55119 ■ "Medium or Marketplace?" in *Tradeshow Week* **(Vol. 34, December 20, 2004, No. 51, pp. 7)**
Pub: Reed Business Information
Ed: Adam Schaffer. **Description:** Chris Meyer of the Las Vegas Convention and Visitors Authority believes tradeshows are a good marketing tool for companies to show goods and services. Statistical data included.

55120 ■ "Meetings & Clubs" in *Bellingham Business Journal* **(January 2007, pp. C3)**
Pub: Sun News Inc.
Description: Calendar of clubs and meetings in the Bellingham area targeting business-minded individuals.

55121 ■ "MGM Mirage Expands: New Project CityCenter Set to Include Space for Convention Meetings" in *Tradeshow Week* **(Vol. 34, December 6, 2004)**
Pub: Reed Business Information
Ed: Heidi Genoist. **Description:** MGM Mirage has announced plans for Project CityCenter, an urban environment that will consist of 18 million square feet of buildings, including a 4,000-room hotel and casino, three 400-room boutique hotels, 550,000 square feet of restaurants and entertainment venues, and 1,650 luxury units for permanent and temporary occupancy.

55122 ■ "Milwaukee, Wis., to Host Biotech Finance Gathering in 2007" in *Milwaukee Journal Sentinel* **(December 14, 2005)**
Pub: Journal Sentinel, Inc.
Ed: Kathleen Gallagher. **Description:** Venture capitalists representing more than $7 billion and biotechnology and medical device startups will meet in Milwaukee in September 2007 for the largest industry event in the Midwest. The BIO Med-America Venture-Forum expects 75 to 100 VCs to attend.

55123 ■ "MIMlist Draws Eclectic Crowd: Online Forums" in *Tradeshow Week* **(Vol. 34, November 29, 2004, No. 48, pp. 52)**
Pub: Reed Business Information
Ed: Rachelle Crum. **Description:** Exhibition industry associations provide a listserve or other online forum exclusively for its members. Profile of MIMlist, a forum of more than 4,000 members is profiled.

55124 ■ "Minorities meet opportunities" in *Hispanic Business* **(Vol. 22, No. 9, September 2000, pp. 14)**
Pub: Hispanic Business
Ed: Scott Williams. **Description:** The marketing expertise of the National Minority Supplier Development Council and the purchasing power of the Latin Business Association have been combined at the Latino Business Expo, held in Los Angeles, California.

55125 ■ "More Bang for Your Buck" in *Entrepreneur* **(Vol. 32)**
Pub: Entrepreneur Media Inc.
Ed: Nichole L. Torres. **Description:** Associated Surplus Dealers/Associated Merchandise Dealers (ASD/MD) Trade Show Las Vegas, produced by VNU Expositions, offers small business entrepreneurs and eBay resellers a cost-effective venue for selling products. The show includes 3,500 exhibitors with products ranging from dollar-store merchandise to general merchandise such as toys, gifts, electronics, health and beauty, and fashion accessories.

55126 ■ "More Change For IAEM: New Magazine Planned, Foundation Mothballed As Unification Talks Continue" in *Tradeshow Week* **(Vol. 34)**
Pub: Reed Business Information
Ed: Heidi Genoist. **Description:** The International Association for Exhibition Management announced plans to publish its own publication at its annual Expo! Expo! Meeting. The magazine will be distributed to members on a bi-monthly basis and will be called, 'Exhibition Management'.

55127 ■ "More versatility and splash can be found at tradeshows" in *Atlanta Business Chronicle* **(Vol. 24, No. 14, September 7, 2001, pp. S10)**
Pub: American City Business Journals Inc.
Ed: Tonya Layman. **Description:** Various company executives discuss the latest trends in tradeshow displays.

55128 ■ "A Multi-Sensory Booth Attraction" in *Tradeshow Week* **(Vol. 34, December 6, 2004, No. 49, pp. S10)**
Pub: Reed Business Information
Description: Profile of Kodak's autosteroscopic display. The system gives tradeshow exhibitors a new way to show products with fine optics for stereo display. The system creates virtual images that eliminate eye strains.

55129 ■ "NAIAS Spotlight Shines on Design" in *Crain's Detroit Business* **(Vol. 23, January 1, 2007, No. 1, pp. 1)**
Pub: Crain Communications Inc. - Detroit
Ed: Jennette Smith. **Description:** Differentiation in design and styling are getting the most attention at the Auto Show in Detroit this year. All brands are about equal in quality and reliability due to engineering advances, so differentiation in styling has moved back to the forefront. Industry cutbacks and layoffs have not affected the design areas.

55130 ■ "Net Gains" in *Incentive* **(Vol. 174, No. 10, October 2000, pp. 9)**
Pub: Bill Communications
Ed: Joan M. Steinauer. **Description:** The Internet has become the top source for planning trade show visits.

55131 ■ "Networking is a Click Away" in *Black Enterprise* **(Vol. 34, No. 6, January 2004, pp. 101)**
Pub: Earl Graves Publishing Co.
Description: Information is given for the 2004 B.E. Entrepreneurs Conference to be held May 12-16, 2004 in Dallas, Texas. Nominations are also being accepted for BE Small Business Awards.

55132 ■ "New Economy Creates New Markets" in *Hispanic Business* **(Vol. 22, No. 1/2, January/February, pp. 24, 26)**
Pub: Hispanic Business
Description: Marketers share strategies at the Se Habla Expanol Market and Media Expo.

55133 ■ "New Products Hit Showfloor: Expo! Expo!" in *Tradeshow Week* **(Vol. 34, November 29, 2004, No. 48, pp. 47)**
Pub: Reed Business Information
Ed: Margo McCall. **Description:** New technology products and services were unveiled at the Expo! Expo! Show. The show's highlights include Accumanage, a new software program that provides an exhibitor management system that can be used by show management or exhibitors to complete company profiles for a directory listing.

55134 ■ "No Biz Like Show Biz" in *Small Business Opportunities* **(Vol. 13, No. 6, November 2001, pp. 18)**
Pub: Harris Publications, Inc.
Ed: Noemi Pollack. **Description:** Advice is given to maximize an investment when exhibiting at a trade show. Costs and a checklist are included.

55135 ■ "Nonprofit Seminar is March 13" in *Crain's Detroit Business* **(Vol. 22, February 13, 2006, No. 7, pp. 26)**
Pub: Crain Communications Inc. - Detroit
Description: The Best Practices from the Best-Managed Nonprofits seminar is scheduled for March 13, 2006 in Detroit, Michigan. Speakers will address topics such as collaboration and alliances and mergers between nonprofits.

55136 ■ "The Opportunity is Knocking" in *Black Enterprise* **(Vol. 34, No. 7, February 2004)**
Pub: Earl Graves Publishing Co.
Description: The 2004 "Black Enterprise/General Motors Entrepreneurs Conference" will be held in Dallas, Texas. This year's theme will be, "Taking Business Beyond Boundaries", and will present industry experts, venture capitalists, and entrepreneurs. The event is geared to provide information and inspiration for African American executives, professionals, entrepreneurs, and wealth-accumulators.

55137 ■ "Organizer's Laud Bigger Javits" in *Tradeshow Week* **(Vol. 34)**
Pub: Reed Business Information
Ed: Margo McCall. **Description:** New York State legislators approved the expansion of the Jacob K. Javits Convention Center. The move is expected to increase the number of shows drawn to the area.

55138 ■ "Overland Park Convention Center Overland Park, KS" in *Tradeshow Week* **(Vol. 34, November 29, 2004, No. 48, pp. S5)**
Pub: Reed Business Information
Description: Profile of the Overland Park Convention Center in Kansas. The center is attached to the Sheraton Overland Park Hotel with 412 rooms and an additional 600 rooms at within walking distance.

55139 ■ "Palm Beach County Convention Center West Palm Beach, FL" in *Tradeshow Week* **(Vol. 34, November 29, 2004, No. 48, pp. S4)**
Pub: Reed Business Information
Description: Profile of the Palm Beach County Convention Center in West Palm Beach, Florida. The center provides a 100,000 square foot exhibition hall, 23,000 square feet of meeting space, and a 25,000 square foot ballroom.

55140 ■ "Pennsylvania RV Show Hits the Road" in *Tradeshow Week* **(Vol. 34)**
Pub: Reed Business Information
Ed: Margo McCall. **Description:** The Pennsylvania RV and Camping Show is moving from the Pennsylvania Farm Show Complex in Harrisburg to the Hershey Park Sports and Entertainment Complex. The show ranks 11th on the Tradeshow Week 200 for 2003.

55141 ■ "Personalized Web Invitations From Exhibitors to Prospects" in *Tradeshow Week* **(Vol. 34, December 6, 2004, No. 49, pp. S10)**
Pub: Reed Business Information
Description: New Media Gateway produces personalized invitations for exhibitors to invite customers to booths or events. Three messages are sent via the Internet two to four weeks prior to an event, along with confirmation and post-event follow-up.

55142 ■ "PGI Closes Offices, Lays Off 50 Employees" in *Tradeshow Week* **(Vol. 34, December 20, 2004, No. 51, pp. 3)**
Pub: Reed Business Information
Description: PGI, an event management service, closes eight of its 26 offices globally; the firm also laid off 50 of its 350 employees. Bob McCormick will take on responsibilities as both president and COO. The company plans to move away from destination marketing and focus on event management services.

55143 ■ "Planes, Tractors and Automobiles" in *Tradeshow Week* (Vol. 34, November 29, 2004, No. 48, pp. 64)
Pub: Reed Business Information
Ed: Heidi Genoist. **Description:** Trade show management is highlighted.

55144 ■ "PMMI Debuts Contracting Service: By Taking Over Services, PACK EXPO Intl" in *Tradeshow Week* (Vol. 34)
Pub: Reed Business Information
Ed: Rachelle Crum. **Description:** Packaging Machinery Manufacturers Institute 27th Expo was held in Chicago, Illinois. The show introduced PACK EXPO Services. The show drew more than 46,000 visitors and 1,600 exhibitors.

55145 ■ "Polk County Convention Complex Des Moines, IA" in *Tradeshow Week* (Vol. 34, November 29, 2004, No. 48, pp. S6)
Pub: Reed Business Information
Description: Profile of Polk County Convention Complex in Des Moines, Iowa. The complex is connected to the downtown skywalk system allowing for a climate-controlled walkway to hotels, restaurants and retail outlets as well as Wells Fargo Arena, Hy-Vee Hall and Veterans Memorial Auditorium.

55146 ■ "Preparation key to conquering overseas exhibits" in *Atlanta Business Chronicle* (Vol. 24, No. 14, September 7, 2001, pp. S16)
Pub: American City Business Journals Inc.
Ed: Jonathan Kalstrom. **Description:** Maren Christensen of the Minnesota Trade Office, Liz DeLuca of Skyline Displays Inc., and Allen Konopacki of Incomm International discuss how to plan overseas tradeshows. Factors to keep in mind are customs and postal regulations, language differences, and freight-forwarding services.

55147 ■ "Pueblo Convention Center Pueblo, CO" in *Tradeshow Week* (Vol. 34, November 29, 2004, pp. S7)
Pub: Reed Business Information
Description: Profile of the Pueblo Convention Center located in Pueblo, Colorado. The center can host up to 1,600 convention attendees and 1,000 banquet guests. The center features a tribute to the U.S. Congressional Medal of Honor recipients in its plaza.

55148 ■ "Reed Acquires Manufacturing Shows" in *Tradeshow Week* (Vol. 34, December 13, 2004, No. 50, pp. 3)
Pub: Reed Business Information
Description: Reed Exhibitions has acquired a series of regional manufacturing tradeshows with the purchase of Advanced Manufacturing and Productivity Exposition series from the Technical Exhibitions and Conferences. The shows focus on automated manufacturing, assembly systems and information technology.

55149 ■ "Reed Jumps Onto the Medical Bandwagon " in *Tradeshow Week* (Vol. 3)
Pub: Reed Business Information
Ed: Rachelle Crum. **Description:** Reed Exhibitions has launched a new show division along with its sister company, publisher Elsevier Health Sciences. The new division will focus on continuing medical education. Reed Medical Education is committed to improving health care delivery.

55150 ■ "Resources: Web Sites, Organizations, Events and More to Grow Your Business" in *Entrepreneur* (Vol. 32, August 2004, No. 8, pp. 8)
Pub: Entrepreneur Media Inc.
Ed: Steve Cooper. **Description:** Showcase of information to help small business include: Global Advisor offers services from United Parcel Service to help companies learn ways to conduct business overseas, including trade tools and terminology, a global time clock and HAP, supply chain management, and a guide to international shipping; a CAN-SPAM Act of 2003 summary; RE:INVENTION INC is a daily blog dedicated to women entrepreneurs; and a directory of venture capital and private equity firms.

55151 ■ "Right Message, Right Time Key for Hospitality Marketing" in *Crain's Detroit Business* (Vol. 21, October 10, 2005, No. 43, pp. 16)
Pub: Crain Communications Inc. - Detroit
Ed: Roger Slavens. **Description:** According to the Meetings & Conventions 2004 Meetings Market Report, meeting planners and hotel executives are the two most lucrative audiences for marketers looking to increase involvement in the hospitality and travel industry.

55152 ■ "Rising Gas Costs Create Pricing Pressure" in *Tradeshow Week* (Vol. 34, November 29, 2004, No. 48, pp. 4)
Pub: Reed Business Information
Ed: Margo McCall. **Description:** Trucking companies and airlines, as well as general service contractors, are increasing the cost of moving exhibition equipment to tradeshows due to the increase in gas prices.

55153 ■ "ROI Drive Spurs New Models: More Choices" in *Tradeshow Week* (Vol. 34, November 29, 2004, No. 48, pp. 58)
Pub: Reed Business Information
Ed: David S. Cohen. **Description:** Tradeshow organizers are experimenting with new ideas in presenting exhibits in order to show measurable return on investment to exhibitors.

55154 ■ "St. Charles Convention Center St. Charles, MO" in *Tradeshow Week* (Vol. 34, November 29, 2004, No. 48, pp. S5)
Pub: Reed Business Information
Description: Profile of the St. Charles Convention Center in Missouri. The new facility will open April 2005, offering high tech conveniences like fiber optic cabling, Wi-Fi technology, and a cyber cafe in the historic district.

55155 ■ "Sales Picture Brightens for Sparks Exhibits and Environments" in *Tradeshow Week* (Vol. 34, December 6, 2004, No. 49, pp. 2)
Pub: Reed Business Information
Description: Sparks Exhibits and Environments attributes its growth in revenue to sales from new and existing customers; Marlton reported a $6 million rise in revenue; Exhibitgroup/Giltspur reported a 5.8 percent third quarter revenue gain.

55156 ■ "Seminars focus on bio-research" in *Hispanic Business* (Vol. 22, No. 6, June 2000, pp. 28)
Pub: Hispanic Business
Description: The U.S. Government will provide $495 million funding for research into nanotechnology in 2001. Small businesses wishing to participate in the new technological revolution are being helped by the National Institutes of Health, which is sponsoring a symposium on nanotechnology.

55157 ■ "Small Firms Emphasize Trade-Show Marketing" in *Crain's Detroit Business* (Vol. 21, February 7, 2005, No. 6, pp. 24)
Pub: Crain Communications Inc. - Detroit
Ed: DeAnna Belger. **Description:** According to a recent survey, more small companies in Michigan rely on trade shows than their larger competitors. Most respondents reported attending trade shows to generate sales leads, increase visibility, and to network.

55158 ■ "Spotlight On" in *Crain's Detroit Business* (Vol. 21, October , 2005, No. 43, pp. 10)
Pub: Crain Communications Inc. - Detroit
Description: Companies specializing in meetings, conventions and tourism are listed. Statistical data included.

55159 ■ "State Farm Signs On As Host" in *Black Enterprise* (Vol. 36, December 2005, No. 5, pp. 166)
Pub: Earl G. Graves Publishing Co. Inc.
Ed: Alysha N. Cryer. **Description:** State Farm Insurance Company has partnered with Black Enterprise to launch the inaugural Women of Pow4er Summit. The professional leadership conference is designed exclusively for women of color executives.

55160 ■ "Stealing the Show: Exhibitors and Show Managers Fight Suitcasing" in *Tradeshow Week* (Vol. 34, December 6, 2004, No. 49, pp. S3)
Pub: Reed Business Information
Ed: Gary Tufel. **Description:** In a tough economy, exhibitors are upset with sales people who walk the aisles of a tradeshow marketing without paying for booth space, called suitcasing. Suitcasers are able to take buyers away from the show to a hotel or restaurant. Industrial espionage is another problem for exhibitors.

55161 ■ "Success Products" in *Black Enterprise* (Vol. 37, February 2007, No. 7, pp. 135)
Pub: Earl G. Graves Publishing Co. Inc.
Ed: Tanisha A. Sykes. **Description:** Using innovative resources that are already at your fingertips instead of trying to reach out to companies first is a great way to discover whether you have a viable idea or product. Be motivated to start an e-newsletter letting people know about your products and attend conferences like The Motivation Show, the world's largest exhibition of motivational products and services related to performance in business.

55162 ■ *The Successful Exhibitor's Handbook: Trade Show Techniques for Beginners and Pros*
Pub: Self-Counsel Press, Inc.
Ed: Barry Siskind. **Released:** 1993, second edition. **Price:** $14.95 (paper).

55163 ■ "Successful Expo! Expo! Mirrors Greater Optimism" in *Tradeshow Week* (Vol. 34, December 13, 2004, No. 50, pp. 1)
Pub: Reed Business Information
Ed: Margo McCall. **Description:** The International Association for Exhibition Management reported increased attendance for its annual Expo! Expo! Meeting, showing optimism for the industry.

55164 ■ "A Super Selling Point" in *Crain's Detroit Business* (Vol. 22, February 13, 2006, No. 7, pp. 11)
Pub: Crain Communications Inc. - Detroit
Ed: Jennette Smith. **Description:** The Detroit Metro Convention & Visitors Bureau and others in the local hospitality sectors, including restaurants and hotels, plan to capitalize on the positive publicity the city received during Super Bowl XL.

55165 ■ "Supplier Diversity" in *Hispanic Business* (September 2004, pp. 18)
Pub: Hispanic Business
Description: The National Minority Supplier Development Council held its annual conference and Business Opportunity Fair in Washington, DC. The council reports more than 15,000 minority-owned businesses it has certified supply nearly $80 billion annually in goods and services to the council's 3,500 corporation members.

55166 ■ "The U.S. Commercial Service: www.export.gov/comm_svc" in *Entrepreneur* (Vol. 32, November 2004, No. 11, pp. 6)
Pub: Entrepreneur Media Inc.
Ed: Steve Cooper. **Description:** U.S. Commercial Service offers global business solutions in the areas of market research, trade events to promote businesses and services, introductions between buyers and distributors, and export counseling.

55167 ■ "Thinking Small: Coca-Cola Shows How the 20'x20' Exhibit Is Done" in *Tradeshow Week* (Vol. 34, December 6, 2004, No. 49, pp. S6)
Pub: Reed Business Information
Ed: Heidi Genoist. **Description:** Small companies are using Coca-Cola's small tradeshow booth as a model for introducing new products to a key buyer group.

55168 ■ *Trade Show Exhibiting: The Insider's Guide for Entrepreneurs*
Pub: The McGraw-Hill Companies
Ed: Diane K. Weintraub. **Released:** 1991. **Price:** $14.95 (paper).

55169 ■ "Trade Show Exhibitors Association: www.tsea.org" in *Entrepreneur* (Vol. 31, No. 12, December 2003, pp. 8)
Pub: Entrepreneur Media Inc.
Ed: Steve Cooper. Description: Profile of the Web site Trade Show Exhibitors Association is presented. The site offers advice for exhibit and event marketing professionals.

55170 ■ *Trade Shows: The Small Business Guide to Successful Exhibiting*
Pub: TAB Books, Inc.
Ed: Diane K. Weintraub. Released: 1991. Price: $14.95 (paper). Description: Published by Liberty Hall Press.

55171 ■ *Trade Shows Worldwide*
Pub: Thomson Gale
Released: Annual, latest edition 22, Published July 2005. Price: $435, individuals. Covers: over 10,800 trade shows and exhibitions, including those held at conferences, conventions, meetings, trade and industrial events, merchandise marts, and national expositions; 6,000 trade show sponsors and organizers; of trade show facilities, services, and information sources, approximately 2,000 conference and convention centers, about 600 visitor and convention bureaus, 400 World Trade Centers; sources of information for the trade show industry, including professional associations, consulting organizations, and publications; and 1,900 trade show industry service suppliers. Entries Include: For shows and exhibitions—Name of convention, exhibit, or show; producer, sponsor, and/or organizer name, address, phone, e-mail, website, toll-free phone, telex, fax, name and title of contact; show frequency; founding date; audience; number of attendees; price for display space; description of exhibits; registration fees; industry programs; social events; square feet/meters of exhibition space; number of meeting rooms needed; number of hotel rooms and nights needed; publications and dates and locations of future shows. For sponsors and organizers—Company or organization name, address, phone, toll-free, e-mail, URL, fax, telex, and alphabetical listing of shows handled. For facilities, suppliers of services, and information sources—Company or organization name, address, phone, toll-free, e-mail, URL, telex, fax, name and title of contact, and description of services. Arrangement: Separate sections for shows and exhibitions, for sponsors/organizers, and for trade show facilities, services, and information sources. Indexes: Chronological (show date), geographical (show location), subject, name and keyword.

55172 ■ *The Tradeshow Week Calendar*
Pub: Tradeshow Week Inc.
Contact: Adam Schaffer, Publisher
E-mail: aschaffer@reedbusiness.com
Released: Annual, December. Price: $10; Free. Publication Includes: About 100 major North American trade shows and expositions for a one-week period six months from the date of the issue and one year from date of the issue; overseas trade shows and expositions for a one-week period eight months from the date of the issue. Entries Include: Exposition name, dates, location, frequency of meeting, number of booths, number of companies exhibiting in show, expected attendance, name, address, phone and fax of show management. Principal content of publication is news and statistics on the tradeshow industry. Arrangement: Chronological.

55173 ■ *Tradeshow Week Data Book*
Pub: Tradeshow Week Inc.
Contact: Adam Schaffer, Publisher
E-mail: aschaffer@reedbusiness.com
Released: Annual. Price: $439, individuals. Covers: Nearly 5,000 trade and public shows with at least 5,000 net square feet of exhibit space scheduled in the United States and Canada up to five years from publication date. Entries Include: Show title, show management and sponsor, show description, location, dates, general contractor, estimated net square feet of exhibit space, number and profile of exhibitors and participants, fees, associated seminars, meetings and

conferences, show history, future dates and sites. Arrangement: Classified by industry category. Indexes: Geographical, alphabetical, chronological, show management, show size, rotation pattern, new shows.

55174 ■ "Trading Spaces" in *Crain's Detroit Business* (Vol. 19, No. 49, December 8, 2003, pp. 20)
Pub: Crain Communications Inc., Detroit
Description: Tips to use while preparing a booth for exhibiting at a trade show are listed.

55175 ■ "Trading spaces" in *Entrepreneur* (Vol. 31, No. 4, April 2003, pp. 140)
Pub: Entrepreneur Media Inc.
Ed: Nichole L. Torres. Description: The importance of setting goals when promoting goods or services at a trade show is covered.

55176 ■ "Vegas Furniture Market Getting Even Hotter" in *Tradeshow Week* (Vol. , pp.)
Pub: Reed Business Information
Ed: Heidi Genoist. Description: The World Market Center and the Association of Woodworking and Furnishings Suppliers have decided to share space at the Las Vegas Convention Center in spring 2005. Four more furniture-related tradeshows will also take place in Las Vegas in 2005.

55177 ■ "Want to Be an Event Planner?" in *Black Enterprise* (Vol. 36, November 2005, No. 4, pp. 132)
Pub: Earl G. Graves Publishing Co. Inc.
Ed: Lee Anna Jackson. Description: According to The Meeting Professional Institute (MPI), 41 percent of American marketing executives surveyed and 56 percent of executives worldwide believe that events are critical to any organization's success. MPI is developing a program to define core competencies for meeting professionals.

55178 ■ "What's In Your Wallet?" in *Tradeshow Week* (Vol. 34, December 13, 2004, No. 50, pp. 1)
Pub: Reed Business Information
Description: Statistical information regarding tradeshow managers is presented. Show manager income rose an average of 3.6 percent in 2004. Statistical data included.

55179 ■ "Who Belongs to IAEM? A Breakdown of Its Membership" in *Tradeshow Week* (Vol. 34, November 29, 2004, No. 48, pp. 18)
Pub: Reed Business Information
Description: Tradeshow Week Custom Research presents statistics and facts about the industry, including strategic information important to leaders in the sector. Statistical data included.

55180 ■ "Wired Right: Ian Kery Is Ready To Take Freeman's New Electrical Division To the West Coast and Beyond" in *Tradeshow Week* (Vol. 34)
Pub: Reed Business Information
Ed: Heidi Genoist. Description: An interview with Ian Kery, owner of Toronto, Canada's largest electrical firm. Kery is selling that firm and moving to Anaheim, California to launch its West Coast Electrical Division. Kery provides tradeshow electrical services.

55181 ■ "Workin' the show" in *BlackEnterprise* (Vol. 32, No. 2, September 2001, pp. 58)
Pub: Earl Graves Publishing Co.
Ed: Pittershawn Palmer. Description: Technical trade shows are a good tool for professionals and consumers to learn the latest in hardware, software, and the Internet.

TRADE PERIODICALS

55182 ■ *Exhibit Builder*
Pub: Exhibit Builder Magazine
Contact: Judy Pomerantz, Managing Editor
E-mail: judyp@exhibitbuilder.net

Released: Periodic, 7/year. Price: $40; $50 Canada; $60 out of country; $80 two years other countries. Description: Magazine covering new product information and research related to the exhibit building, including museums and trade shows.

55183 ■ *Expo*
Pub: EXPO Magazine Inc.
Contact: Donna Sanford, Publisher
E-mail: dsanford@ascendmedia.com
Ed: Danica Tormohlen, Editor, dtormohlen@ascendmedia.com. Released: Monthly, 10 times a year. Description: Trade magazine for those in the exposition industry.

55184 ■ *Successful Meetings*
Pub: Successful Meetings
Contact: Vincent Alonzo, Editor-in-Chief
E-mail: valonzo@succesfulmeetings.com
Ed: Terri Hardin, Editor, thardin@succesfulmeetings.com. Released: Monthly. Price: $79; $95 Canada; $195 other countries. Description: Magazine focusing on conventions, meetings, exhibits, training, trade shows and incentive travel. Includes annual directory issue.

55185 ■ *TradeShow & Exhibit Manager*
Pub: Goldstein & Associates
Contact: Steve Goldstein, President
Ed: Les Plesko, Editor. Released: Bimonthly. Price: $80. Description: Magazine for corporate exhibit managers and independent show organizers who are responsible for all facets of tradeshow activities, management, and expenditures.

55186 ■ *Tradeshow Week*
Pub: Darlene Gudea
Contact: Irene Sperling, Publisher
E-mail: isperling@tsweek.com
Released: Weekly (Mon.), 50/year. Price: $349. Description: Provides coverage of tradeshows, facilities, labor conditions, new exhibit ideas, people, and a comprehensive show calendar.

VIDEOCASSETTES/AUDIOCASSETTES

55187 ■ *It'll Be O.K. on the Day*
Video Arts, Inc.
c/o Aim Learning Group
8238-40 Lehigh
Morton Grove, IL 60053-2615
Free: 877-444-2230
Fax: (416)252-2155
Co. E-mail: service@aimlearninggroup.com
URL: http://www.aimlearninggroup.com
Released: 1989. Price: $695.00. Description: Understand the best way to set up an exhibition booth so that it will be most efficient. Availability: VHS; 3/4U.

55188 ■ *That's Show Business: The Rules of Exhibiting*
Video Arts, Inc.
c/o Aim Learning Group
8238-40 Lehigh
Morton Grove, IL 60053-2615
Free: 877-444-2230
Fax: (416)252-2155
Co. E-mail: service@aimlearninggroup.com
URL: http://www.aimlearninggroup.com
Released: 1991. Price: $790.00. Description: A sensible yet humorous approach to business exhibitions show the most common mistakes and how to avoid them. Availability: VHS; 8mm; 3/4U; Special order formats.

55189 ■ *The Trade Show Advantage*
Creative Training Solutions
5 Timberline Dr.
Voorhees, NJ 08043
Ph:(856)784-3468
Free: 800-515-4114
Fax: (856)784-7087
Co. E-mail: mail@creativetraining.com

URL: http://www.creativetraining.com
Price: $395.00. **Description:** Shows how to set up a booth at a trade show. Includes everything from personal comportment to information on the typical trade show environment. Includes planning guide, handout, and audiocassette. **Availability:** VHS.

55190 ■ *Working the Booth: Trade Show Success*
American Media, Inc.
4621 121st St.
Urbandale, IA 50323-2311
Ph:(515)224-0919
Free: 888-776-8268
Fax: (515)327-2555
Co. E-mail: custsvc@ammedia.com
URL: http://www.ammedia.com
Released: 1992. **Price:** $395.00. **Description:** Details techniques on successfully setting up and maintaining a booth at a trade show. Stresses etiquette, professionalism, positivity, correct prospect handling, and salesmanship. **Availability:** VHS; 3/4U; 8mm.

TRADE SHOWS AND CONVENTIONS

55191 ■ **ABA/BMA National Conference for Community Bankers**
American Bankers Association
1120 Connecticut Ave. NW
Washington, DC 20036
Free: 800-BAN-KERS
Co. E-mail: custserv@aba.com
URL: http://www.aba.com
Released: Annual. **Audience:** Chairmen and presidents, mainly of banks with less than $500 million in assets, community bank CEOs, bank directors, and other community bank executives. **Principal Exhibits:** Products and services related to investment management, customer service improvements, advertising, asset/liability management, bank management, electronic data interchange, employee recruitment/training, insurance, strategic planning models, including preparation for the 21st century, new revenue sources, cost control techniques, mainframe computers, market research, MCIF technology, minicomputers in community banking applications, software: platform, optical disk, and loan pricing, sweep accounts, and relationship banking for community bankers. **Dates and Locations:** 2007 Feb 18-21.

55192 ■ **ABA Sales Management Workshop**
American Bankers Association
1120 Connecticut Ave. NW
Washington, DC 20036
Free: 800-BAN-KERS
Co. E-mail: custserv@aba.com
URL: http://www.aba.com
Released: Annual. **Audience:** Senior community bank executives, marketing directors, mid-level bank retail managers, sales managers. **Principal Exhibits:** Services related to creating and maintaining customers.

55193 ■ **Action Sports Retailer - ASR Trade Expo, Atlantic City**
VNU Expo (Laguna)
310 Broadway
Laguna Beach, CA 92651
Ph:(946)376-6200
Free: 800-486-2701
Fax: (949)497-5290
Co. E-mail: interbike@wyoming.com
URL: http://www.vnuexpo.com
Released: Annual. **Audience:** Surf, skate, swim, urban street war, retailers and media. **Principal Exhibits:** Surf, skate, swim, urban street wear, hard goods and soft goods & accessories.

55194 ■ **Action Sports Retailer - ASR Trade Expo, Long Beach**
VNU Expo (Laguna)
310 Broadway
Laguna Beach, CA 92651
Ph:(946)376-6200

Free: 800-486-2701
Fax: (949)497-5290
Co. E-mail: interbike@wyoming.com
URL: http://www.vnuexpo.com
Released: Annual. **Audience:** Surf, skate, and urban/street wear hard goods and soft goods and accessories buyers. **Principal Exhibits:** Surf, skate, swim, footwear and urban/street wear, hard goods, soft goods and accessories.

55195 ■ **Action Sports Retailer - ASR Trade Expo, San Diego**
VNU Expo (Laguna)
310 Broadway
Laguna Beach, CA 92651
Ph:(946)376-6200
Free: 800-486-2701
Fax: (949)497-5290
Co. E-mail: interbike@wyoming.com
URL: http://www.vnuexpo.com
Released: Annual. **Audience:** Owners and managers of the speciality surf/skate/apparel retail stores. **Principal Exhibits:** Skate, surf and youth culture apparel, gear and accessories. **Dates and Locations:** 2007 Jan 25-27, San Diego, CA.

55196 ■ **American Public Health Association Public Health Expo**
American Public Health Association
800 I St. NW
Washington, DC 20001
Ph:(202)777-2742
Fax: (202)777-2534
Co. E-mail: comments@apha.org
URL: http://www.apha.org/
Released: Annual. **Audience:** Public health professionals, physicians, nurses, and health administrators. **Principal Exhibits:** Medical, products-related and pharmaceutical, health services, publishers, computer/software, educational, government, schools of public health. **Dates and Locations:** 2007 Nov 03-07, Washington, DC; 2008 Oct 25-29, San Diego, CA; 2009 Nov 07-11, Philadelphia, PA.

55197 ■ **American Quilt Study Group Seminar**
American Quilt Study Group
35th & Holdrege, E Campus Loop
PO Box 4737
Lincoln, NE 68504-0737
Ph:(402)472-5361
Fax: (402)472-5428
Co. E-mail: AQSG2@unl.edu
URL: http://www.h-net.org/~aqsg/
Released: Annual. **Principal Exhibits:** Quilt-related articles.

55198 ■ **American Real Estate Society Annual Meeting**
American Real Estate Society
5353 Parkside Dr.
Cleveland State University
College of Business
Department of Finance, UC513
Jupiter, FL 33458
Ph:(561)799-8664
Fax: (561)799-8535
Co. E-mail: dcooper@fau.edu
URL: http://www.aresnet.org
Released: Annual. **Audience:** College and university professors; high-level practicing professionals involved in all aspects real estate. **Principal Exhibits:** Exhibits relating to decision-making within real estate finance, real estate market analysis, investment, valuation, development, and other areas related to real estate in the private sector. Data providers, book publishers, etc. **Dates and Locations:** 2007 Apr 11-14, San Francisco, CA.

55199 ■ **American School Health Association National School Health Conference**
American School Health Association
7263 State Rte. 43
PO Box 708
Kent, OH 44240
Ph:(330)678-1601
Free: 800-445-2742

Fax: (330)678-4526
Co. E-mail: asha@ashaweb.org
URL: http://www.ashaweb.org
Released: Annual. **Audience:** School nurses, health educators, physicians, teachers, school administrators, dentists, school counselors, physical educators, and school health coordinators. **Principal Exhibits:** Publications, pharmaceuticals, clinical and medical equipment and supplies, information on health organizations, and health education methods and materials. **Dates and Locations:** 2007 Jul 09-13, Honolulu, HI.

55200 ■ **American Society for Healthcare Risk Management Convention**
American Society for Healthcare Risk Management
1 N Franklin
Chicago, IL 60606
Ph:(312)422-3980
Fax: (312)422-4580
Co. E-mail: ashrm@aha.org
URL: http://www.ashrm.org
Released: Annual. **Principal Exhibits:** Healthcare industry risk management equipment, supplies, and services.

55201 ■ **American Technical Education Association National Conference on Technical Education**
American Technical Education Association
c/o North Dakota State College of Science
800 N. 6th St.
Wahpeton, ND 58076-0002
Ph:(701)671-2301
Fax: (701)671-2260
URL: http://www.ateaonline.org
Released: Annual. **Audience:** Technical educators and administrators of post-secondary technical education. **Principal Exhibits:** Supplies and services related to post secondary technical education.

55202 ■ **ApEx**
Canadian Restaurant and Food Services Association
316 Bloor St. W., Ste. 1201
Toronto, ON, Canada M5S 1W5
Ph:(416)923-8416
Free: 800-387-5649
Fax: (416)923-1450
Co. E-mail: info@crfa.ca
URL: http://www.crfa.ca
Audience: Trade. **Principal Exhibits:** Products and services for the restaurant and hospitality industry, as well as institutions, convenience stores, delis and bakeries.

55203 ■ **Association for Research on Nonprofit Organizations and Voluntary Action Conference (ACNOVA)**
Association for Research on Nonprofit Organizations and Voluntary Action
550 W N St., Ste. 301
Indianapolis, IN 46202
Ph:(317)684-2120
Fax: (317)684-2128
Co. E-mail: aplotin@indyvax.iupui.edu
URL: http://www.arnova.org
Released: Annual. **Audience:** Scholars and nonprofit organization professionals. **Principal Exhibits:** Exhibits for citizen participation and voluntary action, including social movements, interest groups, consumer groups, political participation, community development, and religious organizations.

55204 ■ **Baltimore Women's Show**
S & L Productions, Inc.
1916 Crain Hwy., Ste. 16
Glen Burnie, MD 21061
Ph:(410)863-1180
Fax: (410)863-1187
URL: http://www.mdhomeandgarden.com
Released: Annual. **Audience:** Women 25-65 yrs. **Principal Exhibits:** Products and services for women.

55205 ■ **BMA Annual Marketing Forum**
American Bankers Association
1120 Connecticut Ave. NW
Washington, DC 20036

Free: 800-BAN-KERS
Co. E-mail: custserv@aba.com
URL: http://www.aba.com
Released: Annual. **Audience:** Bankers including community bank CEO's, marketing directors, sales managers, advertising directors, public relations managers. **Principal Exhibits:** Financial services marketing offering banking solutions in advertising services, bank equipment/systems, computer software, database marketing, direct marketing/sales, incentive/premium programs, insurance services, investment services, marketing consulting, merchandising, publishing, research, retail delivery, sales training, service quality, signage, and telemarketing.

55206 ■ BMA Private Wealth Sales Management Workshop, an ABA Program
American Bankers Association
1120 Connecticut Ave. NW
Washington, DC 20036
Free: 800-BAN-KERS
Co. E-mail: custserv@aba.com
URL: http://www.aba.com
Released: Annual. **Audience:** Trust, private banking and asset management officers, bank brokerage managers, sales managers, business development managers, and regional department managers. **Principal Exhibits:** Provides marketing education and information, professional growth and networking resources to marketing professionals in the financial services industry.

55207 ■ Broadcast Cable Financial Management Association Conference
Broadcast Cable Financial Management Association
550 Frontage Rd., Ste. 3600
Northfield, IL 60093
Ph:(847)716-7000
Fax: (847)716-7004
Co. E-mail: info@bcfm.com
URL: http://www.bcfm.com
Released: Annual. **Audience:** Business managers, CFO's. **Principal Exhibits:** Exhibits relating to the financial management of radio, television, and cable television operations, including issues such as industry - specific software, collection agencies, insurance, investments, banking, accounting firms and musi c licensing.

55208 ■ Cabletelevision Advertising Bureau - Cable Advertising Conference
Cabletelevision Advertising Bureau
830 3rd Ave., 2nd Fl.
New York, NY 10022
Ph:(212)508-1200
Fax: (212)832-3268
URL: http://www.cabletvadbureau.com
Released: Annual. **Audience:** Cable television and advertising trade. **Principal Exhibits:** Cable television and advertising equipment, supplies, and services.

55209 ■ Canadian Real Estate Association Annual Conference and Trade Show
Canadian Real Estate Association
Canada Bldg.
344 Slater St., Ste. 1600
Ottawa, ON, Canada K1R 7Y3
Ph:(613)237-7111
Free: 800-842-2732
Fax: (613)234-2567
Co. E-mail: info@crea.ca
URL: http://www.crea.ca
Released: Annual. **Audience:** Real estate professionals, brokers, managers, corporate representatives from real estate boards across the country. **Principal Exhibits:** Real Estate, financial, printing, and computer business equipment.

55210 ■ Computer Game Developers' Conference
CMP Media LLC (San Mateo)
2800 Campus Dr.
San Mateo, CA 94403
Ph:(650)513-4300
Co. E-mail: cmp@cmp.com
URL: http://www.cmp.com

Released: Annual. **Principal Exhibits:** Equipment, supplies, and services for developers and producers of computer games. **Dates and Locations:** 2007 Mar 05-09, San Jose, CA.

55211 ■ Estuarine Research Federation Conference
Estuarine Research Federation
PO Box 510
University of Southwest Louisiana
Dept. of Biology
Port Republic, MD 20676
Ph:(410)586-0997
Fax: (410)586-9226
Co. E-mail: webmaster@erf.org
URL: http://www.erf.org
Released: Biennial. **Principal Exhibits:** Exhibits for persons actively engaged in biological, hydrographic, or related investigations of estuarine problems.

55212 ■ Event Solutions Expo
Virgo Publishing Inc.
PO Box 40079
Phoenix, AZ 85067-0079
Ph:(480)990-1101
Fax: (480)990-0819
URL: http://www.vpico.com/
Released: Annual. **Audience:** Event planners, hotels, caterers, rental companies, designers, event producers, special event sites, DMCs, and entertainers. **Principal Exhibits:** Products and services for the special events industry, including tents, linens, decor, special effects, entertainment, props, lighting, venues, and food service equipment.

55213 ■ Expo Comm Wireless Korea
E.J. Krause & Associates, Inc.
6550 Rock Spring Dr., Ste. 500
Bethesda, MD 20817
Ph:(301)493-5500
Fax: (301)493-5705
Co. E-mail: ejkinfo@ejkrause.com
URL: http://www.ejkrause.com
Released: Annual. **Principal Exhibits:** Equipment, supplies, and services for computers.

55214 ■ Florida RV Supershow
Florida RV Trade Association
10510 Gibsonton Dr.
Riverview, FL 33569
Ph:(813)741-0488
Free: 888-FLA-RVGO
Fax: (813)741-0688
Co. E-mail: frvta@frvta.org
URL: http://www.frvta.org
Released: Annual. **Audience:** First time buyers as well as current owners. **Principal Exhibits:** Recreational vehicle supplies and accessories.

55215 ■ GMC Philadelphia Home Show
dmg world media (USA) inc. (Philadelphia)
200 Haddonfield-Berlin Rd.
High Ridge Commons
Ste. 302
Gibbsboro, NJ 08026
Ph:(856)784-4774
Free: 800-756-5692
Fax: (856)435-5920
URL: http://www.dmgworldmedia.com
Released: Annual. **Audience:** Home owners and apartment dwellers. **Principal Exhibits:** House and apartment products, supplies, and services.

55216 ■ Great Lakes Industrial Show
North American Exposition Co.
33 Rutherford Ave.
Boston, MA 02129
Ph:(617)242-6092
Free: 800-225-1577
Fax: (617)242-1817
Co. E-mail: naexpo@hotmail.com
URL: http://www.naexpo.com
Released: Annual. **Audience:** Buyers and officers from maintenance, material handling, engineering, production, purchasing, management, shipping and related professionals. **Principal Exhibits:** Industrial

products, machine tools, hand tools, pneumatics, hydraulics, plant engineering, and maintenance, paper and packaging, plastics, rubber products, material handling equipment, and dies and stampings.

55217 ■ Handmade - A Division of the San Francisco International Gift Fair
George Little Management, LLC (New York)
10 Bank St.
White Plains, NY 10606-1954
Ph:(914)421-3200
Free: 800-272-SHOW
Fax: (914)948-6180
Co. E-mail: cathy_steel@glmshows.com
URL: http://www.glmshows.com
Released: Semiannual. **Audience:** Specialty, department, stationery, juvenile, and jewelry stores, interior designers, gift shops, mail order atalogs,importers/distributors of homeproducts. **Principal Exhibits:** Handmade merchandise, including functional and decorative home furnishings, fashion accessories, jewelry plus an array of other unique craft objects. All merchandise is selected by a panel of craft professionals for uniqueness, originality and marketability.

55218 ■ Health and Fitness Expo
Jerry Hanson & Associates
PO Box 200201
303 N. Roberts
Billings, MT 59104-0392
Ph:(406)245-0404
Fax: (406)245-3897
Released: Annual. **Audience:** Health professionals and general public. **Principal Exhibits:** Lawn and garden products, home improvements/repair products, spas, computers, interior decorating, nurseries, entertainment and health related services and products.

55219 ■ Home Entertainment Show
Moorea Marketing
200 E. Joppa Rd., Ste. 403
Towson, MD 21286
Ph:(410)769-8223
Free: 800-830-3976
Fax: (410)769-8112
Co. E-mail: info@mooreamarketing.com
URL: http://www.mooreamarketing.com
Released: Biennial. **Audience:** Consumers, trade & press. **Principal Exhibits:** Home theater and high fidelity audio equipment, supplies, and services.

55220 ■ HSMAI - Affordable Meetings West
George Little Management, LLC (New York)
10 Bank St.
White Plains, NY 10606-1954
Ph:(914)421-3200
Free: 800-272-SHOW
Fax: (914)948-6180
Co. E-mail: cathy_steel@glmshows.com
URL: http://www.glmshows.com
Released: Annual. **Audience:** Trade professionals. **Principal Exhibits:** Equipment, supplies, and services for the hospitality and marketing industry.

55221 ■ The Imprinted Sportswear Show, Atlantic City
VNU Expositions, Inc. - Bill Communications, Inc.
1199 S. Belt Line Rd., Ste. 100
Coppell, TX 75019
Ph:(972)906-6500
Fax: (972)906-6501
Co. E-mail: jlerner@vnuemedia.com
URL: http://www.vnuexpo.com
Released: Annual. **Audience:** Trade only. **Principal Exhibits:** Trade show source for the imprinted sportswear/textile screen printing/embroidery industry; T-shirts, pre-prints, and other apparel; design software; screen printing supplies and equipment; transfers, lettering embroidery equipment and supplies.

55222 ■ International Conference on Fundraising
Association of Fundraising Professionals
222, Block C
04551-065 So Paulo, Sao Paulo, Brazil
Ph:55 11 2148 4700

URL: http://www.afpnet.org
Released: Annual. **Audience:** Decision makers for development offices for nonprofits. **Principal Exhibits:** Fund raising tools.

55223 ■ International Sport Summit
E.J. Krause & Associates, Inc.
6550 Rock Spring Dr., Ste. 500
Bethesda, MD 20817
Ph:(301)493-5500
Fax: (301)493-5705
Co. E-mail: ejkinfo@ejkrause.com
URL: http://www.ejkrause.com
Released: Annual. **Audience:** Trade professionals. **Principal Exhibits:** Equipment, supplies, and services for sports facilities and events.

55224 ■ JAGEN UND FISCHEN - International Exhibition for Hunters, Fishermen and Marksmen
Kallman Worldwide, Inc.
4 North St.
Suite 800
Waldwick, NJ 07463-1842
Ph:(201)251-2600
Fax: (201)251-2760
Co. E-mail: info@kallman.com
URL: http://www.kallman.com
Principal Exhibits: Equipment, supplies, and services for hunters, fishermen, and marksmen.

55225 ■ Maryland Municipal League Convention
Maryland Municipal League
1212 W St.
Annapolis, MD 21401
Ph:(410)268-5514
Free: 800-492-7121
Fax: (410)268-7004
Co. E-mail: mml@mdmunicipal.org
URL: http://www.mdmunicipal.org
Released: Annual. **Audience:** Municipal officials and other county and state officials. **Principal Exhibits:** Office equipment, public works equipment, insurance companies, consulting firms, recreation equipment, computers, engineering firms, police equipment, and code publishers. **Dates and Locations:** 2007 Jun.

55226 ■ Memories Expo
Offinger Management Co.
1100-H Brandywine Blvd.
PO Box 3388
Zanesville, OH 43702-3388
Ph:(740)452-4541
Free: 888-878-6334
Fax: (740)452-2552
Co. E-mail: OMC.Info@Offinger.com
URL: http://www.offinger.com
Released: 5/year. **Audience:** Trade and public. **Principal Exhibits:** Scrapbook supplies.

55227 ■ Michigan Association for Computer Users in Learning Conference
Michigan Association for Computer Users in
   Learning
PO Box 518
Holt, MI 48842-0518
Ph:(517)694-9756
Fax: (517)694-9773
Co. E-mail: macul@macul.org
URL: http://www.macul.org
Released: Annual. **Audience:** Educational technology professionals. **Principal Exhibits:** Computer and educational equipment, supplies, and services. **Dates and Locations:** 2007 Mar 14-16, Detroit, MI; 2008 Mar 05-07, Grand Rapids, MI; 2009 Mar 18-20, Detroit, MI.

55228 ■ Michigan Interscholastic Athletic Administrators Mid-Winter Conference
Michigan Interscholastic Athletic Administrator
   Association
35445 Hathaway
Livonia, MI 48150-2513
Ph:(734)422-3569
Fax: (734)762-9957
Released: Annual. **Audience:** Educators in the field of secondary interscholastic athletic administration.

Principal Exhibits: Sports supplies, athletic equipment, clothing, publications, fund raisers, and athletic training supplies, and awards companies. **Dates and Locations:** 2007 Mar 16-20, Traverse City, MI.

55229 ■ Michigan Restaurant Show
Michigan Restaurant Association
225 W. Washtenaw St.
Lansing, MI 48933
Ph:(517)482-5244
Free: 800-968-9668
Fax: (517)482-7663
URL: http://www.michiganrestaurant.org
Released: Annual. **Audience:** Food service industry professionals. **Principal Exhibits:** Equipment, supplies, and services for the food service industry.

55230 ■ Minneapolis International Motorcycle Show
Advanstar Communications Inc.
One Park Ave.
New York, NY 10016
Ph:(212)951-6600
Fax: (212)951-6793
Co. E-mail: info@advantstar.com
URL: http://www.advanstar.com
Audience: Public: Motorcycle, watercraft and ATV enthusiasts. **Principal Exhibits:** A marketplace where manufacturers and retailers can display and sell their products such as motorcycles, all-terrain vehicles (ATV), scooters, watercraft, apparel, parts and accessories. **Dates and Locations:** 2007 Feb 02-04, Minneapolis, MN.

55231 ■ National Agricultural Bankers Conference
American Bankers Association
1120 Connecticut Ave. NW
Washington, DC 20036
Free: 800-BAN-KERS
Co. E-mail: custserv@aba.com
URL: http://www.aba.com
Released: Annual. **Audience:** Bank CEOs, mainly from community banks in rural areas, executive vice presidents, senior vice presidents, economists, analysts. **Principal Exhibits:** The latest developments in the agricultural lending business, as well as strategies for better market share, profitability and customer service.

55232 ■ Natural Products Expo East
New Hope Natural Media
1401 Pearl St. Ste. 200
Boulder, CO 80302-5346
Ph:(303)939-8440
Free: (303)939-8440
Fax: (303)998-9020
Co. E-mail: info@newhope.com
URL: http://www.newhope.com
Released: Annual. **Audience:** Retailers, wholesalers, distributors, and brokers from the natural products industry. **Principal Exhibits:** Natural, organic and environmentally sound products, including: alternative health care, vegetarian and allergy-free personal care, recycled/recyclable products, biodegradable products, and organic meats.

55233 ■ NCSL - National Conference of State Legislatures Annual Meeting and Exhibition
National Conference of State Legislatures
7700 E 1st Pl.
Denver, CO 80230
Ph:(303)364-7700
Fax: (303)364-7800
Co. E-mail: info@ncsl.org
URL: http://www.ncsl.org
Released: Annual. **Audience:** Key legislators, senior staff, state and federal agency personnel, government relations managers, and business and associations executives. **Principal Exhibits:** Products and technology that have impact on the states. **Dates and Locations:** 2007 Aug 05-09, Boston, MA; 2008 Jul 22-26, New Orleans, LA.

55234 ■ ND/SD Realtors Convention
South Dakota Association of Realtors
204 N. Euclid Ave.
Pierre, SD 57501

Ph:(605)224-0554
Fax: (605)224-8975
Co. E-mail: sdar@sdrealtor.org
URL: http://www.sdrealtor.org
Released: Annual. **Principal Exhibits:** Realty equipment, supplies, and services.

55235 ■ New Jersey League of Municipalities
New Jersey League of Municipalities
407 W State St.
Trenton, NJ 08618
Ph:(609)695-3481
Fax: (609)695-0151
Co. E-mail: league@njslom.com
URL: http://www.njslom.com
Released: Annual. **Audience:** Municipal officials. **Principal Exhibits:** Municipal products and services.

55236 ■ New York Restaurant & Food Service Show
Reed Exhibitions (North American Headquarters)
383 Main Ave.
Norwalk, CT 06851
Ph:(203)840-5337
Fax: (203)840-9570
Co. E-mail: export@reedexpo.com
URL: http://www.reedexpo.com
Released: Annual. **Principal Exhibits:** Equipment, supplies, and services for the food products, foodservice, restaurant, and institutional food service industries. **Dates and Locations:** 2007 Mar 04-06, New York, NY.

55237 ■ North American Association of State and Provincial Lotteries Conference and Trade Show
North American Association of State and Provincial
   Lotteries
2775 Bishop Rd., Ste. B
Willoughby Hills, OH 44092
Ph:(216)241-2310
Fax: (216)241-4350
Co. E-mail: NASPLHQ@aol.com
URL: http://www.naspl.org
Released: Annual. **Audience:** Lottery industry professionals. **Principal Exhibits:** Lottery equipment, supplies, and services. **Dates and Locations:** 2007 Oct 03-07, Louisville, KY.

55238 ■ Old House/New House Home Show
Kennedy Productions, Inc.
1208 Lisle Pl.
Lisle, IL 60532-2262
Ph:(630)515-1160
Fax: (630)515-1165
Co. E-mail: kp@corecomm.net
URL: http://www.kennedyproductions.com
Released: Semiannual. **Audience:** Trade professionals and general public. **Principal Exhibits:** Products and services for home remodeling, improvement, enhancement, decorating, landscaping and more. Hundreds of ideas to improve and beautify every home.

55239 ■ ON DEMAND Digital Printing & Publishing Strategy Conference and Exposition
Advanstar Communications Inc.
One Park Ave.
New York, NY 10016
Ph:(212)951-6600
Fax: (212)951-6793
Co. E-mail: info@advantstar.com
URL: http://www.advanstar.com
Released: Annual. **Audience:** Corporate executives, print providers, government users. **Principal Exhibits:** Addresses the digitalization of workflow in the printing and publishing marketplace. **Dates and Locations:** 2007 Apr 16-19, Boston, MA.

55240 ■ Outdoor Retailer Summer Market
VNU Expo (Laguna)
310 Broadway
Laguna Beach, CA 92651
Ph:(946)376-6200
Free: 800-486-2701
Fax: (949)497-5290
Co. E-mail: interbike@wyoming.com

URL: http://www.vnuexpo.com
Released: Annual. **Audience:** Owners and managers of the specialty sports retail stores. **Principal Exhibits:** Human-powered outdoor sports goods.

55241 ■ Outdoor Retailer Winter Market
VNU Expo (Laguna)
310 Broadway
Laguna Beach, CA 92651
Ph:(946)376-6200
Free: 800-486-2701
Fax: (949)497-5290
Co. E-mail: interbike@wyoming.com
URL: http://www.vnuexpo.com
Released: Annual. **Audience:** Owners and managers of specialty sports retail stores. **Principal Exhibits:** Human-powered outdoor sports goods.

55242 ■ Pittsburgh Women's Show
Moorea Marketing
200 E. Joppa Rd., Ste. 403
Towson, MD 21286
Ph:(410)769-8223
Free: 800-830-3976
Fax: (410)769-8112
Co. E-mail: info@mooreamarketing.com
URL: http://www.mooreamarketing.com
Released: Annual. **Audience:** Trade and public. **Principal Exhibits:** Products and services for women relating to health, fitness, business, career, and finance.

55243 ■ Rocky Mountain Snowmobile & Icefishing Expo
Industrial Expositions, Inc.
1675 Larimer St., No.700
PO Box 480084
Denver, CO 80248-0084
Ph:(303)892-6800
Free: 800-457-2434
Fax: (303)892-6322
Co. E-mail: info@iei-expos.com
URL: http://www.iei-expos.com/
Released: Annual. **Audience:** Snowmobilers. **Principal Exhibits:** Snowmobiles, clothing and accessories, recreational vehicles, travel and accommodations.

55244 ■ Scuba ExtaSea Expo
Industrial Expositions, Inc.
1675 Larimer St., No.700
PO Box 480084
Denver, CO 80248-0084
Ph:(303)892-6800
Free: 800-457-2434
Fax: (303)892-6322
Co. E-mail: info@iei-expos.com
URL: http://www.iei-expos.com/
Released: Annual. **Audience:** General public. **Principal Exhibits:** Scuba diving, snorkeling, travel and accessories.

55245 ■ Society of Craft Designers Educational Seminar (SCD)
Offinger Management Co.
1100-H Brandywine Blvd.
PO Box 3388
Zanesville, OH 43702-3388
Ph:(740)452-4541
Free: 888-878-6334
Fax: (740)452-2552
Co. E-mail: OMC.Info@Offinger.com
URL: http://www.offinger.com
Released: Annual. **Audience:** Designers, manufacturers, editors, and publishers. **Principal Exhibits:** Craft designer showcases and education.

55246 ■ Society for Human Resource Management (SHRM) The HRM Marketplace Exposition
Society for Human Resource Management
1800 Duke St.
Alexandria, VA 22314
Ph:(703)548-3440
Free: 800-283-SHRM
Fax: (703)535-6490
Co. E-mail: shrm@shrm.org

URL: http://www.shrm.org
Released: Annual. **Audience:** Human resource management and related professionals. **Principal Exhibits:** Human resource management products and services; including relocation human resource information systems, recruitment, executive search, temporary/contact personnel employee compensation and benefits, incentive program information, childcare/eldercare, and drug testing information.

55247 ■ Texas Apartment Association Annual Education Conference and Trade Show
Texas Apartment Association, Inc.
606 W. 12th St.
Austin, TX 78701-1718
Ph:(512)479-6252
Fax: (512)479-6291
URL: http://www.taa.org
Released: Annual. **Audience:** Owners and management company reps of multi-housing communities from Texas. **Principal Exhibits:** Goods and services geared to multi-housing professionals, including software, soft goods, and property supplies. **Dates and Locations:** 2007 Apr 19-21, Houston, TX.

55248 ■ TS2 - The Trade Show About Trade Shows
National Trade Productions, Inc.
313 S Patrick St.
Alexandria, VA 22314-3567
Ph:(703)683-8500
Free: 800-687-7469
Fax: (703)836-4486
Co. E-mail: ntpinfo@ntpshow.com
URL: http://www.ntpshow.com
Released: Annual. **Audience:** Exhibit managers. **Principal Exhibits:** Equipment, supplies, and services for the trade show industry, including moving companies, booths and other structures, publications, audiovisual equipment, and related items. **Dates and Locations:** 2007 Jul 31 - Aug 02, Washington, DC.

55249 ■ Virginia Health Care Association Annual Convention and Trade Show
Virginia Health Care Association
2112 W. Laburnum Ave., Ste. 206
Richmond, VA 23227
Ph:(804)353-9101
Fax: (804)353-3098
Co. E-mail: kathy.robertson@vhca.org
URL: http://www.vhca.org
Released: Annual. **Audience:** Nursing homeowners, administrators, purchasing agents, and nurses; dietary, housekeeping, social services, and activities departments heads. **Principal Exhibits:** Equipment, supplies, and services for nursing home operations, including food, medical supplies, furniture, computer systems, linen, medical equipment, insurance, pharmaceuticals, optometrists, psychologists, and transportation.

55250 ■ West Ex: The Rocky Mountain Regional Hospitality Exposition
Colorado Restaurant Association
430 E. 7th Ave.
Denver, CO 80203
Ph:(303)830-2972
Free: 800-522-2972
Fax: (303)830-2973
Co. E-mail: info@coloradorestaurant.com
URL: http://www.coloradorestaurant.com
Released: Annual. **Audience:** Food service and restaurant industry personnel. **Principal Exhibits:** Food service and lodging products, equipment, and services. **Dates and Locations:** 2007 May 15, Denver, CO.

55251 ■ Western Food Service & Hospitality Expo Los Angeles
California Restaurant Association
1011 10th St.
Sacramento, CA 95814
Ph:(916)447-5793
Free: 800-765-4842
Fax: (916)447-6182
URL: http://www.calrest.org

Audience: Food service hospitality and lodging industry professionals. **Principal Exhibits:** Food, equipment, supplies, and services for foodservice and lodging industries.

55252 ■ World Gaming Congress and Expo
Ascend Media Gaming Group
1771 E Flamingo Rd., Ste.208A
Las Vegas, NV 89119
Fax: (702)794-0799
Co. E-mail: sgibbs@ascendmedia.com
URL: http://www.ascendgaming.com
Audience: International gaming and napitality executive. **Principal Exhibits:** Casino operations equipment, supplies, and services. Hotel, & resort systems, services. Decorative furnishings and fixtures.

CONSULTANTS

55253 ■ Featherlite Exhibits
7300 32nd Ave. N
Minneapolis, MN 55427
Ph:(763)537-5533
Free: 800-229-5533
Fax: (763)923-6041
Co. E-mail: marketing@featherlite.com
URL: http://www.featherlite.com

E-mail: marketing@featherlite.com
Scope: Tradeshow consultancy includes full-service rentals, installation and dismantling, accessories and complete graphic design services. **Special Services:** Computer-aided drafting and design service.

55254 ■ International Training and Management Co.
16436 Shaw's Creek Rd.
Caledon, ON, Canada L7K 1K1
Ph:(519)927-9494
Free: 800-358-6079
Fax: 800-358-6084
Co. E-mail: info@siskindtraining.com
URL: http://www.siskindtraining.com

E-mail: info@siskindtraining.com
Scope: Full service exhibitor training company, providing both exhibitor training products as well as consulting services. Industries served: private and public companies who exhibit at trade or consumer shows. **Publications:** "Bumblebees Can't Fly, a Practical Guide to Making Everyday Work," 2002; "Take the stress out of show planning"; "Avoid convention overload "; "Powerful Exhibit Marketing"; "Making Contact"; "Seminars to Build Your Business". **Seminars:** Successful Exhibiting.

55255 ■ Intex Exhibit Systems L.L.C.
7018 NE 40th Ave.
Vancouver, WA 98661
Ph:(360)713-0300
Free: 800-331-6633
Fax: (360)713-0327
Co. E-mail: info@intexexhibits.com
URL: http://www.intexexhibits.com

E-mail: info@intexexhibits.com
Scope: Firm specializes in the design and production of exhibits, displays and pavilions for world fairs, tradeshows and similar events. Services include product design, industrial and engineering design for educational exhibits, museum exhibits and science and technology museology. Serves private industry as well as government agencies. **Publications:** "Trade Show Marketing"; "Exhibitor Times". **Special Services:** Fastpack™; Panelflo™; affordable-1™; the graphic arm™; Expression™; TigerMark™.

55256 ■ Reed–Sendecke–Krebsbach Inc.
701 Deming Way
Madison, WI 53717-1937
Ph:(608)827-0701
Free: 800-373-0043
Fax: (608)827-0702
Co. E-mail: info@rsandk.com
URL: http://www.rsandk.com

E-mail: info@rsandk.com
Scope: Provides marketing, advertising and design. Communications agency that specializes in creating image and awareness programs for business-to-business clients in the life sciences, computer technology, power quality, filtration, medical equipment, financial services and telecommunications industries.

55257 ■ Together Inc.
802 E 6th St.
PO Box 52528
Tulsa, OK 74152
Ph:(918)587-2405
Free: 800-282-0085
Fax: (918)382-0906
Co. E-mail: pinrus@aol.com
URL: http://aquarius.lunarpages.com/~positi5/
positivepins

E-mail: pinrus@aol.com

Scope: Offers services in employee and client self development training, logo development, lapel pin design, fund raising, public relations, conference and exhibit planning, direct marketing, association management, human resource development, and photography. Assists organizations in developing a positive community image and also assists them in developing a donor program. Industries served: government agencies, education, association and business, public and private schools. **Seminars:** Adventures in Attitudes; Diversity and Board Training for non-profits. **Special Services:** The Pin Man®.

ASSOCIATIONS AND OTHER ORGANIZATIONS

55258 ■ Agricultural Producers Union–Union des Producteurs Agricoles
555 Roland-Therrien Blvd., Bureau 100
Longueuil, QC, Canada J4H 3Y9
Ph:(450)679-0530
Co. E-mail: upa@upa.qc.ca
URL: http://www.upa.qc.ca
Contact: Laurent Pellerin, Pres. Gen.
Description: Promotes and supports the interests of agricultural producers throughout Canada. Provides information on updated developments on the farming industry. Works as a communications network among Quebec farmers. Protects the rights of individuals within the agricultural producing community. **Publications:** *Terre de Chez Nous* (weekly).

55259 ■ Association des Aides Familiales du Quebec
1750, Rue St. Andre
Montreal, QC, Canada H2L 3T8
Ph:(514)272-2670
Fax: (514)272-8338
Co. E-mail: aafq@aafq.ca
URL: http://www.aafq.ca
Contact: Louise Dionne, Dir.
Membership: Domestic workers. **Purpose:** Seeks to obtain optimal conditions of employment for members. Advocates for increased recognition of the rights of domestic workers; represents members in negotiations with employers. **Publications:** *Standing Tall* (bimonthly).

55260 ■ Building and Construction Trades Department - Canadian Office–Departement des Metiers de la Construction - Bureau Canadien
No. 1902-130 Albert
Ottawa, ON, Canada K1P 5G4
Ph:(613)236-0653
Fax: (613)230-5138
Co. E-mail: rblakely@buildingtrades.ca
URL: http://www.buildingtrades.ca
Contact: Edward C. Sullivan, Pres.
Membership: Individuals working in the building trades. **Purpose:** Seeks to obtain optimal conditions of employment for members. Represents members in negotiations with employers.

55261 ■ Canadian Association of Labour Media
76 Westmount Ave.
Toronto, ON, Canada M6H 3K1
Ph:(416)656-2256
Free: 888-290-CALM
Fax: (416)656-7649
Co. E-mail: editor@calm.ca
URL: http://www.calm.ca
Contact: Rosemarie Bahr, Ed.
Membership: Media organizations operated by labor unions. **Purpose:** Promotes increased awareness of

the trade union movement and issues affecting workers. Serves as a clearinghouse on trade unionism and labor issues. **Publications:** *CALMideas* (annual).

55262 ■ Canadian Association of Professional Employees–Association Canadienne des employes professionels
100 Queen St., 4th Fl.
Ottawa, ON, Canada K1P 1J9
Ph:(613)236-9181
Free: 800-265-9181
Fax: (613)236-6017
Co. E-mail: general@acep-cape.ca
URL: http://www.acep-cape.ca
Contact: Jose Aggrey, Pres.
Membership: Professional and technical employees. **Purpose:** Seeks to obtain optimal conditions of employment for members. Represents members in negotiations with employers. **Telecommunication Services:** electronic mail, jaggrey@acep-cape.ca.

55263 ■ Canadian Auto Workers
205 Placer Ct.
Toronto, ON, Canada M2H 3H9
Ph:(416)497-4110
Free: 800-268-5763
Fax: (416)495-6559
Co. E-mail: caw@caw.ca
URL: http://www.caw.ca
Contact: Buzz Hargrove, Pres.
Description: Represents the economic and workplace safety interests of Canadian automobile workers. Conducts economic and social action activities; maintains educational, charitable and research programs. Operates speakers' bureau. **Publications:** *Contact* (weekly).

55264 ■ Canadian Industrial Relations Association–Association Canadienne des Relations Industrielles
Department des Relations Industrielles
Universite de Laval, Pavillon J.-A.-DeSeve
Ste.-Foy, QC, Canada G1K 7P4
Ph:(418)656-2468
Fax: (418)656-3175
Co. E-mail: acri-cira@rlt.ulaval.ca
URL: http://www.cira-acri.ca
Contact: Ann Frost, Pres.
Membership: Industrial relations' professionals. **Purpose:** Seeks to advance the study and practice of industrial relations. Serves as a forum for the exchange of ideas and information among members; sponsors research.

55265 ■ Canadian Labour and Business Centre–Centre syndicat et patronal du Canada
55 Metcalfe St., Ste. 1440
Ottawa, ON, Canada K1P 6L5
Ph:(613)234-0505
Fax: (613)234-2482
Co. E-mail: info@clbc.ca
URL: http://www.clbc.ca
Contact: Shirley Seward, CEO
Purpose: Promotes increased industrial productivity through improved cooperation between labor and

business organizations. Serves as liaison linking labor and industrial associations; gathers and disseminates information on business and labor issues; makes available advocacy and consulting services.

55266 ■ Canadian Labour Congress–Congres du travail du Canada
2841 Riverside Dr.
Ottawa, ON, Canada K1V 8X7
Ph:(613)521-3400
Fax: (613)521-4655
Co. E-mail: president@clc-ctc.ca
URL: http://www.clc-ctc.ca
Contact: Ken Georgetti, Pres.
Description: Works to ensure that all Canadians are able to find employment at fair wages, with union representation and the right to collective bargaining, in a safe environment. Seeks to create a just and equitable society. Joins with other organizations for advocacy and action on behalf of working Canadians. Facilitates establishment of grass roots organizations. Conducts research and educational programs; maintains speakers' bureau; compiles statistics. **Publications:** *C.L.C. Fax-Press* (weekly); *Sweatshop Alert* (periodic); *UI Bulletin* (periodic).

55267 ■ Canadian Media Guild–Guilde Canadienne des Medias
144 Front St. W, Ste. 300
Toronto, ON, Canada M5J 2L7
Ph:(416)591-5333
Free: 800-465-4149
Fax: (416)591-7278
Co. E-mail: info@cmg.ca
URL: http://www.cmg.ca
Contact: Lise Lareau, Pres.
Membership: Employees of press and broadcasting companies and other media outlets. **Purpose:** Seeks to secure optimal conditions of employment for members. Represents members in negotiations with employers. **Publications:** *F-Force* (5/year).

55268 ■ Canadian Teachers' Federation–Federation Canadienne des Enseignantes et des Enseignants
2490 Don Reid Dr.
Ottawa, ON, Canada K1H 1E1
Ph:(613)232-1505
Free: (866)283-1505
Fax: (613)232-1886
Co. E-mail: info@ctf-fce.ca
URL: http://www.ctf-fce.ca
Contact: Dr. Julius Buski, Sec.Gen.
Description: Provincial and territorial teachers' organizations. Works to ensure that teachers' opinions are considered when national government bodies debate educational legislation. Facilitates communication and cooperation among members. Conducts research, educational, and lobbying activities. **Publications:** Annual Report (annual).

55269 ■ Canadian Telecommunications Employees' Association–Association Canadienne des Employes de Telephone
PO Box 103
Toronto, ON, Canada M5G 2C8

Ph:(416)977-2251
Free: 800-595-2696
Fax: (416)977-9738
URL: http://www.acet-ctea.com
Contact: Brenda Knight, Pres.
Membership: Telephone company employees. **Purpose:** Seeks to obtain optimal conditions of employment for members. Represents members in negotiations with employers.

55270 ■ Canadian Union of Public Employees–Le Syndicat canadien de la fonction publique
21 Florence St.
Ottawa, ON, Canada K2P 0W6
Ph:(613)237-1590
Fax: (613)237-5508
URL: http://www.cupe.ca
Contact: Paul Moist, Pres.
Membership: Local union organizations representing 500,000 public service employees. **Purpose:** Seeks to protect the rights and improve the conditions of employment of members. Promotes fairness in hiring and promotion without regard to race or gender. Represents members in collective bargaining; makes available legal, educational, research, job evaluation, and communications services. **Publications:** *CUPE: It's Your Union*; *Organize* (periodic).

55271 ■ Communications, Energy and Paperworkers Union of Canada–Syndicat Canadien des Communications, de l'Energie et du Papier
301 Laurier Ave. W
Ottawa, ON, Canada K1P 6M6
Ph:(613)230-5200
Fax: (613)230-5801
Co. E-mail: info@cep.ca
URL: http://www.cep.ca
Contact: Brian Payne, Pres.
Description: Trade union. Organizes and conducts collective bargaining for individuals employed in the telecommunications, electrical, electronics, pulp and paper, energy, print and broadcast media, and chemical industries in Canada.

55272 ■ Confederation of National Trade Unions–Confederation des Syndicats Nationaux
1601 Ave. de Lorimier
Montreal, QC, Canada H2K 4M5
Ph:(514)598-2121
Co. E-mail: international@csn.qc.ca
URL: http://www.csn.qc.ca
Contact: Claudette Carbonneau, Pres.
Membership: National trade unions representing 235,000 workers. **Purpose:** Promotes advancement of the Canadian labor movement. Represents workers in collective bargaining. **Publications:** *Nouvelles CSN* (biweekly).

55273 ■ Editors' Association of Canada–Association canadienne des reviseurs
502-27 Carlton St.
Toronto, ON, Canada M5B 1L2
Ph:(416)975-1379
Free: (866)226-3348
Fax: (416)975-1637
Co. E-mail: info@editors.ca
URL: http://www.editors.ca
Contact: Lynne Massey, Exec. Dir.
Membership: Editors, proofreaders, copy editors, and researchers working on both English and French language printed materials. **Purpose:** Promotes advancement of the profession of editing, and of members' capabilities. Conducts professional development courses for members; makes available to members job hotline services and discount long-term disability, extended health, and dental and life insurance. Sets and enforces editorial standards of practice; establishes payment levels and conditions of employment for editorial work. Cooperates with other organizations pursuing similar goals. **Publications:** *Active Voice* (bimonthly).

55274 ■ International Labor History Association
706 Bruce Ct.
Madison, WI 53705
Ph:(608)231-1886
Contact: Ronald C. Kent, Editor
Membership: Trade unionists, writers, scholars, and other interested individuals. **Purpose:** Seeks to advance the study and teaching of working-class history in each country of the world. Supports progressive labor movements and the cause of world peace. Works to improve critical labor histories in schools, universities, adult education institutions, and trade unions. Opposes racism, antisemitism, fascism, sexism, apartheid, and imperialism. Conducts research and educational programs. Operates speakers' bureau. **Publications:** *ILHA Newsletter* (periodic).

55275 ■ Labor Union Congress of Quebec–Centrale des Syndicats du Quebec
9405 rue Sherbrooke E
Montreal, QC, Canada H1L 6P3
Ph:(514)356-8888
Free: 800-465-0897
Co. E-mail: organisation_syndicale@csq.qc.net
URL: http://www.csq.qc.net
Contact: Gabriel Marchand, Dir. Gen.
Description: Professional unions representing teachers and other educational personnel. Represents members in collective bargaining negotiations; promotes members' professional interests. Conducts union education, political action, and research activities. Serves as liaison between French-speaking educational organizations in the world through the Comite Syndical Francophone de L'Education et de la Formation. **Publications:** *Nouvelles CSQ* (bimonthly); *Journal* (periodic).

55276 ■ Sweatshop Watch
1250 S Los Angeles St., Ste. 212
Los Angeles, CA 90015
Ph:(213)748-5945
Fax: (213)748-5955
Co. E-mail: sweatinfo@sweatshopwatch.org
URL: http://www.sweatshopwatch.org
Contact: Rini Chakraborty, Exec. Dir.
Membership: Labor, community, civil rights, and women's organizations and attorneys and advocates. **Purpose:** Seeks to eliminate "the exploitation that occurs in sweatshops." Conducts public education and public advocacy programs; works to build coalitions among organizations opposing sweatshop working conditions.

55277 ■ TNG Canada/CWA
7B-1050 Baxter Rd.
Ottawa, ON, Canada K2C 3P1
Ph:(613)820-9777
Free: 877-486-4292
Fax: (613)820-8188
Co. E-mail: info@tngcanada.org
URL: http://www.tngcanada.org
Contact: Arnold Amber, Dir.
Description: Primarily union of journalists and media workers in Canada, as well as social workers and employees in the manufacturing industry. **Publications:** *TNG Canada Today* (monthly).

55278 ■ Union of Canadian Transportation Employees
233 Gilmour St., Ste. 702
Ottawa, ON, Canada K2P 0P2
Ph:(613)238-4003
Fax: (613)236-0379
Co. E-mail: ucte@ucte.com
URL: http://www.ucte.com
Contact: Christine Collins, Natl. VP
Membership: Individuals employed in the transportation industries. **Purpose:** Seeks to obtain optimal conditions of employment for members. Represents members in negotiations with employers.

55279 ■ United Steelworkers of America - Canadian Branch–Metallurgistes Unis d'Amerique
234 Eglinton Ave. E, 8th Fl.
Toronto, ON, Canada M4P 1K7

Ph:(416)487-1571
Fax: (416)482-5548
Co. E-mail: kneumann@steelworkers-metallos.ca
URL: http://www.uswa.ca
Contact: Ken Neumann, Dir.
Description: Represents the interests of workers in a variety of sectors in Canada. Maintains charitable program. **Publications:** *Steelabor - Canadian Edition* (monthly); *Steeleader* (periodic); *Unionbuilder* (periodic).

REFERENCE WORKS

55280 ■ "American Airlines' Future Hangs Union Votes" in *Dallas Morning News* (April 11, 2003)
Pub: Knight-Ridder/Tribune Business News
Ed: Eric Torbenson. **Description:** American Airlines and its three major unions reached last-minute deals on March 31, 2003 for $1.62 billion in annual concessions. Details of the negotiations are included.

55281 ■ "America's Labor Federation" in *The Economist* (Vol. 376, July 30-August 5, 2005, No. 8437, pp. 25-26)
Pub: The Economist Newspaper Ltd.
Description: Will the split in the AFL-CIO help or hurt organized labor in the U.S.? Union membership has been on a decline since for the last forty years.

55282 ■ "Automaker-Union Talks Critical to State" in *Crain's Detroit Business* (Vol. 22, November 27, 2006, No. 48, pp. 8)
Pub: Crain Communications Inc. - Detroit
Description: Critical business issue in 2007 for the State of Michigan will be the auto contract talks between the UAW and the Big 3 US automakers. Not only will the results affect the companies themselves, but all the other manufacturers in the region and the ability to draw new manufacturers into the State.

55283 ■ "Better Way for Better Made?" in *Crain's Detroit Business* (Vol. 21, October 3, 2005, No. 43, pp. 3)
Pub: Crain Communications Inc. - Detroit
Ed: Brent Snavely. **Description:** Better Made Snack Foods Inc. is hoping its new products will boost sales for the firm. The company has put together a new executive team and signed a new union contract.

55284 ■ "Checking In? First Pass the Picket Line" in *Business Week* (February 20, 2006, No. 3972, pp. 39)
Pub: McGraw-Hill Companies
Ed: Aaron Bernstein. **Description:** February 15, 2006, hotel workers' unions are expected to kick-off a new national campaigned designed to sign up thousands of employees at Hilton Hotels Corporation and Starwood Hotel & Resorts Worldwide Inc., which owns Sheraton, Westin and four other chains.

55285 ■ "Churn Plagues Wal-Mart Labor Effort" in *Tampa Tribune* (December 23, 2005)
Pub: Media General, Inc.
Ed: Michael Sasso. **Description:** Wal-Mark Workers Association is having difficulty organizing the retailer's workforce due to the high rate of members quitting their jobs with the retailer. The association is backed by two unions, the United Food and Commercial Workers Union and the Service Employees International Union along with the advocacy group, the Association of Community Organizations for Reform Now.

55286 ■ "Clinic shut down as union vote neared" in *Crain's Detroit Business* (Vol. 19, No. 15, April 14, 2003, pp. 30)
Pub: Crain Communications Inc., Detroit
Ed: Robert Ankeny. **Description:** ZLB Plasma Services has shut down its Detroit clinic without warning. The closing affects nearly 30 employees, some who worked for the company for more than 20 years.

55287 ■ "Declaring War On Wal-Mart" in *Business Week* **(February 7, 2005, No. 3919, pp. 31)**
Pub: McGraw-Hill Companies
Ed: Aaron Bernstein. **Description:** Wal-Mart has launched an ad campaign in January with the message: Wal-Mart is working for everyone. The retailer is fighting back against allegations of sex discrimination, poverty-level wages, and non-union workforce.

55288 ■ "Delphos Gets OK to Take $3.4B Cerberus-led offer" in *Crain's Detroit Business* **(Vol. 23, January 15, 2007, No. 3, pp. 1)**
Pub: Crain Communications Inc. - Detroit
Ed: Brent Snaveley. **Description:** US Bankruptcy judge clears way for Delphos to proceed with Cerberus investment package. GM and UAW approval is still required to proceed.

55289 ■ "Digging Deeper and Keeping Up" in *Employment Relations Today* **(Vol. 26, No. 4, Winter 2000, pp. 95)**
Pub: John Wiley & Sons, Inc.
Description: A bibliography of books that deal with the future of work and employment is presented. Topics include the Internet, unemployment, and employee relations.

55290 ■ "Dissident Unions Come to Agreement with AFL-CIO About Local Groups" in *Sacramento Bee* **(November 17, 2005)**
Pub: The Sacramento Bee
Ed: Rachel Osterman. **Description:** Four dissident unions have joined the Change to Win Federation but want to continue participation in local and state labor groups. Disputes over the conditions for remaining in the local organizations kept both sides locked in negotiations. However, the two have agreed to a truce which will allow the dissidents to maintain ties with state and local labor groups.

55291 ■ "Equal Time? Legal" in *Entrepreneur* **(Vol. 31, No. 9, September 2003, pp. 80)**
Pub: Entrepreneur Media, Inc.
Ed: Jane Easter Bahls. **Description:** Labor unions may be able to use company email systems in order to communicate with members. A discussion regarding a recent decision by an administrative judge for the National Labor Relations Board involving Prudential Insurance's Office & Professional Employees International Union is cited.

55292 ■ Essentials of Labor Relations
Pub: Prentice Hall
Ed: Mollie H. Bowers and David A. DeCenzo. **Released:** 1991. **Price:** $22.80 (paper).

55293 ■ "Ethics, Deception and Labor Negotiation" in *Journal of Business Ethics* **(Vol. 28, No. 2, November 15, 2000, pp. 145)**
Pub: Kluwer Academic Publishers
Ed: Chris Provis. **Description:** The importance of trust among all parties in the employment relationship, associated with a call for increased "integrative bargaining", is discussed.

55294 ■ "Guards Unionize" in *San Fernando Valley Business Journal* **(Vol. 12, January 2007, No. 2, pp. 37)**
Pub: San Fernando Valley Business Journal Associates
Ed: Vanessa Herman. **Description:** After talks between a number of security guard companies, building owners and the powerful Service Employees International Union, as many as 10,000 Los Angeles County security guards will be allowed to organize.

55295 ■ "Hicksville-Based KeySpan Trains Managers to Take Over Blue-Collar/Clerical Jobs..." in *Long Island Business News* **(Feb. 20, 2004)**
Pub: Dolan Media Newswires
Ed: Claude Solnik. **Description:** KeySpan Corporation, an energy company in New York, trained managers to assume blue collar and clerical positions in the event of a possible strike by some 3,000 employees.

55296 ■ "Janitors at Safeway Seek Union Contract" in *Sacramento Bee* **(November 23, 2005)**
Pub: The Sacramento Bee
Ed: Rachel Osterman. **Description:** Janitors working for Safeway supermarkets in Northern California want better wages and a union contract. Nearly 200 janitors who met with union staff stated some workers are making $5 an hour, $1.75 under the state's minimum wage law.

55297 ■ Labor Relations and Collective Bargaining
Pub: Macmillan Publishing Co., Inc.
Ed: Michael R. Carrell. **Released:** Revised edition, 1995. **Price:** $104.25. **Description:** Originally titled Collective Bargaining and Labor Relations.

55298 ■ Labor Relations: Development, Structure, Process
Pub: McGraw-Hill Professional Book Group
Ed: John A. Fossum. **Released:** 7th ed. 1999. **Price:** $61.50 (cloth).

55299 ■ "Labor Relations" in *Inc.* **(Volume 27, December 2005, No. 12, pp. 34)**
Pub: Inc. Magazine
Description: Union members have been banned from installing giant inflatable rats in front of businesses and construction sites employing non-union workers.

55300 ■ "Labor's Fate Tied to Delphi's" in *Crain's Detroit Business* **(Vol. 21, October 10, 2005, No. 43, pp. 1)**
Pub: Crain Communications Inc. - Detroit
Ed: Terry Kosdrosky. **Description:** According to industry analysts, if Delphi Corporation gets the wage and benefit concessions it has asked for from its union, the move will impact the entire U.S. supplier industry.

55301 ■ "New Work Rules Will Help Cobo, Auto Show" in *Crain's Detroit Business* **(Vol. 21, October 10, 2005, No. 43, pp. 8)**
Pub: Crain Communications Inc. - Detroit
Description: Exhibit companies for the North American International Auto Show and five skilled-trades unions adopted new work rules to govern labor for preparation and presentation of the show. The new five-year pact could cut costs through reduction in crew sizes and overtime.

55302 ■ "NLRB Finds California Almond Growers Engaged in Anti-Union Activity" in *Sacramento Bee* **(November 1, 2005)**
Pub: The Sacramento Bee
Ed: Rachel Osterman. **Description:** The National Labor Relations Board has filed a complaint against Blue Diamond Growers for illegally threatening, interrogating and firing workers wishing to unionize the cooperative's downtown almond plant. Details of the complaint are outlined.

55303 ■ No Place Like Home: Organizing Home-Based Labor in the Era of Structural Adjustment
Pub: Routledge Inc.
Ed: David Staples. **Released:** November 2006. **Price:** $70.00. **Description:** The book examines the role of home-based women workers in contemporary capitalism.

55304 ■ "Northwest worries labor could harm on-time record" in *Crain's Detroit Business* **(Vol. 16, No. 50, December 11, 2000, pp. 21)**
Pub: Crain Communications, Inc.
Ed: Terry Kosdrosky. **Description:** Northwest Airlines finds another year of labor unrest, this time with the Aircraft Mechanics Fraternal Association. Northwest accused the unionized mechanics of staging a slowdown in 1998 that put the airline at or near the bottom of the industry for on-time performance.

55305 ■ "OCC Starts Negotiations With Unions" in *Crain's Detroit Business* **(Vol. 22, January 23, 2006, No. 4, pp. 5)**
Pub: Crain Communications Inc. - Detroit
Ed: Sherri Begin. **Description:** Oakland Community College has entered preliminary negotiations with four of the six unions representing employees at the college's six sites in Oakland County, Michigan.

55306 ■ "Overtime Reform Overdoses on Politics" in *Inc.* **(July 1, 2004)**
Pub: Inc. Magazine
Ed: Jess McCuan. **Description:** New rules governing overtime will be part of the overhauling of the Fair Labor Standards Act in 2004, but politics are leaving rules unclear.

55307 ■ "Plant Manager Urges Lockheed Martin Employees Not to Strike" in *Atlanta Journal-Constitution* **(March 5, 2005)**
Pub: Knight-Ridder/Tribune Business News
Ed: Dave Hirschman. **Description:** International Association of Machinists Local 709's 2,800 members are poised to reject a tentative three-year contract and authorize a strike. The Lockheed Martin's plant in Marietta, Georgia builds F/A-22 Raptor fighters and C-130J transports. Employees are unhappy about rising health care and retirement insurance costs.

55308 ■ "Ralphs Grocery Co. Indicted on Charges Related to Hiring Striking Union Workers" in *Sacramento Bee* **(December 16, 2005)**
Pub: The Sacramento Bee
Ed: Dale Kasler. **Description:** A federal grand jury has charged Ralphs Grocery Company of secretly hiring non-union workers under false names during a strike by its union workers.

55309 ■ The Rights of Employees & Union Members: The Basic ACLU Guide to the Rights of Employees & Union Members
Pub: Southern Illinois University Press
Ed: Wayne N. Outten. **Released:** Revised edition, 1994. **Price:** $39.95; $14.95 (paper).

55310 ■ "Sex, Drugs, and Career Choices" in *Fortune* **(Vol. 141, No. 7, April 3, 2000, pp. 68)**
Pub: Time Inc.
Ed: Rob Norton. **Description:** When young women first got access to the birth control pill in the late 1960s, their career options, and the future shape of U.S. work force, changed completely.

55311 ■ "Shipbuilders Labor Union Threatens Management Over Layoff Plans in Bath, Maine" in *Portland Press Herald* **(June 22, 2005)**
Pub: Blethen Maine Newspapers, Inc.
Ed: Matt Wickenheiser. **Description:** Bath Iron Works' maintenance workers union is concerned about the firm's move to hire a private firm to clean offices, care for the grounds, run the heating and cooling systems, and perform other tasks; the move would eliminate 24 union jobs.

55312 ■ "South Florida Braces From New Overtime Law" in *South Florida Business Journal* **(Vol. 23, No. 47, June 27, 2003, pp. 1)**
Pub: American City Business Journals
Ed: John T. Fakler. **Description:** New federal laws effecting the rates of payment to employees working overtime are examined.

55313 ■ "Stakes High For Region as Big Three, UAW Sit Down to Talk." in *Crain's Detroit Business* **(Vol. 23, January 1, 2007, No. 1, pp. 3)**
Pub: Crain Communications Inc. - Detroit
Ed: Brent Snaveley. **Description:** Major conflicts loom as contracts expire and must be renegotiated. Financial distress of the North American auto industry is pitted against the declining Union membership and Jobs Bank program. Strikes are possible on these major issues.

55314 ■ "State Of The Unions" in *Entrepreneur* (Vol. 28, No. 10, October 2000, pp. 106)
Pub: Entrepreneur Media Inc.
Ed: Jacquelyn Lynn. **Description:** Unions are eyeing workers in companies with as few as 30 employees.

55315 ■ "Union, Nursing Home Owners in Tense Negotiations" in *Chicago Tribune* (March 2, 2005)
Pub: Knight-Ridder/Tribune Business News
Ed: Barbara Rose. **Description:** Contract negotiations between local nursing union and nursing home owners in the Chicago area are examined. Nursing home owners deny union accusations they collect millions in fees yet deny their lowest paid employees adequate raises.

55316 ■ "Union Paychecks Could Be Bigger in 2005, But At a Cost" in *Kansas City Star* (February 22, 2005)
Pub: Knight-Ridder/Tribune Business News
Ed: Randolph Heaster. **Description:** Employers that are willing to raise wages during union negotiations will most likely cut health benefits at the same time. According to a recent survey, 60 percent of employers would consider wage hikes, while 69 percent reported health insurance and related benefits were top priority in concession gains.

55317 ■ "Unions Buying Amalgamated; CFL, Other Groups Take Stake in Bank Long Tied to Labor" in *Crains Chicago Business* (Vol. 26, No. 51)
Pub: Crain Communications, Inc.
Ed: Steven R. Strahler. **Description:** Amalgamated Bank of Chicago is being sold to a group of unions. Details of the transaction are investigated. Statistical data included.

55318 ■ "Unions Buying Amalgamated" in *Crain's Chicago Business* (Vol. 26, No. 51, December 22, 2003, pp. 3)
Pub: Crain Communications, Inc.
Ed: Steven R. Strahler. **Description:** Amalgamated Bank of Chicago is being sold to a group of unions. Details of the transaction are investigated. Statistical data included.

55319 ■ "Union's Job is to Protect Due Process, Not Bad Teachers" in *Crain's Chicago Business* (Vol. 29, December 2006, No. 51, pp.)
Pub: Crain Communications, Inc.
Ed: Marilyn Stewart. **Description:** Unions do not want to protect professionals who do not perform well. Overview of union member's rights and the reason they can be an important functional institution for employees.

55320 ■ "Unions shouldn't labor in financial secrecy" in *Crain's Detroit Business* (Vol. 18, No. 16, April 22, 2002, pp. 8)
Pub: Crain Communications Inc. - Detroit
DES It is suggested that unions should be required to make financial disclosure statements.

55321 ■ "Use It Or Lose It" in *The Economist* (Vol. 377, October 1-7, 2005, No. 8446, pp. 37)
Pub: The Economist Newspaper Ltd.
Description: The Canadian Broadcasting Corporation locked 5,300 of its 9,000 employees out after 15 months of negotiations. By September 26th, the Canadian labor minister entered negotiations with the television network and its employees.

55322 ■ "Why the Union Can't Win" in *Inc.* (Volume 27, March 2005, No. 3, pp. 55)
Pub: Inc. Magazine
Ed: Norm Brodsky. **Description:** It is suggested in the article that labor union leaders must learn to think more like business leaders in order to be successful.

55323 ■ "The world in your backyard" in *WorkingWoman* (Vol. 25, No. 2, February 2000, pp. 72)
Pub: Lang Communications Inc.

Ed: Caitlin Kelly. **Description:** There are 617 consulates in the U.S., offering services in international marketing, labor and culture.

TRADE PERIODICALS

55324 ■ *Collective Bargaining Negotiations and Contracts*
Pub: Bureau of National Affairs Inc.
Contact: Leslie Goldman, Managing Editor
Released: Biweekly. **Price:** $246. **Description:** Presents news of developments in collective bargaining, including contract settlements, bargaining techniques and trends, and contract interpretations by the courts. Recurring features include columns titled Clause Talk, Arbitrating the Contract, Facts & Figures, and Perspective.

55325 ■ *Daily Labor Report*
Pub: Bureau of National Affairs Inc.
Contact: Susan Sala, Managing Editor
Released: Daily. **Price:** $6,160. **Description:** Covers labor developments in Congress, the courts, federal agencies, unions, management, and the National Labor Relations Board.

55326 ■ *Human Resources Report*
Pub: Bureau of National Affairs Inc.
Contact: Gail Moorstein, Managing Editor
Released: Weekly. **Price:** $875. **Description:** Monitors employee and labor relations in the United States. Follows private sector developments in compensation, health benefits, Equal Employment Opportunity (EEO), labor economics, legislation, and regulatory issues. Recurring features include a calendar of events, and weekly analysis.

55327 ■ *International Journal of Comparative Labour Law and Industrial Relations*
Pub: Kluwer Academic/Plenum Publishing Corp.
Contact: Marco Biagi, Managing Editor
Released: Quarterly. **Price:** $226 Euro; $267 U.S.D; $158 GBP. **Description:** Journal covering comparative labor law and industrial relations worldwide.

55328 ■ *IRC Newsletter*
Pub: Industrial Relations Center (IRC)
Released: Bimonthly. **Description:** Focuses on industrial relations and collective bargaining, with summaries of court decisions in the field and of decisions of the National Labor Relations Board and other boards and commissions. Covers pending legislation pertaining to work, labor-management relations, and similar subjects. Recurring features include bibliographic information, statistics, announcements of appointments, and synopses of significant reports and studies.

55329 ■ *Label Letter*
Pub: Union Label & Services Trades
Ed: Charlie Mercer, Editor. **Released:** Bimonthly. **Price:** Included in membership. **Description:** Provides news and information in support of unionized labor, often highlighting injustices experienced by non-unionized members of the work force. Recurring features include a list of products and companies currently under boycott by the AFL-CIO.

55330 ■ *Labor Center Reporter*
Pub: Center for Labor Research and Education
Released: Quarterly. **Price:** $20 (Donation). **Description:** Supplies economic and social analysis of issues of concern to the trade union community.

55331 ■ *Labor Relations Week*
Pub: Bureau of National Affairs Inc.
Contact: Susan Sala, Managing Editor
Released: Weekly. **Price:** $944. **Description:** Provides a comprehensive overview of developments influencing labor relations in the private sector.

55332 ■ *On the Line: A Guide for Union Stewards*
Pub: Bureau of National Affairs Inc.
Contact: Jeff Day, Managing Editor

Released: Quarterly. **Price:** $2 per copy;. **Description:** Reports on shop floor issues affecting union stewards. Includes summaries of arbitration awards, court cases, and problem-solving tips.

55333 ■ *School of Labor and Industrial Relations eNewsletter*
Pub: School of Labor and Industrial Relations
Ed: Sally Pratt, Editor. **Released:** Semiannual. **Price:** Free. **Description:** Reports news of the School, including the status of various programs and services and statistics on growth. Contains articles on manpower, organizational behavior and personnel management, international and comparative labor and industrial relations, social structure and community organization, and social and industrial psychology. Recurring features include notices of job opportunities for graduates, courses offered, activities of the faculty, and meetings; book reviews; and recent reprints.

55334 ■ *Union Labor Report Weekly Newsletter*
Pub: Bureau of National Affairs Inc.
Contact: Jeff Day, Managing Editor
Released: Weekly. **Price:** $162. **Description:** Provides a roundup of developments of concern to organized labor. Includes summaries of arbitration awards and court cases. Recurring features include sections titled Special Report, Labor Facts, and Grievance Guide. Included with subscription to Union Labor Report (see separate listing) or available separately. Subscription price includes Union Labor Report's On The Line newsletter.

VIDEOCASSETTES/ AUDIOCASSETTES

55335 ■ *Labor Management*
New Dimension Media, Inc.
680 N Lake Shore Dr., Ste. 900
Chicago, IL 60611
Ph:(312)642-9400
Free: 800-288-4456
Fax: (312)642-9805
Co. E-mail: Info@NDMquestar.com
URL: http://www.ndmquestar.com
Released: 1987. **Price:** $50.00. **Description:** Shows the importance of cooperation between union workers and management. Because it supplies solutions for handling employee situations, it is aimed towards management. **Availability:** VHS; 3/4U.

COMPUTERIZED DATABASES

55336 ■ *Collective Bargaining Contract Library*
Bureau of National Affairs Inc.
1231 25th St. NW
Washington, DC 20037
Ph:(202)452-4200
Free: 800-372-1033
Fax: (202)452-4226
Co. E-mail: customercare@bna.com
URL: http://www.bna.com
Contact: Laurel Palmer
Entries Include: Company name, address, union name, local number if applicable, number of employees covered, Standard Industrial Classification (SIC) code, contract expiration date. **Database Covers:** Nearly 5,000 master and local union collective bargaining agreements in the U.S.

55337 ■ *Collective Bargaining Contract Settlements*
Bureau of National Affairs Inc.
1231 25th St. NW
Washington, DC 20037
Ph:(202)452-4200
Free: 800-372-1033
Fax: (202)452-4226
Co. E-mail: customercare@bna.com

URL: http://www.bna.com
Contact: Laurel Palmer
Entries Include: Company name, address, industry, union name and local number, settlement date, effective date, contract length, number of employees covered, wage rate changes, summary of contract provisions. **Database Covers:** summaries of 7,900 collective bargaining agreements covering AFL-CIO affiliates and independent unions in the U.S.

55338 ■ *Construction Labor Report*
The Bureau of National Affairs Inc.
1231 25th St. NW
Washington, DC 20037
Ph:(202)452-4200
Free: 800-372-1033
Fax: (202)452-4226
Co. E-mail: customercare@bna.com
URL: http://www.bna.com
Description: Contains labor and employment issues for all segments of the construction industry, including union, non-union, dual shop, and government officials tracking the industry. Topics include apprentices, arbitration decisions, collective bargaining, contractor associations, court and administrative decisions, EEO, employee benefits, federal and state legislation, government regulations, health and safety, independent contractors, jobsite accidents, jurisdictional disputes, labor laws, union organizing, worker shortages, workers' compensation insurance, workforce demographics, regulatory, legislative, and industry developments impacting the construction industry; legal news, state news, economic statistics, lists of relevant meetings, seminars, and conferences; and full text of court decisions, legislation approved by Congress, minority business enterprises, mixed crews, NLRB decisions, pension and benefits matters, prevailing wage laws, productivity, project labor agreements, substance abuse and control, training, transportation, and union job targeting programs. Includes summaries of all reports covered in each issue. **Availability:** Online: The Bureau of National Affairs Inc., Thomson West. **Type:** Full text.

55339 ■ *Human Resources Report*
The Bureau of National Affairs Inc.
1231 25th St. NW
Washington, DC 20037
Ph:(202)452-4200
Free: 800-372-1033
Fax: (202)452-4226
Co. E-mail: customercare@bna.com
URL: http://www.bna.com
Description: Contains detailed reporting and news of developments and trends affecting human resources and employee relations. Covers relevant national news, legislative and regulatory developments, labor economics, developments in training and technology, health benefits, employee-management relations, compensation, and legal developments. Provides conference reports, status reports on legislation and regulations, and state, local, and international news. Covers issues such as grievances, EEO/diversity, compensation and benefits, comparable worth, job security, flexible employment, right-to-know, maternity/paternity benefits, employment at will, employee privacy rights, pay equity, drug screening, child care benefits, smoking restrictions, early retirement, immigration reform, benefits taxation, and healthcare cost containment. **Availability:** Online: The Bureau of National Affairs Inc. **Type:** Full text.

55340 ■ *Labor Relations Week*
The Bureau of National Affairs Inc.
1231 25th St. NW
Washington, DC 20037
Ph:(202)452-4200
Free: 800-372-1033
Fax: (202)452-4226
Co. E-mail: customercare@bna.com
URL: http://www.bna.com
Description: Contains the latest information on congressional, judicial, legislative, and economic developments affecting private-sector labor relations.

Includes coverage of collective bargaining, National Labor Relations Board (NLRB) and court rulings, Equal Employment Opportunity (EEO) policy, health issues, safety, technology issues, and legislative and regulatory news. Covers state and federal labor trends and laws, contracts and grievances, union organization, labor management, and more. **Availability:** Online: The Bureau of National Affairs Inc. **Type:** Full text; Numeric.

LIBRARIES

55341 ■ Canadian Labour Congress–Library
2841 Riverside Dr.
Ottawa, ON, Canada K1V 8X7
Ph:(613)521-3400
Fax: (613)521-5461
Co. E-mail: ncote@clc-ctc.ca
URL: http://www.canadianlabour.ca
Contact: Nora Lezada Cote, MLS
Scope: Labor, labor history, industrial relations, trade unions, economics. **Services:** Interlibrary loan. **Holdings:** 4000 books; CLC Convention documents. **Subscriptions:** 36 journals and other serials.

55342 ■ Federation des Travailleurs et Travailleuses du Quebec–Centre de Documentation
565 boul Cremazie E. Bureau 12100
Montreal, QC, Canada H2M 2W3
Ph:(514)383-8025
Fax: (514)383-0502
Co. E-mail: ireny@ftq.qc.ca
URL: http://www.ftq.qc.ca
Contact: Isabelle Reny, Doc.
Scope: Work, unions, sociology, economy. **Services:** Copying; Library open to the public. **Holdings:** 10,200 books. **Subscriptions:** 150 journals and other serials; 3 newspapers.

55343 ■ Manitoba Department of Labour–Manitoba Labour Board–Library (258 P)
258 Portage Ave., Rm. 402
Winnipeg, MB, Canada R3C 0B6
Ph:(204)945-3783
Fax: (204)945-1296
Co. E-mail: mlb@gov.mb.ca
URL: http://www.gov.mb.ca/labour/labbrd/
Scope: Labor. **Services:** Library open to the public. **Holdings:** 100 books; 1080 bound periodical volumes. **Subscriptions:** 10 journals and other serials.

55344 ■ York University–Centre for Research in Work and Society
276 York Lanes
4700 Keele St.
Toronto, ON, Canada M3J 1P3
Ph:(416)736-2100 x70494
Co. E-mail: paszter@yorku.ca
URL: http://www.yorku.ca/crws
Contact: Dr. Norene Pupo, Dir.
Scope: Work and society, unions, arbitration. **Services:** Library open to students, faculty and staff; open by appointment only from May to August. **Holdings:** 500 books; journals; primary and secondary documents and sources.

RESEARCH CENTERS

55345 ■ Indiana Labor Department–Planning and Administration–Research and Statistics
402 W Washington St., Rm. W195
Indianapolis, IN 46204
Ph:(317)232-2655
Free: 800–743-3333
Fax: (317)233-3790
URL: http://www.in.gov/labor/statistics/index.html
Scope: Labor.

55346 ■ International Labor Rights Fund
2001 S St. NW, Ste. 420
Washington, DC 20009
Ph:(202)347-4100
Fax: (202)347-4885
Co. E-mail: laborrights@ilrf.org
URL: http://www.laborrights.org
Contact: Terry Collingsworth, Exec.Dir.
E-mail: laborrights@ilrf.org
Scope: Labor rights in the U.S. and abroad, including child labor exploitation, forced labor, attacks on and imprisonment of union leaders, and other violations of international labor standards, trade unions, democracy in developing countries, global trade, and economic integration. **Services:** Information and analyses regarding labor rights conditions internationally. **Publications:** Books and papers (quarterly). **Educational Activities:** Conferences (periodically). **Awards:** Award for leadership in defending labor rights (occasionally).

55347 ■ Labor and Employment Relations Association
121 LIR Bldg.
504 E Armory Ave.
Champaign, IL 61820
Ph:(217)333-0072
Fax: (217)265-5130
Co. E-mail: LERAoffice@uiuc.edu
URL: http://www.lera.uiuc.edu
Contact: Paula D. Wells, Exe.Dir.
E-mail: LERAoffice@uiuc.edu
Scope: Labor, employment, and the workplace, including employer and employee organization, employment and labor relations, human resources, labor markets, income security, and related fields, including international and comparative dimensions in all pertinent disciplines, including industrial relations, history, economics, political science, psychology, sociology, law, management, labor studies, and others. **Services:** IRRA jobs announcement service (weekly). **Publications:** IRRA Newsletter (quarterly); IRRA Proceedings of the Annual Meeting (annually); Perspectives on Work magazine (semiannually); Research Volume (annually). **Educational Activities:** IRRA PhD Student Consortium (annually). **Awards:** IRRA Best Dissertation Award (annually); IRRA Excellence in Education Awards (annually); IRRA Lifetime Achievement Award (annually); IRRA Outstanding Young Practitioner Award (annually); IRRA Outstanding Young Scholar Awards (annually).

55348 ■ Labor Research Association
330 W 42nd St., 13th Fl.
New York, NY 10001
Ph:(212)714-1677
Fax: (212)714-1674
Co. E-mail: info@lra-ny.com
URL: http://www.laborresearch.org
Contact: Jeannine Rudolph, Treas.
E-mail: info@lra-ny.com
Scope: Economic, social, and political conditions, focusing on labor relations.

55349 ■ University of Louisville–Labor-Management Center
Patterson Hall, Rm. 105
Louisville, KY 40292
Ph:(502)852-6482
Fax: (502)852-6453
Co. E-mail: cgdona01@louisville.edu
URL: http://www.louisville.edu/cbpa/lmc/
Contact: Prof. Carrie G. Donald, Dir.
E-mail: cgdona01@louisville.edu
Scope: Labor-management relations, equal employment opportunity, economic development issues, and public perceptions of labor relations. **Services:** Arbitration Advocacy Institute; Institute for ADA Medication; Planning and consulting services. **Publications:** Newsletter (quarterly); Research publications series. **Educational Activities:** Symposia and seminars. **Awards:** Labor-Management Annual Award, honors a workplace where management and the union(s) have promoted and demonstrated positive labor-management relations..

START-UP INFORMATION

55350 ■ "The $50 Million Giveaway" in *Business 2.0* **(Vol. 6, September 2005, No. 8, pp. 76)**
Pub: Time, Inc.
Ed: Michael V. Copeland. **Description:** The visions of eleven venture capital firms are examined; each firm is looking for the right startup to fulfill these visions.

55351 ■ "2005: A Quiet, But Critical Year for Venture Capital" in *Venture Capital Journal* **(January 1, 2005)**
Pub: Thomason Financial Inc.
Description: Some industry experts are predicting a transformation in the venture capital industry for 2005, with a shift toward seed and early stage investing.

55352 ■ "The Amazing, Real-Life Adventures of Microfly" in *Venture Capital Journal* **(Vol. 42, No. 8, August 2002, pp. 30-31)**
Pub: Thomas Venture Economics
Ed: Michael V. Copeland. **Description:** Profile of a robotic fly that weighs less than a paper clip and its promising technological value is discussed.

55353 ■ "American Megatrends vets start a new company" in *Atlanta Business Chronicle* **(Vol. 24, No. 11, August 17, 2001, pp. 2A)**
Pub: American City Business Journals Inc.
Ed: Mary Jane Credeur. **Description:** Two former engineers of American Megatrends Inc. have formed iVivity Inc., which has received over $11 million in venture capital backup. Sukha Ghosh and Sanjay Sehgal are now designing a data storage management storage product they hope will revolutionize the market. Their iDISX (Distributed Intelligent Storage exchange) product will operate, diagnose and repair data storage networks.

55354 ■ "And on your Left" in *Entrepreneur* **(Vol. 28, No. 9, September 2000, pp. 48)**
Pub: Entrepreneur Media Inc.
Ed: Cynthia E. Griffin. **Description:** The things investors are looking at when touring a business are examined.

55355 ■ "Angel Investing Still Alive, Barely, in Chicago Area" in *Chicago Tribune* **(November 10, 2002)**
Pub: Knight Ridder/Tribune Business News
Ed: Rob Kaiser. **Description:** Profile of Bill Maulsby, founder of the Chicago-based BusBank charter bus service, tells how he was able to secure angel investments. The decline in angels to invest in startups is discussed.

55356 ■ "Angel on you Side" in *Entrepreneur* **(Vol. 28, No. 10, October 2000, pp. 171)**
Pub: Entrepreneur Media Inc.
Ed: Pamela Rohland. **Description:** The best place to find angel investors for funding is within your current

circle of contacts: family members, friends and professional associates, as well as, chamber of commerce, banks, accounting firms, universities, business incubators, regional or state economic development agencies, editors of business publications and even potential customers.

55357 ■ "Atlantis Group Plans to Back Start-ups" in *Venture Capital Journal* **(Vol. 40, No. 10, November 2000, pp. 14)**
Pub: Venture Economics
Description: Profile of Robbie Hardy, angel investor and entrepreneur, who founded The Atlantis Group LLC, to back seed-stage companies.

55358 ■ "Battle of the Business Plans: a new march madness" in *Fortune* **(Vol. 141, No. 2, January 24, 2000, pp. 128)**
Pub: Time Inc.
Ed: Eric Nee. **Description:** Some of the most successful technology companies were started by university students. To this end, venture capitals have been scouring college campuses looking for the next big thing.

55359 ■ "Bay State VC pace falls to 1999 level" in *Boston Business Journal* **(Vol. 22, No. 16, May 24, 2002, pp. 1)**
Pub: MCP, Inc.
Ed: Edward Mason. **Description:** Massachusetts venture capital investments declined by 44 percent during first quarter 2002, when compared with same quarter of 2001. A total of $734 million in investments for first quarter 2002 versus a total of $1.3 billion in investments in first quarter 2001 were tabulated.

55360 ■ "Be a Loan Shark" in *Success* **(Vol. 47, No. 3, July 2000, pp. 59)**
Pub: Success Publishing, Inc.
Ed: Michael A. Butler. **Description:** Small business has become huge in America. Each year, more and more entrepreneurs bypass the corporate ladder to take a shot at realizing a dream: owning their own businesses. Without proper preparation, the inspiration may not become reality because of the inability to obtain a small business loan.

55361 ■ "Beacon Telco Aims To Jumpstart Optics" in *Venture Capital Journal* **(Vol. 40, No. 10, November 2000, pp. 6, 8)**
Pub: Venture Economics
Description: Beacon Telco, a venture capital development company, was launched in mid-September 2000, to focus on optical networking and broadband communications. The venture capital firm will provide its portfolio companies with $1 million to $3 million in funding, noting that companies which choose to participate in the incubation program will also need to pay a program cost for incubator services.

55362 ■ "Black Dotcom Shake-Up" in *Black Enterprise* **(Vol. 31, No. 5, December 2000, pp. 134)**
Pub: Earl Graves Publishing Co.
Ed: Sonya A. Donaldson. **Description:** Many Internet start-ups that gambled on a big payoff are now rolling snake-eyes.

55363 ■ "Business Incubator Has a Fish Wriggling Off of the Hook" in *St. Louis Post-Dispatch* **(August 27, 2004)**
Pub: Knight-Ridder/Tribune Business News
Ed: David Nicklaus. **Description:** Marcia Mellitz, founder of Symbiontics Inc., is considering a move to Wisconsin because of lack of funding. The firm is developing treatments for genetic disorders known as lysosomal storage diseases. It was launched with $3.5 million.

55364 ■ "Capital Ventures" in *Black Enterprise* **(Vol. 30, No. 11, July 2000, pp. 235)**
Pub: Earl Graves Publishing Co.
Ed: Eric L. Smith. **Description:** Gaining access to existing sources of financing remains a priority for black-owned firms.

55365 ■ "CapitalSource Nets Largest-Ever Series A Round" in *Venture Capital Journal* **(Vol. 40, No. 10, November 2000, pp. 14)**
Pub: Venture Economics
Description: CapitalSource Holdings LLC, based in Washington, became the most highly capitalized venture-backed start-up in history in October 2000.

55366 ■ "Cover Story" in *Inc.* **(September 2000, pp. 70)**
Pub: The Goldhirsh Group
Description: Ways to avoid pitfalls when filling a term sheet for a venture capitalist are explained.

55367 ■ "Credit card financing: Tempting but risky for small businesses" in *Crain's Detroit Business* **(Vol. 16, No. 33, August 14, 2000, pp. 13)**
Pub: Crain Communications, Inc.
Ed: Brent Snavely. **Description:** Counselors from the Service Corps of Retired Executives believe that entrepreneurs should never use credit cards to finance a business. A variety of resources for advice and funding are investigated.

55368 ■ "David Nicklaus Column" in *St. Louis Post-Dispatch* **(September 19, 2004)**
Pub: Knight-Ridder/Tribune Business News
Ed: David Nicklaus. **Description:** Profile of Arch Angel Investor Network, a group led by the St. Louis Regional Chamber & Growth Association and the Nidus Center for Scientific Enterprise. The group is looking for investors willing to back startup companies in the St. Louis area.

55369 ■ "Day Care for Dot-Coms: Warmer, Fuzzier Venture Capitalism" in *Fortune* **(Vol. 140, No. 11, pp. 72+)**
Pub: Time Inc.
Ed: Eric Nee. **Description:** Today the pace of Internet-startup activity is so intense that a company's chances of survival are directly related to how fast it can bring its brainchild into the world, and to market.

55370 ■ "Dealflow: the most intriguing recent VC fundings" in *Red Herring* (January 2003, pp. 68)
Pub: Herring Communications Inc.
Description: A listing of the ten most intriguing venture fundings is presented, including the company, funding amount and round of funding, prior funding, and monthly burn rate.

55371 ■ "Doing It for Themselves" in *Entrepreneur* (Vol. 28, No. 8, August 2000, pp. 40)
Pub: Entrepreneur Media Inc.
Ed: Cynthia E. Griffin. **Description:** Women investors are aiding women entrepreneurs.

55372 ■ "Dot-Com Deathwatch" in *Fortune* (Vol. 142, No. 3, July 24, 2000, pp. 48)
Pub: Time Inc.
Ed: Katrina Brooker. **Description:** Gloom was in the air at PC Expo in July 2000, because venture capitalists are not funding dot-com entrepreneurs as much as in the past.

55373 ■ "Dot Com Fever Black-Oriented" in *Black Enterprise* (Vol. 30, No. 8, March 2000, pp. 82)
Pub: Earl Graves Publishing Co.
Ed: Tariq K. Muhammad. **Description:** Websites are finally attracting capital. The key is in knowing how to get your share.

55374 ■ "Eat Our Dust: Broadband infrastructure has made Redpoint the hottest VC firm you've never heard of" in *Fortune* (Oct. 9, 2000, pp. 200)
Pub: Time Inc.
Ed: Shawn Tully. **Description:** Entrepreneurial experience, cutting-edge technology, industry-transforming ideas - these are the things that have made the Redpoint partners among the hottest VC's in the land.

55375 ■ "Ellman: Building a VC Empire in the Empire State" in *Venture Capital Journal* (Vol. 40, No. 10, October 2000, pp. 48-49)
Pub: Venture Economics
Description: Profile of Stuart Ellman, 33, founder and general partner at RRE Ventures. Mr. Ellman tells how he and James Robinson IV, together with Robinson's father, created the New York-based venture capital firm.

55376 ■ "Entrepreneurs should be wary of incubators" in *Red Herring* (No. 76, March 2000, pp. 86)
Pub: Herring Communications, Inc.
Ed: Alex Gove. **Description:** Not all incubators are created equal. Some incubators may offer infrastructure benefits, but the true test concerns those who run them.

55377 ■ "Entrepreneurs test start-ups-on the side" in *Wall Street Journal* (May 7, 2002, pp. B6)
Pub: Wall Street Journal
Ed: Jeff Bailey. **Description:** Many entrepreneurs are working fulltime jobs in order to finance their start-ups since venture capital and start-up funding has become more difficult to acquire.

55378 ■ "Fallen Idols" in *Fortune* (Vol. 142, No. 10, October 30, 2000, pp. 108+)
Pub: Time Inc.
Ed: Melanie Warner. **Description:** Along the way people stopped seeing venture capitalists as just money guys. Once considered the gods of the new economy, venture capitalists heartily endorsed some of the most disastrous excesses of the dot-com age.

55379 ■ "Financial Roulette" in *Entrepreneur* (Vol. 28, No. 6, June 2000, pp. 68)
Pub: Entrepreneur Media Inc.
Ed: David R. Evanson. **Description:** Is borrowing from your IRA to fund a business startup a healthy risk or a tragic mistake?

55380 ■ "Financing" in *Crain's Detroit Business* (Vol. 19, No. 49, December 8, 2003, pp. 13)
Pub: Crain Communications Inc., Detroit
Description: Sources of money for startup firms are listed.

55381 ■ "Finding the Fault Line Where A New Business Can Grow" in *Fortune* (Vol. 142, No. 10, October 30, 2000, pp. 294+)
Pub: Time Inc.
Ed: Thomas A. Stewart. **Description:** The new company, 12 Entrepreneuring, an operating company whose mission is to reinvent business, is profiled.

55382 ■ "Finding financing" in *Black Enterprise* (Vol. 32, No. 6, January 2002, pp. 8)
Pub: Earl Graves Publishing Co.
Ed: Bevolyn Williams-Harold. **Description:** Minority entrepreneurs may need to look for more innovative capital resources, such as minority-focused venture capital funds or community-based securitization programs, to maintain cash flow.

55383 ■ "Five things to remember when raising money" in *Red Herring* (No. 76, March 2000, pp. 92)
Pub: Herring Communications, Inc.
Ed: Ross Garber. **Description:** The five most important things to consider when raising venture capital are explained.

55384 ■ "Five Ways to Finance Your Business" in *Black Enterprise* (Vol. 31, No. 3, October 2000, pp. 43)
Pub: Earl Graves Publishing Co.
Ed: Glenn Townes. **Description:** The five best ways to find the cash to make your dream a reality are identified as: personal savings, trade credit, commercial banks, second mortgages, and angel investors.

55385 ■ "Flip Flipowski" in *Internet World* (Vol. 6, No. 13, July 1, 2000, pp. 60)
Pub: Mecklermedia Corporation
Ed: Elizabeth Gardner. **Description:** A profile of Divine Interventures and CEO Andrew 'Flip' Flipowski, who aims to strengthen the reputation of Chicago in the Internet start-up world and move the Midwest into the New Economy. Flipowski, believing that traditional businesses have missed enormous opportunities on the Internet and emphasizing the business-to-business market, has already backed more than a dozen industry-specific online exchanges.

55386 ■ "Fostering Urban Entrepreneurship" in *Black Enterprise* (Vol. 34, No. 4, November 2003, pp. 46)
Pub: Earl Graves Publishing Co.
Ed: Charlene Carter. **Description:** The winners of the third annual Miller Urban Entrepreneurs Business Grant Competition are highlighted. Each winner was awarded $20,000 to fund a business venture or expansion.

55387 ■ "From the Ground Floor: The business paths to nanotech" in *Red Herring* (No. 99, June 15 & July 1, 2001, pp. 42, 44)
Pub: Herring Communications
Ed: Steve Jurvetson. **Description:** A discussion involving nanotechnology and the startup opportunities, which paths will receive U.S. government grants, and which are market-driven businesses that attract venture capital.

55388 ■ "Funding a Franchise Startup" in *Hispanic Business* (Vol. 23, No. 5, May 2001, pp. 52, 54)
Pub: Hispanic Business
Ed: Barbara Beckley. **Description:** Funding sources available for franchise start-ups are presented. The Certified Development Company, a private, non-profit organization licensed by the SBA, the Small Business Investment Companies (SBICs), which provide equity capital and long-term debt financing; and the Community Development Corporations (CDCs) are among the resources profiled.

55389 ■ "Generation W" in *Success* (Vol. 47, No. 4, September 2000, pp. 62)
Pub: Success Publishing, Inc.
Ed: Joan Szabo. **Description:** Women business owners get a shot at venture funding.

55390 ■ "Harley's Angels" in *Success* (Vol. 47, No. 4, September 2000, pp. 66)
Pub: Success Publishing, Inc.
Ed: Juan Hovey. **Description:** The best way to find angel investors is to network among people likely to know them.

55391 ■ "Hello, please give me $9 million" in *WorkingWoman* (Vol. 25, No. 7, August 2000, pp. 72)
Pub: Lang Communications Inc.
Ed: Ashley Craddock. **Description:** American businesswomen are being given the opportunity to invest in business run specifically by other women by venture capitalists running the Springboard 2000 investment showcase.

55392 ■ "Hold'Em" in *Entrepreneur* (Vol. 28, No. 7, July 2000, pp. 78)
Pub: Entrepreneur Media Inc.
Ed: Cynthia Harrington. **Description:** Takes a look at two entrepreneurs balancing the eternal choice between selling equity or borrowing.

55393 ■ "How do Fast Companies Work Now?" in *Fast Company* (September 2001, pp. 134)
Pub: Fast Company
Ed: Keith H. Hammonds. **Description:** Imagine a company started by the best-connected investment bank in the world, by a leading management-consulting firm, and by one of the top venture capital firms - give it $300 million, and set it loose to reinvent big business - that is the formula guiding David Pecaut and his colleagues at Iformation.

55394 ■ *How to Finance Your Business for the 21st Century: Step by Step Guide to Starting & Managing Your Own Business*
Pub: Lewis & Renn Associates
Ed: Jerre G. Lewis. **Released:** 1999. **Price:** $18.95.

55395 ■ "How iWon Won the Web" in *Success* (Vol. 47, No. 6, November 2000, pp. 28)
Pub: Success Publishing, Inc.
Ed: Scott Smith, Paul Gallagher. **Description:** Profile of iWon.com, the Web portal that offers small business e-mail, news, services, and a chance to bag at least $10,000 a day. IWon.com's co-founders and co-CEO's, Bill Daugherty and Jonas Steinman, share some of the key ingredients that have helped them stay ahead of the curve.

55396 ■ "I Want My meVC!: the armchair venture capitalist" in *Fortune* (Vol. 142, No. 1, June 26, 2000, pp. 294)
Pub: Time Inc.
Ed: Lee Clifford. **Description:** Are the newfangled offerings really good news for investors?

55397 ■ "In for the Count" in *Entrepreneur* (Vol. 28, No. 9, September 2000, pp. 60)
Pub: Entrepreneur Media Inc.
Ed: Cynthia E. Griffin. **Description:** Iris J. Burnett and Nell Merlino, developers of the innovative program called Count-Me-In had revolutionized business loans for women.

55398 ■ "In Good Forum" in *Entrepreneur* (Vol. 28, No. 7, July 2000, pp. 97)
Pub: Entrepreneur Media Inc.
Ed: Cynthia E. Griffin. **Description:** You need tons of money. You have no financial contacts. Where can you turn? Many entrepreneurs have found what they need in venture forums.

55399 ■ "It's Not the First Time" in *Entrepreneur* (Vol. 30, No. 2, February 2002, pp. 53)
Pub: Entrepreneur Media Inc.

Ed: Jennifer Pellet. **Description:** Venture capitalists are looking for leadership experience when investing in startup companies.

55400 ■ **"Just Do It"** in *Entrepreneur* (Vol. 28, No. 17, July 2000, pp. 162)
Pub: Entrepreneur Media Inc.
Ed: Don Debelak. **Description:** Putting off applying for that patent? You may regret it later. The 1999 Supreme Court ruling (Pfaff v. Wells Electronics Inc.) is expected to have a huge impact on how quickly inventors apply for a patent.

55401 ■ **"Lightspeed GPs Set To Launch New Fund"** in *Venture Capital Journal* (October 1, 2005)
Pub: Thomason Financial Inc.
Description: Lightspeed's General Partners is creating a new team with a strategy to focus on early stage technology deals. They plan to have the new fund raised by the end of 2005.

55402 ■ **"Making Ideas Fly"** in *Internet World* (Vol. 6, No. 12, June 15, 2000, pp. 31)
Pub: Mecklermedia Corporation
Ed: David Lipschultz. **Description:** Despite some setbacks, dot-com companies continue to pop up. Sometimes a start-up company would do well to go with a business incubator. These incubators can offer all manner of services from business to Web site development, but often take a large part of the company. Some start-ups work with venture capital companies who are eager to invest in Internet companies.

55403 ■ **"Merit Networks offshoot draws $5M in venture capital funding"** in *Crain's Detroit Business* (Vol. 16, No. 37, Sept. 11, 2000, pp. 55)
Pub: Crain Communications, Inc.
Ed: Matt Roush. **Description:** Profile of Merit Networks Inc. and its spin-off company, Interlinks Networks Inc.

55404 ■ **"Mining venture capital"** in *Black Enterprise* (Vol. 32, No. 7, February 2002,)
Pub: Earl Graves Publishing Co.
Ed: Derek T. Dingle. **Description:** Strategies are given to entrepreneurs about finding capital to fund start-ups in today's economy. Statistical data included.

55405 ■ **"Montreal: A Fertile Ground For VC Exploration"** in *Venture Capital Journal* (Vol. 42, No. 5, May 2002, pp. 54)
Pub: Thomas Venture Economics
Description: Montreal, Quebec is becoming the hot spot for technological development, and is supported by a strong investment community and world-class local venture capital environment.

55406 ■ **"Need Money?"** in *Inc.* (November 2006, pp.25-26)
Pub: Gruner & Jahr USA Publishing
Ed: Max Chafkin and Bobbie Gossage. **Description:** Private financial markets are difficult to navigate and dynamic. Various funding alternatives are discussed depending upon size of the venture. Trends are changing and reviewed in this article.

55407 ■ **"Needbucks.com"** in *Forbes* (January 10, 2000, pp. 188)
Pub: Forbes Magazine
Ed: Guy Kawasaki. **Description:** There is plenty of money for raising capital out there, but there are also a lot of bad business plans. Ten tips to improve the odds that your plan is read, and possibly funded, are provided.

55408 ■ **"New venture survival: ignorance, external shocks, and risk reduction strategies"** in *Journal of Business Venturing* (Vol. 15, No. 5-6)
Pub: Elsevier Science, Inc.
Ed: Dean A. Shepherd, Evan J. Douglas, Mark Shanley. **Description:** A theoretical model is proposed that explains the survival of new ventures.

55409 ■ **"New Venture-Capital Group Wants to Keep Entrepreneurs in State"** in *Crain's Detroit Business* (Vol. 18, No. 2, June 3, 2002, pp. 43)
Pub: Crain Communications Inc. - Detroit
Ed: Katie Merx. **Description:** Investors from across the state of Michigan hope that the Michigan Venture Capital Association will attract more venture capitalists to the state and keep entrepreneurs from leaving.

55410 ■ **"Nice work If You Can Get It"** in *Fortune* (Vol. 140, No. 11, December 6, 1999, pp. 177+)
Pub: Time Inc.
Ed: Melanie Warner. **Description:** The venture capital business was once a courtly tennis match. It's now more like a hockey game, and people are losing a few teeth.

55411 ■ **"On the Edge"** in *Red Herring* (No. 106, October 15, 2001, pp. 62-64, 66)
Pub: Herring Communications
Ed: Michael Fitzgerald. **Description:** It could take a giant like Microsoft to get reluctant venture capitalists into funding the new software startups focusing on terminal nodes of networks where data transactions are executed from cellular phones and wireless-enabled handheld devices.

55412 ■ **"On the Internet Nobody Knows You're Not a VC"** in *Red Herring* (No. 75, February 2000, pp. 148-150, 152, 154, 156, 158)
Pub: Herring Communications, Inc.
Ed: Dan Brekke. **Description:** Suddenly, the more desperate entrepreneurs are flocking to the new on-line venture capital firms. The article tells who these firms are, and who is behind their Web sites.

55413 ■ **"One Life To Live: They say starting up is hard to do"** in *Fortune* (Vol. 142, No. 8, October 9, 2000, pp. 180+)
Pub: Time Inc.
Ed: Daniel Roth. **Description:** The article follows a week in the life of a new company unsuccessfully trying to obtain capital for the new venture.

55414 ■ **"Only a Few Sea Turtles Survive"** in *Forbes* (February 21, 2000, pp. 96)
Pub: Forbes Magazine
Ed: James Champy. **Description:** Survival tactics for new technology companies are offered.

55415 ■ **"The opposite sex: women in search of money still face a man's world"** in *Entrepreneur* (Vol. 30, No. 9, September 2002, pp. 36)
Pub: Entrepreneur Media Inc.
Ed: Aliza Pilar Sherman. **Description:** Three women discuss the specific issues women encounter when trying to secure financing for a startup business.

55416 ■ **"PayPal Founders Banking on New VC Firm"** in *Venture Capital Journal* (September 1, 2005)
Pub: Thomason Financial Inc.
Description: PayPal co-founders, Ken Howery and Peter Thiel are forming The Founders Fund with $50 million focused on seed-stage Internet deals.

55417 ■ **"Perceived risks and choices in entrepreneurs' new venture decisions"** in *Journal of Business Venturing* (Vol.15, No.4, Jul.2000, pp.305)
Pub: Elsevier Science, Inc.
Ed: David Forlani, John W. Mullins. **Description:** Issues are presented concerning the evaluation risk, the perception of risk and the willingness of entrepreneurs to make hazardous choices in the pursuit of potentially significant financial gains.

55418 ■ **"Playing favorites"** in *Entrepreneur* (Vol. 31, No. 4, April 2003, pp. 22)
Pub: Entrepreneur Media Inc.
Ed: Julie Monahan. **Description:** Software companies are finding venture capital funding easier because they do not have a high inventory risk, along with the fact that needed changes can be implemented quickly.

55419 ■ **"Podcast Startups Look Doomed from the Start"** in *Venture Capital Journal* (October 1, 2005)
Pub: Thomason Financial Inc.
Description: Podcast service allows the user to get automatic updates of Website audio content and can listen to it on an iPod or other MP3 player. Problems being faced by Podcast startups are discussed.

55420 ■ **"A private space race"** in *Wall Street Journal* (Feb. 5, 2003, pp. B1)
Pub: Dow Jones & Co. Inc.
Ed: J. Lynn Lunsford. **Description:** Entrepreneur Peter Diamandis has founded and helped to fund the St. Louis, Missouri, based X Prize Foundation, which will award a $10 million prize to the first private venture to fund, design and launch a manned space vehicle. Twenty-four entrepreneur-led teams are vying for the prize and the recent accident aboard the Space Shuttle Columbia has not deterred any in that quest. The foundation's rules for the spacecraft say only that it must be able to hold three passengers and must be able to fly 62 miles up and return safely two times in the course of two weeks.

55421 ■ **"The Quebec Story: Low Cost, Low Risk, Tremendous Opportunity"** in *Venture Capital Journal* (Vol. 42, No. 5, May 2002, pp. 48, 50)
Pub: Thomas Venture Economics
Ed: Peter Diekmeyer. **Description:** Canada's venture capital center has become a hotbed of technology startups because of the unique incentives, including tax incentives, low business costs, Montreal's close ties to Europe, and an educated workforce focused on technology.

55422 ■ **"Quebec's Competitive Edge"** in *Venture Capital Journal* (Vol. 42, No. 5, May 2002, pp. 51-52)
Pub: Thomas Venture Economics
Description: U.S. venture capital firms that invest in Quebec, Canada may have a head start on the competition. Statistical data included.

55423 ■ **"Rising money"** in *Entrepreneur* (Vol. 30, No. 1, January 2002, pp. 36)
Pub: Entrepreneur Media Inc.
Ed: Steve Cooper. **Description:** A listing of financial sources used by entrepreneurs in 2001, information about customer trust, and other areas of interest to small business is presented. Statistical data included.

55424 ■ **"Sand Hill Road's Networking Guru Plugs Us In: Vinod Khosla on Cisco, Redback, Juniper, and more"** in *Fortune* (Aug. 14, 2000, pp. 268)
Pub: Time Inc.
Ed: Adam Lashinsky. **Description:** Vinod Khosla will be remembered as the venture capitalist who helped create the next generation of networking companies.

55425 ■ **"Seed Capital for Farm Communities"** in *Inc.* (October 1, 2004)
Pub: Inc. Magazine
Ed: Jess McCuan. **Description:** In June, 2004, the U.S. Department of Agriculture along with the Small Business Administration, launched the Rural Business Investment Program, providing $60 million in early stage funding to companies in small rural communities.

55426 ■ *Seed-Stage Venture Investing: The Ins and Outs for Entrepreneurs, Start-Ups, and Investors on Successfully Starting a New Business*
Pub: Aspatore Books, Incorporated
Ed: William J. Robbins. **Released:** July 2006. **Price:** $199.95. **Description:** Ideas for starting, funding, and managing technology-based firms, also known as, venture capitalists, are featured.

55427 ■ **"Show Me the Money"** in *Home Office Computing* (Vol. 18, No. 11, November 2000, pp. 85)
Pub: Scholastic Inc.
Ed: Steven Van Yoder. **Description:** Raising capital for a small business is a challenge that Robert Luster,

who started a home-based construction company, knows firsthand. The article tells how to tap the right resources to find the cash needed to start and grow a business.

55428 ■ "Silicon Peninsula?" in *Crain's Detroit Business*

Pub: Crain Communications, Inc.

Ed: Matt Roush. **Description:** There's still a lack of venture capital in Michigan to back tech spin-offs.

55429 ■ "Sister, can you share five bucks" in *WorkingWoman* **(Vol. 25, No. 7, August 2000, pp. 20)**

Pub: Lang Communications Inc.

Ed: Kathleen Jacobs. **Description:** Women will be the main beneficiaries of a new organization set up to ensure business women have easier access to enterprise loans by asking every female in America to donate $5.

55430 ■ "Six Degrees of Capitalization" in *Success* **(Vol. 47, No. 1, January 2000, pp. 16)**

Pub: Success Publishing, Inc.

Ed: Elaine Pofeldt. **Description:** Review of Neo Vision Hypersystems and the talk of a public offering for the company.

55431 ■ "Sky Dayton" in *Internet World* **(Vol. 6, No. 7, April 1, 2000, pp. 94)**

Pub: Mecklermedia Corporation

Ed: Brian Caulfield. **Description:** EarthLink Network founder Sky Dayton plans to launch more new Web-based businesses, now that EarthLink has merged with rival MindSpring. Jake Winebaum's and Dayton's eCompanies, a business incubator for new Web companies, generates efficient Web start-ups within 180 days, including funding. Dayton looks for companies that blend commerce, community, and content.

55432 ■ "Small business package passes Congress" in *BlackEnterprise* **(Vol. 31, No. 10, May 2001, pp. 22)**

Pub: Earl Graves Publishing Co.

Ed: Joyce Jones. **Description:** Information regarding the package of small business legislation passed by the 106th Congress will keep some programs intact and secure the future of others. SBA budget agreement appropriations, including venture capital assistance are presented. Statistical data included.

55433 ■ "The stages of investment" in *Crain's Detroit Business* **(Vol. 19, No. 12, March 24, 2003, pp. 12)**

Pub: Crain Communications Inc., Detroit

Description: The five stages of venture capital investment include the initial/seed money, first stage financing, follow-on stages financing, bridge/mezzanine stage, then the Initial Public Offering, when the company is successfully listed and traded on a stock exchange or market.

55434 ■ "Starts Slow, Jobs Grow" in *Business Week* **(No. 3689, July 10, 2000, pp. F8)**

Pub: McGraw-Hill, Inc.

Description: Many banks are tightening credit requirements for small business loans, venture capitalists are growing more demanding, and angel investors may not be feeling so generous in an uncertain stock market.

55435 ■ "Startups, Beware: Obey the Law Of Supply and Demand" in *Fortune* **(Vol. 141, No. 11, May 29, 2000, pp. 278)**

Pub: Time Inc.

Ed: J. William Gurley. **Description:** A venture capitalist comments on the state of the venture capital market and on the outlook for startups in particular.

55436 ■ "A stealthier way to raise money" in *Harvard Business Review* **(Vol. 78, No. 5, September-October 2000, pp. 18)**

Pub: Harvard Business School Publishing Corp.

Ed: David Champion. **Description:** Many entrepreneurs are seeking funding from private investors and corporations rather than from venture capital companies. The dangers from venture capitalists are that they demand control, and because of their networking, they may inadvertently reveal company secrets.

55437 ■ "Success line" in *Success* **(Vol. 47, No. 3, July 2000, pp. 78)**

Pub: Success Publishing, Inc.

Description: Questions are answered on starting a business, including loans and grants, patents, and federal certification for minority- or woman-owned business.

55438 ■ "A Talk With the Net's Financiers" in *Internet World* **(Vol. 6, No. 6, March 15, 2000, pp. 60)**

Pub: Mecklermedia Corporation

Ed: David Lipschultz. **Description:** An interview with five leading venture capitalists to answer questions on the state of the Internet revolution. Questions are related to topics such as the types of businesses that venture capitalists are looking for and the possibility of emergence of another Yahoo or Cisco. The venture capitalists were also asked about the importance of the CEO in a company and predictions regarding when the Internet explosion was likely to end.

55439 ■ "Technology makes a comeback: fizzling dotcoms were last year's news" in *Black Enterprise* **(Vol. 32, No. 8, March 2002, pp. 87)**

Pub: Earl Graves Publishing Co.

Ed: Sonya A. Donaldson. **Description:** How African Americans fit into the discussion of venture capitalists, startups, and the technology industry is discussed. Interviews with various experts tell how African Americans can find the capital needed to fund a business venture.

55440 ■ "TechTalk: Big Bargain: 'Chipless' Semiconductor Startups" in *Venture Capital Journal* **(Vol. 42, No. 10, October 2002, pp. 38-39)**

Pub: Thomas Venture Economics

Ed: Ravi Chiruvolu. **Description:** The 'soft silicon' approach to manufacturing chips give customers absolute control over intellectual property, allowing for a faster time to market, and if there is an error in the chip, it can be corrected quickly and inexpensively.

55441 ■ "10 months, 10 minutes, $10 million" in *The New York Times* **(June 7, 2000, pp. D3, H3)**

Pub: The New York Times Company

Ed: Courtney Barry. **Description:** The Texas Venture Capitalist Conference was held in Austin; WebTaggers, one of 21 startups seeking funding is discussed. Statistical data is included.

55442 ■ "There's Life In Life Science" in *Venture Capital Journal* **(Vol. 42, No. 8, August 2002, pp. 32-35)**

Pub: Thomas Venture Economics

Ed: Adam Reinebach. **Description:** Venture capitalists are taking a real interest in life sciences. Profiles of four venture-backed startups are presented, including PTC Therapeutics Inc., working in small molecule drug discovery; Sensors for Medical Solutions Inc., medical sensors; Medical Scientists Inc., predictive modeling software; and Message Pharmaceuticals, drug discovery focusing on messenger RNA. Statistical data included.

55443 ■ "This VC Firm's Motto: Make Money, Not War" in *Fortune* **(Vol. 142, No. 3, July 24, 2000, pp. 54)**

Pub: Time Inc.

Ed: Jane M. Folpe. **Description:** Military Commercial Technologies, an Orlando venture capital firm and high-tech incubator, has a winning formula for bringing defense technology to the public sector.

55444 ■ "To Do: Determine the Value of My Failed Startup's IP" in *Venture Capital Journal* **(Vol. 42, No. 10, October 2002, pp. 43-44)**

Pub: Thomas Venture Economics

Ed: Thomas D. Halket. **Description:** Investors who have representatives on a company's board have a legal duty to maximize the value of a company's assets.

55445 ■ "Touched by an Angel" in *BlackEnterprise* **(Vol. 31, No. 11, June 2001, pp. 242)**

Pub: Earl Graves Publishing Co.

Ed: Roger Barnes. **Description:** In-depth coverage of venture capital funding programs for African American businesses.

55446 ■ "VC Whispers: Software surges ahead" in *Red Herring* **(No. 105, October 1, 2001, pp. 84)**

Pub: Herring Communications

Ed: Lawrence Aragon. **Description:** With the deflation of the Internet hype, computer software and programming has become one of the top-funded technology sectors. Web-services startups receiving recent funding include Asera, Bowstreet Software, Cape Clear, Grand Central Networks, and Infravio. Statistical data included.

55447 ■ "VCs Build Equity-And Lots of Debt" in *Fortune* **(Vol. 142, No. 5, September 4, 2000, pp. 76)**

Pub: Time Inc.

Ed: Anne Schukat. **Description:** A recent survey of large venture firms by MoneyUnion, an online consumer-loan company, revealed that venture capitalists are six times more likely to know the debt status of their startup companies than of their personal accounts.

55448 ■ "Venture capitalists, venturing beyond capital" in *The New York Times* **(October 15, 2000, pp. BU1)**

Pub: The New York Times Company

Ed: Lynnley Browning. **Description:** Some venture capital firms, like Charles River Ventures, are providing offices, legal advice and temporary chief executives to the start-ups in which they've invested.

55449 ■ "Venture investors start lending a hand" in *Red Herring* **(January 2003, pp. 68)**

Pub: Herring Communications Inc.

Ed: Julie Landry. **Description:** Entrepreneurs are finding it hard to procure seed money for new ventures. Venture Credit, a New York firm, is one of many venture lenders that went out of business in 2002.

55450 ■ "Venture funding down sharply from June" in *Atlanta Business Chronicle* **(Vol. 24, No. 11, August 17, 2001, pp. 11B)**

Pub: American City Business Journals Inc.

Ed: Tony Heffernan. **Description:** Venture firms are remaining cautious about investing, with only three metro Atlanta-based high-tech startups raising $20.6 million in funding in July. This funding is discussed.

55451 ■ "The Village Vanguard: Two new-economy entrepreneurs aim to jump-start businesses in college towns" in *Fortune* **(July 10, 2000, pp.154)**

Pub: Time Inc.

Ed: Andy Serwer. **Description:** Village Ventures wants to build businesses in places that are brainy and bucolic, and overlooked by venture capitalists.

55452 ■ "Waning Risk Tolerance Haunts Tech IPOs" in *Venture Capital Journal* **(Vol. 42, No. 5, May 2002, pp. 6, 8, 10-11)**

Pub: Thomas Venture Economics

Ed: Colleen Marie O'Connor, Robyn Kurdek. **Description:** The level of risk the Initial Public Offering investors are willing to take continues to fall, causing problems for venture-backed technology startups.

55453 ■ "Wanted" in *Black Enterprise* **(Vol. 32, No. 6, January 2002, pp. 3)**

Pub: Earl Graves Publishing Co.

Ed: Bridget McCrea. **Description:** Profile of David Vinson's company, Optate Inc, a Michigan-based online employee-relationship management firm. Vinson explains how his approach to staffing paid off when it came time to seek financing.

55454 ■ "War Doesn't Pay" in *Venture Capital Journal* **(Vol. 42, No. 9, September 2002, pp. 18-23)**

Pub: Thomas Venture Economics

Ed: Michael V. Copeland. **Description:** Although technology to combat terrorism seemed like a good idea to profit from war, neither the government or venture capital firms proceeded with the idea. A listing of anti-terrorism startups funded after September 11 is presented.

55455 ■ "We Found It! The Venture Rebound" in *Fortune* **(Vol. 149, No. 9, May 3, 2004, pp. 115)**
Pub: Time, Inc.
Ed: Ellen Florian. **Description:** Using data from VentureOne, a research firm that tracks over 100 sectors, the article picked the five most funded sectors, proving that VC funding is good in a few key sectors.

55456 ■ "What is venture capital?" in *Crain's Detroit Business* **(Vol. 19, No. 12, March 24, 2003, pp. 12)**
Pub: Crain Communications Inc., Detroit
Description: Venture capital is defined by the National Venture Capital Association as "money provided by professionals who invest alongside management in young companies that have the potential to develop into significant economic contributors."

55457 ■ "Where Seed Money Really Comes From" in *Inc.* **(August 1, 2003)**
Pub: Gruner & Jahr USA Publishing
Ed: Cara Cannella. **Description:** The four "F's" for small business financing are explored: founders, family, friends and foolhardy investors.

55458 ■ "Words to the Wise" in *Entrepreneur* **(Vol. 28, No. 6, June 2000, pp. 180)**
Pub: Entrepreneur Media Inc.
Ed: Don Dedelak. **Description:** One criterion that should be used in any evaluation of an invention is whether a meaningful patent can be obtained for a particular innovation.

55459 ■ "Yamacraw fund broadens its focus" in *Atlanta Business Chronicle* **(Vol. 24, No. 8, July 27, 2001, pp. 3A)**
Pub: American City Business Journals Inc.
Ed: Mary Jane Credeur. **Description:** Due to decreased demand for fiber-optics in the broadband industry, the Yamacraw Seed Capital Fund may invest in one or more of the following areas: antenna and wireless technology, data compression and decompression technology, and efficiency solutions for the cable industry. The $5 million fund was started in 1999 for the purpose of creating jobs in the traditionally high-paying technology sector.

55460 ■ "Yesterday & Today: How DFJ Went From Shrimp to Whale" in *Venture Capital Journal* **(Vol. 42, No. 5, May 2002, pp. 12)**
Pub: Thomas Venture Economics
Ed: Alistair Christopher. **Description:** Profile of Draper Fisher Jurvetson, an early-stage information technology firm that evolved from Draper & Associates. In ten years, Draper went from a $20 million fund to closing on a $640 million fund.

55461 ■ "Your Butt On The Line" in *Entrepreneur* **(Vol. 28, No. 7, July 2000, pp. 70)**
Pub: Entrepreneur Media Inc.
Ed: David R. Evanson and Art Beroff. **Description:** Raising capital for your small business will require risking your own money.

55462 ■ "Your Feature Presentation" in *Entrepreneur* **(Vol. 28, No. 9, September 2000, pp. 82)**
Pub: Entrepreneur Media Inc.
Ed: David R. Evanson and Art Beroff. **Description:** Be a star when you audition in front of investors for a role in their venture-capital portfolios.

ASSOCIATIONS AND OTHER ORGANIZATIONS

55463 ■ Canada's Venture Capital and Private Equity Association–Association Canadienne du Capital de Risque et d'Investissement
MaRS Centre
Heritage Bldg.
101 College St., Ste. 120 J
Toronto, ON, Canada M5G 1L7
Ph:(416)487-0519
Fax: (416)487-5899
Co. E-mail: cvca@cvca.ca
URL: http://www.cvca.ca
Contact: Ms. Lauren Linton, Dir. of Marketing
Membership: Ventures and risks capital companies.
Purpose: Promotes economic growth through provision of capital to emerging businesses. Conducts research; facilitates exchange of information among members; represents the venture capital industry before government agencies, industrial and financial organizations, and the public. **Publications:** *Enterprise* (quarterly).

55464 ■ Center for Venture Research
University of New Hampshire
Whittemore School of Business and Economics
15 College Rd.
Durham, NH 03824-3593
Ph:(603)862-3341
Fax: (603)862-3383
Co. E-mail: cvr@unh.edu
URL: http://www.unh.edu/cvr
Contact: Jeffrey E. Sohl, Dir.
Description: Encourages and conducts research into methods of financing new technology-based industries and firms.

55465 ■ Coleman Foundation
651 W Washington, Ste. 306
Chicago, IL 60661
Ph:(312)902-7120
Fax: (312)902-7124
Co. E-mail: info@colemanfoundation.org
URL: http://www.colemanfoundation.org
Contact: Michael W. Hennessy, Pres./CEO
Description: Strives to support entrepreneurship, cancer research, housing and education for the handicapped, and diverse educational programs.

55466 ■ Commercial Finance Association
225 W 34th St., Ste. 1815
New York, NY 10122
Ph:(212)594-3490
Fax: (212)564-6053
Co. E-mail: info@cfa.com
URL: http://www.cfa.com
Contact: Bruce H. Jones, Exec. Dir.
Membership: Organizations engaged in asset-based financial services including commercial financing and factoring and lending money on a secured basis to small- and medium-sized business firms. **Purpose:** Acts as a forum for information and consideration about ideas, opportunities, and legislation concerning asset-based financial services. Seeks to improve the industry's legal and operational procedures. Offers job placement and reference services for members. Sponsors School for Field Examiners and other educational programs. Compiles statistics; conducts seminars and surveys; maintains Speaker's Bureau and 21 committees. **Publications:** *Secured Lender: Magazine of the Asset-Based Financial Services Industry* (bimonthly).

55467 ■ Council for Art Education
PO Box 479
Hanson, MA 02341-0479
Ph:(781)293-4100
Fax: (781)294-0808
Co. E-mail: sarahs@acminet.org
URL: http://www.acminet.org/cfae.htm
Contact: Deborah M. Fanning CAE, Exec. VP
Purpose: Promotes increased public funding for art education; seeks to publicize the value of art educa-

tion and improve the quality of school art programs. Sponsors National Youth Art Month each March. **Publications:** *YAM News* (quarterly).

55468 ■ Council of Development Finance Agencies
815 Superior Ave., Ste. 1301
Cleveland, OH 44114
Ph:(216)920-3073
Fax: (216)771-4938
Co. E-mail: info@cdfa.net
URL: http://www.cdfa.net
Contact: Toby Rittner, Exec.Dir.
Description: Works for the advancement of development finance concerns and interests. Represents the nation's leading and most knowledgeable members of the development finance community from the public, private and non-profit sectors. **Publications:** *CDFA Update* (monthly).

55469 ■ National Association of Development Companies
6764 Old McLean Village Dr.
McLean, VA 22101
Ph:(703)748-2575
Fax: (703)748-2582
Co. E-mail: merril@nadco.org
URL: http://www.nadco.org
Contact: Christopher L. Crawford, Pres./CEO
Description: Small Business Administration Section 504 certified development companies. Provides long-term financing to small and medium-sized businesses. Represents membership in negotiations with the SBA, Congress, and congressional staff members; negotiates changes in legislation, regulations, operation procedures, and other matters such as prepayments problems, reporting requirements, and loan servicing procedures. Provides technical assistance and information regarding special training programs, marketing techniques, audit checklists, and loan closing and processing procedures. Compiles statistics. **Publications:** *NADCO News* (monthly). Also publishes information packages.

55470 ■ National Association of Equity Source Banks
10451 Mill Run Cir., Ste. 400
Owings Mills, MD 21117
Ph:(410)363-3698
Co. E-mail: nahbb@msn.com
Contact: Rudolph Lewis, Pres.
Membership: Private investors and venture capital firms. **Purpose:** Promotes investments in microeconomic enterprises from urban and rural areas with certified business models and franchises (these models must be third party verified from a business development institution authorized by the Association).

55471 ■ National Association of Investment Companies
1300 Pennsylvania Ave. NW, Ste. 700
Washington, DC 20004
Ph:(202)204-3001
Fax: (202)204-3022
Co. E-mail: rgreene@naicvc.com
URL: http://www.naicvc.com
Contact: Robert L. Greene, Pres./CEO
Description: Aims to: represent the minority small business investment company industry in the public sector; provide industry education; develop research material on the activities of the industry; promote the growth of minority-owned small businesses by informing the public of their contribution to the vitality of the nation's economy; collect and disseminate relevant business and trade information to members; facilitate the exchange of new ideas and financing strategies; assist organizing groups attempting to form or acquire minority enterprise small business investment companies; provide management and technical assistance to members; monitor regulatory agency actions. Conducts three professional seminars; sponsors research; compiles statistics. **Publications:** *NAIC Membership Directory* (annual); *National Association of Investment Companies—Perspective* (monthly).

55472 ■ National Association of Small Business Investment Companies
666 11th St. NW, Ste. 750
Washington, DC 20001
Ph:(202)628-5055
Fax: (202)628-5080
Co. E-mail: nasbic@nasbic.org
URL: http://www.nasbic.org
Contact: Lee W. Mercer, Pres.
Membership: Firms licensed as Small Business Investment Companies (SBICs) under the Small Business Investment Act of 1958. **Publications:** *Layman's Guide to the Legal Aspects of Venture Investments*; *NASBIC Membership Directory* (annual); *NASBIC News* (quarterly); *Today's SBICs: Investing in America's Future*.

55473 ■ National Venture Capital Association
1655 N Ft. Myer Dr., Ste. 850
Arlington, VA 22209
Ph:(703)524-2549
Fax: (703)524-3940
Co. E-mail: mheesen@nvca.org
URL: http://www.nvca.org
Contact: Mark G. Heesen, Pres.
Membership: Venture capital organizations, corporate financiers, and individual venture capitalists who are responsible for investing private capital in young companies on a professional basis. **Purpose:** Fosters a broader understanding of the importance of venture capital to the vitality of the U.S. economy and to stimulate the free flow of capital to young companies. Seeks to improve communications among venture capitalists throughout the country and to improve the general level of knowledge of the venturing process in government, universities, and the business community. **Publications:** *National Venture Capital Association—Annual Membership Directory* (annual); *NVCA Today* (quarterly); *The Venture Capital Review* (semiannual); Yearbook (annual); Report (annual).

REFERENCE WORKS

55474 ■ "3rd Annual LP Survey & Report Card" in *Venture Capital Journal* (October 1, 2005)
Pub: Thomason Financial Inc.
Description: The difference between general partners and limited partners is examined. An overview of the Third Annual LP Survey & Report Card is presented.

55475 ■ "7 Mesh Networking Startups Snag Funding" in *Venture Capital Journal* (September 1, 2005)
Pub: Thomason Financial Inc.
Description: Venture capital firms are investing in mesh network companies who will build or expand wireless technology for the home and workplace. Kiyon Inc. and PacketHop Inc are the two most recent recipients of startup funding.

55476 ■ "The $7B Question" in *Venture Capital Journal* (October 1, 2005)
Pub: Thomason Financial Inc.
Description: Speculations are made regarding Google's next venture-backed company it will buy. Information is outlined on past Google acquisitions.

55477 ■ "75 Most Powerful Blacks on Wall Street" in *Black Enterprise* (Vol. 37, October 2006, No. 3, pp. 136)
Pub: Earl G. Graves Publishing Co. Inc.
Ed: Carolyn M. Brown. **Description:** Profiles of seventy-five African American top executives. The listing is a compilation of the brightest and best venture capitalists, asset managers, CEOs, traders, and investment bankers.

55478 ■ "Access to Capital and Terms of Credit: A Comparison of Men- and Women-Owned Small Businesses" in *Journal of Small Business Management*
Pub: West Virginia University
Ed: Susan Coleman. **Description:** A comparison of access to capital for men- and women-owned small businesses. The study uses data from the 1993 National Survey of Small Business Finances.

55479 ■ "Aether Systems Unveils $125M Venture Arm" in *Venture Capital Journal* (Vol. 40, No. 10, October 2000, pp. 6)
Pub: Venture Economics
Description: In order to expand its markets, Aether Systems Inc., provider of wireless data products and services, launched Aether Capital as its venture capital arm.

55480 ■ "After its dot-bombing, SBVC rebuilds" in *Red Herring* (No. 105, October 1, 2001, pp. 40)
Pub: Herring Communications
Ed: Lawrence Aragon. **Description:** Profile of Softbank Venture Capital (SBVC) and its string of downwardly mobile Internet investments. The company has nearly $1 billion to be invested out of its sixth fund. Statistical data included.

55481 ■ "After the Gold Rush" in *Crain's Chicago Business* (Vol. 26, No. 50, December 15, 2003, pp. 13)
Pub: Crain Communications, Inc.
Ed: Steven R. Strahler. **Description:** Profile of Madison Dearborn Partners Inc., the largest private-equity firm in Chicago, Illinois. John A. Canning, Jr., CEO, speaks confidently about a rebound in deal flow, however a survey by Thomson Venture Economics, an equity information service, and the National Venture Capital Associations do not agree.

55482 ■ "Aftermarket Hits Its Stride" in *Venture Capital Journal* (November 1, 2004)
Pub: Thomason Financial Inc.
Ed: Lawrence Aragon. **Description:** Of the six venture-backed companies listed in September 2004, most posted strong aftermarket performances. Thereavance Inc., a drug company in San Francisco; IntraLase Corporation, maker of software for lasers used in eye surgery; and PlanetOut Inc., which operates gay and lesbian-themed Websites, went public as of October 15, 2004.

55483 ■ "Against the Grain" in *Red Herring* (No. 105, October 1, 2001, pp. 54-57)
Pub: Herring Communications
Ed: Stephan Herrera. **Description:** Agricultural biotechnology's third wave, producing therapeutic proteins from plants, should help the beleaguered field improve its public image. An interview with Mich Hein, president and founder of Epicyte, which produces drugs with molecular farming is included. Statistical data included.

55484 ■ "Alameda high-tech incubator is expanding" in *Kiplinger California Letter* (Vol. 38, No. 17, September 4, 2002)
Pub: Kiplinger Washington Editors, Inc.
Description: Profile of Advancing California's Emerging Technologies high-tech incubator. The high-tech incubator will construct a 40,000 square foot laboratory and offices with $6.5 million in federal money.

55485 ■ "All Funds Aren't Created Equal: When Is It Wise To Get Into a Late-Stage Fund?" in *Venture Capital Journal* (July 1, 2003)
Pub: Thomson Financial Inc.
Description: Analysis of private equity performance, examining performance cycles in the VC and private equity industries is presented. Statistical data included.

55486 ■ "Allegis Capital Markets New Fund" in *Venture Capital Journal* (Vol. 40, No. 10, November 2000, pp. 20, 22)
Pub: Venture Economics
Description: Allegis Capital is back in the fund-raising business with the fourth member of its media technology fund group.

55487 ■ "Alternative Energy Attracts Big Money" in *Altanta Journal-Constitution* (January 24, 2007)
Pub: Cox Newspapers, Inc.
Ed: Dan Chapman. **Description:** Major corporations, venture capitalists, investment banks, hedge funds and farmers spent $71 billion globally on renewable energy research.

55488 ■ "Amount raised by venture funds plunged to $6.9 billion in 2002" in *Wall Street Journal* (February 11, 2003, pp. C5)
Pub: Dow Jones & Co. Inc.
Ed: Raymond Hennessey. **Description:** Reports from Thomson Venture Economics and National Venture Capital Association show venture capital fell to $6.9 billion in 2002.

55489 ■ "Angel Investors Take a Plunge" in *Milwaukee Journal Sentinel* (December 20, 2005)
Pub: Journal Sentinel, Inc.
Ed: Kathleen Gallagher. **Description:** AquaSensors has obtained $360,000 from angel investors for its equipment that can calculate the amount of oxygen in beer or measure bacterial levels for wastewater treatment plants. Details of the deal are presented.

55490 ■ "'Angels' Seek to Expand Territory; Investors Begin to Target Waukesha County" in *Milwaukee Journal Sentinel* (December 12, 2005)
Pub: Journal Sentinel, Inc.
Ed: Kathleen Gallagher. **Description:** IQ Corridor Angel Network is targeting Waukesha County to help develop a series of high-tech companies from Chicago through Milwaukee and Madison onto Minneapolis. The firm is seeking ideas related to manufacturing equipment needed by biotech and other high-tech companies, especially those in Madison, Wisconsin.

55491 ■ "Ann Arbor's QuatRx Pharmaceuticals Files for Stock Offering" in *Crain's Detroit Business* (Vol. 22, February 13, 2006, No. 7, pp. 25)
Pub: Crain Communications Inc. - Detroit
Ed: Andrew Dieterich. **Description:** QuatRx Pharmaceuticals Company, based in Ann Arbor, Michigan, filed an initial public offering in the hopes of raising $86 million. The firm develops and commercializes products in the endocrine, metabolic, and cardiovascular therapeutic areas.

55492 ■ "Anti-Terrorism Startups Funded After Sept. 11" in *Venture Capital Journal* (Vol. 42, No. 10, October 2002, pp. 53)
Pub: Thomas Venture Economics
Description: Due to a data-processing error on the part of the journal, many of the dollar amounts on the chart presented last month were incorrect. A corrected version is presented.

55493 ■ "Apex Venture Partners Preps for Fifth Vehicle" in *Venture Capital Journal* (Vol. 40, No. 10, November 2000, pp. 16)
Pub: Venture Economics
Description: Apex Venture Partners began raising its fifth fund in January 2001. The new fund will invest in about 25-35 companies with initial investments in the $2 million range. Apex mainly backs telecommunications, software, information technology, and consumer-related companies in the U.S.

55494 ■ "Arbortext's windfall" in *Crain's Detroit Business* (Vol. 19, No. 11, March 17, 2003, pp. 3)
Pub: Crain Communications Inc., Detroit
Ed: Andrew Dietderich. **Description:** Arbortext, a company making editing and publishing software for business-related content, has landed an $8.75 round of financing from venture capital firms.

55495 ■ "Arlington, Texas, High-Tech Incubator Gets $2.85 Million Boost" in *Dallas Morning News* (October 27, 2002)
Pub: Knight Ridder/Tribune Business News
Ed: Jenni Smith. **Description:** The Arlington Technology Incubator, a joint venture of the University of Texas at Arlington and the Arlington Chamber of Commerce, received a $150,000 technical assistance grant from the U.S. Economic Development Administration and will get another $2.7 million from the research portion of the defense bill signed by President Bush in October.

55496 ■ "Asia: The VC sum rises in the East" in *Red Herring* (No. 99, June 15 & July 1, 2001, pp. 35-36)
Pub: Herring Communications
Ed: Rebecca Fannin. **Description:** Established U.S. venture capital firms have begun to invest in Asian companies. Cisco Systems, along with Japan's Softbank, raised $2 billion to invest in broadband, wireless, optical networking, and the Internet in Asia.

55497 ■ "Ask the Attorney" in *Red Herring* (No. 105, October 1, 2001, pp. 105)
Pub: Herring Communications
Description: Legal questions are answered, including issues of venture financing, venture capital, software protection, equity, patents, insider trading, and strategic financing.

55498 ■ *Attracting Investors: A Marketing Approach to Finding Funds for Your Business*
Pub: John Wiley & Sons, Incorporated
Ed: Philip Kotler, Hermawan Kartajaya, S. David Young. **Released:** August 2004. **Price:** $29.95 (US), $42.99 (Canadian). **Description:** Marketing experts advise entrepreneurs in ways to find investors in order to raise capital for their companies.

55499 ■ "B-to-B Takes Backseat to Infrastructure Deals" in *Venture Capital Journal* (Vol. 40, No. 10, October 2000, pp. 8, 10)
Pub: Venture Economics
Description: An overview of the B-to-B e-commerce and the fact that infrastructure investments could spark a rebirth to the industry.

55500 ■ "Bayla's Plea: Put Your Money Where Your Mouth Is" in *Fortune* (Vol. 142, No. 4, August 14, 2000, pp. 276+)
Pub: Time Inc.
Ed: Melanie Warner. **Description:** Meg Luttrell, CEO of Bayla Home, an online furniture retailer, shares her experiences searching for funding to save her company.

55501 ■ "Beating the Odds" in *Entrepreneur* (Vol. 27, No. 12, December 1999, pp. 154)
Pub: Entrepreneur Media Inc.
Ed: Geoff Williams. **Description:** Graham McFarland shares his plight to save his company, Express Digital.

55502 ■ "Been there, done that: growing an entrepreneurial empire?" in *Entrepreneur* (Vol. 30, No. 9, September 2002, pp. 25)
Pub: Entrepreneur Media Inc.
Ed: Joshua Kurlantzick. **Description:** Many venture capital entrepreneurs are seeking businesses that have the same qualities that made their own companies successful.

55503 ■ "Before You Do That 'Amazing' Biotech Deal, Read This Story" in *Venture Capital Journal* (Vol. 42, No. 8, August 2002, pp. 36-37)
Pub: Thomas Venture Economics
Ed: Ravi Chiruvolu. **Description:** Biotechnology startups always require a longer incubation period. The author shares his experiences with biotechnology deals.

55504 ■ "Behind the Deals" in *Entrepreneur* (Vol. 28, No. 6, June 2000, pp. 38)
Pub: Entrepreneur Media Inc.
Ed: Cynthia E. Griffin. **Description:** Small Business Investment Companies (SBIC) are the private investors who quietly serve the capital interests of business are discussed.

55505 ■ "Bereinga Starts $150M Fund, Opens China Office" in *Crain's Detroit Business* (Vol. 23, February 5, 2007, No. 6, pp. 23)
Pub: Crain Communications Inc. - Detroit
Ed: Tom Henderson **Description:** Tier one auto supplier acquisition or venture with Chinese is early project justifying Shanghai office; firm also hopes to help keep Southeast Michigan out front of new investments in not only auto-related commerce.

55506 ■ "Beware the Venture Catalyst" in *Inc.* (August 2000, pp. 127)
Pub: The Goldhirsh Group
Description: Newfangled venture catalysts may have great connections to angel investors and venture capitalists, but they may also be breaking the law. A warning from a former counsel for the National Association of Securities Dealers.

55507 ■ "Big Communications Deals Keep On Coming" in *Venture Capital Journal* (Vol. 40, No. 10, October 2000, pp. 10, 12)
Pub: Venture Economics
Description: Venture capital firms are financing communications businesses, with optical switching technology being strongest.

55508 ■ "The Big Guns" in *Entrepreneur* (Vol. 31, No. 11, November 2003, pp. 68)
Pub: Entrepreneur Media, Inc.
Ed: David Worrell. **Description:** Ways to secure venture capital for a small business are explored, including raising money from a venture capitalist who is also an important business partner and potential customer.

55509 ■ "Big Pharma Eyeing Startups" in *Venture Capital Journal* (October 1, 2204)
Pub: Thomason Financial Inc.
Ed: Tom York. **Description:** Larger pharmaceutical companies are seeking more investment deals and partnerships with emerging companies due to patent expirations and new drugs going to market.

55510 ■ "The Big Squeeze Part II: How VC Firms Are Coping" in *Venture Capital Journal* (Vol. 42, No. 5, May 2002, pp. 27, 29-31)
Pub: Thomas Venture Economics
Ed: Dan Primack. **Description:** Venture capitalists have been advising fiscal discipline to portfolio companies for two years, and now see they need to take their own advice for their firms.

55511 ■ "The Big Squeeze" in *Venture Capital Journal* (Vol. 42, No. 5, May 2002, pp. 20-26)
Pub: Thomas Venture Economics
Ed: Dan Primack. **Description:** Market pressures have forced most banks, venture firms, technology companies to scale back and slow growth.

55512 ■ "Bill Woodward: the Hollywood VC with staying power" in *Red Herring* (No. 87, December 18, 2000, pp. 56, 58)
Pub: Herring Communications, Inc.
Ed: Hildy Medina. **Description:** A profile of Bill Woodward, a Hollywood venture capitalist.

55513 ■ "Biographies" in *Venture Capital Journal* (February 1, 2006)
Pub: Thomason Financial Inc.
Description: Profiles of leading venture capital firms including Canaan Partners, BA Venture Partners, Orrick, Alta Partners, Inter West Partners, New Enterprise Associates, and Frazier Healthcare Ventures.

55514 ■ "Biotech Hotbeds: Where Are They, and How Do You Get One?" in *Venture Capital Journal* (October 1, 2004)
Pub: Thomason Financial Inc.
Ed: Dan Primack. **Description:** Boston, San Diego, San Francisco, and Research Triangle Park are earning the reputation in the life sciences sector as biotech hotbeds, clusters or hubs. These centers rely on four things: there is at least one large, nonprofit research institution strong in the field of biomedicine, close proximity to venture capital firms investing in biotech companies, local government officials have an interest in enhancing business environment for biotech companies, and there are a few publicly-traded biotech companies in the area.

55515 ■ "Biotech II Alan Frazier" in *Venture Capital Journal* (January 1, 2005)
Pub: Thomason Financial Inc.
Description: In an interview with Alan Frazier, founder of Frazier Healthcare Ventures in Seattle, Washing-

ton, he discusses the best and worst things that could happen in biotechnology in 2005. Frazier sites a continued IPO market that prices good companies appropriately along with mergers and acquisitions would be positive for the sector.

55516 ■ "Blackstone Breaks Record" in *Venture Capital Journal* (Vol. 42, No. 9, September 2002, pp. 13)
Pub: Thomas Venture Economics
Description: Profile of the new fund-raising king, Blackstone Group, a firm that raised $6.45 billion for Blackstone Capital Partners IV.

55517 ■ "Bonus Round" in *Entrepreneur* (Vol. 31, No. 7, July 2003, pp. 52)
Pub: Entrepreneur Media, Inc.
Ed: David Worrell. **Description:** Venture debt is a loan that earns the lender a small pledge of stock warrants. VC lenders are willing to work with risky, early-stage companies because that small equity gives them a potential to a large upside.

55518 ■ *Borrowing to Build Your Business: Getting Your Banker to Say "Yes"*
Pub: Upstart Publishing Co., Inc.
Ed: George M. Dawson. **Released:** 1997. **Price:** $26.95; $16.95.

55519 ■ *Borrowing for Your Business: Winning the Battle for the Banker's "Yes"*
Pub: Upstart Publishing Co., Inc.
Ed: George M. Dawson. **Price:** $19.95. **Description:** Provides information for borrowers on lenders. Covers selecting a bank and a banker, how bankers look at loans, how to be prepared, and getting a loan renewed.

55520 ■ "Bosco Joins Clarity, Raising $1B Fund" in *Venture Capital Journal* (Vol. 40, No. 10, November 2000, pp. 18)
Pub: Venture Economics
Description: Harry Bosco, former president of Lucent Technologies' Optical Networking Group, will join Clarity Partners on October 16, 2000. The firm will back early- to late-stage network infrastructure, wireless services and applications, e-commerce and broadband media companies.

55521 ■ "Boston Scientific Looks To Expand Its Products Beyond Stents" in *Boston Globe* (February 2, 2005)
Pub: New York Times Company
Ed: Ross Kerber. **Description:** Boston Scientific executives are looking to expand beyond stents into technology areas such as implantable cardiac defibrillators, and small spinal implants for pain management. The company has also developed an endoscopy system that includes a digital camera which could replace other instruments currently used for colonoscopies.

55522 ■ "Briefly" in *Crain's Detroit Business* (Vol. 19, No. 17, April 28, 2003, pp. 26)
Pub: Crain Communications Inc., Detroit
Description: C&G Newspapers has launched its new paper called the Birmingham-Bloomfield Eagle. MBT Financial Corporation, located in Monroe, Michigan is expanding into Wayne County. The University of Michigan will host the 2003 Michigan Growth Capital Symposium.

55523 ■ "Britt's Grit: Why He Left the Safety of JPMorgan in a Down Market" in *Venture Capital Journal* (Vol. 42, No. 10, Oct. 2002, pp. 22)
Pub: Thomas Venture Economics
Ed: Dan Primack. **Description:** Profile of David Britts, partner in ComVentures. Britts left JPMorgan Partners to become a partner at ComVentures in Palo Alto, California.

55524 ■ "Brookfield, Wis., Staffing Firm to Get $3 Million Venture-Capital Infusion" in *Milwaukee Journal Sentinel* (December 7, 2005)
Pub: Journal Sentinel, Inc.
Ed: Kathleen Gallagher. **Description:** Pinstripe LLC, a recruitment-process outsourcing firm that contracts

for large companies in order to recruit, assess, interview and hire new employees. The firm also offers orientation programs and a job satisfaction program. Pinstripe secured $3 million in venture capital from Baird Venture Partners.

55525 ■ "Buoyed by Biotech" in *Venture Capital Journal* **(February 1, 2006)**
Pub: Thomason Financial Inc.
Description: Life science venture capitalists gathered in San Francisco, California recently to discuss backing life sciences startups that are developing drugs and creating innovated medical devices.

55526 ■ "Burning Cash, MannKind is Raising More Money" in *San Fernando Valley Business Journal* **(Vol. 11, December 2006, No. 25, pp. 11)**
Pub: San Fernando Valley Business Journal Associates
Ed: Chris Coates. **Description:** MannKind Corp., the biopharmaceutical developer, plans to raise $400 million to help fund Technosphere, a cornerstone product for diabetes that has been in research and development for over a decade.

55527 ■ *Business Borrowers Complete Success Kit*
Pub: International Wealth Success, Inc.
Ed: Tyler G. Hicks. **Released:** 1st ed. 1999. **Price:** $99.50 (paper).

55528 ■ "Business Owners: Are You Getting Your Share of Investment Capital?" in *Women in Business* **(Vol. 54, No. 5, Sept.-Oct. 2002, pp. 28)**
Pub: The ABWA Company, Inc.
Ed: Mary-Lane Kamberg. **Description:** Sources of funding and techniques to obtain funding are discussed.

55529 ■ *The Business Planner: A Complete Guide to Raising Finances for Your Business*
Pub: Butterworth-Heinemann
Ed: Iain Maitland. **Released:** 1992. **Price:** $36.95 (paper). **Description:** Covers the writing of business plans, including writing the commercial section, drawing up the financial section, adding the appendices, and putting it together.

55530 ■ "Calendar" in *Venture Capital Journal* **(Vol. 42, No. 10, October 2002, pp. 51-52)**
Pub: Thomas Venture Economics
Description: The October 2002 calendar of events is presented by the journal.

55531 ■ "Can Your Company Get VC Funding?" in *Success* **(Vol. 47, No. 2, June 2000, pp. 25)**
Pub: Success Publishing, Inc.
Ed: Susan Mason. **Description:** A venture capitalist discloses the secrets of financing.

55532 ■ "Capital expansion" in *Black Enterprise* **(Vol. 31, No. 5, December 2000, pp. 66)**
Pub: Earl Graves Publishing Co.
Ed: Paula McCoy-Pinderhughes. **Description:** The owner of a 2-1/2 year old women's sportswear and gift company asks where to find angel investors or venture capitalists.

55533 ■ "Cash crunch" in *Entrepreneur* **(Vol. 30, No.2 February 2002, pp. 53)**
Pub: Entrepreneur Media Inc.
Ed: Jennifer Pellet. **Description:** When judging the benefit of potential funding, beware of certain terms demanded by banks and other financing sources.

55534 ■ "Cashflow: August 1-15, 2001" in *Red Herring* **(No. 105, October 1, 2001, pp. 32)**
Pub: Herring Communications
Ed: Mark A. Mowrey. **Description:** Although venture investment in the technology-related sectors remained low, activity in the biotechnology sector was increasing during the period of August 1-15, 2001. Statistical data included.

55535 ■ "Cashflow: August 15-31, 2001" in *Red Herring* **(No. 105, October 1, 2001, pp. 36)**
Pub: Herring Communications
Ed: Mark A. Mowrey. **Description:** Technology venture investing fell to its lowest level in the period of August 15-31, 2001, with only $353 million dollars being offered to young technology firms. Statistical data included.

55536 ■ "Cashflow: September 1-15, 2001" in *Red Herring* **(No. 106, October 15, 2001, pp. 32)**
Pub: Herring Communications
Ed: Mark A. Mowrey. **Description:** With U.S. markets closed in the wake of the September 11 terrorist attacks, public equity-related activity slowed to a standstill, as well as venture investment announcements and IPOs. Statistical data included, with graphs showing global IPOs, venture capital investments by U.S. firms, and global M&A announcements.

55537 ■ "CenterPoint Ventures: 'Hunting Elephants'" in *Venture Capital Journal* **(Vol. 41, No. 8, August 2000, pp. 39-40)**
Pub: Venture Economics
Ed: Jennifer Strauss. **Description:** Profile of the venture capital firm, CenterPoint Ventures, founded in 1996. Active Power, Applied Science Fiction, Chorum Technologies, Globe Ranger Corporation, Medical Present Value, OraMetrix, Scale8, and Silicon Laboratories are some of CenterPoint Ventures portfolio companies.

55538 ■ "Chase Reshapes PE Investments" in *Venture Capital Journal* **(Vol. 40, No. 10, November 2000, pp. 28)**
Pub: Venture Economics
Description: Chase Capital Partners is reorganizing a $5 billion portfolio. In order to free more capital for future investments, Chase will be trimming down its commitments in some leveraged buyout funds.

55539 ■ "China" in *Business Week* **(January 16, 2006, No. 3967, pp. 44)**
Pub: McGraw-Hill Companies
Ed: Frederik Balfour. **Description:** Some of the best venture investments in China might be outside the technology sector, but investors beware of the issues involved in dealing with individuals who have never left home, speak little or no English, and do not understand the marketplace, or venture capital. Statistical data included.

55540 ■ "Cleantech Becomes Catalyst" in *Crain's Detroit Business* **(Vol. 22, November 20, 2006, No. 47, pp. 13)**
Pub: Crain Communications Inc. - Detroit
Ed: Tom Henderson. **Description:** Financial investment firm focuses in on green tech businesses for venture capital and funding. Brighton based firms now has three subsidiaries and holds trade shows in the U.S. and Europe to match investors with companies that market clean products and technology.

55541 ■ "Cloning: Venture capitalists decline a visit to the animal farm" in *Red Herring* **(No. 103, September 1, 2001, pp. 34)**
Pub: Herring Communications
Ed: Lawrence Aragon. **Description:** Profile of Lou Hawthorne, CEO of GS&C, based in Mill Valley, California. Mr. Hawthorne is considering making his gene bank, and eventually pet cloning services, available free of charge.

55542 ■ "Co-production of business assistance in business incubators: An exploratory study" in *Journal of Business Venturing* **(Vol. 17, No. 2)**
Pub: Elsevier Science, Inc.
Ed: Mark P. Rice. **Description:** This study examines the role of a business incubator and the role of the entrepreneurial ventures located within the incubator. The incubator is described as the producer of business assistance programs, while the venture holds a co-producer role. Both roles are discussed.

55543 ■ "Common Cents" in *Entrepreneur* **(Vol. 32, November 2004, No. 11, pp. 72)**
Pub: Entrepreneur Media Inc.
Ed: David Worrell. **Description:** Angel investors tend to invest in industries of similar interest. Angel Strategies coaches entrepreneurs to look for affinity investors.

55544 ■ "Communications Jonathan Silver" in *Venture Capital Journal* **(January 1, 2005)**
Pub: Thomason Financial Inc.
Description: Jonathan Silver, managing director of Core Capital Partners in Washington DC, offers predictions in the communications market for 2005. Silver believes the best thing is that venture capitalists are regaining interest in communications.

55545 ■ "Company Catalyst" in *Boston Business Journal* **(Vol. 23, No. 25, July 25, 2003, pp. 3)**
Pub: American City Business Journals
Ed: Allison Connolly. **Description:** Christoph Westphal of Waltham, Massachusetts Polaris Venture Partners, had no experience in the venture capital sector before being hired as a general partner. Polaris Venture Partners has signed three deals since hiring Mr. Westphal.

55546 ■ "The Compensation Game" in *Venture Capital Journal* **(Vol. 40, No. 10, November 2000, pp. 47-48)**
Pub: Venture Economics
Ed: Alissa Leibowitz. **Description:** While opportunities abound, firms entice partner-level venture capitalists to stick around. Statistical data included.

55547 ■ *The Complete Book of Raising Capital*
Pub: The McGraw-Hill Companies
Ed: Lawrence W. Tuller. **Released:** 1993. **Price:** $59.95. **Description:** Includes 1.44 megabyte 3.5 inch diskette, MS-DOS compatible.

55548 ■ "Congress Waking Up to Stock Options" in *Venture Capital Journal* **(Vol. 40, No. 10, November 2000, pp. 42)**
Pub: Venture Economics
Ed: Howard Cox. **Description:** The importance of stock options to companies is addressed by Howard Cox, General Partner of Greylock in Boston, Massachusetts.

55549 ■ "Connecting Firms with Needed Funds; Financial Assistance" in *Crain's New York Business* **(Vol. 22, November 13, 2006, No. 46, pp. 32)**
Pub: Crain Communications, Inc.
Description: Listing of organizations that provide incentives or financial assistance to firms that are based in New York or are relocating to the area.

55550 ■ "Consumer Tech II Oren Zeev" in *Venture Capital Journal* **(January 1, 2005)**
Pub: Thomason Financial Inc.
Description: In an interview with Oren Zeev, consumer technology investments are discussed. Ultra wide band-wireless technology, primarily used for the home, will have a large impact in 2005. Zeev discusses trends in consumer technology and where he is putting his money.

55551 ■ "The Content Crunch" in *Venture Capital Journal* **(July 1, 2003)**
Pub: Thomson Financial Inc.
Description: The new changes in FCC rules are examined, focusing on how these changes will impact the private equity business.

55552 ■ "Convergent Fund VI Hits $64M Mark" in *Venture Capital Journal* **(Vol. 40, No. 10, November 2000, pp. 26)**
Pub: Venture Economics
Description: Convergent Investors LLC held a $64 million close on Convergent Investors VI LP, Convergent's first traditional venture capital fund.

55553 ■ "Corporate Collateral" in *Entrepreneur* (Vol. 28, No. 7, July 2000, pp. 38)
Pub: Entrepreneur Media Inc.
Ed: Cynthia E. Griffin. **Description:** Where to get money to grow your company, including big companies as resources.

55554 ■ *Corporate Venture Capital: Bridging the Equity Gap in the Small Business Sector*
Pub: Routledge
Ed: Kevin McNally. **Released:** 1997. **Price:** $85.00 (cloth).

55555 ■ "Corporate Venture Capital: Moving to the Head of the Class" in *Venture Capital Journal* (Vol. 40, No. 10, November 2000, pp. 43-46)
Pub: Venture Economics
Ed: Alistair Christopher. **Description:** Ways established venture capital firms are working to differentiate themselves from their competitors are highlighted.

55556 ■ *Corporate Venturing Directory and Yearbook*
Pub: Asset Alternatives
Contact: Jim Beecher, VP & Gen. Mgr.
E-mail: jim.beecher@alternativeinvestor.info
Covers: Approximately 300 corporate investors. **Entries Include:** Company name, address, phone, fax, Web site, and e-mail address; program goals for entrepreneurial finance; investment activity and criteria, board policies, and industry/geographic preferences; and recent investment list.

55557 ■ "Cranking Up the Earnings" in *Inc.* (October 1, 2004)
Pub: Inc. Magazine
Ed: Bobbie Gossage. **Description:** Venture capitalists are less interested in revenue growth as they are in earnings before interest, taxes, depreciation, and amortization (EBITDA) when investing in companies.

55558 ■ "Credit Markets 2000" in *Business Week* (No. 3698, September 11, 2000, pp. F30)
Pub: McGraw-Hill, Inc.
Description: Due to the strong credit market for small business, the July survey by the National Federation of Independent Business found only 5% of business owners identifying credit as their most important problem, as compared to more than 40% in the early 1980s.

55559 ■ "Cross Atlantic Capital Partners" in *Venture Capital Journal* (Vol. 40, No. 10, November 2000, pp. 56-57)
Pub: Venture Economics
Description: Gerry McCrory, an Irish entrepreneur came to America in 1998 to visit venture capitalists in Silicon Valley, California and Boston, Massachusetts. Mr. McCrory presented his plans for a strategic partnership between a seed-stage fund based in Ireland and a U.S. venture capital firm. The results of that visit are explored, along with a listing of some of the Cross Atlantic Partners portfolio companies.

55560 ■ "Cutting the Cord: Investing in Wireless" in *Venture Capital Journal* (February 1, 2005)
Pub: Thomason Financial Inc.
Description: The growth of the wireless industry has created opportunity for private equity investors to expand their portfolios. Current issues facing private equity investment in the wireless sector are discussed.

55561 ■ "Datatrac trucks in $3 million in venture capital funding" in *Atlanta Business Chronicle* (Vol. 25, December 13, 2002, No. 27, pp. A3)
Pub: American City Business Publications, Inc.
Ed: Mary Jane Credeur. **Description:** Datatrac Corporation has raised $3 in venture capital, led by Magunticook Management Inc., Boston, Massachusetts. The funds will allow Datatrac to further develop its eTrac online network providing real-time data for the transportation and logistics industries. Customers have expressed great interest in the eTrac product, and the funding will allow for increased capacity.

55562 ■ "DCM Nears Final Close" in *Venture Capital Journal* (Vol. 40, No. 10, October 2000, pp. 22)
Pub: Venture Economics
Description: Doll Capital plans to invest 20-25 percent of its new fund internationally, with focus in Asia.

55563 ■ "Deal Volume Remains Steady in Q2 But How Bout Some Exits?" in *Venture Capital Journal* (September 1, 2005)
Pub: Thomason Financial Inc.
Description: Second earnings for venture capital firms are reported. Nearly $5.82 billion was invested in 751 deals in second quarter 2005, up from the first quarter, according to The MoneyTree Survey.

55564 ■ "Dealflop: Good night, sweetheart" in *Red Herring* (No. 103, September 1, 2001, pp. 33)
Pub: Herring Communications
Ed: Julie Landry. **Description:** The demise of Tradia, a consumer-to-consumer e-commerce and swapping site, cost Accel Partners, Sequoia Capital, and angels Roger Sippl and Ron Conway $14 million.

55565 ■ "Dealflow: Startup Intelligence" in *Red Herring* (No. 99, June 15 & July 1, 2001, pp. 36)
Pub: Herring Communications
Ed: Julie Landry. **Description:** A compilation of e-learning companies that were able to raise large amounts of venture capital, including Blackboard, Bigchalk, and Logilent.

55566 ■ "Delagardelle Joins Sprout Group" in *Venture Capital Journal* (Vol. 40, No. 10, November 2000, pp. 36)
Pub: Venture Economics
Description: The Sprout Group hired Jeani Delagardelle, former general partner at Weiss, Peck & Greer Venture Partners. Ms. Delagardelle came to Sprout because of their dedication to investments in healthcare technologies.

55567 ■ "Dell, Other Corporations Shut Venture Units" in *Venture Capital Journal* (February 1, 2005)
Pub: Thomason Financial Inc.
Description: Nearly 166 corporate VCs spent $1.3 billion on 476 deals in 2004, compared to 2,155 deals totaling $16.9 billion in 2000. Investing venture capital by U.S. corporations continues to decline.

55568 ■ "Desperate Pension Funds Plan To Put up to $1B into Private Equity" in *Venture Capital Journal* (Vol. 42, No. 10, Oct. 2002)
Pub: Thomas Venture Economics
Ed: Carolina Braunschweig. **Description:** The Missouri legislature has directed its state teachers' pension fund to invest in young companies to stimulate innovation and create jobs. Ted Dintersmith of Charles River Ventures, warns that any LP contemplating entering the private equity or venture capital market should do so with caution.

55569 ■ "Detroit Free Press Small Business Column" in *Detroit Free Press* (May 23, 2005)
Pub: Knight-Ridder/Tribune Business News
Ed: Carol Cain. **Description:** Profile of Detroit-based Mobius Microsystems Inc., a firm that designs and sells patented intellectual property to microchip makers. Co-owners are looking to raise $5.5 million in venture capital to grow the firm.

55570 ■ "Developer raises $200 million to buy buildings" in *Atlanta Business Chronicle* (Vol. 25, December 6, 2002, No. 26, pp. 3A)
Pub: American City Business Publications, Inc.
Ed: Jarred Schenke. **Description:** Industrial Developments International Inc. aims to use the $200 million raised to purchase warehouses and other industrial properties.

55571 ■ "'Devil in the Details' of Chase/J.P. Morgan Merger" in *Venture Capital Journal* (Vol. 40, No. 10, October 2000, pp. 26)
Pub: Venture Economics
Description: An overview of the proposed merger between J.P. Morgan Capital Corporation and Chase Capital Partners, is presented.

55572 ■ "Dialogue Picks Up on St. Louis' Status in IT and Biotech" in *St. Louis Post-Dispatch* (November 3, 2004)
Pub: Knight-Ridder/Tribune Business News
Ed: David Nicklaus. **Description:** St. Louis reports dozens of startup biotechnology companies and venture capital funds to back them. According to a study conducted by the Battelle Institute, St. Louis has become competitive in both life sciences and information technology sectors.

55573 ■ "Digging for Gold" in *Venture Capital Journal* (January 1, 2005)
Pub: Thomason Financial Inc.
Description: Profile of Claire Kendrick, former field geologist who shares insight into how her years working in mining have helped her in her career today as principal and director of private equity investment for Hirtle, Callaghan & Company, a fund of funds in Philadelphia, Pennsylvania.

55574 ■ "Digital Defenses Sector Analysis" in *Red Herring* (January 2003, pp. 64)
Pub: Herring Communications Inc.
Description: An analysis of the digital defense sector in the U.S. is presented. Statistical data includes a listing of private companies, date founded, number of employees, funding, and number of funding rounds. Industry sectors include biological security, digital identity, managed security services, and network security.

55575 ■ *Directory of Operating Small Business Investment Companies*
Pub: Investment Div.
Released: Semiannual, April and October. **Covers:** about 300 operating small business investment companies holding regular licenses and licenses under the section 301(d) of the Small Business Investment Act covering minority enterprise SBICs. **Entries Include:** Company name, address, phone, branch offices, type of ownership, date licensed by SBA, license number, amount of obligation to the Small Business Administration, amount of private capital held, and type of investments made. **Arrangement:** Separate geographical sections for each type of license.

55576 ■ *Directory of Venture Capital*
Pub: John Wiley & Sons Inc.
Contact: Kate Lister, Author
Released: Published April, 2000. **Price:** $45, individuals List price. **Covers:** More than 600 actively investing venture capital firms and funding sources. **Entries Include:** Company name, address, phone, types of investments, geographic preference.

55577 ■ "Dot-com Bust Fallout" in *Hispanic Business* (November 2002, pp. 14)
Pub: Hispanic Business
Description: Startups that received venture-backed funding in 1999 and 2000 are failing at a faster rate than startups initially funded between 1992 and 1998. Statistical data included.

55578 ■ "Dot-Coms Hope To Cash In On IPO Resurgence" in *Venture Capital Journal* (November 1, 2004)
Pub: Thomason Financial Inc.
Description: Twenty-four companies went public in third quarter 2004, raising nearly $3.2 billion, a sign that the Initial Public Offering market is growing. Four dot-coms were backed by a combination of 20 funds. Statistical data included.

55579 ■ "Dotcom Damage" in *Entrepreneur* (Vol. 30, No. 1, January 200)
Pub: Entrepreneur Media Inc.
Ed: Aliza Pilar Sherman. **Description:** Gender issues following the dotcom crash are discussed. Despite what financiers may say, it seems women are still considered an investment risk.

55580 ■ "Down Economy Helps Incubate Small Businesses" in *Crain's Detroit Business* (Vol. 19, No. 45, November 10, 2003, pp. 11)
Pub: Crain Communications Inc., Detroit

Ed: Laura Bailey. **Description:** The State of Michigan reported 8,432 new business entities in 2003, and expects the trend to grow in 2004.

55581 ■ "Drug Importation and the Capital Markets" in *Venture Capital Journal* (November 1, 2004)
Pub: Thomason Financial Inc.
Description: Issues involving the importation of prescription drugs are covered. An examination of the economics behind cross-border shipment of drugs is essential in order to understand the affects of importation. Canadian and European governments are able to name the price they will pay for a particular drug and the Canadian government pays only the cost of manufacturing with a small markup, while American consumers not only pay manufacturing costs, but also research and development, administrative along with a markup.

55582 ■ "Dry Powder Dilemma" in *Venture Capital Journal* (Vol. 42, No. 5, May 2002, pp. 32-35)
Pub: Thomas Venture Economics
Ed: Jesse Reyes. **Description:** A critical look at the issue that is high priority for both general partners and limited partners, un-invested capital. Statistical data included.

55583 ■ "Early Stage Deals Could Come Back" in *Venture Capital Journal* (October 1, 2204)
Pub: Thomason Financial Inc.
Ed: Tom York. **Description:** Life sciences sector is expected to see a surge in investment opportunities in 2005, which will result in turning promising technologies into new companies.

55584 ■ "Early-Stage Loans With A Venture Capital Twist" in *FSB* (Vol. 10, No. 9, December 1, 2000, pp. 38)
Pub: Time Inc.
Description: An interview with Jerry Michaud, Managing Director of GATX Ventures Inc., who lends money to startups between their first and second rounds of venture financing, a time when bankers shun most new businesses.

55585 ■ "Earning Your Wings" in *Inc.* (January 1, 2005)
Pub: Inc. Magazine
Ed: Darren Dahl. **Description:** It's becoming more difficult to obtain seed money from angel investors, who pick up the slack from venture capital funds.

55586 ■ "Eboys: The First Inside Account of Venture Capitalists at Work" in *Harvard Business Review* (Vol. 78, No. 4, July 2000, pp. 152)
Pub: Harvard Business School Publishing Corp.
Ed: John T. Landry. **Description:** Randall E. Stross discusses how venture capitalists have upstaged investment bankers. A review of his new book is included.

55587 ■ "ECD short of cash at critical time as partners pull out of ventures" in *Crain's Detroit Business* (Vol. 19, No. 8, Feb. 24, 2003)
Pub: Crain Communications Inc., Detroit
Ed: Andrew Dietderich. **Description:** Energy Conversion Devices Inc. has lost funding from three companies for joint ventures in fuel-cell development.

55588 ■ "Economy Stephen Levy" in *Venture Capital Journal* (January 1, 2005)
Pub: Thomason Financial Inc.
Description: Stephen Levy, director and co-founder of the Center for Continuing Study of the California Economy, believes an export boom would be the best thing for the 2005 economy, and the continued drop in new company formation the worst.

55589 ■ "Electric Shoes and 'Breadcrumbs' for the Troops" in *Venture Capital Journal* (Vol. 42, No. 9, September 2002, pp. 26-27)
Pub: Thomas Venture Economics
Ed: Michael V. Copeland. **Description:** New defense technologies being developed to protect U.S. troops during wartime are presented.

55590 ■ "Emerging Market Investing Means More Than Just India or China" in *Venture Capital Journal* (November 1, 2004)
Pub: Thomason Financial Inc.
Description: In an interview, Michael Bleyzer, president and chief executive of SigmaBleyzer, has moved from private equity investing in the Ukraine and is focusing on countries like Romania and Bulgaria. Bleyzer sees the Slavic countries as an emerging market.

55591 ■ "Ending Advertising's Spiral" in *Business 2.0* (Vol. 6, September 2005, No. 8, pp. 42)
Pub: Time, Inc.
Ed: John Heilemann. **Description:** Profile of Miles Nadal, chairman and CEO of Toronto-based MDC Partners. Nadal invests in advertising companies.

55592 ■ "Entrepreneur Column" in *Entrepreneur.com* (September 22, 2005)
Pub: Entrepreneur Media Inc.
Ed: James Casparie. **Description:** Strategies for raising money to startup or grow a business are shared with the founder and CEO of The Venture Alliance.

55593 ■ "Entrepreneurial Event at Automation Alley Jan. 12" in *Crain's Detroit Business* (Vol. 22, January 2, 2006, No. 1, pp. 17)
Pub: Crain Communications Inc. - Detroit
Ed: Joanne Scharich. **Description:** Three emerging technology companies, IMX, Check the Crib, and Secure Crossing, are scheduled to present business plans during the fourth Entrepreneurial Initiative of Southeast Michigan. Venture capitalists, bankers, and angel investors will provide feedback after the presentations.

55594 ■ *The Entrepreneur's Guide to Preparing a Winning Business Plan and Raising Venture Capital*
Pub: Prentice Hall
Ed: Keith W. Schilit. **Released:** 1990. **Price:** $32.95 (paper). **Description:** Workbook for developing a business plan. Includes appendix of state-by-state listings of venture capital firms.

55595 ■ "Equation Predicts Returns-Real Math or Wishful Thinking" in *Venture Capital Journal* (Vol. 42, No. 10, October 2002, pp. 8, 10, 12)
Pub: Thomas Venture Economics
Ed: Michael V. Copeland. **Description:** According to Dennis Shasha, computer science professor at New York University, has developed a scientific equation to help venture capitalists invest funding successfully.

55596 ■ "Evaluating and Managing a Potential Clawback Liability, Part 2" in *Venture Capital Journal* (Vol. 42, No. 10, Oct. 2002, pp. 45-46)
Pub: Thomas Venture Economics
Ed: Steven R. Franklin, Stig A. Colberg. **Description:** Alternative for protecting assets, fee options, alternative approaches, economic advantages, risks, and the final steps involved in evaluating and managing a potential clawback liability are discussed.

55597 ■ "Evaluating and Managing a Potential Clawback Liability" in *Venture Capital Journal* (Vol. 42, No. 9, September 2002, pp. 34-35)
Pub: Thomas Venture Economics
Ed: Steven R. Franklin, Stig A. Colberg. **Description:** The trend towards venture capital fund management fee reductions is examined. Two steps for evaluating and managing potential clawback liabilities and ways to best determine who is responsible for the liability are included.

55598 ■ "Evenhandedly Political: VCs Back Candidates in Both Camps" in *Venture Capital Journal* (Vol. 40, No. 10, October 2000, pp. 5)
Pub: Venture Economics
Description: An overview of campaign contributions made by the venture capital community is presented.

55599 ■ "Exposed!" in *Red Herring* (Jan. 2003, pp. 42)
Pub: Herring Communications Inc.
Ed: Tom Stein. **Description:** Venture capital will no longer be the secret society of the past because public opinion demands it of the industry. Pension funds are the largest source of cash for venture capital firms. Statistical data included.

55600 ■ "An eye for a dye" in *Red Herring* (March 2003, pp. 60)
Pub: Herring Communications Inc.
Ed: Michael V. Copeland. **Description:** Optiva's nanotechnology has attracted JP Morgan Partners investment.

55601 ■ "Facts about venture capital firms" in *Crain's Detroit Business* (Vol. 16, No. 19, May 8, 2000, pp. 20)
Pub: Crain Communications, Inc.
Description: Facts about venture capital firms are provided by the National Venture Capital Association located in Arlington, Virginia. A Website for further information is included.

55602 ■ "False Start" in *Venture Capital Journal* (October 1, 2005)
Pub: Thomason Financial Inc.
Ed: Lawrence Aragon. **Description:** A recap of the venture-backed IPO market for 2005 is presented. So far, seven VC-backed companies have gone public and raised $550 million by the end of August 2005. There were 33 IPOs for the first seven months of 2005. Statistical data included.

55603 ■ "Family matters" in *Entrepreneur* (Vol. 30, No. 12, December 2002, pp. 83)
Pub: Entrepreneur Media Inc.
Ed: Jennifer Pellet. **Description:** Difficulties encountered by family-owned businesses when attempting to obtain venture capital backing are discussed.

55604 ■ *Federal Research Report*
Pub: CD Publications
Contact: Leonard Eiserer, CON
Ed: Leonard Eiserer, Editor, eiserer@aol.com. **Released:** Weekly. **Price:** $284 per year. **Covers:** Government and foundation grants and contracts for research, development, and education. **Entries Include:** Grant title; name, address, and phone of contact; deadline; amount. **Arrangement:** Classified by discipline or field of interest.

55605 ■ "Fernandez: An Entrepreneur at Heart" in *Venture Capital Journal* (Vol. 40, No. 11, November 2000, pp. 52)
Pub: Venture Economics
Description: Profile of Manny Fernandez, a managing director at SI Ventures, a technology research firm. Despite working for SI Ventures for nearly ten years, Mr. Fernandez still considers himself an entrepreneur at heart.

55606 ■ "Finance vets bank on bypassed businesses" in *Houston Business Journal* (Vol. 33, No. 48, April 11, 2003, pp. 1A)
Pub: Houston Business Journal
Ed: Jim Greer. **Description:** Briar Capital LP has been formed by Frank Goldberg and Steve Rosencranz, to provide financing to small businesses which have been bypassed by banks.

55607 ■ "Financial Industry Expects Growth Amid Radical Changes" in *Crain's Detroit Business* (Vol. 19, No. 45, November 10, 2003, pp. 24)
Pub: Crain Communications Inc., Detroit
Ed: Katie Merx. **Description:** Southeast Michigan banks are expecting increases across the board in commercial lines of business, credit unions are expected to expand, and mortgage companies and brokers are offering new services to keep business brisk when interest rates rise. Venture capital and mergers-and-acquisition are also projected to do well.

55608 ■ "Financial services firms foresee mixed results" in *Atlanta Business Chronicle* **(Vol. 25, January 10, 2003, No. 31, pp. 18A)**
Pub: American City Business Publications, Inc.
Ed: Tony Heffernan. **Description:** The University of Georgia's Georgia Economic Outlook 2003 indicates that financial services companies will have mixed performances this coming year. One performance issue is that community banks will do better than bigger banks because they are not dependent on venture capital lending.

55609 ■ "Financing" in *Entrepreneur* **(Vol. 28, No. 8, August 2000, pp. 134)**
Pub: Entrepreneur Media Inc.
Ed: Cynthia E. Griffin. **Description:** Nonprofit organizations are testing finance programs to help low-income individuals start and sustain businesses.

55610 ■ *Financing Your Business*
Pub: Prentice Hall
Ed: Iris Lorenz-Fife. **Released:** 1997. **Price:** $13.95.
Description:

55611 ■ *Financing Your Business Dreams with Other People's Money: How & Where to Find Money for Start-Up & Growing Businesses*
Pub: Rhodes & Easton
Ed: Harold R. Lacy. **Released:** 1998. **Price:** $15.95.

55612 ■ *Financing Your Small Business*
Pub: Barron's Educational Series, Incorporated
Ed: Robert Walter. **Released:** March 2004. **Price:** $18.95 (US), $27.50 (Canadian). **Description:** Tips for raising venture capital, dealing with bank officials, and initiating public offerings of stock shares for small business.

55613 ■ *Financing Your Small Business: Techniques for Planning, Acquiring, and Managing Debt*
Pub: Oasis Press
Ed: Art DeThomas. **Released:** 1992. **Price:** $19.95 (paper). **Description:** Provides step-by-step information on small business financing, including debt financing, short-term credit, negotiating long-term loans, and going public.

55614 ■ "Firm Suiting Up for New Space Flights" in *San Fernando Valley Business Journal* **(Vol. 12, January 2007, No. 1, pp. 12)**
Pub: San Fernando Valley Business Journal Associates
Ed: Mark R. Madler. **Description:** Profile on Orbital Outfitters, a company that wants to revolutionize the space industry by designing the next generation of space suits targeting crew and passengers for space travel through commercial and privately funded space flight. The firm also has an administrative office in Washington, D.C. to better deal with the regulations which oversee the New Space industry.

55615 ■ "First-Half Disbursements Continue Venture Capital's Record-Setting Pace" in *Venture Capital Journal* **(Vol. 40, No. 10, Oct. 2000, pp. 47)**
Pub: Venture Economics
Ed: Daniel Primack, Jennifer Strauss. **Description:** Venture capital money is still flowing into innovative new companies. The article includes investment totals by region and by quarter. Statistical data included.

55616 ■ *Fitzroy Dearborn Directory of Venture Capital Funds*
Pub: Fitzroy Dearborn Publishers, Inc.
Ed: A. David Silver. **Released:** 1994. **Price:** $65.00 (library binding).

55617 ■ "Five Angels With Angles" in *Inc.* **(Volume 27, July 2005, No. 7, pp. 92-99)**
Pub: Inc. Magazine
Ed: Jim Melloan. **Description:** Today's early stage angel investors are tougher and smarter than their predecessors. Tips to help work with angel investors are presented.

55618 ■ "Five More VCs Slash Funds, Is There Any Room for More?" in *Venture Capital Journal* **(Vol. 42, No. 8, August 2002, pp. 6, 8, 10)**
Pub: Thomas Venture Economics
Ed: Dan Primack, Michael V. Copeland, Lawrence Aragon. **Description:** Five more venture funds have confirmed they will give back a combined $821 million committed capital to limited partners. The latest firms to cut include BRM Capital Management, Carlyle Europe Venture Partners, Viventures, Walden International and Worldview Technology Partners. Statistical data included.

55619 ■ "Flourishing in the Windy City" in *Hispanic Business* **(January/February 2003, pp. 49)**
Pub: Hispanic Business
Ed: Jonathan J. Higuera. **Description:** Profile of Cyberworks Media Group, located in Chicago, Illinois. Cyberworks, an Internet technology firm, has succeeded when so many other dot-coms have failed, by staying away from venture capital and equity funding.

55620 ■ "Focused Fundraising" in *Entrepreneur.com* **(Vol. 34, February 2006, No. 2, pp. 49)**
Pub: Entrepreneur Media Inc.
Ed: David Worrell. **Description:** Phil Libin discusses his experiences when seeking venture capital for his national security technology firm; Libin also secured million-dollar contracts with the Department of Defense.

55621 ■ "Forecast for IPOs? Wait Till Next Year" in *Venture Capital Journal* **(Vol. 41, No. 8, August 2000, pp. 16-17)**
Pub: Venture Economics
Description: It is predicted that the IPO market will not improve until the economy recovers, but it is a good time to be a venture capitalist.

55622 ■ "Forget Diamonds" in *Entrepreneur* **(Vol. 28, No. 1, January 2000, pp. 42)**
Pub: Entrepreneur Media Inc.
Ed: Cynthia E. Griffin. **Description:** The Women's Business Enterprise National Council (WBENC) identified the Fortune 500 companies that are the most committed to ensuring that women business owners participate in their procurement programs.

55623 ■ "Forget India, Outsource to Oregon!" in *Venture Capital Journal* **(December 1, 2004)**
Pub: Thomason Financial Inc.
Description: Reasons for venture capitals to target investments in Oregon and the Pacific Northwest rather than India or China are presented. Experienced angel investors and venture capitalists are taking the lead in building Oregon's high-tech entrepreneurial community.

55624 ■ "Forget VC: Successful Entrepreneur Says Good Riddance" in *Venture Capital Journal* **(October 1, 2004)**
Pub: Thomason Financial Inc.
Description: In an interview, Harry Gruber, founder and CEO of Kintera Inc., a company providing software and services to help nonprofits conduct fundraising via the Internet. Gruber discusses the advantages, as well as the disadvantages of using venture capital to grow a business, particularly the control venture capitalists gain over a firm.

55625 ■ "Former Nortel VP Joins Enterprise" in *Venture Capital Journal* **(Vol. 40, No. 10, October 2000, pp. 36)**
Pub: Venture Economics
Description: Enterprise Partners Venture Capital recently hired Naser Partovi as a general partner. Partovi will focus on telecommunications, specifically the optical and wireless spaces.

55626 ■ "Former Wrestling Star Body Slams Private Equity" in *Venture Capital Journal* **(Vol. 42, No. 9, September 2002, pp. 15-16)**
Pub: Thomas Venture Economics
Ed: Michael V. Copeland. **Description:** Profile of Ira Lubert, co-founder/principal of Lubert-Alder Management Inc. of Philadelphia, Pennsylvania; Lubert targets his market to mid- to late-stage companies that can't go public and don't want to be sold right away.

55627 ■ "Forum helps firms headed by women raise capital" in *Wall Street Journal* **(June 13, 2000, pp. B4)**
Pub: Dow Jones & Co., Inc.
Ed: Jeffrey Tannenbaum. **Description:** Highlights of the Springboard 2000 Silicon Valley Conference, held in Redwood Shores, California in January.

55628 ■ "Forward: Thomas Middelhoff faces the music at Bertelsmann" in *Red Herring* **(No. 105, October 1, 2001, pp. 30-31)**
Pub: Herring Communications
Ed: Robert LaFranco. **Description:** Despite the pronouncements given by Thomas Middelhoff, CEO of Bertelsmann, only one new-media investment he has spearheaded has paid off. In January 2000, Bertelsmann stated that his company wanted to be Number One in media e-commerce.

55629 ■ "Foundation Puts More Than $12M Behind Push For Design" in *Crain's Detroit Business* **(Vol. 22, November 20, 2006, No. 47, pp. 1)**
Pub: Crain Communications Inc. - Detroit
Ed: Sherri Begin. **Description:** Kresge Foundation is encouraging non-profit businesses to incorporate sustainable design onto their capital projects. Grants to cover the usual extra costs to incorporate green as well as advice and referrals are available through Kresge on a national level.

55630 ■ "4Q venture funding bumps up" in *Crain's Detroit Business* **(Vol. 16, No. 8, February 21, 2000, pp. 3)**
Pub: Crain Communications, Inc.
Ed: Matt Roush. **Description:** According to the quarterly "Money Tree" report, the level of venture capital in Southeast Michigan rose in the fourth quarter 1999. Seventeen Michigan companies attracted more than $43 million, including seven Internet-based companies, three biotechnology companies, three manufacturers, and two software companies receiving funds.

55631 ■ "Franchising, Franchising" in *Inc.* **(Volume 27, June 2005, No. 6, pp. 24, 26)**
Pub: Inc. Magazine
Description: A group of entrepreneurs have launched Franchising Ventures Group, with $10 million to invest. The VC is looking for profitable companies that show franchise potential.

55632 ■ "Freshmen LPs Prep for PE" in *Venture Capital Journal* **(Vol. 42, No. 10, October 2002, pp. 6)**
Pub: Thomas Venture Economics
Description: A list of five new institutional investors with up to $1 billion to invest is presented along with their plans.

55633 ■ "Friends in High Places" in *Hispanic Business* **(Vol. 23, No. 7/8, July/August 2001, pp. 62, 64)**
Pub: Hispanic Business
Ed: Scott Williams. **Description:** Profile of the newly formed Hispanic Network of Entrepreneurs. The group hopes to ease the way for a new generation of Hispanic entrepreneurs in the high-tech industry, business development, venture capital financing, recruiting and exchange of ideas.

55634 ■ "Fund gets boost from Masco connection" in *Crain's Detroit Business* **(Vol. 16, No. 16, April 17, 2000, pp. 27)**
Pub: Crain Communications, Inc.
Ed: Leslie Green. **Description:** Gerard Boylan, former vice president at Masco Corporation, tells how Masco helped him and his partners raise capital for Long Point Capital Inc.

55635 ■ "Fund Profile: Hey, Abbott! FoF Tops Target" in *Venture Capital Journal* **(Vol. 42, No. 9, September 2002, pp. 12)**
Pub: Thomas Venture Economics
Ed: Charles R. Fellers. **Description:** Profile of Abbott Capital Management, the New York-based venture capital firm that closed on a $730 million private equity fund-of-funds in July.

55636 ■ "Fund Profile" in *Venture Capital Journal* (February 1, 2006)
Pub: Thomason Financial Inc.
Description: Profile of Aisling Capital, founded in 2002 as Perseus-Soros BioPharmaceutical Fund. The VC invests in biopharmaceutical companies that require $15M to $30M of new capital.

55637 ■ "Fund-Raising Falters, VCs Keep Cutting Back" in *Venture Capital Journal* (Vol. 42, No. 10, October 2002, pp. 18-20)
Pub: Thomas Venture Economics
Description: Venture capital firms refunded more money to limited partners than they raised in the second quarter 2002, the first time that has happened.

55638 ■ "Fund-Raising Soars 78 Percent, Momentum Builds" in *Venture Capital Journal* (December 1, 2004)
Pub: Thomason Financial Inc.
Description: Venture firms raised more capital in the first three quarters of 2004 than all of 2003, with 125 venture funds taking in nearly $11.25 billion in commitments and the number is expected to grow.

55639 ■ "Funding from the Feds: Local interest in Small Business Investment Corporations is growing" in *Crain's Detroit Business* (Vol.16, No.33)
Pub: Crain Communications, Inc.
Ed: Matt Roush. **Description:** A venture capital program instituted during the Eisenhower administration is growing in Southeast Michigan. Several local groups are studying the creation of Small Business Investment Corporations, or SBICs, that are venture capital-like investment companies chartered by the federal SBA, and matches organizers' money up to $2-for-$1.

55640 ■ "Funds Face Unexpected Antitrust Problem" in *Venture Capital Journal* (January 1, 2005)
Pub: Thomason Financial Inc.
Description: Profile of the Clayton Act Section 8 of federal antitrust law is examined. The Act, which prohibits an end-run around the Sherman Act's ban on monopolization and agreements in restraint of trade by prohibiting the same person from serving on boards of competitive companies, has rarely been enforced by either private litigants or by the federal government.

55641 ■ "Gabriel Venture Partners Fund II Targets $300M" in *Venture Capital Journal* (Vol. 40, No. 10, November 2000, pp. 18, 20)
Pub: Venture Economics
Description: Gabriel Venture Partners plans to back 30-35 communications networking, and information technology companies with it second fund with the target $300M.

55642 ■ "Game On! Game-Makers are Definitely not Sleeping in Seattle" in *Entrepreneur* (Vol. 32, No. 4, April 2004, pp. 22)
Pub: Entrepreneur Media, Inc.
Ed: Nichole L. Torres. **Description:** Game manufacturers are catching the eyes of venture capitalists in the Seattle, Washington area. Profiles of Cranium Inc. (Cranium) founders Richard Tait and Whit Alexander, Screenlife LLC (Scene It) founders Dave Long and Craig Kinzer, and Entspire (Derivation) founders Brad Chase.

55643 ■ *Getting a Business Loan: Your Step-by-Step Guide*
Pub: Crisp Publications, Inc.
Ed: Orlando J. Antonini. **Released:** 1993. **Price:** $15.95 (paper).

55644 ■ "Girls Just Wanna Have Funds" in *Entrepreneur* (Vol. 28, No. 3, March 2000, pp. 38)
Pub: Entrepreneur Media, Inc.
Ed: Cynthia E. Griffin. **Description:** The article looks at ways of changing how venture capital firms look at women.

55645 ■ "Go Small" in *Entrepreneur* (Vol. 28, No. 6, June 2000, pp. 38)
Pub: Entrepreneur Media Inc.
Ed: Cynthia E. Griffin. **Description:** Investing in venture capital funds is explored.

55646 ■ "The Google Effect Kicks In" in *Venture Capital Journal* (December 1, 2004)
Pub: Thomason Financial Inc.
Ed: Lawrence Aragon. **Description:** The average price of venture capital-backed initial public offerings rose 32 percent in aftermarket, the biggest monthly gain in nine months. Statistical data included.

55647 ■ "Google's Banker" in *Fortune* (Vol. 149, No. 9, May 3, 2004, pp. 105)
Pub: Time, Inc.
Ed: Adam Lashinsky. **Description:** Venture capital information is discussed, including the impact of Google going public; Michael Moritz and his partners will likely reap hundreds of millions of dollars.

55648 ■ "GPs Say Valuation Standard Is 'Important' But Can't Agree on One" in *Venture Capital Journal* (Vol. 42, No. 10, Oct. 2002, pp. 47-48)
Pub: Thomas Venture Economics
Ed: Colin Blaydon, Michael Horvath. **Description:** Results from a survey conducted by Foster Center for Private Equity at the Tuck School of Business are presented. The survey was sent to 550 venture capital general partnerships.

55649 ■ "Granite Ventures Chisels Out Its Own Identity" in *Venture Capital Journal* (September 1, 2005)
Pub: Thomason Financial Inc.
Description: San Francisco, Granite Ventures has topped a new fund with $350 million in capital commitments from various investors. Granite was launched as an early stage VC group within Hambrecht & Quest in 1992.

55650 ■ "A grim adventure: Amphion Capital's venture fund loses all" in *Barron's* (Vol. 82, No. 58, February 17, 2003, pp. T8)
Pub: Barron's
Ed: Eric J. Savitz. **Description:** Amphion's portfolio of tech stocks all collapsed in the past two years, as the fund's assets under management dropped from $91.8 million January 30, 2000 to below zero at the end of 2002. Major losses were Axcess and Biocentric Solutions.

55651 ■ "The Growing Number of Female Managers in VC-backed Firms means that Women are seen as Less Risky" in *Inc.* (September 2000, pp. 60)
Pub: The Goldhirsh Group
Ed: D.M. Osborne. **Description:** Catherine Muther created not a separate, women-only network but rather a system for ushering women into the larger venture landscape. Managers of venture funds targeting women stress that they're not interested in special-needs cases.

55652 ■ "Guardian Angel" in *Entrepreneur* (Vol. 33, March 2005, No. 3, pp. 58)
Pub: Entrepreneur Media Inc.
Ed: David Worrell. **Description:** Profile of the ACE-Net, the Angel Capital Electronic Network, which helps entrepreneurs with angel capital. Since it began in 1995, ACE-Net has helped entrepreneurs raise over $100 million.

55653 ■ *Guerrilla Financing: Alternative Techniques to Finance Any Small Business*
Pub: Houghton Mifflin Co.
Ed: Bruce J. Blechman and Jay C. Levinson. **Released:** 1992. PR $10.75. **Description:** Describes innovative approaches to evaluating assets, unearthing alternative finance sources, and marketing yourself and your business.

55654 ■ "Guest Article" in *Venture Capital Journal* (February 1, 2006)
Pub: Thomason Financial Inc.

Description: Section 409A of the Internal Revenue Code for non-qualified deferred compensation plans is outlined. The new rule could hurt venture capital-backed companies.

55655 ■ "Gurus in the garage" in *Harvard Business Review* (Vol. 78, No. 6, November-December 2000, pp. 71)
Pub: Harvard Business School Publishing Corp.
Description: Description of a special type of advisor who helps entrepreneurs with a variety of tasks, including recruiting staff and negotiating seed money.

55656 ■ "A Hand Up: Urban, Minority Entrepreneurs are Hotter Than Ever-So Where is Their Funding?" in *Entrepreneur* (Vol. 31, Sept. 2003)
Pub: Entrepreneur Media, Inc.
Ed: Joshua Kurlantzick. **Description:** Venture capitalists and large financial institutions are investing in minority-owned companies, although smaller banks are cutting commitments to African-American owned firms.

55657 ■ "Has the Free Software Paradox Been Solved?" in *Venture Capital Journal* (September 1, 2005)
Pub: Thomason Financial Inc.
Ed: Tom Stein. **Description:** Open source software is a popular investment for VCs in 2005. Open source is changing the way software is developed and used by corporations.

55658 ■ "Hatching a Better Incubator" in *Red Herring* (No. 87, December 18, 2000, pp. 88-92, 94)
Pub: Herring Communications, Inc.
Ed: Dean Takahashi. **Description:** A profile of Raza Foundries, a venture capital incubator that continues to have tremendous success.

55659 ■ "Have Faith, Not Fear" in *Venture Capital Journal* (Vol. 42, No. 9, September 2002, pp. 31)
Pub: Thomas Venture Economics
Ed: Darryl E. Wash. **Description:** Darryl Wash, managing partner of Ascend Venture Group, a venture capital firm in New York City, feels the entrepreneurial spirit will keep the economy moving in the right direction.

55660 ■ "Hennessey VC company looks for small business" in *Crain's Detroit Business* (Vol. 18, No. 23, June 1)
Pub: Crain Communications Inc. - Detroit
Ed: Michael Strong. **Description:** Owners of small businesses in search of capital may be able to tap a new source: Hennessey Capital LLC, located in Troy, MI. The company provides management services for small businesses with annual revenue ranging from $500,000 to $5 million.

55661 ■ "A Hidden Gem? Quebec Looks To Flex Muscle" in *Venture Capital Journal* (Vol. 42, No. 5, May 2002, pp. 44-45)
Pub: Thomas Venture Economics
Ed: Danielle Fugazy. **Description:** American venture capitalists have not invested much in Quebec's industry in the past, but the continuous growth Quebec is seeing in the fields of engineering, transportation, telecommunications, aeronautics and aerospace technology, medical research, computer science and biotechnology, has American VCs taking a second look.

55662 ■ "Hidden treasure" in *Entrepreneur* (Vol. 30, No. 2, February 2002, pp. 56)
Pub: Entrepreneur Media Inc.
Ed: Sean P. Melvin. **Description:** In a tightened economy, entrepreneurs can look for capital in the nooks, crannies, equipment and real estate the business already owns.

55663 ■ "Hispanic Chamber of Commerce creates venture fund" in *Wall Street Journal* (February 22, 2000, pp. B2)
Pub: Dow Jones & Co., Inc.
Ed: Paulette Thomas. **Description:** Statistical information regarding the venture fund created by the Hispanic Chamber of Commerce is cited.

55664 ■ "Hit Parade" in *Venture Capital Journal* **(September 1, 2005)**
Pub: Thomason Financial Inc.
Ed: Constance Loizos. **Description:** New fund managers need to stress the fact that they can deliver venture-level returns by meeting with potential investors.

55665 ■ "Hollinger Contacts VC Giant" in *Crain's Chicago Business* **(Vol. 26, No. 50, December 15, 2003, pp. 1)**
Pub: Crain Communications, Inc.
Ed: Jeremy Mullman. **Description:** Hicks Muse & Furst Inc., an investment firm located in Texas, is hoping to acquire Conrad Black's controlling interest in Hollinger International Inc., owner of the Chicago Sun-Times. Details of the negotiations are presented. Statistical data included.

55666 ■ "Hollinger Contacts VC Giant; Hicks Muse Could See Synergies with Radio Here" in *Crains Chicago Business* **(Vol. 26, No. 50)**
Pub: Crain Communications, Inc.
Ed: Jeremy Mullman. **Description:** Hicks Muse & Furst Inc., an investment firm located in Texas, is hoping to acquire Conrad Black's controlling interest in Hollinger International Inc., owner of the Chicago Sun-Times. Details of the negotiations are presented. Statistical data included.

55667 ■ "Hollinger VC Unit has Family Ties; Black's Nephew has Few Hits, Many Misses With Fund" in *Crains Chicago Business* **(Vol. 26, No. 51)**
Pub: Crain Communications, Inc.
Ed: Jeremy Mullman. **Description:** Matthew Doullo is the nephew of Conrad Black, chairman of Hollinger International Inc. Doullo runs the venture investment unit of Hollinger International. A profile of Doullo is provided.

55668 ■ "Hollinger VC Unit has Family Ties" in *Crain's Chicago Business* **(Vol. 26, No. 51, December 22, 2003, pp. 3)**
Pub: Crain Communications, Inc.
Ed: Jeremy Mullman. **Description:** Matthew Doullo is the nephew of Conrad Black, chairman of Hollinger International Inc. Doullo runs the venture investment unit of Hollinger International. A profile of Doullo is provided.

55669 ■ *How to Finance a Growing Business: An Insider's Guide to Negotiating the Capital Markets*
Pub: Merritt Publishing
Ed: Royce Diener. **Released:** 5th ed. 1997. **Price:** $24.95.

55670 ■ "How Not To Get Tripped Up by UBTI" in *Venture Capital Journal* **(July 1, 2003)**
Pub: Thomson Financial Inc.
Description: Business plans and projects for portfolio companies and venture capital funds have been weakened by the slow economy, resulting in devaluations, recapitalizations and fewer realizations, along with the need for funds to borrow in order to protect investments, thus raising the prospect of unrelated business taxable income (UBTI). Circumstances that would make borrowing a good option include dry funds, bridging calls, borrowing to pay expenses, or to accelerate realizations.

55671 ■ "How Partnerships Can Avoid Tax Surprises" in *Venture Capital Journal* **(July 1, 2003)**
Pub: Thomson Financial Inc.
Description: Tax planning ideas helpful to the venture capital industry are examined. Issues discussed include establishing a partnership status, contribution requirements, capital account allocation, tax basis allocation, distributions, and state filing requirements.

55672 ■ "How To Create an Entrepreneurial Infrastructure" in *Venture Capital Journal* **(January 1, 2005)**
Pub: Thomason Financial Inc.
Ed: Tom Dickerson. **Description:** Development of a favorable entrepreneurial environment requires an in-

crease in the quantity and quality of each of three critical elements: research and development, capital and entrepreneurs and each of these elements typically grow in relation to the others.

55673 ■ "How To Pick Through the Optics Fire Sale" in *Venture Capital Journal* **(Vol. 42, No. 9, September 2002, pp. 5-6)**
Pub: Thomas Venture Economics
Ed: Danielle Fugazy, Lawrence Aragon. **Description:** In the first half of 2002, 63 optical networking companies secured nearly $950 million from more than 260 venture firms. A listing of the top ten deals are presented.

55674 ■ "How VCs Can Limit Their Liabilities in a Down Round" in *Venture Capital Journal* **(Vol. 42, No. 10, October 2002, pp. 40-42)**
Pub: Thomas Venture Economics
Ed: Christopher Aidun. **Description:** Steps to avoid the pitfalls of a breach of the duty of loyalty, or to minimize the risk of liability in a situation where a breach may be an unavoidable, acceptable risk are presented.

55675 ■ "How Your CFO should Raise Money: What the Experts Say" in *Inc.* **(April 2000, pp. 123)**
Pub: The Goldhirsh Group
Description: There is a new breed of chief financial officers: those who actively network to raise money in addition to handling the paperwork. Some venture capitalists share their thoughts on this approach.

55676 ■ "Huron to Announce $25M Deal, Eyes New $250M Fund" in *Crain's Detroit Business* **(Vol. 23, No. 3, January 15, 2007, pp. 26)**
Pub: Crain Communications Inc. - Detroit
Ed: Tom Henderson. **Description:** Huron Capital Partners L.L.C. is coming off a record year for deal volume. A new $25M deal was announced, two more under letters of intent, and has begun raising funds for large $250M fund by the end of 2007.

55677 ■ "In the Family Way: Adam's Excellent Venture" in *Fortune* **(Vol. 141, No. 12, June 12, 2000, pp. 311+)**
Pub: Time Inc.
Ed: Andy Serwer. **Description:** How does one become a venture capitalist? An interview with Adam Dell, 30 year old brother of Mike Dell, answers this question.

55678 ■ "Innovation and Incentives: VCs Find Partner in Quebec" in *Venture Capital Journal* **(Vol. 42, No. 5, May 2002, pp. 47)**
Pub: Thomas Venture Economics
Ed: Alistair Christopher. **Description:** The Quebec government offers a research and development tax credit to local businesses, which is attracting the attention of U.S. venture capitalists.

55679 ■ "Intellectual Property and Licensing Pitfalls" in *Venture Capital Journal* **(December 1, 2004)**
Pub: Thomason Financial Inc.
Description: Intellectual property and licensing issues can result in restrictions on a company's operations and profitability, as well as reduced flexibility in undertaking liquidity events and impair the value of an investment. Intellectual property and licensing pitfalls are outlined.

55680 ■ "InterWest Fund VIII Nears $750M Mark" in *Venture Capital Journal* **(Vol. 40, No. 10, October 2000, pp. 16)**
Pub: Venture Economics
Description: InterWest Partners is aiming for a post-Labor Day final close on $750 million for the firm's latest vehicle, InterWest Partners VIII. The fund will back companies in the telecommunications/communications infrastructure space, medical technology and the Internet economy.

55681 ■ "Investing in Training Will Yield a Powerful ROI" in *Venture Capital Journal* **(November 1, 2004)**
Pub: Thomason Financial Inc.
Description: Venture capital firms implementing training programs see a return on that investment by creating a competitive advantage as well as improved performance.

55682 ■ "Investment continues to drop" in *Crain's Detroit Business* **(Vol. 19, No. 12, March 24, 2003, pp. 11)**
Pub: Crain Communications Inc., Detroit
Ed: Katie Merx. **Description:** Despite the fact that venture capital investment fell to 1998 levels in 2002, Michigan investors expect the VC market to improve in 2003.

55683 ■ "Investment Firms Forge Partnerships" in *Venture Capital Journal* **(Vol. 41, No. 8, August 2000, pp. 14, 16)**
Pub: Venture Economics
Description: Report of investment firm mergers which includes information about the merger between European incubator inVentures with New York-based search firm Redwood Partners; and the merger between Washington-based Core Capital Parners and GCI Venture Partners.

55684 ■ "Investment Pace Starts To Return to Normal" in *Venture Capital Journal*
Pub: Thomason Financial Inc.
Description: New Enterprise Associates was the most active investor in 2004, doing 70 deals, followed by Draper Fisher Jurvetson, with 55 deals. A listing of the top ten VCs for 2004 is provided.

55685 ■ "Investors don't want their MeVC" in *Red Herring* **(No. 106, October 15, 2001, pp. 36)**
Pub: Herring Communications
Ed: Julie Landry. **Description:** Although MeVC had planned to launch up to twenty funds over five years, the company has launched just one fund in 18 months of business. MeVC has laid off half of its staff, leaving a crew of about 12 workers. The online VC network OffRoad Capital has laid off one-third of its workforce, and Garage.com, once a Web site that linked angels with prospective startups is now a hybrid venture capital firm and investment bank.

55686 ■ "IOP Aftermarket" in *Venture Capital Journal* **(Vol. 42, No. 10, Oct. 2002, pp. 54)**
Pub: Thomas Venture Economics
Description: Odysey HealthCare, providing hospice care, leads the list of Initial Public Offerings with offering price, bid price, percent change, business description, and date of IPO.

55687 ■ "IPO Aftermarket: I'm a Bull! No, I'm a Bear! Wait, I'm a ... Blear!" in *Venture Capital Journal* **(Vol. 42, No. 9, Sept. 2002, pp. 46)**
Pub: Thomas Venture Economics
Description: Information on the confused "blear" market is presented, including a list of Initial Public Offerings with offering price, bid price, percent change, business description, and date of IPO.

55688 ■ "IPO Aftermarket: New Issues Could Start to Gather Momentum in Spring" in *Venture Capital Journal* **(Vol. 42, No. 5, May 2002, pp. 59)**
Pub: Thomas Venture Economics
Description: A list of Initial Public Offerings with offering price, bid price, percent change, business description, and date of IPO is presented. Of the 35 venture-backed companies that went public between April 2001 and March 2002, 54 percent were trading at or above their IPO prices.

55689 ■ "IPO Aftermarket: New Issues Struggle to Overcome the Enron Effect" in *Venture Capital Journal* **(Vol. 42, No. 8, August 2002, pp. 50)**
Pub: Thomas Venture Economics
Description: A list of Initial Public Offerings with offering price, bid price, percent change, business description, and date of IPO is presented.

55690 ■ **"IPO Aftermarket" in** *Venture Capital Journal* **(Vol. 41, No. 8, August 2000, pp. 46-47)**
Pub: Venture Economics
Description: Between July 2000 and June 2001, 136 venture-backed companies went public with 39 trading at or above their initial public offering. Listing of the 136 IPOs is displayed. Statistical data included.

55691 ■ **"IPO Monitor" in** *Venture Capital Journal* **(Vol. 40, No. 10, November 2000, pp. 64)**
Pub: Venture Economics
Description: A listing of the 12 venture-backed companies that went public during the month of September 2000, raising a total of $1.154 billion.

55692 ■ **"IPO Review" in** *Red Herring* **(No. 99, June 15 & July 1, 2001, pp. 61)**
Pub: Herring Communications
Ed: Debbie Gravitz. **Description:** A look at last year's top Initial Public Offerings (IPOs), venture capital firms, and banks, before and after the fall of the economy.

55693 ■ **"IPO Scandal Means Venture Capitalists Need To Be More Vigilant" in** *Venture Capital Journal* **(Vol. 42, No. 10, October 2002, pp. 50)**
Pub: Thomas Venture Economics
Ed: Thomas C. McConnell. **Description:** Initial Public Offering practices are the latest business practices to come under regulatory, Congressional and media scrutiny.

55694 ■ **"IPOs/Recent Issues" in** *Venture Capital Journal* **(Vol. 42, No. 9, September 2002, pp. 44-45)**
Pub: Thomas Venture Economics
Description: Information on recent IPOs for BioDelivery Sciences International Inc., and Healthetech Inc. is provided.

55695 ■ **"IPOs Take a Break After a Big Year" in** *Venture Capital Journal* **(January 1, 2005)**
Pub: Thomason Financial Inc.
Ed: Lawrence Aragon. **Description:** Five venture-backed companies went public November 2004, causing the IPO market to slow some for the month; average deals for 2004 was $110 million, an increase of $38 million from same period 2003.

55696 ■ **"The IT Hot List: Leading VCs Say Where the Smart Money is Headed" in** *Venture Capital Journal* **(Vol. 40, No. 10, October 2000, pp. 4-46)**
Pub: Venture Economics
Ed: Alistair Christopher. **Description:** Forecasts for the next information technology sectors venture capital funds will be focused upon are presented. Wireless communications, optics, semiconductors and nanotechnology are discussed.

55697 ■ **"It's a Stretch" in** *Entrepreneur* **(Vol. 30, No. 1, January 2002, pp. 48)**
Pub: Entrepreneur Media Inc.
Ed: Mark Henricks. **Description:** The difficulty for small businesses to bridge the gap between a good product and enough capacity to fulfill the needs of big customers who can help grow a business. Expansion loans are difficult to procure for small businesses, especially in new technologies areas.

55698 ■ **"It's Time For Venture Capital Firms To Grow Up" in** *Venture Capital Journal* **(Vol. 42, No. 8, August 2002, pp. 38-39)**
Pub: Thomas Venture Economics
Ed: R. David Spreng. **Description:** Venture capital is moving from its beginnings as a cottage industry to a more mainstreamed asset class. The five traits of a next-generation venture capitalist are listed.

55699 ■ **"Jadi's Journey; Move to OU Incubator Could Lead to Funding" in** *Crain's Detroit Business* **(Vol. 22, January 9, 2006, No. 2, pp. 3)**
Pub: Crain Communications Inc. - Detroit

Ed: Sheena Harrison. **Description:** Jadi Inc. should receive $3 million in grants and federal funding for its new navigation systems for military robots. The firm has moved into the SmartZone Business Incubator at Oakland University in Michigan.

55700 ■ **"JSU Receives Record Funding" in** *Mississippi Business Journal* **(Vol. 28, September 2006, No. 36, pp. 23)**
Pub: Venture Publications, Inc.
Description: Jackson State University has been granted a record $56 million in research and other sponsored programs awards for the external funding of 175 projects from federal and state agencies.

55701 ■ **"Junkyard Blues" in** *Forbes* **(October 30, 2000, pp. 282)**
Pub: Forbes Magazine
Ed: Michael Freedman. **Description:** The difficulties small companies face trying to obtain financing are examined.

55702 ■ **"Just a Little Bit Public" in** *Inc.* **(August 2005, pp. 32, 34)**
Pub: Inc. Magazine
Ed: Jennifer Gill. **Description:** Private placements are on the rise as the stock market falters. Private placement expert, Mike Haider, CEO of BioE has raised $22.5 million from investors.

55703 ■ **"Kleiner Perkins Adds Lane As New GP" in** *Venture Capital Journal* **(Vol. 40, No. 10, October 2000, pp. 34)**
Pub: Venture Economics
Description: Raymond Lane, former chief operating officer at Oracle Corporation, has joined Kleiner, Perkins, Caufield & Byers. Lane will invest in all sectors, especially business-to-business, focusing on supply chain management.

55704 ■ **"The Launch" in** *Inc.* **(October 17, 2000, pp. 57)**
Pub: The Goldhirsh Group
Description: This article sites statistics including the Inc. 500 by sector, initial start-up capital, how CEOs raised that start-up capital, and the Top 10 fastest growing companies that were formed in 1995.

55705 ■ **"LDMI gets $15 million in venture capital funding" in** *Crain's Detroit Business* **(Vol. 16, No. 15, April 10, 2000, pp. 26)**
Pub: Crain Communications, Inc.
Ed: Matt Roush. **Description:** A Hamtramck, Michigan-based local and long-distance telephone company has received $15 million more in venture capital funding, to be used to expand services.

55706 ■ *The Lender Liability Deskbook*
Pub: Irwin Professional Publishing
Ed: Peter M. Edelstein. **Released:** 1992. **Price:** $35.00. **Description:** Provides information on the dealings between lenders and borrowers. Covers eight areas of law, including negligence, breach of contract, and fraudulent and nonfraudulent representation.

55707 ■ **"Let's Have Some Funds!" in** *Entrepreneur* **(Vol. 32, July 2004)**
Pub: Entrepreneur Media Inc.
Ed: Aliza Pilar Sherman. **Description:** Vicki Esralew and Shoba Purushothaman share insight into finding venture capital for women entrepreneurs.

55708 ■ **"Life Sciences Span The Globe: U.S. VCs Like to Spend Money in their Backyards" in** *Venture Capital Journal* **(October 1, 2004)**
Pub: Thomason Financial Inc.
Ed: Matthew Sheahan. **Description:** U.S. life science companies took about $3.6 billion in venture capital funding in 2004, more than 70 percent of the worldwide total, but Europe and Canada are working to attract these same companies. The cost advantages in both Canada and Europe are discussed.

55709 ■ **"Liquidity Events" in** *Fast Company* **(March 2005, No. 92, pp. 28)**
Pub: Gruner & Jahr USA Publishing

Ed: Jena McGregor. **Description:** The best bloggers offering insight and information into the world of venture capital are highlighted, including Feld Thoughts that gives information on negotiation techniques to software trends and The J Curve, and Beyond VC who provides advice on dealing with bad customers to running efficient board meetings.

55710 ■ **"Little Things Make a Big Difference at NanoOpto" in** *Venture Capital Journal* **(Vol. 42, No. 10, October 2002, pp. 33-34)**
Pub: Thomas Venture Economics
Ed: Ken Ryan. **Description:** The growing field of nanotechnology is examined.

55711 ■ **"Loan guarantees: costs of default and benefits to small firms" in** *Journal of Business Venturing* **(Vol. 16, No. 6, Nov. 2001, pp. 595)**
Pub: Elsevier Science, Inc.
Ed: Allan L. Riding, George Haines, Jr. **Description:** Research examining types of loan guarantees for the development of small firms is presented. Particular attention is given to international variations in default rates and cost benefits, with focus on the Canadian policy of loan guarantees.

55712 ■ **"Look for Early Stage Returns to Surge" in** *Venture Capital Journal* **(September 1, 2005)**
Pub: Thomasia Financial Inc.
Description: Experts predict an early return on investments for VCs over the next 15 years. Statistical data included.

55713 ■ **"L.P. Confidential" in** *Venture Capital Journal* **(Vol. 42, No. 8, August 2002, pp. 18-29)**
Pub: Thomas Venture Economics
Description: Four anonymous Limited Partners discuss current hot issues in the venture capital sector.

55714 ■ **"LPs Carry Their Weight Beyond Venture Capital" in** *Venture Capital Journal* **(Vol. 42, No. 9, September 2002, pp. 10-11)**
Pub: Thomas Venture Economics
Ed: Carolina Braunschweig. **Description:** A listing of the 10 venture capital firms making the most deals includes information on number of deals, investments and descriptions.

55715 ■ **"LPs Give Redpoint $1.25B Green Light" in** *Venture Capital Journal* **(Vol. 40, No. 10, October 2000, pp. 16, 17)**
Pub: Venture Economics
Description: Redpoint Ventures announced in August that it held a $1.25 billion final close on its second investment vehicle. The fund will focus on the type of Internet infrastructure plays that make up approximately 60 percent of Redpoint's current investments.

55716 ■ **"LPs Reconsider the Value of IRRs" in** *Venture Capital Journal* **(Vol. 42, No. 5, May 2002, pp. 5-6)**
Pub: Thomas Venture Economics
Ed: Carolina Braunschweig. **Description:** The Institutional Limited Partners Association (ILPA) wants to do away with the traditional method of using internal rates of return (IRRs), saying they are meaningless. Instead, the ILPA wants venture capital firms to adopt a "cash-in and cash-out" policy.

55717 ■ **"The Lure of Bay State Technology" in** *Boston Globe* **(February 7, 2005)**
Pub: New York Times Company
Ed: Robert Weisman. **Description:** Overseas investors are seeking acquisitions in Massachusetts, focusing on the state's high-technology and life sciences start-ups. Two deals are presented.

55718 ■ **"M/C Venture Partners Close on $550M" in** *Venture Capital Journal* **(Vol. 40, No. 10, November 2000, pp. 24, 26)**
Pub: Venture Economics
Description: M/C Venture Partners will us its latest vehicle, M/C Venture Partners V LP, to back nearly 30 companies with average initial investments between $15-$20 million. The firm will target early-stage communications services and information technology services companies, splitting capital evenly between the two sectors.

55719 ■ **"Make a List, Check it Twice: Can You Check Off All the Items on Your List?"** in *Entrepreneur* (Vol. 33, February 2005, pp. 92)

Pub: Entrepreneur Media Inc.

Ed: Guy Kawasaki. Description: Guy Kawasaki offers advice to entrepreneurs in developing business skills. His latest book, The Art of the Start: The Time-Tested, Battle-Hardened Guide for Anyone Starting Anything, offers his experience as an evangelist, entrepreneur, investment banker and venture capitalist.

55720 ■ **"Make Your Company an Idea Factory"** in *Fortune* (Vol. 141, No. 12, June 12, 2000, pp. 264N+)

Pub: Time Inc.

Description: Geoff Yang, venture capitalist, says there has never been a better time to back entrepreneurs who think their product or service is going to change the world.

55721 ■ **"Making sense of corporate venture capital"** in *Harvard Business Review* (Vol. 80, No. 3, March 2002, pp. 90)

Pub: Harvard Business School Press

Ed: Henry W. Chesbrough. Description: Corporate venture capital and a new framework that can help identify investments that will yield strategic growth is presented.

55722 ■ **"Making Life Easier Overseas; Export Assistance"** in *Crain's New York Business* (Vol. 22, November 13, 2006, No. 46, pp. 22)

Pub: Crain Communications, Inc.

Description: Listing of agencies that provide financial assistance and technical information for companies that sell goods overseas.

55723 ■ **"Making the Most of What You Have"** in *Success* (Vol. 47, No. 6, November 2000, pp. 26)

Pub: Success Publishing, Inc.

Ed: Scott Smith. Description: The head of the Jay Abraham Group in Los Angeles, who has fueled the growth of more than 10,000 companies in 400 industries around the world by rethinking the assumptions businesses make, shares some thoughts.

55724 ■ **"Marketing Quandary: VCs See a Growing Need for Differentiation"** in *Venture Capital Journal* (Vol. 41, No. 8, August 2000, pp. 31-33)

Pub: Venture Economics

Ed: Charles Fellers. Description: Marketing partners become a new addition to several venture capital firms by focusing on mentoring and promoting portfolio companies.

55725 ■ **"Med Tech Carl Goldfischer"** in *Venture Capital Journal* (January 1, 2005)

Pub: Thomason Financial Inc.

Description: According to Carl Goldfischer, managing director at Bay City Capital, the best thing that could happen to the medical device market in 2005 is that large and small companies continue creating new products that improve disease management.

55726 ■ **"Merger to Join Cambridge, Mass., Rivals in Anti-Aging Work"** in *Boston Globe* (January 14, 2003)

Pub: Knight Ridder/Tribune Business News

Ed: Jeffrey Krasner. Description: Two Cambridge, Massachusetts start-ups with technologies to discover the genetic factors behind aging, have announced a merger to create one single company in order to become a leader in the emerging field that will treat diseases of aging. A second round of venture funding is expected from the firms' original backers, which includes MPM Capital LP, Arch Venture Partners, and Oxford Bioscience Partners.

55727 ■ **"Milwaukee, Wis., to Host Biotech Finance Gathering in 2007"** in *Milwaukee Journal Sentinel* (December 14, 2005)

Pub: Journal Sentinel, Inc.

Ed: Kathleen Gallagher. Description: Venture capitalists representing more than $7 billion and biotech-

nology and medical device startups will meet in Milwaukee in September 2007 for the largest industry event in the Midwest. The BIO Med-America Venture-Forum expects 75 to 100 VCs to attend.

55728 ■ **"Minority Report"** in *Entrepreneur* (Vol. 32, October 2004, No. 10, pp. 59)

Pub: Entrepreneur Media Inc.

Ed: C.J. Prince. Description: Historically, women and minority-owned businesses have received less venture capital, with only 4.2 percent of all venture capital in 2003 going to women-led companies. The Kauffman Fellows Program educates and trains future venture capitalists and is led by 14 fellows, eight of which are from minority groups (two are black, five are Asian, and one is Middle Eastern, three are women).

55729 ■ **"Model behavior"** in *Entrepreneur* (Vol. 30, No. 3, March 2002, pp. 68)

Pub: Entrepreneur Media Inc.

Ed: David Newton. Description: Raising money for a growing company has taken a turn back to basics, opportunity and market share are no longer enough to secure capital; the business model, once again, plays a major role.

55730 ■ **"Mohr, Davidow Names New Partner, East Coast Presence"** in *Venture Capital Journal* (Vol. 40, No. 10, October 2000, pp. 34)

Pub: Venture Economics

Description: The article includes the announcement from Mohr, Davidow Ventures that the firm hired Partner Michael Sheridan to lead the company's effort to establish an East Coast presence.

55731 ■ **"Mohyr, Davidow Hires AOL Exec."** in *Venture Capital Journal* (Vol. 40, No. 10, November 2000, pp. 36)

Pub: Venture Economics

Description: Mohr, Davidow Ventures hired Debby Meredith, former senior vice president and chief of quality officer at America Online Inc, in early September 2000. The firm backs and helps develop start-up companies. Ms. Meredith will focus on Internet companies, software services and infrastructure and business-to-business spaces.

55732 ■ *Money for Entrepreneurs*

Pub: Alpha Publishing, Inc.

Price: $39.95.

55733 ■ **"Money Is Out There, But Where?"** in *Crain's Chicago Business* (Vol. 30, January 2007, No. 1, pp. 12)

Pub: Crain Communications, Inc.

Ed: Dee Gill. Description: Chicago is a great place to start a business and entrepreneurs have a wealth of free help, resources, and information available to them. Unfortunately, most have no idea these services even exist and as a result money set aside for small businesses never gets spent. SourceLink is one such service that can help entrepreneurs find those resources.

55734 ■ **"Money Matters"** in *Small Business Opportunities* (Vol. 13, No. 5, September 2001, pp. 10)

Pub: Harris Publications, Inc.

Ed: Carla Vincent. Description: Ways for small businesses to generate venture capital are explored, including a list of government agencies that provide small business funding.

55735 ■ **"Money Talks to New Economy Firms: More Startups Choose Chicago for Home Base"** in *Crain's Chicago Business* (Vol. 23, Nov. 27, 2000)

Pub: Crain Communications, Inc. Crain Communications, Inc.

Ed: Judith Nemes. Description: More new economy startups are choosing Chicago to headquarter their new businesses, partly because of the huge influx of venture capital targeting that sector.

55736 ■ **"Montana Champion Again, Joins F-of-F"** in *Venture Capital Journal* (Vol. 40, No. 10, November 2000, pp. 8, 9)

Pub: Venture Economics

Description: Champion Ventures, the investment firm that invests in other venture capital funds, was founded in 1999 by San Francisco 49ers Ronnie Lott and Harris Barton. In mid-September 2000, Joe Montana joined the firm as a general partner.

55737 ■ **"The Month in Review: Who Made News?"** in *Venture Capital Journal* (Vol. 42, No. 5, May 2002, pp. 15, 16-17)

Pub: Thomas Venture Economics

Description: Abstracts of stories from the pages of the VCJ's sister publication, Private Equity Week, are presented. A Web address is provided to see entire stories.

55738 ■ **"The Most Successful VC Isn't Who You Think"** in *Fortune* (Vol. 142, No. 10, October 30, 2000, pp. 56)

Pub: Time Inc.

Ed: Melanie Warner. Description: Five years ago, if you asked people to name the Valley's top ten venture capitalists, Vinod Khosla probably would not have made the list. A profile of Vinod Khosla, a partner at Kleiner Perkins, whose investments have been so lucrative that he now holds the unofficial distinction of being the most successful venture capitalist of all times.

55739 ■ **"Mr. Cashman, You're On"** in *Inc.* (Volume 27, July 2005, No. 7, pp. 100-102, 104)

Pub: Inc. Magazine

Ed: Jim Melloan. Description: Entrpreneur, Chris Cashman, is looking for $500,000 in venture capital for his Protez Pharmaceuticals firm. Protez is currently working on four different drug technologies.

55740 ■ **"My Life as a Blogger: A Growing Number of VCs Are Opening Themselves Up in Online Diaries"** in *Venture Capital Journal* (Jan. 1, 2005)

Pub: Thomason Financial Inc.

Ed: Tom Stein. Description: Information about the new blog-related technologies and startup companies emerging is shared. Currently there are about twelve venture-related blogs on the Internet.

55741 ■ **"The Myth of the Superstar CEO"** in *Venture Capital Journal* (November 1, 2004)

Pub: Thomason Financial Inc.

Ed: Ravi Chiruvolu. Description: PeopleSoft, the enterprise software company, replaced its CEO Craig Conway with founder and chairman, Dave Duffield. Whether a superstar CEO is worth the time, effort and additional equity required to retain him or her is addressed.

55742 ■ **"Nanotech Steve Jurvetson"** in *Venture Capital Journal* (January 1, 2005)

Pub: Thomason Financial Inc.

Description: Steve Jurvetson's firm Draper Fisher Jurvetson, has invested in more than 20 nanotech, MEMS and novel materials startups. Jurvetson suggests the best thing to happen to the nanotechnology sector in 2005 would be a major restructuring of immigration and education policy to prioritize science and engineering, the worst, more federal restrictions on immigration or freedom of scientific research like stem cell policy.

55743 ■ *National Venture Capital Association—Membership Directory*

Pub: National Venture Capital Association

Contact: Molly M. Myers, V

Released: Annual, January. Price: $175 hard copy; $300 CD-ROM, one-user license. Covers: 450 venture capital firms, including subsidiaries of banks and insurance companies. Entries Include: Firm name, address, phone, contact names, fax number, investment preferences. Arrangement: Alphabetical. Indexes: Contact name.

55744 ■ "Nature Brings Uncertainty and Opportunity" in *Venture Capital Journal* **(October 1, 2005)**
Pub: Thomason Financial Inc.
Description: Impacts of Hurricane Katrina and the passing of Chief Justice William Rehnquist on the venture capital sector are discussed. In the first half of 2005, VCs had already invested $239.6 million in alternative energy companies up nearly $40 million over last year.

55745 ■ "Navigation-Technology Startup Seeks Investors" in *Portland Press Herald* **(August 5, 2005)**
Pub: Blethen Maine Newspapers, Inc.
Ed: Matt Wickenheiser. **Description:** Profile of Zachariah Conover, founder of CrossRate Technology LLC. Conover returned to his hometown after earning his MBA at Drexel University in Pennsylvania. He hired two childhood friends and is seeking investors for his backup device for a global positioning system.

55746 ■ "NEA Fund 10 $2B Hard Cap" in *Venture Capital Journal* **(Vol. 40, No. 10, October 2000, pp. 18, 20, 22)**
Pub: Venture Economics
Description: NEA will continue targeting start-up companies in the information technology, communications, software, B-to-B e-commerce and semiconductor sectors, as well as medical, biotech and life sciences companies.

55747 ■ "A New Century for Start-ups" in *Hispanic Business* **(Vol. 22, No. 3, March 2000, pp. 54)**
Pub: Hispanic Business
Ed: Christopher D. Lancette. **Description:** The importance of a comprehensive business plan to the successful winning of venture capital backing are explored. The calculation of required start-up capital is often underestimated and often results in business failure.

55748 ■ "New Ethics or No Ethics? Questionable behavior is Silicon Valley's next big thing" in *Fortune* **(Vol. 141, No. 6, Mar. 20, 2000, pp. 82)**
Pub: Time Inc.
Ed: Jerry Useem. **Description:** Eventually our deeper values catch up to the new worlds we create. In the meantime, there will be a lot of shenanigans.

55749 ■ "New Media Venture Partners" in *Venture Capital Journal* **(Vol. 40, No. 10, October 2000, pp. 52-53)**
Pub: Venture Economics
Description: Profile of New Media Venture Partners (NMVP), the fast growing digital media holding company focused on investing in and developing core technologies, the next phase of the Internet - the development and distribution of digital media and content. A listing of NMVP's portfolio companies is included.

55750 ■ "New venture strategy and profitability: a venture capitalist's assessment" in *Journal of Business Venturing* **(Vol. 15, No. 5-6)**
Pub: Elsevier Science, Inc.
Ed: Dean A. Shepherd, Richard Ettenson, Andrew Crouch. **Description:** A new study investigates decision-making policies of venture capitalists.

55751 ■ "New SEC Rules Regarding Selective Disclosure and Insider Trading Increase Risks" in *Venture Capital Journal* **(Vol.40, No.10, Oct. 2000)**
Pub: Venture Economics
Description: In depth report examining the Regulation Fair Disclosure (FD), issued by the Securities and Exchange Commission, and two new insider trading rules.

55752 ■ "A new venue for seeking capital" in *BlackEnterprise* **(Vol. 32, No. 3, October 2001, pp. 56)**
Pub: Earl Graves Publishing Co.
Ed: Paula McCoy-Pinderhughes. **Description:** The first-ever three-day conference aimed at helping African American and other minority technology-based businesses was held in Chantilly, Fairfax County, Virginia, from July 11-13, 2001. The Emerging Business Forum (EBF) will host its second conference next fall.

55753 ■ "New Wireless Service to Debut in 2006" in *Crain's Detroit Business* **(Vol. 21, October 10, 2005, No. 43, pp. 1)**
Pub: Crain Communications Inc. - Detroit
Ed: Andrew Dietderich. **Description:** As part of a $739 million investment in MetroPCS Inc., two buyout and private-equity firms are backing the startup of a new wireless service planned for the Detroit area; the plan also includes opening as many as 12 company-owned stores in metropolitan Detroit, Michigan.

55754 ■ "The Next Big Trend: Cutting Mgmt. Fees" in *Venture Capital Journal* **(Vol. 42, No. 9, September 2002, pp. 6, 8-9)**
Pub: Thomas Venture Economics
Ed: Lawrence Aragon. **Description:** Private equity firms are planning to cut fees or work out new fee arrangements with limited partners. VantagePoint Venture Partners' plans to defer fees for 18 months on its $1.6 billion Fund IV.

55755 ■ "No mercy: are VCs sucking the life out of your business?" in *Entrepreneur* **(Vol. 30, No. 12, December 2002, pp. 79)**
Pub: Entrepreneur Media Inc.
Ed: C.J. Prince. **Description:** Difficulties small businesses encounter in finding venture capital backing during a poor economy are discussed.

55756 ■ "Northern Exposure: American Entrepreneurs are Finding Success by Heading for the Border" in *Entrepreneur* **(Vol. 31, August 2003)**
Pub: Entrepreneur Media, Inc.
Ed: Joshua Kurlantzick. **Description:** Canada is becoming more attractive to entrepreneurs because Canada has recorded the strongest economic growth of any industrialized nation in the past two years. Venture capitalists in Canada are usually more generous than those in the U.S.

55757 ■ "Not So Fast! Raising Money: Seeking an Investor?" in *Entrepreneur* **(Vol. 31, No. 9, September 2003, pp. 55)**
Pub: Entrepreneur Media, Inc.
Ed: David Worrell. **Description:** Profile of Bob Shallenberger, owner of Highland Homes of Saint Louis, who never needed an investor until 2003. Shallenberger stresses the need to take time when finding an investor.

55758 ■ "Nth Power Energizes New $120M Fund" in *Venture Capital Journal* **(Vol. 40, No. 10, November 2000, pp. 26, 28)**
Pub: Venture Economics
Description: With its new close, Nth Power Technologies Inc., intends to maintain its investment focus on distributed energy and storage, energy-related communications, power quality and transmission, and distribution automation.

55759 ■ "NY Metro Gets $388M in Fourth-Quarter Venture Funds, Survey Says" in *Long Island Business News* **(February 20, 2004)**
Pub: Dolan Media Newswires
Ed: Ken Schachter. **Description:** The Money Tree survey conducted by PricewaterhouseCoopers, Venture Economics and the National Venture Capital Association, reported companies received $388 million fourth quarter 2003, up 9 percent over same period 2002. Statistical data included.

55760 ■ "Obesity Whets VC Appetites" in *Inc.* **(Volume 27, June 2005, No. 6, pp. 26)**
Pub: Inc. Magazine
Ed: Michelle Leder. **Description:** Venture capitalists have invested millions in six anti-obesity companies in the past year.

55761 ■ *Obtaining Venture Financing: Principles & Practices*
Pub: The Free Press
Ed: James W. Henderson. **Released:** 1991. **Price:** $16.95 (paper).

55762 ■ "The Old Guard" in *Venture Capital Journal* **(Vol. 42, No. 10, October 2002, pp. 24-30)**
Pub: Thomas Venture Economics
Ed: Peter D. Henig. **Description:** Reid Dennis, Bill Draper, Pitch Johnson, Arthur Rock and Paul Wythes, better known as the "Old Guard" pioneered the venture capital business. The Old Guard offers advice on how to get the venture capital industry back on track.

55763 ■ "Older firm gets venture funds" in *Wall Street Journal* **(March 25, 2003, pp. B4)**
Pub: Dow Jones & Co. Inc.
Ed: Raymond Hennessey. **Description:** Because of the low number of initial public offerings, older firms are receiving venture capital.

55764 ■ "OneLiberty Ventures Wraps On $200M" in *Venture Capital Journal* **(Vol. 40, No. 10, October 2000, pp. 26)**
Pub: Venture Economics
Description: OneLiberty Ventures held a $200 million final close in June on OneLiberty Ventures 2000 LP, and will back early-stage information technology and medical technology companies.

55765 ■ "Online Markets for Private Equity Enter Second Season" in *Venture Capital Journal* **(Vol. 40, No. 10, November 2000, pp. 50)**
Pub: Venture Economics
Ed: George B. Moriarty. **Description:** Several new Web sites have been launched by private equity professionals who intend to take the relationship with the Internet beyond a profit experience.

55766 ■ "Opening the Door to VC" in *Hispanic Business* **(Vol. 23, No. 7/8, July/August 2001, pp. 66)**
Pub: Hispanic Business
Ed: Christopher D. Lancette. **Description:** I-DealFlow, a national coalition of business and organizations, will sponsor a venture capital fair November 2, 2001 in Atlanta, Georgia. The coalition includes such members as AOL Time Warner, the Wall Street Project, the U.S Hispanic Chamber of Commerce (USHCC), and the Telecommunications Development Fund.

55767 ■ "The Opportunity is Knocking" in *Black Enterprise* **(Vol. 34, No. 7, February 2004)**
Pub: Earl Graves Publishing Co.
Description: The 2004 "Black Enterprise/General Motors Entrepreneurs Conference" will be held in Dallas, Texas. This year's theme will be, "Taking Business Beyond Boundaries", and will present industry experts, venture capitalists, and entrepreneurs. The event is geared to provide information and inspiration for African American executives, professionals, entrepreneurs, and wealth-accumulators.

55768 ■ "The Overhand Shrinks, But Does It Matter?" in *Venture Capital Journal* **(July 1, 2003)**
Pub: Thomson Financial Inc.
Description: Because of many fund reductions and little new fundraising, the venture capital overhang dropped by 13 percent to $84 billion in 2002. However, venture capitalists are predicting the overhang to grow smaller over 2003 because of increased deals taking advantaged of the falling valuations.

55769 ■ "Pacific Life Insurance Committed to Secondaries" in *Venture Capital Journal* **(Vol. 41, No. 8, August 2000, pp. 41)**
Pub: Venture Economics
Ed: Alistair Christopher. **Description:** Profile of Pacific Life Insurance located in Newport Beach, California, whose private equity portfolio consisting of 32 percent buyout/growth capital funds, 30 percent venture vehicles, 20 percent international funds, 12 percent specialty sector funds vehicles, and 6 percent mezzanine funds.

55770 ■ "Papermaster in startup mode" in *Austin Business Journal* (Vol. 22, No. 28, September 27, 2002, pp. 1)
Pub: Austin Business Journal Inc.
Ed: Spacey Higginbotham. **Description:** Steve Papermaster's software company Agillion Inc. was sold at auction when dot-com companies crashed. He is back now as chairman of a high tech business company formed through incubator Powershift Ventures LLP, and co-investor with Azure Capital Partners LP, called CooperaTech Inc., which develops risk and opportunity management software.

55771 ■ "Patent Pitfalls for Early Stage Investors" in *Venture Capital Journal* (November 1, 2004)
Pub: Thomason Financial Inc.
Ed: M. Sharon Webb. **Description:** Investors need to understand that a company's patent portfolio might include patents that are not necessarily owned by the firm. It is important for the investor to be sure all patents presented in a portfolio are actually owned by the company they will be investing in.

55772 ■ "Patient Capital: How Life Sciences Investments Touch Us All" in *Venture Capital Journal* (December 1, 2004)
Pub: Thomason Financial Inc.
Description: National Venture Capital Association's report explains the role venture capital plays in the expansion and enhancement of health and medical systems. The venture capital industry has invested almost $41 billion in more than 6,600 biotechnology and medical device companies in the last 20 years. Statistical data included.

55773 ■ "PE Returns Set To Turn Up in 2nd Half" in *Venture Capital Journal* (July 1, 2003)
Pub: Thomson Financial Inc.
Description: An overview of the venture capital industry is presented. Private equity returns are expected to rise in the second half of 2003. Results of the VE/NVCA survey are included.

55774 ■ "A Perfect Match?" in *Entrepreneur* (Vol. 31, No. 10, October 2003, pp. 60)
Pub: Entrepreneur Media, Inc.
Ed: Crystal Detamore-Rodman. **Description:** Profile of Ahmed and Reem Rahim, brother and sister entrepreneurs, and their first step in the half-million dollar expansion of their organic tea company.

55775 ■ "The Perfect Pitch" in *Hispanic Business* (March 2005, pp. 38, 40)
Pub: Hispanic Business
Ed: Scott Williams. **Description:** Tracy Lefteroff, global managing partner of VC arm of PriceWaterhouseCoopers believes it is a great time to be an entrepreneur. Pointers to help entrepreneurs win over private equity investors are shared. Statistical data included.

55776 ■ "Peter Falvey: Whiz Kid: Peter Falvey is Betting the Company on Tech Investment" in *Boston Business Journal* (Vol. 23, July 11, 2003)
Pub: American City Business Journals
Ed: Edward Mason. **Description:** Revolution Partners focuses on high technology investment; profile of the investment bank's co-founder Peter Falvey is included.

55777 ■ "Planning for Gold" in *Entrepreneur* (Vol. 32, November 2004, No. 11, pp. 112)
Pub: Entrepreneur Media Inc.
Ed: Nichole L. Torres. **Description:** Business plan competitions are growing in popularity. In order for entrepreneurs to cash in and win cash, services or venture capital they must understand the process. Many of the competitions are associated with university MBA programs, but there are also those produced by communities, which are open to anyone in the local area or a particular business sector.

55778 ■ "Pond Venture Partners Closes $78M Fund II" in *Venture Capital Journal* (Vol. 40, No. 10, October 2000, pp. 24, 26)
Pub: Venture Economics
Description: Pond Venture Partners Ltd. will focus its investments into early-stage communications companies, including firms in Western Europe.

55779 ■ "Portfolio D&O Insurance Can Leave Outside Directors in the Cold" in *Venture Capital Journal* (October 1, 2005)
Pub: Thomason Financial Inc.
Description: The need for liability insurance to cover directors of public and private portfolio companies is stressed. The article sites a lawsuit against Benchmark Capital.

55780 ■ "The potential of actuarial decision models: can they improve the venture capital investment decision" in *Journal of Business Venturing*
Pub: Elsevier Science, Inc.
Ed: Andrew L. Zacharakis, G. Dale Meyer. **Description:** Issues are presented concerning the ability of venture capitalists to identify the risks associated with hazardous investment opportunities and the benefits of potential future gains. The use of actuarial decision models is discussed.

55781 ■ "Primus Fund V Eyes $250M Close" in *Venture Capital Journal* (Vol. 40, No. 10, October 2000, pp. 22, 24)
Pub: Venture Economics
Description: The Primus Fund V will focus on four industry sectors: telecommunications, Internet/e-commerce, out-sourced business services, and health care.

55782 ■ "Private Equity Firms Help Hurricane Victims" in *Buyouts* (October 3, 2005)
Pub: Thomson Financial Inc.
Ed: Matthew Sheahan. **Description:** Private equity firms, along with their portfolio companies, reached out to help victims of Hurricanes Katrina and Rita through relief efforts.

55783 ■ "Private Investors Purchase a Controlling Stake at Ecoboard Holdings" in *Long Island Business News* (February 13, 2004)
Pub: Dolan Media Newswires
Ed: Ben Abelson. **Description:** Ecoboard Holdings Inc., manufacturer of plastic lumber, has raised nearly $750,000 from Long Island Capital Alliance's annual venture capital forum. The company's products are used mainly for outdoor applications such as decks, bridges, and piers.

55784 ■ "Private Lives" in *Inc.* (October 2005, pp. 84)
Pub: Inc. Magazine
Ed: Lora Koldony. **Description:** Adam Seifer, CEO of Fotolog, the New York City-based photo company, places photos of every meal he's eaten in the last three years on his Internet blog. Seifer started the blog when he launched his business, which hosts millions of photoblogs for other companies.

55785 ■ "Private venture capital sources in Michigan" in *Crain's Detroit Business* (Vol. 16, No. 19, May 8, 2000, pp. 17)
Pub: Crain Communications, Inc.
Description: A list of Michigan offices that make available venture capital and other kinds of private start-up and working capital to small companies. The list includes private venture companies, small-business investment companies, business and industrial development corporations (Bidcos), and other entities.

55786 ■ "Profile: Alan Patricof as entrepreneurial curmudgeon" in *Red Herring* (No. 103, September 1, 2001, pp. 38, 40)
Pub: Herring Communications
Ed: Julia Lawlor **Description:** Profile of venture capitalist, Alan Patricof, the chairman of Patricof & Co. Ventures.

55787 ■ "Public opinion" in *Entrepreneur* (Vol. 30, No. 10, October 2002, pp. 76)
Pub: Entrepreneur Media Inc.
Ed: Jennifer Pellet. **Description:** Issues currently facing companies that wish to file an Initial Public Offering are discussed. The first quarter 2002 saw only 15 firms go from private to public.

55788 ■ "Putting their money where the future is" in *The New York Times* (March 27, 2000, pp. D3, H3)
Pub: The New York Times Company
Ed: Jonathan Burton. **Description:** Venture capitalists and e-commerce is discussed. Statistical data included.

55789 ■ "PVC Index" in *Venture Capital Journal* (October 1, 2005)
Pub: Thomason Financial Inc.
Description: A presentation of the Thomson Venture Economics Post-Venture Capital Index (PVCI) includes a market-valued index measuring the performance of public stocks of companies receiving venture capital or buyout financing. The index represents 667 companies and tracks the stocks from point going public and traded for ten years.

55790 ■ "QuatRx uses $10M in venture capital for psoriasis drug" in *Crain's Detroit Business* (Vol. 19, No. 12, March 24, 2003, pp. 12)
Pub: Crain Communications Inc., Detroit
Ed: Renee Saunders. **Description:** QuatRx, a biopharmaceutical company located in Ann Arbor, Michigan, hopes that the recent $10 million venture capital financing received will help find a cure for psoriasis and other ailments.

55791 ■ "Quest for the Next Great Search Company" in *Venture Capital Journal* (December 1, 2004)
Pub: Thomason Financial Inc.
Ed: Katherine Heires. **Description:** Venture capital firms are investing in Internet search companies to the tune of $67 million in 15 companies for the first part of 2004. Google's initial public offering is fueling the trend to invest in Web search startups.

55792 ■ "Quicker SBA Loans" in *Business Week* (No. 3698, September 11, 2000, pp. F6)
Pub: McGraw-Hill, Inc.
Description: The Small Business Administration plans to enlarge its Community Express pilot program, which aims to streamline loan reviews for companies in low-income areas or those owned by minorities, women, or veterans.

55793 ■ *The Radical New Road to Wealth: How to Raise Venture Capital for a New Business*
Pub: International Wealth Success, Inc.
Ed: David A Silver. **Released:** 1996. **Price:** $15.00.

55794 ■ *Raising Capital*
Pub: Raising Capital
Ed: Andrew J. Sherman. **Price:** $34.95.

55795 ■ *Raising Capital: How to Write a Financing Proposal to Raise Venture Capital*
Pub: PSI Research
Ed: Lawrence Flanagan. **Released:** 1997. **Price:** $39.95 (ringbound); $19.95 (paper).

55796 ■ *Raising Capital for Your Business: By Using Private Placement Offerings, Direct Public Offerings*
Pub: Griffin Publishing
Ed: Michael N. Brette. **Released:** 1998. **Price:** $18.95.

55797 ■ *Raising Money to Start of Expand Your Business Through a SCOR*
Pub: Infoware
Ed: Eileen Savid. **Released:** 1997. **Price:** $34.00 (spiral).

55798 ■ "Ray of hope?" in *Entrepreneur* **(Vol. 31, No. 5, May 2003, pp. 45)**
Pub: Entrepreneur Media Inc.
Ed: C.J. Prince. Description: With $21.2 billion of venture capital invested in 2002, the year finished at the same level as 1998. A greater number of later-stage companies and those seeking expansion capital, rather than startups, received funding.

55799 ■ "Reality Checker" in *Forbes* **(February 19, 2001, pp. 95)**
Pub: Forbes Magazine
Ed: Jennifer Godwin. Description: A profile of Joseph W. Goodman, a retired electrical engineer, who has become a consultant for venture capital firms.

55800 ■ "Rebuilding and Revitalizing Lower Manhattan" in *Venture Capital Journal* **(Vol. 42, No. 9, September 2002, pp. 32)**
Pub: Thomas Venture Economics
Ed: Sheldon Silver. Description: Sheldon Silver, Speaker of the New York State Assembly, and represents the largest part of Silicon Alley, shares insight into the rebuilding and revitalizing of the Lower Manhattan area of New York after the terrorist attacks of September 11.

55801 ■ "Recovering from Tragedy - How Alta Has Coped with Losses" in *Venture Capital Journal* **(Vol. 42, No. 9, September 2002, pp. 24-25)**
Pub: Thomas Venture Economics
Ed: Dan Primack. Description: Ways in which members of Alta Communications has coped in the aftermath of the terrorist attacks of 9/11 are discussed. Along with raising its new fund in a down market, each partner is very proud of their newly created foundation honoring two of their colleagues lost in the tragedy.

55802 ■ "Redleaf, UPenn Launch PenNetWorks" in *Venture Capital Journal* **(Vol. 40, No. 10, October 2000, pp. 6, 8)**
Pub: Venture Economics
Description: The technology operating company, Redleaf Group Inc., partnered with the University of Pennsylvania in August to form PenNetWorks, an on-campus Internet accelerator. The accelerator is owned by the University and managed by Redleaf.

55803 ■ "Relief Is Finally Coming with A Rise in M&A" in *Venture Capital Journal* **(July 1, 2003)**
Pub: Thomson Financial Inc.
Description: According to experts, mergers and acquisitions are expected to rise over the next year and a half, thus reinforcing the role of the venture capitalist by promoting the growth of promising new technology companies, and also making money for entrepreneurs, employees and limited partners. Statistical data included.

55804 ■ "Renal Solutions" in *Pittsburgh Business Times* **(Vol. 22, No. 51, July 4, 2003, pp. 1)**
Pub: Pittsburgh Business Times
Ed: Patty Tascarella. Description: Renal Solutions Inc., led by CEO Peter DeComo, has received $2 million in venture capital funding. The firm raised nearly $16.7 million in first round venture capital funding.

55805 ■ "Reporter's Notebook; The Question of Private Equity" in *Crain's Detroit Business* **(Vol. 23, January 29, 2007, No. 5, pp. 11)**
Pub: Crain Communications Inc. - Detroit
Ed: Brent Snaveley. Description: Many smaller auto suppliers have been purchased by private equity and hedge funds. This may not be in the best interests of the supplier company or the customer, but may be necessary for survival.

55806 ■ "Resources: Web Sites, Organizations, Events and More To Grow Your Business" in *Entrepreneur* **(Vol. 32, September 2004, No. 9, pp. 8)**
Pub: Entrepreneur Media Inc.
Ed: Steve Cooper. Description: Resources to help small business are featured including the Small Busi-

ness Administration's effort to help teen entrepreneurs launch a business; KnockNow an online community of entrepreneurs, executives, venture capitalists, angel investors, service sector companies, and government; the SBA's business Website offering information on small business development, financial assistance, taxes, laws and regulations, international trade, workplace issues, buying and selling and federal forms.

55807 ■ "The Reverse Greenhouse Effect: Why pay another to gardener to cultivate your stock?" in *Fortune* **(Vol.141, No.7, Apr. 3, 2000, pp.302)**
Pub: Time Inc.
Ed: Adam Lashinsky. Description: Incubators are a lot like venture capital firms, at least in what they set out to accomplish. But incubators take a holistic approach by anticipating all of a startup's needs from the get-go.

55808 ■ "RFID Due Diligence: RFID Technologies Hold Great Promise for VCs" in *Venture Capital Journal* **(January 1, 2005)**
Pub: Thomason Financial Inc.
Description: Radio frequency identification (RFID) investing requires an understanding of the markets the technology serves. RFID technology is composed of three components: tags that can store data about anything as well as transmit and receive that data over low or high frequencies; an infrastructure platform that creates a wireless network whereby data can be transmitted and received; and a software solutions component that can then manipulate and analyze that data, store it and share it with existing software systems.

55809 ■ "The Right Fit" in *Entrepreneur* **(Vol. 33, September 2005, No. 9, pp. 58)**
Pub: Entrepreneur Media Inc.
Ed: Description: Word-of-mouth through networking with angel investors, venture capitalists and larger private equity groups will help entrepreneurs to learn about these boutiques who partner with small companies.

55810 ■ "Right on the Money?" in *Fast Company* **(May 2001, pp. 42)**
Pub: Fast Company
Ed: Linda Tischler. Description: Discussions from a bimonthly FastTalk event are featured. The topic for the January meeting was 'Winning in Tough and Turbulent Times', and covered venture capital.

55811 ■ "Riparian Unveils Village Ventures' R.I. Fund" in *Venture Capital Journal* **(Vol. 40, No. 10, November 2000, pp. 20)**
Pub: Venture Economics
Description: The investment banking firm, Riparian Partners, will back technology-related companies in high-growth industries, including telecommunications, Internet plays, some medical technology companies, and marine-related technologies.

55812 ■ "Rising Drug Costs" in *Venture Capital Journal* **(October 1, 2204)**
Pub: Thomason Financial Inc.
Ed: Alastair Goldfisher. Description: With the rising costs of conducting clinical trials of new drugs, technology companies may choose offshore outsourcing of research and development to save money. However, the cost of new drug development is rising worldwide. Statistical data included.

55813 ■ "Running Dry" in *Entrepreneur* **(Vol. 33, August 2005, No. 8, pp. 20)**
Pub: Entrepreneur Media Inc.
Ed: Crystal Detamore-Rodman. Description: The U.S. government's Small Business Investment Company (SBIC) provides equity capital to entrepreneurs. Currently the SBIC Participating Securities Program provides as much as $2 for every $1 of capital raised by venture funds licensed by the SBA; this program is in jeopardy of being discontinued.

55814 ■ "Sarbanes-Oxley: A Guide for Venture Capitalists" in *Venture Capital Journal* **(November 1, 2004)**
Pub: Thomason Financial Inc.
Description: An overview of the Sarbanes Oxley Act (SOX) and how it relates to venture capitalists is presented. SOX is legislation passed by Congress in 2002 to deter and punish corporate accounting fraud and corruption.

55815 ■ "SBA Suspends VC Program, Future in Doubt" in *Venture Capital Journal* **(January 1, 2005)**
Pub: Thomason Financial Inc.
Description: Faced with nearly $2 billion in losses, the Small Business Administration's Small Business Investment Companies (SBIC) program will stop licensing new SBIC firms until October 1, 2005. The program provides about one-fifth of U.S. venture funds.

55816 ■ "SBV Venture Partners Eyes $75M First Fund" in *Venture Capital Journal* **(Vol. 40, No. 10, November 2000, pp. 24)**
Pub: Venture Economics
Description: SBV Venture Partners aimed for a late fall or early 2001 second close for its inaugural fund and the fund's companion vehicle. The two funds Sigefi Burnette & Vallee I and Sigefi, Burnette & Vallee IA, considered one vehicle by the firm, will focus primarily on network infrastructure companies and companies arising from the convergence between communications and computing.

55817 ■ "Secondaries Jay Pierrepont" in *Venture Capital Journal* **(January 1, 2005)**
Pub: Thomason Financial Inc.
Description: In an interview, Jay Pierrepont discusses the secondaries market. Pierrepont makes his predictions for the best and worst things that could happen to the consumer market it 2005.

55818 ■ "Secondaries Ready For The Big Leagues" in *Venture Capital Journal* **(July 1, 2003)**
Pub: Thomson Financial Inc.
Description: The lack of corporate buying and a weak IPO market are leaving funds with little or no opportunity to improve returns. Statistical data included.

55819 ■ "Seeing Green" in *Entrepreneur*
Pub: Entrepreneur Media Inc.
Ed: Tracy T. Lefteroff. Description: An overview of Entrepreneur's 4th Annual Venture Capital 100 is presented. The listing will help entrepreneurs find the best investor for their businesses.

55820 ■ "Seller Expectations" in *Venture Capital Journal* **(July 1, 2003)**
Pub: Thomson Financial Inc.
Description: Seller expectations in the venture capital industry are discussed.

55821 ■ "Semiconductors Pierre Lamond" in *Venture Capital Journal* **(January 1, 2005)**
Pub: Thomason Financial Inc.
Description: Pierre Lamond shares insight into the best and worst that could happen to the semiconductor industry for 2005. Lamond believes continued growth in the global economy is essential.

55822 ■ "Series A, For Arthritis: Proprius Pharmaceuticals Inc." in *San Diego Business Journal* **(Vol. 28, January 15, 2007, No. 3, pp. 38)**
Pub: San Diego Business Journal Associates
Ed: Brad Graves. Description: Atlas Venture of Waltham, Massachusetts and Forward Ventures of San Diego provided venture capital to Proprius Pharmaceuticals Inc. in order to develop a drug to treat osteoarthritis. Series A funding equaled $11 million and may grow to $17 million.

55823 ■ "Show Me the Money!" in *Success* **(Vol. 47, No. 6, November 2000, pp. 60)**
Pub: Success Publishing, Inc.
Ed: Phil Garfinkle. Description: Many companies are unable to secure financing, not because of a flaw in

their business, but because of flaws in how they approach the capital formation process. A listing of some of the most common gaffes, and the steps entrepreneurs should take to avoid them.

55824 ■ "Signal Strength" in *Entrepreneur* (Vol. 33, March 2005, No. 3, pp. 18)
Pub: Entrepreneur Media Inc.
Ed: John F. Ince. **Description:** Venture capital firms are ramping up marketing efforts by hiring public relations firms to promote their portfolio companies and full-time marketing consultants to introduce their names to prospective entrepreneurs.

55825 ■ "Six Degrees of Separation" in *Venture Capital Journal* (October 1, 2005)
Pub: Thomason Financial Inc.
Description: Isaac Applebaum has resigned from Lightspeed Venture Partners in order to form his own firm with two other partners.

55826 ■ "SmaL Camera Technologies Snaps Up $13.5M in V.C." in *Boston Business Journal* (Vol. 23, No. 27, August 8, 2003, pp. 21)
Pub: American City Business Journals
Ed: Tom Witkowski. **Description:** The operations and growth of SmaL Camera Technologies and its securing of $13.5 million in venture capital are discussed.

55827 ■ "Small Business Advisor: Choose kids' or collectors' market" in *Crain's Chicago Business* (Vol. 23, November 13, 2000, pp. SB17)
Pub: Crain Communications, Inc. Crain
Communications, Inc.
Ed: Warren Denniston. **Description:** Checkerboard Toys Inc. faces numerous challenges, including business focus and capital funding.

55828 ■ *Small Business Financing: How & Where to Get It*
Pub: CCH Inc.
Ed: Alice H. Magos, SmallOffice Home Office Editorial Group Staff; illustrated by Tim Kaage, introduction by Martin Bush. **Released:** 1998. **Price:** $17.95.

55829 ■ *Small Business Guide to Borrowing Money*
Pub: Bell Springs Publishing
Ed: R. Rubin and P. Goldberg. **Price:** 18.95. **Description:** Small business owners know that financing is often hard to find, until you know where to look and how to apply. Here are the sources of financing you may never have considered or known about. Includes information about how to prepare a first-class loan application, how to obtain favorable action, and how to settle the best terms.

55830 ■ *The Small Business Money Guide: How to Get It, Use It, Keep It*
Pub: John Wiley & Sons, Inc.
Ed: Terri Lonier and Lisa M. Aldisert. **Released:** 1998.
Price: $16.95.

55831 ■ "Small Business Resource Guide: Service Providers: Part 1 of 2" in *Crain's Detroit Business* (Vol. 15, No. 50, Dec. 13, 1999, pp. E-11)
Pub: Crain Communications, Inc.
Description: The Michigan Economic Development Corporation is the State of Michigan's one-stop resource for businesses seeking growth in the state. Includes a listing of the SBA's programs and contact information.

55832 ■ "Small Business Resource Guide: Service Providers: Part 2 of 2" in *Crain's Detroit Business* (Vol. 15, No. 50, Dec. 13, 1999, pp. E-13)
Pub: Crain Communications, Inc.
Description: More contact information for small and start-up business in the State of Michigan, including information about Michigan State University Extension Service, the public library systems, organizations, IRS publications, regulators, Michigan Unemployment Agency, and the Michigan Department of Environmental Quality.

55833 ■ "Smaller Venture Funds Drive Interest in FoFs" in *Venture Capital Journal* (October 1, 2005)
Pub: Thomason Financial Inc.
Description: Many venture capital firms are raising smaller funds than in the past and looking to fund-of-funds (FoFs) as sound investments.

55834 ■ "Software Companies: Get Real with Revenue" in *Venture Capital Journal* (July 1, 2003)
Pub: Thomson Financial Inc.
Description: Analysts and accounts suggest that software companies should begin to record license fee revenue ratably over time, rather than up-front as they have traditionally done; Wall Street and venture capitalists do not agree.

55835 ■ "Software Gerry Langeler" in *Venture Capital Journal* (January 1, 2005)
Pub: Thomason Financial Inc.
Description: Gerry Langeler, co-founder of Mentor Graphics Corporation and general partner of OVP Venture Partners in Portland, Oregon, makes predictions for the software market in 2005 as well as what happened to the market in 2004.

55836 ■ "Software/Hardware Sector Seconds August VC Spending" in *Venture Capital Journal* (Vol. 40, No. 10, October 2000, pp. 14)
Pub: Venture Economics
Description: Venture capitalists invested in 74 computer software and hardware companies during August, for a total of nearly $1 billion, compared with $500 million for 53 firms in July.

55837 ■ "Software-Maker Bulks up with $20 Million VC Deal" in *Atlanta Business Chronicle* (Vol. 25, No. 21, November 1, 2002, pp. 3A)
Pub: American City Business Publications, Inc.
Ed: Mary Jane Credeur. **Description:** WebTone Technologies Inc. of Georgia, a customer relationship management software producer, has received $20 million in venture capital. Technology Crossover Ventures was the leader of the funding round.

55838 ■ "A Sore Site for Eyes" in *Entrepreneur* (Vol. 28, No. 10, October 2000, pp. 38)
Pub: Entrepreneur Media Inc.
Ed: Doug Hood and Marilea S. Hood. **Description:** If a sloppy Web site is your calling card, don't expect a call from lenders, a polished site will help attract funding.

55839 ■ "Spinoff Doctors" in *Entrepreneur* (Vol. 32, November 2004, No. 11, pp. 18)
Pub: Entrepreneur Media Inc.
Ed: David Worrel. **Description:** Trends in the venture capital industry are spotlighted.

55840 ■ "Spreading The Wealth" in *Forbes* (May 15, 2000, pp. 324)
Pub: Forbes Magazine
Ed: Doug Donovan. **Description:** Venture capital investments in the U.S. rose to $48 billion in 1999. The largest concentration of funds was seen on the two coasts and Texas.

55841 ■ "Start Spreading the News" in *Business 2.0* (Vol. 6, July 2005, No. 6, pp. 40, 42)
Pub: Time, Inc.
Ed: John Heilemann. **Description:** Fred Wilson, venture capitalist and leader of the new firm, Union Square Adventures, is investing in New York. Wilson believes that as the Internet transforms the media, marketing, and finance new technologies will make investing in Internet startups profitable again.

55842 ■ "Start Your Blogs" in *Venture Capital Journal* (January 1, 2005)
Pub: Thomason Financial Inc.
Ed: Lawrence Aragon. **Description:** It is predicted that venture capital firms will use Internet blogs as a means for building business relationships. One byproduct of blogs will be that brands will move away from venture firms to individual partners.

55843 ■ "Starting Up in High Gear" in *Harvard Business Review* (Vol. 78, No. 4, July 2000, pp. 93)
Pub: Harvard Business School Publishing Corp.
Ed: David Champion, Nicholas G. Carr. **Description:** Internet has opened unparalleled opportunities for entrepreneurs according to venture capitalists Vinod Khosla. He now works for Silicon Valley's Kleiner Perkins Caufield and Byers.

55844 ■ *Starting Your Own Big Business with Venture Capital*
Pub: Western Book Journal Press
Ed: William A. Gilmartin. **Released:** 1995. **Price:** $24.95.

55845 ■ "Startups: Microsoft matters again" in *Red Herring* (No. 103, September 1, 2001, pp. 34)
Pub: Herring Communications
Ed: Julie Landry. **Description:** Venture capitalists are looking toward technology that will enable all applications to talk to one another and share data over the Internet, regardless of programming language.

55846 ■ "State to seek VC to ease biotech cuts" in *Crain's Detroit Business* (Vol. 19, No. 8, February 24, 2003, pp. 1)
Pub: Crain Communications Inc., Detroit
Ed: Amy Lane. **Description:** Governor Jennifer Granholm, in an attempt to cut the state's budget, has cut $12.5 million from Michigan life sciences funding and is seeking venture capitalists to pick up the slack.

55847 ■ "Staying Afloat: VCs Raise Annex Funds to Buoy Waning Portfolios" in *Venture Capital Journal* (Vol. 41, No. 8, August 2000, pp. 27-30)
Pub: Venture Economics
Ed: Carolina Braunschweig. **Description:** In an effort to sustain troubled portfolios and reverse negative returns, a few venture capitalists are going back to their LPs to raise annex funds. This latest breed of venture fund, also known as bailout funds, has put some of the nation's largest VC firms in the same predicament as their struggling startups - asking for more funds after recently losing money.

55848 ■ "Sterling Venture, Set to Close Fund I" in *Venture Capital Journal* (Vol. 40, No. 10, October 2000, pp. 24)
Pub: Venture Economics
Description: Sterling Venture prefers to be the first to back a company and work with entrepreneurs.

55849 ■ "Sticky Money" in *Entrepreneur* (Vol. 28, No. 11, November 2000, pp. 38)
Pub: Entrepreneur Media Inc.
Ed: Cynthia E. Griffin. **Description:** A growing number of Web sites connect business owners with financing resources ranging from banks and venture capitalists to private investors looking to purchase stock in direct public offerings.

55850 ■ "Striking Out with VCs?" in *Inc.* (Volume 28, January 2006, No. 1, pp. 34-36)
Pub: Inc. Magazine
Ed: Jennifer Gill. **Description:** A new trend is for small companies to go public without an initial public offering, while tapping the hedge fund market.

55851 ■ "SV Life Sciences Sets Sights on Fourth Fund" in *Venture Capital Journal* (October 1, 2005)
Pub: Thomason Financial Inc.
Description: SV Life Sciences, of Boston, Massachusetts, is looking to raise $400 million for its fourth round of venture funding; it already has 27 portfolio companies.

55852 ■ "Taking Flight: Angel Investors are Flocking Together to Your Advantage" in *Entrepreneur* (Vol. 32, October 2004, No. 10, pp. 34)
Pub: Entrepreneur Media Inc.
Ed: David Worrell. **Description:** Angel investors are partnering to help screen deals and mentor entrepre-

neurs. Thirty member groups of the Angel Capital Association have put an average of $1.85 million into an average of 5.3 investments annually, with each group averaging about 50 individual angels. Deal terms vary, but many report purchasing 20 to 30 percent of a company's stock when investing.

55853 ■ "Targeting Options Threatens Innovation and Growth" in *Venture Capital Journal* **(Vol. 42, No. 5, May 2002, pp. 42)**
Pub: Thomas Venture Economics
Ed: Craig A.T. Jones. **Description:** Stock options are critical in fostering innovation and entrepreneurship; the mandatory expensing of these options would make them too expensive to issue for most organizations.

55854 ■ "Tax Breaks for Angels" in *Inc.* **(September 2005, pp. 30)**
Pub: Inc. Magazine
Ed: Christina Galoozis. **Description:** In order to foster technology transfer, many states are rewarding early-stage investors. Statistical data included.

55855 ■ "Tax Relief Act Is A Boon for VC" in *Venture Capital Journal* **(July 1, 2003)**
Pub: Thomson Financial Inc.
Description: The impact of the Jobs and Growth Tax Relief Reconciliation Act of 2003 is discussed. The Act contains an estimated $330 billion in tax cuts, and implements many basic and revolutionary changes to the Internal Revenue Code which are good for investors.

55856 ■ "Tech Biz. Tough Crowd" in *Boston Business Journal* **(Vol. 23, No. 21, June 27, 2003, pp. 16)**
Pub: American City Business Journals
Description: Silicon Dimensions Inc. (Marlborough, Massachusetts) acquired $3 million in investment from Globespan Capital Partners and Kodiak Venture Partners. Michael Naum, one of the three founders of the company, had to learn how to successfully give effective presentations in order to gain venture capital.

55857 ■ "Tech Detective: Lasers at PARC" in *Venture Capital Journal* **(Vol. 42, No. 10, October 2002, pp. 31-32)**
Pub: Thomas Venture Economics
Ed: Michael V. Copeland. **Description:** Profile of PARC laboratory located at the Palo Alto Research Center in California. PARC is an expert in laser technology.

55858 ■ *Technological Entrepreneurship*
Pub: Edward Elgar Publishing, Incorporated
Ed: Donald Siegel. **Released:** October 2006. **Price:** $230.00. **Description:** Technological entrepreneurship at universities is discussed. The book covers four related topics: university licensing and patenting; science parks and incubators; university-based startups; and the role of academic science in entrepreneurship.

55859 ■ "TechTalk: How Maple Got Out of a Sticky Situation" in *Venture Capital Journal* **(Vol. 42, No. 9, September 2002, pp. 38-39)**
Pub: Thomas Venture Economics
Ed: Ravi Chiuvolu. **Description:** Problems faced by the firm funding Maple Optical, a company building technology for next-generation networks are investigated. Ravi Chiruvolu, general partner of Charter Venture Capital, advises venture capitalists to pay attention to the outside world when investing in companies.

55860 ■ "Tell me no secrets" in *Entrepreneur* **(Vol. 31, No. 5, May 2003, pp. 48)**
Pub: Entrepreneur Media Inc.
Ed: David Worrell. **Description:** The topic of nondisclosure agreements is discussed in the context of venture capital as well as other business negotiations.

55861 ■ "There's Something About Harry" in *Venture Capital Journal* **(Vol. 42, No. 5, May 2002, pp. 18-19)**
Pub: Thomas Venture Economics
Ed: Charles R. Feller. **Description:** Profile of Harry Turner, Director of Park Street Capital. Turner believes he has an inside track on reviewing some of the really good partnerships that have established track records and are rather small.

55862 ■ "These Days, Who Isn't a Venture Capitalist?" in *Fortune* **(Vol. 141, No. 8, April 17, 2000, pp. 532)**
Pub: Time Inc.
Ed: Richard A. Shaffer. **Description:** The venture capital business is more lucrative than ever. Last year almost four times as many venture-financed technology companies went public, thus making more money for the venture capitalists.

55863 ■ "They're Certifiable" in *Entrepreneur* **(Vol. 28, No. 10, October 2000, pp. 36)**
Pub: Entrepreneur Media Inc.
Ed: Cynthia E. Griffin. **Description:** The importance of "accredited investors" when looking for money is reviewed.

55864 ■ "This little drug went to the market" in *Ingram's* **(Vol. 28, No. 6, June 2002, pp. 27)**
Pub: Show Me Publishing, Inc.
Description: Information regarding the funding activity of VasoGenix Pharmaceuticals and the ongoing development of their calitonin gene-related peptide is presented. The company is seeking $5 million in second-round venture capital funding to develop the peptide which has three possible uses, one of which increases blood flow stimulation in balloon angioplasties to decrease strokes and heart attacks.

55865 ■ "The Thrill of the Chase" in *Entrepreneur* **(Vol. 31, No. 7, July 2003, pp. 56)**
Pub: Entrepreneur Media, Inc.
Ed: Tracy T. Lefteroff. **Description:** Despite the drop in venture capital spending in 2002, the trend actually represents a return to historical norms. According to Roger Novak, general partner of Novak-Biddle in McLean, Virginia, entrepreneurs are putting together good business plans with less competitors, making this a good time for VCs.

55866 ■ "Tips on getting a loan" in *Crain's Detroit Business* **(Vol. 16, No. 50, December 11, 2000, pp. E-1)**
Pub: Crain Communications, Inc.
Description: An outline covering all of the information required for a well-written loan proposal.

55867 ■ "Titan May Build Plant" in *Mississippi Business Journal* **(Vol. 28, September 2006, No. 36, pp. 24)**
Pub: Venture Publications, Inc.
Description: Titan Technologies Inc. of Albuquerque N.M. has received $100,000 and an exclusive license agreement from Ally Investment LLE to build recycling facilities in Texas, Oklahoma, Mississippi and Louisiana.

55868 ■ "Tom McConnell: At Service to the Venture Community" in *Venture Capital Journal* **(Vol. 41, No. 8, August 2000, pp. 35-36)**
Pub: Venture Economics
Ed: Ken Ryan. **Description:** Profile of Tom McConnell, general partner with New Enterprise Associates, who also devotes his time to the National Venture Capital Association (NVCA) as its chairman.

55869 ■ "The Top 25 IPOs of 2000" in *Red Herring* **(No 99, June 15 & July 1, 2001, pp. 62, 64)**
Pub: Herring Communications
Ed: Lorraine Fry. **Description:** After a wild ride, the IPO market gets back to basics. The number of tech IPOs fell in the fourth quarter. The article includes a listing of the top 25 IPOs of 2000, including rank, issuer, ticker, issue month, IPO size, and percent change since December.

55870 ■ "The Top 25 VC Firms of 2000" in *Red Herring* **(No. 99, June 15 & July 1, 2001, pp. 68, 69)**
Pub: Herring Communications
Ed: Kate McKinley. **Description:** Venture capital investments in the tech sector fell 41 percent from the third to fourth quarter 2000. A listing of the top 25 venture capital firms is presented, ranked by the average equi-return performance of their IPOs in 2000.

55871 ■ "Top Venture Capital Companies" in *Ingram's* **(Vol. 29, No. 7, July 2003, pp. 20)**
Pub: Show Me Publishing, Inc.
Description: Statistical ranking of the top 25 Kansas City, Missouri venture capital companies is presented.

55872 ■ "Toward Transparency" in *Venture Capital Journal* **(October 1, 2005)**
Pub: Thomason Financial Inc.
Description: Transparency in the venture capital market is defined. Venture firms need to respond to their investors' demands for more openness.

55873 ■ "Trading Private Equity Publicly May not fly" in *Red Herring* **(No. 105, October 1, 2001, pp. 36)**
Pub: Herring Communications
Ed: Julie Landry. **Description:** For venture capital to obtain liquidity, venture capitalists will have to open their long-closed books. Laurence Allen, CEO of NYPPE hopes to change private equity by taking the private out of private equity, thus making it easier to trade restricted securities in private companies and limited partnerships, using his firm's electronic communications network (ECN).

55874 ■ "Trendy VC providers still overlooking Central Ohio" in *Business First Columbus* **(Vol. 18, No. 40, May 24, 2002, pp. A6)**
Pub: Business First Columbus, Inc.
Ed: Laura Newpoff. **Description:** In a comparison between the Cincinnati and Columbus areas, Columbus is not attracting as much private venture capital.

55875 ■ "Triad venture firms invest in Charlotte companies" in *Charlotte Business Journal* **(Vol. 18, No. 1, April 4, 2003, pp. 7)**
Pub: Charlotte Business Journal
Ed: Jen Zoghby. **Description:** Venture capital firms in North Carolina's Triad area provided $3.5 million in financing for Charlotte-based companies in the spring of 2003; Trinity Security received $1.5 million from Venture Capital Solutions and Piedmont Angel Network invested $2 million in AvidXchange.

55876 ■ "Two Companies Find Investment at Long Island VC Forum" in *Long Island Business News* **(February 13, 2004)**
Pub: Dolan Media Newswires
Description: Consolidated Billing Solutions and Motion Imagine Inc. have received venture capital funding as a result of the Long Island Capital Alliance forum.

55877 ■ "2Q venture capital up 75 percent over last year" in *Crain's Detroit Business* **(Vol. 16, No. 33, August 14, 2000, pp. 32)**
Pub: Crain Communications, Inc.
Ed: Joseph Serwach. **Description:** According to PricewaterhouseCoopers Money Tree Survey, venture capitalists poured $52.4 million into Michigan companies during the second quarter of 2000.

55878 ■ "The Ultimate Business Plan" in *Success* **(Vol. 47, No. 1, January 2000, pp. 44)**
Pub: Success Publishing, Inc.
Ed: C.J. Prince. **Description:** Miles Spencer, cofounder of MoneyHunt Properties in Norwalk, Connecticut, and a member of the venture fund Capital Express, advises no one write your business plan but you. Included are informative tips including: The Executive Summary, Management: Who's Running This Thing?, Marketing, Financials, and Your Tone.

55879 ■ "UM prof's laser slices through fear of eye surgery" in *Crain's Detroit Business* **(Vol. 16, No. 16, April 16, 2000, pp. 13)**
Pub: Crain Communications, Inc.
Ed: Jeffrey Kosseff. **Description:** Profile of IntraLase Corporation, founded in Ann Arbor, Michigan in 1997, now headquartered in Irvine, California. The laser manufacturer recently gained FDA approval to sell a more precise laser eye surgery device. The article chronicles how the IntraLase was able to obtain funding.

55880 ■ **"Unhappy LPs Pass on New Mayfield Fund" in** *Venture Capital Journal* (September 1, 2005)
Pub: Thomason Financial Inc.
Description: Mayfield, the venture capital firm founded in 1969, has suffered a blow to its reputation in the VC industry because a departing limited partner has reported Mayfield's arrogant manner used in the handling of a management fee issue.

55881 ■ **"U.S. Needs Help from the Private Sector to Combat Terrorism" in** *Venture Capital Journal* (Vol. 42, No. 9, September 2002, pp. 40)
Pub: Thomas Venture Economics
Ed: Leighton Read. **Description:** The private sector will play a major role in homeland security by developing and producing antiterrorism countermeasures.

55882 ■ **"Vanguard Adds Eilers, Wraps on Fund Seven" in** *Venture Capital Journal* (Vol. 40, No. 10, November 2000, pp. 34)
Pub: Venture Economics
Description: Vanguard Venture Partners hired Daniel Eilers as the firm's fourth general partner. The firm backs early-stage communications equipment, Internet infrastructure and life sciences companies.

55883 ■ *Vankirk's Venture Capital Directory*
Pub: Online Publishing, Inc.
Ed: Clarke V. Simmons, editor. **Released:** 1993. **Price:** $490.00. **Description:** Directory listing 1003 venture capital sources and 1003 organizations. Entries include financing preferences by stage, industry, size, and geography, and compensation methods. Also contains how-to information for targeting venture capital proposals, developing a business plan, and approaching venture capitalists.

55884 ■ **"VC-backed IPOs Roared In Q2, But Whither the Enron Effect?" in** *Venture Capital Journal* (Vol. 42, No. 8, August 2002, pp. 11-14)
Pub: Thomas Venture Economics
Ed: Colleen Marie O'Connor, Lawrence Aragon. **Description:** Accounting scandals, CEO misdeeds and a bear market have put a major crunch on the IPO market, and the near future doesn't look promising. Statistical data included.

55885 ■ **"VC Company to Double One Fund, Add $40M Fund." in** *Crain's Detroit Business* (Vol. 23, January 15,2007, No. 3, pp. 26)
Pub: Crain Communications Inc. - Detroit
Ed: Tom Henderson. **Description:** Local Venture Capital firm adds personnel and expands funds to increase business. First fund is doubled to $20M and began raising money for a second fund of $40M.

55886 ■ **"VC infusions flagged: Tech firms hope year better than tough '01" in** *Business First Columbus* (Vol. 18, No. 25, Feb. 8, 2002, pp. A3)
Pub: Business First Columbus, Inc.
Ed: Laura Newpoff. **Description:** Tech firms in Ohio are hoping that venture capitalists will provide more funding in 2002 than the previous year.

55887 ■ **"VC Goes Institutional: The Hiring of a Chief Operating Officer" in** *Venture Capital Journal* (Vol. 40, No. 10, October 2000, pp. 41-43)
Pub: Venture Economics
Ed: Alissa Leibowitz. **Description:** An overview of venture capital firms who have turned to a Chief Operating Officer to manage the firm's capital. These firms feel this move will enable them to offer more services.

55888 ■ **"The VC Process" in** *Hispanic Business* (March 2004, pp. 36-37)
Pub: Hispanic Business
Ed: Joel Russell. **Description:** Hispanics have lagged behind in the private-equity market, but experts offer ways for them to improve acquiring venture financing.

55889 ■ **"VC Vintage" in** *Entrepreneur* (Vol. 28, No. 6, June 2000, pp. 38)
Pub: Entrepreneur Media Inc.
Ed: Cynthia E. Griffin. **Description:** According to two reports in February 2000, 1999 was a banner year for venture capital.

55890 ■ **"VC & Visas: Foreign Workers After the Fall" in** *Venture Capital Journal* (Vol. 41, No. 8, August 2000, pp. 6, 8, 10)
Pub: Venture Economics
Description: The failure of the dot-com industry has not hurt foreign workers with H-1B visas and venture-backed companies because of the critical need for those worker's expertise. Statistical data included.

55891 ■ **"VC Whispers: Glowing optimism" in** *Red Herring* (No. 103, September 1, 2001, pp. 78)
Pub: Herring Communications
Ed: Lawrence Aragon. **Description:** Despite the fact that venture deals in energy-related companies have slowed, venture capitalists predict a bright future for the sector. Statistical data included.

55892 ■ **"VC Whispers: Optical components shine brightly in a dreary market" in** *Red Herring* (No. 102, August 15, 2001, pp. 76)
Pub: Herring Communications
Ed: Julie Landry. **Description:** Communications investors continue to put money into companies building optical components for carrier networks, because carriers continue to move forward with network upgrades to integrate smaller, cheaper, and more advanced components.

55893 ■ **"VC Whispers: Putting cash into stash" in** *Red Herring* (No. 105, October 1, 2001, pp. 86)
Pub: Herring Communications
Ed: Lawrence Aragon. **Description:** Funding for the storage sector rose in second quarter 2001, largely due to follow-on rounds for previously funded firms.

55894 ■ **"VCFA Closes $250M Fund with LBO Focus" in** *Venture Capital Journal* (September 1, 2005)
Pub: Thomason Financial Inc.
Description: VCFA Group has expanded into the business of buyouts with VCFA Private Equity Partners IV. The firm recently closed with $250 million. VCFA Group is noted for helping to start the secondary market.

55895 ■ **"VCs raid biotechs, nab talent" in** *San Francisco Business Times* (Vol. 16, No. 42, May 24, 2002, pp. 1)
Pub: San Francisco Business Times Inc.
Ed: Brendan Doherty. **Description:** Venture capital companies are hiring scientists and other experts from the biotechnology industry, making it harder for research firms to get good talent.

55896 ■ **"VCs Born in the Bubble Start To Go Pop!" in** *Venture Capital Journal* (Vol. 42, No. 10, October 2002, pp. 14, 16)
Pub: Thomas Venture Economics
Ed: Michael V. Copeland. **Description:** It is estimated that new firms launched two years ago could shrink by one-third. Four first-time venture funds raised during the Internet bubble have stopped doing business, which include Seattle-based Incepta a Bechtel Enterprises Holdings-backed firm; New York City firms Starting-Point Venture Partners and Metropolis Venture Partners; and White Plains, New York iCentennial Ventures.

55897 ■ **"VCs Buoyed by $3B for Stem Cell Research" in** *Venture Capital Journal* (December 1, 2004)
Pub: Thomason Financial Inc.
Description: Proposal 71 in California approves a stem cell research initiative in California, a big win for the venture capital industry.

55898 ■ **"VCs Feel the Love from Wall Street" in** *Venture Capital Journal* (February 1, 2005)
Pub: Thomason Financial Inc.
Description: Despite a slow beginning, 2004 ended a strong year for initial public offerings (IPOs), marking the strongest year since the Internet bubble. Two-hundred sixteen companies went public last year, three times more than 2002.

55899 ■ **"VCs Get Back to Basics" in** *Atlanta Business Chronicle* (Vol. 24, No. 10, August 10, 2001, pp. 3A)
Pub: American City Business Journals Inc.
Ed: Mary Jane Credeur. **Description:** Venture capitalists invested $244.8 million in Georgia companies in the second quarter of 2001, a nearly 13 percent drop from previous quarter, in 23 deals. Nationally, venture capital investing was about $7.5 billion in the second quarter, versus $10 billion in the first quarter. Statistical data included.

55900 ■ **"VCs Investing Their Money in Nontech Firms" in** *Atlanta Business Chronicle* (Vol. 26, No. 14, September 12, 2003, pp. 3A)
Pub: American City Business Publications, Inc.
Ed: Mary Jane Credeur. **Description:** Industry analysts state that venture capital companies are expanding into the non-tech sector. Noro-Moseley has invested $10 million in Cypress Communications Inc.

55901 ■ **"VCs Look for Sweet Deals in Intel Spin-offs" in** *Venture Capital Journal* (Vol. 42, No. 10, October 2002, pp. 12, 14)
Pub: Thomas Venture Economics
Ed: Carolina Braunschweig. **Description:** Because businesses inside large corporations that are not focused on the company's core strengths are often under-funded and under-managed. Venture capital firms are playing a vital role in Intel Corporation's efforts to size down and focus on its core business.

55902 ■ **"VCs Revive Ailing Drkoop.com" in** *Venture Capital Journal* (Vol. 40, No. 10, October 2000, pp. 37)
Pub: Venture Economics
Description: Profile of drkoop.com, the ailing dot. com, and ways new investors are working to save the company.

55903 ■ **"VCs See Bottom, Expect To Do More Deals" in** *Venture Capital Journal* (July 1, 2003)
Pub: Thomson Financial Inc.
Description: According to a survey conducted by Venture Capital Journal, VCs are feeling more optimistic, yet cautious, about the industry and are predicting a slow recovery. More startups are experiencing funding, particularly seed- and early-stage rounds, focusing both by industry and region. Life sciences and nanotechnology are receiving the most interest.

55904 ■ **"VCs See Jumbo Opportunity in Fighting Obesity" in** *Venture Capital Journal* (January 1, 2005)
Pub: Thomason Financial Inc.
Description: Obesity-fighting companies saw $234 million invested from January through November 2004. Obesity is a growing problem, with estimates that one-third of all American adults are obese. Statistical data included.

55905 ■ **"VCs Try Partnering for Successful Incubation" in** *Venture Capital Journal* (February 1, 2005)
Pub: Thomason Financial Inc.
Description: Today, incubator companies comprise small operations sponsored by individual investors, to entrepreneurial clusters housed by venture capitalists, to groups evolving into stand-alone venture funds themselves. An incubator backed by multiple venture firms has become a popular model.

55906 ■ "Venetia Kontogouris: A Uniquely Different VC" in *Venture Capital Journal* (Vol. 41, No. 8, August 2000, pp. 34, 36)
Pub: Venture Economics
Ed: Ken Ryan. **Description:** Profile of Venetia Kontogouris, who works at Trident, the national VC firm that focuses on the information technology sector. Kontogouris says she uses her intuition regarding entrepreneurs.

55907 ■ "Venture-backed IPOs Rebound from Q2 Slump" in *Venture Capital Journal* (Vol. 40, No. 10, November 2000, pp. 10, 12, 14)
Pub: Venture Economics
Description: Venture-backed companies raised more than $7.57 billion in the third quarter of 2000. Statistical data included.

55908 ■ *Venture Capital*
Pub: National Association of Small Business Investment Cos.
Contact: Jamie G. Blake, Dir. Member Svcs.
Released: Annual. **Price:** $35, individuals includes postage. **Covers:** about 420 member firms licensed as small business investment companies (SBICs) under the Small Business Investment Act of 1958; associate and sustaining members who are non-SBIC investors in small businesses or suppliers of services. **Entries Include:** Company name, address, phone, name of principal executive, industries and/or types of situations that are of special interest, preferred limit for loans or investments, investment policy, branch offices. **Arrangement:** By membership type; SBICs are then geographical; others are alphabetical.

55909 ■ "Venture Capital: Arthritic corporations get a chance at a second childhood" in *Red Herring* (No. 87, December 18, 2000, pp. 40)
Pub: Herring Communications, Inc.
Ed: Guy Paisner. **Description:** Ways in which venture capital firms are competing to help dot.com corporations to develop new Internet strategies is discussed.

55910 ■ "Venture Capital Deals Decline in Michigan" in *Crain's Detroit Business* (Vol. 15, No. 49, December 6, 1999, pp. 3)
Pub: Crain Communications, Inc.
Ed: Matt Roush. **Description:** A major accounting and consulting firm's survey show a third straight quarterly decline in Michigan funding. Despite the decline, experts still site a robust climate.

55911 ■ *Venture Capital Directory*
Pub: Forum Publishing Co.
Ed: Raymond Lawrence, Editor. **Released:** Annual, February. **Price:** $12.95. **Covers:** over 400 members of the Small Business Administration and the Small Business Investment Company that provide funding for small and minority businesses. **Entries Include:** Company name, address, phone, names and titles of key personnel, geographical area served, financial data, branch office or subsidiary names, description of services and projects. **Arrangement:** Alphabetical.

55912 ■ "Venture Capital: First-round investments: now for the small and the brave" in *Red Herring* (No. 105, October 1, 2001, pp. 38-39)
Pub: Herring Communications
Ed: Lawrence Aragon, Julie Landry. **Description:** Venture capitalists are taking more time before investing in new investments and spending more time trying to raise follow-on rounds for their existing companies. Statistical data included.

55913 ■ "Venture-capital investing fell to five-year low in 1st quarter" in *Wall Street Journal* (April 29, 2003, pp. C5)
Pub: Dow Jones & Co. Inc.
Ed: Ann Grimes. **Description:** According to the MoneyTree Survey prepared by National Venture Capital Association, Thomson Venture Economics and PricewaterhouseCoopers, venture capital investing fell to a five year low in first quarter 2003.

55914 ■ "Venture Capital: Its' hip to be old" in *Red Herring* (No. 102, August 15, 2001, pp. 32)
Pub: Herring Communications
Ed: Lawrence Aragon, Julie Landry. **Description:** Venture capitalists are growing more conservative since the downfall of dot-coms and are investing in older, self-funded companies.

55915 ■ "Venture Capital is Not For Girlie Men" in *Fortune* (Vol. 152, October 17, 2005, No. 8, pp. 38)
Pub: Time Inc.
Ed: Adam Lashinsky. **Description:** Profile of Tim Draper, whose firm currently has a network of affiliated funds in 28 cities worldwide and 75 partners managing $3.4 billion investing in nearly 500 companies.

55916 ■ *Venture Capital Sourcebook: The Definitive Guide to Finding Start-Up Fuds & Growth Capital*
Pub: Probus Publishing Co., Inc.
Ed: A. David Silver. **Released:** 1994. **Price:** $29.95 (paper).

55917 ■ "Venture Capitalism Inspires Hope in the Face of Tragedy" in *Venture Capital Journal* (Vol. 42, No. 9, September 2002, pp. 30)
Pub: Thomas Venture Economics
Ed: Mark G. Heesen. **Description:** Mark G. Heesen, president of the National Venture Capital Association, representing more than 400 venture capital and private equity firms, shares his views on the hope for the future that venture capital investments provide.

55918 ■ "A Venture Capitalist's View of 9-11" in *Venture Capital Journal* (Vol. 42, No. 9, September 2002, pp. 28-29)
Pub: Thomas Venture Economics
Ed: Alan Patricof. **Description:** Alan Patricof, vice chairman of Apax Partners Inc., an international private equity firm, shares his perspective of New York City after 9-11, including the economic impact of the attacks.

55919 ■ "Venture capitalists get 'clawed'" in *Wall Street Journal* (December 10, 2002, pp. 35)
Pub: Dow Jones & Co. Inc.
Ed: Ann Grimes. **Description:** Investments in venture capital funds continue to fall.

55920 ■ "Venture capitalists show hope" in *Wall Street Journal* (February 28, 2003, pp. C5)
Pub: Dow Jones & Co. Inc.
Ed: Ann Grimes. **Description:** According to a survey conducted by Deloitte and Touche LLP, hope is on the horizon in the area of venture capital.

55921 ■ "Venture Lender Lighthouse Attracts $336M" in *Venture Capital Journal* (July 1, 2003)
Pub: Thomson Financial Inc.
Description: Lighthouse Capital Partners closed its fifth fund with $366, giving a boost to the venture lending business. Lighthouse plans to continue investing in firms that have already received funding from traditional VC firms over the next few years.

55922 ■ "Venture Michigan Makes First Investment Commitments" in *Crain's Detroit Business* (Vol. 23, January 29, 2007, No. 5, pp. 17)
Pub: Crain Communications Inc. - Detroit
Ed: Amy Lane. **Description:** First investment commitments to smaller venture capital fund providers is made by state venture group. Investments are in capital funds that support start-up firms with a Michigan presence that engage in new product development, research, and technology in non-manufacturing sectors.

55923 ■ "Venture funding keeps up pace: First quarter blows away 1999 start" in *Crain's Detroit Business* (Vol. 16, No. 21, May 22, 2000, pp. 3)
Pub: Crain Communications, Inc.
Ed: Matt Roush. **Description:** New figures released by the accounting firm PricewaterhouseCoopers, show a continued surge in capital funding in the first quarter of 2000 for Michigan businesses.

55924 ■ "Venturelab Launches $50M Targeted Fund" in *Venture Capital Journal* (Vol. 40, No. 10, November 2000, pp. 22)
Pub: Venture Economics
Description: Keystone Venture VI LP will back about 25-30 information technology companies, particularly in the wireless, tool, e-commerce and affinity marketing spaces. The firm will target early expansion-stage companies.

55925 ■ "Ventures' valuations decline" in *Wall Street Journal* (June 3, 2003, pp. C5)
Pub: Dow Jones & Co. Inc.
Description: Profile of venture-capital backed companies is presented.

55926 ■ "Venturing Forward?" in *Boston Business Journal* (Vol. 23, No. 33, September 19, 2003, pp. 40)
Pub: American City Business Journals
Ed: Edward Mason. **Description:** Business for venture capital companies is returning after a long dry spell since the stock market crash of 2000. Boston Millennia Partners has recently made four deals.

55927 ■ "A Very British Compromise" in *Red Herring* (No. 105, October 1, 2001, pp. 50-53)
Pub: Herring Communications
Ed: Guy Paisner. **Description:** The United Kingdom's largest venture capital company, 3i, has global ambitions. It aims to succeed where Silicon Valley firms fear to tread. 3i has a network of offices in 43 offices, including locations in the United States. The firm plans to overtake its rivals, especially those in the U.S., by providing risk capital to technology startups.

55928 ■ "Veteran CEO: Don't Fall for These Five Lines" in *Venture Capital Journal* (Vol. 42, No. 5, May 2002, pp. 38-39)
Pub: Thomas Venture Economics
Ed: Dean Goodermote. **Description:** An investigation into the five statements from small technology firms that should set off a red flag to venture capitalists, showing the misconception and the reality of the statement.

55929 ■ "Veteran GPs Launch Maven" *Venture Capital Journal* (February 1, 2006)
Pub: Thomason Financial Inc.
Ed: Constance Loizos. **Description:** In January 2006, Jennifer Gill Roberts and Marc Friend were set to launch fund-raising efforts for $150 million for an inaugural fund. The firm will focus on smart mobile services.

55930 ■ "Vietnam Primed for VC Growth" in *Venture Capital Journal* (February 1, 2006)
Pub: Thomason Financial Inc.
Description: Many experts predict that Vietnam is the next Southeast Asian country to emerge to become an economic powerhouse. The country has 6,000 publicly held companies. Statistical data included.

55931 ■ "Viewpoint: Timing Is Right for Digital Content" in *Venture Capital Journal* (July 1, 2003)
Pub: Thomson Financial Inc.
Description: Although venture capitalists have traditionally stayed away from investing in pure media and content plays, the entertainment and media industries continue to grow at a 6 percent rate in the U.S.

55932 ■ "VoIP; After Years of Hype, a Real Market has Emerged for Voice Over IP." in *Venture Capital Journal* (December 1, 2004)
Pub: Thomason Financial Inc.
Ed: Michael Fitzgerald. **Description:** Voice over Internet Protocol (VoIP) will create new ways to handle

music, videos, video-conferencing and other types of multimedia. Venture capitalists are prepared to ramp up VoIP investments for the next year. In 2004 VCs invested $355 million for 18 companies. Statistical data included.

55933 ■ "Vulture capital gains spotlight after swoon of dot-coms" in *Wall Street Journal* **(October 17, 2000, pp. C1)**
Pub: Dow Jones & Co., Inc.
Ed: Suzanne McGee. **Description:** An overview of deals and deal makers with statistical data included.

55934 ■ "We Need Reform To Curb Corporate Scandals, But Don't Get Excessive" in *Venture Capital Journal* **(Vol. 42, No. 8, August 2002, pp. 40)**
Pub: Thomas Venture Economics
Ed: Mark Heesen. **Description:** The Corporate and Auditing Accountability, Responsibility, and Transparency Act, which creates a new oversight body that will certify accountants and have the authority to punch, is profiled.

55935 ■ "Weiss, Peck & Greer Venture Partners Vanishes in Lightspeed" in *Venture Capital Journal* **(Vol. 40, No. 10, November 2000, pp. 16, 18)**
Pub: Venture Economics
Description: The executives with Weiss, Peck & Greer Venture Partners have left the firm in order to start a new company named Lightspeed Venture Partners. The new company has also formed a charitable initiative named Lightspeed Bright Futures, an ongoing partnership with Plugged In and OpNet, a pair of non-profit organizations working to bridge the digital divide.

55936 ■ *Western Association of Venture Capitalists—Directory of Members*
Pub: Western Association of Venture Capitalists
Contact: Fran Cannon
Released: Annual, February. **Covers:** about 169 venture capital firms; coverage limited to the western United States. **Entries Include:** Company name, address, phone, name and title of contact; years experienced in venture capital field; description of investment preferences, desired maturity of company, desired investment position. **Arrangement:** Alphabetical.

55937 ■ "What is venture capital?" in *Crain's Detroit Business* **(Vol. 16, No. 19, May 8, 2000, pp. 18)**
Pub: Crain Communications, Inc.
Description: An in-depth investigation into all aspects of venture capital funding.

55938 ■ "What Venture Trends Can Tell You" in *Harvard Business Review* **(Vol. 81, No. 7, July 2003, pp. 18)**
Pub: Harvard Business School Press
Ed: William F. Meehan III, Ron Lemmens, Matthew R. Cohler. **Description:** The future of the U.S. venture capital industry and its investments are explored.

55939 ■ "What's a Clawback?" in *Venture Capital Journal* **(September 1, 2005)**
Pub: Thomason Financial Inc.
Description: A clawback clause in a limited partners agreement requires the general partners to return money to their limited partners when the value of the illiquid portion of a portfolio falls after the distribution is made.

55940 ■ "What's a Company Worth? It Depends on Which GP You Ask" in *Venture Capital Journal* **(Vol. 42, No. 5, May 2002, pp. 40-41)**
Pub: Thomas Venture Economics
Ed: Colin Blaydon, Michael Horvath. **Description:** Now, GPs are spending nearly as much time managing LP relationships as their portfolio companies, with valuation reporting being one of the most difficult issues being faced. Venture capitalists may not really understand the value of some portfolio companies.

55941 ■ "What's Next for The Internet" in *Venture Capital Journal* **(July 1, 2003)**
Pub: Thomson Financial Inc.
Description: The future of the Internet is discussed. The value of the Philadelphia Internet Index has doubled since late 2002. One industry expert estimates that so far, the Internet revolution is less than 3 percent complete.

55942 ■ "What's a VC Doing on a Public Board?" in *Venture Capital Journal* **(Vol. 42, No. 8, August 2002, pp. 5-6)**
Pub: Thomas Venture Economics
Ed: Michael V. Copeland. **Description:** The risks taken by venture capitalists sitting on the boards of publicly traded companies are investigated.

55943 ■ "When the Chips are Down" in *Red Herring* **(No. 99, June 15 & July 1, 2001, pp. 122)**
Pub: Herring Communications
Ed: Tom Stein. **Description:** As the semiconductor sector cools off, venture capitalists seek companies with staying power.

55944 ■ "When an Incubator Goes Cold" in *Business Week Online* **()**
Pub: McGraw-Hill, Inc.
Description: Investors in Idealab! want to liquidate the Pasadena high tech incubator, but instead feel they are being offered a fraction of what their shares of stock are worth.

55945 ■ *Where to Find Venture Capital: A Resource Guide*
Pub: Rainbow Books, Inc.
Ed: Philip C. Paul. **Released:** 1995. **Price:** $19.95.

55946 ■ *Where to Get the Money & Management Help for New Business Start-Ups & Small Business Growth: East-North Central Region, IL, IN, MI, OH, WI*
Pub: Special Reports, Inc.
Ed: Richard S. Guyer and Frank J. Domeracki. **Released:** 1998. **Price:** $197.00.

55947 ■ *Where to Get the Money & Management Help for New Business Start-Ups & Small-Business Growth: East-South Central Region, AL, KY, MS, TN*
Pub: Special Reports, Inc.
Ed: Richard S. Guyer and Frank J. Domeracki. **Released:** 1998. **Price:** $197.00.

55948 ■ *Where to Get the Money & Management Help for New Business Start-Ups & Small Business Growth: Mountain Region, AZ, CO, ID, MT, NV, NM, UT, WY*
Pub: Special Reports, Inc.
Ed: Richard S. Guyer and Frank J. Domeracki. **Released:** 1998. **Price:** $197.00.

55949 ■ *Where to Get the Money & Management Help for New Business Start-Ups & Small Business Growth: Pacific Region, AK, CA, HI, OR, WA*
Pub: Richard S. Guyer and Frank J. Domeracki
Ed: Richard S. Guyer and Frank J. Domeracki. **Released:** 1998. **Price:** $197.00.

55950 ■ *Where to Get the Money & Management Help for New Business Start-Ups & Small Business Growth: West-North Central Region, IA, KS, MN, MO, NE, ND, SD*
Pub: Special Reports, Inc.
Ed: Richard S. Guyer and Frank J. Domeracki. **Released:** 1998. **Price:** $197.00.

55951 ■ *Where to Get the Money & Management Help for New Business Start-Ups & Small Growth: West-South Central Region, AR, LA, OK, TX*
Pub: Special Reports, Inc.
Ed: Richard S. Guyer and Frank J. Domeracki. **Released:** 1998. **Price:** $197.00.

55952 ■ "White Joins Pequot, Heads West Coast Ops." in *Venture Capital Journal* **(Vol. 40, No. 10, November 2000, pp. 34, 36)**
Pub: Venture Economics
Description: Pequot Capital Management Inc. hired Karen White, former senior vice president of worldwide business development at Oracle Corporation, as a general partner in the firm's private equity group. Pequot's private equity group backs early- to expansion-stage technology, telecommunications and healthcare companies.

55953 ■ "Why the Old Rules Don't Apply" in *Business Week* **(February 14, 2005, No. 3920, pp. 68)**
Pub: McGraw-Hill Companies
Ed: Stephen Baker, Adam Aston. **Description:** An overview of nanotechnology. Venture capital firm Draper Fisher Jurvetson has invested $95 million in eleven nanotechnology startup companies.

55954 ■ "Why the Small-Business Market is the Internet's new frontier" in *Red Herring* **(No. 76, pp. 185-186, 188, 192, 194, 198-200, 202, 204)**
Pub: Herring Communications, Inc.
Description: Why venture capitalists, retail investors, and many Internet companies think they can make large profits by targeting the small business market. Extensive statistical data is included with charts and graphs.

55955 ■ "Why SPACs Are Luring VCs Into Public Market" in *Venture Capital Journal* **(October 1, 2005)**
Pub: Thomason Financial Inc.
Description: Private non-control investors are increasingly playing a role in public control acquisition equities in order to give the private equity firm a low-risk and low-cost method to leverage the public markets while backing entire management teams.

55956 ■ "Winston-Salem, N.C. Area Attracts $567 Million in Venture Capital" in *Winston-Salem Journal* **(April 11, 2003)**
Pub: Knight-Ridder/Tribune Business News
Ed: Kristi E. Swartz. **Description:** Local investments in the Winston-Salem area helped place North Carolina in the ninth spot for venture capital investments nationally, according to a report by the Council for Entrepreneurial Development.

55957 ■ "Wireless security catches the eye of venture capitalists" in *Red Herring* **(No. 106, October 15, 2001, pp. 34-35)**
Pub: Herring Communications
Ed: Scott Tyler Shafer. **Description:** The future of wireless is discussed. Several obstacles are addressed, including security and network management. Venture capitalists are backing startups creating the key technologies for the wireless industry.

55958 ■ "With dot-coms no longer soaring, financial backers get back to basics" in *The New York Times* **(December 18, 2000, pp. C28)**
Pub: The New York Times Company
Ed: Jonathan Burton. **Description:** An interview with Venture Strategy founder Joanna Rees Gallanter.

55959 ■ "Won't You Be My Neighbor?" in *Entrepreneur* **(Vol. 32, August 2004, No. 8, pp. 52)**
Pub: Entrepreneur Media Inc.
Ed: Jennifer Pellet. **Description:** Community development funds invest in companies that will benefit low-income workers in distressed communities.

55960 ■ "Yazam Taps Coleman, Opens DC Office" in *Venture Capital Journal* **(Vol. 40, No. 10, October 2000, pp. 36)**
Pub: Venture Economics
Description: Yazam hired Sean Coleman as a managing director to head up the firm's new Washington, DC office.

55961 ■ "Year In Review Fund-Raising" in *Venture Capital Journal* **(February 1, 2006)**
Pub: Thomason Financial Inc.
Description: A total of 182 U.S.-based venture funds raised $25.2 billion in 2005, lower in number than in 2005 but a 46 percent surge in dollar amount. Statistical data included.

55962 ■ "Year In Review IPO Market" in *Venture Capital Journal* **(February 1, 2006)**
Pub: Thomason Financial Inc.
Description: Initial public offerings for 2005 was the highest since 2000 with biotechnology and medical technology, semiconductors and computer chips leading the way.

55963 ■ "Year In Review People" in *Venture Capital Journal* **(February 1, 2006)**
Pub: Thomason Financial Inc.
Description: Leading venture capitalists in 2005 include Robert Alexander from Alta Partners, Stewart Alsop from Alsop Louie Partners, and Isaac Applebaum from Opus Capital.

55964 ■ "Your Vote Really Does Count: Changing Political Dynamics of an Evenly Divided Congress" in *Venture Capital Journal* **(Vol. 40, No. 10)**
Pub: Venture Economics
Description: The article points out the importance for business owners to vote during elections.

TRADE PERIODICALS

55965 ■ *SCOR Report*
Pub: SCOR Report
Ed: Tom Stewart-Gordon, Editor, tsg@scor-report. com. **Released:** Monthly, plus 2 issues in Feb/Aug. **Price:** $280, individuals; $400 annual issues with index in Acrobat on a CD. **Description:** Deals with capital formation alternatives for small companies with emphasis on public offerings using the Small Corporate Offering Registration Exemption found under Regulations A and D of the Securities Acts of 1933 as amended. Aims to help small companies, their lawyers, accountants and advisors raise capital by keeping them up to date on changes in state and federal laws, regulations and programs. Also publishes articles on how other companies have raised money.

55966 ■ *Venture Capital Journal*
Pub: Venture Economics Inc.
Contact: Kathleen Devlin, Editor-in-Chief
E-mail: Lawrence.Aragon@thomson.com
Released: Monthly. **Price:** $960, U.S. first year; $1650, elsewhere for combination of print and online edition. **Description:** Hard news, analysis and data on the North American private equity market.

CONSULTANTS

55967 ■ Alimansky Capital Group Inc.
12 E 44th St., Penthouse
New York, NY 10017-3606
Ph:(212)832-7300
Fax: (212)832-7338
Co. E-mail: info@alimansky.com
URL: http://www.alimansky.com

E-mail: info@alimansky.com
Scope: A private investment banking and advisory firm specializing in advising smaller middle-market companies on raising equity and debt for acquisitions, expansion, and restructurings, and in sponsoring such businesses to appropriate sources of capital. Also works with management teams that are seeking leveraged buyout or acquisition financing, and with private and institutional investors. Helps formulate investment strategies and evaluate venture capital and buyout opportunities. Serves companies in a broad range of industries, from leading edge technologies to consumer products and services.

55968 ■ Alpha Capital Partners Ltd.
122 S Michigan Ave., Ste. 1700
Chicago, IL 60603
Ph:(312)322-9800
Fax: (312)322-9808
Co. E-mail: kalnow@alphacapital.com
URL: http://www.alphacapital.com

E-mail: kalnow@alphacapital.com
Scope: A venture capital management organization that provides equity financing for promising growth businesses and buyouts or recapitalization of established companies.

55969 ■ Antares Capital Corp.
7900 Miami Lakes Dr. W
PO Box 410730
Miami Lakes, FL 33016
Ph:(305)894-2888
Fax: (305)894-3227
Co. E-mail: ltrafford@antarescapital.com
URL: http://www.antarescapital.com

E-mail: ltrafford@antarescapital.com
Scope: A private venture capital firm investing equity capital in developmental and expansion stage companies and in management buy-out opportunities.

55970 ■ Avery Business Development Services
2506 St. Michel Ct.
Ponte Vedra Beach, FL 32082
Ph:(904)285-6033
Fax: (904)285-6033
Scope: Offers general business and management consulting of business development from project conception to full commercialization. Scope of activities includes new venture development, business strategy planning, corporate development, licensing, and merger/acquisitions. Industries served: chemical, plastics, and biotechnology coatings. **Seminars:** Constructing the Business Plan and Obtaining Financing For a New Business Venture; Business Strategy Planning.

55971 ■ Samuel E. Bodily
100 Darden Blvd.
Charlottesville, VA 22903
Ph:(434)924-4813
Fax: (434)243-7677
Co. E-mail: bodilys@virginia.edu

E-mail: bodilys@virginia.edu
Scope: Consultant specializes in financial analysis, capital investment, business/product/market planners, financial risk analysis, and decision sciences. **Publications:** "I Can't Get No Satisfaction: How Bundling and Multi-Part Pricing Can Satisfy Consumers and Suppliers," Feb, 2006; "Organizational Use of Decision Analysis," Oct, 2004; "Real Options," Oct, 2004.

55972 ■ Concept Development Associates Inc.
1408 Lark Dr.
PO Box 15245
Evansville, IN 47716-0245
Ph:(812)471-3334
Fax: (812)477-6499
URL: http://www.conceptdevelopmentassociates. com
Scope: A globally-connected venture capital group.

55973 ■ Crosslink Capital
2 Embarcadero Ctr., Ste. 2200
San Francisco, CA 94111
Ph:(415)617-1800
Co. E-mail: info@crosslinkcapital.com
URL: http://www.crosslinkcapital.com

E-mail: info@crosslinkcapital.com
Scope: An independent venture capital and investment firm. Firm focuses on strategic business and technology questions as well as to discuss tactical approaches to addressing these challenges.

55974 ■ Equity Partners Of America Ltd.
1450 W Long Lake Rd., Ste. 340
Troy, MI 48098
Ph:(248)952-0300
Fax: (248)952-0314
Co. E-mail: equitypartners@email.msn.com

E-mail: equitypartners@email.msn.com
Scope: Private investment bank specializes in debt and equity capital procurement; buying and selling businesses; shareholder value enhancement strategies; and litigation and alternative dispute resolution assistance; including expert witness assistance. Serves manufacturing, distribution and service industries. **Seminars:** Preparation of a business plan; Use of financial statements in damage claims; Determining the value of a business; When to sell a family business.

55975 ■ Jenam Securities Inc.
10 Kingsbridge Garden Cir., Ste. 506
Mississauga, ON, Canada L5R 3K6
Ph:(905)890-9245
Fax: (905)890-3229
URL: http://www.thebusinessplace.com
Scope: Assists in the buying and selling of businesses, arranging bank financing, venture capital loans/ investments, mergers, and acquisitions.

55976 ■ Newmarket Capital Advisors
5310 Harvest Hill Rd.
Dallas, TX 75230
Ph:(972)503-1516
Fax: (972)503-1519
Scope: Venture capitalists that offers assistance in strategic decisions and long range planning.

55977 ■ Pacific Century Group Ventures Ltd.
105-150 Crowfoot Cres. NW, Ste. 700
Calgary, AB, Canada T3G 3T2
Ph:(604)871-0452
Fax: (604)871-0451
Co. E-mail: info@pcentury.com
URL: http://www.pcentury.com

E-mail: info@pcentury.com
Scope: Experienced in fund management, venture capital and corporate finance. Specializes in information technology and real estate sectors.

55978 ■ Seacoast Capital
55 Ferncroft Rd., Ste. 110
Danvers, MA 01923
Ph:(978)750-1300
Fax: (978)750-1301
Co. E-mail: gdeli@seacoastcapital.com
URL: http://www.seacoastcapital.com

E-mail: gdeli@seacoastcapital.com
Scope: Invests growth capital in small companies led by strong, entrepreneurial management teams. Invested in U.S. companies in growing or fragmented industries with revenues in excess of $5 million and positive operating earnings. Provides follow-on financing for acquisitions, internal growth or the execution of roll-out strategies. Assists portfolio companies develop and refine strategic plans, recruit additional management or board talent, access debt or equity capital markets, identify and negotiate acquisitions, develop compensation and incentive programs, and maximize value for all stakeholders upon exit.

55979 ■ SG Capital
1925 Century Pk. E, 5th Fl.
Los Angeles, CA 90067
Ph:(310)556-9900
Fax: (310)861-9024
Co. E-mail: info@sgcapital.com
URL: http://www.sgcapital.com

E-mail: info@sgcapital.com
Scope: Venture capital firm providing secured asset based funding to companies experiencing fast growth exceeding normal debt to equity ratios and companies being re-structured due to losses.

55980 ■ Spherix Inc.
12051 Indian Creek Ct.
Beltsville, MD 20705
Ph:(301)419-3900
Fax: (301)210-4909
Co. E-mail: info@spherix.com
URL: http://www.biospherics.com

E-mail: info@spherix.com
Scope: Teleservices, ebusinesses, and IT solutions for the health and information industries.

55981 ■ Sprout Group
11 Madison Ave., Fl. 26
New York, NY 10010-3629
Ph:(212)325-2000
Fax: (212)538-8245
Co. E-mail: info@sproutgroup.com
URL: http://www.sproutgroup.com

E-mail: info@sproutgroup.com
Scope: The firm invests in stages from start-ups through buyouts in high growth areas such as information technology, medical products and services, business services and retail.

55982 ■ Venture Economics Inc.
395 Hudson St.
New York, NY 10014
Ph:(212)807-5000
Free: 888-989-8373
Fax: (212)807-5122
Scope: Venture capital and business development specialists providing customized research for industrial and financial corporations. Services include: identification of high-potential companies for investment, alliance or acquisition; assistance in establishing venture capital or strategic alliance programs; and assistance with specific acquisition searches. Services for institutional investors in venture capital include: basic education and due diligence evaluation of venture capital as an investment; development of venture capital investment strategy; and identification of investment opportunities, portfolio monitoring, analysis, performance; and benchmarking for the venture capital asset class. Serves private industries as well as government agencies. **Seminars:** Venture Capital Forum; Leveraged Buy-out Symposia; Strategic Partnering Symposia; Performance Monitoring Workshop.

55983 ■ Venture Planning Associates Inc.
7119 Tanager Dr.
Carlsbad, CA 92009
Ph:(760)931-5435
Free: 888-404-1212
Fax: (858)457-3388
Co. E-mail: capital@ventureplan.com
URL: http://www.ventureplan.com

E-mail: capital@ventureplan.com
Scope: Provides venture capital consulting services for all phases of business development, from start-ups to IPOs. Investment criteria and participation in projects include: the ability to purchase founders stock convertible preferred or warrants; direct participation in management either on the board of directors or as an officer business market large enough to go national; exit strategy via buyout or acquisition by larger firms; fee for services paid following seed capital funding. Also provides entrepreneurial training, consulting, executive search, marketing assistance and referral services to other professionals.

55984 ■ Western Capital Holdings Inc.
10050 E Applwood Dr.
Parker, CO 80138
Ph:(303)841-1022
Fax: (303)770-1945
Scope: Specialists in all phases of financial and management consulting. Provide strong emphasis in strategic planning and corporate development, financial analysis, acquisitions, investment banking and corporate finance. Projects range in size and duration to fit clients needs. Services can be applied to many diverse financial projects that may include the following: business plan development, budgeting and forecast-

ing, strategic planning, cash flow analysis, cash flow management, corporate development, banking relations, asset management, and financial analysis. Industries served: food industry, manufacturing, distribution, retailing, computer services, agri-business, financial services, insurance, and government agencies. **Seminars:** Buy Low, Sell High, Collect Early and Pay Late; Preparing Your Company for Sale; Venture Capital - Finding an Angel.

FRANCHISES AND BUSINESS OPPORTUNITIES

55985 ■ Advantage Leasing Corp.
324 E Wisconsin Ave.
Milwaukee, WI 53202
Ph:(414)291-3400
Free: 800-949-7040
Fax: (414)291-3406
URL: http://www.advantageleasing.com
Description: Advantage has been providing equipment financing to businesses for twelve years. We are the funding source (not broker) so terms are very attractive and flexible. Financing may be prepaid without penalty. We offer franchisees financing to complement their other sources of capital.

55986 ■ Innovative Lease Services, Inc.
5937 Darwin Ct., Ste. 103
Carlsbad, CA 92008
Ph:(760)438-1470
Free: 800-298-2882
Fax: (760)438-2046
Founded: 1987. **Description:** Equipment financing for franchises.

55987 ■ Leadssolutions.com
Direct Software, LLC
222 Fears St.
PO Box 433
Pineland, TX 75968
Ph:(409)584-3880
Free: (866)584-3880
Founded: 2003. **Description:** Leads, lead management and email campaigns.

55988 ■ Wirth Business Credit
4200 Dahlberg Dr., No. 100
Minneapolis, MN 55422
Ph:(763)520-8500
Fax: (763)520-8501
No. of Franchise Units: 9. **Founded:** 2005. **Franchised:** 2005. **Description:** Equipment leasing and financing. **Equity Capital Needed:** $47,700-$69,500. **Franchise Fee:** $30,000. **Royalty Fee:** None. **Financial Assistance:** No.

COMPUTERIZED DATABASES

55989 ■ *Business and Technical Assistance Programs*
Wheeling Jesuit University
316 Washington Ave.
Wheeling, WV 26003
Ph:(304)243-4341
Free: 800-678-6882
Fax: (304)243-4388
Co. E-mail: technology@nttc.edu
URL: http://www.nttc.edu
Description: Contains detailed information on programs and organizations specializing in technical and financial assistance for small businesses and start-up companies. Includes descriptions and contact information for the organizations. Contains address, phone numbers, and other data. **Availability:** Online: Wheeling Jesuit University. **Type:** Full text; Directory.

55990 ■ *Small Business Innovative Research Awards*
Wheeling Jesuit University
316 Washington Ave.
Wheeling, WV 26003

Ph:(304)243-4341
Free: 800-678-6882
Fax: (304)243-4388
Co. E-mail: technology@nttc.edu
URL: http://www.nttc.edu
Description: Lists Small Business Innovation Research (SBIR) Program award winners and abstracts of their winning projects. Provides information on potentially useful technology under development and products emerging with the aid of SBIR funding. **Type:** Directory; Bibliographic.

55991 ■ *Small Business Innovative Research Current Solicitations*
Wheeling Jesuit University
316 Washington Ave.
Wheeling, WV 26003
Ph:(304)243-4341
Free: 800-678-6882
Fax: (304)243-4388
Co. E-mail: technology@nttc.edu
URL: http://www.nttc.edu
Description: Contains solicitations for the Small Business Innovation Research (SBIR) Program and the Small Business Technology Transfer (STTR) Pilot Program. Programs seek to stimulate U.S. technological innovation by funding small business research projects. The database assists users in exploring topics for which funding is available. **Type:** Full text.

55992 ■ *Small Business Innovative Research Past Solicitations*
Wheeling Jesuit University
316 Washington Ave.
Wheeling, WV 26003
Ph:(304)243-4341
Free: 800-678-6882
Fax: (304)243-4388
Co. E-mail: technology@nttc.edu
URL: http://www.nttc.edu
Description: Contains past solicitations for the Small Business Innovation Research (SBIR) Program and the Small Business Technology Transfer (STTR) Pilot Program. **Availability:** Online: Wheeling Jesuit University. **Type:** Full text.

55993 ■ *Small Business Innovative Research Solicitations and Awards*
Wheeling Jesuit University
316 Washington Ave.
Wheeling, WV 26003
Ph:(304)243-4341
Free: 800-678-6882
Fax: (304)243-4388
Co. E-mail: technology@nttc.edu
URL: http://www.nttc.edu
Description: Combines Small Business Innovation Research (SBIR) Program and the Small Business Technology Transfer (STTR) Pilot Program solicitations, and Small Business Innovative Research (SBIR) awards databases. Provides an overview of all SBIR/STTR activity. **Availability:** Online: Wheeling Jesuit University. **Type:** Full text.

COMPUTER SYSTEMS/ SOFTWARE

55994 ■ *Loan Express*
Entrepreneur, Inc.
2445 McCabe Way
Irvine, CA 92614
Ph:(949)261-2325
Free: 800-421-2300
Fax: (949)261-7729
URL: http://www.entrepreneur.com
Price: $99.95. **Description:** Software program providing step-by-step information for writing a loan proposal.

LIBRARIES

**55995 ■ Innovation Ontario
Corporation–Information Centre**
56 Wellesley St. W, 7th Fl.
Toronto, ON, Canada M7A 2E7
Ph:(416)326-1041
Fax: (416)326-1109
Scope: Venture capital, innovation, new technology licensing. **Services:** Copying; Library not open to the public. **Holdings:** Figures not available.

**55996 ■ Loan Brokers
Association–Information Services**
917 S. Park St.
Owosso, MI 48867-4422
Contact: Ben Campbell, Dir.

Scope: Loan brokers, loan consulting, credit repair, lending, credit cards, venture capital. **Services:** Copying; SDI; Library to members or by permission.

**55997 ■ Sentron Medical Inc.–Senmed
Medical Ventures Library**
4445 Lake Forest Dr., No. 600
Cincinnati, OH 45242-3798
Ph:(513)563-3244
Contact: Rosanne Wohlwender
Scope: Biotechnology, medical devices and diagnostics, technology transfer, pharmaceuticals, venture capital, licensing. **Services:** Library not open to the public. **Holdings:** 800 books; 50 reports. **Subscriptions:** 100 journals and other serials; 2 newspapers.

RESEARCH CENTERS

**55998 ■ St. Louis University–Smurfit-Stone
Center for Entrepreneurship**
John Cook School of Business
3674 Lindell Blvd.
St. Louis, MO 63108
Ph:(314)977-3850
Fax: (314)977-3627
Co. E-mail: ecenter@slu.edu
URL: http://eweb.slu.edu
Contact: Dr. Kevin Schulte, Dir.
E-mail: ecenter@slu.edu
Scope: Venture capital, endowed positions in entrepreneurship. **Educational Activities:** Gateway Series for Entrepreneurship Research (annually), in spring.

Wholesaling

START-UP INFORMATION

55999 ■ "Be Your Own Boss" in *Small Business Opportunities* (July 2005)
Pub: Harris Publications Inc.
Description: Basic tips for starting your own business are outlined. Fifteen startups that can be launched for under $500 are listed, including sunglass sales, customized items, online auctions, children's music education, custom tea, vehicle ramps, waste management, pet businesses, sporting goods and sports merchandise, recipes, home improvement, wholesaling, personalized candy bars, promotional advertising products and more.

56000 ■ "Electric Avenue" in *Small Business Opportunities* (Vol. 13, No. 6, November 2001, pp. 108)
Pub: Harris Publications, Inc.
Ed: Annette Wood. **Description:** Profile of R.S.C. Electronics, Inc., an electronics supply company that began in Wichita, Kansas.

56001 ■ "Fast Track" in *Entrepreneur* (Vol. 28, No. 1, January 2000, pp. 42)
Pub: Entrepreneur Media Inc.
Ed: Cynthia E. Griffin. **Description:** Profile of Patricia Green's Ginger Kids Inc., manufacturer and wholesaler of children's international baking and cooking kits, which also conducts baking and cooking classes for individuals and schools.

56002 ■ *Scrapbooking for Profit: Cashing in on Retail, Home-Based and Internet Opportunities*
Pub: Allworth Press
Ed: Rebecca Pittman. **Released:** June 2005. **Price:** $19.95 (US), $22.95 (Canadian). **Description:** Eleven strategies for starting a scrapbooking business, including brick-and-mortar stores, home-based businesses, and online retail and wholesale outlets.

ASSOCIATIONS AND OTHER ORGANIZATIONS

56003 ■ Distribution Research and Education Foundation
1725 K St. NW, Ste. 300
Washington, DC 20006
Ph:(202)872-0885
Fax: (202)785-0586
Co. E-mail: rschreibman@nawd.org
URL: http://www.naw.org/Template.
   cfm?section=DREF
Contact: Ron Schreibman, Exec.Dir.
Description: Firms that are members of the National Association of Wholesaler-Distributors, wholesalers, and trade associations. Seeks to advance knowledge in the field of wholesale distribution by means of long-range research projects. **Publications:** *The Acquisitive Distributor; Connect with Your Suppliers: A*

Wholesaler-Distributor's Guide to Electronic Communications Systems; Facing the Forces of Change: The Road to Opportunity (triennial); *Price for Success: A Practical Guide for Improving Margins in Wholesale Distribution.*

56004 ■ International Federation of Pharmaceutical Wholesalers
10569 Crestwood Dr.
Manassas, VA 20109
Ph:(703)331-3714
Fax: (703)331-3715
Co. E-mail: info@ifpw.com
URL: http://www.ifpw.com
Contact: William G. Goetz, Pres.
Membership: Wholesalers and distributors of pharmaceutical products. **Purpose:** Promotes efficient delivery of pharmaceuticals to hospitals, physicians, and pharmacists; seeks to increase public awareness of the role played by members in the health care system. Facilitates cooperation and exchange of information among members; represents members' commercial and regulatory interests; sponsors educational and promotional programs. **Publications:** *Focus* (semimonthly).

56005 ■ National Association of Wholesaler-Distributors
1725 K St. NW, Ste. 300
Washington, DC 20006-1419
Ph:(202)872-0885
Fax: (202)785-0586
Co. E-mail: naw@nawd.org
URL: http://www.naw.org
Contact: Dirk Van Dongen, Pres.
Description: Federation of national, state, and regional associations, and individual wholesaler-distributor firms. Represents industry's views to the federal government. Analyzes current and proposed legislation and government regulations affecting the industry. Maintains public relations and media programs and a research foundation. Conducts wholesale executive management courses. **Publications:** *NAW Report* (bimonthly); *SmartBrief.* **Telecommunication Services:** electronic mail, dvandongen@nawd.org.

DIRECTORIES OF EDUCATIONAL PROGRAMS

56006 ■ *The International Directory of Agents, Distributors & Wholesalers*
Pub: Interdata
Released: Annual. **Price:** $385, individuals seamail, includes insured delivery and handling; $455, individuals airmail, includes insured delivery and handling. **Covers:** More than 34,000 agents, distributors and wholesalers in 160 countries. **Entries Include:** Company name, address, phone, fax, contact name, company type, number of employees, year founded, products and services. **Arrangement:** In two sections, alphabetical and classified by product. **Indexes:** Commodity.

REFERENCE WORKS

56007 ■ *American Wholesalers and Distributors Directory*
Pub: Thomson Gale
Contact: Deborah J. Baker
Released: Annual, latest edition 13, published September, 2004; next edition September, 2005. **Price:** $305, individuals. **Covers:** more than 28,000 wholesalers and distributors of consumer products in the U.S. **Entries Include:** Company name, address, phone, fax, e-mail, URLs, names and titles of key personnel, personal e-mail addresses, number of employees, financial data, product line, Standard Industrial Classification (SIC) code, and date established. **Arrangement:** Classified by subject, then alphabetical by company name. **Indexes:** SIC, geographical, alphabetical.

56008 ■ "Barnes & Noble unit is dropped by 2 big chains" in *Wall Street Journal* (February 5, 2003, pp. B4)
Pub: Dow Jones & Co. Inc.
Ed: Jeffrey A. Trachtenberg. **Description:** Sterling Publishing, owned by Barnes & Noble, lost contracts with both Borders Group Inc. and Costco Wholesale Corporation.

56009 ■ "Building Your Business" in *Small Business Opportunities* (Vol. 17, May 2005, No. 3, pp. 12)
Pub: Harris Publications Inc.
Ed: Carla Longley Vincent. **Description:** Seven ways for a small business to tap into customers and increase profits include the development of alliances, franchising, adding wholesale clients, sell to the government, work with nonprofits, market yourself, and create new goods or services.

56010 ■ "Foreign Targets" in *Hispanic Business* (July/August 2004, pp. 48)
Pub: Hispanic Business
Ed: Michael Caplinger. **Description:** Wholesalers and manufactures share insight into winning in a competitive global market. Statistical data included.

56011 ■ "GoWholesale" in *Entrepreneur* (Vol. 33, October 2005, No. 10, pp. 6)
Pub: Entrepreneur Media Inc.
Ed: Steve Cooper. **Description:** Buyers and sellers of goods will love the new Go Wholesale portal offering paid and unpaid content, including pay-per-click advertising, wholesale online auctions, free classified, blogs and small business information.

56012 ■ "Hispanic market pioneer retires" in *Hispanic Business* (Vol. 22, No. 1-2, January-February 2000, pp. 30)
Pub: Hispanic Business
Description: Robert W. Gray, former president of insurance group Allstate Property and Casualty, retired at the end of 1999 after 37 years with the company. Gary had a twin-track approach to marketing, incorporating Spanish-language advertising.

56013 ■ **"Jolting Joe"** in *Washington Business Journal* **(Vol. 22, No. 12, July 25, 2003, pp. 23)**
Pub: Washington Business Journal
Ed: Eleni Kretikos. **Description:** Dwayne Walker, operational chief of M.E. Swing Coffee Roasters, has been working at the 87-year-old coffee company since 1989. The coffee company's retail operations expanded after new city regulations forced it to halt wholesaling roasting.

56014 ■ **"New Site Gives Lipari Foods Room to Continue Growth"** in *Crain's Detroit Business* **(Vol. 23, January 8, 2007, No. 2, pp. 10)**
Pub: Crain Communications Inc. - Detroit
Ed: Brent Snaveley. **Description:** New location doubles size of local wholesale food delivery service. Recent growth with expanded product offerings dictates larger warehouse requirements. Plans are to expand territory to surrounding states in the Midwest.

56015 ■ **"Paper, Printing & Profit"** in *Small Business Opportunities* **(Vol. 16, No. 2, March 2004, pp. 70)**
Pub: Harris Publications, Inc.
Ed: Annette Wood. **Description:** Profile of Eric Jacobsen and Mahlon Regier, owners of Timber Creek Paper of Wichita, Kansas. The owners stay competitive by focusing on customer service, catering to smaller accounts such as churches, small businesses and local printers.

56016 ■ **"Quick Fix: Do SBA Express Loans Really Shortchange Entrepreneurs?"** in *Entrepreneur* **(Vol. 32, No. 4, April 2004, pp. 27)**
Pub: Entrepreneur Media, Inc.
Ed: Julie Monahan. **Description:** Profile of the U.S. Small Business Administration's Express program that guaranteed loans to thousands of entrepreneurs. Retailers with gross sales of $6 million or less, wholesalers with 100 employees or less, and manufacturers with 500 employees or less, are eligible for Express Loans.

56017 ■ **"Top 50 Exporters"** in *Hispanic Business* **(July/August 2004, pp. 50, 51)**
Pub: Hispanic Business
Description: Of the top fifty exporters in the U.S., thirty-five of them are wholesalers and manufacturers, accounting for $1.7 billion in export sales. The fastest growing exporter was Latin Node Inc., with a 400-percent increase in export sales.

56018 ■ **"Wal-Mart Said to Be Weighing Bid for Massachusetts-Based BJ's Wholesale Club"** in *Boston Globe* **(April 11, 2003)**
Pub: Knight-Ridder/Tribune Business News

Ed: Chris Reidy. **Description:** Wal-Mart Stores Inc. is considering a bid to purchase BJ's Wholesale Club Inc., located in Natick, Massachusetts. The chain operates about 140 club stores with sales of nearly $5.9 billion in 2002.

56019 ■ **"Wholesale power for retail agents"** in *Rough Notes* **(Vol. 146, No. 3, March 2003, pp. 108)**
Pub: Rough Notes
Ed: Elisabeth Boone. **Description:** Ernie Telford and Steve DeCarlo formed American Wholesale Insurance which is an independently owned wholesaler with buying power to serve retailers, independent insurance agencies and brokers.

56020 ■ **"Wholesale changes: Mom-and-Pop stores are so passe"** in *Entrepreneur* **(Vol. 30, No. 2, February 2002, pp. 19)**
Pub: Entrepreneur Media Inc.
Ed: Nichole L. Torres. **Description:** Some retailers are revamping the layout of stores to give the look of a warehouse in order to attract more customers.

56021 ■ **"Wholesaler plans Web expansion"** in *Hispanic Business* **(Vol. 22, No. 6, June 2000, pp. 114)**
Pub: Hispanic Business
Ed: Christopher D. Lancette, Scott Williams, Joel Russell. **Description:** Hispanic-owned electronic wholesaler OneSource Distributors Inc. ranks 42nd in the Hispanic Business 500 table with 1999 revenues totaling $81.7 million. The company plans to grow through electronic commerce.

STATISTICAL SOURCES

56022 ■ *RMA Annual Statement Studies*
Pub: Robert Morris Associates (RMA)
Released: Annual. **Price:** $175.00 2004-05 edition, $105.00. **Description:** Contains composite balance sheets and income statements for more than 360 industries, including the accounting, auditing, and bookkeeping industries. Also contains five years of comparative historical data for discerning trends. Includes 16 commonly used ratios, computed for most of the size groupings for nearly every industry.

TRADE PERIODICALS

56023 ■ *The Distributor's & Wholesaler's Advisor*
Pub: Whitaker Newsletters Inc.
Ed: Susan M. Dyckman, Editor, dwaeditor@aol.com. **Released:** Semiannual. **Description:** Provides case

studies, how-to-do-it reports, and industry news of interest to wholesalers and distributors. Covers management strategies, working with manufacturers, logistics and warehousing, finance, personnel issues, sales management, technology, customer service, and law and regulation.

56024 ■ *NAW Report*
Pub: National Association of Wholesaler-Distributors (NAW)
Ed: Greg Erickson, Editor, gerickson@nawd.org. **Released:** Bimonthly. **Description:** Publishes information on government issues and actions affecting wholesaler-distributors specifically and the business community generally. Recurring features include reports on federal legislative and regulatory developments; legal and insurance trends; industry research and statistics; and business services offered through the association's group purchasing program. Remarks: Available online only

FRANCHISES AND BUSINESS OPPORTUNITIES

56025 ■ **Business Cards Tomorrow & Business Cards Tomorrow Satellite**
Business Cards Tomorrow, Inc.
3000 NE 30th Pl., 5th Fl.
Ft. Lauderdale, FL 33306
Ph:(954)563-1224
Free: 800-627-9998
Fax: (954)565-0742
No. of Franchise Units: 83. **No. of Company-Owned Units:** 3. **Founded:** 1975. **Franchised:** 1977. **Description:** Professional, niche wholesale service business. **Equity Capital Needed:** $45,000 minimum cash required, not borrowed. **Franchise Fee:** $35,000. **Financial Assistance:** Yes. **Training:** Yes.

56026 ■ **Worldwide Merchandise**
130 Fifth Ave., 10th Fl.
New York, NY 10011-4399
Ph:(212)242-4399
Description: Business of wholesaling with over 7 different marketing programs to wholesale merchandise including Internet sales from Cyberstore, rack merchandising, mail order, flea markets, wholesaling to retail stores, catalog sales and general merchandising. **Equity Capital Needed:** $140.00-$900.00. **Managerial Assistance:** Custom designed website featuring your merchandise displayed worldwide, full color catalogs imprinted with your company name. **Training:** Provides unlimited consultation and assistance from support staff.

START-UP INFORMATION

56027 ■ "After Eight Years of Dreaming, Tulsa Woman Opens Wedding Chapel" in *Journal Record (Oklahoma City, OK)* (February 5, 2007)
Pub: Journal Record
Ed: Ginger Shepherd. **Description:** Profile of Judy Odum, founder of Vesica Piscis Wedding Chapel. Odum shares her dream of owning her own wedding chapel and shares insight into starting her business.

56028 ■ "Blossom Antique Shop Opens in Frenchtown" in *St. Charles Business Record* (May 4, 2004)
Pub: Dolan Media Company
Description: Profile of Blossom Antiques, a new shop offering unique, shabby chic items. Co-owners Blossom Arcobasso, Susan Rollins, and Vickie Clembronowicz are handling the day-to-day operations without other employees. The three friends each bring their own particular expertise to the business.

56029 ■ "Book Meets Girl" in *Entrepreneur. com* (Vol. 34, February 2006, No. 2, pp. 112)
Pub: Entrepreneur Media Inc.
Ed: Genevieve Jenkins. **Description:** Profile of Ellen Langas Campbell of Nou-Soma Communications, Inc. Campbell has written a series of inspirational books for girls between the ages of 8 and 12. The books encourage self-esteem and career focus.

56030 ■ "Bright Ideas" in *Entrepreneur* (Vol. 27, No. 12, December 1999, pp. 170)
Pub: Entrepreneur Media Inc.
Ed: Don Debelak. **Description:** The success story of Karen Alvarez and her invention of the Baby Comfort Strap, that safely secures a baby in a shopping cart.

56031 ■ "Business Incubator Has a Fish Wriggling Off of the Hook" in *St. Louis Post-Dispatch* (August 27, 2004)
Pub: Knight-Ridder/Tribune Business News
Ed: David Nicklaus. **Description:** Marcia Mellitz, founder of Symbiontics Inc., is considering a move to Wisconsin because of lack of funding. The firm is developing treatments for genetic disorders known as lysosomal storage diseases. It was launched with $3.5 million.

56032 ■ "Business On Her Own Terms" in *Black Enterprise* (Vol. 35, August 2004, No. 1, pp. 57)
Pub: Earl G. Graves Publishing Co. Inc.
Ed: Bridget McCrea. **Description:** Profile of Fay Coleman, president and CEO of her Silver Spring, Maryland firm, Westover Consultants Inc. Coleman started her business in the basement of her home and began developing educational training programs, planning events, creating public outreach programs, and conducting surveys for government agencies. Today, the firm comprises three divisions: Health and Behavior Sciences, Management Support Services, and Information Technology Services.

56033 ■ "Conference Helps Moms Jumpstart Home-Based Business Careers" in *Orange County Register* (January 28, 2005)
Pub: Freedom Communications Inc.
Ed: Nancy Luna. **Description:** The top ten home-based businesses are listed: Internet sales and marketing, Web and graphic design, online research, technical support, virtual assistant, business coach, event planner, children's product development, home services, and direct sales.

56034 ■ "Contest Challenges Teens to Consider Entrepreneurship" in *Kansas City Star* (March 8, 2005)
Pub: Knight-Ridder/Tribune Business News
Ed: Donna Vestal. **Description:** The National Association of Women Business Owners and Adams-Gabbert & Associates Inc. in Kansas City have announced a contest for senior girls to enter. The competition is meant to promote entrepreneurship among young women.

56035 ■ "Crafting a specialty: how to target a pleasant and profitable niche" in *Meetings & Conventions* (Vol. 37, No. 10, Sept. 2002, pp. 49)
Pub: NorthStar Travel Media, LLC
Ed: Sarah J.F. Braley. **Description:** Elizabeth Zielinski, shares her experiences while starting her own marketing service for independent planners.

56036 ■ "Detroit Free Press Macomb Small Business Column" in *Detroit Free Press* (July 21, 2005)
Pub: Knight-Ridder/Tribune Business News
Ed: Carol Cain. **Description:** After taking a buyout from General Motors Corporation, Miriam Muley launched a company that will help other firms tap into the power of women buyers.

56037 ■ "Doing It for Themselves" in *Entrepreneur* (Vol. 28, No. 8, August 2000, pp. 40)
Pub: Entrepreneur Media Inc.
Ed: Cynthia E. Griffin. **Description:** Women investors are aiding women entrepreneurs.

56038 ■ "Electric Avenue" in *Small Business Opportunities* (Vol. 13, No. 6, November 2001, pp. 108)
Pub: Harris Publications, Inc.
Ed: Annette Wood. **Description:** Profile of R.S.C. Electronics, Inc., an electronics supply company that began in Wichita, Kansas.

56039 ■ "Enjoy your meal!" in *Entrepreneur* (Vol. 30, No. 12, December 2002, pp. 32)
Pub: Entrepreneur Media Inc.
Ed: Gisela M. Pedroza. **Description:** Profile of Angela Roth, owner of Peanut Butter & Ellie's, the Portland, Oregon restaurant that caters to youngsters; first year sales are expected to reach $180,000.

56040 ■ "Entrepreneur of the Year: Shoba Purushothaman" in *Inc.* (January 1, 2005)
Pub: Inc. Magazine

Ed: Nadine Heintz. **Description:** Profile of Shoba Purushothaman, founder of NewsMarket, the firm that enables television broadcasters to transmit, watch and download video footage over the Internet. Purushothaman was voted Entrepreneur of the Year for 2004.

56041 ■ "The Entrepreneurial Elite" in *Business Week* (No. 3658, December 6, 1999, pp. F46)
Pub: McGraw-Hill, Inc.
Description: A discussion with various business-affiliated people regarding small businesses, including how women entrepreneurs are changing the workplace and vice versa.

56042 ■ "Eureka! I have an idea - how a business is born" in *Women in Business* (Vol. 54, No. 5, September-October 2002, pp. 30)
Pub: The ABWA Company, Inc.
Ed: Mia Katz. **Description:** The development of several businesses is discussed by the women who established them.

56043 ■ "Explosive Success" in *Small Business Opportunities* (Vol. 14, No. 1, January 2002, pp. 62-64)
Pub: Harris Publications, Inc.
Ed: Annette Wood. **Description:** Profile of Sandy Faust, who launched her circuit board company from her back porch, and has turned the business into a $1 million a year enterprise. Faust has won numerous business awards and plans to grow the business for her family then retire.

56044 ■ "Fast Track" in *Entrepreneur* (Vol. 28, No. 1, January 2000, pp. 42)
Pub: Entrepreneur Media Inc.
Ed: Cynthia E. Griffin. **Description:** Profile of Patricia Green's Ginger Kids Inc., manufacturer and wholesaler of children's international baking and cooking kits, which also conducts baking and cooking classes for individuals and schools.

56045 ■ "Food fair: how one caterer's soiree made her the talk of the town" in *Entrepreneur* (Vol. 31, No. 5, May 2003, pp. 77)
Pub: Entrepreneur Media Inc.
Ed: April Y. Pennington. **Description:** Profile of Connie Chantilis and her catering firm, Two Sisters, located in Dallas, Texas. Chantilis expects 2003 sales to approach the $3 million mark.

56046 ■ "Football Fever" in *Small Business Opportunities* (Vol. 13, No. 6, November 2001, pp. 54-55)
Pub: Harris Publications, Inc.
Ed: Stan Roberts. **Description:** Profile of Charlotte Begley, retailer who earns $500,000 a year selling licensed football products. Ms. Begley attends three trade shows a year to find the latest designs, colors and styles.

56047 ■ "A Franchise of Her Own" in *Entrepreneur* (Vol. 28, No. 6, June 2000, pp. 163)
Pub: Entrepreneur Media Inc.
Ed: Ellen Paris. Description: Meet a few exceptions to the rule that women don't do franchising, and why don't they anyway?

56048 ■ "Generation W" in *Success* (Vol. 47, No. 4, September 2000, pp. 62)
Pub: Success Publishing, Inc.
Ed: Joan Szabo. Description: Women business owners get a shot at venture funding.

56049 ■ "Hanging tough: Wilhelmina Bell-Taylor overcame cancer to launch a successful business" in *Black Enterprise* (Oct. 2002, pp. 55)
Pub: Earl Graves Publishing Co.
Ed: Phaedra Brotherton. Description: Profile of Wilhelmina Bell-Taylor, who was diagnosed with Hodgkin's disease when she was only 19 years old. At age 54, Bell-Taylor is the founder and president of BETAH Associates Inc., a management counseling, communications, information, and administrative services firm located in Bethesda, Maryland. The company started as a home-based operation, incorporated in 1994.

56050 ■ "Health Crisis Inspires Medesto, Calif. Woman to Open Needlework Store" in *Modesto Bee* (January 22, 2003)
Pub: Knight-Ridder/Tribune Business News
Ed: Tim Moran. Description: Lois Mouriski Bear tells how she went from legal secretary to owner of the Elegant Stitch in Modesto, California. Mouriski Bear was diagnosed with breast cancer in 1997 and started her Internet business at home selling high-end needlework patterns and supplies.

56051 ■ "Hello, please give me $9 million" in *WorkingWoman* (Vol. 25, No. 7, August 2000, pp. 72)
Pub: Lang Communications Inc.
Ed: Ashley Craddock. Description: American businesswomen are being given the opportunity to invest in business run specifically by other women by venture capitalists running the Springboard 2000 investment showcase.

56052 ■ "Honor Thy Self" in *Black Enterprise* (Vol. 35, February 2005, No. 7, pp. 156)
Pub: Earl G. Graves Publishing Co. Inc.
Ed: Tanisha A. Sykes. Description: Self-esteem, stress management, and dealing with difficult people are the issues discussed for an aspiring woman entrepreneur.

56053 ■ "How I Did It: Amber Chand" in *Inc.* (September 1, 2004)
Pub: Inc. Magazine
Ed: Hillary Johnson. Description: Profile of Amber Chand, a businesswoman who went from running a museum gift shop to co-founding Eziba with her brother-in-law. Chand's mission to foster social change was the idea behind the artisan handicrafts retailer which provides a market for entrepreneurs worldwide, especially those in war-torn nations.

56054 ■ "I want to start my own business" in *Women in Business* (Vol. 54, No. 5, September-October 2002, pp. 14)
Pub: The ABWA Company, Inc.
Ed: Elizabeth Bradley. Description: The desire to start a business is discussed by several women business owners.

56055 ■ "If at First You Don't Succeed..." in *Black Enterprise* (Vol. 34, No. 4, Nov. 2003, pp. 48)
Pub: Earl Graves Publishing Co.
Ed: Zakiyyah El-Amin. Description: Profile of Linda A. Banks and Terri Michele who, together, attempted various business ventures, but found their true calling when starting a childcare center in Pittsburgh, Pennsylvania.

56056 ■ "In for the Count" in *Entrepreneur* (Vol. 28, No. 9, September 2000, pp. 60)
Pub: Entrepreneur Media Inc.
Ed: Cynthia E. Griffin. Description: Iris J. Burnett and Nell Merlino, developers of the innovative program called Count-Me-In had revolutionized business loans for women.

56057 ■ "The Inside Scoop: What's It Really Like to Buy a Franchise?" in *Entrepreneur* (Vol. 33, January 2005, No. 1, pp. 96)
Pub: Entrepreneur Media Inc.
Ed: Nichole L. Torres. Description: Profile of a woman who purchased a Cold Stone Creamery franchise.

56058 ■ "La Habra, Calif., Resident Builds Needlework Empire" in *Orange County Register* (February 12, 2001)
Pub: Knight-Ridder/Tribune Business News
Ed: Jan Norman. Description: Profile of Candamar Designs, maker of art needlework, including cross-stitch, needlepoint and embroidery kits, both retail and through mail order catalogs and the Internet. Candi Martin began her business venture as a means to stay home with her three daughters.

56059 ■ "Making the grade" in *Entrepreneur* (Vol. 31, No. 5, May 2003, pp. 96)
Pub: Entrepreneur Media Inc.
Ed: Devlin Smith. Description: Profile of Angela F. Norman, owner of The Goddard School of Centerville, a childcare and education center in Ohio. Norman is a former district sales manager for a pharmaceutical company, and does not have a degree in education or early childhood development.

56060 ■ "Millinery Magic" in *Small Business Opportunities* (Vol. 13, No. 6, November 2001, pp. 62, 122)
Pub: Harris Publications, Inc.
Description: Profile of Laura Daly, the home-based entrepreneur who designs and manufactures her own line of one-of-kind hats. In less than one year Ms. Daly is selling her designs at famed Henri Bendel's on Fifth Avenue, New York.

56061 ■ "Money Master" in *Entrepreneur* (Vol. 28, No. 9, September 2000, pp. 60)
Pub: Entrepreneur Media Inc.
Ed: Cynthia E. Griffin. Description: Finance is still an obstacle for businesswomen, and that is why expert Jennifer Openshaw has created a Web site to help women learn about personal finance.

56062 ■ "More Immigrant Women Begin Opening Own Businesses" in *San Jose Mercury News* (February 23, 2005)
Pub: Knight-Ridder/Tribune Business News
Ed: Steve Johnson. Description: San Francisco's Bay Area has become a popular site for immigrant women entrepreneurs.

56063 ■ "New Group Creating Opportunities for Women" in *Atlanta Business Chronicle* (Vol. 25, November 15, 2002, No. 23 pp. 10A)
Pub: American City Business Publications, Inc.
Ed: Wendy Bowman-Littler. Description: Project Tsunami Inc., a nonprofit organization launched with a seed grant from the Ewing Marion Kaufmann Foundation in 2002, aims to provide women entrepreneurs with economic opportunities around the world.

56064 ■ "New Stratford, Conn., Needlework Quickly Gains Fans" in *Connecticut Post* (January 31, 2003)
Pub: Knight-Ridder/Tribune Business News
Ed: Stephania H. Davis. Description: Profile of Janet Kemp Fine Yarns and Needlework. Kemp tells how she and her husband obtained a second mortgage on their home in order to start her business. The store features high quality yarns, patterns, and accessories for the crafts of knitting, embroidery and needlepoint.

56065 ■ "On the Survival Prospects of Men's and Women's New Business Ventures" in *Journal of Business Venturing* (Vol. 15, July 2000, pp. 347)
Pub: Elsevier Science, Inc.
Ed: Richard J. Boden, Jr., Alfred R. Nucci. Description: Issues are presented concerning the success of men and women entrepreneurs. Women were found to use less capital to start their businesses and the success of a business was found to relate directly to the amount of start-up capital employed.

56066 ■ "Opportunity of the Fly" in *Entrepreneur* (Vol. 28, No. 8, August 2000, pp. 40)
Pub: Entrepreneur Media Inc.
Ed: Cynthia E. Griffin. Description: The Air Force has launched an outreach campaign in order to contract with more women business owners.

56067 ■ "The opposite sex: women in search of money still face a man's world" in *Entrepreneur* (Vol. 30, No. 9, September 2002, pp. 36)
Pub: Entrepreneur Media Inc.
Ed: Aliza Pilar Sherman. Description: Three women discuss the specific issues women encounter when trying to secure financing for a startup business.

56068 ■ "Personal Shopper, Concierge Service Removes Clients' Stress" in *Washington Times* (February 4, 2005)
Pub: Washington Times
Ed: Donna DeMarco. Description: While shopping at a women's clothing store, Indra Books was asked by another customer to help her find the right clothing for her. Books attributes that experience to the driving force behind her newly founded personal shopping and concierge service called On the Go 4 U.

56069 ■ "A Plan for Today's Money Market" in *Hispanic Business* (March 2003, pp. 42, 44)
Pub: Hispanic Business
Ed: Andrea Siedsma. Description: A well-crafted business plan is essential for an entrepreneur to obtain capital. The plan must emphasize honesty, credibility, and the details of marketing. Sandra Delarosa, a California female entrepreneur, outlines the details of her business plan for procuring capital. Web sites to assist in writing a business plan are included.

56070 ■ "Powerful forces" in *Black Enterprise* (Vol. 32, No. 6, January 2002, pp. 69)
Pub: Earl Graves Publishing Co.
Ed: Bridget McCrea. Description: Profile of three women entrepreneurs who took on the high tech industry and succeeded with their startup companies. The articles discusses the fact that African American women are forging ahead in this male-dominated field.

56071 ■ "Raising the Woof: Make No Bones About It-This Bakery Takes Dog Food to a Whole New Level" in *Entrepreneur* (Vol. 32, July 2004)
Pub: Entrepreneur Media Inc.
Ed: Jonathan Riggs. Description: Profile of Melanie Superack who founded Just Dogs! with her mother. The franchise, located in a shopping mall, offers gift ideas for dog lovers, including holiday cookies, dog lollipops and flavored barrel treats. Sales for the store are expected to reach nearly $170,000.

56072 ■ "Selling Serenity" in *Small Business Opportunities* (Vol. 13, No. 5, September 2001, pp. 74, 130)
Pub: Harris Publications, Inc.
Ed: Marie Sherlock. Description: Profile of Judy Wallace, who runs a store called Serenity Shop, that sells inspirational products for those struggling with or recovering from addictions.

56073 ■ "She's Got a Brand New Bag: TV Producer's Designs Express Her Inner Child" in *Black Enterprise* (Vol. 35, August 2004, No. 1, pp. 133)
Pub: Earl G. Graves Publishing Co. Inc.

Ed: Maureen Jenkins. **Description:** Profile of Keisha McClellan, founder of Girly Bags & Accessories, a line of urban pillows, purses, backpacks and totes. McClellan is hoping to find a manufacturer interested in licensing and mass-producing her designs on children's pillows, bedding and wallpaper.

56074 ■ "Sister, can you share five bucks" in *WorkingWoman* (Vol. 25, No. 7, August 2000, pp. 20)
Pub: Lang Communications Inc.
Ed: Kathleen Jacobs. **Description:** Women will be the main beneficiaries of a new organization set up to ensure business women have easier access to enterprise loans by asking every female in America to donate $5.

56075 ■ "Small Businesses Fuel Growth" in *Success* (Vol. 47, No. 3, July 2000, pp. 16)
Pub: Success Publishing, Inc.
Description: A study showing that small businesses are getting a boost from ever-cheaper information technology and easier access to financial assistance, and are helping to fuel the U.S. economy's record expansion. The study also predicts that this segment of the American economy will see a shift in management as well as the labor force over the next 15 years. Entrepreneurs will no longer be predominately young, white men. They will be older women, many of whom will also be Hispanic and African-American, reflecting the same shift in the U.S. population as a whole.

56076 ■ "Soothe operator: word-of-mouth was the cure for discouragement" in *Entrepreneur* (Vol. 30, No. 12, December 2002, pp. 112)
Pub: Entrepreneur Media Inc.
Ed: April Y. Pennington. **Description:** Profile of Resheda Hagen, breast-feeding counselor and mother; Hagen began selling lanolin to new mothers for its healing power.

56077 ■ "Special Delivery" in *My Business* (February/March 2003, pp. 54)
Pub: My Business Magazine
Ed: Shannon Scully. **Description:** Profile of Dana Roy, who launched MaternitySolutions.com, an online catalog company specializing in upscale career and special occasion apparel for pregnant women.

56078 ■ "Stress free home office" in *WorkingWoman* (Vol. 25, No. 8, September 2000, pp. 72)
Pub: Lang Communications Inc.
Ed: Lisa Kanarek. **Description:** Advice on how to set up a home office and how to create a working environment within a home is presented.

56079 ■ "Stress Relief" in *Entrepreneur.com* (Vol. 34, February 2006, No. 2, pp. 104)
Pub: Entrepreneur Media Inc.
Ed: Sara Wilson. **Description:** Profile of Jeni Garrett who mastered three businesses by age 27. Garrett sold clothing and jewelry line, raised and sold cattle, and created a new spa brand in 2001. Garrett founded The Woodhouse Day Spa in Victoria, Texas and offers franchising opportunities.

56080 ■ "Success line" in *Success* (Vol. 47, No. 3, July 2000, pp. 78)
Pub: Success Publishing, Inc.
Description: Questions are answered on starting a business, including loans and grants, patents, and federal certification for minority- or woman-owned business.

56081 ■ "Taking the 'dis' out of disability" in *Black Enterprise* (Vol. 32, No. 9, March 2002, pp. 102)
Pub: Earl Graves Publishing Co.
Ed: Alan Hughes. **Description:** Profile of Carmen Jones who triumphed over a crippling car accident and built a marketing firm that serves disabled consumers.

56082 ■ "Ventura County Star, Calif., Business Profile Column" in *Ventura County Star* (June 30, 2994)
Pub: Ventura County Star
Description: Profile of Judy Arnold, owner of the new doggy daycare startup, Judy's Paw Spa. Arnold opened the pet spa in February 2005 and employs two individuals.

56083 ■ "Wanda Wen" in *Entrepreneur* (Vol. 30, No. 10, October 2002, pp. 32)
Pub: Entrepreneur Media Inc.
Ed: April Y. Pennington. **Description:** Profile of Wanda Wen, 39-year-old designer and co-founder of Soolip Inc. located in West Hollywood, California. Soolip retails and wholesales fine papers and customized invitations.

56084 ■ "What's For Dinner?" in *Entrepreneur* (Vol. 31, No. 8, August 2003, pp. 148)
Pub: Entrepreneur Media, Inc.
Ed: April Y. Pennington. **Description:** Profile of Dream Dinners Inc., a home meal-preparation service that has twelve customers, each paying $160, migrate around refrigerated stations, and preparing any 12 of the meals featured monthly. Tina Kuna and Stephanie Firchau, co-founders of Dream Dinners, have five locations in the Washington State area.

56085 ■ *Work@home: A Practical Guide for Women Who Want to Work from Home*
Pub: Woman's Missionary Union
Ed: Glynnis Whitwer. **Released:** March 2007. **Price:** $15.99. **Description:** Fifty-three percent of all small business are home-based. The book provides tips to women for starting a home-based business.

ASSOCIATIONS AND OTHER ORGANIZATIONS

56086 ■ Alliance of Minority Women for Business and Political Development
1316 Fenwick, Ste. 908
Silver Spring, MD 20910
Ph:(301)585-8051
Fax: (301)681-3681
Contact: Brenda Alford, Pres.
Membership: Organizations in support of minority women in business and politics. **Purpose:** Seeks to increase number of minority women business owners as elected officials, especially on the state level. Political action committee supports candidates through fundraising, endorsements, and training. **Publications:** *Power in Color and Gender* (quarterly).

56087 ■ American Academy of Professional Coders
2480 S 3850 W, Ste. B
Salt Lake City, UT 84120
Ph:(801)236-2200
Free: 800-626-2633
Fax: (801)236-2258
Co. E-mail: info@aapc.com
URL: http://www.aapc.com
Contact: Ms. Traci Wood, Marketing Coor.
Description: Works to elevate the standards of medical coding by providing ongoing education, certification, networking and recognition. Represents nearly 50,000 members worldwide. Promotes high standards of physician and outpatient facility coding through education and certification. **Publications:** *ACADEMY CODING EDGE* (monthly).

56088 ■ American Business Women's Association
9100 Ward Pkwy.
PO Box 8728
Kansas City, MO 64114-0728
Ph:(816)361-6621
Free: 800-228-0007
Fax: (816)361-4991
Co. E-mail: abwa@abwa.org
URL: http://www.abwa.org
Contact: Robin Necci, Natl. Pres.

Description: Women in business, including women owning or operating their own businesses, women in professions, and women employed in any level of government, education, or retailing, manufacturing, and service companies. Provides opportunities for businesswomen to help themselves and others grow personally and professionally through leadership, education, networking support, and national recognition. Offers leadership training, business skills training and business education; special membership options for retired businesswomen and the Company Connection for business owners, a resume service, credit card and programs, various travel and insurance benefits. Sponsors American Business Women's Day and National Convention and regional conferences held annually. **Publications:** *The Company Connection* (bimonthly); *The Leadership Edge* (quarterly); *Prime Time Connection* (quarterly) ; *Women in Business* (bimonthly). Also publishes training materials.

56089 ■ American Woman's Economic Development Corporation
216 E 45th St., 10th Fl.
New York, NY 10017
Ph:(917)368-6100
Co. E-mail: info@awed.org
URL: http://www.awed.org
Contact: Roseanne Antonucci, Exec.Dir.
Description: Entrepreneurs and executives from the private sector. Seeks to help entrepreneurial women start and grow their own businesses. Provides formal course instruction, one-on-one business counseling, seminars, special events, and peer group support. Seeks to increase the start-up, survival and expansion rates of small businesses. Represents women from all socio-economic levels, including formerly employed women and women from low-income communities. **Publications:** *AWED's in Business* (bimonthly).

56090 ■ Asian Women in Business
358 5th Ave., Ste. 504
New York, NY 10001
Ph:(212)868-1368
Fax: (212)868-1373
Co. E-mail: info@awib.org
URL: http://www.awib.org
Contact: Bonnie Wong, Pres.
Membership: Asian-American women in business. **Purpose:** Seeks to enable Asian-American women to achieve their entrepreneurial potential. Serves as a clearinghouse on issues affecting small business owners; provides technical assistance and other support to members; sponsors business and entrepreneurial education courses. **Publications:** Newsletter (quarterly).

56091 ■ Canadian Association of Insurance Women–Association Canadienne des Femmes d'Assurance
Purdy's Wharf, No. 601
1969 Upper Water St.
Halifax, NS, Canada B3J 3R7
Ph:(902)429-6813
URL: http://www.caiw-acfa.com
Contact: Glenda Edwardsen, Pres.
Membership: Women employed in the insurance industry. **Purpose:** Promotes professional advancement of members; seeks to insure equality of opportunity for women in the insurance industry. Facilitates communication among members; conducts continuing professional development programs; represents members' interests within the insurance industry.

56092 ■ Canadian Association of Women Executives and Entrepreneurs–Association Canadienne des Femmes Cadres et Entrepreneurs
PO Box 620
Toronto, ON, Canada M5S 2Y4
Ph:(416)756-0000
Fax: (416)929-5256
Co. E-mail: contact@cawee.net
URL: http://www.cawee.net
Contact: Kathryn Quirke, Pres.
Description: Seeks to provide opportunities for women to empower other women in the development

and advancement of their business and professional lives; which fosters financial independence, professional development and personal satisfaction. **Publications:** *Acclaim* (quarterly).

56093 ■ **Canadian Federation of Business and Professional Women's Clubs**
87 Kenilworth St.
Ottawa, ON, Canada K1Y 3Y6
Ph:(905)845-9760
Fax: (905)845-9406
Co. E-mail: darla.dw.campbell@sympatico.ca
URL: http://www.bpwcanada.com
Contact: Darla Campbell, Pres.
Description: Canadian women engaged in business, the professions, or industry. Works to enhance the economic, social, and employment status of women. Encourages women to become active in government at every level. Strives to improve business service standards. Networks with related organizations to promote common concerns. **Publications:** *Business and Professional Women* (quarterly).

56094 ■ **Center for Economic Options**
910 Quarrier St., Ste. 206
Charleston, WV 25301
Ph:(304)345-1298
Fax: (304)342-0641
Co. E-mail: info@economicoptions.org
URL: http://www.centerforeconomicoptions.org
Contact: Pam Curry, Exec.Dir.
Description: Seeks to improve the economic position and quality of life for women, especially low-income and minority women. Works to provide access to job training and employment options to women. Supports self-employed women and small business owners by offering training and technical assistance and information. Advocates women's legal right to employment, training, education, and credit. Seeks to inform the public on economic issues related to women; while activities are conducted on local and state levels, group cooperates with national and international organizations on issues relating to employment and economic justice for women. Maintains speakers' bureau and library. Compiles statistics; conducts research. **Publications:** *Women and Employment News* (quarterly).

56095 ■ **Center for Women's Business Research**
1411 K St. NW, Ste. 1350
Washington, DC 20005
Ph:(202)638-3060
Fax: (202)638-3064
Co. E-mail: info@womensbusinessresearch.org
URL: http://www.cfwbr.org
Contact: Dr. Sharon G. Hadary, Exec. Dir.
Description: Women business owners. Supports the growth of women business owners and their enterprises by conducting research, sharing information and increasing knowledge. Offers marketing consulting and seminars. **Publications:** *News*.

56096 ■ **Commission on the Status of Women**
Division for the Advancement of Women
2 UN Plz., DC2-12th Fl.
New York, NY 10017
Ph:(212)963-3463
Fax: (212)963-3463
Co. E-mail: daw@un.org
URL: http://www.un.org/womenwatch/daw/csw
Contact: Ms. Carmen Maria Gallardo, Chair
Membership: 45 Representatives from United Nations member States. **Purpose:** Promotes women's rights in political, economic, civil, social, and educational fields. Encourages cooperation between organizations seeking to advance the status of women, and advises the U.N. and member bodies on situations requiring immediate attention. Acts as a preparatory body for the world conference on women.

56097 ■ **Educational Foundation for Women in Accounting**
National Headquarters
PO Box 1925
Southeastern, PA 19399-1925
Ph:(610)407-9229

Fax: (610)644-3713
Co. E-mail: info@efwa.org
URL: http://www.efwa.org
Contact: Cynthia Hires, Admin.
Description: Women in the accounting field. Supports the advancement of women in the accounting profession through funding of education, research, career literature, publications, and other projects. **Publications:** *The Educator*.

56098 ■ **National Association for Female Executives**
60 E 42nd St., Ste. 2700
New York, NY 10165
Ph:(212)351-6451
Free: 800-927-6233
Fax: (212)351-6486
Co. E-mail: nafe@nafe.com
URL: http://www.nafe.com
Contact: Ms. Christine Roberts, Operations Mgr.
Description: Represents and supports professional women and women business owners; provides resources and services through education, networking, and public advocacy to empower members to achieve career success and financial security. **Publications:** *NAFE E-Newsletter* (biweekly); *NAFE Magazine* (quarterly).

56099 ■ **National Association of Women Business Owners**
8405 Greensboro Dr., Ste. 800
McLean, VA 22102
Ph:(703)506-3268
Free: 800-556-2926
Fax: (703)506-3266
Co. E-mail: national@nawbo.org
URL: http://www.nawbo.org
Contact: Erin M. Fuller CAE, Exec. Dir.
Description: Represents and promotes women-owned businesses to shape economic and public policy. **Publications:** *Leader Bulletin*; *NAWBOTime* (bimonthly).

56100 ■ **National Association of Women MBAs**
PO Box 2932
Houston, TX 77005
Co. E-mail: director@mbawomen.org
URL: http://www.mbawomen.org
Contact: Laura Wright, Natl. Dir.
Description: Provides networking opportunities for its members. Increases communication among graduate business schools regarding their initiatives to educate and support women in business.

56101 ■ **National Women's Business Council**
409 3rd St. SW, Ste. 210
Washington, DC 20024
Ph:(202)205-3850
Fax: (202)205-6825
Co. E-mail: info@nwbc.gov
URL: http://www.nwbc.gov
Contact: Margaret Mankin Barton, Exec. Dir.
Description: Women business owners. Strives to promote initiatives, policies, and programs designed to support women's business enterprises. **Publications:** *Engage* (bimonthly); *2000 U.S. Case Study: Successful Public and Private Sector Initiatives Fostering the Growth of Women's Business Ownership*.

56102 ■ **Seton Hill University's E-magnify**
Box 389F, Seton Hill University
Seton Hill Dr.
Greensburg, PA 15601
Ph:(724)830-4625
Fax: (724)834-7131
Co. E-mail: info@e-magnify.com
URL: http://www.e-magnify.com
Contact: Ms. Jayne H. Huston, Dir.
Description: Promotes women and business ownership. Offers a variety of entrepreneurial resources, educational programs, advocacy initiatives and networking opportunities to women entrepreneurs. Works "to strengthen the economic impact of women business owners as a collective force and to advance their growth through innovative programming in entre-

preneurship and new venture creation." Provides support, education and encouragement essential for the continued growth of women-owned businesses through its services. **Publications:** *e-magnify Extra!* (weekly). **Telecommunication Services:** electronic mail, huston@setonhill.edu.

56103 ■ **Women Entrepreneurs of Saskatchewan**
112-2100 8th St. E
Saskatoon, SK, Canada S7H 0V1
Ph:(306)477-7173
Free: 800-879-6331
Fax: (306)477-7175
Co. E-mail: info@womenentrepreneurs.sk.ca
URL: http://www.womenentrepreneurs.sk.ca
Contact: Janet Ursu, Chair
Description: Works with women who are considering starting a business, purchasing a business, or operating an existing business. **Publications:** *Women and Business* (semiannual); Bulletin (bimonthly).

56104 ■ **Women in Franchising**
53 W Jackson Blvd., Ste. 1157
Chicago, IL 60604
Ph:(312)431-1467
Fax: (312)431-1469
Co. E-mail: info@womeninfranchising.com
URL: http://www.womeninfranchising.com
Contact: Susan P. Kezios, Pres.
Description: Assists women interested in all aspects of franchise business development including those buying a franchised business and those expanding their businesses via franchising. Provides franchise technical assistance in both of these areas. Surveys the industry on the status of women. **Publications:** *Buying a Franchise: How to Make the Right Choice*; *Growing Your Business: The Franchise Option*.

56105 ■ **Women in Packaging**
4290 Bells Ferry Rd., Ste. 106-17
Kennesaw, GA 30144-1300
Ph:(770)924-3563
Fax: (770)928-2338
Co. E-mail: wpstaff@womeninpackaging.org
URL: http://womeninpackaging.org
Contact: JoAnn R. Hines, Founder
Purpose: Works to promote and encourage women in the packaging industry. Educates the packaging industry about the contributions of women to the industry; helps to eliminate stereotypes and discrimination in the profession; offers networking opportunities; conducts career enhancement programs; compiles statistics; maintains Speaker's Bureau. **Publications:** *Career Hotline* (monthly) ; *Packaging Horizons*; Update.

56106 ■ **Women's Regional Publications of America**
12620-3 Beach Blvd., No. 303
Jacksonville, FL 32246
Ph:(904)992-7228
Co. E-mail: kgreen@womsdigest.net
URL: http://www.womensyellowpages.org
Contact: Karen Green, Pres.
Description: Objectives are: to provide a forum where publishers of women's publications and business directories share information and resources; increase the visibility, authority, influence and status of women's business for the purpose of promoting growth and support of women; educate the general public about the need to support women-owned businesses, including equal opportunity employers and contractors. Directories published annually to reach out to the women's business community.

REFERENCE WORKS

56107 ■ **"$1 Billion Outreach"** in *Hispanic Business* **(April 2005, pp. 14)**
Pub: Hispanic Business
Description: Marriott International Inc. plans to spend $1 billion with minority- and women-owned suppliers over the next five years.

56108 ■ "19th Annual Entrepreneurial Woman's Conference" in *Entrepreneur* (Vol. 33, August 2005, No. 8, pp. 4)
Pub: Entrepreneur Media Inc.
Ed: Steve Cooper. **Description:** The Women's Business Development Center holds its annual Entrepreneurial Women's Conference for women business owners. The event presents a buyer's mart that allows the owners to market products and services to corporate and government buyers. There are also discussions and workshops addressing issues and trends affecting women-owned businesses.

56109 ■ "50 Most Powerful Black Women in Business" in *Black Enterprise* (Vol. 36, February 2006, No. 7, pp. 124)
Pub: Earl G. Graves Publishing Co. Inc.
Ed: Carolyn M. Brown. **Description:** Profiles of Black Enterprise's fifty most powerful black women in business are highlighted. The women represent senior managers of multinational corporations to founders of the largest black-owned businesses in the U.S.

56110 ■ "2005 Elite Women" in *Hispanic Business* (April 2005, pp. 44, 46, 48, 50, 52)
Pub: Hispanic Business
Description: Profiles of the 2005 Elite Women honored by Hispanic Business are presented. The women were chosen for their work in forging new ground in business and beyond.

56111 ■ "The "A" team" in *WorkingWoman* (Vol. 25, No. 5, May 2000, pp. 24)
Pub: Lang Communications Inc.
Ed: Adele M. Stan. **Description:** The work of the President's Interagency Council on Women covers both international and domestic issues, including universal equality for females in education, health care and economic opportunity. It also provides a forum for career-minded women to be publicly noticed.

56112 ■ "ABWA entrepreneurs are making fun their business!" in *Women in Business* (Vol. 54, No. 5, September-October 2002, pp. 18)
Pub: The ABWA Company, Inc.
Description: American Business Women Association members discuss their companies. These businesses include a comedy club, bed and breakfast inn and a direct mail company.

56113 ■ "Access to Capital and Terms of Credit: A Comparison of Men- and Women-Owned Small Businesses" in *Journal of Small Business Management*
Pub: West Virginia University
Ed: Susan Coleman. **Description:** A comparison of access to capital for men- and women-owned small businesses. The study uses data from the 1993 National Survey of Small Business Finances.

56114 ■ "Ahead of Her Time" in *Success* (Vol. 47, No. 3, July 2000, pp. 84)
Pub: Success Publishing, Inc.
Ed: Jane R. Plitt. **Description:** The article uses Victorian entrepreneur Martha Matilda Harper as a teaching model for business education.

56115 ■ "Ambitious business women search for mentors during challenging times" in *San Francisco Business Times* (Vol. 16, No. 42, May 24, 2002)
Pub: San Francisco Business Times Inc.
Ed: Kristen Bole. **Description:** Mentoring Circles, a San Francisco nonprofit, connects women business owners with established women in business. Mentoring programs at San Francisco area companies are also discussed.

56116 ■ "Antigravity investing" in *Working Woman* (Vol. 25, No. 2, February 2000, pp. 32)
Pub: Lang Communications Inc.
Ed: James Pethokoukis. **Description:** Advice is given to select Internet stocks to avoid the roller-coaster effect.

56117 ■ "Art Lover Plays Fair Game" in *Crain's New York Business* (Vol. 23, January 29, 2007, No. 5, pp. F19)
Pub: Crain Communications, Inc.
Ed: Miriam Kreinin Souccar. **Description:** Profile of Helen Allen and her art fairs, including Pulse, a contemporary art fair in Miami which took in more than $10 million. Numerous dealers sold out their inventory on the first day of the fair. Her art fairs which in addition to Pulse include Ramsay and Art 212 are designed for a younger generation and feature more affordable pieces of work.

56118 ■ "The Art of the Woman Warrior" in *Inc.* (August 2005, pp. 26)
Pub: Inc. Magazine
Description: Two former Marines offer management training exclusively for businesswomen. The two sisters have created leadership workshops focusing on ten concepts they learned from the Marines.

56119 ■ "Artascope Carves Out Niche In Arts and Crafts" in *Portland Press Herald* (June 17, 2005)
Pub: Blethen Maine Newspapers, Inc.
Ed: Edward D. Murphy. **Description:** Profile of Catherine Bickford and partner Kendra Haskell, owners of Artascope Studios. The studio offers mostly one-day art events that allow individuals to complete a project in a few hours. Media represented includes metals, paper, fibers, painting and prints and precious metal clay, a malleable material made from silver.

56120 ■ "Asian Persuasion" in *Entrepreneur*
Pub: Entrepreneur Media Inc.
Ed: Nichole L. Torres. **Description:** Profile of Leslie Karen Potter and Lynn Potter Wells, designers of Asian-inspired children's clothing in Longview, Texas. Leslie Potter adopted her daughter from China in 2000 and fell in love with the Chinese culture and wanted to raise her daughter knowing about and being proud of her heritage. That inspired her to create a line of clothing for her daughter and other children.

56121 ■ "At close range" in *WorkingWoman* (Vol. 25, No. 6, June 2000, pp. 32)
Pub: Lang Communications Inc.
Ed: Danielle Svetcov. **Description:** A freelance writer describes the communication difficulties she encountered with her parents when she returned to live near them in San Francisco, California, after living a distance for seven years.

56122 ■ "Atlanta ranked No. 1 in business owner diversity" in *Atlanta Business Chronicle* (Vol. 24, No. 10, August 10, 2001, pp. 45A)
Pub: American City Business Journals Inc.
Ed: G. Scott Thomas. **Description:** Compared to 180 other cities, Atlanta has the most diverse mix of entrepreneurs, according to a study by the Demographics Daily; Miami was second. The index has three components, which are divided along gender and racial lines: women in business, blacks in business, and Hispanics in business.

56123 ■ "Atlanta businesswoman puts ethics over profit" in *Atlanta Business Chronicle* (Vol. 25, No. 22, November 8, 2002, pp. 9B)
Pub: American City Business Publications, Inc.
Ed: Lee Hall. **Description:** Professional Management Resources Inc., a healthcare consulting company, recently carried out its first mass layoffs in the ten years it existed. Although PMR has been experiencing problems, Laverne Poindexter, head, stopped the firm's relationship with an undisclosed customer that frequently failed to comply with government rules. PRM was victorious in getting a Georgia Business Ethics Award from the Society of Financial Service Professionals' Atlanta Chapter.

56124 ■ "Atlanta!" in *Women In Business* (Vol. 52, No. 2, March 2000, pp. 14)
Pub: The ABWA Co., Inc.
Ed: Michele Compton. **Description:** Atlanta, Georgia, which will host the American Business Women's Association convention in November 2000, is a city with a lot of historical attractions.

56125 ■ "Atwater exec parlays experience into success" in *Crain's Detroit Business* (Vol. 19, No. 10, March 10, 2003, pp. 17)
Pub: Crain Communications Inc., Detroit
Ed: Robert Ankeny. **Description:** Profile of Vivian Carpenter, president of Atwater Entertainment Associates LLC., Carpenter began her career at age 26 after suddenly becoming widowed in 1978.

56126 ■ *Avon: Building the World's Premier Company for Women*
Pub: John Wiley & Sons, Incorporated
Ed: Laura Klepacki. **Released:** May 2006. **Price:** $21.99. **Description:** Profile of Avon, the world's largest direct sales company. Avon representatives number four million in over 140 countries.

56127 ■ "Bakery Wishes, Cake-Decorating Dreams" in *Bradenton Herald* (February 12, 2005)
Pub: Bradenton Herald
Ed: Tilde Herrera. **Description:** Profile of Deborah Naids and daughter, Jessica, co-owners of The Pour House. The shop offers four tables for those dining in, a counter across the back with 10 computer connections for laptops; the menu consists of baked goods, coffee, and a few breakfast and lunch-style sandwiches.

56128 ■ "Balance diet" in *Entrepreneur* (Vol. 30, No. 3, March 2002, p)
Pub: Entrepreneur Media Inc.
Ed: Aliza Pilar Sherman. **Description:** Despite the progress being made by women entrepreneurs, balancing work and family remains a major struggle for them.

56129 ■ "Bare Essentials" in *Entrepreneur* (Vol. 31, No. 11, November 2003, pp. 180)
Pub: Entrepreneur Media, Inc.
Ed: April Y. Pennington. **Description:** Profile of Sarah Siegel-Magness, maker of intimate and sportswear apparel. Siegel-Magness projects sales of $3.5-$5.5 million for 2003.

56130 ■ "Bead It! For Johnna Snell, Her Hobby's a Charm" in *Black Enterprise* (Vol. 34, No. 4, November 2003, pp. 171)
Pub: Earl Graves Publishing Co.
Ed: Pamela K. Johnson. **Description:** Profile of Johnna Snell, market director of the American Heart Association in Charlotte, North Carolina. Snell began creating jewelry as a hobby, but now has clients paying between $75 and $400 for her custom creations.

56131 ■ "Bead Store Blends Ancient and Modern to Find Success Downtown" in *San Jose Mercury News* (March 1, 2005)
Pub: Knight-Ridder/Tribune Business News
Ed: Joe Rodriguez. **Description:** Profile of Kathleen McCabe's bead store, Global Beads. McCabe stocks 50,000 kinds of beads in her Castro Street store.

56132 ■ "Beauty and the Bugs" in *Home Business* (Vol. 12, March/April 2005, No. 2, pp. 81)
Pub: Home Business Magazine
Ed: Sandy Larson. **Description:** Profile of Genma Stringer Holmes, founder of a home-based pest control company.

56133 ■ "Bed, Breakfast House in Arcadia, Miss., Reopens with New Owner" in *Sun Herald* (January 11, 2004)
Pub: Knight-Ridder/Tribune Business News
Ed: Dawn Krebs. **Description:** Profile of Audra McMurray, owner of Arcadia's Magnolia House Bed & Breakfast. McMurray always loved staying at bed and breakfasts when traveling and decided it was the right home-based business for her.

56134 ■ "Being strong comes at high cost" in *Women In Business* (Vol. 52, No. 5, September-October 2000, pp. 18)
Pub: The ABWA Co., Inc.
Ed: Penny Shaffer. **Description:** Issues are presented concerning women's ability to cope with balancing careers, family life, and raising children. The increasing occurrence of burnout among women is covered.

56135 ■ "Beth Blake and Sophie Simmons: 34 and 32, Founders of Thread in New York City" in *Entrepreneur* (Vol. 32, July 2004, No. 7, pp. 25)
Pub: Entrepreneur Media Inc.
Ed: Sara Wilson. Description: Profile of Beth Blake and Sophie Simmons, designers and manufacturers of bridesmaids' dresses. Word-of-mouth has helped the women grow their business.

56136 ■ "Bette LaPlante & Diane Cuvelier" in *Entrepreneur* (Vol. 31, No. 4, April 2003, pp. 17)
Pub: Entrepreneur Media Inc.
Description: Profile of Bette LaPlante and Diane Cuvelier, co-founders of Doughmakers LLC, a manufacturer of solid aluminum bakeware with a patented pebble pattern. The two women started their company with $1,000 in 1997 and projected sales for 2003 are estimated at more than $5 million.

56137 ■ "Beyond the resume" in *Women In Business* (Vol. 52, No. 4, July 2000, pp. 36)
Pub: The ABWA Co., Inc.
Ed: Diane Domeyer. Description: Issues regarding the recruitment of personnel are presented. The importance of interpersonal skills, knowledge technology, enthusiasm, and adaptability are discussed.

56138 ■ "Big Plans" in *Entrepreneur* (Vol. 30, No. 2, February 2002, p)
Pub: Entrepreneur Media Inc.
Ed: Aliza Pilar Sherman. Description: A report released in late 2001 by the Center for Women's Business Research (formerly the National Foundation for Women Business Owners), states that women-owned firms formed in the last decade are more growth-oriented than their predecessors.

56139 ■ "A Billion in Baskets" in *Small Business Opportunities* (Vol. 13, No. 6, November 2001, pp. 38, 40)
Pub: Harris Publications, Inc.
Description: Profile of Longaberger Company, the largest handmade basket-making company in the United States. The company grew from a small family business to a billion-dollar empire, and is the 22nd largest woman-owned company in America.

56140 ■ "Biloxi, Miss.-Area Pet Sitting Services Offer Alternative to Kennel Boarding" in *Sun Herald* (November 12, 2004)
Pub: Sun Herald
Ed: Tom Wilemon. Description: Profile of Maureen Rosetti, owner of The Pampered Pet Sitting Service, in Biloxi, Mississippi. Rosetti charges fees starting at $12.50 a visit, where she'll feed the pets, walk the dog, give medication, and water plants if necessary.

56141 ■ "The birth of a web site" in *Women in Business* (Vol. 54, No. 2, March-April 2002, pp. 26)
Pub: The ABWA Co Inc.
Ed: Mary Lou Chandler. Description: An American Business Women's Association member builds a Web site with the assistance of a Web site designer who is not a member of the association. Teamwork accomplished the task.

56142 ■ "Biz By the Book" in *Small Business Opportunities* (Vol. 17, September 2005, No. 5, pp. 58, 60)
Pub: Harris Publications Inc.
Ed: Vicki Gerson. Description: Partners, Ann Christophersen and Linda Bubon sell books for women and children. Women & Children First hosts events and book signings to promote the shop. Steps to open and market a book store are included.

56143 ■ "Blackgirl Rules!" in *Black Enterprise* (Vol. 34, No. 2, September 2003, pp. S4)
Pub: Earl Graves Publishing Co.
Ed: Raelyn C. Johnson. Description: Profile of Kenya Jordana James, teenage publisher of Blackgirl Magazine. The magazine spotlights African American girls at their best.

56144 ■ "Bringing Back a Classic" in *Inc.* (August 1, 2003)
Pub: Gruner & Jahr USA Publishing
Ed: Leigh Buchanan. Description: Profile of Betty Morris, the woman who founded Shrinky Dinks in 1973 and by the 1980s the products were seen everywhere.

56145 ■ "Broad's eye view" in *WorkingWoman* (Vol. 25, No. 8, September 2000, pp. 64)
Pub: Lang Communications Inc.
Description: 85Broads.com founder Janet Tiebout Hanson discussed her aims when starting up the online network aimed at women. The group has over 600 members who have worked for or are currently working for Goldman Sachs.

56146 ■ "The buddy system" in *WorkingWoman* (Vol. 25, No. 5, May 2000, pp. 84)
Pub: Lang Communications Inc.
Ed: JoBeth McDaniel. Description: There is a simple set of rules that enables business travel with a colleague to go smoothly. These rules include avoiding office gossip, flying separately, sharing dinner but not accommodation, and not hold meetings in hotel rooms.

56147 ■ "Building the Minority High-Tech Work Force" in *Hispanic Business* (Vol. 23, No. 7/8, July/August 2001, pp. 116)
Pub: Hispanic Business
Description: The Council on Competitiveness has received a $23 million grant to establish a non-profit organization to address the critical shortage of women and minorities in the high-tech industries sector in the U.S.

56148 ■ "Bus or bust" in *Women in Business* (Vol. 54, No. 5, September-October 2002, pp. 11)
Pub: The ABWA Company, Inc.
Ed: Elizabeth Bradley. Description: An appreciation of bus trips to the American Business Women Association's conferences and conventions is discussed.

56149 ■ "Business Bookshelf" in *Small Business Opportunities* (Vol. 17, September 2005, No. 5, pp. 134)
Pub: Harris Publications Inc.
Description: Reviews of three books of interest to small business owners and entrepreneurs are highlighted. Minding Her Own Business covers tax laws and financial matters to assist female business owners. Never Eat Alone covers networking and other business secrets to success. The Bottom Line On Integrity discusses business ethics and what it means to be honest.

56150 ■ "Business is Bouncin'" in *Home Business* (Vol. 12, October 2005, No. 5, pp. 71)
Pub: Home Business Magazine
Ed: Sandy Larson. Description: Profile of Jill Plumb, former teacher who rents out inflatable play structures from her home-based business in Northern California.

56151 ■ "Business Owners: Are You Getting Your Share of Investment Capital?" in *Women in Business* (Vol. 54, No. 5, Sept.-Oct. 2002, pp. 28)
Pub: The ABWA Company, Inc.
Ed: Mary-Lane Kamberg. Description: Sources of funding and techniques to obtain funding are discussed.

56152 ■ *C-E-O & M-O-M, Same Time, Same Place*
Pub: RB Balch & Associates, Inc.
Ed: Rochelle Balch; illustrated by Running Changes Staff. Released: 1997. Price: $9.95. Description: This quick reading, fun book tells the reader how to turn a downsized and out of work situation, into upsized success, independence and fun. The author, a single mom, started her homebased professional computer consulting business after losing her corporate job.

56153 ■ "Campaigns allow chapters and networks to share ABWA" in *Women In Business* (Vol. 52, No. 1, January-February 2000, pp. 42)
Pub: The ABWA Co., Inc.
Description: Members of the American Business Women's Association (ABWA) have encouraged membership via informal meetings and follow-up calls. Having fun is a priority for a successful membership campaign.

56154 ■ "Capital expansion" in *Black Enterprise* (Vol. 31, No. 5, December 2000, pp. 66)
Pub: Earl Graves Publishing Co.
Ed: Paula McCoy-Pinderhughes. Description: The owner of a 2-1/2 year old women's sportswear and gift company asks where to find angel investors or venture capitalists.

56155 ■ "Carver vs. OneUnited" in *Black Enterprise* (Vol. 35, December 2004, No. 5, pp. 96)
Pub: Earl G. Graves Publishing Co. Inc.
Ed: Sakina P. Spruell. Description: Profile of Deborah Wright, who has set her sights on making her firm a billion dollar giant. Carver was involved in a failed attempt in a takeover bid for Independence Federal Savings Bank.

56156 ■ "Celebrate Success. Embrace Innovation" in *Black Enterprise* (Vol. 37, February 2007, No. 7, pp. 145)
Pub: Earl G. Graves Publishing Co. Inc.
Description: 2007 Women of Power Summit provides networking opportunities, empowerment sessions, and nightly entertainment. More than 500 executive women of color are expected to attend this inspiring summit in Phoenix, February 7-10.

56157 ■ "Central Perks" in *Entrepreneur* (Vol. 33, September 2005, No. 9, pp. 34)
Pub: Entrepreneur Media Inc.
Ed: Aliza Pilar Sherman. Description: Most business women owners offer benefits that balances business needs with the needs of her employees.

56158 ■ "Chamber Kicks Off Weekly Member-Appreciation Program" in *Bellingham Business Journal* (December 2006, pp. 4)
Pub: Sun News Inc.
Description: Bellingham Women Chamber of Commerce and Industry celebrates various businesses within its membership with a member appreciation program.

56159 ■ "Changing for the better through conferences and conventions" in *Women in Business* (Vol. 54, No. 2, March-April 2002, pp. 24)
Pub: The ABWA Co Inc.
Ed: Mary-Lane Kamberg. Description: American Business Women's Association members can change their work lives when attending association conventions. Courses and get-togethers with other members can prove to be beneficial.

56160 ■ "Changing times: tax relief for women business owners" in *Women in Business* (Vol. 54, No. 5, September-October 2002, pp. 12)
Pub: The ABWA Company, Inc.
Ed: Edward Jones. Description: Wise retirement plan changes that could be implemented by women business owners as a result of the passage of the Economic Growth and Tax Relief Reconciliation Act of 2001 are discussed.

56161 ■ "Chatom Offers Wines With Cause Tie-Ins" in *Marketing to Women* (Vol. 19, November 2006, No. 11, pp. 5)
Pub: EPM Communications, Inc.
Description: She Wines, a line of wines created to benefit heart disease and breast cancer research, was introduced by women-owned and run Chatom Vineyards. The winery is based in Calaveras County, California.

56162 ■ "Chick magnet: How can you attract women to your business?" in *Entrepreneur* (Vol. 30, No. 3, March 2002, pp. 93)
Pub: Entrepreneur Media Inc.
Ed: Kim T. Gordon. Description: Nine out of ten households identify women as the primary shopper and in the past five years, women-owned businesses have increased at twice the rate of firms overall, therefore whether targeting businesses or consumers, it is important to improve ways of marketing to women in order to be successful.

56163 ■ "Child's Play" in *Entrepreneur* (Vol. 31, No. 9, September 2003, pp. 119)
Pub: Entrepreneur Media, Inc.
Description: Profile of three moms who left their jobs to start a children's enrichment center where parents can not only drop their children off but can also stay around and take a yoga class, or just enjoy watching their children participate in activities.

56164 ■ "Clone yourself" in *WorkingWoman* (Vol. 25, No. 5, May 2000, pp. 79)
Pub: Lang Communications Inc.
Ed: Russell Wild. Description: Planning for a successor is a good strategy for career development and makes good sense. Issues concerning the training of a replacement and the ability to delegate are presented.

56165 ■ "Commentary: For Women in Management, Communication is King" in *Long Island Business News* (March 12, 2004)
Pub: Dolan Media Newswires
Ed: Natalie Canavor. Description: Reasoning behind women's management skills versus men's are discussed; research studies are used to document opinions.

56166 ■ "Commentary: Three Steps to Becoming a Business Leader in Your Field" in *Long Island Business News* (February 13, 2004)
Pub: Dolan Media Newswires
Description: Interview with Martha Ann Walther, one of the most impressive women in business today. Walther is vice president of operations for Triborough Bridge and Tunnel Authority and believes that being perceived as a leader can be a career-making factor for women in every industry at any stage of her career.

56167 ■ "Common Ground" in *Pittsburgh Business Times* (Vol. 23, No. 7, September 5, 2003, pp. 23)
Pub: Pittsburgh Business Times
Ed: Suzanne Elliott. Description: Profiles of six women-owned businesses on Penn Avenue in Pittsburgh, Pennsylvania are presented.

56168 ■ "Community Crusader" in *Black Enterprise* (Vol. 35, September 2004, No. 2, pp. 67)
Pub: Earl G. Graves Publishing Co. Inc.
Ed: Erin Straker. Description: Profile of Drunia M. Duvivier, owner of a three-level property located in the Bedford-Stuyvesant section of Brooklyn, New York. Duvivier a former executive at Morgan Stanley, turned real estate investor, took advantage of the Neighborhood Housing Services' StoreWorks program. The program is geared toward community rehabilitation and revitalization.

56169 ■ "Competing with the Big Guys" in *Home Business* (Vol. 13, January/February 2006, No. 1, pp. 71)
Pub: Home Business Magazine
Ed: Sandy Larson. Description: Profile of Seema Matia who runs a marketing research firm from her home in Calabasas, California. Matia offers services to small and medium-sized businesses.

56170 ■ "Conference Calendar" in *Marketing to Women* (Vol. 20, January 2007, No. 1, pp. 7)
Pub: EPM Communications, Inc.
Description: Calendar spotlighting women's business conferences through the month of June.

56171 ■ "Connect the daughters: sons aren't the only offspring taking over family businesses" in *Entrepreneur* (Vol. 30, No. 12, Dec. 2002)
Pub: Entrepreneur Media Inc.
Ed: Aliza Pilar Sherman. Description: According to Joseph H. Astrachan, director of the Cox Family Enterprise Center at Kennesaw State University in Georgia, it is often easier for daughters to take over a family business than for sons, because the daughters are not in competition with the father.

56172 ■ "Consulting the Homeland" in *Crain's New York Business* (Vol. 23, January 29, 2007, No. 5, pp. F9)
Pub: Crain Communications, Inc.
Ed: Samantha Marshall. Description: Profile of Wendy Cai, director of Chinese Services Group, Deloitte & Touche USA, and one-time owner of e-commerce company Hagglers.com. She is one of the youngest directors in Deloitte's history and advises Fortune 500 companies on China investments ranging from $10 to $50 million.

56173 ■ "Contrasting restaurateurs stick fork in Mt. Clemens" in *Crain's Detroit Business* (Vol. 19, No. 14, April 7, 2003, pp.)
Pub: Crain Communications Inc., Detroit
Ed: Michael Strong. Description: Profile of Jennifer Hawk and Joann Tocco, founders of La Fondue in downtown Royal Oak, and their new restaurant The Fondue Room located in Mt. Clemens, Michigan.

56174 ■ "Convention Calendar" in *Black Enterprise* (Vol. 37, February 2007, No. 7, pp. 68)
Pub: Earl G. Graves Publishing Co. Inc.
Description: Listing of conventions and trade show of interest to minority and women business leaders.

56175 ■ "Coping with change" in *Women In Business* (Vol. 52, No. 3, May 2000, pp. 22)
Pub: The ABWA Co., Inc.
Ed: Mary M. Witherspoon. Description: Four different personality types are identified and how each type manages change in their personal and/or professional lives.

56176 ■ "Coping secrets for new stay-at-home Moms" in *Women In Business* (Vol. 52, No. 4, July 2000, pp. 18)
Pub: The ABWA Co., Inc.
Ed: Rhonda Reinholtz and Mary Jo Peebles-Kleiger. Description: Many successful businesswomen who remain at home after the birth of a child find it a stressful experience. Advice is given on coping with childcare, housework and the reevaluation of priorities.

56177 ■ "Corporate Elite" in *Hispanic Business* (January/February 2005, pp. 30, 32, 34, 38, 40, 42)
Pub: Hispanic Business
Description: Profiles of leading Hispanic corporate leaders include Richard A. Gonzalez, Abbott Laboratories; Carolos M. Morales, Merrill Lynch; James J. Padilla, Ford Motor Co.; William D. Perez, Nike; Marie Quintana Cummiskey, PepsiCo; and Felicia D. Thornton, Albertsons Inc., as well as others.

56178 ■ "Corporate Ties" in *Black Enterprise* (Vol. 34, July 2004, No. 12, pp. 41)
Pub: Earl G. Graves Publishing Co. Inc.
Ed: Nicole Lewis. Description: Profile of Alice Turner Byrd, owner of Turner Training USA. Byrd's firm provides corporate training to management and staff in CIGNA Corporation's customer service division.

56179 ■ "Courting Trouble" in *Inc.* (October 1, 2003)
Pub: Gruner & Jahr USA Publishing
Ed: Nadine Heintz. Description: Profile of an entrepreneur facing mail fraud charges engaged in a fraudulent scheme to obtain certification as a disadvantaged small business in 2000, in order to procure government road-construction contracts set aside for minorities and women.

56180 ■ "Creating human links" in *Black Enterprise* (Vol. 33, No. 3, October 2002, pp. 66)
Pub: Earl Graves Publishing Co.
Ed: Shani Smothers. Description: Founder of Youth LINKS USA, Alicia R. Jones, wants to eradicate technical literacy for youth in the Detroit, Michigan area. Jones offers training in software programs and A certification for computer repair up to the Microsoft Certified Engineer Training.

56181 ■ "Creature Comfort" in *Inc.* (November 1, 2003)
Pub: Gruner & Jahr USA Publishing
Ed: Riza Cruz. Description: Profile of Myriam Zaoui, cofounder and executive vice president of the Art of Shaving (TAOS); Zaoui uses her own formula for grooming products for men.

56182 ■ "Cutting the Corporate Purse Strings" in *Ingram's* (Vol. 27, No. 7, July 2001, pp. 20)
Pub: Show Me Publishing, Inc.
Description: Techniques and management theory for women small business owners is outlined. Topics include clarifying objectives, refining business ideas, research ideas, budgeting, concept testing, developing a business plan, and securing financing.

56183 ■ "De la Torre Named to Hall of Fame" in *Hispanic Business* (Vol. 23, No. 5, May 2001, pp. 20)
Pub: Hispanic Business
Description: Profile of Martha C. de la Torre, publisher of the Southern California Spanish language weekly El Clasificado. Ms. de la Torre was inducted into the National Association of Women Business Owners Hall of Fame in March 2001.

56184 ■ "Decorating Dollars" in *Small Business Opportunities* (Vol. 16, No. 2, March 2004, pp. 110, 112)
Pub: Harris Publications, Inc.
Description: Profile of Karen Price and Josie Cicerale, founders of Decor & You, a home-based decorating franchise. Professionally trained interior decorators go to client's homes and change the looks of rooms using wall and window coverings, furnishings, carpets and other elements. Currently 24 franchises are operating.

56185 ■ "Departures Raise Questions About Loss of Women" in *Crain's Detroit Business* (Vol. 22, November 27, 2006, No. 48, pp. 12)
Pub: Crain Communications Inc. - Detroit
Ed: Brent Snaveley. Description: Female executives are leaving a void behind them in business and industry when they leave. Most of them leave the auto industry entirely and a few move to tier one and tier two suppliers. Strong message is sent to other women in the organization of the unrest.

56186 ■ "Detroit Free Press Small Business Column" in *Detroit Free Press* (May 12, 2005)
Pub: Knight-Ridder/Tribune Business News
Ed: Carol Cain. Description: Profile of Donna Brinker, floral shop owner. Brinker opened her new shop and features candy and collectibles as well as flowers.

56187 ■ "Detroit Free Press Wayne Small Business Column" in *Detroit Free Press* (July 28, 2005)
Pub: Knight-Ridder/Tribune Business News
Ed: Carol Cain. Description: Profile of Dawn McAlister, owner of Designer's Choice. The firm's studio offers four employees who focus on custom design, while the company's warehouse offers discounts up to 30 percent. The warehouse showcases cabinets, lighting, sofas, artwork and other products.

56188 ■ "The Dimensions of Ping Fu" in *Inc.* (Volume 27, December 2005, No. 12, pp. 90-97, 132, 134-135)
Pub: Inc. Magazine
Ed: John Brant. Description: Profile of Ping Fu, owner of a software firm called Geomagic in Research

Triangle Park, North Carolina. Geomagic has defined and dominated the high-tech field of digital shape sampling and processing or DSSP, which entails scanning an object with optical beams, rendering it on a computer screen three-dimensionally for manufacturing, testing, and inspection purposes.

56189 ■ *Dive Right in - the Sharks Won't Bite: The Entrepreneurial Woman's Guide to Success*
Pub: Dearborn Financial Publishing, Inc.
Ed: Jane Wesman. Released: 1995. Price: $19.95.

56190 ■ "The Diversity Game" in *Forbes* (Vol. 170, No. 12, December 9, 2002, pp. 140)
Pub: Forbes Magazine
Ed: Tomas Kellner. Description: Information about the Small Business Administration's Section 8(a) program and its reform are examined. The program was created by President Nixon to foster black capitalism and sets aside up to $6 billion a year worth of government contracts for small companies owned by minorities or women.

56191 ■ "Do the locomotive" in *WorkingWoman* (Vol. 25, No. 2, February 2000, pp. 76)
Pub: Lang Communications Inc.
Ed: Bob Woods. Description: Business travel on new high-speed trains may be faster by up to 50 percent on Amtrak's Acela service.

56192 ■ "The Doll Maker: Cozbi Cabrera Breaks the Mold" in *Black Enterprise* (Vol. 35, October 2004, No. 3, pp. 203)
Pub: Earl G. Graves Publishing Co. Inc.
Ed: Sonia Alleyne. Description: Profile of Cozbi A. Cabrera, who turned her love for crafts into a home-based business that grew into a boutique in Brooklyn, New York. Her one-of-a-kind dolls are dressed with detailed beading, paint and hand-rolled hems. Cabrera shares information for doll collectors.

56193 ■ "Dotcom Damage" in *Entrepreneur* (Vol. 30, No. 1, January 200)
Pub: Entrepreneur Media Inc.
Ed: Aliza Pilar Sherman. Description: Gender issues following the dotcom crash are discussed. Despite what financiers may say, it seems women are still considered an investment risk.

56194 ■ "Double header" in *WorkingWoman* (Vol. 25, No. 5, May 2000, pp. 38)
Pub: Lang Communications Inc.
Ed: Eilene Zimmerman. Description: The Female Athlete company has 70 percent of its sales generated by catlogs and 30 percent from Web sites sales. Issues concerning marketing strategies to direct customers away from traditional catalog buying to purchasing on-line are presented.

56195 ■ "Doucette Really Gets Around" in *Sarasota Herald-Tribune* (September 16, 2004)
Pub: Sarasota Herald-Tribune
Ed: Amy Abern. Description: Profile of Sheila Doucette, owner of Your Shopper, a four-person transportation system that runs errands for people unable to do so themselves. Doucette started the same kind of company in Michigan, but moved to Florida, where there is a larger senior population.

56196 ■ "Doyenne of Hip Proffers Hot Tips" in *Crain's New York Business* (Vol. 23, January 29, 2007, No. 5, pp. F9)
Pub: Crain Communications, Inc.
Ed: Elisabeth Butler. Description: Profile of Dany Levy and her trendy business, an e-newsletter, Daily Candy. Advertisers are flocking to this Internet publication which expects to generate revenues of $25 million this year.

56197 ■ "The Dream Achievers" in *Women in Business* (Vol. 54, No. 2, March-April 2002, pp. 7)
Pub: The ABWA Co Inc.
Ed: Mia Katz. Description: Brenda L. Lawrence became the first African American and the first woman to be elected mayor of Southfield, Michigan. She is a member of the Millenium Chapter of the American Business Women's Association.

56198 ■ "The Dress Code: How Business Style is Communicated" in *Black Enterprise* (Vol. 34, No. 2, September 2003, pp. 60)
Pub: Earl Graves Publishing Co.
Ed: Laura Egodigwe. Description: Women business leaders tend to set standards by their business style. The basis of any executive's wardrobe is a great suit and wearing the best affordable quality.

56199 ■ "Easy e-commerce" in *WorkingWoman* (Vol. 25, No. 6, June 2000, pp. 107)
Pub: Lang Communications Inc.
Ed: Nancy Henderson. Description: Intensive courses in the business use of the World Wide Web are described, with focus on choosing a course to fit your previous knowledge and your own requirements.

56200 ■ "80 Elite Hispanic Women Directory" in *Hispanic Business* (Vol. 24, No. 4, Apr. 2002, pp. 32)
Pub: Hispanic Business Inc.
Description: A listing the 80 successful Hispanic women listed on the Hispanic Women Directory. A brief profile of each is included.

56201 ■ "The emancipates organization. Insights on gender, leadership, and power" in *Harvard Business Review* (Vol. 80, Sept. 2002, pp. 20)
Pub: Harvard Business School Press
Ed: Gardiner Morse. Description: In an interview with Kim Campbell, former Canadian Prime Minister, Campbell answers questions about being a female in male-dominated managerial jobs.

56202 ■ "An Embarrassment of riches" in *WorkingWoman* (Vol. 25, No. 5, May 2000, pp. 66)
Pub: Lang Communications Inc.
Ed: Marlys Harris. Description: Issues concerning the plethora of books written on financial guides for women are presented, including details on a selection of seven of the more "inspirational" books.

56203 ■ "Employing Her Literary Skills" in *San Diego Business Journal* (Vol. 28, January 8, 2007, No. 2, pp. 10)
Pub: San Diego Business Journal Associates
Ed: Michelle Mowad. Description: Profile of Professor Susan Bisom-Rapp, author of a new book on international and comparative employment law. The book covers laws in nine countries, including labor and employment law regulations.

56204 ■ "Enhance your people skills" in *Women In Business* (Vol. 52, No. 5, September-October 2000, pp. 34)
Pub: The ABWA Co., Inc.
Ed: Diane Domeyer. Description: Issues are presented concerning the benefits of implementing a team-based business environment. The skills that are required by personnel involved in team-based projects are explored.

56205 ■ *Enterprising Women: Lessons from 100 of the Greatest Entrepreneurs of Our Day*
Pub: AMACOM
Ed: A. David Silver. Released: 1994. Price: $21.95.

56206 ■ "Entrepreneur Column" in *Entrepreneur.com* (September 21, 2006)
Pub: Entrepreneur Media Inc.
Ed: Nichole L. Torres. Description: Women starting a business with younger children deal with special issues and concerns. It is difficult to balance the family and the business, but assistance is available and discussed to make this more manageable.

56207 ■ "Entrepreneurial Spirit" in *Black Enterprise* (Vol. 31, No. 4, November 2000, pp. 50)
Pub: Earl Graves Publishing Co.
Ed: Chirstine Albano. Description: Independent literary agent eyes financial freedom with aggressive investment and savings strategies.

56208 ■ "Entrepreneurship on the Rise" in *Home Business* (Vol. 12, March/April 2005, No. 2, pp. 44)
Pub: Home Business Magazine
Description: According to a study by the Office of Advocacy of the U.S. Small Business Administration, entrepreneurship for women, blacks, and Latinos has risen from 1979 to 2003.

56209 ■ "Executive women and the myth of having it all" in *Harvard Business Review* (Vol. 80, No. 4, April 2002, pp. 66)
Pub: Harvard Business School Press
Ed: Sylvia Ann Hewlett. Description: The results of research into the professional and private lives of highly-educated and high-earning women. The research reveals that, while high-achieving men continue to 'have it all', high-achieving women tend to be unable to combine career success and having children.

56210 ■ "Express Personnel Exec Named American Staffing Association Committee Chair" in *Journal Record* (June 25, 2003)
Pub: Dolan Media Company
Description: Profile of Linda C. Haneborg, newly named committee chair for American Staffing Association. Haneborg also serves on the U.S. Chamber of Commerce Labor Relations Board.

56211 ■ "Facing new pressure" in *Atlanta Business Chronicle* (Vol. 25, November 29, 2002, No. 25, pp. 1A)
Pub: American City Business Publications, Inc.
Ed: Walter Woods. Description: Augusta National Golf Club is receiving pressure from several Georgia business leaders to alter its men-only membership policy. Business leaders fear the situation will become more controversial and add to Georgia's poor reputation for diversity.

56212 ■ "Failure Rates for Female-Controlled Businesses: Are They Any Different?" in *Journal of Small Business Management* (Vol. 41, July 2003)
Pub: International Council of Small Business
Ed: John Watson. Description: According to studies, female-owned businesses generally under-perform male-owned businesses on various measures such as revenue, profit, growth, and failure rates. Statistical data included.

56213 ■ "Fast and fun" in *WorkingWoman* (Vol. 25, No. 7, August 2000, pp. 88)
Pub: Lang Communications Inc.
Ed: Jayne O'Donnell. Description: The development of more comfortable, practical, yet stylish sports cars has attracted a large number of women buyers into a predominantly male market.

56214 ■ "Fast Learner" in *My Business* (April/May 2004, pp. 48)
Pub: My Business Magazine
Ed: Lena Basha. Description: Profile of Louise Creager, owner of a gift-basket business she operates from her home in Bellvue, Colorado. Creager addresses inventory issues, assets and balance sheets.

56215 ■ "Father Figure" in *Entrepreneur* (Vol. 33, October 2005, No. 10, pp. 36)
Pub: Entrepreneur Media Inc.
Ed: Aliza Pilar Sherman. Description: Issues faced by daughters who inherit their father's business are discussed.

56216 ■ *Female Enterprise in the New Economy*
Pub: University of Toronto Press
Ed: Karen D. Hughes. Released: December 2005. Price: $24.95 (US), $29.95 (Canadian). Description: Examination of whether the increasingly entrepreneurial economy is offering women more opportunity or increases their risk for poverty and economic insecurity.

56217 ■ *The Female Entrepreneur*
Pub: Crisp Publications, Inc.

Ed: Connie Sitterly. **Released:** 1994. **Price:** $15.95. **Description:** Part of the Small Business & Entrepreneurship Series.

56218 ■ *The Feminine Quest for Success: How to Prosper in Business & Be True to Yourself*
Pub: Berrett-Koehler Publishers
Ed: Nancy H. Bancroft. **Released:** 1995. **Price:** $22.95.

56219 ■ **"Finally, Credit Where Credit is Due"** in *Business Week* (No. 3687, June 26, 2000, pp. 250)
Pub: McGraw-Hill, Inc.
Description: More and more banks are taking note of the unique characteristics and needs of women business owners, and it is getting easier for them to obtain loans.

56220 ■ **"Fire in the belly"** in *WorkingWoman* (Vol. 25, No. 2, February 2000, pp. 48)
Pub: Lang Communications Inc.
Ed: Russell Wild. **Description:** Successful women give secrets for staying motivated, including patting oneself on the back and taking the long view.

56221 ■ **"First to the Starting Line"** in *Black Enterprise* (Vol. 36, December 2005, No. 5, pp. 32)
Pub: Earl G. Graves Publishing Co. Inc.
Ed: Cliff Hocker. **Description:** According to a report by Florida International University, blacks are more inclined to start their own businesses than whites with the same educational backgrounds. However, blacks and Hispanics have more difficulties maintaining a new firm than their white counterparts.

56222 ■ **"Florida Online Dating Service Tries to Find Love Link for Urban Professionals"** in *Miami Herald* (March 1, 2004)
Pub: Knight-Ridder/Tribune Business News
Description: Profile of Beatrice Louissaint and Yolanda Davis and their online dating service and event company, Soul Connections. The service targets urban professionals in search of love. The Website provides a place for users to post photos and information to meet other singles, while an event division organizes functions where singles can socialize.

56223 ■ **"Flower power"** in *Entrepreneur* (Vol. 31, No. 5, May 2003, pp. 104)
Pub: Entrepreneur Media Inc.
Ed: Nichole L. Torres. **Description:** Profile of Tish Ciravolo of Daisy Rock Girl Guitars LLC. Ciravolo started her manufacturing firm in 2000 to make guitars that fit little girl's fingers and have flower and heart designs.

56224 ■ **"Focus on Fundraising"** in *Black Enterprise* (Vol. 35, September 2004, No. 2, pp. 63)
Pub: Earl G. Graves Publishing Co. Inc.
Ed: Sonia Alleyne. **Description:** Advice is given to a black woman pursuing a business management career organizing fundraising events.

56225 ■ **"For Better Or. How Women Entrepreneurs Strike a Balance Between Business and Marriage"** in *Entrepreneur* (Vol. 31, Oct. 2003)
Pub: Entrepreneur Media, Inc.
Ed: Aliza Pilar Sherman. **Description:** Two successful women entrepreneurs discuss marriage and business conflict and ways to deal with it.

56226 ■ **"For the Love of the Game: How One Woman Scores in the Sports Entertainment Industry"** in *Black Enterprise* (Vol. 35, August 2004)
Pub: Earl G. Graves Publishing Co. Inc.
Ed: Zakiyyah El-Amin. **Description:** Profile of Cydni Bickerstaff, founder of Bickerstaff Sports & Entertainment. Bickerstaff is a full-service sports marketing, managing, and event production company, specializing in marketing and promotions, sporting events, athlete appearances, and sponsorships.

56227 ■ **"For Offering Hope and Help to the Parents of Autistic Children"** in *Inc.* (April 1, 2005)
Pub: Inc. Magazine
Description: Profile of Julie Azuma, founder of Different Roads to Learning. After learning that her daughter Miranda was autistic, Azuma created an online retail business offering tools to help teach language and social skills to autistic children.

56228 ■ **"Former Female Weightlifter Opens Yuba City, Calif., Women-Only Fitness Center"** in *Marysville Appeal-Democrat* (January 26, 2003)
Pub: Knight Ridder/Tribune Business News
Ed: Harold Kruger. **Description:** Profile of Sherry Gideons-Martin and her husband Gary, who own the Natural Woman Lifestyle Center, a women-only fitness business in Marysville, California. At age 37, Gideons-Martin is a former fitness model and power lifter, who has fought bulimia, drugs, homelessness and a near-fatal heart attack.

56229 ■ **"Former Flight Attendant Starts Biz & Soars To $1.5 Million"** in *Small Business Opportunities* (Vol. 17, May 2005, No. 3, pp. 72)
Pub: Harris Publications Inc.
Description: Profile of Dawn Adams-Skodney who left her job as a flight attendant and became of medical transcriptionist and grew that profession into the successful Transcription Network, employing 30 employees. Revenue for 2005 should be more than $1.5 million.

56230 ■ **"Former Model Opens Hollywood, Fla. Maternity Clothes Boutique"** in *South Florida Sun-Sentinel* (November 5, 2003)
Pub: Knight Ridder/Tribune Business News
Ed: Gregory Lewis. **Description:** Profile of Velicia Hill, former runway model who decided to open a maternity clothing boutique after finding she could not find quality maternity clothing when she was pregnant.

56231 ■ **"Forum helps firms headed by women raise capital"** in *Wall Street Journal* (June 13, 2000, pp. B4)
Pub: Dow Jones & Co., Inc.
Ed: Jeffrey Tannenbaum. **Description:** Highlights of the Springboard 2000 Silicon Valley Conference, held in Redwood Shores, California in January.

56232 ■ **"Four Starrs Moves, Doubles Size"** in *Bellingham Business Journal* (January 2007, pp. A6)
Pub: Sun News Inc.
Description: Danielle Starr, owner of Four Starrs Boutique is moving to a location double the size of the original. The women's boutique sells cosmetics and clothing lines not readily available to the area.

56233 ■ **"Fredericksburg, Va., Administrative Services Company Lends Firms a Virtual Hand"** in *Free Lance-Star* (November 6, 2004)
Pub: Free Lance-Star Publishing Co.
Ed: Portsia Smith. **Description:** Profile of Kathy McHenry, owner of Your Virtual Advantage, a home-based company. McHenry, a former legal assistant, office manager and loan collector started her company in 2001 and provides services to clients in Virginia, Washington and Chicago.

56234 ■ **"From Mushing to Management"** in *Inc.* (January 1, 2005)
Pub: Inc. Magazine
Ed: Nicole Gull. **Description:** Lisa Wehl learned how to manage her 22 employees through a group of Alaskan husky dogs while competing in competitions such as the Knik 200 and the Klondike 300.

56235 ■ **"Frontier Online"** in *Business Week* (No. 3694, August 14, 2000, pp. F8)
Pub: McGraw-Hill, Inc.
Description: The number of federal contracts awarded to small businesses dropped by 23 percent from 1997 to 1999, from 6.4 million to 4.9 million, with minority- and women-owned companies hardest hit.

56236 ■ **"Generation next"** in *San Francisco Business Times* (Vol. 16, No. 42, May 24, 2002, pp. S4)
Pub: San Francisco Business Times Inc.
Ed: Kristen Bole. **Description:** Changes in society which impact women executives and opportunities for women in business are discussed along with employee benefits. Women in the Bay Area are highlighted.

56237 ■ **"Getting Ahead"** in *Hispanic Business* (June 2005, pp. 18)
Pub: Hispanic Business
Description: According to a study from the Immigration Policy Center, immigrant women play an important role in the growth of women entrepreneurship in the U.S.

56238 ■ **"Getting the Corner Office"** in *Black Enterprise* (Vol. 35, August 2004, No. 1, pp. 78)
Pub: Earl G. Graves Publishing Co. Inc.
Ed: Maureen Jenkins. **Description:** Profiles of African American women who have been successful in various businesses.

56239 ■ **"Getting Props: Awards Can Boost Your Self-Esteem-And Your Business"** in *Entrepreneur* (Vol. 33, March 2005, No. 3, pp. 38)
Pub: Entrepreneur Media Inc.
Ed: Aliza Pilar Sherman. **Description:** Awards focusing on female entrepreneurs can boost self-esteem and grow a business. Many national women's business awards are presented by organizations like the National Association of Women Business Owners and the National Association for Female Executives.

56240 ■ **"Girl Franchising Power"** in *Black Enterprise* (Vol. 36, February 2006, No. 7, pp. 155)
Pub: Earl G. Graves Publishing Co. Inc.
Ed: Bridget McCrea. **Description:** The Women's Franchise Committee (WFC) was created in 1996 by the International Franchise Association. The 18-member committee helps women become leaders in the field through mentoring, education, and training programs.

56241 ■ **"Girl power"** in *Entrepreneur* (Vol. 31, No. 5, May 2003, pp. 28)
Pub: Entrepreneur Media Inc.
Ed: Aliza Pilar Sherman. **Description:** Social entrepreneurship looks at the way a business fits into a community; an interview with business owners who did that and also found ways to help women and girls using their companies in included.

56242 ■ *The Girl's Guide to Being a Boss (Without Being a Bitch): Valuable Lessons, Smart Suggestions, and True Stories for Succeeding*
Pub: Random Housing Publishing Group
Ed: Caitlin Friedman; Kimberly Yorio. **Released:** April 2006.

56243 ■ **"Girls Just Wanna Have Funds"** in *Entrepreneur* (Vol. 28, No. 3, March 2000, pp. 38)
Pub: Entrepreneur Media Inc.
Ed: Cynthia E. Griffin. **Description:** The article looks at ways of changing how venture capital firms look at women.

56244 ■ *Girls & Young Women Entrepreneurs: True Stories about Starting & Running a Business Plus How You Can Do It Yourself*
Pub: Free Spirit Publishing, Inc.
Ed: Frances A. Karnes and Suzanne M. Bean. **Released:** 1997. **Price:** $12.95. **Description:** This book reminds readers that entrepreneurs can be male or female, young or old, experienced or new on the scene. Inspires young people to be creative, take positive risks, and focus on their futures. Includes first-person stories by young entrepreneurs & step-by-step instructions on how to start and run a business.

56245 ■ "Give 'Em the Sack" in *Entrepreneur* (Vol. 31, No. 9, July 2003, pp. 112)
Pub: Entrepreneur Media, Inc.
Ed: Nichole L. Torres. Description: Profile of Debra Scott and Jane Ubell-Meyer, founders of Buzz Bags LLC. The firm provides high-end gift bags to celebrities at trendy events.

56246 ■ "Global financing options" in *BlackEnterprise* (Vol. 31, No. 8, March 2001, pp. 48)
Pub: Earl Graves Publishing Co.
Ed: Paula McCoy-Pinderhughes. Description: Small business services provided by the Export-Import Banks of the United States, are profiled. The Export-Import (Ex-Im) Bank of the U.S. is an independent government agency that offers a number of financing options to minority- and women-owned export companies, including credit insurance and working capital guarantees on commercial loans.

56247 ■ "Going Global: International Business Tips Make a World of Difference" in *Entrepreneur* (Vol. 32, December 2004, No. 12, pp. 34)
Pub: Entrepreneur Media Inc.
Ed: Aliza Pilar Sherman. Description: Tips for women business owners to follow when expanding markets and increasing sales by doing business with overseas vendors and clients.

56248 ■ "Good as Gold" in *Entrepreneur* (Vol. 31, No. 10, October 2003, pp. 120)
Pub: Entrepreneur Media, Inc.
Ed: Nichole L. Torres. Description: Profile of Lindsay Cain of Femmegems, owner of a "design your own jewelry" store.

56249 ■ *Grassroots NGOs by Women for Women: The Driving Force of Development in India*
Pub: SAGE Publications, Incorporated
Ed: Femida Handy; Meenaz Kassam; Suzanne Feeney; Bhagyashree Ranade. Released: July 2006. Price: $29.95. Description: Understanding the role of non-governmental organizations in women's development is offered through interviews with twenty women in India who have founded NGOs serving women.

56250 ■ *Greater Phoenix Chamber Membership List—Women-Owned or Operated Businesses*
Pub: Greater Phoenix Chamber of Commerce
Price: $53, members print; $63, nonmembers print; $55, members diskette; $65, nonmembers diskette; all prices include shipping. Covers: 808 women-owned or operated businesses in the greater Phoenix, Arizona area. Entries Include: Contact details.

56251 ■ "Groups Pick Up Push for Women in Tech World" in *Crain's Detroit Business* (Vol. 22, December 4, 2006, No. 49, pp. 13)
Pub: Crain Communications Inc. - Detroit
Ed: Sheena Harrison. Description: Local groups, such as Ann Arbor Women in Computing, assist in providing opportunities for women in the local technology industry through networking, training, scholarships, job fairs and other means.

56252 ■ "The Growing Number of Female Managers in VC-backed Firms means that Women are seen as Less Risky" in *Inc.* (September 2000, pp. 60)
Pub: The Goldhirsh Group
Ed: D.M. Osborne. Description: Catherine Muther created not a separate, women-only network but rather a system for ushering women into the larger venture landscape. Managers of venture funds targeting women stress that they're not interested in special-needs cases.

56253 ■ *Growth Oriented Women Entrepreneurs and Their Businesses: A Global Research Perspective*
Pub: Edward Elgar Publishing, Incorporated
Ed: Candida G. Brush. Released: June 2006. Price: $135.00. Description: Roles women play in entrepreneurship globally and their economic impact are examined.

56254 ■ "Guide Advises Would-Be Entrepreneurs" in *Marketing to Women* (Vol. 20, January 2007, No. 1, pp. 8)
Pub: EPM Communications, Inc.
Description: Smart Women and Small Business: How to Make the Leap from Corporate Careers to the Right Small Enterprise, a new how-to guide book for women looking to leave their corporate careers and join the entrepreneurial workforce, offers tips on getting loans, starting a business, working with business partners, and finding and closing the right deals.

56255 ■ "Guzman to Head CHCC" in *Hispanic Business* (December 2001, pp. 14)
Pub: Hispanic Business
Description: Profile of Melinda Guzman, the first woman elected president of the California Hispanic Chambers of Commerce. Ms. Guzman recently won the Luminary Award for business leadership from the National Association of Women Business Owners.

56256 ■ *Hardball for Women: Winning at the Game of Business*
Pub: NAL Dutton
Ed: Pat Heim. Released: 1993. Price: $21.95.

56257 ■ "Have a Talent for Sales?" in *Black Enterprise* (Vol. 36, November 2005, No. 4, pp. 60)
Pub: Earl G. Graves Publishing Co. Inc.
Ed: Eve Tahmincioglu. Description: African American women are looking towards direct-selling as a means of empowerment and selling products targeted to African Americans. Our Own Image is a firm that sells Afrocentric products ranging from decor items to cosmetics.

56258 ■ "Health and Female Self-Employment" in *Journal of Small Business Management* (Vol. 41, No. 3, July 2003, pp. 233)
Pub: International Council of Small Business
Ed: Arthur L. Dolinsky, Richard K. Caputo. Description: Data from the Mature Women's Cohort of the National Longitudinal Survey of Labor Market Experience was used to study self-employed, wage earning, and non-employed women showed that self-employment had no significant effect on health status in 1995.

56259 ■ "Healthy prospects" in *Black Enterprise* (Vol. 32, No. 9, April 2002, pp.)
Pub: Earl Graves Publishing Co.
Ed: Wendy Pelle-Beer. Description: Profile of Juanita Simmons, owner of an exercise studio, who worked through the StoreWorks program to purchase a new building for her studio. StoreWorks is a collaborative partnership between the Neighborhood Housing Services Community Development Corp., the City of New York's Department of Housing Preservation and Development, the Department of Housing and Urban Development, and participating private lenders; available only in New York City.

56260 ■ "Heavy Hoop Dreams: Jackson Women, Partner Market New Fitness Twist" in *Business Journal-Milwaukee* (Vol. 20, No. 42, July 4, 2003)
Pub: American City Business Journals, Inc.
Ed: Phill Trewyn. Description: Profile of Wendy Iverson's Heavy Hoop Inc., who uses a heavy hoola hoop and other favorite toys to conduct fitness workouts at her fitness center.

56261 ■ "Help me out, here" in *Entrepreneur* (Vol. 30, No. 10, October 2002, pp. 40)
Pub: Entrepreneur Media Inc.
Ed: Aliza P. Sherman. Description: Successful women business owners discuss ways they are giving back through mentoring, sitting on corporate boards, and investing in their companies.

56262 ■ "Helping each other - one woman at a time" in *Women in Business* (Vol. 53, No. 7, January-February 2002, pp. 9)
Pub: The ABWA Co Inc.
Ed: Carolyn B. Elman. Description: The aims and objectives of the American Business Women's Association are provided. It is important for businesswomen to assist and mentor each other.

56263 ■ "Hispanic Business - Woman of the Year: Making the Case for Small Business" in *Hispanic Business* (March 2003, pp. 26-28)
Pub: Hispanic Business
Ed: Patricia Guadalupe. Description: Profile of Congresswoman Nydia Velazquez, Hispanic Business magazine's first Woman of the Year. Velazquez is known for her uncompromising advocacy on behalf of small businesses.

56264 ■ "Hispanic women taking the reins" in *Hispanic Business* (Vol. 22, No. 6, June 2000, pp. 118)
Pub: Hispanic Business
Ed: Jim Medina. Description: The number of U.S.-based, Hispanic women-owned companies grew by 205.6 percent between 1987 and 1996, according to the National Foundation for Women Business Owners. Their annual sales for the period reached $67.3 billion.

56265 ■ "A Home Court Advantage" in *Hispanic Business* (Vol. 23, No. 11, November 2001, pp. 38, 40)
Pub: Hispanic Business Inc.
Ed: Vivienne Heines. Description: The new American Airlines Center in Dallas, Texas will set a new standard for minority participation in construction and operations. American Airlines has been recognized as a model for its commitment to minority- and women-owned businesses, which won contracts totaling more than $94 million during the sports center's construction.

56266 ■ "Homegrown Business" in *Mail Tribune* (February 21, 2005)
Pub: Knight-Ridder/Tribune Business News
Ed: Greg Stiles. Description: Profile of Elizabeth Bretko, owner of Heartsong Herbal Brewing Company. Bretko offers four varieties of her tea as an alternative to soda, coffee and alcohol. All teas are made from organic ingredients.

56267 ■ "Hot commodities" in *WorkingWoman* (Vol. 25, No. 2, February 2000, pp. 40)
Pub: Lang Communications Inc.
Ed: Joanne Cleaver, Carrie Patton, and Lisa Holton. Description: Corporate recruiters from Time Warner and Yahoo, along with top job applicants, offer job-search secrets.

56268 ■ "Hotlist 05" in *Black Enterprise* (Vol. 36, December 2005, No. 5, pp. 102)
Pub: Earl G. Graves Publishing Co. Inc.
Description: Profiles of the top young powerful African Americans chosen by Black Enterprise to represent their Hotlist for 2005. These professionals and entrepreneurs are all under the age of 40 and have transformed American business using innovative products or practices.

56269 ■ "How to Help Women? Start With an MBA" in *Crain's Detroit Business* (Vol. 22, December 4, 2006, No. 49, pp. 11)
Pub: Crain Communications Inc. - Detroit
Ed: Sheena Harrison Description: Increased percentage of women in MBA programs will lead to more advancement of women in the work place. Women's Initiative is working to increase the enrollment of women in University of Michigan's Ross School of Business through various student organizations and foundations.

56270 ■ "How I Did It" in *Inc.* (October 2005, pp. 132-134)
Pub: Inc. Magazine
Ed: Lora Kolodny. Description: In an interview, Paulette Cole tells how she wants to transform her New York City emporium ABC Home into a 100 percent socially responsible world market without jeopardizing the firm's $80 million in annual revenue.

56271 ■ "How I Did It: Roxanne Quimby" in *Inc.* (January 1, 2004)
Pub: Gruner & Jahr USA Publishing
Ed: Susan Donovan. Description: Profile of Roxanne Quimby, cofounder of Burt's Bees, maker of natural personal care products.

56272 ■ **"How do working parents rate?"** in *Women In Business* **(Vol. 52, No. 4, July 2000, pp. 26)**
Pub: The ABWA Co., Inc.
Ed: Michele Compton. **Description:** The views of children on having parents who work are presented. Advice is given on ways in which to include children in discussions about work and on how to schedule time for work and for children.

56273 ■ *How to Run Your Business Like a Girl: Successful Strategies from Entrepreneurial Women Who Made It Happen*
Pub: Adams Media Corporation
Ed: Elizabeth Cogswell Baskin. **Released:** September 2005. **Price:** $14.95. **Description:** Tour of three women entrepreneurs and their successful companies.

56274 ■ **"I Consider Myself the Visionary Still"** in *Business Week* **(December 19, 2005, No. 3964, pp. 54, 56)**
Pub: McGraw-Hill Companies
Description: Martha Stewart discusses her television shows, her return to work, and her time in jail.

56275 ■ **"I Think I'll Pass: Do Women Have a Tougher Time Delegating Tasks?"** in *Entrepreneur* **(Vol. 32, October 2004, No. 10, pp. 44)**
Pub: Entrepreneur Media Inc.
Ed: Aliza Pilar Sherman. **Description:** Although all entrepreneurs have trouble delegating tasks to employees, women business owners seem to have even more difficulty. Women also tend to be nurturing when delegating.

56276 ■ **"If I knew then what I know now"** in *WorkingWoman* **(Vol. 25, No. 7, August 2000, pp. 48)**
Pub: Lang Communications Inc.
Ed: Jeanne McDowell. **Description:** The views of seven successful American business women are shared, covering early working experience, combining family and work and competing in a male dominated sector.

56277 ■ **"Image is Everything"** in *Entrepreneur* **(Vol. 32, September 2004, No. 9, pp. 106)**
Pub: Entrepreneur Media Inc.
Description: Profile of Sandy Meyers, marketer of materials that incorporate fine art. Meyers uses the process of securing fine art prints and displaying them on items such as luggage tags, postcards, mouse pads, and coffee mugs, instead of a company's logo for marketing purposes. She also runs Visual Promotions, a firm that creates point-of-purchase and trade show banners and displays.

56278 ■ **"Industrious solution"** in *Houston Business Journal* **(Vol. 33, No. 48, April 11, 2003, pp. 19A)**
Pub: Houston Business Journal
Ed: Allison Wollam. **Description:** Profile of Caroline Brown, president and CEO of Magnum Staffing Services Inc., the company is seeing an increase in the hiring of temporary workers.

56279 ■ **"Inside Business"** in *Tribune* **(March 9, 2005)**
Pub: Knight-Ridder/Tribune Business News
Ed: Leslie E. Stevens. **Description:** Profile of Joni Anderson, who wears a pink hardhat when running her commercial construction company.

56280 ■ **"Inspirational Notes"** in *Black Enterprise* **(Vol. 36, December 2005, No. 5, pp. 138)**
Pub: Earl G. Graves Publishing Co. Inc.
Description: Profile of Sheraun Britton-Parris, who launched an inspirational t-shirt company. According to Marketdata Enterprises Inc., Americans are seeking psychological sustenance and motivational products made up 55 percent of retail sales in 2003.

56281 ■ **"Interiors By Design"** in *Black Enterprise* **(Vol. 35, October 2004, No. 3, pp. 54)**
Pub: Earl G. Graves Publishing Co. Inc.
Ed: Virginia Myers Kelly. **Description:** Profile of Denese Guadeloupe Rojas, a laid off direct mail worker, who earned a degree in interior design and is now the successful owner of Interiors By Design. Rojas offers interior and exterior design as well as home accessories to her clients. She started out working from home, but soon found she needed more space.

56282 ■ *International Handbook of Women and Small Business Entrepreneurship*
Pub: Edward Elgar Publishing, Incorporated
Ed: Sandra L. Fielden. **Released:** June 2005. **Price:** $165.00. **Description:** The number of women entrepreneurs is growing at a faster rate than male counterparts worldwide. Insight into the phenomenon is targeted to scholars and students of women in management and entrepreneurship as well as policymakers and small business service providers.

56283 ■ **"Introduction by TS Provides Personal Matchmaking for Long Island and NYC Clientele"** in *Long Island Business News* **(March 5, 2004)**
Pub: Dolan Media Newswires
Ed: Rosmaria Mancini. **Description:** Profile of Terry Sloane, a personal matchmaker on Long Island, New York. Sloane claims a 50 percent success rate helping clients find romance. Before starting her business, Sloan was already considered a matchmaker by friends and family.

56284 ■ **"Invest in the Basics"** in *Women In Business* **(Vol. 52, No. 5, September-October 2000, pp. 44)**
Pub: The ABWA Co., Inc.
Ed: Edward Jones. **Description:** Issues are presented concerning the investment decisions that need to be taken regularly by business owners. The provision of good employee facilities as a means of retaining quality employees is covered.

56285 ■ **"Is There a Secret to Happiness in Retirement?"** in *Women In Business* **(Vol. 52, No. 3, May 2000, pp. 9)**
Pub: The ABWA Co., Inc.
Ed: Kathie Dickenson. **Description:** Radford University Human Development Professor Janette Newhouse suggests good health, sufficient money and close relationships with family and friends will help people to have an enjoyable retirement.

56286 ■ **"It figures"** in *Entrepreneur* **(Vol. 31, No. 6, June 2003, pp. 36)**
Pub: Entrepreneur Media Inc.
Ed: Steve Cooper. **Description:** A compilation of miscellaneous business statistics are presented, including women's wages, Web servers, and consumer confidence.

56287 ■ **"It's in the Bag, Baby"** in *Entrepreneur.com* **(Vol. 34, February 2006, No. 2, pp. 110)**
Pub: Entrepreneur Media Inc.
Ed: James Park. **Description:** Profile of Christie Rein, founder of Diapees & Wipees in Flower Mound, Texas. Rein designs and sells fashionable diaper bags for moms on the go.

56288 ■ **"Jewelry Mixes Fashion and Healing Energies"** in *Marketing to Women* **(Vol. 19, November 2006, No. 11, pp. 5)**
Pub: EPM Communications, Inc.
Description: Body Rocks combines fashion and spirituality in their new line of jewelry and accessories that harness the healing properties of specific stones.

56289 ■ **"The Joy Factory"** in *WorkingWoman* **(Vol. 25, No. 4, April 2000, pp. 48)**
Pub: Lang Communications Inc.
Ed: Susan Caminiti. **Description:** Clincal psychologist, author, and television presenter, Dr. Joy Browne, talks about her move to television from radio broadcasting.

56290 ■ **"Kay Wagner"** in *San Diego Business Journal* **(Vol. 28, January 15, 2007, No. 3, pp. 34)**
Pub: San Diego Business Journal Associates
Ed: Pat Broderick. **Description:** Profile of Kay Wagner, who has been executive director of the Children's Museum/Museo de Los Ninos since 1999. Wagner is responsible for the museum's new 50,000-square-foot complex.

56291 ■ *Kitchen Table Entrepreneurs: How Eleven Women Escaped Poverty and Became Their Own Bosses*
Pub: Westview Press
Ed: Martha Shirk, Anna S. Wadia. **Released:** February 2004. **Price:** $14.95. **Description:** Profile of eleven successful women entrepreneurs.

56292 ■ **"Kitchen Table Entrepreneurs"** in *Small Business Opportunities* **(Vol. 16, November 2004, No. 6, pp. 134)**
Pub: Harris Publications Inc.
Description: Book review of Kitchen Table Entrepreneurs, by Martha Shirk and Anna S. Wadia. The book shows how eleven women pulled themselves from poverty and became successful entrepreneurs.

56293 ■ **"La Habra, Calif., Entrepreneur Starts Errand-Running Service for Busy Workers"** in *San Gabriel Valley Tribune* **(July 8, 2004)**
Pub: San Gabriel Valley Tribune
Ed: Andrew Blazier. **Description:** Profile of Sherri Durbin, owner of Consider It Done!, a new errand service. Durbin charges $32 per hour for services performed by her team of six independent contractors. Durban also founded an international mystery shopping and staffing company that she continues to manage.

56294 ■ **"Latinas' Businesses and Earnings are Seeing Major Growth"** in *Marketing to Women* **(Vol. 19, October 2006, No. 10, pp. 2)**
Pub: EPM Communications, Inc.
Description: According to Hispanic Business Inc., Hispanic woman-owned businesses grew 64 percent between 1997 and 2004. Latinas' median incomes also grew. Statistical data included.

56295 ■ **"Leader of the Pack"** in *Entrepreneur* **(Vol. 32, November 2004, No. 11, pp. 106)**
Pub: Entrepreneur Media Inc.
Ed: Jeri Yoshida. **Description:** Profile of Urmila Patel, the 46-year-old single mother who owns a PostalAnnex franchise. Patel had owned a clothing store in Belgium for 20 years before relocating to the U.S. She bought the franchise without knowing anything about postal, packaging and shipping services, but learned quickly, and now expects sales in 2004 to reach $500,000.

56296 ■ *Leadership Skills for Women*
Pub: Crisp Publications, Inc.
Ed: Marilyn Manning and Patricia Haddock. **Price:** $12.95.

56297 ■ **"Leading the Way"** in *Black Enterprise* **(Vol. 35, February 2005, No. 7, pp. 57)**
Pub: Earl G. Graves Publishing Co. Inc.
Ed: Bridget McCrea. **Description:** Profile of Lisa Williams, one of a few African American women leaders in the high-tech logistics and supply management field. Williams' firm conducts original research and offers technology services to help clients move information, goods, and capital within and between organizations.

56298 ■ **"Leaving a legacy"** in *Women In Business* **(Vol. 52, No. 4, July 2000, pp. 24)**
Pub: The ABWA Co., Inc.
Ed: Rachel Warbington. **Description:** The giving of personal time to charities that help people improve themselves can often be of more benefit than a legacy in a will. The satisfaction gained from helping others is reviewed.

56299 ■ "Lemon Aid" in *WorkingWoman* **(Vol. 25, No. 8, September 2000, pp. 94)**
Pub: Lang Communications Inc.
Ed: JoBeth McDaniel. **Description:** Advice for travelers for getting a good quality hotel room, a safe hire car and a comfortable seat on an aircraft is presented.

56300 ■ "Let's Have Some Funds!" in *Entrepreneur* **(Vol. 32, July 2004)**
Pub: Entrepreneur Media Inc.
Ed: Aliza Pilar Sherman. **Description:** Vicki Esralew and Shoba Purushothaman share insight into finding venture capital for women entrepreneurs.

56301 ■ "Let's Talk About Sexism: Do Sexist Attitudes Still Exist in Business? Women Sound Off" in *Entrepreneur* **(Vol. 32, No. 4, April 2004)**
Pub: Entrepreneur Media, Inc.
Ed: Aliza Pilar Sherman. **Description:** Women entrepreneurs discuss the issues of sexism in business, comparing issues today with those of the past. The article is divided with interviews with these women in each decade starting in the 1970s.

56302 ■ "Life after business" in *Women in Business* **(Vol. 53, No. 2, March-April, 2001, pp. 38)**
Pub: The ABWA Co. Inc.
Ed: Melissa Will. **Description:** Advice and information on participating in group travel are discussed. The advantages of being part of a group and the opportunities available on a cruise sponsored by the American Business Women's Association are discussed.

56303 ■ "Life after business" in *Women In Business* **(Vol. 52, No. 4, July 2000, pp. 21)**
Pub: The ABWA Co., Inc.
Ed: Michele Compton. **Description:** The average life expectancy of U.S. citizens has increased. Fifty thousand centenarians lived in the U.S. in 1999, and it is expected that this number will rise. The importance of diet and exercise in extending longevity is discussed.

56304 ■ "A Lifetime of Perseverance" in *Hispanic Business* **(December 2006, pp. 44)**
Pub: Hispanic Business
Ed: Michael Todd. **Description:** Profile of Terera Zubizarreta, founder of Zubi Advertising, located in Miami, Florida. Zubizarreta was awarded the Eduardo Caballero Lifetime Achievement Award from the Association of Hispanic Advertising Agencies.

56305 ■ "Living the Lifestyle of the Successful Businessperson" in *Hispanic Business* **(March 2005, pp. 62)**
Pub: Hispanic Business
Ed: Leslie A. Westbrook. **Description:** Profile of Watsonville Mayor, Ana Ventura Phares. Her father is the former vice-president of harvesting at Dole.

56306 ■ "Loanworthy Women" in *Business Week* **(June 12, 2000, pp. F8)**
Pub: McGraw-Hill, Inc.
Description: The conditions are favorable for loans for small women-owned companies.

56307 ■ "Local Business Changes Name" in *Bellingham Business Journal* **(January 2007, pp. 3)**
Pub: Sun News Inc.
Description: Profile of bridal self-help e-commerce website, TheSimplyOrganizedBride.com. The business name was changed from Weddings by Deborah to better reflect the nature of the business. Advertising opportunities for local wedding vendors, free tips and wedding articles, and a category for local bridal shows are now included in the content of the site.

56308 ■ "Long-term dare" in *WorkingWoman* **(Vol. 25, No. 7, August 2000, pp. 36)**
Pub: Lang Communications Inc.
Ed: Lisa Holton. **Description:** Issues and advice are given concerning the planning for and selection of long term care financial plans.

56309 ■ "Lowcost Launch" in *Small Business Opportunities* **(Vol. 16, November 2004, No. 6, pp. 76)**
Pub: Harris Publications Inc.
Ed: Vicki Gerson. **Description:** Profile of Jennifer Breen, president of WorkForce Cleaning, Inc. in Illinois. Breen's house cleaning business earns $1.5 million in sales annually. Her first big contract was to care for a 400-unit corporate housing project.

56310 ■ "Maine Women's Fund Makes a Difference With Women Entrepreneurs" in *Portland Press Herald* **(April 26, 2005)**
Pub: Blethen Maine Newspapers, Inc.
Ed: Tux Turkel. **Description:** Maine Women's Fund helps fund startup businesses for women as well as supporting programs to stop domestic violence. The association works with 125 centers in the U.S. that support entrepreneurial development among women.

56311 ■ "Maintaining Momentum" in *Hispanic Business* **(October 2003, pp. 86)**
Pub: Hispanic Business
Description: Profile of Jamie Gutierrez Vela, president of Midwest Maintenance Company, reporting sales that have more than tripled in the last five years. Ms. Gutierrez was named entrepreneur of the year by the University of Nebraska's Center for Entrepreneurship.

56312 ■ "Making ethical business decisions" in *Women in Business* **(Vol. 53, No. 2, March-April, 2001, pp. 22)**
Pub: The ABWA Co. Inc.
Ed: Mary-Lane Kamberg. **Description:** Issues concerning the steps involved in ethical decision-making in business are discussed. The importance of establishing clear guidelines for staff on company policy regarding ethics, honesty, and behavior is stressed.

56313 ■ "Making the Most of Your Network" in *Women In Business* **(Vol. 52, No. 4, July 2000, pp. 20)**
Pub: The ABWA Co., Inc.
Ed: Donna Fisher. **Description:** The importance of networking and the measurement of the benefits of networking to a business are discussed. The positive benefits of involving all staff in networking are considered.

56314 ■ "Making strides, but losing ground?" in *Black Enterprise* **(Vol. 32, No. April 2002, 9, pp. 30)**
Pub: Earl Graves Publishing Co.
Ed: Alan Hughes. **Description:** Female minority-owned businesses are growing at a greater rate than all women-owned firms with Hispanics leading the way, and African American next, then Asian and lastly Native American.

56315 ■ "Making the upgrade" in *Working Woman* **(Vol. 25, No. 6, June 2000, pp. 114)**
Pub: Lang Communications Inc.
Ed: JoBeth McDaniel. **Description:** Advice on upgrading your air ticket from coach class to first class is offered, including always using the same airline, searching for seats on the Internet and plan your business trips well in advance.

56316 ■ "Mane Attraction" in *Inc.* **(August 1, 2003)**
Pub: Gruner & Jahr USA Publishing
Ed: Heather Kenny. **Description:** Profile of Katrina Markoff, owner of a Chicago, Illinois chocolate boutique; Markoff unwinds by riding her horse, Euclide.

56317 ■ "A Man's World?" in *Entrepreneur* **(Vol. 31, No. 8, August 2003, pp. 26)**
Pub: Entrepreneur Media, Inc.
Ed: Aliza Pilar Sherman. **Description:** Interview with three women entrepreneurs examining the challenges women entrepreneurs face in today's marketplace. The panel consisted of Cristi Cristich, CEO and founder of Cristek Interconnects Inc., maker of connectors and cabling for medical and military applications; Sheri L. Parrack, president and CEO of Texas Motor Transportation Consultants, a professional registration, tax and title service company; and Terrie Jones, owner of AGSI, a provider of information technology resource solutions.

56318 ■ "Many happy returns" in *WorkingWoman* **(Vol. 25, No. 2, February 2000, pp. S8)**
Pub: Lang Communications Inc.
Ed: Rebecca Reisner. **Description:** Questions regarding income tax return preparation, including personal income tax exemptions and home office expense deductions, are answered.

56319 ■ *Mary Kay's You Can Have It All: Practical Advice for Doing Well by Doing Good*
Pub: Prima Publishing & Communications
Ed: Mary Kay Ash. **Released:** 1995. **Price:** $22.95.

56320 ■ "Marysville, Calif., Woman Runs Personal Chef Service" in *Marysville Appeal-Democrat* **(August 25, 2002)**
Pub: Knight Ridder/Tribune Business News
Ed: Katherine Tam. **Description:** Profile of Tiffani Williams, who started her own business, Fare & Simple Personal Chef Service, in which she prepares menus geared towards her clients' needs and tastes in their home. Williams can prepare five days' worth of meals at one time, each which can be reheated when ready to serve. Price plans are included.

56321 ■ "Meeting of the Minds: Women-Specific Conferences Have a Lot to Offer" in *Entrepreneur* **(Vol. 33, January 2005, No. 1, pp. 32)**
Pub: Entrepreneur Media Inc.
Ed: Alilza Pilar Sherman. **Description:** A listing of upcoming conferences geared to women entrepreneurs is presented.

56322 ■ "Milwaukee Businesswoman Opens Plus-Size Clothing Store to Fill Need" in *Milwaukee Journal Sentinel* **(November 16, 2003)**
Pub: Journal Sentinel
Ed: Tannette Johnson-Elie. **Description:** Profile of Cynthia Simpson, a plus-size African American woman who opened a store to meet the shopping needs of larger women, focusing on African American women who prefer trendy clothing with an Afrocentric flair.

56323 ■ "Minority Architects Say Reaching Out to Youth Will Help Add Diversity" in *Crain's Detroit Business* **(Vol.16, No.31, July 31,2000, pp.35)**
Pub: Crain Communications, Inc.
Ed: Jennette Smith. **Description:** Detroit-area minority architects are reaching out to raise awareness to women, youth, and minorities in this white-male dominated profession.

56324 ■ "Minority Businesses Look For a Boost From Super Bowl and Beyond" in *Crain's Detroit Business* **(Vol. 21, October 10, 2005, No. 43)**
Pub: Crain Communications Inc. - Detroit
Ed: Sheena Harrison. **Description:** Minority and women business owners are capitalizing on the opportunities presented by the Super Bowl XL coming to Detroit, Michigan. More than 1,100 of these companies have applied or are participating in the Super Bowl's Emerging Business Program open to any certified minority- or woman-owned firm in the state. It also provides training and networking to help compete in contracts.

56325 ■ "Minority Report" in *Entrepreneur* **(Vol. 32, October 2004, No. 10, pp. 59)**
Pub: Entrepreneur Media Inc.
Ed: C.J. Prince. **Description:** Historically, women and minority-owned businesses have received less venture capital, with only 4.2 percent of all venture capital in 2003 going to women-led companies. The Kauffman Fellows Program educates and trains future venture capitalists and is led by 14 fellows, eight of which are from minority groups (two are black, five are Asian, and one is Middle Eastern, three are women).

56326 ■ "More Women Than Men Have Home Offices" in *Marketing to Women* **(Vol. 19, October 2006, No. 10, pp. 12)**
Pub: EPM Communications, Inc.
Description: A survey of business professionals by Intellicontact reflects that women are more likely than men to have home offices. The survey also shows that while men and women both check their e-mail frequently, the two sexes manage their inboxes differently.

56327 ■ "Mrs., Mom, and CEO" in *Black Enterprise* **(Vol. 32, No. 9, April 2)**
Pub: Earl Graves Publishing Co.
Ed: Monique R. Brown. **Description:** Profile of Vickie Clark, owner and founder of a family owned, home-based business that transports kids back and forth to various activities.

56328 ■ "Music Instructor Gives Students Confidence to Get Up On Stage" in *The Record* **(November 13, 2005)**
Pub: New Jersey Media Group
Ed: Michael L. Diamond. **Description:** Profile of Jody Joseph, owner of Jody Joseph Music LLC in Tinton Falls, New Jersey; Joseph teaches her students to sing and perform in a way that connects with the audience.

56329 ■ "My Focus Is My Children" in *Inc.* **(October 1, 2003)**
Pub: Gruner & Jahr USA Publishing
Ed: Rita Cruz. **Description:** Profile of restaurateur, Monica Chitins and her husband who quit their New York careers and moved to Puerto Rico. It was there that Chitins opened her own restaurant, which allows her to spend time with her family.

56330 ■ "My Own Private Way to Go" in *Working Woman* **(Vol. 25, No. 7, August 2000, pp. 86)**
Pub: Lang Communications Inc.
Ed: Bob Woods. **Description:** The price and accessibility of private charter flying is making it a more practical way for business people to travel.

56331 ■ "MyTechTool" in *My Business* **(June/July 2002, pp. 24)**
Pub: My Business Magazine
Description: Profile of Susan Soros, owner of Soap Goddess, a home-based business that makes and sells all-natural handmade soap online.

56332 ■ *The NAFE Guide to Starting Your Own Business: A Handbook for Entrepreneurial Women*
Pub: Irwin Professional Publishing
Ed: Marilyn Manning. **Released:** 1995. **Price:** $16.95 (paper).

56333 ■ *National Directory of Woman-Owned Business Firms*
Pub: Business Research Services Inc.
Ed: Thomas D. Johnson, Editor. **Released:** Annual. **Price:** $295, individuals paperback. **Covers:** 28,000 woman-owned businesses. **Entries Include:** Company name, address, phone, name and title of contact, minority group, certification status, date founded, number of employees, description of products or services, sales volume, government contracting experience, references. **Arrangement:** Standard Industrial Classification (SIC) code, geographical. **Indexes:** Alphabetical by company.

56334 ■ "National Women's Business Council" in *Black Enterprise* **(Vol. 34, No. 4, November 2003, pp. 62)**
Pub: Earl Graves Publishing Co.
Description: Jean Johnson has been appointed to the National Women's Business Council in Houston, Texas. Johnson lists the goals she hopes to implement during her term.

56335 ■ "NAWBO honors top business women" in *Crain's Detroit Business* **(Vol. 16, No. 10, March 6, 2000, pp. 21)**
Pub: Crain Communications, Inc.

Description: The National Association of Women Business Owners announced the winners of the Top 10 Michigan Women Business Owners of Distinction Awards. The awards honor women owners whose businesses are profitable and who have had both ownership interest and involvement in their companies for a minimum of three years.

56336 ■ "Needed on the Frontline" in *Pittsburgh Business Times* **(Vol. 23, No. 8, September 12, 2003, pp. 19)**
Pub: Pittsburgh Business Times
Ed: Lynne Glover. **Description:** Profile of Frontline Healthcare LLC, founded by three local women, provides healthcare products designed by nurses. The firm, founded in 2002, introduced its new Personal Products Caddy Pack for hospital patients.

56337 ■ "Networking know-how" in *Women in Business* **(Vol. 53, No. 7, January-February 2002, pp. 40)**
Pub: The ABWA Co Inc.
Description: Different networking techniques and groups are listed. Networks can be provided by professional business organizations as well as civic organizations.

56338 ■ "Networking for Success" in *Hispanic Business* **(Vol. 24, No. 4, April 2002, pp. 26)**
Pub: Hispanic Business Inc.
Ed: Scott Williams. **Description:** Advanced interpersonal communication skills enable women executives to climb the career ladder. Interviews with successful Hispanic women include Patricia Romero Cronin, VP at IBM; Cari Dominguez, EEOC Chair; and Rebeca Johnson, VP of ethnic and urban marketing at Frito-Lay Inc.

56339 ■ "New Biscotti Company Gets Cooking" in *Bellingham Business Journal* **(December 2006, pp. A5)**
Pub: Sun News Inc.
Description: Profile of Kyoung Croft, owner of Rainy Days Kitchen, a company that produces non-traditional biscotti.

56340 ■ "New Deli Destination Coming to Town" in *Bellingham Business Journal* **(December 2006, pp. A3)**
Pub: Sun News Inc.
Description: Heidi Rosebush, a former Trader Joe's manager, will be opening Destination Deli, a sandwich cart serving sandwiches using local ingredients from bakeries and farms. Heidi will also develop a Web site that allows customers to place and pay for orders online.

56341 ■ "New Entrepreneurs Arise from Bad Breaks" in *Altanta Journal-Constitution* **(January 20, 2007)**
Pub: Cox Newspapers, Inc.
Ed: Jill Young Miller. **Description:** Profile of Kimberly Morrison, owner of A Blue Lady, a floral shop in Georgia. Morrison discusses overcoming depression after her husband filed for divorce and starting her own business.

56342 ■ "New Leadership Breeds New Energy" in *Women In Business* **(Vol. 52, No. 3, May 2000, pp. 18)**
Pub: The ABWA Co., Inc.
Ed: Rachel Warbington. **Description:** Issues concerning the membership of the American Business Women's Association and advice on helping new members develop leadership skills are covered.

56343 ■ "The new pay paradigm" in *WorkingWoman* **(Vol. 25, No. 7, August 2000, pp. 57)**
Pub: Lang Communications Inc.
Ed: Elizabeth Wasserman. **Description:** Issues concerning the pay of women compared to men are discussed and the impact on wages of a large number of electronic commerce-based firms attracting highly paid women away from traditional market-place jobs. An annual review of women's salaries and interviews are included.

56344 ■ "New Portland, Maine, Boutique Sells High-Eng Maternity Clothes" in *Portland Press Herald* **(July 4, 2003)**
Pub: Knight Ridder/Tribune Business News
Ed: Matt Wickenheiser. **Description:** Profile of Lisa Curran, owner of Nine Months, a boutique that sells high-end clothing for pregnant women and infants.

56345 ■ "New Positions Emerging: How You Can Prepare for Them" in *Women In Business* **(Vol. 52, No. 2, March 2000, pp. 30)**
Pub: The ABWA Co., Inc.
Ed: Diane Domeyer. **Description:** Women should plan for the new roles anticipated in the workplace as a result of technological advances.

56346 ■ "New Website for Women's Clothes" in *Marketing to Women* **(Vol. 20, January 2007, No. 1, pp. 8)**
Pub: EPM Communications, Inc.
Description: FrillyGirls.com is a new website catering to women between the ages of 21-45. The site is run by three stay-at-home mothers looking to reenter the workforce and specializes in designer clothing and accessories.

56347 ■ "NFL Reaches Out" in *Crain's Detroit Business* **(Vol. 21, January 3, 2005, No. 1, pp. 12)**
Pub: Crain Communications Inc. - Detroit
Ed: Jennette Smith. **Description:** Super Bowl XL Host Committee and the National Football League have partnered to create an emerging-business program that encourages minority- and women-owned business to participate in the Super Bowl. The committee will also announce plans for a $2 million youth center to be located in Detroit.

56348 ■ "Nice Girls Don't Ask" in *Harvard Business Review* **(Vol. 81, No. 10, October 2003, pp. 14)**
Pub: Harvard Business School Press
Ed: Linda Babcock. **Description:** Three recent studies have shown that women are less likely to engage in negotiations because they are less likely to get what they asked for.

56349 ■ "No Bad Days: Sherry Williams excels as a Mary Kay sales pro while battling breast cancer" in *Black Enterprise* **(Oct. 2002, pp. 175)**
Pub: Earl Graves Publishing Co.
Ed: Shani Smothers. **Description:** Profile of Sherry B. Williams, an independent senior sales director for Mary Kay Cosmetics in Phoenix, Arizona. Williams, diagnosed with cancer for the third time in 2002, says that her business has survived her illnesses, because of its mobility. She can do business from home using the phone, mail and the Internet.

56350 ■ *No More Frogs to Kiss*
Pub: Harper Business
Ed: Joline Godfrey. **Released:** 1995. **Price:** $12.00.

56351 ■ "No More Ms. NiceGuy: Do Nice Girls Really Finish Last in the Business World" in *Entrepreneur* **(Vol. 33, February 2005, No. 2, pp. 34)**
Pub: Entrepreneur Media Inc.
Ed: Alisa Pilar Sherman. **Description:** Lois P. Frankel, corporate coach and author of Nice Girls Don't Get Rich: 75 Avoidable Mistakes Women Make With Money, recommends that female entrepreneurs stand up for themselves while providing services.

56352 ■ "No Small Change" in *Black Enterprise* **(Vol. 32, No. 8, March 2002, pp. 64)**
Pub: Earl Graves Publishing Co.
Ed: Lee Anna Jackson. **Description:** Profile of Joyce Harris, Web page designer.

56353 ■ "Novel Ideas: Two Entrepreneurs Write Books About Their Experiences-And Learn Something in the Process" in *Entrepreneur* **(Vol. 32)**
Pub: Entrepreneur Media Inc.
Ed: Aliza Pilar Sherman. **Description:** Profiles of Lisa Price, president of a manufacturing and retail compa-

ny that specializes in homemade body care products and Lisa Hammons, founder and CEO of Femail Creations, a handcrafted-gift catalog and Website featuring female-focused products created by women. Both entrepreneurs wrote books about their business and personal lives and offer advice for publishing a book.

56354 ■ "OKC Rotary Club Elects First Female President" in *Journal Record* **(June 24, 2003)**
Pub: Dolan Media Company
Description: Profile of Meg Salyer, first woman president of the Rotary Club of Oklahoma City, Oklahoma. Salyer is president of Accel Financial Staffing, a temporary, temp-to-hire and direct placement agency in accounting and finance careers.

56355 ■ "On the road to fitness" in *Women in Business* **(Vol. 54, No. 2, March-April 2002, pp. 30)**
Pub: The ABWA Co Inc.
Ed: Mary-Lane Kamberg. **Description:** Businesswomen should maintain their physical fitness routines and business travel should not interfere.

56356 ■ *On Our Own Terms: Portraits of Women Business Leaders*
Pub: DIANE Publishing Co.
Ed: Liane Enkelis, Karen Olsen, Marion Lewenstein; foreword by Jane Applegate. **Released:** 1998. **Price:** $20.00. **Description:** Profiles women CEOs & presidents of companies with annual revenues of $10 million or more. Their experiences cover a wide range of issues, including: career planning, customer service, employee communications, child day care, growing a business, and managing work and family life.

56357 ■ "On a role" in *WorkingWoman* **(Vol. 25, No. 7, August 2000, pp. 79)**
Pub: Lang Communications Inc.
Ed: Russell Wild. **Description:** Acting classes can improve the performance of top executives who regularly have to make important speeches or give seminars to large groups of people.

56358 ■ *On Your Own: A Woman's Guide to Building a Business*
Pub: Upstart Publishing Co., Inc.
Ed: Laurie B. Zuckerman. **Released:** Second edition, 1993. **Price:** $19.95 (paper). **Description:** Provides information for women who are interested in starting and running a business, covering writing a business plan, working with banks, discrimination, financial statements, and networking. Includes charts and sample worksheets. Lists resources for women business owners and describes how women-owned businesses differ from male-owned businesses.

56359 ■ "One-Track Mind" in *Entrepreneur.com* **(Vol. 34, February 2006, No. 2, pp. 33)**
Pub: Entrepreneur Media Inc.
Ed: Heather Clancy. **Description:** Profile of Ananda Roberts, owner of nFocus Software, the maker of products that track data for the government, educational institutions, and nonprofit organizations. Roberts employs 35 workers at her Phoenix, Arizona company.

56360 ■ "Online Resources: Consultant Keeps Computers Well" in *My Business* **(December/January 2003, pp. 52)**
Pub: My Business Magazine
Description: Short profile of RB Balch and Associates, located in Glendale, Arizona. The company, owned by Rochelle Balch, provides computer support and consulting services.

56361 ■ *Our Wildest Dreams: Women Entrepreneurs Making Money, Having Fun, Doing Good*
Pub: Harper Business
Ed: Joline Godfrey. **Released:** 1993. **Price:** $11.00 (paper).

56362 ■ "Pampering Pets Makes Miami-Area Groomer, Salon Owner Happy" in *Miami Herald* **(June 28, 2004)**
Pub: Knight-Ridder/Tribune Business News

Ed: Wendy Doscher-Smith. **Description:** Erica Richter tells of her love for animals. Richter owns the Salon Poochini in Bay Harbor Islands and spends her days with cats and dogs.

56363 ■ "Passing the bucks" in *WorkingWoman* **(Vol. 25, No. 4, April 2000, pp. 28)**
Pub: Lang Communications Inc.
Ed: Lisa Holton. **Description:** Advice on making a will and estate planning are covered.

56364 ■ "Paulson Changes Name of Business" in *Bellingham Business Journal* **(January 2007, pp. A19)**
Pub: Sun News Inc.
Description: Judith Paulson, certified financial planner, changed the name of her business from Financial Counseling Services to Paulson Financial Services. With the change of the name also comes a new focus in which she plans to provide insurance and tax planning, financial education, and retirement planning.

56365 ■ "People Growers Deals With Personal Growing Pains" in *Business Journal-Portland* **(Vol. 20, No. 22, August 1, 2003, pp. 3)**
Pub: American City Business Journals, Inc.
Ed: Robin J. Moody. **Description:** Profile of Windy Baty, owner of People Growers. The home-based firm helps companies organize on-site health fairs and promotes wellness among employees.

56366 ■ "Pioneers in a Wider World" in *Hispanic Business* **(March 2003, pp. 30-31, 34, 36, 38, 40-42, 44, 46, 48, 50, 52, 54, 56-57)**
Pub: Hispanic Business
Description: The list of Elite Hispanic Women documents the broadening range of female achievement and leadership, and includes a short profile of the 80 women making the list. Statistical data included.

56367 ■ "Plan Events that Will Fill Seats" in *Women In Business* **(Vol. 52, No. 2, March 2000, pp. 32)**
Pub: The ABWA Co., Inc.
Ed: Jane Thomas. **Description:** Kansas City Express Network is a network for professional women which helps them to make contacts, while also considering their lack of time. The group holds 1-1/2 hour monthly lunch meetings and plans meetings quarterly.

56368 ■ "Planning productive programs" in *Women In Business* **(Vol. 52, No. 4, July 2000, pp. 28)**
Pub: The ABWA Co., Inc.
Ed: Rachel Warbington. **Description:** Issues concerning the successful planning of programs to present to staff who are members of the American Business Women's Association are presented. The importance of choosing good educational speakers is discussed.

56369 ■ "Playing Favorites" in *Entrepreneur* **(Vol. 31, Sept. 2003)**
Pub: Entrepreneur Media, Inc.
Ed: Aliza Pilar Sherman. **Description:** Women entrepreneurs report favorite business Web sites they use to run their companies, with Google.com heading the list.

56370 ■ "Portland, Maine, Woman Builds Successful Child-Care Business" in *Portland Press Herald* **(June 10, 2005)**
Pub: Blethen Maine Newspapers, Inc.
Ed: Edward D. Murphy. **Description:** Profile of Cheryl Carrier and her booming child care business, Toddle Inn, in the Portland, Maine area. Carrier also plans a franchise in Brewer, Maine, and also runs an early-stage furniture business.

56371 ■ "Power Shopping" in *Entrepreneur* **(Vol. 28, No. 4, April 2000, pp. 62)**
Pub: Entrepreneur Media Inc.
Ed: Cynthia E. Griffin. **Description:** When it comes to shopping for clothing, household items and cars, studies have shown women wield a tremendous amount of influence.

56372 ■ "Preparing for national leadership" in *Women in Business* **(Vol. 53, No. 4, July-August, 2001, pp. 20)**
Pub: The ABWA Co. Inc.
Ed: Mary-Lane Kamberg. **Description:** Issues concerning leadership development opportunities for women are discussed, with focus on women's opportunities to become national officers or to organize national conferences. Cases of women in leadership positions are examined.

56373 ■ "Priority" in *Inc.* **(Volume 27, March 2005, No. 3, pp. 23-26, 28, 30)**
Pub: Inc. Magazine
Description: Business information discussed includes information about the SEC looking into unlicensed investment brokers, the economy, freight co-ops to help shippers ease costs, hiring, Google, education, SBA assistance to women entrepreneurs, and new inventions.

56374 ■ "Professional athlete credits ABWA with the right 'assist'" in *Women in Business* **(Vol. 54, No. 5, September-October 2002, pp. 10)**
Pub: The ABWA Company, Inc.
Ed: Mia Katz. **Description:** American Business Women's Association member, Jeanette Simonsen, discusses her appreciation of the organization and its members. As a professional volleyball player, she enjoys the professional accomplishments of the other women in the association.

56375 ■ "Professional Organizer Sets Up Shop" in *Bellingham Business Journal* **(January 2007, pp. 4)**
Pub: Sun News Inc.
Description: Profile of Cathy Gersich, a professional organizer and owner of PriOrganize. PriOrganize provides an invaluable organizational service to help individuals simplify their homes and offices.

56376 ■ "Protecting your company from high turnover" in *Women in Busines s* **(Vol. 53, No. 2, March-April, 2001, pp. 30)**
Pub: The ABWA Co. Inc.
Ed: Melissa Will. **Description:** Strategies to attract and retain good caliber employees are addressed. Ways of reducing staff turnover through the use of flexible working hours, employee involvement and fair management practices are explored.

56377 ■ "Publisher Evolves With Technology, Entrepreneurial Talent" in *Portland Press Herald* **(October 21, 2005)**
Pub: Blethen Maine Newspapers, Inc.
Ed: Edward D. Murphy. **Description:** Profile of Nancy Randolph, who started her business Just Write Books after spending years helping others get their books ready for publication. Randolph splits the profits with authors after a book is published.

56378 ■ "Puzzleman to the Rescue" in *My Business* **(December/January 2003, pp. 12-13)**
Pub: My Business Magazine
Ed: Melany Klinck. **Description:** Profile of Cypriana Porter, owner of the educational toy store called The Gingerbread House. Porter invented the superhero Puzzleman to increase sales.

56379 ■ "Raging Beauty: One-Time Female Boxing Champ is Winning Bouts in Sports" in *Black Enterprise* **(Vol. 35, December 2004, No. 5, pp. 55)**
Pub: Earl G. Graves Publishing Co. Inc.
Ed: Zakiyyah El-Amin. **Description:** Profile of husband and wife team Isra Girgrah Wynn and Marry Wynn, owners of Raging Promotions Inc. The former boxing champ and her husband provide sports and entertainment management specializing in boxing events and services clients.

56380 ■ "A Reason to Smile" in *Black Enterprise* **(Vol. 34, No. 2, September 2003, pp. 62)**
Pub: Earl Graves Publishing Co.
Ed: Ashley Gibson. **Description:** Of the 6,000 board certified oral surgeons in the U.S., about 100 are

women. Profile of Dr. Ngozi Etufugh, who was born in Nigeria, operates two practices in New York. Etufugh tells how she empowered herself to become a top oral surgeon despite being black, being a woman, and being petite.

56381 ■ "Recognition for Volunteer" in *San Diego Business Journal* **(Vol. 28, January 15, 2007, No. 3, pp. 33)**
Pub: San Diego Business Journal Associates
Description: Marjorie McLaughlin was named Volunteer of the Year by the San Diego Association of Realtors. McLaughlin has been the director for the California Association of Realtors for twenty years.

56382 ■ "Report Reveals Best Lenders for Black Business" in *Black Enterprise* **(Vol. 36, November 2005, No. 4, pp. 38)**
Pub: Earl G. Graves Publishing Co. Inc.
Ed: Glenn Townes. **Description:** The Greenlining Institute, a public policy research and advocacy group, ranks U.S. financial institutions for the Small Business Administration according to loans to minorities. Bank of America and JPMorgan Chase were at the top of the list. Statistical data included.

56383 ■ "Required Reading" in *Entrepreneur* **(Vol. 31, No. 7, July 2003, pp. 32)**
Pub: Entrepreneur Media, Inc.
Ed: Aliza Pilar Sherman. **Description:** Reviews of books recommended for aspiring and current women entrepreneurs are shared. Many of these successful women are using the wisdom found in these books to improve business strategies.

56384 ■ "Resources: Web Sites, Organizations, Events and More to Grow Your Business" in *Entrepreneur* **(Vol. 32, August 2004, No. 8, pp. 8)**
Pub: Entrepreneur Media Inc.
Ed: Steve Cooper. **Description:** Showcase of information to help small business include: Global Advisor offers services from United Parcel Service to help companies learn ways to conduct business overseas, including trade tools and terminology, a global time clock and HAP, supply chain management, and a guide to international shipping; a CAN-SPAM Act of 2003 summary; RE:INVENTION INC is a daily blog dedicated to women entrepreneurs; and a directory of venture capital and private equity firms.

56385 ■ "Revamping a Retirement Plan" in *Black Enterprise* **(Vol. 35, October 2004, No. 3, pp. 43)**
Pub: Earl G. Graves Publishing Co. Inc.
Ed: Carmen Brown. **Description:** Calvin and Jacqueline McGahee share investment strategies for a better retirement.

56386 ■ "Rich in Tradition" in *Home Business* **(Vol. 12, March/April 2005, No. 2, pp. 63)**
Pub: Home Business Magazine
Ed: Sandy Larson. **Description:** Profile of Michele Ogden, who creates heirloom-type keepsakes for families from her home.

56387 ■ "Right of Fashion" in *Entrepreneur. com* **(Vol. 34, February 2006, No. 2, pp. 30)**
Pub: Entrepreneur Media Inc.
Ed: Sara Wilson. **Description:** Profile of Stacey Pecor of Olive and Bette's Co. Inc., a New York City-based women's retail clothing store.

56388 ■ "The right rewards" in *WorkingWoman* **(Vol. 25, No. 7, August 2000, pp. 40)**
Pub: Lang Communications Inc.
Ed: Carol Leonetti Dannhauser. **Description:** Issues concerning the motivation and retention of employees through means and other pay raises are discussed.

56389 ■ "Robert L. Johnson" in *Black Enterprise* **(Vol. 36, November 2005, No. 4, pp. 34)**
Pub: Earl G. Graves Publishing Co. Inc.
Ed: Matthew S. Scott. **Description:** Profile of Robert L. Johnson, Black entrepreneur who founded the Black Entertainment Television network and sold it to build greater wealth.

56390 ■ "Running on empty?" in *Women in Business* **(Vol. 53, No. 2, March-April, 2001, pp. 32)**
Pub: The ABWA Co. Inc.
Ed: Nancy Cloak. **Description:** Advice on methods of coping with stress is presented. Ways of changing behavior patterns from self-destructive habits to more positive soothing, adaptive, or reflective activities are suggested.

56391 ■ "Sailing On the Crest of the Home Health Care Wave" in *Indianapolis Business Journal* **(Vol. 25)**
Pub: Indianapolis Business Journal Corporation
Ed: Tracy Donhardt. **Description:** Profile of Jan Roberts, owner and CEO of Alliance Home Health Care and Adult Day Services, the twelfth-largest women-owned business in the Indianapolis area. The company, with 200 employees, provides home care, skilled nursing and medical adult day care.

56392 ■ "Same Markets, New Marketplaces" in *Black Enterprise* **(Vol. 35, September 2004, No. 2, pp. 34)**
Pub: Earl G. Graves Publishing Co. Inc.
Ed: Malik Singleton. **Description:** According to a study performed by the Center for Women's Business Research, African American women entrepreneurs in nontraditional sectors rose between 1997 and 2002. Wisconsin, Delaware, and Oregon were among the top states experiencing the rise, with Wisconsin reporting 453 percent growth in the number of African American women-owned businesses. Statistical data included.

56393 ■ "San Diego: Stone Makes Rock-Solid Impression" in *San Diego Business Journal* **(Vol. 28, January 15, 2007, No. 3, pp. 16)**
Pub: San Diego Business Journal Associates
Ed: Amy Yarnall. **Description:** Profile of San Diego-based StoneImpressions and its Make-Mine-a-Million, a program that helps women entrepreneurs develop million dollar businesses.

56394 ■ "Say Cheese, Fairhaven" in *Bellingham Business Journal* **(December 2006, pp. A3)**
Pub: Sun News Inc.
Description: Profile of Rachel Riggs, a lover of artisan cheeses, who opened a new shop in Fairhaven named Quel Fromage. The store will supply restaurants and offers retail customers over 125 varieties of cheese and other specialty items not available locally to customers. It will also feature wine pairings, guest cheesemakers, and more.

56395 ■ "SBA Increases Bond Maximum" in *Hispanic Business* **(Vol. 23, No. 5, May 2001, pp. 24)**
Pub: Hispanic Business
Description: The U.S. Small Business Administration (SBA) has increased the size of surety bonds to increase contracting opportunities for small, minority, and women contractors. In fiscal year 2000, the Surety Bond Guarantee Program backed more than 1,795 final bonds on contracts valued at nearly $328.9 million.

56396 ■ "SBA's Small Business Person of the Year Shares Her Story" in *Portland Press Herald* **(May 6, 2005)**
Pub: Blethen Maine Newspapers, Inc.
Ed: Edward D. Murphy. **Description:** Profile of Marianne Sensale-Guerin, the Small Business Administration's new national Small Business Person of the Year. Sensale-Guerin tells how she started her business two months after her husband was killed in a work-related accident.

56397 ■ "Scrubs in Vogue" in *Home Business* **(Vol. 13, January/February 2006, No. 1, pp. 41)**
Pub: Home Business Magazine
Ed: Sandy Larson. **Description:** Profile of Christina Rojas-Fletes, designer of fashionable scrub uniforms for health care workers.

56398 ■ *Secrets of Millionaire Moms*
Pub: McGraw-Hill
Ed: Tamara Monosoff. **Released:** March 2007. **Price:** $16.95. **Description:** Profiles of successful women/mother entrepreneurs are presented, including Julie Clark, Lane Nemeth, Lillian Vernon, Victoria Knight, Rachel Ashwell and other powerful businesswomen.

56399 ■ "Seeds of success" in *Houston Business Journal* **(Vol. 33, No. 46, March 28, 2003, pp. 17A)**
Pub: Houston Business Journal
Ed: Allison Wollam. **Description:** The leadership style of Suzanne Longley as president of Suzanne Longley Landscapes Inc. is profiled. The company grows its own tress and is planning to add a sprinkler system and a greenhouse in order to grow flowers.

56400 ■ "Shattered Magazine: A Monthly for the Global Businesswoman" in *Marketing to Women* **(Vol. 19, December 2006, No. 2, pp. 6)**
Pub: EPM Communications, Inc.
Ed: Julie Ros. **Description:** Shattered is a glossy magazine distributed monthly and run by veteran financial journalist, Julie Ros. Shattered concentrates its focus on the business world and puts special emphasis on the global impact women are having in the leadership roles of the business community.

56401 ■ "She's not afraid to flex her sales muscles" in *Selling* **(October 2002, pp. 15)**
Pub: Institutional Investor, Inc.
Ed: Jenny McCune. **Description:** Profile of Ann Power, National Franchise Sales Director of Lady of America, a women-only fitness chain with 500 locations worldwide; Power started her career selling for a weight-loss company, and became successful in sales.

56402 ■ "Silence is Golden" in *Small Business Opportunities* **(Vol. 16, No. 2, March 2004, pp. 102, 104)**
Pub: Harris Publications, Inc.
Ed: Chuck Green. **Description:** Profile of Sandy Horwitz, owner Clothes Minded, a clothing boutique in Chicago, Illinois. Thanks to a unique inventory and a staff that allows customers to shop in peace, along with selling for the long-term, the store reports sales totaling $400,000 a year.

56403 ■ "Simply the Best" in *Small Business Opportunities* **(Vol. 16, November 2004, No. 6, pp. 90)**
Pub: Harris Publications Inc.
Description: Profile of Vanessa Best, president and CEO of Precision HealthCare Consultants, a medical billing and consulting company in New York State.

56404 ■ "Sister Act" in *My Business* **(February/March 2004, pp. 28-31)**
Pub: My Business Magazine
Ed: Nancy Mann Jackson. **Description:** Profile of three sisters who started a coffee shop together; profile of a sister and brother who own an office furniture installation and facility management company together; another brother and sister team who run a successful mail sorting firm; and two brothers who own a telecommunications management company. Each team shares advice to others wishing to start a family business.

56405 ■ *Sister CEO: The Black Woman's Guide to Starting Your Own Business*
Pub: Viking Penguin
Ed: Cheryl D. Broussard. **Released:** 1998. **Price:** $12.95.

56406 ■ "Skin Deep" in *Entrepreneur* **(Vol. 33, January 2005, No. 1, pp. 21)**
Pub: Entrepreneur Media Inc.
Ed: Sara Wilson. **Description:** Profile of Rosie Herman, founder of One Minute Manicure, manufacturer and distributor of body care products. Herman mixes a combination of oils, sea salts and organic products to treat dry and overexposed skin.

56407 ■ "Skip the links and head to the gym or the spa" in *Crain's Chicago Business* (Vol. 25, No. 42, October 21, 2002, pp. SR11)
Pub: Crain Communications, Inc.
Ed: Lisa Bertagnoli. **Description:** If you want to find a networking businessman, check the golf course; if you want to find a networking businesswoman, check an upscale bar, a barn, gym, or a beauty salon.

56408 ■ "Small Business Spotlight" in *Small Business Opportunities* (Vol. 16, No. 2, March 2004, pp. 172)
Pub: Harris Publications, Inc.
Description: Profile of Jon Stocking who donates profits from his Endangered Species Chocolate Company to save threatened animals, an environmentally-friendly dry cleaner, and women and franchising.

56409 ■ "Small Businesses Are Engine to American Economy" in *Atlanta Business Chronicle* (Vol. 24, No. 9, August 3, 2001, pp. 10B)
Pub: American City Business Journals Inc.
Ed: Paige Bowers. **Description:** Senator Max Cleland discusses what he has done in support of small business in America. The Senator's support includes reducing taxes on small businesses, broadening health care options and boosting the opportunities for minority and women-owned enterprises.

56410 ■ *The Smart Women's Guide to Starting a Business*
Pub: Career Press, Inc.
Ed: Vickie L. Montgomery. **Released:** 2nd ed. 1998.
Price: $15.99 (paper).

56411 ■ "Sowing seeds for growth" in *Women In Business* (Vol. 52, No. 1, January-February 2000, pp. 20)
Pub: The ABWA Co., Inc.
Description: The criteria for the National Board Award has been amended in an attempt to motivate chapters and encourage membership growth and development. The 1999-2000 chapter year will also include a networking component.

56412 ■ "Speaking volumes on the dollar" in *WorkingWoman* (Vol. 25, No. 2, February 2000, pp. S19)
Pub: Lang Communications Inc.
Ed: Dana Asher. **Description:** Book reviews of various financial books of interest to women in business.

56413 ■ "Spotlight on Retailing" in *The Record* (November 12, 2005)
Pub: New Jersey Media Group
Ed: Joan Verdon. **Description:** Profile of Lee Long and Linda Rogers, owners of The Children's Exchange stores in Bergen County, New Jersey. The partners started their children's used clothing and furniture stores in 1988 and have watched customers grow from buying for their children to buying for their grandchildren.

56414 ■ "Springboard to Success" in *Black Enterprise* (Vol. 35, December 2004, No. 5, pp. 84)
Pub: Earl G. Graves Publishing Co. Inc.
Ed: Nkechi Olisemeka. **Description:** Profile of Pamela G. Carlton, co-founder and president of Springboard, committed to assisting underrepresented groups neglected early in their career.

56415 ■ "Spy Moms" in *Home Business* (Vol. 12, October 2005, No. 5, pp. 92)
Pub: Home Business Magazine
Ed: Sandy Larson. **Description:** Profile of private investigators, Mollie Carman and Valerie Agosta, who run a private investigation firm from their homes in Boise, Idaho.

56416 ■ "Star quality" in *WorkingWoman* (Vol. 28, No. 5, May 2000, pp. 50)
Pub: Lang Communications Inc.
Ed: Betsy Wiesendanger. **Description:** The stories of the winners in the second annual Entrepreneurial Excellence Awards include women who have exploited the technology boom, used innovative staffing solutions to beat labor problems, and offered free training to help women out of the welfare dependence scenario.

56417 ■ "State Farm Signs On As Host" in *Black Enterprise* (Vol. 36, December 2005, No. 5, pp. 166)
Pub: Earl G. Graves Publishing Co. Inc.
Ed: Alysha N. Cryer. **Description:** State Farm Insurance Company has partnered with Black Enterprise to launch the inaugural Women of Pow4er Summit. The professional leadership conference is designed exclusively for women of color executives.

56418 ■ "Study: Women Executives Want Corner Office, Too" in *Miami Herald* (June 24, 2004)
Pub: Knight-Ridder/Tribune Business News
Ed: Gillian Wee. **Description:** According to a recent survey, female officials aspire to be chief executives at the same rate as male counterparts.

56419 ■ "Succeeding in adversity makes success all the sweeter" in *Fast Company* (May 2001, pp. 84)
Pub: Fast Company
Ed: Sheila Wellington. **Description:** Profile of Sheila Wellington, author of the book 'Be Your Own Mentor: Career Strategies for Women', published in February 2001 by Random House. Wellington suggests that during tough economic times, the strong become creative for survival.

56420 ■ "Super Sales in Service" in *Small Business Opportunities* (Vol. 17, September 2005, No. 5, pp. 76, 86)
Pub: Harris Publications Inc.
Ed: Chuck Green. **Description:** Jenny Cooper, owner of a boutique offering bath and body products attributes her success to knowing how to treat her customers. Her boutique also offers a variety of accessories.

56421 ■ "Survey" in *Crain's Detroit Business* (Vol. 21, October 24, 2005, No. 43, pp. 1)
Pub: Crain Communications Inc. - Detroit
Ed: Tom Hdnderson. **Description:** According to the 2005 Michigan Women's Leadership Index, the number of top women executives has fallen by 20 percent over the last two years. The auto industry ranked lowest for upper-management opportunity for its female executives.

56422 ■ "Surviving the ups and downs of corporate restructuring" in *Women In Business* (Vol. 52, No. 3, May 2000, pp. 14)
Pub: The ABWA Co., Inc.
Ed: Mary-Lane Kamberg. **Description:** Advice on how to foresee the possibility of downsizing occurring in a company and information on how to find support and a new job is discussed.

56423 ■ "Surviving Self-Employment" in *Black Enterprise* (Vol. 35, October 2004, No. 3, pp. 84)
Pub: Earl G. Graves Publishing Co. Inc.
Ed: Carolyn M. Brown. **Description:** Profile of Ellen Hendrix tells how she is working as a video editor after being laid off from her job. She has invested in a rental property, but it is only making a small profit.

56424 ■ "Susan McMillan Appointed Executive Director of the Long Island Better Business Bureau" in *Long Island Business News* (Feb. 6, 2004)
Pub: Dolan Media Newswires
Ed: Ryan McCormick. **Description:** Profile of Susan McMillan, newly appointed executive director of the Long Island Better Business Bureau. McMillan also serves on the Consumer Affairs Committee of the Bar Association of the City of New York and is an active member of the Small Business Advisory Committee.

56425 ■ "Sweet Enterprise" in *Small Business Opportunities* (Vol. 17, May 2005, No. 3, pp. 86)
Pub: Harris Publications Inc.
Ed: Chuck Green. **Description:** Profile of Lauren Grill, who relied on customer input when developing and building her business. She experimented with recipes in her kitchen for a few months before selling any of her candy.

56426 ■ "Sweet Expectations: A Recipe for Success: In the Darkest Period of Her Life" in *Black Enterprise* (Vol. 35, December 2004, No. 5)
Pub: Earl G. Graves Publishing Co. Inc.
Ed: Michele Hoskins, Jean A. Williams. **Description:** Profile of Michele Hoskins who decided to become an entrepreneur and founded Michele Foods Inc. after finding a generations-old family recipe for Honey Creme Syrup. Hoskins shares the touching story behind the recipe.

56427 ■ "Sweet Reward: Reaching Out to the Media Really Does Pay Off" in *Entrepreneur* (Vol. 31, No. 9, July 2003, pp. 81)
Pub: Entrepreneur Media, Inc.
Ed: April Y. Pennington. **Description:** Profile of Fran Bigelow, owner of Fran's Chocolates Inc., opened in 1982. Bigelow sent letters to food editors educating them on the fine chocolates she uses and included samples. The editors published articles that gave her store more exposures and Bigelow was named The Best Chocolatier in America by The Book of Chocolate.

56428 ■ "Sweet taste of success" in *WorkingWoman* (Vol. 25, No. 2, February 2000, pp. 34)
Pub: Lang Communications Inc.
Ed: Amanda Walmac. **Description:** Rena Pocrass of Chocolates a la Carte helps her employees by offering a stock plan.

56429 ■ "Take it from me" in *Entrepreneur* (Vol. 31, No. 4, April 2003, pp. 26)
Pub: Entrepreneur Media Inc.
Ed: Aliza Pilar Sherman. **Description:** An interview with two women business owners offering advice in management, business growth, and business downsizing.

56430 ■ "Taking ABWA to the office" in *Women in Business* (Vol. 53, No. 2, March-April, 2001, pp. 28)
Pub: The ABWA Co. Inc.
Ed: Rachel Warbington. **Description:** Ideas on ways of promoting membership of the American Business Women's Association (ABWA) to colleagues are presented. Suggestions on using ABWA logos, clothing and accessories to publicize the organization are given.

56431 ■ "Tampa, Fla., Bike Shop Turns Off Its Engine" in *Tampa Tribune* (November 5, 2005)
Pub: Media General, Inc.
Ed: Randy Diamond. **Description:** Profile of Patsy Ann Lovengreen, a feisty septuagenarian, who ran a motorcycle salvage and repair shop. Lovengreen is closing her store in order to spend more time caring for her collection of orchids and her husband, Bill.

56432 ■ "That's My Baby: Who Says Running a Business and Motherhood Don't Mix?" in *Entrepreneur* (Vol. 32, No. 2, February 2004, pp. 30)
Pub: Entrepreneur Media, Inc.
Ed: Aliza Pilar Sherman. **Description:** Profile of Alison Nelson, co-owner of a candy store called the Chocolate Bar; Caroline Caskey, president and CEO of a DNA identification service; and Adrienne Lumpkin, president of a converged communications firm specializing in business telecommunications tools. The three business women share their ideas and feelings about their pregnancies and ways they will handle being an entrepreneur along with motherhood.

56433 ■ "The Best for Women" in *Crain's Detroit Business* (Vol. 19, No. 42, October 20, 2003, pp. 30)
Pub: Crain Communications Inc., Detroit
Description: A listing of the top-ten scoring companies on the 2003 Michigan Women's Leadership Index, with FNBH Bancorp Inc. finishing first with 24 points, followed by Compuware Corporation and Energy Conversion Devices Inc., respectively.

56434 ■ "The Easy Entree Expands Service to Accommodate Walk-In Customers" in *Bellingham Business Journal* (December 2006, pp. 2)
Pub: Sun News Inc.
Description: Evelyn Turner, owner of The Easy Entree, has expanded her business to now offer a walk-in service for customers. Patrons can create their own entrees or pick up pre-made entrees to take home and cook or freeze.

56435 ■ "The Problem" in *Inc.* (Volume 27, March 2005, No. 3, pp. 44, 46)
Pub: Inc. Magazine
Ed: Nadine Heintz. **Description:** Addie Swartz has created a new brand for pre-teens that empowers girls in a positive way. Swartz started with a book series about girls facing modern-day issues.

56436 ■ "Things I Can't Live Without..." in *Inc.* (August 1, 2003)
Pub: Gruner & Jahr USA Publishing
Description: Profile of Rita Cruz, founder and president of Archive, the parent company of five bath and beauty lines in Colorado. Cruz's fiance and mother both share in the business. The firm has 23 employees and more than 100 sales representatives.

56437 ■ "Thinking Pink? Think Again" in *Entrepreneur* (Vol. 32, No. 2, February 2004, pp. 12)
Pub: Entrepreneur Media, Inc.
Ed: Rieva Lesonsky. **Description:** Female entrepreneurs claim a natural advantage over men when it comes to marketing to women. Because of the growing economic status of women, they have become an important and influential market.

56438 ■ "Through Grieving" in *Success from Failure* (August 2000)
Pub: Vision Quest Publishing, Inc.
Ed: Barbara Parton. **Description:** Barbara Parton, CEO of The Transpective Group, a business coaching and organization transformation firm, tells how she successfully led the family owned company "through grieving" after her husband died.

56439 ■ "To Thine Own Self" in *Entrepreneur* (Vol. 33, August 2005, No. 8, pp. 34)
Pub: Entrepreneur Media Inc.
Ed: Aliza Pilar Sherman. **Description:** Three tactics to boost a women entrepreneur's self-esteem are outlined by Jennifer Read Hawthorne, co-author of "Chicken Soup for the Woman's Soul".

56440 ■ "Too Much Information?" in *Black Enterprise* (Vol. 37, December 2006, No. 5, pp. 59)
Pub: Earl G. Graves Publishing Co. Inc.
Ed: James C. Johnson. **Description:** African American business owners often face the dilemma of whether or not to divulge their minority status when soliciting new customers and financial institutions. The quality of the products or services is always the key factor and race should never define one's business; however, it is appropriate to market oneself as a minority or women-owned business, especially if the company is in an industry where those clients are offered top-tier contracts.

56441 ■ "The top 10 business women of ABWA" in *Women In Business* (Vol. 52, No. 1, January-February 2000, pp. 16)
Pub: The ABWA Co., Inc.
Ed: Michele Compton. **Description:** Fran Amos is one of the top ten business women selected from the 70,000 members of American Business Women's Association (ABWA). Brief career details of the ten top business women are included.

56442 ■ "The top 500 women-owned businesses" in *WorkingWoman* (Vol. 25, No. 6, June 2000, pp. 51)
Pub: Lang Communications Inc.
Description: A survey is presented of the top 500 businesses owned by women in the U.S. with focus on the contribution made by individual women to their enterprises.

56443 ■ "Top ten business women of ABWA!" in *Women in Business* (Vol. 53, No. 7, January-February 2002, pp. 14)
Pub: The ABWA Co Inc.
Ed: Rachel Warbington. **Description:** The Top Ten Businesswoman Award is one of the most prestigious in the American Business Women's Association. A profile of those members who won the award in 2002 is provided.

56444 ■ "Top Dog Enterprise" in *Small Business Opportunities* (Vol. 16, No. 2, March 2004, pp. 134, 138)
Pub: Harris Publications, Inc.
Ed: Annette Wood. **Description:** Profile of Cindy McCarrier, owner of The Dog House, a shop for pet owners in Wichita, Kansas, offering products and grooming services. Requirements for opening a pet-related business are listed.

56445 ■ "Top Ten Program Offers Many Possibilities for Women" in *Women in Business* (Vol. 53, No. 1, January-February, 2001, pp. 16)
Pub: The ABWA Co. Inc.
Ed: Melissa Will. **Description:** The Top Ten Business Women of the American Business Women's Association (ABWA) program and its opportunities for women in business are discussed.

56446 ■ *Tough Choices: A Memoir*
Pub: Penguin Group
Ed: Carly Florina. **Released:** October 2006. **Price:** $24.95. **Description:** Former woman CEO at Hewlett-Packard is profiled.

56447 ■ "Trading faces" in *WorkingWoman* (Vol. 25, No. 4, April 2000, pp. 26)
Pub: Lang Communications Inc.
Ed: Lisa Lee Freeman. **Description:** A journalist, who often appears on the television, describes her experiences with image consultant, Mari Lyn Henry.

56448 ■ "A Trailblazer, Rediscovered" in *Inc.* (September 1, 2003)
Pub: Gruner & Jahr USA Publishing
Ed: Nadine Heintz. **Description:** Profile of Brownie Wise who built the multimillion-dollar Tupperware empire. A new documentary entitled, "In Tupperware!" will be seen on PBS in spring 2003. The film assesses Wise's marketing genius and her ouster in 1958.

56449 ■ "Training Trainers and Leaders" in *Women in Business* (Vol. 53, No. 7, January-February 2002, pp. 30)
Pub: The ABWA Co Inc.
Description: The American Business Women's Association provides the Membership Training and Development Certification Program and the Leadership Certificate Program for developing training and leadership skills. Organization members have used the skills they have learned in the programs at work and in volunteer situations.

56450 ■ "Transform Your Life" in *Black Enterprise* (Vol. 37, January 2007, No. 6, pp. 14)
Pub: Earl G. Graves Publishing Co. Inc.
Description: Through the magazine, television and radio programs, events, and the website, the various platforms of Black Enterprise will provide the tools necessary to achieve success in business ventures, career aspirations, and personal goals.

56451 ■ "Trusting Your Instincts: Crystal Winslow Followed Her Heart to Become an Author" in *Black Enterprise* (Vol. 34, No. 7, February 2004)
Pub: Earl Graves Publishing Co.
Ed: Keisha-Gaye Anderson. **Description:** Profile of Crystal Winslow, writer of novels and owner of a publishing company. Winslow majored in legal studies at New York City Technical College and interned in a law firm before making the decision to follow her dream of writing.

56452 ■ "Twenty Nine Percent of State's Farmers are Female" in *Journal Record* (February 4, 2003)
Pub: Dolan Media Company
Description: According to a report by the U.S. Department of Agriculture's National Agricultural Statistics Service, 29 percent of Oklahoma's agriculture producers are women. Statistical data included.

56453 ■ "Two women's drive opens a closed door" in *Wall Street Journal* (May 13, 2003, pp. B7)
Pub: Dow Jones & Co. Inc.
Ed: Paulette Thomas. **Description:** Profile of Kathy Boyce and Deborah Jones, co-founders of Chix With Stix Golf School.

56454 ■ "Ugly Salt and Pepper Shakers Spur Buffalo, N.Y., Woman's eBay Business" in *Buffalo News* (March 29, 2004)
Pub: Knight-Ridder/Tribune Business News
Ed: Lisa Haarlander. **Description:** Profile of Wendy Merkle, owner of an eBay drop-off center. Drop-off center work like consignment shops where customers drop off merchandise to be sold on eBay and the center collects a commission.

56455 ■ "Uncommon Enterprise: Sinking Ships" in *My Business* (December/January 2003, pp. 54)
Pub: My Business Magazine
Ed: Shannon Scully. **Description:** Profile of Ginger Martus, owner of New Jersey-based Nautical Stars. Martus finds owners for abandoned antique boats through her newsletter that features classified advertising for boat lovers.

56456 ■ "Under Attack? Think Another Woman is Out to Get You? Here's How to Watch Your Back" in *Entrepreneur* (Vol. 32, August 2004, No. 8)
Pub: Entrepreneur Media Inc.
Ed: Aliza Pilar Sherman. **Description:** Do women sabotage other women in business? According to a professional certified executive coach and behavioral analyst, both men and women commit sabotage, however women entrepreneurs understand the importance of a long-term relationship.

56457 ■ "Understanding Women is Key to Biz Success, Author Says" in *Crain's Detroit Business* (Vol. 22, November 20, 2006, No. 47, pp. 6)
Pub: Crain Communications Inc. - Detroit
Ed: Bill Shea. **Description:** Successful companies recognize that women make 80% of all buying decisions. Author also has advice for women-owned businesses with trend and specifics provided.

56458 ■ "Up Front: Supersize It? No Thanks!" in *My Business* (October/November 2003, pp. 10-11)
Pub: My Business Magazine
Ed: Jackie Ross. **Description:** Profile of Sarah Cohen, owner of Route II Potato Chips, located in Middletown, Virginia; Cohen manufactures the snacks in retro packaging. The potato chips are fried in pure, monounsaturated sunflower and peanut oils and are hand-blended with salt and seasonings in order to produce an all natural product.

56459 ■ "Upfront: Be Flexible or Fold" in *My Business* (June/July 2002, pp. 13-14)
Pub: My Business Magazine
Ed: Karen E. Klein. **Description:** Sometimes a small firm needs to steer away from original business plans in order to grow. Martha C. de al Torre, Hispanic Business Woman of the Year 2000, tells how she learned to be flexible and creative with her business plan.

56460 ■ "Upfront: Don't Say That" in *My Business* (April/May 2002, pp. 13-14)
Pub: My Business Magazine
Ed: Ivan Sylvester. **Description:** Market consultant and trainer, Merrie Spaeth, believes that public communication is all about the power of negatives. Spaeth sends out a monthly e-mail known as "The Bimbo Award", that recognizes public comments that cause the listener to believe exactly the opposite of what is said. Spaeth and her employees teach big and small firms how to communicate effectively.

56461 ■ "Use Your Intuition" in *Entrepreneur* (Vol. 33, March 2005, No. 3, pp. 85)
Pub: Entrepreneur Media Inc.
Ed: Kimberly L. McCall. **Description:** Jaye Hersh uses in-home shopping parties to promote her Los Angeles, California clothing store.

56462 ■ "Valuable Cargo" in *Small Business Opportunities* (Vol. 16, November 2004, No. 6, pp. 122)
Pub: Harris Publications Inc.
Ed: Chuck Green. **Description:** Profile of Carolyn Gable, owner of New Age Transportation & Warehousing. The firm helps businesses ship and warehouse inventory.

56463 ■ "Venus's Designs" in *Inc.* (September 1, 2003)
Pub: Gruner & Jahr USA Publishing
Ed: Nicole Gull. **Description:** Profile of Venus Williams' interior design firm V Star Interiors. V Starr has six active accounts and projects gross sales of about $1 million for 2003.

56464 ■ "Video Ventures" in *Small Business Opportunities* (Vol. 17, September 2005, No. 5, pp. 52, 54)
Pub: Harris Publications Inc.
Ed: Mollie Neal. **Description:** Profile of Tamara Carlisle, founder of a film production company that produces entertainment products for children that also educate.

56465 ■ "Vintage Chic" in *New York Times* (November 5, 2006, pp. 109)
Pub: New York Times Company
Ed: Christine Muhlke. **Description:** Profiles of five women from the wine industry is included; all are at the top in this industry.

56466 ■ "Virtual Company Achieves Actual Savings" in *Home Business* (Vol. 12, March/April 2005, No. 2, pp. 48)
Pub: Home Business Magazine
Ed: Sandy Larson. **Description:** Profile of Karlin Sloan, who runs her executive coaching firm from her home using a telecommuting program.

56467 ■ "A Vision for Recycling" in *Business Journal-Milwaukee* (Vol. 20, No. 51, September 5, 2003, pp. A14)
Pub: American City Business Journals, Inc.
Ed: David Schuyler. **Description:** Profile of Elia Lemke and Joe Tate, who formed Sauceda Sanitation LLC, a small woman-owned business. Lemke has limited business background and Tate is the retired chairman and founder of Superior Services Inc.

56468 ■ "Want a Facial With That Steak?" in *Charlotte Observer* (February 5, 2007)
Pub: Knight-Ridder/Tribune Business News
Ed: Jen Aronoff. **Description:** Profile of Burke Myotherapy Massage & Spa and Schell's Bistro. Lynn Shell moved her massage therapy business into a 106-year old home that had been used as a restaurant. She opened her own eatery on the first floor and offers massage therapy upstairs.

56469 ■ "Wanted: Road warrior queen" in *Incentive* (Vol. 174, No. 8, August 2000, pp. 8)
Pub: Bill Communications
Ed: Jeanie Casison. **Description:** Wyndham Hotels and Resorts recognizes women business travelers.

56470 ■ "Warming Up to Cold Calls" in *Inc.* (November 1, 2004)
Pub: Inc. Magazine
Ed: Nicole Gull. **Description:** Samantha Ettus, CEO of Ettus Media Management, a New York City public relations and branding agency spends much of her time making cold calls in order to land new accounts.

56471 ■ "Watching baby grow" in *WorkingWoman* (Vol. 25, No. 4, April 2000, pp. 32)
Pub: Lang Communications Inc.

Ed: Eilene Zimmerman. **Description:** Advice is given to O. Robin Sweet, founder of Well Fed Baby.

56472 ■ "We Have Liftoff" in *Entrepreneur* (Vol. 32, October 2004, No. 10, pp. 104)
Pub: Entrepreneur Media Inc.
Ed: Amanda C. Kooser. **Description:** Profile of Pursenickety's updated Website marketing handbags. Deborah Nail shares the work involved in creating the new site that won the Entrepreneur and Interland's Tech Makeover. The new site manages the company's inventory of purses and baby bags, offers separate wholesale pricing, and handles real-time credit card transactions.

56473 ■ "Weekend warrior" in *Entrepreneur* (Vol. 31, No. 6, June 2003, pp. 160)
Pub: Entrepreneur Media Inc.
Ed: Barbie White, April Y. Pennington. **Description:** Profile of Barbie White, president and co-designer of Japanese Weekend Inc., a San Francisco maternity clothing retailer and wholesaler; sales are expected to hit $10 million in 2003.

56474 ■ "Westinn Kennels: A Phenomenal Growth Story" in *St. Charles Business Record* (September 30, 2004)
Pub: Dolan Media Newswires
Ed: James Monahan. **Description:** Profile of Sharon West, owner of Westinn Kennels. West opened the kennel in 1997 with a client base of 100 dog owners and has grown to 4,000 clients today. West recently opened her new pet facility, Everything Under One Woof, an indoor sports facility that accommodates competitive events and agility exercises for dogs.

56475 ■ "What's In a Name? Quite a Lot, Actually" in *Crain's Detroit Business* (Vol. 21, October 3, 2005, No. 43, pp. 8)
Pub: Crain Communications Inc. - Detroit
Ed: Keith Crain. **Description:** The Detroit Women's Economic Club has changed its name to Inforum.

56476 ■ "What's Up Doc? They May Not be Old Enough for Medical School, But Now Kids Can Look the Part" in *Entrepreneur* (Vol. 32, July 2004)
Pub: Entrepreneur Media Inc.
Ed: Nichole L. Torres. **Description:** Profile of Jacquelyn Aven, founder of MiniScrubs Inc. Aven's company manufactures personalized doctors' scrubs for children to wear both inside and outside the hospital setting.

56477 ■ "When It Comes to Shopping, Safety Comes First" in *Home Business* (Vol. 13, January/February 2006, No. 1, pp. 56)
Pub: Home Business Magazine
Ed: Sandy Larson. **Description:** Profile of Tracy Richter, inventor of a safety strap that secures infant car seats to shopping carts. Mother of three is dedicated to promoting awareness of the safety issues when using infant seats in shopping carts.

56478 ■ "When Your Job Really Makes You Sick" in *Black Enterprise* (Vol. 34, No. 5, December 2003, pp. 63)
Pub: Earl Graves Publishing Co.
Ed: Lee Anna Jackson. **Description:** Profile of Erica Benson, owner of A-Solution, her home-based consulting service offering job coaching among professional and business services.

56479 ■ "When Your Job Really Makes You Sick: Why You Need to Develop a High Adversity Quotient" in *Black Enterprise* (Vol. 34, December 2003)
Pub: Earl Graves Publishing Co.
Ed: Lee Anna Jackson. **Description:** Profile of Erica Benson, owner of A-Solution, her home-based consulting service offering job coaching among professional and business services.

56480 ■ "Where Are You Headed?" in *Women in Business* (Vol. 53, No. 7, January-February 2002, pp. 22)
Pub: The ABWA Co Inc.
Ed: Mary-Lane Kamberg. **Description:** It is important to establish goals and to develop a plan of action to

achieve the goals. An individual must also be flexible because goals could change during their implementation.

56481 ■ "Where It's a Woman's World" in *Inc.* (January 1, 2004)
Pub: Gruner & Jahr USA Publishing
Ed: Bobbie Gossage. **Description:** The U.S. ranked tenth with women entrepreneurs, among countries surveyed by researchers from Babson College, the London School of Economics and the Ewing M. Kauffman Foundation. Statistical data included.

56482 ■ "Whoops! I won't let that happen again!" in *Women in Business* (Vol. 54, No. 5, September-October 2002, pp. 32)
Pub: The ABWA Company, Inc.
Ed: Elizabeth Bradley. **Description:** The mistakes made by several women business owners are recounted.

56483 ■ "Who's the Boss?" in *Success* (Vol. 47, No. 2, June 2000, pp. 76)
Pub: Success Publishing, Inc.
Ed: Sharon Nelton. **Description:** Women-owned businesses are America's fastest-growing employers. Includes a profile of the company, Sheila's Inc., and statistical data.

56484 ■ "With Great Power Tools Comes Great Responsibility" in *Inc.* (May 1, 2005)
Pub: Inc. Magazine
Ed: Allen P. Roberts, Jr. **Description:** Profile of Barbara Kavovit, founder of Barbara K! Enterprises. Kavovit produces tools designed for women; sales were reported at $5 million in 2004.

56485 ■ "Woman Car Dealership Owner Brings Fresh Outlook to Male-Oriented Business" in *Long Island Business News* (February 27, 2004)
Pub: Dolan Media Newswires
Description: Profile of Juliana Curran Terian, president of Rallye Group in Roslyn, New York, a high-end automobile dealership. Terian took over leadership of the firm after the death of her husband Peter Terian.

56486 ■ *The Woman Entrepreneur—Out of Your Mind and into the Marketplace*
Pub: Upstart Publishing Co., Inc.
Ed: Linda Pinson and Jerry Jinnett. **Released:** 1993. **Price:** $14.00 (paper).

56487 ■ *The Woman Entrepreneur: 33 Personal Stories of Success*
Pub: Upstart Publishing Co., Inc.
Ed: Linda Pinson and Jerry Jinnett. **Released:** 1993. **Price:** $14.00 (paper). **Description:** Provides statistical analysis of women in business and information for starting a business. Includes 33 case histories of women who started their own businesses.

56488 ■ *Woman to Woman: Street Smarts for Women Entrepreneurs*
Pub: Prentice Hall
Ed: Geraldine Larkin. **Released:** 1993. **Price:** $14.95. **Description:** Provides information for women entrepreneurs on managing people, time, and money. Includes checklists and work sheets.

56489 ■ "A Woman's Job" in *My Business* (June/July 2004, pp. 50)
Pub: My Business Magazine
Ed: Lena Basha. **Description:** Women franchisees are moving into a traditionally male-dominated market.

56490 ■ "Women Business Owners Get Credit Easily" in *Marketing to Women* (Vol. 19, November 2006, No. 11, pp. 12)
Pub: EPM Communications.
Description: According to a Gallup study commissioned by Wells Fargo, women find it easier to obtain credit than men. Statistical data included.

56491 ■ "Women Business Owners Seek Financing" in *Marketing to Women* (Vol. 19, December 2006, No. 2, pp. 8)
Pub: EPM Communications, Inc.
Description: A study by the Center for Women's Business Research shows that women business owners have become more savvy when seeking financial support for their business ventures. Statistical data included.

56492 ■ Women Business Owners: Selling to the Federal Government
Pub: DIANE Publishing Co.
Released: 1993. **Price:** $20.00 (paper).

56493 ■ "Women of Courage International to hold second women's conference" in *Pueblo Business Journal* (February 28, 2003)
Pub: Dolan Media Newswires
Ed: Lisa Seley. **Description:** The second women's conference in Pueblo, Colorado, hosted by the Women of Courage International, will be held in spring 2003. The conference is designed to give women and teen girls direction and hope in their lives.

56494 ■ "Women integrating workday courage" in *Women in Business* (Vol. 54, No. 2, March-April 2002, pp. 28)
Pub: The ABWA Co Inc.
Ed: Sandra Ford Walston. **Description:** Courage in the workplace is important to utilize. Businesswomen must be accountable and overcome limitations.

56495 ■ "Women" in *Entrepreneur* (Vol. 27, No. 12, December 1999, pp. 44)
Pub: Entrepreneur Media Inc.
Ed: Cynthia E. Griffin. **Description:** A new study underscores the old adage that the most important thing in business is location, location, location. In the top 50 U.S. metropolitan areas, the number of women-owned firms has increased 33 to 59 percent in the past seven years, according to a 1999 report by the National Foundation for Women Business Owners (NFWBO).

56496 ■ Women Entrepreneurs
Pub: Edward Elgar Publishing, Incorporated
Ed: Andrea Smith-Hunter. **Released:** October 2006. **Price:** $120.00. **Description:** Focus is on women entrepreneurs; information includes human capital, network structures and financial capital, with comparative analysis across racial lines.

56497 ■ Women Entrepreneurs: Moving Beyond the Glass Ceiling
Pub: Sage Publications, Inc.
Ed: Dorothy P. Moore and E. Holly Buttner. **Released:** 1997. **Price:** $46.00 (cloth).

56498 ■ "Women Entrepreneurship in the 21st Century" in *Entrepreneur* (Vol. 31, No. 8, August 2003, pp. 6)
Pub: Entrepreneur Media, Inc.
Ed: Steve Cooper. **Description:** A Website created by the U.S. Department of Labor and the U.S. Small Business Administration is featured. The site assists women business owners in finding federal resources and business in general.

56499 ■ "Women Find 'Grass Ceiling' of Men-Only Clubs Impediment to Business" in *Chicago Tribune* (February 3, 2003)
Pub: Knight Ridder/Tribune Business News
Ed: Greg Burns. **Description:** Executive women speak out on the difficulties encountered when golf courses exclude them from grillrooms, member-guest tournaments and Saturday morning tee times. Maureen Grzelakowski decided to solve her problem by purchasing her own nine-hole golf course in the southwest suburbs of Chicago.

56500 ■ "Women of interest" in *WorkingWoman* (Vol. 25, No. 2, February 2000, pp. S10)
Pub: Lang Communications Inc.
Ed: Dana Asher. **Description:** The prediction of death for brick and mortar banks has been made in this age of e-commerce. Bank presidents Kathleen Walsh Carr and Deborah C. Wright discuss the prediction.

56501 ■ Women-Owned & Home-Based Businesses
Pub: DIANE Publishing Co.
Ed: Christopher S. Bond. **Released:** 1999. **Price:** $40.00.

56502 ■ "Women Roll Out Cigar Magazine" in *Tampa Tribune* (November 17, 2005)
Pub: Media General, Inc.
Ed: Richard Mullins. **Description:** Profile of Lisa Figueredo and her cigar magazine, Cigar City. Figueredo believed there was a market for the magazine in an area where cigar-making has traditional roots.

56503 ■ "Women of Substance: Who Says It's a Man's World?" in *Entrepreneur* (Vol. 31, No. 11, November 2003, pp. 104)
Pub: Entrepreneur Media, Inc.
Ed: Devlin Smith. **Description:** Women entrepreneurs share thoughts on ways franchising allows them to balance work and family lives.

56504 ■ "Women mentoring women" in *Women in Business* (Vol. 53, No. 7, January-February 2002, pp. 28)
Pub: The ABWA Co Inc.
Ed: Lisa Keating. **Description:** There are psychological and professional rewards for the mentor and the person who is mentored. Women mentors can assist new businesswomen to learn how to manage job stress and plan their careers or small business.

56505 ■ "Women's Business Centers Fight for Funding" in *Inc.* (August 1, 2004)
Pub: Inc. Magazine
Ed: Bobbie Gossage. **Description:** U.S. Small Business Administration announced the opening of 11 new Women's Business Centers.

56506 ■ "The Women's Business Centers: the help women business owners need?" in *WorkingWoman* (Vol. 25, No. 2, February 2000, pp. S32)
Pub: Lang Communications Inc.
Ed: Joanne Symons. **Description:** Questions regarding the Women's Business Centers Bill are answered.

56507 ■ Women's Business Resource Guide
Pub: McGraw-Hill Professional Publishing Group
Contact: Barbara Littman, Author
Released: Biennial, latest edition 1st. **Price:** $18.95, individuals. **Covers:** Over 600 training, technical assistance, and counseling programs, information sources, government agencies, membership organizations, and other associations of interest to women in business. **Entries Include:** Resource name, address, phone, geographical area served, description. **Arrangement:** Classified by topic. **Indexes:** Product/service, organization name, subject.

56508 ■ "Women's Firms Reach Nearly $2 Trillion in Sales" in *Marketing to Women* (Vol. 19, October 2006, No. 10, pp. 12)
Pub: EPM Communications, Inc.
Description: According to the Center for Women's Business Research, women own a half or majority stake in 40 percent of all businesses in the U.S. and employ 12.8 million people. Statistical data included.

56509 ■ Women's Ventures, Women's Visions: 29 Inspiring Stories from Women Who Started Their Own Business
Pub: The Crossing Press, Inc.
Ed: Shoshana Alexander. **Released:** 1997. **Price:** $14.95.

56510 ■ "Words from the Wise" in *Entrepreneur* (Vol. 28, No. 1, January 2000, pp. 42)
Pub: Entrepreneur Media Inc.
Ed: Cynthia E. Griffin. **Description:** In Tustin, California there is a non-profit organization dedicated to helping women-owned businesses create their first board of directors or advisory board.

56511 ■ Work of Her Own: A Woman's Guide to Success off the Career Track
Pub: The Putnam Publishing Group
Ed: Susan W. Albert. **Released:** 1994. **Price:** $12.95 (paper).

56512 ■ "Work with me" in *WorkingWoman* (Vol. 25, No. 6, June 2000, pp. 40)
Pub: Lang Communications Inc.
Ed: Eilene Zimmerman. **Description:** Georgina Curran and Petra Vester founded Lbdtogo.com in 1999 selling little black dresses. They wish to increase turnover by forming partnerships with other electronic retailers and are seeking advice on the best way of doing this.

56513 ■ "Work Space" in *Tribune* (February 15, 2005)
Pub: Knight-Ridder/Tribune Business News
Ed: AnnMarie Cornejo. **Description:** Profile of Susie Clark who transformed part of South County history by turning a rustic wooden store into a spiritual gift shop selling candles, incense, tarot cards, books, and crystals.

56514 ■ "Working virtually works for her" in *Black Enterprise* (Vol. 32, No. 7, February 2002, pp. 51)
Pub: Earl Graves Publishing Co.
Ed: Bridget McCrea. **Description:** Profile of Victoria Parham, owner and president of Virtual Support Services LLC. Parham's firm provides administrative support, such as email and database management, travel arrangements, scheduling, and customer-relationship management and support to a national client base, all done virtually.

56515 ■ "Working on the Highway: This Entrepreneur Minds Her Cash Flow and the Traffic Flow" in *Black Enterprise* (Vol. 34, January 2004)
Pub: Earl Graves Publishing Co.
Ed: Zakiyyah El-Amin. **Description:** Profile of Bellandra B. Foster, owner of BBF Engineering Services. Foster became an entrepreneur after the birth of her first child. Her firm is located in Southfield, Michigan and offers consulting services, which include construction inspection and testing, construction permit review, traffic and transportation engineering studies, construction engineering, and traffic crash analysis, creating a niche for road and bridge projects.

56516 ■ "Working With Women" in *My Business* (April/May 2003, pp. 14)
Pub: My Business Magazine
Ed: Mardy Fones. **Description:** Ways in which women business owners can grow a business by effectively managing female employees are addressed in a question/answer format.

56517 ■ "Workload S.O.S." in *Women In Business* (Vol. 52, No. 5, September-October 2000, pp. 30)
Pub: The ABWA Co., Inc.
Ed: Mary-Lane Kamberg. **Description:** Issues are presented concerning the solutions to staff shortages which occur as a result of workload fluctuations. The use of temporary staff, outside consultants, and the outsourcing of work are discussed.

56518 ■ "Write Stuff" in *Crain's New York Business* (Vol. 23, January 15, 2007, No. 3, pp. 47)
Pub: Crain Communications, Inc.
Ed: Elisabeth Butler. **Description:** Profile of Karen Levy, a calligrapher, and her company Writer's Camp, a business that inscribes place cards, invitations and menus for individual clients as well as large companies including Saks Fifth Avenue and J.P. Morgan Chase.

56519 ■ "Writing her own e-ticket" in *WorkingWoman* (Vol. 25, No. 8, September 2000, pp. 20)
Pub: Lang Communications Inc.
Ed: Susan Caminiti. **Description:** Priceline.com Chief Financial Officer (CFO) Heidi Miller talks about her plans for new role and of leaving Citigroup where she was also CFO.

56520 ■ "WSJ Honors Economist" in *Hispanic Business* (June 2005, pp. 18)

Pub: Hispanic Business
Description: Maria Fiorini Ramierez, president and CEO of her global economic and financial consulting firm of the same name, was named one of the top two economists in the U.S. in forecasting the actual rate of inflation during the last three years by The Wall Street Journal.

56521 ■ "A Year of Advice is Prize in Woman-Owned Program" in *Crain's Detroit Business* (Vol. 21, December 12, 2005, No. 50, pp. 2)

Pub: Crain Communications Inc. - Detroit
Description: Three Detroit-area woman-owned businesses will receive professional assistance from the Athena PowerLink program. The winners must be companies that are majority-owned by a woman, operating for at least two years, have a minimum of two employees, annual revenue of $250,000 or more in manufacturing or retail, or $100,000 in service business, and have clearly defined goals.

56522 ■ "Yoga Instructor finds peace in classroom" in *Long Island Business News* (Vol. 50, No. 14, March 28, 2003, pp. 23A)

Pub: Dolan Media Newswires
Ed: Adina Genn. **Description:** Profile of Gail Grossman, who provides special training for teaching yoga to children, as well as to adults.

56523 ■ "Young, Female, and Demanding" in *Inc.* (Volume 28, January 2006, No. 1, pp. 27)

Pub: Inc. Magazine
Description: Young Generation X women are burning out in the workplace at increasingly high numbers. Charlotte Shelton, a business professor at Rockhurst University in Missouri, believes changing attitudes placing high expectations on women are partly to blame.

56524 ■ "You've Got Mail" in *WorkingWoman* (Vol. 25, No. 2, February 2000, pp. S23)

Pub: Lang Communications Inc.
Ed: Melissa Wahl. **Description:** A directory of networking services, including member profiles and on-line services, is presented.

56525 ■ "You've got the power!" in *Black Enterprise* (Vol. 31, No. 5, December 2000, pp. 166)

Pub: Earl Graves Publishing Co.
Ed: Robyn D. Clarke. **Description:** The value of communicating with confidence and power through your body language is examined.

TRADE PERIODICALS

56526 ■ *BusinessWoman Magazine*

Pub: Business and Professional Women/USA
Contact: Sherry Saunders
E-mail: ssaunders@bpwusa.org
Released: 3/year. **Description:** Magazine for working women that promotes workplace equity issues.

56527 ■ *CWC Communicator*

Pub: California Women's Caucus
Ed: Dr. Pat Nellor Wickwire, Editor. **Released:** 2-4/year. **Price:** $15, Included in membership. **Description:** Discusses issues affecting women, particularly regarding careers and especially women in counseling careers. Recurring features include news of research, a calendar of events, news of educational opportunities, and notices of publications available.

56528 ■ *The Facilitator*

Pub: Nurre Ink
Contact: Susan M. Nurre, Editor & Publisher
E-mail: snurre@thefacilitator.com
Released: Quarterly. **Price:** $35, U.S.; $35, institutions; $40, out of country. **Description:** Provides articles written by facilitators that are designed to link

facilitators from around the world in a forum of sharing, networking, and communicating. Includes updates on training, automated meeting tools, and resources. Recurring features include tips and techniques, a calendar of events, reports of meetings, news of educational opportunities, book reviews, and notices of publications available.

56529 ■ *Multicultural Marketing News*

Pub: Multicultural Marketing Resources Inc.
Contact: Lisa Skriloff, Editor-in-Chief
Released: Bimonthly. **Price:** $700 for Multicultural Marketing News only; $250 for MMN Online only. **Description:** Covers minority- and women-owned businesses and corporations that sell to them. Provides story ideas, diverse resources for journalists, and contacts for marketing executives. Recurring features include a calendar of events, business profiles, and a feature on a trend in multicultural marketing.

56530 ■ *Women in Business*

Pub: The ABWA Company Inc.
Contact: Cynthia Bell, Advertising Sales
E-mail: cbell@abwa.org
Ed: Kathleen Isaacson, Editor, kisaacson@abwa.org. **Released:** Bimonthly. **Price:** $20; $24 other countries. **Description:** Women's business magazine.

56531 ■ *Women Chemists*

Pub: American Chemical Society
Ed: Teri Quinn Gray, Editor. **Released:** Semiannual. **Description:** Aims "to be leaders in attracting, developing, and promoting women in the chemical sciences." Reports on women's achievements in the chemical sciences, as well as grants available, symposiums, and current events.

56532 ■ *Working Moms & Dads Magazine*

Pub: Corporate Marketing & Publishing
Ed: Patrick McGuire, Editor. **Released:** Monthly. **Description:** Contains national and local news on parenting, childcare, education, and work issues. For professional and working parents.

VIDEOCASSETTES/AUDIOCASSETTES

56533 ■ *American Institute of Small Business: Women in Business*

American Institute of Small Business (AISB)
7515 Wayzata Blvd., Ste. 126
Minneapolis, MN 55426
Ph:(612)545-7001
Free: 800-328-2906
Fax: (612)545-7020
Co. E-mail: AISBOFMN@AOL.COM
URL: http://www.accessil.com/aisb
Released: 199?. **Price:** $69.95. **Description:** Female small business owners discuss success, overcoming stereotypes, obtaining financing, and other issues. **Availability:** VHS.

56534 ■ *Change Your Mind: Inner Training for Women in Business*

American Bar Association
321 N. Clark St.
Chicago, IL 60610
Ph:(312)988-5000
Fax: (312)988-5528
Co. E-mail: abapubed@abanet.org
URL: http://www.abanet.org/publiced/
Released: 1988. **Price:** $495.00. **Description:** Dr. Kay Porter and Judy Foster give steps that will help women become better and more confident in the business world. **Availability:** VHS.

56535 ■ *Enterprising Women*

AIMS Multimedia
20765 Superior St.
Chatsworth, CA 91311-4409
Ph:(818)773-4300
Free: 800-367-2467
Fax: (818)341-6700
Co. E-mail: info@aims.multimedia.com
URL: http://www.aimsmultimedia.com

Released: 1989. **Price:** $395.00. **Description:** Profiles of five different businesses and the women who run them. **Availability:** VHS; 3/4U.

56536 ■ *Inc. Magazine Business Success Programs*

Cambridge Educational
c/o Films Media Group
PO Box 2053
Princeton, NJ 08843-2053
Free: 800-257-5126
Fax: (609)671-0266
Co. E-mail: custserve@filmsmediagroup.com
URL: http://www.cambridgeol.com
Released: 1987. **Price:** $99.95. **Description:** These four programs contain a step-by-step explanation of what must be done to succeed in business. **Availability:** VHS; CC.

56537 ■ *Special Issues for Women Entrepreneurs*

Instructional Video
2219 C St.
Lincoln, NE 68502
Ph:(402)475-6570
Free: 800-228-0164
Fax: (402)475-6500
Co. E-mail: feedback@insvideo.com
URL: http://www.insvideo.com
Price: $89.95. **Description:** Contains panel discussion on the problems women face when starting and running their own business. Includes insight from honored women entrepreneurs. **Availability:** VHS.

56538 ■ *Time Management for Women*

Instructional Video
2219 C St.
Lincoln, NE 68502
Ph:(402)475-6570
Free: 800-228-0164
Fax: (402)475-6500
Co. E-mail: feedback@insvideo.com
URL: http://www.insvideo.com
Price: $79.95. **Description:** Kay Cronkite Waldo offers time management training for women, focusing on behavior patterns, energy cycles, efficiency vs. effectiveness, time wasters, decision-making factors, and the superwoman theory. **Availability:** VHS.

56539 ■ *Woman Entrepreneur: Do You Have What it Takes?*

Cambridge Educational
c/o Films Media Group
PO Box 2053
Princeton, NJ 08843-2053
Free: 800-257-5126
Fax: (609)671-0266
Co. E-mail: custserve@filmsmediagroup.com
URL: http://www.cambridgeol.com
Released: 1987. **Price:** $29.95. **Description:** A motivational look at starting a business for women, featuring interviews with a half-dozen women who have made it. **Availability:** VHS.

TRADE SHOWS AND CONVENTIONS

56540 ■ *Annual NAIW Convention - National Association of Insurance Women International*

National Association of Insurance Women - International
6528 E. 101st St. PMB 750
Tulsa, OK 74133
Free: 800-766-6249
Fax: (918)743-1968
URL: http://www.naiw.org
Released: Annual. **Principal Exhibits:** Equipment, supplies, and services for insurance industry professionals. **Dates and Locations:** 2007 Jun.

CONSULTANTS

56541 ■ Association of Home-Based Women Entrepreneurs
11330 Olive Blvd., Ste. 106
Saint Louis, MO 63141-7161
Ph:(314)995-1455
Fax: (314)909-8179
Co. E-mail: aschaefer@advbizsol.com
URL: http://www.hbwe.org

E-mail: aschaefer@advbizsol.com
Scope: A non-profit womens organization who target the needs of women entrepreneurs/business owners working from home based offices. **Seminars:** Twenty Five Key Steps To Maintaining A Successful Home-Based Business, Nov, 2006; Pyro Marketing, Jan, 2007.

56542 ■ Donna Cornell Enterprises Inc.
68 N Plank Rd., Ste. 204
Newburgh, NY 12550-2122
Ph:(845)565-0088
Fax: (845)565-0084
Co. E-mail: rc@cornellcareercenter.com
URL: http://www.dce.com

E-mail: rc@cornellcareercenter.com
Scope: Offers services in career consultant, professional search, job placement, and national professional search. **Publications:** "The Power of the Woman Within".

56543 ■ Joel Greenstein & Associates
6212 Nethercombe Ct.
McLean, VA 22101
Ph:(703)893-1888
Co. E-mail: jgreenstein@contractmasters.com

E-mail: jgreenstein@contractmasters.com
Scope: Provides services to minority and women-owned businesses and government agencies. Experienced in interpreting federal and agency-specific acquisition regulations and contract terms and conditions. Offers assistance with preparing technical and cost proposals and sealed bids.

FRANCHISES AND BUSINESS OPPORTUNITIES

56544 ■ Fresh Fruit Bouquet Company
130 Fifth Ave., 10th Fl.
New York, NY 10011-4399
Ph:(212)242-4399
Description: Operate from a retail location where you create and offer for sale to customers our variety of fresh fruit bouquets and products. Offers a unique, healthy and alternative to floral arrangements, center pieces, gifts, appetizers and desserts. You offer these products for sale via customer pickup or delivery by refrigerated van. **Equity Capital Needed:** $89,900-$135,450 total investment. **Managerial Assistance:** Equipment ordering and set-up from kitchen appliances to computers, installation of customized software and a complete operations manual. **Training:** An intensive training session, store location selection, store design and layout guidelines, and ongoing personal support and assistance.

56545 ■ Wild Bird Centers of America
130 Fifth Ave., 10th Fl.
New York, NY 10011-4399
Ph:(212)242-4399
Description: Retail store that offers more than just bird feeders and seed. The store offers a wide selection of products including exclusive seed blends that are field-tested and proven to attract a wide variety of wild birds. In addition to an extensive selection of feeders, birdbaths, nest boxes and other bird feeding products, the stores offer a variety of backyard and nature-oriented gifts and books, plus a wide range of binoculars and spotting scopes. **Equity Capital Needed:** $94,900-$152,300 total investment; $30,000-$50,000 cash required. **Training:** You receive a turn-key, proven business system, comprehensive training and support.

COMPUTERIZED DATABASES

56546 ■ *National Directory of Woman-Owned Business Firms*
Business Research Services Inc.
4701 Sangamore Rd., Ste. S-155
Bethesda, MD 20816
Ph:(301)229-5561
Free: 800-845-8420
Fax: (301)229-6133
Co. E-mail: brspubs@sba8a.com
URL: http://www.sba8a.com
Description: Contains information on more than 27,000 woman-owned businesses in the United States. Provides name, address, telephone number, name and title of contact, minority group, certification status, date founded, number of employees, description of products or services, U.S. Standard Industrial Classification (SIC) codes, sales volume, government contracting experience, and references. Regional subsets and custom databases also available. Corresponds to the *National Directory of Woman-Owned Business Firms*. **Availability:** CD-ROM: Business Research Services Inc; Diskette: Business Research Services Inc;Batch: Business Research Services Inc. **Type:** Directory.

RESEARCH CENTERS

56547 ■ HEC Montreal–Group for Women, Management and Organizations
3000 Chemin de la Cote-Sainte-Catherine
Montreal, QC, Canada H3T 2A7
Ph:(514)340-6014
Fax: (514)340-3825
Co. E-mail: louise.st-cyr@hec.ca
URL: http://neumann.hec.ca/groupefge/
Contact: Louise St-Cyr, Dir.
E-mail: louise.st-cyr@hec.ca
Scope: Women in a changing world: sources, development and practices of leadership; women entrepreneurs: characteristics, motivations, management practices and access to financing; women's succession; and reconciling family and career. **Publications:** Research. **Educational Activities:** Seminars, in the fall and winter.

ASSOCIATIONS AND OTHER ORGANIZATIONS

56548 ■ National Safe Workplace Institute/ SafeSpaces.com
3008 Bishops Ridge Ct.
Monroe, NC 28110
Ph:(704)282-1111
Fax: (704)550-5857
Co. E-mail: info@safespaces.com
URL: http://www.safespaces.com
Contact: Joseph A. Kinney, Pres.
Purpose: Provides research and education on issues related to occupational health and safety. Is concerned with safe and healthy work environments and workplace violence. Seeks to make workplace safety and health a priority. Monitors efforts of the public and private sectors in improving workplace safety. Conducts periodic studies of national and regional industry issues. **Publications:** *Electronic Newsletter* (semi-monthly); *Newsletter* (monthly). Also publishes national, regional, and state reports on occupational safety and health issues.

56549 ■ National Safety Council
1121 Spring Lake Dr.
Itasca, IL 60143-3201
Ph:(630)285-1121
Free: 800-621-7619
Fax: (630)285-1315
Co. E-mail: info@nsc.org
URL: http://www.nsc.org
Contact: Alan McMillan, Pres.
Description: Promotes injury reduction by providing a forum for the exchange of safety and health ideas, techniques, and experiences and the discussion of injury prevention methods. Offers courses in first aid, occupational safety and traffic safety. Maintains extensive library on health and safety subjects. **Publications:** *Accident Prevention Manual for Business and Industry; Family Safety and Health* (quarterly); *Injury Facts* (annual); *Safe Driver* (monthly); *Safe Worker* (monthly); *Safety and Health* (monthly); *Traffic Safety* (monthly).

56550 ■ National Safety Management Society
PO Box 4460
Walnut Creek, CA 94596-0460
Free: 800-321-2910
Fax: (573)441-1765
Co. E-mail: nsmsinc@yahoo.com
URL: http://www.nsms.us
Contact: Dr. Jeffrey Chung PhD, Exec.Dir.
Membership: Individuals with managerial responsibilities related to safety/loss control management, including professionals in the fields of education, medicine, computer technology, security, personnel, law, and other disciplines. **Purpose:** Advances new concepts of accident prevention and loss control and promotes the role of safety management in the total management effort. Advises concentration in areas where a favorable cost/benefit return can be achieved with these new concepts while being cognizant of hu-

manitarian considerations. Participates in local, state, and regional safety conferences; conducts regional management improvement and executive safety training seminars. **Publications:** *Digest* (monthly); *Journal of Safety Management* (quarterly). Also contributes to *Occupational Hazards Magazine.*

56551 ■ Voluntary Protection Programs Participants' Association
7600-E Leesburg Pike, Ste. 440
Falls Church, VA 22043-2004
Ph:(703)761-1146
Fax: (703)761-1148
Co. E-mail: administration@vpppa.org
URL: http://www.vpppa.org
Contact: R. Davis Layne, Exec. Dir.
Membership: Companies participating in Voluntary Protection Programs and other workplace environmental protection, health, and safety programs. **Purpose:** Promotes cooperation between labor, management, and government agencies to insure safe and environmentally sustainable workplaces. Works closely with federal environmental and safety agencies to develop and implement cooperative programs; provides information on environmental health and workplace safety to congressional committees considering legislation. **Publications:** *The Leader* (quarterly); *On the Wire* (bimonthly); *Safety News Network* (biweekly); *Washington Update* (monthly).

REFERENCE WORKS

56552 ■ "Adapting to a multicultural workforce" in *Safety & Health* (Vol. 163, No. 3, March 2001, pp. 282)
Pub: National Safety Council
Description: Issues concerning the effectiveness of health and safety measures presented to company employees are discussed, by way of answering the concerns of a safety professional. It is emphasized that all employees' communication needs should be addressed to ensure effectiveness of safety regulations.

56553 ■ *CompControl: Secrets of Reducing Workers' Compensation Costs*
Pub: Oasis Press
Ed: Edward J. Priz. **Released:** 1995. **Price:** $19.95.

56554 ■ "Contingency Planning and Disaster Recovery: a Small Business Guide" in *Entrepreneur* (Vol. 31, No. 12, Dec. 2003, pp. 8)
Pub: Entrepreneur Media Inc.
Ed: Steve Cooper. **Description:** Contingency planning and disaster recovery needs of small businesses are explored.

56555 ■ "Defusing disasters" in *Atlanta Business Chronicle* (Vol. 24, No. 8, July 27, 2001, pp. 1B)
Pub: American City Business Journals Inc.
Ed: Chaundra Frierson. **Description:** Workplace violence has become an important issue facing small businesses. The article offers ways to address workplace violence.

56556 ■ "Duncan Manufacturing Firm to Receive Exemption from OSHA" in *Journal Record* (February 4, 2004)
Pub: Dolan Media Company
Description: Richard's Manufacturing, Duncan, Oklahoma, will be one of 34 businesses exempt from the Occupational Safety and Health Administration inspection. The precision machine shop has been in business since 1976.

56557 ■ "The economics of ergonomics" in *Atlanta Business Chronicle* (Vol. 23, No. 35, February 2, 2001, pp. 51A)
Pub: American City Business Journals Inc.
Ed: Chaundra Frierson. **Description:** A new ergonomics regulation has been enacted recently which requires businesses to set up programs to reduce the amount of work-related injuries that take place. Small businesses oppose the regulation because it will increase costs dramatically. An accompanying sidebar includes an ergonomics timeline, while another provides statistics about who will be covered by this new regulation and its costs.

56558 ■ *Enabling Environments for Jobs and Entrepreneurship: The Role of Policy and Law in Small Enterprise Employment*
Pub: International Labour Office
Ed: Gerhard Reinecke, Simon White. **Released:** February 2004. **Price:** $22.95. **Description:** National policies, laws and regulations governing workplace safety.

56559 ■ "5 Ergonomic Guidelines for Yourself" in *My Business* (April/May 2002, pp. 44)
Pub: My Business Magazine
Description: Five important ergonomic guidelines for individuals who spend most of their day working on computers are outlined.

56560 ■ "The Good Fire" in *Entrepreneur* (Vol. 28, No. 3, March 2000, pp. 127)
Pub: Entrepreneur Media Inc.
Ed: Jacquelyn Lynn. **Description:** Try a kinder, gentler termination to help avoid workplace violence.

56561 ■ "Guiding Light" in *Entrepreneur* (Vol. 31, No. 11, November 2003, pp. 56)
Pub: Entrepreneur Media, Inc.
Ed: Gisela M. Pedroza. **Description:** Profile of Forever Flashlights designed to help keep offices safe in the event of a power outage.

56562 ■ "Hands off small business!" in *My Business* (September/October 2001, pp. 23)
Pub: My Business Magazine
Description: The results of a recent survey by NFIB to its members is displayed. The survey included such issues as taxes, compensatory time off, pay disparities, ergonomics, competition with prisons, federal contract bundling, and Internet taxes.

56563 ■ **"The Healthy Home Office"** in *Home Office Computing* **(Vol. 18, No. 10, October 2000, pp. 58)**
Pub: Scholastic Inc.
Ed: William Van Winkle. **Description:** According to the Occupational Safety & Health Administration (OSHA), approximately 1.8 million U.S workers suffer from repetitive strain injuries (RSIs) each year. A guide to home office ergonomics is provided to prevent such injuries. Web sites describing news, products and services are included.

56564 ■ **"Home Invasion"** in *Business Week* **(No. 3666, January 31, 2000, pp. F8)**
Pub: McGraw-Hill, Inc.
Description: Employer responsibility for at-home workers' safety is explored.

56565 ■ **"How To Prevent Violence At Work"** in *Fortune* **(Vol. 151, February 21, 2005, No. 4, pp. 42)**
Pub: Time Inc.
Ed: Anne Fisher. **Description:** According to the U.S. Bureau of Labor Statistics, 18,104 injuries from assaults and 609 homicides in the workplace were reported in 2002. The U.S. Centers for Disease Control have determined workplace violence as a national epidemic.

56566 ■ **"I Spy...: Workplace Surveillance is Coming to Small and Midsize Businesses"** in *Entrepreneur* **(Vol. 31, No. 8, August 2003, pp. 20)**
Pub: Entrepreneur Media, Inc.
Ed: Nichole L. Torres. **Description:** Nearly 20 percent of small companies actively monitor email and Internet usage, and another 20 percent are considering the process, according to Mallary Tytel, president of Healthy Workplaces LLC. The consulting firm, located in Bolton, Connecticut, state that small to mid-size firms are more likely to use technological surveillance rather than pricier undercover detective agencies.

56567 ■ *Industrial Hygiene Made Easy: A Checklist Approach to Recognizing, Evaluating & Controlling Workplace Hazards*
Pub: Moran Associates
Ed: Darolyn K. Wall. **Released:** 1998. **Price:** $59.95.

56568 ■ **"The language of safety"** in *Rough Notes* **(Vol. 146, No. 4, April 2003, pp. 24)**
Pub: Rough Notes
Ed: Elisabeth Boone. **Description:** Accidents and injuries sustained by non-English speaking workers can be reduced or avoided when they learn by doing. Training industrial workers has been a success with Best Institute Inc., headed by Joseph E. Harcarz, Sr., CEO.

56569 ■ *The Law and Occupational Injury, Disease, and Death*
Pub: Greenwood Publishing Group, Inc.
Ed: Warren Freedman. **Released:** 1990. **Price:** $65.00. **Description:** Discusses common workplace hazards and provides a survey of the applicable statutes, case law, and court decisions. Covers such issues as identifying specific exposures in the workplace, drug testing, the roles of involved parties, and theories of liability.

56570 ■ *Law for the Small and Growing Business*
Pub: Jordans Publishing Limited
Ed: P. Bohm. **Released:** February 2007. **Price:** $59.98. **Description:** Legal and regulatory issues facing small businesses, including employment law, health and safety, commercial property, company law and finance are covered.

56571 ■ *A Manager's Guide to OSHA*
Pub: Crisp Publications, Inc.
Ed: Neville C. Tompkins. **Price:** $9.95.

56572 ■ **"Minimizing the Risk of Violence in the Workplace"** in *Employment Relations Today* **(Vol. 27, No. 1, Spring 2000, pp. 83)**
Pub: John Wiley & Sons, Inc.

Ed: Dannie B. Fogleman. **Description:** The seriousness of employer liability for violence in the workplace and prevention of workplace violence are looked into. Topics addressed include conflict management, policies to maintain workplace integrity, and the profiles and warning signs workers at risk for violence. Statistical data included.

56573 ■ *National Directory of Safety Consultants*
Pub: American Society of Safety Engineers
Contact: Fred Fortman, Exec. Dir.
E-mail: ffortman@asse.org
Released: latest edition 18th ed. **Price:** Free. **Covers:** over 2,000 occupational health and safety consultants who are members of the society's consultants division. **Entries Include:** Name, office address and phone, highest degree held, areas of occupational specialization, memberships, licenses and registrations held. **Arrangement:** Alphabetical. **Indexes:** Geographical, area of expertise.

56574 ■ **"New OSHA Rules to Reduce Injuries"** in *Home Office Computing* **(Vol. 18, No. 8, August 2000, pp. 15)**
Pub: Scholastic Inc.
Ed: William Van Winkle. **Description:** Being ergonomically correct is about to become the law of the land; The Occupational Safety & Health Administration (OSHA) is set to implement new ergonomic rules that could send businesses, both large and small, hurrying for compliance, including companies with teleworkers in home offices.

56575 ■ **"A New Pain in the Neck-OSHA lays down ergonomic standards for businesses great and small"** in *PC Computing* **(April 2000, pp. 44)**
Pub: Ziff-Davis Inc.
Ed: Jennifer Powell. **Description:** The Occupational Safety and Health Administration's (OSHA) move to protect knowledge workers from workplace injuries caused by musculoskeletal disorders (MSD) is facing stiff opposition from businesses and some members of Congress. OSHA estimates that more than 600,000 people suffer from lost-workday MSDs each year and that MSDs account for more than one-third of all occupational injuries. Opponents of the regulations argue that there is not enough scientific data to know what causes injuries due to MSD or what workplace changes will stop them.

56576 ■ *Occupational Hazards—Annual Directory Issue*
Pub: Penton Media Inc.
Ed: Stephen Minter, Editor, SMinter@penton.com.
Released: Annual, Published January, 2004. **Publication Includes:** List of about 1,900 manufacturers of equipment and products, and suppliers of services for industrial safety, health, hygiene, hazardous material control, and plant protection. **Entries Include:** Company name, address, phone, fax, type of product or service. **Arrangement:** Alphabetical. **Indexes:** Product/service.

56577 ■ **"The Occupational Safety & Health Administration (OSHA)"** in *Entrepreneur* **(Vol. 32, No. 1, January 2004, pp. 10)**
Pub: Entrepreneur Media, Inc.
Ed: Steve Cooper. **Description:** Occupational Safety & Health Administration (OSHA) has added information for small businesses regarding workplace emergency preparedness, covering issues of preparing for chemical and biological attacks, personal protective equipment, bioterrorism, training and education, and safety equipment.

56578 ■ *Occupational Safety and Health Standards for General Industry*
Pub: C C H, Inc.
Released: Annual 1992. **Price:** $17.50.

56579 ■ **"Omniplex on the Case"** in *Black Enterprise* **(Vol. 37, December 2006, No. 5, pp. 38)**
Pub: Earl G. Graves Publishing Co. Inc.
Ed: Glenn Townes. **Description:** Office of Personnel Management in Washington D.C. recently awarded a

service contract to Omniplex World Services Corp. Virginia-based, The Chantilly, will perform security investigations and background checks on current and prospective federal employees and military personnel and contractors.

56580 ■ *OSHA Handbook for Small Businesses*
Pub: DIANE Publishing Co.
Ed: Released: 1997. **Price:** $25.00 **Description:** This handbook will assist small business employers to meet the legal requirements imposed by, and under, the authority of the Occupational Safety & Health Act of 1970 and achieve voluntary in-compliance status, prior to inspections.

56581 ■ **"OSHA Ushers Itself Out"** in *Business Week* **(March 27, 2000, pp. F6)**
Pub: McGraw-Hill, Inc.
Description: The Occupational Health and Safety Administration announces that it won't inspect home offices.

56582 ■ *Practical Behavior-Based Safety: Step-by-Step Methods to Improve Your Workplace*
Pub: J. J. Keller & Associates, Inc.
Ed: E. Scott Geller. **Released:** 1997. **Price:** $299.00 (ringbound).

56583 ■ **"Private Sector Soldiers"** in *Fortune* **(Vol. 149, No. 9, May 3, 2004, pp. 33)**
Pub: Time, Inc.
Ed: Jeremy Kahn, Nelson D. Schwartz. **Description:** It is estimated that 20,000 private military contractors are working in Iraq. Given the danger these workers face, little work is being accomplished.

56584 ■ **"Protect Your Profits"** in *Small Business Opportunities* **(Vol. 12, No. 2, March 2000, pp. 20)**
Pub: Harris Publications, Inc.
Ed: Marie Sherlock. **Description:** Criminal sociologist, Rosemary Erickson, provides tips for small business owners to protect their enterprise against robberies.

56585 ■ **"Rhino Products Device Keeps Ladders Stationary"** in *Journal Record* **(June 24, 2003)**
Pub: Dolan Media Company
Ed: Darren Currin. **Description:** Profile of Scott Walker, inventor of Secure Ladder, a device that attaches onto standard extension ladders to keep them stationery.

56586 ■ **"Safety Dance: Get Policies in Place Now, and Avoid Liability Later"** in *Entrepreneur* **(Vol. 31, No. 11, November 2003, pp. 93)**
Pub: Entrepreneur Media, Inc.
Ed: Jacquelyn Lynn. **Description:** Insurance policies designed to address potentially risky situations are important to most small businesses. Procedural policies should include employment practices, equipment management, Internet use, cell phone use, vehicles and workplace safety.

56587 ■ *Safety, Health & Environmental Hazards in the Workplace*
Pub: Cassell Academic
Ed: Alan Dalton. **Released:** 1998. **Price:** $80.00 (cloth); $35.95 (paper).

56588 ■ **"Shed Some Light on Your Work"** in *My Business* **(April/May 2002, pp. 47)**
Pub: My Business Magazine
Ed: Dave Donelson. **Description:** When the workplace is improperly lit, employees can suffer from eyestrain, headache, muscle strain, fatigue, stress and poor morale. Many times efforts to save energy increase safety risks.

56589 ■ *Small Businesses and Workplace Fatality Risk: An Exploratory Analysis*
Pub: RAND Corporation
Ed: John F. Mendelhoff; Christopher Nelson; Kilkon Ko. **Released:** June 2006. **Price:** $20.00. **Description:** According to previous research, small business worksites report higher rates of deaths or serious injuries than larger corporations. Statistical data included.

56590 ■ "Stressed Out" in *PC Computing* (April 2000, pp. 44)
Pub: Ziff-Davis Inc.
Ed: Jennifer Powell. **Description:** The seriousness of musculoskeletal disorders and their impact is covered. Musculoskeletal disorders (MSDs), also known as repetitive strain injuries (RSIs), can begin whenever a part of the body is used in the same way repeatedly, especially when twisting or lifting.

56591 ■ "Tips on managing older workers" in *Crain's Detroit Business* (Vol. 17, No. 44, October 22, 2001, pp. 11)
Pub: Crain Communications, Inc.
Description: Tips for managing an older workforce are covered. Topics covered include compensation benefits, ergonomic equipment, stress management, flexible schedules, conflict resolution, and training.

56592 ■ "Workplace Air 'Unfit'" in *The Record* (November 15, 2005)
Pub: New Jersey Media Group
Description: According to a recent study, air in bars, restaurants, and casinos in New Jersey are unfit for workers due to indoor air quality.

56593 ■ *Workplace Safety and Health Guide*
Pub: Clark Boardman Callaghan
Released: 1995.

56594 ■ *Your Company Safety & Health Manual: Programs, Policies & Procedures for Preventing Accidents & Injuries in the Workplace*
Pub: Government Institutes, Inc.
Ed: O. Dan Nwaelele. **Released:** 1997. **Price:** $79.00.

TRADE PERIODICALS

56595 ■ *Accident Prevention*
Pub: Industrial Accident Prevention Association
Released: Bimonthly. **Description:** Trade magazine for the occupational and environmental safety and health fields.

56596 ■ *Canadian Occupational Safety*
Pub: Clifford/Elliot Ltd.
Contact: Vesna Moore, Circulation Mgr
E-mail: vmoore@clbmedia.ca
Ed: Kerry Knudsen, Editor, kknudsen@clbmedia.ca. **Released:** Bimonthly, 6/yr. **Description:** Industrial safety and health news magazine (tabloid).

56597 ■ *Employment Safety and Health Guide—Summary*
Pub: CCH Inc.
Ed: Diane Ward, Editor. **Released:** Weekly. **Price:** $139, individuals. **Description:** A summary that provides a quick insight into the week's developments on decision rules, regulations and other developments.

56598 ■ *Industrial Safety and Hygiene News*
Pub: BNP Media
Contact: Randy Green, Publisher
E-mail: greenr@bnpmedia.com
Released: Monthly. **Price:** $64; $128 two years; $87 Canada; $173 Canada 2 years; $102 other countries; $204 other countries 2 years. **Description:** Magazine for corporate managers and specialists responsible for employee safety and health, environmental programs, and regulatory compliance.

56599 ■ *Inside OSHA*
Pub: Inside Washington Publishers
Contact: Bob Cusack, Managing Editor
Released: Biweekly, every other Monday. **Price:** $725, U.S. and Canada; $775, elsewhere. **Description:** Reports on news of the Occupational Safety and Health Administration.

56600 ■ *Occupational Hazards*
Pub: Penton Media Inc.
Contact: John DiPaola, Vice President
E-mail: jdipaola@penton.com

Ed: Sandy Smith, Editor, ssmith@penton.com. **Released:** Monthly. **Price:** $72 Canada; $126 two years; $50 Canada digital version; $99 international; $162 international; $80 international digital version. **Description:** Monthly publication for safety professionals featuring information to meet OSHA and EPA compliance requirements, improve management of safety, industrial hygiene and environmental programs and find products and services to protect employees and property.

56601 ■ *Occupational Health & Safety*
Pub: Stevens Publishing Corp.
Contact: Craig S. Stevens, Publisher
Ed: Jerry Laws, Editor. **Released:** Monthly. **Price:** $99. **Description:** Magazine covering federal and state regulation of occupational health and safety.

56602 ■ *OSHA Compliance Advisor*
Pub: Business & Legal Reports Inc.
Contact: Robert L. Brady, Editor-in-Chief
E-mail: rbrady@blr.com
Released: Semimonthly, 24/year. **Price:** $299.95, individuals. **Description:** Provides information on employee safety issues, Occupational Safety and Health Act (OSHA), programs, accident incidents, and job hazards. Recurring features include columns titled Compliance Report, Federal Register Digest, From the States, Washington Watch, News Roundup.

56603 ■ *OSHA Week*
Pub: Stevens Publishing Corp.
Contact: Ralph Jensen, Editor-in-Chief
Ed: Katie Hooten, Editor. **Released:** Weekly, 48/year. **Price:** $399. **Description:** Reports on news and updates on safety issues. Recurring features include news of research and a calendar of events.

56604 ■ *Safety Compliance Alert*
Pub: Progressive Business Publications
Ed: Rebecca Cavanaugh, Editor, cavanaugh@pbp.com. **Released:** Semimonthly. **Price:** $299, individuals. **Description:** Presents real world examples to help safety professionals avoid accidents and fires, reduce costs, and comply with changing OSHA rules. Recurring features include news of research, a calendar of events, news of educational opportunities, and a column titled Sharpen Your Judgment.

56605 ■ *Safety and the Supervisor*
Pub: Clement Communications Inc.
Contact: Eric C. Blomfelt, Senior Contributing Ed.
Released: Biweekly, fortnightly. **Price:** $149.50, individuals. **Description:** Provides supervisors and managers with safety techniques and information to improve the work environment.

56606 ■ *Safety Update*
Pub: Ontario Safety League
Contact: Wendy Williams, Ed.Coor.
Ed: Kira Vermond, Editor. **Released:** Quarterly. **Price:** $30. **Description:** Newsletter on the Ontario Safety League's activities and news related to transportation and safety education.

56607 ■ *Wary Canary*
Pub: Wary Canary Press
Contact: Suzanne Randegger, Editor & Publisher
Released: Quarterly. **Price:** $20; $6, single issue. **Description:** For and about victims of environmental illness. Serves as an educational tool for doctors, legislators, relatives, and employers to promote understanding of environmental illness and/or chemical sensitivities.

56608 ■ *Work & Stress*
Pub: Taylor & Francis
Contact: Mary Tisserand, Asst. Ed.
Ed: Prof. Tom Cox, Editor, Work-and-Stress@nottingham.ac.uk. **Released:** Quarterly, 4/yr. **Price:** $416 institutions online; $219 print; $254 institutions; $132; $438 institutions print & online. **Description:** Journal containing information relating to stress, health and safety, as well as articles for those involved with such issues.

VIDEOCASSETTES/ AUDIOCASSETTES

56609 ■ *Accident Investigation: A Tool for Effective Prevention*
LearnCom HR Consulting and Training
38 Discovery, Ste. 250
Irvine, CA 92618
Ph:(515)440-0890
Free: 800-698-8263
Fax: (515)221-3149
Co. E-mail: nhartline@learncom.com
URL: http://www.learncomhr.com
Released: 1992. **Description:** Provides accident investigation techniques for supervisors and managers. Includes Leader's Guide. **Availability:** VHS; 3/4U.

56610 ■ *Back Injury Prevention Through Ergonomics*
Film Library/Greater Los Angeles Safety Council
600 Wilshire Blvd., No. 1263
Los Angeles, CA 90017
Ph:(213)385-6461
Free: 800-421-9585
Fax: (213)385-8405
URL: http://www.lasafety.org
Released: 198?. **Description:** This is a demonstration of how a total ergonomics program can reduce workers' on-the-job injuries. **Availability:** VHS; 3/4U.

56611 ■ *Brace Your Space: Earthquake Safety in the Work Environment*
University of California Extension Ctr. for Media & Independent Learning
2000 Center St., 4th Fl.
Berkeley, CA 94704
Ph:(510)642-0460
Fax: (510)643-9271
Co. E-mail: mediaservices@ucxonline.berkeley.edu
Released: 1993. **Price:** $150.00. **Description:** Uses earthquake footage from the 1989 Loma Prieta quake to demonstrate the need for seismic safety in the school and business workplace, including the three basic principles of earthquake workplace safety and simple techniques for bracing and securing common office equipment and furnishings. **Availability:** VHS; 3/4U.

56612 ■ *CHEMSAFE*
LearnCom HR Consulting and Training
38 Discovery, Ste. 250
Irvine, CA 92618
Ph:(515)440-0890
Free: 800-698-8263
Fax: (515)221-3149
Co. E-mail: nhartline@learncom.com
URL: http://www.learncomhr.com
Released: 1991. **Price:** $175.00. **Description:** A nine-module program designed to help companies comply with OSHA's Hazard Communication Standard. Each module covers a different type of chemical hazard. A leader's guide and participants' handouts are included. **Availability:** VHS; 3/4U.

56613 ■ *Don't Gamble With Bloodhorne Disease*
LearnCom HR Consulting and Training
38 Discovery, Ste. 250
Irvine, CA 92618
Ph:(515)440-0890
Free: 800-698-8263
Fax: (515)221-3149
Co. E-mail: nhartline@learncom.com
URL: http://www.learncomhr.com
Released: 199?. **Price:** $305. **Description:** Thorough presentation covers safe practices when dealing with infectious materials such as blood, compliance with OSHA standards, avoiding risk and liability of bloodborne disease, and more. Complete with trainer's manual and employee manuals. **Availability:** VHS.

56614 ■ *Don't Panic: Responding to a Hazardous Materials Incident*
LearnCom HR Consulting and Training
38 Discovery, Ste. 250
Irvine, CA 92618

Ph:(515)440-0890
Free: 800-698-8263
Fax: (515)221-3149
Co. E-mail: nhartline@learncom.com
URL: http://www.learncomhr.com
Released: 199?. **Price:** $395. **Description:** Outlines the steps which should be taken in the event of chemical spills. Explains how to identify the source of the material, use of placards and MSDS. Includes leader's guide and workbooks. **Availability:** VHS.

56615 ■ *80% Preventable (Burn Injury Prevention)*
Bergwall Productions, Inc.
1224 Baltimore Pike, Ste. 203
Kennett Square, PA 19317
Ph:(610)361-0334
Free: 800-934-8696
Fax: (610)361-0092
Co. E-mail: bergwall@bergwall.com
URL: http://www.bergwall.com
Released: 1992. **Price:** $99.00. **Description:** Dramatizes what can happen when a lazy and careless worker goofs around once too often. Testimony from a nurse reaffirms the message of the title—that 80% of burn accidents are preventable. **Availability:** VHS.

56616 ■ *Electrical Case Histories*
Audio Graphics Training Systems
503 Gabbettville Rd.
Lagrange, GA 30240
Ph:(706)883-6366
Free: 800-814-9792
Fax: (706)882-3004
Released: 199?. **Price:** $495.00. **Description:** Includes reenactments of actual incidents, reporting unsafe electrical working conditions, personal protective equipment. **Availability:** VHS.

56617 ■ *Electrical Safety in the Lab*
Film Library/Greater Los Angeles Safety Council
600 Wilshire Blvd., No. 1263
Los Angeles, CA 90017
Ph:(213)385-6461
Free: 800-421-9585
Fax: (213)385-8405
URL: http://www.lasafety.org
Released: 1995. **Price:** $99.95. **Description:** Explains how electricity works and its potential hazards. **Availability:** VHS.

56618 ■ *Electrical Safety Related Work Practices*
Gulf Publishing Co.
PO Box 2608
Houston, TX 77252-2608
Ph:(713)520-4448
Free: 800-231-6275
Fax: (713)204-4433
Co. E-mail: csv@gulfpub.com
URL: http://www.gulfpub.com
Released: 1992. **Price:** $1495.00. **Description:** Six-part training program that offers educational material on electrical safety. Centers on the new OSHA requirements for work performed on or near exposed energized and de-energized parts of electrical equipment, the use of electrical protective equipment, and the safe use of electrical equipment. **Availability:** VHS; 3/4U; Special order formats.

56619 ■ *Emergency Evacuation Training: Preparing for the Future*
LearnCom HR Consulting and Training
38 Discovery, Ste. 250
Irvine, CA 92618
Ph:(515)440-0890
Free: 800-698-8263
Fax: (515)221-3149
Co. E-mail: nhartline@learncom.com
URL: http://www.learncomhr.com
Released: 199?. **Price:** $295. **Description:** Illustrates the nature of emergency situations and offers evacuation procedures. Discusses the importance of first responder, pre-planning, exit routes, notification systems, assembly areas, and more. Complete with leader's guide. **Availability:** VHS; CC.

56620 ■ *Emergency Planning and Crisis Management Series*
Gulf Publishing Co.
PO Box 2608
Houston, TX 77252-2608
Ph:(713)520-4448
Free: 800-231-6275
Fax: (713)204-4433
Co. E-mail: csv@gulfpub.com
URL: http://www.gulfpub.com
Released: 1992. **Price:** $995.00. **Description:** Three-part vocational series that helps facilities develop an emergency plan and provide for employee training regarding this plan. Comes with detailed leader's guide. **Availability:** VHS; 3/4U.

56621 ■ *ErgoKinetics: Safety in Motion*
Aspen Publishers
7201 McKinney Circ.
Frederick, MD 21704
Ph:(301)644-3599
Free: 800-638-8437
Fax: (301)644-3550
URL: http://www.aspenpublishers.com
Released: 1994. **Description:** Training program that offers ergonomic solutions for preventing three of the most common types of complaints in the workplace: back and neck injuries; hand, wrist, and arm injuries; and VDT-related visual problems. Contains two separate modules: one for the plant and one for the office. Comes with leader's guide and participants' workbooks. **Availability:** VHS.

56622 ■ *Ergonomics: Low-Cost, Common-Sense Training Solutions*
LearnCom HR Consulting and Training
38 Discovery, Ste. 250
Irvine, CA 92618
Ph:(515)440-0890
Free: 800-698-8263
Fax: (515)221-3149
Co. E-mail: nhartline@learncom.com
URL: http://www.learncomhr.com
Released: 1991. **Description:** A 3-tape guide to reducing cumulative trauma disorders (also known as repetitive motion illnesses), reduce stress, and increase productivity—all without costly engineering controls or job redesigns. A set of three tapes, complete with Leader's Guides and Participant Workbooks. **Availability:** VHS; 3/4U.

56623 ■ *Ergonomics at Work*
Film Library/Greater Los Angeles Safety Council
600 Wilshire Blvd., No. 1263
Los Angeles, CA 90017
Ph:(213)385-6461
Free: 800-421-9585
Fax: (213)385-8405
URL: http://www.lasafety.org
Released: 198?. **Description:** This tape looks at how ergonomics can aid in creating safer working conditions. **Availability:** VHS; 3/4U.

56624 ■ *Explosives*
LearnCom HR Consulting and Training
38 Discovery, Ste. 250
Irvine, CA 92618
Ph:(515)440-0890
Free: 800-698-8263
Fax: (515)221-3149
Co. E-mail: nhartline@learncom.com
URL: http://www.learncomhr.com
Price: $395. **Description:** Employees learn how to prevent accidental fires and explosions while working around highly combustible materials. Includes a trainer's manual and ten handbooks. **Availability:** VHS; 8mm; 3/4U; CC.

56625 ■ *The Extra Step*
Altschul Group Corp.
Health Division
1560 Sherman Ave., Ste. 100
Evanston, IL 60201
Ph:(847)328-6700
Free: 800-323-9084
Fax: (847)328-6706
Price: $445.00. **Description:** A program for both new and veteran employees about the potential danger in handling and working around chemicals. Emphasizes the need for proper safety attitudes and the importance of personal protection from chemical hazards. **Availability:** VHS; 3/4U; Special order formats.

56626 ■ *Facts about OSHA Inspections*
Film Library/Greater Los Angeles Safety Council
600 Wilshire Blvd., No. 1263
Los Angeles, CA 90017
Ph:(213)385-6461
Free: 800-421-9585
Fax: (213)385-8405
URL: http://www.lasafety.org
Released: 1995. **Price:** $195.00. **Description:** Explains compliance procedures for conducting OSHA inspections. Aids workers, supervisors and managers to improve the workplace in order to avoid fines, penalties and citations. **Availability:** VHS.

56627 ■ *Fire Basics in the Workplace*
LearnCom HR Consulting and Training
38 Discovery, Ste. 250
Irvine, CA 92618
Ph:(515)440-0890
Free: 800-698-8263
Fax: (515)221-3149
Co. E-mail: nhartline@learncom.com
URL: http://www.learncomhr.com
Released: 199?. **Price:** $395. **Description:** Introduces employees to the particulars of fire safety in the workplace, including use of fire extinguishers. Complete with leader's guide. **Availability:** VHS; CC.

56628 ■ *First Aid on the Job*
Audio Graphics Training Systems
503 Gabbettville Rd.
Lagrange, GA 30240
Ph:(706)883-6366
Free: 800-814-9792
Fax: (706)882-3004
Released: 199?. **Price:** $395.00. **Description:** Covers when and how to move a victim, stopping bleeding, symptoms of shock and prevention, and bloodborne precautions. **Availability:** VHS.

56629 ■ *Foreman's Accident Protection Series*
Gulf Publishing Co.
PO Box 2608
Houston, TX 77252-2608
Ph:(713)520-4448
Free: 800-231-6275
Fax: (713)204-4433
Co. E-mail: csv@gulfpub.com
URL: http://www.gulfpub.com
Released: 1988. **Price:** $375.00. **Description:** An 11-tape series on setting up an effective industrial safety program. **Availability:** VHS; 3/4U.

56630 ■ *Handle with Care*
Bergwall Productions, Inc.
1224 Baltimore Pike, Ste. 203
Kennett Square, PA 19317
Ph:(610)361-0334
Free: 800-934-8696
Fax: (610)361-0092
Co. E-mail: bergwall@bergwall.com
URL: http://www.bergwall.com
Released: 1992. **Price:** $99.00. **Description:** Short story segments dramatize dangerous situations a variety of people can find themselves in on any given day. Impacts viewers in a more direct way than many lectures devoted to safety. **Availability:** VHS.

56631 ■ *The Hazard Awareness Training Series*
Genium Group Inc.
1171 Riverfront Center
Amsterdam, NY 12010
Ph:(518)842-4111
Free: 800-243-6486
Fax: (518)842-1843
Co. E-mail: info@genium.com
URL: http://www.genium.com
Released: 1989. **Price:** $534.00. **Description:** OSHA laws, how to read and label material safety data sheets, and other industrial health threats are covered in this series. **Availability:** VHS; 3/4U.

56632 ■ *HAZCOM Case Histories*
Audio Graphics Training Systems
503 Gabbettville Rd.
Lagrange, GA 30240
Ph:(706)883-6366
Free: 800-814-9792
Fax: (706)882-3004
Released: 199?. **Price:** $495.00. **Description:** Includes true stories of HAZCOM accidents, and covers warning labels, personal protective equipment, and emergency response. **Availability:** VHS.

56633 ■ *Identifying the UN/DOT Hazard Classes: Labels and Placards (Revised)*
Media Resources, Inc.
2614 Fort Vancouver Way
Vancouver, WA 98661-3997
Ph:(360)693-3344
Free: 800-666-0106
Fax: (360)693-1760
Released: 1992. **Price:** $175.00. **Description:** Helps workers identify hazardous materials with labels and placards. Highlights information on hazard classes, containers, packaging, and emergency information resources. Includes an instructor's guide, discussion questions, a quiz, and a study guide. A discount is available to those who trade-in the original version. **Availability:** VHS.

56634 ■ *Industrial Safety*
Agency for Instructional Technology (AIT)
1800 N. Stonelake Dr.
Box A
Bloomington, IN 47402-0120
Ph:(812)339-2203
Free: 800-457-4509
Fax: (812)333-4218
Co. E-mail: info@ait.net
URL: http://www.ait.net
Released: 1986. **Price:** $1095.00. **Description:** A series of ten programs about things that can be done to make the workplace safer. **Availability:** VHS; 3/4U.

56635 ■ *Laboratory Conditions: Using Chemicals Safely*
LearnCom HR Consulting and Training
38 Discovery, Ste. 250
Irvine, CA 92618
Ph:(515)440-0890
Free: 800-698-8263
Fax: (515)221-3149
Co. E-mail: nhartline@learncom.com
URL: http://www.learncomhr.com
Released: 199?. **Price:** $395. **Description:** Demonstrates proper laboratory techniques, explaining how to detect hazardous materials, health hazards, use of protective equipment and more. Complete with trainer and participant manuals. **Availability:** VHS.

56636 ■ *Lifting Properly*
LearnCom HR Consulting and Training
38 Discovery, Ste. 250
Irvine, CA 92618
Ph:(515)440-0890
Free: 800-698-8263
Fax: (515)221-3149
Co. E-mail: nhartline@learncom.com
URL: http://www.learncomhr.com
Released: 199?. **Price:** $295. **Description:** Demonstrates safe lifting techniques, including handling of drums and cylinders. **Availability:** VHS.

56637 ■ *Making It Better: How Everyone Can Create a Safer Workplace*
LearnCom HR Consulting and Training
38 Discovery, Ste. 250
Irvine, CA 92618
Ph:(515)440-0890
Free: 800-698-8263
Fax: (515)221-3149
Co. E-mail: nhartline@learncom.com
URL: http://www.learncomhr.com
Price: $295.00. **Description:** Shows examples of safety measures created and implemented by employees. Encourages employees to take an active role in workplace safety. Includes leader guide and 10 workbooks. **Availability:** VHS; 3/4U; 8mm.

56638 ■ *The Man from OSHA*
Film Library/Greater Los Angeles Safety Council
600 Wilshire Blvd., No. 1263
Los Angeles, CA 90017
Ph:(213)385-6461
Free: 800-421-9585
Fax: (213)385-8405
URL: http://www.lasafety.org
Released: 198?. **Description:** This is an explanation of the OSHA program and what an OSHA inspector does. **Availability:** VHS; 3/4U.

56639 ■ *Office Safety and Workplace Ergonomics*
Gulf Publishing Co.
PO Box 2608
Houston, TX 77252-2608
Ph:(713)520-4448
Free: 800-231-6275
Fax: (713)204-4433
Co. E-mail: csv@gulfpub.com
URL: http://www.gulfpub.com
Released: 1992. **Price:** $495.00. **Description:** Training program that centers on ways of fostering awareness among office employees regarding safety in the office. **Availability:** VHS; 3/4U.

56640 ■ *OSHA Confined Space Entry*
Williams Learning Network
15400 Calhoun Dr.
Rockville, MD 20855-2762
Ph:(301)315-6700
Free: 800-848-1717
Fax: (301)315-6880
Co. E-mail: mait@willearn.com
URL: http://www.willearn.com
Released: 1993. **Description:** Outlines OSHA regulations for permit required confined spaces covering such topics as isolating, testing, and preparing permit spaces; properly equipping workers; maintaining entry conditions and employee duties. Includes Leader's Guide and 25 Program Guides. **Availability:** VHS; 3/4U.

56641 ■ *OSHA Electrical Safety for Non-Electrical Workers*
Williams Learning Network
15400 Calhoun Dr.
Rockville, MD 20855-2762
Ph:(301)315-6700
Free: 800-848-1717
Fax: (301)315-6880
Co. E-mail: mait@willearn.com
URL: http://www.willearn.com
Description: Describes basic electrical safety for employees with little or no training. Explains basic properties of electricity, avoidance of electrical hazards, and steps to take in an electrical emergency. Helps meet OSHA 29 CFR 1910.331-335 training requirements. Includes Leader's Guide and 25 Program Guides. **Availability:** VHS; 3/4U.

56642 ■ *Right-to-Know Working Around Hazardous Substances*
LearnCom HR Consulting and Training
38 Discovery, Ste. 250
Irvine, CA 92618
Ph:(515)440-0890
Free: 800-698-8263
Fax: (515)221-3149
Co. E-mail: nhartline@learncom.com
URL: http://www.learncomhr.com
Released: 199?. **Price:** $295. **Description:** Hazardous waste handlers learn the importance of labels and are offered guidelines for handling toxic substances. Complete with leader's guide and workbook. **Availability:** VHS.

56643 ■ *The Safety Deck*
LearnCom HR Consulting and Training
38 Discovery, Ste. 250
Irvine, CA 92618
Ph:(515)440-0890
Free: 800-698-8263
Fax: (515)221-3149
Co. E-mail: nhartline@learncom.com
URL: http://www.learncomhr.com

duces workers to the many safety hazards they may encounter at work and how to deal with them, including disposal, storage, and labeling of waste materials. Complete with trainer and employee manuals. **Availability:** VHS; CC.

56644 ■ *Safety Is Caring About Identifying Hazards*
LearnCom HR Consulting and Training
38 Discovery, Ste. 250
Irvine, CA 92618
Ph:(515)440-0890
Free: 800-698-8263
Fax: (515)221-3149
Co. E-mail: nhartline@learncom.com
URL: http://www.learncomhr.com
Released: 199?. **Price:** $295. **Description:** Employees are taught to identify safety hazards, and are offered instruction on avoiding hazards. Complete with leader's guide and workbooks. **Availability:** VHS.

56645 ■ *Safety: Not By Accident*
LearnCom HR Consulting and Training
38 Discovery, Ste. 250
Irvine, CA 92618
Ph:(515)440-0890
Free: 800-698-8263
Fax: (515)221-3149
Co. E-mail: nhartline@learncom.com
URL: http://www.learncomhr.com
Released: 199?. **Price:** $295. **Description:** Introduces employees to safety equipment and clothing, warning signs, labels, and more. Complete with leader's guide and workbooks. **Availability:** VHS.

56646 ■ *Sounding the Alarm: Awareness Level Training*
LearnCom HR Consulting and Training
38 Discovery, Ste. 250
Irvine, CA 92618
Ph:(515)440-0890
Free: 800-698-8263
Fax: (515)221-3149
Co. E-mail: nhartline@learncom.com
URL: http://www.learncomhr.com
Released: 199?. **Price:** $395. **Description:** Workers learn what to do if they are the first on the scene of a HAZMAT incident. Complete with leader's guide and workbooks. **Availability:** VHS.

56647 ■ *Take Two ... for Safety*
DuPont Safety Resources
PO Box 80013
Wilmington, DE 19880-0013
Free: 800-532-7233
Fax: 888-644-7233
Co. E-mail: info@dupont.com
URL: http://www.dupont.com/safety
Released: 1993. **Description:** A series about industrial safety precautions. **Availability:** VHS; 3/4U.

56648 ■ *Thinking Through Safety: The Job Safety and Healthy Analysis*
LearnCom HR Consulting and Training
38 Discovery, Ste. 250
Irvine, CA 92618
Ph:(515)440-0890
Free: 800-698-8263
Fax: (515)221-3149
Co. E-mail: nhartline@learncom.com
URL: http://www.learncomhr.com
Released: 199?. **Price:** $295. **Description:** Supervisors are introduced to ways of improving health and safety processes within the workplace. Offers tips on formulating job safety and health analyses, and more. Complete with leader's guide and workbooks. **Availability:** VHS.

56649 ■ *What's Your Risk?*
Gulf Publishing Co.
PO Box 2608
Houston, TX 77252-2608
Ph:(713)520-4448
Free: 800-231-6275
Fax: (713)204-4433
Co. E-mail: csv@gulfpub.com

URL: http://www.gulfpub.com
Released: 1991. **Price:** $395.00. **Description:** A look at the three categories of risk infection as defined by OSHA, and the safe work practices and protective equipment necessary to minimize exposure. **Availability:** VHS; 3/4U.

TRADE SHOWS AND CONVENTIONS

56650 ■ Ohio Safety Congress and Expo
Bureau of Workers Compensation
30 W. Spring St.
13430 Yarmouth Dr.
Columbus, OH 43215-2256
Ph:800-292-4833
Free: 800-644-6292
Fax: 877-520-6446
Co. E-mail: ombudsperson@bwc.state.oh.us
URL: http://www.ohiobwc.com
Released: Annual. **Audience:** Occupational safety and health professionals. **Principal Exhibits:** Occupational safety and health equipment, supplies, and services. **Dates and Locations:** 2007 Mar 20-22, Cleveland, OH.

56651 ■ Wisconsin Safety and Health Congress/Exposition
Wisconsin Council of Safety, Division WMC
    Foundation
501 E Washington Ave.
PO Box 352
Madison, WI 53703-2944
Ph:(608)258-3400
Fax: (608)258-3413
URL: http://www.wmc.org
Released: Annual. **Audience:** Safety professionals; executives; local representatives; occupational health & industrial hygiene personnel. **Principal Exhibits:** Safety, health and compliance products/services for industry.

CONSULTANTS

56652 ■ American Forensic Engineers
34 Sammis Ln.
White Plains, NY 10605
Ph:(914)949-5978
Fax: (914)949-0350
Scope: Provides industrial, safety, and forensic consulting services. These services include relevant engineering studies, sampling, statistical studies, quality and reliability efforts, industrial hygiene, human factors analysis, industrial experimentation, product safety analysis and product liability causes in the electrical, electronic, electro-chemical, chemical, mechanical, and battery industrial areas. Now offers building inspection services. Serves private industries as well as government agencies in the U.S. **Publications:** Ethics in Quality, published by Marcell Dekker; Standards Column in Quality Engineering, a quarterly by Marcell Dekker and American Society for Quality Control.

56653 ■ Caliche Ltd.
200 Brantley Ln.
PO Box 107
Magnolia, TX 77353-0107
Ph:(281)356-6038
Free: 800-683-1046
Fax: (281)356-6224
Co. E-mail: calicheltd@calicheltd.com
URL: http://www.calicheltd

E-mail: calicheltd@calicheltd.com
Scope: Safety, health and environmental management consulting company. Provides comprehensive environmental services including air, soil and water monitoring and analysis, emission and ventilation studies, asbestos and lead-based paint consulting, environmental site assessments, industrial hygiene and safety audits, indoor air quality and underground storage tank closures. Industries served: all.

56654 ■ Charp Associates Inc.
39 Maple Ave.
Upper Darby, PA 19082-1902
Ph:(610)789-7498
Fax: (610)789-7499
Co. E-mail: charp@seas.upenn.edu

E-mail: charp@seas.upenn.edu
Scope: Consulting engineers providing analysis of designs, technical analyses, investigations and reports primarily on electrical, mechanical and electro-mechanical equipment. Experienced in communications equipment, instrumentation and sensing systems, production processes and controls, quality control and performance characteristics, occupational and industrial safety, statistical data processing and equipment, accident reconstruction, failure analysis, and analysis of causes of fires. Also offers consulting in training and development, especially in relation to the needs and applications of computers in education. Expertise in applications of computers and technology in educational institutions/systems and to commercial suppliers. Industries served: manufacturing and industrial, transportation, occupational safety, legal and insurance industries. **Publications:** Technological Horizons in Education.

56655 ■ Claymore Engineering
1308 Valle Vista Dr.
Fullerton, CA 92831-1944
Ph:(714)870-4521
Fax: (714)870-7051
Scope: Practice limited to solving air pollution and industrial safety compliance problems. Serves private industries as well as government agencies.

56656 ■ Cocciardi & Associates Inc.
4 Kacey Ct.
Mechanicsburg, PA 17055-5596
Ph:(717)766-4500
Free: 800-377-3024
Fax: (717)766-3999
Co. E-mail: jcocciardi@cocciardi.com
URL: http://www.cocciardi.com

E-mail: jcocciardi@cocciardi.com
Scope: Firm provides safety, health and environmental consulting and training. It handles such issues as Hazardous Waste Operations and Emergency Response Regulation (HAZWOPER), asbestos and lead training (for licensing requirements), environmental auditing, and health and safety investigations. It serves all industries worldwide. **Publications:** Cocciardi, JA: Terrorism Response Field Guide, Jones and Bartlett, Boston, MA, 2003. Cocciardi, JA: Terrorism Response Training Manual, Jones and Bartlett, Boston, MA, 2003. Cocciardi, JA: Emergency Response Team Manual, National Fire Protection Association, Boston, MA 2004.

56657 ■ Roy C. Craft
1707 Pecan St.
Bay City, TX 77414
Ph:(979)245-9991
Fax: (979)245-9991
Co. E-mail: rcraft@wcnet.net

E-mail: rcraft@wcnet.net
Scope: A consultant in health physics concerning control, protection, contamination, regulation, and environmental impact.

56658 ■ donphin.com Inc.
5713 Corporate Way, Ste. 101
West Palm Beach, FL 33407
Ph:(561)688-1000
Free: 800-234-3304
Fax: (561)688-1142
Co. E-mail: inquiry@donphin.com
URL: http://www.donphin.com

E-mail: inquiry@donphin.com
Scope: Offers a comprehensive approach to understanding and applying a broad range of business principles: legal compliance issues, management concerns, health and safety, customer service, marketing, information management. Industries served: all developing small businesses. **Publications:** "Doing Business Right!". **Seminars:** Doing Business Right!; HR That Works!.

56659 ■ Environmental Assessment Services Inc.
124 S Main St.
Middletown, OH 45044-4023
Ph:(513)424-3400
Fax: (513)424-2020
Co. E-mail: easdave@aol.com

E-mail: easdave@aol.com
Scope: Offers environmental and health and safety services in compliance auditing, program management and implementation, field services (monitoring/testing), and real estate assessment.

56660 ■ Environmental Support Network Inc.
5376 Fulton Dr. NW
Canton, OH 44718-1808
Ph:(330)494-0905
Fax: (330)494-1650
Co. E-mail: esn@sssnet.com

E-mail: esn@sssnet.com
Scope: Provides environmental, health, and safety consulting and project management services. These include compliance auditing and remediation specifications concerning air, groundwater, and soil quality. Also offers health and safety reviews, asbestos and lead-based paint handling, noise sampling, industrial permitting, and UST management. Industries served: education, finance, industry, and government. **Seminars:** Environmental Health and Safety Management in Ohio; Managing Compliance in Ohio; Environmental Site Remediation in Ohio and Surrounding States; Conducting ESAs by ASTM Standards; Health and Safety Management in the Medical Setting; Exposure Monitoring in Schools and Public Buildings.

56661 ■ Error Analysis Inc.
5811 Amaya Dr., Ste. 205
La Mesa, CA 91942-4156
Ph:(619)464-4427
Fax: (619)464-4992
Co. E-mail: info@erroranalysis.com
URL: http://www.erroranalysis.com

E-mail: info@erroranalysis.com
Scope: Firm dedicated to research and consulting in the fields of human factors, safety and accident reconstruction. Provides consulting and expert witness services to attorneys, the insurance industry and businesses throughout the world. **Publications:** Safety Handbook and numerous articles and papers related to safety. **Seminars:** Safety; Risk Management; Premises and Product Liability.

56662 ■ Jose Fabregas
897 Sorbona University Gardens
San Juan, PR 00923
Ph:(787)751-9019
Fax: (787)751-9019

56663 ■ Foxfire Safety Inc.
407 Lincolnway W
Osceola, IN 46561
Ph:(219)295-4180
Scope: Teaches proper use and placement of hand portable fire extinguishers and the use and types of fire suppression systems. It serves all industries in a 150-mile radius of South Bend, Indiana.

56664 ■ Leonard R. Friedman Risk Management Inc.
170 Great Neck Rd., Ste. 140
Great Neck, NY 11021-3337
Ph:(516)466-0750
Fax: (516)466-0997
Scope: Provides risk and insurance management, and safety and claims managements services to corporations across the country. Analyzes exposure to loss, audits insurance contracts, structures competitive bidding, reviews contracts and leases, imple-

ments and monitors safety and claims management programs, and recommends risk transfer programs to reduce exposure to loss. Industries served: profit and nonprofit companies engaged in retail, manufacturing, distributing, hospitality, real estate, and service.

56665 ■ GA Environmental Services Inc.
15 W State St. Fl-II
Trenton, NJ 08608
Ph:(609)393-4089
Fax: (609)393-7304
Scope: Specializes in environmental audits; remediation planning and coordination; asbestos and lead based paint inspection, abatement, and monitoring; and occupational health investigation and monitoring. The firm serves governments, school boards, commercial building owners, realtors, lending institutions, and attorneys. **Seminars:** Offers seminars on: New Jersey technical requirements for site remediation; preliminary investigation and document review; site inspections; bloodborne pathogens; lead abatement; technical assessments; asbestos abatement; OSHA hazards training. **Special Services:** Full service environmental and contruction consulting. Firm with capabilities including materials testing, structural design and inspection, and construction management.

56666 ■ Humanics ErgoSystems Inc.
PO Box 17388
Encino, CA 91416-7388
Ph:(818)345-3746
Fax: (818)705-3903
Co. E-mail: questions@humanics-es.com
URL: http://www.humanics-es.com

E-mail: questions@humanics-es.com
Scope: Specializes in occupational ergonomics; ergonomic workplace evaluations; ergonomics research; ergonomic seminars and training; psychological and biomechanics testing (EMG, dynamic lumbar motion, strength assessment, nerve conduction); product evaluations; compliance with ergonomic standards; and expert witnessing. Serves all industries in the U.S. and worldwide. **Publications:** "Hard Facts About Soft Machines: The Science of Seated Posture," edited by Lueder, R. and Noro, K., London and Philadelphia: Taylor & Francis, Ltd., 1994; "Work Postures and Ergonomics," R. Lueder, Chiropractic Family Practice. J. Sweere, ed. Aspen Pub., 1992; "The ERgonomics Payoff," Holt Rhinehart and Winston of Canada, (1987). **Seminars:** Presents a variety of seminars, including How to Conduct a Workplace Assessment; How to Reduce Cumulative Trauma in Your Workplace; and How to Evaluate Ergonomic Seats, Workstations, Keyboards, and Other Products. **Special Services:** Accesses variety of online commercial, academic, and government databases. Skilled in the areas of technical ergonomics research and analysis.

56667 ■ Retail Safety Consortium
640 N Main St., Ste. 1256
Salt Lake City, UT 84101
Ph:(801)951-2566
Free: 800-370-9168
Scope: Firm specializes in safety and human factors to retail industry.

56668 ■ Safety Management Services
4012 Santa Nella Pl.
San Diego, CA 92130-2291
Ph:(858)259-0591
Fax: (858)792-2350
Scope: Offers safety consulting services: evaluates safety policies and procedures to determine degree of effectiveness; advises on compliance with OSHA standards; and provides safety programs for managers, supervisors, and workers. Industries served: general contractors in new construction, renovation, and demolition; and tenant improvement companies which hire general contractors to perform construction activities on their premises. Also assists litigation as construction safety expert witness. Safety training programs customized to meet clients needs. **Publications:** "What Can Go Wrong?," International Cranes magazine, Apr 1994; and "Construction Safety - A Study in Failure," EXCEL Newletter, West Virginia University, 1994. **Seminars:** Federal OSHA Construction Safety and Health Course for Trainers, University of California, San Diego; OSHA 10-Hour Construction Safety Course; 90-Hour Construction Safety Management Certificate Course - 1991 to 1993; Fall Protection; Confined Space Standards; Cranes and Rigging; Scaffold or Trenching and Excavation; and Safe Construction Work Practices.

56669 ■ John Smithkey, III, RN
1271 Overland Ave. NE
North Canton, OH 44720-1731
Ph:(330)494-3729
Scope: Specializes in public and occupational health, HIV/AIDS education and prevention programs, grant and proposal writing, and programs for businesses and employees.

56670 ■ Vaccari & Associates Inc.
17 Cypress St.
Marblehead, MA 01945
Ph:(781)639-0946
Fax: (781)639-0946
Co. E-mail: rvaccari1@verizon.net
URL: http://www.vaccari-associates.com

E-mail: rvaccari1@verizon.net
Scope: A provider of appraisals for primary and secondary mortgages; mortgage refinancing; employee relocation; private mortgage insurance removal; estate planning and divorce settlement.

56671 ■ Verk Consultants Inc.
1190 Olive St.
PO Box 11277
Eugene, OR 97440-3477
Ph:(541)687-9170
Fax: (541)687-9758
Co. E-mail: larry@verk.com
URL: http://www.verk.com

E-mail: larry@verk.com
Scope: Specializes in vocational rehabilitation, worksite evaluations for managing workers'compensation and the Americans with Disabilities Act, Title I. **Seminars:** ADA Title I, Workers Compensation, Disability Management.

FRANCHISES AND BUSINESS OPPORTUNITIES

56672 ■ Vocam
Vocam USA LLC
855 E Golf Rd., Ste. 2145
Arlington Heights, IL 60005-5222
Ph:(847)734-3000
Free: 888-388-6226
Fax: (847)734-7159
No. of Franchise Units: 18. **No. of Company-Owned Units:** 4. **Founded:** 1990. **Franchised:** 1994. **Description:** Distribution of interactive safety packages. **Equity Capital Needed:** $35,000-$108,000. **Franchise Fee:** $15,000-$60,000. **Financial Assistance:** No. **Training:** Yes.

COMPUTERIZED DATABASES

56673 ■ *Environment & Safety Library*
The Bureau of National Affairs Inc.
1231 25th St. NW
Washington, DC 20037
Ph:(202)452-4200
Free: 800-372-1033
Fax: (202)452-4226
Co. E-mail: customercare@bna.com
URL: http://www.bna.com
Description: Contains reports on current laws and regulations, news, and developments in the environment and safety field worldwide. Covers air pollution; ANSI standards scopes; Canadian laws and regulations; chemical manufacturing and regulation; compliance deadlines; environmental due diligence; European Union directives and regulations; federal statutes; regulations; guidance/agency documents and executive orders; food and drug regulation; food safety; hazmat transport; international treaties; bilateral agreements; conventions; environmental laws and regulations; contacts; Mexican laws and regulations; mines and mining safety; NAFTA; occupational safety and health; OSWER directives; pesticides; right-to-know; solid, hazardous, and radioactive waste; state environmental statutes and regulations; state safety statutes and regulations for OSHA-approved states; test methods; toxic substances; waste management, disposal, and cleanup; and water pollution. Includes the full text of federal statutes, codified regulations, and the *Federal Register*; the full text of state statutes and regulations; full text of international treaties, Canadian and Mexican laws, country profiles, and European Union directives; legal decisions; BNA analysis; BNA reports; more than 3,000 federal and state forms; and data on more than 80,000 regulated chemical substances. Also contains an index of more than 275,000 cross-referenced entries. **Availability:** Online: The Bureau of National Affairs Inc; CD-ROM: The Bureau of National Affairs Inc. **Type:** Full text.

56674 ■ *Health and Safety Science Abstracts*
CSA
7200 Wisconsin Ave., Ste. 601
Bethesda, MD 20814
Ph:(301)961-6700
Free: 800-843-7751
Fax: (301)961-6720
Co. E-mail: service@csa.com
URL: http://www.csa.com
Description: Contains more than 135,000 citations, with abstracts, to the worldwide literature on safety science and hazard control, with an emphasis on the identification, evaluation, and elimination or control of hazards. Includes coverage of issues related to liability. Sources include books, periodicals, government reports, conference proceedings, patents, and dissertations. Corresponds to *Health and Safety Science Abstracts* and in part to the online Environmental Sciences and Pollution Management Database (described in a separate entry) and Biological Sciences Database (described in a separate entry). **Availability:** Online: CSA, STN International. **Type:** Bibliographic.

56675 ■ *OSH-DB*
Information Ventures Inc. (IVI)
42 S 15th St., Ste. 700
Philadelphia, PA 19102-2299
Ph:(215)569-2300
Fax: (215)569-2575
Co. E-mail: ivi@infoventures.com
URL: http://www.infoventures.com
Description: Contains more than 220,000 bibliographic database records on occupational health and safety from NIOSHTIC in addition to updates prepared by Information Ventures. Includes in-depth summaries of articles from more than 4000 sources, including 160 journals from the past 100 years. Subjects include behavioral sciences, biochemistry, education and training, ergonomics, occupational medicine, hazardous waste, and health physics. Enables users to search by Chemical Abstracts Service (CAS) registry numbers, which are unique numbers assigned by the Chemical Abstracts Service of the American Chemical Society to represent a specific chemical compound; and Standard Industrial Classifications (SIC) codes, which are unique numbers assigned by the Office of Management and Budget to represent specific industrial operations. **Availability:** Online: Information Ventures Inc. (IVI). **Type:** Bibliographic.

56676 ■ *State Health Care Regulatory Developments*
The Bureau of National Affairs Inc.
1231 25th St. NW
Washington, DC 20037
Ph:(202)452-4200
Free: 800-372-1033
Fax: (202)452-4226

Co. E-mail: customercare@bna.com
URL: http://www.bna.com
Description: Contains information on health care regulatory news and developments in the United States. Subjects include community-based care, home care, emergency care, infectious diseases, managed care, insurance, laboratories, Medicaid, mental health, medical waste, nursing homes, pharmaceuticals, physician services, professional licensing, provider relationships, worker protection and compensation. Entries are organized by state, topic, and register citation. **Availability:** Online: The Bureau of National Affairs Inc., Thomson West. **Type:** Full text.

LIBRARIES

56677 ■ Ameren Corporation–Library
1901 Chouteau Ave.
Box 66149
St. Louis, MO 63166-6149
Ph:(314)554-3094
Fax: (314)554-2888
Co. E-mail: khayes2@ameren.com
Contact: Katharine A. Hayes, Info.Rsrcs.
Scope: Business, environment, engineering, occupational safety and health, nuclear power, public utilities, public-private power. **Holdings:** Figures not available. **Subscriptions:** 619 journals and other serials.

56678 ■ Bureau of National Affairs, Inc. –Library
1231 25th St., NW
Washington, DC 20037-1197
Ph:(202)452-4466
Fax: (202)452-4084
Co. E-mail: library@bna.com
URL: http://www.bna.com
Contact: Marilyn M. Bromley, Lib.Dir.
Scope: Law, labor-management relations, economics, government regulation, business, environment, industrial safety and health. **Services:** Interlibrary loan; Library open by special arrangement only. **Holdings:** 20,000 volumes. **Subscriptions:** 850 journals and other serials; 30 newspapers.

56679 ■ CELOTEX Technical Center–Library
10301 9th St., N.
St. Petersburg, FL 33716
Ph:(813)576-4171
Fax: (813)576-0318
Contact: David Brzana, Info.Spec.
Scope: Polymer chemistry, specialty chemicals, building materials, materials science. **Services:** Interlibrary loan; center not open to the public. **Holdings:** 2000 books. **Subscriptions:** 150 journals and other serials.

56680 ■ CIGNA Corporation–Philadelphia Research Library
2 Liberty Pl.
1601 Chestnut St.
Philadelphia, PA 19192
Ph:(215)761-4120
Fax: (215)761-5588
URL: http://www.cigna.com
Contact: Patricia Malahan, Mgr.
Scope: Insurance, management, occupational and environmental safety and health. **Services:** Interlibrary loan; Library not open to the public. **Holdings:** 2000 books. **Subscriptions:** 400 journals and other serials.

56681 ■ Cogswell College–Library
1175 Bordeaux Dr.
Sunnyvale, CA 94089-9772
Ph:(408)541-0100, x144
Fax: (408)747-0764
Co. E-mail: library@cogswell.edu
URL: http://www.cogswell.edu/cgi-local/jobs. cgi?MODE=vlibraryac
Contact: Bruce G. Dahms, Libn.
Scope: Fire science, electrical engineering, software engineering, computer and video imaging, digital motion pictures, digital audio technology. **Services:** In-

terlibrary loan; copying; Library open to the public for reference use only. **Holdings:** 13,024 books. **Subscriptions:** 91 journals and other serials; 3 newspapers.

56682 ■ Consad Research Corporation–Library
121 N. Highland Ave.
Pittsburgh, PA 15206
Ph:(412)363-5500
Fax: (412)363-5509
URL: http://www.consad.com
Contact: Sheila Steger, Libn.
Scope: Social science methodology, statistics, urban planning, drug abuse, healthcare, economics, occupational safety and health. **Services:** Library open to the public with restrictions. **Holdings:** 10,000 books; 10,000 reports. **Subscriptions:** 54 journals and other serials.

56683 ■ Cornell University–School of Industrial and Labor Relations–Martin P. Catherwood Library (239 I)
239 Ives Hall
Ithaca, NY 14853-3901
Ph:(607)255-2184
Fax: (607)255-9641
Co. E-mail: ilrlib@cornell.edu
URL: http://www.ilr.cornell.edu/library/
Contact: Stuart Basefsky, Libn.
Scope: Labor-management relations, labor law and legislation, labor organization, industrial and labor conditions, labor economics, human resources, income security, human resources management, supervision, occupational safety and health, international and comparative labor relations, organizational behavior and negotiation, and conflict resolution. **Services:** Interlibrary loan; Library open to the public. **Holdings:** 204,265 volumes; 44,368 microforms; 18,016 cubic feet of manuscripts; 647 motion pictures; 1016 filmstrips and slides; 878 videotapes; 2123 sound recordings; 373 computer files. **Subscriptions:** 3998 serials; 4 newspapers.

56684 ■ Exxon Research and Engineering Company–Information, Computing, and Business Systems
PO Box 998
Rte. 22 E.
Annandale, NJ 08801
Ph:(908)730-2924
Fax: (908)730-3344
Co. E-mail: mjbarne@erenj.com
Contact: Mary Jo Barnello, Sr.Anl.
Scope: Petroleum refining processes and products, petrochemical processes and products, chemistry, physics, metallurgy, mathematics, industrial safety. **Services:** Services not open to the public. **Holdings:** 35,000 volumes and microforms; patent holdings. **Subscriptions:** 350 journals and other serials.

56685 ■ The Hartford Financial Services Company–Loss Control Library
690 Asylum Ave.
Hartford Plaza
COGS 2-45
Hartford, CT 06105
Ph:(860)547-5000
Fax: (860)547-6004
Co. E-mail: lynn.zweiflet@thehartford.com
URL: http://www.thehartford.com
Contact: Lynn A. Zweifler, MLS
Scope: Safety engineering, toxicology, chemistry, fire protection, transportation, occupational safety and health, industrial hygiene, ergonomics, risk management. **Services:** Interlibrary loan; Library open to the public by special arrangement only. **Holdings:** 2000 books; government documents; 15 VF drawers. **Subscriptions:** 200 journals and other serials.

56686 ■ Industrial Health Foundation, Inc. –Library
34 Penn Cir., W.
Pittsburgh, PA 15206
Ph:(412)363-6600
Fax: (412)363-6605
Co. E-mail: admin@infipcorp.com
Contact: Janice O'Polka, Proj.Mgr., Info.Svcs.

Scope: Industrial hygiene, occupational safety and health, toxicology, environmental issues. **Services:** Interlibrary loan; Library not open to the public. **Holdings:** 3000 books; 100 bound periodical volumes; 78,000 abstracts; 50 VF drawers of pamphlets and reprints. **Subscriptions:** 60 journals and other serials.

56687 ■ Institute for Business and Home Safety–Library
4775 E. Fowler Ave.
Tampa, FL 33617
Ph:(813)286-3400
Fax: (813)286-9960
Co. E-mail: info@ibhs.org
URL: http://www.ibhs.org
Contact: Hilary B. Thomson, Lib.Hd.
Scope: Insurance, natural disasters, building codes, wind and seismic engineering. **Services:** Interlibrary loan; research for member companies. **Holdings:** 3000 books, periodicals, and audio/visuals. **Subscriptions:** 159 journals and other serials; 3 newspapers.

56688 ■ International Union of Operating Engineers–Research Department–Library (1125)
1125 17th St., NW
Washington, DC 20036
Ph:(202)429-9100
URL: http://www.iuoe.org/index.asp
Contact: David Treanor, Dir.
Scope: Union history, productivity of heavy equipment, industrial safety. **Services:** Library not open to the public. **Holdings:** 2000 books; industrial surveys; slides; motion pictures; microfiche.

56689 ■ J.J. Keller & Associates, Inc. –Editorial Resource Center–Research & Technical Library (MS141)
MS1410
PO Box 368
Neenah, WI 54957-0368
Ph:(920)727-7271
Fax: (920)727-7455
URL: http://www.jjkeller.com
Contact: Webb A. Shaw, Corp.Ed.Dir.
Scope: Transportation, motor carrier regulations, workplace safety regulations and practices, hazardous materials, hazardous wastes, industry regulations and compliance, food safety, human resources. **Services:** Copying; Library open to the public by referral. **Holdings:** 7600 books, AV programs, and government documents (Department of Transportation, Environmental Protection Agency, and Department of Labor). **Subscriptions:** 1100 journals and other serials.

56690 ■ Lakehead University–Resource Centre for Occupational Health and Safety
955 Oliver Rd.
Thunder Bay, ON, Canada P7B 5E1
Ph:(807)343-8128
Fax: (807)343-8616
URL: http://www.lakeheadu.ca/~lucas/rcohmain.htm
Contact: Neela Paranjape, Info./Educ.Off.
Scope: Occupational health and safety, environment. **Services:** Interlibrary loan; copying; Library open to the public. **Holdings:** 10,000 books and articles. **Subscriptions:** 10 journals and other serials; 2 newspapers.

56691 ■ Lockheed Martin Utility Services, Inc.–Portsmouth Gaseous Diffusion Plant–X-710 Library MS-2206 (Box 6)
Box 628
Piketon, OH 45661
Ph:(614)897-5797
Fax: (614)897-3595
Contact: James D. Cox, Libn.
Scope: Atomic and nuclear science; chemistry; physics; engineering - chemical, mechanical, electrical; industrial safety; metallurgical science; mathematics. **Services:** Interlibrary loan; Library not open to the public. **Holdings:** 50,000 books; 5000 bound periodical volumes; 22,000 technical reports; 61,000 technical reports in microform. **Subscriptions:** 600 journals and other serials.

56692 ■ Manitoba Department of Labour & Immigration–Workplace Safety and Health Division–Client Resource Centre (200-4)
200-401 York Ave.
Winnipeg, MB, Canada R3C 0P8
Ph:(204)945-3446
URL: http://www.gov.mb.ca/labour/
Scope: Toxicology, occupational health and safety, industrial hygiene. **Services:** Library not open to the public. **Holdings:** Figures not available.

56693 ■ Montana Tech of the University of Montana–Montana Tech Library
1300 W. Park St.
Butte, MT 59701-8997
Ph:(406)496-4281
Fax: (406)496-4133
Co. E-mail: astclair@mtech.edu
URL: http://www.mtech.edu/library
Contact: Ann St. Clair, Dir.
Scope: Geology, mining, mineral processing, geochemistry, geophysics, petroleum, environmental engineering, occupational safety, mineral economics, industrial hygiene. **Services:** Interlibrary loan; copying; Library open to the public. **Holdings:** 59,039 books; 81,794 bound periodical volumes. **Subscriptions:** 394 journals and other serials.

56694 ■ National Safety Council–Library
1121 Spring Lake Dr.
Itasca, IL 60143-3201
Ph:(630)775-2199
Fax: (630)285-0765
Co. E-mail: library@nsc.org
URL: http://www.nsc.org/
Contact: Robert J. Marecek, Mgr.
Scope: Accident prevention, traffic safety, industrial health, all aspects of safety and safety research. **Services:** Interlibrary loan; copying; Library open to the public with prior contact suggested. **Holdings:** 4300 books; 700 bound periodical volumes; 87,000 other cataloged items; 34,000 research reports; 700 reels of microfilm; 5000 microfiche. **Subscriptions:** 125 journals and other serials.

56695 ■ New Mexico (State) Department of Environment–NMED Library
1190 St. Francis Dr., Ste. N4050
PO Box 26110
Santa Fe, NM 87502
Ph:(505)827-2855
Free: 800-219-6157
Fax: (505)827-2818
Co. E-mail: ann_baumgarn@nmenv.state.nm.us
URL: http://www.nmenv.state.nm.us
Contact: Ann Baumgarn, Libn.Sr.
Scope: Ground water protection, surface water protection, hazardous waste disposal, radiation protection, occupational health and safety, air quality protection. **Services:** Copying; Library open to the public for reference use only. **Holdings:** 700 books; 154 bound periodical volumes; 6500 reports and documents. **Subscriptions:** 35 journals and other serials.

56696 ■ New York (State) Department of State–Office of Fire Prevention and Control–Academy of Fire Science - Library (600 C)
600 College Ave.
Montour Falls, NY 14865-9634
Ph:(607)535-7136, x605
Fax: (607)535-4841
Co. E-mail: drobinso@dos.state.ny.us
URL: http://www.dos.state.ny.us/fire/library.html
Contact: Diana Robinson, Libn.
Scope: Fire protection, prevention, and control; occupational safety; fire department administration and management; New York state codes, standards, and regulations; emergency medical services; consumer safety; hazardous materials; arson prevention and investigation; history of fire service in New York State. **Services:** Interlibrary loan; copying; answers to mail and telephone inquiries from patrons in New York state; Library open to the public. **Holdings:** 6000 books; 250 bound periodical volumes; 16 VF drawers; 200 microfiche; 2800 videocassettes. **Subscriptions:** 130 journals and other serials.

56697 ■ North Carolina (State) Department of Labor–Charles H. Livengood, Jr. Memorial Labor Library
Old Revenue Bldg., 5th Fl.
4 W. Edenton St.
1101 Mail Service Center
Raleigh, NC 27699-1101
Ph:(919)807-2848
Fax: (919)807-2849
Co. E-mail: nvincelli@mail.dol.state.nc.us
URL: http://www.nclabor.com/lib/lib2.htm
Contact: Nick Vincelli, Libn.
Scope: Labor law and history, occupational safety, health, and training. **Services:** Interlibrary loan; copying; SDI. **Holdings:** 8000 books; 533 bound periodical volumes; 200 videos; vertical files; state government documents. **Subscriptions:** 50 journals and other serials.

56698 ■ Ohio (State) Bureau of Workers' Compensation–BWC Library
30 W. Spring St., 3rd Fl.
Columbus, OH 43215-2241
Ph:(614)466-7388
Free: 800-644-6292 (press 22
Fax: (614)644-9634 (central
Co. E-mail: library@bwc.state.oh.us
URL: http://www.ohiobwc.com
Contact: Melissa Hatfield, Mgr.
Scope: Occupational safety, industrial hygiene, workers' compensation, occupational rehabilitation. **Services:** Interlibrary loan; copying; Center open to the public. **Holdings:** 4000 books; 850 standards; 200 microfiche; 20 VF drawers of pamphlets; 650 subject headings; 2 VF drawers of clippings. **Subscriptions:** 280 journals and other serials.

56699 ■ PACE International Union–Irene Glaus Memorial Library
3340 Perimeter Hill Dr.
Box 1475
Nashville, TN 37202
Ph:(615)834-8590
Fax: (615)831-6792
Co. E-mail: mdimoff@paceunion.org
URL: http://www.paceunion.org
Contact: Mary Alyce Dimoff, Info.Spec.
Scope: Labor relations, law, and history; occupational safety and health. **Services:** Interlibrary loan; Library open to the public for reference use only. **Holdings:** 10,100 books; 1600 bound periodical volumes; 12,250 microfiche; 60 audiotapes; 310 videotapes; 600 government documents; UPIU archival material (39 linear feet of folders, boxes, bound periodical volumes, microfilm), AIW, IWNA and OCAW archival material. **Subscriptions:** 183 journals and other serials; 44 newspapers.

56700 ■ Triodyne Consulting Engineers and Scientists–Safety Information Center
666 Dundee Rd., Ste. 103
Northbrook, IL 60062
Ph:(847)677-4730
Fax: (847)647-2047
Co. E-mail: infoserv@triodyne.com
URL: http://www.triodyne.com
Contact: Marna S. Sanders, Info.Svcs.Mgr.
Scope: Engineering - forensic, mechanical, automotive, civil; industrial safety; materials science. **Services:** Interlibrary loan; copying; center not open to the public. **Holdings:** 6650 books; 300 VF drawers of technical reports and patents; 143 VF drawers of manufacturers' literature; 45 VF drawers of engineering standards and specifications; 14 VF drawers of catalogs. **Subscriptions:** 212 journals and other serials.

56701 ■ U.S. Army–Center for Health Promotion & Preventive Medicine–Library (Bldg.)
Bldg. E1570
5158 Blackhawk Rd.
Aberdeen Proving Ground, MD 21010-5403
Free: 800-222-9698
URL: http://chppm-www.apgea.army.mil/
Contact: Krishan S. Goel, Libn.
Scope: Occupational medicine, safety and health; chemistry and toxicology; audiology; medical ento-

mology; laser, microwave, and radiological safety and health; air and water pollution; sanitary engineering. **Services:** Interlibrary loan; copying; SDI. **Holdings:** 9000 books; 8000 bound periodical volumes; 8400 R&D reports; 3000 microfiche. **Subscriptions:** 250 journals and other serials.

56702 ■ U.S. Bureau of Mines–Twin Cities Research Center–Library (201 F)
201 Federal Dr.
St. Paul, MN 55111
Ph:(612)725-4503
Fax: (612)725-4784
Contact: Marilynn R. Anderson, Libn.
Scope: Mining engineering, metallurgy, mineral industries, geology, industrial safety, environmental remediation. **Services:** Interlibrary loan; copying; Library open to the public. **Holdings:** 8200 books; 2270 bound periodical volumes; 120 VF drawers of reports, documents, patents. **Subscriptions:** 190 journals and other serials.

56703 ■ U.S. Dept. of Labor–Occupational Safety and Health Administration–Region VIII Library (1999)
1999 Broadway, Ste. 1690
PO Box 46550
Denver, CO 80201-6550
Ph:(303)844-1600
Fax: (303)844-1616
Co. E-mail: leslie.carolyn@dol.gov
Contact: Carolyn Leslie, Libn.
Scope: Industrial hygiene, industrial safety, OSHA regulations. **Services:** Interlibrary loan; copying; Library open to the public for reference use only. **Holdings:** 510 books; 1062 reports. **Subscriptions:** 12 journals and other serials.

56704 ■ U.S. Dept. of Labor–OSHA–Billings Area Office Library (2900)
2900 4th Ave. N., No. 303
Billings, MT 59101-1228
Ph:(406)247-7494
Fax: (406)247-7499
URL: http://www.osha.gov
Contact: Bonnie Albright, Ck.
Scope: Safety and health in the workplace. **Services:** Library open to the public. **Holdings:** 500 books.

56705 ■ U.S. Dept. of Labor–OSHA–Region III Library (Curti)
Curtis Center
170 S. Independence Mall, W.
Ste. 740 W.
Philadelphia, PA 19106-3309
Ph:(215)861-4900
Fax: (215)861-4904
URL: http://www.osha.gov
Contact: Barbara Bray, Libn.
Scope: Occupational health and safety, industrial hygiene, toxic substances. **Services:** Library open to the public. **Holdings:** 2000 books. **Subscriptions:** 12 journals and other serials.

56706 ■ U.S. Dept. of Labor–OSHA–Region X Library (1111)
1111 3rd Ave., Ste. 715
Seattle, WA 98101-3212
Ph:(206)553-7620
Fax: (206)553-6499
URL: http://www.osha.gov/
Scope: Industrial hygiene, toxic substances, industrial safety, toxicology, safety, engineering. **Services:** Interlibrary loan; copying; Library open to the public for reference use only. **Holdings:** 1600 titles. **Subscriptions:** 10 journals and other serials.

56707 ■ U.S. Dept. of Labor–OSHA–Technical Data Center (200 C)
200 Constitution Ave., NW
Rm. N-2625
Washington, DC 20210
Ph:(202)693-2350
Fax: (202)693-1648
URL: http://www.osha.gov/dts/
Contact: Jeff Davidson, Dir.
Scope: Occupational safety, industrial hygiene, toxicology, control technology, hazardous materials, fire

safety, electrical safety, noise, carcinogens, material safety, farm safety, process safety, ergonomics, occupational health nursing, blood-borne pathogens, indoor air quality, Occupational Safety & Health Administration (OSHA) rulemaking docket. **Services:** Interlibrary loan; center open to the public for reference use only. **Holdings:** 12,000 books and bound periodical volumes; 400,000 microfiche; standards from more than 370 organizations and societies. **Subscriptions:** 207 journals and other serials.

56708 ■ U.S. Dept. of Labor–OSHA - Office of Training & Education–H. Lee Saltsgaver Library (2020)
2020 S. Arlington Heights Rd.
Arlington Heights, IL 60005
Ph:(847)759-7736
Fax: (847)759-7748
Co. E-mail: vosburgh.linda@dol.gov
URL: http://www.osha.gov/fso/ote/training/resource-center/loan.html
Contact: Linda Vosburgh, Libn.
Scope: Industrial hygiene, occupational safety, industrial toxicology. **Services:** Library open to the public for reference use only. **Holdings:** 1550 government documents; 1250 standards. **Subscriptions:** 46 journals and other serials.

56709 ■ U.S. National Institute for Occupational Safety & Health–Library C-21
4676 Columbia Pkwy.
Cincinnati, OH 45226
Ph:(513)533-8321
Fax: (513)533-8382
Contact: Lawrence Q. Foster, Hd.Libn.
Scope: Occupational safety and health, industrial hygiene and toxicology. **Services:** Interlibrary loan; Library open to the public. **Holdings:** 8000 books; 10,000 bound periodical volumes. **Subscriptions:** 125 journals and other serials.

56710 ■ University of California, Berkeley–School of Public Health–Labor Occupational Health Program Library (2223)
2223 Fulton St., 4th Fl.
Berkeley, CA 94720-5120
Ph:(510)643-4335
Fax: (510)643-5698
Co. E-mail: andrews2@berkeley.edu
Contact: Karen Andrews
Scope: Chemical and physical occupational hazards, medical and industrial hygiene, standards and regulations, workers' compensation and education. **Services:** Copying; Library open to the public for reference use only; technical assitance by phone. **Holdings:** 2200 books; 180 unbound periodicals; newspaper clipping file. **Subscriptions:** 50 journals and other serials; 110 newspapers.

56711 ■ Workplace Health, Safety and Compensation Commission–Communications Department
PO Box 160
Saint John, NB, Canada E2L 3X9
Ph:(506)633-5660
Co. E-mail: communications@whscc.nb.ca
URL: http://www.whscc.nb.ca/cor3_e.asp
Contact: Debbie Kay, Mgr. of Comm.
Scope: Social affairs, education, occupational health and safety, training, mining safety. **Holdings:** Figures not available.

RESEARCH CENTERS

56712 ■ National Farm Medicine Center
1000 N Oak Ave.
Marshfield, WI 54449
Ph:(715)389-4999
Free: 800—662-6900
Fax: (715)389-4996
Co. E-mail: lee.barbara@mcrf.mfldclin.edu
URL: http://research.marshfieldclinic.org/nfmc/
Contact: Barbara Lee PhD, Dir.
E-mail: lee.barbara@mcrf.mfldclin.edu
Scope: Human health and safety associated with rural and agricultural work, life and environment. **Publications:** Progress Report.

56713 ■ University of Michigan–Center for Ergonomics
1205 Beal Ave.
Ann Arbor, MI 48109-2117
Ph:(734)763-2243
Fax: (734)764-3451
Co. E-mail: rrabourn@umich.edu
URL: http://www.centerforergonomics.org
Contact: Randy Rabourn
E-mail: rrabourn@umich.edu
Scope: Ergonomics and safety engineering, including studies on contemporary techniques and methods necessary to minimize occupational health and safety problems and maximize human-hardware performance capability. **Educational Activities:** 15 one- to five-day courses for engineers, managers, and occupational health professionals (annually).

56714 ■ University of Montreal–Université de Montréal–Health and Prevention Social Research Group
2801 blvd. Edouard-Montpetit, Ste. 16E
PO Box 6128, Downtown Sta.
Montreal, QC, Canada H3C 3J7
Ph:(514)343-6193
Fax: (514)343-2334
Co. E-mail: grasp@umontreal.ca
URL: http://www.grasp.umontreal.ca
Contact: Andre Demers PhD, Dir.
E-mail: grasp@umontreal.ca
Scope: Social determinants of health and social dynamics in illness, health, and services, including collective choices in matters of health policy and health resource allocation; social control and regulation of social and health problems; social and ethical issues related to new medical technologies; sociology of health professions; social dynamics of drinking behavior; mental health policy development and implementation; community-based mental health care; sociology of mental health iatrogenics; psychotropic drug utilization; handicap and stigma; and critical mental health theory. Also studies prevention strategies in occupational work and safety, including development and impact of occupational health and safety policies; organizational factors in occupational health and safety; work organization and mental health; management styles and types of occupational diseases; evaluation of efficacy of preventive measures in occupational health and safety; aging at work. **Services:** Policy consultation, to health and welfare organizations, advocacy groups, and government. **Educational Activities:** Multidisciplinary university seminars (monthly).

56715 ■ University of Utah–Rocky Mountain Center for Occupational and Environmental Health
391 Chipeta Way, Ste. C
Salt Lake City, UT 84108
Ph:(801)581-4800
Fax: (801)581-7224
Co. E-mail: kurt.hegmann@hsc.utah.edu
URL: http://www.rmcoeh.utah.edu/
Contact: Dr. Kurt T. Hegmann, Dir.
E-mail: kurt.hegmann@hsc.utah.edu
Scope: Occupational and environmental health and safety with emphasis on exposure assessment, environmental epidemiology, asbestos-related health problems, musculoskeletal and other injury evaluation and prevention, and ergonomic aspects of the work environment. **Services:** Consulting, for federal, state, and local governments, industry, and other organizations. **Educational Activities:** Continuing education programs, in industrial hygiene, occupational medicine, and occupational safety and ergonomics, with more than 2,000 attendees yearly; Graduate programs in industrial hygiene and occupational medicine; Residency program in occupational medicine.

56716 ■ University of Waterloo–Ergonomics and Safety Consulting Services
200 University Ave. W
Waterloo, ON, Canada N2L 3G1
Ph:(519)888-4567
Fax: (519)886-5488
Co. E-mail: wells@healthy.uwaterloo.ca
URL: http://www.ergonomics.uwaterloo.ca/
Contact: Prof. Richard Wells PhD, Dir.
E-mail: wells@healthy.uwaterloo.ca
Scope: Contract research and consulting for industry and government in occupational safety, and ergonomics. Studies include workplace hazard assessments, personal protective equipment evaluations, repetitive strain and over-exertion injury prevention, ergonomic intervention. **Services:** Information and advisory services, including interpretations and consultations, and other analytical services. **Educational Activities:** Seminars; Short courses; Symposia.

56717 ■ West Virginia University–Institute of Occupational and Environmental Health
3801 Health Sciences South
PO Box 9190
Morgantown, WV 26506-9190
Ph:(304)293-3693
Fax: (304)293-2629
Co. E-mail: cmartin@hsc.wvu.edu
URL: http://www.hsc.wvu.edu/ioeh
Contact: Edward Doyle MD, Dir.
E-mail: cmartin@hsc.wvu.edu
Scope: Occupational and environmental health, including occupational medicine and environmental toxicology. **Services:** Community consultations, on toxic exposure risk; Patient care, for toxic exposure. **Publications:** Occupational Health. **Educational Activities:** Master's degree, in public health; Residencies, in preventive occupational and environmental medicine; Workshops.

START-UP INFORMATION

56718 ■ "Close Up: Teen Sensations" in *Entrepreneur* (Vol. 28, No. 11, November 2000, pp. 24)
Pub: Entrepreneur Media Inc.
Ed: Devlin Smith. **Description:** Teen entrepreneurs give insights regarding teen consumers. A few of their suggestions include to know why a teenager buys a certain product, to set a good example, and to use humor. A listing of the top five magazines for teens is included.

56719 ■ "Contest Challenges Teens to Consider Entrepreneurship" in *Kansas City Star* (March 8, 2005)
Pub: Knight-Ridder/Tribune Business News
Ed: Donna Vestal. **Description:** The National Association of Women Business Owners and Adams-Gabbert & Associates Inc. in Kansas City have announced a contest for senior girls to enter. The competition is meant to promote entrepreneurship among young women.

56720 ■ "Destined for success" in *Hispanic Business* (Vol. 22, No. 6, June 2000, pp. 20)
Pub: Hispanic Business
Ed: Vivienne Heines. **Description:** Profile of Mary Rodas, who began her business career when she was four years old. Ms. Rodas, now 24 years old, is president of Catalyst Toys. Daughter of Salvadoran immigrants, Ms. Rodas says the greatest obstacle to her success is her age, not her ethnicity.

56721 ■ "Eco-Preneuring" in *Small Business Opportunities* (Vol. 12, No. 5, September 2000, pp. 94, 98)
Pub: Harris Publications, Inc.
Ed: Annette Wood. **Description:** A profile of Billy Darnell and Zoobee, the company he founded that makes exotic wildlife-themed watches.

56722 ■ "Fashion's phat cats" in *Black Enterprise* (Vol. 33, No. 3, October 2002, pp. S8)
Pub: Earl Graves Publishing Co.
Ed: Shani Smothers. **Description:** Profiles of Jazmin Ruotolo, Dorothy Antoine, Zareth Edghill, and Kianga Peterson, professional clothing designers. Antoine and Peterson both launched their careers while still teenagers.

56723 ■ "Kid power! Adults need not apply" in *Black Enterprise* (Vol. 32, No. 9, April 2002, pp. 135)
Pub: Earl Graves Publishing Co.
Ed: Kenneth Meeks. **Description:** An overview of the Kidpreneurs Conference sponsored by Black Enterprise. The conference is designed to develop the entrepreneurial potential of young people.

56724 ■ "The Knight's Still Young" in *Home Business* (Vol. 12, October 2005, No. 5, pp. 70)
Pub: Home Business Magazine

Ed: Sandy Larson. **Description:** Profile of Rick Jensen, winner of the NFIB/Visa USA Youth Entrepreneur of the Year award, designs hand-crafted apparel and accessories from a chain mesh he weaves. Jensen sells his goods at craft fairs, Renaissance festivals and on the Internet.

56725 ■ "The Merchant of Bay Ridge" in *Forbes* (Vol. 174, December 27, 2004, No. 13, pp. 80)
Pub: Forbes Magazine Inc.
Ed: Phyllis Berman. **Description:** Profile of Joseph Cohen, the 17-year-old entrepreneur who developed a thriving online retail business called Bay Ridge.

56726 ■ "New Economy" in *Inc.* (November 2000, pp. 37)
Pub: The Goldhirsh Group
Description: Profile of Dave Bell, a senior at Nashua High School, in Nashua, New Hampshire who is hard at work building his new company.

56727 ■ "Organizations" in *Black Enterprise* (Vol. 34, No. 5, December 2003, pp. S5)
Pub: Earl Graves Publishing Co.
Description: Profile of the Future Business Leaders of American (FBLA), a nonprofit for young entrepreneurs and students preparing for careers in business.

56728 ■ "Pilot program to assist young entrepreneurs" in *Black Enterprise* (Vol. 32, No. 6, January 2002, pp. 37)
Pub: Earl Graves Publishing Co.
Ed: Paula McCoy-Pinderhughes. **Description:** Profile of the Prudential Young Entrepreneur Program, a three-year pilot entrepreneurial development project funded by the Prudential Foundation, a nonprofit, grant-making organization of the Newark, New Jersey-based Prudential Insurance Company of America. The program is designed to offer young adults in urban areas opportunity to train to become a small business owner.

56729 ■ "Sweet success" in *Black Enterprise* (Vol. 33, No. 3, October 2002, pp. S6)
Pub: Earl Graves Publishing Co.
Ed: Sonya Kimmble-Ellis. **Description:** Profile of Camilla Amber White, the 15 year old entrepreneur with her own baking business. White offers a wide range of pies, as well as cheesecakes, bread, and rice puddings.

ASSOCIATIONS AND OTHER ORGANIZATIONS

56730 ■ **Entrepreneurs' Organization**
500 Montgomery St., Ste. 500
Alexandria, VA 22314
Ph:(703)519-6700
Fax: (703)519-1864
Co. E-mail: info@eonetwork.org
URL: http://www.eonetwork.org

Contact: Troy Hazard, Pres.
Membership: Entrepreneurs under the age of 40 who have either founded, co-founded, are a controlling shareholders of, or own a firm with annual gross revenues exceeding $1000000. **Purpose:** Serves as a focal point for communication among members; provides educational programs; facilitates small group meetings with leading entrepreneurs. Conducts charitable and educational programs; operates speakers' bureau; compiles statistics. Membership is by invitation only. **Publications:** *Axis* (monthly); *Octane* (quarterly); *Overdrive* (monthly).

56731 ■ **National Foundation for Teaching Entrepreneurship**
120 Wall St., 29th Fl.
New York, NY 10005
Ph:(212)232-3333
Free: 800-367-6383
Fax: (212)232-2244
Co. E-mail: nfte@nfte.com
URL: http://www.nfte.com
Contact: Steve Mariotti, Founder/Pres.
Description: Devoted to teaching entrepreneurship education to low-income young people, ages 11 through 18. **Publications:** *NFTE News* (quarterly).

56732 ■ **Young Presidents' Organization**
600 E Las Colinas Blvd., Ste. 1000
Irving, TX 75039
Ph:(972)587-1500
Free: 800-773-7976
Co. E-mail: askypo@ypo.org
URL: http://www.ypo.org
Contact: Les Ward, CFO/COO
Description: Presidents or chief executive officers of corporations with minimum of 50 employees; each member must have been elected president before his/her 40th birthday and must retire by June 30th the year after his/her 50th birthday. Assists members in becoming better presidents through education and idea exchange. Conducts courses for members and spouses, in business, arts and sciences, world affairs, and family and community life, during a given year at various locations, including graduate business schools. **Publications:** *Worldwide*.

REFERENCE WORKS

56733 ■ "The 2003 Teenpreneur Money Guide" in *Black Enterprise* (Vol. 34, No. 2, September 2003, pp. S10)
Pub: Earl Graves Publishing Co.
Ed: Tanisha A. Sykes. **Description:** Online resources for young entrepreneurs that will teach them how to be financially literate.

56734 ■ "Aerobatic Ace: Young Pilot Flies Plane That's Smaller Than a Car" in *Black Enterprise* (Vol. 34, No. 2, September 2003, pp. S9)
Pub: Earl Graves Publishing Co.
Ed: Raelyn C. Johnson. **Description:** Profile of Jamail Larkins, 19-year-old owner of Larkins Enterprises

Inc. Larkins' aviation and advertising company has gone from selling flight training books to selling satellite navigation systems. He flies himself to speaking engagements and air shows where he advertises for Delta, AeroShell, and Power Serve International.

56735 ■ **"Arthur Andersen announces YoungIT Entrepreneur Award" in** *Crain's Detroit Business* **(Vol. 26, No. 12, March 20, 2000, pp. 37)**
Pub: Crain Communications, Inc.
Description: Arthur Andersen L.L.P. will sponsor the Young IT Entrepreneur Award at the second annual Michigan Information Technology Business Summit. The award will recognize entrepreneurs under 30 who have started Internet-based businesses.

56736 ■ *Biz Kids Guide to Success: Money-Making Ideas for Young Entrepreneurs*
Pub: Barron's Educational Series, Inc.
Ed: Terri Thompson. **Released:** 1992. **Price:** $4.95 (paper).

56737 ■ **"Blackgirl Rules!" in** *Black Enterprise* **(Vol. 34, No. 2, September 2003, pp. S4)**
Pub: Earl Graves Publishing Co.
Ed: Raelyn C. Johnson. **Description:** Profile of Kenya Jordana James, teenage publisher of Blackgirl Magazine. The magazine spotlights African American girls at their best.

56738 ■ *Capitalism for Kids: Growing Up to Be Your Own Boss*
Pub: Bluestocking Press
Ed: Karl Hess. **Released:** June 2006. **Price:** $8.95.
Description: Capitalism, democratic socialism, socialism, communism, and totalitarianism is explained to children. The book explains to young people how to build a profitable business.

56739 ■ **"A Car is Born: Wydens Gabriel Transforms Ordinary Model Cars into Masterpieces" in** *Black Enterprise* **(Vol. 34, No. 5, December 2003)**
Pub: Earl Graves Publishing Co.
Ed: Jennifer L. Smith. **Description:** Profile of Wydens Gabriel, 17-year-old founder of Wydnes Gabriel's Speed Cars, a model car detailing business.

56740 ■ **"Detroit Free Press Small Business Column" in** *Detroit Free Press* **(June 13, 2005)**
Pub: Knight-Ridder/Tribune Business News
Ed: Carol Cain. **Description:** Profile of Paul Sowinski, 19-year-old entrepreneur, who sells computer supplies to 2,100 Michigan customers, with growth projected as far away as Guam and Antigua.

56741 ■ **"Entrepreneurial Enthusiasm" in** *Black Enterprise* **(Vol. 34, No. 7, February 2004, pp. 32)**
Pub: Earl Graves Publishing Co.
Ed: Carolyn M. Brown. **Description:** Approximately 41 percent of American youth feel that owning a business will provide more security than working for a company, and 81 percent believe there is more job satisfaction owning your own company rather working for someone else.

56742 ■ **"Fast Times" in** *Entrepreneur* **(Vol. 32, November 2004, No. 11, pp. 28)**
Pub: Entrepreneur Media Inc.
Ed: Nichole L. Torres. **Description:** Three individuals share how working in fast food restaurants as teenagers actually helped prepare them to become successful entrepreneurs.

56743 ■ *50 Great Businesses for Teens*
Pub: Macmillan Publishing Co., Inc.
Ed: Sarah Riehm. **Released:** 1997. **Price:** $14.95.

56744 ■ **"From Landscaper to Landowner" in** *Black Enterprise* **(Vol. 34, No. 5, December 2003, pp. S4)**
Pub: Earl Graves Publishing Co.
Ed: Sonya Kimble-Ellis. **Description:** Profile of young entrepreneur Airyque Ervin, who started a lawn service with his brother at age 14. Ervin found that owning land, selling it, and buying more was a more profitable venture.

56745 ■ **"Getting No Respect?" in** *Entrepreneur* **(Vol. 33, February 2005, pp. 110)**
Pub: Entrepreneur Media Inc.
Ed: Nichole L. Torres. **Description:** Young college entrepreneurs are offered advice to help them with credibility as business owners.

56746 ■ **"It's all about the profits (you're the boss)" in** *Black Enterprise* **(Vol. 33, No. 3, October 2002, pp. S3)**
Pub: Earl Graves Publishing Co.
Ed: Carolyn M. Brown. **Description:** Financial management advice is given for student-owned businesses. A formula is provided for pricing services or products.

56747 ■ **"Keeping Score" in** *Wall Street Journal* **(September 12, 2002, pp. B8)**
Pub: Dow Jones & Co. Inc.
Description: Kidsway Inc. provides a ranking of businesses run by children in the U.S.

56748 ■ **"Kid-Friendly Business Sources" in** *Black Enterprise* **(Vol. 37, January 2007, No. 6, pp. 40)**
Pub: Earl G. Graves Publishing Co. Inc.
Ed: Carolyn M. Brown. **Description:** Financial or business camps are a great way to encourage a child who interested in starting his or her own business. A number of these camps are available each year including Kidpreneurs Conference and Bull and Bear Investment Camp. Other resources are available online. Resources included.

56749 ■ **"Kid stuff: want to light your child's entrepreneurial fire?" in** *Entrepreneur* **(Vol. 31, No. 5, May 2003, pp. 24)**
Pub: Entrepreneur Media Inc.
Ed: Nichole L. Torres. **Description:** Information on camps focusing on hands-on training for young people to learn to be entrepreneurs is provided. Requirements and contact information for Camp Startup; Excellence in Youth Entrepreneurs; Wise Kid, Wealthy Kid Youth Entrepreneurship Camp, and Youth Entrepreneur Camp is also included.

56750 ■ *Kidbiz: Everything You Need to Start Your Own Business*
Pub: Puffin Books
Ed: Conn McQuinn; illustrated by Mike Reddy. **Released:** 1998. **Price:** $9.99.

56751 ■ *The Kids' Business Book*
Pub: The Lerner Publishing Group
Ed: Arlene Erlbach. **Released:** 1996. **Price:** $22.60.

56752 ■ **"Leading the Pack" in** *Black Enterprise* **(Vol. 34, No. 4, November 2003, pp. 82)**
Pub: Earl Graves Publishing Co.
Ed: Marcia A. Wade. **Description:** The winners of the Black Enterprise Small Business Awards were announced at the 2003 Black Enterprise/Microsoft Entrepreneurs Conference in May. Among the winners were: John Sterling of Synch-Solutions Inc., Colleen Payne-Nabors of Mobile Cardiac Imaging LLC, Orlando Robinson of D&D Innovations Inc., and Kenya James of Blackgirl Magazine. Kenya is a 14-year-old entrepreneur publishing a magazine to improve the self-esteem of young women across the nation.

56753 ■ **"A Lesson Learned" in** *Black Enterprise* **(Vol. 34, No. 2, September 2003, pp. S2)**
Pub: Earl Graves Publishing Co.
Ed: Jennifer Smith. **Description:** Young entrepreneurs share the experiences as small business owners while, at the same time, attending school.

56754 ■ **"Making Cents of It All" in** *Home Business* **(Vol. 12, March/April 2005, No. 2, pp. 70)**
Pub: Home Business Magazine
Ed: Sandy Larson. **Description:** Profile of Trevor Ollivierre, the young entrepreneur helped his family create the new board game, All Around Spending.

56755 ■ **"Mixing Books with Business" in** *Black Enterprise* **(Vol. 34, No. 2, September 2003, pp. S1)**
Pub: Earl Graves Publishing Co.
Description: Kenya Jordana James, Black Enterprise 2003 Teenpreneur of the Year winner. The 14-year-old James publishes the periodical, Blackgirl Magazine.

56756 ■ **"Not On His Watch" in** *Entrepreneur.com* **(Vol. 34, January 2006, No. 1, pp. 35)**
Pub: Entrepreneur Media Inc.
Ed: Sara Wilson. **Description:** Profile of Bryan Hammond, age 21, founder of ExploreAnywhere Software LLC. Hammond's computer-monitoring products cater to parents, employers and educators. The software company projects 2005 sales at more than $1 million.

56757 ■ **"O-Web Design Firm Makes Case for Student Startups" in** *Crain's Cleveland Business* **(Vol. 26, January 10, 2005, No. 2, pp. 7)**
Pub: Crain Communications Inc.
Ed: Henry Gomez. **Description:** After spending $75 to start their own Web design business in 2003, Oleg Fridman, Stan Garber and Alex Yakubovich, grew their business to $60,000 in revenue for 2004.

56758 ■ **"Opportunity knocks at Kauffman" in** *Ingram's* **(Vol. 28, No. 3, March 2002, pp. 17)**
Pub: Show Me Publishing, Inc.
Ed: Jack Cashill. **Description:** The Kauffman Foundation offers young people in the Kansas City area an opportunity to acquire real-world business skills.

56759 ■ **"Putting Pen to Paper: Teen Publisher Uses Poetry to Touch Hearts" in** *Black Enterprise* **(Vol. 34, No. 2, September 2003, pp. S6)**
Pub: Earl Graves Publishing Co.
Ed: Feona Sharhran Huff. **Description:** Profile of Jarad Badinger, writer and publisher of poetry and a three-part series called, Peter Black. The series chronicles the boarding school years of a young man attending the fictional Gideon University.

56760 ■ **"Resources: Web Sites, Organizations, Events and More To Grow Your Business" in** *Entrepreneur* **(Vol. 32, September 2004, No. 9, pp. 8)**
Pub: Entrepreneur Media Inc.
Ed: Steve Cooper. **Description:** Resources to help small business are featured including the Small Business Administration's effort to help teen entrepreneurs launch a business; KnockNow an online community of entrepreneurs, executives, venture capitalists, angel investors, service sector companies, and government; the SBA's business Website offering information on small business development, financial assistance, taxes, laws and regulations, international trade, workplace issues, buying and selling and federal forms.

56761 ■ **"A Risky Business" in** *Kiplinger's Personal Finance Magazine* **(Vol. 54, No. 9, September 2000, pp. 94)**
Pub: The Kiplinger Washington Editors, Inc.
Ed: Catherine Siskos, Matt Popowsky. **Description:** Some college students are quitting school to become Web entrepreneurs.

56762 ■ **"Rotary Club Of Jackson Invests In Metro Students" in** *Mississippi Business Journal* **(Vol. 28, September 2006, No. 36, pp. 3)**
Pub: Venture Publications, Inc.
Ed: Lynne Jeter **Description:** Profile of the Rotary Club of Jackson and it's college scholarship program to aid low income potential students of the Jackson community in attending college.

56763 ■ *Starting Out: Step-by-Step Guide for Teens Succeeding in the '90s*
Pub: Step-by-Step Publications
Ed: Terilyn A. Davenport. **Released:** 1994. **Price:** $29.95; $19.95 (paper).

56764 ■ **"Students of Enterprise" in** *Entrepreneur* **(Vol. 32, November 2004, No. 11, pp. 108)**
Pub: Entrepreneur Media Inc.
Ed: April Y. Pennington, Devlin Smith. **Description:** Collegiate Entrepreneurs' Organization supports college students wanting to start their own businesses. The Chicago-based organization's membership has grown to 14,000 members nationwide. Profile of Fred DeLuca, who started a Subway sandwich shop when he was only seventeen, is included.

56765 ■ **"Teen Biz? Piece of Cake!" in** *Black Enterprise* **(Vol. 34, No. 5, December 2003, pp. S2)**
Pub: Earl Graves Publishing Co.
Ed: Jessica Hopkins. **Description:** Profile of teen entrepreneur, who started her own cake business, selling cakes and cupcakes.

56766 ■ **"Teen Decorating Diva: A Designer Turns Cluttered Corners Into Dream Spaces" in** *Black Enterprise* **(Vol. 34, No. 2, September 2003)**
Pub: Earl Graves Publishing Co.
Ed: Feona Sharhran Huff. **Description:** Profile of Alexis Tiara Hudson, the 17-year-old CEO of Lexica Interior Design. Hudson uses her talent to turn boring bedrooms into soothing sleeping spaces and cluttered corners into stylish rooms.

56767 ■ **"This Is Not About Charity" in** *Forbes* **(August 21, 2000, pp. 70)**
Pub: Forbes Magazine
Ed: Ann Marsh. **Description:** Academy of Business Leadership teaches teenagers to reach for their dreams.

56768 ■ **"Trash to Treasure" in** *Small Business Opportunities* **(Summer 2005)**
Pub: Harris Publications Inc.
Description: Brian Scudamore started his junk removal service while attending college and was awarded a Young Entrepreneur of the Year Award. His firm will remove any non-hazardous items from a home, business, or worksite.

56769 ■ **"Truly 'Small' Business" in** *My Business* **(June/July 2002, pp. 45)**
Pub: My Business Magazine
Ed: Doug McPherson. **Description:** Profile of Evan and Elise Macmillan, age 16 and 13 respectively. Evan and Elise are co-founders of The Chocolate Farm that sells chocolate candies from a Web site, which employs 30-40 part-time workers.

56770 ■ **"Turn classmates into customers" in** *Black Enterprise* **(Vol. 33, No. 3, October 2002, pp. S2)**
Pub: Earl Graves Publishing Co.
Ed: LaToya S. Foye. **Description:** Suggestions are offered for successfully marketing a business, including targeting classmates as customers. The nonprofit organization BUILD (Businesses United in Investing, Lending and Development) encourages young people to develop businesses is highlighted.

56771 ■ **"Websites" in** *Black Enterprise* **(Vol. 34, No. 5, December 2003, pp. S8)**
Pub: Earl Graves Publishing Co.
Ed: Sonya Kimble-Ellis. **Description:** A listing of three Web sites offering startup advice to young entrepreneurs is presented.

56772 ■ **"What Makes Owning a Business Fun? A Lesson Learned" in** *Black Enterprise* **(Vol. 34, No. 5, December 2003, pp. S2)**
Pub: Earl Graves Publishing Co.
Ed: Jennifer L. Smith. **Description:** Young entrepreneurs talk about their companies.

56773 ■ **"Young Entrepreneurs Give the U.S. Mint Their Two Cents" in** *Wall Street Journal* **(March 14, 2000, pp. B4)**
Pub: Dow Jones & Co., Inc.
Ed: Eleena De Lisser. **Description:** An overview of a program with the National Foundation for Teaching Entrepreneurship for marketing new coins.

56774 ■ *Young Entrepreneur's Guide to Creating What Matters Most: Building Attitudes, Behaviors & an Action Plan for Success in Your Own Business*
Pub: Courage Press
Ed: Mary S. Moore. **Released:** 1994. **Price:** $9.95 (paper).

TRADE PERIODICALS

56775 ■ *College & Career Guide News for College Students*
Pub: Corporate Marketing & Publishing
Contact: Patrick McGuire, Editorial Mgr.
Released: Quarterly. **Description:** College and career news source for college and non-traditional students.

56776 ■ *Futures*
Pub: Junior Achievement Inc.
Ed: Jeri Howard, Editor, etaylor@ja.org. **Released:** Quarterly. **Description:** Carries feature articles on various aspects of the Junior Achievement program and the volunteers and funders who support it. Promotes the principles of the free enterprise system. Recurring features include board member and volunteer profiles, and strategic initiatives.

56777 ■ *Working Moms & Dads Magazine*
Pub: Corporate Marketing & Publishing
Ed: Patrick McGuire, Editor. **Released:** Monthly. **Description:** Contains national and local news on parenting, childcare, education, and work issues. For professional and working parents.

VIDEOCASSETTES/ AUDIOCASSETTES

56778 ■ *Baby-Sitting the Responsible Way*
Cambridge Educational
c/o Films Media Group
PO Box 2053
Princeton, NJ 08843-2053
Free: 800-257-5126
Fax: (609)671-0266
Co. E-mail: custserve@filmsmediagroup.com
URL: http://www.cambridgeol.com
Price: $49.00. **Description:** Covers issues in responsible babysitting, including handling emergencies, keeping children on schedule, mealtime, handling behavior problems, and accident avoidance. Outlines behaviors to avoid such as talking extensively on the phone, failing to clean-up, and doing homework. Includes manual. **Availability:** VHS.

State Listings

SMALL BUSINESS DEVELOPMENT CENTER LEAD OFFICE

56779 ■ Alabama SBDC–University of Alabama
2800 Milan Ct., Ste. 124
Birmingham, AL 35211-6908
Ph:(205)943-6750
Co. E-mail: wcampbell@provost.uab.edu
URL: http://www.asbdc.org
Contact: William Campbell Jr., State Dir.

56780 ■ Alabama Small Business Development Consortium–Office of the State Director–University of Alabama at Birmingham (2800)
2800 Milan Court, Ste. 124
Medical Towers Bldg.
Birmingham, AL 35211-6908
Ph:(205)943-6750
Fax: (205)943-6752
URL: http://www.asbdc.org
Contact: John Sandefur, State Director
E-mail: sandefur@uab.edu

SMALL BUSINESS DEVELOPMENT CENTERS

56781 ■ Auburn University–Small Business Development Center
Lowder Business Bldg.
415 W. Magnolia Ave., Ste. 108-B
Auburn, AL 36849
Ph:(334)844-4220
Co. E-mail: bobweb@auburn.edu
URL: http://www.business.auburn.edu/programs/sbdc/
Contact: Jackie DiPofi, Dir.
E-mail: dipofja@auburn.edu

56782 ■ Jacksonville State University–Small Business Development Center–College of Commerce and Business Administration (700 P)
700 Pelham Rd. N.
114 Merrill Hall
Jacksonville, AL 36265
Ph:(256)782-5271
Fax: (256)782-5179
Co. A-mail: sbdc@jsu.edu
URL: http://www.jsu.edu/depart/sbdc/
Contact: Pat Shaddix, Dir.

56783 ■ NEARSBDC–University of Alabama at Huntsville–NE Alabama Regional Small Business Development Center (225 C)
225 Church St.
PO Box 168
Huntsville, AL 35801-0168
Ph:(256)535-2061

Fax: (256)535-2050
URL: http://www.nearsbdc.org
Contact: Larry Crowson, Dir.
E-mail: lcrowson@nearsbdc.org

56784 ■ Small Business Development Center–Alabama State University–College of Business Administration (915 S)
915 S. Jackson St.
Montgomery, AL 36104
Ph:(334)229-4138
Fax: (334)269-1102
URL: http://www.cobanetwork.com/sbdc/index.htm
Contact: Lorenza Patrick, Dir.
E-mail: lpatrick@asunet.alasu.edu

56785 ■ Small Business Development Center–Culverhouse College of Commerce–The University of Alabama (PO Bo)
PO Box 870397
Tuscaloosa, AL 35487-0397
Ph:(205)348-7011
Fax: (205)348-6974
Co. E-mail: phaninen@cba.ua.edu
URL: http://sbdc.cba.ua.edu/
Contact: Brian Davis, Dir.

56786 ■ Troy State University–Small Business Development Center
102 Bibb Graves Hall
Troy, AL 36082
Ph:(334)670-3771
URL: http://sbdc.troy.edu/
Contact: Sandra Lucas, Dir.
E-mail: slucas@troy.edu

56787 ■ University of Alabama at Birmingham–Alabama Small Business Development Consortium–Small Business Development Center (1055)
1055 S. 11th St., Rm. 202
Birmingham, AL 35294
Ph:(205)934-6760
Fax: (205)934-0538
Co. E-mail: sbdc@uab.edu
URL: http://www.business.uab.edu/sbdc/
Contact: John Sandefur, State Dir.
E-mail: sandefur@uab.edu

56788 ■ University of North Alabama–Small Business Development Center
1 Harrizon Plaza
135 Keller Hall
Florence, AL 35632-0001
Ph:(256)765-4629
Fax: (256)765-4813
Co. E-mail: cmlong@una.edu
URL: http://www.business.una.edu/ptac/
Contact: Carolyn Long, Dir.

56789 ■ University of South Alabama–Small Business Development Center
Mitchell College of Business, Rm. 118
307 University Blvd.
Mobile, AL 36688

Ph:(251)460-6004
Fax: (251)460-6246
Co. E-mail: sbdc@usouthal.edu
URL: http://www.southalabama.edu/sbdc/index.html
Contact: Thomas Tucker, Dir.
E-mail: ttucker@usamail.usouthal.edu

56790 ■ University of West Alabama–Small Business Development Center
Station 35
Livingston, AL 35470
Ph:(205)652-3665
Fax: (205)652-3516
URL: http://sbdc.uwa.edu/
Contact: Ken Walker, Dir.
E-mail: kwalker@uwa.edu

SMALL BUSINESS ASSISTANCE PROGRAMS

56791 ■ Alabama Department of Economic and Community Affairs–Planning and Economic Development
401 Adams Ave.
PO Box 5690
Montgomery, AL 36103-5690
Ph:(334)242-5100
Fax: (334)242-5099
URL: http://www.adeca.state.al.us
Contact: Shabbir Olia, Prgm Mgr
Description: Provides consultation services to small and developing businesses; provides information on federal grants and projects; and helps businesses to develop export contacts and markets.

56792 ■ U.S. Small Business Administration
2121 8th Ave. N, Ste. 200
Birmingham, AL 35203-2398
Ph:(205)731-1344
Fax: (205)731-1404
URL: http://www.sba.gov
Description: Assists businesses planning new manufacturing, processing, warehousing, distribution, research, or office facilities, or expanding present facilities. Staff includes experts in research, tax, finance, community data, and other areas. Helps in developing a finance package made up of bonds, grants, and loans. Services offered free of charge.

56793 ■ University of Alabama–Alabama International Trade Center
Box 870396
Tuscaloosa, AL 35487-0396
Ph:(205)348-7621
Free: 800-747-2482
Fax: (205)348-6974
Co. E-mail: aitc@aitc.ua.edu
URL: http://www.aitc.ua.edu
Contact: Brian Davis
Description: Offers consulting services and seminars to help businesses develop international activities. Compiles information on foreign business climates. Services provided free of charge to smaller businesses; others must pay a fee.

SCORE OFFICES

56794 ■ SCORE Alabama Capitol
c/o Raymond Furlong, Chm.
600 S Court St.
Montgomery, AL 36104
Ph:(334)240-6868
Fax: (334)240-6869
Co. E-mail: jklove41@knology.net
URL: http://www.score.org
Description: Provides public service to America by offering small business advice and training.

56795 ■ SCORE Baldwin County
c/o Eastern Shore Chamber of Commerce
327 Fairhope Ave.
Fairhope, AL 36532
Ph:(251)928-6387
Fax: (251)928-6389
Co. E-mail: info@baldwinscore.org
URL: http://www.score.org
Contact: Harry Moreland, Chapter Chm.
Description: Provides public service to America by offering small business advice and training.

56796 ■ SCORE East Alabama
c/o Opelika Chamber of Commerce
PO Box 2366
Opelika, AL 36803
Ph:(334)745-4861
Fax: (334)749-4740
Co. E-mail: jimbicel@sbcglobal.net
URL: http://www.score.org
Description: Provides public service to America by offering business advice and training.

56797 ■ SCORE Mobile
c/o Mobile Area Chamber of Commerce
851 Government St.
Mobile, AL 36652
Ph:(251)431-8614
Fax: (251)431-8646
Co. E-mail: score@mobilechamber.com
Description: Provides professional guidance and information to maximize the success of existing and emerging small businesses. Offers business counseling and workshops.

56798 ■ SCORE North Alabama
c/o UAB Small Business Development Center
1055 - 11th St. S, Ste. 202
Birmingham, AL 35294-2060
Ph:(205)934-6868
Fax: (205)934-0538
Co. E-mail: scorechapter84@att.net
Description: Provides professional guidance and information to maximize the success of existing and emerging small businesses. Offers business counseling and workshops.

56799 ■ SCORE Northeast Alabama
c/o Calhoun County Chamber of Commerce
1330 Quintard Ave.
Anniston, AL 36202
Ph:(256)237-3536
Fax: (256)327-4338
Co. E-mail: score@calhounchamber.com
Description: Provides professional guidance and information to maximize the success of existing and emerging small businesses. Offers business counseling and workshops.

56800 ■ SCORE Tuscaloosa
c/o Chamber of Commerce West Alabama
2200 University Blvd.
Tuscaloosa, AL 35402
Ph:(205)758-7588
Fax: (205)391-0565
Co. E-mail: dontown1000@aol.com
Description: Provides professional guidance and information to maximize the success of existing and emerging small businesses. Offers business counseling and workshops.

BETTER BUSINESS BUREAUS

56801 ■ Better Business Bureau, Birmingham
PO Box 55268
Birmingham, AL 35255-5268
Ph:(205)558-2222
Free: 800-824-5274
Fax: (205)558-2239
Co. E-mail: inquiry@birmingham-al.bbb.org
URL: http://www.birmingham-al.bbb.org
Contact: David C. Smitherman, Pres.

56802 ■ Better Business Bureau, Montgomery
500 Eastern Blvd., Ste. 128
Montgomery, AL 36117
Ph:(334)273-5530
Fax: (334)273-5546
Co. E-mail: inquiry@birmingham-al.bbb.org
URL: http://www.birmingham-al.bbb.org

56803 ■ Better Business Bureau of North Alabama
PO Box 383
Huntsville, AL 35804-0383
Ph:(256)533-1640
Free: 800-239-1642
Fax: (256)533-1177
Co. E-mail: info@northalabama.bbb.org
URL: http://www.northalabama.bbb.org
Contact: Ms. Michele McDaniel, Pres.

56804 ■ Better Business Bureau of South Alabama
PO Box 91419
Mobile, AL 36691-1419
Ph:(251)433-5494
Free: 800-544-4714
Fax: (251)438-3191
Co. E-mail: info@bbsouthal.org
URL: http://www.bbsouthal.org
Contact: Tina Waller, Pres.

CHAMBERS OF COMMERCE

56805 ■ Alabama Gulf Coast Area Chamber of Commerce
3150 Gulf Shores Pkwy.
PO Drawer 3869
Gulf Shores, AL 36547-3869
Ph:(251)968-6904
Fax: (251)968-5332
Co. E-mail: info@alagulfcoastchamber.com
URL: http://www.alagulfcoastchamber.com
Contact: Mark Berson, Pres.

56806 ■ Albertville Chamber of Commerce
316 E Sand Mountain Dr.
PO Box 1457
Albertville, AL 35950-6457
Ph:(256)878-3821
Free: 800-878-3821
Fax: (256)878-3822
Co. E-mail: albertvillechamber@charter.net
Contact: Brian Murphree, Pres.

56807 ■ Alexander City Chamber of Commerce
120 Tallapoosa St.
PO Box 926
Alexander City, AL 35011-0926
Ph:(256)234-3461
Fax: (256)234-0094
Co. E-mail: susan@charter.net
URL: http://www.alexandercity.org
Contact: Susan Foy, Exec.Dir.

56808 ■ Aliceville Area Chamber of Commerce
PO Drawer A
Aliceville, AL 35442

Ph:(205)373-2820
Fax: (205)373-8692
Co. E-mail: commerce@pickens.net
URL: http://www.pickens.net/~commerce
Contact: Gale Ammerman, Chm.

56809 ■ Andalusia Area Chamber of Commerce
1208 W Bypass
PO Box 667
Andalusia, AL 36420
Ph:(334)222-2030
Fax: (334)222-7844
Co. E-mail: chamber@alaweb.com
Contact: Bette D. Reynolds, Exec.VP

56810 ■ Arab Chamber of Commerce
PO Box 626
1157 N Main St.
Arab, AL 35016
Ph:(256)586-3138
Free: 888-403-2722
Fax: (256)586-0233
Co. E-mail: arabchamber@charter.net
URL: http://www.arab-chamber.org
Contact: Melissa Cook, Pres.

56811 ■ Ashford Area Chamber of Commerce
PO Box 463
Ashford, AL 36312
Ph:(334)899-GROW
Fax: (334)899-GROW
Contact: Delores Posey, Exec. Dir.

56812 ■ Athens-Limestone County Chamber of Commerce
101 S Beaty St.
PO Box 150
Athens, AL 35612
Ph:(256)232-2600
Fax: (256)232-2609
Co. E-mail: info@tourathens.com
URL: http://www.tourathens.com
Contact: Hugh Ball, Pres.

56813 ■ Atmore Area Chamber of Commerce
501 S Pensacola Ave.
Atmore, AL 36502
Ph:(251)368-3305
Fax: (251)368-0800
Co. E-mail: atmoreal@frontiernet.net
URL: http://www.atmorechamber.com
Contact: Emilie W. Mims, Exec.Dir.

56814 ■ Auburn Chamber of Commerce
714 E Glenn Ave.
PO Box 1370
Auburn, AL 36831-1370
Ph:(334)887-7011
Fax: (334)821-5500
Co. E-mail: info@auburnchamber.com
URL: http://www.auburnchamber.com
Contact: Lolly Stainer, Pres.

56815 ■ Bayou La Batre Chamber of Commerce
PO Box 486
Bayou La Batre, AL 36509
Ph:(251)824-4088
Fax: (251)824-4088
Co. E-mail: info@bayoulabatrechamber.com
URL: http://www.bayoulabatrechamber.com
Contact: Harold Hodges, Pres.

56816 ■ Bessemer Area Chamber of Commerce
321 N 18th St.
PO Box 648
Bessemer, AL 35021-0648
Ph:(205)425-3253
Free: 888-423-7736
Fax: (205)425-4979
Co. E-mail: mmilan1@bellsouth.net
URL: http://www.bessemerchamber.com
Contact: Ronnie Acker, Pres.

56817 ■ Birmingham Regional Chamber of Commerce
505 20th St. N
Birmingham, AL 35203
Ph:(205)324-2100
Fax: (205)324-2314
Co. E-mail: jcoleman@birminghamchamber.com
URL: http://www.birminghamchamber.com
Contact: Russel Cunningham, Pres/CEO

56818 ■ Blount County-Oneonta Chamber of Commerce
PO Box 1487
Oneonta, AL 35121
Ph:(205)274-2153
Fax: (205)274-2099
Co. E-mail: cvbridge@otelco.net
URL: http://www.coveredbridge.org
Contact: Charles Carr, Pres.

56819 ■ Boaz Chamber of Commerce
100 E Bartlett St.
PO Box 563
Boaz, AL 35957
Ph:(256)593-8154
Free: 800-SHOP-BOAZ
Fax: (256)593-1233
Co. E-mail: boazchamber@charter.net
URL: http://www.boazchamberofcommerce.com
Contact: Keyesta Hopper, Pres.

56820 ■ Center Point Area Chamber of Commerce
PO Box 9474
Birmingham, AL 35220

56821 ■ Central Baldwin Chamber of Commerce
22193 Hwy. 59, Ste. A
PO Box 587
Robertsdale, AL 36567
Ph:(251)947-5932
Fax: (251)947-2626
Co. E-mail: brucesims@yahoo.com
URL: http://www.cbchamber.org
Contact: Bruce Sims, Pres.

56822 ■ Chamber of Commerce-Bessemer Area
321 N 18th St.
Bessemer, AL 35020
Ph:(205)425-3253
Free: 888-423-7736
Fax: (205)425-4979
Co. E-mail: mmilan1@bellsouth.net
URL: http://www.bessemerchamber.com
Contact: Pam Nichols, Chair

56823 ■ Chamber of Commerce of Huntsville/Madison County
PO Box 408
Huntsville, AL 35804-0408
Ph:(256)535-2000
Fax: (256)535-2015
Co. E-mail: hcc@hsvchamber.org
URL: http://www.huntsvillealabamausa.com
Contact: Brian Hilson, Pres./CEO

56824 ■ Chamber of Commerce of Walker County
204 19th St. E, Ste. 101
Jasper, AL 35501
Ph:(205)384-4571
Fax: (205)384-4901
Co. E-mail: walkcham@sonet.net
URL: http://www.walkerchamber.us
Contact: Linda Lewis, Exec. VP

56825 ■ Chamber of Commerce of West Alabama
2200 University Blvd.
Tuscaloosa, AL 35401-1542
Ph:(205)758-7588
Fax: (205)391-0565
Co. E-mail: chamber@dbtech.net
URL: http://www.tuscaloosachamber.com
Contact: Johnnie R. Aycock, Pres.

56826 ■ Cherokee County Chamber of Commerce
801 Cedar Bluff Rd.
PO Box 86
Centre, AL 35960-0086
Ph:(256)927-8455
Fax: (256)927-2768
Co. E-mail: cccoc@tds.net
URL: http://www.cherokee-chamber.org
Contact: Ms. Mel Williams, Pres.

56827 ■ Childersburg Chamber of Commerce
PO Box 527
Childersburg, AL 35044
Ph:(256)378-5482
Fax: (256)378-5833
Co. E-mail: chamber@childersburg.com
URL: http://www.childersburg.com
Contact: George Limbaugh, Exec.Dir.

56828 ■ Chilton County Chamber of Commerce
PO Box 66
Clanton, AL 35046
Ph:(205)755-2400
Free: 800-553-0493
Fax: (205)755-8444
Co. E-mail: chamber@chiltonconcountychamber.
  com
URL: http://www.chiltoncountychamber.com
Contact: Pennie Broussard

56829 ■ Citronelle Area Chamber of Commerce
PO Box 394
Citronelle, AL 36522-0394
Ph:(251)866-7733
Fax: (251)866-7982
Co. E-mail: citronelle@prodigy.net
Contact: Charles S. Belk, Pres.

56830 ■ Clay County Chamber of Commerce
PO Box 85
Lineville, AL 36266
Ph:(256)396-2828
Fax: (256)396-5532
Co. E-mail: staff@claycochamber.com
URL: http://www.claycochamber.com
Contact: Charles Higgins

56831 ■ Cleburne County Chamber of Commerce
PO Box 413
Heflin, AL 36264
Ph:(256)463-2222
Fax: (256)463-4668
Co. E-mail: cleburne-coc@aol.com
URL: http://www.cleburnecounty.org/chamber
Contact: Terri C. Dalton, Pres.

56832 ■ Crenshaw County Chamber of Commerce
PO Box 12
Luverne, AL 36049
Ph:(334)335-2253
Fax: (334)335-3820
Contact: Sherry Richburg, Exec. Dir.

56833 ■ Cullman Area Chamber of Commerce
PO Box 1104
Cullman, AL 35056-1104
Ph:(256)734-0454
Free: 800-313-5114
Fax: (256)737-7443
Co. E-mail: cullman@corrcomm.net
URL: http://www.cullmanchamber.org
Contact: Kirk Mancer, Pres.

56834 ■ Dadeville Area Chamber of Commerce
185 S Tallassee St., Ste. 103
Dadeville, AL 36853
Ph:(256)825-4019
Fax: (256)825-4019
Co. E-mail: chamber@lakemartin.net
URL: http://www.dadeville.com

Contact: Jim Williams, Pres.

56835 ■ Daleville Chamber of Commerce
740 S Daleville Ave.
PO Box 688
Daleville, AL 36322
Ph:(334)598-6331
Fax: (334)598-2333
Co. E-mail: chamber@dalevilleal.com
URL: http://www.dalevilleal.com
Contact: Pam Souders, Exec.Dir.

56836 ■ Decatur Morgan County Chamber of Commerce
515 Sixth Ave. NE
PO Box 2003
Decatur, AL 35602-2003
Ph:(256)353-5312
Fax: (256)353-2384
Co. E-mail: chamber@dcc.org
URL: http://www.dcc.org
Contact: John Seymour, Pres./CEO

56837 ■ Demopolis Area Chamber of Commerce
102 E Washington St.
PO Box 667
Demopolis, AL 36732
Ph:(334)289-0270
Fax: (334)289-1382
Co. E-mail: dacc@westal.net
URL: http://www.demopolischamber.com
Contact: Jay Shows, Pres.

56838 ■ Dothan Area Chamber of Commerce
102 Jamestown Blvd.
PO Box 638
Dothan, AL 36302-0638
Ph:(334)792-5138
Free: 800-221-1027
Fax: (334)794-4796
Co. E-mail: cshippey@dothan.com
URL: http://www.dothan.com
Contact: Matt Parker, Pres.

56839 ■ Eastern Shore Chamber of Commerce
29750 Larry Dee Cawyer Dr.
PO Drawer 310
Daphne, AL 36526
Ph:(251)621-8222
Fax: (251)621-8001
Co. E-mail: office@eschamber.com
URL: http://www.eschamber.com
Contact: Darrelyn J. Bender, Pres.

56840 ■ Elba Chamber of Commerce
200 Buford St.
Elba, AL 36323
Ph:(334)897-3125
Fax: (334)897-1762
Co. E-mail: ecc@alaweb.com
Contact: Kaye Whitworth, Exec.Dir.

56841 ■ Enterprise Chamber of Commerce
PO Box 310577
Enterprise, AL 36331-0577
Ph:(334)347-0581
Free: 800-235-4730
Fax: (334)393-8204
Co. E-mail: chamber@entercomp.com
URL: http://www.enterprisealabama.com
Contact: Kathleen W. Sauer, Pres.

56842 ■ Eufaula - Barbour County Chamber of Commerce
333 E Broad St.
PO Box 697
Eufaula, AL 36072-0697
Ph:(334)687-6664
Free: 800-524-7529
Fax: (334)687-5240
Co. E-mail: ebcchamber@bellsouth.net
URL: http://www.eufaula-barbourchamber.com
Contact: Jim Bradley, Exec.Dir.

56843 ■ Eutaw Area Chamber of Commerce
110 Main St.
PO Box 31
Eutaw, AL 35462
Ph:(205)372-9002
Fax: (205)372-9974
URL: http://www.greenecountyalabama.com
Contact: Don Thompson

56844 ■ Evergreen/Conecuh Chamber of Commerce
100 Depot Sq.
Evergreen, AL 36401
Ph:(251)578-1707
Fax: (251)578-5660
Co. E-mail: emma0916@bellsouth.net
URL: http://www.conecuhchamber.com
Contact: Ms. Emma Johnson, Sec.

56845 ■ Fayette Area Chamber of Commerce
PO Box 247
Fayette, AL 35555
Ph:(205)932-4587
Fax: (205)932-8788
Co. E-mail: fcoc@cyberjoes.com
URL: http://www.fayette.net/chamber/index.html
Contact: Anne Hamner, Dir.

56846 ■ Fort Deposit Chamber of Commerce
PO Box 162
Fort Deposit, AL 36032
Ph:(334)227-4242
Free: 888-437-4242
Fax: (334)227-4272
Contact: Cecille B. Cross III, Pres.

56847 ■ Fort Payne Chamber of Commerce
300 Gault Ave. N
PO Box 680125
Fort Payne, AL 35968
Ph:(256)845-2741
Fax: (256)845-5849
Co. E-mail: fpchambe@adelphia.net
URL: http://www.fortpayne.com
Contact: Larry Hancock, Exec.Dir.

56848 ■ Franklin County Chamber of Commerce
103 N Jackson Ave.
PO Box 44
Russellville, AL 35653
Ph:(256)332-1760
Fax: (256)332-1740
Co. E-mail: franklincounty@charter.net
URL: http://www.franklincountychamber.org
Contact: Lisa Stockton, Exec.Dir.

56849 ■ Gadsden Area Chamber of Commerce
PO Box 185
Gadsden, AL 35902
Ph:(256)543-3472
Free: 800-238-6924
Fax: (256)543-9887
Co. E-mail: info@gadsdenchamber.com
URL: http://www.gadsdenchamber.com
Contact: Tom Quinn, Pres.

56850 ■ Gardendale Chamber of Commerce
945 Grubbs Ave.
PO Box 26
Gardendale, AL 35071
Ph:(205)631-9195
Fax: (205)631-9034
Co. E-mail: gdalechamber@mindspring.com
URL: http://www.gardendalechamberofcommerce.com
Contact: Michael Galloway, Pres.

56851 ■ Gordo Area Chamber of Commerce
PO Box 33
Gordo, AL 35466-0033
Ph:(205)364-7870
Fax: (205)364-7383
Co. E-mail: gordochamber@pickens.net
URL: http://www.pickens.net/gordochamber
Contact: Barbara Dyer, Pres.

56852 ■ Greater Brewton Area Chamber of Commerce
1010 B Douglas Ave.
Brewton, AL 36426
Ph:(251)867-3224
Fax: (251)809-1793
Co. E-mail: jcrane@hotmail.com
URL: http://www.brewtonchamber.com
Contact: Judy Crane, Exec.Dir.

56853 ■ Greater Geneva Area Chamber of Commerce
517 S Commerce St.
PO Box 477
Geneva, AL 36340
Ph:(334)684-6582
Fax: (334)684-2100
Co. E-mail: geneva_chamber@entercomp.com
URL: http://www.genevaalabama.com
Contact: George Lindenmuth, Exec.VP

56854 ■ Greater Irondale Chamber of Commerce
1912 1st Ave. S
Irondale, AL 35210-1503
Ph:(205)956-3104
Free: 877-70T-RAIN
Fax: (205)956-5964
Co. E-mail: caboose500@aol.com
URL: http://www.irondalechamber.org
Contact: Daniel E.J. Devers, Exec.Dir.

56855 ■ Greater Jackson County Chamber of Commerce
PO Box 973
Scottsboro, AL 35768
Ph:(256)259-5500
Free: 800-259-5508
Fax: (256)259-4447
Co. E-mail: chamber@scottsboro.org
URL: http://www.jacksoncountychamber.com
Contact: Rick Roden, Pres./CEO

56856 ■ Greater Leeds Area Chamber of Commerce
933 Thornton Ave.
PO Box 900
Leeds, AL 35094-0900
Ph:(205)699-5001
Fax: (205)699-5893
Co. E-mail: chamber@leedsalabama.com
URL: http://www.leedsalabama.com
Contact: Vickie Padgett, Exec.Dir.

56857 ■ Greater Shelby County Chamber of Commerce
PO Box 324
Pelham, AL 35124
Ph:(205)663-4542
Fax: (205)663-4524
Co. E-mail: info@shelbychamber.org
URL: http://www.shelbychamber.org
Contact: Karen Ream, Pres.

56858 ■ Greater Talladega Area Chamber of Commerce
PO Drawer A
Talladega, AL 35160
Ph:(256)362-9075
Fax: (256)362-9093
Co. E-mail: info@talladegachamber.com
URL: http://www.talladegachamber.com
Contact: Heidi Edwards, Exec.Dir.

56859 ■ Greater Tallassee Area Chamber of Commerce
650 Gilmer Ave.
Tallassee, AL 36078
Ph:(334)283-5151
Fax: (334)252-0774
Co. E-mail: chamber@tallassee.al.us
URL: http://www.tallassee.al.us
Contact: George McCain, Exec.Dir.

56860 ■ Greater Valley Area Chamber of Commerce
PO Box 205
Lanett, AL 36863

Ph:(334)642-1411
Fax: (334)642-1410
Co. E-mail: info@greatervalleyarea.com
URL: http://www.greatervalleyarea.com
Contact: Benita Gunnells, Exec.Dir.

56861 ■ Greenville Area Chamber of Commerce
PO Box 158
Greenville, AL 36037
Ph:(334)382-7111
Free: 800-959-0717
Fax: (334)382-3181
Co. E-mail: gacoc@alaweb.com
URL: http://www.greenville-alabama.com
Contact: Carol C. Lee, Pres./CEO

56862 ■ Grove Hill Area Chamber of Commerce
PO Box 567
Grove Hill, AL 36451-0567
Ph:(251)275-4188
Fax: (251)275-2278
Contact: Cheryl Horton, Sec.

56863 ■ Haleyville Chamber of Commerce
PO Box 634
Haleyville, AL 35565
Ph:(205)486-4611
Fax: (205)486-5074
Co. E-mail: info@haleyvillechamber.org
URL: http://www.haleyvillechamber.org
Contact: Harold Bearden, Exec. Dir.

56864 ■ Hartselle Area Chamber of Commerce
PO Box 817
Hartselle, AL 35640
Ph:(256)773-4370
Free: 800-294-0692
Fax: (256)773-4379
Co. E-mail: susan@hartsellechamber.com
URL: http://www.hartsellechamber.com
Contact: Susan Hines, Pres.

56865 ■ Headland Chamber of Commerce
PO Box 236
Headland, AL 36345
Ph:(334)693-3303
Free: 800-886-9749
Fax: (334)693-3846
Co. E-mail: headlandchamber@centurytel.net
URL: http://www.headlandal.com
Contact: Jones Penny, Chm.

56866 ■ Homewood Chamber of Commerce
1721 Oxmoor Rd.
Homewood, AL 35209
Ph:(205)871-5631
Co. E-mail: director@homewoodchamber.org
URL: http://www.homewoodchamber.com
Contact: Lori Leonard, Exec.Dir.

56867 ■ Hoover Chamber of Commerce
PO Box 36005
Hoover, AL 35236
Ph:(205)988-5672
Co. E-mail: bill@hooverchamber.org
URL: http://www.hooverchamber.org
Contact: Bill Powell, Exec.Dir.

56868 ■ Hueytown Chamber of Commerce
PO Box 3356
Hueytown, AL 35023
Ph:(205)491-8039
Co. E-mail: randydooley@charter.net
URL: http://www.hueytown.org/chamber.htm

56869 ■ Jackson Chamber of Commerce
500 Commerce St.
Jackson, AL 36545
Ph:(251)246-3251
Fax: (251)246-3213
Co. E-mail: jacksonchamber@earthlink.net
URL: http://www.jacksonchamber.net
Contact: Crystal Sebright, Admin.

56870 ■ Lake Guntersville Chamber of Commerce
PO Box 577
Guntersville, AL 35976
Ph:(256)582-3612
Free: 800-869-LAKE
Fax: (256)582-3682
Co. E-mail: gcc@lakeguntersville.org
URL: http://www.lakeguntersville.org
Contact: Morri Yancy, Exec.Dir.

56871 ■ Lawrence County Chamber of Commerce
12001 Alabama Hwy. 157
PO Box 325
Moulton, AL 35650
Ph:(256)974-1658
Fax: (256)974-2400
Co. E-mail: lcc@hiwaay.net
URL: http://www.lawrencealabama.com
Contact: Vicki Morese, Exec.Dir.

56872 ■ Mobile Area Chamber of Commerce
451 Government St.
PO Box 2187
Mobile, AL 36652-2187
Ph:(251)433-6951
Free: 800-422-6952
Fax: (251)432-1143
Co. E-mail: info@mobilechamber.com
URL: http://www.mobilechamber.com
Contact: Mr. Winthrop M. Hallett III, Pres.

56873 ■ Monroeville Area Chamber of Commerce
PO Box 214
Monroeville, AL 36461
Ph:(251)743-2879
Fax: (251)743-2189
Co. E-mail: info@monroecountyal.com
URL: http://www.monroecountyal.com
Contact: Sandy C. Smith, Exec.Dir.

56874 ■ Montevallo Chamber of Commerce
720 Oak St.
Montevallo, AL 35115
Ph:(205)665-1519
Fax: (205)665-0759
Co. E-mail: montevallocc@bellsouth.net
URL: http://www.montevallocc.org
Contact: Ben McCrory, Pres.

56875 ■ Montgomery Area Chamber of Commerce
41 Commerce St.
PO Box 79
Montgomery, AL 36101
Ph:(334)834-5200
Fax: (334)265-4745
Co. E-mail: macoc@montgomerychamber.com
URL: http://www.montgomerychamber.com
Contact: Randall L. George CED, Pres.

56876 ■ North Baldwin Chamber of Commerce
301 McMeans Ave.
PO Box 310
Bay Minette, AL 36507
Ph:(251)937-5665
Fax: (251)937-5670
Co. E-mail: nbcoc@bellsouth.net
URL: http://www.northbaldwinchamber.com
Contact: Bridget L. McDonald, Exec.Dir.

56877 ■ Northwest Alabama Junior Chamber of Commerce
2808 Jackson Hwy.
Sheffield, AL 35660
Ph:(256)740-0255
Co. E-mail: nwajcc@mail.com
URL: http://nwajcc.tripod.com
Contact: Martin Dean, Pres.

56878 ■ Opelika Chamber of Commerce
601 Ave. A
PO Box 2366
Opelika, AL 36803-2366

Ph:(334)745-4861
Fax: (334)749-4740
Co. E-mail: coc@opelika.com
URL: http://www.opelika.com
Contact: Wendi Routhier, Pres.

56879 ■ Opp and Covington County Area Chamber of Commerce
PO Box 148
Opp, AL 36467
Ph:(334)493-3070
Free: 800-239-8054
Fax: (334)493-1060
Co. E-mail: info@oppchamber.com
URL: http://www.oppchamber.com
Contact: James Kelsoe, Exec.Dir.

56880 ■ Ozark Area Chamber of Commerce
294 Painter Ave.
Ozark, AL 36360
Ph:(334)774-9321
Free: 800-582-8497
Fax: (334)774-8736
Co. E-mail: ozarkcc@snowhill.com
Contact: Jeanette Reeves, Exec.Dir.

56881 ■ Phenix City-Russell County Chamber of Commerce
1107 Broad St.
Phenix City, AL 36867
Ph:(334)298-3639
Free: 800-892-2248
Fax: (334)298-3846
Co. E-mail: pcrccham@ldl.net
URL: http://pcrcchamber.com/pcrcchamber.htm
Contact: Victor W. Cross, Pres.

56882 ■ Pike County Chamber of Commerce
PO Box 249
Troy, AL 36081
Ph:(334)566-2294
Fax: (334)566-2298
Co. E-mail: pikecoc@troycable.net
Contact: Jennifer Barner, Pres.

56883 ■ Prattville Area Chamber of Commerce
1002 E Main St.
Prattville, AL 36066-5624
Ph:(334)365-7392
Free: 800-588-2796
Fax: (334)361-1314
Co. E-mail: jprochazka@prattvillechamber.com
URL: http://www.prattvillechamber.com
Contact: Connie Bainbridge, Pres.

56884 ■ Rainsville Chamber of Commerce
PO Box 396
Rainsville, AL 35986
Ph:(256)638-7800
Co. E-mail: timeberhart@farmerstel.com
URL: http://www.rainsville.info/about1.htm
Contact: Tim Eberhart, Publicity Dir.

56885 ■ Saraland Area Chamber of Commerce
939 Hwy. 43 S
Saraland, AL 36571
Ph:(251)675-4444
Fax: (251)675-2307
Co. E-mail: cocsara@bellsouth.net
URL: http://www.saralandcoc.com
Contact: Debbie O'Brien, Chm. of the Board

56886 ■ Selma and Dallas County Chamber of Commerce
912 Selma Ave.
Selma, AL 36701
Ph:(334)875-7241
Free: 800-45S-ELMA
Fax: (334)875-7142
Co. E-mail: info@selmaalabama.com
URL: http://www.inselma.com
Contact: Claire S. Twardy, Exec.Dir.

56887 ■ Shoals Chamber of Commerce
612 S Court St.
PO Box 1331
Florence, AL 35630

Ph:(256)764-4661
Free: 877-764-4661
Fax: (256)766-9017
Co. E-mail: shoals@shoalschamber.com
URL: http://www.shoalschamber.com
Contact: Mr. Stephen B. Holt CCE, Pres.

56888 ■ South Baldwin Chamber of Commerce
104 N Mackenzie St.
PO Box 1117
Foley, AL 36536
Ph:(251)943-3291
Free: 877-588-7137
Fax: (251)943-6810
Co. E-mail: info@southbaldwinchamber.com
URL: http://www.southbaldwinchamber.com
Contact: Donna H. Watts, Pres./CEO

56889 ■ Springville Area Chamber of Commerce
6496 US Hwy. 11
Springville, AL 35146
Ph:(205)467-2339
URL: http://www.stclaircountyal.com
Contact: Cason Catts, Pres.

56890 ■ Sumiton Chamber of Commerce
PO Box 188
Sumiton, AL 35148
Contact: Joeletta Martin, Dir.

56891 ■ Sylacauga Chamber of Commerce
PO Box 185
Sylacauga, AL 35150
Ph:(256)249-0308
Fax: (256)249-0315
Co. E-mail: mcgradyg@sylacauga.net
URL: http://www.sylacauga.net/chamber
Contact: Jeff Ramsland, Exec.Dir.

56892 ■ Tarrant/Pinson Valley Chamber of Commerce
1621 Pinson St.
Birmingham, AL 35217
Ph:(205)849-2803
Fax: (205)849-2805
Co. E-mail: lkeith@cityoftarrant.com
Contact: Ms. Lois B. Carlisle

56893 ■ Tillman's Corner Chamber of Commerce
5055 Carol Plantation Rd.
Mobile, AL 36619
Ph:(251)666-2846
Fax: (251)666-2813
Contact: T. O. Sutton, Pres.

56894 ■ Tri-Cities Chamber of Commerce
1099 5th St.
Florala, AL 36442
Ph:(334)858-6252
Co. E-mail: tricity@gt.net
URL: http://www.gtcom.net
Contact: Carey Stewart, Pres.

56895 ■ Trussville Area Chamber of Commerce
225 Parkway Dr.
Trussville, AL 35173
Ph:(205)655-7535
Free: 800-949-8222
Fax: (205)655-3705
Co. E-mail: trusscoc@hiwaay.net
URL: http://www.trussvillechamber.com
Contact: Delane B. Melvin, Exec.Dir.

56896 ■ Trusville Chamber of Commerce
225 Parkway Dr.
Trussville, AL 35173
Ph:(205)655-7535
Free: 800-949-8222
Fax: (205)655-3705
Co. E-mail: trusscoc@hiwaay.net
URL: http://www.trussvillechamber.com
Contact: Ms. Delane B. Melvin, Exec. Dir.

56897 ■ Union Springs/Bullock County Chamber of Commerce
PO Box 87
Union Springs, AL 36089
Ph:(334)738-5411
Fax: (334)738-5413
Co. E-mail: bcda@ustconline.net
URL: http://www.unionspringsalabama.com
Contact: Betty Helms

56898 ■ Vernon Chamber of Commerce
PO Box 336
Vernon, AL 35592-0336
Ph:(205)695-7718
Fax: (205)695-9287
Co. E-mail: kurth@fayette.net
Contact: Allan V. Chandler, Pres.

56899 ■ Vestavia Hills Chamber of Commerce
1975 Merryvale Rd.
Vestavia Hills, AL 35216
Ph:(205)823-5011
Free: (866)402-VHCC
Fax: (205)823-8974
Co. E-mail: chamber@vestaviahills.org
URL: http://www.vestaviahills.org
Contact: Jim Anderson, Pres.

56900 ■ Wetumpka Area Chamber of Commerce
110 E Bridge St.
PO Box 785
Wetumpka, AL 36092
Ph:(334)567-4811
Fax: (334)567-1811
Co. E-mail: wacc@bellsouth.net
URL: http://www.wetumpkachamber.com
Contact: Jan Wood, Exec.Dir.

56901 ■ Winfield Chamber of Commerce
126 City Hall St.
PO Box 1557
Winfield, AL 35594
Ph:(205)487-8841
Co. E-mail: chamberofcommerce@winfieldcity.org
URL: http://www.winfieldcity.org
Contact: Natalie Maddox

MINORITY BUSINESS ASSISTANCE PROGRAMS

56902 ■ Birmingham Business Resource Center
110 12th St. N
Birmingham, AL 35203
Ph:(205)250-6380
Fax: (205)250-6384
URL: http://www.bbrc.biz
Contact: Andrew Mayo

FINANCING AND LOAN PROGRAMS

56903 ■ 21st Century Health Ventures
One Health South Pky.
Birmingham, AL 35243
Ph:(256)268-6250
Fax: (256)970-8928
Investment Types: First stage and second stage, and leveraged buyout. **Industry Preferences:** Medical and health related. **Geographic Preferences:** U.S.

56904 ■ Bonaventure Capital
820 Shades Creek Pky., Ste. 3100
Birmingham, AL 35209
Ph:(205)870-8050
Fax: (205)870-8052
URL: http://www.bonaventurecapital.com
Contact: Steve Dauphin, Partner
Preferred Investment Size: $500,000 to $1,500,000. **Investment Policies:** Early stage. **Industry Preferences:** Computer software, industrial and energy, financial services, and utilities. **Geographic Preferences:** Southeast.

56905 ■ Cordova Capital (Montgomery)
4121 Carmichael Rd., Ste. 301
Montgomery, AL 36106
Ph:(334)271-6011
Fax: (334)260-0120
URL: http://www.cordovaventures.com
Contact: T. Forcht Dagi, Venture Partner
Preferred Investment Size: $250,000 to $4,000,000. **Investment Types:** Seed, start-up, early, first, second, and late stage, and expansion. **Industry Preferences:** Computer software and services, medical and health, Internet specific, communications and media, other products, biotechnology, industrial and energy, consumer related, semiconductors and other electronics. **Geographic Preferences:** Southeast.

56906 ■ FHL Capital Corp.
600 20th Street N., Ste. 350
Birmingham, AL 35203
Ph:(205)328-3098
Fax: (205)323-0001
URL: http://www.fhlcapital.com
Contact: Kevin Keck, Vice President
Preferred Investment Size: $500,000 to $1,000,000. **Investment Types:** Mezzanine, leveraged buyout, and special situation. **Geographic Preferences:** Southeast.

56907 ■ FJC Growth Capital
PO Box 1290
Huntsville, AL 35807
Ph:(256)964-5201
Fax: (256)964-5209
URL: http://www.collazoenterprises.com
Contact: Francisco Collazo, President
Preferred Investment Size: $300,000 to $500,000. **Investment Policies:** Second stage and mezzanine. **Industry Preferences:** Communications, semiconductors and other electronics, and consumer related. **Geographic Preferences:** Southeast.

56908 ■ FJC Growth Capital Corp.
PO Box 1290
Huntsville, AL 35807
Ph:(256)964-5201
Fax: (256)964-5209
URL: http://www.collazoenterprises.com
Contact: Francisco Collazo, President
Preferred Investment Size: $300,000 to $500,000. **Investment Types:** Mezzanine and second stage. **Industry Preferences:** Communications and media, semiconductors and other electronics, and consumer related. **Geographic Preferences:** Southeast U.S.

56909 ■ Harbert Management Corp.
One Riverchase Pky. S.
Birmingham, AL 35244
Ph:(205)987-5500
Fax: (205)987-5707
URL: http://www.harbert.net
Contact: Charles Miller, Vice President
Investment Types: Leveraged buyout, acquisition, and recapitalizations. **Geographic Preferences:** Mid Atlantic, and Southeastern U.S.

56910 ■ Hickory Venture Capital Corp.
301 Washington St. NW
Suite 301
Huntsville, AL 35801
Ph:(256)539-1931
Fax: (256)539-5130
URL: http://www.hvcc.com
Contact: J. Thomas Noojin, President
Preferred Investment Size: $1,000,000 to $7,000,000. **Investment Types:** First stage, later stage, balanced, and leverage buyout. **Industry Preferences:** Communications and media, computer software and services, computer hardware, Internet specific, consumer related, industrial and energy, semiconductors and other electronics, medical and health, other products, and biotechnology. **Geographic Preferences:** Southeast, Midwest, and Texas.

56911 ■ Jefferson Capital Fund, Ltd.
PO Box 13129
Birmingham, AL 35213

Preferred Investment Size: $1,000,000 minimum. **Investment Types:** Leveraged buyout, special situation and control-block purchases. **Industry Preferences:** Communications and media, semiconductors and other electronics, medical and health, consumer related, industrial and energy, and manufacturing. **Geographic Preferences:** Northeast, Southeast, and Mid Atlantic.

56912 ■ Private Capital Corp.
100 Brookwood Pl., 4th Fl.
Birmingham, AL 35209
Ph:(205)879-2722
Fax: (205)879-5121
Contact: William Acker, Vice President
Preferred Investment Size: $500,000 to $1,000,000. **Investment Types:** Start-up, first and second stage, mezzanine, leveraged buyout, and special situation. **Industry Preferences:** Communications and media, computer software and hardware, Internet specific, semiconductors and other electronics, medical and health, consumer related, industrial and energy, financial services, and manufacturing. **Geographic Preferences:** Southeast.

56913 ■ SBCA / A.G. Bartholomew & Associates
PO Box 231074
Montgomery, AL 36123-1074
Ph:(334)284-3640
Preferred Investment Size: $2,000,000 minimum. **Investment Types:** Start-up, first and second stage, leveraged buyout, and special situation. **Industry Preferences:** Communications and media, computer software and hardware, semiconductors and other electronics, medical and health, consumer related, industrial and energy, transportation, financial and business services, and manufacturing. **Geographic Preferences:** Southeast U.S.

56914 ■ Southeastern Technology Fund
207 East Side Sq.
Huntsville, AL 35801
Ph:(256)883-8711
Fax: (256)883-8558
URL: http://www.selfund.com
Contact: Chris Horgen, Managing Partner
Preferred Investment Size: $500,000 to $5,000,000. **Investment Types:** Early, first and second stage, and expansion. **Industry Preferences:** Communications and media, Internet specific, computer software and services. **Geographic Preferences:** Southeast.

PROCUREMENT ASSISTANCE PROGRAMS

56915 ■ Alabama Department of Finance–Division of Purchasing
100 N Union St., Ste 192
Montgomery, AL 36130-3620
Ph:(334)242-7250
Fax: (334)242-4419
URL: http://www.purchasing.state.al.us
Contact: Isaac Kervin, Purchasing Dir
Description: Contact for the state's list of bidders for government purchasing contracts. A small business representative is available.

56916 ■ Alabama Procurement Center Representatives
Bldg. 5303, Rm. 3135 US SBA
Redstone Arsenal, AL 35898-5150
Ph:(256)842-6240
Fax: (256)842-0091
Co. E-mail: gary.heard@sba.gov
URL: http://www.sba.gov
Contact: Gary Heard, Prgm Rep
E-mail: gary.heard@sba.gov
Description: Covers activities for Army Aviation & Missile Command (Huntsville, AL).

56917 ■ Alabama Small Business Development Consortium
2800 Milan Ct., Ste. 124
Birmingham, AL 35211-6908

Ph:(205)943-6750
Fax: (205)943-6752
URL: http://www.asbdc.org
Contact: Bill Campbell, Dir
Description: Notifies businesses of bidding opportunities. Offers counseling in areas such as bid package preparation, minority programs, military packaging, pricing, bonding, and quality assurance. Holds training seminars and procurement conferences.

INCUBATORS/RESEARCH AND TECHNOLOGY PARKS

56918 ■ Auburn University–Economic Development Institute
3354 Haley Ctr.
Auburn University, AL 36849-5252
Ph:(334)844-4704
Fax: (334)844-4709
Co. E-mail: sumneja@auburn.edu
URL: http://www.auburn.edu/outreach/edi
Contact: Joe A. Sumners PhD, Dir.
E-mail: sumneja@auburn.edu
Scope: Facilitates technology transfer activities through interdisciplinary technology assistance teams and projects. Conducts industrial research and development activities. Serves as a resource for generating projects that link education and economic development by supporting faculty and graduate research opportunities. Assists in implementation of community economic development plans, and in contract and grant development. Also provides assistance to faculty, graduate students, professionals, business and industry, and local and state governments in proposal and project development. **Services:** Technical assistance for entrepreneurs. **Publications:** Annual report.

56919 ■ Auburn University–Office of Vice President for Research
202 Samford Hall
Auburn University, AL 36849
Ph:(334)844-4784
Fax: (334)844-5971
Co. E-mail: moriacm@auburn.edu
URL: http://www.auburn.edu/research/vpr
Contact: Dr. C. Michael Moriarty, VP for Res.
E-mail: moriacm@auburn.edu
Scope: Administers and coordinates all research conducted at the University, including research in biological, physical, and social sciences, the arts, humanities, engineering, space, and related areas. **Publications:** Annual Research Report.

56920 ■ Cummings Research Park
Chamber of Commerce of Huntsville/Madison
    County
225 Church St.
Huntsville, AL 35801
Ph:(256)535-2000
Fax: (256)535-2015
Co. E-mail: bhilson@hsvchamber.org
URL: http://www.HuntsvilleAlabamaUSA.com
Contact: Brian Hilson, Pres./CEO
E-mail: bhilson@hsvchamber.org
Scope: Aerospace, missile defense research and development, electronics, telecommunications, applied optics, artificial intelligence, software development, and data communications. **Publications:** Initiatives (monthly).

56921 ■ The Entrepreneurial Center
110 12th St. N
Birmingham, AL 35203
Ph:(205)250-8000
Fax: (205)250-8013
Co. E-mail: ecinfo@entrepreneurialctr.com
URL: http://www.entrepreneurialctr.com
Contact: William Goodrich, Chairman
Description: Entrepreneurial center offering its tenants business plan guidance, business breaks seminars, networking opportunities, and mentoring from BBAN staff and board of directors. Formerly, Birmingham Business Assistance Network (BBAN).

56922 ■ Montgomery Area Center for Economic - Small Business Incubator
600 S Court St.
Montgomery, AL 36101
Ph:(334)837-4790
Fax: (334)240-6869
Co. E-mail: info@montgomeryincubator.org
URL: http://www.montgomeryincubator.org/
Description: A non-profit small business incubator program for new service and light manufacturing businesses in the Montgomery area.

56923 ■ Northeast Alabama Entrepreneurial System
1400 Commerce Blvd., Ste. 1
Anniston, AL 36207
Ph:(256)831-5215
Fax: (256)831-8728
Co. E-mail: giles@neaes.org
URL: http://www.neaes.org
Contact: Greg Brown, Chairman

56924 ■ Tuskegee University–Center for Biomedical Research - RCMI Carver Research Foundation
Old Montgomery Rd., Rm. 6
Tuskegee, AL 36088
Ph:(334)727-8287
Fax: (334)727-2069
Co. E-mail: wsapp@tuskegee.edu
Contact: Dr. Walter J. Sapp, Prog.Dir.
E-mail: wsapp@tuskegee.edu
Scope: Administers, conducts, and coordinates extramurally supported research in agricultural, behavioral, and natural science areas. **Services:** Technical assistance, through the Cooperative Extension Service and the Center for Continuing Education. **Publications:** Annual Report; Newsletter.

56925 ■ University of Alabama–Office for Sponsored Programs
PO Box 870104
Tuscaloosa, AL 35487-0104
Ph:(205)348-5152
Fax: (205)348-8882
Co. E-mail: chopejones@fu.ua.edu
URL: http://www.osp.ua.edu/
Contact: Cindy Hope Jones, Dir.
E-mail: chopejones@fu.ua.edu
Scope: Coordinates contract and grant-sponsored research and development activities on campus of the University located in Tuscaloosa in engineering, mathematics, physics, chemistry, biology, sociology, psychology, business, highway engineering, computer science, geology, nutrition, child development, nursing, communications, law, community health, mining, energy, natural resources, social work, music, public administration, and archeology.

56926 ■ University of Alabama–Research Advisory Committee
Rose Administration Bldg., Rm. 152, Box 870104
Office for Sponsored Programs
Tuscaloosa, AL 35487-0104
Ph:(205)348-5152
Fax: (205)348-8882
Co. E-mail: dbackman@aalan.ua.edu
Contact: Douglas B. Backman, Dir.
E-mail: dbackman@aalan.ua.edu
Scope: Provides grants for individual research of any full-time, permanent faculty or staff member.

56927 ■ University of Alabama at Birmingham–Office of Grants and Contracts Administration
AB 1170
1530 3rd Ave. S
Birmingham, AL 35294-0111
Ph:(205)934-5266
Fax: (205)975-5977
Co. E-mail: ccchrist@uab.edu
URL: http://www.uab.edu/uabra/ogca/ogca.htm
Contact: Cynthia Christian, Actg.Dir.
E-mail: ccchrist@uab.edu
Scope: Administers and coordinates extramurally sponsored research conducted in all units of the University located in Birmingham.

LEGISLATIVE ASSISTANCE

56928 ■ Alabama State House of Representatives–Bill Status Office
Alabama State House, Rm. 512
11 S. Union St. 5th Fl.
Montgomery, AL 36130
Ph:(334)242-7627
Free: 800-499-3051
Fax: (334)353-9040
Co. E-mail: alsenate@mindspring.com
URL: http://www.legislature.state.al.us
Contact: Jennifer Dabbou, Bill Status Clerk

56929 ■ Alabama State House of Representatives–House Commerce Committee
Alabama State House, Rm. 522-B
11 S. Union St., Rm. 522-B
c/o Frank McDaniel
Montgomery, AL 36130
Ph:(334)242-7697
Fax: (334)353-0828
Co. E-mail: house3@mindspring.com
URL: http://www.legislature.state.al.us
Contact: Frank McDaniel, Chair

PUBLICATIONS

56930 ■ *Atlanta Business Chronicle*
1801 Peachtree St., Ste. 150
Atlanta, GA 30309
Ph:(404)249-1000
Fax: (404)249-1048
Co. E-mail: atlanta@amcity.com
URL: http://www.amcity.com/atlanta

56931 ■ *Business Alabama Monthly*
P.O. Box 66200
Mobile, AL 36660
Ph:(205)473-6269
Fax: (205)479-8822

56932 ■ *Business First: Newspaper of Birmingham*
2100 Riverchase Center, Ste. 110
Birmingham, AL 35244
Ph:(205)979-0004

56933 ■ *Starting and Operating a Business in Alabama: A Step-by-Step Guide*
PSI Research
300 N. Valley Dr.
Grants Pass, OR 97526
Ph:(503)479-9464
Free: 800-228-2275
Fax: (503)476-1479
Co. E-mail: psi2@magick.net
Ed: Michael D. Jenkins. **Released:** Revised edition, 1992. **Price:** $29.95 (looseleaf binder); $24.95 (paper). **Description:** Part of the Successful Business Library series.

PUBLISHERS

56934 ■ Modern Press
964 Martinwood Rd.
Birmingham, AL 35235
Ph:(205)833-7923
Contact: Donald F. Cashman, President
Description: Publishes reports dealing with small home-based business ventures including import/export and other aspects of foreign trade. Reaches market through direct mail. **Founded:** 1980.

56935 ■ Penn & Pearl Publishers L.L.C.
PO Box 148
Logan, AL 35098-0148
Free: 877-403-0991
Fax: (801)697-4955
Co. E-mail: editor@pennpearl.com
URL: http://www.pennpearl.com

Description: Publishes business, professional and general interest books.

SMALL BUSINESS DEVELOPMENT CENTER LEAD OFFICE

56936 ■ Alaska SBDC–University of Alaska - Anchorage
430 W. 7th Ave., Ste. 110
Anchorage, AK 99501
Ph:(907)274-7232
Fax: (907)274-9524
URL: http://www.aksbdc.org
Contact: Jean R. Wall, State Dir.
E-mail: anjaf@uaa.sbdc.alaska.edu

56937 ■ University of Alaska (Anchorage)–Small Business Development Center
430 W. 7th Ave., Ste. 110
Anchorage, AK 99501-3550
Ph:(907)274-7232
Free: 800-478-7232
Fax: (907)274-9524
Co. E-mail: anjaf@uaa.alaska.edu
Contact: Jan Fredericks, Director

SMALL BUSINESS DEVELOPMENT CENTERS

56938 ■ Juneau SBDC–University of Alaska at Anchorage
3100 Channel Dr., Ste. 306
Juneau, AK 99801
Ph:(907)463-3789
Fax: (907)463-3489
URL: http://www.aksbdc.org
Contact: Jackie Stewart, Dir.
E-mail: anjas3@uaa.alaska.edu

56939 ■ Kenai Peninsula Small Business Development Center
43335 Kalifornsky Beach Rd., Ste. 12
43335 Kalifornsky Beach Rd., Ste. 16
Soldotna, AK 99669
Ph:(907)260-5629
Fax: (907)260-1695
URL: http://www.aksbdc.org
Contact: Mark Gregory, Dir.
E-mail: inmeg@uaa.alaska.edu

56940 ■ Mat-su–Small Business Development Center
201 N. Lucille St., Ste. 2-A
Wasilla, AK 99654
Ph:(907)373-7232
Fax: (907)373-7234
URL: http://www.aksbdc.org/
Contact: Timothy Sullivan, Dir.
E-mail: antjs@uaa.alaska.edu

56941 ■ University of Alaska (Fairbanks)–Small Business Development Center
613 Cushman St., Ste. 209
Fairbanks, AK 99701-4655
Ph:(907)456-7232
Fax: (907)456-7233
Co. E-mail: fnjm1@uaf.edu
URL: http://www.aksbdc.org
Contact: James McDermott, Dir.

SMALL BUSINESS ASSISTANCE PROGRAMS

56942 ■ Alaska Department of Commerce, Community, and Economic Development
PO Box 110800
Juneau, AK 99811-0809
Ph:(907)465-2500
Fax: (907)465-3767
Co. E-mail: gonorth@dced.state.ak.us
URL: http://www.commerce.state.ak.us
Description: Assists entrepreneurs in starting new businesses or expanding existing businesses. Helps prepare applications for economic development programs. Holds seminars and workshops on various aspects of business management.

SCORE OFFICES

56943 ■ SCORE Anchorage
c/o Ed Ratliff, Chm.
510 L St., Ste. 310
Anchorage, AK 99501-1952
Ph:(907)271-4022
Free: 800-755-7034
Fax: (907)271-4545
Co. E-mail: score@akscore.org
URL: http://www.akscore.org
Contact: Ed Ratliff, Chm.
Description: Provides professional guidance and information to maximize the success of existing and emerging small businesses. Offers business counseling and workshops.

BETTER BUSINESS BUREAUS

56944 ■ Better Business Bureau of Alaska
3601 C St., Ste. 1378
Anchorage, AK 99503
Ph:(907)562-0704
Free: 888-244-0704
Fax: (907)562-4061
Co. E-mail: info@thebbb.org
URL: http://www.alaska.bbb.org
Contact: Robert W.G. Andrew, Pres./CEO

CHAMBERS OF COMMERCE

56945 ■ Alaska State Chamber of Commerce
217 2nd St., Ste. 201
Juneau, AK 99801-1267
Ph:(907)586-2323
Fax: (907)463-5515
Co. E-mail: info@alaskachamber.com
URL: http://www.alaskachamber.com
Contact: Wayne A. Stevens, Pres.

56946 ■ Anchor Point Chamber of Commerce
PO Box 610
Anchor Point, AK 99556-0610
Ph:(907)235-2600
Fax: (907)235-2600
Co. E-mail: info@anchorpointchamber.org
URL: http://www.anchorpointalaska.info
Contact: Joanne Collins, Exec.Sec.

56947 ■ Anchorage Chamber of Commerce
441 W 5th Ave., Ste. 300
Anchorage, AK 99501-2309
Ph:(907)272-2401
Fax: (907)272-4117
Co. E-mail: info@anchoragechamber.org
URL: http://www.anchoragechamber.org
Contact: Stacy Schubert, Pres.

56948 ■ Bethel Chamber of Commerce
PO Box 329
Bethel, AK 99559
Ph:(907)543-2911
Fax: (907)543-2255
Co. E-mail: bethelchamber1@alaska.org
Contact: Bonnie Bradbury

56949 ■ Big Lake Chamber of Commerce
PO Box 520067
Big Lake, AK 99652
Ph:(907)892-6109
Fax: (907)892-6189
Co. E-mail: biglake@mtaonline.net
URL: http://www.biglake-ak.com
Contact: Randi Perlman, Pres.

56950 ■ Chugiak-Eagle River Chamber of Commerce
11401 Old Glenn Hwy., Ste. 105
PO Box 770353
Eagle River, AK 99577-0353
Ph:(907)694-4702
Fax: (907)694-1205
Co. E-mail: info@cer.com
URL: http://www.cer.org
Contact: Susan Gorski, Exec.Dir.

56951 ■ City of Barrow Chamber of Commerce
PO Box 629
Barrow, AK 99723
Ph:(907)852-5211
Fax: (907)852-5871

Co. E-mail: webmaster@cityofbarrow.org
URL: http://www.cityofbarrow.org
Contact: Nathaniel Olemaun Jr., Mayor

56952 ■ Cordova Chamber of Commerce
PO Box 99
Cordova, AK 99574
Ph:(907)424-7260
Fax: (907)424-7259
Co. E-mail: cchamber@ctcak.net
URL: http://www.cordovachamber.com
Contact: J.R. Lewis, Pres.

56953 ■ Delta Chamber of Commerce
PO Box 987
Delta Junction, AK 99737-0987
Ph:(907)895-5068
Free: 877-895-5068
Fax: (907)895-5141
Co. E-mail: deltacc@deltachamber.org
URL: http://www.deltachamber.org
Contact: Brenda Peterson, Exec.Dir.

56954 ■ Dillingham Chamber of Commerce
PO Box 348
Dillingham, AK 99576
Ph:(907)842-5115
Fax: (907)842-4097
Co. E-mail: info@dillinghamak.com
URL: http://www.dillinghamak.com/
Contact: Cheryl A. Hinkes, Pres.

56955 ■ Funny River Chamber of Commerce
35850 Pioneer Rd.
Soldotna, AK 99669
Ph:(907)262-0879
Contact: Warren Hoflich, Pres.

56956 ■ Greater Copper Valley Chamber of Commerce
PO Box 469
Glennallen, AK 99588-0469
Ph:(907)822-5558
Fax: (907)822-5555
Co. E-mail: info@traveltoalaska.com
URL: http://www.traveltoalaska.com
Contact: Liz Rice, Exec.Dir.

56957 ■ Greater Fairbanks Chamber of Commerce
800 Cushman St., Ste. 114
Fairbanks, AK 99701
Ph:(907)452-1105
Fax: (907)456-6968
Co. E-mail: lanien.livingston@fairbankschamber.org
URL: http://www.fairbankschamber.org
Contact: Lanien Livingston, Pres./CEO

56958 ■ Greater Healy-Denali Chamber of Commerce
PO Box 437
Healy, AK 99743-0437
Ph:(907)683-4636
Co. E-mail: postmaster@denalichamber.com
URL: http://www.denalichamber.com

56959 ■ Greater Ketchikan Chamber of Commerce
PO Box 5957
Ketchikan, AK 99901
Ph:(907)225-3184
Fax: (907)225-3187
Co. E-mail: info@ketchikanchamber.com
URL: http://www.ketchikanchamber.com
Contact: Danielle Miller, Exec.Dir.

56960 ■ Greater Palmer Chamber of Commerce
PO Box 45
Palmer, AK 99645
Ph:(907)745-2880
Fax: (907)746-4164
Co. E-mail: info@palmerchamber.org
URL: http://www.palmerchamber.org
Contact: Dusty Silva, Pres.

56961 ■ Greater Sitka Chamber of Commerce
PO Box 638
Sitka, AK 99835
Ph:(907)747-8604
Fax: (907)747-7613
Co. E-mail: chamber@ptialaska.net
URL: http://www.sitkacoc.com
Contact: Lawrence Blood, Exec. Dir.

56962 ■ Greater Soldotna Chamber of Commerce
44790 Sterling Hwy.
Soldotna, AK 99669
Ph:(907)262-9814
Fax: (907)262-3566
Co. E-mail: director@soldotnachamber.com
URL: http://www.soldotnachamber.com
Contact: Evy Gebhardt, Pres.

56963 ■ Greater Wasilla Chamber of Commerce
415 E Railroad Ave.
Wasilla, AK 99654
Ph:(907)376-1299
Fax: (907)373-2560
Co. E-mail: info@wasillachamber.org
URL: http://www.wasillachamber.org
Contact: Chas St. George, Pres.

56964 ■ Haines Chamber of Commerce
PO Box 1449
Haines, AK 99827-1449
Ph:(907)766-2202
Fax: (907)766-2271
Co. E-mail: chamber@haineschamber.org
URL: http://www.haineschamber.org
Contact: Joan Carlson, Office Mgr.

56965 ■ Homer Chamber of Commerce
PO Box 541
Homer, AK 99603
Ph:(907)235-7740
Fax: (907)235-8766
Co. E-mail: info@homeralaska.org
URL: http://www.homeralaska.org
Contact: Derotha Ferraro, Exec.Dir.

56966 ■ Juneau Chamber of Commerce
3100 Channel Dr., Ste. 300
Juneau, AK 99801
Ph:(907)463-3488
Fax: (907)463-3489
Co. E-mail: jcc@alaska.com
URL: http://www.juneauchamber.com
Contact: Chris Wyatt, Exec.Dir.

56967 ■ Kenai Chamber of Commerce
402 Overland St.
Kenai, AK 99611
Ph:(907)283-7989
Fax: (907)283-7183
Co. E-mail: info@kenaichamber.org
URL: http://www.kenaichamber.org
Contact: Roy Wells, Pres.

56968 ■ Kodiak Area Chamber of Commerce
100 E Marine Way, Ste. 300
Kodiak, AK 99615-1485
Ph:(907)486-5557
Fax: (907)486-7605
Co. E-mail: chamber@kodiak.org
URL: http://www.kodiak.org
Contact: Norman D. Wooten, Exec.Dir.

56969 ■ Nenana Chamber of Commerce
PO Box 00070
Nenana, AK 99760
Ph:(907)832-5442
Co. E-mail: milesofalaska@hotmail.com
URL: http://www.auriuswebdesign.com/sites/
    nenanachamber
Contact: Mr. Miles Martin, Sec.

56970 ■ Nome Chamber of Commerce
PO Box 250
Nome, AK 99762
Ph:(907)443-3879

Fax: (907)443-3892
Co. E-mail: nomechamber@gci.net
URL: http://www.nomechamber.org
Contact: Mitch Erickson, Exec.Dir.

56971 ■ Petersburg Chamber of Commerce
PO Box 649
Petersburg, AK 99833
Ph:(907)772-3646
Fax: (907)772-2453
Co. E-mail: chamber@petersburg.org
URL: http://www.petersburg.org
Contact: Karen Ellingstad, Mgr.

56972 ■ Prince of Wales Chamber of Commerce
PO Box 490
Klawock, AK 99925-0490
Ph:(907)755-2526
Fax: (907)755-2627
Co. E-mail: info@princeofwalescoc.org
URL: http://www.princeofwalescoc.org
Contact: Stu Vincent, Pres.

56973 ■ Seldovia Chamber of Commerce
PO Drawer F
Seldovia, AK 99663
Ph:(907)234-7803
Fax: (907)234-7612
Co. E-mail: maryg@seldovia.com
URL: http://www.xyz.net/~seldovia
Contact: Mary Glover, Pres.

56974 ■ Seward Chamber of Commerce
PO Box 749
Seward, AK 99664-0749
Ph:(907)224-8051
Fax: (907)224-5353
Co. E-mail: director@seward.net
URL: http://www.sewardak.org
Contact: Richard Blythe, Pres.

56975 ■ Skagway Chamber of Commerce
PO Box 194
Skagway, AK 99840-0194
Ph:(907)983-1898
Fax: (907)983-2031
Co. E-mail: chamber@aptalaska.net
URL: http://www.skagwaychamber.org
Contact: Sylvia Fields, Office Admin.

56976 ■ Talkeetna Chamber of Commerce
PO Box 334
Talkeetna, AK 99676-0334
Ph:(907)733-2330
Fax: (907)733-4578
Co. E-mail: info@talkeetnachamber.org
URL: http://www.talkeetnachamber.org
Contact: Alice Bergdoll, Sec.

56977 ■ Tok Chamber of Commerce
PO Box 389
Tok, AK 99780-0389
Ph:(907)883-5775
Co. E-mail: info@tokalaskainfo.com
URL: http://www.tokalaskainfo.com
Contact: Bonnie Jenkins, Mgr.

56978 ■ Willow Chamber of Commerce
PO Box 183
Willow, AK 99688
Ph:(907)495-6800
Fax: (907)495-6800
Co. E-mail: mail@willowchamber.org
URL: http://www.willowchamber.org
Contact: Mr. Barry Stanley, VP

56979 ■ Wrangell Chamber of Commerce
PO Box 49
Wrangell, AK 99929
Ph:(907)874-3901
Free: 800-367-9745
Fax: (907)874-3905
Co. E-mail: wchamber@gci.net
URL: http://www.wrangellchamber.org
Contact: Jim Leslie, Pres.

MINORITY BUSINESS ASSISTANCE PROGRAMS

56980 ■ Alaska Minority Business Development Center–Tanana Chief Conference, Inc.
122 First Ave., Ste. 600
Fairbanks, AK 99701
Ph:(907)452-8251
Fax: (907)459-3851
Co. E-mail: info@tananachiefs.org
URL: http://www.tananachiefs.org

PROCUREMENT ASSISTANCE PROGRAMS

56981 ■ University of Alaska Anchorage–Small Business Development Center
430 W 7th Ave., Ste. 110
Anchorage, AK 99501
Ph:(907)274-7232
Fax: (907)274-9524
Co. E-mail: anmec2@uaa.alaska.edu
URL: http://www.aksbdc.org
Contact: Jean Wall, Dir

56982 ■ University of Alaska (Fairbanks)–Procurement Technical Assistance Center Program
613 Cushman St., Ste. 209
Fairbanks, AK 99701
Ph:(907)456-7232
Fax: (907)456-7233
Co. E-mail: fnmaw@uaf.edu

URL: http://www.ptacalaska.org

INCUBATORS/RESEARCH AND TECHNOLOGY PARKS

56983 ■ University of Alaska Fairbanks–Office of Sponsored Programs
212 W Ridge Research Bldg.
PO Box 757270
Fairbanks, AK 99775-7270
Ph:(907)474-6000
Fax: (907)474-5444
Co. E-mail: fnamg@uaf.edu
URL: http://www.uaf.edu/osp
Contact: Dr. Andrew Parkerson-Gray, Dir.
E-mail: fnamg@uaf.edu
Scope: Responsible for coordination of research programs of the University involving geophysics, marine science, water resources, energy resources, agriculture, biology, social and economic concerns, education, environmental data, anthropology, archeology, fisheries, wildlife, forests, and minerals, emphasizing Northern, cold, and arctic regions. Approves all proposals for grants, locates funding sources, and maintains contact with federal and state agencies and private foundations interested in research. Administers special research projects not allocated to research institutes, centers, or laboratories; supervises support services, including aircraft, ships, land vehicles, and a rocket-launching facility; and operates numerous observational field sites in Alaska, its adjacent territories, and overseas. **Services:** Extension services, in agriculture, fisheries, mining, and small business development. **Educational Activities:** National and international symposia; Seminars, organized through research of the University.

EDUCATIONAL PROGRAMS

56984 ■ Matanuska-Susitna College
PO Box 2889
Palmer, AK 99645
Ph:(907)745-9774
Fax: (907)745-9711
Co. E-mail: info@matsu.alaska.edu
URL: http://www.matsu.alaska.edu
Description: Two-year college offering a program in small business management.

PUBLICATIONS

56985 ■ *Alaska Business Monthly*
P.O. Box 241288
Anchorage, AK 99524-1288
Ph:(907)276-4373
Fax: (907)279-2900
Co. E-mail: info@akbizmag.com
URL: http://www.akbizmag.com

56986 ■ *Starting and Operating a Business in Alaska: A Step-by-Step Guide*
PSI Research
300 N. Valley Dr.
Grants Pass, OR 97526
Ph:(503)479-9464
Free: 800-228-2275
Fax: (503)476-1479
Co. E-mail: psi2@magick.net
Ed: Michael D. Jenkins. **Released:** Revised edition, 1992. **Price:** $29.95 (looseleaf binder); $24.95 (paper). **Description:** Part of the Successful Business Library series.

SMALL BUSINESS DEVELOPMENT CENTER LEAD OFFICE

56987 ■ Arizona Small Business Development Center Network–Maricopa County Community College–SBDC (2411)
2411 W 14th St., Ste. 132
Tempe, AZ 85281
Ph:(480)731-8722
Fax: (480)731-8729
URL: http://www.dist.maricopa.edu/sbdc
Contact: Michael York, State Director
E-mail: mike.york@domail.maricopa.edu

56988 ■ Arizona Small Business Development Center Network–Maricopa County Community Colleges
2411 W. 14th St., Ste. 132
Tempe, AZ 85281
Ph:(480)731-8720
Fax: (489)731-8729
URL: http://www.dist.maricopa.edu.sbdc
Contact: Michael York, State Dir.
E-mail: mike.york@domail.maricopa.edu

56989 ■ Maricopa County Community College–Arizona Small Business Development Center–Lead Center (2411)
2411 W. 14th St., Ste. 114
Tempe, AZ 85281-6941
Ph:(480)784-0590
Fax: (480)230-7989
URL: http://www.dist.maricopa.edu.sbdc
Contact: Rich Senopole, Actg. State Dir.
E-mail: rich.senopole@domail.maricopa.edu

SMALL BUSINESS DEVELOPMENT CENTERS

56990 ■ Arizona Western College–Small Business Development Center
1351 S. Redondo Ctr. Dr., Ste. 101
Yuma, AZ 85365
Ph:(928)317-6151
Fax: (928)317-6154
Co. E-mail: randy.nelson@azwestern.edu
URL: http://sbdc.azwestern.edu/
Contact: Randy Nelson, Dir.
E-mail: randy.nelson@azwestern.edu

56991 ■ Central Arizona College–Pinal County Small Business Development Center
8470 N. Overfield Rd.
Coolidge, AZ 85228
Ph:(520)494-5444
Free: 800-237-9814
Fax: (520)494-5141
Co. E-mail: sbdc@centralaz.edu
Contact: Bennett Curry, Dir.

56992 ■ Cochise College–Small Business Development Center
901 N. Colombo, Rm. 308
Sierra Vista, AZ 85635
Ph:(520)515-5478
Free: 800-966-7943
Fax: (520)515-5437
URL: http://www.cochise.edu/conteducation/sbdc/
Contact: Mignonne Hollis, Dir.
E-mail: hollism@cochise.edu

56993 ■ Coconino County Community College–Small Business Development Center
3000 N. 4th St.
Flagstaff, AZ 86004
Ph:(928)526-5653
Free: 800-350-7122
Fax: (928)526-8693
Co. E-mail: sbdc@coconino.edu
URL: http://www.coconino.edu/sbdc/
Contact: Rick Leibowitz, Dir.
E-mail: rick.leibowitz@cocnino.edu

56994 ■ Eastern Arizona College–Small Business Development Center
615 N. Stadium Ave.
Thatcher, AZ 85552-0769
Ph:(928)428-8590
Free: 888-322-5780
Fax: (928)428-8591
Co. E-mail: sbdc@eac.eu
URL: http://www.eac.edu/sbdc/
Contact: Michael Fox, Dir.

56995 ■ Mohave Community College–Small Business Development Center
1971 Jagerson Ave.
Kingman, AZ 86401
Ph:(928)757-0894
Fax: (928)692-3087
URL: http://www.mohave.edu/
Contact: Kelley Marsh, Dir.

56996 ■ Northland Pioneer College–Small Business Development Center
1001 W. Deuce of Clubs
PO Box 610
Holbrook, AZ 86025
Ph:(928)532-6170
Free: 800-266-7232
Fax: (928)532-6171
Co. E-mail: npcsbdc@cybertrails.com
Contact: Jessica Covey, Dir.
E-mail: sbdcjess@yahoo.com

56997 ■ Pima Community College–Small Business Training and Development Center
4905 E. Broadway Blvd.
Tucson, AZ 85709-1010
Ph:(520)206-4500
Free: 800-860-PIMA
Co. E-mail: infocenter@pima.edu
URL: http://www.pima.edu/business/training-dev/
Contact: Joe Donato, Dir.
E-mail: jdonato@pimcc.pima.edu

56998 ■ Yavapai College–Small Business Development Center
Building 30
1100 E. Sheldon St.
Prescott, AZ 86301
Ph:(928)776-2008
Free: 800-922-6787
Fax: (928)771-4815
URL: http://www.2.yc.edu/content/sbdc/
Contact: Rick Marcum, Dir.

SMALL BUSINESS ASSISTANCE PROGRAMS

56999 ■ Arizona Department of Commerce
1700 W Washington, Ste. 600
Phoenix, AZ 85007
Ph:(602)280-1300
Fax: (602)771-1202
URL: http://www.azcommerce.com
Description: Offers assistance to businesses in various stages of growth; helps businesses establishing operations in Arizona; packages expansion financing for established companies; and helps with export financing.

SCORE OFFICES

57000 ■ SCORE East Valley
1201 S Alma School Rd., Ste. 4800
Mesa, AZ 85210
Ph:(480)833-9020
Fax: (480)833-6009
Co. E-mail: info@scoreaz.org
URL: http://www.scoreaz.org
Description: Provides professional guidance and information to maximize the success of existing and emerging small businesses. Offers business counseling and workshops.

57001 ■ SCORE Lake Havasu
Bank of America Bldg.
10 Acoma Blvd.
Lake Havasu City, AZ 86405
Ph:(928)453-5951
Fax: (928)453-5951
Co. E-mail: havasu@scoreaz.org
URL: http://scoreaz.org
Description: Provides professional guidance and information to maximize the success of existing and emerging small businesses. Offers business counseling and workshops.

57002 ■ SCORE Northern Arizona
1228 Willow Creek Rd., Ste. 2
Prescott, AZ 86301
Ph:(928)778-7438
Free: 800-410-2260
Fax: (928)778-4129
Co. E-mail: score@northlink.com
URL: http://scoreaz.org

Description: Provides professional guidance and information to maximize the success of existing and emerging small businesses. Offers business counseling and workshops.

57003 ■ SCORE Phoenix
2828 N Central Ave., No. 800
Central & One Thomas
Phoenix, AZ 85004
Ph:(602)745-7250
Fax: (602)745-7210
Co. E-mail: info@scorephoenix.org
URL: http://www.scorephoenix.org
Description: Provides expertise to help Phoenix area entrepreneurs prepare business plans, complete loan applications, protect their intellectual property, develop marketing strategies and gather valuable information about doing business.

57004 ■ SCORE Tucson
10 E Broadway, Ste. 208
Tucson, AZ 85701
Ph:(520)670-5008
Fax: (520)670-5011
Co. E-mail: score@dakotacom.net
URL: http://www.scoreaz.org
Contact: Mr. Bill Roach, Chm.
Description: Counselors to America's small business. Provides business advice, business planning assistance, business counseling and training.

BETTER BUSINESS BUREAUS

57005 ■ Better Business Bureau, Central/Northern Arizona
4428 N 12th St.
Phoenix, AZ 85014-4585
Ph:(602)264-1721
Free: 877-291-6222
Fax: (602)263-0997
Co. E-mail: info@arizonabbb.org
URL: http://www.phoenix.bbb.org
Contact: Matthew Fehling, Pres./CEO

57006 ■ Better Business Bureau of Tucson
434 S Williams Blvd., Ste. 102
Tucson, AZ 85711
Ph:(520)888-5353
Fax: (520)888-6262
Co. E-mail: info@tucson.bbb.org
URL: http://www.tucson.bbb.org
Contact: Tom Collier, Pres.

CHAMBERS OF COMMERCE

57007 ■ Ahwatukee Foothills Chamber of Commerce
10235 S 51st St., No. 185
Phoenix, AZ 85044
Ph:(480)753-7676
Fax: (480)753-3898
Co. E-mail: info@ahwatukeechamber.com
URL: http://www.ahwatukeechamber.com
Contact: John McComish, Exec.Dir.

57008 ■ Ajo District Chamber of Commerce
400 Taladro St.
Ajo, AZ 85321
Ph:(520)387-7742
Fax: (520)387-3641
Co. E-mail: ajocofc@tabletoptelephone.com
URL: http://www.ajochamber.com
Contact: Silvia Howard, Exec.Dir.

57009 ■ Alpine Chamber of Commerce
PO Box 410
Alpine, AZ 85920
Ph:(928)339-4330
Fax: (928)339-1887
Co. E-mail: chamber@alpinearizona.com
URL: http://www.alpinearizona.com

Contact: Mary Phelan, Pres.

57010 ■ Apache Junction Chamber of Commerce
PO Box 1747
Apache Junction, AZ 85217-1747
Ph:(480)982-3141
Free: 800-252-3141
Fax: (480)982-3234
Co. E-mail: ajchamber@qwest.net
URL: http://www.apachejunctioncoc.com
Contact: Rayna Palmer, Pres./CEO

57011 ■ Arizona Chamber of Commerce
1221 E Osborn Rd., Ste. 100
Phoenix, AZ 85014
Ph:(602)248-9172
Free: 800-498-6973
Fax: (602)265-1262
Co. E-mail: japperson@azchamber.com
URL: http://www.azchamber.com
Contact: James J. Apperson, Pres./CEO

57012 ■ Arizona City Chamber of Commerce
PO Box 5
Arizona City, AZ 85223-0005
Ph:(520)466-5141
Fax: (520)466-8204
Co. E-mail: azchamber@cgmailbox.com
URL: http://www.azcchamber.com

57013 ■ Arizona Hispanic Chamber of Commerce
255 E Osborne Rd., Ste. 201
Phoenix, AZ 85012
Ph:(602)279-1800
Fax: (602)279-8900
Co. E-mail: info@azhcc.com
URL: http://www.azhcc.com
Contact: Harry Garewal, Pres./CEO

57014 ■ Asian Chamber of Commerce
1219 E Glendale Ave., No. 25
Phoenix, AZ 85020
Ph:(602)222-2009
Fax: (602)870-7562
Co. E-mail: asiansun@aol.com
URL: http://www.asianchamber.org
Contact: Madeline Ong-Sakata, Exec.Dir./Sec.

57015 ■ Benson - San Pedro Valley Chamber of Commerce
PO Box 2255
249 E 4th
Benson, AZ 85602
Ph:(520)586-2842
Fax: (520)586-1972
Co. E-mail: info@bensonchamberaz.com
URL: http://www.bensonchamberaz.com
Contact: Beverly E. Stepp, Exec.Dir.

57016 ■ Bisbee Chamber of Commerce and Visitor Center
PO Box BA
Bisbee, AZ 85603
Ph:(520)432-5421
Free: (866)224-7233
Fax: (520)432-3308
Co. E-mail: info@bisbeearizona.com
URL: http://www.bisbeearizona.com
Contact: Selly Grant, Dir.

57017 ■ Bouse Chamber of Commerce
PO Box 817
Bouse, AZ 85325
Ph:(928)851-2174
Co. E-mail: bousechamber@redrivernet.com
URL: http://www.bouseazchamber.com
Contact: Clyde Praast, Pres.

57018 ■ Buckeye Valley Chamber of Commerce
508 E Monroe Ave.
Buckeye, AZ 85326
Ph:(623)386-2727
Free: 877-850-2600
Fax: (623)386-7527

Co. E-mail: info@buckeyevalleychamber.org
URL: http://www.buckeyevalleychamber.org
Contact: Deanna Kupcik, Exec.Dir.

57019 ■ Bullhead Area Chamber of Commerce
1251 Hwy. 95
Bullhead City, AZ 86429
Ph:(928)754-4121
Free: 800-987-7457
Fax: (928)754-5514
Co. E-mail: info@bullheadchamber.com
URL: http://www.bullheadchamber.com
Contact: Michael K. Conner, Pres./CEO

57020 ■ Camp Verde Chamber of Commerce
385 S Main St.
Camp Verde, AZ 86322
Ph:(928)567-9294
Fax: (928)567-4793
Co. E-mail: info@campverde.org
URL: http://www.campverde.org
Contact: Roy Gugliotta, Exec.Dir.

57021 ■ Chandler Chamber of Commerce
25 S Arizona Pl., No. 201
Chandler, AZ 85225
Ph:(480)963-4571
Free: 800-963-4571
Fax: (480)963-0188
Co. E-mail: becky@chandlerchamber.com
URL: http://www.chandlerchamber.com
Contact: Becky Jackson, Pres./CEO

57022 ■ Chino Valley Area Chamber of Commerce
PO Box 419
Chino Valley, AZ 86323
Ph:(928)636-2493
Free: 877-523-1988
Fax: (928)636-4112
Co. E-mail: chamber@chinovalley.org
URL: http://www.chinovalley.org
Contact: Karrie Blum, Pres.

57023 ■ Chloride Chamber of Commerce
PO Box 268
Chloride, AZ 86431-0268
Ph:(928)565-2204
Co. E-mail: contact@chloridearizona.com
URL: http://www.chloridearizona.com
Contact: Christine Brown, Sec.

57024 ■ Clarkdale Chamber of Commerce
PO Box 161
Clarkdale, AZ 86324
Ph:(928)634-4296
Co. E-mail: ccc@clarkdalechamber.com
URL: http://www.clarkdalechamber.com
Contact: Katy Canon, Pres.

57025 ■ Coolidge Chamber of Commerce
PO Box 943
Coolidge, AZ 85228
Ph:(520)723-3009
Fax: (520)723-9410
Co. E-mail: coolidgeaz@cybertrails.com
Contact: Kandi Hastings

57026 ■ Copper Basin Chamber of Commerce
PO Box 206
Kearny, AZ 85237
Ph:(520)363-7607
Fax: (520)363-9663
Co. E-mail: cbc@copperbasinaz.com
URL: http://www.copperbasinaz.com
Contact: Myra Fontes Warren, Exec.Dir.

57027 ■ Cottonwood Chamber of Commerce
1010 S Main St.
Junction 89A and 260
Cottonwood, AZ 86326
Ph:(928)634-7593
Fax: (928)634-7594
Co. E-mail: cottonwoodchamber@verdeonline.com
URL: http://cottonwood.verdevalley.com

Contact: Peter A. Sesow, Exec.Dir.

57028 ■ Dolan Springs Chamber of Commerce
PO Box 274
Dolan Springs, AZ 86441
Ph:(928)767-4473
Co. E-mail: webmaster@dsiaz.com
URL: http://www.dolanspringschamber.com
Contact: Norty Turchen, Pres.

57029 ■ Eloy Chamber of Commerce
305 N Stuart Blvd.
Eloy, AZ 85231
Ph:(520)466-3411
Fax: (520)466-4698
Co. E-mail: info@eloychamber.com
URL: http://www.eloychamber.com
Contact: Al Gramando, Pres.

57030 ■ Flagstaff Chamber of Commerce
101 W Rte. 66
Flagstaff, AZ 86001
Ph:(928)774-4505
Fax: (928)779-1209
Co. E-mail: info@flagstaffchamber.com
URL: http://www.flagstaffchamber.com
Contact: Julie Pastrick, Pres./CEO

57031 ■ Fountain Hills Chamber of Commerce
PO Box 17598
Fountain Hills, AZ 85269-7598
Ph:(480)837-1654
Fax: (480)837-3077
Co. E-mail: frank@fountainhillschamber.com
URL: http://www.fountainhillschamber.com
Contact: Frank S. Ferrara, Pres./CEO

57032 ■ Gilbert Chamber of Commerce
PO Box 527
Gilbert, AZ 85299-0527
Ph:(480)892-0056
Fax: (480)892-1980
Co. E-mail: info@gilbertchamber.com
URL: http://www.gilbertaz.com
Contact: Kathy Langdon, Pres./CEO

57033 ■ Glendale Chamber of Commerce
PO Box 249
Glendale, AZ 85311
Ph:(623)937-4754
Free: 800-437-8669
Fax: (623)937-3333
Co. E-mail: info@glendaleazchamber.org
URL: http://www.glendaleazchamber.org
Contact: Don Rinehart, Pres./CEO

57034 ■ Globe-Miami Regional Chamber of Commerce and Economic Development Corporation
1360 N Broad St.
Globe, AZ 85501
Ph:(928)425-4495
Free: 800-804-5623
Fax: (928)425-3410
Co. E-mail: gmr@cableone.net
URL: http://www.globemiamichamber.com
Contact: Mrs. Mary A. Moreno, CEO

57035 ■ Golden Valley Chamber of Commerce
3395 Verde
Golden Valley, AZ 86413
Ph:(928)565-3311
Fax: (928)565-3133
Co. E-mail: goldenvalleychamber@azconnect.com
URL: http://www.goldenvalleychamber.com
Contact: Ms. Chris Crow, Pres.

57036 ■ Graham County Chamber of Commerce
1111 Thatcher Blvd.
Safford, AZ 85546
Ph:(928)428-2511
Free: 888-837-1841
Fax: (928)428-0744

Co. E-mail: info@graham-chamber.com
URL: http://www.graham-chamber.com
Contact: Sheldon Miller, Exec.Dir.

57037 ■ Grand Canyon Chamber of Commerce
PO Box 3007
Grand Canyon, AZ 86023
Ph:(928)638-2901
Co. E-mail: info@grandcanyonchamber.org
URL: http://www.grandcanyonchamber.com

57038 ■ Greater Casa Grande Chamber of Commerce
575 N Marshall St.
Casa Grande, AZ 85222-5246
Ph:(520)836-2125
Free: 800-916-1515
Fax: (520)836-6233
Co. E-mail: chamber@cgmailbox.com
URL: http://www.casagrandechamber.org
Contact: Ms. Helen Neuharth, Pres./CEO

57039 ■ Greater Florence Chamber of Commerce
291 N. Bailey St.
PO Box 929
Florence, AZ 85232-0929
Ph:(520)868-9433
Free: 800-437-9433
Fax: (520)868-5797
Co. E-mail: info@florenceaz.org

57040 ■ Greater Phoenix Black Chamber of Commerce
201 E Washington St., Ste. 350
Phoenix, AZ 85004
Ph:(602)307-5200
Fax: (602)307-5204
Co. E-mail: cody@phoenixblackchamber.com
URL: http://www.phoenixblackchamber.com/cgi-bin/WebObjects/gpbcc
Contact: Mr. Cody Williams, Pres./CEO

57041 ■ Greater Phoenix Chamber of Commerce
201 N Central Ave., 27th Fl.
Phoenix, AZ 85073
Ph:(602)254-5521
Fax: (602)495-8913
Co. E-mail: info@phoenixchamber.com
URL: http://www.phoenixchamber.com
Contact: Katie Pushor, Pres./CEO

57042 ■ Greater Sierra Vista Area Chamber of Commerce
21 E Wilcox Dr.
Sierra Vista, AZ 85635
Ph:(520)458-6940
Fax: (520)452-0878
Co. E-mail: info@sierravistachamber.org
URL: http://www.sierravistachamber.org
Contact: Susan Tegmeyer, Exec.Dir.

57043 ■ Heber - Overgaard Chamber of Commerce
PO Box 1926
Overgaard, AZ 85933
Ph:(928)535-5777
Fax: (928)535-3254
Co. E-mail: coc@heberovergaard.org
URL: http://www.heberovergaard.org
Contact: Gale Lewis, Pres.

57044 ■ Holbrook Chamber of Commerce
100 E Arizona St.
Holbrook, AZ 86025
Ph:(520)524-6558
Free: 800-524-2459
Fax: (520)524-1719
Co. E-mail: holbrookchamb@cybertrails.com
Contact: Art Standiford, Exec.Dir.

57045 ■ Jerome Chamber of Commerce
PO Box 236
Dewey, AZ 86327
Ph:(928)634-2900

Co. E-mail: staff@jeromechamber.com
URL: http://www.jeromechamber.com
Contact: Christine Barag, Pres.

57046 ■ Kingman Area Chamber of Commerce
PO Box 1150
Kingman, AZ 86402-1150
Ph:(928)753-6253
Fax: (928)753-1049
Co. E-mail: kgmncofc@ctaz.com
URL: http://www.kingmanchamber.org
Contact: Beverly J. Liles, Pres./CEO

57047 ■ Lake Havasu Area Chamber of Commerce
314 London Bridge Rd.
Lake Havasu City, AZ 86403-5772
Ph:(928)855-4115
Fax: (928)680-0010
Co. E-mail: lisak@havasuchamber.com
URL: http://www.havasuchamber.com
Contact: Lisa Krueger, Pres./CEO

57048 ■ Marana Chamber of Commerce
13881 N Casa Grande Hwy.
Marana, AZ 85653-9312
Ph:(520)682-4314
Fax: (520)682-2303
Co. E-mail: maranachamber@comcast.net
URL: http://www.maranachamber.com
Contact: Ed Stolmaker, Exec.Dir.

57049 ■ McMullen Valley Chamber of Commerce
PO Box 700
Salome, AZ 85348-0700
Ph:(928)859-3846
Fax: (928)859-4399
Co. E-mail: mcmullenchamber@tds.net
URL: http://www.azoutback.com
Contact: Tom Overman, Dir.

57050 ■ Mesa Chamber of Commerce
120 N Center St.
Mesa, AZ 85201
Ph:(480)969-1307
Fax: (480)827-0727
Co. E-mail: info@mesachamber.org
URL: http://www.mesachamber.org
Contact: Charles Deaton, Pres./CEO

57051 ■ Mohave Valley Chamber of Commerce
5630 Hwy. 95, Ste. 5
PO Box 9101
Fort Mohave, AZ 86427-9101
Ph:(928)768-2777
Fax: (928)768-2777
Co. E-mail: info@mohavevalleychamber.com
URL: http://www.mohavevalleychamber.com
Contact: Judy Gaston, Admin.

57052 ■ Nogales-Santa Cruz County Chamber of Commerce
123 W Kino Park Way
Nogales, AZ 85621
Ph:(520)287-3685
Fax: (520)287-3688
Co. E-mail: info@nogaleschamber.com
URL: http://www.nogaleschamber.com
Contact: Dr. Marcelino Varona, Chm.

57053 ■ North Phoenix Chamber of Commerce
2737 E Greenway Rd., Ste. No. 10
Phoenix, AZ 85032-4391
Ph:(602)482-3344
Fax: (602)482-2261
Co. E-mail: solutions@northphoenixchamber.com
URL: http://www.northphoenixchamber.com
Contact: Don Sprigings, Pres./CEO

57054 ■ Northwest Valley Chamber of Commerce
12801 W Bell Rd., Ste. 14
Surprise, AZ 85374

Ph:(623)583-0692
Fax: (623)583-0694
Co. E-mail: chamber@northwestvalley.com
URL: http://www.northwestvalley.com
Contact: Debbie Wilden, Pres./CEO

57055 ■ Oatman-Goldroad Chamber of Commerce
PO Box 423
Oatman, AZ 86433
Ph:(928)768-6222
Co. E-mail: oatman@oatmangoldroad.com
URL: http://www.oatmangoldroad.com
Contact: Jackie Rowland

57056 ■ Page-Lake Powell Chamber of Commerce
PO Box 727
Page, AZ 86040
Ph:(928)645-2741
Free: 888-261-PAGE
Fax: (928)645-3181
Co. E-mail: chamber@pagelakepowellchamber.org
URL: http://www.pagelakepowellchamber.org
Contact: Joan Nevills-Stavely, Exec.Dir.

57057 ■ Parker Area Chamber of Commerce
1217 S California Ave.
Parker, AZ 85344
Ph:(928)669-2174
Fax: (928)669-6304
Co. E-mail: info@parkerareachamberofcommerce.com
URL: http://www.parkerareachamberofcommerce.com
Contact: Tammy Thorn, Pres.

57058 ■ Pearce - Sunsites Chamber of Commerce
PO Box 308
Pearce, AZ 85625
Ph:(520)826-3535
Fax: (520)826-3446
URL: http://www.vtc.net/~seariz
Contact: John Edmonton, Pres.

57059 ■ Peoria Chamber of Commerce
10601 N 83rd Dr.
PO Box 70
Peoria, AZ 85380
Ph:(623)979-3601
Free: 800-580-2645
Fax: (623)486-4729
Co. E-mail: info@peoriachamber.com
URL: http://www.peoriachamber.com
Contact: Robert Ware, Exec.Dir.

57060 ■ Pinetop-Lakeside Chamber of Commerce
PO Box 4220
Pinetop, AZ 85935
Ph:(928)367-4290
Free: 800-573-4031
Fax: (928)367-1247
Co. E-mail: info@pinetoplakesidechamber.com
URL: http://www.pinetoplakesidechamber.com
Contact: Elaine Szemesi, Exec.Dir.

57061 ■ Prescott Chamber of Commerce
117 W Goodwin St.
PO Box 1147
Prescott, AZ 86302-1147
Ph:(928)445-2000
Free: 800-266-7534
Fax: (928)445-0068
Co. E-mail: dmaurer@prescott.org
URL: http://www.prescott.org
Contact: David Maurer, CEO

57062 ■ Prescott Valley Chamber of Commerce
3001 N Main St., Ste. 2A
Prescott Valley, AZ 86314
Ph:(928)772-8857
Fax: (928)772-4267
Co. E-mail: info@pvchamber.org
URL: http://www.pvchamber.org

Contact: Lew Rees, Exec.Dir.

57063 ■ Quartzsite Chamber of Commerce
PO Box 85
Quartzsite, AZ 85346-0085
Ph:(928)927-5600
Fax: (928)927-7438
Co. E-mail: qtzchamber@redrivernet.com
URL: http://www.quartzsitechamber.com
Contact: Jean Barney, Exec.Dir./Exec.VP

57064 ■ Rim Country Regional Chamber of Commerce
100 W Main St.
PO Box 1380
Payson, AZ 85547
Ph:(928)474-4515
Free: 800-672-9766
Fax: (928)474-8812
Co. E-mail: chamber@npgcable.com
URL: http://www.rimcountrychamber.com
Contact: Tina Bruess, Exec.Dir.

57065 ■ St. Johns Regional Chamber of Commerce
PO Box 929
St. Johns, AZ 85936
Ph:(928)337-2000
Fax: (928)337-2020
Co. E-mail: office@stjohnschamber.com
URL: http://www.stjohnschamber.com
Contact: Kelly Gunnels, Exec.Dir.

57066 ■ Scottsdale Area Chamber of Commerce
7343 Scottsdale Mall
Civic Ctr. Mall Area
Scottsdale, AZ 85251-4498
Ph:(480)945-8481
Free: 800-877-1117
Fax: (480)947-4523
Co. E-mail: info@scottsdalechamber.com
URL: http://www.scottsdalechamber.com
Contact: Virginia L. Korte, Pres./CEO

57067 ■ Sedona-Oak Creek Canyon Chamber of Commerce
PO Box 478
Sedona, AZ 86336
Ph:(928)282-7722
Free: 800-288-7336
Fax: (928)204-1064
Co. E-mail: info@sedonachamber.com
URL: http://www.sedonachamber.com
Contact: Char Beltran, Pres./CEO

57068 ■ Show Low Regional Chamber of Commerce
81 E Deuce of Clubs
Show Low, AZ 85901
Ph:(928)537-2326
Free: 888-SHO-WLOW
Fax: (928)532-7610
Co. E-mail: info@showlowchamberofcommerce.com
URL: http://www.showlowchamberofcommerce.com
Contact: Barbara Bruce, Pres./CEO

57069 ■ SMOR Chamber of Commerce
PO Box 1886
Oracle, AZ 85623
Ph:(520)896-9322
Fax: (520)385-4593
Co. E-mail: smorcoc@theriver.com
Contact: Janice Rapp, Dir.

57070 ■ Snowflake - Taylor Chamber of Commerce
110 N Main St.
Snowflake, AZ 85937
Ph:(928)536-4331
Fax: (928)536-5208
Co. E-mail: info@snowflaketaylorchamber.com
URL: http://snowflaketaylorchamber.com
Contact: Cari Garrigus, Exec.Dir.

57071 ■ Sonoita - Elgin Chamber of Commerce
PO Box 607
Sonoita, AZ 85637
Ph:(520)455-5498
URL: http://www.sonoitaelginchamber.org
Contact: Pat Carnevale, Treas.

57072 ■ Southwest Valley Chamber of Commerce
289 N Litchfield Rd.
Goodyear, AZ 85338
Ph:(623)932-2260
Fax: (623)932-9057
Co. E-mail: info@southwestvalleychamber.org
URL: http://www.southwestvalleychamber.org
Contact: Sharolyn Hohman, CEO/Pres.

57073 ■ Springerville-Eagar Regional Chamber of Commerce
PO Box 31
318 E Main St.
Springerville, AZ 85938-0031
Ph:(928)333-2123
Free: 800-733-2123
Fax: (928)333-5690
Co. E-mail: tourist@cybertrails.com
URL: http://www.springerville-eagar.com

57074 ■ Superior Chamber of Commerce
PO Box 95
Superior, AZ 85273-0095
Ph:(520)689-0200
Fax: (520)689-0200
Co. E-mail: jcoffman@copper.net
URL: http://www.superiorazchamber.net
Contact: John Coffman, Pres.

57075 ■ Tempe Chamber of Commerce
PO Box 28500
Tempe, AZ 85285-8500
Ph:(480)967-7891
Fax: (480)966-5365
Co. E-mail: info@tempechamber.org
URL: http://www.tempechamber.org
Contact: Mary Ann Miller, Pres./CEO

57076 ■ Tombstone Chamber of Commerce
PO Box 995
Tombstone, AZ 85638
Ph:(520)457-9317
Free: 888-457-3929
Fax: (520)457-2458
Co. E-mail: info@tombstone.org
URL: http://tombstone.org
Contact: Jean Sullivan, Exec.Dir.

57077 ■ Tubac Chamber of Commerce
PO Box 1866
Tubac, AZ 85646
Ph:(520)398-2704
Co. E-mail: assistance@tubacaz.com
URL: http://www.tubacaz.com
Contact: Carol Cullen, Exec.Dir.

57078 ■ Tucson Metropolitan Chamber of Commerce
PO Box 991
Tucson, AZ 85701
Ph:(520)792-2250
Fax: (520)882-5704
Co. E-mail: info@tucsonchamber.org
URL: http://www.tucsonchamber.org
Contact: John C. Camper CCE, Pres.

57079 ■ Wickenburg Chamber of Commerce
216 N Frontier St.
Wickenburg, AZ 85390
Ph:(928)684-5479
Fax: (928)684-5470
Co. E-mail: info@wickenburgchamber.com
URL: http://www.wickenburgchamber.com
Contact: Julia Brooks, Exec.Dir.

57080 ■ Willcox Chamber of Commerce and Agriculture
1500 N Cir. I Rd.
Willcox, AZ 85643

Ph:(520)384-2272
Free: 800-200-2272
Fax:(520)384-0293
Co. E-mail: willcoxchamber@vtc.net
URL: http://www.willcoxchamber.com
Contact: Kathy Smith, Exec.Dir.

57081 ■ Williams-Grand Canyon Chamber of Commerce
200 W Railroad Ave.
Williams, AZ 86046
Ph:(928)635-1418
Fax: (928)635-1417
Co. E-mail: info@williamschamber.com
URL: http://www.williamschamber.com
Contact: Ms. Donna Eastman, Pres./CEO

57082 ■ Winslow Chamber of Commerce
PO Box 460
Winslow, AZ 86047
Ph:(928)289-2434
Fax: (928)289-5660
Co. E-mail: winslowchamber@cableone.net
URL: http://www.winslowarizona.org
Contact: Mr. Bob Hall, Exec.Dir.

57083 ■ Yarnell - Peeples Valley Chamber of Commerce
PO Box 275
Yarnell, AZ 85362-0275
Ph:(928)427-6424
Fax: (520)427-3867
Co. E-mail: ypvcoc@hotmail.com
Contact: Roxie Barringer, Pres.

57084 ■ Yuma County Chamber of Commerce
180 W 1st St., Ste. A
Yuma, AZ 85364
Ph:(928)782-2567
Free: 877-782-0438
Fax: (928)343-0038
Co. E-mail: info@yumachamber.org
URL: http://www.yumachamber.org
Contact: Ken Rosevear, Exec.Dir.

MINORITY BUSINESS ASSISTANCE PROGRAMS

57085 ■ Arizona Minority Business Development Center
255 E Osborn Rd., Ste. 202
Phoenix, AZ 85012
Ph:(602)248-0007
Fax: (602)279-8900
Co. E-mail: info@azmbdc.org
URL: http://www.azmbdc.org/
Contact: Roy Laos, Dir

57086 ■ Arizona Native American Business Development Center–National Center for American Indian Enterprise Development Center
953 E Juanita Ave.
953 E. Juanita Ave.
Mesa, AZ 85204
Ph:(480)545-1298
Fax: (480)545-4208
Co. E-mail: ncaiedcln@aol.com
URL: http://www.ncaied.org

FINANCING AND LOAN PROGRAMS

57087 ■ The Columbine Venture Funds
9449 North 90th St., Ste. 200
Scottsdale, AZ 85258
Ph:(602)661-9222
Fax: (602)661-6262
Preferred Investment Size: $300,000 to $800,000.
Investment Types: Seed, research and development, start-up, and first stage. **Geographic Preferences:** Southwest, Rocky Mountains, and West Coast.

57088 ■ Coronado Venture Fund
PO Box 65420
Tucson, AZ 85728-5420
Ph:(520)577-3764
Fax: (520)299-8491
Preferred Investment Size: $100,000 to $500,000.
Investment Types: Seed, start-up, first and second stage. **Industry Preferences:** Communications and media, computer software and hardware, semiconductors and other electronics, biotechnology, medical and health, consumer related, and industrial and energy.

57089 ■ Estreetcapital.com
660 South Mill Ave., Ste. 315
Tempe, AZ 85281
Ph:(480)968-8400
Fax: (480)968-9966
URL: http://www.estreetcapital.com
Contact: Doug Newell, Chief Financial Officer
Investment Types: Early stage. **Industry Preferences:** Internet specific. **Geographic Preferences:** Arizona.

57090 ■ Koch Ventures
5950 Berkshire Ln., Ste. 1000
Dallas, TX 75225
Ph:(214)891-3010
Fax: (214)891-3012
URL: http://www.kochventures.com
Contact: Ray Gary, President
Preferred Investment Size: $300,000 to $10,000,000. **Investment Types:** Seed and early stage. **Industry Preferences:** Communications and media, computer software and services, Internet specific, semiconductors and other electronics, medical and health, other products, and biotechnology. **Geographic Preferences:** Southwest and Texas.

57091 ■ McKee & Co.
PMB 187
7119 E. Shea Blvd., Ste. 109
Scottsdale, AZ 85254
Preferred Investment Size: $1,000,000 minimum.
Investment Types: Second stage, mezzanine, and leveraged buyout. **Industry Preferences:** Communications and media, computer software and hardware, Internet specific, semiconductors and other electronics, biotechnology, medical and health, consumer related, industrial and energy, transportation, and financial services. **Geographic Preferences:** U.S.

57092 ■ Merita Capital Ltd.
8912 E. Pinnacle Peak Rd.
PMB 493
Scottsdale, AZ 85255
Ph:(480)947-8700
Fax: (480)947-8766
URL: http://www.gwynnfinancial.com
Contact: David Gwynn, President
Investment Types: First and second stage, mezzanine, and special situation. **Geographic Preferences:** Midwest, Northwest, Rocky Mountains, Southwest and West Coast.

57093 ■ Miller Capital Corp.
4909 E. McDowell Rd.
Phoenix, AZ 85008
Ph:(602)225-0504
Fax: (602)225-9024
URL: http://www.themillergroup.net
Contact: Rudy R. Miller, President, CEO and Chairman
Preferred Investment Size: $1,000,000 to $5,000,000. **Investment Types:** Second stage. **Industry Preferences:** Consumer related. **Geographic Preferences:** U.S.

57094 ■ Valley Ventures / Arizona Growth Partners, L.P.
80 East Salado Pky., Ste. 705
Tempe, AZ 85281
Ph:(480)661-6600
Fax: (480)661-6262
Contact: Jock Holliman, General Partner
Investment Types: Seed, early and second stage, balanced, expansion, mezzanine, private placement,

recapitalizations, and leveraged buyout. **Industry Preferences:** Computer software, Internet specific, semiconductors and other electronics, biotechnology, and medical and health. **Geographic Preferences:** Arizona, Colorado, Nevada, New Mexico, Southern California, Southwest, Texas, and Utah.

PROCUREMENT ASSISTANCE PROGRAMS

57095 ■ Arizona Procurement Technical Assistance Center–The National Center for AIED
National Center Headquarters
953 E Juanita Ave.
Mesa, AZ 85204
Ph:(480)545-1298
Free: 800-462-2433
Fax: (480)454-4208
Co. E-mail: ken.robbins@ncaied.org
URL: http://www.ncaied.org
Contact: Elaine Young, Prgm Dir

57096 ■ Maricopa County Procurement Technical Assistance Center–APTAN - Bid Source
201 N Central Ave., 27th Fl.
Phoenix, AZ 85073
Ph:(602)495-6467
Fax: (602)495-8913
Co. E-mail: bidsource@phoenixchamber.com
URL: http://www.phoenixchamber.com
Contact: Cyndi McCroskey
E-mail: cmccroskey@phoenixchamber.com

INCUBATORS/RESEARCH AND TECHNOLOGY PARKS

57097 ■ Arizona State University Research Park
8750 S Science Dr.
Tempe, AZ 85284
Ph:(408)752-1000
Fax: (408)491-2273
Co. E-mail: michele.pino@asu.edu
URL: http://researchpark.asu.edu
Contact: Michele Pino, Exec.Dir.
E-mail: michele.pino@asu.edu
Scope: Seeks to link technological results of university and individual research with private industry. The Park provides tenants with leased land for construction of research and development facilities, laboratories, offices, pilot plants, facilities for production or assembly of prototype products, University and government research facilities, education and training facilities, and corporate regional or national headquarters facilities related to these functions. **Educational Activities:** Conferences.

57098 ■ Association of University Research Parks
12100 Sunset Hills Rd., Ste. 130
Reston, VA 20190
Ph:(703)234-4088
Fax: (703)435-4390
Co. E-mail: info@aurp.net
URL: http://www.aurp.net
Contact: William M. Drohan, Exec.Dir.
E-mail: info@aurp.net
Scope: Serves as forum for the exchange of information on planning, construction, marketing, and managing of university-related research parks, particularly information on university-industry relations, innovation, technology incubators, and technology transfer to the private sector. Monitors legislative and regulatory actions affecting the development and operation of research parks. Acts as a clearinghouse for career opportunities. **Publications:** The Research Park Forum (bimonthly). **Educational Activities:** Annual conference; Seminars; Workshops.

57099 ■ Research Corporation Technologies
101 N Wilmot Rd., Ste. 600
Tucson, AZ 85711-3365
Ph:(520)748-4400
Fax: (520)748-0025
Co. E-mail: attention@rctech.com
URL: http://www.rctech.com
Contact: Dr. Paul M. Grand, Dir.
E-mail: attention@rctech.com
Scope: Appraises, protects, develops, and commercializes inventions from colleges, universities, medical research organizations, and other research laboratories. Among the variety of inventions that have been developed and marketed are agricultural and other chemicals, chemical processes, biotechnologies, bioprocessing, diagnostics, foods and additives, pharmaceuticals, plants, vaccines, veterinary products, agricultural equipment, analytical instruments, chemicals, electronics, materials, industrial processes, machines, medical/surgical diagnostics, and optics/ optical instruments. Provides incentives for invention disclosure, funds selected applied research, new business formation. **Publications:** Brochures; News Releases; Year in Review (annually).

57100 ■ University of Arizona–Office of Vice President for Research and Graduate Studies
601 Administration Bldg.
Tucson, AZ 85721-0066
Ph:(520)621-3513
Fax: (520)621-7507
Co. E-mail: tolbert@email.arizona.edu
URL: http://www.vpr.arizona.edu/
Contact: Prof. Leslie P. Tolbert PhD, VP
E-mail: tolbert@email.arizona.edu
Scope: Responsible for coordinating and administering extramurally supported research programs conducted in various departments and organized research units of the University. **Publications:** Report on Research (semiannually); UA Outreach (semiannually). **Educational Activities:** Faculty Community Lecture Series.

57101 ■ University of Arizona Foundation
1111 N Cherry Ave.
PO Box 210105
Tucson, AZ 85721-0109
Ph:(520)621-9061
Fax: (520)621-8820
Co. E-mail: brenda@al.arizona.edu
URL: http://www.al.arizona.edu/foundation/
Contact: James H. Moore Jr., Pres./CEO
E-mail: brenda@al.arizona.edu
Scope: Seeks private funds for support of educational and research programs at the University. **Publications:** Foundation report (semiannually). **Educational Activities:** Conferences.

EDUCATIONAL PROGRAMS

57102 ■ Eastern Arizona College
615 N Stadium Ave.
Thatcher, AZ 85552-0769
Ph:(928)428-8472
Free: 800-678-3808
Fax: (928)428-8462
URL: http://www.eac.edu
Description: Two-year college offering a small business management program.

57103 ■ Rio Salado Community College
2323 W 14th St.
Tempe, AZ 85281
Ph:(480)517-8000
Free: 800-729-1197
Fax: (480)517-8519
URL: http://www.rio.maricopa.edu
Description: Two-year college offering a program in small business management.

PUBLICATIONS

57104 ■ *Starting and Operating a Business in Arizona: A Step-by-Step Guide*
PSI Research
300 N. Valley Dr.
Grants Pass, OR 97526
Ph:(503)479-9464
Free: 800-228-2275
Fax: (503)476-1479
Co. E-mail: psi2@magick.net
Ed: Michael D. Jenkins. **Released:** Revised edition, 1992. **Price:** $29.95 (looseleaf binder); $24.95 (paper). **Description:** Part of the Successful Business Library series.

PUBLISHERS

57105 ■ Agritech Publishing Group Inc.
12515 N Eliese Ave.
Marana, AZ 85653-9434
Ph:(520)616-9520
Co. E-mail: aggiebookman@msn.com
Contact: Robert P. Griset, CEO & Pres
Description: Wholesaler and distributor. Speciality publisher. Reaches market through distributors including The Intelligent Cowboy and Western Supply Company Inc. **Founded:** 1979.

57106 ■ Center for Business Research/AZB
College of Business
Box 874406
Tempe, AZ 85287-4406
Ph:(602)965-3961
Fax: (602)965-5458
Co. E-mail: nancy.maneely@asu.edu
URL: http://www.cob.asu.edu/seid/cbr
Contact: Tom R. Rex, Research Mgr.
E-mail: tom.rex@asu.edu
Description: Public service bureau that conducts special projects in the areas of economics, real estate, consumer price index, and demographics. Business and economics information center for local community. Also publishes the monthly periodical *Arizona Business*. Reports and documents in microform distributed by University Microfilms, Information Access Company, and the Institute for Scientific Information. Printed publications available from the Center. Does not accept unsolicited manuscripts. **Founded:** 1954.

57107 ■ Marketing Methods Press
2811 N 7th Ave.
Phoenix, AZ 85007-1125
Ph:(602)266-9344
Fax: (602)266-9478
Contact: Barbara Lambesis, Gen Mgr
Description: Publishes books on starting and operating small businesses. Offers a business guidebook.

Accepts unsolicited manuscripts for business titles. Reaches market through telephone sales, trade sales, Ingram Book Co., Baker & Taylor, Quality Books, Inc., and Login Publishers Consortium. **Founded:** 1989.

57108 ■ Positive Potentials
9699 N Hayden Rd., Ste. 108
PMB 232
Scottsdale, AZ 85258-5805
Ph:(480)922-9699
Free: 877-547-3713
Fax: (480)922-4961
URL: http://www.positivepotentials.com
Contact: Michelle Cubas
E-mail: mcubas@positivepotentials.com
Description: Publishes on business-related coaching, training, and consulting via newsletters, electronic magazines, and media articles.

57109 ■ Sohnen-Moe Associates Inc.
3906 W Ina Rd., Ste. 200-367
Tucson, AZ 85741-2995
Ph:(520)743-3936
Free: 800-786-4774
Fax: (520)743-3656
Co. E-mail: info@sohnen-moe.com
URL: http://www.sohnen-moe.com
Contact: Cherie Sohnen-Moe, Owner
E-mail: cherie@sohnen-moe.com
Description: Publishes materials for small business owners, especially health care practitioners. Offers workshops and training programs. Does not accept unsolicited manuscripts. Distributes for Nolo Press, and Bell Springs, among others. Reaches market through direct mail, telephone and trade sales, and distributors and wholesalers, including New Leaf Distributing Co., Baker & Taylor, and BookPeople. **Founded:** 1984.

57110 ■ Success Showcase Publishing
PO Box 27946
Scottsdale, AZ 85255-0149
Ph:(480)634-7691
Free: 800-359-4544
Fax: (480)419-8912
Co. E-mail: info@confessionsofshameless.com
URL: http://www.confessionsofshameless.com
Contact: Debbie Allen, President
E-mail: debbie@debbieallen.com
Description: Publishes general business and marketing titles. Does not accept unsolicited manuscripts. Reaches market through direct mail, reviews and listings. **Founded:** 1996.

57111 ■ World Economic Processing Zones Association
C/O The Flagstaff Institute
PO Box 986
Flagstaff, AZ 86002-0986
Ph:(928)779-0052
Fax: (928)774-8589
Co. E-mail: instflag@aol.com
URL: http://www.wepza.org
Contact: Robert Haywood, Director
E-mail: director@wepza.org
Description: Publishes materials on free zones, export processing zones, economic development zones, research parks, multinational manufacturing, and international development agencies. Does not accept unsolicited manuscripts. **Founded:** 1978.

SMALL BUSINESS DEVELOPMENT CENTER LEAD OFFICE

57112 ■ Arkansas SBDC–University of Arkansas
2801 S. University Ave.
Little Rock, AR 72204
Ph:(501)324-9043
Fax: (501)324-9049
URL: http://asbdc.ualr.edu
Contact: Janet M. Roderick, State Dir.
E-mail: jmroderick@ualr.edu

57113 ■ University of Arkansas at Little Rock–Small Business Development Center
Little Rock Technology Center Bldg.
100 S. Main, Ste. 401
Little Rock, AR 72201
Ph:(501)324-9043
Free: 800-862-2040
Fax: (501)324-9049
URL: http://www.ualr.edu/~sbdcdept/
Contact: Janet Nye, State Director
E-mail: jmnye@ualr.edu

SMALL BUSINESS DEVELOPMENT CENTERS

57114 ■ Arkansas State University, Jonesboro Center–Small Business Development Center
PO Box 2650
Jonesboro, AR 72467
Ph:(870)972-3517
Co. E-mail: hlawrenc@astate.edu
URL: http://www.deltaced.astate.edu/sbdc.htm
Contact: Herb Lawrence, Center Dir.

57115 ■ Fort Smith Regional Office–Small Business Development Center
UA Fort Smith
Fort Smith, AR 72903
Ph:(479)788-7755
Co. E-mail: vvanzant@ualr.edu
URL: http://www.uafortsmith.edu/SBDC/
Contact: Vonelle Vanzant, Center Dir.

57116 ■ Henderson State University–Small Business Development Center
PO Box 7624
Arkadelphia, AR 71999
Ph:(870)230-5184
Co. E-mail: liux@hsu.edu
URL: http://www.hsu.edu/sbdc/
Contact: Lonnie Jackson, Center Dir.
E-mail: jacksol@hsu.edu

57117 ■ Southern Arkansas University–Small Business Development Center
PO Box 9192
Magnolia, AR 71754-9379

Ph:(870)235-5033
URL: http://www.saumag.edu/sbdc/
Contact: T. Paul Considine, Center Dir.
E-mail: tpconsidine@saumag.edu

57118 ■ University of Arkansas–Small Business Development Center
Donald W. Reynolds Center for Enterprise
    Development, Ste. 2
145 Buchanan
Fayetteville, AR 72701
Ph:(479)575-5148
Fax: (479)575-4013
Co. E-mail: tjeffers@walton.uark.edu
URL: http://sbdc.waltoncollege.uark.edu/
Contact: Tracy Jeffers, Center Dir.

57119 ■ University of Arkansas at Little Rock–Small Business Development Center
2801 S. University Ave.
Little Rock, AR 72204
Ph:(501)682-7760
Free: 800-862-2040
Fax: (501)683-7720
URL: http://asbdc.ualr.edu
Contact: Janet Roderick, Exec. Dir.
E-mail: jmroderick@ualr.edu

57120 ■ University of Arkansas - Monticello–Small Business Development Center–College of Technology - McGehee (PO Bo)
PO Box 747
McGehee, AR 71654
Ph:(870)222-4900
URL: http://www.uamont.edu/McGehee/SBDC/
    SBDChome.htm
Contact: Kathryn Peacock, Center Dir.
E-mail: peacockk@uamont.edu

SCORE OFFICES

57121 ■ SCORE Garland County
659 Quachita
Hot Springs, AR 71902
Ph:(501)321-1700
Fax: (501)321-3551
Co. E-mail: score@hotspringschamber.com
Contact: Jimmy Mayes, Chm.
Description: Provides professional guidance and information to maximize the success of existing and emerging small businesses. Offers business counseling and workshops.

57122 ■ SCORE Little Rock
2120 Riverfront Dr.
SBA Rm. 100
Little Rock, AR 72202-1747
Ph:(501)324-7379
Fax: (501)324-5199
Co. E-mail: littlerockscore@sbcglobal.net
Description: Provides professional guidance and information to maximize the success of existing and emerging small businesses. Offers business counseling and workshops.

57123 ■ SCORE Northwest Arkansas
614 E Emma St., Rm. M412
Springdale, AR 72764
Ph:(479)725-1809
Co. E-mail: score@jtlshop.jonesnet.org
Description: Provides professional guidance and information to maximize the success of existing and emerging small businesses. Offers business counseling and workshops.

57124 ■ SCORE South Central
c/o El Dorado Chamber of Commerce
201 N Jackson Ave.
El Dorado, AR 71730-5803
Ph:(870)863-6113
Fax: (870)863-6115
Co. E-mail: score@boomtown.org
URL: http://www.scorearkansas.org/eldorado
Contact: Bob Barr, Chm.
Description: Provides free technical and managerial guidance to small business owners, non-profit organizations and prospective business owners.

57125 ■ SCORE Southeast Arkansas
510 Main St.
Pine Bluff, AR 71611
Ph:(870)535-0110
Fax: (870)535-1643
Co. E-mail: pinebluffscore@sbcglobal.net
Description: Provides professional guidance and information to maximize the success of existing and emerging small businesses. Offers business counseling and workshops.

BETTER BUSINESS BUREAUS

57126 ■ Better Business Bureau of Arkansas
12521 Kanis Rd.
Little Rock, AR 72211-2605
Ph:(501)664-7274
Fax: (501)664-0024
Co. E-mail: info@bbbarkansas.org
URL: http://www.arkansas.bbb.org
Contact: Janet J. Robb, Pres.

CHAMBERS OF COMMERCE

57127 ■ Alma Area Chamber of Commerce
PO Box 2607
Alma, AR 72921
Ph:(479)632-4127
Fax: (479)632-4037
Co. E-mail: almachamber@valuelinx.net
URL: http://almachamber.com
Contact: Mr. Eldon Mushrush, Exec.Dir.

57128 ■ Arkadelphia Area Chamber of Commerce
PO Box 38
Arkadelphia, AR 71923-0038

Ph:(870)246-5542
Free: 800-874-4289
Fax: (870)246-5543
Co. E-mail: blain@cityofarkadelphia.com
URL: http://www.arkadelphia.org
Contact: Mr. Blain Smith, Exec.Dir.

57129 ■ Arkansas State Chamber of Commerce
PO Box 3645
Little Rock, AR 72203-3645
Ph:(501)374-9225
Fax: (501)372-2722
Co. E-mail: rrussell@ascc-aia.org
URL: http://statechamber-aia.dina.org
Contact: Ron Russell, Pres./CEO

57130 ■ Bald Knob Area Chamber of Commerce
PO Box 338
Bald Knob, AR 72010
Ph:(501)724-3140
Fax: (501)724-8100
Co. E-mail: baldknobchamber@centurytel.net
URL: http://www.baldknobchamber.com
Contact: Charles Holt, Pres.

57131 ■ Batesville Area Chamber of Commerce
409 Vine St.
Batesville, AR 72501
Ph:(870)793-2378
Fax: (870)793-3061
Co. E-mail: info@mybatesville.org
URL: http://www.mybatesville.org
Contact: Larry Sandage, Pres./CEO

57132 ■ Benton Chamber of Commerce
607 N Market St.
Benton, AR 72015
Ph:(501)315-8272
Fax: (501)315-8290
Co. E-mail: mgillis@bentonchamber.com
URL: http://www.bentonchamber.com
Contact: Mark Gillis, Exec.Dir.

57133 ■ Bentonville-Bella Vista Chamber of Commerce
412 S Main
Bentonville, AR 72712
Ph:(479)273-2841
Fax: (479)273-2180
Co. E-mail: info@bbvchamber.com
URL: http://www.bbvchamber.com
Contact: Ed Clifford, Pres./CEO

57134 ■ Berryville Chamber of Commerce
PO Box 402
Berryville, AR 72616-0402
Ph:(870)423-3704
Co. E-mail: chamber@hbeark.com
URL: http://www.berryvillear.com
Contact: Mike Ellis, Dir.

57135 ■ Blytheville-Gosnell Area Chamber of Commerce
PO Box 485
Blytheville, AR 72316-0485
Ph:(870)762-2012
Fax: (870)762-0551
Co. E-mail: blygoscc@sbcglobal.net
URL: http://blytheville.dina.org
Contact: Elizabeth Smith, Exec.Dir.

57136 ■ Booneville Development Corporation - South Logan County Chamber of Commerce
PO Box 55
Booneville, AR 72927
Ph:(479)675-2666
Fax: (479)675-5158
Co. E-mail: info@booneville.com
URL: http://www.booneville.com
Contact: Stacey McCollough, Exec.Dir.

57137 ■ Bradley County Chamber of Commerce
104 N Myrtle St.
Warren, AR 71671
Ph:(870)226-5225
Fax: (870)226-6285
Co. E-mail: bccc@cei.net
URL: http://www.bradleycountychamberofcommerce.com
Contact: Joel Tolefree, Pres.

57138 ■ Brinkley Chamber of Commerce
1501 Weatherby Dr.
Brinkley, AR 72021
Ph:(870)734-2262
Fax: (870)589-2020
Co. E-mail: brinkleyc@futura.net
URL: http://www.brinkleyar.com
Contact: Sandra Kemmer, Sec.

57139 ■ Bryant Chamber of Commerce
PO Box 261
Bryant, AR 72089-0261
Ph:(501)847-4702
Fax: (501)847-7576
Co. E-mail: bryantcofc@aristotle.net
URL: http://www.bryant-ar.com
Contact: Rae Ann Fields, Exec.Dir.

57140 ■ Bull Shoals Lake - White River Chamber of Commerce
PO Box 354
Bull Shoals, AR 72619
Ph:(870)445-4443
Free: 800-447-1290
Co. E-mail: havefun@bullshoals.org
URL: http://www.bullshoals.org

57141 ■ Cabot Chamber of Commerce
PO Box 631
Cabot, AR 72023
Ph:(501)843-2136
Fax: (501)843-1861
Co. E-mail: julia@cabotarkansas.us
URL: http://www.cabotarkansas.us
Contact: Mary Jane Sawyer, Exec.Dir.

57142 ■ Camden Area Chamber of Commerce
314 Adams Ave.
Camden, AR 71701
Ph:(870)836-6426
Fax: (870)836-6400
Co. E-mail: info@growingcamden.com
URL: http://www.growingcamden.com
Contact: Beth Osteen, Exec.Dir.

57143 ■ Cave City Chamber of Commerce
PO Box 493
Cave City, AR 72521-0493
Ph:(870)283-7333
Free: (866)351-7333
Co. E-mail: laura@frontiercs.com
URL: http://www.cavecityarkansas.info
Contact: James Street, Pres.

57144 ■ Charleston Chamber of Commerce
PO Box 456
Charleston, AR 72933
Ph:(479)965-2201
Fax: (479)965-2205
Contact: Alice Wood, Sec.-Treas.

57145 ■ Clarendon Chamber of Commerce
PO Box 153
Clarendon, AR 72029-0153
Ph:(870)747-5414
Co. E-mail: info@clarendon-ar.com
URL: http://www.clarendon-ar.com
Contact: Valerie Davenport, Sec.-Treas.

57146 ■ Clarksville-Johnson County Chamber of Commerce
101 N Johnson St.
Clarksville, AR 72830
Ph:(479)754-2340
Fax: (479)754-4923

Co. E-mail: cjccofc@centurytel.net
URL: http://www.clarksvillearchamber.com
Contact: Vicki Lyons, Exec.Dir.

57147 ■ Clinton Chamber of Commerce
PO Box 52
Clinton, AR 72031
Ph:(501)745-6500
Fax: (501)745-6500
Co. E-mail: office@clintonchamber.com
URL: http://www.clintonchamber.com
Contact: Linda Fisher, Exec.Dir.

57148 ■ Conway Area Chamber of Commerce
900 Oak St.
Conway, AR 72032-4402
Ph:(501)327-7788
Fax: (501)327-7790
Co. E-mail: info@conwayarkcc.org
URL: http://www.conwayarkcc.org
Contact: Nancy Elphingstone, Pres./CEO

57149 ■ Corning Area Chamber of Commerce
PO Box 93
Corning, AR 72422-0093
Ph:(870)857-3874
Co. E-mail: cacoc@neark.net
Contact: John Schooley, Sec.-Treas.

57150 ■ Cotter Chamber of Commerce
PO Box 489
Cotter, AR 72626-0489
Ph:(870)435-4455
Co. E-mail: chamber@cotterarkansas.com
URL: http://www.cotterarkansas.com
Contact: John Berry, Pres.

57151 ■ Cross County Chamber of Commerce and Economic Development Corporation
PO Box 234
Wynne, AR 72396
Ph:(870)238-2601
Fax: (870)238-7844
Co. E-mail: crossccc@sbcglobal.net
URL: http://www.crosscountychamber.com
Contact: Bill Thomas, Exec.VP

57152 ■ Crossett Area Chamber of Commerce
101 W 1st Ave.
Crossett, AR 71635
Ph:(870)364-6591
Fax: (870)364-7488
Co. E-mail: info@crossettchamber.com
Contact: Abbey Ebarb, Exec.Dir.

57153 ■ De Queen/Sevier County Chamber of Commerce
PO Box 67
De Queen, AR 71832-0067
Ph:(870)584-3225
Fax: (870)642-5533
Co. E-mail: dqscoc@ipa.net
URL: http://www.dequeenchamberofcommerce.com
Contact: Chad Mullins, Pres.

57154 ■ Delight Area Chamber of Commerce
PO Box 147
Delight, AR 71940
Ph:(870)379-2020
Contact: Becky Woods, Pres.

57155 ■ Dermott Area Chamber of Commerce
PO Box 147
Dermott, AR 71638
Ph:(870)538-5656
Fax: (870)538-5493
Co. E-mail: email@dermottchamber.com
URL: http://www.dermottchamber.com
Contact: Frank Henry Jr., Exec. Dir.

57156 ■ Diamond City Chamber of Commerce
PO Box 1161
Diamond City, AR 72630
Ph:(870)422-7575
Co. E-mail: dchamber@diamondcity.net
URL: http://www.diamondcity.org
Contact: Sandy Beaver, Pres.

57157 ■ Dierks Chamber of Commerce
PO Box 292
Dierks, AR 71833-0292
Ph:(870)286-2928
Fax: (870)286-2105
Contact: Brandi Misty, Pres.

57158 ■ Dover Chamber of Commerce
PO Box 731
Dover, AR 72837-0731
Ph:(479)967-2838
Fax: (479)331-4151
Contact: Mr. Alan Boatright, Pres.

57159 ■ Dumas Chamber of Commerce
PO Box 431
Dumas, AR 71639-0431
Ph:(870)382-5447
Fax: (870)382-3031
URL: http://www.dumasar.org
Contact: Ramona Weatherford, Exec.Dir.

57160 ■ El Dorado Chamber of Commerce
201 N Jackson
El Dorado, AR 71730
Ph:(870)863-6113
Fax: (870)863-6115
Co. E-mail: chamber@boomtown.org
URL: http://www.boomtown.org
Contact: Don Wales, Pres./CEO

57161 ■ Eudora Chamber of Commerce
PO Box 325
Eudora, AR 71640
Ph:(870)355-8443
Fax: (870)355-4373
Co. E-mail: eudoracofc@sbcglobal.net
Contact: Mack Ball Jr., Pres.

57162 ■ Fairfield Bay Area Chamber of Commerce
PO Box 1159
Fairfield Bay, AR 72088-1159
Ph:(501)884-3324
Free: 888-224-4386
Fax: (501)884-6250
Co. E-mail: ffb@ffbchamber.org
URL: http://www.ffbchamber.org
Contact: Sue Kelly, Exec.Dir.

57163 ■ Fayetteville Chamber of Commerce
PO Box 4216
Fayetteville, AR 72702-4216
Ph:(479)521-1710
Fax: (479)521-1791
Co. E-mail: questions@fayettevillear.com
URL: http://www.fayettevillear.com
Contact: Bill Ramsey, Pres./CEO

57164 ■ Flippin Chamber of Commerce
PO Box 118
Flippin, AR 72634-0118
Ph:(870)453-8480
Fax: (870)453-2280
Co. E-mail: sanders@flippinchamber.com
URL: http://www.flippinchamber.com
Contact: Randy Livingston, Pres.

57165 ■ Fordyce Chamber of Commerce
119 W Third St.
PO Box 588
Fordyce, AR 71742
Ph:(870)352-3520
Fax: (870)352-8090
Co. E-mail: fordyce@ipa.net
URL: http://www.fordycearkansas.org
Contact: Barbara M. Finley, Exec. Dir.

57166 ■ Forrest City Area Chamber of Commerce
203 N Izard
Forrest City, AR 72335
Ph:(870)633-1651
Fax: (870)633-9500
Co. E-mail: info@forrestcitychamber.com
URL: http://www.forrestcitychamber.com
Contact: Danny Ferguson, Exec.Dir.

57167 ■ Fort Smith Chamber of Commerce
PO Box 1668
Fort Smith, AR 72902
Ph:(479)783-6118
Fax: (479)783-6110
Co. E-mail: info@fortsmithchamber.com
URL: http://www.fschamber.com
Contact: Tom Manskey, Pres.

57168 ■ Gentry Main Street - Chamber of Commerce
PO Box 642
Gentry, AR 72734-0642
Ph:(479)736-2555
Fax: (479)736-2877
Co. E-mail: gentrymscc@hotmail.com
Contact: Candice Miller

57169 ■ Grant County Chamber of Commerce
202 N Oak St.
Sheridan, AR 72150-2132
Ph:(870)942-3021
Fax: (870)942-3378
Co. E-mail: info@grantcountychamber.com
URL: http://www.grantcountychamber.com
Contact: Trudy Lape, Exec.Sec.

57170 ■ Greater Eureka Springs Chamber of Commerce
PO Box 551
Eureka Springs, AR 72632-0551
Ph:(479)253-8737
Free: 800-6-EUREKA
Fax: (479)253-5037
Co. E-mail: escoc@eurekaspringschamber.com
URL: http://www.eurekaspringschamber.com
Contact: Ben Carson, Pres.

57171 ■ Greater Hot Springs Chamber of Commerce
PO Box 6090
Hot Springs, AR 71902-6090
Ph:(501)321-1700
Free: 800-467-INFO
Fax: (501)321-3551
Co. E-mail: hscc@hotsprings.net
URL: http://www.hotspringchamber.com
Contact: Jay Chesshir, Pres.

57172 ■ Greater Pine Bluff Chamber of Commerce
PO Box 5069
Pine Bluff, AR 71611-5069
Ph:(870)535-0110
Fax: (870)535-1643
Co. E-mail: info@pinebluffchamber.com
URL: http://www.pinebluffchamber.com
Contact: Jim V. Crider, Pres./CEO

57173 ■ Greenwood Chamber of Commerce
PO Box 511
Greenwood, AR 72936
Ph:(479)996-6357
Fax: (479)996-1162
Co. E-mail: info@greenwoodchamber.net
URL: http://www.greenwoodarkansas.com
Contact: Jimmy Gossett, Pres.

57174 ■ Greers Ferry Area Chamber of Commerce
PO Box 1534
Greers Ferry, AR 72067
Ph:(501)825-7188
Free: 888-825-7199
Co. E-mail: chamber@greersferry.com
URL: http://greersferry.com

Contact: Dave Blasingim, Pres.

57175 ■ Gurdon Chamber of Commerce
PO Box 187
Gurdon, AR 71743-0187
Ph:(870)353-2661
Contact: Laurie Pilgreen, Pres.

57176 ■ Hamburg Area Chamber of Commerce
PO Box 460
Hamburg, AR 71646
Ph:(870)853-8345
Fax: (870)853-8134
Co. E-mail: hchamber@seark.net
URL: http://www.ashleycountyledger.com/chamber
Contact: Robin LaCaze, Exec.Dir.

57177 ■ Harrisburg Area Chamber of Commerce
PO Box 265
Harrisburg, AR 72432
Ph:(870)578-5461
Free: (866)495-8495
Fax: (870)578-4113
Co. E-mail: hbgchamber@pcsii.com
URL: http://www.harrisburgchamber.com
Contact: Mildred Traynom, Sec.-Treas.

57178 ■ Harrison Chamber of Commerce
621 E Rush
Harrison, AR 72601
Ph:(870)741-2659
Free: 800-880-6265
Fax: (870)741-9059
Co. E-mail: cocinfo@harrison-chamber.com
URL: http://www.harrison-chamber.com
Contact: Layne Wheeler, Pres.

57179 ■ Hazen Chamber of Commerce
PO Box 907
Hazen, AR 72064-0907
Ph:(870)255-4915
Fax: (501)255-3772
Contact: Connie Swaim, Pres.

57180 ■ Heber Springs Area Chamber of Commerce
1001 W Main
Heber Springs, AR 72543
Ph:(501)362-2444
Free: 800-774-3237
Fax: (501)362-9953
Co. E-mail: chamber@heber-springs.com
URL: http://www.heber-springs.com
Contact: Jo Price, Exec. Dir.

57181 ■ Hope-Hempstead County Chamber of Commerce
PO Box 250
Hope, AR 71802-0250
Ph:(870)777-3640
Fax: (870)722-6154
Co. E-mail: hopeark@arkansas.net
URL: http://www.hopemelonfest.com
Contact: Mark Keith, Dir.

57182 ■ Horseshoe Bend Area Chamber of Commerce
811 2nd St., No. 18
Horseshoe Bend, AR 72512
Ph:(870)670-5433
Free: 800-239-9338
Co. E-mail: info@horseshoebendar.com
URL: http://www.horseshoebendar.com
Contact: Paul Sulser, Pres.

57183 ■ Huntsville Chamber of Commerce
PO Box 950, On the Sq.
Huntsville, AR 72740-0950
Ph:(479)738-6000
Co. E-mail: chamber@madisoncounty.net
URL: http://www.huntsvillear.com
Contact: Mr. Terry Fuller, Pres.

57184 ■ Jonesboro Regional Chamber of Commerce
PO Box 789
Jonesboro, AR 72403-0789
Ph:(870)932-6691
Fax: (870)933-5758
Co. E-mail: jonesboroinfo@jonesborocofc.org
URL: http://www.jonesborochamber.org
Contact: Henry P. Jones III, Pres./CEO

57185 ■ Lake Village Chamber of Commerce
PO Box 752
Lake Village, AR 71653
Ph:(870)265-5997
Fax: (870)265-5254
Co. E-mail: director@lakevillagechamber.com
URL: http://www.lakevillagechamber.com
Contact: Lisa V. Raby, Dir.

57186 ■ Little River Chamber of Commerce
PO Box 160
Ashdown, AR 71822
Ph:(870)898-2758
Fax: (870)898-6699
Co. E-mail: lrcoc0436@sbcglobal.net
URL: http://www.littlerivercounty.org
Contact: Fonda Hawthorne, Dir.

57187 ■ Little Rock Regional Chamber of Commerce
One Chamber Plz.
Little Rock, AR 72201-2486
Ph:(501)374-2001
Fax: (501)374-6018
Co. E-mail: chamber@littlerockchamber.com
URL: http://www.littlerockchamber.com
Contact: Paul H. Harvel, Pres./CEO

57188 ■ Lonoke Area Chamber of Commerce
102 1/2 NW Front St.
PO Box 294
Lonoke, AR 72086
Ph:(501)676-4399
Fax: (501)676-4399
Co. E-mail: uni1mac55@yahoo.com
URL: http://www.lonoke.com
Contact: Pat Dickinson, Exec.Dir.

57189 ■ Magnolia-Columbia County Chamber of Commerce
202 N Pine
PO Box 866
Magnolia, AR 71754-0866
Ph:(870)234-4352
Free: 800-482-3330
Fax: (870)234-7937
Co. E-mail: magcoc@arkansas.net
URL: http://www.magnoliachamber.com

57190 ■ Malvern and Hot Springs County Chamber of Commerce
PO Box 266
Malvern, AR 72104
Ph:(501)332-2721
Fax: (501)332-8558
Co. E-mail: rdarrow@malvernar.com
Contact: Marla Hunter, Mgr.

57191 ■ Marion Chamber of Commerce
PO Box 652
Marion, AR 72364-0652
Ph:(870)739-6041
Fax: (870)739-5448
Co. E-mail: chamber@marionarkansas.org
URL: http://www.marionarkansas.org
Contact: Linda Basser, Exec.Dir.

57192 ■ Marked Tree Chamber of Commerce
1 Elm St.
Marked Tree, AR 72365
Ph:(870)358-3000
Fax: (870)358-7867
Contact: Pam Wright, Exec. Sec.

57193 ■ Maumelle Area Chamber of Commerce
PO Box 13099
Maumelle, AR 72113-0099

Ph:(501)851-9700
Fax: (501)851-6690
Co. E-mail: info@maumellechamber.com
URL: http://www.maumellechamber.com
Contact: Pam Rantisi, Exec.Dir.

57194 ■ McGehee Chamber of Commerce
PO Box 521
McGehee, AR 71654
Ph:(870)222-4451
Fax: (870)222-5729
Co. E-mail: paula@mcgeheechamber.com
URL: http://www.mcgeheechamber.com
Contact: Paula Mote, Mgr.

57195 ■ Melbourne Area Chamber of Commerce
PO Box 128
Melbourne, AR 72556
Ph:(870)368-4215
Fax: (870)368-4721
Contact: James Miller, Pres.

57196 ■ Mena/Polk County Chamber of Commerce
524 Sherwood Ave.
Mena, AR 71953
Ph:(479)394-2912
Fax: (479)394-5394
Co. E-mail: menapolkcofc@voltage.net
Contact: Lynn Oglesby, Exec.VP

57197 ■ Monticello Drew County Chamber of Commerce
335 E Gaines St.
Monticello, AR 71655
Ph:(870)367-6741
Fax: (870)367-0050
Co. E-mail: monticellochamber@sbcglobal.net
URL: http://www.montdrewchamber.com
Contact: Glenda Nichols-Bolin, Exec.Dir.

57198 ■ Morrilton Area Chamber of Commerce
PO Box 589
Morrilton, AR 72110
Ph:(501)354-2393
Fax: (501)354-8642
Co. E-mail: johngibson@cox-internet.com
URL: http://www.morrilton.com
Contact: John Gibson, Pres.

57199 ■ Mount Ida Area Chamber of Commerce
PO Box 6
Mount Ida, AR 71957-0006
Ph:(870)867-2723
Fax: (870)867-5099
Co. E-mail: director@mtichamber.com
URL: http://www.mtidachamber.com
Contact: Phillip Carr, Pres.

57200 ■ Mountain Home Area Chamber of Commerce
PO Box 488
Mountain Home, AR 72654-0488
Ph:(870)425-5111
Free: 800-822-3536
Fax: (870)425-4446
Co. E-mail: visitus@mtnhomechamber.com
URL: http://www.mtnhomechamber.com
Contact: Barbara Fouts, Exec.Dir.

57201 ■ North Little Rock Chamber of Commerce
100 Main St.
PO Box 5288
North Little Rock, AR 72114
Ph:(501)372-5959
Fax: (501)372-5955
Co. E-mail: nlrchamber@nlrchamber.org
URL: http://www.nlrchamber.org
Contact: Terry Hartwick, Pres./CEO

57202 ■ Osceola-South Mississippi County Chamber of Commerce
PO Box 174
Osceola, AR 72370-0174

Ph:(870)563-2281
Fax: (870)563-5385
Co. E-mail: info@osceolachamber.net
URL: http://www.osceolachamber.net
Contact: Lynnette Trail, Exec.Dir.

57203 ■ Ozark Area Chamber of Commerce
300 W Commercial
Ozark, AR 72949
Ph:(479)667-2525
Free: 800-951-2525
Fax: (479)667-5750
Co. E-mail: info@ozarkareacoc.com
URL: http://www.ozarkareacoc.com
Contact: Dale Abbott, Mgr.

57204 ■ Paragould - Greene County Chamber of Commerce
PO Box 124
Paragould, AR 72450
Ph:(870)236-7684
Fax: (870)236-1517
Co. E-mail: ceo@paragould.org
URL: http://www.paragould.org
Contact: Sue McGowan, Dir./CEO

57205 ■ Paris Area Chamber of Commerce
301 W Walnut
Paris, AR 72855-3731
Ph:(479)963-2244
Fax: (479)963-8321
Co. E-mail: parischamber@centurytel.net
URL: http://www.paris-ar.com
Contact: Rick Allen, Pres.

57206 ■ Philips County Chamber of Commerce
111 Hickory Hill Dr.
PO Box 447
Helena, AR 72342
Ph:(870)338-8327
Fax: (870)338-6445
Co. E-mail: pcchamber@cox-internet.com
URL: http://www.phillipscountychamber.com
Contact: Mrs. Barbara King, Pres.

57207 ■ Piggott Chamber of Commerce
PO Box 96
Piggott, AR 72454
Ph:(870)598-3167
Co. E-mail: cchamber@piggott.net
Contact: Gayla Donner, Pres.

57208 ■ Prairie Grove Chamber of Commerce
PO Box 23
Prairie Grove, AR 72753
Ph:(479)846-2197
Co. E-mail: info@pgchamber.com
URL: http://www.pgchamber.com
Contact: Tom Willcutt, Pres.

57209 ■ Randolph County Chamber of Commerce
PO Box 466
Pocahontas, AR 72455-0466
Ph:(870)892-3956
Fax: (870)892-5399
Co. E-mail: chamber@tcac.net
URL: http://www.randolphchamber.com
Contact: Mr. Wayne Gearhart, Exec.Dir.

57210 ■ Rector Chamber of Commerce
PO Box 307
Rector, AR 72461-0307
Ph:(870)595-3549
Fax: (870)595-3611
Co. E-mail: ccd@rectorarkansas.com
URL: http://www.dina.org/resources/chambers.html
Contact: Ms. Nancy J. Kemp, Pres.

57211 ■ Rogers Lowell Area Chamber of Commerce
317 W Walnut
Rogers, AR 72756-4566
Ph:(479)636-1240
Fax: (479)636-5485

Co. E-mail: info@rogerslowell.com
URL: http://www.rogerslowell.com
Contact: Mr. Raymond M. Burns CCE, Pres./CEO

57212 ■ Russellville Chamber of Commerce
708 W Main St.
Russellville, AR 72801-3617
Ph:(479)968-2530
Fax: (479)968-5894
Co. E-mail: chamber@russellville.org
URL: http://www.russellvillechamber.org
Contact: Jeff Pipkin, Pres./CEO

57213 ■ Searcy Chamber of Commerce
2323 S Main St.
Searcy, AR 72143
Ph:(501)268-2458
Fax: (501)268-9530
Co. E-mail: scc@cswnet.com
URL: http://www.searcyarkansas.org
Contact: Buck C. Layne Jr., Pres.

57214 ■ Searcy County Chamber of Commerce
PO Box 1385
Marshall, AR 72650
Ph:(870)448-5788
Fax: (870)448-5788
Co. E-mail: information@searcycountychamber.com
URL: http://www.searcycountychamber.com

57215 ■ Sherwood Chamber of Commerce
PO Box 6082
Sherwood, AR 72124
Ph:(501)835-7600
Fax: (501)835-2326
Co. E-mail: shwdchamber@cityofsherwood.net
URL: http://www.cityofsherwood.net
Contact: Pat Layton, Exec. Dir.

57216 ■ Siloam Springs Chamber of Commerce
PO Box 476
Siloam Springs, AR 72761-0476
Ph:(479)524-6466
Fax: (479)549-3032
Co. E-mail: info@siloamchamber.com
URL: http://www.siloamchamber.com
Contact: Paul Joseph, Pres.

57217 ■ Spring River Area Chamber of Commerce
PO Box 1234
Hardy, AR 72542
Ph:(870)856-3210
Fax: (870)856-5678
Co. E-mail: info@sracc.com
URL: http://www.sracc.com
Contact: Clint Wiles, Pres.

57218 ■ Springdale Chamber of Commerce
PO Box 166
Springdale, AR 72765-0166
Ph:(479)872-2222
Free: 800-972-7261
Fax: (479)751-4699
Co. E-mail: info@springdale.com
URL: http://www.springdale.com
Contact: Perry Webb CCE, Pres./CEO

57219 ■ Stephens Chamber of Commerce
PO Box 572
Stephens, AR 71764
Ph:(870)786-5221
Fax: (870)786-5749
Contact: Margie L. Wagnon, Sec./Mgr.

57220 ■ Stuttgart Chamber of Commerce
507 S Main St.
PO Box 1500
Stuttgart, AR 72160
Ph:(870)673-1602
Fax: (870)673-1604
Co. E-mail: chamber@stuttgartarkansas.org
URL: http://stuttgartarkansas.com
Contact: Mr. Stephen R. Bell, Exec.VP

57221 ■ Sulphur Springs Community Chamber of Commerce
PO Box 115
Sulphur Springs, AR 72768-0115
Ph:(479)298-3297
Fax: (479)298-3562
Contact: Steve Sevak, Pres.

57222 ■ Trumann Area Chamber of Commerce
PO Box 215
Trumann, AR 72472
Ph:(870)483-5424
Fax: (870)483-6660
Co. E-mail: tchamber@bscn.com
Contact: Mr. Jackie Ross, Exec.Dir.

57223 ■ Tuckerman Chamber of Commerce
PO Box 1117
Tuckerman, AR 72473
Ph:(870)349-5313
Fax: (870)349-5336
Co. E-mail: cityoftuckerman@yahoo.com
Contact: Gerald Jackson, Pres.

57224 ■ Van Buren Chamber of Commerce
1103 E End Plz.
Van Buren, AR 72956
Ph:(479)474-2761
Fax: (479)474-6259
Co. E-mail: dorvan@vanburenchamber.org
URL: http://www.vanburenchamber.org
Contact: Dorvan Wiley, Exec.Dir.

57225 ■ Waldron Area Chamber of Commerce
323 Washington St.
PO Box 1985
Waldron, AR 72958
Ph:(479)637-2775
Fax: (479)637-0041
Co. E-mail: info@waldronar.com
URL: http://www.waldronar.com
Contact: Shana Slaten, Exec. Dir.

57226 ■ Walnut Ridge/Lawrence County Chamber of Commerce
PO Box 842
Walnut Ridge, AR 72476-0842
Ph:(870)886-3232
Fax: (870)886-1736
Co. E-mail: lawrencecofc@cox-internet.com
Contact: Mr. Ted Moskal, Exec.Dir.

57227 ■ Ward Chamber of Commerce
80 S 2nd St.
Ward, AR 72176
Ph:(501)843-6533
Contact: Ginny Sue Woods

57228 ■ Watson Chamber of Commerce
PO Box 143
Watson, AR 71674
Ph:(870)644-3893
Fax: (870)644-3254
Contact: Sherrie Ferguson, Sec.

57229 ■ Weiner Area Chamber of Commerce
PO Box 361
Weiner, AR 72479
Ph:(870)684-2221
Contact: Marjorie Huber, Pres.

57230 ■ White Hall Chamber of Commerce
102 Anderson St.
White Hall, AR 71602
Ph:(870)247-5502
Co. E-mail: dburdick@pbjc-lib.state.ar.us
URL: http://www.whitehallarkansas.org
Contact: David Matheny, Pres.

57231 ■ Yellville Area Chamber of Commerce
PO Box 369
Yellville, AR 72687
Ph:(870)449-4676
Free: 800-832-1414
Fax: (870)449-4671

Co. E-mail: chamber@yellville.com
URL: http://www.yellville.com
Contact: Joy Copeland, Pres.

MINORITY BUSINESS ASSISTANCE PROGRAMS

57232 ■ Arkansas Department Of Economic Development–Small and Minority Business Division
1 State Capitol Mall
Little Rock, AR 72201
Ph:(501)682-6105
Fax: (501)324-9856
Co. E-mail: info@1800arkansas.com
URL: http://www.1800arkansas.com
Contact: Larry Walther, Dir
Description: Provides financial assistance, training seminars, and technical and management assistance to new and expanding minority businesses. Also refers these businesses to other organizations that offer assistance.

FINANCING AND LOAN PROGRAMS

57233 ■ Alltel Ventures
1 Allied Dr.
Little Rock, AR 72202
Ph:(501)905-8970
Fax: (501)905-8589
URL: http://www.alltel.com

57234 ■ Arkansas Capital Corp.
225 South Pulaski St.
Little Rock, AR 72201
Ph:(501)374-9247
Fax: (501)374-9425
URL: http://www.arcapital.com
Contact: Sam Walls, Chairman and CEO
Investment Types: Expansion.

PROCUREMENT ASSISTANCE PROGRAMS

57235 ■ Arkansas Procurement Assistance Center (APAC)
127 W 5th St.
Malvern, AR 72104
Ph:(501)337-5355
Fax: (501)337-5045
Co. E-mail: apac@uaex.edu
URL: http://www.arcommunities.org/
Contact: Sue Coates, Prgm Dir
E-mail: aptan@primenet.com

INCUBATORS/RESEARCH AND TECHNOLOGY PARKS

57236 ■ Arkansas Biotechnology Incubator–Biomedical Biotechnology Center
4301 W Markham St.
Little Rock, AR 72205
Ph:(501)686-6696
Fax: (501)686-8501
Co. E-mail: biotech@uams.edu
URL: http://www.uamsbiotech.com
Contact: Timothy O'Brien, Dir
Description: The BBC was established to promote Arkansas' biotechnology. The Center seeks to support technology transfer and startup company development as well as forge alliances between industry and research institutions.

57237 ■ Genesis Technology Incubator
Engineering Research Center
University of Arkansas
700 Research Center Blvd.
Fayetteville, AR 72701

Ph:(479)575-7227
Fax: (479)575-7446
URL: http://www.genesis.uark.edu
Contact: Phil Stafford, Dir
Description: GENESIS provides office space and shared services to technology-based entrepreneurs, enhanced by the resources of the University of Arkansas.

57238 ■ University of Arkansas–Arkansas Center for Technology Transfer
700 Research Center Blvd.
Fayetteville, AR 72701
Ph:(501)575-7227
Fax: (501)575-6615
Co. E-mail: mcl3@engr.uark.edu
Contact: Dr. Marcus C. Langston, Dir.
E-mail: mcl3@engr.uark.edu
Scope: Provides research and technical facilities to analyze factors such as production, workforce motivation and training, and technical problems. Facilitates research and technology transfer in the areas of manufacturing technology, interactive technology, productivity, and industrial efficiency. Specific projects include bar-code reading of trucks at weigh stations, scales to weigh-in-motion, tactile sensing, and advanced brakes, clutches, and transmissions. **Services:** Technical assistance, to entrepreneurs and small businesses statewide; Technical seminars, on automation, productivity, quality, and computer-aided-design and computer-aided-manufacturing. **Awards:** Graduate research assistantships.

57239 ■ University of Arkansas–Research Support and Sponsored Programs
120 Ozark Hall
Fayetteville, AR 72701
Ph:(479)575-3845
Fax: (479)575-3846
Co. E-mail: rsspinfo@uark.edu
URL: http://www.uark.edu/admin/rsspinfo
Contact: Dr. Rosemary Ruff, Dir.
E-mail: rsspinfo@uark.edu
Scope: Administers all contract and grant research and other sponsored programs conducted at the University. Oversees patent and copyright administration and technology transfer. Assists faculty members in preparing proposals for submission to prospective sponsors of research projects and serves as liaison with extramural sponsors. Also provides administrative support to research workers, including reproduction, computer, shop, and special equipment services. The office is also responsible for research compliance. **Publications:** Monthly; On-line newsletter. **Educational Activities:** Seminar/workshop, for faculty members on research opportunities.

LEGISLATIVE ASSISTANCE

57240 ■ Arkansas House and Senate Committees on Insurance and Commerce
State Capitol Bldg, Rm. 315
Little Rock, AR 72201

Ph:(501)682-1937
Fax: (501)682-1936
URL: http://www.arkleg.state.ar.us
Contact: Toni Minicozzi

PUBLICATIONS

57241 ■ *Arkansas Business*
201 E. Markham, Ste. 220
Little Rock, AR 72201-1651
Ph:(501)372-1443
Fax: (501)375-0933
Co. E-mail: abnews@abnews.com
URL: http://abnews.com

57242 ■ *Starting and Operating a Business in Arkansas: A Step-by-Step Guide*
PSI Research
300 N. Valley Dr.
Grants Pass, OR 97526
Ph:(503)479-9464
Free: 800-228-2275
Fax: (503)476-1479
Co. E-mail: psi2@magick.net
Ed: Michael D. Jenkins. **Released:** Revised edition, 1992. **Price:** $29.95 (looseleaf binder); $24.95 (paper). **Description:** Part of the Successful Business Library series.

SMALL BUSINESS DEVELOPMENT CENTER LEAD OFFICE

57243 ■ California Small Business Development Center–California Trade and Commerce Agency
801 K St., Ste 1700
Sacramento, CA 95814
Ph:(916)324-5068
Fax: (916)322-5084
URL: http://commerce.ca.gov/business/small/ starting/sb_sbdcl.html
Contact: Kim Neri, State Director

57244 ■ Fresno SBDC–UC Merced Lead Center–University of California at Merced (550 E)
550 E. Shaw, Ste. 105-A
Fresno, CA 93710
Ph:(559)241-6590
Fax: (559)241-7422
URL: http://sbdc.ucmerced.edu
Contact: Chris Rosander, State Dir.
E-mail: crosander@ucmerced.edu

57245 ■ Los Angeles Region SBDC–Long Beach Community College District
3950 Paramount Blvd., Ste. 101
Lakewood, CA 90712
Ph:(562)938-5004
Fax: (562)938-5030
URL: http://www.lasbdcnet.org
Contact: Sheneui Sloan, Interim Lead Center Dir.
E-mail: ssloan@lbcc.edu

57246 ■ San Francisco SBDC–Northern California SBDC Lead Center–Humboldt State University (Offic)
Office of Economic Development
Siemens Hall
1 Harpst St., 2006A
Arcata, CA 95521
Ph:(707)445-9720
Fax: (707)445-9652
URL: http://www.norcalsbdc.org
Contact: Kristin Johnson, Regional Dir.
E-mail: johnson@northcoastsbdc.org

57247 ■ Santa Ana SBDC–Tri-County Lead SBDC–California State University at Fullerton (800 N)
800 N. State College Blvd., LH640
Fullerton, CA 92834
Ph:(714)278-2719
Fax: (714)278-7858
URL: http://www.leadsbdc.org
Contact: Vi Pham, Lead Center Dir.
E-mail: vpham@fullerton.edu

SMALL BUSINESS DEVELOPMENT CENTERS

57248 ■ Alliance Small Business Development Center–Merced Satellite
Merced Tri College Center
Bldg. TC-3, Rm. D
PO Box 1029
Merced, CA 95341
Ph:(209)381-6557
Fax: (209)381-6552
URL: http://www.alliancesbdc.com
Contact: Mike Souza, Satellite Mgr.
E-mail: msouza@alliancesbdc.com

57249 ■ Amador County Outreach - Satellite SBDC
1500 S. Hwy. 49
PO Box 1077
Jackson, CA 95642
Ph:(209)223-0351
Fax: (209)223-2261

57250 ■ Butte College–Small Business Development Center
19 Williamsburg Ln.
Chico, CA 95926
Ph:(530)895-9017
Fax: (530)566-9851
URL: http://www.bcsbdc.org
Contact: Sophie Konuwa, Dir.
E-mail: Konuwaso@butte.edu

57251 ■ Cascade Small Business Development Center
1420 Butte St.
Redding, CA 96001
Ph:(530)245-7348
Fax: (530)225-3904
URL: http://www3.shastacollege.edu/sbdc/ CascadeSBDC/Welcome.html
Contact: Brad Banghart, Dir.
E-mail: bbanghart@shastacollege.edu

57252 ■ Central California–Small Business Development Center
3302 N. Blackstone Ave., Ste. 225
Fresno, CA 93726
Ph:(559)230-4056
URL: http://www.ccsbdc.org
Contact: Richard T. Wheeler, Dir.

57253 ■ Central California /Visalia Satellite–SBDC
220 N. Santa Fe Ave.
Visalia, CA 93292
Ph:(559)625-3051
Fax: (559)625-3053
Co. E-mail: wendim@ccsbdc.org
URL: http://www.ccsbdc.org
Contact: Brian Moe, Satellite Mgr.
E-mail: blmoe@ccsbdc.org

57254 ■ Central Coast Small Business Development Center–Cabrillo College
6500 Soquel Dr.
Aptos, CA 95003
Ph:(831)479-6136
Fax: (831)479-6166
URL: http://www.centralcoastsbdc.org
Contact: Teresa Thomae, Dir.
E-mail: tethomae@cabrillo.cc.ca.us

57255 ■ Contra Costa SBDC
2425 Bisso Ln., Ste. 200
Concord, CA 94520
Ph:(925)646-5377
Fax: (925)646-5299
Co. E-mail: info@ContraCostaSBDC.com
URL: http://www.ContraCostaSBDC.com
Contact: Beverly Hamile, Dir.

57256 ■ East Bay Small Business Development Center
475 14th. St., Ste. 150
Oakland, CA 94612
Ph:(510)208-0410
Fax: (510)208-0413
Co. E-mail: info@eastbaysbdc.org
Contact: Raj George, Dir.
E-mail: fhameed@ebsbdc.org

57257 ■ El Centro SBDC Service Center
301 N. Imperial Ave., Ste. B
El Centro, CA 92248
Ph:(760)312-9800
Fax: (760)312-9838
URL: http://www.ivsbdc.org
Contact: Ben Solomon, Dir.
E-mail: ben.solomon@imperial.edu

57258 ■ Export SBDC of Southern California
222 N. Sepulveda, Ste. 1690
El Segundo, CA 90245
Ph:(310)606-0166
Fax: (310)606-0155
Co. E-mail: info@exportsbdc.org
URL: http://www.exportsbdc.org
Contact: Gladys Moreau, Dir.

57259 ■ Gavilan College–Small Business Development Center
8351 Church St., Bldg. E
Gilroy, CA 95020
Ph:(408)847-0373
Fax: (408)847-0393
URL: http://www.gavilansbdc.org
Contact: Richard Gillis, Dir.
E-mail: rgillis@dsldesigns.net

57260 ■ Greater Sacramento SBDC
1410 Ethan Way
Sacramento, CA 95825-2205
Ph:(916)563-3220
Fax: (916)563-3266
URL: http://www.sbdc.net
Contact: Molly Stuart
E-mail: stuartmo@losrios.edu

57261 ■ Greater San Diego Chamber of Commerce–Small Business Development Center
4275 Executive Sq., Ste. 920
La Jolla, CA 92037
Ph:(619)453-9388
Fax: (619)450-1997
Co. E-mail: sbdc@smallbiz.org
URL: http://www.smallbiz.org
Contact: Hal Lefkowitz, Dir.

57262 ■ Inland Empire North SBDC–Satellite Center
15490 Civic Dr., Ste. 102
Victorville, CA 92392
Ph:(760)951-1592
Fax: (760)951-8929
URL: http://www.iesbdc.org
Contact: Louisa Miller, Business Consultant
E-mail: lmiller@iesbdc.org

57263 ■ Inland Empire SBDC Coachella Valley SBDC–Coachella Valley Satellite Center
500 S. Palm Canyon Dr., Ste. 222
Palm Springs, CA 92264
Ph:(760)864-1311
Fax: (760)864-1319
URL: http://www.iesbdc.org
Contact: Brad Mix, Consultant
E-mail: bmix@iesbdc.org

57264 ■ Inland Empire Small Business Development Center
1201 Research Park Dr., Ste. 100
Riverside, CA 92507
Ph:(951)781-2345
Free: 800-750-2353
Fax: (951)781-2353
URL: http://www.iesbdc.org
Contact: Vincent McCoy, Dir.
E-mail: jhoff@iesbdc.org

57265 ■ Mt. San Antonio College SBDC
363 S. Park Ave., Ste. 101
Pomona, CA 91766
Free: 800-450-7232
Fax: (909)629-8310
Contact: Mike Brady, Dir.
E-mail: mbrady@mtsac.edu

57266 ■ Napa Valley College–Small Business Development Center
1556 First St., Ste. 103
Napa, CA 94559
Ph:(707)253-3210
Fax: (707)253-3068
Co. E-mail: nvcsbdc@napasbdc.org
URL: http://www.napasbdc.org/
Contact: Elizabeth Pratt, Dir.
E-mail: apratt@napavalley.edu

57267 ■ North Coast–Small Business Development Center
520 E St.
Eureka, CA 95501
Ph:(707)445-9720
Fax: (707)445-9652
URL: http://www.northcoastsbdc.org
Contact: Kristin Johnson, Dir.

57268 ■ Orange County–Small Business Development Center
2323 N. Broadway, Ste. 201
Santa Ana, CA 92706
Ph:(714)564-5200
Fax: (714)647-1168
URL: http://www.ocsbdc.com/
Contact: Leila Mozaffari, Dir.
E-mail: mozaffari_leila@rsccd.org

57269 ■ Redwood Empire–Small Business Development Center
606 Healdsburg Ave.
Santa Rosa, CA 95401
Ph:(707)524-1770
Fax: (707)524-1772

URL: http://www.santarosa.edu/sbdc
Contact: Lorraine DuVerney, Dir.
E-mail: lduverney@santarosa.edu

57270 ■ Sacramento SBDC–California State University at Chico
PO Box 765
Chico, CA 95929-0765
Ph:(530)898-4598
Fax: (530)898-4734
URL: http://qsbdc.csuchico.edu
Contact: Dan Ripke, Interim Regional Dir.
E-mail: dripke@csuchico.edu

57271 ■ San Diego SBDC–Southwestern Community College District
900 Otey Lakes Rd.
Chula Vista, CA 91910
Ph:(619)482-6388
Fax: (619)482-6402
URL: http://www.sbditc.org
Contact: Debbie P. Trujillo, Regional Dir.

57272 ■ San Francisco SBDC
455 Market St., 6th Fl.
San Francisco, CA 94105-2420
Ph:(415)908-7501
Fax: (415)974-6035
Contact: Albert Dixon, Director
E-mail: al@sfsbdc.org

57273 ■ San Joaquin Delta College–Small Business Development Center
445 N. San Joaquin St.
Stockton, CA 95202
Ph:(209)943-5089
Fax: (209)943-8325
URL: http://www.asbdc-us.org/
Contact: Gillian Murphy, Dir.
E-mail: gmurphy@deltacollege.edu

57274 ■ Sierra College–Small Business Development Center
11930 Heritage Oak Place, Ste. 1
Auburn, CA 95603
Ph:(530)885-5488
Fax: (530)823-2831
Co. E-mail: sbdcinfo@sbdcsierra.org
URL: http://www.sbdcsierra.org
Contact: Indria Gillespie, Dir.
E-mail: igillspie@sierracollege.edu

57275 ■ Silicon Valley SBDC–De Anza College
84 W. Santa Clara St., Ste. 100
San Jose, CA 95113-1815
Ph:(408)494-0240
Fax: (408)494-0245
URL: http://www.siliconvalley-sbdc.org/
Contact: Becky Walker, Dir.
E-mail: beckw@siliconvalley-sbdc.org

57276 ■ Southwestern College–Small Business Development and International Trade Center
900 Otay Lakes Rd., Bldg. 1600
Chula Vista, CA 91910
Ph:(619)482-6391
Fax: (619)482-6402
Co. E-mail: support@sbditc.org
URL: http://www.sbditc.org
Contact: Victor M. Castillo, Dir.
E-mail: vcastillo@swccd.edu

57277 ■ Stanislaus Economic Development and Workplace Alliance–Small Business Development Center
1010 10th St. Pl.
PO Box 3091
Modesto, CA 95354
Ph:(209)567-4985
Fax: (209)567-4944
URL: http://www.alliancesbdc.com
Contact: Kurtis Clark, Dir.

57278 ■ Weill Institute SBDC at Bakersfield
2100 Chester Ave., 1st Fl.
Bakersfield, CA 93301

Ph:(661)395-4125
Fax: (661)395-4134
Co. E-mail: weill@slightspeed.net
URL: http://www.weill-sbdc.com
Contact: Peter DeArmond, Dir.
E-mail: pdearmon@bakersfieldcollege.edu

57279 ■ Yuba College SBDC
330 9th St.
PO Box 262
Marysville, CA 95901
Ph:(530)-749-0153
Fax: (530)749-0155
URL: http://www.yubasbdc.org
Contact: Ken Freeman, Dir.

SMALL BUSINESS ASSISTANCE PROGRAMS

57280 ■ California Trade and Commerce Agency–Office of Business Development
801 K St., Ste. 1700
Sacramento, CA 95814
Ph:(916)322-1394
Fax: (916)323-7481
URL: http://www.commerce.ca.gov
Description: Assists new and expanding businesses by providing economic and employment information for various locations, and aiding them in finding financing. Also acts as an advocate for business.

57281 ■ California Trade and Commerce Agency–Office of Economic Research
801 K St., Ste. 1700
Sacramento, CA 95814
Ph:(916)322-3539
Fax: (916)322-0669
URL: http://www.commerce.ca.gov
Description: Conducts research and compiles economic and demographic data on communities inside and outside California. Provides information to the public upon request.

57282 ■ California Trade and Commerce Agency–Office of Small Business
1102 Q St.
Sacramento, CA 95814
Ph:(916)322-5790
Fax: (916)322-5084
URL: http://www.commerce.ca.gov
Description: Provides information on business regulations and licenses, how to start a business, and sources of financing; sells guidebooks and manuals; advocates on behalf of small businesses; provides management and technical counseling; and offers seminars. Coordinates loan programs, such as the Small Business Loan Guarantee Program for small firms that are unable to obtain loans at a reasonable cost; the New Product Development Program; Energy Reduction Loans; the Hazardous Waste Reduction Loan Program; the Farm Loan Program; and loans from Business and Industrial Development Corporations. Holds annually a small business conference, which provides information to current and prospective small business owners, and the Governor's Women-in-Business Conference.

SCORE OFFICES

57283 ■ SCORE Antelope Valley
c/o Mr. Harry Brodock, Chm.
1212 East Ave. S
Palmdale, CA 93550
Ph:(661)947-7679
Co. E-mail: avscore@antelecom.net
URL: http://www.score.av.org
Contact: Mr. Harry Brodock, Chm.
Description: Assists individuals with their decisions to begin or to operate small businesses. Provides educational seminars and business counseling.

57284 ■ SCORE Central California
2719 N Air Fresno Dr., Ste. 200
Fresno, CA 93727-1547
Ph:(559)487-5605
Fax: (559)487-5636
Co. E-mail: jonestiii@aol.com
Description: Provides professional guidance and information to maximize the success of existing and emerging small businesses. Offers business counseling and workshops.

57285 ■ SCORE Central Coast
509 W Morrison Ave.
Santa Maria, CA 93454
Ph:(805)739-8928
Fax: (805)739-8928
Co. E-mail: score491@best1.net
Description: Provides professional guidance and information to maximize the success of existing and emerging small businesses. Offers business counseling and workshops.

57286 ■ SCORE - Counselors to America's Small Business
550 W C St., Ste. 550
San Diego, CA 92101
Ph:(619)557-7272
Fax: (619)557-5894
Co. E-mail: sd.score@sba.gov
URL: http://www.score-sandiego.org
Contact: Rodney D. Means, Pres.
Description: Provides free business counseling and management training programs for small business owners/managers, and for those who plan to start a new business.

57287 ■ SCORE East Bay
519 17th St., Ste. 240
Oakland, CA 94612
Ph:(510)273-6611
Fax: (510)273-6015
Co. E-mail: eastbayscore@yahoo.com
URL: http://www.eastbayscore.org
Contact: Pat Lopez
Description: Provides professional guidance and information to maximize the success of existing and emerging small businesses. Offers business counseling and workshops.

57288 ■ SCORE Golden Empire
2100 Chester Ave., Ste. 167
Bakersfield, CA 93301
Ph:(661)395-4126
Fax: (661)395-4134
Co. E-mail: thiesen777@cs.com
URL: http://www.bakersfield.org/score
Contact: Paul Leung, Chapter Chm.
Description: Assists individuals with their decisions to begin or to operate small businesses. Provides educational seminars and business counseling.

57289 ■ SCORE Greater Chico Area
1324 Mangrove St., Ste. 114
Chico, CA 95926
Ph:(530)342-8932
Fax: (530)342-8932
Co. E-mail: counsel@scorechico.org
Description: Assists individuals with their decisions to begin or to operate small businesses. Provides educational seminars and business counseling.

57290 ■ SCORE Inland Empire Chapter 503
1700 E Florida Ave.
Hemet, CA 92544-4679
Ph:(909)652-4390
Fax: (909)929-8543
Co. E-mail: score503@netzero.com
URL: http://www.iescore503.org
Contact: Mr. Herbert R. Carter, Chm.
Description: Provides business counseling to help meet the needs of small business owners and entrepreneurs. Offers workshops and guidance to small business owners and start-up entrepreneurs.

57291 ■ SCORE Los Angeles
330 N Brand Blvd., Ste. 190
Glendale, CA 91203-2304

Ph:(818)552-3206
Fax: (818)547-1220
Co. E-mail: 09@scorela.org
URL: http://www.scorela.org
Contact: Steve Pinard, Sec.
Description: Provides professional guidance and information to maximize the success of existing and emerging small businesses. Offers business counseling and workshops.

57292 ■ SCORE Monterey Bay
c/o Monterey Peninsula Chamber of Commerce
380 Alvarado St.
Monterey, CA 93940
Ph:(831)648-5360
Co. E-mail: montereybayscore@aol.com
URL: http://www.bayscore.org
Description: Assists individuals with their decisions to begin or to operate small businesses. Provides educational seminars and business counseling.

57293 ■ SCORE North Coast
777 Sonoma Ave., Rm. 115 B
Santa Rosa, CA 95404
Ph:(707)571-8342
Fax: (707)541-0331
Co. E-mail: score450@iscweb.com
URL: http://www.scorenorthcoastca.org
Description: Provides assistance to both existing and start-up small businesses. Offers workshops and counseling.

57294 ■ SCORE Orange City
200 W Santa Ana Blvd., 7th Fl.
Santa Ana, CA 92701
Ph:(714)550-7369
Fax: (714)550-0191
Co. E-mail: information@score114.org
URL: http://www.score114.org
Contact: Bill Morland, Chm.
Description: Provides professional guidance and information to maximize the success of existing and emerging small businesses. Offers business counseling and workshops.

57295 ■ SCORE Palm Springs
901 E Tahquitz Canyon Way, Ste. A-103
Palm Springs, CA 92262-6706
Ph:(760)320-6682
Fax: (760)323-9426
Co. E-mail: srichrich@aol.com

57296 ■ SCORE Sacramento
4990 Stockton Blvd.
Sacramento, CA 95820
Ph:(916)635-9085
Fax: (916)455-9089
Co. E-mail: info@sacscore.org
URL: http://www.sacscore.org
Contact: Tim Melson, Pres.
Description: Provides counseling, training, and resource material for businesses throughout Sacramento and the surrounding region. Conducts seminars and workshops for small business owners.

57297 ■ SCORE San Francisco
c/o Al Pose, Chm.
455 Market St. 6th Fl.
San Francisco, CA 94105
Ph:(415)744-6827
Free: 800-310-4357
Fax: (415)744-6750
Co. E-mail: sfscore@sfscore.com
URL: http://www.sfscore.com
Contact: Al Pose, Chm.

57298 ■ SCORE San Luis Obispo
4111 Broad St., Ste. A
San Luis Obispo, CA 93401
Ph:(805)547-0779
Co. E-mail: info@sloscore.org
URL: http://www.sloscore.org
Description: Assists individuals with their decisions to begin or to operate small businesses. Provides educational seminars and business counseling.

57299 ■ SCORE Santa Barbara
c/o Mr. Gerald W. Harter, Chm.
PO Box 30602
Santa Barbara, CA 93130-0602
Ph:(805)563-0084
Co. E-mail: info@score-santabarbara.org
URL: http://www.score-santabarbara.org
Contact: Mr. Gerald W. Harter, Chm.
Description: Provides professional guidance and information to maximize the success of existing and emerging small businesses. Offers business counseling and workshops.

57300 ■ SCORE Shasta
c/o Carol Starnes, Chair
737 Auditorium Dr.
Redding, CA 96099
Ph:(530)225-2770
URL: http://www.score.org

57301 ■ SCORE Silicon Valley
c/o Wally Dale, Chm.
84 W Santa Clara St., Ste. 100, Entrepreneur Ctr.
San Jose, CA 95113
Ph:(408)288-8479
Fax: (408)494-0214
Co. E-mail: svscore@hotmail.com
URL: http://www.svscore.org
Contact: Mr. Robert W. Goedjen, Marketing Mgr.
Description: Previous owners or senior managers of businesses. Works to provide counseling to small businesses and startups. Conducts regular workshop in starting and managing a business. Offers e-mail counseling on various topics, assessment of businesses, and mentoring of clients.

57302 ■ SCORE Stockton
401 N San Joaquin St., Rm. 114
Stockton, CA 95202
Ph:(209)946-6293
Fax: (209)946-6294
Co. E-mail: scoreca463@aol.com
URL: http://www.scorestockton.org
Description: Promotes entrepreneur education and the formation, growth and success of the nation's small business.

57303 ■ SCORE Tuolumne County
c/o Tuolome Chamber of Commerce
222 S Shephard St.
Sonora, CA 95370
Ph:(209)588-0128
Fax: (209)588-0673
Co. E-mail: score@mlode.com
Description: Assists individuals with their decisions to begin or to operate small businesses. Provides educational seminars and business counseling.

57304 ■ SCORE Ventura
400 E Esplanade Dr., Ste. 300
Oxnard, CA 93036-2146
Ph:(805)676-7500
Fax: (805)650-1414
Co. E-mail: scoreven@dslextreme.com
URL: http://www.scoreventura.org
Contact: Steve Sarchett, Chm.
Description: Provides professional guidance and information to maximize the success of existing and emerging small businesses. Offers business counseling and workshops.

57305 ■ SCORE Yosemite
c/o Modesto Chamber of Commerce
1114 J St.
Modesto, CA 95354
Ph:(209)577-5757
Fax: (209)577-2673
Co. E-mail: chapter@score556.org
URL: http://www.score556.org
Description: Assists individuals with their decisions to begin or to operate small businesses. Provides educational seminars and business counseling.

BETTER BUSINESS BUREAUS

57306 ■ Better Business Bureau
1000 Broadway, Ste. 625
Oakland, CA 94607-4042
Ph:(510)844-2000
Free: (866)411-2221
Fax: (510)844-2100
Co. E-mail: info@oakland.bbb.org
URL: http://bbbgoldengate.org
Contact: Gene O'Neil, Pres.

57307 ■ Better Business Bureau of Central California
4201 W Shaw Ave., Ste. 107
Fresno, CA 93722
Ph:(559)222-8111
Fax: (559)228-6518
Co. E-mail: info@bbbcencal.org
URL: http://www.cencal.bbb.org
Contact: Doug Broten, CEO

57308 ■ Better Business Bureau, Encino
17609 Ventura Blvd., Ste. LL03
Encino, CA 91316-5138
Ph:(818)386-5510
Fax: (818)386-5513
Co. E-mail: info@labbb.org
URL: http://www.labbb.org
Contact: Joanne Smith

57309 ■ Better Business Bureau of Northeast California
400 South St.
Sacramento, CA 95814-6997
Ph:(916)443-6843
Fax: (916)443-0376
Co. E-mail: info@northeastcalifornia.bbb.org
URL: http://www.sacramento.bbb.org
Contact: Barry Goggin, Pres./CEO

57310 ■ Better Business Bureau of San Diego
5050 Murphy Canyon Rd., Ste. 110
San Diego, CA 92123
Ph:(858)496-2131
Fax: (858)496-2141
Co. E-mail: info@sandiego.bbb.org
URL: http://www.sandiego.bbb.org
Contact: Sheryl Charleston, Pres./CEO

57311 ■ Better Business Bureau of San Mateo County
510 Broadway, Ste. 200
Millbrae, CA 94030-1966
Ph:(650)552-9222
Free: (866)411-2221
Fax: (650)652-1748
Co. E-mail: info@sanmateo.bbb.org
URL: http://www.sanmateo.bbb.org
Contact: Gene O'Neil, Pres.

57312 ■ Better Business Bureau of Silicon Valley
700 Empey Way, Ste. No. 110
San Jose, CA 95128
Ph:(408)278-7400
Fax: (408)278-7444
Co. E-mail: info@bbbsilicon.org
URL: http://www.bbbsilicon.org

57313 ■ Better Business Bureau of the Southland
315 N La Cadena Dr.
Colton, CA 92324
Ph:(909)835-6064
Co. E-mail: info@labbb.org
URL: http://www.labbb.org
Contact: William G. Mitchell, Pres.

57314 ■ Better Business Bureau of Tri-Counties
PO Box 129
Santa Barbara, CA 93102

Ph:(805)963-8657
Fax: (805)962-8557
Co. E-mail: info@santabarbara.bbb.org
URL: http://www.santabarbara.bbb.org
Contact: Rick Copelan, Pres.

CHAMBERS OF COMMERCE

57315 ■ Acton Chamber of Commerce
PO Box 81
Acton, CA 93510
Ph:(661)269-5785
Fax: (661)269-4121
Co. E-mail: actoncoc@copper.net
URL: http://cityofacton.org
Contact: Farzad Tafreshi, Pres.

57316 ■ Adelanto Chamber of Commerce
11600 Air Expressway
PO Box 712
Adelanto, CA 92301-0712
Ph:(760)246-5711
Fax: (760)246-4019
Co. E-mail: adelantocc@mscomm.com
Contact: Becki States, Pres.

57317 ■ Agoura - Oak Park - Las Virgenes Chamber of Commerce
30101 Agoura Ct., Ste. 115
Agoura Hills, CA 91301
Ph:(818)889-3150
Fax: (818)889-3366
Co. E-mail: info@agourachamber.org
URL: http://www.agourachamber.org
Contact: Louis Masry, Pres.

57318 ■ Alameda Chamber of Commerce
1416 Park Ave.
Alameda, CA 94501-4579
Ph:(510)522-0414
Fax: (510)522-7677
Co. E-mail: connect@alamedachamber.com
URL: http://www.alamedachamber.com
Contact: Ms. Melody Marr, CEO

57319 ■ Albany Chamber of Commerce
1108 Solano Ave.
Albany, CA 94706
Ph:(510)525-1771
Fax: (510)525-6068
Co. E-mail: albanychamber@bigplanet.com
URL: http://www.albanychamber.org
Contact: James Carter, Exec.Dir.

57320 ■ Alhambra Chamber of Commerce
104 S 1st St.
Alhambra, CA 91801
Ph:(626)282-8481
Fax: (626)282-5596
Co. E-mail: alhambrachamber@yahoo.com
URL: http://www.alhambrachamber.org
Contact: Michael Carney, Pres.

57321 ■ Alpine Chamber of Commerce
2157 Alpine Blvd.
PO Box 69
Alpine, CA 91901
Ph:(619)445-2722
Fax: (619)445-2871
Co. E-mail: info@alpinechamber.com
URL: http://www.alpinechamber.com
Contact: Pat Cannon, CEO/Pres.

57322 ■ Alpine County Chamber of Commerce
PO Box 265
Markleeville, CA 96120
Ph:(530)694-2475
Fax: (530)694-2478
Co. E-mail: alpinecounty@alpinecounty.com
URL: http://www.alpinecounty.com
Contact: Teresa Burkhauser, Exec.Dir.

57323 ■ Altadena Chamber of Commerce
Altadena Community Center Bldg.
730 E Altadena Dr.
Altadena, CA 91001

Ph:(626)794-3988
Fax: (626)794-6015
Co. E-mail: altadenachamber@earthlink.net
URL: http://www.abacus-es.com/altadena
Contact: Eraca Allen, Pres.

57324 ■ Alturas Chamber of Commerce
522 S Main St.
Alturas, CA 96101-4115
Ph:(530)233-4434
Fax: (530)233-4434
Co. E-mail: contactus@alturaschamber.org
URL: http://www.alturaschamber.org
Contact: Micki Dodds, Pres.

57325 ■ Amador County Chamber of Commerce and Visitors Bureau
125 Peek St., Ste. B
PO Box 596
Jackson, CA 95642-0596
Ph:(209)223-0350
Free: 800-649-4988
Fax: (209)223-4425
Co. E-mail: info@amadorcountychamber.com
URL: http://www.amadorcountychamber.com
Contact: Jacqueline Lucido, Exec.Dir.

57326 ■ Anaheim Chamber of Commerce
201 E Center St.
Anaheim, CA 92805
Ph:(714)758-0222
Fax: (714)758-0468
Co. E-mail: info@anaheimchamber.org
URL: http://www.anaheimchamber.org
Contact: Todd Ament, Pres./CEO

57327 ■ Anderson Chamber of Commerce
2994 Ventura St.
PO Box 1144
Anderson, CA 96007-1144
Ph:(530)365-8095
Fax: (530)365-4561
Co. E-mail: lassenview@charter.net
Contact: Debe Hopkins, Exec.Dir.

57328 ■ Anderson Valley Chamber of Commerce
PO Box 275
Boonville, CA 95415
Ph:(707)895-2379
Co. E-mail: info@andersonvalleychamber.com
URL: http://www.andersonvalleychamber.com
Contact: Karen Newman, Pres.

57329 ■ Angwin Community Council
PO Box 747
Angwin, CA 94508
Ph:(707)965-2047
Co. E-mail: hford@puc.edu
URL: http://www.angwincouncil.org
Contact: Dr. Herbert Ford, Pres.

57330 ■ Antelope Highlands Chamber of Commerce
PO Box 20
5945A Watt Ave.
North Highlands, CA 95660
Ph:(916)821-5758
Fax: (916)991-5134
Co. E-mail: ahchamber@juno.com
URL: http://www.antelopehighlandschamber.com
Contact: Keith Weber, Pres.

57331 ■ Antelope Valley Board of Trade
548 W Lancaster Blvd., Ste. 103
Lancaster, CA 93534-2534
Ph:(661)942-9581
Fax: (661)723-9279
Co. E-mail: cathy@avbot.org
URL: http://www.avbot.org
Contact: Cathy Hart, Exec.Dir.

57332 ■ Antelope Valley Chambers of Commerce - Rosamond
PO Box 365
Rosamond, CA 93560
Ph:(661)256-3248

Fax: (661)256-3249
Co. E-mail: steve@avchambers.com
URL: http://www.avchambers.com
Contact: Steve Malicot, Pres./CEO

57333 ■ Antioch Chamber of Commerce
324 G St.
Antioch, CA 94509-1255
Ph:(925)757-1800
Fax: (925)757-5286
Co. E-mail: info@antiochchamber.com
URL: http://www.antiochchamber.com
Contact: Devi Lanphere, Pres./CEO

57334 ■ Anza Valley Chamber of Commerce
PO Box 391460
Anza, CA 92539
Ph:(909)763-4164
URL: http://www.anzavalleychamber.com
Contact: Robyn Garrison, Pres.

57335 ■ Apple Valley Chamber of Commerce
17852 Hwy. 18
PO Box 1073
Apple Valley, CA 92307
Ph:(760)242-2753
Fax: (760)242-0303
Co. E-mail: info@avchamber.org
URL: http://www.avchamber.org
Contact: Janice Moore, Pres.CEO

57336 ■ Aptos Chamber of Commerce
7605A Old Dominion Ct.
Aptos, CA 95003
Ph:(831)688-1467
Fax: (831)688-6961
Co. E-mail: info@aptos.com
URL: http://www.aptoschamber.com
Contact: Karen Hibble, Dir.

57337 ■ Arcadia Chamber of Commerce
388 W Huntington Dr.
Arcadia, CA 91007-3402
Ph:(626)447-2159
Fax: (626)445-0273
Co. E-mail: arcadiac@pacbell.net
URL: http://www.arcadiachamber.com
Contact: Beth Costanza, Exec.Dir.

57338 ■ Arcata Chamber of Commerce
1635 Heindon Rd.
Arcata, CA 95521
Ph:(707)822-3619
Fax: (707)822-3515
Co. E-mail: chamber@arcatachamber.com
URL: http://www.arcatachamber.com
Contact: Ms. Jenny Bowen, Exec.Dir.

57339 ■ Arroyo Grande Chamber of Commerce
800 W Branch St.
Arroyo Grande, CA 93420-1999
Ph:(805)489-1488
Fax: (805)489-2239
Co. E-mail: agcoc@arroyograndecc.com
URL: http://www.arroyograndecc.com
Contact: Heather Jensen, Pres./CEO

57340 ■ Arvin Chamber of Commerce
PO Box 645
Arvin, CA 93203
Ph:(661)854-2265
Fax: (661)854-2265
Contact: Raymond Kincy, Pres.

57341 ■ Atascadero Chamber of Commerce
6550 El Camino Real
Atascadero, CA 93422
Ph:(805)466-2044
Fax: (805)466-9218
Co. E-mail: info@atascaderochamber.org
URL: http://www.atascaderochamber.org
Contact: Joanne Main, Pres./CEO

57342 ■ Atwater Chamber of Commerce
1181 3rd St.
Atwater, CA 95301

Ph:(209)358-4251
Fax: (209)358-0934
Co. E-mail: info@atwater-chamber.com
URL: http://www.atwater-chamber.com
Contact: Dr. Joe Keller, Pres.

57343 ■ Auburn Area Chamber of Commerce
601 Lincoln Way
Auburn, CA 95603
Ph:(530)885-5616
Free: 800-971-1888
Fax: (530)885-5854
Co. E-mail: info@auburnchamber.net
URL: http://www.auburnchamber.net
Contact: Bruce L. Cosgrove, Exec.Dir.

57344 ■ Australian-American Chamber of Commerce, Orange County
2525 Ocean Blvd., Apt. 1F
Corona Del Mar, CA 92625-2824
Ph:(949)675-9588
Contact: Alan Cameron

57345 ■ Azusa Chamber of Commerce
240 W Foothill Blvd.
Azusa, CA 91702
Ph:(626)334-1507
Fax: (626)334-5217
Co. E-mail: info@azusachamber.org
URL: http://www.azusachamber.org
Contact: Evelyn Kahn, Exec.Dir.

57346 ■ Baldwin Park Chamber of Commerce
14327 Ramona Blvd.
Baldwin Park, CA 91706
Ph:(626)960-4848
Fax: (626)960-2990
Co. E-mail: baldwinparkchamber@msn.com
Contact: Elena Fernandez, Admin.Asst.

57347 ■ Banning Chamber of Commerce
123 E Ramsey St.
Banning, CA 92220
Ph:(951)849-4695
Fax: (951)849-9395
Co. E-mail: info@banningchamber.org
URL: http://www.banningchamber.org
Contact: Jack Holden, Exec.Dir.

57348 ■ Barstow Area Chamber of Commerce
PO Box 698
Barstow, CA 92312-0698
Ph:(760)256-8617
Free: 888-4-BARSTOW
Fax: (760)256-7675
Co. E-mail: bacc@barstowchamber.com
URL: http://www.barstowchamber.com
Contact: Darla Gerner, Exec.Dir.

57349 ■ Bass Lake Chamber of Commerce
PO Box 126
Bass Lake, CA 93604
Ph:(559)642-3676
Co. E-mail: chamber@basslake.com
URL: http://www.basslakechamber.com
Contact: Vaden Savage, Pres.

57350 ■ Beaumont Chamber of Commerce
726 Beaumont Ave.
PO Box 637
Beaumont, CA 92223
Ph:(951)845-9541
Fax: (951)769-9080
Co. E-mail: info@beaumontcachamber.com
URL: http://www.beaumontcachamber.com
Contact: Joan Taylor, Exec.Dir.

57351 ■ Bell Chamber of Commerce
PO Box 294
Bell, CA 90201-0294
Ph:(323)560-8755
Fax: (323)560-2060
Co. E-mail: bellcchamber@sbcglobal.net
Contact: Julie Gonzalez, Gen.Mgr.

57352 ■ Bell Gardens Association of Merchants and Commerce
6006 Shull St.
Bell Gardens, CA 90201-4502
Ph:(562)806-2355
Fax: (568)806-1585
Co. E-mail: bellgardens1@earthlink.net
URL: http://www.bellgardenschamber.org
Contact: Dennis Grizzle, Exec.Dir.

57353 ■ Bellflower Chamber of Commerce
16730 Bellflower Blvd., Ste. A
Bellflower, CA 90706
Ph:(562)867-1744
Fax: (562)866-7545
Co. E-mail: bellflowercoc@yahoo.com
Contact: Michele Moore, Mgr.

57354 ■ Belmont Chamber of Commerce
1070 6th Ave., Ste. 102
Belmont, CA 94002-3866
Ph:(650)595-8696
Fax: (650)595-8731
Co. E-mail: director@belmontchamber.org
URL: http://www.belmontchamber.org
Contact: Deanna Meredith, Exec.Dir.

57355 ■ Benicia Chamber of Commerce and Visitors' Center
601 1st St., Ste. 100
PO Box 185
Benicia, CA 94510-3211
Ph:(707)745-2120
Free: 800-559-7377
Fax: (707)745-2275
Co. E-mail: beniciachamber@aol.com
URL: http://www.beniciachamber.com
Contact: Stephanie Christiansen, CEO/Pres.

57356 ■ Berkeley Chamber of Commerce
1834 University Ave.
Berkeley, CA 94703-1516
Ph:(510)549-7000
Fax: (510)549-1789
Co. E-mail: info@berkeleychamber.com
URL: http://www.berkeleychamber.com
Contact: Rachel A. Rupert, CEO

57357 ■ Bethel Island Chamber of Commerce
PO Box 263
Bethel Island, CA 94511
Ph:(925)684-3220
Fax: (925)684-9025
Co. E-mail: bicc@cctrap.com
URL: http://www.bethelisland-chamber.com
Contact: Linda Nowak, Office Mgr.

57358 ■ Beverly Hills Chamber of Commerce
239 S Beverly Dr.
Beverly Hills, CA 90212
Ph:(310)248-1000
Fax: (310)248-1020
Co. E-mail: denny_fitzpatrick@hilton.com
URL: http://www.beverlyhillscc.org
Contact: Dan Walsh, CEO

57359 ■ Beverly Hills Chamber of Commerce and Civic Association
239 S Beverly Dr.
Beverly Hills, CA 90212
Ph:(310)248-1000
Free: 800-345-2210
Fax: (310)248-1020
Co. E-mail: lynch@beverlyhillschamber.com
URL: http://www.beverlyhillscc.org
Contact: James D. Lynch, CEO

57360 ■ Big Bear Chamber of Commerce
630 Bartlett Rd.
PO Box 2860
Big Bear Lake, CA 92315-2860
Ph:(909)866-4607
Free: 877-866-5253
Fax: (909)866-5412
Co. E-mail: info@bigbearchamber.com
URL: http://www.bigbearchamber.com
Contact: Jerri Boone, Exec.Dir.

57361 ■ Bishop Area Chamber of Commerce and Visitors Bureau
690 N Main St.
Bishop, CA 93514
Ph:(760)873-8405
Free: 888-395-3952
Fax: (760)873-6999
Co. E-mail: info@bishopvisitor.com
URL: http://www.bishopvisitor.com
Contact: Wayne Carpenter, Exec.Dir.

57362 ■ Black Business Association of Los Angeles
PO Box 43159
Los Angeles, CA 90043
Ph:(323)291-9334
Fax: (323)291-9234
Co. E-mail: admin@bbala.net
URL: http://www.bbala.org
Contact: Earl "Skip" Cooper II, Pres./CEO

57363 ■ Black Chamber of Commerce of Orange County
2323 N. Broadway, Ste. 330
Santa Ana, CA 92706-1652
Ph:(714)547-2646
Co. E-mail: ibdmac13@aol.com
URL: http://www.ocblackchamber.com

57364 ■ Blythe Area Chamber of Commerce
201 S Broadway
Blythe, CA 92225
Ph:(760)922-8166
Fax: (760)922-4010
Co. E-mail: blythecoc@yahoo.com
URL: http://www.blytheareachamberofcommerce.com
Contact: Mark Fulton, Exec.VP

57365 ■ Bodega Bay Area Chamber of Commerce
PO Box 146
Bodega Bay, CA 94923
Ph:(707)875-3422
Fax: (707)875-4200
URL: http://www.bodegabay.com

57366 ■ Bonsall Chamber of Commerce
PO Box 1142
Bonsall, CA 92003
Ph:(760)630-1933
Fax: (760)758-4484
URL: http://www.bonsallchamber.org
Contact: Leigh Ann Howard, Pres.

57367 ■ Boron Chamber of Commerce
26922 Twenty Mule Team Rd.
Boron, CA 93516
Ph:(760)762-5810
Fax: (760)762-4400
Co. E-mail: chamber@boronchamber.org
URL: http://www.boronchamber.org
Contact: F.O. Roe, Pres.

57368 ■ Borrego Springs Chamber of Commerce
786 Palm Canyon Dr.
PO Box 420
Borrego Springs, CA 92004-0420
Ph:(760)767-5555
Free: 800-559-5524
Fax: (760)767-5976
Co. E-mail: info@borregospringschamber.com
URL: http://www.borregosprings.org
Contact: Gwenn Marie, Pres.

57369 ■ Brawley Chamber of Commerce and Economic Development Commission
204 S Imperial Ave.
PO Box 218
Brawley, CA 92227
Ph:(760)344-3160
Fax: (760)344-7611
Co. E-mail: chamber@brawleychamber.com
URL: http://www.brawleychamber.com
Contact: Nicole Nicholas Gilles, Exec.Dir.

57370 ■ Brea Chamber of Commerce
1 Civic Center Cir.
Brea, CA 92821
Ph:(714)529-4938
Fax: (714)529-6103
Co. E-mail: nona@breachamber.com
URL: http://www.breachamber.com
Contact: Nona Watson, Exec.Dir.

57371 ■ Brentwood Chamber of Commerce
240 Oak St.
PO Box 773
Brentwood, CA 94513
Ph:(925)634-3344
Fax: (925)634-3731
Co. E-mail: bcoc240@sbcglobal.net
URL: http://www.brentwoodchamber.com
Contact: Bonnie Lucchese, Office Mgr.

57372 ■ Bridgeport Chamber of Commerce
PO Box 541
Bridgeport, CA 93517
Ph:(760)932-7500
Fax: (760)932-7500
Co. E-mail: info@bridgeportcalifornia.com
URL: http://www.bridgeportcalifornia.com
Contact: Kelly Annett, Pres.

57373 ■ Brisbane Chamber of Commerce
50 Park Pl.
Brisbane, CA 94005
Ph:(415)467-7283
Fax: (415)467-5421
Co. E-mail: info@brisbanechamber.com
URL: http://www.brisbanechamber.com
Contact: Burton H. Alberts, Exec.Dir.

57374 ■ Buena Park Chamber of Commerce
6601 Beach Blvd.
Buena Park, CA 90620
Ph:(714)521-0261
Fax: (714)521-1851
Co. E-mail: info@buenaparkchamber.org
URL: http://www.buenaparkchamber.org
Contact: Gail S. Dixon, CEO/Pres.

57375 ■ Builders Industry Association Southern California-Baldy View Chapter
8711 Monroe Ct., Ste. B
Rancho Cucamonga, CA 91730-4804
Ph:(909)945-1884
Fax: (909)948-9631
Co. E-mail: frank@biabuild.com

57376 ■ Burbank Chamber of Commerce
200 W Magnolia Blvd.
Burbank, CA 91502-1724
Ph:(818)846-3111
Fax: (818)846-0109
Co. E-mail: info@burbankchamber.org
URL: http://www.burbankchamber.org
Contact: Gary Olson, Exec.Dir.

57377 ■ Burlingame Chamber of Commerce
290 California Dr.
Burlingame, CA 94010
Ph:(650)344-1735
Fax: (650)344-1763
Co. E-mail: info@burlingamechamber.org
URL: http://burlingamechamber.org
Contact: Georgette Naylor, Pres./CEO

57378 ■ Burney Chamber of Commerce
PO Box 36
Burney, CA 96013
Ph:(530)335-2111
Fax: (530)335-2711
Co. E-mail: burneycc@c-zone.net
URL: http://www.burneychamber.com
Contact: Sherri Quinlan, Exec.Dir.

57379 ■ Buttonwillow Chamber of Commerce
104 W 2nd St.
PO Box 251
Buttonwillow, CA 93206
Ph:(661)764-5406
Fax: (661)764-5406

Contact: Mike Torigiani, Acting Pres.

57380 ■ Calabasas Chamber of Commerce
23564 Calabasas Rd., Ste. 101
Calabasas, CA 91302
Ph:(818)222-5680
Fax: (818)222-5690
Co. E-mail: info@calabasaschamber.com
URL: http://www.calabasaschamber.com
Contact: Carol Wasburn, Pres./CEO

57381 ■ Calaveras County Chamber of Commerce
1211 S Main St.
PO Box 1145
Angels Camp, CA 95222
Ph:(209)736-2580
Fax: (209)736-2576
Co. E-mail: chamber@calaveras.org
URL: http://www.calaveras.org
Contact: Diane Gray, Exec.Dir.

57382 ■ Calexico Chamber of Commerce
1100 Imperial Ave.
Calexico, CA 92231
Ph:(760)357-1166
Fax: (760)357-9043
Co. E-mail: calexicochamber@hotmail.com
URL: http://www.calexicochamber.org
Contact: Hildy Carrillo-Rivera, Exec.Dir.

57383 ■ California Chamber of Commerce
PO Box 1736
Sacramento, CA 95812-1736
Ph:(916)444-6670
Fax: (916)325-1272
Co. E-mail: debi.hobson@calchamber.com
URL: http://www.calchamber.com
Contact: Allan Zaremberg, Pres./CEO

57384 ■ California Chamber of Commerce, Southern California Office
PO Box 8230
La Verne, CA 91750-8230
Ph:(909)593-0449
Fax: (909)593-0498
Co. E-mail: marlene.carney@calchamber.com
URL: http://www.calchamber.com
Contact: Marlene Carney, Dir., Local Chamber Services

57385 ■ California City Chamber of Commerce
8001 California City Blvd.
California City, CA 93505
Ph:(760)373-8676
Fax: (760)373-1414
Co. E-mail: chamber@ccis.com
Contact: Dottie Helton, Mgr.

57386 ■ California Israel Chamber of Commerce
20883 Stevens Creek Blvd.
Cupertino, CA 95014
Ph:(408)343-0917
Fax: (408)343-1197
Co. E-mail: info@ca-israelchamber.org
URL: http://www.ca-israelchamber.org
Contact: Shuly Galili, Exec. Dir.

57387 ■ Calimesa Chamber of Commerce
PO Box 246
Calimesa, CA 92320
Ph:(909)795-7612
Fax: (909)795-2822
Co. E-mail: calimesachamber@cybertime.net
Contact: Brenda Hyatt, Exec.Dir.

57388 ■ Calistoga Chamber of Commerce
1458 Lincoln Ave., No. 9
Calistoga, CA 94515
Ph:(707)942-6333
Free: (866)306-5588
Fax: (707)942-9287
Co. E-mail: office@calistogachamber.com
URL: http://www.calistogachamber.com
Contact: Sue Mauro, Exec.Dir.

57389 ■ Camarillo Chamber of Commerce
2400 E Ventura Blvd.
Camarillo, CA 93010
Ph:(805)484-4383
Fax: (805)484-1395
Co. E-mail: info@camarillochamber.org
URL: http://www.camarillochamber.org
Contact: Thomas P. Kelley, Pres./CEO

57390 ■ Cambria Chamber of Commerce
767 Main St.
Cambria, CA 93428
Ph:(805)927-3624
Fax: (805)927-9426
Co. E-mail: info@cambriachamber.org
URL: http://cambriachamber.org
Contact: Mary Carson, Mgr.

57391 ■ Campbell Chamber of Commerce
1628 W Campbell Ave.
Campbell, CA 95008
Ph:(408)378-6252
Fax: (408)378-0192
Co. E-mail: ccoc@pacbell.net
URL: http://www.campbellchamber.com
Contact: Betty C. Deal, Exec.Dir.

57392 ■ Canoga Park - West Hills Chamber of Commerce
7248 Owensmouth Ave.
Canoga Park, CA 91303
Ph:(818)884-4222
Fax: (818)884-4604
Co. E-mail: cpwhchamber@socal.rr.com
Contact: Carol Gendler, Exec.Dir.

57393 ■ Capitola-Soquel Chamber of Commerce
716-G Capitola Ave.
Capitola, CA 95010
Ph:(831)475-6522
Fax: (831)475-6530
Co. E-mail: capcham@capitolachamber.com
URL: http://www.capitolachamber.com
Contact: Mrs. Toni Castro, CEO

57394 ■ Cardiff-by-the-Sea Chamber of Commerce
PO Box 552
Cardiff-by-the-Sea, CA 92007
Ph:(760)436-0431
Co. E-mail: info@cardiffbythesea.org
URL: http://www.cardiffbythesea.org
Contact: Jim Clark, Pres.

57395 ■ Carlsbad Chamber of Commerce
5934 Priestly Dr.
Carlsbad, CA 92008
Ph:(760)931-8400
Fax: (760)931-9153
Co. E-mail: chamber@carlsbad.org
URL: http://www.carlsbad.org
Contact: Ted Owen, Pres./CEO

57396 ■ Carmel Chamber of Commerce
PO Box 4444
Carmel, CA 93921
Ph:(831)624-2522
Free: 800-550-4333
Fax: (831)624-1329
Co. E-mail: info@carmelchamber.org
URL: http://www.carmelcalifornia.org
Contact: Monta Potter, CEO

57397 ■ Carmel Valley Chamber of Commerce
PO Box 288
Carmel Valley, CA 93924
Ph:(831)659-4000
Fax: (831)659-8415
Co. E-mail: info@carmelvalleychamber.com
URL: http://www.carmelvalleychamber.com
Contact: Astrid Coleman, Exec.Dir.

57398 ■ Carmichael Chamber of Commerce
6825 Fair Oaks Blvd., Ste. 100
Carmichael, CA 95608

Ph:(916)481-1002
Fax: (916)481-1003
Co. E-mail: information@carmichaelchamber.com
URL: http://www.carmichaelchamber.com
Contact: Jan Bass Otto, Exec.VP

57399 ■ Carpinteria Valley Chamber of Commerce
PO Box 956
Carpinteria, CA 93013
Ph:(805)684-5479
Fax: (805)684-3477
Co. E-mail: info@carpchamber.org
URL: http://www.carpchamber.org
Contact: Lin Graf, Pres./CEO

57400 ■ Carson Chamber of Commerce
530 E Del Amo Blvd.
PO Box 4626
Carson, CA 90746
Ph:(310)217-4590
Fax: (310)217-4591
Co. E-mail: wogan@carsonchamber.com
URL: http://www.carsonchamber.com
Contact: Walter Neil, Chm.

57401 ■ Castro Valley Chamber of Commerce
3467 Castro Valley Blvd.
PO Box 2312
Castro Valley, CA 94546
Ph:(510)537-5300
URL: http://www.mycastrovalley.com/chamber_of_commerce
Contact: Valorie Robles, Exec. Dir.

57402 ■ Castroville Chamber of Commerce
PO Box 744
Castroville, CA 95012
Ph:(831)633-6545
Fax: (831)633-0485
Co. E-mail: castrovillechamber@redshift.com
URL: http://www.artichoke-festival.org
Contact: Catherine Lindstrom, Exec.Dir.

57403 ■ Catalina Island Chamber of Commerce and Visitors' Bureau
1 Green Pier
PO Box 217
Avalon, CA 90704-0217
Ph:(310)510-1520
Fax: (310)510-7606
Co. E-mail: info@catalinachamber.com
URL: http://www.catalinachamber.com
Contact: Wayne G. Griffin ACE, Pres./CEO

57404 ■ Cathedral City Chamber of Commerce
68-845 Perez Rd., Ste. 6
Cathedral City, CA 92234-7254
Ph:(760)328-1213
Fax: (760)321-0659
Co. E-mail: info@cathedralcitycc.com
URL: http://www.cathedralcitycc.com
Contact: Greg Wetmore, Pres./CEO

57405 ■ Cayucos Chamber of Commerce
PO Box 141
Cayucos, CA 93430
Ph:(805)995-1200
Free: 800-563-1878
Fax: (805)995-2086
Co. E-mail: info@cayucoschamber.com
URL: http://www.cayucoschamber.com
Contact: Breck Smith, Pres.

57406 ■ Central California Hispanic Chamber of Commerce
2331 Fresno St., Ste. 114
Fresno, CA 93721
Ph:(559)495-4817
Fax: (559)495-4811
Co. E-mail: directorlorena@cchcc.net
URL: http://www.cchcc.net
Contact: Lorena Martinez, Exec.Dir.

57407 ■ Century City Chamber of Commerce
2029 Century Park E, Concourse Level
Los Angeles, CA 90067
Ph:(310)553-2222
Fax: (310)553-4623
Co. E-mail: contact@centurycitycc.com
URL: http://www.centurycitycc.com
Contact: Robyn Ritter Simon, Pres./CEO

57408 ■ Ceres Chamber of Commerce
2904 4th St.
Ceres, CA 95307
Ph:(209)537-2601
Fax: (209)537-2699
Co. E-mail: chamber@cereschamber.org
URL: http://www.cereschamber.org
Contact: Terri Tillman, CEO

57409 ■ Cerritos Chamber of Commerce
13259 South St.
Cerritos, CA 90703
Ph:(562)467-0800
Fax: (562)467-0840
Co. E-mail: info@cerritos.org
URL: http://www.cerritos.org
Contact: Catherine Gaughen, Exec.Dir.

57410 ■ Chamber of Commerce of Dana Point
PO Box 12
Dana Point, CA 92629-0012
Ph:(949)496-1555
Free: 800-290-DANA
Fax: (949)496-1555
Co. E-mail: chamber@beach.net
URL: http://www.danapoint-chamber.com
Contact: Penny Maynard, Pres./CEO

57411 ■ Chamber of Commerce of Huntington Beach, Women of Action
19891 Beach Blvd., No. 140
Huntington Beach, CA 92648-2461
Ph:(714)536-8888
Contact: Joyce Riddell, Pres.

57412 ■ Chamber of Commerce of La Habra
321 E La Habra Blvd.
La Habra, CA 90631-5493
Ph:(562)697-1704
Fax: (562)697-8359
Co. E-mail: info@lahabrachamber.com
URL: http://www.lahabrachamber.com

57413 ■ Chamber of Commerce Mountain View
580 Castro St.
Mountain View, CA 94041
Ph:(650)968-8378
Fax: (650)968-5668
Co. E-mail: info@chambermv.org
URL: http://www.mountainviewchamber.org
Contact: Carol Olson, Pres./CEO

57414 ■ Chatsworth - Porter Ranch Chamber of Commerce
10038 Old Depot Plz. Rd.
Chatsworth, CA 91311
Ph:(818)341-2428
Fax: (818)341-4930
Co. E-mail: info@chatsworthchamber.com
URL: http://www.chatsworthchamber.com
Contact: Ivy Weiss, CEO

57415 ■ Chester/Lake Almanor Chamber of Commerce
PO Box 1198
Chester, CA 96020
Ph:(530)258-2426
Free: 800-350-4838
Fax: (530)258-2760
Co. E-mail: almanor@chester-lakealmanor.com
URL: http://chester-lakealmanor.com
Contact: Suki Hock, Mgr.

57416 ■ Chico Chamber of Commerce
300 Salem St.
Chico, CA 95928

Ph:(530)891-5556
Free: 800-852-8570
Fax: (530)891-3613
Co. E-mail: info@chicochamber.com
URL: http://www.chicochamber.com
Contact: Jim Goodwin, Pres./CEO

57417 ■ Chinese Chamber of Commerce
730 Sacramento St.
San Francisco, CA 94108
Ph:(415)982-3000
Fax: (415)982-4720
Contact: David Lem, Pres.

57418 ■ Chino Valley Chamber of Commerce
13150 7th St.
Chino, CA 91710
Ph:(909)627-6177
Fax: (909)627-4180
Co. E-mail: info@chinovalleychamber.com
URL: http://www.chinovalleychamber.com
Contact: Jeanne Batista, Exec.Dir.

57419 ■ Chowchilla District Chamber of Commerce
228 Trinity Ave.
Chowchilla, CA 93610
Ph:(559)665-5603
Fax: (559)665-0896
Co. E-mail: chamberofcommerce@ci.chowchilla.ca.
us
Contact: Jan DuBose, Exec.Dir./Mgr.

57420 ■ Chula Vista Chamber of Commerce
233 4th Ave.
Chula Vista, CA 91910
Ph:(619)420-6603
Fax: (619)420-1269
Co. E-mail: info@chulavistachamber.org
URL: http://www.chulavistachamber.org
Contact: Kevin Carlson, Pres.

57421 ■ Citrus Heights Chamber of Commerce
PO Box 191
Citrus Heights, CA 95611
Ph:(916)722-4545
Fax: (916)722-4543
Co. E-mail: chamber@chchamber.com
URL: http://www.chchamber.com
Contact: Bettie Cosby, CEO

57422 ■ City of Tulelake Chamber of Commerce
800 S Main St.
Tulelake, CA 96134
Ph:(530)667-5312
Fax: (530)667-5351
Co. E-mail: tulefair@cot.net
URL: http://www.tulelakecalifornia.com
Contact: Cindy Wright, Pres.

57423 ■ Claremont Chamber of Commerce
205 Yale Ave.
Claremont, CA 91711
Ph:(909)624-1681
Fax: (909)624-6629
Co. E-mail: info@claremontchamber.org
Contact: Maureen Aldridge, Exec.Dir.

57424 ■ Clear Lake Chamber of Commerce
4700 Golf Ave.
Clearlake, CA 95422
Ph:(707)994-3600
Fax: (707)994-3603
Co. E-mail: clearlakechamber@mchsi.com
URL: http://www.clearlakechamber.com
Contact: Gary Briggs, Pres.

57425 ■ Clements Lockeford Chamber of Commerce
18980 N Hwy. 88, Ste. A
Lockeford, CA 95237
Ph:(209)727-3142
Fax: (209)727-3365
Co. E-mail: clemlockchamber@cctonline.net
URL: http://www.clementslockefordchamber.org

Contact: Bill Ferraro, Pres.

57426 ■ Cloverdale Chamber of Commerce
PO Box 356
Cloverdale, CA 95425-0356
Ph:(707)894-4470
Fax: (707)894-9568
Co. E-mail: cchamber@vbbn.net
URL: http://www.cloverdale.net
Contact: Linda C. Brown ACE, CEO/Pres.

57427 ■ Clovis District Chamber of Commerce
325 Pollasky Ave.
Clovis, CA 93612-1139
Ph:(559)299-7363
Fax: (559)299-2969
Co. E-mail: info@clovischamber.com
URL: http://www.clovischamber.com
Contact: Jim Ware, Pres./CEO

57428 ■ Colfax Area Chamber of Commerce
2 S Railroad Ave.
PO Box 86
Colfax, CA 95713
Ph:(530)346-8888
Fax: (530)346-8888
Co. E-mail: info@colfaxarea.com
URL: http://www.colfaxarea.com
Contact: Michelle Peerson, Exec.Dir.

57429 ■ Colton Chamber of Commerce
655 N La Cadena Dr.
Colton, CA 92324
Ph:(909)825-2222
Fax: (909)824-1650
Co. E-mail: coltonchamber@aol.com
Contact: Eufemia Reyes, Exec.Dir.

57430 ■ Commerce Industrial Council Chamber of Commerce
6055 E Washington Blvd., Ste. 120
Commerce, CA 90040
Ph:(323)728-7222
Fax: (323)728-7565
URL: http://www.industrialcouncil.org
Contact: Pat Monroy

57431 ■ Compton Chamber of Commerce
310 N Willowbrook Ave., Ste. 4A
Compton, CA 90220
Ph:(310)631-8611
Fax: (310)631-2066
Co. E-mail: cptchamber@aol.com
Contact: Ms. Lestean M. Johnson, Pres.

57432 ■ Corcoran Chamber of Commerce
1099 Otis Ave.
PO Box 459
Corcoran, CA 93212
Ph:(559)992-4514
Fax: (559)992-2341
Co. E-mail: corcoran@savy2k.net
Contact: Kelly Fowler, Exec.Asst.

57433 ■ Corning District Chamber of Commerce
1110 Solano St.
PO Box 871
Corning, CA 96021
Ph:(530)824-5550
Fax: (530)824-9499
Co. E-mail: info@corningchamber.com
URL: http://corningchamber.org
Contact: Valanne de Bourg, Exec.Dir.

57434 ■ Corona Chamber of Commerce
904 E 6th St.
Corona, CA 92879
Ph:(951)737-3350
Fax: (951)737-3531
Co. E-mail: mail@coronachamber.org
URL: http://www.coronachamber.org
Contact: John Cleghorn, Exec.VP

57435 ■ Corona Del Mar Chamber of Commerce
2855 E Coast Hwy., Ste. 101
PO Box 72
Corona Del Mar, CA 92625
Ph:(949)673-4050
Fax: (949)673-3940
Co. E-mail: info@cdmchamber.com
URL: http://www.cdmchamber.com
Contact: Linda Leonhard, Dir.

57436 ■ Coronado Chamber of Commerce
1313 Ynez Pl.
Coronado, CA 92118
Ph:(619)435-9260
Fax: (619)522-6577
Co. E-mail: info@coronadochamber.com
URL: http://www.coronadochamber.com
Contact: Karen Finch, CEO

57437 ■ Corte Madera Chamber of Commerce
129 Town Ctr.
Corte Madera, CA 94925
Ph:(415)924-0441
Fax: (415)924-1839
Co. E-mail: chamber@cortemadera.org
URL: http://www.cortemadera.org

57438 ■ Costa Mesa Chamber of Commerce
1700 Adams Ave., Ste. 101
Costa Mesa, CA 92626
Ph:(714)885-9090
Fax: (714)885-9094
Co. E-mail: rquinn@costamesachamber.com
URL: http://www.costamesachamber.com
Contact: Ed Fawcett, Pres./CEO

57439 ■ Cotati Chamber of Commerce
PO Box 592
Cotati, CA 94931
Ph:(707)795-5508
Fax: (707)795-5868
Co. E-mail: chamber@cotati.org
URL: http://www.cotati.org
Contact: Suzanne Whipple, Exec.Dir.

57440 ■ Cottonwood Chamber of Commerce
PO Box 584
Cottonwood, CA 96022-0584
Ph:(530)347-6800
Fax: (530)347-6800
Co. E-mail: lionmax@juno.com

57441 ■ Covina Chamber of Commerce
935 W Badillo St., Ste. 100
Covina, CA 91722
Ph:(626)967-4191
Fax: (626)966-9660
Co. E-mail: chamber@covina.org
URL: http://www.covina.org
Contact: Dawn Nelson, Pres./CEO

57442 ■ Crescent City-Del Norte County Chamber of Commerce
1001 Front St.
Crescent City, CA 95531
Ph:(707)464-3174
Free: 800-343-8300
Fax: (707)464-9676
Co. E-mail: chamber@northerncalifornia.net
URL: http://www.northerncalifornia.net
Contact: Jeff Russell, Exec.Dir.

57443 ■ Crescenta Valley Chamber of Commerce
3131 Foothill Blvd., Ste. D
La Crescenta, CA 91214
Ph:(818)248-4957
Fax: (818)248-9625
Co. E-mail: cvcoc@aol.com
URL: http://www.lacrescenta.org
Contact: Jean Maluccio, Exec.Dir.

57444 ■ Crestline Chamber of Commerce
PO Box 926
24385 Lake Dr.
Crestline, CA 92325

Ph:(909)338-2706
Fax: (909)338-6588
Co. E-mail: info@crestlinechamber.net
URL: http://www.crestlinechamber.net
Contact: Mike Chilson, Pres.

57445 ■ Crockett Chamber of Commerce
PO Box 191
Crockett, CA 94525
Ph:(510)787-1155
Co. E-mail: heidi@throughglass.com
URL: http://www.crockettca-chamber.org
Contact: Heidi Petty, Pres.

57446 ■ Culver City Chamber of Commerce
4249 Overland Ave.
PO Box 707
Culver City, CA 90232-0707
Ph:(310)287-3850
Fax: (310)287-1350
Co. E-mail: ssssteve@culvercitychamber.com
URL: http://www.culvercitychamber.com
Contact: Steven J. Rose, Pres.

57447 ■ Cupertino Chamber of Commerce
20455 Silverado Ave.
Cupertino, CA 95014-4439
Ph:(408)252-7054
Fax: (408)252-0638
Co. E-mail: info@cupertino-chamber.org
URL: http://www.cupertino-chamber.org
Contact: Christine Giusiana, CEO

57448 ■ Cypress Chamber of Commerce
5550 Cerritos Ave., Ste. D
Cypress, CA 90630
Ph:(714)827-2430
Fax: (714)827-1229
Co. E-mail: info@cypresschamber.org
URL: http://www.cypresschamber.org
Contact: Ed Munson, Exec.Dir.

57449 ■ Daggett Chamber of Commerce
PO Box 327
Daggett, CA 92327
Ph:(760)254-2427
Contact: J. David Linn, Sec.

57450 ■ Daly City - Colma Chamber of Commerce
355 Gellert Blvd., No. 138
Daly City, CA 94015-2665
Ph:(650)755-3900
Fax: (650)755-5160
Co. E-mail: staff@dalycity-colmachamber.org
URL: http://www.dalycity-colmachamber.org
Contact: Mario C. Panoringan, CEO

57451 ■ Danville Area Chamber of Commerce
117E Town and Country Dr.
Danville, CA 94526
Ph:(925)837-4400
Fax: (925)837-5709
Co. E-mail: danvillecachamber@danvillecachamber.
com
URL: http://www.danvillecachamber.com
Contact: Melony Newman, Pres./CEO

57452 ■ Davis Chamber of Commerce
130 G St., Ste. B
Davis, CA 95616-4630
Ph:(530)756-5160
Fax: (530)756-5190
Co. E-mail: askus@davischamber.com
URL: http://www.davischamber.com
Contact: Sherry Richter, CEO

57453 ■ Death Valley Chamber of Commerce
PO Box 157
Shoshone, CA 92384
Ph:(760)852-4524
Fax: (760)852-4354
Co. E-mail: deathvalleych@earthlink.net
URL: http://www.deathvalleychamber.org
Contact: Kari Coughlin, Dir.

57454 ■ Del Mar Regional Chamber of Commerce
1104 Camino Del Mar, Ste. 1
Del Mar, CA 92014
Ph:(858)755-4844
Fax: (858)356-0595
Co. E-mail: info@delmarchamber.org
URL: http://www.delmarchamber.org
Contact: Nancy Wasko, CEO

57455 ■ Delano Chamber of Commerce
931 High St.
Delano, CA 93215-1704
Ph:(661)725-2518
Fax: (661)725-4743
Co. E-mail: delanocc@lightspeed.net
URL: http://www.chamberofdelano.com
Contact: Sandra Bello, Exec.Dir.

57456 ■ Desert Hot Springs Chamber of Commerce
11711 W Dr.
Desert Hot Springs, CA 92240-3652
Ph:(760)329-6403
Fax: (760)329-2833
Co. E-mail: info@deserthotsprings.com
URL: http://www.deserthotsprings.com
Contact: Carole Farm, CEO

57457 ■ Diamond Bar Chamber of Commerce
21845 E Copley Dr., Ste. 1170
Diamond Bar, CA 91765-6401
Ph:(909)860-1904
Fax: (909)860-6064
Co. E-mail: info@diamondbarchamber.com
URL: http://www.diamondbarchamber.com
Contact: Steve Smith, CEO

57458 ■ Dinuba Chamber of Commerce
210 N L St.
Dinuba, CA 93618
Ph:(559)591-2707
Fax: (559)591-2712
Co. E-mail: dinuba@theworks.com
URL: http://www.dinubacommerce.org
Contact: Terri Mejorado, Exec.Dir.

57459 ■ Dixon District Chamber of Commerce
110 E Mayes St.
Dixon, CA 95620-3401
Ph:(707)678-2650
Fax: (707)678-3654
Co. E-mail: info@dixonchamber.org
URL: http://www.dixonchamber.org
Contact: Ms. Saeuntel Allen, Office Mgr.

57460 ■ Downey Chamber of Commerce
11131 Brookshire Ave.
Downey, CA 90241-3860
Ph:(562)923-2191
Fax: (562)869-0461
Co. E-mail: downeycc@verizon.net
URL: http://www.downeychamber.com
Contact: Ms. Joan Warner-Plettinck, Exec.Dir.

57461 ■ Duarte Chamber of Commerce
1634 3rd St.
PO Box 1438
Duarte, CA 91010
Ph:(626)357-3333
Fax: (626)357-3645
Co. E-mail: janduartechamber@charter.net
URL: http://www.duartechamber.com
Contact: Jan Wight, Exec.Dir.

57462 ■ Dublin Chamber of Commerce
7080 Donlon Way, Ste. 110
Dublin, CA 94568
Ph:(925)828-6200
Fax: (925)828-4247
Co. E-mail: info@dublinchamberofcommerce.org
URL: http://www.dublinchamberofcommerce.org
Contact: Nancy Feeley, CEO/Pres.

57463 ■ Dunsmuir Chamber of Commerce
4118 Pine St.
Dunsmuir, CA 96025

Ph:(530)235-2177
Free: 800-386-7684
Fax: (530)235-0911
Co. E-mail: chamber@dunsmuir.com
URL: http://www.dunsmuir.com
Contact: Laura Leach, Pres.

57464 ■ Eagle Rock Chamber of Commerce
PO Box 41354
Eagle Rock, CA 90041
Ph:(323)257-2197
Fax: (323)254-3208
Co. E-mail: erccwebguy@aol.com
URL: http://www.eaglerockchamberofcommerce.com
Contact: Michael Nogueira Jr., Pres.

57465 ■ East Los Angeles Chamber of Commerce
PO Box 63220
Los Angeles, CA 90063-0220
Ph:(323)722-2005
Fax: (323)722-2405
Co. E-mail: elacoc@pacbell.net
URL: http://www.
eastlosangeleschamberofcommerce.com
Contact: Michelle Mestas

57466 ■ Eastern Plumas Chamber of Commerce
PO Box 1379
Portola, CA 96122-1379
Ph:(530)836-6811
Free: 800-995-6057
Fax: (530)836-6809
Co. E-mail: epluchmb@psln.com
URL: http://www.easternplumaschamber.com
Contact: Betty J. Heck, Mgr.

57467 ■ El Centro Chamber of Commerce and Visitors Bureau
1095 S 4th St.
PO Box 3006
El Centro, CA 92244-3006
Ph:(760)352-3681
Fax: (760)352-3246
Co. E-mail: generalinfo@elcentrochamber.org
URL: http://www.elcentrochamber.org
Contact: Cathy Kennerson, CEO

57468 ■ El Cerrito Chamber of Commerce
10848 San Pablo Ave.
PO Box 538
El Cerrito, CA 94530
Ph:(510)233-7040
URL: http://www.elcerritochamber.org
Contact: Tracy Giles, Pres.

57469 ■ El Dorado County Chamber of Commerce
542 Main St.
Placerville, CA 95667-5610
Ph:(530)621-5885
Free: 800-457-6279
Fax: (530)642-1624
Co. E-mail: chamber@eldoradocounty.org
URL: http://www.eldoradocounty.org
Contact: Laurel Brent-Bumb, CEO

57470 ■ El Dorado Hills Chamber of Commerce
PO Box 5055
981 Governor, Ste. 103
El Dorado Hills, CA 95762
Ph:(916)933-1335
Fax: (916)933-5908
Co. E-mail: chamber@eldoradohillschamber.com
URL: http://www.eldoradohillschamber.com
Contact: Debbie Manning, Pres./CEO

57471 ■ El Monte-South El Monte Chamber of Commerce
10505 Valley Blvd., Ste. 312
PO Box 5866
El Monte, CA 91734-1866
Ph:(626)443-0180
Fax: (626)443-0463
Co. E-mail: chamber@ksb8.com

URL: http://dbdla.com/chamber
Contact: Richard Nichols, Exec. Dir.

57472 ■ El Segundo Chamber of Commerce
427 Main St.
El Segundo, CA 90245
Ph:(310)322-1220
Fax: (310)322-6880
Co. E-mail: awyant@elsegundochamber.org
URL: http://www.elsegundochamber.org
Contact: David A. Herbst, Pres.

57473 ■ El Sobrante Chamber of Commerce
3769 San Pablo Dam Rd., No. B
El Sobrante, CA 94803
Ph:(510)223-0757
Contact: Marie Carayanis, Pres.

57474 ■ Elk Grove Chamber of Commerce
9280 W Stockton Blvd., Ste. 104
Elk Grove, CA 95758
Ph:(916)691-3760
Fax: (916)691-3810
Co. E-mail: chamber@elkgroveca.com
URL: http://www.elkgroveca.com
Contact: Janet Toppenberg, Exec.Dir.

57475 ■ Emeryville Chamber of Commerce
3980 Harlan St.
Emeryville, CA 94608-3771
Ph:(510)652-5223
Fax: (510)652-4223
Co. E-mail: info@emeryvillechamber.com
URL: http://www.emeryvillechamber.com
Contact: Bob Canter, Pres./CEO

57476 ■ Encinitas Chamber and Visitors Center
138 Encinitas Blvd.
Encinitas, CA 92024
Ph:(760)753-6041
Fax: (760)753-6270
Co. E-mail: info@encinitaschamber.com
URL: http://www.encinitaschamber.com
Contact: Keith Turner, CEO

57477 ■ Encino Chamber of Commerce
4933 Balboa Blvd.
Encino, CA 91316-3497
Ph:(818)789-4711
Fax: (818)789-2485
Co. E-mail: info@encinochamber.org
URL: http://www.encinochamber.org
Contact: John Stiegler Jr., Pres.

57478 ■ Escalon District Chamber of Commerce
2001 Main St., Ste. A
PMB 1333
Escalon, CA 95320
Ph:(209)838-2793
Fax: (209)838-6707
Contact: Linda Martin, Treas.

57479 ■ Escondido Chamber of Commerce
720 N Broadway
Escondido, CA 92025-1893
Ph:(760)745-2125
Fax: (760)745-1183
Co. E-mail: info@escondidochamber.org
URL: http://www.escondidochamber.org
Contact: Harvey Mitchell, CEO

57480 ■ Esparto District Chamber of Commerce
PO Box 194
Esparto, CA 95627
Ph:(530)787-3242
Fax: (530)787-4804
Co. E-mail: info@espartochamber.org
URL: http://www.espartochamber.com

57481 ■ Exeter Chamber of Commerce
101 W Pine St.
Exeter, CA 93221
Ph:(559)592-2919
Fax: (559)592-3720

Co. E-mail: chamber@exeterchamber.com
URL: http://www.exeterchamber.com
Contact: Carlos Aleman, Chm.

57482 ■ Fair Oaks Chamber of Commerce
10224 Fair Oaks Blvd.
PO Box 352
Fair Oaks, CA 95628
Ph:(916)967-2903
Fax: (916)967-8536
Co. E-mail: info@fairoakschamber.com
URL: http://www.fairoakschamber.com
Contact: Marsha A. Karley, Exec.Dir.

57483 ■ Fallbrook Chamber of Commerce
233 E Mission Rd., Ste. A
Fallbrook, CA 92028-2146
Ph:(760)728-5845
Fax: (760)728-4031
Co. E-mail: fallbrook@primemail.com
URL: http://www.fallbrookca.org
Contact: Robert K. Leonard, Exec.Dir.

57484 ■ Farmersville Chamber of Commerce
4376 N Farmersville Blvd.
Farmersville, CA 93223
Ph:(559)747-0223
Contact: Don Mason, Pres.

57485 ■ Ferndale Chamber of Commerce
PO Box 325
Ferndale, CA 95536-0325
Ph:(707)786-4477
Fax: (707)786-4477
Co. E-mail: ferncofc@cox.net
URL: http://www.victorianferndale.org/chamber

57486 ■ Filipino American Chamber of Commerce of Orange County
215 E Orangethorpe Ave., No. 288
Fullerton, CA 92832-3017
Ph:(714)280-4729
Co. E-mail: lindasarno@aol.com
Contact: Ms. Maria Erlinda Sarno Atty., Pres.

57487 ■ Fillmore Chamber of Commerce
275 Central Ave.
Fillmore, CA 93015
Ph:(805)524-0351
Fax: (805)524-2551
Co. E-mail: info@fillmorechamber.com
URL: http://www.fillmorechamber.com
Contact: Cindy Jackson-Bires, Past Pres.

57488 ■ Finnish American Chamber of Commerce
PO Box 3058
Tustin, CA 92781-3058
Ph:(310)457-8381
Co. E-mail: info@faccpacific.com
URL: http://www.FACCpacific.com

57489 ■ Firebaugh District Chamber of Commerce
PO Box 517
Firebaugh, CA 93622
Ph:(559)659-3701
Contact: Dorice Fannon, Pres.

57490 ■ Folsom Chamber of Commerce
200 Wool St.
Folsom, CA 95630
Ph:(916)985-2698
Free: 800-377-1414
Fax: (916)985-4117
Co. E-mail: information@folsomchamber.com
URL: http://www.folsomchamber.com
Contact: Joseph P. Gagliardi, CEO

57491 ■ Fontana Chamber of Commerce
8491 Sierra Ave.
Fontana, CA 92335-3860
Ph:(909)822-4433
Fax: (909)822-6238
Co. E-mail: fontanac@sbcglobal.net
Contact: David G. Pulido, Exec.Dir.

57492 ■ Foresthill Divide Chamber of Commerce
PO Box 346
Foresthill, CA 95631
Ph:(530)367-2474
Fax: (530)367-2474
Co. E-mail: info@foresthillchamber.org
URL: http://www.foresthillchamber.org
Contact: Larry Mobley, Treas.

57493 ■ Forestville Chamber of Commerce
PO Box 546
Forestville, CA 95436
Ph:(707)887-1111
Fax: (707)887-0106
Co. E-mail: vesta@sonic.net
URL: http://www.forestvillechamber.org
Contact: Earl Stephens, Pres.

57494 ■ Fort Bragg - Mendocino Coast Chamber of Commerce
PO Box 1141
Fort Bragg, CA 95437
Ph:(707)961-6300
Free: 800-726-2780
Fax: (707)964-2056
Co. E-mail: chamber@mcn.org
URL: http://www.mendocinocoast.com
Contact: Debra DeGraw, Exec.Dir.

57495 ■ Fortuna Chamber of Commerce
735 14th St.
Fortuna, CA 95540-2113
Ph:(707)725-3959
Fax: (707)725-4766
Co. E-mail: chamber@sunnyfortuna.com
URL: http://www.chamber.sunnyfortuna.com
Contact: Cliff Chapman, Exec.Dir.

57496 ■ Foster City Chamber of Commerce
989 E Hillsdale Blvd., Ste. 160
Foster City, CA 94404
Ph:(650)573-7600
Fax: (650)573-5201
Co. E-mail: info@fostercitychamber.com
URL: http://www.fostercitychamber.com
Contact: Carol Torgerson, Pres./CEO

57497 ■ Fountain Valley Chamber of Commerce
11100 Warner Ave., Ste. 204
Fountain Valley, CA 92708
Ph:(714)668-0542
Fax: (714)668-9164
Co. E-mail: bwhite@fvchamber.com
URL: http://www.fvchamber.com
Contact: Beverly White, Business Mgr.

57498 ■ Fowler Chamber of Commerce
412 E Merced St.
PO Box 412
Fowler, CA 93625
Ph:(559)834-3869
Fax: (559)834-5319
Co. E-mail: ccoffowler@earthlink.net
Contact: Curtis Leroy, Pres.

57499 ■ Fremont Chamber of Commerce
39488 Stevenson Pl., Ste. 100
Fremont, CA 94539-3085
Ph:(510)795-2244
Fax: (510)795-2240
Co. E-mail: fmtcc@fremontbusiness.com
URL: http://www.fremontbusiness.com
Contact: Cindy Bonior, Pres./CEO

57500 ■ Fullerton Chamber of Commerce
444 N Harbor Blvd., No. 200
Fullerton, CA 92832
Ph:(714)871-3100
Fax: (714)871-2871
Co. E-mail: tharvey@fullertonchamber.com
URL: http://www.fullertonchamber.com
Contact: Theresa Harvey, Exec.Dir.

57501 ■ Galt District Chamber of Commerce
PO Box 1446
Galt, CA 95632

Ph:(209)745-2529
Fax: (209)745-0840
Co. E-mail: info@galtchamber.com
URL: http://www.galtchamber.com
Contact: Barbara Clare, Exec.Dir./CEO

57502 ■ Garberville-Redway Area Chamber of Commerce
PO Box 445
773 Redwood Dr., Ste. E
Garberville, CA 95542
Ph:(707)923-2613
Free: 800-923-2613
Fax: (707)923-4789
Co. E-mail: chamber@garberville.org
URL: http://www.garberville.org
Contact: Janis Tillery, Exec.Dir.

57503 ■ Garden Grove Chamber of Commerce
12866 Main St., Ste. 102
Garden Grove, CA 92840-5298
Ph:(714)638-7950
Free: 800-959-5560
Fax: (714)636-6672
Co. E-mail: connie.margolin@gardengrovechamber.
   org
URL: http://gardengrovechamber.org
Contact: Connie Margolin, CEO/Pres.

57504 ■ Gardena Valley Chamber of Commerce
1204 W Gardena Blvd., Ste. E & F
Gardena, CA 90247
Ph:(310)532-9905
Fax: (310)329-7307
Co. E-mail: gardenavalleycc@aol.com
URL: http://www.gardenachamber.com
Contact: Fred Davis, Pres.

57505 ■ Geyserville Chamber of Commerce
PO Box 276
Geyserville, CA 95441
Ph:(707)857-3745
Co. E-mail: moreinfo@geyservillecc.com
URL: http://www.geyservillecc.com
Contact: Cosette Trautman-Scheiber, Pres.

57506 ■ Gilroy Chamber of Commerce
7471 Monterey St.
Gilroy, CA 95020
Ph:(408)842-6437
Fax: (408)842-6010
Co. E-mail: chamber@gilroy.org
URL: http://www.gilroy.org
Contact: Susan Valenta ACE, Pres./CEO

57507 ■ Glendale Chamber of Commerce
200 S Louise St.
Glendale, CA 91205
Ph:(818)240-7870
Fax: (818)240-2872
Co. E-mail: info@glendalechamber.com
URL: http://www.glendalechamber.com
Contact: Sharon Beauchamp, Exec.VP

57508 ■ Glendora Chamber of Commerce
131 E Foothill Blvd.
Glendora, CA 91741-3336
Ph:(626)963-4128
Fax: (626)914-4822
Co. E-mail: info@glendora-chamber.org
URL: http://www.glendora-chamber.org
Contact: D.J. Jafari, Pres.

57509 ■ Golden Triangle Chamber of Commerce
6235 Lusk Blvd.
San Diego, CA 92121
Ph:(858)866-0676
Co. E-mail: johnwalsh@yahoo.com
URL: http://goldentrianglechamber.com
Contact: John Walsh, Pres.

57510 ■ Golden Valley Chamber of Commerce
37167 Ave. 12, Ste. 5C
Madera, CA 93638-8710

Ph:(559)645-4001
Fax: (559)645-4002
Contact: Dana Bell, Office Mgr.

57511 ■ Goleta Valley Chamber of Commerce
PO Box 781
Goleta, CA 93116
Ph:(805)967-4618
Free: 800-646-5382
Fax: (805)967-4615
Co. E-mail: info@goletavalley.com
URL: http://goletavalley.com
Contact: Kristen Miller Amyx, Pres./CEO

57512 ■ Gonzales Chamber of Commerce
PO Box 216
Gonzales, CA 93926
Ph:(831)675-9019
Co. E-mail: email@gonzaleschamber.org
URL: http://www.gonzaleschamber.org
Contact: Frances Muma, Sec.-Treas.

57513 ■ Granada Hills Chamber of Commerce
17723 Chatsworth St.
Granada Hills, CA 91344
Ph:(818)368-3235
Fax: (818)366-7425
Co. E-mail: email@granadachamber.com
URL: http://www.granadachamber.com
Contact: Della Carroll, Admin.

57514 ■ Grand Terrace Area Chamber of Commerce
21900 Barton Rd., Ste. 102
Grand Terrace, CA 92313
Ph:(909)783-3581
Fax: (909)370-2906
Co. E-mail: office@gtchamber.com
URL: http://www.gtchamber.com
Contact: Bobbie Kay Forbes, Pres.

57515 ■ Greater Bakersfield Chamber of Commerce
1725 Eye St.
PO Box 1947
Bakersfield, CA 93301
Ph:(661)327-4421
Fax: (661)327-8751
Co. E-mail: info@bakersfieldchamber.org
URL: http://www.bakersfieldchamber.org
Contact: Sheryl Barbich, Chair

57516 ■ Greater Clairemont Chamber of Commerce
4230 Genesee Ave., No. 103-122
San Diego, CA 92117
Ph:(858)472-1694
Co. E-mail: john@investwithjohn.com
URL: http://www.clairemont.com/chamber
Contact: John Mc Dermott, Pres.

57517 ■ Greater Concord Chamber of Commerce
2280 Diamond Blvd., Ste. 200
Concord, CA 94520
Ph:(925)685-1181
Fax: (925)685-5623
Co. E-mail: info@concordchamber.com
URL: http://www.concordchamber.com
Contact: Marilyn Fowler, Office and Accounting Mgr.

57518 ■ Greater Eureka Chamber of Commerce
2112 Broadway
Eureka, CA 95501
Ph:(707)442-3738
Free: 800-356-6381
Fax: (707)442-0079
Co. E-mail: chamber@eurekachamber.com
URL: http://www.eurekachamber.com
Contact: J. Warren Hockaday, Exec.Dir.

57519 ■ Greater Fresno Area Chamber of Commerce
2331 Fresno St.
Fresno, CA 93721

Ph:(559)495-4800
Fax: (559)495-4811
Co. E-mail: info@fresnochamber.com
URL: http://www.fresnochamber.com
Contact: Al Smith, Interim CEO

57520 ■ Greater Huntington Park Area Chamber of Commerce
6330 Pacific Blvd., Ste. 208
Huntington Park, CA 90255
Ph:(323)585-1155
Fax: (323)585-2176
Co. E-mail: efren@hpchamber1.com
URL: http://www.hpchamber1.com
Contact: Dante D'Eramo, Exec.Mgr.

57521 ■ Greater Merced Chamber of Commerce
690 W 16th St.
Merced, CA 95340
Ph:(209)384-7092
Free: 800-446-5353
Fax: (209)384-8472
Co. E-mail: info@merced-chamber.com
URL: http://www.merced-chamber.com
Contact: Jennifer Krumm, Office Mgr.

57522 ■ Greater Redding Chamber of Commerce
747 Auditorium Dr.
Redding, CA 96001
Ph:(530)225-4433
Fax: (530)225-4398
Co. E-mail: info@reddingchamber.com
Contact: Frank J. Strazzarino Jr., Pres./CEO

57523 ■ Greater Riverside Chamber of Commerce
3985 University Ave.
Riverside, CA 92501
Ph:(951)683-7100
Fax: (951)683-2670
Co. E-mail: croth@riverside-chamber.com
URL: http://www.riverside-chamber.com
Contact: Cindy Roth, Pres./CEO

57524 ■ Greater Sherman Oaks Chamber of Commerce
14827 Ventura Blvd., Ste. 207
Sherman Oaks, CA 91403-5224
Ph:(818)906-1951
Fax: (818)783-3100
Co. E-mail: ourchamber@aol.com
URL: http://www.shermanoakschamber.org
Contact: Sondra Frohlich, Exec.Dir.

57525 ■ Greater Stockton Chamber of Commerce
445 W Weber Ave., Ste. 220
Stockton, CA 95203
Ph:(209)547-2770
Fax: (209)466-5271
Co. E-mail: schamber@stocktonchamber.org
URL: http://www.stocktonchamber.org
Contact: Douglass W. Wilhoit Jr., CEO

57526 ■ Greater Tehachapi Chamber of Commerce
PO Box 401
209 E Tehachapi Blvd.
Tehachapi, CA 93581-0401
Ph:(661)822-4180
Fax: (661)822-9036
Co. E-mail: chamber@tehachapi.com
URL: http://www.tehachapi.com/chamber
Contact: Ida Rennie, Pres.

57527 ■ Greater Trinidad Chamber of Commerce
PO Box 356
Trinidad, CA 95570
Ph:(707)677-1610
Co. E-mail: info@trinidadcalif.com
URL: http://www.trinidadcalif.com
Contact: Dave Jones, Pres.

57528 ■ Greater Ukiah Chamber of Commerce
200 S School St.
Ukiah, CA 95482
Ph:(707)462-4705
Fax: (707)462-2088
Co. E-mail: info@ukiahchamber.com
URL: http://www.ukiahchamber.com
Contact: Ms. Cherie Blower, CEO

57529 ■ Greenfield Chamber of Commerce
PO Box 387
Greenfield, CA 93927
Ph:(831)674-3222
Fax: (831)674-3149
Co. E-mail: postmaster@ci.greenfield.ca.us
URL: http://www.greenfieldchamber.info
Contact: Joe Kolnick, Pres.

57530 ■ Gridley Area Chamber of Commerce
613 Kentucky St.
Gridley, CA 95948
Ph:(530)846-3142
Fax: (530)846-7165
Co. E-mail: gridleychamber@hotmail.com
URL: http://gridleyareachamber.com
Contact: Devona Pace, Sec.

57531 ■ Guadalupe Chamber of Commerce and Visitor Center
873 Guadalupe St.
Guadalupe, CA 93434
Ph:(805)343-2236
Fax: (805)343-2236
Co. E-mail: info@guadalupechamber.org
URL: http://www.guadalupechamber.org
Contact: Rhonda Walker, Pres.

57532 ■ Gustine Chamber of Commerce
375 5th St.
Gustine, CA 95322
Ph:(209)854-6975
Fax: (209)854-3511
Co. E-mail: gustinechamber@inreach.com
URL: http://www.gustinechamberofcommerce.com
Contact: Pam Bluett, Pres.

57533 ■ Half Moon Bay - Coastside Chamber of Commerce and Visitors' Bureau
520 Kelly Ave., 1st Fl.
Half Moon Bay, CA 94019
Ph:(650)726-8380
Fax: (650)726-8389
Co. E-mail: info@halfmoonbaychamber.org
URL: http://www.halfmoonbaychamber.org
Contact: Charise Hale McHugh, Pres./CEO

57534 ■ Hanford Chamber of Commerce
200 Santa Fe, Ste. D
Hanford, CA 93230
Ph:(559)582-0483
Fax: (559)582-0960
Co. E-mail: hope@hanfordchamber.com
URL: http://www.hanfordchamber.com
Contact: Hope Williams-Morikawa, CEO

57535 ■ Harbor City - Harbor Gateway Chamber of Commerce
19401 S Vermont Ave., Ste. G104
Torrance, CA 90502
Ph:(310)516-7933
Fax: (310)516-7734
Co. E-mail: hchgchamber@sbcglobal.net
URL: http://www.hchgchamber.com
Contact: Joeann Valle, Exec.Dir.

57536 ■ Hawthorne Chamber of Commerce
4444 El Segundo Blvd.
Hawthorne, CA 90250
Ph:(310)676-1163
Fax: (310)676-7661
Co. E-mail: info@hawthorne-chamber.com
URL: http://www.hawthorne-chamber.com
Contact: David S. Villegas, Office Mgr.

57537 ■ Hayward Chamber of Commerce
22561 Main St.
Hayward, CA 94541

Ph:(510)537-2424
Fax: (510)537-2730
Co. E-mail: info@hayward.org
Contact: Scott Raty, Pres./CEO

57538 ■ Healdsburg Chamber of Commerce and Visitors Bureau
217 Healdsburg Ave.
Healdsburg, CA 95448-4103
Ph:(707)433-6935
Free: 800-648-9922
Fax: (707)433-7562
Co. E-mail: info@healdsburg.org
URL: http://www.healdsburg.org
Contact: Lynn Woznicki, Pres./CEO

57539 ■ Helendale Chamber of Commerce
PO Box 1449
Helendale, CA 92342-1449
Ph:(760)952-2231
Fax: (760)952-2231
Contact: Kristie Rosman, Pres.

57540 ■ Hemet San Jacinto Valley Chamber of Commerce
615 N San Jacinto St.
Hemet, CA 92543
Ph:(951)658-3211
Free: 800-334-9344
Fax: (951)766-5013
Co. E-mail: info@hemetsanjacintochamber.org
URL: http://hemetsanjacintochamber.com
Contact: Patti Drusky, Pres./CEO

57541 ■ Hercules Chamber of Commerce
PO Box 5283
Hercules, CA 94547
Ph:(510)741-7945
Fax: (510)741-8965
Co. E-mail: office@herculeschamber.com
URL: http://www.herculescc.com
Contact: Shirley Gotelli, Exec.Dir.

57542 ■ Hermosa Beach Chamber of Commerce and Visitors Bureau
1007 Hermosa Ave.
Hermosa Beach, CA 90254
Ph:(310)376-0951
Fax: (310)798-2594
Co. E-mail: info@hbchamber.net
URL: http://www.hbchamber.net
Contact: Carla Merriman, Exec.Dir.

57543 ■ High Desert Hispanic Chamber of Commerce
14443 Park Ave., Ste. A3
Victorville, CA 92392
Ph:(760)241-6661
Fax: (760)241-2281
URL: http://www.hdhcc.org
Contact: Rudy Cabriales, Pres./CEO

57544 ■ Highland Area Chamber of Commerce
PO Box 455
Highland, CA 92346
Ph:(909)864-4073
Fax: (909)864-4583
Co. E-mail: hcoc@highlandchamber.org
URL: http://www.highlandchamber.org
Contact: Karen Gaffney, Exec.Dir.

57545 ■ Hilmar Chamber of Commerce
PO Box 385
Hilmar, CA 95324
Ph:(209)632-2028
Contact: Gloria Bettencourt, Pres.

57546 ■ Hispanic Chamber of Commerce of Orange County
888 W Santa Ana Blvd., Ste. 150
Santa Ana, CA 92701
Ph:(714)953-4289
Fax: (714)953-0273
Co. E-mail: mail@hcoc.org
URL: http://www.hcoc.org
Contact: Joel Ayala, Pres./CEO

57547 ■ Hispanic Chamber of Commerce of Santa Barbara
PO Box 6592
Santa Barbara, CA 93160-6592
Ph:(805)637-3680
Fax: (805)681-1260
Co. E-mail: lvillegas@sbhcc.com
URL: http://www.sbhcc.com
Contact: Luis Villegas, Pres./CEO

57548 ■ Hispanic Chamber of Commerce of Sonoma County
PO Box 11392
Santa Rosa, CA 95406
Ph:(707)577-7129
Fax: (707)577-7075
Co. E-mail: execdirectorhccsc@hotmail.com
URL: http://www.hccsc.com
Contact: Alexandra Baquero, Chamber Dir.

57549 ■ Historic Sonora Chamber of Commerce
PO Box 884
Sonora, CA 95370-0251
Ph:(209)588-9625
Fax: (209)588-9625
Co. E-mail: info@sonorachamber.com
URL: http://www.sonorachamber.com
Contact: Mrs. Margaret Taylor-Kahl, Exec. Dir.

57550 ■ Hollywood Chamber of Commerce
7018 Hollywood Blvd.
Hollywood, CA 90028
Ph:(323)469-8311
Fax: (323)469-2805
Co. E-mail: info@hollywoodchamber.net
URL: http://hollywoodchamber.net
Contact: Leron Gubler, Pres./CEO

57551 ■ Holtville Chamber of Commerce
101 W 5th St.
Holtville, CA 92250
Ph:(760)356-2923
Fax: (760)356-2925
Co. E-mail: info@holtvillechamber.ca.gov
URL: http://www.holtvillechamber.ca.gov
Contact: Laura Goodsell, Dir.

57552 ■ Hughson Chamber of Commerce
7135 Hughson Ave.
PO Box 1520
Hughson, CA 95326-1520
Ph:(209)883-2800
Fax: (209)883-1808
Co. E-mail: apryl@hughsonchamber.com
URL: http://www.hughsonchamber.com
Contact: Apryl Azevedo-Stanhope, Exec.Dir.

57553 ■ Huntington Beach Chamber of Commerce
19891 Beach Blvd., Ste. 140
Huntington Beach, CA 92648
Ph:(714)536-8888
Fax: (714)960-7654
Co. E-mail: lmartin@hbcoc.com
URL: http://www.hbchamber.org
Contact: Joyce Riddell CCE, Pres.

57554 ■ Idyllwild Chamber of Commerce
PO Box 304
Idyllwild, CA 92549
Ph:(951)659-3259
Free: 888-659-3259
Fax: (951)659-6216
Co. E-mail: info@idyllwildchamber.com
URL: http://www.idyllwildchamber.com
Contact: Dr. Betty Jandl, Pres.

57555 ■ Imperial Beach Chamber of Commerce and Visitor's Bureau
702 Seacoast Dr.
Imperial Beach, CA 91932
Ph:(619)424-3151
Fax: (619)424-3008
Co. E-mail: infor@ib-chamber.org
URL: http://www.ib-chamber.com
Contact: Pat Hutchins, Pres.

57556 ■ Imperial Chamber of Commerce
101 E 4th St.
Imperial, CA 92251-1611
Ph:(760)355-1609
Fax: (760)355-3920
Co. E-mail: info@imperialchamber.org
URL: http://www.imperialchamber.org
Contact: Shelley Rivers, Exec.Dir.

57557 ■ Indian Valley Chamber of Commerce
408 Main St.
PO Box 516
Greenville, CA 95947
Ph:(530)284-6633
Fax: (530)284-6907
Co. E-mail: indianvalleychamber@psln.com
URL: http://www.indianvalley.net
Contact: Alicia Knadler, Pres.

57558 ■ Indio Chamber of Commerce
82-921 Indio Blvd.
Indio, CA 92201
Ph:(760)347-0676
Free: 800-44-INDIO
Fax: (760)347-6069
Co. E-mail: info@indiochamber.org
URL: http://www.indiochamber.org
Contact: Sherry I. Johnson, CEO

57559 ■ Industry Manufacturers Council
255 N Hacienda Blvd., Ste. 100
City of Industry, CA 91744
Ph:(626)968-3737
Fax: (626)330-5060
Co. E-mail: dsachs@cityofindustry.org
URL: http://www.cityofindustry.org
Contact: Donald Sachs, Exec.Dir.

57560 ■ Inglewood/Airport Area Chamber of Commerce
330 E Queen St.
Inglewood, CA 90301-1817
Ph:(310)677-1121
Fax: (310)677-1001
Co. E-mail: inglewoodchamber@sbcglobal.net
URL: http://www.inglewoodchamber.com
Contact: Shannon R. Howe, Exec.VP

57561 ■ Inland Empire Hispanic Chamber of Commerce
320 NE St., Ste. 211
San Bernardino, CA 92401
Ph:(909)888-2188
Fax: (909)888-1151
Co. E-mail: members@iehcc.org
URL: http://www.iehcc.org
Contact: Rita Arias, Pres.

57562 ■ Irvine Chamber of Commerce
2485 McCabe Way, Ste. 150
Irvine, CA 92614
Ph:(949)660-9112
Fax: (949)660-0829
Co. E-mail: icc@irvinechamber.com
URL: http://www.irvinechamber.com
Contact: Jacquie Ellis, Pres./CEO

57563 ■ Irwindale Chamber of Commerce
PO Box 2307
16102 Arrow Hwy.
Irwindale, CA 91706
Ph:(626)960-6606
Fax: (626)960-3868
Co. E-mail: info@irwindalechamber.org
URL: http://www.irwindalechamber.org
Contact: Lisa Bailey, Pres./CEO

57564 ■ Isleton Chamber of Commerce
PO Box 758
Isleton, CA 95641
Ph:(916)777-5880
Fax: (916)777-4330
Co. E-mail: isletoncoc@citilink.net
URL: http://www.isletoncoc.org
Contact: Olivia Glavin, Mgr.

57565 ■ Japanese Chamber of Commerce of Southern California
244 San Pedro, Ste. 504
Los Angeles, CA 90012
Ph:(213)626-3067
Fax: (213)626-3067
Co. E-mail: office@jccsc.com
URL: http://www.jccsc.com
Contact: Shinji Abe, Pres.

57566 ■ Joshua Tree Chamber of Commerce
PO Box 600
61325-29 Palms Hwy., Ste. F
Joshua Tree, CA 92252
Ph:(760)366-3723
Fax: (760)366-2573
Co. E-mail: jtcoc@cci-29palms.com
URL: http://joshuatreechamber.com
Contact: Ms. Nancy Karl, Exec.Dir.

57567 ■ Julian Chamber of Commerce
PO Box 1866
2129 Main St.
Julian, CA 92036
Ph:(760)765-1857
Fax: (760)765-2544
Co. E-mail: chamber@julianca.com
URL: http://www.julianca.com
Contact: Dick Thilken, Pres.

57568 ■ June Lake Chamber of Commerce
PO Box 2
June Lake, CA 93529
Ph:(760)648-7584
Co. E-mail: jlchamber@qnet.com
URL: http://www.junelakechamber.org
Contact: Ron Black, Pres.

57569 ■ Jurupa Chamber of Commerce
7920 Limonite Ave., Ste. C115
Riverside, CA 92509
Ph:(909)681-9242
Fax: (909)681-2720
Co. E-mail: jurupachamber@aol.com
Contact: Bob Shovah, Exec.Dir.

57570 ■ Kerman District Chamber of Commerce
783 S Madera Ave.
Kerman, CA 93630-1744
Ph:(559)846-6343
Fax: (559)846-6344
Co. E-mail: krmchmbr@kermantel.net
URL: http://www.kermanchamber.org
Contact: Linda Geringer, Exec. Dir.

57571 ■ Kern River Valley Chamber of Commerce
PO Box 567
Lake Isabella, CA 93240
Ph:(760)379-5236
Free: (866)578-4386
Fax: (760)379-5457
Co. E-mail: office@kernrivervalley.com
URL: http://www.kernrivervalley.com
Contact: Ms. Sue Weis, Office Mgr.

57572 ■ Kernville Chamber of Commerce
11447 Kernville Rd.
PO Box 397
Kernville, CA 93238-0397
Ph:(760)376-2629
Free: (866)KERNVILLE
Fax: (760)376-4371
Co. E-mail: office@kernvillechamber.org
URL: http://www.kernvillechamber.org
Contact: Michael Ludiker, Pres.

57573 ■ Kettleman City Chamber of Commerce
101 4th St.
PO Box 66
Kettleman City, CA 93239-0066
Ph:(559)386-5850
Contact: Joy Ewalt, Pres./Sec.

57574 ■ King City and Southern Monterey Chamber of Commerce and Agriculture
200 Broadway, Ste. 40
King City, CA 93930
Ph:(831)385-3814
Fax: (831)386-9462
Co. E-mail: kcchamber@tcsn.net
URL: http://www.kingcitychamber.com
Contact: Scott Brennan, Pres.

57575 ■ Kingsburg District Chamber of Commerce
1475 Draper St.
Kingsburg, CA 93631
Ph:(559)897-1111
Fax: (559)897-4621
Co. E-mail: jessatkingsburg@aol.com
URL: http://www.kingsburgchamberofcommerce.com
Contact: Jess Chambers, Exec. Dir.

57576 ■ Korean Chamber of Commerce
9562 Garden Grove Blvd., Ste. O
Garden Grove, CA 92844
Ph:(714)638-1440
Fax: (714)638-7507
Co. E-mail: kccocusa@yahoo.com
Contact: Annie Choie, Pres.

57577 ■ La Canada - Flintridge Chamber of Commerce
4529 Angeles Crest Hwy., Ste. 102
La Canada, CA 91011
Ph:(818)790-4289
Fax: (818)790-8930
Co. E-mail: exec@lacanadaflintridge.com
URL: http://www.lacanadaflintridge.com
Contact: Patricia A. Anderson, Exec.Dir.

57578 ■ La Habra Area Chamber of Commerce
321 E La Habra Blvd.
La Habra, CA 90631
Ph:(562)697-1704
Fax: (562)697-8359
Co. E-mail: info@lahabrachamber.com
URL: http://www.lahabrachamber.com
Contact: Mark Sturdevant, Exec.Dir.

57579 ■ La Jolla Town Council
PO Box 1101
La Jolla, CA 92038
Ph:(858)454-1444
Fax: (858)454-1848
Co. E-mail: brookeatljtc@aol.com
Contact: Brooke Patterson, Mgr.

57580 ■ La Mirada Chamber of Commerce
13714 La Mirada Blvd.
La Mirada, CA 90638
Ph:(562)902-3130
Co. E-mail: info@lmchamber.org
URL: http://lmchamber.org
Contact: Stacey Cripe, Exec.Dir.

57581 ■ La Palma Chamber of Commerce
7861 Valley View St.
La Palma, CA 90623
Ph:(714)228-1488
Fax: (714)228-2208
Co. E-mail: lpcc@lapalmachamber.org
Contact: Sally Mabbott, Exec.Dir.

57582 ■ La Quinta Chamber of Commerce
78-371 Hwy. 111
La Quinta, CA 92253
Ph:(760)564-3199
Fax: (760)564-3111
Co. E-mail: contactus@laquintachamberofcommerce.com
URL: http://www.laquintachamberofcommerce.com
Contact: Valerie J. Smith, Exec.Dir.

57583 ■ La Verne Chamber of Commerce
2078 Bonita Ave.
La Verne, CA 91750
Ph:(909)593-5265
Fax: (909)596-0579

Co. E-mail: tassin@lavernechamber.org
URL: http://www.lavernechamber.org
Contact: LaDonna Tassin, Pres./CEO

57584 ■ Lafayette Chamber of Commerce
100 Lafayette Cir., Ste. 103
Lafayette, CA 94549
Ph:(925)284-7404
Fax: (925)284-3109
Co. E-mail: info@lafayettechamber.org
URL: http://www.lafayettechamber.org
Contact: Jay Lifson, Exec.Dir.

57585 ■ Laguna Beach Chamber of Commerce
357 Glenneyre Ave.
Laguna Beach, CA 92651
Ph:(949)494-1018
Fax: (949)376-8916
Co. E-mail: info@lagunabeachchamber.org
URL: http://www.lagunabeachchamber.org
Contact: Verlaine Crawford, Exec.Dir.

57586 ■ Laguna Niguel Chamber of Commerce
30011 Ivy Glenn Dr., Ste. 125
Laguna Niguel, CA 92677
Ph:(949)363-0136
Fax: (949)363-9026
Co. E-mail: info@lagunaniguelchamber.net
URL: http://lagunaniguelchamber.net
Contact: Debbie Newman, CEO

57587 ■ Lake Arrowhead Communities Chamber of Commerce
PO Box 219
Lake Arrowhead, CA 92352
Ph:(909)337-3715
Fax: (909)336-1548
Co. E-mail: info@lakearrowhead.net
URL: http://www.lakearrowhead.net
Contact: Lewis Murray, Exec.Dir.

57588 ■ Lake Elsinore Valley Chamber of Commerce
132 W Graham Ave.
Lake Elsinore, CA 92530
Ph:(951)245-8848
Fax: (951)245-9127
Co. E-mail: info@lakeelsinorechamber.com
URL: http://www.lakeelsinorechamber.com
Contact: Kim Joseph Cousins, Pres./CEO

57589 ■ Lake Los Angeles Chamber of Commerce
PO Box 500071
Lake Los Angeles, CA 93591-0071
Ph:(661)264-2786
Fax: (661)264-3470
Co. E-mail: lakela@lakelachamber.org
URL: http://www.lakelachamber.org
Contact: Pete Cordera, Pres.

57590 ■ Lakeport Regional Chamber of Commerce
PO Box 295
Lakeport, CA 95453-0295
Ph:(707)263-5092
Free: (866)525-3767
Fax: (707)263-5104
Co. E-mail: lakeport@pacific.net
URL: http://www.lakeportchamber.com
Contact: Melissa Fulton, Exec.Dir.

57591 ■ Lakeside Chamber of Commerce
9924 Vine St.
Lakeside, CA 92040
Ph:(619)561-1031
Fax: (619)561-7951
Co. E-mail: lksdchbr@pacbell.net
URL: http://www.lakesideca.com
Contact: Jeannette Perez, Exec.Dir.

57592 ■ Larkspur Chamber of Commerce
PO Box 315
Larkspur, CA 94977
Ph:(415)838-0038

Co. E-mail: info@larkspurchamber.org
URL: http://www.larkspurchamber.org
Contact: Donna Craft, Exec.Sec.

57593 ■ Lassen County Chamber of Commerce
PO Box 338
84 N Lassen St.
Susanville, CA 96130-0338
Ph:(530)257-4323
Fax: (530)251-2561
Co. E-mail: director@lassencountychamber.org
URL: http://www.lassencountychamber.org
Contact: Patricia Hagata, Exec.Dir.

57594 ■ Lathrop Chamber of Commerce
PO Box 313
Lathrop, CA 95330
Ph:(209)858-9466
Fax: (209)234-2327
Co. E-mail: info@lathropchamber.org
URL: http://www.lathropchamber.org
Contact: Jon J. Serafin DC, Pres.

57595 ■ Lawndale Chamber of Commerce
15424 S Hawthorne Blvd., Ste. 102
Lawndale, CA 90260
Ph:(310)679-3306
Fax: (310)679-5661
Contact: Steve Drasil, Exec.Dir.

57596 ■ Lee Vining Chamber of Commerce
PO Box 130
Lee Vining, CA 93541
Ph:(760)647-6629
Fax: (760)647-6377
Co. E-mail: info@leevining.com
URL: http://www.leevining.com
Contact: Nancy Boman, Pres.

57597 ■ Lemon Grove Chamber of Commerce
3443 Main St.
PO Box 1076
Lemon Grove, CA 91946-1076
Ph:(619)469-9621
Fax: (619)469-0035
Co. E-mail: info@lemongrovechamber.com
URL: http://www.lemongrovechamber.com
Contact: Pam Watt, Dir.

57598 ■ Lemoore District Chamber of Commerce
218 W D St.
Lemoore, CA 93245-2940
Ph:(559)924-6401
Fax: (559)924-4520
Co. E-mail: exec@lemoorechamber.com
Contact: Laura Thompson, CEO

57599 ■ Lincoln Area Chamber of Commerce
511 5th St.
Lincoln, CA 95648
Ph:(916)645-2035
Fax: (916)645-9455
Co. E-mail: info@lincolnchamber.com
URL: http://www.lincolnchamber.com
Contact: Harvi Callahan, CEO

57600 ■ Lincoln Heights Chamber of Commerce
2716 N Broadway, Ste. 210
Los Angeles, CA 90031
Ph:(323)221-6571
Fax: (323)221-1513
Co. E-mail: lhchamber@earthlink.net
Contact: Steven Kastes, Pres.

57601 ■ Linden-Peters Chamber of Commerce
PO Box 557
Linden, CA 95236
Ph:(209)547-3046
Contact: Frank DeBenedetti, Pres.

57602 ■ Lindsay Chamber of Commerce
PO Box 989
Lindsay, CA 93247

Ph:(559)562-4929
Fax: (559)562-5219
Co. E-mail: lindsaychamber@lindsay.ca.us
URL: http://chamber.lindsay.ca.us
Contact: Carolyn Callison, Exec.Dir.

57603 ■ Littlerock Chamber of Commerce
PO Box 326
Littlerock, CA 93543
Ph:(661)944-6990
Fax: (661)944-2199
Co. E-mail: s8f230@aol.com
URL: http://www.littlerock-ca.com
Contact: Penney Lynn Gertz, Pres.

57604 ■ Live Oak District Chamber of Commerce
PO Box 391
Live Oak, CA 95953
Ph:(530)695-1519
Co. E-mail: liveoakchamber@syix.com
URL: http://www.liveoakchamber.org
Contact: Annette Bertolini, Pres./Treas.

57605 ■ Livermore Chamber of Commerce
2157 1st St.
Livermore, CA 94550
Ph:(925)447-1606
Fax: (925)447-1641
Co. E-mail: lccinfo@livermorechamber.org
URL: http://www.livermorechamber.org
Contact: Dale Kaye, Pres./CEO

57606 ■ Lodi Chamber of Commerce
35 S School St.
Lodi, CA 95240
Ph:(209)367-7840
Fax: (209)334-0528
Co. E-mail: info@lodichamber.com
URL: http://www.lodichamber.com
Contact: Pat Patrick, Pres./CEO

57607 ■ Loleta Chamber of Commerce
PO Box 327
Loleta, CA 95551
Ph:(707)733-5731
Co. E-mail: loletachamber@yahoo.com
Contact: Barbara Petersen, Pres.

57608 ■ Loma Linda Chamber of Commerce
PO Box 343
Loma Linda, CA 92354-0343
Ph:(909)799-2828
Fax: (909)799-2825
Co. E-mail: info@lomalindachamber.com
URL: http://www.lomalindachamber.com
Contact: Peg Karsick, CEO

57609 ■ Lomita Chamber of Commerce
25332 Narbonne Ave., Ste. 250
Lomita, CA 90717
Ph:(310)326-6378
Fax: (310)326-2904
Co. E-mail: chuck@lomitacoc.com
URL: http://lomitacoc.com
Contact: Chuck Taylor, Exec.Dir.

57610 ■ Lompoc Valley Chamber of Commerce and Visitors' Bureau
PO Box 626
Lompoc, CA 93438-0626
Ph:(805)736-4567
Free: 800-240-0999
Fax: (805)737-0453
Co. E-mail: chamber@lompoc.com
URL: http://www.lompoc.com
Contact: C. Dennis Anderson, Pres./CEO

57611 ■ Lone Pine Chamber of Commerce
PO Box 749
Lone Pine, CA 93545
Ph:(760)876-4444
Free: 877-253-8981
Fax: (760)876-9205
Co. E-mail: info@lonepinechamber.org
URL: http://www.lonepinechamber.org
Contact: Kathleen New, Exec.Dir.

57612 ■ Long Beach Area Chamber of Commerce
1 World Trade Ctr., Ste. 206
Long Beach, CA 90831-0206
Ph:(562)437-8823
Fax: (562)432-2061
Co. E-mail: info@lbchamber.com
URL: http://www.lbchamber.com
Contact: Randy Gordon, Pres./CEO

57613 ■ Loomis Basin Chamber of Commerce
5911 King Rd., Ste. C
Loomis, CA 95650
Ph:(916)652-7252
Fax: (916)652-7211
Co. E-mail: manager@loomischamber.com
URL: http://www.loomischamber.com
Contact: Brenda Newsom, Exec.Dir.

57614 ■ Los Alamitos Area Chamber of Commerce
3231 Katella Ave.
PO Box 111
Los Alamitos, CA 90720
Ph:(562)598-6659
Fax: (562)598-7035
Co. E-mail: info@losalchamber.org
URL: http://www.losalchamber.org
Contact: Connie Pedenko, CEO

57615 ■ Los Altos Chamber of Commerce
321 University Ave.
Los Altos, CA 94022
Ph:(650)948-1455
Fax: (650)948-6238
Co. E-mail: info@losaltoschamber.org
URL: http://www.losaltoschamber.org
Contact: Julie Rose, Pres.

57616 ■ Los Angeles Area Chamber of Commerce
350 S Bixel St.
Los Angeles, CA 90017
Ph:(213)580-7500
Fax: (213)580-7511
Co. E-mail: info@lachamber.org
URL: http://www.lachamber.org
Contact: Russell J. Hammer, Pres./CEO

57617 ■ Los Banos Chamber of Commerce
PO Box 2117
Los Banos, CA 93635
Ph:(209)826-2495
Free: 800-336-6354
Fax: (209)826-9689
Co. E-mail: lbcofc@losbanos.com
URL: http://www.losbanos.com
Contact: Rhonda Lowe, Pres.

57618 ■ Los Osos/Baywood Park Chamber of Commerce
PO Box 6282
Los Osos, CA 93412-6282
Ph:(805)528-4884
Fax: (805)528-8401
Co. E-mail: chamber@fix.net
URL: http://www.losososbaywoodpark.org
Contact: Ms. Annie Mueller, Exec.Dir.

57619 ■ Lucerne Valley Chamber of Commerce
PO Box 491
Lucerne Valley, CA 92356
Ph:(760)248-7215
Fax: (760)248-2024
Co. E-mail: chamber@lucernevalley.net
URL: http://www.lucernevalley.net
Contact: Lloyd Schultz, Pres.

57620 ■ Lynwood Chamber of Commerce
3651 E Imperial Hwy.
PO Box 763
Lynwood, CA 90262
Ph:(310)537-6484
Fax: (310)537-8143
Co. E-mail: lynwoodchamber@aol.com

URL: http://www.lynwoodchamber.org
Contact: Donna Terrell, Pres.

57621 ■ Madera Chamber of Commerce
120 NE St.
Madera, CA 93638
Ph:(559)673-3563
Fax: (559)673-5009
Co. E-mail: dbray@maderachamber.com
URL: http://www.maderachamber.com
Contact: Debi Bray, Exec.VP

57622 ■ Malibu Chamber of Commerce
23805 Stuart Ranch Rd., Ste. 100
Malibu, CA 90265
Ph:(310)456-9025
Fax: (310)456-0195
Co. E-mail: info@malibu.org
URL: http://malibu.wliinc3.com/index.asp
Contact: Pam Brady, Pres.

57623 ■ Manhattan Beach Chamber of Commerce
425 15th St.
PO Box 3007
Manhattan Beach, CA 90266
Ph:(310)545-5313
Fax: (310)545-7203
Co. E-mail: info@manhattanbeachchamber.net
URL: http://www.mb-chamber.com
Contact: Helen Duncan, Exec.Dir.

57624 ■ Manteca Chamber of Commerce
107 N Lincoln Ave.
Manteca, CA 95336
Ph:(209)823-6121
Fax: (209)823-9959
Co. E-mail: chamber@manteca.org
URL: http://www.manteca.org
Contact: Debby Moorhead, Exec.Dir.

57625 ■ Marina Chamber of Commerce
PO Box 425
Marina, CA 93933
Ph:(831)384-9155
URL: http://www.marinachamber.com
Contact: Cecil Potter, Pres.

57626 ■ Mariposa County Chamber of Commerce
PO Box 425
5158 Hwy. 140
Mariposa, CA 95338
Ph:(209)966-2456
Fax: (209)966-4193
Co. E-mail: commerce@yosemite.net
URL: http://www.mariposa.org
Contact: Dorothy Kuhnel, Exec.Dir.

57627 ■ Mark West Area Chamber of Commerce
642 Larkfield Shopping Ctr.
Santa Rosa, CA 95403
Ph:(707)578-7975
Fax: (707)578-0397
Co. E-mail: markwest@markwest.org
URL: http://www.markwest.org
Contact: Doug Williams, Pres.

57628 ■ Martinez Area Chamber of Commerce and Visitors and Information Center
603 Marina Vista
Martinez, CA 94553
Ph:(925)228-2345
Fax: (925)259-2356
Co. E-mail: lou@martinezchamber.com
URL: http://www.martinezchamber.com
Contact: Lou Schoeneman, Exec.Dir.

57629 ■ Maywood Chamber of Commerce
PO Box 645
5720 Heliothrope Ave.
Maywood, CA 90270
Ph:(323)562-3373
Fax: (323)562-2905
Co. E-mail: sjimenez@cityofmaywood.com

URL: http://www.cityofmaywood.com
Contact: Susan Jimenez, Gen.Mgr.

57630 ■ McCloud Chamber of Commerce
PO Box 372
McCloud, CA 96057
Ph:(530)964-3113
Fax: (530)964-2808
Co. E-mail: contact@mccloudchamber.com
URL: http://www.mccloudchamber.com/chamber.
   html
Contact: Sheri Burris, Pres.

57631 ■ McKinleyville Chamber of Commerce
1640 Central Ave.
McKinleyville, CA 95519
Ph:(707)839-2449
Fax: (707)839-1205
URL: http://www.mckinleyvillechamber.com
Contact: Andre Carey, Pres.

57632 ■ Menifee Valley Chamber of Commerce
27070 Sun City Blvd.
Sun City, CA 92586
Ph:(951)672-1991
Fax: (951)672-4022
Co. E-mail: info@menifeevalleychamber.org
URL: http://www.menifeevalleychamber.com
Contact: Bob Duistermars, Chm.

57633 ■ Menlo Park Chamber of Commerce
1100 Merrill St.
Menlo Park, CA 94025-4386
Ph:(650)325-2818
Fax: (650)325-0920
Co. E-mail: info@menloparkchamber.com
URL: http://www.menloparkchamber.com
Contact: Fran Dehn, Pres./CEO

57634 ■ Merced County Chamber of Commerce
646 S Hwy. 59
PO Box 1112
Merced, CA 95341-1112
Ph:(209)722-3864
Fax: (209)722-2406
Co. E-mail: info@mercedcountychamber.com
URL: http://www.mercedcountychamber.com
Contact: Julius Pekar, Exec.Dir.

57635 ■ Mid Valley Chamber of Commerce
7120 Hayvenhurst Ave., Ste. 114
Van Nuys, CA 91406-3813
Ph:(818)989-0300
Fax: (818)989-3836
Co. E-mail: info@midvalleychamber.com
URL: http://www.midvalleychamber.com
Contact: Nancy Hoffman Vanyek, CEO

57636 ■ Mill Valley Chamber of Commerce
85 Throckmorton Ave.
PO Box 5123
Mill Valley, CA 94942
Ph:(415)388-9700
Fax: (415)388-9770
Co. E-mail: chamber@millvalley.org
URL: http://www.millvalley.org
Contact: Kathy Severson, CEO

57637 ■ Millbrae Chamber of Commerce
50 Victoria Ave., Ste. 103
Millbrae, CA 94030-2622
Ph:(650)697-7324
Fax: (650)259-7918
Co. E-mail: info@millbrae.com
URL: http://www.millbrae.com
Contact: John Ford, Pres./CEO

57638 ■ Milpitas Chamber of Commerce
828 N Hillview Dr.
Milpitas, CA 95035-4544
Ph:(408)262-2613
Fax: (408)262-2823
Co. E-mail: info@milpitaschamber.com
URL: http://www.milpitaschamber.com

Contact: Don Ryan, VP for Programs

57639 ■ Modesto Chamber of Commerce
1114 J St.
PO Box 844
Modesto, CA 95353-0844
Ph:(209)577-5757
Fax: (209)577-2673
Co. E-mail: info@modchamber.org
URL: http://www.modchamber.org
Contact: Joy Madison, Pres./CEO

57640 ■ Modesto Junior Chamber of Commerce
PO Box 76
Modesto, CA 95354
Ph:(209)573-7979
Co. E-mail: info@jayceesmodesto.org
URL: http://www.jayceesmodesto.org
Contact: Annette McDonnell, Pres.

57641 ■ Monrovia Chamber of Commerce
620 S Myrtle Ave.
Monrovia, CA 91016-2805
Ph:(626)358-1159
Fax: (626)357-6036
Co. E-mail: chamber@monroviacc.com
URL: http://www.monroviacc.com
Contact: Karin Crehan, Exec.Dir.

57642 ■ Montclair Chamber of Commerce
5220 Benito St.
Montclair, CA 91763
Ph:(909)624-4569
Fax: (909)625-2009
URL: http://www.montclairchamber.com
Contact: Dana Cox, Pres.

57643 ■ Monte Rio Chamber of Commerce
PO Box 220
Monte Rio, CA 95462-0220
Ph:(707)865-1533
Fax: (707)865-2181
Co. E-mail: mrcc@sonic.net
URL: http://monterio.org
Contact: Mary Baker, Board Sec.

57644 ■ Montebello Chamber of Commerce
817 W Whittier Blvd., Ste. 200
Montebello, CA 90640
Ph:(323)721-1153
Fax: (323)721-7946
Co. E-mail: info@montebellochamber.org
URL: http://www.montebellochamber.org
Contact: Andrea Wagg, Pres.

57645 ■ Monterey Park Chamber of Commerce
700 El Mercado
PO Box 387
Monterey Park, CA 91754-0387
Ph:(626)570-9429
Fax: (626)570-9491
Co. E-mail: mpcc@montereypark.com
Contact: Lucy Kelley, Exec.Dir.

57646 ■ Monterey Peninsula Chamber of Commerce
380 Alvarado St.
Monterey, CA 93940
Ph:(831)648-5360
Fax: (831)649-3502
Co. E-mail: info@mpcc.com
URL: http://www.mpcc.com
Contact: Brenda Roncarati, CEO/Pres.

57647 ■ Montrose-Verdugo City Chamber of Commerce
3516 N Verdugo Rd.
Glendale, CA 91208
Ph:(818)249-7171
Fax: (818)249-8919
Co. E-mail: mvcc@montrosechamber.org
URL: http://www.montrosechamber.org
Contact: Liz Church, Exec.Dir.

57648 ■ Morgan Hill Chamber of Commerce
PO Box 786
Morgan Hill, CA 95038-0786
Ph:(408)779-9444
Fax: (408)779-5405
Co. E-mail: mchh@morganhill.org
URL: http://www.morganhill.org
Contact: Dan Ehler, Exec.Dir.

57649 ■ Morro Bay Chamber of Commerce
845 Embarcadero Rd., Ste. D
Morro Bay, CA 93442
Ph:(805)772-4467
Free: 800-231-0592
Fax: (805)772-6038
Co. E-mail: baywatch@morrobay.org
URL: http://www.morrobay.org
Contact: Kim Kimball, Exec.Dir./CEO

57650 ■ Moss Landing Chamber of Commerce
PO Box 41
Moss Landing, CA 95039
Ph:(831)633-4501
Fax: (831)633-4501
URL: http://www.mosslandingchamber.com
Contact: Carole Kettman, Admin. Asst.

57651 ■ Mount Shasta Chamber of Commerce
300 Pine St.
Mount Shasta, CA 96067
Ph:(530)926-4865
Free: 800-926-4865
Fax: (530)926-0976
Co. E-mail: info@mtshastachamber.com
URL: http://www.mtshastachamber.com
Contact: Larry Montgomery, Pres.

57652 ■ Murrieta Chamber of Commerce
26396 Beckman Ct., Ste. C
Murrieta, CA 92562
Ph:(951)677-7916
Fax: (951)677-9976
Co. E-mail: roliver@murrietachamber.org
Contact: Mr. Rex Oliver IOM, CEO & Pres.

57653 ■ Napa Chamber of Commerce
1556 1st St.
PO Box 636
Napa, CA 94559-0636
Ph:(707)226-7455
Fax: (707)226-1171
Co. E-mail: info@napachamber.com
URL: http://www.napachamber.com
Contact: Kate King ACE, Pres./CEO

57654 ■ National City Chamber of Commerce
901 National City Blvd.
National City, CA 91950-3203
Ph:(619)477-9339
Free: 800-292-4624
Fax: (619)477-5018
Co. E-mail: thechamber@nationalcitychamber.org
URL: http://www.nationalcitychamber.org
Contact: John Webster, Pres.

57655 ■ Needles Area Chamber of Commerce
PO Box 705
Needles, CA 92363-0705
Ph:(760)326-2050
Fax: (760)326-2194
Co. E-mail: needlescofc@rraz.net
URL: http://www.needleschamber.com
Contact: Sue Godnick, Exec.Dir.

57656 ■ Networkers of the Costa Mesa Chamber of Commerce
1700 Adams Ave., Ste. 101
Costa Mesa, CA 92626-4865
Ph:(714)885-9090
Fax: (714)885-9094
Co. E-mail: rquinn@costamesachamber.com
URL: http://www.costamesachamber.com
Contact: Ed Fawcett, Pres./CEO

57657 ■ Nevada City Chamber of Commerce
132 Main St.
Nevada City, CA 95959-2520
Ph:(530)265-2692
Free: 800-655-NJOY
Fax: (530)265-3892
Co. E-mail: info@nevadacitychamber.com
URL: http://www.nevadacitychamber.com
Contact: Bob Buhlis, Pres.

57658 ■ Newark Chamber of Commerce
6066 Civic Terr. Ave., Ste. 8
Newark, CA 94560
Ph:(510)744-1000
Fax: (510)744-1003
Co. E-mail: info@newark-chamber.com
URL: http://www.newark-chamber.com
Contact: Lt. Tom Milner, Pres.

57659 ■ Newman Chamber of Commerce
PO Box 753
Newman, CA 95360
Ph:(209)862-1000
Fax: (209)862-4133
Contact: Sean McNaughton, Pres.

57660 ■ Newport Harbor Area Chamber of Commerce
1470 Jamboree Rd.
Newport Beach, CA 92660
Ph:(929)729-4400
Fax: (929)729-4417
Co. E-mail: info@newportbeach.com
URL: http://www.newportbeach.com
Contact: Richard R. Luehrs, Pres./CEO

57661 ■ Niland Chamber of Commerce
8031 Hwy. 111
PO Box 97
Niland, CA 92257
Ph:(760)359-0870
Contact: Kenny Koon, Pres.

57662 ■ Nipomo Chamber of Commerce
671 W Tefft St., Ste. 8
Nipomo, CA 93444
Ph:(805)929-1583
Fax: (805)929-5835
Co. E-mail: nipomochamber@yahoo.com
URL: http://www.nipomochamber.org
Contact: Clyde Cruise, Pres.

57663 ■ Norco Chamber of Commerce
2816 Hamner Ave.
Norco, CA 92860
Ph:(951)737-2531
Fax: (951)737-2574
Co. E-mail: staff@norcochamber.com
URL: http://www.norcochamber.com
Contact: Robert Shine, Pres.

57664 ■ North Fork Chamber of Commerce
PO Box 426
North Fork, CA 93643
Ph:(559)877-2410
Fax: (559)877-2332
Co. E-mail: info@north-fork-chamber.com
URL: http://www.north-fork-chamber.com
Contact: Bob McKee, Pres.

57665 ■ North Monterey County Chamber of Commerce
PO Box 1744
Castroville, CA 95012
Ph:(831)633-2465
Fax: (831)633-0485
Co. E-mail: info@northmontereycountychamber.org
URL: http://www.prunedale.org
Contact: Gary DeAmaral, VP

57666 ■ North of the River Chamber of Commerce
PO Box 5551
Bakersfield, CA 93388
Ph:(661)871-4555
Fax: (661)871-4555
Co. E-mail: norchamber@bak.rr.com

Contact: Stan Shires, Exec.Dir.

57667 ■ North Sacramento Chamber of Commerce
492 Arden Way
Sacramento, CA 95815
Ph:(916)925-6773
Fax: (916)925-2176
Co. E-mail: franklin.burris@potter-taylor.com
URL: http://northsacramentochamber.org
Contact: Franklin Burris, Pres.

57668 ■ North Valley Regional Chamber of Commerce
9401 Reseda Blvd., Ste. 100
Northridge, CA 91324
Ph:(818)349-5676
Fax: (818)349-4343
Co. E-mail: info@nvrcc.com
URL: http://www.nvrcc.com
Contact: Wayne Adelstein, Pres./CEO

57669 ■ Northeast San Fernando Valley Chamber of Commerce
601 S Brand Blvd., No. 20
San Fernando, CA 91340
Ph:(818)361-1184
Fax: (818)898-1986
Co. E-mail: mail@nesfvcc.org
Contact: Ramiro G. Estrada, Exec.Dir.

57670 ■ Norwalk Chamber of Commerce
12040 Foster Rd.
Norwalk, CA 90650
Ph:(562)864-7785
Fax: (562)864-8539
Co. E-mail: ceo@norwalkchamber.com
URL: http://www.norwalkchamber.com
Contact: John E. Hackney, CEO

57671 ■ Novato Chamber of Commerce
807 DeLong Ave.
Novato, CA 94945
Ph:(415)897-1164
Fax: (415)898-9097
Co. E-mail: info@novatochamber.com
URL: http://www.novato.org
Contact: Coy Smith, Exec.Dir.

57672 ■ Oakdale District Chamber of Commerce
590 N Yosemite Ave.
Oakdale, CA 95361-2732
Ph:(209)847-2244
Fax: (209)847-0826
Co. E-mail: info@yosemite-gateway.net
URL: http://www.yosemite-gateway.net
Contact: Mary Guardiola, CEO

57673 ■ Oakhurst Area Chamber of Commerce
49074 Civic Circle Dr.
Oakhurst, CA 93644-8713
Ph:(559)683-7766
Fax: (559)658-2942
Co. E-mail: kmccorry@oakhurstchamber.com
URL: http://www.oakhurstchamber.com
Contact: Kathy McCorry, Exec.Dir.

57674 ■ Oakland African-American Chamber of Commerce
PO Box 5790
Oakland, CA 94605-5790
Ph:(510)567-1307
Fax: (510)567-1709
Co. E-mail: info@oaacc.org
URL: http://www.oaklandblackchamber.com
Contact: Robert Bobb, Founding Pres.

57675 ■ Oakland Chinatown Chamber of Commerce
Pacific Renaissance Plz.
388 9th St., Ste. 258
Oakland, CA 94607
Ph:(510)893-8979
Fax: (510)893-8988
Co. E-mail: oaklandctchamber@aol.com

URL: http://www.oaklandchinatownstreetfest.com
Contact: Jenny Ong, Exec.Dir.

57676 ■ Oakland Metropolitan Chamber of Commerce
475 14th St.
Oakland, CA 94612-1903
Ph:(510)874-4800
Fax: (510)839-8817
Co. E-mail: jharaburda@oaklandchamber.com
URL: http://www.oaklandchamber.com
Contact: Joseph Haraburda, Pres./CEO

57677 ■ Oakley Chamber of Commerce
PO Box 1340
Oakley, CA 94561
Ph:(925)625-1035
Fax: (925)625-4051
Co. E-mail: oakley@ecis.com
URL: http://www.oakleychamber.com
Contact: Gene Buchholz, Pres.

57678 ■ Occidental Chamber of Commerce
PO Box 159
Occidental, CA 95465
Ph:(707)874-3279
Co. E-mail: occidentalcc@bigplanet.com
Contact: Cheri Keel ASID, Pres.

57679 ■ Oceanside Chamber of Commerce
928 N Coast Hwy.
Oceanside, CA 92054
Ph:(760)722-1534
Free: 800-350-7873
Fax: (760)722-8336
Co. E-mail: info@oceansidechamber.com
URL: http://www.oceansidechamber.com
Contact: David L. Nydegger, CEO

57680 ■ Ojai Valley Chamber of Commerce
PO Box 1134
150 W Ojai Ave.
Ojai, CA 93023
Ph:(805)646-8126
Fax: (805)646-9762
Co. E-mail: info@ojaichamber.com
URL: http://www.ojaichamber.org
Contact: Bret Bradigan, Pres.

57681 ■ Ontario Chamber of Commerce
421-B N Euclid Ave.
Ontario, CA 91762
Ph:(909)984-2458
Fax: (909)984-6439
Co. E-mail: info@ontario.org
URL: http://www.ontario.org
Contact: Mark Smiley, Pres./CEO

57682 ■ Orange Chamber of Commerce and Visitor Bureau
439 E Chapman Ave.
Orange, CA 92866
Ph:(714)538-3581
Free: 800-938-0073
Fax: (714)532-1675
Co. E-mail: info@orangechamber.com
URL: http://www.orangechamber.com
Contact: Barbara deBoom ACE, Pres./CEO

57683 ■ Orange County Business Council
2 Park Plz., Ste. 100
Irvine, CA 92614-5904
Ph:(949)476-2242
Fax: (949)476-9240
Co. E-mail: pbluck@ocbc.org
URL: http://www.ocbc.org
Contact: Stan Oftelie, Pres./CEO/Sec.

57684 ■ Orange County Chamber of Commerce Profit Connection
439 E Chapman Ave.
Orange, CA 92866-1509
Ph:(714)538-3581
Fax: (714)532-1675
Co. E-mail: info@orangechamber.com
URL: http://www.orangechamber.com
Contact: Heide Larkin-Reed, Pres./CEO

57685 ■ Orange County Chinese-American Chamber of Commerce
4605 Barranca Pkwy., No. 101-J
Irvine, CA 92604
Ph:(949)681-0380
Fax: (949)551-3501
Co. E-mail: info@occacc.org
URL: http://www.occacc.org

57686 ■ Orangevale Chamber of Commerce
9267 Greenback Ln., Ste. B91
Orangevale, CA 95662
Ph:(916)988-0175
Fax: (916)988-1049
Co. E-mail: info@orangevalechamber.com
URL: http://www.orangevalechamber.com
Contact: Karen Adams, Exec.Dir.

57687 ■ Orick Chamber of Commerce
PO Box 234
Orick, CA 95555
Ph:(707)488-2885
Fax: (707)488-5295
Co. E-mail: orick@orick.net
URL: http://www.orick.net
Contact: Donna Hufford, Sec.-Treas.

57688 ■ Orinda Chamber of Commerce
PO Box 2271
Orinda, CA 94563
Ph:(925)254-3909
Fax: (925)254-1635
Co. E-mail: orinda@silcon.com
URL: http://www.orindachamber.org
Contact: Valerie Hotz, Exec.Dir.

57689 ■ Orland Area Chamber of Commerce
636 Third St.
Orland, CA 95963
Ph:(530)865-2311
Fax: (530)865-8171
Co. E-mail: info@orlandchamber.com
URL: http://www.orlandchamber.com
Contact: Arlene Dobson, Mgr.

57690 ■ Oroville Area Chamber of Commerce
1789 Montgomery St.
Oroville, CA 95965
Ph:(530)538-2542
Free: 800-655-GOLD
Fax: (530)538-2546
Co. E-mail: info@orovillechamber.net
URL: http://www.orovillechamber.net
Contact: Linda Dahlmeier, Pres.

57691 ■ Otay Mesa Chamber of Commerce
9163 Siempre Viva Rd., Ste. I-2
San Diego, CA 92154-7608
Ph:(619)661-6111
Fax: (619)661-6178
Co. E-mail: jluken@otaymesa.org
URL: http://www.otaymesa.org
Contact: Alejandra Teran Mier, Exec.Dir.

57692 ■ Oxnard Chamber of Commerce
400 E Esplanade Dr., Ste. 301
Oxnard, CA 93036
Ph:(805)983-6118
Fax: (805)604-7331
Co. E-mail: info@oxnardchamber.org
URL: http://www.oxnardchamber.org
Contact: Nancy Lindholm, Pres./CEO

57693 ■ Pacific Grove Chamber of Commerce
PO Box 167
Pacific Grove, CA 93950
Ph:(831)373-3304
Free: 800-656-6650
Fax: (831)373-3317
Co. E-mail: chamber@pacificgrove.org
URL: http://www.pacificgrove.org
Contact: Moe Ammar, Pres.

57694 ■ Pacific Palisades Chamber of Commerce
15330 Antioch St.
Pacific Palisades, CA 90272

Ph:(310)459-7963
Fax: (310)459-9534
Co. E-mail: palisadeschamber@earthlink.net
URL: http://www.palisadeschamber.com
Contact: Arnie Wishnick, Exec.Dir.

57695 ■ Pacifica Chamber of Commerce and Visitor Center
225 Rockaway Beach, Ste. 1
Pacifica, CA 94044
Ph:(650)355-4122
Fax: (650)355-6949
Co. E-mail: don@pacificachamber.org
URL: http://www.pacificachamber.com
Contact: Don Eagleston, Exec.VP

57696 ■ Pajaro Valley Chamber of Commerce
444 Main St.
PO Box 1748
Watsonville, CA 95077-1748
Ph:(831)724-3900
Fax: (831)728-5300
Co. E-mail: info@pajarovalleychamber.com
URL: http://www.pajarovalleychamber.com
Contact: Kristen Collins, Pres./CEO

57697 ■ Palm Desert Chamber of Commerce
73-710 Fred Waring Dr., Ste. 114
Palm Desert, CA 92260-2553
Ph:(760)346-6111
Fax: (760)346-3263
Co. E-mail: info@pdcc.org
URL: http://www.palmdesert.org
Contact: Susan E. Harvey, Pres./CEO

57698 ■ Palm Springs Chamber of Commerce
190 W Amado Rd.
Palm Springs, CA 92262
Ph:(760)325-1577
Fax: (760)325-8549
Co. E-mail: pschamber@pschamber.org
URL: http://www.pschamber.org
Contact: Janet Cook, CEO

57699 ■ Palmdale Chamber of Commerce
817 E Ave. Q9
Palmdale, CA 93550-4732
Ph:(661)273-3232
Fax: (661)273-8508
Co. E-mail: ibarcelona@palmdalechamber.org
URL: http://www.palmdalechamber.org
Contact: Isaac Barcelona, Pres./CEO

57700 ■ Palo Alto Chamber of Commerce
122 Hamilton Ave.
Palo Alto, CA 94301
Ph:(650)324-3121
Fax: (650)324-1215
Co. E-mail: info@paloaltochamber.com
URL: http://www.paloaltochamber.com
Contact: Sandra Lonnquist, Pres./CEO

57701 ■ Palos Verdes Peninsula Chamber of Commerce
707 Silver Spur Rd., Ste. 100
Rolling Hills Estates, CA 90274
Ph:(310)377-8111
Fax: (310)377-0614
Co. E-mail: info@palosverdeschamber.com
URL: http://palosverdeschamber.com
Contact: Kay Finer, Pres./CEO

57702 ■ Paradise Ridge Chamber of Commerce
5550 Skyway, No. 1
Paradise, CA 95969
Ph:(530)877-9356
Free: 800-845-2769
Fax: (530)877-1865
Co. E-mail: pchamber@c-zone.net
URL: http://www.paradisechamber.com
Contact: Ed Salome, Exec.Dir.

57703 ■ Paramount Chamber of Commerce
15357 Paramount Blvd.
Paramount, CA 90723-4338

Ph:(562)634-3980
Fax: (562)634-0891
Co. E-mail: plemons@paramountchamber.com
URL: http://www.paramountchamber.org
Contact: Peggy Lemons, Exec.Dir.

57704 ■ Parlier Chamber of Commerce
PO Box 453
Parlier, CA 93648
Ph:(559)646-3545
URL: http://www.fresnocog.org/city1/city_of_parlier.htm
Contact: Israel Lara, Pres.

57705 ■ Pasadena Chamber of Commerce and Civic Association
865 E Del Mar Blvd.
Pasadena, CA 91101
Ph:(626)795-3355
Fax: (626)795-5603
Co. E-mail: pasadenacoc@earthlink.net
URL: http://www.pasadena-chamber.org
Contact: Lynne C. Hess, Pres./CEO

57706 ■ Paso Robles Chamber of Commerce
1225 Park St.
Paso Robles, CA 93446
Ph:(805)238-0506
Free: 800-406-4040
Fax: (805)238-0527
Co. E-mail: info@pasorobleschamber.com
URL: http://www.pasorobleschamber.com
Contact: Mike Gibson, Pres./CEO

57707 ■ Patterson-Westley Chamber of Commerce
PO Box 365
Patterson, CA 95363
Ph:(209)892-2821
Fax: (209)892-2821
Co. E-mail: chamberofcommerce@gvni.com
URL: http://www.patterson-westleychamber.com
Contact: Mark Lynch, Pres.

57708 ■ Pearblossom Chamber of Commerce
PO Box 591
Pearblossom, CA 93553
Ph:(661)944-6435
Contact: Chuck Milner, Pres.

57709 ■ Peninsula Chamber of Commerce
PO Box 7018
San Diego, CA 92167-0018
Ph:(619)225-8200
Co. E-mail: billk@seaportrealtors.com
URL: http://www.peninsulachamber.com

57710 ■ Perris Valley Chamber of Commerce
11 South D St.
Perris, CA 92571
Ph:(951)657-3555
Fax: (951)657-3085
Co. E-mail: perrischamber@puhsd.org
URL: http://www.perrischamber.com
Contact: Mark Howison, Pres.

57711 ■ Petaluma Area Chamber of Commerce
800 Baywood Dr.
Petaluma, CA 94954
Ph:(707)762-2785
Fax: (707)762-4721
Co. E-mail: pacc@petalumachamber.com
URL: http://www.petalumachamber.com
Contact: David King, Pres.

57712 ■ Phelan Chamber of Commerce
PO Box 290010
Phelan, CA 92329-0010
Ph:(760)868-3291
Fax: (760)868-3291
Co. E-mail: info@phelanchamber.org
URL: http://www.phelanchamber.org
Contact: Tony Inglese, Pres.

57713 ■ Pico Rivera Chamber of Commerce
6771 Passons Blvd.
Pico Rivera, CA 90660-3647

Ph:(562)949-2473
Fax: (562)949-8320
Co. E-mail: hartter@picoriverachamber.org
URL: http://www.picoriverachamber.com
Contact: Roger Hartter, Exec.Dir.

57714 ■ Pinole Chamber of Commerce
PO Box 1
Pinole, CA 94564
Ph:(510)724-4484
Fax: (510)724-4408
Co. E-mail: pinolechamber@msn.com
URL: http://www.pinolechamber.org
Contact: Ivette Ricco, Exec.Dir.

57715 ■ Pinon Hills Chamber of Commerce
PO Box 720095
Pinon Hills, CA 92372
Ph:(760)868-4309
Fax: (760)868-5801
URL: http://www.ph.qnet.com/~mojave/phelan/pinhill.htm

57716 ■ Pismo Beach Chamber of Commerce and Visitors' Information Center
581 Dolliver St.
Pismo Beach, CA 93449
Ph:(805)773-4382
Free: 800-443-7778
Fax: (805)773-6772
Co. E-mail: pbcoc@charter.net
URL: http://www.pismochamber.com
Contact: Rebecca McMurry, Exec.Dir.

57717 ■ Pittsburg Chamber of Commerce
485 Railroad Ave.
Pittsburg, CA 94565
Ph:(925)432-7301
Fax: (925)427-5555
Co. E-mail: mconig@pittsburg.org
URL: http://www.pittsburg.org
Contact: Mary P. Coniglio, Exec.VP/CEO

57718 ■ Placentia Chamber of Commerce
201 E Yorba Linda Blvd., Ste. C
Placentia, CA 92870-3418
Ph:(714)528-1873
Fax: (714)528-1879
Co. E-mail: info@placentiachamber.com
URL: http://www.placentiachamber.com
Contact: Glenn Baldwin, Pres.

57719 ■ Pleasant Hill Chamber of Commerce
91 Gregory Ln., Ste. 11
Pleasant Hill, CA 94523-4914
Ph:(925)687-0700
Fax: (925)676-7422
Co. E-mail: info@pleasanthillchamber.com
URL: http://www.pleasanthillchamber.com
Contact: Charley Daly, Exec.Dir.

57720 ■ Pleasanton Chamber of Commerce
777 Peters Ave.
Pleasanton, CA 94566-6500
Ph:(925)846-5858
Fax: (925)846-9697
Co. E-mail: info@pleasanton.org
URL: http://www.pleasanton.org
Contact: David Bouchard, Pres./CEO

57721 ■ Pomona Chamber of Commerce
PO Box 1457
Pomona, CA 91769-1457
Ph:(909)622-1256
Fax: (909)620-5986
Co. E-mail: info@pomonachamber.org
URL: http://www.pomonachamber.org
Contact: Ms. Pamela A. Morgan, Exec.Dir./CEO

57722 ■ Port Hueneme Chamber of Commerce
220 N Market St.
Port Hueneme, CA 93041-3204
Ph:(805)488-2023
Fax: (805)488-6993
Co. E-mail: phc@huenemechamber.com
URL: http://www.huenemechamber.com

Contact: Arlene Fraser, Exec.Dir.

57723 ■ Porterville Chamber of Commerce
93 N Main St., Ste. A
Porterville, CA 93257
Ph:(559)784-7502
Fax: (559)784-0770
Co. E-mail: chamber@porterville.com
URL: http://www.chamber.porterville.com
Contact: Donnette Silva Carter, Pres./CEO

57724 ■ Poway Chamber of Commerce
PO Box 868
Poway, CA 92074-0868
Ph:(858)748-0016
Fax: (858)748-1710
Co. E-mail: chamber@poway.com
URL: http://www.poway.com
Contact: Toni Kraft, Pres./CEO

57725 ■ Quartz Hill Chamber of Commerce
42043 50th St. W
Quartz Hill, CA 93536
Ph:(661)722-4811
Fax: (661)722-3235
Co. E-mail: info@quartzhillchamber.org
URL: http://www.quartzhillchamber.org
Contact: Mr. Rod Jacobson, Pres.

57726 ■ Quincy Chamber of Commerce
464 W Main St.
Quincy, CA 95971
Ph:(530)283-0188
Free: 877-283-0188
Fax: (530)283-5864
Co. E-mail: office@quincychamber.com
URL: http://www.quincychamber.com
Contact: Myrna Berry, Admin. Asst.

57727 ■ Ramona Chamber of Commerce
960 Main St.
Ramona, CA 92065
Ph:(760)789-1311
Fax: (760)789-1317
Co. E-mail: info@ramonachamber.com
URL: http://www.ramonachamber.com
Contact: Nelson MacWilliams, Exec.Dir./Chamber
    Mgr.

**57728 ■ Rancho Cordova Chamber of
Commerce**
3328 Mather Field Rd.
Rancho Cordova, CA 95670
Ph:(916)361-8700
Fax: (916)361-3049
Co. E-mail: ralbright@ranchocordova.org
URL: http://www.ranchocordova.org
Contact: Rex Albright, Exec.Dir./CEO

**57729 ■ Rancho Cucamonga Chamber of
Commerce**
7945 Vineyard Ave., Ste. D-5
Rancho Cucamonga, CA 91730-2314
Ph:(909)987-1012
Fax: (909)987-5917
Co. E-mail: info@ranchochamber.org
URL: http://www.ranchochamber.org
Contact: Norm MacKenzie, Pres./CEO

**57730 ■ Rancho Mirage Chamber of
Commerce**
42-464 Rancho Mirage Ln.
Rancho Mirage, CA 92270
Ph:(760)568-9351
Fax: (760)779-9684
Co. E-mail: info@ranchomirage.org
URL: http://www.ranchomirage.org
Contact: Stuart W. Ackley, Pres./CEO

**57731 ■ Red Bluff-Tehama County Chamber
of Commerce**
100 Main St.
PO Box 850
Red Bluff, CA 96080
Ph:(530)527-6220
Free: 800-655-6225
Fax: (530)527-2908

Co. E-mail: rbchamber@tco.net
URL: http://www.redbluffchamberofcommerce.com
Contact: Rod Wright, Pres.

57732 ■ Redlands Chamber of Commerce
1 E Redlands Blvd.
Redlands, CA 92373
Ph:(909)793-2546
Fax: (909)335-6388
Co. E-mail: info@redlandschamber.org
URL: http://www.redlandschamber.org
Contact: Kathie Thurston, Exec.Dir.

**57733 ■ Redondo Beach Chamber of
Commerce and Visitors Bureau**
200 N Pacific Coast Hwy.
Redondo Beach, CA 90277
Ph:(310)376-6911
Fax: (310)374-7373
Co. E-mail: marna@redondochamber.org
URL: http://www.redondochamber.org
Contact: Marna Smeltzer, Pres./CEO

57734 ■ Reseda Chamber of Commerce
7033 Reseda St.
Reseda, CA 91335
Ph:(818)345-1920
Fax: (818)345-1925
Contact: Ann Kinzle, Exec.Dir.

57735 ■ Rialto Chamber of Commerce
120 N Riverside Ave.
Rialto, CA 92376
Ph:(909)875-5364
Fax: (909)875-6790
Co. E-mail: roslyn@rialtochamber.com
URL: http://www.rialtochamber.org
Contact: Roslyn Garner, Pres.

57736 ■ Richmond Chamber of Commerce
3925 Macdonald Ave.
Richmond, CA 94805
Ph:(510)234-3512
Fax: (510)234-3540
Co. E-mail: staff@rcoc.com
URL: http://www.rcoc.com
Contact: Ms. Judith Morgan, Pres./CEO

57737 ■ Ridgecrest Chamber of Commerce
128-B E California Ave., Ste. B
Ridgecrest, CA 93555
Ph:(760)375-8331
Fax: (760)375-0365
Co. E-mail: chamber@ridgecrest.ca.us
URL: http://www.ridgecrestchamber.com
Contact: Mary Booster, Pres.

**57738 ■ Rio Linda-Elverta Chamber of
Commerce**
PO Box 75
Rio Linda, CA 95673
Ph:(916)991-9344
Fax: (916)922-9074
Co. E-mail: info@rlechamber.com
URL: http://www.rlechamber.com
Contact: Jeff Culley, Pres.

57739 ■ Rio Vista Chamber of Commerce
50 N 2nd St.
Rio Vista, CA 94571
Ph:(707)374-2700
Fax: (707)374-2424
Co. E-mail: cocinfo@riovista.org
URL: http://www.riovista.org
Contact: Denise Rubiaco, Exec.Dir.

57740 ■ Ripon Chamber of Commerce
929 W Main St.
PO Box 327
Ripon, CA 95366
Ph:(209)599-7519
Fax: (209)599-2286
Co. E-mail: boothd@charterinternet.com
URL: http://www.riponchamber.org
Contact: Dorothy Booth, Exec.Dir.

57741 ■ Riverbank Chamber of Commerce
3300 Santa Fe St.
Riverbank, CA 95367
Ph:(209)869-4541
Fax: (209)869-4639
Co. E-mail: riverbankchamber@charter.net
URL: http://www.riverbankchamber.com
Contact: Kimilyn Velasquez, Mgr.

57742 ■ Rocklin Area Chamber of Commerce
5055 Pacific St.
Rocklin, CA 95677
Ph:(916)624-2548
Fax: (916)624-5743
Co. E-mail: info@rocklinchamber.com
URL: http://www.rocklinchamber.com
Contact: Mary Jo Edmondson, Exec.Dir.

**57743 ■ Rohnert Park Chamber of
Commerce**
6050 Commerce Blvd., Ste. 211
Rohnert Park, CA 94928
Ph:(707)584-1415
Fax: (707)584-2945
Co. E-mail: info@rpchamber.org
URL: http://www.rohnertparkchamber.org
Contact: Carla Howell, Pres./CEO

57744 ■ Rosemead Chamber of Commerce
3953 Muscatel Ave.
PO Box 425
Rosemead, CA 91770
Ph:(626)288-0811
Fax: (626)288-2514
Co. E-mail: maryjo@rosemeadcc.org
URL: http://www.rosemeadcc.org
Contact: Lee Ann Dalessio, Exec.Dir.

57745 ■ Roseville Chamber of Commerce
650 Douglas Blvd.
Roseville, CA 95678
Ph:(916)783-8136
Fax: (916)783-5261
Co. E-mail: admin@rosevillechamber.com
URL: http://www.rosevillechamber.com
Contact: Carol Powell, Admin.Asst.

**57746 ■ Rough and Ready Chamber of
Commerce**
PO Box 801
Rough and Ready, CA 95975
Ph:(530)272-4320
Co. E-mail: evburka@cwnet.com
URL: http://www.roughandreadychamber.com
Contact: Charles Crecilius, Pres.

**57747 ■ Running Springs Area Chamber of
Commerce**
PO Box 96
Running Springs, CA 92382-0096
Ph:(909)867-2411
Fax: (909)867-5571
Co. E-mail: info@runningspringschamber.com
URL: http://www.runningspringschamber.com
Contact: Walt Schaedle, Chm.

**57748 ■ Russian River Chamber of
Commerce and Visitor Center**
16209 1st St.
PO Box 331
Guerneville, CA 95446
Ph:(707)869-9000
Free: 877-644-9001
Fax: (707)869-9009
Co. E-mail: info@russianriver.com
URL: http://www.russianriver.com
Contact: Jim Maresca, Exec.Dir.

**57749 ■ Sacramento Black Chamber of
Commerce**
2655 Del Monte St.
West Sacramento, CA 95691
Ph:(916)374-9355
Fax: (916)374-9366
Co. E-mail: info@sacblackchamber.org
URL: http://www.sacblackchamber.org
Contact: Richard Nelson, Pres./CEO

57750 ■ Sacramento Hispanic Chamber of Commerce
2848 Arden Way, Ste. 230
Sacramento, CA 95825
Ph:(916)486-7700
Fax: (916)486-7728
Co. E-mail: diana@sachcc.org
URL: http://www.sachcc.org
Contact: Ms. Diana M. Borroel, Pres./CEO

57751 ■ Sacramento Metro Chamber of Commerce
917 7th St.
Sacramento, CA 95814
Ph:(916)552-6800
Fax: (916)443-2672
Co. E-mail: chamber@metrochamber.org
URL: http://www.metrochamber.org
Contact: Matthew R. Mahood, CEO/Pres.

57752 ■ St. Helena Chamber of Commerce
1010 Main St., Ste. A
St. Helena, CA 94574
Ph:(707)963-4456
Free: 800-799-6456
Fax: (707)963-5396
Co. E-mail: rex@sthelena.com
URL: http://www.sthelena.com/chamber
Contact: Rex Stults, CEO

57753 ■ Salinas Valley Chamber of Commerce
119 E Alisal St.
PO Box 1170
Salinas, CA 93902-1170
Ph:(831)424-7611
Fax: (831)424-8639
Co. E-mail: info@salinaschamber.com
URL: http://www.salinaschamber.com
Contact: Beverly Meamber, CEO/Pres.

57754 ■ San Anselmo Chamber of Commerce
PO Box 2844
San Anselmo, CA 94979-2844
Ph:(415)454-2510
Fax: (415)258-9458
Co. E-mail: info@sananselmochamber.org
URL: http://www.sananselmochamber.org
Contact: Connie S. Rodgers, Pres./CEO

57755 ■ San Benito County Chamber of Commerce
650 San Benito St., Ste. 130
Hollister, CA 95023-3988
Ph:(831)637-5315
Fax: (831)637-1008
Co. E-mail: info@sanbenitocountychamber.com
URL: http://www.sanbenitocountychamber.com
Contact: Liz Sparling, Exec.Dir.

57756 ■ San Bernardino Area Chamber of Commerce
PO Box 658
San Bernardino, CA 92402
Ph:(909)885-7515
Fax: (909)384-9979
Co. E-mail: sba.chamber@verizon.net
URL: http://www.sbachamber.org
Contact: Judi Penman, Pres./CEO

57757 ■ San Bruno Chamber of Commerce
618 San Mateo Ave.
San Bruno, CA 94066
Ph:(650)588-0180
Fax: (650)588-6473
Co. E-mail: sbchamber@sanbrunocable.com
Contact: Karin Cunningham, Pres.

57758 ■ San Carlos Chamber of Commerce
1500 Laurel St., Ste. B
San Carlos, CA 94070-5103
Ph:(650)593-1068
Fax: (650)593-9108
Co. E-mail: staff@sancarloschamber.org
URL: http://www.sancarloschamber.org
Contact: Sheryl Pomerenk, CEO

57759 ■ San Clemente Chamber of Commerce
1100 N El Camino Real
San Clemente, CA 92672-4653
Ph:(949)492-1131
Fax: (949)492-3764
Co. E-mail: info@scchamber.com
URL: http://www.scchamber.com
Contact: Lynn Wood, Pres./CEO

57760 ■ San Diego County Hispanic Chamber of Commerce
1250 6th Ave., Ste. 550
San Diego, CA 92101
Ph:(619)702-0790
Fax: (619)696-3282
Co. E-mail: lindacm@sdchcc.com
URL: http://www.sdchcc.com
Contact: Linda Caballero-Merritt, Pres./CEO

57761 ■ San Diego East County Chamber of Commerce
201 S Magnolia Ave.
El Cajon, CA 92020-4525
Ph:(619)440-6161
Fax: (619)440-6164
Co. E-mail: terry@eastcountychamber.org
URL: http://www.eastcountychamber.org
Contact: Terry Saverson, CEO/Pres.

57762 ■ San Diego North Chamber of Commerce
11650 Iberia Pl., Ste. 220
San Diego, CA 92128
Ph:(858)487-1767
Fax: (858)487-8051
Co. E-mail: infodesk@sdncc.com
URL: http://www.sdncc.com
Contact: Mr. Gary Powers, Pres./CEO

57763 ■ San Diego Regional African American Chamber of Commerce
1727 Euclid Ave.
San Diego, CA 92105-5414
Ph:(619)262-2121
Co. E-mail: sdcbcc@pacbell.net
URL: http://www.sdraacc.org
Contact: Gerri Warren, Pres.

57764 ■ San Diego Regional Chamber of Commerce
402 W Broadway, Ste. 1000
San Diego, CA 92101-3585
Ph:(619)544-1300
Co. E-mail: webinfo@sdchamber.org
URL: http://www.sdchamber.org
Contact: Richard Vortmann, Pres./CEO

57765 ■ San Dimas Chamber of Commerce
PO Box 175
San Dimas, CA 91773-0175
Ph:(909)592-3818
Fax: (909)592-8178
Co. E-mail: info@sandimaschamber.com
URL: http://www.sandimaschamber.com
Contact: Ted Powl, Pres./CEO

57766 ■ San Francisco Chamber of Commerce
235 Montgomery St., 12th Fl.
San Francisco, CA 94104
Ph:(415)392-4520
Fax: (415)392-0485
Co. E-mail: sfalk@sfchamber.com
URL: http://www.sfchamber.com
Contact: Steve Falk, Pres./CEO

57767 ■ San Gabriel Chamber of Commerce
620 W Santa Anita St.
San Gabriel, CA 91776
Ph:(626)576-2525
Fax: (626)289-2901
Co. E-mail: debsgcofc@yahoo.com
URL: http://www.sangabrielchamber.com
Contact: Molly Jones, Pres.

57768 ■ San Jose - Silicon Valley Chamber of Commerce
310 S 1st St.
San Jose, CA 95113
Ph:(408)291-5250
Fax: (408)286-5019
Co. E-mail: info@sjchamber.com
URL: http://www.sjchamber.com
Contact: Pat Dando, Pres./CEO

57769 ■ San Juan Bautista Chamber of Commerce
PO Box 1037
San Juan Bautista, CA 95045-1037
Ph:(831)623-2454
Fax: (831)623-0674
Co. E-mail: sjbcc@sbcglobal.net
URL: http://www.sjbchamber.com
Contact: Denise Cauthen-Wright, Exec.Dir.

57770 ■ San Juan Capistrano Chamber of Commerce
PO Box 1878
San Juan Capistrano, CA 92675-1878
Ph:(949)493-4700
Fax: (949)489-2695
Co. E-mail: info@sanjuanchamber.com
URL: http://www.sanjuanchamber.com
Contact: Mr. Stan Wylazlowski, Exec.Dir.

57771 ■ San Leandro Chamber of Commerce
262 Davis St.
San Leandro, CA 94577
Ph:(510)351-1481
Fax: (510)351-6740
Co. E-mail: jmaraglia@sanleandrochamber.com
URL: http://www.sanleandrochamber.com
Contact: Debra Vandiver, Interim CEO

57772 ■ San Luis Obispo Chamber of Commerce
1039 Chorro St.
San Luis Obispo, CA 93401
Ph:(805)781-2777
Fax: (805)543-1255
Co. E-mail: slochamber@slochamber.org
URL: http://www.slochamber.org
Contact: Dave Garth, CEO/Pres.

57773 ■ San Marcos Chamber of Commerce
939 Grand Ave.
San Marcos, CA 92078
Ph:(760)744-1270
Fax: (760)744-5230
Co. E-mail: info@sanmarcoschamber.com
URL: http://www.sanmarcoschamber.com
Contact: Patricia Melvin, CEO

57774 ■ San Marino Chamber of Commerce
2304 Huntington Dr., Ste. 202
San Marino, CA 91108
Ph:(626)286-1022
Fax: (626)286-7765
Co. E-mail: snmarinocofc@earthlink.net
Contact: Barbara Veenstra, Pres.

57775 ■ San Mateo Chamber of Commerce
POB 936
San Mateo, CA 94403
Ph:(650)341-5679
Fax: (650)341-0679
Co. E-mail: info@sanmateoca.org
URL: http://www.sanmateoca.org
Contact: Linda Ashbury, Pres./CEO

57776 ■ San Pablo Chamber of Commerce
PO Box 6204
San Pablo, CA 94806
Ph:(510)234-2067
Fax: (510)234-0604
URL: http://www.ci.san-pablo.ca.us/main/
   chamberofcommerce.htm
Contact: William R. Erwin, Pres.

57777 ■ San Pedro Peninsula Chamber of Commerce
390 W 7th St.
San Pedro, CA 90731

Ph:(310)832-7272
Fax: (310)832-0685
Co. E-mail: info@sanpedrochamber.com
URL: http://www.sanpedrochamber.com
Contact: Elizabeth Brazil, Exec.Dir.

57778 ■ San Rafael Chamber of Commerce
817 Mission Ave.
San Rafael, CA 94901
Ph:(415)454-4163
Free: 800-454-4163
Fax: (415)454-7039
Co. E-mail: srcc@sanrafaelchamber.com
URL: http://www.sanrafael.org
Contact: Talia Hart, Pres./CEO

57779 ■ San Ramon Chamber of Commerce
12667 Alcosta Blvd., Ste. 160
Bishop Ranch 15
San Ramon, CA 94583
Ph:(925)242-0600
Fax: (925)242-0603
Co. E-mail: info@sanramon.org
URL: http://www.sanramon.org
Contact: Toby Brinks, Pres./CEO

57780 ■ San Simeon Chamber of Commerce
250 San Simeon, Ste. 3A
San Simeon, CA 93452
Ph:(805)927-3500
Free: 800-342-5613
Fax: (805)927-6453
Co. E-mail: sansimeonchamber@yahoo.com
URL: http://www.sansimeonchamber.org
Contact: Helen Leopold, Coor.

**57781 ■ San Ysidro Chamber of Commerce
and Visitor Information Center**
663 E San Ysidro Blvd.
San Ysidro, CA 92173
Ph:(619)428-1281
Fax: (619)428-1294
Co. E-mail: info@sanysidrochamber.org
URL: http://www.sanysidrochamber.org
Contact: Israel Adato, Pres.

**57782 ■ Sanger District Chamber of
Commerce**
1789 Jensen Ave., Ste. B
Sanger, CA 93657-2860
Ph:(559)875-4575
Fax: (559)875-0745
Co. E-mail: sanger@psnw.com
URL: http://www.sanger.org
Contact: Clarence Harvey, Pres./CEO

57783 ■ Santa Ana Chamber of Commerce
PO Box 205
Santa Ana, CA 92702-0205
Ph:(714)541-5353
Fax: (714)541-2238
Co. E-mail: mmetzler@santaanachamber.com
URL: http://www.santaanachamber.com
Contact: Mr. Michael Metzler, Pres./CEO

**57784 ■ Santa Barbara Region Chamber of
Commerce**
924 Anacapa St., Ste. 1
Santa Barbara, CA 93101
Ph:(805)965-3023
Fax: (805)966-5954
Co. E-mail: info@sbchamber.org
URL: http://www.sbchamber.org
Contact: Steve Cushman, Exec.Dir.

**57785 ■ Santa Clara Chamber of Commerce
and Convention and Visitors Bureau**
1850 Warburton Ave.
Santa Clara, CA 95050
Ph:(408)244-9660
Free: 800-272-6822
Fax: (408)244-7830
Co. E-mail: steve.vandorn@santaclara.org
URL: http://www.santaclara.org
Contact: Steve VanDorn, Pres./Gen.Mgr.

**57786 ■ Santa Clarita Valley Chamber of
Commerce**
28460 Ave. Stanford., Ste. 100
Santa Clarita, CA 91355
Ph:(661)702-6977
Fax: (661)702-6980
Co. E-mail: info@scvchamber.com
URL: http://www.scvchamber.com
Contact: Larry Mankin, Pres./CEO

57787 ■ Santa Cruz Chamber of Commerce
611 Ocean St., Ste. 1
Santa Cruz, CA 95060
Ph:(831)457-3713
Fax: (831)423-1847
Co. E-mail: greg@santacruzchamber.org
URL: http://www.santacruzchamber.org
Contact: Greg Carter, Exec.Dir.

**57788 ■ Santa Fe Springs Chamber of
Commerce and Industrial League**
12016 E Telegraph Rd., Ste. 100
Santa Fe Springs, CA 90670
Ph:(562)944-1616
Fax: (562)946-3976
Co. E-mail: mail@sfschamber.com
URL: http://www.sfschamber.com
Contact: Leslie Hamrick, CEO

**57789 ■ Santa Maria Valley Chamber of
Commerce**
614 S Broadway
Santa Maria, CA 93454-5111
Free: 800-331-3779
Fax: (805)928-7559
Co. E-mail: smvcc@santamaria.com
URL: http://www.santamaria.com
Contact: Robert P. Hatch, CEO/Pres.

**57790 ■ Santa Monica Chamber of
Commerce**
1234 6th St., Ste. 100
Santa Monica, CA 90401
Ph:(310)393-9825
Fax: (310)394-1868
Co. E-mail: info@smchamber.com
URL: http://www.smchamber.com
Contact: Kathryn Dodson, Exec.Dir./CEO

57791 ■ Santa Paula Chamber of Commerce
200 N 10th St.
PO Box 1
Santa Paula, CA 93061
Ph:(805)525-5561
Fax: (805)525-8950
Co. E-mail: info@santapaulachamber.com
URL: http://www.santapaulachamber.com
Contact: Ken Brookes, Mgr.

57792 ■ Santa Rosa Chamber of Commerce
637 1st St.
Santa Rosa, CA 95404
Ph:(707)545-1414
Fax: (707)545-6914
Co. E-mail: chamber@santarosachamber.com
URL: http://www.santarosachamber.com
Contact: Michael Hauser, Pres.

57793 ■ Santee Chamber of Commerce
10315 Mission Gorge Rd.
Santee, CA 92071-3031
Ph:(619)449-6572
Fax: (619)562-7906
Co. E-mail: info@santee-chamber.org
URL: http://www.santee-chamber.org
Contact: Warren H. Savage Jr., Exec.Dir.

57794 ■ Saratoga Chamber of Commerce
14485 Big Basin Way
Saratoga, CA 95070
Ph:(408)867-0753
Fax: (408)867-5213
Co. E-mail: info@saratogachamber.org
URL: http://www.saratogachamber.org
Contact: Kathy Phelan, Exec.Dir.

57795 ■ Sausalito Chamber of Commerce
10 Liberty Ship Way, Bay 2, Ste. 250
Sausalito, CA 94965
Ph:(415)331-7262
Fax: (415)332-0323
Co. E-mail: chamber@sausalito.org
URL: http://www.sausalito.org
Contact: Greg Christie, Pres.

57796 ■ Scotts Valley Chamber of Commerce
4 Camp Evers Ln.
Scotts Valley, CA 95066
Ph:(831)438-1010
Fax: (831)438-6544
Co. E-mail: info@svchamber.org
URL: http://www.scottsvalleychamber.com
Contact: Mr. Clyde Vaughn, Exec.Dir.

**57797 ■ Seal Beach Chamber of Commerce,
California**
201 8th St., Ste. 120
Seal Beach, CA 90740
Ph:(562)799-0179
Fax: (562)795-5637
Co. E-mail: info@sealbeachchamber.org
URL: http://sealbeachchamber.com
Contact: Matt Murphree, Pres.

**57798 ■ Seaside-Sand City Chamber of
Commerce**
505 Broadway Ave.
Seaside, CA 93955-4202
Ph:(831)394-6501
Fax: (831)394-1977
Co. E-mail: contact@seaside-sandcity.com
URL: http://www.seaside-sandcity.com
Contact: Chely Schwartz, Pres.

**57799 ■ Sebastopol Area Chamber of
Commerce and Visitors Center**
PO Box 178
265 S Main St.
Sebastopol, CA 95473-0178
Ph:(707)823-3032
Free: 877-828-4748
Fax: (707)823-8439
Co. E-mail: apples@sebastopol.org
URL: http://www.sebastopol.org
Contact: Teresa Ramondo, Exec.Dir./Sec.

**57800 ■ Selma District Chamber of
Commerce**
1821 Tucker St.
Selma, CA 93662
Ph:(559)891-2235
Fax: (559)896-7075
Co. E-mail: cindyh@cityofselma.com
URL: http://www.cityofselma.com/chamber/index.htm
Contact: Cindy L. Howell, Exec.Dir.

57801 ■ Shafter Chamber of Commerce
336 Pacific Ave.
Shafter, CA 93263
Ph:(661)746-2600
Fax: (661)746-0607
URL: http://www.shafter.com
Contact: Karen Wilkins, Dir.

**57802 ■ Shingle Springs/Cameron Park
Chamber of Commerce**
PO Box 341
Cameron Park, CA 95682
Ph:(530)677-8000
Fax: (530)676-8313
Co. E-mail: info@sscpchamber.org
URL: http://www.sscpchamber.org
Contact: Carolyn Doty, CEO

57803 ■ Sierra Madre Chamber of Commerce
78 W Sierra Madre Blvd.
Sierra Madre, CA 91024
Ph:(626)355-5111
Fax: (626)306-1150
Co. E-mail: info@sierramadrechamber.org
URL: http://www.sierramadrechamber.com
Contact: Kathy Buchan, Office Mgr.

57804 ■ Signal Hill Chamber of Commerce
PO Box 138
2201 E Willow St., Ste. D
Signal Hill, CA 90755
Ph:(562)424-6489
Fax: (562)989-0833
Co. E-mail: shillchamber@aol.com
URL: http://www.signalhillchamber.com
Contact: Jane Fallon, Exec.Dir.

57805 ■ Simi Valley Chamber of Commerce
40 W Cochran St., Ste. 100
Simi Valley, CA 93065
Ph:(805)526-3900
Fax: (805)526-6234
Co. E-mail: info@simichamber.org
URL: http://simivalleychamber.org
Contact: Leigh Nixon, Pres./CEO

57806 ■ Solana Beach Chamber of Commerce
PO Box 623
210 W Plz. St.
Solana Beach, CA 92075-0623
Ph:(858)755-4775
Fax: (858)755-4889
Co. E-mail: info@solanabeachchamber.com
URL: http://www.solanabeachchamber.com
Contact: Bruce Goad, Acting Pres.

57807 ■ Solvang Chamber of Commerce
PO Box 465
Solvang, CA 93464
Ph:(805)688-0701
Co. E-mail: linda@solvangcc.org
URL: http://www.solvangcc.org
Contact: Linda Johansen, VP

57808 ■ Sonoma Valley Chamber of Commerce
651A Broadway
Sonoma, CA 95476
Ph:(707)996-1033
Fax: (707)996-9402
Co. E-mail: info@sonomachamber.com
URL: http://www.sonomachamber.com
Contact: Jennifer Yankovich, Exec.Dir.

57809 ■ South Gate Chamber of Commerce
3350 Tweedy Blvd.
South Gate, CA 90280
Ph:(323)567-1203
Fax: (323)567-1204
URL: http://www.southgatechamber.com
Contact: Ted Chandler, Exec. Dir.

57810 ■ South Lake Tahoe Chamber of Commerce
3066 Lake Tahoe Blvd.
South Lake Tahoe, CA 96150
Ph:(530)541-5255
Fax: (530)541-7121
Co. E-mail: sltcc@sierra.net
URL: http://www.tahoeinfo.com
Contact: Duane Wallace, Exec.Dir.

57811 ■ South Orange County Regional Chambers of Commerce
26111 Antonio Pkwy., Ste. 400
Rancho Santa Margarita, CA 92688
Ph:(949)635-5800
Fax: (949)635-1635
Co. E-mail: info@socchambers.com
URL: http://www.socchambers.com
Contact: Tanya McElhaney, CEO

57812 ■ South San Francisco Chamber of Commerce
213 Linden Ave.
South San Francisco, CA 94080
Ph:(650)588-1911
Fax: (650)588-1529
Co. E-mail: info@ssfchamber.com
URL: http://www.ssfchamber.com
Contact: Greg Cochran, Exec.Dir.

57813 ■ Spring Valley Chamber of Commerce
3322 Sweetwater Springs Blvd., Ste. 202
PO Box 1211
Spring Valley, CA 91979-1211
Ph:(619)670-9902
Fax: (619)670-9924
Co. E-mail: info@springvalleychamber.org
URL: http://www.springvalleychamber.org
Contact: Connie Rodriguez, Pres.

57814 ■ Springville Chamber of Commerce
PO Box 104
Springville, CA 93265-0104
Co. E-mail: chamber@springville.ca.us
URL: http://springville.ca.us
Contact: Mr. Del Pengilly, Pres.

57815 ■ Stanton Chamber of Commerce
PO Box 353
8381 Katella Ave., Ste. H
Stanton, CA 90680
Ph:(714)995-1485
Fax: (714)995-1184
Co. E-mail: stanton1@ix.netcom.com
URL: http://www.stanton-chamber.org
Contact: Billie Jean Turner, Exec.Dir.

57816 ■ State of Jefferson Chamber of Commerce
PO Box 521
Seiad Valley, CA 96086
Ph:(530)496-3325
URL: http://jeffersonstate.com
Contact: Brian Helsaple, Pres.

57817 ■ Studio City Chamber of Commerce
4024 Radford Ave., Ed. 2, Ste. F
Studio City, CA 91604
Ph:(818)655-5916
Fax: (818)655-8392
Co. E-mail: sccc@mptp.com
URL: http://www.studiocitychamber.com
Contact: Sandra Reed-Funnell, Exec.Dir.

57818 ■ Sun Valley Area Chamber of Commerce
8133-A San Fernando Rd.
Sun Valley, CA 91352
Ph:(818)768-2014
Fax: (818)767-1947
Co. E-mail: executivedirector@chambersunvalleyca.org
URL: http://www.chambersunvalleyca.org
Contact: Vinita McClennon, Exec.Dir.

57819 ■ Sunland-Tujunga Chamber of Commerce
7314 Foothill Blvd.
Tujunga, CA 91043
Ph:(818)352-4433
Co. E-mail: stchamberofcomm@aol.com
URL: http://www.verdugo-online.com/clubs/chamber.htm
Contact: Kathy Anthony, Pres.

57820 ■ Sunnyvale Chamber of Commerce
101 W Olive Ave.
Sunnyvale, CA 94086-6193
Ph:(408)736-4971
Fax: (408)736-1919
Co. E-mail: info@svcoc.org
URL: http://www.svcoc.org
Contact: Suzi Blackman, Pres./CEO

57821 ■ Swedish-American Chamber of Commerce, San Diego/Tijuana
1020 Symphony Towers, 750 B St.
San Diego, CA 92101
Ph:(619)338-4020
Fax: (619)233-9890
Co. E-mail: info@sacc-sandiego.org
URL: http://www.sacc-sandiego.org

57822 ■ Taft District Chamber of Commerce
400 Kern St.
Taft, CA 93268

Ph:(661)765-2165
Fax: (661)765-6639
Co. E-mail: taftchamber@bak.rr.com
URL: http://www.taftchamber.com
Contact: Charmayne Brooks, Exec.Dir.

57823 ■ Tarzana Chamber of Commerce
PO Box 570414
Tarzana, CA 91356
Ph:(818)343-3687
Fax: (818)705-0127
Co. E-mail: info.chamber@sbcglobal.net
URL: http://www.tarzanachamber.com
Contact: Steve Hornstein Esq., Pres.

57824 ■ Temecula Valley Chamber of Commerce
26790 Ynez Ct.
Temecula, CA 92591
Free: (866)676-5090
Fax: (951)676-5090
Co. E-mail: info@temecula.org
URL: http://www.temecula.org
Contact: Alice Sullivan, Pres./CEO

57825 ■ Temple City Chamber of Commerce
9050 Las Tunas Dr.
Temple City, CA 91780
Ph:(626)286-3101
Fax: (626)286-2590
Co. E-mail: info@templecitychamber.org
URL: http://www.templecitychamber.org
Contact: Linda Payne, Pres./CEO

57826 ■ Templeton Chamber of Commerce
PO Box 701
Templeton, CA 93465
Ph:(805)434-1789
Co. E-mail: info@templetonchamber.com
URL: http://www.templetonchamber.com
Contact: Fritz Hermann, Pres.

57827 ■ Thousand Oaks - Westlake Village Regional Chamber of Commerce
600 Hampshire Rd., Ste. 200
Westlake Village, CA 91361-2571
Ph:(805)370-0035
Fax: (805)370-1083
Co. E-mail: info@towlvchamber.org
URL: http://www.towlvchamber.org
Contact: Janet Levett, Pres./CEO

57828 ■ Thousand Palms Chamber of Commerce
72-715 La Canada Way
Thousand Palms, CA 92276-0365
Ph:(760)343-1988
Fax: (760)343-1988
Contact: Monett Schwartz, Admin.

57829 ■ Tiburon Peninsula Chamber of Commerce
PO Box 563
96 B Main St.
Tiburon, CA 94920
Ph:(415)435-5633
Fax: (415)435-1132
Co. E-mail: info@tiburonchamber.org
Contact: Georgia Kirchmaier, Exec.Mgr.

57830 ■ Torrance Area Chamber of Commerce Foundation
3400 Torrance Blvd., Ste. 100
Torrance, CA 90503
Ph:(310)540-5858
Fax: (310)540-7662
Co. E-mail: barbara@torrancechamber.com
URL: http://www.torrancechamber.com
Contact: Barbara Glennie, Pres./CEO

57831 ■ Town of Los Gatos Chamber of Commerce
349 N Santa Cruz Ave.
Los Gatos, CA 95030
Ph:(408)354-9300
Fax: (408)399-1594
Co. E-mail: chamber@losgatosweb.com

URL: http://www.losgatosweb.com
Contact: Ronee Nassi, Exec.Dir.

57832 ■ Tracy Chamber of Commerce
223 E 10th St.
Tracy, CA 95376
Ph:(209)835-2131
Fax: (209)833-9526
Co. E-mail: info@tracychamber.org
URL: http://www.tracychamber.org
Contact: Steve Hartje, Exec.Dir.

57833 ■ Trinity County Chamber of Commerce
211 Trinity Lakes Blvd.
PO Box 517
Weaverville, CA 96093-0517
Ph:(530)623-6101
Free: 800-4-TRINITY
Fax: (530)623-3753
Co. E-mail: chamber@trinitycounty.com
URL: http://www.trinitycounty.com
Contact: Carol Eli, Exec.Dir.

57834 ■ Truckee-Donner Chamber of Commerce
10065 Donner Pass Rd.
Truckee, CA 96161
Ph:(530)587-2757
Fax: (530)587-2439
Co. E-mail: info@truckee.com
URL: http://www.truckee.com
Contact: Lynn Saunders, Pres./CEO

57835 ■ Tulare Chamber of Commerce
PO Box 1435
Tulare, CA 93275-1435
Ph:(559)686-1547
Fax: (559)686-4915
Co. E-mail: info@tularechamber.org
URL: http://www.tularechamber.org
Contact: Jennifer McCoun, Pres./CEO

57836 ■ Tuolumne County Chamber of Commerce
222 S Shepherd St.
Sonora, CA 95370
Ph:(209)532-4212
Fax: (209)532-8068
Co. E-mail: info@tcchamber.com
URL: http://www.tcchamber.com
Contact: George Segarini, Pres./CEO

57837 ■ Turlock Chamber of Commerce
115 S Golden State Blvd.
Turlock, CA 95380
Ph:(209)632-2221
Fax: (209)632-5289
Co. E-mail: info@turlockchamber.com
URL: http://www.turlockchamber.com
Contact: Sharon Silva, Pres./CEO

57838 ■ Tustin Chamber of Commerce
399 El Camino Real
Tustin, CA 92780-3605
Ph:(714)544-5341
Fax: (714)544-2083
Co. E-mail: mcharette@tustinchamber.org
URL: http://tustinchamber.org
Contact: Marisa L. Charette, Exec.Dir.

57839 ■ Tustin Women in Chamber of Commerce
PO Box 1524
Tustin, CA 92781-1524
Ph:(714)838-3366
Co. E-mail: bikerider7@aol.com
Contact: Mary Elaine Gustafson, Pres.

57840 ■ Twain Harte Area Chamber of Commerce
PO Box 404
Twain Harte, CA 95383
Ph:(209)586-4482
Fax: (209)586-0360
Co. E-mail: info@twainhartecc.com
URL: http://www.twainhartecc.com

Contact: Shirley Vierth, Pres.

57841 ■ Twentynine Palms Chamber of Commerce
73660 Civic Ctr., Ste. C and D
Twentynine Palms, CA 92277
Ph:(760)367-3445
Fax: (760)367-3366
Co. E-mail: 29coc@29chamber.com
URL: http://www.29chamber.com
Contact: Christina Dooley, Exec.Dir.

57842 ■ Union City Chamber of Commerce
33412 Alvarado Niles Rd.
Union City, CA 94587
Ph:(510)471-3115
Fax: (510)471-6011
Co. E-mail: info@unioncitychamber.com
URL: http://www.unioncitychamber.com
Contact: Donna Mize, Chair

57843 ■ Universal City-North Hollywood Chamber of Commerce
11335 Magnolia Blvd., Ste. 2D
North Hollywood, CA 91601-3706
Ph:(818)508-5155
Fax: (818)508-5156
Co. E-mail: info@noho.org
URL: http://www.noho.org

57844 ■ Upland Chamber of Commerce
433 N 2nd Ave.
Upland, CA 91786
Ph:(909)931-4108
Fax: (909)931-4184
Co. E-mail: realpeople@uplandchamber.org
URL: http://www.uplandchamber.org
Contact: Sonnie S. Faires, Pres./CEO

57845 ■ Vacaville Chamber of Commerce
300 Main St., Ste. A
Vacaville, CA 95688
Ph:(707)448-6424
Fax: (707)448-0424
Co. E-mail: jennifer@vacavillechamber.com
URL: http://www.vacavillechamber.com
Contact: Gary H. Tatum, Pres./CEO

57846 ■ Vallejo Chamber of Commerce
2 Florida St.
Vallejo, CA 94590
Ph:(707)644-5551
Fax: (707)644-5590
Co. E-mail: info@vallejochamber.com
URL: http://www.vallejochamber.com
Contact: Rick Wells, Pres./CEO

57847 ■ Valley Center Chamber of Commerce
27818 Valley Center Rd.
PO Box 793
Valley Center, CA 92082
Ph:(760)749-8472
Co. E-mail: info@vcchamber.com
URL: http://www.vcchamber.com
Contact: Tom Bumgardner, Pres.

57848 ■ Venice Area Chamber of Commerce
PO Box 202
Venice, CA 90294
Ph:(310)822-5425
Fax: (310)314-7641
Co. E-mail: info@venicechamber.net
URL: http://www.venicechamber.org
Contact: Robert Feist, Pres.

57849 ■ Ventura Chamber of Commerce
801 S Victoria Ave., Ste. 200
Ventura, CA 93003
Ph:(805)676-7500
Fax: (805)650-1414
Co. E-mail: info@ventura-chamber.org
URL: http://www.ventura-chamber.org
Contact: Zoe J. Taylor ACE, CEO/Pres.

57850 ■ Vernon Chamber of Commerce
3801 Santa Fe Ave.
Vernon, CA 90058

Ph:(323)583-3313
Fax: (323)583-0704
Co. E-mail: molguin@vernonchamber.org
URL: http://www.vernonchamber.org
Contact: Marisa Olguin, Exec.Dir.

57851 ■ Victorville Chamber of Commerce
14174 Green Tree Blvd.
Victorville, CA 92395
Ph:(760)245-6506
Fax: (760)245-6505
Co. E-mail: vvchamber@vvchamber.com
URL: http://vvchamber.com
Contact: Michele Spears, Pres./CEO

57852 ■ Vietnamese Chamber of Commerce
9121 Bolsa Ave., Ste. 203
Westminster, CA 92683
Ph:(714)892-6928
Fax: (714)892-6938
Co. E-mail: vaccoc@yahoo.com
URL: http://www.businessfinance.com/coc_List.
    asp?low=92138&amp
Contact: Lynn Lien Dangter, Exec.Dir.

57853 ■ Visalia Chamber of Commerce
303 E Acequia
Visalia, CA 93291
Ph:(559)734-5876
Free: 877-VIS-ALIA
Fax: (559)734-7479
Co. E-mail: info@visaliachamber.org
URL: http://www.visaliachamber.org
Contact: Michael Cully, Pres./CEO

57854 ■ Vista Chamber of Commerce
201 Washington St.
Vista, CA 92084
Ph:(760)726-1122
Fax: (760)726-8654
Co. E-mail: info@vistachamber.com
URL: http://www.vistachamber.com
Contact: Jim Baumann, CEO

57855 ■ Walnut Creek Chamber of Commerce
1777 Botelho Dr., Ste. 103
Walnut Creek, CA 94596-4233
Ph:(925)934-2007
Fax: (925)934-2404
Co. E-mail: chamber@walnut-creek.com
URL: http://www.walnut-creek.com
Contact: Jay Hoyer, Pres./CEO

57856 ■ Walnut Valley Chamber of Commerce
18800 Amar Rd., No. C14
Walnut, CA 91789
Ph:(626)965-1707
Fax: (626)965-1709
Co. E-mail: walnutchamber@juno.com
URL: http://www.walnutchamber.com
Contact: Claudette Willhite, Exec.Sec.

57857 ■ Wasco Chamber of Commerce and Agriculture
675 Oak Ave.
PO Box 783
Wasco, CA 93280
Ph:(661)758-2746
Fax: (661)758-4939
Co. E-mail: vhight@ci.wasco.ca.us
URL: http://www.ci.wasco.ca.us
Contact: Vickie Hight, Office Mgr.

57858 ■ Weed Chamber of Commerce
34 Main St.
Weed, CA 96094-2522
Ph:(530)938-4624
Free: 877-938-4624
Fax: (530)938-1658
Co. E-mail: weedchamber@ncen.org
URL: http://www.weedchamber.com
Contact: Karen Heiser, Mgr.

57859 ■ West Covina Chamber of Commerce
811 S Sunset Ave.
West Covina, CA 91790-5512

Ph:(626)338-8496
Free: 888-763-3232
Fax: (626)960-0511
Co. E-mail: sdunn@westcovinachamber.com
URL: http://www.westcovinachamber.com
Contact: Sue Dunn, Exec.Dir.

57860 ■ West Los Angeles Chamber of Commerce
10850 W Pico Blvd., Ste. 405
Los Angeles, CA 90064
Ph:(310)475-8806
Fax: (310)475-8316
Co. E-mail: info@westlachamber.org
URL: http://www.westlachamber.org
Contact: Jay Handal, Pres.

57861 ■ West Marin Chamber of Commerce
PO Box 1045
Point Reyes Station, CA 94956
Ph:(415)663-9232
Co. E-mail: info@pointreyes.org
URL: http://www.pointreyes.org
Contact: Frank Borodic, Pres.

57862 ■ West Sacramento Chamber and Visitors Bureau
PO Box 404
West Sacramento, CA 95691-3209
Ph:(916)371-7042
Fax: (916)371-7007
Co. E-mail: kay@westsacramentochamber.com
URL: http://www.westsacramentochamber.com
Contact: W. Kay Fenrich, Exec.Dir.

57863 ■ West Shores Chamber of Commerce of the Salton Sea
4112 Haven Ave.
PO Box 5185
Salton City, CA 92275-5185
Ph:(760)394-4112
Fax: (760)394-4303
URL: http://www.westshoreschamber.org
Contact: Ron Spears, Pres.

57864 ■ Westchester-LAX/ Marina del Rey Chamber of Commerce
6151 W Century Blvd., No. 514
Westchester, CA 90045
Ph:(310)645-5151
Fax: (310)645-0130
Co. E-mail: christina@wlaxmdrchamber.com
URL: http://www.wlaxmdrchamber.com
Contact: Tony Ciancimino, Exec.Dir.

57865 ■ Western Association of Chamber Executives
PO Box 1736
Sacramento, CA 95812-1736
Ph:(916)442-2223
Fax: (916)444-6685
Co. E-mail: info@waceonline.com
URL: http://www.waceonline.com
Contact: Kate King, Chair

57866 ■ Westminster Chamber of Commerce
14491 Beach Blvd.
Westminster, CA 92683
Ph:(714)898-9648
Fax: (714)373-1499
Co. E-mail: info_westminsterchamber@bizla.rr.com
URL: http://westminsterchamber.org
Contact: Crystal R. Wadsworth, Exec.Dir.

57867 ■ Westwood Area Chamber of Commerce
PO Box 1247
Westwood, CA 96137
Ph:(530)256-2456
Fax: (530)256-2456
Co. E-mail: wacc1@citilink.net
Contact: Dianna Desfosses, Sec.

57868 ■ Whittier Area Chamber of Commerce
8158 Painter Ave.
Whittier, CA 90602
Ph:(562)698-9554

Fax: (562)693-2700
Co. E-mail: info@whittierchamber.com
URL: http://www.whittierchamber.com
Contact: Carol Crosby, Exec.Dir.

57869 ■ Wildomar Chamber of Commerce
PO Box 885
Wildomar, CA 92595
Ph:(909)245-0437
URL: http://www.wildomarcity.com/wchamber.html

57870 ■ Willits Chamber of Commerce
239 S Main St.
Willits, CA 95490
Ph:(707)459-7910
Fax: (707)459-7914
Co. E-mail: info@willits.org
URL: http://www.willits.org
Contact: Lynn R. Kennelly, Exec.Dir.

57871 ■ Willow Creek Chamber of Commerce
PO Box 704
Willow Creek, CA 95573
Ph:(530)629-2693
Free: 800-628-5156
Fax: (530)629-4051
Co. E-mail: info@willowcreekchamber.com
URL: http://www.willowcreekchamber.com
Contact: Tom O'Gorman, Pres.

57872 ■ Willows Area Chamber of Commerce
118 W Sycamore
Willows, CA 95988
Ph:(530)934-8150
Free: 888-799-4254
Fax: (530)934-8710
Co. E-mail: willowschamber@dcsi.net
URL: http://www.willowschamber.org

57873 ■ Wilmington Chamber of Commerce
PO Box 90
544 N Avalon Blvd., No. 104
Wilmington, CA 90744
Ph:(310)834-8586
Fax: (310)834-8887
Co. E-mail: info@wilmington-chamber.com
URL: http://www.wilmington-chamber.com
Contact: Dan Hoffman, Exec.Dir.

57874 ■ Wilshire Center Chamber of Commerce
3600 Wilshire Blvd., Ste. 1032
Los Angeles, CA 90010
Ph:(213)386-8224
Fax: (213)386-1655
Co. E-mail: chamber@wilshirecenter.com
URL: http://www.wilshirecenter.com
Contact: Gary Russell, Pres.

57875 ■ Windsor Chamber of Commerce and Visitors Center
PO Box 367
Windsor, CA 95492
Ph:(707)838-7285
Fax: (707)838-2778
Co. E-mail: info@windsorchamber.com
URL: http://www.windsorchamber.com
Contact: Gary Howell, Exec.Dir.

57876 ■ Winters District Chamber of Commerce
PO Box 423
201 Railroad Ave.
Winters, CA 95694
Ph:(530)795-2329
Fax: (530)795-3202
Co. E-mail: winterschamber@yahoo.com
URL: http://www.winterschamber.com
Contact: Dan Maguire, Exec.Dir.

57877 ■ Women in Business Roundtable
235 Montgomery St., 12th Fl.
San Francisco, CA 94104
Ph:(415)392-4520
Fax: (415)392-0485
Co. E-mail: nchan@sfchamber.com
URL: http://www.sfchamber.com

Contact: Karen Dana

57878 ■ Woodland Area Chamber of Commerce
307 1st St.
Woodland, CA 95695-3412
Ph:(530)662-7327
Free: 888-843-2636
Fax: (530)662-4086
Co. E-mail: wchamber@woodlandchamber.org
URL: http://www.woodlandchamber.com
Contact: Kristy Wright, CEO

57879 ■ Woodland Hills Chamber of Commerce
PO Box 1
Woodland Hills, CA 91364
Ph:(818)347-4737
Fax: (818)347-3321
Co. E-mail: info@woodlandhillscc.net
URL: http://www.woodlandhillscc.net
Contact: Ms. Rhonda Weinstein, Exec.Admin.Asst.

57880 ■ Wrightwood Chamber of Commerce
PO Box 416
Wrightwood, CA 92397
Ph:(760)249-4320
Fax: (760)249-6822
Co. E-mail: info@wrightwoodchamber.org
URL: http://www.wrightwoodchamber.org
Contact: Mr. Leo Van Kampen, Pres.

57881 ■ Yorba Linda Chamber of Commerce
17670 Yorba Linda Blvd.
Yorba Linda, CA 92886
Ph:(714)993-9537
Fax: (714)993-7764
Co. E-mail: phyllisylcc@sbcglobal.net
URL: http://www.yorbalindachamber.com
Contact: Phyllis A. Coleman, Exec.Dir.

57882 ■ Yountville Chamber of Commerce
6484 Washington St., Ste. F
Yountville, CA 94599
Ph:(707)944-0904
Fax: (707)944-4465
Co. E-mail: info@yountville.com
URL: http://www.yountville.com
Contact: Vicky Baxter, Pres.

57883 ■ Yreka Chamber of Commerce
117 W Miner St.
Yreka, CA 96097
Ph:(530)842-1649
Fax: (530)842-7086
Co. E-mail: yrekachamber@nctv.com
URL: http://www.yrekachamber.com
Contact: Mark Dean, Exec.Dir.

57884 ■ Yuba-Sutter Chamber of Commerce
PO Box 1429
Marysville, CA 95901
Ph:(530)743-6501
Fax: (530)741-8645
Co. E-mail: chamber@yubasutterchamber.com
URL: http://www.yubasutterchamber.com
Contact: Evelyn Cosner, Admin.Asst.

57885 ■ Yucaipa Valley Chamber of Commerce
PO Box 45
Yucaipa, CA 92399-0045
Ph:(909)790-1841
Fax: (909)790-3484
Co. E-mail: info@yucaipachamber.org
URL: http://www.yucaipachamber.org
Contact: Ms. Pamela Grigg, Exec.Dir.

57886 ■ Yucca Valley Chamber of Commerce
56711 29 Palms Hwy.
Yucca Valley, CA 92284-2942
Ph:(760)365-6323
Fax: (760)365-0763
Co. E-mail: chamber@yuccavalley.org
URL: http://www.yuccavalley.org
Contact: Cheryl Nankervis, Exec.Dir.

MINORITY BUSINESS ASSISTANCE PROGRAMS

57887 ■ Asian, Inc.
1670 Pine St.
San Francisco, CA 94109
Ph:(415)928-5910
Fax: (415)921-0182
Co. E-mail: info@asianinc.org
URL: http://www.asianinc.org

57888 ■ California Indian Business Development Center–National Center for American Indian Enterprise
11138 Valley Mall, Ste. 200
11138 Valley Mall Ste. 200
El Monte, CA 91731
Ph:(626)442-3701
Fax: (626)442-7115
Co. E-mail: schambers@ncaied.org
URL: http://www.ncaied.org
Contact: Sharon Chambers, Dir

57889 ■ Central Valley Minority Business Development Center
5528 N Palm Ave., Ste. 114
Fresno, CA 93702
Ph:(559)449-0875
Fax: (559)447-1374
Co. E-mail: mbdc@lightspeed.net
URL: http://www.cvmbdc.com

57890 ■ East Los Angeles Minority Business Development Center
5271 E Beverly Blvd.
Los Angeles, CA 90022
Ph:(323)726-7734
Fax: (323)721-9794
Co. E-mail: eastlambdc@ibm.net

57891 ■ Los Angeles Metro Minority Business Development Center
3550 Wilshire Blvd., Ste. 905
Los Angeles, CA 90010
Ph:(213)368-1450
Fax: (213)368-1454
Co. E-mail: info@lambdc.org
URL: http://www.lambdc.org
Contact: Ramesh Swamy

57892 ■ Los Angeles Minority Business Opportunity Committee–Mayor's Office of Economic Development
Mayor's Office of Economic Development
200 N Spring St., 14th Fl.
Los Angeles, CA 90012
Ph:(213)978-0671
Fax: (213)978-0690
URL: http://www.lamboc.org

57893 ■ Small & Minority Business - OSMB–Department of General Services–Small and Minority Business Office (707 3)
707 3rd St.
West Sacramento, CA 95605
Ph:(916)322-5060
Fax: (916)442-7855
URL: http://www.dgs.ca.gov/osbcr
Description: Offers technical assistance to small and minority business and promotes their procurement of government contracts for purchases, construction, and services.

57894 ■ South Los Angeles Minority Business Development Center
Los Angeles Urban League
110 S Labea Ave.
Inglewood, CA 90301
Ph:(310)419-8755
Fax: (310)419-8755
Co. E-mail: laulrbbc@pacbell.net
URL: http://www.laul.org

FINANCING AND LOAN PROGRAMS

57895 ■ 2 M Invest Inc.
1875 S. Grant St., Ste. 750
San Mateo, CA 94402-2667
Ph:(650)231-1210
Fax: (650)372-9107
Co. E-mail: 2minfo@2minvest.com
URL: http://www.2minvest.com
Contact: Ari Kaaro, Managing Director
Investment Types: Start-up, early stage and expansion. **Industry Preferences:** Internet specific, computer software, hardware and services, semiconductors and other electronics, communications and media, medical and health, and consumer related. **Geographic Preferences:** U.S. and West Coast.

57896 ■ 5AM Ventures / 5AM Partners
3000 Sand Hill Rd.
Bldg. 4, Ste. 230
Menlo Park, CA 94025
Ph:(650)233-8600
Fax: (650)233-8923
URL: http://www.5amventures.com
Contact: Carin Mueller, Principal
Investment Policies: Seed and early stage. **Industry Preferences:** Biotechnology. **Geographic Preferences:** East and West Coast.

57897 ■ 21st Century Internet Venture Partners
2 South Park, 2nd Fl.
San Francisco, CA 94107
Ph:(415)512-1221
Fax: (415)512-2650
URL: http://www.21vc.com
Contact: J. Neil Weintraut, General Partner
Preferred Investment Size: $3,000,000 minimum. **Investment Types:** Start-up and early stage. **Industry Preferences:** Internet specific, Computer software and services, communications and media, and consumer related. **Geographic Preferences:** U.S. and Canada.

57898 ■ Aberdare Ventures
1 Embarcadero Ctr., Ste. 4000
San Francisco, CA 94111
Ph:(415)392-7442
Fax: (415)392-4264
URL: http://www.aberdare.com
Contact: Paul Klingenstein, General Partner
Preferred Investment Size: $500,000 to $7,000,000. **Investment Types:** Start-up, first and second stage, and expansion. **Industry Preferences:** Internet specific, biotechnology, medical and health. **Geographic Preferences:** U.S.

57899 ■ ACACIA Venture Partners
101 California St., Ste. 3160
San Francisco, CA 94111
Ph:(415)433-4200
Fax: (415)433-4250
URL: http://www.acaciavp.com
Contact: David Heer, Managing Director
Preferred Investment Size: $5,000,000 minimum. **Investment Policies:** Seed, start-up, first and second stage, leveraged buyout, and mezzanine. **Industry Preferences:** Internet specific, medical and health, computer software and services, industrial and energy, and communications and media. **Geographic Preferences:** U.S.

57900 ■ Accel-kkr, LLC
2500 Sand Hill Rd., Ste. 100
Menlo Park, CA 94025
Ph:(650)289-2460
Fax: (650)289-2461
URL: http://www.accel-kkr.com
Contact: Andy Hammann, Principal
Preferred Investment Size: $10,000,000 to $75,000,000. **Investment Types:** Later stage, leveraged buyout, generalist PE, and management buyouts. **Industry Preferences:** Communications and media, Internet specific, computer related, and semiconductors and other electronics. **Geographic Preferences:** Canada.

57901 ■ Accel Partners
428 University Ave.
Palo Alto, CA 94301
Ph:(650)614-4800
Fax: (650)614-4880
URL: http://www.accel.com
Contact: Fearghal O. Riordain, Principal
Preferred Investment Size: $1,000,000 minimum. **Investment Policies:** Seed, start-up, and early stage. **Industry Preferences:** Internet specific, computer software and services, communications and media, semiconductors and other electronics, other products, medical and health, computer hardware, biotechnology, industrial and energy, and consumer related. **Geographic Preferences:** U.S.

57902 ■ Accenture Technology Ventures
1661 Page Mill Rd.
Palo Alto, CA 94304
Ph:(650)213-2500
Fax: (650)213-2222
URL: http://www.accenturetechventures.com
Preferred Investment Size: $2,000,000 to $10,000,000. **Investment Types:** Start-up, early and later stage, balanced, expansion, and mezzanine. **Industry Preferences:** Internet specific, computer software, hardware and services, communications and media. **Geographic Preferences:** U.S.

57903 ■ Access Venture Partners
8787 Turnpike Dr., Ste. 2260
Westminster, CO 80030
Ph:(303)426-8899
Fax: (303)426-8828
URL: http://www.accessventurepartners.com
Contact: Jay Campion, Managing Director
Preferred Investment Size: $250,000 to $2,000,000. **Investment Types:** Seed and early stage. **Industry Preferences:** Internet specific, communications and media, biotechnology, computer software and services, semiconductors and other electronics, industrial and energy. **Geographic Preferences:** Northern California, Rocky Mountains, and Southwest.

57904 ■ Acer Technology Ventures
5201 Great America Pky., Ste. 270
Santa Clara, CA 95054
Ph:(408)894-7900
Fax: (408)894-7939
URL: http://www.acervc.com
Contact: James Lu, Managing Director
Preferred Investment Size: $1,000,000 to $7,000,000. **Investment Types:** Seed, start-up, first and second stage, early and later stage, mezzanine, and balanced. **Industry Preferences:** Communications and media, computer software and hardware, Internet specific, semiconductors and other electronics, consumer related, and financial services. **Geographic Preferences:** U.S. and Canada.

57905 ■ Acorn Campus
6 Results Way
Cupertino, CA 95014-5924
Ph:(408)777-8090
Fax: (408)777-8091
URL: http://www.acorncampus.com
Contact: Wu-fu Chen, Chairman and Managing Director
Preferred Investment Size: $250,000 to $5,000,000. **Investment Policies:** Seed, start-up, and early stage. **Industry Preferences:** Communications, computer software, semiconductors and other electronics. **Geographic Preferences:** Northern California.

57906 ■ Acorn Ventures, Inc.
268 Bush St., Ste. 2829
San Francisco, CA 94014
Ph:(650)994-7801
Fax: (925)249-1748
URL: http://www.acornventures.com
Contact: Cliff Girard, Chief Executive Officer
Preferred Investment Size: $3,000 to $10,000,000. **Investment Types:** Seed, first and second stage, early and later stage, fund of funds, acquisition, turnaround, and leveraged buyout. **Industry Preferences:** Communications and media, Internet specific,

computer software and services, semiconductors and other electronics, other products, computer hardware, biotechnology, industrial and energy, medical and health. **Geographic Preferences:** West Coast.

57907 ■ Acuity Ventures
1960 The Alameda, Ste. 200
San Jose, CA 95126-1493
Ph:(408)261-4286
Fax: (408)557-6555
URL: http://www.acuityventures.com
Investment Policies: Early stage.

57908 ■ Advanced Technology Ventures (Palo Alto)
485 Ramona St.
Palo Alto, CA 94301
Ph:(650)321-8601
Fax: (650)321-0934
URL: http://www.atvcapital.com
Contact: Steven Baloff, General Partner
Preferred Investment Size: $15,000,000 to $35,000,000. **Investment Types:** Seed, first, and second stage, early and later stage, and balanced. **Industry Preferences:** Internet specific, computer software and services, computer hardware, semiconductors and other electronics, communications and media, medical and health, biotechnology, industrial and energy, consumer related, and other products. **Geographic Preferences:** U.S. and Canada.

57909 ■ Advent International (Palo Alto)
525 University Ave., Ste. 700
Palo Alto, CA 94301
Ph:(650)233-7500
Fax: (650)233-7515
URL: http://www.adventinternational.com
Contact: Andrew Fillat, Managing Director
Preferred Investment Size: $1,000,000 minimum. **Investment Types:** Seed, start-up, early, first, second, and later stage, control-block purchases, balanced, mezzanine, leveraged buyout, special situation, recapitalizations, research and development, public companies, industry rollups, generalist PE, and acquisitions. **Industry Preferences:** Communications and media, consumer related, Internet specific, industrial and energy, medical and health, computer software and services, computer hardware, semiconductors and other electronics, and biotechnology, and other products. **Geographic Preferences:** U.S and Canada.

57910 ■ Agilent Ventures
395 Page Mill Rd.
MS A3-08
Palo Alto, CA 94303-0870
Ph:(650)752-5000
Fax: (650)752-5772
URL: http://www.agilentventures.com
Contact: Maximilian Schroeck, Managing Director
Preferred Investment Size: $500,000 to $10,000,000. **Investment Types:** Start-up, early, first, and second stage. **Industry Preferences:** Communications and media, semiconductors and other electronics, biotechnology, medical and health, and industrial and energy. **Geographic Preferences:** U.S and Canada.

57911 ■ Al Shugart International (ASI)
920 41st Ave.
Santa Cruz, CA 95062
Ph:(831)464-4740
Fax: (831)464-4778
URL: http://www.alshugart.com
Contact: Al Shugart, General Partner
Investment Types: Seed, start-up, and early stage.

57912 ■ Alcatel Ventures
3530 Wilshire Blvd. Ste. 360
Los Angeles, CA 90010
Ph:(213)351-6880
Fax: (213)739-7882
URL: http://www.alcatelventures.com
Contact: Steven Kim, Managing Partner
Preferred Investment Size: $500 to $6,000,000. **Investment Types:** Early stage and seed. **Industry**

Preferences: Computer software and services, Internet specific, communications and media, computer hardware, semiconductors and other electronics. **Geographic Preferences:** U.S.

57913 ■ Allegis Capital / Media Technology Ventures
100 Hamilton Ave., Ste. 250
Palo Alto, CA 94301
Ph:(650)687-0500
Fax: (650)687-0234
URL: http://www.allegiscapital.com
Contact: Barry Weinman, Managing Partner
Preferred Investment Size: $3,000,000 to $7,000,000. **Investment Policies:** Seed, start-up, early stage, and research and development. **Industry Preferences:** Internet specific, computer software and services, communications and media, semiconductors and other electronics, computer hardware, and other products. **Geographic Preferences:** West Coast.

57914 ■ Alliance Venture Management, LLC
2575 Augustine Dr.
Santa Clara, CA 95054
Ph:(408)855-4900
Fax: (408)855-4999
URL: http://www.alliancevm.com
Preferred Investment Size: Investment Policies: Seed and start-up. **Industry Preferences:** Communications and media, Internet specific, and semiconductors and other electronics.

57915 ■ Alloy Ventures
480 Cowper St., 2nd Fl.
Palo Alto, CA 94301
Ph:(650)687-5000
Fax: (650)687-5010
URL: http://www.alloyventures.com
Contact: Peter Loukianoff, Partner
Investment Types: Start-up, seed, and early stage. **Industry Preferences:** Internet specific, computer software and services, medical and health, biotechnology, communications and media, semiconductors and other electronics, computer hardware, and industrial and energy. **Geographic Preferences:** U.S.

57916 ■ Alpine Technology Ventures
20300 Stevens Creek Blvd., Ste. 495
Cupertino, CA 95014
Ph:(408)725-1810
Fax: (408)725-1207
URL: http://www.alpineventures.com
Contact: Chuck Chan, General Partner
Preferred Investment Size: $2,000,000 to $4,000,000. **Investment Types:** Seed, start-up, research and development, first and second stage. **Industry Preferences:** Internet specific, computer software and services, computer hardware, communications and media, semiconductors and other electronics, other products, industrial and energy. **Geographic Preferences:** California.

57917 ■ Alta Partners
1 Embarcadero Ctr., Ste. 4050
San Francisco, CA 94111
Ph:(415)362-4022
Fax: (415)362-6178
URL: http://www.altapartners.com
Contact: Allison De Bord, Principal
Preferred Investment Size: $2,000,000 to $15,000,000. **Investment Types:** Seed, start-up, first and second stage, early and later stage, mezzanine, and expansion. **Industry Preferences:** Internet specific, computer software and services, industrial and energy, consumer related, communications and media, medical and health, computer hardware, biotechnology, semiconductors and other electronics, and other products. **Geographic Preferences:** West Coast.

57918 ■ Alterlayer Venture Services
510 3rd St., Ste. 515
San Francisco, CA 94107
Ph:(415)358-4074
Fax: (415)358-4074
URL: http://www.alterlayer.com

Contact: Kris Jacob, Chief Executive Officer and Managing Dir
Investment Policies: Early stage.

57919 ■ Altos Ventures
2882 Sand Hill Rd., Ste. 100
Menlo Park, CA 94025
Ph:(650)234-9771
Fax: (650)233-9821
URL: http://www.altosvc.com
Contact: Anthony Lee, Principal
Preferred Investment Size: $1,000,000 to $5,000,000. **Investment Types:** Start-up, seed, first, second, and later stage. **Industry Preferences:** Internet specific, computer software and services, other products, consumer related, communications and media, and medical and health. **Geographic Preferences:** Northern California and West Coast.

57920 ■ Altotech Ventures
1 Lagoon Dr., Ste. 100
Redwood City, CA 94065
Ph:(650)631-8080
Fax: (650)631-8081
URL: http://www.altotechventures.com
Contact: Gloria Wahl, General Partner
Investment Policies: Early stage. **Industry Preferences:** Communications, computer software, Internet specific, semiconductors and other electronics, and biotechnology. **Geographic Preferences:** U.S.

57921 ■ American River Ventures
2270 Douglas Blvd., Ste. 212
Roseville, CA 95661
Ph:(916)780-2828
Fax: (916)780-5443
URL: http://www.arventures.com
Contact: Barbara Grant, Partner
Preferred Investment Size: $500,000 to $2,000,000. **Investment Policies:** Start-up, seed, early, first and second stage. **Industry Preferences:** Communications, computer software and hardware, Internet specific, semiconductors and other electronics, and business service. **Geographic Preferences:** Arizona, California, Colorado, Idaho, Nevada, New Mexico, Oregon, Utah, Washington, and West Coast.

57922 ■ Amgen, Inc.
1 Amgen Ctr. Dr.
Thousand Oaks, CA 91320
Ph:(805)447-1000
Fax: (805)447-1010
URL: http://www.amgen.com
Contact: Kevin Sharer, Chief Executive Officer
Investment Policies: Early stage. **Industry Preferences:** Biotechnology. **Geographic Preferences:** U.S.

57923 ■ Amidzad, LLC
353 University Ave.
Palo Alto, CA 94301
Ph:(650)323-4777
Fax: (650)323-4044
URL: http://www.amidzad.com
Contact: Pejman Nozad, General Partner
Investment Policies: Start-up and balanced.

57924 ■ Angel Investors, LP
817 Orange Blossom Way
Danville, CA 94526
URL: http://www.svangel.com
Contact: Bob Bozeman, General Partner
Investment Types: Early stage. **Industry Preferences:** Internet specific, computer hardware, computer software and services, communications and media, consumer related, and other products. **Geographic Preferences:** California and Northern California.

57925 ■ Angels Forum & the Halo Fund
PO Box 1605
Los Altos, CA 94023
Ph:(650)857-0700
Fax: (650)857-0773
URL: http://www.angelsforum.com
Contact: Mei Xu, Chief Financial Officer
Preferred Investment Size: $100,000 to $750,000. **Investment Policies:** Start-up, seed, early, first and

second stage, and balanced. **Industry Preferences:** Communications, Internet specific, computer related, semiconductors and other electronics, biotechnology, medical and health, consumer related, industrial and energy, transportation, financial services, business service, manufacturing, and environment. **Geographic Preferences:** California and Northern California.

57926 ■ Anila.org, LLC

400 Channing Ave.
Palo Alto, CA 94301
Ph:(650)833-5790
Fax: (650)833-0590
URL: http://www.anila.com
Contact: Moses Joseph, Managing Partner
Investment Types: Early stage, and expansion. **Industry Preferences:** Communications and media, and Internet specific, and computer software. **Geographic Preferences:** California and U.S.

57927 ■ Anthem Venture Partners

225 Arizona Ave., Ste. 200
Santa Monica, CA 90401
Ph:(310)899-6225
Fax: (310)899-6234
URL: http://www.anthemvp.com
Contact: William Woodward, Managing Director
Preferred Investment Size: $1,000,000 to $500,000,000. **Investment Policies:** Early and later stage.

57928 ■ Applied Materials Ventures

1142 Crane St.
Menlo Park, CA 94025
Ph:(650)833-0400
URL: http://www.appliedvc.com
Contact: Joshua Segal, Principal
Investment Policies: Seed and early stage. **Industry Preferences:** Communications.

57929 ■ Applied Technology

1010 El Camino Real, Ste. 300
Menlo Park, CA 94025
Ph:(415)326-8622
Fax: (415)326-8163
Contact: David Boucher, General Partner
Investment Types: Seed, start-up, first and second stage, research and development, and leveraged buyout. **Industry Preferences:** Computer software, hardware, and services, Internet specific, semiconductors and other electronics, communications and media, industrial and energy, and consumer related. **Geographic Preferences:** U.S.

57930 ■ APV Technology Partners

2370 Watson Ct., Ste. 200
Menlo Park, CA 94025
Ph:(650)354-3200
Fax: (650)813-1244
URL: http://www.apvtp.com
Contact: Paul Sestili, Principal
Preferred Investment Size: $5,000,000 to $15,000,000. **Investment Types:** Early stage and expansion. **Industry Preferences:** Internet specific, computer software, hardware, and services, semiconductors and other electronics, communications and media. **Geographic Preferences:** Northeast, Northern California, Northwest, Rocky Mountains, Southwest, and West Coast.

57931 ■ Artemis Ventures

207 2nd St.
Ste. E, 3rd Fl.
Sausalito, CA 94965
Ph:(415)289-2500
Fax: (415)289-1789
URL: http://www.artemisventures.com
Investment Types: Seed, first and second stage. **Industry Preferences:** Internet specific, computer software and services, semiconductors and other electronics. **Geographic Preferences:** California, Northeast, Northern California, Northwest, and West Coast.

57932 ■ Aspen Ventures

1000 Fremont Ave., Ste. 200
Los Altos, CA 94024

Ph:(650)917-5670
Fax: (650)917-5677
URL: http://www.aspenventures.com
Contact: Alexander Cilento, General Partner
E-mail: alex@aspenventures.com
Preferred Investment Size: $300,000 to $500,000. **Investment Types:** Seed, early, first, and second stage. **Industry Preferences:** Communications and media, computer software and services, Internet specific, computer hardware, biotechnology, medical and health, semiconductors and other electronics, industrial and energy, and consumer related. **Geographic Preferences:** West Coast.

57933 ■ Asset Management Company Venture Capital

2100 Geng Rd., Ste. 200
Palo Alto, CA 94303
Ph:(650)494-7400
Fax: (650)856-1826
URL: http://www.assetman.com
Contact: Evgeny Zaytsev, Principal
Preferred Investment Size: $100,000 to $2,000,000. **Investment Types:** Seed, start-up, early and first stage. **Industry Preferences:** Computer software and services, medical and health, biotechnology, computer hardware, semiconductors and other electronics, Internet specific, communications and media, consumer related, industrial and energy, and other products. **Geographic Preferences:** West Coast.

57934 ■ Athena Technology Ventures

310 University Ave., Ste. 202
Palo Alto, CA
Ph:(650)470-0370
Fax: (650)470-0378
URL: http://www.athenatv.com
Contact: Perry Ha, Partner
Investment Types: Seed, start-up, early, and first stage. **Industry Preferences:** Internet specific, communications and media, computer software and services, computer hardware, semiconductors and other electronics, and consumer related. **Geographic Preferences:** West Coast.

57935 ■ August Capital Management

2480 Sand Hill Rd., Ste. 101
Menlo Park, CA 94025
Ph:(650)234-9900
Fax: (650)234-9910
URL: http://www.augustcap.com
Contact: Andrew Rappaport, General Partner
Investment Types: Start-up, seed, first stage, early stage, and special situation. **Industry Preferences:** Internet specific, computer software, and services, communications and media, computer hardware, semiconductors and other electronics. **Geographic Preferences:** Northwest, Southwest, Rocky Mountains and West Coast.

57936 ■ Authosis

226 Airport Pky., Ste. 405
San Jose, CA 95110
Ph:(650)814-3603
URL: http://www.authosis.com
Contact: Danny Lui, Co-Founder
Investment Types: Seed, first and second stage. **Industry Preferences:** Computer software. **Geographic Preferences:** U.S.

57937 ■ AVI Capital L.P.

One First St., Ste. 2
Los Altos, CA 94022
Ph:(650)949-9862
Fax: (650)949-8510
URL: http://www.avicapital.com
Contact: Brian J. Grossi, General Partner
E-mail: grossi@avicapital.com
Preferred Investment Size: $1,000,000 to $2,000,000. **Investment Types:** Seed, start-up, first and second stage, and special situation. **Industry Preferences:** Computer software, hardware, and services Internet specific, communications and media, semiconductors and other electronics, industrial and energy, and medical and health. **Geographic Preferences:** West Coast.

57938 ■ Baccharis Capital, Inc.

2420 Sand Hill Rd., Ste. 100
Menlo Park, CA 94025
Ph:(650)324-6844
Fax: (650)854-3025
Preferred Investment Size: $1,000,000 minimum. **Investment Types:** Start-up, first and second stage, mezzanine, special situation, leveraged buyout, and control-block purchases. **Industry Preferences:** Computer software, biotechnology, consumer related, industrial and energy, manufacturing, agriculture, forestry and fishing. **Geographic Preferences:** West Coast.

57939 ■ BancBoston Capital / BancBoston Ventures (Palo Alto)

435 Tasso St., Ste. 250
Palo Alto, CA 94305
Ph:(650)470-4184
Fax: (650)853-1425
URL: http://www.bancbostoncapital.com
Preferred Investment Size: $1,000,000 to $15,000,000. **Investment Types:** Seed, early stage, acquisition, expansion, later stage, management buyouts, fund of funds, generalist PE, mezzanine, and recapitalizations. **Industry Preferences:** Communications and media, Internet specific, computer hardware, other products, consumer related, industrial and energy, computer software and services, semiconductors and other electronics, biotechnology, medical and health. **Geographic Preferences:** U.S. and Eastern Canada.

57940 ■ Band of Angels

275 Middlefield Rd.
Menlo Park, CA 94025
Ph:(650)321-0854
Fax: (650)321-1968
URL: http://www.bandangels.com
Contact: Tim Massey, Principal
Preferred Investment Size: $300,000 to $2,000,000. **Investment Policies:** Seed, early stage, and balanced. **Industry Preferences:** Communications, computer software, semiconductors and other electronics, biotechnology, industrial and energy. **Geographic Preferences:** California.

57941 ■ BankAmerica Ventures / BA Venture Partners

950 Tower Ln., Ste. 700
Foster City, CA 94404
Ph:(650)378-6000
Fax: (650)378-6040
URL: http://www.baventurepartners.com
Contact: Eric Sigler, Principal
Preferred Investment Size: $5,000,000 to $15,000,000. **Investment Types:** Start-up, first and second stage, early and later stage, balanced, and expansion. **Industry Preferences:** Computer software and services, Internet specific, medical and health, communications and media, biotechnology, other products, consumer related, industrial and energy, semiconductors and other electronics. **Geographic Preferences:** U.S.

57942 ■ The Barksdale Group

2730 Sand Hill Rd., Ste. 100
Menlo Park, CA 94025
Ph:(650)234-5200
Fax: (650)234-5201
URL: http://www.barksdalegroup.com
Investment Types: Early stage and balanced. **Industry Preferences:** Internet specific, computer software and services, communications and media, other products, industrial and energy. **Geographic Preferences:** U.S.

57943 ■ Barrington Partners

1001-1/2 Alameda de las Pulgas
Belmont, CA 94002
Ph:(650)802-0500
Fax: (650)637-1917
URL: http://www.barvc.com
Contact: James Baker, General Partner
Investment Policies: Seed. **Industry Preferences:** Internet specific, other products, communications and media.

57944 ■ Bastion Capital Corp.
1901 Avenue of the Stars, Ste. 400
Los Angeles, CA 90067
Ph:(310)788-5700
Fax: (310)277-7582
URL: http://www.bastioncapital.com
Contact: James Villanueva
Preferred Investment Size: $10,000,000 minimum.
Investment Types: Leveraged buyout, special situation and control-block purchases. **Industry Preferences:** Communications and media, semiconductors and other electronics, medical and health, consumer related, industrial and energy, transportation, financial services, and manufacturing. **Geographic Preferences:** U.S. and Canada.

57945 ■ Bay Partners
10600 North De Anza Blvd., Ste. 100
Cupertino, CA 95014-2031
Ph:(408)725-2444
Fax: (408)446-4502
URL: http://www.baypartners.com
Contact: Robert Williams, General Partner
Preferred Investment Size: $1,000,000 to $10,000,000. **Investment Types:** Early stage. **Industry Preferences:** Communications and media, Internet specific, computer software and services, computer hardware, semiconductors and other electronics, industrial and energy, consumer related, medical and health, and biotechnology. **Geographic Preferences:** West Coast and Canada.

57946 ■ Benchmark Capital
2480 Sand Hill Rd., Ste. 200
Menlo Park, CA 94025
Ph:(650)854-8180
Fax: (650)854-8183
URL: http://www.benchmark.com
Contact: Alexandre Balkanski, General Partner
Investment Types: Seed, early stage, research and development, start-up, first and second stage, expansion, leveraged buyout, research and development, and special situation. **Industry Preferences:** Internet specific, communications and media, computer software and services, computer hardware, industrial and energy, semiconductors and other electronics, and consumer related. **Geographic Preferences:** Southwest and West Coast.

57947 ■ Berkeley International Capital Corp.
650 California St., Ste. 2800
San Francisco, CA 94108-2609
Ph:(415)249-0450
Fax: (415)392-3929
URL: http://www.berkeleyvc.com
Preferred Investment Size: $20,000,000 minimum.
Investment Types: Second stage, mezzanine, leveraged buyout, and special situation. **Industry Preferences:** Semiconductors and other electronics, communications and media, computer software and services, computer hardware, biotechnology, medical and health, other products, Internet specific, industrial and energy. **Geographic Preferences:** U.S.

57948 ■ Bessemer Venture Partners (Menlo Park)
535 Middlefield Rd., Ste. 245
Menlo Park, CA 94025
Ph:(650)853-7000
Fax: (650)853-7001
URL: http://www.bessemervp.com
Contact: Jeremy Levine, Principal
Preferred Investment Size: $1,000,000 to $10,000,000. **Investment Types:** Seed, research and development, startup, first, early and second stage, leveraged buyout, special situation, control-block purchases, and expansion. **Industry Preferences:** Communications and media, Internet specific, computer software and services, semiconductors and other electronics, consumer related, medical and health, industrial and energy, and biotechnology, computer hardware, and other products. **Geographic Preferences:** U.S.

57949 ■ Blueprint Ventures LLC
601 Gateway Blvd., Ste. 1140
South San Francisco, CA 94080
Ph:(415)901-4000
Fax: (415)901-4035
URL: http://www.blueprintventures.com
Contact: Bart Schachter, Managing Partner
Preferred Investment Size: $500,000 to $3,000,000.
Investment Types: Seed, Early, first and second stage. **Industry Preferences:** Communications and media, computer related, and semiconductors and other electronics. **Geographic Preferences:** West Coast.

57950 ■ Blumberg Capital Ventures
580 Howard St., Ste. 401
San Francisco, CA 94105
Ph:(415)905-5007
Fax: (415)357-5027
URL: http://www.blumberg-capital.com
Contact: David Blumberg, Managing Partner
Preferred Investment Size: $500,000 to $3,000,000.
Investment Types: Seed, early and first stage. **Industry Preferences:** communications and media, computer software, Internet specific. **Geographic Preferences:** U.S.

57951 ■ Bowman Capital
1875 S. Grant St., Ste. 600
San Mateo, CA 94402
Ph:(650)287-2200
Fax: (650)572-1844
URL: http://www.bowmancapital.com
Contact: Richard Chang, Principal
Investment Types: Early and later stage, and expansion. **Industry Preferences:** Communications and media, Internet specific, computer software and services, semiconductors and other electronics, computer hardware, biotechnology, and other products. **Geographic Preferences:** U.S.

57952 ■ Brad Peery Capital, Inc.
145 Chapel Pky.
Mill Valley, CA 94941
Ph:(415)389-0625
Fax: (415)389-1336
URL: http://www.peery-inc.com
Contact: Brad Peery, Chairman
Preferred Investment Size: $100,000 to $300,000.
Investment Types: Second stage. **Industry Preferences:** Communications and media, and Internet specific. **Geographic Preferences:** U.S. and Canada.

57953 ■ Brentwood Venture Capital
11150 Santa Monica Blvd., Ste. 1200
Los Angeles, CA 90025
Ph:(310)477-7678
Fax: (310)312-1868
URL: http://www.brentwoodvc.com
Contact: Brian Atwood, General Partner
Investment Policies: Seed, start-up, and second stage. **Industry Preferences:** Communications and media, computer software, Internet specific, biotechnology, and medical and health. **Geographic Preferences:** West Coast.

57954 ■ Burr, Egan, Deleage, and Co. (San Francisco)
1 Embarcadero Center, Ste. 4050
San Francisco, CA 94111
Ph:(415)362-4022
Fax: (415)362-6178
Description: Private venture capital supplier. Invests start-up, expansion, and acquisitions capital nationwide. Principal concerns are strength of the management team; large, rapidly expanding markets; and unique products for services. Past investments have been made in the fields of biotechnology and pharmaceuticals, cable TV, chemicals/plastics, communications, software, computer systems and peripherals, distributorships, radio common carriers, electronics and electrical components, environmental control, health services, medical devices and instrumentation, and radio and cellular telecommunications. Primarily interested in medical, electronics, and media industries.

57955 ■ Burrill & Company
1 Embarcadero Ctr., Ste. 2700
San Francisco, CA 94111-3776
Ph:(415)591-5400
Fax: (415)591-5401
URL: http://www.burrillandco.com
Contact: Ann Hanham, Managing Director
Preferred Investment Size: $1,000,000 to $11,000,000. **Investment Types:** Seed, early, first and second stage, and mezzanine. **Industry Preferences:** Biotechnology, medical and health, Internet specific, computer software and services, and consumer related. **Geographic Preferences:** U.S. and Canada.

57956 ■ BV Capital / Bertelsmann Ventures, LP (Santa Barbara)
111 El Paseo
Santa Barbara, CA 93101
Ph:(805)568-1514
Fax: (805)568-1534
URL: http://www.bvfund.com
Contact: Jan Buettner, Managing General Partner
Preferred Investment Size: $1,000,000 to $5,000,000. **Investment Types:** Early, first and second stage, and expansion. **Industry Preferences:** Communications and media, computer software and services, and Internet specific. **Geographic Preferences:** West Coast.

57957 ■ California Technology Ventures LLC
1111 S. Arroyo Pky., Ste. 220
Pasadena, CA 91105
Ph:(626)403-6632
Fax: (626)403-6634
URL: http://www.ctventures.com
Contact: Alexander Suh, Managing Director
Preferred Investment Size: $100,000 to $5,000,000.
Investment Policies: Early, first and second stage.
Industry Preferences: Communications, computer software and hardware, Internet specific, semiconductors and other electronics, biotechnology, medical and health, and industrial and energy. **Geographic Preferences:** California, Northern California, and Southern California.

57958 ■ The Cambria Group
1600 El Camino Real, Ste. 155
Menlo Park, CA 94025
Ph:(650)329-8600
Fax: (650)329-8601
URL: http://www.cambriagroup.com
Contact: Christopher Sekula, Principal
Investment Types: Second stage, mezzanine, leveraged buyout, special situation, and control-block purchases. **Industry Preferences:** Communications and media, semiconductors and other electronics, medical and health, consumer related, industrial and energy, transportation, business service, manufacturing, agriculture, forestry and fishing. **Geographic Preferences:** U.S.

57959 ■ Cambrian Ventures
201 San Antonio Cir., Ste. 235
Mountain View, CA 94040
Ph:(650)917-6630
Fax: (650)917-6636
URL: http://www.cambrianventures.com
Contact: Anand Rajaraman, Founding Partner
Investment Types: Seed and early stage. **Industry Preferences:** Internet specific. **Geographic Preferences:** U.S.

57960 ■ Campsix
600 Townsend St., Ste. 170e
San Francisco, CA
Free: 800-226-7749
Contact: David Wamsley, Chief Executive Director
Investment Policies: Early stage. **Industry Preferences:** Internet specific.

57961 ■ Campventures
280 2nd St., Ste. 280
Los Altos, CA 94022
Ph:(650)949-0843
Fax: (650)618-1719
URL: http://www.campventures.com
Contact: Jerome Camp, Managing General Partner
Preferred Investment Size: $300,000 to $500,000.
Investment Policies: Seed and early stage. **Industry**

Preferences: Communications and media, computer software, and semiconductors and other electronics. **Geographic Preferences:** California.

57962 ■ Canaan Partners (Menlo Park)
2884 Sand Hill Rd., Ste. 115
Menlo Park, CA 94025
Ph:(650)854-8092
Fax: (650)854-8127
URL: http://www.canaan.com
Contact: Andrew Firlik, Principal
Preferred Investment Size: $3,00,000 to $25,000,000. **Investment Types:** Early stage, first stage, and expansion. **Industry Preferences:** Internet specific, computer software and services, computer hardware, medical and health, communications and media, biotechnology, semiconductors and other electronics, consumer related, and industrial and energy. **Geographic Preferences:** Northeast, West Coast, and U.S.

57963 ■ Capstone Ventures
3000 Sand Hill Rd., Bldg. 1, Ste. 290
Menlo Park, CA 94025
Ph:(650)854-2523
Fax: (650)854-9010
URL: http://www.capstonevc.com
Contact: Brian Santry, General Partner
Preferred Investment Size: $1,000,000 to $2,000,000. **Investment Types:** Start-up, first and second stage, early stage, and expansion. **Industry Preferences:** Communications and media, computer software and services, computer hardware, semiconductors and other electronics, biotechnology, medical and health, and other products. **Geographic Preferences:** Midwest and West Coast.

57964 ■ Cascade Communications Ventures, LLC
60 East Sir Francis Drake Blvd., Ste. 300
Larkspur, CA 94939
Ph:(415)925-6500
Fax: (415)925-6501
Contact: Dennis Brush, Managing Partner
Investment Types: Leveraged buyout, acquisition, mezzanine, recapitalizations, and turnaround. **Industry Preferences:** Communications and media, consumer related, and business service. **Geographic Preferences:** U.S and Canada.

57965 ■ Charter Life Sciences
525 University Ave., Ste. 1400
Palo Alto, CA 94301
Ph:(650)325-6953
Fax: (650)325-4762
URL: http://www.charterls.com
Contact: Andrew Klatt, Chief Financial Officer
Preferred Investment Size: $500,000 to $8,000,000. **Investment Policies:** Early stage. **Industry Preferences:** Biotechnology, and medical and health. **Geographic Preferences:** Midwest and West Coast.

57966 ■ Charter Venture Capital / Charter Ventures
525 University Ave., Ste. 1400
Palo Alto, CA 94301
Ph:(650)325-6953
Fax: (650)325-4762
URL: http://www.charterventures.com
Contact: A. Barr Dolan, General Partner
Preferred Investment Size: $500,000 to $10,000,000. **Investment Policies:** Early stage. **Industry Preferences:** Internet specific, biotechnology, medical and health, computer software and services, communications and media, computer hardware, semiconductors and other electronics, other products, and other products. **Geographic Preferences:** U.S.

57967 ■ Charter Ventures /Charter Venture Capital
525 University Ave., Ste. 1400
Palo Alto, CA 94301
Ph:(650)325-6953
Fax: (650)325-4762
URL: http://www.charterventures.com
Contact: A. Barr Dolan, General Partner
Preferred Investment Size: $500,000 to $10,000,000. **Investment Types:** Early stage. **Indus-**

try Preferences: Biotechnology, Internet specific, medical and health, communications and media, computer software and services, computer hardware, other products, semiconductors and other electronics, industrial and energy. **Geographic Preferences:** U.S.

57968 ■ Clearstone Venture Partners / Idealab! Capital Partners
1351 4th St., 4th Fl.
Santa Monica, CA 90401
Ph:(310)460-7900
Fax: (310)460-7901
URL: http://www.clearstone.com
Contact: Erik Lassila, Managing Director
Preferred Investment Size: $2,000,000 to $10,000,000. **Investment Types:** Early Stage. **Industry Preferences:** Internet specific, computer software and services, computer hardware, communications and media, industrial and energy, semiconductors and other electronics, and other products. **Geographic Preferences:** Northern and Southern California, California, and West Coast.

57969 ■ CMEA Ventures / Chemicals & Materials Enterprise Association
1 Embarcadero Ctr., Ste. 3250
San Francisco, CA 94111
Ph:(415)352-1520
Fax: (415)352-1524
URL: http://www.cmeaventures.com
Contact: Thomas Baruch, General Partner
E-mail: tom@cmeaventures.com
Preferred Investment Size: $250,000 to $10,000,000. **Investment Types:** Early, start-up, first, second, and later stage, balanced, and mezzanine. **Industry Preferences:** Medical and health, biotechnology, communications and media, computer software and services, semiconductors and other electronics, Internet specific, industrial and energy, computer hardware, other products. **Geographic Preferences:** Northwest and West Coast.

57970 ■ Comdisco Venture Group (Silicon Valley)
3000 Sand Hill Rd., Bldg. 1, Ste. 155
Menlo Park, CA 94025
Ph:(650)854-9484
Fax: (650)854-4026
Preferred Investment Size: $300,000 to $20,000,000. **Investment Types:** Seed, start-up, first and second stage. **Geographic Preferences:** No preference.

57971 ■ Commerce One Ventures
4440 Rosewood Dr.
Plesanton, CA 94588
Ph:(925)520-6000
Fax: (925)520-6060
URL: http://www.commerceone.com
Contact: Katie Nittler, Partner
Preferred Investment Size: $3,000,000 to $15,000,000. **Investment Types:** Early and later stage. **Industry Preferences:** Internet specific. **Geographic Preferences:** U.S.

57972 ■ Commtech International
535 Middlefield Rd., Ste. 200
Menlo Park, CA 94025
Ph:(650)328-0190
Fax: (650)328-6442
Preferred Investment Size: $300,000 to $500,000. **Investment Types:** Seed, start-up, early stage, and research and development. **Industry Preferences:** Communications and media, computer software, Internet specific, semiconductors and other electronics, biotechnology, medical and health. **Geographic Preferences:** West Coast.

57973 ■ Communications Ventures
305 Lytton Ave., Ste. 305
Palo Alto, CA 94301
Ph:(650)325-9600
Fax: (650)325-9608
URL: http://www.comven.com
Contact: Clifford Higgerson, General Partner
Preferred Investment Size: $500,000 to $25,000,000. **Investment Types:** Seed, start-up,

early, first, and second stage. **Industry Preferences:** Communications and media, Internet specific, semiconductors and other electronics, computer software, hardware and services. **Geographic Preferences:** U.S.

57974 ■ Compass Technology Partners
1550 El Camino Real, Ste. 275
Menlo Park, CA 94025-4111
Ph:(650)322-7595
Fax: (650)322-0588
URL: http://www.compasstechpartners.com
Contact: Alain Harrus, Partner
Preferred Investment Size: $250,000 to $1,250,000. **Investment Types:** Early stage, seed, start-up, first stage, private placement, public companies, and expansion. **Industry Preferences:** Internet specific, medical and health, communications and media, semiconductors and other electronics, computer software and services. **Geographic Preferences:** California and U.S.

57975 ■ Convergence Partners
3000 Sand Hill Rd., Bldg. 2, Ste. 235
Menlo Park, CA 94025
Ph:(650)854-3010
Fax: (650)854-3015
URL: http://www.convergencepartners.com
Contact: Eric DiBenedetto, General Partner
Preferred Investment Size: $2,000,000 to $10,000,000. **Investment Types:** Seed, early and first stage. **Industry Preferences:** Internet specific, computer software and services, semiconductors and other electronics, computer hardware, other products, industrial and energy, communications and media. **Geographic Preferences:** U.S.

57976 ■ Crocker Capital
1 Post St., Ste. 2500
San Francisco, CA 94101
Ph:(415)956-5250
Fax: (415)959-5710
Investment Types: Start-up, second stage, and leveraged buyout. **Industry Preferences:** Communications and media, semiconductors and other electronics, medical and health, consumer related, industrial and energy, manufacturing, and environment. **Geographic Preferences:** West Coast.

57977 ■ Crosslink Capital / Omega Venture Partners
2 Embarcadero Ctr., Ste. 2200
San Francisco, CA 94111
Ph:(415)617-1800
Fax: (415)617-1801
URL: http://www.crosslinkcapital.com
Contact: Bill Nolan, General Partner
Preferred Investment Size: $3,000,000 to $10,000,000. **Investment Types:** Early, first, second, and later stage, seed, mezzanine, leveraged buyout, private placement, balanced, and expansion. **Industry Preferences:** Internet specific, computer software and services, semiconductors and other electronics, communications and media, biotechnology, computer hardware, other products, consumer related, medical and health, industrial and energy. **Geographic Preferences:** California and U.S.

57978 ■ The Dakota Group
PO Box 1025
Menlo Park, CA 94025
Ph:(650)853-0600
Fax: (650)851-4899
Co. E-mail: info@dakota.com
Preferred Investment Size: $300,000 to $500,000. **Investment Types:** First and second stage, start-up, seed, recapitalizations, and special situation. **Industry Preferences:** Communications and media, computer software, consumer related, and manufacturing. **Geographic Preferences:** U.S.

57979 ■ Davis Group
PO Box 69953
Los Angeles, CA 90069-0953
Ph:(323)654-2510
Contact: Roger W. Davis, Chief Executive Officer
Preferred Investment Size: $100,000 minimum. **Investment Types:** Seed, start-up, first and early stage,

leveraged buyout, joint ventures, management buyouts, expansion, distressed debt, acquisition, and turnaround. **Geographic Preferences:** U.S. and Canada.

57980 ■ De Novo Ventures
1550 El Camino Real, Ste. 150
Menlo Park, CA 94025
Ph:(650)329-1999
Fax: (650)329-1315
URL: http://www.denovovc.com
Contact: Ken Pereira, Chief Financial Officer
Preferred Investment Size: $1,000,000 to $3,000,000. **Investment Policies:** Start-up, seed, first and early stage, and expansion. **Industry Preferences:** Internet specific, biotechnology, and medical and health. **Geographic Preferences:** Northwest, Rocky Mountains, Southwest, and West Coast.

57981 ■ Defta Partners
111 Pine St., Ste. 1410
San Francisco, CA 94111
Ph:(415)433-2262
Fax: (415)433-2264
URL: http://www.defta-partners.com
Contact: Masa Isono, Principal
Preferred Investment Size: $500,000 to $3,000,000. **Investment Policies:** Start-up, seed, and early stage. **Industry Preferences:** computer software and services, semiconductors and other electronics, Internet specific, communications and media, medical and health, and computer hardware. **Geographic Preferences:** National.

57982 ■ Delphi Ventures
3000 Sand Hill Rd.
Bldg. 1, Ste. 135
Menlo Park, CA 94025
Ph:(650)854-9650
Fax: (650)854-2961
URL: http://www.delphiventures.com
Contact: David Douglass, General Partner
Preferred Investment Size: $1,000,000 to $7,000,000. **Investment Types:** Seed, start-up, first and second stage, early stage, expansion, and balanced. **Industry Preferences:** medical and health, Internet specific, biotechnology, computer software and services, computer hardware, industrial and energy, communications and media. **Geographic Preferences:** U.S.

57983 ■ Denali Venture Capital
1925 Woodland Ave.
Santa Clara, CA 95050
Ph:(408)690-4838
Fax: (408)247-6979
URL: http://www.denaliventurecapital.com
Preferred Investment Size: $100,000 to $5,000,000. **Investment Types:** Early stage. **Industry Preferences:** Medical and health. **Geographic Preferences:** West Coast.

57984 ■ Deucalion Venture Partners
19501 Brookline
Sonoma, CA 95476
Ph:(707)938-4974
Fax: (707)938-8921
Preferred Investment Size: $500,000 minimum. **Investment Types:** Seed, start-up, first and second stage. **Industry Preferences:** Computer software, biotechnology, medical and health, consumer related, industrial and energy, transportation, financial services, and manufacturing. **Geographic Preferences:** West Coast.

57985 ■ Developers Equity Corp.
1880 Century Park E., Ste. 211
Los Angeles, CA 90067
Ph:(213)277-0300
Investment Types: Seed, start-up, and leverage buyout. **Industry Preferences:** Industrial and energy, transportation, and financial services.

57986 ■ DFJ Frontier
302 Olive St.
Santa Barbara, CA 93101
Ph:(805)560-6796

Fax: (805)564-1381
URL: http://www.dfjfrontier.com
Contact: David Cremin, Managing Director
Preferred Investment Size: $100,000 to $500,000. **Investment Policies:** Seed and early stage. **Industry Preferences:** Communications and media, computer software, Internet specific, semiconductors and other electronics, biotechnology, consumer related, industrial and energy, financial services, agriculture, forestry and fishing. **Geographic Preferences:** California.

57987 ■ Diamondhead Ventures, L.P.
2200 Sand Hill Rd., Ste. 110
Menlo Park, CA 94025
Ph:(650)233-7526
Fax: (650)233-7527
URL: http://www.dhven.com
Contact: Pete Hartigan, Principal
Investment Types: Seed, start-up, early, first and second stage. **Industry Preferences:** Communications and media, computer software, Internet specific, semiconductors and other electronics. **Geographic Preferences:** Northern California and West Coast.

57988 ■ Digital Media Campus
2221 Park Pl.
El Segundo, CA 90245
Ph:(310)426-8000
Fax: (310)426-8010
URL: http://www.digitalmediacampus.com
Contact: Leonard Amato, Chairman and Chief Executive Officer
Investment Types: Seed and early stage. **Industry Preferences:** Consumer related and business service.

57989 ■ Doll Capital Management
3000 Sand Hill Rd., Bldg. 3, Ste. 225
Menlo Park, CA 94025
Ph:(650)233-1400
Fax: (650)854-9159
URL: http://www.dcmvc.com
Contact: Ruby Lu, Principal
Preferred Investment Size: $3,000,000 to $15,000,000. **Investment Types:** Seed, early, first, second and later stage, and mezzanine. **Industry Preferences:** Internet specific, computer software and services, communications and media, semiconductors and other electronics, computer hardware, other products, and consumer related. **Geographic Preferences:** Northern California, Northwest, and West Coast.

57990 ■ Domain Associates, L.L.C.
28202 Cabot Rd., Ste. 200
Laguna Niguel, CA 92677
Ph:(949)347-2446
Fax: (949)347-9720
URL: http://www.domainvc.com
Contact: Akiko Shibata, Principal
Preferred Investment Size: $1,000,000 to $20,000,000. **Investment Types:** Start-up, seed, first and second stage, early and later stage, expansion, private placement, research and development, public companies, mezzanine, and balanced. **Industry Preferences:** Consumer related, computer software and services, biotechnology, Internet specific, medical and health, industrial and energy, semiconductors and other electronics. **Geographic Preferences:** U.S.

57991 ■ Dominion Ventures, Inc.
1656 N. California Blvd., Ste. 300
Walnut Creek, CA 94596
Ph:(925)280-6300
Fax: (925)280-6338
URL: http://www.dominion.com
Contact: Brian Smith, General Partner
Preferred Investment Size: $2,000,000 to $4,000,000. **Investment Types:** Start-up, first, and second stage. **Industry Preferences:** Internet specific, computer software and services, computer hardware, other products, medical and health, semiconductors and other electronics, communications and media, consumer related, biotechnology, industrial and energy. **Geographic Preferences:** U.S.

57992 ■ Dorset Capital
Pier 1
Bay 2
San Francisco, CA 94111
Ph:(415)398-7101
Fax: (415)398-7141
URL: http://www.dorsetcapital.com
Contact: John Berg, Managing Partner
Preferred Investment Size: $5,000,000 to $30,000,000. **Investment Types:** First, second and later stage, expansion, generalist PE, leveraged buyout, management buyouts, and recapitalizations. **Industry Preferences:** Consumer related, financial services, business service, and manufacturing. **Geographic Preferences:** U.S.

57993 ■ Dot Edu Ventures
514 Bryant St., Ste. 108
Palo Alto, CA 94301
Ph:(650)321-3804
Fax: (650)321-3808
URL: http://www.doteduventures.com
Contact: Asha Jadeja, Managing Partner
Investment Types: Early stage and seed. **Industry Preferences:** Internet specific. **Geographic Preferences:** U.S.

57994 ■ Dotcom Ventures LP
3945 Freedom Cir., Ste. 740
Santa Clara, CA 95045
Ph:(408)919-9855
Fax: (408)919-9857
URL: http://www.dotcomventuresatl.com
Investment Types: Early, first stage, and seed. **Industry Preferences:** Telecommunications and Internet related. **Geographic Preferences:** U.S.

57995 ■ Dougery Ventures
165 Santa Ana Ave.
San Francisco, CA 94127
Ph:(415)566-5226
Fax: (415)566-5757
Preferred Investment Size: $1,000,000 minimum. **Investment Types:** Seed, start-up, first and second stage, and leveraged buyout. **Industry Preferences:** Communications and media, industrial and energy, computer hardware, software and services, semiconductors and other electronics, medical and health, biotechnology, consumer related, computer software and services, and other products. **Geographic Preferences:** West Coast.

57996 ■ Draper, Fisher, Jurvetson / Draper Associates
2882 Sand Hill Rd., Ste. 150
Menlo Park, CA 94025
Ph:(650)233-9000
Fax: (650)233-9233
URL: http://www.dfj.com
Contact: Jennifer Fonstad, Managing Director
Preferred Investment Size: $500,000 to $20,000,000. **Investment Types:** Seed, early, start-up, first and second stage, balanced, and expansion. **Industry Preferences:** Computer software and services, communications and media, semiconductors and other electronics, industrial and energy, consumer related, medical and health, Internet specific, computer hardware, other products, and biotechnology. **Geographic Preferences:** Northeast U.S. and Canada.

57997 ■ Draper International
50 California St., Ste. 2925
San Francisco, CA 94111
Ph:(415)616-4050
Fax: (415)616-4060
URL: http://www.draperintl.com
Contact: William Draper, Managing Director
Preferred Investment Size: $250,000 to $1,000,000. **Investment Types:** Early and first stage. **Industry Preferences:** Internet specific, computer hardware, computer software and services, consumer related, communications and media. **Geographic Preferences:** Mid Atlantic, Northeast, Northwest, Southeast, and West Coast.

57998 ■ Draper Richards L.P.
50 California St., Ste. 2925
San Francisco, CA 94111
Ph:(415)616-4050
Fax: (415)616-4060
URL: http://www.draperrichards.com
Contact: William Draper, General Partner
Investment Types: Early, first and second stage. **Industry Preferences:** Internet specific, computer software and services, communications and media, consumer related, semiconductors and other electronics, biotechnology, and other products. **Geographic Preferences:** Mid Atlantic, Northeast, Northern California, and West Coast.

57999 ■ Drysdale Enterprises
177 Bovet Rd., Ste. 600
San Mateo, CA 94402
Ph:(650)341-6336
Fax: (650)341-1329
Preferred Investment Size: $3,000,000 minimum. **Investment Types:** First and second stage, mezzanine, leveraged buyout, and special situation. **Industry Preferences:** Communications and media, computer software and hardware, semiconductors and other electronics, biotechnology, medical and health, industrial and energy, consumer related, financial services, transportation, business service, manufacturing, agriculture, forestry and fishing. **Geographic Preferences:** West Coast.

58000 ■ Dynafund Ventures LLC
21515 Hawthorne Blvd., Ste. 1200
Torrance, CA 90503
Ph:(310)543-5477
Fax: (310)543-8733
URL: http://www.dynafundventures.com
Contact: James Ko, Principal
Preferred Investment Size: $1,000,000 to $4,000,000. **Investment Types:** Early, first and second stage. **Industry Preferences:** Semiconductors and other electronics, communications and media, Internet specific, computer software and services, computer hardware, and biotechnology. **Geographic Preferences:** U.S.

58001 ■ E4E, Inc.
4699 Old Ironside Dr., Ste. 350
Santa Clara, CA 95054
Ph:(408)764-5100
Fax: (408)982-5401
URL: http://www.e4einc.com
Contact: Sridhar Mitta, President
Preferred Investment Size: $1,000,000 to $20,000,000. **Investment Types:** Seed, start-up, and early stage. **Industry Preferences:** Internet specific. **Geographic Preferences:** U.S.

58002 ■ Eaglestone Investment Partners
400 Oceangate, Ste. 1125
Long Beach, CA 90802
Ph:(562)590-6377
Fax: (562)590-6382
Contact: Joseph Schuchert, President
Preferred Investment Size: $1,000,000 to $5,000,000. **Investment Policies:** Early stage and balanced. **Industry Preferences:** Medical and health, consumer related, and manufacturing.

58003 ■ Eastwest Venture Group / Eastwest Capital Associates
10900 Wilshire Blvd., Ste. 950
Los Angeles, CA 90024
Fax: (310)209-6160
URL: http://www.eastwestvg.com
Contact: Merv Adelson, Chairman and Chief Executive Officer
Investment Types: Early stage. **Industry Preferences:** Internet specific, computer software and services, communications and media, computer hardware, semiconductors and other electronics.

58004 ■ E*Capital Corporation
1000 Wilshire Blvd., 9th Fl.
Los Angeles, CA 90017
Ph:(213)688-8080
Fax:(213)688-8095

URL: http://www.e-cap.com
Contact: Eric Wedbush, Managing Director
Preferred Investment Size: $500,000 to $3,000,000. **Investment Types:** Early and later stage, leveraged buyout, and public companies. **Geographic Preferences:** Southern California.

58005 ■ Ecompanies
2120 Colorado Ave.
Santa Monica, CA 90404
Ph:(310)586-4000
Fax: (310)586-4425
URL: http://www.ecompanies.com
Contact: Steve Ledger, Managing General Partner
Investment Types: Early stage. **Industry Preferences:** Internet specific, computer software and services, industrial and energy, and other products.

58006 ■ El Dorado Ventures
2884 Sand Hill Rd., Ste. 121
Menlo Park, CA 94025
Ph:(650)854-1200
Fax: (650)854-1202
URL: http://www.eldoradoventures.com
Contact: Scott Irwin, Principal
Preferred Investment Size: $500,000 to $4,000,000. **Investment Types:** Seed, start-up, first and early stage. **Industry Preferences:** Internet specific, computer software and services, computer hardware, communications and media, semiconductors and other electronics, medical and health, other products, consumer related, and biotechnology. **Geographic Preferences:** West Coast.

58007 ■ Electronics for Imaging / EFI
303 Velocity Way
Foster City, CA 94404
Ph:(650)357-3500
Fax: (650)357-3907
URL: http://www.efi.com
Contact: Guy Gecht, Chief Executive Officer
Investment Types: Early stage.

58008 ■ Emerald Venture Group
12396 World Trade Dr., Ste. 116
San Diego, CA 92128
Ph:(858)451-1001
Fax: (858)451-1003
URL: http://www.emeraldventure.com
Contact: Cherie Simoni
Preferred Investment Size: $100,000 to $50,000,000. **Investment Types:** Start-up, seed, first and second stage, leveraged buyout, mezzanine, and research and development. **Industry Preferences:** Diversified. **Geographic Preferences:** No preference.

58009 ■ Emergence Capital Partners, L.L.C.
1 Bay Plz., Ste. 700
1350 Old Bayshore Hwy.
Burlingame, CA 94010
Ph:(650)347-9500
Fax: (650)347-9525
URL: http://www.emergencecap.com
Contact: Brian Jacobs, General Partner
Preferred Investment Size: $1,000,000 to $8,000,000. **Investment Policies:** Start-up, seed, early stage, and expansion. **Industry Preferences:** Computer software, Internet specific, consumer related, financial services, and business service. **Geographic Preferences:** U.S.

58010 ■ Encore Venture Partners, LP
c/o Dr. Horton
1901 Ascension, Ste. 350
Arlington, TX 76006
Ph:(817)436-6052
Fax: (817)436-6053
URL: http://www.encorevp.com
Contact: Stephen Perison, Principal
Preferred Investment Size: $1,000,000 to $5,000,000. **Investment Types:** Early stage. **Industry Preferences:** Internet specific, computer hardware, and other products. **Geographic Preferences:** California.

58011 ■ Enterprise Partners Venture Capital / EPVC
2223 Avenida de la Playa, Ste. 300
La Jolla, CA 92037
Ph:(858)731-0300
Fax: (858)731-0235
URL: http://www.epvc.com
Contact: Naser Partovi, Managing Director
Preferred Investment Size: $2,000,000 to $20,000,000. **Investment Types:** Seed and early stage. **Industry Preferences:** Communications and media, computer software and services, Internet specific, computer hardware, other products, medical and health, biotechnology, semiconductors and other electronics, consumer related, industrial and energy. **Geographic Preferences:** Southern California and Southwest.

58012 ■ Falcon Fund
100 N. Barranca St., Ste., 920
West Covina, CA 91791
Ph:(626)966-6235
Fax: (626)966-0193
URL: http://www.falconfund.com
Contact: Edward Tuck, Principal
Investment Policies: Early stage. **Industry Preferences:** Communications, computer software, and transportation.

58013 ■ Far East Capital Corp.
350 S. Grand Ave., Ste. 4100
Los Angeles, CA 90071
Ph:(213)687-1361
Fax: (213)617-7939
Co. E-mail: free@fareastnationalbank.com
Preferred Investment Size: $100,000 to $300,000. **Investment Types:** First and second stage, mezzanine, and special situation. **Industry Preferences:** Communications and media, computer software and hardware, Internet specific, semiconductors and other electronics, medical and health. **Geographic Preferences:** West coast.

58014 ■ Finaventures
3000 Ocean Park Blvd., Ste. 1022
Santa Monica, CA 90405
Ph:(310)399-5011
Fax: (310)452-5492
URL: http://www.finaventures.com
Contact: Abdou Bensouda, Managing Director
Preferred Investment Size: $500,000 to $3,000,000. **Investment Policies:** Early, first, and second stage, balanced, and expansion. **Industry Preferences:** Communications, computer software, and semiconductors and other electronics. **Geographic Preferences:** Northern and Southern California.

58015 ■ Flynn Ventures, LLC
1 Flynn Ctr.
825 Van Ness Ave.
San Francisco, CA 94109
Ph:(415)673-5900
Fax: (415)673-6093
URL: http://www.flynnventures.com
Contact: Barry Lewis, Principal
Preferred Investment Size: $200,000 to $1,000,000. **Investment Types:** Early stage. **Industry Preferences:** Communications and media, Internet specific, and consumer related. **Geographic Preferences:** West Coast, and Western Canada.

58016 ■ Flywheel Ventures
3000 Sand Hill Rd.
Bldg. 1, Ste. 205
Menlo Park, CA 94025
Ph:877-810-8104
Fax: 877-810-8104
URL: http://www.flywheelventures.com
Contact: Trevor Loy, Managing Director
Investment Policies: Seed and early stage. **Industry Preferences:** Communications, computer software, and semiconductors and other electronics. **Geographic Preferences:** New Mexico, Rocky Mountains, and West Coast.

58017 ■ Forrest, Binkley & Brown
19900 MacArthur Blvd., Ste. 570
Irvine, CA 92660

Ph:(949)222-1987
Fax: (949)222-1988
URL: http://www.fbbvc.com
Contact: Greg Yurkovich, Principal
Investment Policies: $250,000 to $4,000,000. **Investment Types:** Later stage, expansion, acquisition, generalist PE, leveraged buyout, and management buyouts. **Industry Preferences:** Computer software and services, Internet specific, semiconductors and other electronics, biotechnology, communications and media, other products, computer hardware, medical and health, and consumer related. **Geographic Preferences:** U.S.

58018 ■ Forward Ventures
9393 Towne Centre Dr.
San Diego, CA 92121
Ph:(858)677-6077
Fax: (858)452-8799
URL: http://www.forwardventure.com
Contact: David Urso, Principal
Preferred Investment Size: $500,000 to $10,000,000. **Investment Types:** Seed, first and second stage, early and later stage. **Industry Preferences:** Biotechnology, medical and health, and Internet specific. **Geographic Preferences:** Northern and Southern California, and Eastern Canada.

58019 ■ Foundation Capital
70 Willow Rd., Ste. 200
Menlo Park, CA 94025
Ph:(650)614-0500
Fax: (650)614-0505
URL: http://www.foundationcapital.com
Contact: Adam Grosser, General Partner
Investment Types: Start-up, seed, first and second stage, early stage, research and development, and balanced. **Industry Preferences:** Internet specific, communications and media, computer software and services, computer hardware, semiconductors and other electronics, industrial and energy, other products, industrial and energy, medical and health, and consumer related. **Geographic Preferences:** West Coast.

58020 ■ Gabriel Venture Partners
350 Marine Pky., Ste. 200
Redwood Shores, CA 94065
Ph:(650)551-5000
Fax: (650)551-5001
URL: http://www.gabrielvp.com
Contact: Rick Bolander, Managing General Partner
Preferred Investment Size: $250,000 to $7,000,000. **Investment Types:** Seed, early and first stage. **Industry Preferences:** Internet specific, computer software and services, communications and media, computer hardware, semiconductors and other electronics, medical and health. **Geographic Preferences:** California, Mid Atlantic, Northeast, Northern California, and West Coast.

58021 ■ Garage Technology Ventures / Garage.com
3300 Hillview Ave., Ste. 150
Palo Alto, CA 94304
Ph:(650)354-1800
Fax: (650)354-1801
URL: http://www.garage.com
Contact: Bill Reichert, President
Preferred Investment Size: $100,000 to $1,000,000. **Investment Policies:** Seed, early, first and second stage. **Industry Preferences:** Communications, computer software, Internet specific, and semiconductors and other electronics. **Geographic Preferences:** California and West Coast.

58022 ■ Gatx Capital
4 Embarcadero Ctr., Ste. 2200
San Francisco, CA 94904
Ph:(415)955-3200
Fax: (415)955-3449
Preferred Investment Size: $500,000 to $5,000,000. **Investment Types:** Early and later stages, and leveraged buyouts. **Industry Preferences:** Diversified technologies, forestry, and agriculture. **Geographic Preferences:** National and Canada.

58023 ■ GATX Ventures / Meier Mitchell & Co.
3687 Mount Diablo Blvd., Ste. 200
Lafayette, CA 94549
Ph:(925)258-6000
Fax: (925)258-6020
URL: http://www.gatxventures.com
Contact: Robert Pomeroy, President
Preferred Investment Size: $500,000 minimum. **Investment Policies:** Seed, start-up, first and second stage, research and development, and mezzanine. **Industry Preferences:** Communications, computer hardware and software, semiconductors and other electronics, biotechnology, medical and health, industrial and energy, and manufacturing. **Geographic Preferences:** U.S.

58024 ■ Geneva Venture Partners
4 Embarcadero Ctr., Ste. 1400
San Francisco, CA 94111
Ph:(415)732-5672
Fax: (415)433-6635
URL: http://www.genevaventurepartners.com
Contact: Igor Sill, General Partner
Investment Types: Seed and early stage. **Industry Preferences:** Communications and media, Internet specific, computer software and services, industrial and energy, and other products. **Geographic Preferences:** California.

58025 ■ Global Crossing
960 Hamlin Ct.
Sunnyvale, CA 94089
Ph:(408)542-0100
Fax: (405)541-0429
URL: http://www.gcventures.com
Preferred Investment Size: $2,000,000 to $10,000,000. **Investment Types:** Early, first, and second stage. **Industry Preferences:** Communications and media, Internet specific, semiconductors and other electronics, computer software, hardware and services. **Geographic Preferences:** U.S.

58026 ■ Glynn Ventures
3000 Sand Hill Rd.
Bldg. 4, Ste. 235
Menlo Park, CA 94025
Ph:(650)854-2215
Fax: (650)854-8083
Preferred Investment Size: $300,000 to 500,000. **Investment Types:** Start-up, first and second stage, leveraged buyout, and mezzanine. **Industry Preferences:** Internet specific, communications and media, medical and health, computer software and services. **Geographic Preferences:** Northeast, Northwest, Southeast and West Coast.

58027 ■ Greylock (San Mateo)
2929 Campus Dr., Ste. 400
San Mateo, CA 94403
Ph:(650)493-5525
Fax: (650)493-5575
URL: http://www.greylock.com
Contact: Michele Law, Principal
Preferred Investment Size: $250,000 minimum. **Investment Types:** Seed, start-up, early and first stage, and expansion. **Industry Preferences:** Internet specific, computer hardware, computer software and services, communications and media, semiconductors and other electronics, medical and health, biotechnology, consumer related, industrial and energy, and other products. **Geographic Preferences:** U.S.

58028 ■ GRP Partners / Global Retail Partners
2121 Avenue of the Stars, Ste. 1630
Los Angeles, CA 90067
Ph:(310)785-5100
Fax: (310)785-5111
URL: http://www.grpvc.com
Contact: Dana Kibler, Vice President
Preferred Investment Size: $3,000,000 to $25,000,000. **Investment Types:** First and second stage, early and later stage, expansion, and balanced. **Industry Preferences:** Internet specific, consumer related, computer hardware, computer software and services, communications and media, and other products. **Geographic Preferences:** U.S.

58029 ■ Hallador Venture Partners
740 University Ave., Ste. 110
Sacramento, CA 95825-6710
Ph:(916)920-0191
Fax: (916)920-5188
Contact: Chris Branscum, Managing Director
E-mail: chris@shallador.com
Preferred Investment Size: $500,000 to $1,000,000. **Investment Types:** Seed, start-up, first and second stage, and research and development. **Industry Preferences:** Communications and media, computer software, Internet specific, semiconductors and other electronics. **Geographic Preferences:** West Coast.

58030 ■ Hamilton Bioventures / Hamilton Apex Technology Ventures
12555 High Bluff Dr., Ste. 310
San Diego, CA 92130
Ph:(858)314-2350
Fax: (858)314-2355
URL: http://www.hamiltonbioventures.com
Contact: David Coats, Managing Director
Preferred Investment Size: $1,000,000 to $5,600,000. **Investment Policies:** Early, first and second stage. **Industry Preferences:** Biotechnology, and medical and health. **Geographic Preferences:** Northern and Southern California, and West Coast.

58031 ■ Headland Ventures, LP / Sterling Payot Capital
65 Cloudview Rd.
Sausalito, CA 94965
Ph:(415)289-2590
Fax: (415)289-2591
URL: http://www.headlandventures.com
Contact: Larry Stites, Chief Financial Officer
Investment Policies: Early stage. **Industry Preferences:** Computer software, Internet specific, and consumer related. **Geographic Preferences:** U.S.

58032 ■ Health Capital Group
6371 Royal Grove Dr.
Hunnington Beach, CA 92648
Ph:(714)536-0367
Fax: (714)536-3056
Preferred Investment Size: $5,000,000 minimum. **Investment Types:** Start-up, first and second stage, leveraged buyout, and mezzanine. **Industry Preferences:** Communications and media, computer hardware and software, semiconductors and other electronics, biotechnology, medical and health, consumer related, industrial and energy, financial services, business service, and manufacturing. **Geographic Preferences:** West Coast.

58033 ■ Hewlett Packard / Compaq Computer Corporation
3000 Hanover St.
Palo Alto, CA 94304
Ph:(650)857-1501
Fax: (650)857-5518
URL: http://www.hp.com
Contact: Michael Duggan, Managing Director
Investment Policies: Early stage. **Industry Preferences:** Biotechnology. **Geographic Preferences:** National.

58034 ■ Highbar Ventures
1151 Werth Ave.
Menlo Park, CA 94025
Contact: Roy Sardina, General Partner
Investment Policies: Early stage.

58035 ■ HMS Group
730 North Pastoria Ave.
Sunnyvale, CA 94085
Ph:(408)992-0320
Contact: Richard Grey, General Partner
Industry Preferences: Communications and media, computer software and services, computer hardware, semiconductors and other electronics, Internet specific, industrial and energy, and other products.

58036 ■ Horizon Ventures
Four Main St., Ste. 50
Los Altos, CA 94022
Ph:(650)917-4100

Fax: (650)917-4109
URL: http://www.horizonvc.com
Contact: Doug Tsui, Managing Director
Preferred Investment Size: $500,000 to $3,500,000.
Investment Types: Seed, start-up, early, first and second stage. **Industry Preferences:** Internet specific, computer hardware, computer software and services, semiconductors and other electronics, medical and health, communications and media, and other products. **Geographic Preferences:** West Coast.

58037 ■ Icon Venture Advisors / Icon Ventures
2480 Sand Hill Rd., Ste. 201
Menlo Park, CA 94025
Ph:(650)234-9500
Fax: (650)234-9508
Preferred Investment Size: $3,000,000 to $6,000,000. **Industry Preferences:** Communications and media, computer software, Internet specific, and semiconductors and other electronics. **Geographic Preferences:** West Coast.

58038 ■ Idanta Partners, Ltd. (San Diego)
4660 La Jolla Village Dr., Ste. 775
San Diego, CA 92122
Ph:(619)452-9690
URL: http://www.idanta.com
Contact: David Dunn, Managing Partner
Preferred Investment Size: $1,000,000 to $10,000,000. **Investment Types:** Seed, early stage, first and second stage, balanced, acquisition, and management buyouts. **Industry Preferences:** Semiconductors and other electronics, communications and media, computer software and services, Internet specific, computer hardware, consumer related, medical and health, and other products. **Geographic Preferences:** U.S.

58039 ■ Idealab!
130 West Union St.
Pasadena, CA 91103
Ph:(626)585-6900
Fax: (626)535-2701
URL: http://www.idealab.com
Contact: Howard Morgan, President
Investment Policies: Early stage. **Industry Preferences:** Internet specific.

58040 ■ IDG Ventures (San Francisco)
650 California St., 24th Fl.
San Francisco, CA 94108
Ph:(415)439-4420
Fax: (415)439-4424
URL: http://www.idgventures.com
Contact: Anil Hansjee, Principal
Preferred Investment Size: $44,000 to $4,000,000.
Investment Types: Seed, first stage, early and later stage, mezzanine, and balanced. **Industry Preferences:** Internet specific, computer software and services, computer hardware, communications and media, medical and health, semiconductors and other electronics, biotechnology, consumer related, and other products. **Geographic Preferences:** U.S.

58041 ■ The Ignite Group / Ignite Associates, LLC
255 Shoreline Dr., Ste. 510
Redwood City, CA 94065
Ph:(650)622-2000
Fax: (650)622-2015
URL: http://www.ignitegroup.com
Contact: Nobuo Mii, Managing Partner
Preferred Investment Size: $2,000,000 to $10,000,000. **Investment Types:** Seed, start-up, early, first, and second stage. **Industry Preferences:** Internet specific, communications and media, computer software and services, computer hardware, semiconductors and other electronics, medical and health. **Geographic Preferences:** Northern and Southern California.

58042 ■ IMinds
135 Main St., Ste. 1350
San Francisco, CA 94105
Ph:(415)547-0000
Fax: (415)547-0010

URL: http://www.iminds.com
Preferred Investment Size: $500,000 to $5,000,000.
Investment Types: Seed, start-up, early and first stage. **Industry Preferences:** Internet specific, computer software and services. **Geographic Preferences:** Northern California and West Coast.

58043 ■ Imperial Ventures Inc.
9920 S. La Cienega Boulevar, 14th Fl.
Inglewood, CA 90301
Ph:(310)417-5409
Fax: (310)338-6115
Contact: H. Wayne Snaveley, President
Preferred Investment Size: $500,000 to $2,000,000.
Investment Types: Second stage and leveraged buyout.

58044 ■ Indosuez Ventures
2180 Sand Hill Rd., Ste. 450
Menlo Park, CA 94025
Ph:(650)854-0587
Fax: (650)323-5561
URL: http://www.indosuezventures.com
Preferred Investment Size: $250,000 to $4,000,000.
Investment Types: Start-up, first and early stage, and mezzanine. **Industry Preferences:** Computer software and services, computer hardware, medical and health, semiconductors and other electronics, Internet specific, communications and media, consumer related, industrial and energy, biotechnology, and other products. **Geographic Preferences:** West Coast.

58045 ■ Infinity Capital LLC
100 Hamilton Ave., Ste. 400
Palo Alto, CA 94301
Ph:(650)462-8400
Fax: (650)462-8415
URL: http://www.infinityllc.com
Contact: Bruce Graham, Managing Director
Preferred Investment Size: $275,000 to $10,000,000. **Investment Types:** Early stage. **Industry Preferences:** Internet specific, communications and media, computer hardware, medical and health, other products, computer software and services, semiconductors and other electronics. **Geographic Preferences:** U.S.

58046 ■ Information Technology Ventures
100 Hamilton Ave., Ste. 400
Palo Alto, CA 94301
Ph:(650)462-8400
Fax: (650)462-8415
URL: http://www.itventures.com
Contact: George Kitagawa, Chief Financial Officer
Investment Types: Start-up. **Industry Preferences:** Internet specific, computer software and services, communications and media, semiconductors and other electronics, computer hardware, industrial and energy, and other products. **Geographic Preferences:** Northeast, Northwest, and West Coast.

58047 ■ Inglewood Ventures
12526 Highbluff Dr., Ste. 300
San Diego, CA 92130
Ph:(858)792-3579
Fax: (858)792-3417
URL: http://www.inglewoodventures.com
Contact: Killu Tougu Sanborn, Principal
Preferred Investment Size: $500,000 to $2,600,000.
Investment Types: Seed and early stage. **Industry Preferences:** Biotechnology, medical and health. **Geographic Preferences:** Northern and Southern California, and West Coast.

58048 ■ Inman and Bowman
4 Orinda Way, Bldg. D, Ste. 150
Orinda, CA 94563
Ph:(925)253-1611
Fax: (925)253-9037
Preferred Investment Size: $1,000,000 minimum.
Investment Types: Start-up, first and second stage, leveraged buyout, and special situation. **Industry Preferences:** Computer software and hardware, semiconductors and other electronics, medical and health. **Geographic Preferences:** West Coast.

58049 ■ Innocal Venture Capital
Plaza Tower, Ste. 1270
600 Anton Blvd.
Costa Mesa, CA 92626
Ph:(714)850-6784
Fax: (714)850-6798
URL: http://www.innocal.com
Contact: James Houlihan, Managing Director
Preferred Investment Size: $1,000,000 to $5,000,000. **Investment Types:** Early, first, and second stage, expansion, recapitalizations, and turn-around. **Industry Preferences:** Computer software and services, Internet specific, medical and health, communications and media, industrial and energy, semiconductors and other electronics, and biotechnology. **Geographic Preferences:** Northern and Southern California, and the West Coast.

58050 ■ Institutional Venture Partners
3000 Sand Hill Rd.
Bldg. 2, Ste. 290
Menlo Park, CA 94025
Ph:(650)854-0132
Fax: (650)854-2009
URL: http://www.ivp.com
Contact: Dennis Phelps, Partner
Preferred Investment Size: $2,000,000 to $10,000,000. **Investment Types:** Later stage, expansion, public companies, private placement, open market, and mezzanine. **Industry Preferences:** Internet specific, communications and media, medical and health, computer hardware, computer software and services, semiconductors and other electronics, biotechnology, consumer related, industrial and energy, and other products. **Geographic Preferences:** West Coast and U.S.

58051 ■ Integrated Consortium Inc.
50 Ridgecrest Rd.
Kentfield, CA 94904
Ph:(415)925-0386
Fax: (415)461-2726
Preferred Investment Size: $1,000,000. **Investment Types:** First and second stage, control-block purchases, industry rollups, leveraged buyouts, and mezzanine. **Industry Preferences:** Entertainment and leisure, retail, computer stores, franchises, food/beverage, consumer products and services. **Geographic Preferences:** West Coast.

58052 ■ Interwest Partners (Menlo Park)
2710 Sand Hill Rd., 2nd Fl.
Menlo Park, CA 94025
Ph:(650)854-8585
Fax: (650)854-4706
URL: http://www.interwest.com
Contact: Doug Pepper, Principal
Preferred Investment Size: $2,000,000 to $25,000,000. **Investment Types:** Seed, research and development, start-up, first and second stage, early and later stage, balanced, and expansion. **Industry Preferences:** Medical and health, Internet specific, consumer related, biotechnology, communications and media, computer hardware, computer software and services, semiconductors and other electronics, industrial and energy, and other products. **Geographic Preferences:** U.S.

58053 ■ Invencor, Inc.
PO Box 7355
Menlo Park, CA 94026
Ph:(650)330-1210
Fax: (650)330-1222
URL: http://www.invencor.com
Contact: Debra Guerin, Managing Director
Preferred Investment Size: $300,000 to $2,000,000.
Investment Types: Seed, start-up, early and first stage. **Geographic Preferences:** Arizona, California, Hawaii, Northern California, Northwest, New Mexico, and Utah.

58054 ■ Jafco Ventures
505 Hamilton Ave., Ste. 310
Palto Alto, CA 94301
Ph:(650)463-8800
Fax: (650)463-8801
URL: http://www.jafco.com

Contact: Joseph Horowitz, Managing General Partner
Preferred Investment Size: $2,000,000 to $6,000,000. **Investment Types:** Early, second stage, and expansion. **Industry Preferences:** Communications and media, computer software and services, and semiconductors and other electronics. **Geographic Preferences:** U.S.

58055 ■ Jolson Merchant Partners Group, LLC
1 Embarcadero Ctr., Ste. 2100
San Francisco, CA 94111
Ph:(415)835-8900
Fax: (415)263-1337
URL: http://www.jolsonmp.com
Contact: Joseph Jolson, Chief Executive Director
Investment Policies: Early stage.

58056 ■ Kaiser Permanente Ventures
1800 Harrison St., 22nd Fl.
Oakland, CA 94612
Ph:(510)625-4001
Fax: (510)625-4036
URL: http://www.kpventures.com
Contact: Chris Grant, Vice President
Preferred Investment Size: $500,000 to $2,000,000. **Investment Types:** Early, first, and second stage, balanced, strategic alliances, and expansion. **Industry Preferences:** Biotechnology, and medical and health. **Geographic Preferences:** Canada.

58057 ■ Kingsbury Associates
4401 Eastgate Mall
San Diego, CA 92122
Ph:(858)677-0600
Fax: (858)677-0800
Contact: Timothy Wollaeger, Partner
Preferred Investment Size: $500,000 to $1,000,000. **Investment Types:** Start-up, early, first and second stage. **Industry Preferences:** Medical and health, biotechnology, computer software and services, and other products. **Geographic Preferences:** West Coast.

58058 ■ Kleiner Perkins Caufield & Byers (Menlo Park)
2750 Sand Hill Rd.
Menlo Park, CA 94025
Ph:(650)233-2750
Fax: (650)233-0300
URL: http://www.kpcb.com
Contact: John Denniston, Chief Operating Officer
Preferred Investment Size: $500,000 minimum. **Investment Types:** Seed, start-up, first stage, and balanced. **Industry Preferences:** Internet specific, computer software and services, computer hardware, communications and media, semiconductors and other electronics, medical and health, biotechnology, industrial and energy, consumer related, and other products. **Geographic Preferences:** West Coast.

58059 ■ Kline Hawkes & Co.
11726 San Vicente Blvd., Ste. 300
Los Angeles, CA 90049
Ph:(310)442-4700
Fax: (310)442-4707
URL: http://www.klinehawkes.com
Contact: Frank Kline, Managing Partner
Preferred Investment Size: $3,000,000 to $15,000,000. **Investment Types:** Second and later stage, private placement, expansion, acquisition, generalist PE, industry rollups, leveraged buyout, management buyouts, private placement, turnaround, and recapitalizations. **Industry Preferences:** Communications and media, Internet specific, medical and health, semiconductors and other electronics, computer software, and services, computer hardware, biotechnology, industrial and energy, and other products. **Geographic Preferences:** Northwest, Southwest, and West Coast.

58060 ■ KLM Capital Group
10 Almaden Blvd., Ste. 988
San Jose, CA 95113
Ph:(408)970-8888
Fax: (408)970-8887

URL: http://www.klmtech.com
Contact: Ron Cao, Principal
Preferred Investment Size: $500,000 to $5,000,000. **Investment Types:** Seed, expansion, early stage, and acquisition. **Industry Preferences:** Semiconductors and other electronics, Internet specific, computer software and services, communications and media, and consumer related. **Geographic Preferences:** U.S. and Canada.

58061 ■ KTB Ventures / KTB Venture Capital
720 University Ave., Ste. 100
Palo Alto, CA 94301
Ph:(650)324-4681
Fax: (650)324-4682
URL: http://www.ktbvc.com
Contact: Sung Yoon, Managing Partner
Preferred Investment Size: $500,000 to $5,000,000. **Investment Types:** Start-up, first and early stage, and balanced. **Industry Preferences:** Internet specific, semiconductors and other electronics, communications and media, computer software and services, computer hardware, industrial and energy. **Geographic Preferences:** U.S.

58062 ■ Kyocera International, Inc.
Corporate Development
8611 Balboa Ave.
San Diego, CA 92123
Ph:(858)576-2600
Fax: (858)492-1456
Preferred Investment Size: $300,000 to $500,000. **Investment Types:** Second stage. **Industry Preferences:** Communications and media, computer related, semiconductors and other electronics, biotechnology, medical and health, consumer related, industrial and energy, business service, agriculture, forestry and fishing. **Geographic Preferences:** West Coast.

58063 ■ Labrador Ventures
101 University Ave., 4th Fl.
Palo Alto, CA 94301
Ph:(650)366-6000
Fax: (650)366-6430
URL: http://www.labrador.com
Contact: Nina Kubal, Chief Financial Officer
Preferred Investment Size: $500,000 to $6,000,000. **Investment Policies:** Start-up, seed, early and first stage. **Industry Preferences:** Communications, computer software, and semiconductors and other electronics. **Geographic Preferences:** Northern California and West Coast

58064 ■ Latterell Venture Partners
4 Embarcadero Centre, Ste. 2500
San Francisco, CA 94111-4106
Ph:(415)399-9880
Fax: (415)399-9879
URL: http://www.lvpcapital.com
Contact: Patrick Latterell, Managing Director
Investment Policies: Early stage and balanced. **Industry Preferences:** Biotechnology, and medical and health. **Geographic Preferences:** U.S.

58065 ■ Lawrence Financial Group
701 Teakwood
PO Box 491773
Los Angeles, CA 90049
Ph:(310)471-4060
Fax: (310)472-3155
URL: http://www.lawrencefinancial.com
Contact: Larry Hurwitz
Preferred Investment Size: $500,000 to $1,000,000. **Investment Types:** Second stage. **Industry Preferences:** Communications and media, computer related, semiconductors and other electronics, biotechnology, medical and health, consumer related, industrial and energy, financial services, business service, agriculture, forestry and fishing. **Geographic Preferences:** West Coast.

58066 ■ Leapfrog Ventures
Ph:(650)926-9900
Fax: (650)233-9063
URL: http://www.leapfrogventures.com
Contact: Alan Mello, Chief Financial Officer

Preferred Investment Size: $700,000 to $5,000,000. **Investment Policies:** Start-up, seed, early and first stage. **Industry Preferences:** Communications and media, computer software, and Internet specific. **Geographic Preferences:** Northern California and West Coast.

58067 ■ Legacy Venture
550 Lytton Ave., 2nd Fl.
Palo Alto, CA 94301
Ph:(650)324-5980
Fax: (650)324-5982
URL: http://www.legacyventure.com
Contact: Chris Eyre, Principal
Preferred Investment Size: $3,000,000 to $10,000,000. **Investment Policies:** Early stage, and fund of funds. **Geographic Preferences:** U.S.

58068 ■ Leonard Mautner Associates
1434 Sixth St., Ste. 10
Santa Monica, CA 90401
Ph:(213)393-9788
Fax: (310)459-9918
Contact: Leonard Mautner
Preferred Investment Size: $100,000 to $300,000. **Investment Types:** Seed, start-up, first stage, and special situation. **Industry Preferences:** Communications and media, computer software and hardware, semiconductors and other electronics, medical and health. **Geographic Preferences:** West Coast.

58069 ■ LF International, Inc.
360 Post St., Ste. 705
San Francisco, CA 94108
Ph:(415)399-0110
Fax: (415)399-9222
URL: http://www.lfvc.com
Contact: Michael Hsieh, President
Preferred Investment Size: $5,000,000 to $10,000,000. **Investment Types:** Private placement, later, management buyouts, and expansion. **Industry Preferences:** Consumer related. **Geographic Preferences:** U.S.

58070 ■ Liberty Environmental Partners
220 Montgomery St.
Penthouse 10
San Francisco, CA 94104
Ph:(415)834-1600
Fax: (415)834-1603
Contact: Tim Woodward, Principal
Preferred Investment Size: $300,000 to $500,000. **Investment Types:** Start-up, first and second stage. **Industry Preferences:** Industrial and energy, biotechnology, semiconductors and other electronics, and Internet specific. **Geographic Preferences:** Rocky Mountains and West Coast.

58071 ■ Lighthouse Capital Partners
500 Drake's Landing Rd.
Greenbrae, CA 94904
Ph:(415)464-5900
Fax: (415)925-3387
URL: http://www.lcpartners.com
Contact: Dennis Ryan, Chief Operating Officer
Preferred Investment Size: $1,000,000 to $10,000,000. **Investment Types:** Seed, start-up, first and second stage, early stage, and expansion. **Industry Preferences:** Internet specific, computer software and services, other products, semiconductors and other electronics, communications and media. **Geographic Preferences:** California and Massachusetts.

58072 ■ Lightspeed Venture Partners / Weiss, Peck and Greer
2200 Sand Hill Rd.
Menlo Park, CA 94025
Ph:(650)234-8300
Fax: (650)234-8333
URL: http://www.lightspeedvp.com
Contact: Eric O'Brien, Principal
Preferred Investment Size: $500,000 to $20,000,000. **Investment Types:** Seed, first, second and later stage. **Industry Preferences:** Communications and media, Internet specific, computer software and services, computer hardware, semiconductors and other electronics, medical and health, industrial and energy, biotechnology, consumer related, and other products. **Geographic Preferences:** U.S.

58073 ■ Lucent Venture Partners, Inc.
600 Mountain Ave.
Rm. 6A-406
Murray Hill, NJ 07974
Ph:(908)852-8538
Fax: (908)852-8048
URL: http://www.lucentventurepartners.com
Contact: Mark Rappaport, Chief Financial Officer
Preferred Investment Size: $500,000 to $5,000,000.
Investment Types: Early stage. **Industry Preferences:** Communications and media, semiconductors and other electronics, Internet specific, computer software and services, and computer hardware. **Geographic Preferences:** U.S.

58074 ■ Magic Venture Capital LLC
1010 El Camino Real, Ste. 300
Menlo Park, CA 94025
Ph:(650)327-7719
Contact: Erin McGurk, Managing Director
Preferred Investment Size: $300,000 to $1,000,000.
Investment Types: Seed, start-up, and first stage. **Industry Preferences:** Medical and health. **Geographic Preferences:** West Coast.

58075 ■ Manitou Ventures, LLC
460 Bush St., 2nd Fl.
San Francisco, CA 94108
Ph:(415)288-0727
Fax: (415)627-9079
URL: http://www.manitouventures.com
Contact: Chris Wadsworth, Partner
Preferred Investment Size: $500,000 to $1,500,000.
Investment Policies: Early stage. **Geographic Preferences:** National.

58076 ■ Marwit Capital, LLC
180 Newport Center Dr., Ste. 200
Newport Beach, CA 92660
Ph:(949)640-6234
Fax: (949)720-8077
URL: http://www.marwit.com
Contact: Chris Britt, President
Preferred Investment Size: $250,000 minimum. **Investment Types:** Leveraged buyout, management buyouts, and acquisition. **Industry Preferences:** Medical and health, transportation, business service, and manufacturing. **Geographic Preferences:** California, Southern California, and West Coast.

58077 ■ Maton Venture
16615 Lark Ave., Ste. 108
Los Gatos, CA 95032
Ph:(408)358-8567
Fax: (408)358-8275
URL: http://www.maton.com
Contact: James Chen, Managing Partner
Preferred Investment Size: $250,000 to $2,500,000.
Investment Types: Seed, start-up, early stage, first and second stage, expansion, private placement, research and development, and turnaround. **Industry Preferences:** Communications and media, computer software and hardware, Internet specific, semiconductors and other electronics. **Geographic Preferences:** Northern California.

58078 ■ Matrix Partners (Menlo Park)
2500 Sand Hill Rd., Ste. 113
Menlo Park, CA 94025
Ph:(650)854-3131
Fax: (650)854-3296
URL: http://www.matrixpartners.com
Contact: Andrew Verlahen, General Partner
Preferred Investment Size: $100,000 to $10,000,000. **Investment Types:** Start-up, early, first and second stage, balanced, and leveraged buyout. **Industry Preferences:** Communications and media, Internet specific, computer software and services, computer hardware, semiconductors and other electronics, consumer related, medical and health, industrial and energy, biotechnology, and other products. **Geographic Preferences:** California and Massachusetts.

58079 ■ Mayfield Fund
2800 Sand Hill Rd., Ste. 250
Menlo Park, CA 94025

Ph:(650)854-5560
Fax: (650)854-5712
URL: http://www.mayfield.com
Contact: Harvey Schloss, Chief Operating Officer
Preferred Investment Size: $250,000 minimum. **Investment Types:** Early, second, and later stage, acquisition, joint ventures, management buyouts, private placement, research and development, and strategic alliances. **Industry Preferences:** Computer software and services, computer hardware, Internet specific, communications and media, semiconductors and other electronics, biotechnology, medical and health, consumer related, industrial and energy, and other products. **Geographic Preferences:** Northwest, Rocky Mountains, and West Coast.

58080 ■ McCown De Leeuw and Co. (Menlo Park)
3000 Sand Hill Rd., Bldg. 3, Ste. 290
Menlo Park, CA 94025-7111
Ph:(650)854-6000
Fax: (650)854-0853
URL: http://www.mdcpartners.com
Contact: George McCown, Managing Director
Preferred Investment Size: $20,000,000 to $50,000,000. **Investment Types:** Leveraged buyout. **Industry Preferences:** Consumer related, computer software and services, medical and health, Internet specific, communications and media, computer hardware, semiconductors and other electronics, industrial and energy, and other products. **Geographic Preferences:** U.S.

58081 ■ McGoodwin James & Co.
611 Anton Blvd.
Costa Mesa, CA 92626
Ph:(714)434-7150
Investment Policies: Start-up and seed. **Geographic Preferences:** U.S.

58082 ■ Media Technology Ventures
100 Hamilton Ave., Ste. 250
Palo Alto, CA 94301
Ph:(650)687-0500
Fax: (650)687-0234
URL: http://www.allegiscapital.com
Contact: Robert Ackerman, Managing Director
Investment Types: Start-up, seed, early stage, and research and development. **Industry Preferences:** Communications and media, Internet specific, and computer software and services, other products, computer hardware, semiconductors and other electronics. **Geographic Preferences:** U.S.

58083 ■ Media Venture Partners
111 San Pablo Ave.
San Francisco, CA 94127
Ph:(415)661-3818
Fax: (415)661-2542
Preferred Investment Size: $500,000 to $1,000,000.
Investment Types: Seed, start-up, first and second stage, leveraged buyout, control-block purchases, and special situation. **Industry Preferences:** Communications and media, computer software and hardware, consumer related, and manufacturing. **Geographic Preferences:** U.S. and Canada.

58084 ■ Medicus Venture Partners (Burlingame)
800 Airport Blvd., Ste. 508
Burlingame, CA 94010
Ph:(650)375-0200
Fax: (650)375-0230
URL: http://www.medicusvc.com
Contact: Frederick Dotzler, General Partner
Investment Types: Early stage. **Industry Preferences:** Medical and health, biotechnology, Internet specific, computer software and services, computer hardware. **Geographic Preferences:** Northwest, Rocky Mountains, Southwest, and West Coast.

58085 ■ Medventure Associates
5980 Horton St., Ste. 390
Emeryville, CA 94608
Ph:(510)597-7979
Fax: (510)597-9920
URL: http://www.medven.com

Contact: Annette Campbell-White, Managing Partner
Preferred Investment Size: $200,000 to $500,000.
Investment Types: Seed and early stage. **Industry Preferences:** Medical and health, Internet specific, biotechnology, communications and media, computer software and services. **Geographic Preferences:** West Coast.

58086 ■ Menlo Ventures
3000 Sand Hill Rd.
Bldg. 4, Ste. 100
Menlo Park, CA 94025
Ph:(650)854-8540
Fax: (650)854-7059
URL: http://www.menloventures.com
Contact: H. DuBose Montgomery, Managing Director
E-mail: dubose@menloventures.com
Preferred Investment Size: $5,000,000 to $25,000,000. **Investment Types:** Start-up, early, first, second, and later stage, expansion, and balanced. **Industry Preferences:** Internet specific, communications and media, computer software and services, computer hardware, medical and health, semiconductors and other electronics, biotechnology, consumer related, industrial and energy, and other products. **Geographic Preferences:** U.S.

58087 ■ Merrill Pickard Anderson & Eyre
556 Mowry Ave.
Fremont, CA 94025
Ph:(510)574-0150
Fax: (510)574-0155
Preferred Investment Size: $1,000,000 minimum.
Investment Types: Seed, start-up, first and second stage. **Industry Preferences:** Computer software, hardware and services, communications and media, semiconductors and other electronics, Internet specific, medical and health, consumer related, industrial and energy, and biotechnology.

58088 ■ Millennium Hanson
9551 Wilshire Blvd.
Beverly Hills, CA 90212
Ph:(310)550-1995
Fax: (310)550-8213
URL: http://www.millhanson.com
Investment Policies: Early stage. **Industry Preferences:** Internet specific. **Geographic Preferences:** National.

58089 ■ Mission Ventures
11512 El Camino Real, Ste. 215
San Diego, CA 92130
Ph:(858)259-0100
Fax: (858)259-0112
URL: http://www.missionventures.com
Contact: David Ryan, Managing Partner
Preferred Investment Size: $2,000,000 to $20,000,000. **Investment Types:** Seed, early, first and second stage, and research and development. **Industry Preferences:** Internet specific, communications and media, computer software and services, medical and health, consumer related, semiconductors and other electronics, and other products. **Geographic Preferences:** Southern California.

58090 ■ Mobius Venture Capital / Softbank Venture Capital
2 Palo Alto Sq., Ste. 500
3000 El Camino Real
Palo Alto, CA 94306
Ph:(650)319-2700
Fax: (650)319-2730
URL: http://www.mobiusvc.com
Contact: Aaron Cheatham, Principal
Preferred Investment Size: $2,000,000 to $100,000,000. **Investment Types:** Seed, start-up, early and first stage. **Industry Preferences:** Internet specific, computer software and services, computer hardware, communications and media, consumer related, semiconductors and other electronics, biotechnology, industrial and energy, and other products. **Geographic Preferences:** California, East and West Coast.

58091 ■ Mohr Davidow Ventures (Menlo Park)
2775 Sand Hill Rd.
Bldg. 3, Ste. 240
Menlo Park, CA 94025
Ph:(650)854-7236
Fax: (650)854-7365
URL: http://www.mdv.com
Contact: Jim Smith, General Partner
Preferred Investment Size: $500,000 to $10,000,000. **Investment Types:** Seed, early, first and second stage. **Industry Preferences:** Internet specific, computer software and services, computer hardware, semiconductors and other electronics, communications and media, medical and health, consumer related, biotechnology, industrial and energy, and other products. **Geographic Preferences:** Northwest, Mid Atlantic, and West Coast.

58092 ■ Montgomery Associates, Inc.
425 California St., Ste. 200
PO Box 2230
San Francisco, CA 94126
Ph:(415)421-4200
Fax: (415)981-3601
Preferred Investment Size: $500,000 minimum. **Investment Types:** Seed, start-up, first and second stage, leveraged buyout, research and development, and special situation. **Industry Preferences:** Communications and media, semiconductors and other electronics, medical and health, consumer related, industrial and energy, transportation, and financial services. **Geographic Preferences:** West Coast.

58093 ■ National Investment Management, Inc.
PO Box 3095
Palos Verdes Estates, CA 90274
Ph:(310)784-7600
Co. E-mail: robins621@aol.com
Contact: Richard Robins, President
Preferred Investment Size: $1,000,000 minimum. **Investment Types:** Leveraged buyout. **Industry Preferences:** Internet specific, computer software and services, consumer related, industrial and energy, communications and media, semiconductors and other electronics, computer hardware, and other products. **Geographic Preferences:** U.S.

58094 ■ Netcatalyst
PO Box 25028
Los Angeles, CA 90025
URL: http://www.netcatalyst.com
Contact: Chris Karkenny, Chief Executive Officer
Investment Policies: Early stage. **Industry Preferences:** Internet specific. **Geographic Preferences:** National.

58095 ■ Netfuel Inc.
19 Alpine Ave.
Los Gatos, CA 95030
Ph:(408)354-8138
Fax: (408)865-0668
URL: http://www.netfuel.com
Contact: Jennifer Forsyth, Principal
Investment Policies: Seed and start-up. **Industry Preferences:** Internet specific. **Geographic Preferences:** Midwest.

58096 ■ New Enterprise Associates (Menlo Park)
2490 Sand Hill Rd.
Menlo Park, CA 94025
Ph:(650)854-9499
Fax: (650)854-9397
URL: http://www.nea.com
Contact: Aaron Vermut, Principal
Preferred Investment Size: $200,000 to $20,000,000. **Investment Types:** Seed, early, start-up, first and second stage, and mezzanine. **Industry Preferences:** Communications and media, Internet specific, medical and health, computer software and services, computer hardware, semiconductors and other electronics, biotechnology, consumer related, industrial and energy, and other products. **Geographic Preferences:** U.S.

58097 ■ New Vista Capital, LLC
540 Cowper St., Ste. 200
Palo Alto, CA 94301
Ph:(650)566-2200
Fax: (650)833-6889
URL: http://www.nvcap.com
Contact: Frank Greene, Managing Partner
E-mail: fgreene@nvcap.com
Investment Types: Seed, start-up, early, first and second stage. **Industry Preferences:** Internet specific, computer software and services, computer hardware, semiconductors and other electronics, communications and media, consumer related, and other products. **Geographic Preferences:** Northwest, Rocky Mountains, Southwest, and West Coast.

58098 ■ Newbury Ventures
4 Orinda Way, Ste. 150A
Orinda, CA 94563
Ph:(925)258-1400
Fax: (925)258-1404
URL: http://www.newburyven.com
Contact: Bruce Bauer, Managing Partner
Preferred Investment Size: $10,000,000 to $10,000,000. **Investment Types:** First and second stage. **Industry Preferences:** Internet specific, semiconductors and other electronics, communications and media, computer software and services, computer hardware, medical and health. **Geographic Preferences:** Northwest U.S. and Eastern Canada.

58099 ■ Newtek Ventures
500 Washington St., Ste. 720
San Francisco, CA 94111
Ph:(415)986-5711
Fax: (415)986-4618
URL: http://www.newtekventure.com
Preferred Investment Size: $1,000,000 minimum. **Investment Types:** Seed, start-up, first and second stage. **Industry Preferences:** Computer software and services, medical and health, industrial and energy, Internet specific, semiconductors and other electronics, biotechnology, communications and media, and computer hardware. **Geographic Preferences:** Rocky Mountains, Southwest, and West Coast.

58100 ■ NextGen Partners LLC
1114 State St., Ste. 247
Santa Barbara, CA 93101
Ph:(805)564-3156
URL: http://www.nextgenpartners.com
Contact: Anthony Cheetham, Managing Director
Preferred Investment Size: $100,000 to $3,000,000. **Investment Types:** Seed, start-up, early, first and second stage, expansion, and research and development. **Industry Preferences:** Communications and media, semiconductors and other electronics, biotechnology, industrial and energy. **Geographic Preferences:** U.S. and Canada.

58101 ■ Nextreme Ventures
4350 La Jolla Village Dr., Ste. 450
San Diego, CA 92122
Ph:(858)623-1331
Fax: (858)623-1333
URL: http://www.nextremeventures.com
Contact: Taher Behbehani, Chief Executive Officer
Investment Types: Early stage. **Industry Preferences:** Communications and media. **Geographic Preferences:** U.S.

58102 ■ NIF Ventures USA, Inc.
2300 Geng Rd., Ste. 220
Palo Alto, CA 94303
Ph:(650)461-5000
Fax: (650)858-0892
URL: http://www.nifusa.com
Contact: James Timmins, Partner
Preferred Investment Size: $1,000,000 to $10,000,000. **Investment Types:** Early and later stage, and expansion. **Industry Preferences:** Internet specific, communications and media, computer hardware, computer software and services, semiconductors and other electronics, biotechnology, medical and health, and other products. **Geographic Preferences:** U.S. and Canada.

58103 ■ Nokia Venture Partners
545 Middlefield Rd., Ste 210
Menlo Park, CA 94025
Ph:(650)462-7250
Fax: (650)462-7252
URL: http://www.nokiaventurepartners.com
Contact: Jui Tan, President
Preferred Investment Size: $1,000,000 to $10,000,000. **Investment Types:** Seed, start-up, early, first and second stage. **Industry Preferences:** Computer software, hardware and services, communications and media, and Internet specific. **Geographic Preferences:** U.S. and Canada.

58104 ■ Norwest Venture Partners
525 University Ave., Ste. 800
Palo Alto, CA 94301
Ph:(650)321-8000
Fax: (650)321-8010
URL: http://www.nvp.com
Contact: Promod Haque, Managing General Partner
Preferred Investment Size: $1,000,000 to $25,000,000. **Investment Types:** Seed, early stage, and expansion. **Industry Preferences:** Internet specific, computer software and services, communications and media, semiconductors and other electronics, consumer related, industrial and energy, medical and health, computer hardware, other products, and biotechnology. **Geographic Preferences:** U.S.

58105 ■ Novus Ventures
20111 Stevens Creek Blvd., Ste. 130
Cupertino, CA 95014
Ph:(408)252-3900
Fax: (408)252-1713
URL: http://www.novusventures.com
Contact: Daniel Tompkins, General Partner
Preferred Investment Size: $25,000 to $10,000,000. **Investment Types:** First, early and second stage, and expansion. **Industry Preferences:** Communications and media, computer software and services, Internet specific, semiconductors and other electronics, medical and health. **Geographic Preferences:** California and West Coast.

58106 ■ Nu Capital Access Group, Ltd.
7677 Oakport St., Ste. 105
Oakland, CA 94621
Preferred Investment Size: $500,000 to $1,000,000. **Investment Types:** First and second stage, leveraged buyout, industry rollups, and special situation. **Industry Preferences:** Consumer related, industrial and energy, and manufacturing. **Geographic Preferences:** Northwest, Southwest, and West Coast.

58107 ■ Oak Investment Partners (Palo Alto)
525 University Ave., Ste. 1300
Palo Alto, CA 94301
Ph:(650)614-3700
Fax: (650)328-6345
URL: http://www.oakvc.com
Contact: Iftikar Ahmed, Vice President
Preferred Investment Size: $1,000,000 to $60,000,000. **Investment Types:** Later stage, balanced, expansion, management buyouts, private placement, and special situation. **Industry Preferences:** Communications and media, Internet specific, computer software and services, semiconductors and other electronics, computer hardware, consumer related, medical and health, biotechnology, industrial and energy, and other products. **Geographic Preferences:** U.S.

58108 ■ Omninet Capital, LLC
9420 Wilshire Blvd., Ste. 400
Beverly Hills, CA 90212
Ph:(310)300-4100
Fax: (310)300-4101
URL: http://www.omninet.com
Contact: Benjamin Nazarian, President
Investment Policies: Start-up and early stage. **Industry Preferences:** Communications, and Internet specific. **Geographic Preferences:** U.S.

58109 ■ Onset Ventures
2400 Sand Hill Rd., Ste. 150
Menlo Park, CA 94025

Ph:(650)529-0700
Fax: (650)529-0777
URL: http://www.onset.com
Contact: Nicole Walker, Principal
Preferred Investment Size: $1,000,000 to $12,000,000. **Investment Types:** Seed and early stage. **Industry Preferences:** Computer software and services, computer hardware, Internet specific, communications and media, semiconductors and other electronics, medical and health, other products, and biotechnology. **Geographic Preferences:** West Coast and U.S.

58110 ■ Opportunity Capital Partners
2201 Walnut Ave., Ste. 210
Fremont, CA 94538
Ph:(510)795-7000
Fax: (510)494-5439
URL: http://www.ocpcapital.com
Contact: J. Peter Thompson, Managing Partner
Preferred Investment Size: $2,000,000 to $8,000,000. **Investment Types:** Second and later stage, mezzanine, leveraged buyout, balanced, and industry rollups. **Industry Preferences:** Communications and media, computer software and services, computer hardware, consumer related, Internet specific, medical and health, industrial and energy, other products, and semiconductors and other electronics. **Geographic Preferences:** California and West Coast.

58111 ■ Oracle Venture Fund
500 Oracle Pky.
Redwood Shores, CA 94065
Ph:(650)506-7000
Fax: (650)633-0272
URL: http://www.oracle.com/corporate/venturefund.com
Contact: Laurent Sandrolini, Managing Director
Preferred Investment Size: $2,000,000 to $5,000,000. **Investment Types:** Early and later stage, and balanced. **Industry Preferences:** Internet specific, computer software and services, medical and health, biotechnology, communications and media, computer hardware, and other products. **Geographic Preferences:** U.S.

58112 ■ Orange Ventures
1 Market Plz.
Spear Tower, 35th Fl.
San Francisco, CA 94105
Ph:(415)293-8300
Fax: (415)293-7719
URL: http://www.orangeventures.com
Contact: Mateusz Szeszkowski, Principal
Investment Policies: Start-up and early stage. **Industry Preferences:** Communications and media. **Geographic Preferences:** National.

58113 ■ Osprey Ventures, L.P.
2500 Sand Hill Rd., Ste. 215
Menlo Park, CA 94025
Ph:(650)854-4555
Fax: (650)854-4331
URL: http://www.ospreyventures.com
Contact: David Stastny, Managing Director
Investment Types: Balanced, early stage, and expansion. **Industry Preferences:** Internet specific, semiconductors and other electronics, communications and media, computer software and services, computer hardware, medical and health. **Geographic Preferences:** West Coast.

58114 ■ Outlook Ventures / Iminds, Interactive Minds
135 Main St., Ste. 1350
San Francisco, CA 94105
Ph:(415)547-0000
Fax: (415)547-0010
URL: http://www.outlookventures.com
Contact: Carl Nichols
Preferred Investment Size: $500,000 to $5,000,000. **Investment Policies:** Start-up, seed, early and first stage. **Industry Preferences:** Internet specific, computer software and services, computer hardware, and other products. **Geographic Preferences:** Northern California and West Coast.

58115 ■ Pacifica Fund
480 S. California Ave., Ste. 104
Palo Alto, CA 94306
Ph:(650)289-0063
Fax: (650)289-0290
URL: http://www.pacificafund.com
Contact: Tim Oren, Managing Director
Preferred Investment Size: $250,000 to $1,500,000. **Investment Types:** Start-up, early, first and second stage, and expansion. **Industry Preferences:** Communications and media, computer hardware and software, Internet specific, semiconductors and other electronics, and industrial and energy. **Geographic Preferences:** Northern California and West Coast.

58116 ■ Pacrim Venture Management
605 Cowper St.
Palo Alto, CA 94301
Ph:(650)330-0880
Fax: (650)330-0785
URL: http://www.pacrimpartners.com
Contact: Thomas Toy, Managing Director
Preferred Investment Size: $100,000 to $2,000,000. **Investment Types:** Seed, start-up, early and first stage. **Industry Preferences:** Communications and media, computer hardware and software, Internet specific, semiconductors and other electronics. **Geographic Preferences:** West Coast.

58117 ■ Palm Ventures
400 N. McCarthy Blvd.
Milpitas, CA 95035
Ph:(408)503-7000
Fax: (408)503-2750
URL: http://www.palm.com
Contact: Judy Bruner, Chief Financial Officer
Preferred Investment Size: $1,000,000 to $5,000,000. **Investment Policies:** Early stage. **Industry Preferences:** Communications. **Geographic Preferences:** U.S. S.

58118 ■ Palo Alto Venture Partners / 21VC Oartners
151 Lytton Ave.
Palo Alto, CA 94301
Ph:(650)462-1221
Fax: (650)462-1227
URL: http://www.pavp.com
Contact: Neil Weintraut, Partner
Preferred Investment Size: $1,000,000 to $10,000,000. **Investment Policies:** Start-up, seed, early and first stage. **Industry Preferences:** Internet specific, computer software and services, communications and media, other products, and consumer related. **Geographic Preferences:** U.S.

58119 ■ Palomar Ventures
100 Wilshire Blvd., Ste. 450
Santa Monica, CA 90401
Ph:(310)260-6050
Fax: (310)656-4150
URL: http://www.palomarventures.com
Contact: Amanda Reed, Partner
Preferred Investment Size: $250,000 to $15,000,000. **Investment Types:** Seed, start-up, first and early stage, and expansion. **Industry Preferences:** Communications and media, Internet specific, computer software and services, computer hardware, consumer releated, and other products. **Geographic Preferences:** Northern California, Southwest, West Coast, and U.S.

58120 ■ Paragon Venture Partners
3000 Sand Hill Rd.
Bldg. 1, Ste. 275
Menlo Park, CA 94025
Ph:(650)854-8000
Fax: (650)854-7260
Preferred Investment Size: $500,000 to $1,500,000. **Investment Types:** Start-up, seed, first and second stage, and special situation. **Industry Preferences:** Medical and health, computer software, hardware and services, communications and media, biotechnology, consumer related, semiconductors and other electronics, industrial and energy, and Internet specific.

58121 ■ Partech International
50 California St., Ste. 3200
San Francisco, CA 94111
Ph:(415)788-2929
Fax: (415)788-6763
URL: http://www.partechvc.com
Contact: Colin Born, Principal
Preferred Investment Size: $1,000,000 to $15,000,000. **Investment Types:** Seed, early and later stage. **Industry Preferences:** Internet specific, computer software, hardware and services, communications and media, semiconductors and other electronics, medical and health, consumer related, biotechnology, industrial and energy. **Geographic Preferences:** U.S.

58122 ■ Pathfinder Venture Capital Funds (Menlo Park)
3000 Sand Hill Rd.
Bldg. 3, Ste. 255
Menlo Park, CA 94025
Ph:(650)854-0650
Fax: (650)854-4706
Preferred Investment Size: $2,000,000 minimum. **Investment Types:** Seed, start-up, first and second stage, mezzanine, leveraged buyout, and special situation. **Industry Preferences:** Medical and health, computer software and services, semiconductors and other electronics, communications and media, biotechnology, industrial and energy, computer hardware, other products, and consumer related. **Geographic Preferences:** U.S. and Canada.

58123 ■ Patricof & Co. Ventures, Inc. (Palo Alto)
2100 Geng Rd., Ste. 150
Palo Alto, CA 94303
Ph:(650)494-9944
Fax: (650)494-6751
URL: http://www.patricof.com
Preferred Investment Size: $5,000,000 minimum. **Investment Types:** Seed, start-up, first and second stage, mezzanine, and leveraged buyout. **Industry Preferences:** Diversified. **Geographic Preferences:** No preference.

58124 ■ Peninsula Equity Partners
3000 Sand Hill Rd.
Bldg. 3, Ste. 125
Menlo Park, CA 94025
Ph:(650)854-0314
Fax: (650)854-0670
URL: http://www.peninsulaequity.com
Contact: Gregory Robinson, Principal
Investment Policies: First and second stage. **Industry Preferences:** Computer software, and medical and health.

58125 ■ Phoenix Growth Capital
2401 Kerner Blvd.
San Rafael, CA 94901
Ph:(415)485-4519
Fax: (415)485-4663
URL: http://www.phoenixgrowthcapital.com
Preferred Investment Size: $250,000 to $1,000,000. **Investment Types:** First and second stage, and mezzanine. **Industry Preferences:** Communications, computer related, consumer retailing, distribution, electronics, genetic engineering, medical and health related, education, publishing, and transportation. **Geographic Preferences:** U.S.

58126 ■ Prescient Capital
535 Pacific Ave., Ste. 400
San Francisco, CA 94133
Ph:(415)675-6750
Fax: (415)675-6755
URL: http://www.prcap.com
Contact: Eric Mathewson, Managing Director
Investment Types: Early stage. **Industry Preferences:** Communications and media, computer hardware and software, Internet specific, and consumer related. **Geographic Preferences:** Colorado and Northern California.

58127 ■ Prospect Venture Partners / Prospect Management LLC
435 Tasso, Ste. 200
Palo Alto, CA 94301
Ph:(650)470-8116
Fax: (650)324-8838
Contact: Alexander Barkas, Managing Director
Preferred Investment Size: $1,000,000 to $50,000,000. **Investment Types:** Seed, start-up, first and second stage, early and later stage, expansion, and special situation. **Industry Preferences:** Biotechnology, medical and health, computer software and services, semiconductors and other electronics. **Geographic Preferences:** U.S.

58128 ■ Putnam Lovell NBF Capital Partners, L.P.
550 Deep Valley Dr., Ste. 293
Rolling Hills Estates, CA 90274
Ph:(310)750-3620
Fax: (310)265-1920
URL: http://www.putnamlovell.com
Contact: Donald Putnam, Chief Executive Officer
Preferred Investment Size: $5,000,000 to $50,000,000. **Investment Types:** Seed, start-up, early, first, second and later stage, acquisition, balanced, expansion, leveraged buyout, management buyouts, and special situation. **Industry Preferences:** Financial services. **Geographic Preferences:** U.S. and Canada.

58129 ■ Quest Ventures
601 Montgomery, Ste. 700
San Francisco, CA 94111
Ph:(415)782-1414
Fax: (415)782-1415
Preferred Investment Size: $300,000 to $1,000,000. **Investment Types:** Seed, start-up, early, first and second stage, and special situation. **Industry Preferences:** Communications and media, computer related, semiconductors and other electronics, biotechnology, medical and health, consumer related, industrial and energy, financial services, and manufacturing. **Geographic Preferences:** Southwest and West Coast.

58130 ■ Red Rock Ventures
180 Lytton Ave.
Palo Alto, CA 94301
Ph:(650)325-3111
Fax: (650)853-7044
URL: http://www.redrockventures.com
Contact: Carol Pereira, Chief Financial Officer
Preferred Investment Size: $500,000 to $5,000,000. **Investment Policies:** Seed, early and first stage. **Industry Preferences:** Computer software and services, Internet specific, communications and media, computer hardware, and industrial and energy. **Geographic Preferences:** West Coast.

58131 ■ Redleaf Group, Inc.
14395 Saratoga Ave., Ste. 130
Saratoga, CA 95070
Ph:(408)868-0800
Fax: (408)868-0810
URL: http://www.redleaf.com
Contact: Charles Sum, Managing Director
Preferred Investment Size: $1,000,000 to $20,000,000. **Investment Types:** Seed and first stage. **Industry Preferences:** Computer software and services, Internet specific, medical and health, communications and media, consumer related, and other products. **Geographic Preferences:** California.

58132 ■ Redrock Ventures
180 Lytton Ave.
Palo Alto, CA 94301
Ph:(650)325-3111
Fax: (650)853-7044
URL: http://www.redrockventures.com
Contact: Carol Pereira, Chief Financial Officer
Preferred Investment Size: $500,000 to $5,000,000. **Investment Types:** Seed, early and first stage. **Industry Preferences:** Internet specific, computer software and services, computer hardware, communications and media, industrial and energy, medical and health. **Geographic Preferences:** West Coast.

58133 ■ Rembrandt Venture Partners
2200 Sand Hill Rd., Ste. 160
Menlo Park, CA 94025
Ph:(650)326-7070
Fax: (650)326-3780
URL: http://www.rembrandtvc.com
Contact: Heather Alexander, Chief Financial Officer
Investment Policies: Early stage. **Industry Preferences:** Communications, and Internet specific. **Geographic Preferences:** U.S.

58134 ■ Ridge Ventures
1728 Union St., Ste. 205
San Francisco, CA 94123
Ph:(415)674-1357
Fax: (650)652-1504
Contact: Eric Hautemont, Managing Director
Preferred Investment Size: $20,000 to $2,000,000. **Investment Policies:** Seed and early stage. **Geographic Preferences:** West Coast.

58135 ■ Riordan Lewis & Haden
300 South Grand Ave., 29th Fl.
Los Angeles, CA 90071
Ph:(213)229-8500
Fax: (213)229-8597
Preferred Investment Size: $2,000,000 minimum. **Investment Types:** First and second stage, start-up, leveraged buyout, and special situation. **Industry Preferences:** Computer software, medical and health, consumer related, industrial and energy, transportation, business service, and manufacturing. **Geographic Preferences:** West Coast.

58136 ■ Robertson-Stephens Co.
555 California St., Ste. 2600
San Francisco, CA 94104
Ph:(415)781-9700
Fax: (415)781-2556
URL: http://www.omegaadventures.com
Description: Private venture capital firm. Considers investments in any attractive merging-growth area, including product and service companies. Key preferences include health care, communications and technology, biotechnology, software, and information services. Maximum investment is $5 million.

58137 ■ Rocket Ventures
3000 Sand Hill Rd., Ste. 240
Menlo Park, CA 94025
Ph:(650)566-1565
Fax: (650)853-1748
URL: http://www.rocketventures.com
Contact: David Adams, Managing Director
Preferred Investment Size: $1,000,000 to $8,000,000. **Investment Types:** Seed, start-up, and early stage. **Industry Preferences:** Communications and media, computer software, and Internet specific. **Geographic Preferences:** California and West Coast.

58138 ■ Rosewood Capital, L.P.
1 Maritime Plz., Ste. 1330
San Francisco, CA 94111-3503
Ph:(415)362-5526
Fax: (415)362-1192
URL: http://www.rosewoodvc.com
Contact: Kevin Reilly, Principal
E-mail: kevin@rosewoodvc.com
Preferred Investment Size: $5,000,000 to $20,000,000. **Investment Types:** Second stage, leveraged buyout, special situation and control-block purchases. **Industry Preferences:** Consumer related, Internet specific, Computer software and services, communications and Media, biotechnology, and other products. **Geographic Preferences:** U.S.

58139 ■ RWI Group
835 Page Mill Rd.
Palo Alto, CA 94304-1011
Ph:(650)251-1800
Fax: (650)213-8660
URL: http://www.rwigroup.com
Contact: Donald Lucas, Managing Director
Preferred Investment Size: $500,000 to $8,000,000. **Investment Types:** Start-up, early, first and second

stage. **Industry Preferences:** Internet specific, computer software and services, computer hardware, communications and media, semiconductors and other electronics, medical and health, other products, industrial and energy. **Geographic Preferences:** U.S.

58140 ■ Saderling Ventures
2730 Sand Hill Rd., Ste. 200
Menlo Park, CA 94025
Ph:(650)854-9855
Fax: (650)854-9855
URL: http://www.saderling.com
Contact: Timothy Wollaeger, Managing Director
Preferred Investment Size: $500,000 to $5,000,000. **Investment Types:** Seed, start-up, early stage, and mezzanine. **Industry Preferences:** Biotechnology, medical and health, Internet specific, computer software and services, computer hardware, semiconductors and other electronics, industrial and energy, communications and media, and consumer related. **Geographic Preferences:** U.S. and Canada.

58141 ■ Saints Ventures
475 Sansome St., Ste. 1850
San Francisco, CA 94111
Ph:(415)773-2080
Fax: (415)835-5970
URL: http://www.saintsvc.com
Contact: Kenneth Sawyer, Managing Director
Investment Policies: Early stage. **Industry Preferences:** Communications, computer software, and Internet specific. **Geographic Preferences:** U.S.

58142 ■ Sanderling Ventures
400 S. El Camino Real, Ste. 1200
San Mateo, CA 94402
Ph:(650)401-2000
Fax: (650)375-7077
URL: http://www.sanderling.com
Contact: Donald Huffman, Chief Financial Officer
Preferred Investment Size: $2,000,000 to $5,000,000. **Investment Policies:** Seed, start-up, early and later stage. **Industry Preferences:** Biotechnology, medical and health, industrial and energy, Internet specific, computer software and services, other products, communications and media, computer hardware, and semiconductors and other electronics. **Geographic Preferences:** National.

58143 ■ Sandton Financial Group
6320 Canoga Ave., Ste. 1500
Woodland Hills, CA 91367
Ph:(818)702-9283
Contact: Lawrence Gaiber, President
Preferred Investment Size: $250,000 to $20,000,000. **Investment Types:** Seed, start-up, early and first stage, turnaround, expansion, mezzanine, private placement, distressed debt, joint ventures, recapitalizations, and special situation. **Geographic Preferences:** U.S. and Canada.

58144 ■ SBV Venture Partners / Sigefi, Burnette & Vallee
1400 Fashion Island Blvd., Ste. 600
San Mateo, CA 94404
Ph:(650)522-0085
Fax: (650)522-0087
URL: http://www.sbvpartners.com
Contact: James Burnette, General Partner
Preferred Investment Size: $500,000 to $2,500,000. **Investment Policies:** Seed, start-up, research and development, early and first stage. **Industry Preferences:** Communications, computer hardware and software, Internet specific, semiconductors and other electronics, biotechnology, and medical and health. **Geographic Preferences:** West Coast.

58145 ■ Selby Venture Partners
3500 Alameda de las Pulgas, Ste. 200
Menlo Park, CA 94025
Ph:(650)854-7399
Fax: (650)854-7039
URL: http://www.selbyventures.com
Contact: Robert Marshall, Managing Partner
Preferred Investment Size: $500,000 to $7,000,000. **Investment Types:** Seed, early and first stage. **In-**

dustry Preferences: Internet specific, communications and media, consumer related, computer software, and services, computer hardware, semiconductors and other electronics. Geographic Preferences: Northern California, Southern California, and West Coast.

58146 ■ Semper Ventures
325M Sharon Park Dr., Ste. 200
Menlo Park, CA 94025
Ph:(847)589-4197
URL: http://www.semperventures.com
Contact: Victor Lee, Managing Partner
Preferred Investment Size: $500,000 to $2,000,000. Investment Policies: Early and later stage. Industry Preferences: Computer software. Geographic Preferences: National.

58147 ■ Sequoia Capital
3000 Sand Hill Rd.
Bldg. 4, Ste. 180
Menlo Park, CA 94025
Ph:(650)854-3927
Fax: (650)854-2977
URL: http://www.sequoiacap.com
Contact: Greg McAdoo, Partner
Preferred Investment Size: $50,000 to $10,000,000. Investment Types: Early, seed, start-up, first and second stage and expansion. Industry Preferences: Internet specific, communications and media, computer software and services, computer hardware, other products, semiconductors and other electronics, medical and health, consumer related, biotechnology, industrial and energy. Geographic Preferences: West Coast.

58148 ■ Shoreline Venture Management, LLC
675 Mariners Island Blvd., Ste. 109
San Mateo, CA 94404
Ph:(650)854-6685
Fax: (415)389-6757
URL: http://www.shorelineventures.com
Contact: Peter Craddock, Managing Director
Investment Policies: Seed and early stage. Industry Preferences: Consumer related. Geographic Preferences: National.

58149 ■ Sienna Ventures / Sienna Holdings Inc.
2330 Marinship Way, Ste. 130
Sausalito, CA 94965
Ph:(415)339-2800
Fax: (415)339-2805
URL: http://www.siennaventures.com
Contact: Daniel Skaff, Managing Director
Preferred Investment Size: $35,000,000 minimum. Investment Types: Start-up, early, first and second stage, and balanced. Industry Preferences: Internet specific, computer software and services, consumer related, computer hardware, communications and media, other products, and semiconductors and other electronics. Geographic Preferences: U.S. and Canada.

58150 ■ Sierra Ventures
3000 Sand Hill Rd., Ste. 100
Menlo Park, CA 94025
Ph:(650)854-1000
Fax: (650)854-5593
URL: http://www.sierraventures.com
Preferred Investment Size: $10,000,000 to $15,000,000. Investment Types: Seed, start-up, early, first and second stage. Industry Preferences: Internet specific, computer software and services, computer hardware, communications and media, medical and health, semiconductors and other electronics, industrial and energy, biotechnology, and consumer related. Geographic Preferences: West Coast.

58151 ■ Sigma Partners (Menlo Park)
1600 El Camino Real, Ste. 280
Menlo Park, CA 94025
Ph:(650)853-1700
Fax: (650)853-1717
URL: http://www.sigmapartners.com
Contact: Lawrence Finch, Managing Director

Preferred Investment Size: $1,000,000 minimum. Investment Types: Start-up, early stage, and expansion. Industry Preferences: Internet specific, computer hardware, computer software and services, communications and media, semiconductors and other electronics, industrial and energy, consumer related, medical and health, and other products. Geographic Preferences: U.S.

58152 ■ Signia Ventures
411 Borel Ave., Ste. 510
San Mateo, CA 94402
Ph:(650)372-1200
Fax: (650)372-1212
URL: http://www.signiaventures.com
Contact: Lawrence Braitman, Managing Director
Investment Types: Early stage. Industry Preferences: Internet specific. Geographic Preferences: Northern California.

58153 ■ Silicon Valley Bancventures / Silicon Valley Bank (Menlo Park)
3000 Sand Hill Rd.
Bldg. 3, Ste. 150
Menlo Park, CA 94025
Ph:(650)233-7420
Fax: (650)233-9061
URL: http://www.svb.com
Contact: Aaron Gershenberg, Managing Director
Preferred Investment Size: $500,000 to $1,000,000. Investment Types: Start-up, first and second stage, and mezzanine. Industry Preferences: Internet specific, communications and media, semiconductors and other electronics, computer software and services, medical and health, consumer related, computer hardware, and other products. Geographic Preferences: U.S.

58154 ■ Skyline Ventures
125 University Ave.
Palo Alto, CA 94301
Ph:(650)462-5800
Fax: (650)329-1090
URL: http://www.skylineventures.com
Contact: John Freund, Managing Director
Investment Types: Early stage. Industry Preferences: Medical and health, biotechnology, computer software and services, Internet specific, semiconductors and other electronics. Geographic Preferences: U.S.

58155 ■ Sofinnova Ventures
140 Geary St., 10th Fl.
San Francisco, CA 94108
Ph:(415)228-3380
Fax: (415)228-3390
URL: http://www.sofinnova.com
Contact: Eric Buatois, Managing Director
Preferred Investment Size: $5,000,000 to $9,000,000. Investment Types: Seed, start-up, early, first and second stage, and mezzanine. Industry Preferences: Internet specific, computer software and services, computer hardware, biotechnology, medical and health, communications and media, semiconductors and other electronics, industrial and energy, and other products. Geographic Preferences: Northeast and West Coast.

58156 ■ Sorrento Ventures
4370 LaJolla Village Dr., Ste. 1040
San Diego, CA 92122
Ph:(619)452-3100
Fax: (619)452-7607
URL: http://www.sorrentoventures.com
Contact: Robert Jaffe, President/Founder
Preferred Investment Size: $1,000,000 to $3,000,000. Investment Types: Early, first and second stage. Industry Preferences: Medical and health, computer software and services, Internet specific, biotechnology, communications and media, consumer related, computer hardware, industrial and energy. Geographic Preferences: Southern California.

58157 ■ Southern California Ventures
406 Amapola Ave. Ste. 125
Torrance, CA 90501

Ph:(310)787-4381
Fax: (310)787-4382
Preferred Investment Size: $300,000 to $1,000,000. Investment Types: Seed, start-up, and first stage. Industry Preferences: Communications and media, medical and health. Geographic Preferences: West Coast.

58158 ■ Sprout Group (Menlo Park)
3000 Sand Hill Rd.
Bldg. 3, Ste. 170
Menlo Park, CA 94025
Ph:(650)234-2700
Fax: (650)234-2779
URL: http://www.sproutgroup.com
Contact: Simon Guenzl, Vice President
Preferred Investment Size: $5,000,000 to $50,000,000. Investment Types: Start-up, early and later stage, expansion, leveraged buyout, and management buyouts. Industry Preferences: Medical and health, computer hardware, Internet specific, communications and media, biotechnology, consumer related, computer software and services, semiconductors and other electronics, industrial and energy, and other products. Geographic Preferences: U.S.

58159 ■ Starting Point Partners
45 Glengarry Way
Hillsborough, CA 94010
Ph:(650)722-1035
URL: http://www.startingpointpartners.com
Contact: John Chang, General Partner
Preferred Investment Size: $200,000 to $1,000,000. Investment Types: Early stage.

58160 ■ Summit Partners (Palo Alto)
499 Hamilton Ave., Ste. 200
Palo Alto, CA 94301
Ph:(650)321-1166
Fax: (650)321-1188
URL: http://www.summitpartners.com
Contact: C.J. Fitzgerald, Principal
Preferred Investment Size: $10,000,000 to $150,000,000. Investment Types: Second and later stage, balanced, mezzanine, generalist PE, leveraged buyout, special situation, and control-block purchases. Industry Preferences: Computer software and services, computer hardware, communications and media, Internet specific, semiconductors and other electronics, medical and health, consumer related, biotechnology, industrial and energy, and other products. Geographic Preferences: U.S. and Canada.

58161 ■ Sundance Venture Partners, L.P.
100 Clocktower Place, Ste. 130
Carmel, CA 93923
Preferred Investment Size: $800,000 minimum. Investment Types: First and second stage, mezzanine, leveraged buyout, and special situations. Geographic Preferences: Southwest and West Coast.

58162 ■ Sutter Hill Ventures
755 Page Mill Rd., Ste. A-200
Palo Alto, CA 94304
Ph:(650)493-5600
Fax: (650)858-1854
URL: http://www.shv.com
Contact: David Anderson, Managing Director
Preferred Investment Size: $100,000 to $10,000,000. Investment Types: Seed, start-up, early, and first stage. Industry Preferences: Computer software and services, Internet specific, computer hardware, communications and media, medical and health, biotechnology, semiconductors and other electronics, consumer related, industrial and energy, and other products. Geographic Preferences: U.S.

58163 ■ Sybase, Inc.
5000 Hacienda Dr.
Dublin, CA 94568
Ph:(925)236-6215
Fax: (925)236-6815
URL: http://www.sybase.com
Contact: John Chen, President, Chief Executive Officer, Chai
Preferred Investment Size: $500,000 to $5,000,000. Investment Types: Seed, early stage, and expan-

sion. **Industry Preferences:** Computer software, and Internet specific. **Geographic Preferences:** U.S.

58164 ■ Synopsys, Inc.
700 E. Middlefield Rd.
MVA-23
Mountain View, CA 94043
Ph:(650)584-1481
URL: http://www.synopsys.com/corporate/venture.
  html
Contact: Michael O Brien, Vice President
Preferred Investment Size: $500,000 to $5,000,000. **Investment Types:** Seed, start-up, early, first, second, and later stage, and expansion. **Industry Preferences:** Semiconductors and other electronics, computer software and services, and computer hardware.

58165 ■ TA Associates, Inc. (Menlo Park)
70 Willow Rd., Ste. 100
Menlo Park, CA 94025
Ph:(650)328-1210
Fax: (650)326-4933
URL: http://www.ta.com
Contact: Michael C. Child, Managing Director
E-mail: mchild@ta.com
Preferred Investment Size: $30,000,000 to $300,000,000. **Investment Types:** Later stage, leveraged buyout, management buyouts, mezzanine, expansion, and recapitalizations. **Industry Preferences:** Computer Software and services, computer hardware, communications and media, Internet specific, medical and health, semiconductors and other electronics, consumer related, industrial and energy, biotechnology, and other products. **Geographic Preferences:** U.S. and Canada.

58166 ■ Tallwood Venture Capital
635 Waverly St.
Palo Alto, CA 94301
Ph:(650)473-6750
URL: http://www.tallwoodvc.com
Contact: Dado Banatao, Managing Partner
Investment Policies: start-up, early stage, and balanced. **Industry Preferences:** Communications, and semiconductors and other electronics. **Geographic Preferences:** U.S.

58167 ■ Taylor and Turner
220 Montgomery St.
Penthouse 10
San Francisco, CA 94104-3402
Ph:(415)398-6325
Fax: (415)398-3220
Preferred Investment Size: $300,000 to $500,000. **Investment Types:** Seed, start-up, first stage, control-block purchases, leveraged buyout, and special situation. **Industry Preferences:** Communications and media, computer hardware and software, medical and health, and consumer related. **Geographic Preferences:** West Coast.

58168 ■ Techfarm Ventures / Techfund Capital
4750 Patrick Henry Dr.
Santa Clara, CA 95054
Ph:(408)492-0142
Fax: (408)492-0182
URL: http://www.techfarm.com
Contact: Gordon Campbell, Managing Director
Preferred Investment Size: $1,500,000 to $10,000,000. **Investment Types:** Seed, early, first, and later stage. **Industry Preferences:** Semiconductors and other electronics, computer software and services, Internet specific, communications and media. **Geographic Preferences:** Northern California and U.S.

58169 ■ Technology Crossover Ventures (TCV)
528 Ramona St.
Palo Alto, CA 94301
Ph:(650)614-8200
Fax: (650)614-8222
URL: http://www.tcv.com
Contact: A. Brooke Seawell, Venture Partner
Preferred Investment Size: $10,000 to $60,000,000. **Investment Types:** Start-up, first and second stage,

and mezzanine. **Industry Preferences:** Internet specific, computer software, hardware and services, communications and media, consumer related, semiconductors and other electronics, and biotechnology. **Geographic Preferences:** U.S and Canada.

58170 ■ Technology Funding
1107 Investment Blvd., Ste. 180
El Dorado Hills, CA 95762
Ph:(916)941-1400
Fax: (916)941-7551
Contact: Charles Kokesh, Managing General
  Partner
Preferred Investment Size: $500,000 to $2,000,000. **Investment Types:** Early stage, expansion, and joint ventures. **Industry Preferences:** Industrial and energy, biotechnology, medical and health, computer software and services, computer hardware, other products, Internet specific, semiconductors and other electronics, communications and media. **Geographic Preferences:** Northern California.

58171 ■ Technology Partners
550 University Ave.
Palo Alto, CA 94301
Ph:(650)289-9000
Fax: (650)289-9001
URL: http://www.technologypartners.com
Contact: Ira Ehrenpreis, General Partner
Preferred Investment Size: $2,000,000 to $8,000,000. **Investment Types:** Seed, early and first stage. **Industry Preferences:** Internet specific, medical and health, communications and media, computer software and services, consumer related, biotechnology, semiconductors and other electronics, computer hardware, industrial and energy, and other products. **Geographic Preferences:** West Coast.

58172 ■ Telos Venture Partners
835 Page Mill Rd.
Palo Alto, CA 94304
Ph:(650)251-1850
Fax: (650)213-9060
URL: http://www.telosvp.com
Contact: Bruce Bourbon, Managing General Partner
Preferred Investment Size: $1,000,000 to $3,000,000. **Investment Types:** Early, first and second stage. **Industry Preferences:** Internet specific, computer software and services, computer hardware, semiconductors and other electronics, communications and media, and other products. **Geographic Preferences:** Northern California, Northwest, and West Coast.

58173 ■ Thompson Clive & Partners Limited (Menlo Park)
3000 Sand Hill Rd.
Bldg. 1, Ste. 185
Menlo Park, CA 94025
Ph:(650)854-0314
Fax: (650)854-0670
URL: http://www.tcvc.com
Contact: Greg Ennis, Principal
Preferred Investment Size: $500,000 to $2,000,000. **Investment Types:** Early stage, expansion, management buyouts, recapitalizations, and turnaround. **Industry Preferences:** Communications and media, computer software and services, Internet specific, computer hardware, semiconductors and other electronics, biotechnology, medical and health, consumer related, industrial and energy, and manufacturing. **Geographic Preferences:** U.S.

58174 ■ Ticonderoga Capital Inc.
40 William St., Ste., G20
Wellesley, MA 02481
Ph:(781)416-3400
Fax: (781)416-9868
Contact: Craig Jones, Managing Partner
Preferred Investment Size: $5,000,000 to $10,000,000. **Investment Types:** Later stage. **Industry Preferences:** Computer software, and services, industrial and energy, biotechnology, computer hardware, consumer related, semiconductors and other electronics, medical and health, communications and media, Internet specific, and other products. **Geographic Preferences:** U.S. and Canada.

58175 ■ Trinity Ventures
3000 Sand Hill Rd.
Bldg. 4, Ste. 160
Menlo Park, CA 94025
Ph:(650)854-9500
Fax: (650)854-9501
URL: http://www.trinityventures.com
Contact: Patricia Nakache, Principal
Preferred Investment Size: $5,000,000 to $20,000,000. **Investment Types:** Early stage. **Industry Preferences:** Internet specific, computer software and services, computer hardware, communications and media, consumer related, semiconductors and other electronics, medical and health, industrial and energy, and other products. **Geographic Preferences:** U.S.

58176 ■ Triune Capital
19925 Stevens Creek Blvd., Ste. 200
Cupertino, CA 95014
Ph:(310)284-6800
Fax: (310)284-3290
Preferred Investment Size: $1,000,000 minimum. **Investment Types:** Start-up, first and second stage, mezzanine, and special situation. **Industry Preferences:** Communications and media, computer software and hardware, Internet specific, semiconductors and other electronics, biotechnology, medical and health, consumer related, industrial and energy, and manufacturing. **Geographic Preferences:** West Coast.

58177 ■ Union Venture Corp.
445 S. Figueroa St., 9th Fl.
Los Angeles, CA 90071
Ph:(213)236-4092
Fax: (213)236-6329
Preferred Investment Size: $300,000 to $500,000. **Investment Types:** Second stage, mezzanine, leveraged buyout, and special situation. **Industry Preferences:** Communications and media. **Geographic Preferences:** U.S.

58178 ■ U.S. Venture Partners
2180 Sand Hill Rd., Ste. 300
Menlo Park, CA 94025
Ph:(650)854-9080
Fax: (650)854-3018
URL: http://www.usvp.com
Contact: William K. Bowes Jr., Founding Partner
E-mail: bbowes@usvp.com
Preferred Investment Size: $250,000 to $25,000,000. **Investment Types:** Seed, start-up, first and second stage, early and later stage, and expansion. **Industry Preferences:** Internet specific, computer software and services, computer hardware, communications and media, semiconductors and other electronics, consumer related, medical and health, biotechnology, industrial and energy, and other products. **Geographic Preferences:** U.S.

58179 ■ USVP-Schlein Marketing Fund
2180 Sand Hill Rd., Ste. 300
Menlo Park, CA 94025
Ph:(415)854-9080
Fax: (415)854-3018
URL: http://www.usvp.com
Description: Venture capital fund. Prefers specialty retailing/consumer products companies.

58180 ■ Vanguard Ventures
525 University Ave., Ste. 1200
Palo Alto, CA 94301
Ph:(650)321-2900
Fax: (650)321-2902
URL: http://www.vanguardventures.com
Contact: Donald Wood, General Partner
Preferred Investment Size: $500,000 to $10,000,000. **Investment Types:** Seed, early, and first stage, research and development. **Industry Preferences:** Communications and media, Internet specific, medical and health, semiconductors and other electronics, computer software and services, biotechnology, computer hardware, semiconductors and other electronics, industrial and energy, and other products. **Geographic Preferences:** U.S.

58181 ■ Venrock Associates (Menlo Park)
2494 Sand Hill Rd., Ste. 200
Menlo Park, CA 94025
Ph:(650)561-9580
Fax: (650)561-9180
URL: http://www.venrock.com
Contact: Anthony Sun, Managing General Partner
Preferred Investment Size: $5,000,000 to
$15,000,000. **Investment Types:** Seed, start-up, first,
early, and later stage. **Industry Preferences:** Biotechnology, Internet specific, computer software and
services, computer hardware, communications and
media, medical and health, semiconductors and other
electronics, industrial and energy, consumer related,
and other products. **Geographic Preferences:** U.S.

58182 ■ Ventana Capital Management, Inc.
(Irvine)
18881 Von Karman Ave.
Tower 17, Ste. 330
Irvine, CA 92612
Ph:(949)476-2204
Fax: (949)752-0223
URL: http://www.ventanaglobal.com
Contact: Elliot Parks, Managing Director
Preferred Investment Size: $1,000,000 minimum.
Investment Types: Early stage. **Industry Prefer-
ences:** Communications and media, semiconductors
and other electronics, biotechnology, medical and
health, and industrial and energy. **Geographic Pref-
erences:** Southern California.

58183 ■ Venture Growth Associates
2479 East Bayshore Rd., Ste. 710
Palo Alto, CA 94303
Ph:(650)855-9100
Fax: (650)855-9104
Contact: James Berdell, Managing Partner
Preferred Investment Size: $1,000,000 to
$2,000,000. **Investment Types:** Start-up, first and
second stage. **Industry Preferences:** Communications and media, computer software, semiconductors
and other electronics, computer related, and biotechnology. **Geographic Preferences:** Southwest.

58184 ■ VK Ventures
600 California St., Ste. 1700
San Francisco, CA 94111
Ph:(415)391-5600
Fax: (415)397-2744
Preferred Investment Size: $100,000 to $300,000.
Investment Types: Second stage, mezzanine, and
leveraged buyout. **Industry Preferences:** Communications and media, computer software, semiconductors and other electronics, biotechnology, medical and
health, consumer related, industrial and energy. **Geographic Preferences:** West Coast.

58185 ■ Walden International
1 California St., Ste. 2800
San Francisco, CA 94111
Ph:(415)765-7100
Fax: (415)765-7200
URL: http://www.waldenintl.com
Contact: Tzu-Hwa Hsu, Managing Director
Preferred Investment Size: $10,000,000 to
$25,000,000. **Investment Types:** Seed, start-up,
early and first stage. **Industry Preferences:** Communications and media, computer hardware, other products, Internet specific, semiconductors and other
electronics, computer Software and services, medical
and health, biotechnology, consumer related, industrial and energy. **Geographic Preferences:** U.S.

58186 ■ Wedbush Capital Partners
1000 Wilshire Blvd.
Los Angeles, CA 90017
Ph:(213)688-4545
Fax: (213)688-6642
URL: http://www.wedbush.com
Preferred Investment Size: $500,000 minimum. **In-
vestment Types:** Second stage, mezzanine, recapi-
talizations, and leveraged buyout. **Industry
Preferences:** Computer software and hardware, In-
ternet specific, medical and health, consumer related,
and business service. **Geographic Preferences:**
West Coast.

58187 ■ Westar Capital (Costa Mesa)
949 South Coast Dr., Ste. 650
Costa Mesa, CA 92626
Ph:(714)481-5160
Fax: (714)481-5166
URL: http://www.westarcapital.com
Contact: C. Rick Goolsby, Principal
Preferred Investment Size: $5,000,000 to
$10,000,000. **Investment Types:** Leveraged buy-
outs, special situation, control-block purchases, and
industry rollups. **Industry Preferences:** Communications and media, computer related, semiconductors
and other electronics, medical and health, consumer
related, industrial and energy, transportation, financial
services, and manufacturing. **Geographic Preferences:** Northwest, Southwest, Rocky Mountains, and
West Coast.

58188 ■ Western States Investment Group
9191 Towne Ctr. Dr., Ste. 310
San Diego, CA 92122
Ph:(858)678-0800
Fax: (858)678-0900
URL: http://www.wsig.com
Contact: William Patch, Vice President
Preferred Investment Size: $1,000,000 minimum.
Investment Types: Seed, start-up, first stage, re-
search and development, and leveraged buyout. **In-
dustry Preferences:** Industrial and energy, medical
and health, communications and media, semiconduc-
tors and other electronics, computer software and ser-
vices, and biotechnology. **Geographic Preferences:**
Southwest and West Coast.

58189 ■ Western Technology Investment
2010 N. First St., Ste. 310
San Jose, CA 95131
Ph:(408)436-8577
Fax: (408)436-8625
Preferred Investment Size: $500,000 to
$25,000,000. **Investment Types:** Seed, research and
development, start-up, first and second stage, mezzanine, balanced, and special situation. **Industry Preferences:** Communications and media,
semiconductors and other electronics, biotechnology,
medical and health, and manufacturing. **Geographic
Preferences:** U.S.

58190 ■ Windward Ventures (Westlake
Village)
717-A Lakefield Rd.
Westlake Village, CA 91361
Ph:(805)497-3222
Fax: (805)497-9331
Contact: James Cole, Managing Partner
Preferred Investment Size: $250,000 to $5,000,000.
Investment Types: Start-up, early, first, and second
stage. **Industry Preferences:** Medical and health, In-
ternet specific, computer software and services, com-
munications and media, semiconductors and other
electronics, and other products. **Geographic Prefer-
ences:** Southern California.

58191 ■ Woodside Fund
350 Marine Pky., Ste. 300
Redwood City, CA 94065
Ph:(650)610-8050
Fax: (650)610-8051
URL: http://www.woodsidefund.com
Contact: Thomas Shields, Principal
Preferred Investment Size: $3,000,000 to
$15,000,000. **Investment Types:** Seed, start-up,
early, and first stage. **Industry Preferences:** Computer software and services, biotechnology, communications and media, Internet specific, consumer related,
industrial and energy, medical and health, computer
hardware, other products, semiconductors and other
electronics. **Geographic Preferences:** Northern California and West Coast.

58192 ■ Worldview Technology Partners
435 Tasso St., Ste. 120
Palo Alto, CA 94301
Ph:(650)322-3200
Fax: (650)322-3880
URL: http://www.worldview.com
Contact: Terence Tan, Managing Director

Investment Types: Seed, research and development, start-up, first and second stage, balanced, and
mezzanine. **Industry Preferences:** Communications
and media, Internet specific, semiconductors and
other electronics, computer software, and services,
computer hardware, and other products. **Geographic
Preferences:** U.S.

PROCUREMENT
ASSISTANCE PROGRAMS

58193 ■ California Procurement Technical
Assistance Center–Federal Technology
Center Procurement Technical Assistance
Center
4600 Roseville Rd., Ste 100
Sacramento, CA 95660
Ph:(209)385-7686
Fax: (209)383-4959
Co. E-mail: jack@theftc.org
URL: http://www.theftc.org/PTAC
Contact: Jack Toney

58194 ■ California Procurement Technical
Assistance Center–Riverside Community
College District
14745 Riverside Dr.
Riverside, CA 92518
Ph:(951)571-6475
Fax: (951)653-1051
Co. E-mail: deborah.slayton@rcc.edu
URL: http://www.rcchelpsbusiness.com
Contact: Deborah Slayton

58195 ■ California Procurement Technical
Assistance Center–San Diego Contracting
Opportunities Center
4007 Camino Del S Rio, Ste 210
San Diego, CA -92108
Ph:(619)285-7022
Fax: (619)285-7030
Co. E-mail: gschalin@ptac-sandiego.org
URL: http://www.ptac-sandiego.org
Contact: Gunnar Schalin

INCUBATORS/RESEARCH
AND TECHNOLOGY PARKS

58196 ■ Business Technology Center of Los
Angeles County
2400 N Lincoln Ave.
West Altadena, CA 91001
Ph:(626)296-6300
Fax: (626)296-6301
Co. E-mail: info@labtc.org
URL: http://www.labtc.org
Contact: Mark Loeberman, Administrator
Description: The BTC committed to developing high
technology firms by providing financial, technical, and
business management assistance.

58197 ■ California Institute of
Technology–Office of Sponsored Research
1200 E California Blvd., MC 201-15
Pasadena, CA 91125
Ph:(626)395-6357
Fax: (626)795-4571
Co. E-mail: richard.seligman@caltech.edu
URL: http://www.atc.caltech.edu/osr
Contact: Richard P. Seligman, Dir.
E-mail: richard.seligman@caltech.edu
Scope: Responsible for administrative and financial
aspects of extramurally sponsored research conduct-
ed by faculty members and graduate students of the
Institute.

58198 ■ California State University,
Fresno–Office of Research and Sponsored
Programs
4910 N Chestnut Ave.
Fresno, CA 93726-1852
Ph:(559)278-0840

Fax: (559)278-0992
URL: http://www.csufresno.edu/grants/
Contact: Daniel J. Griffin, Assoc.Dir.
Scope: Supports research programs in academic and professional schools in the fields of agriculture, business, engineering, humanities, health and social work, physical and natural sciences, education, and behavioral and social sciences. **Publications:** Brochure; Reports. **Educational Activities:** Research symposium (annually), on current campus and community research.

58199 ■ California State University Fresno Foundation
4910 N Chestnut
Fresno, CA 93726-1852
Ph:(559)278-0850
Fax: (559)278-0992
Co. E-mail: kkompsi@csufresno.edu
URL: http://www.auxiliary.com/Foundation/index.htm
Contact: Keith Kompsi, Dir.
E-mail: kkompsi@csufresno.edu
Scope: Chemistry, biology, business, and agriculture. Administers grants and contracts for sponsored research performed by faculty members and graduate students of the University and generally promotes the interests of the University.

58200 ■ California State University, Long Beach–Office of University Research
1250 Bellflower Blvd.
Long Beach, CA 90840
Ph:(562)985-5314
Fax: (562)985-8665
Co. E-mail: research@csulb.edu
URL: http://www.csulb.edu/misc/research/
Contact: Dr. Jim Till, Dir.
E-mail: research@csulb.edu
Scope: Responsible for development and administration of research and creative activity in more than 70 academic departments and programs of the University conducted under grants and contracts funded by external public and private sources. Administers instructional innovation research and improvement funded by governmental agencies, private foundations, and industry. Also responsible for coordination of protection of human subjects, animal welfare, patent and copyright, and innovation policies. **Publications:** Annual Report; Research Notes (monthly).

58201 ■ California State University, Long Beach Foundation
6300 State University Dr. E, Ste. 332
Long Beach, CA 90815
Ph:(562)985-5537
Fax: (562)985-7951
Co. E-mail: rbehm@csulb.edu
URL: http://www.foundation.csulb.edu
Contact: Robert Behm, Exec.Dir.
E-mail: rbehm@csulb.edu
Scope: Responsible for financial administration of extramural grants to the University for research, campus programs, operations of performing arts center, and other activities.

58202 ■ California State University, Northridge–Office of Research and Sponsored Projects
18111 Nordhoff St.
Northridge, CA 91330-8232
Ph:(818)677-2901
Fax: (818)677-4691
Co. E-mail: mack.johnson@csun.edu
URL: http://www.csun.edu/graduatestudies/research.html
Contact: Mack I. Johnson, Assoc.VP
E-mail: mack.johnson@csun.edu
Scope: Administers and coordinates research at the University and provides support in all fields of scholarly activities for general faculty research projects and application efforts. **Publications:** Research Newsletter. **Awards:** Faculty Research and Creative Activity Awards Competition (annually).

58203 ■ Communications Technology Cluster (CTC)
300 Frank H. Ogawa Plaza, Ste. 210
Oakland, CA 94612-1932

Ph:(510)903-1902
Fax: (510)903-1952
Co. E-mail: info@ctcluster.com
URL: http://www.ctcluster.com
Contact: Joe Gross, Pres & CEO
Description: CTC provides services for startup and fledgling businesses within a broad definition of for-profit communications technology. Examples include radio and television, internet access, satellite technology, and many other types of firms.

58204 ■ The Greater Antelope Valley Economic Alliance
42060 10th. St W
Lancaster, CA 93534
Ph:(661)945-2741
Free: 800-888-7483
Fax: (661)945-7711
Co. E-mail: gavea@aveconomy.org
URL: http://www.aveconomy.org

58205 ■ Humboldt State University Foundation
PO Box 1185
Arcata, CA 95518-1185
Ph:(707)826-4189
Fax: (707)826-4783
Co. E-mail: hsuf@humboldt.edu
URL: http://www.humboldt.edu/~hsuf
Contact: Jacob Varkey, Pres.
E-mail: hsuf@humboldt.edu
Scope: Administers extramurally sponsored research and training projects conducted at the University in such areas as education, fisheries, forestry, wildlife management, oceanography, endangered species, mathematics, economics, computer information systems, business management, social welfare, psychology, geology, environmental resources engineering, and native American studies. Also raises funds and makes grants to the University. **Publications:** The Humboldt Stater (quarterly).

58206 ■ San Diego State University Research Foundation
Gateway Center
5250 Campanile Dr.
San Diego, CA 92182
Ph:(619)594-1900
Fax: (619)582-9164
Co. E-mail: sdsuf@foundation.sdsu.edu
URL: http://www.foundation.sdsu.edu
Contact: Frea Sladek, CEO
E-mail: sdsuf@foundation.sdsu.edu
Scope: Works with faculty and staff to develop and administer grants and contracts and community-service programs; develops and administers major centers, institutes, community partnerships and programs; administers a technology transfer program; administers student scholarship, loan funds and financially manages and invests gifts, trusts and endowments, most on behalf of the University's philanthropic foundation; and acquires, develops, and manages real property to provide space for sponsored programs.

58207 ■ San Francisco State University–Office of Research and Sponsored Programs
Administration Bldg., Rm. 471
1600 Holloway Ave.
San Francisco, CA 94132
Ph:(415)338-7094
Fax: (415)338-2493
Co. E-mail: kenp@sfsu.edu
URL: http://www.sfsu.edu/~orspwww/
Contact: Dr. Kenneth Paap, Assoc.VP
E-mail: kenp@sfsu.edu
Scope: Facilitates faculty research and scholarly and creative activities and assists faculty members in securing extramural funding by locating potential research sponsors and providing all budget, pre-award services, and post-award grant and contract management. Administers grant development and sponsored research activities funded by foundations and corporations. **Services:** Consultation, regarding the conceptualization, planning, networking, critiquing, and

editing of a proposal; National funding searches, by computer. **Publications:** Research News (quarterly). **Educational Activities:** Conferences, on federal and non-federal funding sources for faculty, grant office administrators, and the general public; Workshops, on proposal development and identification of funding sources, open to faculty members, University staff.

58208 ■ San Francisco State University Foundation, Inc.
PO Box 320160
San Francisco, CA 94132-0160
Ph:(415)338-2297
Fax: (415)338-7949
Co. E-mail: tthomas@sfsu.edu
URL: http://www.foundation.sfsu.edu
Contact: Don Scoble, Exec.Dir.
E-mail: tthomas@sfsu.edu
Scope: Administers a portion of research done at or in connection with San Francisco State University.

58209 ■ San Jose Software Business Cluster
2 N First St., Fourth Fl.
San Jose, CA 95113
Ph:(408)535-2701
Fax: (408)535-2711
Co. E-mail: info@sjsbc.org
URL: http://www.sjsbc.org
Contact: Chuck Erickson, Managing Director
Description: Small business incubator with capacity for 20 to 30 emerging software firms.

58210 ■ San Jose State University Foundation
210 N Franklin St., 4th Fl.
San Jose, CA 95112
Ph:(408)924-1400
Fax: (408)924-1499
Co. E-mail: jcarmo@foundation.sjsu.edu
URL: http://www.sjsu.foundation.org/
Contact: Jerri Carmo, Dir., Off. of Sponsored Prog.
E-mail: jcarmo@foundation.sjsu.edu
Scope: Develops, administers, and coordinates extramurally sponsored research and training, special projects, conferences, and short courses. Also administers a faculty research grant, provides seed support to faculty members, and develops campus policy with respect to research and advanced studies of the University with assistance of faculty-administrative research committees.

58211 ■ Stanford University–Office of Research and Graduate Policy
Bldg. 10, 2nd Fl.
Stanford, CA 94305-2061
Ph:(650)723-0977
Fax: (650)725-1653
Co. E-mail: charles.kruger@stanford.edu
Contact: Charles H. Kruger, Vice Provost/Dean
E-mail: charles.kruger@stanford.edu
Scope: Develops University research policy and manages independent research laboratories and centers.

58212 ■ Stanford University–Office of Sponsored Research
651 Serra St.Rm.260
Stanford, CA 94305-4125
Ph:(650)724-6613
Fax: (650)723-1654
Co. E-mail: pwebb@stanford.edu
URL: http://www.stanford.edu/dept/ORA/osr
Contact: Pamela Webb, Dir.
E-mail: pwebb@stanford.edu
Scope: Administers and coordinates extramurally sponsored research, education, and training programs conducted at the University. **Publications:** Sponsored Projects Proposal Preparation Manual.

58213 ■ Stanford University–Office of Technology Licensing
1705 El Camino Real
Palo Alto, CA 94306-1106
Ph:(650)723-0651
Fax: (650)725-7295
Co. E-mail: info@otlmail.stanford.edu
URL: http://otl.stanford.edu
Contact: Katharine Ku, Dir.

E-mail: info@otlmail.stanford.edu
Scope: Licenses technology in the fields of scientific and medical instruments, pharmaceuticals, chemicals, computer software and databases, integrated circuit technology, optics, and microbiology. Evaluates, markets, and negotiates licensing agreements with industry.

58214 ■ Stanford University–Stanford Research Park
2770 Sand Hill Rd.
Menlo Park, CA 94025
Ph:(650)926-0200
Fax: (650)926-2000
Co. E-mail: jsnider@stanford.edu
URL: http://www.stanfordmanage.org/smc_srp.html
Contact: Jean Snider
E-mail: jsnider@stanford.edu
Scope: 704-acre site linking research resources of the University with Park tenants, particularly in the areas of electronics, software, space, publishing, pharmaceutics, and biotechnology. Activities between park tenants and the University community include cooperative research ventures, instruction, and consulting.

58215 ■ University Auxiliary Services, Inc.
ADM 306
5151 State University Dr.
Los Angeles, CA 90032
Ph:(323)343-2526
Fax: (323)226-0436
Contact: Dean Calvo, Exec.Dir.
Scope: Administers research and other grants and contracts for projects conducted at the University. **Educational Activities:** Conferences; Workshops, both of noncredit.

58216 ■ University of California–Office of Technology Transfer
1111 Franklin St., 5th Fl.
Oakland, CA 94607-5200
Ph:(510)587-6000
Fax: (510)587-6090
Co. E-mail: william.tucker@ucop.edu
URL: http://www.ucop.edu/ott
Contact: William T. Tucker, Exec.Dir.
E-mail: william.tucker@ucop.edu
Scope: Facilitates technology transfer and research activities in biotechnology, health care, engineering, and chemical materials at the Berkeley, Davis, Irvine, Los Angeles, Merced, Riverside, San Diego, San Francisco, Santa Barbara, and Santa Cruz campuses.

58217 ■ University of California–State Governmental Relations Office
1130 K St., Ste. 340
Sacramento, CA 95814-3968
Ph:(916)445-9924
Fax: (916)445-1426
Co. E-mail: kristen.grodeon@ucop.edu
URL: http://ucop.edu/uer/state/welcome.html
Contact: Stephen A. Arditti, Asst. VP/Dir.
E-mail: kristen.grodeon@ucop.edu
Scope: Responsible for relations with executive and legislative branches of state government, both with respect to legislation and the University's research response to potential state policy problems.

58218 ■ University of California at Berkeley–Sponsored Projects Office
336 Sproul Hall, No. 5940
Berkeley, CA 94720-5940
Ph:(510)642-0120
Fax: (510)642-8236
Co. E-mail: pgates@berkeley.edu
URL: http://www.spo.berkeley.edu
Contact: Patricia Gates, Actg.Dir.
E-mail: pgates@berkeley.edu
Scope: Administers extramurally funded research contracts and grants at the University.

58219 ■ University of California, Davis–Office of Research
402 Mrak Hall
1 Shields Ave.
Davis, CA 95616

Ph:(530)752-6374
Fax: (530)754-7391
Co. E-mail: bmklein@ucdavis.edu
URL: http://www.research.ucdavis.edu
Contact: Barry M. Klein, Vice Chancellor
E-mail: bmklein@ucdavis.edu
Scope: Administers contracts, grants, and sponsored research activities. **Publications:** Supports for Teaching and Research.

58220 ■ University of California, Irvine–Office of Research and Graduate Studies
155 Administration Bldg.
Irvine, CA 92697
Ph:(949)824-5796
Fax: (949)824-2095
Co. E-mail: whparker@uci.edu
URL: http://www.rgs.uci.edu/
Contact: Prof. William H. Parker, Vice Chancellor for Res.
E-mail: whparker@uci.edu
Scope: Administers research programs and units at the University; fosters research development; obtains oversees grants, contracts, and research equipment; and sponsors technology transfer activities and animal and human research projects.

58221 ■ University of California, Irvine–Office of Technology Alliances
380 University Tower
Irvine, CA 92697-7700
Ph:(949)824-7295
Fax: (949)824-2899
Co. E-mail: schetter@uci.edu
URL: http://www.ota.uci.edu
Contact: David G. Schetter, Asst. Vice Chancellor
E-mail: schetter@uci.edu
Scope: University and industry partnership and cooperative research development, including industrial contract development, review, and approval; science and technology research identification; consortia participation; new consortia initiation; and federal and state science and technology center participation. **Services:** Technology transfer services (weekly), on licensed and emerging technologies and other materials.

58222 ■ University of California, San Diego–Office of Contract and Grant Administration
MC 0934
9500 Gilman Dr.
La Jolla, CA 92093-0934
Ph:(858)534-3330
Fax: (858)534-0280
Co. E-mail: ldale@ucsd.edu
URL: http://ocga2.ucsd.edu/
Contact: Linda Dale, Dir.
E-mail: ldale@ucsd.edu
Scope: Coordinates grants and contracts at the University.

58223 ■ University of California, Santa Barbara–Office of Research
3227 Cheadle Hall
Santa Barbara, CA 93106-2050
Ph:(805)893-4188
Fax: (805)893-2611
Co. E-mail: moore@research.ucsb.edu
URL: http://research.ucsb.edu
Contact: Louise Moore, Exec.Dir.
E-mail: moore@research.ucsb.edu
Scope: Responsible for administration of organized research units on Santa Barbara campus of the University, and for planning, developing, and supporting other research activities on campus. Present research plan stresses development of strengths in physical, mathematical and biological sciences and developments in marine biotechnology, ocean engineering and coastal zone, geological sciences, biomedical and neurosciences, remote sensing, special education, polymers, microelectronics, artificial intelligence, advanced materials, and society and culture. **Publications:** Research Newsletter (monthly).

58224 ■ University of Southern California–Office of Technology Licensing
3716 S Hope St., Ste. 313
Los Angeles, CA 90007
Ph:(213)743-2282
Fax: (213)744-1832
Co. E-mail: otl@usc.edu
URL: http://www.usc.edu/academe/otl
Contact: Roseanne Dutton, Dir.
E-mail: otl@usc.edu
Scope: Transfers technology from the University to the private sector, including the areas of medicine, engineering, pharmacy, and gerontology. **Publications:** Newsletter. **Educational Activities:** Seminars, for faculty and students.

58225 ■ US Market Access Center
111 N Market St., Ste. 600
San Jose, CA 95113-1101
Ph:(408)351-3300
Fax: (408)351-3330
Co. E-mail: info@usmarketaccess.com
URL: http://www.usmarketaccess.com
Contact: Bob Vander Woude, CEO
Description: IBI is a non-profit business incubator sponsored by a collaboration of business, government, and academic organizations. IBI is also qualified to assist business representatives new to the United States.

EDUCATIONAL PROGRAMS

58226 ■ American River College
4700 College Oak Dr.
Sacramento, CA 95841-4286
Ph:(916)484-8011
Fax: (916)484-8673
URL: http://www.arc.losrios.edu
Description: Two-year college offering small business management classes.

58227 ■ Chabot College
25555 Hesperian Blvd.
Hayward, CA 94545
Ph:(510)723-6700
Fax: (510)723-7510
URL: http://www.chabotcollege.edu
Description: Two-year college offering a program in entrepreneurship.

58228 ■ Cypress College
Business Office
9200 Valley View St.
Cypress, CA 90630
Ph:(714)484-7000
Fax: (714)527-4733
URL: http://www.cypress.cc.ca.us
Description: Regular business program includes courses on small business management, human relations, and related topics.

58229 ■ De Anza College
21250 Stevens Creek Blvd.
Cupertino, CA 95014
Ph:(408)864-5678
Fax: (408)864-5433
URL: http://www.deanza.fhda.edu
Description: Two-year college offering a small business management program. Certificate program includes marketing, finance, and management.

58230 ■ Empire College–School of Business
3035 Cleveland Ave.
Santa Rosa, CA 95403
Ph:(707)546-4000
Fax: (707)546-4058
Co. E-mail: rhurd@empcol.com
URL: http://www.empcol.com

E-mail: rhurd@empcol.com
Description: College offering a small business management program.

58231 ■ Lake Tahoe Community College
1 College Dr.
South Lake Tahoe, CA 96150-4524

Ph:(530)541-4660
Fax: (530)541-7852
URL: http://www.ltcc.cc.ca.us
Description: Two-year college offering a small business management program.

58232 ■ Ohlone College
43600 Mission Blvd.
Fremont, CA 94539
Ph:(510)659-6000
Fax: (510)659-7321
URL: http://www.ohlone.cc.ca.us
Description: Two-year college offering a small business management program.

58233 ■ Saddleback College
28000 Marguerite Pky.
Mission Viejo, CA 92692
Ph:(949)582-4500
Fax: (949)347-0438
URL: http://www.saddleback.cc.ca.us
Description: Two-year college offering a small business management program.

58234 ■ Santa Ana College
1530 W 17th St.
Santa Ana, CA 92706
Ph:(714)564-6000
Fax: (714)564-6370
URL: http://www.sac.edu
Description: Two-year college offering a small business management program.

58235 ■ Southwestern College
900 Otay Lakes Rd.
Chula Vista, CA 91910
Ph:(619)421-6700
Fax: (619)482-6402
URL: http://www.swc.cc.ca.us
Description: Two-year college offering a program in small business management.

TRADE PERIODICALS

58236 ■ *California Employer Advisor*
Pub: Employer Resource Institute Inc.
Ed: Larry J. Shapiro, Esq., Editor, lshapiro@arthcink. net. **Released:** Monthly. **Price:** $177, individuals. **Description:** The award-winning guide to California employment law and employee relations.

58237 ■ *California Labor and Employment ALERT Newsletter*
Pub: Castle Publications Ltd.
Contact: Richard Simmons, President
Released: Bimonthly. **Price:** $75; $85 includes 3-ring binder. **Description:** Reports on current developments in California and federal laws concerning personnel and employment issues. Recurring features include notices of publications available.

58238 ■ *California Labor and Employment Law Quarterly*
Pub: State Bar of California
Contact: Marty Fassler, Managing Editor
Released: Quarterly. **Description:** Contains information and news on California's labor and employment laws and regulations.

PUBLICATIONS

58239 ■ *The Business Journal Serving San Jose and Silicon Valley*
96 N. 3rd St., Ste. 100
San Jose, CA 95112-5560
Ph:(408)295-3800
Fax: (408)295-5028
Co. E-mail: sanjose@amcity.com
URL: http://www.amcity.com

58240 ■ *California Corporation Formation Package and Minute Book*
Oasis Press
300 N. Valley Dr.
Grants Pass, OR 97526

Ph:(541)479-9464
Free: 800-228-2275
Fax: (541)476-1479
Co. E-mail: psi2@magick.net
Ed: Kevin W. Finck. **Released:** Seventh edition, 1992. **Price:** $29.95 (paper); $39.95 (ringbound).

58241 ■ *How to Form Your Own California Corporation*
Nolo Press
950 Parker St.
Berkeley, CA 94710
Ph:(510)549-1976
Free: 800-992-6656
Fax: 800-645-0895
URL: http://www.nolo.com
Ed: Anthony Mancuso. **Released:** Seventh edition, 1988. **Price:** $29.95 (paper).

58242 ■ *Orange County Business Journal*
4590 McArthur, Ste. 100
Newport Beach, CA 92660
Ph:(714)833-8373
Fax: (714)833-8751
Co. E-mail: ocbj@ocbj.com
URL: http://ocbj@ocbj.com

58243 ■ *Sacramento Business Journal*
1401 21st St., Ste. 200
Sacramento, CA 95814-3120
Ph:(916)447-7661
Fax: (916)444-7779
Co. E-mail: tbj@ns.net
URL: http://www.amcity.com/sacramento

58244 ■ *San Diego Business Journal*
4909 Murphy Canyon Rd., Ste. 200
San Diego, CA 92123-4300
Ph:(619)277-6359
Fax: (619)571-3628
Co. E-mail: sdbj@sdbj.com
URL: http://www.sdbj.com

58245 ■ *Small Business Success*
Pacific Bell Directory
101 Spear St., Rm. 429
San Francisco, CA 94105
Ph:(415)995-3899
Ed: Andrea Hine, editor. **Price:** Free. **Description:** Contains articles on small business development in California. Includes a resource directory.

58246 ■ *Starting and Operating a Business in California: A Step-by-Step Guide*
PSI Research
300 N. Valley Dr.
Grants Pass, OR 97526
Ph:(503)479-9464
Free: 800-228-2275
Fax: (503)476-1479
Co. E-mail: psi2@magick.net
Ed: Michael D. Jenkins. **Released:** Revised edition, 1992. **Price:** $29.95 (looseleaf binder); $24.95 (paper). **Description:** Part of the Successful Business Library series.

PUBLISHERS

58247 ■ Adams-Blake Company Inc.
8041 Sierra St., Ste. 102
Fair Oaks, CA 95628-7530
Ph:(916)962-9296
Fax: (916)962-9296
Co. E-mail: info@adams-blake.com
URL: http://www.adams-blake.com
Contact: Alan N. Canton, President
E-mail: acanton@adams-blake.com
Description: Publishes business, career, and technology books. Accepts unsolicited manuscripts. Reaches market through direct mail, and wholesalers and distributors, including Baker & Taylor Books and Ingram Books. **Founded:** 1990.

58248 ■ Advisor Media Inc.
4849 Viewridge Ave.
PO Box 429002
San Diego, CA 92123

Ph:(858)278-5600
Free: 800-336-6060
Fax: (858)278-0300
Co. E-mail: CustomerService5Q3@Advisor.com
URL: http://www.advisormedia.com
Description: Publishes business related materials. **Founded:** 1983.

58249 ■ Ashar Press
1002 Elk Hills Dr.
PO Box 524
Galt, CA 95632
Ph:(209)745-4703
Free: 877-342-7427
Fax: (209)745-7776
Co. E-mail: Beverly@asharpress.com
URL: http://www.asharpress.com/
Contact: Beverly M. Breakey, President
Description: Publishes books on "health and healing." Titles include *Choose Life! Living Consciously in an Unconscious World.* **Founded:** 1999.

58250 ■ Association of Area Business Publications
4929 Wilshire Blvd., Ste. 428
Los Angeles, CA 90010-3817
Ph:(323)937-5514
Fax: (323)937-0959
Co. E-mail: info@alliancebizpubs.com
URL: http://www.bizpubs.org
Contact: C. James Dowden, Exec. Dir.
E-mail: jdowden@alliancebizpubs.com
Description: Publishes guides to local and regional business publications. Also publishes a monthly newsletter distributed by FAX to members and print industry personnel. Reaches market through commission representatives, direct mail, and advertisements. **Founded:** 1979.

58251 ■ Bay Tree Publishing
721 Creston Rd.
Berkeley, CA 94708
Ph:(510)526-2916
Fax: (510)525-0842
URL: http://www.baytreepublish.com/
Contact: David Cole, Editor
E-mail: dcole@baytreepublish.com
Description: Publishes nonfiction in the areas of current affairs, business, and psychology. **Founded:** 2002

58252 ■ Bell Springs Publishing
PO Box 1240
Willits, CA 95490
Ph:(707)459-6372
Free: 800-515-8050
Fax: (707)459-8614
Co. E-mail: info@bellsprings.com
URL: http://www.bellsprings.com
Contact: Bernard Kamoroff, Publisher
E-mail: kamoroff@saber.net
Description: Publishes small business guidebooks and pinball machine repair manuals. Reaches market through trade sales and wholesalers. Does not accept unsolicited manuscripts. **Founded:** 1976.

58253 ■ BizBest Media Corp.
860 Via de la Paz, Ste. D-4
Pacific Palisades, CA 90272
Ph:(310)230-6868
Free: 800-873-5205
Fax: (310)454-6130
Co. E-mail: info@bizbest.com
URL: http://bizbest.com
Contact: Daniel Kehrer, CEO
Description: Publishes a small business resources directory. **Founded:** 1999.

58254 ■ Blueprint Books
PO Box 10757
Pleasanton, CA 94588
Ph:800-605-2913
Fax: 800-605-2914
Co. E-mail: info@BlueprintBooks.com
URL: http://blueprintbooks.com
Contact: Bette Daoust
Description: Publishes business books.

58255 ■ Books on Business
5482 Burlingame Ave.
PO Box 313-G
Buena Park, CA 90621
Ph:(714)523-0357
Fax: (714)523-0357
Contact: James E. Kristy, Pub.
Description: Publishes on business topics. Also produces computer software. Reaches market through direct mail. Does not accept unsolicited manuscripts. **Founded:** 1970.

58256 ■ California State University Press
5241 N Maple Ave.
Fresno, CA 93740-8024
Ph:(559)278-3056
Fax: (559)278-6758
Co. E-mail: press@csufresno.edu
URL: http://www.csufresno.edu
Description: Publishes books on art, drama, music, film, the media, architecture, politics, business, and autobiography. Reaches market through Southern Illinois University Press. Does not accept unsolicited manuscripts. **Founded:** 1982.

58257 ■ CMP Books
6600 Silacci Way
Gilroy, CA 95020
Ph:(408)848-3854
Free: 800-500-6875
Fax: (408)848-5784
Co. E-mail: cmp@rushorder.com
URL: http://www.cmpbooks.com
Contact: Matthew Kelsey, Publisher
E-mail: mkelsey@cmp.com
Description: Publishes information on computing, design and communications solutions.

58258 ■ Collins Publications
3233 Grand Ave., Ste. N-294C
Chino Hills, CA 91709
Ph:(909)590-2471
Free: 800-795-8999
Fax: (909)628-9330
Co. E-mail: collins@collinspub.com
URL: http://www.collinspub.com
Contact: Ann Collins, President
Description: Publishes how-to, business, and self-help products. Offers an array of software training materials, such as videos, books and CD-ROMs. Also offers self publishing services. Reaches market through commission representatives, direct mail, trade sales, and wholesalers and distributors, including Baker & Taylor and Brodart. Does not accept unsolicited manuscripts. **Founded:** 1991.

58259 ■ Frontal Lobe
836 Starlite Ln.
Los Altos, CA 94024
Ph:(650)941-8561
Co. E-mail: masonc2@earthlink.net
URL: http://masonc.home.netcom.com
Contact: Mason A. Clark, Editor
E-mail: masonc2@earthlink.net
Description: Publishes small business management, entrepreneurship, religion and how-to books. **Founded:** 1978.

58260 ■ GifTech Corp.
2961 Industrial Rd., Ste. 731
Las Vegas, NV 89109
Free: 800-594-9829
Co. E-mail: taxmama@taxmama.com
URL: http://www.taxmama.com
Contact: Eva Rosenberg, Director
E-mail: taxwriter@taxmama.com
Description: Publishes information about tax, business, women, networking and e-books. Offers videotapes and calendars. Also offers a weekly newsletter. Does not accept unsolicited manuscripts. Reaches market through reviews, listings and the Internet. **Founded:** 1984.

58261 ■ Hunter Arts Publishing
PO Box 66578E
Los Angeles, CA 90066
Ph:(310)842-8864

Free: 877-443-2348
Fax: (310)842-8868
Co. E-mail: publisher@hunterarts.com
URL: http://www.hunterarts.com/
Contact: Darrell W. Gurney, Publisher
E-mail: careermeister@careersecrets.com
Description: Publishes *Headhunters Revealed! Career Secrets for Choosing and Using Professional Recruiters*-an executive recruiter that exposes the mind and mechanics of the search industry to job-seeking professionals. Does not accept unsolicited manuscripts. Reaches market through commission representatives, telephone sales, online, wholesalers and distributors, including Ingram, Baker and Taylor, Quality Books, and Partners Publishers Group. **Founded:** 1999.

58262 ■ IBIS/Business Information Services, International
PO Box 3271
Tustin, CA 92781-3271
Ph:(949)552-8494
Fax: (501)432-5112
Contact: Gabriel Z. Sopos, Gen Mgr
Description: Publishes book, audio-tape and video sets on various business topics for entrepreneurs and enterprising managers, business students, and business groups. Also publishes business manuals on a variety of topics. Reaches market through direct mail, trade sales, and through the distributor. Does not accept unsolicited manuscripts. **Founded:** 1980.

58263 ■ Ingram Micro Inc.
1600 E St. Andrew Pl.
PO Box 25125
Santa Ana, CA 92799-5125
Ph:(714)566-1000
Free: 800-456-8000
Fax: (714)566-7940
Co. E-mail: customer.service@ingrammicro.com
URL: http://www.ingrammicro.com
Contact: Kent Foster, CEO
Description: Wholesaler. **Founded:** 1983.

58264 ■ International Business & Management Institute
IBMI Ctr.
PO Box 3271
Tustin, CA 92781-3271
Ph:(949)552-8494
Fax: (501)432-5112
Co. E-mail: ibmi-books@juno.com
Contact: T. R. Balla, Dir. of Services
Description: Publishes on diverse business and management topics focusing on international trade and finance for entrepreneurs and managers. Also publishes booklets. Offers consulting and in-house educational programs. Distributes IBIS Business Reports. Reaches market through direct mail, internet, and trade promotions. Does not accept unsolicited manuscripts. **Founded:** 1970.

58265 ■ Janco Associates Inc.
11 Eagle Landing
Park City, UT 84060
Ph:(435)940-9300
Co. E-mail: information@e-janco.com
URL: http://www.e-janco.com
Description: Publishes paperless books on the Internet which focuses on management information systems. **Founded:** 1982.

58266 ■ Juice Gallery Multimedia
2042 Big Oak Ave.
PO Box 151
Chino Hills, CA 91709
Ph:(909)597-0791
Free: 800-710-8163
Fax: (909)597-0791
Co. E-mail: info@juicegallery.com
URL: http://www.juicegallery.com
Contact: Dan Titus, President
Description: Publishes materials related to staring a restaurant business. Accepts unsolicited manuscripts. Reaches market through direct mail, reviews, listings, telephone sales, and wholesalers Ingram and Baker & Taylor. **Founded:** 1992.

58267 ■ Ketab Bookstore
1419 Westwood Blvd.
Los Angeles, CA 90024
Ph:(310)477-7477
Fax: (310)444-7176
Co. E-mail: ketab1@ketab.com
URL: http://www.ketab.com
Contact: Bijan Khalili, Owner
Description: Distributes Persian books, music, videos, and posters. **Founded:** 1981.

58268 ■ Learning Forum
1725 S Coast Hwy.
Oceanside, CA 92054
Ph:(760)722-0072
Free: 800-285-3276
Fax: (760)722-3507
Co. E-mail: info@learningforum.com
URL: http://www.learningforum.com/
Contact: Bobbi DePorter
Description: Publishes books on teaching methods for educators and business training. **Founded:** 1981

58269 ■ Madson Group Inc.
PO Box 2489
Yelm, WA 98597
Ph:(360)446-5348
Free: 800-556-5131
Fax: (360)446-5234
Co. E-mail: findagroomer@atsearthlink.net
URL: http://www.mygroomingbusiness.com
Contact: Madeline Bright Ogle, President
E-mail: maddie2@earthlink.net
Description: Publishes on careers and business, pets, travel, education and management. Also publishes newsletters. Offers online services. Accepts unsolicited manuscripts. Reaches market through direct mail. **Founded:** 1987.

58270 ■ Mendham Publishing
515 S Figueroa St., Ste. 1800
Los Angeles, CA 90071
Ph:(213)622-0862
Free: 888-253-4710
Fax: (213)622-0842
URL: http://www.thepersonalbrandinggroup.com
Contact: Timothy P. O'Brien, CEO
E-mail: tob@thepersonabrandinggroup.com
Description: Publishes a book about personal branding. Does not accept unsolicited manuscripts. Reaches market through commission representatives, direct mail, and telephone sales. **Founded:** 1999

58271 ■ Monterey Media Inc.
566 St. Charles Dr.
Thousand Oaks, CA 91360
Ph:(805)494-7199
Free: 800-424-2593
Fax: (805)496-6061
Co. E-mail: orderenquiry@montereymedia.com
URL: http://www.montereymedia.com
Contact: Mr. Jerr Rae Mansfield, CFO
Description: Publishes educational audio and video cassettes. Does not accept unsolicited manuscripts. Reaches market through wholesalers, distributors, and direct to store sales. **Founded:** 1979.

58272 ■ Motivision Media
9528 Blossom Valley Rd.
El Cajon, CA 92021
Ph:(619)390-6700
Fax: (619)390-6628
Co. E-mail: sales@motivisionmedia.com
URL: http://www.motivisionmedia.com/
Contact: John Cordova
Description: Publishes books on business and Internet commerce.

58273 ■ Out of Your Mind. . .and into the Marketplace
13381 White Sand Dr.
Tustin, CA 92780-4565
Ph:(714)544-0248
Free: 800-419-1513
Fax: (714)730-1414
Co. E-mail: lpinson@business-plan.com
URL: http://www.business-plan.com

Contact: Linda Pinson
E-mail: LPinson@business-plan.com
Description: Publishes on small and home-based business concerns, stressing step-by-step, hands-on approach to business start-up, recordkeeping, marketing and business plan preparation. Offers a business plan software program for windows. Reaches market through commission representatives, direct mail, trade sales and wholesalers. Does not accept unsolicited manuscripts. **Founded:** 1987.

58274 ■ Paton Press L.L.C.
PO Box 44
Chico, CA 95927
Ph:(530)342-5480
Fax: (530)342-5471
Co. E-mail: info@patonpress.com
URL: http://www.patonpress.com
Description: Publishes books on business topics for professionals. Offers monthly newsletter via email. Accepts unsolicited manuscripts; send book proposal for initial review.

58275 ■ PCS86 Co.
2798 B S Bascom Ave.
San Jose, CA 95124
Ph:(408)559-1581
Fax: (408)559-1581
Co. E-mail: pcs86co@yahoo.com
Description: Publishes books relating to high tech, medical/health, financial/business, real estate, auto/aerospace, and law. Reaches market through direct mail. Does not accept unsolicited manuscripts. **Founded:** 1986.

58276 ■ Pele Productions
PO Box 4165
Mountain View, CA 94040
Ph:(650)962-1389
Free: 877-735-3782
Fax: (650)962-1546
Co. E-mail: publisher@pelepubs.com
URL: http://www.pelepubs.com
Contact: Catherine Kitcho, Author
Description: Publishes books on business technology. Does not accept unsolicited manuscripts. Reaches market through through website. **Founded:** 1998

58277 ■ Phillip B. Chute Corp.
4100 Central Ave., Ste. 201
Riverside, CA 92506
Ph:(909)686-6970
Fax: (909)686-6990
Contact: Phillip B. Chute, President
Description: Publishes a textbook and workbook on small business management. Reaches market through commission representatives, telephone sales and wholesalers. Presently inactive. **Founded:** 1985.

58278 ■ Pleasanton Publishing
PO Box 1257
Pleasanton, CA 94566
Ph:(925)249-9112
Fax: (925)249-1807
URL: http://www.drmira.com/index.html
Contact: Dr. Mira Kaplan MD., President
E-mail: mira@drmira.com
Description: Publishes literary works for holistic and natural healing using a teddy bear metaphor to con-

nect reader, including *The Teddy Bear Guide to Self-Healing*. For adults and children. Does not accept unsolicited manuscripts. Reaches market through distributors, including Ingram, New Leaf, De Vorss, Quality Books, and Baker & Taylor. **Founded:** 2000.

58279 ■ Power2BE Media
2975 Seahorse
Ventura, CA 93001
Ph:(805)650-1248
Fax: (805)650-1249
Co. E-mail: info@powerselling.com
URL: http://www.powerselling.com
Contact: Steven Power, President
E-mail: spower@powerselling.com
Description: Publishes business books about power selling. Does not accept unsolicited manuscripts. Reaches market through commission representatives, direct mail and via e-mail. **Founded:** 2002.

58280 ■ Puma Publishing Co.
1670 Coral Dr.
Santa Maria, CA 93454
Ph:(805)925-3216
Free: 800-255-5730
Fax: (805)925-2656
Co. E-mail: pumapub871@aol.com
Contact: William M. Alarid, President
Description: Publishes how-to books for small business. Distributes for Nolo Press, Upstart, and Bell Springs. Does not accept unsolicited manuscripts. Reaches market through trade sales and wholesalers and distributors, including LPC (login) and Quality Books. **Founded:** 1986.

58281 ■ Rampant Lion Publishers Inc.
c/o L. H. Joseph, Jr.
8344 Melrose Ave., No. 23
Los Angeles, CA 90069
Contact: Lawrence H. Joseph Jr., President
Description: Publishes management and how-to books for business people. Reaches market through business organizations. **Founded:** 1980.

58282 ■ Rhino's Press
PO Box 3520
Laguna Hills, CA 92654
Free: 800-872-3274
Fax: (714)244-3256
Contact: Scott Alexander, Owner
Description: Publishes books. **Founded:** 1980.

58283 ■ Sanai Publishing
1140 Brockman Dr.
Sonoma, CA 95476
Ph:(707)935-7798
Fax: (707)935-3642
URL: http://www.sanaipublishing.com
Contact: Lorien Fenton, Business & Project Mgr.
E-mail: lfenton@sanaipublishing.com
Description: Publishes books on nonfiction including business leadership and ethics, spirituality, holistic health, and music.

58284 ■ Sun Publications
300 Carlsbad Village Dr., Ste. 108A-78
Carlsbad, CA 92008
Ph:(619)884-7505

Free: 888-786-3777
Fax: (760)434-7076
Co. E-mail: eagles10@pacbell.net
Contact: Steve Pestrak, President
Description: Publishes business leadership and women's issues books and tapes. They are concerned with helping business people succeed and reach their goals. Does not accept unsolicited manuscripts. Reaches market through direct mail, wholesalers and distributors, seminars and speaking engagements. **Founded:** 2000.

58285 ■ Thomson Crisp Learning
1200 Hamilton Ct.
Menlo Park, CA 94025
Ph:(650)323-6100
Free: 800-442-7477
Fax: (650)323-5800
Co. E-mail: courseiltcrisp@thomsonlearning.com
URL: http://www.courseilt.com
Contact: Michael Crisp, President
E-mail: mcrisp@crisplearning.com
Description: Publishes self-study books on business skills. Also offers video cassettes, audio cassettes, and CD-ROMs. Offers online learning via the internet. Provides customized products for corporate training. Does not accept unsolicited manuscripts. Reaches market through commission representatives, direct mail, reviews and listings, telephone sales, and distributors including NBN. **Founded:** 1984.

58286 ■ Vince Emery Productions
781 Prague St.
PO Box 460279
San Francisco, CA 94112
Ph:(415)337-6000
Fax: (415)337-6070
Co. E-mail: postmaster@emery.com
URL: http://www.emery.com
Contact: Vince Emery, Owner
E-mail: vince@emery.com
Description: Publishes books on internet businesses.

58287 ■ WBusiness Books
9682 Telstar Ave., Ste. 110
El Monte, CA 91731
Ph:(626)448-3448
Fax: (626)602-3817
Co. E-mail: info@academiclearningcompany.com
URL: http://www.wbusinessbooks.com
Contact: Arthur Chou, Mgr
Description: Publishes business books. Accepts unsolicited manuscripts. Reaches market through commission representatives. **Founded:** 2005.

58288 ■ Women's Yellow Pages "Referral Guide"
13547 Ventura Blvd., Ste. 374
Sherman Oaks, CA 91423
Ph:(818)995-6646
Co. E-mail: info@referral-guide.com
URL: http://www.wypwrs.com
Description: Publishes an annual directory of women-owned businesses, professional women, and their organizations and services. Reaches market through marketing representatives, direct mail, and telephone sales. Does not accept unsolicited manuscripts. **Founded:** 1977.

SMALL BUSINESS DEVELOPMENT CENTER LEAD OFFICE

58289 ■ Colorado Office of Economic Development–Small Business Development Center
1625 Broadway, Ste. 1710
Denver, CO 80202
Ph:(303)892-3840
Fax: (303)892-3848
URL: http://www.state.co.us/gov_dir/oed/sbdc/sbdc-list.html
Contact: Ms. Virginia "Gin" Butler, Deputy Director

58290 ■ Colorado SBDC–Office of Economic Development
1625 Broadway, Ste. 170
Denver, CO 80202
Ph:(303)892-3864
Fax: (303)892-3848
URL: http://www.state.co.us/oed/sbdc
Contact: Kelly Manning, State Dir.
E-mail: kelly.manning@state.co.us

SMALL BUSINESS DEVELOPMENT CENTERS

58291 ■ Adams State College–Alamosa Small Business Development Center
208 Edgemont St., Business Bldg. 105
Alamosa, CO 81102
Ph:(719)587-7011
Free: 800-824-6494
Fax: (719)587-7522
URL: http://www.sbdc.adams.edu
Contact: Mary Hoffman, Dir.
E-mail: mchoffma@adams.edu

58292 ■ Boulder Small Business Development Center–Boulder Chamber of Commerce
2440 Pearl St.
PO Box 73
Boulder, CO 80302
Ph:(303)442-1475
Fax: (303)938-8837
URL: http://www.boulderchamber.com/
Contact: Sharon King, Dir.
E-mail: sharon.king@boulderchamber.com

58293 ■ Canon City Small Business Development Center
3080 E. Main St.
Canon City, CO 81212
Ph:(719)275-5335
Fax: (719)269-7334
Contact: Rich Hunter, Dir.
E-mail: hunter@pcc.cccoes.edu

58294 ■ Colorado Springs Small Business Development Center–University of Colorado at Colorado Springs
1420 Austin Buffs Pkwy.
PO Box 7150
Colorado Springs, CO 80933-7150
Ph:(719)262-3844
Fax: (719)262-3878
Co. E-mail: sbdc@uccs.edu
URL: http://www.cssbdc.org/
Contact: Matt Barrett, Dir.
E-mail: matthew.barrett@uccs.edu

58295 ■ Community College of Aurora–Aurora Small Business Development Center
9801 E. Colfax Ave., Ste. 200
Aurora, CO 80010-2154
Ph:(303)326-8690
Fax: (303)361-2953
Co. E-mail: info@aurorabdc.com
URL: http://www.aurorasbdc.com
Contact: Santos Blan, Business Specialist

58296 ■ Craig-Satellite Glenwood Springs Small Business Development Center–Colorado Mountain College and Northwestern Community College
601 Yampa Ave.
Craig, CO 81625
Ph:(970)824-7078
Fax: (970)824-5004
Co. E-mail: sbdc@cmn.net
URL: http://www.coloradomtn.edu/sbdc/
Contact: 800621-8559 Kaye Jacobson, Regional Dir.
E-mail: kjacobson@coloradomtn.edu

58297 ■ Delta SBDC–Region 10
League for Economic Assistance and Planning, Inc.
300 N. Cascade, Ste. 1
Montrose, CO 81401
Ph:(970)240-1109
Fax: (970)249-2488
Contact: Jim Kidd
E-mail: jim@region10.net

58298 ■ Delta Small Business Development Center
1765 US Hwy. 50
Delta, CO 81416
Ph:(970)874-7671
Free: 888-393-5252
Fax: (970)874-8796
Co. E-mail: mba1st@aol.com
URL: http://www.dmavtc.tec.co.us/sbdc/index.html
Contact: Bob Marshall, Dir.

58299 ■ Denver Small Business Development Center–Community College of Denver–Denver Metro Chamber of Commerce (1445)
1445 Market St.
Denver, CO 80202
Ph:(303)620-8076
Fax: (303)534-3200

Co. E-mail: sbdc@den-chamber.org
URL: http://www.denversbdc.org/
Contact: Tameka Montgomery, Dir.
E-mail: tameka.montgomery@den-chamber.org

58300 ■ Durango Small Business Development Center–Fort Lewis College
1000 Rim Dr., EBB 140
Durango, CO 81301-3999
Ph:(970)247-7009
Fax: (970)247-7205
URL: http://soba.fortlewis.edu/sbdc
Contact: Joe Keck, Dir.
E-mail: keck_j@fortlewis.edu

58301 ■ Fort Morgan Small Business Development Center–Morgan Community College
300 Main St.
Fort Morgan, CO 80701
Ph:(970)542-3263
Fax: (970)867-3352
Co. E-mail: merle.rhoades@morgancc.edu
URL: http://www.morgancc.edu/sbdc.htm
Contact: Merle Rhoades, Dir.

58302 ■ Glenwood Springs Small Business Development Center–Colorado Mountain College
831 Grand Ave.
PO Box 1376
Glenwood Springs, CO 81602
Ph:(970)384-8522
Free: 800-621-1647
Fax: (970)384-8525
Co. E-mail: kjacobson@coloradomtn.edu
URL: http://www.coloradomtn.edu/sbdc/
Contact: Kaye Jacobson, Dir.

58303 ■ Grand Junction Small Business Development Center–Western Colorado Business Development Corp.
2591 B 3/4 Rd.
Grand Junction, CO 81503
Ph:(970)243-5242
Fax: (970)241-0771
Co. E-mail: jmorey@gjincubator.org
URL: http://www.gjincubator.org/
Contact: Julie Morey, Dir.
E-mail: jmorey@gjincubator.org

58304 ■ Greeley Small Business Development Center–Aims Community College–Greeley and Weld Chamber of Commerce (902 7)
902 7th Ave.
Greeley, CO 80631
Ph:(970)352-3661
Fax: (970)352-3572
URL: http://www.aimsced.com/sbdc/smbusiness.htm
Contact: Patrice Gapen, Dir.
E-mail: patrice.gapen@aims.edu

58305 ■ La Junta SBDC–Otero Junior College
1802 Colorado Ave.
La Junta, CO 81050

Ph:(719)384-6959
Fax: (719)384-6960
Contact: Bryan Bryant
E-mail: bryan.bryant@ojc.edu

58306 ■ LaJunta Small Business Development Center
1802 Colorado
LaJunta, CO 81050
Ph:(719)384-6959
Fax: (719)354-6960
Co. E-mail: Bryant.bryant@ojc.cccoes.edu
URL: http://www.ojc.edu/home.asp
Contact: Bryant Bryant, Dir.

58307 ■ Lakewood Small Business Development Center–Denver satellite Office
1667 Cole Blvd., Bldg. 19, Ste. 400
Golden, CO 80407
Ph:(303)233-5555
Fax: (303)237-7633
Co. E-mail: sbdcrrcc@rmii.com
URL: http://www.sbdcredrocks.org
Contact: Jayne Reiter, Dir.
E-mail: jayne.reiter@den-chamber.org

58308 ■ Larimer County Small Business Development Center–Front Range Community College
125 S. Howes, Ste. 150
Fort Collins, CO 80521
Ph:(970)498-9295
Fax: (970)498-8924
Co. E-mail: sbdc@frii.com
URL: http://www.state.co.us/oed/sbdc
Contact: Mary Fischer, Dir.

58309 ■ Pueblo Small Business Development Center–Pueblo Community College
900 W. Orman Ave.
Pueblo, CO 81004
Ph:(719)549-3224
Fax: (719)549-3139
Co. E-mail: allan.mcconnell@pcc.cccoes.edu
URL: http://www.pueblocc.edu/sbdc/welcome.htm

58310 ■ South Metro Small Business Development Center
South Metro Chamber of Commerce
6840 S. University Blvd.
Centennial, CO 80122
Ph:(303)548-5300
Fax: (303)795-7250
Contact: Selma Kristel
E-mail: skristel@bestchamber.com

58311 ■ Trinidad Small Business Development Center
136 W. Main St.
Trinidad, CO 81082
Ph:(719)846-5644
Fax: (719)846-4550
URL: http://www.trinidadstate.edu/sbdc/
Contact: Donna Watkins, Dir.
E-mail: donna.watkins@trinidadstate.edu

58312 ■ Westminster Small Business Development Center–Front Range Community College
3645 W., 112th Ave.
Box 6
Westminster, CO 80030
Ph:(303)460-1032
Fax: (303)469-7143
URL: http://www.coloradosbdc.com
Contact: Chris Luchs, Dir.
E-mail: chris.luchs@frontrange.edu

SMALL BUSINESS ASSISTANCE PROGRAMS

58313 ■ Colorado Office of Economic Development and International Trade–Small Business Development Center
1625 Broadway, Ste. 1700
Denver, CO 80202

Ph:(303)892-3840
Free: 800-333-7798
Fax: (303)892-3848
Co. E-mail: kelly.manning@state.co.us
URL: http://www.advancecolorado.com
Contact: Kelly Manning, State Dir
Description: Answers small business inquiries or refers them to an appropriate resource. Provides information on starting a business, marketing, financing, and other aspects of running a business.

58314 ■ Colorado University Business Advancement Centers
5353 Manhattan Circle, Ste. 202
Boulder, CO 80303
Ph:(303)554-9493
Fax: (303)554-9605
URL: http://www.colorado.edu/cubac/
Description: Provides consulting on management, marketing, financing, procuring government contracts, and exporting. Also offers BRAIN, a technology transfer service available through NASA's Industrial Application Center. Holds seminars. Has branches in Grand Junction, Durango, Colorado Springs, Trinidad, and Burlington.

58315 ■ Denver Metro Chamber of Commerce–Small Business Development Center
1445 Market St.
Denver, CO 80202
Ph:(303)620-8076
Fax: (303)534-3200
Co. E-mail: denver.sbdc@den-chamber.org
URL: http://www.denversbdc.org
Contact: Steve Ambriz, Training Coordinator
Description: Assists companies with 100 or fewer employees. The Management Education Division provides management education and training; the Information/Networking Division sponsors meetings for small business chief executive officers for the exchange of information; and the Special Services Division is involved in such activities as legislative lobbying and sponsoring group health insurance programs for small businesses.

58316 ■ International Trade Office–Governor's office of International Trade
1625 Broadway, Ste. 1700
Denver, CO 80202
Ph:(303)892-3840
Fax: (303)892-3848
Co. E-mail: ito@state.co.us
URL: http://www.state.co.us/oed
Contact: Brain Vogt, Dir
Description: Promotes the export of Colorado's products and assists businesses in many aspects of exporting.

SCORE OFFICES

58317 ■ SCORE Colorado Springs
2 N Cascade Ave., Ste. 110
Colorado Springs, CO 80903
Ph:(719)636-3074
Fax: (719)635-1571
Co. E-mail: score@cscc.org
URL: http://www.coloradospringsscore.org
Contact: Harold Larson, Chm.
Description: Provides free business counseling as well as related workshops.

58318 ■ SCORE Denver
721 19th St., 4th Fl., Rm. 426
Denver, CO 80202-2517
Ph:(303)844-3985
Co. E-mail: score62@scoredenver.org
URL: http://www.scoredenver.org
Description: Assists individuals with their decisions to begin or to operate small businesses. Provides educational seminars and business counseling.

58319 ■ SCORE Grand Junction
2591 B 3/4 Rd.
Grand Junction, CO 81503

Ph:(970)243-5242
Co. E-mail: bob@ahinet.com
URL: http://www.score.org

58320 ■ SCORE Pueblo
c/o Chamber of Commerce
302 N Santa Fe
Pueblo, CO 81003
Ph:(719)542-1704
Fax: (719)542-1624
Co. E-mail: score@puebloscore.org
URL: http://score.pueblo.org
Contact: William Sprouse, Chm.
Description: Assists individuals with their decisions to begin or to operate small businesses. Provides educational seminars and business counseling.

BETTER BUSINESS BUREAUS

58321 ■ Better Business Bureau of Denver
1020 Cherokee St.
Denver, CO 80204-4032
Ph:(303)758-2100
Fax: (303)758-8321
Co. E-mail: info@denverbbb.org
URL: http://www.denverbbb.org
Contact: Jean Herman, Pres./CEO

58322 ■ Better Business Bureau of the Mountain States
8020 S County Rd. 5, Ste. 100
Fort Collins, CO 80528-8994
Ph:(970)484-1348
Fax: (970)221-1239
Co. E-mail: info@mountainstates.bbb.org
URL: http://www.fortcollins.bbb.org
Contact: Pamela King, Pres./CEO

58323 ■ Better Business Bureau of Southern Colorado
25 N Wahsatch
Colorado Springs, CO 80903
Ph:(719)636-1155
Free: (866)206-1800
Fax: (719)636-5078
Co. E-mail: info@bbbsc.org
URL: http://www.bbbsc.org

CHAMBERS OF COMMERCE

58324 ■ Alamosa County Chamber of Commerce
300 Chamber Dr.
Cole Park
Alamosa, CO 81101-2601
Ph:(719)589-3681
Fax: (719)589-1773
Co. E-mail: info@alamosachamber.com
URL: http://www.alamosachamber.com
Contact: Patricia Skroch, Exec.Dir.

58325 ■ Antonito Chamber of Commerce
PO Box 427
220 Main St.
Antonito, CO 81120-0427
Ph:(719)376-2277
Fax: (719)376-2277
Co. E-mail: antonitocofc@surfbest.net
Contact: Bill Laurell, Pres.

58326 ■ Arvada Chamber of Commerce
7305 Grandview Ave.
Arvada, CO 80002-9960
Ph:(303)424-0313
Fax: (303)424-5370
Co. E-mail: director@arvadachamber.org
URL: http://www.arvadachamber.org
Contact: Lynn J. Kensinger, Pres.

58327 ■ Aspen Chamber Resort Association
425 Rio Grande Pl.
Aspen, CO 81611

Ph:(970)925-1940
Fax: (970)920-1173
Co. E-mail: info@aspenchamber.org
URL: http://www.aspenchamber.org
Contact: Debbie Contini Braun, Pres./CEO

58328 ■ Aurora Chamber of Commerce
562 Sable Blvd., Ste. 200
Aurora, CO 80011-0809
Ph:(303)344-1500
Fax: (303)344-1564
Co. E-mail: info@aurorachamber.org
URL: http://www.aurorachamber.org
Contact: Kevin Hougen, Pres./CEO

58329 ■ Basalt Chamber of Commerce
PO Box 514
Basalt, CO 81621-0514
Ph:(970)927-4031
Fax: (970)927-2833
Co. E-mail: bchamber@rof.net
URL: http://www.basaltchamber.com
Contact: Elizabeth Phillips, Exec.Dir.

58330 ■ Berthoud Area Chamber of Commerce
748 Mountain Ave.
PO Box 1709
Berthoud, CO 80513
Ph:(970)532-4200
Fax: (970)532-7690
Co. E-mail: bcc@berthoudcolorado.com
URL: http://www.berthoudcolorado.com
Contact: Michele Jurs, Exec.Dir.

58331 ■ Boulder Chamber of Commerce
PO Box 73
Boulder, CO 80302
Ph:(303)442-1044
Fax: (303)938-8837
Co. E-mail: info@boulderchamber.com
URL: http://www.boulderchamber.com
Contact: Susan Graf, Pres.

58332 ■ Breckenridge Resort Chamber of Commerce
PO Box 1909
Breckenridge, CO 80424-1909
Ph:(970)453-2913
Fax: (970)453-7238
Co. E-mail: gobreck@gobreck.com
URL: http://www.gobreck.com
Contact: Corry Mihm, Exec.Dir.

58333 ■ Broomfield Chamber of Commerce
350 Interlocken Blvd., Ste. 250
PO Box 301
Broomfield, CO 80038
Ph:(303)466-1775
Fax: (303)466-4481
Co. E-mail: info@broomfieldchamber.com
URL: http://www.broomfieldchamber.com
Contact: Rick Roberts, Pres./CEO

58334 ■ Brush Chamber of Commerce
1215 Edison St.
Brush, CO 80723
Ph:(970)842-2666
Free: 800-354-8659
Fax: (970)842-3828
Co. E-mail: brush@brushchamber.org
URL: http://www.brushchamber.org
Contact: Dr. Ronald Prascher, Exec.Dir.

58335 ■ Buena Vista Area Chamber of Commerce
343 Hwy. 24 S
PO Box 2021
Buena Vista, CO 81211
Ph:(719)395-6612
Fax: (719)395-8035
Co. E-mail: buenavista@vtinet.com
URL: http://www.buenavistacolorado.org
Contact: Judy Hassell, Exec.Dir.

58336 ■ Canon City Chamber of Commerce
403 Royal Gorge Blvd.
Canon City, CO 81212

Ph:(719)275-2331
Free: 800-876-7922
Fax: (719)275-2332
Co. E-mail: chamber@canoncity.com
URL: http://www.canoncitychamber.com
Contact: Dorothy Day, Pres.

58337 ■ Carbondale Community Chamber of Commerce
PO Box 1645
Carbondale, CO 81623
Ph:(970)963-1890
Fax: (970)963-4719
Co. E-mail: chamber@carbondale.com
URL: http://www.carbondale.com
Contact: Ms. Randi Lowenthal, Exec.Dir.

58338 ■ Castle Rock Chamber of Commerce
420 Jerry St.
PO Box 282
Castle Rock, CO 80104
Ph:(303)688-4597
Fax: (303)688-2688
Co. E-mail: info@castlerock.org
URL: http://www.castlerock.org
Contact: Pam Ridler, Pres.

58339 ■ Cedaredge Area Chamber of Commerce
PO Box 278
245 W Main St.
Cedaredge, CO 81413
Ph:(970)856-6961
Fax: (970)856-7292
Co. E-mail: cedaredgech@tds.net
URL: http://www.cedaredgecolorado.com
Contact: Anne Chastain, Exec.Dir.

58340 ■ Chamber of Commerce of Highlands Ranch
541 W Highlands Ranch Pkwy., No. 105
Highlands Ranch, CO 80129
Ph:(303)791-3500
Fax: (303)791-3522
Co. E-mail: staff@highlandsranchchamber.org
Contact: Julie Bautista, Admin.Mgr.

58341 ■ Cherry Creek Chamber of Commerce
288 Clayton St.,Ste.303
Denver, CO 80206
Ph:(303)388-6022
Fax: (303)355-9894
Co. E-mail: staff@cherrycreekchamber.org
Contact: Mr. Greg Riddell, Exec.Dir.

58342 ■ Conifer Chamber of Commerce
PO Box 127
Conifer, CO 80433
Ph:(303)838-5711
Fax: (303)838-5712
Co. E-mail: info@coniferchamber.org
URL: http://www.coniferchamber.org
Contact: Dave Watts, Pres.

58343 ■ Cortez Area Chamber of Commerce
928 E Main
PO Box 968
Cortez, CO 81321
Ph:(970)565-3414
Fax: (970)565-8373
Co. E-mail: cacc@fone.net
URL: http://www.cortezchamber.org
Contact: Reuben Hammond, Pres.-Elect

58344 ■ Costilla County Chamber of Commerce
PO Box 428
Fort Garland, CO 81133
Ph:(719)379-3512
Co. E-mail: sanluis2@fone.net
URL: http://www.slvguide.com/Costilla
Contact: Glenda Maes, Admin.

58345 ■ Craig Chamber of Commerce
360 E Victory Way
Craig, CO 81625

Ph:(970)824-5689
Free: 800-864-4405
Fax: (970)824-0231
Co. E-mail: info@craig-chamber.com
URL: http://www.craig-chamber.com
Contact: Cathy J. Vanatta, Exec.Dir.

58346 ■ Crawford Area Chamber of Commerce
PO Box 22
Crawford, CO 81415
Ph:(970)921-4000
Co. E-mail: info@crawfordcountry.org
URL: http://www.crawfordcountry.org
Contact: Alowetta Terrien, Pres.

58347 ■ Creede - Mineral County Chamber of Commerce
PO Box 580
1207 N Main St.
Creede, CO 81130-0580
Ph:(719)658-2374
Free: 800-327-2102
Fax: (719)658-2717
Co. E-mail: creede@my.amigo.net
URL: http://www.creede.com
Contact: Pat Richmond, Exec.Dir.

58348 ■ Crested Butte/Mount Crested Butte Chamber of Commerce
601 Elk Ave.
PO Box 1288
Crested Butte, CO 81224
Ph:(970)349-6438
Free: 800-545-4505
Fax: (970)349-1023
Co. E-mail: info@cbchamber.com
URL: http://www.cbchamber.com
Contact: Rebecca Thompson, Dir.

58349 ■ Cripple Creek Chamber of Commerce
PO Box 650
Cripple Creek, CO 80813
Ph:(719)689-2169
Free: 877-858-4653
Fax: (719)689-2774
Co. E-mail: info@cripple-creek.co.us
URL: http://www.cripple-creek.co.us
Contact: Steph Hilliard, Mgr.

58350 ■ Custer County Merchants and Chamber of Commerce
PO Box 81
Westcliffe, CO 81252-0081
Ph:(719)783-9163
Free: 877-793-3170
Co. E-mail: custco@ris.net
URL: http://www.custercountyco.com
Contact: Paul Wenke, Pres.

58351 ■ Del Norte Chamber of Commerce
PO Box 148
Del Norte, CO 81132
Ph:(719)657-2845
Free: 888-616-4638
Co. E-mail: info@delnortechamber.info
URL: http://www.delnortechamber.org
Contact: Jessica Salavar, Sec.

58352 ■ Delta Area Chamber of Commerce
301 Main St.
Delta, CO 81416-1881
Ph:(970)874-8616
Fax: (970)874-8618
Co. E-mail: chamber@deltacolorado.org
URL: http://www.deltacolorado.org
Contact: Dale Hukle, Exec.Dir.

58353 ■ Denver Hispanic Chamber of Commerce
924 W Colfax Ave.
Denver, CO 80204
Ph:(303)534-7783
Fax: (303)595-8977
Co. E-mail: info@dhcc.com
URL: http://www.dhcc.com

Contact: Jeffrey Campos, Pres./CEO

**58354 ■ Denver Metro Chamber of
Commerce**
1445 Market St.
Denver, CO 80202
Ph:(303)534-8500
Fax: (303)534-2145
Co. E-mail: dmcc@den-chamber.org
URL: http://www.denverchamber.org
Contact: Joe Blake, Pres./CEO

58355 ■ Dolores Chamber of Commerce
201 Railroad Ave.
PO Box 602
Dolores, CO 81323
Ph:(970)882-4018
Free: 800-807-4712
Co. E-mail: info@doloreschamber.com
URL: http://www.doloreschamber.com
Contact: Edward Merritt, Treas.

58356 ■ Durango Chamber of Commerce
PO Box 2587
111 S Camino Del Rio
Durango, CO 81302
Ph:(970)247-0312
Free: 800-525-8855
Fax: (970)385-7884
Co. E-mail: chamber@durangobusiness.org
URL: http://www.durango.org
Contact: Bobby Lieb, Exec.Dir.

58357 ■ Eads Chamber of Commerce
PO Box 163
Eads, CO 81036-0163
Ph:(719)438-5590
Co. E-mail: dennis.pearson@state.co.us
URL: http://www.kiowacountycolo.com/
    chamberofcommerce.htm
Contact: Dennis Pearson, Pres.

58358 ■ Eagle Valley Chamber of Commerce
100 Fairgrounds Rd.
PO Box 965
Eagle, CO 81631
Ph:(970)328-5220
Fax: (970)328-1120
Co. E-mail: evcc@eaglevalley.org
URL: http://www.eaglevalley.org
Contact: Randy Goodwin, Pres.

**58359 ■ Elizabeth Area Chamber of
Commerce**
146 N Elbert St.
Elizabeth, CO 80107
Ph:(303)646-4287
Fax: (303)646-9806
Co. E-mail: info@elizabethchamber.org
URL: http://www.elizabethchamber.org
Contact: Ed Robinson, Pres.

58360 ■ Erie Chamber of Commerce
PO Box 97
235 Wells St.
Erie, CO 80516
Ph:(303)828-3440
Fax: (303)828-3330
Co. E-mail: info@eriechamber.org
URL: http://www.eriechamber.org
Contact: Tammy Thomas, Exec.Dir.

58361 ■ Estes Park Chamber of Commerce
500 Big Thompson Ave.
Estes Park, CO 80517
Free: 800-378-3708
Co. E-mail: staff@estesparkresort.com
URL: http://www.estesparkresort.com
Contact: Deeva Boleman, Exec.Dir.

58362 ■ Evans Area Chamber of Commerce
3700 Golden St.
Evans, CO 80620
Ph:(970)330-4204
Fax: (970)330-7561
Co. E-mail: ecc@bwn.net
Contact: Jack J. Meakins, Exec.Dir.

**58363 ■ Evergreen Area Chamber of
Commerce**
28055 Hwy. 74, Ste. 201
PO Box 97
Evergreen, CO 80437-0097
Ph:(303)674-3412
Fax: (303)674-8463
Co. E-mail: info@evergreenchamber.org
URL: http://www.evergreenchamber.org
Contact: Melanie Nuchols, Pres.

58364 ■ Florence Chamber of Commerce
117 S Pikes Peak Ave.
PO Box 145
Florence, CO 81226
Ph:(719)784-3544
Fax: (719)784-9324
Co. E-mail: florencecolorado@aol.com
URL: http://www.florencecolorado.net
Contact: Darrell Lindsey, Exec. Dir.

**58365 ■ Fort Collins Area Chamber of
Commerce**
225 S Meldrum St.
Fort Collins, CO 80521
Ph:(970)482-3746
Fax: (970)482-3774
Co. E-mail: general@fcchamber.org
URL: http://www.fortcollinschamber.com
Contact: David L. May CCE, Pres./CEO

**58366 ■ Fort Morgan Area Chamber of
Commerce**
300 Main St.
PO Box 971
Fort Morgan, CO 80701
Ph:(970)867-6702
Free: 800-354-8660
Fax: (970)867-6121
Co. E-mail: fortmorganchamber@flci.net
URL: http://www.fortmorganchamber.org
Contact: Marti Vocke, Pres.

**58367 ■ Fountain Valley Chamber of
Commerce**
PO Box 201
Fountain, CO 80817-0201
Ph:(719)382-3190
Fax: (719)322-9395
Co. E-mail: fvcc@qwest.net
URL: http://www.fountaincolorado.org/chamber
Contact: Lorene Moore, Pres.

58368 ■ Fruita Chamber of Commerce
432 E Aspen Ave.
Fruita, CO 81521
Ph:(970)858-3894
Fax: (970)858-3121
Co. E-mail: info@fruitachamber.org
URL: http://www.fruitachamber.org
Contact: Christy Hovland, Dir.

58369 ■ Georgetown Promotions Committee
PO Box 426
Georgetown, CO 80444
Ph:(303)569-2555
Free: 888-569-1130
Fax: (303)569-2705
URL: http://www.town.georgetown.co.us
Contact: Jeannette Peterson, Chair

58370 ■ Granby Chamber of Commerce
PO Box 35
Granby, CO 80446
Ph:(970)887-2311
Free: 800-325-1661
Fax: (970)887-3895
Co. E-mail: grcoc@rkymtnhi.com
URL: http://granbychamber.com
Contact: Sharon Brenner, Exec.Dir.

**58371 ■ Grand Junction Area Chamber of
Commerce**
360 Grand Ave.
Grand Junction, CO 81501
Ph:(970)242-3214
Free: 800-352-5286

Fax: (970)242-3694
Co. E-mail: info@gjchamber.org
URL: http://www.gjchamber.org
Contact: Diane Schwenke, Pres./CEO

**58372 ■ Grand Lake Area Chamber of
Commerce**
PO Box 57
Grand Lake, CO 80447-0057
Ph:(970)627-3372
Free: 800-531-1019
Fax: (970)627-8007
Co. E-mail: glinfo@grandlakechamber.com
URL: http://www.grandlakechamber.com

**58373 ■ Greater Brighton Area Chamber of
Commerce**
36 S Main St.
Brighton, CO 80601
Ph:(303)659-0223
Fax: (303)659-5115
Co. E-mail: mjkilker@qwest.net
URL: http://www.brightonchamber.com
Contact: Mary Kilker, Admin.

**58374 ■ Greater Colorado Springs Chamber
of Commerce**
2 N Cascade Ave., Ste. 110
Colorado Springs, CO 80903
Ph:(719)635-1551
Fax: (719)635-1571
Co. E-mail: info@cscc.org
URL: http://www.coloradospringschamber.org
Contact: Will Temby, Pres./CEO

**58375 ■ Greater Englewood Chamber of
Commerce**
3501 S Broadway
2nd Fl., Colonial Bank Bldg.
Englewood, CO 80110-3629
Ph:(303)789-4473
Fax: (303)789-0098
Co. E-mail: englewoodchamber@mho.net
URL: http://www.greatenglewoodchamber.com
Contact: Cristin Penning, Exec.Dir.

**58376 ■ Greater Golden Chamber of
Commerce**
PO Box 1035
Golden, CO 80401
Ph:(303)279-3113
Free: 800-590-3113
Fax: (303)279-0332
Co. E-mail: info@goldencochamber.org
URL: http://www.goldencochamber.org
Contact: Gary L. Wink, Pres./CEO

**58377 ■ Greater Pueblo Chamber of
Commerce**
302 N Santa Fe Ave.
Pueblo, CO 81003-4102
Ph:(719)542-1704
Free: 800-233-3446
URL: http://www.pueblochamber.org
Contact: Rod Slyhoff, Pres./CEO

**58378 ■ Greater Woodland Park Chamber of
Commerce**
Ute Pass Cultural Ctr.
PO Box 9022
Woodland Park, CO 80866-9022
Ph:(719)687-9885
Free: 800-551-7886
Fax: (719)687-8216
Co. E-mail: info@gwpcc.biz
URL: http://www.woodlandparkchamber.com
Contact: Carol Beck, Exec.Dir.

**58379 ■ Greeley/Weld Chamber of
Commerce**
902 7th Ave.
Greeley, CO 80631-4603
Ph:(970)352-3566
Fax: (970)352-3572
Co. E-mail: info@greeleychamber.com
URL: http://www.greeleychamber.com
Contact: Sarah MacQuiddy, Pres.

58380 ■ Gunnison County Chamber of Commerce
500 E Tomichi Ave.
Gunnison, CO 81230-0036
Ph:(970)641-1501
Co. E-mail: info@gunnisonchamber.com
URL: http://www.gunnison-co.com
Contact: Tammy Scott, Exec.Dir.

58381 ■ Haxtun Chamber of Commerce
PO Box 535
Haxtun, CO 80731
Ph:(970)774-6104
Fax: (970)774-5875
Contact: Gordon Smith, Pres.

58382 ■ Heart of the Rockies Chamber of Commerce
406 W Hwy. 50
Salida, CO 81201
Ph:(719)539-2068
Free: 877-772-5432
Fax: (719)539-7844
Co. E-mail: info@salidachamber.org
URL: http://salidachamber.org
Contact: Bonnie Swyers, Exec.Dir.

58383 ■ Holyoke Chamber of Commerce
212 S Interocean
PO Box 134
Holyoke, CO 80734-0134
Ph:(970)854-3517
Fax: (970)854-3514
Co. E-mail: holyokec@pctc.net
URL: http://www.holyokechamber.org
Contact: Mary Tomky, Dir.

58384 ■ Hotchkiss Chamber of Commerce
PO Box 158
Hotchkiss, CO 81419-0158
Ph:(970)872-3226
Fax: (970)872-4050
Co. E-mail: info@hotchkisschamber.com
URL: http://www.hotchkisschamber.com
Contact: Linda Perry, Pres.

58385 ■ I-70 Corridor Chamber of Commerce
401 S 1st St.
Bennett, CO 80102
Ph:(303)644-4607
Fax: (303)644-3271
Co. E-mail: coc_170corridor@tds.net
Contact: Marilyn Elliott, Pres.

58386 ■ Idaho Springs Chamber of Commerce
PO Box 97
Idaho Springs, CO 80452
Ph:(303)567-4382
URL: http://www.idahospringschamber.com
Contact: Deb Davies, Exec.Dir.

58387 ■ Johnstown-Milliken Chamber of Commerce
PO Box 501
Johnstown, CO 80534-0501
Ph:(970)587-7042
Co. E-mail: info@johnsontownmillikenchamber.com
URL: http://www.johnstownmillikenchamber.com
Contact: Olivia Eldred, Pres.

58388 ■ Kersey Area Chamber of Commerce
PO Box 397
Kersey, CO 80644-0397
Ph:(970)356-8669
Co. E-mail: contact@kerseycolorado.com
URL: http://www.kerseycolorado.com
Contact: Steve Kramer, Pres.

58389 ■ Kremmling Area Chamber of Commerce and Economic Development Commission
PO Box 471
Kremmling, CO 80459
Ph:(970)724-3472
Free: 877-573-4263
Fax: (970)724-0397

Co. E-mail: chamber@kremmlingchamber.com
URL: http://www.kremmlingchamber.com
Contact: Katrina Wright, Exec.Dir.

58390 ■ La Junta Chamber of Commerce
110 Santa Fe Ave.
La Junta, CO 81050
Ph:(719)384-7411
Fax: (719)384-2217
Co. E-mail: ljcc@centurytel.net
URL: http://www.lajuntachamber.com
Contact: Meriann Grasmick, Office Mgr.

58391 ■ La Veta/Cuchara Chamber of Commerce
PO Box 32
La Veta, CO 81055
Ph:(719)742-3676
Free: (866)615-3676
Co. E-mail: email@lavetacucharachamber.com
URL: http://www.lavetacucharachamber.com
Contact: Sandy Helwig, Co-Pres.

58392 ■ Lafayette Chamber of Commerce
309 S Public Rd.
Lafayette, CO 80026
Ph:(303)666-9555
Fax: (303)666-4392
Co. E-mail: info@lafayettecolorado.com
URL: http://www.lafayettecolorado.com
Contact: Vicki Trumbo, Exec.Dir.

58393 ■ Lake City - Hinsdale County Chamber of Commerce
800 N Gunnison Ave.
PO Box 430
Lake City, CO 81235
Ph:(970)944-2527
Free: 800-569-1874
Co. E-mail: info@lakecityco.com
URL: http://www.lakecityco.com
Contact: Alena Martinez, Exec.Dir.

58394 ■ Lamar Chamber of Commerce
109A E Beech St.
Lamar, CO 81052
Ph:(719)336-4379
Fax: (719)336-4370
Co. E-mail: lamarchamber@bresnan.net
URL: http://www.lamarchamber.com
Contact: Chana Reed, Office Mgr.

58395 ■ Las Animas - Bent County Chamber of Commerce
332 Ambassador Thompson Blvd.
Las Animas, CO 81054
Ph:(719)456-0453
Fax: (719)456-0455
Co. E-mail: chamber@bentcounty.org
URL: http://bentcounty.org
Contact: Russell Smith, Exec.Dir.

58396 ■ Leadville/Lake County Chamber of Commerce
PO Box 861
Leadville, CO 80461-0861
Ph:(719)486-3900
Free: 888-532-3845
Fax: (719)486-8478
Co. E-mail: leadville@leadvilleusa.com
URL: http://www.leadvilleusa.com
Contact: Ms. Amy Ellis, Chamber Business Dir.

58397 ■ Limon Chamber of Commerce
PO Box 101
Limon, CO 80828
Ph:(719)775-9418
Fax: (719)775-9513
Co. E-mail: happylibrn@hotmail.com
URL: http://www.limonchamber.com
Contact: Tim Anderson, Pres.

58398 ■ Logan County Chamber of Commerce
PO Box 1683
109 N Front St.
Sterling, CO 80751

Ph:(970)522-5070
Free: (866)522-5070
Fax: (970)522-4082
Co. E-mail: loganccc@logancountychamber.com
URL: http://www.logancountychamber.com
Contact: Mr. Timothy Edgar, Exec.Dir.

58399 ■ Longmont Area Chamber of Commerce
528 Main St.
Longmont, CO 80501-5537
Ph:(303)776-5295
Fax: (303)776-5657
Co. E-mail: staff@longmontchamber.org
URL: http://www.longmontchamber.org
Contact: Kathy Millisor, CEO/Pres.

58400 ■ Louisville Chamber of Commerce
PO Box 271
901 Main St.
Louisville, CO 80027
Ph:(303)666-5747
Fax: (303)666-4285
Co. E-mail: chamber@h2net.net
URL: http://www.louisvillechamber.com
Contact: Eugene A. Caranci, Exec.Dir.

58401 ■ Loveland Chamber of Commerce and Visitors Center
5400 Stone Creek Cir.
Loveland, CO 80538-8838
Ph:(970)667-6311
Fax: (970)667-5211
Co. E-mail: info@loveland.org
URL: http://www.loveland.org
Contact: Ms. Gaye Stockman, Pres./CEO

58402 ■ Loveland Info Chamber of Commerce
5400 Stone Creek Cir.
Loveland, CO 80538
Ph:(970)667-6311
Fax: (970)667-5211
Co. E-mail: gstockman@loveland.org
URL: http://www.loveland.org
Contact: Gaye Stockman, Pres./CEO

58403 ■ Lyons Chamber of Commerce
PO Box 426
Lyons, CO 80540
Ph:(303)823-5215
Free: 877-LYONS-CO
Co. E-mail: info@lyons-colorado.com
URL: http://www.lyons-colorado.com
Contact: Chastidee Bolkovatz, Exec.Dir.

58404 ■ Manitou Springs Chamber of Commerce
354 Manitou Ave.
Manitou Springs, CO 80829
Ph:(719)685-5089
Free: 800-642-2567
Fax: (719)685-0355
Co. E-mail: manitou@pikes-peak.com
URL: http://www.manitousprings.org
Contact: Leslie Lewis, Exec. Dir.

58405 ■ Meeker Chamber of Commerce
PO Box 869
Meeker, CO 81641-0869
Ph:(970)878-5510
Fax: (970)878-0271
Co. E-mail: meekerchamber@nctelecom.net
URL: http://www.meekerchamber.com
Contact: Betty Morlan, Pres.

58406 ■ Metro North Chamber of Commerce
2921 W 120th Ave., Ste. 210
Westminster, CO 80234
Ph:(303)288-1000
Fax: (303)227-1050
Co. E-mail: info@metronorthchamber.com
URL: http://www.metronorthchamber.com
Contact: Deborah Obermeyer, Pres./CEO

58407 ■ Monte Vista Chamber of Commerce
1035 Park Ave.
Monte Vista, CO 81144

Ph:(719)852-2731
Free: 800-562-7085
Fax: (719)852-9382
Co. E-mail: chamber@monte-vista.org
URL: http://www.monte-vista.org
Contact: Stacy Bliss, Pres.

58408 ■ Montrose Chamber of Commerce
1519 E Main St.
Montrose, CO 81401-3807
Ph:(970)249-5000
Free: 800-923-5515
Fax: (970)249-2907
Co. E-mail: info@montrosechamber.com
URL: http://www.montrosechamber.com
Contact: Marge Keehfuss, Exec.Dir.

58409 ■ Nederland Area Chamber of Commerce
PO Box 85
Nederland, CO 80466
Ph:(303)258-3936
Free: 800-221-0044
Co. E-mail: info@nederlandchamber.org
URL: http://www.nederlandchamber.org
Contact: Kay Lorenz, Pres.

58410 ■ New Castle Area Chamber of Commerce
PO Box 983
New Castle, CO 81647
Ph:(970)984-0455
Co. E-mail: info@newcastlechamber.org
URL: http://www.newcastlechamber.org
Contact: Russell Talbott, Pres.

58411 ■ North Park Chamber of Commerce
416 4th St.
PO Box 68
Walden, CO 80480-0068
Ph:(970)723-4600
Fax: (970)723-4600
Co. E-mail: northparkcoc@cs.com
Contact: Rae Redman, Office Mgr.

58412 ■ Nucla-Naturita Area Chamber of Commerce
PO Box 425
Naturita, CO 81422
Ph:(970)865-2350
Fax: (970)864-7600
Co. E-mail: csbterri@fone.net
URL: http://nucla-naturita.com
Contact: Terri Tooker, Pres.

58413 ■ Ouray Chamber Resort Association
1230 Main St.
PO Box 145
Ouray, CO 81427-0145
Ph:(970)325-4746
Free: 800-228-1876
Fax: (970)325-4868
Co. E-mail: ouray@ouraycolorado.com
URL: http://www.ouraycolorado.com
Contact: Rennie Ross, Dir.

58414 ■ Pagosa Springs Area Chamber of Commerce
PO Box 787
Pagosa Springs, CO 81147
Ph:(970)264-2360
Free: 800-252-2204
URL: http://www.pagosaspringschamber.com
Contact: Sally Hameister, Exec. Dir.

58415 ■ Palisade Chamber of Commerce
319 S Main St.
PO Box 729
Palisade, CO 81526
Ph:(970)464-7458
Fax: (970)464-4757
Co. E-mail: info@palisadecoc.com
URL: http://www.palisadecoc.com
Contact: Ms. Christine Jasper, Exec.Dir.

58416 ■ Paonia Chamber of Commerce
PO Box 366
Paonia, CO 81428-0366

Ph:(970)527-3886
Co. E-mail: chamber@paonia.com
URL: http://www.paoniachamber.com

58417 ■ Parker Chamber of Commerce
20118 E Main St., Ste. A
Parker, CO 80138-7334
Ph:(303)841-4268
Fax: (303)841-8061
Co. E-mail: director@parkerchamber.com
URL: http://www.parkerchamber.com
Contact: Dawna Callahan, Exec.Dir.

58418 ■ Rangely Area Chamber of Commerce
209 E Main St.
Rangely, CO 81648
Ph:(970)675-5290
Fax: (970)675-8471
Co. E-mail: rangelycoc@rangelygovt.com
URL: http://www.rangely.com
Contact: Jane Miller, Pres.

58419 ■ Rifle Area Chamber of Commerce
200 Lions Park Circle
Rifle, CO 81650-0809
Ph:(970)625-2085
Free: 800-842-2085
Fax: (970)625-4757
Co. E-mail: mail@riflechamber.com
URL: http://www.riflechamber.org
Contact: Patty Lambert, Exec.Dir.

58420 ■ Rocky Ford Chamber of Commerce
105 N Main St.
Rocky Ford, CO 81067-1268
Ph:(719)254-7483
Fax: (719)254-6756
Co. E-mail: rfchamber@rockyfordchamber.com
Contact: Julie Worley, Exec.Dir.

58421 ■ Sedgwick County Chamber of Commerce
100 W 2nd St.
Julesburg, CO 80737
Ph:(970)474-3504
Fax: (970)474-4008
Co. E-mail: sced@kci.net
Contact: Patricia Stever, Exec.Dir.

58422 ■ Silverton Chamber of Commerce
PO Box 565
Silverton, CO 81433-0565
Ph:(970)387-5654
Free: 800-752-4494
Fax: (970)387-0282
Co. E-mail: chamber@silvertoncolorado.net
URL: http://www.silvertoncolorado.com
Contact: Amy Gass, Exec.Dir.

58423 ■ Snowmass Village Resort Association
PO Box 5010
Snowmass Village, CO 81615-5420
Ph:(970)922-2297
Free: 800-SNOWMASS
Fax: (970)922-1139
Co. E-mail: info@snowmassvillage.com
URL: http://www.snowmassvillage.com
Contact: Mr. Brett Huske, Pres.

58424 ■ South Fork Chamber of Commerce and Visitors Center
PO Box 1030
South Fork, CO 81154
Ph:(719)873-5512
Free: 800-571-0881
Fax: (719)873-5693
Co. E-mail: southfrk@amigo.net
URL: http://www.southfork.org
Contact: Josephine Pierce, Dir.

58425 ■ South Metro Denver Chamber of Commerce
6840 S University Blvd.
Centennial, CO 80122
Ph:(303)795-0142

Fax: (303)795-7520
Co. E-mail: jbrackney@bestchamber.com
URL: http://www.bestchamber.com
Contact: John Brackney, Pres.

58426 ■ South Platte Area Chamber of Commerce
PO Box 606
Platteville, CO 80651
Ph:(970)737-2916
Fax: (970)785-2236
Co. E-mail: spachamberofcomm@aol.com
URL: http://www.southplattechamber.com
Contact: John Taylor, Pres.

58427 ■ Southern Colorado Women's Chamber of Commerce
PO Box 49218
Colorado Springs, CO 80949
Ph:(719)442-2007
Co. E-mail: sec@scwcc.com
URL: http://www.scwcc.com
Contact: Lynda Carmichael, Pres.

58428 ■ Springfield Chamber of Commerce
PO Box 12
Springfield, CO 81073
Ph:(719)523-4061
Co. E-mail: cospringfieldchamber@yahoo.com
URL: http://www.springfieldco.info
Contact: Cecil Wade, Pres.

58429 ■ Steamboat Springs Chamber Resort Association
PO Box 774408
1255 S Lincoln Ave.
Steamboat Springs, CO 80477-4408
Ph:(970)879-0882
Fax: (970)879-2543
Co. E-mail: info@steamboatchamber.com
URL: http://www.steamboatchamber.com
Contact: Sandy Evans Hall, Exec.VP

58430 ■ Summit County Chamber of Commerce
PO Box 2010
Frisco, CO 80443
Ph:(970)668-2051
Free: 800-530-3099
Fax: (970)668-1515
Co. E-mail: info@summitchamber.org
URL: http://www.summitchamber.org
Contact: Constance Jones, Exec.Dir.

58431 ■ Tri-Lakes Chamber of Commerce
300 Hwy. 105
PO Box 147
Monument, CO 80132
Ph:(719)481-3282
Fax: (719)481-1638
Co. E-mail: info@trilakeschamber.com
URL: http://www.trilakeschamber.com
Contact: Mr. Steve Spry, Exec.Dir.

58432 ■ Trinidad-Las Animas Chamber of Commerce
309 Nevada Ave.
Trinidad, CO 81082-2557
Ph:(719)846-9285
Free: (866)480-4750
Fax: (719)846-3545
Co. E-mail: chamber@amigo.net
Contact: Kimberly Pacheco, Exec.Dir.

58433 ■ Vallecito Lake Chamber of Commerce
PO Box 804
Bayfield, CO 81122
Ph:(970)247-1573
Co. E-mail: info@vallecitolakechamber.com
URL: http://www.vallecitolakechamber.com
Contact: Burt Armstrong, Pres.

58434 ■ West Chamber of Commerce Serving Jefferson County
PO Box 280748
Lakewood, CO 80228-0748

Ph:(303)233-5555
Fax: (303)237-7633
Co. E-mail: info@westchamber.org
URL: http://www.westchamber.org
Contact: Amy Sherman, Pres./CEO

58435 ■ West Yuma County Chamber of Commerce
215 S Main St.
Yuma, CO 80759
Ph:(970)848-2704
Fax: (970)848-5700
Co. E-mail: chamber@seeyuma.com
URL: http://www.seeyuma.com
Contact: Crystal Cliff, Asst. Dir./Office Mgr.

58436 ■ Windsor Chamber of Commerce
421 Main St.
Windsor, CO 80550
Ph:(970)686-7189
Fax: (970)686-0352
Co. E-mail: michal@windsorchamber.net
URL: http://www.windsorchamber.net
Contact: Michal Connors, Office Mgr.

58437 ■ Winter Park/Fraser Valley Chamber of Commerce
78841 U.S. Hwy. 40
PO Box 3236
Winter Park, CO 80482-3236
Ph:(970)726-4118
Free: 800-903-7275
Fax: (970)726-9449
Co. E-mail: visitorcenter@winterpark-info.com
URL: http://www.winterpark-info.com
Contact: Catherine Ross, Exec.Dir.

58438 ■ Wray Chamber of Commerce
PO Box 101
110 E 3rd St.
Wray, CO 80758
Ph:(970)332-3484
Co. E-mail: wraychambercomm@centurytel.net
URL: http://www.wrayco.net
Contact: Linda Ellerd, Dir.

MINORITY BUSINESS ASSISTANCE PROGRAMS

58439 ■ Colorado Office of Business Development–Minority Business Office
1625 Broadway, Ste. 1700
Denver, CO 80202
Ph:(303)892-3840
Fax: (303)892-3848
URL: http://www.state.co.us/oed/MBO/
Contact: Brian Vogt, Dir
Description: Provides information and assistance to women-owned businesses in Colorado.

58440 ■ Colorado Office of Economic Development International Trade–Minority Business Office
1625 Broadway, Ste. 1700
Denver, CO 80202
Ph:(303)892-3850
Fax: (303)892-3848
Co. E-mail: ito@state.co.us
URL: http://www.advancecolorado.com
Contact: Brian Vogt, Dir
Description: Provides information and assistance to minority-owned businesses in Colorado.

58441 ■ Denver Business Associates
3840 York St Ste 230B
Denver, CO 80205
Ph:(303)455-3099
Fax: (303)455-3076
Co. E-mail: info@denverba.com
URL: http://www.denverba.com

FINANCING AND LOAN PROGRAMS

58442 ■ 5280 Partners
360 S. Monroe St., Ste. 600
Denver, CO 80209
Ph:(303)333-1215
Fax: (303)322-3553
Contact: Jeffrey Bennis, Principal
Preferred Investment Size: $1,000,000 to $2,000,000. **Investment Policies:** First and second stage. **Industry Preferences:** Communications, computer software, and Internet specific. **Geographic Preferences:** Rocky Mountains.

58443 ■ Access Venture Partners
8787 Turnpike Dr., Ste. 260
Westminster, CO 80030
Ph:(303)426-8899
Fax: (303)426-8828
URL: http://www.accessventurepartners.com
Contact: Jay Campion, Managing Director
Preferred Investment Size: $250,000 to $2,000,000. **Investment Policies:** Seed and early stage. **Industry Preferences:** Communications and media, biotechnology, Internet specific, semiconductors and other electronics, computer software and services, industrial and energy. **Geographic Preferences:** Northern California, Rocky Mountains, and Southwest.

58444 ■ Altira Group LLC
1625 Broadway, Ste. 2450
Denver, CO 80202
Ph:(303)592-5500
Fax: (303)592-5519
URL: http://www.altiragroup.com
Contact: Dick McDermott, Managing Partner
Preferred Investment Size: $500,000 to $5,000,000. **Investment Types:** Early stage. **Industry Preferences:** Industrial and energy, and environment. **Geographic Preferences:** U.S. and Canada.

58445 ■ Appian Ventures
1700 Lincoln St.
Denver, CO 80203
Ph:(303)830-2450
Fax: (303)830-2449
URL: http://www.appianvc.com
Contact: Chris Onan, Principal
Preferred Investment Size: $500,000 to $5,000,000. **Investment Policies:** Seed, early and later stage. **Industry Preferences:** Communications, and computer software. **Geographic Preferences:** Colorado, Rocky Mountains, and West Coast.

58446 ■ Aweida Capital Management LLP
500 Discovery Pky., Ste. 300
Superior, CO 80027
Ph:(303)664-9520
Fax: (303)664-9530
URL: http://www.aweida.com
Contact: Daniel Aweida, Managing Partner
Preferred Investment Size: $500,000 to $1,000,000. **Investment Types:** Seed, start-up, and early stage. **Industry Preferences:** Computer software and hardware, Internet specific, biotechnology, and medical and health. **Geographic Preferences:** Rocky Mountains.

58447 ■ Boranco Management, L.L.C.
1528 Hillside Dr.
Fort Collins, CO 80524-1969
Ph:(970)221-2297
Preferred Investment Size: $100,000. **Investment Types:** Seed, start-up, first and second stage, research and development. **Industry Preferences:** Consumer related.

58448 ■ Centennial Ventures
1428 15th St.
Denver, CO 80202-1318
Ph:(303)405-7500
Fax: (303)405-7575
URL: http://www.centennial.com
Contact: Sean White, President

Preferred Investment Size: $100,000 minimum. **Investment Types:** Seed, start-up, early, later, first stage, and balanced. **Industry Preferences:** Communications and media, Internet specific, computer hardware, computer software and services, semiconductors and other electronics, medical and health, biotechnology, consumer related, other products, and industrial and energy. **Geographic Preferences:** U.S.

58449 ■ Colorado Venture Management / CVM Equity Funds
2575 Park Ln., Ste. 200
Lafayette, CO 80026
Ph:(303)440-4055
Fax: (303)440-4636
URL: http://www.cvmequity.com
Contact: Gary Bloomer, President and Chief Operating Officer
Preferred Investment Size: $50,000 to $1,000,000. **Investment Types:** Seed, start-up, and early stage. **Industry Preferences:** Computer software and services, medical and health, Internet specific, computer hardware, communications and media, consumer related, biotechnology, industrial and energy, semiconductors and other electronics, and other products. **Geographic Preferences:** Rocky Mountains and Midwest.

58450 ■ The Columbine Venture Funds
7000 E. Belleview Ave., Ste. 150
Englewood, CO 80111
Ph:(303)694-3222
Fax: (303)694-9007
Contact: Carl Stutts, General Partner
Preferred Investment Size: $300,000 to $800,000. **Investment Types:** Seed, research and development, start-up, and first stage. **Industry Preferences:** Medical and health, biotechnology, industrial and energy, semiconductors and other electronics, computer software, hardware and services, Internet specific, communications and media. **Geographic Preferences:** Southwest, Rocky Mountains, and West Coast.

58451 ■ Dean & Associates
4362 Apple Way
Boulder, CO 80301
Fax: (303)473-9900
Preferred Investment Size: $5,000,000 to $10,000,000. **Investment Types:** First and second stage, and mezzanine. **Industry Preferences:** Internet specific. **Geographic Preferences:** West Coast.

58452 ■ Hanifen Imhoff Capital
1125 17th St., Ste. 2260
Denver, CO 80202
Ph:(303)297-1701
Fax: (303)297-1702
URL: http://www.rockycapital.com
Contact: Edward Brown, Managing Partner
Preferred Investment Size: $3,000,000 to $7,000,000. **Investment Types:** Mezzanine, management buyouts, acquisition, and recapitalizations. **Industry Preferences:** Communications and media, consumer related, industrial and energy, medical and health, semiconductors and other electronics, computer software and services, Internet specific, and other products. **Geographic Preferences:** California, Midwest, Rocky Mountains, Northwest, West Coast, and Southwest.

58453 ■ Ibelay
1701 Pearl St., Ste. 200
Boulder, CO 80302
Ph:(720)406-1100
Fax: (720)406-1101
URL: http://www.ibelay.com
Contact: Ben Addoms, Managing Partner
Investment Policies: Seed.

58454 ■ Investment Securities of Colorado, Inc.
4605 Denice Dr.
Englewood, CO 80111
Ph:(303)796-9192
Investment Types: Seed and start-up. **Industry Preferences:** Semiconductors and other electronics,

medical and health. **Geographic Preferences:** Rocky Mountains.

58455 ■ Kinship Partners
6300 S. Syracuse Way, Ste. 484
Englewood, CO 80111
Ph:(303)694-0268
Fax: (303)694-1707
Preferred Investment Size: $500,000 to $1,000,000.
Investment Types: Seed, start-up, and first stage. **Industry Preferences:** Communications and media, computer software and hardware, biotechnology, medical and health.

58456 ■ Meritage Private Equity Funds
1600 Wynkoop St., Ste. 300
Denver, CO 80202
Ph:(303)352-2040
Fax: (303)352-2050
URL: http://www.meritagefunds.com
Contact: Laura Beller, Managing Director
Preferred Investment Size: $1,000,000 to $50,000,000. **Investment Types:** Seed, early and later stage, balanced, expansion, industry rollups, public companies, recapitalizations, special situation, and turnaround. **Industry Preferences:** Internet specific, communications and media, computer hardware, and computer software and services. **Geographic Preferences:** U.S.

58457 ■ New Venture Resources
445C E. Cheyenne Mtn. Blvd.
PMB 342
Colorado Springs, CO 80906-4570
Ph:(719)598-9272
Fax: (719)598-9272
Contact: Jeffrey M. Cooper, Managing Director
E-mail: jmcooper3@aol.com
Preferred Investment Size: $100,000 to $300,000.
Investment Types: Seed and start-up. **Industry Preferences:** Communications and media, computer related, semiconductors and other electronics, biotechnology, medical and health, consumer related, industrial and energy. **Geographic Preferences:** Southwest and Rocky Mountains.

58458 ■ Quest Capital
2344 Washington St.
Newton, MA 02462
Ph:(617)332-7227
Fax: (617)332-3113
URL: http://www.questcapitalinc.com
Contact: Ed Slade, Co-Founder
Investment Policies: Early stage. **Industry Preferences:** Consumer related.

58459 ■ Rockmountain Ventures
1840 Deer Creek, Ste. 300
Monument, CO 80132
Ph:(714)488-3900
URL: http://www.rockventures.com
Contact: Barton Skalla, Managing Director
Investment Types: Start-up. **Industry Preferences:** Communications and media, computer software, Internet specific, semiconductors and other electronics. **Geographic Preferences:** Colorado and Texas.

58460 ■ Roser Ventures LLC
1105 Spruce St.
Boulder, CO 80302
Ph:(303)443-6436
Fax: (303)443-1885
URL: http://www.roserventures.com
Contact: Christopher Roser, Partner
Preferred Investment Size: $250,000 to $3,000,000.
Investment Types: Early stage and expansion. **Industry Preferences:** Internet specific, communications and media, industrial and energy, semiconductors and other electronics, computer software and services, medical and health, computer hardware, other products, biotechnology, and consumer related. **Geographic Preferences:** Rocky Mountains.

58461 ■ Sandlot Capital LLC
600 S. Cherry St., Ste. 525
Denver, CO 80246

Ph:(303)893-3400
Fax: (303)893-3403
URL: http://www.sandlotcapital.com
Contact: Candace Newman
Preferred Investment Size: $250,000 to $20,000,000. **Investment Types:** Seed, start-up, early and first stage, and special situation. **Industry Preferences:** Communications and media, computer software and hardware, and Internet specific.

58462 ■ Sequel Venture Partners
4430 Arapahoe Ave., Ste. 220
Boulder, CO 80303
Ph:(303)546-0400
Fax: (303)546-9728
Co. E-mail: tom@sequelvc.com
URL: http://www.sequelvc.com
Contact: Thomas Washing, Partner
Preferred Investment Size: $2,000,000 to $12,000,000. **Investment Types:** Seed, early, and first stage. **Industry Preferences:** Internet specific, computer software and services, medical and health, semiconductors and other electronics, biotechnology, communications and media, computer hardware, and other products. **Geographic Preferences:** Colorado and Rocky Mountains.

58463 ■ Telecom Partners / Telecom Management LLC
4600 S. Syracuse St., Ste. 1000
Denver, CO 80237
Ph:(303)874-1100
Fax: (303)874-1110
URL: http://www.telecompartners.com
Contact: Mark Adolph, Chief Operating Officer
Preferred Investment Size: $1,000,000 to $75,000,000. **Investment Types:** Seed and early stage. **Industry Preferences:** Internet specific, communications and media, semiconductors and other electronics, computer software and services, and consumer related. **Geographic Preferences:** U.S.

58464 ■ Wolf Ventures / Wolf Asset Management Corp.
1600 Stout St., Ste. 1510
Denver, CO 80202
Ph:(303)321-4800
Fax: (303)321-4848
Co. E-mail: businessplan@wolfventures.com
URL: http://www.wolfventures.com
Contact: David Wolf, Managing Partner
Preferred Investment Size: $500,000 to $2,500,000.
Investment Types: Early, first and second stage, and expansion. **Industry Preferences:** Computer software and services, semiconductors and other electronics, Internet specific, communications and media, medical and health, computer hardware, other products, industrial and energy, and consumer related. **Geographic Preferences:** Rocky Mountains.

PROCUREMENT ASSISTANCE PROGRAMS

58465 ■ Colorado Procurement Technical Assistance Center–Denver Small Business Development Procurement Center
1445 Market St.
Denver, CO 80202
Ph:(303)620-8082
Fax: (303)620-8076
URL: http://www.colorado.sbdc.com
Contact: Tom Foster

INCUBATORS/RESEARCH AND TECHNOLOGY PARKS

58466 ■ Colorado State University–Office of Vice President for Research
203 Administration Bldg.
Fort Collins, CO 80523-2001
Ph:(970)491-7194
Fax: (970)491-5541

Co. E-mail: hank.gardner@research.colostate.edu
URL: http://www.vprit.colostate.edu
Contact: Dr. Hank Gardner, Interim VP,Res.
E-mail: hank.gardner@research.colostate.edu
Scope: Administers and coordinates research activities in the various colleges, departments, and special research units at the University. **Publications:** Research at Colorado State University. **Educational Activities:** Conference services; Research colloquia.

58467 ■ Colorado State University Research Foundation
PO Box 483
Fort Collins, CO 80522
Ph:(970)482-2916
Fax: (970)484-0354
Co. E-mail: Kathleen@csurf.org
URL: http://www.csurf.org
Contact: Kathleen Henry, Pres./CEO
E-mail: Kathleen@csurf.org
Scope: Assists Colorado State University and the other universities governed by the Colorado Board of Governors State Board of Agriculture through the management of patents and licenses, acquisition of research equipment and facilities, and the acquisition and management of land. Acts as a support organization in tax-exempt debt financing, which takes the form of municipal bonds, notes, mortgages, revolving lines of credit, and equipment leasing.

58468 ■ Colorado Technology Incubator
2400 Trade Center
Longmont, CO 80501
Ph:(303)678-8000
Fax: (303)678-8505
Co. E-mail: alex@ctek.biz
URL: http://www.ctek.biz
Contact: Alex Sammoury, Exec Dir
Description: BTI assists startup companies in the technology industry by offering services such as business planning, management development, and executive suites.

58469 ■ The Denver Enterprise Center
3003 Arapahoe St.
Denver, CO 80205
Ph:(303)296-9400
Fax: (303)296-5542
Co. E-mail: decinfo@thedec.org
URL: http://www.thedec.org/
Contact: Pat Durand, Exec Dir
Description: A small business incubator that assists entrepreneurs in the business start-up process and gives aid to new businesses to help ensure their survival.

58470 ■ Fremont County Business Development Center
402 Valley Rd.
Canon City, CO 81212
Ph:(719)275-8601
Free: 800-426-4794
Fax: (719)275-4400
Co. E-mail: fedc@piopc.net
URL: http://www.fremontedc.org
Description: A small business incubator that assists entrepreneurs in the business start-up process and gives aid to new businesses to help ensure their survival.

58471 ■ Pueblo Business and Technology Center
301 N Main St.
Pueblo, CO 81003
Ph:(719)546-1133
Free: 800-522-1120
Fax: (719)546-1942
Co. E-mail: btc@amigo.net
URL: http://www.btc-pueblo.com
Description: A small business incubator that assists entrepreneurs in the business start-up process and gives aid to new businesses to help ensure their survival.

58472 ■ University of Colorado at Boulder–Research Park
CB 317
Boulder, CO 80309-0317

Ph:(303)492-1525
Fax: (303)492-7186
Co. E-mail: lipton@colorado.edu
Contact: Jeffrey Lipton, Dir.
E-mail: lipton@colorado.edu
Scope: Fosters the interaction between the University research community and tenants, particularly in the areas of information technologies, space sciences, biotechnology, telecommunications, computer science, chemistry, biochemistry, and environmental sciences.

58473 ■ University of Colorado at Boulder–Technology Transfer Office
588 UCB
4740 Walnut St., Ste. 100
Boulder, CO 80309-0588
Ph:(303)735-3711
Fax: (303)735-3831
Co. E-mail: david.allen@cu.edu
URL: http://www.cusys.edu/techtransfer
Contact: David Allen
E-mail: david.allen@cu.edu
Scope: Administers and coordinates sponsored research proposals and post-award administrative activities of the University, provides administrative and accounting services, assists faculty members conducting research, and serves as liaison and negotiator with extramural sponsors of research conducted at the University and with governmental auditors. **Publications:** Technology Transfer Office Annual Report; TTO Newsletter (monthly). **Awards:** Proof-of-Concept Grants (semiannually), to CU researchers working to develop the commercial potential of CU inventions.

58474 ■ Western Colorado Business Development Corp.
2591B 3/4 Rd.
Grand Junction, CO 81503
Ph:(970)243-5242
Fax: (970)241-0771
Co. E-mail: administrative@gjincubator.org
URL: http://www.gjincubator.org
Contact: Thea Chase-Gilman, Exec Dir
Description: Assists entrepreneurs in the business start-up process and in managing new businesses.

EDUCATIONAL PROGRAMS

58475 ■ Aims Community College
PO Box 69
Greeley, CO 80632
Ph:(970)330-8008
Free: 800-745-0650
Fax: (970)330-5705
URL: http://www.aims.edu
Description: Two-year college offering a small business management program.

58476 ■ Colorado Northwestern Community College (Craig)
50 College Dr.
Craig, CO 81625
Ph:(970)824-7071
Fax: (970)824-1134
URL: http://www.cncc.edu
Description: Two-year college offering a small business management program.

58477 ■ Emily Griffith Opportunity School
1250 Welton St.
Denver, CO 80204
Ph:(720)423-4700
Fax: (720)575-4840
URL: http://www.egos-school.com
Description: Trade and technical school offering classes in entrepreneurship.

58478 ■ Lamar Community College
2401 S Main St.
Lamar, CO 81052

Ph:(719)336-2248
Free: 800-968-6920
Fax: (719)336-2448
Co. E-mail: angela.woodward@lcc.cccoes.edu
URL: http://www.lcc.cccoes.edu
Description: Two-year college offering a small business management program.

LEGISLATIVE ASSISTANCE

58479 ■ Colorado Senate Committee on Business Affairs and Labor
State Capitol
200 E Colfax Ave.
Denver, CO 80203
Ph:(303)866-3521
Free: 888-811-7647
Fax: (303)866-2316
Co. E-mail: access from website
URL: http://www.state.co.us
Contact: Jeanette Chapman

TRADE PERIODICALS

58480 ■ *Colorado Job Finder*
Pub: Colorado Municipal League
Released: Semimonthly, 1st and 3rd Wednesday of each month. **Price:** individuals; $30 for 6 months. **Description:** Consists of local government employment opportunities in Colorado and surrounding area.

PUBLICATIONS

58481 ■ *The Denver Business Journal*
1700 Broadway, Ste. 515
Denver, CO 80290
Ph:(303)837-3500
Fax: (303)837-3535
URL: http://www.amcity.com/denver

58482 ■ *Smart Start your Colorado Business*
PSI Research
300 N. Valley Dr.
Grants Pass, OR 97526
Ph:(503)479-9464
Free: 800-228-2275
Fax: (503)476-1479
Co. E-mail: info@psi-research.com
URL: http://www.psi-research.com
Ed: Michael D. Jenkins. **Released:** Revised edition, 1992. **Price:** $29.95 (looseleaf binder); $24.95 (paper). **Description:** Part of the Successful Business Library series.

58483 ■ *Starting and Operating a Business in Colorado: A Step-by-Step Guide*
PSI Research
300 N. Valley Dr.
Grants Pass, OR 97526
Ph:(503)479-9464
Free: 800-228-2275
Fax: (503)476-1479
Co. E-mail: psi2@magick.net
Ed: Michael D. Jenkins. **Released:** Revised edition, 1992. **Price:** $29.95 (looseleaf binder); $24.95 (paper). **Description:** Part of the Successful Business Library series.

PUBLISHERS

58484 ■ Center for Self-Sufficiency–Publishing Div.
Prosperity & Profits Unlimited
PO Box 416
Denver, CO 80201-0416

Ph:(303)575-5676
Co. E-mail: mail@gumbomedia.com
URL: http://www.centerforselfsufficiency.org
Contact: A. C. Doyle, Founder
Description: Publishes how-to, consumer, recycling, and small business titles. Does not accept unsolicited manuscripts. Reaches market through direct mail. **Founded:** 1982.

58485 ■ Lifestar
2244 S Olive St.
Denver, CO 80224
Ph:(303)756-9144
Free: 888-468-1537
Fax: (303)756-3107
Co. E-mail: lifestar@rmi.net
URL: http://www.qimacros.com/
Contact: Jay Arthur
Description: Publishes materials on improving business operations and employee stress involving conflict and communication issues.

58486 ■ Restaurant Publishing
c/o Prosperity & Profit Unlimited, Distribution Services
PO Box 416
Denver, CO 80201-0416
Ph:(303)575-5676
Fax: (303)575-1187
Co. E-mail: mail@prosperityandprofitsunlimited.com
URL: http://www.prosperityandprofitsunlimited.com
Contact: A. Doyle, President
Description: Publishes and distributes cookbooks, food how-to books, and newsletters for restaurants, cafes, and catering services. Distributes *Recipe Greetings, Recipe Multiplication Forms,* and *Herbal Verbal* cassettes. Reaches market through direct mail, trade sales, and Prosperity and Profits Unlimited. Does not accept unsolicited manuscripts. **Founded:** 1989.

58487 ■ Rollaway Bay Publications Inc.
6334 S Racine Cir., Ste. 100
Centennial, CO 80111-6405
Ph:(303)799-8320
Fax: (303)799-4220
Co. E-mail: publisher@rollawaybay.com
URL: http://www.rollawaybay.com
Contact: Rick Elliott
Description: Publishes business titles. **Founded:** 2003

58488 ■ Thimband
c/o Continnuus
PO Box 416
Denver, CO 80201-0416
Ph:(303)575-5676
Fax: (303)575-1187
Co. E-mail: mail@thimbland.com
URL: http://www.thimband.com
Contact: A. Doyle, President
Description: Publishes resources for cottages industries. **Founded:** 1997.

58489 ■ Update Publicare Co.
c/o Prosperity & Profits Unlimited
PO Box 416
Denver, CO 80201-0416
Ph:(303)575-5676
Fax: (303)575-1187
Co. E-mail: mail@breadpudding.net
Contact: A. C. Doyle, Editor
E-mail: mail@gumbomedia.com
Description: Publishes for consumers and businesses. Offers newsletters on recycling, self employment, publishing, and small business. Does not accept unsolicited manuscripts. **Founded:** 1989.

SMALL BUSINESS DEVELOPMENT CENTER LEAD OFFICE

58490 ■ Connecticut Small Business Development Center–University of Connecticut
1376 Storrs Rd., Unit 4094
Storrs, CT 06269-1094
Ph:(860)870-6370
Fax: (860)870-6374
Co. E-mail: csbdcinformation@sba.uconn.edu
URL: http://www.sbdc.uconn.edu

E-mail: richard.cheney@uconn.edu/

58491 ■ University of Connecticut–Small Business Development Center
2 Bourn Place, U - 49
Storrs, CT 06269-5094
Ph:(860)486-4135
Fax: (860)486-1576
Co. E-mail: CSBDCinformation@sba.uconn.edu
URL: http://www.sbdc.uconn.edu
Contact: Dennis Gruell, State Director
E-mail: statedirector@ct.sbdc.uconn.edu

SMALL BUSINESS DEVELOPMENT CENTERS

58492 ■ Bridgeport Economic Resource Center–Small Business Development Center
10 Middle St., 6th Fl.
Bridgeport, CT 06604-4229
Ph:(203)330-4813
Fax: (203)335-1297
Co. E-mail: bridgeportcsbdc@sba.uconn.edu
URL: http://www.sbdc.uconn.edu
Contact: Juan Scott, Regional Dir.
E-mail: juan.scott@uconn.edu

58493 ■ Connecticut SBDC–Asnuntuck Community College
170 Elm St.
Enfield, CT 06082
Ph:(860)253-3125
Fax: (860)253-3067
Contact: Sean McGuire
E-mail: smcguire@acc.commnet.edu

58494 ■ CSBDC Groton, Norwich and New London–University of Connecticut–Small Business Development Center (Admin)
Administration Bldg., Rm. 104
1084 Shennecossett Rd.
Groton, CT 06340-6097
Ph:(860)405-9002
Fax: (860)405-9041
URL: http://www.sbdc.uconn.edu
Contact: Peter Pappas, Regional Dir.
E-mail: peter.pappas@uconn.edu

58495 ■ Eastern Connecticut State University–Small Business Development Center
83 Windham St.
Willimantic, CT 06226-2295
Ph:(860)465-5349
Fax: (860)465-5143
Co. E-mail: willimanticcsbdc@easternct.edu
URL: http://www.asbdc-us-org

E-mail: twissd@easternct.edu

58496 ■ Greater New Haven Chamber of Commerce–Small Business Development Center
900 Chapel St., 10th Fl.
New Haven, CT 06510-2009
Ph:(203)782-4390
Fax: (203)782-4329
Co. E-mail: newhavencsbdc@sba.uconn.edu
URL: http://www.sbdc.uconn.edu
Contact: Pete Rivera, Regional Dir.
E-mail: pedro.rivera@uconn.edu

58497 ■ Middlesex County Chamber of Commerce–Small Business Development Center
393 Main St.
Middletown, CT 06457-3309
Ph:(860)344-2158
Co. E-mail: middletowncsbdc@sba.uconn.edu
URL: http://www.sbdc.uconn.edu
Contact: Paul Hughes, Business Counselor
E-mail: paul.hughes@uconn.edu

58498 ■ Quinebaug Valley Community College–CSBDC Danielson–Small Business Development Center (742 U)
742 Upper Maple St.
Danielson, CT 06239-1440
Ph:(860)774-1133
Fax: (860)774-6737
Co. E-mail: danielsoncsbdc@sba.uconn.edu
URL: http://www.sbdc.uconn.edu
Contact: Jack Derby, Regional Director
E-mail: jderby@qvcc.commnet.edu

58499 ■ Southwestern Area Commerce and Industry Association (SACIA)–Small Business Development Center
1 Landmark Sq.
Stamford, CT 06901
Ph:(203)359-3220
Fax: (203)967-8294
Co. E-mail: stamfordcsbdc@sba.uconn.edu
URL: http://www.sbdc.uconn.edu
Contact: Harry Bloomberg, Regional Dir.
E-mail: harvey.bloomberg@uconn.edu

58500 ■ University of Connecticut (Greater Hartford Campus)–Small Business Development Center
1800 Asylum Ave.
West Hartford, CT 06117
Ph:(860)570-9109
Fax: (860)570-9107

Co. E-mail: westhartfordcsbdc@sba.uconn.edu
Contact: Ben Chepovsky
E-mail: benjamin_chepovsky@uconn.edu

SMALL BUSINESS ASSISTANCE PROGRAMS

58501 ■ Connecticut Economic Development Commission–Business Response Center
805 Brook St. Bldg. 4
Rocky Hill, CT 06067-3405
Ph:(860)571-7136
Free: 800-392-2122
Fax: (860)571-7150
Co. E-mail: solutions@cerc.com
URL: http://www.cerc.com
Contact: Connie Maffeo, Dir
Description: Provides managerial assistance and assists in preparing applications for financing.

58502 ■ Department of Economic Development & Community Development–Small Business Assistance
505 Hudson St.
Hartford, CT 06106
Ph:(860)270-8000
Free: 800-392-2122
Fax: (860)270-8070
Co. E-mail: DECD@po.state.ct.us
URL: http://www.decd.org
Description: Promotes trade; publishes a brochure on licensing and joint ventures; and administers the Exporters Revolving Loan Fund for small and medium-sized businesses.

SCORE OFFICES

58503 ■ SCORE Fairfield City
24 Belden Ave., 5th Fl.
Norwalk, CT 06850
Ph:(203)847-7348
Fax: (203)849-9308
Co. E-mail: score41@aol.com
Description: Assists individuals with their decisions to begin or to operate small businesses. Provides educational seminars and business counseling.

58504 ■ SCORE Greater Bridgeport
c/o Charles Lipetz, Chm.
230 Park Ave.
Bridgeport, CT 06604
Ph:(203)576-4369
Fax: (203)576-4388
Co. E-mail: score471@bridgeport.edu
URL: http://scorebridgeportct.org
Contact: Charles Lipetz, Chm.

58505 ■ SCORE Greater Danbury
246 Federal Rd.
Brookfield, CT 06804
Ph:(203)775-1151

Co. E-mail: danburyscore@earthlink.net
URL: http://www.danbury.org/org/score
Description: Promotes entrepreneur education and the formation, growth and success of the nation's small business.

58506 ■ SCORE Greater Hartford City
330 Main St.
Hartford, CT 06106
Ph:(860)240-4700
Fax: (860)524-1611
Co. E-mail: r.s.hager@snet.net
URL: http://www.score56.org
Contact: Bob Hager, Chm.
Description: Provides professional guidance and information to maximize the success of existing and emerging small businesses. Promotes entrepreneur education in Greater Hartford area, Connecticut.

58507 ■ SCORE New Haven
c/o Gateway Community College
60 Sargent Dr., Rm. 207A
New Haven, CT 06511
Ph:(203)865-7645
Co. E-mail: jbrander@aol.com
URL: http://www.newhavenscore.com
Contact: Julie Brander, Chair
Description: Provides professional guidance and information to maximize the success of existing and emerging small businesses. Promotes entrepreneur education in New Haven County area, Connecticut.

58508 ■ SCORE Old Saybrook
c/o Old Saybrook Chamber of Commerce
146 Main St.
Old Saybrook, CT 06475
Ph:(860)388-9508
Fax: (860)388-9433
Co. E-mail: score579@hotmail.com

BETTER BUSINESS BUREAUS

58509 ■ Better Business Bureau, Connecticut
94 S Turnpike Rd.
Wallingford, CT 06492
Ph:(203)269-2700
Fax: (203)269-3124
Co. E-mail: info@ctbbb.org
URL: http://www.connecticut.bbb.org
Contact: Paulette Hotton, Pres./CEO

CHAMBERS OF COMMERCE

58510 ■ Avon Chamber of Commerce
412 W Avon Rd.
Avon, CT 06001
Ph:(860)677-4832
Fax: (860)675-0469
Co. E-mail: avonchamber@sbcglobal.net
URL: http://www.avonchamber.com
Contact: Ronald Evans, Pres.

58511 ■ Berlin Chamber of Commerce
Ferndale Ctr., 40 Chamberlain Hwy.
Kensington, CT 06037
Ph:(860)829-1033
Fax: (860)829-1243
Co. E-mail: director@berlinctchamber.org
URL: http://www.berlinctchamber.org
Contact: Katherine A. Fuechsel, Exec.Dir.

58512 ■ Bethel Chamber of Commerce
16 P.T. Barnum Sq.
Bethel, CT 06801
Ph:(203)743-6500
Fax: (203)744-5265
Co. E-mail: bethelchamber@aol.com
URL: http://www.bethelchamber.com
Contact: Violet Mattone, Exec. Dir.

58513 ■ Bloomfield Chamber of Commerce
330 Park Ave., 2nd Fl.
Bloomfield, CT 06002
Ph:(860)242-3710
Fax: (860)242-6129
Co. E-mail: director@bloomfieldchamber.org
URL: http://www.bloomfieldchamber.org
Contact: Ms. Vera Smith-Winfree, Exec.Dir.

58514 ■ Branford Chamber of Commerce
239 N Main St.
Branford, CT 06405
Ph:(203)488-5500
Fax: (203)488-5046
Co. E-mail: info@branfordct.com
URL: http://www.branfordct.com
Contact: John F. Cushing, Pres.

58515 ■ Bridgeport Regional Business Council
10 Middle St., 4th Fl.
Bridgeport, CT 06604
Ph:(203)335-3800
Fax: (203)366-0105
Co. E-mail: info@brbc.org
URL: http://www.brbc.org
Contact: Paul S. Timpanelli, Pres./CEO

58516 ■ Canton Chamber of Commerce
PO Box 704
Canton, CT 06019
Ph:(860)693-0405
Fax: (860)693-9105
Co. E-mail: cantoncofc@msn.com
URL: http://www.cantonchamberofcommerce.com
Contact: Philip E. Worley, Exec.Dir.

58517 ■ Chamber of Commerce of Eastern Connecticut
PO Box 726
Gales Ferry, CT 06335
Ph:(860)464-7373
Free: (866)274-5587
Fax: (860)464-7374
Co. E-mail: tsheridan@chamberect.com
URL: http://www.chamberect.com
Contact: Thomas A. Sheridan, Pres.

58518 ■ Chamber of Commerce of Newtown
PO Box 314
Newtown, CT 06470
Ph:(203)426-2695
Fax: (203)426-2695
Co. E-mail: ramooreod@cs.com
URL: http://www.newtown-ct.com
Contact: Jack Rosenthal, Admin.Sec.

58519 ■ Chamber of Commerce of Northwest Connecticut
PO Box 59
Torrington, CT 06790
Ph:(860)482-6586
Fax: (860)489-8851
Co. E-mail: joann@nwctchamberofcommerce.org
URL: http://www.nwctchamberofcommerce.org
Contact: JoAnn Ryan, Pres.

58520 ■ Chamber of Commerce of Southeastern Connecticut
105 Huntington St.
New London, CT 06320-6622
Ph:(860)443-8332
Fax: (860)444-1529
Co. E-mail: stevens@chamberect.com
URL: http://www.chamberect.com
Contact: Cynthia H. Clegg, Pres.

58521 ■ Chamber of Commerce, Windham Region
PO Box 43
Willimantic, CT 06226-0043
Ph:(860)423-6389
Fax: (860)423-8235
Co. E-mail: info@windhamchamber.com
URL: http://www.windhamchamber.com
Contact: Roger Adams, Exec.Dir.

58522 ■ Cheshire Chamber of Commerce
195 S Main St.
Cheshire, CT 06410
Ph:(203)272-2345
Fax: (203)271-3044
Co. E-mail: info@cheshirechamber.com
URL: http://www.cheshirechamber.com
Contact: Sheldon Dill, Exec.Dir.

58523 ■ Clinton Chamber of Commerce
PO Box 334
Clinton, CT 06413
Ph:(860)669-3889
Fax: (860)669-3889
Co. E-mail: chamber@clintonct.com
URL: http://clintonct.com
Contact: Ellen Cavanagh, Exec.Dir.

58524 ■ Connecticut Business and Industry Association
350 Church St.
Hartford, CT 06103-1126
Ph:(860)244-1900
Fax: (860)278-8562
URL: http://www.cbia.com
Contact: Kenneth O. Decko, Pres./CEO

58525 ■ Darien Chamber of Commerce
17 Old Kings Hwy. S
Darien, CT 06820
Ph:(203)655-3600
Fax: (203)655-2074
Co. E-mail: darienchamber@optonline.net
URL: http://dcc.darien.org
Contact: Carol Wilder Tamme, Exec.Dir.

58526 ■ East Granby Chamber of Commerce
PO Box 1335
East Granby, CT 06026
Ph:(860)651-3833
Fax: (860)651-3818
Co. E-mail: eastgranbycoc@eastgranbycoc.org
URL: http://www.eastgranbycoc.org
Contact: Dave Peichert, Pres.

58527 ■ East Hartford Chamber of Commerce
1137 Main St.
East Hartford, CT 06108
Ph:(860)289-0239
Fax: (860)289-0230
Co. E-mail: ehcoc@aol.com
URL: http://www.ehcoc.com
Contact: Mary Beth Reid, Exec.Dir.

58528 ■ East Haven Chamber of Commerce
PO Box 120055
East Haven, CT 06512
Ph:(203)467-4305
Fax: (203)469-2299
Co. E-mail: ehchamber@ehchamber.org
URL: http://ehchamber.org
Contact: Mary W. Cacace, Exec.Dir.

58529 ■ Fairfield Chamber of Commerce
1597 Post Rd.
Fairfield, CT 06824
Ph:(203)255-1011
Fax: (203)256-9990
Co. E-mail: info@fairfieldctchamber.com
URL: http://www.fairfieldctchamber.com
Contact: Patricia L. Ritchie, Pres./CEO

58530 ■ Farmington Chamber of Commerce
827 Farmington Ave.
Farmington, CT 06032
Ph:(860)676-8490
Fax: (860)677-8332
Co. E-mail: raygagnon@farmingtonchamber.com
URL: http://www.farmingtonchamber.com
Contact: Ray Gagnon, Membership Dir.

58531 ■ Glastonbury Chamber of Commerce
2400 Main St.
Glastonbury, CT 06033
Ph:(860)659-3587
Fax: (860)659-0102

URL: http://www.glastonburychamber.com
Contact: Mary Ellen Dombrowski, Exec. Dir.

58532 ■ Granby Chamber of Commerce
PO Box 211
Granby, CT 06035
Ph:(860)653-5085
Co. E-mail: info@granbycoc.org
URL: http://www.granbycoc.org
Contact: Bruce Johnston, Administrator

58533 ■ Greater Danbury Chamber of Commerce
39 West St.
Danbury, CT 06810
Ph:(203)743-5565
Fax: (203)794-1439
Co. E-mail: info@danburychamber.com
URL: http://www.danburychamber.com
Contact: Stephen A. Bull, Pres.

58534 ■ Greater Manchester Chamber of Commerce
20 Hartford Rd.
Manchester, CT 06040
Ph:(860)646-2223
Fax: (860)646-5871
Co. E-mail: staffgmcc@manchesterchamber.com
URL: http://www.manchesterchamber.com
Contact: Sue O'Connor, Pres.

58535 ■ Greater Meriden Chamber of Commerce
3 Colony St., Ste. 301
Meriden, CT 06450
Ph:(203)235-7901
Fax: (203)686-0172
Co. E-mail: info@meridenchamber.com
URL: http://www.meridenchamber.com
Contact: Sean W. Moore, Pres.

58536 ■ Greater New Haven Chamber of Commerce
900 Chapel St., 10th Fl.
New Haven, CT 06510
Ph:(203)787-6735
Fax: (203)782-4329
Co. E-mail: info@gnhcc.com
URL: http://www.newhavenchamber.com
Contact: Anthony P. Rescigno, Pres.

58537 ■ Greater New Milford Chamber of Commerce
11 Railroad St.
New Milford, CT 06776-2717
Ph:(860)354-6080
Fax: (860)354-8526
Co. E-mail: nmcc@newmilford-chamber.com
URL: http://www.newmilford-chamber.com
Contact: Denise Del Mastro, Exec.Dir.

58538 ■ Greater Norwalk Chamber of Commerce
PO Box 668
Norwalk, CT 06852-0668
Ph:(203)866-2521
Fax: (203)852-0583
Co. E-mail: info@norwalkchamberofcommerce.com
URL: http://www.norwalkchamberofcommerce.com
Contact: Edward J. Musante Jr., Pres.

58539 ■ Greater Southington Chamber of Commerce
1 Factory Sq.
Southington, CT 06489
Ph:(860)628-8036
Fax: (860)276-9696
Co. E-mail: info@southingtoncoc.com
URL: http://www.southingtoncoc.com
Contact: Art Secondo, Pres.

58540 ■ Greater Valley Chamber of Commerce
900 Bridgeport Ave.
Shelton, CT 06484
Ph:(203)925-4981
Fax: (203)925-4984

Co. E-mail: info@greatervalleychamber.com
URL: http://greatervalleychamber.com
Contact: William E. Purcell CCE, Pres.

58541 ■ Greenwich Chamber of Commerce
45 E Putnam Ave., No. 121
Greenwich, CT 06830
Ph:(203)869-3500
Fax: (203)869-3502
Co. E-mail: info@greenwichchamber.com
URL: http://www.greenwichchamber.com
Contact: Mary Ann Morrison, Pres./CEO

58542 ■ Guilford Chamber of Commerce
63 Whitfield St.
Guilford, CT 06437-2640
Ph:(203)453-9677
Fax: (203)453-6022
Co. E-mail: chamber@guilfordct.com
URL: http://www.guilfordct.com
Contact: Joanna Martin, Pres.

58543 ■ Hamden Chamber of Commerce
2969 Whitney Ave.
Hamden, CT 06518
Ph:(203)288-6431
Fax: (203)288-4499
Co. E-mail: hcc@hamdenchamber.com
URL: http://www.hamdenchamber.com
Contact: Nancy Dudchik, Exec.Dir.

58544 ■ Kent Chamber of Commerce
PO Box 124
Kent, CT 06757-0124
Ph:(860)927-1463
Co. E-mail: president@kentct.com
URL: http://www.kentct.com
Contact: Geraldine Woodruff, Pres.

58545 ■ Killingworth Chamber of Commerce
PO Box 780
Killingworth, CT 06419
Co. E-mail: killingworthonline@hotmail.com
URL: http://www.killingworthct.com

58546 ■ Madison Chamber of Commerce
22 Scotland Ave.
Madison, CT 06443
Ph:(203)245-7394
Fax: (203)245-4279
Co. E-mail: chamber@madisonct.com
URL: http://www.madisonct.com
Contact: Eileen Speed, Exec.Dir.

58547 ■ MetroHartford Chamber of Commerce
31 Pratt St., 5th Fl.
Hartford, CT 06103
Ph:(860)525-4451
Fax: (860)293-2592
Co. E-mail: info@metrohartford.com
URL: http://www.metrohartford.com
Contact: Oz Griebel, Pres./CEO

58548 ■ Middlesex County Chamber of Commerce
393 Main St.
Middletown, CT 06457
Ph:(860)347-6924
Fax: (860)346-1043
Co. E-mail: info@middlesexchamber.com
URL: http://www.middlesexchamber.com
Contact: Larry McHugh, Pres.

58549 ■ Milford Chamber of Commerce
5 Broad St.
Milford, CT 06460
Ph:(203)878-0681
Fax: (203)876-8517
Co. E-mail: chamber@milfordct.com
URL: http://www.milfordct.com
Contact: Kathleen Alagno, Pres./CEO

58550 ■ Monroe Chamber of Commerce
477 Main St.
Monroe, CT 06468
Ph:(203)268-6518

Fax: (203)268-3337
Co. E-mail: info@monroe-chamber.com
URL: http://www.monroe-chamber.com
Contact: Jo-Ellen Stipak, Exec.Dir.

58551 ■ Mystic Chamber of Commerce
14 Holmes St.
PO Box 143
Mystic, CT 06355
Ph:(860)572-9578
Fax: (860)572-9273
Co. E-mail: linnea@mysticchamber.org
URL: http://www.mysticchamber.org
Contact: Linnea Lindstrom, Exec.Dir.

58552 ■ Naugatuck Chamber of Commerce
195 Water St.
Naugatuck, CT 06770
Ph:(203)729-4511
Fax: (203)729-4512
Co. E-mail: lward@waterburychamber.com
Contact: Lynn Ward, Dir.

58553 ■ New Britain Chamber of Commerce
1 Court St.
New Britain, CT 06051
Ph:(860)229-1665
Fax: (860)223-8341
Co. E-mail: bill@newbritainchamber.com
URL: http://www.newbritainchamber.com
Contact: William F. Millerick, Pres.

58554 ■ New Canaan Chamber of Commerce
111 Elm St.
New Canaan, CT 06840
Ph:(203)966-2004
Fax: (203)966-3810
Co. E-mail: director@newcanaanchamber.com
URL: http://www.newcanaanchamber.com
Contact: Pamela B. Ogilvie, Exec.Dir.

58555 ■ Newington Chamber of Commerce
1046 Main St.
Newington, CT 06111
Ph:(860)666-2089
Fax: (860)665-7551
Co. E-mail: office@newingtonchamber.com
URL: http://www.newingtonchamber.com
Contact: Gail Whitney, Exec.Dir.

58556 ■ North Central Connecticut Chamber of Commerce
73 Hazard Ave.
Enfield, CT 06083
Ph:(860)741-3838
Fax: (860)741-3512
Co. E-mail: chamber@ncccc.org
URL: http://www.ncccc.org
Contact: Mr. Richard Schaefer, Pres.

58557 ■ Northeastern Connecticut Chamber of Commerce
3 Central St.
Danielson, CT 06239
Ph:(860)774-8001
Fax: (860)774-4299
Co. E-mail: info@nectchamber.com
URL: http://www.nectchamber.com
Contact: Elizabeth Kuszaj, Exec.Dir.

58558 ■ Old Saybrook Chamber of Commerce
146 Main St.
PO Box 625
Old Saybrook, CT 06475-0625
Ph:(860)388-3266
Co. E-mail: info@oldsaybrookchamber.com
URL: http://www.oldsaybrookct.com
Contact: Linanne Lee, Exec.Dir.

58559 ■ Orange Chamber of Commerce
605A Orange Center Rd.
Orange, CT 06477
Ph:(203)795-3328
Fax: (203)795-5926
Co. E-mail: orange.commerce@sbcglobal.net
URL: http://www.orangectchamber.com

Contact: Ms. Patricia Sikeritzky, Exec.Dir.

58560 ■ Prospect Chamber of Commerce
4 Summit Rd.
Prospect, CT 06712-0132
Ph:(203)758-6640
Fax: (203)758-0766
Co. E-mail: prospectchmbrcom@aol.com
URL: http://www.prospectchamber.com
Contact: Ann LaVorgna, Pres.

58561 ■ Quinnipiac Chamber of Commerce
100 S Turnpike Rd.
Wallingford, CT 06492
Ph:(203)269-9891
Fax: (203)269-1358
Co. E-mail: robin@quinncham.com
URL: http://www.quinncham.com
Contact: Robin Wilson, Pres./CEO

58562 ■ Ridgefield Chamber of Commerce
9 Bailey Ave.
Ridgefield, CT 06877
Ph:(203)438-5992
Fax: (203)438-9175
Co. E-mail: phoffman@ridgefieldchamber.org
URL: http://www.ridgefieldchamber.org
Contact: Penny S. Hoffman, Pres.

58563 ■ Rocky Hill Chamber of Commerce
33 Church St.
Rocky Hill, CT 06067
Ph:(860)258-7633
Fax: (860)258-7637
Co. E-mail: chamber@rockyhillchamberofcommerce.com
URL: http://www.rhchamber.org
Contact: John L. Swingen Jr., Sec.

58564 ■ Simsbury Chamber of Commerce
PO Box 224
Simsbury, CT 06070
Ph:(860)651-7307
Fax: (860)651-1933
Co. E-mail: info@simsburycoc.org
URL: http://www.simsburycoc.org
Contact: Charity P. Folk, Exec.Dir.

58565 ■ Stamford Chamber of Commerce
733 Summer St.
Stamford, CT 06901-1019
Ph:(203)359-4761
Fax: (203)363-5069
Co. E-mail: jcondlin@stamfordchamber.com
URL: http://www.stamfordchamber.com
Contact: Jack Condlin, Pres.

58566 ■ Suffield Chamber of Commerce
PO Box 741
Suffield, CT 06078
Ph:(860)668-4848
Fax: (860)668-4848
Co. E-mail: info@suffieldchamber.com
URL: http://www.suffieldchamber.com
Contact: Fred Ardery, Pres.

58567 ■ Tolland County Chamber of Commerce
30 Lafayette Sq.
Vernon, CT 06066-4527
Ph:(860)872-0587
Fax: (860)872-0588
Co. E-mail: tccc@tollandcountychamber.org
URL: http://www.tollandcountychamber.org
Contact: Candice Corcione, Exec.Dir.

58568 ■ Town of Portland Chamber of Commerce
33 E Main St.
PO Box 71
Portland, CT 06480-0071
Ph:(860)342-6700
Fax: (860)342-6714
URL: http://www.portlandct.org
Contact: Susan Bransfield, First Selectwoman

58569 ■ Tri-State Chamber of Commerce
PO Box 368
Lakeville, CT 06039
Ph:(860)435-0740
Co. E-mail: info@tristatechamber.com
Contact: John Lannen, Pres.

58570 ■ Waterbury Regional Chamber
PO Box 1469
Waterbury, CT 06721
Ph:(203)757-0701
Fax: (203)756-3507
Co. E-mail: info@waterburychamber.com
URL: http://www.waterburychamber.org
Contact: Stephen R. Sasala II, Pres./CEO

58571 ■ West Hartford Chamber of Commerce
948 Farmington Ave.
West Hartford, CT 06107
Ph:(860)521-2300
Fax: (860)521-1996
Co. E-mail: info@whchamber.com
URL: http://www.whchamber.com
Contact: Edward C. Pilkington, Pres./CEO

58572 ■ West Haven Chamber of Commerce
334 Main St.
West Haven, CT 06516
Ph:(203)933-1500
Co. E-mail: info@westhavenchamber.com
URL: http://www.westhavenchamber.com
Contact: Nicholas DeMatties, Exec.Dir.

58573 ■ Westport/Weston Chamber of Commerce
60 Church Ln.
Westport, CT 06880
Ph:(203)227-9234
Fax: (203)454-4019
Co. E-mail: info@westportchamber.com
URL: http://www.westportchamber.com
Contact: Barbara Sweet, Exec.Dir.

58574 ■ Wethersfield Chamber of Commerce
860B Silas Deane Hwy.
Wethersfield, CT 06109
Ph:(860)721-6200
Fax: (860)721-8703
Co. E-mail: connfda@aol.com
URL: http://www.wethersfieldchamber.com
Contact: John Cascio, Pres.

58575 ■ Wilton Chamber of Commerce
PO Box 7094
Wilton, CT 06897-7094
Ph:(203)762-0567
Fax: (203)762-9096
Co. E-mail: wiltoncoc@snet.net
URL: http://www.wiltonchamber.com
Contact: Ms. Stephanie R. Barksdale, Exec.Dir.

58576 ■ Windsor Chamber of Commerce
261 Broad St.
Windsor, CT 06095
Ph:(860)688-5165
Fax: (860)688-0809
Co. E-mail: wseligjr@aol.com
URL: http://www.windsorcc.org
Contact: Sharran S. Bennett, Pres.

58577 ■ Windsor Locks Chamber of Commerce
PO Box 257
Windsor Locks, CT 06096-0257
Ph:(860)623-9319
Free: (866)WIN-LOCKS
Fax: (860)623-9319
Co. E-mail: wlchamber@juno.com
URL: http://www.wmch.com/chamber/commerce.htm
Contact: Fred Stroiney, Pres.

FINANCING AND LOAN PROGRAMS

58578 ■ ABP Acquisition Corporation
115 Maple Ave.
Greenwich, CT 06830
Ph:(203)625-8287
Fax: (203)552-5346
Contact: George Skakel, Chief Executive Officer
Preferred Investment Size: $250,000 to $50,000,000. **Investment Types:** Acquisition. **Industry Preferences:** Semiconductors and other electronics, consumer related, industrial and energy, transportation, financial services, business service, manufacturing and utilities. **Geographic Preferences:** Mid Atlantic, Northeast, Southeast, and Canada.

58579 ■ Advanced Materials Partners, Inc.
45 Pine St., E. Wing
PO Box 1022
New Canaan, CT 06840
Ph:(203)966-6415
Fax: (203)966-8448
Investment Types: Seed, start-up, first and second stage, early and late stage, generalist PE, joint ventures, mezzanine, leveraged buyout, research and development, and private placement. **Industry Preferences:** Semiconductors and other electronics, biotechnology, medical and health, consumer related, industrial and energy, transportation, business service, manufacturing, utilities, and other products. **Geographic Preferences:** U.S. and Canada.

58580 ■ Axiom Venture Partners, L.P.
City Place II
185 Asylum St., 17th Fl.
Hartford, CT 06103
Ph:(860)548-7799
Fax: (860)548-7797
URL: http://www.axiomventures.com
Contact: Marc Fogassa, Principal
Preferred Investment Size: $1,000,000 to $5,000,000. **Investment Types:** Early and later stage, and expansion. **Industry Preferences:** Communications and media, biotechnology, computer software and services, medical and health, Internet specific, consumer related, semiconductors and other electronics, computer hardware, other products, industrial and energy. **Geographic Preferences:** U.S. and Canada.

58581 ■ Baxter Associates, Inc.
PO Box 1333
Stamford, CT 06904
Ph:(203)323-3143
Fax: (203)348-0622
Preferred Investment Size: $2,000,000 minimum. **Investment Types:** Seed, start-up, first stage, research and development, leveraged buyout, and special situation. **Industry Preferences:** Communications and media, computer software, biotechnology, medical and health, consumer related, industrial and energy, business service, agriculture, forestry and fishing.

58582 ■ Beacon Partners Inc.
6 Landmark Sq., Ste. 400
Stamford, CT 06901-2704
Ph:(203)348-8858
Fax: (203)323-3188
Preferred Investment Size: $300,000 to $1,000,000. **Investment Types:** Second stage, turnaround, mezzanine, recapitalizations, and leveraged buyout. **Industry Preferences:** Consumer related, industrial and energy, Internet specific, other products, medical and health, semiconductors and other electronics, communications and media, computer software and services. **Geographic Preferences:** Northeast.

58583 ■ Bev Capital / Brand Equity Ventures
263 Tresser Blvd.
1 Stamford Plz., Ste. 1600
Stamford, CT 06901
Ph:(203)724-1100

Fax: (203)724-1155
URL: http://www.bevcapital.com
Contact: Chris Kirchen, Managing General Partner
Preferred Investment Size: $1,000,000 to $5,000,000. **Investment Types:** Early, second and later stage, expansion, balanced, and private placement. **Industry Preferences:** Internet specific, consumer related, semiconductors and other electronics, computer software and services, and other products. **Geographic Preferences:** Mid Atlantic and Northeast.

58584 ■ Canaan Partners
105 Rowayton Ave.
Rowayton, CT 06853
Ph:(203)855-0400
Fax: (203)854-9117
URL: http://www.canaan.com
Contact: Brent Ahrens, General Partner
Preferred Investment Size: $3,000,000 to $20,000,000. **Investment Types:** Seed, first and early stage. **Industry Preferences:** Internet specific, computer software and services, medical and health, communications and media, biotechnology, other products, computer hardware, semiconductors and other electronics, consumer related, industrial and energy. **Geographic Preferences:** Northeast, West Coast, and U.S.

58585 ■ Catterton Partners
599 W. Putnam Ave., No. 200
Greenwich, CT 06830
Ph:(203)629-4901
Fax: (203)629-4903
URL: http://www.cpequity.com
Contact: Craig Sakin, Managing Partner
Preferred Investment Size: $5,000,000 minimum. **Investment Types:** Acquisition, expansion, leveraged buyout, recapitalizations, and turnaround. **Industry Preferences:** Consumer related, Internet specific, and biotechnology. **Geographic Preferences:** U.S. and Canada.

58586 ■ Collinson, Howe, and Lennox
1055 Washington Blvd., 5th Fl.
Stamford, CT 06901
Ph:(203)324-7700
Fax: (203)324-3636
Co. E-mail: info@chlmedical.com
URL: http://www.chlmedical.com
Contact: Gregory Weinhoff, Principal
Preferred Investment Size: $2,000,000 to $12,000,000. **Investment Types:** Start-up and early stage. **Industry Preferences:** Medical and health, biotechnology, and Internet specific. **Geographic Preferences:** U.S.

58587 ■ Connecticut Innovations, Inc.
999 West St.
Rocky Hill, CT 06067
Ph:(860)563-5851
Fax: (860)563-4877
URL: http://www.ctinnovations.com
Contact: Lisa Dondy, Managing Director
Preferred Investment Size: $100,000 to $2,000,000. **Investment Types:** Seed, first, second and early stage. **Industry Preferences:** Internet specific, computer software and services, semiconductors and other electronics, biotechnology, medical and health, industrial and energy, communications and media, other products, computer hardware, and consumer related. **Geographic Preferences:** Connecticut.

58588 ■ Conning Capital Partners
100 Pearl St., 17th Fl.
Hartford, CT 06103
Ph:(860)761-8220
Fax: (860)761-8299
URL: http://www.conning.com
Contact: John Clinton, Managing Partner
Preferred Investment Size: $4,000,000 to $40,000,000. **Investment Types:** Balanced and expansion. **Industry Preferences:** Other products, Internet specific, computer software and services, consumer related, medical and health, and computer hardware. **Geographic Preferences:** U.S. and Canada.

58589 ■ Consumer Venture Partners
22 Baldwin Farms S.
Greenwich, CT 06831
Ph:(203)629-8800
Fax: (203)869-6694
Contact: Chris Kirchen, Managing Director
Preferred Investment Size: $10,000,000 minimum. **Investment Types:** Start-up, first and second stage, and leveraged buyout. **Industry Preferences:** Consumer related, Internet specific, communications and media, and other products. **Geographic Preferences:** U.S.

58590 ■ The Crestview Financial Group
431 Post Rd. E, Ste. 1
Westport, CT 06880-4403
Ph:(203)222-0333
Fax: (203)222-0000
Preferred Investment Size: $500,000 to $3,000,000. **Investment Types:** Seed, research and development, first and second stage, and mezzanine. **Industry Preferences:** Communications and media, computer software and hardware, Internet specific, semiconductors and other electronics, biotechnology, medical and health, consumer related, industrial and energy, financial services, business service, manufacturing, agriculture, forestry and fishing. **Geographic Preferences:** U.S. and Canada.

58591 ■ Cullinane & Donnelly Venture Partners, L.P.
970 Farmington Ave.
West Hartford, CT 06107
Ph:(860)521-7811
Fax: (860)521-7911
Preferred Investment Size: $300,000 to $1,000,000. **Investment Types:** Seed, first and second stage, and recapitalizations. **Industry Preferences:** Communications and media, computer software and hardware, semiconductors and other electronics, medical and health, consumer related, and financial services. **Geographic Preferences:** Northeast.

58592 ■ Endeavor Capital Management
830 Post Rd. E.
Westport, CT 06880
Ph:(203)341-7788
Fax: (203)341-7799
URL: http://www.endeavor.com
Contact: Anthony Buffa, Managing General Partner
Preferred Investment Size: $50,000 to $10,000,000. **Investment Types:** Early stage and expansion. **Industry Preferences:** Other products, communications and media, Internet specific, consumer related, medical and health, computer hardware, computer software and services, and industrial and energy. **Geographic Preferences:** U.S. and Canada.

58593 ■ First New England Capital, L.P.
100 Pearl St.
Hartford, CT 06103
Ph:(860)293-3333
Fax: (860)293-3338
URL: http://www.firstnewenglandcapital.com
Contact: Lawrence Stillman, Vice President
Preferred Investment Size: $100,000 to $4,500,000. **Investment Types:** Mezzanine, leveraged buyout, management buyouts, private placement, recapitalizations, later stage, industry rollups, and acquisition. **Industry Preferences:** Consumer related, industrial and energy, transportation, business service, manufacturing, and other products. **Geographic Preferences:** U.S.

58594 ■ Generation Capital Partners
1 Greenwich Office Park
Greenwich, CT 06831
Ph:(203)422-8200
Fax: (203)422-8250
URL: http://www.generation.com
Contact: Erich Vaden, Vice President
Preferred Investment Size: $5,000,000 minimum. **Investment Types:** Start-up, first and second stage, and leveraged buyout. **Industry Preferences:** Computer software and services, Internet specific, communications and media, consumer related, industrial and energy. **Geographic Preferences:** U.S. and Canada.

58595 ■ Insurance Venture Partners, Inc.
31 Brookside Dr., Ste. 211
Greenwich, CT 06830
Ph:(203)861-0030
Fax: (203)861-2745
URL: http://www.imms.com
Contact: Bernard Brown, Managing Director
Preferred Investment Size: $500,000 to $50,000,000. **Investment Types:** First and second stage, and leveraged buyout. **Industry Preferences:** Financial services.

58596 ■ James B. Kobak & Co.
6 Hale Ln.
Darien, CT 06820
Ph:(203)656-3471
Fax: (203)655-2905
Investment Types: First stage. **Industry Preferences:** Manufacturing.

58597 ■ Jerome Capital LLC
5 Timrod Ln.
West Hartford, CT 06107
Ph:(860)206-1616
Fax: (860)561-1781
Contact: Halley Faust, Managing Director
Preferred Investment Size: $50,000,000 to $250,000,000. **Investment Policies:** Seed, start-up, early, first and second stage. **Industry Preferences:** Semiconductors and other electronics, biotechnology, medical and health, consumer related, and financial services. **Geographic Preferences:** Connecticut.

58598 ■ Landmark Partners, Inc.
10 Mill Pond Ln.
Simsbury, CT 06070
Ph:(860)651-9760
Fax: (860)408-4608
URL: http://www.landmarkpartners.com
Contact: Lance Whitehead, Managing Director
Preferred Investment Size: $500,000 minimum. **Investment Types:** Fund of funds, fund of funds of second. **Industry Preferences:** Other products, computer software and services, computer hardware, semiconductors and other electronics, Internet specific, biotechnology, medical and health, consumer related, industrial and energy. **Geographic Preferences:** U.S. and Canada.

58599 ■ LTI Ventures Leasing Corp.
221 Danbury Rd.
Wilton, CT 06897
Ph:(203)563-1100
Fax: (203)563-1111
URL: http://www.ltileasing.com
Contact: Richard Livingston, Vice President
Preferred Investment Size: $500,000 to $2,000,000. **Investment Types:** Early, first, second, and later stage, mezzanine, and special situation. **Industry Preferences:** Communications and media, computer hardware and software, Internet specific, semiconductors and other electronics, biotechnology, medical and health, consumer related, industrial and energy. **Geographic Preferences:** U.S.

58600 ■ Marketcorp Venture Associates, L.P. (MCV)
274 Riverside Ave.
Westport, CT 06880
Ph:(203)222-3030
Fax: (203)222-3033
Contact: E. Bulkeley Griswold, General Partner
Preferred Investment Size: $500,000 to $1,000,000. **Investment Types:** First and second stage, mezzanine, and leveraged buyout. **Industry Preferences:** Computer software, and consumer related. **Geographic Preferences:** U.S.

58601 ■ Medmax Ventures L.P.
1 Northwestern Dr., Ste. 203
Bloomfield, CT 06002
Ph:(860)286-2960
Fax: (860)286-9960
Contact: Noam Karstaedt
Preferred Investment Size: $500,000 minimum. **Investment Types:** Seed, start-up, first and second stage, research and development. **Industry Preferences:** Biotechnology, medical and health. **Geographic Preferences:** Northeast.

58602 ■ Meyer, Duffy & Associates
125 Elm St., Ste. 6
New Canaan, CT 06840
Ph:(203)972-0331
Fax: (203)972-0229
URL: http://www.meyerduffy.com
Contact: Teddy Kaplan, Vice President
Investment Policies: First and second stage. **Industry Preferences:** Computer software and services, communications and media, computer hardware, and other products.

58603 ■ Northeast Ventures
1 State St., Ste. 1720
Hartford, CT 06103
Ph:(860)547-1414
Fax: (860)246-8755
Preferred Investment Size: $1,000,000 minimum. **Industry Preferences:** Communications and media, computer software and hardware, semiconductors and other electronics, biotechnology, medical and health, consumer related, industrial and energy. **Geographic Preferences:** U.S.

58604 ■ The NTC Group
3 Pickwick Plz., Ste. 200
Greenwich, CT 06830
Ph:(203)862-2800
Fax: (203)622-6538
Preferred Investment Size: $1,000,000 minimum. **Investment Types:** Seed, first stage, control-block purchases, and leveraged buyout. **Industry Preferences:** Semiconductors and other electronics, and industrial and energy. **Geographic Preferences:** U.S.

58605 ■ Oak Investment Partners
1 Gorham Island
Westport, CT 06880
Ph:(203)226-8346
Fax: (203)227-0372
URL: http://www.oakvc.com
Preferred Investment Size: $1,000,000 to $60,000,000. **Investment Types:** Balanced, expansion, later stage, management buyouts, private placement, and special situation. **Industry Preferences:** Communications and media, Internet specific, computer software and services, semiconductors and other electronics, consumer related, medical and health, computer hardware, other products, biotechnology, industrial and energy. **Geographic Preferences:** U.S.

58606 ■ Orien Ventures
14523 Westlake Dr., Ste. 6
Lake Oswego, OR 97035
Ph:(203)259-9933
Fax: (203)259-5288
Contact: Anthony Miadich, Managing General
  Partner
Preferred Investment Size: $500,000 minimum. **Investment Types:** Start-up, seed, early and first stage. **Industry Preferences:** Communications and media, computer software, Internet specific, semiconductors and other electronics, medical and health.

58607 ■ Oxford Bioscience Partners (Westport)
315 Post Rd. W.
Westport, CT 06880
Ph:(203)341-3300
Fax: (203)341-3309
URL: http://www.oxbio.com
Contact: Jonathan Fleming, Managing Partner
Preferred Investment Size: $25,000 to $20,000,000. **Investment Types:** Start-up, early and first stage, and research and development. **Industry Preferences:** Biotechnology, medical and health, Internet specific, computer software and services, consumer related, and semiconductors and other electronics. **Geographic Preferences:** U.S. and Canada.

58608 ■ Prime Capital Management Co., Inc.
107 John St.
Southport, CT 06490
Ph:(203)259-8287
Fax: (203)964-0862
Contact: Dean Fenton

Preferred Investment Size: $500,000 to $1,500,000. **Investment Types:** Acquisition, expansion, mezzanine, and turnaround. **Industry Preferences:** Semiconductors and other electronics, biotechnology, medical and health, consumer related, financial services, business service, and manufacturing. **Geographic Preferences:** Northeast and Southeast.

58609 ■ Prince Ventures
303 W. Madison St., Ste. 1900
Chicago, IL 60606
Ph:(312)419-1909
Fax: (314)419-9502
Investment Types: Seed, start-up, first and second stage, and leveraged buyout. **Industry Preferences:** Medical and health, biotechnology, computer software and services, semiconductors and other electronics, industrial and energy, computer hardware, communications and media, and other products.

58610 ■ Regulus International Capital Co., Inc.
140 Greenwich Ave.
Greenwich, CT 06830
Ph:(203)625-9700
Fax: (203)625-9706
Co. E-mail: lee@chaossystems.com
Preferred Investment Size: $100,000 to $500,000. **Investment Types:** Start-up, seed, research and development. **Industry Preferences:** Computer software, industrial and energy, and manufacturing.

58611 ■ RFE Investment Partners
36 Grove St.
New Canaan, CT 06840
Ph:(203)966-2800
Fax: (203)966-3109
URL: http://www.rfeip.com
Contact: James A. Parsons, General Partner
Preferred Investment Size: $5,000,000 to $24,000,000. **Investment Types:** Later stage, acquisition, leveraged buyout, management buyouts, and recapitalizations. **Industry Preferences:** Other products, medical and health, industrial and energy, consumer related, computer software and services, computer hardware, communications and media, semiconductors and other electronics, and biotechnology. **Geographic Preferences:** U.S.

58612 ■ SAE Ventures
125 Elm St.
New Canaan, CT 06840
Ph:(203)972-3100
Fax: (203)966-4197
URL: http://www.
Preferred Investment Size: $5,000,000 minimum. **Investment Types:** Start-up, first and second stage, control-block purchases, leveraged buyout, mezzanine, research and development, and special situation. **Industry Preferences:** Computer hardware and software, Internet specific, semiconductors and other electronics, biotechnology, medical and health. **Geographic Preferences:** U.S.

58613 ■ Saugatuck Capital Company
1 Canterbury Green
Stamford, CT 06901
Ph:(203)348-6669
Fax: (203)324-6995
URL: http://www.saugatuckcapital.com
Contact: Barbara Parker, Managing Director
Preferred Investment Size: $4,000,000 to $7,000,000. **Investment Types:** Leveraged buyout, management buyouts, and later stage. **Industry Preferences:** Other products, medical and health, consumer related, communications and media, industrial and energy, computer hardware, semiconductors and other electronics, computer software and services, and Internet specific. **Geographic Preferences:** U.S.

58614 ■ Signal Lake Management LLC
606 Post Rd. E., Ste. 667
Westport, CT 06880
Ph:(203)454-1133
Fax: (203)454-7142
URL: http://www.signallake.com
Contact: Bart Stuck, Managing Director

Preferred Investment Size: $500,000 to $5,000,000. **Investment Types:** Early stage and balanced. **Industry Preferences:** Internet specific, semiconductors and other electronics, communications and media, computer hardware, computer software and services. **Geographic Preferences:** Northeast and U.S.

58615 ■ Soundview Financial Group, Inc.
1700 E. Putnam Ave.
Old Greenwich, CT 06902
Ph:(203)321-7000
Fax: (203)321-7300
URL: http://www.sndv.com
Contact: Jason Wright, Principal
E-mail: bbristol@soundview.com
Preferred Investment Size: $1,000,000 to $10,000,000. **Investment Types:** Second stage and mezzanine. **Industry Preferences:** Semiconductors and other electronics, communications and media, Internet specific, computer software and services. **Geographic Preferences:** U.S. and Canada.

58616 ■ Sweeney & Co., Inc.
PO Box 567
Southport, CT 06490
Ph:(203)255-0220
Fax: (203)255-0220
Preferred Investment Size: $1,000,000 minimum. **Investment Types:** Seed, start-up, first and second stage, mezzanine, research and development, and leveraged buyout. **Industry Preferences:** Communications and media, computer software and hardware, semiconductors and other electronics, biotechnology, medical and health, consumer related, industrial and energy, financial services, business service, and manufacturing. **Geographic Preferences:** Mid Atlantic and Northeast U.S.; Eastern Canada, Ontario, and Quebec.

58617 ■ TSG Capital Group, L.L.C.
177 Broad St., 12th Fl.
Stamford, CT 06901
Ph:(203)541-1500
Fax: (203)406-1590
URL: http://www.tsgequitypartners.com
Contact: Cleveland Christophe, Managing Partner
Preferred Investment Size: $30,000,000 minimum. **Investment Types:** Second stage, expansion, and leveraged buyout. **Industry Preferences:** Communications and media, consumer related, other products, industrial and energy, and Internet specific. **Geographic Preferences:** U.S. and Canada.

58618 ■ Whitney and Co.
177 Broad St.
Stamford, CT 10111
Ph:(212)332-2400
Fax: (212)332-2422
URL: http://www.whitney.com
Contact: Robert Warden, Vice President
Preferred Investment Size: $1,000,000 minimum. **Investment Types:** Leveraged buyout, expansion, balanced, and mezzanine. **Industry Preferences:** Consumer related, Internet specific, communications and media, medical and health, computer hardware, software and services, biotechnology, semiconductors and other electronics, industrial and energy. **Geographic Preferences:** U.S.

58619 ■ Windward Holdings
38 Sylvan Rd.
Madison, CT 06443
Ph:(203)245-6870
Fax: (203)245-6865
Preferred Investment Size: $300,000 minimum. **Investment Types:** Leveraged buyouts, mezzanine, recaps, and special situations. **Industry Preferences:** Electronics, food/beverage, and industrial products. **Geographic Preferences:** Northeastern U.S.

PROCUREMENT ASSISTANCE PROGRAMS

58620 ■ Connecticut Procurement Technical Assistance Center–Small Business Development Procurement Center
190 Governor Winthrop Blvd., Ste. 300
New London, CT 06320
Ph:(860)437-4659
Fax: (860)437-4662
Co. E-mail: secter@secter.org
URL: http://www.ctptap.org
Contact: Brien Robertson, Prgm Dir

58621 ■ Southeastern Connecticut Enterprise Region–Connecticut Procurement Center
190 Governor Winthrop Blvd., Ste. 300
New London, CT 06320
Ph:(860)437-4659
Fax: (860)437-4662
Co. E-mail: secter@secter.org
URL: http://www.secter.org
Contact: John Markowicz, Exec Dir
E-mail: lawrence.steele@sba.gov
Description: Covers activities for the VA Medical Center (West Haven, CT), Naval Submarine base (Groton, CT), and the U.S. Coast Guard Academy (New London, CT).

58622 ■ State of Connecticut Procurement Services–Purchasing Services Division
165 Capitol Ave., 5th Fl. S
Hartford, CT 06106
Ph:(860)713-5095
Fax: (860)713-7457
Co. E-mail: carol.wilson@po.state.ct.us
URL: http://www.das.state.ct.us/busopp.asp
Contact: Carol Wilson, Mgr

INCUBATORS/RESEARCH AND TECHNOLOGY PARKS

58623 ■ Bridgeport Innovation Center
955 Connecticut Ave., Ste 5103
Bridgeport, CT 6607
Ph:(203)333-9000
Fax: (203)333-9008
Co. E-mail: reneesand@hotmail.com
URL: http://www.bridgeportinnovationcenter.com
Contact: Carleton Pierpont, Gen Mgr

58624 ■ Ceebraid Signal
112 Hoyt St.
Stamford, CT 6905
Ph:(203)406-1300
Fax: (203)406-1305
URL: http://www.ceebraidsignal.com

58625 ■ Fairfield University–Office of Grants and Sponsored Programs
1073 N Benson Rd.
Fairfield, CT 06824-5195
Ph:(203)254-4000
Fax: (203)254-4101
Co. E-mail: slafrance@mail.fairfield.edu
Contact: Susan La France
E-mail: slafrance@mail.fairfield.edu
Scope: Encourages, facilitates, sponsors, and coordinates research at the university in all branches of the natural and social sciences, business, arts, humanities, education, and allied fields.

58626 ■ University of Connecticut–Research Foundation
438 Whitney Rd.
Storrs, CT 06269-1221
Ph:(860)486-0517
Fax: (860)486-5381
Co. E-mail: ilze.krisst@uconn.edu
URL: http://www.rac.uconn.edu/
Contact: Ilze Krisst PhD, Asst. Vice Provost
E-mail: ilze.krisst@uconn.edu
Scope: Reviews and approves research program in all departments of the University, including physical, life, and social sciences, engineering, agriculture, fine arts, and the humanities. Offers advisory service on externally sponsored research opportunities. Manages intellectual properties of the University, including licensing and patenting. Serves as a liaision for faculty with industry.

58627 ■ Yale University–Office of Cooperative Research
433 Temple St.
PO Box 208336
New Haven, CT 06520-8336
Ph:(203)436-8096
Fax: (203)436-8086
Co. E-mail: ocr@yale.edu
URL: http://www.yale.edu/ocr
Contact: Dr. E. Jonathan Saderstrom, Dir.
E-mail: ocr@yale.edu
Scope: Facilitates the transfer of technology from the University to business and industry. Patents and licenses University inventions in the areas of physical sciences and engineering, medicine and biotechnology, and computer sciences. Administers industrial liasion programs in computer science.

EDUCATIONAL PROGRAMS

58628 ■ Housatonic Community College
900 Lafayette Blvd.
Bridgeport, CT 06604
Ph:(203)332-5000
Fax: (203)332-5123
URL: http://www.hcc.commnet.edu
Description: Two-year college offering a small business management program.

PUBLICATIONS

58629 ■ *Starting and Operating a Business in Connecticut: A Step-by-Step Guide*
PSI Research
300 N. Valley Dr.
Grants Pass, OR 97526
Ph:(503)479-9464
Free: 800-228-2275
Fax: (503)476-1479
Co. E-mail: psi2@magick.net
Ed: Michael D. Jenkins. **Released:** Revised edition, 1992. **Price:** $29.95 (looseleaf binder); $24.95 (paper). **Description:** Part of the Successful Business Library series.

PUBLISHERS

58630 ■ Aspen Publishers Inc.
125 Eugene O'Neill Dr., Ste. 103
New London, CT 06320
Ph:(860)442-4365
Free: 800-876-9105
Fax: (860)437-3150
Co. E-mail: customer.service@aspenpubl.com
URL: http://www.aspenpublishers.com

Description: Publishes business and professional development information in a variety of formats, including newsletters, books and manuals, posters, videos, and electronic format. Accepts unsolicited manuscripts. Reaches market through direct mail, commission representatives, and telephone sales. **Founded:** 1917.

58631 ■ Business Books International
194 Putnam Rd.
New Canaan, CT 06840
Ph:(203)966-9645
Fax: (203)966-6018
Co. E-mail: editor@businessbooksusa.com
URL: http://www.businessbooksusa.com
Contact: Les de Villiers, President
E-mail: lesdu@businessbooksusa.com
Description: Publishes reference books for business and library use on regions of the world. Reaches market through advertising, direct mail, trade sales and wholesalers. Does not accept unsolicited manuscripts. **Founded:** 1982.

58632 ■ Grolier
90 Old Sherman Tpke.
Danbury, CT 06816
Ph:(203)797-3500
Free: 800-621-1115
Fax: (203)797-3657
Co. E-mail: custserv@scholastic.com
URL: http://librarypublishing.scholastic.com
Contact: Mark Cummings, Vice President
Description: Publishes encyclopedias and reference materials in print and online for public libraries and school libraries. Does not accept unsolicited manuscripts. Reaches market through commission representatives, direct mail, reviews, listings, and telephone sales. **Founded:** 1960.

58633 ■ Hannacroix Creek Books Inc.
1127 High Ridge Rd., Ste. 110B
Stamford, CT 06905-1203
Ph:(203)321-8674
Fax: (203)968-0193
Co. E-mail: hannacroix@aol.com
URL: http://www.hannacroixcreekbooks.com
Contact: Dr. Jan Yager Ph.D., Founder
Description: Publishes books and audio cassettes in the areas of deafness, friendship, business, time management and relationships. **Founded:** 1996.

58634 ■ Hunt-Scanlon Publishing
700 Fairfield Ave.
Stamford, CT 06902
Ph:(203)352-2920
Free: 800-477-1199
Fax: (203)352-2930
Co. E-mail: info@hunt-scanlon.com
URL: http://www.hunt-scanlon.com
Contact: Christopher Hunt, President
E-mail: hayes@hunt-scanlon.com
Description: Publishes business directories for business-to-business applications. Also publishes CD-ROMs and software, as well as a newsletter. Reaches market through direct mail. **Founded:** 1989.

58635 ■ RDS Associates Inc.
41 Brainard Rd.
Niantic, CT 06357-1722
Ph:(860)691-0081
Free: 800-363-8867
Fax: (860)691-1145
Co. E-mail: rds@businessbookpress.com
URL: http://www.businessbookpress.com
Contact: Russell L. Brown, President
E-mail: r.brown@businessbookpress.com
Description: Publishes reference and business books relating to buying, selling, valuing, starting or improving a business. Accepts unsolicited manuscripts. Reaches market through direct mail and Book-World Services. **Founded:** 1996.

SMALL BUSINESS DEVELOPMENT CENTER LEAD OFFICE

58636 ■ Delaware SBDC–Small Business Development Center
Delaware Technology Park
1 Innovation Way, Ste. 301
Newark, DE 19711
Ph:(302)831-2747
Fax: (302)831-1423
URL: http://www.delawaresbdc.org
Contact: Clinton Tymes, State Dir.
E-mail: clinton.tymes@mvs.udel.edu

58637 ■ University of Delaware–Delaware Small Business Development Center Network
102 MBNA America Hall
Newark, DE 19716-2711
Ph:(302)831-1555
Fax: (302)831-1423
Co. E-mail: newark@delawaresbdc.org
URL: http://www.be.udel.edu/sbdc
Contact: Clinton Tymes, State Director
E-mail: Clinton.Tymes@mvs.udel.edu

SMALL BUSINESS DEVELOPMENT CENTERS

58638 ■ Delaware State University–Small Business Resource and Information Center–SBDC (1200)
1200 N. DuPont Hwy., Ste. 108
Dover, DE 19901
Ph:(302)678-1555
Fax: (302)857-6950
URL: http://www.delaware.sbdc.org
Contact: Al Paoli, Director

58639 ■ University of Delaware–Delaware SBDC Network
100 W. 10th St., Ste. 812
Wilmington, DE 19801
Ph:(302)831-2770
URL: http://www.delawaresbdc.org
Contact: Barbara Necarsulmer, Assoc. State Dir.

58640 ■ University of Delaware–Small Business Development Center
103 W. Pine St.
Georgetown, DE 19947
Ph:(302)856-1555
Fax: (302)854-6979
URL: http://www.delawaresbdc.org
Contact: William F. Pfaff, Dir.

SMALL BUSINESS ASSISTANCE PROGRAMS

58641 ■ Delaware Economic Development Office–Business Finance Section
99 Kings Hwy.
Dover, DE 19901
Ph:(302)739-4271
Fax: (302)739-2028
URL: http://www.delaware.gov
Description: Promotes the development and growth of new and existing businesses; trains workers, assists employers with recruiting, and develops training programs; conducts research on the state's business and economic climate; and provides publications entitled *Small Business Start-Up Guide, Selling to the State, Solutions for Delaware Small Business,* and *The Workforce Resource.* The Small Business Advocate acts as a liaison between small businesses and local, state, and federal agencies; helps businesses get into state programs; and provides information on permits, regulations, financing, and procurement programs.

58642 ■ Delaware Economic Development Office–International Section–Exporter Assistance Program (Carve)
Carvel State Office Bldg., 10th Fl.
820 N French St.
Wilmington, DE 19801
Ph:(302)577-8477
Fax: (302)577-8499
Co. E-mail: john.pastor@state.de.us
URL: http://www.state.de.us/dedo
Description: Provides counseling, seminars, and contacts for businesses seeking to engage in international trade.

SCORE OFFICES

58643 ■ SCORE Wilmington
1007 N Orange St., Ste. 1120
Wilmington, DE 19801
Ph:(302)573-6552
Fax: (302)573-6092
Co. E-mail: info@scoredelaware.org
URL: http://www.score.org
Description: Provides public service to America by offering business advice and training.

BETTER BUSINESS BUREAUS

58644 ■ Better Business Bureau of Delaware
Foulkstone Plz.
1415 Foulk Rd., Ste. 202
Wilmington, DE 19803
Ph:(302)230-0108
Fax: (302)230-0116

Co. E-mail: info@delaware.bbb.org
URL: http://www.delaware.bbb.org
Contact: Christine R. Sauers, Pres.

CHAMBERS OF COMMERCE

58645 ■ Bethany-Fenwick Area Chamber of Commerce
PO Box 1450
Bethany Beach, DE 19930-1450
Ph:(302)539-2100
Free: 800-962-7873
Fax: (302)539-9434
Co. E-mail: info@bethany-fenwick.org
URL: http://www.bethany-fenwick.org
Contact: Karen McGrath, Exec.Dir.

58646 ■ Central Delaware Chamber of Commerce
435 N DuPont Hwy.
Dover, DE 19901
Ph:(302)678-0892
Fax: (302)678-0189
Co. E-mail: info@cdcc.net
URL: http://www.cdcc.net
Contact: Judy Diogo, Pres.

58647 ■ Chamber of Commerce for Greater Milford
PO Box 805
Milford, DE 19963
Ph:(302)422-3344
Fax: (302)422-7503
Co. E-mail: milford@milfordchamber.com
URL: http://www.milfordchamber.com
Contact: Ruth Abbate, Pres.

58648 ■ Delaware State Chamber of Commerce
PO Box 671
Wilmington, DE 19899-0671
Ph:(302)655-7221
Free: 800-292-9507
Fax: (302)654-0691
Co. E-mail: dscc@dscc.com
URL: http://www.dscc.com
Contact: James A. Wolfe, Pres./CEO

58649 ■ Greater Seaford Chamber of Commerce
PO Box 26
Seaford, DE 19973
Ph:(302)629-9690
Free: 800-416-GSCC
Fax: (302)629-0281
Co. E-mail: admin@seafordchamber.com
URL: http://www.seafordchamber.com
Contact: Paula K. Gunson, Exec.Dir.

58650 ■ Lewes Chamber of Commerce
PO Box 1
120 Kings Hwy.
Lewes, DE 19958
Ph:(302)645-8073

Free: 877-465-3937
Fax: (302)645-8412
Co. E-mail: inquiry@leweschamber.com
URL: http://www.leweschamber.com
Contact: Betsy Reamer, Exec.Dir.

58651 ■ New Castle County Chamber of Commerce
PO Box 11247
Wilmington, DE 19850-1247
Ph:(302)737-4345
Fax: (302)737-8450
Co. E-mail: info@ncccc.com
URL: http://www.ncccc.com
Contact: Ronald E. Walker, Pres.

58652 ■ Rehoboth Beach-Dewey Beach Chamber of Commerce
501 Rehoboth Ave.
PO Box 216
Rehoboth Beach, DE 19971-0216
Ph:(302)227-2233
Free: 800-441-1329
Fax: (302)227-8351
Co. E-mail: rehoboth@beach-fun.com
URL: http://www.beach-fun.com
Contact: Carol Everhart, Exec.Dir.

MINORITY BUSINESS ASSISTANCE PROGRAMS

58653 ■ Wilmington Minority Business Enterprise Office
800 French St., 3rd Fl.
Wilmington, DE 19801-3537
Ph:(302)576-2121
Fax: (302)573-5557
URL: http://www.ci.wilmington.de.us/dbe.htm
Contact: Larraine Watson, Dir

FINANCING AND LOAN PROGRAMS

58654 ■ Blue Rock Capital
5803 Kennett Pike
Wilmington, DE 19807-1135
Ph:(302)426-1767
Fax: (302)426-0982
URL: http://www.bluerockcapital.com
Contact: James Zucco, Partner
Investment Types: Seed, start-up, and first stage. **Industry Preferences:** Internet specific, semiconductors and other electronics, communications and media, consumer related, computer software and services, and computer hardware. **Geographic Preferences:** Northeast and Mid Atlantic.

INCUBATORS/RESEARCH AND TECHNOLOGY PARKS

58655 ■ University of Delaware–Office of the Vice Provost for Research
210 Hullihen Hall
Newark, DE 19716
Ph:(302)831-2136
Fax: (302)831-2828
Co. E-mail: ctgood@udel.edu
URL: http://www.udel.edu/OVPR/
Contact: Carolyn Thoroughgood, Vice Provost, Res.
E-mail: ctgood@udel.edu
Scope: Reviews proposals from university units to external agencies and manages the resulting grants and contracts for the life of the research projects. Also manages the university's intellectual property holdings, including licensing. research, colloidal studies, climatic research, historic architecture and engineering, and disaster research.

58656 ■ University of Delaware Research Foundation
210 Hullihen Hall
University of Delaware
Newark, DE 19716

Ph:(302)831-2136
Fax: (302)831-2828
Contact: Dr. T.W. Fraser Russell, Vice Provost
Scope: Supports University research in science and engineering by awarding grants to faculty members.

LEGISLATIVE ASSISTANCE

58657 ■ Delaware House Committee on Small Business
Legislative Hall
Senate Majority
Dover, DE 19903
Ph:(302)744-4286
Free: 800-282-8545
Fax: (302)739-6890
URL: http://www.delaware.gov/
Contact: Sen. Robert Chair, Chair

58658 ■ Delaware Senate Committee on Small Business
Legislative Hall
Dover, DE 19901
Ph:(302)744-4298
Free: 800-282-8545
Fax: (302)739-6890
URL: http://www.delaware.gov/

PUBLICATIONS

58659 ■ *Starting and Operating a Business in Delaware: A Step-by-Step Guide*
PSI Research
300 N. Valley Dr.
Grants Pass, OR 97526
Ph:(503)479-9464
Free: 800-228-2275
Fax: (503)476-1479
Co. E-mail: psi2@magick.net
Ed: Michael D. Jenkins. **Released:** Revised edition, 1992. **Price:** $29.95 (looseleaf binder); $24.95 (paper). **Description:** Part of the Successful Business Library series.

SMALL BUSINESS DEVELOPMENT CENTER LEAD OFFICE

58660 ■ Howard University–Small Business Development Center
2600 6th St., NW
Rm. 128
Washington, DC 20059
Ph:(202)806-1550
Fax: (202)806-1777
Contact: Henry J. Turner, Exec. Dir.

58661 ■ Howard University School of Business–Small Business Development Center
2600 6th St. NW, Rm. 128
Washington, DC 20059
Ph:(202)806-1550
Fax: (202)806-1777
URL: http://www.dcsbdc.com
Contact: Henry J. Turner, Exec. Dir.

SMALL BUSINESS DEVELOPMENT CENTERS

58662 ■ Marshall Heights Community Development Organization–SBDC
3917 Minnesota Ave., NE
Washington, DC 20019
Ph:(202)396-1200
Fax: (202)396-4106
Contact: Terry Strong, Financing Specialist

58663 ■ Washington District Office–Business Information Center–SBDC (1110)
1110 Vermont Ave., NW, 9th Fl.
PO Box 34346
Washington, DC 20043
Ph:(202)606-4000
Fax: (202)606-4225
URL: http://www.scoredc.org
Contact: Johnetta Hardy, Marketing Specialist

SMALL BUSINESS ASSISTANCE PROGRAMS

58664 ■ District of Columbia Office of Economic Development–Revenue Bonds and Enterprise Zone
John A Wilson Bldg.
1350 Pennsylvania Ave NE Suite 317
Washington, DC 20004
Ph:(202)727-6365
Fax: (202)727-6703
URL: http://www.dcbiz.dc.gov
Description: Works to attract new businesses and retain existing ones. The Financial Services Division of-

fers SBA 503/504 loans and other loan programs. The Small Business Incubator Facility Program provides affordable facilities and management assistance to new and small businesses. The Neighborhood Commercial Services Division provides loans and technical assistance to encourage the revitalization of neighborhood commercial districts.

SCORE OFFICES

58665 ■ SCORE Washington DC
c/o Mr. Ralph N. Johanson, Jr., Chm.
740 15th St. NW, 3rd Fl.
Washington, DC 20005
Ph:(202)272-0390
Fax: (202)638-7670
Co. E-mail: chapter1@scoredc.org
URL: http://www.scoredc.org
Contact: Mr. Ralph N. Johanson Jr., Chm.
Description: Works to provide counseling to small businesses.

BETTER BUSINESS BUREAUS

58666 ■ Better Business Bureau of Metropolitan Washington
1411 K St. NW, Ste. 1000
Washington, DC 20005
Ph:(202)393-8000
Fax: (202)393-1198
Co. E-mail: info@mybbb.org
URL: http://www.dc.bbb.org
Contact: Edward J. Johnson III, Pres./CEO

CHAMBERS OF COMMERCE

58667 ■ District of Columbia Chamber of Commerce
1213 K St., NW
Washington, DC 20005
Ph:(202)347-7201
Fax: (202)638-6762
Co. E-mail: dedwards@dcchamber.org
URL: http://www.dcchamber.org
Contact: Barbara Lang, Pres./CEO

MINORITY BUSINESS ASSISTANCE PROGRAMS

58668 ■ Government of the District of Columbia–Department of Small and Local Business Development
441 4th St. NW, Ste. 970N
Washington, DC 20001
Ph:(202)727-3900

Fax: (202)724-3786
Co. E-mail: mboc@dchomepage.net
URL: http://www.olbd.washingtondc.gov
Contact: Jacquelyn Flowers, Dir

FINANCING AND LOAN PROGRAMS

58669 ■ Allied Capital Corporation
1919 Pennsylvania Ave. NW, 3rd Fl.
Washington, DC 20006-3434
Ph:(202)331-1112
Fax: (202)659-2053
URL: http://www.alliedcapital.com
Contact: William Walton, President and Chief Executive Officer
Preferred Investment Size: $10,000,000 to $99,999,000. **Investment Types:** Mezzanine, leveraged buyout, management buyouts, acquisition, expansion, later stage, generalist PE, private placement, and recapitalizations. **Industry Preferences:** Other products, consumer related, industrial and energy, communications and media, medical and health, Internet specific, computer software and services, computer hardware, biotechnology, semiconductors and other electronics. **Geographic Preferences:** U.S.

58670 ■ Atlantic Coastal Ventures, L.P.
3101 South St. NW
Washington, DC 20007
Ph:(202)293-1166
Fax: (202)293-1181
URL: http://www.atlanticcv.com
Contact: Patrick Hall, Partner
Preferred Investment Size: $300,000 minimum. **Investment Types:** Leveraged buyout, mezzanine, and special situation. **Industry Preferences:** Communications and media, computer hardware, semiconductors and other electronics.

58671 ■ Bailey Capital
1155 15th St., NW, Ste. 302
Washington, DC 20005
Ph:(202)223-3222
URL: http://www.baileycapital.com
Preferred Investment Size: $500,000 minimum. **Investment Policies:** First and second stage. **Industry Preferences:** Communications, computer software, and Internet specific. **Geographic Preferences:** Southeast.

58672 ■ Capital Investors
901 15th St., NW
Washington, DC 20005
Ph:(202)589-0090
Fax: (202)589-0010
URL: http://www.capitalinvestors.com
Contact: Andrew Sachs, President
Preferred Investment Size: $50,000 to $1,000,000. **Investment Types:** Seed, early, first and second stage. **Industry Preferences:** Communications, computer software, and Internet specific. **Geographic Preferences:** District of Columbia.

58673 ■ **Columbia Capital Group, Inc.**
1660 L St. NW, Ste. 308
Washington, DC 20036
Ph:(202)775-8815
Fax: (202)223-0544
URL: http://www.columbiacapitalgroup.com
Contact: Loyd Arrington, President
Investment Types: First and second stage, and mezzanine. **Industry Preferences:** Communications and media, and computer software and services. **Geographic Preferences:** District of Columbia.

58674 ■ **Core Capital Partners**
901 15th St., NW, Ste. 950
Washington, DC 20005
Ph:(202)589-0090
Fax: (202)589-0091
URL: http://www.core-capital.com
Contact: Pascal Luck, Principal
Preferred Investment Size: $1,000,000 to $10,000,000. **Investment Types:** Start-up, early, first, second, and later stage, and expansion. **Industry Preferences:** Communications and media, computer software and computer related. **Geographic Preferences:** Mid Atlantic, Northeast, Southeast, and West Coast.

58675 ■ **The Grosvenor Funds**
1808 Eye St. NW, Ste. 900
Washington, DC 20006
Ph:(202)861-5650
Fax: (202)861-5653
URL: http://www.grosvenorfund.com
Contact: Bruce Dunnan, Managing Partner
Preferred Investment Size: $1,000,000 to $3,000,000. **Investment Types:** Seed, early and later stage. **Industry Preferences:** Communications, Internet specific, semiconductors and other electronics, and biotechnology.

58676 ■ **Next Point Partners, L.P.**
701 Pennsylvania Ave. NW, Ste. 900
Washington, DC 20004
Ph:(202)434-7319
Fax: (202)434-7400
URL: http://www.nextpointvc.com
Contact: Michael Faber, Managing General Partner
Preferred Investment Size: $250,000 to $6,000,000. **Investment Types:** Seed, start-up, early stage, and research and development. **Industry Preferences:** Communications and media, computer software, computer related, Internet specific, semiconductors and other electronics, industrial and energy, and other. **Geographic Preferences:** Mid Atlantic, Midwest, Northeast, and Southeast.

58677 ■ **Potomac Ventures**
1054 31st St. NW, Ste. 410
Washington, DC 20007
Ph:(202)295-3046
URL: http://www.potomacventures.com
Contact: Tom Ross, Managing Partner
Preferred Investment Size: $400,000 to $1,000,000. **Investment Types:** Early stage. **Industry Preferences:** Internet specific. **Geographic Preferences:** Mid Atlantic.

58678 ■ **Telecommunications Development Fund (TDF)**
1850 K St. NW, Ste. 1075
Washington, DC 20006
Ph:(202)293-8840
Fax: (202)293-8850
URL: http://www.tdfund.com
Contact: James Pastoriza, Managing Partner
Preferred Investment Size: $350,000 to $1,000,000. **Investment Types:** First, second, and early stage. **Industry Preferences:** Computer software and services, Internet specific, computer hardware, communications and media, semiconductors and other electronics. **Geographic Preferences:** U.S.

58679 ■ **Wachtel & Co., Inc.**
1101 4th St., NW
Washington, DC 20005-5680
Ph:(202)898-1144
Preferred Investment Size: $100,000 to $300,000. **Investment Types:** Start-up, first and second stage, and recapitalizations. **Industry Preferences:** Communications, computer hardware and software, semiconductors and other electronics, medical and health, consumer related, industrial and energy, financial services, business service, and manufacturing. **Geographic Preferences:** U.S. and District of Columbia.

58680 ■ **Winslow Partners LLC**
1300 Connecticut Ave., NW
Washington, DC 20036-1748
Ph:(202)530-5000
Fax: (202)530-5010
URL: http://www.winslowpartners.cz
Contact: Robert Chartener, Partner
Preferred Investment Size: $5,000,000 minimum. **Investment Types:** Early and later stage, acquisition, control-block purchases, expansion, managements, and leverage buyout. **Industry Preferences:** Communications, semiconductors and other electronics, medical and health, consumer related, industrial and energy, transportation, financial services, business service, and manufacturing. **Geographic Preferences:** U.S.

58681 ■ **Womens Growth Capital Fund**
1054 31st St., NW, Ste. 110
Washington, DC 20007
Ph:(202)342-1431
Fax: (202)342-1203
URL: http://www.wgcf.com
Contact: Patty Abramson, Managing Director
Preferred Investment Size: $100,000 to $1,800,000. **Investment Types:** First, second, and later stage. **Industry Preferences:** Internet specific, computer software and services, communications and media, consumer related, biotechnology, medical and health. **Geographic Preferences:** Mid Atlantic, Northeast, and Southeast.

PROCUREMENT ASSISTANCE PROGRAMS

58682 ■ **Procurement Center Representative**
Department of Health & Human Services
200 Independence Ave. SW, Rm. 300
Washington, DC 20201
Ph:(202)690-8330
Fax: (202)690-8772
Contact: Malda SBA Representative, SBA Representative
E-mail: rlewis@os.dhhs.gov
Description: Covers activities for Department of Health and Human Services (Washington, DC), Army Corps of Engineers (Baltimore, MD), Social Security Administration (Baltimore, MD).

58683 ■ **Washington, DC, Metropolitan Area Procurement Center–Department of Transportation**
400 7th St. SW, Rm. 9410
Washington, DC 20590
Ph:(202)366-5325
Fax: (202)366-7538
URL: http://www.osdbuweb.dot.gov
Contact: Reginald SBA Representative, SBA Representative
E-mail: reggie.holloway@ost.dot.gov
Description: Covers activities for Department of Transportation (Washington, DC), Department of Commerce (Washington, DC), Department of Veterans Affairs (Washington, DC), Small Business Administration (Washington, DC), GSA/Regional Office (Washington, DC), Department of Housing and Urban Development (Washington, DC).

INCUBATORS/RESEARCH AND TECHNOLOGY PARKS

58684 ■ **American University–Office of Sponsored Programs**
Nebraska Hall, Rm. 105
4400 Massachusetts Ave. NW
Washington, DC 20016-8066
Ph:(202)885-3442
Fax: (202)885-3453
Contact: Liz Kirby, Dir.
Scope: Coordinates and facilitates externally sponsored research and other special educational activities of the University.

58685 ■ **Howard University–Office of University Research and Planning**
1400 Shepard NE
Washington, DC 20017
Ph:(202)806-0977
Fax: (202)806-5467
Co. E-mail: rmanning@research.howard.edu
Contact: Ranimor A. Manning III, Interim Dir.
E-mail: rmanning@research.howard.edu
Scope: Primarily responsible for examining the university from an institutional perspective relative to efficient utilization of available resources. Provides analytical services to facilitate formulation of university policy and management decisions. Continuously studies, analyzes, and evaluates existing programs, administrative divisions, units or departments, and all university administrative procedures. Responds to information and data requests from internal and external sources. **Publications:** Facts (annually); Howard University Factbook (annually). **Educational Activities:** Conference (annually); University Data Conference (quarterly).

58686 ■ **Joint Oceanographic Institutions**
1201 New York Ave. NW, Ste. 400
Washington, DC 20005
Ph:(202)232-3900
Fax: (202)265-4409
Co. E-mail: sbohlen@joiscience.org
URL: http://www.joiscience.org
Contact: Dr. Steven Bohlen, Pres.
E-mail: sbohlen@joiscience.org
Scope: Responsible for the program management of the U.S. ship in the Integrated Ocean Drilling Program (IODP) which is an international partnership of scientists and research institutions organized to explore the structure and history of the Earth. JOI has contracted with Texas A&M University to serve as science operator and with Lamont-Doherty Earth Observatory of Columbia University to provide downhole logging services for IODP. JOI is responsible for the management and administration of the JOI-U.S. Science Support Program, a long-term program that supports activities to be carried out by the U.S. scientific community as an integral part of IODP. JOI is also responsible for the coordination of other large oceanographic research programs. **Publications:** JOIDES Journal (semiannually); ODP Proceedings Part A & B (semiannually). **Educational Activities:** Educational CD-Roms; JOI/USSAC Distinguished Lecturer Series.

LEGISLATIVE ASSISTANCE

58687 ■ **Council of the District of Columbia**
John A Wilson Bldg
1350 Pennsylvania Ave., NW
Washington, DC 20004
Ph:(202)724-8052
Fax: (202)724-8120
Co. E-mail: Afenty@dccouncil.us
URL: http://www.dccouncil.us

TRADE PERIODICALS

58688 ■ *DMAW Marketing Advents*
Pub: Direct Marketing Association of Washington, DC
Ed: Nancy Scott, Editor. **Released:** Monthly. **Price:** $165, Included in membership. **Description:** Spotlights direct marketing topics for members in the Washington, DC area. Recurring features include interviews, a calendar of events, news of educational opportunities, and job listings.

PUBLICATIONS

58689 ■ *Starting and Operating a Business in District of Columbia: A Step-by-Step Guide*
PSI Research
300 N. Valley Dr.
Grants Pass, OR 97526
Ph:(503)479-9464
Free: 800-228-2275
Fax: (503)476-1479
Co. E-mail: psi2@magick.net
Ed: Michael D. Jenkins. **Released:** Revised edition, 1992. **Price:** $29.95 (looseleaf binder); $24.95 (paper). **Description:** Part of the Successful Business Library series.

PUBLISHERS

58690 ■ **Friends of the Earth**
1717 Massachusetts Ave. NW, Ste. 600
Washington, DC 20036-2002
Free: 877-843-8687
Fax: (202)783-0444
Co. E-mail: foe@foe.org
URL: http://www.foe.org
Contact: Brent Blackwelder, President
Description: Publishes quarterly and annual reports on environmental degradation and studies. **Founded:** 1969.

58691 ■ **Gallaudet University Press**
800 Florida Ave. NE
Washington, DC 20002-1205
Ph:(202)651-5488
Fax: (202)651-5489
Co. E-mail: gupress@gallaudet.edu
URL: http://gupress.gallaudet.edu
Contact: Ivey B. Wallace, Man. Ed.

E-mail: ivey.wallace@gallaudet.edu
Description: Publishes reference books, biographies for and about deaf and hard of hearing people, deaf culture, and deaf studies. Accepts unsolicited manuscripts. Reaches market through direct mail, reviews, listings, wholesalers and distributors. **Founded:** 1980.

58692 ■ **International Franchise Association**
1501 K St. NW, Ste. 350
Washington, DC 20005
Ph:(202)628-8000
Free: 800-543-1038
Fax: (202)628-0812
Co. E-mail: ifa@franchise.org
URL: http://www.franchise.org
Contact: Matthew R. Shay, President
E-mail: don@franchise.org
Description: Publishes educational tools for members, public, press and governments to describe the workings and advantages of franchising as a method of doing business. Offers audio cassettes, video tapes, computer diskettes. Distributes for Commerce Clearing House. **Founded:** 1960.

58693 ■ **Kiplinger Books and Tapes**
1729 H St. NW
Washington, DC 20006
Ph:(202)887-6400
Free: 800-544-0155
Fax: (202)223-8990
Co. E-mail: books@kiplinger.com
URL: http://www.kiplinger.com
Contact: Ted Miller, Editorial Dir.
E-mail: tmiller@kiplinger.com
Description: Publishes personal finance and business forecasting books for both professionals and the public. Reaches market through distributors. Does not accept unsolicited manuscripts. **Founded:** 1920.

58694 ■ **National Association for Business Economics**
1233 20th St. NW, Ste. 505
Washington, DC 20036

Ph:(202)463-6223
Fax: (202)463-6239
Co. E-mail: nabe@nabe.com
URL: http://www.nabe.com
Contact: Susan Doolittle, Exec. Dir.
E-mail: doolittle@nabe.com
Description: Publishes journals and newsletters. Provides a means of communication and exchange of experience and ideas between the business community and schools, government, and economists. Also offers placement assistance, economic surveys, annual meetings, seminars, and training programs. Reaches market through direct mail. Does not accept unsolicited manuscripts. **Founded:** 1959.

58695 ■ **National Small Business Association**
1156 15th St. NW, Ste. 1100
Washington, DC 20005
Ph:(202)293-8830
Fax: (202)872-8543
Co. E-mail: nsbu@nsbu.org
URL: http://www.nsba.biz
Contact: Paul Hense, Chairman of the Board
Description: Publishes information pertinent to small business. Also operates an Export Opportunity Hot line providing trade information to small firms. Reaches market through direct mail. **Founded:** 1937.

58696 ■ **U.S. Small Business Administration**
409 3rd St. SW
Washington, DC 20416
Ph:(202)205-6740
Free: 800-827-5722
Fax: (202)205-6913
URL: http://www.sba.gov/
Contact: Melanie R. Sabelhaus, Dep. Admin.
Description: Government agency that publishes books and videotapes on starting and financing your own business and on international trade.

SMALL BUSINESS DEVELOPMENT CENTER LEAD OFFICE

58697 ■ Florida Small Business Development Center–University of West Florida
UWF Downtown Center
19 W. Garden St., Ste. 300
Pensacola, FL 32501
Ph:(850)595-6060
Fax: (850)595-6070
Co. E-mail: fsbdc@uwf.edu
URL: http://www.floridasbdc.edu
Contact: Jerry Cartwright, Director
E-mail: jcartwri@uwf.edu

58698 ■ University of West Florida–Florida SBDC
401 E. Chase St., Ste. 100
Pensacola, FL 32502
Ph:(850)473-7800
Fax: (850)473-7813
URL: http://www.floridasbdc.com
Contact: Jerry Cartwright, State Dir.
E-mail: jcartwright@uwf.edu

SMALL BUSINESS DEVELOPMENT CENTERS

58699 ■ Brevard Community College (Melbourne)–Small Business Development Center
3865 N. Wickham Rd., Rm. 122
Bldg. 10
Melbourne, FL 32935
Ph:(321)433-5570
Fax: (321)433-5708
URL: http://www.brevardcc.edu
Contact: Victoria Peak, Director
E-mail: peake.v@brevardcc.edu

58700 ■ Daytona Beach Community College–Small Business Development Center
Bldg. 10, Rm. 223
1200 W. International Speedway Blvd.
Daytona Beach, FL 32114-2817
Ph:(386)506-4723
Fax: (386)258-4465
Co. E-mail: sbdc@dbcc.edu
URL: http://www.sbdcdaytona.com
Contact: Ned Harper, Dir.
E-mail: lburgwin@bellsouth.net

58701 ■ Florida Agricultural and Mechanical University–Small Business Development Center
1157 E. Tennessee St.
Tallahassee, FL 32308
Ph:(850)599-3407
Fax: (850)561-2049
URL: http://www.famu/edu/sbdc

Contact: Patricia McGowan, Dir.
E-mail: pmcgowan@famu.edu

58702 ■ Florida Atlantic University–Small Business Development Center
1515 W. Commercial Blvd., Rm. 111-112
Ft. Lauderdale, FL 33309-3009
Ph:(954)229-4216
URL: http://www.fausbdc.com
Contact: Marty Zients, Mgr.

58703 ■ Florida Gulf Coast University–Small Business Development Center
Bldg. 3, Ste. 8
12751 Westlinks Dr.
Fort Myers, FL 33913-8615
Ph:(239)225-4220
Fax: (239)225-4221
URL: http://di.fqcu.edu/sbdc
Contact: Dan Regelski, Regional Dir.
E-mail: dregelsk@fgcu.edu

58704 ■ Florida Gulf Coast University–Small Business Development Center–Center for Leadership & Innovation (Bldg.)
Bldg. III, Unit 7
12751 Westlinks Dr.
Fort Myers, FL 33913
Ph:(239)225-4200
Free: 800-225-4220
Co. E-mail: cli@fgcu.edu
URL: http://www.fgcu.edu/cob/sbdc
Contact: Dan Regelski, Dir.
E-mail: dregelsk@fgcu.edu

58705 ■ Florida International University–Small Business Development Center
University Park
CEAS-2620
Miami, FL 33199
Ph:(305)348-2272
Fax: (305)348-2965
Contact: Marvin Nesbit, Dir.

58706 ■ Gulf Coast Community College–Small Business Development Center
2500 Minnesota Ave.
Lynn Haven, FL 32444
Ph:(850)271-1108
Free: 800-542-7232
Fax: (850)271-1109
Co. E-mail: gcccsbdc@knology.net
URL: http://www.northfloridabiz.com
Contact: Stephen Whitt, Dir.

58707 ■ Indian River Community College–Small Business Development Center
3209 Virginia Ave., Rm. 110
Ft. Pierce, FL 34981-5541
Ph:(772)462-4756
Fax: (772)462-4796
Contact: Marsha Thompson, Dir.
E-mail: mthompso@ircc.edu

58708 ■ Manatee Community College–Small Business Development Center
8000 Tamiami Trail, S.
Venice, FL 34293-5113
Ph:(941)408-1412
Fax: (941)497-6433
URL: http://www.mccfl.edu
Contact: Carolyn Griffin, Asst. Dir.
E-mail: griffic2@mccfl.edu

58709 ■ Okaloosa-Walton Community College–Small Business Development Center
922 Mar Walt Dr., Ste. 203
Ft. Walton Beach, FL 32547
Ph:(850)833-9400
Co. E-mail: fwbsbdc@uwf.edu
Contact: Jane Briere Mgr., Mgr.

58710 ■ Polk County Board of County Commissioners–Small and Minority Business Development Center
600 N. Broadway Ave., Ste. 300
Bartow, FL 33830
Ph:(863)534-2503
Fax: (863)519-8997
Co. E-mail: info@polksbdc.org
URL: http://www.polksbdc.org
Contact: Doretha Brooks, Director

58711 ■ SBDC at Seminole Community College–Seminole Technology Business Incubation Center–Small Business Development Center (1445)
1445 Dolgner Pl.
Sanford, FL 32771
Ph:(407)321-3495
Fax: (407)321-4184
URL: http://sbdc.scc-fl.edu
Contact: Wayne T. Hardy, Regional Mgr.
E-mail: hardyw@scc-fl.edu

58712 ■ Small Business Development Center–Gainesville Technology Enterprise Center
2153 SE Hawthorne Rd., Ste. 126
Gainesville, FL 32641
Ph:(352)334-7230
Fax: (352)334-7233
Co. E-mail: sbdcgnv@atlantic.net
URL: http://www.sbdc.unf.edu
Contact: Lalla Sheehy, Program Mgr.

58713 ■ University of Central Florida–Kissimmee/Osceola Chamber of Commerce–Small Business Development Center (1425)
1425 E. Vine St.
Kissimmee, FL 34744-3621
Ph:(407)847-2452
Fax: (407)847-5971
URL: http://www.bus.ucf.edu/sbdc/
Contact: Ben Dobson, Asst. Dir.
E-mail: cen.dobson@bus.ucf.edu

58714 ■ University of Central Florida–Small Business Development Center
College of Business Administration, Ste. 309
315 E. Robinson St., Ste. 100
12565 Research Parkway, Ste. 300
Orlando, FL 32801
Ph:(407)420-4850
Fax: (407)420-4862
Co. E-mail: sbdcucf@bus.ucf.edu
URL: http://www.bus.ucf.edu/sbdc
Contact: Eunice Choi, Interim Dir.
E-mail: Eunice.Choi@bus.ucf.edu

58715 ■ University of North Florida–Ocala Small Business Development Center
110 E. Silver Springs Blvd.
Ocala, FL 34470
Ph:(352)622-8763
Fax: (352)351-1031
Co. E-mail: sbdcoca@atlantic.net
URL: http://www.sbdc.unf.edu
Contact: Philip Geist, Program Dir.

58716 ■ University of North Florida–Small Business Development Center
12000 Alumni Dr.
Jacksonville, FL 32224-2677
Ph:(904)620-2476
Free: 800-450-4624
Fax: (904)620-2567
Co. E-mail: smallbiz@unf.edu
URL: http://www.sbdc.unf.edu
Contact: Lowell Salter, Regional Dir.
E-mail: lsalter@unf.edu

58717 ■ University of South Florida–Small Business Development Center
1101 Channelside Dr., Ste. 210
Tampa, FL 33620-3613
Ph:(813)905-5800
Fax: (813)905-5801
URL: http://www.coba.usf.edu/centers/sbdc
Contact: Irene Hurst, Dir.
E-mail: hurst@coba.usf.edu

58718 ■ University of West Florida–Small Business Development Center
401 E. Chase St., Ste. 100
Pensacola, FL 32502
Ph:(850)473-7830
Fax: (850)473-7831
URL: http://www.sbdc.uwf.edu
Contact: Larry Strain, Regional Dir.
E-mail: lstrain@uwf.edu

SMALL BUSINESS ASSISTANCE PROGRAMS

58719 ■ Enterprise Florida, Inc.–Marketing And Development Division
390 N. Orange Ave., Ste. 1300
Orlando, FL 32801
Ph:(407)316-4600
Fax: (407)316-4599
URL: http://www.floridabusiness.com
Description: Administers the Business Supplier Program, which helps businesses locate suppliers of goods and services in Florida.

58720 ■ NASA/Southern Technology Applications Center
1900 SW 34th St.
Gainesville, FL 32608
Ph:(352)294-7822
Fax: (352)294-7802
URL: http://www.4stac.org
Description: Provides information on technology, science, industry, management, marketing, economics, and business.

SCORE OFFICES

58721 ■ Pasco-Hernando County SCORE - Chapter 439
Bank of America Bldg.
6014 US Hwy. 19, Ste. 302
New Port Richey, FL 34652
Ph:(727)842-4638
Fax: (727)841-7266
Co. E-mail: score439@verizon.net
URL: http://www.score439.org
Description: Represents businessmen and women, small business owners, senior corporate executives and experienced professionals. Provides professional guidance and information to maximize the success of existing and emerging small businesses.

58722 ■ SCORE Bay County
2500 Minnesota Ave.
Lynn Haven, FL 32444
Ph:(407)420-4844
Fax: (850)271-1109
Co. E-mail: score@floridanec.org
Description: Promotes entrepreneur education and the formation, growth and success of the nation's small business.

58723 ■ SCORE Central Florida
5410 S Florida Ave., No. 3
Lakeland, FL 33813
Ph:(863)619-5783
Co. E-mail: score122@verizon.net
Description: Provides resources and expertise to maximize the success of existing and emerging small businesses. Offers business counseling and workshops.

58724 ■ SCORE Charlotte County
1777 Tamiami Trail, Ste. 411
Port Charlotte, FL 33948
Ph:(941)743-6179
Co. E-mail: score0318@aol.com
URL: http://www.charlotte-florida.com/business/scorepg01.htm
Description: Provides resources and expertise to maximize the success of existing and emerging small businesses. Offers business counseling and workshops.

58725 ■ SCORE Citrus County
3810 S Lecanto Hwy., Bldg. P1-101
Lecanto, FL 34461
Ph:(352)621-0775
Co. E-mail: score.citrus@gmail.com
URL: http://www.scorecitrus.org
Description: Provides professional guidance and information to maximize the success of existing and emerging small businesses. Promotes entrepreneur education in Citrus County area, FL.

58726 ■ SCORE Dade
100 S Biscayne Blvd., 7th Fl.
Miami, FL 33131-2011
Ph:(786)217-6729
Fax: (305)536-5058
Co. E-mail: scoremiami@gmail.com
URL: http://www.scoremiami.org
Description: Provides professional guidance and information to maximize the success of existing and emerging small businesses. Offers business counseling and workshops.

58727 ■ SCORE Fort Lauderdale
c/o Leonard Kulakofsky, Chm.
299 E Broward Blvd., No. 123
Fort Lauderdale, FL 33301
Ph:(954)356-7263
Fax: (954)356-7145
Co. E-mail: mail@score17.org
URL: http://www.score17.org
Contact: Leonard Kulakofsky, Chm.
Description: Provides professional guidance and information to maximize the success of existing and emerging small businesses. Promotes entrepreneur education in Fort Lauderdale area, Florida.

58728 ■ SCORE Hillsborough
c/o Corporate Square
7402 N 56th St., Bldg. 400, Ste. 425
Tampa, FL 33617
Ph:(813)988-1435
Co. E-mail: counselor@tampascore.com
URL: http://www.tampascore.com
Description: Provides resources and expertise to maximize the success of existing and emerging small businesses. Offers business counseling and workshops.

58729 ■ SCORE Jacksonville
c/o Bryce Sovereign, Chm.
7825 Baymeadows Way
Jacksonville, FL 32256
Ph:(904)443-1900
Fax: (904)443-1980
Co. E-mail: info@scorejax.org
URL: http://www.scorejax.org
Contact: Bryce Sovereign, Chm.
Description: Provides professional guidance and information to maximize the success of existing and emerging small businesses. Offers business counseling and workshops.

58730 ■ SCORE Lake-Sumter
Lake Technical Center
2001 Kurt St.
Eustis, FL 32726
Ph:(352)589-2250
Co. E-mail: askscore@score414.org
URL: http://www.score414.org
Contact: Jerry Benedict, Chm.
Description: Creates opportunities for small business owners and potential small business owners to achieve success. Provides in-depth, industry-specific business assistance to help evaluate a business idea or plan, stimulate business growth and ensure long-term stability.

58731 ■ SCORE Manasota
c/o Mr. Ed Piekarz, Chm.
2801 Fruitville Rd., Ste. 280
Sarasota, FL 34237
Ph:(941)955-1029
Fax: (941)955-5581
Co. E-mail: scorech116@verizon.net
URL: http://www.score-suncoast.org
Contact: Mr. Ed Piekarz, Chm.
Description: Works for the formation, growth, and success of small businesses. Provides on-line business counseling and business improvement activities.

58732 ■ SCORE Naples of Collier
c/o Ekkehard Grampp, CHR, Chm.
900 Goodlette Rd. N
Naples, FL 34102
Ph:(239)430-0081
Fax: (239)430-0082
Co. E-mail: score@scorenaples.org
URL: http://www.scorenaples.org
Contact: Mr. Ekkehard Grampp CHR, Chm.
Description: Creates opportunities for small business owners and potential small business owners to achieve success. Provides entrepreneur education in Naples area, in Florida. Offers individual counseling, workshops, seminars and literature.

58733 ■ SCORE Ocala
110 E Silver Spring Blvd.
Ocala, FL 34470
Ph:(352)629-5959
Co. E-mail: scoreocala@cox.net
Description: Creates opportunities for small business owners and potential business owners to achieve success. Provides entrepreneur education in Ocala area, Florida.

58734 ■ SCORE Orlando
National Entrepreneur Ctr.
Landmark One Bldg.
315 E Robinson St., Ste. 100
Orlando, FL 32801
Ph:(407)420-4844
Fax: (407)420-4849
Co. E-mail: score@floridanec.org

URL: http://www.scoreorlando.org
Contact: Mr. Skip Honigstein, Chm.
Description: All-volunteer resource partner of the Small Business Administration. Provides business management counselors for present and future small business owners in need of expert advice. Offers free and confidential one-on-one and email counseling, in addition to numerous educational seminars appropriate for entrepreneurs.

58735 ■ SCORE Palm Beach
c/o Mr. James J. Kubie, Chm.
500 Australian Ave. S, Ste. 115
West Palm Beach, FL 33401
Ph:(561)833-1672
Fax: (561)833-1470
Co. E-mail: wpbscore@us-it.net
URL: http://www.wpbscore.org
Contact: Mr. James J. Kubie, Chm.
Description: Represents retired entrepreneurs and corporate executives. Provides free business counseling to start-ups and small businesses. Includes primary counseling areas such as; business planning, business structure, marketing, distribution, home businesses, accounting, budgeting, personnel, operation issues, etc.

58736 ■ SCORE South Broward
3475 Sheridian St., Ste. 203
Hollywood, FL 33021
Ph:(954)966-8415
Fax: (954)966-2313
Co. E-mail: sbascore@aol.com
Description: Provides resources and expertise to maximize the success of existing and emerging small businesses. Offers business counseling and workshops.

58737 ■ SCORE South Palm Beach
7999 N Federal Hwy., Ste. 201
Boca Raton, FL 33487
Ph:(561)981-5180
Fax: (561)981-5391
Co. E-mail: mail@score-chapter412.org
URL: http://www.score-chapter412.org
Description: Strives for the formation, growth and success of small businesses. Provides professional guidance and information, accessible to all, to maximize the success of existing and emerging small businesses. Promotes entrepreneur education in South Palm Beach area, Florida.

58738 ■ SCORE Southwest Florida
Social Security Bldg.
10100 Deer Run Farms Rd., Ste. 231
Fort Myers, FL 33912
Ph:(239)489-2935
Fax: (239)489-1170
Co. E-mail: score219@msn.com
URL: http://www.score219.org
Contact: Dennis Weimer, Chm.
Description: Provides resources and expertise to maximize the success of existing and emerging small businesses. Offers business counseling and workshops.

58739 ■ SCORE Space Coast
Melbourne Professional Complex
1600 Sarno, Ste. 205
Melbourne, FL 32935
Ph:(321)254-2288
Fax: (321)254-2288
Co. E-mail: scorechapter400@nebutel.com
URL: http://www.spacecoastscore.org
Contact: James C. Robertson, Chm.
Description: Strives for the formation, growth, and success of small businesses. Offers educational seminars and business counseling.

58740 ■ SCORE Suncoast/Pinellas
Airport Business Ctr.
4707 140th Ave. N, No. 311
Clearwater, FL 33762
Ph:(727)532-6800
Fax: (727)532-6800
Co. E-mail: score115@ij.net
URL: http://www.score115.org

Description: Provides professional guidance and information to maximize the success of existing and emerging small businesses. Offers business counseling and workshops.

58741 ■ SCORE Tallahassee
c/o Gordon Clifford, Chm.
200 W Park Ave.
Tallahassee, FL 32302
Ph:(850)487-2665
URL: http://www.score.org

58742 ■ SCORE Treasure Coast
3220 S US Hwy. 1, Ste. No. 2
Fort Pierce, FL 34982
Ph:(772)489-0548
Fax: (772)489-0548
Co. E-mail: score308@bellsouth.net
URL: http://www.score308.com
Description: Provides resources and expertise to maximize the success of existing and emerging small businesses. Offers business counseling and workshops.

58743 ■ SCORE Volusia/Flagler Co
c/o Nathaniel Kosak, Chm.
921 N Nova Rd., Ste. A
Holly Hill, FL 32117
Ph:(386)255-6889
Fax: (386)255-0229
Co. E-mail: score87@earthlink.net
URL: http://www.score87.org
Contact: Nathaniel Kosak, Chm.
Description: Provides professional guidance and information to maximize the success of existing and emerging small businesses. Offers business counseling and workshops.

BETTER BUSINESS BUREAUS

58744 ■ Better Business Bureau of Central Florida
1600 S Grant St.
Longwood, FL 32750
Ph:(407)621-3300
Free: 800-275-6614
Fax: (407)786-2625
Co. E-mail: info@orlando.bbb.org
URL: http://www.orlando.bbb.org
Contact: Judy Pepper, Pres./CEO

58745 ■ Better Business Bureau of Northeast Florida
4417 Beach Blvd., Ste. 202
Jacksonville, FL 32207
Ph:(904)721-2288
Fax: (904)721-7373
Co. E-mail: info@bbbnefla.org
URL: http://www.bbbnortheastflorida.org
Contact: Tom Stephens, Pres.

58746 ■ Better Business Bureau of Northwest Florida
912 E Gadsden St.
Pensacola, FL 32501
Ph:(850)429-0002
Free: 800-729-9226
Fax: (850)429-0006
Co. E-mail: info@nwfl.bbb.org
URL: http://www.nwfl.bbb.org
Contact: Norman Wright, Pres.

58747 ■ Better Business Bureau of Port St. Lucie
1950 SE Port St. Lucie Blvd., Ste. 211
Port St. Lucie, FL 34952-5579
Ph:(772)878-2010
Fax: (772)335-9486

58748 ■ Better Business Bureau of West Florida
PO Box 7950
Clearwater, FL 33758-7950

Ph:(727)535-5522
Fax: (727)539-6301
Co. E-mail: info@bbbwestflorida.org
URL: http://www.clearwater.bbb.org
Contact: Karen Nalven, Pres.

CHAMBERS OF COMMERCE

58749 ■ Alachua Chamber of Commerce
PO Box 387
Alachua, FL 32616
Ph:(386)462-3333
Fax: (386)462-1992
Co. E-mail: info@alachua.com
URL: http://www.alachua.com
Contact: Sonya Counce, Pres.

58750 ■ Anna Maria Island Chamber of Commerce
5313 Gulf Dr.
Holmes Beach, FL 34217
Ph:(941)778-1541
Fax: (941)778-9679
Co. E-mail: amichamber@aol.com
URL: http://www.annamariaislandchamber.org
Contact: Mary Ann Brockman, Exec.Dir.

58751 ■ Apalachicola Bay Chamber of Commerce
122 Commerce St.
Apalachicola, FL 32320
Ph:(850)653-9419
Fax: (850)653-8219
Co. E-mail: info@apalachicolabay.org
URL: http://www.apalachicolabay.org
Contact: Anita Gregory-Grove, Exec.Dir.

58752 ■ Apollo Beach Chamber of Commerce
6432 Hwy. 41 N
Apollo Beach, FL 33572
Ph:(813)645-1366
Free: 800-309-9360
Fax: (813)641-2612
Co. E-mail: abeachcham@verizon.net
URL: http://www.apollobeachchamber.com
Contact: Joanne C. Gadek, Exec.Dir.

58753 ■ Apopka Area Chamber of Commerce
180 E Main St.
Apopka, FL 32703
Ph:(407)886-1441
Fax: (407)886-1131
Co. E-mail: staff@apopkachamber.org
URL: http://www.apopkachamber.org
Contact: Andy Gardiner, Exec.Dir.

58754 ■ Auburndale-Mainstreet Chamber of Commerce
111 E Park St.
Auburndale, FL 33823
Ph:(863)967-3400
Fax: (863)967-0880
Co. E-mail: information@auburndalechamber.com
URL: http://www.auburndalefl.com
Contact: Dru Wilson, Exec.Dir.

58755 ■ Avon Park Chamber of Commerce
28 E Main St.
Avon Park, FL 33825
Ph:(863)453-3350
Fax: (863)453-0973
Co. E-mail: apcc@apfla.com
URL: http://www.apfla.com
Contact: David Greenslade, Exec.Dir.

58756 ■ Baker County Chamber of Commerce
20 E MacClenny Ave.
MacClenny, FL 32063
Ph:(904)259-6433
Fax: (904)259-2737
Co. E-mail: gbarber@bakerchamberfl.com
URL: http://www.bakerchamberfl.com
Contact: Ginger Barber, Exec.Dir.

58757 ■ Bay County Chamber of Commerce
PO Box 1850
235 W 5th St.
Panama City, FL 32402-1850
Ph:(850)785-5206
Fax: (850)763-6229
Co. E-mail: info@panamacity.org
URL: http://www.panamacity.org
Contact: Carol Roberts, Exec.Dir.

58758 ■ Belle Glade Chamber of Commerce
540 S Main St.
Belle Glade, FL 33430
Ph:(561)996-2745
Fax: (561)996-2252
Co. E-mail: bgchamber@aol.com
URL: http://www.bellegladechamber.com
Contact: Brenda Bunting, Exec.Dir.

58759 ■ Belleview-South Marion Chamber of Commerce
5301 SE Abshier Blvd.
Belleview, FL 34420
Ph:(352)245-2178
Fax: (352)245-7673
Co. E-mail: info@bsmcc.org
URL: http://www.bsmcc.org
Contact: Sheila Lister, Exec.Dir.

58760 ■ Boca Grande Area Chamber of Commerce
PO Box 704
Boca Grande, FL 33921
Ph:(941)964-0568
Fax: (941)964-0620
Co. E-mail: info@bocagrandechamber.com
URL: http://www.bocagrandechamber.com
Contact: Craig Lutz, Exec.Dir.

58761 ■ Bonita Springs Area Chamber of Commerce
25071 Chamber of Commerce Dr.
Bonita Springs, FL 34135
Ph:(239)992-2943
Free: 800-226-2943
Fax: (239)992-5011
Co. E-mail: info@bonitaspringschamber.com
URL: http://www.bonitaspringschamber.com
Contact: Nancy P. Keefer, Pres.

58762 ■ Calhoun County Chamber of Commerce
20816 Central Ave. E, Ste. 2
Blountstown, FL 32424
Ph:(850)674-4519
Fax: (850)674-4962
Co. E-mail: cchamber@yahoo.com
URL: http://www.calhounco.org
Contact: Samantha Taylor, Dir.

58763 ■ Camara de Comercio Hispana de Hialeah
4410 W 16th Ave., Ste. 62
Hialeah, FL 33013
Ph:(305)557-5060
Fax: (305)556-7333
Contact: Vicente Rodriguez, Pres.

58764 ■ Cedar Key Chamber of Commerce
PO Box 610
Cedar Key, FL 32625
Ph:(352)543-5600
Fax: (352)543-5600
Co. E-mail: info@cedarkey.org
URL: http://www.cedarkey.org
Contact: Joni Ellis, Pres.

58765 ■ Central Pasco Chamber of Commerce
2810 Land O'Lakes Blvd.
PO Box 98
Land O' Lakes, FL 34639-0098
Ph:(813)909-2722
Fax:(813)909-0827
Co. E-mail: office@centralpascochamber.com
URL: http://centralpascochamber.com
Contact: Kathy Dunkley, Exec.Dir.

58766 ■ Chamber of Commerce of Cape Coral
PO Box 100747
Cape Coral, FL 33910
Ph:(239)549-6900
Free: 800-226-9609
Fax: (239)549-9609
Co. E-mail: info@capecoralchamber.com
URL: http://www.capecoralchamber.com
Contact: Michael Quaintance, Pres.

58767 ■ Chamber of Commerce of the Palm Beaches
401 N Flagler Dr.
West Palm Beach, FL 33401
Ph:(561)833-3711
Fax: (561)833-5582
Co. E-mail: chamber@palmbeaches.org
URL: http://www.palmbeaches.org
Contact: Dennis Grady, Pres.

58768 ■ Chamber of Commerce of West Volusia
520 N Volusia Ave.
Orange City, FL 32763-4802
Ph:(386)775-2793
Fax: (386)775-4575
Co. E-mail: info@chamberofcommerceofwestvolusia.com
URL: http://www.chamberofcommerceofwestvolusia.com
Contact: Pat Northey, Pres./CEO

58769 ■ Chamber South
6410 SW 80th St.
South Miami, FL 33143
Ph:(305)661-1621
Fax: (305)666-0508
Co. E-mail: info@chambersouth.com
URL: http://www.chambersouth.com
Contact: Donna G. Masson, Pres.

58770 ■ Charlotte County Chamber of Commerce
326 W Marion Ave., Ste. 112
Punta Gorda, FL 33950-4417
Ph:(941)639-2222
Fax: (941)639-6330
Co. E-mail: askus@charlottecountychamber.org
URL: http://www.charlottecountychamber.org
Contact: Julie Mathis, Exec.Dir.

58771 ■ Citrus County Chamber of Commerce
3495 S Suncoast Blvd.
PO Box 709
Homosassa Springs, FL 34447-0709
Ph:(352)628-2666
Fax: (352)621-0920
Co. E-mail: ccommerce1@tampabay.rr.com
URL: http://www.citruscountychamber.com
Contact: Kevin Cunningham, Pres.

58772 ■ Citrus County Chamber of Commerce - Crystal River Office
28 NW Hwy. 19
Crystal River, FL 34429-3900
Ph:(352)795-3149
Fax: (352)795-4260
Co. E-mail: ccommerce1@tampabay.rr.com
URL: http://www.citruscountychamber.com
Contact: Kitty Barnes, Exec.Dir.

58773 ■ Clay County Chamber of Commerce
1734 Kingsley Ave.
Orange Park, FL 32073
Ph:(904)264-2651
Fax: (904)264-0070
Co. E-mail: kjkilberg@claychamber.com
URL: http://www.claychamber.org
Contact: Kellie Jo Kilberg, Pres./Chief Economic Officer

58774 ■ Clearwater Regional Chamber of Commerce
1130 Cleveland St.
Clearwater, FL 33755

Ph:(727)461-0011
Fax: (727)449-2889
Co. E-mail: info@clearwaterflorida.org
URL: http://www.clearwaterflorida.org
Contact: Beth Coleman, Pres./CEO

58775 ■ Clewiston Chamber of Commerce
PO Box 275
109 Central Ave.
Clewiston, FL 33440
Ph:(863)983-7979
Fax: (863)983-7108
Co. E-mail: clewistonchamber@earthlink.net
URL: http://www.clewiston.org
Contact: Jeff Barwick, Exec.Dir.

58776 ■ Cocoa Beach Area Chamber of Commerce
400 Fortenberry Rd.
Merritt Island, FL 32952
Ph:(321)459-2200
Fax: (321)459-2232
Co. E-mail: kschillo@cocoabeachchamber.com
URL: http://www.cocoabeachchamber.com
Contact: Kathi Schillo, Pres./CEO

58777 ■ Coconut Grove Chamber of Commerce
2820 McFarlane Rd.
Coconut Grove, FL 33133
Ph:(305)444-7270
Fax: (305)444-2498
Co. E-mail: info@coconutgrove.com
URL: http://www.coconutgrove.com
Contact: Charity Johnson, Exec.Dir.

58778 ■ Coral Gables Chamber of Commerce
PO Box 347555
Coral Gables, FL 33234
Ph:(305)446-1657
Fax: (305)446-9900
Co. E-mail: info@coralgableschamber.org
URL: http://www.coralgableschamber.org
Contact: Lettie J. Bien, Pres./CEO

58779 ■ Coral Springs Chamber of Commerce
11805 Heron Bay Blvd.
Coral Springs, FL 33076
Ph:(954)752-4242
Fax: (954)827-0543
Co. E-mail: info@cschamber.com
URL: http://www.cschamber.com
Contact: David Margolis, Chm.

58780 ■ Crestview Area Chamber of Commerce
502 S Main St.
Crestview, FL 32536-4222
Ph:(850)682-3212
Fax: (850)682-7413
Co. E-mail: info@crestviewchamber.com
URL: http://www.crestviewchamber.com
Contact: Wayne Harris, Exec.Dir.

58781 ■ Davie-Cooper City Chamber of Commerce
4185 Davie Rd.
Davie, FL 33314
Ph:(954)581-0790
Fax: (954)581-9684
Co. E-mail: dcch@davie-coopercity.org
URL: http://www.davie-coopercity.org
Contact: Alice Harrington, Exec.Dir.

58782 ■ Daytona Beach - Halifax Area Chamber of Commerce
126 E Orange Ave.
Daytona Beach, FL 32114
Ph:(386)255-0981
Free: 800-854-1234
Fax: (386)258-5104
Co. E-mail: info@daytonachamber.com
URL: http://www.daytonachamber.com
Contact: George Mirabal, Pres./CEO

58783 ■ Daytona Beach Shores Chamber of Commerce
3048 S Atlantic Ave.
Daytona Beach, FL 32118
Ph:(386)761-7163
Fax: (386)788-9497
Co. E-mail: dbschamber@bellsouth.net
URL: http://www.dbschamber.com
Contact: Tracy Flint, Exec.Dir.

58784 ■ DeLand Area Chamber of Commerce
336 N Woodland Blvd.
DeLand, FL 32720
Ph:(386)734-4331
Fax: (386)734-4333
Co. E-mail: welcome@delandchamber.org
URL: http://www.delandchamber.org
Contact: Jenny Stumbras, Exec.Dir.

58785 ■ DeSoto County Chamber of Commerce
16 S Volusia Ave.
Arcadia, FL 34266
Ph:(863)494-4033
Fax: (863)494-3312
Co. E-mail: dawnballard@desotochamber.net
URL: http://www.desotochamber.net
Contact: Dawn Ballard

58786 ■ Destin Area Chamber of Commerce
4484 Legendary Dr., Ste. A
Destin, FL 32541
Ph:(850)837-6241
Fax: (850)654-5612
Co. E-mail: mail@destinchamber.com
URL: http://www.destinchamber.com
Contact: Shane Moody, Pres./CEO

58787 ■ Dixie County Chamber of Commerce
PO Box 547
Cross City, FL 32628
Ph:(352)498-5454
Fax: (352)498-2601
Co. E-mail: dixiechamber@usa.net
URL: http://www.dixiecounty.org
Contact: Gary Poore, VP

58788 ■ Dundee Area Chamber of Commerce
PO Box 241
Dundee, FL 33838-4213
Ph:(863)439-3261
Fax: (863)439-3261
Co. E-mail: ccommer6@tampabay.rr.com
Contact: Becky Baker, Exec.Dir.

58789 ■ Dunedin Chamber of Commerce
301 Main St.
Dunedin, FL 34698
Ph:(727)733-3197
Fax: (727)734-8942
Co. E-mail: chamber@dunedin-fl.com
URL: http://www.dunedin-fl.com
Contact: Lynn Wargo, Pres./CEO

58790 ■ Dunnellon Area Chamber of Commerce
20500 E Pennsylvania Ave.
PO Box 868
Dunnellon, FL 34432
Ph:(352)489-2320
Free: 800-830-2087
Fax: (352)489-6846
Co. E-mail: dchamber@atlantic.net
URL: http://www.dunnellonchamber.org
Contact: Don Koppler, Exec.Dir.

58791 ■ East Lake County Chamber of Commerce
PO Box 774
Sorrento, FL 32776-0774
Ph:(352)383-8801
Fax: (352)383-9343
Co. E-mail: chamber@elcchamber.com
URL: http://www.elcchamber.com
Contact: Theresa Salamone, Office Mgr.

58792 ■ East Orlando Chamber of Commerce
10111 E Colonial Dr.
Orlando, FL 32817-4370
Ph:(407)277-5951
Fax: (407)381-1720
Co. E-mail: eocc@eocc.org
URL: http://www.eocc.org
Contact: Sherry Melville, Exec.Asst.

58793 ■ Englewood-Cape Haze Area Chamber of Commerce
601 S Indiana Ave.
Englewood, FL 34223-3788
Ph:(941)474-5511
Free: 800-603-7198
Fax: (941)475-9257
Co. E-mail: info@englewoodchamber.com
URL: http://www.englewoodchamber.com
Contact: Karen W. Maurer, Exec.Dir.

58794 ■ Estero Chamber of Commerce
PO Box 588
Estero, FL 33928
Ph:(239)948-7990
Fax: (239)947-9968
Co. E-mail: info@esterochamber.org
URL: http://www.esterochamber.org
Contact: Eileen Glavin, Exec.Dir.

58795 ■ Eustis Area Chamber of Commerce
1 W Orange Ave.
PO Box 1210
Eustis, FL 32727-1210
Ph:(352)357-3434
Fax: (352)357-1392
Co. E-mail: eustischamber@mpinet.net
URL: http://www.eustischamber.org
Contact: Nancy Muenzmay, Pres.

58796 ■ Everglades Area Chamber of Commerce
PO Box 130
Everglades City, FL 34139-0130
Ph:(239)695-3941
Free: 800-914-6355
Fax: (239)695-3172
Co. E-mail: info@evergladeschamber.com
URL: http://www.florida-everglades.com
Contact: Winnie Thomas, Mgr.

58797 ■ Flagler Beach Chamber of Commerce
PO Box 5
Flagler Beach, FL 32136-0005
Ph:(386)439-0995
Free: 800-298-0995
Fax: (386)439-0998
Co. E-mail: fbcc@flaglercounty.com
URL: http://www.flaglercounty.com/fbcc
Contact: Mary Stetler, Pres.

58798 ■ Flagler County Palm Coast Chamber of Commerce
20 Airport Rd.
Bunnell, FL 32110
Ph:(386)437-0106
Free: 800-881-1022
Fax: (386)437-5700
Co. E-mail: info@flaglerchamber.org
URL: http://www.flaglerpcchamber.org
Contact: Richard E. Morris, Exec.Dir.

58799 ■ Florida Chamber of Commerce
136 S Bronough St.
PO Box 11309
Tallahassee, FL 32302-3309
Ph:(850)521-1200
Fax: (850)521-1219
Co. E-mail: info@flchamber.com
URL: http://www.flchamber.com
Contact: Frank M. Ryll Jr., Pres.

58800 ■ Frostproof Chamber of Commerce
118 E Wall St.
PO Box 968
Frostproof, FL 33843-0968
Ph:(863)635-9112

Co. E-mail: info@frostproofchamber.com
URL: http://www.frostproofchamber.com

58801 ■ Gadsden County Chamber of Commerce
PO Box 389
Quincy, FL 32353-0389
Ph:(850)627-9231
Free: 800-627-9231
Fax: (850)875-3299
Co. E-mail: gadsdencc@tds.net
URL: http://www.gadsdencc.com
Contact: David A. Gardner, Exec.Dir.

58802 ■ Gainesville Area Chamber of Commerce
300 E Univ. Ave., Ste. 100
PO Box 1187
Gainesville, FL 32602-1187
Ph:(352)334-7100
Fax: (352)334-7141
Co. E-mail: info@gainsvillechamber.com
URL: http://www.gainsvillechamber.com
Contact: Brent Christensen, Pres./CEO

58803 ■ Gilchrist County Chamber of Commerce
220 S Main St.
Trenton, FL 32693
Ph:(352)463-3467
Fax: (352)463-3469
Co. E-mail: chamber@gilchristcounty.com
URL: http://www.gilchristcounty.com
Contact: Maureen Gentry, Exec. Dir.

58804 ■ Glades County Chamber of Commerce
PO Box 490
Moore Haven, FL 33471
Ph:(863)946-0440
Fax: (863)946-2282
Co. E-mail: gccommerce@gladesonline.com
URL: http://www.gladesonline.com
Contact: Lisa Langdale, Exec.Dir.

58805 ■ Goldenrod Area Chamber of Commerce
PO Box 61
Goldenrod, FL 32733
Ph:(407)667-5980
Fax: (407)667-4928
Co. E-mail: smiller@goldenrodchamber.com
URL: http://www.goldenrodchamber.com
Contact: Sarah Miller, Exec. Dir.

58806 ■ Greater Bartow Chamber of Commerce
510 N Broadway Ave.
Bartow, FL 33830-3918
Ph:(863)533-7125
Fax: (863)533-3793
Co. E-mail: discoverbartow@bartowchamber.com
URL: http://www.bartowchamber.com
Contact: Jeff Clark, Exec.Dir.

58807 ■ Greater Boca Raton Chamber of Commerce
1800 N Dixie Hwy.
Boca Raton, FL 33432
Ph:(561)395-4433
Fax: (561)392-3780
Co. E-mail: info@bocaratonchamber.com
URL: http://www.bocaratonchamber.com
Contact: M. J. Arts, Pres./CEO

58808 ■ Greater Boynton Beach Chamber of Commerce
639 E Ocean Ave., Ste. 108
Boynton Beach, FL 33435
Ph:(561)732-9501
Fax: (561)734-4304
Co. E-mail: chamber@boyntonbeach.org
URL: http://www.boyntonbeach.org
Contact: Diana H. Johnson, Pres./CEO

58809 ■ Greater Brandon Chamber of Commerce
808 Oakfield Dr.
Brandon, FL 33511
Ph:(813)689-1221
Fax: (813)689-9440
Co. E-mail: info@brandonchamber.com
URL: http://www.brandonchamber.com
Contact: Ms. Tammy C. Bracewell, Pres./CEO

58810 ■ Greater Chiefland Area Chamber of Commerce
PO Box 1397
Chiefland, FL 32644
Ph:(352)493-1849
Fax: (352)493-0282
Co. E-mail: info@chieflandchamber.com
URL: http://www.chieflandchamber.com
Contact: Resa Jerrel, Exec.Dir.

58811 ■ Greater Dade City Chamber of Commerce
14112 8th St.
Dade City, FL 33525
Ph:(352)567-3769
Fax: (352)567-3770
Co. E-mail: info@dadecitychamber.org
URL: http://www.dadecitychamber.org
Contact: Phyllis S. Smith, Exec.Dir.

58812 ■ Greater Dania Beach Chamber of Commerce
PO Box 1017
Dania Beach, FL 33004
Ph:(954)926-2323
Fax: (954)926-2384
Co. E-mail: greaterdania@earthlink.net
URL: http://www.greaterdania.org
Contact: Morris Stowers, Exec.Dir.

58813 ■ Greater Deerfield Beach Chamber of Commerce
1601 E Hillsboro Blvd.
Deerfield Beach, FL 33441-4386
Ph:(954)427-1050
Fax: (954)427-1056
Co. E-mail: info@deerfieldchamber.com
URL: http://www.deerfieldchamber.com
Contact: Janyce Becker, Exec.Dir.

58814 ■ Greater Delray Beach Chamber of Commerce
64-A SE 5th Ave.
Delray Beach, FL 33483
Ph:(561)278-0424
Co. E-mail: bwood@delraybeach.com
URL: http://www.delraybeach.com
Contact: William Wood, Pres./CEO

58815 ■ Greater Fort Lauderdale Chamber of Commerce
512 NE 3rd Ave.
Fort Lauderdale, FL 33301-3236
Ph:(954)462-6000
Fax: (954)527-8766
Co. E-mail: info@ftlchamber.com
URL: http://www.ftlchamber.com
Contact: Christopher Pollock, Pres./CEO

58816 ■ Greater Fort Myers Chamber of Commerce
PO Box 9289
Fort Myers, FL 33902
Ph:(239)332-3624
Free: 800-366-3622
Fax: (239)332-7276
Co. E-mail: fortmyers@fortmyers.org
URL: http://www.fortmyers.org
Contact: Marietta Mudgett, Exec.Dir.

58817 ■ Greater Fort Walton Beach Chamber of Commerce
PO Box 640
Fort Walton Beach, FL 32549
Ph:(850)244-8191
Fax: (850)244-1935
Co. E-mail: info@fwbchamber.org

URL: http://www.fwbchamber.org
Contact: Ted Corcoran, Pres./CEO

58818 ■ Greater Hernando County Chamber of Commerce
101 E Ft. Dade Ave.
Brooksville, FL 34601
Ph:(352)796-0697
Fax: (352)796-3704
Co. E-mail: info@hernandochamber.com
URL: http://www.hernandochamber.com
Contact: Pat Crowley, Exec.Dir.

58819 ■ Greater Hollywood Chamber of Commerce
330 N Federal Hwy.
Hollywood, FL 33020
Ph:(954)923-4000
Free: 800-231-5562
Fax: (954)923-8737
Co. E-mail: information@hollywoodchamber.org
URL: http://www.hollywoodchamber.org
Contact: Don Dalton, Exec.Dir.

58820 ■ Greater Homestead/Florida City Chamber of Commerce
43 N Krome Ave.
Homestead, FL 33030
Ph:(305)247-2332
Free: 888-352-4891
Fax: (305)246-1100
Co. E-mail: info@chamberinaction.com
URL: http://www.chamberinaction.com
Contact: Mary Finlan, Exec.Dir.

58821 ■ Greater LaBelle Chamber of Commerce
PO Box 456
LaBelle, FL 33975-0456
Ph:(863)675-0125
Fax: (863)675-6160
Co. E-mail: labelle.chamber@olsusa.com
Contact: Leeann Frost, Exec.Sec.

58822 ■ Greater Lake Worth Chamber of Commerce
501 Lake Ave.
Lake Worth, FL 33460
Ph:(561)582-4401
Fax: (561)547-8300
URL: http://www.lwchamber.com
Contact: Thomas Ramiccio, Pres./CEO

58823 ■ Greater Lantana Chamber of Commerce
212 Iris St.
Lantana, FL 33462-3219
Ph:(561)585-8664
Fax: (561)585-0644
Co. E-mail: info@lantanachamber.com
Contact: Ron Washam, Pres.

58824 ■ Greater Marathon Chamber of Commerce
12222 Overseas Hwy.
Marathon, FL 33050
Ph:(305)743-5417
Free: 800-262-7284
Fax: (305)289-0183
Co. E-mail: visitus@floridakeysmarathon.com
URL: http://www.floridakeysmarathon.com
Contact: Audrey Moir, Exec.Dir.

58825 ■ Greater Miami Chamber of Commerce
1601 Biscayne Blvd.
Ballroom Level
Miami, FL 33132-1260
Ph:(305)350-7700
Fax: (305)374-6902
Co. E-mail: info@miamichamber.com
URL: http://www.greatermiami.com
Contact: George Foyo, Pres./CEO

58826 ■ Greater Miami Chamber of Commerce, Women in Business Group
Omni International Complex
1601 Biscayne Blvd.
Miami, FL 33132-1260

Ph:(305)577-5427
Fax: (305)374-6902
Co. E-mail: reception@miamichamber.com
URL: http://www.greatermiami.com
Contact: Lisa Showers, Exec. Asst.

58827 ■ Greater Miami Shores Chamber of Commerce
9701 NE 2nd Ave.
Miami Shores, FL 33138-2310
Ph:(305)754-5466
Fax: (305)759-8872
Co. E-mail: shoreschamber@bellsouth.net
URL: http://www.miamishores.com
Contact: Lew Soli, Exec.Dir.

58828 ■ Greater Mulberry Chamber of Commerce
400 N Church Ave.
PO Box 254
Mulberry, FL 33860
Ph:(863)425-4414
Fax: (863)425-3837
Co. E-mail: mulberrychamber@verizon.net
URL: http://www.mulberrychamber.org
Contact: Corine Waters, Exec.Dir.

58829 ■ Greater Naples Chamber of Commerce
3620 Tamiami Trail N
Naples, FL 34103-3724
Ph:(239)262-6141
Fax: (239)262-8374
Co. E-mail: visitorscenter@napleschamber.org
URL: http://www.napleschamber.org
Contact: Mike Reagen PhD, Pres.

58830 ■ Greater Nassau County Chamber of Commerce
PO Box 98
45383 Dixie Ave.
Callahan, FL 32011
Ph:(904)879-1441
Fax: (904)879-4033
Co. E-mail: gncc@juno.com
URL: http://www.greaternassaucounty.com
Contact: Louise Banks, Exec.Dir.

58831 ■ Greater North Miami Chamber of Commerce
13100 W Dixie Hwy.
North Miami, FL 33161
Ph:(305)891-7811
Fax: (305)893-8522
Co. E-mail: info@northmiamichamber.com
URL: http://www.northmiamichamber.com
Contact: Carol F. Keys, Pres.

58832 ■ Greater Oviedo Chamber of Commerce
PO Box 621236
200 W Broadway
Oviedo, FL 32762-1236
Ph:(407)365-6500
Fax: (407)365-6587
Co. E-mail: fay@oviedochamber.org
URL: http://www.oviedochamber.org
Contact: Melissa O. King, Exec.Dir.

58833 ■ Greater Palm Bay Chamber of Commerce
1153 Malabar Rd. NE, Ste. 18
Palm Bay, FL 32907
Ph:(321)951-9998
Free: 800-276-9130
Fax: (321)951-0012
Co. E-mail: dobusiness@palmbaychamber.com
URL: http://www.palmbaychamber.com
Contact: Kathleen Bishop, Pres./CEO

58834 ■ Greater Palm Harbor Area Chamber of Commerce
1151 Nebraska Ave.
Palm Harbor, FL 34683
Ph:(727)784-4287
Fax: (727)786-2336
Co. E-mail: phchamber@palmharborcc.org

URL: http://www.palmharborcc.org
Contact: Connie Davis, Pres./CEO

58835 ■ Greater Panama City Beaches Chamber of Commerce
415 Beckrich Rd., Ste. 200
Panama City Beach, FL 32407
Ph:(850)234-3193
Fax: (850)235-2301
Co. E-mail: chamber@pcbeach.org
URL: http://www.pcbeach.org
Contact: Debi Knight, Pres.

58836 ■ Greater Pine Island Chamber of Commerce
PO Box 525
Matlacha, FL 33993
Ph:(239)283-0888
Fax: (239)283-0336
Co. E-mail: info@pineislandchamber.org
URL: http://www.pineislandchamber.org
Contact: Sally Topager, Pres.

58837 ■ Greater Plant City Chamber of Commerce
106 N Evers St.
PO Drawer CC
Plant City, FL 33564-9021
Ph:(813)754-3707
Free: 800-760-2315
Fax: (813)752-8793
Co. E-mail: info@plantcity.org
URL: http://www.plantcity.org
Contact: Marion Smith, Pres.

58838 ■ Greater Plantation Chamber of Commerce
7401 NW 4th St.
Plantation, FL 33317
Ph:(954)587-1410
Fax: (954)587-1886
Co. E-mail: info@plantationchamber.org
URL: http://www.plantationchamber.org
Contact: Siobhan Edwards, Pres.

58839 ■ Greater Pompano Beach Chamber of Commerce
2200 E Atlantic Blvd.
Pompano Beach, FL 33062
Ph:(954)941-2940
Fax: (954)785-8358
Co. E-mail: pompano@pompanobeachchamber.com
URL: http://www.pompanobeachchamber.com
Contact: Anne Dufresne, CEO/Pres.

58840 ■ Greater Riverview Chamber of Commerce
PO Box 128
Riverview, FL 33568
Ph:(813)643-8000
Fax: (813)643-8500
Co. E-mail: riverviewchamber@aol.com
URL: http://www.riverviewchamber.com
Contact: Connie Lesko, Exec.Dir.

58841 ■ Greater Sarasota Chamber of Commerce
1945 Fruitville Rd.
Sarasota, FL 34236
Ph:(941)955-8187
Fax: (941)366-5621
Co. E-mail: pmorgan@sarasotachamber.org
URL: http://www.sarasotachamber.org
Contact: Steve Queior CCE, Pres./CEO

58842 ■ Greater Sebring Chamber of Commerce
309 Circle Park Dr.
Sebring, FL 33870-3314
Ph:(863)385-8448
Free: 877-844-6007
Fax: (863)385-8810
Co. E-mail: information@sebringflchamber.com
URL: http://www.sebringflchamber.com
Contact: Mr. Daniel F. Andrews, Exec.Dir./CEO

58843 ■ Greater Seffner Area Chamber of Commerce
PO Box 1920
Seffner, FL 33583-1920
Ph:(813)627-8686
Co. E-mail: info@seffnerchamber.com
URL: http://www.seffnerchamber.com
Contact: Mr. Barrett Smith, Pres.

58844 ■ Greater Seminole Area Chamber of Commerce
8400 113th St. N
Seminole, FL 33772
Ph:(727)392-3245
Fax: (727)397-7753
Co. E-mail: ljolley@ij.net
URL: http://seminolechamber.net
Contact: Jimmy Johnson, Exec.Dir.

58845 ■ Greater Sunrise Chamber of Commerce
Sawgrass Mills Mall, No. 101
12801 W Sunrise Blvd.
Sunrise, FL 33323
Ph:(954)835-2428
Fax: (954)835-2431
Co. E-mail: director@greatersunrisechamber.org
URL: http://www.greatersunrisechamber.org
Contact: Steve Solomon, Chm.

58846 ■ Greater Tallahassee Chamber of Commerce
PO Box 1639
100 N Duval St.
Tallahassee, FL 32302
Ph:(850)224-8116
Fax: (850)561-3860
Co. E-mail: info@talchamber.com
URL: http://www.talchamber.com
Contact: Sue Dick, Pres.

58847 ■ Greater Tampa Chamber of Commerce
PO Box 420
Tampa, FL 33601
Ph:(813)228-7777
Free: 800-298-2672
Fax: (813)223-7899
Co. E-mail: info@tampachamber.com
URL: http://www.tampachamber.com
Contact: Mr. Kim Scheeler, Pres./CEO

58848 ■ Greater Temple Terrace Chamber of Commerce
9385 N 56th St.
Temple Terrace, FL 33617
Ph:(813)989-7004
Fax: (813)989-7005
Co. E-mail: cdonohue@templeterracechamber.com
URL: http://www.templeterracechamber.com
Contact: Cheri Donohue, Exec.Dir.

58849 ■ Greater Winter Haven Chamber of Commerce
401 Ave. B, NW
PO Box 1420
Winter Haven, FL 33881
Ph:(863)293-2138
Free: 800-871-7027
Fax: (863)297-5818
Co. E-mail: chamber1@winterhavenfl.com
URL: http://www.winterhavenfl.com
Contact: Bob Gernert Jr., Exec.Dir.

58850 ■ Gulf Breeze Area Chamber of Commerce
PO Box 337
Gulf Breeze, FL 32562-0337
Ph:(850)932-7888
Fax: (850)934-4601
Co. E-mail: info@gulfbreezechamber.com
URL: http://www.gulfbreezechamber.com
Contact: Sandra Kimbrough, Exec.Dir.

58851 ■ Gulf County Chamber of Commerce
155 Captain Fred's Pl.
PO Box 964
Port St. Joe, FL 32457-0964

Ph:(850)227-1223
Free: 800-239-9553
Fax: (850)227-9684
Co. E-mail: info@gulfchamber.org
URL: http://www.gulfchamber.org
Contact: Sandra B. Chafin, Exec. Dir.

58852 ■ Haines City Chamber of Commerce
PO Box 986
Haines City, FL 33845-0986
Ph:(863)422-3751
Fax: (863)422-4704
Co. E-mail: info@hainescity.com
URL: http://www.hainescity.com
Contact: Ms. Jane Patton, Exec.Dir.

58853 ■ Hamilton County Chamber of Commerce
PO Box 366
Jasper, FL 32052
Ph:(386)792-1300
Fax: (386)792-0559
Co. E-mail: hamiltoncoc@alltel.net
URL: http://www.hamiltoncountyflorida.com
Contact: Jack Vinson, Chm.

58854 ■ Hardee County Chamber of Commerce
225 E Main St.
PO Box 683
Wauchula, FL 33873
Ph:(863)773-6967
Fax: (863)773-0229
Co. E-mail: hardeecc@strato.net
URL: http://www.hardeecc.com
Contact: Janet Hendry, Exec.Dir.

58855 ■ Hawthorne Area Chamber of Commerce
PO Box 125
Hawthorne, FL 32640-0125
Ph:(352)481-4436
Fax: (352)481-4593
Co. E-mail: rpotter@ms-bank.com
URL: http://www.HawthorneFlorida.org
Contact: Regina Potter, Pres.

58856 ■ Hialeah Chamber of Commerce and Industry
1840 W 49th St., Ste. 700
Hialeah, FL 33012
Ph:(305)828-9898
Fax: (305)828-9777
Co. E-mail: info@hialeahchamber.com
URL: http://www.hialeahchamber.com
Contact: Daniel Hernandez, Pres.

58857 ■ High Springs Chamber of Commerce
PO Box 863
High Springs, FL 32655
Ph:(386)454-3120
Co. E-mail: chamber@highsprings.com
URL: http://www.highsprings.com
Contact: Tony Boothby, Pres.

58858 ■ Hobe Sound Chamber of Commerce
8994 SE Bridge Rd.
PO Box 1507
Hobe Sound, FL 33475
Ph:(772)546-4724
Fax: (772)546-9969
Co. E-mail: info@hobesound.org
URL: http://hobesound.org
Contact: Jennifer Ferrari, Exec.Dir.

58859 ■ Holly Hill Chamber of Commerce
1056 Ridgewood Ave.
Holly Hill, FL 32117
Ph:(386)255-7311
Fax: (386)255-6433
Co. E-mail: ryan.ochipa.gw26@statefarm.com
URL: http://www.hollyhillchamber.com
Contact: Ryan Ochipa, Sec.

58860 ■ Holmes County Chamber of Commerce
106 E Byrd Ave.
PO Box 779
Bonifay, FL 32425

Ph:(850)547-4682
Fax: (850)547-4206
Co. E-mail: hcdc@wfeca.net
Contact: Jyl Eickmann, Exec.Dir.

58861 ■ Immokalee Chamber of Commerce
720 N 15th St.
Immokalee, FL 34142
Ph:(239)657-3237
Fax: (239)657-5450
Co. E-mail: info@immokaleechamber.org
URL: http://www.immokaleechamber.org
Contact: H.B. Starling Jr., Exec.Dir.

58862 ■ Indian River County Chamber of Commerce
1216 21st St.
PO Box 2947
Vero Beach, FL 32960
Ph:(772)567-3491
Fax: (772)778-3181
Co. E-mail: info@indianriverchamber.com
URL: http://www.indianriverchamber.com
Contact: Penny Chandler, Exec.Dir.

58863 ■ Indiantown Western Martin County Chamber of Commerce
PO Box 602
15935 SW Warfield Blvd.
Indiantown, FL 34956-0602
Ph:(772)597-2184
Fax: (772)597-6063
Co. E-mail: itowncc@onearrow.net
URL: http://indiantownfl.org
Contact: Allon R. Fish, Pres./CEO

58864 ■ Islamorada Chamber of Commerce
PO Box 915
Islamorada, FL 33036-0915
Ph:(305)664-4503
Free: 800-FAB-KEYS
Fax: (305)664-4289
Co. E-mail: info@islamoradachamber.com
URL: http://www.islamoradachamber.com
Contact: Eva Scott, Exec.Dir.

58865 ■ Jackson County Chamber of Commerce
4318 Lafayette St.
PO Box 130
Marianna, FL 32447-0130
Ph:(850)482-8060
Fax: (850)482-8002
Co. E-mail: info@jacksoncounty.com
URL: http://www.jcflchamber.com
Contact: Art Kimbrough, Pres./CEO

58866 ■ Jacksonville Regional Chamber of Commerce
3 Independent Dr.
Jacksonville, FL 32202
Ph:(904)366-6600
Co. E-mail: info@jacksonvillechamber.org
URL: http://www.myjaxchamber.com
Contact: Walter M. Lee III, Pres.

58867 ■ Jacksonville Regional Chamber of Commerce - Beaches Division
325 Jacksonville Dr.
Jacksonville Beach, FL 32250
Ph:(904)249-3868
Fax: (904)241-7556
Co. E-mail: beaches@myjaxchamber.com
URL: http://www.myjaxchamber.com
Contact: Jill Sprowell, Exec.Dir.

58868 ■ Jensen Beach Chamber of Commerce
1900 Ricou Terr.
Jensen Beach, FL 34957-7236
Ph:(772)334-3444
Fax: (772)334-0817
Co. E-mail: info@jensenbeachchamber.com
URL: http://www.jensenbeachchamber.org
Contact: Tammy Simoneau, Pres.

58869 ■ Jupiter-Tequesta-Juno Beach Chamber of Commerce
800 N U.S. Hwy. 1
Jupiter, FL 33477-4440
Ph:(561)746-7111
Free: 800-616-7402
Fax: (561)746-7715
Co. E-mail: roxy@jupiterfl.org
URL: http://www.jupiterfl.org
Contact: Louise Murtaugh APRP, Pres.

58870 ■ Key Biscayne Chamber of Commerce
88 W McIntyre St., Ste. 100
Key Biscayne, FL 33149
Ph:(305)361-5207
Fax: (305)361-9411
Co. E-mail: info@keybiscaynechamber.org
Contact: Kathye Susnjer, Exec.Dir.

58871 ■ Key Largo Chamber of Commerce
106000 Overseas Hwy.
Key Largo, FL 33037
Ph:(305)451-4747
Free: 800-822-1088
Fax: (305)451-4726
Co. E-mail: info@keylargochamber.org
URL: http://www.keylargochamber.org
Contact: Karen Tiedemann, Pres.

58872 ■ Key West Chamber of Commerce
402 Wall St.
Key West, FL 33040
Ph:(305)294-2587
Free: 800-LAST-KEY
Fax: (305)294-7806
Co. E-mail: info@keywestchamber.org
URL: http://www.keywestchamber.org
Contact: Virginia A. Panico, Pres.

58873 ■ Kissimmee - Osceola County Chamber of Commerce
1425 E Vine St.
Kissimmee, FL 34744
Ph:(407)847-3174
Fax: (407)870-8607
Co. E-mail: info@kissimmeechamber.com
URL: http://www.kissimmeechamber.com
Contact: Mike Horner, Pres.

58874 ■ Lady Lake Area Chamber of Commerce
PO Box 1430
Lady Lake, FL 32158-1430
Ph:(352)753-6029
Fax: (352)753-8029
Co. E-mail: info@ladylakechamber.com
URL: http://www.ladylakechamber.com
Contact: Betty Bernard, Exec.Dir.

58875 ■ Lafayette County Chamber of Commerce
PO Box 416
Mayo, FL 32066
Ph:(386)294-2705
Fax: (386)294-3073
Co. E-mail: lafayettecnty@aol.com
URL: http://www.lafayettecounty.net
Contact: Bob Skomp, Pres.

58876 ■ Lake Alfred Chamber of Commerce
210 N Seminole Ave.
PO Box 956
Lake Alfred, FL 33850
Ph:(863)291-5380
Fax: (863)291-5317
Co. E-mail: lachamber@lake-alfred.com
URL: http://www.lake-alfred.com
Contact: Dave Emerson, Pres.

58877 ■ Lake City - Columbia County Chamber of Commerce
162 S Marion Ave.
Lake City, FL 32025-4354
Ph:(386)752-3690
Fax: (386)755-7744
Co. E-mail: info@lakecitychamber.com

URL: http://www.lakecitychamber.com
Contact: Jim Poole, Exec.Dir.

58878 ■ Lake Placid Chamber of Commerce
18 N Oak St.
Lake Placid, FL 33852
Ph:(863)465-4331
Fax: (863)465-2588
Co. E-mail: chamber@lpfla.com
URL: http://www.lpfla.com
Contact: Eileen M. May, Exec.Dir.

58879 ■ Lake Wales Area Chamber of Commerce
340 W Central Ave.
PO Box 191
Lake Wales, FL 33859-0191
Ph:(863)676-3445
Fax: (863)676-3446
Co. E-mail: info@lakewaleschamber.com
URL: http://www.lakewaleschamber.com
Contact: Betty Wojcik, Exec. Dir.

58880 ■ Lake Weir Chamber of Commerce
PO Box 817
Ocklawaha, FL 32183
Ph:(352)288-3751
Fax: (352)288-3980
Co. E-mail: lakeweirchamcom@juno.com
URL: http://welcome.to/lwccc
Contact: Ernie Ayotte, VP

58881 ■ Lakeland Area Chamber of Commerce
35 Lake Morton Dr.
PO Box 3607
Lakeland, FL 33802-3607
Ph:(863)688-8551
Fax: (863)683-7454
Co. E-mail: info@lakelandchamber.com
URL: http://lakelandchamber.com
Contact: Kathleen L. Munson, Pres.

58882 ■ Lauderdale By The Sea Chamber of Commerce
4201 Ocean Dr.
Lauderdale By The Sea, FL 33308
Ph:(954)776-1000
Free: 800-699-6764
Fax: (954)776-6203
Co. E-mail: info@lbts.com
URL: http://www.lbts.com
Contact: Judy Swaggerty, Exec.Dir.

58883 ■ Leesburg Area Chamber of Commerce
PO Box 490309
Leesburg, FL 34749-0309
Ph:(352)787-2131
Fax: (352)787-3985
Co. E-mail: staff@leesburgchamber.com
URL: http://www.leesburgchamber.com
Contact: Bill Deese, Exec.Dir.

58884 ■ Lehigh Acres Chamber of Commerce
PO Box 757
Lehigh Acres, FL 33970-0757
Ph:(239)369-3322
Fax: (239)368-0500
Co. E-mail: ollie.lehighchamber@comcast.net
URL: http://www.lehighacreschamber.org
Contact: Oliver B. Conover, Exec. Dir.

58885 ■ Liberty County Chamber of Commerce
PO Box 523
Bristol, FL 32321
Ph:(850)643-2359
Fax: (850)643-3334
Co. E-mail: jbe@gtcom.net
Contact: Johnny Eubanks, Dir.

58886 ■ Longboat Key Chamber of Commerce
6960 Gulf of Mexico Dr.
Longboat Key, FL 34228

Ph:(941)383-2466
Fax: (941)383-8217
Co. E-mail: gloefgren@longboatkeychamber.com
URL: http://longboatkeychamber.com
Contact: Gail Loefgren, Pres.

58887 ■ Lower Keys Chamber of Commerce
PO Box 430511
31020 Overseas Hwy.
Big Pine Key, FL 33043-0511
Ph:(305)872-2411
Free: 800-872-3722
Fax: (305)872-0752
Co. E-mail: lkchamber@aol.com
URL: http://www.lowerkeyschamber.com
Contact: Carole Stevens, Chamber Mgr.

58888 ■ Madison County Chamber of Commerce
105 N Range St.
Madison, FL 32340
Ph:(850)973-2788
Fax: (850)973-8864
Co. E-mail: parnold@madisonfl.org
URL: http://www.madisonfl.org
Contact: Ms. Paula Arnold, Pres.

58889 ■ Maitland Area Chamber of Commerce
110 N Maitland Ave.
Maitland, FL 32751
Ph:(407)644-0741
Fax: (407)539-2529
Co. E-mail: info@maitlandchamber.com
URL: http://www.maitlandchamber.com
Contact: Mary F. Hodge, Exec.Dir.

58890 ■ Manatee Chamber of Commerce
PO Box 321
222 10th St. W
Bradenton, FL 34206-0321
Ph:(941)748-3411
Fax: (941)745-1877
Co. E-mail: info@manateechamber.com
URL: http://www.manateechamber.com
Contact: Robert P. Bartz, Pres.

58891 ■ Marco Island Area Chamber of Commerce
1102 N Collier Blvd.
Marco Island, FL 34145
Ph:(239)394-7549
Free: 800-788-6272
Fax: (239)394-3061
Co. E-mail: info@marcoislandchamber.org
URL: http://www.marcoislandchamber.org
Contact: Sandi Riedemann, Exec.Dir.

58892 ■ Melbourne-Palm Bay Area Chamber of Commerce
1005 E Strawbridge Ave.
Melbourne, FL 32901-4782
Ph:(321)724-5400
Free: 800-771-9922
Fax: (321)725-2093
Co. E-mail: chamber@metrolink.net
URL: http://www.melpb-chamber.org
Contact: Jim L. Ridenour, Chm.

58893 ■ Miami Beach Chamber of Commerce
1920 Meridian Ave.
Miami Beach, FL 33139-1818
Ph:(305)674-1300
Fax: (305)538-4336
Co. E-mail: wkallergis@miamibeachchamber.com
URL: http://www.miamibeachchamber.com
Contact: Wendy Kallergis, Pres./CEO

58894 ■ Miami-Dade County Chamber of Commerce
11380 NW 27th Ave., Bldg. 1, Ste. 1328
Miami, FL 33167
Ph:(305)751-8648
Fax: (305)758-3839
Co. E-mail: mdcc@m-dcc.org
URL: http://www.m-dcc.org
Contact: Robert Beatty, Chm.

58895 ■ Miramar-Pembroke Pines Regional Chamber of Commerce
10100 Pines Blvd., 4th Fl.
Pembroke Pines, FL 33026-3900
Ph:(954)432-9808
Fax: (954)432-9193
Co. E-mail: info@miramarpembrokepines.org
URL: http://www.miramarpembrokepines.org
Contact: Stella J. Tokar, Exec.Dir.

58896 ■ Monticello-Jefferson County Chamber of Commerce
420 W Washington St.
Monticello, FL 32344
Ph:(850)997-5552
Fax: (850)997-1020
Co. E-mail: info@monticellojeffersonfl.com
URL: http://www.monticellojeffersonfl.com
Contact: Mary Frances Drawdy, Dir.

58897 ■ Mount Dora Area Chamber of Commerce
PO Box 196
Mount Dora, FL 32756-0196
Ph:(352)383-2165
Fax: (352)383-1668
Co. E-mail: chamber@mountdora.com
URL: http://www.mountdora.com
Contact: Cathy Hoechst, Exec.Dir.

58898 ■ Navarre Beach Area Chamber of Commerce
PO Drawer 5430
Navarre, FL 32566
Ph:(850)939-3267
Free: 800-480-7263
Fax: (850)939-0085
Co. E-mail: membership@navarrefl.com
URL: http://www.navarrefl.com
Contact: Dorothy Slye, Pres.

58899 ■ Newberry Area Chamber of Commerce
PO Box 495
Newberry, FL 32669
Ph:(352)472-6611
Co. E-mail: info@newberrychamber.com
URL: http://www.newberrychamber.com
Contact: Jeff Rizzo, Pres.

58900 ■ Niceville-Valparaiso Bay Area Chamber of Commerce
1055 E John Sims Pkwy.
Niceville, FL 32578
Ph:(850)678-2323
Fax: (850)678-2602
Co. E-mail: info@nicevillechamber.com
URL: http://www.nicevillechamber.com
Contact: Martha Miller, Pres.

58901 ■ North Dade Regional Chamber of Commerce
1300 NW 167th St., Ste. 1
Miami, FL 33169
Ph:(305)690-9123
Fax: (305)690-9124
Co. E-mail: thechamber@thechamber.cc
URL: http://www.thechamber.cc
Contact: R. Terry Cuson, Pres./CEO

58902 ■ North Florida Regional Chamber of Commerce
PO Box 576
Starke, FL 32091-0576
Ph:(904)964-5278
Fax: (904)964-2863
Co. E-mail: commerce@atlantic.net
URL: http://www.northfloridachamber.com
Contact: Ron Lilly, Pres./CEO

58903 ■ North Fort Myers Chamber of Commerce
3323 N Key Dr., Ste. 1, Plz. 41
North Fort Myers, FL 33903
Ph:(239)997-9111
Fax: (239)997-4026
Co. E-mail: info@northfortmyerschamber.com

URL: http://www.northfortmyerschamber.org
Contact: Walt Tumiati, Pres.

58904 ■ North Miami Beach Chamber of Commerce
1870 NE 171 St.
North Miami Beach, FL 33162
Ph:(305)944-8500
Fax: (305)944-8191
Co. E-mail: chamber@nmbchamber.com
URL: http://www.nmbchamber.com
Contact: Drew Landmeier, Pres.

58905 ■ North Palm Beach County Chamber of Commerce
3970 RCA Blvd., Ste. 7010
Palm Beach Gardens, FL 33410-4231
Ph:(561)694-2300
Fax: (561)694-0126
Co. E-mail: info@npbchamber.com
URL: http://www.npbchamber.com
Contact: Casey Steinbacher, Pres./CEO

58906 ■ North Port Area Chamber of Commerce
15141 Tamiami Trail
North Port, FL 34287-2711
Ph:(941)423-5040
Fax: (941)423-5042
Co. E-mail: info@northportareachamber.com
URL: http://www.northportareachamber.com
Contact: Patricia Foster, Exec.Dir.

58907 ■ North Tampa Chamber of Commerce
Relocation Town Ctr.
11778 N Dale Mabry Hwy.
Tampa, FL 33618
Ph:(813)961-2420
Fax: (813)961-2903
Co. E-mail: info@northtampachamber.com
URL: http://www.northtampachamber.com
Contact: Lawrence Siegel, Exec.Dir.

58908 ■ Ocala-Marion County Chamber of Commerce
110 Silver Springs Blvd.
Ocala, FL 34470-6613
Ph:(352)629-8051
Fax: (352)629-7651
Co. E-mail: ourguest@ocalacc.com
URL: http://www.ocalacc.com
Contact: Ms. Jaye Baillie APR, Pres./CEO

58909 ■ Okeechobee Chamber of Commerce
55 S Parrott Ave.
Okeechobee, FL 34972
Ph:(863)763-6464
Fax: (863)763-3531
Co. E-mail: commerce@strato.net
URL: http://okeechobeechamberofcommerce.com
Contact: Brenda O'Connor, Exec. Dir.

58910 ■ Oldsmar/Upper Tampa Bay Regional Chamber of Commerce
163 State Rd. 580 W
Oldsmar, FL 34677
Ph:(813)855-4233
Fax: (813)854-1237
Co. E-mail: kgartland@utbchamber.com
URL: http://www.oldsmarchamber.com
Contact: Kevin Gartland, Pres./CEO

58911 ■ Orlando Regional Chamber of Commerce
PO Box 1234
75 S Ivanhoe Blvd.
Orlando, FL 32802-1234
Ph:(407)425-1234
Fax: (407)835-2500
Co. E-mail: info@orlando.org
URL: http://www.orlando.org
Contact: Jacob V. Stuart, Pres.

58912 ■ Ormond Beach Chamber of Commerce
165 W Granada Blvd.
Ormond Beach, FL 32174

Ph:(386)677-3454
Fax: (386)677-4363
Co. E-mail: obchamber@ormondchamber.com
URL: http://www.ormondchamber.com
Contact: Lorry Garafolo, Pres.

58913 ■ Pahokee Chamber of Commerce
115 E Main St.
Pahokee, FL 33476
Ph:(561)924-5579
Fax: (561)924-8116
Co. E-mail: info@pahokee.com
URL: http://www.pahokee.com
Contact: Lewis Pope, Pres.

58914 ■ Palm Beach Chamber of Commerce
400 Royal Palm Way, Ste. 106
Palm Beach, FL 33480
Ph:(561)655-3282
Fax: (561)655-7191
Co. E-mail: info@palmbeachchamber.com
URL: http://www.palmbeachchamber.com
Contact: Laurel Baker, Exec.Dir.

58915 ■ Palm City Chamber of Commerce
880 SW Martin Downs Blvd.
Palm City, FL 34990
Ph:(772)286-8121
Fax: (772)286-3331
Co. E-mail: info@palmcitychamber.com
URL: http://www.palmcitychamber.com
Contact: Carolyn Davi, Exec.Dir.

58916 ■ Palms West Chamber of Commerce
13901 Southern Blvd.
PO Box 1062
Loxahatchee, FL 33470-1062
Ph:(561)790-6200
Free: 800-790-2364
Fax: (561)791-2069
Co. E-mail: info@palmswest.com
URL: http://www.palmswest.com
Contact: Vivian Palmer, CEO

**58917 ■ Pensacola Area Chamber of
Commerce**
117 W Garden St.
Pensacola, FL 32502
Ph:(850)438-4081
Fax: (850)438-6369
Co. E-mail: eemerson@pensacolachamber.com
URL: http://www.pensacolachamber.com
Contact: Evon Emerson, Pres./CEO

**58918 ■ Pensacola Beach Chamber of
Commerce and Visitor Information Center**
735 Pensacola Beach Blvd.
Pensacola Beach, FL 32561
Ph:(850)932-1500
Free: 800-635-4803
Fax: (850)932-1551
Co. E-mail: penbeach@bellsouth.net
URL: http://www.visitpensacolabeach.com
Contact: Sandy Johnston, Exec.Dir.

**58919 ■ Pinellas Park/Mid-County Chamber
of Commerce**
Park Sta.
5851 Park Blvd.
Pinellas Park, FL 33781
Ph:(727)544-4777
Fax: (727)209-0837
Co. E-mail: info@pinellasparkchamber.com
URL: http://www.pinellasparkchamber.com
Contact: Stan McKenzie, Pres.

**58920 ■ Port Orange/South Daytona
Chamber of Commerce**
3431 Ridgewood Ave.
Port Orange, FL 32129
Ph:(386)761-1601
Fax: (386)788-9165
Co. E-mail: info@pschamber.com
URL: http://www.pschamber.com
Contact: Jill Geddy, Exec. Dir.

**58921 ■ Putnam County Chamber of
Commerce**
PO Box 550
1100 Reid St.
Palatka, FL 32178-0550
Ph:(386)328-1503
Fax: (386)328-7076
Co. E-mail: pcccfla@bellsouth.net
URL: http://www.putnamcountychamber.org
Contact: Mr. C.W. Larson II, Pres.

**58922 ■ Putnam County Chamber of
Commerce - South Putnam Branch**
PO Box 550
Palatka, FL 32178-0550
Ph:(386)328-1503
Fax: (386)328-7076
Co. E-mail: pcccfla@bellsouth.net
URL: http://www.putnamcountychamber.org
Contact: Mr. C.W. Larson Jr., Pres.

58923 ■ Ruskin Chamber of Commerce
315 S Tamiami Trail
Ruskin, FL 33570-4660
Ph:(813)645-3808
Fax: (813)645-2099
Co. E-mail: ruskinchamber@earthlink.net
URL: http://www.ruskinchamber.org
Contact: Suzy Lacey, Exec.Dir.

**58924 ■ Safety Harbor Chamber of
Commerce**
200 Main St.
Safety Harbor, FL 34695
Ph:(727)726-2890
Fax: (727)726-2733
Co. E-mail: info@safetyharborchamber.com
URL: http://www.safetyharborchamber.com
Contact: Cynthia O'Donnel, Exec.Dir.

**58925 ■ St. Cloud Greater Osceola County
Chamber of Commerce**
1200 New York Ave.
St. Cloud, FL 34769
Ph:(407)892-3671
Fax: (407)892-5289
Co. E-mail: info@stcloudflchamber.com
URL: http://www.stcloudchamber.cc
Contact: David C. Lane, Pres./CEO

**58926 ■ St. Lucie County Chamber of
Commerce**
2200 Virginia Ave.
Fort Pierce, FL 34982
Ph:(772)595-9999
Fax: (772)461-9084
Co. E-mail: info@stluciechamber.org
URL: http://www.stluciechamber.org
Contact: Linda W. Cox, Exec. VP/Exec. Dir.

**58927 ■ St. Petersburg Area Chamber of
Commerce**
PO Box 1371
100 2nd Ave. N, Ste. 150
St. Petersburg, FL 33701
Ph:(727)821-4069
Fax: (727)895-6326
Co. E-mail: mbaker@stpete.com
URL: http://www.stpete.com
Contact: Russ Sloan, Pres./CEO

**58928 ■ Sanford - Seminole County Chamber
of Commerce**
400 E First St.
Sanford, FL 32771-1408
Ph:(407)322-2212
Fax: (407)322-8160
Co. E-mail: info@sanfordchamber.com
URL: http://www.sanfordchamber.com
Contact: Angelia L. Gordon, Pres./CEO

**58929 ■ Sanibel-Captiva Islands Chamber of
Commerce**
1159 Causeway Rd.
Sanibel, FL 33957
Ph:(239)472-1080
Fax: (239)472-1070

Co. E-mail: island@sanibel-captiva.org
URL: http://www.sanibel-captiva.org
Contact: Steven Greenstein, Exec.Dir.

**58930 ■ Santa Rosa County Chamber of
Commerce**
5247 Stewart St.
Milton, FL 32570-4737
Ph:(850)623-2339
Fax: (850)623-4413
Co. E-mail: director@srcchamber.com
URL: http://www.srcchamber.com
Contact: Donna Tucker, Exec.Dir.

**58931 ■ Sebastian River Area Chamber of
Commerce**
700 Main St.
Sebastian, FL 32958
Ph:(772)589-5969
Free: 888-881-7568
Fax: (772)589-5993
Co. E-mail: info@sebastianchamber.com
URL: http://www.sebastianchamber.com
Contact: Beth L. Mitchell, Exec.Dir.

**58932 ■ Seminole County Regional Chamber
of Commerce**
725 Primera Blvd., Ste. 100
Lake Mary, FL 32746
Ph:(407)333-4748
Fax: (407)829-2100
Co. E-mail: lreynolds@seminolebusiness.org
URL: http://www.seminolebusiness.org
Contact: Diane Parker, Pres.

58933 ■ Siesta Key Chamber of Commerce
5118 Ocean Blvd.
Siesta Key, FL 34242
Ph:(941)349-3800
Free: 888-831-7778
Fax: (941)349-9699
Co. E-mail: info@siestakeychamber.com
URL: http://www.siestakeychamber.com
Contact: Peter W. Kiziu, Exec. Dir.

58934 ■ South Lake Chamber of Commerce
PO Box 120417
Clermont, FL 34711
Ph:(352)394-4191
Fax: (352)394-5799
Co. E-mail: office@southlakechamber-fl.com
URL: http://www.southlakechamber-fl.com
Contact: Ray San Fratello, Exec.Dir.

**58935 ■ South Tampa Chamber of
Commerce**
PO Box 13342
Tampa, FL 33681-3342
Ph:(813)637-0156
Fax: (813)637-0644
Co. E-mail: executivedirector@southtampachamber.
org
URL: http://www.southtampachamber.org
Contact: Ms. Leigh S. Humes, Exec. Dir.

**58936 ■ Southeast Volusia Chamber of
Commerce**
115 Canal St.
New Smyrna Beach, FL 32168-7003
Ph:(386)428-2449
Free: 877-460-8410
Fax: (386)423-3512
Co. E-mail: lsdennis@sevchamber.com
URL: http://www.sevchamber.com
Contact: Steve Dennis, Exec.VP

**58937 ■ Southwest Florida Hispanic
Chamber of Commerce**
10051 McGregor Blvd., Ste. 204
Fort Myers, FL 33919
Ph:(239)418-1441
Fax: (239)418-1475
Co. E-mail: hispanicchamber.lg@earthlink.net
Contact: Leonardo Garcia, Exec.Dir.

58938 ■ Stuart-Martin County Chamber of Commerce
1650 S Kanner Hwy.
Stuart, FL 34994-7199
Ph:(772)287-1088
Fax: (772)220-3437
Co. E-mail: kferguson@goodnature.org
URL: http://www.goodnature.org
Contact: Joseph A. Catrambone, Pres./CEO

58939 ■ Sumter County Chamber of Commerce
PO Box 100
Sumterville, FL 33585-0100
Ph:(352)793-3099
Fax: (352)793-2120
Co. E-mail: sumter-coc@sum.net

58940 ■ Sun City Center Area Chamber of Commerce
1651 Sun City Center Plz.
Sun City Center, FL 33573
Ph:(813)634-5111
Fax: (813)634-8438
Co. E-mail: sccchamber@aol.com
URL: http://www.suncitycenterchamber.org
Contact: Elaine Brad, Exec.Dir.

58941 ■ Suwannee County Chamber of Commerce
816 S Ohio Ave.
PO Drawer C
Live Oak, FL 32064
Ph:(386)362-3071
Fax: (386)362-4758
Co. E-mail: staff@suwanneechamber.com
URL: http://www.suwanneechamber.com
Contact: Dennis Cason, Pres.

58942 ■ Tampa Bay Beaches Chamber of Commerce
6990 Gulf Blvd.
St. Petersburg, FL 33706
Ph:(727)360-6957
Free: 800-944-1847
Fax: (727)360-2233
Co. E-mail: info@tampabaybeaches.com
URL: http://www.tampabaybeaches.com
Contact: Missy Pike, Pres.

58943 ■ Tarpon Springs Chamber of Commerce
11 E Orange St.
Tarpon Springs, FL 34689-3439
Ph:(727)937-6109
Fax: (727)937-2879
Co. E-mail: chamber@tarponsprings.com
URL: http://www.tarponsprings.com
Contact: Tj Davis, Pres.

58944 ■ Titusville Area Chamber of Commerce
2000 S Washington Ave.
Titusville, FL 32780
Ph:(321)267-3036
Fax: (321)264-0127
Co. E-mail: gaedcke@titusville.org
URL: http://www.titusville.org
Contact: Marcia Gaedcke, Pres.

58945 ■ Umatilla Chamber of Commerce
PO Box 300
Umatilla, FL 32784
Ph:(352)669-3511
Fax: (352)669-8900
Co. E-mail: umatilla@umatillachamber.org
URL: http://www.umatillachamber.org
Contact: Nancy Skorski

58946 ■ Upper Tampa Bay Regional Chamber of Commerce
7512 Paula Dr., Ste. 105
Tampa, FL 33615
Ph:(813)884-5344
Fax: (813)885-2093
Co. E-mail: dpaul@utbchamber.com
URL: http://www.utbchamber.com

Contact: Diane Paul, Mgr.

58947 ■ Venice Area Chamber of Commerce
597 Tamiami Trail S
Venice, FL 34285
Ph:(941)488-2236
Fax: (941)484-5903
Co. E-mail: vchamber@venicechamber.com
URL: http://www.venicechamber.com
Contact: John G. Ryan, Pres./CEO

58948 ■ Villages Chamber of Commerce
996 Alverez Ave.
The Villages, FL 32159
Ph:(352)259-4800
Free: (866)489-1856
Fax: (352)259-4819
Co. E-mail: info@thevillageschamberofcommerce.
    org
URL: http://www.thevillageschamberofcommerce.org
Contact: Gary Lester, Pres.

58949 ■ Wakulla County Chamber of Commerce
23 High Dr.
PO Box 598
Crawfordville, FL 32326
Ph:(850)926-1848
Fax: (850)926-2050
Co. E-mail: wakullacochamber@earthlink.net
Contact: Beverly Halstead, Office Mgr.

58950 ■ Walton County Chamber of Commerce
95 Circle Dr.
Defuniak Springs, FL 32435
Ph:(850)892-3191
Fax: (850)892-9588
Co. E-mail: info@waltoncountychamber.com
URL: http://www.waltoncountychamber.com
Contact: Dawn Moliterno, Pres./CEO

58951 ■ Washington County Chamber of Commerce
685 7th St.
PO Box 457
Chipley, FL 32428
Ph:(850)638-4157
Fax: (850)638-8770
Co. E-mail: wcchamber@wfeca.net
URL: http://www.washcomall.com
Contact: Tommy McDonald, Exec.Dir.

58952 ■ Wellington Chamber of Commerce
12230 Forest Hill Blvd., Ste. 183
Wellington, FL 33414
Ph:(561)792-6525
Fax: (561)792-6200
Co. E-mail: info@wellingtonchamber.com
URL: http://www.wellingtonchamber.com
Contact: Ms. Michela Perillo-Green, Exec.Dir.

58953 ■ West Orange Chamber of Commerce
12184 W Colonial Dr.
Winter Garden, FL 34787
Ph:(407)656-1304
Fax: (407)656-0221
Co. E-mail: info@wochamber.com
URL: http://www.wochamber.com
Contact: Stina D'Uva, Pres.

58954 ■ West Pasco Chamber of Commerce
5443 Main St.
New Port Richey, FL 34652
Ph:(727)842-7651
Fax: (727)842-0202
Co. E-mail: chamber@westpasco.com
URL: http://www.westpasco.com
Contact: Joe Alpine, Pres.

58955 ■ Weston Area Chamber of Commerce
1290 Weston Rd., Ste. 200
Weston, FL 33326-1909
Ph:(954)389-0600
Fax: (954)384-6133
Co. E-mail: jack@westonchamber.com
URL: http://www.westonchamber.com

Contact: Jack Miller, Pres./CEO

58956 ■ Williston Area Chamber of Commerce
PO Box 369
Williston, FL 32696
Ph:(352)528-5552
Fax: (352)528-4342
Co. E-mail: wcoc@willistonfl.com
URL: http://www.willistonfl.com

58957 ■ Winter Park Chamber of Commerce
507 N New York Ave., Ste. 102
Winter Park, FL 32789
Ph:(407)644-8281
Fax: (407)644-7826
Co. E-mail: wpcc@winterpark.org
URL: http://www.winterpark.org
Contact: Sam Stark, Pres./CEO

58958 ■ Ybor City Chamber of Commerce
1800 E 9th Ave.
Tampa, FL 33605-9998
Ph:(813)248-3712
Fax: (813)247-1764
Co. E-mail: info@ybor.org
URL: http://www.ybor.org
Contact: Thomas P. Keating, Pres./CEO

58959 ■ Zephyrhills Chamber of Commerce
38550 5th Ave.
Zephyrhills, FL 33542
Ph:(813)782-1913
Fax: (813)783-6060
Co. E-mail: info@zephyrhillschamber.org
URL: http://zephyrhillschamber.org
Contact: Susan Frimmel, Pres.

MINORITY BUSINESS ASSISTANCE PROGRAMS

58960 ■ Florida Black Business Investment Board
2019 Centre Pointe Blvd., Ste. 101
Tallahassee, FL 32308
Ph:(850)878-0826
Fax: (850)878-4578
Co. E-mail: hillmon.sorey@fbbib.com
URL: http://www.fbbib.com
Contact: Hillmon Sorey Jr.
Description: Obtains and provides loans for Black-owned and -operated businesses.

58961 ■ Florida Minority Supplier Development Council
6880 Lake Ellenor Dr., Ste. 104-A
Orlando, FL 32809
Ph:(407)245-6062
Fax: (407)857-8647
Co. E-mail: info@fmsdc.org
URL: http://www.nmsdcfl.com
Contact: Malik Ali, Pres

58962 ■ Florida Regional Minority Business Council
9499 NE 2nd Ave., Ste. 201
Miami, FL 33138
Ph:(305)762-6151
Free: 800-79F-RMPC
Fax: (305)762-6158
Co. E-mail: frmbc@frmbc.org
URL: http://www.frmbc.org
Contact: Beatrice Louissaint, Pres & CEO
Description: Private-sector corporation that promotes the procurement of goods and services from minority businesses. Provides technical assistance and referral services to minority businesses.

58963 ■ Minority Business Development Center
3050 Biscayne Blvd., Ste 201
Miami, FL 33137
Ph:(786)316-0888
Fax: (786)316-0090

Co. E-mail: info@mbdcsouthflorida.org
URL: http://www.mbdcsouthflorida.org
Contact: Financial Specialist

58964 ■ Palm Beach County Resource Center, Inc.
2001 Broadway, Ste. 250
Riviera Beach, FL 33404
Ph:(561)863-0895
Fax: (561)863-0897
Co. E-mail: p_skyers@pbcrc.org
URL: http://www.pbcrc.org
Contact: Paul Skyers, Dir

FINANCING AND LOAN PROGRAMS

58965 ■ Avery Business Development Services
2506 St. Michel Ct.
Ponte Vedra, FL 32082
Ph:(904)285-6033
Fax: (904)280-8840
Contact: Henry Avery, President
Preferred Investment Size: $50,000 to $5,000,000.
Investment Types: Research and development, start-up, first and second stage, early and later stage, management buyouts, special situation, expansion, acquisition, joint ventures, and turnaround. **Industry Preferences:** Communications, computer software, biotechnology, medical and health, Consumer related, industrial and energy, business service, agriculture, forestry and fishing. **Geographic Preferences:** Southeast.

58966 ■ CEO Advisors
1061 Maitland Ctr. Commons, Ste. 209
Maitland, FL 32751
Ph:(407)660-9327
Fax: (407)660-2109
Contact: G. Arthur Herbert, Principal
Preferred Investment Size: $300,000 to $500,000.
Investment Types: Seed, start-up, first stage, and research and development. **Industry Preferences:** Communications and media, computer hardware and software, semiconductors and other electronics, biotechnology, medical and health, consumer related. **Geographic Preferences:** Southeast.

58967 ■ Chartwell Capital Management Co., Inc.
1 Independent Dr., Ste. 3120
Jacksonville, FL 32202
Ph:(904)355-3519
Fax: (904)353-5833
Co. E-mail: info@chartwellcap.com
Contact: Mindy Lanigan, Chief Financial Officer
Preferred Investment Size: $5,000,000 minimum.
Investment Types: First and second stage, and leveraged buyout. **Industry Preferences:** Consumer related, Internet specific, computer software and services, communications and media, medical and health. **Geographic Preferences:** Northwest and Southeast.

58968 ■ CMB Capital, LLC (CMBC)
7650 W. Courtney Campbell, Ste. 1120
Tampa, FL 33607
Ph:(813)387-4087
Fax: (813)835-4197
URL: http://www.cmbcapital.com
Contact: Clay Biddinger, Chief Executive Officer
Preferred Investment Size: $2,000,000 minimum.
Investment Types: Early and later stage, and expansion. **Industry Preferences:** Communications and Internet specific. **Geographic Preferences:** Southeast.

58969 ■ Florida Capital Ventures, Ltd.
325 Florida Bank Plaza
100 W. Kennedy Blvd.
Tampa, FL 33622
Ph:(813)229-2294
Fax: (813)229-2028
Contact: Warren Miller

Preferred Investment Size: $500,000 minimum. **Investment Types:** Start-up, first and second stage, leveraged buyout, and special situation. **Industry Preferences:** Communications and media, computer related, semiconductors and other electronics, biotechnology, medical and health, consumer related, industrial and energy, transportation, business service, manufacturing, agriculture, forestry and fishing. **Geographic Preferences:** Southeast.

58970 ■ Grace Venture Partners
200 S. Orange Ave.
Sun Trust Ctr., Ste. 1850
Orlando, FL 32801
Ph:(407)835-7900
Fax: (407)835-7901
URL: http://www.graceventure.com
Contact: Edward Grace
Preferred Investment Size: $500,000 to $2,000,000.
Investment Policies: Seed, start-up, early, first, and second stage. **Industry Preferences:** Communications, computer software, semiconductors and other electronics, and consumer related. **Geographic Preferences:** East Coast, Northeast, and Southeast.

58971 ■ Henry & Co.
8201 Peters Rd., Ste. 1000
Plantation, FL 33324
Ph:(847)735-9973
Contact: June Knaudt
Preferred Investment Size: $500,000 to $1,000,000.
Investment Policies: First and second stage. **Industry Preferences:** Medical and health. **Geographic Preferences:** West Coast.

58972 ■ LM Capital Corp.
120 S. Olive Ave., Ste. 400
West Palm Beach, FL 33401
Ph:(561)833-9700
Fax: (561)655-6587
URL: http://www.lmcapitalsecurities.com
Contact: Leslie Corley, President
Preferred Investment Size: $5,000,000 minimum.
Investment Types: Leveraged buyout. **Industry Preferences:** Computer hardware, semiconductors and other electronics, medical and health, consumer related, industrial and energy, and financial services.

58973 ■ Lovett Miller & Co. Incorporated
1 Independent Sq., Ste. 1600
Jacksonville, FL 32202
Ph:(904)634-0077
Fax: (904)634-0633
URL: http://www.lovettmiller.com
Contact: David Smoley, Vice President
Preferred Investment Size: $2,000,000 to $10,000,000. **Investment Types:** Seed, start-up, early and later stage, leveraged buyout, and mezzanine. **Industry Preferences:** Computer software and services, Internet specific, communications and media, consumer related, medical and health, and other products. **Geographic Preferences:** U.S.

58974 ■ New South Ventures
5053 Ocean Blvd.
Sarasota, FL 34242
Ph:(941)358-6000
Fax: (941)358-6078
URL: http://www.newsouthventures.com
Contact: Gary Arnold, Managing Partner
Preferred Investment Size: $250,000 to $3,000,000.
Investment Types: Seed and early stage. **Geographic Preferences:** Florida and Southeast.

58975 ■ North American Business Development Co., L.L.C.
135 S. LaSalle St., Ste. 4000
Chicago, IL 60603
Ph:(312)332-4950
Fax: (312)332-1540
URL: http://www.northamericanfund.com
Contact: Robert Underwood, Partner
Preferred Investment Size: $10,000,000 minimum.
Investment Types: Leveraged buyout, special situation, control-block purchases, and industry rollups.

58976 ■ Quantum Capital Partners
339 S. Plant Ave.
Tampa, FL 33606
Ph:(813)250-1999
Fax: (813)250-1998
URL: http://www.qcpventures.com
Contact: N. John Simmons, President
Preferred Investment Size: $500,000 to $3,000,000.
Investment Types: Later stage. **Industry Preferences:** Computer software, Internet specific, semiconductors and other electronics, medical and health, consumer related, industrial and energy, business service, and manufacturing. **Geographic Preferences:** Florida.

58977 ■ SI Ventures
12600 gateway Blvd.
Ft. Myers, FL 33913
Ph:(239)561-4760
Fax: (239)561-4916
URL: http://www.siventures.com
Contact: Brian Beach, Managing Director
Preferred Investment Size: $3,000,000 to $10,000,000. **Investment Types:** Early stage and expansion. **Industry Preferences:** Internet specific, computer software, hardware and services, communications and media, medical and health, semiconductors and other electronics. **Geographic Preferences:** U.S.

58978 ■ Sigma Capital Corp.
22668 Caravelle Cir.
Boca Raton, FL 33433
Ph:(561)368-9783
Preferred Investment Size: $100,000 to $300,000.
Investment Types: Second stage. **Industry Preferences:** Communications, computer hardware and software, semiconductors and other electronics, biotechnology, medical and health, consumer related, industrial and energy, financial services, and manufacturing. **Geographic Preferences:** Southeast.

58979 ■ South Atlantic Venture Funds, L.P.
614 W. Bay St.
Tampa, FL 33606-2704
Ph:(813)253-2500
Fax: (813)253-2360
URL: http://www.southatlantic.com
Contact: Sandra Barber, Managing Director
Preferred Investment Size: $1,500,000 to $7,500,000. **Investment Types:** First and second stage, acquisition, expansion, later stage, recapitalizations, and management buyouts. **Industry Preferences:** Communications and media, medical and health, Other products, Internet specific, consumer related, semiconductors and other electronics, computer software and services, computer hardware, industrial and energy. **Geographic Preferences:** Southeast, Florida, and Texas.

58980 ■ Venture Capital Management Corp.
PO Box 2626
Satellite Beach, FL 32937
Ph:(407)777-1969
Preferred Investment Size: $100,000 to $300,000.
Investment Types: First and second stage, and leveraged buyout. **Industry Preferences:** Communications and media, computer hardware, semiconductors and other electronics, biotechnology, medical and health, consumer related, industrial and energy, transportation, financial services, manufacturing, agriculture, forestry and fishing.

PROCUREMENT ASSISTANCE PROGRAMS

58981 ■ Florida Department of Management Services–Division of Purchasing
4050 Esplanade Way
Tallahassee, FL 32399-0950
Ph:(850)488-8440
Fax: (850)488-5498
URL: http://dms.myflorida.com

Contact: Russ Rothman, Dir
Description: Publishes *Doing Business with the State of Florida*. Potential vendors should contact each state agency's purchasing office, since the Department of General Services does not make purchases for all agencies.

58982 ■ Florida Procurement Center Representatives
Naval Air Warfare Center
Training Systems Division
12350 Research Pky.
Orlando, FL 32826-3224
Ph:(407)380-8252
Fax: (407)380-8232
Co. E-mail: walter.wallace@sba.gov
URL: http://www.sba.gov
Contact: Walter Wallace, PCR Rep
E-mail: walter.wallace@sba.gov
Description: Covers activities for Naval Training Systems Center (Orlando, FL). McDill Air Force Base (Tampa, FL), Patrick Air Force Base (Cocoa Beach, FL), and NASA, Kennedy Space Flight Center (Cape Canaveral, FL).

58983 ■ Florida Procurement Technical Assistance Center
401 E Chase St., Ste 100
Pensacola, FL 32502-6160
Ph:(850)473-7806
Fax: (850)473-7813
Co. E-mail: lsubel@uwf.edu
URL: http://www.fptac.org
Contact: Laura Subel, Prgm Mgr
E-mail: lsubel@uwf.edu

INCUBATORS/RESEARCH AND TECHNOLOGY PARKS

58984 ■ Central Florida Research Park
12424 Research Pky., Ste. 100
Orlando, FL 32826
Ph:(407)282-3944
Fax: (407)282-1988
URL: http://www.cfrp.org
Contact: Joe Wallace, Exec.Dir.
Scope: 1,027-acre site zoned for commercial and light manufacturing adjacent to the University. Established to create an environment which promotes and fosters relationships between industry and the University. **Publications:** Central Florida Research Park Update.

58985 ■ Enterprise North Florida Corporation, Inc. (ENFC)
4905 Belfort Rd. Ste.110
Jacksonville, FL 32256
Ph:(904)730-4700
Fax: (904)730-4711
Co. E-mail: admin@enfc.org
URL: http://www.enfc.org
Contact: Alan Rossiter, Pres & CEO
Description: ENFC is a non-profit corporation that assists emerging high technology firms in northern Florida.

58986 ■ Florida Atlantic Research and Development Park
3701 FAU Blvd., Ste. 208
Boca Raton, FL 33431
Ph:(561)416-6092
Fax: (561)620-8493
Co. E-mail: scott@research-park.org
URL: http://www.research-park.org
Contact: Scott Ellington, Exec.Dir.
E-mail: scott@research-park.org
Scope: Serves as a bridge between the research interests of the tenant companies and research activities of the university community. The park features an innovation center and incubator to aid in transferring technology. **Awards:** Research award, $25,000.

58987 ■ Florida/NASA Business Incubation Center–Technology Research and Development Authority
TRDA
5195 S Washington Ave.
Titusville, FL 32780
Ph:(321)269-6330
Fax: (321)383-5260
Co. E-mail: admin@trda.org
URL: http://www.trda.org/fnbic/
Description: The goal of this incubator is to increase the number of successful technology-based small companies in Brevard County, Florida. Tenants must be producing a technology-intensive product or be commercializing a NASA technology.

58988 ■ Florida State University–Center for Arts Administration Program
123 Carothers Hall
Tallahassee, FL 32306-4480
Ph:(850)644-2158
Fax: (850)644-5067
Co. E-mail: cdorn@mailer.fsu.edu
Contact: Prof. Charles M. Dorn
E-mail: cdorn@mailer.fsu.edu
Scope: Serves as an administrative and resource base for the development of research, service, and education in arts administration. Provides psychological, social, business, governance, and art related information to private and public arts agencies. Administers research capabilities at the University in arts, business, and public administration. **Services:** Consultation, to local arts agencies and organizations specializing in rural and minority groups. **Educational Activities:** Technical assistance workshops, for small arts organizations; Workshops; Conferences.

58989 ■ Florida State University–Institute of Science and Public Affairs
C2200 University Center
Tallahassee, FL 32306-2641
Ph:(850)644-2007
Fax: (850)644-7360
Co. E-mail: rbradley@admin.fsu.edu
URL: http://www.ispa.fsu.edu
Contact: Dr. Robert B. Bradley, Dir.
E-mail: rbradley@admin.fsu.edu
Scope: Biology, chemistry, geography, education, human trafficking, maternal and child health, planning, public administration, physics, economics, law, and social issues. **Services:** Consulting; Data processing; Geographic information system application; Library marketing and citing analysis; Software development. **Publications:** Atlases; Curricula; Maps. **Educational Activities:** Teacher training and workshops.

58990 ■ Florida State University–Office of Research
109 Westcott Bldg.
Tallahassee, FL 32306-1330
Ph:(850)644-9694
Fax: (850)645-0108
Co. E-mail: kkemper@research.fsu.edu
URL: http://www.research.fsu.edu
Contact: Dr. Kirby W. Kemper, VP,Res.
E-mail: kkemper@research.fsu.edu
Scope: Administers and coordinates extramurally sponsored research in natural sciences, social sciences, the humanities, and professional schools conducted by faculty members and graduate students of the University. Also administers the University's patenting, copyrighting, and technology transfer functions. **Publications:** Office of Research Newsletter (monthly); Research in Review (3/year). **Educational Activities:** Cornerstone Research Program.

58991 ■ Innovation Park
1736 W Paul Dirac Dr.
Tallahassee, FL 32310-3673
Ph:(850)575-0343
Fax: (850)575-0355
Co. E-mail: innpark@earthlink.net
URL: http://www.innovation-park.com
Contact: Linda Nicholsen, Exec.Dir.
E-mail: innpark@earthlink.net
Scope: Fosters research partnerships between the Universities and industry tenants.

58992 ■ Progress Corporate Park
13709 Progress Blvd.
PO Box 10
Alachua, FL 32615
Ph:(386)462-4040
Free: 877—457-6489
Fax: (386)462-3932
Co. E-mail: sandy@progresscorporatepark.com
URL: http://progresscorporatepark.com
Contact: Sandra Burgess, Mgr.
E-mail: sandy@progresscorporatepark.com
Scope: 200-acre research and technology park open to both public and private research and manufacturing organizations emphasizing high-technology development, including electronics, biotechnology, advanced materials, pharmacology, and agriculture. Center provides a link between University researchers and industry and transfers new technologies from the laboratory to the marketplace. **Services:** Assistance, in entrepreneurial development, commercialization of scientific and technological innovations, and international marketing.

58993 ■ University of Central Florida–Office of Research and Commercialization
12201 Research Pky., Ste. 501
Orlando, FL 32826
Ph:(407)823-3778
Fax: (407)823-3299
Co. E-mail: webmasteroor@mail.ucf.edu
URL: http://www.research.ucf.edu
Contact: Dr. Tom O'Neal, Assoc.VP
E-mail: webmasteroor@mail.ucf.edu
Scope: Administers and coordinates contract and grant research conducted at the departmental level and in University research centers and institutes. Specializations include simulation and training, fiber optics, laser electronics, computer hardware and software development, solar energy, alternative energy development, and human factors. **Publications:** Annual report. **Educational Activities:** Seminars, in grant writing and contract/grant administration.

58994 ■ University of Florida–Biotechnology Development Incubator
12085 Research Dr.
Alachua, FL 32615
Ph:(386)462-0880
Fax: (386)462-0875
Co. E-mail: dlday@ufl.edu
URL: http://www.biotech.ufl.org
Contact: David L. Day, Dir.
E-mail: dlday@ufl.edu
Scope: Biotechnology development. **Educational Activities:** Biotechnological techniques training, in cooperation with the Interdisciplinary Center for Biotechnology Research.

58995 ■ University of Florida–Division of Sponsored Research
Grinter Hall
PO Box 115500
Gainesville, FL 32611-5500
Ph:(352)392-1582
Fax: (352)846-0491
Co. E-mail: wphil@ufl.edu
URL: http://rgp.ufl.edu/research/
Contact: Dr. Winfred M. Phillips, VP
E-mail: wphil@ufl.edu
Scope: Administers and stimulates the growth of research and graduate education; creates significant relationships between government, industry, and other research sponsors and the university; promotes economic development in Alachua County, the State of Florida and the nation through technology transfer opportunities. **Publications:** Explore Research Magazine (semiannually); Graduate Catalog (annually); RGP Annual Report. **Awards:** Supplemental Retention Awards.

58996 ■ University of Miami–Office of Research
School of Medicine
PO Box 016960 (R-64)
Miami, FL 33136
Ph:(305)243-6415
Fax: (305)243-3549

Co. E-mail: naltman@miami.edu
URL: http://www.miami.edu/research
Contact: Norman H. Altman VMD, Vice Provost
E-mail: naltman@miami.edu
Scope: Promotes and encourages research at the University and assists and coordinates research programs carried out in individual departments and divisions of the University.

58997 ■ University of North Florida–First Coast Technology Park
4567 St. Johns Bluff Rd. S
Jacksonville, FL 32224-2645
Ph:(904)620-1260
Fax: (904)620-1980
Co. E-mail: traynham@unf.edu
Contact: Earle C. Traynham PhD
E-mail: traynham@unf.edu
Scope: Facilitates cooperative research and development activities between Park tenants and the University community.

58998 ■ University of South Florida–Office of Research
4202 E Fowler Ave., ADM 200
Tampa, FL 33620-5950
Ph:(813)974-5570
Fax: (813)974-3348
Co. E-mail: research@research.usf.edu
URL: http://www.research.usf.edu
Contact: Robert Chang PhD, VP
E-mail: research@research.usf.edu
Scope: Administers activities involving both sponsored and non-sponsored research conducted at the university, including research compliance, intellectual property, and research park development. **Services:** Technical assistance. **Publications:** Annual Report. **Awards:** Internal awards program.

58999 ■ University of West Florida–Office of Research and Sponsored Programs
11000 University Pky.
Pensacola, FL 32514
Ph:(850)474-2824
Fax: (850)474-2082
Co. E-mail: research@uwf.edu
URL: http://research.uwf.edu/
Contact: Richard S. Podemski PhD, Assoc.VP
E-mail: research@uwf.edu
Scope: Administers and coordinates sponsored research programs at the University, including software engineering, behavioral medicine, and bioremediation. **Publications:** Guide to Graduate Student Funding; Perspectives on Research and Creative Activity; Research: Guide to Fellowships. **Educational Activities:** Grant writing workshops; Intellectual property forums; Sponsored research forums.

EDUCATIONAL PROGRAMS

59000 ■ Florida Department of Education–Division of Workforce Development
Florida Dep. of Education
Florida Education
325 W Gaines St., Rm. 744
Tallahassee, FL 32399-0400
Ph:(850)488-2601
Fax: (850)487-0419
URL: http://www.firn.edu/doe/workforce
Description: Trains employees of new, expanding, and diversifying industries.

59001 ■ Florida Keys Community College
5901 College Rd.
Key West, FL 33040
Ph:(305)296-9081
Fax: (305)292-5155
URL: http://www.fkcc.edu
Description: Two-year college offering degree and certificate programs in small business management program.

59002 ■ St. Johns River Community College
5001 St. Johns Ave.
Palatka, FL 32177

Ph:(386)312-4200
Fax: (386)312-4292
URL: http://www.sjrcc.cc.fl.us
Description: Two-year college offering a small business management program.

59003 ■ Santa Fe Community College
3000 NW 83rd St., Rm. 112
Gainesville, FL 32606
Ph:(352)395-5443
Fax: (352)395-5922
Co. E-mail: information@sfcc.edu
URL: http://www.santafe.cc.fl.us
Description: Two-year college offering a program in small business management.

59004 ■ Seminole Community College
100 Weldon Blvd.
Sanford, FL 32773-6199
Ph:(407)328-4722
Fax: (407)328-2029
URL: http://www.scc-fl.com
Description: Two-year college offering a small business Administration program.

PUBLICATIONS

59005 ■ *Business in Broward*
PO Box 460669
Ft. Lauderdale, FL 33346-0669
Ph:(954)763-3338
Co. E-mail: sfbiz@mindspring.com

59006 ■ *Daily Business Review*
1 SE 3rd Ave., Ste. 900
Miami, FL 33131-1820
Ph:(305)377-3721
Fax: (305)347-6678

59007 ■ *Florida Trend*
PO Box 611
St. Petersburg, FL 33731
Ph:(813)822-5083

59008 ■ *How to Form a Simple Corporation in Florida*
Sphinx Publishing
3908 East Miami
Phoenix, AZ 85040
Ph:(602)437-0208
Ed: Mark Warda. **Released:** 1991. **Price:** $19.95.

59009 ■ *How to Form Your Own Florida Corporation*
Nolo Press
950 Parker St.
Berkeley, CA 94710
Ph:(510)549-1976
Free: 800-992-6656
Fax: (510)548-5902
URL: http://www.nolo.com
Ed: Anthony Mancuso. **Released:** Third edition, 1990. **Price:** $24.95.

59010 ■ *Incorporation and Business Guide for Florida*
Self-Counsel Press, Inc.
1704 N. State St.
Bellingham, WA 98225
Ph:(360)676-4530
Free: 800-663-3007
Fax: (360)676-4549
Ed: Robert C. Waters. **Released:** 1992. **Price:** $21.95. **Description:** Includes forms to help entrepreneurs incorporate in Florida.

59011 ■ *Silver River Marine Institute*
1519 NE 22nd Ave.
Ocala, FL 34470
Ph:(352)620-3601
Fax: (352)620-3604

59012 ■ *Starting and Operating a Business in Florida: A Step-by-Step Guide*
PSI Research
300 N. Valley Dr.
Grants Pass, OR 97526

Ph:(503)479-9464
Free: 800-228-2275
Fax: (503)476-1479
Co. E-mail: psi2@magick.net
Ed: Michael D. Jenkins. **Released:** Revised edition, 1992. **Price:** $29.95 (looseleaf binder); $24.95 (paper). **Description:** Part of the Successful Business Library series.

PUBLISHERS

59013 ■ DC Press
2445 River Tree Cir.
Sanford, FL 32771
Ph:(407)688-1156
Free: (866)602-1476
Fax: (407)688-1135
Co. E-mail: info@focusonethics.com
URL: http://www.focusonethics.com
Contact: Dennis McClellan, President
E-mail: dennis@focusonethics.com
Description: Publishes ethical books in a variety of areas. **Founded:** 2001.

59014 ■ Donald Wade Johnson
7911 Old Kings Rd. S
Jacksonville, FL 32217-4107
Ph:(904)737-4901
Fax: (904)737-4570
Co. E-mail: dowajo@aol.com
Contact: Donald Wade Johnson, Publisher
Description: Publishes a manual on piano care. **Founded:** 1999.

59015 ■ Downtown Book Center Inc. Spanish Div.
247 SE 1st St.
Miami, FL 33131
Ph:(305)377-9939
Free: 800-599-8712
Fax: (305)371-5926
Co. E-mail: raxdown@aol.com
Contact: Raquel Roque, CEO
Description: Distributor. Reaches market through direct mail, reviews, listings, telephone sales, and wholesalers, including Baker & Taylor. **Founded:** 1965.

59016 ■ Famaco Publishers
PO Box 440665
Jacksonville, FL 32244-0665
Ph:(904)434-5901
Fax: (904)777-5901
Co. E-mail: famapub@aol.com
URL: http://www.members.aol.com/famapub
Contact: D.A. Miller, President
Description: Publishes scholarly non-fiction works on religion, politics, and social commentary. Does not accept unsolicited manuscripts. Reaches market through commission representatives, direct mail, telephone sales, wholesalers and distributors, and Broadcast Internet. **Founded:** 1996.

59017 ■ Financial Research Associates Inc.
203 Avenue A NW, Ste. 202
Winter Haven, FL 33881
Ph:(863)299-3969
Fax: (863)299-2131
Co. E-mail: sales@frafssb.com
URL: http://www.frafssb.com
Contact: Grant Lacerte, President
Description: Publishes financial ratio analysis for small business, which is useful for bank loan officers, CPA's, business consultants, leasing companies, and individual business owners. Reaches market through direct mail and wholesalers. **Founded:** 1976.

59018 ■ GoalsGuy Learning Systems
36181 E Lake Rd., Ste. 139
Palm Harbor, FL 34685
Free: 877-462-5748
Fax: (813)435-2022
Co. E-mail: info@goalsguy.com
URL: http://www.goalsguy.com
Contact: Gary Blair, Owner

E-mail: gary@goalsguy.com
Description: Distributor of motivational business-related products for personal development.

59019 ■ Hibel Studio Inc.
PO Box 9967
Riviera Beach, FL 33419
Ph:(561)848-9633
Free: 800-275-3426
Fax: (561)848-9640
Co. E-mail: sales@hibel.com
URL: http://www.hibel.com
Contact: Theodore Plotkin, President
Description: Wholesaler of Edna Hibel's fine arts and gifts. **Founded:** 1960.

59020 ■ Liberty Publishing Company Inc.
PO Box 4248
Deerfield Beach, FL 33442-4248
Ph:(561)395-3750
Co. E-mail: jblittle@bellsouth.net
URL: http://www.libertypub.com
Contact: Judith A. Little, Secretary
Description: Distributes of nonfiction for small presses. Reaches market through sales representatives and direct mail. **Founded:** 1977.

59021 ■ Rei America Inc.
10049 NW 89th Ave., Unit 13-14
Medley, FL 33178-1443
Ph:(305)805-0771
Free: 800-726-5337
Fax: (305)887-4138
Co. E-mail: contacto@reiamericainc.com
URL: http://www.reiamericainc.com
Contact: Javier Castro, Mktg Mgr
E-mail: jcastro@reiamericainc.com
Description: Distributes and publishes Spanish language textbooks for grades K-12. Offers audio cassettes and software. Reaches market through commission representatives and direct mail. **Founded:** 1989.

59022 ■ Socrates Media L.L.C.
227 W Monroe St., Ste. 500
Chicago, IL 60606
Ph:(312)762-5600
Free: 800-822-4566
Fax: (312)762-5601
Co. E-mail: customerservice@socrates.com
URL: http://www.socrates.com
Contact: William A. Lederer, CEO & Chm Bd
Description: Distributes and Publishes business, finance, real estate, law and human resources. **Founded:** 1987.

59023 ■ Thomson Delmar Learning–Solitaire Publishing
Executive Woods, 5 Maxwell Dr.
PO Box 8007
Clifton Park, NY 12065-8007
Ph:(518)348-2300
Free: 800-998-7498
Fax: 800-487-8488
Co. E-mail: info@delmar.com
URL: http://www.delmarlearning.com
Contact: Greg Burnell, President
E-mail: gburnell@delmar.com
Description: Wholesaler of various media for career development. **Founded:** 1982.

59024 ■ Virtual Word Publishing
PO Box 938504
Margate, FL 33093
Ph:(954)971-4025
Fax: (954)971-4025
URL: http://www.virtualwordpublishing.com
Contact: Diana Ennen
Description: Publishes books on how to become a work-at-home virtual assistant and start word processing businesses.

SMALL BUSINESS DEVELOPMENT CENTER LEAD OFFICE

59025 ■ University of Georgia–Small Business Development Center
Chicopee Complex
1180 E. Broad St.
Athens, GA 30602-5412
Ph:(706)542-6762
Fax: (706)542-6776
URL: http://www.sbdc.uga.edu
Contact: Hank Logan, State Director
E-mail: hlogan@sbdc.uga.edu

SMALL BUSINESS DEVELOPMENT CENTERS

59026 ■ Clayton State University–Small Business Development Center
2000 Clayton State Blvd.
Morrow, GA 30260-0285
Ph:(678)466-5100
Fax: (678)466-5109
URL: http://www.sbdc.uga.edu
Contact: Cecil McDaniel, Area Dir.
E-mail: cmcdaniel@mail.clayton.edu

59027 ■ Georgia Highlands College–Small Business Development Center
415 E. Third Ave.
Rome, GA 30161
Ph:(706)295-6326
Fax: (706)295-6732
URL: http://www.sbdc.uga.edu
Contact: Peter R. Matthews, Area Dir.
E-mail: peter_matthews@mail.fc.peachnet.edu

59028 ■ Georgia Southern University–Small Business Development Center
PO Box 8156
Statesboro, GA 30460-8156
Ph:(912)681-5194
Fax: (912)681-0648
URL: http://www.sbdc.uga.edu
Contact: Lori Durden, Area Dir.
E-mail: ldurden@gsvms2.cc.gasou.edu

59029 ■ Georgia State University - Atlanta Office–Small Business Development Center
10 Park Place S., Ste. 450
PO Box 3986
Atlanta, GA 30303-3986
Ph:(404)651-3550
Fax: (404)651-1035
Co. E-mail: sbdbjm@langate.gsu.edu
URL: http://www.sbdc.uga.edu
Contact: Bernie Meineke, Area Dir.

59030 ■ Kennesaw State University–Small Business Development Center
1000 Chastain Rd., No. 0409
Burruss Bldg., Rm. 405
KSU Ctr. - Busbee Pkwy.
Kennesaw, GA 30144-5591
Ph:(770)423-6450
Fax: (770)423-6564
Contact: Lydia Jones, Area Dir.
E-mail: ljones@ksumail.kennesaw.edu

59031 ■ University of Georgia - Albany Office–Small Business Development Center
230 S. Jackson St., Ste. 333
Albany, GA 31701-2885
Ph:(229)420-2885
Fax: (229)420-3933
URL: http://www.sbdc.uga.edu
Contact: Sue Ford, Regional Dir.
E-mail: sford@sbdc.uga.edu

59032 ■ University of Georgia - Augusta Office–Small Business Development Center
1054 Claussen Rd., Ste. 301
Augusta, GA 30907-0305
Ph:(706)737-1790
Fax: (706)731-7937
URL: http://www.sbdc.uga.edu
Contact: Debra McKenzie, Area Dir.
E-mail: dmckenzie@sbdc.uga.edu

59033 ■ University of Georgia - Brunswick Office–Small Business Development Center
501 Gloucester St., Ste. 200
Brunswick, GA 31520-7014
Ph:(912)264-7343
Fax: (912)262-3095
URL: http://www.sbdc.uga.edu
Contact: David Lewis, Area Dir.
E-mail: dlewis@sbdc.uga.edu

59034 ■ University of Georgia - Columbus Office–Small Business Development Center
3100 Gentian Blvd., Ste. 119
Columbus, GA 31907
Ph:(706)569-2651
Fax: (706)569-2657
URL: http://www.sbdc.uga.edu
Contact: Lori Canterbury, Area Dir.
E-mail: loric@sbdc.uga.edu

59035 ■ University of Georgia - Decatur Office–Small Business Development Center
1 Decatur Towncenter
150 E. Ponce de Leon Ave.
Decatur, GA 30030
Ph:(404)371-7399
Fax: (404)371-7484
URL: http://www.sbdc.uga.edu
Contact: Sharon Macaluso, Area Dir.
E-mail: macaluso@sbdc.uga.edu

59036 ■ University of Georgia - Gainesville Office–Small Business Development Center
604 Washington St. W., Ste. B-2
Gainesville, GA 30501-8545

Ph:(770)531-5681
Fax: (770)531-5684
URL: http://www.sbdc.uga.edu
Contact: Ron Simmons, Area Dir.
E-mail: resimmon@sbdc.uga.edu

59037 ■ University of Georgia - Macon Office–Small Business Development Center
111 3rd St., Ste. 201
Macon, GA 31201
Ph:(478)751-6592
Fax: (478)751-6607
URL: http://www.sbdc.uga.edu
Contact: Donald Rhodes, Area Dir.
E-mail: drhodes@sbdc.uga.edu

59038 ■ University of Georgia - Savannah Office–Small Business Development Center
111 E. Liberty St., Ste. 200
Savannah, GA 31401-4410
Ph:(912)651-3200
Fax: (912)651-3209
URL: http://www.sbdc.uga.edu
Contact: Lynn Vos, Area Dir.
E-mail: lvos@sbdc.uga.edu

59039 ■ Valdosta State University–Small Business Development Center
College of Business Administration
Thaxton Hall
Valdosta, GA 3168-0065
Ph:(229)245-3738
Fax: (229)245-3741
Contact: Suzanne Barnett, Area Dir.
E-mail: sbarnett@valdosta.edu

59040 ■ Georgia SBDC Network State Office–University of Georgia Business SBDC–SBDC (Chico)
Chicopee Complex
1180 E. Broad St.
Athens, GA 30602-5412
Ph:(706)542-2762
Fax: (706)542-6776
URL: http://ww.sbdc.uga.edu
Contact: Allan Adams, Interim State Dir.

SMALL BUSINESS ASSISTANCE PROGRAMS

59041 ■ Georgia Department of Community Affairs–Department of Economic Development
60 Executive Park South, NE
Atlanta, GA 30329
Ph:(404)679-4940
Free: 800-359-4663
Fax: (404)679-0572
Co. E-mail: jthompso@dca.state.ga.us
URL: http://www.dca.state.ga.us
Contact: James Thompson, Mgr
Description: Coordinates technical and financial assistance programs for rural development.

59042 ■ Georgia Department of Economic Development–Entrepreneur and Small Business Development
75 5th NW, Ste. 1200
Atlanta, GA 30308
Ph:(404)962-4000
Fax: (404)962-4096
Co. E-mail: rcardoza@georgia.org
URL: http://www.georgia.org
Contact: Gilda Watters, Dir
Description: Promotes the interests of small businesses at trade fairs.

SCORE OFFICES

59043 ■ SCORE Atlanta
c/o Mr. Robert F. Tuve, VC Admin.
Harris Tower
233 Peachtree St., Ste. 1900
Atlanta, GA 30303
Ph:(404)331-0121
Fax: (404)331-0108
Co. E-mail: office@scoreatlanta.org
URL: http://www.scoreatlanta.org
Contact: Mr. Robert F. Tuve, VC Admin.
Description: Works to provide free counseling to small business community.

59044 ■ SCORE Dalton-Whitfield
c/o Dalton-Whitfield Chamber of Commerce
890 College Dr.
Dalton, GA 30720
Ph:(706)279-3383
Co. E-mail: score@daltonchamber.org
Description: Provides professional guidance and information to maximize the success of existing and emerging small businesses. Promotes entrepreneur education in Dalton area, Georgia.

59045 ■ SCORE Savannah
111 E Liberty St.
Savannah, GA 31401
Ph:(912)652-4335
Fax: (912)652-4184
Co. E-mail: info@scoresav.org
URL: http://www.scoresav.org
Contact: Al Torpie, Chm.
Description: Provides professional guidance and information to maximize the success of existing and emerging small businesses. Develops business plans and evaluates financial projections. Identifies problems and potential solutions.

BETTER BUSINESS BUREAUS

59046 ■ Better Business Bureau, Augusta
301 7th St.
PO Box 2085
Augusta, GA 30901
Ph:(706)722-1574
Fax: (706)724-0969
Co. E-mail: info@augusta-ga.bbb.org

59047 ■ Better Business Bureau of Central Georgia
277 Martin Luther King Jr. Blvd., Ste. 102
Macon, GA 31201-3495
Ph:(478)742-7999
Fax: (478)742-8191
Co. E-mail: info@centralgeorgia.bbb.org
URL: http://www.centralgeorgia.bbb.org
Contact: Kelvin Collins, CEO

59048 ■ Better Business Bureau of Metro Atlanta, Athens and Northeast Georgia
503 Oak Pl., Ste. 590
College Park, GA 30349
Ph:(404)766-0875
Free: (866)225-1090
Fax: (404)768-1085
Co. E-mail: info@atlanta.bbb.org

URL: http://www.atlanta.bbb.org
Contact: Mr. Fred Elsberry Jr., Pres./CEO

59049 ■ Better Business Bureau Southeast Atlantic
6606 Abercorn St., Ste. 108C
Savannah, GA 31405
Ph:(912)354-7521
Free: 800-353-1192
Fax: (912)354-5068
Co. E-mail: bbbsea@bellsouth.net
URL: http://www.bbbsoutheastatlantic.org
Contact: Ross Howard, Pres./CEO

59050 ■ Better Business Bureau of Southwest Georgia
PO Box 808
Albany, GA 31702
Ph:(229)883-0744
Fax: (229)438-8222
Co. E-mail: albgabbb@mchsi.com
URL: http://www.columbus-ga.bbb.org
Contact: Leonard Crain, Pres.

59051 ■ Better Business Bureau of West Georgia - East Alabama
PO Box 2587
Columbus, GA 31902
Ph:(706)324-0712
Fax: (706)324-2181
Co. E-mail: info@columbus-ga.bbb.org
URL: http://www.columbus-ga.bbb.org
Contact: Leonard Crain, Pres.

CHAMBERS OF COMMERCE

59052 ■ Adel-Cook County Chamber of Commerce
100 S Hutchinson Ave.
Adel, GA 31620
Ph:(229)896-2281
Fax: (229)896-8201
Co. E-mail: cookcochamber@alltel.net
URL: http://www.adel-cookchamber.org
Contact: Marietta Brown, Chair

59053 ■ Airport Area Chamber of Commerce
Regions Bank Bldg.
600 S Central Ave., Ste. 100
Atlanta, GA 30354
Ph:(404)209-0910
Fax: (404)209-0910
Co. E-mail: mike@airportchamber.com
URL: http://www.airportchamber.com
Contact: Mike Simpson, Exec.Dir.

59054 ■ Albany Area Chamber of Commerce
225 W Broad Ave.
Albany, GA 31701
Ph:(229)434-8700
Free: 800-475-8700
Fax: (229)434-8716
Co. E-mail: info@albanyga.com
URL: http://www.albanyga.com
Contact: Tim Martin, Pres./CEO

59055 ■ Alma-Bacon County Chamber of Commerce
PO Box 450
Alma, GA 31510
Ph:(912)632-5859
Fax: (912)632-7710
Co. E-mail: abcchamber@accessatc.net
URL: http://www.abcchamber.org

59056 ■ American-Israel Chamber of Commerce, Southeast Region
1150 Lake Hearn Dr., Ste. 130
Atlanta, GA 30342
Ph:(404)843-9426
Fax: (404)843-1416
Co. E-mail: aiccse@aiccse.org
URL: http://www.aiccse.org
Contact: Tom Glaser, Pres.

59057 ■ Americus-Sumter County Chamber of Commerce
400 W Lamar St.
PO Box 724
Americus, GA 31709-0724
Ph:(229)924-2646
Fax: (229)924-8784
Co. E-mail: rachael@americus.net
URL: http://www.americus-sumterchamber.com
Contact: Rachael Gresham, Membership Dir.

59058 ■ Ashburn - Turner County Chamber of Commerce
238 E College Ave.
Ashburn, GA 31714
Ph:(229)567-9696
Free: 800-471-9696
Co. E-mail: szorn@alltel.net
URL: http://www.turnerchamber.com
Contact: Shelly Zorn, Pres./Economic Developer

59059 ■ Athens Area Chamber of Commerce
246 W Hancock Ave.
Athens, GA 30601
Ph:(706)549-6800
Fax: (706)549-5636
Co. E-mail: info@athenschamber.net
URL: http://www.athenschamber.net
Contact: Larry McKinney, Pres.

59060 ■ Augusta Metro Chamber of Commerce
PO Box 1837
Augusta, GA 30903
Ph:(706)821-1300
Free: 888-639-8188
Fax: (706)821-1330
Co. E-mail: smacgregor@augustagausa.com
URL: http://www.augustagausa.com
Contact: Scott MacGregor, VP

59061 ■ Bainbridge-Decatur County Chamber of Commerce
PO Box 755
Bainbridge, GA 39818
Ph:(229)246-4774
Free: 800-243-4774
Co. E-mail: info@bainbridgechamber.org
URL: http://www.bainbridgegachamber.com
Contact: Cile G. Warr, Pres.

59062 ■ Banks County Chamber of Commerce
PO Box 57
105 US Hwy. N
Homer, GA 30547-0057
Ph:(706)677-2108
Free: 800-638-5004
Fax: (706)677-2109
Co. E-mail: bankscountychamber@alltel.net
URL: http://www.bankscountyga.org
Contact: Sherry L. Ward, Exec.Dir.

59063 ■ Barnesville-Lamar County Chamber of Commerce
PO Box 506
100 Commerce Pl.
Barnesville, GA 30204
Ph:(770)358-5884
Fax: (770)358-0006
Co. E-mail: chamber@barnesville.org
URL: http://www.barnesville.org
Contact: Melissa Kinnard, Exec.Dir.

59064 ■ Barrow County Chamber of Commerce
6 Porter St.
PO Box 456
Winder, GA 30680-1731
Ph:(770)867-9444
Fax: (770)867-6366
Co. E-mail: mwalker@barrowchamber.com
URL: http://www.barrowchamber.com
Contact: Carolyn Delamont, Pres.

59065 ■ Baxley-Appling County Chamber of Commerce
PO Box 413
305 W Parker St.
Baxley, GA 31515
Ph:(912)367-7731
Fax: (912)367-2073
Co. E-mail: glennkk@bellsouth.net
URL: http://www.baxley.org
Contact: Karen Glenn, Exec.Dir.

59066 ■ Blairsville - Union County Chamber of Commerce
PO Box 789
Blairsville, GA 30514
Ph:(706)745-5789
Free: 877-745-5789
Fax: (706)745-1382
Co. E-mail: negamtns@alltel.net
URL: http://www.blairsvillechamber.com
Contact: Renai Brock, Pres.

59067 ■ Blakely-Early County Chamber of Commerce
PO Box 189
Blakely, GA 39823
Ph:(229)723-3741
Fax: (229)723-6876
Co. E-mail: info@blakelyearlychamber.com
URL: http://www.blakelyearlychamber.com
Contact: Wanda Hudson, Pres./CEO

59068 ■ Brunswick-Golden Isles Chamber of Commerce
4 Glynn Ave.
Brunswick, GA 31520
Ph:(912)265-0620
Fax: (912)265-0629
Co. E-mail: chamber@bgicoc.com
URL: http://www.brunswick-georgia.com/chamber

59069 ■ Butts County Chamber of Commerce
PO Box 147
Jackson, GA 30233-0147
Ph:(770)775-4839
Fax: (770)775-4868
Co. E-mail: matha2@bellsouth.net
Contact: Melinda Atha, Exec.Dir.

59070 ■ Camden-Kings Bay Area Chamber of Commerce
2603 Osborne Rd., Ste. R
St. Marys, GA 31558
Ph:(912)729-5840
Fax: (912)576-7924
Co. E-mail: information@camdenchamber.com
URL: http://www.camdenchamber.com
Contact: Mr. Jeff Barker, Chm.

59071 ■ Camilla Chamber of Commerce
PO Box 226
212 E Broad St.
Camilla, GA 31730
Ph:(229)336-5255
Fax: (229)336-5256
Co. E-mail: charla@camillageorgia.com
URL: http://www.camillageorgia.com
Contact: Charla A. Thornton, Exec.Asst.

59072 ■ Carroll County Chamber of Commerce
200 Northside Dr.
Carrollton, GA 30117
Ph:(770)832-2446
Fax: (770)832-1300
Co. E-mail: info@carroll-ga.org
URL: http://www.carroll-ga.org
Contact: Kenneth J. O'Neill, Pres./CEO

59073 ■ Cartersville-Bartow County Chamber of Commerce
PO Box 307
122 W Main St.
Cartersville, GA 30120
Ph:(770)382-1466
Fax: (770)382-2704

Co. E-mail: reception@cartersvillechamber.com
URL: http://www.cartersvillechamber.com
Contact: Molly Grover, Pres./CEO

59074 ■ Catoosa County Chamber of Commerce
PO Box 52
Ringgold, GA 30736
Ph:(706)965-5201
Free: 877-965-5201
Fax: (706)965-8224
Co. E-mail: chamber@catt.com
URL: http://www.gatewaytogeorgia.com
Contact: Tammy Cole, Pres.

59075 ■ Chamber of Commerce for the City of Loganville
254 Main St., Ste. 200
PO Box 2390
Loganville, GA 30052
Ph:(770)466-1601
Fax: (770)466-1668
Co. E-mail: info@loganvillechamber.com
URL: http://loganvillechamber.com
Contact: Betty McCullers, Pres.

59076 ■ Chatsworth-Murray County Chamber of Commerce
PO Box 327
116 N 3rd Ave.
Chatsworth, GA 30705
Ph:(706)695-6060
Fax: (706)517-0198
Co. E-mail: mchamber@northga.net
Contact: Dinah Rowe, Pres.

59077 ■ Chattooga County Chamber of Commerce
44 Hwy. 48
PO Box 217
Summerville, GA 30747
Ph:(706)857-4033
Fax: (706)857-6963
Co. E-mail: chattoogachamber@alltel.net
Contact: Susan B. Spivey, Pres.

59078 ■ Cherokee County Chamber of Commerce
PO Box 4998
3605 Marietta Hwy.
Canton, GA 30114
Ph:(770)345-0400
Fax: (770)345-0030
Co. E-mail: pam@cherokeechamber.com
URL: http://www.cherokee-chamber.com
Contact: Pamela W. Carnes, Pres./CEO

59079 ■ Claxton-Evans County Chamber of Commerce - Welcome Center
4 N Duval St.
Claxton, GA 30417
Ph:(912)739-1391
Fax: (912)739-3827
Co. E-mail: info@claxtonevanschamber.com
URL: http://www.claxtonevanschamber.com
Contact: Tammi Rogers Hall, Exec.Dir.

59080 ■ Clayton County Chamber of Commerce
2270 Mt. Zion Rd.
Jonesboro, GA 30236
Ph:(678)610-4021
Fax: (678)610-4025
Co. E-mail: info@claytoncham.org
URL: http://www.claytoncham.org
Contact: Matt Carlson, Pres.

59081 ■ Cobb Chamber of Commerce
PO Box 671868
Marietta, GA 30006-0032
Ph:(770)980-2000
Fax: (770)980-9510
Co. E-mail: info@cobbchamber.org
URL: http://www.cobbchamber.org
Contact: Bill Cooper, Pres./CEO

59082 ■ Colquitt - Miller County Chamber of Commerce
302 E College St.
Colquitt, GA 39837
Ph:(229)758-2400
Fax: (229)758-8140
Co. E-mail: cmccoc@bellsouth.net
URL: http://www.colquitt-georgia.com/site
Contact: Veryl Garland, Pres.

59083 ■ Conyers-Rockdale Chamber of Commerce
PO Box 483
1186 Scott St.
Conyers, GA 30012
Ph:(770)483-7049
Fax: (770)922-8415
Co. E-mail: fred@conyers-rockdale.com
URL: http://www.conyers-rockdale.com
Contact: Fred Boscarino, Pres.

59084 ■ Cordele-Crisp Chamber of Commerce
PO Box 158
302 E 16th Ave.
Cordele, GA 31015
Ph:(229)273-3526
Fax: (229)273-5132
Co. E-mail: info@cordele-crisp-chamber.com
URL: http://www.cordele-crisp-chamber.com
Contact: Monica G. Simmons, Pres.

59085 ■ Cumming-Forsyth County Chamber of Commerce
212 Kelly Mill Rd.
Cumming, GA 30040
Ph:(770)887-6461
Fax: (770)781-8800
Co. E-mail: jmccoy@cummingforsythchamber.org
URL: http://wwws.cummingforsythchamber.org
Contact: James McCoy, Pres./CEO

59086 ■ Dade County Chamber of Commerce
111 Railway Ln.
PO Box 1014
Trenton, GA 30752
Ph:(706)657-4488
Fax: (706)657-7513
Co. E-mail: dcoc@tvn.net
URL: http://www.dadecogachamber.com
Contact: Mr. David Carroll, Exec.Dir.

59087 ■ Dahlonega Lumpkin County Chamber of Commerce
13 S Park St.
Dahlonega, GA 30533-2082
Ph:(706)864-3711
Free: 800-231-5543
Fax: (706)864-7917
Co. E-mail: dahlonega@alltel.net
URL: http://www.dahlonega.org
Contact: Dale Steenbergen, Pres.

59088 ■ Dalton-Whitfield Chamber of Commerce
524 Holiday Ave.
Dalton, GA 30720
Ph:(706)278-7373
Fax: (706)226-8739
Co. E-mail: info@daltonchamber.org
URL: http://www.daltonchamber.org
Contact: George Woodward, Pres./CEO

59089 ■ Dawson County Chamber of Commerce
PO Box 299
Dawsonville, GA 30534
Ph:(706)265-6278
Free: 877-302-9271
Fax: (706)265-6279
Co. E-mail: info@dawson.org
URL: http://www.dawson.org
Contact: Linda Williams, Pres.

59090 ■ DeKalb Chamber of Commerce
150 E Ponce De Leon Ave., Ste. 400
1 Towne Ctr.
Decatur, GA 30030

Ph:(404)378-8000
Fax: (404)378-3397
Co. E-mail: info@dekalbchamber.org
URL: http://www.dekalbchamber.org
Contact: Mr. Leonardo McClarty, Pres.

59091 ■ Donalsonville-Seminole County Chamber of Commerce
PO Box 713
Donalsonville, GA 39845
Ph:(229)524-2588
Fax: (229)524-8406
Co. E-mail: dosemcc@surfsouth.com
URL: http://www.donalsonvillega.com
Contact: Brenda H. Broome, Pres.

59092 ■ Dooly County Chamber of Commerce
117 E Union St.
PO Box 308
Vienna, GA 31092
Ph:(229)268-8275
Fax: (229)268-8200
Co. E-mail: dccoc@sowega.net
URL: http://www.doolychamber.com
Contact: Judy Ledford, CEO & Pres.

59093 ■ Douglas - Coffee County Chamber of Commerce
PO Box 2470
Douglas, GA 31534-2470
Ph:(912)384-1873
Fax: (912)383-6304
Co. E-mail: chamber@douglasga.org
URL: http://www.douglasga.org
Contact: JoAnne Lewis, Pres.

59094 ■ Douglas County Chamber of Commerce
6658 Church St.
Douglasville, GA 30134
Ph:(770)942-5022
Fax: (770)942-5876
Co. E-mail: info@douglascountygeorgia.com
URL: http://www.douglascountygeorgia.com
Contact: Kali Boatright, Pres./CEO

59095 ■ Dublin - Laurens County Chamber of Commerce
PO Box 818
Dublin, GA 31040-0818
Ph:(478)272-5546
Fax: (478)275-0811
Co. E-mail: chamber@dublin-georgia.com
URL: http://www.dublin-georgia.com
Contact: Willie Paulk, Pres.

59096 ■ Eastman - Dodge County Chamber of Commerce
116 9th Ave.
PO Box 550
Eastman, GA 31023
Ph:(478)374-4723
Fax: (478)374-4626
Co. E-mail: fjfenn@eastman-georgia.com
URL: http://www.eastman-georgia.com
Contact: F.J. Fenn, Pres./CEO/Economic Developer

59097 ■ Eatonton-Putnam County Chamber of Commerce
105 S Washington St.
PO Box 4088
Eatonton, GA 31024
Ph:(706)485-7701
Fax: (706)485-3277
Co. E-mail: epchamber@eatonton.com
URL: http://www.eatonton.com
Contact: Roddie Anne Blackwell, Pres.

59098 ■ Effingham County Chamber of Commerce
520 W 3rd St.
Springfield, GA 31329
Ph:(912)754-3301
Fax: (912)754-1236
Co. E-mail: effingham@effinghamcounty.com
URL: http://www.effinghamcounty.com

Contact: Brad Lofton, Exec.Dir.

59099 ■ Elbert County Chamber of Commerce
148 College Ave.
PO Box 537
Elberton, GA 30635
Ph:(706)283-5651
Fax: (706)283-5722
Co. E-mail: chamber@elbertga.com
Contact: Phyllis Brooks, Pres.

59100 ■ Ellaville - Schley County Chamber of Commerce
PO Box 4
Ellaville, GA 31806
Ph:(229)937-2262
Fax: (229)937-2262
Co. E-mail: schley@alltel.net

59101 ■ Fannin County Chamber of Commerce
3990 Appalachian Hwy.
Blue Ridge, GA 30513
Ph:(706)632-5680
Free: 800-899-MTNS
Fax: (706)632-2241
Co. E-mail: chamber@blueridgemountains.com
URL: http://www.blueridgemountains.com
Contact: Jan Hackett, Exec.Dir.

59102 ■ Fayette County Chamber of Commerce
200 Courthouse Sq.
Fayetteville, GA 30214
Ph:(770)461-9983
Fax: (770)461-9622
Co. E-mail: fayettechamber@mindspring.com
URL: http://www.fayettechamber.org
Contact: Virginia Gibbs, Pres.

59103 ■ Forsyth-Monroe County Chamber of Commerce
PO Box 811
267 Tift College Dr.
Forsyth, GA 31029
Ph:(478)994-9239
Free: 888-642-4628
Fax: (478)994-9240
Co. E-mail: pchristo@forsythcable.com
URL: http://www.forsyth-monroechamber.com
Contact: Pamela L. Christopher, Pres./CEO

59104 ■ Georgia Association of Chamber of Commerce Executives
PO Box 888401
Atlanta, GA 30356-0401
Ph:(770)698-9668
Fax: (770)730-8852
Co. E-mail: info@gacce.org
URL: http://www.gacce.org
Contact: Tiffany Fulmer, Administrator

59105 ■ Georgia Chamber of Commerce
235 Peachtree St. NE, Ste. 900
Atlanta, GA 30303-1402
Ph:(404)233-2264
Free: 800-241-2286
Fax: (404)233-2290
Co. E-mail: lga@gachamber.com
URL: http://www.gachamber.com
Contact: George M. Israel III, Pres./CEO

59106 ■ Georgia Hispanic Chamber of Commerce
2801 Buford Hwy., Ste. 500
Atlanta, GA 30329
Ph:(404)929-9998
Fax: (404)929-9908
Co. E-mail: info@ghcc.org
URL: http://www.ghcc.org
Contact: Sara J. Gonzalez, Pres./CEO

59107 ■ Gilmer County Chamber of Commerce
PO Box 505
368 Craig St., Ste. 4
Ellijay, GA 30540

Ph:(706)635-7400
Fax: (706)635-7410
Co. E-mail: chamber@ellijay.com
URL: http://www.gilmerchamber.com
Contact: Brenda Johnson, Exec.Dir.

59108 ■ Gordon County Chamber of Commerce
300 S Wall St.
Calhoun, GA 30701
Ph:(706)625-3200
Fax: (706)625-5062
Co. E-mail: contact@gordonchamber.org
URL: http://www.gordonchamber.org
Contact: Jimmy Phillips, Pres.

59109 ■ Greater Columbus Chamber of Commerce
PO Box 1200
1200 6th Ave.
Columbus, GA 31902-1200
Ph:(706)327-1566
Free: 800-360-8552
Fax: (706)327-7512
Co. E-mail: mgaymon@columbusgachamber.com
URL: http://www.columbusgachamber.com
Contact: Mike Gaymon, Pres./CEO

59110 ■ Greater Hall Chamber of Commerce
230 EE Butler Pkwy.
Gainesville, GA 30501
Ph:(770)532-6206
Fax: (770)535-8419
Co. E-mail: info@ghcc.com
URL: http://www.ghcc.com
Contact: Kit Dunlap, Pres./CEO

59111 ■ Greater Helen Area Chamber of Commerce
PO Box 192
Helen, GA 30545
Ph:(706)878-1908
Fax: (706)878-3064
Co. E-mail: office@helenchamber.com
URL: http://www.helenchamber.com
Contact: Kay Mathea, Asst. to the Pres.

59112 ■ Greater Macon Chamber of Commerce
PO Box 169
305 Coliseum Dr.
Macon, GA 31202-0169
Ph:(478)621-2000
Fax: (478)621-2021
Co. E-mail: info@maconchamber.com
URL: http://www.maconchamber.com
Contact: Charles Bishop, Chm.

59113 ■ Greater North Fulton Chamber of Commerce
11605 Haynes Bridge Rd., Ste. 100
Alpharetta, GA 30004
Ph:(770)993-8806
Fax: (770)594-1059
Co. E-mail: info@gnfcc.com
URL: http://www.gnfcc.com
Contact: Brandon L. Beach, Pres./CEO

59114 ■ Greater Tattnall Chamber of Commerce
PO Box 399
Reidsville, GA 30453
Ph:(912)557-4119
Fax: (912)557-3046
URL: http://www.tattnall.com
Contact: Jeanette DeLoach, Pres.

59115 ■ Greene County Chamber of Commerce
PO Box 741
111 N Main St.
Greensboro, GA 30642
Ph:(706)453-7592
Free: 800-886-5253
Fax: (706)453-1430
Co. E-mail: chamber@greeneccoc.org
URL: http://www.greeneccoc.org

Contact: Becky Cronic, Dir.

59116 ■ Griffin-Spalding Chamber of Commerce
143 N Hill St.
Griffin, GA 30223
Ph:(770)228-8200
Fax: (770)228-8031
Co. E-mail: griffinchamber@cityofgriffin.com
URL: http://www.griffinchamber.com
Contact: Bonnie Pfrogner, Exec. Dir.

59117 ■ Gwinnett Chamber of Commerce
6500 Sugarloaf Pkwy.
Duluth, GA 30097
Ph:(770)232-3000
Fax: (770)232-8807
Co. E-mail: info@gwinnettchamber.org
URL: http://www.gwinnettchamber.org
Contact: James J. Maran, Pres./CEO

59118 ■ Habersham County Chamber of Commerce
PO Box 366
668 Clarkesville St.
Cornelia, GA 30531
Ph:(706)778-4654
Free: 800-835-2559
Fax: (706)776-1416
Co. E-mail: stephaniesnow@alltel.net
URL: http://www.habershamchamber.com
Contact: Stephanie Snow, Exec.Asst.

59119 ■ Haralson County Chamber of Commerce
70 Murphy Campus Blvd.
Waco, GA 30182
Ph:(770)537-5594
Fax: (770)537-5873
Co. E-mail: hccoc@haralson.org
URL: http://www.haralson.org
Contact: Jennie West, Pres.

59120 ■ Harris County Chamber of Commerce
PO Box 426
Hamilton, GA 31811
Ph:(706)628-4381
Free: 800-381-4381
Fax: (706)628-4381
Co. E-mail: info@harriscountychamber.org
URL: http://www.harriscountychamber.org
Contact: Ms. Kim W. Russell, Exec.Dir.

59121 ■ Hart County Chamber of Commerce
PO Box 793
31 E Howell St.
Hartwell, GA 30643
Ph:(706)376-8590
Fax: (706)376-5177
Co. E-mail: hartchamber@hartcom.net
URL: http://www.hart-chamber.org
Contact: Ginger Johnson, Exec.Dir.

59122 ■ Hawkinsville-Pulaski County Chamber of Commerce
PO Box 300
Hawkinsville, GA 31036
Ph:(478)783-1717
Fax: (478)783-1700
Co. E-mail: lauragahawk@cstel.net

59123 ■ Hazlehurst-Jeff Davis County Chamber of Commerce
95 E Jarman St.
PO Box 546
Hazlehurst, GA 31539-0546
Ph:(912)375-4543
Fax: (912)375-7948
Co. E-mail: hazjdcoc@altamaha.net
Contact: Rebecca Burnette, Exec.Dir.

59124 ■ Henry County Chamber of Commerce
1709 Hwy. 20 W
Westridge Business Center
McDonough, GA 30253

Ph:(770)957-5786
Fax: (770)957-8030
Co. E-mail: executivedirector@henrycounty.com
URL: http://www.henrycounty.com
Contact: Kay Pippin, Exec.Dir.

59125 ■ Homerville - Clinch County Chamber of Commerce
23 W Plant Ave.
Homerville, GA 31634
Ph:(912)487-2360
Co. E-mail: clinchchamber1@clinchcountychamber.org
URL: http://www.clinchcountychamber.org
Contact: Lottie Bruce, Asst. Exec. Dir.

59126 ■ Jackson County Area Chamber of Commerce
PO Box 1444
1655 S Elm St.
Commerce, GA 30529
Ph:(706)335-1896
Fax: (706)335-3312
Co. E-mail: jcmembers@alltel.net
URL: http://www.jacksoncountyga.com
Contact: Pepe Cummings, Pres./CEO

59127 ■ Jefferson County Chamber of Commerce
PO Box 630
302 E Broad St.
Louisville, GA 30434
Ph:(478)625-8134
Free: (866)527-2642
Fax: (478)625-9060
Co. E-mail: info@jeffersoncounty.org
URL: http://www.jeffersoncounty.org
Contact: Lillian E. Agel, Pres.

59128 ■ Jenkins County Chamber of Commerce and Development Authority
548 Cotton Ave.
Millen, GA 30442
Ph:(478)982-5595
Fax: (478)982-5512
Co. E-mail: jenkinsdepot@jeffersonenergy.com
Contact: Paula Herrington, Exec.Dir.

59129 ■ LaGrange - Troup County Chamber of Commerce
PO Box 636
LaGrange, GA 30241
Ph:(706)884-8671
Fax: (706)882-8012
Co. E-mail: assistant@lagrangechamber.com
URL: http://www.lagrangechamber.com
Contact: Jane L. Fryer, Pres.

59130 ■ Lake Park Area Chamber of Commerce and Visitors Center
5208 Jewel Futch Rd.
Lake Park, GA 31636
Ph:(229)559-5302
Fax: (229)559-0828
Co. E-mail: info@lakeparkga.com
URL: http://www.lakeparkga.com
Contact: Rhonda Barnes, Exec.Dir.

59131 ■ Lavonia Chamber of Commerce
1629 E Main St.
Lavonia, GA 30553
Ph:(706)356-8202
Co. E-mail: lavoniacofc@alltel.net
URL: http://www.lavonia-ga.com
Contact: Toni Childress, Exec.Sec.

59132 ■ Liberty County Chamber of Commerce
500 E Oglethorpe Hwy.
Hinesville, GA 31313-2804
Ph:(912)368-4445
Fax: (912)368-4677
Co. E-mail: awilsoncoc@coastalnow.net
URL: http://www.libertycounty.org
Contact: Ronald Tolley, Pres./CEO

59133 ■ Lincolnton - Lincoln County Chamber of Commerce and Development Authority
112 N Washington St.
PO Box 490
Lincolnton, GA 30817-0490
Ph:(706)359-7970
Fax: (706)359-5477
Co. E-mail: lincolncham@nu-z.net
URL: http://www.lincolncountyga.org
Contact: Ms. Ginger D. Parham, Exec.Asst.

59134 ■ Madison County Chamber of Commerce and Industrial Authority
PO Box 381
Danielsville, GA 30633-0381
Ph:(706)795-3473
Fax: (706)795-3262
Co. E-mail: chamber@madisoncountyga.org
URL: http://www.madisoncountyga.org
Contact: Marvin White, Pres.

59135 ■ Madison-Morgan County Chamber of Commerce
PO Box 826
115 E Jefferson St.
Madison, GA 30650-0826
Ph:(706)342-4454
Free: 800-709-7406
Fax: (706)342-4455
Co. E-mail: welcomecenter@madisonga.org
URL: http://www.madisonga.org
Contact: Frederick J. Boscarino, Pres./CEO

59136 ■ McIntosh County Chamber of Commerce
PO Box 1497
Darien, GA 31305
Ph:(912)437-6684
Fax: (912)437-5251
Co. E-mail: chamber@darientel.net
URL: http://www.mcintoshcounty.com
Contact: Fred Stregles, Dir.

59137 ■ Meriwether County Chamber of Commerce
PO Box 9
Warm Springs, GA 31830
Ph:(706)655-2558
Fax: (706)655-2812
Co. E-mail: sandrahudson@alltel.net
URL: http://www.meriwethercountychamberofcommerce.com
Contact: Sandra Hudson, Exec.Dir.

59138 ■ Metro Atlanta Chamber of Commerce
235 Andrew Young Intl. Blvd. NW
Atlanta, GA 30303-2718
Ph:(404)880-9000
Fax: (404)586-8464
Co. E-mail: samwilliams@macoc.com
URL: http://www.metroatlantachamber.com
Contact: Sam A. Williams, Pres.

59139 ■ Metter-Candler Chamber of Commerce
PO Box 497
Metter I-16 Welcome Ctr.
Metter, GA 30439-0497
Ph:(912)685-2159
Free: 888-573-7960
Fax: (912)685-2108
Co. E-mail: ebim@pineland.net
URL: http://www.metter-candler.com
Contact: Mr. Billy Patterson, Chm.

59140 ■ Milledgeville-Baldwin County Chamber of Commerce
PO Box 751
130 S Jefferson St.
Milledgeville, GA 31059-0751
Ph:(478)453-9311
Fax: (478)453-0051
Co. E-mail: mbcchamber@alltel.net
URL: http://www.milledgevillega.com
Contact: Tara Peters, Pres./CEO

59141 ■ Monticello-Jasper County Chamber of Commerce
PO Box 133
Monticello, GA 31064
Ph:(706)468-8994
Fax: (706)468-1041
URL: http://www.monticelloga.org
Contact: Jennifer Nash, Dir.

59142 ■ Moultrie-Colquitt County Chamber of Commerce
116 1st Ave. SE
PO Box 487
Moultrie, GA 31776-0487
Ph:(229)985-2131
Fax: (229)890-2638
Co. E-mail: contact@moultriechamber.com
URL: http://www.moultriechamber.com
Contact: Darrell Moore, Pres.

59143 ■ Nashville-Berrien Chamber of Commerce
PO Box 217
201 N Jefferson St.
Nashville, GA 31639
Ph:(229)686-5123
Fax: (229)686-7196
Co. E-mail: berrienchamber@alltel.net
URL: http://www.berrienchamber.com
Contact: Mary Alice McGee, Exec.Dir.

59144 ■ Newnan-Coweta Chamber of Commerce
23 Bullsboro Dr.
Newnan, GA 30263
Ph:(770)253-2270
Fax: (770)253-2271
Co. E-mail: info@ncchamber.org
Contact: Candace LaForge, Pres.

59145 ■ Ocilla - Irwin Chamber of Commerce
PO Box 104
Ocilla, GA 31774
Ph:(229)468-9114
Fax: (229)468-4452
Co. E-mail: irwinchamber@alltel.net
Contact: Hazel McCranie, Pres.

59146 ■ Oconee County Chamber of Commerce
55 Nancy Dr.
PO Box 348
Watkinsville, GA 30677
Ph:(706)769-7947
Fax: (706)769-7948
Co. E-mail: cgrimes@occoc.org
URL: http://www.occoc.org
Contact: Charles Grimes, Pres.

59147 ■ Okefenokee Chamber of Commerce and Folkston and Charlton County Development Authority
PO Box 756
202 W Main St.
Folkston, GA 31537
Ph:(912)496-2536
Fax: (912)496-4601
Co. E-mail: folkstonauth@alltel.net
URL: http://www.folkston.com
Contact: Doug Vaught, Exec.Dir.

59148 ■ Paulding Chamber of Commerce
455 Jimmy Campbell Pkwy.
Dallas, GA 30132
Ph:(770)445-6016
Fax: (770)445-3050
Co. E-mail: steaster@thepcoc.com
URL: http://www.pauldingcountygeorgia.com
Contact: Mr. Lloyd B. Teaster Jr., Pres./CEO

59149 ■ Peach County Chamber of Commerce
PO Box 1238
201 Oakland Heights Pkwy.
Fort Valley, GA 31030
Ph:(478)825-3733
Fax: (478)825-2501

Co. E-mail: chamber@peachcountyga.com
URL: http://www.peachcountyga.com
Contact: Steve Humphry, Pres./CEO

59150 ■ Pelham Chamber of Commerce
PO Box 151
Pelham, GA 31779
Ph:(229)294-4924
Fax: (229)294-1583
Co. E-mail: pelhamchamber@bellsouth.net
Contact: Danny Singleton, Exec.Dir.

59151 ■ Perry Area Chamber of Commerce
101 Gen. Courtney Hodges Blvd.
PO Box 592
Perry, GA 31069
Ph:(478)987-1234
Fax: (478)988-1234
Co. E-mail: mail@perrygachamber.com
URL: http://www.perrygachamber.com
Contact: Megan Smith, Pres./CEO

59152 ■ Pierce County Chamber of Commerce
200 S Central Ave.
PO Box 47
Blackshear, GA 31516
Ph:(912)449-7044
Fax: (912)449-7045
Co. E-mail: pierceco@accessatc.net
Contact: Debra Lee, Exec.Coor.

59153 ■ Pine Mountain Chamber of Commerce
PO Box 483
Pine Mountain, GA 31822
Ph:(706)663-8850
Co. E-mail: tourism@pinemountain.org
URL: http://www.pinemountainchamber.com
Contact: Dirk Steenbergen, Pres.

59154 ■ Quitman-Brooks County Chamber of Commerce
900 E Screven St.
Quitman, GA 31643
Ph:(229)263-4841
Fax: (229)263-4822
Co. E-mail: brookscochamber@alltel.net
URL: http://www.quitmangeorgia.org
Contact: LaDon Toole, Pres.

59155 ■ Rabun County Chamber of Commerce
PO Box 750
323 Hwy. 441
Clayton, GA 30525-0019
Ph:(706)782-4812
Fax: (706)782-4810
Co. E-mail: rabunchamber@gamountains.com
URL: http://www.gamountains.com/content
Contact: Rhonda Lunsford, Pres.

59156 ■ Roberta - Crawford County Chamber of Commerce
38 Wright Ave.
PO Box 417
Roberta, GA 31078-0417
Ph:(478)836-3825
Fax: (478)836-4509
Co. E-mail: rcccoc@pstel.net
Contact: Mona Lowe, Exec.Dir.

59157 ■ Savannah Area Chamber of Commerce
PO Box 1628
101 E Bay St.
Savannah, GA 31402-1628
Ph:(912)644-6400
Fax: (912)644-6499
Co. E-mail: ebrowne@savcvb.com
URL: http://www.savannahchamber.com
Contact: William W. Hubbard, Pres./CEO

59158 ■ Screven County Chamber of Commerce
101 S Main St.
Sylvania, GA 30467

Ph:(912)564-7878
Free: 800-972-7887
Fax: (912)564-7245
Co. E-mail: scrcoc@planters.net
URL: http://www.screvencounty.com
Contact: Nancy Edenfield, Exec.Dir.

59159 ■ Soperton - Treutlen Chamber of Commerce
402 2nd St.
Soperton, GA 30457
Ph:(912)529-6868
Fax: (912)529-4385
URL: http://www.soperton.org
Contact: Tammi Walraven, Sec.

59160 ■ South Fulton Chamber of Commerce
6400 Shannon Pkwy.
Union City, GA 30291
Ph:(770)964-1984
Fax: (770)969-1969
Co. E-mail: info@sfcoc.org
URL: http://www.southfultonchamber.org
Contact: John Boothby, Pres./CEO

59161 ■ Southwest Georgia Chamber of Commerce
201 N Lumpkin St.
PO Box 31
Cuthbert, GA 39840
Ph:(229)732-2683
Fax: (229)732-6590
Co. E-mail: rigsby@alltel.net
Contact: Beryl Rigsby, Exec.Dir.

59162 ■ Statesboro-Bulloch Chamber of Commerce
PO Box 303
102 S Main St.
Statesboro, GA 30459
Ph:(912)764-6111
Fax: (912)489-3108
Co. E-mail: chamber1@frontiernet.net
URL: http://www.statesboro-chamber.org
Contact: Peggy Chapman, Pres.

59163 ■ Swainsboro-Emanuel County Chamber of Commerce
102 S Main St.
Swainsboro, GA 30401
Ph:(478)237-6426
Fax: (478)237-7460
Co. E-mail: swainsborochambr@bellsouth.net
URL: http://www.emanuelchamber.org
Contact: Sonny Stephens, Chm.

59164 ■ Telfair County Chamber of Commerce
120 E Oak St.
Mc Rae, GA 31055
Ph:(229)868-6365
Fax: (229)868-7970
Co. E-mail: info@telfairco.com
URL: http://www.telfairco.com
Contact: Mr. Ryan Waldrep, Pres.

59165 ■ Terrell County Chamber of Commerce
PO Box 405
Dawson, GA 39842-0405
Ph:(229)995-2011
Fax: (229)995-3971
Co. E-mail: tccc@alltel.net
URL: http://www.terrellcountygeorgia.org
Contact: Ms. Gina Hobbs, Exec.Dir.

59166 ■ Thomaston - Upson Chamber of Commerce
213 E Gordon St.
PO Box 827
Thomaston, GA 30286
Ph:(706)647-9686
Fax: (706)647-1703
Co. E-mail: thomaston@alltel.net
URL: http://www.thomastonchamber.com
Contact: Betsy W. Hueber, Pres.

59167 ■ Thomasville-Thomas County Chamber of Commerce
401 S Broad St.
PO Box 560
Thomasville, GA 31799
Ph:(229)226-9600
Fax: (229)226-9603
Co. E-mail: chamber@rose.net
URL: http://www.thomasvillechamber.com
Contact: Donald P. Sims, Pres.

59168 ■ Toombs-Montgomery Chamber of Commerce
2805 E 1st St.
Vidalia, GA 30474
Ph:(912)537-4466
Fax: (912)537-1805
Co. E-mail: information@toombschamber.com
URL: http://www.toombsmontgomerychamber.com
Contact: Bill Mitchell, Pres.

59169 ■ Towns County Chamber of Commerce
1411 Fuller Cir.
Young Harris, GA 30582
Ph:(706)896-4966
Free: 800-984-1543
Fax: (706)896-5441
Co. E-mail: townscoc@brmemc.net
URL: http://www.mountaintopga.com
Contact: Candace Lee, Pres.

59170 ■ Valdosta-Lowndes County Chamber of Commerce
PO Box 790
Valdosta, GA 31603
Ph:(229)247-8100
Fax: (229)245-0071
Co. E-mail: chamber@valdostachamber.com
URL: http://www.valdostachamber.com
Contact: Myrna Ballard, Pres.

59171 ■ Walker County Chamber of Commerce
PO Box 430
10052 Hwy. 27 N
Rock Spring, GA 30739
Ph:(706)375-7702
Fax: (706)375-7797
Co. E-mail: angie@walkercochamber.com
URL: http://www.walkercochamber.com
Contact: Angie Meeks, Dir. of Programs and Events

59172 ■ Walton County Chamber of Commerce
PO Box 89
Monroe, GA 30655
Ph:(770)267-6594
Fax: (770)267-0961
Co. E-mail: teri@waltonchamber.org
URL: http://www.waltonchamber.org
Contact: Teri H. Wommack, Pres.

59173 ■ Warner Robins Area Chamber of Commerce
1420 Watson Blvd.
Warner Robins, GA 31093
Ph:(478)922-8585
Fax: (478)328-7745
Co. E-mail: info@warner-robins.com
URL: http://www.warner-robins.com
Contact: Frank Feild, Pres.

59174 ■ Warren County Chamber of Commerce
PO Box 27
Warrenton, GA 30828
Ph:(706)465-9604
Fax: (706)465-1789
Co. E-mail: chamber@warrencountyga.com
URL: http://www.warrencountyga.org
Contact: O.B. McCorkle, Exec.Dir.

59175 ■ Washington County Chamber of Commerce
PO Box 582
131 W Haynes St.
Sandersville, GA 31082

Ph:(478)552-3288
Fax: (478)552-1449
Co. E-mail: wacocofc@bellsouth.net
URL: http://www.washingtoncounty-ga.com
Contact: Theo McDonald, Pres.

59176 ■ Washington-Wilkes Chamber of Commerce
104 E Liberty St.
PO Box 661
Washington, GA 30673
Ph:(706)678-2013
Fax: (706)678-1932
Co. E-mail: washcham@washingtonwilkes.org
URL: http://www.washingtonwilkes.com
Contact: Sandy White, Exec.Dir.

59177 ■ Wayne County Chamber of Commerce
124 NW Broad St.
Jesup, GA 31545-2708
Ph:(912)427-2028
Free: 888-224-5983
Fax: (912)427-2778
Co. E-mail: web@waynechamber.com
URL: http://www.waynechamber.com
Contact: Hary Yeomans, Exec.Dir.

59178 ■ Wheeler County Chamber of Commerce
PO Box 654
Alamo, GA 30411
Ph:(912)568-7808
Fax: (912)568-7808
Co. E-mail: wchamber1@alltel.net
URL: http://www.wheelercounty.org
Contact: Mike Hayes, Pres.

59179 ■ White County Chamber of Commerce and Development Authority
122 N Main St.
Cleveland, GA 30528
Ph:(706)865-5356
Fax: (706)865-0758
Co. E-mail: judy@whitecountychamber.org
URL: http://www.whitecountychamber.org
Contact: Judy Walker, Pres.

59180 ■ Wrightsville - Johnson County Chamber of Commerce
PO Box 94
Wrightsville, GA 31096
Ph:(478)864-7200
Fax: (478)864-7207
Co. E-mail: commerce@wrightsville-johnsoncounty.com
URL: http://www.wrightsville-johnsoncounty.com
Contact: Charlene Milligan, Exec.Sec.

MINORITY BUSINESS ASSISTANCE PROGRAMS

59181 ■ Governor's Small Business Center
State Bldg.
1102 West Tower
200 Piedmont Ave.
1306 West Tower
Atlanta, GA 30334
Ph:(404)656-6315
Free: 800-495-0053
Fax: (404)657-4681
Co. E-mail: gsbc@doas.ga.gov
URL: http://www.doas.ga.gov
Contact: Charlet Taylor
Description: Assists the development of small and minority-owned businesses.

FINANCING AND LOAN PROGRAMS

59182 ■ Accuitive Medical Ventures LLC / AMV Partners
2750 Premiere Pky., Ste. 200
Duluth, GA 30097
Ph:(678)417-7626
Fax: (678)417-7325
URL: http://www.amvpartners.com
Contact: Charles Larsen, Managing Director
Investment Policies: Early stage and expansion. **Industry Preferences:** Medical and health. **Geographic Preferences:** Southeast.

59183 ■ Advanced Technology Development Fund
1000 Abernathy, Ste. 1420
Atlanta, GA 30328-5614
Ph:(404)668-2333
Fax: (404)668-2333
Preferred Investment Size: $500,000 to $1,500,000.
Investment Types: Seed, start-up, first and second stage, and leveraged buyout.

59184 ■ Alliance Technology Ventures
2400 Lakeview Pky., Ste. 675
Alpharetta, GA 30004
Ph:(678)336-2000
Fax: (678)336-2001
URL: http://www.atv.com
Contact: William Lyman, General Partner
Preferred Investment Size: $500,000 to $5,000,000.
Investment Types: Seed and first stage. **Industry Preferences:** Internet specific, semiconductors and other electronics, biotechnology, communications and media, computer software and services, computer hardware, medical and health. **Geographic Preferences:** U.S.

59185 ■ Brainworks Ventures
1700 Water Pl, Ste. 190
Atlanta, GA 30339
Ph:(404)272-9811
URL: http://www.brainworksvc.com
Contact: Donald Ratajczak, Chief Operating Officer
Investment Types: Balanced and early stage. **Industry Preferences:** Communications and media, and computer hardware. **Geographic Preferences:** U.S.

59186 ■ CB Capital Investors, L.P.
4200 Northside Pky., NW, Bldg. 1, Ste., 100
Atlanta, GA 30327
Ph:(404)841-3131
Fax: (404)841-3135
URL: http://www.croft-bender.com
Contact: Edward Croft, Managing Director
Investment Types: Early stage, acquisition, expansion, and recapitalizations. **Industry Preferences:** Internet specific, computer software and services, medical and health, communications and media. **Geographic Preferences:** Southeast.

59187 ■ CGW Southeast Partners / Cravey, Green, & Wahlen
12 Piedmont Ctr., Ste. 210
Atlanta, GA 30305
Ph:(404)816-3255
Fax: (404)816-3258
URL: http://www.cgwlp.com
Contact: Edwin Wahlen, Managing Partner
Preferred Investment Size: $25,000,000 to $200,000,000. **Investment Types:** Acquisition and recapitalizations. **Industry Preferences:** Other products, industrial and energy, consumer related, medical and health, and communications and media. **Geographic Preferences:** U.S.

59188 ■ Cordova Ventures / Cordova Capital (Alpharetta)
2500 North Winds Pky., Ste. 475
Alpharetta, GA 30004
Ph:(678)942-0300
Fax: (678)942-0301
URL: http://www.cordovaventures.com

Contact: T. Forcht Dagi, Venture Partner
Preferred Investment Size: $250,000 to $4,000,000.
Investment Types: Seed, start-up, early, first, second and later stage, and expansion. **Industry Preferences:** Computer software and services, medical and health, Internet specific, communications and media, other products, industrial and health, biotechnology, consumer related, semiconductors and other electronics. **Geographic Preferences:** Southeast.

59189 ■ Cyberstarts
1900 Emery St., NW, 3rd Fl.
Atlanta, GA 30318
Ph:(404)267-5000
Fax: (404)267-5200
URL: http://www.cyberstarts.com
Investment Types: Seed and start-up. **Industry Preferences:** Internet and financial services. **Geographic Preferences:** U.S.

59190 ■ EGL Ventures
10 Piedmont Ctr., Ste. 412
3495 Piedmont Rd.
Atlanta, GA 30305
Ph:(404)949-8300
Fax: (404)949-8311
URL: http://www.eglventures.com
Contact: Salvatore Massaro, Managing Partner
E-mail: samassaro@eglholdings.com
Preferred Investment Size: $500,000 to $6,000,000.
Investment Types: Early and later stage, balanced, and expansion. **Industry Preferences:** Communications, computer hardware and software, Internet specific, semiconductors and other electronics, medical and health, industrial and energy, and manufacturing. **Geographic Preferences:** Mid Atlantic, Midwest, Northeast, Midwest, and Southeast.

59191 ■ EHatchery, LLC
1175 Peachtree St. NE
100 Colony Sq., Ste. 2250
Atlanta, GA 30361
Ph:(404)487-1380
Fax: (404)487-1380
URL: http://www.ehatchery.com
Contact: Larry Honig, Managing Director
Investment Policies: Start-up, seed, and early stage.

59192 ■ Equity-South Advisors, LLC / Grubb & Williams Ltd.
1790 The Lenox Bldg.
3399 Peachtree Rd., NE
Atlanta, GA 30326
Ph:(404)237-6222
Fax: (404)261-1578
URL: http://www.equity-south.com
Contact: Douglas Diamond, Managing Director
Preferred Investment Size: $1,000,000 to $6,000,000. **Investment Types:** Acquisition, expansion, leveraged buyout, management buyouts, recapitalizations, generalist PE, later stage, and special situation. **Industry Preferences:** Communications, computer software, semiconductors and other electronics, medical and health, consumer related, industrial and energy, business service, and manufacturing. **Geographic Preferences:** Mid Atlantic, Midwest, and Southeast.

59193 ■ Financial Capital Resources, Inc.
21 Eastbrook Bend, Ste. 116
Peachtree City, GA 30269
Ph:(404)487-6650
Preferred Investment Size: $5,000,000 minimum.
Investment Types: Leveraged buyout. **Industry Preferences:** Industrial and energy.

59194 ■ First Growth Capital, Inc.
Best Western Plaza, Ste. 105
PO Box 815
Forsyth, GA 31029
Ph:(912)781-7131
Fax: (912)781-0066
Contact: Vidya Patel, Vice President
Preferred Investment Size: $100,000 to $300,000.
Investment Types: Second stage and special situation.

59195 ■ Five Paces Ventures
3400 Peachtree Rd., Ste. 102
Atlanta, GA 30326
Ph:(404)926-3484
Fax: (404)926-3494
URL: http://www.fivepaces.com
Contact: Alan Quarterman, Partner
Investment Types: Early stage and balanced. **Geographic Preferences:** U.S. and Southeast.

59196 ■ Frontline Capital, Inc.
3475 Lenox Rd., Ste. 400
Atlanta, GA 30326
Ph:(404)240-7280
Fax: (404)240-7281
Preferred Investment Size: $1,000,000 minimum.
Investment Types: First stage. **Industry Preferences:** Diversified communication and computer technology, consumer products and services, distribution, electronics, business and financial services, and publishing. **Geographic Preferences:** Southeast.

59197 ■ Fuqua Ventures LLC
1201 W. Peachtree St., NW, Ste. 5000
Atlanta, GA 30309
Ph:(404)815-4500
Fax: (404)815-4528
URL: http://www.fuquaventures.com
Contact: John Huntz, Managing Director
Preferred Investment Size: $500,000 to $2,500,000.
Investment Types: Balanced. **Industry Preferences:** Internet specific, computer software and services, biotechnology, computer hardware, communications and media. **Geographic Preferences:** Mid Atlantic and Southeast.

59198 ■ Gray Ventures
3330 Cumberland Blvd., Ste. 625
Atlanta, GA 30339
Ph:(678)589-7610
Fax: (678)589-7721
URL: http://www.grayventures.com
Preferred Investment Size: $500,000 to $2,000,000.
Investment Types: Early and first stage. **Industry Preferences:** Internet specific, computer software and services, communications and media, semiconductors and other electronics, and computer hardware. **Geographic Preferences:** Georgia and North Carolina.

59199 ■ Healthcare Capital Partners
6065 Roswell Rd., Ste. 800
Atlanta, GA 30328
Ph:(678)244-5874
Fax: (404)250-9431
URL: http://www.healthcarecp.com
Preferred Investment Size: $250,000 to $3,000,000.
Investment Policies: Early stage. **Industry Preferences:** Medical and health. **Geographic Preferences:** Southeast.

59200 ■ Liveoak Equity Partners
1266 Park Vista Dr.
Atlanta, GA 30319
Ph:(404)790-2666
Fax: (404)842-1502
URL: http://www.liveoakequity.com
Contact: James Gilbert, Managing Partner
Preferred Investment Size: $500,000 to $6,000,000.
Investment Types: Seed, first and second stage, early and later stage. **Industry Preferences:** Computer software and services, Internet specific, communications and media, medical and health, biotechnology, semiconductors and other electronics. **Geographic Preferences:** Southeast.

59201 ■ Noro-Moseley Partners
9 N. Pkwy. Sq.
4200 Northside Pky., NW
Atlanta, GA 30327
Ph:(404)233-1966
Fax: (404)239-9280
URL: http://www.noro-moseley.com
Contact: Alan Taetle, General Partner
Preferred Investment Size: $3,000,000 to $15,000,000. **Investment Types:** Start-up, seed, early stage, leveraged buyout, management buyouts, expansion, acquisition, generalist PE, and recapitalizations. **Industry Preferences:** Internet specific, computer software and services, medical and health, consumer related, other products, communications and media, computer hardware, semiconductors and other electronics, industrial and energy, and biotechnology. **Geographic Preferences:** Southeast.

59202 ■ Ptek Ventures
3399 Peachtree Rd., NE, Ste. 600
Atlanta, GA 30326
Ph:(404)262-8400
Fax: (404)504-2347
URL: http://www.ptekventures.com
Contact: Donald Gasgarth, Partner
Investment Types: Early stage. **Industry Preferences:** Internet specific, computer hardware, and computer software and services. **Geographic Preferences:** Southeast.

59203 ■ Renaissance Capital Corp.
34 Peachtree St. NW, Ste. 2230
Atlanta, GA 30303
Ph:(404)658-9061
Fax: (404)658-9064
Contact: Larry Edler
Preferred Investment Size: $300,000 minimum. **Investment Types:** Second stage, mezzanine, and leveraged buyout. **Industry Preferences:** Communications and media, computer hardware and software, Internet specific, semiconductors and other electronics, medical and health, consumer related, industrial and energy, financial services, and manufacturing. **Geographic Preferences:** Southeast.

59204 ■ River Capital
2 Midtown Plz.
1360 Peachtree St., Ste. 1430
Atlanta, GA 30309
Ph:(404)873-2166
Fax: (404)873-2158
URL: http://www.river-capital.com
Contact: Jon Van Tuin, Vice President
Preferred Investment Size: $3,000,000 minimum.
Investment Types: Mezzanine, recapitalizations, and leveraged buyout. **Industry Preferences:** Semiconductors and other electronics, medical and health, consumer related, industrial and energy, transportation, and manufacturing. **Geographic Preferences:** Southeast, Southwest, Midwest, and Mid Atlantic.

59205 ■ State Street Bank & Trust Co.
3414 Peachtree Rd. NE, Ste. 1010
Atlanta, GA 30326
Ph:(404)364-9500
Fax: (404)261-4469
Preferred Investment Size: $10,000,000 minimum.
Investment Types: Leveraged buyout and special situations. **Industry Preferences:** Diversified technology. **Geographic Preferences:** National.

59206 ■ Technology Ventures, L.L.C.
PO Box 550168
Atlanta, GA 30355
Ph:(404)869-7537
Fax: (404)231-0706
URL: http://www.techven.com
Contact: Joe McCall, Managing Partner
Investment Types: Seed, start-up, and early stage. **Industry Preferences:** Computer software, and Internet specific. **Geographic Preferences:** Southeast.

59207 ■ UPS Strategic Enterprise Fund
55 Glenlake Pky., NE
Bldg. 1, 4th Fl.
Atlanta, GA 30328
Ph:(404)828-8814
Fax: (404)828-8088
URL: http://www.ups.com/sef/sef_home.html
Preferred Investment Size: $250,000 to $1,500,000.
Investment Types: Start-up, first stage, and expansion. **Industry Preferences:** Internet specific, computer software and services, other products, computer hardware, communications and media, semiconductors and other electronics. **Geographic Preferences:** U.S. and Canada.

59208 ■ Venture First Associates (Acworth)
4811 Thornwood Dr.
Acworth, GA 30101
Ph:(770)928-3733
Fax: (770)928-6455
Contact: J. Douglas Mullins, Partner
Preferred Investment Size: $500,000 to $10,000,000. **Investment Types:** Seed, start-up, early and first stage. **Industry Preferences:** Communications, semiconductors and other electronics, medical and health. **Geographic Preferences:** Southeast.

59209 ■ Wachovia Capital Associates, Inc. (WCA)
191 Peachtree St., NE, 26th Fl.
Atlanta, GA 30303
Ph:(404)332-5000
Fax: (404)332-1392
URL: http://www.wachovia.com/wca
Contact: Andy Rose, Vice President
Preferred Investment Size: $5,000,000 to $15,000,000. **Investment Types:** Expansion, leveraged buyout, later stage, and recapitalizations. **Industry Preferences:** Communications and media, industrial and energy, consumer related, other products, medical and health, Internet specific, computer software and services, semiconductors and other electronics, and computer hardware. **Geographic Preferences:** Southeast.

PROCUREMENT ASSISTANCE PROGRAMS

59210 ■ Department of Administrative Services–Office of Small and Minority Business Division
200 Piedmont Ave., Ste 1804, W Tower
Atlanta, GA 30334
Ph:(404)656-5514
Free: 800-495-0053
Fax: (404)651-9595
Co. E-mail: customerservice@doas.ga.gov
URL: http://doas.georgia.gov
Description: Helps small and minority businesses secure government procurement contracts.

59211 ■ Georgia Procurement Technical Assistance Center–Georgia Institute of Technology (ATDC)
151 Osigian Blvd.
Warner Robins, GA 31088
Ph:(478)953-3155
Fax: (478)953-3169
URL: http://www.edi.gatech.edu/gtpac
Contact: Zach Osborne, Prgm Dir
E-mail: zack.osborne@edi.gatech.edu

59212 ■ US Small Business Administration
PO Box 611
Warner Robins, GA 31099-0611
Ph:(478)926-7446
Fax: (478)926-3832
Co. E-mail: thomas.hollingsworth@robins.mil
URL: http://www.sba.gov/
Contact: T.C. Hollingsworth, PCR
E-mail: tholling@wrdisol.robins.af.mil
Description: Covers activities for Warner Robins ALC (Warner Robins, GA) and the Marine Corps Logistics Command (Albany, GA).

INCUBATORS/RESEARCH AND TECHNOLOGY PARKS

59213 ■ Advanced Technology Development Center
Georgia Institute of Technology
75 5th St. NW, Ste. 100
Atlanta, GA 30308
Ph:(404)894-3575
Fax: (404)894-4545
URL: http://www.atdc.org

Contact: Simah Benyamin, Building Cor.

59214 ■ Computer Link Professional Services and Software Training Center
3140 Augusta Tech Dr.
Augusta, GA 30906
Ph:(706)792-1118
Fax: (706)792-9905
Co. E-mail: RAStokes@setechctr.org
URL: http://www.computerlinkaugusta.com
Description: This small business incubator supports entrepreneurs and small/disadvantaged technology-based firms. STC offers managerial and technical assistance to tenants, as well as affordable office space, shared office services, and equipment.

59215 ■ Foundation for Agronomic Research
107 S State St., Ste. 300
Monticello, IL 61856
Ph:(217)762-2074
Fax: (217)762-8655
Co. E-mail: hreetz@farmresearch.com
URL: http://www.farmresearch.com
Contact: Dr. Harold F. Reetz Jr., Pres.
E-mail: hreetz@farmresearch.com
Scope: Encourages multidisciplinary crop production research by developing funding strategies to capitalize on research opportunities at existing institutions. **Publications:** FAR Letter (quarterly). **Educational Activities:** Research workshops (periodically).

59216 ■ Georgia Institute of Technology–Advanced Technology Development Center
75 5th St., NW Ste. 100
Atlanta, GA 30308
Ph:(404)894-3575
Fax: (404)894-4545
Co. E-mail: wayne.hodges@edi.gatech.edu
URL: http://www.atdc.org
Contact: H. Wayne Hodges, Dir.
E-mail: wayne.hodges@edi.gatech.edu
Scope: Promotes the development of advanced technology-based companies throughout Georgia. including firms involved in advanced structural materials, electronic equipment, biotechnology, health and medical products, artificial intelligence, environmental sciences, telecommunications, aerospace systems, instrumentation and test equipment, robotics, and related technolgies. **Services:** Business assistance, to start-up technology companies; General management consulting; Technical and business management services, to entrepreneurs. **Publications:** Technology Partners (quarterly).

59217 ■ Georgia Tech Research Corp.
505 10th St.
Atlanta, GA 30332-0415
Ph:(404)894-3870
Fax: (404)385-2078
Co. E-mail: jilda.garton@gtrc.gatech.edu
URL: http://www.gatech.edu/gtrc
Contact: Jilda Diehl Garton, Gen.Mgr.
E-mail: jilda.garton@gtrc.gatech.edu
Scope: Serves as contracting agency for extramurally sponsored projects conducted by Georgia Institute of Technology; also as a corporate depository for patents on discoveries and inventions developed in the course of such research.

59218 ■ South DeKalb Business Incubator
1599-A Memorial Dr.
Atlanta, GA 30317
Ph:(404)329-4500
Fax: (404)378-0768
URL: http://www.sdbusinc.org
Contact: Tonya Weaver, Office Mgr

59219 ■ University of Georgia–Office of Vice President for Research
Boyd Graduate Studies Research Center, Ste. 609
Athens, GA 30602-7411
Ph:(706)542-5969
Co. E-mail: dclee@uga.edu
URL: http://www.ovpr.uga.edu
Contact: Dr. David Lee, VP for Res.
E-mail: dclee@uga.edu

Scope: Administers and coordinates externally sponsored research in all University academic disciplines. **Publications:** Research Reporter Magazine (semiannually).

EDUCATIONAL PROGRAMS

59220 ■ East Georgia College
131 College Cir.
Swainsboro, GA 30401
Ph:(478)289-2017
Fax: (478)289-2038
URL: http://www.ega.edu
Description: Two-year college offering a program in small business management.

59221 ■ Emory University–Center for Lifelong Learning
Center For Longlife Learning Mailstop 1256/001/1AD
Atlanta, GA 30322-1790
Ph:(404)727-6000
Fax: (404)727-6001
Co. E-mail: evening@emory.edu
URL: http://www.cll.emory.edu
Description: Offers courses for owners—or potential owners—of small business enterprises. Also offers courses through the School of Business Administration.

59222 ■ Georgia Highlands College–Floyd Campus
3175 Cedartown Hwy.
Rome, GA 30162-1864
Ph:(706)802-5000
Free: 800-332-2406
Fax: (706)295-6341
URL: http://www.highlands.edu
Description: Two-year college offering a small business management program.

59223 ■ University of West Georgia–Richards College of Business
1601 Maple St.
Carrollton, GA 30118
Ph:(678)839-6467
Fax: (678)839-6774
Co. E-mail: busn@westga.edu
URL: http://www.westga.edu

E-mail: dhovey@westga.edu
Description: Presents business-related courses, seminars, and workshops to persons interested in professional and staff development. Also provides counseling, databases, and case studies to those interested in starting or building a small business.

LEGISLATIVE ASSISTANCE

59224 ■ Georgia House of Representatives
State Capitol
Atlanta, GA 30334
Ph:(404)656-0305
Fax: (404)656-6897
Co. E-mail: skelly@legis.state.ga.us
URL: http://www.legis.state.ga.us

PUBLICATIONS

59225 ■ *Atlanta Magazine*
1330 West Peachtree St., Ste. 450
Atlanta, GA 30309-3214
Ph:(404)872-3100
Fax: (404)870-6230
Co. E-mail: atlmag@atlanta.com
URL: http://atlantamag.atlanta.com

59226 ■ *The Atlanta Small Business Monthly*
6129 Oakbrook Pkwy.
Norcross, GA 30093
Ph:(770)446-5434

Fax: (770)446-3970
Co. E-mail: asbm@bellsouth.net

59227 ■ Starting and Operating a Business in Georgia: A Step-by-Step Guide
PSI Research
300 N. Valley Dr.
Grants Pass, OR 97526
Ph:(503)479-9464
Free: 800-228-2275
Fax: (503)476-1479
Co. E-mail: psi2@magick.net

Ed: Michael D. Jenkins. **Released:** Revised edition, 1992. **Price:** $29.95 (looseleaf binder); $24.95 (paper). **Description:** Part of the Successful Business Library series.

PUBLISHERS

59228 ■ Franklin-Sarrett Publishers L.L.C.
3761 Vineyard Trace NE
Marietta, GA 30062-5227
Ph:(770)578-9410

Free: 800-346-0656
Fax: (770)973-2222
Co. E-mail: info@franklin-sarrett.com
URL: http://www.franklin-sarrett.com
Contact: Kay Borden, President
E-mail: kborden@mindspring.com
Description: Publishes material for small business. Accepts unsolicited manuscripts. Reaches market through reviews and listings. Wholesalers include Baker & Taylor, Amazon.com., Barnes & Noble, and Borders. **Founded:** 1992.

SMALL BUSINESS DEVELOPMENT CENTER LEAD OFFICE

59229 ■ University of Hawaii at Hilo–Hawaii SBDC
308 Kamehameha Ave., Ste. 201
Hilo, HI 96720
Ph:(808)974-7515
Fax: (808)974-7683
URL: http://www.hawaii-sbdc.org
Contact: Darryl Mleynek, State Dir.
E-mail: darrylm@interpac.net

SMALL BUSINESS DEVELOPMENT CENTERS

59230 ■ Business Research Library–Maui Research and Technology Park–SBDC (590 L)
590 Lipoa Pkwy., Ste. 136
Kihei, HI 96753
Ph:(808)875-2400
Fax: (808)875-2406
URL: http://www.hawaii-sbdc.org
Contact: Ruth Corn, Library Dir.
E-mail: ruth.corn@hawaii-sbdc.org

59231 ■ Honolulu SBDC
1041 Nuuanu Ave., Ste. A
Honolulu, HI 96817
Ph:(808)523-6499
Fax: (808)550-0724
URL: http://www.hawaii-sbdc.org
Contact: Caroline Kim, Dir.
E-mail: Caroline.Kim@hawaii-sbdc.org

59232 ■ Kaua'i Community College–Small Business Development Center
3-1901 Kaumuali'i Hwy.
Lihu'e, HI 96766
Ph:(808)246-1748
Fax: (808)241-3229
URL: http://www.hawaii-sbdc.org
Contact: Susan Tai, Actg. Center Dir.
E-mail: susan.tai@hawaii-sbdc.org

59233 ■ Maui Small Business Development Center
590 Lipoa Pkwy.
Kihei, HI 96753
Ph:(808)875-2402
Fax: (808)875-2406
URL: http://www.hawaii-sbdc.org
Contact: David Fisher, Center Dir.
E-mail: david.fisher@hawaii-sbdc.org

59234 ■ University of Hawaii at Hilo–Small Business Development Center
200 W. Kawili St.
Hilo, HI 96720-4091

Ph:(808)974-7515
Fax: (808)974-7683
URL: http://www.hawaii-sbdc.org
Contact: Dr. Darryl Mleynek, State Director
E-mail: darrylm@interpac.net

SMALL BUSINESS ASSISTANCE PROGRAMS

59235 ■ Chamber of Commerce of Hawaii–Small Business Council
1132 Bishop St., Ste. 402
Honolulu, HI 96813
Ph:(808)545-4300
Fax: (808)545-4369
Co. E-mail: info@cochawaii.org
URL: http://www.cochawaii.org
Contact: Jim Tollefson, Pres & CEO
Description: Offers business referrals, financial planning, loan packaging, and business, marketing, and entrepreneurship counseling.

59236 ■ Hawaii Department of Business, Economic Development, and Tourism–Strategic Marketing & Support
PO Box 2359
Honolulu, HI 96804
Ph:(808)586-2423
Fax: (808)587-2790
Co. E-mail: library@dbedt.hawaii.gov
URL: http://www.hawaii.gov/dbedt
Contact: Theodore Liu, Dir
Description: Promotes new enterprise development in Hawaii from the U.S. mainland and international business centers.

59237 ■ University of Hawaii–Pacific Business Center Program
2404 Maile Way A413
Pacific Business Ctr.
College of Business Administration
University of Hawaii
Honolulu, HI 96822
Ph:(808)956-6286
Fax: (808)956-6278
URL: http://www.cba.hawaii.edu
Description: Provides counseling and referral services to businesses. Conduct some research for program clients.

SCORE OFFICES

59238 ■ SCORE of Hawaii
c/o D.J. Halcro, Chm.
300 Ala Moana Blvd., Rm. 2-235
Honolulu, HI 96850
Ph:(808)547-2700
Fax: (808)541-2950
Co. E-mail: bobsouza@hawaiiscore.org
URL: http://www.score.org
Contact: D.J. Halcro, Chm.

Description: Creates opportunities for small business owners and potential business owners to achieve success. Provides business assistance to develop business plans, stimulate business growth and identify problems and potential solutions. Promotes entrepreneur education in Hawaii.

BETTER BUSINESS BUREAUS

59239 ■ Better Business Bureau of Hawaii
1132 Bishop St., Ste. 1507
Honolulu, HI 96813-2813
Ph:(808)536-6956
Free: 877-222-6551
Fax: (808)523-2335
Co. E-mail: info@hawaii.bbb.org
URL: http://www.hawaii.bbb.org
Contact: Bonnie Horibata, Interim CEO

CHAMBERS OF COMMERCE

59240 ■ Australian/American Chamber of Commerce - Hawaii
1000 Bishop St., Penthouse
Honolulu, HI 96813
Ph:(808)526-2242
Fax: (808)534-0475
Co. E-mail: aacc@lava.net
Contact: Richard J. Dahl, Pres.

59241 ■ Chamber of Commerce of Hawaii
1132 Bishop St., Ste. 402
Honolulu, HI 96813
Ph:(808)545-4300
Fax: (808)545-4369
Co. E-mail: info@cochawaii.org
URL: http://www.cochawaii.com
Contact: Jim Tollefson, Pres./CEO

59242 ■ Chinese Chamber of Commerce of Hawaii
42 N King St.
Honolulu, HI 96813
Ph:(808)533-3181
Fax: (808)533-6967
Co. E-mail: info@chinesechamber.com
URL: http://www.ccchi.org
Contact: Edward Pei, Pres.

59243 ■ Filipino Chamber of Commerce
905 Umi St., Rm. 306
Honolulu, HI 96819
Ph:(808)792-8876
Fax: (808)847-6089
Co. E-mail: fcch@aloha.net
Contact: Nelly Liu

59244 ■ Hawaii Island Chamber of Commerce
106 Kamehameha Ave.
Hilo, HI 96720

Ph:(808)935-7178
Fax: (808)961-4435
Co. E-mail: admin@hicc.biz
URL: http://www.hicc.biz
Contact: Mr. Richard Nelson, Pres.

59245 ■ Hawaii Island Portuguese Chamber of Commerce
PO Box 1839
Hilo, HI 96721
Ph:(808)982-7317
Co. E-mail: dmorgado@hawaii.rr.com
URL: http://www.hipcc.org
Contact: Dianne Morgado, Pres.

59246 ■ Hawaii Korean Chamber of Commerce
PO Box 2296
Honolulu, HI 96804
Ph:(808)524-7441
Fax: (808)528-0470
Co. E-mail: hkcc@hkccweb.org
URL: http://www.hkccweb.org
Contact: Rex K.C. Kim, Pres.

59247 ■ Hispanic Chamber of Commerce of Hawaii
PO Box 235263
Honolulu, HI 96823
Ph:(808)545-4344
Fax: (808)521-1496
Co. E-mail: hhcc1992@yahoo.com
Contact: Mrs. Susana G. Ho, Pres.

59248 ■ Honolulu Japanese Chamber of Commerce
2454 S Beretania St., Ste. 201
Honolulu, HI 96826
Ph:(808)949-5531
Fax: (808)949-3020
Co. E-mail: info@honolulujapanesechamber.org
URL: http://www.honolulujapanesechamber.org
Contact: Sharon Narimatsu, Pres.

59249 ■ Honolulu Japanese Junior Chamber of Commerce
2454 S Beretania St., Ste. 201
Honolulu, HI 96826
Ph:(808)949-5531
Fax: (808)949-3020
Co. E-mail: info@honolulujapanesechamber.org
URL: http://www.honolulujapanesechamber.org
Contact: Sharon S. Narimatsu, Pres.

59250 ■ Kailua Chamber of Commerce
600 Kailua Rd., Ste. 103
PO Box 1496
Kailua, HI 96734
Ph:(808)261-2727
Fax: (808)261-2676
Co. E-mail: kcoc@kailuachamber.com
URL: http://www.kailuachamber.com
Contact: David Earles, Pres.

59251 ■ Kauai Chamber of Commerce
PO Box 1969
Lihue, HI 96766
Ph:(808)245-7363
Fax: (808)245-8815
Co. E-mail: info@kauaichamber.org
URL: http://www.kauaichamber.org
Contact: Randall Francisco, Pres.

59252 ■ Kona Kohala Chamber of Commerce
75-5737 Kaukini Hwy., Ste. 208
Kailua-Kona, HI 96740-1735
Ph:(808)329-1758
Fax: (808)329-8564
Co. E-mail: info@kona-kohala.com
URL: http://www.kona-kohala.com

59253 ■ Leeward Oahu Junior Chamber of Commerce
PO Box 273
Pearl City, HI 96782

59254 ■ Maui Chamber of Commerce
313 Ano St.
Kahului, HI 96732
Ph:(808)871-7711
Fax: (808)871-0706
Co. E-mail: rossel@mauichamber.com
URL: http://www.mauichamber.com
Contact: Pamela Tumpap, Pres.

59255 ■ Moloka'i Chamber of Commerce
PO Box 515
Kaunakakai, HI 96748-0515
Ph:(808)553-4482
Fax: (808)553-4482
Co. E-mail: mkkcham@mobettah.net
URL: http://www.molokaichamber.org
Contact: Barbara Haliniak, Pres.

59256 ■ Native Hawaiian Chamber of Commerce
PO Box 597
Honolulu, HI 96809
Ph:(808)531-3744
Fax: (808)732-7059
Co. E-mail: robson@hawaii.rr.com
URL: http://www.nativehawaiian.cc
Contact: Warren Ahsing, Pres.

59257 ■ Small Business Council of the Chamber of Commerce of Hawaii
1132 Bishop St., No. 402
Honolulu, HI 96813
Ph:(808)545-4300
Fax: (808)545-4369
Co. E-mail: sbc@cochawaii.org
Contact: Jim Tollefson, Pres./CEO

MINORITY BUSINESS ASSISTANCE PROGRAMS

59258 ■ Honolulu Minority Business Development Center
2404 Maile Way, D-307
Honolulu, HI 96822
Ph:(808)956-0850
Fax: (808)956-0851
Co. E-mail: info@honolulu-mbdc.org
URL: http://www.honolulu-mbdc.org

FINANCING AND LOAN PROGRAMS

59259 ■ HMS Hawaii Management Partners
Davies Pacific Ctr.
841 Bishop St., Ste. 860
Honolulu, HI 96813
Ph:(808)545-3755
Fax: (808)531-2611
Contact: Richard Grey, General Partner
Preferred Investment Size: $500,000 to $1,500,000.
Investment Types: Seed, start-up, early stage, and joint ventures. **Industry Preferences:** Communications and media, Internet specific, medical and health, other products, and industrial and energy. **Geographic Preferences:** Hawaii and West Coast.

INCUBATORS/RESEARCH AND TECHNOLOGY PARKS

59260 ■ Manoa Innovation Center (MIC)
2800 Woodlawn Dr., Ste. 100
Honolulu, HI 96822
Ph:(808)539-3806
Fax: (808)539-3614
Co. E-mail: htdc@htdc.org
URL: http://www.htdc.org
Contact: Philip Bossert, Exec Dir
Description: The MIC is a high technology small business incubator that forges ties between entrepreneurs and university-oriented research and development.

59261 ■ Maui Research and Technology Park
590 Lipoa Pky., Ste. 103
Kihei, HI 96753
Free: 800—298-6284
Fax: (808)879-0011
Co. E-mail: info@medb.org

E-mail: info@medb.org
Scope: 415-acre research park fostering research activities between the academic sector and Park tenants, particularly in the areas of fiber-optic systems, electronics design and assembly, information systems and telecommunications, biotechnology, and alternate energy. **Publications:** Proceedings of Symposium. **Educational Activities:** Distinguished lecture series; Partners in Planning, a symposium/workshop on the integrated land use/transportation planning process.

59262 ■ Research Corporation of the University of Hawaii
2800 Woodlawn Dr., Ste. 200
Honolulu, HI 96822
Ph:(808)988-8300
Fax: (808)988-8349
Co. E-mail: rcuhed@rcuh.com
URL: http://www.rcuh.com
Contact: Michael P. Hamnett, Exec.Dir.
E-mail: rcuhed@rcuh.com
Scope: Provides administrative support services for university, state, and private sector research. Assist in promoting and implementing scientific, educational, and economic development activities in the state, Pacific Island areas, and other countries. Administers grants, contracts, and bequests. **Services:** Accounting, fiscal, personnel and purchasing support. **Publications:** Annual report (annually). **Educational Activities:** Conferences; Lectures; Seminars.

LEGISLATIVE ASSISTANCE

59263 ■ Hawaii House Labor and Public Employment Committee
State Capitol, House of Reps
415 S. Beretania St. Rm. 438
Honolulu, HI 96813
Ph:(808)586-8485
Fax: (808)586-8489
Co. E-mail: repsaiki@capitol.hawaii.gov
URL: http://www.capitol.hawaii.gov

59264 ■ Hawaii Senate Consumer Protection Committee
State Capitol, Rm. 219
Honolulu, HI 96813
Ph:(808)586-6740
Fax: (808)586-6829
Co. E-mail: senmenor@capitol.hawaii.gov
URL: http://www.capitol.hawaii.gov

59265 ■ Hawaii Senate Water and Land Use Planning Committee
State Capitol Bldg., Rm. 201
415 S. Beretania St.
Honolulu, HI 96813
Ph:(808)586-7335
Fax: (808)586-7339
Co. E-mail: seninouye@capital.hawaii.gov
URL: http://www.capitol.hawaii.gov
Contact: Sen. Lorraine Inoye

TRADE PERIODICALS

59266 ■ *Pacific Magazine with Islands Business*
Pub: PacificBasin Communications
Contact: Giff Johnson, Managing Editor
Released: Monthly. **Price:** $15; $55 other countries airmail; $25 two years. **Description:** Magazine covering business in Hawaii.

PUBLICATIONS

59267 ■ *Business Basics in Hawaii: Secrets of Starting Your Own Business in Our State*
University of Hawaii Press (Editorial Department)
2840 Kolowalu St.
Honolulu, HI 96822
Ph:(808)956-8694
Fax: (808)988-6052
Co. E-mail: uhpbook@hawaii.edu
Ed: Dennis K. Kondo. **Released:** 1988. **Price:** $14.95.

59268 ■ *Hawaii Business*
825 Keeaumoku
PO Box 913
Honolulu, HI 96808
Ph:(808)537-9500
Fax: (808)537-6455

Co. E-mail: hawbus@pixi.com
URL: http://www.hawaiibusinessmagizine.com

59269 ■ *Pacific Business News*
P.O. Box 833
Honolulu, HI 96808-0833
Ph:(808)596-2021
Fax: (808)591-2321
URL: http://www.amcity.com

59270 ■ *Smart Start your Hawaii Business*
PSI Research
300 N. Valley Dr.
Grants Pass, OR 97526
Ph:(503)479-9464
Free: 800-228-2275
Fax: (503)476-1479
Co. E-mail: info@psi-research.com
URL: http://www.psi-research.com

Ed: Michael D. Jenkins and Franklin Forbes. **Released:** Revised edition, 1992. **Price:** $29.95 (looseleaf binder); $24.95 (paper). **Description:** Part of the Successful Business Library series.

59271 ■ *Starting and Operating a Business in Hawaii: A Step-by-Step Guide*
PSI Research
300 N. Valley Dr.
Grants Pass, OR 97526
Ph:(503)479-9464
Free: 800-228-2275
Fax: (503)476-1479
Co. E-mail: psi2@magick.net
Ed: Michael D. Jenkins. **Released:** Revised edition, 1992. **Price:** $29.95 (looseleaf binder); $24.95 (paper). **Description:** Part of the Successful Business Library series.

SMALL BUSINESS DEVELOPMENT CENTER LEAD OFFICE

59272 ■ Boise State University–Small Business Development Center
College of Business
1910 University Dr.
Boise, ID 83725
Ph:(208)426-1640
Free: 800-225-3815
Fax: (208)426-3877
URL: http://www.idahosbdc.org
Contact: James Hogge, State Director
E-mail: jhogge@boisestate.edu

59273 ■ Boise State University (Region III)–Small Business Development Center
1910 University Dr.
Boise, ID 83725
Ph:(208)426-3875
Free: 800-225-3815
Fax: (208)426-3877
Co. E-mail: jhogge@boisestate.edu
URL: http://www.idahosbdc.org
Contact: Jim Hogge, State Dir.
E-mail: rvycital@boisestate.edu

SMALL BUSINESS DEVELOPMENT CENTERS

59274 ■ Boise State University (Region III)–Small Business Development Center–McCall Satellite Office (299 S)
299 S. 3rd St.
PO Box 1901
McCall, ID 83638
Ph:(208)634-7102
Fax: (208)634-2965
Co. E-mail: klabrum@boisestate.edu
URL: http://www.idahosbdc.org
Contact: Allen Quimby, Business Consultant
E-mail: allenquimby@boisestate.edu

59275 ■ College of Southern Idaho (Region IV)–Small Business Development Center
315 Falls Ave.
PO Box 1238
Twin Falls, ID 83303-1238
Ph:(208)733-9554
Fax: (208)733-9316
Co. E-mail: srust@csi.edu
URL: http://www.csi.edu/isbdc
Contact: Bryan Matsuoka, Co-Dir.
E-mail: bmatsuoka@csi.edu

59276 ■ Idaho State University (Region V)–Small Business Development Center
1651 Alvin Ricken Dr.
Pocatello, ID 83201
Ph:(208)232-4921

Free: 800-225-3815
Fax: (208)282-4813
Co. E-mail: dittmike@isu.edu
URL: http://www.idahosbdc.org
Contact: Matthew Creamer, Regional Dir.
E-mail: creamatt@isu.edu

59277 ■ Idaho State University (Region VI)–Small Business Development Center
2300 N. Yellowstone
Idaho Falls, ID 83401
Ph:(208)523-1087
Free: 800-658-3829
Fax: (208)528-7127
Co. E-mail: kellyn@iictr.com
URL: http://www.idahosbdc.org
Contact: David Noack, Regional Dir.
E-mail: noacdavi@isu.edu

59278 ■ Lewis-Clark State College (Region II)–Small Business Development Center
500 8th Ave.
Lewiston, ID 83501
Ph:(208)799-2465
Free: 800-933-5272
Fax: (208)799-2878
Co. E-mail: adanttila@lcsc.edu
Contact: Jill Thomas-Jorgenson, Regional Dir.
E-mail: jjorgenson@lcsc.edu

59279 ■ North Idaho College (Region 1)–Small Business Development Center
525 W. Clearwater Loop
Post Falls, ID 83854
Ph:(208)666-8009
Fax: (208)769-3223
Co. E-mail: leslie_dawson@nic.edu
URL: http://www.nic.edu/wft/default.asp?
Contact: William Jhung, Regional Dir.
E-mail: william_jhung@nic.edu

SMALL BUSINESS ASSISTANCE PROGRAMS

59280 ■ Idaho Department of Commerce and Labor–Department of Economic Development
PO Box 83720-0093
Boise, ID 83720-0093
Ph:(208)334-2470
Free: 800-842-5858
Fax: (208)334-2631
URL: http://www.idoc.state.id.us
Description: Provides information on regulations, permits, and licenses. Sponsors the Idaho Business Network. Offers international trade assistance, and travel and tourism promotion.

SCORE OFFICES

59281 ■ SCORE Eastern Idaho
c/o Charles M. Rice
2300 N Yellowstone, Ste. 119
Idaho Falls, ID 83401
Ph:(208)523-1022
Fax: (208)528-7127
Co. E-mail: score295@iictr.com
URL: http://www.score.org
Contact: Charles M. Rice

59282 ■ SCORE Treasure Valley
380 E Parkcenter Blvd., Ste. 330
Boise, ID 83706
Ph:(208)334-1696
Fax: (208)334-9353
Co. E-mail: info@idahotvscore.org
URL: http://www.idahotvscore.org
Contact: Allen Quimby
Description: Provides professional guidance and information to maximize the success of existing and merging small businesses. Promotes entrepreneur education in Treasure Valley area, Idaho.

BETTER BUSINESS BUREAUS

59283 ■ Better Business Bureau of Eastern Idaho and Western Wyoming
320 Memorial Dr., Ste. 2
Idaho Falls, ID 83402-3615
Ph:(208)523-9754
Fax: (208)227-1603
Co. E-mail: bbb@bbb4u.com
URL: http://www.idahofalls.bbb.org
Contact: Kathryn Jones, Pres.

59284 ■ Better Business Bureau of Southwest Idaho and Eastern Oregon
4355 Emerald, Ste. 290
Boise, ID 83706
Ph:(208)342-4649
Fax: (208)342-5116
Co. E-mail: info@boise.bbb.org
URL: http://www.boise.bbb.org
Contact: Brian Smith, Pres.

CHAMBERS OF COMMERCE

59285 ■ American Falls Chamber of Commerce
239 Idaho St.
American Falls, ID 83211
Ph:(208)226-7214
Co. E-mail: afchamber@dcdi.net
Contact: Paul Sonnen, Pres.

59286 ■ Bayview Chamber of Commerce
PO Box 121
Bayview, ID 83803-0121

Ph:(208)683-2963
Fax: (208)683-6223
Co. E-mail: bviewchmbr@hotmail.com
URL: http://www.bayview-idaho.org
Contact: Doug Landwehr, Pres.

59287 ■ Boise Metro Chamber of Commerce
250 S 5th St., Ste. 800
PO Box 2368
Boise, ID 83701
Ph:(208)472-5200
Fax: (208)472-5201
Co. E-mail: info@boisechamber.org
URL: http://www.boisechamber.org
Contact: Nancy Vannorsdel, Pres./CEO

59288 ■ Buhl Chamber of Commerce
716 U.S. Hwy. 30 E
Buhl, ID 83316-5039
Ph:(208)543-6682
Fax: (208)543-2185
Co. E-mail: linda@buhlchamber.myrf.net
URL: http://www.buhlidaho.us
Contact: Charlotte Frazier, Exec. Dir.

59289 ■ Butte County Chamber of Commerce
PO Box 719
Arco, ID 83213
Ph:(208)527-8977
Fax: (208)527-3036
Co. E-mail: bic@atcnet.net
Contact: Jeff Simpson, Pres.

59290 ■ Caldwell Chamber of Commerce
PO Box 819
Caldwell, ID 83606
Ph:(208)459-7493
Fax: (208)454-1284
Co. E-mail: chamber@ci.caldwell.id.us
URL: http://chamber.cityofcaldwell.com
Contact: Diana Brown, Exec.Dir.

59291 ■ Cascade Chamber of Commerce
PO Box 571
Cascade, ID 83611
Ph:(208)382-3833
Fax: (208)382-3833
Co. E-mail: info@cascadechamber.com
URL: http://www.cascadechamber.com
Contact: Steve Loder, Pres.

59292 ■ Coeur d'Alene Area Chamber of Commerce
PO Box 850
Coeur d'Alene, ID 83816
Ph:(208)664-3194
Free: 877-782-9232
Fax: (208)667-9338
Co. E-mail: info@cdachamber.com
URL: http://www.coeurdalenechamber.com
Contact: Jonathan S. Coe, Pres./Gen.Mgr.

59293 ■ Council Chamber of Commerce
Hwy. 95, 108 Illinois Ave.
Council, ID 83612
Ph:(208)253-6830
Fax: (208)253-4851
Co. E-mail: councilidaho@ctcweb.net
URL: http://www.councilidaho.net
Contact: Linda Rogers, Pres./Events Coor.

59294 ■ Donnelly Area Chamber of Commerce
PO Box 83
Donnelly, ID 83615-0083
Ph:(208)325-3000
Co. E-mail: info@donnellychamber.org
URL: http://www.donnellychamber.org
Contact: Julie Leslie

59295 ■ Fruitland Chamber of Commerce
PO Box 408
Fruitland, ID 83619
Ph:(208)452-4350
Fax: (208)452-5028
Co. E-mail: chamber@fmtc.com

URL: http://www.fruitlandidaho.org
Contact: Kay Ernst, Sec.

59296 ■ Gem County Chamber of Commerce
127 E Main
PO Box 592
Emmett, ID 83617
Ph:(208)365-3485
Fax: (208)365-3220
Co. E-mail: chamber@emmettidaho.com
URL: http://www.emmettidaho.com
Contact: Wisti Rosenthal, Exec.Dir.

59297 ■ Glenns Ferry Chamber of Commerce
PO Box 317
Glenns Ferry, ID 83623
Ph:(208)366-7345
Fax: (208)366-2238
URL: http://www.glennsferryidaho.org
Contact: Jimi Orr, Pres.

59298 ■ Grangeville Chamber of Commerce
PO Box 212
Grangeville, ID 83530
Ph:(208)983-0460
Fax: (208)983-1429
Co. E-mail: chamber@grangevilleidaho.com
URL: http://www.grangevilleidaho.com
Contact: Melinda Fischer, Dir.

59299 ■ Greater Bear Lake Valley Chamber of Commerce
PO Box 265
Montpelier, ID 83254
Ph:(208)847-0067
Free: 800-448-2327
Co. E-mail: chamber@dcdi.net
URL: http://www.bearlakechamber.org
Contact: Beth Tafoya, Exec.Dir.

59300 ■ Greater Blackfoot Area Chamber of Commerce
130 N W Main
PO Box 801
Blackfoot, ID 83221-0801
Ph:(208)785-0510
Fax: (208)785-7974
Co. E-mail: chamber@blackfootchamber.org
URL: http://www.blackfootchamber.org
Contact: Merlin Wright, Exec.Dir.

59301 ■ Greater Bonners Ferry Chamber of Commerce
PO Box X
Bonners Ferry, ID 83805
Ph:(208)267-5922
Fax: (208)267-5922
Co. E-mail: bfchamber@coldreams.com
URL: http://www.bonnersferrychamber.com
Contact: Margaret Mouat, Dir. of Visitor Center

59302 ■ Greater Pocatello Chamber of Commerce
343 W Center
Pocatello, ID 83204
Ph:(208)233-1525
Fax: (208)233-1527
Co. E-mail: aseiler@pocatelloidaho.com
URL: http://www.pocatelloidaho.com
Contact: Mr. Matt Hunter, Exec.Dir.

59303 ■ Greater St. Anthony Chamber of Commerce
420 N Bridge St., Ste. C
St. Anthony, ID 83445
Ph:(208)624-4870
Fax: (208)624-3711
Co. E-mail: sachamber@fretel.com
URL: http://www.stanthonychamber.com
Contact: Linda Bates, Pres.

59304 ■ Greater Sandpoint Chamber of Commerce
PO Box 928
Sandpoint, ID 83864
Ph:(208)263-0887
Free: 800-800-2106

Fax: (208)265-5289
Co. E-mail: info@sandpointchamber.com
URL: http://sandpointchamber.org
Contact: Judy Baird, Exec.Dir.

59305 ■ Greater Weiser Area Chamber of Commerce
309 State St.
Weiser, ID 83672-2530
Ph:(208)414-0452
Co. E-mail: weisercc@ruralnetwork.net
URL: http://www.ruralnetwork.net/~weisercc
Contact: Anne Oglevie, Pres.

59306 ■ Hagerman Valley Chamber of Commerce
PO Box 599
Hagerman, ID 83332-0599
Ph:(208)837-9131
Co. E-mail: angjones@pmt.org
URL: http://www.hagermanchamber.com
Contact: Angie Jones, Pres.

59307 ■ Hailey Chamber of Commerce
PO Box 100
Hailey, ID 83333
Ph:(208)788-3484
Fax: (208)578-1595
Co. E-mail: info@haileyidaho.com
URL: http://www.haileyidaho.com
Contact: Jim Spinelli, Exec.Dir.

59308 ■ Historic Silver Valley Chamber of Commerce
10 Station Ave.
Kellogg, ID 83837
Ph:(208)784-0821
Fax: (208)783-4343
Co. E-mail: info@
historicsilvervalleychamberofcommerce.com
URL: http://www.
historicsilvervalleychamberofcommerce.com
Contact: Doris Miller, Sec./Dir.

59309 ■ Homedale Chamber of Commerce
PO Box 845
Homedale, ID 83628
Ph:(208)337-3161
Fax: (208)337-5304
Contact: Tammy Giedd, Sec.-Treas.

59310 ■ Jerome Chamber of Commerce
1731 S Lincoln Ave., Ste. A
Jerome, ID 83338
Ph:(208)324-2711
Fax: (208)324-6881
Co. E-mail: chamber@visitjerome.com
URL: http://www.visitjerome.com
Contact: Elizabeth Thomas, Exec.Dir.

59311 ■ Kamiah Chamber of Commerce
PO Box 1124
518 Main St.
Kamiah, ID 83536-1124
Ph:(208)935-2290
Fax: (208)935-2290
Co. E-mail: info@kamiahchamber.com
URL: http://www.kamiahchamber.com
Contact: Linda Thomas, Pres.

59312 ■ Kuna Chamber of Commerce
PO Box 123
Kuna, ID 83634
Ph:(208)922-9254
Co. E-mail: admin@kunachamber.com
URL: http://www.kunachamber.com
Contact: Travis Walthall, Pres.

59313 ■ Lava Hot Springs Chamber of Commerce
PO Box 238
Lava Hot Springs, ID 83246
Ph:(208)776-5500
Co. E-mail: findout@lavahotsprings.org
URL: http://www.lavahotsprings.org
Contact: Nathleen Rife, Pres.

59314 ■ Lewiston Chamber of Commerce
111 Main St., Ste. 120
Lewiston, ID 83501
Ph:(208)743-3531
Free: 800-473-3543
Fax: (208)743-2176
Co. E-mail: info@lewistonchamber.org
URL: http://www.lewistonchamber.org
Contact: Keith Havens, Exec. Dir.

59315 ■ McCall Area Chamber of Commerce
102 N 3rd St.
PO Box 350
McCall, ID 83638-0350
Ph:(208)634-7631
Free: 800-260-5130
Fax: (208)634-7752
Co. E-mail: info@mccallchamber.org
URL: http://www.mccall-idchamber.org
Contact: Jim Hinson, Pres.

59316 ■ Meridian Chamber of Commerce
215 E Franklin Rd.
PO Box 7
Meridian, ID 83680-0007
Ph:(208)888-2817
Fax: (208)888-2682
Co. E-mail: info@meridianchamber.org
URL: http://www.meridianchamber.org
Contact: Teri Sackman, Exec.Dir.

59317 ■ Mini-Cassia Chamber of Commerce
1177 7th St.
PO Box 640
Heyburn, ID 83336
Ph:(208)679-4793
Fax: (208)679-4794
Co. E-mail: visitorinfo@pmt.org
URL: http://www.minicassiachamber.org
Contact: Matthew D. Flygare, Exec. Dir.

59318 ■ Moscow Chamber of Commerce
411 S Main St.
PO Box 8936
Moscow, ID 83843-0180
Ph:(208)882-1800
Free: 800-380-1801
Fax: (208)882-6186
Co. E-mail: info@moscowchamber.com
URL: http://www.moscowchamber.com
Contact: Paul Kimmell, Exec.Dir.

59319 ■ Mountain Home Chamber of Commerce
205 N 3rd St. E
Mountain Home, ID 83647
Ph:(208)587-4334
Fax: (208)587-0042
Co. E-mail: chamber@mountain-home.org
URL: http://www.mountain-home.org/chamber
Contact: Debbie Shoemaker, Exec.Dir.

59320 ■ Nampa Chamber of Commerce
312 13th Ave. S
Nampa, ID 83651
Ph:(208)466-4641
Free: 877-20-NAMPA
Fax: (208)466-4677
Co. E-mail: info@nampa.com
URL: http://www.nampa.com
Contact: Georgia Gunstream, Pres./CEO

59321 ■ Post Falls Chamber of Commerce
PO Box 908
Post Falls, ID 83877
Ph:(208)773-5016
Free: 800-292-2553
Fax: (208)773-3843
Co. E-mail: info@postfallschamber.com
URL: http://www.postfallschamber.com
Contact: Ms. Angela Alexander, Pres./CEO

59322 ■ Preston Chamber of Commerce
49 N State, Ste. A
Preston, ID 83263
Ph:(208)852-2703
Co. E-mail: pacc@dcdi.net

URL: http://www.prestonidaho.org
Contact: Penny Christensen, Exec.Dir.

59323 ■ Priest Lake Chamber of Commerce
PO Box 174
Coolin, ID 83821
Ph:(208)443-3191
Free: 888-774-3785
Fax: (208)443-4061
Co. E-mail: plcc@povn.com
URL: http://www.priestlake.org
Contact: Teri Hill, Pres.

59324 ■ Priest River Chamber of Commerce
PO Box 929
Priest River, ID 83856
Ph:(208)448-2721
Co. E-mail: prchamber@povn.com
URL: http://www.priestriver.org
Contact: Linda Kingery, Pres.

59325 ■ Rexburg Chamber of Commerce
420 W 4th S
Cotton Tree Conference Ctr.
Rexburg, ID 83440
Ph:(208)356-5700
Free: 888-INF-O880
Fax: (208)356-5799
Co. E-mail: info@rexcc.com
URL: http://www.rexcc.com
Contact: Donna Benfield, Exec. Dir.

59326 ■ St. Maries Chamber of Commerce
PO Box 162
St. Maries, ID 83861
Ph:(208)245-3563
Co. E-mail: manager@stmarieschamber.org
URL: http://www.stmarieschamber.org
Contact: Lorrie Yearout, Office Mgr.

59327 ■ Salmon River Chamber of Commerce
PO Box 289
Riggins, ID 83549
Ph:(208)628-3778
Co. E-mail: cfriend@ctcweb.net
URL: http://www.rigginsidaho.com
Contact: Dawn Shepherd, Pres.

59328 ■ Salmon Valley Chamber of Commerce
200 Main St., Ste. 1
Salmon, ID 83467
Ph:(208)756-2100
Free: 800-727-2540
Co. E-mail: info@salmonchamber.com
URL: http://www.salmonchamber.com
Contact: Karen Sholes, Administrator

59329 ■ Shelley Chamber of Commerce
101 S Emerson Ave. A
Shelley, ID 83274
Ph:(208)357-3390
Contact: Kevin Donyes, Pres.

59330 ■ Snake River Territory Convention and Visitors Bureau
630 W Broadway
PO Box 50498
Idaho Falls, ID 83405-0498
Ph:(208)523-1010
Free: (866)365-6943
Fax: (208)523-2255
Co. E-mail: info@visitidahofalls.com
Contact: Robb Chiles, CEO

59331 ■ Soda Springs Chamber of Commerce
PO Box 697
9 W 2nd S - City Hall
Soda Springs, ID 83276
Ph:(208)547-4964
Fax: (208)547-2601
Co. E-mail: sodacoc@sodachamber.com
URL: http://www.sodachamber.com
Contact: Bob Ward, Pres.

59332 ■ Stanley - Sawtooth Chamber of Commerce
PO Box 8
Stanley, ID 83278-0008
Ph:(208)774-3411
Free: 800-878-7950
Co. E-mail: info@stanleycc.org
URL: http://www.stanleycc.org
Contact: Greg Edson, Exec.Dir.

59333 ■ Sun Valley-Ketchum Chamber and Visitors Bureau
PO Box 2420
Sun Valley, ID 83353
Ph:(208)725-2111
Free: (866)305-0408
Co. E-mail: chamberinfo@visitsunvalley.com
URL: http://www.visitsunvalley.com
Contact: Carol Waller, Exec.Dir.

59334 ■ Teton Valley Chamber of Commerce
PO Box 250
Driggs, ID 83422
Ph:(208)354-2500
Fax: (208)354-2517
Co. E-mail: tvcc@tetonvalleychamber.com
URL: http://www.tetonvalleychamber.com
Contact: C. Reid Rogers, Pres.

59335 ■ Twin Falls Area Chamber of Commerce
858 Blue Lakes Blvd. N
Twin Falls, ID 83301
Ph:(208)733-3974
Free: (866)TWIN-FALLS
Fax: (208)733-9216
Co. E-mail: info@twinfallschamber.com
URL: http://www.twinfallschamber.com
Contact: Shawn Barigar, Pres./CEO

59336 ■ Wallace Chamber of Commerce
10 River St., Exit 61
Wallace, ID 83873
Ph:(208)753-7151
Free: 800-434-4204
Fax: (208)753-7151
Co. E-mail: director@wallaceidahochamber.com
URL: http://www.wallaceidahochamber.com
Contact: Colleen Pettis, Dir.

FINANCING AND LOAN PROGRAMS

59337 ■ Akers Capital LLC
223 N. 6th St., Ste. 310
Boise, ID 83702
Ph:(208)345-3456
Fax: (208)345-3427
URL: http://www.akerscapital.com
Contact: Roger Akers, Managing Partner
Preferred Investment Size: $500,000 to $3,000,000.
Investment Policies: Early, first, and second stage.
Industry Preferences: Communications, software, and Internet specific. **Geographic Preferences:** Northern California and Northwest.

59338 ■ Sun Valley Ventures (Ketchum)
160 2nd St.
Ketchum, ID 83340
Ph:(208)726-5005
Fax: (208)726-5094
Contact: Daniel Styles
Preferred Investment Size: $5,000,000 minimum.
Investment Types: Second stage, leveraged buyout, control-block purchases, and special situation. **Industry Preferences:** Computer software, Internet specific, semiconductors and other electronics, medical and health, consumer related, industrial and energy, financial services, business service, and manufacturing.
Geographic Preferences: U.S. and Canada.

PROCUREMENT ASSISTANCE PROGRAMS

59339 ■ Idaho Procurement Technical Assistance Center–Idaho Department of Commerce
PO Box 83720
Boise, ID 83720-0093
Ph:(208)334-2470
Fax: (208)334-2631
URL: http://www.clidaho.gov
Contact: Pat Receptionist, Receptionist

INCUBATORS/RESEARCH AND TECHNOLOGY PARKS

59340 ■ Bonner Business Center (BBC)
804 Airport Way
Sandpoint, ID 83864
Ph:(208)263-4073
Fax: (208)263-4609
Co. E-mail: pride@netw.com
URL: http://www.sandpoint.org/bbc/
Contact: Wally Schmidt, Mgr
Description: A small business incubator assisting the development of new firms in northern Idaho. The BBC is also equipped with a fully licensed shared-use food production facility.

59341 ■ College of Southern Idaho–Business Incubator
315 Falls Ave
PO Box 1238
Twin Falls, ID 83303-1238
Ph:(208)733-9554
Fax: (208)733-9316
URL: http://www.csi.edu
Contact: Cindy Bond Ph.D, Dir
Description: Using the resources of the College of Southern Idaho, this small business incubator offers emerging firms affordable office space, business consulting, and a variety of other services.

59342 ■ East Central Idaho Planning Development Association–Upper Snake River Valley Incubator
310 N 2nd E
Rexburg, ID 83440
Ph:(208)356-4524
Fax: (208)356-4544
URL: http://www.ecipda.org
Contact: Ted Hendricks, Mgr

59343 ■ Idaho Innovation Center, Inc.
2300 N Yellowstone Hwy.
Idaho Falls, ID 83401
Ph:(208)523-1026
Fax: (208)528-7127
URL: http://www.iictr.com
Contact: Jeff Krantz, Exec Dir
Description: A small business incubator.

59344 ■ Idaho State University Research Park
1651 Alvin Ricken Dr.
Pocatello, ID 83201
Ph:(208)282-3600
Fax: (208)282-5960
Co. E-mail: blicphil@isu.edu
Contact: Philip Blick, Mgr.
E-mail: blicphil@isu.edu
Scope: Facilitates the interaction of University research community with Park tenants and other professional organizations, particularly in the areas of health professions, biological and physical sciences, pharmacy, nuclear engineering, hazardous waste management, and state of the art decision support systems. Collaborates on technology transfer programs with the Idaho National Engineering Laboratory. **Services:** Technical assistance, to early state companies. **Publications:** An Environment for Innovation.

59345 ■ North Central Idaho Business Technology Incubator
121 W Sweet Ave.
Moscow, ID 83843
Ph:(208)885-3800
Fax: (208)885-3803
Co. E-mail: edc@moscow.com
Contact: Barbara Crouch, Dir
Description: A small business incubator offering affordable space for emerging technology-based firms. Space can be configured to suit the needs of tenants.

59346 ■ Panhandle Area Council–Business Center for Innovation and Development
11100 N Airport Dr.
Hayden, ID 83835
Ph:(208)772-0584
Fax: (208)772-6196
URL: http://www.pacni.org
Contact: Jeff Deffenbaugh, Exec Dir
Description: A small business incubator that assists entrepreneurs in the business start-up process and gives aid to new businesses to help ensure their survival.

59347 ■ University of Idaho–Idaho Research Foundation
Morrill Hall, 414
PO Box 443003
Moscow, ID 83844-3003
Ph:(208)885-4550
Fax: (208)885-4551
Co. E-mail: irf@uidaho.edu
URL: http://www.irf.uro.uidaho.edu
Contact: Gene A. Merrell PhD, Dir.
E-mail: irf@uidaho.edu
Scope: Technology transfer/commercialization agent for the University of Idaho.

59348 ■ University of Idaho–University Research Office
PO Box 443010
Moscow, ID 83844-3010
Ph:(208)885-6651
Fax: (208)885-6198
Co. E-mail: info@uidaho.edu
URL: http://www.uro.uidaho.edu/
Contact: Dr. Charles R. Hatch, VP
E-mail: info@uidaho.edu
Scope: Coordinates research in various fields at the University, including agriculture, anthropology, education, chemical, civil, electrical, mechanical, transportation and general engineering, forestry, geology, humanities, law, life sciences, physical sciences, social sciences, water resources, materials, aquaculture, microelectronics, metallurgy, mining, computer science, wildlife and wilderness. **Publications:** Idaho Research. **Educational Activities:** Grant seeking workshops; K-12 teacher/student research experiences.

EDUCATIONAL PROGRAMS

59349 ■ BYU Idaho
525 S Center St.
Rexburg, ID 83460-0800
Ph:(208)496-2411
Fax: (208)356-1185
Co. E-mail: infodesk@byui.edu
URL: http://www.byui.edu
Description: General studies associates degrees.

59350 ■ College of Southern Idaho–School of Vo-Tech Education
PO Box 1238
Twin Falls, ID 83303
Ph:(208)732-6621
Free: 800-680-0274
Fax: (208)736-3015
Co. E-mail: info@csi.edu
URL: http://www.csi.edu
Description: Vocation-technical school offering customized training; industry-specific upgrade training; independent business and agribusiness management training; entry/re-entry training; and retraining for displaced workers.

59351 ■ Eastern Idaho Technical College
1600 South 25th East
Idaho Falls, ID 83404
Ph:(208)524-3000
Free: 800-662-0261
Fax: (208)524-3007
URL: http://www.eitc.edu
Description: Vocation-technical school offering customized training; industry-specific upgrade training; independent business and agribusiness management training; entry/re-entry training; and retraining for displaced workers.

59352 ■ Idaho State University–College of Technology
Campus Box 8380
Pocatello, ID 83209
Ph:(208)282-2622
Fax: (208)282-5195
Co. E-mail: ctech@isu.edu
URL: http://www.isu.edu/ctech
Description: Vocation-technical school offering customized training; industry-specific upgrade training; independent business and agribusiness management training; entry/re-entry training; and retraining for displaced workers.

59353 ■ Lewis-Clark State College–School of Technology
500 8th Ave.
Lewiston, ID 83501
Ph:(208)792-5272
Free: 800-933-5272
Fax: (208)792-2816
URL: http://www.lcsc.edu
Description: Vocation-technical school offering customized training; industry-specific upgrade training; independent business and agribusiness management training; entry/re-entry training; and retraining for displaced workers.

59354 ■ North Idaho College–Professional -Technical Education
1000 W Garden Ave.
Coeur D'Alene, ID 83814
Ph:(208)769-3300
Free: 877-404-4536
Fax: (208)769-3459
URL: http://www.nic.edu
Description: Vocation-technical school offering customized training; industry-specific upgrade training; independent business and agribusiness management training; entry/re-entry training; and retraining for displaced workers.

LEGISLATIVE ASSISTANCE

59355 ■ Idaho Department of Commerce
700 W State St.
PO Box 83720
Boise, ID 83720-0093
Ph:(208)334-2470
Free: 800-842-5858
Fax: (208)334-2631
URL: http://cl.idaho.gov

PUBLICATIONS

59356 ■ *The Idaho Business Review*
PO Box 8866
Boise, ID 83707
Ph:(208)336-3768
Fax: (208)336-5534

59357 ■ *North Idaho Business Journal*
201 N., Second St.
Coeur D'Alene, ID 83814
Ph:(208)664-8176
Fax: (208)664-0212
Co. E-mail: editor@cbapress.com

59358 ■ Starting and Operating a Business in Idaho: A Step-by-Step Guide
PSI Research
300 N. Valley Dr.
Grants Pass, OR 97526

Ph:(503)479-9464
Free: 800-228-2275
Fax: (503)476-1479
Co. E-mail: psi2@magick.net
Ed: Michael D. Jenkins. **Released:** Revised edition, 1992. **Price:** $29.95 (looseleaf binder); $24.95

(paper). **Description:** Part of the Successful Business Library series.

SMALL BUSINESS DEVELOPMENT CENTER LEAD OFFICE

59359 ■ Department of Commerce and Economic Opportunity–Illinois SBDC
620 East Adams, S-4
Springfield, IL 62701-1696
Ph:(217)524-5700
Fax: (217)524-0171
URL: http://www.commerce.state.il.us/
doingbusiness/First_Stop/SBDCServices.htm
Contact: Mark Petrilli, State Dir.
E-mail: mark.petrill@illinois.gov

59360 ■ Illinois Department of Commerce and Community Affairs–Small Business Development Center
620 E. Adams St., 3rd Fl.
Springfield, IL 62701-1696
Ph:(217)524-5700
Fax: (217)524-0171
Co. E-mail: mpetrill@commerce.state.il.us
URL: http://www.commerce.state.il.us/
doingbusiness/First_Stop/SBDCServices.htm
Contact: Mark Petrilli, State Director

SMALL BUSINESS DEVELOPMENT CENTERS

59361 ■ Asian American Alliance–SBDC
2169B S. China Pl.
Chicago, IL 60616
Ph:(312)225-9320
Fax: (312)225-9340
Co. E-mail: info@asianamericanalliance.com
URL: http://www.asianamericanalliance.com
Contact: George Mui, Dir.

59362 ■ Back of the Yards Neighborhood Council–Small Business Development Center
1751 W. 47th St.
Chicago, IL 60609-3889
Ph:(773)523-4419
Fax: (773)254-3525
Co. E-mail: sbdc@bync.org
Contact: Joseph Montgomery, Dir.

59363 ■ Black Hawk College–Small Business Development Center
4703 16th St., Ste. G
Moline, IL 61265-7066
Ph:(309)764-2213
Fax: (309)797-9344
URL: http://www.bhc.edu/BIC/sbdc/index.htm
Contact: Donna Scalf, Dir.
E-mail: scalfd@bhcl.bhc.edu

59364 ■ Bradley University–Small Business Development Center
141 Jobst Hall
1501 W. Bradley Ave.
Peoria, IL 61625-0001

Ph:(309)677-2992
Fax: (309)677-3386
Co. E-mail: sbdc@bradley.edu
URL: http://www.bradley.edu/turnercenter/about_us/
centers/sbdc.html
Contact: Ken Klotz, Dir.

59365 ■ College of DuPage–Small Business Development Center
425 Fawell Blvd.
Glen Ellyn, IL 60137-6599
Ph:(630)942-2771
Fax: (630)942-3789
URL: http://www.cod.edu/BPI/BPI_SBDC.htm
Contact: David Gay, Dir.
E-mail: gaydav@cdnet.cod.edu

59366 ■ College of Lake County–Small Business Development Center
19351 W. Washington St.
Grayslake, IL 60030-1198
Ph:(847)543-2033
Fax: (847)223-9371
Co. E-mail: clcsbdc@clcillinois.edu
URL: http://www.clc.cc.il.us/dept/cee/sbd/index.htm
Contact: Alese Campbell, Dir.

59367 ■ Danville Area Community College–Small Business Development Center
28 W. North St.
Danville, IL 61832-5729
Ph:(217)442-7232
Fax: (217)442-1897
Co. E-mail: sbdc@dacc.cc.il.us
URL: http://www.dacc.cc.il.us/sbdc
Contact: Ed Adrain, Dir.

59368 ■ Eighteenth Street Development Corp.–Small Business Development Center
1843 S. Carpenter
Chicago, IL 60608-3347
Ph:(312)733-2287
Fax: (312)733-8242
Co. E-mail: esdc1839@aol.com
Contact: John Chavez-Pederson, Dir.

59369 ■ Elgin Community College–Small Business Development Center
1700 Spartan Dr.
Elgin, IL 60123-7193
Ph:(847)214-7488
Fax: (847)931-3911
URL: http://www.elgin.edu
Contact: Kriss Knowles, Dir.
E-mail: kknowles@elgin.edu

59370 ■ Evanston Business and Technology Innovation Center–Small Business Development Center
820 Davis St., Ste. 137
Evanston, IL 60201-3670
Ph:(847)866-1817
Fax: (847)866-1808
URL: http://www.sbdc-evanston.org
Contact: Victoria Montes, Dir.
E-mail: v.gheorge@sbdc-evanston.org

59371 ■ Governors State University–Small Business Development Center
College of Business, Rm. 3300
University Park, IL 60466-0975
Ph:(708)534-4928
Fax: (708)534-1646
URL: http://www.centerpointgsu.com
Contact: Hilary Burkinshaw, Dir.
E-mail: h-burkinshaw@govst.edu

59372 ■ Greater North Pulaski Development Corp.–Small Business Development Center
6600 W. Armitage
Chicago, IL 60607
Ph:(773)637-2768
Co. E-mail: gnpdcsbdc@sbcglobal.net
URL: http://www.gnpdc.org/sbdc.html
Contact: Tom Laures, Dir.

59373 ■ Illinois Eastern Community College–Small Business Development Center
702 High St.
Olney, IL 62450
Ph:(618)395-3011
Fax: (618)395-1922
URL: http://www.ieccsbdc.com/
Contact: Barney Brumfiel, Dir.
E-mail: brumfielb@iecc.edu

59374 ■ Illinois Valley Community College–Small Business Development Center
815 N. Orlando Smith Ave., Bldg. 11
Oglesby, IL 61348-9692
Ph:(815)224-0212
Fax: (815)223-1780
URL: http://www.ivcc.edu/sbdc/
Contact: Bev Malooley, Dir.
E-mail: bev_malooley@ivcc.edu

59375 ■ Industrial Council of Nearwest Chicago–Small Business Development Center
2010 W. Fulton, Ste. 280
Chicago, IL 60612
Ph:(312)433-2373
Fax: (312)421-1871
Co. E-mail: sbdc@industrialcouncil.com
URL: http://www.industrialcouncil.com
Contact: Bryan Stubbs, Dir.

59376 ■ John A. Logan College–Small Business Development Center
700 Logan College Rd.
Carterville, IL 62918
Ph:(618)985-2828
Free: 800-851-4720
Co. E-mail: logan@jalc.edu
Contact: Chris Barr, Dir.
E-mail: chrisbarr@jalc.edu

59377 ■ Joliet Junior College–Small Business Development Center
214 N. Ottawa St., Rm. 400
Joliet, IL 60432-4077
Ph:(815)280-1400
Fax: (815)280-1292

Co. E-mail: sbdc@jjc.edu
URL: http://www.jjciet.org/sbdc.asp
Contact: Bob Hansen, Dir.

59378 ■ Kankakee Community College–Small Business Development Center
River Rd., Box 888
Kankakee, IL 60901-7878
Ph:(815)933-0376
Fax: (815)933-0217
URL: http://www.kcc.edu/biz/empsolutions/sbdc/
index.asp
Contact: Ken Crite, Dir.
E-mail: kcrite@kcc.edu

59379 ■ Kaskaskia College–Small Business Development Center
27210 College Rd.
Centralia, IL 62801
Ph:(618)545-3000
Free: 800-642-0859
Co. E-mail: kcsbdc@kaskaskia.edu
URL: http://www.kaskaskia.edu
Contact: Nancy Michael, Dir.
E-mail: nmichael@kaskaskia.edu

59380 ■ Latin American Chamber of Commerce–Small Business Development Center
3512 W. Fullerton St.
Chicago, IL 60647-2418
Ph:(773)252-5211
Fax: (773)252-7065
Co. E-mail: sbdc@
latinamericanchamberofcommerce.com
URL: http://www.latinamericanchamberofcommerce.
com
Contact: Andres Cerritos, Dir.

59381 ■ Lincoln Land Community College–Small Business Development Center
Greater Springfield Chamber of Commerce
3 S. Old State Capitol Plaza
Springfield, IL 62701
Ph:(217)789-1017
Fax: (217)522-3512
Co. E-mail: sbdc@llcc.edu
URL: http://www.llcc.cc.il.us/sbdc/
Contact: Kevin Lust, Dir.

59382 ■ McHenry County College–Small Business Development Center
8900 U.S. Hwy. 14
Crystal Lake, IL 60012-2761
Ph:(815)455-6098
Fax: (815)455-9319
Co. E-mail: sbdc@mchenry.edu
URL: http://www.ccedtraining.machinery.edu/sbdc.
asp
Contact: Catherine Jones, Dir.

59383 ■ Moraine Valley Community College–Small Business Development Center
10900 S. 88th Ave.
Palos Hills, IL 60465-0937
Ph:(708)974-5468
Fax: (708)974-0078
URL: http://www.morainevalley.edu/SBDC/default.
htm
Contact: Wesley Christensen, Dir.
E-mail: christensen@morainevalley.edu

59384 ■ North Business and Industrial Council (NORBIC)–SBDC
5353 W. Armstrong Ave.
Chicago, IL 60646-6509
Ph:(773)594-9292
Fax: (773)594-9416
URL: http://www.norbic.org/
Contact: Colette Buscemi, Dir.
E-mail: cbuscemi@norbic.org

59385 ■ Rend Lake College–Small Business Development Center
327 Potomac Blvd., Ste. A
Mt. Vernon, IL 62864
Ph:(618)242-5813

Fax: (618)242-8220
URL: http://www.rlc.edu
Contact: Curt Mowrer, Dir.
E-mail: mowrer@rlc.edu

59386 ■ Rock Valley College–Small Business Development Center
Technology Center, Eiger Lab
605 Fulton, Rm. E-109
Rockford, IL 61103
Ph:(815)921-2081
Fax: (815)921-2089
URL: http://www.rockvalleycollege.edu/show.
cfm?durki=294
Contact: Louis Saldarriaga, Dir.
E-mail: l.saldarriaga@rvc.cc.il.us

59387 ■ Sauk Valley Community College–Small Business Development Center
173 Illinois, Rte. 2
Dixon, IL 61021-9188
Ph:(815)288-5511
Fax: (815)288-5958
URL: http://www.svcc.cc.il.us
Contact: Michelle Miller, Dir.
E-mail: millerm@svcc.edu

59388 ■ Shawnee Community College–Small Business Development Center
8364 Shawnee College Rd.
Ullin, IL 62992-2206
Ph:(618)634-3371
Fax: (618)634-2347
Co. E-mail: sccsbdc@shawneecc.edu
URL: http://www.shawneecc.edu/communit/sbdc.asp
Contact: Don Denny, Dir.

59389 ■ Southeastern Illinois College–Small Business Development Center
303 S. Commercial
Harrisburg, IL 62946-2125
Ph:(618)252-5001
Fax: (618)252-0210
URL: http://www.sic.edu
Contact: Lori Cox, Dir.
E-mail: lori.cox@sic.edu

59390 ■ Southern Illinois University at Carbondale–Small Business Development Center
Dunn-Richmond Economic Development Center
150 E. Pleasant Hill Rd.
Carbondale, IL 62901-4300
Ph:(618)536-2424
Fax: (618)453-5040
Co. E-mail: sbdc@siu.edu
URL: http://www.siuc.edu/~sbdc
Contact: Robyn Laur Russell, Dir.

59391 ■ Southern Illinois University at Edwardsville–Small Business Development Center
Alumni Hall 2126
Campus Box 1107
Edwardsville, IL 62026
Ph:(618)650-2929
Fax: (618)650-2647
URL: http://www.siue.edu/UNIVERSITYPARK/
tenants.htm
Contact: Michelle Kosteck, Dir.
E-mail: mkostec@iue.edu

59392 ■ Southern Illinois University at St. Louis
Bldg. D, Rm. 1017
601 James R. Thompson Blvd.
East St. Louis, IL 62201
Ph:(618)482-8330
Fax: (618)482-8341
URL: http://www.siue.edu/BUSINESS/sbdc/
Contact: Theresa Ebeler, Dir.
E-mail: tebeler@siue.edu

59393 ■ University of Illinois Extension at Decatur–SBDC
Building 11, Ste. 1105
2525 E. Federal Dr.
Decatur, IL 62526-2184

Ph:(217)875-4004
Fax: (217)875-4334
URL: http://web.extension.uiuc.edu
Contact: Al aluchett@uiuc.edu, Dir.

59394 ■ Waubonsee Community College (Aurora Campus)–Small Business Development Center
5 E. Galena Blvd.
Aurora, IL 60506-4178
Ph:(630)906-4143
Fax: (630)892-4668
URL: http://www.wcc.il.us/sbdc
Contact: Harriet Parker, Dir.
E-mail: hparker@waubonsee.edu

59395 ■ Western Illinois University–Small Business Development Center
510 N. Pearl St., Ste. 1400
Macomb, IL 61455
Ph:(309)836-2640
Fax: (309)837-4688
Co. E-mail: SB-Center@wiu.edu
URL: http://www.wiusbdc.org
Contact: Dan Voorhis, Dir.

59396 ■ Women's Business Development Center–Small Business Development Center
8 S. Michigan, Ste. 400
Chicago, IL 60603-3302
Ph:(312)853-3477
Fax: (312)853-0145
URL: http://www.wbdc.org
Contact: Mary Ann Angle, Dir.
E-mail: mangle@wbdc.org

SMALL BUSINESS ASSISTANCE PROGRAMS

59397 ■ Illinois Department of Commerce and Community Affairs–Illinois Enterprise Zone Program
620 E Adams St.
Springfield, IL 62701
Ph:(217)524-0166
Free: 800-252-2923
Fax: (217)524-4145
Co. E-mail: thenders@commerce.state.il.us
URL: http://www.commerce.state.il.us
Description: Provides various tax credits, exemptions, and deductions as an incentive to locate a business in one of 59 enterprise zones targeted for economic development throughout the state.

59398 ■ Illinois Department of Commerce and Community Affairs–Small Business Office
620 E Adams St.
Springfield, IL 62701
Ph:(217)524-5856
Free: 800-252-3998
Fax: (217)524-0171
URL: http://www.commerce.state.il.us
Description: Provides management, technical, and financial assistance through its Advocacy, Program Evaluation, Business Development, and Business Finance and Energy Assistance Division.

59399 ■ Illinois Department of Commerce and Economic Opportunity–Small Business Division
100 W Randolph St., Ste. 3-400
Chicago, IL 60601
Ph:(312)814-1346
Fax: (312)814-5247
URL: http://www.commerce.state.il.us
Contact: Jack Lavin, Dir.
Description: Intervenes in the utility rate-setting process and in disputes between small businesses and utility companies. Assists in financing energy conservation measures.

SCORE OFFICES

59400 ■ SCORE Central Illinois
402 N Hershey Rd.
Bloomington, IL 61704
Ph:(309)664-0549
Fax: (309)663-8270
Co. E-mail: webmaster@central-illinois-score.org
URL: http://www.central-illinois-score.org
Contact: John Robinson, Chm.
Description: Provides free consulting services to both start-up and existing small businesses in Central Illinois service area.

59401 ■ SCORE Chicago
500 W Madison St., Ste. 1250
Chicago, IL 60661-2511
Ph:(312)353-7724
Fax: (312)886-4879
Co. E-mail: scorechi@sbcglobal.net
URL: http://www.chicagoscore.org
Description: Works to strengthen the formation, growth and success of small businesses nationwide.

59402 ■ SCORE Decatur
Millikin University
1184 W Main St.
Decatur, IL 62522
Ph:(217)424-6296
Fax: (217)424-3523
Co. E-mail: score@decaturscore.org
URL: http://www.decaturscore.org
Contact: Gail Weinrich, District Dir.
Description: Works to strengthen the formation, growth and success of small businesses nationwide.

59403 ■ SCORE Fox Valley
1444 N Farnsworth Ave., Rm. 504
Aurora, IL 60505
Ph:(630)692-1162
Fax: (630)852-3127
Co. E-mail: mckaydonald@cs.com
URL: http://www.scorefoxvalley.org
Contact: Don McKay, Chm.
Description: Strives for the formation, growth and success of small businesses. Provides professional guidance and information to maximize the success of existing and emerging small businesses. Promotes entrepreneur education in Fox Valley area, Illinois.

59404 ■ SCORE Northern Illinois
c/o Marion Wilke, Chm.
515 N Court St.
Rockford, IL 61103-6807
Ph:(815)962-0122
Fax: (815)962-0806
Co. E-mail: marwid@juno.com
URL: http://www.northernillinoisscore.org
Contact: Ms. Marion Wilke, Chm.
Description: Counsels small businesses on start-up, writing a business plan, addressing problems with cash flow, inventory control, and other business-related issues.

59405 ■ SCORE Peoria
c/o Peoria Chamber of Commerce
124 SW Adams, Ste. 300
Peoria, IL 61602
Ph:(309)676-0755
Fax: (309)676-7534
Co. E-mail: score@score.h-p.org
Description: Strives for the formation, growth and success of small businesses. Provides professional guidance and information to maximize the success of existing and emerging small businesses. Promotes entrepreneur education in Peoria area, Illinois.

59406 ■ SCORE Quad Cities
622 19th St.
Moline, IL 61265
Ph:(309)797-0082
Fax: (309)757-5435
Co. E-mail: info@quadcitiesscore.org
URL: http://www.qconline.com/business/score
Contact: Richard Weeks, Chm.
Description: Provides professional guidance and information to maximize the success of existing and

emerging small businesses. Develops business plans and evaluate financial projections. Promotes entrepreneur education in Moline, IL.

59407 ■ SCORE Quincy Tri-State
c/o Quincy Area Chamber of Commerce
300 Civic Center Plz., Ste. 245
Quincy, IL 62301
Ph:(217)222-8093
Fax: (217)222-3033
Co. E-mail: score@adams.net
URL: http://www.score-tristate.org
Contact: Ralph Mortimore, Chm.
Description: Provides counseling to persons wanting to go into business as well as those already in the business. Sponsors seminars and workshops.

59408 ■ SCORE Southern Illinois
150 E Pleasant Hill Rd.
Carbondale, IL 62901
Ph:(618)453-6654
Fax: (618)453-5040
Co. E-mail: siuscore@siu.edu
URL: http://silscore.org
Description: Provides professional guidance and information to maximize the success of existing and emerging small businesses. Promotes entrepreneur education in Southern Illinois.

59409 ■ SCORE Springfield
3330 Ginger Creek Dr., Ste. B, S
Springfield, IL 62711
Ph:(217)793-5020
Fax: (217)793-5027
Co. E-mail: score571@aol.com
URL: http://www.scorespi.org

59410 ■ SCORE SW Illinois
c/o Ned Wuellner, Chm.
5800 Godfrey Rd.
Alden Hall
Godfrey, IL 62035-2466
Ph:(618)467-2280
Fax: (618)466-8289
Co. E-mail: score@lc.edu
Contact: Mr. Ned H. Wuellner, Chapter Chm.

BETTER BUSINESS BUREAUS

59411 ■ Better Business Bureau of Central Illinois
112 Harrison
Peoria, IL 61602
Ph:(309)688-3741
Fax: (309)681-7290
Co. E-mail: bbb@heart.net
URL: http://www.peoria.bbb.org
Contact: Bonnie Bakin, CEO

59412 ■ Better Business Bureau of Chicago and Northern Illinois
330 N Wabash Ave., Ste. 2006
Chicago, IL 60611
Ph:(312)832-0500
Fax: (312)832-9985
Co. E-mail: info@chicago.bbb.org
URL: http://www.chicago.bbb.org
Contact: James E. Baumhart, Pres./CEO

CHAMBERS OF COMMERCE

59413 ■ Abingdon Chamber of Commerce
902 W Jackson St.
Abingdon, IL 61410-1276
Ph:(309)462-3234
Co. E-mail: palmerh1@gallatinriver.net
URL: http://www.abingdon.net
Contact: Hollis Palmer, Treas.

59414 ■ Addison Chamber of Commerce and Industry
777 Army Trail Rd., Ste. D
Addison, IL 60101
Ph:(630)543-4300
Fax: (630)543-4355
Co. E-mail: addisonchamber@sbcglobal.net
URL: http://www.addisonaic.org
Contact: Bernadette Hanrahan, Exec.Dir.

59415 ■ Albany Park Chamber of Commerce
4745 N Kedzie Ave.
Chicago, IL 60625
Ph:(773)478-0202
Fax: (773)478-0282
Co. E-mail: mmcdaniel@northrivercommission.com
URL: http://www.albanyparkchamber.org
Contact: Melissa McDaniel, Exec.Dir.

59416 ■ Aledo Area Chamber of Commerce
PO Box 261
Aledo, IL 61231
Ph:(309)582-5373
Fax: (309)582-8822
Contact: Peggy Smith, Sec.

59417 ■ Algonquin - Lake in the Hills Chamber of Commerce
106 S Main St.
PO Box 7283
Algonquin, IL 60102
Ph:(847)658-5300
Fax: (847)658-6546
Co. E-mail: info@algonquin-lith-chamber.com
URL: http://www.algonquin-lith-chamber.com
Contact: Sandy Oslance, Exec.Dir.

59418 ■ Alsip Chamber of Commerce and Economic Development
12159 S Pulaski Rd.
Alsip, IL 60803
Ph:(708)597-2668
Free: 800-INA-LSIP
Fax: (708)597-5962
Co. E-mail: info@alsipevents.com
URL: http://www.alsipevents.com
Contact: Mary Schmidt, Exec.Dir.

59419 ■ Altamont Chamber of Commerce
202 N 2nd St.
Altamont, IL 62411
Ph:(618)483-5714
Co. E-mail: chamber@altamontil.net
URL: http://www.altamontil.net
Contact: Butch Roedl, Pres.

59420 ■ Amboy Area Chamber of Commerce
PO Box 163
Amboy, IL 61310
Ph:(815)857-3814
Contact: Julie Kessel Jr., Pres.

59421 ■ Antioch Chamber of Commerce and Industry
882 Main St.
Antioch, IL 60002
Ph:(847)395-2233
Fax: (847)395-8954
Co. E-mail: info@antiochchamber.org
URL: http://www.antiochchamber.org
Contact: Barbara Porch, Exec. Dir.

59422 ■ Arcola Chamber of Commerce
PO Box 274
Arcola, IL 61910
Ph:(217)268-4530
Free: 800-336-5456
Co. E-mail: arcolachamber@consolidated.net
URL: http://www.arcola-il.org
Contact: Susan Foster, Exec. Dir.

59423 ■ Arlington Heights Chamber of Commerce
311 S Arlington Heights Rd., Ste. 20
Arlington Heights, IL 60005
Ph:(847)253-1703
Fax: (847)253-9133

Co. E-mail: info@arlingtonhtschamber.com
URL: http://www.arlingtonhtschamber.com
Contact: Jon S. Ridler, Exec.Dir.

59424 ■ Arthur Association of Commerce
106 E Progress St.
Arthur, IL 61911
Ph:(217)543-2242
Free: 800-722-6474
Fax: (217)543-2004
Co. E-mail: tourismarthur@consolidated.net
URL: http://www.illinoisamishcountry.com
Contact: Jim Jurgens, Pres.

59425 ■ ATHENA International
70 E Lake St., Ste. 1220
Chicago, IL 60601-5939
Ph:(312)580-0111
Free: 800-548-8247
Fax: (312)580-0110
Co. E-mail: athena@athenainternational.org
URL: http://www.athenafoundation.org
Contact: Dorothy Huisman, Exec. Dir.

59426 ■ Barrington Area Chamber of Commerce
325 N Hough St.
Barrington, IL 60010-3026
Ph:(847)381-2525
Fax: (847)381-2540
Co. E-mail: email@barringtonchamber.com
URL: http://www.barringtonchamber.com
Contact: Janet Meyer, Pres.

59427 ■ Bartlett Chamber of Commerce
138 S Oak Ave.
Bartlett, IL 60103
Ph:(630)830-0324
Fax: (630)830-9724
Co. E-mail: info@bartlettchamber.com
URL: http://www.bartlettchamber.com
Contact: Diane Hubberts, Exec.Dir.

59428 ■ Batavia Chamber of Commerce
100 N Island Ave.
Batavia, IL 60510-1931
Ph:(630)879-7134
Fax: (630)879-7215
Co. E-mail: chamber@cityofbatavia.net
URL: http://www.bataviachamber.org
Contact: Mr. Roger Breisch, Exec.Dir.

59429 ■ Beardstown Chamber of Commerce
121 S State St.
Beardstown, IL 62618
Ph:(217)323-3271
Fax: (217)323-3271
Co. E-mail: info@beardstownil.org
URL: http://www.beardstownil.org

59430 ■ Beecher Chamber of Commerce
PO Box 292
Beecher, IL 60401
Ph:(708)946-6803
Co. E-mail: bchamber@villageofbeecher.org
URL: http://www.villageofbeecher.org/chamber
Contact: Chuck Hoehn, Pres.

59431 ■ Bellwood Chamber of Commerce and Industry
PO Box 86
Bellwood, IL 60104
Ph:(708)547-5030
Fax: (708)547-5030
Co. E-mail: slthompson73@yahoo.com
URL: http://www.bellwoodchamber.org
Contact: Vera Douglas, Pres.

59432 ■ Belmont-Central Chamber of Commerce
3250 N Central Ave., 2nd Fl.
Chicago, IL 60634
Ph:(773)202-9923
Co. E-mail: belmontcentralcc@aol.com
URL: http://www.belmontcentral.org
Contact: Larry Lynch, Pres.

59433 ■ Belvidere Area Chamber of Commerce
200 S State St.
Belvidere, IL 61008
Ph:(815)544-4357
Fax: (815)547-7654
Co. E-mail: tlassandro@belviderechamber.com
URL: http://www.belviderechamber.com
Contact: Thomas Lassandro, Exec.Dir.

59434 ■ Bensenville Chamber of Commerce
PO Box 905
Bensenville, IL 60106-0315
Ph:(630)860-3800
Fax: (630)860-3814
Co. E-mail: info@bensenvillechamber.org
URL: http://www.bensenvillechamber.org
Contact: Rich Johnson, Dir.

59435 ■ Benton-West City Area Chamber of Commerce
211 N Main St.
PO Box 574
Benton, IL 62812
Ph:(618)438-2121
Free: (866)536-8423
Fax: (618)438-8011
Co. E-mail: chamber@bentonwestcity.com
URL: http://www.bentonwestcity.com
Contact: Gloria Atchison, Exec.Sec.

59436 ■ Bloomingdale Chamber of Commerce
109 W Franklin St.
Bloomingdale, IL 60108
Ph:(630)980-9082
Fax: (630)980-9092
Co. E-mail: bloomcham@sbcglobal.net
URL: http://www.BloomingdaleChamber.com
Contact: Mrs. Richa Wennerholm, Admin.

59437 ■ Blue Island Area Chamber of Commerce and Industry
2434 Vermont St.
Blue Island, IL 60406
Ph:(708)388-1000
Fax: (708)388-1062
Co. E-mail: blueislandchamber@sbcglobal.net
URL: http://www.bichamber.org
Contact: Eda Schrimple, Exec.Dir.

59438 ■ Bolingbrook Area Chamber of Commerce
375 W Briarcliff Rd.
Bolingbrook, IL 60440
Ph:(630)226-8420
Fax: (630)759-9937
Co. E-mail: info@bolingbrookchamber.org
URL: http://www.bolingbrookchamber.org
Contact: Peg Kenyon, Exec.Dir.

59439 ■ Bradley-Bourbonnais Chamber of Commerce
1690 Newtowne Dr.
Bourbonnais, IL 60914
Ph:(815)932-2222
Fax: (815)932-3294
Co. E-mail: bbcc@bbchamber.com
URL: http://bbchamber.com
Contact: Ed Munday, Pres./CEO

59440 ■ Breese Chamber of Commerce
PO Box 132
Breese, IL 62230-0132
Ph:(618)526-7731
URL: http://www.breese.org/Chamber.htm

59441 ■ Bridgeview Chamber of Commerce
7300 W 87th St.
Bridgeview, IL 60455
Ph:(708)598-1700
Fax: (708)598-1709
Co. E-mail: bvchamber@aol.com
URL: http://www.bridgeviewchamber.com
Contact: Roseann Bautista, Exec.Dir.

59442 ■ Brookfield Chamber of Commerce
3724 Grand Blvd.
Brookfield, IL 60513
Ph:(708)485-1434
Co. E-mail: matthew.joseph@wamu.net
URL: http://www.brookfieldchamberofcommerce.org
Contact: Mr. Matthew Joseph, Pres.

59443 ■ Buffalo Grove Area Chamber of Commerce
50 1/2 Raupp Blvd.
PO Box 7124
Buffalo Grove, IL 60089
Ph:(847)541-7799
Fax: (847)541-7819
Co. E-mail: info@bgacc.org
URL: http://www.bgacc.org
Contact: Lynne Schneider, Exec.Dir.

59444 ■ Burbank Chamber of Commerce
5501 W 79th St.
Burbank, IL 60459
Ph:(708)425-4668
Fax: (708)424-9492
Contact: Judy M. Balestri, Exec. Sec.

59445 ■ Bushnell Chamber of Commerce
PO Box 111
Bushnell, IL 61422
Ph:(309)772-2171
Fax: (309)772-3616
Co. E-mail: chamber@bushnellchamber.com
URL: http://www.bushnellchamber.com
Contact: Don Swartzbaugh, Pres.

59446 ■ Byron Area Chamber of Commerce
110 N Union
PO Box 405
Byron, IL 61010-0405
Ph:(815)234-5500
Fax: (815)234-7114
Co. E-mail: byronchamber@byronil.net
URL: http://byronchamber.com
Contact: Caryn Huber, Exec.Dir.

59447 ■ Cahokia Area Chamber of Commerce
905 Falling Springs Rd.
Cahokia, IL 62206
Ph:(618)332-1900
Fax: (618)337-1597
Co. E-mail: business@cahokiachamber.com
URL: http://www.cahokiachamber.com
Contact: Wendi Sellers, Pres.

59448 ■ Cairo Chamber of Commerce
220 8th St.
Cairo, IL 62914-2135
Ph:(618)734-2737
Co. E-mail: cairochamber@earthlink.net
Contact: Ms. Mickey Blackburn, Sec.

59449 ■ Calumet City Chamber of Commerce
1243 Hirsch Ave.
Calumet City, IL 60409
Ph:(708)891-5888
Fax: (708)891-9451
Co. E-mail: cccham2000@aol.com
Contact: Frank Orsini, Pres.

59450 ■ Canton Area Chamber of Commerce
45 E Side Sq., Ste. 303
Canton, IL 61520
Ph:(309)647-2677
Fax: (309)647-2712
Co. E-mail: cantonareacc@sbcglobal.net
URL: http://www.cantonillinois.org
Contact: Rod Ahitow, Exec.Dir.

59451 ■ Carbondale Chamber of Commerce
PO Box 877
Carbondale, IL 62903
Ph:(618)549-2146
Fax: (618)529-5063
Co. E-mail: info@carbondalechamber.com
URL: http://www.carbondalechamber.com
Contact: Mary Mechler, Pres.

59452 ■ Carlinville Community Chamber of Commerce
126 E Main St.
Carlinville, IL 62626
Ph:(217)854-2141
Fax: (217)854-8548
Co. E-mail: info@carlinvillechamber.com
URL: http://www.carlinvillechamber.com

59453 ■ Carlyle Lake Chamber of Commerce
PO Box 246
Carlyle, IL 62231
Ph:(618)594-7666
Co. E-mail: resort@onemain.com
URL: http://www.carlyle.il.us
Contact: Mark Sugars, Pres.

59454 ■ Carmi Chamber of Commerce
225 E Main St.
Carmi, IL 62821
Ph:(618)382-7606
Co. E-mail: ccc@cityofcarmi.com
URL: http://www.cityofcarmi.com
Contact: Paula Pierson, Exec.Dir.

59455 ■ Carol Stream Chamber of Commerce
150 S Gary Ave.
Carol Stream, IL 60188-2079
Ph:(630)665-3325
Fax: (630)665-6965
Co. E-mail: info@carolstreamchamber.com
URL: http://www.carolstreamchamber.com
Contact: Ms. Luanne Triolo, Exec.Dir.

59456 ■ Carrollton Chamber of Commerce
PO Box 69
Carrollton, IL 62016
Ph:(217)942-3187
Co. E-mail: fieldsteve@hotmail.com
Contact: Steve Field, Pres.

59457 ■ Carterville Chamber of Commerce
PO Box 262
Carterville, IL 62918-0262
Ph:(618)985-6942
Fax: (618)985-4205
Co. E-mail: chamber@midamer.net
URL: http://www.cartervillechamber.com
Contact: Tracey Glenn, Exec.Dir.

59458 ■ Carthage Area Chamber of Commerce
PO Box 247
Carthage, IL 62321
Ph:(217)357-3024
Fax: (217)357-3024
Co. E-mail: chamber@carthage-il.com
URL: http://www.carthage-il.com
Contact: Cyndi Huffman, Sec.-Treas.

59459 ■ Cary/Grove Area Chamber of Commerce
27 E Main St.
PO Box 302
Cary, IL 60013
Ph:(847)639-2800
Fax: (847)639-2168
Co. E-mail: info@carygrovechamber.com
URL: http://www.carygrovechamber.com
Contact: Jack Ehlers, Pres.

59460 ■ Caseyville Chamber of Commerce
PO Box 470
Caseyville, IL 62232
Ph:(618)345-2452
Fax: (618)345-0188
Contact: Jim Eisele, Pres.

59461 ■ Chamber of Commerce for Decatur and Macon County
243 S Water St., Ste. 100
Decatur, IL 62523
Ph:(217)422-2200
Fax: (217)422-4576
Co. E-mail: chamber@decaturchamber.com
URL: http://www.decaturchamber.com
Contact: Randy Prince, Pres.

59462 ■ Champaign County Chamber of Commerce
1817 S Neil St., Ste. 201
Champaign, IL 61820-7269
Ph:(217)359-1791
Fax: (217)359-1809
Co. E-mail: info@champaigncounty.org
URL: http://www.ccchamber.org
Contact: Laura E. Weis IOM, Exec.Dir.

59463 ■ Charleston Area Chamber of Commerce
501 Jackson Ave.
PO Box 77
Charleston, IL 61920-0077
Ph:(217)345-7041
Fax: (217)345-7042
Co. E-mail: caccinfo@charlestonchamber.com
URL: http://www.charlestonchamber.com
Contact: Cindy Titus, Exec.Dir.

59464 ■ Chester Chamber of Commerce
PO Box 585
Chester, IL 62233
Ph:(618)826-2721
Co. E-mail: chesterc@egyptian.net
URL: http://www.chesterill.com
Contact: Linda Sympson, Exec.Dir.

59465 ■ Chicago Area Gay and Lesbian Chamber of Commerce
1210 W Rosedale
Chicago, IL 60660
Ph:(773)303-0167
Fax: (773)303-0168
Co. E-mail: info@glchamber.org
URL: http://www.glchamber.org
Contact: Christee L. Snell, Exec.Dir.

59466 ■ Chicago Chinatown Chamber of Commerce
2169B S China Pl.
Chicago, IL 60616
Ph:(312)326-5320
Fax: (312)326-5668
Co. E-mail: info@chicagochinatown.org
URL: http://www.chicagochinatown.org
Contact: Jimmy D. Lee, Exec.Dir.

59467 ■ Chicago Ridge - Worth Business Association
PO Box 356
Worth, IL 60482
Ph:(708)923-2050
Contact: Jack Murray, Pres.

59468 ■ Chicagoland Chamber of Commerce
One IBM Plz.
330 N Wabash, Ste. 2800
Chicago, IL 60611-3605
Ph:(312)494-6700
Fax: (312)494-0196
Co. E-mail: staff@chicagolandchamber.org
URL: http://www.chicagolandchamber.org
Contact: Robert Wislow, Pres./CEO

59469 ■ Chillicothe Chamber of Commerce
1028 N 2nd St.
Chillicothe, IL 61523
Ph:(309)274-4556
Fax: (309)274-3303
Co. E-mail: info@chillicothechamber.com
URL: http://www.chillicothechamber.com
Contact: Sarah Williamson, Pres.

59470 ■ Cicero Chamber of Commerce and Industry
5801 W Cermak Rd., 2nd Fl.
Cicero, IL 60804
Ph:(708)863-6000
Fax: (708)863-8981
URL: http://www.cicerochamber.org
Contact: Mary Esther Rodriguez, Exec. Dir.

59471 ■ Clinton Area Chamber of Commerce
100 S Center St., Ste. 101
Clinton, IL 61727-1945

Ph:(217)935-3364
Free: (866)4DE-WITT
Fax: (217)935-0064
Co. E-mail: info@clintonilchamber.com
URL: http://www.clintonilchamber.com
Contact: Steve Vandiver, Exec.Dir.

59472 ■ Collinsville Chamber of Commerce
221 W Main St.
Collinsville, IL 62234
Ph:(618)344-2884
Fax: (618)344-7499
Co. E-mail: info@discovercollinsville.com
URL: http://www.discovercollinsville.com

59473 ■ Cook County Chamber of Commerce
One Westbrook Corporate Center, Ste. 300
Westchester, IL 60154-5701
Ph:(708)531-1117
Fax: (630)968-9038
Co. E-mail: gmurph@xnet.com
Contact: Gerald L. Murphy, Pres.

59474 ■ Cosmopolitan Chamber of Commerce
560 W Lake St., 5th Fl.
Chicago, IL 60661
Ph:(312)786-0212
Fax: (312)786-9079
Co. E-mail: hildafontaine@cchamber.org
URL: http://www.cchamber.org
Contact: Gloria Bell, Exec.Dir.

59475 ■ Crete Area Chamber of Commerce
PO Box 263
Crete, IL 60417-0263
Ph:(708)672-9216
Fax: (708)672-7640
Co. E-mail: cretechamber@sbcglobal.net
URL: http://www.cretechamber.com
Contact: Patricia C. Herbert, Exec.Dir.

59476 ■ Crystal Lake Chamber of Commerce
427 Virginia St.
Crystal Lake, IL 60014-5959
Ph:(815)459-1300
Fax: (815)459-0243
Co. E-mail: info@clchamber.com
URL: http://www.clchamber.com
Contact: Bob Blazier, Pres.

59477 ■ Darien Chamber of Commerce
1702 Plainfield Rd.
Darien, IL 60561-5080
Ph:(630)968-0004
Fax: (630)968-2474
Co. E-mail: info@darienchamber.com
URL: http://www.darienchamber.com
Contact: Tom Sailer, Pres.

59478 ■ Deerfield, Bannockburn, Riverwoods Chamber of Commerce
601 Deerfield Rd., Ste. 200
Deerfield, IL 60015
Ph:(847)945-4660
Fax: (847)940-0381
Co. E-mail: info@dbrchamber.com
URL: http://www.dbrchamber.com
Contact: Victoria Case, Exec.Dir.

59479 ■ DeKalb Chamber of Commerce
164 E Lincoln Hwy.
DeKalb, IL 60115
Ph:(815)756-6306
Fax: (815)756-5164
Co. E-mail: chamber@dekalb.org
URL: http://www.dekalb.org
Contact: Chuck Siebrasse, Exec.Dir.

59480 ■ Des Plaines Chamber of Commerce and Industry
1401 Oakton St.
Des Plaines, IL 60018
Ph:(847)824-4200
Fax: (847)824-7932
Co. E-mail: info@dpchamber.com
URL: http://www.dpchamber.com

Contact: Barbara Ryan, Exec.Dir.

59481 ■ Dixon Area Chamber of Commerce and Industry
101 W Second St., Ste. 301
Dixon, IL 61021
Ph:(815)284-3361
Fax: (815)284-3675
Co. E-mail: dchamber@essex1.com
URL: http://www.dixonillinoischamber.com
Contact: John R. Thompson, CEO/Pres.

59482 ■ Dolton Chamber of Commerce
PO Box 823
Dolton, IL 60419-0823
Ph:(708)841-4810
Fax: (708)841-4833
Contact: Larceeda Jefferson, Admin. Asst.

59483 ■ Downers Grove Area Chamber of Commerce and Industry
1015 Curtiss St.
Downers Grove, IL 60515
Ph:(630)968-4050
Fax: (630)968-8368
Co. E-mail: chamber@downersgrove.org
URL: http://www.downersgrove.org
Contact: Barbara L. Wysocki, Pres./CEO

59484 ■ Du Quoin Chamber of Commerce
PO Box 57
Du Quoin, IL 62832-0057
Ph:(618)542-9570
Free: 800-455-9570
Co. E-mail: dqchamber@onecliq.net
URL: http://www.duquoin.org
Contact: Joe Davis, Pres.

59485 ■ Dwight Area Chamber of Commerce
119 W Main St.
Dwight, IL 60420
Ph:(815)584-2091
Free: 800-554-6635
Fax: (815)584-2096
Co. E-mail: dwightchamber@fyidwight.net
Contact: Judy Piskule, Admin.

59486 ■ East Peoria Chamber of Commerce and Tourism
111 W Washington St., Ste. 290
East Peoria, IL 61611-2532
Ph:(309)699-6212
Fax: (309)699-6220
Co. E-mail: epcc@epcc.org
URL: http://www.epcc.org
Contact: Charlie Moore, Exec.Dir.

59487 ■ East Side Chamber of Commerce
3658 E 106th St.
Chicago, IL 60617-6611
Ph:(773)721-7948
Fax: (773)721-7446
Co. E-mail: eastsidechamber@aol.com
Contact: Joann Caporale, Exec.Sec.

59488 ■ Edgebrook Chamber of Commerce
6440 N Central Ave.
Chicago, IL 60646
Ph:(773)775-0378
Fax: (773)775-0371
URL: http://www.edgebrookchamber.com
Contact: Barbara A. Copeland, Exec. Dir.

59489 ■ Edwardsville - Glen Carbon Chamber of Commerce
200 University Park Dr., Ste. 260
Edwardsville, IL 62025
Ph:(618)656-7600
Fax: (618)656-7611
Co. E-mail: cforeman@edglenchamber.com
URL: http://www.edglenchamber.com
Contact: Carol Foreman, Exec.Dir.

59490 ■ El Paso Chamber of Commerce
475 W Front St.
El Paso, IL 61738
Ph:(309)527-4005

Fax: (309)527-4717
Co. E-mail: mroberts@hbtbank.com
URL: http://www.elpasoil.org/chamber
Contact: Mindy Roberts, Sec.

59491 ■ Elgin Area Chamber of Commerce
31 S Grove Ave.
PO Box 648
Elgin, IL 60120
Ph:(847)741-5660
Fax: (847)741-5677
Co. E-mail: info@elginchamber.com
URL: http://www.elginchamber.com
Contact: Leo Nelson, Pres.

59492 ■ Elizabeth Chamber of Commerce
PO Box 371
Elizabeth, IL 61028
Ph:(815)858-2221
Fax: (815)858-3881
Co. E-mail: info@elizabeth-il.com
URL: http://www.elizabeth-il.com
Contact: Lyndsay Plath, Pres.

59493 ■ Elmhurst Chamber of Commerce and Industry
113 Adell Pl.
PO Box 752
Elmhurst, IL 60126-0752
Ph:(630)834-6060
Fax: (630)834-6002
Co. E-mail: info@elmhurstchamber.org
URL: http://www.elmhurstchamber.org
Contact: John R. Quigley, Pres.

59494 ■ Evanston Chamber of Commerce
1 Rotary Ctr.
1560 Sherman Ave., Ste. 860
Evanston, IL 60201
Ph:(847)328-1500
Fax: (847)328-1510
Co. E-mail: info@evchamber.com
URL: http://www.evchamber.com
Contact: Jonathan D. Perman, Exec.Dir.

59495 ■ Evergreen Park Chamber of Commerce
3960 W 95th St., 3rd Fl.
Evergreen Park, IL 60805-1905
Ph:(708)423-1118
Fax: (708)423-1859
Co. E-mail: epchamber@sbcglobal.net
URL: http://www.evergreenparkchamber.com
Contact: Timothy J. Clark, Pres.

59496 ■ Fairbury Chamber of Commerce
101 E Locust
PO Box 86
Fairbury, IL 61739
Ph:(815)692-3899
Fax: (815)692-4273
Co. E-mail: fac@fairburyil.com
URL: http://www.fairburyil.org
Contact: Cathi Coppinger, Exec.Sec.

59497 ■ Fairview Heights Chamber of Commerce
10003 Bunkum Rd.
Fairview Heights, IL 62208-1703
Ph:(618)397-3127
Fax: (618)397-5563
Co. E-mail: office@fairviewheightschamber.org
URL: http://www.fairviewheightschamber.org
Contact: Ms. Terri Isenhart, Exec.Dir.

59498 ■ Flora Chamber of Commerce
122 N Main St.
Flora, IL 62839
Ph:(618)662-5646
Fax: (618)662-5646
Co. E-mail: fchamber@bspeedy.com
URL: http://www.florachamber.com
Contact: Belinda Davis, Pres.

59499 ■ Forest Park Chamber of Commerce
7344 W Madison St.
PO Box 617
Forest Park, IL 60130

Ph:(708)366-2543
Fax: (708)366-3373
Co. E-mail: more@forestparkchamber.org
URL: http://www.forestparkchamber.org
Contact: Laurie Kokenes, Exec.Dir.

59500 ■ Fox Lake Area Chamber of Commerce and Industry
PO Box 203
Fox Lake, IL 60020
Ph:(847)587-7474
Fax: (847)587-1725
Co. E-mail: discoverfoxlake@yahoo.com
URL: http://www.discoverfoxlake.com
Contact: Mary Randall, Exec.Sec.

59501 ■ Frankfort Chamber of Commerce
123 Kansas St.
Frankfort, IL 60423
Ph:(815)469-3356
Free: 877-469-3356
Fax: (815)469-4352
Co. E-mail: info@frankfortchamber.com
URL: http://www.frankfortchamber.com
Contact: Lynne Doogan, Exec.Dir.

59502 ■ Franklin Park/Schiller Park Chamber of Commerce
PO Box 186
Franklin Park, IL 60131
Ph:(708)865-9510
Fax: (708)865-9520
Co. E-mail: info@chamberbyohare.org
URL: http://www.chamberbyohare.org
Contact: Patricia Letarte, Pres.

59503 ■ Freeburg Chamber of Commerce
PO Box 179
Freeburg, IL 62243
Ph:(618)539-6075
Contact: Mr. Gregory Nold, Pres.

59504 ■ Freeport Area Chamber of Commerce
27 W Stephenson St.
Freeport, IL 61032
Ph:(815)233-1350
Fax: (815)233-3226
Co. E-mail: kim.grimes@aeroinc.net
URL: http://www.freeportilchamber.com
Contact: Mr. Kim Grimes, Exec.Dir.

59505 ■ Fulton Chamber of Commerce
PO Box 253
Fulton, IL 61252-0253
Ph:(815)589-4545
Co. E-mail: chamber@cityoffulton.us
URL: http://www.cityoffulton.us/chamber.php
Contact: Heather Bennett, Exec.Dir.

59506 ■ Galena Area Chamber of Commerce
101 Bouthillier St.
Galena, IL 61036
Ph:(815)777-9050
Fax: (815)777-8465
Co. E-mail: office@galenachamber.com
URL: http://www.galenachamber.com
Contact: Nancy Lewis, Exec.Dir.

59507 ■ Galesburg Area Chamber of Commerce
471 E Main St.
PO Box 749
Galesburg, IL 61402-0749
Ph:(309)343-1194
Fax: (309)343-1195
Co. E-mail: chamber@galesburg.org
URL: http://www.galesburg.org
Contact: Robert C. Maus, CEO/Pres.

59508 ■ Geneseo Chamber of Commerce
100 W Main
Geneseo, IL 61254-1518
Ph:(309)944-2686
Fax: (309)944-2647
Co. E-mail: geneseo@geneseo.net
Contact: Dawn Tubbs, Exec.Dir.

59509 ■ Geneva Chamber of Commerce
8 S 3rd St.
PO Box 481
Geneva, IL 60134-0481
Ph:(630)232-6060
Free: (866)4-GENEVA
Fax: (630)232-6083
Co. E-mail: chamberinfo@genevachamber.com
URL: http://www.genevachamber.com
Contact: Jean Gaines, Pres.

59510 ■ Genoa Chamber of Commerce
327 W Main St., Upper Level
Genoa, IL 60135
Ph:(815)784-2212
Fax: (815)784-2212
Co. E-mail: genoachamb@tbcnet.com
Contact: Susan J. Drendel, Exec.Dir.

59511 ■ Gibson Area Chamber of Commerce
126 N Sangamon Ave.
Gibson City, IL 60936
Ph:(217)784-5217
Fax: (217)784-4119
Co. E-mail: chamber@gibsoncityillinois.com
URL: http://gibsoncityillinois.com/default.asp
Contact: Pam Bradbury, Sec.-Treas.

59512 ■ Gilman Chamber of Commerce
PO Box 13
Gilman, IL 60938
Ph:(815)265-4818
Contact: Jeff McMillan, Pres.

59513 ■ Girard Chamber of Commerce
PO Box 92
Girard, IL 62640
Ph:(217)627-3441
Fax: (217)627-3528
Co. E-mail: girardchamber@girardilusa.com
URL: http://www.girardilusa.com
Contact: Debra Burnett, Sec.

59514 ■ Glen Ellyn Chamber of Commerce
490 Pennsylvania Ave.
Glen Ellyn, IL 60137
Ph:(630)469-0907
Fax: (630)469-0426
Co. E-mail: kay@glenellynchamber.com
URL: http://www.glenellynchamber.com
Contact: Kay C. Kendall, Exec.Dir.

59515 ■ Glencoe Chamber of Commerce
PO Box 575
Glencoe, IL 60022
Ph:(847)835-3333
Fax: (847)835-9823
Co. E-mail: info@glencoechamber.org
URL: http://www.glencoechamber.org
Contact: Lenna Scott, Exec. Dir.

59516 ■ Glenview Chamber of Commerce
2320 Glenview Rd.
Glenview, IL 60025-2711
Ph:(847)724-0900
Fax: (847)724-0202
Co. E-mail: gcstaff@glenviewchamber.com
URL: http://glenviewchamber.com
Contact: Kathleen Miles, Pres.

59517 ■ GLMV Area Chamber of Commerce
1123 S Milwaukee Ave.
Libertyville, IL 60048
Ph:(847)680-0750
Fax: (847)680-0760
Co. E-mail: info@glmvchamber.org
URL: http://www.glmvchamber.org
Contact: B. Dwight Houchins, Pres.

59518 ■ Grayslake Area Chamber of Commerce
10 S Seymour Ave.
PO Box 167
Grayslake, IL 60030
Ph:(847)223-6888
Fax: (847)223-6895
Co. E-mail: business@grayslakechamber.com

URL: http://www.grayslakechamber.com
Contact: Shirley A. Christian, Exec.Dir.

59519 ■ Grayville Chamber of Commerce
PO Box 117
Grayville, IL 62844
Ph:(618)375-7518
Contact: Steve Hartsock, Pres.

59520 ■ Greater Aurora Chamber of Commerce
43 W Galena Blvd.
Aurora, IL 60506
Ph:(630)897-9214
Fax: (630)897-7002
Co. E-mail: jhenning@aurora-il.org
URL: http://www.aurorachamber.com
Contact: Joseph Henning, Exec.Dir.

59521 ■ Greater Belleville Chamber of Commerce
216 E A St.
Belleville, IL 62221
Ph:(618)233-2015
Fax: (618)233-2077
Co. E-mail: info@bellevillechamber.org
URL: http://www.bellevillechamber.org
Contact: Kathleen Kaiser, Exec. Dir.

59522 ■ Greater Centralia Chamber of Commerce
130 S Locust St.
Centralia, IL 62801
Ph:(618)532-6789
Free: 888-533-2600
Fax: (618)533-7305
Co. E-mail: gccoc@centraliail.com
URL: http://www.centraliail.com
Contact: Bob Kelsheimer, Exec.Dir.

59523 ■ Greater Channahon-Minooka Area Chamber of Commerce
408 Mondamin St.
PO Box 444
Minooka, IL 60447
Ph:(815)521-9999
Fax: (815)521-0903
Co. E-mail: cmchamber@cbcast.com
URL: http://www.cmchamber.org

59524 ■ Greater East St. Louis Chamber of Commerce
327 Missouri Ave., Ste. 602
East St. Louis, IL 62201
Ph:(618)271-2855
Fax: (618)271-4622
Co. E-mail: nrosscsac@yahoo.com
Contact: Norman Ross, Exec.Dir.

59525 ■ Greater Effingham Chamber of Commerce and Industry
PO Box 643
Effingham, IL 62401
Ph:(217)342-4147
Fax: (217)342-4228
Co. E-mail: chamber@effinghamchamber.org
URL: http://www.effinghamchamber.org
Contact: Norma Lansing, Pres.

59526 ■ Greater Fairfield Area Chamber of Commerce
121 E Main St.
Fairfield, IL 62837
Ph:(618)842-6116
Co. E-mail: chamber@wabash.net
URL: http://www.fairfieldillinoischamber.com
Contact: Patsy J. Cooper, Exec.Sec.

59527 ■ Greater Harvard Area Chamber of Commerce
62 N Ayer St., Ste. B
Harvard, IL 60033
Ph:(815)943-4404
Fax: (815)943-4410
Co. E-mail: info@harvcc.net
URL: http://www.harvcc.net
Contact: Pamela Hayes, Exec.Dir.

59528 ■ Greater Lincolnshire Chamber of Commerce
175 Olde Half Day Rd., Ste. 125
Lincolnshire, IL 60069-3061
Ph:(847)793-2409
Fax: (847)793-2405
Co. E-mail: tglcc@aol.com
URL: http://www.lincolnshirechamber.org
Contact: Jane Meloy, Exec. Dir.

59529 ■ Greater Salem Chamber of Commerce
615 W Main St.
Salem, IL 62881
Ph:(618)548-3010
Fax: (618)548-3014
Co. E-mail: visitus@salemilchamber.com
URL: http://www.salemilchamber.com
Contact: Jon Ashby, Pres.

59530 ■ Greater Springfield Chamber of Commerce
3 S Old State Capitol Plaza
Springfield, IL 62701-1593
Ph:(217)525-1173
Fax: (217)525-8768
Co. E-mail: gplummer@gscc.org
URL: http://www.gscc.org
Contact: Gary Plummer, CEO/Pres.

59531 ■ Greenville Chamber of Commerce
PO Box 283
Greenville, IL 62246
Ph:(618)664-9272
Free: 888-862-8201
Co. E-mail: greenville@gcctv.com
URL: http://greenvilleusa.com
Contact: Ms. Julia Jenner, Exec.Dir.

59532 ■ Hamilton County Chamber of Commerce and Economic Development Commission
PO Box 456
McLeansboro, IL 62859
Ph:(618)643-3971
URL: http://www.mcleansboro.com
Contact: Mark Becker

59533 ■ Hampshire Area Chamber of Commerce
PO Box 157
Hampshire, IL 60140
Ph:(847)683-1122
Fax: (847)683-1146
URL: http://www.hampshireillinois.com
Contact: Lynn Klein, Pres.

59534 ■ Havana Area Chamber of Commerce
PO Box 116
Havana, IL 62644
Ph:(309)543-7385
Free: 888-236-8406
Co. E-mail: mcdemo@havanaprint.com
URL: http://www.havanail.net
Contact: Mary Layton, Pres.

59535 ■ Henry Area Chamber of Commerce
514 Front St.
River Park Ctr.
Henry, IL 61537-0211
Ph:(309)364-3261
Fax: (309)364-3261
Co. E-mail: s1939@ocslink.com
URL: http://www.cc.henry.il.us
Contact: Jerry Read, Pres.

59536 ■ Herrin Chamber of Commerce
3 S Park Ave.
Herrin, IL 62948
Ph:(618)942-5163
Co. E-mail: herrincc@herrinillinois.com
URL: http://www.herrinillinois.com
Contact: Sue Douglas, Exec. Dir.

59537 ■ Herscher Chamber of Commerce
PO Box 437
Herscher, IL 60941

Ph:(815)426-2131
URL: http://www.herscher.net
Contact: Tim Feller, Pres.

59538 ■ Highland Chamber of Commerce
907 Main St.
Highland, IL 62249
Ph:(618)654-3721
Fax: (618)654-8966
Co. E-mail: jami@highlandillinois.com
URL: http://www.highlandillinois.com
Contact: Jami Jansen, Exec.Dir.

59539 ■ Highland Park Chamber of Commerce
508 Central Ave., Ste. 206
Highland Park, IL 60035
Ph:(847)432-0284
Fax: (847)432-2802
Co. E-mail: chamber@ehighlandpark.com
URL: http://www.ehighlandpark.com/default2.asp
Contact: Ginny Anzelmo Glasner, Exec.Dir.

59540 ■ Hills Chamber of Commerce
PO Box 1164
Bridgeview, IL 60455-0164
Ph:(708)364-7739
Contact: Arlene Kasper, Pres.

59541 ■ Hillsboro Area Chamber of Commerce
PO Box 6
Hillsboro, IL 62049-0006
Ph:(217)532-3711
Fax: (217)532-5567
Co. E-mail: hillsborochamber@consolidated.net
Contact: Yvonne Purcell, Exec.Sec.

59542 ■ Hinsdale Chamber of Commerce
22 E 1st St.
Hinsdale, IL 60521
Ph:(630)323-3952
Fax: (630)323-3953
Co. E-mail: hinsdalechamber@earthlink.net
URL: http://www.hinsdalechamber.com
Contact: Jim Slonoff, Pres.

59543 ■ Hoffman Estates Chamber of Commerce
2200 W Higgins Rd., Ste. 201
Hoffman Estates, IL 60195-2400
Ph:(847)781-9100
Fax: (847)781-9172
Co. E-mail: info@hechamber.com
URL: http://www.hechamber.com
Contact: Ms. Jill Blodgett, Exec.Dir.

59544 ■ Homewood Area Chamber of Commerce
18300 Dixie Hwy.
Charter One Bank Bldg.
Homewood, IL 60430
Ph:(708)206-3384
Fax: (708)206-3605
Co. E-mail: kyle@homewoodareachamber.com
URL: http://www.homewoodareachamber.com
Contact: Mr. Kyle Storjohann IOM, Administrator

59545 ■ Huntley Area Chamber of Commerce and Industry
PO Box 157
Huntley, IL 60142
Ph:(847)669-0166
Fax: (847)669-0170
Co. E-mail: info@huntleychamber.org
URL: http://www.huntleychamber.org
Contact: Rita Slawek, Exec.Dir.

59546 ■ Hyde Park Chamber of Commerce
5211 S Harper, Ste. D
Chicago, IL 60615
Ph:(773)288-0124
Fax: (773)288-0464
Co. E-mail: hpchamber@juno.com
URL: http://www.hpchamber.com
Contact: Cheryl Heads, Exec.Dir.

59547 ■ Illinois Association of Chamber of Commerce Executives
215 E Adams St.
Springfield, IL 62701
Ph:(217)522-5512
Fax: (217)522-5518
Co. E-mail: info@iacce.org
URL: http://www.iacce.org
Contact: Elizabeth D. Fiala, Pres.

59548 ■ Illinois Quad City Chamber of Commerce
622 19th St.
Moline, IL 61265-2142
Ph:(309)757-5416
Fax: (309)757-5435
Co. E-mail: rbaker@quadcitychamber.com
URL: http://www.quadcitychamber.com
Contact: Rick L. Baker, Pres./CEO

59549 ■ Illinois River Area Chamber of Commerce
135 Washington St.
Marseilles, IL 61341-0326
Ph:(815)795-2323
Fax: (815)795-4546
Co. E-mail: iracc@mtco.com
URL: http://www.
Contact: John F. Henning, Exec.Dir.

59550 ■ Illinois State Chamber of Commerce
311 S Wacker Dr., Ste. 1500
Chicago, IL 60606-6619
Ph:(312)983-7100
Fax: (312)983-7101
Co. E-mail: info@ilchamber.org
URL: http://www.ilchamber.org
Contact: Douglas L. Whitley, Pres./CEO

59551 ■ Illinois Valley Area Chamber of Commerce and Economic Development
300 Bucklin
PO Box 446
La Salle, IL 61301-0446
Ph:(815)223-0227
Fax: (815)223-4827
Co. E-mail: ivaced@ivaced.org
URL: http://www.ivaced.org
Contact: Ms. Barb Koch, Exec. Dir./CEO

59552 ■ Jacksonville Area Chamber of Commerce
155 W Morton
Jacksonville, IL 62650
Ph:(217)245-2174
Fax: (217)245-0661
Co. E-mail: chamber@jacksonvilleareachamber.org
URL: http://www.jacksonvilleareachamber.org
Contact: Ginny Fanning, Pres.

59553 ■ Jasper County Chamber of Commerce
207 1/2 Jourdan St.
Newton, IL 62448
Ph:(618)783-3399
Fax: (618)783-4556
Co. E-mail: jasperchamber@psbnewton.com
URL: http://www.newtonillinois.com
Contact: Beverly Worthey, Exec.Dir.

59554 ■ Jefferson County Chamber of Commerce
200 Potomac Blvd.
Mount Vernon, IL 62864
Ph:(618)242-5725
Fax: (618)242-5130
Co. E-mail: chamber@mvn.net
URL: http://www.southernillinois.com
Contact: Floyd Brookman, Exec.Dir.

59555 ■ Jefferson Park Chamber of Commerce
4849 N Milwaukee Ave., Ste. 305
Chicago, IL 60630-2171
Ph:(773)736-6991
Fax: (773)736-3508
Co. E-mail: carol@jeffersonpark.net
URL: http://www.jeffersonpark.net

Contact: Carol Gawron, Exec.Dir.

59556 ■ Jersey County Business Association
209 N State St.
Jerseyville, IL 62052-1755
Ph:(618)639-5222
Co. E-mail: ann@jcba-il.us
URL: http://www.jerseycounty.org
Contact: Ann Rice, Admin.Asst.

59557 ■ Joliet Region Chamber of Commerce and Industry
63 N Chicago St.
PO Box 752
Joliet, IL 60434-0752
Ph:(815)727-5371
Fax: (815)727-5374
Co. E-mail: info@jolietchamber.com
URL: http://www.jolietchamber.com
Contact: Russ Slinkard, Pres./CEO

59558 ■ Kankakee River Valley Chamber of Commerce
PO Box 905
Kankakee, IL 60901
Ph:(815)933-7721
Fax: (815)933-7675
Co. E-mail: sara.segur@krvcc.org
URL: http://www.kankakee.org
Contact: Sara Segur Barzantny

59559 ■ Kewanee Chamber of Commerce
113 E 2nd St.
Kewanee, IL 61443
Ph:(309)852-2175
Fax: (309)852-2176
Co. E-mail: chamber@kewanee-il.com
URL: http://www.kewanee-il.com
Contact: Mark Mikenas, Exec.VP

59560 ■ Lake County Chamber of Commerce
5221 W Grand Ave.
Gurnee, IL 60031-1818
Ph:(847)249-3800
Fax: (847)249-3892
Co. E-mail: info@lakecountychamber.com
URL: http://www.lakecounty-il.org
Contact: Mr. Steve Robinson, Pres.

59561 ■ Lake Forest - Lake Bluff Chamber of Commerce
695 N Western Ave.
Lake Forest, IL 60045
Ph:(847)234-4282
Co. E-mail: info@lflbchamber.com
URL: http://www.lakeforestonline.com
Contact: Joanna Rolek, Exec.Dir.

59562 ■ Lake View East Chamber of Commerce
3138 N Broadway
Chicago, IL 60657-5316
Ph:(773)348-8608
Fax: (773)348-7409
Co. E-mail: info@lakevieweast.com
URL: http://www.lakevieweast.com
Contact: Maureen Martino, Exec.Dir.

59563 ■ Lake Zurich Area Chamber of Commerce
1st Bank Plz., Ste. 304
Lake Zurich, IL 60047
Ph:(847)438-5572
Fax: (847)438-5574
Co. E-mail: info@lzacc.com
URL: http://www.lzacc.com
Contact: Dale Perrin, Exec.Dir.

59564 ■ Lansing Chamber of Commerce
3404 Lake St.
Lansing, IL 60438
Ph:(708)474-4170
Contact: Joyce Tiltges, Exec. Dir.

59565 ■ Lawrence County Chamber of Commerce
619 12th St.
Lawrenceville, IL 62439

Ph:(618)943-3516
Fax: (618)943-4748
Co. E-mail: lccc@midwest.net
URL: http://www.lawrencecountyillinois.com/
   chamber.html
Contact: Delilah Gray, Exec.Dir.

59566 ■ Lebanon Chamber of Commerce
221 W St. Louis St.
Lebanon, IL 62254
Ph:(618)537-8420
URL: http://www.lebanonil.org/chamber.htm

59567 ■ Lemont Area Chamber of Commerce
101 Main St.
Lemont, IL 60439-3675
Ph:(630)257-5997
Fax: (630)257-3238
Co. E-mail: lacc@core.com
URL: http://www.lemontchamber.com
Contact: Mr. Pat O'Brien, Pres.

59568 ■ Lewistown Chamber of Commerce
119 S Adams
Lewistown, IL 61542
Ph:(309)547-4300
Contact: Anna Raines, Pres.

59569 ■ Limestone Area Chamber of Commerce
PO Box 4043
Bartonville, IL 61607
Ph:(309)697-1031
Co. E-mail: email@limestonechamber.com
URL: http://www.limestonechamber.com
Contact: Alan Getz, Pres.

59570 ■ Lincoln - Logan County Chamber of Commerce
1555 Fifth St.
Lincoln, IL 62656
Ph:(217)735-2385
Fax: (217)735-9205
Co. E-mail: chamber@lincolnillinois.com
URL: http://www.lincolnillinois.com
Contact: Bobbi Abbott, Exec.Dir.

59571 ■ Lincoln Park Chamber of Commerce
2534 N Lincoln Ave., Ste. 301
Chicago, IL 60614-2354
Ph:(773)880-5200
Fax: (773)880-0266
Co. E-mail: info@lincolnparkchamber.com
URL: http://www.lincolnparkchamber.com
Contact: Kim Klausmeier, Pres./CEO

59572 ■ Lincolnwood Chamber of Commerce and Industry
7001 N Lawndale Ave.
Lincolnwood, IL 60712
Ph:(847)679-5760
Fax: (847)679-5790
Co. E-mail: dlass@lincolnwoodchamber.org
URL: http://www.lincolnwoodchamber.org
Contact: Diana Lass, Exec.Dir.

59573 ■ Lindenhurst - Lake Villa Chamber of Commerce
500 Grand Ave.
PO Box 6075
Lindenhurst, IL 60046-6075
Ph:(847)356-8446
Fax: (847)356-8561
Co. E-mail: llvchamber@llvchamber.com
URL: http://www.llvchamber.com
Contact: Connie Meadie, Exec.Dir.

59574 ■ Lisle Chamber of Commerce
4733 Main St.
Lisle, IL 60532
Ph:(630)964-0052
Fax: (630)964-2726
Co. E-mail: info@lislechamber.com
URL: http://www.lislechamber.com
Contact: Tom Althoff, Pres./CEO

59575 ■ Litchfield Chamber of Commerce
311 N Madison
PO Box 334
Litchfield, IL 62056
Ph:(217)324-2533
Fax: (217)324-3559
Co. E-mail: chamber@litchfieldil.com
URL: http://www.litchfieldil.com/chamber
Contact: Charlene Pigg, Exec.VP

59576 ■ Lockport Chamber of Commerce
921 S State St.
Lockport, IL 60441-3435
Ph:(815)838-3357
Fax: (815)838-2653
Co. E-mail: office@lockportchamber.com
URL: http://www.lockportchamber.com
Contact: Ms. Sharon Hannah, Exec. Dir.

59577 ■ Lombard Area Chamber of Commerce and Industry
225 W St. Charles Rd.
Lombard, IL 60148
Ph:(630)627-5040
Fax: (630)627-5519
Co. E-mail: info@lombardchamber.com
URL: http://www.lombardchamber.com
Contact: Tom Ploke, Pres.

59578 ■ Loves Park - Machesney Park Chamber of Commerce
100 Heart Blvd.
Loves Park, IL 61111
Ph:(815)633-3999
Fax: (815)633-4057
Co. E-mail: info@parkschamber.com
URL: http://www.parkschamber.com
Contact: Kurt Cottier, Pres.

59579 ■ Macomb Area Chamber of Commerce & Downtown Development Corporation
214 N. Lafayette St.
PO Box 274
Macomb, IL 61455-0274
Ph:(309)837-4855
Fax: (309)837-4857
Co. E-mail: chamber@macomb.com
Contact: Becky Paulsen, Pres.

59580 ■ Mahomet Chamber of Commerce
PO Box 1031
Mahomet, IL 61853-1031
Ph:(217)586-3165
Co. E-mail: mahchbrcomm@netscape.net
URL: http://www.mahometchamberofcommerce.com
Contact: Jim Fialkowski, Pres.

59581 ■ Manhattan Chamber of Commerce
PO Box 357
Manhattan, IL 60442-0357
Ph:(815)478-3811
Fax: (815)478-7761
Co. E-mail: chamber@manhattan-il.com
URL: http://www.manhattan-il.com
Contact: Jeane Wade, Pres.

59582 ■ Manito Area Chamber of Commerce
PO Box 143
Manito, IL 61546
Ph:(309)968-7200
Contact: Rayeann Meeker, Board Member

59583 ■ Marengo-Union Chamber of Commerce
116 S State St.
Marengo, IL 60152
Ph:(815)568-6680
Fax: (815)568-6879
Co. E-mail: info@marengo-union.com
URL: http://www.marengo-union.com
Contact: Candice W. Delger, Exec.Dir.

59584 ■ Marion Chamber of Commerce
PO Box 307
Marion, IL 62959
Ph:(618)997-6311

Free: 800-699-1760
Fax: (618)997-4665
Co. E-mail: marionchamber@marionillinois.com
URL: http://www.marionillinois.com
Contact: Rose Mary Crear, Exec.Sec.

59585 ■ Marshall Area Chamber of Commerce
708 Archer Ave.
Marshall, IL 62441
Ph:(217)826-2034
Fax: (217)826-2034
Co. E-mail: marshall.chamber@abcs.com
URL: http://www.marshall-il.com
Contact: George Dallmier, Pres.

59586 ■ Martinsville Chamber of Commerce
PO Box 429
Martinsville, IL 62442-0429
Ph:(217)382-4323
Fax: (217)382-4726
Contact: Gary Haignman, Pres.

59587 ■ Matteson Area Chamber of Commerce
600 Holiday Plaza Dr., Ste. 110
PO Box 106
Matteson, IL 60443
Ph:(708)747-6000
Fax: (708)747-6054
URL: http://www.macclink.com
Contact: Georgia C. O'Neill, Pres./CEO

59588 ■ Mattoon Chamber of Commerce
500 Broadway Ave.
Mattoon, IL 61938-3911
Ph:(217)235-5661
Fax: (217)234-6544
Co. E-mail: matchamber@consolidated.net
URL: http://www.mattoonchamber.com
Contact: Mary Wetzel, Exec.Dir.

59589 ■ Maywood Chamber of Commerce
PO Box 172
Maywood, IL 60153
Ph:(708)345-7077
Fax: (708)345-9455
Co. E-mail: info@maywoodchamber.org
Contact: Edwin H. Walker IV, Pres.

59590 ■ McHenry Area Chamber of Commerce
1257 N Green St.
McHenry, IL 60050
Ph:(815)385-4300
Fax: (815)385-9142
Co. E-mail: info@mchenrychamber.com
URL: http://www.mchenrychamber.com
Contact: Kay Rial Bates, Membership Dir.

59591 ■ McLean County Chamber of Commerce
210 S East St.
PO Box 1586
Bloomington, IL 61702-1586
Ph:(309)829-6344
Fax: (309)827-3940
Co. E-mail: info@mcleancochamber.org
URL: http://www.mcleancochamber.org
Contact: Michael Malone, Exec.Dir.

59592 ■ Melrose Park Chamber of Commerce
1718 W Lake St.
Melrose Park, IL 60160-3819
Ph:(708)338-1007
Fax: (708)338-9924
Co. E-mail: info@melroseparkchamber.org
URL: http://www.melroseparkchamber.org
Contact: Mrs. Cathy K. Stenberg, Exec.Dir.

59593 ■ Mendota Area Chamber of Commerce
800 Washington St.
PO Box 620
Mendota, IL 61342-0620
Ph:(815)539-6507
Fax: (815)539-6025

Co. E-mail: mendotachamber@yahoo.com
URL: http://mendotachamber.com
Contact: Valerie Corrigan, Exec.Dir.

59594 ■ Metropolis Area Chamber of Commerce
607 Market St.
PO Box 188
Metropolis, IL 62960-0188
Ph:(618)524-2714
Free: 800-949-5740
Fax: (618)524-4780
Co. E-mail: metrochamber@hcis.net
URL: http://www.metropolischamber.com
Contact: Lindsay Pankey, Sec.

59595 ■ Mokena Chamber of Commerce
19820 S Wolf Rd.
PO Box 67
Mokena, IL 60448-9998
Ph:(708)479-2468
Fax: (708)479-7144
Co. E-mail: joann@mokena.com
URL: http://www.mokena.com
Contact: Jo Ann McGowan, Exec. Dir.

59596 ■ Momence Chamber of Commerce
203 E River
Momence, IL 60954
Ph:(815)472-4620
Fax: (815)472-6453
Co. E-mail: membership@momence.net
URL: http://www.momence.net
Contact: Patrick Dryer, Pres.

59597 ■ Monmouth Area Chamber of Commerce
90 Public Sq.
PO Box 857
Monmouth, IL 61462-0857
Ph:(309)734-3181
Co. E-mail: macc@maplecity.com
URL: http://www.ci.monmouth.il.us/coc
Contact: Angie McElwee, Exec.Dir.

59598 ■ Mont Clare - Elmwood Park Chamber of Commerce
11 Conti Pkwy.
Elmwood Park, IL 60707
Ph:(708)456-8000
Fax: (708)456-8680
Co. E-mail: info@mcepchamber.org
URL: http://www.mcepchamber.org
Contact: Walter Saranecki Jr., Pres.

59599 ■ Monticello Chamber of Commerce
PO Box 313
Monticello, IL 61856-0313
Ph:(217)762-7921
Free: 800-952-3396
Fax: (217)762-2711
Co. E-mail: info@monticellochamber.org
URL: http://www.monticellochamber.org
Contact: Sue Gortner, Exec.Dir.

59600 ■ Morrison Chamber of Commerce
202 E Lincoln Way
Morrison, IL 61270
Ph:(815)772-3757
Fax: (815)772-3757
Co. E-mail: morrcham@essex1.com
URL: http://www.thecity1.com/biz/morrisoncc/index.
php
Contact: Roann Porter, Administrator

59601 ■ Morton Chamber of Commerce
415 W Jefferson
Morton, IL 61550-1817
Ph:(309)263-2491
Free: 888-765-6588
Fax: (309)263-2401
Co. E-mail: pumpkin@mtco.com
URL: http://mortonchamber.org
Contact: Mike Badgerow, Exec.Dir.

59602 ■ Morton Grove Chamber of Commerce and Industry
6101 Capulina Ave., Lower Level
Morton Grove, IL 60053
Ph:(847)965-0330
Fax: (847)965-0349
Co. E-mail: info@mgcci.org
URL: http://www.mgcci.org
Contact: Suzanne Archer, Acting Exec.Dir.

59603 ■ Mount Carroll Chamber of Commerce
PO Box 94
Mount Carroll, IL 61053
Ph:(815)244-2255
URL: http://www.mount-carroll.il.us
Contact: Kathy Cyr, Pres.

59604 ■ Mount Greenwood Chamber of Commerce
3052 W 111th St.
Chicago, IL 60655
Ph:(773)238-6103
Contact: Darlene Larsen, Exec. Dir.

59605 ■ Mount Prospect Chamber of Commerce
107 S Main St.
Mount Prospect, IL 60056
Ph:(847)398-6616
Fax: (847)398-6780
Co. E-mail: jim@mountprospect.com
URL: http://www.mountprospectchamber.org
Contact: James Uszler, Exec.Dir.

59606 ■ Mount Zion Chamber of Commerce
PO Box 84
Mount Zion, IL 62549
Ph:(217)864-2526
Fax: (217)864-6115
Co. E-mail: contact@mtzionchamberofcommerce.
com
Contact: Judy Kaiser, Admin.

59607 ■ Murphysboro Chamber of Commerce
PO Box 606
Murphysboro, IL 62966
Ph:(618)684-6421
Fax: (618)684-2010
Co. E-mail: executive@globaleyes.net
URL: http://www.murphysboro.com/chamber/index.
html
Contact: Robert Wurster MS Ed., Exec.Dir.

59608 ■ Naperville Area Chamber of Commerce
55 S Main St., Ste. 351
Naperville, IL 60540
Ph:(630)355-4141
Fax: (630)355-8335
Co. E-mail: chamber@naperville.net
URL: http://www.naperville.net
Contact: Mike Skarr, Pres./CEO

59609 ■ Nauvoo Chamber of Commerce
PO Box 41
1295 Mulholland St.
Nauvoo, IL 62354
Ph:(217)453-6648
Free: 877-NAUVOO-1
Fax: (217)453-2032
Co. E-mail: chamber@nauvoo.net
URL: http://www.nauvoochamber.org
Contact: David C. Miller, Pres.

59610 ■ New Lenox Chamber of Commerce
PO Box 42
New Lenox, IL 60451-0042
Ph:(815)485-4241
Fax: (815)485-5001
Co. E-mail: bev@newlenoxchamber.com
URL: http://www.newlenoxchamber.com
Contact: Beverly J. Ferris, Exec.Dir.

59611 ■ Niles Chamber of Chamber of Commerce and Industry
8060 Oakton St.
Niles, IL 60714
Ph:(847)268-8180
Fax: (847)268-8186
Co. E-mail: info@nileschamber.org
URL: http://www.nileschamber.org
Contact: Katie DiMaria, Exec.Dir.

59612 ■ Northbrook Chamber of Commerce and Industry
2002 Walters Ave.
Northbrook, IL 60062
Ph:(847)498-5555
Fax: (847)498-5510
Co. E-mail: info@northbrookchamber.com
URL: http://www.northbrookchamber.org
Contact: Tensley Garris, Pres.

59613 ■ Northlake Chamber of Commerce
PO Box 2067
Northlake, IL 60164
Ph:(708)562-3110
Contact: Natalie Bradford, Pres.

59614 ■ Norwood Park Chamber of Commerce and Industry
6097 N NW Hwy.
Chicago, IL 60631
Ph:(773)763-3606
Fax: (773)763-3620
Co. E-mail: info@norwoodpark.org
URL: http://www.norwoodpark.org
Contact: Helen I. Brown, Pres.

59615 ■ Oak Brook Area Association of Commerce and Industry
One Lincoln Ctr., 10th Fl., Ste. 1000
18 W 140 Butterfield Rd.
Oakbrook Terrace, IL 60181
Ph:(630)705-9991
Fax: (630)705-9992
Co. E-mail: ltadams@oakbrookbiz.com
Contact: Laurie Teschner Adams, Pres. & CEO

59616 ■ Oak Forest Chamber of Commerce
15440 S Central Ave.
Oak Forest, IL 60452
Ph:(708)687-4600
Fax: (708)687-7878
Co. E-mail: ofchamber@oakforest.org
URL: http://www.oakforest.org
Contact: Mr. Terence Quinn, Interim Exec.Dir.

59617 ■ Oak Lawn Chamber of Commerce
5314 W 95th St.
Oak Lawn, IL 60453
Ph:(708)424-8300
Fax: (708)229-2236
Co. E-mail: oaklawnchamber@sbcglobal.net
URL: http://www.oaklawnchamber.com
Contact: Jennifer Busk, Exec.Dir.

59618 ■ Oak Park-River Forest Chamber of Commerce
1110 N Blvd.
Oak Park, IL 60301
Ph:(708)848-8151
Fax: (708)848-8182
Co. E-mail: oprf@oprfchamber.org
URL: http://www.oprfchamber.org
Contact: Jim Doss, Exec.Dir.

59619 ■ O'Fallon Chamber of Commerce
PO Box 371
O'Fallon, IL 62269
Ph:(618)632-3377
Fax: (618)632-8162
Co. E-mail: chamber@ofallonchamber.com
URL: http://www.ofallonchamber.com
Contact: Kathy Federico, Pres.

59620 ■ Okawville Chamber of Commerce
PO Box 345
Okawville, IL 62271
Ph:(618)243-5694

Co. E-mail: tokawville@earthlink.net
URL: http://www.okawvillecc.com

59621 ■ Olney and the Greater Richland County Chamber of Commerce
201 E Chestnut
Olney, IL 62450
Ph:(618)392-2241
Fax: (618)392-4179
Co. E-mail: olneychamber@otbnet.com
URL: http://www.olneychamber.com
Contact: Gwen Gassmann, Exec.Dir.

59622 ■ Oregon Chamber of Commerce
124 1/2 N 4th St.
Oregon, IL 61061
Ph:(815)732-2100
Fax: (815)732-2177
Co. E-mail: ococ@oglecom.com
URL: http://www.oregonil.com
Contact: Dr. Michael Nelson

59623 ■ Orland Park Area Chamber of Commerce
8799 W 151st St.
Orland Park, IL 60462
Ph:(708)349-2972
Fax: (708)349-7454
Co. E-mail: info@orlandparkchamber.org
URL: http://www.orlandparkchamber.org
Contact: Keloryn Putnam, Exec.Dir.

59624 ■ Oswego Chamber of Commerce
22 W VanBuren
Oswego, IL 60543-0863
Ph:(630)554-3505
Fax: (630)554-0050
Co. E-mail: info@oswegochamber.org
URL: http://www.oswegochamber.org
Contact: Kim Rosebraugh, Exec.Dir.

59625 ■ Ottawa Area Chamber of Commerce and Industry
100 W Lafayette St.
Ottawa, IL 61350
Ph:(815)433-0084
Fax: (815)433-2405
Co. E-mail: info@ottawachamberillinois.com
URL: http://www.ottawachamberillinois.com
Contact: Boyd Palmer, Exec.Dir.

59626 ■ Palatine Area Chamber of Commerce
625 North Ct., Ste. 320
Palatine, IL 60067
Ph:(847)359-7200
Fax: (847)359-7246
Co. E-mail: info@palatinechamber.com
URL: http://www.palatinechamber.com
Contact: Mindy Phillips, Dir.

59627 ■ Palestine Chamber of Commerce
PO Box 155
Palestine, IL 62451
Ph:(618)586-2222
Fax: (618)586-9477
Co. E-mail: plstnecc@shawneelink.net
URL: http://www.pioneercity.com/
    chamberofcommerce
Contact: Brad Surrells, Pres.

59628 ■ Palestine Development Association
PO Box 101
Palestine, IL 62451
Co. E-mail: pda@pioneercity.com
URL: http://pioneercity.com/pda

59629 ■ Palos Hills Chamber of Commerce
10335 S Roberts Rd.
Palos Hills, IL 60465
Ph:(708)598-3400
URL: http://www.paloshillsweb.org
Contact: Phyllis Majka, Pres.

59630 ■ Pana Chamber of Commerce
City Hall
120 E 3rd St.
Pana, IL 62557-1646

Ph:(217)562-4240
Fax: (217)562-3823
Co. E-mail: panail@consolidated.net
URL: http://www.panaillinois.com
Contact: Jim Deere, Sec.-Treas.

59631 ■ Paris Area Chamber of Commerce and Tourism
105 N Central Ave.
Paris, IL 61944
Ph:(217)465-4179
URL: http://www.parisilchamber.com
Contact: Brenda Buckley, Exec. Dir.

59632 ■ Park Ridge Chamber of Commerce
140 Euclid
Park Ridge, IL 60068
Ph:(847)825-3121
Fax: (847)825-3122
Co. E-mail: email@parkridgeilchamber.com
URL: http://www.parkridgeilchamber.com
Contact: Richard E. Brayer, Exec.Dir.

59633 ■ Paxton Area Chamber of Commerce
PO Box 75
148 N Market St.
Paxton, IL 60957
Ph:(217)379-4655
Co. E-mail: pacc@illicom.net
URL: http://www.paxtonil.com/chamber.html
Contact: Madge Mullinax, Exec. Sec.

59634 ■ Pekin Area Chamber of Commerce
402 Court St.
PO Box 636
Pekin, IL 61555-0636
Ph:(309)346-2106
Fax: (309)346-2104
Co. E-mail: chamber@pekin.net
URL: http://www.pekin.net
Contact: Bill Fleming, Exec.Dir.

59635 ■ Peoria Area Chamber of Commerce
124 SW Adams St., Ste. 300
Peoria, IL 61602-1388
Ph:(309)676-0755
Fax: (309)676-7534
Co. E-mail: chamber@chamber.h-p.org
URL: http://www.peoriachamber.org
Contact: Roberta M. Parks, Senior VP/COO

59636 ■ Peoria Heights Chamber of Commerce
1203 E Kingman
Peoria, IL 61616
Ph:(309)685-4812
Co. E-mail: phcc@bwsys.net
Contact: Susan Watters, Sec.

59637 ■ Petersburg Chamber of Commerce
PO Box 452
Petersburg, IL 62675
Ph:(217)632-7363
Fax: (217)632-7363
Co. E-mail: dsk@petersburgil.com
URL: http://www.petersburgil.com/pcoc
Contact: Betty Winchester, Pres.

59638 ■ Pike County Chamber of Commerce
224 W Washington
PO Box 283
Pittsfield, IL 62363
Ph:(217)285-2971
Fax: (217)285-5251
Co. E-mail: info@pikeil.org
URL: http://www.pikeil.org
Contact: Ms. Alicia Smith, Exec.Dir.

59639 ■ Pinckneyville Chamber of Commerce
4 S Walnut St.
Pinckneyville, IL 62274-0183
Ph:(618)357-3243
Co. E-mail: pvllecoc@midwest.net
URL: http://chamber.pinckneyville.com
Contact: Joan Smith, Exec.Coor.

59640 ■ Plainfield Area Chamber of Commerce
530 W Lockport St., No. 108
Plainfield, IL 60544-1583
Ph:(815)436-4431
Fax: (815)436-0520
Co. E-mail: etcollins@plainfieldchamber.com
URL: http://www.plainfieldchamber.com
Contact: Liz Collins, Pres./CEO

59641 ■ Plano Commerce Association
101 W Main St.
PO Box 81
Plano, IL 60545-0081
Ph:(630)552-7272
Fax: (630)552-0165
Co. E-mail: pedco@indianvalley.com
URL: http://planocommerce.org
Contact: William Negley, Exec.Dir.

59642 ■ Polo Chamber of Commerce
115 S Franklin Ave.
Polo, IL 61064
Ph:(815)946-3131
Fax: (815)946-2004
Co. E-mail: webmaster@poloil.net
URL: http://www.poloil.net
Contact: Susie Corbitt, Sec.

59643 ■ Pontiac Area Chamber of Commerce
PO Box 534
Pontiac, IL 61764
Ph:(815)844-5131
Fax: (815)844-2600
Co. E-mail: clambert@pontiacchamber.org
URL: http://www.pontiacchamber.org
Contact: Cheri Lambert, Pres./CEO

59644 ■ Portage Park Chamber of Commerce
4849 A Irving Park Rd.
Chicago, IL 60641-2719
Ph:(773)777-2020
Fax: (773)777-0202
Co. E-mail: beebuilding@aol.com
URL: http://www.portageparkchamber.org
Contact: George S. Borovik, Exec. Dir.

59645 ■ Princeton Area Chamber of Commerce and Main Street
435 S Main St.
Princeton, IL 61356
Ph:(815)875-2616
Free: 877-730-4306
Fax: (815)875-1156
Co. E-mail: ptoncham@theramp.net
URL: http://www.princeton-il.com
Contact: Woody Wendt, Exec.Dir.

59646 ■ Prophetstown-Lyndon Area Chamber of Commerce
5 Victoria Dr.
Prophetstown, IL 61277-1401
Ph:(815)499-0201
Co. E-mail: ptownms@frontiernet.net
URL: http://www.prophetstownil.com/organizations.
    html
Contact: Sena Warkins

59647 ■ Quincy Area Chamber of Commerce
300 Civic Center Plz., Ste. 245
Quincy, IL 62301
Ph:(217)222-7980
Fax: (217)222-3033
Co. E-mail: amyl@adams.net
URL: http://www.quincychamber.org
Contact: Amy Looten, Exec.Dir.

59648 ■ Rantoul Area Chamber of Commerce
100 W Sangamon Ave., Ste. 101
Rantoul, IL 61866
Ph:(217)893-3323
Co. E-mail: dir@pdnt.com
URL: http://www.rantoulchamber.com/RACC
Contact: Joe Bolser, Exec.Dir.

59649 ■ Richmond/Spring Grove Area Chamber of Commerce
10906 Main St.
PO Box 475
Richmond, IL 60071
Ph:(815)678-7742
Fax: (815)678-2070
Co. E-mail: chamber@rsg.org
URL: http://www.rsgchamber.com
Contact: Loretta Podeszwa, Exec. Dir.

59650 ■ Riverdale Chamber of Commerce
208 W 144th St.
Riverdale, IL 60827
Ph:(708)841-3311
Fax: (708)841-1805
Co. E-mail: rdpl2@earthlink.net
URL: http://www.district148.net/rcoc
Contact: Adelle Swanson, Sec.

59651 ■ Riverside Chamber of Commerce
PO Box 7
Riverside, IL 60546
Ph:(708)802-1631
Co. E-mail: business@
    riversidechamberofcommerce.com
URL: http://www.riversidechamberofcommerce.com
Contact: David Moravecek, Pres.

59652 ■ Rochelle Area Chamber of Commerce
350 May Mart Dr.
Rochelle, IL 61068-0220
Ph:(815)562-4189
Fax: (815)562-4180
Co. E-mail: chamber@rochelle.net
URL: http://www.rochellechamber.org
Contact: Jeana Abbott, Exec.Dir.

59653 ■ Rock Falls Chamber of Commerce
601 W 10th St.
Rock Falls, IL 61071-1576
Ph:(815)625-4500
Fax: (815)625-4558
Co. E-mail: rockfallschamber@essex1.com
URL: http://www.rockfallschamber.com/index.html
Contact: Doug Wiersema, Pres./CEO

59654 ■ Rockford Regional Chamber of Commerce
515 N Court St.
Rockford, IL 61103
Ph:(815)987-8100
Fax: (815)987-8122
Co. E-mail: cservice@rockfordchamber.com
URL: http://www.rockfordchamber.com
Contact: Verla Sterett, Customer Service

59655 ■ Rockford Regional Chamber of Commerce Business Women's Council
308 W State St., Ste. 190
Rockford, IL 61101
Ph:(815)987-8100
Fax: (815)987-8122
Co. E-mail: info@rockfordchamber.com
URL: http://www.rockfordchamber.com
Contact: Teri Watts, Sr. Mgr. of Leadership
    Rockford

59656 ■ Rockton Chamber of Commerce
119 Blackhawk Blvd.
PO Box 237
Rockton, IL 61072
Ph:(815)624-7625
Fax: (815)624-7385
Co. E-mail: info@rocktonchamber.com
URL: http://www.rocktonchamber.com
Contact: Ms. Carol Lamb, Exec.Dir.

59657 ■ Rolling Meadows Chamber of Commerce
2775 Algonquin Rd., Ste. 310
Rolling Meadows, IL 60008
Ph:(847)398-3730
Fax: (847)398-3745
Co. E-mail: office@rmchamber.org
URL: http://www.rmchamber.org

Contact: Linda Liles Ballantine, Exec.Dir.

59658 ■ Romeoville Chamber of Commerce
27 Montrose Dr.
Romeoville, IL 60446-1329
Ph:(815)886-2076
Fax: (815)886-2096
Co. E-mail: info@romeovillechamber.org
URL: http://www.romeovillechamber.org
Contact: Tony Marquez, Pres.

59659 ■ Roselle Chamber of Commerce and Industry
81 E Devon Ave.
Roselle, IL 60172
Ph:(630)894-3010
Fax: (630)894-3042
Co. E-mail: execdir@rosellechamber.com
URL: http://www.rosellechamber.com
Contact: Gail Croson, Exec.Dir.

59660 ■ Round Lake Area Chamber of Commerce and Industry
1777 N Cedar Lake Rd.
Round Lake Beach, IL 60073
Ph:(847)546-2002
Co. E-mail: rlchamber@sbcglobal.net
URL: http://www.rlchamber.org
Contact: Monica Marr, Exec.Dir.

59661 ■ Rushville Area Chamber of Commerce and Main Street
PO Box 171
117 S Congress St.
Rushville, IL 62681
Ph:(217)322-3689
Fax: (217)322-3689
Co. E-mail: racc_mst@frontiernet.net
URL: http://www.rushville.org
Contact: Ms. Kathy Love, Chamber Office Mgr./
    Exec.Dir.

59662 ■ St. Charles Area Chamber of Commerce
10 State Ave.
St. Charles, IL 60174
Ph:(630)584-8384
Fax: (630)584-6065
Co. E-mail: info@stcharleschamber.com
URL: http://www.stcharleschamber.com
Contact: Lori G. Hewitt, Exec.Dir.

59663 ■ Saline County Chamber of Commerce
303 S Commercial St.
Harrisburg, IL 62946
Ph:(618)252-4192
Fax: (618)252-0210
Co. E-mail: chamber@salinecountychamber.org
URL: http://www.salinecountychamber.org
Contact: Katrinka Stevers, Dir.

59664 ■ Sandwich Chamber of Commerce
PO Box 214
128 E Railroad St.
Sandwich, IL 60548
Ph:(815)786-9075
Fax: (815)786-2505
Co. E-mail: info@sandwich-il.org
URL: http://www.sandwich-il.org
Contact: Pat Voga, Admin.

59665 ■ Sauk Valley Area Chamber of Commerce
211 Locust St.
Sterling, IL 61081-3536
Ph:(815)625-2400
Fax: (815)625-9361
Co. E-mail: chamber@essex1.com
URL: http://www.saukvalleyareachamber.com
Contact: Heather Sotelo, Exec.Dir.

59666 ■ Savanna Chamber of Commerce
PO Box 315
Savanna, IL 61074
Ph:(815)273-2722
Fax: (815)273-2754

Co. E-mail: savchamber@grics.net
URL: http://www.savanna-il.com
Contact: Karen Wallace, Exec.Dir.

59667 ■ Shelbyville Area Chamber of Commerce
124 N Morgan St.
Shelbyville, IL 62565
Ph:(217)774-2221
Fax: (217)774-2221
Co. E-mail: chamber01@consolidated.net
URL: http://www.shelbyvillechamberofcommerce.
    com
Contact: Joe Hampton

59668 ■ Skokie Chamber of Commerce
5002-5006 Oakton St.
Skokie, IL 60077
Ph:(847)673-0240
Fax: (847)673-0249
Co. E-mail: chamber@skokiechamber.org
URL: http://www.skokiechamber.org
Contact: Sandi Stamp, Sec.

59669 ■ Southwestern Madison County Chamber of Commerce
3600 Nameoki Rd., Ste. 202
Granite City, IL 62040-0370
Ph:(618)876-6400
Fax: (618)876-6448
Co. E-mail: chamber@chamberswmadisoncounty.
    com
URL: http://www.chamberswmadisoncounty.com
Contact: Rosemarie Brown, Exec. Dir.

59670 ■ Sparta Area Chamber of Commerce
PO Box 93
Sparta, IL 62286-0093
Ph:(618)443-2151
Contact: Nathan Lee, Pres.

59671 ■ Staunton Chamber of Commerce
229 W Main St.
Staunton, IL 62088
Ph:(618)635-8356
URL: http://www.stauntonil.com
Contact: Ray Duda, Pres.

59672 ■ Streamwood Chamber of Commerce
22 W Streamwood Blvd.
Streamwood, IL 60107
Ph:(630)837-5200
Fax: (630)837-5251
Co. E-mail: staff@streamwoodchamber.com
URL: http://www.streamwoodchamber.com
Contact: Ann Townsend, Exec.Sec.

59673 ■ Streator Area Chamber of Commerce and Industry
PO Box 360
Streator, IL 61364
Ph:(815)672-2921
Fax: (815)672-1768
Co. E-mail: sacci@streatorchamber.com
URL: http://www.streatoril.com
Contact: Michael Neuenkirchen, Exec. Dir.

59674 ■ Sullivan Chamber and Economic Development
112 W Harrison St.
Sullivan, IL 61951
Ph:(217)728-4223
Fax: (217)728-4064
Co. E-mail: info@sullivanchamber.com
URL: http://www.sullivanchamber.com
Contact: Kathy Woodworth, Administrator

59675 ■ Swansea Chamber of Commerce
1501 Caseyville Ave.
Swansea, IL 62226
Ph:(618)233-3938
Fax: (618)233-3936
Co. E-mail: swansea@swanseachamber.org
URL: http://www.swanseachamber.org
Contact: Amy Melinder, Exec.Dir.

59676 ■ Sycamore Chamber of Commerce
407 W State St., Ste. 10
Sycamore, IL 60178
Ph:(815)895-3456
Fax: (815)895-0125
Co. E-mail: info@sycamorechamber.com
URL: http://www.sycamorechamber.com
Contact: Rose Treml, Exec.Dir.

59677 ■ Tinley Park Chamber of Commerce
17316 S Oak Park Ave.
Tinley Park, IL 60477
Ph:(708)532-5700
Fax: (708)532-1475
Co. E-mail: info@tinleychamber.org
URL: http://www.tinleychamber.org
Contact: Ms. Bernadette Shanahan-Haas, Exec.Dir.

59678 ■ Troy Area Chamber of Commerce
647 E US Hwy. 40
Troy, IL 62294
Ph:(618)667-8769
Free: 888-667-8769
Fax: (618)667-8759
Co. E-mail: info@troycoc.com
URL: http://www.troycoc.com
Contact: Dawn Mushill, Exec.Dir.

59679 ■ Turkish American Chamber of Commerce
PO Box 06238
Chicago, IL 60606-6238
Co. E-mail: info@turkishchamber.org
URL: http://www.turkishchamber.org

59680 ■ Tuscola Chamber of Commerce
PO Box 434
Tuscola, IL 61953
Ph:(217)253-5013
Co. E-mail: tourism@tuscola.org
URL: http://www.tuscola.org
Contact: Dedee Hoel, Pres.

59681 ■ Union County Chamber of Commerce
330 S Main St.
Anna, IL 62906
Ph:(618)833-6311
Fax: (618)833-1903
Co. E-mail: uccc@shawneelink.net
URL: http://www.shawneeheartland.com
Contact: Jeannie Toler, Exec. Dir.

59682 ■ Uptown Chamber of Commerce
4753 N Broadway, Ste. 822
Chicago, IL 60640
Ph:(773)878-1184
Fax: (773)878-3678
Co. E-mail: info@uptownchamber.com
URL: http://www.uptownchamber.com
Contact: Wally Rozak, Interim Exec.Dir.

59683 ■ Vandalia Chamber of Commerce
1408 N 5th St.
PO Box 238
Vandalia, IL 62471
Ph:(618)283-2728
Fax: (618)283-4439
URL: http://www.vandaliaillinois.com
Contact: Pat Click, Dir.

59684 ■ Vermilion Advantage-Chamber of Commerce Division
28 W North St.
Danville, IL 61832-5729
Ph:(217)442-1887
Free: 800-373-6201
Fax: (217)442-6228
Co. E-mail: gkietzmann@vermilionadvantage.com
URL: http://www.vermilionadvantage.com
Contact: Glenda Kietzman, Exec.Dir.

59685 ■ Villa Park Chamber of Commerce
10 W Park Blvd.
Villa Park, IL 60181
Ph:(630)941-9133
Fax: (630)941-9134

Co. E-mail: vpchamber@sbcglobal.net
URL: http://www.villaparkchamber.org
Contact: Rhonda M. Hartman, Exec.Dir.

59686 ■ Village of Itasca Chamber of Commerce
550 W Irving Park Rd.
Itasca, IL 60143
Ph:(630)773-0835
Fax: (630)773-2505
URL: http://www.itasca.com
Contact: Claudia Gruber

59687 ■ Wabash County Chamber of Commerce
219 Market St., Ste. 1A
Mount Carmel, IL 62863-1698
Ph:(618)262-5116
Fax: (618)262-2424
Co. E-mail: mtcarmelchamber@mt-carmel.net
Contact: Tanja Bingham, Exec.Dir.

59688 ■ Walnut Chamber of Commerce
105 S Main St.
Walnut, IL 61376
Ph:(815)379-2141
Co. E-mail: walnutchamber@villageofwalnut.com
URL: http://www.villageofwalnut.com
Contact: Ms. Donna L. Manak, Exec. Dir.

59689 ■ Washington Chamber of Commerce
112 Washington Sq.
Washington, IL 61571-2657
Ph:(309)444-9921
Co. E-mail: wcoc@mtco.com
Contact: Denise Magnuson, Dir.

59690 ■ Waterloo Chamber of Commerce
PO Box 1
Waterloo, IL 62298
Ph:(618)939-5300
Fax: (618)939-1805
Co. E-mail: chamber@enjoywaterloo.com
URL: http://www.enjoywaterloo.com
Contact: Debbie Ruggeri, Exec.Dir.

59691 ■ Watseka Area Chamber of Commerce
206 E Walnut St.
Watseka, IL 60970
Ph:(815)432-2416
Fax: (815)432-2762
Co. E-mail: office@watsekachamber.org
URL: http://www.watsekachamber.org
Contact: Darcey Smith, Exec.Dir.

59692 ■ Wauconda Chamber of Commerce
100 Main St.
Wauconda, IL 60084
Ph:(847)526-5580
Fax: (847)526-3059
Co. E-mail: info@waucondachamber.org
URL: http://www.waucondachamber.org
Contact: Debra Ogorzaly, Exec.Dir.

59693 ■ West Chicago Chamber of Commerce and Industry
306 Main St.
West Chicago, IL 60185-2839
Ph:(630)231-3003
Fax: (630)231-3009
Co. E-mail: wchicagochamber@cs.com
Contact: Joe Castelluccio, Pres.

59694 ■ West Lawn Chamber of Commerce
4021 W 63rd St., Unit 2-B
Chicago, IL 60629-3711
Ph:(773)735-7690
Fax: (773)284-8110
Co. E-mail: wstlwncc@aol.com
URL: http://www.westlawnchamber.org
Contact: Mrs. Edie Cavanaugh, Exec. Dir.

59695 ■ West Suburban Chamber of Commerce and Industry
47 S 6th Ave.
La Grange, IL 60525

Ph:(708)352-0494
Fax: (708)352-0620
Co. E-mail: info@westsuburbanchamber.org
URL: http://www.westsuburbanchamber.org
Contact: Lisa Zeigler, Exec.Dir.

59696 ■ Westchester Chamber of Commerce
PO Box 7309
Westchester, IL 60154
Ph:(708)562-7747
Fax: (708)223-8475
Co. E-mail: brat6169@aol.com
URL: http://www.westchesterchamber.org
Contact: Ms. Kathy Sheldon, Pres.

59697 ■ Westmont Chamber of Commerce and Tourism Bureau
1 S Cass Ave.
Westmont, IL 60559
Ph:(630)960-5553
Fax: (630)960-5554
Co. E-mail: information@westmontchamber.com
URL: http://www.westmontchamber.com
Contact: Janelle Fallan, Exec.Dir.

59698 ■ Westridge Chamber of Commerce
2720 W Devon, Ste. B
Chicago, IL 60659
Ph:(773)743-6022
Fax: (773)743-2893
Co. E-mail: westridgechamber@sbcglobal.net
URL: http://westridgechamber.org
Contact: Neal Gallo, Pres.

59699 ■ Wheaton Chamber of Commerce
108 E Wesley St.
Wheaton, IL 60187
Ph:(630)668-6464
Fax: (630)668-2744
Co. E-mail: wccinfo@ewheaton.com
URL: http://www.ewheaton.com
Contact: Glenn Keller, Chm.

59700 ■ Wheeling - Prospect Heights Area Chamber of Commerce and Industry
395 E Dundee Rd., Ste. 300
Wheeling, IL 60090
Ph:(847)541-0170
Fax: (847)541-0296
Co. E-mail: info@wphchamber.com
URL: http://www.wphchamber.com
Contact: Catherine Powers, Exec. Dir.

59701 ■ Will County Center for Economic Development
116 N Chicago St., Ste. 101
Joliet, IL 60432-4204
Ph:(815)774-6060
Fax: (815)723-6972
Co. E-mail: john.greuling@willcountyced.com
URL: http://www.willcountyced.com
Contact: Mr. John E. Greuling, Pres./CEO

59702 ■ Willowbrook - Burr Ridge Chamber of Commerce and Industry
8300 S Madison
Burr Ridge, IL 60527
Ph:(630)654-0909
Fax: (630)654-0922
Co. E-mail: info@wbbrchamber.org
URL: http://www.wbbrchamber.org
Contact: Ron Isdonas, Pres.

59703 ■ Wilmette Chamber of Commerce
1150 Wilmette Ave., Ste. A
Wilmette, IL 60091
Ph:(847)251-3800
Fax: (847)251-6321
Co. E-mail: info@wilmettechamber.org
URL: http://www.wilmettechamber.org
Contact: Julie Yusim, Exec.Dir.

59704 ■ Wilmington Chamber of Commerce
PO Box 724
Wilmington, IL 60481
Ph:(815)476-5991
Fax: (815)476-7002

Co. E-mail: fpnads@cbcast.com
URL: http://www.wilmingtonchamberofcommerce.org
Contact: Eric Fisher, Pres.

59705 ■ Winfield Chamber of Commerce
OS 125 Church St.
PO Box 209
Winfield, IL 60190
Ph:(630)682-3712
Fax: (630)682-3726
Co. E-mail: winfieldchamber@sbcglobal.net
URL: http://www.winfield-chamber.com
Contact: Rich Bysina, Exec.Dir.

59706 ■ Winnetka Chamber of Commerce
841 Spruce St., Ste. 204
Winnetka, IL 60093
Ph:(847)446-4451
Fax: (847)446-4452
Co. E-mail: wcc@winnetkachamber.com
URL: http://www.winnetkachamber.com
Contact: Cicely Clarke Michalak, Exec.Dir.

59707 ■ Wood Dale Chamber of Commerce
PO Box 353
Wood Dale, IL 60191-0353
Ph:(630)595-0505
Fax: (630)595-0677
Co. E-mail: info@wooddalechamber.com
URL: http://www.wooddalechamber.com
Contact: Lorrie Heggaton, Pres.

59708 ■ Woodridge Area Chamber of Commerce
5 Plaza Dr., Ste. 212
Woodridge, IL 60517-5014
Ph:(630)960-7080
Fax: (630)852-2316
Co. E-mail: chamber@woodridgechamber.org
URL: http://www.woodridgechamber.org
Contact: Shawnna Donovan, Pres./CEO

59709 ■ Woodstock Chamber of Commerce and Industry
136 Cass St.
Woodstock, IL 60098
Ph:(815)338-2436
Fax: (815)338-2927
Co. E-mail: chamber@woodstockilchamber.com
URL: http://www.woodstockilchamber.com
Contact: Quinn Keefe, Exec.Dir.

59710 ■ Wyanet Chamber of Commerce
PO Box 373
Wyanet, IL 61379
Ph:(815)699-2631
Fax: (815)699-2631
Contact: John Gordon

59711 ■ Yorkville Area Chamber of Commerce
26 W Countryside Pkwy., Ste. 101
Yorkville, IL 60560
Ph:(630)553-6853
Fax: (630)553-0702
Co. E-mail: yorkvillechamber@sbcglobal.net
URL: http://www.yorkvillechamber.org

59712 ■ Zion Chamber of Commerce
2671 Sheridan Rd.
Zion, IL 60099
Ph:(847)872-5405
Fax: (847)872-9309
Co. E-mail: info@zionchamber.com
URL: http://www.zionchamber.com
Contact: Diana Gornik, Exec.Dir.

MINORITY BUSINESS ASSISTANCE PROGRAMS

59713 ■ Chicago Minority Business Development Center
1 East Wacker Dr. Ste. 1200
Chicago, IL 60601

Ph:(312)755-8889
Fax: (312)755-8891
Co. E-mail: mbdclacc@ix.netcom.com
URL: http://www.mbda.gov

59714 ■ Latin American Chamber of Commerce
3512 W Fullerton Ave.
Chicago, IL 60647
Ph:(773)252-5211
Fax: (773)252-7065
Co. E-mail: bsantana@bussysam.com
URL: http://www.latinamericanchamberofcommerce.com
Contact: Bennet Santana, Pres

FINANCING AND LOAN PROGRAMS

59715 ■ Aarbor Industries, Inc.
PO Box 168
Deerfield, IL 60015
Ph:(847)945-0767
Fax: (847)945-1282
Contact: Robert Morris, President
Investment Policies: Acquisition, leveraged buyout, management buyouts, and turnaround. **Geographic Preferences:** Midwest.

59716 ■ ABN AMRO Private Equity
208 S. La Salle St., 10th Fl.
Chicago, IL 60604
Ph:(312)855-7292
Fax: (312)553-6648
URL: http://www.abnequity.com
Contact: David Foreman, Managing Director
Preferred Investment Size: $1,000,000 to $10,000,000. **Investment Types:** Expansion. **Industry Preferences:** Consumer related, computer software and services, other products, communications and media, Internet specific, medical and health, semiconductors and other electronics, and biotechnology. **Geographic Preferences:** U.S. and Canada.

59717 ■ Allstate Private Equity
3075 Sanders Rd., Ste. G5D
Northbrook, IL 60062
Ph:(847)402-8247
Fax: (847)402-0880
Preferred Investment Size: $5,000,000 minimum. **Investment Types:** Start-up, first and second stage, mezzanine, leveraged buyout, and special situation. **Industry Preferences:** Communications and media, computer hardware and software, semiconductors and other electronics, biotechnology, medical and health, consumer related, industrial and energy, financial services, and manufacturing. **Geographic Preferences:** U.S.

59718 ■ Alpha Capital Partners, Ltd.
122 S. Michigan Ave., Ste. 1700
Chicago, IL 60603
Ph:(312)322-9800
Fax: (312)322-9808
Co. E-mail: acp@alphacapital.com
URL: http://www.alphacapital.com
Contact: Andrew Kalnow, President
Preferred Investment Size: $750,000 to $5,000,000. **Investment Types:** First, second, and later stage, leveraged buyout, expansion, and special situation. **Industry Preferences:** Computer software and services, consumer related, other products, communications and media, medical and health, biotechnology, semiconductors and other electronics, Internet specific, industrial and energy, and computer hardware. **Geographic Preferences:** Midwest.

59719 ■ Ameritech Development Corp.
30 S. Wacker Dr., 37th Fl.
Chicago, IL 60606
Free: 800-257-0902
Fax: (312)207-1601
Contact: Craig Lee, Managing Director
Preferred Investment Size: $5,000,000 minimum. **Investment Types:** Start-up, first and second stage.

Industry Preferences: Communications, computer hardware and software, semiconductors and other electronics. **Geographic Preferences:** U.S.

59720 ■ Apex Venture Partners
225 W. Washington, Ste. 1500
Chicago, IL 60606
Ph:(312)857-2800
Fax: (312)857-2024
URL: http://www.apexvc.com
Contact: Amando Pauker, General Partner
Preferred Investment Size: $5,000,000 to $15,000,000. **Investment Types:** Seed, start-up, and early stage. **Industry Preferences:** Internet specific, computer software and services, other products, communications and media, semiconductors and other electronics, consumer related, medical and health, industrial and energy, and biotechnology. **Geographic Preferences:** U.S.

59721 ■ Arch Venture Partners
8725 W. Higgins Rd., Ste. 290
Chicago, IL 60631
Ph:(773)380-6600
Fax: (773)380-6606
URL: http://www.archventure.com
Contact: Steven Lazarus, Managing Director
Preferred Investment Size: $500,000 to $10,000,000. **Investment Types:** Seed, start-up, and early stage. **Industry Preferences:** Internet specific, semiconductors and other electronics, computer software and services, medical and health, biotechnology, communications and media, computer hardware, industrial and energy, consumer related, and other products. **Geographic Preferences:** Midwest, Mid Atlantic, Northeast, Northern and Southern California, Northwest, Rocky Mountains, Southwest, and West Coast.

59722 ■ The Bank Funds
208 South LaSalle St., Ste. 1680
Chicago, IL 60604
Ph:(312)855-6020
Fax: (312)855-8910
Contact: Charles Moore, President
Investment Types: Control-block purchases, later stage, leveraged buyout, second stage, and special situation. **Industry Preferences:** Computer hardware, communications and media. **Geographic Preferences:** U.S.

59723 ■ Batterson Venture Partners (BVP)
303 W. Madison St., Ste. 1625
Chicago, IL 60606
Ph:(312)269-0300
Fax: (312)269-0021
URL: http://www.battersonvp.com
Contact: Leonard Batterson, Chairman and Chief Executive Officer
Preferred Investment Size: $500,000 to $3,000,000. **Investment Types:** Seed, start-up, early and later stage. **Industry Preferences:** Computer software and services, medical and health, Internet specific, communications and media, biotechnology, industrial and energy, computer hardware, other products, semiconductors and other electronics, and consumer related. **Geographic Preferences:** U.S.

59724 ■ Beecken, Petty & Company LLC (Lisle)
901 Warrenville Rd., Ste. 205
Lisle, IL 60532
Ph:(630)435-0300
Fax: (630)435-0370
URL: http://www.beeckenpetty.com
Contact: Dave Beecken, Managing Director
Preferred Investment Size: $1,000,000 to $15,000,000. **Investment Types:** Early and later stage, leveraged buyout, management buyouts, expansion, and recapitalizations. **Industry Preferences:** Medical and health, computer software and services, Internet specific, other products, communications and media. **Geographic Preferences:** U.S. and Canada.

59725 ■ Bluestar Ventures L.P.
208 S. LaSalle St., Ste. 1020
Chicago, IL 60604

Ph:(312)384-5000
Fax: (312)384-5005
URL: http://www.bluestarventures.com
Contact: Patrick Pollard, Managing Director
Preferred Investment Size: $500,000 to $3,000,000.
Investment Types: Start-up, early, first, and second stage. **Industry Preferences:** Communications, computer software, and Internet specific. **Geographic Preferences:** Mid Atlantic, Midwest, Northwest, Southeast, and Southwest.

59726 ■ The Capital Strategy Management Co.
233 S. Wacker Dr.
Box 06334
Chicago, IL 60606
Ph:(312)444-1170
Contact: Eric Von Bauer, President
Preferred Investment Size: $200,000 to $50,000,000. **Investment Types:** Start-up, first, second, early and later stage, acquisition, balanced, distressed debt, control-block purchases, industry rollups, leveraged buyout, private placement, public companies, strategic alliance, management buyouts, expansion, generalist PE, joint ventures, mezzanine, recapitalizations, turnaround, and special situation. **Industry Preferences:** Communications, computer hardware and software, Internet specific, semiconductors and other electronics, biotechnology, medical and health, consumer related, industrial and energy, transportation, business service, manufacturing, agriculture, forestry and fishing, environment, and utilities. **Geographic Preferences:** Mid Atlantic, Midwest, Rocky Mountains, Southwest, and Southeast.

59727 ■ Cerulean Fund / WGC Enterprises
1701 E. Lake Ave., Ste. 170
Glenview, IL 60025
Ph:(708)657-8002
Fax: (708)657-8168
Contact: Brian Dettmann, Partner
Preferred Investment Size: $5,000,000 minimum. **Investment Types:** Seed, start-up, control-block purchases, leveraged buyout, research and development, and special situation. **Industry Preferences:** communications and media, computer hardware and software, semiconductors and other electronics, biotechnology, medical and health, consumer related, industrial and energy, financial services, business service, and manufacturing. **Geographic Preferences:** Midwest.

59728 ■ Divine Interventures / Platinum Venture Partners
3333 Warrenville Rd., Ste. 800
Lisle, IL 60532
Ph:(630)799-7500
Fax: (630)799-3858
URL: http://www.divineinterventures.com
Contact: Scott Hartkopf, President
Investment Types: Start-up, first and second stage. **Industry Preferences:** Computer software and services, Internet specific, consumer related, medical and health, other products, and communications and media. **Geographic Preferences:** U.S.

59729 ■ DN Partners LLC
77 W. Wacker Dr., Ste. 4040
Chicago, IL 60601
Ph:(312)332-7960
Fax: (312)332-7979
URL: http://www.dnpartners.com
Contact: Maury Bell, Managing Director
Preferred Investment Size: $500,000 to $3,000,000.
Investment Types: Control-block purchases, generalist PE, industry rollups, later stage, leveraged buyout, management buyouts, and recapitalizations. **Industry Preferences:** Communications, computer hardware, Internet specific, semiconductors and other electronics, medical and health, consumer related, industrial and energy, transportation, financial services, business service, manufacturing, agriculture, forestry and fishing. **Geographic Preferences:** Midwest and U.S.

59730 ■ Dresner Capital Resources, Inc.
20 N. Clark St., Ste. 3550
Chicago, IL 60602

Ph:(312)726-3600
Fax: (312)726-7448
URL: http://www.dresnerco.com
Preferred Investment Size: $500,000 to $1,000,000.
Investment Types: Leveraged buyout, mezzanine, and second stage. **Industry Preferences:** Communications, computer hardware and software, Internet specific, semiconductors and other electronics, medical and health, consumer related, industrial and energy, financial services, business service, and manufacturing.

59731 ■ Duchossois Technology Partners LLC (DTEC)
845 Larch Ave.
Elmhurst, IL 60126
Ph:(630)993-8647
Fax: (630)993-8644
URL: http://www.duchtec.com
Contact: Dan Phelps, Partner
Preferred Investment Size: $2,000,000 to $7,000,000. **Investment Types:** Early, and first stage. **Industry Preferences:** Communications, computer software, semiconductors and other electronics, **Geographic Preferences:** U.S.

59732 ■ Eblast Ventures LLC
11 South LaSalle St., 5th Fl.
Chicago, IL 60603
Ph:(312)372-2600
Fax: (312)372-5621
URL: http://www.eblastventures.com
Preferred Investment Size: $100,000 to $500,000.
Investment Types: Early, seed, start-up, and turnaround. **Industry Preferences:** Diversified. **Geographic Preferences:** Midwest.

59733 ■ Evanston Business Investment Corp.
20 N. Wacker Dr., Ste. 2200
Chicago, IL 60606
Ph:(312)357-9600
Fax: (312)855-0488
Co. E-mail: t-parkinson@nwu.com
URL: http://www.ebic.com
Preferred Investment Size: $100,000 to $150,000.
Investment Types: Seed. **Industry Preferences:** Communications, computer software, Internet specific, semiconductors and other electronics, medical and health, consumer related, and industrial and energy. **Geographic Preferences:** Illinois.

59734 ■ First Analysis Corp.
233 S. Wacker Dr., Ste. 9500
Chicago, IL 60606
Ph:(312)258-1400
Fax: (312)258-0334
URL: http://www.firstanalysis.com
Contact: Allan Cohen, Managing Director
Preferred Investment Size: $3,000,000 to $10,000,000. **Investment Types:** Early and later stage, expansion, and balanced. **Industry Preferences:** Industrial and energy, Internet specific, other products, computer software and services, communications and media, consumer related, medical and health, computer hardware, semiconductors and other electronics, and biotechnology. **Geographic Preferences:** U.S.

59735 ■ Frontenac Company
135 S. LaSalle St., Ste. 3800
Chicago, IL 60603
Ph:(312)368-0044
Fax: (312)368-9520
URL: http://www.frontenac.com
Contact: David Katz, Managing Director
Preferred Investment Size: $10,000,000 to $50,000,000. **Investment Types:** Leveraged buyout, expansion, acquisition, later stage, management buyouts, and recapitalizations. **Industry Preferences:** Consumer related, other products, Internet specific, computer software and services, medical and health, communications and media, industrial and energy, computer hardware, semiconductors and other electronics, and biotechnology. **Geographic Preferences:** U.S.

59736 ■ GTCR Golder Rauner LLC
6100 Sears Tower
Chicago, IL 60606
Ph:(312)382-2200
Fax: (312)382-2201
URL: http://www.gtcr.com
Contact: Barry Dunn, Principal
Preferred Investment Size: $10,000,000 to $300,000,000. **Investment Types:** Acquisition, expansion, leveraged buyout, management buyouts, industry rollups, generalist PE, and recapitalizations. **Industry Preferences:** Communications, other products, computer software and services, consumer related, semiconductors and other electronics, medical and health, Internet specific, industrial and energy, computer hardware. **Geographic Preferences:** U.S.

59737 ■ High Street Capital
11 South LaSalle St., 5th Fl.
Chicago, IL 60603
Ph:(312)423-2650
Fax: (312)346-8450
URL: http://www.highstr.com
Contact: Joseph Katcha, Principal
Preferred Investment Size: $2,000,000 to $7,000,000. **Investment Types:** Acquisition, control-block purchases, expansion, generalist PE, leveraged buyout, industry rollups, management buyouts, mezzanine, strategic alliances, recapitalizations, and special situation. **Industry Preferences:** Communications, computer software, semiconductors and other electronics, medical and health, industrial and energy, business service, and manufacturing. **Geographic Preferences:** U.S.

59738 ■ IEG Venture Management, Inc.
70 West Madison St., 14th Fl.
Chicago, IL 60602
Ph:(312)644-0890
Fax: (312)454-0369
URL: http://www.iegventure.com
Investment Types: Seed, start-up, first and second stage. **Industry Preferences:** Communications, computer hardware and software, Internet specific, semiconductors and other electronics, biotechnology, medical and health, industrial and energy, transportation, manufacturing, agriculture, forestry and fishing. **Geographic Preferences:** Midwest.

59739 ■ Inroads Capital Partners, L.P.
1603 Orrington Ave., Ste. 2050
Evanston, IL 60201-3841
Ph:(847)864-2000
Fax: (847)864-9692
URL: http://www.inroadsvc.com
Contact: Jerrold Carrington, General Partner
Preferred Investment Size: $1,000,000 to $5,000,000. **Investment Types:** Expansion and later stage. **Industry Preferences:** Internet specific, semiconductors and other electronics, computer Software and services, semiconductors and other electronics, industrial and energy, other products, medical and health, and consumer related. **Geographic Preferences:** U.S.

59740 ■ JK&B Capital
180 N. Stetson Ave., Ste. 4500
Chicago, IL 60601
Ph:(312)946-1200
Fax: (312)946-1103
URL: http://www.jkbcapital.com
Contact: Albert DaValle, Partner
Preferred Investment Size: $5,000,000 to $30,000,000. **Investment Types:** Early, first, second, and later stage, and expansion. **Industry Preferences:** Internet specific, communications and media, computer software and services, semiconductors and other electronics, industrial and energy, and consumer related. **Geographic Preferences:** U.S.

59741 ■ KB Partners LLC
1101 Skokie Blvd., Ste. 260
Northbrook, IL 60062
Ph:(847)714-0444
Fax: (847)714-0445
Co. E-mail: keith@kbpartners.com
URL: http://www.kbpartners.com

Contact: Keith Bank, Managing Director
E-mail: keith@kppartners.com
Preferred Investment Size: $1,000,000 to $5,000,000. **Investment Types:** Early stage and expansion. **Industry Preferences:** Internet specific, computer software and services, industrial and energy, communications and media, semiconductors and other electronics, and medical and health. **Geographic Preferences:** Midwest and Rocky Mountains.

59742 ■ Kettle Partners
350 W. Hubbard St., Ste. 350
Chicago, IL 60610
Ph:(312)329-9300
Fax: (312)329-9310
URL: http://www.kettlevc.com
Contact: David Semmel, Managing Partner
Preferred Investment Size: $1,000,000 to $5,000,000. **Investment Types:** Seed, early, first and second stage. **Industry Preferences:** Internet specific, other products, computer software and services, communications and media. **Geographic Preferences:** U.S.

59743 ■ Lake Capital Partners, Inc.
676 N. Michigan Ave., Ste. 3900
Chicago, IL 60611
Ph:(312)640-7050
Fax: (312)640-7051
URL: http://www.lakecapital.com
Contact: Joseph Karczewski, Principal
Preferred Investment Size: $50,000,000 to $75,000,000. **Investment Types:** Start-up, expansion, acquisition, and leveraged buyout. **Industry Preferences:** Financial services, and business service. **Geographic Preferences:** U.S.

59744 ■ Lake Shore Capital Partners
20 N. Wacker Dr., Ste. 2807
Chicago, IL 60606
Ph:(312)803-3536
Fax: (312)803-3534
Preferred Investment Size: $1,000,000 to $10,000,000. **Investment Types:** First and second stage, mezzanine, and leveraged buyout. **Industry Preferences:** Diversified. **Geographic Preferences:** National.

59745 ■ LaSalle Capital Group, Inc.
3 First National Plz., Ste. 5710
Chicago, IL 60602
Ph:(312)236-6150
Fax: (312)236-0720
URL: http://www.lasallecapitalgroup.com
Contact: Jeff Walters, Partner
Preferred Investment Size: $5,000,000 to $50,000,000. **Investment Types:** Leveraged buyout, acquisition, turnaround, management buyouts, industry rollups, and recapitalizations. **Industry Preferences:** Communications, consumer related, semiconductors and other electronics, medical and health, industrial and energy, business service, manufacturing, and agriculture, forestry and fishing. **Geographic Preferences:** U.S.

59746 ■ Linc Capital, Inc.
303 E. Wacker Dr., Ste. 1000
Chicago, IL 60601
Ph:(312)946-2670
Fax: (312)938-4290
Co. E-mail: bdemars@linccap.com
Contact: Martin E. Zimmerman, Chief Executive Officer
Preferred Investment Size: $500,000 to $2,000,000. **Investment Types:** Seed, start-up, early and late stage, mezzanine, research and development, leveraged, and special situation. **Industry Preferences:** Communications and media, computer related, semiconductors and other electronics, medical and health, industrial and energy. **Geographic Preferences:** U.S.

59747 ■ Madison Dearborn Partners LLC
3 First National Plz., Ste. 3800
Chicago, IL 60602
Ph:(312)895-1000
Fax: (312)895-1001

URL: http://www.mdcp.com
Contact: Benjamin Chereskin, Managing Director
Preferred Investment Size: $50,000,000 to $600,000,000. **Investment Types:** Leveraged buyout, management buyouts, expansion, acquisition, and recapitalizations. **Industry Preferences:** Communications and media, Internet specific, consumer related, semiconductors and other electronics, medical and health, industrial and energy, computer software and services, computer hardware, and other products. **Geographic Preferences:** U.S. and Canada.

59748 ■ Marquette Venture Partners
676 N. Michigan Ave., Ste. 3120
Deerfield, IL 60611
Ph:(312)932-9230
Fax: (312)787-5907
URL: http://www.marquetteventures.com
Contact: Chip Ruth, General Partner
Preferred Investment Size: $1,000,000 to $5,000,000. **Investment Types:** Start-up, first and second stage. **Industry Preferences:** Medical and health, consumer related, computer software and services, communications and media, biotechnology, Internet specific, semiconductors and other electronics, industrial and energy, and computer hardware. **Geographic Preferences:** Mid Atlantic, Midwest, Rocky Mountains, and West Coast.

59749 ■ Mesirow Private Equity Investments, Inc.
350 N. Clark St.
Chicago, IL 60610
Ph:(312)595-6000
Fax: (312)595-6211
URL: http://www.meisrowfinancial.com
Contact: Daniel Howell, Senior Managing Director
Preferred Investment Size: $2,000,000 to $10,000,000. **Investment Types:** Later stage, mezzanine, generalist PE, leveraged buyout, management buyouts, fund of funds, acquisition, expansion, and recapitalizations. **Industry Preferences:** Computer software and services, other products, computer hardware, consumer related, Internet specific, communications and media, industrial and energy, semiconductors and other electronics, medical and health. **Geographic Preferences:** U.S. and Canada.

59750 ■ Mosaix Ventures
1822 N. Mohawk
Chicago, IL 60614
Ph:(312)274-0988
Fax: (773)913-2792
URL: http://www.mosaixventures.com
Contact: Ranjan Lal, Managing Partner
Preferred Investment Size: $1,000,000 to $4,000,000. **Investment Types:** Balanced. **Industry Preferences:** Medical and health, and biotechnology. **Geographic Preferences:** U.S. and Canada.

59751 ■ Motorola Ventures
1303 E. Algonquin Rd., 6th Fl.
Schaumburg, IL 60196
Ph:(847)576-4929
Fax: (847)576-2569
URL: http://www.motorola.com
Contact: John O. Donohue, Managing Director
Investment Types: Second stage. **Industry Preferences:** Communications and media, Internet specific, computer software and services, semiconductors and other electronics, Internet specific, medical and health, computer hardware, biotechnology, consumer related, and other products. **Geographic Preferences:** U.S.

59752 ■ Nesbitt Burns
111 West Monroe St.
Chicago, IL 60603
Ph:(312)416-3855
Fax: (312)765-8000
URL: http://www.harrisbank.com
Contact: I. David Burn
Investment Types: Control-block purchases, leveraged buyout, and special situation. **Industry Preferences:** Diversified. **Geographic Preferences:** U.S. and Canada.

59753 ■ New World Ventures
1603 Orrington Ave., Ste. 1600
Evanston, IL 60201
Ph:(847)328-0300
Fax: (847)328-8297
URL: http://www.newworldvc.com
Contact: Christopher Girgenti, Managing Director
Preferred Investment Size: $2,000,000 to $4,000,000. **Investment Types:** Early stage. **Industry Preferences:** Internet specific, communications and media, and computer software and services. **Geographic Preferences:** U.S.

59754 ■ Open Prairie Ventures
115 N. Neil St., Ste. 209
Champaign, IL 61820
Ph:(217)351-7000
Fax: (217)351-7051
URL: http://www.openprairie.com
Contact: Dennis Beard, Chief Financial Officer
Preferred Investment Size: $250,000 to $2,500,000. **Investment Types:** Early stage. **Industry Preferences:** Communications and media, computer hardware and software, Internet specific, computer related, semiconductors and other electronics, biotechnology, medical and health, industrial and energy. **Geographic Preferences:** Midwest.

59755 ■ Polestar Capital, Inc.
180 N. Michigan Ave., Ste. 1905
Chicago, IL 60601
Ph:(312)984-9090
Fax: (312)984-9877
URL: http://www.polestarvc.com
Investment Types: Start-up, first and second stage. **Industry Preferences:** Communications and media, computer software, computer related, and manufacturing. **Geographic Preferences:** U.S.

59756 ■ Portage Venture Partners / Graystone Venture Partners
1 Northfield Plz., Ste. 530
Northfield, IL 60093
Ph:(847)446-9460
Fax: (847)446-9470
URL: http://www.portageventures.com
Contact: Mathew McCall, Managing Director
Preferred Investment Size: $1,000,000 to $4,000,000. **Investment Types:** Early stage. **Industry Preferences:** Internet specific, computer software and services, biotechnology, communications and media, medical and health, other products, semiconductors and other electronics, and consumer related. **Geographic Preferences:** U.S.

59757 ■ Prince Ventures
303 W. Madison St., Ste. 1900
Chicago, IL 60606
Ph:(312)419-1909
Fax: (312)419-9502
Investment Types: Seed, start-up, first and second stage, and leveraged buyout. **Industry Preferences:** Medical and health, biotechnology, computer software and services, semiconductors and other electronics, industrial and energy, communications and media, computer hardware, and other products.

59758 ■ Prism Capital
444 N. Michigan Ave., Ste. 1910
Chicago, IL 60611
Ph:(312)464-7900
Fax: (312)464-7915
URL: http://www.prismfund.com
Contact: John Hoesley, Principal
Preferred Investment Size: $500,000 to $7,000,000. **Investment Types:** Later stage, mezzanine, leveraged buyout, acquisition, and expansion. **Industry Preferences:** Computer software and services, Internet specific, and consumer related, medical and health, semiconductors and other electronics, computer hardware, and other products. **Geographic Preferences:** U.S.

59759 ■ Robotic Ventures
875 N. Michigan Ave., Ste. 1560
Chicago, IL 60611
Ph:(312)867-3470

Fax: (312)751-0769
URL: http://www.roboticventures.com
Contact: Brian Friedman, Managing Director
Preferred Investment Size: $500,000 to $1,000,000.
Investment Policies: Early stage. **Geographic Preferences:** National.

59760 ■ Third Coast Capital
900 N. Franklin St., Ste. 850
Chicago, IL 60610
Ph:(312)337-3303
Fax: (312)337-2567
URL: http://www.thirdcoastcapital.com
Contact: Brad Wheatley, Managing Director
Preferred Investment Size: $1,000,000 to $5,000,000. **Investment Types:** Start-up, early and second stage. **Industry Preferences:** Communications, computer software, Internet specific, biotechnology, medical and health, and consumer related. **Geographic Preferences:** U.S.

59761 ■ Thoma Cressey Equity Partners
Sears Tower, 92nd Fl.
233 S. Wacker Dr.
Chicago, IL 60606
Ph:(312)777-4444
Fax: (312)777-4445
URL: http://www.thomacressey.com
Contact: D. Jeanne Plessinger, Principal
Preferred Investment Size: $20,000,000 to $100,000,000. **Investment Types:** Later stage, leveraged buyout, and recapitalizations. **Industry Preferences:** Other products, medical and health, computer software and services, Internet specific, consumer related, computer hardware, and biotechnology. **Geographic Preferences:** U.S. and Canada.

59762 ■ Transcap Associates Inc.
900 Skokie Blvd., Ste. 210
Northbrook, IL 60062
Ph:(847)753-9600
Fax: (847)753-9090
URL: http://www.transcaptrade.com
Preferred Investment Size: $500,000 to $5,000,000.
Investment Types: Mezzanine, second stage, and special situation. **Industry Preferences:** Communications, computer hardware, semiconductors and other electronics, medical and health, consumer related, industrial and energy. **Geographic Preferences:** U.S.

59763 ■ Tribune Ventures
435 N. Michigan Ave., Ste. 600
Chicago, IL 60611
Ph:(312)222-9100
Fax: (312)222-5993
URL: http://www.tribuneventures.com
Contact: Andy Oleszczuk, President
Preferred Investment Size: $2,000,000 to $10,000,000. **Investment Types:** Early, first and second stage, and expansion. **Industry Preferences:** Internet specific, computer software and services, communications and media, and other products. **Geographic Preferences:** Midwest, Northeast, an West Coast.

59764 ■ Ventana Financial Resources, Inc.
249 Market Sq.
Lake Forest, IL 60045
Ph:(847)234-3434
Preferred Investment Size: $5,000,000 minimum.
Investment Types: Seed, start-up, first and second stage, research and development, leveraged buyout, and mezzanine. **Industry Preferences:** Communications, computer hardware and software, semiconductors and other electronics, biotechnology, medical and health, consumer related, industrial and energy, and manufacturing. **Geographic Preferences:** Midwest, Southeast, and Southwest.

59765 ■ William Blair Capital Partners
227 W. Monroe St., Ste. 3500
Chicago, IL 60606
Ph:(312)364-8250
Fax: (312)236-1042
Co. E-mail: privateequity@wmblair.com
URL: http://www.wmblair.com

Contact: Mio Stojkovich, Vice President
Preferred Investment Size: $7,000,000 to $35,000,000. **Investment Types:** Early and later stage, expansion, generalist PE, management and leveraged buyouts, recapitalizations, and special situation. **Industry Preferences:** Consumer related, medical and health, computer software, hardware and services, biotechnology, industrial and energy, communications and media, semiconductors and other electronics. **Geographic Preferences:** U.S.

59766 ■ Wind Point Partners (Chicago)
676 N. Michigan Ave., Ste. 330
Chicago, IL 60611
Ph:(312)255-4800
Fax: (312)255-4820
URL: http://www.wppartners.com
Contact: Nathan Brown, Principal
Preferred Investment Size: $10,000,000 to $60,000,000. **Investment Types:** Later stage, leveraged buyout, and management buyouts, balanced, generalist PE, acquisition, expansion, and recapitalizations. **Industry Preferences:** Industrial and energy, consumer related, other products, communications and media, medical and health, Internet specific, biotechnology, computer software and services, computer hardware, semiconductors and other electronics. **Geographic Preferences:** U.S.

PROCUREMENT ASSISTANCE PROGRAMS

59767 ■ Disa Conas
c/o DITCO/DO4DT
Small Business Administration/PCR
2300 East Dr., Bldg. 3189, R
Scott Air Force B, IL 62225-5406
Ph:(618)229-8935
Fax: (618)229-8936
Co. E-mail: chut@scott.disa.mil
Contact: Tung Shing Chu, TPCR Supervisor
Description: Covers activities for Defense Information & Technological Contracting (Scott Air Force Base, IL), 375th Airlift Wing (Scott Air Force Base, IL), and USAF AMC Contracting Flight (Scott Air Force Base, IL).

59768 ■ Illinois Procurement Technical Assistance Center–State of Illinois Department of Commerce & Community Affairs
620 E Adams St., 4th Fl.
Springfield, IL 62701
Ph:(217)557-7808
Fax: (217)524-0171
Co. E-mail: ralton@ildceo.net
URL: http://www.commerce.state.il.us/dceo/
Contact: Richard Alton
E-mail: lvanmete@commerce.state.il.us

59769 ■ Latin American Chamber of Commerce–Latin American Chamber of Commerce
3512 W Fullerton Ave
Chicago, IL 60647
Ph:(773)252-5211
Fax: (773)252-7065
Co. E-mail: lacc@latinamericanchamberofcommerce.com
URL: http://www.latinamericanchamberofcommerce.com
Contact: Andrea Cerritos, Small Bus Dir

INCUBATORS/RESEARCH AND TECHNOLOGY PARKS

59770 ■ Argonne National Laboratory–Office of Technology Transfer
9700 S Cass Ave.
Argonne, IL 60439
Ph:(630)252-8111
Free: 800—627-2596

Fax: (630)252-5230
Co. E-mail: sdban@anl.gov
URL: http://www.anl.gov/techtransfer
Contact: Stephen Ban, Dir.
E-mail: sdban@anl.gov
Scope: Facilitates the exchange of Argonne research resources and inventions with U.S. industry and develops partnerships with industry. **Publications:** Argonne News (biweekly); Resources for Technology-Based Small Businesses in the Midwest Region (annually); TransForum (quarterly). **Educational Activities:** Community roundtable.

59771 ■ Bradley University–Office for Teaching Excellence and Faculty Development
Olin Hall 149
1501 W Bradley Ave.
Peoria, IL 61625
Ph:(309)676-7611
Fax: (309)677-3558
Co. E-mail: eks@bradley.edu
URL: http://www.bradley.edu/otefd/
Contact: Dr. Erich Stabenau, Dir.
E-mail: eks@bradley.edu
Scope: Internal research mechanisms are coordinated by the Teaching Excellence Committee and Research Excellence Committee. Development activities of foundational nature are coordinated under the direction of Vice President for Development and University Relations. **Services:** Business Technology Incubator; International Trade Center; Small Business Development Center. **Publications:** Catalyst. **Educational Activities:** Proposal Development Workshop (annually), open to University staff and faculty; Student Research/Creative Production Exhibition and Competition (annually), open to students and faculty involved in collaborative research and creative production activity.

59772 ■ Business Center of Decatur
2121 S Imboden Ct.
Decatur, IL 62521
Ph:(217)423-2832
Fax: (217)423-7214
Co. E-mail: bcd@decaturcenter.com
URL: http://www.decaturcenter.com
Contact: Jim Seaberg, Gen Mgr

59773 ■ Business and Technology Center (Champaign)
701 Devonshire Dr., C-2
Champaign, IL 61820
Ph:(217)398-5759
Fax: (217)398-0413
Contact: Cindy Somers, Owner

59774 ■ Chicago Southland Enterprise Center
1655 Union St
Chicago Heights, IL 60411
Ph:(708)754-6960
Fax: (708)754-8779
Description: Owned by a not-for-profit corporation, this small business incubator fosters collaboration among its tenants, businesses ranging from service to light manufacturing.

59775 ■ Chicago State University–Institutional Research and Academic Evaluation
Cook Administrative Bldg., Rm. 319
9501 S King Dr.
Chicago, IL 60628
Ph:(773)995-2382
Fax: (773)995-2543
Co. E-mail: s-miari@csu.edu
Contact: Dr. Samir Miari, Assoc.VP
E-mail: s-miari@csu.edu
Scope: Compiles academic and other data relating to the University. Provides technical assistance to faculty for various research projects.

59776 ■ Chicago Technology Park
2201 W Campbell Park Dr.
Chicago, IL 60612
Ph:(312)829-7252

Fax: (312)829-4069
Co. E-mail: harvey.reiter@sbcglobal.net
URL: http://www.techpark.com
Contact: Harvey Reiter, Pres.
E-mail: harvey.reiter@sbcglobal.net
Scope: Seeks to coordinate industry, university, and government partnerships to stimulate the formation of science-based companies and economic development in the Chicago area. Provides access to university and hospital resources, offers assistance in the creation of new venture companies, and provides space in an incubator building.

59777 ■ Fulton Carroll Center Incubator
2010 W Fulton St., Ste 280
Suite 200
Chicago, IL 60612
Ph:(312)421-3941
Fax: (312)421-1871
URL: http://www.industrialcouncil.com

59778 ■ Galesburg Business and Technology Center
3000 Log City Tr.
Galesburg, IL 61401
Ph:(309)345-3501
Fax: (309)345-3526
Co. E-mail: info@galesburgbtc.org
URL: http://www.galesburgbtc.org

59779 ■ Greater Sterling Development Corporation
1741 Industrial Dr.
Sterling, IL 61081
Ph:(815)625-5255
Fax: (815)625-5094
Co. E-mail: info@sterlingdevelopment.org
URL: http://www.sterlingdevelopment.org
Contact: David Barajas Jr., Exec Dir

59780 ■ Illinois State University–University Research Office
Havey 310, CB 3040
Normal, IL 61790-3040
Ph:(309)438-2528
Fax: (309)438-7912
Co. E-mail: gmcginn@ilstu.edu
Contact: Gary McGinnis PhD, Assoc.VP
E-mail: gmcginn@ilstu.edu
Scope: Various biological and sociological research projects, including studies on general and special education. Assists in preparation of research proposals and project reports. **Educational Activities:** Faculty seminars.

59781 ■ Macomb Area Economic Development Corporation
Western Illinois University
510 N Pearl St.
Macomb, IL 61455
Ph:(309)837-4684
Fax: (309)837-4688
Co. E-mail: maedco@wiu.edu
URL: http://www.maedco.org

59782 ■ Maple City Business and Technology Center Incubator–Technology Center Incubator
620 S Main St.
Monmouth, IL 61462
Ph:(309)734-8544
Fax: (309)734-8579

59783 ■ Michael Reese Hospital and Medical Center–Research and Education Foundation
2929 E Ellis Ave.
Cummings Pavilion Rm. 411
Chicago, IL 60616-3390
Ph:(312)791-2830
Fax: (312)791-2927
Co. E-mail: waclark@michaelreesefoundation.org
URL: http://www.michaelreesefoundation.org
Contact: William A. Clark PhD, Dir.
E-mail: waclark@michaelreesefoundation.org
Scope: Administers and coordinates contracts and grants for biomedical research conducted in the vari-

ous departments of the Michael Reese Hospital and Medical Center. Research projects are funded by the government, private philanthropy, and outside sources and include studies on cancer, heart disease, stroke, neurological disorders, arthritis, birth defects, schizophrenia, and other afflictions.

59784 ■ Northern Illinois University–Technology Commercialization Office
DeKalb, IL 60115
Ph:(815)753-2117
Fax: (815)753-1631
Co. E-mail: lkscherer@niu.edu
URL: http://www.grad.niu.edu/tco/
Contact: Czail Michell, Assoc.Dir.
E-mail: lkscherer@niu.edu
Scope: Assists faculty at NIU with technical and commercial assessments, patent applications and licensing. **Publications:** Newsletter for faculty (semiannually). **Educational Activities:** Seminars on commercialization process, intellectual property matters.

59785 ■ Northwestern University–Evanston Research Park
820 Church St., Ste. 300
Evanston, IL 60201
Ph:(847)864-9334
Fax: (847)475-7380
Co. E-mail: r-kysiak@northwestern.edu
URL: http://www.researchpark.com/
Contact: Ron Kysiak, Exec.VP/CEO
E-mail: r-kysiak@northwestern.edu
Scope: Encourages the exchange of research activities between the University and Research Park tenants and the transfer of technological advances to industry. Major tenants include the Center for Biotechnology; The Institute for International Entrepreneurship, and the Institute for the Learning Sciences, an artificial intelligence center. The Research Park provides a small-business incubator system to support newly developing, high-technology companies, offers technical assistance, and administers a seed capital fund. **Publications:** Park Progress Annual Report; Researchpark.com Newsletter. **Educational Activities:** Seminars, on computer training and business assistance; Technology Executive Round Table (monthly).

59786 ■ Northwestern University–Office for Research
Rebecca Crown Center, Rm. 2-223
633 Clark St.
Evanston, IL 60208-1108
Ph:(847)491-3485
Fax: (847)467-4620
Co. E-mail: vp-research@northwestern.edu
URL: http://www.northwestern.edu/research/
Contact: C. Bradley Moore PhD, VP
E-mail: vp-research@northwestern.edu
Scope: Provides support for interdisciplinary research centers. Oversees Center for Comparative Medicine, the Office of Research Safety, Office of Sponsored Research, Office for the Protection of Research Subjects, Office for Research Integrity, Office for Research Planning, Finance and Communications, and the Office for Research Information Systems. Administers interdisciplinary research service centers of the University. **Publications:** Annual report; CenterPiece magazine (quarterly).

59787 ■ Northwestern University–The Technology Innovation Center
820 Davis St.
Evanston, IL 60201
Ph:(847)864-0800
Fax: (847)866-1808
Co. E-mail: t-lavengood@nwu.edu
URL: http://www.theincubator.com
Contact: Tim Lavengood, Dir.
E-mail: t-lavengood@nwu.edu
Scope: Matches University resources with the needs of businesses, including assisting faculty entrepreneurs to commercialize their new technologies. The Center maintains three administrative offices: the in-

cubator component leases space to technology-based small companies; the Small Business Development Center provides technical and business assistance companies in the Research Park and northern Cook County, manages the Evanston Business Investment Corporation (a seed capital fund) and links companies to campus expertise; and the Minority Business Development Office administers special training projects. **Publications:** Park Facts.

59788 ■ Shetland Properties Limited Partnership
5400 W Roosevelt Rd.
Chicago, IL 60644
Ph:(773)921-5400
Fax: (773)921-6680
Co. E-mail: slate@shetland.com
URL: http://www.shetland.com
Contact: Andrew Lappin, Pres

59789 ■ Southern Illinois Research Park Inc.
150 E Pleasant Hill Rd., MC 6891
Carbondale, IL 62901
Ph:(618)536-4451
Fax: (618)453-5040
Co. E-mail: lenzi@siu.edu
URL: http://www.sirpark.com
Contact: Dr. Raymond C. Lenzi, Exec.Dir./CEO
E-mail: lenzi@siu.edu
Scope: Facilitates the retention, expansion, and creation of businesses in research park to diversify the southern Illinois region. Serves as a catalyst for economic, community, and regional development in Southern Illinois. **Services:** Grant writing assistance, to incubator tenants and clients within Illinois; Grant writing assistance, to incubator tenants and clients within Illinois. **Publications:** Carbondale Forum (monthly); Connections (quarterly). **Educational Activities:** Conferences, forums; Seminars; Workshops, both on business startup and applications.

59790 ■ Southern Illinois University at Carbondale–Office of Research Development and Administration
MC 4709
Woody Hall C-206
Carbondale, IL 62901
Ph:(618)453-4540
Fax: (618)453-8038
Co. E-mail: orda@siu.edu
URL: http://www.siu.edu/orda/
Contact: Dr. Prudence M. Rice, Dir.
E-mail: orda@siu.edu
Scope: Serves as central administrative coordinating agency for organized research; supports a variety of research facilities, and administers special internal grants programs conducted by the University; acts as a comprehensive information source about grant programs, and provides logistical support and service to faculty and staff seeking and administering grants. **Publications:** Perspectives Research Magazine (semiannually); Research Matters (monthly); Sponsored Project Guide.

59791 ■ Southern Illinois University at Edwardsville–Office of Research and Projects
Edwardsville, IL 62026-1046
Ph:(618)692-3162
Fax: (618)692-3523
Co. E-mail: shansen@siue.edu
URL: http://www.siue.edu/graduate
Contact: Dr. Stephen Hansen, Dean
E-mail: shansen@siue.edu
Scope: Serves as coordinating unit between the University and agencies and foundations that provide support for research, training, and other programs at the University. Functions as a service facility to assist faculty members in obtaining outside support for their projects. **Publications:** Research and Creative Activities (biennially); Research Highlights (quarterly). **Educational Activities:** Seminars and workshops, on grant development.

59792 ■ University of Illinois at Chicago–Office of Research Services
310 Administrative Office Bldg., MC 672
1737 W Polk St.
Chicago, IL 60612

Ph:(312)996-2862
Fax: (312)996-9005
Co. E-mail: bhelms@uic.edu
URL: http://www.uic.edu/depts/ovcr/ors/index.html
Contact: Byron Helms, Dir.
E-mail: bhelms@uic.edu
Scope: Administers and coordinates extramurally supported research conducted by faculty members of various departments of the University.

59793 ■ University of Illinois at Chicago–Office of Technology Management
312 Administrative Office Bldg., MC 682
1737 W Polk St.
Chicago, IL 60612
Ph:(312)996-7018
Fax: (312)996-1995
Co. E-mail: mdicig@uic.edu
URL: http://www.uic.edu/depts/ovcr/otm/
Contact: Mary E. Dicig, Dir.
E-mail: mdicig@uic.edu
Scope: Assists in the support, development, and commercialization of University inventions and discoveries, and coordinates campus-developed intellectual property, including copyrights, patents, and licensing. **Publications:** Technology Transfer (annually). **Educational Activities:** Workshops.

59794 ■ University of Illinois at Urbana-Champaign–Office of Technology Management
319 Ceramics Bldg.
105 S Goodwin Ave.
Urbana, IL 61801
Ph:(217)333-7862
Fax: (217)265-5530
Co. E-mail: otm@uiuc.edu
URL: http://www.otm.uiuc.edu
Contact: Lesley Millar, Interim Dir.
E-mail: otm@uiuc.edu
Scope: Transfers technology from the university to business and industry, particularly in the areas of engineering, agriculture and computing. particularly in the areas of engineering, agriculture and computing.

59795 ■ Western Illinois University–Office of Sponsored Projects
Sherman Hall 320
1 University Cir.
Macomb, IL 61455
Ph:(309)298-1191
Fax: (309)298-2091
Co. E-mail: B-Seaton@wiu.edu
URL: http://www.wiu.edu/SponsoredProjects/council
Contact: Beth Seaton, Dir.
E-mail: B-Seaton@wiu.edu
Scope: Serves as a coordinating agency for sponsored projects at the University in life, physical, and social sciences, agriculture, and education. Coordinates all sources of external funds for research, institutes, workshops, and other extramurally supported activities at the University. **Publications:** Sponsored Projects News & Notes (5/year).

EDUCATIONAL PROGRAMS

59796 ■ Black Hawk College–Quad-Cities Campus
6600 34th Ave.
Moline, IL 61265
Ph:(309)796-5000
Free: 800-334-1311
Fax: (309)792-5976
URL: http://www.bhc.edu
Description: Two-year college offering a small business management program.

59797 ■ Chicago State University–Office of Continuing Education
9501 S King Dr.
Robinson University Center Rm 200
Chicago, IL 60628-1598
Ph:(773)995-2545
Fax: (773)995-2941
Co. E-mail: conted@csu.edu

URL: http://www.csu.edu/continuingeducation
Description: Offers mature students career-updating and business-related courses, seminars, and workshops for degree, nondegree, credit, or noncredit status. Conducts course work in advanced business, management, human relations, and small business management. Also provides on-site training and development for employees of small businesses involved in computer operation, budgeting, marketing, and personnel management. Additional courses are presented through the College of Business Administration.

59798 ■ Loyola University Chicago–School of Professional Studies
820 N Michigan Ave., Ste. 401
Chicago, IL 60611
Ph:(312)915-6501
Fax: (312)915-6508
Co. E-mail: sps@luc.edu
URL: http://www.luc.edu
Description: Sponsors several programs of interest to small business professionals: The Weekend College is a concentrated program for men and women who wish to attend college while working full time. The program offers 11 majors, with residence opportunity. The Continuing Education Program serves women interested in beginning or continuing their college careers through day classes. Other courses of study are offered through the Business Administration Department.

59799 ■ Rend Lake College
468 N Ken Gray Pky.
Ina, IL 62846
Ph:(618)437-5321
Fax: (618)437-5677
URL: http://www.rlc.cc.il.us
Description: Two-year college offering a small business management program.

59800 ■ Rock Valley College
3301 N Mulford Rd.
Rockford, IL 61114
Ph:(815)921-7821
Free: 800-973-7821
Fax: (815)636-4074
URL: http://www.rockvalleycollege.edu
Description: Two-year college offering a small business management program.

59801 ■ Sauk Valley Community College
173 IL., Rte. 2
Dixon, IL 61021
Ph:(815)288-5511
Fax: (815)288-1880
URL: http://www.svcc.edu
Description: Two-year college offering small business management classes.

PUBLICATIONS

59802 ■ *Being an Entrepreneur in Illinois*
Multi Business Concepts
615 Griswold, Ste. 1410
Detroit, MI 48226
Ph:(313)961-2665
Fax: (313)963-6797
Ed: Anthony Brogdon. **Released:** 1991. **Price:** $12. 95. **Description:** Concentrates on the legal aspects of starting a business in the state of Illinois.

59803 ■ *How to Form Your Own Illinois Corporation Before the Inc. Dries!: A Step by Step Guide, With Forms*
P. Gaines Publishing Co.
333 S. Taylor Ave.
PO Box 2253
Oak Park, IL 60302
Ph:(708)524-9033
Fax: (708)524-9038
Ed: Phillip Williams. **Released:** Fourth edition, 1994. **Price:** $26.95. **Description:** Volume 1 of the Small Business Incorporation series. Explains the advan-

tages and disadvantages of incorporation and shows, step-by-step, how the small business owners can incorporate at low cost. Covers Illinois profit and nonprofit corporations, Illinois professional service corporations, subchapter S corporations, and Delaware corporations. Includes forms necessary for incorporation.

59804 ■ *Smart Start your Illinois Business*
PSI Research
300 N. Valley Dr.
Grants Pass, OR 97526
Ph:(503)479-9464
Free: 800-228-2275
Fax: (503)476-1479
Co. E-mail: info@psi-research.com
URL: http://www.psi-research.com
Ed: Michael D. Jenkins. **Released:** Revised edition, 1992. **Price:** $29.95 (looseleaf binder); $24.95 (paper). **Description:** Part of the Successful Business Library series.

59805 ■ *Starting and Operating a Business in Illinois: A Step-by-Step Guide*
PSI Research
300 N. Valley Dr.
Grants Pass, OR 97526
Ph:(503)479-9464
Free: 800-228-2275
Fax: (503)476-1479
Co. E-mail: psi2@magick.net
Ed: Michael D. Jenkins. **Released:** Revised edition, 1992. **Price:** $29.95 (looseleaf binder); $24.95 (paper). **Description:** Part of the Successful Business Library series.

PUBLISHERS

59806 ■ Blackman Kallick Bartelstein L.L.P.
10 S Riverside Plz., 9th Fl.
Chicago, IL 60606
Ph:(312)207-1040
Fax: (312)207-1066
Co. E-mail: bkinfo@blackmankallick.com
URL: http://www.bkadvice.com
Contact: Irving L. Blackman, Founding Ptr.
Description: Publishes on personal taxes and tax information for closely held businesses. Also produces cassettes. Reaches market through direct mail. **Founded:** 1962.

59807 ■ Dearborn Trade Publishing Inc.
30 S Wacker Dr., Ste. 2500
Chicago, IL 60606
Ph:(312)836-4400
Free: 800-245-2665
Fax: (312)836-1021
Co. E-mail: ContactKaplanFinancial@kaplan.com
URL: http://www.dearborn.com
Contact: Cynthia Zigmund, Vice President
E-mail: zigmund@dearborn.com
Description: Publishes books for consumers and professionals on finance, business, real estate, and marketing sales. Accepts proposals for new books. Reaches market through commission representatives, direct mail, and telephone sales. Accepts unsolicited manuscripts. **Founded:** 1959.

59808 ■ Distribooks Inc.
8120 N Ridgeway Ave.
Skokie, IL 60076-2911
Ph:(847)676-1596
Free: 888-266-5713
Fax: (847)676-1195
Co. E-mail: info@distribooks.com
Contact: Nicolas Mengin, CEO
E-mail: n.mengin@distribooks.com
Description: Distributor of titles on foreign language instruction and related dictionaries. **Founded:** 1989.

59809 ■ Institute of Real Estate Management
430 North Michigan Ave.
Chicago, IL 60611
Ph:(312)329-6000
Free: 800-837-0706

Co. E-mail: custserv@irem.org
URL: http://www.irem.org
Description: Publishes an array of publications, software and a journal geared toward real estate professionals.

59810 ■ McGraw-Hill/Irwin
1333 Burr Ridge Pky.
Burr Ridge, IL 60527-6423
Ph:(630)789-4000
Free: 800-338-3987
Fax: (630)789-6944
Co. E-mail: jim_kelly@mcgraw-hill.com
URL: http://www.mhhe.com
Contact: John Paul Lenney, President
E-mail: john_paul_lenney@mcgraw-hill.com
Description: Publishes books on accounting, advertising, business law, business math and statistics, computer information technology, economics, finance, management information systems, marketing and organizational behavior. **Founded:** 1933.

59811 ■ Nicholas Brealey Publishing
100 City Hall Plaza, Ste. 501
Boston, MA 02108
Ph:(617)523-3801
Fax: (617)523-3708
Co. E-mail: info@nicholasbrealey.com
URL: http://www.nbrealey-books.com
Contact: Nicholas Brealey, Owner
E-mail: rights@nbrealey-books.com
Description: Publishes trade and professional books in business, intelligent self-help and popular psychology. Accepts unsolicited manuscripts. Reaches market

through commission representatives, direct mail, reviews, listings and distributors. **Founded:** 1992.

59812 ■ PivotPoint Press
PO Box 577468
Chicago, IL 60657-7468
Ph:(773)561-1512
Co. E-mail: info@PirvoitPointPress.com
URL: http://www.PirvoitPointPress.com
Contact: Robert Logan
Description: Publishes nonfiction books on business, economics, and family. **Founded:** 2003

59813 ■ Pride Publications Inc.
4 N Wilshire Ln.
Arlington Heights, IL 60004
Fax: (847)398-0670
Co. E-mail: ginnodo@pridepublications.com
URL: http://www.pridepublications.com
Description: Publishes nonfiction books.

59814 ■ ProdigalPen Publishing Inc.
3023 N Clark St., No. 236
Chicago, IL 60613
Ph:(312)375-7141
Co. E-mail: info@knockthehustle.com
URL: http://www.prodigalpen.com
Contact: Hadji Williams, Author
E-mail: author@knockthehustle.com
Description: Publishes religious books by writers of color. Reaches market through Baker & Taylor.

59815 ■ Productivity Press
2427 Bond St.
University Park, IL 60466-3101
Ph:(708)587-4152

Free: 888-319-5852
Fax: (708)534-7803
Co. E-mail: info@productivitypress.com
URL: http://www.productivitypress.com
Contact: Ralph Bernstein, Editor
Description: Publishes materials on lean manufacturing and business improvement.

59816 ■ Sourcebooks Inc.
1935 Brookdale Rd., Ste. 139
Naperville, IL 60563
Ph:(630)961-3900
Free: 800-432-7444
Fax: (630)961-2168
Co. E-mail: info@sourcebooks.com
URL: http://www.sourcebooks.com
Contact: Dominique Raccah, CEO
E-mail: dominique@sourcebooks.com
Description: Publishes general trade. Accepts unsolicited manuscripts; query first with a chapter outline and sample chapters. Reaches market through direct mail, trade sales, and wholesalers and distributors, including Baker & Taylor Books, Ingram Book Co., and Quality Books. **Founded:** 1987.

59817 ■ World Exonumia
PO Box 4143CPA
Rockford, IL 61110-0643
Ph:(815)226-0771
Fax: (815)397-7662
Co. E-mail: hartzog@exonumia.com
URL: http://www.exonumia.com
Contact: Rich Hartzog, President
Description: Wholesaler. Reaches market through direct mail. **Founded:** 1972.

Indiana

SMALL BUSINESS DEVELOPMENT CENTER LEAD OFFICE

59818 ■ Indiana SBDC–Indiana Economic Development Corporation
1 North Capitol, Ste. 900
Indianapolis, IN 46204
Ph:(317)232-2464
Fax: (317)232-8874
Co. E-mail: sthrash@in.net
URL: http://www.isbdc.org
Contact: Bruce Kid, State Dir.
E-mail: bkidd@iedc.in.gov

SMALL BUSINESS DEVELOPMENT CENTERS

59819 ■ Bedford Chamber of Commerce–SBDC
1116 16th St.
Bedford, IN 47421
Ph:(812)275-4493

59820 ■ Brown County Chamber of Commerce–SBDC
37 W. Main St.
Nashville, IN 47448
Ph:(812)988-6647

59821 ■ Central Indiana SBDC
2126 N. Meridian St., Ste. 120
Indianapolis, IN 46202
Ph:(317)233-7232
Fax: (317)926-2829
Co. E-mail: centralindiana@isbdc.org
URL: http://www.isbdc.org

59822 ■ East Central Indiana SBDC
500 S. A St.
Richmond, IN 47374
Ph:(765)962-2887
Free: 877-962-2887
Fax: (765)966-0882
Co. E-mail: eastcentral@isbdc.org

59823 ■ Entrepreneurial Center of Michigan City–SBDC Satellite Office
422 Franklin St.
Michigan City, IN 46360
Ph:(219)809-4200
Fax: (219)809-4210

59824 ■ Greater Lafayette Area SBDC
Burton D. Morgan Ctr. For Entrepreneurship
1201 W. State St.
West Lafayette, IN 47907
Ph:(765)496-6491
Fax: (765)494-9870
Co. E-mail: grlafayette@isbdc.org

59825 ■ Greater Lafayette Community Development Corp.–SBDC
337 Columbia
PO Box 277
Lafayette, IN 47902
Ph:(765)742-1984
Fax: (765)742-6276
Contact: Susan Davis, Dir.

59826 ■ Greater LaPorte Chamber of Commerce–Small Business Development Center
414 Lincoln Way
La Porte, IN 46352
Ph:(219)326-3178
URL: http://www.lpchamber.com

59827 ■ Kendallville Chamber of Commerce–SBDC Satellite Office
122 S. Main St.
Kendallville, IN 46755
Ph:(219)347-1554
URL: http://www.isbdc.org

59828 ■ Linton/Stockton Chamber of Commerce–SBDC
159 1st St., NW
Linton, IN 47441
Ph:(812)847-4846

59829 ■ North Central Indiana–Small Business Development Center
700 E. Firmin St., Ste. 106
Kokomo, IN 46902-2350
Ph:(765)454-7922
Fax: (765)854-0438
Co. E-mail: northcentral@isbdc.org
URL: http://www.isbdc.org
Contact: Mary Giangiordano, Dir.

59830 ■ Northeast Indiana Regional Office–Small Business Development Center
Hobson Ctr.
4312 Hobson Rd., Ste. B
Fort Wayne, IN 46815
Ph:(260)481-0500
Fax: (260)481-0500
Co. E-mail: northeast@isbdc.org
URL: http://www.nisbdc.org
Contact: Jomare Bowers-Mizzell, Dir.

59831 ■ Northwest Indiana Regional Development Company–Small Business Development Center
5997 Carlson Ave., Ste. B
Portage, IN 46368
Ph:(219)764-2700
Fax: (219)764-2890
URL: http://www.rdc504.org
Contact: Tony Rodriguez, Exec. Dir

59832 ■ Northwest Indiana SBDC
2646 Highway Ave., 1st Fl.
Highland, IN 46322
Ph:(219)838-0176
Fax: (219)838-0554

Co. E-mail: northwest@isbdc.org
URL: http://www.nwisbdc.org

59833 ■ Project Future, Inc.–SBDC
Commerce Center
401 Colfax, Ste. 305
South Bend, IN 46617
Ph:(574)234-6590
Free: 800-228-8086
Fax: (574)236-1060
URL: http://www.projectfuture.org

E-mail: pmcmahon@projectfuture.org

59834 ■ Purdue University–SBDC
1058 Hovde Hall
610 Purdue Mall
West Lafayette, IN 47907-2040
Ph:(317)494-5858

59835 ■ Randolph County Economic Development Foundation–SBDC
111 S. Main St.
Winchester, IN 47394
Free: 800-905-0514

59836 ■ South Bend Area SBDC
401 E. Colfax Ave., Ste. 120
South Bend, IN 46617-2735
Ph:(219)282-4350
Fax: (219)236-1056
Co. E-mail: southbend@isbdc.org
URL: http://www.southbendbcg.com
Contact: Janet Fye, Dir.

59837 ■ South Central Indiana
501 N. Morton St., Ste. 106
Bloomington, IN 47404
Ph:(812)339-8937
Fax: (812)335-7352
Co. E-mail: southcentral@isbdc.org
URL: http://www.gowayfinder.com/products/
Contact: David Miller, Dir.

59838 ■ South Central Indiana SBDC
501 N. Morton St., Ste. 106
Bloomington, IN 47404-3731
Ph:(812)339-8937
Fax: (812)335-7352
Co. E-mail: southcentral@isbdc.org
URL: http://www.isbdc.org
Contact: Brian Kleber, Dir.

59839 ■ Southeastern Indiana SBDC
975 Industrial Dr.
Madison, IN 47250
Ph:(812)265-3127
Free: 800-595-3127
Fax: (812)265-5544
Co. E-mail: southeastern@isbdc.org
URL: http://www.isbdc.org
Contact: Linda Wood, Dir.

59840 ■ Southeastern Indiana SBDC at Connersville–Satellite Office
115 E. 6th St.
Connersville, IN 47331
Ph:(765)825-8328
Fax: (765)825-4613
URL: http://www.isbdc.org

59841 ■ Southwestern Indiana Regional Small Business Development Center
100 NW 2nd St., Ste. 100
Evansville, IN 47708
Ph:(812)425-7232
Fax: (812)421-5883
Co. E-mail: southwestern@isbdc.org
URL: http://www.isbdc.org
Contact: Kim Howard, Dir.

59842 ■ Tipton County Economic Development Corp.–SBDC
136 E. Jefferson
Tipton, IN 46072
Free: 800-461-4907
URL: http://www.tiptonedc.com

59843 ■ Wabash Area Chamber of Commerce–SBDC (111 S)
111 S. Wabash
Wabash, IN 46992
Ph:(219)563-1168
URL: http://www.wabashchamber.org

59844 ■ West Central Indiana SBDC
Indiana State University College of Business, Rm. 510
800 Sycamore St.
Terre Haute, IN 47809
Ph:(812)237-7676
Fax: (812)237-7675
Co. E-mail: westcentral@isbdc.org
URL: http://www.isbdc.org
Contact: Tara Lane, Dir.

SMALL BUSINESS ASSISTANCE PROGRAMS

59845 ■ Indiana Department of Commerce–Department of Economic Development
1 N Capitol Ave., Ste. 700
Indianapolis, IN 46204-2288
Ph:(317)232-8888
Fax: (317)232-4146
URL: http://www.indianacommerce.com
Description: Coordinates business services offered by the Department of Commerce and other agencies. Serves as a switchboard for access to those services, such as export promotion, defense procurement, minority business development, and regulatory assistance.

59846 ■ Indiana Department of Commerce–Energy Policy Division
1 N Capitol Ave., Ste. 700
Indianapolis, IN 46204-2288
Ph:(317)232-8940
Free: 800-382-4631
Fax: (317)232-8995
URL: http://www.indianacommerce.com
Description: Provides information on energy conservation. Gives free energy audits for small businesses. Provides some loan subsidies for energy conservation measures.

59847 ■ Indiana Department of Commerce–International Trade Division
1 N Capitol Ave., Ste. 700
Indianapolis, IN 46204
Ph:(317)232-8845
Fax: (317)233-1680
URL: http://www.indianacommerce.com
Description: Helps businesses interested in foreign trade to establish contacts and leads. Organizes trade missions.

59848 ■ Indiana Institute of Technology–McMillen Productivity and Design Center
1600 E Washington Blvd.
Ft. Wayne, IN 46803
Ph:(260)422-5561
Free: 800-937-2448
Fax: (260)422-7696
URL: http://www.indianatech.edu
Description: Offers industrial-quality production-level hardware and software, and staff expertise. Provides consulting and seminars in computer-aided design.

59849 ■ Indiana State University–Small Business Development Center
Ninth & Sycamore St.
Terre Haute, IN 47809
Ph:(812)237-7676
Free: 800-227-7232
Fax: (812)237-7675
Co. E-mail: westcentral@isbdc.org
URL: http://www.indstate.edu/schbus/sbdc/
Description: Provides consulting, seminars, training, and access to economic databases.

59850 ■ Indiana University–Indiana Business Research Center
Kelley School of Business
1275 E 10th St., Ste. 3110
Bloomington, IN 47405
Ph:(812)855-5507
Fax: (812)855-7763
Co. E-mail: ibrc@iupui.edu
URL: http://www.ibrc.indiana.edu
Contact: Jerry Conover, Dir
Description: Collects and analyses business and economic data in the state. Information is accessible through the Indiana Information Retrieval System at libraries, universities, and public agencies. Puts out two bimonthly publications. Presents a Business Outlook Panel annually in several cities.

59851 ■ Indiana University–Indiana Molecular Biology Institute
Myers Hall
915 E 3rd St., Ste. 150
Bloomington, IN 47405
Ph:(812)855-4183
Fax: (812)855-6082
Co. E-mail: freemanr@indiana.edu
URL: http://imbi.bio.indiana.edu
Contact: Rhea Freeman, Admn Asst
Description: Offers expertise and use of its facilities for industrial research in molecular and cellular biology.

59852 ■ Purdue University–Technical Assistance Program
1435 Win Hentschel Blvd., No. B-110
Technical Assistance Program
West Lafayette, IN 47906-4145
Ph:(765)494-6258
Fax: (765)494-9187
Co. E-mail: tap@purdue.edu
URL: http://www.purdue.edu/tap
Contact: David McKinnis, Ph. D., Dir
Description: Provides technology transfers to businesses free of charge.

SCORE OFFICES

59853 ■ SCORE Anderson
c/o Anderson Chamber of Commerce
PO Box 469
Anderson, IN 46015
Ph:(765)642-0264
Co. E-mail: postmaster@scoreanderson.org
URL: http://www.scoreanderson.org
Contact: Jim Alexander
Description: Provides counseling to persons wanting to go into business as well as those already in the business. Sponsors seminars and workshops.

59854 ■ SCORE Bloomington
c/o James Rusie, Chm.
216 W Allen St., Ste. 133
Bloomington, IN 47403

Ph:(812)335-7344
Co. E-mail: score527@sbcglobal.net
URL: http://www.bloomingtonscore.org

59855 ■ SCORE Chapter 50
0130 Federal Bldg.
1300 S Harrison St.
Fort Wayne, IN 46802
Ph:(260)422-2601
Fax: (260)422-2601
Co. E-mail: score@fwi.com
URL: http://www.score-fortwayne.org
Contact: Al Kruetzman, Chm.
Description: Volunteer businessmen and women. Provides free small business management assistance to individuals in Northeast Indiana.

59856 ■ SCORE Elkhart
c/o Greater Elkhart Chamber of Commerce
418 S Main St.
Elkhart, IN 46515
Ph:(574)293-1531
Fax: (219)294-1859
Co. E-mail: score@elkhart.org
Description: Provides professional guidance and information to America's small businesses.

59857 ■ SCORE Evansville
c/o Tom Koetting, Chm.
1100 W Lloyd Expy., Ste. 314
Evansville, IN 47708-1146
Ph:(812)426-6144
Fax: (812)426-6144
Co. E-mail: scoreevv@aol.com
URL: http://www.scoreevansville.com

59858 ■ SCORE Kokomo/Howard Counties
325 N Main St.
Kokomo, IN 46901
Ph:(765)457-5301
Fax: (765)452-4564
Co. E-mail: chair543@kokomoscore.org
Contact: Mr. Bob Straub, Chm.
Description: Represents Business professionals and Counselors. Seeks to provide assistant and counsel to existing and newly opened small businesses.

59859 ■ SCORE Logansport
2815 E Market St., Rm. 112
Logansport, IN 46947
Ph:(574)753-5101
Free: (866)753-5102
Fax: (574)735-5103
Co. E-mail: score@clss.net
URL: http://www.score615logansport.org
Contact: Mrs. Chris Coon, Chair

59860 ■ SCORE Marion/Grant Co
215 S Adams St.
Marion, IN 46952
Ph:(765)664-5107
Co. E-mail: score550@nxco.com
URL: http://www.bloomington.in.us/~mscore
Description: Provides free business counseling and management training programs for small business owners/managers, and for those who plan to start a new business.

59861 ■ SCORE South Bend
401 E Colfax Ave., Ste. 120
South Bend, IN 46601
Ph:(574)282-4350
Fax: (574)236-1056
Co. E-mail: chair@southbend-score.org
URL: http://www.southbend-score.org
Contact: George Stump, Chm.
Description: Provides counseling to persons wanting to go into business as well as those already in the business. Sponsors seminars and workshops.

59862 ■ SCORE South Central Indiana
702 E Market St.
New Albany, IN 47150
Ph:(812)944-9178
Co. E-mail: 522score@netpointe.com
Description: Provides counseling to persons wanting to go into business as well as those already in the business. Sponsors seminars and workshops.

59863 ■ SCORE South East Indiana
500 Franklin St.
Columbus, IN 47201
Ph:(812)379-4457
Co. E-mail: score419@tls.net
URL: http://www.score.org

59864 ■ Service Corps of Retired Executives-Chapter 6
8500 Keystone Crossing, Ste. 401
Indianapolis, IN 46240
Ph:(317)226-7264
Fax: (317)226-7259
Co. E-mail: score@indyscore.org
URL: http://www.score-indianapolis.org
Description: Consults those who want to start a new business or grow an existing business.

BETTER BUSINESS BUREAUS

59865 ■ Better Business Bureau of Central Indiana
22 E Washington St., Ste. 200
Indianapolis, IN 46204
Ph:(317)488-2222
Free: (866)IND-YBBB
Fax: (317)488-2224
Co. E-mail: info@central-in.bbb.org
URL: http://www.indybbb.org
Contact: Linda R. Carmody, Pres./CEO

59866 ■ Better Business Bureau of Elkhart County
722 W Bristol St.
Elkhart, IN 46514
Ph:(219)262-8996
Free: 800-552-4631
Fax: (219)266-2026
Co. E-mail: info@neindianabbb.org
URL: http://www.elkhart.bbb.org
Contact: Dreama Jensen

59867 ■ Better Business Bureau of Northeastern Indiana
4011 Parnell Ave.
Fort Wayne, IN 46805
Ph:(260)423-4433
Free: 800-552-4631
Fax: (260)423-3301
Co. E-mail: info@neindianabbb.org
URL: http://www.neindiana.bbb.org
Contact: Mike Coil, Pres.

59868 ■ Better Business Bureau of Northwest Indiana
6111 Harrison St., Ste. 101
Merrillville, IN 46410
Ph:(219)980-1511
Fax: (219)884-2123
Co. E-mail: info@nwin.bbb.org
URL: http://www.nwin.bbb.org
Contact: Morris W. Cochran, Pres./CEO

59869 ■ Central Indiana Better Business Bureau
22 E Washington St., Ste. 200
Indianapolis, IN 46204
Ph:(317)488-2222
Fax: (317)488-2224
Co. E-mail: info@central-in.bbb.org
URL: http://www.indybbb.org
Contact: Linda Carmody, Pres./CEO

59870 ■ Tri-State Better Business Bureau
1139 Washington Sq.
Evansville, IN 47715
Ph:(812)473-0202
Fax: (812)473-3080
Co. E-mail: info@evansville.bbb.org
URL: http://www.evansville.bbb.org
Contact: Cathy Eichele, Pres.

CHAMBERS OF COMMERCE

59871 ■ Alexandria - Monroe Chamber of Commerce
119 N Harrison St.
Alexandria, IN 46001-2017
Ph:(765)724-3144
Fax: (765)724-3144
Co. E-mail: kimberly.chamber@sbcglobal.net
URL: http://alexandriachamber.com
Contact: Kimberly Kirtley, Dir./Pres.

59872 ■ Angola Area Chamber of Commerce
211 E Maumee St., Ste. B
Angola, IN 46703
Ph:(260)665-3512
Fax: (260)665-7418
Co. E-mail: info@angolachamber.org
URL: http://www.angolachamber.org
Contact: Jill Boggs, Exec.Dir.

59873 ■ Auburn Chamber of Commerce
PO Box 168
208 S Jackson St.
Auburn, IN 46706-0168
Ph:(260)925-2100
Fax: (260)925-2199
Co. E-mail: chamber@locl.net
URL: http://www.chamberinauburn.com
Contact: Kelly Knox, Exec.Dir.

59874 ■ Batesville Area Chamber of Commerce
132 S Main St.
Batesville, IN 47006
Ph:(812)934-3101
Fax: (812)932-0202
Co. E-mail: chamberexec@batesvillein.com
URL: http://www.batesvillein.com
Contact: Lydia S. Woodward, Exec.Dir.

59875 ■ Bedford Area Chamber of Commerce
1116 16th St.
Bedford, IN 47421
Ph:(812)275-4493
Fax: (812)279-5998
Co. E-mail: bedford@bedfordchamber.com
URL: http://www.bedfordchamber.com
Contact: Adele Bowden-Purlee, Pres.

59876 ■ Berne Chamber of Commerce
PO Box 85
175 W Main St.
Berne, IN 46711-0085
Ph:(260)589-8080
Fax: (260)589-8384
Co. E-mail: tourism@bernein.com
URL: http://www.bernein.com
Contact: Connie Potter, Exec.Dir.

59877 ■ Bloomfield Chamber of Commerce
PO Box 144
Bloomfield, IN 47424
Ph:(812)384-9286
Fax: (812)384-8936
Contact: R. Michael Johnson, Pres.

59878 ■ Boone County Chamber of Commerce
221 N Lebanon St.
Lebanon, IN 46052
Ph:(765)482-1320
Fax: (765)482-3114
Co. E-mail: info@boonechamber.org
URL: http://www.boonechamber.org
Contact: Christa Childers, Exec.VP

59879 ■ Bremen Chamber of Commerce
PO Box 125
Bremen, IN 46506
Ph:(574)546-2044
Fax: (574)546-5487
Co. E-mail: townbremenin@skyenet.net
Contact: D. Elliott, Operations Dir.

59880 ■ Brookville-Franklin County Chamber of Commerce
PO Box 211
Brookville, IN 47012-0211
Ph:(765)647-3177
Co. E-mail: fcedc@cnz.com
Contact: Lois E. Clark, Exec.Dir.

59881 ■ Brown County Chamber of Commerce
37 W Main St.
PO Box 164
Nashville, IN 47448-0164
Ph:(812)988-6647
Fax: (812)988-1547
Co. E-mail: commerce@browncounty.org
URL: http://www.browncounty.org

59882 ■ Brownsburg Chamber of Commerce
104 E Main St.
PO Box 82
Brownsburg, IN 46112-0082
Ph:(317)852-7885
Fax: (317)852-8688
Co. E-mail: chamber@brownsburg.com
URL: http://www.brownsburg.com
Contact: Walter Duncan, Exec.Dir.

59883 ■ Carmel Clay Chamber of Commerce
41 E Main St.
PO Box 1
Carmel, IN 46032
Ph:(317)846-1049
Fax: (317)844-6843
Co. E-mail: chamberinfo@carmelchamber.com
URL: http://www.carmelchamber.com
Contact: Mo Merhoff, Pres.

59884 ■ Cedar Lake Chamber of Commerce
PO Box 101
Cedar Lake, IN 46303-0101
Ph:(219)374-6157
Fax: (219)374-6157
Co. E-mail: clchamber@eternalisp.com
Contact: Diane Jostes, Exec.Dir.

59885 ■ Chamber of Commerce for Anderson and Madison County
PO Box 469
205 W 11th St.
Anderson, IN 46015-0469
Ph:(765)642-0264
Fax: (765)642-0266
Co. E-mail: andersonchamber@ameritech.net
URL: http://www.andersoninchamber.com
Contact: Keith J. Pitcher, Pres./CEO

59886 ■ Chamber of Commerce of Harrison County
310 N Elm St.
Corydon, IN 47112
Ph:(812)738-2137
Free: 888-738-2137
Fax: (812)738-6438
Co. E-mail: dvoelker@harrisonchamber.org
URL: http://www.harrisonchamber.org
Contact: Darrell R. Voelker, Economic Developmental Dir.

59887 ■ Chamber of Commerce in Pendleton
PO Box 542
Pendleton, IN 46064-0542
Ph:(765)778-1741
Fax: (765)778-1741
Contact: Suzanne Hagan, Mgr.

59888 ■ Chamber of Commerce of St. Joseph County
401 E Colfax Ave., Ste. 310
PO Box 1677
South Bend, IN 46634-1677
Ph:(574)234-0051
Fax: (574)289-0358
Co. E-mail: info@sjchamber.org
URL: http://www.sjchamber.org
Contact: Mark N. Eagan CCE, Pres./CEO

59889 ■ Chesterton and Duneland Chamber of Commerce
220 Broadway
Chesterton, IN 46304
Ph:(219)926-5513
Fax: (219)926-7593
Co. E-mail: info@chestertonchamber.org
URL: http://www.chestertonchamber.org
Contact: Ms. Bonnie Trout, Exec.Dir.

59890 ■ Cicero Area Chamber of Commerce
70 N Byron St.
PO Box 466
Cicero, IN 46034
Ph:(317)984-4079
Fax: (317)984-4079
Co. E-mail: jane@hamiltonnorthchamber.com
URL: http://www.belong2it.com/cicerochamber
Contact: Jane Hunter, Exec.Dir.

59891 ■ Clay County Chamber of Commerce
PO Box 23
Brazil, IN 47834-0023
Ph:(812)448-8457
Fax: (812)448-9957
Co. E-mail: claycoc@claynet.com
Contact: Cheryl Myers, Sec.

59892 ■ Clinton County Chamber of Commerce
259 E Walnut St.
Frankfort, IN 46041
Ph:(765)654-5507
Fax: (765)654-9592
Co. E-mail: chamber@ccinchamber.org
URL: http://ccinchamber.org
Contact: Gina L. Sheets, CEO

59893 ■ Cloverdale Area Chamber of Commerce
PO Box 83
Cloverdale, IN 46120
Ph:(765)795-3993
Co. E-mail: chamber@ccrtc.com
URL: http://www.cloverdale.in.us/chamber/index.htm
Contact: Steve Walters

59894 ■ Columbia City Area Chamber of Commerce
201 N Line St.
PO Box 166
Columbia City, IN 46725-0166
Ph:(260)248-8131
Fax: (260)248-8162
Co. E-mail: info@columbiacity.org
URL: http://www.columbiacity.org
Contact: Patricia Hatcher, Exec. Dir.

59895 ■ Columbus Area Chamber of Commerce
500 Franklin St.
Columbus, IN 47201-6214
Ph:(812)379-4457
Fax: (812)378-7308
Co. E-mail: info@columbusareachamber.com
URL: http://www.columbusareachamber.com
Contact: Richard A. Stenner, Pres.

59896 ■ Connersville - Fayette County Chamber of Commerce
115 E 6th St.
Connersville, IN 47331-2046
Ph:(765)825-2561
Fax: (765)825-4613
Co. E-mail: chamber@ydial.com
Contact: Katrina Griffin, Exec.Dir.

59897 ■ Crawford County Chamber of Commerce
6225 E Industrial Ln., Ste. C
Leavenworth, IN 47137
Ph:(812)365-2443
Free: 888-739-7911
Fax: (812)739-4180
Co. E-mail: stroud1942@aol.com
URL: http://www.cccn.net
Contact: Patricia A. Stroud, Pres.

59898 ■ Crawfordsville - Montgomery County Chamber of Commerce
309 N Green St.
Crawfordsville, IN 47933
Ph:(765)362-6800
Fax: (765)362-6900
Co. E-mail: info@crawfordsvillechamber.com
URL: http://www.crawfordsvillechamber.com
Contact: Dave Long, Exec. VP

59899 ■ Culver Chamber of Commerce
PO Box 129
Culver, IN 46511-0129
Ph:(574)842-5253
Free: 888-252-5253
Fax: (574)842-5253
Co. E-mail: djdodge@culcom.net
URL: http://www.culverchamber.com
Contact: Judi Dodge, Pres.

59900 ■ Daviess County Chamber of Commerce
1 Train Depot St.
PO Box 430
Washington, IN 47501-0430
Ph:(812)254-5262
Free: 800-449-5262
Fax: (812)254-4003
Co. E-mail: chamber@dmrtc.net
Contact: Elke Guratzsch, Exec.Asst.

59901 ■ Dearborn County Chamber of Commerce
320 Walnut St.
Lawrenceburg, IN 47025
Ph:(812)537-0814
Free: 800-322-8198
Fax: (812)537-0845
Co. E-mail: maryc@seidata.com
URL: http://www.dearborncountychamber.org
Contact: Debbie Smith, Dir.

59902 ■ Decatur Chamber of Commerce
125 E Monroe St.
Decatur, IN 46733-1732
Ph:(260)724-2604
Fax: (260)724-3104
Co. E-mail: wkuntzman@decaturchamber.org
URL: http://www.decaturchamber.org
Contact: Wes Kuntzman, Exec. Dir.

59903 ■ Demotte Chamber of Commerce
PO Box 721
Demotte, IN 46310
Ph:(219)987-5800
URL: http://www.townofdemotte.com
Contact: Pat Kopanda, Outreach Dir.

59904 ■ Dunkirk Area Chamber of Commerce
Box 291
Dunkirk, IN 47336
Ph:(765)768-6225
Co. E-mail: samjhub@aol.com
Contact: Sam J. Hubbard, Exec.Dir

59905 ■ Dyer Chamber of Commerce
PO Box 84
Dyer, IN 46311
Ph:(219)865-1045
Co. E-mail: chamber@townofdyer.com
Contact: Ms. Tammy Hedrick

59906 ■ Elwood Chamber of Commerce
108 S Anderson St.
Elwood, IN 46036
Ph:(765)552-0180
Fax: (765)552-1277
Co. E-mail: elwoodchamber@yahoo.com
Contact: Jerry Mendenhall, Exec.Dir.

59907 ■ Ferdinand Chamber of Commerce
PO Box 101
Ferdinand, IN 47532-0101
Ph:(812)367-0550
Fax: (812)367-1303
Co. E-mail: btretter@psci.net
URL: http://www.ferdinandinchamber.org

Contact: Brian Tretter, Exec.Dir.

59908 ■ Fishers Chamber of Commerce
11601 Municipal Dr.
PO Box 353
Fishers, IN 46038-0353
Ph:(317)578-0700
Fax: (317)578-1097
Co. E-mail: info@fisherschamber.com
URL: http://www.fisherschamber.com
Contact: Christi J. Wolf, Pres.

59909 ■ Fowler Chamber of Commerce
PO Box 293
Fowler, IN 47944-0293
Ph:(765)884-0222
Contact: Mike Brewer, Pres.

59910 ■ Franklin Chamber of Commerce
370 E Jefferson St.
Franklin, IN 46131
Ph:(317)736-6334
Fax: (317)736-9553
Co. E-mail: franklincoc@franklincoc.org
URL: http://www.franklincoc.org
Contact: Tricia E. Bechman, Exec. Dir.

59911 ■ Fremont Area Chamber of Commerce
PO Box 462
Fremont, IN 46737
Ph:(260)495-9010
Fax: (260)495-2070
Co. E-mail: fremontc@locl.net
URL: http://www.fremontchamber.org
Contact: Darci Gaff, Exec.Dir.

59912 ■ French Lick - West Baden Chamber of Commerce
PO Box 347
French Lick, IN 47432
Ph:(812)936-2405
Co. E-mail: trichardson@flwbcc.com
URL: http://www.frenchlick-westbadencc.org
Contact: Teresa Richardson

59913 ■ Garrett Chamber of Commerce
111 W Keyser St.
Garrett, IN 46738-1462
Ph:(260)357-4600
Fax: (260)357-5634
Contact: Amy Demske, Pres.

59914 ■ Gary Chamber of Commerce
839 Broadway, 1st Fl., Rear
Gary, IN 46402
Ph:(219)885-7407
Fax: (219)885-7408
Co. E-mail: info@garychamber.com
URL: http://www.garychamber.com
Contact: Jeffrey Q. Williams, Exec. Dir.

59915 ■ Goshen Chamber of Commerce
232 S Main St.
Goshen, IN 46526-3723
Ph:(574)533-2102
Free: 800-307-4204
Fax: (574)533-2103
Co. E-mail: goshenchamber@goshen.org
URL: http://www.goshen.org
Contact: Brent Randall, VP

59916 ■ Greater Avon Chamber of Commerce
8244 E Hwy. 36, Ste. 140
Avon, IN 46123
Ph:(317)272-4333
Fax: (317)272-7217
Co. E-mail: info@avonchamber.org
URL: http://www.avonchamber.org
Contact: Tom Downard, Exec.Dir.

59917 ■ Greater Bloomington Chamber of Commerce
400 W 7th St., Ste. 102
PO Box 1302
Bloomington, IN 47402-1302

Ph:(812)336-6381
Fax: (812)336-0651
Co. E-mail: csteele@chamberbloomington.org
URL: http://www.chamber.bloomington.in.us
Contact: Christy Steele, Pres.

59918 ■ Greater Danville Chamber of Commerce
56 W Main St.
PO Box 273
Danville, IN 46122
Ph:(317)745-0670
Fax: (317)745-0682
Co. E-mail: chamber@danville.org
URL: http://www.danville.org
Contact: Sandy Teer, Exec. Dir.

59919 ■ Greater Edinburgh Community Chamber of Commerce
PO Box 128
Edinburgh, IN 46124
Ph:(812)373-4016
URL: http://www.edinburgh-in.com
Contact: Kathy Richmond, Pres.

59920 ■ Greater Elkhart County Chamber of Commerce
418 S Main St.
Elkhart, IN 46515-0428
Ph:(574)293-1531
Fax: (574)294-1859
Co. E-mail: info@elkhart.org
URL: http://www.elkhart.org
Contact: Philip Penn, Pres./CEO

59921 ■ Greater Fort Wayne Chamber of Commerce
826 Ewing St.
Fort Wayne, IN 46802
Ph:(260)424-1435
Fax: (260)426-7232
Co. E-mail: ppl@fwchamber.org
URL: http://www.fwchamber.org
Contact: Philip P. Laux, Pres./CEO

59922 ■ Greater Greencastle Chamber of Commerce
2 S Jackson St.
PO Box 389
Greencastle, IN 46135
Ph:(765)653-4517
Co. E-mail: gchamber@ccrtc.com
URL: http://www.gogreencastle.com
Contact: Tammy Amor, Exec. Dir.

59923 ■ Greater Greenfield Chamber of Commerce
1 Courthouse Plz.
Greenfield, IN 46140-2300
Ph:(317)477-4188
Fax: (317)477-4189
Co. E-mail: gfdchamb@greenfieldcc.org
URL: http://www.greenfieldcc.org
Contact: Linda Imel, Pres.

59924 ■ Greater Greenwood Chamber of Commerce
550 U.S. Hwy. 31 S
Greenwood, IN 46142-3063
Ph:(317)888-4856
Fax: (317)865-2609
Co. E-mail: gail@greenwoodchamber.com
URL: http://www.greenwood-chamber.com
Contact: Gail W. Richards, Exec. Dir.

59925 ■ Greater Indianapolis Chamber of Commerce
Chase Tower
111 Monument Cir., Ste. 1950
Indianapolis, IN 46204
Ph:(317)464-2200
Fax: (317)464-2217
Co. E-mail: rdorson@indylink.com
URL: http://www.indychamber.com
Contact: Roland M. Dorson, Pres.

59926 ■ Greater La Porte Chamber of Commerce
414 Lincolnway
PO Box 486
La Porte, IN 46352-0486
Ph:(219)362-3178
Fax: (219)324-7349
Co. E-mail: info@lpchamber.com
URL: http://www.lpchamber.com
Contact: Michael B. Seitz, Pres.

59927 ■ Greater Martinsville Chamber of Commerce
109 E Morgan St.
PO Box 1378
Martinsville, IN 46151
Ph:(765)342-8110
Fax: (765)342-5713
Co. E-mail: info@martinsvillechamber.com
URL: http://www.scican.net/~chamber
Contact: Jamie Thompson, Interim Exec. Dir.

59928 ■ Greater Mitchell Chamber of Commerce
PO Box 216
Mitchell, IN 47446
Ph:(812)849-4441
Free: 800-580-1985
Fax: (812)849-4619
Co. E-mail: mitchell@kiva.net
Contact: Debra Webster, Exec.Dir.

59929 ■ Greater Monticello Chamber of Commerce and Visitors Bureau
116 N Main St.
Monticello, IN 47960
Ph:(574)583-7220
Co. E-mail: janet.dold@monticelloin.com
URL: http://www.monticelloin.com
Contact: Janet Dold, Exec.Dir.

59930 ■ Greater Portage Chamber of Commerce
2642 Eleanor St.
PO Box 1098
Portage, IN 46368-3634
Ph:(219)762-3300
Fax: (219)763-2450
Co. E-mail: gpcoc@netnitco.net
Contact: Terry A. Hufford, Exec.Dir.

59931 ■ Greater Scott County Chamber of Commerce
PO Box 404
Scottsburg, IN 47170
Ph:(812)752-4080
Fax: (812)752-4307
Co. E-mail: scottcom@c3bb.com
URL: http://www.greatscottindiana.org/Scott_County/
    chamber/chamber.htm
Contact: Keith Colbert, Exec.Dir.

59932 ■ Greater Seymour Chamber of Commerce
105 S Chestnut St.
Seymour, IN 47274
Ph:(812)522-3681
Fax: (812)524-1800
Co. E-mail: seycoc@comcast.net
URL: http://www.seymourchamber.org
Contact: Bill Bailey, Pres.

59933 ■ Greater Terre Haute Chamber of Commerce
643 Wabash Ave.
PO Box 689
Terre Haute, IN 47808-0689
Ph:(812)232-2391
Fax: (812)232-2905
Co. E-mail: jlatta@terrehautechamber.com
URL: http://www.terrehautechamber.com
Contact: G. Roderick Henry, Pres.

59934 ■ Greater Valparaiso Chamber of Commerce
PO Box 330
Valparaiso, IN 46384-0330

Ph:(219)462-1105
Fax: (219)462-5710
Co. E-mail: info@valparaisochamber.org
URL: http://www.valparaisochamber.org
Contact: Rex G. Richards, Pres.

59935 ■ Greater Zionsville Chamber of Commerce
135 S Elm St.
PO Box 148
Zionsville, IN 46077
Ph:(317)873-3836
Fax: (317)873-3836
Co. E-mail: info@zionsvillechamber.org
URL: http://www.zionsvillechamber.org
Contact: Debbie Cranfill, Exec.Dir.

59936 ■ Greensburg Decatur County Chamber of Commerce
115 E North St.
Greensburg, IN 47240
Ph:(812)663-2832
Fax: (812)663-4275
Co. E-mail: info@greensburgchamber.com
URL: http://www.greensburgchamber.com
Contact: Jennifer Sturges, Exec.Dir.

59937 ■ Griffith Chamber of Commerce
PO Box 204
201 S Broad St.
Griffith, IN 46319-0204
Ph:(219)838-2401
Fax: (219)838-2661
Co. E-mail: griffithchamber@dopplerexpress.net
URL: http://griffithchamber.org
Contact: Michael Longmiller, Pres.

59938 ■ Hamilton Area Chamber of Commerce
PO Box 66
Hamilton, IN 46742
Ph:(205)921-7786
Fax: (205)921-2220
Co. E-mail: chamber@hamiltonchamber.com
URL: http://www.hamiltonchamber.com
Contact: Holly Law, Pres.

59939 ■ Hamilton Chamber of Commerce
PO Box 66
Hamilton, IN 46742
Ph:(260)488-3607
Co. E-mail: chamber@hamiltonchamber.com
URL: http://www.hamiltonchamber.com
Contact: Tracy Thornbrugh, Pres.

59940 ■ Hartford City Chamber of Commerce
PO Box 286
Hartford City, IN 47348
Ph:(765)348-1905
Fax: (765)348-4945
Co. E-mail: cbrown@blackfordcounty.com
Contact: Chris Brown, Sec.Mgr.

59941 ■ Highland Chamber of Commerce
8536 Kennedy Ave.
Highland, IN 46322
Ph:(219)923-3666
Co. E-mail: mary@highlandchamber.com
URL: http://www.highlandchamber.com
Contact: Mary Luptak, Exec.Dir.

59942 ■ Hobart Chamber of Commerce
1001 Lillian St.
Hobart, IN 46342
Ph:(219)942-5774
Fax: (219)942-4928
Co. E-mail: info@hobartchamber.com
URL: http://www.hobartchamber.com
Contact: Brenda Clemmons, Exec. Dir.

59943 ■ Huntingburg Chamber of Commerce
309 N Geiger St.
Huntingburg, IN 47542
Ph:(812)683-5699
Fax: (812)683-3524
Co. E-mail: info@huntingburgchamber.org
URL: http://www.huntingburgchamber.org

Contact: Christine Prior, Exec.Dir.

59944 ■ Huntington County Chamber of Commerce
305 Warren St.
Huntington, IN 46750
Ph:(260)356-5300
Fax: (260)356-5434
Co. E-mail: manager@huntington-chamber.com
URL: http://www.huntington-chamber.com
Contact: Robert C. Brown Jr., Pres.

59945 ■ Indiana Chamber of Commerce
115 W Washington St., Ste. 850 S
Indianapolis, IN 46204-3420
Ph:(317)264-3110
Fax: (317)264-6855
Co. E-mail: inchamber@indianachamber.com
URL: http://www.indianachamber.com
Contact: Kevin Brinegar, Pres.

59946 ■ Indiana State Hispanic Chamber of Commerce
2511 E 46th St.
Corporate Sq., S-U3
Indianapolis, IN 46205
Ph:(317)547-0200
Fax: (317)547-0210
Co. E-mail: mgon@ishcc.com
URL: http://www.ishcc.com
Contact: Manuel T. Gonzalez, Pres./CEO

59947 ■ Jasper Chamber of Commerce
302 W 6th St.
PO Box 307
Jasper, IN 47547-0307
Ph:(812)482-6866
Fax: (812)482-1883
Co. E-mail: chamber@jasperin.org
URL: http://www.jasperin.org

59948 ■ Jennings County Chamber of Commerce
PO Box 340
North Vernon, IN 47265
Ph:(812)346-2339
Fax: (812)346-2065
Co. E-mail: jheath@jenningscountychamber.org
URL: http://www.jenningscountychamber.org
Contact: Judy Heath, Admin.Asst.

59949 ■ Kendallville Area Chamber of Commerce
122 S Main St.
Kendallville, IN 46755-1716
Ph:(260)347-1554
Free: 877-347-1554
Fax: (260)347-1575
Co. E-mail: kchamber@locl.net
URL: http://www.kendallvillechamber.com
Contact: Kimm Hunt, Exec. Dir.

59950 ■ Kentland Area Chamber of Commerce
PO Box 273
Kentland, IN 47951-0273
Ph:(219)474-6665
Fax: (219)474-5071
Co. E-mail: knochel@kentlandbank.com
URL: http://www.kentlandindiana.org/Business/kaindex.html
Contact: Sue Knochel, Membership/Welcoming Committee

59951 ■ Knightstown Indiana Chamber of Commerce
PO Box 44
Knightstown, IN 46148-0044
Ph:(765)345-5290
Free: 800-668-1895
Co. E-mail: info@knightstownchamber.com
URL: http://www.knightstownchamber.com
Contact: Rex Pasco, Pres.

59952 ■ Knox County Chamber of Commerce
102 N 3rd St.
PO Box 553
Vincennes, IN 47591-0553

Ph:(812)882-6440
Free: 888-895-6622
Fax: (812)882-6441
Co. E-mail: info@knoxcountychamber.com
URL: http://www.knoxcountychamber.com
Contact: Mark A. McNeece, Pres./CEO

59953 ■ Kokomo - Howard County Chamber of Commerce
325 N Main St.
Kokomo, IN 46901-4621
Ph:(765)457-5301
Co. E-mail: info@kokomochamber.com
URL: http://www.kokomochamber.com
Contact: Rick Hamilton, Pres.

59954 ■ Kouts Chamber of Commerce
PO Box 330
Kouts, IN 46347
Ph:(219)766-2867
Fax: (219)766-3152
Co. E-mail: koutschamber@verizon.net
URL: http://www.kouts.org
Contact: Julie Jones, Exec.Dir.

59955 ■ Lafayette - West Lafayette Chamber of Commerce
337 Columbia St.
PO Box 348
Lafayette, IN 47902-0348
Ph:(765)742-4041
Fax: (765)742-6276
Co. E-mail: dana@lafayettechamber.com
URL: http://www.lafayettechamber.com
Contact: Mr. David Williams, Chm.

59956 ■ Lagrange County Chamber of Commerce
901 S Detroit St., Ste. A
Lagrange, IN 46761
Ph:(260)463-2443
Free: 877-735-0340
Fax: (260)463-2683
Co. E-mail: info@lagrangechamber.org
URL: http://www.lagrangechamber.org
Contact: Jack Dold, Exec.Dir.

59957 ■ Lake Station Chamber of Commerce
PO Box 5191
Lake Station, IN 46405
Ph:(219)962-4878
URL: http://www.lakestationchamber.com/members002.shtml
Contact: Jim Bradford, Sec.

59958 ■ Lakeshore Chamber of Commerce
5246 Hohman Ave., Ste. 100
Hammond, IN 46320
Ph:(219)931-1000
Fax: (219)937-8778
Co. E-mail: info@lakeshorechamber.com
URL: http://www.lakeshorechamber.com
Contact: Joseph A. Kosina, Pres.

59959 ■ Liberty - Union County Chamber of Commerce
5 W High St.
Liberty, IN 47353-1121
Ph:(765)458-5976
Fax: (765)458-5976
Co. E-mail: ucdc@dslmyway.com
URL: http://www.ucdc.us
Contact: Blanche G. Stelle, Exec. Dir.

59960 ■ Ligonier Chamber of Commerce
PO Box 121
Ligonier, IN 46767-0121
Ph:(260)894-9909
URL: http://www.ligonierindianachamber.org
Contact: Mike Corner, Pres.

59961 ■ Linton-Stockton Chamber of Commerce
159 1st St. NW
PO Box 208
Linton, IN 47441
Ph:(812)847-4846

Fax: (812)847-0246
Co. E-mail: chamber@joink.com
URL: http://www.lintonchamber.org
Contact: Tammy Martin, Exec.Dir.

59962 ■ Logansport - Cass County Chamber of Commerce
300 E Broadway, Ste. 103
Logansport, IN 46947-3185
Ph:(574)753-6388
Co. E-mail: info@logan-casschamber.com
URL: http://www.logan-casschamber.com
Contact: Brain Shafer, Pres.

59963 ■ Lowell Chamber of Commerce
428 E Commercial Ave.
Lowell, IN 46356
Ph:(219)696-0231
Fax: (219)696-0383
Co. E-mail: lowellchamber@xvi.net
URL: http://Lowell.net
Contact: Ruth Dunn, Office Mgr.

59964 ■ Madison Area Chamber of Commerce
975 Industrial Dr., Ste. 1
Madison, IN 47250
Ph:(812)265-3135
Fax: (812)265-5544
Co. E-mail: info@madisonchamber.org
URL: http://www.madisonchamber.org
Contact: Mr. Galen L. Bremmer, Exec.VP

59965 ■ Marion-Grant County Chamber of Commerce
215 S Adams St.
Marion, IN 46952-3895
Ph:(765)664-5107
Fax: (765)668-5443
Co. E-mail: info@marionchamber.org
URL: http://www.marionchamber.org
Contact: Aaron DeWeese, Pres.

59966 ■ Martin County Chamber of Commerce
PO Box 257
Loogootee, IN 47553
Ph:(812)295-4142
Fax: (812)295-5425
Contact: Laura Albertson, Pres.

59967 ■ Mentone Chamber of Commerce
PO Box 366
Mentone, IN 46539
Ph:(574)353-7417
Co. E-mail: valley@medt.com
URL: http://www.mentoneeggcity.com
Contact: Rita Simpson, Pres.

59968 ■ Merrillville Chamber of Commerce
255 W 80th Pl.
Merrillville, IN 46410
Ph:(219)769-8180
Fax: (219)736-6223
Co. E-mail: geninq@merrillvillecoc.org
URL: http://www.merrillvillecoc.org
Contact: John J. Janik, Pres./CEO

59969 ■ Metropolitan Evansville Chamber of Commerce
100 NW 2nd St., Ste. 100
Evansville, IN 47708-2101
Ph:(812)425-8147
Fax: (812)421-5883
Co. E-mail: info@evansvillechamber.com
URL: http://www.evansvillechamber.com
Contact: Matt Meadors, Pres./CEO

59970 ■ Michigan City Area Chamber of Commerce
200 E Michigan Blvd.
Michigan City, IN 46360-3270
Ph:(219)874-6221
Fax: (219)873-1204
Co. E-mail: info@mcachamber.com
URL: http://www.michigancitychamber.com
Contact: Tim Bietry, Pres.

59971 ■ Monon Chamber of Commerce
PO Box 777
Monon, IN 47959
Ph:(219)253-6441
Contact: Troy Geisler, Pres.

59972 ■ Mooresville Chamber of Commerce
26 S Indiana St.
PO Box 62
Mooresville, IN 46158
Ph:(317)831-6509
Fax: (317)831-9548
Co. E-mail: mrsvlcoc@mooresvillechamber.org
Contact: Julie Kyle-Lee, Ofc.Admin.

59973 ■ Muncie-Delaware County Chamber of Commerce
401 S High St.
PO Box 842
Muncie, IN 47308-0842
Ph:(765)288-6681
Free: 800-336-1373
Fax: (765)751-9151
Co. E-mail: chamber@muncie.com
URL: http://www.muncie.com
Contact: Dan Allen, Pres.

59974 ■ Munster Chamber of Commerce
1040 Ridge Rd.
Munster, IN 46321
Ph:(219)836-5549
Fax: (219)836-5551
Co. E-mail: info@munsterchamber.com
URL: http://www.munsterchamber.com
Contact: Rhonda Damjanovich, Pres.

59975 ■ Nappanee Area Chamber of Commerce
451 N Main St.
Nappanee, IN 46550
Ph:(574)773-7812
Fax: (574)773-4961
Co. E-mail: info@nappaneechamber.com
URL: http://www.nappaneechamber.com
Contact: Larry Andrews, Exec.Dir.

59976 ■ New Castle-Henry County Chamber of Commerce
100 S Main St., Ste. 108
New Castle, IN 47362
Ph:(765)529-5210
Fax: (765)521-7404
Co. E-mail: info@nchcchamber.com
URL: http://www.nchcchamber.com
Contact: Betty Lou Heintz, Exec.Dir.

59977 ■ New Haven Chamber of Commerce
428 Broadway
PO Box 66
New Haven, IN 46774-0066
Ph:(260)749-4484
Fax: (260)749-4484
Co. E-mail: nhchamber@aol.com
Contact: Ron Oetting, Pres.

59978 ■ New Palestine Area Chamber of Commerce
PO Box 541
New Palestine, IN 46163
Ph:(317)861-2345
Fax: (317)861-4201
Co. E-mail: info@newpalchamber.com
URL: http://www.newpalchamber.com
Contact: Rebecca Gaines, Sec.

59979 ■ Noblesville Chamber of Commerce
54 N 9th St., Ste. 100
Noblesville, IN 46060
Ph:(317)773-0086
Fax: (317)773-1966
Co. E-mail: info@noblesvillechamber.com
URL: http://www.noblesvillechamber.com
Contact: Sharon McMahon, Pres.

59980 ■ North Manchester Chamber of Commerce
109 N Market St.
North Manchester, IN 46962-1518

Ph:(260)982-7644
Fax: (260)982-8718
Co. E-mail: nmcc@kconline.com
URL: http://www.northmanchesterchamber.com
Contact: Kathy Roberts, Exec.Dir.

59981 ■ North Newton Area Chamber of Commerce
PO Box 268
Roselawn, IN 46372
Ph:(219)345-2525
Fax: (219)345-2121
Contact: John Morgin, Pres.

59982 ■ North Webster - Tippecanoe Township Chamber of Commerce
301 N Main St., Ste. F
North Webster, IN 46555
Ph:(574)834-1600
URL: http://www.northwebster.com/homepage.html
Contact: Chris Bruno, Pres.

59983 ■ Orleans Chamber of Commerce
PO Box 9
Orleans, IN 47452-0009
Ph:(812)865-9930
URL: http://www.town.orleans.in.us
Contact: Robert F. Henderson, Pres./CEO

59984 ■ Owen County Chamber of Commerce and Economic Development Corporation
205 E Morgan St., Ste. D
PO Box 87
Spencer, IN 47460
Ph:(812)829-3245
Fax: (812)829-0936
Co. E-mail: oced@ccrtc.com
URL: http://www.owencountyindiana.org
Contact: Denise Shaw, Exec.Dir.

59985 ■ Paoli Chamber of Commerce
210 SW Court St.
Paoli, IN 47454
Ph:(812)723-4769
Co. E-mail: paolichamber@verizon.net
URL: http://www.paolichamber.com
Contact: Beverly Dillard, Pres.

59986 ■ Parke County Chamber of Commerce
105 N Market St., Ste. A
Rockville, IN 47872
Ph:(765)569-5565
Co. E-mail: info@parkecountychamber.com
URL: http://www.parkecountychamber.com
Contact: Chris Leach, Exec.Dir.

59987 ■ Perry County Chamber of Commerce
645 Main St., Ste. 200
PO Box 82
Tell City, IN 47586-0082
Ph:(812)547-2385
Fax: (812)547-8378
Co. E-mail: info@perrycountychamber.com
URL: http://www.perrycountychamber.com
Contact: Cheri Cronin, Admin.Asst.

59988 ■ Peru - Miami County Chamber of Commerce
13 E Main St.
Peru, IN 46970
Ph:(765)472-1923
Fax: (765)472-7099
Co. E-mail: info@miamicochamber.com
URL: http://www.miamicochamber.com
Contact: Sandy Chittum, Exec. Dir.

59989 ■ Pike County Chamber of Commerce
714 E Main St.
PO Box 291
Petersburg, IN 47567-0291
Ph:(812)354-8155
Fax: (812)354-2335
Co. E-mail: chamber@verizon.net
URL: http://pikecountyin.org

Contact: Alycia Church, Exec.Dir.

59990 ■ Plainfield Chamber of Commerce
210 W Main St.
PO Box 14
Plainfield, IN 46168-0014
Ph:(317)839-3800
Fax: (317)839-9670
Co. E-mail: plainfieldchamber@ameritech.net
URL: http://www.plainfield-in.com
Contact: Jeff Banning, Pres.

59991 ■ Plymouth Area Chamber of Commerce
120 N Michigan St.
Plymouth, IN 46563
Ph:(574)936-2323
Fax: (574)936-6584
Co. E-mail: plychamber@plychamber.org
URL: http://www.plychamber.org
Contact: Doug Anspach, Exec.Dir.

59992 ■ Portland Area Chamber of Commerce
118 S Meridian St., Ste. A
Portland, IN 47371
Ph:(260)726-4481
Fax: (260)726-3372
Co. E-mail: chamber@jayco.net
URL: http://portlandchamber.jayco.net
Contact: Vicki L. Tague, Exec.Dir.

59993 ■ Posey County Chamber of Commerce
915 E 4th St.
PO Box 633
Mount Vernon, IN 47620-0633
Ph:(812)838-3639
Fax: (812)838-6358
Co. E-mail: poseychamber@sbcglobal.net
URL: http://www.mtvernonposeycochamber.com
Contact: Sally A. Dennning, Admin.Dir.

59994 ■ Princeton Area Chamber of Commerce
202 E Broadway
Princeton, IN 47670
Ph:(812)385-2134
Fax: (812)385-2401
Co. E-mail: paccoffice@insightbb.com
URL: http://www.princetonin.org
Contact: B. Todd Mosby, Exec.Dir.

59995 ■ Rensselaer - Remington Chamber of Commerce
PO Box 194
Rensselaer, IN 47978
Ph:(219)866-8223
Fax: (219)866-8593
Co. E-mail: chamber@nwiis.com
Contact: Renee Bruscemi, Dir.

59996 ■ Richmond-Wayne County Chamber of Commerce
33 S 7th St., Ste. 2
Richmond, IN 47374
Ph:(765)962-1511
Fax: (765)966-0882
Co. E-mail: info@rwchamber.org
URL: http://www.rwchamber.org
Contact: Dennis Andrews, Pres./CEO

59997 ■ Ripley County Chamber of Commerce
102 N Main St.
PO Box 576
Versailles, IN 47042
Ph:(812)689-6654
Fax: (812)689-3934
Co. E-mail: ripleycc@ripleycountychamber.org
URL: http://ripleycountychamber.org
Contact: Darla Westerfield, Pres.

59998 ■ Rochester and Lake Manitou Chamber of Commerce
822 Main St.
Rochester, IN 46975

Ph:(574)224-2666
Fax: (574)224-2329
Co. E-mail: chamber@rtcol.com
Contact: Alison Heyde, Exec.Dir.

59999 ■ Rush County Chamber of Commerce
315 N Main St.
Rushville, IN 46173-1635
Ph:(765)932-2880
Co. E-mail: rccc@lightbound.com
URL: http://www.rushcounty.com/chamber
Contact: Pamela C. Leisure, Exec.Dir.

60000 ■ St. John Chamber of Commerce
PO Box 592
St. John, IN 46373
Ph:(219)365-4686
Fax: (219)365-4602
Co. E-mail: boricrs@jorsm.com
URL: http://www.stjohnchamber.com
Contact: Jim Betowski, Pres.

60001 ■ Schererville Chamber of Commerce
13 W Joliet St.
Schererville, IN 46375
Ph:(219)322-5412
Fax: (219)322-0598
Co. E-mail: info@scherervillechamber.com
URL: http://www.scherervillechamber.com
Contact: Mary Watson, Pres.

60002 ■ Shakamak Chamber of Commerce
PO Box 101
Jasonville, IN 47438
Ph:(812)665-3622
Contact: Brad Dunchon, Pres.

60003 ■ Shelby County Chamber of Commerce
501 N Harrison St.
Shelbyville, IN 46176
Ph:(317)398-6647
Free: 800-318-4083
Fax: (317)392-3901
Co. E-mail: chamberinfo@shelbychamber.net
URL: http://www.shelbychamber.net
Contact: Tim Barrick, Pres.

60004 ■ Southern Indiana Chamber of Commerce
4100 Charlestown Rd.
New Albany, IN 47150-9538
Ph:(812)945-0266
Fax: (812)948-4664
Co. E-mail: greg@sicc.org
URL: http://www.sicc.org
Contact: Greg Fitzloff, Pres.

60005 ■ Spencer County Regional Chamber of Commerce
2792 N U.S. Hwy. 231, Ste. 100
Rockport, IN 47635
Ph:(812)649-2186
Fax: (812)649-2246
Co. E-mail: scrcc@psci.net
URL: http://www.spencercoin.org
Contact: Barbie Brown, Exec.Dir.

60006 ■ Starke County Chamber of Commerce
PO Box 5
Knox, IN 46534
Ph:(574)772-5548
Fax: (574)772-0867
Co. E-mail: info@starkechamber.com
URL: http://www.starkechamber.com
Contact: Linda Molenda, Exec. Sec.

60007 ■ Sullivan County Chamber of Commerce
4 N. Court St.
PO Box 325
Sullivan, IN 47882
Ph:(812)268-4836
Fax: (812)268-4836
Co. E-mail: bunny@abcs.com
Contact: Joan Smith, Coor.

60008 ■ Syracuse-Wawasee Chamber of Commerce
PO Box 398
Syracuse, IN 46567-0398
Ph:(574)457-5637
Fax: (574)528-6040
Co. E-mail: info@swchamber.com
URL: http://www.swchamber.com
Contact: Kristi E. Plikerd, Exec. Dir.

60009 ■ Tipton County Chamber of Commerce
136 E Jefferson St.
Tipton, IN 46072
Ph:(765)675-7533
Fax: (765)675-8917
Co. E-mail: ditimm@tds.net
URL: http://www.tiptonchamber.com
Contact: Diane R. Timm, Exec. Dir.

60010 ■ Union City Chamber of Commerce
PO Box 424
Union City, IN 47390
Ph:(765)964-5409
Fax: (765)964-5409
Co. E-mail: ucchamber@jayco.net
Contact: Darlene Wymer, Exec.Dir.

60011 ■ Upland Chamber of Commerce
PO Box 157
Upland, IN 46989
Ph:(765)998-2579
Contact: Kevin Crawford, Pres.

60012 ■ Van Buren Chamber of Commerce
PO Box 484
Van Buren, IN 46991
Ph:(765)934-4646
Contact: Dean Baker, Pres.

60013 ■ Vermillion County Chamber of Commerce
PO Box 7
Clinton, IN 47842-0007
Ph:(765)832-3844
Fax: (765)828-1619
Contact: Chadwanna Jukes, Exec.Asst.

60014 ■ Wabash Area Chamber of Commerce
111 S Wabash St.
PO Box 371
Wabash, IN 46992-0371
Ph:(260)563-1168
Fax: (260)563-6920
Co. E-mail: wacc@wabashchamber.org
URL: http://www.wabashchamber.org
Contact: Ms. Kimberly A. Pinkerton, Pres.

60015 ■ Wakarusa Chamber of Commerce
100 W Waterford St.
PO Box 291
Wakarusa, IN 46573
Ph:(574)862-4344
Fax: (574)862-2245
Co. E-mail: chamber@wakarusachamber.com
URL: http://www.wakarusachamber.com
Contact: Doris Biller, Exec.Sec.

60016 ■ Walkerton Area Chamber of Commerce
612 Roosevelt Rd.
Walkerton, IN 46574-1218
Ph:(574)586-3100
Fax: (574)586-3469
Co. E-mail: louzons@1stsource.com
URL: http://www.walkerton.org
Contact: Phil Buckmaster, Pres.

60017 ■ Warrick County Chamber of Commerce
224 W Main St.
PO Box 377
Boonville, IN 47601-0377
Ph:(812)897-2340
Fax: (812)897-2360
Co. E-mail: warco@sigecom.net

URL: http://www.warrickcounty.com
Contact: Tracy Holder, Exec.Dir.

60018 ■ Warsaw - Kosciusko County Chamber of Commerce
313 S Buffalo St.
Warsaw, IN 46580-4304
Ph:(574)267-6311
Free: 800-776-6311
Fax: (574)267-7762
Co. E-mail: jmccarthy-sessing@wkchamber.com
URL: http://www.wkchamber.com
Contact: Joy McCarthy-Sessing, Pres.

60019 ■ Wells County Chamber of Commerce
211 W Water St.
Bluffton, IN 46714
Ph:(260)824-0510
Fax: (260)824-5871
Co. E-mail: coc@blufftonwellschamber.com
URL: http://www.blufftonwellschamber.com
Contact: Suzanne Huffman, Dir.

60020 ■ Westfield Washington Chamber of Commerce
322 W Main St.
PO Box 534
Westfield, IN 46074
Ph:(317)896-2378
Fax: (317)867-2523
Co. E-mail: info@westfield-chamber.org
URL: http://www.westfield-chamber.org
Contact: Julieann Sole, Exec.Dir.

60021 ■ Westville Area Chamber of Commerce
PO Box 215
Westville, IN 46391-0215
Ph:(219)785-2824
Contact: Yvonne Lundwall, Pres.

60022 ■ Whiting - Robertsdale Chamber of Commerce
1442 119th St.
Whiting, IN 46394
Ph:(219)659-0292
Fax: (219)659-5851
Co. E-mail: puccini99@aol.com
URL: http://www.whitingindiana.com
Contact: Gayle Faulkner-Kosalko, Exec.Dir.

60023 ■ Winchester Area Chamber of Commerce
112 W Washington St.
Winchester, IN 47394
Ph:(765)584-3731
Fax: (765)584-5544
Co. E-mail: chamber@globalsite.net
URL: http://www.winchesterchamber.org
Contact: Vicki Phenis, Exec.Dir.

MINORITY BUSINESS ASSISTANCE PROGRAMS

60024 ■ Indiana Business Diversity Council
2126 N Meridian St.
Indianapolis, IN 46202
Ph:(317)923-2110
Fax: (317)923-2204
Co. E-mail: rkhenderson@inbdc.org
URL: http://www.inbdc.org
Contact: Reginald Henderson, Pres
Description: Promotes purchases by corporations from minority businesses through training programs, a Business Opportunity Fair, meetings, and supplier and purchaser directories.

60025 ■ Indiana Department of Transportation–Economic Opportunity Division–Disadvantaged Business Enterprise Program (State)
State Office Bldg.
100 N Senate Ave, Rm.904
Indianapolis, IN 46204-2218

Ph:(317)232-5093
Fax: (317)233-0891
URL: http://www.in.gov/dot/
Description: Promotes the securing of Department of Highways contracts by minority and women-owned businesses. Provides certification for these companies.

60026 ■ Indiana Small Business Development Center
1 N Capitol Ave., Ste. 900
Indianapolis, IN 46204-2026
Ph:(317)234-2082
Fax: (317)232-8872
Co. E-mail: leadcenter@isdc.org
URL: http://www.isbdc.org
Contact: Debbie Bishop-Trocha

FINANCING AND LOAN PROGRAMS

60027 ■ 1st Source Capital Corp.
100 North Michigan St.
PO Box 1602
South Bend, IN 46601
Ph:(219)235-2180
Fax: (219)235-2227
Contact: Eugene L. Cavanaugh, Vice President
Preferred Investment Size: $300,000 to $500,000.
Investment Types: Second stage, mezzanine, leveraged buyout, and special situation. **Industry Preferences:** Communications and media, computer hardware and software, semiconductors and other electronics, medical and health, consumer related, industrial and energy, and transportation. **Geographic Preferences:** Midwest.

60028 ■ Cambridge Venture Partners
4181 E. 96th St., Ste. 200
Indianapolis, IN 46240
Ph:(317)814-6192
Fax: (317)844-9815
Contact: Jean Wojtowicz, President
Investment Types: Mezzanine, later stage, acquisition, and recapitalizations. **Geographic Preferences:** Midwest.

60029 ■ CID Equity Partners
1 American Sq., Ste. 2850
Box 82074
Indianapolis, IN 46282
Ph:(317)269-2350
Fax: (317)269-2355
URL: http://www.cidequity.com
Contact: Eric Bruun, Principal
Preferred Investment Size: $500,000 to $10,000,000. **Investment Types:** Start-up, first and second stage, early and later stage, industry rollups, leveraged buyout, mezzanine, balanced, and special situation. **Industry Preferences:** Computer software, hardware and services, medical and health, biotechnology, consumer related, industrial and energy, communications and media, Internet specific, semiconductors and other electronics. **Geographic Preferences:** Indiana, Midwest, and Rocky Mountains.

60030 ■ Gazelle Techventures
6325 Digital Way, Ste. 460
Indianapolis, IN 46278
Ph:(317)275-6800
Fax: (317)275-1100
URL: http://www.gazellevc.com
Contact: Don Aquilano
Preferred Investment Size: $1,000,000 to $3,000,000. **Investment Types:** Early and later stage, and expansion. **Industry Preferences:** Communications and media, computer hardware and software, biotechnology, medical and health, consumer related, industrial and energy, agriculture, forestry, and fishing. **Geographic Preferences:** Indiana, Illinois, Kentucky, Michigan, Midwest, and Ohio.

60031 ■ Irwin Ventures LLC / Irwin Ventures Incorporated
500 Washington St.
Columbus, IN 47202
Ph:(812)373-1434
Fax: (812)376-1709
URL: http://www.irwinventures.com
Contact: Thomas Washburn, President
Investment Types: Seed, early and first stage, start-up, and joint ventures. **Industry Preferences:** Communications, computer related, financial services, and business service. **Geographic Preferences:** Mid Atlantic, Northeast, Northern California, Northwest, and West Coast.

60032 ■ Monument Advisors, Inc.
Bank One Tower
111 Monument Cir., Ste. 4500
Indianapolis, IN 46204-5172
Ph:(317)656-5065
Fax: (317)656-5060
URL: http://www.monumentadv.com
Contact: Larry Wechter, Chief Executive Officer and Managing Dir
Preferred Investment Size: $1,000,000 to $3,000,000. **Investment Types:** Leveraged buyout, later stage, management buyouts, expansion, acquisition, recapitalizations, generalist PE. **Industry Preferences:** Computer software and services, other products, industrial and energy, communications and media, consumer related, medical and health. **Geographic Preferences:** Midwest.

60033 ■ MWV Capital Partners
201 N. Illinois St., Ste. 300
Indianapolis, IN 46204
Ph:(317)237-2323
Fax: (317)237-2325
URL: http://www.mwvcapital.com
Contact: Garth Dickey, Managing Director
Preferred Investment Size: $1,000,000 to $5,000,000. **Investment Types:** Balanced, second and later stage. **Industry Preferences:** Geographic Preferences: Midwest.

PROCUREMENT ASSISTANCE PROGRAMS

60034 ■ Indiana Small Business Development Center
1 N Capitol Ave., Ste. 900
Indianapolis, IN 46204-2248
Ph:(317)234-2082
Free: 888-472-3244
Fax: (317)232-8872
Co. E-mail: leadcenter@isbdc.org
URL: http://www.isbdc.org
Contact: Debbie Trocha, State Dir
Description: Helps businesses seeking government contracts. Provides marketing assistance, a library of federal specifications, and counseling and workshops on such topics as quality control, packaging, and proposal writing.

60035 ■ Partners in Contracting Corporation–Partners in Contracting Corporation
2646 Highway Ave.
Highland, IN 46322
Ph:(219)838-0176
Fax: (219)838-0554
Co. E-mail: picc@piccorp.org
URL: http://www.piccorp.org
Contact: Dennis Terry, Pres
E-mail: kdfox@netnitco.net

INCUBATORS/RESEARCH AND TECHNOLOGY PARKS

60036 ■ Ball State University–Academic Research and Sponsored Programs
2100 W. Riverside Ave.
Muncie, IN 47306

Ph:(765)285-1600
Fax: (765)285-1624
Co. E-mail: jpyle@bsu.edu
URL: http://www.bsu.edu/research
Contact: James Pyle, Asst.VP
E-mail: jpyle@bsu.edu
Scope: Encourages and facilitates research at the University by assisting individual investigators in developing research proposals, obtaining outside support for their research projects, and providing assistance in research design. **Services:** Consulting with Indiana nonprofit organizations. **Publications:** Bene Facta (annually); Information Newsletter (monthly). **Educational Activities:** Benefacta Day; Focus on Excellence; Seminars; Student symposium; Workshops.

60037 ■ Purdue Research Foundation
3000 Kent Ave.
West Lafayette, IN 47906
Ph:(765)494-8645
Fax: (765)496-1146
Co. E-mail: jbhornett@purdueresearchfoundation.edu
URL: http://www.purdueresearchfoundation.org
Contact: Joseph Hornett, Sr. VP/Treas.
E-mail: jbhornett@purdueresearchfoundation.edu
Scope: Serves as contracting agency for the University in acceptance of research grants and contracts from government, industry, and other foundations. Its Division of Sponsored Programs, established in 1966, serves the University and the Foundation in review, approval, and submission of proposals for research, instructional, and other externally sponsored programs. The Foundation acts as the University's agency in processing and managing patents and copyrights which grow out of research projects and provides research grants and fellowships from its own funds to faculty members and graduate students of the University.

60038 ■ Purdue Research Park
Purdue Research Foundation
3000 Kent Ave.
West Lafayette, IN 47906
Ph:(765)494-8645
Fax: (765)496-1146
Co. E-mail: gwdeason@prf.org
URL: http://www.purdueresearchpark.com
Contact: Greg Deason, VP
E-mail: gwdeason@prf.org
Scope: Provides facilities and University research and technical support services to research and development tenants. **Services:** Own and manage an incubator. **Publications:** Purdue Research Park Newsletter (quarterly).

60039 ■ Purdue University–Division of Sponsored Program Development
610 Purdue Mall
West Lafayette, IN 47907-1021
Ph:(765)494-6200
Fax: (765)496-2589
Co. E-mail: chipr@purdue.edu
Contact: Dr. Charles O. Ruttledge, Interim Vice Provost
E-mail: chipr@purdue.edu
Scope: Assists faculty in contacting potential research sponsors, negotiates research agreements with industrial sponsors, and communicates University interests to the Indiana Congressional delegation. Acts for the Purdue Research Foundation and University regarding research proposals and projects. Serves the instructional programs at the University with grant assistance for fellowships, training, institutes, curriculum development, equipment, and institutional development.

60040 ■ St. Joseph Station
Business Center
300 N Main St.
South Bend, IN 46601
Ph:(574)289-5471
Fax: (574)289-7105

60041 ■ University of Notre Dame–Office of Research of The Graduate School
511 Main Bldg.
Notre Dame, IN 46556-5602
Ph:(574)631-7432
Fax: (574)631-6630
Co. E-mail: research@nd.edu
URL: http://www.nd.edu/~research
Contact: Michael T. Edwards, Dir.
E-mail: research@nd.edu
Scope: Responsible for coordination and administration of sponsored research in all academic departments of the University and for awards received from U.S. government agencies, industrial and business organizations, philanthropic foundations, nonprofit organizations, professional societies, and individuals.

EDUCATIONAL PROGRAMS

60042 ■ Ball State University–Small Business Entrepreneurship Program
2000 W University Ave
Department of Management
Muncie, IN 47306
Ph:(765)289-1241
Free: 800-382-8540
Fax: (765)285-8024
URL: http://www.bsu.edu
Description: Offers a degree program, courses, seminars, and conferences for entrepreneurs and small business professionals. Covers financial and legal aspects of business ownership as well as small business assistance. Includes courses on business plan preparation and microcomputer use. 1-800-382-8540

60043 ■ Ivy Tech State College of Indiana–Columbus
4475 Central Ave.
Columbus, IN 47203
Ph:(812)372-9925
Free: 800-922-4838
Fax: (812)372-0311
URL: http://www.ivytech.edu/columbus
Description: Trade and technical college offering a business administration program, and a small business management program.

60044 ■ Ivy Tech State College of Indiana–Fort Wayne
3800 N Anthony Blvd.
Ft. Wayne, IN 46805
Ph:(260)482-9171
Fax: (260)480-4177
URL: http://www.ivytech.edu/fortwayne
Description: Trade and technical school offering a program in small business management. 1-888-489-5463

60045 ■ Ivy Tech State College of Indiana–Gary
1440 E 35th Ave.
Gary, IN 46409
Ph:(219)981-1111
Free: 800-843-4882
Fax: (219)981-4415
URL: http://www.gary.ivytech.edu
Description: Trade and technical school offering a program in small business management.

LEGISLATIVE ASSISTANCE

60046 ■ Indiana Chamber of Commerce–Indiana Small Business Council–Small Business Legislative Network (115 W)
115 W Washington St., Ste. 850S
Indianapolis, IN 46204
Ph:(317)264-3110
Fax: (317)264-6855
URL: http://www.indianachamber.com/

60047 ■ Indiana Senate Committee on Agriculture and Small Business
523 Eads Pky.
Lawrenceburg, IN 47025
Ph:(812)537-0628
Fax: (812)537-0636
Co. E-mail: nugentts@one.net
Contact: Johnny Nejent

PUBLICATIONS

60048 ■ *How to Form Your Own Indiana Corporation Before the Inc. Dries!: A Step by Step Guide, With Forms*
P. Gaines Publishing Company
333 S. Taylor Ave.
PO Box 2253
Oak Park, IL 60302
Ph:(708)524-9033
Fax: (708)524-9038
Ed: Phillip Williams. Released: 1992. Price: $19.95 (paper). Description: Volume 4 of the Small Business Incorporation series. Explains the advantages and disadvantages of incorporation and shows, step-by-step, how the small business owners can incorporate at low cost. Covers Indiana profit and nonprofit corporations, Indiana professional service corporations, subchapter S corporations, and Delaware corporations. Includes forms necessary for incorporation.

60049 ■ *Smart Start your Indiana Business*
PSI Research
300 N. Valley Dr.
Grants Pass, OR 97526
Ph:(503)479-9464
Free: 800-228-2275
Fax: (503)476-1479
Co. E-mail: info@psi-research.com
URL: http://www.psi-research.com
Ed: Michael D. Jenkins. Released: Revised edition, 1992. Price: $29.95 (looseleaf binder); $24.95 (paper). Description: Part of the Successful Business Library series.

PUBLISHERS

60050 ■ Macmillan Online USA
c/o Nature America Inc.
345 Park Ave. S
New York, NY 10010-1707
Ph:(212)726-9200
Fax: (212)696-9006
Co. E-mail: a.thomas@nature.com
URL: http://www.thomson.com
Contact: Annette Thomas, CEO
E-mail: a.thomas@nature.com
Description: Publishes Internet titles. Founded: 1869.

Iowa

SMALL BUSINESS DEVELOPMENT CENTER LEAD OFFICE

60051 ■ Iowa SBDC–Iowa State University
340 Gerdin Business Bldg.
Ames, IA 50011-1350
Ph:(515)294-2037
Fax: (515)294-6522
URL: http://www.iabusnet.org
Contact: Jon Ryan, State Dir.
E-mail: jonryan@iastate.edu

60052 ■ Iowa State University–Small Business Development Center
137 Lynn Ave.
Ames, IA 50014-7198
Ph:(515)292-6351
Free: 800-373-7232
Fax: (515)292-0020
URL: http://www.iabusnet.org/sbdc/
Contact: Ronald Manning, State Director
E-mail: rmanning@iastate.edu

SMALL BUSINESS DEVELOPMENT CENTERS

60053 ■ Drake University–Small Business Development Center
2507 University Ave.
Des Moines, IA 50311-4505
Ph:(515)271-2655
Fax: (515)271-1899
URL: http://www.iowasbdc.org/sbdc/drake.cfm
Contact: Sherry Shafer, Dir.
E-mail: sbdc01s@drake.edu

60054 ■ Eastern Iowa Community College–Small Business Development Center
331 W. 3rd St., Ste. 100
Davenport, IA 52801
Ph:(563)336-3401
Free: 800-462-3255
Fax: (563)336-3479
URL: http://www.eicc.edu/sbdc/
Contact: Ann Hutchinson, Dir.
E-mail: ahutchinson@eicc.edu

60055 ■ Indian Hills Community College–Small Business Development Center
651 Indian Hills Dr., Bldg. 17
Ottumwa, IA 52501
Ph:(641)683-5127
Free: 800-726-2585
Fax: (641)683-5296
URL: http://www.ihcc.cc.ia.us/ihbirc/sbdc.ap
Contact: Bryan Ziegler, Dir.
E-mail: bziegler@ott1.ihcc.cc.ia.us

60056 ■ Iowa Central Community College–SBDC
VoTech Bldg., Rm. 110
330 Ave. M
Ft. Dodge, IA 50501
Ph:(515)576-5090
Free: 800-362-2793
Fax: (515)576-0826
URL: http://www.iabusnet.org/sbdc/directory/iowacentral.cfm
Contact: Lisa Schorzmann, Dir.
E-mail: schorzmann@triton.iccc.cc.ia.us

60057 ■ Iowa Lakes Community College (Spencer)–Small Business Development Center
1900 N. Grand Ave., Ste. 8
Spencer, IA 51301
Ph:(712)262-4213
Fax: (712)262-4047
URL: http://www.iabusnet.org/sbdc/centers.cfm
Contact: Kelly McCarty, Dir.
E-mail: kmccarty@iowalakes.edu

60058 ■ Iowa State University–Small Business Development Center
Bldg. 1, Ste. 1615
2501 N. Loop Dr.
Ames, IA 50010-8283
Ph:(515)296-7828
Fax: (515)296-6714
URL: http://www.isupjenter/org/assistance/sbdc/
Contact: Mike Upah, Dir.
E-mail: mjupah@iastate.edu

60059 ■ Iowa Western Community College–Small Business Development Center
2700 College Rd., Box 4C
Council Bluffs, IA 51502
Ph:(712)325-3350
Free: 800-432-5852
Fax: (712)325-3408
URL: http://www.iwcc.edu/ewd/sbdc.asp
Contact: Sue Pitts, Dir.
E-mail: spitts@iwcc.edu

60060 ■ Kirkwood Community College–Small Business Development Center
3375 Armar Dr.
Marion, IA 52302
Ph:(319)377-8256
Fax: (319)398-5698
URL: http://www.kirdwood.edu/ktos/sbdc/index.html
Contact: Steve Sprague, Dir.
E-mail: sspragu@kirkwood.cc.ia.us

60061 ■ North Iowa Area–Small Business Development Center
500 College Dr.
Mason City, IA 50401
Ph:(641)422-4342
Free: 888-466-4222
Fax: (641)422-4129
URL: http://www.niacc.edu/pappajohn/smbusdev.html
Contact: Ted Bair, Dir.

E-mail: bairted@niacc.edu

60062 ■ Northeast Iowa–Small Business Development Center
608 Main St.
Dubuque, IA 52001-6944
Ph:(563)588-3350
Fax: (563)588-8033
URL: http://www.dubuquechamber.com/Public/Business_Assistance.cfm
Contact: Terry Sullivan, Dir.
E-mail: sullivant@nicc.edu

60063 ■ Southeastern Community College–Small Business Development Center
River Park Pl.
610 N. 4th St., Ste. 201
West Burlington, IA 52655
Ph:(319)752-2731
Free: (866)722-4692
Fax: (319)752-3407
URL: http://www.scciowa.edu/cbis/smallbus.html
Contact: Janine Clover, Dir.
E-mail: jclover@secc.cc.ia.us

60064 ■ Southwestern Community College–Small Business Development Center
1501 W. Townline Rd.
Creston, IA 50801
Ph:(641)782-4161
Fax: (641)782-1334
Contact: Bill Taylor, Dir.
E-mail: taylor@swcc.cc.ia.us

60065 ■ University of Iowa–Small Business Development Center
108 Pappajohn Business Bldg., Ste. S-160
S-160
Iowa City, IA 52242-1000
Ph:(319)335-3742
Fax: (319)353-2445
URL: http://www.iowajpec.org/entreps/smallbus.html
Contact: Paul Heath, Dir.
E-mail: paul-heath@uiowa.edu

60066 ■ University of Northern Iowa–Small Business Development Center
212 E. 4th St.
Waterloo, IA 50703
Ph:(319)236-8123
Fax: (319)236-8240
URL: http://www.uni.edu/rbc/
Contact: Maureen Collins-Williams, Dir.
E-mail: maureen.collins-williams@uni.edu

60067 ■ Western Iowa Tech Community College–Small Business Development Center
4647 Stone Ave.
PO Box 5199
Sioux City, IA 51102-5199
Ph:(712)274-6418
Free: 800-352-4649
Fax: (712)274-6429
URL: http://www.iowasbdc.org
Contact: Jackie Nohr, Dir.
E-mail: nohrj@witcc.com

SMALL BUSINESS ASSISTANCE PROGRAMS

60068 ■ Iowa Department of Economic Development–Department of Economic Development
200 E Grand Ave.
Des Moines, IA 50309
Ph:(515)242-4700
Free: 800-532-1216
Fax: (515)242-4809
Co. E-mail: info@iowalifechanging.com
URL: http://www.iowalifechanging.com
Description: Works with the private sector to promote policies and implement programs that will expand the economy and increase job opportunities for Iowans.

60069 ■ Iowa Department of Economic Development–International Division
200 E Grand Ave.
Des Moines, IA 50309
Ph:(515)242-4700
Free: 800-532-1216
Fax: (515)242-4918
Co. E-mail: info@iowalifechanging.com
URL: http://www.iowalifechanging.com
Description: Provides information and consulting to companies interested in international trade. Organizes booth space at international trade shows; publishes directories of products to be exported from Iowa.

60070 ■ Iowa Department of Economic Development–Small Business Services
200 E Grand Ave.
Des Moines, IA 50309
Ph:(515)242-4700
Free: 800-532-1216
Fax: (515)242-4809
Co. E-mail: info@iowalifechanging.com
URL: http://www.iowalifechanging.com
Description: Strives to further the economic well being of Iowa small business and to provide them with growth opportunities by offering services and coordinating efforts with existing programs.

SCORE OFFICES

60071 ■ SCORE Burlington
Federal Bldg.
300 N Main St.
Burlington, IA 52601
Ph:(319)752-2967
Co. E-mail: riverscore@lisco.com
Description: Provides professional guidance and information to maximize the success of existing and merging small businesses. Promotes entrepreneur education in Burlington area, Iowa.

60072 ■ SCORE Cedar Rapids
2750 1st Ave. NE, Ste. 350
Cedar Rapids, IA 52402-4831
Ph:(319)362-6405
Fax: (319)362-7861
Co. E-mail: score@scorecr.org
URL: http://www.scorecr.org
Description: Provides professional guidance and information to maximize the success of existing and emerging small businesses. Offers business assistance to develop business idea or plan and identify problems and potential solutions. Promotes entrepreneur education in Cedar Rapids area.

60073 ■ SCORE Des Moines
c/o Paul Whitmore, Chm.
Federal Bldg./Rm. 749
210 Walnut St.
Des Moines, IA 50309-2186
Ph:(515)284-4760

60074 ■ SCORE Fort Dodge
Federal Bldg., Rm. 256
205 S 8th St.
Fort Dodge, IA 50501
Ph:(515)955-2622
Co. E-mail: scorefd@yahoo.com
Description: Provides professional guidance and information to maximize the success of existing and emerging small businesses. Promotes entrepreneur education in Fort Dodge area, Iowa.

60075 ■ SCORE Illowa
333 4th Ave. S
Clinton, IA 52732
Ph:(563)242-5702
Co. E-mail: illowascoreclinton0541@yahoo.com
Description: Provides professional guidance and information to maximize the success of existing and emerging small businesses. Promotes entrepreneur education in Illowa area.

60076 ■ SCORE Iowa City
c/o William Suiters, Chm.
PO Box 1853
Iowa City, IA 52240-1853
Ph:(319)338-1662
Contact: Keith Kafer

60077 ■ SCORE Iowa Lakes
c/o C. Arnold Walker, Chm.
PO Box 7937
122 W 5th St.
Spencer, IA 51301
Ph:(712)262-3059
Co. E-mail: scoreil@smunet.net
URL: http://www.score.org
Contact: C. Arnold Walker, Chm.
Description: Provides professional guidance and information to maximize the success of existing and emerging small businesses. Promotes entrepreneur education in Spencer area, Iowa.

60078 ■ SCORE Northeast Iowa
613 North St.
Decorah, IA 52101
Ph:(563)382-6222
Co. E-mail: raenco123@aol.com
Description: Provides professional guidance and information to maximize the success of existing and emerging small businesses. Promotes entrepreneur education in Northeast Iowa.

60079 ■ SCORE River City
c/o Clarence Wagler, Chm.
PO Box 1128
Mason City, IA 50401
Ph:(641)423-5724
Co. E-mail: oldonphyl@netins.net
URL: http://www.score.org
Contact: Clarence Wagler, Chm.
Description: Provides public service to America by offering small business advice and training.

60080 ■ SCORE Sioux City
320 6th St.
Federal Bldg., Rm. 186
Sioux City, IA 51101
Ph:(712)277-2324
Fax: (712)277-2325
Co. E-mail: score104@iw.net
URL: http://www.iw.net/~score104
Description: Provides professional guidance and information to maximize the success of existing and emerging small businesses. Promotes entrepreneur education in Sioux area, Iowa.

60081 ■ SCORE South Central
SBDC, Indian Hills Community College
525 Grandview Ave.
Ottumwa, IA 52501
Ph:(641)683-5127
Description: Provides professional guidance and information to maximize the success of existing and emerging small businesses. Promotes entrepreneur education in Ottumwa area, Iowa.

60082 ■ SCORE Vista
c/o Storm Lake Chamber of Commerce
119 W 6th St.
Storm Lake, IA 50588
Ph:(712)732-3780
Fax: (712)732-1511
Co. E-mail: darelb50588@yahoo.com
Description: Provides entrepreneur education for the formation, growth and success of small businesses in the area.

60083 ■ SCORE Waterloo
Regional Business Center
212 E 4th St.
Waterloo, IA 50703
Ph:(319)236-8123
Description: Provides professional guidance and information to maximize the success of existing and emerging small businesses. Promotes entrepreneur education in Waterloo area, Iowa.

BETTER BUSINESS BUREAUS

60084 ■ Better Business Bureau of Central and Eastern Iowa
505 5th Ave., Ste. 950
Des Moines, IA 50309-2375
Ph:(515)243-8137
Free: 800-222-1600
Fax: (515)243-2227
Co. E-mail: info@dm.bbb.org
URL: http://www.desmoines.bbb.org
Contact: Chris Coleman, Pres.

60085 ■ Better Business Bureau of the Greater Sioux Region
600 4th St., Terra Centre No. 904
Sioux City, IA 51101
Ph:(712)252-4501
Free: 888-845-4222
Fax: (712)252-0285
Co. E-mail: general@siouxlandbbb.org
Contact: Stephanie Hageman, CEO

CHAMBERS OF COMMERCE

60086 ■ Adel Partners Chamber of Commerce
1129 Main St.
PO Box 73
Adel, IA 50003
Ph:(515)993-5472
Fax: (515)993-3384
Co. E-mail: adel@netins.net
URL: http://www.adeliowa.org
Contact: John Standley, Pres.

60087 ■ Algona Area Chamber of Commerce
123 E State St.
Algona, IA 50511
Ph:(515)295-7201
Fax: (515)295-5920
Co. E-mail: info@algona.org
URL: http://www.algona.org
Contact: Vicki Mallory, Exec.Dir.

60088 ■ Alta Chamber of Commerce
106 W Railroad St.
Storm Lake, IA 50588
Ph:(712)732-7594
URL: http://www.altaiowa.com/chamber.htm
Contact: Joe Aube, Pres.

60089 ■ Altoona Area Chamber of Commerce
119 2nd St.
Altoona, IA 50009
Ph:(515)967-3366
Fax: (515)967-3346
Co. E-mail: altoona@netins.net
URL: http://www.altoonachamber.org
Contact: Paulette Franklin, Exec.VP

60090 ■ Ames Chamber of Commerce
1601 Golden Aspen Dr., Ste. 110
Ames, IA 50010
Ph:(515)232-2310

Fax: (515)232-6716
Co. E-mail: dmaahs@ameschamber.com
URL: http://www.chamber.ames.ia.us
Contact: Daniel A. Culhane, Exec.Dir.

60091 ■ Anamosa Chamber of Commerce
124 E Main St.
Anamosa, IA 52205
Ph:(319)462-4879
Fax: (319)462-2209
Co. E-mail: anachamb@ia.net
URL: http://www.anamosachamber.com
Contact: K.C. Kiner, Exec.Dir.

60092 ■ Ankeny Area Chamber of Commerce
803 SW 3rd St.
PO Box 488
Ankeny, IA 50021
Ph:(515)964-0685
Fax: (515)964-0487
Co. E-mail: chamber@ankeny.org
URL: http://www.ankeny.org
Contact: Julie Cooper, Exec.Dir.

60093 ■ Atlantic Area Chamber of Commerce
102 Chestnut St.
Atlantic, IA 50022-1451
Ph:(712)243-3017
Free: 877-283-2124
Fax: (712)243-4404
Co. E-mail: atlanticchamber@a-m-u.net
URL: http://www.atlanticiowa.com
Contact: Ann Pross, Exec.Dir.

60094 ■ Audubon Chamber of Commerce
PO Box 66
Audubon, IA 50025-0066
Ph:(712)563-3780
Fax: (712)563-2537
Co. E-mail: audchamber@iowatelecom.net
Contact: Barbara Smith, Sec.

60095 ■ Bedford Chamber of Commerce
307 Main St.
Bedford, IA 50833
Ph:(712)523-3637
Fax: (712)523-3663
Co. E-mail: bedfordchamber@frontiernet.net
URL: http://www.bedford-iowa.com
Contact: Amber Reed, Pres.

60096 ■ Belle Plaine Chamber of Commerce
PO Box 163
Belle Plaine, IA 52208
Ph:(319)444-2541
Co. E-mail: tvriherd@netins.net
Contact: Suzanne Riherd, Sec.-Treas.

60097 ■ Bellevue Area Chamber of Commerce
PO Box 12
Bellevue, IA 52031
Ph:(563)872-5830
Fax: (563)872-3611
Co. E-mail: chamber@bellevueia.com
URL: http://www.bellevueia.com
Contact: Jennifer Dema

60098 ■ Belmond Area Chamber of Commerce
327 E Main St., Ste. 100
Belmond, IA 50421-1143
Ph:(641)444-3937
Fax: (641)444-3944
Co. E-mail: belmond@kalnet.com
URL: http://www.belmond.com
Contact: Cindy M. Rabe, Exec.Dir.

60099 ■ Bettendorf Chamber of Commerce
2117 State St.
Bettendorf, IA 52722
Ph:(563)355-4753
Fax: (563)355-7913
Co. E-mail: scott.tunnicliff@bettendorfchamber.com
URL: http://www.bettendorfchamber.com
Contact: Scott Tunnicliff, Pres./CEO

60100 ■ Boone Area Chamber of Commerce
903 Story St.
Boone, IA 50036
Ph:(515)432-3342
Fax: (515)432-3343
Co. E-mail: boonechamber@iowatelecom.net
URL: http://www.booneiowa.com
Contact: Jeffrey C. Brittain, Exec.Dir.

60101 ■ Britt Chamber of Commerce
PO Box 63
Britt, IA 50423
Ph:(641)843-3867
Fax: (641)843-4004
Co. E-mail: brittcoc@wctatel.net
URL: http://www.brittchamberofcommerce.com
Contact: Tamara Becker, Dir.

60102 ■ Burlington/West Burlington Area Chamber of Commerce
River Park Pl.
610 N 4th St., Ste. 200
Burlington, IA 52601-5069
Ph:(319)752-6365
Free: 800-82-RIVER
Fax: (319)752-6454
Co. E-mail: chamber@growburlington.com
URL: http://www.growburlington.com
Contact: Michael Brouwer, Pres.

60103 ■ Carroll Chamber of Commerce
223 W 5th St.
PO Box 307
Carroll, IA 51401
Ph:(712)792-4383
Free: (866)586-4383
Fax: (712)792-4384
Co. E-mail: chamber@carrolliowa.com
URL: http://www.carrolliowa.com
Contact: Jim Gossett, Exec.Dir.

60104 ■ Cedar Falls Chamber of Commerce
PO Box 367
10 Main St.
Cedar Falls, IA 50613-0367
Ph:(319)266-3593
Fax: (319)277-4325
Co. E-mail: cfchamber@cfu.net
URL: http://www.cedarfalls.org
Contact: Bob Justis, Pres.

60105 ■ Cedar Rapids Area Chamber of Commerce
424 1st Ave. NE
Cedar Rapids, IA 52401-1196
Ph:(319)398-5317
Fax: (319)398-5228
Co. E-mail: chamber@cedarrapids.org
URL: http://www.cedarrapids.org
Contact: Lee Clancey, Pres./CEO

60106 ■ Centerville Area Chamber of Commerce
128 N 12th St.
Centerville, IA 52544-1703
Ph:(641)437-4102
Free: 800-611-3800
Fax: (641)437-0527
Co. E-mail: cntrvlle@lisco.net
URL: http://www.iowachamber.net/directory.html
Contact: Joyce Bieber, Exec.Dir.

60107 ■ Chamber of Commerce of Corydon and Allerton
PO Box 253
Corydon, IA 50060-0253
Ph:(641)872-1338
Contact: Dr. Brenna Davis, Exec. Sec.

60108 ■ Chamber-Main Street Sac City
615 W Main St.
Sac City, IA 50583-1701
Ph:(712)662-7316
Fax: (712)662-7399
Co. E-mail: cmssc@pionet.net
URL: http://www.saccity.org
Contact: Laura Zimmerman, Program Dir.

60109 ■ Chariton Chamber and Development Corp.
104 N Grand St.
PO Box 488
Chariton, IA 50049
Ph:(641)774-4059
Fax: (641)774-2801
Co. E-mail: ccdc@iowatelecom.net
URL: http://www.charitonchamber.com
Contact: Ruth Comer, Exec.Dir.

60110 ■ Cherokee Chamber of Commerce
416 W Main St.
Cherokee, IA 51012
Ph:(712)225-6414
Fax: (712)225-2803
Co. E-mail: cofccherokee@ncn.net
URL: http://www.cherokeeiowachamber.com
Contact: Joni DeVos, Exec.Dir.

60111 ■ Clarinda Chamber of Commerce
115 E Main St.
Clarinda, IA 51632
Ph:(712)542-2166
Fax: (712)542-4113
Co. E-mail: chamber@clarinda.org
URL: http://www.clarinda.org
Contact: Elaine Farwell, Exec.Dir.

60112 ■ Clarion Area Chamber of Commerce
302 S Main
PO Box 6
Clarion, IA 50525-0006
Ph:(515)532-2256
Fax: (515)532-2511
Co. E-mail: clchamber@goldfieldaccess.net
Contact: Cheryl Ketelsen, Exec.Dir.

60113 ■ Clear Lake Area Chamber of Commerce
205 Main Ave.
PO Box 188
Clear Lake, IA 50428
Ph:(641)357-2159
Free: 800-285-5338
Fax: (641)357-8141
Co. E-mail: chamber@netins.net
URL: http://www.clearlakeiowa.com
Contact: David W. Collins, Exec.Dir.

60114 ■ Clinton Area Chamber of Commerce
333 4th Ave. S
PO Box 1024
Clinton, IA 52733-1024
Ph:(563)242-5702
Fax: (563)242-5803
Co. E-mail: clintonchamber@mcleodusa.net
URL: http://www.clintonia.com
Contact: Dennis W. Lauver, Pres.

60115 ■ Colfax Chamber of Commerce
PO Box 62
Colfax, IA 50054
Ph:(515)674-3565
Fax: (515)674-4194
Co. E-mail: info@colfaxiowachamber.com
URL: http://www.colfaxiowachamber.com
Contact: J.D. Smith, Pres.

60116 ■ Conrad Chamber of Commerce
PO Box 10
Conrad, IA 50621
Ph:(641)366-2165
Fax: (641)366-3505
Co. E-mail: jamjar@netins.net
URL: http://www.conradchamber.com
Contact: Julie McNair

60117 ■ Council Bluffs Area Chamber of Commerce
7 N 6th St.
Council Bluffs, IA 51503
Ph:(712)325-1000
Free: 800-228-6878
URL: http://www.councilbluffsiowa.com
Contact: Bob Mundt, Pres./CEO

60118 ■ Cresco Area Chamber of Commerce
PO Box 403
Cresco, IA 52136
Ph:(563)547-3434
Free: 800-373-6293
Fax: (563)547-2056
Co. E-mail: chamber@crescoia.com
URL: http://www.crescoia.com
Contact: Laura Ollendick, Exec.Dir.

60119 ■ Creston Chamber of Commerce
208 W Taylor St.
PO Box 471
Creston, IA 50801
Ph:(641)782-7021
Fax: (641)782-9927
Co. E-mail: chamber@crestoniowachamber.com
URL: http://www.mddc.com/chamber
Contact: Ellen Gerharz, Exec.Dir.

60120 ■ DavenportOne
130 W 2nd St.
Davenport, IA 52801
Ph:(563)322-1706
Fax: (563)322-7804
Co. E-mail: dhuber@davenportone.com
URL: http://www.davenportone.com
Contact: Dan Huber, Pres./CEO

60121 ■ De Witt Chamber of Commerce
524 10th St.
De Witt, IA 52742
Ph:(563)659-8500
Fax: (563)659-2410
Co. E-mail: info@dewitt.org
URL: http://www.dewitt.org
Contact: JoElla O'Connell, Exec.Dir.

60122 ■ Decorah Area Chamber of Commerce
300 W Water St.
Decorah, IA 52101
Ph:(563)382-3990
Free: 800-463-4692
Fax: (563)382-5515
Co. E-mail: info@decorah-iowa.com
URL: http://www.decorah-iowa.com
Contact: Nikki Brevig, Exec.Dir.

60123 ■ Denison Chamber of Commerce
18 S Main
Denison, IA 51442
Ph:(712)263-5621
Fax: (712)263-5238
Co. E-mail: chamber@denisonia.com
URL: http://www.denisonia.com
Contact: Dave Pauling, Exec.VP

60124 ■ Dubuque Area Chamber of Commerce
300 Main St., Ste. 200
PO Box 705
Dubuque, IA 52004-0705
Ph:(563)557-9200
Free: 800-798-4748
Fax: (563)557-1591
Co. E-mail: office@dubuquechamber.com
URL: http://www.dubuquechamber.com
Contact: Steward Sandstrom, Pres./CEO

60125 ■ Dyersville Area Chamber of Commerce
1100 16th Ave. Ct. SE
Dyersville, IA 52040
Ph:(563)875-2311
Fax: (563)875-8391
Co. E-mail: dyersvillechamber@dyersville.org
URL: http://www.dyersville.org
Contact: Karla Thompson, Exec.Dir.

60126 ■ Eagle Grove Area Chamber of Commerce
120 N Lucas
PO Box 2
Eagle Grove, IA 50533
Ph:(515)448-4821
Fax: (515)448-4821

Co. E-mail: egchambr@goldfieldaccess.net
URL: http://www.eaglegrove.com
Contact: Sara Tokheim, Exec.Dir.

60127 ■ Eldora Area Chamber and Development Council
1442 Washington St.
Eldora, IA 50627
Ph:(641)939-3241
Fax: (641)939-5667
Co. E-mail: eacdc@netins.net
URL: http://www.eldoraiowa.com/eacdc/eacdc.htm
Contact: Bill Grove, Pres.

60128 ■ Elkader Area Chamber of Commerce
305 High St.
PO Box 599
Elkader, IA 52043-0599
Ph:(563)245-2857
Free: (866)334-2857
Fax: (563)245-2857
Co. E-mail: elkader@alpinecom.net
URL: http://www.elkader-iowa.com
Contact: Linda Beck, Exec.Sec.

60129 ■ Emmetsburg Chamber of Commerce
1121 Broadway
Emmetsburg, IA 50536
Ph:(712)852-2283
Fax: (712)852-2156
Co. E-mail: eburgwelcome@kemb.org
URL: http://www.emmetsburg.com
Contact: Kathy Fank, Dir.

60130 ■ Essex Commercial Club
PO Box 334
Essex, IA 51638
Ph:(712)379-3485
Contact: Susie Tillman, Exec.Sec.

60131 ■ Estherville Area Chamber of Commerce
620 First Ave. S
Estherville, IA 51334
Ph:(712)362-3541
Fax: (712)362-7742
Co. E-mail: echamber@ncn.net
URL: http://www.ncn.net/~echamber/indexmaineville.
html
Contact: Dusty Heland, Exec.Dir.

60132 ■ Fairfield Area Chamber of Commerce
204 W Broadway
Fairfield, IA 52556
Ph:(641)472-2111
Fax: (641)472-6510
Co. E-mail: bphipps@fairfieldiowa.com
URL: http://fairfieldiowa.com
Contact: Robert E. Phipps, Exec.VP

60133 ■ Fayette Chamber of Commerce
PO Box 28
Fayette, IA 52142-0028
Ph:(563)425-4316
Co. E-mail: fayettecityhall@mchsi.com
URL: http://www.fayetteia.com

60134 ■ Fort Dodge Area Chamber of Commerce
1406 Central Ave.
PO Box T
Fort Dodge, IA 50501
Ph:(515)955-5500
Fax: (515)955-3245
Co. E-mail: chamber@dodgenet.com
URL: http://www.fortdodgechamber.com
Contact: Robert Singer, Exec.Dir.

60135 ■ Fort Madison Area Chamber of Commerce
614 9th St.
PO Box 277
Fort Madison, IA 52627
Ph:(319)372-5471
Fax: (319)372-6404
Co. E-mail: chamber@fortmadison.com

URL: http://www.fortmadison.com
Contact: Tracy R. Vance, Exec.Dir.

60136 ■ Garner Chamber of Commerce
211 State St.
Garner, IA 50438
Ph:(641)923-3993
Fax: (641)923-3993
Co. E-mail: chamberoffice@trvnet.net
URL: http://www.garner.govoffice2.com
Contact: Barb Eisenmenger, Pres.

60137 ■ Glenwood/Mills County Chamber of Commerce and Economic Development
32 1/2 N Walnut St.
Glenwood, IA 51534
Ph:(712)527-3298
Fax: (712)527-4349
Co. E-mail: glenwoodia@glenwoodcs.com
URL: http://www.millscountyiowa.com
Contact: Linda Washburn, Exec.Dir.

60138 ■ Greater Cedar Valley Chamber of Commerce - Waterloo
315 E 5th St.
Waterloo, IA 50703
Ph:(319)233-8431
Fax: (319)233-4580
Co. E-mail: bjustis@cfu.net
URL: http://www.waterloochamber.org
Contact: Bob Justis, Pres./CEO

60139 ■ Greater Des Moines Partnership
700 Locust St., Ste. 100
Des Moines, IA 50309
Ph:(515)286-4950
Free: 800-451-2625
Fax: (515)286-4974
Co. E-mail: info@desmoinesmetro.com
URL: http://www.desmoinesmetro.com
Contact: Martha A. Willits, Pres./CEO

60140 ■ Greater Eldora Chamber of Commerce
PO Box 303
Eldora, IA 50627
Ph:(641)939-3000
Co. E-mail: president@eldorachamber.com
URL: http://www.eldorachamber.com
Contact: Wanda Estes

60141 ■ Greater Muscatine Chamber of Commerce and Industry
319 E 2nd St., Ste. 102
Muscatine, IA 52761-4100
Ph:(563)263-8895
Fax: (563)263-8896
Co. E-mail: chamber@muscatine.com
URL: http://www.muscatine.com
Contact: Jane L. Daufeldt, Exec. Dir.

60142 ■ Greenfield Chamber/Main Street and Community Development Corporation
201 S 1st St.
PO Box 61
Greenfield, IA 50849
Ph:(641)743-8444
Fax: (641)743-8205
Co. E-mail: grfld_cc_ms_dev@iowatelecom.net
URL: http://www.greenfieldiowa.com
Contact: Ginny Kuhfus

60143 ■ Grinnell Area Chamber of Commerce
833 4th Ave.
PO Box 538
Grinnell, IA 50112
Ph:(641)236-6555
Fax: (641)236-3499
Co. E-mail: gcrec@grinnellchamber.org
URL: http://www.grinnellchamber.org
Contact: Larry R. Goodrich, Pres.

60144 ■ Grundy Center Chamber of Commerce and Development
705 F Ave.
Grundy Center, IA 50638

Ph:(319)825-3838
Fax: (319)825-6471
Co. E-mail: chamber@gcmuni.net
URL: http://www.grundycenter.com
Contact: Ms. Joyce Schmidt, Exec.Dir.

60145 ■ Guthrie Center Chamber of Commerce
203 Newton St.
Guthrie Center, IA 50115
Ph:(641)332-2190
Fax: (641)332-2192
URL: http://www.guthriecenter.com
Contact: Marie See, Sec.-Treas.

60146 ■ Guttenberg Civic and Commerce Club
PO Box 536
323 S River Park Dr.
Guttenberg, IA 52052-0536
Ph:(563)252-2323
Free: 877-252-2323
Fax: (563)252-2378
Co. E-mail: gutnberg@alpinecom.net
URL: http://www.guttenberg-iowa.org
Contact: Connie Backes, Sec.-Treas.

60147 ■ Hampton Area Chamber of Commerce
5 1st St. SW
Hampton, IA 50441
Ph:(641)456-5668
Fax: (641)456-5660
Co. E-mail: hacc@hamptoniowa.org
URL: http://www.hamptoniowa.org
Contact: Jennifer Gruelke, Dir.

60148 ■ Hartley Chamber of Commerce
11 S Central Ave.
Hartley, IA 51346
Ph:(712)928-2240
Co. E-mail: hart2020@tcaexpress.net
URL: http://www.hartleyiowa.com
Contact: Carole Klein, Sec.-Treas.

60149 ■ Hawarden Area Partnership for Progress
1150 Central Ave.
PO Box 266
Hawarden, IA 51023
Ph:(712)551-4433
Fax: (712)551-4433
Co. E-mail: happ@cityofhawarden.com
URL: http://www.cityofhawarden.com
Contact: Dan Cain, Pres.

60150 ■ Holstein Chamber of Commerce
PO Box 254
Holstein, IA 51025
Ph:(712)368-4898
Fax: (712)368-2782
Co. E-mail: holstein@netllc.net
Contact: Kathy Vollmar, Pres.

60151 ■ Hudson Chamber of Commerce
PO Box 493
Hudson, IA 50643-0493
Ph:(319)988-4655
Co. E-mail: admin@hudsoniachamber.org
URL: http://www.hudsoniachamber.org
Contact: Mark Nading, Sec.

60152 ■ Humboldt-Dakota City Chamber of Commerce
29 S 5th St.
PO Box 247
Humboldt, IA 50548-0247
Ph:(515)332-1481
Fax: (515)332-1496
Co. E-mail: chamber@trvnet.net
URL: http://www.ci.humboldt.ia.us
Contact: Sara Tokheim, Exec.Dir.

60153 ■ Independence Area Chamber of Commerce
PO Box 104
Independence, IA 50644

Ph:(319)334-7178
Fax: (319)334-7394
Co. E-mail: indycommerce@indytel.com
URL: http://www.indycommerce.com
Contact: Tammy Shaffer, Exec. Dir.

60154 ■ Indianola Chamber of Commerce
515 N Jefferson, Ste. D
Indianola, IA 50125
Ph:(515)961-6269
Co. E-mail: chamber@indianolachamber.com
URL: http://www.indianolachamber.com
Contact: Lynette Corkery, Exec.Dir.

60155 ■ Iowa City Area Chamber of Commerce
325 E Washington St., No. 100
PO Box 2358
Iowa City, IA 52244-2358
Ph:(319)337-9637
Fax: (319)338-9958
Co. E-mail: nancy@iowacityarea.com
URL: http://www.iowacityarea.com
Contact: Nancy Quellhorst, Pres.

60156 ■ Iowa Falls Chamber of Commerce - Main Street
520 Rockysylvania
Iowa Falls, IA 50126-2313
Ph:(641)648-5549
Fax: (641)648-3702
Co. E-mail: chamber@iafalls.com
URL: http://www.iafalls.com
Contact: Diana Thies, Exec.Dir.

60157 ■ Iowa Great Lakes Area Chamber of Commerce
243 W Broadway
PO Box 9
Arnolds Park, IA 51331-0009
Ph:(712)332-2107
Free: 800-839-9987
Fax: (712)332-7714
Co. E-mail: tom@okobojichamber.com
URL: http://www.iowachamber.net
Contact: Tom Kuhlman, Exec.VP

60158 ■ Jefferson Area Chamber of Commerce
220 N Chestnut St.
Jefferson, IA 50129
Ph:(515)386-2155
Fax: (515)386-2156
Co. E-mail: chamber@jeffersoniowa.com
URL: http://www.jeffersoniowa.com
Contact: Tracie Miller, Exec.Dir.

60159 ■ Jesup Chamber of Commerce
PO Box 592
Jesup, IA 50648
Ph:(319)827-1522
Fax: (319)827-3510
Co. E-mail: todd.rohlfsen@fsb1879.com
URL: http://www.jesupiowa.com
Contact: Rodney Duroe, Pres.

60160 ■ Johnston Chamber of Commerce
PO Box 61
Johnston, IA 50131
Ph:(515)276-9064
Fax: (515)309-0144
Co. E-mail: heather@growjohnston.com
Contact: Heather Wilcox, Mgr.

60161 ■ Kalona Area Chamber of Commerce
514 B Ave.
PO Box 615
Kalona, IA 52247
Ph:(319)656-2660
Fax: (319)656-2263
Co. E-mail: chamber@kctc.net
URL: http://www.kalonachamber.org
Contact: Mary Brennerman, Office Mgr.

60162 ■ Keokuk Area Chamber of Commerce
329 Main St.
Keokuk, IA 52632

Ph:(319)524-5055
Fax: (319)524-5016
Co. E-mail: keokukcc@interl.net
URL: http://keokuk-ia.com/chamber
Contact: Katie O'Brien, Exec. Dir.

60163 ■ Knoxville Chamber of Commerce and Economic Development
309 E Main St.
PO Box 71
Knoxville, IA 50138
Ph:(641)828-7555
Fax: (641)828-7978
Co. E-mail: chamber@harenet.net
URL: http://www.knoxville-iowa.com
Contact: Brian Stickel, Exec.Dir.

60164 ■ La Porte City Chamber of Commerce
PO Box 82
La Porte City, IA 50651
Ph:(319)342-2850
Contact: Mike Chingren, Pres.

60165 ■ Lake City Betterment Association
113 E Main St.
Lake City, IA 51449
Ph:(712)464-7611
Co. E-mail: betterment@lakecityiowa.com
URL: http://www.lakecityiowa.com
Contact: Janelle Nesbitt, Exec.Sec.

60166 ■ Laurens Chamber of Commerce
PO Box 33
Laurens, IA 50554
Ph:(712)845-2620
Fax: (712)845-2544
Contact: Ken Kunickis, Pres.

60167 ■ Leon Chamber of Commerce
PO Box 210
Leon, IA 50144
Ph:(641)446-6221
Fax: (641)446-7500
Contact: Janet Busch, Pres.

60168 ■ Logan Chamber of Commerce
PO Box 187
Logan, IA 51546
Ph:(712)644-3208
Fax: (712)644-3124
URL: http://www.loganiowa.com
Contact: Chris Hartwig, Treas.

60169 ■ Madison County Chamber of Commerce
73 Jefferson St.
Winterset, IA 50273
Ph:(515)462-1185
Free: 877-770-4438
Fax: (515)462-1393
Co. E-mail: chamber@madisoncounty.com
URL: http://www.madisoncounty.com

60170 ■ Main Street Chamber of Commerce - Adel Partners
PO Box 73
Adel, IA 50003
Ph:(515)993-5472
Fax: (515)993-3384
Co. E-mail: adel@netins.net
URL: http://www.adeliowa.org/Partners
Contact: Julie Bailey, Program Dir.

60171 ■ Manchester Area Chamber of Commerce
200 E Main St.
Manchester, IA 52057
Ph:(563)927-4141
Fax: (563)927-2958
Co. E-mail: macc@manchesteriowa.org
URL: http://www.manchesteriowa.org
Contact: Jack Klaus, Exec.Dir.

60172 ■ Manning Chamber of Commerce
PO Box 354
Manning, IA 51455-0354
Ph:(712)655-3541

Fax: (712)655-2478
Co. E-mail: ddoyel@iowatelecom.net
URL: http://www.manningia.com
Contact: Jodi Tyrrel, VP

60173 ■ Manson Economic Development Corp. and Chamber of Commerce
PO Box 561
Manson, IA 50563
Ph:(712)469-3311
Co. E-mail: arice@iowatelecom.net
URL: http://www.mansoniowa.org
Contact: Pat Essing, Chm.

60174 ■ Maquoketa Area Chamber of Commerce
117 S Main St.
Maquoketa, IA 52060
Ph:(563)652-4602
Free: 800-989-4602
Fax: (563)652-3020 .
Co. E-mail: maqchamber@qwest.net
URL: http://www.maquoketachamber.com
Contact: Stacy Driscoll, Exec.Dir.

60175 ■ Marengo Chamber of Commerce
PO Box 251
Marengo, IA 52301
Ph:(319)741-5241
Fax: (319)642-3232
Contact: Lee Slaymaker, Pres.

60176 ■ Marshalltown Area Chamber of Commerce
709 S Center St.
PO Box 1000
Marshalltown, IA 50158
Ph:(641)753-6645
Fax: (641)752-8373
Co. E-mail: info@marshalltown.org
URL: http://www.marshalltown.org
Contact: Ken Anderson, Pres.

60177 ■ Mason City Area Chamber of Commerce
25 W State St.
Mason City, IA 50401
Ph:(641)423-5724
Fax: (641)423-5725
Co. E-mail: chamber@masoncityia.com
URL: http://www.masoncityia.com
Contact: Robin Anderson, Exec.Dir.

60178 ■ McGregor/Marquette Chamber of Commerce
146 Main St.
PO Box 105
McGregor, IA 52157
Ph:(563)873-2186
Free: 800-896-0910
Fax: (563)873-2847
Co. E-mail: mac-marq@alpinecom.net
URL: http://www.mcgreg-marq.org
Contact: Kaye Morel, Exec.Dir.

60179 ■ Missouri Valley Chamber of Commerce
PO Box 130
Missouri Valley, IA 51555
Ph:(712)642-2553
Fax: (712)642-3771
Co. E-mail: chamberofcommerce1@juno.com
URL: http://www.missourivalley.com
Contact: Mr. Jeff Snyder, Exec.Dir.

60180 ■ Monticello Area Chamber of Commerce
306 E 1st St.
Monticello, IA 52310
Ph:(319)465-5626
Fax: (319)465-6194
Co. E-mail: chamber@ci.monticello.ia.us
URL: http://www.monticello.ia.us
Contact: Tara Fall, Sec.

60181 ■ Mount Pleasant Area Chamber of Commerce
124 S Main St.
PO Box 109
Mount Pleasant, IA 52641
Ph:(319)385-3101
Free: 800-436-7619
Fax: (319)385-3012
Co. E-mail: jdaly@mountpleasantiowa.org
URL: http://www.mtpleasantiowa.com
Contact: Jennifer Daly, Exec.VP

60182 ■ Mount Vernon Area Chamber of Commerce
311 1st St. W
PO Box 281
Mount Vernon, IA 52314-0281
Ph:(319)895-8214
Free: 877-895-8214
Fax: (319)895-4046
Co. E-mail: johnbardsley@mountvernoniowa.org
URL: http://www.mountvernoniowa.org
Contact: John Bardsley, Community Coor.

60183 ■ Nevada Chamber of Commerce
1015 6th St.
Nevada, IA 50201
Ph:(515)382-6538
Free: 800-558-2288
Fax: (515)382-3803
Co. E-mail: chamber@midiowa.net
URL: http://www.nevadaiowa.org
Contact: Sara Clausen, Exec.Dir.

60184 ■ New Horizons-Chamber/MainStreet
15 W Main
New Hampton, IA 50659
Ph:(641)394-2021
Fax: (641)394-2494
Co. E-mail: nhc@iowatelecom.net
URL: http://www.newhamptoniowa.com
Contact: Ms. Jeannine Burgart, Exec.Dir.

60185 ■ Northwood Area Chamber of Commerce
PO Box 71
Northwood, IA 50459
Ph:(641)324-1420
Contact: Teresa George, VP

60186 ■ Norwalk Area Chamber of Commerce
PO Box 173
Norwalk, IA 50211
Ph:(515)981-0619
Fax: (515)981-1890
Co. E-mail: norwalkchamber@smsn.com
URL: http://www.norwalkchamber.org
Contact: Jon Niemeyer, Pres.

60187 ■ Oelwein Chamber and Area Development
25 W Charles St.
Oelwein, IA 50662
Ph:(319)283-1105
Fax: (319)283-2890
Co. E-mail: ocad@oelwein.com
URL: http://www.oelwein.com
Contact: Sally Falb, Exec.Dir.

60188 ■ Onawa Chamber of Commerce
1009 Iowa Ave.
Onawa, IA 51040
Ph:(712)423-1801
Fax: (712)423-2626
Co. E-mail: chamber@onawa.com
URL: http://www.onawa.com
Contact: Fran Tramp

60189 ■ Orange City Chamber of Commerce
509 8th St. SE
PO Box 36
Orange City, IA 51041
Ph:(712)707-4510
Fax: (712)707-4523
Co. E-mail: octulip@frontiernet.net
URL: http://orangecityiowa.com

Contact: Mary Lou Vander Wel, Exec.Dir.

60190 ■ Osage Chamber of Commerce
808 Main St.
Osage, IA 50461
Ph:(641)732-3163
Fax: (641)732-3163
Co. E-mail: chamber@osage.net
URL: http://www.osage.net/~chamber
Contact: Ms. Wendy Heuton, Exec.Coor.

60191 ■ Osceola Chamber of Commerce
100 S Fillmore
Osceola, IA 50213
Ph:(641)342-4200
Co. E-mail: ocms@iowatelecom.net
URL: http://www.osceolachamber.com
Contact: Becky Persels, Mgr.

60192 ■ Oskaloosa Area Chamber and Development Group
124 N Market St.
Oskaloosa, IA 52577-2827
Ph:(641)672-2591
Fax: (641)672-2047
Co. E-mail: oskycofc@oacdg.org
URL: http://www.oskaloosachamber.org

60193 ■ Ottumwa Area Chamber of Commerce
217 E Main St.
PO Box 308
Ottumwa, IA 52501
Ph:(641)682-3465
Co. E-mail: info@ottumwaiowa.com
URL: http://www.ottumwaiowa.com/chamber/index.html
Contact: Joy Johnston, Dir.

60194 ■ Pella Chamber of Commerce
518 Franklin St.
Pella, IA 50219-1636
Ph:(641)628-2626
Free: 888-746-3882
Fax: (641)628-9697
Co. E-mail: pellacoc@pella.org
URL: http://www.pella.org
Contact: David Vollmar, Exec. Dir.

60195 ■ Perry Chamber of Commerce
1226 2nd St.
Perry, IA 50220-1556
Ph:(515)465-4601
Fax: (515)465-2256
Co. E-mail: perrychmbr@aol.com
URL: http://www.perryia.org
Contact: Ms. Sara Truesdell, Exec.Dir.

60196 ■ Pocahontas Chamber of Commerce
PO Box 125
Pocahontas, IA 50574
Ph:(712)335-3223
Co. E-mail: chamber@pocahontasiowa.com
URL: http://www.pocahontasiowa.com
Contact: Jan Stoulil, Exec.Sec.

60197 ■ Red Oak Chamber of Commerce
307 E Reed St.
Red Oak, IA 51566
Ph:(712)623-4821
Fax: (712)623-4822
Co. E-mail: adminasst@redoakiowa.com
URL: http://www.redoakiowa.com
Contact: Jodie Smith, Admin.Asst.

60198 ■ Rock Rapids Community Affairs Corporation
206 1st Ave.
PO Box 403
Rock Rapids, IA 51246
Ph:(712)472-3456
Fax: (712)472-2126
Co. E-mail: linda@rockrapids.com
URL: http://www.rockrapids.com
Contact: Linda Pribyl

60199 ■ Rock Valley Chamber of Commerce
PO Box 89
Rock Valley, IA 51247
Ph:(712)476-9300
Fax: (712)476-9116
Co. E-mail: curt@cityofrockvalley.com
URL: http://www.cityofrockvalley.com
Contact: Curt Strouth, Community Activities Dir.

60200 ■ Rockwell City Chamber and Development
2790 290th St.
Rockwell City, IA 50579
Ph:(712)297-8874
Fax: (712)297-8874
Co. E-mail: rcdev@iowatelecom.net
URL: http://www.rockwellcity.com
Contact: Susan Carlson, Coor.

60201 ■ St. Ansgar Chamber of Commerce
PO Box 533
St. Ansgar, IA 50472-0533
Ph:(641)713-4921
Co. E-mail: stansgar@stansgar.org
URL: http://www.stansgar.org
Contact: Brenda Esdohr, Pres.

60202 ■ Schaller Chamber of Commerce
PO Box 129
Schaller, IA 51053
Ph:(712)275-4229
Contact: Theresa Bailey, Sec.-Treas.

60203 ■ Shelby County Chamber of Commerce
1101 7th St.
Harlan, IA 51537
Ph:(712)755-2114
Free: 888-876-1774
Fax: (712)755-2115
Co. E-mail: info@exploreshelbycounty.com
URL: http://www.exploreshelbycounty.com
Contact: Dawn Cundiff, Dir.

60204 ■ Sheldon Chamber and Development Corp.
416 9th St.
PO Box 276
Sheldon, IA 51201-0276
Ph:(712)324-2813
Fax: (712)324-4602
Co. E-mail: rachelk@sheldoniowa.com
URL: http://www.sheldoniowa.com
Contact: Mark Gaul, Dir.

60205 ■ Shenandoah Chamber and Industry Association
100 Maple St.
PO Box 38
Shenandoah, IA 51601
Ph:(712)246-3455
Fax: (712)246-3456
Co. E-mail: chamber@simplyshenandoah.com
URL: http://shenandoahiowa.net
Contact: Shelly Smith, Marketing Dir.

60206 ■ Sibley Chamber of Commerce
848 3rd Ave.
Sibley, IA 51249
Ph:(712)754-3212
Fax: (712)754-3212
Co. E-mail: chamber@sibleyiowa.net
URL: http://www.sibleyiowa.net
Contact: Christina Greenfield, Exec.Dir.

60207 ■ Sidney Chamber of Commerce
PO Box 401
Sidney, IA 51652
Ph:(712)374-2801
Fax: (712)374-2622
URL: http://www.aboutsidney.net
Contact: Randy Moreland, Pres.

60208 ■ Sigourney Main Street Chamber
112 E Washington
Sigourney, IA 52591-1445
Ph:(641)622-2288

Fax: (641)622-2396
Co. E-mail: sadc@se-iowa.net
URL: http://www.sigourney.com
Contact: Ms. Sue Martin, Exec.Dir.

60209 ■ Sioux Center Chamber of Commerce
303 N Main Ave.
Sioux Center, IA 51250
Ph:(712)722-3457
Free: 800-SXC-ENTR
Fax: (712)722-3465
Co. E-mail: scchambr@mtcnet.net
URL: http://www.siouxcenterchamber.com
Contact: Ardith Lein, Exec.Dir.

60210 ■ Siouxland Chamber of Commerce
101 Pierce St.
Sioux City, IA 51101
Ph:(712)255-7903
Free: 800-228-7903
Fax: (712)258-7578
Co. E-mail: chamber@siouxlandchamber.com
URL: http://www.siouxlandchamber.com
Contact: Debi Durham, Pres.

60211 ■ Spencer Chamber of Commerce
122 W 5th St.
PO Box 7937
Spencer, IA 51301-7937
Ph:(712)262-5680
Fax: (712)262-5747
Co. E-mail: spencerchamber@smunet.net
URL: http://www.spenceriowachamber.org
Contact: Robert Rose, Exec.Dir.

60212 ■ Storm Lake Chamber of Commerce
119 W 6th St.
PO Box 864
Storm Lake, IA 50588
Ph:(712)732-3780
Free: 888-752-4692
Fax: (712)732-1511
Co. E-mail: slc@stormlake.org
URL: http://www.stormlakechamber.com
Contact: Gary Lalone, Exec.Dir.

60213 ■ Story City Chamber of Commerce
618 Broad St.
Story City, IA 50248
Ph:(515)733-4214
Fax: (515)733-4504
Co. E-mail: chamber@storycity.net
URL: http://www.storycity.net

60214 ■ Strawberry Point Chamber of Commerce
PO Box 404
Strawberry Point, IA 52076
Ph:(563)933-4400
Contact: Gene Rima, Sec.

60215 ■ Tama/Toledo Area Chamber of Commerce
PO Box 367
Toledo, IA 52342
Ph:(641)484-6661
Fax: (641)484-6540
Co. E-mail: charlotte@tamatoledo.com
URL: http://www.tamatoledo.com
Contact: Elmer Baier, Pres.

60216 ■ Tipton Chamber of Commerce
PO Box 5
Tipton, IA 52772
Ph:(563)886-6350
Fax: (563)886-3762
Co. E-mail: ccedco@jeonet.com
Contact: Daisy Wingert, Pres.

60217 ■ Traer Chamber of Commerce
545 2nd St.
PO Box 431
Traer, IA 50675
Ph:(319)478-8899
Co. E-mail: traercc@netins.net
Contact: Brenda Huntley, Pres.

60218 ■ Urbandale Chamber of Commerce
3600 8th St.
Urbandale, IA 50322
Ph:(515)331-6855
Fax: (515)278-3927
Co. E-mail: info@urbandalechamber.com
URL: http://www.uniquelyurbandale.com
Contact: Tiffany Menke, Exec.Dir.

60219 ■ Villisca Chamber of Commerce
601 S Third Ave.
Villisca, IA 50864
Ph:(712)826-2282
Contact: Gayle Heard, Treas.

60220 ■ Walcott Chamber of Commerce
128 W Lincoln
Walcott, IA 52773-0000
Ph:(563)284-6571

60221 ■ Wall Lake Chamber of Commerce
PO Box 302
Wall Lake, IA 51466
Ph:(712)664-2311
URL: http://www.walllake.com
Contact: Dawn Potthoff, Sec.Treas.

60222 ■ Washington Chamber of Commerce
212 N Iowa Ave.
Washington, IA 52353
Ph:(319)653-3272
Fax: (319)653-5805
Co. E-mail: washcofc@iowatelecom.net
URL: http://www.washingtoniowachamber.com
Contact: Susan Wellington, Dir.

60223 ■ Waukon Chamber of Commerce
101 W Main St.
Waukon, IA 52172
Ph:(563)568-4110
Fax: (563)568-6990
Co. E-mail: waukoncc@acegroup.cc
URL: http://www.waukon.org
Contact: Danny Schlitter, Dir.

60224 ■ Waverly Area Development Group
112 W Bremer Ave., Ste. A
Waverly, IA 50677
Ph:(319)352-4526
Fax: (319)352-0136
Co. E-mail: waverly@wl-p.net
URL: http://wadg.waverlyia.com/index.asp
Contact: Tara Harn, Retail-Commercial Dir.

60225 ■ Webster City Area Association of Business and Industry
628 2nd St.
PO Box 310
Webster City, IA 50595-0310
Ph:(515)832-2564
Free: 800-535-8341
Fax: (515)832-5130
Co. E-mail: info@webstercity-iowa.com
URL: http://www.webstercity-iowa.com
Contact: Jennifer Asa, Dir.

60226 ■ West Bend Chamber of Commerce
PO Box 366
West Bend, IA 50597
Ph:(515)887-2181
Fax: (515)887-4721
URL: http://www.westbendiowa.com
Contact: Darla Winkerhurst, Sec.

60227 ■ West Branch Chamber of Commerce
108 W Main St.
PO Box 810
West Branch, IA 52358
Ph:(319)643-2111
Co. E-mail: wbchamb@lcom.net
Contact: Claudia Wallick, Pres.

60228 ■ West Des Moines Chamber of Commerce
PO Box 65320
West Des Moines, IA 50265
Ph:(515)225-6009

Fax: (515)225-7129
Co. E-mail: info@wdmchamber.org
URL: http://www.wdmchamber.org
Contact: Linda Hulleman, Exec.Dir.

60229 ■ West Liberty Chamber of Commerce
405 N Elm St.
West Liberty, IA 52776
Ph:(319)627-4876
Fax: (319)627-3087
Co. E-mail: wlchamber@lcom.net
URL: http://www.westlibertyiowa.org
Contact: Gwen Kessler, Exec.Sec.

60230 ■ West Union Chamber of Commerce
101 N Vine St.
West Union, IA 52175-0071
Ph:(563)422-3070
Co. E-mail: wuchamber@alpinecom.net
URL: http://www.westunion.com
Contact: Robin Bostrom, Exec.Dir.

60231 ■ Williamsburg Chamber of Commerce
PO Box 982
Williamsburg, IA 52361
Ph:(319)668-1500
URL: http://www.williamsburgiowa.org
Contact: Barb Hopp

60232 ■ Wilton Chamber of Commerce
118 W 4th St.
PO Box 280
Wilton, IA 52778-0005
Ph:(563)732-2330
Fax: (563)732-2332
Co. E-mail: wiltoncc@netins.net
URL: http://www.wiltoniowa.org
Contact: Mrs. Eva Belitz, Exec. VP

60233 ■ Winfield Chamber of Commerce
PO Box 73
Winfield, IA 52659
Ph:(319)257-6661
Contact: Klay Edwards, Pres.

FINANCING AND LOAN PROGRAMS

60234 ■ Aavin Equity Advisors, LLC
118 3rd St., Ste. 630
Cedar Rapids, IA 52401
Ph:(319)247-1072
Fax: (319)363-9519
URL: http://www.aavin.com
Contact: James Thorp, Managing Director
Preferred Investment Size: $500,000 to $3,000,000.
Investment Policies: Start-up, first, second, and later stage, acquisition, expansion, leveraged buyout, management buyouts, recapitalizations, and turnaround.
Industry Preferences: Communications and media, computer software and hardware, semiconductors and other electronics, medical and health, consumer related, industrial and energy, transportation, financial services, business service, manufacturing, agriculture, forestry, and fishing, utilities, and environment.
Geographic Preferences: Midwest.

60235 ■ Allsop Venture Partners
118 3rd Ave. SE, Ste. 837
Cedar Rapids, IA 52401
Ph:(319)368-6675
Fax: (319)363-9515
Preferred Investment Size: $500,000 minimum. **Investment Types:** First stage, industry rollups, leveraged buyout, mezzanine, second stage, and special situation. **Industry Preferences:** communications and media, computer hardware and software, semiconductors and other electronics, medical and health, consumer related, industrial and energy, transportation, financial services, business service, and manufacturing. **Geographic Preferences:** U.S.

60236 ■ Berthel Fisher & Company Planning, Inc.
701 Tama St., Bldg. B
PO Box 609
Marion, IA 52302
Ph:800-356-5234
Fax: (319)447-4250
URL: http://www.berthel.com
Contact: Henry Royer, Managing Director
Investment Types: Later stage. **Geographic Preferences:** Midwest.

60237 ■ InvestAmerica Venture Group, Inc.
101 2nd St. SE, Ste. 800
Cedar Rapids, IA 52401
Ph:(319)363-8249
Fax: (319)363-9683
URL: http://www.investam.com
Contact: David Schroder, President
Preferred Investment Size: $500,000 to $1,000,000.
Investment Types: First and second stage, leveraged buyout, and special situation. **Industry Preferences:** Other products, industrial and energy, Internet specific, communications and media, consumer related, computer hardware, computer software and services, semiconductors and other electronics, biotechnology, medical and health. **Geographic Preferences:** U.S.

60238 ■ Pappajohn Capital Resources
2116 Financial Ctr.
Des Moines, IA 50309
Ph:(515)244-5746
Fax: (515)244-2346
URL: http://www.pappajohn.com
Preferred Investment Size: $500,000 to $1,000,000.
Investment Types: Seed, start-up, first and second stage, leveraged buyout, and special situation. **Industry Preferences:** Computer software and services, biotechnology, Internet specific, medical and health, consumer related, other products, communications and media, industrial and energy, semiconductors and other electronics. **Geographic Preferences:** U.S.

PROCUREMENT ASSISTANCE PROGRAMS

60239 ■ Iowa Procurement Outreach Center
2701 SE Convenience Blvd., Ste. 13
2272 Howe Hall, CIRAS, Ste. 2620
Ankeny, IA 50021
Ph:(515)289-0281
Free: 800-458-4465
Fax: (515)294-4483
Co. E-mail: bconey@ciras.iastate.edu
URL: http://www.ciras.iastate.edu
Description: Helps small businesses secure federal government contracts.

60240 ■ Iowa Procurement Technical Assistance Center–Outreach Center
2701 SE Convenience Blvd., Ste. 13
Ankeny, IA 50021
Ph:(515)289-0281
Free: 800-458-4465
Fax: (515)294-4483
Co. E-mail: bconey@ciras.iastate.edu
URL: http://www.ciras.iastate.edu
Contact: Ronald Cox, Dir
E-mail: bconey@ided.state.ia.us

INCUBATORS/RESEARCH AND TECHNOLOGY PARKS

60241 ■ Iowa State University Research Park
2711 S Loop Dr., Ste. 4050
Ames, IA 50010-8648
Ph:(515)296-7275
Fax: (515)296-9924
Co. E-mail: isupark@iastate.edu
URL: http://www.isupark.org

Contact: Steven T. Carter, Pres.
E-mail: isupark@iastate.edu
Scope: 195-acre site on the University's South Campus facilitating interaction between corporate research laboratories and the University research community.

60242 ■ Iowa State University of Science and Technology–ISU Foundation
2505 Elwood Dr.
Ames, IA 50010-8644
Ph:(515)294-4607
Free: (866)-419-6768
Fax: (515)294-9402
Co. E-mail: dansaftig@foundation.iastate.edu
URL: http://www.foundation.iastate.edu
Contact: Dan Saftig, Pres.
E-mail: dansaftig@foundation.iastate.edu
Scope: Supports research and educational activities at the University through the administration of grants, gifts, and bequests to the University. **Publications:** Partners.

60243 ■ University of Iowa–Division of Sponsored Programs
100 Gilmore Hall
Iowa City, IA 52242-1320
Ph:(319)353-2123
Fax: (319)335-2130
Co. E-mail: dap@uiowa.edu
URL: http://www.uiowa.edu/~vpr/
Contact: Twila Fisher Reighley, Dir.
E-mail: dap@uiowa.edu
Scope: Serves as coordinating agency and institutional representative for external funding of educational and scientific research and development at the University. Maintains a reference center on funding resources and government policy on research.

60244 ■ University of Iowa–Technology Innovation Center
100 Oakdale Campus,Rm. 109 TIC
Iowa City, IA 52242-5000
Ph:(319)335-4063
Fax: (319)335-4489
Co. E-mail: thomas_bauer@uiowa.edu
URL: http://research.uiowa.edu/techtransfer/tic_main.htm
Contact: Thomas K. Bauer, Interim Dir.
E-mail: thomas_bauer@uiowa.edu
Scope: Fosters collaborative applied research involving faculty and corporate investigators in developing new business ventures in technological areas. Provides referral to research capabilities of University faculty, access to equipment, instruments, and computing facilities, office help, grant and contract assistance, and capital and business advice to new business. Leases space to new and existing research-oriented firms.

EDUCATIONAL PROGRAMS

60245 ■ Des Moines Area Community College–Urban Campus
1100 7th St.
Des Moines, IA 50314
Ph:(515)244-4226
Free: 800-362-2127
Fax: (515)248-7253
URL: http://www.dmacc.org
Description: A wide variety of courses and workshops are offered to the working student wishing to develop or update specific occupational skills. Programs emphasize both fundamental concepts and practical experience to assure thorough competence in the chosen field. The Small Business Management Education Program offers a number of courses for credit and noncredit status—designed to meet the educational needs of the small business owner.

60246 ■ Iowa Lakes Community College (Estherville)
300 S 18th St.
Estherville, IA 51334
Ph:(712)362-2604

Free: 800-242-5106
Fax: (712)362-8363
Co. E-mail: info@iowalakes.edu
URL: http://www.ilcc.cc.ia.us
Description: Two-year college offering a small business management program.

60247 ■ Marshalltown Community College
3700 S Center St.
Marshalltown, IA 50158
Ph:(641)752-7106
Fax: (641)752-8149
Co. E-mail: mccinfo@iavalley.edu
URL: http://www.iavalley.cc.ia.us/mcc
Description: Two-year college offering a small business course through the continuing education program.

LEGISLATIVE ASSISTANCE

60248 ■ Iowa Senate Committee on Small Business, Economic Development and Tourism
State Capitol
1007 E Grand St.
Des Moines, IA 50319
Ph:(515)281-5381
Fax: (319)938-2659
URL: http://www.legis.state.ia.us

Contact: Sen. Kitty Rehberg

PUBLICATIONS

60249 ■ *Business Record*
100 4th St.
Des Moines, IA 50309
Ph:(515)288-3336
Fax: (515)288-0309

60250 ■ *Innovation in Iowa*
Iowa State University
Small Business Development Center
137 Lynn Ave.
Ames, IA 50014-7198
Free: 800-373-7232
Fax: (515)292-0020
URL: http://www.Iowsbe.org/
Ed: Bryan Ziegler. **Price:** $7.00. **Description:** Offers information on developing and marketing products.

60251 ■ *Smart Start your Iowa Business*
PSI Research
300 N. Valley Dr.
Grants Pass, OR 97526
Ph:(503)479-9464
Free: 800-228-2275
Fax: (503)476-1479
Co. E-mail: info@psi-research.com

URL: http://www.psi-research.com
Ed: Michael D. Jenkins. **Released:** Revised edition, 1992. **Price:** $29.95 (looseleaf binder); $24.95 (paper). **Description:** Part of the Successful Business Library series.

60252 ■ *Starting and Operating a Business in Iowa: A Step-by-Step Guide*
PSI Research
300 N. Valley Dr.
Grants Pass, OR 97526
Ph:(503)479-9464
Free: 800-228-2275
Fax: (503)476-1479
Co. E-mail: psi2@magick.net
Ed: Michael D. Jenkins. **Released:** Revised edition, 1992. **Price:** $29.95 (looseleaf binder); $24.95 (paper). **Description:** Part of the Successful Business Library series.

60253 ■ *Starting a Small Business in Iowa*
Iowa State University
Small Business Development Center
137 Lynn Ave.
Ames, IA 50014-7198
Free: 800-373-7232
Fax: (515)292-0020
Ed: Bryan Ziegler. **Price:** $10.00. **Description:** Provides details on Iowa resources and requirements, from marketing surveys to insurance needs and licensing permits.

SMALL BUSINESS DEVELOPMENT CENTER LEAD OFFICE

60254 ■ Fort Hayes State University–Kansas Small Business Development Center State Office
214 SW 6th St., Ste. 301
Topeka, KS 66603-3719
Ph:(785)296-6514
Fax: (785)291-3261
Contact: Brenda O'Gorman, State Director
E-mail: ksbdc.bogorman@fhsu.edu

60255 ■ KSBDC Lead Center–Fort Hays State University
214 SW 6th St., Ste. 301
Topeka, KS 66603
Ph:(785)296-6514
Free: 877-625-7232
Fax: (785)291-3261
Co. E-mail: ksbdc@fhsu.edu
URL: http://www.ksbdc.biz/
Contact: Wally Kearns, State Dir.
E-mail: ksbdc.wkearns@fhsu.edu

60256 ■ Wichita State University–Small Business Development Center
1845 Fairmount, Campus Box 148
Wichita, KS 67260-0148
Ph:(316)978-3193
Fax: (316)978-3647
Contact: Marcia Stevens, Regional Dir.
E-mail: mstevens@twsu.edu

SMALL BUSINESS DEVELOPMENT CENTERS

60257 ■ Cloud County Community College–Small Business Development Center
2221 Campus Dr.
PO Box 1002
Concordia, KS 66901
Ph:(785)243-1435
Free: 800-729-5101
Fax: (785)243-9321
URL: http://www.webs.wichita.edu/ksbdc
Contact: Linda Sutton, Consultant
E-mail: lsutton@cloud.edu

60258 ■ Emporia State University–Small Business Development Center
1320 C of E Dr.
Emporia, KS 66801-2584
Ph:(620)341-5308
Fax: (620)341-5418
URL: http://www.emporia.edu/sbdc
Contact: Lisa Brumbaugh, Regional Dir.
E-mail: brumbaul@emporia.edu

60259 ■ Fort Hays State University–Small Business Development Center
109 W. 10th St.
Hays, KS 67601-3602
Ph:(785)628-6786
Fax: (785)628-0533
URL: http://www.fhsu.edu/sbdc
Contact: Sheryl Davis, Actg. Dir.

60260 ■ Garden City Community College–Small Business Development Center
801 Campus Dr.
Garden City, KS 67846-6333
Ph:(620)276-9632
Fax: (620)275-3249
URL: http://www.westernkansas.net/sbdc
Contact: Paat Veesart, Regional Dir.
E-mail: pveesart@gcnet.com

60261 ■ Johnson County Community College–Small Business Development Center
Carlsen Ctr., Rm. 309
Overland Park, KS 66210-1299
Ph:(913)469-3878
Fax: (913)469-2547
Co. E-mail: sbdc@icc.net
URL: http://www.centerforbusiness.org
Contact: Cheri Streeter, Regional Dir.
E-mail: cstreet@iccc.net

60262 ■ Manhattan Area Chamber of Commerce (MACC)–Small Business Development Center
501 Poyntz Ave.
Manhattan, KS 66502-6605
Ph:(785)587-9917
Fax: (785)776-0679
Contact: Chad Jackson
E-mail: chad.jackson@washburn.edu

60263 ■ Pittsburg State University–Small Business Development Center
Shirk Hall
1501 S. Joplin
Pittsburg, KS 66762-7560
Ph:(620)235-4920
Fax: (316)235-4919
Co. E-mail: ksbdc@pittstate.edu
URL: http://www.faculty.pittstate.edu/bti/
Contact: Kathryn Richard, Regional Dir.
E-mail: krichard@pittstate.edu

60264 ■ Seward County Community College–Small Business Development Center
1801 N. Kansas
PO Box 1137
Liberal, KS 67905-1137
Ph:(316)624-1951
Free: 800-626-3009
Fax: (316)629-2689
URL: http://www.sccc.edu
Contact: 800626-3009 Dale Reed, Dir.

60265 ■ University of Kansas–Small Business Development Center
734 Vermont St., Ste. 104
Lawrence, KS 66044-2370
Ph:(785)843-8844
Fax: (785)843-8878
Co. E-mail: office@kusbdc.net
URL: http://www.kusbdc.net
Contact: Will Katz, Regional Dir.

60266 ■ Washburn University of Topeka–Small Business Development Center
120 SE 6th St., Ste. 110
Topeka, KS 66603
Ph:(785)234-3235
Fax: (785)234-8656
Co. E-mail: sbdc@washburn.edu
URL: http://www.washburn.edu
Contact: Rick LeJuerrne, Dir.
E-mail: rick.lejuerrne@washburn.edu

60267 ■ Wichita State University–Small Business Development Center
1845 Fairmont, Campus Box 248
Wichita, KS 67260-0148
Ph:(316)978-3193
Fax: (316)978-3647
URL: http://www.webs.wichita.edu/ksbdc
Contact: Marcia Stevens, Regional Dir.
E-mail: marcia.stevens@twichita.edu

SMALL BUSINESS ASSISTANCE PROGRAMS

60268 ■ Business and Technology Institute–Department of Economic Development
Pittsburg State University
1501 South Joplin St.
Pittsburg, KS 66762
Ph:(620)235-4920
Fax: (620)235-4919
Co. E-mail: bti@pittstate.edu
URL: http://www.pittstate.edu/bti
Description: Provides one-stop managerial, financial, and technical assistance to new and expanding businesses in Southeast Kansas, Missouri, Oklahoma, and Arkansas.

60269 ■ Kansas Department of Commerce–Agriculture Marketing
1000 SW Jackson St., Ste. 100
Topeka, KS 66612
Ph:(785)296-3481
Fax: (785)296-5055
URL: http://www.kansascommerce.com
Description: Provides marketing assistance through food shows, seminars, and media promotions.

60270 ■ Kansas Department of Commerce–Business Development Division
1000 SW Jackson St., Ste. 100
Topeka, KS 66612

Ph:(785)296-5298
Fax: (785)296-3490
URL: http://www.kansascommerce.com
Description: Promotes the growth, diversification, and retention of business and industry in Kansas. Advocates on behalf of small businesses. Act as a clearinghouse for information on permits and licenses. Maintains six regional offices to provide assistance to small businesses.

60271 ■ Kansas Department of Commerce–Division of Trade Development
1000 SW Jackson St., Ste. 100
Topeka, KS 66612
Ph:(785)296-3481
Fax: (785)296-5055
URL: http://www.kansascommerce.com
Description: Provides information and assistance to businesses interested in international trade. Services offered include identifying agents and distributors worldwide, assisting in market development, providing technical information, offering world trade statistical data, and trade lead information services.

60272 ■ Kansas Department of Commerce–Kansas Technology Enterprise Corp.
214 SW 6th St., 1st Fl.
Topeka, KS 66603
Ph:(785)296-5272
Fax: (785)296-1160
Co. E-mail: ktec@ktec.com
URL: http://www.ktec.com
Contact: Tracy Taylor, Pres & CEO
Description: Provides technical information and referral services. Provides funds for technology-based research.

60273 ■ Wichita State University–Center for Technology Application (MAMTC)
8441 E 32nd St., N, Ste. 100
Niar Bldg.
Wichita, KS 67226
Ph:(316)978-3525
Fax: (316)978-3677
URL: http://www.mamtc.com
Description: Provides training, seminars, and technical information to engineers, managers, and other employees.

SCORE OFFICES

60274 ■ SCORE Ark Valley
205 E Ninth St.
Winfield, KS 67156
Ph:(316)221-1617
Co. E-mail: arkvalleyscore317@yahoo.com
URL: http://www.geocities.com/arkvalleyscore317/home.html
Contact: Wally Bell, Chm.
Description: Provides free business counseling and management training programs for small business owners/managers, and for those who plan to start a new business.

60275 ■ SCORE Emporia
c/o Evora Wheeler, Chair
1320 C of E Dr.
Emporia, KS 66801
Ph:(316)341-5308
Fax: (316)341-5418
Co. E-mail: emporiascore@hotmail.com
URL: http://www.score.org

60276 ■ SCORE Hutchinson
One E 9th
Hutchinson, KS 67501
Ph:(620)665-8468
Fax: (620)665-7619
Co. E-mail: score@hutchquest.com
Description: Provides professional guidance and information to America's small businesses.

60277 ■ SCORE McPherson
c/o Chamber of Commerce
306 N Main
McPherson, KS 67460

Ph:(316)241-3303
Co. E-mail: glenwood@cox.net
URL: http://www.score.org

60278 ■ SCORE North Central Kansas
c/o Concordia Chamber of Commerce
606 Washington St.
Concordia, KS 66901
Ph:(785)527-5784
Fax: (785)243-1833
Co. E-mail: dmswen1955@yahoo.com
Description: Provides professional guidance and information to America's small businesses.

60279 ■ SCORE Southwest Kansas
c/o Dodge City Senior Center
2408 Central
Dodge City, KS 67801
Ph:(620)225-5253
Co. E-mail: dcscore@rurallink.com
Contact: Leo Dickinson, Chm.
Description: Provides professional guidance and information to America's small businesses.

60280 ■ SCORE Topeka
c/o Washburn University Small Business Development Center
120 SE 6th, Ste. 110
Topeka, KS 66603
Ph:(785)234-3049
Co. E-mail: score@topekachamber.org
URL: http://www.scoretopeka.org
Contact: Shirley Gorman, Chair
Description: Helps people in planning small business operations.

BETTER BUSINESS BUREAUS

60281 ■ Better Business Bureau of Northeast Kansas
501 SE Jefferson, Ste. 24
Topeka, KS 66607-1190
Ph:(785)232-0454
Fax: (785)232-9677
Co. E-mail: topekabbb@kansasone.com
URL: http://www.topeka.bbb.org
Contact: Joyce Woodard, Pres.

60282 ■ Better Business Bureau, Wichita
328 Laura
Wichita, KS 67211-1707
Ph:(316)263-3146
Free: 800-856-2417
Fax: (316)263-3063
Co. E-mail: info@wichita.bbb.org
URL: http://www.wichita.bbb.org
Contact: Linda Schroer, Pres.

CHAMBERS OF COMMERCE

60283 ■ Abilene Area Chamber of Commerce
500 N Buckeye
Abilene, KS 67410
Ph:(785)263-1770
Free: (866)224-5357
Co. E-mail: visitus@abileneks.com
URL: http://www.abileneks.com
Contact: Lynda Lowry, Exec.VP

60284 ■ Alma Chamber of Commerce
PO Box 234
Alma, KS 66401
Ph:(785)765-3327
Fax: (785)765-3384
Contact: Trish Ringel, Sec.

60285 ■ Americus Chamber of Commerce
PO Box 459
Americus, KS 66835
Ph:(620)443-5550
Contact: Mike Pearson, Pres.

60286 ■ Andover Area Chamber of Commerce and Convention and Visitors' Bureau
310 W Central, Ste. D
PO Box 339
Andover, KS 67002-0339
Ph:(316)733-0648
Fax: (316)733-8808
Co. E-mail: achamber@swbell.net
URL: http://www.andoverks.com
Contact: Judy Ulmer, Exec.Dir.

60287 ■ Anthony Chamber of Commerce
PO Box 354
Anthony, KS 67003
Ph:(620)842-5456
Fax: (620)842-5753
Co. E-mail: acc@midway.net
URL: http://www.anthonychamber.com
Contact: Gwen Warner, Exec.Dir.

60288 ■ Arkansas City Area Chamber of Commerce
106 S Summit
PO Box 795
Arkansas City, KS 67005
Ph:(620)442-0230
Fax: (620)441-0048
Co. E-mail: ywood@arkansascityks.gov
URL: http://www.arkcity.org
Contact: Ms. Yazmin Wood, CEO/Pres.

60289 ■ Ashland Chamber of Commerce
PO Box 37
Ashland, KS 67831-0037
Ph:(620)635-2680
Co. E-mail: pioneer@ucom.net
URL: http://users.ucom.net/~pioneer
Contact: Mr. Tony Maphet, Sec./Coor.

60290 ■ Atchison Area Chamber of Commerce
PO Box 126
Atchison, KS 66002
Ph:(913)367-2427
Free: 800-234-1854
Fax: (913)367-2485
Co. E-mail: ccpresident@atchisonkansas.net
URL: http://www.atchisonkansas.net
Contact: Glenda Purkis, Pres./CEO

60291 ■ Atwood Chamber of Commerce
416 Main
PO Box 152
Atwood, KS 67730-2042
Ph:(785)626-9630
Free: 800-422-9630
Fax: (785)626-9630
URL: http://www.atwoodkansas.com
Contact: Cathy Domsch, Dir.

60292 ■ Baldwin City Chamber of Commerce
720 High St.
PO Box 501
Baldwin City, KS 66006-0501
Ph:(785)594-3200
Co. E-mail: chamber@baldwin-city.com
URL: http://www.baldwincitychamber.com

60293 ■ Baxter Springs Chamber of Commerce
1004 Military Ave.
Baxter Springs, KS 66713-1547
Ph:(620)856-3131
Fax: (620)856-3185
Co. E-mail: chamber@baxtersprings.us
URL: http://www.baxtersprings.org
Contact: Carolyn Pendleton, Exec.Dir.

60294 ■ Belle Plaine Area Chamber of Commerce
PO Box 721
Belle Plaine, KS 67013-0721
Ph:(620)488-2645
Fax: (620)488-3517
Co. E-mail: joanderson_98@yahoo.com
URL: http://www.belleplainechamber.com

Contact: Jay White, Pres.

60295 ■ Belleville Chamber of Commerce
1819 L St.
PO Box 280
Belleville, KS 66935-0280
Ph:(785)527-5524
Free: (866)527-2355
Fax: (785)527-2334
Co. E-mail: bellevcham@nckcn.com
URL: http://www.bellevilleks.org
Contact: Mary Kolsky, Sec.-Treas.

60296 ■ Beloit Area Chamber of Commerce
123 N Mill
PO Box 582
Beloit, KS 67420-0582
Ph:(785)738-2717
Co. E-mail: beloitchamber@nckcn.com
URL: http://skyways.lib.ks.us/towns/Beloit
Contact: Erma J. Cikanek, Exec. VP

60297 ■ Bird City Community Club
PO Box 41
Bird City, KS 67731
Ph:(785)734-2609
URL: http://www.opencountry.com
Contact: Larry Henry, Pres.

60298 ■ Bonner Springs/Edwardsville Area Chamber of Commerce
PO Box 403
Bonner Springs, KS 66012-0403
Ph:(913)422-5044
Fax: (913)441-1366
Co. E-mail: bilesc@hotmail.com
URL: http://www.bonnersprings.org/chamber.html
Contact: Charlene A. Biles, Exec.Sec.

60299 ■ Caldwell Area Chamber of Commerce
PO Box 42
Caldwell, KS 67022
Ph:(620)845-6666
Co. E-mail: caldwell@kanokla.net
URL: http://caldwellkansas.com
Contact: LuAnn Jamison, Sec.

60300 ■ Caney Chamber of Commerce
PO Box 211
Caney, KS 67333
Ph:(620)879-5131
Co. E-mail: dcarey@caney.com
URL: http://www.caney.com
Contact: Beverly Spradling, Sec.

60301 ■ Cedar Vale Chamber of Commerce
PO Box 112
Cedar Vale, KS 67024
Ph:(620)758-2221
Contact: Allen Zadorozny, Pres.

60302 ■ Chanute Area Chamber of Commerce and Office of Tourism
21 N Lincoln Ave.
PO Box 747
Chanute, KS 66720
Ph:(620)431-3350
Free: 877-431-3350
Fax: (620)431-7770
Co. E-mail: information@chanutechamber.com
URL: http://www.chanutechamber.com
Contact: Jodi Lucke, Exec.Dir.

60303 ■ Chase County Chamber of Commerce
PO Box 362
Cottonwood Falls, KS 66845
Ph:(620)273-8469
Free: 800-431-6344
Fax: (620)273-6578
Co. E-mail: chamber@kansas.net
Contact: Diana Sigel, Adm.Dir.

60304 ■ Cheney Chamber of Commerce
PO Box 716
Cheney, KS 67025

Ph:(316)542-0054
Co. E-mail: tlasher@cheneyks.org
URL: http://www.cheneyks.org/chamber.html
Contact: Marie Davis

60305 ■ Cherryvale Chamber of Commerce
PO Box 112
Cherryvale, KS 67335
Ph:(620)336-2108
Fax: (620)336-2225
Contact: Linda Ellison, Mgr.

60306 ■ Chetopa Chamber of Commerce
917 Locust St.
Chetopa, KS 67336
Ph:(620)236-7511
URL: http://www.chetopacity.org
Contact: Mary Jane Houston, Pres.

60307 ■ Cimarron Chamber of Commerce
102 East Ave. A
Cimarron, KS 67835
Ph:(620)855-2507
URL: http://skyways.lib.ks.us/towns/Cimarron
Contact: Joanne Koehn, Sec.-Treas.

60308 ■ Clay Center Area Chamber of Commerce
Depot Plz.
308 Court St.
Clay Center, KS 67432-2420
Ph:(785)632-5674
Fax: (785)632-5674
Co. E-mail: ccchamber@cebridge.net
URL: http://www.claycenterkschamber.org
Contact: Sharon Brown, Exec. Dir.

60309 ■ Clifton Chamber of Commerce
PO Box 189
Clifton, KS 66937-0189
Ph:(785)455-3345
Fax: (785)455-2269
Contact: Janelle Wohler

60310 ■ Coffey County Chamber of Commerce
110 N 4th St.
Burlington, KS 66839-1602
Ph:(620)364-2002
Free: 877-364-2002
Fax: (620)364-3048
Co. E-mail: countychamber@earthlink.net
URL: http://www.coffeycountychamber.com
Contact: Mary Walker, Exec.Dir.

60311 ■ Coffeyville Chamber of Commerce
PO Box 457
Coffeyville, KS 67337-0457
Ph:(620)251-2550
Fax: (620)251-5448
Co. E-mail: chamber@coffeyville.com
URL: http://www.coffeyville.com
Contact: Karen Strimple, Exec. Dir.

60312 ■ Colby - Thomas County Chamber of Commerce
350 S Range, Ste. 10
Colby, KS 67701
Ph:(785)460-7643
Free: 800-611-8835
Fax: (785)462-4509
Co. E-mail: cvb@thomascounty.com
URL: http://www.colbychamber.com
Contact: Jada Tubbs, Exec.Dir.

60313 ■ Coldwater Chamber of Commerce
PO Box 333
Coldwater, KS 67029-0333
Ph:(620)582-2546
Co. E-mail: kkpitzer@carrollsweb.com
URL: http://www.coldwaterkansas.com/bd.html
Contact: Kenneth Pitzer, Pres.

60314 ■ Columbus Chamber of Commerce
320 E Maple
Columbus, KS 66725
Ph:(620)429-1492

Fax: (620)429-1674
Co. E-mail: columbuschamber@columbus-ks.com
URL: http://www.columbus-ks.com
Contact: Jean Pritchett, Mgr.

60315 ■ Concordia Area Chamber of Commerce
606 Washington St.
Concordia, KS 66901-2816
Ph:(785)243-4290
Free: 800-343-4290
Fax: (785)243-2014
Co. E-mail: chamber@dustdevil.com
Contact: Roberta Lowrey, Pres./CEO

60316 ■ Decatur County Area Chamber of Commerce
132 S Penn
Oberlin, KS 67749
Ph:(785)475-3441
Co. E-mail: dcacc@kans.com
URL: http://www.oberlinkansas.org
Contact: Glenva Nichols, Office Mgr.

60317 ■ Derby Chamber of Commerce
330 E Madison St., Ste. 150
Derby, KS 67037
Ph:(316)788-3421
Fax: (316)788-6861
Co. E-mail: chamber@derbyks.com
URL: http://www.derbyks.com
Contact: Rhonda Cott, Pres.

60318 ■ Dodge City Area Chamber of Commerce
311 W Spruce
PO Box 939
Dodge City, KS 67801-0939
Ph:(620)227-3119
Fax: (620)227-2957
Co. E-mail: info@dodgechamber.com
URL: http://www.dodgechamber.com
Contact: Cindy Malek, Exec.VP

60319 ■ Doniphan County Chamber of Commerce and Economic Development Commission
209 Roseport Rd.
PO Box 325
Elwood, KS 66024-0325
Ph:(913)365-2604
Fax: (913)365-0203
Co. E-mail: gweiland@highlandcc.edu
URL: http://www.dpcountyks.com
Contact: Galen Weiland, Exec.Dir.

60320 ■ Douglass Chamber of Commerce
PO Box 401
Douglass, KS 67039
Ph:(316)746-3135
Contact: Jim Davis, Pres.

60321 ■ Edwards County Chamber of Commerce
PO Box 161
Kinsley, KS 67547
Ph:(620)659-2711
Free: 877-464-3929
Fax: (620)659-2711
Co. E-mail: ecedcweb@sbcglobal.net
URL: http://www.edwardscounty.org
Contact: Fred Burgess, Dir.

60322 ■ El Dorado Chamber of Commerce
201 E Central
PO Box 509
El Dorado, KS 67042
Ph:(316)321-3150
Fax: (316)321-5419
Co. E-mail: eldoradochamber@powwwer.net
URL: http://www.eldoradochamber.com
Contact: Linda Jolly, Exec.Dir.

60323 ■ Elkhart Area Chamber of Commerce
PO Box 696
Elkhart, KS 67950
Ph:(620)697-4600

Contact: Karen Brady, Pres.

60324 ■ Ellinwood Area Chamber of Commerce
PO Box 482
Ellinwood, KS 67526-0482
Ph:(620)564-3300
Co. E-mail: ellinwoodchamberofcommerce@yahoo.
com
URL: http://www.ellinwoodkschamberofcommerce.
org
Contact: Monte Strecker, Pres.

60325 ■ Ellis Chamber of Commerce
PO Box 229
Ellis, KS 67637
Ph:(785)726-3636
Fax: (785)726-3636
Co. E-mail: chrysler@eaglecom.net
Contact: Robert Redger, Pres.

60326 ■ Ellsworth-Kanopolis Area Chamber of Commerce
114-1/2 N Douglas
PO Box 315
Ellsworth, KS 67439
Ph:(785)472-4071
Fax: (785)472-5668
Co. E-mail: ecofc@classicnet.net
URL: http://www.ellsworthks.net/Chamber.htm
Contact: Mr. Nick V. Slechta, Dir.

60327 ■ Emporia Chamber of Commerce and Convention and Visitors Bureau
719 Commercial St.
PO Box 703
Emporia, KS 66801-0703
Ph:(620)342-1600
Free: 800-279-3730
Fax: (620)342-3223
Co. E-mail: chamber@emporiakschamber.org
URL: http://www.emporiakschamber.org
Contact: Jeanine McKenna, Pres./CEO

60328 ■ Eureka Area Chamber of Commerce
Memorial Bldg.
PO Box 563
Eureka, KS 67045
Ph:(620)583-5452
Fax: (620)583-5452
Co. E-mail: eurekacofc@eurekaherald.com
URL: http://www.eurekakansas.com
Contact: Mary Ann Thornton, Coor.

60329 ■ Florence Chamber of Commerce
423 Main
Florence, KS 66851
Ph:(620)878-4478
Contact: Vicki Turner, Sec.

60330 ■ Fort Scott Area Chamber of Commerce
231 E Wall St.
PO Box 205
Fort Scott, KS 66701-0205
Ph:(620)223-3566
Free: 800-245-3678
Fax: (620)223-3574
Co. E-mail: fschamber@fortscott.com
URL: http://www.fortscott.com
Contact: Gary Emry, Pres.

60331 ■ Fredonia Chamber of Commerce
PO Box 449
Fredonia, KS 66736-0449
Ph:(620)378-3221
Fax: (620)378-4833
Co. E-mail: fredoniakschamber@twinmounds.com
URL: http://www.fredoniachamber.com
Contact: Byron L. Schroder, Exec.Dir.

60332 ■ Galena Chamber of Commerce
PO Box 465
Galena, KS 66739
Ph:(620)783-1395
Contact: Kathleen Anderson, Pres.

60333 ■ Garden City Area Chamber of Commerce
1511 E Fulton Terr.
Garden City, KS 67846-6165
Ph:(620)276-3264
Fax: (620)276-3290
Co. E-mail: chamber@gcnet.com
URL: http://www.gardencity.net/chamber
Contact: Carol Meyer, Pres.

60334 ■ Gardner Area Chamber of Commerce
900 E Main
PO Box 402
Gardner, KS 66030
Ph:(913)856-6464
Fax: (913)856-5274
Co. E-mail: gardnerchamb@kcnet.com
URL: http://www.gardnerchamber.com
Contact: Peter Solie, Pres.

60335 ■ Garnett Area Chamber of Commerce
420 S Oak
Garnett, KS 66032
Ph:(785)448-6767
Fax: (785)448-6767
Co. E-mail: garnettchamber@earthlink.net
URL: http://www.garnettchamber.org
Contact: Ms. Jennifer Hughes, Pres.

60336 ■ Girard Area Chamber of Commerce
PO Box 41
Girard, KS 66743-0041
Ph:(620)724-4715
Fax: (620)724-8060
Co. E-mail: girardchamber@ckt.net
Contact: Maxine B. Harris, Exec.Dir.

60337 ■ Glasco Chamber Pride
PO Box 572
Glasco, KS 67445-0572
Ph:(785)568-2515
URL: http://skyways.lib.ks.us/kansas/towns/Glasco
Contact: Claude Harwood MD

60338 ■ Goodland Area Chamber of Commerce
1002 Main St., Ste. 101
PO Box 628
Goodland, KS 67735
Ph:(785)899-7130
Fax: (785)890-8411
Co. E-mail: gdlchmbr@eaglecom.net
URL: http://www.goodlandnet.com
Contact: Courtney Warden, Dir.

60339 ■ Grant County Chamber of Commerce
113B S Main
Ulysses, KS 67880
Ph:(620)356-4700
Fax: (620)424-2437
Co. E-mail: uchamber@pld.com
URL: http://www.ulysseschamber.com
Contact: Tim Nemechek, Chm.

60340 ■ Great Bend Chamber of Commerce
PO Box 400
Great Bend, KS 67530
Ph:(620)792-2401
Co. E-mail: gbcc@greatbend.org
URL: http://www.greatbend.org
Contact: Jan Peters, Pres./CEO

60341 ■ Greater Topeka Chamber of Commerce
120 SE 6th St., Ste. 110
Topeka, KS 66603-3515
Ph:(785)234-2644
Fax: (785)234-8656
Co. E-mail: dkinsinger@topekachamber.org
URL: http://www.topekachamber.org
Contact: Douglas S. Kinsinger, Pres./CEO

60342 ■ Greensburg Chamber of Commerce
315 S Sycamore
Greensburg, KS 67054

Ph:(620)723-2261
Free: 800-207-7369
Fax: (620)723-3299
Co. E-mail: tourism@bigwell.org
URL: http://www.bigwell.org
Contact: Lana Swisher, Pres.

60343 ■ Halstead Chamber of Commerce
PO Box 328
Halstead, KS 67056
Ph:(316)835-2662
Co. E-mail: coc@halsteadkansas.com
URL: http://chamberofcommerce.halsteadkansas.
com
Contact: Stacey Weesner, Sec.-Treas.

60344 ■ Harper Chamber of Commerce
201 W Main St.
Harper, KS 67058
Ph:(620)896-2511
Co. E-mail: cityofharper@cyberlodge.com
URL: http://skyways.lib.ks.us/towns/Harper/index.
html
Contact: Andy Sona, Sec.-Treas.

60345 ■ Hays Area Chamber of Commerce
1301 Pine St.
Hays, KS 67601
Ph:(785)628-8201
Fax: (785)628-1471
Co. E-mail: hayscc@discoverhays.com
URL: http://www.discoverhays.com
Contact: Gina Riedel, Exec.Dir.

60346 ■ Haysville Chamber of Commerce
PO Box 372
Haysville, KS 67060
Ph:(316)529-2461
Fax: (316)524-0091
Co. E-mail: hvcoc@sbcglobal.net
URL: http://www.haysville-ks.com/chamber
Contact: Rebecca Ladd, Admin.Asst.

60347 ■ Hesston Community Chamber of Commerce
115 E Smith St.
Hesston, KS 67062
Ph:(620)327-4102
Free: 800-442-1563
Fax: (620)327-4595
Co. E-mail: chamber@hesstonks.org
URL: http://www.hesstonks.org
Contact: Shana Smith, Exec.Dir.

60348 ■ Hiawatha Chamber of Commerce and Visitors Bureau
602 Oregon St.
Hiawatha, KS 66434
Ph:(785)742-7136
Fax: (785)742-3510
Co. E-mail: hiawathachamber@rainbowtel.net
Contact: Nancy Petty, Admin.

60349 ■ Hillsboro Chamber of Commerce
109 S Main
Hillsboro, KS 67063-1525
Ph:(620)947-3458
Fax: (620)947-2585
Co. E-mail: hillsborochamber@dtnspeed.net
URL: http://www.hillsboro-kansas.com
Contact: Megan Kilgore, Exec.Dir.

60350 ■ Hoisington Chamber of Commerce
123 N Main
Hoisington, KS 67544-2357
Ph:(620)653-4311
Fax: (620)653-4311
Co. E-mail: hoisingtoncofc@earthlink.net
Contact: Ms. Stacey Bressler, Exec. VP

60351 ■ Holton Chamber of Commerce
416 Pennsylvania Ave.
Holton, KS 66436
Ph:(785)364-3963
Co. E-mail: dwilson@holtonks.net
URL: http://www.holtonks.net/city/chamber/chamber.
htm

Contact: Dianna Wilson, Administrator

60352 ■ Horton Chamber of Commerce
126 W 8th St.
Horton, KS 66439
Ph:(785)486-3321
Co. E-mail: hortonchamber@rainbowtel.net
URL: http://www.hortonkansas.net/chamber.html
Contact: Sue Korthanke, Pres.

60353 ■ Hoxie Area Chamber of Commerce and EDC
PO Box 839
Hoxie, KS 67740
Ph:(785)675-3016
Co. E-mail: bmosier@ruraltel.net
Contact: Bert Mosier, Dir.

60354 ■ Hugoton Area Chamber of Commerce
630 S Main
Hugoton, KS 67951
Ph:(620)544-4305
Fax: (620)544-4610
Co. E-mail: ecodevo@pld.com
Contact: Vicki Hewitt, Dir.

60355 ■ Humboldt Chamber of Commerce
PO Box 133
Humboldt, KS 66748-0133
Ph:(620)473-2325
Co. E-mail: humboldtks@cox.net
URL: http://www.humboldtks.com
Contact: Don Copley, Pres.

60356 ■ Hutchinson/Reno County Chamber of Commerce
117 N Walnut
PO Box 519
Hutchinson, KS 67504-0519
Ph:(620)662-3391
Co. E-mail: info@hutchchamber.com
URL: http://www.hutchchamber.com
Contact: Jon R. Daveline, Pres./CEO

60357 ■ Independence Chamber of Commerce
322 N Penn
PO Box 386
Independence, KS 67301
Ph:(620)331-1890
Free: 800-882-3606
Fax: (620)331-1899
Co. E-mail: gwen@indkschamber.org
URL: http://www.indkschamber.org
Contact: Gwen Wilburn, Pres. & CEO

60358 ■ Iola Area Chamber of Commerce
208 W Madison
Iola, KS 66749
Ph:(620)365-5252
Fax: (620)365-8078
Co. E-mail: chamber@iolaks.com
URL: http://www.cityofiola.com
Contact: Barbara Chalker Collins, Exec.Dir.

60359 ■ Jewell Chamber of Commerce
PO Box 235
Jewell, KS 66949
Ph:(785)428-3600
Fax: (785)428-3600
Contact: Heather Mather, Sec.

60360 ■ Junction City Area Chamber of Commerce
814 N Washington Ave.
PO Box 26
Junction City, KS 66441
Ph:(785)762-2632
Fax: (785)762-3353
Co. E-mail: jcchamberoffice@jcks.com
URL: http://www.junctioncitychamber.org
Contact: Ms. Cheryl Lyn Higgins, Pres./CEO

60361 ■ Kansas Chamber of Commerce and Industry
835 SW Topeka Blvd.
Topeka, KS 66612-1671

Ph:(785)357-6321
Fax: (785)357-4732
Co. E-mail: info@kansaschamber.org
URL: http://www.kansaschamber.org
Contact: David Kerr, Chm.

60362 ■ Kansas City, Kansas Area Chamber of Commerce
727 Minnesota Ave.
PO Box 171337
Kansas City, KS 66117
Ph:(913)371-3070
Fax: (913)371-3732
Co. E-mail: chamber@kckchamber.com
URL: http://kckchamber.com
Contact: Cindy Cash, Pres./CEO

60363 ■ Kingman Area Chamber of Commerce
322 N Main St.
Kingman, KS 67068
Ph:(620)532-1853
Co. E-mail: kingmanchamber@copper.net
URL: http://www.skyways.org/towns/Kingman/chamber.html
Contact: Ron Mason, Pres.

60364 ■ La Crosse Chamber of Commerce
PO Box 716
La Crosse, KS 67548-0716
Ph:(785)222-2639
Co. E-mail: chamber67548@yahoo.com
Contact: Diane Morse, Sec.-Treas.

60365 ■ Lane County Area Chamber of Commerce
147 E Long
PO Box 942
Dighton, KS 67839-0942
Ph:(620)397-2211
Co. E-mail: lcacc@st-tel.net
Contact: Chelle Anderson, Sec.

60366 ■ Larned Area Chamber of Commerce
502 Broadway
Larned, KS 67550
Ph:(620)285-6916
Free: 800-747-6919
Co. E-mail: chamber@larned.org
URL: http://larned.org
Contact: Linda Henderson, Exec.Dir.

60367 ■ Lawrence Chamber of Commerce
734 Vermont St., Ste. 101
Lawrence, KS 66044-0586
Ph:(785)865-4411
Co. E-mail: lawrencechamber@lawrencechamber.com
URL: http://www.lawrencechamber.com
Contact: Lavern D. Squier, Pres./CEO

60368 ■ Leavenworth-Lansing Area Chamber of Commerce
518 Shawnee
PO Box 44
Leavenworth, KS 66048
Ph:(913)682-4112
Fax: (913)682-8170
Co. E-mail: lindsey.chamber@sbcglobal.net
URL: http://www.leavenworth-lansingareachamberofcommerce.com
Contact: Charlie H. Gregor Jr., Exec.VP

60369 ■ Leawood Chamber of Commerce
11300 Tomahawk Creek Pkwy., No. 240
Leawood, KS 66211
Ph:(913)498-1514
Fax: (913)491-0134
Co. E-mail: chamber@leawoodchamber.org
URL: http://www.leawoodchamber.org
Contact: Kevin Jeffries, Pres./CEO

60370 ■ Lebanon Hub Club
PO Box 125
Lebanon, KS 66952
Ph:(785)389-3261
Contact: Lori LaDow, Pres.

60371 ■ Lenexa Chamber of Commerce
11180 Lackman Rd.
Lenexa, KS 66219
Ph:(913)888-1414
Fax: (913)888-3770
Co. E-mail: bschreck@lenexa.org
URL: http://www.lenexa.org
Contact: Blake Schreck, Pres.

60372 ■ Lenora Chamber of Commerce
125 E Washington
Lenora, KS 67645
Ph:(785)567-4860
Co. E-mail: lenoraco@ruraltel.net
URL: http://skyways.lib.ks.us/towns/Lenora/index.html
Contact: Gayle James

60373 ■ Liberal Area Chamber of Commerce
4 Rock Island Rd.
PO Box 676
Liberal, KS 67905
Ph:(620)624-3855
Fax: (620)624-8851
Co. E-mail: liberalcoc@adelphia.net
URL: http://www.liberalkschamber.com
Contact: Jack Taylor, Exec.VP

60374 ■ Lincoln Area Chamber of Commerce
137 W Lincoln Ave.
Lincoln, KS 67455
Ph:(785)524-4934
Fax: (785)524-4934
Co. E-mail: lcoc137@sbcglobal.net
URL: http://www.lincolnkansaschamber.com
Contact: Leann Hillmer, Exec. Dir.

60375 ■ Lindsborg Chamber of Commerce
104 E Lincoln
Lindsborg, KS 67456-2416
Ph:(785)227-3706
Free: 888-227-2227
Fax: (785)227-4128
Co. E-mail: chamber@lindsborg.org
URL: http://www.lindsborg.org
Contact: Kathy Malm, Exec.Dir.

60376 ■ Louisburg Chamber of Commerce
PO Box 245
Louisburg, KS 66053
Ph:(913)837-2826
Co. E-mail: chamber@louisburgkansas.com
URL: http://www.louisburgkansas.com
Contact: Patsey Bortner, Administrator

60377 ■ Lucas Area Chamber of Commerce
201 S Main
PO Box 186
Lucas, KS 67648
Ph:(785)525-6288
Co. E-mail: lucascoc@wtciweb.com
URL: http://lucaskansas.com
Contact: Connie Dougherty, Dir.

60378 ■ Lyndon Chamber of Commerce
PO Box 523
Lyndon, KS 66451
Ph:(785)828-4931
Contact: Cathy Allen, Pres.

60379 ■ Madison Area Chamber of Commerce
PO Box 58
Madison, KS 66860-0058
Ph:(620)437-3463
Co. E-mail: madisonchamber@madtel.net
URL: http://www.madisonkschamber.org
Contact: Karen McIlvain

60380 ■ Manhattan Area Chamber of Commerce
501 Poyntz Ave.
Manhattan, KS 66502-6005
Ph:(785)776-8829
Fax: (785)776-0679
Co. E-mail: chamber@manhattan.org
URL: http://www.manhattan.org

Contact: Lyle Butler III, Pres./CEO

60381 ■ Mankato Chamber of Commerce
City Office, Box 2
Mankato, KS 66956
Ph:(785)378-3652
Co. E-mail: mankato@nckcn.com
Contact: Lori Brown, Sec.

60382 ■ Marysville Chamber of Commerce
101 N 10th
PO Box 16
Marysville, KS 66508
Ph:(785)562-3101
Free: 800-752-3965
Fax: (785)562-3101
Co. E-mail: marysvillechamber@sbcglobal.net
URL: http://skyways.lib.ks.us/towns/Marysville
Contact: Judy Kracht, Sec.

60383 ■ McPherson Chamber of Commerce
306 N Main
PO Box 616
McPherson, KS 67460-0616
Ph:(620)241-3303
Fax: (620)241-8708
Co. E-mail: chamber@mcphersonks.org
URL: http://www.mcphersonks.org
Contact: Ms. Jennifer Burch, Exec.Dir.

60384 ■ Meade Chamber of Commerce
PO Box 576
Meade, KS 67864-0576
Ph:(620)873-2359
Co. E-mail: lpodrebarac@sbcglobal.net
URL: http://www.meadechamber.com
Contact: Louis Podrebarac, Sec.

60385 ■ Medicine Lodge Area Chamber of Commerce
108 W 1st St.
Medicine Lodge, KS 67104
Ph:(316)886-3417
Co. E-mail: mlchamber@cyberlodg.com
URL: http://www.cyberlodge.com/mlchamber
Contact: Karen Larson, Pres.

60386 ■ Miltonvale Chamber of Commerce
102 SW 6th
Miltonvale, KS 67466
Ph:(785)427-3372
Contact: Carl Kennedy, Pres.

60387 ■ Minneapolis Area Chamber of Commerce
200 W 2nd
Minneapolis, KS 67467
Ph:(785)392-3068
Co. E-mail: mplschamber@yahoo.com
URL: http://www.minneapolisks.org
Contact: Yvonne Martin, Exec.Dir.

60388 ■ Mound City Chamber of Commerce
PO Box 10
Mound City, KS 66056
Ph:(913)795-2200
Fax: (913)795-3089
Contact: Elle Hurt

60389 ■ Moundridge Community Chamber of Commerce
PO Box 312
Moundridge, KS 67107-0312
Ph:(620)345-6300
Fax: (620)345-2877
Co. E-mail: images@mtelco.net
URL: http://www.moundridge.com
Contact: Kevin Wiens, Pres.

60390 ■ Mulvane Chamber of Commerce
PO Box 67
Mulvane, KS 67110-0067
Ph:(316)777-4850
URL: http://www.mulvanekansas.com
Contact: Diane Paul, Pres.

60391 ■ Ness City Chamber of Commerce
102 W Main
PO Box 262
Ness City, KS 67560-0262
Ph:(785)798-2413
Co. E-mail: nesscitycofc@yahoo.com
URL: http://skyways.lib.ks.us/kansas/towns/nesscity/index.html
Contact: Yvette Schlegel, Exec.Dir.

60392 ■ Newton Area Chamber of Commerce and Visitors Bureau
500 N Main, Ste. 101
Newton, KS 67114
Ph:(316)283-2560
Free: 800-868-2560
Fax: (316)283-8732
Co. E-mail: info@thenewtonchamber.org
URL: http://www.thenewtonchamber.org
Contact: Virgil Penner, Exec.VP/CEO

60393 ■ Northeast Johnson County Chamber of Commerce
5800 Foxridge Dr., Ste. 100
Mission, KS 66202
Ph:(913)262-2141
Fax: (913)262-2146
Co. E-mail: info@nejcchamber.com
URL: http://www.nejcchamber.com
Contact: Pamela Ducas, Pres./CEO

60394 ■ Norton Area Chamber of Commerce
PO Box 97
Norton, KS 67654
Ph:(785)877-2501
Co. E-mail: nortoncc@ruraltel.net
URL: http://www.us36.net/nortonkansas
Contact: Karla Reed, Exec.Dir.

60395 ■ Oakley Area Chamber of Commerce
313 Center
Oakley, KS 67748
Ph:(785)672-4862
Fax: (785)672-4766
Co. E-mail: oakleycc@ruraltel.net
URL: http://www.discoveroakley.com
Contact: Margie Broeckelman, Exec.VP

60396 ■ Olathe Chamber of Commerce
142 N Cherry
PO Box 98
Olathe, KS 66051-0098
Ph:(913)764-1050
Fax: (913)782-4636
Co. E-mail: chamber@olathe.org
URL: http://www.olathe.org
Contact: L. Franklin Taylor, Pres.

60397 ■ Osage City Chamber of Commerce
PO Box 250
Osage City, KS 66523
Ph:(785)528-3112
Co. E-mail: ckerns@banklandmark.com
URL: http://www.osagecity.com
Contact: Cherity L. Kerns, Pres.

60398 ■ Osawatomie Chamber of Commerce
PO Box 63
Osawatomie, KS 66064
Ph:(913)755-4114
Fax: (913)755-4114
Co. E-mail: chamber@osawatomiechamber.org
URL: http://www.osawatomiechamber.org
Contact: Linda Dalton, Exec.Dir.

60399 ■ Osborne Area Chamber of Commerce
130 N 1st St.
Osborne, KS 67473-2002
Ph:(785)346-2881
Free: (866)346-2670
Fax: (785)346-2522
Co. E-mail: ochamber@ruraltel.net
URL: http://www.discoverosborne.com
Contact: Von Rothenberger, Exec.Dir.

60400 ■ Oswego Chamber of Commerce and Visitors Center
515 Commercial St.
Oswego, KS 67356
Ph:(620)795-2600
Free: 877-750-2600
Fax: (620)795-4267
Contact: Linda Rife, Pres.

60401 ■ Ottawa Area Chamber of Commerce
109 E 2nd
Ottawa, KS 66067
Ph:(785)242-1000
Fax: (785)242-4792
Co. E-mail: chamber@ottawakansas.org
URL: http://www.ottawakansas.org
Contact: Tom Weigand, Pres./CEO

60402 ■ Overland Park Chamber of Commerce
9001 W 110th, Ste. 150
Overland Park, KS 66210
Ph:(913)491-3600
Fax: (913)491-0393
Co. E-mail: opcc@opks.org
URL: http://www.opks.org
Contact: Tracey Osborne, Pres.

60403 ■ Paola Chamber of Commerce
3 W Wea
Paola, KS 66071-1403
Ph:(913)294-4335
Fax: (913)294-4336
Co. E-mail: mgr@paolachamber.org
URL: http://www.paolachamber.org
Contact: Carol Everhart

60404 ■ Parsons Chamber of Commerce
1715 Corning
Parsons, KS 67357
Ph:(620)421-6500
Free: 800-280-6401
Fax: (620)421-6501
Co. E-mail: chamber@parsonschamber.org
URL: http://www.parsonschamber.org
Contact: Whitney Yoder, Exec.VP/Dir.

60405 ■ Phillipsburg Area Chamber of Commerce
270 State St.
PO Box 326
Phillipsburg, KS 67661-0326
Ph:(785)543-2321
Fax: (785)543-0038
Co. E-mail: cvbcham@ruraltel.net
URL: http://www.phillipsburgks.us
Contact: Jackie L. Swatzell, Mgr.

60406 ■ Pittsburg Area Chamber of Commerce
117 W 4th St.
PO Box 1115
Pittsburg, KS 66762
Ph:(620)231-1000
Fax: (620)231-3178
Co. E-mail: pres@pittsburgkschamber.com
URL: http://www.pittsburgkschamber.com
Contact: Anissa Lomshek, Pres.

60407 ■ Pratt Area Chamber of Commerce
114 N Main
Pratt, KS 67124
Ph:(620)672-5501
Free: 888-886-1164
Co. E-mail: chamberofcommerce_pratt@yahoo.com
URL: http://www.prattkan.com
Contact: Kristen Veverka, Exec.Dir.

60408 ■ Quinter Chamber of Commerce
PO Box 35
Quinter, KS 67752
Ph:(785)754-3538
Contact: Carolyn Tuttle, Sec.

60409 ■ Russell Area Chamber of Commerce
610 N Main
Russell, KS 67665

Ph:(785)483-6960
Co. E-mail: chamber@russellks.org
URL: http://www.russellks.org
Contact: Juli Reiss, Exec. Dir.

60410 ■ Sabetha Chamber of Commerce
808 Main St.
Sabetha, KS 66534
Ph:(785)284-2408
Fax: (785)284-2408
Co. E-mail: chamber@mewlan.com
URL: http://skyways.lib.ks.us/towns/Sabetha/
chamber.htm
Contact: Emma Boltz, Operations Dir.

60411 ■ St. Francis Area Chamber of Commerce
212 E Washington
St. Francis, KS 67756
Ph:(785)332-2961
Co. E-mail: coc@cityofstfrancis.net
URL: http://www.stfranciskansas.com
Contact: Gloria Bracelin, Dir./Sec.

60412 ■ Salina Area Chamber of Commerce
120 W Ash St.
PO Box 586
Salina, KS 67402-0586
Ph:(785)827-9301
Fax: (785)827-9758
Co. E-mail: gcook@salinakansas.org
URL: http://www.salinakansas.org
Contact: Gerald Cook, Pres.

60413 ■ Satanta Chamber of Commerce
Box 98
Satanta, KS 67870-0098
Ph:(620)649-2258
Co. E-mail: chamber@satanta.org
URL: http://www.satanta.org
Contact: Terri Rankin, Sec.

60414 ■ Scott City Area Chamber of Commerce
221 W 5th
Scott City, KS 67871
Ph:(620)872-3525
Fax: (620)872-3391
Co. E-mail: sccc@pld.com
URL: http://www.scottcity.com
Contact: Anne Lampe, Exec.Dir.

60415 ■ Sedan Chamber of Commerce
PO Box 182
Sedan, KS 67361
Ph:(620)725-4033
Fax: (620)725-4023
Contact: Rhonda Davis, Pres.

60416 ■ Seneca Chamber of Commerce
PO Box 135
Seneca, KS 66538-0135
Ph:(785)336-2294
Fax: (785)336-6344
Contact: Penny Zeller, Exec. Dir.

60417 ■ Shawnee Area Chamber of Commerce
15100 W 67th St., Ste. 202
Shawnee, KS 66217-9344
Ph:(913)631-6545
Free: 888-550-7252
Fax: (913)631-9628
Co. E-mail: info@shawneekschamber.com
URL: http://shawneekschamber.com
Contact: Linda Leeper, Pres.

60418 ■ Smith Center Chamber of Commerce
219 S Main
Smith Center, KS 66967
Ph:(785)282-3895
Fax: (785)282-3895
Co. E-mail: scchamber@ruraltel.net
URL: http://www.smithcenterks.com
Contact: Mrs. Irene Baumann, Office Mgr.

60419 ■ Spring Hill Chamber of Commerce
PO Box 15
Spring Hill, KS 66083
Ph:(913)592-3893
Fax: (913)592-3893
Co. E-mail: chamber@springhillks.org
URL: http://www.springhillks.org
Contact: Pamela E. Martell

60420 ■ Stafford Area Chamber of Commerce
PO Box 24
Stafford, KS 67578
Ph:(620)234-5614
Contact: Carolyn Claypool, Sec.-Treas.

60421 ■ Sterling Chamber of Commerce
PO Box 56
Sterling, KS 67579
Ph:(620)278-3727
Co. E-mail: lcbuckman@cm.kscoxmail.com
URL: http://www.sterling-kansas.org
Contact: Ben Marshall, Pres.

60422 ■ Stockton Chamber of Commerce
PO Box 1
Stockton, KS 67669
Ph:(785)425-6162
Fax: (785)425-6424
Co. E-mail: tkeas@kans.com
URL: http://www.stocktonkansas.net
Contact: Denise Murchie, Pres.

60423 ■ Syracuse-Hamilton County Chamber of Commerce
PO Box 678
Syracuse, KS 67878-0678
Ph:(620)384-5459
Fax: (620)384-7585
Co. E-mail: schamber@pld.com
URL: http://skyways.lib.ks.us/towns/Syracuse
Contact: Sandy Dikeman, Exec.VP

60424 ■ Tri-County Area Chamber of Commerce
106 N Broadway
Herington, KS 67449
Ph:(785)258-2115
Fax: (785)258-2799
Co. E-mail: hrngtnch@tctelco.net
URL: http://skyways.lib.ks.us/towns/Herington/
chamber.html
Contact: Phyllis Smith, Exec.Dir.

60425 ■ Valley Center Chamber of Commerce
214 W Main St.
PO Box 382
Valley Center, KS 67147
Ph:(316)755-7340
Fax: (316)755-7319
Co. E-mail: vccc67147@yahoo.com
URL: http://www.valleycenterkschamber.org
Contact: Virginia Boyd, Pres.

60426 ■ Valley Falls Chamber of Commerce
PO Box 162
Valley Falls, KS 66088
Ph:(785)945-3245
Fax: (785)945-6269
Co. E-mail: pheinen@grasshoppernet.com
Contact: Robert Zieg, Pres.

60427 ■ Wa Keeney Chamber of Commerce
117 N Main St., No. B
PO Box 295
Wa Keeney, KS 67672
Ph:(785)743-2077
Fax: (785)743-5530
URL: http://www.wakeeney.org
Contact: Teri Aaron, Dir.

60428 ■ Wallace County Area Chamber of Commerce
PO Box 642
Sharon Springs, KS 67758-0642
Ph:(785)852-4935

Co. E-mail: wallacecoeda@yahoo.com
URL: http://www.wallacecounty.net

60429 ■ Wamego Area Chamber of Commerce
PO Box 34
Wamego, KS 66547
Ph:(785)456-7849
Fax: (785)456-2016
Co. E-mail: wchamber@kansas.net
URL: http://www.wamegochamber.com
Contact: Chad Bunger, Dir.

60430 ■ Waterville Chamber of Commerce
PO Box 173
Waterville, KS 66548
Ph:(785)363-2515
Fax: (785)363-2368
URL: http://watervillekansas.com

60431 ■ Wellington Area Chamber of Commerce
207 S Washington Ave.
Wellington, KS 67152-3037
Ph:(620)326-7466
Fax: (620)326-7467
Co. E-mail: ccccwell@idir.net
Contact: Carter Green, Exec.Dir.

60432 ■ Wellsville Area Chamber of Commerce
PO Box 472
Wellsville, KS 66092
Ph:(785)883-2296
URL: http://www.wellsvillechamber.com
Contact: Roy Baker, Pres.

60433 ■ Wichita Area Chamber of Commerce
350 W Douglas Ave.
Wichita, KS 67202-2970
Ph:(316)265-7771
Fax: (316)265-7502
Co. E-mail: info@wichitachamber.org
URL: http://www.wichitakansas.org
Contact: Bryan Derreberry, Pres./CEO

60434 ■ Winfield Area Chamber of Commerce
205 E 9th Ave.
PO Box 640
Winfield, KS 67156
Ph:(620)221-2420
Fax: (620)221-2958
Co. E-mail: win@winfieldchamber.org
URL: http://winfieldchamber.org
Contact: Seth Bate, Exec.Dir.

60435 ■ Winona Chamber of Commerce
PO Box 54
Winona, KS 67764
Ph:(785)846-7702
Contact: Louise Smith, Treas.

60436 ■ Women's Chamber of Commerce
PO Box 171337
Kansas City, KS 66117-0337
Ph:(913)371-3165
Fax: (913)371-3732
Contact: Carol Lever, Pres.

60437 ■ Woodson County Chamber of Commerce
108 S Main
PO Box 233
Yates Center, KS 66783
Ph:(620)625-3235
Fax: (620)625-2416
Co. E-mail: chamber@wccc.kscoxmail.com
URL: http://www.woodsoncounty.net
Contact: Shelia Lampe, Exec.Dir.

MINORITY BUSINESS ASSISTANCE PROGRAMS

60438 ■ Kansas Department of Commerce–Office of Minority Business
1000 SW Jackson St., Ste. 100
Topeka, KS 66612
Ph:(785)296-5298
Fax: (785)296-3490
URL: http://www.kansascommerce.com
Description: Provides counseling, technical assistance, and procurement counseling. Conducts low-cost business seminars, workshops, and conferences. Offers business reference materials.

FINANCING AND LOAN PROGRAMS

60439 ■ Child Health Investment Company, LLC
6803 W. 64th St., Ste. 208
Shawnee Mission, KS 66202
Ph:(913)262-1436
Fax: (913)262-1575
URL: http://www.chca.com
Contact: Don Black, President
Investment Types: Balanced, early stage, first stage, seed, and start-up. **Industry Preferences:** Medical and health, biotechnology, other products, Internet specific, computer software and services, computer hardware, and semiconductors and other electronics. **Geographic Preferences:** U.S.

60440 ■ Enterprise Merchant Bank
9150 Glenwood St.
Shawnee Mission, KS 66201
Ph:(913)652-9315
Fax: (913)652-9305
Preferred Investment Size: $1,000,000 minimum. **Investment Types:** Second stage, leveraged buyout, mezzanine, and special situation. **Geographic Preferences:** Midwest.

60441 ■ Kansas Technology Enterprise Corporation
214 SW 6th, 1st Fl.
Topeka, KS 66603-3719
Ph:(785)296-5272
Fax: (785)296-1160
URL: http://www.ktec.com
Contact: Michael Peck, Vice President
Preferred Investment Size: $250,000 to $500,000. **Investment Types:** Seed, start-up, first and early stage. **Industry Preferences:** Communications, computer hardware and software, Internet specifics, semiconductors and other electronics, biotechnology, transportation, medical and health, consumer related, industrial and energy, and business service, and manufacturing. **Geographic Preferences:** Midwest.

60442 ■ Kansas Venture Capital, Inc.
6700 Antioch Plz., Ste. 460
Overland Park, KS 66204
Ph:(913)262-7117
Fax: (913)262-3509
Contact: Thomas Blackburn, President
Preferred Investment Size: $500,000 to $250,000,000. **Investment Types:** Later stage, mezzanine, leveraged buyout, management buyouts, acquisition, expansion, turnaround, and recapitalizations. **Industry Preferences:** Communications and media, computer related, semiconductors and other electronics, medical and health, consumer related, industrial and energy, business service, and manufacturing. **Geographic Preferences:** Midwest.

PROCUREMENT ASSISTANCE PROGRAMS

60443 ■ Kansas Department of Administration–Division of Purchases
102 N Landon State Office Bldg.
900 Jackson St.
Topeka, KS 66612-1286
Ph:(785)296-2376
Fax: (785)296-7240
Co. E-mail: purchweb@da.state.ks.us
URL: http://www.da.state.ks.us/purch
Contact: Christopher Howe, Purchasing Dir
Description: In cooperation with the Division of Existing Industry Development, provides assistance to businesses seeking procurement opportunities with the state.

INCUBATORS/RESEARCH AND TECHNOLOGY PARKS

60444 ■ Johnson County Community College–Office of Institutional Research
12345 College Blvd.
Overland Park, KS 66210
Ph:(913)469-8500
Fax: (913)469-4481
Co. E-mail: jseybert@jccc.net
Contact: Dr. Jeffrey A. Seybert, Dir.
E-mail: jseybert@jccc.net
Scope: Conducts assessments of student learning outcomes and institutional effectiveness, program evaluation for instructional programs, student services, and support services. Provides decision support and assistance to College planning processes through analysis of management information. Conducts market research for enrollment management and program development. Offers information resource services and consulting services. Provides research and technical support services to public and private agencies and various consortia, including Kansas Association of Community Colleges and the League for Innovation in the Community College. **Educational Activities:** National Community College Benchmark Conference.

60445 ■ Kansas State University–Office of the Vice Provost for Research
Anderson Hall, Rm. 108
Manhattan, KS 66506
Ph:(785)532-5110
Fax: (785)532-6507
Co. E-mail: trewyn@ksu.edu
URL: http://www.ksu.edu/kstateresearch
Contact: Prof. Ronald W. Trewyn, Vice Provost & Dean
E-mail: trewyn@ksu.edu
Scope: Administers all University related research projects and intellectual property activities at Kansas State University. Also administers research projects supported by extramural agencies in all units of the University, including the physical, biological, behavioral sciences, agriculture, engineering, and humanities. Monitors university compliance with federal regulations. **Publications:** Funding Bulletin (weekly); Proposal Manual; Research Notes (bimonthly). **Educational Activities:** Seminars (periodically); Training workshops, open to the general public; Workshops, for faculty and graduate students. **Awards:** Distinguished Graduate Faculty Award; Travel awards.

60446 ■ Kansas State University Research Foundation
1500 Hayes Dr.
Manhattan, KS 66502-5068
Ph:(785)532-5720
Fax: (785)532-3920
Co. E-mail: tech.transfer@ksu.edu
URL: http://www.ksu.edu/tech.transfer
Contact: Prof. Ronald W. Trewyn, Pres.
E-mail: tech.transfer@ksu.edu
Scope: Provides patenting and licensing assistance to KSU researchers. **Educational Activities:** Seminars, on patent and technology transfer.

60447 ■ Pittsburg State University–Kansas Polymer Research Center–Business and Technology Institute
1701 S Broadway
Pittsburg, KS 66762-7560
Ph:(620)235-4920
Fax: (620)235-4919
Co. E-mail: bti@pittstate.edu
URL: http://www.pittstate.edu/bti
Contact: R. Steve Robb, Exec/Dir.
E-mail: bti@pittstate.edu
Scope: Conducts applied research, transfers technology, and provides assistance to industry through its research associates, staff, and through the School of Technology. Emphasis in polymer/plastics, secondary wood processing, and rapid prototyping. **Educational Activities:** Training programs, in advanced technology in manufacturing, production problem solving, product design, and prototype development.

EDUCATIONAL PROGRAMS

60448 ■ Coffeyville Community College
400 W 11th St.
Coffeyville, KS 67337
Ph:(620)251-7700
Fax: (620)252-7098
URL: http://www.ccc.cc.ks.us
Description: Two-year college offering a small business management program.

60449 ■ Labette Community College
200 S 14th St.
Parsons, KS 67357
Ph:(620)421-6700
Free: 888-522-3883
Fax: (620)421-0180
Co. E-mail: juliusg@labette.edu
URL: http://www.labette.cc.ks.us
Description: Two-year college offering a small business management program.

60450 ■ Wichita State University–Center for Entrepreneurship
Devlin Hall, 2nd Fl.
1845 N Fairmount
Wichita, KS 67260-0147
Ph:(316)978-3000
Fax: (316)978-3687
URL: http://www.cfe.wichita.edu
Description: Offers degreed courses for entrepreneurs and small business management.

LEGISLATIVE ASSISTANCE

60451 ■ Kansas House Standing Committee on Economic Development
Statehouse, Rm. 545 N
Kansas Legis. Research Department
300 SW 10th Ave
Topeka, KS 66612
Ph:(785)296-3181
Fax: (785)296-3824
Co. E-mail: aprilh@klrd.state.ks.us
URL: http://skyway.lib.ks.us/ksleg/KLRD/klrd.html
Contact: April Holman

PUBLICATIONS

60452 ■ *Smart Start your Washington D.C. Business*
PSI Research
300 N. Valley Dr.
Grants Pass, OR 97526
Ph:(503)479-9464
Free: 800-228-2275
Fax: (503)476-1479
Co. E-mail: info@psi-research.com
URL: http://www.psi-research.com
Ed: Michael D. Jenkins. **Released:** Revised edition, 1992. **Price:** $29.95 (looseleaf binder); $24.95 (paper). **Description:** Part of the Successful Business Library series.

SMALL BUSINESS DEVELOPMENT CENTER LEAD OFFICE

60453 ■ Kentucky SBDC–University of Kentucky–Kentucky SBDC (225 G)
225 Gatton College of Business Economics Bldg.
Lexington, KY 40506-0034
Ph:(859)257-7744
Free: 888-475-SBDC
Fax: (859)323-1907
URL: http://www.ksbdc.org
Contact: Becky Naugle, State Dir.
E-mail: lrnaug0@pop.uky.edu

60454 ■ University of Kentucky–Center for Business Development
225 Gatton College of Business and Economics
Lexington, KY 40506-0034
Ph:(859)257-7668
Free: 888-475-SBDC
Fax: (859)323-1907
Contact: Becky Naugle, State Director
E-mail: lrnaug0@pop.uky.edu

SMALL BUSINESS DEVELOPMENT CENTERS

60455 ■ Eastern Kentucky University–Small Business Development Center
675 Monticello St., Ste. A
Somerset, KY 42501
Ph:(606)678-3042
Free: 877-358-7232
Fax: (859)622-1413
URL: http://www.ksbdc.org
Contact: Kathleen Moats, Dir.
E-mail: kathy.moats@eku.edu

60456 ■ Greater Louisville–Small Business Development Center
123 E. Main St.
Louisville, KY 40202
Ph:(502)625-0145
Free: 888-475-SBDC
Fax: (502)625-1181
URL: http://www.louisvillesmallbiz.org/
Contact: Kathleen Hoye, Dir.
E-mail: khoye@greaterlouisville.com

60457 ■ Greater Louisville SBDC
123 E. Main St.
Louisville, KY 40202
Ph:(502)625-0145
Free: 888-475-SBDC
Fax: (502)625-1181
URL: http://www.louisvillesmallbiz.org/
Contact: Kathleen Hoye, Director
E-mail: khoye@greaterlouisville.com

60458 ■ Lexington Area Small Business Development Center
Central Library Bldg., 4th Fl.
140 E. Main St.
Lexington, KY 40507-1376
Ph:(859)257-7666
Fax: (859)257-1751
URL: http://www.ksbdc.org
Contact: Shirie Mack, Dir.
E-mail: smack3@uky.edu

60459 ■ Morehead State University–Morehead Small Business Development Center
150 University Blvd.
Box 667
Morehead, KY 40351
Ph:(606)783-2895
Fax: (606)783-5020
URL: http://www.moreheadstate.edu/sbdc/
Contact: David Barber, Consultant
E-mail: d.barber@moreheadstate.edu

60460 ■ Morehead State University–Pikeville Small Business Development Center
3455 N. Mayo Trail, No. 4
Pikeville, KY 41501
Ph:(606)432-5848
Fax: (606)432-8924
URL: http://www.ksbdc.org
Contact: Michael Morley, District Dir.
E-mail: m.morley@moreheadstate.edu

60461 ■ Morehead State University (Boyd County)–Ashland SBDC–SBDC (1645)
1645 Winchester Ave., 2nd Fl.
207 15th St.
Ashland, KY 41101
Ph:(606)329-8011
Fax: (606)324-4570
URL: http://www.ksbdc.org
Contact: Kimberly A. Jenkins, Dir.
E-mail: k.jenkins@moreheadstate.edu

60462 ■ Murray State University–Owensboro SBDC
3860 U.S. Hwy. 60 W.
Owensboro, KY 42301
Ph:(270)926-8085
Fax: (270)684-0714
URL: http://www.ksbdc.org
Contact: Mickey Johnson, District Dir.
E-mail: mickeyjohnson@gradd.com

60463 ■ Murray State University–West Kentucky SBDC
Business Bldg. S., Rm. 253
Murray, KY 42071-3314
Ph:(270)809-2856
Fax: (270)809-3049
URL: http://www.ksbdc.org
Contact: Rosemary Miller, Dir.
E-mail: rosemary.miller@murraystate.edu

60464 ■ Murray State University (Hopkinsville)–Small Business Development Center
2800 Ft. Campbell Blvd.
Hopkinsville, KY 42240
Ph:(270)886-8666
Fax: (270)881-9366
URL: http://www.ksbdc.org
Contact: Roy Keller, Dir.
E-mail: roy.keller@murraystate.edu

60465 ■ Northern Kentucky University–SBDC
305 Johns Hill Rd.
Highland Heights, KY 41099-0506
Ph:(859)442-4281
Fax: (859)442-4285
URL: http://www.nku.edu/~sbdc/
Contact: Tom Burke, Dir.
E-mail: burket1@nku.edu

60466 ■ Southeast Community College - Bell County Campus–SBDC
1300 Chichester Ave.
Middlesboro, KY 40965-2265
Ph:(606)248-0563
Free: 888-225-7232
Fax: (606)242-4514
URL: http://www.SoutheastSBDC.com
Contact: Sam Coleman, Dir.
E-mail: samuel.coleman@cktcs.net

60467 ■ University of Kentucky (Elizabethtown)–Small Business Development Center
1105 Juliana Court No. 6
Elizabethtown, KY 42701
Ph:(270)765-6737
Fax: (270)769-5095
URL: http://www.ksbdc.org
Contact: Patricia Krausman, Dir.
E-mail: pksbdc@kvnet.org

60468 ■ Western Kentucky University (Warren County)–Bowling Green Small Business Development Center
Vanmeter Rm. 203
1 Big Red Way
Bowling Green, KY 42104
Ph:(270)745-1905
Fax: (270)745-1931
URL: http://www.wku.edu/Dept/Support/AcadAffairs/IED/SBDC/
Contact: Richard S. Horn, Dir.
E-mail: rick.horn@wku.edu

SMALL BUSINESS ASSISTANCE PROGRAMS

60469 ■ Kentucky Cabinet for Economic Development–Business and Entrepreneurship Development Division
2200 Capitol Plaza Tower, 22nd Fl.
500 Mero St.
Frankfort, KY 40601

Ph:(502)564-4252
Fax: (502)564-5932
Co. E-mail: rmbrown@mail.state.ky.us
URL: http://www.thinkkentucky.com
Description: Offers new and existing businesses a centralized information source on business regulation; assists businesses in securing necessary permits; and acts as an ombudsman and referral service.

60470 ■ Kentucky Cabinet for Economic Development–International Trade Division–Department for Existing Business Development (Old C)
Old Capital Annex Building
300 W Broadway
Frankfort, KY 40601
Ph:(502)564-7140
Fax: (502)564-3256
Co. E-mail: mark.peachey@ky.gov
URL: http://www.thinkkentucky.com
Contact: Mark Peachey, Dir
Description: Preserves and increases employment opportunities through foreign investment within the state, and increased export of Kentucky's manufactured products. Operates a Far East office in Japan and a European office in England.

60471 ■ Kentucky Cabinet for Economic Development–New Business Development Division
Old Capital Annex Building
300 W Broadway
Frankfort, KY 40601
Ph:(502)564-7140
Fax: (502)564-9758
URL: http://www.thinkkentucky.com
Contact: John McCarty, Commissioner
Description: Provides site selection assistance and information. Focuses on new job creation and job retention through an Existing Industries Branch, an Industrial Marketing Branch, an Enterprise Zone Program, and a Site Evaluation Branch.

60472 ■ Kentucky Cabinet for Economic Development–Office of Business Technology
2200 Capitol Plaza Tower, 22nd Fl., Rm. 2224
500 Mero St.
Frankfort, KY 40601
Ph:(502)564-4252
Fax: (502)564-5932
URL: http://www.thinkkentucky.com
Description: Serves as a link between businesses and the technological resources and research capabilities of the state universities. Provides coordination of technology transfer to the private sector and works with the federal Small Business Innovation Research program.

60473 ■ Kentucky Cabinet for Economic Development–Small and Minority Business Division–Office of Export Development (67 Wi)
67 Wilkinson Blvd.
Frankfort, KY 40601
Ph:(502)564-2064
Fax: (502)564-9758
URL: http://www.thinkkentucky.com
Description: Provides exporting assistance to small manufacturers.

60474 ■ Kentucky Cabinet for Economic Development–Small and Minority Business Division–Small and Minority Business Division (67 Wi)
67 Wilkinson Blvd.
Frankfort, KY 40601
Ph:(502)564-2064
Fax: (502)564-9758
URL: http://www.thinkkentucky.com
Description: Serves as an advocate and ombudsman for small business. Works with the Legislative Small Business Task Force, provides information on programs of interest, and provides information on specialized resource assistance.

SCORE OFFICES

60475 ■ SCORE Lexington
389 Waller Ave., Ste. 130
Lexington, KY 40504-2900
Ph:(859)231-9902
Fax: (859)253-3190
Co. E-mail: scorelex@pdgweb.com
Description: Provides professional guidance and information to America's small businesses.

60476 ■ SCORE Paducah
c/o Arthur Feather, CHR
Federal Office Bldg.
501 Broadway, Rm. B-36
Paducah, KY 42001
Ph:(270)442-5685
URL: http://www.score.org

BETTER BUSINESS BUREAUS

60477 ■ Better Business Bureau of Central and Eastern Kentucky
1460 Newtown Pike
Lexington, KY 40511
Ph:(859)259-1008
Free: 800-866-6668
Fax: (859)259-1639
Co. E-mail: info@ky.bbb.org
URL: http://www.ky.bbb.org
Contact: Roger Grigsby, Chm.

60478 ■ Better Business Bureau - Louisville, Southern Indiana and Western Kentucky
844 S 4th St.
Louisville, KY 40203-2186
Ph:(502)583-6546
Free: 800-388-2222
Fax: (502)589-9940
Co. E-mail: info@ky-in.bbb.org
URL: http://www.bbbkyin.org
Contact: Charlie Mattingly, Pres./CEO

CHAMBERS OF COMMERCE

60479 ■ Adairville - South Logan Chamber of Commerce
PO Box 266
Adairville, KY 42202
Ph:(270)539-6731
Contact: Ms. Donna Blake, Pres.

60480 ■ Anderson County Chamber of Commerce
PO Box 543
Lawrenceburg, KY 40342-0543
Ph:(502)839-5564
Fax: (502)839-5106
Co. E-mail: commdevlpmt@adelphia.net
URL: http://www.lawrenceburgky.org
Contact: Tami Vater, Exec.Dir.

60481 ■ Ashland Alliance
1733 Winchester Ave.
PO Box 830
Ashland, KY 41105-0830
Ph:(606)324-5111
Fax: (606)325-4607
Co. E-mail: bhammond@inicity.net
URL: http://www.ashlandalliance.com
Contact: Bob Hammond, Dir. of Business Development

60482 ■ Bardstown-Nelson County Chamber of Commerce
1 Court Sq.
Bardstown, KY 40004
Ph:(502)348-9545
Fax: (502)348-6478
Co. E-mail: chamber@bardstown.com

URL: http://www.bardstownchamber.com
Contact: Dorothy White, Exec.Dir.

60483 ■ Bell County Chamber of Commerce
215 N 20th St.
PO Box 788
Middlesboro, KY 40965
Ph:(606)248-1075
Fax: (606)248-8851
Co. E-mail: chamber@bellcountychamber.com
URL: http://www.bellcountyworks.com
Contact: Nioma Lawson, Exec.Dir.

60484 ■ Bowling Green Area Chamber of Commerce
812 State St.
PO Box 51
Bowling Green, KY 42102
Ph:(270)781-3200
Fax: (270)843-0458
Co. E-mail: info@bgchamber.com
URL: http://www.bgchamber.com
Contact: James N. Hizer CEcD, Pres./CEO

60485 ■ Bracken County Chamber of Commerce
PO Box 7
Brooksville, KY 41004
Ph:(606)735-3176
Fax: (606)735-3103
Contact: Perry Poe, Pres.

60486 ■ Bullitt County Chamber of Commerce
505 Buffalo Run Rd., Ste. 101
Shepherdsville, KY 40165
Ph:(502)543-6727
Fax: (502)543-1765
Co. E-mail: bcchamber@alltel.net
URL: http://www.travelbullitt.org
Contact: Beth Cassity, Exec. Dir.

60487 ■ Burkesville Cumberland County Chamber of Commerce
PO Box 312
Burkesville, KY 42717
Ph:(270)864-5890
Co. E-mail: chamber@burkesville.com
URL: http://www.burkesville.com/chamber
Contact: Jeremy White, Pres.

60488 ■ Cadiz-Trigg County Chamber of Commerce
PO Box 647
Cadiz, KY 42211
Ph:(270)522-3892
Fax: (270)522-6343
Co. E-mail: cadizky@apex.net
URL: http://www.barkleylake.com
Contact: Donna Bryan, Pres.

60489 ■ Campbellsville - Taylor County Chamber of Commerce
107 W Broadway
Campbellsville, KY 42718
Ph:(270)465-8601
Fax: (270)465-0607
Co. E-mail: chamber@teamtaylorcounty.com
URL: http://www.campbellsvillechamber.com
Contact: Frieda Sandidge, Pres.

60490 ■ Carlisle - Nicholas County Chamber of Commerce
PO Box 201
Carlisle, KY 40311
Ph:(859)289-6489
Fax: (859)289-6611
Co. E-mail: cncchamber@hotmail.com
Contact: Grant Mathes, Pres.

60491 ■ Carroll County Chamber of Commerce
511 Highland Ave.
Carrollton, KY 41008
Ph:(502)732-7034
Fax: (502)732-7028
Co. E-mail: chamber@carrollcountyky.com

URL: http://www.carrollcountyky.com
Contact: Stephen Jones, Pres.

60492 ■ Cave City Chamber of Commerce
PO Box 460
Cave City, KY 42127
Ph:(270)773-5159
Fax: (270)773-5159
Co. E-mail: ccchamber@scrtc.com
Contact: Gina Lyon, Pres.

60493 ■ Central City Chamber of Commerce
203 N. 2nd St.
Central City, KY 42330
Ph:(270)754-2360
Fax: (270)754-2365
Co. E-mail: chamber@muhlon.com
URL: http://www.centralcitykychamber.com
Contact: Shelia Bivins, Sec.

60494 ■ Columbia-Adair County Chamber of Commerce
PO Box 116
Columbia, KY 42728
Ph:(270)384-6020
Fax: (270)384-2056
Co. E-mail: coladair@duo-county.com
Contact: Sue Stivers, Exec.Dir.

60495 ■ Crittenden County Chamber of Commerce
217 S Main St.
Marion, KY 42064
Ph:(270)965-5015
Free: 800-755-0361
Co. E-mail: chamber@marionkentucky.us
URL: http://www.marionkentucky.us/chamber
Contact: Renee James, Sec.

60496 ■ Cynthiana-Harrison County Chamber of Commerce
203 W Pike St.
Cynthiana, KY 41031
Ph:(859)234-5236
Fax: (859)234-9102
Co. E-mail: cynchamber@se-tel.com
URL: http://www.cynthianaky.com/chamber
Contact: Tonya Coleman, Exec.Dir.

60497 ■ Danville-Boyle County Chamber of Commerce
304 S Fourth St.
Danville, KY 40422-2005
Ph:(859)236-2361
Fax: (859)236-3197
Co. E-mail: info@danvilleboylechamber.com
URL: http://www.danvilleboylechamber.com
Contact: Paula Fowler Kilby, Exec.Dir.

60498 ■ Dawson Springs Chamber of Commerce
PO Box 403
Dawson Springs, KY 42408
Ph:(270)797-2781
Co. E-mail: whi@dawsonspringsky.com
URL: http://www.dawsonspringsky.com
Contact: Rick Hendrickson, Pres.

60499 ■ Edmonton - Metcalfe County Chamber of Commerce
PO Box 42
Edmonton, KY 42129
Ph:(270)432-3222
Fax: (270)432-3224
Co. E-mail: metchamb@scrtc.com
URL: http://www.metcalfechamber.com
Contact: Gaye Shaw, Exec.Dir.

60500 ■ Elizabethtown-Hardin County Chamber of Commerce
111 W Dixie Ave.
Elizabethtown, KY 42701
Ph:(270)765-4334
Fax: (270)737-0690
Co. E-mail: etownchamber@kvnet.org
URL: http://www.elizabethtownchamber.org
Contact: Edith Dupin, Pres.

60501 ■ Estill County Development Alliance
PO Box 421
Irvine, KY 40336
Ph:(606)723-2450
Fax: (606)726-9713
Co. E-mail: estilldevelopment@yahoo.com
URL: http://www.estillcountyky.net
Contact: Jeffrey Crowe, Pres./CEO

60502 ■ Fleming County Chamber of Commerce
PO Box 24
Flemingsburg, KY 41041
Ph:(606)845-1223
Fax: (606)845-1223
Co. E-mail: flemingchamber@pqisp.net
URL: http://www.flemingkychamber.com
Contact: Mary Jo Litton, Exec.Dir.

60503 ■ Floyd County Chamber of Commerce
113 S Central Ave.
PO Box 1508
Prestonsburg, KY 41653
Ph:(606)886-0364
Co. E-mail: floydchamber@setel.com
URL: http://www.floydcountykentucky.com
Contact: Dr. George Edwards, Chm.

60504 ■ Frankfort Area Chamber of Commerce
100 Capital Ave.
Frankfort, KY 40601
Ph:(502)223-8261
Fax: (502)223-5942
Co. E-mail: chamber@frankfortky.info
URL: http://www.frankfortky.info
Contact: Carmen Inman, Exec.Dir.

60505 ■ Franklin-Simpson County Chamber of Commerce
201 S Main St.
PO Box 513
Franklin, KY 42135-0513
Ph:(270)586-7609
Fax: (270)586-5438
Co. E-mail: keaton@fschamber.com
URL: http://www.f-schamber.com
Contact: Karen Eaton, Exec.Dir.

60506 ■ Garrard County Chamber of Commerce
656 Stanford Rd.
Lancaster, KY 40444
Ph:(859)792-2282
Fax: (859)792-2282
Co. E-mail: garcocham@earthlink.net
URL: http://www.garrardchamber.com
Contact: Susan Ledford, Sec.-Treas.

60507 ■ Georgetown-Scott County Chamber of Commerce
160 E Main St.
Georgetown, KY 40324
Ph:(502)863-5424
Fax: (502)863-5756
Co. E-mail: info@gtown.org
URL: http://www.gtown.org
Contact: Jack Conner, Exec. Dir.

60508 ■ Glasgow-Barren County Chamber of Commerce
118 E Public Sq.
Glasgow, KY 42141
Ph:(270)651-3161
Fax: (270)651-3122
Co. E-mail: chamber@glasgow-ky.com
URL: http://www.glasgowbarren.com
Contact: Ernie Myers, Exec.VP

60509 ■ Grand Rivers Tourism Commission
PO Box 181
Grand Rivers, KY 42045
Ph:(270)362-0152
Free: 888-493-0152
Co. E-mail: info@grandrivers.com
URL: http://www.grandrivers.com

Contact: Ms. Kim Kraemer, Exec.Dir.

60510 ■ Grant County Chamber of Commerce
PO Box 365
Williamstown, KY 41097-0365
Ph:(859)824-3322
Free: 800-824-2858
Fax: (859)824-7082
Co. E-mail: wgutman@grantcommerce.com
URL: http://www.grantcommerce.com
Contact: Wade Gutman, Exec. Dir.

60511 ■ Grayson Area Chamber of Commerce
PO Box 612
Grayson, KY 41143
Ph:(606)474-4401
Fax: (606)474-4401
Co. E-mail: graysonchamber@yahoo.com
URL: http://www.graysonchamber.org
Contact: Rebecca Justice, Exec.Asst.

60512 ■ Grayson County Chamber of Commerce
425 S Main St.
Leitchfield, KY 42754
Ph:(270)259-5587
Free: 800-667-5934
Fax: (270)259-9278
Co. E-mail: chamberinfo@graysoncountychamber.com
URL: http://www.graysoncountychamber.com
Contact: Caryn Lewis, Exec.Dir.

60513 ■ Greater Breckinridge County Chamber of Commerce
PO Box 725
Hardinsburg, KY 40143-0725
Ph:(270)756-0268
Co. E-mail: chamber@breckinridgeco.com
URL: http://www.breckinridgeco.com
Contact: Sherry D. Stith, Exec.Dir.

60514 ■ Greater Corbin Chamber of Commerce
805 S Main St.
Corbin, KY 40701
Ph:(606)528-6390
Fax: (606)528-1583
Co. E-mail: chamberofcommerce@corbinkentucky.us
URL: http://www.corbinkentucky.us
Contact: Bruce Carpenter, Pres.

60515 ■ Greater Lexington Chamber of Commerce
330 E Main St., Ste. 100
PO Box 1968
Lexington, KY 40507
Ph:(859)254-4447
Fax: (859)233-3304
Co. E-mail: info@commercelexington.com
Contact: Robert L. Quick, CEO & Pres.

60516 ■ Greater Louisville Inc. - The Metro Chamber of Commerce
614 W Main St., Ste. 6000
Louisville, KY 40202
Ph:(502)625-0000
Fax: (502)625-0010
Co. E-mail: sfarnsworth@greaterlouisville.com
URL: http://www.greaterlouisville.com
Contact: Joe Reagan, Pres./CEO

60517 ■ Greensburg-Green County Chamber of Commerce
PO Box 327
Greensburg, KY 42743
Ph:(270)932-4298
Fax: (270)932-7778
Co. E-mail: greenchamber@earthlink.net
URL: http://greensburgky.com
Contact: John Henderson, Pres.

60518 ■ Greenville-Muhlenberg County Chamber of Commerce
200 Court St.
PO Box 313
Greenville, KY 42345
Ph:(270)338-5422
Fax: (270)338-5440
Co. E-mail: gchamber@muhlon.com
Contact: Dorothy Walker, Exec.Sec.

60519 ■ Hancock County Chamber of Commerce
PO Box 404
Hawesville, KY 42348
Ph:(270)927-8223
Fax: (270)927-8223
Co. E-mail: erice@hancockcounty-ky.com
URL: http://www.hancockcounty-ky.com/coc/index. html
Contact: Edna Rice, Exec.Dir.

60520 ■ Hart County Chamber of Commerce
PO Box 688
Munfordville, KY 42765
Ph:(270)524-2892
Fax: (270)524-1127
Co. E-mail: hart_co@scrtc.com
URL: http://www.hartcountyky.org
Contact: Virgina Davis, Exec.Dir.

60521 ■ Hazard-Perry County Chamber of Commerce
229 Argil Ct.
Hazard, KY 41701
Ph:(606)439-2659
Fax: (606)436-6074
URL: http://www.cityofhazard.com
Contact: Mr. Tony Whitaker, Pres.

60522 ■ Henderson - Henderson County Chamber of Commerce
201 N Main St.
Henderson, KY 42420
Ph:(270)826-9531
Fax: (270)827-4461
Co. E-mail: info@hendersonchamber.org
URL: http://www.hendersonky.com
Contact: George H. Warren, Pres.

60523 ■ Henry County Chamber of Commerce
PO Box 355
137 S Main
New Castle, KY 40050
Ph:(502)845-0806
Fax: (502)845-5313
Co. E-mail: henrychamber@insightbb.com
URL: http://www.henrycountyky.com
Contact: Ms. Pat Wallace, Exec.Dir.

60524 ■ Hickman Chamber of Commerce
808 Moscow Ave.
PO Box 166
Hickman, KY 42050
Ph:(270)236-2902
Co. E-mail: hickmanchamber@mygalaxyexpress. com
URL: http://www.hickmankychamber.org
Contact: Velva Yarbro, Exec.Dir.

60525 ■ Hopkinsville-Christian County Chamber of Commerce
2800 Ft. Campbell Blvd.
Hopkinsville, KY 42240
Ph:(270)885-9096
Free: 800-842-9959
Fax: (270)886-2059
Co. E-mail: chamber@commercecenter.org
URL: http://www.commercecenter.org/chamber
Contact: Betsy Shelton, Pres./CEO

60526 ■ Jackson - Breathitt County Chamber of Commerce
99 Snowden Branch Rd.
Jackson, KY 41339
Ph:(606)666-7183
Contact: Mr. Mark Mullins, Pres.

60527 ■ Jeffersontown Chamber of Commerce
10434 Watterson Trail
Jeffersontown, KY 40299
Ph:(502)267-1674
Fax: (502)267-2070
Co. E-mail: info@jtownchamber.com
URL: http://www.jtownchamber.com
Contact: Vicky Weber, Pres.

60528 ■ Jessamine County Chamber of Commerce
508 N Main St.
Nicholasville, KY 40356
Ph:(859)887-4351
Fax: (859)887-1211
Co. E-mail: jessaminechamber@aol.com
URL: http://www.jessaminechamber.com
Contact: Nancy Stone, Exec. Dir.

60529 ■ Kentucky Chamber of Commerce
464 Chenault Rd.
Frankfort, KY 40601
Ph:(502)695-4700
Fax: (502)695-6824
Co. E-mail: info@kychamber.com
URL: http://www.kychamber.com
Contact: Dave Adkisson, Pres./CEO

60530 ■ Knox County Chamber of Commerce
196 Daniel Boone Dr., Ste. 205
Barbourville, KY 40906
Ph:(606)546-4300
Fax: (606)546-4300
Co. E-mail: chamber@barbourville.com
URL: http://www.knoxcochamber.com
Contact: Janet Jones, Sec./Office Mgr.

60531 ■ LaRue County Chamber of Commerce
60 Lincoln Sq.
PO Box 176
Hodgenville, KY 42748-0176
Ph:(270)358-3411
Fax: (270)358-3411
Co. E-mail: info@laruecountychamber.org
URL: http://www.laruecountychamber.org
Contact: Robin Terry, Exec.Dir.

60532 ■ Lebanon-Marion County Chamber of Commerce
239 N Spalding Ave., Ste. 201
Lebanon, KY 40033-1518
Ph:(270)692-9594
Fax: (270)692-2661
Co. E-mail: chamber@hamdays.com
URL: http://www.hamdays.com
Contact: Steve Downs, Pres.

60533 ■ Letcher County Chamber of Commerce
PO Box 127
Whitesburg, KY 41858-0127
Ph:(606)633-0310
Contact: Tracy Fraizer Jr., Exec.Dir.

60534 ■ Liberty-Casey County Chamber of Commerce
PO Box 278
Liberty, KY 42539-0278
Ph:(606)787-6463
Fax: (606)787-9835
Co. E-mail: libcas1@alltel.net
Contact: Linda K. Gosser, Exec.Dir.

60535 ■ Lincoln County Chamber of Commerce
201 E Main St., No. 5
Stanford, KY 40484
Ph:(606)365-4118
Fax: (606)365-4118
Co. E-mail: director@lincolncountychamber.com
URL: http://www.lincolncountychamber.com
Contact: Mrs. Andrea E. Miller, Exec. Dir.

60536 ■ Logan County Chamber of Commerce
116 S Main St.
Russellville, KY 42276
Ph:(270)726-2206
Fax: (270)726-2237
Co. E-mail: logancounty@logantele.com
URL: http://www.loganchamber.com
Contact: Lisa Browning, Exec. Dir.

60537 ■ London-Laurel County Chamber of Commerce
529 S Main St.
London, KY 40741
Ph:(606)864-4789
Fax: (606)864-7300
Co. E-mail: bengefarm@alltel.net
URL: http://www.londonlaurelchamber.com
Contact: Randy L. Smith, Exec.Dir.

60538 ■ Madisonville-Hopkins County Chamber of Commerce
15 E Center St.
Madisonville, KY 42431
Ph:(270)821-3435
Fax: (270)821-9190
Co. E-mail: c.commerce@charter.net
URL: http://www.hopkinschamber.com
Contact: Frank Williams, Chm.

60539 ■ Marshall County Chamber of Commerce
17 U.S. Hwy. 68 W
Benton, KY 42025
Ph:(270)527-7665
Co. E-mail: info@marshallcounty.net
URL: http://www.marshallcounty.net
Contact: William J. Butler, Pres./CEO

60540 ■ Mayfield-Graves County Chamber of Commerce
201 E College St.
Mayfield, KY 42066
Ph:(270)247-6101
Fax: (270)247-6110
Co. E-mail: chamber@mayfieldchamber.com
URL: http://www.mayfieldchamber.com
Contact: Donna Davenport, Exec.Dir.

60541 ■ Maysville-Mason County Area Chamber of Commerce
15 W 2nd St.
Maysville, KY 41056
Ph:(606)564-5534
Free: 888-875-MAYS
Fax: (606)564-5535
Co. E-mail: chamber@maysvilleky.net
URL: http://www.maysvillekentucky.com
Contact: John D. Carpenter, Exec. Dir.

60542 ■ McCreary County Chamber of Commerce
PO Box 548
Whitley City, KY 42653-0548
Ph:(606)376-5004
Co. E-mail: chamber7@highland.net
URL: http://mccrearychamber.com
Contact: Tim Duncan, Pres.

60543 ■ McLean County Chamber of Commerce
170 E 2nd
PO Box 303
Calhoun, KY 42327
Ph:(270)273-9760
Fax: (270)273-9760
Co. E-mail: chamfond@owensboro.net
Contact: Mr. Charles Mann Jr., Pres.

60544 ■ Meade County Area Chamber of Commerce
PO Box 483
Brandenburg, KY 40108
Ph:(270)422-3626
Fax: (270)422-1389
Co. E-mail: chamber@bbtel.com
URL: http://www.meadekychamber.org

Contact: Russ Powell, Exec.Dir.

60545 ■ Mercer County Chamber of Commerce
104 W Poplar St.
Harrodsburg, KY 40330
Ph:(859)734-2365
Fax: (859)734-2067
Co. E-mail: info@mercerchamber.com
URL: http://www.mercerchamber.com
Contact: Brenda Sexton, Exec.Dir.

60546 ■ Middletown Chamber of Commerce
12556 Shelbyville Rd.
PO Box 13259
Middletown, KY 40253
Ph:(502)244-8086
Fax: (502)244-0185
Co. E-mail: judy@middletownchamber.com
URL: http://www.middletownchamber.com
Contact: Judy Francis, Pres./CEO

60547 ■ Monticello/Wayne County Chamber of Commerce
PO Box 566
157 S Main St.
Monticello, KY 42633
Ph:(606)348-3064
Co. E-mail: info@monticellokychamber.com
URL: http://www.monticellokychamber.com
Contact: Penny Thompson, Admin.Asst.

60548 ■ Morehead-Rowan County Chamber of Commerce
150 E 1st St.
Morehead, KY 40351
Ph:(606)784-6221
Free: 800-654-1944
Fax: (606)783-1373
Co. E-mail: tcwilliams@moreheadchamber.com
URL: http://www.moreheadchamber.com
Contact: Tracy C. Williams, Exec.Dir.

60549 ■ Morganfield Chamber of Commerce
PO Box 66
Morganfield, KY 42437
Ph:(270)389-3396
Co. E-mail: bgreenw2@bellsouth.net
URL: http://www.morganfieldchamber.org
Contact: Becky Greenwell, Sec.

60550 ■ Morgantown-Butler County Chamber of Commerce
PO Box 408
Morgantown, KY 42261
Ph:(270)526-6827
Co. E-mail: butlerco@logantele.com
URL: http://www.morgantownbutlerco.com
Contact: Lisa Marie Fields, Sec.

60551 ■ Mount Sterling-Montgomery County Chamber of Commerce
126 W Main St.
Mount Sterling, KY 40353
Ph:(859)498-5343
Fax: (859)498-3947
Co. E-mail: contact@mtsterlingchamber.com
URL: http://www.mtsterlingchamber.com
Contact: Mike Beverly, Pres.

60552 ■ Murray-Calloway County Chamber of Commerce
805 N 12th St.
PO Box 190
Murray, KY 42071-0190
Ph:(270)753-5171
Free: 800-900-5171
Fax: (270)753-0948
Co. E-mail: chamber@murray-ky.net
URL: http://www.mymurray.com

60553 ■ Northern Kentucky Chamber of Commerce
PO Box 17416
300 Buttermilk Pike, Ste. 330
Fort Mitchell, KY 41017-0416
Ph:(859)578-8800

Fax: (859)578-8802
Co. E-mail: info@nkychamber.com
URL: http://www.nkychamber.com
Contact: Gary L. Toebben CCE, Pres.

60554 ■ Ohio County Chamber of Commerce
PO Box 3
Hartford, KY 42347-0003
Ph:(270)298-3551
Fax: (270)298-3331
URL: http://www.ohiocounty.com
Contact: David Lanham, Pres.

60555 ■ Oldham County Chamber of Commerce
PO Box 366
La Grange, KY 40031-0366
Ph:(502)222-1635
Fax: (502)222-3159
Co. E-mail: connie@oldhamcountychamber.com
URL: http://www.oldhamcountychamber.com
Contact: Joseph Schoenbaechler, Pres./CEO

60556 ■ Owensboro-Daviess County Chamber of Commerce
200 E 3rd St.
PO Box 825
Owensboro, KY 42302-0825
Ph:(270)926-1860
Fax: (270)926-3364
Co. E-mail: chamber@owensboro.com
URL: http://www.owensboro.com
Contact: Jody Wassmer, Pres.

60557 ■ Owingsville-Bath County Chamber of Commerce
PO Box 360
Owingsville, KY 40360
Ph:(606)674-2531
Co. E-mail: info@owingsville.com
URL: http://www.owingsville.com
Contact: Mike Ray, Pres.

60558 ■ Paducah Area Chamber of Commerce
PO Box 810
Paducah, KY 42002-0810
Ph:(270)443-1746
Fax: (270)442-9152
Co. E-mail: info@paducahchamber.org
URL: http://www.paducahchamber.org
Contact: Elaine Spalding, Pres.

60559 ■ Paintsville - Johnson County Chamber of Commerce
304 Main St.
PO Box 629
Paintsville, KY 41240
Ph:(606)789-5688
Fax: (606)789-3396
Co. E-mail: tourpvil@foothills.net
Contact: R. T. Daniel, Exec.Dir.

60560 ■ Paris-Bourbon County Chamber of Commerce
525 High St., Ste. 114
Paris, KY 40361
Ph:(859)987-3205
Free: 888-987-3205
Fax: (859)987-4640
Co. E-mail: paboch@adelphia.net
URL: http://www.parisky.com
Contact: Lucy Cooper, Exec. Dir.

60561 ■ Pendleton County Chamber of Commerce
230 Main St.
Falmouth, KY 41040
Ph:(859)654-4189
Co. E-mail: pclore@pccoc.org
URL: http://www.pccoc.org
Contact: Patrick Clore, Pres.

60562 ■ Pike County Chamber of Commerce
787 Hambley Blvd.
Pikeville, KY 41501
Ph:(606)432-5504

Fax: (606)432-7295
Co. E-mail: info@pikecountychamber.org
URL: http://www.pikecountychamber.org
Contact: Kitty White, Exec. Dir.

60563 ■ Princeton-Caldwell County Chamber of Commerce
110 W Washington St.
PO Box 47
Princeton, KY 42445
Ph:(270)365-5393
Co. E-mail: caldwellchamber@ziggycom.net
URL: http://www.princetonky.com
Contact: Sherry S. Noel, Exec.Sec.

60564 ■ Radcliff-Hardin County Chamber of Commerce
306 N Wilson Rd.
Radcliff, KY 40160
Ph:(270)351-4450
Fax: (270)352-4449
Co. E-mail: jo@radcliffchamber.org
URL: http://www.radcliffchamber.org
Contact: Jo Emary, Exec. Dir.

60565 ■ Richmond Chamber of Commerce
201 E Main St.
Richmond, KY 40475
Ph:(859)623-1720
Fax: (859)623-0839
Co. E-mail: rchamber@richmondchamber.com
URL: http://www.richmondchamber.com
Contact: Robert Rumpke, Exec. Dir.

60566 ■ Russell County Chamber of Commerce
PO Box 64
Russell Springs, KY 42642-0064
Ph:(270)866-4333
Fax: (270)866-4304
Co. E-mail: lake@duo-county.com
URL: http://www.russellcountyky.com
Contact: Portia Flowers Grosser, Exec. Dir.

60567 ■ Scottsville-Allen County Chamber of Commerce
102 Public Sq.
PO Box 416
Scottsville, KY 42164-0416
Ph:(270)237-4782
Fax: (270)237-5498
Co. E-mail: chamber@scottsvilleky.info
URL: http://www.scottsvilleky.info
Contact: Sue Shaver, Exec. Dir.

60568 ■ Sebree Chamber of Commerce
PO Box 326
Sebree, KY 42455
Ph:(270)835-2201
Fax: (270)835-7811
Contact: Jeremy Bradford, Pres.

60569 ■ Shelby County Chamber of Commerce
PO Box 335
Shelbyville, KY 40066-0335
Ph:(502)633-1636
Fax: (502)633-7501
Co. E-mail: info@shelbycountykychamber.com
URL: http://www.shelbycountykychamber.com
Contact: Shelley Goodwin, Exec.Dir.

60570 ■ Somerset-Pulaski County Chamber of Commerce
445 S Hwy. 27, Ste. 301
Somerset, KY 42501
Ph:(606)679-7323
Fax: (606)679-1744
Co. E-mail: info@spcchamber.com
URL: http://www.spcchamber.com
Contact: Jack Keeney, Dir.

60571 ■ Springfield-Washington County Chamber of Commerce
124 W Main St.
Springfield, KY 40069
Ph:(859)336-3810

Fax: (859)336-9410
Co. E-mail: wasngtns@belsouth.net
URL: http://www.washingtoncochamber.com
Contact: Mr. Craig Arnold, Pres.

60572 ■ Sturgis Chamber of Commerce
PO Box 125
Sturgis, KY 42459
Ph:(270)333-9316
Fax: (270)333-9319
Co. E-mail: sturgisrally@bellsouth.net
URL: http://www.littlesturgisrally.net
Contact: Paul Hart, Pres.

60573 ■ Taylorsville - Spencer County Chamber of Commerce
PO Box 555
Taylorsville, KY 40071
Ph:(502)477-8369
Contact: Wesley Martin, Pres.

60574 ■ Tompkinsville - Monroe County Chamber of Commerce
202 N Magnolia St.
Tompkinsville, KY 42167
Ph:(270)487-1314
Fax: (270)487-0975
Co. E-mail: monroemoney@centernetwork.net
URL: http://www.monroecountyky.com
Contact: Barry Burnette, Pres.

60575 ■ Tri-City Chamber of Commerce
506 W Main St.
PO Box J
Cumberland, KY 40823
Ph:(606)589-5812
Fax: (606)589-5812
URL: http://www.kingdomcome.org
Contact: W. Bruce Ayers, Exec. Dir.

60576 ■ West Point Chamber of Commerce
PO Box 33
West Point, KY 40177
Ph:(502)922-4560
Co. E-mail: roszelleh@hotmail.com
Contact: Pat Shambo, Pres.

60577 ■ Winchester-Clark County Chamber of Commerce
2 S Maple St.
Winchester, KY 40391
Ph:(859)744-6420
Fax: (859)744-9229
Co. E-mail: chamber@winchesterky.com
URL: http://www.winchesterky.com
Contact: Charmagne Castle, Pres.

60578 ■ Woodford County Chamber of Commerce
141 N Main St.
Versailles, KY 40383
Ph:(859)873-5122
Fax: (859)873-4576
Co. E-mail: woodford@woodfordchamber-ky.com
URL: http://www.woodfordchamber-ky.com
Contact: David Cordell, Exec. Dir.

MINORITY BUSINESS ASSISTANCE PROGRAMS

60579 ■ Kentucky Cabinet for Economic Development–Community Development Department–Small and Minority Business Division (300 W)
300 W Broadway
Frankfort, KY 40601
Ph:(502)564-7140
Fax: (502)564-9758
URL: http://www.thinkkentucky.com
Description: Coordinates minority enterprise activities throughout the state's administrative structure. Acts as an advocate. Mobilizes resources and information. Develops marketing resources and provides individual guidance. Also administers a public-sector purchasing assistance program.

FINANCING AND LOAN PROGRAMS

60580 ■ Chrysalis Ventures
101 S. Fifth St., Ste., 1650
Louisville, KY 40202
Ph:(502)583-7644
Fax: (502)583-7648
URL: http://www.chrysalisventures.com
Contact: David Jones, Chairman and Managing Director
Preferred Investment Size: $1,000,000 to $9,000,000. **Investment Types:** First and second stage, early and later stage, and expansion. **Industry Preferences:** Internet specific, medical and health, computer software and services, other products, communications and media, consumer related, biotechnology, and industrial and energy. **Geographic Preferences:** Southeast, Mid Atlantic, and Midwest.

60581 ■ Humana Venture Capital
500 W. Main St.
Louisville, KY 40202
Ph:(502)580-3665
Fax: (502)580-2051
Co. E-mail: gemont@humana.com
Contact: Thomas Liston, Managing Director
Preferred Investment Size: $1,000,000 to $10,000,000. **Investment Types:** Balanced. **Industry Preferences:** Medical and health, Internet specific, biotechnology, computer software and services, computer hardware, and other products. **Geographic Preferences:** U.S.

60582 ■ Iceberg Ventures
124 N. 1st St.
Louisville, KY 40202
Ph:(502)583-6810
Fax: (502)583-6810
URL: http://www.icebergventures.com
Contact: Keith Williams, President and Chief Operating Officer
Investment Policies: Early stage. **Geographic Preferences:** U.S.

60583 ■ K–Kentucky Highlands Investment Corporation
362 Old Whitley Rd.
PO Box 1738
London, KY 40741
Ph:(606)864-5175
Fax: (606)864-5194
URL: http://www.khic.org
Contact: Brenda McDaniel, Chief Financial Officer
Investment Policies: Start-up, second stage, and special situation. **Industry Preferences:** Manufacturing. **Geographic Preferences:** Kentucky.

60584 ■ Kentucky Highlands Investment Corporation
362 Old Whitley Rd.
PO Box 1738
London, KY 40741
Ph:(606)864-5175
Fax: (606)864-5194
URL: http://www.khic.org
Contact: Brenda McDaniel, Chief Financial Officer
Investment Types: Second stage, special situation, and start-up. **Industry Preferences:** Manufacturing. **Geographic Preferences:** Kentucky.

60585 ■ Summit Capital Group
6510 Glenridge Park Pl., Ste. 8
Louisville, KY 40222
Ph:(502)332-2700
URL: http://www.summit-cap.com
Contact: Monica Benton, Managing Director
Preferred Investment Size: $10,000,000 to $40,000,000. **Investment Types:** Control-block purchases, expansion, leveraged and management buyouts. **Industry Preferences:** Computer software and services, communications and media, industrial and energy, biotechnology, consumer related. **Geographic Preferences:** Southeast and Southwest.

PROCUREMENT ASSISTANCE PROGRAMS

60586 ■ Kentucky Procurement Assistance Program
Cabinet for Economic Development
2300 Capital Tower Plaza
500 Mero St.
Frankfort, KY 40601
Ph:(502)564-4252
Free: 800-838-3266
Fax: (502)564-5932
Co. E-mail: debbie.mcknight@ky.gov
URL: http://www.thinkkentucky.com
Contact: Debbie McKnight, Mgr
Description: Helps Kentucky businesses tap the federal procurement market.

60587 ■ Kentucky & Tennessee Procurement Center
600 Dr. MLK Jr. Pl.
Louisville, KY 40202
Ph:(502)582-6662
Fax: (502)582-5547
Co. E-mail: kathleen.hyatt@sba.gov
URL: http://www.sba.gov
Contact: Kathleen Hyatt, PCR
E-mail: kathleen.hyatt@sba.gov
Description: Covers activities for Army Corps of Engineers (Louisville, KY), Fort Knox (Fort Knox, KY), Fort Campbell (Fort Campbell, KY), and Army Corps of Engineers (Nashville, TN).

INCUBATORS/RESEARCH AND TECHNOLOGY PARKS

60588 ■ Morehead State University–Office of Research, Grants and Contracts
Division of Academic Affairs
901 Ginger Hall
Morehead, KY 40351
Ph:(606)783-2010
Fax: (606)783-2130
Co. E-mail: c.morella@morehead-st.edu
URL: http://www.morehead-st.edu/units/research/index.html
Contact: Carole C. Morella, Dir.
E-mail: c.morella@morehead-st.edu
Scope: Teacher education, public policy, regional analysis, adult education, and pre-school education. Also coordinates faculty research of the university, including studies on alcohol investigations, histoplasmosis research, corrections, educational assessment, social and behavioral sciences, and science and mathematics. **Publications:** Annual Report on Proposals Submitted and Funded; MSU Today: Focus Edition of Research and Creative Productions (annually). **Educational Activities:** Conferences (periodically); Special programs, both for University personnel.

60589 ■ Northern Kentucky University Foundation Inc.
Lucas Administrative Ctr., Ste. 221
Nunn Dr.
Highland Heights, KY 41099
Ph:(859)572-5126
Fax: (859)572-6005
Co. E-mail: wmbaker@nku.edu
URL: http://foundation.nku.edu
Contact: W. Michael Baker, Exec.Dir.
E-mail: wmbaker@nku.edu
Scope: Solicits, records, and administers gifts in support of research and educational activities at the University.

60590 ■ University of Louisville–Sponsored Program Development
Belknap Campus
Louisville, KY 40292
Ph:(502)852-6512
Fax: (502)852-8361
Co. E-mail: sponprog@gwise.louisville.edu

Contact: Kim Lalley, Dir.
E-mail: sponprog@gwise.louisville.edu
Scope: Coordinates research grants and contracting for the University in the following schools both on the main campus and at the Health Sciences Center: Medicine; Dentistry; Nursing; Health and Social Services; Arts and Sciences; Engineering; Business and Public Administration; Law; Music; Education; and Graduate Schools. **Publications:** Impact.

EDUCATIONAL PROGRAMS

60591 ■ Bowling Green Community College of Western Kentucky University
2355 Nashville Rd., Ste. B
Bowling Green, KY 42101
Ph:(270)780-2550
Fax: (270)745-2011
URL: http://www.wku.edu/Dept/Academic/BGCC
Description: Two-year college offering a small business management program.

60592 ■ Morehead State University
Small Business Development Center
College of Business
150 E First St.
Morehead, KY 40351
Ph:(606)783-2895
Fax: (606)783-5020
URL: http://www.morehead-st.edu

E-mail: k.moore@morehead-st.edu
Description: Provides training programs that benefit the small business community.

60593 ■ National College of Business and Technology
7627 Ewing Blvd.
Florence, KY 41042
Ph:(859)525-6510

Fax: (859)525-8961
URL: http://www.ncbt.edu
Description: Business college offering a small business management program.

LEGISLATIVE ASSISTANCE

60594 ■ Office of the Governor–Legislative Liaison Office
700 Capitol Ave.
Frankfort, KY 40601
Ph:(502)564-2611
Fax: (502)564-2735
URL: http://www.governor.ky.gov/
Description: Assists the governor in formulating small business policies.

PUBLICATIONS

60595 ■ *Business Bulletin*
464 Chenault Rd.
PO Box 817
Frankfort, KY 40602
Ph:(502)695-4700
Fax: (502)695-6824
Co. E-mail: kccmis.net
URL: http://www.kychamber.com

60596 ■ *Business First*
111 W. Washington St.
P.O. Box 249
Louisville, KY 40202
Ph:(502)583-1731
Fax: (502)587-1703
URL: http://www.ancity.com-louiseville

60597 ■ *Smart Start your Kentucky Business*
PSI Research
300 N. Valley Dr.
Grants Pass, OR 97526

Ph:(503)479-9464
Free: 800-228-2275
Fax: (503)476-1479
Co. E-mail: info@psi-research.com
URL: http://www.psi-research.com
Ed: Michael D. Jenkins. **Released:** Revised edition, 1992. **Price:** $29.95 (looseleaf binder); $24.95 (paper). **Description:** Part of the Successful Business Library series.

PUBLISHERS

60598 ■ Hatfield House Books
7710 Commonwealth Dr.
Crestwood, KY 40014
Ph:(502)241-5950
Contact: Kenneth Hatfield, President
E-mail: kenhat@aol.com
Description: Publishes books for small business owners. Reviews books on business related topics and acts as a literary agent. Reaches market through commission representatives and direct mail. Does not accept unsolicited manuscripts. **Founded:** 1984.

60599 ■ Kentucky Cabinet for Economic Development–Small & Minority Business Div.
Old Capitol Annex, 300 W Broadway
Frankfort, KY 40601
Ph:(502)564-7140
Free: 800-626-2930
Fax: (502)564-3256
Co. E-mail: econdev@ky.gov
URL: http://www.thinkkentucky.com
Contact: Marvin E. Strong Jr., Secretary
E-mail: Gene.Strong@ky.gov
Description: Publishes on Kentucky-based small, minority and women-owned businesses. **Founded:** 1972.

Louisiana

SMALL BUSINESS DEVELOPMENT CENTER LEAD OFFICE

60600 ■ Louisiana SBDC–University of Louisiana at Monroe
College of Business Administration
700 University Ave.
Monroe, LA 71209
Ph:(318)342-5506
Fax: (318)342-5510
URL: http://www.lsbdc.org
Contact: Mary Lynn Wilkerson, State Dir.
E-mail: wilkerson@ulm.edu

SCORE OFFICES

60601 ■ SCORE Baton Rouge
c/o Hillar Moore, Jr., Chm.
564 Laurel St.
PO Box 3217
Baton Rouge, LA 70801
Ph:(225)381-7130
Fax: (225)336-4306
Co. E-mail: scorebr@juno.com
Contact: Hillar Moore Jr., Chm.

60602 ■ SCORE Central Louisiana
PO Box 992
Alexandria, LA 71309
Ph:(318)442-6671
Fax: (318)442-6734
URL: http://www.cenlachamber.org
Contact: Elton Pody, Exec.VP

60603 ■ SCORE, Chapter 44
c/o John Coles, Chm.
U.S. Small Business Administration
365 Canal St., Ste. 2820
New Orleans, LA 70130
Ph:(504)589-2356
Fax: (504)589-2339
Co. E-mail: admin@scorenola.org
Contact: John Coles, Chm.
Description: Free counseling and mentoring for people starting a small business or those already in business.

60604 ■ SCORE Lafayette
Lafayette Job Ctr.
706 E Vermillion St.
Lafayette, LA 70501
Ph:(337)262-5533
Fax: (337)262-5520
Co. E-mail: score_lafayette@prodigy.net
Description: Provides public service to America by offering small business advice and training.

60605 ■ SCORE Lake Charles
c/o Jeff Davis Bank
1535 Kirby St.
Lake Charles, LA 70601

Ph:(337)480-1199
URL: http://www.score.org

60606 ■ SCORE Northeast Louisiana
1810 Auburn Ave., Ste. 102
Monroe, LA 71201
Ph:(318)323-0878
Fax: (318)323-9492
Co. E-mail: smilesviv@bellsouth.net
Contact: Miles K. Luke, Chm.
Description: Serves as volunteer program in which working and retired business management professionals provide free business counseling to men and women who are considering starting a small business, encountering problems with their business, or expanding their business. Offers free one-on-one counseling, online counseling and low cost workshops on a variety of business topics.

60607 ■ SCORE Northshore
c/o Eunice Paddio-Johnson, CHR
2 West Thomas
Hammond, LA 70401
Ph:(985)345-4457
Fax: (985)345-4749
URL: http://www.score.org

60608 ■ SCORE Shreveport
400 Edwards St.
Shreveport, LA 71101
Ph:(318)677-2536
Fax: (318)677-2548
Co. E-mail: terridyer@shreveportchamber.org
Description: Provides professional guidance and information to America's small businesses.

BETTER BUSINESS BUREAUS

60609 ■ Better Business Bureau of Acadiana
4007 W Congress St., Ste. B
Lafayette, LA 70506
Ph:(337)981-3497
Fax: (337)981-7559
Co. E-mail: info@acadiana.bbb.org
URL: http://www.lafayette.bbb.org
Contact: Sharane A. Gott, Pres./CEO

60610 ■ Better Business Bureau of Central Louisiana
5220-C Rue Verdun
Alexandria, LA 71303
Ph:(318)473-4494
Free: 800-372-4222
Fax: (318)473-8906
Co. E-mail: info@alexandria-la.bbb.org
URL: http://www.alexandria-la.bbb.org
Contact: Mrs. Teeter Pate, Exec. Dir.

60611 ■ Better Business Bureau of Northeast Louisiana
212 Walnut St., Ste. 210
Monroe, LA 71201-7345

Ph:(318)361-0461
Fax: (318)361-0461
Co. E-mail: info@bbbnela.org
URL: http://www.bbbnela.org
Contact: Amy Lawson, Pres.

60612 ■ Better Business Bureau, Shreveport
401 Edwards St., Ste. 135
Shreveport, LA 71101
Ph:(318)222-7575
Free: 800-372-4222
Fax: (318)222-7576
Co. E-mail: info@shreveport.bbb.org
URL: http://www.shreveport.bbb.org
Contact: Denise Swenson, Office Mgr./Operations Dir.

60613 ■ Better Business Bureau of South Central Louisiana
748 Main St.
Baton Rouge, LA 70802
Ph:(225)346-5222
Fax: (225)346-1029
Co. E-mail: info@batonrouge.bbb.org
URL: http://www.batonrouge.bbb.org
Contact: James E. Stalls Jr., Pres./CEO

60614 ■ Better Business Bureau of Southwest Louisiana
2309 E Prien Lake Rd.
PO Box 7314
Lake Charles, LA 70605
Ph:(337)478-6253
Free: 800-542-7085
Fax: (337)474-8981
Co. E-mail: swlabbb@cox-internet.com
URL: http://www.lakecharles.bbb.org
Contact: Mrs. Carmen Million, Pres./CEO

CHAMBERS OF COMMERCE

60615 ■ Amite Chamber of Commerce
101 SE Central Ave.
Amite, LA 70422
Ph:(985)748-5537
Fax: (985)748-5537
Contact: Larry Reid, Pres.

60616 ■ Ascension Chamber of Commerce
1006 W Hwy. 30
PO Box 1204
Gonzales, LA 70707-1204
Ph:(225)647-7487
Fax: (225)647-5124
Co. E-mail: info@ascensionchamber.com
URL: http://www.ascensionchamber.com
Contact: Sherrie Despino, Pres.

60617 ■ Assumption Area Chamber of Commerce
PO Box 718
4751 Hwy. 1
Napoleonville, LA 70390
Ph:(985)369-2816

Fax: (985)369-2811
Co. E-mail: assumption@charter.net
URL: http://www.assumptionchamber.org
Contact: Ella Metrejean, Exec.Dir.

60618 ■ Baker Chamber of Commerce
3439 Groom Rd.
Baker, LA 70714
Ph:(225)775-3547
Fax: (225)775-8060
Co. E-mail: bakerchamber@yahoo.com
URL: http://www.baker-chamber.com
Contact: Sherri Cobb, Exec.Dir.

60619 ■ Bogalusa Chamber of Commerce
608 Willis Ave.
Bogalusa, LA 70427-3002
Ph:(985)735-5731
Fax: (985)735-6707
Co. E-mail: bogalusachamber@bellsouth.net
URL: http://www.bogalusachamber.cc
Contact: Marilyn G. Bateman, Exec. Dir.

60620 ■ Bossier Chamber of Commerce
710 Benton Rd.
Bossier City, LA 71111-3797
Ph:(318)746-0252
Fax: (318)746-0357
Co. E-mail: info@bossierchamber.com
URL: http://www.bossierchamber.com
Contact: Wanda Bennett, Pres.

60621 ■ Breaux Bridge Area Chamber of Commerce
134 E Bridge St.
PO Box 88
Breaux Bridge, LA 70517
Ph:(337)332-5406
Fax: (337)332-5424
Co. E-mail: bbcc@centurytel.net
URL: http://www.breauxbridgelive.com
Contact: Jennifer P. Angelle, Exec. Dir.

60622 ■ Bunkie Chamber of Commerce
110 NW Main St.
PO Box 70
Bunkie, LA 71322-0070
Ph:(318)346-2575
Fax: (318)346-2576
Co. E-mail: bunkiechamber@kricket.net
Contact: Phyllis O'Quin, Dir.

60623 ■ Central Louisiana Chamber of Commerce
PO Box 992
Alexandria, LA 71309
Ph:(318)442-6671
Fax: (318)442-6734
Co. E-mail: eltonpody@cenlachamber.org
URL: http://www.cenlachamber.org
Contact: Elton Pody, Pres.

60624 ■ Chamber of Commerce of Lafourche and the Bayou Region
107 W 26th St.
PO Box 1462
LaRose, LA 70373
Ph:(985)693-6700
Fax: (985)693-6702
Co. E-mail: lafchamber@lafourchechamber.com
URL: http://www.lafourchechamber.com
Contact: Lin Kiger, Pres./CEO

60625 ■ Chamber - Southwest Louisiana
PO Box 3110
120 W Pujo St.
Lake Charles, LA 70602-3110
Ph:(337)433-3632
Fax: (337)436-3727
Co. E-mail: mail@chamberswla.org
URL: http://www.chamberswla.org
Contact: Donna Addkison, Pres./CEO

60626 ■ Church Point Area Chamber of Commerce
216 N Main St.
Church Point, LA 70525

Ph:(337)684-3030
Fax: (337)684-3802
Co. E-mail: cpcityhall@aol.com
Contact: Tammy Richard, Exec.Dir.

60627 ■ Claiborne Chamber of Commerce
519 S Main St.
Homer, LA 71040
Ph:(318)927-3271
Fax: (318)927-3271
URL: http://www.claiborneone.org/homer/coc/index.
  html
Contact: Mr. John Watson, Exec. Dir.

60628 ■ Clairborne Chamber of Commerce
519 S Main St.
Homer, LA 71040
Ph:(318)927-3271
Co. E-mail: claibornecoc@claiborneone.org
URL: http://www.claiborneone.org/homer/coc/index1.
  html
Contact: John Watson, Exec.Dir.

60629 ■ Coushatta-Red River Chamber of Commerce
PO Box 333
Coushatta, LA 71019
Ph:(318)932-3289
Fax: (318)932-6919
Co. E-mail: redriverchamber@bellsouth.net
URL: http://www.chamber.coushatta.net
Contact: Marsha Loftin, Exec. Dir.

60630 ■ Crowley Chamber of Commerce
114 E 1st St.
PO Box 2125
Crowley, LA 70527-2125
Ph:(337)788-0177
Fax: (337)783-9507
Co. E-mail: crowleychamber@aol.com
URL: http://www.crowleychamber-la.org
Contact: Sarah Hebert, CEO & Pres.

60631 ■ Desoto Parish Chamber of Commerce
101 N Washington
PO Box 928
Mansfield, LA 71052
Ph:(318)872-1310
Fax: (318)871-1875
Co. E-mail: desotoc@wnonline.net
Contact: Mr. James R. May, Interim Dir.

60632 ■ Donaldsonville Area Chamber of Commerce
714 Railroad Ave.
PO Box 646
Donaldsonville, LA 70346
Ph:(225)473-4814
Fax: (225)473-4817
Co. E-mail: dvillecoc@bellsouth.net
URL: http://www.donaldsonvillecoc.org
Contact: Becky Katz, Exec. Dir.

60633 ■ Eunice Chamber of Commerce
200 S CC Duson
PO Box 508
Eunice, LA 70535
Ph:(337)457-2565
Fax: (337)546-0278
URL: http://www.eunicechamber.com
Contact: Betty A. Pousson, Admin. Asst.

60634 ■ Feliciana Chamber of Commerce
PO Box 667
Jackson, LA 70748
Ph:(225)634-7155
Fax: (225)634-7155
Co. E-mail: tourism1@bellsouth.net
URL: http://www.felicianatourism.org
Contact: Audrey Faciane, Exec. Dir.

60635 ■ Greater Abbeville-Vermilion Chamber of Commerce
1907 Veterans Memorial Dr.
Abbeville, LA 70510
Ph:(337)893-2491

Fax: (337)893-1807
Co. E-mail: abbevillechamber@abbevillechamber.
  com
URL: http://www.abbevillechamber.com
Contact: Rebecca V. Shirley, Exec. VP

60636 ■ Greater Baton Rouge Chamber of Commerce
564 Laurel St.
PO Box 3217
Baton Rouge, LA 70821-3217
Ph:(225)381-7125
Fax: (225)336-4306
Co. E-mail: info@brchamber.org
URL: http://www.brchamber.org
Contact: Stephen Moret, Pres. and CEO

60637 ■ Greater Beauregard Area Chamber of Commerce
111 N Washington Ave.
PO Box 309
DeRidder, LA 70634
Ph:(337)463-5533
Fax: (337)463-2244
Co. E-mail: deridder@wnonline.net
Contact: Frances Jouban, Exec.VP

60638 ■ Greater Denham Springs Chamber of Commerce
PO Box 591
Denham Springs, LA 70727-0591
Ph:(225)665-8155
Fax: (225)665-2411
Co. E-mail: info@dschamber.org
URL: http://www.dschamber.org
Contact: Ms. Sonya Allen, Pres.

60639 ■ Greater Iberia Chamber of Commerce
111 W Main St.
New Iberia, LA 70560
Ph:(337)364-1836
Fax: (337)367-7405
Co. E-mail: chamber@mail.msis.net
URL: http://www.iberia.org
Contact: Mary Ellen Wilke, Pres./CEO

60640 ■ Greater Jennings Chamber of Commerce
246 N Main St.
PO Box 1209
Jennings, LA 70546
Ph:(337)824-0933
Fax: (337)824-0934
Co. E-mail: info@jdbusinessalliance.com
URL: http://www.jenningschamber.com
Contact: Cynthia Hoffpauir, Pres./CEO

60641 ■ Greater Lafayette Chamber of Commerce
804 E Saint Mary Blvd.
PO Box 51307
Lafayette, LA 70503-1307
Ph:(337)233-2705
Fax: (337)234-8671
Co. E-mail: rob@lafchamber.org
URL: http://www.lafchamber.org
Contact: Robert M. Guidry, Pres./CEO

60642 ■ Greater Pointe Coupee Chamber of Commerce
PO Box 555
New Roads, LA 70760
Ph:(225)638-3500
Fax: (225)638-9858
Co. E-mail: gpcchamber@yahoo.com
URL: http://www.pcchamber.org
Contact: Fran Bartee, Pres.

60643 ■ Greater St. Francisville Chamber of Commerce
U.S. Hwy. 61 and River Bend Power Station Dr.
PO Box 545
St. Francisville, LA 70775-0545
Ph:(225)635-6717
Fax: (225)635-6885
Co. E-mail: wfcd@bsf.net

Contact: Mary Ann Bilowich, Bus.Coor.

60644 ■ Greater Shreveport Chamber of Commerce
400 Edwards St.
Shreveport, LA 71101
Ph:(318)677-2500
Free: 800-448-5432
Fax: (318)677-2541
Co. E-mail: info@shreveportchamber.org
URL: http://www.shreveportchamber.org
Contact: Mr. Dick Bremer, Pres.

60645 ■ Greater Slidell Area Chamber of Commerce
118 W Hall Ave.
Slidell, LA 70460-2633
Ph:(985)643-5678
Free: 800-471-3758
Fax: (985)649-2460
Co. E-mail: info@slidellchamber.com
URL: http://www.slidellchamber.com
Contact: Jay Hebert, Exec.Dir.

60646 ■ Greater Vernon Chamber of Commerce
PO Box 1228
Leesville, LA 71496-1228
Ph:(337)238-0349
Free: 877-234-0349
Fax: (337)238-0340
Co. E-mail: chamber@chambervernonparish.com
URL: http://www.chambervernonparish.com
Contact: Eddie Wise, Exec. Dir.

60647 ■ Hammond Chamber of Commerce
400 NW Railroad Ave.
PO Box 1455
Hammond, LA 70401
Ph:(985)345-4457
Fax: (985)345-4749
Co. E-mail: chamber@i-55.com
URL: http://www.hammondchamber.net
Contact: Guy Recotta Jr., Chm.

60648 ■ Houma-Terrebonne Chamber of Commerce
6133 Hwy. 311
Houma, LA 70360-6664
Ph:(985)876-5600
Fax: (985)876-5611
Co. E-mail: info@houmachamber.com
URL: http://www.houmachamber.com
Contact: Kandy Theriot, Pres./CEO

60649 ■ Iberville Chamber of Commerce
23675 Church St.
PO Box 248
Plaquemine, LA 70764
Ph:(225)687-3560
Fax: (225)687-3575
Co. E-mail: hankgrace@premier.net
URL: http://www.ibervillechamber.com
Contact: Hank Grace, Exec.Dir.

60650 ■ Jackson Parish Chamber of Commerce
102 4th St.
PO Box 220
Jonesboro, LA 71251
Ph:(318)259-4693
Fax: (318)259-5039
Contact: Nancy Zuber, Dir.

60651 ■ Jeanerette Chamber of Commerce
500 E Main St.
PO Box 31
Jeanerette, LA 70544
Ph:(337)276-4293
Fax: (337)276-5911
Co. E-mail: sugarcity@msis.net
Contact: Peggy Parker, Exec.Dir.

60652 ■ Jefferson Chamber of Commerce
3421 N Causeway Blvd., Ste. 203
Metairie, LA 70002
Ph:(504)835-3880

Fax: (504)835-3828
Co. E-mail: info@jeffersonchamber.org
URL: http://www.jeffersonchamber.org
Contact: Angelle LaBorde IOM, Pres./CEO

60653 ■ Kaplan Area Chamber of Commerce
701 N Cushing Ave.
Kaplan, LA 70548
Ph:(337)643-2400
Fax: (337)643-8811
Contact: Jackie Faulk, Exec. Dir.

60654 ■ Kentwood Chamber of Commerce
PO Box 685
Kentwood, LA 70444
Ph:(985)229-4656
Fax: (985)230-0841
Co. E-mail: sreed@i-55.com
URL: http://www.kentwoodla.org
Contact: Beryl Billiot, Pres.

60655 ■ Logansport Chamber of Commerce
PO Box 320
Logansport, LA 71049
Ph:(318)697-0076
Fax: (318)697-0076
Contact: Edith Williams, Treas.

60656 ■ Marksville Chamber of Commerce
PO Box 767
Marksville, LA 71351
Ph:(318)253-9222
Fax: (318)253-0457
URL: http://www.marksvillechamberofcommerce.
   com
Contact: Eleanor Gremillion, Sec.-Treas.

60657 ■ Minden/South Webster Chamber of Commerce
110 Sibley Rd.
PO Box 819
Minden, LA 71058-0819
Ph:(318)377-4240
Free: 800-264-6336
Fax: (318)377-4215
Co. E-mail: suegruber@minden.org
URL: http://www.minden.org
Contact: Sue Gruber, Pres.

60658 ■ Monroe Chamber of Commerce
212 Walnut St., Ste. 100
Monroe, LA 71201-6707
Ph:(318)323-3461
Fax: (318)322-7594
Co. E-mail: chamber@monroe.org
URL: http://www.monroe.org
Contact: Sue Edmunds, Pres./CEO

60659 ■ Natchitoches Area Chamber of Commerce
550 2nd St.
PO Box 3
Natchitoches, LA 71457
Ph:(318)352-6894
Fax: (318)352-5385
Co. E-mail: chamber@natchitoches.net
URL: http://www.natchitocheschamber.com
Contact: Nick Pollacia Jr., Pres.

60660 ■ Oakdale Area Chamber of Commerce
205 S 10th St.
PO Box 1138
Oakdale, LA 71463
Ph:(318)335-1729
Fax: (318)215-1729
Co. E-mail: oakdale@wnonline.net
Contact: Brenda Fontenot, Ofc.Mgr.

60661 ■ Oberlin Chamber of Commerce
PO Box 237
Oberlin, LA 70655-0237
Ph:(337)639-2288
Fax: (337)639-2702
Contact: Abbey Musselwhite, VP

60662 ■ Opelousas-St. Landry Chamber of Commerce
109 W Vine St.
Opelousas, LA 70570
Ph:(337)942-2683
Fax: (337)942-2684
Co. E-mail: opelousaschamber@charter.net
URL: http://www.opelousaschamber.org
Contact: Ms. Frankie Bertrand, Pres./CEO

60663 ■ Ponchatoula Chamber of Commerce
109 W Pine St.
PO Box 306
Ponchatoula, LA 70454
Ph:(985)386-2533
Co. E-mail: info@ponchatoulachamber.com
URL: http://www.ponchatoulachamber.com
Contact: Cheri Viola, Pres.

60664 ■ Rayne Chamber of Commerce
PO Box 383
Rayne, LA 70578
Ph:(337)334-2332
Fax: (337)334-8341
Co. E-mail: raynechamber@earthlink.net
URL: http://www.rayne.org/chamber.html
Contact: Debbie Foreman, Dir.

60665 ■ Ruston - Lincoln Chamber of Commerce
PO Box 1383
Ruston, LA 71273-1383
Ph:(318)255-2031
Fax: (318)255-3481
Co. E-mail: mail@rustonlincoln.org
URL: http://www.rustonlincoln.org
Contact: Andy Halbrook, Pres.

60666 ■ Sabine Parish Chamber of Commerce
1601 Texas Hwy.
Many, LA 71449
Ph:(318)256-5880
Fax: (318)256-4137
Co. E-mail: chamber@sabineparish.com
URL: http://www.sabineparish.com
Contact: Bill Adams, Pres.

60667 ■ St. Martinville Chamber of Commerce
PO Box 436
St. Martinville, LA 70582
Ph:(337)394-7578
Fax: (337)394-4497
URL: http://stmartinparish-la.org/
   chamberofcommerce.htm
Contact: Marian Melancon, Exec. Dir.

60668 ■ St. Mary Chamber of Commerce
7332 Hwy. 90 E
PO Box 2606
Morgan City, LA 70381
Ph:(985)384-3830
Fax: (985)384-0771
Co. E-mail: chamber@petronet.net
Contact: Emile Babin, Pres./CEO

60669 ■ St. Tammany West Chamber of Commerce
610 Hollycrest Blvd.
Covington, LA 70433
Ph:(985)892-3216
Fax: (985)893-4244
Co. E-mail: info@sttammanychamber.org
URL: http://www.sttammanychamber.org
Contact: Lacey Toledano, Pres./CEO

60670 ■ Springhill - North Webster Chamber of Commerce
400 N Giles St.
Springhill, LA 71075
Ph:(318)539-4717
Fax: (318)539-2500
Co. E-mail: tstewart@springhilllouisiana.com
URL: http://www.springhilllouisiana.com
Contact: Dianne Stephens, Pres.

60671 ■ Thibodaux Chamber of Commerce
318 E Bayou Rd.
Thibodaux, LA 70301
Ph:(985)446-1187
Fax: (985)446-1191
Co. E-mail: info@thibodauxchamber.com
URL: http://www.thibodauxchamber.com
Contact: Kathy Terracina, Pres./CEO

60672 ■ Union Parish Chamber of Commerce
PO Box 67
Farmerville, LA 71241
Ph:(318)368-3947
Fax: (318)368-3945
Co. E-mail: upcoc@bayou.com
URL: http://unionparishchamber.org
Contact: Rhonda Aulds, Administrator

60673 ■ Vidalia Chamber of Commerce
2003 Billy Deal Ln.
Vidalia, LA 71373
Ph:(318)336-8223
Co. E-mail: vidaliachamber@telepak.net
URL: http://www.vidaliala.com
Contact: Kathy Nunnery, Dir.

60674 ■ Ville Platte Chamber of Commerce
PO Box 331
Ville Platte, LA 70586
Ph:(337)363-1878
Fax: (337)363-1894
Co. E-mail: vpcoc@asbank.com
Contact: Becky Buller, Exec.VP

60675 ■ Welsh Chamber of Commerce
PO Box 786
Welsh, LA 70591
Ph:(337)734-2231
Contact: Shirley Berken, Pres.

60676 ■ West Baton Rouge Chamber of Commerce
PO Box 72
Port Allen, LA 70767-0072
Ph:(225)383-3140
Fax: (225)343-1389
Co. E-mail: wbrcc@wbrchamber.org
URL: http://www.wbrchamber.org
Contact: Larry Durbin, Exec.Dir.

60677 ■ West Carroll Chamber of Commerce
PO Box 1336
Oak Grove, LA 71263
Ph:(318)428-4700
Fax: (318)428-4421
Contact: Charlotte Hamilton, Pres.

60678 ■ West Monroe-West Ouachita Chamber of Commerce
112 Professional Dr.
PO Box 427
West Monroe, LA 71294-0427
Ph:(318)325-1961
Fax: (318)325-4296
Co. E-mail: info@westmonroechamber.org
URL: http://www.westmonroechamber.org
Contact: MaryAnn Newton, Pres.

60679 ■ Winn Chamber of Commerce
PO Box 565
Winnfield, LA 71483-0565
Ph:(318)628-4461
Fax: (318)628-2551
Co. E-mail: info@winnchamberofcommerce.com
URL: http://www.winnchamberofcommerce.com
Contact: Dorothy Skains, Sec.

60680 ■ Winnsboro - Franklin Parish Chamber of Commerce
3830 Front St.
PO Box 1574
Winnsboro, LA 71295
Ph:(318)435-4488

Co. E-mail: info@winnsborochamber.com
URL: http://www.winnsborochamber.com
Contact: Richard Mahoney, Pres.

60681 ■ Zachary Chamber of Commerce
4633 Main St.
Zachary, LA 70791
Ph:(225)654-6777
Fax: (225)654-3957
Co. E-mail: lrioux@zacharyla.com
Contact: Lisa V. Rioux, Exec. Dir.

PUBLICATIONS

60682 ■ *Smart Start your Connecticut Business*
PSI Research
300 N. Valley Dr.
Grants Pass, OR 97526
Ph:(503)479-9464
Free: 800-228-2275
Fax: (503)476-1479
Co. E-mail: info@psi-research.com
URL: http://www.psi-research.com
Ed: Michael D. Jenkins. **Released:** Revised edition, 1992. **Price:** $29.95 (looseleaf binder); $24.95 (paper). **Description:** Part of the Successful Business Library series.

PUBLISHERS

60683 ■ Trost Publishing
400 Poydras St., Ste. 1850
New Orleans, LA 70130
Ph:(504)680-6754
URL: http://www.trostpublishing.com
Contact: Katherine Moody
Description: Publishes nonfiction books on business and economics. **Founded:** 2004

SMALL BUSINESS DEVELOPMENT CENTER LEAD OFFICE

60684 ■ University of Southern Maine–Maine SBDC State Office
96 Falmouth St.
PO Box 9300
Portland, ME 04103-9300
Ph:(207)780-4420
Fax: (207)780-4810
Co. E-mail: mainesbdc@usm.maine.edu
URL: http://www.mainesbdc.org
Contact: John Massaua, State Dir.
E-mail: jrmassaua@maine.edu

60685 ■ University of Southern Maine–Small Business Development Center
96 Falmouth St.
PO Box 9300
Portland, ME 04103
Ph:(207)780-4420
Fax: (207)780-4810
Contact: John Massaua, State Director
E-mail: jrmassaua@maine.edu

SMALL BUSINESS DEVELOPMENT CENTERS

60686 ■ Androscoggin Valley Council of Governments–Small Business Development Center
125 Manley Rd.
Auburn, ME 04210-3600
Ph:(207)783-9186
Fax: (207)783-5211
URL: http://www.mainesbdc.org
Contact: Bob Kasputes
E-mail: bkasputes@avcog.org

60687 ■ Coastal Enterprises Inc. (CEI)–Maine SBDC
Weston Bldg.
7 N. Chestnut St.
Augusta, ME 04330-5012
Ph:(207)621-0245
Fax: (207)622-9739
URL: http://www.mainesbdc.org
Contact: Brad Swanson, Counselor
E-mail: wbs@ceimaine.org

60688 ■ Eastern Maine Development Corp. –Maine SBDC Service Center at Bangor
40 Harlow St.
Bangor, ME 04401
Ph:(207)942-1744
Free: 800-339-6389
Fax: (207)942-3548
Co. E-mail: info@emdc.org
URL: http://www.mainesbdc.org
Contact: Steve Richard

E-mail: srichard@emdc.org

60689 ■ Main SBDC Outreach Office at Limestone–ATDC Agriculture–Maine's Applied Technology Development Centers (191 D)
191 Development Dr.
Limestone, ME 04750-6114
Ph:(207)498-8736
URL: http://www.mainesbdc.org
Contact: Rod Thompson, Center Dir.
E-mail: rthompson@nmdc.org

60690 ■ Maine SBCD Service Center at Midcoast East–Coastal Enterprises, Inc.
Water St.
PO Box 268
Wiscasset, ME 04578-0268
Ph:(207)882-4340
Fax: (207)882-4456
URL: http://www.mainesbdc.org
Contact: David Hill, Counselor
E-mail: dhill@ceimaine.org

60691 ■ Maine SBDC Outreach Office at Belfast–Hutchinson Center
80 Belmont Ave.
Belfast, ME 04915-7350
Ph:(207)882-4340
Fax: (207)882-4456
URL: http://www.mainesbdc.org
Contact: David Hill, Center Dir.
E-mail: drhill@ceimaine.org

60692 ■ Maine SBDC Outreach Office at Bingham–Municipal Bldg., Town of Bingham
13 Murray St.
PO Box 652
Bingham, ME 04920-0652
Ph:(207)453-4258
Fax: (207)453-4264
URL: http://www.mainesbdc.org
Contact: Ted Wirth, Counselor
E-mail: trw@ceimanie.org

60693 ■ Maine SBDC Outreach Office at Bridgton–Greater Bridgton Lakes Region Chamber of Commerce
Portland Rd.
Bridgton, ME 04009-1256
Ph:(207)647-3472
URL: http://www.mainesbdc.org
Contact: Bob Kasputes, Counselor
E-mail: bkasputes@avcog.org

60694 ■ Maine SBDC Outreach Office at Bucksport–Bucksport Town Hall
264 Maine St.
Bucksport, ME 04614
Ph:(207)664-2990
Fax: (207)667-3416
URL: http://www.mainesbdc.org
Contact: Steve Richard, Counselor
E-mail: srichard@emdc.org

60695 ■ Maine SBDC Outreach Office at Calais–Washington County Community College
1 College Dr.
Calais, ME 04619-4046
Ph:(207)255-8811
Fax: (207)667-3416
URL: http://www.mainesbdc.org
Contact: Steve Richard
E-mail: srichard@emdc.org

60696 ■ Maine SBDC Outreach Office at Dover-Foxcroft–Penquis Higher Education Center
50 Mayo St.
Dover-Foxcroft, ME 04226-1231
Ph:(207)942-1744
Free: 800-339-6389
Fax: (207)942-3548
URL: http://www.mainesbdc.org
Contact: Steve Richard, Counselor
E-mail: srichard@emdc.org

60697 ■ Maine SBDC Outreach Office at Fort Kent–Aroostock County Registry of Deeds
22 Hall St., Ste. 201
Fort Kent, ME 04743-1126
Ph:(207)498-8736
Free: 800-427-8736
Fax: (207)493-3108
URL: http://www.mainesbdc.org
Contact: David Spooner, Counselor
E-mail: dspooner@nmdc.org

60698 ■ Maine SBDC Outreach Office at Houlton–Ward Log Homes Executive Suites
Superior Court House
Court St.
Houlton, ME 04730
Ph:(207)498-8736
Fax: (207)498-3108

60699 ■ Maine SBDC Outreach Office at Rumford–ATD Manufacturing
Applied Technology Development Centers
60 Lowell St.
PO Box 559
Rumford, ME 04276-2048
Ph:(207)783-9186
Fax: (207)783-5211
URL: http://www.mainesbdc.org
Contact: Bob Kasputes, Counselor
E-mail: bkasputes@avcog.org

60700 ■ Maine SBDC Outreach Office at Saco–Biddeford-Saco Area Economic Development–SBDC (190 M)
190 Main St., 3rd Fl.
Saco, ME 04072
Ph:(207)282-1748
Fax: (207)282-9574
URL: http://www.mainesbdc.org
Contact: Gordon Platt, Counselor
E-mail: gplatt@usm.maine.edu

60701 ■ Maine SBDC Outreach Office at Skowhegan–University of Maine Cooperative Extension
Norridgewock Ave.
Skowhegan, ME 04976-9734
Ph:(207)453-4258
Fax: (207)453-4264
URL: http://www.mainesbdc.org
Contact: Ted Wirth, Counselor
E-mail: trw@ceimaine.org

60702 ■ Maine SBDC Outreach Office at South Paris–Oxford Hills Chamber of Commerce
213 Main St.
South Paris, ME 04281-1629
Ph:(207)743-5297
Fax: (207)783-5211
URL: http://www.mainesbdc.org
Contact: Bob Kasputes, Center Dir.
E-mail: bkasputes@avcog.org

60703 ■ Maine SBDC Outreach Office at Wilton–Career Center
865 U.S. Rte. 2E
Wilton, ME 04294-6649
Ph:(207)645-5824
Fax: (207)783-5211
URL: http://www.mainesbdc.org
Contact: Gregory Gould, Counselor
E-mail: ggould@avcog.org

60704 ■ Maine SBDC Outreach Office at York–York Chamber of Commerce–SBDC (1 Sto)
1 Stonewall Ln.
York, ME 03909-1662
Ph:(207)363-4422
Fax: (207)324-2958
URL: http://www.mainesbdc.org
Contact: Gordon Platt, Counselor
E-mail: gplatt@usm.maine.edu

60705 ■ Maine SBDC Service Center at Bangor–Eastern Maine Development Corp. (EMDC)
40 Harlow St.
Bangor, ME 04401
Ph:(207)942-1744
Free: 800-339-6389
Fax: (207)942-3548
URL: http://www.mainesbdc.org
Contact: Steve Richard, Counselor
E-mail: srichard@emdc.org

60706 ■ Maine SBDC Service Center at Ellsworth
125 High St.
Ellsworth, ME 04605-1711
Ph:(207)664-2990
Fax: (207)667-3416
URL: http://www.mainesbdc.org
Contact: Steve Richard, Counselor
E-mail: srichard@emdc.org

60707 ■ Maine SBDC Service Center at Fairfield–CEI at Kennebec Valley Council of Governments
17 Main St.
Fairfield, ME 04937-1119
Ph:(207)453-4258
Fax: (207)453-4264
URL: http://www.mainesbdc.org
Contact: Ted Wirth, Counselor
E-mail: trw@ceimaine.org

60708 ■ Maine SBDC Service Center at Gardiner–Maine Technology Institute
405 Water St., Ste. 300
Gardiner, ME 04345-2104
Ph:(207)582-4790
Fax: (207)582-4772
URL: http://www.mainesbdc.org
Contact: Meriby Sweet, Counselor
E-mail: meriby@usm.maine.edu

60709 ■ Maine SBDC Service Center at Machias–Sunrise County Economic Council–SBDC (1 Sta)
1 Stackpole Rd.
Machias, ME 04654-0679
Ph:(207)255-8811
Fax: (207)677-3416
URL: http://www.mainesbdc.org
Contact: Steve Richard, Counselor
E-mail: srichard@emdc.org

60710 ■ Maine SBDC Service Center at Midcoast-West–CEI at MidCoast Council for Business Development and Planning
7 Park St.
Bath, ME 04530-2828
Ph:(207)443-5790
Fax: (207)443-8675
URL: http://www.mainesbcd.org
Contact: Jim Burbank, Counselor
E-mail: jburbank@gwi.net

60711 ■ Maine SBDC Service Center at Portland–University of Southern Maine
68 High St., 2nd Fl.
PO Box 9300
Portland, ME 04104-9300
Ph:(207)780-4949
Fax: (207)780-4810
URL: http://www.mainesbdc.org
Contact: Brian Burwell, Counselor
E-mail: burwell@usm.maine.edu

60712 ■ Maine SBDC Service Center at Sanford/Springvale–Southern Maine Regional Planning Commission
21 Bradeen St., Ste. 304
Springvale, ME 04083-1925
Ph:(207)324-0316
Fax: (207)324-2958
URL: http://www.mainesbdc.org
Contact: Gordon Platt, Counselor
E-mail: gplatt@usm.maine.edu

60713 ■ Northern Maine Development Commission–Maine SBDC Service Center at Caribou
11 W. Presque Isle
PO Box 779
Caribou, ME 04736-0779
Ph:(207)498-8736
Free: 800-427-8736
Fax: (207)498-3108
URL: http://www.mainesbdc.org
Contact: Rod Thompson, Counselor
E-mail: rthompson@nmdc.org

60714 ■ Rockland Satellite–SBDC
331 Main St.
KeyBank of Maine
Rockland, ME 04841-3303
Ph:(207)882-4340
Fax: (207)882-4456
URL: http://www.mainesbdc.org
Contact: Tyrell Russell, Technical Asst.
E-mail: tar@ceimaine.org

60715 ■ Southern Maine Regional Planning Commission–Small Business Development Center
21 Bradeen St., Ste. 304
Springvale, ME 04083
Ph:(207)324-2952
URL: http://www.mainesbdc.org/hosts.cfm

60716 ■ Thomas College–Waterville Satellite–SBDC (Admin)
Administrative Bldg. - Library
180 W. River Rd.
Waterville, ME 04901
Ph:(207)859-1111
Fax: (207)859-1114
Co. E-mail: postmaster@thomas.edu
URL: http://www.thomas.edu

SMALL BUSINESS ASSISTANCE PROGRAMS

60717 ■ Maine Department of Economic and Community Development
State House Sta. 59
Augusta, ME 04333
Ph:(207)624-9804
Fax: (207)287-5701
Co. E-mail: biz.growth@state.me.us
URL: http://www.econdevmaine.com
Description: Provides business planning, financing, information, and networking assistance to existing Maine businesses that need financing for expansion purposes. Utilizes programs offered through the Maine WEET and JTPA offices. Assists in identifying funding sources, including federal, state, and private. Also runs the Job Opportunity Zone Program which focuses attention on four designated depressed areas.

60718 ■ Maine Department of Economic and Community Development–Office of Business Development
State House Sta. 59
Augusta, ME 04333
Ph:(207)624-9804
Fax: (207)287-5701
Co. E-mail: biz.growth@state.me.us
URL: http://www.econdevmaine.com
Description: Encourages investment in new Maine businesses and provides technical assistance to businesses in labor training, financing, site selection, and state licenses, and permits. Includes Maine Products Marketing Program which promotes regional and national awareness of Maine's products.

60719 ■ Maine Development Foundation
45 Memorial Cir., Ste. 302
Augusta, ME 04333
Ph:(207)622-6345
Fax: (207)622-6346
Co. E-mail: mdf@mdf.org
URL: http://www.mdf.org
Description: Nonprofit corporation that assists Maine businesses. Services include coordination of joint public-private projects; research and long-range planning for future economic development; and economic education.

60720 ■ Maine International Trade Center
511 Congress St., Ste. 100
Portland, ME 04101-3428
Ph:(207)541-7400
Fax: (207)541-7420
Co. E-mail: info@mitc.com
URL: http://www.mitc.com
Contact: Ashleigh Arledge, Prgm Mgr
Description: A private, nonprofit organization offering extensive export services to Maine businesses. Also includes a library of information on world trade.

SCORE OFFICES

60721 ■ SCORE Augusta
68 Sewall St., Rm. 512
Augusta, ME 04330
Ph:(207)622-8509
Co. E-mail: score305@gwi.net
URL: http://www.scoremaine.org
Description: Provides entrepreneur education and the formation, growth and success of small business nationwide. Provides free counseling and low-cost workshops.

60722 ■ SCORE Bangor
354 Hogan Rd.
Bangor, ME 04401
Ph:(207)825-3819
Description: Provides public service by offering small business advice and training.

60723 ■ SCORE Central and Northern Aroostock
24 Sweden St., Ste. 101
Caribou, ME 04736
Ph:(207)492-8010
Co. E-mail: cci@cariboumaine.net
Contact: Wendy Landes, Business Developer

60724 ■ SCORE Lewiston-Auburn
Career Center
5 Mollison Way
Lewiston, ME 04240-7764
Ph:(207)782-3708
Fax: (207)783-7745
Co. E-mail: contact@lascore.org
URL: http://www.lascore.org
Contact: R. Tuttle, Chm.
Description: Serves as volunteer program in which working and retired business management professionals provide free business counseling to men and women who are considering starting a small business, encountering problems with their business, or expanding their business. Offers free one-on-one counseling, online counseling and low cost workshops on a variety of business topics.

60725 ■ SCORE Maine Coastal
Mill Mall
248 State St.
Ellsworth, ME 04605-5352
Ph:(207)667-5800
Fax: (207)667-8367
Co. E-mail: scoredowneastmaine@verizon.net
Contact: Ann Anda, Chair
Description: Offers free, confidential business counseling and advice for regional small business owners, in association with the U.S. Small Business Administration.

60726 ■ SCORE Oxford Hills
2 Market Sq.
South Paris, ME 04281
Ph:(207)743-0499
Co. E-mail: oxscore@prexar.com
URL: http://www.scoremaine.org
Description: Serves as volunteer program in which working and retired business management professionals provide free business counseling to men and women who are considering starting a small business, encountering problems with their business, or expanding their business. Offers free one-on-one counseling, online counseling and low cost workshops on a variety of business topics.

60727 ■ SCORE Portland
East Tower, 2nd Fl.
100 Middle St.
Portland, ME 04101
Ph:(207)772-1147
Fax: (207)772-5581
Co. E-mail: score@score53.org
URL: http://www.score53.org

60728 ■ SCORE Western Mountains
c/o Oxford Federal Credit Union
PO Box 252
255 River St.
Mexico, ME 04257-0252
Ph:(207)369-9976
Co. E-mail: lkimball@megalink.net
URL: http://www.scoremaine.org
Description: Serves as volunteer program in which working and retired business management professionals provide free business counseling to men and women who are considering starting a small business, encountering problems with their business, or expanding their business. Offers free one-on-one counseling, online counseling and low cost workshops on a variety of business topics.

CHAMBERS OF COMMERCE

60729 ■ Androscoggin County Chamber of Commerce
179 Lisbon St.
PO Box 59
Lewiston, ME 04243-0059
Ph:(207)783-2249
Fax: (207)783-4481
Co. E-mail: info@androscoggincounty.com
URL: http://www.androscoggincounty.com
Contact: Charles Morrison, Pres.

60730 ■ Bangor Regional Chamber of Commerce
519 Main St.
PO Box 1443
Bangor, ME 04401
Ph:(207)947-0307
Fax: (207)990-1427
Co. E-mail: chamber@bangorregion.com
URL: http://www.bangorregion.com
Contact: Candace Guerette, Pres./CEO

60731 ■ Bar Harbor Chamber of Commerce
PO Box 158
Bar Harbor, ME 04609
Ph:(207)288-5103
Free: 800-288-5103
Fax: (207)288-2565
Co. E-mail: visitors@barharborinfo.com
URL: http://www.barharbormaine.com
Contact: Clare Bingham, CEO

60732 ■ Belfast Area Chamber of Commerce
PO Box 58
Belfast, ME 04915
Ph:(207)338-5900
Fax: (207)338-3808
Co. E-mail: info@belfastmaine.org
URL: http://www.belfastmaine.org
Contact: Jayne Crosby-Giles, Pres.

60733 ■ Bethel Area Chamber of Commerce
Bethel Train Sta.
8 Station Pl.
PO Box 1247
Bethel, ME 04217-1247
Ph:(207)824-2282
Free: 800-442-5826
Fax: (207)824-7123
Co. E-mail: info@bethelmaine.com
URL: http://www.bethelmaine.com
Contact: Ms. Robin Zinchuk, Exec. Dir.

60734 ■ Biddeford-Saco Chamber of Commerce and Industry
110 Main St., Ste. 1202
Saco, ME 04072
Ph:(207)282-1567
Fax: (207)282-3149
Co. E-mail: info@biddefordsacochamber.org
URL: http://www.biddefordsacochamber.org
Contact: Jeanne Innes, Admin.Asst.

60735 ■ Blue Hill Peninsula Chamber of Commerce
PO Box 520
28 Water St.
Blue Hill, ME 04614
Ph:(207)374-3242
Fax: (207)374-3242
Co. E-mail: chamber@bluehillpeninsula.org
URL: http://www.bluehillpeninsula.org
Contact: Mike Sealander, Pres.

60736 ■ Boothbay Harbor Region Chamber of Commerce
192 Townsend Ave.
PO Box 356
Boothbay Harbor, ME 04538-0356
Ph:(207)633-2353
Fax: (207)633-7448
Co. E-mail: seamaine@boothbayharbor.com
URL: http://www.boothbayharbor.com
Contact: Jaimie A. Kleinstiver, Exec.Dir.

60737 ■ Bucksport Bay Area Chamber of Commerce
PO Box 1880
Bucksport, ME 04416
Ph:(207)469-6818
Fax: (207)469-2054
Co. E-mail: director@bucksportbaychamber.com
URL: http://www.bucksportchamber.org
Contact: Cindy Kimball, Dir.

60738 ■ Caribou Chamber of Commerce and Industry
24 Sweden St., Ste. 101
Caribou, ME 04736-2132
Ph:(207)498-6156
Fax: (207)492-1362
Co. E-mail: info@cariboumaine.net
URL: http://www.cariboumaine.net
Contact: Richard Scott, Exec.Dir.

60739 ■ China Area Chamber of Commerce
PO Box 189
South China, ME 04358
Ph:(207)445-3183
Contact: Marlene Menger, Sec.

60740 ■ Cobscook Bay Area Chamber of Commerce
PO Box 42
Whiting, ME 04691-0042
Ph:(207)733-2201
Co. E-mail: info@cobscookbay.com
URL: http://www.cobscookbay.com
Contact: Michael McCabe, Pres.

60741 ■ Damariscotta Region Chamber of Commerce
PO Box 13
Damariscotta, ME 04543
Ph:(207)563-8340
Fax: (207)563-2690
Co. E-mail: info@damariscottaregion.com
URL: http://www.damariscottaregion.com
Contact: Heather O'Bryan, Exec. Dir.

60742 ■ Deer Isle - Stonington Chamber of Commerce
PO Box 490
Deer Isle, ME 04627
Ph:(207)348-6124
Co. E-mail: deerisle-stoningtonchamber@verizon.net
URL: http://www.deerislemaine.com
Contact: Darwin Davidson

60743 ■ Eastport Area Chamber of Commerce
PO Box 254
Eastport, ME 04631
Ph:(207)853-4644
Co. E-mail: chamber@eastport.net
URL: http://www.eastport.net
Contact: Roland Lavelle, Pres.

60744 ■ Ellsworth Area Chamber of Commerce
163 High St.
PO Box 267
Ellsworth, ME 04605
Ph:(207)667-5584
Fax: (207)667-2617
Co. E-mail: eacc@midmaine.com
URL: http://www.ellsworthchamber.org
Contact: Margaret Sumpter, Exec.Dir.

60745 ■ Fort Fairfield Chamber of Commerce
232 Main St., Ste. 4
PO Box 607
Fort Fairfield, ME 04742
Ph:(207)472-3802
Fax: (207)472-3886
Co. E-mail: fortcc@mfx.net
URL: http://www.fortcc.org
Contact: Michael Eisensmith, Exec. Dir.

60746 ■ Franklin County Chamber of Commerce
575 Wilton Rd.
Farmington, ME 04938
Ph:(207)778-4215
Fax: (207)778-2438
Co. E-mail: info@fwcoc.org
URL: http://www.farmingtonwiltonchamber.org

60747 ■ Freeport Merchants Association
23 Depot St.
PO Box 452
Freeport, ME 04032-0452
Ph:(207)865-1212
Free: 800-865-1994
Co. E-mail: chamber@freeportusa.com
URL: http://www.freeportusa.com
Contact: Dick Collins, Exec.Dir.

60748 ■ Greater Bridgton-Lakes Region Chamber of Commerce
PO Box 236
Bridgton, ME 04009-0236
Ph:(207)647-3472
Co. E-mail: info@mainelakeschamber.com
URL: http://www.mainelakeschamber.com
Contact: Michael McClellan, Exec.Dir.

60749 ■ Greater Fort Kent Area Chamber of Commerce
291 W Main St., Ste. 101
Fort Kent, ME 04743
Ph:(207)834-5354
Free: 800-733-3563
Fax: (207)834-6868
Co. E-mail: info@fortkentchamber.com
URL: http://www.fortkentchamber.com
Contact: Jody Marston, Exec. Dir.

60750 ■ Greater Houlton Chamber of Commerce
109 Main St.
Houlton, ME 04730
Ph:(207)532-4216
Fax: (207)532-4961
Co. E-mail: chamber@greaterhoulton.com
URL: http://www.greaterhoulton.com
Contact: Chris Batby, Administrator

60751 ■ Greater Limestone Chamber of Commerce
291 Main St.
Limestone, ME 04750
Ph:(207)325-4707
Fax: (207)325-3330
Co. E-mail: chamber@limestonemaine.org
Contact: Mrs. Grace O'Neal, Pres.

60752 ■ Greater Madawaska Chamber of Commerce
PO Box 144
Madawaska, ME 04756
Ph:(207)728-7000
Fax: (207)728-4696
Co. E-mail: valleyvisit@pwless.net
URL: http://www.townofmadawaska.com
Contact: Dennis Paul Michaud, Exec. Dir.

60753 ■ Greater Portland Chamber of Commerce
60 Pearl St.
Portland, ME 04101
Ph:(207)772-2811
Fax: (207)772-1179
Co. E-mail: chamber@portlandregion.com
URL: http://www.portlandregion.com
Contact: W. Godfrey Wood, Pres./CEO

60754 ■ Greater Van Buren Chamber of Commerce
51 Main St., Ste. 101
Van Buren, ME 04785
Ph:(207)868-5059
Fax: (207)868-2222
Co. E-mail: vbchamber@pwless.net
URL: http://www.greatervanburenchamber.com
Contact: Ann Roy, Pres.

60755 ■ Katahdin Area Chamber of Commerce
1029 Central St.
Millinocket, ME 04462
Ph:(207)723-4443
Fax: (207)723-4459
Co. E-mail: info@katahdinmaine.com
URL: http://www.katahdinmaine.com

Contact: Brenda Wheaton, Exec.Dir.

60756 ■ Kennebec Valley Chamber of Commerce
PO Box 676
Augusta, ME 04332-0676
Ph:(207)623-4559
Fax: (207)626-9342
Co. E-mail: info@augustamaine.com
URL: http://www.augustamaine.com
Contact: Peter G. Thompson, Pres./CEO

60757 ■ Kennebunk-Kennebunkport Chamber of Commerce
PO Box 740
Kennebunk, ME 04043
Ph:(207)967-0857
Fax: (207)967-2867
Co. E-mail: info@visitthekennebunks.com
URL: http://www.visitthekennebunks.com
Contact: Dick Leeman, Exec. Dir.

60758 ■ Lincoln Lakes Region Chamber of Commerce
PO Box 164
Lincoln, ME 04457
Ph:(207)794-8065
Free: 888-794-8065
Fax: (207)794-8065
Co. E-mail: glacc@midmaine.com
URL: http://www.lincolnmechamber.org
Contact: Cheri Archer, Office Mgr.

60759 ■ Madison - Anson Chamber of Commerce
PO Box 91
Madison, ME 04950
Ph:(207)696-8341
Fax: (207)696-3055
Contact: Joan Black, Pres.

60760 ■ Maine State Chamber of Commerce
7 University Dr.
Augusta, ME 04330
Ph:(207)623-4568
Fax: (207)622-7723
Co. E-mail: pfournier@mainechamber.org
URL: http://www.mainechamber.org
Contact: Patience Fournier, Admin. Asst./Database Mgr.

60761 ■ Mid-Maine Chamber of Commerce
1 Post Office Sq.
PO Box 142
Waterville, ME 04901-6651
Ph:(207)873-3315
Fax: (207)877-0087
Co. E-mail: info@midmainechamber.com
URL: http://www.midmainechamber.com
Contact: Kimberly N. Lindlof, Pres.

60762 ■ Moosehead Lake Region Chamber of Commerce
PO Box 581
Greenville, ME 04441-0581
Ph:(207)695-2702
Free: 888-876-2778
Fax: (207)695-3440
Co. E-mail: info@mooseheadlake.org
URL: http://www.mooseheadlake.org
Contact: Sarah Holman, Exec.Dir.

60763 ■ Mount Desert Chamber of Commerce
PO Box 675
Northeast Harbor, ME 04662-0675
Ph:(207)276-5040
Co. E-mail: info@mountdesertchamber.org
URL: http://www.mountdesertchamber.org
Contact: W. A. Shaw, Pres.

60764 ■ Northern Kathadin Valley Region Chamber of Commerce
PO Box 374
Island Falls, ME 04747
Ph:(207)463-2077
Fax: (207)463-2139

Co. E-mail: nkvrcc@mfx.net
URL: http://www.allmaine.com/nkvrcc
Contact: Heidi Hollis, Pres.

60765 ■ Ogunquit Chamber of Commerce
PO Box 2289
Ogunquit, ME 03907
Ph:(207)646-2939
Fax: (207)641-0856
Co. E-mail: director@ogunquit.org
URL: http://www.ogunquit.org
Contact: Eleanor Vadenais, Exec.Dir.

60766 ■ Old Orchard Beach Chamber of Commerce
PO Box 600
Old Orchard Beach, ME 04064
Ph:(207)934-2500
Fax: (207)934-4994
Co. E-mail: info@oldorchardbeachmaine.com
URL: http://www.oldorchardbeachmaine.com
Contact: James Harmon, Exec. Dir.

60767 ■ Oxford Hills Chamber of Commerce
PO Box 167
4 Western Ave.
South Paris, ME 04281
Ph:(207)743-2281
Fax: (207)743-0687
Co. E-mail: info@oxfordhillsmaine.com
URL: http://www.oxfordhillsmaine.com
Contact: Rich Livingston, Pres./CEO

60768 ■ Penobscot Bay Regional Chamber of Commerce
Harbor Park
PO Box 508
Rockland, ME 04841-0508
Ph:(207)596-0376
Free: 800-562-2529
Fax: (207)596-6549
Co. E-mail: info@therealmaine.com
URL: http://www.therealmaine.com
Contact: Bob Hastings, Exec. Dir./CEO

60769 ■ Presque Isle Area Chamber of Commerce
3 Houlton Rd.
PO Box 672
Presque Isle, ME 04769
Ph:(207)764-6561
Fax: (207)764-6571
Co. E-mail: piacc@mfx.net
URL: http://www.pichamber.com
Contact: Allen Deeves, Exec.Dir.

60770 ■ Rangeley Lakes Region Chamber of Commerce
PO Box 317
Rangeley, ME 04970
Ph:(207)864-5571
Free: 800-MT-LAKES
Fax: (207)864-5366
Co. E-mail: info@rangeleymaine.com
URL: http://www.rangeleymaine.com
Contact: Evelyn McAllister, Exec. Dir.

60771 ■ River Valley Chamber of Commerce
60 Lowell St.
Rumford, ME 04276
Ph:(207)364-3241
Fax: (207)369-0356
Co. E-mail: info@rivervalleychamber.com
URL: http://www.rivervalleychamber.com

60772 ■ Rockport-Camden-Lincolnville Chamber of Commerce
PO Box 919
Camden, ME 04843
Ph:(207)236-4404
Free: 800-223-5459
Fax: (207)236-4315
Co. E-mail: chamber@camdenme.org
URL: http://www.visitcamden.com
Contact: Andy McPherson, Pres.

60773 ■ St. Croix Valley Chamber of Commerce
Downeast Heritage Museum Bldg.
39 Union St.
Calais, ME 04619
Ph:(207)454-2308
Free: 888-422-3112
Fax: (207)454-7979
Co. E-mail: visitstcroixvalley@verizon.net
URL: http://www.visitcalais.com
Contact: Mr. Jim Thompson, Exec. Dir.

60774 ■ Schoodic Peninsula Area Chamber of Commerce
PO Box 381
Winter Harbor, ME 04693
Ph:(207)963-7658
Free: 800-231-3008
Fax: (207)963-7495
Co. E-mail: info@acadia-schoodic.org
URL: http://www.acadia-schoodic.org
Contact: Megan Moshier, Pres.

60775 ■ Sebago Lakes Region Chamber of Commerce
PO Box 1015
Windham, ME 04062
Ph:(207)892-8265
Fax: (207)893-0110
Co. E-mail: info@sebagolakeschamber.com
URL: http://www.sebagolakeschamber.com
Contact: Barbara Clark, Exec.Dir.

60776 ■ Skowhegan Area Chamber of Commerce
23 Commercial St.
Skowhegan, ME 04976
Ph:(207)474-3621
Free: 888-772-4392
Fax: (207)474-3306
Co. E-mail: info@skowheganchamber.com
URL: http://www.skowheganchamber.com
Contact: Michelle Tuttle, Exec. Dir.

60777 ■ Southern Midcoast Maine Chamber
59 Pleasant St.
Brunswick, ME 04011
Ph:(207)725-8797
Free: 877-725-8797
Fax: (207)725-9787
Co. E-mail: chamber@midcoastmaine.com
URL: http://www.midcoastmaine.com
Contact: Catherine Glover, Pres./CEO

60778 ■ Southern Piscataquis County Chamber of Commerce
PO Box 376
Dover Foxcroft, ME 04426
Ph:(207)564-7533
Co. E-mail: dennis@spccc.org
URL: http://www.spccc.org
Contact: Dennis Lyford, Exec.Dir.

60779 ■ Upper Kennebec Valley Chamber of Commerce
PO Box 491
Bingham, ME 04920
Ph:(207)672-4100
Contact: Chet Hibbard, Pres.

60780 ■ Wells Chamber of Commerce
136 Post Rd.
PO Box 356
Wells, ME 04090-0356
Ph:(207)646-2451
Fax: (207)646-8104
Co. E-mail: wellschamber@wellschamber.org
URL: http://www.wellschamber.org
Contact: Sandee Mariner, Exec.Sec.

60781 ■ Yarmouth Chamber of Commerce
162 Main St.
Yarmouth, ME 04096
Ph:(207)846-3984
Fax: (207)846-5419
Co. E-mail: info@yarmouthmaine.org
URL: http://www.yarmouthmaine.org
Contact: Carolyn Schuster, Managing Dir.

60782 ■ York Chamber of Commerce
1 Stonewall Ln.
York, ME 03909
Ph:(207)363-4422
Fax: (207)363-7320
Co. E-mail: info@yorkme.org
URL: http://www.gatewaytomaine.org
Contact: Catherine R. Goodwin, Exec.Dir.

FINANCING AND LOAN PROGRAMS

60783 ■ CEI Ventures, Inc. / CVI
2 Portland Fish Pier, Ste. 201
Portland, ME 04101
Ph:(207)772-5356
Fax: (207)772-5503
URL: http://www.ceiventures.com
Contact: Nathaniel Henshaw, President
Preferred Investment Size: $250,000 to $2,000,000
Investment Types: Balanced. **Geographic Preferences:** Northeast.

60784 ■ Commwealth Bioventures, Inc.
4 Milk St.
Portland, ME 04101
Ph:(207)780-0904
Fax: (207)780-0913
Co. E-mail: cbi4milk@aol.com
Investment Types: Seed. **Industry Preferences:** Biotechnology, medical and health.

60785 ■ North Atlantic Capital Corporation
2 City Ctr., 5th Fl.
Portland, ME 04101
Ph:(207)772-4470
Fax: (207)772-3257
URL: http://www.northatlanticcapital.com
Contact: Kimberly Miles, Chief Financial Officer
Preferred Investment Size: $2,000,000 - $10,000,000. **Investment Types:** Later stage, acquisition, expansion, leveraged buyout, mezzanine, management buyouts, and recapitalizations. **Industry Preferences:** Internet specific, computer hardware, other products, consumer related, industrial and energy, computer software and services, communications and media, medical and health, semiconductors and other electronics, and biotechnology. **Geographic Preferences:** Northeast and Mid Atlantic.

PROCUREMENT ASSISTANCE PROGRAMS

60786 ■ Maine Procurement Technical Assistance Center–Eastern Maine Development Corporation–Market Development Center (40 Ha)
40 Harlow St.
Bangor, ME 04441
Ph:(207)942-6389
Fax: (207)942-3548
Co. E-mail: info@emdc.org
URL: http://www.emdc.org
Contact: Pat Rice, Dir
E-mail: ralexander@emdc.org

60787 ■ US SBA Office of Government Contracting for Maine and New Hampshire
68 Sewall St.
Augusta, ME 4330
Ph:(207)622-8274
Fax: (207)622-8277
Co. E-mail: sean.crean@sba.gov
URL: http://www.sba.gov
Contact: Sean Crean, SBA Representative
E-mail: sean.crean@sba.gov
Description: Covers activities for the VA Hospital (Togus, ME), the Portsmouth Naval Shipyard (Portsmouth, NH), and the Naval Air Station (Brunswick, ME).

INCUBATORS/RESEARCH AND TECHNOLOGY PARKS

60788 ■ University of Maine–Office of the Vice President for Research
5703 Alumni Hall, Rm. 209
Orono, ME 04469-5703
Ph:(207)581-1506
Fax: (207)581-1300
Co. E-mail: lynrrec@maine.edu
URL: http://www.umaine.edu/research/
Contact: Michael Eckardt PhD, VP, Res.
E-mail: lynrrec@maine.edu
Scope: Responsible for research at the university and for administration and coordination of research activities of various departments, colleges, and specialized research units, including extramurally supported projects.

EDUCATIONAL PROGRAMS

60789 ■ University of Maine at Machias
9 O'Brien Ave.
Machias, ME 04654-1397
Ph:(207)255-1200
Free: 888-468-6866
Fax: (207)255-4864
Co. E-mail: ummwebmaster@maine.edu
URL: http://www.umm.maine.edu
Description: Offers programs in small business management.

PUBLICATIONS

60790 ■ *Smart Start your Arizona Business*
PSI Research
300 N. Valley Dr.
Grants Pass, OR 97526
Ph:(503)479-9464
Free: 800-228-2275
Fax: (503)476-1479
Co. E-mail: info@psi-research.com
URL: http://www.psi-research.com
Ed: Michael D. Jenkins. **Released:** Revised edition, 1992. **Price:** $29.95 (looseleaf binder); $24.95 (paper). **Description:** Part of the Successful Business Library series.

PUBLISHERS

60791 ■ Trionics International Inc.
66 Upper Oak Point
Winterport, ME 04496
Fax: (207)848-5649
Co. E-mail: info@trionicsusa.com
URL: http://www.trionicsusa.com
Contact: Bernhoff A. Dahl M.D.
Description: Publishes business books on the design and dynamics of organizations and also includes interactive worksheets on CD-ROM. **Founded:** 1981.

SMALL BUSINESS DEVELOPMENT CENTER LEAD OFFICE

60792 ■ Maryland Small Business Development Center
7100 Baltimore Ave., Ste. 401
College Park, MD 20740-3627
Ph:(301)403-8300
Free: 877-787-SBDC
Fax: (301)403-8303
Contact: Renee C. Sprow, State Dir.
E-mail: rsprow@sbdc.umd.edu

60793 ■ Maryland Small Business Development Center–University of Maryland
7100 Baltimore Ave., Ste. 401
College Park, MD 20740-3627
Ph:(301)403-8300
Free: 877—787-SBDC
Fax: (301)403-8303
URL: http://www.mdsbdc.umd.edu
Contact: Renee Sprow, State Dir.
E-mail: rsprow@sbdc.umd.edu

SMALL BUSINESS DEVELOPMENT CENTERS

60794 ■ Baltimore County Chamber of Commerce–SBDC
102 W. Pennsylvania Ave., Ste. 101
Towson, MD 21204
Ph:(410)832-6200
Fax: (410)821-9901
URL: http://www.baltcountycc.com
Contact: Shuraie L. Mackin, Consultant
E-mail: smackinsbdrc@baltcountycc.com

60795 ■ Carrol County Economic Development Office–SBDC
225 N. Center St., Ste. 101
Westminster, MD 21157
Ph:(410)386-2070
Fax: (410)876-8471
Co. E-mail: info@carrollbiz.org

60796 ■ College of Southern Maryland–Southern Maryland SBDC–SBDC (8730)
8730 Mitchell Rd.
PO Box 910
LaPlata, MD 20646
Ph:(301)934-7583
Free: 800-762-7232
Fax: (301)934-7681
URL: http://www.mdsbdc.umd.edu
Contact: Danita Boonschaisri, Exec. Dir.
E-mail: danitab@csm.cc.md.us

60797 ■ Garrett Community College–Small Business Development Center–Satellite Office (687 M)
687 Mosser Rd.
McHenry, MD 21541
Ph:(301)387-6666
Fax: (301)387-3096
Co. E-mail: sbdc@sbdc-wmd.com
URL: http://www.sbdc.wmd.com
Contact: Sandy Major, Business Analyst

60798 ■ Howard County Center for Business and Technology Development–SBDC Central Region
9250 Bendix Rd., N.
Columbia, MD 21045-1800
Ph:(410)313-6190
Fax: (410)313-7515
URL: http://www.hceda.org
Contact: Anthony Ruiz, Counselor
E-mail: aruiz@towson.edu

60799 ■ Prince George's County Minority Business Opportunities Commission–Suburban Washington Region Small Business Development Center
1400 McCormick Dr., Ste. 281
Largo, MD 20774
Ph:(301)883-6480
Fax: (301)883-6479
URL: http://www.princegeorgescountymd.gov
Contact: Jack B. Johnson, Actg. Exec. Dir.

60800 ■ Salisbury State University–Eastern SBDC
Power Professional Bldg., Ste. 170
Salisbury, MD 21801
Ph:(410)548-4419
Free: 800-999-7232
Fax: (410)548-5389
Co. E-mail: sbdcuser@salisbury.edu
URL: http://www.salisbury.edu/community/sbdc
Contact: Dennis Hebert, Exec.Dir.
E-mail: djhebert@ssu.edu

60801 ■ Towson University–Baltimore County Small Business Development Center
Terrace Dale Office Complex
7801 York Rd.
Towson, MD 21204
Ph:(410)704-5001
Fax: (410)704-5009
URL: http://www.towson.edu
Contact: Leonard R. Lee, Counselor
E-mail: lrlee@towson.edu

60802 ■ Western Maryland Region–Small Business Development
14701 National Hwy, Ste. 1
LaVale, MD 21502
Ph:(301)687-1080
Fax: (301)687-1008
URL: http://www.mdsbdc.umd.edu
Contact: Sam LaManna, Exec.Dir.
E-mail: lamanna@sbdc-wmd.com

SMALL BUSINESS ASSISTANCE PROGRAMS

60803 ■ Maryland Department of Business and Economic Development–Business Development Division
217 E Redwood St.
Baltimore, MD 21202-3316
Ph:(410)767-6300
Free: 800-811-0051
Fax: (410)333-6792
Co. E-mail: jposey@choosemaryland.org
URL: http://www.choosemaryland.org

60804 ■ Maryland Economic Development Corp.
100 N Charles St., Ste. 630
Baltimore, MD 21201
Ph:(410)625-0051
Fax: (410)625-1848
Contact: Robert Brennan, Exec Dir
Description: Develops vacant or under-utilized industrial sites and other facilities and economic resources that would serve the public interest. Assists in the expansion, modernization, and retention of existing Maryland businesses. Provides marketing, financing, and networking information.

SCORE OFFICES

60805 ■ SCORE Frederick County
43A S Market St., Ste. 202
Frederick, MD 21701
Ph:(301)662-8723
Fax: (301)846-4427
Co. E-mail: rich@frederickscore.com
URL: http://www.frederickscore.com

60806 ■ SCORE Greater Baltimore
The City Crescent Bldg., 6th Fl.
10 S Howard St.
Baltimore, MD 21201
Ph:(410)962-2233
Fax: (410)962-1805
Co. E-mail: score.balt@erols.com
URL: http://www.scorebaltimore.org
Contact: Joseph Babinski, Chm.
Description: Serves as volunteer program in which working and retired business management professionals provide free business counseling to men and women who are considering starting a small business, encountering problems with their business, or expanding their business. Offers free one-on-one counseling, online counseling and low cost workshops on a variety of business topics.

60807 ■ SCORE Hagerstown
c/o Bob Poor, Chm.
28 W Washington St., Ste. 200
Hagerstown, MD 21740
Ph:(301)739-2015
Fax: (301)739-1278

Co. E-mail: score@hagerstown.org
URL: http://www.scorehagerstown.org
Contact: Bob Poor, Chm.
Description: Aims to help emerging businesses succeed and stay active in the local and national small business marketplace.

60808 ■ SCORE Salisbury
Salisbury Area Chamber of Commerce Bldg.
144 E Main St.
Salisbury, MD 21801
Ph:(410)749-0185
Fax: (410)860-9925
Co. E-mail: score@salisburyarea.com
URL: http://www.salisburyarea.com/score.htm
Contact: Ed Heath, Chm.
Description: Serves as volunteer program in which working and retired business management professionals provide free business counseling to men and women who are considering starting a small business, encountering problems with their business, or expanding their business. Offers free one-on-one counseling, online counseling and low cost workshops on a variety of business topics.

60809 ■ SCORE Southern Maryland
49 Old Solomons Island Rd., Ste. 204
Annapolis, MD 21401
Ph:(410)266-9553
Fax: (410)573-0981
Co. E-mail: score390@aol.com
Contact: Ms. Mary Aleese Schreiber, Chair
Description: Provides no cost business counseling and workshops on starting and growing small businesses to entrepreneurs and individuals interested to start a small business in Anne Arundel, Calvert, Charles, and St. Mary's Counties in Maryland.

60810 ■ SCORE Upper Shore
c/o Kent City Chamber of Commerce
122 N Cross St.
Chestertown, MD 21620-1547
Ph:(410)810-0021
Co. E-mail: chapter670@easternshorescore.org
URL: http://www.easternshorescore.org/chapter670.
   php
Description: Serves as volunteer program in which working and retired business management professionals provide free business counseling to men and women who are considering starting a small business, encountering problems with their business, or expanding their business. Offers free one-on-one counseling, online counseling and low cost workshops on a variety of business topics.

BETTER BUSINESS BUREAUS

60811 ■ Better Business Bureau of Greater Maryland
1414 Key Hwy., Ste. 100
Baltimore, MD 21230
Ph:(410)347-3990
Fax: (410)347-3936
Co. E-mail: info@bbbmd.org
URL: http://www.baltimore.bbb.org
Contact: David Wilson, Pres./CEO

CHAMBERS OF COMMERCE

60812 ■ Aberdeen Chamber of Commerce
115 N Parke St.
PO Box 292
Aberdeen, MD 21001
Ph:(410)272-2580
Co. E-mail: aberdeen115@comcast.net
URL: http://www.aberdeencc.com
Contact: Janet Emmons, Dir.

60813 ■ Allegany County Chamber of Commerce
Bell Tower Bldg.
24 Frederick St.
Cumberland, MD 21502

Ph:(301)722-2820
Fax: (301)722-5995
Co. E-mail: info@alleganycountychamber.com
URL: http://www.alleganycountychamber.com
Contact: Ms. Barbara G. Buehl, Exec. Dir.

60814 ■ Annapolis and Anne Arundel County Chamber of Commerce
49 Old Solomons Island Rd., Ste. 204
Annapolis, MD 21401
Ph:(410)266-3960
Fax: (410)266-8270
Co. E-mail: info@aaaccc.org
URL: http://www.annapolischamber.com
Contact: Robert W. Burdon, Pres./CEO

60815 ■ Baltimore City Chamber of Commerce
312 N Martin Luther King Jr. Blvd.
Baltimore, MD 21201
Ph:(410)837-7101
Fax: (410)837-7104
Co. E-mail: baltcham@aol.com
URL: http://www.baltimorecitychamber.com
Contact: Francel M. Smith, Chm.

60816 ■ Baltimore County Chamber of Commerce
102 W Pennsylvania Ave., Ste. 101
Towson, MD 21204-4526
Ph:(410)825-6200
Fax: (410)821-9901
Co. E-mail: jhatfield@baltcountycc.com
URL: http://www.baltcountycc.com
Contact: Joan G. Hatfield, Pres./CEO

60817 ■ Baltimore - Washington Corridor Chamber of Commerce
312 Marshall Ave., Ste. 104
Laurel, MD 20707-4824
Ph:(410)792-9714
Fax: (301)725-0776
Co. E-mail: bwcc@baltwashchamber.org
URL: http://www.baltwashchamber.com
Contact: H. Walter Townshend III, Pres./CEO

60818 ■ Calvert County Chamber of Commerce
120 Dares Beach Rd.
PO Box 9
Prince Frederick, MD 20678
Ph:(410)535-2577
Fax: (410)257-3140
Co. E-mail: calvertchamber@calvertchamber.org
URL: http://www.calvertchamber.org
Contact: Carolyn McHugh, Pres./CEO

60819 ■ Caroline County Chamber of Commerce
PO Box 494
Denton, MD 21629-0494
Ph:(410)479-4638
Fax: (410)479-4638
Contact: Robert Clendaniel, Pres.

60820 ■ Carroll County Chamber of Commerce
700 Corporate Center Ct., Ste. L
PO Box 871
Westminster, MD 21158-0871
Ph:(410)848-9050
Fax: (410)876-1023
Co. E-mail: info@carrollcountychamber.org
URL: http://www.carrollcountychamber.org
Contact: Richard Hadda, Pres.

60821 ■ Cecil County Chamber of Commerce
233 E Main St.
PO Box 96
Elkton, MD 21922-0096
Ph:(410)392-3833
Fax: (410)392-6225
Co. E-mail: chamber@cecilchamber.org
URL: http://www.cecilchamber.org
Contact: Tari Moore, Exec.Dir.

60822 ■ Chamber of Commerce of Frederick County
43A S Market St.
Frederick, MD 21701-5524
Ph:(301)662-4164
Fax: (301)846-4427
Co. E-mail: kbusz@frederickchamber.org
URL: http://www.frederickchamber.org
Contact: Kenneth Busz, Pres./CEO

60823 ■ Charles County Chamber of Commerce
101 Centennial Ave., Ste. A
La Plata, MD 20646-4208
Ph:(301)932-6500
Fax: (301)932-3945
Co. E-mail: info@charlescountychamber.org
URL: http://www.charlescountychamber.org
Contact: Sally Jameson, Exec.Dir.

60824 ■ Crisfield Area Chamber of Commerce
PO Box 292
Crisfield, MD 21817-0292
Ph:(410)968-2500
Free: 800-782-3913
Fax: (410)968-0524
Co. E-mail: info@crisfieldchamber.com
URL: http://www.crisfieldchamber.com
Contact: Steve Marshall, Pres.

60825 ■ Dorchester Chamber of Commerce
528 Poplar St.
Cambridge, MD 21613
Ph:(410)228-3575
Fax: (410)228-6848
Co. E-mail: chamber@dorchesterchamber.org
URL: http://www.dorchesterchamber.org
Contact: John Nussear, Exec.Dir.

60826 ■ Elkton Chamber and Alliance
101 E Main St.
Elkton, MD 21921-6109
Ph:(410)398-5076
Fax: (410)398-4971
Co. E-mail: info@elktonalliance.org
URL: http://www.elktonalliance.org
Contact: Ms. Mary Jo Jablonski, Mgr.

60827 ■ Essex - Middle River - White Marsh Chamber of Commerce
435-C Eastern Blvd.
Essex, MD 21221
Ph:(410)686-2233
Fax: (410)687-9081
Co. E-mail: info@emrchamber.org
URL: http://www.emrchamber.org
Contact: Alexander B. Page III, Pres.

60828 ■ Gaithersburg-Germantown Chamber of Commerce
4 Professional Dr., Ste. 132
Gaithersburg, MD 20879-3426
Ph:(301)840-1400
Fax: (301)963-3918
Co. E-mail: info@ggchamber.org
URL: http://www.ggchamber.org
Contact: Marilyn Balcombe PhD, Pres./CEO

60829 ■ Garrett County Chamber of Commerce
15 Visitors Center Dr.
McHenry, MD 21541
Ph:(301)387-4386
Fax: (301)387-2080
Co. E-mail: info@garrettchamber.com
URL: http://www.visitdeepcreek.com
Contact: Charlie Ross, Pres.

60830 ■ Greater Bethesda-Chevy Chase Chamber of Commerce
7910 Woodmont Ave., Ste. 1204
Bethesda, MD 20814-3015
Ph:(301)652-4900
Fax: (301)657-1973
Co. E-mail: staff@bccchamber.org
URL: http://www.bccchamber.org

Contact: Ginanne M. Italiano, Pres.

60831 ■ Greater Bowie Chamber of Commerce
6911 Laurel Bowie Rd., Ste. 302
Bowie, MD 20715
Ph:(301)262-0920
Fax: (301)262-0921
Co. E-mail: info@bowiechamber.org
URL: http://www.bowiechamber.org
Contact: Art Widmann, Pres.

60832 ■ Greater Crofton Chamber of Commerce
PO Box 4146
Crofton, MD 21114-4146
Ph:(410)721-9131
Fax: (410)721-0785
Co. E-mail: coachops@aol.com
URL: http://www.croftonchamber.com
Contact: John Hollywood, Pres.

60833 ■ Greater Severna Park Chamber of Commerce
1 Holly Ave.
Severna Park, MD 21146
Ph:(410)647-3900
Fax: (410)647-3999
Co. E-mail: info@severnaparkchamber.com
URL: http://www.severnaparkchamber.com
Contact: Linda Zahn, Exec.Dir.

60834 ■ Greater Silver Spring Chamber of Commerce
8601 Georgia Ave., Ste. 203
Silver Spring, MD 20910-3458
Ph:(301)565-3777
Fax: (301)565-3377
Co. E-mail: info@gsscc.org
URL: http://www.silverspringchamber.com
Contact: Jane Redicker, Pres.

60835 ■ Hagerstown-Washington County Chamber of Commerce
28 W Washington St., Ste. 200
Hagerstown, MD 21740
Ph:(301)739-2015
Fax: (301)739-1278
Co. E-mail: chamber@hagerstown.org
URL: http://www.hagerstown.org
Contact: Brien J. Poffenberger, Pres./CEO/Sec.

60836 ■ Harford County Chamber of Commerce
108 S Bond St.
Bel Air, MD 21014
Ph:(410)838-2020
Free: 800-682-8536
Fax: (410)893-4715
Co. E-mail: info@harfordchamber.org
URL: http://www.harfordchamber.org
Contact: William B. Seccurro, CEO/Pres.

60837 ■ Havre De Grace Chamber of Commerce
450 Pennington Ave.
Havre De Grace, MD 21078
Ph:(410)939-3303
Fax: (410)939-3490
Co. E-mail: hdegchamber1@comcast.net
URL: http://www.hdgchamber.com
Contact: Cathy L. Vincenti, Exec.Dir.

60838 ■ Howard County Chamber of Commerce
5560 Sterrett Pl., Ste. 105
Columbia, MD 21044-2616
Ph:(410)730-4111
Fax: (410)730-4584
Co. E-mail: info@howardchamber.com
URL: http://www.howardchamber.com
Contact: Pamela J. Klahr CCE, Pres./CEO

60839 ■ Kent County Chamber of Commerce
122 N Cross St.
PO Box 146
Chestertown, MD 21620

Ph:(410)810-2968
Fax: (410)778-1406
Co. E-mail: kentchamber@verizon.net
URL: http://www.kentchamber.org
Contact: Judith Reveal, Exec.Dir.

60840 ■ Maryland Chamber of Commerce
60 West St., Ste. 100
Annapolis, MD 21401
Ph:(410)269-0642
Fax: (410)269-5247
Co. E-mail: ksnyder@mdchamber.org
URL: http://www.mdchamber.org
Contact: Kathleen T. Snyder CCE, Pres./CEO

60841 ■ Montgomery County Chamber of Commerce
51 Monroe St., Ste. 1609
Rockville, MD 20850
Ph:(301)738-0015
Fax: (301)738-8792
Co. E-mail: info@montgomerycountychamber.com
URL: http://www.montgomerycountychamber.com
Contact: Richard N. Parsons, Pres./CEO

60842 ■ North East Chamber of Commerce
PO Box 787
North East, MD 21901
Free: 800-CE-CIL95
Fax: (410)287-2571
Co. E-mail: info@northeastchamber.org
URL: http://www.northeastchamber.org
Contact: Ray Heidel, Pres.

60843 ■ Northern Anne Arundel County Chamber of Commerce
7477 Baltimore-Annapolis Blvd., No. 203
Glen Burnie, MD 21061
Ph:(410)766-8282
Fax: (410)766-5722
Co. E-mail: info@naaccc.com
URL: http://www.naaccc.com
Contact: Ms. Frances Schmidt, Exec. Dir.

60844 ■ Ocean City Chamber of Commerce
12320 Ocean Gateway
Ocean City, MD 21842
Ph:(410)213-0552
Fax: (410)213-7521
Co. E-mail: info@oceancity.org
URL: http://www.oceancity.org
Contact: Dan Balufardi, Exec.Dir.

60845 ■ Ocean Pines Area Chamber of Commerce
11073 Cathell Rd., Unit 202
Ocean Pines, MD 21811-1911
Ph:(410)641-5306
Fax: (410)641-6176
Co. E-mail: info@oceanpineschamber.org
URL: http://www.oceanpineschamber.org
Contact: JoAnn Unger, Exec.Dir.

60846 ■ Olney Chamber of Commerce
PO Box 550
Olney, MD 20830
Ph:(301)924-3555
Fax: (301)774-4944
Co. E-mail: olneycoc@aol.com
URL: http://www.olneymd.org
Contact: Virginia Mauk, Exec.Dir.

60847 ■ Pikesville Chamber of Commerce
7 Church Ln.
Pikesville, MD 21208
Ph:(410)484-2337
Fax: (410)484-4151
Co. E-mail: pikescoc@toad.net
URL: http://www.pikesvillechamber.org
Contact: Eddie Steinberg, Pres.

60848 ■ Pocomoke City Chamber of Commerce
144 Market St.
PO Box 356
Pocomoke City, MD 21851-0356
Ph:(410)957-1919

Fax: (410)957-4784
Co. E-mail: pchamber@ixpres.com
URL: http://www.pocomoke.com
Contact: Carol Johnsen, Sec./Dir.

60849 ■ Poolesville Area Chamber of Commerce
PO Box 256
Poolesville, MD 20837-0256
Ph:(301)349-5753
Fax: (301)349-4701
Co. E-mail: tom.maggie@verizon.net
URL: http://www.pacc.cc
Contact: Maggie Nightingale, Exec.Sec.

60850 ■ Potomac Chamber of Commerce
9812 Falls Rd., Ste. 114, Box 320
Potomac, MD 20854
Ph:(301)299-2170
Fax: (301)299-4650
Co. E-mail: pcc@potomacchamber.org
URL: http://potomacchamber.org
Contact: Ms. Jennifer Matheson, Sec.

60851 ■ Prince George's Chamber of Commerce
4640 Forbes Blvd., Ste. 130
Lanham, MD 20706
Ph:(301)731-5000
Fax: (301)731-5013
Co. E-mail: pgcoc@pgcoc.org
URL: http://www.pgcoc.org
Contact: William Shipp, Chm.

60852 ■ Princess Anne Chamber of Commerce
PO Box 642
Princess Anne, MD 21853-0642
Ph:(410)651-2961
Fax: (410)651-3836
Contact: David Donohoe, Pres.

60853 ■ Queen Anne's County Chamber of Commerce
PO Box 511
Chester, MD 21619-0511
Ph:(410)643-8530
Fax: (410)643-8477
Co. E-mail: business@qacchamber.com
URL: http://www.qacchamber.com
Contact: Linda Friday, Pres.

60854 ■ Reisterstown - Owings Mills - Glyndon Chamber of Commerce
66 Painters Mill Rd.
Owings Mills, MD 21117
Ph:(410)356-2888
Fax: (410)356-5112
Co. E-mail: romg@romgchamber.org
URL: http://www.romgchamber.org
Contact: Brian Ditto, Exec.Dir.

60855 ■ Rockville Chamber of Commerce
255 Rockville Pike, Ste. L-10
Rockville, MD 20850-4165
Ph:(301)424-9300
Fax: (301)762-7599
Co. E-mail: rockville@rockvillechamber.org
URL: http://www.rockvillechamber.org
Contact: Joy E. Young, Exec.Dir.

60856 ■ St. Mary's County Chamber of Commerce
44200 Airport Rd., Ste. B
California, MD 20619
Ph:(301)737-3001
Fax: (301)737-0089
Co. E-mail: info@smcchamber.com
URL: http://www.smcchamber.com
Contact: Willam E. Scarafia, Pres./CEO

60857 ■ Salisbury Area Chamber of Commerce
144 E Main St.
PO Box 510
Salisbury, MD 21801
Ph:(410)749-0144

Fax: (410)860-9925
Co. E-mail: chamber@salisburyarea.com
URL: http://www.salisburyarea.com
Contact: Timothy L. Feist, Pres.

60858 ■ Snow Hill Chamber of Commerce
PO Box 176
Snow Hill, MD 21863
Ph:(410)632-0809
URL: http://www.atbeach.com/cities/snowhill/
snowcomm.asp
Contact: Tammy Simpson, Pres.

60859 ■ West Anne Arundel County Chamber of Commerce
8379 Piney Orchard Pkwy., Ste. E
Odenton, MD 21113-1531
Ph:(410)672-3422
Fax: (410)672-3475
Co. E-mail: info@waaccc.org
URL: http://www.waaccc.org
Contact: Ms. Bridget Boardman, Exec.Dir.

FINANCING AND LOAN PROGRAMS

60860 ■ Abell Venture Fund
111 S. Calvert St., Ste. 2300
Baltimore, MD 21202
Ph:(410)547-1300
Fax: (410)539-6579
URL: http://www.abellventurefund.com
Preferred Investment Size: $100,000 to $3,000,000. **Investment Policies:** Early stage and expansion. **Industry Preferences:** Internet specific, semiconductors and other electronics, communications and media, computer software and services, and medical and health. **Geographic Preferences:** Mid Atlantic.

60861 ■ ABS Ventures
1 South St.
Baltimore, MD 21202
Ph:(410)895-3895
Fax: (410)895-3899
URL: http://www.absventures.com
Contact: Scott Yaphe, Principal
Preferred Investment Size: $3,000,000 to $15,000,000. **Investment Policies:** Later stage, fund of funds, and expansion. **Industry Preferences:** Computer software and services, medical and health, communications and media, Internet specific, computer hardware, biotechnology, other products, industrial and energy, consumer related, semiconductors and other electronics. **Geographic Preferences:** U.S.

60862 ■ Annapolis Ventures LLC
151 West St., Ste. 302
Annapolis, MD 21401
Ph:(443)482-9555
Fax: (443)482-9565
URL: http://www.annapolisventures.com
Contact: Douglas Hickman, President
Preferred Investment Size: $2,000,000 to $5,000,000. **Investment Types:** Later stage. **Industry Preferences:** Communications and media, computer software, Internet specific, biotechnology, medical and health, consumer related, financial services, and business service. **Geographic Preferences:** Midwest, Northeast, and Southeast.

60863 ■ Anthem Capital Management
The Mangels Bldg.
1414 Key Hwy., Ste. 300
Baltimore, MD 21230
Ph:(410)625-1510
Fax: (410)625-1735
URL: http://www.anthemcapital.com
Contact: William Gust, Managing Partner
Preferred Investment Size: $1,000,000 to $5,000,000. **Investment Types:** Seed, early and first stage. **Industry Preferences:** Computer software and services, Internet specific, biotechnology, industrial and energy, medical and health, communications and media, and other products. **Geographic Preferences:** Mid Atlantic.

60864 ■ Beacon Venture Capital
4550 Montgomery Ave., Ste. 302 N.
Bethesda, MD 20814
Ph:(301)664-5600
Fax: (301)664-5615
Co. E-mail: bvc@beaconventurecapital.com
URL: http://www.beaconventurecapital.com
Contact: John Groth, Managing Director
Preferred Investment Size: $500,000 to $20,000,000. **Investment Policies:** Early and later stage, and balanced. **Industry Preferences:** Communications and media, computer software, semiconductors and other electronics, biotechnology, medical and health, and financial services.

60865 ■ Boulder Ventures, Ltd.
4750 Owings Mills Blvd.
Owings Mills, MD 21117
Ph:(410)998-3114
Fax: (410)356-5492
URL: http://www.boulderventures.com
Contact: Andy Jones, General Partner
Preferred Investment Size: $2,000,000 to $5,000,000. **Investment Types:** Start-up, first and second stage. **Industry Preferences:** Communications and media, Internet specific, computer software and services, consumer related, semiconductors and other electronics, other products, consumer related, biotechnology, and medical and health. **Geographic Preferences:** Colorado and Mid Atlantic.

60866 ■ Bridge Partners, LLC
16 W. Madison St.
Baltimore, MD 21201
Ph:(410)625-0560
Fax: (410)752-2978
Contact: Jim Heerwagen, Managing Partner
Investment Types: Early Stage. **Industry Preferences:** Communications and media. **Geographic Preferences:** Mid Atlantic.

60867 ■ Catalyst Ventures
1119 St. Paul St.
Baltimore, MD 21202
Ph:(410)244-0123
Fax: (410)752-7721
Preferred Investment Size: $500,000 maximum. **Investment Policies:** Equity. **Investment Types:** Research and development, and early stage. **Industry Preferences:** Data communications, biotechnology, and medical related. **Geographic Preferences:** Middle Atlantic.

60868 ■ Delmag Ventures
220 Wardour Dr.
Annapolis, MD 21401
Ph:(410)267-8196
Fax: (410)267-8017
URL: http://www.delmagventures.com
Contact: Denis Seynhaeve, President
Preferred Investment Size: $250,000 to $1,000,000. **Investment Types:** Early stage and seed. **Industry Preferences:** Communications and media, computer software, Internet specific, semiconductors and other electronics. **Geographic Preferences:** Mid Atlantic.

60869 ■ Embryon Capital
7903 Sleaford Pl.
Bethesda, MD 20814
Ph:(301)656-6837
Fax: (301)656-8056
Contact: Timothy Webb, General Partner
Preferred Investment Size: $300,000 to $1,000,000.

60870 ■ Grace Venture Capital / Grace Internet Capital
405 Ocean Pky.
No. 4-390
Ocean Pines, MD 21811
URL: http://www.gracevc.com
Contact: Gregory Grace, Chief Executive Officer
Investment Policies: Seed, early and first stage. **Industry Preferences:** Internet specific. **Geographic Preferences:** Northeast U.S.; and National.

60871 ■ Grotech Capital Group
9690 Deereco Rd., Ste. 800
Timonium, MD 21093

Ph:(410)560-2000
Fax: (410)560-1910
URL: http://www.grotech.com
Contact: Frank Adams, Managing General Partner
Preferred Investment Size: $3,000,000 to $40,000,000. **Investment Types:** Early, first, second and later stage, mezzanine, management buyouts, leveraged buyout, private placement, industry rollups, acquisition, expansion, turnaround, recapitalizations, and special situation. **Industry Preferences:** Internet specific, medical and health, consumer related, communications and media, other products, computer software, and services, biotechnology, industrial and energy, and semiconductors and other electronics, and other products. **Geographic Preferences:** Southeast and Mid Atlantic.

60872 ■ Hatch Group, LLC
PO Box 10708
Gaithersburg, MD 20898
Ph:(202)777-2648
Fax: (202)777-2648
URL: http://www.thehatchgroup.com
Contact: Peter Minihane, Managing Partner
Investment Policies: Start-up and early stage. **Industry Preferences:** Computer software, and Internet specific. **Geographic Preferences:** U.S.

60873 ■ Kinetic Ventures LLC
2 Wisconsin Cir., Ste. 620
Chevy Chase, MD 20815
Ph:(301)652-8066
Fax: (301)652-8310
URL: http://www.kineticventures.com
Contact: Nelson Chu, Principal
Preferred Investment Size: $2,000,000 to $5,000,000. **Investment Types:** Early and first stage. **Industry Preferences:** Internet specific, communications and media, computer software and services, industrial and energy, semiconductors and other electronics, other products, industrial and energy, computer hardware, medical and health, and biotechnology. **Geographic Preferences:** U.S.

60874 ■ Market Street Capital, LLC
38 S. Market St., Ste. 1
Fredrick, MD 21701
Ph:(301)668-6226
Fax: (301)668-6229
URL: http://www.marketstreetcapital.com
Investment Policies: Start-up, seed, and first stage. **Industry Preferences:** Financial services, and business service. **Geographic Preferences:** Mid Atlantic.

60875 ■ Maryland Venture Capital Trust
217 E. Redwood St., Ste. 2200
Baltimore, MD 21202
Ph:(410)767-6361
Fax: (410)333-6931
Investment Types: Fund of funds. **Industry Preferences:** Medical and health, computer software and services, other products, industrial and energy, semiconductors and other electronics, consumer related, biotechnology, and computer hardware. **Geographic Preferences:** Maryland.

60876 ■ New Enterprise Associates (Baltimore)
1119 St. Paul St.
Baltimore, MD 21202
Ph:(410)244-0115
Fax: (410)752-7721
URL: http://www.nea.com
Contact: Frank Bonsal, Founding Partner
E-mail: frank@nea.com
Preferred Investment Size: $200,000 to $20,000,000. **Investment Types:** Seed, early, start-up, first and second stage, and mezzanine. **Industry Preferences:** Communications and media, Internet specific, medical and health, computer software and services, semiconductors and other electronics, biotechnology, computer hardware, other products, consumer related, industrial and energy. **Geographic Preferences:** U.S.

60877 ■ Novak Biddle Venture Partners, L.P.
7501 Wisconsin Ave., E. Tower, Ste. 1380
Bethesda, MD 20814

Ph:(240)497-1910
Fax: (240)223-0255
Co. E-mail: roger@novakbiddle.com
URL: http://www.novakbiddle.com
Contact: Roger Novak, Founding Partner
Preferred Investment Size: $100,000 to $10,000,000. **Investment Types:** Seed and early stage. **Industry Preferences:** Internet specific, communications and media, computer software and services, semiconductors and other electronics, computer hardware, other products, and medical and health . **Geographic Preferences:** Mid Atlantic, Northeast, and Southeast.

60878 ■ Spring Capital Partners, L.P.
Latrobe Bldg., 5th Fl.
2 E. Read St.
Baltimore, MD 21202
Ph:(410)685-8000
Fax: (410)545-0015
Co. E-mail: mailbox@springcap.com
URL: http://www.springcap.com
Contact: Robert M. Stewart, General Manager
Preferred Investment Size: $2,000,000 minimum. **Investment Types:** Second and later stage, acquisition, industry rollups, balanced, mezzanine, and leveraged buyout. **Industry Preferences:** Communications and media, computer related, semiconductors and other electronics, medical and health, consumer related, industrial and energy, transportation, and manufacturing. **Geographic Preferences:** Mid Atlantic.

60879 ■ Sterling Capital Limited
111 S. Calvert St., Ste. 2810
Baltimore, MD 21202
Ph:(410)347-2919
Fax: (410)347-3140
URL: http://www.sterlingcap.com
Contact: Eric Becker, Managing Partner
Investment Types: Early stage and leveraged buyout. **Industry Preferences:** Communications and media, computer software, medical and health, consumer related, business service, and manufacturing. **Geographic Preferences:** Mid Atlantic and Midwest.

60880 ■ T. Rowe Price Threshold Partnerships
100 E. Pratt St.
Baltimore, MD 21202
Ph:(410)345-2000
Fax: (410)345-2800
URL: http://www.troweprice.com
Preferred Investment Size: $3,000,000 to $5,000,000. **Investment Types:** Mezzanine, turnaround, leveraged buyout, later stage, expansion, and special situation. **Industry Preferences:** Computer software and services, Internet specific, consumer related, medical and health, other products, semiconductors and other electronics, communications and media, industrial and energy, biotechnology, and other products. **Geographic Preferences:** U.S.

60881 ■ Toucan Capital
7600 Wisconsin Ave., 7th Fl.
Bethesda, MD 20814
Ph:(240)497-4060
Fax: (240)497-4065
URL: http://www.toucancapital.com
Contact: Linda Powers, Managing Director
Preferred Investment Size: $100,000 to $5,000,000. **Investment Types:** Early stage, seed, and start-up. **Industry Preferences:** Biotechnology, industrial and energy. **Geographic Preferences:** Mid Atlantic and Northeast.

60882 ■ Walker Ventures SBIC / Walker Ventures
3060 Washington Rd.
Glenwood, MD 21738
Ph:(301)854-6850
Fax: (301)854-6235
URL: http://www.walkerventures.com
Contact: Rusty Griffith, Principal
Preferred Investment Size: $250,000 to $3,000,000. **Investment Types:** Early stage. **Industry Prefer-**

ences: Internet specific, computer software and services, communications and media, medical and health, other products, and semiconductors and other electronics. **Geographic Preferences:** Mid Atlantic.

PROCUREMENT ASSISTANCE PROGRAMS

60883 ■ Maryland Department of Business and Economic Development Center–Administration Division–Contracts and Procurement Office (217 E)
217 East Redwood, Ste. 1501
Baltimore, MD 21202
Ph:(410)767-2211
Fax: (410)767-2031
Co. E-mail: dchronister@mdbusiness.state.m
URL: http://www.dop.state.md.us

60884 ■ Offfice Of Goverment Contacting
National Aeronautics and Space Administration
Goddard Space Flight Center
Code 210,
Greenbelt, MD 20771
Ph:(301)286-4378
Fax: (301)286-0237
URL: http://www.sba.gov
Contact: Michael Killick, SBA Representative
E-mail: bkilyk@pop200.gsfc.nasa.gov
Description: Covers activities for NASA, Goddard Space Flight Center (Greenbelt, MD), NASA Headquarters (Washington, DC), LABCOM Adelphi Lab Center (Adelphi, MD), and Navy Surface Warfare Center (Indian Head, MD).

60885 ■ Regional Contracting Assistance Center–Ranson
150 E Burr Blvd.
Kearneysville, WV -25430
Ph:(304)724-7547
Fax: (304)728-3068
Co. E-mail: ctodd@rcacwv.com
URL: http://www.rcacwv.com
Contact: Christine Todd, Marketing Assistance Specialist

INCUBATORS/RESEARCH AND TECHNOLOGY PARKS

60886 ■ Maryland Advanced Development Laboratory
University Research Foundation
6411 Ivy Ln., Ste. 110
Greenbelt, MD 20770
Ph:(301)345-8664
Fax: (301)345-7305
Co. E-mail: krone@urf.com
URL: http://www.urf.com/madl/index.html
Contact: Dr. Norris J. Krone Jr., Pres.
E-mail: krone@urf.com
Scope: Science, engineering, and business. Research and development activities focus on advanced aircraft avionics, optics, lasers, and advanced computer systems such as high speed parallel processing. Performs contract research and development involving classified or proprietary research, complex program management, and quick reaction contracting.

60887 ■ Maryland Technology Extension Service
University of Maryland, College Park
Potomac Bldg. No. 092
College Park, MD 20742
Ph:(301)405-3883
Free: 800-245-5810
Fax: (301)314-1994
URL: http://www.erc.umd.edu
Description: Assists in problem identification, provides support, and formulates solutions. Also performs information searches. Reviews and critiques new ideas, products, and designs.

60888 ■ R&D Village
Montgomery County Office of Economic Development
101 Monroe St., Ste. 1500
Rockville, MD 20850
Ph:(240)777-2000
Fax: (240)777-2001
Co. E-mail: david.edgerley@montgomerycountymd.gov
Contact: David W. Edgerley, Dir.
E-mail: david.edgerley@montgomerycountymd.gov
Scope: 1,200-acre site linking biomedical research and development activities between government, park tenants, and academia. Houses the Center for Advanced Research in Biotechnology, a joint research venture between the National Institute of Standards and Technology, University of Maryland, and Montgomery county government; also houses a Johns Hopkins University facility focusing on advanced study programs in computer science, electrical engineering, and technical management, and the University's campus at Shady Grove. The Village also includes the Shady Grove Life Sciences Center, Shady Grove Executive Center, Decoverly, and The Washingtonian. **Services:** Site location assistance. **Publications:** Newsletter (quarterly). **Educational Activities:** Conferences; Meetings (monthly), of Biotechnology Network and Telecommunications Network; Workshops.

60889 ■ The Rural Development Center
Richard A. Henson Center
Rm. 2145, UMES
Princess Anne, MD 21853
Ph:(410)651-6183
Fax: (410)651-6512
Co. E-mail: dskuennen@mail.umes.edu
URL: http://www.umes.edu
Contact: Daniel Kuennen, Dir
Description: The RDC is a community-based incubator serving the needs of people in rural communities. It is located on the campus of the University of Maryland Eastern Shore.

60890 ■ Technology Advancement Program
387 Technology Dr., Ste. 1105
College Park, MD 20742
Ph:(301)314-7805
Fax: (301)226-5378
Co. E-mail: smagids@umd.edu
URL: http://www.tap.umd.edu/
Contact: Scott Magids, Dir
Description: The TAP is a program of the Engineering Research Center utilizing the extensive resources of the University of Maryland at College Park.

60891 ■ Towson University–Office of University Research Services
7800 York Rd., Rms. 225-220
Towson, MD 21252-0001
Ph:(410)704-2236
Fax: (410)704-4494
Co. E-mail: healy@towson.edu
URL: http://www.towson.edu/ours
Contact: Mary Louise Healy, Dir.
E-mail: healy@towson.edu
Scope: Identifies funding agencies, collaborates with faculty on proposal submissions, administers externally funded grants and contracts, negotiates research contracts, advises University administration on federal regulations affecting research, and develops university policies and procedures for sponsored research. **Educational Activities:** Proposal-writing workshops.

60892 ■ University of Maryland–Biotechnology Institute
9600 Gudelsky Dr.
Rockville, MD 20850
Ph:(240)314-6161
Fax: (240)314-6250
Co. E-mail: hunterce@umbi.umd.edu
URL: http://www.umbi.umd.edu
Contact: Dr. Jennie Hunter-Cevera, Pres.
E-mail: hunterce@umbi.umd.edu
Scope: Coordinates basic biotechnology research in the following areas: protein engineering, structure,

and function; molecular biology of plant and animal protection; bioprocess engineering; legal, and ethical issues raised by biotechnology and its applications; marine molecular biology and molecular genetics; human virology; and medical biotechnology. **Publications:** Annual Report; mMBI; Scientific Proceedings. **Educational Activities:** Research seminars; Science and technology courses, for middle school students; Short courses; Specialized workshops; Symposium; Tours for local industry.

EDUCATIONAL PROGRAMS

60893 ■ University of Baltimore–Merrick School of Business
1420 N Charles St.
Baltimore, MD 21201
Ph:(410)837-4200
Fax: (410)837-5652
URL: http://www.ubalt.edu
Description: Undergraduate and graduate business courses, institutes, and conferences are offered in flexible evening and weekend schedules. Programs are designed for persons already in positions of executive responsibility, as well as for those about to enter into managerial positions.

PUBLICATIONS

60894 ■ *Baltimore Business Journal*
111 Market Place, Ste. 720
Baltimore, MD 21202
Ph:(410)576-1161
Fax: (410)752-3112
URL: http://www.amcity.com/baltimore

60895 ■ *Smart Start your Maryland Business*
PSI Research
300 N. Valley Dr.
Grants Pass, OR 97526
Ph:(503)479-9464
Free: 800-228-2275
Fax: (503)476-1479
Co. E-mail: info@psi-research.com
URL: http://www.psi-research.com
Ed: Michael D. Jenkins. **Released:** Revised edition, 1992. **Price:** $29.95 (looseleaf binder); $24.95 (paper). **Description:** Part of the Successful Business Library series.

PUBLISHERS

60896 ■ ABS Consulting Training Services
16855 Northchase Dr.
Houston, TX 77060
Ph:(281)673-2800
Free: 800-462-6420
Co. E-mail: info@absconsulting.com
URL: http://www.absconsulting.com/svc_training.cfm
Contact: G. David William, COO
Description: Publishes law, regulatory and technical books on subjects that include federal safety and code regulations. **Founded:** 1973.

60897 ■ Charles River Media
25 Thomson Pl.
Boston, MA 02210
Ph:(859)647-5963
Free: 800-347-7707
Fax: (617)757-7969
Co. E-mail: info@charlesriver.com
URL: http://www.charlesriver.com/books/Features.aspx
Contact: David Pallai, President
E-mail: dpallai@charlesriver.com
Description: Publishes books and software on game development, web development, networking and computer graphics. Accepts unsolicited manuscripts. Reaches market through commission representatives, as wells as wholesalers and distributors. **Founded:** 1994.

60898 ■ IBEX Publishers Inc.
PO Box 30087
Bethesda, MD 20824
Ph:(301)718-8188
Free: 888-718-8188
Fax: (901)907-8707
Co. E-mail: info@ibexpub.com
URL: http://www.ibexpub.com
Contact: Shirzad Farhad, Publisher
E-mail: farhad@ibexpub.com
Description: Distributes and publishes books on Middle East. Distributor. Reaches market through direct mail, reviews and listings. **Founded:** 1979.

60899 ■ Posterity Press
PO Box 71081
Chevy Chase, MD 20813
Ph:(301)652-2384
Fax: (301)652-2543
Co. E-mail: publisher@posteritypress.com

URL: http://www.posteritypress.com
Contact: Philip Kopper
Description: Publishes books on nonfiction including religion, history, memoirs, animals, and business along with fictional titles such as for children and thrillers. Accepts unsolicited manuscripts; must call the editorial office to discuss book proposal. Reaches market through distributors including Baker & Taylor and Ingram. **Founded:** 1995

60900 ■ Rolling Hills Publishing
PO Box 724
New Windsor, MD 21776
Ph:(410)635-3233
Co. E-mail: info@rollinghillspublishing.com
URL: http://www.rollinghillspublishing.com
Contact: Michael Gray
Description: Publishes educational and how-to books. **Founded:** 2003

60901 ■ Schreiber Publishing Inc.
51 Monroe St., Ste. 101
PO Box 4193
Rockville, MD 20850
Ph:(301)424-7737
Free: 800-822-3213
Fax: (301)424-2336
Co. E-mail: spbooks@aol.com
URL: http://www.schreiberpublishing.com
Contact: Mordecai Schreiber, Owner
E-mail: mschreiber@schreiberpublishing.com
Description: Publishes language and translation books and books relating to art, the Holocaust, history and children. Publishes reference books and fiction books. Accepts unsolicited manuscripts. Reaches market through commission reps, direct mail, reviews, listings, telephone sales, as well as distributors. **Founded:** 1994.

60902 ■ Union Communication Services Inc.
165 Conduit St.
Annapolis, MD 21401
Ph:(410)626-1400
Free: 800-321-2545
Fax: (410)626-1353
Co. E-mail: ucs@unionist.com
URL: http://www.unionist.com
Contact: David Prosten
Description: Publishes books on union-related topics for members such as labor laws, negotiator resources, health and safety. **Founded:** 1981

SMALL BUSINESS DEVELOPMENT CENTER LEAD OFFICE

60903 ■ University of Massachusetts–Massachusetts SBDC
School of Management, Rm. 205
Amherst, MA 01003-4935
Ph:(413)545-6301
Fax: (413)545-1273
URL: http://msbdc.som.umass.edu
Contact: Georgianna Parkin, State Dir.
E-mail: gep@msbdc.umass.edu

60904 ■ University of Massachusetts–Small Business Development Center
205 Isenberg School of Management
Amherst, MA 01003-4935
Ph:(413)545-6301
Contact: Ms. Georgianna Parkin, Acting State Director
E-mail: gep@msbdc.umass.edu

SMALL BUSINESS DEVELOPMENT CENTERS

60905 ■ Clark University–Small Business Development Center
950 Main St.
Worcester, MA 01610
Ph:(508)793-7615
Fax: (508)793-8890
Co. E-mail: sbdc@clarku.edu
URL: http://www.clarku.edu/offices/sbdc/
Contact: Larry March, Regional Dir.
E-mail: lmarsh@clarku.edu

60906 ■ Massachusetts Export Center–Small Business Development Center Network
State Transportation Bldg.
10 Park Plz., Ste. 4510
Boston, MA 02216
Ph:(617)973-8664
Fax: (617)973-8681
URL: http://www.mass.gov/export
Contact: Paula Murphy, Dir.
E-mail: paula.murphy@state.ma.us

60907 ■ Metropolitan Boston Regional Office–Boston College SBDC
142 Beacon St.
Chestnut Hill, MA 02467
Ph:(617)552-4091
Fax: (617)552-2730
Co. E-mail: sbdcmail@bc.edu
URL: http://www.bc.edu
Contact: Dr. Jack McKiernan, Regional Dir.
E-mail: john.mckiernan@bc.edu

60908 ■ Minority Business Center–SBDC
University of Massachusetts (Boston)
100 Morrissey Blvd.
Boston, MA 02125
Ph:(617)287-7750
Fax: (617)287-7767
URL: http://www.sbdc.umb.edu
Contact: Mark Allio, Dir.
E-mail: mark.allio@umb.edu

60909 ■ Southeastern Massachusetts Regional Office–Small Business Development Center
200 Pocasset St.
Fall River, MA 02721
Ph:(508)673-9783
Fax: (508)674-1929
Co. E-mail: sbdc@meganet.net
URL: http://www.msbdc.org/semass/
Contact: James Sullivan, Interim Regional Dir.
E-mail: sullivan@msbdc.umass.edu

60910 ■ Western Massachusetts Regional Office–Scibelli Enterprise Center
One Federal St., Bldg. 101-R
Springfield, MA 01105-1160
Ph:(413)737-6712
Fax: (413)737-2312
URL: http://www.msbdc.org/wmass/
Contact: Dianne Fuller Doherty, Regional Dir.
E-mail: ddoherty@msbdc.umass.edu

SMALL BUSINESS ASSISTANCE PROGRAMS

60911 ■ Massachusetts Export Center (Headquarters)–Trade Development Unit–Massachusetts Small Business Export Program (State)
State Transportation Bldg.
10 Park Plaza, Ste. 4510
Boston, MA 02116
Ph:(617)973-8664
Fax: (617)973-8681
Co. E-mail: pmurphy@massport.com
URL: http://www.mass.gov/export
Description: Provides assistance in market analysis, training, advice on export practices and financing for participation in foreign trade missions, export counseling, and market research. Also identifies foreign contacts for exporting firms and organizes and conducts trade events.

60912 ■ Massachusetts Office of Business Development
1 Ashton Pl., Ste. 2101
Boston, MA 02108
Ph:(617)788-3670
Free: 800-CAP-ITAL
Fax: (617)973-8797
URL: http://www.mass.gov
Description: Provides assistance and information on relocating and expanding businesses in Massachusetts.

60913 ■ Massachusetts Office of International Trade and Investment
State Transportation Bldg.
10 Park Plaza, Ste. 4510
Boston, MA 02116
Ph:(617)367-1830
Fax: (617)227-3488
Co. E-mail: moiti@state.ma.us
URL: http://www.mass.gov/moiti
Description: Oversees the state's international trade activities. Also monitors the degree of foreign investment in Massachusetts.

60914 ■ University of Massachusetts–Small Business Development Center
227 Isenberg School of Management
Amherst, MA 01003
Ph:(413)545-6301
Fax: (413)545-1273
URL: http://www.msbdc.org
Contact: Georgianna Parkin, Dir
Description: Provides program assistance and counseling to small businesses

SCORE OFFICES

60915 ■ SCORE Boston
10 Causeway St., Rm. 265
Boston, MA 02222-1093
Ph:(617)565-5591
Fax: (617)565-5597
Co. E-mail: boston-score-20@verizon.net
URL: http://www.scoreboston.org
Description: Serves as volunteer program in which working and retired business management professionals provide free business counseling to men and women who are considering starting a small business, encountering problems with their business, or expanding their business. Offers free one-on-one counseling, online counseling and low cost workshops on a variety of business topics.

60916 ■ SCORE Cape Cod
270 Communications Way
Independence Park, Ste. 5-B
Hyannis, MA 02601
Ph:(508)775-4884
Fax: (508)790-2540
Co. E-mail: capecodscore@verizon.net
URL: http://www.scorecapecod.com
Contact: John Caspole, Chm.
Description: Serves as volunteer program in which working and retired business management professionals provide free business counseling to men and women who are considering starting a small business, encountering problems with their business, or expanding their business. Offers free one-on-one counseling, online counseling and low cost workshops on a variety of business topics.

60917 ■ SCORE Franklin County
1 Federal St.
Springfield Ent. Ctr.
Springfield, MA 01105

Ph:(413)785-0314
Co. E-mail: score@stcc.edu
URL: http://www.scorechapter14.org

60918 ■ SCORE Northeast Massachusetts
Danvers Savings Bank
100 Cummings Ctr., Ste. 101 K
Beverly, MA 01915
Ph:(978)922-9441
Co. E-mail: scorene411@yahoo.com
URL: http://www.scorenemass.org
Contact: Peter McGarry, Chm.
Description: Serves as volunteer program in which working and retired business management professionals provide free business counseling to men and women who are considering starting a small business, encountering problems with their business, or expanding their business. Offers free one-on-one counseling, online counseling and low cost workshops on a variety of business topics.

60919 ■ SCORE Southeast Massachusetts
60 School St.
Brockton, MA 02301
Ph:(508)587-2673
Fax: (508)587-1340
Co. E-mail: score@metrosouthchamber.com
Contact: Bruce Young, Chm.
Description: Serves as volunteer program in which working and retired business management professionals provide free business counseling to men and women who are considering starting a small business, encountering problems with their business, or expanding their business. Offers free one-on-one counseling, online counseling and low cost workshops on a variety of business topics.

60920 ■ SCORE Worcester
339 Main St.
Worcester, MA 01608
Ph:(508)753-2929
Fax: (508)754-8560
Co. E-mail: score@worcesterchamber.org
URL: http://www.scoreworcester.org
Description: Works to facilitate the formation, success and growth of small business. Provides free, confidential business counseling to individuals just starting a business and to existing small businesses. Offers low cost educational workshops on business topics.

BETTER BUSINESS BUREAUS

60921 ■ Better Business Bureau of Central New England
339 Main St.
Worcester, MA 01608-1900
Free: (866)566-9222
Fax: (508)754-4158
Co. E-mail: info@cne.bbb.org
URL: http://www.cne.bbb.org
Contact: Mr. C.J. Pederson

60922 ■ Better Business Bureau Serving Eastern Massachusetts, Maine and Vermont
235 W Central St., Ste. 1
Natick, MA 01760
Ph:(508)652-4800
Fax: (508)652-4820
Co. E-mail: info@bosbbb.org
URL: http://www.bosbbb.org
Contact: Mr. Kevin J. Sanders, Pres./CEO

CHAMBERS OF COMMERCE

60923 ■ Affiliated Chambers of Commerce of Greater Springfield
1441 Main St., Ste. 136
Springfield, MA 01103-1449
Ph:(413)787-1555
Fax: (413)731-8530

Co. E-mail: denver@myonlinechamber.com
URL: http://www.myonlinechamber.com
Contact: Russell F. Denver, Pres.

60924 ■ Alliance for Amesbury
5 Market Sq.
Amesbury, MA 01913
Ph:(978)388-3178
Fax: (978)388-4952
Co. E-mail: alliance@amesburymass.com
URL: http://www.amesburymass.com
Contact: Raymond Shockey, Exec.Dir.

60925 ■ Amherst Area Chamber of Commerce
28 Amity St.
Amherst, MA 01002
Ph:(413)253-0700
Fax: (413)256-0771
Co. E-mail: info@amherstarea.com
URL: http://www.amherstarea.com
Contact: John Coull, Exec.Dir.

60926 ■ Arlington Chamber of Commerce
1 Whittemore Park
Arlington, MA 02474
Ph:(781)643-4600
Fax: (781)646-5581
Co. E-mail: info@arlcc.org
URL: http://www.arlcc.org
Contact: Michele M. Meagher, Pres.

60927 ■ Assabet Valley Chamber of Commerce
18 Church St.
PO Box 578
Hudson, MA 01749
Ph:(978)568-0360
Fax: (978)562-4118
Co. E-mail: info@assabetvalleychamber.org
URL: http://www.assabetvalleychamber.org
Contact: Sarah B. Cressy, Pres./CEO

60928 ■ Bedford Chamber of Commerce
Town Center Bldg.
12 Mudge Way (2-2)
Bedford, MA 01730
Ph:(781)275-8503
Co. E-mail: bcoc@bedfordchamber.org
URL: http://www.bedfordchamber.org
Contact: Maureen McAulifee Sullivan, Exec.Dir.

60929 ■ Berkshire Chamber of Commerce
6 W Main St.
North Adams, MA 01247
Ph:(413)449-4000
Fax: (413)664-1049
Co. E-mail: info@berkshirechamber.com
URL: http://www.berkshirechamber.com
Contact: David R. Bissaillon, Pres./CEO

60930 ■ Berkshires Chamber of Commerce
75 N St., Ste. 360
Pittsfield, MA 01201
Ph:(413)499-4000
Fax: (413)447-9641
Co. E-mail: info@berkshirechamber.com
URL: http://www.berkshirechamber.com
Contact: Ms. Stephanie L. French, Dir. of Marketing and Communications

60931 ■ Beverly Chamber of Commerce
28 Cabot St.
Beverly, MA 01915
Ph:(978)232-9559
Fax: (978)232-9372
Co. E-mail: info@beverlychamber.com
URL: http://www.gobeverly.com
Contact: Susan Mueller, Exec.Dir.

60932 ■ Billerica Chamber of Commerce
574 Boston Rd., Unit 1
Billerica, MA 01821
Ph:(978)663-0036
Fax: (978)670-1020
Co. E-mail: info@billericachamberofcommerce.com
URL: http://www.billericachamberofcommerce.com

Contact: Edna M. Chalmers, Pres.

60933 ■ Blackstone Valley Chamber of Commerce
110 Church St.
Whitinsville, MA 01588
Ph:(508)234-9090
Fax: (508)234-5152
Co. E-mail: ndesrosiers@blackstonevalley.org
URL: http://www.blackstonevalley.org
Contact: Jeff Ritter, Exec.Dir.

60934 ■ Brookline Chamber of Commerce
1101 Beacon St., Lower Level
Brookline, MA 02446-3202
Ph:(617)739-1330
Fax: (617)739-1200
Co. E-mail: info@brooklinechamber.com
URL: http://www.brooklinechamber.com
Contact: John F. Heffernan, Exec.Dir.

60935 ■ Cambridge Chamber of Commerce
859 Massachusetts Ave.
Cambridge, MA 02139
Ph:(617)876-4100
Fax: (617)354-9874
Co. E-mail: ccinfo@cambridgechamber.org
URL: http://www.cambridgechamber.org
Contact: Kelly Thompson Clark, Pres./CEO

60936 ■ Cape Ann Chamber of Commerce
33 Commercial St.
Gloucester, MA 01930-5087
Ph:(978)283-1601
Fax: (978)283-4740
Co. E-mail: info@capeannchamber.com
URL: http://www.capeannchamber.com
Contact: Michael Costello, Exec. Dir.

60937 ■ Cape Cod Canal Regional Chamber of Commerce
70 Main St.
Buzzards Bay, MA 02532
Ph:(508)759-6000
Fax: (508)759-6965
Co. E-mail: info@capecodcanalchamber.org
URL: http://www.capecodcanalchamber.org
Contact: Marie Oliva, Exec.Dir.

60938 ■ Chamber of Commerce of the Attleboro Area
42 Union St.
Attleboro, MA 02703-2911
Ph:(508)222-0801
Fax: (508)222-1498
Co. E-mail: officemanager@attleborochamber.com
URL: http://www.attleborochamber.com
Contact: Roy M. Nascimento, Pres.

60939 ■ Chatham Chamber of Commerce
PO Box 793
Chatham, MA 02633-0793
Ph:(508)945-5199
Free: 800-715-5567
Co. E-mail: chamber@chathaminfo.com
URL: http://www.chathaminfo.com
Contact: Scott D. Hamilton, Pres.

60940 ■ Chelsea Chamber of Commerce
308 Broadway
Chelsea, MA 02150
Ph:(617)884-4877
Fax: (617)884-4878
URL: http://www.chelseachamber.com
Contact: Donald M. Harney, Exec. Dir.

60941 ■ Chicopee Chamber of Commerce
264 Exchange St.
Chicopee, MA 01013
Ph:(413)594-2101
Fax: (413)594-2103
Co. E-mail: info@chicopeechamber.org
URL: http://www.chicopeechamber.org
Contact: Gail Sherman, Pres.

60942 ■ Cohasset Chamber of Commerce
PO Box 336
Cohasset, MA 02025-0336

Ph:(781)383-1010
Co. E-mail: info@cohassetchamber.com
URL: http://www.cohassetchamber.org
Contact: Michael Conlon, Pres.

60943 ■ Concord Chamber of Commerce
15 Walden St., Ste. 7
Concord, MA 01742-2504
Ph:(978)369-3120
Fax: (978)369-1515
Co. E-mail: info@concordchamberofcommerce.org
URL: http://www.concordchamberofcommerce.org
Contact: Stephanie Stillman, Exec.Dir.

60944 ■ Cranberry Country Chamber of Commerce
PO Box 409
Middleboro, MA 02346-0409
Ph:(508)947-1499
Fax: (508)947-1446
Co. E-mail: info@cranberrycountry.org
URL: http://www.cranberrycountry.org
Contact: Jean Scarborough, Pres.

60945 ■ East Boston Chamber of Commerce
296 Bennington St., 2nd Fl.
East Boston, MA 02128
Ph:(617)569-5000
Fax: (617)569-1945
Co. E-mail: info@eastbostonchamber.com
URL: http://www.eastbostonchamber.com
Contact: Lisa Loiacono, Exec.Dir.

60946 ■ Eastham Chamber of Commerce
PO Box 1329
Eastham, MA 02642
Ph:(508)240-7211
Co. E-mail: info@easthamchamber.com
URL: http://www.easthamchamber.com
Contact: Janet Demetri, Pres.

60947 ■ Easthampton Chamber of Commerce
33 Union St.
Easthampton, MA 01027
Ph:(413)527-9414
Fax: (413)527-1445
Co. E-mail: ehamp@valinet.com
Contact: Mr. Eric A. Snyder, Exec.Dir.

60948 ■ Everett Chamber of Commerce
467 Broadway
Everett, MA 02149
Ph:(617)387-9100
Fax: (617)389-6655
Co. E-mail: ecocoffice@aol.com
Contact: Colin Kelly, Exec.Dir.

60949 ■ Fall River Area Chamber of Commerce and Industry
200 Pocasset St.
Fall River, MA 02721-1585
Ph:(508)676-8226
Fax: (508)675-5932
Co. E-mail: info@fallriverchamber.com
URL: http://www.fallriverchamber.com
Contact: Peter F. Kortright AICP, Pres./CEO

60950 ■ Falmouth Chamber of Commerce
20 Academy Ln.
Falmouth, MA 02540
Ph:(508)548-8500
Free: 800-526-8532
Fax: (508)548-8521
URL: http://www.falmouthchamber.com
Contact: Christine Ross, Exec. Dir.

60951 ■ Franklin County Chamber of Commerce
PO Box 898
Greenfield, MA 01302
Ph:(413)773-5463
Fax: (413)773-7008
Co. E-mail: fccc@crocker.com
URL: http://www.co.franklin.ma.us
Contact: Ann L. Hamilton, Pres.

60952 ■ Greater Boston Chamber of Commerce
75 State St., 2nd Fl.
Boston, MA 02109
Ph:(617)227-4500
Fax: (617)227-7505
Co. E-mail: info@bostonchamber.com
URL: http://www.bostonchamber.com
Contact: Paul Guzzi, Pres./CEO

60953 ■ Greater Gardner Chamber of Commerce
210 Main St.
Gardner, MA 01440
Ph:(978)632-1780
Fax: (978)630-1767
Co. E-mail: ggcc@gardnerma.com
URL: http://www.gardnerma.com
Contact: Michael F. Ellis, Pres./CEO

60954 ■ Greater Haverhill Chamber of Commerce
87 Winter St.
Haverhill, MA 01830
Ph:(978)373-5663
Fax: (978)373-8060
Co. E-mail: info@haverhillchamber.com
URL: http://www.haverhillchamber.com
Contact: Sally L. Cerasuolo-O'Rorke, Pres./CEO

60955 ■ Greater Holyoke Chamber of Commerce
177 High St.
Holyoke, MA 01040-6504
Ph:(413)534-3376
Fax: (413)534-3385
Co. E-mail: ransford@holycham.com
URL: http://www.holyokechamber.com
Contact: Doris M. Ransford, Pres.

60956 ■ Greater Lowell Chamber of Commerce
144 Merrimack St.
Lowell, MA 01852
Ph:(978)459-8154
Fax: (978)452-4145
Co. E-mail: info@greaterlowellchamber.org
URL: http://www.glcc.biz
Contact: Jeanne Osborn, Pres./CEO

60957 ■ Greater Newburyport Chamber of Commerce
38R Merrimac St.
Newburyport, MA 01950
Ph:(978)462-6680
Fax: (978)465-4145
Co. E-mail: info@newburyportchamber.org
URL: http://www.newburyportchamber.org
Contact: Mr. William K. Piercey, Pres.

60958 ■ Greater Northampton Chamber of Commerce
99 Pleasant St.
Northampton, MA 01060
Ph:(413)584-1900
Fax: (413)584-1934
Co. E-mail: suzanneb@northamptonuncommon.com
URL: http://northamptonuncommon.com
Contact: Suzanne Beck, Exec.Dir.

60959 ■ Hanover Chamber of Commerce
PO Box 68
Hanover, MA 02339-0068
Ph:(781)826-8865
Fax: (781)826-7721
Co. E-mail: chamber@hanovermachamber.com
URL: http://www.hanovermachamber.com
Contact: Susannah Leslie, Exec.Dir.

60960 ■ Harwich Chamber of Commerce
One Schoolhouse Rd.
Harwich Port, MA 02646
Ph:(508)432-1600
Free: 800-4-HARWICH
Fax: (508)430-2105
Co. E-mail: info@harwichcc.com
URL: http://www.harwichcc.com

Contact: Sandra Davidson, Exec.Dir.

60961 ■ Holden Area Chamber of Commerce
1174 Main St.
Holden, MA 01520-0377
Ph:(508)829-9220
Fax: (508)829-9220
Co. E-mail: info@holdenareachamber.org
URL: http://www.holdenareachamber.org
Contact: Ms. Jennifer Stanovich, Exec.Dir.

60962 ■ Hyannis Area Chamber of Commerce
1481 Rte. 132
PO Box 100
Hyannis, MA 02601
Ph:(508)362-5230
Free: 877-HYA-NNIS
Fax: (508)362-9499
Co. E-mail: chamber@hyannis.com
URL: http://www.hyannischamber.com
Contact: Monica Parker, Exec.Dir.

60963 ■ Lenox Chamber of Commerce
Curtis Five Walker St.
Lenox, MA 01240-0646
Ph:(413)637-3646
Fax: (413)637-0041
Co. E-mail: info@lenox.org
URL: http://www.lenox.org
Contact: Shannon McNulty, Exec. Dir.

60964 ■ Lexington Chamber of Commerce
1875 Massachusetts Ave.
Lexington, MA 02420
Ph:(781)862-2480
Fax: (781)862-5995
Co. E-mail: jterhune@lexingtonchamber.org
URL: http://www.lexingtonchamber.org
Contact: Mary Jo Bohart, Exec.Dir.

60965 ■ Lynn Area Chamber of Commerce
100 Oxford St.
Lynn, MA 01901
Ph:(781)592-2900
Fax: (781)592-2903
Co. E-mail: info@lynnareachamber.com
URL: http://www.lynnareachamber.com
Contact: Rich Gorham, Pres.

60966 ■ Malden Chamber of Commerce
200 Pleasant St., Ste. 416
Malden, MA 02148-4884
Ph:(781)322-4500
Fax: (781)322-4866
Co. E-mail: info@maldenchamber.org
URL: http://www.maldenchamber.org
Contact: Maurene J. Campbell, Exec.Dir.

60967 ■ Marblehead Chamber of Commerce
62 Pleasant St.
PO Box 76
Marblehead, MA 01945
Ph:(781)631-2868
Fax: (781)639-8582
Co. E-mail: info@marbleheadchamber.org
URL: http://www.marbleheadchamber.org
Contact: Leslie Gould, Exec.Dir.

60968 ■ Marlborough Regional Chamber of Commerce
11 Florence St.
Marlborough, MA 01752-2822
Ph:(508)485-7746
Fax: (508)481-1819
Co. E-mail: info@marlboroughchamber.org
URL: http://www.marlboroughchamber.org
Contact: Susanne Morreale-Leeber, Pres./CEO

60969 ■ Martha's Vineyard Chamber of Commerce
PO Box 1698
Vineyard Haven, MA 02568-1698
Ph:(508)693-0085
Free: 800-505-4815
Fax: (508)693-7589
Co. E-mail: info@mvy.com

URL: http://www.mvy.com
Contact: Gary Cogley, Exec.Dir.

60970 ■ Medford Chamber of Commerce
One Shipyard Way, Ste. 302-304
Medford, MA 02155
Ph:(781)396-1277
Fax: (781)396-1278
Co. E-mail: director@medfordchamberma.com
URL: http://www.medfordchamberma.com
Contact: Cheryl White, Exec.Dir.

60971 ■ Melrose Chamber of Commerce
1 W Foster St.
Melrose, MA 02176
Ph:(781)665-3033
Co. E-mail: info@melrosechamber.org
URL: http://www.melrosechamber.org
Contact: Elizabeth W. McNelis, Exec. Dir.

60972 ■ Merrimack Valley Chamber of Commerce
264 Essex St.
Lawrence, MA 01840-1496
Ph:(978)686-0900
Fax: (978)794-9953
Co. E-mail: thechamber@merrimackvalleychamber.com
URL: http://www.merrimackvalleychamber.com
Contact: Joseph J. Bevilacqua, Pres./CEO

60973 ■ Metro South Chamber of Commerce
60 School St.
Brockton, MA 02301-4087
Ph:(508)586-0500
Fax: (508)587-1340
Co. E-mail: info@metrosouthchamber.com
URL: http://www.metrosouthchamber.com
Contact: Christopher Cooney, Pres./CEO

60974 ■ MetroWest Chamber of Commerce
1671 Worchester Rd., Ste. 201
Framingham, MA 01701-5400
Ph:(508)879-5600
Fax: (508)875-9325
Co. E-mail: chamber@metrowest.org
URL: http://www.metrowest.org
Contact: A. Theodore Welte, Pres./CEO

60975 ■ Middlesex West Chamber of Commerce
77 Great Rd., Ste. 214
Acton, MA 01720-5603
Ph:(978)263-0010
Fax: (978)264-0303
Co. E-mail: info@mwcoc.com
URL: http://www.mwcoc.com
Contact: Sarah Fletcher, Exec.Dir.

60976 ■ Milford Area Chamber of Commerce
258 Main St., Ste. 306
PO Box 621
Milford, MA 01757
Ph:(508)473-6700
Fax: (508)473-8467
Co. E-mail: chamber@milfordchamber.org
URL: http://www.milfordchamber.org
Contact: Barry Feingold, Pres./CEO

60977 ■ Nantucket Island Chamber of Commerce
48 Main St.
Nantucket, MA 02554-3595
Ph:(508)228-1700
Fax: (508)325-4925
Co. E-mail: info@nantucketchamber.org
URL: http://www.nantucketchamber.org
Contact: Ms. Tracy Bakalar, Exec.Dir.

60978 ■ Nashoba Valley Chamber of Commerce
100 Sherman Ave., Ste. 3
Devens, MA 01434
Ph:(978)772-6976
Fax: (978)772-3503
Co. E-mail: director@nvcoc.com
URL: http://www.nvcoc.com

Contact: Andrew Syiek, Exec.Dir.

60979 ■ Neponset Valley Chamber of Commerce
190 Vanderbilt Ave., Ste. 1
Norwood, MA 02062-5047
Ph:(781)769-1126
Fax: (781)769-0808
Co. E-mail: doug@nvcc.com
URL: http://www.nvcc.com
Contact: Douglas R. Wynne CAE, Pres./CEO

60980 ■ New Bedford Area Chamber of Commerce
794 Purchase St.
New Bedford, MA 02740
Ph:(508)999-5231
Fax: (508)999-5237
Co. E-mail: info@newbedfordchamber.com
URL: http://www.newbedfordchamber.com
Contact: James H. Mathes, Pres.

60981 ■ Newton - Needham Chamber of Commerce
281 Needham St.
Newton, MA 02464
Ph:(617)244-5300
Fax: (617)244-5302
Co. E-mail: torourke@nnchamber.com
URL: http://www.nnchamber.com
Contact: Tom O'Rourke, Pres.

60982 ■ North Attleboro and Plainville Chamber of Commerce
PO Box 1071
North Attleboro, MA 02761
Ph:(508)695-6011
Fax: (508)695-6096
Co. E-mail: shirley@napcc.org
URL: http://www.napcc.org
Contact: Shirley Nolin, Pres.

60983 ■ North Central Massachusetts Chamber of Commerce
860 South St.
Fitchburg, MA 01420
Ph:(978)353-7600
Fax: (978)353-4896
Co. E-mail: mckeehan@massweb.org
URL: http://www.northcentralmass.com
Contact: David L. McKeehan, Pres.

60984 ■ North Quabbin Chamber of Commerce
PO Box 157
Athol, MA 01331
Ph:(978)249-3849
Fax: (978)249-7151
Co. E-mail: nqcc1@verizon.net
URL: http://www.northquabbinchamber.com
Contact: Thomas J. Kussy, Exec. Dir.

60985 ■ North Shore Chamber of Commerce
5 Cherry Hill Dr., Ste. 100
Danvers, MA 01923-4395
Ph:(978)774-8565
Fax: (978)774-3418
Co. E-mail: info@northshorechamber.org
URL: http://www.northshorechamber.org
Contact: Malcolm MacLean, Chm.

60986 ■ North Suburban Chamber of Commerce
76R Winn St., Ste. 3D
Woburn, MA 01801
Ph:(781)933-3499
Fax: (781)933-1071
Co. E-mail: info@northsuburbanchamber.com
URL: http://www.northsuburbanchamber.com
Contact: Maureen A. Rogers, Pres.

60987 ■ Peabody Chamber of Commerce
24 Main St.
Peabody, MA 01960-5593
Ph:(978)531-0384
Fax: (978)532-7227
Co. E-mail: pcc@peabodychamber.com

URL: http://www.peabodychamber.com
Contact: Anthony Picano, Pres.

60988 ■ Plymouth Area Chamber of Commerce
10 Cordage Park Cir., Ste. 231
Plymouth, MA 02360
Ph:(508)830-1620
Fax: (508)830-1621
Co. E-mail: info@plymouthchamber.com
URL: http://www.plymouthchamber.com
Contact: Denis Hanks, Exec.Dir.

60989 ■ Provincetown Chamber of Commerce
PO Box 1017
Provincetown, MA 02657-1017
Ph:(508)487-3424
Fax: (508)487-8966
Co. E-mail: info@ptownchamber.com
URL: http://www.ptownchamber.com
Contact: Candice Collins-Boden, Exec.Dir.

60990 ■ Quaboag Valley Chamber of Commerce
3 Converse St., Ste. 103
Palmer, MA 01069-0269
Ph:(413)283-2418
Fax: (413)289-1355
Co. E-mail: lenny@quaboagvalley.org
URL: http://www.quaboagvalley.org
Contact: Leonard N. Weake, Pres.

60991 ■ Reading-North Reading Chamber of Commerce
PO Box 771
Reading, MA 01867
Ph:(781)944-8824
Fax: (781)944-6125
Co. E-mail: rnrchambercom@aol.com
URL: http://www.readingnreadingchamber.org
Contact: Carol Hughes, Exec. Dir.

60992 ■ Revere Chamber of Commerce
270 Broadway, Ste. 10
Revere, MA 02151
Ph:(781)289-8009
Fax: (781)289-2166
Co. E-mail: reverechamber@verizon.net
URL: http://www.reverechamber.org
Contact: Bob Silverman, Pres.

60993 ■ Rockland Chamber of Commerce
PO Box 45
Rockland, MA 02370
Ph:(781)792-2845
Contact: Maureen Shnider, Pres.

60994 ■ Salem Chamber of Commerce
265 Essex St., Ste. 101
Salem, MA 01970
Ph:(978)744-0004
Fax: (978)745-3855
Co. E-mail: scc@salem-chamber.org
URL: http://www.salem-chamber.org
Contact: Rinus Oosthoek, Exec.Dir.

60995 ■ Salisbury By the Sea Chamber of Commerce
Town Hall
Beach Rd.
PO Box 1000
Salisbury, MA 01952
Ph:(978)465-3581
Fax: (978)465-3581
Co. E-mail: mmiles7488@aol.com
Contact: Maria Miles, Pres.

60996 ■ Saugus Chamber of Commerce
335 Central St.
Saugus, MA 01906
Ph:(781)233-8407
Fax: (781)231-1145
Co. E-mail: sauguschamber@verizon.net
URL: http://www.sauguschamber.org
Contact: Desiree McKelvey, Exec.Dir.

60997 ■ Scituate Chamber of Commerce
PO Box 401
Scituate, MA 02066-0401
Ph:(781)545-4000
Co. E-mail: info@scituatechamber.org
URL: http://www.scituatechamber.org
Contact: Dan Taylor, Pres.

60998 ■ Somerville Chamber of Commerce
PO Box 440343
Somerville, MA 02144
Ph:(617)776-4100
Fax: (617)776-1157
Co. E-mail: info@somervillechamber.org
URL: http://www.somervillechamber.org
Contact: Stephen Mackey, Pres./CEO

60999 ■ South Hadley Chamber of Commerce
116 Main St., Ste. 4
South Hadley, MA 01075
Ph:(413)532-6451
Fax: (413)532-6451
Co. E-mail: mail@shchamber.com
URL: http://www.shchamber.com
Contact: Susan Stockman, Exec. Dir.

61000 ■ South Shore Chamber of Commerce
36 Miller Stile Rd.
PO Box 690625
Quincy, MA 02269
Ph:(617)479-1111
Fax: (617)479-9274
Co. E-mail: info@southshorechamber.org
URL: http://www.southshorechamber.org
Contact: Peter Forman, Pres./CEO

61001 ■ Southern Berkshire Chamber of Commerce
40 Railroad St., No. 2
PO Box 810
Great Barrington, MA 01230-0810
Ph:(413)528-4284
Free: 800-269-4825
Fax: (413)528-2200
Co. E-mail: sbcoc@bcn.net
URL: http://www.southernberkshirechamber.com
Contact: Sharon Palma, Exec. Dir.

61002 ■ Stockbridge Chamber of Commerce
6 Elm St.
PO Box 224
Stockbridge, MA 01262-0224
Ph:(413)298-5200
Fax: (413)298-4321
Co. E-mail: info@stockbridgechamber.org
URL: http://www.stockbridgechamber.org
Contact: Barbara Zanetti, Exec.Dir.

61003 ■ Stoneham Chamber of Commerce
269 Main St.
Stoneham, MA 02180
Ph:(781)438-0001
Fax: (781)438-0007
Co. E-mail: info@stonehamchamber.org
URL: http://www.stonehamchamber.org
Contact: Sharon A. Iovanni, Exec.Dir.

61004 ■ Stoughton Chamber of Commerce
PO Box 41
Stoughton, MA 02072
Ph:(781)297-7450
Fax: (781)344-1747
Co. E-mail: chamber@stoughtonma.com
URL: http://www.stoughtonma.com
Contact: Terry Schneider, Pres.

61005 ■ Taunton Area Chamber of Commerce
12 Taunton Green, Ste. 201
Taunton, MA 02780-3227
Ph:(508)824-4068
Fax: (508)884-8222
Co. E-mail: info@tauntonareachamber.org
URL: http://www.tauntonareachamber.org
Contact: Diana L. Shearstone, Pres./CEO

61006 ■ Three Rivers Chamber of Commerce
PO Box 233
Three Rivers, MA 01080
Ph:(413)283-8321
Contact: Roger Dugay, Exec. Sec.

61007 ■ Tri-Community Area Chamber of Commerce
380 Main St.
Sturbridge, MA 01566
Ph:(508)347-2761
Free: 888-788-7274
Fax: (508)347-5218
Co. E-mail: info@sturbridge.org
URL: http://www.tricomchamber.org
Contact: Robert P. Chartier, Pres.

61008 ■ Tri-Town Chamber of Commerce
15 West St.
Mansfield, MA 02048
Ph:(508)339-5655
Fax: (508)339-8333
Co. E-mail: chamber@tri-townchamber.org
URL: http://www.tri-townchamber.org
Contact: Tricia White, Exec.Dir.

61009 ■ United Chamber of Commerce
PO Box 354
Franklin, MA 02038
Ph:(508)528-2800
Fax: (508)520-7864
Co. E-mail: ucc@unitedchamber.org
URL: http://www.unitedchamber.org
Contact: Thomas J. Fleming III, Pres./CEO

61010 ■ Wachusett Chamber of Commerce
1 Green St.
Clinton, MA 01510
Ph:(978)368-7687
Fax: (978)368-7689
Co. E-mail: info@wachusettchamber.com
URL: http://www.wachusettchamber.com
Contact: Maegen McCaffrey, Exec.Dir.

61011 ■ Wakefield Chamber of Commerce
PO Box 585
Wakefield, MA 01880
Ph:(781)245-0741
Fax: (781)245-1544
Co. E-mail: chamber@wakefieldma.org
URL: http://www.wakefieldma.org
Contact: Sue Worden, Pres.

61012 ■ Walpole Chamber of Commerce
PO Box 361
Walpole, MA 02081
Ph:(508)668-0081
Co. E-mail: office@walpolechamber.com
URL: http://walpolechamber.com
Contact: Beth Pelick, Pres.

61013 ■ Waltham West Suburban Chamber of Commerce
84 South St.
Waltham, MA 02453
Ph:(781)894-4700
Fax: (781)894-1708
Co. E-mail: info@walthamchamber.com
URL: http://www.walthamchamber.com
Contact: John C. Peacock, Exec.Dir.

61014 ■ Watertown - Belmont Chamber of Commerce
182 Main St.
Watertown, MA 02471
Ph:(617)926-1017
Fax: (617)926-2322
Co. E-mail: info@wbcc.org
URL: http://www.wbcc.org
Contact: Brenda Fanara, Exec.Dir.

61015 ■ Wellesley Chamber of Commerce
1 Hollis St., Ste. 111
Wellesley, MA 02482-4671
Ph:(781)235-2446
Fax: (781)235-7326
Co. E-mail: mobrien@wellesleychamber.org

URL: http://www.wellesleychamber.org
Contact: Maura M. O'Brien, Pres./CEO

61016 ■ Wellfleet Chamber of Commerce
PO Box 571
Wellfleet, MA 02667-0571
Ph:(508)349-2510
Fax: (508)349-3740
Co. E-mail: info@wellfleetchamber.com
URL: http://www.wellfleetchamber.com
Contact: Maureen Schraut, Exec.Sec.

61017 ■ Williamstown Chamber of Commerce
PO Box 357
Williamstown, MA 01267
Ph:(413)458-9077
Free: 800-214-3799
Fax: (413)458-2666
Co. E-mail: info@williamstownchamber.com
URL: http://www.williamstownchamber.com
Contact: Amber Braman, Exec.Dir.

61018 ■ Wilmington Chamber of Commerce
PO Box 463
Wilmington, MA 01887-0463
Ph:(978)657-7211
Fax: (978)657-0139
Co. E-mail: wilmingtonchmbr@earthlink.net
URL: http://www.wilmingtonbusiness.com
Contact: Arthur Hayden, Pres.

61019 ■ Winchester Chamber of Commerce
25 Waterfield St.
Winchester, MA 01890
Ph:(781)729-8870
URL: http://www.winchesterchamber.com
Contact: Catherine S. Alexander, Dir.

61020 ■ Winthrop Chamber of Commerce
207 Hagman Rd.
Winthrop, MA 02152-0005
Ph:(617)846-9898
Fax: (617)846-9922
Co. E-mail: info@winthropchamber.com
URL: http://www.winthropchamber.com
Contact: Eric Gaynor, Exec.Dir.

61021 ■ Worcester Regional Chamber of Commerce
339 Main St.
Worcester, MA 01608-1581
Ph:(508)753-2924
Fax: (508)754-8560
Co. E-mail: rkennedy@worcesterchamber.org
URL: http://www.worcesterchamber.org
Contact: Richard B. Kennedy, Pres./CEO

MINORITY BUSINESS ASSISTANCE PROGRAMS

61022 ■ Umass Boston Small Business Development Center & Minority Business Center
College of Management
100 Morresy Blvd., M-5-403
Boston, MA 02125
Ph:(617)287-7750
Fax: (617)287-7767
URL: http://www.sbdc.umb.edu
Contact: Mark Allio, Dir

FINANCING AND LOAN PROGRAMS

61023 ■ 100 X
880 Winter St., Ste 300
North Waltham, MA 02451
Ph:(781)529-1000
Fax: (781)529-1098
URL: http://www.100x.com
Contact: Ken Lang, Chief Executive Officer

Investment Types: Seed, start-up, and first stage. **Industry Preferences:** Internet specific.

61024 ■ Abry Partners, LLC
111 Huntington Ave., 30th Fl.
Boston, MA 02199
Ph:(617)859-2959
Fax: (617)859-2959
URL: http://www.abry.com
Contact: Dan Budde, Partner
Investment Policies: Leveraged buyout, and mezzanine. **Industry Preferences:** Communications and media. **Geographic Preferences:** U.S.

61025 ■ Adams, Harkness & Hill, Inc.
60 State St.
Boston, MA 02109
Ph:(617)788-1670
Fax: (617)788-1663
URL: http://www.ahhventures.com
Contact: Timothy McMahan, President
Preferred Investment Size: $500,000 to $2,500,000.
Investment Types: Second stage and expansion. **Industry Preferences:** Communications and media, computer software, semiconductors and other electronics. **Geographic Preferences:** U.S.

61026 ■ ADL Ventures / Arthur D. Little Enterprises, Inc.
68 Fargo St.
Boston, MA 02210
Ph:(617)443-0309
Fax: (617)443-0166
URL: http://www.arthurlittle.com
Contact: Pamela McNamara, Chief Executive Officer
Investment Policies: Seed, start-up, first and second stage. **Industry Preferences:** Medical and health, consumer related, agriculture, forestry and fishing.

61027 ■ Advanced Technology Ventures (ATV)
Bay Colony Corporate Ctr.
281 Winter St., Ste. 3700
North Waltham, MA 02451
Ph:(781)290-0707
Fax: (781)768-3825
URL: http://www.atvcapital.com
Contact: Jack Harrington, General Director
Preferred Investment Size: $15,000,000 to $35,000,000. **Investment Types:** Start-up, seed, first and second stage, early and later stage, and balanced. **Industry Preferences:** Internet specific, computer software and services, computer hardware, other products, semiconductors and other electronics, communications and media, medical and health, biotechnology, industrial and energy, and consumer related. **Geographic Preferences:** U.S. and Canada.

61028 ■ Advent International
75 State St., 29th Fl.
Boston, MA 02109
Ph:(617)951-9400
Fax: (617)951-0566
URL: http://www.adventinternational.com
Contact: William Schmidt, Managing Director
Preferred Investment Size: $1,000,000 minimum.
Investment Types: Seed, early, later, first and second stage, balanced, control-block purchases, expansion, generalist PE, industry rollups, leveraged buyout, mezzanine, public companies, recapitalizations, research and development, and special situation. **Industry Preferences:** Other products, consumer related, communications and media, Internet specific, industrial and energy, medical and health, computer software and services, computer hardware, semiconductors and other electronics, and biotechnology. **Geographic Preferences:** U.S. and Canada.

61029 ■ American Research and Development Corporation
30 Federal St.
Boston, MA 02110-2508
Ph:(617)423-7500
Fax: (617)423-9655
Contact: Francis Hughes, President
Preferred Investment Size: $100,000 minimum. **Investment Types:** Seed, start-up, first and second

stage. **Industry Preferences:** Communications, computer hardware and software, Internet specific, semiconductors and other electronics. **Geographic Preferences:** Northeast.

61030 ■ Ampersand Ventures
55 William St., Ste. 240
Wellesley, MA 02481
Ph:(617)239-0700
Fax: (617)239-0824
URL: http://www.ampersandventures.com
Contact: Richard Charpie, Managing General Partner
Preferred Investment Size: $5,000,000 to $10,000,000. **Investment Types:** Early and later stage, first and second stage, expansion, generalist PE, industry rollups, management buyouts, mezzanine, private placement, recapitalizations, special situation, and turnaround. **Industry Preferences:** Biotechnology, semiconductors and other electronics, Internet specific, communications and media, computer software and services, industrial and energy, other products, medical and health, consumer related, and computer hardware. **Geographic Preferences:** U.S.

61031 ■ Applied Technology
1 Cranberry Hill
Lexington, MA 02421-7397
Ph:(617)862-8622
Fax: (617)862-8367
Contact: Eugene Flath, Partner
Investment Types: Seed, start-up, first and second stage, leveraged buyout, and research and development. **Industry Preferences:** Computer software, hardware and services, Internet specific, semiconductors and other electronics, communications and media, industrial and energy, and consumer related. **Geographic Preferences:** U.S.

61032 ■ Argo Global Capital
210 Broadway, Ste. 101
Lynnfield, MA 01940
Ph:(781)592-5250
Fax: (781)592-5230
URL: http://www.gsmcapital.com
Investment Types: Balanced and expansion. **Industry Preferences:** Communications, computer, and Internet related. **Geographic Preferences:** No preference.

61033 ■ Ascent Venture Partners
255 State St., 5th Fl.
Boston, MA 02109
Ph:(617)270-9400
Fax: (617)270-9401
URL: http://www.ascentvp.com
Contact: Matt Fates, Principal
Preferred Investment Size: $2,000,000 to $6,000,000. **Investment Types:** Balanced. **Industry Preferences:** Internet specific, medical and health, computer software and services, communications and media, medical and health, computer hardware, consumer related, industrial and energy, semiconductors and other electronics. **Geographic Preferences:** East Coast, Mid Atlantic, and Northeast.

61034 ■ Atlantic Capital
164 Cushing Hwy.
Cohasset, MA 02025
Ph:(617)383-9449
Fax: (617)383-6040
Co. E-mail: info@atlanticcap.com
URL: http://www.atlanticcap.com
Preferred Investment Size: $300,000 to $500,000.
Investment Types: Start-up and first stage. **Industry Preferences:** Diversified. **Geographic Preferences:** National.

61035 ■ Atlas Venture
222 Berkeley St., Ste. 1950
Boston, MA 02116
Ph:(617)488-2200
Fax: (617)859-9292
URL: http://www.atlasventure.com
Contact: Robert Badavas, Chief Operating Officer
Preferred Investment Size: $1,000,000 to $20,000,000. **Investment Types:** Seed, start-up, re-

search and development, first and second stage, mezzanine, and balanced. **Industry Preferences:** Internet specific, computer software, hardware and services, biotechnology, communications and media, medical and health, semiconductors and other electronics, industrial and energy. **Geographic Preferences:** U.S. and Canada.

61036 ■ Axxon Capital, LP
28 State St., 37th Fl.
Boston, MA 02109
Ph:(617)722-0980
Fax: (617)557-6014
URL: http://www.axxoncapital.com
Contact: Paula Groves, Founding Partner
Preferred Investment Size: $500,000 to $3,500,000.
Investment Types: Early later, first, and second stage, and expansion. **Industry Preferences:** Communications, and business service. **Geographic Preferences:** Northeast.

61037 ■ BancBoston Capital/BancBoston Ventures
175 Federal St., 10th Fl.
Boston, MA 02110
Ph:(617)434-2509
Fax: (617)434-1153
URL: http://www.bancbostoncapital.com
Preferred Investment Size: $1,000,000 to $15,000,000. **Investment Types:** Seed, early stage, acquisition, recapitalizations, later stage, management buyouts, expansion, fund of funds, generalist PE, and mezzanine. **Industry Preferences:** Other products, communications and media, Internet specific, consumer related, industrial and energy, computer software, hardware and services, semiconductors and other electronics, biotechnology, medical and health, and computer hardware. **Geographic Preferences:** U.S. and Eastern Canada.

61038 ■ Battery Ventures, L.P. (Wellesley)
20 William St., Ste. 200
Wellesley, MA 02481
Ph:(781)577-1000
Fax: (781)577-1001
URL: http://www.battery.com
Contact: Michael Brown, Partner
Preferred Investment Size: $3,000,000 to $35,000,000. **Investment Types:** Seed, start-up, first stage, balanced, mezzanine, and leveraged buyout. **Industry Preferences:** Internet specific, computer software and services, communications and media, other products, semiconductors and other electronics, computer hardware, industrial and energy. **Geographic Preferences:** U.S. and Canada.

61039 ■ Beacon Technology Ventures
8 Saint Mary's St., Ste. 910
Boston, MA 02215
Ph:(617)358-1600
Fax: (617)358-1536
URL: http://www.btechventures.com
Contact: Alok Prasad, President
Preferred Investment Size: $250,000 to $3,000,000.
Investment Policies: Start-up, seed, early, first and second stage. **Industry Preferences:** Communications and media, computer related, semiconductors and other electronics, biotechnology, medical and health. **Geographic Preferences:** Northeast.

61040 ■ Bedrock Capital Partners
c/o Aueer, Mason & Zajac
29 Dean Ave.
PO Box 347
Franklin, MA 02038
URL: http://www.bedrockcapital.com
Contact: James McLean, Managing Director
Preferred Investment Size: $175,000 to $5,580,000.
Investment Policies: Seed and early stage. **Industry Preferences:** Internet specific, computer software and services, communications and media, medical and health, computer hardware, and other products.

61041 ■ Berkshires Capital Investors
296 Main St., 2nd Fl.
Williamstown, MA 01267
Ph:(413)458-9683

Fax: (413)458-5603
URL: http://www.berkshirescap.com
Contact: Russell Howard, Managing Director
Preferred Investment Size: $33,000,000 minimum.
Investment Policies: Seed and early stage. **Industry Preferences:** Communications, computer software, Internet specific, and business service. **Geographic Preferences:** Massachusetts and New York.

61042 ■ Bessemer Venture Partners (Wellesley Hills)
83 Walnut St.
Wellesley Hills, MA 02481
Ph:(781)237-6050
Fax: (781)237-7576
URL: http://www.bessemervp.com
Contact: Jeremy Levine, Principal
Preferred Investment Size: $1,000,000 to $10,000,000. **Investment Types:** Seed, start-up, early, first and second stage, research and development, expansion, control-block purchases, leveraged buyout, and special situation. **Industry Preferences:** Internet specific, communications and media, computer software and services, semiconductors and other electronics, consumer related, medical and health, industrial and energy, other products, and biotechnology. **Geographic Preferences:** U.S.

61043 ■ Bioventures Investors
245 1st St., 14th Fl.
Cambridge, MA 02142
Ph:(617)252-3443
Fax: (617)621-7993
URL: http://www.bioventuresinvestors.com
Contact: Mickey Kim, Principal
Preferred Investment Size: $500,000 to $7,500,000. **Investment Policies:** Seed, early, first and second stage, balanced, and private placement. **Industry Preferences:** Biotechnology, and medical and health. **Geographic Preferences:** East Coast U.S.; and Canada.

61044 ■ Boardman Ventures
40 Beach St., Ste. 104
Manchester, MA 01944
Ph:(978)525-9000
Fax: (978)526-9999
URL: http://www.boardmanventures.com
Investment Policies: Early stage. **Industry Preferences:** Computer software. **Geographic Preferences:** East Coast.

61045 ■ Boston Capital Ventures
114 State St., 6th Fl.
Boston, MA 02109
Ph:(617)227-6550
Fax: (617)227-3847
URL: http://www.bcv.com
Contact: Alex Wilmerding, Partner
Preferred Investment Size: $500,000 to $3,000,000. **Investment Types:** Start-up, first and second stage, recapitalizations, expansion, and leveraged buyout. **Industry Preferences:** Internet specific, communications and media, other products, medical and health, computer software and services, consumer related, industrial and energy, semiconductors and other electronics, industrial and energy, biotechnology, and computer hardware. **Geographic Preferences:** Northeast and Canada.

61046 ■ Boston Financial & Equity Corp.
20 Overland St.
PO Box 15071
Boston, MA 02215
Ph:(617)267-2900
Fax: (617)437-7601
Co. E-mail: debbie@bfec.com
Contact: Deborah J. Monosson, Senior Vice President
Preferred Investment Size: $500,000 to $1,000,000. **Investment Types:** Seed, start-up, first and second stage, leveraged buyout, mezzanine, and research and development. **Industry Preferences:** Diversified. **Geographic Preferences:** National.

61047 ■ Boston Millennia Partners
30 Rowes Wharf, Ste. 500
Boston, MA 02110

Ph:(617)428-5150
Fax: (617)428-5160
URL: http://www.bmpvc.com
Contact: Dana Callow, Managing General Partner
E-mail: dana@milleniapartners.com
Preferred Investment Size: $3,000,000 to $15,000,000. **Investment Types:** First and second stage, start-up, later stage, and expansion. **Industry Preferences:** Internet specific, computer software and services, biotechnology, communications and media, semiconductors and other electronics, other products, computer hardware, consumer related, medical and health. **Geographic Preferences:** All U.S., East Coast, and Canada.

61048 ■ Boston University Community Technology Fund
108 Bay State Rd.
Boston, MA 02215
Ph:(617)353-4550
Fax: (617)353-6141
URL: http://www.bu.edu/ctf
Contact: Matthew Crowley, Managing Director
Preferred Investment Size: $250,000 to $1,000,000. **Investment Types:** Seed, start-up, early, first and second stage, and expansion. **Industry Preferences:** Medical and health, biotechnology, Internet specific, semiconductors and other electronics, computer software and services, computer hardware, communications and media, industrial and energy, consumer related, and other products. **Geographic Preferences:** Northeast.

61049 ■ Bristol Investment Trust
842A Beacon St.
Boston, MA 02215-3199
Ph:(617)566-5212
Fax: (617)267-0932
Investment Types: First and second stage, and mezzanine. **Industry Preferences:** Medical and health, consumer related, and financial services. **Geographic Preferences:** Northeast.

61050 ■ Brook Venture Partners, L.L.C.
301 Edgewater Pl., Ste. 425
Wakefield, MA 01880
Ph:(781)295-4000
Fax: (781)295-4007
URL: http://www.brookventure.com
Contact: Edward Williams, Partner
Preferred Investment Size: $1,000,000 to $3,000,000. **Investment Types:** Early, first, and second stage, and expansion. **Industry Preferences:** Communications, computer software, Internet specific, semiconductors and other electronics, medical and health, industrial and energy, transportation, and manufacturing. **Geographic Preferences:** Northeast, New York, and District of Columbia.

61051 ■ Burr, Egan, Deleage, and Co. (Boston)
200 Clarendon St., Ste. 3800
Boston, MA 02116
Ph:(617)262-7770
Fax: (617)262-9779
Preferred Investment Size: $2,000,000. **Investment Types:** No preference. **Industry Preferences:** Communications, computer, and medical/health related. **Geographic Preferences:** Entire U.S.

61052 ■ Cambridge Samsung Partners
1 Exeter Plz., 9th Fl.
Boston, MA 02116
Ph:(617)262-4440
Fax: (617)262-5562
URL: http://www.cspartners.com
Contact: Sundar Subramaniam, Managing Director
Investment Types: First stage. **Geographic Preferences:** U.S.

61053 ■ Cambridgelight Partners
3 Bow St., 4th Fl.
Cambridge, MA 02138
Ph:(617)497-6310
URL: http://www.cambridgelight.com
Contact: Dan Alexander, Co-Founder
Preferred Investment Size: $50,000 to $2,000,000. **Investment Policies:** Seed and early stage. **Industry**

Preferences: Communications, computer software, Internet specific, and semiconductors and other electronics. **Geographic Preferences:** Massachusetts.

61054 ■ Castile Ventures
890 Winter St., Ste. 140
Waltham, MA 02451
Ph:(781)890-0060
Fax: (781)890-0065
URL: http://www.castileventures.com
Contact: Roger Walton, Partner
Preferred Investment Size: $1,000,000 to $10,000,000. **Investment Types:** Seed and early stage. **Industry Preferences:** Communications and media, and Internet specific. **Geographic Preferences:** Mid Atlantic and Northeast.

61055 ■ Charles River Ventures
1000 Winter St., Ste. 3300
Waltham, MA 02451
Ph:(781)768-6000
Fax: (781)768-6100
URL: http://www.crv.com
Contact: Austin Westerling, Principal
Preferred Investment Size: $1,000,000 to $15,000,000. **Investment Types:** Start-up and first stage. **Industry Preferences:** Internet specific, communications and media, computer software and services, computer hardware, other products, industrial and energy, semiconductors and other electronics, medical and health, consumer related, and biotechnology. **Geographic Preferences:** U.S.

61056 ■ Chestnut Street Partners, Inc.
75 State St., Ste. 2500
Boston, MA 02109
Ph:(617)345-7220
Fax: (617)345-7201
Co. E-mail: chestnut@chestnutp.com
Contact: David Croll, Vice President
Investment Types: Seed, research and development, start-up, and first stage. **Industry Preferences:** Communications, computer software, Internet specific, semiconductors and other electronics, medical and health, consumer related, and industrial and energy.

61057 ■ Claflin Capital Management, Inc.
10 Liberty Sq., Ste. 300
Boston, MA 02109
Ph:(617)426-6505
Fax: (617)482-0016
URL: http://www.claflincapital.com
Contact: Thomas Claflin, Managing Partner
Preferred Investment Size: $250,000 to $1,000,000. **Investment Types:** Early stage and start-up. **Industry Preferences:** Computer software and services, computer hardware, Internet specific, medical and health, communications and media, semiconductors and other electronics, biotechnology, consumer related, industrial and energy, and other products. **Geographic Preferences:** Northeast.

61058 ■ Clarity Capital
45 Fairfield St., 5th Fl.
Boston, MA 02116
Ph:(617)262-6800
Fax: (617)262-6030
URL: http://www.claritycap.com
Preferred Investment Size: $1,000,000 to $5,000,000. **Investment Types:** Early stage. **Industry Preferences:** Communications and media. **Geographic Preferences:** U.S.

61059 ■ Comdisco Venture Group (Waltham)
Totton Pond Office Ctr.
400-1 Totten Pond Rd., 3rd Fl.
Waltham, MA 02451
Ph:(617)672-0250
Fax: (617)398-8099
URL: http://www.comdisco.com
Contact: Jim Labe, Chief Executive Officer
Preferred Investment Size: $300,000 to $20,000,000. **Investment Types:** Seed, early and later stage, mezzanine, and expansion. **Industry Preferences:** Internet specific, computer hardware, software and services, communications and media, medical and health, consumer related, semiconductors and other electronics. **Geographic Preferences:** U.S.

61060 ■ Commonwealth Capital Ventures
950 Winter St., Ste. 4100
Wellesley, MA 02451
Ph:(781)890-5554
Fax: (781)890-3414
URL: http://www.commonwealthvc.com
Contact: Jeffrey Hurst, General Partner
Preferred Investment Size: $1,000,000 to $10,000,000. **Investment Types:** Early, first and second stage. **Industry Preferences:** Computer software and services, Internet specific, communications and media, industrial and energy, medical and health, consumer related, semiconductors and other electronics, biotechnology, and other products. **Geographic Preferences:** U.S.

61061 ■ Copley Venture Partners
99 Summer St., Ste. 1720
Boston, MA 02110
Ph:(617)737-1253
Fax: (617)439-0699
Preferred Investment Size: $1,000,000 minimum.
Investment Types: Start-up, first and second stage.

61062 ■ Corning Capital / Corning Technology Ventures
121 High St., Ste. 400
Boston, MA 02110
Ph:(617)338-2656
Fax: (617)261-3864
URL: http://www.corningventures.com
Contact: Barney Corning, Partner
Investment Policies: Early stage. **Industry Preferences:** Internet specific, computer software and services medical and health, consumer related, computer hardware, communications and media, semiconductors and other electronics, biotechnology, industrial and energy. **Geographic Preferences:** Northeast.

61063 ■ Dhunn-Carr Venture
530 Atlantic Ave., 3rd Fl.
Boston, MA 02210
Ph:(617)426-6401
Fax: (617)426-1422
URL: http://www.dhunn-carr.com
Contact: Gul Iqbal, Managing Director
Investment Policies: Seed and early stage. **Industry Preferences:** Communications, computer software, Internet specific, and semiconductors and other electronics. **Geographic Preferences:** National.

61064 ■ Dover Medical Ventures
75 Federal St., 9th Fl.
Boston, MA 02110
Ph:(617)912-5128
URL: http://www.dovermedicalventures.com
Contact: Edward Hamilton, Chief Financial Officer
Investment Policies: Seed and early stage. **Industry Preferences:** Medical and health.

61065 ■ Downer & Company
211 Congress St.
Boston, MA 02110
Ph:(617)482-6200
Fax: (617)482-6201
Co. E-mail: cdowner@downer.com
URL: http://www.downer.com
Contact: Charles Downer, Chief Executive Officer
Preferred Investment Size: $300,000 to $500,000.
Investment Types: Start-up, first and second stage, and mezzanine. **Industry Preferences:** Computer hardware and software, semiconductors and other electronics, medical and health, consumer related, industrial and energy, and manufacturing. **Geographic Preferences:** Northeast and Canada.

61066 ■ Draper Fisher Jurvetson New England / DFJ/NE
1 Broadway, 14th Fl.
Cambridge, MA 02142
Ph:(617)758-4275
Fax: (617)758-4101
URL: http://www.dfjne.com
Contact: Scott Johnson, Managing Director
Preferred Investment Size: $500,000 to $1,250,000.
Investment Policies: Start-up, seed, second, early

and later stage. **Industry Preferences:** Communications, computer hardware and software, Internet specific, semiconductors and other electronics, consumer related, industrial and energy, and business service. **Geographic Preferences:** Northeast.

61067 ■ Echelon Ventures LLC
234 Lewis Wharf
Boston, MA 02110
Ph:(617)624-3880
Fax: (617)624-0280
URL: http://www.echelonventures.com
Contact: Alfred Woodworth, Managing Director
Preferred Investment Size: $1,000,000 to $5,000,000. **Investment Policies:** Early, first, and second stage, and expansion. **Industry Preferences:** Computer software, semiconductors and other electronics, biotechnology, and medical and health. **Geographic Preferences:** Northeast.

61068 ■ Egan-Managed Capital
30 Federal St.
Boston, MA 02110-2508
Ph:(617)695-2600
Fax: (617)695-2699
URL: http://www.egancapital.com
Contact: John Egan, Managing Partner
Preferred Investment Size: $2,000,000 to $5,000,000. **Investment Types:** Seed, start-up, Early, and first stage. **Industry Preferences:** Computer software and services, Internet specific, semiconductors and other electronics, communications and media, and computer hardware. **Geographic Preferences:** Northeast.

61069 ■ Fidelity Ventures
82 Devonshire St., E16B
Boston, MA 02109
Ph:(617)392-2448
Fax: (617)385-2692
URL: http://www.fidelityventures.com
Contact: Larry Cheng, Principal
Preferred Investment Size: $1,000,000 to $10,000,000. **Investment Types:** Seed, start-up, early, first and second stage, and expansion. **Industry Preferences:** Internet specific, computer software, and services, communications and media, computer hardware, consumer related, semiconductors and other electronics, and other products. **Geographic Preferences:** U.S. and Canada.

61070 ■ Flagship Ventures
1 Memorial Dr., 7th Fl.
Cambridge, MA 02142
Ph:(617)868-1888
Fax: (617)868-1115
URL: http://www.flagshipventures.com
Contact: Noubar Afeyan, Chief Executive Officer and Managing Dir
Preferred Investment Size: $1,000,000 to $22,000,000. **Investment Policies:** Start-up, seed, research and development, early and first stage, and balanced. **Industry Preferences:** Computer software and services, communications and media, biotechnology, Internet specific, medical and health, semiconductors and other electronics, other products, computer hardware, and industrial and energy. **Geographic Preferences:** Mid Atlantic, Northeast, and West Coast.

61071 ■ Fletcher Spaght Associates
222 Berkeley St., 20th Fl.
Boston, MA 02116
Ph:(617)247-7757
Fax: (617)247-7757
URL: http://www.fletcherspaght.com
Contact: Peary Spaght, President
Investment Policies: Early stage. **Industry Preferences:** Communications, computer hardware and software, Internet specific, semiconductors and other electronics, medical and health, industrial and energy, transportation, and financial services. **Geographic Preferences:** U.S.

61072 ■ Fowler, Anthony & Co.
20 Walnut St., 3rd. Fl.
Wellesley, MA 02481-2104

Ph:(781)237-4201
Fax: (781)237-7718
Contact: John Quagliaroli, President
Preferred Investment Size: $4,000,000 to $5,000,000. **Investment Types:** Early, first, second and later stage, acquisition, control-block purchases, expansion, generalist PE, mezzanine, management buyouts, private placement, recapitalizations, special situation, and turnaround. **Industry Preferences:** Communications and media, computer software and hardware, Internet specific, semiconductors and other electronics, biotechnology, medical and health, consumer related, industrial and energy, transportation, financial services, business service, manufacturing, agriculture, forestry and fishing. **Geographic Preferences:** U.S. and Canada.

61073 ■ Gemini Investors / GMN Investors
20 William St., Ste. 250
Wellesley, MA 02481
Ph:(781)237-7001
Fax: (781)237-7233
URL: http://www.gemini-investors.com
Contact: James Goodman, President
Preferred Investment Size: $3,000 to $8,000. **Investment Types:** Expansion, generalist PE, later stage, private placement, and recapitalizations. **Industry Preferences:** Communications and media, medical and health, computer software and services, Internet specific, other products, computer hardware, and consumer related. **Geographic Preferences:** U.S.

61074 ■ General Catalyst Partners / General Catalyst Group LLC
20 University Rd., Ste. 450
Cambridge, MA 02138
Ph:(617)234-7000
Fax: (617)234-7040
URL: http://www.generalcatalyst.com
Contact: William Fitzgerald, Managing Director and Chief Financial Of
Preferred Investment Size: $1,000,000 to $25,000,000. **Investment Types:** Seed, start-up, early, and first stage. **Industry Preferences:** Internet specific, computer software and services, communications and media, other products, industrial and energy, semiconductors and other electronics, and consumer related. **Geographic Preferences:** Northeast.

61075 ■ Great Hill Equity Partners, LLC
1 Liberty Sq.
Boston, MA 02109
Ph:(617)790-9400
Fax: (617)790-9401
URL: http://www.greathillpartners.com
Contact: Christopher Gaffney, Managing Partner
Preferred Investment Size: $10,000,000 to $40,000,000. **Investment Types:** Balanced. **Industry Preferences:** Internet specific, communications and media, computer hardware, software and services, semiconductors and other electronics, and other products. **Geographic Preferences:** U.S.

61076 ■ Greylock Management Corp. (Boston)
1 Federal St.
Boston, MA 02110-2065
Ph:(617)423-5525
Fax: (617)482-0059
Contact: Chris Surowiec
Preferred Investment Size: $250,000 minimum. **Investment Types:** Seed, start-up, first and early stage, and expansion. **Industry Preferences:** Diversified. **Geographic Preferences:** No preference.

61077 ■ Grove Street Advisors LLC
20 William St., Ste. 230
Wellesley, MA 02481
Ph:(781)263-6100
Fax: (781)263-6101
URL: http://www.grovestreetadvisors.com
Contact: Clinton Harris, Managing General Partner
Preferred Investment Size: $1,000,000 to $7,500,000. **Investment Types:** Early and later

stage, mezzanine, special situation, fund of funds, expansion, and other. **Industry Preferences:** Communications and media, computer software and hardware, Internet specific, semiconductors and other electronics, consumer related, industrial and energy, and business service.

61078 ■ Gryphon Ventures
222 Berkeley St., Ste.1600
Boston, MA 02116
Ph:(617)267-9191
Fax: (617)267-4293
Co. E-mail: all@gryphoninc.com
Contact: Andrew J. Atkinson, Vice President
Preferred Investment Size: $1,000,000 minimum.
Investment Types: Start-up, first stage, second stage. **Industry Preferences:** Biotechnology, industrial and energy. **Geographic Preferences:** U.S.

61079 ■ Halpern, Denny & Co.
500 Boylston St., Ste. 1880
Boston, MA 02116
Ph:(617)536-6602
Fax: (617)536-8535
URL: http://www.halperndenny.com
Contact: David Malm, Partner
Preferred Investment Size: $5,000,000 to $40,000,000. **Investment Types:** Seed, early, first, second, and later stage, acquisition, balanced, control-block purchases, management buyouts, leveraged buyout, expansion, generalist PE, joint ventures, mezzanine, recapitalizations, and turnaround. **Industry Preferences:** Consumer related, Internet specific, other products, communications and media, computer software and services, industrial and energy, medical and health, and computer hardware. **Geographic Preferences:** U.S.

61080 ■ Harbourvest Partners, LLC
1 Financial Ctr., 44th Fl.
Boston, MA 02111
Ph:(617)348-3707
Fax: (617)350-0305
URL: http://www.harbourvest.com
Contact: Brett Delbridge, Managing Director
Preferred Investment Size: $5,000,000 to $80,000,000. **Investment Types:** Later stage, balanced, fund of funds, fund of funds of second, generalist PE, and leveraged buyout, recapitalizations, mezzanine, and acquisition. **Industry Preferences:** Other products, Internet specific, communications and media, computer software and services, consumer related, computer hardware, semiconductors and other electronics, industrial and energy, biotechnology, medical and health. **Geographic Preferences:** Mid Atlantic, Northeast, Rocky Mountains, and West Coast.

61081 ■ High Peaks Venture Partners, LLC / Berkshires Capital Invest
125 High Rock Ave.
Saratoga Springs, NY 12866
Ph:(518)306-3048
Fax: (518)580-9843
URL: http://www.berkshirescap.com
Contact: Russell Howard, Managing Director
Investment Types: Early stage. **Geographic Preferences:** New York and Northeast.

61082 ■ Highland Capital Partners
92 Hayden Ave.
Lexington, MA 02421
Ph:(781)861-5500
Fax: (781)861-5499
URL: http://www.hcp.com
Contact: Corey Mulloy, General Partner
Preferred Investment Size: $100,000 to $20,000,000. **Investment Types:** Seed, early, and later stage. **Industry Preferences:** Internet specific, computer software and services, communications and media, medical and health, other products, biotechnology, semiconductors and other electronics, computer hardware, and industrial and energy. **Geographic Preferences:** U.S. and Canada.

61083 ■ Industry Ventures (Newburyport)
6 Bayne Ln.
Newburyport, MA 01950

Ph:(978)499-7606
Fax: (978)499-0686
URL: http://www.industryventures.com
Contact: Thomas Litle, Managing Director
Preferred Investment Size: $250,000 to $250,000,000. **Investment Types:** Seed, start-up, early, first, and second stage, and acquisition. **Industry Preferences:** Communications and media, computer software, Internet specific, consumer related, and business service. **Geographic Preferences:** Mid Atlantic, Northeast, Northern California, and West Coast.

61084 ■ Kestrel Venture Management / Corning Venture Management
Ph:(617)451-6722
Fax: (617)451-3321
URL: http://www.kestrelvm.com
Contact: R. Gregg Stone, Principal
Preferred Investment Size: $250,000 minimum. **Investment Policies:** Early stage. **Industry Preferences:** Internet specific, biotechnology, Computer software and services, semiconductors and other electronics, other products, consumer related, computer hardware, communications and media, medical and health, and industrial and energy. **Geographic Preferences:** Northeast.

61085 ■ Lee Munder Venture Partners
John Hancock Tower T-28
200 Clarendon St.
Boston, MA 02116
Ph:(617)380-5600
Fax: (617)380-5601
URL: http://www.leemunder.com
Contact: Murray Metcalfe, Managing Director
Preferred Investment Size: $500,000 to $3,000,000.
Investment Types: Early, first stage, and expansion.
Industry Preferences: Communications, computer software, industrial and energy, semiconductors and other electronics, and financial services. **Geographic Preferences:** Mid Atlantic, Northeast, and Southeast.

61086 ■ Longworth Venture Partners, L.P.
1050 Winter St., Ste. 2600
Waltham, MA 02451
Ph:(781)663-3600
Fax: (781)663-3691
URL: http://www.longworth.com
Contact: JOHN Lawrence, Chief Financial Officer
Preferred Investment Size: $500,000 to $4,000,000.
Investment Types: Seed, start-up, first, and second stage. **Industry Preferences:** Computer software, Internet specific, financial services, and business service. **Geographic Preferences:** Mid Atlantic, Midwest, Northeast, and Southeast.

61087 ■ M/C Venture Partners
75 State St., Ste. 2500
Boston, MA 02109
Ph:(617)345-7200
Fax: (617)345-7201
URL: http://www.mcventurepartners.com
Contact: Russell Pyle, Vice President
Preferred Investment Size: $5,000,000 to $50,000,000. **Investment Types:** Early stage and leveraged buyout. **Industry Preferences:** Communications and media, Internet specific, semiconductors and other electronics, computer software and services, and consumer related. **Geographic Preferences:** U.S. and Canada.

61088 ■ Manulife Capital Corporation
175 Federal St., Ste. 825
Boston, MA 02110
Ph:(617)426-1154
URL: http://www.manulife.com
Investment Policies: Early stage. **Industry Preferences:** Biotechnology. **Geographic Preferences:** National.

61089 ■ Marconi Ventures
890 Winter St., Ste. 310
Waltham, MA 02451
Ph:(781)839-7177
Fax: (781)522-7477
URL: http://www.marconi.com

Contact: Philip Wilson, Managing Director
Preferred Investment Size: $1,000,000 to $10,000,000. **Investment Types:** Balanced, first, second, and later stage, and start-up. **Industry Preferences:** Communications and media, computer software, Internet specific, semiconductors and other electronics, medical and health. **Geographic Preferences:** U.S. and Canada.

61090 ■ Massachusetts Capital Resource Co.
420 Boylston St.
Boston, MA 02116
Ph:(617)536-3900
Fax: (617)536-7930
Contact: William J. Torpey Jr., President
Preferred Investment Size: $500,000 to $1,000,000.
Investment Types: Second stage, leveraged buyout, and mezzanine. **Industry Preferences:** Industrial and energy, semiconductors and other electronics, computer software, hardware and services, consumer related, communications and media, medical and health, and Internet specific. **Geographic Preferences:** Northeast.

61091 ■ Massachusetts Technology Development Corp. (MTDC)
148 State St.
Boston, MA 02109
Ph:(617)723-4920
Fax: (617)723-5983
Co. E-mail: jhodgman@mtdc.com
URL: http://www.mtdc.com
Contact: John F. Hodgman, President
Preferred Investment Size: $350,000 to $500,000.
Investment Types: Early, seed, and start-up. **Industry Preferences:** Computer software, hardware and services, semiconductors and other electronics, Internet specific, biotechnology, medical and health, industrial and energy, communications and media. **Geographic Preferences:** Massachusetts.

61092 ■ Masthead Venture
55 Cambridge Pky., Ste. 103
Cambridge, MA 02142
Ph:(617)621-3000
Fax: (617)621-3055
URL: http://www.mvpartners.com
Contact: John O'Sullivan, Principal
Preferred Investment Size: $500,000 to $5,000,000.
Investment Policies: Early stage. **Industry Preferences:** Communications, computer software, semiconductors and other electronics, biotechnology, and medical and health. **Geographic Preferences:** Northeast.

61093 ■ Matrix Partners
Bay Colony Corporate Ctr.
1000 Winter St., Ste. 4500
Waltham, MA 02451
Ph:(781)890-2244
Fax: (781)890-2288
URL: http://www.matrixpartners.com
Contact: Andrew Marcuvitz, General Partner
Preferred Investment Size: $100,000 to $10,000,000. **Investment Types:** Start-up, early, first and second stage, balanced, and leveraged buyout.
Industry Preferences: Communications and media, Internet specific, computer software and services, computer hardware, semiconductors and other electronics, consumer related, medical and health, industrial and energy, other products, and biotechnology.
Geographic Preferences: California and Massachusetts.

61094 ■ MDT Advisers, Inc.
125 Cambridge Park Dr.
Cambridge, MA 02140
Ph:(617)234-2200
Fax: (617)234-2210
URL: http://www.mdtai.com
Contact: Jay Senerchia, Principal
Preferred Investment Size: $500,000 to $5,000,000.
Investment Types: Early stage and expansion. **Industry Preferences:** Consumer related, other products, Internet specific, communications and media, computer software and services, semiconductors and other electronics, industrial and energy, medical and health, computer hardware, and biotechnology. **Geographic Preferences:** Northeast.

61095 ■ Medical Science Partners
200 W. St., Ste. 403
Waltham, MA 02451
Ph:(781)890-8797
Fax: (781)250-2101
URL: http://www.medsci.com
Contact: Andre Lamotte, Managing General Partner
Preferred Investment Size: $300,000 to $2,500,000.
Investment Policies: Start-up, seed, first and second stage. **Industry Preferences:** Biotechnology, medical and health, and industrial and energy. **Geographic Preferences:** National.

61096 ■ Mediphase Venture Partners / EHealth Technology Fund
2180 Washington St., Ste. 200
Newton, MA 02462
Ph:(617)332-3408
Fax: (617)332-8463
URL: http://www.mediphaseventure.com
Contact: Lawrence Miller, Partner
Investment Types: Early stage. **Industry Preferences:** Internet specific, medical and health. **Geographic Preferences:** U.S.

61097 ■ Mees Pierson Investeringsmaat. B.V. / BOA 2 Management
20 William St., Ste. 210
Wellesley, MA 02482
Ph:(781)239-7600
Fax: (781)239-0377
Investment Types: First and second stage, start-up, and balanced. **Industry Preferences:** Communications and media, Internet specific, semiconductors and other electronics. **Geographic Preferences:** U.S. and Canada.

61098 ■ Megunticook Management
137 Newbury St., Fl. 2
Boston, MA 02116
Ph:(617)986-3000
Fax: (617)986-3100
URL: http://www.megunticook.com
Contact: Grant Gund, Principal
Preferred Investment Size: $1,000,000 to $8,000,000. **Investment Types:** Early and second stage stage. **Industry Preferences:** Internet specific, communications and media, computer software and services, semiconductors and other electronics, consumer related, computer hardware, and other products. **Geographic Preferences:** Northeast.

61099 ■ MPM Capital / MPM Asset Management LLC
111 Huntington Ave., 31st Fl.
Boston, MA 02199
Ph:(617)425-9200
Fax: (617)425-9201
URL: http://www.mpmcapital.com
Contact: Ed Mascioli, Principal
Preferred Investment Size: $5,000,000 to $50,000,000. **Investment Types:** Start-up, first and early stage, balanced, expansion, other, and mezzanine. **Industry Preferences:** Biotechnology, medical and health, computer software and services, and Internet specific. **Geographic Preferences:** U.S.

61100 ■ Navigator Technology Ventures / NTV
4 Cambridge Ctr., 2nd Fl.
Cambridge, MA 02142
Ph:(617)494-0111
Fax: (617)225-2080
URL: http://www.ntven.com
Contact: Alan Hanover, Chief Executive Officer and Managing Dir
Preferred Investment Size: $200,000 to $2,000,000.
Investment Policies: Early stage. **Industry Preferences:** Communications, semiconductors and other electronics, and biotechnology. **Geographic Preferences:** Northeast.

61101 ■ Neocarta Ventures, Inc.
45 Fairfield St., 4th Fl.
Boston, MA 02116
Ph:(617)239-9000
Fax: (617)266-4107

URL: http://www.neocarta.com
Contact: Andre Turenne, Managing Director
Preferred Investment Size: $1,000,000 to $5,000,000. **Investment Types:** Start-up, early, second, and later stage. **Industry Preferences:** Internet specific, communications and media, computer software and services, semiconductors and other electronics, computer hardware, and other products. **Geographic Preferences:** U.S.

61102 ■ New England Partners
1 Boston Pl., Ste. 3630
Boston, MA 02108
Ph:(617)624-8400
Fax: (617)624-8416
URL: http://www.nepartners.com
Contact: Tom Hancock, Principal
Preferred Investment Size: $500,000 to $6,000,000.
Investment Types: First and second stage. **Industry Preferences:** Biotechnology, consumer related, communications and media, computer software and services, medical and health, Internet specific, semiconductors and other electronics, other products, and industrial and energy. **Geographic Preferences:** Northeast, Southeast, and Mid Atlantic.

61103 ■ North Bridge Venture Partners
950 Winter St. Ste. 4600
Waltham, MA 02451
Ph:(781)290-0004
Fax: (781)290-0999
URL: http://www.nbvp.com
Contact: Edward Anderson, Managing General Partner
Preferred Investment Size: $2,000,000 to $3,000,000. **Investment Types:** Early stage. **Industry Preferences:** Communications and media, Internet specific, computer software and services, computer hardware, semiconductors and other electronics, medical and health, other products, and biotechnology. **Geographic Preferences:** Northeast and Southeast.

61104 ■ North Hill Ventures
10 Post Office Sq., 11th Fl.
Boston, MA 02109
Ph:(617)788-2150
Fax: (617)788-2152
URL: http://www.northhillventures.com
Contact: Benjamin Malka, Principal
Preferred Investment Size: $1,000,000 to $5,000,000. **Investment Types:** Expansion, second, and later stage. **Industry Preferences:** Consumer related, financial services, and business service. **Geographic Preferences:** U.S.

61105 ■ Norwest Equity Partners
80 S. 8th St., Ste. 3600
Minneapolis, MA 55402
Ph:(612)215-1600
Fax: (612)215-1601
URL: http://www.nep.com
Contact: Steve Farsht, Principal
Preferred Investment Size: $10,000,000 to $60,000,000. **Investment Types:** Later stage, acquisition, leveraged buyout, management buyouts, mezzanine, recapitalizations, and expansion. **Industry Preferences:** Computer software, communications and media, semiconductors and other electronics, consumer related, industrial and energy, business service, and manufacturing. **Geographic Preferences:** U.S.

61106 ■ OneLiberty Ventures
150 Cambridge Park Dr., 10th Fl.
Cambridge, MA 02140
Ph:(617)868-1888
Fax: (617)868-1115
URL: http://www.oneliberty.com
Contact: Edwin Kania, Senior Managing Director
Preferred Investment Size: $1,000,000 to $10,000,000. **Investment Types:** Early stage. **Industry Preferences:** Communications and media, computer software, hardware and services, Internet specific, biotechnology, medical and health, semiconductors and other electronics, industrial and energy. **Geographic Preferences:** Northeast and Southeast.

61107 ■ Osborn Capital LLC
171 Grove St.
Lexington, MA 02420
Ph:(781)402-1790
Fax: (781)402-1793
URL: http://www.osborncapital.com
Contact: Eric Janszen, Managing Director
Investment Types: Seed and start-up.

61108 ■ Palmer Partners, L.P.
200 Unicorn Park Dr.
Woburn, MA 01801
Ph:(781)933-5445
Fax: (781)933-0698
Investment Types: Start-up, first and second stage, recapitalizations, and special situation. **Industry Preferences:** Communications and media, computer related, industrial and energy, financial services, and manufacturing. **Geographic Preferences:** Mid Atlantic, Midwest, Northeast, Southeast and Southwest U.S.; Central and Eastern Canada.

61109 ■ Polaris Venture Partners
1000 Winter St., Ste. 3500
Waltham, MA 02451
Ph:(781)290-0770
Fax: (781)290-0880
URL: http://www.polarisventures.com
Contact: Alan Spoon, Managing Partner
Preferred Investment Size: $250,000 to $15,000,000. **Investment Types:** Seed, start-up, early, first and second stage, expansion, research and development, and balanced. **Industry Preferences:** Internet specific, computer software services, computer hardware, biotechnology, communications and media, medical and health, and other products. **Geographic Preferences:** U.S.

61110 ■ Prism Venture Partners
100 Lowder Brook Dr., Ste. 2500
Westwood, MA 02090
Ph:(781)302-4000
Fax: (781)302-4040
URL: http://www.prismventure.com
Contact: Steve Weintein, Principal
Preferred Investment Size: $5,000,000 to $15,000,000. **Investment Types:** Early stage. **Industry Preferences:** Internet specific, medical and health, communications and media, computer software and services, biotechnology, semiconductors and other electronics, and computer hardware. **Geographic Preferences:** Mid Atlantic, Northeast, and West Coast U.S.; and Canada.

61111 ■ RCT Bioventures NE LLC
30 Monument Sq., Ste. 215
Concord, MA 01742
Ph:(978)371-7100
Fax: (978)371-2371
URL: http://www.rctbvne.com
Preferred Investment Size: $500,000 to $750,000
Investment Types: Seed, start-up, early stage, and research and development. **Industry Preferences:** Biotechnology, medical and health, industrial and energy. **Geographic Preferences:** West Coast and Northeast.

61112 ■ Rockport capital Partners
160 Federal St., 18th Fl.
Boston, MA 02110
Ph:(617)912-1420
Fax: (617)912-1449
URL: http://www.rockportcap.com
Contact: Charles McDermott, Partner
Preferred Investment Size: $1,000,000 to $10,000,000. **Investment Policies:** Early, first, second, and later stage. **Industry Preferences:** Semiconductors and other electronics, industrial and energy, utilities, and environmental. **Geographic Preferences:** U.S.

61113 ■ Royan Capital Fund, L.P.I. / Royalty Capital Management, Inc.
5 Downing Rd.
Lexington, MA 02421-6918
Ph:(781)861-8490
Fax: (781)674-2363

Preferred Investment Size: $57,000,000 to $300,000,000. **Investment Types:** Start-up, first and second stage, leveraged buyout, and special situation. **Industry Preferences:** Communications, computer hardware and software, Internet specific, semiconductors and other electronics, biotechnology, medical and health, consumer related, industrial and energy, and manufacturing. **Geographic Preferences:** Northeast.

61114 ■ RSA Capital
174 Middlesex Tpke.
Bedford, MA 01730
Ph:(781)515-5000
Fax: (781)301-5170
URL: http://www.rsasecurity.com
Contact: Barry Rosenbaum, Managing Director
Preferred Investment Size: $2,000,000 to $5,000,000. **Investment Types:** Seed, expansion and early stage. **Industry Preferences:** Communications, computer software, and Internet specific. **Geographic Preferences:** U.S.

61115 ■ Sage Management Group
The John Simpson House
39 Elm St.
Newport, RI 02840
Ph:(401)849-6622
Fax: (401)849-4622
Preferred Investment Size: $500,000 to $1,000,000. **Investment Types:** First and second stage, leveraged buyout, mezzanine, and special situation. **Industry Preferences:** Communications and media, computer hardware and software, Internet specific, semiconductors and other electronics, medical and health, industrial and energy, and manufacturing. **Geographic Preferences:** U.S.

61116 ■ Schroder Ventures
Life Sciences
60 State St., Ste. 3650
Boston, MA 02109
Ph:(617)367-8100
Fax: (617)367-1590
URL: http://www.shroderventures.com
Contact: Nobuo Matsuki, Managing General Partner
Preferred Investment Size: $250,000 minimum. **Investment Types:** Balanced, first stage, leveraged buyout, mezzanine, second stage, special situation, and start-up. **Industry Preferences:** Medical and health, computer software, hardware and services, biotechnology, consumer related, Internet specific, communications and media, industrial and energy, semiconductors and other electronics. **Geographic Preferences:** U.S. and Canada.

61117 ■ Seacoast Capital
55 Ferncroft Rd.
Danvers, MA 01923
Ph:(978)750-1300
Fax: (978)750-1301
URL: http://www.seacoastcapital.com
Contact: Eben Moulton, Managing Director
Preferred Investment Size: $2,000,000 to $10,000,000. **Investment Types:** Mezzanine. **Industry Preferences:** Other products, Internet specific, consumer related, semiconductors and other electronics, medical and health, industrial and energy, computer software and services. **Geographic Preferences:** U.S.

61118 ■ Seaflower Ventures
Bay Colony Corporate Ctr.
1000 Winter St., Ste. 1000
Waltham, MA 02451
Ph:(781)466-9552
Fax: (781)466-9553
URL: http://www.seaflower.com
Contact: James Sherblom, Managing General Partner
Preferred Investment Size: $200,000 to $3,000,000. **Investment Types:** Seed, start-up, early, first and second stage. **Industry Preferences:** Medical and health, biotechnology, Internet specific, computer hardware, industrial and energy, and other products. **Geographic Preferences:** Illinois, Michigan, Mid Atlantic, Midwest, Northeast, Northeast, Southeast, and Wisconsin U.S.; Central Canada, Ontario and Quebec.

61119 ■ Shawmut Capital Partners
75 Federal St., 18th Fl.
Boston, MA 02110
Ph:(617)368-4900
Fax: (617)368-4910
URL: http://www.shawmutcapital.com
Contact: Daniel Doyle, Managing Director
Preferred Investment Size: $5,000,000 minimum. **Investment Types:** Start-up, first and second stage, mezzanine, leveraged buyout, industry rollups, control-block purchases, and special situation. **Industry Preferences:** Financial services. **Geographic Preferences:** U.S. and Canada.

61120 ■ Softbank Capital Partners
1188 Centre St.
Newton Center, MA 02459
Ph:(617)928-9300
Fax: (617)928-9305
URL: http://www.sbcap.com
Contact: Eric Hippeau, Managing Director
Investment Types: Seed, start-up, first and second stage, early and later stage, mezzanine, leveraged buyout, and special situation. **Industry Preferences:** Internet specific, consumer related, computer software and services, communications and media, computer hardware, semiconductors and other electronics, and industrial and energy. **Geographic Preferences:** U.S. and Canada.

61121 ■ Solstice Capital
15 Broad St., 3rd Fl.
Boston, MA 02109-4216
Ph:(617)523-7733
Fax: (617)523-5827
URL: http://www.solcap.com
Contact: Harry George, Principal
Preferred Investment Size: $500,000 to $1,500,000. **Investment Types:** Seed, early, and first stage. **Industry Preferences:** Computer software and services, industrial and energy, Internet specific, biotechnology, medical and health, semiconductors and other electronics, computer hardware, communications and media, consumer related, and other products. **Geographic Preferences:** Northeast and Southwest.

61122 ■ Sparkventures, LLC
10 Wilson Rd., Ste. 3
Cambridge, MA 02138
URL: http://www.sparkventures.com
Contact: Andrew Robbins, Managing Director
Investment Types: Early stage. **Industry Preferences:** Computer software and Internet specific. **Geographic Preferences:** Northeast. .

61123 ■ Spectrum Equity Investors
333 Middlefield Rd., Ste. 200
Menlo Park, CA 94025
Ph:(415)464-4600
Fax: (415)464-4601
URL: http://www.spectrumequity.com
Contact: Benjamin Coughlin, Principal
Preferred Investment Size: $5,000,000 minimum. **Investment Types:** Start-up, seed, first, second, early and later stage, balanced, acquisition, expansion, leveraged buyout, mezzanine, and recapitalizations. **Industry Preferences:** Communications and media, Internet specific, computer software and services, other products, semiconductors and other electronics, and consumer related. **Geographic Preferences:** U.S. and Canada.

61124 ■ Spray Venture Partners
1 Walnut St.
Boston, MA 02108
Ph:(617)305-4140
Fax: (617)305-4144
URL: http://www.spraypartners.com
Contact: Joseph Ciffolillo, Venture Partner
Preferred Investment Size: $50,000 to $6,000,000. **Investment Types:** Seed, start-up, first, and second stage. **Industry Preferences:** Medical and health, biotechnology, and Internet specific. **Geographic Preferences:** U.S.

61125 ■ The Still River Fund
10 Liberty Sq., Ste. 300
Boston, MA 02109
Ph:(617)426-3325
Fax: (617)426-6226
URL: http://www.stillriverfund.com
Contact: Mary Ellen Brayton, Vice President
Preferred Investment Size: $500,000 to $3,000,000. **Investment Types:** Seed and early stage. **Industry Preferences:** Other products, communications and media, Internet specific, semiconductors and other electronics, computer software and services, biotechnology, and consumer related. **Geographic Preferences:** Northeast.

61126 ■ Summit Partners
222 Berkeley, 18th Fl.
Boston, MA 02116
Ph:(617)824-1000
Fax: (617)824-1100
URL: http://www.summitpartners.com
Contact: C.J. Fitzgerald, Principal
Preferred Investment Size: $10,000,000 to $150,000,000. **Investment Types:** Second and later stage, mezzanine, leveraged buyout, special situation, control-block purchases, balanced, generalist PE. **Industry Preferences:** Other products, computer software and other services, communications and media, Internet specific, computer hardware, semiconductors and other electronics, medical and health, consumer related, biotechnology, industrial and energy. **Geographic Preferences:** U.S. and Canada.

61127 ■ TA Associates, Inc. (Boston)
125 High St., Ste. 2500
Boston, MA 02110
Ph:(617)574-6700
Fax: (617)574-6728
URL: http://www.ta.com
Contact: Brian Conway, Managing Director
E-mail: bconway@ta.com
Preferred Investment Size: $30,000,000 to $300,000,000. **Investment Types:** Later stage, leveraged buyout, management buyouts, expansion, mezzanine, and recapitalizations. **Industry Preferences:** Computer software and services, other products, communications and media, Internet specific, medical and health, semiconductors and other electronics, consumer related, computer hardware, industrial and health, and biotechnology. **Geographic Preferences:** U.S. and Canada.

61128 ■ TTC Ventures
1 Station Pl.
Stamford, CT 06902
Ph:(203)969-8700
Fax: (203)977-8354
URL: http://www.ttcventures.com
Investment Types: Seed, start-up, first and second stage, and mezzanine. **Industry Preferences:** Internet specific, computer software and services, communications and media, and computer hardware. **Geographic Preferences:** U.S.

61129 ■ TVM Techno Venture Management
101 Arch St., Ste. 1950
Boston, MA 02110
Ph:(617)345-9320
Fax: (617)345-9377
Co. E-mail: info@tvmvc.com
URL: http://www.tvmvc.com
Contact: Helmut Schuehsler, Managing Partner
Preferred Investment Size: $2,000 to $5,000. **Investment Types:** Seed, start-up, early and later stage. **Industry Preferences:** Biotechnology, medical and health, computer software, hardware and services, Internet specific, communications and media, semiconductors and other electronics, consumer related, industrial and energy. **Geographic Preferences:** U.S.

61130 ■ UNC Ventures
64 Buroughs St.
Boston, MA 02130-4017
Ph:(617)552-2160
Fax: (617)522-2176
Preferred Investment Size: $500,000 to $1,000,000. **Investment Types:** Leveraged buyout, mezzanine,

and second stage. **Industry Preferences:** Communications and media, industrial and energy, and financial services. **Geographic Preferences:** U.S.

61131 ■ The Venture Capital Fund of New England
30 Washington St.
Wellesley Hills, MA 02481-2175
Ph:(781)431-8400
Fax: (781)237-6578
Contact: Kevin J. Dougherty, Managing Director
Preferred Investment Size: $500,000 to $3,000,000.
Investment Types: Early stage. **Industry Preferences:** Computer software and services, communications and media, medical and health, industrial and energy, semiconductors and other electronics, computer hardware, other products, Internet specific, biotechnology, and consumer related. **Geographic Preferences:** Northeast.

61132 ■ Venture Investment Management Company LLC (VIMAC)
177 Milk St.
Boston, MA 02190-3410
Ph:(617)292-3300
Fax: (617)292-7979
Co. E-mail: bzeisig@vimac.com
URL: http://www.vimac.com
Contact: John Evans, Managing Director
Preferred Investment Size: $500,000 to $2,500,000.
Investment Types: Seed and early stage. **Industry Preferences:** Internet specific, computer software, hardware and services, communications and media, semiconductors and other electronics, medical and health, and consumer related. **Geographic Preferences:** Ontario and Quebec, Canada.

61133 ■ Ventures
200 Brickstone, 2nd Fl.
Andover, MA 01810
Ph:(978)684-7500
Fax: (978)684-7520
URL: http://www.venture.com
Contact: Peter Mills, Managing Partner
Preferred Investment Size: $1,000,000 to $20,000,000. **Investment Policies:** Early and later stage, expansion, generalist PE, industry rollups, recapitalizations, and special situation. **Industry Preferences:** Internet specific. **Geographic Preferences:** U.S. and Canada.

61134 ■ Yankeetek Ventures
1 Memorial Dr., 12th Fl.
Cambridge, MA 01242
Ph:(617)250-0500
Fax: (617)250-0501
URL: http://www.yankeetek.com
Contact: Howard Anderson, Senior Managing Director
Preferred Investment Size: $500,000 to $6,000,000.
Investment Types: Seed and first stage. **Industry Preferences:** Communications, computer software, Internet specific, semiconductors and other electronics, and business service. **Geographic Preferences:** Northeast.

61135 ■ Zero Stage Capital Co., Inc.
101 Main St., 17th Fl.
Cambridge, MA 02142-1519
Ph:(617)876-5355
Fax: (617)876-1248
URL: http://www.zerostage.com
Contact: Ben Bronstein, Managing Director
Preferred Investment Size: $2,000 to $10,000,000.
Investment Types: Seed, start-up, first and second stage, early and later stage, and fund of funds. **Industry Preferences:** Computer software and services, Internet specific, communications and media, medical and health, biotechnology, semiconductors and other electronics, industrial and energy, consumer related, and other products. **Geographic Preferences:** East Coast and Northeast.

PROCUREMENT ASSISTANCE PROGRAMS

61136 ■ Small Business Administration
Electronic Systems Center
Hanscom AFB
275 Randolf Rd., Bldg. 1101
275 Randolf Rd.
Bedford, MA 01731-2818
Ph:(781)377-4448
Fax: (781)377-3015
URL: http://www.sba.gov
Contact: Arvind Patel
E-mail: keith.hubbard@sba.gov
Description: Covers activities for Hanscom Air Force Base (Bedford, MA), Army Corps of Engineers (Waltham, MA), Army Soldiers Systems Command (Natick, MA), Transportation Systems Control (Cambridge, MA).

INCUBATORS/RESEARCH AND TECHNOLOGY PARKS

61137 ■ Babson College–Board of Research
Babson Hall 204
Babson Park, MA 02457-0310
Ph:(781)239-5339
Fax: (781)239-6416
Co. E-mail: chern@babson.edu
URL: http://www.babson.edu/bor/
Contact: Susan Chern, Coord.
E-mail: chern@babson.edu
Scope: Encourage and support the research activities of the college. **Publications:** Research at Babson College (quarterly); Working papers (annually). **Educational Activities:** Research forums, featuring research related topics; Research Chats (10/year), featuring faculty research projects. **Awards:** Babson faculty summer stipends; Grants, for research related expenses.

61138 ■ Boston College–Office for Sponsored Programs
140 Commonwealth Ave.
Chestnut Hill, MA 02467
Ph:(617)552-3344
Fax: (617)552-0747
Co. E-mail: john.carfora@bc.edu
URL: http://www.bc.edu/research/osp.html
Contact: John M. Carfora, Dir.
E-mail: john.carfora@bc.edu
Scope: Administers and coordinates extramurally sponsored research in biology, business, chemistry, economics, education, English, geology, geophysics, law, mathematics, nursing, physics, psychology, social work, and sociology conducted in various academic and research units of the College. **Publications:** OSP Newsletter.

61139 ■ Boston University–Office of Sponsored Programs
25 Buick St., 2nd Fl.
Boston, MA 02215
Ph:(617)353-4365
Fax: (617)353-6660
Co. E-mail: joank@bu.edu
URL: http://www.bu.edu/osp
Contact: Joan Kirkendall, Dir.
E-mail: joank@bu.edu
Scope: Responsible for coordination of University funding efforts with government and foundation sources and for administration of all grant/contract awards received at the University.

61140 ■ Harvard University–Office for Sponsored Research
Holyoke Center, 6th Fl.
1350 Massachusetts Ave.
Cambridge, MA 02138
Ph:(617)495-5501
Fax: (617)496-2524
Co. E-mail: elizabeth_mora@harvard.edu
URL: http://vpf-web.harvard.edu/osr/

Contact: Elizabeth Mora, Dir.
E-mail: elizabeth_mora@harvard.edu
Scope: Administers and coordinates all extramurally sponsored research conducted at the University.

61141 ■ Harvard University–Office of Technology Development
Holyoke Center, Rm. 727
1350 Massachusetts Ave.
Cambridge, MA 02138
Ph:(617)495-3067
Fax: (617)495-9568
Co. E-mail: isaac_kohlberg@harvard.edu
URL: http://www.techtransfer.harvard.edu/
Contact: I.T. Kohlberg
E-mail: isaac_kohlberg@harvard.edu
Scope: Facilitates University-industry relations through technology licensing in the areas of applied sciences, recombinant DNA, hybridoma technology, software and courseware, chemistry, therapeutics, vaccines, bioprocesses, and medical, veterinary, and agricultural diagnostics.

61142 ■ Massachusetts Institute of Technology–Office of Sponsored Programs
77 Massachusetts Ave.
Bldg. E19-750
Cambridge, MA 02139
Ph:(617)253-2762
Fax: (617)253-4734
Co. E-mail: pwf@mit.edu
URL: http://web.mit.edu/org/o/osp/www/
Contact: Patrick W. Fitzgerald, Dir.
E-mail: pwf@mit.edu
Scope: Administers sponsored research program of the Institute, negotiating research contracts, taking care of business and contractual obligations, and serving as liaison with research sponsors.

61143 ■ Massachusetts Institute of Technology–Real Estate Office
238 Main St., Ste. 200
Cambridge, MA 02142
Ph:(617)253-4304
Fax: (617)258-6675
Co. E-mail: scmarsh@mit.edu
Contact: Steven C. Marsh, Mng.Dir.
E-mail: scmarsh@mit.edu
Scope: Fosters interaction between the Institute's research community and park tenants.

61144 ■ Massachusetts Institute of Technology–Technology Licensing Office
5 Cambridge Center, Kendall Sq.
Rm. NE25-230
Cambridge, MA 02142-1493
Ph:(617)253-6966
Fax: (617)258-6790
Co. E-mail: tlo-www@mit.edu
URL: http://web.mit.edu/tlo/www/
Contact: Lita Nelsen, Dir.
E-mail: tlo-www@mit.edu
Scope: Commercializes technology from the Institute in the areas of biotechnology, biomedicine, ceramics, chemistry, computers, electrooptics, integrated circuits, and polymers. Markets inventions and software developed at Lincoln Laboratory.

61145 ■ Massinnovation, LLC
250 Merrimack St.
Lawrence, MA 1843
Ph:(978)683-2901
Fax: (978)683-2837
Co. E-mail: info@massinnovation.com
URL: http://www.massinnovation.com
Contact: Robert Ansin, Pres & CEO
Description: The MIC supports entrepreneurs with facilities for offices, laboratories, and light manufacturing as well as access to venture capital.

61146 ■ Northeastern University–Division of Research Management
405 Lake Hall
360 Huntington Ave.
Boston, MA 02115
Ph:(617)373-2124
Fax: (617)373-4595

Co. E-mail: l.barnett@neu.edu
Contact: Larry Barnett, Assoc.Dir.
E-mail: l.barnett@neu.edu
Scope: Administers and coordinates research activities for the entire University and handles research grants and contracts for extramurally sponsored research conducted by faculty members in the various academic disciplines. Administers University Invention, Patent and Licensing Program, develops programmatic initiatives, coordinates new research efforts, and manages technology transfer. **Educational Activities:** Colloquia; Seminars (occasionally); Workshops.

61147 ■ Office of Economic and Community Development–Office of Economic Development
3 City Hall Sq., Rm 307
Rm 307
Lynn, MA 1901
Ph:(781)581-9399
Fax: (781)581-9731
URL: http://www.lynndevelopment.com
Contact: Mary Jane Smalley, Admin Ass

61148 ■ Smith College–Office of Institutional Research
32 College Hall
50 Elm St.
Northampton, MA 01063
Ph:(413)585-3021
Fax: (413)585-3026
Co. E-mail: dcuneo@smith.edu
URL: http://www.smith.edu/ir
Contact: Diane O. Cuneo, Dir.
E-mail: dcuneo@smith.edu
Scope: Institutional planning.

61149 ■ Tufts University–Office of the Associate Provost for Research
Ballou Hall
Medford, MA 02155
Ph:(617)627-3417
Fax: (617)627-3673
Co. E-mail: peggy.newell@tufts.edu
URL: http://www.tufts.edu/central/research/index. html
Contact: Margaret E. Newell, Assoc. Provost for Res.
E-mail: peggy.newell@tufts.edu
Scope: Coordinates research activities in all units and divisions of the University, including arts and sciences, medicine, dentistry, veterinary, nutrition and international affairs. Activities are carried out through two offices: one in Medford, Massachusetts, and one in Boston, Massachusetts.

61150 ■ University of Massachusetts at Amherst–Office of Research Affairs
70 Butterfield Terr.
Amherst, MA 01003-9242
Ph:(413)545-3428
Fax: (413)545-3754
Co. E-mail: mccandless@ora.umass.edu
URL: http://www.umass.edu/research/ora
Contact: Bruce McCandless, Dir.
E-mail: mccandless@ora.umass.edu
Scope: Provides coordination, funds, and information for research efforts of the University. Serves as faculty liaison on research grant proposals.

61151 ■ Worcester Polytechnic Institute–Division of Academic Affairs
100 Institute Rd.
Worcester, MA 01609-2280
Ph:(508)831-5065
Fax: (508)831-5774
Co. E-mail: wwdurgin@wpi.edu
URL: http://www.wpi.edu/Admin/Provost
Contact: William W. Durgin, VP, Res.
E-mail: wwdurgin@wpi.edu
Scope: Administers research activities for Intelligent Materials Processing Multidisciplinary Research Center, Center for Image Understanding, Center for Inorganic Membrane Studies, Artificial Intelligence Research Group, Center for Holographic Studies and

Laser Technology, Aluminum Casting Research Laboratory, Applied Bioengineering Multidisciplinary Research Center, Carl Gunnard Johnson Powder Metallurgy Research Center, Center for Wireless Information Network Studies, and Magnetic Resonance Imaging Center, Metal Processing Institute. **Services:** Consulting; Technical assistance.

EDUCATIONAL PROGRAMS

61152 ■ Becker College
61 Sever St.
Worcester, MA 01609
Ph:(508)791-9241
Free: 877-5-BECKER
Fax: (508)831-7505
URL: http://www.beckercollege.edu
Description: Four and two year college offering a small business management programs.

61153 ■ Bunker Hill Community College
250 New Rutherford Ave.
Boston, MA 02129-2925
Ph:(617)228-2000
Fax: (617)228-2082
URL: http://www.bhcc.mass.edu
Description: Two-year college offering a small business management course.

61154 ■ Dean College
99 Main St.
Franklin, MA 02038
Ph:(508)541-1508
Free: 800-852-7702
Fax: (508)541-8726
Co. E-mail: admissions@dean.edu
URL: http://www.dean.edu
Description: Two-year college offering a small business management program.

61155 ■ MassBay Community College
50 Oakland St.
Wellesley Hills, MA 02481
Ph:(781)239-3000
Fax: (781)239-1047
URL: http://www.massbay.edu
Description: College offering a two-year small business management program.

61156 ■ Mt. Ida College–Division of Continuing Education
777 Dedham St.
Newton Centre, MA 02459
Ph:(617)928-4500
Fax: (617)928-4760
URL: http://www.mountida.edu
Description: Offers certificate and/or associate degree programs in business administration and paralegal studies. Also provides noncredit professional development programs to small business owners.

TRADE PERIODICALS

61157 ■ Quincy Business News
Pub: John R. Graham Inc.
Ed: Michael Maynard, Editor, m_maynard@grahamcomm.com. **Released:** Monthly, 3/year. **Price:** Free. **Description:** Provides information on Quincy businesses. Includes one feature business per issue. One restaurant review each issue. Recurring features include columns titled Cracker Barrel and Commentary.

PUBLICATIONS

61158 ■ Boston Business Journal
200 High St.
Boston, MA 02110
Ph:(617)330-1000
Fax: (617)330-1016
URL: http://www.amcity.com/boston

61159 ■ New England Economic Review
PO Box 2076
Boston, MA 02106-2076
Ph:(617)973-3403
Fax: (617)973-3957

61160 ■ Smart Start your Massachusetts Business
PSI Research
300 N. Valley Dr.
Grants Pass, OR 97526
Ph:(503)479-9464
Free: 800-228-2275
Fax: (503)476-1479
Co. E-mail: info@psi-research.com
URL: http://www.psi-research.com
Ed: Michael D. Jenkins. **Released:** Revised edition, 1992. **Price:** $29.95 (looseleaf binder); $24.95 (paper). **Description:** Part of the Successful Business Library series.

61161 ■ Worcester Business Journal
172 Shrewsbury St.
Worcester, MA 01604
Ph:(508)755-8004
Free: 800-925-8004
Fax: (508)755-8860
URL: http://www.wbjournal.com

PUBLISHERS

61162 ■ Boomerang Software Inc.
90 Concord Ave.
Belmont, MA 02478
Ph:(617)489-3000
URL: http://www.boomerangsoftware.com
Description: Publishes software on business and web design for large and small business owners. **Founded:** 1991

61163 ■ DBA Books
291 Beacon St., Ste. 8
Boston, MA 02116
Ph:(617)262-0411
Contact: Diane Bellavance, Owner
E-mail: dbellava@lynx.neu.edu
Description: Publishes books for small business owners. Reaches market through direct mail and internet bookstores. Does not accept unsolicited manuscripts. **Founded:** 1979.

61164 ■ HRD Press
22 Amherst Rd.
Amherst, MA 01002-9709
Ph:(413)253-3488
Free: 800-822-2801
Fax: (413)253-3490
Co. E-mail: info@hrdpress.com
URL: http://www.hrdpress.com
Contact: R.W. Carkhuff, President
Description: Publishes textbooks and workshops on human resources development, management and training. Reaches market through direct mail and telephone sales. **Founded:** 1972.

61165 ■ Jeffrey Lant Associates Inc.
50 Follen St., Ste. 507
PO Box 38-2767
Cambridge, MA 02138-3509
Ph:(617)547-6372
Fax: (617)547-0061
Co. E-mail: drjlant@worldprofit.com
URL: http://www.jeffreylant.com
Contact: Jeffrey Lant, President
E-mail: drjlant@worldprofit.com
Description: Publishes technical assistance books for nonprofit organizations, consultants, independent professionals and small and home-based businesses. Offers audio cassettes, workshops and consultation services. Also publishes twice monthly Worlgram newsletter. Reaches market through commission representatives, direct mail, telephone sales and the internet. Accepts unsolicited manuscripts. **Founded:** 1979.

61166 ■ JLA Publications
50 Follen St., Ste. 507
Cambridge, MA 02138
Ph:(617)547-6372
Fax: (617)547-0061
Contact: Dr. Jeffrey L. Lant, President
E-mail: drjlant@worldprofit.com

Description: Publishes guides and books on small business topics. Accepts unsolicited manuscripts.
Founded: 1979.

61167 ■ Standish Press
105 Standish St.
Duxbury, MA 02332
Ph:(781)934-9570
Fax: (781)934-9570

Co. E-mail: standish@verizon.net
Contact: Dick Rothschild, President
Description: Publishes health and fitness for self-help, medical care, writing, home improvement, humor, business, travel and fiction for an adult audience. Does not accept unsolicited manuscripts. Reaches market through reviews and listings as well as wholesalers and distributors. **Founded:** 1999.

SMALL BUSINESS DEVELOPMENT CENTER LEAD OFFICE

61168 ■ 1st Step, Inc.–Michigan Small Business and Technology Development Center
2415 14th Ave., S.
Escanaba, MI 49829
Ph:(906)786-9634
Fax: (906)786-4442
Co. E-mail: 1ststep@chartermi.net
URL: http://www.misbtdc.org/region1
Contact: Joel Schultz, Dir.

61169 ■ Grand Valley State University–Michigan Small Business Development Center
510 W. Fulton
Grand Rapids, MI 49504
Ph:(616)336-7480
Fax: (616)336-7485
Contact: Carol Lopucki, State Director
E-mail: lopuckic@gvsu.edu

SMALL BUSINESS DEVELOPMENT CENTERS

61170 ■ Allegan County Economic Alliance–SBDC
2891 116th Ave., M-222 E.
PO Box 2777
Allegan, MI 49010
Ph:(616)673-8442
Fax: (616)686-2232
Co. E-mail: aceda@accn.org
Contact: Chuck Birr, Dir.

61171 ■ Alpena Community College–Huron Shores Campus–SBDC (5800)
5800 Skeel Ave.
Oscoda, MI 48750
Ph:(517)739-1445
Fax: (517)739-1161
Contact: Dave Wentworth, Dir.
E-mail: wentword@alpena.cc.mi.us

61172 ■ Alpena Community College–SBTDC
Newport Center, Rm. 108
Alpena, MI 49707
Ph:(989)358-7383
Fax: (989)358-7554
URL: http://www.misbtdc.org/region3/
Contact: Carl Bourdelais, Dir.
E-mail: bourdelc@alpena.cc.edu

61173 ■ Arenac County Extension Service–SBDC
120 N. Grove St.
PO Box 745
Standish, MI 48658
Ph:(517)846-4111
Co. E-mail: arenac@msue.msu.edu
Contact: Ken Kernstock, Dir.

61174 ■ Association of Commerce and Industry–SBDC
1 S. Harbor
PO Box 509
Grand Haven, MI 49417
Ph:(616)846-3153
Fax: (616)842-0379
Co. E-mail: acisbdc@hotmail.com
Contact: Karen K. Benson, Dir.

61175 ■ Battle Creek Area Chamber of Commerce–SBDC
4 Riverwalk Centre
34 W. Jackson, Ste. A
Battle Creek, MI 49017
Ph:(616)962-8996
Fax: (616)962-2692
Co. E-mail: bizstorenetwork-link.net
Contact: Kevin Wells, Dir.

61176 ■ Bay Area Chamber of Commerce–SBDC
901 Saginaw Rd.
Bay City, MI 48708
Ph:(517)893-4567
Fax: (517)893-7016
Contact: Deb Wieland, Dir.

61177 ■ Branch County Economic Growth Alliance–SBDC
20 Division St.
Coldwater, MI 49036
Ph:(517)369-2239
Fax: (517)279-8936
Co. E-mail: bcega@orion.brance-co.lib
Contact: Harry Adamson, Dir.
E-mail: eric@bcega.com

61178 ■ Buchanan Chamber of Commerce–SBDC
119 Main St.
Buchanan, MI 49107
Ph:(616)695-3291
Fax: (616)695-4250
Contact: Brent Miller, Dir.

61179 ■ Central Michigan University–Small Business Development Center
256 Applied Business Studies Complex
Mt. Pleasant, MI 48859
Ph:(517)774-3270
Fax: (517)774-7992
Co. E-mail: 34ntjen@cmuvm.csv.cmich.edu
Contact: Charles Fitzpatrick, Dir.

61180 ■ Community Capital Development Corp.–SBDC
711 N. Saginaw, Ste. 102
Flint, MI 48503
Ph:(810)239-5847
Fax: (810)239-5575
Co. E-mail: ccdc@tir.com

Contact: Kim Yarber, Regional Dir.

61181 ■ Dakota County Technical College–SBDC
1300 145th St. E.
Rosemount, MN 55068
Ph:(612)423-8262
Fax: (612)423-8761
Contact: Tom Trutna, Dir.

61182 ■ Delta College Corporate Services–Small Business Technology Development Center
1961 Delta Rd.
University Center, MI 48710-0002
Ph:(989)686-9597
Fax: (989)667-2222
Co. E-mail: sbtdc@corpserv.delta.edu
URL: http://www.misbtdc.org/region5
Contact: Christine M. Greve

61183 ■ Downriver Community Conference Small Business Development Center
15100 Northline Rd.
Southgate, MI 48195
Ph:(734)362-3477
Fax: (734)281-0301
URL: http://www.misbtdc.org/region9
Contact: Paula Boase, Dir.
E-mail: paulab@dccwf.org

61184 ■ Eastern Michigan University–Small Business Technology Development Center
306 Gary M. Owen Bldg.
300 W. Michigan Ave.
Ypsilanti, MI 48197
Ph:(734)487-0355
Fax: (734)481-3354
URL: http://www.misbtdc.org/region9
Contact: Richard King, Dir.
E-mail: richard.king@emich.edu

61185 ■ Economic Development Alliance of St. Clair County
735 Erie St., Ste. 250
Port Huron, MI 48060
Ph:(810)982-9511
Fax: (810)982-9531
URL: http://www.edaofstclaircounty.com
Contact: Amy Deprez, Business Consultant
E-mail: adeprez@edascc.com

61186 ■ Ferris State University–Small Business Development Center
330 Oak St.
330 Oak St. West 025
Big Rapids, MI 49307
Ph:(616)592-2082
Fax: (616)592-3539
Contact: Lora Swenson, Dir.
E-mail: yc26@ferris.bitnet

61187 ■ First Step, Inc.–Small Business Development Center
2415 14th Ave., S.
Escanaba, MI 49829

Ph:(906)786-9234
Free: 800-562-4442
Fax: (906)786-4442
Co. E-mail: cuppad@up.net
Contact: David Gillis, Regional Dir.

61188 ■ Grand Valley State University–Small Business Technology Development Center
401 W. Fulton Ave.
DeVos Center, 3rd Fl.
Grand Rapids, MI 49504
Ph:(616)331-7370
Fax: (616)331-7195
URL: http://www.misbtdc.org/region7
Contact: Nancy S. Boese, Dir.
E-mail: boesen@gvsu.edu

61189 ■ Gratiot Area Chamber of Commerce–SBDC
110 W. Superior St.
PO Box 516
Alma, MI 48801-0516
Ph:(517)463-5525
Fax: (517)463-6588
Contact: Debbie Sitts, Dir.

61190 ■ Greater Gratiot Development, Inc. –Small Business Center
136 S. Main
Ithaca, MI 48847
Ph:(517)875-2083
Fax: (517)875-2990
Contact: Don Schurr, Dir.
E-mail: don.schurr@gratiot.com

61191 ■ Greater Niles Economic Development Fund–SBDC
1105 N. Front St.
Niles, MI 49120
Ph:(616)683-1833
Fax: (616)683-7515
Contact: Sharon Witt, Dir.

61192 ■ Greater South Haven Chamber of Commerce–SBDC
300 Broadway
South Haven, MI 49090
Ph:(616)637-5171
Fax: (616)639-1570
Co. E-mail: cofc@southhavenmi.com
Contact: Larry King, Dir.

61193 ■ Harbor Country Chamber of Commerce–SBDC
530 S. Whittaker St., Ste. F
New Buffalo, MI 49117
Ph:(616)469-5409
Fax: (616)469-2257
Co. E-mail: hccc@hc.cns.net
Contact: Peggy King, Office Mgr.

61194 ■ Hastings Industrial Incubator–SBDC
1035 E. State St.
Hastings, MI 49058
Ph:(616)948-2305
Fax: (616)948-2947
Co. E-mail: edohast@voyager.net
Contact: Joe Rahn, Dir.

61195 ■ Host Site in Transition–Small Business Technology Development Center
510 W. Fulton
Grand Rapids, MI 49504
Ph:(616)331-7480
Fax: (616)331-7485
Co. E-mail: sbtdchq@gvsu.edu
URL: http://www.misbtdc.org/region6

61196 ■ Huron County Economic Development Corp.–Small Business Development Center
250 E. Huron, Ste. 303
Bad Axe, MI 48413
Ph:(989)269-6431
Fax: (989)269-8209
URL: http://www.misbtdc.org/region6
Contact: Carl Osentoski, Dir.

E-mail: carl@huroncounty.com

61197 ■ Jackson Business Development Center–SBDC
414 N. Jackson St.
Jackson, MI 49201-1249
Ph:(517)787-0442
Fax: (517)787-3960
Co. E-mail: jbdc@jacksonmi.com
Contact: Duane Miller, Dir.

61198 ■ Kalamazoo College–Small Business Technology Development Center
Stryker Center
1327 Academy St.
Kalamazoo, MI 49006-3200
Ph:(269)337-7350
Fax: (269)337-7352
Co. E-mail: sbtdc@kzoo.edu
URL: http://www.misbtdc.org/region11
Contact: Steve Dobbs, Dir.

61199 ■ Kirtland Community College–SBDC
10775 N. St. Helen Rd.
Roscommon, MI 48653
Ph:(517)275-5121
Fax: (517)275-8745
Contact: John Loiacano, Dir.
E-mail: loiacanj@k2.kirtland.cc.mi.us

61200 ■ Lake Michigan College Satellite Office–Small Business Development Center (2755)–Corporate and Community Involvement (E. Napier)
2755 E. Napier
Benton Harbor, MI 49022
Ph:(616)927-8179
Fax: (616)927-8103
Contact: Milton E. Richter, Dir.
E-mail: richter@lmc.cc.mi.us

61201 ■ Lansing Community College–Small Business Development Center
315 N. Grand Ave., Rm. 202
PO Box 40010
Lansing, MI 48901
Ph:(517)483-1921
Fax: (517)483-1675
Co. E-mail: sbtdc@lcc.edu
URL: http://www.misbtdc.org/region8
Contact: Bo Garcia, Regional Dir.
E-mail: bgarcia@llc.edu

61202 ■ Lapeer Development Corp.–Small Business Development Center
449 McCormick Dr.
Lapeer, MI 48446
Ph:(810)667-0080
Fax: (810)667-3541
Contact: Patricia Lucas, Dir.
E-mail: patricia@lapeerdevelopment.com

61203 ■ Livingston County Economic Development Center–SBDC Satellite Office
131 S. Hyne St.
Brighton, MI 48116
Ph:(810)227-3556
Fax: (810)227-3080
Co. E-mail: livibusi@bizserve.com
Contact: Dennis Whitney, Dir.

61204 ■ Macomb Community College–Center for Continuing Education-Macomb Community College–SBDC (32101)
32101 Caroline
Fraser, MI 48026
Ph:(810)296-3516
Fax: (810)293-0427
Contact: Donald Amboyer, Dir.

61205 ■ Macomb Community College–SBDC
14500 12 Mile Rd.
Warren, MI 48088
Ph:(586)445-7999
Free: (866)622-6621
Fax: (586)45—7140
URL: http://www.macomb.edu

Contact: Geary Maiurini, Dir.

61206 ■ Macomb County Department of Planning and Economic Development–Small Business Technology Development Center
1 S. Main St., 7th Fl.
Mt. Clemens, MI 48043
Ph:(586)469-5118
Fax: (586)469-6787
Co. E-mail: SBTDC@macombcountymi.gov
URL: http://www.misbtdc.org/region10
Contact: Donald L. Morandi, Dir.

61207 ■ Michigan Manufacturing Technology Center–SBDC Specialty Center
2901 Hubbard Rd.
PO Box 1485
Ann Arbor, MI 48106-1485
Ph:(734)769-4110
Fax: (734)769-4064
Co. E-mail: wrl@iti.org
Contact: Bill Loomis, Dir.

61208 ■ Mid-Michigan Community College–Small Business Technology Development Center
M-Tec Bldg.
1375 S. Clare Ave.
Harrison, MI 48625
Ph:(989)386-6630
Fax: (989)802-0971
URL: http://www.misbtdc.org/region4
Contact: Anthony E. Fox, Dir.
E-mail: aefox@midmich.edu

61209 ■ Midland Chamber of Commerce–SBDC Satellite Office
300 Rodd St.
Midland, MI 48640-6596
Ph:(517)839-9522
Fax: (517)835-3701
Co. E-mail: chamber@macc.org
URL: http://www.midlandedc.org
Contact: Christine Greve, Dir.
E-mail: greve@midlandedc.org

61210 ■ Monroe County Industrial Development Corp.–SBDC
111 Conant Ave.
Monroe, MI 48161
Ph:(313)243-5947
Fax: (313)242-0009
Co. E-mail: mcidc@ic.net
Contact: Randy Thelan, Dir.

61211 ■ Muskegon Economic Growth Alliance–Small Business Development Center Satellite Office
230 Terrace Plz.
PO Box 1087
Muskegon, MI 49443-1087
Ph:(616)724-3180
Fax: (616)728-7251
Contact: Eddie Garner, Dir.

61212 ■ Northern Lakes Economic Alliance–SBDC
1048 East Main St.
Boyne City, MI 49712-0008
Ph:(231)582-6482
Fax: (231)582-3213
URL: http://www.misbtdc.org
Contact: Thomas Johnson, Dir.

61213 ■ Northwest Michigan Council of Governments–Small Business Development Center
2194 S. Garfield Ave., Ste. C
PO Box 506
Traverse City, MI 49685-0506
Ph:(231)922-3780
Fax: (231)929-5042
URL: http://www.misbtdc.org/region8
Contact: Deb Donovan, Business Consultant
E-mail: ddonovan@nwm.cog.mi.us

61214 ■ Northwestern Michigan College MTEC–Small Business Development Center
1701 E. Front St.
Traverse City, MI 49686
Ph:(231)995-2023
Fax: (231)995-2022
URL: http://www.misbtdc.org
Contact: Kirk Hornberg, Dir.
E-mail: khornburg@nmc.edu

61215 ■ Oceana County Economic Development Corp.–SBDC
100 State St.
PO Box 168
Hart, MI 49420-0168
Ph:(616)873-7141
Fax: (616)873-5914
Co. E-mail: edc@oceana.net
Contact: Charles Persenaire, Dir.

61216 ■ Ottawa County Economic Development Office, Inc.–Small Business Development Center
6676 Lake Michigan Dr.
PO Box 539
Allendale, MI 49401-0539
Ph:(616)892-4120
Fax: (616)895-6670
URL: http://www.misddc.org/region7
Contact: Ken Rizzio, Dir.
E-mail: krizzio@altelco.net

61217 ■ The Right Place Program–SBDC
161 Ottawa Ave. NW, Ste. 400
Grand Rapids, MI 49503-2701
Ph:(616)771-0325
Fax: (616)771-0555
Co. E-mail: info@rightplace.org
URL: http://rightplace.org
Contact: Raymond P. DeWinkle, Dir.
E-mail: dewinkler@rightplace.org

61218 ■ Saginaw County Chamber of Commerce–SBDC
515 N. Washington Ave., 2nd Fl.
Saginaw, MI 48607-1370
Ph:(989)752-7161
Fax: (989)752-9055
Co. E-mail: info@saginawchamber.org
URL: http://www.saginawchamber.org/
Contact: James Bockelman, Dir.

61219 ■ Saginaw Future, Inc.–Small Business Development Center
301 E. Genesee, 3rd Fl.
Saginaw, MI 48607
Ph:(517)754-8222
Fax: (517)754-1715
Contact: Steven Black, Dir.
E-mail: sblack@compuserve.delta.edu

61220 ■ Saginaw Valley State University–Small Business Development Center
7400 Bay Rd.
Wickes 387
University Center, MI 48710
Ph:(517)790-4388
Fax: (517)790-4983
Contact: Charles Curtiss, Regional Dir.

61221 ■ Sterling Heights Chamber of Commerce–Small Business Development Center
12900 Hall Rd., Ste. 110
Sterling Heights, MI 48313
Ph:(586)731-5400
Fax: (586)731-3521
URL: http://www.suscc.com
Contact: Lillian Adams, Dir.
E-mail: ladams@suscc.com

61222 ■ Traverse Bay Economic Development Corp.–Small Business Development Center
202 E. Grandview Pkwy.
Traverse City, MI 49684

Ph:(231)995-7105
Fax: (231)946-2565
Co. E-mail: tbbest@tcchamber.org
URL: http://www.tcchamber.org
Contact: Matthew Meadors, Regional Dir.
E-mail: matt@tcchamber.org

61223 ■ Traverse City Area Chamber of Commerce–Small Business Development Center
109 6th St.
PO Box 387
Traverse City, MI 49685-0387
Ph:(231)947-5075
Fax: (231)946-2565
Co. E-mail: infor@tcchamber.org
URL: http://www.misbtdc.org
Contact: Charles Blankenship, Dir.
E-mail: tbedc@gtii.com

61224 ■ Tuscola County Economic Development Corp.–Small Business Development Center
157 N. State St.
Caro, MI 48723
Ph:(989)673-2849
Fax: (989)673-2517
Co. E-mail: tuscolaedc@centurytel.net
URL: http://www.misbtdc.org/region6
Contact: James McLoskey, Dir.

61225 ■ University of Detroit-Mercy–Small Business Development Center Satellite Office
College of Business Administration., Rm. 105
4001 W. McNichols
PO Box 19900
Detroit, MI 48219-0900
Ph:(313)993-1115
Fax: (313)993-1052
Contact: Ram Kesavan, Dir.
E-mail: kesavar@udmercy.edu

61226 ■ Warren - Centerline - Sterling Heights Chamber of Commerce–Small Business Development Center
30500 Van Dyke, Ste.118
Warren, MI 48093
Ph:(810)751-3939
Fax: (810)751-3995
Contact: Janet Masi, Dir.
E-mail: janetmorris@chambercom.com

61227 ■ Washtenaw Community College–SBDC
301 W. Michigan Ave., Ste. 101
Ypsilanti, MI 48197
Ph:(734)547-9170
Fax: (734)547-9178
Co. E-mail: sbtdc@wccnet.org
URL: http://www.misbtdc.org/region12
Contact: Charles Penner, Regional Dir.
E-mail: rking@wccnet.org

61228 ■ Wayne State University–Michigan SBDC
2727 Second Ave., Ste. 121
Detroit, MI 48201
Ph:(313)964-1798
Fax: (313)964-3648
Co. E-mail: stateoffice@misbdc.wayne.edu
Contact: Ronald R. Hall, State Dir.
E-mail: ron@misbdc.wayne.edu

61229 ■ West Shore Community College–Small Business Development Center
Business and Industrial Development Institute
3000 N. Stiles Rd.
PO Box 277
Scottville, MI 49454-0277
Ph:(616)845-0211
Fax: (616)845-0207
Contact: Mark Bergstrom, Dir.
E-mail: bergstr@westshore.cc.mi.us

61230 ■ Grand Valley State University–Michigan SBTDC
510 W. Fulton Ave.
Grand Rapids, MI 49504
Ph:(616)331-7485
Fax: (616)331-7389
URL: http://www.misbtdc.org
Contact: Carol Lopucki, State Dir.
E-mail: lopuckic@gvsu.edu

SMALL BUSINESS ASSISTANCE PROGRAMS

61231 ■ Michigan Economic Development Corp.
300 N Washington Sq.
Lansing, MI 48913
Ph:(517)373-9808
Fax: (517)335-0198
URL: http://www.michigan.org
Description: Assists firms in developing foreign markets.

61232 ■ Michigan Economic Development Corp.–Michigan Economic Development Corp.
300 N Washington Sq.
Lansing, MI 48913
Ph:(517)373-9808
Fax: (517)335-0198
URL: http://www.michigan.org
Description: Advocate for businesses in Michigan that have a conflict with state agencies or that need assistance in getting attention from state agencies.

61233 ■ Michigan Economic Development Corp.–Small Business Services
300 N Washington Sq.
Lansing, MI 48913
Ph:(517)373-9808
Fax: (517)335-0198
URL: http://www.michigan.org

61234 ■ Midland Economic Development Council
300 Rodd St., Ste. 201
Midland, MI 48640-6596
Ph:(989)839-0340
Fax: (989)839-7372
URL: http://www.midlandedc.org/

SCORE OFFICES

61235 ■ SCORE Ann Arbor Area Chapter
425 S Main St., Ste. 103
Ann Arbor, MI 48104
Ph:(734)665-4433
Fax: (734)665-4191
Co. E-mail: info@annarborchamber.org
Description: Provides public service by offering small business advice and training.

61236 ■ SCORE Cadillac
222 N Lake St.
Cadillac, MI 49601
Ph:(231)775-9776
Fax: (231)775-1440
Co. E-mail: score@cadillac.org
Description: Serves as volunteer program in which working and retired business management professionals provide free business counseling to men and women who are considering starting a small business, encountering problems with their business, or expanding their business. Offers free one-on-one counseling, online counseling and low cost workshops on a variety of business topics.

61237 ■ SCORE Detroit
c/o Emily Olivero, CHR
477 Michigan Ave., Rm. 515-SBA
Detroit, MI 48226
Ph:(313)226-7947

Fax: (313)226-3448
Co. E-mail: detscore@sbcglobal.net
URL: http://scoredetroit.org
Contact: Ms. Emily Olivero, Chair
Description: Seeks to provide counseling for new and small business.

61238 ■ SCORE Grand Rapids
c/o Judith K. Thome, Chair
111 Pearl St. NW
Grand Rapids, MI 49503
Ph:(616)771-0305
Fax: (616)771-0328
Co. E-mail: score@grandrapids.org
URL: http://scoregr.org
Contact: Judith K. Thome, Chapter Chair
Description: Dedicated to entrepreneur education and the formation, growth and success of small businesses nationwide.

61239 ■ SCORE Muskegon
c/o Muskegon Area Chamber of Commerce
900 Third St., Ste. 200
Muskegon, MI 49443-1087
Ph:(231)722-3751
Fax: (231)728-7251
Co. E-mail: score@muskegon.org
URL: http://www.scoremuskegon.org
Description: Serves as volunteer program in which working and retired business management professionals provide free business counseling to men and women who are considering starting a small business, encountering problems with their business, or expanding their business. Offers free one-on-one counseling, online counseling and low cost workshops on a variety of business topics.

61240 ■ SCORE Petoskey
401 E Mitchell
Petoskey, MI 49770
Ph:(231)347-4150
Fax: (231)348-1810
Co. E-mail: chamber@petoskey.com
URL: http://www.score.org

61241 ■ SCORE Traverse City
c/o Pat Hobson
202 E Grandview Pkwy.
Traverse City, MI 49684
Ph:(231)947-5075
Fax: (231)946-2565
Co. E-mail: score@tcchamber.org
URL: http://www.score-traversecity.org
Contact: Pat Hobson
Description: Provides entrepreneurs with free, confidential, face-to-face and email business counseling.

BETTER BUSINESS BUREAUS

61242 ■ Better Business Bureau of Detroit and Eastern Michigan
30555 Southfield Rd., Ste. 200
Southfield, MI 48076-7751
Ph:(248)644-9100
Fax: (248)644-5026
Co. E-mail: info@easternmichiganbbb.org
URL: http://www.easternmichiganbbb.org
Contact: Fred Hoffecker, Pres.

61243 ■ Better Business Bureau of Western Michigan
354 Trust Bldg.
40 Pearl St. NW, Ste. 354
Grand Rapids, MI 49503
Ph:(616)774-8236
Free: 800-684-3222
Fax: (616)774-2014
Co. E-mail: bbbinfo@iserv.net
URL: http://www.grandrapids.bbb.org
Contact: Kenneth J. Vander Meeden, Pres./CEO

CHAMBERS OF COMMERCE

61244 ■ Alger Chamber of Commerce
PO Box 405
Munising, MI 49862
Ph:(906)387-2138
Fax: (906)387-1858
Co. E-mail: chamber@algercounty.org
URL: http://www.algercounty.org
Contact: Kay LeVeque, Dir.

61245 ■ Allegan Area Chamber of Commerce
882 Marshall St., Ste. B
Allegan, MI 49010
Ph:(269)673-2479
Fax: (269)673-7190
Co. E-mail: chamber@allegan.net
URL: http://www.chamber.allegan.net
Contact: Lynda Ferris, Dir.

61246 ■ Allendale Chamber of Commerce
PO Box 539
Allendale, MI 49401
Ph:(616)895-6295
Fax: (616)895-6670
Co. E-mail: aacc@allendalechamber.org
URL: http://www.allendalechamber.org
Contact: Julie Van Dyke, Exec.Dir.

61247 ■ Anchor Bay Chamber of Commerce
35054 23 Mile Rd., Ste. 110
New Baltimore, MI 48047
Ph:(586)725-5148
Fax: (586)725-5369
Co. E-mail: info@anchorbaychamber.com
URL: http://www.anchorbaychamber.com
Contact: Lisa Edwards, Exec.Dir.

61248 ■ Ann Arbor Area Chamber of Commerce
425 S Main St., Ste. 103
Ann Arbor, MI 48104-2303
Ph:(734)665-4433
Fax: (734)665-4191
Co. E-mail: info@annarborchamber.org
Contact: Ms. Sabrina Keeley, Pres.

61249 ■ Atlanta Area Chamber of Commerce
PO Box 410
Atlanta, MI 49709
Ph:(989)785-3400
Fax: (989)785-3400
Co. E-mail: chamber_office@atlantamichigan.com
URL: http://www.atlantamichigan.com
Contact: Betty Comoford, Pres.

61250 ■ Au Gres Chamber of Commerce
PO Box 455
Au Gres, MI 48703
Ph:(989)876-6688
Contact: Eric Forton, Pres.

61251 ■ Auburn Area Chamber of Commerce
PO Box 215
Auburn, MI 48611
Ph:(989)662-4001
Co. E-mail: cornfest@auburnchambermi.com
URL: http://www.auburnchambermi.com
Contact: Dave Hill, Pres.

61252 ■ Bad Axe Chamber of Commerce
PO Box 87
Bad Axe, MI 48413
Ph:(989)269-6936
Free: 800-469-5146
Fax: (989)269-2611
Co. E-mail: badaxemi@yahoo.com
Contact: Charlene Kramer, Sec.-Treas.

61253 ■ Barry County Area Chamber of Commerce
221 W State St.
Hastings, MI 49058
Ph:(269)945-2454
Free: 800-510-2922
Fax: (269)945-3839

Co. E-mail: barrychamber@sbcglobal.net
URL: http://www.barrychamber.com
Contact: Julie DeBoer, Exec.Dir.

61254 ■ Battle Creek Area Chamber of Commerce
77 E Michigan Ave., Ste. 80
Commerce Pointe
Battle Creek, MI 49017
Ph:(269)962-4076
Fax: (269)962-6309
Co. E-mail: kmechem@battlecreek.org
URL: http://www.battlecreek.org
Contact: Kathleen L. Mechem, Pres./CEO

61255 ■ Bay Area Chamber of Commerce
901 Saginaw St.
Bay City, MI 48708
Ph:(989)893-4567
Fax: (989)995-5594
Co. E-mail: chamber@baycityarea.com
URL: http://www.baycityarea.com
Contact: Michael D. Seward CCE, Pres./CEO

61256 ■ Bellaire Area Chamber of Commerce
PO Box 205
Bellaire, MI 49615
Ph:(231)533-6023
Fax: (231)533-6023
Co. E-mail: info@bellairemichigan.com
URL: http://www.bellairemichigan.com
Contact: Pat DuBois, Exec.Dir.

61257 ■ Belleville Area Chamber of Commerce
248 Main St.
Belleville, MI 48111
Ph:(734)697-7151
Fax: (734)697-1415
Co. E-mail: bellechamber@sbcglobal.net
URL: http://www.bellevillech.com
Contact: Janet Millard, Exec.Dir.

61258 ■ Benzie County Chamber of Commerce
826 Michigan Ave.
PO Box 204
Benzonia, MI 49616
Ph:(231)882-5801
Free: 800-882-5801
Fax: (231)882-9249
Co. E-mail: chamberinfo@benzie.org
URL: http://www.benzie.org
Contact: Carol Davidson, Exec.Dir.

61259 ■ Birch Run Area Chamber of Commerce
PO Box 153
Birch Run, MI 48415
Ph:(989)624-9193
Free: 888-624-9193
Fax: (989)624-5337
Co. E-mail: info@birchrunchamber.com
URL: http://www.birchrunchamber.com
Contact: Tammey S. Inman, Exec.Dir.

61260 ■ Birmingham-Bloomfield Chamber of Commerce
124 W Maple Rd.
Birmingham, MI 48009-3322
Ph:(248)644-1700
Fax: (248)644-0286
Co. E-mail: thechamber@bbcc.com
URL: http://www.bbcc.com
Contact: Pamela Iacobelli, Pres.

61261 ■ Blissfield Area Chamber of Commerce
PO Box 25
Blissfield, MI 49228-0025
Ph:(517)486-3642
Fax: (517)486-4328
Co. E-mail: info@blissfieldchamber.com
URL: http://www.blissfield.net
Contact: Beth Borchardt, Pres.

61262 ■ Boyne Area City Chamber of Commerce
28 S Lake St.
Boyne City, MI 49712
Ph:(231)582-6222
Fax: (231)582-6963
Co. E-mail: boynechamber@boynechamber.com
URL: http://www.boynecity.com
Contact: Scott MacKenzie, Exec.Dir.

61263 ■ Branch County Area Chamber of Commerce
20 Division St.
Coldwater, MI 49036-1966
Ph:(517)278-5985
Fax: (517)278-8369
Co. E-mail: info@branch-county.com
URL: http://www.branch-county.com
Contact: Hillary Eley, Pres.

61264 ■ Brooklyn - Irish Hills Chamber of Commerce
221 N Main St.
Brooklyn, MI 49230-8999
Ph:(517)592-8907
Fax: (517)592-8907
Co. E-mail: bihcc@frontiernet.net
URL: http://www.brooklynmi.com
Contact: Linda Reynolds, Exec.Dir.

61265 ■ Buchanan Area Chamber of Commerce
103 W Front St.
Buchanan, MI 49107-1410
Ph:(269)695-3291
Fax: (269)695-3813
Co. E-mail: bacc@buchanan.mi.us
URL: http://www.buchanan.mi.us
Contact: Michelle Klarich, Exec.Dir.

61266 ■ Cadillac Area Chamber of Commerce
222 Lake St.
Cadillac, MI 49601-1874
Ph:(231)775-9776
Fax: (231)775-1440
Co. E-mail: info@cadillac.org
URL: http://www.cadillac.org
Contact: Bill Tencza, Pres.

61267 ■ Canton Chamber of Commerce
45525 Hanford Rd.
Canton, MI 48187
Ph:(734)453-4040
Fax: (734)453-4503
Co. E-mail: info@cantonchamber.com
URL: http://www.cantonchamber.com
Contact: Dianne Cojei, Pres.

61268 ■ Capac Area Chamber of Commerce
PO Box 520
Capac, MI 48014
Ph:(810)395-4359
Contact: Rosy Cousins

61269 ■ Caro Chamber of Commerce
157 N State St.
Caro, MI 48723
Ph:(989)673-5211
Fax: (989)672-4098
Co. E-mail: executivedirector@carochamber.org
URL: http://www.carochamber.org
Contact: Susan Steinhoff, Exec.Dir.

61270 ■ Cass City Chamber of Commerce
6506 Main St.
Cass City, MI 48726-1524
Ph:(989)872-4618
Free: (866)266-3822
Fax: (989)872-4855
Co. E-mail: chamber@cass-city.net
URL: http://www.casscity.org
Contact: Kay Warner, Administrator

61271 ■ Central Lake Chamber of Commerce
2587 N M-88 Hwy.
Central Lake, MI 49622

Ph:(231)544-3322
Co. E-mail: clcc@torchlake.com
URL: http://www.central-lake.com
Contact: Jackie White, Pres.

61272 ■ Central Macomb County Chamber of Commerce
49 Macomb Pl.
Mount Clemens, MI 48043
Ph:(586)493-7600
Fax: (586)493-7602
Co. E-mail: info@central-macomb.com
URL: http://www.central-macomb.com
Contact: Grace M. Shore, Pres.

61273 ■ Chamber - Grand Haven, Spring Lake, Ferrysburg
PO Box 509
1 S Harbor Dr.
Grand Haven, MI 49417-0509
Ph:(616)842-4910
Fax: (616)842-0379
Co. E-mail: areainfo@grandhavenchamber.org
URL: http://www.grandhavenchamber.org
Contact: Joy A. Gaasch, Pres.

61274 ■ Charlevoix Area Chamber of Commerce
408 Bridge St.
PO Box 358
Charlevoix, MI 49720-1417
Ph:(231)547-2101
Free: 800-951-2101
Fax: (231)547-6633
Co. E-mail: info@charlevoix.org
URL: http://www.charlevoix.org
Contact: Jacqueline Merta, Pres.

61275 ■ Charlotte Chamber of Commerce
PO Box 356
Charlotte, MI 48813
Ph:(517)543-0400
Fax: (517)543-9638
Co. E-mail: charlotte@ia4u.net
Contact: Ann Garvey, Dir.

61276 ■ Cheboygan Area Chamber of Commerce
124 N Main St.
PO Box 69
Cheboygan, MI 49721
Ph:(231)627-7183
Free: 800-968-3302
Fax: (231)627-2770
Co. E-mail: mgrisdale@cheboygan.com
URL: http://www.cheboygan.com
Contact: Michael Grisdale, Exec.Dir.

61277 ■ Chelsea Area Chamber of Commerce
522 N Main St.
Chelsea, MI 48118
Ph:(734)475-1145
Fax: (734)475-6102
Co. E-mail: info@chelseamichamber.org
URL: http://www.chelseamichamber.org
Contact: Bob Pierce, Exec.Dir.

61278 ■ Chesaning Chamber of Commerce
218 N Front St.
PO Box 83
Chesaning, MI 48616
Ph:(989)845-3055
Free: 800-255-3055
Fax: (989)845-6006
Co. E-mail: info@chesaningchamber.org
URL: http://www.chesaningchamber.org
Contact: Sandi Richardson, Exec.Dir.

61279 ■ Clare Area Chamber of Commerce
429 N McEwan St.
Clare, MI 48617
Ph:(989)386-2442
Free: 888-ATC-LARE
Fax: (989)386-3173
Co. E-mail: chamberoffice@claremichigan.com
URL: http://www.claremichigan.com

Contact: Ann Doherty, Pres.

61280 ■ Clarkston Area Chamber of Commerce
5856 S Main
Clarkston, MI 48346
Ph:(248)625-8055
Fax: (248)625-8041
Co. E-mail: info@clarkston.org
URL: http://www.clarkston.org
Contact: Penny Shanks, Exec.Dir.

61281 ■ Coloma-Watervliet Area Chamber of Commerce
PO Box 418
Coloma, MI 49038
Ph:(269)468-9160
Fax: (269)468-7088
Co. E-mail: info@coloma-watervliet.org
URL: http://www.coloma-watervliet.org
Contact: Sandy Kraemer, Pres.

61282 ■ Coopersville Area Chamber of Commerce
289 Danforth St.
Coopersville, MI 49404
Ph:(616)997-9731
Fax: (616)997-6679
Co. E-mail: jrichardson@cityofcoopersville.com
URL: http://www.coopersville.com
Contact: Mrs. Jan Richardson, Exec. Dir.

61283 ■ Davison Area Chamber of Commerce
105 E 2nd St., Ste. 7
Davison, MI 48423
Ph:(810)653-6266
Fax: (810)653-0669
Co. E-mail: dcofcomm@yahoo.com
Contact: Phil Becker, Exec.Dir.

61284 ■ Dearborn Chamber of Commerce
15544 Michigan Ave.
Dearborn, MI 48126
Ph:(313)584-6100
Fax: (313)584-9818
Co. E-mail: info@dearbornchamber.org
URL: http://www.dearbornchamber.org

61285 ■ Delta County Area Chamber of Commerce
230 Ludington St.
Escanaba, MI 49829
Ph:(906)786-2192
Free: 800-DEL-TAMI
Fax: (906)786-8830
Co. E-mail: info@deltami.org
URL: http://www.deltami.org
Contact: Vickie Micheau, Exec.Dir.

61286 ■ Detroit Black Chamber of Commerce
3011 W Grand Blvd., Ste. 1200
Detroit, MI 48202-3013
Ph:(313)664-2000
Co. E-mail: info@detroitblackchamber.com
Contact: Kathi Dones-Carson, Pres.

61287 ■ Detroit Regional Chamber
PO Box 33840
Detroit, MI 48232-0840
Free: (866)MBR-LINE
Fax: (313)964-0183
Co. E-mail: members@detroitchamber.com
URL: http://www.detroitchamber.com
Contact: Richard E. Blouse Jr., Pres./CEO

61288 ■ Durand Area Chamber of Commerce
100 W Clinton St.
Durand, MI 48429
Ph:(989)288-3715
Fax: (989)288-3922
Co. E-mail: office@durandchamber.com
URL: http://www.durandchamber.com
Contact: Candalee Rathbun, Exec. Sec.

61289 ■ East Jordan Area Chamber of Commerce
PO Box 137
100 Main St., Ste. B
East Jordan, MI 49727
Ph:(231)536-7351
Fax: (231)536-0966
Co. E-mail: info@ejchamber.org
URL: http://www.ejchamber.org
Contact: Mary H. Faculak, Exec.Dir.

61290 ■ Eastpointe Chamber of Commerce
23801 Gratiot Ave.
PO Box 24
Eastpointe, MI 48021-0024
Ph:(586)776-5520
Fax: (586)776-7808
URL: http://www.epchamber.com
Contact: Catherine Green, Exec. Dir.

61291 ■ Edwardsburg Area Chamber of Commerce
PO Box 575
Edwardsburg, MI 49112
Ph:(269)663-6344
Free: 800-942-8413
Fax: (269)663-5344
Co. E-mail: administration@edwardsburg.biz
URL: http://www.edwardsburg.biz
Contact: Karen Sinkiewicz, Admin.

61292 ■ Elk Rapids Area Chamber of Commerce
305 U.S. 31 N
PO Box 854
Elk Rapids, MI 49629-0854
Ph:(231)264-8202
Free: 800-626-7328
Fax: (231)264-6591
Co. E-mail: info@elkrapidschamber.org
URL: http://www.elkrapidschamber.org
Contact: Terri Crandall-Kimble, Exec.Dir.

61293 ■ Evart Area Chamber of Commerce
PO Box 688
Evart, MI 49631-0688
Ph:(231)734-6119
Fax: (231)734-2055
Co. E-mail: chamber@evart.org
URL: http://www.evart.org
Contact: Roger Elkins, Pres.

61294 ■ Farmington - Farmington Hills Chamber of Commerce
30903 W Ten Mile Rd., Ste. B
Farmington Hills, MI 48336
Ph:(248)474-3440
Fax: (248)474-9235
Co. E-mail: atopouzian@ffhchamber.com
URL: http://ffhchamber.com
Contact: Ara Topouzian, Pres./CEO

61295 ■ Farwell Area Chamber of Commerce
PO Box 771
Farwell, MI 48622-0771
Ph:(989)588-0580
Fax: (989)588-0580
Co. E-mail: facc@farewellareachamber.com
URL: http://www.farwellareachamber.com
Contact: Janice Jenkins, Chair

61296 ■ Fenton Area Chamber of Commerce
114 N Leroy St.
Fenton, MI 48430
Ph:(810)629-5447
Fax: (810)629-6608
Co. E-mail: info@fentonchamber.com
URL: http://www.fentonchamber.com
Contact: Mrs. Shelly Day, Pres.

61297 ■ Flint Area Chamber of Commerce
519 S Saginaw St., Ste. 200
Flint, MI 48502-1802
Ph:(810)232-7101
Fax: (810)233-7437
Co. E-mail: flintchamber@flint.org
URL: http://www.flintchamber.org/home.htm

Contact: Larry Ford, Pres.

61298 ■ Flushing Area Chamber of Commerce
133 E Main St.
PO Box 44
Flushing, MI 48433
Ph:(810)659-4141
Fax: (810)659-6964
Co. E-mail: flushingchamber@sbcglobal.net
URL: http://www.flushingchamber.com
Contact: Susan Little, Exec.Dir.

61299 ■ Four Flags Area Chamber of Commerce
321 E Main St.
Niles, MI 49120-0010
Ph:(269)683-3720
Fax: (269)683-3722
Co. E-mail: nileschamber@qtm.net
URL: http://www.nilesmi.com
Contact: Ronald J. Sather, Pres./CEO

61300 ■ Frankenmuth Chamber of Commerce and Convention and Visitors Bureau
635 S Main St.
Frankenmuth, MI 48734
Free: 800-FUN-TOWN
Fax: (989)652-3841
Co. E-mail: chamber@frankenmuth.org
URL: http://www.frankenmuth.org
Contact: Jennifer Tebedo CAE, Pres./CEO

61301 ■ Frankfort - Elberta Area Chamber of Commerce
PO Box 566
Frankfort, MI 49635
Ph:(231)352-7251
Fax: (231)352-6750
Co. E-mail: fcofc@frankfort-elberta.com
URL: http://www.frankfort-elberta.com
Contact: Alice Fewins, Exec.Dir.

61302 ■ Fremont Area Chamber of Commerce
7 E Main St.
Fremont, MI 49412
Ph:(231)924-0770
Fax: (231)924-9248
Co. E-mail: fchamber@ncats.net
URL: http://www.fremontcommerce.com
Contact: Ron Vliem, Exec.Dir.

61303 ■ Garden City Chamber of Commerce
30120 Ford Rd., Ste. D
Garden City, MI 48135
Ph:(734)422-4448
Fax: (734)422-1601
URL: http://www.gardencity.org
Contact: Sandra Wheatley, Pres.

61304 ■ Gaylord - Otsego County Chamber of Commerce
101 W Main St.
PO Box 513
Gaylord, MI 49734
Ph:(989)732-6333
Free: 800-345-8621
Fax: (989)732-7990
Co. E-mail: info@gaylordchamber.com
URL: http://www.gaylordchamber.com
Contact: Bob Kasprzak, Exec.Dir.

61305 ■ Gladwin County Chamber of Commerce
608 W. Cedar Ave.
Gladwin, MI 48624-2028
Ph:(989)426-5451
Free: 800-789-4812
Fax: (989)426-1074
Co. E-mail: chamber@ejourney.com
Contact: Tom Tucholski, Exec.Dir.

61306 ■ Grand Blanc Chamber of Commerce
512 E Grand Blanc Rd.
Grand Blanc, MI 48439

Ph:(810)695-4222
Fax: (810)695-0053
Co. E-mail: jet@grandblancchamber.org
URL: http://www.grandblancchamber.org
Contact: Jet Kilmer, Pres.

61307 ■ Grand Ledge Area Chamber of Commerce
121 S Bridge St.
Grand Ledge, MI 48837
Ph:(517)627-2383
Fax: (517)627-5006
Co. E-mail: glacc@grandledgemi.com
URL: http://www.grandledgemi.com
Contact: Norman Snyder, Exec.Dir.

61308 ■ Grand Rapids Area Chamber of Commerce
111 Pearl St. NW
Grand Rapids, MI 49503-2831
Ph:(616)771-0300
Fax: (616)771-0318
Co. E-mail: info@grandrapids.org
URL: http://grandrapids.org
Contact: Ms. Jeanne Englehart, Pres./CEO

61309 ■ Grandville Chamber of Commerce
2905 Wilson Ave., Ste. 202-A
Grandville, MI 49418
Ph:(616)531-8890
Fax: (616)531-8896
Co. E-mail: gcc@grandvillechamber.org
URL: http://www.grandvillechamber.org
Contact: Chris Konyndyk, Exec.Dir.

61310 ■ Gratiot Area Chamber of Commerce
110 W Superior St.
PO Box 516
Alma, MI 48801
Ph:(989)463-5525
Fax: (989)463-6588
Co. E-mail: chamber@gratiot.org
URL: http://www.gratiot.org/chamber/chamber.html
Contact: Patricia F. Nelson, Exec.Dir.

61311 ■ Grayling Regional Chamber of Commerce
213 N James St.
PO Box 406
Grayling, MI 49738
Ph:(989)348-2921
Free: 800-937-8837
Fax: (989)348-7315
Co. E-mail: director@graylingchamber.com
URL: http://www.grayling-mi.com
Contact: Timothy E. Zigila, Exec.Dir.

61312 ■ Greater Albion Chamber of Commerce
416 S Superior St.
PO Box 238
Albion, MI 49224
Ph:(517)629-5533
Fax: (517)629-4284
Co. E-mail: gacoc@forks.org
URL: http://www.greateralbionchamber.org
Contact: Sue Marcos, Pres.

61313 ■ Greater Algonac Chamber of Commerce
1396 St. Clair River Dr.
PO Box 375
Algonac, MI 48001
Ph:(810)794-5511
Fax: (810)794-5511
Co. E-mail: execdirector@algonacchamber.com
URL: http://www.algonacchamber.com
Contact: Lisa M. Edwards, Exec.Dir.

61314 ■ Greater Berkley Chamber of Commerce
PO Box 72-1253
Berkley, MI 48072
Ph:(248)414-9157
Co. E-mail: kees.hiatt@nationalcity.com
URL: http://berkleychamber.com
Contact: Kees Hiatt, Pres.

61315 ■ Greater Brighton Area Chamber of Commerce
131 Hyne St.
Brighton, MI 48116
Ph:(810)227-5086
Fax: (810)227-5940
Co. E-mail: info@brightoncoc.org
URL: http://www.brightoncoc.org
Contact: Pam McConeghy, Exec.Dir.

61316 ■ Greater Croswell - Lexington Chamber of Commerce
PO Box 142
Lexington, MI 48450
Ph:(810)359-2262
Co. E-mail: croslex@greatlakes.net
URL: http://www.cros-lex-chamber.com
Contact: Marleen Reynolds, Pres.

61317 ■ Greater Decatur Chamber of Commerce
PO Box 211
Decatur, MI 49045
Ph:(269)423-2411
Co. E-mail: info@decaturmi.org
URL: http://www.decaturmi.org
Contact: Dave Moormann, Pres.

61318 ■ Greater Dowagiac Area Chamber of Commerce
200 Depot Dr.
Dowagiac, MI 49047
Ph:(269)782-8212
Fax: (269)782-6701
Co. E-mail: vickie@dowagiacchamber.com
URL: http://www.dowagiacchamber.com
Contact: Vickie Phillipson, Program Dir.

61319 ■ Greater Jackson Chamber of Commerce
One Jackson Sq., 11th Fl.
PO Box 80
Jackson, MI 49204-0080
Ph:(517)782-8221
Fax: (517)782-0061
Co. E-mail: smilhoan@enterprisegroup.org
URL: http://www.gjcc.org
Contact: Susan L. Milhoan, Pres.

61320 ■ Greater Paw Paw Chamber of Commerce
804 S Kalamazoo St., Ste. 4
PO Box 105
Paw Paw, MI 49079
Ph:(269)657-5395
Fax: (269)655-8755
Co. E-mail: mary@pawpawchamber.com
URL: http://www.pawpawmi.com
Contact: Mary Springer, Community Relations Representative

61321 ■ Greater Port Huron Area Chamber of Commerce
920 Pine Grove Ave.
Port Huron, MI 48060
Ph:(810)985-7101
Free: 800-361-0526
Fax: (810)985-7311
Co. E-mail: info@porthuron-chamber.org
URL: http://www.porthuron-chamber.org
Contact: Lisa Hatch, Exec.Dir.

61322 ■ Greater Romulus Chamber of Commerce
9191 Wickham
Romulus, MI 48174
Ph:(734)326-4290
Fax: (734)326-3489
Co. E-mail: info@romuluschamber.org
URL: http://www.romuluschamber.org
Contact: David B. Goodwin, Pres.

61323 ■ Greater Royal Oak Chamber of Commerce
200 S Washington Ave.
Royal Oak, MI 48067-3821
Ph:(248)547-4000

Fax: (248)547-0504
Co. E-mail: coc@virtualroyaloak.com
URL: http://www.virtualroyaloak.com
Contact: Mrs. Liz Tillander, Exec.Dir.

61324 ■ Greater South Haven Area Chamber of Commerce
606 Phillips St.
South Haven, MI 49090
Ph:(616)637-5171
Fax: (616)639-1570
Co. E-mail: cofc@southhavenmi.com
URL: http://www.southhavenmi.com

61325 ■ Greater West Bloomfield Chamber of Commerce
6668 Orchard Lake Rd., Ste. 207
West Bloomfield, MI 48322
Ph:(248)626-3636
Fax: (248)626-4218
Co. E-mail: wbcc@sbcglobal.net
URL: http://www.westbloomfieldchamber.com
Contact: Maureen Malone, Exec. Dir.

61326 ■ Greenville Area Chamber of Commerce
108 N Lafayette St., Ste. C
Greenville, MI 48838
Ph:(616)754-5697
Fax: (616)754-4710
Co. E-mail: info@greenvillechamber.net
URL: http://www.greenvillechamber.net
Contact: Jeff Cook, Chm.

61327 ■ Harbor Beach Chamber of Commerce
PO Box 113
Harbor Beach, MI 48441
Ph:(989)479-6477
Free: 800-HBM-ICH5
Fax: (989)479-6477
Co. E-mail: visitor@harborbeachchamber.com
URL: http://www.harborbeachchamber.com
Contact: Bill Duerr, Exec.Sec.

61328 ■ Harbor Country Chamber of Commerce
530 S Whittaker, Ste. F
New Buffalo, MI 49117
Ph:(269)469-5409
Fax: (269)469-2257
Co. E-mail: info@harborcountry.org
URL: http://www.harborcountry.org
Contact: Karen Gear, Pres.

61329 ■ Harbor Springs Chamber of Commerce
368 E Main St.
Harbor Springs, MI 49740-0037
Ph:(231)526-7999
Free: (866)526-7999
Fax: (231)526-5593
Co. E-mail: info@harborspringschamber.com
URL: http://www.harborspringschamber.com
Contact: Kathy Lott, Exec.Dir.

61330 ■ Harrison Chamber of Commerce
809 N 1st St.
PO Box 682
Harrison, MI 48625-0682
Ph:(989)539-6011
Fax: (989)539-6099
Co. E-mail: harrisonchamber@sbcglobal.net
URL: http://www.harrisonchamber.com
Contact: Debbie Gadberry, Pres.

61331 ■ Hart - Silver Lake Mears Chamber of Commerce
2388 N Comfort Dr.
Hart, MI 49420
Ph:(231)873-2247
Free: 800-870-9786
Fax: (231)873-1683
Co. E-mail: info@hartsilverlakemears.com
URL: http://www.hartsilverlakemears.com
Contact: Tom Rickhoff, Pres.

61332 ■ Hillman Area Chamber of Commerce
PO Box 506
Hillman, MI 49746
Ph:(989)742-3739
Fax: (989)742-4757
URL: http://www.hillmanmichigan.org/chamber.html
Contact: Ms. Margaret Kirby, Pres.

61333 ■ Hillsdale County Chamber of Commerce
22 N Manning St.
Hillsdale, MI 49242
Ph:(517)437-6401
Fax: (517)437-6408
Co. E-mail: info@hillsdalecountychamber.com
URL: http://www.hillsdalecountychamber.com
Contact: Karri Doty, Exec.Dir./Pres.

61334 ■ Holland Area Chamber of Commerce
272 E 8th St.
Holland, MI 49423
Ph:(616)392-2389
Fax: (616)392-7379
Co. E-mail: info@hollandchamber.org
URL: http://www.hollandchamber.org
Contact: Jane Clark, Pres.

61335 ■ Holly Area Chamber of Commerce
202 S Saginaw St., 2nd Fl.
Holly, MI 48442
Ph:(248)215-7099
Fax: (248)215-7106
Co. E-mail: staff@hollymi.com
URL: http://www.hollymi.com/index.htm
Contact: Aaron Oppenheimer, Pres.

61336 ■ Houghton Lake Chamber of Commerce
1625 W Houghton Lake Dr.
Houghton Lake, MI 48629
Ph:(989)366-5644
Free: 800-248-5253
Fax: (989)366-9472
Co. E-mail: hlcc@houghtonlakemichigan.net
URL: http://www.houghtonlakechamber.org
Contact: Georgetta Garner

61337 ■ Howell Area Chamber of Commerce
123 E Washington St.
Howell, MI 48843
Ph:(517)546-3920
Fax: (517)546-4115
Co. E-mail: pconvery@howell.org
URL: http://www.howell.org
Contact: Ms. Pat Convery, Pres.

61338 ■ Hudson Area Chamber of Commerce
300 W Main St.
Hudson, MI 49247
Ph:(517)448-6666
URL: http://www.hudsonmich.com
Contact: Brian Golden, Pres.

61339 ■ Hudsonville Area Chamber of Commerce
PO Box 216
Hudsonville, MI 49426
Ph:(616)662-0900
Fax: (616)662-4557
Co. E-mail: hcc@netpenny.net
Contact: Laurie Van Haitsma, Dir.

61340 ■ Huron Shores Chamber of Commerce
PO Box 581
Harrisville, MI 48740
Ph:(989)724-5107
Free: 800-432-2823
Fax: (989)724-5107
Co. E-mail: info@huronshoreschamber.com
URL: http://www.huronshoreschamber.com
Contact: Cheryl Peterson, Pres.

61341 ■ Huron Township Chamber of Commerce
19132 Huron River Dr.
PO Box 247
New Boston, MI 48164

Ph:(734)753-4220
Fax: (734)753-4602
Co. E-mail: township@provide.net
URL: http://www.members.tripod.com/htcc48164
Contact: Teresa Trosin, Exec. Office Sec.-Treas.

61342 ■ Huron Valley Chamber of Commerce
317 Union St., Ste. F
Milford, MI 48381
Ph:(248)685-7129
Fax: (248)685-9047
Co. E-mail: info@huronvcc.com
URL: http://www.huronvcc.com
Contact: Susan Happel, Exec.Dir.

61343 ■ Indian River Resort Region Chamber of Commerce
3435 S Straits Hwy.
PO Box 57
Indian River, MI 49749-0057
Ph:(231)238-9325
Free: 800-EXIT-310
Fax: (231)238-0949
Co. E-mail: info@irchamber.com
URL: http://www.irchamber.com
Contact: Jeff Comps, Pres.

61344 ■ Inkster Chamber of Commerce
29150 Carlysle St.
Inkster, MI 48141-2807
Ph:(734)722-5146
Contact: Ernestine Williams, Pres.

61345 ■ Interlochen Area Chamber of Commerce
PO Box 13
Interlochen, MI 49643
Ph:(231)276-7141
Co. E-mail: interlochenchamber@juno.com
URL: http://www.interlochenchamber.org
Contact: Laura M. Franke, Dir.

61346 ■ Ionia Area Chamber of Commerce
434 W Main St.
Ionia, MI 48846
Ph:(616)527-2560
Fax: (616)527-0894
Co. E-mail: info@ioniachamber.net
URL: http://www.ioniachamber.org
Contact: Dawn Ketchum, Exec. Dir.

61347 ■ Iron County Chamber of Commerce
50 E Genesee St.
Iron River, MI 49935
Ph:(906)265-3822
Free: 888-TRY-IRON
Fax: (906)265-5605
Co. E-mail: info@iron.org
URL: http://www.tryiron.org
Contact: Gayle Dae, Exec.Dir.

61348 ■ Ironwood Area Chamber of Commerce
PO Box 45
Ironwood, MI 49938
Ph:(906)932-1122
Fax: (906)932-2756
Co. E-mail: chamber@ironwoodmi.org
URL: http://www.ironwoodmi.org
Contact: Kim Kolesar, Exec.Dir.

61349 ■ Ishpeming Office of Lake Superior Community Partnership
610 Palms Ave.
Ishpeming, MI 49849
Ph:(906)486-4841
Free: 888-57-UNITY
Fax: (906)486-4850
Co. E-mail: mqtinfo@marquette.org
URL: http://www.marquette.org
Contact: Amy Clickner, Dir. of Chamber Operations

61350 ■ Kalamazoo Regional Chamber of Commerce
346 W Michigan Ave.
Kalamazoo, MI 49007
Ph:(269)381-4000

Fax: (269)343-0430
Co. E-mail: info@kazoochamber.com
URL: http://www.kazoochamber.com
Contact: David P. Sanford, Interim Pres./CEO

61351 ■ Kalkaska Area Chamber of Commerce
353 S Cedar St.
PO Box 291
Kalkaska, MI 49646
Ph:(231)258-9103
Free: 800-487-6880
Fax: (231)258-6155
Co. E-mail: chamber@kalkaskami.com
URL: http://www.kalkaskami.com
Contact: Sharon Coppock, Office Mgr.

61352 ■ Keweenaw Peninsula Chamber of Commerce
902 College Ave.
PO Box 336
Houghton, MI 49931-0336
Ph:(906)482-5240
Free: (866)304-5722
Fax: (906)482-5241
Co. E-mail: info@keweenaw.org
URL: http://www.keweenaw.org
Contact: Mr. Richard L. Baker, Exec.Dir.

61353 ■ Lake City Area Chamber of Commerce
PO Drawer H
Lake City, MI 49651
Ph:(231)839-4969
Fax: (231)839-5991
Co. E-mail: info@lakecitymich.com
URL: http://www.lakecitymich.com
Contact: Kim Mosher, Admin.Asst.

61354 ■ Lake Gogebic Area Chamber of Commerce
PO Box 114
Bergland, MI 49910-0114
Ph:(906)842-3611
Free: 888-464-3242
Fax: (906)842-3653
Co. E-mail: info@lakegogebicarea.com
URL: http://www.lakegogebicarea.com
Contact: Carol Peterson, Sec.

61355 ■ Lakes Area Chamber of Commerce
305 N Pontiac Trail, Ste. B
Walled Lake, MI 48390-3479
Ph:(248)624-2826
Fax: (248)624-2892
Co. E-mail: info@lakesareachamber.com
URL: http://www.lakesareachamber.com
Contact: Jo Louise Alley, Exec.Dir.

61356 ■ Lakeshore Chamber of Commerce
PO Box 93
Stevensville, MI 49127-0093
Ph:(269)429-1170
Fax: (269)429-8882
Co. E-mail: information@lakeshorechamber.org
URL: http://www.lakeshorechamber.org
Contact: Susan Hardy, Sec.

61357 ■ Lakeview Area Chamber of Commerce
PO Box 57
Lakeview, MI 48850
Ph:(989)352-1200
Co. E-mail: fssinc@pathwaynet.com
URL: http://www.lakeviewmi.org
Contact: April Finup, Sec.

61358 ■ Lansing Regional Chamber of Commerce
PO Box 14030
Lansing, MI 48901
Ph:(517)487-6340
Fax: (517)484-6910
Co. E-mail: klane@lansingchamber.org
URL: http://www.lansingchamber.org
Contact: Bill Sepic, Pres.

61359 ■ Lapeer Area Chamber of Commerce
108 W Park St.
Lapeer, MI 48446
Ph:(810)664-6641
Fax: (810)664-4349
Co. E-mail: staff@lapeerareachamber.org
URL: http://www.lapeerareachamber.org
Contact: Diana Faught, Exec.Dir.

61360 ■ Leelanau Peninsula Chamber of Commerce
5046 SW Bayshore Dr., Ste. G
Suttons Bay, MI 49682
Ph:(231)271-9895
Free: 800-980-9895
Fax: (231)271-9896
Co. E-mail: info@leelanauchamber.com
URL: http://www.leelanauchamber.com
Contact: Richard Stearns, Pres.

61361 ■ Lenawee County Chamber of Commerce
5282 W US Hwy. 223, Ste. A
Adrian, MI 49221
Ph:(517)265-5141
Fax: (517)263-6065
Co. E-mail: cphipp@lenaweechamber.com
URL: http://www.lenaweechamber.com
Contact: David B. Munson CEE, Pres./CEO

61362 ■ Lewiston Area Chamber of Commerce
2946 Kneeland St.
PO Box 656
Lewiston, MI 49756
Ph:(989)786-2293
Fax: (989)786-4515
Co. E-mail: lewistonchamber@i2k.net
URL: http://lewistonchamber.com

61363 ■ Lincoln Park Chamber of Commerce
1335 Southfield Rd.
PO Box 382
Lincoln Park, MI 48146
Ph:(313)386-0140
Fax: (313)386-0140
Co. E-mail: lpchamberofcommerce@juno.com
Contact: Karen Maniaci, Exec.Dir.

61364 ■ Linden Argentine Chamber of Commerce
PO Box 219
Linden, MI 48451-0128
Ph:(810)735-1277
Fax: (810)735-7738
Co. E-mail: info@lindenchamber.com
URL: http://www.lindenchamber.com
Contact: Brian E. Chidsey, Pres.

61365 ■ Litchfield Chamber of Commerce
PO Box 343
Litchfield, MI 49252
Ph:(517)542-2921
Fax: (517)542-2491
Co. E-mail: litchcity@chartermi.net
URL: http://www.ci.litchfield.mi.us
Contact: Marge Delaney, Pres.

61366 ■ Livonia Chamber of Commerce
33233 Five Mile Rd.
Livonia, MI 48154
Ph:(734)427-2122
Fax: (734)427-6055
Co. E-mail: chamber@livonia.org
URL: http://www.livonia.org
Contact: Wes Graff, Pres.

61367 ■ Lowell Area Chamber of Commerce
113 Riverwalk Plz.
PO Box 224
Lowell, MI 49331
Ph:(616)897-9161
Fax: (616)897-9101
Co. E-mail: info@lowellchamber.org
URL: http://www.lowellchamber.org
Contact: Liz Baker, Exec.Dir.

61368 ■ Ludington Area Chamber of Commerce
5300 W U.S. 10
Ludington, MI 49431
Ph:(231)845-0324
Fax: (231)845-6857
Co. E-mail: ludington@ludington.org
URL: http://www.ludington.org
Contact: Alberta L. Muzzin, Pres./CEO

61369 ■ Mackinac Island Tourism Bureau
PO Box 451
Mackinac Island, MI 49757
Ph:(906)847-6418
Free: 800-454-5227
Fax: (906)847-3571
Co. E-mail: info@mackinacisland.org
URL: http://www.mackinacisland.org
Contact: Mrs. Mary McGuire Slevin, Exec.Dir.

61370 ■ Mackinaw City Chamber of Commerce
216 E Central Ave.
PO Box 856
Mackinaw City, MI 49701
Ph:(231)436-5574
Free: 888-455-8100
Co. E-mail: dedwards@mackinawchamber.com
URL: http://www.mackinawchamber.com
Contact: Dawn Edwards, Exec.Dir.

61371 ■ Macomb Chamber
31201 Chicago Rd., Ste. C-102
Chicago Plz.
Warren, MI 48093
Ph:(586)268-6430
Fax: (586)268-6397
Co. E-mail: info@macombchamber.com
URL: http://www.macombchamber.com
Contact: Melanie D. Davis, Pres.

61372 ■ Madison Heights - Hazel Park Chamber of Commerce
724 W 11 Mile Rd.
Madison Heights, MI 48071
Ph:(248)542-5010
Fax: (248)542-6821
Co. E-mail: info@madisonheightschamber.org
URL: http://www.madisonheightschamber.org
Contact: Mary Lou Sames, Exec. Dir.

61373 ■ Mancelona Area Chamber of Commerce
PO Box 558
Mancelona, MI 49659
Ph:(231)587-5500
Fax: (231)587-5500
Co. E-mail: info@mancelonachamber.org
URL: http://www.mancelonachamber.org

61374 ■ Manchester Area Chamber of Commerce
PO Box 521
Manchester, MI 48158
Ph:(734)428-6222
Co. E-mail: president@manchestermi.org
URL: http://www.manchestermi.org
Contact: Bill Chizmar, Pres.

61375 ■ Manistee Area Chamber of Commerce
11 Cypress St.
Manistee, MI 49660
Ph:(231)723-2575
Free: 800-288-2286
Fax: (231)723-1515
Co. E-mail: chamber@manistee.com
URL: http://www.manisteecountychamber.com
Contact: Dave Yarnell, Exec.Dir.

61376 ■ Marine City Chamber of Commerce
PO Box 38
113 E St. Clair St.
Marine City, MI 48039
Ph:(810)765-4501
Fax: (810)765-4501
Co. E-mail: marinecitychamber@yahoo.com

URL: http://www.marinecitychamber.com
Contact: Bill Senk, Dir.

61377 ■ Marion Area Chamber of Commerce
PO Box 294
Marion, MI 49665
Ph:(231)743-2461
Fax: (231)743-2461
Co. E-mail: rebeccainmarion@hotmail.com
Contact: Rebecca Martinson, VP

61378 ■ Marquette Area Chamber of Commerce- Lake Superior Community Partnership
501 S Front St.
Marquette, MI 49855
Ph:(906)226-6591
Free: 888-57U-NITY
Fax: (906)226-2099
Co. E-mail: mqtinfo@marquette.org
URL: http://www.marquette.org
Contact: Amy Clickner, Exec.Dir.

61379 ■ Marshall Area Chamber of Commerce
424 E Michigan Ave.
Marshall, MI 49068
Ph:(269)781-5163
Free: 800-877-5163
Co. E-mail: chamber@marshallmi.org
URL: http://www.marshallmi.org
Contact: Monica Anderson, Pres.

61380 ■ Marysville Chamber of Commerce
2055 Gratiot Blvd., Ste. D
Marysville, MI 48040
Ph:(810)364-6180
Fax: (810)364-9388
Co. E-mail: chamber@marysvillechamber.com
URL: http://www.marysvillechamber.com
Contact: Laura J. Crawford, Exec.Dir.

61381 ■ Mason Area Chamber of Commerce
148 E Ash St.
Mason, MI 48854-1646
Ph:(517)676-1046
Fax: (517)676-8504
Co. E-mail: masonchamber@masonchamber.org
URL: http://www.masonchamber.org
Contact: Mr. Douglas Klein APR, Exec.Dir.

61382 ■ McBain Area Chamber of Commerce
PO Box 203
McBain, MI 49657-0203
Ph:(231)825-2893
Fax: (231)825-8008
Co. E-mail: info@mcbainmichigan.com
URL: http://www.mcbainmichigan.com
Contact: Paula Dykhouse, Pres.

61383 ■ Mecosta County Area Chamber of Commerce
246 N State St.
Big Rapids, MI 49307
Ph:(231)796-7649
Fax: (231)796-1625
Co. E-mail: mcacc@mecostacounty.com
URL: http://www.mecostacounty.com
Contact: Anja J. Wing, Exec.Dir.

61384 ■ Memphis Chamber of Commerce
PO Box 41006
Memphis, MI 48041
Ph:(810)392-2394
Fax: (810)392-3600
Contact: Nina Powers, Pres.

61385 ■ Mesick Area Chamber of Commerce
PO Box 548
Mesick, MI 49668
Ph:(231)885-3200
Fax: (231)885-2650
Co. E-mail: jkjellens@netscape.net
URL: http://www.mesick-michigan.org
Contact: Jeff Ellens, Pres.

61386 ■ Metro East Chamber of Commerce
27601 Jefferson Ave.
St. Clair Shores, MI 48081
Ph:(586)777-2741
Fax: (586)777-4811
Co. E-mail: info@metroeastchamber.org
URL: http://www.metroeastchamber.org
Contact: Jeffrey W. Pakulski, Chm.

61387 ■ Michigan Chamber of Commerce
600 S Walnut St.
Lansing, MI 48933
Ph:(517)371-2100
Free: 800-748-0266
Fax: (517)371-7224
Co. E-mail: info@michamber.com
URL: http://www.michamber.com
Contact: Jim Barrett, Pres./CEO

61388 ■ Midland Area Chamber of Commerce
300 Rodd St., Ste. 101
Midland, MI 48640
Ph:(989)839-9901
Fax: (989)835-3701
Co. E-mail: chamber@macc.org
URL: http://www.macc.org
Contact: Mr. Sid Allen, Pres./CEO

61389 ■ Milan Area Chamber of Commerce
PO Box 164
Milan, MI 48160-0164
Ph:(734)439-7932
Fax: (734)241-3520
Co. E-mail: info@milanchamber.org
URL: http://www.milanchamber.org
Contact: Jean Wilson, Pres.

61390 ■ Monroe County Chamber of Commerce
1122 W Front St.
Monroe, MI 48161
Ph:(734)242-3366
Fax: (734)242-7253
Co. E-mail: chamber@monroecountychamber.com
URL: http://www.monroecountychamber.com
Contact: Michelle S. Nisley, Pres.

61391 ■ Mount Pleasant Area Chamber of Commerce
114 E Broadway
Mount Pleasant, MI 48858
Ph:(989)772-2396
Fax: (989)773-2656
Co. E-mail: jkostrava@mt-pleasant.net
URL: http://www.mt-pleasant.net
Contact: James E. Kostrava CAE, Pres./CEO

61392 ■ Muskegon Area Chamber of Commerce
900 Third St., Ste. 200
Muskegon, MI 49440
Ph:(231)722-3751
Fax: (231)728-7251
Co. E-mail: macc@muskegon.org
URL: http://www.muskegon.org
Contact: Cindy Larsen, Pres.

61393 ■ Newberry Area Chamber of Commerce
4947 E County Rd., No. 460
PO Box 308
Newberry, MI 49868
Ph:(906)293-5562
Free: 800-831-7292
Fax: (906)293-5739
Co. E-mail: newberry@sault.com
Contact: Melissa Ronquist, Exec.Dir.

61394 ■ Northville Chamber of Commerce
195 S Main St.
Northville, MI 48167
Ph:(248)349-7640
Fax: (248)349-8730
Co. E-mail: chamber@northville.org
URL: http://www.northville.org
Contact: Jody Humphries, Pres.

61395 ■ Novi Chamber of Commerce
47601 Grand River Ave., Ste. A 208
Novi, MI 48374
Ph:(248)349-3743
Fax: (248)349-4523
Co. E-mail: info@novichamber.com
URL: http://www.novichamber.com
Contact: Nora Champion, Pres.

61396 ■ Ontonagon County Chamber of Commerce
PO Box 266
Ontonagon, MI 49953
Ph:(906)884-4735
Co. E-mail: ontcofc@up.net
URL: http://www.ontonagonmi.com
Contact: Edith Basile, Corresponding Sec.

61397 ■ Orion Area Chamber of Commerce
PO Box 484
Lake Orion, MI 48361
Ph:(248)693-6300
Fax: (248)693-9227
Co. E-mail: oacc@msn.com
URL: http://www.orion.lib.mi.us/orion
Contact: Donna Heyniger, Managing Dir.

61398 ■ Otsego Area Chamber of Commerce
135 E Allegan St.
Otsego, MI 49078
Ph:(269)694-6880
Co. E-mail: chamber@mei.net
URL: http://otsegochamber.org
Contact: Tracy Allard, Exec.Dir.

61399 ■ Oxford Area Chamber of Commerce
PO Box 142
Oxford, MI 48371-0142
Ph:(248)628-0410
Fax: (248)628-0430
Co. E-mail: info@oxfordchamber.com
URL: http://oxfordchamber.com
Contact: Jennifer Duncan, Exec.Dir.

61400 ■ Pentwater Chamber of Commerce
PO Box 614
Pentwater, MI 49449
Ph:(231)869-4150
Fax: (231)869-5286
Co. E-mail: travelinfo@pentwater.org
URL: http://www.pentwater.org
Contact: Julie Shaw, Exec.Dir.

61401 ■ Petoskey Regional Chamber of Commerce
401 E Mitchell St.
Petoskey, MI 49770-2623
Ph:(231)347-4150
Fax: (231)348-1810
Co. E-mail: chamber@petoskey.com
URL: http://www.petoskey.com
Contact: Carlin Smith, Exec.Dir.

61402 ■ Pigeon Chamber of Commerce
PO Box 618
Pigeon, MI 48755
Ph:(989)453-7400
Co. E-mail: pgncofc@avci.net
URL: http://www.pigeonchamber.com
Contact: Bill Esch, Pres.

61403 ■ Pinconning Area Chamber of Commerce
PO Box 628
Pinconning, MI 48650
Ph:(989)879-2816
Co. E-mail: admin@cheesetown.org
URL: http://www.mypinconning.com
Contact: Tina Bergeron, Pres.

61404 ■ Plainwell Chamber of Commerce
131 S Main St., Ste. A
Plainwell, MI 49080-1684
Ph:(269)685-8877
Fax: (269)685-1844
Co. E-mail: plchcom@aol.com
URL: http://www.michamber.com

Contact: Lori Sanyder, Exec.Dir.

61405 ■ Plymouth Community Chamber of Commerce
850 W Ann Arbor Trail
Plymouth, MI 48170
Ph:(734)453-1540
Fax: (734)453-1724
Co. E-mail: chamber@plymouthmi.org
URL: http://www.plymouthchamber.org
Contact: Fran Toney, Exec.Dir.

61406 ■ Pontiac Regional Chamber
402 N Telegraph Rd.
Pontiac, MI 48341
Ph:(248)335-9600
Fax: (248)335-9601
Co. E-mail: info@pontiacchamber.com
URL: http://www.pontiacchamber.com
Contact: Rosemary Gallardo, Pres.

61407 ■ Portland Area Chamber of Commerce
PO Box 303
Portland, MI 48875
Ph:(517)647-2100
Fax: (517)647-2100
Co. E-mail: portlandmichamber@yahoo.com
Contact: Terry Schrauben, Pres.

61408 ■ Quincy Chamber of Commerce
PO Box 132
Quincy, MI 49082
Ph:(517)639-8369
Fax: (517)639-5757
Contact: Michelle Street, Pres.

61409 ■ Redford Township Chamber of Commerce
26050 5 Mile Rd.
Redford, MI 48239-3289
Ph:(313)535-0960
Fax: (313)535-6356
Co. E-mail: rtcc@htdconnect.com
URL: http://redfordchamber.org
Contact: Dan Lis, Pres.

61410 ■ Reed City Area Chamber of Commerce
PO Box 27
Reed City, MI 49677
Ph:(231)832-5431
Free: 877-832-7332
Fax: (231)832-5431
Co. E-mail: sally.rccc@charter.net
URL: http://www.reedcitycrossroads.com
Contact: Mr. David Langworthy, Pres.

61411 ■ Reese Chamber of Commerce
PO Box 113
Reese, MI 48757
Ph:(989)868-9810
Contact: Rick Keyser, Pres.

61412 ■ Richmond Area Chamber of Commerce
68371 Oak St.
Richmond, MI 48062
Ph:(586)727-3266
Fax: (586)727-3635
Co. E-mail: kim@racc-online.org
URL: http://www.racc-online.org
Contact: Kim Galante, Exec.Dir.

61413 ■ River Cities Regional Chamber of Commerce
PO Box 427
Menominee, MI 49858
Ph:(906)863-2679
Fax: (906)863-3288
Co. E-mail: info@rivercities.net
Contact: Sylvia Nelson, Pres.

61414 ■ Rockford Area Chamber of Commerce
PO Box 520
12 Squires St.
Rockford, MI 49341

Ph:(616)866-2000
Fax: (616)866-2141
Co. E-mail: info@rockfordmichamber.com
URL: http://www.rockfordmichamber.com
Contact: Brenda Davis, Exec.Dir.

61415 ■ Rogers City Chamber of Commerce
PO Box 55
Rogers City, MI 49779
Ph:(989)734-2535
Free: 800-622-4148
Fax: (989)734-7767
Co. E-mail: rcchamber@lhi.net
URL: http://www.rogerscitychamber.com
Contact: William Hanchett, Exec.Dir.

61416 ■ Romeo-Washington Chamber of Commerce
228 N Main, Ste. D
PO Box 175
Romeo, MI 48065-0175
Ph:(586)752-4436
Fax: (586)752-2835
Co. E-mail: joyce@rwchamber.com
URL: http://www.rwchamber.com
Contact: Joyce E. Dych, Exec.Dir.

61417 ■ Saginaw County Chamber of Commerce
515 N Washington Ave., 2nd Fl.
Saginaw, MI 48607-1370
Ph:(989)752-7161
Fax: (989)752-9055
Co. E-mail: info@saginawchamber.org
URL: http://www.saginawchamber.org
Contact: Bob Van Deventer, Pres./CEO

61418 ■ St. Ignace Chamber of Commerce
560 N State St.
St. Ignace, MI 49781-1429
Ph:(906)643-8717
Free: 800-970-8717
Fax: (906)643-9380
Co. E-mail: info@stignace.com
URL: http://www.stignace.com
Contact: Janet Peterson, Exec.Dir.

61419 ■ St. Johns Area Chamber of Commerce
1013 S US 27
PO Box 61
St. Johns, MI 48879
Ph:(989)224-7248
Fax: (989)224-7667
Co. E-mail: ccchamber@power-net.net
URL: http://www.stjohnschamber.org
Contact: Brenda Terpening, Exec.Dir.

61420 ■ Saline Area Chamber of Commerce
141 E Michigan Ave.
PO Box 198
Saline, MI 48176-0198
Ph:(734)429-4494
Fax: (734)944-6835
Co. E-mail: salinechamber@aol.com
URL: http://www.salinechamber.com
Contact: Mr. Larry Osterling, Exec.Dir.

61421 ■ Sault Area Chamber of Commerce
2581 I-75 Business Spur
Sault Ste. Marie, MI 49783
Ph:(906)632-3301
Fax: (906)632-2331
Co. E-mail: info@saultstemarie.org
URL: http://www.saultstemarie.org
Contact: Virginia R. Zinser, Exec.Dir.

61422 ■ Schoolcraft County Chamber of Commerce
1000 W Lakeshore Dr.
Manistique, MI 49854
Ph:(906)341-5010
Fax: (906)341-1549
Co. E-mail: chamber@upmail.com
URL: http://www.manistique.com
Contact: Ms. Lenore Heminger, Exec.Dir.

61423 ■ Scottville Area Chamber of Commerce
140 S Main St.
PO Box 224
Scottville, MI 49454-0224
Ph:(231)757-4304
Fax: (231)757-4341
Co. E-mail: chamber@scottville.org
URL: http://www.scottville.org
Contact: Albert Muzzin, Exec.Dir.

61424 ■ Sebewaing Chamber of Commerce
PO Box 622
Sebewaing, MI 48759
Ph:(989)883-2683
Fax: (989)883-9367
Contact: Jeff Sigmund, Pres.

61425 ■ Shiawassee Regional Chamber of Commerce
215 N Water St.
Owosso, MI 48867-2875
Ph:(989)723-5149
Fax: (989)723-8353
Co. E-mail: customerservice@shiawasseechamber.org
URL: http://www.shiawasseechamber.org
Contact: Marsha Lyttle, Interim Pres.

61426 ■ Silver Lake Sand Dunes Area Chamber of Commerce
1951 N 24th Ave.
Mears, MI 49436-9687
Ph:(231)873-2778

61427 ■ Sleeping Bear Area Chamber of Commerce
PO Box 217
Glen Arbor, MI 49636
Ph:(231)334-3238
Fax: (231)334-3238
Co. E-mail: gullinglen@aol.com
URL: http://www.sleepingbeararea.com
Contact: Bill Thompson, Pres.

61428 ■ South Lyon Area Chamber of Commerce
125 N Lafayette (Pontiac Trail)
South Lyon, MI 48178
Ph:(248)437-3257
Fax: (248)437-4116
Co. E-mail: greeter@southlyonchamber.com
URL: http://www.southlyonchamber.com
Contact: Michele Tucholke, Co-Exec.Dir.

61429 ■ Southern Wayne County Regional Chamber
20600 Eureka Rd., Ste. 315
Taylor, MI 48180-5306
Ph:(734)284-6000
Fax: (734)284-0198
Co. E-mail: info@swccc.org
URL: http://www.swccc.org
Contact: James Williams, Chm.

61430 ■ Southfield Area Chamber of Commerce
17515 W 9 Mile Rd., Ste. 750
Southfield, MI 48075
Ph:(248)557-6661
Fax: (248)557-3931
Co. E-mail: southfieldchamber@yahoo.com
URL: http://www.southfieldchamber.com
Contact: Ed Powers, Exec.Dir.

61431 ■ Sterling Heights Area Chamber of Commerce
12900 Hall Rd., Ste. 190
Sterling Heights, MI 48313
Ph:(586)731-5400
Fax: (586)731-3521
Co. E-mail: ladams@suscc.com
URL: http://www.suscc.com
Contact: Lil Adams, Exec.Dir.

61432 ■ Sturgis Area Chamber of Commerce
200 W Main
PO Box 189
Sturgis, MI 49091-0189
Ph:(269)651-5758
Fax: (269)651-4124
Co. E-mail: sturgischamber@charter.net
URL: http://www.sturgischamber.com
Contact: Cathi Garn, Exec.Dir.

61433 ■ Suttons Bay Chamber of Commerce
PO Box 46
Suttons Bay, MI 49682-0046
Ph:(231)271-5077
URL: http://www.suttonsbayarea.com
Contact: Piper Goldson, Pres.

61434 ■ Swedish American Chamber of Commerce - Detroit Chapter
PO Box 0396
Birmingham, MI 48012-0396
Ph:(248)644-8170
Co. E-mail: sacc-detroit@atsprodigy.net
Contact: Melissa Mark, Exec.Dir

61435 ■ Tawas Area Chamber of Commerce
402 E Lake St.
PO Box 608
Tawas City, MI 48764-0608
Ph:(989)362-8643
Free: 800-55T-AWAS
Fax: (989)362-7880
Co. E-mail: info@tawas.com
URL: http://www.tawas.com
Contact: Jamie Gentry, Exec.Dir.

61436 ■ Three Rivers Area Chamber of Commerce
57 N Main St.
Three Rivers, MI 49093
Ph:(616)278-8193
Fax: (616)273-1751
Co. E-mail: info@trchamber.com
URL: http://www.trchamber.com
Contact: Bruce Snook, Gen.Mgr.

61437 ■ Traverse City Area Chamber of Commerce
202 E Grandview Pkwy.
PO Box 387
Traverse City, MI 49685-0387
Ph:(231)947-5075
Co. E-mail: info@tcchamber.org
URL: http://www.tcchamber.org
Contact: Douglas R. Luciani, Pres.

61438 ■ Troy Chamber of Commerce
4555 Investment Dr., 3rd Fl., Ste. 300
Troy, MI 48098-6338
Ph:(248)641-8151
Fax: (248)641-0545
Co. E-mail: theteam@troychamber.com
URL: http://www.troychamber.com
Contact: Michele Hodges, Pres.

61439 ■ Trufant Area Chamber of Commerce
PO Box 129
Trufant, MI 49347-0129
Ph:(616)984-2555
Fax: (616)984-6311
Contact: Russ Krant, Pres.

61440 ■ Wayne Chamber of Commerce
35122 W Michigan Ave.
Wayne, MI 48184
Ph:(734)721-0100
Fax: (734)721-3070
Co. E-mail: gayle@waynechamber.net
URL: http://www.waynechamber.net
Contact: Gayle Rediske, Dir.

61441 ■ West Branch Area Chamber of Commerce
422 W Houghton Ave.
West Branch, MI 48661
Ph:(989)345-2821
Free: 800-755-9091
Co. E-mail: chamber@westbranch.com
URL: http://www.wbacc.com
Contact: Steven G. Leonard, Exec.Dir.

61442 ■ Westland Chamber of Commerce
36900 Ford Rd.
Westland, MI 48185-2231
Ph:(734)326-7222
Fax: (734)326-6040
Co. E-mail: info@westlandchamber.com
URL: http://www.westlandchamber.com
Contact: Lori Brist, Pres./CEO

61443 ■ White Cloud Area Chamber of Commerce
12 N Charles
White Cloud, MI 49349
Ph:(231)689-6607
Co. E-mail: ladams@gtlakes.net
URL: http://www.whitecloudchamber.org
Contact: Ms. Sherry Adams, Sec.

61444 ■ White Lake Area Chamber of Commerce
124 W Hanson St.
Whitehall, MI 49461
Ph:(231)893-4585
Free: 800-879-9702
Fax: (231)893-0914
Co. E-mail: info@whitelake.org
URL: http://www.whitelake.org
Contact: Carol Wood, Exec.Dir.

61445 ■ Williamston Area Chamber of Commerce
PO Box 53
369 W Grand River
Williamston, MI 48895
Ph:(517)655-1549
Fax: (517)655-8859
Co. E-mail: info@williamston.org
URL: http://www.williamston.org
Contact: Ms. Barbara Burke, Exec.Dir.

61446 ■ Wyoming Kentwood Area Chamber of Commerce
590-32nd St. SE
Wyoming, MI 49548-2345
Ph:(616)531-5990
Fax: (616)531-0252
Co. E-mail: john@southkent.org
URL: http://www.southkent.org
Contact: John J. Crawford, Pres./CEO

61447 ■ Ypsilanti Area Chamber of Commerce
301 W Michigan Ave., Ste. 101
Ypsilanti, MI 48197-5450
Ph:(734)482-4920
Fax: (734)482-2021
Co. E-mail: keith@ypsichamber.org
URL: http://www.ypsichamber.org
Contact: Keith Peters, Pres.

61448 ■ Zeeland Chamber of Commerce
149 Main Pl.
Zeeland, MI 49464-1735
Ph:(616)772-2494
Fax: (616)772-0065
Co. E-mail: zchamber@zeelandcofc.org
URL: http://www.zeelandcofc.org
Contact: Ann L. Query, Pres.

MINORITY BUSINESS ASSISTANCE PROGRAMS

61449 ■ Michigan Economic Development Corporation–Office of Small Business Group
300 N Washington Sq.
Lansing, MI 48913
Ph:(517)373-8431
Fax: (517)373-9143
URL: http://medc.michigan.org
Contact: James Epolito, Pres & CEO
Description: Encourages greater minority enterprise development by providing financial and business education programs. Assists in state certification processes, reviews the impact of legislation, and increases awareness of minority businesses.

61450 ■ Michigan Economic Development Corp.–Office of Women Business Owners Services
300 N Washington Sq., 4th Fl.
Lansing, MI 48913
Ph:(517)335-2877
Fax: (517)335-0198
URL: http://www.michigan.org
Description: Provides advocacy, technical assistance, and references to outside sources for financial counseling for women entrepreneurs.

61451 ■ Michigan Minority Business Development Council
3011 W Grand Blvd., Ste. 230
Detroit, MI 48202-3011
Ph:(313)873-3200
Fax: (313)873-4783
Co. E-mail: mail@mmbdc.org
URL: http://www.mmbdc.com
Contact: Louis Green, Pres & CEO

61452 ■ Michigan Small Business and Technology Development Center
Grand Valley State University
510 W Fulton St.
Grand Rapids, MI 49504
Ph:(616)331-7480
Fax: (616)331-7485
Co. E-mail: sbtdchq@gvsu.edu
URL: http://www.misbtdc.org
Contact: Carol Lopucki, Dir
Description: Provides a full-range of services for a variety of small businesses including: counseling; training; programs for a variety of needs, from how to get started, to financing; effective selling and e-commerce as well as how to develop business plans. Also provides research help and advocacy.

FINANCING AND LOAN PROGRAMS

61453 ■ Arbor Partners LLC
130 S. 1st St., 2nd Fl.
Ann Arbor, MI 48104
Ph:(734)668-9000
Fax: (734)669-4195
URL: http://www.arborpartners.com
Contact: Donald Walker, Managing Director
Preferred Investment Size: $500,000 to $2,000,000. **Investment Policies:** Early stage and expansion. **Industry Preferences:** Internet specific, computer software and services, consumer related, communications and media. **Geographic Preferences:** Michigan and Midwest.

61454 ■ Arboretum Ventures
944 N. Main St.
Ann Arbor, MI 48104
Ph:(734)998-3688
Fax: (734)988-3689
URL: http://www.arboretumvc.com
Contact: Jan Garfinkle, Managing Partner
Investment Policies: Seed and early stage. **Industry Preferences:** Biotechnology, medical and health. **Geographic Preferences:** Illinois, Indiana, Michigan, Midwest, and Ohio.

61455 ■ Camelot Ventures
100 Galleria Officentre, Ste. 419
Southfield, MI 48034
Ph:(248)827-7799
Fax: (248)352-5973
URL: http://www.camelotventures.com
Contact: David Katzman, Managing Partner
Preferred Investment Size: $5,000,000 to $150,000,000. **Investment Types:** Balanced, early, second and later stage, expansion, generalist PE, mezzanine, and private placement. **Industry Preferences:** Communications and media, computer software and hardware, Internet specific, semiconductors and other electronics, consumer related, financial services, and business service. **Geographic Preferences:** U.S. and Canada.

61456 ■ EDF Ventures / Enterprise Development Fund
425 N. Main St.
Ann Arbor, MI 48104
Ph:(734)663-3213
Fax: (734)663-7358
URL: http://www.edfvc.com
Contact: Beau Laskey, Partner
Preferred Investment Size: $1,500,000 to $6,000,000. **Investment Types:** Seed, start-up, first, second and early stage, and research and development. **Industry Preferences:** Internet specific, computer software and services, medical and health, biotechnology, semiconductors and other electronics, communications and media, consumer and related, other products, and computer hardware. **Geographic Preferences:** Midwest.

61457 ■ Investcare Partners L.P. / GMA Capital LLC
32330 W. Twelve Mile Rd.
Farmington Hills, MI 48334
Ph:(248)489-9000
Fax: (248)489-8819
Co. E-mail: gma@gmacapital.com
URL: http://www.gmacapital.com
Contact: Malcolm Moss, Managing Director
E-mail: mmoss@gmacapital.com
Investment Types: Second stage and leveraged buyout. **Industry Preferences:** Medical and health related. **Geographic Preferences:** National.

61458 ■ Liberty Bidco Investment Corporation
30833 Northwestern Hwy., Ste. 211
Farmington Hills, MI 48334
Ph:(248)352-9342
Fax: (248)626-6072
Contact: James Zabriskie, Vice President
E-mail: jzabriski@ibico.com
Preferred Investment Size: $500,000 minimum. **Investment Types:** Second stage, leveraged buyout, mezzanine, and special situation. **Industry Preferences:** Communications and media, and consumer related. **Geographic Preferences:** Midwest, U.S.; Ontario, Canada.

61459 ■ Ralph Wilson Equity Fund LLC
15400 E. Jefferson Ave.
Gross Pointe Park, MI 48230
Ph:(313)821-9122
Fax: (313)821-9101
URL: http://www.rwequity.com
Contact: J. Skip Simms, President
Preferred Investment Size: $500,000 to $1,500,000. **Investment Types:** Eearly stage, expansion, fund of funds, and second stage. **Industry Preferences:** Communications and media, computer software, Internet specific, semiconductors and other electronics, biotechnology, medical and health, consumer related, industrial and energy, and business service. **Geographic Preferences:** Michigan and Midwest.

61460 ■ Seaflower Ventures (Fowlerville)
5170 Nicholson Rd.
PO Box 474
Fowlerville, MI 48836
Ph:(517)223-3335
Fax: (517)223-3337
URL: http://www.seaflower.com
Contact: Zach Jonasson, Principal
Preferred Investment Size: $200,000 to $3,000,000. **Investment Types:** Seed, start-up, early, first and second stage. **Industry Preferences:** Medical and health, biotechnology, Internet specific, computer hardware, industrial and energy, and other products. **Geographic Preferences:** Michigan, Illinois, Mid Atlantic, Midwest, Northeast, and Southeast U.S.; Central Canada, Ontario, and Quebec, Canada.

61461 ■ Venture Funding, Ltd.
Fisher Bldg.
3011 W. Grand Blvd., Ste. 321
Detroit, MI 48202
Ph:(313)871-3606
Fax: (313)873-4935
Preferred Investment Size: $1,000,000 minimum. **Investment Types:** Start-up, seed, leveraged buyout,

research and development, and special situation. **Industry Preferences:** Biotechnology, medical and health, and consumer related. **Geographic Preferences:** U.S.

61462 ■ Wellmax, Inc.
3541 Bendway Blvd., Ste. 100
Bloomfield Hills, MI 48301
Ph:(248)646-3554
Fax: (248)646-6220
Preferred Investment Size: $100,000 to $1,000,000. **Investment Types:** Start-up, first and second stage, leveraged buyout, and special situation. **Industry Preferences:** Semiconductors and other electronics, medical and health, consumer related, industrial and energy, agriculture, forestry and fishing. **Geographic Preferences:** Midwest and Southeast.

61463 ■ White Pines Management, L.L.C.
900 Victors Way, Ste. 280
Ann Arbor, MI 48108
Ph:(734)747-9401
Fax: (734)747-9704
URL: http://www.whitepines.com
Preferred Investment Size: $1,000,000 to $4,000,000. **Investment Types:** Second stage, mezzanine, expansion and special situation. **Industry Preferences:** Internet specific, communications and media, medical and health, computer software and services, biotechnology, consumer related, and other products. **Geographic Preferences:** Southeast and Midwest.

PROCUREMENT ASSISTANCE PROGRAMS

61464 ■ Genesee County Metropolitan Planning Commission
1101 Beach St., Rm. 223
Flint, MI 48502-1420
Ph:(810)257-3010
Fax: (810)257-3185
Co. E-mail: gcmpc@co.genesee.mi.us
URL: http://www.gcmpc.org
Contact: Sheila Auten, Senior Planner

61465 ■ Michigan Procurement Technical Assistance Center–Business Development Center
Schoolcraft College
18600 Haggerty Rd.
Livonia, MI 48152-2696
Ph:(734)462-4438
Fax: (734)462-4673
Co. E-mail: inforeq@schoolcraft.edu
URL: http://www.schoolcraft.edu
Contact: Tammy Puskarz, Counselor

61466 ■ Michigan Procurement Technical Assistance Center–Downriver Community Conference
15100 Northline, Rm. 135
Southgate, MI 48195
Ph:(734)362-7070
Fax: (734)281-0276
Co. E-mail: paulaa@dccwf.org
URL: http://www.dccwf.org
Contact: Paula Boase, Dir

61467 ■ Michigan Procurement Technical Assistance Center–Economic Development Alliance of St. Clair County
735 Erie St., Ste. 250
Port Huron, MI 48060
Ph:(810)982-9511
Fax: (810)982-9531
Co. E-mail: eda@edascc.com
URL: http://www.edascc.com
Contact: Doug Alexander, Exec Dir

61468 ■ Michigan Procurement Technical Assistance Center–Jackson County Metropolitan Planning Commission
1 Jackson Sq., Ste. 1100
Jackson, MI 49201

Ph:(517)788-4680
Fax: (517)782-0061
Co. E-mail: pennie@enterprisegroup.org
URL: http://www.gjcc.org
Contact: Pennie Southwell
E-mail: pennie@jacksonalliance.com

61469 ■ Michigan Procurement Technical Assistance Center–Macomb Community College PTAC
7900 Tank Ave.
Warren, MI 48092
Ph:(586)498-4122
Fax: (586)498-4101
Co. E-mail: oliverr@macomb.edu
URL: http://www.macombchamber.com
Contact: Rosanne Oliver, Work Studies Group
E-mail: janet_masi@chambercom.com

61470 ■ Michigan Procurement Technical Assistance Center–Muskegon Area First
900 Third St., Ste. 112
Muskegon, MI 49440
Ph:(231)722-7700
Free: 800-528-8776
Fax: (231)722-6182
Co. E-mail: psvander@wmis.net
URL: http://www.muskegon.org
Contact: Pamela Vanderlaan, Dir
E-mail: psvander@gte.net

61471 ■ Michigan Procurement Technical Assistance Center–Northwest Michigan Council of Governments
1209 S Garfield Ave.
Traverse City, MI 49685-0506
Ph:(231)929-5000
Free: 800-692-7774
Fax: (231)929-5012
Co. E-mail: jhasling@nwm.cog.mi.us
URL: http://www.nwm.cog.mi.us
Contact: Jim Haslinger
E-mail: jhasling@nwm.cog.mi.us

61472 ■ Michigan Procurement Technical Assistance Center–West Central Michigan Employment & Training Consor
110 Elm St.
Big Rapids, MI 49307
Ph:(231)796-4891
Fax: (231)796-8316
URL: http://www.michworkswc.org
Contact: Paul Griffith, Executive Director

61473 ■ Southwestern Michigan Technical Assistance Center–Western Michigan University
4717 Campus Drive, Box 100
Kalamazoo, MI 49008
Ph:(269)372-3941
Fax: (269)353-5569
Co. E-mail: jcampbell@southwestmichiganfirst.com
Contact: Michael Black, Director W.S.M.I.T.A
E-mail: sledbett@sabien.net

INCUBATORS/RESEARCH AND TECHNOLOGY PARKS

61474 ■ Albion Economic Development Corp.
309 N Superior
PO Box 725
Albion, MI 49224
Ph:(517)629-3926
Fax: (517)629-3929
Co. E-mail: psindt@albionedc.org
URL: http://www.albionedc.org
Contact: Peggy Sindt, Pres & CEO

61475 ■ Altarum
3520 Green Ct., Ste. 300
Ann Arbor, MI 48105
Ph:(734)302-4600
Fax: (734)302-4991
Co. E-mail: mail@altarum.org

URL: http://www.altarum.org
Contact: Ken Baker, Pres & CEO
Description: Research and development facility emphasizing electronics, computer sciences, and optics and their applications. Provides analytical and experimental investigations and technical assistance.

61476 ■ Andrews University–Office of Scholarly Research
Administration 210
Berrien Springs, MI 49104-0355
Ph:(269)471-6361
Fax: (269)471-6246
Co. E-mail: stout@andrews.edu
URL: http://www.andrews.edu/GRAD/OSR/
Contact: Dr. John Stout, Dean, Scholarly Res.
E-mail: stout@andrews.edu
Scope: Administers research grants and contracts for the University. Oversees human subject involvement in research. **Publications:** Brief Guidelines for Human Subjects Research; Grants Guidebook.

61477 ■ Ann Arbor Area Chamber of Commerce
425 S Main, Ste. 103
Ann Arbor, MI 48104
Ph:(734)665-4433
Fax: (734)665-4191
Co. E-mail: info@annarborchamber.org
URL: http://www.annarborchamber.org
Contact: Administrative Ass.

61478 ■ Delta Properties
401 Hall St.
PO Box 95
Grand Rapids, MI 49503
Ph:(616)243-9000
Fax: (616)243-1013
URL: http://www.deltapropertiesinc.com
Contact: David Reed, Operations Mgr

61479 ■ Eastern Michigan University–Office of Research Development
Starkweather Hall, 2nd Fl.
Ypsilanti, MI 48197
Ph:(734)487-3090
Fax: (734)481-0650
Co. E-mail: brian.anderson@emich.edu
URL: http://www.gradord.emich.edu
Contact: Brian D. Anderson, Dir.
E-mail: brian.anderson@emich.edu
Scope: Administers activities in geographic information systems, coatings and paint research, industrial hygiene, entrepreneurship, statistical process control, inventory management, computer-assisted instruction, remote sensing, finite element analysis, child and family research, reproductive toxicology, bilingual education, immunology, microbiology, exercise physiology, instructional effectiveness, teacher education, economic development, environmental assessment, information systems, toxic waste management, and security. **Services:** Outreach and liaison services, to business and government agencies for matches with University resources. **Publications:** Annual report. **Educational Activities:** Workshops (monthly), on proposal development.

61480 ■ Institute for Food Laws and Regulations–Michigan State University
165 National Food Safety and Toxicology Center
East Lansing, MI 48824
Ph:(517)355-8295
Fax: (517)432-1492
Co. E-mail: vhegarty@msu.edu
URL: http://www.iflr.msu.edu
Contact: Dr. Vincent Hegarty, Dir
Description: Provides workshops/seminars.

61481 ■ Michigan Biotechnology Institute International
PO Box 27609
Lansing, MI 48909
Ph:(517)337-3181
Fax: (517)337-2122
Co. E-mail: info@mbi.org
URL: http://www.mbi.org
Contact: Dr. Mark Stowers, Pres & CEO

Description: Coordinates the development of biotechnology research and technology transfer to businesses; provides in-house research and development; and provides technology transfer to biotechnology businesses.

61482 ■ Michigan Molecular Institute & Impact Analytical
1910 W St Andrews Rd.
Midland, MI 48640
Ph:(989)832-5555
Fax: (989)832-5560
Co. E-mail: mmiinfo@mmi.org
URL: http://www.mmi.org
Contact: Dr. Robert Nowak, Pres & CEO
E-mail: wood@impactanalytical.org
Description: Performs advanced research and development, and graduate-level education in polymer science and composite technology. Provides technical assistance and consulting services. Develops new information on the molecular structure and behavior of non-metallic materials. Also performs proprietary research.

61483 ■ Michigan Technological University–Office of Vice President for Research
302 Administration Bldg.
1400 Townsend Dr.
Houghton, MI 49931
Ph:(906)487-3043
Fax: (906)487-2245
Co. E-mail: ddreed@mtu.edu
URL: http://www.admin.mtu.edu/research/vpr/
Contact: Dr. David D. Reed, VP,Res.
E-mail: ddreed@mtu.edu
Scope: Administers and develops University research programs; manages grants and contracts; and administers intellectual property trademark, and licensing program. Serves as a clearing and coordinating agency for interdepartmental research at the University and for other assistance to faculty members engaged in research and graduate education. **Publications:** Michigan Tech Research Magazine (annually); Office of Research and Graduate School Annual Report. **Educational Activities:** Grant workshops, open to all faculty and staff members of the University.

61484 ■ Michigan Technological University–Research and Sponsored Programs
Administration Bldg., 3rd Fl.
1400 Townsend Dr.
Houghton, MI 49931
Ph:(906)487-2225
Fax: (906)487-2245
Co. E-mail: aquinn@mtu.edu
URL: http://www.admin.mtu.edu/research/vpr/rsp.htmlmeetteam
Contact: Anita Quinn, Dir.
E-mail: aquinn@mtu.edu
Scope: Administers and coordinates research conducted by academic programs at the University. Manages all grants and contracts for externally funded programs. Negotiates research contracts, acts as clearing house for all proposal submission and provides budget preparation and review.

61485 ■ Oak Business Center
2712 N Saginaw St.
Flint, MI 48505
Ph:(810)235-5555
Fax: (810)235-5852
Contact: Wesley Grey, Mgr

61486 ■ Southwestern Michigan Economic Growth Alliance, Inc.
1105 N Front St., Unit 1
Niles, MI 49120
Ph:(269)683-1833
Fax: (269)683-7515
Co. E-mail: switt@michigan-business.info
URL: http://www.michigan-business.info
Contact: Sharon Witt, Exec Dir

**61487 ■ University of Detroit
Mercy–Sponsored Research Administration**
4001 W McNichols
Detroit, MI 48221-3038
Ph:(313)993-1585
Fax: (313)993-1534
Co. E-mail: barbara.schirmer@udmercy.edu
URL: http://www.udmercy.edu/ospra/
Contact: Barbara R. Schirmer, VP/Acad. Affairs
E-mail: barbara.schirmer@udmercy.edu
Scope: Serves as a central bureau of information for sources of funds for supporting research projects at the University and assists faculty members and administration in preparation and submission of proposals for such support.

**61488 ■ University of Michigan–Business
and Industrial Assistance Division**
Business Sch.
506 E Liberty St., 3rd Fl.
Ann Arbor, MI 48104-2210
Ph:(734)998-6201
Fax: (734)998-6202
Co. E-mail: mjsk@umich.edu
URL: http://www.bus.umich.edu/FacultyResearch/
 ResearchCenters/ProgramsPartnerships/Biad /
Contact: Dr. Marian Krzyzowski, Dir.
E-mail: mjsk@umich.edu
Scope: Transfers technology from the University to businesses and industry, particularly in the area of automated manufacturing. Emphasizes common problems of manufacturers, manufacturing facilities at risk of closing, and revitalization of closed industrial facilities. **Services:** Technical assistance.

**61489 ■ University of Michigan–College of
Engineering–Office of Technology Transfer
(3003)–Industrial Development Division (S
State St)**
3003 S State St.
Wolverine Tower, Rm. 2071
Ann Arbor, MI 48109-2016
Ph:(734)763-0614
Fax: (734)936-1330
URL: http://www.techtransfer.umich.edu
Contact: Ken Nisbet, Exec Dir
Description: Involved with industry liaison and direct assistance, conferences, workshops, and economic development. Service programs are designed to retain and create employment by expanding and strengthening industry. Supports the Michigan Industrial Developers Association with practitioners training, community economic profiles, and target industry research using national databases.

**61490 ■ University of Michigan–Division of
Research Development and Administration**
3003 S State St.
Ann Arbor, MI 48109-1274
Ph:(734)764-5500
Fax: (734)764-8510
Co. E-mail: mgparnes@umich.edu
URL: http://www.research.umich.edu/contacts/drda/
 drda_contact.html
Contact: Marvin G. Parnes, Dir.
E-mail: mgparnes@umich.edu
Scope: Administers and coordinates extramurally sponsored research and other scholarly activities conducted in all departments and special research units of the University. **Publications:** Administration of Sponsored Programs; The DRDA Reporter; Nongovernmental Research Grant and Fellowship Opportunities in the Health Sciences; Project Director's Guide; Proposal Writer's Guide; Research News; Research Opportunities for Minorities and Women; University of Michigan Research Resources.

**61491 ■ Wayne State University–Sponsored
Program Administration**
656 W Kirby, Rm. 4002
Detroit, MI 48202
Ph:(313)577-2294
Fax: (313)577-2653
Co. E-mail: cbach@med.wayne.edu
URL: http://www.spa.wayne.edu
Contact: Carol Bach, Dir.
E-mail: cbach@med.wayne.edu

Scope: Administers and coordinates extramurally sponsored research conducted at the University. Serves as liaison between research faculty and research-funding organizations. Under the general administrative direction of the Vice President for Research, the office oversees fulfillment of contractual obligations by individual investigators. **Publications:** New Science (annually).

**61492 ■ Western Michigan University–Office
of the Vice President for Research**
240 W Walwood Hall
Kalamazoo, MI 49008-5456
Ph:(269)387-8298
Fax: (269)387-8276
Co. E-mail: leonard.ginsbery@wmich.edu
URL: http://www.wmich.edu/research/
Contact: Dr. Leonard C. Ginsbery, Interim VP
E-mail: leonard.ginsbery@wmich.edu
Scope: Coordinates proposal submission and grant and contract administration for all individual research projects conducted throughout the University in such areas as health and human survices, education, engineering, applied sciences, humanities, social sciences, and business. Research venues exist in the areas of educational evaluation, school reform, biological sciences, geology, physics, math and science education, aviation, paper and printing science and engineering, medieval studies, and rehabilitation/intervention science in health and human services. The University fosters research initiatives in nanotechnology enabling technology, geographic information systems, and the body's response to envi. **Publications:** Annual report; Newsletter. **Educational Activities:** Grantmanship workshops. **Awards:** Research Development Award Program.

EDUCATIONAL PROGRAMS

61493 ■ Alpena Community College
666 Johnson St.
Alpena, MI 49707-1495
Ph:(989)356-9021
Free: 888-468-6222
Fax: (989)358-7561
URL: http://www.alpenacc.org
Description: Two-year college offering a small business management program.

61494 ■ Baker College–Owosso Campus
1020 S Washington St.
Owosso, MI 48867
Ph:(989)729-3300
Free: 800-879-3797
Fax: (989)729-3330
URL: http://www.baker.edu
Description: Vocational school offering a small business management program.

61495 ■ Mid Michigan Community College
1375 S Clare Ave.
Harrison, MI 48625
Ph:(989)386-6622
Fax: (989)386-9088
Co. E-mail: bmather@midmich.cc.mi.us
URL: http://www.midmich.cc.mi.us
Description: Two-year college offering a small business management program.

61496 ■ Montcalm Community College
2800 College Dr. SW
Sidney, MI 48885-0300
Ph:(989)328-2111
Fax: (989)328-2950
URL: http://www.montcalm.cc.mi.us
Description: Two-year college offering a small business management program.

61497 ■ North Central Michigan College
1515 Howard St.
Petoskey, MI 49770
Ph:(231)348-6600
Free: 888-298-6605
Fax: (231)348-6628
URL: http://www.ncmc.cc.mi.us

Description: Two-year college offering a program in small business management.

**61498 ■ Southwestern Michigan
College–Business Development and
Corporate Services**
2229 U.S. 12 E
Niles, MI 49120
Ph:(269)782-1000
Free: 800-456-8675
Fax: (269)687-5655
Co. E-mail: m-tec@smc.cc.mi.us
URL: http://www.smc.cc.mi.us
Description: Offers programs/classes in small business/small business management.

**61499 ■ Wayne State University–School of
Business Administration**
Business Management Office
5201 Cass Ave.
Detroit, MI 48202
Ph:(313)577-4515
Fax: (313)993-7664
URL: http://www.wayne.edu
Description: Schedules business and management courses. Also provides free management consulting to small business managers in the metropolitan Detroit area.

TRADE PERIODICALS

61500 ■ *Leader's Edge*
Pub: Michigan Association of CPAs
Ed: Marla Janness, Editor, mjanness@ix.netcom.com. **Released:** Bimonthly, 10/year. **Price:** $20. **Description:** Contains professional and technical information for certified public accountants.

61501 ■ *MIOSHA News*
Pub: Michigan Department of Consumer and
 Industry Services
Contact: Judith M. Simons, Communications
 Specialist
E-mail: judith.simons@cis.state.mi.us
Released: Quarterly. **Price:** Free. **Description:** Contains information relevant to occupational safety and health in relation to Michigan's employers and employees.

61502 ■ *The Writer's Voice*
Pub: The YMCA of Metropolitan Detroit
Contact: Mary Ann Wehler, Director
E-mail: wehler@home.com
Released: 10/year. **Description:** Focuses on the activities and issues of the Writer's Voice of the Metropolitan Detroit YMCA. Provides information on local poetry workshops, writer's seminars, and open mic nights. Recurring features include a calendar of events.

PUBLICATIONS

**61503 ■ *How to Form Your Own Michigan
Corporation Before the Inc. Dries!: A Step by
Step Guide, With Forms***
P. Gaines Publishing Company
333 S. Taylor Ave.
PO Box 2253
Oak Park, IL 60302
Ph:(708)524-9033
Fax: (708)524-9038
Ed: Phillip Williams. **Released:** Second edition, 1993.
Price: $24.95. **Description:** Volume 3 of the Small Business Incorporation series. Explains the advantages and disadvantages of incorporation and shows, step-by-step, how the small business owners can incorporate at low cost. Covers Michigan profit and nonprofit corporations, Michigan professional service corporations, subchapter S corporations, and Delaware corporations. Includes forms necessary for incorporation.

61504 ■ *Smart Start your Michigan Business*
PSI Research
300 N. Valley Dr.
Grants Pass, OR 97526
Ph:(503)479-9464
Free: 800-228-2275
Fax: (503)476-1479
Co. E-mail: info@psi-research.com
URL: http://www.psi-research.com
Ed: Michael D. Jenkins. **Released:** Revised edition, 1992. **Price:** $29.95 (looseleaf binder); $24.95 (paper). **Description:** Part of the Successful Business Library series.

PUBLISHERS

61505 ■ Agnes Press
2 Brambleberry Dr.
Howell, MI 48843
Ph:(517)546-3799
Fax: (517)546-9565
Contact: Peter H. Burgher, Owner
E-mail: pete@marelco.com
Description: Publishes business books. Offers seminars and consulting. Does not accept unsolicited manuscripts. Reaches market through direct mail. **Founded:** 1986.

61506 ■ Delta Alpha Publishing Ltd.
35 Ash Dr.
Kimball, MI 48074
Ph:(810)885-1165
Free: 800-292-5544
Fax: (810)985-1168
Co. E-mail: contact@deltaalpha.com
URL: http://www.deltaalpha.com
Description: Publishes on real estate, business and travel. Reaches market through direct mail, exhibitions and the internet. **Founded:** 1997.

61507 ■ Jenkins Group Inc.
1129 Woodmere Ave., Suite B
Traverse City, MI 49684-2206
Ph:(231)933-0445
Free: 800-706-4636
Fax: (231)933-0448
URL: http://www.jenkinsgroupinc.com/
Contact: Jerrold R. Jenkins, CEO & Chm Bd
E-mail: jrj@bookpublishing.com&nm
Description: Publishes on business, motivational and professional improvement, health, fitness, non-fiction and children's titles. **Founded:** 1988.

61508 ■ OI Publishing
2675 Rumberland
Berkley, MI 48072
Ph:(313)506-2570
Description: Publishes books on jobs, careers and salaries. Titles include *Get a Job Now with the Salary You Want.*

61509 ■ Teacher's Discovery
2741 Paldan Dr.
Auburn Hills, MI 48326
Ph:(248)340-7210
Free: 800-832-2437
Fax: (248)340-7212
Co. E-mail: english@teachers-discovery.com
URL: http://www.teachersdiscovery.com
Contact: Judy Gatton, Dir of Sales
E-mail: judyg@tir.com
Description: Distributes educational supplemental materials.

61510 ■ Thomson Gale
27500 Drake Rd.
Farmington Hills, MI 48331-3535
Ph:(248)699-4253
Free: 800-877-4253
Fax: (248)699-8065
Co. E-mail: galeord@gale.com
URL: http://www.gale.com
Contact: Gordon T. Macomber, President
Description: Publishes reference books, as well as CD-ROMS, databases, and mailing lists. Distributes for West, CBD Research, Euromonitor Publications, Europa Publications, Macmillan (London), Oceano Grupo. Reaches market through direct mail, commission sales representatives, and telephone sales. Accepts unsolicited manuscripts. **Founded:** 1954.

SMALL BUSINESS DEVELOPMENT CENTER LEAD OFFICE

61511 ■ Minnesota Department of Trade and Economic Development–Small Business Development Center
500 Metro Square
121 7th. Pl. E
St. Paul, MN 55101-2146
Ph:(651)297-5770
Fax: (651)296-1290
Contact: Mary Kruger, State Director
E-mail: mary.kruger@dted.state.mn.us

61512 ■ Minnesota SBDC–Minnesota Small Business Development Center
1st National Bank Bldg.
332 Minnesota St., Ste. E200
St. Paul, MN 55101-1351
Ph:(651)297-5773
Fax: (651)296-5287
URL: http://www.mnsbdc.com
Contact: Michael Myhre, State Dir.
E-mail: michael.myhre@state.mn.us

61513 ■ University of St. Thomas–College of Business–SBDC (Schul)
Schulze Hall 103
46 S. 11th St.
Minneapolis, MN 55403
Ph:(651)962-4500
Free: 800-328-6819
Fax: (651)962-4508
Co. E-mail: smallbus@stthomas.edu
URL: http://www.stthomas.edu/cob/centers/sbdc/

SMALL BUSINESS DEVELOPMENT CENTERS

61514 ■ Albert Lea Business Development Center–Small Business Development Center
2610 Y.H. Hanson Ave.
PO Box 370
Albert Lea, MN 56007
Ph:(507)373-3930
Fax: (507)377-1354
Contact: Dave Lundak, SBDC Specialist
E-mail: drlundak@albertlea.org

61515 ■ Anoka Ramsey Community College–St. Thomas College of Business–Small Business Development Center (11200)
11200 Mississippi Blvd., NW
Coon Rapids, MN 55433
Ph:(763)422-3395

61516 ■ Cambridge area Chamber of Commerce–Small Business Development Center
PO Box 343
Cambridge, MN 55008
Ph:(763)689-2505
Fax: (763)552-2505
Co. E-mail: cambchbr@sherbtel.net
URL: http://www.cambridge-chamber.com
Contact: Kathi Schaff, Dir.

61517 ■ Central Lakes College–Small Business Development Center
501 W. College Dr.
Brainerd, MN 56401
Ph:(218)855-8142
URL: http://www.clcmn.edu/smallbusiness
Contact: Jan Sterner, Program Asst.
E-mail: jsterner@clcmn.edu

61518 ■ Dakota County Technical College–St. Thomas College of Business–Small Business Development Center (14200).
14200 Cedar Ave.
Apple Valley, MN 55124
Ph:(952)997-9550

61519 ■ Department of Trade and Economic Development–Minnesota SBDC
500 Metro Sq.
121 7th Pl. E.
St. Paul, MN 55101-2146
Ph:(651)297-5770
Fax: (651)296-1290
Contact: Mary Kruger, State Dir.
E-mail: mary.kruger@ted.state.mn.us

61520 ■ East Central Regional Development Commission–Small Business Development Center
100 Park St., S.
Mora, MN 55051
Ph:(320)679-4065
Fax: (320)679-4120
URL: http://www.region7erdc.org/
Contact: Robert Voss, Exec. Dir.
E-mail: robert.voss@ecrdc.org

61521 ■ Hibbing Community College–Small Business Development Center
1515 E. 25th St.
Hibbing, MN 55746
Ph:(218)262-6703
Fax: (218)262-6717
URL: http://www.umdced.com
Contact: Terry Rupar, Asst. Business Development Specialist
E-mail: j.antilla@hi.cc.mn.us

61522 ■ Itasca Development Corp.–Small Business Development Center
12 NW 3rd St.
Grand Rapids, MN 55744
Ph:(218)327-2241
Fax: (218)327-2242

Co. E-mail: idsbdc@uslink.net
URL: http://www.umdced.com
Contact: Michael D. Andrews, Dir.

61523 ■ Minnesota Project Innovation–Small Business Development Center
111 3rd Ave. S., Ste. 100
Minneapolis, MN 55401
Ph:(612)338-3280
Fax: (612)338-3483
Contact: Pat Dillon, Dir.
E-mail: pdillon@mpi.org

61524 ■ Minnesota Technology, Inc.–Small Business Development Center
Olcott Plaza Office Bldg.
820 N. 9th St.
Virginia, MN 55792
Ph:(218)741-4251
Fax: (218)741-4249

61525 ■ Minnesota University–Small Business Development Center
1104 7th Ave., S.
MSU Box 132
Moorhead, MN 56563
Ph:(218)236-2289
Fax: (218)236-2280
URL: http://www.mnsbdc.com
Contact: Leonard Sliwoski, Dir.
E-mail: sliwoski@mnstate.edu

61526 ■ Normandale Community College (Bloomington)–Small Business Development Center
9700 France Ave. S
Bloomington, MN 55431
Ph:(612)832-6221
Fax: (612)832-6352
Contact: Scott Harding, Dir.

61527 ■ Northfield Enterprise Center–SBDC for Rice County
1705 Cannon Ln.
Northfield, MN 55057
Ph:(507)664-0933
URL: http://www.northfieldenterprisecenter.com
Contact: Lynda Grady

61528 ■ Northwest Technical College–SBDC
905 Grant Ave., SE
Bemidji, MN 56601
Ph:(218)755-4286
Fax: (218)755-4289
Contact: Susan Kozojed, Dir.

61529 ■ Owatonna Incubator, Inc.–SBDC
1065 SW, 24th Ave.
PO Box 505
Owatonna, MN 55060
Ph:(507)451-0517
Fax: (507)455-2788
Co. E-mail: obi@owatonnaincubator.com
Contact: Ken Henrickson, Dir.

61530 ■ Pine Technical College–Small Business Development Center
1000 4th St.
Pine City, MN 55063
Ph:(320)629-7340
Fax: (320)629-7603
Contact: John Sparling, Dir.
E-mail: sparlinj@ptc.tec.mn.us

61531 ■ Rainy River Community College–Small Business Development Center
1501 Hwy. 71
International Falls, MN 56649
Ph:(218)285-2255
Fax: (218)285-2239
URL: http://www.umdced.com
Contact: Julie Schumacher, Counselor

61532 ■ Region Nine Development Commission–SBDC
1961 Premier Dr., Ste. 268
Mankato, MN 56001
Ph:(507)389-8893
URL: http://www.rndc.org
Contact: Bob Klanderud, Dir.
E-mail: robertk@rndc.mankato.mn.us

61533 ■ Rochester Community and Tech. College–Small Business Development Center
Riverland Hall
851 30th Ave. SE
Rochester, MN 55904
Ph:(507)285-7536
Fax: (507)285-7110
URL: http://www.rochestersbdc.com
Contact: Kay Wiegert, Regional Coord.
E-mail: kay.wiegert@roch.edu

61534 ■ St. Cloud State University–Small Business Development Center
616 Roosevelt Rd., Ste. 100
St. Cloud, MN 56301
Ph:(320)255-4842
Fax: (320)255-4957
URL: http://www.mnsbdc.com
Contact: Dawn Jensen-Ragnier, Dir.
E-mail: djensen@stcloudstate.edu

61535 ■ Southeast Minnesota Development Corp.–SBDC
111 W. Jessie St.
PO Box 684
Rushford, MN 55971
Ph:(507)864-7557
Fax: (507)864-2091
Contact: Terry Erickson, Dir.

61536 ■ Southwest State University–Small Business Development Center
Science and Technical Resource Center, Ste. 105
1501 State St., Ste. 105
Marshall, MN 56258
Ph:(507)537-7386
Fax: (507)387-6094
Co. E-mail: sbdc@southwestMSU.edu
URL: http://www.swsbdc.org
Contact: Liz Struve, Regional Dir.

61537 ■ Twin Cities Regional Office–University of St. Thomas–College of Business (Schul)–Small Business Development Center (ze Hall No)
Schulze Hall No. 103
1000 La Salle Ave.
Minneapolis, MN 55403
Ph:(651)962-4500
Free: 800-328-6819
Fax: (651)962-4408
Co. E-mail: smallbus@stthomas.edu
URL: http://www.stthomas.edu/cob/centers/sbdc/
Contact: Gregg Schneider, Dir.
E-mail: gwschneider@stthomas.edu

61538 ■ University of Minnesota at Duluth–Small Business Development Center
Duluth Technology Village
11 E. Superior St., Ste. 210
Duluth, MN 55802

Ph:(218)726-6192
Free: 888-387-4594
Fax: (218)726-6338
URL: http://www.umdced.com
Contact: Elaine Hansen, Regional Dir.
E-mail: ehansen@umdced.com

61539 ■ Wadena Area Chamber of Commerce–SBDC
5 Aldrich Ave., SE
PO Box 107
Wadena, MN 56482
Ph:(218)631-7704
Fax: (218)631-7705
URL: http://www.wadena.org
Contact: Jenny Munyer, Dir.
E-mail: jmunyer@mnchamber.com

SMALL BUSINESS ASSISTANCE PROGRAMS

61540 ■ Minnesota Department of Employment and Economic Development
First National Bank Bldg
332 Minnesota Suite E200
St. Paul, MN 55101-2146
Ph:(651)297-1291
Free: 800-657-3858
Fax: (651)296-1290
URL: http://www.deed.state.mn.us
Description: Coordinates state government information and resources available to small businesses. Provides information relating to start-up, operation, and expansion of businesses. Offers several free publications.

61541 ■ Minnesota Department of Employment and Economic Development–Business and Community Development Division and Trade
First National Bank Bldg
332 Minnesota Suite E200
St. Paul, MN 55101-2146
Ph:(651)297-1291
Free: 800-657-3858
Fax: (651)296-1290
URL: http://www.deed.state.mn.us
Description: Provides grants to cities, townships and counties

61542 ■ Minnesota Department of Employment and Economic Development–Minnesota Trade Office
First National Bank Bldg
332 Minnesota Suite E200
St. Paul, MN 55101-1351
Ph:(651)297-4222
Free: 800-657-3858
Fax: (651)296-3555
Co. E-mail: mto@state.mn.us
URL: http://www.exportminnesota.com
Contact: Tony Lorusso, Dir
Description: Promotes Minnesota goods and services through export and attraction of foreign investors. Efforts concentrate on small business through several divisions, including Export Development Division, International Marketing and Investment Division, and Export Finance Division.

SCORE OFFICES

61543 ■ SCORE Central Area (St. Cloud)
c/o Mr. John Wertz, Chm.
616 Roosevelt Rd., Ste. 100
St. Cloud, MN 56301-1332
Ph:(320)240-1332
Co. E-mail: stcloud@scoreminn.org
URL: http://www.stcloudscore.org
Contact: Mr. John Wertz, Chm.
Description: Provides one-on-one confidential business consultation, at no cost. Offers low-cost workshops to current and potential entrepreneurs on business planning, finance, marketing, and similar topics.

61544 ■ SCORE Counselors to America's Small Business
220 S Broadway, Ste. 100
Rochester, MN 55904
Ph:(507)288-8103
Fax: (507)282-8960
Co. E-mail: rochester@scoremn.org
URL: http://SCOREmn.org
Contact: Charmaine Flen, Chair
Description: Volunteer businessmen and women. Provides free small business management assistance to individuals in the Rochester, MN area. Sponsors workshops.

61545 ■ SCORE Minneapolis
Bremer Bank Bldg., Ste. 103
8800 Hwy. 7
Minneapolis, MN 55426
Ph:(952)938-4570
Fax: (952)938-2651
Co. E-mail: minneapolis@score-mn.org
URL: http://www.score-minneapolis.org
Contact: Arlen Nissen, Chm.
Description: Serves as volunteer program in which working and retired business management professionals provide free business counseling to men and women who are considering starting a small business, encountering problems with their business, or expanding their business. Offers free one-on-one counseling, online counseling and low cost workshops on a variety of business topics.

61546 ■ SCORE New Ulm Area
c/o New Ulm Chamber of Commerce
1 N Minnesota St.
PO Box 384
New Ulm, MN 56073
Ph:(507)233-4300
Co. E-mail: newulm@score-mn.org
URL: http://www.score-newulm.org
Contact: William J. Fenske, Chm.
Description: Serves as volunteer program in which working and retired business management professionals provide free business counseling to men and women who are considering starting a small business, encountering problems with their business, or expanding their business. Offers free one-on-one counseling, online counseling and low cost workshops on a variety of business topics.

61547 ■ SCORE St. Paul
176 N Snelling Ave., Ste. 300
St. Paul, MN 55104-4707
Ph:(651)632-8937
Fax: (651)632-8938
Co. E-mail: stpaul@score-mn.org
URL: http://www.score-stpaul.org
Contact: Robert Baynton, Dir.
Description: Serves as volunteer program in which working and retired business management professionals provide free business counseling to men and women who are considering starting a small business, encountering problems with their business, or expanding their business. Offers free one-on-one counseling, online counseling and low cost workshops on a variety of business topics.

61548 ■ SCORE South Metro
c/o Steven Saefke, Chm.
101 W Burnsville Pkwy., Ste. 152
Burnsville, MN 55337
Ph:(952)890-7020
Fax: (952)890-7019
Co. E-mail: southmetro@scoreminn.org
Contact: Steven Saefke, Chm.

BETTER BUSINESS BUREAUS

61549 ■ Better Business Bureau Serving Minnesota and North Dakota
2706 Gannon Rd.
St. Paul, MN 55116-2600
Ph:(612)699-1111

Free: 800-646-6222
Fax: (612)699-7665
Co. E-mail: ask@mnd.bbb.org
URL: http://www.mnd.bbb.org
Contact: Jane Driggs, Pres.

CHAMBERS OF COMMERCE

61550 ■ Ada Chamber of Commerce
PO Box 1
Ada, MN 56510-0001
Ph:(218)784-3542
Fax: (218)784-2108
Co. E-mail: leeannko@loretel.net
URL: http://www.ci.ada.mn.us
Contact: Lee Ann Konkin, Sec.

61551 ■ Aitkin Area Chamber of Commerce
PO Box 127
Aitkin, MN 56431-0127
Ph:(218)927-2316
Free: 800-526-8342
Fax: (218)927-4494
Co. E-mail: upnorth@aitkin.com
URL: http://www.aitkin.com
Contact: Sue Marxen, Exec. Dir.

61552 ■ Albany Chamber of Commerce
PO Box 634
Albany, MN 56307-0634
Ph:(320)845-7777
Fax: (320)845-2346
Co. E-mail: albanycc@albanytel.com
URL: http://www.albanymnchamber.com
Contact: Tom Schneider, Pres.

61553 ■ Albert Lea - Freeborn County Chamber of Commerce
701 Marshall St.
Albert Lea, MN 56007
Ph:(507)373-3938
Fax: (507)373-0344
Co. E-mail: susiep@albertlea.org
URL: http://www.albertlea.org

61554 ■ Alexandria Lakes Area Chamber of Commerce
206 Broadway
Alexandria, MN 56308
Ph:(320)763-3161
Free: 800-235-9441
Fax: (320)763-6857
Co. E-mail: alexrecr@rea-alp.com
URL: http://www.alexandriamn.org
Contact: Coni McKay, Exec. Dir.

61555 ■ Anoka Area Chamber of Commerce
12 Bridge Sq.
Anoka, MN 55303
Ph:(763)421-7130
Fax: (763)421-0577
Co. E-mail: mail@anokaareachamber.com
URL: http://www.anokaareachamber.com
Contact: Peter Turok, Pres.

61556 ■ Apple Valley Chamber of Commerce
14800 Galaxie Ave. W, Ste. 301
Apple Valley, MN 55124
Ph:(952)432-8422
Free: 800-301-9435
Fax: (952)432-7964
Co. E-mail: info@applevaleychamber.com
URL: http://www.applevalleychamber.com
Contact: Edward Kearney, Pres.

61557 ■ Arlington Area Chamber of Commerce
PO Box 650
Arlington, MN 55307
Ph:(507)964-2256
Fax: (507)964-5550
Co. E-mail: trisha_rosenfield@hotmail.com
Contact: Trisha Rosenfield, Pres.

61558 ■ Austin Area Chamber of Commerce
329 N Main St., Ste. 102
Austin, MN 55912
Ph:(507)437-4561
Free: 888-319-5655
Fax: (507)437-4869
Co. E-mail: execdir@austincoc.com
URL: http://www.austincoc.com
Contact: Sandy Forstner, Exec. Dir.

61559 ■ Baudette-Lake of the Woods Chamber of Commerce
PO Box 659
Baudette, MN 56623-0659
Ph:(218)634-1174
Free: 800-382-3474
Fax: (218)634-2915
Co. E-mail: lakwoods@wiktel.com
URL: http://www.lakeofthewoodsmn.com
Contact: Jane Sindelir, Office Mgr.

61560 ■ Bemidji Area Chamber of Commerce
300 Bemidji Ave.
PO Box 850
Bemidji, MN 56601
Ph:(218)444-3521
Free: 800-458-2223
Fax: (218)444-4276
Co. E-mail: chamber@paulbunyan.net
URL: http://www.bemidji.org
Contact: Lori Paris, Exec. Dir.

61561 ■ Big Stone Lake Area Chamber of Commerce
987 U.S. Hwy. 12
Ortonville, MN 56278
Ph:(320)839-3284
Free: 800-568-5722
Fax: (320)839-2621
Co. E-mail: chamber@bigstonelake.com
URL: http://www.bigstonelake.com

61562 ■ Blooming Prairie Chamber of Commerce
138 Hwy. 218 S
PO Box 805
Blooming Prairie, MN 55917
Ph:(507)583-4472
Fax: (507)583-4520
Co. E-mail: bpcofc@smig.net
Contact: Becky Noble, Exec.Dir.

61563 ■ Blue Earth Area Chamber of Commerce
118 E 6th St.
Blue Earth, MN 56013-2002
Ph:(507)526-2916
Fax: (507)526-2244
Co. E-mail: chamber@bevcomm.net
Contact: Shelly Greimann, Dir.

61564 ■ Brainerd Lakes Area Chambers of Commerce
124 N 6th St.
PO Box 356
Brainerd, MN 56401-0356
Ph:(218)829-2838
Free: 800-450-2838
Fax: (218)829-8199
Co. E-mail: info@explorebrainerdlakes.com
URL: http://www.explorebrainerdlakes.com
Contact: Lisa Paxton, CEO

61565 ■ Buffalo Area Chamber of Commerce
9 Central Ave.
Buffalo, MN 55313
Ph:(763)682-4902
Fax: (763)682-5677
Co. E-mail: info@buffalochamber.org
URL: http://www.buffalochamber.org
Contact: Sally Custer, Pres.

61566 ■ Burnsville Chamber of Commerce
101 W Bursnville Pkwy., Ste. 150
Burnsville, MN 55337-2571
Ph:(952)435-6000
Fax: (952)435-6972

Co. E-mail: chamber@burnsvillechamber.com
URL: http://www.burnsvillechamber.com
Contact: Daron Van Helden, Pres.

61567 ■ Cambridge Area Chamber of Commerce
PO Box 343
Cambridge, MN 55008
Ph:(763)689-2505
Fax: (763)552-2505
Co. E-mail: cambchbr@sherbtel.net
URL: http://www.cambridge-chamber.com
Contact: Kathi Schaff, Exec.Dir.

61568 ■ Canby Area Chamber of Commerce
123 1st St. E
Canby, MN 56220
Ph:(507)223-7775
Co. E-mail: josh@prairiehub.net
URL: http://canbychamber.com
Contact: Pat Stanley, Pres.

61569 ■ Cannon Falls Area Chamber of Commerce
PO Box 2
Cannon Falls, MN 55009
Ph:(507)263-2289
Fax: (507)263-2785
Co. E-mail: tourism@cannonfalls.org
URL: http://www.cannonfalls.org
Contact: Patricia A. Anderson, Pres.

61570 ■ Chamber of Commerce of Fargo Moorhead
202 1st Ave. N
Moorhead, MN 56560
Ph:(218)233-1100
Fax: (218)233-1200
Co. E-mail: info@fmchamber.com
URL: http://www.fmchamber.com
Contact: David K. Martin, Pres.

61571 ■ Chisholm Area Chamber of Commerce
223 W Lake St.
Chisholm, MN 55719
Ph:(218)254-7930
Free: 800-422-0806
Fax: (218)254-7932
Co. E-mail: chisholm@cpinternet.com
URL: http://www.chisholmchamber.com
Contact: Shannon Kishel Roche, Exec. Dir.

61572 ■ Cloquet Carlton Area Chamber of Commerce
225 Sunnyside Dr.
Cloquet, MN 55720-1149
Ph:(218)879-1551
Free: 800-554-4350
Fax: (218)878-0223
Co. E-mail: chamber@cloquet.com
URL: http://www.cloquet.com
Contact: Della D. Schmidt, Pres.

61573 ■ Cokato Chamber of Commerce
255 Broadway Ave.
PO Box 819
Cokato, MN 55321
Ph:(320)286-5505
Fax: (320)286-5876
Co. E-mail: depclerk@cokato.mn.us
URL: http://www.cokato.mn.us
Contact: Louann Worden, Exec. Sec.

61574 ■ Cold Spring Area Chamber of Commerce
312 1st St. N
PO Box 328
Cold Spring, MN 56320-0328
Ph:(320)685-4186
Fax: (320)685-4186
Co. E-mail: scacc@netlinkcom.com
Contact: David Olson, Exec.Dir.

61575 ■ Cook Area Chamber of Commerce
PO Box 296
Cook, MN 55723

Ph:(218)666-5850
Free: 800-648-5897
Fax: (218)666-0022
Co. E-mail: info@cookminnesota.com
URL: http://www.cookminnesota.com
Contact: Lee Phillips, Pres.

61576 ■ Cottage Grove Area Chamber of Commerce
PO Box 16
Cottage Grove, MN 55016-0016
Ph:(651)458-8334
Fax: (651)458-8383
Co. E-mail: cgchambr@rconnect.com
URL: http://www.cottagegrovechamber.org
Contact: Mary Slusser, Pres.

61577 ■ Crookston Convention and Visitors Bureau
118 Fletcher St.
Crookston, MN 56716
Ph:(218)281-4320
Free: 800-809-5997
Fax: (218)281-4349
Co. E-mail: crookstoncvb@rrv.net
URL: http://www.visitcrookston.com
Contact: Jeannine Windels, CEO/Pres.

61578 ■ Delano Area Chamber of Commerce
PO Box 27
Delano, MN 55328-0027
Ph:(763)972-6756
Fax: (763)972-9326
Co. E-mail: info@delanochamber.com
URL: http://www.delanochamber.com
Contact: Lisa Blodgett, Exec.Dir.

61579 ■ Detroit Lakes Regional Chamber of Commerce
700 Washington Ave.
PO Box 348
Detroit Lakes, MN 56502-0348
Ph:(218)847-9202
Free: 800-542-3992
Fax: (218)847-9082
Co. E-mail: dlchamber@lakesnet.net
URL: http://www.visitdetroitlakes.com
Contact: David E. Hochhalter, Pres.

61580 ■ Duluth Area Chamber of Commerce
5 W First St., Ste. 101
Duluth, MN 55802
Ph:(218)722-5501
Fax: (218)722-3223
Co. E-mail: inquiry@duluthchamber.com
URL: http://www.duluthchamber.com
Contact: David M. Ross, Pres./CEO

61581 ■ East Grand Forks Chamber of Commerce
218 4th St. NW
East Grand Forks, MN 56721
Ph:(218)773-7481
Fax: (218)773-7482
Co. E-mail: info@eastgrandforkschamber.com
Contact: Diane Blair, Pres.

61582 ■ East Lake County Chamber of Commerce
PO Box 26
1026 7th Ave.
Two Harbors, MN 55616
Ph:(218)226-4408
Fax: 800-777-7384
Contact: Marvil LaCroix, Sec.

61583 ■ Eden Prairie Chamber of Commerce
11455 Viking Dr., Ste. No. 270
Eden Prairie, MN 55344
Ph:(952)944-2830
Fax: (952)944-0229
Co. E-mail: pat.mulqueeny@epchamber.org
URL: http://www.epchamber.org
Contact: Pat MulQueeny, Pres.

61584 ■ Elk River Area Chamber of Commerce
509 Hwy. 10
Elk River, MN 55330-1415
Ph:(763)441-3110
Fax: (763)441-3409
Co. E-mail: eracc@elkriverchamber.org
URL: http://www.elkriverchamber.org
Contact: Jeffrey A. Gongoll, Pres.

61585 ■ Ely Chamber of Commerce
1600 E Sheridan St.
Ely, MN 55731
Ph:(218)365-6123
Free: 800-777-7281
Fax: (218)365-5929
Co. E-mail: fun@ely.org
URL: http://www.ely.org
Contact: Linda Fryer, Admin.Dir.

61586 ■ Fairmont Area Chamber of Commerce
323 E Blue Earth Ave.
PO Box 826
Fairmont, MN 56031-0826
Ph:(507)235-5547
Fax: (507)235-8411
Co. E-mail: chamber@fairmont.org
URL: http://www.fairmont.org
Contact: Bob Wallace, Pres.

61587 ■ Faribault Area Chamber of Commerce
530 Wilson Ave.
PO Box 434
Faribault, MN 55021-0434
Ph:(507)334-4381
Free: 800-658-2354
Fax: (507)334-1003
Co. E-mail: chamber@faribaultmn.org
URL: http://www.faribaultmn.org
Contact: Kymn Anderson, Pres.

61588 ■ Farmington Area Chamber of Commerce
PO Box 252
Farmington, MN 55024
Ph:(651)460-6444
Fax: (651)460-2434
Co. E-mail: fgtncham@frontiernet.net
Contact: Marg Van Dale, Co-Chm.

61589 ■ Fergus Falls Area Chamber of Commerce
202 S Court St.
Fergus Falls, MN 56537
Ph:(218)736-6951
Fax: (218)736-6952
Co. E-mail: chamber@prtel.com
URL: http://www.fergusfalls.com
Contact: Stephanie Hoff, Exec. Dir.

61590 ■ Forest Lake Area Chamber of Commerce
56 E Broadway Ave., Ste. 108
PO Box 474
Forest Lake, MN 55025-0474
Ph:(651)464-3200
Fax: (651)464-3201
Co. E-mail: chamber@flacc.org
URL: http://www.flacc.org
Contact: Vicky Savage, Treas.

61591 ■ Glencoe Area Chamber of Commerce
630 E 10th St.
Glencoe, MN 55336
Ph:(320)864-3650
Fax: (320)864-6405
Co. E-mail: chamber@glencoechamber.com
URL: http://www.glencoechamber.com
Contact: Larry Anderson, Pres.

61592 ■ Glenwood Area Chamber of Commerce
202 N Franklin St.
Glenwood, MN 56334

Ph:(320)634-3636
Free: (866)634-3636
Fax: (320)634-3637
Co. E-mail: glenstar@akeva.com
URL: http://www.glenwood-starbuck.org
Contact: Brenda Baumler, Office Mgr.

61593 ■ Grand Marais Chamber of Commerce
PO Box 805
Grand Marais, MN 55604-0805
Ph:(218)387-9112
Co. E-mail: gmcc@boreal.org
URL: http://www.grandmaraismn.com
Contact: Bev Wolke, Exec.Dir.

61594 ■ Grand Rapids Area Chamber of Commerce
1 NW 3rd St.
Grand Rapids, MN 55744-2718
Ph:(218)326-6619
Free: 800-472-6366
Fax: (218)326-4825
Co. E-mail: answers@grandmn.com
URL: http://www.grandmn.com
Contact: Bud Stone, Pres.

61595 ■ Granite Falls Area Chamber of Commerce
646 Prentice St.
Granite Falls, MN 56241
Ph:(320)564-4039
Fax: (320)564-3210
Co. E-mail: gfchamber@kilowatt.net
URL: http://www.granitefalls.com
Contact: Rachel Kimball, Exec. Dir.

61596 ■ Greater Mankato Chamber of Commerce
112 S Riverfront Dr.
PO Box 999
Mankato, MN 56002-1269
Ph:(507)345-4519
Free: 800-657-4733
Fax: (507)345-4451
Co. E-mail: info@greatermankato.com
URL: http://www.greatermankato.com
Contact: Mike King, Chm.

61597 ■ Greater Stillwater Chamber of Commerce
106 S Main St.
PO Box 516
Stillwater, MN 55082
Ph:(651)439-4001
Fax: (651)439-4035
Co. E-mail: info@ilovestillwater.com
URL: http://www.ilovestillwater.com
Contact: Curt Geissler, Pres.

61598 ■ Greater Wayzata Area Chamber of Commerce
402 E Lake St.
Wayzata, MN 55391-1651
Ph:(952)473-9595
Fax: (952)473-6266
Co. E-mail: info@wayzatachamber.com
URL: http://www.wayzatachamber.com
Contact: Diane Wilson, Pres.

61599 ■ Hastings Area Chamber of Commerce and Tourism Bureau
111 E 3rd St.
Hastings, MN 55033-1211
Ph:(651)437-6775
Free: 888-612-6122
Fax: (651)437-2697
Co. E-mail: info@hastingsmn.org
URL: http://www.hastingsmn.org
Contact: Michelle Jacobs, Pres.

61600 ■ Hermantown Chamber of Commerce
4940 Lightning Dr.
Hermantown, MN 55811-1447
Ph:(218)729-6843
Fax: (218)729-7132
Co. E-mail: hermcham@uslink.net

URL: http://www.hermantownchamber.com
Contact: Kay Knight, Exec.Dir.

61601 ■ Hibbing Area Chamber of Commerce
211 E Howard St.
PO Box 727
Hibbing, MN 55746-1763
Ph:(218)262-3895
Fax: (218)262-3897
Co. E-mail: hibbcofc@hibbing.org
URL: http://www.hibbing.org
Contact: Lory Fedo, Pres./CEO

61602 ■ Hispanic Chamber of Commerce of Minnesota
3000 N 2nd St.
Minneapolis, MN 55411
Ph:(612)312-1692
Fax: (612)312-1693
Co. E-mail: info@hispanicmn.org
URL: http://www.hispanicmn.org

61603 ■ Hutchinson Area Chamber of Commerce
2 Main St. S
Hutchinson, MN 55350
Ph:(320)587-5252
Free: 800-572-6689
Fax: (320)587-4752
Co. E-mail: info@explorehutchinson.com
URL: http://www.explorehutchinson.com

61604 ■ I-94 West Chamber of Commerce
21370 John Milless Dr.
PO Box 95
Rogers, MN 55374-0095
Ph:(763)428-2921
Fax: (763)428-9068
Co. E-mail: requests@i94westchamber.org
URL: http://www.i94westchamber.org
Contact: Kathleen Poate, Pres.

61605 ■ International Falls Area Chamber of Commerce
301 2nd Ave.
International Falls, MN 56649
Ph:(218)283-9400
Free: 800-325-5766
Fax: (218)283-3572
Co. E-mail: chamber@intlfalls.org
URL: http://www.internationalfallsmn.us
Contact: Kallie L. Briggs, Exec. Dir.

61606 ■ Jackson Area Chamber of Commerce
82 W Ashley St.
Jackson, MN 56143-1669
Ph:(507)847-3867
Fax: (507)847-3869
Co. E-mail: chamber@cityofjacksonmn.com
URL: http://jacksonmn.com
Contact: Cari Boell, Exec.Dir.

61607 ■ Kanabec Area Chamber of Commerce
805 W Forest
Mora, MN 55051
Ph:(320)679-5792
Free: 800-291-5792
Co. E-mail: macc@ncis.com
URL: http://www.moramn.com
Contact: Madolyn Amundson, Pres.

61608 ■ La Crescent Chamber of Commerce
PO Box 132
La Crescent, MN 55947
Ph:(507)895-2800
Free: 800-926-9480
Fax: (507)895-2619
Co. E-mail: lacrescent.chamber@acegroup.com
URL: http://www.lacrescent.com
Contact: Beverly Jiardina, Exec.Sec.

61609 ■ Lake Benton Area Chamber of Commerce and Convention and Visitors Bureau
110 S Center St.
PO Box 205
Lake Benton, MN 56149

Ph:(507)368-9577
Fax: (507)368-9577
Co. E-mail: lbenton@itctel.com
URL: http://www.itctel.com/lbenton
Contact: Ms. Heather Ulrich, Exec.Dir.

61610 ■ Lake City Area Chamber of Commerce
101 W Center St.
Lake City, MN 55041
Ph:(651)345-4123
Free: 800-369-4123
Fax: (651)345-4195
Co. E-mail: lcchamber@earthlink.net
URL: http://www.lakecity.org
Contact: Mary Huselid, Exec.Dir.

61611 ■ Lake Crystal Area Chamber of Commerce
PO Box 27
Lake Crystal, MN 56055
Ph:(507)726-6088
Fax: (507)726-2045
Co. E-mail: lcchambr@hickorytech.net
URL: http://www.lakecrystalchamber.com
Contact: Sara Nilson, Exec.Coor.

61612 ■ Lake Minnetonka Chamber of Commerce
3600 Shoreline Dr.
PO Box 115
Navarre, MN 55392
Ph:(952)471-0768
Fax: (952)471-0577
Co. E-mail: chamber@lakeminnetonkachamber.com
URL: http://www.lakeminnetonkachamber.com
Contact: Patsy Kiesow, Exec.Dir.

61613 ■ Lake Vermilion Area Chamber of Commerce
Box 776-B
Tower, MN 55790
Ph:(218)753-2301
Free: 800-869-3766
Co. E-mail: info@lakevermilionchamber.com
URL: http://www.lakevermilionchamber.com
Contact: Betsy Clark, Pres.

61614 ■ Laurentian Chamber of Commerce
403 1st St. N
PO Box 1072
Virginia, MN 55792-1072
Ph:(218)741-2717
Fax: (218)749-4913
Co. E-mail: ppilney@laurentianchamber.org
URL: http://laurentianchamber.org
Contact: James Currie, Pres./CEO

61615 ■ Le Sueur Area Chamber of Commerce
500 N Main St.
Le Sueur, MN 56058
Ph:(507)665-2501
Fax: (507)665-4372
Co. E-mail: info@lesueurchamber.org
URL: http://www.lesueurchamber.org
Contact: Julie Boyland, Exec.Dir.

61616 ■ Leech Lake Area Chamber of Commerce
PO Box 1089
Walker, MN 56484-1089
Ph:(218)547-1313
Free: 800-833-1118
Fax: (218)547-1338
Co. E-mail: walker@eot.com
URL: http://www.leech-lake.com
Contact: Cindy Wannarka, Exec.Dir.

61617 ■ Litchfield Chamber of Commerce
219 N Sibley Ave.
PO Box 820
Litchfield, MN 55355-0820
Ph:(320)693-8184
Fax: (320)593-8184
Co. E-mail: litch@litch.com
URL: http://www.litch.com

Contact: Christian Lenz, Exec.Dir.

61618 ■ Little Falls Area Chamber of Commerce
200 NW 1st St.
Little Falls, MN 56345-1365
Ph:(320)632-5155
Fax: (320)632-2122
Co. E-mail: assistance@littlefallsmnchamber.com
URL: http://littlefallsmnchamber.com
Contact: Debora K. Boelz, Pres./CEO

61619 ■ Long Prairie Area Chamber of Commerce
9 Central Ave., Ste. 3
Long Prairie, MN 56347
Ph:(320)732-2514
Fax: (320)732-2514
Co. E-mail: lpchambr@rea-alp.com
URL: http://www.longprairie.org
Contact: Toni Tebben, Pres.

61620 ■ Luverne Area Chamber of Commerce
211 E Main St.
Luverne, MN 56156
Ph:(507)283-4061
Free: 888-283-4061
Fax: (507)283-4061
Co. E-mail: info@luvernemn.com
URL: http://www.luvernemn.com
Contact: Dave Smith, Exec.Dir.

61621 ■ Madelia Area Chamber of Commerce
PO Box 171
Madelia, MN 56062
Ph:(507)642-8822
Free: 888-941-7283
Fax: (507)642-8556
Co. E-mail: mchamber@madeliamn.com
URL: http://www.madeliamn.com/chamber.htm
Contact: Tara Mueller, Exec.Dir.

61622 ■ Madison Area Chamber of Commerce
623 W 3rd St.
PO Box 70
Madison, MN 56256-0070
Ph:(320)598-7301
Fax: (320)598-7955
Co. E-mail: loutfisk@yahoo.com
URL: http://www.madisonmn.info
Contact: Maynard R. Meyer, Coor.

61623 ■ Marshall Area Chamber of Commerce
317 W Main St.
PO Box 352B
Marshall, MN 56258
Ph:(507)532-4484
Fax: (507)532-4485
Co. E-mail: chamber@starpoint.net
URL: http://www.marshall-mn.org
Contact: Tracy Veglahn, Pres./CEO

61624 ■ Melrose Chamber of Commerce
407 E Main St.
PO Box 214
Melrose, MN 56352
Ph:(320)256-7174
Fax: (320)256-7177
Co. E-mail: chamber@meltel.net
URL: http://www.melrosemn.org
Contact: Kelly Neu, Exec.Dir.

61625 ■ MetroNorth Chamber of Commerce
21st Century Bank Bldg.
9380 Central Ave. NE, Ste. 320
Blaine, MN 55434
Ph:(763)783-3553
Fax: (763)783-3557
Co. E-mail: chamber@metronorthchamber.org
URL: http://www.metronorthchamber.org
Contact: Thomas Snell, Exec. Dir.

61626 ■ Milaca Chamber of Commerce
PO Box 155
255 1st St. SE
Milaca, MN 56353

Ph:(320)983-3140
Fax: (320)983-3142
Co. E-mail: chamber@milacacity.com
URL: http://www.cityofmilaca.org
Contact: Heather Jones, Pres.

61627 ■ Minneapolis Regional Chamber of Commerce
81 S 9th St., Ste. 200
Minneapolis, MN 55402-3223
Ph:(612)370-9100
Fax: (612)370-9195
Co. E-mail: info@minneapolischamber.org
URL: http://www.minneapolischamber.org
Contact: Todd Klingel, Pres./CEO

61628 ■ Minnesota American Indian Chamber of Commerce
1508 E Franklin Ave., Ste. 100
Minneapolis, MN 55404
Ph:(612)870-4533
Fax: (612)870-1060
Co. E-mail: info@maicc.org
URL: http://www.maicc.org

61629 ■ Minnesota State Chamber of Commerce
400 Robert St. N, Ste. 1500
St. Paul, MN 55101
Ph:(651)292-4650
Free: 800-821-2230
Fax: (651)292-4656
Co. E-mail: dolson@mnchamber.com
URL: http://www.mnchamber.com
Contact: David Olson, Pres.

61630 ■ Montevideo Area Chamber of Commerce
110 N 1st St.
Montevideo, MN 56265
Ph:(320)269-5527
Free: 800-269-5527
Fax: (320)269-5586
Co. E-mail: generalinfo@montechamber.com
URL: http://www.montechamber.com
Contact: Lori Evenstad, Exec.Dir.

61631 ■ Monticello Area Chamber of Commerce
PO Box 192
Monticello, MN 55362
Ph:(763)295-2700
Fax: (763)295-2705
Co. E-mail: info@monticellochamber.com
URL: http://www.monticellochamber.com
Contact: Dr. Susie Wojchouski, Dir.

61632 ■ Moose Lake Area Chamber of Commerce
PO Box 110
Moose Lake, MN 55767
Ph:(218)485-4145
Free: 800-635-3680
Co. E-mail: mlchamber@moose-tec.com
URL: http://www.mooselake-mn.com
Contact: Dean Paulson, Exec. Dir.

61633 ■ Morris Area Chamber of Commerce and Agriculture
507 Atlantic Ave.
Morris, MN 56267
Ph:(320)589-1242
Fax: (320)585-4814
Co. E-mail: mchamber@info-link.net
URL: http://www.morrismnchamber.org
Contact: Carolyn Peterson, Exec.Dir.

61634 ■ New Prague Chamber of Commerce
101 E Main St.
PO Box 191
New Prague, MN 56071
Ph:(952)758-4360
Fax: (952)758-5396
Co. E-mail: npcofc@bevcomm.net
URL: http://www.newprague.com
Contact: Kim Gassner, Exec.Dir.

61635 ■ New Ulm Area Chamber of Commerce
1 N Minnesota St.
PO Box 384
New Ulm, MN 56073
Ph:(507)233-4300
Free: 888-463-9856
Fax: (507)354-1504
Co. E-mail: nuchamber@newulmtel.net
URL: http://www.newulm.com
Contact: Sharon Weinkauf, Pres./CEO

61636 ■ Nisswa Chamber of Commerce
25532 Main St.
PO Box 185
Nisswa, MN 56468
Ph:(218)963-2620
Free: 800-950-9610
Fax: (218)963-1420
Co. E-mail: requests@nisswa.com
URL: http://www.nisswa.com
Contact: Susan Mezzenga, Exec.Dir.

61637 ■ North Branch Area Chamber of Commerce
PO Box 577
6372 Main St., Ste. D
North Branch, MN 55056
Ph:(651)674-4077
Fax: (651)674-2600
Co. E-mail: nbchamber@sherbtel.net
URL: http://www.northbranchchamber.com
Contact: Kathy Lindo, Exec. Dir.

61638 ■ North Hennepin Area Chamber of Commerce
229 1st Ave. NE
Osseo, MN 55369-1201
Ph:(763)424-6744
Fax: (763)424-6927
Co. E-mail: info@nhachamber.com
URL: http://www.nhachamber.com
Contact: David Looby, Pres./CEO

61639 ■ Northern Dakota County Chamber of Commerce
1121 Town Center Dr., Ste. 102
Eagan, MN 55123
Ph:(651)452-9872
Fax: (651)452-8978
Co. E-mail: info@ndcchambers.com
URL: http://www.ndcchambers.com
Contact: Ruthe Batulis, Pres.

61640 ■ Northfield Area Chamber of Commerce
205 3rd St. W, Ste. A
PO Box 198
Northfield, MN 55057-0198
Ph:(507)645-5604
Free: 800-658-2548
Fax: (507)663-7782
Co. E-mail: info@northfieldchamber.com
URL: http://www.northfieldchamber.com
Contact: Kathy Feldbrugge, Exec.Dir.

61641 ■ Northwest Suburban Chamber of Commerce
8200 County Rd. 116, Ste. 100
Corcoran, MN 55340-9303
Ph:(763)420-3242
Fax: (763)420-5964
Co. E-mail: info@nwschamber.com
URL: http://www.nwschamber.com
Contact: Barbara Lantsberger, Exec.Dir.

61642 ■ Olivia Area Chamber of Commerce
PO Box 37
Olivia, MN 56277-0037
Ph:(320)523-1350
Free: 888-265-CORN
Fax: (320)523-1827
Co. E-mail: oliviachamber@tds.net
URL: http://www.olivia.mn.us
Contact: Libby Revier, Exec. Dir.

61643 ■ Owatonna Area Chamber of Commerce and Tourism
320 Hoffman Dr.
Owatonna, MN 55060
Ph:(507)451-7970
Free: 800-423-6466
Fax: (507)451-7972
Co. E-mail: oacct@owatonna.org
URL: http://www.owatonna.org
Contact: Brad Meier, Pres./CEO

61644 ■ Park Rapids Area Chamber of Commerce
1204 S Park, Hwy. 71 S
PO Box 249
Park Rapids, MN 56470-0249
Ph:(218)732-4111
Free: 800-247-0054
Fax: (218)732-4112
Co. E-mail: chamber@parkrapids.com
URL: http://www.parkrapids.com
Contact: Katherine Magozzi, Exec.Dir.

61645 ■ Paynesville Area Chamber of Commerce
PO Box 4
Paynesville, MN 56362-0004
Ph:(320)243-3233
Free: 800-547-9034
Co. E-mail: sherylf@centralmnfcu.org
URL: http://www.paynesvillechamber.org
Contact: Sheryl Fuchs, Pres.

61646 ■ Pelican Rapids Area Chamber of Commerce
PO Box 206
Pelican Rapids, MN 56572-0206
Ph:(218)863-1221
Free: 800-545-3711
Fax: (218)863-2662
Co. E-mail: tourism@loretel.net
URL: http://www.pelicanrapidschamber.com
Contact: Jane Aschnewitz, Exec.Dir.

61647 ■ Perham Area Chamber of Commerce
135 E Main St.
Perham, MN 56573
Ph:(218)346-7710
Free: 800-634-6112
Fax: (218)346-7712
Co. E-mail: chamber@perham.com
URL: http://www.perham.com
Contact: Sue Huebsch, Pres.

61648 ■ Pine City Area Chamber of Commerce
610 2nd Ave. SW
Pine City, MN 55063
Ph:(320)629-3861
Fax: (320)629-3861
Co. E-mail: info@pinecitychamber.com
URL: http://www.pinecitychamber.com
Contact: Bonnie Garrett, Exec.Sec.

61649 ■ Pipestone Area Chamber of Commerce
117 8th Ave. SE
PO Box 8
Pipestone, MN 56164
Ph:(507)825-3316
Fax: (507)825-3317
Co. E-mail: pipecham@pipestoneminnesota.com
URL: http://www.pipestoneminnesota.com
Contact: Mick Myers, Exec.Dir.

61650 ■ Princeton Area Chamber of Commerce
705 N 2nd St.
Princeton, MN 55371-1550
Ph:(763)389-1764
Co. E-mail: pacc@sherbtel.net
URL: http://www.princetonmnchamber.org
Contact: Nancy Campbell, Pres.

61651 ■ Prior Lake Area Chamber of Commerce
PO Box 114
Prior Lake, MN 55372

Ph:(952)440-1000
Fax: (952)440-1611
Co. E-mail: priorlakechamber@integraonline.com
URL: http://www.priorlakechamber.org
Contact: Sandi Fleck, Exec.Dir.

61652 ■ Red Wing Area Chamber of Commerce
439 Main St.
Red Wing, MN 55066
Ph:(651)388-4719
Free: 800-762-9516
Fax: (651)388-6991
Co. E-mail: chamber@redwingchamber.com
URL: http://www.redwingchamber.com
Contact: Arne Skyberg, Pres.

61653 ■ Redwood Area Chamber and Tourism
200 S Mill St.
PO Box 21
Redwood Falls, MN 56283
Ph:(507)637-2828
Free: 800-657-7070
Fax: (507)637-5202
Co. E-mail: chamber@redwoodfalls.org
URL: http://www.redwoodfalls.org
Contact: Beth Anderson, Exec.Dir.

61654 ■ Richfield Chamber of Commerce
6601 Lyndale Ave. S, Ste. 106
Richfield, MN 55423
Ph:(612)866-5100
Fax: (612)861-8302
Co. E-mail: info@richfieldchambercvb.org
Contact: Steven Lindgren, Pres.

61655 ■ River Heights Chamber of Commerce
5782 Blackhire Path
Inver Grove Heights, MN 55076
Ph:(651)451-2266
Fax: (651)451-0846
Co. E-mail: info@riverheights.com
URL: http://www.riverheights.com
Contact: Jennifer Gale, Pres.

61656 ■ Robbinsdale Chamber of Commerce
PO Box 22646
Robbinsdale, MN 55422-0646
Ph:(763)531-1279
Co. E-mail: dkiser@twelve.tv
URL: http://www.robbinsdalemn.com/chamber.htm
Contact: D. Kiser, Sec.

61657 ■ Rochester Area Chamber of Commerce
220 S Broadway, Ste. 100
Rochester, MN 55904-6517
Ph:(507)288-1122
Fax: (507)282-8960
Co. E-mail: chamber@rochestermnchamber.com
URL: http://www.rochestermnchamber.com
Contact: John Wade, Pres.

61658 ■ St. Cloud Area Chamber of Commerce
110 S 6th Ave.
PO Box 487
St. Cloud, MN 56302-0487
Ph:(320)251-2940
Fax: (320)251-0081
Co. E-mail: information@stcloudareachamber.com
URL: http://www.stcloudareachamber.com
Contact: Teresa Bohnen, Pres.

61659 ■ St. Joseph Chamber of Commerce
PO Box 696
St. Joseph, MN 56374
Ph:(320)363-7721
Co. E-mail: janel@fsbstjoseph.com
URL: http://www.stjosephchamber.com
Contact: Jane Litchy, Pres.

61660 ■ St. Paul Area Chamber of Commerce
401 N Robert St., Ste. 150
St. Paul, MN 55101

Ph:(651)223-5000
Fax: (651)223-5119
Co. E-mail: larry@saintpaulchamber.com
URL: http://www.saintpaulchamber.com
Contact: Larry S. Dowell, Pres.

61661 ■ St. Peter Area Chamber of Commerce
101 S Front St.
St. Peter, MN 56082
Ph:(507)934-3400
Free: 800-473-3404
Fax: (507)934-8960
Co. E-mail: spchamb@hickorytech.net
URL: http://www.tourism.st-peter.mn.us
Contact: Larry Haugen

61662 ■ Sandstone Chamber of Commerce
402 N Main
Sandstone, MN 55072
Ph:(320)245-2271
Co. E-mail: information@sandstonechamber.com
URL: http://www.sandstonechamber.com
Contact: Irene Sandell, Sec.-Treas.

61663 ■ Sauk Centre Area Chamber of Commerce
PO Box 222
Sauk Centre, MN 56378
Ph:(320)352-5201
Fax: (320)352-5202
Co. E-mail: chamber@saukcentrechamber.com
URL: http://www.saukcentrechamber.com
Contact: Christine Brinkman, Exec.Dir.

61664 ■ Savage Chamber of Commerce
First Community Bank Bldg.
14141 Glendale Rd., Ste. 210
Savage, MN 55378
Ph:(952)894-8876
Fax: (952)894-9906
Co. E-mail: mail@savagechamber.com
URL: http://www.savagechamber.com
Contact: Lori Anderson, Exec.Dir.

61665 ■ Shakopee Chamber of Commerce
1801 County Rd. 101 E
PO Box 717
Shakopee, MN 55379-0717
Ph:(952)445-1660
Free: 800-574-2150
Fax: (952)445-1669
Co. E-mail: chamber@shakopee.org
URL: http://www.shakopee.org
Contact: Carol Schultz, Exec.Dir.

61666 ■ Slayton Area Chamber of Commerce
2635 Broadway Ave.
Slayton, MN 56172
Ph:(507)836-6902
Fax: (507)836-6650
Co. E-mail: slaytoncham@iw.net
Contact: Ms. April Gangestad, Exec.Dir.

61667 ■ Sleepy Eye Area Chamber of Commerce
232 E Main St.
Sleepy Eye, MN 56085
Ph:(507)794-4731
Free: 800-290-0588
Fax: (507)794-4732
Co. E-mail: secofc@sleepyeyetel.net
URL: http://sleepyeye-mn.com
Contact: Mrs. Julie Schmitt, Exec.Dir.

61668 ■ Springfield Area Chamber of Commerce
33 S Cass
Springfield, MN 56087
Ph:(507)723-3508
Fax: (507)723-4270
Co. E-mail: spfdchamber@newulmtel.net
URL: http://www.springfieldmnchamber.org
Contact: Alan Fritch, VP

61669 ■ Stewartville Chamber of Commerce
417 1/2 S Main St.
PO Box 52
Stewartville, MN 55976

Ph:(507)533-6006
Free: (866)293-8107
Fax: (507)533-6006
Co. E-mail: stewchamber@stewartville.com
Contact: Jodi Beck, Admin.

61670 ■ Thief River Falls Chamber of Commerce
2017 Hwy. 59 SE
Thief River Falls, MN 56701
Ph:(218)681-3720
Free: 800-827-1629
Co. E-mail: trfchamb@wiktel.com
URL: http://www.visitthiefriverfalls.com
Contact: Stacy Myhrer, Pres.

61671 ■ Tracy Area Chamber of Commerce
372 Morgan St.
Tracy, MN 56175
Ph:(507)629-4021
Fax: (507)629-4345
Co. E-mail: tracychamber@iw.net
URL: http://www.tracymnchamber.com
Contact: Kayla Hussong, Chair

61672 ■ Twin Cities North Chamber of Commerce
5394 Edgewood Dr., Ste. 100
Mounds View, MN 55112
Ph:(763)571-9781
Fax: (763)572-7950
Co. E-mail: info@twincitiesnorth.org
URL: http://www.twincitiesnorth.org
Contact: Bruce Nustad, Pres.

61673 ■ Twin Cities Quorum
1821 University Ave., Ste. S-306A
St. Paul, MN 55104
Ph:(651)646-1029
Co. E-mail: sam@twincitiesquorum.com
URL: http://www.twincitiesquorum.com
Contact: Sam McClure, Pres.

61674 ■ TwinWest Chamber of Commerce
10550 Wayzata Blvd.
Minnetonka, MN 55305-5504
Ph:(952)540-0234
Fax: (952)540-0237
Co. E-mail: info@twinwest.com
URL: http://www.twinwest.com
Contact: Barbara Obershaw, Pres.

61675 ■ Two Harbors Area Chamber of Commerce
1026 7th Ave.
Two Harbors, MN 55616-1149
Ph:(218)834-2600
Free: 800-777-7384
Fax: (218)834-4012
Co. E-mail: thchamber@twoharborschamber.com
URL: http://www.twoharbors.com/chamber
Contact: Gordy Anderson, Pres./CEO

61676 ■ Wabasha-Kellogg Area Chamber of Commerce
160 Main St.
PO Box 105
Wabasha, MN 55981-0105
Ph:(651)565-4158
Free: 800-565-4158
Fax: (651)565-2808
Co. E-mail: info@wabashamn.org
URL: http://www.wabashamn.org
Contact: Randy Voth, Pres.

61677 ■ Waconia Area Chamber of Commerce
209 S Vine St.
Waconia, MN 55387
Ph:(952)442-5812
Fax: (952)856-4476
Co. E-mail: dmcmillan@waconiachamber.org
URL: http://www.waconiachamber.org
Contact: Deb McMillan, Pres.

61678 ■ Waseca Area Chamber of Commerce
111 N State St.
Waseca, MN 56093

Ph:(507)835-3260
Free: 888-820-1243
Fax: (507)835-3267
Co. E-mail: wchamber@hickorytech.net
URL: http://www.wasecamncc.com
Contact: Larry Dukes, Pres.

61679 ■ Wells Area Chamber of Commerce
28 S Broadway
PO Box 134
Wells, MN 56097
Ph:(507)553-6450
Free: (866)553-6450
Fax: (507)553-6451
Co. E-mail: wellscc@bevcomm.net
URL: http://wells.govoffice.com
Contact: Andrea Christensen, Exec.Dir.

61680 ■ Wheaton Area Chamber of Commerce
PO Box 493
Wheaton, MN 56296-0493
Ph:(320)563-8271
Fax: (320)563-8274
URL: http://www.redrivermall.com
Contact: Mary Fox, Sec.

61681 ■ White Bear Area Chamber of Commerce
4801 Hwy. 61, Ste. 109
White Bear Lake, MN 55110
Ph:(651)429-8593
Fax: (651)429-8592
Co. E-mail: info@whitebearchamber.com
URL: http://www.whitebearchamber.com
Contact: Patricia A. Brannan, Pres.

61682 ■ Willmar Lakes Area Chamber of Commerce
2104 E Hwy. 12
Willmar, MN 56201
Ph:(320)235-0300
Fax: (320)231-1948
Co. E-mail: chamber@willmarareachamber.com
URL: http://www.willmarareachamber.com
Contact: Ken Warner, Pres.

61683 ■ Windom Area Chamber of Commerce and Visitors Bureau
303 9th St.
PO Box 8
Windom, MN 56101-0008
Ph:(507)831-2752
Free: 800-7W1-NDOM
Fax: (507)831-2755
Co. E-mail: windomchamber@qwest.net
URL: http://www.winwacc.com
Contact: Cheryl Hanson, Pres.

61684 ■ Winona Area Chamber of Commerce
67 Main St.
PO Box 870
Winona, MN 55987-0870
Ph:(507)452-2272
Fax: (507)454-8814
Co. E-mail: info@winonachamber.com
URL: http://www.winonachamber.com
Contact: Della Schmidt, Pres.

61685 ■ Winthrop Area Chamber of Commerce
PO Box 594
Winthrop, MN 55396
Ph:(507)647-2627
Free: 800-647-9461
Fax: (507)647-2627
Co. E-mail: winthropchamber@hotmail.com
Contact: Julie Trebelhorn, Exec.Sec.

61686 ■ Woodbury Chamber of Commerce
7650 Currell Blvd., Ste. 360
Woodbury. MN 55125
Ph:(651)578-0722
Fax: (651)578-7276
Co. E-mail: chamber@woodburychamber.org
URL: http://www.woodburychamber.org
Contact: Tim Fallon, Chm.

61687 ■ Worthington Area Chamber of Commerce
1121 Third Ave.
Worthington, MN 56187-2435
Ph:(507)372-2919
Free: 800-279-2919
Fax: (507)372-2827
Co. E-mail: wcofc@frontiernet.net
URL: http://www.worthingtonmnchamber.com
Contact: Darlene S. Macklin

61688 ■ Zumbrota Chamber of Commerce
PO Box 2
Zumbrota, MN 55992-0002
Ph:(507)732-4282
URL: http://www.zumbrota.com

MINORITY BUSINESS ASSISTANCE PROGRAMS

61689 ■ Metropolitan Economic Development Association
250 Second Ave. S, Ste. 106
Minneapolis, MN 55401
Ph:(612)332-6332
Fax: (612)317-1002
Co. E-mail: info@meda.net
URL: http://www.meda.net
Contact: Yvonne Cheung Ho

61690 ■ Native American Business Development Center
PO Box 217
Cass Lake, MN 56633
Ph:(218)335-8583
Fax: (218)335-8496
Co. E-mail: info@nabdc.org
URL: http://www.nabdc.org
Contact: Vernon Barsness Jr.

FINANCING AND LOAN PROGRAMS

61691 ■ Affinity Capital Management
901 Marquette Ave., Ste. 1810
Minneapolis, MN 55402
Ph:(612)252-9900
Fax: (612)252-9911
URL: http://www.affinitycapital.net
Contact: Edson W. Spencer, Managing Partner
Investment Types: Seed, early, first and second stage. **Industry Preferences:** Internet specific, medical and health, computer software and services, biotechnology, semiconductors and other electronics. **Geographic Preferences:** Midwest.

61692 ■ Alley Ventures LLC
1550 Utica Ave. S.
Minneapolis, MN 55416
Ph:(952)542-3077
Contact: Kevin Hennessey, Managing Director
Preferred Investment Size: $50,000 to $1,000,000. **Investment Policies:** Seed and early stage. **Industry Preferences:** Medical and health. **Geographic Preferences:** Minnesota.

61693 ■ Artesian Capital
1550 Utica Ave., S.
Saint Louis Park, MN 55416
Ph:(952)738-9388
Fax: (952)345-0303
URL: http://www.artesian.com
Contact: Frank Bennett, President
Preferred Investment Size: $300,000 to $500,000. **Investment Types:** Seed, start-up, second stage, research and development, and leveraged buyout. **Industry Preferences:** Communications and media, medical and media, industrial and energy. **Geographic Preferences:** Midwest.

61694 ■ Bluestream Ventures
225 S. 6th St., Ste. 4350
Minneapolis, MN 55402

Ph:(612)333-8110
Fax: (612)766-4040
URL: http://www.bluestreamventures.com
Contact: John Orcutt, Venture Partner
Preferred Investment Size: $1,000,000 to $10,000,000. **Investment Types:** Early, second, and later stage, and expansion. **Industry Preferences:** Communications, computer software, Internet specific, semiconductors and other electronics. **Geographic Preferences:** U.S.

61695 ■ Cherry Tree Investments, Inc.
301 Carlson Pky., Ste. 103
Minnetonka, MN 55305
Ph:(952)893-9012
Fax: (952)893-9036
URL: http://www.cherrytree.com
Contact: Charles Gorman, Managing Director
Preferred Investment Size: $250,000 to $1,000,000. **Investment Types:** Start-up, early, first and second, and later stage, management buyouts, mezzanine, special situation, turnaround, private placement, and recapitalizations. **Industry Preferences:** Communications, computer hardware and software, Internet specific, semiconductors and other electronics, biotechnology, medical and health, consumer related, financial services, business service, agriculture, forestry and fishing. **Geographic Preferences:** Midwest.

61696 ■ Coral Ventures
60 S. 6th St., Ste. 3510
Minneapolis, MN 55402
Ph:(612)335-8666
Fax: (612)335-8668
URL: http://www.coralventures.com
Contact: Peter McNerney, Managing Partner
Preferred Investment Size: $1,000,000 to $10,000,000. **Investment Types:** Seed, start-up, early, first and second stage, and balanced. **Industry Preferences:** Communications and media, medical and media, computer software, hardware and services, Internet specific, biotechnology, semiconductors and other electronics, industrial and energy, and consumer related. **Geographic Preferences:** U.S.

61697 ■ Crescendo Venture Management, LLC (Minneapolis)
800 LaSalle Ave., Ste. 2250
Minneapolis, MN 55402
Ph:(612)607-2800
Fax: (612)607-2801
URL: http://www.crescendoventures.com
Contact: David Spreng, Managing General Partner
Preferred Investment Size: $5,000,000 to $30,000,000. **Investment Types:** Start-up, seed, first and early stage. **Industry Preferences:** Internet specific, communications and media, semiconductors and other electronics, other products, computer hardware, computer software and services, medical and health, biotechnology, industrial and energy. **Geographic Preferences:** U.S.

61698 ■ Development Corp. of Austin
1900 Eighth Ave., NW
Austin, MN 55912
Ph:(507)433-0346
Fax: (507)433-0361
Co. E-mail: dca@smig.net
URL: http://www.spamtownusa.com
Preferred Investment Size: $100,000. **Investment Types:** Start-up, seed, and first stage. **Industry Preferences:** Diversified. **Geographic Preferences:** No preference.

61699 ■ The Food Fund, Ltd. Partnership
5720 Smatana Dr., Ste. 300
Minnetonka, MN 55343
Ph:(612)939-3950
Fax: (612)939-8106
Contact: John Trucano, General Partner
Preferred Investment Size: $800,000 minimum. **Investment Types:** Start-up, first and second stage, leveraged buyout, and special situation. **Industry Preferences:** Consumer related, industrial and energy, semiconductors and other electronics. **Geographic Preferences:** U.S.

61700 ■ Gideon Hixon Fund
1900 Foshay Tower
821 Marquette Ave.
Minneapolis, MN 55402
Ph:(612)904-2314
Fax: (612)204-0913
Contact: Benson Whitney, Managing Partner
Preferred Investment Size: $300,000 to $500,000.
Investment Policies: Start-up, seed, first and second
stage. **Industry Preferences:** Internet specific, medical and health, computer software and services, other
products, and semiconductors and other electronics.
Geographic Preferences: West Coast.

61701 ■ Gideon Hixon Venture
1900 Foshay Tower
821 Marquette Ave.
Minneapolis, MN 55402
Ph:(612)904-2314
Fax: (612)204-0913
Preferred Investment Size: $300,000 to $500,000.
Investment Types: Start-up, seed, first and second
stage. **Industry Preferences:** Internet specific, medical and health, computer software and services, other
products, semiconductors and other electronics. **Geographic Preferences:** West Coast.

61702 ■ Mayo Medical Ventures
200 First St. SW
Rochester, MN 55905
Ph:(507)284-2511
Fax: (507)284-5410
URL: http://www.mayo.edu
Preferred Investment Size: $250,000 to $1,000,000.
Investment Types: Seed and early stage. **Industry
Preferences:** Biotechnology, medical and health, Internet specific, industrial and energy. **Geographic
Preferences:** U.S.

61703 ■ Medical Innovation Partners
610 Menke Ave.
Shakopee, MN 55344-3245
Ph:(952)828-9616
Fax: (952)828-9596
Contact: Mark Knudson, Managing Partner
Preferred Investment Size: $100,000 minimum. **Investment Types:** Seed, early stage, and research
and development. **Industry Preferences:** Communications and media, medical and health, biotechnology, other products, computer software and services.
Geographic Preferences: Midwest.

61704 ■ Northeast Ventures Corporation
747 Sellwood Bldg.
202 W. Superior
Duluth, MN 55802
Ph:(218)722-9915
Fax: (218)722-9871
Contact: Mark Phillips, Vice President
Preferred Investment Size: $100,000 to $500,000.
Investment Types: Seed, start-up, first and second
stage, mezzanine, leveraged buyout, and research
and development. **Industry Preferences:** Other products, semiconductors and other electronics, computer
software and services, medical and health, communications and media, and consumer related. **Geographic Preferences:** Midwest.

61705 ■ Norwest Equity Partners
80 S. 8th St., Ste. 3600
Minneapolis, MN 55402
Ph:(612)215-1600
Fax: (612)215-1601
URL: http://www.norwestvp.com
Contact: Dorian Faust, Principal
Preferred Investment Size: $10,000,000 to
$60,000,000. **Investment Types:** Expansion, later
stage, acquisition, leveraged buyout, management
buyouts, mezzanine, and recapitalizations. **Industry
Preferences:** Computer software and services, communications and media, consumer related, industrial
and energy, manufacturing, and business service.
Geographic Preferences: U.S.

**61706 ■ Oak Investment Partners
(Minneapolis)**
4550 Wells Fargo Ctr.
90 S. 7th St.
Minneapolis, MN 55402

Ph:(612)339-9322
Fax: (612)337-8017
URL: http://www.oakvc.com
Contact: Scot Javis, Venture Partner
Preferred Investment Size: $1,000,000 to
$60,000,000. **Investment Types:** Balanced, expansion, later stage, management buyouts, private placement, and special situation. **Industry Preferences:**
Communications and media, Internet specific, computer software and services, semiconductors and
other electronics, consumer related, computer hardware, other products, medical and health, biotechnology, industrial and energy. **Geographic Preferences:**
U.S.

**61707 ■ Pathfinder Venture Capital Funds
(Minneapolis)**
7300 Metro Blvd., Ste. 585
Minneapolis, MN 55439
Ph:(612)835-1121
Fax: (612)835-8389
Preferred Investment Size: $2,000,000 minimum.
Investment Types: Seed, start-up, first and second
stage, mezzanine, leveraged buyout, and special situation. **Industry Preferences:** Medical and health,
computer hardware, semiconductors and other electronics, other products, consumer software and services, Internet specific, communications and media,
biotechnology, industrial and energy, and consumer
related. **Geographic Preferences:** U.S. and Canada.

61708 ■ St. Paul Venture Capital, Inc.
10400 Viking Dr., Ste. 550
Eden Prairie, MN 55344
Ph:(952)995-7474
Fax: (952)995-7475
URL: http://www.stpaulvc.com
Contact: Alex Tosheff, Venture Partner
Preferred Investment Size: $2,000,000 to
$40,000,000. **Investment Types:** Early stage. **Industry Preferences:** Internet specific, computer software
and services, communications and media, medical
and health, consumer related, computer hardware,
semiconductors and other electronics, biotechnology,
other products, industrial and energy. **Geographic
Preferences:** California, Massachusetts, and Minnesota.

61709 ■ Shared Ventures, Inc.
6550 York Ave. S.
Edina, MN 55435
Ph:(612)925-3411
Contact: Howard Weiner
Preferred Investment Size: $100,000 to $300,000.
Investment Types: First and second stage, start-up,
leveraged buyout, control-block purchases, and special situation. **Industry Preferences:** Semiconductors
and other electronics, medical and health, consumer
related, industrial and energy, agriculture, forestry and
fishing. **Geographic Preferences:** Midwest.

61710 ■ Sherpa Partners LLC
5050 Lincoln Dr., Ste. 490
Edina, MN 55436
Ph:(952)942-1070
Fax: (952)942-1071
URL: http://www.sherpapartners.com
Contact: Richard Brimacomb, Partner
Preferred Investment Size: $250,000 to $2,000,000.
Investment Types: Seed, start-up, early and first
stage. **Industry Preferences:** Communications and
media, computer software, semiconductors and other
electronics. **Geographic Preferences:** Midwest and
Minnesota.

**61711 ■ U.S. Bancorp Piper Jaffray Private
Capital**
800 Nicollet Mall, Ste. 800
Minneapolis, MN 55402
Ph:(612)303-6000
Fax: (612)303-1350
URL: http://www.piperjaffrey.com
Contact: Barry Nordstrand, Managing Director
Investment Types: Fund of funds, and leveraged
buyout. **Geographic Preferences:** U.S.

PROCUREMENT ASSISTANCE PROGRAMS

**61712 ■ Metropolitan Economic Development
Association (MEDA)–Procurement Techical
Assistance Center**
250 2nd Ave. S, Ste. 106
Minneapolis, MN 55401
Ph:(612)332-6332
Fax: (612)317-1002
Co. E-mail: gjohnson@meda.net
URL: http://www.meda.net
Contact: George Johnson, Dir
E-mail: gjohnson@mpi.org

**61713 ■ Minnesota Procurement Technical
Assistance Center–Metropolitan Economic
Development Association (MEDA)**
250 2nd Ave. S, Ste. 106
Minneapolis, MN 55401
Ph:(612)259-6581
Fax: (612)317-1002
Co. E-mail: rmcqee@meda.net
URL: http://www.meda.net
Contact: Rodney McGee, Mgr
E-mail: rmcgee@mpi.org

**61714 ■ Minnesota Procurement Technical
Assistance Center–Minnesota Project
Innovation, Inc.**
250 2nd Ave. S, Ste 106
Minneapolis, MN 55401
Ph:(612)332-6332
Fax: (612)317-1002
URL: http://www.ptac-meda.net
Contact: Liz Receptionist, Receptionist

**61715 ■ Minnesota Procurement Technical
Assistance Center–Minnesota Project
Innovation, Inc.–Hennepin Technical College
(250 S)**
250 Second Ave. S, Ste. 106
Minneapolis, MN 55401-2551
Ph:(612)338-3280
Fax: (612)349-2603
Co. E-mail: bnelson@mpi.org
URL: http://www.mpi.org
Contact: Rodney McGee
E-mail: tcallen@mpi.org

INCUBATORS/RESEARCH AND TECHNOLOGY PARKS

61716 ■ Ceridian Corp.
3311 East Old Shakopee
Minneapolis, MN 55425
Ph:(952)853-8100
URL: http://www.ceridian.com
Contact: Ron Turner, CEO

61717 ■ Genesis Business Centers, Ltd.
3989 Central Ave. NE, Ste. 630
Columbia Heights, MN 55421
Ph:(763)782-8576
Fax: (763)782-8578
Co. E-mail: harlanjacobs@genesiscenters.com
URL: http://www.genesiscenters.com
Contact: Harlan Jacobs, Pres
Description: An incubator specially designed for
emerging high-tech businesses.

61718 ■ Time Share Systems
511 11th Ave.
Minneapolis, MN 55415
Ph:(612)332-2071
Fax: (612)332-2249

**61719 ■ University of Minnesota–Center for
the Development of Technological
Leadership**
Institute of Technology
1300 S 2nd St., Ste. 510
Minneapolis, MN 55454

Ph:(612)624-5747
Fax: (612)624-7510
Co. E-mail: amin-cdtl@umn.edu
URL: http://www.cdtl.umn.edu/
Contact: Dr. Massoud Amin, Dir.
E-mail: amin-cdtl@umn.edu
Scope: Issues in the management of technology and technology forecasting. **Services:** Consulting, in areas of innovation, technology foresight, intellectual property management for technology-intensive companies; Technical services, in global transition dynamics to enhance resilience, security, and efficiency of national critical infrastructures. **Publications:** Management of Technology follow-up study; Miscellaneous reports; Newsletter. **Educational Activities:** Annual Technology Futures Forum; Short courses and seminars.

61720 ■ University of Minnesota–Office of Sponsored Projects Administration
450 McNamara Alumni Center
200 Oak St. SE
Minneapolis, MN 55455
Ph:(612)624-5599
Fax: (612)624-4843
Co. E-mail: ewink@umn.edu
URL: http://www.ospa.umn.edu
Contact: Edward F. Wink, Assoc.VP
E-mail: ewink@umn.edu
Scope: Serves as the research support unit for University of Minnesota faculty members by administering non-programmatic aspects of all research, training, and public service projects funded by external sources. Reviews and processes all proposals and awards for research, training, and public service projects. **Publications:** Research Review Newsletter.

61721 ■ University of Minnesota–Office for Technology Commercialization
1000 W Gate Dr., Ste. 160
St. Paul, MN 55114-8658
Ph:(612)624-0550
Fax: (612)624-6554
Co. E-mail: umotc@umn.edu
URL: http://www.research.umn.edu/techcomm
Contact: Michael F. Moore
E-mail: umotc@umn.edu
Scope: Transfers technology from the University to business and industry in the areas of health sciences, engineering, biotechnology, and agriculture. **Educational Activities:** Paid internships in technology evaluation and marketing.

61722 ■ University Technology Center (Minneapolis)
1313 5th St. SE
Minneapolis, MN 55414
Ph:(612)379-3800
Fax: (612)379-3875

EDUCATIONAL PROGRAMS

61723 ■ Alexandria Technical College
1601 Jefferson St.
Alexandria, MN 56308
Ph:(320)762-0221
Free: 888-234-1222
Fax: (320)762-4501
URL: http://www.alextech.org
Description: Trade and technical school offering a program in small business management.

61724 ■ Central Lakes College
501 W College Dr.
Brainerd, MN 56401
Ph:(218)855-8000
Free: 800-933-0346
Fax: (218)855-8220
URL: http://www.clc.mnscu.edu
Description: Trade and technical school offering a program in entrepreneurship and small business management.

61725 ■ Hibbing Community College
1515 E 25th St.
Hibbing, MN 55746

Ph:(218)262-7200
Free: 800-224-4422
Fax: (218)262-6717
Co. E-mail: admissions@hibbing.edu
URL: http://www.hibbing.edu
Description: Vocational school offering a small business management program.

61726 ■ Minneapolis Community and Technical College–Business Management Program
1501 Hennepin Ave. S
Minneapolis, MN 55403-1778
Ph:(612)659-6000
Free: 800-247-0911
Fax: (612)359-1357
URL: http://www.mctc.mnscu.edu
Description: Offers long-term instruction at an individual's place of business. Conducts seminars and individualized instruction to improve the management skills of prospective and current business owners.

61727 ■ Minnesota Small Business Management Program
State Board of Technical Colleges
700 World Trade Center
30 E 7th Street
St. Paul, MN 55101
Ph:(651)296-2600
Fax: (651)296-3214
URL: http://www.nnsau.edu
Description: Offers small business owners education through technical institutes in individualized or group sessions. Topics include business planning, record systems, financial analysis, marketing, inventory management, payroll, negotiating for money, computer applications, and others.

61728 ■ Minnesota State Community and Technical College–Detroit Lakes
900 Hwy. 34 E
Detroit Lakes, MN 56501
Ph:(218)846-3700
Free: 800-492-4836
Fax: (218)846-3710
URL: http://www.minnesota.edu
Description: Trade and technical school offering a program in small business management.

61729 ■ Minnesota State Community and Technical College–Fergus Falls
1414 College Way
Fergus Falls, MN 56537
Ph:(218)736-1500
Free: 877-450-3322
Fax: (218)736-1510
URL: http://www.minnesota.edu
Description: Two-year college offering a small business management program.

61730 ■ Minnesota West Community & Technical College
1314 N Hiawatha Ave.
PO Box 250
Pipestone, MN 56164-0250
Ph:800-658-2330
Free: 800-658-2330
Fax: (507)825-4656
URL: http://www.mnwest.mnscu.edu
Description: Vocational school offering a small business management program.

61731 ■ Normandale Community College
9700 France Ave. S
Bloomington, MN 55431
Ph:(952)487-8200
Free: (886)880-8740
Fax: (612)832-6571
URL: http://www.nr.cc.mn.us
Description: Two-year college offering a business and marketing management program, covering management skills, cash management, and marketing techniques used in business.

LEGISLATIVE ASSISTANCE

61732 ■ Minnesota Technology, Inc. –Minnesota Department of Trade and Economic Development Center
111 3rd Ave., S Ste. 120
Minneapolis, MN 55401
Ph:(612)373-2900
Free: 800-325-3073
Fax: (612)373-2901
URL: http://www.minnesotatechnology.org/
Description: Coordinates and develops technology initiatives and policy recommendations. Advises the legislature, the governor, and the commissioner of trade and economic development on the state's science and technology policy.

PUBLICATIONS

61733 ■ *Smart Start your Arkansas Business*
PSI Research
300 N. Valley Dr.
Grants Pass, OR 97526
Ph:(503)479-9464
Free: 800-228-2275
Fax: (503)476-1479
Co. E-mail: info@psi-research.com
URL: http://www.psi-research.com
Ed: Michael D. Jenkins. **Released:** Revised edition, 1992. **Price:** $29.95 (looseleaf binder); $24.95 (paper). **Description:** Part of the Successful Business Library series.

PUBLISHERS

61734 ■ American Institute of Small Business
426 2nd St.
Excelsior, MN 55331
Ph:(952)545-7001
Free: 800-328-2906
Fax: (952)545-7020
Co. E-mail: info@aisb.biz
URL: http://www.aisb.biz/
Contact: Kris Solie Johnson, President
Description: Publishes books on setting up a small business and entrepreneurship. Offers a bimonthly newsletter, video cassettes, and software packages. Accepts unsolicited manuscripts. Reaches market through direct mail, trade sales, telephone sales, wholesalers and distributors. **Founded:** 1984.

61735 ■ Expert Publishing Inc.
14314 Thrush St. NW
Andover, MN 55304
Ph:(763)755-4966
Co. E-mail: harry@expertpublishinginc.com
URL: http://www.expertpublishinginc.com
Contact: Sharron Stockhausen, CEO
Description: Publishes nonfiction titles on subjects such as business.

61736 ■ Little Leaf Press Inc.
1089 Suburban Ave.
Saint Paul, MN 55106
Ph:(651)774-3770
Free: 877-548-2431
Co. E-mail: littleleaf@maxminn.com
URL: http://www.littleleafpress.com
Contact: Beth E. Koch-Blasczyk, CEO
E-mail: bethkoch@msn.com
Description: Publishes children's, history, hobby, and academic books. Accept works from uniquely talented, aspiring authors. Also distributes for Conal & Gavin. Books included are *Pelican's Belly Can*, *Remembering Armegeddon*, and *Dulcimer Building Start to Finish*. Accepts unsolicited manuscripts. Reaches market through direct mail, telephone sales, wholesalers and distributors, including Ingram, The BookMen, Inc., Quality books, Inc., Barnes & Noble, Inc., Amazon.com, Internet, catalogs, premium sales, libraries, bookstores, and museums. **Founded:** 1998.

61737 ■ Nasus Publishing
PO Box 641
Prior Lake, MN 55372
Ph:(952)484-4262
Fax: (952)226-1419
Co. E-mail: nasuspublishing@successideas.com
URL: http://www.successideas.com/
Contact: Susan Carter
E-mail: susancarter@successideas.com

Description: Publishes books aimed to help small business owners "do more with less." Also publishes an online ezine.

61738 ■ Thomson Legal & Regulatory
610 Opperman Dr.
Eagan, MN 55123
Ph:(651)687-7000
Free: 800-328-9378
Co. E-mail: tlrcorporate.communications@thomson.com

URL: http://www.thomson.com
Contact: Brian H. Hall, CEO & Pres
Description: "Thomson Legal & Regulatory is a leading provider of integrated information solutions to legal, tax, accounting, intellectual property, compliance, business and government professionals around the world." Among the flagship legal and regulatory solutions are: Elite, FindLaw, Karnov, La Ley Online, and ProLaw.

SMALL BUSINESS DEVELOPMENT CENTER LEAD OFFICE

61739 ■ Mississippi SBDC–University of Mississippi
B-19 Jeanette Phillips Dr.
PO Box 1848
University, MS 38677
Ph:(662)915-5001
Fax: (662)915-5650
URL: http://olemiss.edu/depts./mssbdc
Contact: Doug Gurley Jr., State Dir.
E-mail: wgurley@olemiss.edu

61740 ■ University of Mississippi–Small Business Development Center
B-19 Jeanette Phillips Dr.
PO Box 1848
University, MS 38677-1848
Ph:(601)232-5001
Free: 800-725-7232
Fax: (601)232-5650
Co. E-mail: msbdc@olemiss.edu
URL: http://www.olemiss.edu/depts/mssbdc
Contact: Walter "Doug" Gurley Jr., Director
E-mail: wgurley@olemiss.edu

SMALL BUSINESS DEVELOPMENT CENTERS

61741 ■ Alcorn State University–SBDC
1000 ASU Dr.
PO Box 90
Lorman, MS 39096
Ph:(601)877-6684
Fax: (601)877-3900
Contact: Sharon Witty, Dir.
E-mail: sawitty@lorman.alcorn.edu

61742 ■ Copiah-Lincoln Community College–Small Business Development Center
11 Co-Lin Circle
Natchez, MS 39120-4452
Ph:(601)446-1254
Fax: (601)446-1221
Co. E-mail: sbdc@colin.edu
URL: http://www.colin.edu/workforceed/SBDC
Contact: Jeff Waller, Dir.
E-mail: jeff.waller@colin.edu

61743 ■ Delta State University–SBDC Business Assistance Center–Greenville Higher Education Center (2900)
2900 A Highway 1 S.
Greenville, MS 38701
Ph:(662)378-8589
Co. E-mail: astout@deltastate.edu

61744 ■ Delta State University–Small Business Development Center
PO Box 3235 DSU
Broom Hall 271
Cleveland, MS 38733-0002
Ph:(662)846-4236
Fax: (662)846-4235
Co. E-mail: dsusbdc@deltastate.edu
URL: http://deltast.edu/pages/294.asp
Contact: Betty Mixon, Sec.
E-mail: bmixon@deltastate.edu

61745 ■ Delta State University Business Assistance Center–Coahoma Co. Higher Education Center
Clarksdale, MS 38614
Ph:(662)627-2930
Contact: Donald Brown, Counselor
E-mail: djuan76@hotmail.com

61746 ■ East Central Community College–SBDC
275 Broad St.
PO Box 129
Decatur, MS 39327-0129
Ph:(601)635-2111
Fax: (601)635-4031
Co. E-mail: sbdc@eccc.edu
URL: http://www.eccc.edu/sbdc/
Contact: Ronald Westbrook, Dir.
E-mail: rwestbrook@eccc.edu

61747 ■ Gulf Coast SBDC
Hancock Chamber of Commerce
412 Hwy. 90, Ste. 6
Bay St. Louis, MS 39520
Ph:(228)466-9145
Fax: (228)467-6033
Co. E-mail: gcsbdc@olemiss.edu
Contact: Teresa Speir, Interim Dir.
E-mail: taspeir@olemiss.edu

61748 ■ Hinds Community College–SBDC Business Assistance Center at Pearl
Rankin Campus
3805 Hwy. 80E
Pearl, MS 39208
Ph:(601)936-1817
Contact: James Bennett, Counselor
E-mail: jbbennett@hindscc.edu

61749 ■ Hinds Community College–Small Business Development Center/International Trade Center
1500 Raymond Lake Rd., 3rd Fl.
PO Box 1100
Raymond, MS 39154-1100
Ph:(601)857-3536
Fax: (601)857-3474
Co. E-mail: sbdc@hindscc.edu
URL: http://www.hindscc.edu/Departments/RCU/SBDC-ITC/
Contact: James Harper, Dir.
E-mail: jeharper@hindscc.edu

61750 ■ Holmes Community College–SBDC
413 W. Ridgeland Ave.
Ridgeland, MS 39157-1518
Ph:(601)835-0827
Fax: (601)853-0844
Contact: John Deddens, Dir.
E-mail: jdeddens@holmes.cc.ms.us

61751 ■ Itawamba Community College–Small Business Development Center
2176 S. Eason Blvd.
Tupelo, MS 38801
Ph:(662)871-1588
Contact: Frank Wiebe, Counselor
E-mail: fawiebe@olemiss.edu

61752 ■ Jackson State University–Small Business Development Center
JSU Mississippi E-Center
1230 Raymond Rd.
Box 500
Jackson, MS 39204
Ph:(601)979-2795
Fax: (601)914-0833
Co. E-mail: jsusbdc@jsums.edu
URL: http://www.jsums.edu/bnusiness/sbdc/index.shtml
Contact: Henry Thomas, Dir.
E-mail: bbreazea@ccaix.jsums.edu

61753 ■ Jones County Junior College–SBDC
900 S. Court St.
Ellisville, MS 39437-3901
Ph:(601)477-4235
Fax: (601)477-4239
Co. E-mail: sbdc@jcjc.edu
URL: http://www.jcjc.edu/depts/sbdc/index.htm
Contact: Greg Butler, Dir.
E-mail: greg.butler@jcjc.edu

61754 ■ Mississippi Contract Procurement Center–SBDC
1636 Popps Ferry Rd., Ste. 229
Biloxi, MS 39532
Ph:(601)396-1288
Fax: (601)396-2520
Co. E-mail: mprogoff@aol.com
Contact: Richard Speights, Exec.Dir.

61755 ■ Mississippi Delta Community College–Small Business Development Center
1656 E. Union
PO Box 5607
Greenville, MS 38704-5607
Ph:(601)378-8183
Fax: (601)378-5349
Co. E-mail: mdccsbdc@tecinfo.com
Contact: Chuck Herring, Dir.

61756 ■ Mississippi Gulf Coast Community College–SBDC
Jackson County Campus
2300 Hwy. 90
PO Box 100
Gautier, MS 39553-5298
Ph:(601)497-7723

Fax: (601)497-7788
Contact: Janice Mabry, Dir.
E-mail: janice.mabry@mgccc.cc.ms.us

61757 ■ Mississippi State University–Small Business Development Center
1 Research Blvd., Ste 201
PO Drawer 5288
Mississippi State, MS 39762-5288
Ph:(662)325-8684
Fax: (662)325-4016
Co. E-mail: sbdc@cobilan.msstate.edu
URL: http://www.cbi.msstate.edu/cobi/sbdc/sbdc.html
Contact: Sonny Fisher, Dir.
E-mail: sfisher@cobilan.msstate.edu

61758 ■ Mississippi Valley State University–Affiliate SBDC
14000 Hwy. 82 W.
Itta Bena, MS 38941
Ph:(601)254-3601
Fax: (601)254-3600
Contact: Jim Breyley, Dir.
E-mail: jbreyley@fielding.mvsu.edu

61759 ■ MSU SBDC Business Assistance Center–Meridian Community College at Webb Center
910 Hwy. 19 N.
Meridian, MS 39307
Ph:(601)482-0602
Fax: (601)482-5803
Contact: Doc Braswell, Counselor
E-mail: dbraswell@mcc.cc.ms.us

61760 ■ Northeast Mississippi Community College–SBDC
Holliday Hall, Rm. 315
101 Cunningham Blvd.
Booneville, MS 38829-1700
Ph:(662)720-7448
Contact: Katie Drewry, Counselor
E-mail: kcdrewry@olemiss.edu

61761 ■ Northwest Mississippi Community College–SBDC
DeSoto Ctr.
5197 W.E. Ross Pkwy., Rm. 208
Southaven, MS 38671-8403
Ph:(601)280-1421
Fax: (601)342-7648
Co. E-mail: smbusdev@nwcc.cc.ms.us
Contact: Jody Dunning, Dir.
E-mail: jodydunning@hotmail.com

61762 ■ Pearl River Community College–Small Business Development Center
5448 U.S. Hwy. 49 S.
Hattiesburg, MS 39401-7806
Ph:(601)544-9133
Fax: (601)544-9149
Contact: Heidi McDuffe, Dir.
E-mail: hmcduffe@prcc.cc.ms.us

61763 ■ Southwest Mississippi Community College–SBDC
College Dr.
Summit, MS 39666-1036
Ph:(601)276-3890
Fax: (601)276-3883
Co. E-mail: sbdc@bears.smcc.cc.ms.us
Contact: Sissy Whittington, Dir.

61764 ■ University of Southern Mississippi–Small Business Development Center
136 Beach Park Pl.
Long Beach, MS 39560-2699
Ph:(601)865-4578
Fax: (601)865-4581
Contact: Lucy Betcher, Dir.
E-mail: lbetcher@medea.gp.usm.edu

SMALL BUSINESS ASSISTANCE PROGRAMS

61765 ■ Mississippi Development Authority–Mississippi Department of Economic and Community Development
501 NW St.
PO Box 849
Jackson, MS 39201
Ph:(601)359-3593
Fax: (601)359-2832
URL: http://www.mississippi.org
Description: Provides assistance to the state's businesses and industries, including loans and loan guarantees to small businesses, and an outreach program.

61766 ■ Mississippi Enterprise for Technology–Mississippi Technology Transfer Office
John C. Stennis Space Center, Bldg. 1103, Rm. 143
Stennis Space Center, MS 39529-6000
Ph:(228)688-3144
Fax: (228)688-1064
URL: http://www.mset.org
Contact: Greg Hinkebein, Pres & CEO
Description: Helps advanced technology companies locate or expand in Mississippi.

61767 ■ Mississippi University for Women–Career Services
218 Hogarth
1100 College St., MUW-1624
Columbus, MS 39701
Ph:(662)241-7619
Fax: (662)329-9192
Co. E-mail: dre,u@muw.edu
URL: http://www.muw.edu/career
Contact: Towanda Williams, Asst Dir

SCORE OFFICES

61768 ■ SCORE Delta
c/o Bess Hicks Condon, CHR
Greenville Chamber/915 Washington A
P.O. Drawer 933
Greenville, MS 38702
Ph:(662)378-3141
Fax: (662)378-3143
URL: http://www.score.org

61769 ■ SCORE Gulfcoast
Hancock Bank Plz.
2510 14th St., Ste. 101-A
Gulfport, MS 39501
Ph:(228)863-0054
Co. E-mail: scoregulfportv@peoplepc.com
URL: http://www.score.org
Contact: Dave Philo, Chm.
Description: Provides public service to America by offering small business advice and training.

BETTER BUSINESS BUREAUS

61770 ■ Better Business Bureau of Mississippi
PO Box 3302
Ridgeland, MS 39158
Ph:(601)977-1020
Free: 800-987-8280
Fax: (601)997-0704
Co. E-mail: info@bbbmississippi.org
URL: http://www.bbbmississippi.org
Contact: Bill Moak, Pres./CEO

CHAMBERS OF COMMERCE

61771 ■ Area Development Partnership
One Convention Ctr. Plz.
PO Box 751
Hattiesburg, MS 39401
Ph:(601)296-7500
Free: 800-238-4288
Fax: (601)296-7505
Co. E-mail: adp@theadp.com
URL: http://www.theadp.com
Contact: Dr. Angie Dvorak, Pres.

61772 ■ Baldwyn Area Chamber of Commerce
PO Box D
Baldwyn, MS 38824
Ph:(662)365-1050
Fax: (662)365-2387
Co. E-mail: chamber@baldwyn.ms
URL: http://www.baldwyn.ms
Contact: Hilary Hamblin, Exec.Dir.

61773 ■ Belzoni - Humphreys Development Foundation
111 Magnolia St.
PO Box 145
Belzoni, MS 39038
Ph:(662)962-3101
Free: 800-408-4838
Co. E-mail: catfish@catfishcapitalonline.com
URL: http://www.catfishcapitalonline.com
Contact: Lee Parker, Pres.

61774 ■ Biloxi Bay Chamber of Commerce
PO Box 889
Biloxi, MS 39533-0889
Ph:(228)435-6149
Fax: (228)435-6334
Co. E-mail: info@biloxibaychamber.com
Contact: Susan Hunt, Exec.Dir.

61775 ■ Biloxi Chamber of Commerce
12284 Intraplex Pkwy.
Gulfport, MS 39503
Ph:(228)604-0014
Fax: (228)374-2764
Co. E-mail: exec@biloxi.org
URL: http://www.biloxi.org
Contact: Kimberly Nastasi Crim, Exec.Dir.

61776 ■ Booneville Area Chamber of Commerce
100 W Church St.
Booneville, MS 38829
Ph:(662)728-4130
Free: 800-300-9302
Fax: (662)728-4134
Co. E-mail: rgreening@boonevillemississippi.com
URL: http://boonevillemississippi.com
Contact: Rhonda Greening, Exec.Dir.

61777 ■ Brookhaven - Lincoln County Chamber of Commerce
230 S Whitworth Ave.
PO Box 978
Brookhaven, MS 39602-0978
Ph:(601)833-1411
Free: 800-613-4667
Fax: (601)833-1412
Co. E-mail: chb@brookhavenchamber.com
URL: http://www.brookhavenchamber.com
Contact: Cliff Brumfield, Exec.VP

61778 ■ Bruce Chamber of Commerce
North Side of the Square
PO Box 1013
Bruce, MS 38915
Ph:(662)983-2222
Fax: (662)983-7300
Co. E-mail: chamber@brucetelephone.com
Contact: Faye Morris, Exec.Sec.

61779 ■ Calhoun City Chamber of Commerce
102 S Monroe St.
PO Box 161
Calhoun City, MS 38916-0161

Ph:(662)628-6990
Fax: (662)628-8931
URL: http://www.calhouncity.net
Contact: James Franklin, Pres.

61780 ■ Canton Chamber of Commerce
PO Box 74
Canton, MS 39046-0074
Ph:(601)859-5816
Fax: (601)855-0149
Co. E-mail: ccoc@canton-mississippi.com
URL: http://www.canton-mississippi.com
Contact: Deborah Anderson, Exec.Dir.

61781 ■ City of Ridgeland Chamber of Commerce
754 Pear Orchard Rd.
PO Box 194
Ridgeland, MS 39158-0194
Ph:(601)991-9996
Fax: (601)991-9997
Co. E-mail: admin@ridgelandchamber.com
URL: http://www.ridgelandchamber.com
Contact: Linda T. Bynum, Exec.Dir.

61782 ■ Clarke County Chamber of Commerce
PO Box 172
Quitman, MS 39355-0172
Ph:(601)776-5701
Fax: (601)776-5745
Co. E-mail: clarkech@netpathway.com
URL: http://www.netpathway.com/~clarkech
Contact: Patty Combest, Sec.

61783 ■ Clarksdale - Coahoma County Chamber of Commerce and Industry Foundation
PO Box 160
Clarksdale, MS 38614
Ph:(662)627-7337
Free: 800-626-3764
Fax: (662)627-1313
Co. E-mail: chamberofcommerce@clarksdale-ms. com
URL: http://www.clarksdale.com/chamber
Contact: Ronald E. Hudson, Exec.Dir.

61784 ■ Cleveland-Bolivar County Chamber of Commerce
600 3rd St.
PO Box 490
Cleveland, MS 38732
Ph:(662)843-2712
Fax: (662)843-2718
Co. E-mail: jthigpen@cableone.net
URL: http://www.clevelandmschamber.com
Contact: Judson Thigpen, Exec.Dir.

61785 ■ Clinton Chamber of Commerce
100 E Leake
PO Box 143
Clinton, MS 39060-0143
Ph:(601)924-5912
Free: 800-611-9980
Fax: (601)925-4009
Co. E-mail: info@clintonchamber.org
URL: http://www.clintonchamber.org
Contact: Dianne Newman, Exec.Dir.

61786 ■ Columbus-Lowndes Chamber of Commerce
318 7th St. N, Ste. A
PO Box 1016
Columbus, MS 39703-1016
Ph:(662)328-4491
Free: 800-232-8990
Fax: (662)327-0976
Co. E-mail: chamber@columbusmississippi.com
Contact: Jay Jordan, Chm.

61787 ■ Community Development Foundation
300 W Main St.
PO Box A
Tupelo, MS 38802-1210
Ph:(662)842-4521

Free: 800-523-3463
Fax: (601)841-0693
Co. E-mail: info@cdfms.org
URL: http://www.cdfms.org
Contact: David P. Rumbarger, Pres./CEO

61788 ■ Community Development Partnership
PO Box 330
Philadelphia, MS 39350
Ph:(601)656-1000
Fax: (601)656-1066
Co. E-mail: info@neshoba.org
URL: http://www.neshoba.org
Contact: David Vowell, Pres.

61789 ■ Covington County Chamber of Commerce
PO Box 1595
Collins, MS 39428-1595
Ph:(601)765-6012
Fax: (601)765-1740
Co. E-mail: contact@covingtonchamber.com
URL: http://www.covingtonchamber.com
Contact: Marie Shoemake, Exec.Dir.

61790 ■ Crystal Springs Chamber of Commerce
210 E Railroad Ave.
PO Box 519
Crystal Springs, MS 39059-0519
Ph:(601)892-2711
Fax: (601)892-4870
Co. E-mail: cschamber@bellsouth.net
Contact: Donna Y. Wells, Exec.Dir.

61791 ■ D'Iberville-St. Martin Chamber of Commerce
PO Box 6054
Diberville, MS 39540
Ph:(228)392-2293
Fax: (228)396-3216
URL: http://www.dsmchamber.com
Contact: Sharon Seymour, Exec. Dir.

61792 ■ Forest Area Chamber of Commerce
120 S Davis St.
PO Box 266
Forest, MS 39074
Ph:(601)469-4332
Fax: (601)469-3224
Co. E-mail: chamberguide@mail.localink4.com
Contact: Patsy Nicholson, Exec.Dir.

61793 ■ Greater Picayune Area Chamber of Commerce
201 Hwy. 11 N
PO Box 448
Picayune, MS 39466
Ph:(601)798-3122
Fax: (601)798-3122
Co. E-mail: chamber@datastar.net
URL: http://www.picayunechamber.org
Contact: Claiborne McDonald, Pres.

61794 ■ Greenville Area Chamber of Commerce
915 Washington Ave.
Greenville, MS 38701
Ph:(662)378-3141
Fax: (662)378-3143
Co. E-mail: director@greenvilleareachamber.com
URL: http://www.greenvilleareachamber.com
Contact: Betty Lynn Cameron, Exec.Dir.

61795 ■ Greenwood-Leflore Chamber of Commerce
PO Box 848
Greenwood, MS 38935-0848
Ph:(662)453-4152
Fax: (662)453-8003
Co. E-mail: chmbr5@bellsouth.net
URL: http://www.greenwoodms.com
Contact: Beth Henderson, Exec.VP

61796 ■ Grenada County Chamber of Commerce
PO Box 628
Grenada, MS 38902-0628
Ph:(662)226-2571
Free: 800-373-2571
Fax: (662)226-9745
Co. E-mail: phillipheard@yahoo.com
URL: http://www.grenadamississippi.com
Contact: Phillip Heard, Exec.Dir.

61797 ■ Hancock County Chamber of Commerce
412 Hwy. 90, Ste. 6
Bay St. Louis, MS 39520
Ph:(228)467-9048
Fax: (228)467-6033
Co. E-mail: lynne@hancockchamber.org
URL: http://www.hancockchamber.org
Contact: Ms. Tish Williams, Exec.Dir.

61798 ■ Hernando Area Chamber of Commerce
2465 Hwy., 51 S
Hernando, MS 38632
Ph:(662)429-9055
Fax: (662)429-2909
Co. E-mail: chamber@hernandoms.org
URL: http://www.hernandoms.org
Contact: Brian K. Goff, Exec.Dir.

61799 ■ Holly Springs Chamber of Commerce
148 E College Ave.
Holly Springs, MS 38635
Ph:(662)252-2943
Fax: (662)252-2934
Co. E-mail: hollyspringscc@bellsouth.net
URL: http://www. hollyspringsmschamberofcommerce.org
Contact: Susan Jordan, Exec.Dir.

61800 ■ Horn Lake Chamber of Commerce
3040 Goodman Rd. W, Ste. 2A
Horn Lake, MS 38637
Ph:(662)393-9897
Fax: (662)393-2942
Co. E-mail: info@hornlakechamber.com
URL: http://www.hornlakechamber.com
Contact: Larry Witherspoon, Exec.Dir.

61801 ■ Indianola Chamber of Commerce
PO Box 151
Indianola, MS 38751
Ph:(662)887-4454
Free: 877-816-7581
Fax: (662)887-4454
Co. E-mail: icoc@tecinfo.com
URL: http://www.indianolams.org
Contact: Beth A. Lyon, Mgr.

61802 ■ Itawamba County Development Council
PO Box 577
Fulton, MS 38843
Ph:(662)862-4571
Free: 800-371-8642
Fax: (662)862-5637
Co. E-mail: icdc@nexband.com
URL: http://www.itawamba.com/icdc/icdc_about_us. html
Contact: Ms. Carol Farris Upton, Exec. Dir.

61803 ■ Jackson County Chamber of Commerce
720 Krebs Ave.
PO Box 480
Pascagoula, MS 39568-0480
Ph:(228)762-3391
Fax: (228)769-1726
Co. E-mail: chamber@jcchamber.com
URL: http://www.jcchamber.com
Contact: Carla Todd, Pres./CEO

61804 ■ Jones County Chamber of Commerce
PO Box 527
Laurel, MS 39441-0527

Ph:(601)649-3031
Fax: (601)428-2047
Co. E-mail: info@edajones.com
URL: http://www.edajones.com
Contact: Sandy Holifield, Dir.

61805 ■ Kosciusko-Attala Chamber of Commerce
124 N Jackson St.
Kosciusko, MS 39090
Ph:(662)289-2981
Fax: (662)289-2986
Co. E-mail: kosychamber@yahoo.com
URL: http://www.kosciuskotourism.com
Contact: Willa G. Sanders, Exec.Dir.

61806 ■ Lawrence County Chamber of Commerce
517 E Broad St.
PO Box 996
Monticello, MS 39654
Ph:(601)587-3007
Fax: (601)587-0765
Co. E-mail: info@lawrencecounty.org
URL: http://www.lawrencecounty.org
Contact: Bob Smira, Pres.

61807 ■ Leake County Chamber of Commerce
103 N Pearl St.
PO Box 209
Carthage, MS 39051-0209
Ph:(601)267-9231
Fax: (601)267-8123
Co. E-mail: director@leakems.com
URL: http://www.leakems.com
Contact: Renodda Dorman, Exec.Dir.

61808 ■ Leland Chamber of Commerce
PO Box 67
Leland, MS 38756
Ph:(662)686-2687
Fax: (662)686-2689
Co. E-mail: lcoc@tecinfo.com
URL: http://www.lelandms.com
Contact: Ashley Zepponi, Exec. Dir.

61809 ■ Liberty Area Chamber of Commerce
PO Box 18
Liberty, MS 39645
Ph:(601)657-8077
Contact: Mary Nation, Pres.

61810 ■ Louisville-Winston County Chamber of Commerce
PO Box 551
Louisville, MS 39339
Ph:(662)773-3921
Fax: (662)773-8909
Co. E-mail: info@winstoncounty.com
URL: http://www.winstoncounty.com
Contact: Linda Skelton, Mgr.

61811 ■ Madison Chamber of Commerce
2168 Main St.
PO Box 544
Madison, MS 39130-0544
Ph:(601)856-7060
Free: 800-824-2833
Fax: (601)856-4852
Co. E-mail: info@madisonthecitychamber.com
URL: http://www.madisonthecity.com
Contact: Rosie Vassallo, Exec. Dir.

61812 ■ Magee Chamber of Commerce
117 NW 1st Ave.
Magee, MS 39111-3500
Ph:(601)849-2517
Fax: (601)849-2517
Co. E-mail: mcoc2@juno.com
Contact: Beulah Stephens, Dir.

61813 ■ Marion County Development Partnership
PO Box 272
Columbia, MS 39429
Ph:(601)736-6385

Fax: (601)736-6392
Co. E-mail: info@marionpartnership.org
URL: http://www.marionpartnership.org
Contact: Carolyn Burton, VP

61814 ■ Mendenhall Area Chamber of Commerce
PO Box 635
Mendenhall, MS 39114-0635
Ph:(601)847-1725
Contact: Marsha Bracter, Sec.

61815 ■ MetroJackson Chamber of Commerce
PO Box 22548
Jackson, MS 39225
Ph:(601)948-7575
Fax: (601)352-5539
Co. E-mail: contact@metrochamber.com
URL: http://www.metrochamber.com
Contact: Duane O'Neill, Pres.

61816 ■ Mississippi Gulf Coast Chamber of Commerce
12284 Intraplex Pkwy.
Gulfport, MS 39503
Ph:(228)604-0014
Fax: (228)374-2764
Co. E-mail: ceo@mscoastchamber.com
URL: http://www.mscoastchamber.com
Contact: Kimberly Nastasi Crim, CEO

61817 ■ Monroe County Chamber of Commerce
1619 Hwy. 25 N
PO Box 128
Amory, MS 38821
Ph:(662)256-7194
Fax: (662)256-9671
Co. E-mail: chamber@gomonroe.org
URL: http://www.gomonroe.org
Contact: Stephen Surles, Pres.

61818 ■ Morton Chamber of Commerce
PO Box 530
Morton, MS 39117-0530
Ph:(601)732-6135
Fax: (601)732-7188
Contact: Brenda M. McCaughn, Exec. Dir.

61819 ■ Natchez-Adams County Chamber of Commerce
211 Main St., Ste. A
Natchez, MS 39120
Ph:(601)445-4611
Fax: (601)445-9361
Co. E-mail: info@natchezchamber.com
URL: http://www.natchezchamber.com
Contact: Laura Godfrey, Pres./CEO

61820 ■ Newton Chamber of Commerce
PO Box 301
Newton, MS 39345
Ph:(601)683-2201
Fax: (601)683-2201
Co. E-mail: chambernewton@bellsouth.net
URL: http://www.ci.newton.ms.us
Contact: Angie Burkes, Exec.Dir.

61821 ■ Noxubee County Chamber of Commerce
503 S Washington St.
Macon, MS 39341
Ph:(662)726-4456
Fax: (662)726-1041
Co. E-mail: noxubeecountychamber@yahoo.com
URL: http://www.noxubeecounty.org
Contact: Jim Robbins, Pres.

61822 ■ Ocean Springs Chamber of Commerce
1000 Washington Ave.
PO Box 187
Ocean Springs, MS 39564
Ph:(228)875-4424
Fax: (228)875-0332
Co. E-mail: mail@oceanspringschamber.com

URL: http://www.oceanspringschamber.com
Contact: Margaret Miller, Exec.VP

61823 ■ Okolona Area Chamber of Commerce-Main Street Program
219 Main St.
PO Box 446
Okolona, MS 38860
Ph:(662)447-5913
Fax: (662)447-0254
Co. E-mail: patsyg@okolona.org
URL: http://www.okolona.org
Contact: Patsy Gregory, Dir.

61824 ■ Olive Branch Chamber of Commerce
PO Box 608
Olive Branch, MS 38654-0608
Ph:(662)895-2600
Fax: (662)895-2625
Co. E-mail: info@olivebranchms.com
URL: http://www.olivebranchms.com
Contact: Vickie DuPree, Exec.Dir.

61825 ■ Oxford-Lafayette County Chamber of Commerce
299 W Jackson
PO Box 147
Oxford, MS 38655
Ph:(662)234-4651
Free: 800-880-6967
Fax: (662)234-4655
Co. E-mail: info@oxfordms.com
URL: http://www.oxfordms.com
Contact: Max D. Hipp, Pres./CEO

61826 ■ Panola Partnership
150 A Public Sq.
Batesville, MS 38606-2219
Ph:(662)563-3126
Free: 888-872-6652
Fax: (662)563-0704
Co. E-mail: pcalexander@cableone.net
Contact: Paul Connor Alexander, CEO

61827 ■ Pearl Chamber of Commerce
110 George Wallace Dr.
PO Box 54125
Pearl, MS 39288-4125
Ph:(601)939-3338
Fax: (601)936-5717
Co. E-mail: fred@pearlms.org
URL: http://www.pearlms.org
Contact: Fred Rendfrey, Exec.Dir.

61828 ■ Pike County Chamber of Commerce and Economic Development District
112 N Railroad Blvd.
McComb, MS 39648
Ph:(601)684-2291
Co. E-mail: pcdee@pikeinfo.com
URL: http://www.pikeinfo.com
Contact: J. Britt Herrin, Exec.Dir.

61829 ■ Pontotoc County Chamber of Commerce
109 N Main St.
Pontotoc, MS 38863
Ph:(662)489-5042
Co. E-mail: chamber@pontotocchamber.com
URL: http://www.pontotocchamber.com
Contact: William Wardlaw, Exec.Dir.

61830 ■ Port Gibson-Claiborne County Chamber of Commerce
1601 Church St.
PO Box 491
Port Gibson, MS 39150
Ph:(601)437-4351
Co. E-mail: jcruggs@portgibson.org
URL: http://www.portgibsononthemississippi.com/chamber_of_commerce.html
Contact: Judith M. Scruggs, Exec.Dir.

61831 ■ Rankin County Chamber of Commerce
101 Service Dr.
PO Box 428
Brandon, MS 39043-0428

Ph:(601)825-2268
Fax: (601)825-1977
Co. E-mail: gmartin@rankinchamber.com
URL: http://www.rankinchamber.com
Contact: Gale Martin, Exec.Dir.

61832 ■ Sardis - Sardis Lake Chamber of Commerce
PO Box 377
Sardis, MS 38666-3411
Ph:(662)487-3451
Fax: (662)487-3451
Co. E-mail: sardiscc@panola.com
Contact: Patty Carter, Exec.Sec.

61833 ■ Southaven - Horn Lake Area Chamber of Commerce
8700 NW Dr.
PO Box 211
Southaven, MS 38671
Ph:(662)342-6114
Free: 800-272-6551
Fax: (662)342-6365
Co. E-mail: info@southavenchamber.com
URL: http://www.southavenchamber.com
Contact: Sheryl Burchett, Dir.

61834 ■ Starkville Area Chamber of Commerce
1 Research Blvd., Ste. 204
Starkville, MS 39759
Ph:(662)323-3322
Free: 800-649-8687
Fax: (662)323-5815
Co. E-mail: info@starkville.org
URL: http://www.starkville.org
Contact: Kristi V. Brown, VP

61835 ■ Tate County Chamber of Commerce
135 N Front St.
Senatobia, MS 38668
Ph:(662)562-8715
Fax: (662)562-5786
Contact: J.E. Mortimer, Exec. Dir.

61836 ■ Tunica County Chamber of Commerce
PO Box 1888
Tunica, MS 38676
Ph:(662)363-2865
Fax: (662)357-0378
Co. E-mail: marketing@tunicachamber.com
URL: http://www.tunicachamber.com
Contact: Lyn Arnold, Pres./CEO

61837 ■ Union Chamber of Commerce
PO Box 90
Union, MS 39365
Ph:(601)774-9586
Co. E-mail: unioncommerce@bellsouth.net
Contact: Ralph Gordon, Exec.Dir.

61838 ■ Vicksburg-Warren County Chamber of Commerce
2020 Mission 66
PO Box 709
Vicksburg, MS 39181-0709
Ph:(601)636-1012
Fax: (601)636-4422
Co. E-mail: beverly@canufly.net
URL: http://www.vicksburgliving.com
Contact: James B. Heidel, Exec.VP

61839 ■ Walthall County Chamber of Commerce
PO Box 227
Tylertown, MS 39667
Ph:(601)876-2680
Co. E-mail: walthallchamber@bellsouth.net
URL: http://www.walthallcountychamber.org
Contact: Fred Bonner, Pres.

61840 ■ Wesson Chamber of Commerce
PO Box 557
Wesson, MS 39191
Ph:(601)643-8316
Contact: Joy Wesbrookes, Sec.-Treas.

61841 ■ Yazoo County Chamber of Commerce
212 E Broadway
PO Box 172
Yazoo City, MS 39194-0172
Ph:(662)746-1273
Free: 800-748-8875
Fax: (662)746-7238
Co. E-mail: yazoocc@tecinfo.com
Contact: Gerald P. Fraiser, Pres./CEO

MINORITY BUSINESS ASSISTANCE PROGRAMS

61842 ■ City of Jackson–Economic Development Division
PO Box 17
Jackson, MS 39205
Ph:(601)960-1055
Fax: (601)960-2403
URL: http://www.city.jackson.ms.us
Description: Provides assistance in the development of minority entrepreneurs.

61843 ■ Mississippi Development Authority
501 NW St., Woolfolk Bldg.
Jackson, MS 39201
Ph:(601)359-3449
Fax: (601)359-2832
URL: http://www.mississippi.org

PROCUREMENT ASSISTANCE PROGRAMS

61844 ■ Mississippi Contract Procurement Center, Inc.–Delta Contract Procurement Center, Inc. (DCPC)
PO Box 1179
Greenville, MS 38702-1179
Ph:(662)334-2656
Fax: (662)334-2709
Co. E-mail: dcpc2@tecinfo.com
URL: http://www.mscpc.com
Contact: Lee Woodyard, Dir
E-mail: dcpc@juno.com

61845 ■ Mississippi Contract Procurement Center, Inc.–Northeast Mississippi Contract Procurement Center, Inc. (NMCPC)
PO Box 1805
Columbus, MS 39703
Ph:(662)329-1077
Fax: (662)327-6600
Co. E-mail: nmcpc@tilc.com
URL: http://www.mscpc.com
Contact: Bill Burge, Dir

61846 ■ Mississippi Contract Procurement Center, Inc.–South Mississippi Contract Procurement Center, Inc. (SMCPC)
1636 Pops Ferry Rd., Ste. 229
Biloxi, MS 39532
Ph:(228)396-1288
Fax: (228)396-2520
Co. E-mail: mprogoff@mscpc.com
URL: http://www.mscpc.com
Contact: Marcia McDowell, Dir
Description: Provides information and direct assistance to firms wishing to do business with the federal government.

INCUBATORS/RESEARCH AND TECHNOLOGY PARKS

61847 ■ The Golden Triangle Enterprise Center
One Research Blvd., Ste. 201
Starkville, MS 39759
Ph:(662)323-3322

Fax: (662)320-3999
Co. E-mail: info@gtec.org
URL: http://www.gtec.org
Description: GTEC is a high-tech incubator program that benefits from its proximity to Mississippi State University.

61848 ■ Jackson Enterprise Center
931 Hwy. 80 W
Jackson, MS 39204
Ph:(601)352-0957
Fax: (601)948-3250
Co. E-mail: jec@riby.com
Contact: Fred LaRue, Dir

61849 ■ John C. Stennis Space Center–Institute for Technology Development
Bldg. 1103, Ste. 118
Stennis Space Center, MS 39529
Ph:(228)688-2509
Fax: (228)688-2861
Co. E-mail: b.roelfson@iftd.org
Contact: Dr. George May, Pres.
E-mail: b.roelfson@iftd.org
Scope: Identifies national and state technological needs in the areas products and services for older americans, microelectronics, and space remote sensing and coordinates the commercialization of research and development from the state's university, government, small business laboratories, and internal resources. Conducts applied technology development for internal purposes and external sponsors. **Publications:** Innovations.

61850 ■ Mississippi Action for Community Education, Inc. (MACE)
119 S Theobald St.
Greenville, MS 38701
Ph:(662)335-3523
Free: 888-812-5837
Fax: (662)334-2939
Co. E-mail: mace@tecinfo.com
URL: http://www.deltamace.org
Contact: Receptionist

61851 ■ Mississippi Research and Technology Park
1 Research Blvd., Ste. 204
Starkville, MS 39759
Ph:(662)323-3322
Fax: (662)323-5815
Co. E-mail: krichardson@starkville.org
Contact: Kim Richardson, VP
E-mail: krichardson@starkville.org
Scope: Research laboratories, incubator and multitenant facilities, professional and business services, and office space to foster high technology research collaboration between the University and industry tenants. **Educational Activities:** Mississippi State University Graduate Student Internship Program.

61852 ■ Mississippi State University–Office of the Vice President for Research and Graduate Studies
PO Box 6343
Mississippi State, MS 39762
Ph:(662)325-3570
Fax: (662)325-8028
Co. E-mail: scanes@research.msstate.edu
URL: http://www.msstate.edu/dept/research/research.html
Contact: Dr. Colin Scanes, VP
E-mail: scanes@research.msstate.edu
Scope: Coordinates research programs of the University in engineering, business, education, physical and biological sciences, social sciences, water resources, and computer science through specialized research centers and institutes administratively responsible to the Office of the Vice President for Research. **Publications:** Summaries of University Research Programs.

61853 ■ University of Southern Mississippi–Sponsored Programs Administration
Bond Hall, 2nd Fl., West Wing, Box 5157
Hattiesburg, MS 39406-0001

Ph:(601)266-4119
Fax: (601)266-4312
Co. E-mail: connie.wyldmon@usm.edu
URL: http://www.usm.edu/spa/
Contact: Connie Wyldmon, Dir.
E-mail: connie.wyldmon@usm.edu
Scope: Responsible for administration of externally sponsored research and training at the University. **Publications:** Newsletter (monthly). **Educational Ac-**

tivities: Activities related to proposal development; Workshops.

PUBLICATIONS

61854 ■ *Smart Start your Florida Business*
PSI Research
300 N. Valley Dr.
Grants Pass, OR 97526

Ph:(503)479-9464
Free: 800-228-2275
Fax: (503)476-1479
Co. E-mail: info@psi-research.com
URL: http://www.psi-research.com
Ed: Carl R. Sniffen and Michael D. Jenkins. **Released:** Revised edition, 1992. **Price:** $29.95 (looseleaf binder); $24.95 (paper). **Description:** Part of the Successful Business Library series.

SMALL BUSINESS DEVELOPMENT CENTER LEAD OFFICE

61855 ■ Missouri SBDC–University of Missouri–SBDC
1205 University Ave., Ste. 300
Columbia, MO 65211
Ph:(573)882-1348
Fax: (573)884-4297
URL: http://www.mo-sbdc.org/index.shtml
Contact: Max Summers, State Dir.
E-mail: summersm@missouri.edu

61856 ■ University of Missouri—Columbia–Small Business Development Center
1205 University Ave., Ste. 300
Columbia, MO 65211
Ph:(573)882-0344
Fax: (573)884-4297
Co. E-mail: sbdcmso@missouri.edu
Contact: Max E. Summers, State Director

SMALL BUSINESS DEVELOPMENT CENTERS

61857 ■ Audrain County Extension Center–SBDC
Courthouse, Rm. 304
101 N. Jefferson
Mexico, MO 65265
Ph:(573)581-3231
Fax: (573)581-2766
Co. E-mail: audrainco@missouri.edu
URL: http://extension.missouri.edu/audrain/biz
Contact: Virgil Woolridge, Business Specialist
E-mail: arendsj@missouri.edu

61858 ■ Boone County Extension Center–SBDC
1012 N. Hwy. UU
Columbia, MO 65203
Ph:(573)445-9792
Fax: (573)445-9807
Contact: Casey Venters, Business Specialist

61859 ■ Cape Girardeau County University of Missouri–SBDC Extension Center
684 W. Jackson Trail
PO Box 408
Jackson, MO 63755
Ph:(573)243-3581
Fax: (573)243-1606
Co. E-mail: capegira@missouri.edu
URL: http://extension.missouri.edu/capegirardeau/index.shtml
Contact: Richard D. Proffer, Business Development Specialist
E-mail: profferrd@missouri.edu

61860 ■ Center for Entrepreneurship and Outreach–University of Missouri at Rolla–Small Business Development Center (203 U)
203 University Center
1870 Miner Cir.
Rolla, MO 65409-1110
Ph:(573)341-4690
Free: 800-522-0938
Co. E-mail: webmaster@umr.edu
URL: http://www.umrceo.net/
Contact: Barry White, Program Mgr.
E-mail: bwhite@umr.edu

61861 ■ Central Missouri State University SBTDC–Center for Technology and Small Business Development
Dockery, Ste. 102
Warrensburg, MO 64093
Ph:(660)543-4402
Fax: (660)543-8159
Co. E-mail: sbdc@cmsu1.cmsu.edu
URL: http://www.cmsu.edu/
Contact: Wes Savage, Dir.

61862 ■ Chillicothe Satellite Center–SBDC
City Hall
715 Washington St.
Chillicothe, MO 64601-2229
Ph:(660)646-6920
Fax: (660)646-6811
Co. E-mail: sbdchill@greenhills.net
Contact: Jeanne Dau, Dir.
E-mail: jcdau@greenhills.net

61863 ■ Cole County Extension Center–SBDC
2436 Tanner Bridge Rd.
Jefferson City, MO 65101
Ph:(573)634-2824
Fax: (573)634-5463
Co. E-mail: coleco@missouri.edu
URL: http://extension.missouri.edu/cole/index.shtml
Contact: Mark Stillwell, Dir.
E-mail: stillwellm@umsystem.edu

61864 ■ East Central Missouri/St. Louis County–Extension Center
121 S. Meramac, Ste. 501
Clayton, MO 63105
Ph:(314)615-2911
Fax: (314)615-8147
Co. E-mail: stlouisco@missouri.edu
URL: http://extension.missouri.edu/stlouis/
Contact: Lee B. Fox, Specialist
E-mail: foxlb@missouri.edu

61865 ■ Franklin County–SBDC Extension Center
116 W. Main St.
Union, MO 63084
Ph:(636)583-5141
Fax: (636)583-5145
Co. E-mail: franklinco@missouri.edu
URL: http://extension.missouri.edu/franklin/
Contact: Kenneth A. Bolte, Program Dir.

E-mail: boltek@missouri.edu

61866 ■ Greene County Extension SBDC
833 Boonville Ave.
Springfield, MO 65806
Ph:(417)862-9284
Co. E-mail: greeneco@missouri.edu
URL: http://extension.missouri.edu/greene/biz.shtml
Contact: Verna E. Lorton, Specialist
E-mail: lortonv@missouri.edu

61867 ■ Howell County–SBDC Extension Center
217 S. Aid Ave.
West Plains, MO 65775
Ph:(417)256-2391
Fax: (417)256-8569
Co. E-mail: howellco@missouri.edu
Contact: Willis Mushrush, Business Development Specialist
E-mail: mushrushw@missouri.edu

61868 ■ Mineral Area College–SBDC
5270 Flat River Rd.
PO Box 1000
Park Hills, MO 63601-1000
Ph:(573)518-2169
Fax: (573)518-2163
Co. E-mail: sbdcph@missouri.edu
Contact: Eugene Cherry, Dir.

61869 ■ Missouri PAC - Southeastern Missouri State University–SBDC
222 N. Pacific
Cape Girardeau, MO 63701
Ph:(314)290-5965
Fax: (314)651-5005
Contact: George Williams, Dir.

61870 ■ Missouri Southern State College–Small Business Development Center
3950 E. Newman Rd.
Joplin, MO 64801-1595
Ph:(417)625-3128
Fax: (417)625-9782
Co. E-mail: sbdcj@missouri.edu
Contact: Jim Krudwig, Dir.
E-mail: krudwig-j@mssu.edu

61871 ■ Monroe County Extension Center–Small Business Development Center
208 N. Main St.
Paris, MO 65275
Ph:(660)327-4158
Fax: (660)327-1376
Co. E-mail: monroeco@missouri.edu
URL: http://extension.missouri.edu/Monroe/biz.shtml
Contact: Wendy Harrington, Business Development Specialist
E-mail: harringtonw@missouri.edu

61872 ■ Montgomery County Extension–Small Business Development Center
310 Salisbury St., Ste. E
Montgomery City, MO 63361

Ph:(573)564-3733
Fax: (573)564-6145
Co. E-mail: montgomeryco@missouri.edu
URL: http://outreach.missouri.edu/montgomery/
Contact: Muthoni Grace Njeru, County Program Dir.
E-mail: njerum@missouri.edu

61873 ■ Northwest Missouri State University–Small Business Development Center
423 N. Market St.
Maryville, MO 64468-1614
Ph:(660)562-1701
Fax: (660)562-1890
Co. E-mail: sbdc@mail.nwmissouri.edu
URL: http://www.nwmissouri.edu/sbdc/
Contact: Jim Hunt, Center Dir.

61874 ■ Pettis County–Extension Center–Central Missouri Region (1012A)
1012A Thompson Blvd.
Sedalia, MO 65301
Ph:(660)827-0591
Fax: (660)827-4888
Co. E-mail: pettisco@missouri.edu
Contact: Eva I. Kabler, Office Mgr.
E-mail: kablere@umsystem.edu

61875 ■ Rockhurst College–Small Business Development Center
1100 Rockhurst Rd.
Kansas City, MO 64110-2599
Ph:(816)501-4572
Fax: (816)501-4646
Co. E-mail: sbdckc@missouri.edu
Contact: Lisa Stubbendick, Dir.

61876 ■ St. Charles County–SBDC University of Missouri Extension Center
260 Brown Rd.
St. Peters, MO 63376
Ph:(636)970-3000
Fax: (636)279-3310
Co. E-mail: stcharlesco@missouri.edu
URL: http://extension.missouri.edu/stcharles/
Contact: Scott Killpack, Program Dir.
E-mail: killpacks@missouri.edu

61877 ■ St. Louis County–Extension Center
724 N. Union
St. Louis, MO 63108
Ph:(314)367-2585
Fax: (314)367-8137
Co. E-mail: StLouisCity@missouri.edu
URL: http://outreach.missouri.edu/stlouis/
Contact: Jody J. Squires, Specialist
E-mail: squiresj@missouri.edu

61878 ■ St. Louis Regional–Small Business Development Center–SBDC (Saint)
Saint Louis University
3750 Lindell Blvd.
St. Louis, MO 63108-3412
Ph:(314)977-7232
Fax: (314)977-7241
Co. E-mail: sbdcstl@ext.missouri.edu
Contact: Virginia Campbell, Dir.

61879 ■ Small Business Research and Information Center–University of Missouri-Rolla
104 Nagogami Ter.
Rolla, MO 65409-1340
Ph:(573)341-4559
Fax: (573)341-6495
Co. E-mail: sbdcr@missouri.edu
Contact: Fred Goss, Dir.

61880 ■ Southeast Missouri State University–Small Business Development Center
One University Plaza
MS 0110
Cape Girardeau, MO 63701
Ph:(573)986-6084
Fax: (573)986-6083
Co. E-mail: sbdccg@missouri.edu

Contact: Frank "Buz" Sutherland, Dir.
E-mail: bsutherland@semo.net

61881 ■ Southwest Missouri State University–College of Business Administration–Small Business Development Center (901 S)
901 S. National
Springfield, MO 65897
Ph:(417)836-5685
Fax: (417)836-7666
Co. E-mail: sbdcs@missouri.edu
URL: http://www.sbdc.missouristate.edu
Contact: Jane Cargill, Dir.
E-mail: janecargill@missouristate.edu

61882 ■ Taney County Extension SBDC
122 Felkins Ave.
PO Box 598
Forsyth, MO 65653
Ph:(417)546-4431
Co. E-mail: taneyco@missouri.edu
URL: http://extension.missouri.edu/taney/index.shtml
Contact: Thomas E. Keohan, Specialist
E-mail: keohant@missouri.edu

61883 ■ Telecommunications Community Resource Center–University of Missouri Extension–Small Business Development Center (200 E)
200 E.K. Porter Bldg.
2080 Three Rivers Blvd.
Poplar Bluff, MO 63901
Ph:(573)840-9450
Fax: (573)840-9456
Co. E-mail: pbtcrc@missouri.edu
URL: http://telecenter.missouri.edu/poplarbluff/
Contact: Kevin Anderson, Extension Assoc.
E-mail: andersonkl@missouri.edu

61884 ■ Thomas Hill Enterprise Satellite Center–Southeast Missouri State University–SBDC (1709)
1709 N. Prospect Dr.
Macon, MO 63552-2602
Ph:(660)385-6550
Fax: (660)385-6568
Co. E-mail: sbdcth@missouri.edu
URL: http://www2.semo.edu/SESBDC/Offices/Thomas.html
Contact: Buz Sutherland, Dir.

61885 ■ Truman State University–Small Business Development Center
100 E. Normal
Kirksville, MO 63501-4221
Ph:(660)785-4307
Fax: (660)785-4357
Co. E-mail: sbdc@truman.edu
URL: http://sbdc.truman.edu/
Contact: Glen Giboney, Dir.

61886 ■ University of Missouri–SBDC Extension Center–Phelps County (Court)
Courthouse
200 N. Main, Ste. G-8
Rolla, MO 65401
Ph:(573)458-6260
Fax: (573)458-6264
URL: http://www.extension.missouri.edu
Contact: Tracy Bowen, Regional Specialist
E-mail: bowent@missouri.edu

61887 ■ University of Missouri at Columbia–Small Business Development Center
1800 University Pl.
Columbia, MO 65211-7946
Ph:(573)882-9931
Fax: (573)882-6156
Co. E-mail: sbdcc@missouri.edu
Contact: Frank Siebert, Dir.

61888 ■ University of Missouri Extension–Camden County–Small Business Development Center (34 Ro)
34 Roofener St.
PO Box 1405
Camdenton, MO 65020

Ph:(573)346-2644
Fax: (573)346-2694
Contact: Jackie Rasmussen, Business Development Specialist
E-mail: rasmussenj@missouri.edu

61889 ■ University of Missouri Extension at Camden County–SBDC
34 Roofener St.
PO Box 1405
Camdenton, MO 65020
Ph:(573)346-2644
Fax: (573)346-2694
Co. E-mail: camdenco@missouri.edu
URL: http://extension.missouri.edu/camden/
Contact: Charli Allee, Business Consultant
E-mail: alleec@missouri.edu

61890 ■ Warren County Extension–Small Business Development Center
107 W. Walton
Warrenton, MO 63383
Ph:(636)456-3444
Fax: (636)456-4108
Co. E-mail: warrenco@missouri.edu
URL: http://outreach.missouri.edu/warren/
Contact: Dale L. Davis, Development Program Asst.
E-mail: davisdal@missouri.edu

61891 ■ Washington County SBDC Extension
113 N. Missouri, Ste. A
Potosi, MO 63664
Ph:(573)438-2671
Fax: (573)438-3068
Co. E-mail: washingtonco@missouri.edu
URL: http://outreach.missouri.edu/Washington/
Contact: Maude Elaine Kelly, County Program Dir.
E-mail: kellyme@missouri.edu

61892 ■ West Plains Satellite Center–Missouri State University–Small Business Development Center (128 G)
128 Garfield
West Plains, MO 65775-2715
Ph:(417)255-7966
Contact: Lyle Wright
E-mail: lylewright@missouristate.edu

SMALL BUSINESS ASSISTANCE PROGRAMS

61893 ■ Central Missouri State University–Center for Technology and Small Business Development
Dockery 102
Warrensburg, MO 64093-5037
Ph:(660)543-4402
Fax: (660)543-8159
Co. E-mail: sbdc@cmsu.edu
URL: http://www.cmsu.edu/sbdc/
Contact: Shirley Krzesinski

61894 ■ Missouri Department of Economic Development–Business Services
PO Box 118
Jefferson City, MO 65102
Ph:(573)751-2863
Free: 800-523-1434
Fax: (573)526-2416
Co. E-mail: nbac@mail.state.mo.us
URL: http://www.econdev.state.mo.us/nbac/
Description: Provides access to all state forms, regulations, requirements, permits, and other information necessary to do business in Missouri.

61895 ■ Missouri Department of Economic Development–Office of International Marketing
Truman State Office Bldg., Rm. 720
PO Box 118
Jefferson City, MO 65102
Ph:(573)751-4999
Free: 800-523-1434
Fax: (573)526-1567

Co. E-mail: akinwort@mail.state.mo.us
URL: http://www.ecodev.state.mo.us/intermark
Description: Provides assistance to international firms. Works to stimulate direct foreign investment in the state and develop export possibilities.

61896 ■ University of Missouri Columbia–Small Business Development Center
W1052 Lafferre Hall
Columbia, MO 65211-7935
Ph:(573)882-7096
Fax: (573)882-9931
URL: http://www.missouribusiness.net
Description: Provides assistance to company officials and local community leaders in their efforts to retain existing jobs and create additional jobs through business expansion. Provides technical assistance and information. People wanting to start small business.

61897 ■ University of Missouri—Rolla–Small Business Research and Information Center
Nagogami Ter., Rm. 104
Rolla, MO 65401-2171
Ph:(573)341-4559
Fax: (573)341-6495
Co. E-mail: cfrank@umr.edu
URL: http://www.umr.edu/~outreach

SCORE OFFICES

61898 ■ SCORE Kansas City
c/o Gary Brickman, Chm.
Business Resource Ctr.
4747 Troost Ave., Ste. 128
Kansas City, MO 64110
Ph:(816)235-6675
Fax: (816)235-6590
Co. E-mail: chapter19@scorekc.org
URL: http://www.scorekc.org
Contact: Gary Brickman, Chm.
Description: Provides consulting services to individuals wishing to start a new business or who have problems with established businesses.

61899 ■ SCORE Lake Ozark
University Extension
113 Kansas St.
Camdenton, MO 65020
Ph:(573)346-2644
Fax: (573)346-2694
Co. E-mail: score@lakeozarkscore.org
URL: http://www.lakeozarkscore.org
Contact: Kenneth Schaeffer, Chm.
Description: Serves as volunteer program in which working and retired business management professionals provide free business counseling to men and women who are considering starting a small business, encountering problems with their business, or expanding their business. Offers free one-on-one counseling, online counseling and low cost workshops on a variety of business topics.

61900 ■ SCORE Mid Missouri
9875 E Vemers Ford Rd.
Columbia, MO 65201
Ph:(573)874-1132
Co. E-mail: scorecol340@aol.com
Description: Provides public service by offering small business advice and training.

61901 ■ SCORE Ozark-Gateway
1486 Glassey Rd.
Cuba, MO 65453-1640
Ph:(573)885-4954
Co. E-mail: score438@fidnet.com
Description: Serves as volunteer program in which working and retired business management professionals provide free business counseling to men and women who are considering starting a small business, encountering problems with their business, or expanding their business. Offers free one-on-one counseling, online counseling and low cost workshops on a variety of business topics.

61902 ■ SCORE Poplar Bluff Area
c/o James W. Carson, VP
806 Emma St.
Poplar Bluff, MO 63901
Ph:(573)686-8892
URL: http://www.score.org
Contact: James Carson, VP

61903 ■ SCORE St. Joseph
c/o Paul Jenner, CHR
4524 Alpha Ln.
St. Joseph, MO 64506
Ph:(816)279-5091
URL: http://www.score.org

61904 ■ SCORE St. Louis
200 N Broadway, Ste. 1500
St. Louis, MO 63102
Ph:(314)539-6600
Fax: (314)539-6200
Co. E-mail: counselors@stlscore.org
URL: http://www.stlscore.org
Contact: Mr. Bill Deemer, Chm.
Description: Serves as volunteer program in which working and retired business management professionals provide free business counseling to men and women who are considering starting a small business, encountering problems with their business, or expanding their business. Offers free one-on-one counseling, online counseling and low cost workshops on a variety of business topics.

61905 ■ SCORE Springfield
830 E Primrose, Ste. 101
Springfield, MO 65809
Ph:(417)890-8501
Fax: (417)889-0074
Co. E-mail: scoreusa@aol.com
URL: http://www.springfieldscore.org
Contact: Nick Weinsaft, Chm.
Description: Serves as volunteer program in which working and retired business management professionals provide free business counseling to men and women who are considering starting a small business, encountering problems with their business, or expanding their business. Offers free one-on-one counseling, online counseling and low cost workshops on a variety of business topics.

BETTER BUSINESS BUREAUS

61906 ■ Better Business Bureau of Eastern Missouri and Southern Illinois
15 Sunnen Dr., Ste. 107
St. Louis, MO 63143
Ph:(314)645-3300
Fax: (314)645-2666
Co. E-mail: bbb@contactbbb.org
URL: http://www.stlouis.bbb.org
Contact: Michelle L. Corey, Pres./CEO

61907 ■ Better Business Bureau of Greater Kansas City
8080 Ward Pkwy.
Kansas City, MO 64114
Ph:(816)421-7800
Fax: (816)472-5442
Co. E-mail: info@kansascity.bbb.org
URL: http://www.kansascity.bbb.org
Contact: David Buckley, Pres.

61908 ■ Better Business Bureau of Southwest Missouri
1516 St. Louis St.
Springfield, MO 65802
Ph:(417)862-4222
Fax: (417)869-5544
Co. E-mail: info@springfield-mo.bbb.org
URL: http://www.springfield-mo.bbb.org
Contact: Ms. Judy Mills, Pres./CEO

CHAMBERS OF COMMERCE

61909 ■ Affton Chamber of Commerce
10203 Gravois Rd.
Affton, MO 63123-4029
Ph:(314)849-6499
Fax: (314)849-6399
Co. E-mail: info@afftonchamber.com
URL: http://www.afftonchamber.com
Contact: Ms. Joan Edleson, Exec.Dir.

61910 ■ Arcadia Valley Chamber of Commerce
PO Box 343
Ironton, MO 63650-0343
Ph:(573)546-7117
Fax: (573)546-3905
Co. E-mail: drwoolley@centurytel.net
Contact: Doug Woolley

61911 ■ Arnold Chamber of Commerce
PO Box 1156
Arnold, MO 63010
Ph:(636)296-1910
Fax: (636)296-1910
Co. E-mail: contact@arnoldchamber.org
URL: http://www.arnoldchamber.org
Contact: Margie Sammons, Pres.

61912 ■ Aurora Chamber of Commerce
121 E Olive
PO Box 257
Aurora, MO 65605-1666
Ph:(417)678-4150
Fax: (417)678-1387
Co. E-mail: auroracoc@mo-net.com
URL: http://www.auroramochamber.com

61913 ■ Ava Area Chamber of Commerce
PO Box 1103
Ava, MO 65608
Ph:(417)683-4594
Fax: (417)683-9464
Co. E-mail: info@avachamber.org
URL: http://avachamber.org
Contact: Teresa Blakey, Exec.Dir.

61914 ■ Barton County Chamber of Commerce
PO Box 577
Lamar, MO 64759
Ph:(417)682-3595
Fax: (417)682-9566
Co. E-mail: tiffany@bartoncounty.com
URL: http://www.bartoncounty.com
Contact: Tiffany Owings, Exec.Dir.

61915 ■ Belton Chamber of Commerce
512 Main St.
PO Box 350
Belton, MO 64012-0350
Ph:(816)331-2420
Fax: (816)331-8736
Co. E-mail: bcoc@beltonmochamber.com
URL: http://beltonmochamber.com
Contact: Ms. Danette Baker, Exec.Dir.

61916 ■ Bethany Area Chamber of Commerce
116 N 16th St.
Bethany, MO 64424
Ph:(660)425-6358
Fax: (660)425-0123
Contact: Susie Rollheiser, Pres.

61917 ■ Black Chamber of Commerce of Greater Kansas City
16 E 18th St.
Historic Lincoln Bldg.
Kansas City, MO 64108
Ph:(816)474-9901
Fax: (816)842-1748
Co. E-mail: bcckc@swbell.net
URL: http://www.bcckc.org
Contact: A. Marie Young, Exec.Dir.

61918 ■ Blue Springs Chamber of Commerce
1000 Main St.
Blue Springs, MO 64015
Ph:(816)229-8558
Fax: (816)229-1244
Co. E-mail: d_whisler@comcast.net
URL: http://www.bluespringschamber.com
Contact: Debbie Whisler, Pres.

61919 ■ Bolivar Area Chamber of Commerce
PO Box 202
Bolivar, MO 65613-0202
Ph:(417)326-4118
Fax: (417)777-9080
Co. E-mail: bolchamb@alltel.net
URL: http://www.bolivarchamber.com
Contact: Diana Leslie, Exec.Dir.

61920 ■ Bonne Terre Chamber of Commerce
11 SW Main St.
PO Box 175
Bonne Terre, MO 63628
Ph:(573)358-4000
Free: 888-358-7350
Fax: (573)358-0071
Co. E-mail: dldirector@yahoo.com
Contact: Kris Black, Pres.

61921 ■ Bowling Green Chamber of Commerce
106 W Main St.
Bowling Green, MO 63334
Ph:(573)324-6800
Fax: (573)324-0152
Co. E-mail: bgchamber@scbglobal.net
URL: http://www.bgchamber.org
Contact: Kathy Engel, Dir.

61922 ■ Branson - Lakes Area Chamber of Commerce
269 State Hwy. 248
PO Box 1897
Branson, MO 65615-1897
Ph:(417)334-4084
Free: 800-214-3661
Fax: (417)334-4139
Co. E-mail: info@bransoncvb.com
URL: http://www.explorebranson.com
Contact: Ross Summers, Pres./CEO

61923 ■ Braymer Chamber of Commerce
115 Main St.
Braymer, MO 64624
Ph:(660)645-2015
Co. E-mail: cgorham@greenhills.net
Contact: Jerry Gorham, Pres.

61924 ■ Brentwood Chamber of Commerce
PO Box 6726
Brentwood, MO 63144-0726
Ph:(314)963-9007
Co. E-mail: brentwoodchamber@aol.com
Contact: Carol Eagelston, Sec.

61925 ■ Brookfield Area Chamber of Commerce
300 N Main St.
Brookfield, MO 64628-1601
Ph:(660)258-7255
Fax: (660)258-7564
Co. E-mail: chamber@shighway.com
URL: http://www.brookfieldmochamber.com
Contact: Patricia Smith, Dir.

61926 ■ Buckner Chamber of Commerce
PO Box 325
Buckner, MO 64016
Ph:(816)650-6103
Fax: (816)650-3888
Co. E-mail: ssmith@fortosage.net
URL: http://www.discoverynet.com/~ajsnead/
mycomm/chamber.html
Contact: Ms. Stephanie Smith, Pres.

61927 ■ Buffalo Area Chamber of Commerce
101 N Maple St.
PO Box 258
Buffalo, MO 65622

Ph:(417)345-2852
Fax: (417)345-2852
Co. E-mail: chamber@buffalococ.com
URL: http://www.buffalococ.com
Contact: Kathy Kesler, Exec.Sec.

61928 ■ Butler Area Chamber of Commerce
7 W Dakota
Butler, MO 64730
Ph:(660)679-3380
Free: 888-679-3380
Fax: (660)679-6636
Co. E-mail: chamberadmin@butlerareachamber.org
Contact: Kendra Welston, Exec.Dir.

61929 ■ Cabool Area Chamber of Commerce
PO Box 285
Cabool, MO 65689-0285
Ph:(417)962-3002
Fax: (417)962-3136
Co. E-mail: cccabool@ozarkshowcase.com
Contact: Betty Tate, Pres.

61930 ■ California Chamber of Commerce
500 S Oak St., Ste. A
PO Box 85
California, MO 65018
Ph:(573)796-3040
Fax: (573)796-8309
Co. E-mail: chamber@calmo.com
URL: http://www.calmo.com
Contact: Ruth Ellis, Exec.Sec.

61931 ■ Camdenton Area Chamber of Commerce
PO Box 1375
Camdenton, MO 65020-1375
Ph:(573)346-2227
Free: 800-769-1004
Fax: (573)346-3496
Co. E-mail: cchamber@thelake.com
URL: http://www.camdentonchamber.com
Contact: Bruce Mitchell, Exec.Dir.

61932 ■ Cameron Chamber of Commerce
PO Box 252
Cameron, MO 64429
Ph:(816)632-2005
Fax: (816)632-8861
Co. E-mail: cameroncoc@hotmail.com
URL: http://www.cameron-mo.com
Contact: Artis Stoebener, Exec.Dir.

61933 ■ Cape Girardeau Area Chamber of Commerce
1267 N Mt. Auburn Rd.
Cape Girardeau, MO 63701
Ph:(573)335-3312
Fax: (573)335-4686
Co. E-mail: info@capechamber.com
URL: http://www.capechamber.com
Contact: John E. Mehner, Pres./CEO

61934 ■ Carrollton Chamber of Commerce
111 N Mason
Carrollton, MO 64633
Ph:(660)542-0922
Fax: (660)542-3489
Co. E-mail: info@carrolltonareachamber.com
URL: http://www.carrolltonareachamber.com
Contact: Brandy Gregg, Exec.Dir.

61935 ■ Carthage Chamber of Commerce
402 S Garrison Ave.
Carthage, MO 64836
Ph:(417)358-2373
Fax: (417)358-7479
Co. E-mail: info@carthagechamber.com
URL: http://www.carthagechamber.com
Contact: Max McKnight, Pres.

61936 ■ Cassville Area Chamber of Commerce
504 Main St.
Cassville, MO 65625-1418
Ph:(417)847-2814
Fax: (417)847-0804

Co. E-mail: info@cassville.com
URL: http://www.cassville.com
Contact: Kevin Bolling, Pres.

61937 ■ Centralia Area Chamber of Commerce
PO Box 235
Centralia, MO 65240
Ph:(573)682-2272
Fax: (573)682-1111
Co. E-mail: ginny@midamerica.net
URL: http://centralia.missouri.org
Contact: Ginny Zoellers, Exec. Dir.

61938 ■ Chaffee Chamber of Commerce
PO Box 35
Chaffee, MO 63740
Ph:(573)887-3558
Co. E-mail: information@chaffeechamber.com
URL: http://spicecat.com/chaffee_chamber
Contact: Rhonda Wessel, Pres.

61939 ■ Charleston Chamber of Commerce
110 E Commercial St.
Charleston, MO 63834
Ph:(573)683-6509
Fax: (573)683-6799
Co. E-mail: charleston@ldd.net
URL: http://www.charlestonmo.org
Contact: Lisa Hillhouse, Exec.Dir.

61940 ■ Chesterfield Chamber of Commerce
101 Chesterfield Business Pkwy.
Chesterfield, MO 63005
Ph:(636)532-3399
Free: 888-242-4262
Fax: (636)532-7446
Co. E-mail: info@chesterfieldmochamber.com
URL: http://www.chesterfieldmotourism.com
Contact: Joan Schmelig, Pres.

61941 ■ Chillicothe Area Chamber of Commerce
514 Washington St.
PO Box 407
Chillicothe, MO 64601
Ph:(660)646-4050
Free: 877-C-CHILLI
Fax: (660)646-3309
Co. E-mail: chamber@chillicothemo.com
URL: http://www.chillicothemo.com
Contact: Barb Burton, Exec.VP

61942 ■ Clarksville Chamber of Commerce
PO Box 238
Clarksville, MO 63336
Ph:(573)242-3993
URL: http://www.clarksvillemo.com/index.html
Contact: Linda Blakely, Pres.

61943 ■ Clayton Chamber of Commerce
225 S Meramec, Ste. 300
Clayton, MO 63105
Ph:(314)726-3033
Fax: (314)726-0637
Co. E-mail: tzupon@claytoncommerce.com
URL: http://www.claytoncommerce.com
Contact: Trish Zupon, Membership Dir.

61944 ■ Clinton Area Chamber of Commerce
200 S Main
Clinton, MO 64735
Ph:(660)885-8166
Free: 800-222-5251
Fax: (660)885-8168
Co. E-mail: sandi@chamberofclinton.org
URL: http://www.chamberofclinton.org
Contact: Sandi Cox, Exec.Dir.

61945 ■ Columbia Chamber of Commerce
PO Box 1016
Columbia, MO 65205-1016
Ph:(573)874-1132
Fax: (573)443-3986
Co. E-mail: admin@columbiamochamber.com
URL: http://chamber.columbia.mo.us
Contact: Don Laird, Pres.

61946 ■ Concordia Chamber of Commerce
702 Main St.
PO Box 143
Concordia, MO 64020-0143
Ph:(660)463-2454
Fax: (660)463-2842
Co. E-mail: concordiachamber@centurytel.net
URL: http://www.concordiamo.com
Contact: Dale Kulssman

61947 ■ Crane Area Chamber of Commerce
PO Box 287
Crane, MO 65633
Ph:(417)669-7294
Co. E-mail: cranechamber@aol.com
URL: http://www.cranemo.com
Contact: Gerald W. Coenen

61948 ■ Creve Coeur - Olivette Chamber of Commerce
677 N New Ballas, Ste. 214
Creve Coeur, MO 63141
Ph:(314)569-3536
Fax: (314)569-3073
Co. E-mail: ccochamb@swbell.net
URL: http://www.ccochamber.com
Contact: Mike Peterson, Pres.

61949 ■ Cuba Chamber of Commerce and Visitor Center
71 Hwy. P (I-44 & Hwy. 19)
PO Box 405
Cuba, MO 65453
Ph:(573)885-2531
Free: 877-212-8429
Fax: (573)885-4954
Co. E-mail: score438@fidnet.com
URL: http://www.cubamochamber.com
Contact: Norma Bretz, Sec.

61950 ■ Desloge Chamber of Commerce
209 N Desloge Dr.
Desloge, MO 63601
Ph:(573)431-3006
Contact: Debbie Kester, Pres.

61951 ■ Dexter Chamber of Commerce
515 W Market St.
PO Box 21
Dexter, MO 63841
Ph:(573)624-7458
Free: 800-332-8857
Co. E-mail: info@dexterchamber.com
URL: http://www.dexterchamber.com
Contact: Janet Coleman, Exec.Dir.

61952 ■ East Prairie Chamber of Commerce
106 S Washington
East Prairie, MO 63845
Ph:(573)649-5243
Fax: (573)649-2024
URL: http://www.eastprairiemo.net/COC/index.html
Contact: Keith Grissom, Pres.

61953 ■ El Dorado Springs Chamber of Commerce
121 W Spring St., Ste. 2
El Dorado Springs, MO 64744-0276
Ph:(417)876-4154
Fax: (417)876-4154
Co. E-mail: info@eldomo-cofc.org
URL: http://www.eldomo-cofc.org
Contact: Ms. Lynette Rush, Exec.Sec.

61954 ■ Eldon Chamber of Commerce
203 E 1st St.
PO Box 209
Eldon, MO 65026
Ph:(573)392-3752
Fax: (573)392-0634
Co. E-mail: wayne@eldonchamber.com
URL: http://www.eldonchamber.com
Contact: Wayne Morgan, Exec.Dir.

61955 ■ Ellington Chamber of Commerce
PO Box 515
Ellington, MO 63638-0515

Ph:(573)663-7997
Fax: (573)663-7873
Co. E-mail: chamber@ellingtonmo.com
URL: http://www.ellingtonmo.com
Contact: Paula DeMent, Pres.

61956 ■ Elsberry Chamber of Commerce
PO Box 32
Elsberry, MO 63343
Ph:(573)898-9124
Co. E-mail: chamber.info@elsberrycofc.org
URL: http://elsberrycofc.org
Contact: Jerry Callahan, Pres.

61957 ■ Eminence Chamber of Commerce
PO Box 415
Eminence, MO 65466
Ph:(573)226-3318
Co. E-mail: chamber@eminencemo.com
URL: http://www.eminencemo.com
Contact: Nancy Brewer, Pres.

61958 ■ Eureka Chamber of Commerce
PO Box 11
Eureka, MO 63025
Ph:(636)938-6062
Fax: (636)938-9983
Co. E-mail: office@eurekachamber.us
URL: http://www.eurekachamber.us
Contact: Patrick Feder, Pres.

61959 ■ Excelsior Springs Area Chamber of Commerce
PO Box 632
461 S Thompson Ave.
Excelsior Springs, MO 64024
Ph:(816)630-6161
Co. E-mail: escoc@sbcglobal.net
URL: http://www.exspgschamber.com
Contact: Mr. Terry Smelcer, Exec.Dir.

61960 ■ Farmington Chamber of Commerce
302 N Washington St.
PO Box 191
Farmington, MO 63640-0191
Ph:(573)756-3615
Fax: (573)756-1003
Co. E-mail: ursalak@farmingtonmo.org
URL: http://www.farmingtonmo.org
Contact: Ursala Kthiri, Exec.Dir.

61961 ■ Fenton Area Chamber of Commerce
1720-F W Park Ctr.
Fenton, MO 63026
Ph:(636)717-0200
Fax: (636)717-0214
Co. E-mail: exdir@fentonmochamber.com
URL: http://www.fentonmochamber.com
Contact: Jeannie Braun, Exec.Dir.

61962 ■ Florissant Valley Chamber of Commerce
420 W Washington St.
Florissant, MO 63031
Ph:(314)831-3500
Fax: (314)831-9682
Co. E-mail: info@florissantvalleycc.com
URL: http://www.florissantvalleycc.com
Contact: Diana Weidinger, Pres.

61963 ■ Forsyth Chamber of Commerce
PO Box 777
Forsyth, MO 65653
Ph:(417)546-2741
Fax: (417)546-4192
Co. E-mail: forsythchamber@inter-linc.net
URL: http://www.forsythmissouri.net
Contact: Mr. Darrell Wells, Exec.Dir.

61964 ■ Fredericktown Chamber of Commerce
137 W Main
PO Box 505
Fredericktown, MO 63645
Ph:(573)783-2604
Fax: (573)783-2645
Co. E-mail: ftown@clas.net

URL: http://www.fredericktownchamber.com
Contact: Terry Sikes, Exec.Sec.

61965 ■ Gerald Area Chamber of Commerce
PO Box 274
Gerald, MO 63037
Ph:(573)764-4627
Contact: Dr. Jennifer Scheer, Pres.

61966 ■ Grandview Area Chamber of Commerce
12500 S 71 Hwy.
Grandview, MO 64030
Ph:(816)761-6505
Fax: (816)763-8460
Co. E-mail: ksc@grandview.org
URL: http://www.grandview.org
Contact: Kim Curtis, Pres.

61967 ■ Greater Kansas City Chamber of Commerce
2600 Commerce Tower
911 Main St., Ste. 2600
Kansas City, MO 64105
Ph:(816)221-2424
Fax: (816)221-7440
Co. E-mail: waltz@kcchamber.com
URL: http://www.kcchamber.com
Contact: Peter Levi, Pres.

61968 ■ Greater Poplar Bluff Area Chamber of Commerce
1111 W Pine St.
Poplar Bluff, MO 63901
Ph:(573)785-7761
Fax: (573)785-1901
Co. E-mail: info@poplarbluffchamber.org
URL: http://www.poplarbluffchamber.org
Contact: Ken Parrett, Pres.

61969 ■ Greater Warrensburg Area Chamber of Commerce
100 S Holden St.
Warrensburg, MO 64093-2331
Ph:(660)747-3168
Free: 877-OLD-DRUM
Fax: (660)429-5490
Co. E-mail: chamber@warrensburg.org
URL: http://www.warrensburg.org
Contact: Mrs. Tamara Long, Exec.Dir.

61970 ■ Greater West Plains Area Chamber of Commerce
401 Jefferson Ave.
West Plains, MO 65775-2659
Ph:(417)256-4433
Fax: (417)256-8711
Co. E-mail: info@wpchamber.com
URL: http://wpchamber.com
Contact: Kris K. Norman, Pres.

61971 ■ Hannibal Area Chamber of Commerce
623 Broadway
PO Box 230
Hannibal, MO 63401
Ph:(573)221-1101
Fax: (573)221-3389
Co. E-mail: info@hannibalchamber.org
URL: http://www.hannibalchamber.org
Contact: Larry B. Craig, Exec.Dir.

61972 ■ Harrisonville Area Chamber of Commerce
400 E Mechanic
Harrisonville, MO 64701
Ph:(816)380-5271
Fax: (816)884-4291
Co. E-mail: harrisonvillechamber@earthlink.net
URL: http://www.harrisonvillechamber.com
Contact: Ann Britt, Exec.Dir.

61973 ■ Hermann Area Chamber of Commerce
312 Market St.
Hermann, MO 65041
Ph:(573)486-2313

Free: 800-932-8687
Fax: (573)486-8995
Co. E-mail: chamber@hermannmo.com
URL: http://www.hermannmo.info
Contact: June Diebal, Mgr.

61974 ■ Higginsville Chamber of Commerce
1919 Main St., Ste. 101
PO Box 164
Higginsville, MO 64037
Ph:(660)584-3030
Fax: (660)584-3033
Co. E-mail: chamber@ctcis.net
URL: http://www.higginsvillechamber.org
Contact: Donald Knehans, Pres.

61975 ■ Holden Chamber of Commerce
100 E 2nd
Holden, MO 64040
Ph:(816)732-6844
Co. E-mail: info@holdenchamber.com
URL: http://www.holdenchamber.com
Contact: Sam Raber, Pres.

61976 ■ Houston Area Chamber of Commerce
PO Box 374
Houston, MO 65483
Ph:(417)967-2220
Fax: (417)967-2178
Co. E-mail: chamber@train.missouri.org
Contact: Brenda Senter, Exec.Dir.

61977 ■ Independence Chamber of Commerce
210 W Truman Rd.
PO Box 1077
Independence, MO 64051
Ph:(816)252-4745
Fax: (816)252-4917
Co. E-mail: info@independencechamber.org
URL: http://www.independencechamber.com
Contact: Rick Hemmingsen, Pres.

61978 ■ Jackson Chamber of Commerce
125 E Main St.
PO Box 352
Jackson, MO 63755
Ph:(573)243-8131
Free: 888-501-8827
Fax: (573)243-0725
Co. E-mail: chamber@jacksonmo.com
URL: http://www.jacksonmo.com
Contact: Marybeth Williams, Exec.Dir.

61979 ■ Jefferson City Area Chamber of Commerce
PO Box 776
213 Adams St.
Jefferson City, MO 65101
Ph:(573)634-3616
Fax: (573)634-3805
Co. E-mail: linda@jcchamber.org
URL: http://www.jcchamber.org
Contact: Randall G. Allan, Pres./CEO

61980 ■ Joplin Area Chamber of Commerce
320 E 4th St.
Joplin, MO 64801
Ph:(417)624-4150
Co. E-mail: robrian@joplincc.com
URL: http://www.joplincc.com
Contact: Rob O'Brian, Pres.

61981 ■ Kahoka - Clark County Chamber of Commerce
250 N Morgan St.
Kahoka, MO 63445
Ph:(660)727-3143
Contact: Beverly Lasfoon, Pres.

61982 ■ Kearney Chamber of Commerce
PO Box 242
Kearney, MO 64060
Ph:(816)628-4229
Fax: (816)902-1234
Co. E-mail: kearneychamber@exop.net

URL: http://www.kearneychamber.org
Contact: Ms. Siouxsan Eisen, Exec.Dir.

61983 ■ Kennett Chamber of Commerce
1601 1st St.
PO Box 61
Kennett, MO 63857
Ph:(573)888-5828
Free: (866)848-5828
Fax: (573)888-9802
Co. E-mail: info@kennettmo.com
URL: http://www.kennettmo.com
Contact: Jan McElwrath, Exec. Dir.

61984 ■ Kingdom of Callaway Chamber of Commerce
409 Court St.
Fulton, MO 65251-1724
Ph:(573)642-3055
Free: 800-257-3554
Fax: (573)642-5182
Co. E-mail: debcoc@sbcgloabl.net
URL: http://www.callawaychamber.com
Contact: Nancy Lewis, Exec. Dir.

61985 ■ Kirksville Area Chamber of Commerce
304 S Franklin
PO Box 251
Kirksville, MO 63501-3581
Ph:(660)665-3766
Fax: (660)665-3767
Co. E-mail: kvacoc@kirksvillechamber.com
URL: http://www.kirksvillechamber.com
Contact: Alisa R. Kigar, Exec.Dir.

61986 ■ Kirkwood Area Chamber of Commerce
108 W Adams
Kirkwood, MO 63122
Ph:(314)821-4161
Fax: (314)821-5229
Co. E-mail: thechamber@thechamber.us
URL: http://www.kirkwoodarea.com
Contact: Jim Wright, Pres.

61987 ■ Knob Noster Chamber of Commerce
PO Box 278
Knob Noster, MO 65336
Ph:(660)563-3011
Fax: (660)563-3196
Contact: Laurie Massengale, Pres.

61988 ■ Lake of the Ozarks West Chamber of Commerce
PO Box 340
Sunrise Beach, MO 65079-0340
Ph:(573)374-5500
Free: 877-227-4086
Fax: (573)374-8576
Co. E-mail: info@lakewestchamber.com
URL: http://www.lakewestchamber.com
Contact: Mr. Michael Kenagy, Exec. Dir.

61989 ■ Lebanon Area Chamber of Commerce
PO Box 505
Lebanon, MO 65536
Ph:(417)588-3256
Fax: (417)588-3251
Co. E-mail: stephanie@lebanonmissouri.com
URL: http://www.lebanonmissouri.com
Contact: Debbie Wikowsky, Exec.Dir.

61990 ■ Lexington Area Chamber of Commerce
1029 Franklin Ave.
PO Box 457
Lexington, MO 64067
Ph:(660)259-3082
Fax: (660)259-7776
Co. E-mail: lexcofc@iland.net
URL: http://www.historiclexington.com
Contact: Ann Crume, Exec. Dir.

61991 ■ Liberty Area Chamber of Commerce
9 S Leonard
Liberty, MO 64068

Ph:(816)781-5200
Fax: (816)781-4901
Co. E-mail: info@libertychamber.com
URL: http://www.libertychamber.com
Contact: Gayle Potter, Pres.

61992 ■ Louisiana Chamber of Commerce
202 S 3rd St., Ste. 120
Louisiana, MO 63353
Ph:(573)754-5921
Free: 888-642-3800
Fax: (573)754-5921
Co. E-mail: chamber@louisiana.mo.us
URL: http://www.louisianamo.com
Contact: Linda Hallows, Office Admin.

61993 ■ Macon Area Chamber of Commerce
1407 N Missouri St.
Macon, MO 63552-1562
Ph:(660)385-2811
Fax: (660)385-6543
Co. E-mail: macc@missvalley.com
URL: http://maconmochamber.com
Contact: Linda Mohn, Exec.Dir.

61994 ■ Malden Chamber of Commerce
PO Box 352
123 W Main
Malden, MO 63863
Ph:(573)276-4519
Fax: (573)276-4925
Co. E-mail: info@maldenchamber.com
URL: http://www.maldenchamber.com
Contact: Bill Hampton, Dir.

61995 ■ Marceline Chamber of Commerce
PO Box 93
Marceline, MO 64658
Ph:(660)376-3528
Fax: (660)376-3881
Co. E-mail: goddards@cvalley.net
URL: http://www.marceline.com
Contact: Pat Kussman, Pres.

61996 ■ Mark Twain Lake Chamber of Commerce
PO Box 182
Monroe City, MO 63456-0182
Ph:(573)735-2105
Fax: (573)735-2105
Co. E-mail: mtlcoc@socket.net
URL: http://www.marktwainlake.com
Contact: Debra Hinds, Exec.Dir.

61997 ■ Marshall Chamber of Commerce
214 N Lafayette
Marshall, MO 65340-1700
Ph:(660)886-3324
Fax: (660)831-0349
Co. E-mail: marshcoc@cdsinet.net
URL: http://www.marshallchamber.com
Contact: Mr. Ken Yowell, Exec.Dir.

61998 ■ Maryland Heights Chamber of Commerce
545 Wesport Plz.
St. Louis, MO 63146-3007
Ph:(314)576-6603
Fax: (314)576-6855
Co. E-mail: kim@mhcc.com
URL: http://www.mhcc.com
Contact: Kim Braddy, Exec.Dir.

61999 ■ Maryville Chamber of Commerce
423 N Market
Maryville, MO 64468
Ph:(660)582-8643
Fax: (660)582-3071
Co. E-mail: chamber@asde.net
URL: http://www.maryvillechamber.com
Contact: Lisa Luke, Exec.Dir.

62000 ■ Mexico Area Chamber of Commerce
100 W Jackson St.
PO Box 56
Mexico, MO 65265
Ph:(573)581-2765

Free: 800-581-2765
Fax: (573)581-6226
Co. E-mail: scaine@mexico-chamber.org
URL: http://www.mexico-chamber.org
Contact: Sue Caine, Exec.VP

62001 ■ Monett Chamber of Commerce
PO Box 47
Monett, MO 65708-0047
Ph:(417)235-7919
Fax: (417)235-4076
Co. E-mail: chamber@monett-mo.com
URL: http://www.monett-mo.com
Contact: Vicki McCormick, Board Pres.

62002 ■ Monroe City Area Chamber of Commerce
314 S Main
Monroe City, MO 63456
Ph:(573)735-4391
URL: http://www.marktwainlake.com/monroecity/mcchamber.html
Contact: Shelia Kandrick, Pres.

62003 ■ Montgomery City Area Chamber of Commerce
PO Box 31
Montgomery City, MO 63361
Ph:(573)564-2712
Free: 800-242-8829
Fax: (573)564-3802
Co. E-mail: byjones@ktis.net
URL: http://www.montgomerycity.org
Contact: Benjamin Jones, Dir.

62004 ■ Mound City Chamber of Commerce
601 State St.
Mound City, MO 64470-1146
Ph:(660)442-3262
URL: http://www.mochamber.org
Contact: Pam Smith, Pres.

62005 ■ Mount Vernon Chamber of Commerce
PO Box 373
Mount Vernon, MO 65712
Ph:(417)466-7654
Fax: (417)466-7654
Co. E-mail: mtvchamber@corpranet.net
URL: http://www.mtvernonchamber.com
Contact: Doris McBride, Exec.Sec.

62006 ■ Mountain Grove Chamber of Commerce
PO Box 434
Mountain Grove, MO 65711
Ph:(417)926-4135
Co. E-mail: chamber@mountaingrovechamber.com
URL: http://www.mountaingrovechamber.com
Contact: Joe Ivory, Pres.

62007 ■ Mountain View Chamber of Commerce
117 E 2nd St.
Mountain View, MO 65548
Ph:(417)934-2794
Free: 877-266-8706
Fax: (417)934-2882
Co. E-mail: mvcoc@townsqr.com
Contact: Linda Lewis, Exec.Dir.

62008 ■ Nevada-Vernon County Chamber of Commerce
201 E Cherry, Ste. 204
Nevada, MO 64772-3163
Ph:(417)667-5300
Fax: (417)667-2157
Co. E-mail: chamber@nevada-mo.com
URL: http://www.nevada-mo.com
Contact: Kathi Wysong, Exec.Dir.

62009 ■ New Madrid Chamber of Commerce
PO Box 96
New Madrid, MO 63869
Ph:(573)748-5300
Free: 877-748-5300
Fax: (573)748-5402

Co. E-mail: chambernm@yahoo.com
URL: http://www.new-madrid.mo.us
Contact: Margaret Palmer, Exec.Dir.

62010 ■ Nixa Area Chamber of Commerce
105 Sherman Way, Ste. 108
Nixa, MO 65714
Ph:(417)725-1545
Fax: (417)725-4532
Co. E-mail: info@nixachamber.com
URL: http://www.nixachamber.com
Contact: Sharon Whitehill Gray, Exec.Dir.

62011 ■ North County Chamber of Commerce
119 Church St., Ste. 135
Ferguson, MO 63135-2459
Ph:(314)521-6000
Fax: (314)521-2897
Co. E-mail: nccferg@msn.com
URL: http://www.northcountycc.com
Contact: Ms. Jean Montgomery, Exec.Dir.

62012 ■ Northland Regional Chamber of Commerce
634 NW Englewood Rd.
Kansas City, MO 64118
Ph:(816)455-9911
Fax: (816)455-9933
Co. E-mail: northland@northlandchamber.com
URL: http://www.northlandchamber.com
Contact: Sheila Tracy, Pres.

62013 ■ Northwest Chamber of Commerce
11965 St. Charles Rock Rd., Ste. 203
Bridgeton, MO 63044
Ph:(314)291-2131
Fax: (314)291-2153
Co. E-mail: info@nwcommchamber.org
URL: http://www.nwcommchamber.org
Contact: Pat Watson, Sec.

62014 ■ Oak Grove Chamber of Commerce
103 SE 12th St.
Oak Grove, MO 64075
Ph:(816)690-4147
Co. E-mail: wanda@oakgrovechamber.org
URL: http://www.oakgrovechamber.org
Contact: Wanda Sandman, Exec.Dir.

62015 ■ Odessa Chamber of Commerce
1236 W Old 40 Hwy.
Odessa, MO 64076
Ph:(816)633-4044
Fax: (816)633-4044
Co. E-mail: director@odessamochamber.com
URL: http://www.odessamochamber.com
Contact: Terri Peel, Exec.Dir.

62016 ■ O'Fallon Chamber of Commerce
2897 Hwy. K, Ste. 200
O'Fallon, MO 63368
Ph:(636)240-1818
Fax: (636)281-8288
Co. E-mail: info@ofallonchamber.org
URL: http://www.ofallonchamber.org
Contact: Bill Mocca, Chm.

62017 ■ Owensville Chamber of Commerce
PO Box 77
Owensville, MO 65066
Ph:(573)437-4270
Co. E-mail: office@owensvillemissouri.com
URL: http://www.owensvillemissouri.com/chamber.html
Contact: Ellen Adams, Pres.

62018 ■ Ozark Chamber of Commerce
191 N 17th St.
PO Box 1450
Ozark, MO 65721
Ph:(417)581-6139
Fax: (417)581-0639
Co. E-mail: ozarkchamber@aol.com
URL: http://www.ozarkchamber.com
Contact: Sue Larimer, Pres.

62019 ■ Pacific Area Chamber of Commerce
333 Chamber Dr.
Pacific, MO 63069
Ph:(636)271-6639
Co. E-mail: icetab@fidmail.com
URL: http://www.pacificchamber.com
Contact: Tim Baker, Pres.

62020 ■ Paris Area Chamber of Commerce
208 N Main St.
Paris, MO 65275-1397
Ph:(660)327-4450
Fax: (660)327-4280
Co. E-mail: chamber@parismo.net
URL: http://www.parismo.net
Contact: Lenice Dunlap, Exec.Dir.

62021 ■ Park Hills Chamber of Commerce
5 Municipal Dr.
Park Hills, MO 63601-2064
Ph:(573)431-1051
Fax: (573)431-2327
Co. E-mail: phcc1@i1.net
URL: http://parkhillscoc.brick.net
Contact: Mrs. Tamara Burns, Exec.Dir.

62022 ■ Perryville Chamber of Commerce
2 W Ste. Maries St.
Perryville, MO 63775
Ph:(573)547-6062
Fax: (573)547-6071
Co. E-mail: perryvillemo@sbcglobal.net
URL: http://www.perryvillemo.com
Contact: Melissa Hemmann, Exec.Dir.

62023 ■ Piedmont Area Chamber of Commerce
PO Box 101
Piedmont, MO 63957
Ph:(573)223-4046
Free: 800-818-4046
Fax: (573)223-4046
Contact: Kawanda Brinkley, Pres.

62024 ■ Platte City Chamber of Commerce
PO Box 650
Platte City, MO 64079
Ph:(816)858-5270
Co. E-mail: chamber@plattecitymo.com
URL: http://www.plattecitymo.com
Contact: Karen E. Wagoner, Exec. Dir.

62025 ■ Plattsburg Chamber of Commerce
101 S Main
Plattsburg, MO 64477
Ph:(816)539-2649
Fax: (816)539-3539
Co. E-mail: info@plattsburgchamber.org
URL: http://www.plattsburgchamber.org
Contact: Linda Stotts, Dir.

62026 ■ Portageville Chamber of Commerce
PO Box 409
Portageville, MO 63873
Ph:(573)379-5390
Fax: (573)379-3080
Co. E-mail: mdell@sheltonbbs.com
Contact: Sandy Stewart, Pres.

62027 ■ Raymore Chamber of Commerce
PO Box 885
Raymore, MO 64083
Ph:(816)322-0599
Fax: (816)322-7127
Co. E-mail: info@raymorechamber.com
URL: http://www.raymorechamber.com
Contact: Brent Ewert, Pres.

62028 ■ Raytown Area Chamber of Commerce
5909 Raytown Trafficway
Raytown, MO 64133-3860
Ph:(816)353-8500
Fax: (816)353-8525
Co. E-mail: staff@raytownchamber.com
URL: http://www.raytownchamber.com
Contact: Kathie Schutte, Pres.

62029 ■ Republic Area Chamber of Commerce
225 US Hwy. 60 W
Republic, MO 65738
Ph:(417)732-5200
Fax: (417)732-2851
Co. E-mail: chamber@republicmo.com
URL: http://www.republicmo.com
Contact: Jennifer Birkenfield, Exec.Dir.

62030 ■ Richmond Chamber of Commerce
107 N Thornton
Richmond, MO 64085
Ph:(816)776-6916
Fax: (816)776-6917
Co. E-mail: cofcommerce@mchsi.com
URL: http://www.richmondchamber.org
Contact: Jerry McCarter, Exec.Dir.

62031 ■ Ripley County Chamber of Commerce
101 Washington St.
Doniphan, MO 63935
Ph:(573)996-2212
Fax: (573)996-2212
Co. E-mail: ripleyco@semo.net
URL: http://www.ripleycountymissouri.org
Contact: Ms. Tracey Holden, Exec. Dir.

62032 ■ Rock Port Chamber of Commerce
PO Box 130
Rock Port, MO 64482
Ph:(660)744-2222
Contact: Jack Mayer, Pres.

62033 ■ Rolla Area Chamber of Commerce
1301 Kingshighway
Rolla, MO 65401
Ph:(573)364-3577
Free: 888-809-3817
Fax: (573)364-5222
Co. E-mail: rollacc@rollachamber.org
URL: http://rollachamber.org
Contact: Ms. Linda Kuenzie, Exec.Dir.

62034 ■ St. Charles Chamber of Commerce
2201 1st Capitol Dr.
St. Charles, MO 63301-5805
Ph:(636)946-0633
Fax: (636)946-0301
Co. E-mail: info@stcharleschamber.org
URL: http://www.stcharleschamber.org
Contact: Claire Felder, Membership Dir.

62035 ■ St. Clair Area Chamber of Commerce
920F St. Clair Plaza Dr.
St. Clair, MO 63077
Ph:(636)629-1889
Fax: (636)629-5510
Co. E-mail: webmaster@stclairmo.com
URL: http://www.stclairmo.com
Contact: Terry Triphahn, Exec.Dir.

62036 ■ Ste. Genevieve Chamber of Commerce
251 Market St.
Ste. Genevieve, MO 63670
Ph:(573)883-3686
Fax: (573)883-7092
Co. E-mail: stegenchamber@sbcgobal.net
URL: http://www.saintegenevieve.org
Contact: Ron Armbruster, Pres.

62037 ■ St. James Chamber of Commerce
PO Box 358
St. James, MO 65559
Ph:(573)265-3899
Free: 800-480-3899
Co. E-mail: chamberofcommerce@stjames-mo.org
URL: http://www.stjamesmissouri.org
Contact: Angie Nappier, Pres.

62038 ■ St. Joseph Area Chamber of Commerce
3003 Frederick Ave.
St. Joseph, MO 64506

Ph:(816)232-4461
Free: 800-748-7856
Fax: (816)364-4873
Co. E-mail: chamber@saintjoseph.com
URL: http://www.saintjoseph.com
Contact: Mr. R. Patt Lilly, Pres./CEO

62039 ■ St. Mary Chamber of Commerce
PO Box 38
St. Mary, MO 63673
Ph:(573)543-2230
Contact: Robert Bartels, Pres.

62040 ■ St. Peters Chamber of Commerce
1236 Jungermann Rd., Ste. C
St. Peters, MO 63376-6962
Ph:(636)447-3336
Fax: (636)447-9575
Co. E-mail: stpeterschamber@stpeterschamber.com
URL: http://www.stpeterschamber.com
Contact: Ed Weeks, Pres./CEO

62041 ■ Salem Area Chamber of Commerce
200 S Main St.
Salem, MO 65560
Ph:(573)729-6900
Fax: (573)729-6741
Co. E-mail: chamber@salemmo.com
URL: http://www.salemmo.com
Contact: Becki Godi, Dir.

62042 ■ Savannah Area Chamber of Commerce
PO Box 101
Savannah, MO 64485
Ph:(816)324-3976
Fax: (816)324-5728
Co. E-mail: sacc@savannahmochamber.com
URL: http://www.savannahmochamber.com
Contact: Christy Sipes, Coor.

62043 ■ Sedalia Area Chamber of Commerce
600 E 3rd St.
Sedalia, MO 65301-4499
Ph:(660)826-2222
Fax: (660)826-2223
Co. E-mail: tballard@visitsedaliamo.com
URL: http://www.sedaliachamber.com
Contact: Deborah L. Biermann, Exec.VP

62044 ■ Sikeston Area Chamber of Commerce
One Industrial Dr.
Sikeston, MO 63801-5216
Ph:(573)471-2498
Fax: (573)471-2499
Co. E-mail: chamber@sikeston.net
URL: http://www.sikeston.net
Contact: Missy Marshall, Exec.Dir.

62045 ■ South Kansas City Chamber of Commerce
5908 E Bannister Rd.
Kansas City, MO 64134-1141
Ph:(816)761-7660
Fax: (816)761-7340
Co. E-mail: skccc@southkcchamber.com
URL: http://www.southkcchamber.com
Contact: Barb Engel, Exec.Dir.

62046 ■ Springfield Area Chamber of Commerce
202 S John Q. Hammons Pkwy.
Springfield, MO 65806
Ph:(417)862-5567
Fax: (417)862-1611
Co. E-mail: jim@springfieldchamber.com
URL: http://www.springfieldchamber.com
Contact: Jim Anderson, Pres.

62047 ■ Steelville Chamber of Commerce
PO Box 956
Steelville, MO 65565
Ph:(573)775-5533
Fax: (573)775-5521
Co. E-mail: chamber@misn.com
URL: http://www.steelville.com/chamberofcommerce

Contact: Becky Teed, Pres.

62048 ■ Stockton Area Chamber of Commerce
PO Box 410
Stockton, MO 65785
Ph:(417)276-5213
Co. E-mail: scofc@microcore.net
Contact: Charlotte Haden, Exec. Dir.

62049 ■ Stover Chamber of Commerce
Blue Lion Promotions
109 W 4th St.
Stover, MO 65078
Ph:(573)377-2137
Co. E-mail: vchandler@blueliondesigns.com
URL: http://www.stovermissouri.org
Contact: Tom Chandler, Pres.

62050 ■ Sullivan Area Chamber of Commerce
2 W Springfield
PO Box 536
Sullivan, MO 63080-0536
Ph:(573)468-3314
Fax: (573)860-2313
Co. E-mail: chamber@sullivanmo.com
URL: http://www.sullivanmo.com
Contact: Sally Jo Schatz, Exec.Dir.

62051 ■ Summersville Chamber of Commerce
PO Box 251
Summersville, MO 65571
Ph:(417)932-5900
Fax: (417)932-4358
Contact: Faye Terrill, Pres.

62052 ■ Table Rock Lake - Kimberling City Area Chamber of Commerce
14226 State Hwy. 13
PO Box 495
Kimberling City, MO 65686
Ph:(417)739-2564
Free: 800-595-0393
Co. E-mail: trlchamber@visittablerocklake.com
URL: http://www.visittablerocklake.com
Contact: Ms. Cindy L. Morris, Pres.

62053 ■ Thayer Area Chamber of Commerce
PO Box 14
Thayer, MO 65791
Ph:(417)264-7324
Fax: (417)264-7291
Co. E-mail: jim.hart@pneumatek.com
URL: http://www.thayerchamber.com
Contact: Jim Hart, Pres.

62054 ■ Tipton Chamber of Commerce
PO Box 307
Tipton, MO 65081-0307
Ph:(660)433-6377
Co. E-mail: chamber@tiptonmo.com
URL: http://www.tiptonmo.com
Contact: Dan Ramsey, Pres.

62055 ■ Trenton Area Chamber of Commerce
617 Main St.
Trenton, MO 64683
Ph:(660)359-4234
Fax: (660)359-4325
Co. E-mail: trentonmochamber@grundyec.net
URL: http://www.trentonmochamber.com
Contact: Terri Henderson, Pres.

62056 ■ Troy Area Chamber of Commerce
112 Professional Pkwy.
Troy, MO 63379
Ph:(636)462-8769
Fax: (636)528-3731
Co. E-mail: info@troyonthemove.com
URL: http://www.troyonthemove.com
Contact: Kerry M. Klump, Exec.Dir.

62057 ■ Twin City Area Chamber of Commerce
114 Main St.
Festus, MO 63028

Ph:(314)937-7697
Fax: (636)937-0925
Co. E-mail: cofc@jcn.net
Contact: Claudia Kirn, Admin.

62058 ■ Union Chamber of Commerce
103 S Oak St.
PO Box 168
Union, MO 63084-0168
Ph:(636)583-8979
Fax: (636)583-3237
Co. E-mail: director@unionmochamber.org
URL: http://www.unionmochamber.org
Contact: Tammy Stowe, Exec.Dir.

62059 ■ Van Buren Area Chamber of Commerce
PO Box 356
Van Buren, MO 63965
Ph:(573)323-4782
Free: 800-692-7582
Fax: (573)323-4696
Co. E-mail: vanburen@semo.net
URL: http://www.semo.net/vanburen
Contact: Dale Kerkvliet, Pres.

62060 ■ Versailles Area Chamber of Commerce
101 N Monroe St.
PO Box 256
Versailles, MO 65084
Ph:(573)378-4401
Fax: (573)378-2499
Co. E-mail: vchamber@sbcglobal.net
URL: http://www.versailleschamber.com
Contact: Sherri Johnson Bauman, Dir.

62061 ■ Warrenton Area Chamber of Commerce
122 E Booneslick Rd.
Warrenton, MO 63383
Ph:(636)456-2530
Fax: (636)456-2329
Co. E-mail: warrentoncoc@socket.net
URL: http://warrentoncoc.com
Contact: Allan Dreyer, Pres.

62062 ■ Warsaw Area Chamber of Commerce
PO Box 264
Warsaw, MO 65355
Free: 800-WARSAW-4
Co. E-mail: warsawcc@iland.net
URL: http://warsawmo.org
Contact: Jill Keehn, Exec.VP

62063 ■ Washington Area Chamber of Commerce
323 W Main St.
Washington, MO 63090
Ph:(636)239-2715
Free: 888-7-WASHMO
Fax: (636)239-1381
Co. E-mail: wluther@washmo.org
URL: http://www.washmo.org
Contact: Walt Luther, Pres./CEO

62064 ■ Waynesville-St. Robert Area Chamber of Commerce
137 St. Robert Blvd.
St. Robert, MO 65584
Ph:(573)336-5121
Fax: (573)336-5472
Co. E-mail: wschamber@earthlink.net
URL: http://www.waynesville-strobertchamber.com
Contact: Bob Chapman, Pres.

62065 ■ Webb City Area Chamber of Commerce
555 S Main St.
PO Box 287
Webb City, MO 64870
Ph:(417)673-1154
Fax: (417)673-2856
Co. E-mail: dixie@webbcitychamber.com
URL: http://www.webbcitychamber.com
Contact: Dixie Meredith, Exec. Dir.

62066 ■ Webster Groves-Shrewsbury Area Chamber of Commerce
46 W Lockwood
St. Louis, MO 63119-2932
Ph:(314)962-4142
Fax: (314)962-9398
Co. E-mail: chamberinfo@go-webster.com
URL: http://www.webstershrewsburychamber.com

62067 ■ Wentzville Chamber of Commerce
PO Box 11
Wentzville, MO 63385
Ph:(636)327-6914
Co. E-mail: info@wentzvillechamber.com
URL: http://www.wentzvillechamber.com

62068 ■ West St. Louis County Chamber of Commerce
14811 Manchester Rd., Ste. 100
Ballwin, MO 63011
Ph:(636)230-9900
Fax: (636)230-9912
Co. E-mail: info@westcountychamber.com
URL: http://www.westcountychamber.com
Contact: Nancy Gray, Exec.Dir.

62069 ■ Willow Springs Area Chamber of Commerce
112 E Main St.
Willow Springs, MO 65793
Ph:(417)469-5519
Fax: (417)469-3192
Co. E-mail: wscoc@townsgr.com
URL: http://www.willowspringscoc.com
Contact: Pat Dunivin, Exec.Dir.

62070 ■ Windsor Area Chamber of Commerce
102 N Main
Windsor, MO 65360
Ph:(660)647-2318
Co. E-mail: windsorm@iland.net
URL: http://www.windsormo.org
Contact: Jennifer Martinez, Exec.Dir.

62071 ■ Wright City Area Chamber of Commerce
PO Box 444
Wright City, MO 63390
Ph:(636)745-7855
Co. E-mail: webmaster@wrightcity.org
URL: http://www.wrightcitychamber.com
Contact: Melissa Springmeyer, Pres.

MINORITY BUSINESS ASSISTANCE PROGRAMS

62072 ■ Kansas City Minority Business Development Center–KCMO Of-DHCD-Small Business Division
1601 E 18th St., Ste. 200
Kansas City, MO 64108
Ph:(816)513-6817
Fax: (816)513-6820
Co. E-mail: span_peoples@kcmo.org

62073 ■ Missouri Department of Economic Development–Office of Minority Business
PO Box 1157
PO Box 118
Jefferson City, MO 65102
Ph:(573)751-4962
Free: 800-523-1434
Fax: (573)751-7258
Co. E-mail: ecodev@ded.mo.gov
URL: http://www.ded.mo.gov
Description: Provides information on obtaining technical and financial assistance, offers education programs, and advocates on the behalf of minority businesses.

62074 ■ St. Louis Minority Business Council
308 N 21st St., Ste. 700
St. Louis, MO 63103
Ph:(314)241-1143

Fax: (314)241-1073
Co. E-mail: info@simbc
URL: http://www.slmbc.org

FINANCING AND LOAN PROGRAMS

62075 ■ A.G. Edwards & Sons
1 N. Jefferson
Saint Louis, MO 63103
Ph:(314)955-3000
Fax: (314)955-2890
URL: http://www.agedwards.com
Contact: Chris Redmond, Managing Director
Investment Policies: Fund of funds. **Industry Preferences:** Agriculture, forestry, and fishing. **Geographic Preferences:** Missouri.

62076 ■ Bankers Capital Corp.
3100 Gillham Rd.
Kansas City, MO 64109
Ph:(816)531-1600
Fax: (816)531-1334
Contact: Lee Glasnapp, Vice President
Preferred Investment Size: $100,000 minimum. **Investment Types:** Leveraged buyout. **Industry Preferences:** Semiconductors and other electronics, consumer related, industrial and energy. **Geographic Preferences:** Midwest.

62077 ■ Bome Investors, Inc.
8000 Maryland Ave., Ste. 1190
St. Louis, MO 63105
Ph:(314)721-5707
Fax: (314)721-5135
URL: http://www.gatewayventures.com
Contact: Gregory R. Johnson
Preferred Investment Size: $500,000 to $1,000,000.
Investment Types: Start-up, early and late stage. **Industry Preferences:** Diversified. **Geographic Preferences:** Midwest.

62078 ■ Broadband Investment Group (BIG)
12444 Powerscourt Rd., Ste. 300
Saint Louis, MO 63131
Ph:(314)984-2520
Fax: (415)974-5310
URL: http://www.bigcorp.com
Contact: David Aiello, Managing Director
Investment Policies: Early stage. **Industry Preferences:** Internet specific. **Geographic Preferences:** U.S.

62079 ■ Capital for Business, Inc. (Clayton)
11 S. Meramac St., Ste. 1430
Clayton, MO 63105
Ph:(314)746-7427
Fax: (314)746-8739
URL: http://www.capitalforbusiness.com
Contact: Wes Hampp, Vice President
Preferred Investment Size: $1,000,000 to $5,000,000. **Investment Types:** Leveraged buyout, management buyouts, mezzanine, acquisition, and later stage. **Industry Preferences:** Industrial and energy, other products, Internet specific, medical and health, consumer related, semiconductors and other electronics, computer hardware, communications and media, and biotechnology. **Geographic Preferences:** Midwest.

62080 ■ Capital for Business, Inc. (Kansas City)
1000 Walnut St., 18th Fl.
Kansas City, MO 64106
Ph:(816)234-2375
Fax: (816)234-2952
URL: http://www.capitalforbusiness.com
Contact: Wess Hampp, Vice President
Preferred Investment Size: $1,000,000 to $5,000,000. **Investment Types:** Leveraged buyout, management buyouts, acquisition, mezzanine, and later stage. **Industry Preferences:** Industrial and energy, other products, Internet specific, medical and health, consumer related, semiconductors and other electronics, computer hardware, communications and media, and biotechnology. **Geographic Preferences:** Midwest.

62081 ■ Crown Capital Corporation
540 Maryville Ctr. Dr., Ste. 120
Saint Louis, MO 63141
Ph:(314)576-1201
Fax: (314)576-1525
URL: http://www.crown-cap.com
Preferred Investment Size: $1,000,000 minimum.
Investment Types: Management buyouts, acquisition, controlblock purchases, distressed debt, expansion, later stage, leveraged buyout, private placement, and recapitalizations. **Industry Preferences:** Communications, computer software, Internet specific, semiconductors and other electronics, medical and health, consumer related, industrial and energy, financial services, business service, agriculture, forestry and fishing, and other. **Geographic Preferences:** U.S.

62082 ■ De Vries, Snedeker & Duncan LLC
10955 Lowell St., Ste. 1056
Kansas City, MO 66210
Ph:(913)906-0055
Fax: (913)906-0056
Contact: Robert De Vries, Management Director
Preferred Investment Size: $1,500,000 minimum.
Investment Types: Acquisition, expansion, second and later stage, leveraged buyout, management buyouts, mezzanine, private placement, and recapitalizations. **Industry Preferences:** Computer software and services. **Geographic Preferences:** U.S.

62083 ■ Gateway Associates, L.P.
8000 Maryland Ave., Ste. 1190
St. Louis, MO 63105
Ph:(314)721-5707
Fax: (314)721-5135
URL: http://www.gatewayventures.com
Contact: Mark Lewis, Partner
Preferred Investment Size: $500,000 to $2,000,000.
Investment Types: Second stage, mezzanine, leveraged buyout, expansion, and special situation. **Industry Preferences:** Internet specific, computer software and services, biotechnology, communications and media, medical and health, semiconductors and other electronics, other products, industrial and energy, computer hardware. **Geographic Preferences:** Midwest.

62084 ■ Harbison Corporation
8112 Maryland Ave., Ste. 250
Saint Louis, MO 63105
Ph:(314)727-8200
Fax: (314)727-0249
Preferred Investment Size: $500,000 minimum. **Investment Types:** Control-block purchases, leveraged buyout, and special situation. **Geographic Preferences:** Mid Atlantic and Southeast, U.S.; Ontario and Quebec, Canada.

62085 ■ Iemerge Ventures
1700 Wyandotte St.
Kansas City, MO 64108
Ph:(819)960-3456
Preferred Investment Size: $300,000 to $500,000.
Investment Policies: Seed.

62086 ■ InvestAmerica Venture Group, Inc. (Kansas City)
Commerce Tower
911 Main St.
Kansas City, MO 64105
Ph:(816)842-0114
Fax: (816)471-7339
Contact: David Schroder, President
Preferred Investment Size: $500,000 to $1,000,000.
Investment Types: First and second stage, leveraged buyout, and special situation. **Industry Preferences:** Other products, industrial and energy, Internet specific, communications and media, consumer related, computer software, and services, semiconductors and other electronics, computer hardware, biotechnology, medical and health. **Geographic Preferences:** U.S.

62087 ■ Kansas City Equity Partners
233 W. 47th St.
Kansas City, MO 64112

Ph:(816)960-1771
Fax: (816)960-1777
URL: http://www.kcep.com
Contact: Abel Mojica, Principal
Preferred Investment Size: $2,000,000 to $6,000,000. **Investment Types:** First and second stage, expansion, leveraged buyout, and management buyouts. **Industry Preferences:** Internet specific, communications and media, consumer related, industrial and energy, computer software and services, semiconductors and other electronics. **Geographic Preferences:** Mid Atlantic, Midwest, Northeast, Rocky Mountains, and West Coast.

62088 ■ Rivervest Venture Partners
7733 Forsyth Blvd., Ste. 1650
Saint Louis, MO 63150
Ph:(314)726-6700
Fax: (314)726-6715
URL: http://www.rivervest.com
Contact: Andrew Craig, Managing Director
Preferred Investment Size: $500,000 to $6,000,000.
Investment Types: Start-up, seed, early and later stage, and expansion. **Industry Preferences:** Biotechnology, medical and health. **Geographic Preferences:** U.S.

PROCUREMENT ASSISTANCE PROGRAMS

62089 ■ Missouri Procurement Technical Assistance Center
300 University Place
Columbia, MO 65211
Ph:(573)882-3597
Fax: (573)884-4297
Co. E-mail: hudsonm@missouri.edu
URL: http://www.missouribusiness.net/ptac
Contact: Morris Hudson

62090 ■ Missouri Procurement Technical Assistance Center–Western Region PTAC–University of Missouri, Kansas City (4747)
4747 Troost Bldg., Rm. 105
Kansas City, MO 64111
Ph:(816)235-2891
Fax: (816)235-2947
Co. E-mail: leonardd@umkc.edu
URL: http://www.missouribusiness.net/ptac
Contact: Donna Leonard

62091 ■ Missouri Southern State University–Heartland Procurment Technical Assistance Center–Institute for Procurement Assistance (3950)
3950 E Newman Rd.
Mattews Hall Rm. 108
Joplin, MO 64801-1595
Ph:(417)625-9538
Fax: (417)625-9782
Co. E-mail: heartlandptac@mssu.edu
URL: http://www.heartlandptac.org
Contact: Terrie Bennett, Dir
Description: Covers activities for Kansas.

62092 ■ St. Louis County Economic Council
121 S Meramec, Ste. 900
Clayton, MO 63105
Ph:(314)615-7663
Fax: (314)615-7666
URL: http://www.slcec.com
Contact: Dennis Coleman, Pres & CEO

INCUBATORS/RESEARCH AND TECHNOLOGY PARKS

62093 ■ A.T. Still University of Health Sciences–Research Support Services
800 W Jefferson
Kirksville, MO 63501
Ph:(660)626-2237

Fax: (660)626-2099
Co. E-mail: jheard@atsu.edu
URL: http://www.kcom.edu
Contact: John Heard PhD, VP
E-mail: jheard@atsu.edu
Scope: Supports and coordinates university research in biomedicine. Also provides educational service.
Publications: Grants and You (monthly). **Educational Activities:** Rural Elderly Research and Education Conference.

62094 ■ Central Missouri State University–Office of Sponsored Programs
Ward Edward 1800
Warrensburg, MO 64093
Ph:(660)543-4264
Fax: (660)543-4778
Co. E-mail: mstone@cmsu.edu
URL: http://www.cmsu.edu/osp
Contact: Dr. Margaret Stone, Dir.
E-mail: mstone@cmsu.edu
Scope: Establishes, administers, and coordinates programs that guide Central Missouri State University's research, scholarly activity, and creative endeavors. **Publications:** Central Research (annually); Research News Comments (monthly). **Educational Activities:** Two workshops, per academic year for faculty and students.

62095 ■ Growth Opportunity Connection–Center for Business Innovation
4747 Troost Ave.
Kansas City, MO 64110
Ph:(816)235-6146
Fax: (816)235-6586
Co. E-mail: info@goconnection.org
URL: http://www.goconnection.org

62096 ■ Missouri Enterprise Business Center
1706 E Tenth St.
Rolla, MO 65401
Ph:(573)341-0117
Free: 800-95M-AMTC
Fax: (573)341-0135
URL: http://www.missourienterprise.org
Contact: Mary Dean, Pres

62097 ■ St. Louis University–Office of Research Services Administration
3634 Lindell Blvd.
St. Louis, MO 63108-3395
Ph:(314)977-2241
Fax: (314)977-2026
Co. E-mail: knightcl@slu.edu
URL: http://www.slu.edu/research/
Contact: Dr. Carole Knight, Dir.
E-mail: knightcl@slu.edu
Scope: Administers and coordinates research conducted at the University.

62098 ■ The Thomas Hill Enterprise Center
PO Box 276
Macon, MO 63552
Ph:(660)385-6550
URL: http://www.e-center.org
Description: The Center describes itself as an internet/intranet incubator that offers entrepreneurs skills training, government forms, and other services.

62099 ■ University of Missouri–Missouri Research Park
14 Research Pk. Dr., Ste. 200
St. Charles, MO 63304
Ph:(636)441-7701
Fax: (636)441-7761
Co. E-mail: finholtr@umsystem.edu
URL: http://www.um-mrp.org
Contact: Rick Finholt PhD, Exec.Dir.
E-mail: finholtr@umsystem.edu
Scope: A 750-acre research park designed to be a link between academia and industry as a center for research and development in such fields as advanced manufacturing, medical technology, and agriculture.

62100 ■ University of Missouri–Columbia–Office of Research Administration
205 Jesse Hall
Columbia, MO 65211

Ph:(573)882-9500
Fax: (573)884-8371
Co. E-mail: colemanjs@missouri.edu
URL: http://www.research.missouri.edu
Contact: James S. Coleman, Vice Provost for Res.
E-mail: colemanjs@missouri.edu
Scope: Coordinates and administers research, especially extramurally sponsored research, performed in various departments and research units of the University, including Dalton Cardiovascular Research Center, Missouri Resource Assessment Partnership, and Research Reactor Facility. **Publications:** Illumination.

62101 ■ University of Missouri—Kansas City–Office of Research Services
5211 Rockhill Rd.
Kansas City, MO 64110-2499
Ph:(816)235-5600
Fax: (816)235-6532
Co. E-mail: research@umkc.edu
URL: http://www.umkc.edu/research/
Contact: Dr. John R. Baumann, Dir.
E-mail: research@umkc.edu
Scope: Serves as information and coordinating center for research activities of Kansas City campus of the University. **Publications:** Research Notes (monthly).

62102 ■ University of Missouri—St. Louis–Office of Research Administration
341 Woods Hall
8001 Natural Bridge Rd.
St. Louis, MO 63121-4400
Ph:(314)516-5897
Fax: (314)516-6759
Co. E-mail: ora@umsl.edu
URL: http://www.umsl.edu/services/ora/
Contact: Nassar Arshadi PhD, Vice Chancellor, Res.
E-mail: ora@umsl.edu
Scope: Responsible for formulation and implementation of research policies at the University of Missouri—St. Louis.

62103 ■ Washington University in St. Louis–Office of Technology Management
CB 8013
660 S Euclid Ave.
St. Louis, MO 63110
Ph:(314)747-0920
Fax: (314)362-5872
Co. E-mail: otm@msnotes.wustl.edu
URL: http://otm.wustl.edu
Contact: Dr. Michael Douglas, Dir.
E-mail: otm@msnotes.wustl.edu
Scope: Transfers technology from the University to business and industry in the area of biotechnology.

EDUCATIONAL PROGRAMS

62104 ■ Jefferson College–Extended Learning
1000 Viking Dr.
Hillsboro, MO 63050
Ph:(636)789-3000
Fax: (636)789-4012
URL: http://www.jeffco.edu
Description: Offers a program/classes in small business/small business management.

62105 ■ St. Louis Community College–Institute for Continuing Education
300 S Broadway
St. Louis, MO 63102
Ph:(314)539-5000
Fax: (314)539-5170
URL: http://www.stlcc.cc.mo.us
Description: Small Business Program offers courses designed for small business owners.

LEGISLATIVE ASSISTANCE

62106 ■ Missouri Department of Economic Development–Economic Development Office
Harry S. Truman State Office Bldg., Rm. 680
Jefferson City, MO 65102
Ph:(573)751-4962
Free: 800-523-1434
Fax: (573)751-7258
URL: http://www.ded.mo.gov
Description: Works to identify and solve problems specific to small business.

PUBLICATIONS

62107 ■ How to Form Your Own Missouri Corporation Before the Inc. Dries!: A Step by Step Guide, With Forms
P. Gaines Publishing Company
333 S. Taylor Ave.
PO Box 2253
Oak Park, IL 60302
Ph:(708)524-9033
Fax: (708)524-9038
Ed: Phillip Williams. **Released:** 1992. **Price:** $19.95 (paper). **Description:** Volume 5 of the Small Business Incorporation series. Explains the advantages and disadvantages of incorporation and shows, step-by-step, how the small business owners can incorporate at low cost. Covers Missouri profit and nonprofit corporations, Missouri professional service corporations, subchapter S corporations, and Delaware corporations. Includes forms necessary for incorporation.

62108 ■ Ingram's
306 E. 12th St., Ste. 1014
Kansas City, MO 64106
Ph:(816)842-9994
Fax: (816)474-1111

62109 ■ Kansas City Business Journal
1101 Walnut, Ste. 800
Kansas City, MO 64106
Ph:(816)421-5900
Fax: (816)472-4010
Co. E-mail: kcbj@unicom.net
URL: http://www.amcity.com

62110 ■ Missouri Business
65101 E. Capitol
PO Box 149
Jefferson City, MO 65102
Ph:(573)634-3511
Fax: (573)634-8855
Co. E-mail: mchamber@computerland.net
URL: http://mochambar.org

62111 ■ St. Louis Business Journal
One Metropolitan Sq., Ste. 2170
St. Louis, MO 63102
Ph:(314)421-6200
Fax: (314)621-5031
Co. E-mail: stlouis@amcity.com
URL: http://amcity.com/stlouis

62112 ■ Smart Start your Missouri Business
PSI Research
300 N. Valley Dr.
Grants Pass, OR 97526
Ph:(503)479-9464
Free: 800-228-2275
Fax: (503)476-1479
Co. E-mail: info@psi-research.com
URL: http://www.psi-research.com
Ed: Michael D. Jenkins. **Released:** Revised edition, 1992. **Price:** $29.95 (looseleaf binder); $24.95 (paper). **Description:** Part of the Successful Business Library series.

PUBLISHERS

62113 ■ American Kennel Club Museum of the Dogs
1721 S Mason Rd.
Saint Louis, MO 63131
Ph:(314)821-3647
Free: 800-533-7323
Fax: (314)821-7381
Co. E-mail: dogarts@aol.com
URL: http://www.akc.org
Contact: Barbara Jedda, Exec. Dir.
Description: Wholesaler. Publishes magazines about dog care. **Founded:** 1982.

62114 ■ International Council for Small Business
The George Washington University
School of Business, Dept. of Management
2201 G St. NW, Funger 315
Washington, DC 20052
Ph:(202)994-0704
Fax: (202)994-4930
Co. E-mail: icsb@gwu.edu
URL: http://www.icsb.org
Contact: Colin Dunn, President
E-mail: colin.dunn@rmit.edu.au
Description: Publishes periodicals and proceedings for members and other persons interested in helping small businesses. **Founded:** 1956.

62115 ■ Three House Publishing
PO Box 6672
Chesterfield, MO 63006-6672
Ph:(314)277-4560
Contact: Ray Goldman
Description: Publishes course materials. Also publishes novels and short stories.

Montana

SMALL BUSINESS DEVELOPMENT CENTER LEAD OFFICE

62116 ■ Montana Department of Commerce–Montana SBDC
301 S. Park Ave., Rm. 114
PO Box 200505
Helena, MT 59620
Ph:(406)814-2746
Fax: (406)444-1872
URL: http://sbdc.mt.gov/
Contact: Ann Desch, State Dir.
E-mail: adesch@state.mt.us

62117 ■ Montana Department of Commerce–Small Business Development Center
1424 9th Ave.
Helena, MT 59620
Ph:(406)444-4780
Fax: (406)444-1872
Contact: Robyn Hampton, State Director
E-mail: rhampton@state.mt.us

SMALL BUSINESS DEVELOPMENT CENTERS

62118 ■ Big Sky Economic Development Authority–Small Business Development Center
222 N. 32nd St., Ste. 200
Billings, MT 59101
Ph:(406)254-6014
Fax: (406)256-6877
Contact: Deanna South, Dir.
E-mail: south@bigskyeda.org

62119 ■ Bozeman Small Business Development Center–Gallatin Development Corporation
222 E. Main St., Ste. 102
Bozeman, MT 59715
Ph:(406)587-3113
Fax: (406)587-9565
Co. E-mail: botmline@bozeman.org
URL: http://www.bozeman.org/cgi-bin/gdc/index.html
Contact: Tracey Jette, Dir.

62120 ■ Butte Small Business Development Center–Southwest Montana Service Center
305 W. Mercury, Ste. 211
Butte, MT 59701
Ph:(406)782-7333
Fax: (406)782-2990
URL: http://www.headwatersrcd.org/redisbdc.htm
Contact: Deanna Johnson, Dir.
E-mail: djohnson@bigskyhsd.com

62121 ■ Gateway Economic Development Corporation–Helena Small Business Development Center
225 Cruise Ave.
Helena, MT 59601
Ph:(406)447-1512
Fax: (406)447-1514
URL: http://www.gatewayedc.org/sbdc.htm
Contact: Dan Anderson, Dir.
E-mail: dan@gatewayedc.org

62122 ■ Great Falls Development Authority–Great Falls SBDC
710 1st. Ave. N.
Great Falls, MT 59401
Ph:(406)453-8834
Fax: (406)454-2995
Contact: Rebecca Engum, Dir.
E-mail: rengum@gfdevelopment.org

62123 ■ Havre Small Business Development Center–Bear Paw Development Corporation
48 2nd Ave.
PO Box 170
Havre, MT 59501
Ph:(406)265-4945
Fax: (406)265-5602
Contact: Tracey Jette, Dir.
E-mail: tjette@bearpaw.org

62124 ■ Kalispell Small Business Development Center–Kalispell Area Chamber of Commerce
15 Depot Park
Kalispell, MT 59901
Ph:(406)758-2802
Fax: (406)758-2805
Co. E-mail: kalsbdc@centurytel.net
Contact: Lad Barney, Dir.

62125 ■ Montana Community Development Corporation–Missoula Small Business Development Center
110 E. Broadway, 2nd Fl.
Missoula, MT 59802
Ph:(406)728-9234
Fax: (406)542-6671
URL: http://www.mtcdc.org
Contact: Anne Iverson, Dir.
E-mail: aiverson@mtcdc.org

62126 ■ Southeastern Montana Development Corporation–Colstrip Small Business Development Center
6200 Main St.
PO Box 1935
Colstrip, MT 59323
Ph:(406)748-2990
Fax: (406)748-2900
Co. E-mail: sbdc@bhwi.net
URL: http://www.semdc.org/
Contact: Michelle Jutila, Dir.

SMALL BUSINESS ASSISTANCE PROGRAMS

62127 ■ Big Sky Economic Development Authority
222 N 32nd St.
Billings, MT 59101-1911
Ph:(406)256-6871
Fax: (406)256-6877
Co. E-mail: langman@bigskyeda.org
URL: http://www.bigskyeda.org
Description: Offers U.S. Customs services, bonded and general warehouse storage, no inventory tax, and licensing brokerage services to shippers, wholesalers, and manufacturers. Access is provided to international and domestic shippers.

62128 ■ Montana Department of Agriculture–Agriculture Development Division
PO Box 200201
Helena, MT 59620-0201
Ph:(406)444-3144
Fax: (406)444-5409
Co. E-mail: agr@mt.gov
URL: http://www.agr.state.mt.us
Contact: Nancy Peterson, Dir
Description: Provides market research and other assistance to Montana's agricultural producers through identification, analysis, and direction in development of both foreign and domestic markets.

62129 ■ Montana Department of Commerce–Business Resources Division
301 S Park Ave.
Helena, MT 59620
Ph:(406)841-2700
Fax: (406)841-2701
Co. E-mail: gness@state.mt.us
URL: http://www.commerce.mt.gov
Description: Publicizes and advertises Montana to firms planning relocations or expansions.

62130 ■ Montana Department of Commerce–Census and Economic Information Center
301 S Park Ave.
Helena, MT 59620
Ph:(406)841-2700
Fax: (406)841-2701
Co. E-mail: ceic@state.mt.us
URL: http://www.commerce.mt.gov
Description: Provides population and economic information to businesses, government agencies, and the general public for research, planning, and decision-making purposes.

62131 ■ Montana Department of Commerce–Certified Communities Program
301 S Park Ave
Helena, MT 59620
Ph:(406)841-2700
Fax: (406)841-2701
Co. E-mail: gness@state.mt.us

URL: http://www.commerce.mt.gov
Description: Provides assistance to cities, towns, counties, and tribal governments in planning and carrying out effective economic development programs specifically designed to meet local needs.

62132 ■ Montana Department of Commerce–Economic Development Division–Marketing Assistance and Made in Montana Program (301 S)
301 S Park Ave.
Helena, MT 59601
Ph:(406)444-4392
Fax: (406)444-2903
Co. E-mail: bbauman@state.mt.us
URL: http://www.commerce.state.mt.us
Description: Works with individual small businesses to develop and expand outlets for products manufactured or processed in Montana.

62133 ■ Montana Department of Commerce–International Trade Program
301 S Park Ave.
Helena, MT 59620
Ph:(406)841-2700
Fax: (406)841-2701
URL: http://www.commerce.mt.gov
Description: Enhances sales of Montana goods and services in international markets and encourages tourism promotion and reverse investment opportunities. Also offers one-stop technical assistance to businesses wishing to enter foreign markets.

62134 ■ Montana Department of Commerce–Montana Science and Technology Alliance Division
301 S Park Ave.
Helena, MT 59601
Ph:(406)841-2700
Fax: (406)841-2701
Co. E-mail: bpomery@state.mt.us
URL: http://www.commerce.state.mt.us
Description: Encourages innovative scientific and technical development within the state. Aids in the creation of new jobs. Assists in financing the establishment of technology-intensive businesses and finances projects that it believes have outstanding technological and commercial potential. Has four complementary investment programs for financial assistance: seed capital investment, applied technology research, technical assistance and technology transfer, and research capability development.

62135 ■ University of Montana–Montana Business Connection
Gallagher Business Bldg., Ste. 242
Missoula, MT 59801
Ph:(406)243-4009
Fax: (406)243-2086
Co. E-mail: bob.campbell@business.umt.edu
URL: http://www.mbc.umt.edu
Description: Seeks to use the Montana University System to link business owners and entrepreneurs with information, resources, and expertise.

SCORE OFFICES

62136 ■ SCORE Billings
815 S 27th St.
Billings, MT 59101
Ph:(406)245-4111
Co. E-mail: djohnson@crowleylaw.com
Description: Serves as volunteer program in which working and retired business management professionals provide free business counseling to men and women who are considering starting a small business, encountering problems with their business, or expanding their business. Offers free one-on-one counseling, online counseling and low cost workshops on a variety of business topics.

62137 ■ SCORE Bozeman
2000 Commerce Way
Bozeman, MT 59715
Ph:(406)586-5421

Fax: (406)586-8286
Co. E-mail: bznscore@bozemanchamber.com
URL: http://www.scorebozeman.org
Contact: Robert Macdonald, Chm.
Description: Serves as volunteer program in which working and retired business management professionals provide free business counseling to men and women who are considering starting a small business, encountering problems with their business, or expanding their business. Offers free one-on-one counseling, online counseling and low cost workshops on a variety of business topics.

62138 ■ SCORE Butte
1000 George St.
Butte, MT 59701
Ph:(406)723-3177
Co. E-mail: buttescore@yahoo.com
Contact: Daniel Berube, Chm.
Description: Serves as volunteer program in which working and retired business management professionals provide free business counseling to men and women who are considering starting a small business, encountering problems with their business, or expanding their business. Offers free one-on-one counseling, online counseling and low cost workshops on a variety of business topics.

62139 ■ SCORE Great Falls
601 10th Ave. N
Great Falls, MT 59403
Ph:(406)761-4434
Co. E-mail: score@sofast.net
Contact: Elvin Ballance, Chm.
Description: Serves as volunteer program in which working and retired business management professionals provide free business counseling to men and women who are considering starting a small business, encountering problems with their business, or expanding their business. Offers free one-on-one counseling, online counseling and low cost workshops on a variety of business topics.

62140 ■ SCORE Havre
c/o Chamber of Commerce
130 5th Ave.
Havre, MT 59501
Ph:(406)265-4383
Co. E-mail: korbg@msun.edu
Description: Serves as volunteer program in which working and retired business management professionals provide free business counseling to men and women who are considering starting a small business, encountering problems with their business, or expanding their business. Offers free one-on-one counseling, online counseling and low cost workshops on a variety of business topics.

62141 ■ SCORE Helena
10 W 15th St., Ste. 1100
Federal Office Bldg.
Helena, MT 59626
Ph:(406)441-1081
Co. E-mail: helenascore@yahoo.com
Contact: Charles Rolling, Chm.
Description: Serves as volunteer program in which working and retired business management professionals provide free business counseling to men and women who are considering starting a small business, encountering problems with their business, or expanding their business. Offers free one-on-one counseling, online counseling and low cost workshops on a variety of business topics.

62142 ■ SCORE Kalispell
2 Main St.
Kalispell, MT 59901
Ph:(406)756-5271
Co. E-mail: bruce_sneddon@member.phideltaphi.org
URL: http://www.score.org

62143 ■ SCORE Missoula
PO Box 632
Missoula, MT 59806
Ph:(406)327-8806
Co. E-mail: craig@safeshop.com

URL: http://www.missoulascore.org
Contact: Jerry Dirnberger, Chm.
Description: Serves as volunteer program in which working and retired business management professionals provide free business counseling to men and women who are considering starting a small business, encountering problems with their business, or expanding their business. Offers free one-on-one counseling, online counseling and low cost workshops on a variety of business topics.

CHAMBERS OF COMMERCE

62144 ■ Anaconda Chamber of Commerce
306 E Park St.
Anaconda, MT 59711
Ph:(406)563-2400
Fax: (406)563-2400
Co. E-mail: anachamber@aol.com
URL: http://www.anacondamt.org
Contact: Edith Fransen, Exec.Dir.

62145 ■ Baker Chamber of Commerce and Agriculture
PO Box 849
Baker, MT 59313-0849
Free: (866)862-2537
Fax: (406)778-2266
URL: http://www.bakermt.com
Contact: Roger Schmidt, Pres.

62146 ■ Beaverhead Chamber of Commerce
10 W Reeder
PO Box 425
Dillon, MT 59725
Ph:(406)683-5511
Fax: (406)683-9233
Co. E-mail: chamber@bmt.net
URL: http://www.bmt.net/~chamber
Contact: Judy Siring, Exec.Dir.

62147 ■ Belgrade Chamber of Commerce
10 E Main
Belgrade, MT 59714
Ph:(406)388-1616
Fax: (406)388-2090
Co. E-mail: info@belgradechamber.org
URL: http://www.belgradechamber.org
Contact: Debra Youngberg IOM, Exec.Dir.

62148 ■ Bigfork Area Chamber of Commerce
PO Box 237
Bigfork, MT 59911
Ph:(406)837-5888
Fax: (406)837-5808
Co. E-mail: chamber@bigfork.org
URL: http://www.bigfork.org
Contact: Andrea M. Goff, Exec.Dir.

62149 ■ Billings Area Chamber of Commerce
815 S 27th St.
PO Box 31177
Billings, MT 59107-1177
Ph:(406)245-4111
Co. E-mail: info@billingschamber.com
URL: http://www.billingschamber.com
Contact: John Brewer, Pres./CEO

62150 ■ Bitter Root Valley Chamber of Commerce
105 E Main St.
Hamilton, MT 59840
Ph:(406)363-2400
Fax: (406)363-2402
Co. E-mail: localinfo@bvchamber.com
URL: http://www.bvchamber.com
Contact: Diane Wolfe, Exec.Dir.

62151 ■ Bozeman Area Chamber of Commerce
2000 Commerce Way
Bozeman, MT 59715
Ph:(406)586-5421
Free: 800-228-4224
Fax: (406)586-8286

Co. E-mail: info@bozemanchamber.com
URL: http://www.bozemanchamber.com
Contact: David R. Smith, Pres./CEO

62152 ■ Butte-Silver Bow Chamber of Commerce
1000 George St.
Butte, MT 59701
Ph:(406)723-3177
Free: 800-735-6814
Co. E-mail: chamber@buttecvb.com
URL: http://www.butteinfo.org
Contact: Marko Lucich, Exec. Dir.

62153 ■ Carter County Chamber of Commerce
PO Box 108
Ekalaka, MT 59324
Ph:(406)775-8714
Co. E-mail: mhutch@midrivers.com
URL: http://www.ekalakachamber.com
Contact: Marilyn Hutchinson, Treas.

62154 ■ Circle Chamber of Commerce and Agriculture
PO Box 321
Circle, MT 59215
Ph:(406)485-2741
Co. E-mail: circle@visitmt.com
URL: http://www.circle.visitmt.com
Contact: Jana Hance, Pres.

62155 ■ Columbia Falls Area Chamber of Commerce
PO Box 312
Columbia Falls, MT 59912
Ph:(406)892-2072
Fax: (406)892-2725
Co. E-mail: info@columbiafallschamber.com
URL: http://www.columbiafallschamber.com
Contact: Carol Pike, Exec.Dir.

62156 ■ Columbia Falls Area Chamber Foundation
PO Box 312
Columbia Falls, MT 59912-0312
Ph:(406)892-2072
Fax: (406)892-2725
Co. E-mail: info@columbiafallschamber.com
URL: http://www.columbiafallschamber.com
Contact: Carol Pike, Exec. Dir.

62157 ■ Conrad Area Chamber of Commerce
702 S Main St., Ste. 1
Conrad, MT 59425
Ph:(406)271-7791
Fax: (406)221-2924
Co. E-mail: chamber@conradmt.com
URL: http://www.conradmt.com
Contact: Misty Redlin, Exec.Sec.

62158 ■ Culbertson Chamber of Commerce
PO Box 351
Culbertson, MT 59218
Ph:(406)787-6120
Fax: (406)787-5271
Co. E-mail: culbertsonmt@hotmail.com
URL: http://www.culbertsonmt.com
Contact: Bruce Houle

62159 ■ Cut Bank Area Chamber of Commerce
PO Box 1243
Cut Bank, MT 59427
Ph:(406)873-4041
Co. E-mail: cbchambe@northerntel.net
URL: http://www.cutbankchamber.com
Contact: Byron Beley, Pres.

62160 ■ Daniels County Chamber of Commerce and Agriculture
PO Box 91
Scobey, MT 59263
Ph:(406)487-2061
Co. E-mail: scobey@nemontel.net
URL: http://www.scobey.org
Contact: Julie French, Pres.

62161 ■ East Glacier Chamber of Commerce
PO Box 260
East Glacier Park, MT 59434
Ph:(406)226-4403
Fax: (406)226-4403
URL: http://www.eastglacierpark.org
Contact: Terry Sherburne, Pres.

62162 ■ Ennis Area Chamber of Commerce
PO Box 291
Ennis, MT 59729
Ph:(406)682-4388
Fax: (406)682-4328
Co. E-mail: info@ennischamber.com
URL: http://www.ennischamber.com
Contact: John Duncan, Pres.

62163 ■ Eureka Area Chamber of Commerce
PO Box 186
Eureka, MT 59917
Ph:(406)889-4636
Contact: Joanne Cuff, Pres.

62164 ■ Fairfield Chamber of Commerce
PO Drawer 9
Fairfield, MT 59436
Ph:(406)467-2341
Co. E-mail: justice@3rivers.net
Contact: Bill Harris, Pres.

62165 ■ Fort Benton Chamber of Commerce
PO Box 12
Fort Benton, MT 59442
Ph:(406)622-3864
Co. E-mail: info@fortbenton.com
URL: http://www.fortbenton.com/chamber
Contact: Valerie Morger, Pres.

62166 ■ Gardiner Chamber of Commerce
PO Box 81
Gardiner, MT 59030
Ph:(406)848-7971
Fax: (406)848-2446
Co. E-mail: info@gardinerchamber.com
URL: http://www.gardinerchamber.com
Contact: Mr. Chris Waters, Sec.

62167 ■ Garfield County Chamber of Commerce
PO Box 370
Jordan, MT 59337
Ph:(406)557-6158
Fax: (406)557-6158
Co. E-mail: chamber@garfieldcounty.com
URL: http://www.garfieldcounty.com
Contact: Rocky Nelson, Pres.

62168 ■ Glasgow Area Chamber of Commerce and Agriculture
PO Box 832
Glasgow, MT 59230-0832
Ph:(406)228-2222
Fax: (406)228-2244
Co. E-mail: chamber@glasgowmt.net
URL: http://www.glasgowmt.net
Contact: Ms. Diane Brandt, Exec.Dir.

62169 ■ Glendive Chamber of Commerce and Agriculture
313 S Merrill
Glendive, MT 59330
Ph:(406)377-5601
Fax: (406)377-5602
Co. E-mail: chamber@midrivers.com
URL: http://www.glendivechamber.com
Contact: Kim Trangmoe, Exec.Dir.

62170 ■ Great Falls Area Chamber of Commerce
100 1 Ave. N
PO Box 2127
Great Falls, MT 59401
Ph:(406)761-4434
Fax: (406)761-6129
Co. E-mail: jmedina@greatfallschamber.org
URL: http://www.greatfallschamber.org
Contact: Rick Evans, Pres.

62171 ■ Greater Stillwater County Chamber of Commerce
PO Box 783
Columbus, MT 59019
Ph:(406)322-4505
Co. E-mail: info@stillwater-chamber.org
URL: http://www.stillwater-chamber.org
Contact: Nancy Brown

62172 ■ Hardin Area Chamber of Commerce and Agriculture
PO Box 446
Hardin, MT 59034
Ph:(406)665-1672
Free: 888-450-3577
Fax: (406)665-2917
Co. E-mail: hardinchamber@bhwi.net
URL: http://www.custerslaststand.org
Contact: Dick Crockford, Pres.

62173 ■ Havre Area Chamber of Commerce
518 1st St.
PO Box 308
Havre, MT 59501-0308
Ph:(406)265-4383
Fax: (406)265-7748
Co. E-mail: chamber@havremt.net
URL: http://www.havremt.com
Contact: Debbie Vandeberg, Exec.Dir.

62174 ■ Helena Area Chamber of Commerce
225 Cruse Ave.
Helena, MT 59601
Ph:(406)447-1530
Free: 800-743-5362
Fax: (406)447-1532
Co. E-mail: info@helenachamber.com
URL: http://www.helenachamber.com
Contact: Cathy Burwell, Pres./CEO

62175 ■ Hot Springs Chamber of Commerce
PO Box 580
Hot Springs, MT 59845
Ph:(406)741-2662
Co. E-mail: hscofc@hotsprgs.net
Contact: Sandra Prongua, Sec.

62176 ■ Kalispell Area Chamber of Commerce
15 Depot Park
Kalispell, MT 59901
Ph:(406)758-2800
Fax: (406)758-2805
Co. E-mail: info@kalispellchamber.com
URL: http://kalispellchamber.com
Contact: Joe Unterreiner, Pres./CEO

62177 ■ Lakeside-Somers Chamber of Commerce
PO Box 177
Lakeside, MT 59922
Ph:(406)844-3715
Co. E-mail: info@lakesidesomers.org
URL: http://www.lakesidesomers.org
Contact: Dee Kirk Boon, Sec.

62178 ■ Laurel Chamber of Commerce
108 E Main
Laurel, MT 59044-0395
Ph:(406)628-8105
Fax: (406)628-8105
Co. E-mail: chamber@laurelmontana.org
URL: http://www.laurelmontana.org
Contact: Dee Dee Crider, Pres.

62179 ■ Lewistown Area Chamber of Commerce
408 NE Main
PO Box 818
Lewistown, MT 59457-0818
Ph:(406)538-5436
Fax: (406)538-5437
Co. E-mail: lewchamb@lewistown.net
URL: http://www.lewistownchamber.com
Contact: Connie Fry, Exec.Dir.

62180 ■ Libby Area Chamber of Commerce
PO Box 704
905 W 9th
Libby, MT 59923
Ph:(406)293-4167
Fax: (406)293-2197
Co. E-mail: libbyacc@libbychamber.org
URL: http://www.libbychamber.org
Contact: Louise Rice, Exec. Dir.

62181 ■ Liberty County Chamber of Commerce
PO Box 632
Chester, MT 59522
Ph:(406)759-5674
Fax: (406)759-5523
Co. E-mail: libcocc@mtintouch.net
Contact: Barb Wolfe, Pres.

62182 ■ Lincoln Valley Chamber of Commerce
PO Box 985
Lincoln, MT 59639-0985
Ph:(406)362-4949
Fax: (406)362-4632
Co. E-mail: lauran@montana.com
URL: http://www.lincolnmontana.com
Contact: Susan Mason, Pres.

62183 ■ Livingston Area Chamber of Commerce
303 E Park St.
Livingston, MT 59047
Ph:(406)222-0850
Fax: (406)222-0852
Co. E-mail: info@livingston-chamber.com
URL: http://www.yellowstone-chamber.com
Contact: Lou Ann Nelson, Office Mgr.

62184 ■ Malta Area Chamber of Commerce
PO Box 1420
Malta, MT 59538
Ph:(406)654-1776
Fax: (406)654-1776
Co. E-mail: malta@ttc-cmc.net
URL: http://www.maltachamber.com
Contact: Anne Boothe, Sec.

62185 ■ Manhattan Area Chamber of Commerce
PO Box 606
Manhattan, MT 59741
Ph:(406)284-4162
Fax: (406)284-3040
Co. E-mail: manhattanmontana@yahoo.com
URL: http://www.manhattanmontana.com
Contact: Tom Shallcorss, Pres.

62186 ■ Miles City Area Chamber of Commerce
511 Pleasant St.
Miles City, MT 59301
Ph:(406)234-2890
Fax: (406)234-6914
Co. E-mail: mcchamber@mcchamber.com
URL: http://www.mcchamber.com
Contact: Linda Wolff, Exec. Dir.

62187 ■ Mineral County Chamber of Commerce
PO Box 483
Superior, MT 59872
Ph:(406)822-4891
Fax: (406)822-4891
Co. E-mail: mccoc@blackfoot.net
URL: http://www.montanarockies.org
Contact: Patricia Nichols, Pres.

62188 ■ Missoula Area Chamber of Commerce
825 E Front St.
Missoula, MT 59802-4704
Ph:(406)543-6623
Fax: (406)543-6625
Co. E-mail: info@missoulachamber.com
URL: http://www.missoulachamber.com
Contact: Bill Samsoe, Membership Dir.

62189 ■ Montana Chamber of Commerce
PO Box 1730
2030 11th Ave., Ste. 21
Helena, MT 59624-1730
Ph:(406)442-2405
Free: 888-442-6688
Fax: (406)442-2409
Co. E-mail: schaefer@3rivers.net
URL: http://www.montanachamber.com
Contact: Webb Scott Brown, Pres.

62190 ■ Musselshell Valley Chamber of Commerce
PO Box 751
Roundup, MT 59072-0751
Ph:(406)323-1966
Co. E-mail: roundupc@midrivers.com
Contact: Bob Snively, Pres.

62191 ■ Philipsburg Chamber of Commerce
PO Box 661
Philipsburg, MT 59858
Ph:(406)859-3388
Fax: (406)859-5151
Co. E-mail: chamber@philipsburgmt.com
URL: http://www.philipsburgmt.com
Contact: Karyn Byhre Hansen, Sec.

62192 ■ Plains-Paradise Chamber of Commerce
PO Box 1531
Plains, MT 59859
Ph:(406)826-4700
Fax: (406)826-3236
Co. E-mail: dacy.holland@coldwellbanker.com
Contact: Dacy Holland, Sec.

62193 ■ Polson Chamber of Commerce
4 2nd Ave. E
PO Box 667
Polson, MT 59860
Ph:(406)883-5969
Fax: (406)883-1716
Co. E-mail: info@polsonchamber.com
URL: http://www.polsonchamber.com
Contact: Michelle Cope, Exec.Dir.

62194 ■ Powder River Chamber of Commerce
PO Box 484
Broadus, MT 59317-0484
Ph:(406)436-2778
Contact: Anne Gergen

62195 ■ Powell County Chamber of Commerce
1109 Main St.
Deer Lodge, MT 59722
Ph:(406)846-2094
Fax: (406)846-2094
Co. E-mail: chamber@powellcountymontana.com
URL: http://www.powellcountymontana.com
Contact: Mrs. Patty Cowan, Exec.Sec.

62196 ■ Prairie County Chamber of Commerce
PO Box 667
Terry, MT 59349-0667
Ph:(406)635-5513
Fax: (406)635-2149
Co. E-mail: pcchamber@midrivers.com
Contact: Dale Galland, Treas.

62197 ■ Red Lodge Area Chamber of Commerce
601 N Broadway
PO Box 988
Red Lodge, MT 59068
Ph:(406)446-1718
Free: 888-281-0625
Fax: (406)446-1718
Co. E-mail: information@redlodge.com
URL: http://www.redlodge.com
Contact: Denise Parsons, Exec. Dir.

62198 ■ Shelby Area Chamber of Commerce
PO Box 865
Shelby, MT 59474-0865

Ph:(406)434-7184
Fax: (406)434-9151
Co. E-mail: shelbymtchamber@sofast.net
URL: http://www.shelbymtchamber.org
Contact: Sean Pahut, Pres.

62199 ■ Sheridan County Chamber of Commerce
PO Box 104
Plentywood, MT 59254-0104
Ph:(406)765-1733
Fax: (406)765-2106
Co. E-mail: chamber@plentywood.com
URL: http://www.plentywood.com
Contact: Richard Rice, Pres.

62200 ■ Sidney Area Chamber of Commerce and Agriculture
909 S Central Ave.
Sidney, MT 59270
Ph:(406)433-1916
Fax: (406)433-1127
Co. E-mail: schamber@midrivers.com
URL: http://www.sidneymt.com
Contact: Laura Schieber, Exec. Dir.

62201 ■ Sweet Grass County Chamber of Commerce
PO Box 1012
Big Timber, MT 59011
Ph:(406)932-5131
Fax: (406)932-5131
Co. E-mail: info@bigtimber.com
URL: http://www.bigtimber.com
Contact: Tracy Bolstad, Mgr.

62202 ■ Thompson Falls Chamber of Commerce
1013 Main St.
Thompson Falls, MT 59873
Ph:(406)827-4930
Fax: (406)827-4430
Co. E-mail: tfl3728@montana.com
URL: http://www.mbc.umt.edu/rdb/detail.
    ASP?num=3994
Contact: Ben Leafkens, Pres.

62203 ■ Three Forks Chamber of Commerce
PO Box 1103
Three Forks, MT 59752-1103
Ph:(406)285-4753
Fax: (406)285-4380
Co. E-mail: chamber@threeforksmontana.com
URL: http://www.threeforksmontana.com
Contact: Linda Larson, Pres.

62204 ■ Townsend Area Chamber of Commerce
PO Box 947
Townsend, MT 59644-0947
Ph:(406)266-3911
Fax: (406)266-3360
Co. E-mail: townsendchamber@montana.net
Contact: Marcia Fider, Pres.

62205 ■ West Yellowstone Chamber of Commerce
30 Yellowstone Ave.
PO Box 458
West Yellowstone, MT 59758-0458
Ph:(406)646-7701
Fax: (406)646-9691
Co. E-mail: visitorsservices@
    westyellowstonechamber.com
URL: http://www.westyellowstonechamber.com
Contact: Marysue Costello, Exec.Dir.

62206 ■ Whitefish Chamber of Commerce
520 E 2nd St.
Whitefish, MT 59937
Ph:(406)862-3501
Free: 877-862-3548
Fax: (406)862-9494
Co. E-mail: emily@whitefishchamber.org
URL: http://www.whitefishchamber.org
Contact: Sheila Bowen, Pres./CEO

62207 ■ Wibaux County Chamber of Commerce
PO Box 159
Wibaux, MT 59353
Ph:(406)796-2412
Co. E-mail: wibaux@midrivers.com
Contact: David Bertelsen, Pres.

62208 ■ Wolf Point Chamber of Commerce and Agriculture
218 3rd Ave. S, Ste. B
Wolf Point, MT 59201
Ph:(406)653-2012
Fax: (406)653-2028
Co. E-mail: wpchmber@nemontel.net
Contact: Christy Stensland, Exec.Dir.

PROCUREMENT ASSISTANCE PROGRAMS

62209 ■ Montana Department of Administration–Procurement Bureau
Purchasing Bureau
Mitchell Bldg., Rm. 165
Helena, MT 59620-0135
Ph:(406)444-2575
Fax: (406)444-2529
URL: http://www.mt.gov
Description: Offers current government procurement information to interested small business bidders. Also provides technical assistance.

62210 ■ Montana Procurement Technical Assistance Center–Government Marketing Assistance Group–Big Sky Economic Development Authority (222 N)
222 N 32nd St., Ste. 200
Billings, MT 59101
Ph:(406)256-6871
Fax: (406)256-6877
Co. E-mail: jewell@bigskyeda.org
URL: http://www.bigskyeda.org
Contact: Maureen Jewell
E-mail: jewell@bigskyeda.org

62211 ■ Montana Procurement Technical Assistance Center–Great Falls Development Authority
710 1st Ave. N
Great Falls, MT 59403
Ph:(406)454-1934

Fax: (406)454-2995
Co. E-mail: kdehn@gfdevelopment.org
URL: http://www.gfdevelopment.org
Contact: Karl Dehn, Dir
E-mail: karl@mt.net

INCUBATORS/RESEARCH AND TECHNOLOGY PARKS

62212 ■ Advanced Technology Park
1711 W College
Bozeman, MT 59715
Ph:(406)587-4480
Fax: (406)587-4480
Co. E-mail: info@bozemantechpark.com
URL: http://www.bozemantechpark.com
Contact: Roger N. Flair, Pres.
E-mail: info@bozemantechpark.com
Scope: Provides access for park tenants to the research community and facilities at the University.
Publications: Montana State University Resources Catalog.

62213 ■ College of Forestry and Conservation–Institute for Tourism and Recreation Research
University of Montana, ITRR
Bldg 32 Campus Dr.
Missoula, MT 59812
Ph:(406)243-5521
Fax: (406)243-4845
Co. E-mail: request@forestry.umt.edu
URL: http://www.forestry.umt.edu/
Contact: Adminastrative Ass.
Description: Scope: Provides research data needed to support the state's tourism industry.

62214 ■ Montana State University-Bozeman–Office of Vice President for Research, Creativity, and Technology Transfer
207 Montana Hall
Bozeman, MT 59717-2460
Ph:(406)994-2891
Fax: (406)994-2893
Co. E-mail: research@montana.edu
URL: http://www.montana.edu/wwwvr/
Contact: Dr. Thomas J. McCoy, VP
E-mail: research@montana.edu
Scope: Coordinates research and creative activities in all departments and colleges of the University, oper-

ating through its subsidiary, Office of Research and Creative Activity, which provides technology transfer management, pre-award services, and coordinates interdisciplinary and multidisciplinary research projects, and its office of Sponsored Programs, which provides fiscal and contract arrangement services. Publications: Discovery (quarterly); Research & Creative Activities (annually). Awards: Best Awards; Block grants; MONTS (Montanans on a New Track for Science) Awards.

PUBLICATIONS

62215 ■ *Big Sky Business Journal*
PO Box 3262
Billings, MT 59103
Ph:(406)259-2309
Fax: (406)259-7040
Co. E-mail: bsbj@imt.net
URL: http://www.montanamarket.com/bsbj

62216 ■ *Livingston Enterprise*
PO Box 665
Livingston, MT 59047
Ph:(406)222-2000
Fax: (406)222-8580
Co. E-mail: enterprise@ycsi.net

62217 ■ *Montana Magazine*
PO Box 5630
Helena, MT 59604
Ph:(406)443-2842
Fax: (406)443-5480
Co. E-mail: magedit@montmang.mt.net
URL: http://www.montanamagazine.com

62218 ■ *Smart Start Your California Business*
PSI Research
300 N. Valley Dr.
Grants Pass, OR 97526
Ph:(503)479-9464
Free: 800-228-2275
Fax: (503)476-1479
Co. E-mail: info@psi-research.com
URL: http://www.psi-research.com
Ed: Michael D. Jenkins. Released: Revised edition, 1992. Price: $29.95 (looseleaf binder); $24.95 (paper). Description: Part of the Successful Business Library series.

SMALL BUSINESS DEVELOPMENT CENTER LEAD OFFICE

62219 ■ University of Nebraska at Omaha–Nebraska Small Business Development Center
College of Business Administration, Rm. 407
60th & Dodge Sts.
Omaha, NE 68182
Ph:(402)554-2521
Fax: (402)554-3473
URL: http://nbdc.unomaha.edu
Contact: Robert Bernier, State Dir.
E-mail: rberniew@unomaha.edu

SMALL BUSINESS DEVELOPMENT CENTERS

62220 ■ Chadron State College–SBDC
Administration Bldg.
Chadron, NE 69337
Ph:(308)432-6282
Fax: (308)432-6430
Contact: Cliff Hanson, Dir.
E-mail: chanson@cscl.csc.edu

62221 ■ EntrepreneurShop at Omaha–Small Business Development Center
13006 W. Center Rd.
Omaha, NE 68144
Ph:(402)595-1158
Fax: (402)595-1194
Co. E-mail: NBDCOmaha@aol.com
Contact: Cliff Mosteller, Dir.

62222 ■ Lincoln Service Center–Small Business Development Center
285 S. 68th St. Pl., Ste. 550
City Campus Mailbox 0224
Lincoln, NE 68588-0224
Ph:(402)472-3358
Fax: (402)472-3363
Contact: Felipe Valdivia, Dir.
E-mail: lvaldivia@mail.unomaha.edu

62223 ■ Mid-Plains Community College–SBDC
416 N. Jeffers, Rm. 26
North Platte, NE 69101
Ph:(308)534-5115
Fax: (308)534-5117
Contact: Dean Kurth, Dir.
E-mail: mdkurth@unomaha.edu

62224 ■ North Platte Center–Small Business Development Center
300 E. 3rd St., Rm. 275
North Platte, NE 69101
Ph:(308)534-5115
Fax: (308)534-5115

Contact: Jason Tuller, Dir.
E-mail: jtuller@mail.unomaha.edu

62225 ■ Omaha Business and Technology Center–Procurement Technical Assistance Center–SBDC (2505)
2505 N. 24 St., Ste. 103
Omaha, NE 68110
Ph:(402)595-3511
Fax: (402)595-3832
Contact: Jerry Dalton, Mgr.
E-mail: gd9203@navix.net

62226 ■ Peru State College–SBDC
T.J. Majors Hall, Rm. 248
Peru, NE 68421
Ph:(402)872-2274
Fax: (402)872-2422
Contact: Jerry Breazile, Dir.
E-mail: breazile@pscosf.peru.edu

62227 ■ Scottsbluff Small Business Development Center–SBDC
Nebraska Public Power Bldg.
1620 Broadway, Ste. 201
Scottsbluff, NE 69361
Ph:(308)635-7513
Fax: (308)635-6682
Contact: Ingrid Battershell, Dir.
E-mail: ibatters@unomaha.edu

62228 ■ University of Nebraska at Kearney–SBDC
West Center Bldg., Rm. 135-C
1917 W. 24th St.
Kearney, NE 68849-4440
Ph:(308)865-8344
Fax: (308)865-8153
URL: http://administration/related_org/nbdc/index.html
Contact: Odee Ingersoll, Dir.
E-mail: ingersollo@unk.edu

62229 ■ University of Nebraska at Omaha–Small Business Development Center
Roskens Hall, Rm. 308
Omaha, NE 68182
Ph:(402)554-6253
URL: http://ptac.unomaha.edu
Contact: Joe Breault, Procurement Assistance
E-mail: jbreault@mail.unomaha.edu

62230 ■ Wayne State College–SBDC
Gardner Hall
1111 Main St.
Wayne, NE 68787
Ph:(402)375-7575
Fax: (402)375-7574
Contact: Loren Kucera, Dir.
E-mail: LoKucer1@wsc.edu

SMALL BUSINESS ASSISTANCE PROGRAMS

62231 ■ Nebraska Ombudsman's Office
State Capitol, Rm. 807
PO Box 94604
Lincoln, NE 68509-4712
Ph:(402)471-2035
Free: 800-742-7690
Fax: (402)471-4277
Co. E-mail: ombud@unicam.state.ne.us
Contact: Marshall Lux, Ombudsman
Description: Receives complaints against state agencies.

SCORE OFFICES

62232 ■ SCORE Central Nebraska
c/o Mr. Robert E. Hobbs, Chm.
PO Box 2288
16 W 11th St.
Kearney, NE 68848-2288
Ph:(308)865-5675
Co. E-mail: rhobbs@scorecentralnebraska.org
URL: http://www.score.org
Contact: Mr. Robert E. Hobbs, Chm.
Description: Provides technical assistance and counseling for new and existing business owners.

62233 ■ SCORE Columbus
c/o Ronald J. Fairbairn
2821 15th St.
Columbus, NE 68601
Ph:(402)564-2769
Co. E-mail: dlux@cccneb.edu
URL: http://www.score.org

62234 ■ SCORE Lincoln
285 S 62th Street Pl.
Lincoln, NE 68510
Ph:(402)437-2409
Co. E-mail: nescore39@aol.com
URL: http://www.score39.org
Description: Provides entrepreneur education for the formation, growth and success of small businesses in the area.

62235 ■ SCORE North Platte
502 S Dewey St.
North Platte, NE 69101
Ph:(308)534-5115
Co. E-mail: mbhonerman@charter.net
Description: Provides entrepreneur education for the formation, growth and success of small businesses in the area.

62236 ■ SCORE Omaha
11141 Mill Valley Rd.
Omaha, NE 68154
Ph:(402)221-3606
Fax: (402)221-7221
Co. E-mail: score@scoreomaha.org

URL: http://www.tandt.com/score
Contact: Richard Halvorson
Description: Provides entrepreneur education for the formation, growth and success of small businesses in the area.

62237 ■ SCORE Panhandle
c/o Chamber of Commerce
1517 Broadway
Scottsbluff, NE 69361
Ph:(308)632-2133
Co. E-mail: chamber@scottsbluffgering.net
URL: http://score-chapter301.org
Contact: Marlene Huston, Chair
Description: Provides entrepreneur education for the formation, growth and success of small businesses in the area.

BETTER BUSINESS BUREAUS

62238 ■ Cornhusker Better Business Bureau
11811 P St.
Omaha, NE 68137
Ph:(402)436-2345
Free: 800-649-6814
Fax: (402)391-7535
Co. E-mail: info@bbbnebraska.org
URL: http://www.bbbnebraska.org
Contact: Roseanna Schulte, Operations Mgr.

CHAMBERS OF COMMERCE

62239 ■ Ainsworth Area Chamber of Commerce and North Central Development Center
335 N Main St.
Ainsworth, NE 69210
Ph:(402)387-2740
Free: (866)387-2740
Fax: (402)387-2740
Co. E-mail: ainsworthchamber@ainsworthlinks.com
URL: http://www.ainsworthlinks.com
Contact: Linda O'Hare, Exec.Sec.

62240 ■ Albion Chamber of Commerce
420 W Market
Albion, NE 68620-1241
Ph:(402)395-6012
Fax:(402)395-6723
Co. E-mail: ccalbn@megavision.com
URL: http://www.albionne.org
Contact: Larry Lambert, Pres.

62241 ■ Alliance Area Chamber of Commerce
111 W 3rd St.
PO Box 571
Alliance, NE 69301
Ph:(308)762-1520
Free: 800-738-0648
Fax: (308)762-4919
Co. E-mail: chamber@bbc.net
Contact: Misty Graham, Exec.Dir.

62242 ■ Alma Chamber of Commerce
PO Box 52
Alma, NE 68920-0052
Ph:(308)928-2992
Fax:(308)928-2683
Co. E-mail: alma@megavision.com
URL: http://www.ci.alma.ne.us
Contact: Dee Mietzner, Acting Pres.

62243 ■ Arapahoe Chamber of Commerce
PO Box 624
Arapahoe, NE 68922
Ph:(308)962-7777
Co. E-mail: chamber@arapahoe-ne.com
URL: http://arapahoe-ne.com
Contact: Tammie Middagh, Sec.-Treas.

62244 ■ Ashland Area Chamber of Commerce
PO Box 5
Ashland, NE 68003
Ph:(402)944-2050
Fax: (402)944-2113
URL: http://www.ashland-ne.com/business/index.htm
Contact: Rod Reisen, Pres.

62245 ■ Auburn Chamber of Commerce
1211 J St.
Auburn, NE 68305
Ph:(402)274-3521
Fax: (402)274-4020
Co. E-mail: cc60618@alltel.net
URL: http://www.ci.auburn.ne.us
Contact: Terry Giles, Mgr.

62246 ■ Aurora Area Chamber and Development
1604 L St.
PO Box 146
Aurora, NE 68818-0146
Ph:(402)694-6911
Fax: (402)694-5766
Co. E-mail: chamber@hamilton.net
URL: http://www.auroracofc.org
Contact: Brad Maul, Exec.Dir.

62247 ■ Beatrice Area Chamber of Commerce
226 S 6th St.
Beatrice, NE 68310-4401
Ph:(402)223-2338
Fax: (402)223-2339
Co. E-mail: info@beatricechamber.com
URL: http://www.beatricechamber.com
Contact: Marian Borland, Office Mgr.

62248 ■ Bellevue Chamber of Commerce
204 West Mission Ave.
Bellevue, NE 68005
Ph:(402)898-3000
Fax: (402)291-8729
Co. E-mail: bellevue@bellevuenebraska.com
URL: http://www.bellevuenebraska.com
Contact: Tom Richards, Chm.

62249 ■ Blair Area Chamber of Commerce
1526 Washington St.
Blair, NE 68008-1600
Ph:(402)533-4455
Fax: (402)533-4456
Co. E-mail: mail@blairchamber.org
URL: http://www.blairchamber.org
Contact: Harriet Waite, Exec.Dir.

62250 ■ Broken Bow Chamber of Commerce
444 S 8th Ave.
Broken Bow, NE 68822
Ph:(308)872-5691
Fax: (308)872-6137
Co. E-mail: info@brokenbow-ne.com
URL: http://www.brokenbow-ne.com
Contact: Denise Russell, Exec.Dir.

62251 ■ Burwell Chamber of Commerce
PO Box 131
Burwell, NE 68823
Ph:(308)346-5210
Free: 888-328-7935
Fax: (308)346-5121
Co. E-mail: burwellinfo@nctc.net
URL: http://www.burwellnebr.com
Contact: Lynn Kratky, Dir.

62252 ■ Cambridge Chamber of Commerce
PO Box Q
Cambridge, NE 69022
Ph:(308)697-3711
Fax: (308)697-3253
URL: http://www.cambridgene.org/government/chamber.html
Contact: Bev Smith, Sec.

62253 ■ Central City Area Chamber of Commerce
PO Box 418
Central City, NE 68826
Ph:(308)946-3897
Fax: (308)946-3334
Co. E-mail: cchamber@cconline.net
URL: http://www.centralcityne.org
Contact: Kay Wimmer, Dir.

62254 ■ Chadron - Dawes County Area Chamber of Commerce
706 W 3rd St.
PO Box 646
Chadron, NE 69337-0646
Ph:(308)432-4401
Free: 800-603-2937
Fax: (308)432-4757
URL: http://www.chadron.com
Contact: Joy C. Omelanuk, Exec. Dir.

62255 ■ Chappell Chamber of Commerce
PO Box 121
Chappell, NE 69129-0121
Ph:(308)874-9912
Fax: (308)874-3459
Co. E-mail: chamber69129@yahoo.com
URL: http://www.chappellne.org/chamber.htm
Contact: G. Konruff, Pres.

62256 ■ Cheyenne County Chamber of Commerce
740 Illinois
Sidney, NE 69162-1748
Ph:(308)254-5851
Free: 800-421-4769
Fax: (308)254-3081
Co. E-mail: ccchamber@hamilton.net
URL: http://www.sidney-nebraska.com
Contact: Ms. Megan McGown, Exec.Dir.

62257 ■ Columbus Area Chamber of Commerce
764 33rd Ave.
PO Box 515
Columbus, NE 68601-0515
Ph:(402)564-2769
Fax: (402)564-2026
Co. E-mail: chamber@megavision.com
URL: http://www.thecolumbuspage.com
Contact: K.C. Belitz, Pres.

62258 ■ Crete Chamber of Commerce
1341 Main Ave.
Crete, NE 68333
Ph:(402)826-2136
Fax: (402)826-2136
Co. E-mail: cretechamber@neb.rr.com
URL: http://www.crete-ne.com
Contact: Sharlyn Sieck, Exec.Dir.

62259 ■ David City Area Chamber of Commerce
449 D St.
David City, NE 68632
Ph:(402)367-4238
Fax: (402)367-4239
Co. E-mail: davidcitychamber@dtnspeed.net
URL: http://www.davidcityne.com
Contact: Pam Siroky, Pres.

62260 ■ Fairbury Chamber of Commerce
518 E St.
PO Box 274
Fairbury, NE 68352-0274
Ph:(402)729-3000
Fax: (402)729-3076
Co. E-mail: fairburychamber@diodecom.net
URL: http://www.fairburychamber.org
Contact: Sharon Priefert, Exec.Dir.

62261 ■ Falls City Area Chamber of Commerce
PO Box 158
Falls City, NE 68355
Ph:(402)245-2105
Fax: (402)245-2741

Co. E-mail: fcecondev@sentco.net
URL: http://www.ci.falls-city.ne.us
Contact: Donna Landis

62262 ■ Fremont Area Chamber of Commerce
605 N Broad St.
PO Box 182
Fremont, NE 68026-0182
Ph:(402)721-2641
Fax: (402)721-9359
Co. E-mail: info@fremontne.org
URL: http://www.fremontne.org
Contact: Allan Hale, Pres./CEO

62263 ■ Gordon Chamber of Commerce
PO Box 160
Gordon, NE 69343
Ph:(308)282-0730
Fax: (308)282-0119
Co. E-mail: gcc@gordonchamber.com
URL: http://www.gordonchamber.com
Contact: Larry Turnbull, Pres.

62264 ■ Gothenburg Area Chamber of Commerce
1021 Lake Ave.
PO Box 263
Gothenburg, NE 69138-0263
Ph:(308)537-3505
Fax: (308)537-2541
Co. E-mail: annea@cozadtel.net
URL: http://www.ci.gothenburg.ne.us
Contact: Anne Anderson, Exec. Dir.

62265 ■ Grand Island Area Chamber of Commerce
309 W 2nd St.
PO Box 1486
Grand Island, NE 68802-1486
Ph:(308)382-9210
Fax: (308)382-1154
Co. E-mail: info@gichamber.com
URL: http://www.gichamber.com
Contact: Cindy K. Johnson, Pres.

62266 ■ Greater Omaha Chamber of Commerce
1301 Harney St.
Omaha, NE 68102
Ph:(402)346-5000
Fax: (402)346-7050
Co. E-mail: info@omahachamber.org
URL: http://www.omahachamber.org
Contact: David G. Brown, Pres./CEO

62267 ■ Greater York Area Chamber of Commerce
116 S Lincoln Ave., Ste. 1
York, NE 68467-4222
Ph:(402)362-5531
Free: 888-SEE-YORK
Fax: (402)362-5953
Co. E-mail: yc03219@alltel.net
URL: http://www.yorkchamber.org
Contact: Brenda Janzen, Dir.

62268 ■ Hartington Area Chamber of Commerce
PO Box 742
Hartington, NE 68739
Ph:(402)254-6357
Fax: (402)254-6391
Co. E-mail: devcoor@hartel.net
URL: http://www.ci.hartington.ne.us/chamber.asp
Contact: Dennis Sturek, Pres.

62269 ■ Hastings Area Chamber of Commerce
301 S Burlington
PO Box 1104
Hastings, NE 68902-1104
Ph:(402)461-8400
Fax: (402)461-4400
Co. E-mail: info@hastingschamber.com
URL: http://www.hastingschamber.com
Contact: Tom Hastings, Pres.

62270 ■ Hebron Chamber of Commerce
PO Box 172
Hebron, NE 68370
Ph:(402)768-7156
Fax: (402)768-6176

62271 ■ Holdrege Area Chamber of Commerce
423 E Ave.
PO Box 200
Holdrege, NE 68949-0200
Ph:(308)995-4444
Fax: (308)995-4445
Co. E-mail: chamber@holdrege.org
URL: http://www.holdrege.org
Contact: Don Lien, Pres.

62272 ■ Imperial Chamber of Commerce
PO Box 87
Imperial, NE 69033
Ph:(308)882-5444
URL: http://www.imperialchamber.com

62273 ■ Kearney Area Chamber of Commerce
PO Box 607
1007 2nd Ave.
Kearney, NE 68848-0607
Ph:(308)237-3101
Free: 800-652-9435
Fax: (308)237-3103
Co. E-mail: info@kearneycoc.org
URL: http://www.kearneycoc.org
Contact: Roger Jasnoch, Pres.

62274 ■ Kimball - Banner County Chamber of Commerce
111 E 2nd St.
Kimball, NE 69145
Ph:(308)235-3782
Fax: (308)235-3825
Co. E-mail: kbccc@megavision.com
URL: http://www.ci.kimball.ne.us
Contact: Kim Baliman, Mgr.

62275 ■ Lavista Area Chamber of Commerce
7536 S 84th St., Ste. B
La Vista, NE 68128
Ph:(402)339-2078
Fax: (402)339-2026
Co. E-mail: info@lavistachamber.org
URL: http://www.lavistachamber.org
Contact: Tina Foehlinger, Exec.Dir.

62276 ■ Lexington Area Chamber of Commerce
302 E 6th St., Ste. 2
PO Box 97
Lexington, NE 68850-0097
Ph:(308)324-5504
Fax: (308)324-5505
Co. E-mail: info@lexcoc.com
URL: http://www.lexcoc.com
Contact: Vicki Gilpin, Exec.Dir.

62277 ■ Lincoln Chamber of Commerce
1135 M St., Ste. 200
PO Box 83006
Lincoln, NE 68501-3006
Ph:(402)436-2350
Fax: (402)436-2360
Co. E-mail: info@lcoc.com
URL: http://www.lcoc.com
Contact: Wendy Birdsall, Interim Pres.

62278 ■ Lincoln Women's Chamber of Commerce
237 S 70th St., Ste. 206
Lincoln, NE 68510
Ph:(402)488-2034
Fax: (402)488-2034
Co. E-mail: lincolnlwcc@juneau.com
Contact: Shirley McDaniel, Pres.

62279 ■ Loup City Chamber of Commerce
PO Box 24
Loup City, NE 68853-0024

Ph:(308)745-0430
Co. E-mail: lcchamber@cornhusker.net
URL: http://www.loupcity.com
Contact: Joe Milner, Pres.

62280 ■ McCook Area Chamber of Commerce
107 Norris Ave.
PO Box 337
McCook, NE 69001-0337
Ph:(308)345-3200
Free: 800-657-2179
Fax: (308)345-3201
Co. E-mail: director@aboutmccook.com
URL: http://aboutmccook.com
Contact: Pamela C. Harsh, Exec.Dir.

62281 ■ Minden Chamber of Commerce
PO Box 375
Minden, NE 68959-0375
Ph:(308)832-1811
Fax: (308)832-1811
Co. E-mail: mindenchamber@gtmc.net
URL: http://www.mindenne.org
Contact: Dena R. Beck, Mgr.

62282 ■ Nebraska Chamber of Commerce and Industry
PO Box 95128
1320 Lincoln Mall
Lincoln, NE 68509-5128
Ph:(402)474-4422
Fax: (402)474-5681
Co. E-mail: nechamber@nechamber.com
URL: http://www.nechamber.com
Contact: Barry L. Kennedy CAE, Pres.

62283 ■ Nebraska City Tourism and Commerce
806 1st Ave.
Nebraska City, NE 68410
Ph:(402)873-6654
Free: 800-514-9113
Fax: (402)873-6701
Co. E-mail: tourism@nebraskacity.com
URL: http://www.nebraskacity.com
Contact: Jim Johnston, Exec.Dir.

62284 ■ Norfolk Area Chamber of Commerce
405 Madison Ave.
Norfolk, NE 68701
Ph:(402)371-4862
Fax: (402)371-0182
Co. E-mail: members@norfolk.ne.us
URL: http://www.norfolk.ne.us
Contact: Dan Mauk, Pres.

62285 ■ North Platte Area Chamber of Commerce
502 S Dewey
North Platte, NE 69101
Ph:(308)532-4966
Fax: (308)532-4827
Co. E-mail: shelley@northplattechamber.com
URL: http://www.northplattechamber.com
Contact: David Bernard-Stevens, Pres.

62286 ■ Ogallala - Keith County Chamber of Commerce
204 E A St.
Ogallala, NE 69153-2640
Ph:(308)284-4066
Free: 800-658-4390
Fax: (308)284-3126
Co. E-mail: info@visitogallala.com
URL: http://www.visitogallala.com
Contact: Marion Kroeker, Exec.Dir.

62287 ■ O'Neill Area Chamber of Commerce
125 S 4th St.
Oneill, NE 68763-1813
Ph:(402)336-2355
Fax: (402)336-4563
Co. E-mail: oneill@morcomm.net
URL: http://www.oneillchamber.org
Contact: Pat Fritz, Exec.Dir.

62288 ■ Ord Area Chamber of Commerce
1514 K St.
Ord, NE 68862
Ph:(308)728-7875
Fax: (308)728-7691
Co. E-mail: valleycountyed@frontiernet.net
URL: http://www.ordneusa.com
Contact: Bethanne Kunz, Exec.Dir.

62289 ■ Orleans Chamber of Commerce
PO Box 464
Orleans, NE 68966
Ph:(308)473-4825
Contact: Charlene Hunt, Pres.

62290 ■ Plainview Chamber of Commerce
306 W Park Ave.
Plainview, NE 68769-0813
Ph:(402)582-3636
Fax: (402)582-4433
URL: http://www.plvwtelco.net/chamber-commerce.
   html
Contact: Audrey Green, Exec.Sec.

62291 ■ Plattsmouth Chamber of Commerce
918 Washington Ave.
Plattsmouth, NE 68048
Ph:(402)296-6021
Fax: (402)296-6974
Co. E-mail: plattsmouthchamber@hotmail.com
URL: http://www.plattsmouthchamber.com
Contact: Jeanene Wehrbein, Exec.Dir.

62292 ■ Ralston Area Chamber of Commerce
5505 Miller Ave.
Ralston, NE 68127
Ph:(402)339-7737
Co. E-mail: chamber@cityofralston.com
URL: http://www.cityofralston.com
Contact: Marlene Hansen, Exec.Dir.

62293 ■ Ravenna Area Chamber of Commerce
PO Box 56
Ravenna, NE 68869
Ph:(308)452-3225
Co. E-mail: ravchamber@towncountrybank.net
URL: http://www.ci.ravenna.ne.us
Contact: Liz Swenson, Exec.Dir.

62294 ■ St. Paul Area Chamber of Commerce
PO Box 153
619 Howard Ave.
St. Paul, NE 68873
Ph:(308)754-5558
Co. E-mail: stpaulcham@cornhusker.net
Contact: Mary Ann Fredrick, Exec.Dir.

62295 ■ Sarpy County Chamber of Commerce
501 Olson Dr., Ste. 4
Papillion, NE 68046
Ph:(402)339-3050
Fax: (402)339-9968
Co. E-mail: jane@sarpychamber.org
URL: http://www.sarpychamber.org
Contact: Jane Nielsen, Pres.

62296 ■ Schuyler Area Chamber of Commerce
1107 B St.
Schuyler, NE 68661
Ph:(402)352-5472
Fax: (402)352-2754
Co. E-mail: cocommerce1002@qwest.com
URL: http://www.ci.schuyler.ne.us
Contact: Marlene Moore, Dir.

62297 ■ Scottsbluff - Gering United Chamber of Commerce
1517 Broadway, Ste. 104
Scottsbluff, NE 69361-3184
Ph:(308)632-2133
Fax: (308)632-7128
Co. E-mail: chamber@scottsbluffgering.net
URL: http://www.scottsbluffgering.net
Contact: Karen Anderson, Exec.Dir.

62298 ■ Seward Area Chamber of Commerce
616 Bradford
Seward, NE 68434
Ph:(402)643-4189
Fax: (402)643-4713
Co. E-mail: sewcham@sewardne.com
URL: http://www.sewardne.com
Contact: Jessica Manley, Admin. Asst.

62299 ■ South Sioux City Area Chamber of Commerce
3900 Dakota Ave., Ste. 11
South Sioux City, NE 68776
Ph:(402)494-1626
Fax: (402)494-5010
Co. E-mail: patmanderson@sscableone.net
Contact: Pat Anderson, Pres.

62300 ■ Superior Area Chamber of Commerce
354 N Commercial Ave.
Superior, NE 68978-1724
Ph:(402)879-3419
Fax: (402)879-3419
Co. E-mail: superiorcc@alltel.net
URL: http://www.superiorne.com/chamber.htm
Contact: Sherry Kniep, Administrator

62301 ■ Tecumseh Chamber of Commerce
PO Box 126
Tecumseh, NE 68450-0126
Ph:(402)335-3400
Co. E-mail: tecumsehchamber@alltel.net
URL: http://www.tecumsehne.com
Contact: Eloise Bartels, Sec.-Treas.

62302 ■ Tekamah Chamber of Commerce
PO Box 231
Tekamah, NE 68061
Ph:(402)374-2225
Fax: (402)374-1392
Co. E-mail: joezink@lee.net
URL: http://www.ci.tekamah.ne.us
Contact: Harriet Schafer, Sec.

62303 ■ Valentine Chamber of Commerce
239 S Main St.
PO Box 201
Valentine, NE 69201
Ph:(402)376-2969
Free: 800-658-4024
Fax: (402)376-2688
Co. E-mail: tourism@valentine-ne.com
URL: http://www.heartcity.com
Contact: Dean Jacobs, Exec.Dir.

62304 ■ Wahoo Chamber of Commerce and Economic Development
640 N Broadway
PO Box 154
Wahoo, NE 68066-0154
Ph:(402)443-4001
Fax: (402)443-3077
Co. E-mail: wahoo@wahoo.ne.us
URL: http://www.wahoo.ne.us
Contact: Doug Watts, Exec.Dir.

62305 ■ Wayne Area Chamber of Commerce
108 W 3rd St.
Wayne, NE 68787-1915
Ph:(402)375-2240
Fax: (402)375-2246
Co. E-mail: waynechamber@hotmail.com
Contact: Leo Ahmann, Interim Dir.

62306 ■ West Point Chamber of Commerce
PO Box 125
West Point, NE 68788-0125
Ph:(402)372-2981
Fax: (402)372-5832
Co. E-mail: info@westpointchamber.com
URL: http://www.westpointchamber.com
Contact: Staci Jensen, Exec.Dir.

62307 ■ Western Douglas County Chamber of Commerce
701 Ctr. St.
Elkhorn, NE 68022

Ph:(402)289-9560
Fax: (402)289-9560
Co. E-mail: jill@wdccc.org
URL: http://www.wdccc.org
Contact: Jill Magers, Exec.Dir.

62308 ■ Wilber Area Chamber of Commerce
PO Box 1164
Wilber, NE 68465
Ph:(402)821-2732
Free: 888-494-5237
Fax: (402)821-2691
URL: http://www.ci.wilber.ne.us

FINANCING AND LOAN PROGRAMS

62309 ■ Fenix Enterprises
1416 Dodge St., Rm. 1230
Omaha, NE 68179
Ph:(402)271-3077
URL: http://www.fexixenterprises.com
Investment Policies: Start-up.

62310 ■ Heartland Capital Fund, Ltd.
PO Box 642117
Omaha, NE 68164
Ph:(402)445-2358
Fax: (402)445-2370
URL: http://www.heartlandcapitalfund.com
Contact: Bradley Edwards, General Partner
Preferred Investment Size: $500,000 to $3,000,000.
Investment Types: First and second stage, and expansion. **Industry Preferences:** Communications, computer software, Internet specific, medical and health. **Geographic Preferences:** Southwest and Midwest.

62311 ■ Odin Capital Group
1625 Farnam St., Ste. 700
Omaha, NE 68102
Ph:(402)827-9900
Fax: (402)342-9311
URL: http://www.odincapital.com
Contact: John Gustafson, Principal
Preferred Investment Size: $500,000 to $3,000,000.
Investment Types: Early, first, and second stage, and expansion. **Industry Preferences:** Communications, computer software, Internet specific, medical and health, industrial and energy, financial services, and business service. **Geographic Preferences:** Midwest, Rocky mountains, and Southwest.

PROCUREMENT ASSISTANCE PROGRAMS

62312 ■ Nebraska Procurement Technical Assistance Center–Nebraska Business Development Center
University of Nebraska at Omaha
RH 308
Omaha, NE 68182-0072
Ph:(402)554-6253
Fax: (402)554-6260
Co. E-mail: mikehall@mail.unomaha.edu
URL: http://www.nbdc.uhomaha.edu
Contact: Mike Hall, Dir

INCUBATORS/RESEARCH AND TECHNOLOGY PARKS

62313 ■ Business and Technology Centre (Omaha)
2505 N 24th St.
Omaha, NE 68110
Ph:(402)453-5336
Fax: (402)451-2876
Co. E-mail: info@osbntc.org
Contact: Vicki Wilson, Exec Dir

62314 ■ University of Nebraska—
Lincoln–Office of Sponsored Programs
Alexander Bldg, West, Rm. 111
312 N 14th St.
Lincoln, NE 68588-0430
Ph:(402)472-3171
Fax: (402)472-9323
Co. E-mail: nbraaten1@unl.edu
URL: http://www.unl.edu/osp/home.html
Contact: Norman O. Braaten, Dir., Pre-Award Devel.
E-mail: nbraaten1@unl.edu
Scope: Administers and coordinates sponsored research at the University, negotiates research grants and contracts with outside agencies for the University, and serves as liaison between research sponsors, the University administration, individual faculty members, and University of Nebraska Foundation. Maintains files on research in progress at the University, government and foundation sources of research support, and application procedures. **Publications:** Annual report; Funding Announcements (weekly). **Educational Activities:** Workshops, on grantsmanship and patenting.

62315 ■ University of Nebraska Technology
Park
University of Nebraska Technology Park
4701 Innovation Dr.
Lincoln, NE 68521-5330
Ph:(402)472-4200
Fax: (402)472-4203
Co. E-mail: info@unebtechpark.com
URL: http://www.unebtechpark.com
Contact: Stephen Frayser, Pres
Description: This small business incubator is a master-planned development with a variety of amenities and services to offer its tenants.

EDUCATIONAL PROGRAMS

62316 ■ Nebraska Department of Economic
Development–Industrial Training Programs
301 Centennial Mall S
PO Box 94666
Lincoln, NE 68509-4666
Ph:800-426-6505
Free: 800-426-6505
Fax: (402)471-3778

URL: http://www.neded.org
Description: Customized job training programs.

62317 ■ University of Nebraska at
Lincoln–Center for Entrepreneurship
Office of Entrepreneurship
University of Nebraska Lincoln CBA 209
Lincoln, NE 68588-0487
Ph:(402)472-3353
Fax: (402)472-5855
Co. E-mail: tsebora1@unl.edu
URL: http://www.cba.unl.edu/outreach/ent
Description: Offers a program/classes in small business/small business management.

PUBLISHERS

62318 ■ GHC Business Books
4214 N Post Rd.
Omaha, NE 68112
Ph:(402)453-1769
Contact: Ray Gustafson, President
Description: Publishes book on small business development. Services include a business brokerage. Reaches market through direct mail. **Founded:** 1982.

SMALL BUSINESS DEVELOPMENT CENTER LEAD OFFICE

62319 ■ Nevada Small Business Development Center–University of Nevada at Reno
College of Business Administration/032
Business Bldg., Rm. 411
Reno, NV 89557-0100
Ph:(702)784-1717
Fax: (702)784-4337
Contact: Sam Males, State Director

62320 ■ University of Nevada at Reno–Small Business Development Center
College of Business Administration, Rm. 411
Reno, NV 89557-0100
Ph:(775)784-1717
Fax: (775)784-4337
URL: http://www.nsbdc.org
Contact: Sam Males, State Dir.
E-mail: males@unr.edu

SMALL BUSINESS DEVELOPMENT CENTERS

62321 ■ Carson City Chamber of Commerce–Small Business Development Center
1900 S. Carson St., Ste. 100
Carson City, NV 89701-4514
Ph:(775)882-1565
Fax: (775)882-4179
Contact: Larry Osborne, Exec. Dir.

62322 ■ Carson Valley Chamber of Commerce and Visitors Authority–SBDC
1512 Hwy. 395 N., Ste. 1
Gardnerville, NV 89410
Ph:(775)782-8144
Fax: (775)782-1025
Co. E-mail: khalbard@earthlink.net

62323 ■ Churchill County Economic Development Authority (CEDA)–SBDC
98 S. Carson St.
PO Box 927
Fallon, NV 89406
Ph:(775)423-8587
Fax: (775)423-1759
Co. E-mail: sbdc@ceda-nv.org
URL: http://www.ceda-nv.org
Contact: Juliette Taylor, Exec. Dir.
E-mail: jtaylor@ceda-nv.org

62324 ■ Great Basin College–Small Business Development Center
723 Railroad St.
Elko, NV 89801
Ph:(775)753-2245

Fax: (775)753-2242
Contact: John Pryor, Dir.

62325 ■ Henderson Nevada SBDC
112 Water St.
Henderson, NV 89015
Ph:(702)992-7208
Fax: (702)992-7245
Contact: Larry Vierra, Business Specialist
E-mail: vierral2@unlv.nevada.edu

62326 ■ Incline Village Chamber of Commerce–SBDC
969 Tahoe Blvd.
Incline Village, NV 89451
Ph:(702)831-4440
Fax: (702)832-1605
Contact: Sheri Woods, Exec. Dir.

62327 ■ Las Vegas SBDC–SBDC
3720 Howard Hughes Pkwy., Ste. 130
Las Vegas, NV 89109
Ph:(702)734-7575
Fax: (702)734-7633
Contact: Robert Holland, Business Specialist

62328 ■ Mineral County High School–SBDC
601 A St.
Box 717
Hawthorne, NV 89415
Ph:(775)945-2405
Fax: (775)845-3621
Contact: Louis Thompson, Business Consultant
E-mail: shirlou@gbis.com

62329 ■ North Las Vegas Small Business Development Center
19 W. Brooks Ave., Ste. B
North Las Vegas, NV 89030
Ph:(702)399-6300
Fax: (702)895-4095
Contact: Janis Stevenson, Business Development Specialist

62330 ■ Rural Nevada Development Center–Ely Nevada SBDC
1320 E. Aultman St.
Ely, NV 89301
Ph:(775)289-8519
Free: 800-404-5204
URL: http://www.rndcnv.org
Contact: Robin Bartlett, Consultant
E-mail: robin@rndcnv.org

62331 ■ Rural Nevada Development Corporation–Pahrump Nevada SBDC
NSB Bldg., 2nd Fl.
1301 S. Hwy. 160
Pahrump, NV 89048
Ph:(775)751-1947
Fax: (775)751-1933
Contact: Allan Parker, Business Consultant
E-mail: alparker@rndcnva.org

62332 ■ Tri-County Development Authority–Small Business Development Center
PO Box 820
Winnemucca, NV 89446
Ph:(702)623-5777
Fax: (702)623-5999
Contact: Teri Williams, Dir.

62333 ■ University of Nevada at Las Vegas–Small Business Development Center
4505 Maryland Pkwy.
Box 456011
Las Vegas, NV 89154-6011
Ph:(702)895-4270
Fax: (702)895-4273
Contact: Nancy Buist, Business Development Specialist

62334 ■ Winnemucca Nevada SBDC
90 W. 4th St.
Winnemucca, NV 89446
Ph:(775)623-1064
Fax: (775)623-1664
Contact: Bill Sims, Specialist
E-mail: bills@unr.edu

SMALL BUSINESS ASSISTANCE PROGRAMS

62335 ■ Economic Development Commission–DEAL WITH VARIOUS ISSUES OF SMALL BUSINESSES
108 E Proctor St.
Carson City, NV 89701
Ph:(775)687-4325
Free: 800-336-1600
Fax: (775)687-4450
URL: http://www.expand2nevada.com

62336 ■ Nevada Department of Business and Industry–DEAL WITH VARIOUS ISSUES OF SMALL BUSINESSES
788 Fairview, Ste. 100
Carson City, NV 89706
Ph:(775)687-4250
Fax: (775)687-4266
URL: http://www.dbi.state.nv.us

SCORE OFFICES

62337 ■ SCORE Las Vegas
City Ctre. Pl.
400 S Fourth St., Ste. 250A
Las Vegas, NV 89101
Ph:(702)388-6104
Co. E-mail: scorelv@coam.net

62338 ■ SCORE Northern Nevada
Nevada Small Business Development Center
College of Business Administration - University of Nevada
Reno, NV 89557

Ph:(775)784-4436
Fax: (775)784-4337
Co. E-mail: score@unr.nevada.edu
URL: http://www.score-reno.org
Contact: John Diedenhofen, Chm.
Description: Offers free and confidential business advice, mentoring and information.

BETTER BUSINESS BUREAUS

62339 ■ Better Business Bureau of Southern Nevada
2301 Palomino Ln.
Las Vegas, NV 89107-4503
Ph:(702)320-4500
Fax: (702)320-4560
Co. E-mail: info@vegasbbb.org
URL: http://www.vegasbbb.org
Contact: Sylvia Campbell, Pres./CEO

CHAMBERS OF COMMERCE

62340 ■ Battle Mountain Chamber of Commerce
PO Box 333
Battle Mountain, NV 89820
Ph:(775)635-8245
Fax: (775)635-8064
Co. E-mail: battlemtncc@hotmail.com
Contact: Sara Burkhart, Exec. Dir.

62341 ■ Beatty Chamber of Commerce
PO Box 956
Beatty, NV 89003
Ph:(775)553-2424
Fax: (775)553-2225
Co. E-mail: beattychamber@beattynv.com
URL: http://www.governet.net/nv/as/bea
Contact: Peggy Johnson, Pres.

62342 ■ Boulder City Chamber of Commerce
465 Nevada Way
Boulder City, NV 89005-2613
Ph:(702)293-2034
Fax: (702)293-0574
Co. E-mail: info@bouldercitychamber.com
URL: http://www.bouldercitychamber.com
Contact: Jill Rowland-Lagan, Exec.Dir.

62343 ■ Caliente Chamber of Commerce
PO Box 553
Caliente, NV 89008
Ph:(775)726-3129
Fax: (775)726-3447
URL: http://www.lincolncountynevada.com
Contact: Michael Taylor, Pres.

62344 ■ Carson City Area Chamber of Commerce
1900 S Carson St.
Carson City, NV 89701
Ph:(775)882-1565
Fax: (775)882-4179
Co. E-mail: ccchamber@carsoncitychamber.com
URL: http://www.carsoncitychamber.com
Contact: Ronni Hannaman, Exec.Dir.

62345 ■ Carson Valley Chamber of Commerce and Visitors Authority
1513 U.S. Hwy. 395 N
Gardnerville, NV 89410
Ph:(775)782-8144
Free: 800-727-7677
Fax: (775)782-1025
Co. E-mail: info@carsonvalleynv.org
URL: http://www.carsonvalleynv.org
Contact: Mr. Skip Sayre, Exec.Dir.

62346 ■ Dayton Area Chamber of Commerce
PO Box 2408
Dayton, NV 89403

Ph:(775)246-7909
Fax: (775)246-5838
Co. E-mail: info@daytonnvchamber.org
URL: http://www.daytonnvchamber.org
Contact: Cary Dyer, Exec. Dir.

62347 ■ Elko Chamber of Commerce
1405 Idaho St.
Elko, NV 89801
Ph:(775)738-7135
Free: 800-428-7143
Fax: (775)738-7136
Co. E-mail: chamber@elkonevada.com
URL: http://www.elkonevada.com
Contact: Patty Rowe, CEO

62348 ■ Eureka Chamber of Commerce and Visitors Center
11 N Main
PO Box 1078
Eureka, NV 89316
Ph:(775)237-5279
Co. E-mail: econdev_eureka@eurekanv.org
Contact: Dan Green, Pres.

62349 ■ Fernley Chamber of Commerce
70 N West St.
Fernley, NV 89408
Ph:(775)575-4459
Fax: (775)575-2626
Co. E-mail: fernleychamber@sbcglobal.net
URL: http://www.fernleychamber.org
Contact: Robert Bidlake, Pres.

62350 ■ Greater Austin Chamber of Commerce
PO Box 212
Austin, NV 89310-0212
Ph:(775)964-2200
Fax: (775)964-2447
Co. E-mail: austinnvchamber@yahoo.com
URL: http://www.austinnevada.com
Contact: Joy K. Brandt, Pres.

62351 ■ Greater Fallon Area Chamber of Commerce
85 N Taylor
Fallon, NV 89406
Ph:(775)423-2544
Fax: (775)423-0540
Co. E-mail: info@fallonchamber.com
URL: http://www.fallonchamber.com
Contact: Michelle Single, Exec.Dir.

62352 ■ Henderson Chamber of Commerce
590 S Boulder Hwy.
Henderson, NV 89015-7512
Ph:(702)565-8951
Fax: (702)565-3115
Co. E-mail: info@hendersonchamber.com
URL: http://www.hendersonchamber.com
Contact: Alice Martz, CEO

62353 ■ Humboldt County Chamber of Commerce
30 W Winnemucca Blvd.
Winnemucca, NV 89445
Ph:(775)623-2225
Free: 877-326-1916
Fax: (775)623-6478
Co. E-mail: chamber@winnemucca.net
URL: http://www.humboldtcountychamber.com
Contact: Paul Thurman, Pres.

62354 ■ Incline Village - Crystal Bay Chamber of Commerce
969 Tahoe Blvd.
Incline Village, NV 89451
Ph:(775)831-4440
Free: 800-519-1584
Fax: (775)832-1625
Co. E-mail: tahoecofc@aol.com
URL: http://www.laketahoechamber.com
Contact: Jim Jeffers, Exec.Dir.

62355 ■ Las Vegas Chamber of Commerce
3720 Howard Hughes Pkwy.
Las Vegas, NV 89109-0937

Ph:(702)735-1616
Fax: (702)735-2011
Co. E-mail: info@lvchamber.com
URL: http://www.lvchamber.com
Contact: Kara J. Kelley, Pres./CEO

62356 ■ Latin Chamber of Commerce of Nevada
300 N 13th St.
Las Vegas, NV 89101
Ph:(702)385-7367
Fax: (702)385-2614
Co. E-mail: info@lvlcc.com
URL: http://www.lasvegaslatincc.com
Contact: Otto Merida, Pres./CEO

62357 ■ Laughlin Chamber of Commerce
PO Box 77777
Laughlin, NV 89028
Ph:(702)298-2214
Free: 800-227-5245
Fax: (702)298-5708
Co. E-mail: chamberrelations@cmaaccess.com
URL: http://www.laughlinchamber.com
Contact: JoElle Hurns, Exec.Dir.

62358 ■ Lovelock/Pershing County Chamber of Commerce
350 Main St.
PO Box 821
Lovelock, NV 89419-0821
Ph:(775)273-7213
Fax: (775)273-1732
Co. E-mail: pcchamber@sbcglobal.net
URL: http://www.zplace2b.com/pccofc
Contact: Kirsten Hertz, Operations Mgr.

62359 ■ Mesquite Area Chamber of Commerce
12 W Mesquite Blvd., Ste. 107
Mesquite, NV 89027
Ph:(702)346-2902
Fax: (702)346-6138
Co. E-mail: meschamber@cascadeaccess.com
URL: http://www.mesquite-chamber.com

62360 ■ Mineral County Chamber of Commerce
314 5th St.
PO Box 2250
Hawthorne, NV 89415
Ph:(775)945-2507
Co. E-mail: info@mineralcountychamber.com
URL: http://www.mineralcountychamber.com
Contact: Jessica Black, Exec. Dir.

62361 ■ Moapa Valley Chamber of Commerce
PO Box 361
Overton, NV 89040
Ph:(702)398-7160
Co. E-mail: loriwaters@mvdsl.com
URL: http://www.moapavalley.com
Contact: Lori Waters, Pres.

62362 ■ Nevada Chamber of Commerce Association
One E First St., No. 1600
PO Box 3499
Reno, NV 89501
Ph:(775)337-3030
Fax: (775)337-3038
Co. E-mail: info@reno-sparkschamber.org
URL: http://www.reno-sparkschamber.org
Contact: Harry York, CEO

62363 ■ North Las Vegas Chamber of Commerce
3345 W Craig Rd., Ste. B
North Las Vegas, NV 89032
Ph:(702)642-9595
Fax: (702)642-0439
Co. E-mail: contact@nlvchamber.org
URL: http://www.nlvchamber.org
Contact: Sharon Powers, Pres./CEO

62364 ■ Pahrump Valley Chamber of Commerce
1301 S Hwy. 160, 2nd Fl.
PO Box 42
Pahrump, NV 89041
Ph:(775)727-5800
Fax: (775)727-3909
Co. E-mail: info@pahrumpchamber.com
URL: http://www.pahrumpchamber.com
Contact: Kari Frilot, CEO

62365 ■ Pioche Chamber of Commerce
PO Box 127
Pioche, NV 89043-0127
Ph:(775)962-5544
Co. E-mail: chamber@piocheneveda.com
URL: http://www.piochenevada.com
Contact: Bob Rowe, Pres.

62366 ■ Reno-Sparks Chamber of Commerce
1 E 1st St., 16th Fl.
PO Box 3499
Reno, NV 89505
Ph:(775)337-3030
Fax: (775)337-3038
Co. E-mail: info@renosparkschamber.org
URL: http://www.renosparkschamber.org
Contact: Harry York, CEO

62367 ■ Sparks Chamber of Commerce
831 Victorian Ave.
PO Box 1776
Sparks, NV 89432-1776
Ph:(775)358-1976
Fax: (775)358-1992
Co. E-mail: info@sparkschamber.org
URL: http://www.sparkschamber.org
Contact: Len Stevens, Exec.Dir.

62368 ■ Tonopah Chamber of Commerce
301 W Brougher Ave.
PO Box 869
Tonopah, NV 89049
Ph:(775)482-3859
Fax: (775)482-3932
URL: http://www.tonopahnevada.com
Contact: Kathleen Hill, Exec.Dir.

62369 ■ Virginia City/Gold Hill Chamber of Commerce
PO Box 920
Virginia City, NV 89440
Ph:(775)847-0311
Fax: (775)847-7915
Co. E-mail: virginiacity@earthlink.net
URL: http://www.virginiacity-nv.com
Contact: Kristin Hamlet, Admin.

62370 ■ Wells Chamber of Commerce
PO Box 615
Wells, NV 89835
Ph:(775)752-3540
Fax: (775)752-2172
Co. E-mail: coc@californiatrailinterpretivecenter.com
URL: http://wellsnevada.com
Contact: Pat Kelly, Pres.

62371 ■ White Pine Chamber of Commerce
636 Aultman St.
Ely, NV 89301-1555
Ph:(775)289-8877
Fax: (775)289-6144
Co. E-mail: elycc@whitepinechamber.com
URL: http://www.whitepinechamber.com
Contact: Evie Pinneo, Exec.Dir.

FINANCING AND LOAN PROGRAMS

62372 ■ The Benefit Capital Companies Inc.
PO Box 542
Logandale, NV 89021
Ph:(702)398-3222
Fax: (702)398-3700

Contact: Robert Smiley
Preferred Investment Size: $2,500,000 minimum. **Investment Types:** Leveraged buyout and mezzanine. **Industry Preferences:** Diversified. **Geographic Preferences:** Entire U.S.

62373 ■ Edge Capital Investment Co., LLC (Las Vegas)
1350 E. Flamingo Rd., Ste. 3000
Las Vegas, NV 89119
Ph:(702)438-3343
Fax: 888-354-4455
URL: http://www.edgecapital.net
Contact: John Yeomans, Managing Director
E-mail: JohnYatsedgcapital.net
Preferred Investment Size: $500,000 to $15,000,000. **Investment Types:** Seed, start-up, first, second, and later stage, mezzanine, leveraged buyout, and special situation. **Industry Preferences:** Communications, computer hardware and software, Internet specific, computer related, semiconductors and other electronics, biotechnology, medical and health, consumer related, industrial and energy, transportation, and financial services. **Geographic Preferences:** U.S. and Canada.

62374 ■ Millennium Three Venture Group LLC
6880 South McCarran Blvd., Ste. A-11
Reno, NV 89509
Ph:(775)954-2020
Fax: (775)954-2023
URL: http://www.m3vg.com
Preferred Investment Size: $500,000 to $2,000,000. **Investment Types:** Early stage, expansion, first stage, mezzanine, second stage, and seed. **Industry Preferences:** Diversified. **Geographic Preferences:** West Coast.

PROCUREMENT ASSISTANCE PROGRAMS

62375 ■ Nevada Commission on Economic Development–Procurement Outreach Program–Northern Nevada Regional Office (108 E)
108 E Proctor St.
Carson City, NV 89701-4240
Ph:(775)687-4325
Free: 800-336-1600
Fax: (775)687-4450
URL: http://www.nvoutreachcenter.com
Contact: Rick Horn, Dir
Description: Assists small and disadvantaged businesses in Nevada obtain and complete federal government contracts. Also encourages the expansion of the manufacturing and service sectors into government contracting.

62376 ■ Nevada Commission on Economic Development–Procurement Outreach Program–Southern Nevada Regional Office (555 E)
555 E Washington Ave., Ste. 5400
Las Vegas, NV 89101
Ph:(702)486-2716
Fax: (702)486-2701
URL: http://www.nvoutreachcenter.com
Contact: Rick Horn, Dir
Description: Assists small and disadvantaged businesses in Nevada obtain and complete federal government contracts. Also encourages the expansion of the manufacturing and service sectors into government contracting.

62377 ■ Nevada Procurement Technical Assistance Center–Economic Development
108 E Proctor St.
Carson City, NV 89701-4240
Ph:(775)687-1813
Free: 800-336-1600
Fax: (775)687-4450
Co. E-mail: cedpop@bizopp.state.nv.us
URL: http://www.nvoutreachcenter.com
Contact: Rick Horn, Dir

INCUBATORS/RESEARCH AND TECHNOLOGY PARKS

62378 ■ Dandini Research Park
DRI Research Parks Ltd.
2215 Raggio Pky.
Reno, NV 89512-1095
Ph:(775)673-7300
Fax: (702)862-5406
Co. E-mail: information@dri.edu
URL: http://www.dri.edu
Contact: Dr. Stephen G. Wells, Pres.
E-mail: information@dri.edu
Scope: 470-acre site that links the research and development activities of Park tenants with the Desert Research Institute's technological equipment, personnel, laboratories, and training programs. Instrument design, environmental testing, and research and development services may be done in cooperation with DRI staff.

EDUCATIONAL PROGRAMS

62379 ■ Community College of Southern Nevada–Cheyenne Campus
3200 E Cheyenne Ave.
North Las Vegas, NV 89030
Ph:(702)651-4000
Free: 800-492-5728
Fax: (702)643-1474
URL: http://www.ccsn.nevada.edu
Description: Offers a program/classes in small business/small business management.

62380 ■ Truckee Meadows Community College–Institute for Business and Industry
5270 Neil Rd.
4001 S Virginia St.
Reno, NV 89502
Ph:(775)829-9000
Fax: (775)829-9009
URL: http://www.tmcc.edu/
Description: Offers a program designed to bring courses to the workplace; in addition, curriculum can be customized for the particular needs of a company.

PUBLICATIONS

62381 ■ *Smart Start your Georgia Business*
PSI Research
300 N. Valley Dr.
Grants Pass, OR 97526
Ph:(503)479-9464
Free: 800-228-2275
Fax: (503)476-1479
Co. E-mail: info@psi-research.com
URL: http://www.psi-research.com
Ed: Michael D. Jenkins. **Released:** Revised edition, 1992. **Price:** $29.95 (looseleaf binder); $24.95 (paper). **Description:** Part of the Successful Business Library series.

62382 ■ *Tax Freedom: The Business Guide to Incorporating in Nevada*
TAB Books, Inc. (McGraw Hill)
860 Taylor Station
Blacklick, OH 43004
Free: 800-822-8138
Ed: Barber. **Released:** 1990. **Price:** $12.95 (paper).

PUBLISHERS

62383 ■ Everett L. Gracey
3288 Alum Creek Ct.
PO Box 6000
Reno, NV 89509
Ph:(775)324-3290
Fax: (775)324-3289
Co. E-mail: Ev@EverettGacey.com

URL: http://www.EverettGracey.com
Contact: Everett L. Gracey, Publisher
Description: Publishes business related books. Reaches market through wholesalers Ingram and Baker & Taylor. Does not accept unsolicited manuscripts. **Founded:** 1994.

62384 ■ Long & Silverman Publishing Inc.
800 N Rainbow Blvd., 208
Las Vegas, NV 89107
Ph:(702)948-5073

Free: 800-99L-SPUB
URL: http://www.lspub.com
Contact: Rebecca Stein
Description: Publishes books on business, economics, finances, inspirational, marketing, motivation, success, real estate, self-help, and taxes **Founded:** 2003

SMALL BUSINESS DEVELOPMENT CENTER LEAD OFFICE

62385 ■ University of New Hampshire–Small Business Development Center
108 McConnell Hall
Durham, NH 03824-3593
Ph:(603)862-4879
Fax: (603)862-4876
URL: http://www.nhsbdc.org
Contact: Mary Collins, State Dir.
E-mail: mary.collins@unh.edu

SMALL BUSINESS DEVELOPMENT CENTERS

62386 ■ Chamber of Commerce–SBDC–Seacoast Regional Office (18 S.)
18 S. Main St., Ste. 2A
Rochester, NH 03867-2702
Ph:(603)330-1929
Fax: (603)330-1948
Contact: Warren Daniel, Regional Mgr.
E-mail: wdaniel@cisunix.unh.edu

62387 ■ Keene State College–Small Business Development Center
Mailstop 2101
Keene, NH 03435-2101
Ph:(603)358-2602
Fax: (603)358-2612
URL: http://www.nhsbdc.org
Contact: Gary Oden, Regional Mgr.
E-mail: goden@keene.edu

62388 ■ Littleton Small Business Development Center
120 Main St.
Littleton, NH 03561
Ph:(603)444-1053
Fax: (603)444-5463
Co. E-mail: nh.sbdc@unh.edu
URL: http://www.nhsbdc.org
Contact: Elizabeth Ward, Regional Mgr.

62389 ■ Manchester Small Business Development Center
33 S. Commercial St.
Manchester, NH 03101-1796
Ph:(603)624-2000
Fax: (603)647-4410
Co. E-mail: nh.sbdc@unh.edu
URL: http://www.nhsbdc.org
Contact: Bob Ebberson, Regional Mgr.

62390 ■ Office of Economic Initiatives–SBDC
172 Pembroke Rd.
Concord, NH 03301
Ph:(603)227-0417

Fax: (603)226-4132
Contact: Janice Kitchen, Dir.
E-mail: jkitchen@unh.edu

62391 ■ Plymouth State College–Small Business Development Center
Outreach Center
MSC No. 24A
Plymouth, NH 03264
Ph:(603)535-2523
Fax: (603)535-2850
Contact: Gary Chabot, Regional Mgr.

62392 ■ Rivier College–Small Business Development Center
420 Main St.
Nashua, NH 03060-5086
Ph:(603)897-8587
Fax: (603)897-8884
Co. E-mail: rmcmillan@rivier.edu
URL: http://www.nhsbdc.org
Contact: Hollis McGuire, Regional Mgr.

SMALL BUSINESS ASSISTANCE PROGRAMS

62393 ■ New Hampshire Department of Resources and Economic Development–Business Resource Center
172 Pembroke Rd.
PO Box 1856
Concord, NH 03302-1856
Ph:(603)271-2591
Fax: (603)271-6784
Co. E-mail: sarnett@dred.state.nh.us
URL: http://www.ded.state.nh.us/obid
Contact: Stuart Arnett, Dir
Description: Assists companies considering locating in New Hampshire in their review of staffing and facility requirements, marketing considerations, support services, and other services. Also offers complete, current, and reliable information on those sections of the state best able to support a specific project. Also helps existing businesses.

SCORE OFFICES

62394 ■ Mount Washington Valley SCORE
1620 E Main St.
Center Conway, NH 03813
Ph:(603)447-4388
Fax: (603)447-9947
Co. E-mail: info@score641.org
URL: http://www.score641.org
Contact: Michael Kline, Chm.
Description: Provides professional guidance and information to America's small business in order to strengthen the local and national economy.

62395 ■ SCORE Concord
c/o George Fearnley, CHR
JC Cleveland Federal Bldg.
55 Pleasant St., Ste. 3101
Concord, NH 03301

Ph:(603)225-1400
Fax: (603)225-1409
Co. E-mail: score518@tolalnetnh.net
URL: http://www.score.org

62396 ■ SCORE Merrimack Valley, NH, Chapter 199
1000 Elm St., 6th Fl.
Manchester, NH 03101
Ph:(603)666-7561
Fax: (603)666-7925
Co. E-mail: chairman@score199.mv.com
URL: http://www.score-manchester.org
Contact: Mr. Jim Hanley, Chm.
Description: Represents business people supported by and affiliated with the U.S. Small Business Administration. Provides free, confidential and professional business counseling for small business and those wishing to start their own business.

62397 ■ SCORE Monadnock
34 Mechanic St.
Keene, NH 03431-3421
Ph:(603)352-0320
Co. E-mail: info@monadnockscore.org
URL: http://www.monadnockscore.org
Contact: Wallace Reney, Chm.
Description: Works to provide quality business counseling without charge to residents and business area.

62398 ■ Seacoast SCORE Chapter 185
195 Commerce Way, Ste. A
Portsmouth, NH 03801
Ph:(603)433-0575
Fax: (603)433-0576
Co. E-mail: info@scorehelp.org
URL: http://www.scorehelp.org/chapter_185.html
Description: Represents the interests of retired business professionals who volunteer their experience and knowledge to help small business owners and potential small business owners achieve success. Provides free business counseling and seminars.

62399 ■ Upper Valley SCORE
Citizens Bank Bldg., Rm. 316
20 W Park St.
Lebanon, NH 03766
Ph:(603)448-3491
Fax: (603)448-1908
Co. E-mail: score@valley.net
URL: http://www.uppervalleyscore.org
Description: Provides free and confidential business counseling tailored to meet the needs of small business and personal objectives.

BETTER BUSINESS BUREAUS

62400 ■ Better Business Bureau of New Hampshire
25 Hall St., Ste. 102
Concord, NH 03301-3483
Ph:(603)224-1991

Fax: (603)228-9035
Co. E-mail: info@bbbnh.org
URL: http://www.concord.bbb.org
Contact: Robert Shomphe, Pres.

CHAMBERS OF COMMERCE

62401 ■ Bethlehem Chamber of Commerce
2182 Main St.
PO Box 748
Bethlehem, NH 03574-0748
Free: 888-845-1957
Co. E-mail: info@bethlehemwhitemtns.com
URL: http://www.bethlehemwhitemtns.com
Contact: Charles Crannell, Pres.

62402 ■ Conway Village Area Chamber of Commerce
PO Box 1019
Conway, NH 03818
Ph:(603)447-2639
Fax: (603)447-3692
Co. E-mail: info@conwaychamber.com
URL: http://www.conwaychamber.com
Contact: Ms. LaRoche Melissa, Administrator

62403 ■ Exeter Area Chamber of Commerce
120 Water St.
Exeter, NH 03833
Ph:(603)772-2411
Fax: (603)772-9965
Co. E-mail: info@exeterarea.org
URL: http://www.exeterarea.org
Contact: Tracey E. McGrail, Pres.

62404 ■ Franconia Notch Chamber of Commerce
PO Box 780
Franconia, NH 03580-0780
Ph:(603)823-5661
Free: 800-237-9007
Fax: (603)823-8479
Co. E-mail: info@franconianotch.org
URL: http://www.franconianotch.org
Contact: Jane Portanaui, Dir.

62405 ■ Greater Claremont Chamber of Commerce
Moody Bldg.
24 Tremont Sq., Ste. 100
Claremont, NH 03743
Ph:(603)543-1296
Fax: (603)542-1469
Co. E-mail: chamber@adelphia.net
URL: http://www.newhampshire.com/
Contact: Theresa Novak Chabot, Exec.Dir.

62406 ■ Greater Derry Chamber of Commerce
29 W Broadway
Derry, NH 03038
Ph:(603)432-8205
Fax: (603)432-7938
Co. E-mail: derrychamber@earthlink.net
URL: http://www.derry-chamber.org
Contact: Gina Gulino-Payne, Exec.Dir.

62407 ■ Greater Dover Chamber of Commerce
299 Central Ave.
Dover, NH 03820-4127
Ph:(603)742-2218
Fax: (603)749-6317
Co. E-mail: info@dovernh.org
URL: http://www.dovernh.org
Contact: Jack Story, Pres./CEO

62408 ■ Greater Franklin Chamber of Commerce
PO Box 464
Franklin, NH 03235
Ph:(603)934-6909
Co. E-mail: info@franklinnhchamber.com
URL: http://www.franklinnhchamber.com
Contact: Michael Seymour, Pres.

62409 ■ Greater Hudson Chamber of Commerce
71 Lowell Rd.
Hudson, NH 03051
Ph:(603)889-4731
Fax: (603)889-7939
Co. E-mail: info@hudsonchamber.com
URL: http://www.hudsonchamber.com
Contact: Brenda Collins, Office Mgr.

62410 ■ Greater Keene Chamber of Commerce
48 Central Sq.
Keene, NH 03431
Ph:(603)352-1303
Fax: (603)358-5341
Co. E-mail: info@keenechamber.com
URL: http://www.keenechamber.com
Contact: Tom Dowling, Pres.

62411 ■ Greater Laconia/Weirs Beach Chamber of Commerce
383 S Main St.
Laconia, NH 03246
Ph:(603)524-5531
Fax: (603)524-5534
Co. E-mail: info@laconia-weirs.org
URL: http://www.laconia-weirs.org
Contact: Theresa Lamson, Exec. Dir.

62412 ■ Greater Manchester Chamber of Commerce
889 Elm St.
Manchester, NH 03101
Ph:(603)666-6600
Fax: (603)626-0910
Co. E-mail: info@manchester-chamber.org
URL: http://www.manchester-chamber.org
Contact: Robin Comstock, Pres./CEO

62413 ■ Greater Nashua Chamber of Commerce
151 Main St.
Nashua, NH 03060
Ph:(603)881-8333
Fax: (603)881-7323
Co. E-mail: chamber@nashuachamber.com
URL: http://www.nashuachamber.com
Contact: Christopher K. Hodgdon, Pres.

62414 ■ Greater Ossipee Area Chamber of Commerce
PO Box 323
Center Ossipee, NH 03814
Ph:(603)539-6201
Co. E-mail: info@ossipeevalley.org
URL: http://www.ossipeevalley.org
Contact: Bill Grover, Pres.

62415 ■ Greater Peterborough Chamber of Commerce
PO Box 401
10 Wilton Rd.
Peterborough, NH 03458
Ph:(603)924-7234
Fax: (603)924-7235
Co. E-mail: info@peterboroughchamber.com
URL: http://www.peterboroughchamber.com
Contact: Deb Blair, Exec.Dir.

62416 ■ Greater Portsmouth Chamber of Commerce
500 Market St.
PO Box 239
Portsmouth, NH 03802-0239
Ph:(603)436-3988
Fax: (603)436-5118
Co. E-mail: info@portsmouthchamber.org
URL: http://www.portsmouthchamber.org
Contact: Dick Ingram, Pres.

62417 ■ Greater Rochester Chamber of Commerce
18 S Main St.
Rochester, NH 03867-2702
Ph:(603)332-5080
Fax: (603)332-5216

Co. E-mail: chamber@rochesternh.org
URL: http://www.rochesternh.org
Contact: Laura A. Ring, Pres.

62418 ■ Greater Salem Chamber of Commerce
224 N Broadway
PO Box 304
Salem, NH 03079-0304
Ph:(603)893-3177
Fax: (603)894-5158
Co. E-mail: chamber@salemnhchamber.com
URL: http://www.salemnhchamber.com
Contact: Donna Morris, Exec.Dir.

62419 ■ Greater Somersworth Chamber of Commerce
58 High St.
PO Box 615
Somersworth, NH 03878-0615
Ph:(603)692-7175
Fax: (603)692-4501
Co. E-mail: info@somersworthchamber.com
URL: http://www.somersworthchamber.com
Contact: Janet Gagne, Admin.Asst.

62420 ■ Hampton Beach Area Chamber of Commerce
1 Park Ave., Ste. 3G
PO Box 790
Hampton, NH 03843
Ph:(603)926-8718
Fax: (603)926-9977
Co. E-mail: info@hamptonchamber.com
URL: http://www.hamptonchamber.com
Contact: B.J. Noel, Pres.

62421 ■ Hanover Area Chamber of Commerce
216 Nugget Bldg.
PO Box 5105
Hanover, NH 03755
Ph:(603)643-3115
Fax: (603)643-5606
Co. E-mail: hacc@valley.net
URL: http://www.hanoverchamber.org
Contact: Clint Bean, Pres./CEO

62422 ■ Hillsborough Chamber of Commerce
PO Box 541
Hillsborough, NH 03244-0541
Ph:(603)464-5858
Fax: (603)464-9166
Co. E-mail: hcofc@conknet.com
URL: http://www.hillsboroughnhchamber.com
Contact: Karen Johnson, Admin.Asst.

62423 ■ Jaffrey Chamber of Commerce
PO Box 2
Jaffrey, NH 03452-0002
Ph:(603)532-4549
Fax: (603)532-8233
Co. E-mail: info@jaffreychamber.com
URL: http://www.jaffreychamber.com
Contact: Bruce Edwards, Pres.

62424 ■ Lebanon Chamber of Commerce
1 School St.
PO Box 97
Lebanon, NH 03766
Ph:(603)448-1203
Fax: (603)448-6489
Co. E-mail: lebanonchamber@lebanonchamber.com
URL: http://www.lebanonchamber.com
Contact: Paul R. Boucher, Pres./CEO

62425 ■ Lincoln-Woodstock Chamber of Commerce
Rte. 112, Kancamagus Scenic Hwy.
PO Box 1017
Lincoln, NH 03251-0358
Ph:(603)745-6621
Fax: (603)745-4908
Co. E-mail: info@lincolnwoodstock.com
URL: http://www.lincolnwoodstock.com
Contact: Mark LaClair, Pres.

62426 ■ Lisbon Area Chamber of Commerce
6 S Main St.
Lisbon, NH 03585
Ph:(603)838-2200
Co. E-mail: lisbonnh@adelphia.net
URL: http://www.lisbonnh.org/public_documents/
    LisbonNH_WebDocs
Contact: John Northrop, Pres.

62427 ■ Littleton Area Chamber of Commerce
PO Box 105
Littleton, NH 03561
Ph:(603)444-6561
Fax: (603)444-2427
Co. E-mail: info@lacc.mv.com
URL: http://www.littletonareachamber.com
Contact: Barbara A. Ashley, Exec.Dir.

62428 ■ Meredith Area Chamber of Commerce
PO Box 732
Meredith, NH 03253-0732
Ph:(603)279-6121
Free: 877-279-6121
Fax: (603)279-4525
Co. E-mail: meredith@lr.net
URL: http://www.meredithcc.org
Contact: Susan Cerutti, Exec.Dir.

62429 ■ Meredith Chamber of Commerce
PO Box 732
Meredith, NH 03253
Ph:(603)279-6121
Free: 877-279-6121
Fax: (603)279-4525
Co. E-mail: meredith@lr.net
URL: http://www.meredithcc.org
Contact: Susan Cerutti, Exec.Dir.

62430 ■ Merrimack Chamber of Commerce
301 Daniel Webster Hwy.
PO Box 254
Merrimack, NH 03054-0254
Ph:(603)424-3669
Fax: (603)429-4325
Co. E-mail: info@merrimackchamber.org
URL: http://www.merrimackchamber.org
Contact: Linda Bonetti, Exec.Dir.

62431 ■ Mount Washington Valley Chamber of Commerce and Visitor's Bureau
PO Box 2300
North Conway, NH 03860
Ph:(603)356-5701
Free: 800-367-3364
Fax: (603)356-7069
Co. E-mail: visitor@mtwashingtonvalley.org
URL: http://www.mtwashingtonvalley.org
Contact: Janice Crawford, Exec. Dir.

62432 ■ New London - Lake Sunapee Region Chamber of Commerce
PO Box 532
New London, NH 03257-0532
Ph:(603)526-6575
Free: 877-526-6575
Co. E-mail: chamberinfo@nhvt.net
URL: http://www.lakesunapeenh.org
Contact: Lorie McClory, Information Dir.

62433 ■ Newfound Region Chamber of Commerce
PO Box 454
Bristol, NH 03222
Ph:(603)744-2150
Co. E-mail: nwfndcoc@worldpath.net
URL: http://www.newfoundchamber.com
Contact: Phyllis Burton, Exec. Dir.

62434 ■ Newport Area Chamber of Commerce
2 N Main St.
Newport, NH 03773
Ph:(603)863-1510
Fax: (603)863-9486
Co. E-mail: chamber@newportnhchamber.org

URL: http://www.newportnhchamber.org
Contact: Ella M. Casey, Exec.Dir.

62435 ■ North Country Chamber of Commerce
PO Box 1
Colebrook, NH 03576
Ph:(603)237-8939
Free: 800-698-8939
Fax: (603)237-4573
Co. E-mail: nccoc@ncia.net
URL: http://www.northcountrychamber.org
Contact: Ms. Gloria Bunnell, Office Mgr.

62436 ■ Northern Gateway Chamber of Commerce
PO Box 537
Lancaster, NH 03584-0537
Ph:(603)788-2530
Free: 877-788-2530
Co. E-mail: info@northerngatewaychamber.org
URL: http://www.northerngatewaychamber.org
Contact: Pamela Remick, Pres.

62437 ■ Northern White Mountain Chamber of Commerce
164 Main St.
Berlin, NH 03570
Ph:(603)752-6060
Free: 800-992-7480
Fax: (603)752-1002
Co. E-mail: nwmcc@ncia.net
URL: http://www.northernwhitemtnchamber.org
Contact: Mrs. Michelle Pimentel, Admin.Asst.

62438 ■ Plymouth Chamber of Commerce
1 Foster St.
PO Box 65
Plymouth, NH 03264
Ph:(603)536-1001
Free: 800-386-3678
Fax: (603)536-4017
Co. E-mail: info@plymouthnh.org
URL: http://plymouthnh.org
Contact: Becki DeVall, Exec. Asst.

62439 ■ Souhegan Valley Chamber of Commerce
89 State Rte. 101A
Amherst, NH 03031
Ph:(603)673-4360
Fax: (603)673-5018
Co. E-mail: chamber@souhegan.net
URL: http://www.souhegan.net
Contact: Lynda Derby, Exec.Dir.

62440 ■ Waterville Valley Region Chamber of Commerce
12 Vintinner Rd.
Campton, NH 03223
Ph:(603)726-3804
Free: 800-237-2307
Fax: (603)726-4058
Co. E-mail: info@watervillevalleyregion.com
URL: http://www.watervillevalleyregion.com
Contact: Chris Bolan, Exec.Dir.

FINANCING AND LOAN PROGRAMS

62441 ■ Arete Corporation
PO Box 1299
Center Harbor, NH 03226
Ph:(603)253-9797
Fax: (603)253-9799
URL: http://www.arete-microgen.com
Contact: Robert Shaw, President
Preferred Investment Size: $500,000 to $3,000,000.
Investment Types: Seed, start-up, early and first stage, and research and development. **Industry Preferences:** Industrial and energy. **Geographic Preferences:** U.S. and Canada.

PROCUREMENT ASSISTANCE PROGRAMS

62442 ■ New Hampshire Procurement Technical Assistance Center–State of New Hampshire–Economic Development (PO Bo)
PO Box 1856
172 Pembroke Rd.
Concord, NH 03302-1856
Ph:(603)271-7581
Fax: (603)271-7583
Co. E-mail: mkeene@dred.state.nh.us
URL: http://www.nheconomy.com
Contact: Martha Keene, Program Ass.

INCUBATORS/RESEARCH AND TECHNOLOGY PARKS

62443 ■ University of New Hampshire–Office of Vice President for Research and Public Service
Thompson Hall, Rm. 107
105 Main St.
Durham, NH 03824-3547
Ph:(603)862-1948
Fax: (603)862-3617
Co. E-mail: office.vicepresident.rps@unh.edu
URL: http://www.unh.edu/orps/
Contact: Dr. John D. Aber, VP
E-mail: office.vicepresident.rps@unh.edu
Scope: Promotes research and development relationships between the private sector and the University. Organizes problem solving teams and makes available University instrumentation and computer facilities and research and development laboratories. Assists business and industry with product development, process development, long-range research and planning, modeling, software development, technical troubleshooting, feasibility studies, development of laboratory testing procedures, market analysis, risk analysis, and planning and educational programs. Develops patents and licenses technology and other intellectual property of the University.

EDUCATIONAL PROGRAMS

62444 ■ Chester College of New England
40 Chester St.
Chester, NH 03036
Ph:(603)887-4401
Free: 800-974-6372
Fax: (603)887-1777
Co. E-mail: admissions@chestercollege.edu
URL: http://www.chestercollege.edu
No longer offers a small business management program.

62445 ■ Hesser College
3 Sundial Ave.
Manchester, NH 03103
Ph:(603)668-6660
Free: 800-526-9231
Fax: (603)666-4722
URL: http://www.hesser.edu
Description: Two-year college offering a small business management program.

PUBLICATIONS

62446 ■ *BNH: The Business of New Hampshire*
404 Chestnut St., Ste. 201
Manchester, NH 03101
Ph:(603)626-6354
Fax: (603)626-6359
Co. E-mail: businessnh@nh.interwebb.com

62447 ■ *New Hampshire Business Review*
150 Dow St.
Manchester, NH 03101-1151
Ph:(603)624-1442
Fax: (603)624-1310
Co. E-mail: nhbr@aol.com
URL: http://www.nhbr.com

62448 ■ *New Hampshire Department of Resources and Economic Development—Agenda*
New Hampshire Division of Economic Development
PO Box 1856
Concord, NH 03302-1856
Ph:(603)271-2341
Fax: (603)271-6784
URL: http://www.dred.state.nh.us/ded/
Ed: Kristi Forrest. **Description:** Presents news on business and industrial development in New Hampshire. Focuses on technology, workers compensation, business awards, legislation, and international trade.

62449 ■ *Smart Start your New Hampshire Business*
PSI Research
300 N. Valley Dr.
Grants Pass, OR 97526
Ph:(503)479-9464
Free: 800-228-2275
Fax: (503)476-1479
Co. E-mail: info@psi-research.com
URL: http://www.psi-research.com
Ed: Michael D. Jenkins. **Released:** Revised edition, 1992. **Price:** $29.95 (looseleaf binder); $24.95 (paper). **Description:** Part of the Successful Business Library series.

PUBLISHERS

62450 ■ Mann Publishing Group
710 Main St., 6th Fl.
PO Box 580
Rollinsford, NH 03869

Ph:(603)601-0325
Fax: (603)601-0334
Co. E-mail: sales@mannpublishing.com
URL: http://www.mannpublishing.com/mannpub/
Description: Publishes books on business, technology, and computer programs and servers. **Founded:** 2002

62451 ■ New Hampshire Small Business Development Center
Whittemore School of Business and Economics, 108 Mconnell Ha
Durham, NH 03824
Ph:(603)862-2200
Fax: (603)862-4876
URL: http://www.nhsbdc.org
Contact: Warren Daniel, Director
Description: Publishes guidebooks of business and marketing data. Reaches market through direct mail. Does not accept unsolicited manuscripts. **Founded:** 1984.

SMALL BUSINESS DEVELOPMENT CENTER LEAD OFFICE

62452 ■ New Jersey Small Business Development Center–Rutgers Graduate School of Management
49 Bleeker St.
Newark, NJ 07102-1993
Ph:(973)353-5950
Fax: (973)353-1110
URL: http://www.njsbdc.com/home
Contact: Brenda Hopper, State Dir.
E-mail: bhopper@njsbdc.com

SMALL BUSINESS DEVELOPMENT CENTERS

62453 ■ Bergen Community College–SBDC
Ciarco Learning Center
355 Main St., Rm. 121
Hackensack, NJ 07601
Ph:(201)447-7841
Fax: (201)447-9405
Co. E-mail: sbcd@bergen.edu
Contact: Vincent D'Elia, Regional Dir.
E-mail: vdelia@bergen.edu

62454 ■ Brookdale Community College–Small Business Development Center
765 Newman Springs Rd.
Lincroft, NJ 07738
Ph:(732)842-8685
Fax: (732)842-0203
Contact: Bill Nunnally, Regional Dir.
E-mail: wnunnally@brookdalecc.edu

62455 ■ Greater Atlantic City Chamber of Commerce–Small Business Development Center
1125 Atlantic Ave.
Atlantic City, NJ 08401
Ph:(609)345-5600
Fax: (609)345-1666
Contact: William R. McGinley, Regional Dir.

62456 ■ Kean University–Small Business Development Center
Willis Hall
301 Morris
Union, NJ 07083
Ph:(908)737-4220
Fax: (908)737-4223
URL: http://www.sba.gov/nj/nj_njsbdc.html
Contact: Mira Kostak, Regional Dir.
E-mail: mkostak@kean.edu

62457 ■ Mercer County Community College–Small Business Development Center
West Windsor Campus
1200 Old Trenton Rd.
PO Box B
Trenton, NJ 08690

Ph:(609)586-4800
Fax: (609)890-6338
Co. E-mail: hss@mccc.edu
Contact: Herb Spiegel, Regional Dir.

62458 ■ Rutgers University at Camden–Small Business Development Center
325 Cooper St.
Camden, NJ 08102
Ph:(856)225-6221
Fax: (856)225-6621
Co. E-mail: rsbdc@camden.rutgers.edu
URL: http://www.rsbdc.org
Contact: Gary Rago, Regional Dir.
E-mail: rago@camden.rutgers.edu

62459 ■ Warren County Community College–Skylands Small Business Development Center
475 Rte. 57 W.
Washington, NJ 07882-9605
Ph:(908)689-9620
Fax: (908)689-2247
Contact: James Smith, Dir.
E-mail: jhsmith@nac.net

SMALL BUSINESS ASSISTANCE PROGRAMS

62460 ■ New Jersey Commerce Economic Growth and Tourism Commission–Office of Business Advocate
Mary G. Roebling Bldg.
20 W State St., 12th Fl.
PO Box 820
Trenton, NJ 08625-0835
Ph:(609)292-2146
Fax: (609)292-9145
URL: http://www.newjerseycommerce.org
Description: Certify Minority, women- owned and small businesses.

62461 ■ New Jersey Commerce Economic Growth and Tourism Commission–Office of Business Services
Mary G. Roebling Bldg.
20 W State St., 12th Fl.
PO Box 820
Trenton, NJ 08625-0835
Ph:(609)292-2146
Fax: (609)292-9145
URL: http://www.newjerseycommerce.org
Description: Provides a central resource for small, women-owned, and minority-owned businesses in dealing with federal, state, and local governments. Also provides financial, marketing, procurement, technical, and managerial assistance.

62462 ■ New Jersey Commerce Economic Growth and Tourism Commission–Office of International Trade
Mary G. Roebling Bldg.
20 W State St. ,12th Fl.
PO Box 820
Trenton, NJ 08625-0835

Ph:(609)633-3606
Fax: (609)292-5509
URL: http://www.newjerseycommerce.org
Description: Helps New Jersey companies in export development and expansion. Also encourages foreign investment in the state.

62463 ■ New Jersey Commerce Economic Growth and Tourism Commission–Office of Marketing
Mary G. Roebling Bldg.
20 W State St., 4th Fl.
PO Box 820
Trenton, NJ 08625-0835
Ph:(609)292-0700
Fax: (609)292-9145
URL: http://www.newjerseycommerce.org
Description: Acts as an ombudsman, handling complaints and problems of small business owners. Also serves as an advocate for small businesses and administers the One Stop Permit Identification System.

62464 ■ New Jersey Economic Development Department
1 River Front Plaza
Newark, NJ 07102
Ph:(973)565-5502
Fax: (973)565-5556
URL: http://www.panynj.gov
Description: Provides complete assistance packages, including financing, site selection, and construction. Package may also include labor recruitment and training.

SCORE OFFICES

62465 ■ SCORE Newark
Small Business Administration
2 Gateway Ctr., 15th Fl.
Newark, NJ 07102
Ph:(973)645-3982
Fax: (973)645-2375
Co. E-mail: newarkscore@yahoo.com
URL: http://www.scoremetronj.org
Description: Provides personalized, confidential counseling to help people start and operate a successful small business.

62466 ■ SCORE Somerset
c/o Robert Lerner, Chair
United Trust Bank
675 Franklin Blvd.
Somerset, NJ 08875
Ph:(732)745-5050

BETTER BUSINESS BUREAUS

62467 ■ Better Business Bureau of Central New Jersey
1700 Whitehorse-Hamilton Square Rd., Ste. D-5
Trenton, NJ 08690-3540

Ph:(609)588-0808
Fax: (609)588-0546
Co. E-mail: info@trenton.bbb.org
URL: http://www.trenton.bbb.org
Contact: Elizabeth Merkel, Pres.

62468 ■ Better Business Bureau of New Jersey
1700 Whitehorse-Hamilton Sq. Rd., Ste. D-5
Trenton, NJ 08690
Ph:(609)588-0808
Fax: (609)588-0546
Co. E-mail: info@trenton.bbb.org
URL: http://www.newjersey.bbb.org
Contact: Ms. Elizabeth Merkel, Pres.

62469 ■ Better Business Bureau of Northern New Jersey
400 Lanidex Plaza
Parsippany, NJ 07054-2797
Ph:(973)581-1313
Fax: (973)581-7022
Co. E-mail: bbb.nj@att.net

62470 ■ Better Business Bureau Serving Ocean County
1700 Whitehorse-Hamilton Square Rd., Ste. D-5
Trenton, NJ 08690
Ph:(609)588-0808
Fax: (609)588-0546
Co. E-mail: info@trenton.bbb.org
URL: http://www.westmont.bbb.org
Contact: Elizabeth Merkel, Pres.

CHAMBERS OF COMMERCE

62471 ■ Atlantic City Regional Chamber of Commerce
1125 Atlantic Ave.
Atlantic City, NJ 08401-4806
Ph:(609)345-4524
Fax: (609)345-1666
Co. E-mail: info@atlanticcitychamber.com
URL: http://www.atlanticcitychamber.com
Contact: Joseph Kelly, Pres.

62472 ■ Atlantic County Mainland Chamber of Commerce
1125 Atlantic Ave., Ste. 105
Atlantic City, NJ 08401
Ph:(609)646-2214
Fax: (609)646-2433
Co. E-mail: info@atlanticcitychamber.com
URL: http://www.atlanticcountychamber.com
Contact: Joseph Kelly, Pres.

62473 ■ Avalon Chamber of Commerce
30th & Ocean Dr.
PO Box 22
Avalon, NJ 08202-0022
Ph:(609)967-3936
Co. E-mail: chamber@avalonbeach.com
URL: http://www.avalonbeach.com
Contact: Allan Dechert, Pres.

62474 ■ Bayonne Chamber of Commerce
PO Box 266
Bayonne, NJ 07002-0266
Ph:(201)436-4333
Fax: (201)436-8546
Co. E-mail: bcc266@bellatlantic.net
Contact: Janis Demellier, Gen.Mgr.

62475 ■ Belmar Chamber of Commerce
PO Box 297
Belmar, NJ 07719
Ph:(732)681-2900
Fax: (732)681-8471
Co. E-mail: info@belmarchamber.com
URL: http://www.belmarchamber.com
Contact: Alice A. Farr-Leonard, Pres.

62476 ■ Bound Brook Area Chamber of Commerce
PO Box 227
Bound Brook, NJ 08805

Ph:(732)356-7273
URL: http://www.boundbrook.com
Contact: Lynn R. Fazen, Exec.Dir.

62477 ■ Brick Township Chamber of Commerce
270 Chambers Bridge Rd., Ste. 6
Brick, NJ 08723
Ph:(732)477-4949
Fax: (732)477-5788
Co. E-mail: info@brickchamber.org
URL: http://www.brickchamber.org
Contact: Michele Eventoff, Exec.Dir.

62478 ■ Bridgeton Area Chamber of Commerce
53 S Laurel St.
PO Box 1063
Bridgeton, NJ 08302
Ph:(856)455-1312
Fax: (856)453-9795
Co. E-mail: bacc@baccnj.com
URL: http://www.baccnj.com
Contact: Anthony Stanzione, Exec.Dir.

62479 ■ Brigantine Beach Chamber of Commerce
PO Box 484
Brigantine, NJ 08203
Ph:(609)266-3437
Co. E-mail: info@brigantinechamber.com
URL: http://www.brigantinechamber.com
Contact: Betty Dillon, Pres.

62480 ■ Burlington County Chamber of Commerce
900 Briggs Rd., Ste. 110
Mount Laurel, NJ 08054
Ph:(856)439-2520
Fax: (856)439-2523
Co. E-mail: bccoc@bccoc.com
URL: http://bccoc.com
Contact: Kristi Howell-Ikeda, Pres.

62481 ■ Butler Tri-Boro Area Chamber of Commerce
PO Box 100
Bloomingdale, NJ 07403
Ph:(973)838-5678
Contact: Jerald Vinci, Pres.

62482 ■ Cape May County Chamber of Commerce
PO Box 74
Cape May Court House, NJ 08210-0074
Ph:(609)465-7181
Fax: (609)465-5017
Co. E-mail: inquiry@cmccofc.com
URL: http://www.cmccofc.com
Contact: Vickie Clark, Exec.Dir.

62483 ■ Central Jersey Chamber of Commerce
PO Box 300
Elizabeth, NJ 07207-0300
Ph:(908)352-0900
Fax: (908)352-0865
Co. E-mail: info@gatewaychamber.com
URL: http://www.gatewaychamber.com
Contact: James R. Coyle, Pres.

62484 ■ Chamber of Commerce of Greater Cape May
609 Lafayette, 2nd Fl.
PO Box 556
Cape May, NJ 08204-0556
Ph:(609)884-5508
Fax: (609)884-2054
Co. E-mail: request@capemaychamber.com
URL: http://www.capemaychamber.com
Contact: Mr. David Ellenberg, Exec.Dir.

62485 ■ Chamber of Commerce Serving Old Bridge, Sayerville and South Amboy
PO Box 5241
Old Bridge, NJ 08857
Ph:(732)607-6340

Fax: (732)607-6341
Contact: Patricia Salcone, Pres.

62486 ■ Chamber of Commerce Southern New Jersey
6014 Main St.
Voorhees, NJ 08043-4659
Ph:(856)424-7776
Fax: (856)424-8180
Co. E-mail: info@chambersnj.com
URL: http://www.chambersnj.com
Contact: Debra P. DiLorenzo, Pres./CEO

62487 ■ Chatham Area Chamber of Commerce
PO Box 231
Chatham, NJ 07928-0231
Ph:(973)635-2444
Fax: (973)635-2953
Co. E-mail: chathamchamber@optonline.net
URL: http://www.chathamarea.com
Contact: Carolyn A. Cherry, Exec.Dir.

62488 ■ Cherry Hill Regional Chamber of Commerce
1060 Kings Hwy. N, Ste. 200
Cherry Hill, NJ 08034
Ph:(856)667-1600
Fax: (856)667-1464
Co. E-mail: chamber@cherryhillregional.com
URL: http://www.cherryhillregional.com
Contact: Arthur C. Campbell, Pres./CEO

62489 ■ Cranford Chamber of Commerce
8 Springfield Ave.
PO Box 165
Cranford, NJ 07016
Ph:(908)272-6114
Fax: (908)272-3742
Co. E-mail: cranfordchamber@comcast.net
URL: http://www.cranford.com/chamber
Contact: Kurt Petschow, Pres.

62490 ■ Dennis Township Chamber of Commerce
PO Box 85
Ocean View, NJ 08230
Ph:(609)624-2276
Fax: (609)624-9110
Co. E-mail: info@dennistwpchamber.com
URL: http://www.dennistwpchamber.com
Contact: Kimberly Schiela, Pres.

62491 ■ Denville Chamber of Commerce
PO Box 333
Denville, NJ 07834
Ph:(973)625-1171
Co. E-mail: gba58@aol.com
URL: http://www.denville-nj.com
Contact: Jennifer Adkins, Pres.

62492 ■ Dover Area Chamber of Commerce
PO Box 506
Dover, NJ 07802
Ph:(973)989-4000
Fax: (973)673-5828
Co. E-mail: email@doverareachamber.com
URL: http://www.doverareachamber.com
Contact: Susan Konight, Pres.

62493 ■ East Brunswick Regional Chamber of Commerce
21 Brunswick Woods Dr.
PO Box 56
East Brunswick, NJ 08816-0056
Ph:(732)257-3009
Fax: (732)257-0949
Co. E-mail: communityedge@ebnjchamber.org
URL: http://ebnjchamber.org
Contact: Marianne Wehrenberg, Exec.Dir.

62494 ■ East Orange Chamber of Commerce
PO Box 2418
East Orange, NJ 07019-2418
Ph:(973)674-0900
Fax: (973)673-5828
Co. E-mail: info@eastorangechamber.biz

URL: http://www.eastorangechamber.biz
Contact: Ron Butler, Exec. Dir.

62495 ■ Eastern Monmouth Area Chamber of Commerce
170 Broad St.
Red Bank, NJ 07701
Ph:(732)741-0055
Fax: (732)741-6778
Co. E-mail: lynda@emacc.org
URL: http://www.emacc.org
Contact: Lynda Rose, Pres./COO

62496 ■ Edison Chamber of Commerce
629 Amboy Ave., 1st Fl.
Edison, NJ 08837
Ph:(732)738-9482
Fax: (732)738-9485
Co. E-mail: edisonchamber@att.net
URL: http://www.edisonchamber.com
Contact: Gloria S. Dittman, Pres./CEO

62497 ■ Egg Harbor City Chamber of Commerce
PO Box 129
Egg Harbor City, NJ 08215
Ph:(609)965-0001
Contact: Toni Baxter, Sec.

62498 ■ Englewood Chamber of Commerce
2-10 N Van Brunt St.
Englewood, NJ 07631-3485
Ph:(201)567-2381
Fax: (201)871-4549
URL: http://www.englewood-chamber.com
Contact: Karen L. Rawl, Exec. Dir.

62499 ■ Fair Lawn Chamber of Commerce
18-00 Fair Lawn Ave.
Fair Lawn, NJ 07410
Ph:(201)796-7050
Co. E-mail: info@fairlawnchamber.org
URL: http://www.fairlawnchamber.org
Contact: Debbie Berowitz, Mgr.

62500 ■ Franklin Lakes Chamber of Commerce
PO Box 81
Franklin Lakes, NJ 07417
Ph:(201)560-1289
Co. E-mail: info@flcoc.org
URL: http://www.flcoc.org
Contact: Mina Kozma, Exec. Admin.

62501 ■ Glen Rock Chamber of Commerce
PO Box 176
Glen Rock, NJ 07452
Ph:(201)447-3434
Contact: Pam Wolak, Pres.

62502 ■ Greater Asbury Park Chamber of Commerce
PO Box 649
Asbury Park, NJ 07712
Ph:(732)775-7676
Fax: (732)775-7675
Co. E-mail: info@asburyparkchamber.com

62503 ■ Greater Bordentown Chamber of Commerce
PO Box 65
Bordentown, NJ 08505
Ph:(609)298-7774
Fax: (609)298-3549
Co. E-mail: information@gbacc.org
URL: http://www.gbacc.org
Contact: Barbara Parmigiani, Exec.Sec.

62504 ■ Greater Elizabeth Chamber of Commerce
456 N Broad St.
Elizabeth, NJ 07208
Ph:(908)355-7600
Fax: (908)436-2054
Co. E-mail: info@elizabethchamber.com
URL: http://www.elizabethchamber.com
Contact: Gordon Haas, Exec.Dir.

62505 ■ Greater Fort Lee Chamber of Commerce
210 Whiteman St.
Fort Lee, NJ 07024-6267
Ph:(201)944-7575
Fax: (201)944-5168
Co. E-mail: fortleechamber@verizon.net
URL: http://www.fortleechamber.us
Contact: Frank Patti, Pres.

62506 ■ Greater Glassboro Chamber of Commerce
PO Box 651
Glassboro, NJ 08028
Ph:(856)881-7900
Co. E-mail: info@glassborochamber.com
URL: http://www.glassborochamber.com
Contact: Michael A. Penk, Pres.

62507 ■ Greater Hackensack Chamber of Commerce
5 University Plaza Dr.
Hackensack, NJ 07601
Ph:(201)489-3700
Fax: (201)489-1741
Co. E-mail: chamberhacknj@aol.com
URL: http://www.hackensackchamber.org
Contact: Darlene Damstrom, Exec.Dir.

62508 ■ Greater Hammonton Chamber of Commerce
10 S Egg Harbor Rd.
PO Box 554
Hammonton, NJ 08037-0554
Ph:(609)561-9080
Fax: (609)561-9411
URL: http://www.hammontonnj.us
Contact: Irma L. Nettleton, Exec. Dir.

62509 ■ Greater Long Branch Chamber of Commerce
PO Box 628
228 Broadway
Long Branch, NJ 07740
Ph:(732)222-0400
Fax: (732)571-3385
Co. E-mail: longbranchchamber@verizon.net
URL: http://www.longbranchchamber.org
Contact: Nancy Kleiberg, Exec.Dir.

62510 ■ Greater Mahwah Chamber of Commerce
67 Ramapo Valley Rd., Ste. 104
Mahwah, NJ 07430
Ph:(201)529-5566
Fax: (201)529-8122
Co. E-mail: info@mahwah.com
URL: http://www.mahwah.com
Contact: Sharon Rounds, Exec.Dir.

62511 ■ Greater Millville Chamber of Commerce
4 City Park Dr.
PO Box 831
Millville, NJ 08332
Ph:(856)825-2600
Fax: (856)825-5333
Co. E-mail: info@millville-nj.com
URL: http://www.millville-nj.com
Contact: Earl Sherrick, Exec.Dir.

62512 ■ Greater Paramus Chamber of Commerce
58 E Midland Ave.
PO Box 325
Paramus, NJ 07652-0325
Ph:(201)261-3344
Fax: (201)261-3346
Co. E-mail: staff@paramuschamber.com
URL: http://www.paramuschamber.com
Contact: Teri Duda, Chair

62513 ■ Greater Paterson Chamber of Commerce
100 Hamilton Plz., Ste. 1201
Paterson, NJ 07505
Ph:(973)881-7300

Fax: (973)881-8233
Co. E-mail: gpcc@greaterpatersoncc.org
URL: http://www.greaterpatersoncc.org
Contact: Charles T. Miller, Associate Dir.

62514 ■ Greater Vineland Chamber of Commerce
2115 S Delsea Dr.
Vineland, NJ 08360
Ph:(856)691-7400
Fax: (856)691-2113
Co. E-mail: chamber@vineland.org
URL: http://chamber.vineland.org/index
Contact: Paige Desiere, Exec.Dir.

62515 ■ Greater Wildwood Chamber of Commerce
3306 Pacific Ave.
Wildwood, NJ 08260-4824
Ph:(609)729-4000
Fax: (609)729-4003
Co. E-mail: info@gwcoc.com
URL: http://www.gwcoc.com
Contact: Andrew J. Cripps, Exec.Dir.

62516 ■ Hillside Chamber of Commerce
PO Box 965
Hillside, NJ 07205-0965
Ph:(908)964-5130
Fax: (973)926-1632
Co. E-mail: ccoelho@ecdwire.com
Contact: Cheryl Coelho, Pres.

62517 ■ Howell Chamber of Commerce
PO Box 196
Howell, NJ 07731
Ph:(732)363-4114
Fax: (732)363-8747
Co. E-mail: info@howellchamber.com
URL: http://www.howellchamber.com
Contact: Susan Dominguez, Exec.Dir.

62518 ■ Hudson County Chamber of Commerce
660 Newark Ave., Ste. 220
Jersey City, NJ 07306
Ph:(201)386-0699
Fax: (201)386-8480
Co. E-mail: info@hudsonchamber.org
URL: http://www.hudsonchamber.org
Contact: Joanne VanDorn, Pres.

62519 ■ Hunterdon County Chamber of Commerce
2200 Rte. 31, Ste. 15
Lebanon, NJ 08833
Ph:(908)735-5955
Fax: (908)730-6580
Co. E-mail: info@hunterdon-chamber.org
URL: http://www.hunterdon-chamber.org
Contact: Suzanne Lagay, Pres.

62520 ■ Irvington Chamber of Commerce
PO Box 323
Irvington, NJ 07111
Ph:(973)372-4100
Fax: (973)673-5828
URL: http://www.irvington-nj.com/ICC.html
Contact: Herb Ramo, Field Coor.

62521 ■ Lakewood Chamber of Commerce
395 Rte. 70 W, Ste. 125
Lakewood, NJ 08701
Ph:(732)363-0012
Fax: (732)367-4453
Co. E-mail: info@mylakewoodchamber.com
URL: http://www.mylakewoodchamber.com
Contact: Ms. Maureen Stankowitz, Exec.Dir.

62522 ■ Lambertville Area Chamber of Commerce
60 Wilson St.
Lambertville, NJ 08530
Ph:(609)397-0055
Fax: (609)397-1530
Co. E-mail: info@lambertville.org
URL: http://www.lambertville.org

Contact: Tom Martin, Pres.

62523 ■ Livingston Area Chamber of Commerce
154 S Livingston Ave., No. 207
Livingston, NJ 07039
Ph:(973)992-4343
Fax: (973)992-8024
Co. E-mail: info@livingstonchambernj.com
URL: http://www.livingstonchambernj.com
Contact: Beth Lippman, Exec.Dir./Administrator

62524 ■ Madison Chamber of Commerce
PO Box 152
Madison, NJ 07940
Ph:(973)377-7830
Fax: (973)377-7810
Co. E-mail: info@madisonnjchamber.org
URL: http://www.madisonnjchamber.org
Contact: Nicole Francouer, Pres.

62525 ■ Maplewood Chamber of Commerce
PO Box 423
Maplewood, NJ 07040
Ph:(973)761-4333
Fax: (973)762-9105
Co. E-mail: contact11@mindspring.com
URL: http://www.maplewoodchamber.org
Contact: Rene Conlon, Exec. Sec.

62526 ■ Matawan - Aberdeen Chamber of Commerce
PO Box 522
Matawan, NJ 07747-0522
Ph:(732)290-1125
Fax: (732)290-1125
Contact: Harold Sherman, Pres.

62527 ■ Maywood Chamber of Commerce
140 W Pleasant Ave.
Maywood, NJ 07607
Ph:(201)843-3111
Fax: (201)843-3111
Co. E-mail: teustace@aol.com
Contact: Dr. Timothy Eustace

62528 ■ Meadowlands Regional Chamber of Commerce
201 Rte. 17 N
Rutherford, NJ 07070
Ph:(201)939-0707
Fax: (201)939-0522
Co. E-mail: office@meadowlands.org
URL: http://www.meadowlands.org
Contact: Jo-Ann VonRapacki, Admin.Dir.

62529 ■ Mercer Regional Chamber of Commerce
214 W State St.
Trenton, NJ 08608
Ph:(609)393-4143
Fax: (609)393-1032
Co. E-mail: info@mercerchamber.org
URL: http://www.mercerchamber.org
Contact: Michele N. Siekerka Esq., Pres.

62530 ■ Metuchen Area Chamber of Commerce
323 Main St., Ste. B
Metuchen, NJ 08840-2433
Ph:(732)548-2964
Fax: (732)548-4094
Co. E-mail: metuchenchamber@metuchenchamber.com
URL: http://www.metuchenchamber.com
Contact: Caroline Woodruff, Office Administrator

62531 ■ Middle Township Chamber of Commerce
PO Box 6
Cape May Court House, NJ 08210
Ph:(609)463-1655
Co. E-mail: middletownshipchamberofcom@middletownshipchamberofcommerce.org
URL: http://www.middletownshipchamberofcommerce.org
Contact: Bob Noel, Pres.

62532 ■ Middlesex County Regional Chamber of Commerce
1 Distribution Way, Ste. 101
Monmouth Junction, NJ 08852
Ph:(732)821-1700
Fax: (732)821-5852
Co. E-mail: info@mcrcc.org
URL: http://www.mcrcc.org
Contact: Christopher J. Phelan, Pres.

62533 ■ Midland Park Chamber of Commerce
PO Box 267
Midland Park, NJ 07432
Ph:(973)423-5815
Co. E-mail: crossi@insurance-nj.com
Contact: Christopher Rossi, Pres.

62534 ■ Millburn-Short Hills Chamber of Commerce
343 Millburn Ave., Ste. 303
PO Box 651
Millburn, NJ 07041
Ph:(973)379-1198
Fax: (973)376-5678
Co. E-mail: info@millburnchamber.com
URL: http://www.millburnchamber.com
Contact: Carrie Lemerman, Exec.Dir.

62535 ■ Montville Township Chamber of Commerce
195 Change Bridge Rd.
Montville, NJ 07045
Ph:(973)263-3310
Co. E-mail: info@montvillechamber.com
URL: http://montvillechamber.com
Contact: Angelina C. Thomas, Sec.

62536 ■ Morris County Chamber of Commerce
25 Lindsley Dr.
Morristown, NJ 07960-4454
Ph:(973)539-3882
Fax: (973)539-3960
Co. E-mail: marggie@morrischamber.org
URL: http://www.morrischamber.org
Contact: Marggie Colburn, Office Mgr.

62537 ■ Mount Olive Area Chamber of Commerce
PO Box 192
Budd Lake, NJ 07828-0192
Ph:(973)691-0109
Fax: (973)691-0110
Co. E-mail: info@mtolivechambernj.com
URL: http://www.mtolivechambernj.com
Contact: Richard J. Murray, Pres.

62538 ■ North Essex Chamber of Commerce
3 Fairfield Ave.
West Caldwell, NJ 07006-7692
Ph:(973)226-5500
Fax: (973)403-9335
Co. E-mail: email@northessexchamber.com
URL: http://www.northessexchamber.com
Contact: Meryl Layton, Exec.Dir.

62539 ■ North Jersey Regional Chamber of Commerce
1033 Rte. 46 E, Ste. A103
Clifton, NJ 07013
Ph:(973)470-9300
Fax: (973)470-9245
Co. E-mail: staff@njrcc.org
URL: http://www.njrcc.org
Contact: Gloria Martini, Pres.

62540 ■ Northern Monmouth Chamber of Commerce
1041 State Hwy. 36
PO Box 521
Navesink, NJ 07752
Ph:(732)291-7870
Fax: (732)291-7871
Co. E-mail: nmcc@comcast.net
URL: http://www.northernmonmouth.org
Contact: Crissy Van Siclen-Tomaine, Exec.Dir.

62541 ■ Nutley Chamber of Commerce
610 Franklin Ave.
Nutley, NJ 07110
Ph:(973)667-5300
Fax: (973)667-0854
Co. E-mail: information@nutleychamber.com
URL: http://www.nutleychamber.com
Contact: Dr. Donna Pontoriero DC, Pres.

62542 ■ Oakland Chamber of Commerce
PO Box 8
Oakland, NJ 07436
Ph:(201)337-9282
URL: http://www.oakland-nj.org
Contact: David Mital, Pres.

62543 ■ Ocean City Chamber of Commerce
854 Asbury Ave.
Ocean City, NJ 08226
Ph:(609)399-1412
Free: 800-BEA-CHNJ
Fax: (609)398-3932
Co. E-mail: info@oceancitychamber.com
URL: http://www.oceancityvacation.com
Contact: Joann DelVescio, Exec.Dir.

62544 ■ Ocean Grove Chamber of Commerce
PO Box 415
Ocean Grove, NJ 07756
Ph:(732)774-1391
Free: 800-388-4768
Fax: (732)774-3799
Co. E-mail: info@oceangrovenj.com
URL: http://oceangrovenj.com
Contact: Lois Hetfield, Administrator

62545 ■ Parsippany Area Chamber of Commerce
12-14 N Beverwyck Rd.
Lake Hiawatha, NJ 07034
Ph:(973)402-6400
Fax: (973)334-2242
Co. E-mail: njpacc@yahoo.com
URL: http://www.pacc-nj.org
Contact: Robert J. Peluso, Pres.

62546 ■ Perth Amboy Chamber of Commerce
PO Box 1546
Perth Amboy, NJ 08861
Ph:(732)442-7400
Fax: (732)442-7450
Co. E-mail: email@perthamboychamber.com
URL: http://www.perthamboychamber.com
Contact: Marilyn Drepaul, Administrator

62547 ■ Phillipsburg Area Chamber of Commerce
675 Corliss Ave.
Phillipsburg, NJ 08865-1698
Ph:(908)859-5161
Fax: (908)859-6861
Co. E-mail: pacc@ptd.net
URL: http://www.phillipsburgnj.com
Contact: Deborah N. Russo, Exec.Dir.

62548 ■ Piscataway/Middlesex/South Plainfield Area Chamber of Commerce
1315 Stelton Rd.
Piscataway, NJ 08854
Ph:(732)394-0220
Fax: (732)394-0223
Co. E-mail: info@pmcoc.org
URL: http://www.pmcoc.org
Contact: Frank Zatika Jr., Pres.

62549 ■ Point Pleasant Beach Chamber of Commerce
517A Arnold Ave.
Point Pleasant Beach, NJ 08742-2501
Ph:(732)899-8076
Free: 888-772-3862
Fax: (732)899-0103
Co. E-mail: info@pointpleasantbeachnj.com
URL: http://www.pointpleasantbeachnj.com
Contact: Marge Pennell, Pres.

62550 ■ Pompton Lakes Chamber of Commerce
PO Box 129
Pompton Lakes, NJ 07442
Ph:(973)839-0187
Contact: Herb Newman, Pres.

62551 ■ Princeton Regional Chamber of Commerce
9 Vandeventer Ave.
Princeton, NJ 08542
Ph:(609)924-1776
Fax: (609)924-5776
Co. E-mail: info@princetonchamber.org
URL: http://www.princetonchamber.org
Contact: Joseph Steiner, Pres./CEO

62552 ■ Randolph Area Chamber of Commerce
PO Box 391
Mount Freedom, NJ 07970-0391
Ph:(973)361-3462
Fax: (973)895-3297
URL: http://www.randolphchamber.org
Contact: William F. Burke Jr., Pres.

62553 ■ Ridgewood Chamber of Commerce
199 Dayton St.
Ridgewood, NJ 07450
Ph:(201)445-2600
Fax: (201)251-1958
Co. E-mail: info@ridgewoodchamber.com
URL: http://www.ridgewoodchamber.com
Contact: Angela Cautillo, Exec.Dir.

62554 ■ Ringwood Chamber of Commerce
PO Box 62
Ringwood, NJ 07456
Ph:(973)835-7998
Co. E-mail: ringchamber@aol.com
URL: http://www.ringwoodchamber.com
Contact: Kathy C. Heck, Pres.

62555 ■ Roxbury Area Chamber of Commerce
PO Box 436
Ledgewood, NJ 07852
Ph:(973)770-0740
Fax: (973)770-0740
Co. E-mail: jrousseau@techsoftit.com
URL: http://www.roxburychamber.org
Contact: Joanne Bohrer, Sec.

62556 ■ Rutherford Chamber of Commerce
PO Box 216
Rutherford, NJ 07070
Ph:(201)933-5230
Fax: (201)507-7077
Co. E-mail: info1@rutherfordchamber.com
URL: http://www.rutherfordchamber.com
Contact: Herbert L. Cutter, Exec. Sec.

62557 ■ Salem County Chamber of Commerce
91 A. South Virginia Ave.
Carneys Point, NJ 08069
Ph:(856)299-6699
Fax: (856)299-0299
Co. E-mail: sccoc@verizon.net
URL: http://salemnjchamber.homestead.com
Contact: Jennifer A. Jones, Exec.Dir.

62558 ■ South Orange Chamber of Commerce
PO Box 621
South Orange, NJ 07079
Ph:(973)762-4333
Fax: (973)673-5828
Co. E-mail: aloehner@gmail.com
URL: http://www.southorangechamber.com
Contact: Adam Loehner, Exec. Dir.

62559 ■ Southern Monmouth Chamber of Commerce
PO Box 1305
Wall, NJ 07719-1305
Ph:(732)280-8800

Fax: (732)280-8505
Co. E-mail: info@smcconline.org
URL: http://www.smcconline.org
Contact: Ms. Evelyn Mars, Exec.Dir.

62560 ■ Southern Ocean County Chamber of Commerce
265 W 9th St.
Ship Bottom, NJ 08008-4614
Ph:(609)494-7211
Free: 800-292-6372
Fax: (609)494-5807
Co. E-mail: info@discoversouthernocean.com
URL: http://www.discoversouthernocean.com
Contact: Ellen R. Johnson, Exec.Dir.

62561 ■ Stone Harbor Chamber of Commerce
PO Box 422
Stone Harbor, NJ 08247-0422
Ph:(609)368-6101
Co. E-mail: joe@wjse.com
URL: http://stoneharborbeach.com
Contact: Deb Orzech, Pres.

62562 ■ Suburban Chamber of Commerce
71 Summit Ave.
Summit, NJ 07901
Ph:(908)522-1700
Fax: (908)522-9252
Co. E-mail: info@suburbanchambers.org
URL: http://www.suburbanchambers.org
Contact: Mort O'Shea, Chm.

62563 ■ Suburban Essex Chamber of Commerce
256 Broad St., Rm. 2F
Bloomfield, NJ 07003
Ph:(973)748-2000
Fax: (973)248-2450
Co. E-mail: admin@suburbanessexchamber.com
URL: http://www.suburbanessexchamber.com
Contact: Joseph Sandora, Pres.

62564 ■ Sussex County Chamber of Commerce
120 Hampton House Rd.
Newton, NJ 07860
Ph:(973)579-1811
Fax: (973)579-3031
Co. E-mail: mail@sussexcountychamber.org
URL: http://www.sussexcountychamber.org
Contact: Tammie Horsfield, Pres.

62565 ■ Teaneck Chamber of Commerce
555 Cedar Ln., Ste. 4
Teaneck, NJ 07666
Ph:(201)801-0012
Fax: (201)907-0870
Co. E-mail: teaneckchamber@aol.com
URL: http://www.teaneckchamber.org
Contact: Karen Careccio, Exec.Dir.

62566 ■ Toms River - Ocean County Chamber of Commerce
1200 Hooper Ave.
Toms River, NJ 08753-3324
Ph:(732)349-0220
Fax: (732)349-1252
Co. E-mail: info@oc-chamber.com
URL: http://www.oc-chamber.com
Contact: Lucy Greene, Pres.

62567 ■ Tri-Town Chamber of Commerce
PO Box 496
Boonton, NJ 07005
Ph:(973)334-4117
Fax: (973)263-4164
Co. E-mail: info@tritownchamber.org
URL: http://www.tritownchamber.com
Contact: Ann Krawiec, Exec. Dir.

62568 ■ Union Township Chamber of Commerce
355 Chestnut St., 2nd Fl.
Union, NJ 07083-9405
Ph:(908)688-2777

Fax: (908)688-0338
Co. E-mail: info@unionchamber.com
URL: http://www.unionchamber.com
Contact: James R. Brody, Exec.Dir.

62569 ■ Vernon Chamber of Commerce
PO Box 308
Vernon, NJ 07462
Ph:(973)764-0764
Free: 888-663-9989
Co. E-mail: info@vernonchamber.com
URL: http://www.vernonchamber.com
Contact: Mary Enilius

62570 ■ Warren County Regional Chamber of Commerce
10 Brass Castle Rd.
Washington, NJ 07882
Ph:(908)835-9200
Fax: (908)835-9296
Co. E-mail: info@warrencountychamber.org
URL: http://www.warrencountychamber.org
Contact: Robert L. Goltz, Pres./CEO

62571 ■ West Milford Chamber of Commerce
PO Box 234
West Milford, NJ 07480
Ph:(973)728-3150
Co. E-mail: westmilford@westmilford.com
URL: http://www.westmilford.com
Contact: JoAnn TenHoeve, Pres.

62572 ■ West New York Chamber of Commerce
PO Box 1145
West New York, NJ 07093
Ph:(201)295-5065
Fax: (201)295-5065
URL: http://www.westnewyork.com
Contact: Michael Parks, Pres.

62573 ■ Western Monmouth Chamber of Commerce
17 Broad St.
Freehold, NJ 07728-1703
Ph:(732)462-3030
Fax: (732)462-2123
Co. E-mail: info@atswmchamber.com
URL: http://www.wmchamber.com
Contact: Arthur R. Kondrup, Pres.

62574 ■ Westfield Area Chamber of Commerce
173 Elm St.
Westfield, NJ 07090
Ph:(908)233-3021
Fax: (908)654-8183
Co. E-mail: info@westfieldchamber.com
URL: http://westfieldchamber.com
Contact: Alison O'Hara, Exec.Dir.

62575 ■ Woodbridge Metro Chamber of Commerce
52 Main St.
Woodbridge, NJ 07095-2892
Ph:(732)636-4040
Fax: (732)636-3492
Co. E-mail: help@woodbridgechamber.org
URL: http://www.woodbridgechamber.org
Contact: Carole S. Hila, Pres.

62576 ■ Wyckoff Chamber of Commerce
PO Box 2
Wyckoff, NJ 07481-0002
Ph:(201)891-3616
Co. E-mail: info@wyckoffchamber.com
URL: http://www.wyckoffchamber.com
Contact: Mina Kozma, Business Administrator

MINORITY BUSINESS ASSISTANCE PROGRAMS

62577 ■ New Jersey Department of Commerce and Economic Development–Division of Small, Women, and Minority Business
20 W State St., 4th Fl.
Mary G. Roebling Bldg. 4th Fl.
Trenton, NJ 08625
Ph:(609)292-2146
Free: 888-239-1288
Fax: (609)292-9145
Co. E-mail: cevramb@commerce.state.nj.us
URL: http://www.state.nj.us/commerce
Contact: Technical Assistant
Description: Assists minority businesses in financing, procurement, and management training.

62578 ■ New Jersey Department of Commerce and Economic Development–Set-Aside and Certification Office
20 W State St., 4th Fl.
Mary G. Roebling Bldg.
PO Box 820
Trenton, NJ 08625
Ph:(609)292-2146
Fax: (609)292-9145
URL: http://www.state.nj.us/commerce
Contact: Office Manager
Description: Responsible for administering the Set-Aside Act for small, women-, and minority-owned businesses. Also helps these businesses compete for government contracts.

62579 ■ Newark Minority Business Development Center
744 Broad St., Ste. 1812
Newark, NJ 07102
Ph:(973)297-1142
Fax: (973)297-1439
URL: http://www.mbda.gov
Contact: Loraine Kelsey, Asst Dir

FINANCING AND LOAN PROGRAMS

62580 ■ Aberlyn Capital Management Co., Inc.
701 Mohican Ct.
Morganville, NJ 07751
Ph:(732)332-1170
Fax: (732)332-1172
Preferred Investment Size: $25,000,000 minimum.
Investment Types: Start-up, first and second stage, leveraged buyout, and special situation. **Industry Preferences:** Computer software, semiconductors and other electronics, biotechnology, medical and health, and consumer related.

62581 ■ Ablesoft
8550 Remington Ave., Ste. E
Pennsauken, NJ 08110
Ph:(856)488-8220
Fax: (856)488-8886

62582 ■ Accel Partners
428 University Ave.
Palo Alto, CA 94301
Ph:(650)614-4800
Fax: (650)614-4880
URL: http://www.accel.com
Contact: James Breyer, Managing Partner
Preferred Investment Size: $1,000,000 minimum.
Investment Types: Seed, start-up and early stage.
Industry Preferences: Internet specific, communications and media, computer software and services, computer hardware, medical and health, biotechnology, semiconductors and other electronics, industrial and energy, other products, and consumer related.
Geographic Preferences: U.S.

62583 ■ Alan I. Goldman & Associates
497 Ridgewood Ave.
Glen Ridge, NJ 07028
Ph:(973)857-5680
Fax: (973)509-8856
Preferred Investment Size: $250,000 minimum. **Investment Types:** Control-block purchases, leveraged buyout, mezzanine, second stage, management buyouts, and special situation. **Industry Preferences:** Communications and media, computer related, semiconductors and other electronics, biotechnology, medical and health, consumer related, industrial and energy, transportation, financial services, business service, manufacturing, agriculture, forestry and fishing. **Geographic Preferences:** U.S.

62584 ■ Basecamp Ventures
1 Executive Dr., Ste. 8
Moorestown, NJ 08057
Ph:(856)813-1100
Fax: (856)793-4242
URL: http://www.basecampventures.com
Contact: Mel Baiada, Managing Director
Investment Policies: Early and first stage. **Industry Preferences:** Communications, computer software, and Internet specific. **Geographic Preferences:** Mid Atlantic.

62585 ■ BCI Partners
Glenpointe Ctr. W.
Teaneck, NJ 07666
Ph:(201)836-3900
Fax: (201)836-6368
URL: http://www.bcipartners.com
Contact: Donald Remey, Managing Director
Preferred Investment Size: $10,000,000 to $50,000,000. **Investment Types:** Expansion, second and later stage. **Industry Preferences:** Communications and media, Internet specific, other products, consumer related, computer software and services, medical and health, industrial and energy, semiconductors and other electronics, computer hardware, and biotechnology. **Geographic Preferences:** U.S.

62586 ■ BD Ventures / Becton, Dickinson and Co.
1 Becton Dr.
Franklin Lakes, NJ 07417
Ph:(201)847-5643
Fax: (201)847-4874
URL: http://www.bd.com
Contact: Clateo Castellini, Chairman and Chief Executive Director
Investment Types: Early stage. **Industry Preferences:** Biotechnology.

62587 ■ Capital Express, L.L.C.
1100 Valleybrook Ave.
Lyndhurst, NJ 07071
Ph:(201)438-8228
Fax: (201)438-5131
Co. E-mail: niles@capitalexpress.com
URL: http://www.capitalexpress.com
Contact: Niles Cohen
E-mail: nilescohen@capitalexpress.com
Preferred Investment Size: $300,000 to $500,000.
Investment Types: Start-up, first and second stage, and recapitalizations. **Industry Preferences:** Internet specific, consumer related, and manufacturing.

62588 ■ Cardinal Partners / Cardinal Health Partners
221 Nassau St.
Princeton, NJ 08542
Ph:(609)924-6452
Fax: (609)683-0174
URL: http://www.cardinalhealthpartners.com
Contact: John Clarke, Managing General Partner
Preferred Investment Size: $1,000,000 to $8,000,000. **Investment Types:** Start-up, seed, first and early stage. **Industry Preferences:** Computer software and services, medical and health, Internet specific, biotechnology, computer hardware, semiconductors and other electronics, communications and media, industrial and energy, other products, and consumer related. **Geographic Preferences:** U.S.

62589 ■ The CIT Group/Venture Capital, Inc.
650 CIT Dr.
Livingston, NJ 07039
Ph:(973)740-5429
Fax: (973)740-5555
URL: http://www.cit.com
Preferred Investment Size: $3,000,000 minimum.
Investment Types: First and second stage, mezzanine, and leveraged buyout. **Industry Preferences:** Diversified. **Geographic Preferences:** Entire U.S.

62590 ■ CS Capital Partners, LLC
328 Second St., Ste. 200
Lakewood, NJ 08701
Ph:(732)901-1111
URL: http://www.cs-capital.com
Contact: Charles Nebenzahl, Managing Partner
Preferred Investment Size: $500,000 to $3,000,000.
Investment Types: Early, first and second stage, expansion, control-block purchases, generalist PE, distressed debt, recapitalizations, and private placement.
Industry Preferences: Internet specific, computer software and services, other products, communications and media, medical and health. **Geographic Preferences:** Mid Atlantic, Northeast, and Southeast.

62591 ■ DFW Capital Partners / Demuth, Folger & Wetherill
Glenpointe Ctr. E., 5th Fl.
300 Frank W. Burr Blvd.
Teaneck, NJ 07666
Ph:(201)836-6000
Fax: (201)836-5666
URL: http://www.dfwcapital.com
Contact: Donald DeMuth, General Partner
Preferred Investment Size: $5,000,000 to $10,000,000. **Investment Types:** Acquisition, control-block purchases, later stage, expansion, leveraged and management buyouts, recapitalizations, and special situation. **Industry Preferences:** Medical and health, consumer related, communications and media, computer hardware, Internet specific, semiconductors and other electronics, computer software and services, other products, industrial and energy. **Geographic Preferences:** U.S.

62592 ■ Domain Associates L.L.C.
1 Palmer Sq., Ste. 515
Princeton, NJ 08542
Ph:(609)683-5656
Fax: (609)683-9789
URL: http://www.domainvc.com
Contact: Brian Dovey, Principal
Preferred Investment Size: $1,000,000 to $20,000,000. **Investment Types:** Seed, start-up, early, first, second, and later stage, balanced, expansion, mezzanine, private placement, research and development, and private placement. **Industry Preferences:** Biotechnology, medical and health, Internet specific, computer software and services, industrial and energy, semiconductors and other electronics, and consumer related. **Geographic Preferences:** U.S.

62593 ■ Early Stage Enterprises, L.P.
995 Rte. 518
Skillman, NJ 08558
Ph:(609)921-8896
Fax: (609)921-8703
URL: http://www.esevc.com
Contact: Ronald R. Hahn, Partner
E-mail: ron@esevc.com
Preferred Investment Size: $500,000 to $1,000,000.
Investment Types: Seed, start-up, first and early stage. **Industry Preferences:** Internet specific, computer software and services, other products, communications and media, medical and health, and biotechnology. **Geographic Preferences:** Mid Atlantic.

62594 ■ Edelson Technology Partners
300 Tice Blvd.
Woodcliff Lake, NJ 07677
Ph:(201)930-9898
Fax: (201)930-8899
URL: http://www.edelsontech.com
Contact: Harry Edelson, General Partner

E-mail: harry@edelsontech.com
Preferred Investment Size: $500,000 to $1,000,000. **Investment Types:** Generalist PE. **Industry Preferences:** Communications and media, industrial and energy, computer software and services, consumer related, computer hardware, semiconductors and other electronics, other products, medical and health, Internet specific, and biotechnology.

62595 ■ Edison Venture Fund
1009 Lenox Dr., No. 4
Lawrenceville, NJ 08648
Ph:(609)896-1900
Fax: (609)896-0066
URL: http://www.edisonventure.com
Contact: Chris Martinson, Managing Partner
Preferred Investment Size: $3,000,000 to $6,000,000. **Investment Types:** First and second stage, acquisition, expansion, and management buyouts. **Industry Preferences:** Computer software and services, Internet specific, industrial and energy, communications and media, medical and health, consumer related, other products, computer hardware, semiconductors and other electronics. **Geographic Preferences:** District of Columbia, Delaware, Maryland, Mid Atlantic, New Jersey, New York, Northeast, Pennsylvania, and Virginia.

62596 ■ First Princeton Capital Corp.
189 Berdan Ave., No. 131
Wayne, NJ 07470-3233
Ph:(973)278-3233
Fax: (973)278-4290
URL: http://www.lytellcatt.net
Preferred Investment Size: $200,000 minimum. **Investment Types:** First and second stage, mezzanine, recapitalizations, control-block purchases, and leveraged buyout. **Industry Preferences:** Computer hardware, medical and health, consumer related, industrial and energy, financial services, business service, and manufacturing. **Geographic Preferences:** Northeast.

62597 ■ Geocapital Partners, LLC
1 executive Dr., Ste. 160
Fort Lee, NJ 07024
Ph:(201)461-9292
Fax: (201)461-7793
URL: http://www.geocapital.com
Contact: Lawrence Lepard, Managing General Partner
Preferred Investment Size: $2,000,000 to $20,000,000. **Investment Types:** Seed, start-up, early, first and later stage, expansion, and private placement. **Industry Preferences:** Internet specific, computer software and services, communications and media, other products, consumer related, industrial and energy, medical and health. **Geographic Preferences:** U.S. and Canada.

62598 ■ Healthcare Ventures LLC / Healthcare Investments
44 Nassau St.
Princeton, NJ 08542-4506
Ph:(609)430-3900
Fax: (609)430-9525
URL: http://www.hcven.com
Contact: Harold Werner, General Partner
Preferred Investment Size: $500,000 to $10,000,000. **Investment Types:** Seed, start-up, early, first, second and later stage, expansion, mezzanine, and public companies. **Industry Preferences:** Biotechnology, medical and health, Internet specific, and consumer related. **Geographic Preferences:** Mid Atlantic and Northeast.

62599 ■ Johnston Associates, Inc.
181 Cherry Valley Rd.
Princeton, NJ 08540
Ph:(609)924-3131
Fax: (609)683-7524
Contact: Robert Johnston, President
Preferred Investment Size: $500,000 to $5,000,000. **Investment Types:** Start-up and early stage. **Industry Preferences:** Biotechnology, medical and health. **Geographic Preferences:** Northeast.

62600 ■ Kemper Ventures
Princeton Forrestal Village
155 Village Blvd.
Princeton, NJ 08540
Ph:(609)936-3133
Fax: (609)936-3180
URL: http://www.kemperventures.com
Contact: John Reynolds, Managing General Partner
Preferred Investment Size: $1,000,000 to $5,000,000. **Investment Types:** Seed, research and development, startup, first and second stage. **Industry Preferences:** Computer hardware and software, Internet specific, medical and health, industrial and energy, financial services, and manufacturing. **Geographic Preferences:** U.S.

62601 ■ MBW Management Inc.
1 Springfield Ave.
Summit, NJ 07901
Ph:(908)273-4060
Fax: (908)273-4430
Preferred Investment Size: $1,000,000 minimum. **Investment Types:** First stage, leveraged buyout, second stage, special situation, and start-up.

62602 ■ New Jersey Technology Council / NJTC
101 Briggs Rd., Ste. 280
Mount Laurel, NJ 08054
Ph:(856)273-6800
Fax: (856)273-0990
Contact: James Gunton, General Partner
Preferred Investment Size: $1,000,000 to $2,000,000. **Investment Types:** Seed, start-up, early, first and second stage, and expansion. **Industry Preferences:** Communications, computer software, Internet specific, semiconductors and other electronics, biotechnology, medical and health, and financial services. **Geographic Preferences:** New Jersey, New York, and Pennsylvania.

62603 ■ New Venture Partners LLC
98 Floral Ave., Ste. 201
Murray Hill, NJ 07974
Ph:(908)464-0900
Fax: (908)464-8129
URL: http://www.nvpllc.com
Contact: Andrew Garman, Managing Partner
Investment Policies: Seed and early stage. **Industry Preferences:** Communications and media, computer software, and semiconductors and other electronics. **Geographic Preferences:** U.S.

62604 ■ Origin Partners
1200 Rte. 22 E., Ste. 2000
Bridgewater, NJ 08807
Ph:(908)595-9100
Fax: (908)595-9763
URL: http://www.originpartners.com
Contact: James Hutchens, Managing Director
Preferred Investment Size: $500,000 to $2,000,000. **Investment Policies:** Start-up, seed, early and first stage. **Industry Preferences:** Communications and media, computer software, Internet specific, semiconductors and other electronics, and medical and health. **Geographic Preferences:** Northeast and Southwest.

62605 ■ Penny Lane Parnters
1 Palmer Sq., Ste. 309
Princeton, NJ 08542
Ph:(609)497-4646
Fax: (609)497-0611
URL: http://www.pennylanepartners.com
Contact: Gregory Trautman, Partner
Preferred Investment Size: $1,000,000 minimum. **Investment Types:** Second stage, leveraged buyouts, and recapitalizations. **Industry Preferences:** Internet specific, other products, semiconductors and other electronics, biotechnology, computer hardware, computer software and services, medical and health, and consumer related. **Geographic Preferences:** Mid Atlantic and Northeast.

62606 ■ Proquest Investments
600 Alexander Park, Ste. 204
Princeton, NJ 08540
Ph:(609)919-3567

Fax: (609)375-1047
URL: http://www.proquestvc.com
Contact: Joyce Tsang, Principal
Preferred Investment Size: $5,000,000 to $15,000,000. **Investment Types:** Seed, start-up, early, first, second, and later stage, balanced, expansion, mezzanine, research and development, and private placement. **Industry Preferences:** Medical and health, biotechnology, and Internet specific. **Geographic Preferences:** U.S. and Canada.

62607 ■ Ridgewood Capital Management, LLC
Ridgewood Commons
947 Linwood Ave.
Ridgewood, NJ 07450
Ph:(201)447-9000
Fax: (201)447-0474
URL: http://www.ridgewoodcapital.com
Contact: Elton Sherwin, Senior Managing Director
Preferred Investment Size: $3,000,000 to $7,000,000. **Investment Types:** Early and later stage, and expansion. **Industry Preferences:** Internet specific, semiconductors and other electronics, communications and media, computer software and services, computer hardware, other products, industrial and energy, and biotechnology. **Geographic Preferences:** Mid Atlantic, Northeast, and West Coast.

62608 ■ Tappan Zee Capital Corp.
201 Lower Notch Rd.
PO Box 416
Little Falls, NJ 07424
Ph:(973)256-8280
Fax: (973)256-2841
Contact: Jeffrey Birnberg, President
Investment Types: Leveraged buyout. **Industry Preferences:** Communications, semiconductors and other electronics, consumer related, industrial and energy.

62609 ■ The Vertical Group
25 DeForest Ave.
Summit, NJ 07901
Ph:(908)277-3737
Fax: (908)273-9434
URL: http://www.vertical-group.com
Contact: Jack Lasersohn, General Partner
Preferred Investment Size: $250,000 to $3,000,000. **Investment Types:** Early and later stage, leveraged buyout, mezzanine, and special situation. **Industry Preferences:** Medical and health, biotechnology, Internet specific, semiconductors and other electronics, computer software and services, communications and media, and industrial and energy.

62610 ■ Westford Technology Ventures, L.P.
17 Academy St.
Newark, NJ 07102
Ph:(973)624-2131
Fax: (973)624-2008
Contact: Jeffrey Hamilton, General Partner
Preferred Investment Size: $300,000 to $500,000. **Investment Types:** Start-up, early, first and second stage. **Industry Preferences:** Communications, computer hardware and software, semiconductors and other electronics, industrial and energy, and manufacturing. **Geographic Preferences:** Mid Atlantic, Midwest, Northeast, and Southeast.

PROCUREMENT ASSISTANCE PROGRAMS

62611 ■ Air Services Development Office of New Jersey
Newark Liberty International Airport
Bldg. 80, 2nd Fl.
Newark, NJ 07114
Ph:(973)961-4278
Fax: (973)961-4282
Co. E-mail: njasdo@asdoaonline.com
URL: http://www.asdoonline.com
Contact: Helene Gibbs, Prgm Mgr
Description: A procurement facility funded by the Port Authority of New York and New Jersey to assist

small firms in Essex, Hudson, and Union counties in obtaining contracts with airlines and other businesses at Newark International Airport.

62612 ■ Defense Procurement Technical Assistance Center–New Jersey Institute of Technology
University Heights
Newark, NJ 07102
Ph:(973)596-3105
Fax: (973)596-5806
Co. E-mail: chaplin@njit.edu
URL: http://www.njit.edu/DPTAC/
Contact: Dolcey Chaplin, Dir
E-mail: chaplin@admin.njit.edu

62613 ■ New Jersey Procurement Technical Assistance Center–Union County Economic Development Corporation (UCEDC)
1085 Morris Ave
Union, NJ 07083
Ph:(908)527-1166
Fax: (908)527-1207
Co. E-mail: info@ucedc.com
URL: http://www.ucedc.com
Contact: Sashee Joshi, Dir

62614 ■ Rutgers School of Management–New Jersey Small Business Development Centers–New Jersey Procurement Technical Assistance Center (49 BI)
49 Bleeker St.
Newark, NJ 07102
Ph:(973)353-1927
Fax: (973)353-1110
Co. E-mail: sburroughs@njsbdc.com
URL: http://www.njsbdc.com
Contact: Stephanie Burroughs
E-mail: britman@andromeda.rutgers.edu

62615 ■ United States Small Business Administration
Attn: SBA-PCR
ATTN: Small Business Administration-PCR, Bldg. 1208
Ft. Monmouth, NJ 7703
Ph:(732)532-3419
Fax: (732)532-8732
Co. E-mail: larry.hanson@sba.gov
URL: http://www.sba.gov
Contact: Martha Magrino, Porocurement Ass.
E-mail: larry.hansen@sba.gov
Description: Covers activities for Communications & Electronics Command (Fort Monmouth, NJ), Army Training Center (Fort Dix, NJ), McGuire Air Force Base (Wrightstown, NJ), and Naval Air Warfare Center (Lakehurst, NJ).

62616 ■ US Small Business Administation
US Army Ardec
Bldg. 1610
Picatinny Arsenal, NJ 07806-5000
Ph:(973)724-6574
Fax: (973)724-5704
URL: http://www.sba.gov
Contact: Michael Cecere, Procurement An.
E-mail: michael.cecere@sba.gov
Description: Covers activities for Research and Development Command (Picatinny Arsenal, NJ), Military Traffic Management Command (Bayonne, NJ), and the Medical Center (East Orange, NJ).

INCUBATORS/RESEARCH AND TECHNOLOGY PARKS

62617 ■ Princeton University–Council of the Humanities
John Henry House
Princeton, NJ 08544
Ph:(609)258-4717
Fax: (609)258-2783
Co. E-mail: humcounc@princeton.edu
URL: http://www.princeton.edu/~humcounc/
Contact: Prof. Anthony Grafton, Chm.

E-mail: humcounc@princeton.edu
Scope: Coordinates various special programs, administers interdisciplinary courses, and selects visiting fellows of the Council. **Publications:** Brochure. **Educational Activities:** Long- and short-term visiting fellows; Old Dominion Faculty Fellows; Old Dominion Faculty Seminars; Princeton Society of Fellows; Visiting Professors of Journalism (annually).

62618 ■ Princeton University–Office of Research and Project Administration
PO Box 36
4 New S Bldg.
Princeton, NJ 08544
Ph:(609)258-3090
Fax: (609)258-1159
Co. E-mail: pieterr@princeton.edu
URL: http://www.princeton.edu/~orpa1/
Contact: Michelle Christy, Dir.
E-mail: pieterr@princeton.edu
Scope: Administers and coordinates all extramurally sponsored research and other projects conducted at the University. Assists faculty members in obtaining financial support for their research or other projects and in fulfilling their contractual obligations to sponsors.

62619 ■ Princeton University–Princeton Forrestal Center
105 College Rd. E
Princeton, NJ 08540
Ph:(609)452-7720
Fax: (609)452-7485
Co. E-mail: picus@picusassociates.com
Contact: David H. Knights, Mktg.Dir.
E-mail: picus@picusassociates.com
Scope: Planned multiuse development area creating an interdependent mix of academic and business enterprise in the Princeton area.

62620 ■ Rutgers University–Office of Corporate Liaison and Technology Transfer
ASB III
3 Rutgers Plz.
New Brunswick, NJ 08901
Ph:(732)932-0115
Fax: (732)932-0146
Co. E-mail: adams@ocltt.rutgers.edu
URL: http://ocltt.rutgers.edu
Contact: William T. Adams, Dir.
E-mail: adams@ocltt.rutgers.edu
Scope: Serves as University liaison for corporate and industrial firms supporting graduate and faculty researchers in departments and centers throughout the University. **Educational Activities:** Conferences; Seminars (occasionally), for industrial clients.

62621 ■ Rutgers University–Office of Research and Sponsored Programs
ASB III
3 Rutgers Plz.
New Brunswick, NJ 08901
Ph:(732)932-0150
Fax: (732)932-0162
Co. E-mail: breton@orsp.rutgers.edu
URL: http://orsp.rutgers.edu
Contact: Dr. Michael E. Breton, Assoc.VP
E-mail: breton@orsp.rutgers.edu
Scope: Coordinates intramural research activities, including programs designed to maximize faculty incentive to seek external funds. Administers programs on protection of human subjects in research, use of animals in research; and pre-award procedures for proposals to external funding agencies. Advises central administration on research policies. Serves as a clearinghouse for information on sources of research support. Administers the Research Council, which awards grants and fellowships to faculty. **Publications:** Annual Report; GrantNet Electronics Newsletter (monthly). **Educational Activities:** Colloquia; Workshops, on grantsmanship.

62622 ■ Stevens Institute of Technology–Office of Research
Castle Point on the Hudson
Hoboken, NJ 07030
Ph:(201)216-5000
Fax: (201)216-8044

URL: http://www.stevens-tech.edu
Contact: Prof. Glenn S. Davis, Dir.
Scope: Administratively responsible for all research conducted at the Institute, including civil engineering, electrical engineering, mechanical engineering, ocean engineering, telecommunications, chemistry and chemical engineering, materials, environmental engineering, computer science, mathematics, physics, and management. **Educational Activities:** Seminars.

62623 ■ Stevens Technology Ventures Incubator
Stevens Institute
Castle Point on Hudson
Hoboken, NJ 07030-5053
Ph:(201)216-5263
Fax: (201)216-8909
Co. E-mail: gboesch@stevens_tech.edu
URL: http://www.soe.stevens-tech.edu
Contact: Marta Boesch, Ex. Assistant
Description: Stevens Technology Ventures Incubator (TVI) seeks to assist entrepreneurs with commercially viable technology innovations and products.

62624 ■ William Paterson University of New Jersey–Office of Institutional Research and Assessment
College Hall, Rm.242
358 Hamburg Tpke.
PO Box 913
Wayne, NJ 07470-0913
Ph:(973)720-2379
Fax: (973)720-3624
Co. E-mail: zeffj@wpunj.edu
URL: http://ww2.wpunj.edu/IRA/default.htm
Contact: Dr. Jane Zeff, Dir.
E-mail: zeffj@wpunj.edu
Scope: Collects and analyzes data on the operation of the University and provides assistance in institutional planning and policy decisions especially those pertaining to the assessment of student learning outcomes.

EDUCATIONAL PROGRAMS

62625 ■ Bergen Community College
400 Paramus Rd.
Paramus, NJ 07652
Ph:(201)447-7100
Fax: (201)670-7973
URL: http://www.bergen.cc.edu
Description: Two-year college offering a small business management program.

62626 ■ Brookdale Community College
765 Newman Springs Rd.
Lincroft, NJ 07738-1597
Ph:(732)224-2345
Fax: (732)224-2772
URL: http://www.brookdale.cc.nj.us
Description: Two-year college offering a program in small business management.

62627 ■ Burlington County College
601 Pemberton-Browns Mills Rd.
Pemberton Browns Mills Rd.
Pemberton, NJ 08068
Ph:(609)894-9311
Fax: (609)894-0764
URL: http://www.bcc.edu
Description: Two-year college offering a certificate in small business management.

TRADE PERIODICALS

62628 ■ *Linux Business Week*
Pub: SYS-CON Media
Contact: Jeremy Geelan, Group Publisher
E-mail: jeremy@sys-con.com
Released: Monthly. **Description:** Professional journal covering Linux news and issues.

PUBLICATIONS

62629 ■ *Mercer Business*
2550 Kuser Rd.
P.O. Box 8307
Trenton, NJ 08650
Ph:(609)586-2056
Fax: (609)586-8052
Co. E-mail: WEgraphics@aol.com

62630 ■ *New Jersey Business*
New Jersey Business and Industry Association
310 Passaic Ave.
Fairfield, NJ 07004
Ph:(973)882-5004
Fax: (973)882-4648
Co. E-mail: njbmag@intac.com
URL: http://www.njbmagazine.com

62631 ■ *New Jersey Monthly*
55 Park Pl.
P.O. Box 920
Morristown, NJ 07963-0920
Ph:(973)539-8230
Fax: (973)538-2953
URL: http://www.njmonthly.com

62632 ■ *Smart Start your New Jersey Business*
PSI Research
300 N. Valley Dr.
Grants Pass, OR 97526
Ph:(503)479-9464
Free: 800-228-2275
Fax: (503)476-1479
Co. E-mail: info@psi-research.com
URL: http://www.psi-research.com
Ed: Michael D. Jenkins. **Released:** Revised edition, 1992. **Price:** $29.95 (looseleaf binder); $24.95 (paper). **Description:** Part of the Successful Business Library series.

PUBLISHERS

62633 ■ **Dow Jones Reuters Business Interactive L.L.C.**
Us Hwy. 1 N
PO Box 300
Princeton, NJ 08540
Ph:(609)627-2000
Free: 800-522-3567
Fax: (609)520-4660
URL: http://www.factiva.com
Contact: Carl M. Valenti, President
Description: Offers almost 70 databases listing current financial and investment material and general news and information. Also produces software. Databases accessible through personal computers, communicating word processors and terminals, and teletypewriters. Reaches market through direct mail, telephone sales, advertising, and trade sales. **Founded:** 1974.

62634 ■ **Dun's Marketing Services**
103 JFK Pkwy.
Short Hills, NJ 07078
Ph:(973)921-5500
Free: 800-526-0651
URL: http://www.dnb.com
Description: Publishes business directories.

62635 ■ **Fictionwise Inc.**
407 Main St.
Chatham, NJ 07928
Ph:(973)701-6773
Fax: (973)701-6774
Co. E-mail: info@fictionwise.com
URL: http://www.fictionwise.com
Contact: Scott Pendergrast, President
Description: Publishes fiction in ebook format and also publishes nonfiction, erotica, humor, horror and romance.

62636 ■ **Passaic County Department of Community and Economic Development**
Admin. Bldg., 401 Grand St., Ste. 511
Paterson, NJ 07505
Ph:(973)881-4427
Fax: (973)684-2042
Co. E-mail: pcupdate@passaiccountynj.org

URL: http://www.passaiccountynj.org
Contact: Deborah Hoffman, Director
Description: Publishes materials to inform developers, business owners, and companies relocating on the economic developments, financing and employment assistance, and general information on economic climate in Passaic County. Offers a newsletter, *Economic Perspective* and the brochures *A Passport to Passaic County* and *Everything You Wanted to Know About Starting or Maintaining a Small Business but Didn't Know Who to Ask.* Reaches market through direct mail. **Founded:** 1978.

62637 ■ **Prentice Hall Business Publishing**
1 Lake St.
Upper Saddle River, NJ 07458
Ph:(201)236-7000
Free: 800-227-1816
Fax: (201)236-7696
URL: http://phbusiness.prenhall.com
Contact: Jerome Grant, President
Description: Publishes business books.

62638 ■ **Prentice Hall Press**
1 Lake St.
Upper Saddle River, NJ 07458
Ph:(201)236-7000
Free: 800-745-8489
Fax: (201)909-6360
URL: http://vig.prenhall.com/
Contact: Sally Wood, Mgr
Description: Publishes books on business, education, and self-help in publishing.

62639 ■ **Two-Can Publishing**
11571 K-Tel Dr.
PO Box 86
Minnetonka, MN 55343
Ph:(952)933-7537
Free: 888-255-9989
Fax: (952)933-3630
Co. E-mail: sales@tnkidsbooks.com
URL: http://www.tnkidsbooks.com/twocan.asp
Contact: Allan Lang, Publishing Dir.
E-mail: AllanLang@two-canpublishingllc.com
Description: Publishes multimedia products and books. Does not accept unsolicited manuscripts. Reaches market through commission representatives, reviews and listings. **Founded:** 2000.

SMALL BUSINESS DEVELOPMENT CENTER LEAD OFFICE

62640 ■ New Mexico SBDC–Santa Fe Community College
6401 Richards Ave.
Santa Fe, NM 87505
Ph:(505)428-1362
Fax: (505)471-9469
URL: http://www.nmsbdc.org
Contact: Roy Miller, State Dir.
E-mail: rmiller@santa-fe.cc.nm.us

62641 ■ Santa Fe Community College–New Mexico Small Business Development Center
6401 Richards Ave.
Santa Fe, NM 87505
Ph:(505)428-1362
Free: 800-281-7232
Fax: (505)428-1469
URL: http://www.nmsbdc.org
Contact: J. Roy Miller, State Director

SMALL BUSINESS DEVELOPMENT CENTERS

62642 ■ Albuquerque SBDC
2501 Yale Blvd. SE, Ste. 302
Albuquerque, NM 87106
Ph:(505)225-5250
Fax: (505)224-5256
Co. E-mail: sbdc@cnm.edu
URL: http://www.cnm.edu/abqsbdc
Contact: Ray Garcia, Dir.

62643 ■ Albuquerque Technical Vocational Institute–Small Business Development Center
801 University SE, Ste. 300
Albuquerque, NM 87106
Ph:(505)272-7980
Fax: (505)272-7969
Contact: Ray Garcia, Dir.

62644 ■ Clovis Community College–Small Business Development Center
417 Schepps Blvd.
Clovis, NM 88101-8381
Ph:(505)769-4136
Fax: (505)769-4135
Co. E-mail: sbdc@clovis.cc.nm.us
URL: http://www.clovis.cc.nm.us
Contact: Dr. Sandra Taylor-Smith

62645 ■ Clovis/Curry County Chamber of Commerce–Small Business Development Center
105 E. Grand St.
Clovis, NM 88101
Ph:(505)763-3435

Fax: (505)763-7266
Co. E-mail: clovisnm@clovisnm.org
URL: http://www.clovisnm.org
Contact: Ernie Kos, Dir.
E-mail: ernie@clovisnm.org

62646 ■ Eastern New Mexico University at Roswell–Small Business Development Center
20 W. Mathis
PO Box 6000
Roswell, NM 88202-6000
Ph:(505)624-7133
Fax: (505)624-7132
URL: http://www.roswell.enmu.edu
Contact: Eugene D. Simmons, Dir.
E-mail: eugene.simmons@roswell.enmu.edu

62647 ■ Luna Community College–Small Business Development Center
366 Luna Dr.
Las Vegas, NM 87701
Ph:(505)454-2582
Fax: (505)454-5326
URL: http://www.luna.edu
Contact: Don Bustos, Dir.
E-mail: dbustos@luna.edu

62648 ■ Mesalands Community College–Small Business Development Center
911 S. 10th St.
Tucumcari, NM 88401
Ph:(505)461-4413
Fax: (505)461-4318
Co. E-mail: sbcd@mesalands.edu
URL: http://www.mesalands.edu
Contact: David Buchen, Dir.

62649 ■ New Mexico Junior College–Small Business Development Center
5317 Lovington Hwy.
Hobbs, NM 88240
Ph:(505)392-5549
Fax: (505)492-1493
URL: http://www.nmjc.edu/sbdc/
Contact: Gloria D. Munoz, Dir.

62650 ■ New Mexico State University at Alamogordo–Small Business Development Center
2230 Lawrence Blvd.
Alamogordo, NM 88310
Ph:(505)434-5272
Fax: (505)434-1432
URL: http://www.alamosbdc.org
Contact: Dwight Harp, Dir.
E-mail: dharp@nmsua.nmsu.edu

62651 ■ New Mexico State University at Carlsbad–Small Business Development Center
221 S. Canyon St.
Carlsbad, NM 88220
Ph:(505)885-9531
Fax: (505)885-1515
Contact: Larry Coalson, Dir.

E-mail: lcoalson@cavern.nmsu.edu

62652 ■ New Mexico State University/Dona Ana SBDC–Small Business Development Center
2345 E. Nevada Ave.
Las Cruces, NM 88001-3902
Ph:(505)527-7676
Fax: (505)528-7432
Co. E-mail: fowensby@nmsu.edu
URL: http://dabcc-www.nmsu.edu/comm/sbdc
Contact: Fred K. Owensby, Dir.

62653 ■ New Mexico State University at Grants–Small Business Development Center
709 E. Roosevelt Ave.
Grants, NM 87020
Ph:(505)287-8221
Fax: (505)287-2125
Co. E-mail: sbdcgrnt@7cities.net
Contact: Clemente Sanchez, Dir.

62654 ■ Northern New Mexico College–Small Business Development Center
921 Paseo de Onate St.
Espanola, NM 87532
Ph:(505)747-2236
Fax: (505)757-2234
URL: http://www.nnmc.edu
Contact: Julianna Barbee, Dir.
E-mail: jbarbee@nnmc.edu

62655 ■ San Juan College–Small Business Development Center
5101 College Blvd.
Farmington, NM 87402
Ph:(505)566-3528
Fax: (505)566-3698
URL: http://www.sjc.cc.nm.us/qcb/sbdc.html
Contact: Larry Armstrong, Dir.
E-mail: armstrongl@sanjuancollege.edu

62656 ■ Sandoval County SBDC
237 S. Camino del Pueblo
PO Box 374
Bernalillo, NM 87004
Ph:(505)867-5066
Fax: (505)867-3746
Co. E-mail: sandovalsbdc@la.unm.edu
Contact: Ward Hickey, Dir.

62657 ■ Santa Fe Business Incubator–Small Business Development Center
3900 Paseo del Sol
Santa Fe, NM 87507
Ph:(505)424-1140
Fax: (505)424-1144
Co. E-mail: info@sfbi.net
URL: http://www.sfbi.net
Contact: Sheila Stalder, Program Mgr.

62658 ■ South Valley SBDC–SBDC
1309 4th St. SW, Ste. A
Albuquerque, NM 87102
Ph:(505)248-0132
Fax: (505)248-0127

Co. E-mail: svsbdc@abq.com
Contact: Steven Becerra, Dir.

62659 ■ University of New Mexico at Gallup–Small Business Development Center
103 W. Hwy. 66
Gallup, NM 87301
Ph:(505)722-2220
Fax: (505)863-6006
Co. E-mail: sbdc@gallup.unm.edu
URL: http://www.gallup.unm.edu
Contact: Elsie Sanchez, Dir.
E-mail: esanchez@cia-g.com

62660 ■ University of New Mexico at Los Alamos–Small Business Development Center
901 18th St., Ste. 11800
PO Box 715
Los Alamos, NM 87544
Ph:(505)662-0001
Fax: (505)662-0099
Co. E-mail: sbdc@losalamos.org
URL: http://www.losalamos.org/lacdc/unmla.htm
Contact: Kevin Holsapple, Dir.

62661 ■ University of New Mexico at Valencia–Small Business Development Center
280 La Entrada
Los Lunas, NM 87031
Ph:(505)925-8980
Fax: (505)925-8981
URL: http://www.unm.edu/~vcsbdc/
Contact: Roberta Scott, Dir.
E-mail: robscott@unm.edu

62662 ■ Western New Mexico University–Small Business Development Center
Besse-Forward Global Resource Center
817 W. 12th St.
PO Box 680
Silver City, NM 88062
Ph:(505)538-6320
Fax: (505)538-6341
Co. E-mail: sbdc@wnmu.edu
URL: http://www.wnmu.edu
Contact: Mary Vigil-Tarazoff, Dir.
E-mail: vigiltarazoffm@wnmu.edu

SMALL BUSINESS ASSISTANCE PROGRAMS

62663 ■ New Mexico Center for Business Research and Services
New Mexico State University
MSC 3CR PO 30001
Las Cruces, NM 88011
Ph:(505)646-1434
Fax: (505)646-7037
Co. E-mail: kboberg@nmsu.edu
Description: Provides research services and a data bank for economic and business related information. Also provides business and economic research to public and private sectors.

62664 ■ New Mexico Department of Agriculture–Marketing and Development Division
3190 S Espina
MSC 5600 1st PO 30005
Las Cruces, NM 88003-8005
Ph:(505)646-5055
Fax: (505)646-3303
Co. E-mail: nmagsec@nmda.nmsu.edu
URL: http://nmdaweb.nmsu.edu/
Contact: Dr. I. Miley Gonzalez Ph.D
Description: Provides technical assistance to agricultural producers and processors who export both domestically and internationally.

62665 ■ New Mexico Economic Development Department–Economic Development Department
1100 St. Francis Dr.
Santa Fe, NM 87505

Ph:(505)827-0300
Free: 800—374-3060
Fax: (505)827-0328
Co. E-mail: edd.info@state.nm.us
URL: http://www.newmexicodevelopment.com
Description: Formulates and implements statewide economic development. Also provides assistance to various individuals and groups.

62666 ■ New Mexico Procurement Assistance Program–General Assistance Department
PO Drawer 26110
Santa Fe, NM 87502-0110
Ph:(505)827-0472
Fax: (505)827-0499
URL: http://www.state.nm.us/spd
Description: Promotes and assists small, minority-owned, and women-owned businesses in marketing their goods and services to government, especially to the state of New Mexico.

SCORE OFFICES

62667 ■ SCORE Las Cruces
Loretto Towne Center
505 S Main St., Ste. 125
Las Cruces, NM 88001
Ph:(505)523-5627
Fax: (505)524-2101
Co. E-mail: score.397@zianet.com
URL: http://www.zianet.com/score.397
Contact: Gabriel Fusco, Chm.
Description: Provides entrepreneur education for the formation, growth and success of small businesses in the area.

BETTER BUSINESS BUREAUS

62668 ■ Better Business Bureau of New Mexico
2625 Pennsylvania NE, Ste. 2050
Albuquerque, NM 87110-3657
Ph:(505)346-0110
Fax: (505)346-0696
Co. E-mail: bureau@bbbsw.org
URL: http://www.bbbnm.com
Contact: Jerry Shipman, Pres.

62669 ■ Better Business Bureau Serving Four Corners and Western Slope
308 N Locke
Farmington, NM 87401-5855
Ph:(505)326-6501
Fax: (505)327-7731
Co. E-mail: bbbfcws@digii.net
URL: http://www.farmington.bbb.org
Contact: Joyce Donald, Pres./CEO

CHAMBERS OF COMMERCE

62670 ■ Alamogordo Chamber of Commerce
1301 N White Sands Blvd.
Alamogordo, NM 88310
Ph:(505)437-6120
Free: 888-843-3441
Fax: (505)437-6334
Co. E-mail: chamber@alamogordo.com
URL: http://www.alamogordo.com
Contact: Ed Carr, Exec.Dir.

62671 ■ Angel Fire Chamber of Commerce
PO Box 547
Angel Fire, NM 87710
Ph:(505)377-6661
Free: 800-446-8117
Fax: (505)377-3034
Co. E-mail: askus@angelfirechamber.org
URL: http://www.angelfirechamber.org

Contact: Don Borgeson, Pres.

62672 ■ Aztec Chamber of Commerce and Visitor Center
110 N Ash
Aztec, NM 87410
Ph:(505)334-9551
Free: 888-838-9551
Fax: (505)334-7648
Co. E-mail: aztec@digii.net
URL: http://www.aztecchamber.com
Contact: Ms. Annette Tidwell, Interim Dir.

62673 ■ Belen Chamber of Commerce
712 Dalies Ave.
Belen, NM 87002-3618
Ph:(505)864-8091
Fax: (505)864-7461
Co. E-mail: belenchamber@belennm.com
URL: http://www.belennm.com
Contact: Cindy Clark, Exec.Dir.

62674 ■ Bloomfield Chamber of Commerce
224 W Broadway
Bloomfield, NM 87413
Ph:(505)632-0880
Free: 800-461-1245
Fax: (505)634-1431
Co. E-mail: askus@bloomfieldnm.info
URL: http://www.bloomfieldnm.info
Contact: Sherry Galloway, Exec.Dir.

62675 ■ Capitan Chamber of Commerce
433 Smokey Bear Blvd.
PO Box 441
Capitan, NM 88316-0441
Ph:(505)354-2273
Co. E-mail: capitancoc@aol.com
URL: http://www.villageofcapitan.com
Contact: Shirley Pavlovic, Pres.

62676 ■ Carrizozo Chamber of Commerce
PO Box 567
Carrizozo, NM 88301
Ph:(505)648-2732
Co. E-mail: zozoccc@tularosa.net
URL: http://www.townofcarrizozo.org
Contact: Dean Lollar, Pres.

62677 ■ Chama Valley Chamber of Commerce
PO Box 306-RB
Chama, NM 87520
Ph:(505)756-2306
Free: 800-477-0149
Fax: (505)756-2892
Co. E-mail: info@chamavalley.com
URL: http://www.chamavalley.com
Contact: Teresa Smith, Pres.

62678 ■ Cimarron Chamber of Commerce
104 N Lincoln
PO Box 604
Cimarron, NM 87714
Ph:(505)376-2417
Free: 888-376-2417
Fax: (505)376-2417
Co. E-mail: chamber@springercoop.com
URL: http://www.cimarronnm.com
Contact: Tracy Boyce, Pres.

62679 ■ Clayton-Union County Chamber of Commerce
PO Box 476
Clayton, NM 88415-0476
Ph:(505)374-9253
Free: 800-390-7858
Fax: (505)374-9253
Co. E-mail: cuchamber@plateautel.net
URL: http://www.claytonnewmexico.org
Contact: Audra Poling, Exec.Dir.

62680 ■ Cloudcroft Chamber of Commerce
PO Box 1290
Cloudcroft, NM 88317
Ph:(505)682-2733
Fax: (505)682-6028

Co. E-mail: cloudcroft@cloudcroft.net
URL: http://www.cloudcroft.net
Contact: Jason Baldwin, Dir.

62681 ■ Clovis - Curry County Chamber of Commerce
105 E Grand St.
Clovis, NM 88101
Ph:(505)763-3435
Fax: (505)763-7266
Co. E-mail: clovisnm@clovisnm.org
URL: http://www.clovisnm.org
Contact: Mrs. Ernie Kos, Exec.Dir.

62682 ■ Columbus Chamber of Commerce
201 Broadway Ave., Ste. 3
PO Box 365
Columbus, NM 88029-0365
Ph:(505)531-2479
Fax: (505)531-2479
Co. E-mail: info@discovercolumbusnewmexico.com
Contact: Norma Gomez, Pres.

62683 ■ Deming-Luna County Chamber of Commerce
800 E Pine
PO Box 8
Deming, NM 88031-0008
Ph:(505)546-2674
Free: 800-848-4955
Fax: (505)546-9569
Co. E-mail: chamber@demingchamber.com
URL: http://www.demingchamber.com
Contact: Linda Wallace, Exec.Dir.

62684 ■ Eagle Nest Chamber of Commerce
PO Box 322
Eagle Nest, NM 87718
Ph:(505)377-2420
Free: 800-494-9117
Fax: (505)377-2420
Co. E-mail: chamber@eaglenest.org
URL: http://www.eaglenest.org/chamber
Contact: Ken Younger, Exec.Dir.

62685 ■ Elephant Butte Chamber of Commerce
PO Box 1355
Elephant Butte, NM 87935
Ph:(505)744-4708
Free: 877-744-4900
Fax: (505)744-0044
Co. E-mail: info@elephantbuttecoc.com
URL: http://www.elephantbuttecoc.com
Contact: Kim Skinner, Pres.

62686 ■ Espanola Valley Chamber of Commerce
710 Paseo de Onate
PO Box 190
Espanola, NM 87532-0190
Ph:(505)753-2831
Fax: (505)753-1252
Co. E-mail: info@espanolanmchamber.com
URL: http://www.espanolanmchamber.com
Contact: Connie Thompson, Exec.Dir.

62687 ■ Farmington Chamber of Commerce
100 W Broadway
Farmington, NM 87401
Ph:(505)325-0279
Free: 888-325-0279
Fax: (505)327-7556
Co. E-mail: chamber@gofarmington.com
URL: http://www.gofarmington.com
Contact: Melissa Bateman-Lane, Pres./CEO

62688 ■ Fort Sumner Chamber of Commerce
PO Box 28
Fort Sumner, NM 88119-0028
Ph:(505)355-7705
Fax: (505)355-2850
Co. E-mail: ftsumnercoc@plateautel.net
URL: http://www.ftsumnerchamber.com
Contact: Sandy Paul, Exec.Dir.

62689 ■ Gallup-McKinley County Chamber of Commerce
103 W Hwy. 66
Gallup, NM 87301
Ph:(505)722-2228
Free: 800-380-4989
Co. E-mail: hwy66@cia-g.com
Contact: Dr. Greg Orphey, Pres.

62690 ■ Grants/Cibola County Chamber of Commerce
PO Box 297
Grants, NM 87020-0297
Ph:(505)287-4802
Free: 800-748-2142
Fax: (505)287-8224
Co. E-mail: discover@grants.org
URL: http://www.grants.org
Contact: Mike Stokes, Exec.Dir.

62691 ■ Greater Albuquerque Chamber of Commerce
PO Box 25100
Albuquerque, NM 87125-0100
Ph:(505)764-3700
Fax: (505)764-3714
Co. E-mail: gacc@abqchamber.com
URL: http://www.gacc.org
Contact: Mrs. Terri L. Cole, Pres./CEO

62692 ■ Greater Artesia Chamber of Commerce
107 N 1st St.
PO Box 99
Artesia, NM 88210-2101
Ph:(505)746-2744
Free: 800-658-6251
Fax: (505)746-2745
Co. E-mail: commerce@pvtnetworks.net
URL: http://www.artesiachamber.com
Contact: Richard Price, Exec.Dir.

62693 ■ Greater Bernalillo Chamber of Commerce
PO Box 1776
Bernalillo, NM 87004
Ph:(505)867-1185
Free: 888-374-0267
Fax: (505)867-3596
Co. E-mail: bernalillochambr@aol.com
URL: http://www.bernalillochamber.org

62694 ■ Greater Las Cruces Chamber of Commerce
760 W Picacho Ave.
PO Drawer 519
Las Cruces, NM 88004-0519
Ph:(505)524-1968
Fax: (505)527-5546
Co. E-mail: chamber@lascruces.org
URL: http://www.lascruces.org
Contact: Jim Berry, Pres.

62695 ■ Hatch Valley Chamber of Commerce
PO Box 38
Hatch, NM 87937
Ph:(505)267-5050
Fax: (505)267-5050
Co. E-mail: mncrdyke@zianet.com
URL: http://www.villageofhatch.org
Contact: Ms. Marcia Nordyke, Sec.

62696 ■ Hispano Chamber of Commerce de Las Cruces
PO Box 1964
Las Cruces, NM 88005
Ph:(505)523-2681
Fax: (505)523-4639
Co. E-mail: office@lascruceshispanochamber.org
URL: http://www.lascruceshispanochamber.org
Contact: John Vasquez, VP

62697 ■ Hobbs Chamber of Commerce
400 N Marland Blvd.
Hobbs, NM 88240-6330
Ph:(505)397-3202
Free: 800-658-6291

Fax: (505)397-1689
Co. E-mail: hobbschamber@leaconet.com
URL: http://www.hobbschamber.org
Contact: Raymond Battaglini, Exec.VP

62698 ■ Las Vegas-San Miguel Chamber of Commerce
701 Grand Ave.
PO Box 128
Las Vegas, NM 87701-0128
Ph:(505)425-8631
Free: 800-832-5947
Fax: (505)425-3057
Co. E-mail: lvsmcc@zialink.com
URL: http://www.lasvegasnm.org

62699 ■ Lordsburg - Hidalgo County Chamber of Commerce
117 E Second St.
Lordsburg, NM 88045-1926
Ph:(505)542-9864
Fax: (505)542-9059
Co. E-mail: lordsburgcoc@aznex.net

62700 ■ Los Alamos Chamber of Commerce
109 Central Park Sq.
Los Alamos, NM 87544-0460
Ph:(505)662-8105
Fax: (505)662-8399
Co. E-mail: chamber@losalamos.com
URL: http://www.losalamoschamber.com
Contact: Kevin Holsapple, Exec.Dir.

62701 ■ Los Alamos Commerce and Development Corporation
PO Box 715
Los Alamos, NM 87544
Ph:(505)662-0001
Fax: (505)662-0099
Co. E-mail: lacdc@losalamos.org
URL: http://www.losalamos.org/lacdc
Contact: Kevin Holsapple, Exec. Dir.

62702 ■ Lovington Chamber of Commerce
201 S Main
Lovington, NM 88260-4222
Ph:(505)396-5311
Fax: (505)396-2823
Co. E-mail: lchamber@valornet.com
URL: http://www.lovington.net

62703 ■ Magdalena Chamber of Commerce
PO Box 281
Magdalena, NM 87825-0281
Free: (866)854-3217
Fax: (505)854-3092
Co. E-mail: info@magdalena-nm.com
URL: http://www.magdalena-nm.com
Contact: Lee Scholes, Pres.

62704 ■ Melrose Chamber of Commerce
PO Box 216
Melrose, NM 88124
Ph:(505)253-4274
Fax: (505)253-4592
Contact: Doyle Young, Pres.

62705 ■ Moriarty Chamber of Commerce
PO Box 96
777 Rte. 66
Moriarty, NM 87035
Ph:(505)832-4087
Co. E-mail: amickeymmm@aol.com
URL: http://www.moriartychamber.com
Contact: Larry Cox, Pres.

62706 ■ Mountainair Chamber of Commerce
PO Box 595
Mountainair, NM 87036-0595
Ph:(505)847-2795
Fax: (505)847-0907
Co. E-mail: mcc@mountainairchamber.com
URL: http://www.mountainairchamber.com
Contact: Dorothy Cole, Pres.

62707 ■ Red River Chamber of Commerce
PO Box 870
Red River, NM 87558

Ph:(505)754-2366
Free: 800-348-6444
Fax: (505)754-3104
Co. E-mail: rrinfo@redriverchamber.org
URL: http://www.redrivernewmex.com
Contact: Emily Kohn, Events Coor.

62708 ■ Rio Rancho Chamber of Commerce
4001 Southern Blvd. SE
Rio Rancho, NM 87124-2069
Ph:(505)892-1533
Fax: (505)892-6157
Co. E-mail: dmoore@rrchamber.org
URL: http://www.rrchamber.org
Contact: Debbi Moore, Exec.Dir.

62709 ■ Roosevelt County Chamber of Commerce
100 S Ave. A
Portales, NM 88130
Ph:(505)356-8541
Free: 800-635-8036
Fax: (505)356-8542
Co. E-mail: chamber@portales.com
URL: http://www.portales.com
Contact: Kim Huffman, Exec.Dir.

62710 ■ Roswell Chamber of Commerce
131 W 2nd St.
PO Box 70
Roswell, NM 88202-0070
Ph:(505)623-5695
Free: 877-849-7679
Fax: (505)624-6870
Co. E-mail: information@roswellnm.org
URL: http://www.roswellnm.org
Contact: Bernarr Treat, Exec.Dir.

62711 ■ Ruidoso Valley Chamber of Commerce
720 Sudderth Dr.
PO Box 698
Ruidoso, NM 88355-0698
Ph:(505)257-7395
Free: 877-RUI-DOSO
Fax: (505)257-4693
Co. E-mail: info@ruidosonow.com
URL: http://ruidosonow.com
Contact: Brad Treptow, Exec.Dir.

62712 ■ Santa Fe Chamber of Commerce
PO Box 1928
8380 Cerillos Rd., Ste. 302
Santa Fe, NM 87507
Ph:(505)988-3279
Fax: (505)984-2205
Co. E-mail: trish@santafechamber.com
URL: http://www.santafechamber.com
Contact: Simon Brackley, Interim Pres.

62713 ■ Silver City-Grant County Chamber of Commerce
201 N Hudson Ave.
Silver City, NM 88061
Ph:(505)538-3785
Free: 800-548-9378
Co. E-mail: info@silvercity.org
URL: http://www.silvercity.org
Contact: Holley Hudgins, Pres.

62714 ■ Taos County Chamber of Commerce
1139 Paseo del Pueblo Sur
PO Drawer I
Taos, NM 87571
Ph:(505)758-3873
Free: 800-732-8267
Fax: (505)758-3872
Co. E-mail: info@taoschamber.com
URL: http://www.taoschamber.com
Contact: Gayle Martinez, Exec. Dir.

62715 ■ Tatum Chamber of Commerce
PO Box 355
Tatum, NM 88267
Ph:(505)398-5455
Fax: (505)398-8288
Co. E-mail: mburns@little.net

Contact: Marilyn Burns, Pres.

62716 ■ Truth or Consequences/Sierra County Chamber of Commerce
400 W 4th St.
PO Box 31
Truth or Consequences, NM 87901
Ph:(505)894-3536
Fax: (505)894-3536
Co. E-mail: cofc@riolink.com
URL: http://www.truthorconsequencesnm.net
Contact: Alice Gutshall, Office Mgr.

62717 ■ Tucumcari-Quay County Chamber of Commerce
404 W Rte. 66
PO Box E
Tucumcari, NM 88401-7005
Ph:(505)461-1694
Free: 888-664-7255
Fax: (505)461-3884
Co. E-mail: chamber@tucumcarinm.com
URL: http://www.tucumcarinm.com
Contact: Virginia Wright, Exec.Dir.

62718 ■ Whites City Chamber of Commerce
PO Box 128
Whites City, NM 88268
Ph:(505)785-2291
Fax: (505)785-2283
Co. E-mail: whitescity@whitescity.com
URL: http://www.whitescity.com
Contact: Tom Dugger

MINORITY BUSINESS ASSISTANCE PROGRAMS

62719 ■ NEDA Business Consultants–New Mexico Statewide Minority Business Enterprise Center
718 Central Ave. SW
Albuquerque, NM 87102
Ph:(505)843-7114
Fax: (505)242-2030
Co. E-mail: info@nedainc.net
URL: http://www.nm-mbdc.com
Contact: Ann Muller, Pres & Project Dir

FINANCING AND LOAN PROGRAMS

62720 ■ Bruce F. Glaspell & Associates
10400 Academy Rd. NE, Ste. 313
Albuquerque, NM 87111
Ph:(505)292-4505
Fax: (505)292-4258
Contact: Bruce Glaspell, Managing Director
Preferred Investment Size: $500,000 to $15,000,000. **Investment Types:** Balanced. **Industry Preferences:** Communications, computer hardware and software, Internet specific, semiconductors and other electronics, biotechnology, medical and health, consumer related, industrial and energy, transportation, financial services, business service, manufacturing, agriculture, forestry and fishing, and other.

62721 ■ High Desert Ventures, Inc.
6101 Imparata St. NE, Ste. 1721
Albuquerque, NM 87111
Ph:(505)797-3330
Fax: (505)338-5147
Co. E-mail: zilenziger@aol.com
Preferred Investment Size: $500,000 to $2,500,000. **Investment Types:** Start-up and early stage. **Industry Preferences:** Diversified. **Geographic Preferences:** Northeast and Southwest.

62722 ■ New Business Capital Fund, Ltd.
5805 Torreon NE
Albuquerque, NM 87109
Ph:(505)822-8445
Investment Types: Seed, start-up, and first stage. **Industry Preferences:** Computer hardware, semiconductors and other electronics, medical and health, consumer related, industrial and energy, and manufacturing.

62723 ■ SBC Ventures
10400 Academy Rd. NE, Ste. 313
Albuquerque, NM 87111
Ph:(505)292-4505
Fax: (505)292-4258
Contact: Viviana Cloninger, General Partner
Preferred Investment Size: $300,000 to $3,000,000.
Investment Types: First stage, research and development, seed, and start-up. **Industry Preferences:** Diversified. **Geographic Preferences:** Entire U.S. and Canada.

62724 ■ Technology Ventures Corp.
1155 University Blvd. SE
Albuquerque, NM 87106
Ph:(505)246-2882
Fax: (505)246-2891
Contact: Beverly Bendicksen
Investment Types: Seed, start-up, first and second stage. **Industry Preferences:** Diversified. **Geographic Preferences:** Southwest.

PROCUREMENT ASSISTANCE PROGRAMS

62725 ■ New Mexico Procurement Technical Assistance Center
PO Box 26110
Santa Fe, NM 87502-0110
Ph:(505)827-0425
Fax: (505)827-0499
URL: http://www.state.nm.us/spd/
Contact: Charles Marquez
E-mail: cmarquez@state.nm.us

INCUBATORS/RESEARCH AND TECHNOLOGY PARKS

62726 ■ Albuquerque Technology Incubator
1009 Bradbury Dr. SE
Albuquerque, NM 87109
Ph:(505)272-7500
Fax: (505)272-7271
Co. E-mail: sfisher@wer-eas.com
Contact: Asst.

62727 ■ Eastern New Mexico University–Office of Grant and Contract Management
Station 9
Quay Hall, Rm. 113
Portales, NM 88130
Ph:(505)562-2677
Fax: (505)562-2578
Co. E-mail: Sharon.King@enmu.edu
Contact: Sharon King, Coord.
E-mail: Sharon.King@enmu.edu
Scope: Administers and coordinates both intramurally and extramurally supported research projects conducted in various units of the University, particularly in environmental sciences, education, and Southwestern archeology. Encourages faculty scholarship in bilingual and multicultural education, archeology, chemistry, fish and game, paleobotany, lipoproteins, and rocket propellents. Performs archeological surveys and excavations for government and private agencies through its subdivision, Agency for Conservation Archaeology. **Publications:** Contributions in Anthropology.

62728 ■ Lea County Economic Development Corporation
2702 N Grimes, Ste. B
Hobbs, NM 88240
Ph:(505)397-2039
Free: 800-443-2236
Fax: (505)392-2300
Co. E-mail: edclea@leaco.net
URL: http://www.leanm.org
Contact: Bethe Cunningham, Exec Dir

62729 ■ Los Alamos Commerce and Economic Development Corp.
PO Box 715
Los Alamos, NM 87544-0715
Ph:(505)662-0001
Fax: (505)662-0099
Co. E-mail: lacdc@losalamos.org
URL: http://www.losalamos.org/lacdc
Contact: Adminatrative Ass.

62730 ■ New Mexico State University–Office of the Vice Provost for Research
MSC 3RES
PO Box 30001
Las Cruces, NM 88003-8001
Ph:(505)646-3734
Fax: (505)646-2480
Co. E-mail: ovprweb@nmsu.edu
URL: http://www.nmsu.edu/docs/human/human.html
Contact: Donald L. Birx PhD, VP, Res.
E-mail: ovprweb@nmsu.edu
Scope: Serves as a coordinating office for all externally supported research at the University.

62731 ■ New Mexico Tech Research/ Industrial Park
801 Leroy Pl.
Socorro, NM 87801-4796
Ph:(505)835-5880
Fax: (505)835-5899
Co. E-mail: vpinst@admin.nmt.edu
Contact: Prof. John Juarez, VP
E-mail: vpinst@admin.nmt.edu
Scope: Facilitates the exchange of research resources between the Institute's research community and Park tenants.

62732 ■ Santa Fe Business Incubator
3900 Paseo del Sol
Santa Fe, NM 87507
Ph:(505)424-1140
Fax: (505)424-1144
Co. E-mail: info@sfbi.net
URL: http://www.sfbi.net
Contact: Marie Longserre, Pres & CEO
Description: The SFBI seeks to enhance the quality of life in Santa Fe County by supporting emerging businesses through shared resources.

62733 ■ University of New Mexico–Office of Vice Provost Research
MSC05 3370
Scholes Hall, 102/105
Albuquerque, NM 87131-6003
Ph:(505)277-2256
Fax: (505)277-5567
Co. E-mail: vpr@unm.edu
URL: http://research.unm.edu/
Contact: Terry L. Yates PhD, Vice Provost, Res.
E-mail: vpr@unm.edu
Scope: Provides general administrative support to all sponsored activities at the University for the Colleges

of Arts and Sciences, Education, Engineering, Fine Arts, Law, Business Administration, Architecture, and various institutes and divisions. Supplies information on external sources of funds for all types of research, service, and training activities; assists with preparation of proposals; approves proposal budgets; and retains files on all proposals submitted to external sources. Provides general support in the area of inventions/patents/licensing to faculty and staff. **Publications:** Research Notes (monthly).

EDUCATIONAL PROGRAMS

62734 ■ Albuquerque Technical-Vocational Institute
525 Buena Vista SE
Albuquerque, NM 87106
Ph:(505)224-3000
Fax: (505)224-4556
URL: http://www.tvi.cc.nm.us
Description: Trade and technical school offering a program in entrepreneurship.

62735 ■ Eastern New Mexico University— Roswell
PO Box 6000
Roswell, NM 88202-6000
Ph:(505)624-7000
Fax: (505)624-7119
URL: http://www.roswell.enmu.edu
Description: Part of a small business assistance center system that provides a variety of training programs, including self-paced, evening, and business courses. 1800-243-6687

62736 ■ New Mexico Junior College–Business Assistance Center
5317 Lovington Hwy.
Hobbs, NM 88240
Ph:(505)392-4510
Free: 800-657-6260
Fax: (505)392-2526
URL: http://www.nmjc.cc.nm.us
Description: Part of a small business system that provides a variety of training, including self-paced, evening, and business courses. 1-800-657-6260.

62737 ■ Northern New Mexico Community College
921 Paso de Onate
Espanola, NM 87532
Ph:(505)747-2100
Fax: (505)747-2180
URL: http://www.nnmcc.edu
Description: Part of a small business assistance center system that provides a variety of training, including self-paced, evening, and business courses.

62738 ■ Santa Fe Community College
6401 Richards Ave.
Santa Fe, NM 87505
Ph:(505)428-1000
Fax: (505)428-1237
URL: http://www.sfccnm.edu
Description: Two-year college offering programs in small business management and entrepreneurship.

LEGISLATIVE ASSISTANCE

62739 ■ Commission on the Status of Women
4001 Indian School Rd. NE, Ste. 300
Albuquerque, NM 87110
Ph:(505)841-8920
Free: 800-432-9168
Fax: (505)841-8926
URL: http://www.state.nm.us/womenscommission
Description: Assesses the needs of women in business in the state of New Mexico and formulates plans to meet those needs.

PUBLICATIONS

62740 ■ *Smart Start your New Mexico Business*
PSI Research
300 N. Valley Dr.
Grants Pass, OR 97526
Ph:(503)479-9464
Free: 800-228-2275
Fax: (503)476-1479
Co. E-mail: info@psi-research.com
URL: http://www.psi-research.com
Ed: Michael D. Jenkins. **Released:** Revised edition, 1992. **Price:** $29.95 (looseleaf binder); $24.95 (paper). **Description:** Part of the Successful Business Library series.

PUBLISHERS

62741 ■ Sun Books - Sun Publishing
PO Box 5588
Santa Fe, NM 87502-5588
Ph:(505)471-5177
Fax: (505)473-4458
Co. E-mail: info@sunbooks.com
URL: http://www.sunbooks.com
Contact: Skip Whitson, Director
Description: Publishes self-help, motivational, astrology, business, history, art, philosophy, and art books. Distributes for Far West Publishing Co. and Sun Books. **Founded:** 1973.

SMALL BUSINESS DEVELOPMENT CENTER LEAD OFFICE

62742 ■ State University of New York–New York SBDC
SUNY Plaza, S-523
Albany, NY 12246-0001
Ph:(518)443-5398
Free: 800-732-SBDC
Fax: (518)443-5398
URL: http://www.nyssbdc.org
Contact: Jim King, State Dir.
E-mail: j.king@nyssbdc.org

62743 ■ State University of New York–New York Small Business Development Center
State University Plz.
41 State St.
Albany, NY 12246-0001
Ph:(518)443-5398
Free: 800-732-7232
Fax: (518)465-5275
Contact: James L. King, State Director
E-mail: kingjl@nyssbdc.org

SMALL BUSINESS DEVELOPMENT CENTERS

62744 ■ Baruch College–Mid-town Manhattan SBDC–SBDC (Field)
Field Center
55 Lexington Ave./24th St.
New York, NY 10010-0010
Ph:(646)312-4790
Fax: (646)312-4781
Co. E-mail: Lendynette_Pacheco@baruch.suny.edu
URL: http://www.baruch.suny.edu
Contact: Monica Dean, Dir.

62745 ■ Binghamton University–Small Business Development Center
Artco Bldg., 3rd Fl.
Binghamton, NY 13901-2705
Ph:(607)777-4024
Fax: (607)777-4029
Co. E-mail: sbdc@binghamtom.edu
URL: http://www.nyssbdc.org
Contact: Douglas Boyce, Dir.

62746 ■ Boricua College–Small Business Development Center
9 Graham Ave.
Brooklyn, NY 11206
Ph:(718)963-2031
Fax: (718)963-2031
Co. E-mail: boricuasbdc@mindspring.com
URL: http://www.nyssbdc.org
Contact: Angel Roman, Dir.

62747 ■ Bronx Community College–Small Business Development Center
McCracken Hall, Rm. 14
W. 181st St. & University Ave.
Bronx, NY 10453
Ph:(718)563-3570
Fax: (718)563-3572
Contact: Adi Israeli, Dir.

62748 ■ Bronx Outreach Center–Con Edison–SBDC (560 C)
560 Cortlandt Ave.
Bronx, NY 10451
Ph:(718)563-9204
Contact: David Bradley

62749 ■ Buffalo State College–Small Business Development Center
Buffalo State College, GC206
Buffalo, NY 14222-4222
Ph:(716)878-4030
Fax: (716)878-4067
Co. E-mail: buffalosbdc@yahoo.com
URL: http://www.nyssbdc.org
Contact: Susan McCartney, Dir.

62750 ■ Clinton Community College–SBDC
Lake Shore Rd., Rte. 9 S.
136 Clinton Point Dr.
Plattsburgh, NY 12901
Ph:(518)562-4260
Fax: (518)563-9759
Contact: Nancy Sullivan, Dir.

62751 ■ Cobleskill Outreach Center–SBDC–SUNY Cobleskill (Harri)
Harrison Business Center, Bldg. A
1220 Washington Ave.
Cobleskill, NY 12043
Ph:(518)485-7647
Fax: (518)485-8223
Contact: Peter Desmond, Business Advisor

62752 ■ College of Staten Island–SBDC
Bldg. 2A, Rm. 300
2800 Victory Blvd.
Staten Island, NY 10314-9806
Ph:(718)982-2560
Fax: (718)982-2323
Co. E-mail: sleap@mail.csi.cuny.edu
URL: http://www.csi.cuny.edu
Contact: Dean Balsamini, Dir.

62753 ■ Corning Community College–Small Business Development Center
24 Denison Pkwy. W.
Corning, NY 14830-2607
Ph:(607)962-9461
Fax: (607)936-6642
URL: http://www.corning-cc.edu
Contact: Bonnie Gestwicki, Dir.
E-mail: gestwicki@corning-cc.edu

62754 ■ Downtown Rochester SBDC Outreach Center–SBDC
SUNY Brockport MetroCenter
Sibley Tower Bldg.

55 Paul St.
Rochester, NY 14604-1007
Ph:(585)395-8410
Fax: (585)395-8674
Contact: Jan Pisanczyn

62755 ■ Dunkirk Satellite–Jamestown Community College–SBDC (10807)
10807 Bennett Rd.
Dunkirk, NY 14048
Free: 800-522-7232
URL: http://www.nyssbdc.org

62756 ■ East Harlem Outreach Center–SBDC
205 E. 122nd St., 2nd Fl.
New York, NY 10035
Ph:(212)987-1806
Contact: Anthony Sanchez, Coordinator

62757 ■ Farmingdale State University of New York–Small Business Development Center
Campus Commons
2350 Rte. 110
Farmingdale, NY 11735-1735
Ph:(631)420-2765
Fax: (631)370-8895
URL: http://www.nyssbdc.org
Contact: Lucille Wesnofske, Dir.
E-mail: wesnofl@farmingdale.edu

62758 ■ Fishkill SBDC Satellite–Marist College Extension
400 Westgate Business Ctr.
Fishkill, NY 12524-2947
Ph:(845)897-3945
Fax: (845)897-4653
Contact: Arnaldo Sehwerert

62759 ■ Harlem Outreach Center–SBDC
163 W. 125th St., Rm. 1307
New York, NY 10038
Ph:(212)346-1900
Fax: (212)534-4576
Contact: Anthony Sanchez, Coordinator

62760 ■ Hempstead Outreach Center–SBDC
EOC Hempstead Outreach Center
269 Fulton Ave.
Hempstead, NY 11550-3900
Ph:(516)564-8672
Fax: (516)564-1895
Contact: Lucille Wesnofske, Asst. Dir.

62761 ■ Jamestown Community College–Small Business Development Center
525 Falconer St.
PO Box 20
Jamestown, NY 14702-0020
Ph:(716)665-5754
Free: 800-522-7232
Fax: (716)338-1476
URL: http://www.sunyjcc.edu
Contact: Irene Dobies, Dir.
E-mail: irenedobies@mail.sunyjcc.edu

62762 ■ Jefferson Community College–Small Business Development Center
1220 Coffeen St.
Watertown, NY 13601-1897
Ph:(315)782-9262
Fax: (315)782-0901
Co. E-mail: sbdc@sunnyjefferson.edu
URL: http://www.sunnyjefferson.edu
Contact: F. Eric Constance, Dir.

62763 ■ LaGuardia Community College–SBDC
29-10 Thomson Ave., 9th Fl.
Long Island City, NY 11101
Ph:(718)482-5303
Fax: (718)609-2091
Co. E-mail: sbdc@lagcc.cuny.edu
URL: http://www.lagcc.cuny.edu
Contact: Joyce Moy, Dir.

62764 ■ Lake Placid Satellite–Essex City Business Council–North Country SBDC (Lake)
Lake Placid Visitor's Bureau
216 Main St.
Lake Placid, NY 12946
Ph:(518)564-2042
URL: http://www.nyssbdc.org

62765 ■ Lehman College–Small Business Development Center
Old Gym Bldg., Rm. 007
250 Bedford Park Blvd. W.
Bronx, NY 10468-1589
Ph:(718)960-8806
Fax: (718)960-7340
Contact: Clarence Stanley, Dir.
E-mail: clarence.stanley@lehman.cuny.edu

62766 ■ Lehman College SBDC
250 Bedford Park Blvd., W.
Bronx, NY 10468-1589
Ph:(718)960-8806
Fax: (718)960-7340
URL: http://www.nyssbdc.org
Contact: Clarence Stanley, Dir.
E-mail: clarence.stanley@lehman.cuny.edu

62767 ■ Long Island University at Southhampton/Southampton Outreach Center–SBDC
Abney Peak, Montauk Hwy.
Southampton, NY 11968-4103
Ph:(631)287-0059
Fax: (631)287-8287
Contact: George Telmany, Business Advisor

62768 ■ Malone Satellite–North Country SBDC Outreach Office–OneWorkSource (158 F)
158 Finney Blvd.
Malone, NY 12953
Ph:(518)564-2042
URL: http://www.nyssbdc.org

62769 ■ Mercy College–SBDC Outreach
Mercy Hall, Rm. 39
555 Broadway
Dobbs Ferry, NY 10522
Ph:(914)674-7485
Fax: (914)693-4996
Co. E-mail: Sbusiness@mercy.edu
URL: http://www.mercy.edu
Contact: Thomas Morley, Coordinator

62770 ■ Mid-Hudson Region SBDC at Kingston
Business Resource Center
1 Development Ct.
Kingston, NY 12401-1949
Ph:(845)339-0025
Fax: (845)339-1631
Co. E-mail: sbdc@sunyulster.edu
URL: http://www.sunyulster.edu
Contact: Arnaldo Sehwerert, Dir.

62771 ■ Mid-Town Manhattan Outreach Center–Baruch College–SBDC (55 Le)
55 Lexington, Ste. 2-140
New York, NY 10010-0010
Ph:(646)312-4790
Fax: (646)312-4781
URL: http://www.midtownmanhattan.nyssbdc.org
Contact: Monica Rivera, Dir.
E-mail: monica_dean@baruch.cuny.edu

62772 ■ Niagara County Community College–International Trade Center–SBDC (50 Ma)
50 Main St.
Lockport, NY 14094-4529
Ph:(716)434-3815
Fax: (716)433-5155
Co. E-mail: sbdc@niagaracc.suny.edu
Contact: Richard Gorko, Dir.
E-mail: gorko@niagaracc.suny.edu

62773 ■ Niagara County Community College–SBDC
50 Main St.
Lockport, NY 14094
Ph:(716)434-3815
Fax: (716)433-5155
Co. E-mail: sbdc@niagaracc.suny.edu
URL: http://www.nyssbdc.org
Contact: Richard Gorko, Dir.

62774 ■ Niagara County Community College at Sanborn–Small Business Development Center
3111 Saunders Settlement Rd.
Sanborn, NY 14132-9460
Ph:(716)614-6480
Fax: (716)614-6825
Co. E-mail: sbdc@niagaracc.suny.edu
URL: http://www.sunyniagara.cc.ny.us
Contact: Richard Gorko, Dir.

62775 ■ Onondaga Community College–Small Business Development Center
Ralph & Fay Whitney Applied Technology Center
4941 Onondaga Rd., Ste. W-210
Syracuse, NY 13215-2099
Ph:(315)498-6070
Fax: (315)492-3704
Co. E-mail: sbdc@sunyocc.edu
URL: http://www.sunyocc.edu
Contact: Patricia Higgins, Dir.

62776 ■ Oswego State University–SBDC Oswego Outreach
103 Rich Hall
Oswego, NY 13126-3599
Ph:(315)312-3492
Fax: (315)312-3374
URL: http://www.nyssbdc.org

62777 ■ Pace University–Small Business Development Center
163 William St., 16th Fl.
New York, NY 10038
Ph:(212)618-6655
Fax: (212)618-6669
Co. E-mail: SBDC@Pace.edu
URL: http://www.pace.edu
Contact: Ira Davidson, Dir.
E-mail: IDavidson@PACE.edu

62778 ■ Rensselaer Polytechnical Institute–Manufacturing Technology Center–SBDC (Renss)
Rensselaer Technology Park
385 Jordan Rd.
Troy, NY 12180-8347
Ph:(518)286-1014
Fax: (518)286-1006
Contact: Bill Brigham, Dir.

62779 ■ Rockland Community College–Small Business Development Center
145 College Rd.
Suffern, NY 10901-3620
Ph:(914)356-0370

Fax: (915)356-0381
URL: http://www.sba.gov/SBDC
Contact: Thomas J. Morley, Dir.

62780 ■ Small Business Development Center at SUNY Brockport
350 New Campus Dr.
Morgan 3205
Brockport, NY 14420
Ph:(585)395-2334
Fax: (585)395-2467
Co. E-mail: sbdc@brockport.edu
URL: http://www.nyssbdc.org
Contact: Jan Pisanczyn, Dir.

62781 ■ Southern Dutchess Chamber of Commerce–SBDC Outreach Center
300 Westgate Business Ctr.
Fishkill, NY 12524-2001
Ph:(914)897-2607
Fax: (914)897-4653

62782 ■ State University Institute of Technology at Utica/Rome–Small Business Development Center
Kunsela Hall, Rm. C101
Rte. 12, N.
PO Box 3050
Utica, NY 13504-3050
Ph:(315)792-7547
Fax: (315)792-7554
URL: http://www.sunyit.edu
Contact: David Mallen, Dir.
E-mail: mallend@sunyit.edu

62783 ■ State University of New York–SUNY College at Plattsburgh–North Country SBDC (Ward)
Ward Hall 118
101 Broad St.
Plattsburgh, NY 12901
Ph:(518)564-2042
Fax: (518)564-2043
Co. E-mail: sbdc@plattsburgh.edu
URL: http://www.plattsburgh.edu
Contact: Delena Clark, Dir.

62784 ■ State University of New York at Albany–Small Business Development Center
Harriman Business Center, Bldg. 7A
1220 Washington Ave., Ste. 500
Albany, NY 12222
Ph:(518)442-5577
Fax: (518)442-5582
URL: http://www.nyssbdc.org
Contact: William Brigham, Dir.
E-mail: wbrigham@uamail.albany.edu

62785 ■ State University of New York at Buffalo–Small Business Development Center
Grover Cleveland Hall, Rm. 206
1300 Elmwood Ave.
Buffalo, NY 14222-4222
Ph:(716)878-4030
Fax: (716)878-4067
Contact: Susan McCartney, Dir.
E-mail: sue_mccartney@yahoo.com

62786 ■ Suffolk County Community College–Riverhead Outreach Center–SBDC (Orien)
Orient Bldg.
Riverhead, NY 11901
Ph:(631)287-0059
Fax: (631)287-8787
URL: http://www.nypl.org/research/sibl/smallbus/
sbdcnyc.htm
Contact: Al Falkowski

62787 ■ SUNY Canton College
Faculty Office Bldg., Rm. 202
34 Cornell Dr.
Canton, NY 13617-1098
Ph:(315)386-7312
Fax: (315)379-3814
Co. E-mail: sbdc@canton.edu
URL: http://www.canton.edu

Contact: Dale Rice, Dir.
E-mail: riced@canton.edu

62788 ■ SUNY Geneseo Outreach Center–SBDC
South Hall, Rm. 111
1 College Circle
Geneseo, NY 14454-1401
Ph:(585)245-5429
Fax: (585)245-5430
Co. E-mail: sbdc@geneseo.edu
URL: http://www.geneseo.edu
Contact: George Gotcsik, Dir.

62789 ■ SUNY at Oswego–Center for Business and Community Development–SBDC (103 R)
103 Rich Hall
Oswego, NY 13126
Ph:(315)312-5696
Fax: (315)312-3374
URL: http://www.oswego.edu/about/centers/cbcd/sbdc/index.html
Contact: Larry Perras, Senior Business Advisor
E-mail: perras@oswega.edu

62790 ■ SUNY at Stony Brook–State University of New York–SBDC (Harri)
Harriman Hall, Rm. 109
Stony Brook, NY 11794-3777
Ph:(631)632-9070
Fax: (631)632-7176
Co. E-mail: lynne.schmidt.sunysb.edu
URL: http://www.nyssbdc.org
Contact: Edward Fritz, Dir.
E-mail: efritz@notes.cc.sunysb.edu

62791 ■ Westchester SBDC
Westchester I-Park, Bldg. 3
Yonkers, NY 10701-2752
Ph:(914)375-2107
Fax: (914)375-9276
URL: http://www.nyssbdc.org
Contact: Thomas Morley, Dir.
E-mail: tmorley@mercy.edu

62792 ■ White Plains Outreach–Westchester Small Business Development Center
108 Corporate Park Dr., Ste. 101
White Plains, NY 10604
Ph:(914)948-2110
URL: http://www.nyssbdc.org

62793 ■ York College/City University of New York–Small Business Development Center
Science Bldg., Rm. 107
94-50 159th St.
Jamaica, NY 11451-9902
Ph:(718)262-2881
Fax: (718)262-2881
Co. E-mail: atitone@york.cuny.edu
URL: http://www.york.cuny.edu
Contact: Alfred Titone, Asst. Dir.

SMALL BUSINESS ASSISTANCE PROGRAMS

62794 ■ New Jersey Economic Development Department
1 River Front Plaza
Newark, NJ 07102
Ph:(973)565-5502
Fax: (973)565-5556
URL: http://www.panynj.gov
Description: Provides complete assistance packages, including financing, site selection, and construction. Package may also include labor recruitment and training.

62795 ■ New York Department of Economic Development–Division for Minority and Women Business Development
30 S Pearl St., 2nd Fl.
Albany, NY 12207
Ph:(518)292-5253

Free: 800-STA-TENY
Fax: (518)292-5803
URL: http://www.empire.state.ny.us
Description: Certify minority and women owned businesses. Monitor the compliance of state agencies. Meet the goals that the agency sets for the utility of minority and women owned businesses.

62796 ■ New York Department of Economic Development–Division for Small Business–Business Service Ombudsman (30 S)
30 S Pearl St., 7th Fl.
Albany, NY 12207
Ph:(518)292-5220
Free: 800-STA-TENY
Fax: (518)292-5884
URL: http://www.empire.state.ny.us
Description: Assists businesses in resolving red tape difficulties with all levels of government.

62797 ■ New York State Office of Science Technology and Academic Research–New York Science and Technology Foundation
30 S Pearl St., 11th Fl.
Albany, NY 12207
Ph:(518)292-5700
Fax: (518)292-5780
URL: http://www.nystar.state.ny.us
Description: Provides major services, including conducting special training programs, awarding research and development grants for university-based research, encouraging high technology, and providing grants and other services to the Centers for Advanced Technology.

62798 ■ New York State Office of Science Technology and Academic Research–New York Science and Technology Foundation–Technology Development Organizations (30 S)
30 S Pearl St., 11th Fl.
Albany, NY 12207
Ph:(518)292-5700
Fax: (518)292-5780
URL: http://www.nystar.state.ny.us
Description: Provides established small and medium-sized manufacturing businesses with knowledge, attitudes, and skills so they can address issues of technology based productivity improvements. Assistance is provided on an individualized basis.

62799 ■ State University of New York at Plattsburgh–Economic Development and Technical Assistance
Redcay, Rm. 213
101 Broad St.
Plattsburgh, NY 12901
Ph:(518)564-2214
Fax: (518)564-3220
Co. E-mail: tac@plattsburgh.edu
URL: http://www.tacsuny.com
Description: Provides technical support and data to the business community and develops and promotes new venture capital formation. Specializes in short-term management, marketing, financial packaging, and feasibility analysis services.

SCORE OFFICES

62800 ■ SCORE 588, Queens New York
c/o Anne Grant, Chair
120-55 Queens Blvd., Rm. 333
Kew Gardens, NY 11415
Ph:(718)263-8961
Fax: (718)263-9032
Co. E-mail: score588@aol.com
Contact: Anne Grant, Chair

62801 ■ SCORE Buffalo - Niagara
540 Niagara Ctr.
130 S Elmwood Ave.
Buffalo, NY 14202
Ph:(716)551-4301
Free: 800-745-0355

Fax: (716)551-4418
Co. E-mail: scorebuffalo@adelphia.net
URL: http://www.scorebuffalo.org
Description: Aims to assist entrepreneurs in the startup and growth of small businesses. Includes services such as free, confidential counseling and low-cost management workshops. Acts as a resource partner in association with the Small Business Administration.

62802 ■ SCORE Dutchess
c/o Poughkeepsie Area Chamber of Commerce
1 Civic Center Plz.
Poughkeepsie, NY 12601
Ph:(845)454-1700
Co. E-mail: scoredcny@hotmail.com
URL: http://www.scoredutchessny.org
Contact: Nancy Kappler-Foster, Chair
Description: Provides resources and expertise to maximize the success of existing and emerging small businesses. Offers business counseling and workshops.

62803 ■ SCORE Northeast
1 Computer Dr. S
Albany, NY 12205
Ph:(518)446-1118
Fax: (518)446-1228
Co. E-mail: info@scorealbany.org
URL: http://www.scorealbany.org
Contact: Elli Benno, Chm.
Description: Strives for the formation, growth, and success of small businesses. Promotes entrepreneur education in Albany area, New York.

62804 ■ SCORE Syracuse
401 S Salina St., 5th Fl.
Syracuse, NY 13202
Ph:(315)471-9393
Co. E-mail: syracusescore@juno.com
URL: http://www.score.org

62805 ■ SCORE Westchester
120 Bloomingdale Rd.
White Plains, NY 10605
Ph:(914)948-3907
Fax: (914)948-4645
Co. E-mail: scoreinfo@scorewestchester.com
URL: http://www.scorewestchester.com
Contact: Joe Brakl, Co-Chm.
Description: Strives for the formation, growth, and success of small businesses. Promotes entrepreneur education in Westchester area, New York.

BETTER BUSINESS BUREAUS

62806 ■ Better Business Bureau, Buffalo
741 Delaware Ave., Ste. 100
Buffalo, NY 14209
Ph:(716)881-5222
Free: 800-828-5000
Fax: (716)883-5349
Co. E-mail: geninquiries@upstatenybbb.org
URL: http://www.buffalo.bbb.org

62807 ■ Better Business Bureau of Metropolitan New York
257 Park Ave. S
New York, NY 10010-7384
Ph:(212)533-6200
Fax: (212)477-4912
Co. E-mail: inquiry@newyork.bbb.org
URL: http://www.newyork.bbb.org
Contact: Ronna D. Brown, Pres.

62808 ■ Better Business Bureau, Rochester
55 St. Paul St.
Rochester, NY 14604
Free: 800-828-5000
Co. E-mail: bcolmerauer@upstatenybbb.org
URL: http://www.rochester.bbb.org

62809 ■ Long Island Better Business Bureau
399 Conklin St.
Farmingdale, NY 11735-2618

Ph:(212)533-6200
Fax: (516)420-1095
Co. E-mail: longisland@newyork.bbb.org
URL: http://www.newyork.bbb.org
Contact: Ronna D. Brown, Pres.

62810 ■ Mid-Hudson Better Business Bureau
150 White Plains Rd., Ste. 107
Tarrytown, NY 10591
Ph:(212)533-6200
Fax: (914)333-7519
Co. E-mail: mhinquiries@newyork.bbb.org
URL: http://www.newyork.bbb.org
Contact: Ronna D. Brown, Pres.

CHAMBERS OF COMMERCE

62811 ■ 1000 Islands - Clayton Region Chamber of Commerce
517 Riverside Dr.
Clayton, NY 13624
Ph:(315)686-3771
Free: 800-252-9806
Fax: (315)686-5564
Co. E-mail: info@1000islands-clayton.com
URL: http://www.1000islands-clayton.com
Contact: Karen Goetz, Exec.Dir.

62812 ■ Adirondack Regional Chamber of Commerce
5 Warren St.
PO Box 158
Glens Falls, NY 12801
Ph:(518)798-1761
Free: 888-516-7247
Fax: (518)792-4147
Co. E-mail: mail@adirondackchamber.org
URL: http://www.adirondackchamber.org
Contact: Marshall Bishop, Pres.

62813 ■ Adirondacks-Speculator Region Chamber of Commerce
Routes 30 & 8
PO Box 184
Speculator, NY 12164
Ph:(518)548-4521
Fax: (518)548-4905
Co. E-mail: adrkmts@frontiernet.net
URL: http://www.adrkmts.com
Contact: Cathleen Connolly, Pres.

62814 ■ African American Chamber of Commerce of Westchester and Rockland Counties
100 Stevens Ave., Ste. 202
Mount Vernon, NY 10550
Ph:(914)699-9050
Fax: (914)699-6279
Co. E-mail: robinlisadouglas@cs.com
URL: http://www.
    africanamericanchamberofcommercenys.org
Contact: Ms. Robin L. Douglas, Pres./CEO

62815 ■ Albany-Colonie Regional Chamber of Commerce
107 Washington Ave.
Albany, NY 12210
Ph:(518)431-1400
Fax: (518)434-1339
Co. E-mail: info@ac-chamber.org
URL: http://www.ac-chamber.org
Contact: Lyn Taylor, Pres.

62816 ■ Alexandria Bay Chamber of Commerce
PO Box 365
Alexandria Bay, NY 13607
Ph:(315)482-9531
Free: 800-541-2110
Co. E-mail: info@alexbay.org
URL: http://www.alexbay.org
Contact: Thomas Weldon, Exec.Dir.

62817 ■ Amherst Chamber of Commerce
325 Essjay Rd., Ste. 200
Williamsville, NY 14221-8214

Ph:(716)632-6905
Fax: (716)632-0548
Co. E-mail: cdipirro@amherst.org
URL: http://www.amherst.org
Contact: Colleen C. DiPirro, Pres./CEO

62818 ■ Andover Chamber of Commerce
PO Box 721
Andover, NY 14806
Ph:(607)478-8455
Contact: Barbara Walker, Sec.-Treas.

62819 ■ Arcade Area Chamber of Commerce
278 Main St.
Arcade, NY 14009
Ph:(585)492-2114
Fax: (585)492-5103
Co. E-mail: lkempf@arcadechamber.org
URL: http://www.arcadechamber.org
Contact: Claudia Miller, Exec.Sec.

62820 ■ Bainbridge Chamber of Commerce
PO Box 2
Bainbridge, NY 13733
Ph:(607)967-8700
Fax: (607)967-3207
Co. E-mail: helen@mkl.com
URL: http://www.bainbridgechamberny.org
Contact: Helen Hernandez, Pres.

62821 ■ Baldwin Chamber of Commerce
PO Box 813
Baldwin, NY 11510
Ph:(516)223-8080
Fax: (516)546-8877
URL: http://www.baldwinchamber.com
Contact: Kathleen Healy Englehart, Sec.

62822 ■ Bedford Hills Chamber of Commerce
PO Box 162
Bedford Hills, NY 10507-0162
Ph:(914)381-3356
Fax: (914)241-8719
Co. E-mail: msprint@aol.com
URL: http://www.bedfordhills.org
Contact: Marcy Furman, Pres.

62823 ■ Bethlehem Chamber of Commerce
318 Delaware Ave., Main Sq.
Delmar, NY 12054-1911
Ph:(518)439-0512
Fax: (518)475-0910
Co. E-mail: info@bethlehemchamber.com
URL: http://www.bethlehemchamber.com
Contact: Marty DeLaney, Pres.

62824 ■ Blooming Grove - Washingtonville Chamber of Commerce
PO Box 454
Washingtonville, NY 10992
Ph:(845)496-5449
Fax: (845)497-7718
Contact: Carole McCann, Pres.

62825 ■ Blue Mountain Lake Association
PO Box 245
Blue Mountain Lake, NY 12812
Ph:(518)352-7659
Contact: John Collins, Pres.

62826 ■ Boonville Area Chamber of Commerce
PO Box 163
Boonville, NY 13309
Ph:(315)942-5112
Fax: (315)942-6823
Co. E-mail: info@boonvillechamber.org
URL: http://www.boonvillechamber.org

62827 ■ Brewster Chamber of Commerce
31 Main St.
Brewster, NY 10509-1528
Ph:(845)279-2477
Fax: (845)278-8349
Co. E-mail: brewster@suscom.net
URL: http://www.brewsterchamber.com
Contact: Beth R. Murtha, Exec.Dir.

62828 ■ Bronx Chamber of Commerce
1200 Waters Pl.
Bronx, NY 10461
Ph:(718)828-3900
Co. E-mail: mail@bronxchamber.org
URL: http://www.bronxmall.com
Contact: Nick Lugo, Pres.

62829 ■ Bronxville Chamber of Commerce
81 Pondfield Rd.
Bronxville, NY 10708
Ph:(914)337-6040
Fax: (914)337-6040
Co. E-mail: cocbville@aol.com
URL: http://www.bronxvillechamber.com
Contact: Sheryl Donner, Exec.Dir.

62830 ■ Brooklyn Chamber of Commerce
25 Elm Pl., Ste. 200, 2nd Fl.
Brooklyn, NY 11201
Ph:(718)875-1000
Fax: (718)237-4274
Co. E-mail: info@brooklynchamber.com
URL: http://www.ibrooklyn.com
Contact: Kenneth Adams, Pres.

62831 ■ Buffalo Niagara Partnership
665 Main St., Ste. 200
Buffalo, NY 14203
Ph:(716)852-7100
Free: 800-241-0474
Fax: (716)852-2761
Co. E-mail: info@thepartnership.org
URL: http://www.thepartnership.org
Contact: Dr. Andrew J. Rudnick, Pres./CEO

62832 ■ Business Council of Westchester
108 Corporate Park Dr., Ste. 101
White Plains, NY 10604
Ph:(914)948-2110
Fax: (914)948-0122
Co. E-mail: mgordon@westchesterny.org
URL: http://www.westchesterny.org
Contact: Dr. Marsha Gordon, Pres./CEO

62833 ■ Cairo Chamber of Commerce
PO Box 515
Cairo, NY 12413-0515
Ph:(518)622-3939
Fax: (518)622-3939
Co. E-mail: info@caironychamber.com
URL: http://caironychamber.com
Contact: M.A. Tarpinian, Admin.

62834 ■ Camden Area Chamber of Commerce
PO Box 134
Camden, NY 13316
Ph:(315)245-5000
Co. E-mail: contact@camdennychamber.com
URL: http://www.camdennychamber.com
Contact: Darrin Smith, Pres.

62835 ■ Canandaigua Chamber of Commerce
113 S Main St.
Canandaigua, NY 14424-1903
Ph:(585)394-4400
Fax: (585)394-4546
Co. E-mail: chamber@canandaigua.com
URL: http://www.canandaigua.com/chamber
Contact: Mary Beth Truini, Office Mgr.

62836 ■ Canastota Chamber of Commerce
222 S Peterboro St.
PO Box 206
Canastota, NY 13032
Ph:(315)697-3677
Co. E-mail: sales@ricksrags.com
URL: http://www.canastota.org
Contact: Rick Stevens, Co-Pres.

62837 ■ Canton Chamber of Commerce
PO Box 369
Canton, NY 13617
Ph:(315)386-8255
Fax: (315)386-8255
Co. E-mail: cantoncc@northnet.org

URL: http://www.cantonnychamber.org
Contact: Sally Roberson, Exec.Dir.

62838 ■ Cape Vincent Chamber of Commerce
175 N James St.
PO Box 482
Cape Vincent, NY 13618-0482
Ph:(315)654-2481
Fax: (315)654-4141
Co. E-mail: thecape@tds.net
URL: http://www.capevincent.org
Contact: Shelley Higgins, Exec.Dir.

62839 ■ Carmel - Kent Chamber of Commerce
PO Box 447
Carmel, NY 10512
Ph:(845)441-9623
Co. E-mail: info@carmelkentchamber.com
URL: http://www.carmelkentchamber.com
Contact: Pat Roitero, Pres.

62840 ■ Carthage Area Chamber of Commerce
313 State St., 2nd Fl.
Carthage, NY 13619
Ph:(315)493-3590
Co. E-mail: carthage@gisco.net
URL: http://www.carthageny.com
Contact: Tammy Trowbridge, Exec.Sec.

62841 ■ Cayuga County Chamber of Commerce
36 South St.
Auburn, NY 13021-3930
Ph:(315)252-7291
Fax: (315)255-3077
Co. E-mail: contact@cayugacountychamber.com
URL: http://www.cayugacountychamber.com
Contact: Terri Bridenbecker, Exec.Dir.

62842 ■ Central Islipislandia Chamber of Commerce
PO Box 542
Central Islip, NY 11749
Ph:(631)581-0510

62843 ■ Chamber of Commerce of the Bellmores
PO Box 861
Bellmore, NY 11710-0861
Ph:(516)679-1875
Fax: (516)409-0544
Co. E-mail: bellmorecc@aol.com
URL: http://www.bellmorechamber.com
Contact: Ms. Joni Caputo, Exec.Dir.

62844 ■ Chamber of Commerce of the Borough of Queens
7520 Astoria Blvd., Ste. 140
East Elmhurst, NY 11370-1131
Ph:(718)898-8500
Fax: (718)898-8599
Co. E-mail: info@queenschamber.org
URL: http://www.queenschamber.org
Contact: William R. Egan, Exec.VP

62845 ■ Chamber of Commerce of Greater Bay Shore
PO Box 5110
Bay Shore, NY 11706
Ph:(631)665-7003
Fax: (631)665-5204
URL: http://www.bayshorecommerce.com
Contact: Donna Periconi, Exec. Dir.

62846 ■ Chamber of Commerce of the Greater Ronkonkoma
PO Box 2546
Ronkonkoma, NY 11779
Ph:(631)471-0302
Co. E-mail: info@ronkonkomachamber.com
URL: http://www.ronkonkomachamber.com
Contact: Arnold Quaranta, Pres.

62847 ■ Chamber of Commerce of the Massapequas
674 Broadway
Massapequa, NY 11758
Ph:(516)541-1443
Fax: (516)541-8625
Co. E-mail: webmaster@massapequachamber.com
URL: http://www.massapequachamber.com
Contact: Joyce Hewston, Pres.

62848 ■ Chamber of Commerce of the Mastics and Shirley
PO Box 4
Mastic, NY 11950
Ph:(631)399-2228
Co. E-mail: info@maticsshirleychamber.com
URL: http://www.masticshirleychamber.com
Contact: Barbara Giaccone, Pres.

62849 ■ Chamber of Commerce of the Nyacks
PO Box 677
Nyack, NY 10960-0677
Ph:(845)353-2221
Fax: (845)353-4204
Co. E-mail: info@nyack-ny.com
URL: http://www.nyack-ny.com
Contact: Lorie Reynolds, Exec. Dir.

62850 ■ Chamber of Commerce of Olean and Vicinity
319 N Union St.
Olean, NY 14760
Ph:(716)373-4230
Free: 800-381-5463
Fax: (716)372-1204
Co. E-mail: margek9061@aol.com
URL: http://oleanny.org
Contact: Margaret Kenney, Pres.

62851 ■ Chamber of Commerce of the Rockaways
253 Beach 116th St.
Rockaway Park, NY 11694
Ph:(718)634-1300
Fax: (718)634-9623
Co. E-mail: rockawaychamber@aol.com
URL: http://www.rockawaychamberofcommerce.com
Contact: Joanie Omeste, Exec.Dir.

62852 ■ Chamber of Commerce of the Tonawandas
15 Webster St.
North Tonawanda, NY 14120
Ph:(716)692-5120
Fax: (716)692-1867
Co. E-mail: chamber@the-tonawandas.com
URL: http://www.the-tonawandas.com
Contact: Paul D. Flash, Exec. Dir.

62853 ■ Chamber of Commerce of Ulster County
55 Albany Ave.
Kingston, NY 12401
Ph:(845)338-5100
Fax: (845)338-0968
Co. E-mail: info@ulsterchamber.org
URL: http://ulsterchamber.org
Contact: Ward Todd, Pres.

62854 ■ Chamber of Commerce of the Willistons
PO Box 207
Williston Park, NY 11596
Ph:(516)739-1943
Co. E-mail: info@chamberofthewillistons.org
URL: http://www.chamberofthewillistons.org
Contact: Maura Clancy, Pres.

62855 ■ Chautauqua County Chamber of Commerce
10785 Bennett Rd.
Dunkirk, NY 14048
Ph:(716)366-6200
Fax: (716)366-4276
Co. E-mail: cccc@chautauquachamber.org
URL: http://www.chautauquachamber.org

Contact: Pamela S. Lydic, Pres./CEO

62856 ■ Cheektowaga Chamber of Commerce
Apple Tree Business Park
2875 Union Rd., Ste. 50
Cheektowaga, NY 14227
Ph:(716)684-5838
Fax: (716)684-5571
Co. E-mail: chamber@cheektowaga.org
URL: http://www.cheektowaga.org
Contact: Debra S. Liegl, Pres./CEO

62857 ■ Chemung County Chamber of Commerce
400 E Church St.
Elmira, NY 14901-2803
Ph:(607)734-5137
Free: 800-MARK-TWAIN
Fax: (607)734-4490
Co. E-mail: info@chemungchamber.org
URL: http://www.chemungchamber.org
Contact: Kevin D. Keeley, Pres./CEO

62858 ■ Clarence Chamber of Commerce
8975 Main St.
Clarence, NY 14031
Ph:(716)631-3888
Fax: (716)631-3946
Co. E-mail: info@clarence.org
URL: http://www.clarence.org
Contact: Jamie Keller, Pres.

62859 ■ Clifton Springs Area Chamber of Commerce
PO Box 86
Clifton Springs, NY 14432
Ph:(315)462-8200
Co. E-mail: info@cliftonspringschamber.com
URL: http://www.cliftonspringschamber.com
Contact: Michael Fullerton, Pres.

62860 ■ Clinton - Oneida County Chamber of Commerce
PO Box 142
Clinton, NY 13323-0142
Ph:(315)853-1735
Fax: (315)853-1735
Co. E-mail: info@clintonnychamber.org
URL: http://www.clintonnychamber.org
Contact: Ferris J. Betrus, Exec.VP

62861 ■ Cold Spring - Garrison Area Chamber of Commerce
PO Box 36
Cold Spring, NY 10516
Ph:(845)265-3200
Co. E-mail: info@csgchamber.org
URL: http://www.hvgateway.com/CHAMBER.HTM
Contact: Cathryn Fadde, Pres.

62862 ■ Colonie Chamber of Commerce
950 New Loudon Rd.
Latham, NY 12110
Ph:(518)785-6995
Fax: (518)785-7173
Co. E-mail: info@coloniechamber.org
URL: http://www.lathamchamber.org
Contact: Jay Cloutier, Exec.Dir.

62863 ■ Columbia County Chamber of Commerce
507 Warren St.
Hudson, NY 12534-2801
Ph:(518)828-4417
Co. E-mail: mail@columbiachamber-ny.com
URL: http://www.columbiachamber-ny.com
Contact: David B. Colby, Pres.

62864 ■ Coney Island Chamber of Commerce
1015 Surf Ave.
Brooklyn, NY 11224
Ph:(718)266-1234
Fax: (718)714-0379
Co. E-mail: info@coneyislandchamberofcommerce.
com
URL: http://www.coneyislandchamberofcommerce.
com

Contact: Al O'Hagan, Chm.

62865 ■ Cooperstown Chamber of Commerce
31 Chestnut St.
Cooperstown, NY 13326
Ph:(607)547-9983
Fax: (607)547-6006
Co. E-mail: info1@cooperstownchamber.org
URL: http://www.cooperstownchamber.org
Contact: Polly Renckens, Exec. Dir.

62866 ■ Cortland County Chamber of Commerce
37 Church St.
Cortland, NY 13045
Ph:(607)756-2814
Fax: (607)756-4698
Co. E-mail: info@cortlandchamber.com
URL: http://www.cortlandchamber.com
Contact: Garry L. VanGorder, Exec.Dir.

62867 ■ Council of Dedicated Merchants Chamber of Commerce
PO Box 512
Miller Place, NY 11764-0512
Ph:(631)821-1313
Fax: (631)928-6504
Co. E-mail: cdmchamber@yahoo.com
URL: http://www.cdmlongisland.com
Contact: Michael Poveromo, Exec.Dir.

62868 ■ Croton Chamber of Commerce
PO Box 111
Croton on Hudson, NY 10520
Ph:(914)271-2196
Contact: Dr. Gregory Schmidt, Pres.

62869 ■ Cutchogue - New Suffolk Chamber of Commerce
PO Box 610
Cutchogue, NY 11935
Ph:(631)734-2335
Co. E-mail: jimtrent22@aol.com
URL: http://www.cutchoguenewsuffolk.org
Contact: Jim Trentalange, Pres.

62870 ■ Dansville Chamber of Commerce
PO Box 105
126 Main St.
Dansville, NY 14437-0105
Ph:(585)335-6920
Free: 800-949-0174
Fax: (585)335-6920
Co. E-mail: dansvillechamber@hotmail.com
URL: http://www.dansvilleny.net
Contact: Richard D. De Asis, Pres.

62871 ■ Delaware County Chamber of Commerce
114 Main St.
Delhi, NY 13753
Ph:(607)746-2281
Fax: (607)746-3571
Co. E-mail: info@delawarecounty.org
URL: http://www.delawarecounty.org
Contact: Mary Beth Silano, Exec.Dir.

62872 ■ Deposit Chamber of Commerce
PO Box 222
Deposit, NY 13754
Ph:(607)467-2556
Co. E-mail: miltpetzold@tds.net
URL: http://www.depositchamber.com
Contact: Jeanne Owens, Pres.

62873 ■ East Hampton Chamber of Commerce
79A Main St.
East Hampton, NY 11937-2730
Ph:(631)324-0362
Fax: (631)329-1642
Co. E-mail: info@easthamptonchamber.com
URL: http://easthamptonchamber.com
Contact: Marina Van, Exec. Dir.

62874 ■ Eastchester - Tuckahoe Chamber of Commerce
PO Box 66
Eastchester, NY 10709
Ph:(914)779-7344
Contact: Elena Marie Teruso, Pres.

62875 ■ Ellenville - Wawarsing Chamber of Commerce
PO Box 227
Ellenville, NY 12428
Ph:(845)647-4620
Co. E-mail: chamberofcommerce2@hvc.rr.com
URL: http://ellenvillewawarsingchamberofcommerce.
    com
Contact: Red Roudis, Office Sec.

62876 ■ Ellicottville Chamber of Commerce
PO Box 456
Ellicottville, NY 14731
Free: 800-349-9099
Fax: (716)699-5637
Co. E-mail: info@ellicottvilleny.com
URL: http://www.ellicottvilleny.com
Contact: Brian McFadden, Exec.Dir.

62877 ■ Fair Haven Area Chamber of Commerce
PO Box 13
Fair Haven, NY 13064
Ph:(315)947-6037
Fax: (315)947-6037
Co. E-mail: info@shawnsmarina.com
URL: http://www.fairhavenny.com
Contact: Dave Wray, Pres.

62878 ■ Farmington Chamber of Commerce
1000 County Rd. 8
Farmington, NY 14425
Ph:(315)986-8100
Fax: (315)986-4377
Contact: Rose M. Kleman, Pres.

62879 ■ Fort Edward Chamber of Commerce
119 Broadway
PO Box 267
Fort Edward, NY 12828-0267
Ph:(518)747-3000
Fax: (518)747-2493
Contact: Joanne Fuller, Pres.

62880 ■ Fredonia Chamber of Commerce
5 E Main St.
Fredonia, NY 14063-1827
Ph:(716)679-1565
Fax: (716)672-5240
Co. E-mail: fredcham@netsync.net
URL: http://www.fredoniachamber.org
Contact: Mary Beth Fagan, Exec.Dir.

62881 ■ Fulton County Regional Chamber of Commerce and Industry
2 N Main St.
Gloversville, NY 12078
Ph:(518)725-0641
Free: 800-676-3858
Fax: (518)725-0643
Co. E-mail: info@fultoncountyny.org
URL: http://www.fultoncountyny.org
Contact: Mr. Wally Hart, Pres.

62882 ■ Garden City Chamber of Commerce
45 Seventh St.
Garden City, NY 11530
Ph:(516)747-3000
Free: 877-549-0400
Co. E-mail: gcchamber@verizon.net
URL: http://www.gardencitychamber.org
Contact: Althea Robinson, Exec. Dir.

62883 ■ Genesee County Chamber of Commerce
210 E Main St.
Batavia, NY 14020-2227
Ph:(585)343-7440
Free: 800-622-2686
Fax: (585)343-7487

Co. E-mail: chamber@geneseeny.com
URL: http://www.geneseeny.com
Contact: Lynn Freeman, Pres.

62884 ■ Geneva Area Chamber of Commerce
35 Lakefront Dr.
PO Box 587
Geneva, NY 14456
Ph:(315)789-1776
Free: 877-543-6382
Fax: (315)789-3993
Co. E-mail: info@genevany.com
URL: http://www.genevany.com
Contact: Rob Gladden, Pres./CEO

62885 ■ Glen Cove Chamber of Commerce
PO Box 721
Glen Cove, NY 11542
Ph:(516)676-6666
Fax: (516)676-5490
Co. E-mail: info@glencovechamber.org
URL: http://www.glencovechamber.org
Contact: Craig Goldstein, Pres.

62886 ■ Goshen Chamber of Commerce
44 Park Pl.
PO Box 506
Goshen, NY 10924-0506
Ph:(845)294-7741
Fax: (845)294-3998
Co. E-mail: chamber@goshennychamber.com
URL: http://www.goshennychamber.com
Contact: Pip Klein, Exec.Dir.

62887 ■ Gowanda Area Chamber of Commerce
PO Box 45
Gowanda, NY 14070-0045
Ph:(716)532-2834
Co. E-mail: gowandausa@yahoo.com
URL: http://www.gowandachamber.org
Contact: Dale M. Kosh, Pres.

62888 ■ Grand Island Chamber of Commerce
2257 Grand Island Blvd.
Grand Island, NY 14072
Ph:(716)773-3651
Fax: (716)773-3316
Co. E-mail: info@gichamber.org
URL: http://www.gichamber.org
Contact: Beverly Kinney, Pres.

62889 ■ Great Neck Chamber of Commerce
643 Middle Neck Rd.
Great Neck, NY 11023
Ph:(516)487-2000
Fax: (516)829-5472
Co. E-mail: info@greatneckchamber.org
URL: http://www.greatneckchamber.org
Contact: David L. Lurie, Admin.Sec.

62890 ■ Greater Baldwinsville Chamber of Commerce
50 Oswego St.
Baldwinsville, NY 13027
Ph:(315)638-0550
Co. E-mail: bchamber@gisco.net
URL: http://www.baldwinsvillechamber.com
Contact: Charlie Farrell, Pres.

62891 ■ Greater Bath Area Chamber of Commerce
10 Pulteney Sq. W
Bath, NY 14810
Ph:(607)776-7122
Co. E-mail: email@bathnychamber.com
URL: http://www.bathnychamber.com
Contact: Faye Ballantine, Pres.

62892 ■ Greater Binghamton Chamber of Commerce
Metrocentre
49 Court St.
PO Box 995
Binghamton, NY 13902-0995
Ph:(607)772-8860
Fax: (607)772-4513

Co. E-mail: chamber@binghamtonchamber.com
URL: http://www.binghamtonchamber.com
Contact: Alex S. DePersis, Pres./CEO

62893 ■ Greater Brockport Chamber of Commerce
PO Box 119
Brockport, NY 14420
Ph:(585)234-1512
URL: http://www.brockportchamber.org
Contact: Nancy Duff

62894 ■ Greater Cazenovia Area Chamber of Commerce
59 Albany St.
Cazenovia, NY 13035
Ph:(315)655-9243
Free: 888-218-6305
Fax: (315)655-9244
Co. E-mail: cazchamber@alltel.net
URL: http://www.cazenoviachamber.com
Contact: Mr. Paul C. Brooks, Chm.

62895 ■ Greater Corning Area Chamber of Commerce
1 W Market St., Ste. 302
Corning, NY 14830
Ph:(607)936-4686
Free: (866)463-6264
Fax: (607)936-4685
Co. E-mail: info@corningny.com
URL: http://www.corningny.com
Contact: Coleen Fabrizi, Pres.

62896 ■ Greater East Aurora Chamber of Commerce
431 Main St.
East Aurora, NY 14052-1783
Ph:(716)652-8444
Free: 800-441-2881
Fax: (716)652-8384
Co. E-mail: eanycc@choiceonemail.com
URL: http://www.eanycc.com
Contact: Gary D. Grote, Exec.Dir.

62897 ■ Greater Fulton Chamber of Commerce
41 S 2nd St.
PO Box 148
Fulton, NY 13069
Ph:(315)598-4231
Free: 800-FUL-TON1
Fax: (315)592-9050
Co. E-mail: bsaunder@twcny.rr.com
Contact: Betsy Sherman-Saunders, Pres.

62898 ■ Greater Gouverneur Chamber of Commerce
214 E Main St.
Lawrence Manor Bldg.
Gouverneur, NY 13642
Ph:(315)287-0331
Fax: (315)287-3694
Co. E-mail: gouvcofc@northnet.org
URL: http://www.gouverneurchamber.net
Contact: Donna M. Lawrence, Exec. Dir.

62899 ■ Greater Greenwich Chamber of Commerce
6 Academy St.
Greenwich, NY 12834-1002
Ph:(518)692-7979
Fax: (518)692-7979
Co. E-mail: info@greenwichchamber.org
URL: http://www.greenwichchamber.org
Contact: Kathy Nichols-Tomkins, Sec.

62900 ■ Greater Harlem Chamber of Commerce
200A W 136th St.
New York, NY 10030
Ph:(212)862-7200
Fax: (212)862-8745
Co. E-mail: info@harlemdiscover.com
URL: http://www.chamber.harlemdiscover.com
Contact: Lloyd Williams, Pres./CEO

62901 ■ Greater Liverpool Chamber of Commerce
314 2nd St.
Liverpool, NY 13088
Ph:(315)457-3895
Fax: (315)234-3226
Co. E-mail: chamber@liverpoolchamber.com
URL: http://www.liverpoolchamber.com
Contact: Mary F. Price, Exec.Dir.

62902 ■ Greater Mahopac-Carmel Chamber of Commerce
953 S Lake Blvd.
PO Box 160
Mahopac, NY 10541-0160
Ph:(845)628-5553
Fax: (845)628-5962
Co. E-mail: mchamber@computer.net
URL: http://www.mahopacchamber.com
Contact: Kevin Bailey, Exec. Dir.

62903 ■ Greater Massena Chamber of Commerce
50 Main St.
Massena, NY 13662
Ph:(315)769-3525
Fax: (315)769-5295
Co. E-mail: chamber@massenaworks.com
URL: http://www.massenany.com
Contact: Paul Haggett, Exec.Dir.

62904 ■ Greater Mexico Chamber of Commerce
PO Box 158
Mexico, NY 13114
Ph:(315)963-1042
Co. E-mail: bj2green@aol.com
URL: http://www.greatermexicochamber.com
Contact: Steve Miller, Pres.

62905 ■ Greater New York Chamber of Commerce
172 Madison Ave., 17th Fl.
New York, NY 10016
Ph:(212)686-7220
Fax: (212)686-7232
Co. E-mail: info@chamber.com
URL: http://www.chamber.com
Contact: Mark S. Jaffe, Pres./CEO

62906 ■ Greater Ogdensburg Chamber of Commerce
1020 Park St.
Ogdensburg, NY 13669
Ph:(315)393-3620
Fax: (315)393-1380
Co. E-mail: chamber@gisco.net
URL: http://www.ogdensburgny.com
Contact: Sandra Porter, Exec. Dir.

62907 ■ Greater Olean Area Chamber of Commerce
120 N Union St.
Olean, NY 14760
Ph:(716)372-4433
Fax: (716)372-7912
Co. E-mail: info@oleanny.com
URL: http://www.oleanny.com
Contact: John Sayegh, COO

62908 ■ Greater Oneida Chamber of Commerce
136 Lenox Ave.
Oneida, NY 13421
Ph:(315)363-4300
Fax: (315)361-4558
Co. E-mail: executivedirector@oneidachamber.com
URL: http://www.oneidachamber.com
Contact: Brett N. Bogardus, Exec. Dir.

62909 ■ Greater Ossining Chamber of Commerce
PO Box 382
Ossining, NY 10562
Ph:(914)941-0009
Fax: (914)381-3131
Co. E-mail: mail@ossiningchamber.org

URL: http://www.ossiningchamber.org
Contact: Maureen Redmond, Pres.

62910 ■ Greater Oswego Chamber of Commerce
44 E Bridge St.
Oswego, NY 13126
Ph:(315)343-7681
Fax: (315)342-0831
Co. E-mail: gocc@oswegochamber.com
URL: http://oswegochamber.com
Contact: Jennifer B. Hill, Exec. Dir.

62911 ■ Greater Patchogue Chamber of Commerce
15 N Ocean Ave.
Patchogue, NY 11772-2001
Ph:(631)475-0121
Co. E-mail: info@patchoguechamber.com
URL: http://www.patchoguechamber.com
Contact: Charles Baker, Sec.-Treas.

62912 ■ Greater Port Jefferson Chamber of Commerce
118 W Broadway
Port Jefferson, NY 11777-1314
Ph:(631)473-1414
Fax: (631)474-4540
Co. E-mail: gpjchamber@optonline.net
URL: http://www.portjeffchamber.com
Contact: Samir Nizam, Pres.

62913 ■ Greater Rochester Metro Chamber of Commerce, International Business Council
55 St. Paul St.
Rochester, NY 14604-1391
Ph:(716)454-2220
Fax: (716)263-3679

62914 ■ Greater Rochester Metro Chamber of Commerce, Retail Rochester
55 St. Paul St.
Rochester, NY 14604-1391
Ph:(716)454-2220
Fax: (716)263-3679

62915 ■ Greater Southern Dutchess Chamber of Commerce
Nussbickel Bldg.
2582 S Ave.
Wappingers Falls, NY 12590
Ph:(845)296-0001
Fax: (845)296-0006
Co. E-mail: annm@gsdcc.org
URL: http://www.gsdcc.org
Contact: Ann Meagher, Pres./CEO

62916 ■ Greater Syracuse Chamber of Commerce
572 S Salina St.
Syracuse, NY 13202-3320
Ph:(315)470-1800
Fax: (315)471-8545
Co. E-mail: info@syracusechamber.com
URL: http://www.syracusechamber.com
Contact: Ms. Darlene Kerr, Pres.

62917 ■ Greater Warsaw Chamber of Commerce
PO Box 221
Warsaw, NY 14569
Co. E-mail: couriernews@frontiernet.net
URL: http://www.warsawchamber.com
Contact: Dolly Pierson, Pres.

62918 ■ Greater Watertown - North Country Chamber of Commerce
1241 Coffeen St.
Watertown, NY 13601
Ph:(315)788-4400
Fax: (315)788-3369
Co. E-mail: chamber@watertownny.com
URL: http://www.watertownny.com
Contact: Karen K. Delmonico, Pres./CEO

62919 ■ Greater Westhampton Chamber of Commerce
PO Box 1228
Westhampton Beach, NY 11978
Ph:(631)288-3337
Fax: (631)288-3322
Co. E-mail: info@whbcc.org
URL: http://www.whbcc.org
Contact: Jennifer Truscott, Pres.

62920 ■ Greene County Chamber of Commerce
1 Bridge St.
Catskill, NY 12414
Ph:(518)943-4222
Fax: (518)943-1700
Co. E-mail: chamber@greenecounty-chamber.com
URL: http://www.greenecounty-chamber.com
Contact: Tracy McNally, Exec. Dir.

62921 ■ Greenport Southold Chamber of Commerce
PO Box 1415
Southold, NY 11971
Ph:(631)765-3161
Co. E-mail: info@greenportsoutholdchamber.org
URL: http://www.greenportsoutholdchamber.org
Contact: Sal Saporito, Pres.

62922 ■ Greenvale Chamber of Commerce
PO Box 123
Greenvale, NY 11548
Ph:(516)621-2110
URL: http://www.greenvalechamber.com
Contact: Michael Lucarelli, Sec.

62923 ■ Greenwich Village-Chelsea Chamber of Commerce
853 Broadway, Ste. 800
New York, NY 10003
Ph:(212)255-5811
Fax: (212)255-5058
Co. E-mail: info@villagechelsea.com
URL: http://www.villagechelsea.com
Contact: Mr. Sean Oakley, Project Mgr.

62924 ■ Guilderland Chamber of Commerce
Pega Plz., Ste. 105
2021 Western Ave.
Albany, NY 12203
Ph:(518)456-6611
Fax: (518)456-6690
Co. E-mail: info@guilderlandchamber.com
URL: http://www.guilderlandchamber.com
Contact: Jane Schramm, Exec.Dir.

62925 ■ Hamburg Chamber of Commerce
8 S Buffalo St.
Hamburg, NY 14075-6261
Ph:(716)649-7917
Free: 877-322-6890
Fax: (716)649-6362
Co. E-mail: mail@hamburg-chamber.org
URL: http://www.hamburg-chamber.org
Contact: Betty B. Newell, Pres./CEO

62926 ■ Hampton Bays Chamber of Commerce
140 W Main St., Ste. 1
Hampton Bays, NY 11946
Ph:(631)728-2211
Fax: (631)728-0308
Co. E-mail: hamptonbayschamber@verizon.net
URL: http://www.hamptonbayschamber.com
Contact: Stan Glinka, Pres.

62927 ■ Harrison Chamber of Commerce
1 Heineman Pl.
Harrison, NY 10528
Ph:(914)835-7039
Fax: (914)835-7039
Co. E-mail: harrisoncc04@yahoo.com
URL: http://www.theharrisoncofc.org
Contact: Ada B. Angarano, Pres./CEO

62928 ■ Hastings-on-Hudson Chamber of Commerce
PO Box 405
Hastings-on-Hudson, NY 10706
Ph:(914)478-0900
Fax: (914)478-1720
Contact: Joseph R. LoCascio Jr., Pres.

62929 ■ Heart of Catskill Association - Catskill Chamber of Commerce
362 Main St.
PO Box 248
Catskill, NY 12414
Ph:(518)943-0989
Fax: (518)943-0989
Co. E-mail: hoca@mhonline.net
Contact: Linda Overbaugh, Exec.Dir.

62930 ■ Hempstead Chamber of Commerce
PO Box 4264
1776 Nichols Ct.
Hempstead, NY 11550
Ph:(516)483-2000
Fax: (516)489-5997
Co. E-mail: president@hempsteadchamber.com
URL: http://www.hempsteadchamber.org
Contact: Spence Kerniss, Pres.

62931 ■ Herkimer County Chamber of Commerce
28 W Main St.
PO Box 129
Mohawk, NY 13407-0129
Ph:(315)866-7820
Fax: (315)866-7833
Co. E-mail: hcccomm@ntcnet.com
Contact: Matthew Stubley, Exec.Dir.

62932 ■ Hicksville Chamber of Commerce
10 W Marie St.
Hicksville, NY 11801-3804
Ph:(516)931-7170
Fax: (516)931-8546
Co. E-mail: hicksvillechamber@earthlink.net
URL: http://www.hicksvillechamber.com
Contact: Judith K. Lombardi, Exec.Sec.

62933 ■ Hudson Falls-Kingsbury Chamber of Commerce
PO Box 346
Hudson Falls, NY 12839
Ph:(518)747-3290
Fax: (518)746-9002
Co. E-mail: info@hudsonfallsnewyork.net
URL: http://www.hudsonfallsnewyork.net/chamber
Contact: Dennis Monahan, Pres.

62934 ■ Hudson Valley Gateway Chamber of Commerce
1 S Division St.
Peekskill, NY 10566
Ph:(914)737-3600
Fax: (914)737-0541
Co. E-mail: info@hvgatewaychamber.com
URL: http://www.hvgatewaychamber.com
Contact: Robin Alexander, Office Mgr.

62935 ■ Huntington Township Chamber of Commerce
164 Main St.
Huntington, NY 11743-3383
Ph:(631)423-6100
Fax: (631)351-8276
Co. E-mail: ellen@chamberli.com
URL: http://www.huntingtonchamber.com
Contact: Ellen O'Brien, Dir. of Administration

62936 ■ Hyde Park Chamber of Commerce
PO Box 17
Hyde Park, NY 12538
Ph:(845)229-8612
Fax: (845)229-8638
Co. E-mail: info@hydeparkchamber.org
URL: http://www.hydeparkchamber.org
Contact: Elizabeth L. Roger, Pres.

62937 ■ Inlet Information Office
160 Rte. 28
PO Box 266
Inlet, NY 13360-0266
Ph:(315)357-5501
Free: (866)GOI-NLET
Fax: (315)357-3570
Co. E-mail: inletny@eagle-wireless.com
URL: http://www.inletny.com
Contact: Adele Burnett, Tourism Dir.

62938 ■ Islip Chamber of Commerce
PO Box 112
Islip, NY 11751-0112
Ph:(631)581-2720
Fax: (631)581-2720
Co. E-mail: info@islipchamberofcommerce.com
URL: http://www.islipchamberofcommerce.com
Contact: Eric S. Buehler, Pres.

62939 ■ Jamaica Chamber of Commerce
90-25 161st St., Ste. 505
Jamaica, NY 11432
Ph:(718)657-4800
Fax: (718)658-4642
Co. E-mail: jamaicachamber@earthline.com
Contact: Robert M. Richards, Pres.

62940 ■ Japanese Chamber of Commerce and Industry of New York
145 W 57th St.
New York, NY 10019
Ph:(212)246-8001
Fax: (212)246-8002
Co. E-mail: info@jcciny.org
URL: http://www.jcciny.org
Contact: Motoatsu Sakurai, Pres.

62941 ■ Kenmore-Town of Tonawanda Chamber of Commerce
3411 Delaware Ave.
Kenmore, NY 14217-1422
Ph:(716)874-1202
Free: 888-281-1680
Fax: (716)874-3151
Co. E-mail: info@ken-ton.org
URL: http://www.ken-ton.org
Contact: Ms. Tracey Longboat, Exec.Dir.

62942 ■ Kings Park Chamber of Commerce
PO Box 322
Kings Park, NY 11754
Ph:(631)269-7678
Fax: (631)269-5575
Co. E-mail: kingsparkchamber@kingsparkli.com
URL: http://www.kingsparkli.com
Contact: Charles Gardner, Pres.

62943 ■ Lackawanna Area Chamber of Commerce
638 Ridge Rd.
Lackawanna, NY 14218
Ph:(716)823-8841
Free: 800-747-8841
Fax: (716)823-8848
Co. E-mail: info@lackawannachamber.com
URL: http://www.lackawannachamber.com
Contact: Edy Molly, Administrator

62944 ■ Lake George Regional Chamber of Commerce
PO Box 272
2176 State Rte. 9
Lake George, NY 12845-0272
Ph:(518)668-5755
Free: 800-705-0059
Fax: (518)668-4286
Co. E-mail: info@lakegeorgechamber.com
URL: http://www.lakegeorgechamber.com

62945 ■ Lake Placid Chamber of Commerce
2610 Main St., Ste. 2
Lake Placid, NY 12946
Ph:(518)523-2445
Free: 800-447-5224
Fax: (518)523-2605
Co. E-mail: visitorservice@lakeplacid.com

URL: http://www.lakeplacid.com
Contact: James McKenna, Pres./CEO

62946 ■ Lancaster Area Chamber of Commerce
PO Box 284
Lancaster, NY 14086
Ph:(716)681-9755
Fax: (716)684-3385
Co. E-mail: info@laccny.org
URL: http://www.laccny.org
Contact: Kathy Konst, Pres./CEO

62947 ■ Lewis County Chamber of Commerce
7383-C Utica Blvd.
Lowville, NY 13367
Ph:(315)376-2213
Fax: (315)376-0326
Co. E-mail: lcchambr@northnet.org
URL: http://www.lewiscountychamber.org
Contact: Bethany Yost, Interim Exec.Dir.

62948 ■ Livingston County Chamber of Commerce
4635 Millennium Dr.
Geneseo, NY 14454
Ph:(585)243-2222
Fax: (585)243-4824
Co. E-mail: coswald@frontiernet.net
URL: http://livchamber.com
Contact: Cynthia Oswald, Pres.

62949 ■ Long Beach Chamber of Commerce
350 National Blvd.
Long Beach, NY 11561-3312
Ph:(516)432-6000
Fax: (516)432-0273
URL: http://www.longbeachnychamber.com
Contact: Michael J. Kerr, Exec. Dir.

62950 ■ Long Island Association
300 Broadhollow Rd., Ste. 110W
Melville, NY 11747-4840
Ph:(631)499-4400
Fax: (631)499-2194
Co. E-mail: info@longislandassociation.org
URL: http://www.longislandassociation.org
Contact: Matthew T. Crosson, Pres.

62951 ■ Lyons Chamber of Commerce
PO Box 39
Lyons, NY 14489
Ph:(315)573-8170
Co. E-mail: videomark@gmail.com
URL: http://www.lyonsny.com
Contact: Mark De Cracker, Pres.

62952 ■ Malone Chamber of Commerce
170 E Main St.
Malone, NY 12953
Ph:(518)483-3760
Free: 877-625-6631
Fax: (518)483-3172
Co. E-mail: info@malonenychamber.com
URL: http://www.malonenychamber.com
Contact: Stephanie Hall, Exec.Dir.

62953 ■ Mamaroneck Chamber of Commerce
430 Center Ave.
Mamaroneck, NY 10543
Ph:(914)698-4400
Fax: (914)698-4541
Contact: Jo Loden, Exec.Dir.

62954 ■ Manhasset Chamber of Commerce
PO Box 754
Manhasset, NY 11030-2333
Ph:(516)627-1098
Fax: (516)365-7644
Co. E-mail: chamber@manhasset.org
URL: http://www.manhasset.org
Contact: Diane Harragan, Co-Pres.

62955 ■ Manhattan Chamber of Commerce
215 Park Ave. S, Ste. 1255
New York, NY 10003

Ph:(212)479-7772
Fax: (212)473-8074
Co. E-mail: info@manhattancc.org
URL: http://www.manhattancc.org
Contact: Nancy Ploeger, Pres.

62956 ■ Mattituck Chamber of Commerce
PO Box 1056
Mattituck, NY 11952
Ph:(631)298-5757
Co. E-mail: info@mattituckchamber.org
URL: http://www.mattituckchamber.org
Contact: Domenico Mautarelli, Pres.

62957 ■ Mayville - Chatauqua Area Chamber of Commerce
PO Box 22
Mayville, NY 14757-0022
Ph:(716)753-3113
Fax: (716)753-3113
Co. E-mail: mccc@madbbs.com
URL: http://mayville-chautauquachamber.org
Contact: Deborah Marsala, Coor.

62958 ■ Mechanicville Area Chamber of Commerce
221 Park Ave.
PO Box 205
Mechanicville, NY 12118
Ph:(518)664-7791
Fax: (518)664-0826
Co. E-mail: mechcham@msn.com
Contact: Sharon Zappola, Pres.

62959 ■ Mineola Chamber of Commerce
PO Box 62
Mineola, NY 11501
Ph:(516)408-3554
Co. E-mail: info@mineolachamber.com
URL: http://www.mineolachamber.com
Contact: Carmela Bernacchio, Pres.

62960 ■ Mohawk Valley Chamber of Commerce
520 Seneca St., 3rd Fl.
Utica, NY 13502
Ph:(315)724-3151
Fax: (315)724-3177
Co. E-mail: info@mvchamber.org
URL: http://www.mvchamber.org
Contact: Matt Stubley, Pres.

62961 ■ Montgomery County Chamber of Commerce at Guy Park Manor
366 W Main
Amsterdam, NY 12010
Ph:(518)842-8200
Free: 800-743-7337
Fax: (518)843-8327
Co. E-mail: chamber@montgomerycountyny.com
URL: http://www.montgomerycountyny.com
Contact: Deborah Auspelmyer, Pres.

62962 ■ Mount Kisco Chamber of Commerce
3 N Moger Ave.
Mount Kisco, NY 10549
Ph:(914)666-7525
Fax: (914)666-7663
Co. E-mail: mtkiscochamber@aol.com
URL: http://www.mtkisco.com
Contact: Anne S. Feldman, Exec.Dir.

62963 ■ Mount Vernon Chamber of Commerce
PO Box 351
Mount Vernon, NY 10550-2009
Ph:(914)667-7500
Fax: (914)699-0139
Co. E-mail: mvny.coc@verizon.net
URL: http://www.mvnycoc.org
Contact: Gerrie Post, Pres.

62964 ■ New City Chamber of Commerce
PO Box 2021
New City, NY 10956
Ph:(845)638-1395
Fax: (845)638-1395

Co. E-mail: martreal@aol.com
Contact: Gillian Ballard, Exec.Dir.

62965 ■ New Hartford Chamber of Commerce
PO Box 372
New Hartford, NY 13413
Ph:(315)735-1974
Fax: (315)266-1231
Co. E-mail: info@newhartfordchamber.com
URL: http://www.newhartfordchamber.com
Contact: Mark A. Turnbull, Pres.

62966 ■ New Paltz Chamber of Commerce
124 Main St.
New Paltz, NY 12561-1610
Ph:(845)255-0243
Fax: (845)255-5189
Co. E-mail: info@newpaltzchamber.org
URL: http://www.newpaltzchamber.org
Contact: Joyce M. Minard, Exec.Dir.

62967 ■ New Rochelle Chamber of Commerce
459 Main St.
New Rochelle, NY 10801-6412
Ph:(914)632-5700
Fax: (914)632-0708
Co. E-mail: chamber@newrochellechamber.org
URL: http://www.newrochellechamber.org
Contact: Denise Lally, Exec.Dir.

62968 ■ New Yorktown Chamber of Commerce
PO Box 632
Yorktown Heights, NY 10598
Ph:(914)245-4599
Fax: (914)734-7171
Co. E-mail: info@yorktownchamber.org
URL: http://www.yorktownchamber.org
Contact: Michael Turton, Exec.Dir.

62969 ■ Newark Chamber of Commerce
203 W Miller St.
Newark, NY 14513
Ph:(315)331-2705
Fax: (315)331-2705
Co. E-mail: newarkcc@redsuspenders.com
URL: http://www.cgazette.com
Contact: Melissa Kline, Admin.

62970 ■ Newcomb Chamber of Commerce
PO Box 222
Newcomb, NY 12852-0222
Ph:(518)582-4255
URL: http://www.newcombny.com
Contact: Robert F. Smith

62971 ■ Niagara USA Chamber
Vantage Ctre.
6311 Inducon Corporate Dr.
Sanborn, NY 14132
Ph:(716)285-9141
Free: 800-808-8198
Fax: (716)285-0941
Co. E-mail: tkraus@niagarachamber.org
URL: http://www.niagarachamber.org
Contact: Thomas J. Kraus, Pres.

62972 ■ Northern Tier Chamber of Commerce
PO Box 44
Rouses Point, NY 12979
Ph:(518)297-3040
Fax: (518)297-2762
Contact: Frank Shambo, Pres.

62973 ■ Oceanside Chamber of Commerce
PO Box 1
Oceanside, NY 11572
Ph:(516)763-9177
Co. E-mail: info@oceansidechamber.org
URL: http://www.oceansidechamber.org
Contact: Robert E. Towers, Pres.

62974 ■ Ontario Chamber of Commerce
PO Box 100
Ontario, NY 14519

Ph:(315)524-5886
Fax: (315)524-9709
Co. E-mail: jswitzer@rochester.rr.com
Contact: Gail Adair, Dir.

62975 ■ Orchard Park Chamber of Commerce
4211 N Buffalo Rd., Ste. 14
Orchard Park, NY 14127-2401
Ph:(716)662-3366
Fax: (716)662-5946
Co. E-mail: opcc@orchardparkchamber.com
URL: http://www.orchardparkchamber.com
Contact: Nancy L. Conley, Exec.Dir.

62976 ■ Orleans County Chamber of Commerce
121 N Main St., Ste. 110
Albion, NY 14411
Ph:(585)589-7727
Fax: (585)589-7326
Co. E-mail: thill@orleanschamber.com
URL: http://www.orleanschamber.com
Contact: Dr. Tango R. Hill, Interim Exec. Dir.

62977 ■ Otsego County Chamber of Commerce
12 Carbon St.
Oneonta, NY 13820-2535
Ph:(607)432-4500
Free: 877-5OT-SEGO
Fax: (607)432-4506
Co. E-mail: tocc@otsegocountychamber.com
URL: http://www.otsegocountychamber.com
Contact: Marie Wiles, Chair

62978 ■ Oxford Chamber of Commerce
Promote Oxford Now
PO Box 11
Oxford, NY 13830
Ph:(607)843-5062
Fax: (607)843-9731
URL: http://www.artmakers.com/oxford
Contact: Tim Ryan, Pres.

62979 ■ Partnership for New York City
1 Battery Park Plz., 5th Fl.
New York, NY 10004
Ph:(212)493-7400
Fax: (212)344-3344
Co. E-mail: info@pfnyc.org
URL: http://www.nycp.org
Contact: Kathryn Wylde, Pres./CEO

62980 ■ Patterson Chamber of Commerce
PO Box 316
Patterson, NY 12563-0316
Ph:(845)878-4696
Fax: (845)278-6256
Co. E-mail: info@pcofc.org
URL: http://www.pcofc.org
Contact: Marsha Thompson, Pres.

62981 ■ Pawling Chamber of Commerce
PO Box 19
Pawling, NY 12564
Ph:(845)855-0500
Co. E-mail: pawlingcoc@aol.com
Contact: Marie Stewart, Pres.

62982 ■ Pelham Chamber of Commerce
PO Box 965
Pelham, NY 10803-0965
Ph:(914)738-7380
Fax: (914)738-1875
Co. E-mail: tina@efk.com
Contact: Dennis Brooks, Pres.

62983 ■ Pittsford Chamber of Commerce
PO Box 576
Pittsford, NY 14534-0576
Ph:(585)234-0308
Co. E-mail: info@pittsfordchamber.org
Contact: Dr. Shirley Joseph, Pres.

62984 ■ Plank Road Chamber of Commerce
PO Box 324
North Syracuse, NY 13212

Ph:(315)458-4181
Co. E-mail: smay@twcny.rr.com
URL: http://www.northsyracuse.org
Contact: Sharon A. May, Sec.

62985 ■ Plattsburgh - North Country Chamber of Commerce
7061 Rte. 9
PO Box 310
Plattsburgh, NY 12901
Ph:(518)563-1000
Fax: (518)563-1028
Co. E-mail: chamber@westelcom.com
URL: http://www.northcountrychamber.com
Contact: Garry Douglas, Pres.

62986 ■ Port Chester - Rye Brook Chamber of Commerce
110 Willett Ave.
Port Chester, NY 10573
Ph:(914)939-1900
Fax: (914)939-2733
Co. E-mail: info@portchesterryebrookchamber.com
URL: http://www.portchesterryebrookchamber.com
Contact: Peter Iasillo, Exec. Dir.

62987 ■ Port Washington Chamber of Commerce
329 Main St.
PO Box 121
Port Washington, NY 11050
Ph:(516)883-6566
Fax: (516)883-6591
Co. E-mail: pwcoc@optionline.net
URL: http://www.portwashington.org
Contact: Bobbie Polay

62988 ■ Potsdam Chamber of Commerce
Potsdam Civic Ctr.
2 Park St.
PO Box 717
Potsdam, NY 13676-0717
Ph:(315)265-5440
Fax: (315)268-0330
Co. E-mail: potsdam@slic.com
URL: http://www.potsdam.ny.us
Contact: Abigail D. Lee, Exec.Coor.

62989 ■ Poughkeepsie Area Chamber of Commerce
1 Civic Center Plz.
Poughkeepsie, NY 12601
Ph:(845)454-1700
Fax: (845)454-1702
Co. E-mail: office@pokchamb.org
URL: http://www.pokchamb.org
Contact: Charles S. North, Pres./CEO

62990 ■ Pulaski - Eastern Shore Chamber of Commerce
PO Box 34
Pulaski, NY 13142
Ph:(315)298-2213
Co. E-mail: pulaski@dreamscape.com
URL: http://www.pulaskinychamber.com
Contact: Margaret Clerkin, Sec.

62991 ■ Red Hook Area Chamber of Commerce
PO Box 254
Red Hook, NY 12571-0254
Ph:(845)758-0824
Co. E-mail: info@redhookchamber.org
URL: http://www.redhookchamber.org
Contact: Ryan McCann, Pres.

62992 ■ Rensselaer County Regional Chamber of Commerce
255 River St.
Troy, NY 12180
Ph:(518)274-7020
Fax: (518)272-7729
Co. E-mail: info@renscochamber.com
URL: http://www.renscochamber.com
Contact: Linda Hillman, Pres.

62993 ■ Rhinebeck Chamber of Commerce
PO Box 42
Rhinebeck, NY 12572
Ph:(845)876-5904
Fax: (845)876-8624
Co. E-mail: info@rhinebeckchamber.com
URL: http://rhinebeckchamber.com
Contact: Ms. Susan Linn, Exec. Dir.

62994 ■ Richfield Area Chamber of Commerce
PO Box 909
Richfield Springs, NY 13439-0909
Ph:(315)858-2553
Co. E-mail: elbudro@aol.com
Contact: Mr. E. Lawrence Budro, Exec. Dir.

62995 ■ Riverhead Chamber of Commerce
542 E Main St., Ste. 2
PO Box 291
Riverhead, NY 11901
Ph:(631)727-7600
Fax: (631)727-7946
Co. E-mail: info@riverheadchamber.com
URL: http://www.riverheadchamber.com
Contact: Thomas Lennon, Pres.

62996 ■ Rochester Business Alliance
150 State St.
Rochester, NY 14614
Ph:(585)244-1800
Fax: (585)263-3679
Co. E-mail: andriap@rballiance.com
Contact: Thomas T. Mooney, Pres.

62997 ■ Rochester Business Alliance, Women's Council
150 State St.
Rochester, NY 14614
Ph:(585)263-3653
Fax: (585)263-3679
Co. E-mail: susan.george@rballiance.com
URL: http://www.grwc.com
Contact: Susan George

62998 ■ Rockland Chamber of Commerce
PO Box 2001
New City, NY 10956
Ph:(845)634-4646
Fax: (914)634-6481
Co. E-mail: martreal@aol.com
Contact: Martin Bernstein, Pres.

62999 ■ Rockville Centre Chamber of Commerce
PO Box 226
Rockville Centre, NY 11571-0226
Ph:(516)766-0666
Fax: (516)706-2236
Co. E-mail: mailbox@rvcchamber.org
URL: http://www.rockvillecentrechamber.com
Contact: Michael J. Shenker CPA, Pres.

63000 ■ Rome Area Chamber of Commerce
139 W Dominick St.
Rome, NY 13440-5809
Ph:(315)337-1700
Fax: (315)337-1715
Co. E-mail: info@romechamber.com
URL: http://www.romechamber.com
Contact: William K. Guglielmo, Pres.

63001 ■ Roscoe-Rockland Chamber of Commerce
PO Box 443
Roscoe, NY 12776-0443
Ph:(607)498-5765
Co. E-mail: info@roscoeny.com
URL: http://www.roscoeny.com
Contact: Eliot Kornhauser, Pres.

63002 ■ Rye Merchants Association
43 Purchase St.
Rye, NY 10580
Ph:(914)565-1783
URL: http://www.ryemerchantsassociation.com
Contact: Lisa McKiernan, Pres.

63003 ■ Sag Harbor Chamber of Commerce
PO Box 2810
Sag Harbor, NY 11963
Ph:(631)725-0011
Fax: (631)725-3028
Co. E-mail: sagchamber@peconic.net
URL: http://www.sagharborchamber.com
Contact: Mr. Robert Evjen, Pres.

63004 ■ St. James Chamber of Commerce
PO Box 286
St. James, NY 11780
Ph:(631)584-8510
Fax: (631)862-9839
Co. E-mail: info@stjameschamber.org
URL: http://www.stjameschamber.org
Contact: Eddie Banks, Pres.

63005 ■ St. Lawrence County Chamber of Commerce
101 Main St. 1st Fl.
Canton, NY 13617-1248
Ph:(315)386-4000
Free: 877-228-7810
Fax: (315)379-0134
Co. E-mail: slccoc@northnet.org
URL: http://www.northcountryguide.com
Contact: Ms. Karen St. Hilaire, Exec.Dir.

63006 ■ Salamanca Area Chamber of Commerce
26 Main St.
Salamanca, NY 14779-1516
Ph:(716)945-2034
Fax: (716)945-2034
Co. E-mail: sal.cofc@verizon.net
URL: http://www.salamancacofc.homestead.com
Contact: Joelle A. Eddy, Administrator

63007 ■ Saranac Lake Area Chamber of Commerce
39 Main St.
Saranac Lake, NY 12983
Ph:(518)891-1990
Free: 800-347-1992
Fax: (518)891-7042
Co. E-mail: snelson@saranaclake.com
URL: http://www.saranaclake.com
Contact: Sylvie D. Nelson, Exec. Dir.

63008 ■ Saratoga County Chamber of Commerce
28 Clinton St.
Saratoga Springs, NY 12866-2143
Ph:(518)584-3255
Fax: (518)587-0318
Co. E-mail: info@saratoga.org
URL: http://www.saratoga.org
Contact: Joseph W. Dalton Jr., Pres.

63009 ■ Schenectady County Chamber of Commerce
306 State St.
Schenectady, NY 12305-2302
Ph:(518)372-5656
Free: 800-962-8007
Fax: (518)370-3217
Co. E-mail: info@schenectadychamber.org
URL: http://www.schenectadychamber.org
Contact: Charles P. Steiner, Pres.

63010 ■ Schoharie County Chamber of Commerce
315-1 Main St.
PO Box 400
Schoharie, NY 12157-0400
Ph:(518)295-6550
Free: 800-41V-ISIT
Fax: (518)295-7453
Co. E-mail: info@schohariechamber.com
URL: http://www.schohariechamber.com
Contact: Jodie Rutt, Acting Exec. Dir.

63011 ■ Schroon Lake Area Chamber of Commerce
PO Box 726
Schroon Lake, NY 12870-0726

Ph:(518)532-7675
Free: 888-724-7666
Fax: (518)532-7675
Co. E-mail: schroon@capital.net
URL: http://schroonlakechamber.com

63012 ■ Schuyler County Chamber of Commerce
100 N Franklin St., Rte. 14
Watkins Glen, NY 14891
Ph:(607)535-4300
Free: 800-607-4552
Fax: (607)535-6243
Co. E-mail: chamber@schuylerny.com
URL: http://www.schuylerny.com
Contact: Mary Suits, Office Mgr.

63013 ■ Seneca County Chamber of Commerce
PO Box 70
Seneca Falls, NY 13148-0070
Ph:(315)568-2906
Free: 800-732-1848
Fax: (315)568-1730
Co. E-mail: windmill@flare.net
URL: http://www.senecachamber.org
Contact: Mr. Fred Gaffney, Exec. Dir.

63014 ■ Sidney Chamber of Commerce
PO Box 2295
Sidney, NY 13838
Ph:(607)561-2642
Fax: (607)561-2644
Co. E-mail: chambersidneyny@mkl.com
URL: http://www.sidneychamber.org
Contact: Greg Hitchcock, Pres.

63015 ■ Skaneateles Area Chamber of Commerce
22 Jordan St.
PO Box 199
Skaneateles, NY 13152
Ph:(315)685-0552
Fax: (315)685-0552
Co. E-mail: skanchamber@adelphia.net
URL: http://www.skaneateles.com
Contact: Susan Dove, Exec.Dir.

63016 ■ Sleepy Hollow Chamber of Commerce
54 Main St.
Tarrytown, NY 10591
Ph:(914)631-1705
Fax: (914)366-4291
Co. E-mail: info@sleepyhollowchamber.com
URL: http://www.sleepyhollowchamber.com
Contact: Linda Rey, Pres.

63017 ■ Smithtown Chamber of Commerce
79 E Main St., Ste. E
PO Box 1216
Smithtown, NY 11787
Ph:(631)979-8069
Fax: (631)979-2206
Co. E-mail: info@smithtownchamber.com
URL: http://www.smithtownchamber.org
Contact: Barbara Franco, Exec. Dir.

63018 ■ Sodus Town Chamber of Commerce
PO Box 187
Sodus, NY 14551-0187
Ph:(315)483-7256
Fax: (315)483-0059
Co. E-mail: chamber14551@yahoo.com
URL: http://www.sodusny.com
Contact: Mary Jane Mumby, Sec.

63019 ■ Southampton Chamber of Commerce
76 Main St.
Southampton, NY 11968
Ph:(631)283-0402
Fax: (631)283-8707
Co. E-mail: info@southamptonchamber.com
URL: http://www.southamptonchamber.com
Contact: Millie A. Fellingham, Exec. Dir.

63020 ■ Southern Saratoga County Chamber of Commerce
PO Box 399
Clifton Park, NY 12065-0399
Ph:(518)371-7748
Fax: (518)371-5025
Co. E-mail: info@southernsaratoga.org
URL: http://www.ssccc.org
Contact: Peter L. Aust, Pres./CEO

63021 ■ Southern Ulster County Chamber of Commerce
33 Main St.
Highland, NY 12528-1407
Ph:(845)691-6070
Fax: (845)691-9194
Co. E-mail: info@southernulsterchamber.org
URL: http://www.southernulsterchamber.org
Contact: William J. Farrell, Pres.

63022 ■ Staten Island Chamber of Commerce
130 Bay St.
Staten Island, NY 10301-2503
Ph:(718)727-1900
Fax: (718)727-2295
Co. E-mail: info@sichamber.com
URL: http://www.sichamber.com
Contact: Ms. Linda Baran, Pres./CEO

63023 ■ Suffern Chamber of Commerce
PO Box 291
Suffern, NY 10901
Ph:(845)357-8424
Fax: (845)357-8424
Contact: Michael Malandri, Pres.

63024 ■ Sullivan County Chamber of Commerce
59 N Main St., Ste. 300
Liberty, NY 12754-1832
Ph:(845)292-8500
Fax: (845)292-5366
Co. E-mail: chamber@catskills.com
URL: http://www.catskills.com
Contact: Terri Hess, Pres./CEO

63025 ■ Syosset Chamber of Commerce
36 Church St.
Syosset, NY 11791
Ph:(516)346-7150
Fax: (516)364-7151
Co. E-mail: agallo.scoc@verizon.net
URL: http://www.syossetchamber.com
Contact: Michael A. Biggiani Esq., Pres.

63026 ■ Ticonderoga Area Chamber of Commerce
94 Montcalm St., Ste. 1
Ticonderoga, NY 12883
Ph:(518)585-6619
Fax: (518)585-9184
Co. E-mail: chamberinfo@bluemoo.net
URL: http://www.ticonderogany.com
Contact: Debra Malaney, Exec.Dir.

63027 ■ Tioga County Chamber of Commerce
188 Front St.
Owego, NY 13827
Ph:(607)687-2020
Fax: (607)687-9028
Co. E-mail: business@tiogachamber.com
URL: http://www.tiogachamber.com
Contact: Martha Sauerbrey, Pres./CEO

63028 ■ Tompkins County Chamber of Commerce
904 E Shore Dr.
Ithaca, NY 14850-1026
Ph:(607)273-7080
Fax: (607)272-7617
Co. E-mail: jean@tompkinschamber.org
URL: http://tompkinschamber.org
Contact: Jean McPheeters, Pres.

63029 ■ Town of Hunter Chamber of Commerce
PO Box 177
Hunter, NY 12442
Ph:(518)263-4900
Fax: (518)589-0117
Co. E-mail: info@hunterchamber.org
URL: http://www.hunterchamber.org
Contact: Michael McCrary, Pres.

63030 ■ Town of Montgomery Chamber of Commerce
2365 Albany Post Rd.
Walden, NY 12586
Ph:(845)778-0514
Fax: (845)778-6346
Contact: Florence Valk, Admin.

63031 ■ Tri-State Chamber of Commerce
PO Box 121
Port Jervis, NY 12771-0121
Ph:(845)856-6694
Fax: (845)856-6695
Co. E-mail: info@tristatechamber.org
URL: http://www.tristatechamber.org
Contact: Susan Burrows, Exec. Dir.

63032 ■ Tupper Lake Chamber of Commerce
60 Park St.
Tupper Lake, NY 12986
Ph:(518)359-3328
Free: 888-887-5253
Fax: (518)359-2507
Co. E-mail: tuppercc@adelphia.net
URL: http://www.tupperlakeinfo.com
Contact: Jon Kopp, Exec.Dir.

63033 ■ Victor Chamber of Commerce
31 E Main St.
PO Box 86
Victor, NY 14564-0086
Ph:(585)742-1476
Fax: (585)924-0523
Co. E-mail: wstehling@aol.com
URL: http://www.victorchamber.com
Contact: Susan Stehling, Pres.

63034 ■ Waddington Area Chamber of Commerce
PO Box 291
Waddington, NY 13694-0291
Ph:(315)388-5576
Co. E-mail: nputney@twcny.rr.com
URL: http://www.waddingtonny.us/chamber
Contact: Nancy Putney, Pres.

63035 ■ Walton Chamber of Commerce
129 N St.
Walton, NY 13856
Ph:(607)865-6656
Co. E-mail: walton_chamber@yahoo.com
Contact: Keath Davis, Pres.

63036 ■ Warrensburg Chamber of Commerce
3847 Main St.
Warrensburg, NY 12885
Ph:(518)623-2161
Fax: (518)623-2184
Co. E-mail: info@warrensburgchamber.com
URL: http://www.warrensburgchamber.com
Contact: Larry Stephenson, Pres.

63037 ■ Warwick Valley Chamber of Commerce
PO Box 202
Warwick, NY 10990
Ph:(914)986-2720
Fax: (914)986-6982
Co. E-mail: info@warwickcc.org
URL: http://www.warwickcc.org
Contact: Linda Glohs, Exec.Dir.

63038 ■ Webster Chamber of Commerce
26 E Main St.
Webster, NY 14580-3280
Ph:(585)265-3960
Fax: (585)265-3702

Co. E-mail: bbernard@websterchamber.com
URL: http://www.websterchamber.com
Contact: Elizabeth Bernard, Administrator

63039 ■ Wellsville Area Chamber of Commerce
114 N Main St.
Wellsville, NY 14895
Ph:(585)593-5080
Fax: (585)593-5088
Co. E-mail: wlsvchamber@adelphia.net
URL: http://www.wellsvilleareachamber.com
Contact: Steven Havey, Exec.Dir.

63040 ■ West Seneca Chamber of Commerce
950A Union Rd., Ste. 5
West Seneca, NY 14224
Ph:(716)674-4900
Co. E-mail: cdillchamber@westseneca.org
URL: http://www.westseneca.org
Contact: Carol J. Dill, Admin.Dir.

63041 ■ West Side Chamber of Commerce
1841 Broadway, Ste. 701
New York, NY 10023-7603
Ph:(212)541-8880
Fax: (212)541-8883
Co. E-mail: mail@westsidechamber.org
URL: http://www.westsidechamber.org
Contact: Andrew Albert, Exec. Dir.

63042 ■ Whitehall Chamber of Commerce
PO Box 97
Whitehall, NY 12887
Ph:(518)499-2292
Fax: (518)499-0798
Co. E-mail: mail@whitehallchamber.com
URL: http://www.whitehallchamber.com
Contact: Stan Woodruff, Pres.

63043 ■ Woodstock Chamber of Commerce and Arts
PO Box 36
Woodstock, NY 12498
Ph:(845)679-6234
Co. E-mail: info@woodstockchamber.com
URL: http://woodstockchamber.com
Contact: Mr. Barry Samuels, Pres.

63044 ■ Wyoming County Chamber of Commerce
6470 Rte. 20A, Ste. 2
Perry, NY 14530-9798
Ph:(585)237-0230
Free: 800-951-9774
Fax: (585)237-0231
Co. E-mail: info@wycochamber.org
URL: http://www.wycochamber.org
Contact: James Pierce, Exec. Dir.

63045 ■ Yonkers Chamber of Commerce
20 S Broadway, Ste. 1207
Yonkers, NY 10701
Ph:(914)963-0332
Fax: (914)963-0455
Co. E-mail: info@yonkerschamber.com
URL: http://www.yonkerschamber.com
Contact: Kevin T. Cacace, Pres.

MINORITY BUSINESS ASSISTANCE PROGRAMS

63046 ■ Brooklyn Minority Business Development Center–Opportunity Development Association (ODA)
12 Heyward St.
Brooklyn, NY 11211
Ph:(718)522-5620
Fax: (718)522-5931
Co. E-mail: oda@odabdc.org
URL: http://www.odabdc.org
Contact: Zvi Kestenbaum, Dir

63047 ■ Jamaica Business Resource Center–Queens/Brooklyn Minority Development Center
160th St.
Jamaica, NY 11432
Ph:(718)206-2255
Fax: (718)206-3693
Co. E-mail: jbrc@jbrc.org
URL: http://www.jbrc.org
Contact: Timothy Marshall, Pres & CEO

63048 ■ New York State Department of Economic Development–Minority and Women's Business Division
Empire State Development
633 3rd Ave., 33rd Fl.
New York, NY 10017
Ph:(212)803-2411
Free: 800-STA-TENY
Fax: (212)803-2459
URL: http://www.empire.state.ny.us
Contact: Maggie Seymour
Description: Assists in obtaining statewide certification, financing, business development and technical assistance, permit and regulatory assistance, market and sales expansion, and employment and training.

63049 ■ New York State Offices General Services–Minority and Women-Owned Business
Corning 2nd Tower, Rm. 3566, 35th Fl.
Empire State Plaza
Albany, NY 12242
Ph:(518)473-7083
Fax: (518)486-2679
Co. E-mail: l.jones@ogs.state.ny.us
URL: http://www.ogs.state.ny.us
Contact: Elaine Whitehead, Dir

63050 ■ Williamsburg Minority Business Development Center–Opportunity Development Association (ODA)
12 Heyward St.
Brooklyn, NY 11211
Ph:(718)522-5620
Fax: (718)522-5931
Co. E-mail: oda@odabdc.org
URL: http://www.odabdc.org
Contact: Zvi Kestenbaum, Dir

FINANCING AND LOAN PROGRAMS

63051 ■ 4C Ventures / Olivetti Holding, N.V.
21 E. 94th St., 3rd Fl.
New York, NY 10128
Ph:(212)996-3133
Fax: (212)996-1838
URL: http://www.4cventures.com
Contact: Alexandra Giurgiu, Partner
Preferred Investment Size: $500,000 to $1,000,000.
Investment Types: Seed, research and development, start-up, first and second stage. **Industry Preferences:** Computer hardware, computer software and services, communications and media, semiconductors and other electronics, consumer related, Internet specific, other products, and industrial and energy. **Geographic Preferences:** U.S. and Canada.

63052 ■ 550 Digital Media Ventures
555 Madison Ave., 5th Fl.
New York, NY 10022
URL: http://www.550dmv.com
Investment Types: Early stage. **Industry Preferences:** Consumer related, and business service. **Geographic Preferences:** U.S.

63053 ■ Adler & Co.
342 Madison Ave., Ste. 807
New York, NY 10173
Ph:(212)599-2535
Fax: (212)599-2526
Contact: Jay Nickse, Chief Financial Officer
Preferred Investment Size: $1,000,000 minimum.
Investment Types: Start-up, first and second stage,

leveraged buyout, and control-block purchases. **Industry Preferences:** Computer software and services, computer hardware, semiconductors and other electronics, communications and media, medical and health, biotechnology, other products, industrial and energy, consumer related, and Internet specific. **Geographic Preferences:** U.S.

63054 ■ Alimansky Capital Group, Inc.
14 E. 44th St., Ste. 400
New York, NY 10017
Ph:(212)832-7300
Fax: (212)832-7338
URL: http://www.alimansky.com
Contact: Burt Alimansky, Managing Director
Preferred Investment Size: $2,000,000. **Investment Types:** First and second stage, mezzanine, leveraged buyout, and special situation. **Industry Preferences:** Communications and media, computer, related, semiconductors and other electronics, biotechnology, medical and health, consumer related, industrial and energy, transportation, financial services, business service, manufacturing, agriculture, forestry and fishing. **Geographic Preferences:** U.S. and Canada.

63055 ■ Allegra Partners / Lawrence, Smith & Horey
320 Park Ave., 18th Fl.
New York, NY 10022
Ph:(212)277-1526
Fax: (212)277-1533
Contact: Larry Lawrence, General Partner
Preferred Investment Size: $5,000,000 minimum. **Investment Types:** Early, expansion, and later stage. **Industry Preferences:** Computer software and services, communications and media, other products, Internet specific, consumer related, medical and health. **Geographic Preferences:** U.S.

63056 ■ Amphion Capital Management, LLC / Wolfensohn Associates
350 Madison Ave.
New York, NY 10022
Ph:(212)210-6200
Fax: (212)210-6271
Contact: Richard Morgan, Managing Partner
Preferred Investment Size: $3,000,000 to $20,000,000. **Investment Types:** Start-up, first and second stage, acquisition, and leveraged buyout. **Industry Preferences:** Communications and media, computer related, semiconductors and other electronics, medical and health. **Geographic Preferences:** U.S.

63057 ■ The Argentum Group
60 Madison, Ste. 701
New York, NY 10010
Ph:(212)949-6262
Fax: (212)949-8294
URL: http://www.argentumgroup.com
Preferred Investment Size: $10,000,000 minimum. **Investment Types:** Second stage, mezzanine, leveraged buyout, other products, and special situation. **Industry Preferences:** Internet specific, medical and health, computer software and services, communications and media, industrial and energy, and computer hardware. **Geographic Preferences:** U.S.

63058 ■ Arthur P. Gould & Co.
1 Wilshire Dr.
Lake Success, NY 11020
Ph:(914)723-2560
Fax: (914)723-1756
Contact: Andrew Gould, Vice President
Preferred Investment Size: $5,000,000 minimum. **Investment Types:** Seed, start-up, first and second stage, research and development, mezzanine, generalist PE, and leveraged buyout. **Industry Preferences:** Communications, computer hardware and software, semiconductors and other electronics, biotechnology, medical and health, consumer related, industrial and energy, transportation, financial services, manufacturing, agriculture, forestry and fishing.

63059 ■ Axavision, Inc.
14 Wall St., 26th Fl.
New York, NY 10005

Ph:(212)619-4000
Fax: (212)619-7202
Preferred Investment Size: $100,000 to $300,000. **Investment Types:** Seed and start-up. **Industry Preferences:** Computer software, Internet specific, and financial services.

63060 ■ B2B-Hive, LLC
75 Broadway, 32nd Fl.
New York, NY 10003
Ph:(212)763-6018
Fax: (212)763-6020
URL: http://www.b2b-hive.com
Contact: George Israel, Principal
Preferred Investment Size: $1,000,000 to $5,000,000. **Investment Types:** Start-up, seed, and early stage. **Industry Preferences:** Financial and business services. **Geographic Preferences:** New York.

63061 ■ Baker Capital Corp.
540 Madison Ave., 29th Fl.
New York, NY 10022
Ph:(212)848-2000
Fax: (212)468-0660
URL: http://www.bakercapital.com
Contact: James Cosgrove, Chief Executive Officer
Investment Types: Early and later stage. **Industry Preferences:** Internet specific, communications and media, computer software and services, computer hardware, semiconductors and other electronics. **Geographic Preferences:** U.S.

63062 ■ Bangert Dawes Reade Davis & Thom
605 3rd. Ave., Ste. 424
New York, NY 10158
Ph:(212)573-6716
Contact: K. Deane Reade, President
Preferred Investment Size: $200,000 to $1,500,000. **Investment Types:** other. **Industry Preferences:** Medical and health.

63063 ■ Bedford Capital Corp.
18 E. 48th St., Ste. 1800
New York, NY 10017
Ph:(212)688-5700
Fax: (212)754-4699
URL: http://www.bedfordnyc.com
Preferred Investment Size: $100,000 to $300,000. **Investment Types:** First and second stage, industry rollups, recapitalizations, and leveraged buyout. **Industry Preferences:** Internet specific, medical and health, consumer related, industrial and energy, financial services, and manufacturing. **Geographic Preferences:** Midwest.

63064 ■ Bessemer Venture Partners (Larchmont)
1865 Palmer Ave., Ste. 104
Larchmont, NY 10538
Ph:(914)833-5300
Fax: (914)833-5499
URL: http://www.bessemervp.com
Contact: Jeremy Levine, Principal
Preferred Investment Size: $1,000,000 to $10,000,000. **Investment Types:** Seed, start-up, early, first and second stage, research and development, leveraged buyout, special situation, control-block purchases, and expansion. **Industry Preferences:** Internet specific, communications and media, computer software and services, computer hardware, semiconductors and other electronics, consumer related, medical and health, industrial and energy, biotechnology, and other products. **Geographic Preferences:** U.S.

63065 ■ Bloom & Co.
950 3rd Ave.
New York, NY 10022
Ph:(212)838-1858
Fax: (212)838-1843
Preferred Investment Size: $3,000,000 minimum. **Investment Types:** Seed, start-up, first and second stage, control-block purchases, leveraged buyout, mezzanine, and special situation.

63066 ■ Bluecar Partners
787 7th Ave., 9th Fl.
New York, NY 10019
Ph:(917)797-8782
Fax: (917)796-3875
URL: http://www.bluecarpartners.com
Contact: Granger Whitelaw, Managing Director
Investment Policies: Seed and early stage. **Industry Preferences:** Communications, Internet specific, biotechnology, medical and health, and transportation. **Geographic Preferences:** U.S.

63067 ■ Bluefish Ventures
990 Avenue of the Americas, Ste., 17J
New York, NY 10018
Ph:(212)290-5317
Fax: (212)695-3449
URL: http://www.bluefishventures.com
Contact: Alex Miller, Partner
Preferred Investment Size: $250,000 to $2,000,000. **Investment Policies:** Seed, start-up, early, first, and second stage. **Industry Preferences:** Communications, computer software, industrial and energy, and business service. **Geographic Preferences:** Northeast and Northwest.

63068 ■ Bristol Capital Management
135 E. 57th St., 15th Fl.
New York, NY 10022
Ph:(212)593-3157
Fax: (212)202-5022
URL: http://www.bristolcap.com
Contact: Arthur Whitcomb, Managing Director
Preferred Investment Size: $1,000,000 to $10,000,000. **Investment Types:** Generalist PE, later stage, leveraged buyout, management buyouts, mezzanine, private placement, public companies, recapitalizations, second stage, and special situation.

63069 ■ Carlin Ventures LLC
575 Madison Ave., 10th Fl.
New York, NY 10022
Ph:(212)605-0409
URL: http://www.carlinventures.com
Contact: Dillon Cohen, President
Investment Types: Early stage. **Industry Preferences:** Internet specific. **Geographic Preferences:** U.S.

63070 ■ Carrot Capital LLC
140 W. 57th St., Ste. 3B
New York, NY 10019
Ph:(212)586-2226
Fax: (212)586-2246
URL: http://www.carrotcapital.com
Contact: David Geliebter, Managing Partner
Preferred Investment Size: $50,000 to $1,000,000. **Investment Policies:** Seed, start-up, and early stage. **Industry Preferences:** Communications, computer hardware and software, semiconductors and other electronics, biotechnology, medical and health, and industrial and energy. **Geographic Preferences:** Canada.

63071 ■ Citicorp Venture Capital Ltd. (New York City)
399 Park Ave., 14th Fl.
New York, NY 10043
Ph:(212)559-1127
Fax: (212)888-2940
Contact: Thomas McWilliams, Managing Director
Preferred Investment Size: $50,000,000 minimum. **Investment Types:** Leveraged buyout, second stage, and special situation. **Industry Preferences:** Semiconductors and other electronics, computer hardware, computer software and services, communications and media, industrial and energy, other products, Internet specific, consumer related, medical and health, and biotechnology. **Geographic Preferences:** U.S.

63072 ■ CM Equity Partners, L.P.
135 E. 57th St., 27th Fl.
New York, NY 10022
Ph:(212)909-8400
Fax: (212)829-0553
URL: http://www.cmequity.com
Contact: Joel Levy, Managing Partner

Preferred Investment Size: $2,000,000 minimum. **Investment Types:** Acquisition, leveraged buyout, and recapitalizations. **Industry Preferences:** Communications and media, and Internet specific. **Geographic Preferences:** U.S. and Canada.

63073 ■ Cohen & Co., L.L.C.
800 3rd Ave.
New York, NY 10022
Ph:(212)317-2250
Fax: (212)317-2255
Preferred Investment Size: $10,000,000 minimum. **Investment Types:** Start-up, seed, first and second stage, mezzanine, leveraged buyout, control-block purchases, and special situation. **Industry Preferences:** Communications and media, computer software, semiconductors and other electronics, medical and health, consumer related, industrial and energy, and business service.

63074 ■ Coleman Venture Group
5909 Northern Blvd.
PO Box 224
East Norwich, NY 11732
Ph:(516)626-3642
Fax: (516)626-9722
Preferred Investment Size: $100,000 to $1,000,000. **Investment Types:** First stage, recapitalizations, seed, start-up, and special situation. **Industry Preferences:** Semiconductors and other electronics, consumer related, industrial and energy. **Geographic Preferences:** Northeast and West Coast, and Canada.

63075 ■ Cornerstone Equity Investors, LLC
717 5th Ave., Ste. 1100
New York, NY 10022
Ph:(212)753-0901
Fax: (212)826-6798
URL: http://www.cornerstone-equity.com
Contact: Mark Rossi, Managing Director
Preferred Investment Size: $50,000,000 minimum. **Investment Types:** Leveraged buyout, management buyouts, and special situation. **Industry Preferences:** Consumer related, medical and health, communications and media, semiconductors and other electronics, computer software and services, Internet specific, semiconductors and other electronics, other products, computer hardware, industrial and energy, and biotechnology.

63076 ■ Corporate Venture Partners L.P.
200 Sunset Park
Ithaca, NY 14850
Ph:(607)257-6323
Fax: (607)257-6128
Preferred Investment Size: $500,000 to $1,000,000. **Investment Types:** First stage. **Industry Preferences:** Communications and media, computer hardware and software, semiconductors and other electronics, biotechnology, medical and health, consumer related, industrial and energy, and manufacturing. **Geographic Preferences:** Northeast.

63077 ■ CW Group, Inc.
1041 3rd Ave., 2nd fl.
New York, NY 10021
Ph:(212)308-5266
Fax: (212)644-0354
URL: http://www.cwventures.com
Contact: Charles Hartman, General Partner
Preferred Investment Size: $500,000 to $5,000,000. **Investment Types:** Seed, start-up, first and second stage, leveraged buyout, research and development, special situation, control block purchases, and balanced. **Industry Preferences:** Medical and health, biotechnology, Internet specific, computer software and services, industrial and energy, other products, computer hardware, semiconductors and other electronics. **Geographic Preferences:** U.S.

63078 ■ Dauphin Capital Partners
108 Forest Ave.
Locust Valley, NY 11560
Ph:(516)759-3339
Fax: (516)759-3322
URL: http://www.dauphincapital.com

Contact: James Hoover, Managing Partner
Preferred Investment Size: $1,000,000 to $10,000,000. **Investment Types:** First and second stage, acquisition, expansion, and management buyouts. **Industry Preferences:** Medical and health. **Geographic Preferences:** Mid Atlantic, Northeast, and Southeast.

63079 ■ Dawntreader Ventures
520 Madison Ave., 9th Fl.
New York, NY 10022
Ph:(646)452-6100
Fax: (646)452-6101
URL: http://www.dtventures.com
Contact: Sang Ahn, Principal
Preferred Investment Size: $1,000,000 to $15,000,000. **Investment Policies:** Seed, early, first and second stage. **Industry Preferences:** Internet specific, computer software and services, semiconductors and other electronics, communications and media, other products, and consumer related.

63080 ■ DH Blair Investment Banking Corp.
44 Wall St., 2nd Fl.
New York, NY 10005
Ph:(212)495-5000
Fax: (212)269-1438
Contact: J. Morton Davis, Chairman
Preferred Investment Size: $100,000 minimum. **Investment Types:** Start-up, first stage, leveraged buyout, and research and development. **Industry Preferences:** Communications and media, computer hardware and software, semiconductors and other electronics, biotechnology, medical and health, consumer related, industrial and energy, financial services, and manufacturing.

63081 ■ Dresdner Kleinwort Capital (New York)
75 Wall St., 24th Fl.
New York, NY 10005
Ph:(212)429-3131
Fax: (212)429-3139
URL: http://www.dresdnerkb.com
Contact: Christopher Wright, President
Investment Types: Early stage, expansion, fund of funds, later stage, leveraged buyout, mezzanine, and turnaround. **Industry Preferences:** Computer software, communications and media, computer related, semiconductors and other electronics, biotechnology, medical and health, consumer related, industrial and energy, business service, and manufacturing.

63082 ■ EA Capital LLC
122 E. 61st St., Ste. 2A
New York, NY 10021
Ph:(212)482-3131
Fax: (212)482-0679
URL: http://www.eacapital.com
Contact: Tony Lent, Managing Director
Investment Policies: Early stage and expansion. **Industry Preferences:** Internet specific, industrial and energy, transportation, agriculture, forestry and fishing. **Geographic Preferences:** U.S.

63083 ■ EarlyBirdCapital.com Inc.
1 State St. Plz.
New York, NY 10004
Ph:(212)792-8100
Fax: (212)269-3787
URL: http://www.EarlyBirdCapital.com
Contact: Peter Kent, President
Investment Types: Early stage. **Industry Preferences:** Internet specific, medical and health, and business service.

63084 ■ East River Ventures, L.P.
645 Madison Ave., 22nd Fl.
New York, NY 10022
Ph:(212)644-2322
Fax: (212)644-5498
URL: http://www.eastrivervc.com
Investment Types: First and second stage, and mezzanine. **Industry Preferences:** Internet specific, medical and health, computer software and services, computer hardware, communications and media, industrial and energy, semiconductors and other electronics, biotechnology, and other products. **Geographic Preferences:** U.S. and Canada.

63085 ■ Easton Hunt Capital Partners
641 Lexington Ave., 21st Fl.
New York, NY 10022
Ph:(212)702-0950
Fax: (212)702-0952
URL: http://www.eastoncapital.com
Contact: Ed Meyer, Managing Director
Preferred Investment Size: $1,000,000 to $8,000,000. **Investment Types:** Balanced, early and later stage, management buyouts, and private placements. **Industry Preferences:** Computer software, industrial and energy, business service, and manufacturing. **Geographic Preferences:** U.S.

63086 ■ Eastport Partners
841 Broadway, Ste. 504
New York, NY 10003
Ph:(212)674-1900
Fax: (212)674-6821
URL: http://www.eastportlp.com
Contact: J. Andrew McWethy, Partner
Investment Policies: Leveraged buyout and management buyouts. **Industry Preferences:** Other products. **Geographic Preferences:** U.S.

63087 ■ Elk Associates Funding Corp.
747 3rd Ave., Ste. 4C
New York, NY 10017
Ph:(212)355-2449
Fax: (212)759-3338
Contact: Gary Granoff, President
E-mail: garyatelk@aol.com
Preferred Investment Size: $100,000 to $300,000. **Investment Types:** Second stage and leveraged buyout. **Industry Preferences:** Communications and media, consumer related, and transportation. **Geographic Preferences:** Southeast and Midwest.

63088 ■ EOS Partners, L.P.
320 Park Ave., 22nd Fl.
New York, NY 10022
Ph:(212)832-5800
Fax: (212)832-5815
URL: http://www.eospartners.com
Contact: Mark First, Managing Director
Preferred Investment Size: $3,000,000. **Investment Types:** Start-up, first, second, and later stage, industry rollups, acquisition, expansion, recapitalizations, leveraged buyout, mezzanine, and special situation. **Industry Preferences:** Communications and media, other products, consumer related, medical and health, semiconductors and other electronics, computer software and services, Internet specific, industrial and energy. **Geographic Preferences:** U.S. and Canada.

63089 ■ Euclidsr Partners
45 Rockefeller Plz., Ste. 3240
New York, NY 10111
Ph:(212)218-6880
Fax: (212)218-6877
URL: http://www.euclidsr.com
Contact: Barbara Dalton, General Partner
Investment Types: First, later and second stage. **Industry Preferences:** Internet specific, computer software and services, medical and health, biotechnology, semiconductors and other electronics, computer hardware, industrial and energy, communications and media, other products, and consumer related. **Geographic Preferences:** U.S.

63090 ■ Evergreen Capital Partners Inc.
150 E. 58th St.
New York, NY 10155
Ph:(212)813-0758
Fax: (212)813-0754
Preferred Investment Size: $300,000,000 minimum. **Investment Types:** Later stage, expansion, private placement, acquisition, generalist PE, leveraged buyout, management buyouts, and private placement. **Industry Preferences:** Computer related, medical and health, biotechnology, semiconductors and other electronics, industrial and energy, communications and media, consumer related, transportation, financial services, business services, and manufacturing. **Geographic Preferences:** U.S and Canada.

63091 ■ Exeter Capital Partners
10 E. 53rd St., 32nd Fl.
New York, NY 10022
Ph:(212)872-1175
Fax: (212)872-1198
URL: http://www.exeterfunds.com
Contact: Keith Fox, President
Preferred Investment Size: $2,000,000 to $20,000,000. **Investment Types:** Management buyouts, leveraged buyout, mezzanine, later stage, expansion, and balanced. **Industry Preferences:** Consumer related, Internet specific, medical and health, computer software and services, communications and media, computer hardware, other products. **Geographic Preferences:** U.S.

63092 ■ Exponential Business Development Co.
216 Walton St.
Syracuse, NY 13202-1227
Ph:(315)474-4500
Fax: (315)474-4682
Co. E-mail: dirksonn@aol.com
URL: http://www.exponential-ny.com
Contact: Dirk Sonneborn, Managing Partner
Preferred Investment Size: $100,000 to $600,000. **Investment Types:** Early and first stage. **Geographic Preferences:** New York.

63093 ■ FA Technology Ventures
30 S. Pearl St.
Albany, NY 12207
Ph:(518)447-8200
Fax: (518)447-8139
URL: http://www.fatechventures.com
Contact: George McNamee, Managing Partner
Preferred Investment Size: $2,500,000 to $8,000,000. **Investment Policies:** Early stage and expansion. **Industry Preferences:** Communications, computer software, and industrial and energy. **Geographic Preferences:** New York.

63094 ■ Financial Technology Research Corp.
518 Broadway
Penthouse
New York, NY 10012
Ph:(212)625-9100
Fax: (212)431-0300
Co. E-mail: fintek@financier.com
Contact: Neal Bruckman, President
Preferred Investment Size: $300,000 to $500,000. **Investment Types:** Seed, research and development, start-up, first and second stage, and special situation. **Industry Preferences:** Communications and media, computer related, semiconductors and other electronics, biotechnology, medical and health, consumer related, industrial and energy, transportation, financial services, business service, manufacturing, agriculture, forestry and fishing. **Geographic Preferences:** U.S. and Canada.

63095 ■ Flatiron Partners
1221 Avenue of the Americas, 39th Fl.
New York, NY 10020-1080
Ph:(212)899-3400
Fax: (212)899-3401
URL: http://www.flatironpartners.com
Contact: Philip Summe, Principal
Investment Types: Early stage. **Industry Preferences:** Internet specific, computer software and services, communications and media, other products, and consumer related. **Geographic Preferences:** New York and Northeast.

63096 ■ Fusient Media Ventures
62 Chelsea Piers, Rm. 316
New York, NY 10011
Ph:(212)986-7570
Fax: (212)342-8899
URL: http://www.fusient.com
Preferred Investment Size: $500,000 to $3,000,000. **Investment Types:** Early and first stage, and seed. **Industry Preferences:** Internet specific, consumer related, and business service.

63097 ■ Gabelli Multimedia Partners
1 Corporate Ctr.
Rye, NY 10580
Ph:(914)921-5395
Fax: (914)921-5031
Co. E-mail: fsommer@gabelli.com
Contact: Robert Zuccaro, Chief Financial Officer
Investment Types: Seed, start-up, first and second stage. **Industry Preferences:** Communications and media. **Geographic Preferences:** Northeast.

63098 ■ Genesee Funding, Inc.
70 Linden Oaks, 3rd Fl.
Rochester, NY 14625
Ph:(716)383-5550
Fax: (716)383-5305
Preferred Investment Size: $200,000 minimum. **Investment Types:** Second stage, mezzanine, and leveraged buyout. **Industry Preferences:** Communications and media, computer hardware, semiconductors and other electronics, medical and health, consumer related, industrial and energy, business service, and manufacturing. **Geographic Preferences:** Northeast.

63099 ■ Genesys Partners
126 5th Ave.
New York, NY 10011
Ph:(212)686-2828
Fax: (212)686-5155
URL: http://www.genesyspartners.com
Contact: James Kollegger, Chief Executive Officer
Investment Types: Early stage. **Industry Preferences:** Internet specific. **Geographic Preferences:** U.S.

63100 ■ Globalnet Management LLC
521 5th Ave., Ste. 1703
New York, NY 10175
Ph:(212)292-4407
Fax: (212)292-4408
URL: http://www.globalnet-advisors.com
Contact: Jonathan Adler, Managing Director
Investment Policies: Early and first stage. **Industry Preferences:** Communications and media, computer software, Internet specific, and industrial and energy.

63101 ■ GMS Capital Partners
405 Park Ave., 16th Fl.
New York, NY 10022
Ph:(212)832-4013
Fax: (212)980-1695
URL: http://www.gmgcapitalpartners.com
Contact: Joachim Gfoeller, Managing General Partner
Investment Types: Early stage. **Industry Preferences:** Communications and media, and Internet specific. **Geographic Preferences:** U.S.

63102 ■ Golub Associates
555 Madison Ave., 30th Fl.
New York, NY 10022
Ph:(212)750-6060
Fax: (212)750-5505
URL: http://wwwgolubassoc.com
Contact: Andrew Steuerman, Managing Director
Preferred Investment Size: $4,000,000 to $25,000,000. **Investment Types:** Later stage, mezzanine, generalist PE, recapitalizations, and private placement. **Industry Preferences:** Medical and health, consumer related, industrial and energy, transportation, business service, and manufacturing. **Geographic Preferences:** U.S.

63103 ■ Hambro America Biosciences, Inc.
650 Madison Ave., 21st Fl.
New York, NY 10022
Ph:(212)223-7400
Fax: (212)223-0305
Investment Policies: First and second stage, and special situation. **Industry Preferences:** Biotechnology, medical and health, and industrial and energy. **Geographic Preferences:** U.S.

63104 ■ Hanover Capital Corp.
505 Park Ave., 15th Fl.
New York, NY 10022

Ph:(212)755-1222
Fax: (212)935-1787
Contact: Michael Wainstein
Preferred Investment Size: $300,000 minimum. **Investment Types:** Leveraged buyout, mezzanine, and second stage. **Industry Preferences:** Communications and media, computer hardware and software, medical and health, industrial and energy, transportation, financial services, business service, and manufacturing. **Geographic Preferences:** U.S.

63105 ■ Harris & Harris Group, Inc.
111 W. 57th St., Ste. 1100
New York, NY 10019
Ph:(212)582-0900
Fax: (212)582-9563
URL: http://www.tinytechvc.com
Contact: Douglas Jamison, President and Chief Operating Officer
Preferred Investment Size: $100,000 to $2,500,000. **Investment Policies:** Early stage. **Industry Preferences:** Communications, semiconductors and other electronics, biotechnology, medical and health, and industrial and energy. **Geographic Preferences:** U.S.

63106 ■ Harvest Partners, Inc.
280 Park Ave., 33rd Fl.
New York, NY 10017
Ph:(212)559-6300
Fax: (212)812-0100
URL: http://www.harvpart.com
Contact: Harvey Mallement, Senior Managing Director
Preferred Investment Size: $40,000,000 to $500,000,000. **Investment Types:** Acquisition, leveraged buyout, management buyouts, and later stage. **Industry Preferences:** Other products, industrial and energy, consumer related, communications and media, and Internet specific. **Geographic Preferences:** U.S.

63107 ■ Herbert Young Securities, Inc.
98 Cuttermill Rd.
Great Neck, NY 11021
Ph:(516)487-8300
Fax: (516)487-8319
Contact: Herbert Levine, President
Preferred Investment Size: $1,000,000 minimum. **Investment Types:** First and second stage, leveraged buyout, mezzanine, and special situation. **Industry Preferences:** Communications, computer hardware and software, Internet specific, semiconductors and other electronics, biotechnology, medical and health, consumer related, industrial and energy, financial services, business service, manufacturing, agriculture, forestry and fishing.

63108 ■ Holding Capital Group, Inc.
630 3rd Ave., 7th Fl.
New York, NY 10017
Ph:(212)486-6670
Fax: (212)486-0843
URL: http://www.holdingcapital.com
Preferred Investment Size: $5,000,000 minimum. **Investment Types:** Leveraged buyout. **Geographic Preferences:** U.S.

63109 ■ Hollinger Capital
270 Lafayette St., Ste. 600
New York, NY 10012
Ph:(212)334-5944
Fax: (212)586-0010
URL: http://www.hollingercapital.com
Contact: Doug Lamb, Partner
Preferred Investment Size: $2,000,000 to $15,000,000. **Investment Types:** Early, first, second and later stage, and expansion. **Industry Preferences:** Communications, computer software, Internet specific, and business service. **Geographic Preferences:** Northeast and Canada.

63110 ■ Hudson Venture Partners
660 Madison Ave., 14th Fl.
New York, NY 10021
Ph:(212)644-9797
Fax: (212)644-7430

URL: http://www.hudsonptr.com
Contact: Lawrence Howard, Senior Managing Director
Preferred Investment Size: $2,000,000 to $8,000,000. **Investment Types:** First, Early, second and later stage. **Industry Preferences:** Internet specific, computer software and services, communications and media, computer hardware, biotechnology, medical and health, other products, semiconductors and other electronics. **Geographic Preferences:** Mid Atlantic and Northeast.

63111 ■ I-Hatch Ventures, LLC
599 Broadway, 11th Fl.
New York, NY 10166
Ph:(212)651-1750
Fax: (212)208-2576
URL: http://www.i.hatch.com
Contact: Brad Farkas, Principal
Investment Types: Seed and early stage. **Industry Preferences:** Internet specific, computer software, hardware and services, consumer related, communications and media. **Geographic Preferences:** Northeast.

63112 ■ IBJS Capital Corp.
1 State St., 9th Fl.
New York, NY 10004
Ph:(212)858-2018
Fax: (212)858-2768
Contact: George Zombeck, Chief Operating Officer
Preferred Investment Size: $2,000,000 minimum. **Investment Types:** Mezzanine, leveraged buyout, and special situation. **Industry Preferences:** Semiconductors and other electronics, consumer related, industrial and energy. **Geographic Preferences:** Midwest, Northeast, and Southwest.

63113 ■ Impact Venture Partners
599 Broadway, 11th Fl.
New York, NY 10019
Ph:(212)219-3931
Fax: (212)214-0909
URL: http://www.impactvp.com
Contact: Jay Brichke, Chief Financial Officer
Preferred Investment Size: $3,000,000 to $5,000,000. **Investment Policies:** Early stage. **Industry Preferences:** Internet specific, computer software and services, communications and media, and computer hardware. **Geographic Preferences:** Northeast and Texas.

63114 ■ Impex Venture Management Co.
PO Box 1570
Green Island, NY 12183
Ph:(518)271-8008
Fax: (518)271-9101
Contact: Jay Banker
Preferred Investment Size: $1,000,000 minimum. **Investment Types:** Start-up, first and second stage, leveraged buyout, and special situation. **Industry Preferences:** Communications, computer hardware, Internet specific, semiconductors and other electronics, biotechnology, consumer related, industrial and energy, and financial services. **Geographic Preferences:** Mid Atlantic and Northeast, U.S.; and Quebec, Canada.

63115 ■ Information Group
875 3rd Ave., 5th Fl.
New York, NY 10022
Ph:(212)548-6300
URL: http://www.informationgroup.com
Contact: Clifton Robbins, Managing Director
Investment Policies: Start-up and expansion. **Industry Preferences:** Internet specific. **Geographic Preferences:** National.

63116 ■ Insight Venture Partners / Insight Capital Partners
680 5th Ave., 8th Fl.
New York, NY 10019
Ph:(212)230-9200
Fax:(212)230-9272
URL: http://www.insightpartners.com
Contact: Deven Parekh, Managing Director
Preferred Investment Size: $5,000,000 to $30,000,000. **Investment Types:** Early stage and ex-

pansion. **Industry Preferences:** Internet specific, computer software and services, other products, consumer related, computer hardware, communications and media. **Geographic Preferences:** U.S and Canada.

63117 ■ InterEquity Capital Partners, L.P.
220 5th Ave., 12th Fl.
New York, NY 10001
Ph:(212)779-2022
Fax: (212)779-2103
URL: http://www.interequity-capital.com
Contact: Irwin Schlass, President
Preferred Investment Size: $1,000,000 to $3,000,000. **Investment Types:** First and second stage, mezzanine, leveraged buyout, and special situation. **Industry Preferences:** Internet specific, medical and health, computer software and services, consumer related, other products, industrial and energy, communications and media. **Geographic Preferences:** U.S.

63118 ■ Jegi Capital, LLC
150 E. 52nd St., 18th Fl.
New York, NY 10022
Ph:(212)754-0710
Fax: (212)754-0337
URL: http://www.jegi.com
Contact: Bill Hitzig, Chief Operating Officer
Preferred Investment Size: $2,000,000 to $5,000,000. **Investment Policies:** Early, first and second stage. **Industry Preferences:** Computer hardware and software, Internet specific, and semiconductors and other electronics. **Geographic Preferences:** U.S.

63119 ■ Jerusalem Venture Partners /JVP
41 Madison Ave., 25th Fl.
New York, NY 10010
Ph:(212)479-5100
Fax: (212)213-1776
URL: http://www.jvpvc.com
Contact: Erel Margalit, Managing Partner
Preferred Investment Size: $2,000,000 to $35,000,000. **Investment Types:** Early stage. **Industry Preferences:** Internet specific, semiconductors and other electronics, communications and media, computer software and services, computer hardware, industrial and energy.

63120 ■ The Jordan Edmiston Group Inc.
150 East 52nd St., 18th Fl.
New York, NY 10022
Ph:(212)754-0710
Fax: (212)754-0337
Contact: Richard Mead, Managing Director
Preferred Investment Size: $1,000,000 minimum. **Investment Types:** Leveraged buyout, mezzanine, second stage, and special situation. **Industry Preferences:** Manufacturing.

63121 ■ Josephberg, Grosz and Co., Inc.
633 3rd Ave., 13th Fl.
New York, NY 10017
Ph:(212)974-9926
Fax: (212)397-5832
Contact: Richard Josephberg
Preferred Investment Size: $1,000,000 minimum. **Investment Types:** Early, second and later stage, expansion, control-block purchases, generalist PE, joint ventures, leveraged buyout, and management buyouts, mezzanine, open market, private placement, turnaround, recapitalizations, and special situation. **Geographic Preferences:** U.S.

63122 ■ J.P. Morgan Capital Corp.
1221 Avenue of the Americas
New York, NY 10020
Ph:(212)899-3400
Fax: (212)899-3401
URL: http://www.jpmorgan.com
Contact: John Mayer, Chief Executive Officer
Preferred Investment Size: $10,000,000 to $20,000,000. **Investment Types:** Balanced and early stage. **Industry Preferences:** Other products, communications and media, Internet specific, computer

software and services, semiconductors and other electronics, consumer related, medical and health, computer hardware, biotechnology, industrial and energy. **Geographic Preferences:** U.S. and Canada.

63123 ■ KBL Healthcare Ventures
645 Madison Ave., 14th Fl.
New York, NY 10022
Ph:(212)319-5555
Fax: (212)319-5591
URL: http://www.kblhealthcare.com
Contact: Marlene Krauss, Managing Director
Preferred Investment Size: $500,000 to $6,000,000. **Investment Types:** Seed, start-up, early, first, second and later stage, expansion, mezzanine, private placement, public companies, recapitalizations, research and development, and turnaround. **Industry Preferences:** Medical and health, biotechnology, Internet specific, communications and media, computer software and services. **Geographic Preferences:** U.S.

63124 ■ The Lambda Funds
147 E. 48th St.
New York, NY 10017
Ph:(212)230-9835
Fax: (212)230-9886
Contact: Anthony Lamport, General Partner
Preferred Investment Size: $100,000 to $1,000,000. **Investment Types:** First stage. **Industry Preferences:** Biotechnology, computer hardware, computer software and services, industrial and energy, consumer related, other products, semiconductors and other electronics, medical and health, communications and media, and Internet specific. **Geographic Preferences:** Mid Atlantic, Northeast, and West Coast.

63125 ■ Lazard Technology Partners
30 Rockefeller Plz., 48th Fl.
New York, NY 10020
Ph:(212)632-2626
Fax: (212)332-8677
URL: http://www.lazardtp.com
Contact: Manu Rana, Principal
Preferred Investment Size: $1,000,000 to $10,000,000. **Investment Types:** Early, first, second and later stage, and expansion. **Industry Preferences:** Internet specific, computer software and services, computer hardware, communications and media, semiconductors and other electronics, and consumer related. **Geographic Preferences:** District of Columbia, East Coast, and New York.

63126 ■ LC39 Venture Group LLC
405 Park Ave.
New York, NY 10022
Ph:(212)759-1775
Fax: (212)759-9773
URL: http://www.lc39.com
Contact: Albert Wenger, Chief Executive Officer
Investment Types: Early stage. **Industry Preferences:** Internet specific. **Geographic Preferences:** U.S.

63127 ■ Lepercq Capital Management, Inc. / Lepercq de Neuflize in
1675 Broadway
New York, NY 10019
Ph:(212)698-0795
Fax: (212)262-0155
URL: http://www.lepercq.com
Preferred Investment Size: $1,000,000 to $10,000,000. **Investment Types:** Control-block purchases, leveraged buyout, and second stage. **Industry Preferences:** Communications, computer hardware and software, Internet specific, and consumer related.

63128 ■ Linux Global Partners
41 E. 11th St., 11th Fl.
New York, NY 10003
Ph:(212)699-3622
Fax: (212)233-1160
URL: http://www.linuxglobalpartners.com
Investment Policies: Start-up, seed, and early stage. **Geographic Preferences:** U.S.

63129 ■ Loeb Partners Corp.
61 Broadway, Ste. 2400
New York, NY 10006
Ph:(212)483-7000
Fax: (212)574-2001
Contact: Thomas Kempner, Chief Executive Officer
Preferred Investment Size: $100,000 minimum. **Investment Types:** Early stage, acquisition, expansion, leveraged buyout, and management buyouts. **Industry Preferences:** Internet specific, biotechnology, medical and health, Internet specific, computer software and services, semiconductors and other electronics. **Geographic Preferences:** U.S.

63130 ■ M31 Ventures, LLC
712 5th Ave., 22nd Fl.
New York, NY 10019
Ph:(212)581-3143
Fax: (212)581-2433
URL: http://www.m31ventures.com
Contact: Adam Pelzman, Managing Partner
Investment Types: Early and later stage, and expansion. **Industry Preferences:** Internet specific. **Geographic Preferences:** U.S.

63131 ■ Madison Investment Partners, Inc.
660 Madison Ave.
New York, NY 10021
Ph:(212)223-2600
Fax: (212)223-8208
Contact: Emile Geisenheimer, President
Preferred Investment Size: $5,000,000 minimum. **Investment Types:** Second stage, leveraged buyout, and industry roll ups. **Industry Preferences:** Communications and media, semiconductors and other electronics, medical and health, consumer related, industrial and energy, financial services, and manufacturing. **Geographic Preferences:** U.S.

63132 ■ MC Capital, Inc.
520 Madison Ave., 16th Fl.
New York, NY 10022
Ph:(212)644-0841
Fax: (212)644-2926
Contact: Katsuhiko Oba, Chief Financial Officer
Preferred Investment Size: $1,000,000 to $30,000,000. **Investment Types:** Acquisition, expansion, first stage, fund of funds, generalist PE, joint ventures, later stage, leveraged buyout, private placement, second stage, special situation, and turnaround. **Industry Preferences:** Communications and media, computer hardware, semiconductors and other electronics, biotechnology, medical and health. **Geographic Preferences:** U.S. and Canada.

63133 ■ McCown, De Leeuw and Co. (New York)
Park Ave. Tower
900 3rd Ave.
New York, NY 10022
Ph:(212)355-5500
Fax: (212)355-6283
URL: http://www.mdcpartners.com
Contact: George McCown, Managing Director
Preferred Investment Size: $20,000,000 to $50,000,000. **Investment Types:** Leveraged buyout. **Industry Preferences:** Consumer related, other products, computer hardware, computer software and services, medical and health, Internet specific, communications and media, semiconductors and other electronics, industrial and energy. **Geographic Preferences:** U.S.

63134 ■ McGraw-Hill Ventures /McGraw-Hill Capital Corp.
1221 Avenue of the Americas, 47th Fl.
New York, NY 10020-1095
Ph:(212)512-2000
Fax: (212)512-6797
URL: http://www.mcgraw-hill.com
Contact: Brian Casey, Vice President
Preferred Investment Size: $500,000 to $5,000,000. **Investment Types:** Early, second and later stage, and expansion. **Industry Preferences:** Communications and media, computer software, Internet specific, medical and health, industrial and energy, financial services, business service, and manufacturing. **Geographic Preferences:** U.S.

63135 ■ Medical Venture Holdings, Inc.
c/o CIBC-Openheimer, Inc.
200 Liberty St.
New York, NY 10281
Ph:(212)667-5053
Fax: (212)667-8148
URL: http://www.
Preferred Investment Size: $1,000,000 minimum. **Investment Types:** Seed, start-up, first and second stage, and mezzanine. **Industry Preferences:** Biotechnology, and medical and health. **Geographic Preferences:** U.S.

63136 ■ Metropolitan Venture Partners (METVP)
257 Park Ave. S., 15th Fl.
New York, NY 10010
Ph:(212)844-3677
Fax: (212)844-3699
URL: http://www.metvp.com
Contact: Michael Levin, Managing Director
Preferred Investment Size: $500,000 to $5,000,000. **Investment Types:** Early, first, and second stage, expansion, management buyouts, recapitalizations, and special situation. **Industry Preferences:** Communications, computer software, semiconductors and other electronics, and Internet specific. **Geographic Preferences:** Northeast.

63137 ■ Milestone Venture Partners
551 Madison Ave., 7th Fl.
New York, NY 10022
Ph:(212)223-7400
Fax: (212)223-0315
URL: http://www.milestonevp.com
Contact: Richard Dumler, General Partner
Preferred Investment Size: $250,000 to $1,000,000. **Investment Types:** Early stage. **Industry Preferences:** Communications and media, computer software, and Internet specific. **Geographic Preferences:** Connecticut, Mid Atlantic, New Jersey, New York, and Northeast.

63138 ■ Mitsui and Co. Venture Partners (MCVP)
200 Park Avenue, 36th Fl.
New York, NY 10166-0130
Ph:(212)878-4050
Fax: (212)878-4070
URL: http://www.mitsuivp.com
Contact: Yoichiro Endo, Chief Executive Officer and Managing Dir
Investment Types: Seed, start-up, first, second, and early stage, and research and development. **Industry Preferences:** Internet specific, semiconductors and other electronics, computer software and other services, communications and media, medical and health, computer hardware, biotechnology, and other products. **Geographic Preferences:** U.S. and Canada.

63139 ■ Morgan Stanley Venture Partners / MSDW
1585 Broadway
New York, NY 10036
Ph:(212)761-6003
Fax: (212)761-9606
URL: http://www.msvp.com
Contact: Debra Abramovitz, Chief Operating Officer
Preferred Investment Size: $5,000,000 to $25,000,000. **Investment Types:** Second and later stage, mezzanine, leveraged buyout, and industry rollups. **Industry Preferences:** Internet specific, computer software and services, medical and health, communications and media, semiconductors and other electronics, industrial and energy, biotechnology, computer hardware, other products, and consumer related. **Geographic Preferences:** U.S. and Canada.

63140 ■ Murphy and Partners, L.P.
45 Rockefeller Plz., Ste. 1960
New York, NY 10111
Ph:(212)332-1000
Fax: (212)332-2920
URL: http://www.murphy-partners.com
Contact: John Murphy, Managing General Partner

Preferred Investment Size: $1,000,000 to $10,000,000. **Investment Types:** Seed, early, first and second stage, leveraged buyout, expansion, and control-block purchases. **Industry Preferences:** Communications, medical and health, and consumer related. **Geographic Preferences:** U.S.

63141 ■ Nazem and Co.
645 Madison Ave., 12th Fl.
New York, NY 10022
Ph:(212)371-7900
Fax: (212)371-2150
Co. E-mail: nazem@msn.com
Contact: Fred F. Nazem, Managing Partner
Preferred Investment Size: $1,000,000 minimum. **Investment Types:** Seed, start-up, first, second, and later stage, mezzanine, leveraged buyout, special situation, expansion, recapitalizations, and turnaround. **Industry Preferences:** Computer hardware, computer software and services, medical and health, communications and media, biotechnology, semiconductors and other electronics, Internet specific, industrial and energy, other products, and consumer related. **Geographic Preferences:** U.S.

63142 ■ Needham Asset Management
445 Park Ave.
New York, NY 10022
Ph:(212)705-0311
Fax: (212)705-0455
URL: http://www.needhamfunds.com
Contact: George Needham, Chief Executive Officer
Preferred Investment Size: $2,000,000 to $10,000,000. **Investment Types:** Later stage, leveraged buyout, management buyouts, and mezzanine. **Industry Preferences:** Semiconductors and other electronics, computer software and services, communications and media, Internet specific, medical and health, computer hardware, other products, consumer related, industrial and energy. **Geographic Preferences:** U.S.

63143 ■ New York State Science & Technology Foundation
90 Washington St., Ste. 1730
Albany, NY 12210
Ph:(518)474-4349
Fax: (518)473-6876
Preferred Investment Size: $100,000 to $300,000. **Investment Types:** Seed, start-up, first and second stage. **Industry Preferences:** Communications, computer related, semiconductors and other electronics, biotechnology, medical and health, consumer related, industrial and energy, agriculture, forestry and fishing. **Geographic Preferences:** Northeast.

63144 ■ Northwood Ventures
485 Underhill Blvd., Ste. 205
Syosset, NY 11791
Ph:(516)364-5544
Fax: (516)364-0879
URL: http://www.northwoodventures.com
Contact: Henry Wilson, Managing Director
Preferred Investment Size: $1,000,000 to $5,000,000. **Investment Types:** Early, first, second, early, and later stage, acquisition, expansion, leveraged buyout, management buyouts, private placement, special situation, balanced, generalist PE, industry rollups, and recapitalizations. **Industry Preferences:** Communications and media, Internet specific, consumer related, biotechnology, industrial and energy, semiconductors and other electronics, computer software and services, and computer hardware. **Geographic Preferences:** U.S. and Canada.

63145 ■ Norwood Venture Corp.
1430 Broadway, Ste. 1607
New York, NY 10018
Ph:(212)783-1117
Fax: (212)869-5331
URL: http://www.norven.com
Contact: Mark Littell
Preferred Investment Size: $500,000 to $1,000,000. **Investment Types:** Mezzanine, leveraged buyout, balanced, and special situation. **Geographic Preferences:** U.S.

63146 ■ Noveltek Venture Corp.
521 5th Ave., Ste. 1700
New York, NY 10175
Ph:(212)286-1963
Preferred Investment Size: $1,000,000 minimum.
Investment Types: Control-block purchases, first stage, mezzanine, second stage, special situation, and start-up. **Industry Preferences:** Communications and media, computer hardware, computer related, semiconductors and other electronics, biotechnology, medical and health, consumer related, industrial and energy. **Geographic Preferences:** U.S. and Canada.

63147 ■ Onondaga Venture Capital Fund, Inc.
241 W. Fayette St.
Syracuse, NY 13202
Ph:(315)478-0157
Fax: (315)478-0158
URL: http://www.onex.com
Contact: Michael Schattner, President
Preferred Investment Size: $50,000 to $300,000. **Investment Types:** Early, first, and second stage, and expansion. **Industry Preferences:** Communications, computer software, semiconductors and other electronics, biotechnology, medical and health, consumer related, and manufacturing. **Geographic Preferences:** Northeast.

63148 ■ Opticality Ventures
29 Country Club Ln., S.
Briarcliff Manor, NY 10510
Ph:(914)923-0003
Fax: (413)487-2114
URL: http://www.opticality.com
Contact: Hadar Pedhazur, Founder
Preferred Investment Size: $1,000,000 to $5,000,000. **Investment Policies:** Early stage. **Industry Preferences:** Computer software and Internet specific.

63149 ■ Ovation Capital Partners
120 Bloomingdale Rd., 4th Fl.
White Plains, NY 10605
Ph:(914)258-0011
Fax: (914)684-0848
URL: http://www.ovationcapital.com
Preferred Investment Size: $500,000 to $4,000,000. **Investment Types:** Early stage. **Industry Preferences:** Internet related. **Geographic Preferences:** Northeast.

63150 ■ Paribas Principal, Inc.
787 7th Ave., 32nd Fl.
New York, NY 10019
Ph:(212)841-2005
Fax: (212)841-3558
URL: http://www.bnpparibas.com
Contact: Miles Alexander, President
Preferred Investment Size: $50,000,000 minimum. **Investment Types:** Leveraged buyout, special situation, and control block purchases. **Industry Preferences:** Communications, computer software, semiconductors and other electronics, medical and health, consumer related, industrial and energy, transportation, business service, and manufacturing. **Geographic Preferences:** U.S.

63151 ■ Patricof & Co. Ventures, Inc. (New York)
445 Park Ave.
New York, NY 10022
Ph:(212)753-6300
Fax: (212)319-6155
URL: http://www.patricof.com
Preferred Investment Size: $500,000 minimum. **Investment Types:** Seed, start-up, first and second stage, mezzanine, and leveraged buyout. **Industry Preferences:** Diversified. **Geographic Preferences:** No preference.

63152 ■ Pennell Venture Partners
332 Bleecker St., No. K-67
New York, NY 10014
Ph:(212)206-1295
Fax: (646)365-3195

URL: http://www.pennell.com
Contact: Thomas Pennell, Managing Partner
Preferred Investment Size: $300,000 to $1,500,000. **Investment Policies:** Early stage. **Industry Preferences:** Computer software. **Geographic Preferences:** New York.

63153 ■ The Pittsford Group, Inc.
8 Lodge Pole Rd.
Pittsford, NY 14534
Ph:(716)223-3523
Preferred Investment Size: $100,000 to $300,000. **Investment Types:** Start-up, first and second stage, and control-block purchases. **Industry Preferences:** Communications and media, computer software, Internet specific, semiconductors and other electronics, biotechnology, consumer related, industrial and energy. **Geographic Preferences:** Northeast and Southeast U.S.; Central, Eastern, Ontario, and Quebec, Canada

63154 ■ The Platinum Group, Inc.
350 Fifth Ave., 71st Fl.
New York, NY 10118
Ph:(212)736-4300
Fax: (212)736-6086
URL: http://www.platinumgroup.com
Investment Types: Start-up, first and second stage, and leveraged buyout. **Industry Preferences:** Communications, computer hardware and software, Internet specific, semiconductors and other electronics, biotechnology, medical and health, consumer related, industrial and energy, and manufacturing. **Geographic Preferences:** U.S.

63155 ■ Poly Ventures
901 Rte. 110
Farmingdale, NY 11735
Ph:(516)249-4710
Preferred Investment Size: $500,000 to $1,000,000. **Investment Policies:** Start-up, seed, first and second stage. **Industry Preferences:** Communications and media, Internet specific, computer software and services, computer hardware, industrial and energy, other products, and semiconductors and other electronics. **Geographic Preferences:** National.

63156 ■ Pomona Capital
780 3rd Ave., 28th Fl.
New York, NY 10017
Ph:(212)593-3639
Fax: (212)593-3987
URL: http://www.pomonacapital.com
Contact: Mark Marusezewski, Principal
Preferred Investment Size: $1,000,000 minimum. **Investment Types:** Fund of funds, and fund of funds of second. **Industry Preferences:** Communications and media, computer hardware and software, biotechnology, medical and health, consumer related, industrial and energy, financial services, and manufacturing. **Geographic Preferences:** U.S. and Canada.

63157 ■ Prospect Street Ventures
10 East 40th St., 44th Fl.
New York, NY 10016
Ph:(212)448-0702
Fax: (212)448-9652
URL: http://www.prospectstreet.com
Contact: John Barry, Senior Managing Director
Preferred Investment Size: $5,000,000 to $25,000,000. **Investment Types:** Seed, start-up, early, first, second, and later stage, expansion, generalist PE, joint ventures, leveraged buyout, and management buyouts. **Industry Preferences:** Internet specific, computer software and services, other products, communications and media, medical and health. **Geographic Preferences:** U.S. and Canada.

63158 ■ Rand Capital Corporation
2200 Rand Bldg.
Buffalo, NY 14203
Ph:(716)853-0802
Fax: (716)854-8480
URL: http://www.randcapital.com
Contact: Allen Grum, President, Chief Executive Officer, and

E-mail: pgrum@randcorp.com
Preferred Investment Size: $50,000 to $5,000,000. **Investment Types:** Early, later and second stage, and expansion. **Industry Preferences:** Industrial and energy, other products, communications and media, computer software and services, Internet specific, medical and health, industrial and energy, consumer related, semiconductors and other electronics, computer hardware, and biotechnology. **Geographic Preferences:** Northeast and New York.

63159 ■ Regent Capital Management
505 Park Ave., Ste. 1700
New York, NY 10022
Ph:(212)735-9900
Fax: (212)735-9908
Contact: Richard Hochman, Chief Executive Officer
Preferred Investment Size: $3,500,000 minimum. **Investment Types:** Second stage, mezzanine, and leveraged buyout. **Industry Preferences:** Consumer related, communications and media, and other products. **Geographic Preferences:** U.S.

63160 ■ Rothschild Ventures, Inc.
1251 Avenue of the Americas, 51st Fl.
New York, NY 10020
Ph:(212)403-3500
Fax: (212)403-3652
URL: http://www.nmrothschild.com
Contact: Bob Andrew, Chief Financial Officer
Investment Types: Seed, start-up, first and second state, research and development, mezzanine, and leveraged buyout. **Industry Preferences:** Computer hardware, software and services, industrial and energy, communications and media, biotechnology, medical and health, consumer related, semiconductors and other electronics, and Internet specific. **Geographic Preferences:** U.S. and Canada.

63161 ■ Sandler Capital Management
767 Fifth Ave., 45th Fl.
New York, NY 10153
Ph:(212)754-8100
Fax: (212)826-0280
URL: http://www.sandlercap.com
Contact: Andrew Sandler, Managing Director
Preferred Investment Size: $20,000,000 minimum. **Investment Policies:** Equity. **Investment Types:** Seed, start-up, first and second stage, control-block purchases, leveraged buyout, mezzanine, research and development, and special situation. **Industry Preferences:** Internet specific, communications and media, other products, computer software and services, consumer related, medical and health, semiconductors and other electronics. **Geographic Preferences:** U.S. and Canada.

63162 ■ Scripps Ventures
200 Madison Ave., 4th Fl.
New York, NY 10010
Ph:(212)293-8709
Fax: (212)293-8716
URL: http://www.scrippsventures.com
Preferred Investment Size: $5,000,000 minimum. **Investment Policies:** First and second stage. **Industry Preferences:** Internet specific, consumer related, computer software and services, computer hardware, and other products. **Geographic Preferences:** U.S. and Canada.

63163 ■ Seed Capital Partners
620 Main St.
Buffalo, NY 14202
Ph:(716)845-7520
Fax: (716)845-7539
URL: http://www.seedcp.com
Contact: Jordan Levy, Managing Partner
Preferred Investment Size: $250 to $2,500,000. **Investment Types:** Seed and early stage. **Industry Preferences:** Computer software and services, communications and media, Internet specific, semiconductors and other electronics, and other products. **Geographic Preferences:** Northeast U.S.; and Ontario and Quebec, Canada..

63164 ■ Siguler Guff & Company
630 Fifth Ave., 16th Fl.
New York, NY 10111

Ph:(212)332-5100
Fax: (212)332-5120
URL: http://www.sigulerguff.com
Contact: Drew Guff, Managing Director
Investment Types: Start-up, first and second stage, control-block purchases, mezzanine, leveraged buyout, special situations, distressed debt, fund of funds. **Industry Preferences:** Communications, computer software and hardware, Internet specific, semiconductors and other electronics, biotechnology, medical and health, consumer related, industrial and energy, transportation, financial services, business service, manufacturing, agriculture, forestry and fishing. **Geographic Preferences:** U.S.

63165 ■ Silicon Alley Venture Partners LLC / SAVP
152 W. 57th St., 20th Fl.
New York, NY 10019
Ph:(212)967-6545
Fax: (212)898-9044
URL: http://www.savp.com
Contact: Brian Model, Principal
Preferred Investment Size: $100,000 to $5,000,000. **Investment Policies:** Start-up, seed, first, early and second stage. **Industry Preferences:** Computer software, and Internet specific. **Geographic Preferences:** Northeast.

63166 ■ Spencer Trask Ventures, Inc. / Spencer Trask Securities
535 Madison Ave.
New York, NY 10022
Ph:(212)326-9000
Fax: (212)751-3362
URL: http://www.spencertrask.com
Contact: William Dioguardi, President
Preferred Investment Size: $1,000,000 to $20,000,000. **Investment Types:** Start-up, first, early and second stage. **Industry Preferences:** Communications and media, computer hardware and software, Internet specific, semiconductors and other electronics, biotechnology, medical and health, consumer related, industrial and energy, financial services, and manufacturing. **Geographic Preferences:** U.S.

63167 ■ Sprout Group (New York City)
11 Madison Ave., 26th Fl.
New York, NY 10010
Ph:(212)538-3600
Fax: (212)538-8245
URL: http://www.sproutgroup.com
Contact: Alexander Rosen, General Partner
Preferred Investment Size: $5,000,000 to $50,000,000. **Investment Types:** Start-up, early and later stage, expansion, leveraged buyout, and management buyouts. **Industry Preferences:** Medical and health, Internet specific, communications and media, biotechnology, consumer related, computer software and services, semiconductors and other electronics, industrial and energy, other products, and computer hardware. **Geographic Preferences:** U.S.

63168 ■ Stamford Financial Consulting
108 Main St.
Stamford, NY 12167
Ph:(607)652-3311
Fax: (607)652-6301
URL: http://www.stamfordfinancial.com
Preferred Investment Size: $2,000,000 to $5,000,000. **Investment Types:** Expansion, mezzanine, early stage, management buyouts, private placement, and turnaround. **Industry Preferences:** Communications, semiconductors and other electronics, consumer related, medical and health, industrial and energy, financial services, and business service. **Geographic Preferences:** U.S.

63169 ■ Sterling/Carl Marks Capital / Sterling Capital
175 Great Neck Rd., Ste. 408
Great Neck, NY 11021
Ph:(516)482-7374
Fax: (516)487-0781
URL: http://www.serlingcarlmarks.com
Contact: Debra Glickman
Preferred Investment Size: $1,000,000 to $2,000,000. **Investment Types:** Second stage, ex-

pansion, management buyouts, and mezzanine. **Industry Preferences:** Internet specific, computer software and services, consumer related, other products, consumer related, medical and health. **Geographic Preferences:** New York and Northeast.

63170 ■ US Trust Private Equity
114 W.47th St.
New York, NY 10036
Ph:(212)852-3949
Fax: (212)852-3759
URL: http://www.ustrust.com/privateequity
Contact: Jim Ruler
E-mail: jruler@ustrust.com
Preferred Investment Size: $5,000,000 minimum. **Investment Types:** Early, first stage, and second stage. **Industry Preferences:** Diversified. **Geographic Preferences:** National.

63171 ■ Vega Capital Corp.
45 Knollwood Rd.
Elmsford, NY 10523
Ph:(914)345-9500
Fax: (914)345-9505
Contact: Ronald Linden
Preferred Investment Size: $300,000 minimum. **Investment Types:** Second stage, mezzanine, leveraged buyout, and special situation. **Industry Preferences:** Communications and media, computer hardware, semiconductors and other electronics, medical and health, consumer related, industrial and energy, transportation, financial services, manufacturing, agriculture, forestry and fishing. **Geographic Preferences:** Northeast, Southeast, and Mid Atlantic.

63172 ■ Vencon Management, Inc.
301 West 53rd St., Ste. 10F
New York, NY 10019
Ph:(212)581-8787
Fax: (212)397-4126
Co. E-mail: vencon@worldnet.att.net
URL: http://www.venconinc.com
Contact: Alina Hamza
Preferred Investment Size: $500,000 to $10,000,000. **Investment Types:** First and second stage, leveraged buyout, seed, special situation, and start-up. **Industry Preferences:** Communications, computer software, Internet specific, semiconductors and other electronics, biotechnology, medical and health. **Geographic Preferences:** U.S. and Canada.

63173 ■ Venrock Associates
30 Rockefeller Plz., Ste. 5508
New York, NY 10112
Ph:(212)649-5600
Fax: (212)649-5788
URL: http://www.venrock.com
Contact: Anthony Sun, Managing General Partner
Preferred Investment Size: $5,000,000 to $15,000,000. **Investment Types:** Seed, start-up, early, first, and later stage. **Industry Preferences:** Biotechnology, Internet specific, computer software and services, communications and media, medical and health, semiconductors and other electronics, industrial and energy, computer hardware, other products, and consumer related. **Geographic Preferences:** U.S.

63174 ■ Venture Capital Fund of America, Inc. / VCFA Group
509 Madison Ave., Ste. 812
New York, NY 10022
Ph:(212)838-5577
Fax: (212)838-7614
URL: http://www.vcfa.com
Contact: Dayton Carr, Managing Director
E-mail: carr@vcfa.com
Preferred Investment Size: $1,000,000 to $100,000,000. **Investment Types:** Fund of funds of second. **Geographic Preferences:** U.S and Canada.

63175 ■ Venture Opportunities Corp.
150 E. 58th St.
New York, NY 10155
Ph:(212)832-3737
Fax: (212)980-6603
Co. E-mail: jerryvoc@aol.com

Contact: A. Fred March, President
Preferred Investment Size: $2,000,000 minimum. **Investment Types:** Start-up, first and second stage, mezzanine, leveraged buyout, and special situation. **Industry Preferences:** Communications and media, computer related, semiconductors and other electronics, biotechnology, medical and health, consumer related, industrial and energy, transportation, and manufacturing. **Geographic Preferences:** U.S.

63176 ■ Warburg Pincus LLC
466 Lexington Ave., 11th Fl.
New York, NY 10017
Ph:(212)878-0600
Fax: (212)878-9100
URL: http://www.warburgpincus.com
Contact: Barry Taylor, Managing Director
Preferred Investment Size: $1,000,000 minimum. **Investment Types:** Seed, start-up, first, early, second, and later stage, mezzanine, leveraged buyout, management buyouts, private placements, acquisition, expansion, generalist PE, open market, research and development, turnaround, recapitalizations, and special situation. **Industry Preferences:** Other products, communications and media, medical and health, Internet specific, computer hardware computer software and services, consumer related, industrial and energy, biotechnology, semiconductors and other electronics. **Geographic Preferences:** U.S. and Canada.

63177 ■ Wasserstein, Perella & Co. Inc.
31 W. 52nd St., 27th Fl.
New York, NY 10019
Ph:(212)702-5691
Fax: (212)969-7879
Contact: Perry W. Steiner
Investment Types: Leveraged buyout. **Industry Preferences:** Diversified. **Geographic Preferences:** National.

63178 ■ Welsh, Carson, Anderson, & Stowe
320 Park Ave., Ste. 2500
New York, NY 10022-6815
Ph:(212)893-9500
Fax: (212)893-9575
Contact: John Almeida, Principal
Preferred Investment Size: $100,000,000 to $500,000,000. **Investment Types:** Leveraged buyout, management buyouts, expansion, joint ventures, mezzanine, turnaround, and special situation. **Industry Preferences:** Medical and health, other products, communications and media, Internet specific, computer software and services, computer hardware, consumer related, semiconductors and other electronics, industrial and energy.

63179 ■ Winthrop Ventures
266 West End Ave., Ste. 600
New York, NY 10023-2666
Ph:(212)873-7958
Contact: Cyrus Brown, President
Preferred Investment Size: $1,000,000 minimum. **Investment Types:** Start-up, first and second stage, and leveraged buyout. **Industry Preferences:** Communications, computer hardware and software, semiconductors and other electronics, biotechnology, medical and health, consumer related, industrial and energy, transportation, financial services, and manufacturing.

PROCUREMENT ASSISTANCE PROGRAMS

63180 ■ Empire State Development–Division for Small Business–Procurement Assistance Program (30 S)
30 S Pearl St. 7th Fl.
Albany, NY 12245
Ph:(518)292-5220
Free: 800-STA-TENY
Fax: (518)592-5884
URL: http://www.empire.state.ny.us
Contact: Arlene Germain

Description: Assists businesses in obtaining contracts and subcontracts from federal and state agencies, departments, and authorities, and from prime contractors in the private sector. Offers training, technical, management, and marketing assistance. Also assists New York state small businesses to compete for Federal research and development grants. The Procurement Assistance Unit also puts out a publication entitled *Selling to Government: Finding New Customers for New York's Businesses.*

63181 ■ New York City Department of Business Services–New York City Procurement Outreach Program
110 William St., Fl.9
New York, NY 10038
Ph:(212)513-6444
Fax: (212)618-8899
Co. E-mail: grichards@sbs.nyc.gov
URL: http://www.nyc.gov
Contact: Gordon Richards

63182 ■ New York Procurement Center
U.S. Army Corps of Engineers
26 Federal Plaza, Rm. 1843
New York, NY 10278
Ph:(212)264-4395
Fax: (212)264-3013
Co. E-mail: debra.libow@sba.gov
URL: http://www.sba.gov
Contact: Debra B. Libow, SBA Representative
E-mail: debra.libow@sba.gov
Description: Covers activities for GSA, Federal Supply Service (New York, NY), GSA, Public Buildings Service (New York, NY), Army Corps of Engineers (New York, NY), U.S. Military Academy (West Point, NY).

63183 ■ New York Procurement Technical Assistance Center–Cattaraugus County
303 Court St.
Little Valley, NY 14755
Ph:(716)938-9111
Free: 800-331-0543
Fax: (716)938-9431
Co. E-mail: jjwilliams@cattco.com
URL: http://www.cattco.org
Contact: Joseph Williams

63184 ■ New York Procurement Technical Assistance Center–Long Island Development Corporation
45 Seaman Ave.
Bethpage, NY 11714
Ph:(516)433-5000
Fax: (516)433-5046
Co. E-mail: gov-contracts@lidc.org
URL: http://www.lidc.org
Contact: Soloman Soskin

63185 ■ New York Procurement Technical Assistance Center–Rockland Economic Development Corporation
One Blue Hill Plaza, Ste 1110
Pearl River, NY 10965
Ph:(845)735-7040
Fax: (845)735-5736
Co. E-mail: info@redc.org
URL: http://www.redc.org
Contact: Mary Ann Williams

63186 ■ New York Procurement Technical Assistance Center–South Bronx Overall Economic Development Corporation
555 Bergen Ave., Fl.3
Bronx, NY 10455
Ph:(718)292-3113
Fax: (718)292-3115
Co. E-mail: mjohnson@sobro.org
URL: http://www.sobro.org
Contact: Miriam Johnson

INCUBATORS/RESEARCH AND TECHNOLOGY PARKS

63187 ■ Broome County Industrial Development Agency
225 Water St.
PO Box 1510
Binghamton, NY 13902-0995
Ph:(607)584-9000
Free: 800-836-6740
Fax: (607)584-9009
Co. E-mail: info@bcida.com
URL: http://www.bcida.com

63188 ■ The Case Center
2-212 Center for Science and Technology
Syracuse University
Syracuse, NY 13244
Ph:(315)443-1060
Fax: (315)443-4745
Co. E-mail: tlbritto@syr.edu
URL: http://www.case.syr.edu
Contact: Shiu-Kai Chin, Dir
Description: Located at Syracuse University, the CASE Center has emphasized its collaboration with industry and outside sponsors.

63189 ■ Center for Environmental Sciences and Technology Management
University at Albany
251 Fuller Rd.
CESTM B110
Albany, NY 12203
Ph:(518)437-8686
Fax: (518)437-8610
URL: http://www.albanynanotech.org
Contact: Jackie DiStefano, Director Of Operations
Description: This incubator for emerging technology firms offers abundant resources to its tenants, including the University's Nuclear Accelerator Laboratory, electron microscopes, cluster tools, and much more.

63190 ■ City University of New York–Sponsored Research
Graduate School & University Center
365 Fifth Ave.
New York, NY 10016-4309
Ph:(212)817-7523
Fax: (212)817-1629
Co. E-mail: hfisher@gc.cuny.edu
URL: http://inside.gc.cuny.edu/orup/
Contact: Hilry Fisher, Dir.
E-mail: hfisher@gc.cuny.edu
Scope: Administers and coordinates research and project planning in speech and hearing, anthropology, art history, biology, chemistry, comparative literature, computer science, criminal justice, earth and environmental sciences, economics, physics, political science, sociology, Spanish, theatre, child development, mathematics, environmental and social-personality psychologies, education, special education, mental health, linguistics, French, classics, history, and urban education.

63191 ■ Colgate University–Research Council
Department of Political Science
13 Oak Dr.
Hamilton, NY 13346
Ph:(315)228-7922
Fax: (315)228-7883
Co. E-mail: nmoore@colgate.edu
URL: http://www.colgate.edu/desktopdefault1.
    aspx?tabid=1947
Contact: Nina Moore, Ch.
E-mail: nmoore@colgate.edu
Scope: Administers the University's research funds, receiving applications from faculty members and making awards each spring for amounts between $1,000-$4,000, plus the possibility of a two-course sabbatical leave. Throughout the year, some money is reserved to support incidental expenses incurred by faculty and costs associated with hiring student assistants.

63192 ■ Columbia University–Office of Projects and Grants
1210 Amsterdam Ave., Mail Code 2205
Rm. 254 Engineering Terrace
New York, NY 10027
Ph:(212)854-6851
Fax: (212)854-2738
Co. E-mail: dc2272@columbia.edu
URL: http://www.columbia.edu/cu/opg
Contact: Daniel Caito, Dir.
E-mail: dc2272@columbia.edu
Scope: Solicits, administers, and coordinates extramurally sponsored research conducted in various departments and special research units of the University and assists faculty members in preparation of applications for research contracts and grants-in-aid.

63193 ■ Columbia University–Science and Technology Ventures
80 Claremont Ave.
Mailcode 9606
New York, NY 10027
Ph:(212)854-8444
Fax: (212)854-8463
Co. E-mail: mc1378@columbia.edu
URL: http://www.stv.columbia.edu
Contact: Ofra Weinberger, Dir.
E-mail: mc1378@columbia.edu
Scope: Transfers technology from the University to business and industry, especially in the area of biotechnology.

63194 ■ Cooper Union Research Foundation
Albert Nerkin School of Engineering
51 Astor Pl.
New York, NY 10003
Ph:(212)353-4291
Fax: (212)353-4341
Co. E-mail: ahmad@cooper.edu
URL: http://www.cooper.edu/curf
Contact: Jameel Ahmad, Res.Dir.
E-mail: ahmad@cooper.edu
Scope: Promotes and supports cooperative scientific and applied research between Cooper Union faculty and students and industry, government, and other sponsors. Services provided include proposal planning, preparation, and submission; contract negotiation and proposal monitoring; project management, including technical and financial reporting; and postgrant institutional responsibilities. Projects are supported in the areas of computer engineering, telecommunication and information processing, energy generation and conservation, environmental planning, management and technology, chemical and industrial processes, and biomedical engineering. **Educational Activities:** Conferences; Lectures; Seminars.

63195 ■ Cornell University–Cornell Business and Technology Park
Real Estate Department
15 Thornwood Dr.
Ithaca, NY 14850
Ph:(607)266-7866
Fax: (607)266-7876
Co. E-mail: jem21@cornell.edu
URL: http://www.cornellbtp.com
Contact: John E. Majeroni, Dir.
E-mail: jem21@cornell.edu
Scope: The Park serves as a conduit between Cornell University and business, especially in electronics, computer manufacturing, and biotechnology and is a home for the independent development of technologies resulting from efforts by Cornell researchers. Leases space for business incubator activities and start-up companies. **Publications:** The Park Light.

63196 ■ Cornell University–Cornell Center for Technology, Enterprise and Commercialization
20 Thornwood Dr., Ste. 105
Ithaca, NY 14850
Ph:(607)257-1081
Fax: (607)257-1015
Co. E-mail: rsc5@cornell.edu
URL: http://www.cctec.cornell.edu
Contact: Richard S. Cahoon, Actg.Dir.
E-mail: rsc5@cornell.edu

Scope: Patent and technology marketing arm of the University. Activities include technology transfer, evaluating legal and business contracts, and assisting with patenting and licensing. Holds title to patents and promotes technology transfer to industry. **Publications:** Selected Technology Available for Licensing (semiannually).

63197 ■ Cornell University–Office of Sponsored Programs
120 Day Hall
Ithaca, NY 14853
Ph:(607)255-2945
Fax: (607)255-5058
Co. E-mail: slj15@cornell.edu
URL: http://www.osp.cornell.edu
Contact: Susane Jones
E-mail: slj15@cornell.edu
Scope: Administratively responsible for all extramurally sponsored research and training conducted at the University.

63198 ■ Fordham University–Office of Research and Sponsored Programs
441 E Fordham Rd., Bldg. 540
Bronx, NY 10458
Ph:(718)817-4650
Fax: (718)817-5575
Co. E-mail: belsole@fordham.edu
URL: http://www.fordham.edu/Academics/Office_of_
    Research/index.html
Contact: Angela M. Belsole, Interim Dir.
E-mail: belsole@fordham.edu
Scope: Provides coordination and administrative services for extramurally sponsored research by faculty members of the University, including studies on urban education problems, psychological processes in human creativity, problems of juvenile delinquency, drug addiction in urban areas, social tensions in urban communities, models of religious education systems, the abortion process, and basic investigations in chemistry, physics, and biology.

63199 ■ Local Development Corporation of East New York–East Brooklyn Enterprise Center
80 Jamaica Ave.
Brooklyn, NY 11207
Ph:(718)385-6700
Fax: (718)385-7505
Co. E-mail: ldceny@hotmail.com
URL: http://www.ldceny.org
Contact: Sherry Roberts, Exec Dir

63200 ■ Long Island High Technology Incubator
25 Health Sciences Drive
Box 100
Stony Brook, NY 11790-3350
Ph:(631)444-8800
Fax: (631)444-8825
Co. E-mail: inbox@lihti.org
URL: http://www.lihti.org
Contact: Judith McEvoy, Pres & Treas
Description: The LIHTI offers tenants a place to start up companies without the difficulties normally associated with emerging businesses. The incubator also provides numerous services through its alliances with both public and private sector organizations.

63201 ■ Long Island University–Development Services
University Center
700 Northern Blvd.
Brookville, NY 11548
Ph:(516)299-3835
Fax: (516)299-3101
Co. E-mail: susan.shebar@liu.edu
Contact: Susan Shebar, Dir.
E-mail: susan.shebar@liu.edu
Scope: Supports University research activities. Provides staff services in development of corporate, foundation, and government grants for all major units of the University, including C.W. Post Campus, Southampton Campus, Brooklyn Campus, and Pharmacy. **Educational Activities:** Grant workshops. **Awards:** Polk Awards.

63202 ■ New York University–Office of Sponsored Programs
15 Washington Pl., No. 1-H
New York, NY 10003
Ph:(212)998-2121
Fax: (212)995-4029
Co. E-mail: osp.agency@nyu.edu
URL: http://www.nyu.edu/osp
Contact: Richard Louth, Dir.
E-mail: osp.agency@nyu.edu
Scope: Serves as central coordinating agency for sponsored activities at the University (exclusive of Medical Center), advises on matters of research policy, recommends operating guidelines for administration of sponsored programs, provides information and assistance to faculty and research staff, maintains records on sponsored research, and allocates some funds internally in support of research programs.

63203 ■ Queens College of City University of New York–Office of Research and Sponsored Programs
65-30 Kissena Blvd.
Flushing, NY 11367
Ph:(718)997-5400
Fax: (718)997-5409
Co. E-mail: Michael_Prasad@qc.cuny.edu
URL: http://www.qc.edu/ORSP
Contact: Gautama M. Prasad, Dir.
E-mail: Michael_Prasad@qc.cuny.edu
Scope: Coordinates all research activities conducted at the College, including extramurally supported projects. **Publications:** Annual Report.

63204 ■ Rensselaer Incubator Program
1223 Peoples Ave.
Troy, NY 12180
Ph:(518)276-6658
Fax: (518)276-6380
Co. E-mail: info@incubator.com
URL: http://www.incubator.com
Contact: Michael Tentnowski, Dir
Description: This program, located at Rensselaer Polytechnic Institute, seeks to nurture new technological ventures. It offers tenants affordable offices space, laboratories, and light manufacturing space as well as other services.

63205 ■ Rensselaer Polytechnic Institute–Office of Contracts and Grants
West Hall, 4th Fl.
110 8th St.
Troy, NY 12180
Ph:(518)276-6281
Fax: (518)276-4820
Co. E-mail: scammr@rpi.edu
URL: http://www.ocg.rpi.edu
Contact: Richard E. Scammell, Dir.
E-mail: scammr@rpi.edu
Scope: Administers research projects at the Institute conducted in such areas as bioenvironmental engineering, machines and structures, materials, electrophysics, mechanics, systems engineering, fluid, chemical, and thermal processes, architecture, economics, history and political sciences, anthropology and sociology, language and literature, philosophy, psychology, management, biology, chemistry, geology, mathematics, computer science, nuclear science, physics, and astronomy.

63206 ■ Rensselaer Polytechnic Institute–Rensselaer Technology Park
100 Jordan Rd.
Troy, NY 12180
Ph:(518)283-7102
Fax: (518)283-0695
Co. E-mail: wachom@rpi.edu
URL: http://www.rpi.edu/dept/rtp
Contact: Michael Wacholder, Dir.
E-mail: wachom@rpi.edu
Scope: Serves as a conduit for joint research activities, consultancies, refresher studies, associate programs, and human interactions between Park tenants and the Institute.

63207 ■ Research Foundation of the City University of New York
230 W 41st St.
New York, NY 10036
Ph:(212)417-8300
Fax: (212)417-8510
Co. E-mail: richard_rothbard@rfcuny.org
URL: http://www.rfcuny.org
Contact: Richard F. Rothbard, Pres.
E-mail: richard_rothbard@rfcuny.org
Scope: Receives, holds, and administers grants, contracts, and gifts for constituent colleges and works to maximize usage of faculty skills as a resource to the community, private industry, government, and the media. **Publications:** Research Foundation Annual Report.

63208 ■ State University of New York at Binghamton–Division of Research
Innovative Technologies Complex
PO Box 6000
Binghamton, NY 13902-6000
Ph:(607)777-4181
Fax: (607)777-3339
Co. E-mail: sgilje@binghamton.edu
URL: http://research.binghamton.edu
Contact: Stephen A. Gilje, Assoc.VP
E-mail: sgilje@binghamton.edu
Scope: Facilitates faculty research funding searches, helps faculty manage funded projects, helps faculty keep current on research policies and practices, enhances awareness of and appreciation for the process and products of discovery. **Services:** Research development services; Laboratory animal services; Technology transfer. **Publications:** Binghamton Research (annually); Discover-E (bimonthly).

63209 ■ State University of New York at Buffalo–Vice President for Research
516 Capen Hall
Buffalo, NY 14260
Ph:(716)645-3321
Fax: (716)645-6792
Co. E-mail: rjgenco@research.buffalo.edu
URL: http://www.research.buffalo.edu/
Contact: Dr. Robert J. Genco, Interim VP
E-mail: rjgenco@research.buffalo.edu
Scope: Administers and coordinates extramurally sponsored research conducted in various departments and research units of the University. **Publications:** Research report.

63210 ■ State University of New York College at Cortland–Office of Sponsored Programs
Jiller Bldg., Rm. 402
PO Box 2000
Cortland, NY 13045
Ph:(607)753-2511
Fax: (607)753-5590
Co. E-mail: amyh@em.courtland.edu
URL: http://www.cortland.edu/osp/
Contact: Amy Henderson-Harr, Dir.
E-mail: amyh@em.courtland.edu
Scope: Serves as liaison for matters pertaining to extramurally funded research at the College, including such projects as the basidiomycetes of the Greater Antilles, especially the Luquillo LTER site; wetland-lake connections and amphibian communities of the Onondaga Lake; trail-based communication in tent caterpillars; and the thermodynamics of binding of simple cationic lipids to DNA. **Publications:** Research News.

63211 ■ State University of New York College at Fredonia–Grants Administration/ Research Services Office
E230 Thompson Hall
Fredonia, NY 14063
Ph:(716)673-3528
Fax: (716)673-3802
Co. E-mail: maggie.bryan-peterson@fredonia.edu
URL: http://www.fredonia.edu/grants
Contact: Maggie Bryan Peterson, Dir.
E-mail: maggie.bryan-peterson@fredonia.edu
Scope: Administers grants and contracts at the University through the processing of grant proposals, as-

sistance in finding funding sources, services for faculty proposal and budget development, and manuscript typing for publications. **Publications:** Newsletter (quarterly). **Educational Activities:** Workshops, in community grant writing.

63212 ■ State University of New York Health Science Center at Brooklyn–Office of Research Administration
450 Clarkson Ave., Box 69
Brooklyn, NY 11203
Ph:(718)270-1178
Fax: (718)270-1407
Co. E-mail: anthony.selvadurah@downstate.edu
Contact: Antony Selvadurai, Dir.
E-mail: anthony.selvadurah@downstate.edu
Scope: Administers sponsors programs, extramural funding, and contracts for research in medical and basic sciences. Also transfers technology from the University to business and industry.

63213 ■ State University of New York at Stony Brook–Department of Technology and Society
347A Harriman
Stony Brook, NY 11794-3760
Ph:(631)632-8765
Fax: (631)632-7809
Co. E-mail: david.ferguson@stonybrook.edu
URL: http://www.sunysb.edu/est/
Contact: David Ferguson, Ch.
E-mail: david.ferguson@stonybrook.edu
Scope: Development of technology planning, technology management and technology assessment to improve learning and teaching of science, technology, engineering, and mathematics, particularly the use of educational technologies and the engagement of underrepresented groups. **Publications:** Journal of Educational Technology Systems (quarterly); Journal of Environmental Systems (quarterly). **Educational Activities:** Professional development programs.

63214 ■ University of Rochester–Office of Research and Project Administration
518 Hylan Bldg.
PO Box 270140
Rochester, NY 14627
Ph:(585)275-4031
Fax: (585)275-9492
Co. E-mail: gunta.liders@rochester.edu
URL: http://www.rochester.edu/orpa
Contact: Gunta J. Liders, Assoc.VP for Res.
E-mail: gunta.liders@rochester.edu
Scope: Serves as central administrative unit for coordination of research programs and extramurally sponsored activities conducted at the University in physical and life sciences, education, engineering, medicine, management, social sciences, the humanities, music, and art. Administrative activities include research administration, legislative liaison, and intellectual property management. **Publications:** Annual Report. **Educational Activities:** Regular workshops (quarterly), for administrators and faculty in areas of sponsored program activity.

63215 ■ Western New York Technology Development Center
726 Exchange St., Ste. 620
Buffalo, NY 14210
Ph:(716)636-3626
Fax: (716)845-6418
URL: http://www.wnytdc.com

EDUCATIONAL PROGRAMS

63216 ■ Board of Cooperative Educational Services–Adult and Continuing Education
63 Gibson Rd.
Goshen, NY 10924-9777
Ph:(845)291-0100
Fax: (845)291-0498
Co. E-mail: adulted@ouboces.mhrcc.org
URL: http://www.ouboces.org/
Description: Offers a ten-session class in small business organization.

63217 ■ Bryant and Stratton Business Institute–Henrietta Campus
1225 Jefferson Rd.
Henrietta, NY 14623
Ph:(585)292-5627
Fax: (585)292-6015
URL: http://www.bryantstratton.edu
Description: Business college offering programs in business management and business operations.

63218 ■ Bryant and Stratton Business Institute–Syracuse Campus
953 James St.
Syracuse, NY 13203
Ph:(315)472-6603
Fax: (315)474-4383
URL: http://www.bryantstratton.edu
Description: Business college offering programs in business management and business operations.

63219 ■ Bryant and Stratton College–Buffalo Campus
465 Main St., Ste. 400
Buffalo, NY 14203
Ph:(716)884-9120
Fax: (716)884-0091
URL: http://www.bryantstratton.edu
Description: Business college offering programs in business management and business operations.

63220 ■ C. W Post Campus of Long Island University–Long Island University
720 Northern Blvd.
Brookville, NY 11548
Ph:(516)299-2000
Free: 800-LIU-PIAW
Fax: (516)299-3829
Co. E-mail: enroll@cwpost.liu.edu
URL: http://www.liu.edu
Description: Offers programs in small business management and entrepreneurship.

63221 ■ Erie Community College, City Campus
121 Ellicott St.
Buffalo, NY 14203
Ph:(716)842-2770
Fax: (716)851-1129
URL: http://www.ecc.edu/
Description: Two-year college offering a certificate in small business management.

63222 ■ Fiorello H. LaGuardia Community College of the City University of New York–Division of Adult and Continuing Education–Center for Corporate Education (31-10)
31-10 Thomson Ave., Rm. E-405
c/o Mr. Wilford Saunders
31-10 Thomson Ave.
Long Island City, NY 11101
Ph:(718)482-7200
Fax: (718)482-5176
Co. E-mail: lagcc@cuny.edu
URL: http://www.lagcc.cuny.edu
Contact: Timothy Rucinsky, Director
Description: Offers courses in supervisory skills and management, microcomputer applications, communication and interpersonal skills, specialized business workshops, and technical training and workshops in retailing skills for small business owners. Maintains an interest in small business by offering programs at no cost to the community through funding by the New York State Department of Education. Small business courses cover personal selling, customer service, merchandise management, accounting, time and stress management, and microcomputers.

63223 ■ Herkimer County Community College
100 Reservoir Rd.
Herkimer, NY 13350
Ph:(315)866-0300
Fax: (315)866-7253
URL: http://www.hccc.ntcnet.com
Description: Two-year college offering a small business management program.

63224 ■ SUNY Canton College
34 Cornell Dr.
Canton, NY 13617
Ph:(315)386-7011
Free: 800-388-7123
Fax: (315)393-5940
URL: http://www.canton.edu/
Description: Two-year college offering a small business management program.

LEGISLATIVE ASSISTANCE

63225 ■ New York Assembly Standing Committee on Small Business
Legislative Office Bldg., Rm. 626
Albany, NY 12248
Ph:(518)455-5806
Fax: (518)455-3976
Co. E-mail: sweeney@assembly.state.ny.us
URL: http://www.assembly.state.ny.us
Contact: Robert Sweeney

63226 ■ New York Senate Standing Committee
Legislative Office Bldg., Rm. 905
Albany, NY -12247
Ph:(518)455-2015
Fax: (518)426-6968
Co. E-mail: alesi@senate.state.ny.us
URL: http://www.senatoralesi.com
Small Business

TRADE PERIODICALS

63227 ■ *Proof*
Pub: Direct Marketing Club of New York
Contact: Stuart Boysen
E-mail: stuboysen@earthlink.net
Released: 10/year. **Description:** Provides information concerning direct marketing to members of the Direct Marketing Club of New York. Recurring features include a calendar of events, news of members, news of educational opportunities, book reviews, and various columns on direct marketing techniques and advancements.

63228 ■ *Queensborough*
Pub: Queens Chamber of Commerce
Ed: Eric Robinson, Editor. **Released:** 5/year. **Price:** Included in membership. **Description:** Focuses on business trends in Queens County, New York.

PUBLICATIONS

63229 ■ *Business First of Buffalo*
472 Delaware Ave.
Buffalo, NY 14202-1378
Ph:(716)882-3020

63230 ■ *Capital District Business Review*
2 Computer Dr. W.
PO Box 15081
Albany, NY 12212-5081
Ph:(518)437-9855
Fax: (518)438-9219
Co. E-mail: cdbr@logical.net
URL: http://www.amcity.com/albany

63231 ■ *Crain's New York Business*
220 E. 42nd St.
New York, NY 10017-5846
Ph:(212)210-0100
Fax: (212)210-0799
URL: http://www.crainsny.com

63232 ■ *How to Form Your Own New York Corporation*
Nolo Press
950 Parker St.
Berkeley, CA 94710
Ph:(510)549-1976

Free: 800-992-6656
URL: http://www.nolo.com
Ed: Anthony Mancuso. **Released:** 1989. **Price:** $24.95. **Description:** Also available for use on IBM PC 3 (1/4 inch disk), IBM PC 5 (disk), and Macintosh (1/2 inch disk).

63233 ■ Hudson Valley Business Journal
P.O. Box 339
Pine Island, NY 10969
Ph:(914)258-4008
Fax: (914)258-4111
Co. E-mail: hvbsnjnl@warwick.net
URL: http://www.hubj.com

63234 ■ Long Island Business News
2150 Smithtown Ave.
Ronkonkoma, NY 11779-7358
Ph:(516)737-1700
Fax: (516)737-1890
Co. E-mail: editor@libn.com
URL: http://www.libn.com

63235 ■ Long Island Magazine
80 Hauppauge Rd.
Commack, NY 11725
Ph:(516)493-3020
Fax: (516)499-2194
URL: http://www.liassoc.com

63236 ■ Rochester Business Journal
55 St. Paul St.
Rochester, NY 14604
Ph:(716)546-8303
Fax: (716)546-3398
Co. E-mail: rbjournal@aol.com
URL: http://www.rbj.net

63237 ■ Rochester Business Magazine
1600 Lyell Ave.
Rochester, NY 14606-2395
Ph:(716)458-8280

63238 ■ Smart Start your New York Business
PSI Research
300 N. Valley Dr.
Grants Pass, OR 97526
Ph:(503)479-9464
Free: 800-228-2275
Fax: (503)476-1479
Co. E-mail: info@psi-research.com
URL: http://www.psi-research.com
Ed: Michael D. Jenkins. **Released:** Revised edition, 1992. **Price:** $29.95 (looseleaf binder); $24.95 (paper). **Description:** Part of the Successful Business Library series.

63239 ■ Westchester County Business Journal
3 Gannett Dr.
White Plains, NY 10604
Ph:(914)694-3600
Fax: (914)694-3699

PUBLISHERS

63240 ■ Allworth Press
10 E 23 St., Ste. 510
New York, NY 10010
Ph:(212)777-8395
Free: 800-491-2808
Fax: (212)777-8261
Co. E-mail: pub@allworth.com
URL: http://www.allworth.com
Contact: Mr. Tad Crawford, Publisher
E-mail: crawford@allworth.com
Description: Publishes practical business and self-help information for photographers, designers, artists, authors, and performing artists. Classic and comtemporary critical writings on art and graphic design. Accepts unsolicited manuscripts. Reaches market through direct and special sales programs; the internet; Watson-Guptill Publications distribution to the trade. **Founded:** 1989.

63241 ■ American Booksellers Association
200 White Plains Rd.
Tarrytown, NY 10591
Ph:(914)591-2665
Free: 800-637-0037
Fax: (914)591-2720
Co. E-mail: info@bookweb.org
URL: http://www.bookweb.org
Contact: Avin Mark Domnitz, CEO
E-mail: avin@bookweb.org
Description: Publishes a book buyer's handbook and returns handbooks. Also offers information, interaction, education and advocacy in bookselling. Hosts an annual convention and BookExpo America. **Founded:** 1900.

63242 ■ America's Hobby Center Inc.
263 W 30th St.
New York, NY 10001-2801
Ph:(212)244-0525
Fax: (212)675-0600
URL: http://www.ahc1931.com
Contact: Peter R. Winston, President
Description: Distributes books. Also distributors of accessories. **Founded:** 1931.

63243 ■ Business Resource Network Inc.
197 Puritan Ave.
Forest Hills, NY 11375
Ph:(718)263-4143
Contact: James Freeley, President
Description: Publishes on small businesses and entrepreneurship. Reaches market through direct mail and distributors. **Founded:** 1982.

63244 ■ Center for Entrepreneurial Management Inc.
180 Varick St., Penthouse Ste.
New York, NY 10014-4606
Ph:(212)633-0060
Fax: (212)633-0063
Contact: Joseph R. Mancuso, President
Description: Publishes business and management information targeted for officials of small and medium businesses. Many titles available on audio and video cassettes. Also produces newsletters and magazines. Reaches market through direct mail. Does not accept unsolicited manuscripts. **Founded:** 1978.

63245 ■ Dafina Books
850 3rd Ave.
New York, NY 10022
Free: 877-422-3665
URL: http://www.kensingtonbooks.com
Contact: LaToya Smith, Editorial Assistant
Description: Publishes a line of African-American themed books.

63246 ■ D.M.R. Consulting Group
225 S Lake Ave., Ste. 300
Pasadena, CA 91101-3005
Ph:(626)440-8365
Contact: Mark Dunnet, President
Description: Publishes home-based business success manuals and other specialized information on various subjects. Distributes for premier Publishers. Reaches market through commission representatives, direct mail, and telephone and trade sales. **Founded:** 1980.

63247 ■ Doubleday Broadway Publishing Group
1745 Broadway
New York, NY 10019
Ph:(212)782-9000
Free: 800-733-3000
Fax: (212)302-7985
Co. E-mail: ddaypub@randomhouse.com
URL: http://www.randomhouse.com/doubleday
Contact: Stephen Rubin, President
Description: Publishes mysteries, romances, westerns, and science fiction. Publishes nonfiction books in many areas including biographies, cookbooks, business, parenting, science, technology, parenting, child care, finance, gay and lesbian studies, money management, and psychology. **Founded:** 1897.

63248 ■ Forum Publishing Co.
383 E Main St.
Centerport, NY 11721
Ph:(631)754-5000
Free: 800-635-7654
Fax: (631)754-0630
Co. E-mail: forumpublishing@aol.com
URL: http://www.forum123.com
Contact: Martin Stevens, CEO
Description: Publishes books and directories on business start-ups and expansions. Offers audio cassettes. Accepts unsolicited manuscripts. Distributes for PSI Research, Tab Books, Nolo Press, Self-Counsel Press and Writer's Digest Books. Reaches market through direct mail. **Founded:** 1981.

63249 ■ The Genesis Society Inc.
102-19 Metropolitan Ave.
Forest Hills, NY 11375
Ph:(718)544-5997
Free: 800-780-6030
Fax: (718)544-5488
Co. E-mail: treeoflife@genesissociety.com
URL: http://www.genesissociety.org
Contact: Rene David Alkalay, CEO & Pres
E-mail: david@genesissociety.org
Description: Publishes health-related hand books. **Founded:** 1999.

63250 ■ HarperBusiness
10 E 53rd St.
New York, NY 10022
Ph:(212)207-7969
Free: 800-242-7737
Fax: (212)207-6961
Co. E-mail: harperbiz@harpercollins.com
URL: http://www.harpercollins.com
Contact: Lisa Berkowitz, Dir of Mktg
E-mail: lisa.berkowitz@harpercollins.com
Description: Publishes business, professional books on finance, management, and human resources. Reaches market through commission representatives, direct mail, and wholesalers. Accepts unsolicited manuscripts. **Founded:** 1992.

63251 ■ The H.W. Wilson Co.
950 University Ave.
Bronx, NY 10452-4224
Ph:(718)588-8400
Free: 800-367-6770
Fax: (718)590-1617
Co. E-mail: intlsales@hwwilson.com
URL: http://www.hwwilson.com
Contact: James Phelan, Vice President
Description: Publishes reference tools for libraries and book trade. Also offers videotapes, computer software, CD-ROMs and online databases. **Founded:** 1898.

63252 ■ Info Press Inc.
728 Center St.
PO Box 826
Lewiston, NY 14092
Ph:(716)754-4669
Free: 888-806-2665
Fax: (905)688-7728
Co. E-mail: infopress@infonews.com
Contact: Edward L. Dixon Jr., Publisher
Description: Publishes an annual directory of business franchising and a monthly newsletter on the same subject. **Founded:** 1969.

63253 ■ International Trademark Association
655 3rd Ave., 10th Fl.
New York, NY 10017-5617
Ph:(212)642-1700
Fax: (212)768-7796
Co. E-mail: info@inta.org
URL: http://www.inta.org
Contact: Alan C. Drewsen, Director
E-mail: rrolfe@inta.org
Description: Obtains, collects and disseminates information on the use, registration and protection of trademarks in the U.S. and abroad. Reaches market through direct mail. Does not accept unsolicited manuscripts; proposals only. **Founded:** 1878.

63254 ■ International Wealth Success Inc.
PO Box 186
Merrick, NY 11566-0186
Ph:(516)766-5850
Free: 800-323-0548
Fax: (516)766-5919
Co. E-mail: admin@iwsmoney.com
URL: http://www.iwsmoney.com
Contact: Tyler G. Hicks, President
E-mail: tyghicks@aol.com
Description: Publishes on capital sources, mail order, import/export and real estate. Also shows how and where to raise money for any type of business. Offers audio and video tapes. Accepts unsolicited manuscripts; include a self-addressed, stamped envelope. Reaches market through commission representatives, direct mail and trade sales. **Founded:** 1967.

63255 ■ JMW Group Inc.
5 W Cross St.
Hawthorne, NY 10532-1259
Ph:(914)769-6400
Fax: (914)769-0250
Co. E-mail: bdiedrick@att.net
Contact: Brice Diedrick, President
Description: Publishes both fiction and nonfiction books. **Founded:** 1950.

63256 ■ Mark A. Adams Inc.
425 Riverside Dr.
New York, NY 10025
Ph:(212)864-0416
Fax: (212)316-6496
Co. E-mail: mail@markadamsinc.com
Contact: Mark A. Adams, Owner
Description: Distributes general books. Wholesaler.

63257 ■ Matthew Bender and Company Inc.
744 Broad St.
Newark, NJ 07102-3885
Ph:(973)820-2000
Free: 800-252-9257
Fax: (973)820-2007
Co. E-mail: corpcomm@lexisnexis.com
URL: http://www.lexisnexis.com/matthewbender
Description: Publishes newsletters, periodicals, manuals, and other materials in the areas of law, accounting, insurance, banking, and other professions. **Founded:** 1887.

63258 ■ The McGraw-Hill Companies Inc.
1221 Avenue of the Americas, 10th Fl.
New York, NY 10020-1095
Ph:(212)904-2000
Free: (866)436-8502
Fax: (212)512-3840
Co. E-mail: customer.service@mcgraw-hill.com
URL: http://www.mcgraw-hill.com
Contact: Harold W. McGraw III, CEO, Pres & Chm Bd
Description: Publishes in three key areas: financial, education, and information and media services. Offers independent investment information, online learning and multimedia tools, and business intelligence, analysis and solutions. **Founded:** 1888.

63259 ■ McGraw-Hill Inc.
1221 Avenue of the Americas
New York, NY 10020

Ph:(212)512-2000
Fax: (212)512-2000
Co. E-mail: customer.service@mcgraw-hill.com
URL: http://www.mcgraw-hill.com/
Contact: Harold McGraw III, CEO, Pres & Chm Bd
Description: Publishes about education, financial sectors, information and media. **Founded:** 1888.

63260 ■ McGraw-Hill Trade
2 Penn Plz.
New York, NY 10121-0101
Ph:(212)904-2000
Fax: (212)904-4760
Co. E-mail: customer.service@mcgraw-hill.com
URL: http://www.mcgraw-hill.com
Contact: Philip Ruppel, Group Pub.
Description: Publishes business and general reference books.

63261 ■ Morgan James Publishing L.L.C.
1225 Franklin Ave., Ste. 325
Garden City, NY 11530-1693
Ph:(516)620-2528
Free: 800-485-4943
Fax: (516)908-4496
Co. E-mail: customerservice@
  morganjamespublishing.com
URL: http://www.morganjamespublishing.com/
Description: Publishes books on business, children's, guerrilla marketing, inspirational, and self-help.

63262 ■ The Passion Profit Co.
PO Box 618, Church Street Sta.
New York, NY 10008-0618
Ph:(212)831-1854
Co. E-mail: info@passionprofit.com
URL: http://www.passionprofit.com
Contact: Walt Goodridge
Description: Publishes how-to books primarily. **Founded:** 1992.

63263 ■ Productivity Press
444 Park Ave. S
New York, NY 10016
Ph:(212)686-5900
Free: 888-319-5852
Fax: (212)686-5411
Co. E-mail: info@productivitypress.com
URL: http://www.productivitypress.com
Contact: Maura May, Publisher
Description: Publishes materials on productivity, quality improvement, product development, corporate management, profit management and employee involvement. Publishes translations into English from Japan. **Founded:** 1983.

63264 ■ PubEasy
630 Central Ave.
New Providence, NJ 07974
Ph:(908)219-0053
Free: 877-782-6111
Fax: (908)219-0191
Co. E-mail: help@pubeasy.com
URL: http://www.pubeasy.com
Contact: John Phillips, Dir of Sales
E-mail: john.phillips@pubeasy.com
Description: Publishes online services to facilitate, speed and connect publishers, booksellers, distributors and wholesalers.

63265 ■ Rock Beach Press
1255 University Ave.
Rochester, NY 14607
Ph:(716)442-0888
Free: 800-235-1005
Fax: (716)442-8353
Contact: William J. Stolze, President
Description: Self-publishes a book about entrepreneurship. Reaches market through direct mail, Baker & Taylor, and MacLean Hunter. **Founded:** 1989.

63266 ■ SelectBooks Inc.
1 Union Sq. W, Ste. 909
New York, NY 10003
Ph:(212)206-1997
Fax: (212)206-3815
Co. E-mail: info@selectbooks.com
URL: http://www.selectbooks.com
Contact: Kenzi Sugihara, Publisher
Description: Publishes nonfiction in the areas of biography, politics, business administration, and alternative medicine. **Founded:** 2001.

63267 ■ Standard & Poor's
55 Water St.
New York, NY 10041
Ph:(212)438-1000
Free: 800-852-1641
Fax: (212)438-3396
Co. E-mail: questions@standardandpoors.com
URL: http://www.standardandpoors.com
Contact: Harold W. McGraw III, President
Description: Publishes on financial information. Offers more than 50 publications and services, disseminates information electronically and produces historical data on microfiche. Offers periodicals and software. Reaches market through commission representatives, direct mail and telephone sales. **Founded:** 1860.

63268 ■ Tokyo Stock Exchange Inc.
New York Representative Office, 45 Broadway, 12th Fl.
New York, NY 10006
Ph:(212)363-2350
Fax: (212)363-2354
Co. E-mail: contact@tsenyrep.com
URL: http://www.tse.or.jp/english/about/oversea.html
Contact: Takuo Tsurushima, CEO & Pres
Description: Publishes on business and statistics. **Founded:** 1870.

63269 ■ Vault.com Inc.
150 W 22nd St., 5th Fl.
New York, NY 10011
Ph:(212)366-4212
Free: 888-562-8285
Fax: (212)366-4212
Co. E-mail: questions@staff.vault.com
URL: http://www.vault.com
Contact: Mark Oldman, Owner
Description: Publishes insider career development books for professionals and recruiters. Accepts unsolicited manuscripts. Reaches market through commission representatives, direct mail, reviews, listing, telephone sales and C.D.S. **Founded:** 1996.

SMALL BUSINESS DEVELOPMENT CENTER LEAD OFFICE

63270 ■ NC Small Business and Technology Development Center–University of North Carolina
333 Fayetteville Street Mall, Ste. 1150
Raleigh, NC 27601-1742
Ph:(919)715-7272
Free: 800-2580-UNC
Fax: (919)715-7777
URL: http://www.sbtdc.org
Contact: Scott R. Daugherty, Executive Director
E-mail: sdaugherty@sbtdc.org

63271 ■ North Carolina SBDTC–University of North Carolina
5 W. Hargett St., Ste. 600
Raleigh, NC 27601
Ph:(919)715-7272
Fax: (919)715-7777
URL: http://www.sbtdc.org
Contact: Scott Daugherty, State Dir.
E-mail: sdaugherty@sbtdc.org

63272 ■ Small Business and Technology Development Center at Raleigh–Capital Region SBTDC–SBDC
900 Main Campus Dr., Ste. 101
Raleigh, NC 27606
Ph:(919)424-4450
Free: 800-258-0862
Co. E-mail: info@sbtc.org
URL: http://www.sbtdc.org/
Contact: Scott R. Daugherty, Exec. Dir.

SMALL BUSINESS DEVELOPMENT CENTERS

63273 ■ Appalachian State University–Small Business and Technology Development Center (Northwestern Region)
Walker College of Business
2018 Raley Hall
Boone, NC 28608-2114
Ph:(828)262-2492
Fax: (828)262-2027
Contact: William Parrish, Dir.
E-mail: wparrish@sbtdc.org

63274 ■ Appalachian State University at Hickory Office–SBTDC
514 Hwy. 321 NW, Ste. A
Hickory, NC 28601-4738
Ph:(828)345-1110
Fax: (828)326-9117
Contact: Blair Abee, Dir.
E-mail: babee@sbtdc.org

63275 ■ Asheville SBTDC
Bank of America Bldg.
68 Patton Ave., Ste. 1
Asheville, NC 28801
Ph:(828)251-6025
Fax: (828)232-6126
Contact: Sandra Trivett, Asst. Dir.
E-mail: strivett@sbtdc.org

63276 ■ East Carolina University–Small Business and Technology Development Center (Eastern Region)–SBDC (Willi)
Willis Bldg.
300 East 1st St.
Greenville, NC 27858-4353
Ph:(252)328-6157
Fax: (252)328-6992
Contact: Carolyn Wilburn, Dir.
E-mail: cwilburn@sbtdc.org

63277 ■ Elizabeth City State University–Small Business and Technology Development Center (Northeastern Region)
1704 Weeksville Rd.
PO Box 874
Elizabeth City, NC 27909-7806
Ph:(252)335-3247
Fax: (252)335-3648

63278 ■ Fayetteville State University–Cape Fear Small Business and Technology Development Center
1200 Murchinson Rd., Ste. 6
PO Box 1334
Fayetteville, NC 28302-1334
Ph:(910)672-1727
Fax: (910)672-1949
Contact: Greg Taylor, Dir.
E-mail: gtaylor@sbtdc.org

63279 ■ North Carolina A&T State University–Small Business and Technology Development Center
Nusbaum Entrepreneurial Center
2007 Yanceyville St., Ste. 300
PO Box D-22
Greensboro, NC 27405
Ph:(336)334-7005
Fax: (336)334-7073
Contact: Tim Janke, Dir.
E-mail: tjanke@sbtdc.org

63280 ■ North Carolina Wesleyan College–SBDC
3400 N. Wesleyan Blvd.
Rocky Mount, NC 27804-9906
Ph:(252)985-5130
Free: 800-488-6292
Fax: (252)977-3701
Contact: Joe Reeves

63281 ■ University of North Carolina–SBDC
5 W. Hargett St., Ste. 600
Raleigh, NC 27601-1348
Ph:(919)715-7272
Free: 800-258-0862

Fax: (919)715-7777
URL: http://www.sbtdc.org
Contact: Scott R. Daugherty, Exec. Dir.
E-mail: sdaugherty@sbtdc.org

63282 ■ University of North Carolina at Chapel Hill–Central Carolina Regional Small Business Development Center
608 Airport Rd., Ste. B
Chapel Hill, NC 27514-5703
Ph:(919)962-0389
Fax: (919)962-3291
Contact: Dr. Ron Ilinitch, Dir.
E-mail: rilinitch@sbtdc.org

63283 ■ University of North Carolina at Charlotte–Small Business and Technology Development Center (Southern Piedmont Region)
The Ben Craig Center
8701 Mallard Creek Rd.
Charlotte, NC 28262-9705
Ph:(704)548-1090
Fax: (704)548-9050
Contact: George McAllister, Dir.
E-mail: gmcallister@sbtdc.org

63284 ■ University of North Carolina at Pembroke–SBTDC
COMtech Livermore Dr.
PO Box 1510
Pembroke, NC 28372-1510
Ph:(910)775-4000
Fax: (910)775-4005
Contact: Johnnie Marshburn, Business Counselor
E-mail: jmarshburn@sbtdc.com

63285 ■ University of North Carolina at Wilmington–Small Business Technology Development Center
601 S. College Rd.
Wilmington, NC 28403-3297
Ph:(910)962-3744
Fax: (910)962-3014
Contact: Leslie Langer, Dir.
E-mail: llanger@sbtdc.org

63286 ■ Western Carolina University–Small Business and Technology Development Center (Western Region)
204 Forsyth Bldg.
Cullowhee, NC 28779
Ph:(828)227-3504
Fax: (828)227-7414
Contact: Wendy Cagle, Dir.
E-mail: wcagle@sbtdc.org

63287 ■ Winston-Salem State University–Small Business Technology Development Center–Northwest Piedmont Region (Ander)–SBDC (son Ctr.,)
Anderson Ctr., Rm. 117C
PO Box 19483
Winston Salem, NC 27110-0001
Ph:(336)750-2030
Fax: (336)750-2031

Contact: Tony Johnson, Dir.
E-mail: tjohnson@sbtdc.org

SMALL BUSINESS ASSISTANCE PROGRAMS

63288 ■ Council for Entrepreneurial Development
100 Capital Dr., Ste. 101
Durham, NC 27713
Ph:(919)549-7500
Fax: (919)549-7405
Co. E-mail: info@cednc.org
URL: http://www.cednc.org
Contact: Monica Doss, Pres
Description: Council of entrepreneurs, business and financial service providers, public policy makers, and university faculty, united to promote the enhancement of entrepreneurial development in North Carolina through monthly programs, newsletters, consultation programs, membership directories, seminars and workshops, and an annual venture capital conference.

63289 ■ East Carolina University–Center for Applied Technology
Science and Technology Building
Ste. 100
Greenville, NC 27858-4353
Ph:(252)328-6708
Fax: (252)328-1545
URL: http://www.sit.ecu.edu
Description: Provides technical and scientific assistance through contract research for industries, businesses, and municipalities.

63290 ■ Frank Hawkins Kenan Institute for Private Enterprise
Campus Box 3490
The Kenan Center
Chapel Hill, NC 27599-3440
Ph:(919)962-8201
Fax: (919)962-8202
Co. E-mail: kenan_institute@unc.edu
URL: http://www.kenan-flagler.unc.edu/KI/
Description: National center for private enterprise research focusing on entrepreneurial development, new venture management, and coursework development.

63291 ■ North Carolina Department of Agriculture and Consumers Services–Division of Marketing
2 W Edenton St. RM.402
Raleigh, NC 27601
Ph:(919)733-7887
Fax: (919)733-0999
URL: http://www.agr.state.nc.us/markets
Description: Provides small businesses with information on doing business internationally.

63292 ■ North Carolina Department of Commerce–Business/Industry Development Division
301 N Wilmington
Raleigh, NC 27601
Ph:(919)733-4151
Fax: (919)733-9265
URL: http://www.commerce.state.nc.us
Contact: Bo Gregory
Description: Assists international, national, and state firms in locating new or expanded facilities in North Carolina.

63293 ■ North Carolina Department of Community Colleges–Small Business Center Network
Caswell Bldg.
200 W Jones St.
Raleigh, NC 27603-5003
Ph:(919)807-7100
Fax: (919)807-7164
Co. E-mail: harveyg@ncccs.cc.nc.us
URL: http://www.nc.community colleges.edu
Description: Offers consultations and referrals, including business planning. Operates a resource and information center containing printed and electronic resources. Sponsors business and computer expos in cooperation with business and community organizations. Offers workshops to potential and existing small businesses on business topics, including business plans, basics of business, motivation, management, financial planning, computer and software applications, customer relations, farm recordkeeping, and franchising.

63294 ■ North Carolina Rural Economic Development Center–Micro Enterprise Loan Program
4021 Carya Dr.
Raleigh, NC 27610
Ph:(919)250-4314
Fax: (919)250-4325
Co. E-mail: info@ncruralcenter.org
URL: http://www.ncruralcenter.org
Contact: Thomas Lambeth, Chairman
Description: Provides and is involved in research and demonstration efforts to identify new ideas, strategies, or programs that will generate economic development in rural North Carolina.

63295 ■ North Carolina Small Business Partnership
5003 Mail Service Ctr.
Raleigh, NC 27699-5003
Ph:(919)807-7100
Fax: (919)807-7164
Co. E-mail: dickens@ncccs.cc.nc.us
URL: http://www.nccs.cc.nc.us
Description: Consists of eleven state and state-supported organizations united to promote cooperation and collaboration in meeting economic concerns. Purposes include serving as an advocate for smaller business interests, and informing public policy makers of small business assistance resources and services.

63296 ■ North Carolina Small Business and Technology Development Center–Western Carolina Small Business and Technology Development Center
Western Carolina University
204 Forsythe Bldg.
Cullowhee, NC 28723
Ph:(828)227-3459
Free: 800-621-0008
Fax: (828)227-7422
URL: http://www.sbtdc.org
Contact: Wendy Cagle, Dir.
Description: Goals are to increase job opportunities and capital investments; to assist in the creation or retention of jobs; to expand economic opportunities; to reduce the incidence of business failure; to assist in community development efforts; and to assist in the development, growth, and expansion of commercial, industrial, and business activities.

63297 ■ North Carolina State University–Industrial Extension Service
Campus Box 7902
Raleigh, NC 27695-7902
Ph:(919)515-2358
Fax: (919)515-6159
Co. E-mail: ies_services@ncsu.edu
URL: http://www.ies.ncsu.edu
Description: Provides assistance to North Carolina industries to help them have a competitive advantage through better utilization of engineering technologies.

SCORE OFFICES

63298 ■ SCORE Asheboro/Randolph
c/o Talmadge Baker, Chm.
Asheboro/Randolph Chamber of Commerce
317 E Dixie Dr.
Asheboro, NC 27203
Ph:(336)626-2626
Fax: (336)626-7077
Co. E-mail: chamber@asheboro.com
URL: http://www.score.org
Description: Provides public service to America by offering small business advice and training.

63299 ■ SCORE Asheville
Federal Bldg., Rm. 259
151 Patton Ave.
Asheville, NC 28801
Ph:(828)271-4786
Fax: (828)271-4786
Co. E-mail: info@ashevillescore.org
URL: http://www.ashevillescore.org
Contact: Mr. Bob Bond, Chm.
Description: Serves as volunteer program in which working and retired business management professionals provide free business counseling to men and women who are considering starting a small business, encountering problems with their business, or expanding their business. Offers free one-on-one counseling, online counseling and low cost workshops on a variety of business topics.

63300 ■ SCORE Chapel Hill
c/o Chapel Hill/Carrboro Chamber of Commerce
104 S Estes Dr.
Chapel Hill, NC 27514
Ph:(919)968-6894
Fax: (919)967-7000
Co. E-mail: info@scorechapelhill.org
URL: http://www.scorechapelhill.org
Contact: Mr. Jay Baker
Description: Provides in-depth, industry-specific business assistance to evaluate a business idea or plan, stimulates business growth and ensure long-term stability.

63301 ■ SCORE Charlotte
One Fairview Center
6302 Fairview Rd., Ste. 300
Charlotte, NC 28210
Ph:(704)344-6576
Fax: (704)344-6769
Co. E-mail: charlottescore47@carolina.rr.com
URL: http://www.charlottescore.org
Contact: Mr. Jerry Byrnes, Chm.
Description: Serves as volunteer program in which working and retired business management professionals provide free business counseling to men and women who are considering starting a small business, encountering problems with their business, or expanding their business. Offers free one-on-one counseling, online counseling and low cost workshops on a variety of business topics.

63302 ■ SCORE Down East
PO Box 790
New Bern, NC 28563
Ph:(252)633-6688
Fax: (252)638-1819
Co. E-mail: score@esisnet.com
URL: http://www.scorenewbern.org
Description: Provides entrepreneur education for the formation, growth and success of small businesses in the area.

63303 ■ SCORE Durham
411 W Chapel Hill St.
Durham, NC 27701
Ph:(919)541-2171
Co. E-mail: alnabb@aol.com
Contact: Alan McNabb, Chm.
Description: Serves as volunteer program in which working and retired business management professionals provide free business counseling to men and women who are considering starting a small business, encountering problems with their business, or expanding their business. Offers free one-on-one counseling, online counseling and low cost workshops on a variety of business topics.

63304 ■ SCORE Greensboro
2007 Yanceyville St.
Box 48
Greensboro, NC 27405
Ph:(336)333-5399
Fax: (336)333-5399
Co. E-mail: info@scoregso.org
URL: http://www.scoregso.org
Description: Serves as volunteer program in which working and retired business management profes-

sionals provide free business counseling to men and women who are considering starting a small business, encountering problems with their business, or expanding their business. Offers free one-on-one counseling, online counseling and low cost workshops on a variety of business topics.

63305 ■ SCORE Hendersonville
Federal Bldg., Ste. 108
W 4th Ave. and Church St.
Hendersonville, NC 28792
Ph:(828)693-8702
Co. E-mail: hendscore@brinet.com
URL: http://www.scorewnc.org
Contact: Fred Henneke, Chm.
Description: Serves as volunteer program in which working and retired business management professionals provide free business counseling to men and women who are considering starting a small business, encountering problems with their business, or expanding their business. Offers free one-on-one counseling, online counseling and low cost workshops on a variety of business topics.

63306 ■ SCORE High Point
PO Box 5025
High Point, NC 27262
Ph:(336)882-8625
Fax: (336)889-9499
Co. E-mail: contact@highpointscore.org
URL: http://www.highpointscore.org
Contact: B. Harrison, Sec.
Description: Serves as volunteer program in which working and retired business management professionals provide free business counseling to men and women who are considering starting a small business, encountering problems with their business, or expanding their business. Offers free one-on-one counseling, online counseling and low cost workshops on a variety of business topics.

63307 ■ SCORE Outer Banks
c/o Bill Burnett, Chm.
Outer Banks Chamber of Commerce
PO Box 1757
Kill Devil Hills, NC 27948
Ph:(252)441-8144
Co. E-mail: mail@score497.org
URL: http://www.score497.org

63308 ■ SCORE Raleigh
PO Box 406
Raleigh, NC 27602
Ph:(919)856-4739
Fax: (919)856-4466
Co. E-mail: contactus@raleighscore.org
URL: http://www.raleighscore.org
Contact: Chuck Goins, Chm.
Description: Serves as volunteer program in which working and retired business management professionals provide free business counseling to men and women who are considering starting a small business, encountering problems with their business, or expanding their business. Offers free one-on-one counseling, online counseling and low cost workshops on a variety of business topics.

63309 ■ SCORE Sandhills Area - No. 364
c/o Sand Hills Area Chamber of Commerce
10677 US 15-501 Hwy.
Southern Pines, NC 28387
Ph:(910)692-3926
Co. E-mail: info@sandhillsscore.org
URL: http://www.sandhillsscore.org
Contact: Judith Kelley
Description: Serves as volunteer program in which working and retired business management professionals provide free business counseling to men and women who are considering starting a small business, encountering problems with their business, or expanding their business. Offers free one-on-one counseling, online counseling and low cost workshops on a variety of business topics.

63310 ■ SCORE Wilmington
4010 Oleander Dr.
Wilmington, NC 28411

Ph:(910)452-5395
Fax: (910)452-5369
Co. E-mail: counselor@wilmingtonscore.org
URL: http://www.wilmingtonscore.org
Contact: John Cowan, Chm.
Description: Serves as volunteer program in which working and retired business management professionals provide free business counseling to men and women who are considering starting a small business, encountering problems with their business, or expanding their business. Offers free one-on-one counseling, online counseling and low cost workshops on a variety of business topics.

BETTER BUSINESS BUREAUS

63311 ■ Better Business Bureau
3608 W Friendly Ave.
Greensboro, NC 27410-4895
Ph:(336)852-4240
Fax: (336)852-7540
Co. E-mail: info@greensboro.bbb.org
URL: http://www.greensboro.bbb.org
Contact: Ms. Pauline S. Morrison, Pres.

63312 ■ Better Business Bureau of Asheville/ Western North Carolina
One W Pack Sq., Ste. 1601
Asheville, NC 28801-3418
Ph:(828)253-2392
Fax: (828)252-5039
Co. E-mail: info@asheville.bbb.org
URL: http://www.asheville.bbb.org
Contact: Ms. Norma Messer, Pres.

63313 ■ Better Business Bureau of Eastern North Carolina
5540 Munford Rd., Ste. 130
Raleigh, NC 27612
Ph:(919)277-4222
Free: 800-222-0950
Fax: (919)277-4221
Co. E-mail: info@raleigh.bbb.org
URL: http://www.bbbenc.org
Contact: Beverly Baskin, Pres.

63314 ■ Better Business Bureau of Northwest North Carolina
500 W 5th St., Ste. 202
Winston-Salem, NC 27101-2728
Ph:(336)725-8348
Free: 800-777-8348
Fax: (336)777-3727
Co. E-mail: info@nwncbbb.com
URL: http://www.winstonsalem.bbb.org
Contact: David W. Dalrymple, Pres./CEO

63315 ■ Better Business Bureau of Southern Piedmont
13860 Ballantyne Corporate Pl., Ste. 225
Charlotte, NC 28277
Ph:(704)927-8611
Fax: (704)927-8615
Co. E-mail: info@charlotte.bbb.org
URL: http://www.charlotte.bbb.org
Contact: Tom Bartholomy, Pres./CEO

CHAMBERS OF COMMERCE

63316 ■ Alamance County Area Chamber of Commerce
610 S Lexington Ave.
PO Box 450
Burlington, NC 27216-0450
Ph:(336)228-1338
Fax: (336)228-1330
Co. E-mail: info@alamancechamber.com
URL: http://www.alamancechamber.com
Contact: Mac Williams, Pres.

63317 ■ Alexander County Chamber of Commerce
16 W Main Ave.
Taylorsville, NC 28681
Ph:(828)632-8141
Fax: (828)632-1096
Co. E-mail: delder@alexandercountychamber.com
URL: http://www.alexandercountychamber.com
Contact: Denise Elder, Exec.Dir.

63318 ■ Alleghany County Chamber of Commerce
58 S Main St.
PO Box 1237
Sparta, NC 28675-1237
Ph:(336)372-5473
Free: 800-372-5473
Fax: (336)372-8251
Co. E-mail: director@sparta-nc.com
URL: http://www.sparta-nc.com
Contact: Bob Bamberg, Exec.Dir.

63319 ■ Andrews Chamber of Commerce
PO Box 800
Andrews, NC 28901
Ph:(828)321-3584
Free: 877-558-0005
Fax: (828)321-3584
Co. E-mail: andrewschamber@webworkz.net
URL: http://www.andrewschambercommerce.com
Contact: Pat Love, Dir. of Tourism

63320 ■ Angier Chamber of Commerce
19 W Depot St.
PO Box 47
Angier, NC 27501-0047
Ph:(919)639-2500
Fax: (919)639-8826
Co. E-mail: angiercc@angierchamber.org
URL: http://www.angierchamber.org
Contact: Jamie Strickland, Exec.Dir.

63321 ■ Anson County Chamber of Commerce
PO Box 305
107-A E Wade St.
Wadesboro, NC 28170-0305
Ph:(704)694-4181
Fax: (704)694-3830
Co. E-mail: ansonchamber@alltel.net
URL: http://www.ansoncounty.org
Contact: Elbert Marshall Jr., Exec.Dir.

63322 ■ Apex Chamber of Commerce
220 N Salem St.
Apex, NC 27502
Ph:(919)362-6456
Free: 800-345-4504
Fax: (919)362-9050
Co. E-mail: info@apexchamber.com
URL: http://www.apexchamber.com
Contact: Sheryl Bynum, Exec.Dir.

63323 ■ Archdale-Trinity Chamber of Commerce
213 Balfour Dr.
Archdale, NC 27263
Ph:(336)434-2073
Fax: (336)431-5845
Co. E-mail: beverly@archdaletrinitychamber.com
URL: http://www.archdaletrinitychamber.com
Contact: Beverly M. Nelson, Pres.

63324 ■ Ashe County Chamber of Commerce and Visitors Center
303 E Second St.
PO Box 31
West Jefferson, NC 28694-0031
Ph:(336)846-9550
Free: 888-343-2743
Fax: (336)846-8671
Co. E-mail: info@ashechamber.com
URL: http://www.ashechamber.com
Contact: Cabot Hamilton, Pres.

63325 ■ Asheboro/Randolph Chamber of Commerce
317 E Dixie Dr.
Asheboro, NC 27203
Ph:(336)626-2626
Fax: (336)626-7077
Co. E-mail: chamber@asheboro.com
URL: http://chamber.asheboro.com
Contact: George Gusler Jr., Pres.

63326 ■ Asheville Area Chamber of Commerce
36 Montford Ave.
PO Box 1010
Asheville, NC 28802-1010
Ph:(828)258-6101
Fax: (828)251-0926
Co. E-mail: contactus@ashevillechamber.org
URL: http://www.ashevillechamber.org
Contact: Rick Lutovsky, Pres./CEO

63327 ■ Ayden Chamber of Commerce
PO Box 31
Ayden, NC 28513
Ph:(252)746-2266
Fax: (252)746-2266
Co. E-mail: chamber@ayden.com
URL: http://www.aydenchamber.com
Contact: Misty Shirley, Exec.Dir.

63328 ■ Beech Mountain Area Chamber of Commerce
403A Beech Mountain Pkwy.
Beech Mountain, NC 28604
Free: 800-468-5506
Co. E-mail: chamber@beechmtn.com
URL: http://www.beechmtn.com
Contact: Barry Schorr, Exec.Dir.

63329 ■ Belhaven Community Chamber of Commerce
125 W Main St.
PO Box 147
Belhaven, NC 27810-0147
Ph:(252)943-3770
Fax: (252)943-3769
Co. E-mail: info@belhavenchamber.com
URL: http://www.belhavenchamber.com
Contact: Margie Miller, Exec.Dir.

63330 ■ Benson Area Chamber of Commerce
303 E Church St.
PO Box 246
Benson, NC 27504-0246
Ph:(919)894-3825
Fax: (919)894-1052
Co. E-mail: info@benson-chamber.com
URL: http://www.benson-chamber.com
Contact: Loretta Byrd, Exec.Dir.

63331 ■ Black Mountain-Swannanoa Chamber of Commerce
201 E State St.
Black Mountain, NC 28711
Ph:(828)669-2300
Free: 800-669-2301
Fax: (828)669-1407
Co. E-mail: info@blackmountain.org
URL: http://www.blackmountain.org
Contact: Bob McMurray, Exec.Dir.

63332 ■ Blowing Rock Chamber of Commerce
PO Box 406
Blowing Rock, NC 28605
Ph:(828)295-7851
Free: 800-295-7851
Fax: (828)295-4643
Co. E-mail: info@blowingrock.com
URL: http://www.blowingrock.com
Contact: Howard Gray, Exec.Dir.

63333 ■ Boone Area Chamber of Commerce
208 Howard St.
Boone, NC 28607-4032
Ph:(828)264-2225
Free: 800-852-9506

Fax: (828)264-6644
Co. E-mail: info@boonechamber.com
URL: http://www.boonechamber.com
Contact: Dan Meyer, Pres./CEO

63334 ■ Brevard - Transylvania Chamber of Commerce
35 W Main St.
Brevard, NC 28712-0589
Ph:(828)883-3700
Free: 800-648-4523
Fax: (828)883-8550
Co. E-mail: brevchamber@citcom.net
URL: http://www.brevardncchamber.org
Contact: Ms. Beth Carden, Pres.

63335 ■ Brunswick County Chamber of Commerce
4948 Main St.
PO Box 1185
Shallotte, NC 28459
Ph:(910)754-6644
Free: 800-426-6644
URL: http://www.brunswickcountychamber.org
Contact: Mitzi York, Pres./CEO

63336 ■ Burke County Chamber of Commerce
110 E Meeting St.
Morganton, NC 28655
Ph:(828)437-3021
Fax: (828)437-1613
Co. E-mail: burkecoc@hci.net
URL: http://www.burkecounty.org
Contact: Michael Jackson, Pres.

63337 ■ Caldwell County Chamber of Commerce
1909 Hickory Blvd. SE
Lenoir, NC 28645
Ph:(828)726-0616
Fax: (828)726-0385
Co. E-mail: visitors@caldwellcochamber.org
URL: http://www.caldwellcochamber.org
Contact: Deborah Ashley, Pres./CEO

63338 ■ Carteret County Chamber of Commerce
801 Arendell St.
Morehead City, NC 28557
Ph:(252)726-6350
Free: 800-622-6278
Fax: (252)726-3505
Co. E-mail: info@nccoastchamber.com
URL: http://www.nccoastchamber.com
Contact: Mike Wagoner, Pres.

63339 ■ Cary Chamber of Commerce
307 N Academy St.
PO Box 4351
Cary, NC 27519-4351
Ph:(919)467-1016
Free: 800-919-CARY
Fax: (919)469-2375
Co. E-mail: info@carychamber.com
URL: http://www.carychamber.com
Contact: Howard S. Johnson, Pres.

63340 ■ Cashiers Area Chamber of Commerce
PO Box 238
Cashiers, NC 28717-0238
Ph:(828)743-5941
Fax: (828)743-9446
Co. E-mail: cashcham@dnet.net
URL: http://www.cashiers-nc.com
Contact: Sue Bumgarner, Exec.Dir.

63341 ■ Caswell County Chamber of Commerce
PO Box 29
Yanceyville, NC 27379
Ph:(336)694-6106
Fax: (336)694-9983
Co. E-mail: caswellchamber@esinc.net
URL: http://www.esinc.net/caswellchamber
Contact: Robert Hillman, Exec.Dir.

63342 ■ Catawba County Chamber of Commerce
PO Box 1828
Hickory, NC 28603-1828
Ph:(828)328-6111
Fax: (828)328-1175
Co. E-mail: info@catawbachamber.org
URL: http://www.catawbachamber.org
Contact: Danny Hearn, Pres.

63343 ■ Chapel Hill - Carrboro Chamber of Commerce
104 S Estes Dr.
PO Box 2897
Chapel Hill, NC 27515-2897
Ph:(919)967-7075
Fax: (919)968-6874
Co. E-mail: anelson@carolinachamber.org
URL: http://www.carolinachamber.org
Contact: Aaron Nelson, Exec.Dir.

63344 ■ Charlotte Chamber of Commerce
330 S Tryon St.
PO Box 32785
Charlotte, NC 28232
Ph:(704)378-1300
Fax: (704)338-6946
Co. E-mail: awilliams@charlottechamber.com
URL: http://www.charlottechamber.org
Contact: Mr. Bob Morgan, Pres.

63345 ■ Chatham County United Chamber of Commerce
1609 E 11th St.
Siler City, NC 27344-2823
Ph:(919)742-3333
Fax: (919)742-1333
Co. E-mail: info@ccucc.net
URL: http://www.ccucc.net
Contact: Jane J. Wrenn, Exec.Dir.

63346 ■ Cherokee Chamber of Commerce
PO Box 460
Cherokee, NC 28719-0460
Free: 800-438-1601
Fax: (828)497-8196
Co. E-mail: chero@dnet.net
URL: http://www.cherokee-nc.com
Contact: Mary Jane Ferguson, Dir.

63347 ■ Cherokee County Chamber of Commerce
805 W U.S. 64
Murphy, NC 28906
Ph:(828)837-2242
Fax: (828)837-6012
Co. E-mail: info@cherokeecountychamber.com
URL: http://www.cherokeecountychamber.com
Contact: David Hilton, Pres.

63348 ■ Cherryville Chamber of Commerce EDC
220 E Main St.
Cherryville, NC 28021
Ph:(704)435-3451
Fax: (704)435-4200
Co. E-mail: cherryvi@bellsouth.net
Contact: Mr. Richard Randall, Exec. Dir.

63349 ■ Clay County Chamber of Commerce
388 Business Hwy. 64
PO Box 88
Hayesville, NC 28904
Ph:(828)389-3704
Co. E-mail: info@claycounty-nc-chamber.com
URL: http://www.claycounty-nc-chamber.com
Contact: Debbie Jackson, Exec.Dir.

63350 ■ Clayton Chamber of Commerce
301 E Main St.
PO Box 246
Clayton, NC 27520
Ph:(919)553-6352
Fax: (919)553-1758
Co. E-mail: info@claytonchamber.com
URL: http://www.claytonchamber.com
Contact: Sally Schlindwein, Exec.Dir.

63351 ■ Cleveland County Chamber of Commerce
PO Box 879
Shelby, NC 28151-0879
Ph:(704)487-8521
Fax: (704)487-7458
Co. E-mail: info@clevelandchamber.org
URL: http://www.clevelandchamber.org
Contact: Stuart Gilbert, Pres.

63352 ■ Clinton-Sampson Chamber of Commerce
414 Warsaw Rd.
PO Box 467
Clinton, NC 28329-0467
Ph:(910)592-6177
Fax: (910)592-5770
Co. E-mail: clintonareacoc@intrstar.net
Contact: Ms. Amber Cava, Exec. Dir.

63353 ■ Davie County Chamber of Commerce
135 S Salisbury St.
Mocksville, NC 27028-2331
Ph:(336)751-3304
Fax: (336)751-5697
Co. E-mail: chamber@daviecounty.com
URL: http://www.daviecounty.com
Contact: Tracey Gibson, Pres.

63354 ■ Dunn Area Chamber of Commerce
209 W Divine St.
PO Box 548
Dunn, NC 28335
Ph:(910)892-4113
Fax: (910)892-4071
Co. E-mail: tammy@dunnchamber.com
URL: http://www.dunnchamber.com
Contact: Tammy Williams, Exec.VP

63355 ■ Eden Chamber of Commerce
678 S Van Buren Rd.
Eden, NC 27288
Ph:(336)623-3336
Fax: (336)623-8800
Co. E-mail: info@edenchamber.com
URL: http://www.edenchamber.com
Contact: Cindy Adams, Pres.

63356 ■ Edenton-Chowan Chamber of Commerce
116 E King St.
PO Box 245
Edenton, NC 27932-0245
Ph:(252)482-3400
Free: 800-775-0111
Fax: (252)482-7093
Co. E-mail: richard.bunch@ncmail.net
URL: http://www.chowancounty-nc.gov
Contact: Richard Bunch, Exec.Dir.

63357 ■ Elizabeth City Area Chamber of Commerce
PO Box 426
Elizabeth City, NC 27907-0426
Ph:(252)335-4365
Fax: (252)335-5732
Co. E-mail: info@elizabethcitychamber.org
URL: http://www.elizabethcitychamber.org
Contact: Jamie Holland, Membership Dir.

63358 ■ Elizabethtown-White Lake Area Chamber of Commerce
103 E Broad St.
PO Box 306
Elizabethtown, NC 28337-0306
Ph:(910)862-4368
Fax: (910)862-4368
Co. E-mail: chamber28337@earthlink.net
URL: http://www.elizabethtownwhitelake.com
Contact: Ms. Elaine Lomax, Exec.Sec.

63359 ■ Erwin Area Chamber of Commerce
PO Box 655
Erwin, NC 28339
Ph:(910)897-7300
Fax: (910)897-5543

Co. E-mail: erwinchamber@surrealnet.net
Contact: Debbie Chestnut, Exec.Sec.

63360 ■ Farmville Chamber of Commerce
PO Box 150
Farmville, NC 27828-0150
Ph:(252)753-4670
Fax: (252)753-7313
Co. E-mail: lrdrake@earthlink.net
Contact: Ms. Lori Drake, Exec.Dir.

63361 ■ Fayetteville Chamber of Commerce
201 Hay St.
PO Box 9
Fayetteville, NC 28302-0009
Ph:(910)483-8133
Fax: (910)483-0263
Co. E-mail: bmartin@ccbusinesscouncil.org
URL: http://www.fayettevillencchamber.org
Contact: William A. Martin, Pres.

63362 ■ Franklin Area Chamber of Commerce
425 Porter St.
Franklin, NC 28734
Ph:(828)524-3161
Free: (866)372-5546
Fax: (828)369-7516
Co. E-mail: facc@franklin-chamber.com
URL: http://www.franklin-chamber.com
Contact: Linda Harbuck, Exec.Dir.

63363 ■ Franklin County Chamber of Commerce
PO Box 62
Louisburg, NC 27549
Ph:(919)496-3056
Fax: (919)496-0422
Co. E-mail: mail@franklin-chamber.org
URL: http://www.franklin-chamber.org
Contact: Shana Filter, Exec.Dir.

63364 ■ Fuquay-Varina Area Chamber of Commerce
121 N Main St.
Fuquay Varina, NC 27526
Ph:(919)552-4947
Fax: (919)552-1029
Co. E-mail: andrew@fuquay-varina.com
URL: http://www.fuquay-varina.com
Contact: Andrew T. Tate, Exec. Dir.

63365 ■ Garner Chamber of Commerce
401 Circle Dr.
Garner, NC 27529
Ph:(919)772-6440
Fax: (919)772-6443
Co. E-mail: info@garnerchamber.org
URL: http://www.garnerchamber.com
Contact: Neal Padgett, Pres.

63366 ■ Gaston Chamber of Commerce
601 W Franklin Blvd.
Gastonia, NC 28052
Ph:(704)864-2621
Free: 800-348-8461
Fax: (704)854-8723
Co. E-mail: jennifer@gastonchamber.com
URL: http://www.gastonchamber.com
Contact: Jennifer Harkey, Finance Dir.

63367 ■ Granville County Chamber of Commerce
PO Box 820
Oxford, NC 27565
Ph:(919)693-6125
Fax: (919)693-6126
Co. E-mail: granvillechamber@earthlink.net
URL: http://www.granville-chamber.com
Contact: Vickie Bailey, Pres.

63368 ■ Greater Chadbourn Chamber of Commerce
PO Box 200
Chadbourn, NC 28431
Ph:(910)654-3445
Contact: Bryan Edwwards, Pres.

63369 ■ Greater Durham Chamber of Commerce
PO Box 3829
Durham, NC 27702-3829
Ph:(919)682-2133
Fax: (919)688-8351
Co. E-mail: info@durhamchamber.org
URL: http://www.durhamchamber.org
Contact: Libby Barnes, Pres./CEO

63370 ■ Greater Hampstead Chamber of Commerce
PO Box 211
Hampstead, NC 28443
Ph:(910)270-9642
Free: 800-833-2483
Fax: (910)270-4000
Co. E-mail: hampsteadcoc1@bellsouth.net
URL: http://www.hampsteadchamber.com
Contact: Susan Forbes, Exec.Dir.

63371 ■ Greater Hendersonville Chamber of Commerce
330 N King St.
Hendersonville, NC 28792
Ph:(828)692-1413
Fax: (828)693-8802
Co. E-mail: chamber@hendersonvillechamber.org
URL: http://www.hendersonvillechamber.org
Contact: Mr. Bob Williford, Pres.

63372 ■ Greater Mount Airy Chamber of Commerce
200 N Main St.
PO Box 913
Mount Airy, NC 27030-0913
Ph:(336)786-6116
Free: 800-948-0949
Fax: (336)786-1488
Co. E-mail: admin@mtairyncchamber.org
URL: http://www.mtairyncchamber.org
Contact: Yvonne Nichols, Exec.Asst.

63373 ■ Greater Raleigh Chamber of Commerce
800 S Salisbury St.
Raleigh, NC 27601
Ph:(919)664-7000
Fax: (919)664-7099
Co. E-mail: hschmitt@the-chamber.org
URL: http://www.raleighchamber.org
Contact: Harvey A. Schmitt, Pres./CEO

63374 ■ Greater Smithfield-Selma Area Chamber of Commerce
1115 Industrial Park Dr.
PO Box 467
Smithfield, NC 27577-0467
Ph:(919)934-9166
Fax: (919)934-1337
Co. E-mail: rchildrey@smithfieldselma.com
URL: http://www.smithfieldselma.com
Contact: Richard Childrey, Pres.

63375 ■ Greater Tabor City Chamber of Commerce
104 Tabor Industrial Park Rd.
PO Box 446
Tabor City, NC 28463
Ph:(910)653-2031
Fax: (910)653-2031
Co. E-mail: tccofc@tpinter.net
Contact: Cynthia Nelson, Exec.VP

63376 ■ Greater Topsail Area Chamber of Commerce and Tourism
PO Box 2486
Surf City, NC 28445
Ph:(910)329-4446
Free: 800-626-2780
Fax: (910)329-4432
Co. E-mail: info@topsailcoc.com
URL: http://www.topsailcoc.com
Contact: Allan W. Libby, Pres.

63377 ■ Greater Whiteville Chamber of Commerce
601 S Madison St.
Whiteville, NC 28472
Ph:(910)642-3171
Free: 888-533-7196
Fax: (910)642-6047
Co. E-mail: chambercow@weblnk.net
URL: http://www.whitevillechamber.org
Contact: Mrs. Janice Young, Exec. VP

63378 ■ Greater Wilmington Chamber of Commerce
1 Estell Lee Pl.
Wilmington, NC 28401
Ph:(910)762-2611
Fax: (910)762-9765
Co. E-mail: info@wilmingtonchamber.org
URL: http://www.wilmingtonchamber.org
Contact: Connie Majure-Rhett CCE, Pres./CEO

63379 ■ Greater Winston-Salem Chamber of Commerce
601 W 4th St.
PO Box 1408
Winston-Salem, NC 27102
Ph:(336)728-9200
Fax: (336)721-2209
Co. E-mail: anderson@winstonsalem.com
URL: http://www.winstonsalem.com
Contact: Gayle N. Anderson, Pres./CEO

63380 ■ Greensboro Area Chamber of Commerce
342 N Elm St.
PO Box 3246
Greensboro, NC 27402
Ph:(336)275-8675
Fax: (336)275-9299
Co. E-mail: msamet@greensboro.org
URL: http://www.greensborochamber.com
Contact: Mindy Samet, Account Exec.

63381 ■ Greenville - Pitt County Chamber of Commerce
302 S Greene St.
Greenville, NC 27834-1564
Ph:(252)752-4101
Fax: (252)752-5934
Co. E-mail: chamber@greenvillenc.org
URL: http://www.greenvillenc.org
Contact: Susanne D. Sartelle CCE, Pres.

63382 ■ Havelock Chamber of Commerce
201 Tourist Ctr. Dr.
PO Box 21
Havelock, NC 28532
Ph:(252)447-1101
Fax: (252)447-0241
Co. E-mail: info@havelockchamber.net
URL: http://www.havelockchamber.net
Contact: Joy Mason, Exec.Dir.

63383 ■ Haywood County Chamber of Commerce
1482 Russ Ave.
PO Drawer 600
Waynesville, NC 28786-0600
Ph:(828)456-3021
Free: 877-456-7265
Fax: (828)452-7265
Co. E-mail: info@haywood-nc.com
URL: http://www.haywood-nc.com
Contact: Ms. CeCe Hipps, Exec.Dir.

63384 ■ Henderson-Vance County Chamber of Commerce
414 S Garnett St.
PO Box 1302
Henderson, NC 27536
Ph:(252)438-8414
Fax: (252)492-8989
Co. E-mail: info@hendersonvance.org
URL: http://www.hendersonvance.org
Contact: Bill Edwards, Pres.

63385 ■ Hickory Nut Gorge Chamber of Commerce
PO Box 32
Chimney Rock, NC 28720
Ph:(828)625-2725
Free: 877-625-2725
Fax: (828)625-9601
Co. E-mail: griffinmichael@bellsouth.net
URL: http://www.thehickorynutgorge.com
Contact: Judy Beeson, Exec.Dir.

63386 ■ High Point Chamber of Commerce
PO Box 5025
High Point, NC 27262-5025
Ph:(336)889-8151
Fax: (336)889-9499
Co. E-mail: info@highpointchamber.org
URL: http://www.highpointchamber.org
Contact: Tom Dayvault, Pres.

63387 ■ Highlands Area Chamber of Commerce
269 Oak St.
PO Box 62
Highlands, NC 28741
Ph:(828)526-5841
Fax: (828)526-5803
Co. E-mail: highlandscofc@smnet.net
URL: http://www.highlandschamber.org
Contact: William F. Bassham, Pres./CEO

63388 ■ Hillsborough/Orange County Chamber of Commerce
121 W Margaret Ln., Ste. A
Hillsborough, NC 27278
Ph:(919)732-8156
Fax: (919)732-4566
Co. E-mail: info@hillsboroughchamber.com
URL: http://www.hillsboroughchamber.com
Contact: Margaret Wood Cannell, Exec.Dir.

63389 ■ Jackson County Chamber of Commerce
773 W Main St.
Sylva, NC 28779-8211
Ph:(828)586-2155
Free: 800-962-1911
Fax: (828)586-4887
Co. E-mail: jctta@nc-mountains.com
URL: http://www.mountainlovers.com
Contact: Julie Spiro, Dir.

63390 ■ Jacksonville - Onslow Chamber of Commerce
PO Box 765
Jacksonville, NC 28541-0765
Ph:(910)347-3141
Fax: (910)347-4705
Co. E-mail: info@jacksonvilleonline.org
URL: http://www.jacksonvilleonline.org
Contact: Mona Padrick, Pres.

63391 ■ Kernersville Chamber of Commerce
136 E Mountain St.
Kernersville, NC 27284-2939
Ph:(336)993-4521
Fax: (336)993-3756
Co. E-mail: kchamber@kernersvillenc.com
URL: http://www.kernersvillenc.com
Contact: Bruce Boyer, Pres./CEO

63392 ■ King Chamber of Commerce
PO Box 863
King, NC 27021
Ph:(336)983-9308
Fax: (336)983-9526
Co. E-mail: kcoc@alltel.net
URL: http://www.kingnc.com
Contact: Deanne M. Moore, Exec.Dir.

63393 ■ Kings Mountain - Branch of Cleveland County Chamber of Commerce
600 York Rd.
PO Box 794
Kings Mountain, NC 28086
Ph:(704)739-4755
Fax: (704)739-8149

Co. E-mail: shirley@clevelandchamber.org
URL: http://www.clevelandchamber.org
Contact: Shirley Brutko, Admin. Asst.

63394 ■ Kinston-Lenoir County Chamber of Commerce
301 N Queen St.
PO Box 157
Kinston, NC 28502-0157
Ph:(252)527-1131
Fax: (252)527-1914
Co. E-mail: cbrochure@kinstonchamber.com
URL: http://www.kinstonchamber.com
Contact: Joyce Cherry, Pres.

63395 ■ Knightdale Chamber of Commerce
207 Main St.
PO Box 601
Knightdale, NC 27545-0601
Ph:(919)266-4603
Fax: (919)266-8010
Co. E-mail: knightdalechamber@knightdalechamber.com
URL: http://www.knightdalechamber.com
Contact: Jennifer Bryan, Exec.Dir.

63396 ■ Lake Gaston Chamber of Commerce
2475 Eaton Ferry Rd.
Littleton, NC 27850
Ph:(252)586-5711
Free: (866)730-5711
Fax: (252)586-3152
Co. E-mail: info@lakegastonchamber.com
URL: http://www.lakegastonchamber.com
Contact: Almira Papierniak, Exec.Dir.

63397 ■ Lake Norman Chamber and Convention and Visitors Bureau
19900 W Catawba Ave.
Cornelius, NC 28031
Ph:(704)892-1922
Fax: (704)892-5313
Co. E-mail: chamber@lakenorman.org
URL: http://www.lakenormanchamber.org
Contact: Bill Russell, Pres.

63398 ■ Laurinburg - Scotland County Area Chamber of Commerce
606 Atkinson St.
PO Box 1025
Laurinburg, NC 28353-1025
Ph:(910)276-7420
Fax: (910)277-8785
Co. E-mail: scotcoc@carolina.net
URL: http://www.laurinburgchamber.org
Contact: Mr. James F. Henderson Jr., Pres.

63399 ■ Lillington Area Chamber of Commerce
PO Box 967
Lillington, NC 27546
Ph:(910)893-3751
Co. E-mail: contact@lillingtonchamber.org
URL: http://www.lillingtonchamber.org
Contact: Jinx Averitte, Chamber Coor.

63400 ■ Lincolnton-Lincoln County Chamber of Commerce
101 E Main St.
PO Box 1617
Lincolnton, NC 28093-1617
Ph:(704)735-3096
Fax: (704)735-5449
Co. E-mail: lincolnchambernc@bellsouth.net
URL: http://www.lincolnchambernc.org
Contact: Ken Kindley, Pres.

63401 ■ Lumberton Area Chamber of Commerce
PO Box 1008
Lumberton, NC 28359-1008
Ph:(910)739-4750
Fax: (910)671-9722
Co. E-mail: lumbertonchamber@bellsouth.net
URL: http://www.lumbertonchamber.com
Contact: Cindy S. Kern, Exec.Dir.

63402 ■ Maggie Valley Area Chamber of Commerce and Convention and Visitors' Bureau
2487 Soco Rd.
PO Box 279
Maggie Valley, NC 28751-0087
Ph:(828)926-1686
Free: 800-624-4431
Fax: (828)926-9398
Co. E-mail: cmaggie@maggievalley.org
URL: http://www.maggievalley.org
Contact: Ms. Lynn Collins, Exec.Dir.

63403 ■ Marshville Chamber of Commerce
PO Box 337
Marshville, NC 28103
Ph:(704)624-3183
Contact: Lisa Ammons, Pres.

63404 ■ Martin County Chamber of Commerce
PO Box 311
Williamston, NC 27892
Ph:(252)792-4131
Fax: (252)792-1013
Co. E-mail: mcchamber@martincountync.com
URL: http://www.martincountync.com
Contact: Billi J. Wynn, Exec.Dir.

63405 ■ Matthews Chamber of Commerce
PO Box 601
Matthews, NC 28106-0601
Ph:(704)847-3649
Fax: (704)847-3364
Co. E-mail: info@matthewschamber.com
URL: http://www.matthewschamber.com
Contact: Tina Whitley, Exec.Dir.

63406 ■ McDowell Chamber of Commerce
1170 W Tate St.
Marion, NC 28752-4487
Ph:(828)652-4240
Fax: (828)659-9620
Co. E-mail: mountains@mcdowellchamber.com
URL: http://www.mcdowellchamber.com
Contact: Rod Birdsong, Exec.Dir.

63407 ■ Mitchell County Chamber of Commerce
PO Box 858
Spruce Pine, NC 28777
Ph:(828)765-9483
Free: 800-227-3912
Fax: (828)765-9034
Co. E-mail: info@mitchell-county.com
URL: http://www.mitchell-county.com
Contact: Shirley Hise, Dir.

63408 ■ Montgomery County Chamber of Commerce
444 N Main St.
PO Box 637
Troy, NC 27371-0637
Ph:(910)572-4300
Fax: (910)572-5193
Co. E-mail: chamber@montgomery-county.com
URL: http://montgomery-county.com
Contact: Judy Stevens, Dir.

63409 ■ Moore County Chamber of Commerce
10677 Hwy. 15-501
Southern Pines, NC 28387
Ph:(910)692-3926
Fax: (910)692-0619
Co. E-mail: moorecountychamber@ncrrbiz.com
URL: http://www.moorecountychamber.com
Contact: Elyse C. Hillegass, Pres./CEO

63410 ■ Mooresville-South Iredell Chamber of Commerce
PO Box 628
Mooresville, NC 28115
Ph:(704)664-3898
Fax: (704)664-2549
Co. E-mail: info@mooresvillenc.org
URL: http://www.mooresvillenc.org

Contact: Leah Mitcham, Membership Coor.

63411 ■ Morrisville Chamber of Commerce
260 Town Hall Dr., Ste. A
PO Box 548
Morrisville, NC 27560-0548
Ph:(919)380-9026
Fax: (919)380-9021
Co. E-mail: chamber@morrisvillenc.com
URL: http://www.morrisvillenc.com
Contact: Jodi Ann LaFreniere, Pres.

63412 ■ Mount Olive Area Chamber of Commerce
123 N Center St.
Mount Olive, NC 28365
Ph:(919)658-3113
Fax: (919)658-3125
Co. E-mail: moacc@bellsouth.net
Contact: Patricia E. O'Donoghue, Pres.

63413 ■ Murfreesboro Chamber of Commerce
116 E Main St.
PO Box 393
Murfreesboro, NC 27855
Ph:(252)398-4886
Fax: (252)398-5871
Contact: Mrs. Jennifer Moore, Exec. Dir.

63414 ■ New Bern Area Chamber of Commerce
PO Drawer C
New Bern, NC 28563-8503
Ph:(252)637-3111
Fax: (252)637-7541
Co. E-mail: kroberts@newbernchamber.com
URL: http://www.newbernchamber.com
Contact: Kevin Roberts, Pres.

63415 ■ Outer Banks Chamber of Commerce
101 Town Hall Dr.
PO Box 1757
Kill Devil Hills, NC 27948-1757
Ph:(252)441-8144
Fax: (252)441-0338
Co. E-mail: chamber@outer-banks.com
URL: http://www.outerbankschamber.com
Contact: John Bone, Pres.

63416 ■ Perquimans County Chamber of Commerce
118 W Market St.
Hertford, NC 27944
Ph:(252)426-5657
Fax: (252)426-7542
Co. E-mail: chamber@perquimans.com
URL: http://www.perquimans.com
Contact: Sid Eley, Dir.

63417 ■ Pleasure Island, Carolina Beach, and Kure Beach Chamber of Commerce
1121 N Lake Park Blvd.
Carolina Beach, NC 28428
Ph:(910)458-8434
Fax: (910)458-7969
Co. E-mail: chamber@carolinabeach.org
URL: http://pleasureislandchambernc.org
Contact: Gail McCloskey, Admin.Mgr.

63418 ■ Polk County Chamber of Commerce
2753 Lynn Rd., Ste. A
Tryon, NC 28782
Ph:(828)859-6236
Fax: (828)859-2301
Co. E-mail: info@polkchamber.org
URL: http://www.polkchamber.org
Contact: Janet Wooley, Exec.Dir.

63419 ■ Raeford - Hoke Chamber of Commerce
101 N Main St.
Raeford, NC 28376
Ph:(910)875-5929
Fax: (910)875-1010
Co. E-mail: chamberofcommercerae@earthlink.net
URL: http://www.hoke-raeford.com/chamber.htm

63420 ■ Randleman Chamber of Commerce
PO Box 207
Randleman, NC 27317
Ph:(336)495-1100
Fax: (336)495-1133
URL: http://www.randlemanchamber.com
Contact: David Caughron, Exec. Dir.

63421 ■ Richmond County Chamber of Commerce
505 Rockingham Rd.
PO Box 86
Rockingham, NC 28380-0086
Ph:(910)895-9058
Fax: (910)895-9056
Co. E-mail: chamber@carolina.rr.com
URL: http://www.richmondcountychamber.com
Contact: Emily Tucker, Pres.

63422 ■ Roanoke Valley Chamber of Commerce
1640 Julian R. Allsbrook Hwy.
PO Box 519
Roanoke Rapids, NC 27870
Ph:(252)537-3513
Fax: (252)535-5767
Co. E-mail: bblackburn@rvchamber.com
URL: http://www.rvchamber.com
Contact: Brenda Blackburn, Pres.

63423 ■ Rocky Mount Area Chamber of Commerce
PO Box 392
Rocky Mount, NC 27802-0392
Ph:(252)446-0323
Free: 800-849-6825
Fax: (252)446-5103
Co. E-mail: rmacc@rockymountchamber.org
URL: http://www.rockymountchamber.org
Contact: Eddie Baysden, Exec.Dir.

63424 ■ Rowan County Chamber of Commerce
204 E Innes St.
PO Box 559
Salisbury, NC 28145-0559
Ph:(704)633-4221
Fax: (704)639-1200
Co. E-mail: info@rowanchamber.com
URL: http://www.rowanchamber.com
Contact: Robert H. Wright, Pres.

63425 ■ Roxboro Area Chamber of Commerce
211 N Main St.
PO Box 209
Roxboro, NC 27573
Ph:(336)599-8333
Fax: (336)599-8335
Co. E-mail: chamber@roxboronc.com
URL: http://www.roxboronc.com
Contact: Marcia O'Neil, Pres./CEO

63426 ■ Rutherford County Chamber of Commerce
162 N Main St.
Rutherfordton, NC 28139-2502
Ph:(828)287-3090
Fax: (828)287-0799
Co. E-mail: info@rutherfordcoc.org
URL: http://www.rutherfordcoc.org
Contact: William L. Hall, Exec.Dir.

63427 ■ Southport-Oak Island Area Chamber of Commerce
4841 Long Beach Rd. SE
Southport, NC 28461
Ph:(910)457-6964
Free: 800-457-6964
Fax: (910)457-0598
Co. E-mail: info@southport-oakisland.com
URL: http://www.southport-oakisland.com
Contact: Trisha Howarth, Pres.

63428 ■ Southport-Oak Island Chamber of Commerce
4841 Long Beach Rd. SE
Southport, NC 28461-8712

Ph:(910)457-6964
Free: 800-457-6964
Fax: (910)457-0598
Co. E-mail: info@southport-oakisland.com
URL: http://www.southport-oakisland.com
Contact: Karen Sphar, Exec.VP

63429 ■ Spring Lake Area Chamber of Commerce
PO Box 333
Spring Lake, NC 28390
Ph:(910)497-8821
Fax: (910)497-1897
Co. E-mail: sprlkchamber@faynet.com
URL: http://www.springlakenc.org
Contact: Evelena Keller-Mullens, Pres.

63430 ■ Stanly County Chamber of Commerce
116 E North St.
Albemarle, NC 28002-4048
Ph:(704)982-8116
Fax: (704)983-5000
Co. E-mail: info@stanlychamber.org
URL: http://www.stanlychamber.org
Contact: Tom Ramseur, Pres./CEO

63431 ■ Swain County Chamber of Commerce
16 Everett St.
PO Box 509
Bryson City, NC 28713
Ph:(828)488-3681
Free: 800-867-9246
Fax: (828)488-6858
Co. E-mail: chamber@greatsmokies.com
URL: http://www.greatsmokies.com
Contact: Gwen Bushyhead, Dir.

63432 ■ Tarboro - Edgecombe Chamber of Commerce
PO Drawer F
Tarboro, NC 27886
Ph:(252)823-7241
Fax: (252)823-1499
Co. E-mail: tarboroedgecombechamber@earthlink.net
URL: http://www.tarborochamber.com
Contact: Cherry Bass, Pres.

63433 ■ Thomasville Area Chamber of Commerce
PO Box 1400
Thomasville, NC 27361-1400
Ph:(336)475-6134
Fax: (336)475-4802
Co. E-mail: tvillecoc@northstate.net
Contact: Doug Croft, Pres.

63434 ■ Union County Chamber of Commerce
903 Skyway Dr.
Monroe, NC 28110-3181
Ph:(704)289-4567
Fax: (704)282-0122
Co. E-mail: info@unioncountycoc.com
URL: http://www.unioncountycoc.com
Contact: Jim Carpenter, Pres.

63435 ■ Wake Forest Chamber of Commerce
350 S White St.
Wake Forest, NC 27587
Ph:(919)556-1519
Fax: (919)556-8570
Co. E-mail: info@wakeforestchamber.org
URL: http://www.wakeforestchamber.org
Contact: Mark Fleming, Exec.Dir.

63436 ■ Wallace Chamber of Commerce
PO Box 427
Wallace, NC 28466
Ph:(910)285-4044
Fax: (910)285-4044
Co. E-mail: lou@wallacechamber.com
URL: http://www.wallacechamber.com
Contact: Lou N. Powell, Dir.

63437 ■ Warsaw Chamber of Commerce
PO Box 585
Warsaw, NC 28398
Ph:(910)293-7804
Fax: (910)293-6773
Co. E-mail: warsawchamber@earthlink.net
URL: http://www.townofwarsawnc.com
Contact: Linda F. Kitchen, Exec.Dir.

63438 ■ Washington - Beaufort County Chamber of Commerce
PO Box 665
Washington, NC 27889
Ph:(252)946-9168
Fax: (252)946-9169
Co. E-mail: info@wbcchamber.com
URL: http://www.wbcchamber.com
Contact: Lee Hemink, Exec.Dir.

63439 ■ Washington County Chamber of Commerce
701 Washington St.
Plymouth, NC 27962
Ph:(252)793-4804
Fax: (252)793-2143
Co. E-mail: chamber@washconc.org
Contact: Sarah Higgins, Exec.Dir

63440 ■ Wayne County Chamber of Commerce
PO Box 1107
Goldsboro, NC 27533-1107
Ph:(919)734-2241
Fax: (919)734-2247
Co. E-mail: steveh@waynecountychamber.com
URL: http://www.waynecountychamber.com
Contact: Steve Hicks, Exec.Dir.

63441 ■ Wendell Chamber of Commerce
115 N Pine St.
PO Box 562
Wendell, NC 27591-0562
Ph:(919)365-6318
Fax: (919)366-2010
Co. E-mail: wendellcc@bellsouth.net
URL: http://www.wendellchamber.com
Contact: Lesia McKenzie, Chair

63442 ■ Western Rockingham Chamber of Commerce
112 W Murphy St.
Madison, NC 27025-1924
Ph:(336)548-6248
Fax: (336)548-4466
Co. E-mail: wrcc1@earthlink.net
URL: http://www.westernrockinghamchamber.com
Contact: Donnie Joyce, Exec.Dir.

63443 ■ Wilkes Chamber of Commerce
717 Main St.
PO Box 727
North Wilkesboro, NC 28659
Ph:(336)838-8662
Fax: (336)838-3728
Co. E-mail: info@wilkesnc.org
URL: http://www.wilkesnc.org
Contact: Linda S. Cheek, Pres.

63444 ■ Wilson Chamber of Commerce
200 W Nash St.
PO Box 1146
Wilson, NC 27894-1146
Ph:(252)237-0165
Fax: (252)243-7931
Co. E-mail: lsoprun@wilsonncchamber.com
URL: http://www.wilsonncchamber.com
Contact: Lucille Soprun, Office Mgr.

63445 ■ Windsor/Bertie County Chamber of Commerce
102 N York St.
PO Box 572
Windsor, NC 27983-0572
Ph:(252)794-4277
Fax: (252)794-5070
Co. E-mail: windsorchamber@gate811.net
URL: http://www.windsor-bertie.com

Contact: Sharon Davis, Exec. Dir.

63446 ■ Yadkin County Chamber of Commerce
205 S Jackson St.
PO Box 1840
Yadkinville, NC 27055-1840
Ph:(336)679-2200
Fax: (336)679-3034
Co. E-mail: btodd@yadkinchamber.org
URL: http://www.yadkinchamber.org
Contact: Robert J. Todd, Dir.

63447 ■ Yadkin Valley Chamber of Commerce
PO Box 496
Elkin, NC 28621
Ph:(336)526-1111
Fax: (336)526-1879
Co. E-mail: mmatthews@yadkinvalley.org
URL: http://www.yadkinvalley.org
Contact: Ann Ashman, Chair

63448 ■ Yancey County/Burnsville Chamber of Commerce
106 W Main St.
Burnsville, NC 28714
Ph:(828)682-7413
Free: 800-948-1632
Fax: (828)682-6599
Co. E-mail: info@yanceychamber.com
URL: http://www.yanceychamber.com
Contact: Miki Pontorno, Exec.Dir.

63449 ■ Zebulon Chamber of Commerce
PO Box 546
Zebulon, NC 27597
Ph:(919)269-6320
Fax: (919)269-6350
Co. E-mail: zebcoc@bellsouth.net
URL: http://www.zebulonchamber.org
Contact: Tammy J. Russo, Exec. Dir.

MINORITY BUSINESS ASSISTANCE PROGRAMS

63450 ■ Asheville Branch of Cherokee Native American Indian Business Development
70 Woodfin Pl., Ste. 312
Asheville, NC 28801
Ph:(828)252-2516
Fax: (828)252-6047
Co. E-mail: ashevillebdc@yahoo.com
URL: http://www.mbda.gov Center

FINANCING AND LOAN PROGRAMS

63451 ■ Academy Funds / Longleaf Venture Fund LLC
633 Davis Dr., Ste. 500
Durham, NC 27713
Ph:(919)991-5420
Fax: (919)991-5421
URL: http://www.academyfunds.com
Contact: Glenn Kline, Managing Partner
Investment Policies: Seed, start-up, early and first stage, and research and development. **Industry Preferences:** Communications and media, computer software and hardware, Internet specific, semiconductors and other electronics, biotechnology, medical and health, consumer related, industrial and energy, and transportation. **Geographic Preferences:** North Carolina and Southeast.

63452 ■ A.M. Pappas & Associates LLC
7030 Kit Creek Rd.
PO Box 110287
Research Triangle Park, NC 27709
Ph:(919)998-3300
Fax: (919)998-3301
URL: http://www.ampappas.com

Contact: Art Pappas, Managing Partner
Preferred Investment Size: $100,000 to $6,000,000.
Investment Policies: Balanced, first, early, later, and second stage, and mezzanine. **Industry Preferences:** Medical and health, biotechnology, computer software and services, and Internet specific. **Geographic Preferences:** Mid Atlantic, Northeast, Northern California, Southeast, and West Coast U.S.; Ontario and Quebec, Canada.

63453 ■ Aurora Funds, Inc.
2525 Meridian Pky., Ste. 220
Durham, NC 27713
Ph:(919)484-0400
Fax: (919)484-0444
URL: http://www.aurorafunds.com
Contact: M. Scott Albert, Managing General Partner
Preferred Investment Size: $100,000 to $2,000,000.
Investment Types: Seed, start-up, and early stage.
Industry Preferences: Medical and health, Internet specific, computer software and services, biotechnology, semiconductors and other electronics, communications and other media, industrial and energy.
Geographic Preferences: Mid Atlantic and Southeast.

63454 ■ Carolinas Capital Investment Corp.
1408 Biltmore Dr.
Charlotte, NC 28207
Ph:(704)375-3888
Fax: (704)375-6226
Co. E-mail: ed@carolinacapital.com
Contact: Edward Goode
Preferred Investment Size: $200,000 to $1,000,000.
Investment Types: Seed, research and development, leveraged buyout, start-up, first and second stage. **Industry Preferences:** Communications and media, semiconductors and other electronics.

63455 ■ Catalysta Partners
1822 E. Hwy. 54, Ste. 250
Durham, NC 27713
Ph:(919)484-0370
Fax: (919)484-0364
URL: http://www.catalystapartners.com
Contact: Brian Kinahan, General Partner
Preferred Investment Size: $50,000 to $4,000,000.
Investment Policies: Seed, early stage, acquisition, and special situation. **Industry Preferences:** Medical and health. **Geographic Preferences:** Northern California.

63456 ■ First Union Capital Partners
1 1st Union Center, 12th Fl.
301 S. College St.
Charlotte, NC 28288-0732
Ph:(704)383-0000
Fax: (704)374-6711
URL: http://www.fucp.com
Contact: L. Watts Hamrick III, Partner
Preferred Investment Size: $5,000,000 minimum.
Investment Types: Seed, start-up, first and second stage, mezzanine, expansion, leveraged buyout, special situations, and control block purchases. **Industry Preferences:** Diversified. **Geographic Preferences:** No preference.

63457 ■ Frontier Capital, LLC
1900 S. Blvd., Ste. 300
Charlotte, NC 28203
Ph:(704)414-2880
Fax: (704)414-2881
URL: http://www.frontierfunds.com
Contact: Michael Ramich, Principal
Preferred Investment Size: $1,000,000 to $3,000,000. **Investment Types:** First and second stage, expansion, and balanced. **Industry Preferences:** Communications, computer software, financial services, and business service. **Geographic Preferences:** Mid Atlantic and Southeast.

63458 ■ Geneva Merchant Banking Partners
PO Box 21962
Greensboro, NC 27420
Ph:(336)275-7002
Fax: (336)275-9155
URL: http://www.genevamerchantbank.com

Preferred Investment Size: $1,000,000 to $7,000,000. **Investment Types:** Distressed debt, expansion, leveraged buyout, management buyouts, mezzanine, second stage, generalist PE, and special situation. **Industry Preferences:** Communications and media, computer hardware, software and services, Internet specific, consumer related, medical and health, industrial and energy, semiconductors and other electronics. **Geographic Preferences:** Mid Atlantic, Midwest, and Southeast.

63459 ■ Intersouth Partners
406 Blackwell St., Ste. 200
Durham, NC 27701
Ph:(919)493-6640
Fax: (919)493-6649
URL: http://www.intersouth.com
Contact: Dennis Dougherty, Venture Partner
Preferred Investment Size: $500,000 to $12,000,000. **Investment Types:** Seed and early stage. **Industry Preferences:** Medical and health, biotechnology, Internet specific, computer software and services, industrial and energy, semiconductors and other electronics, other products, computer hardware, communications and media, and consumer related. **Geographic Preferences:** Southeast.

63460 ■ Kitty Hawk Capital
2700 Coltsgate Rd., Ste. 202
Charlotte, NC 28211
Ph:(704)362-3909
Fax: (704)362-2774
Contact: Chris Hegele, General Partner
Preferred Investment Size: $1,000,000 to $10,000,000. **Investment Policies:** Start-up, seed, and early stage. **Industry Preferences:** Medical and health, industrial and energy, Internet specific, other products, computer software and services, biotechnology, communications and media, consumer related, semiconductors and other electronics, and computer hardware. **Geographic Preferences:** Southeast.

63461 ■ MCNC Ventures LLC
3021 Cornwallis Rd.
PO Box 12889
Research Triangle Park, NC 27709
Ph:(919)248-1800
Fax: (919)248-1455
URL: http://www.mcnc.org
Investment Policies: Seed and early stage. **Industry Preferences:** Communications. **Geographic Preferences:** North Carolina.

63462 ■ The North Carolina Enterprise Fund, L.P.
3600 Glenwood Ave., Ste. 107
Raleigh, NC 27612
Ph:(919)781-2691
Fax: (919)783-9195
URL: http://www.ncef.com
Preferred Investment Size: $2,000,000 minimum.
Investment Types: Start-up, first stage, and mezzanine. **Industry Preferences:** Medical and health, communications and media, computer software and services, biotechnology, computer hardware, other products, Internet specific, semiconductors and other electronics, and consumer related. **Geographic Preferences:** North Carolina and Southeast.

63463 ■ North Carolina Technological Development Authority, Inc.
2 Davis Dr.
PO Box 13169
Triangle Park, NC 27709-3169
Ph:(919)990-8558
Fax: (919)558-0156
Investment Types: Seed, start-up, first and second stage, and research and development. **Industry Preferences:** Communications, computer hardware and software, Internet specific, semiconductors and other electronics, biotechnology, medical and health, industrial and energy. **Geographic Preferences:** Southeast.

63464 ■ Piedmont Venture Partners
1 Morrocroft Ctr.
6805 Morisson Blvd., Ste. 380
Charlotte, NC 28211

Ph:(704)731-5200
Fax: (704)365-9733
URL: http://www.piedmontvp.com
Contact: William Neal, Managing Partner
Preferred Investment Size: $500,000 to $3,000,000.
Investment Types: Early, first and second stage. **Industry Preferences:** Internet specific, computer software and services, biotechnology, medical and health, consumer related, and other products. **Geographic Preferences:** Southeast.

63465 ■ Ruddick Investment Co.
1800 2 First Union Ctr.
Charlotte, NC 28282
Ph:(704)372-5404
Fax: (704)372-6409
Contact: Richard Brigden, Vice President
Preferred Investment Size: $500,000 to $1,000,000.
Investment Types: First and second stage, and mezzanine. **Geographic Preferences:** Southeast.

63466 ■ The Shelton Companies, Inc.
4201 Congress St., Ste. 470
Charlotte, NC 28209
Ph:(704)557-2200
Contact: Charles Shelton, Partner
Preferred Investment Size: $1,000,000 to $10,000,000. **Investment Types:** Control-block purchases, leveraged buyout, recapitalizations, and second stage. **Industry Preferences:** Communications, semiconductors and other electronics, medical and health, consumer related, industrial and energy, transportation, financial services, business service, and manufacturing. **Geographic Preferences:** Mid Atlantic, Midwest, Southeast, and Southwest.

63467 ■ Southern Capitol Ventures
21 Glenwood Ave., Ste. 107
Raleigh, NC 27603
Ph:(919)858-7580
Fax: (919)863-2394
URL: http://www.southerncapitolventures.com
Contact: Benjamin Brooks, Founding Partner
Preferred Investment Size: $100,000 to $1,000,000.
Investment Types: Seed and early stage. **Geographic Preferences:** North Carolina and Southeast.

63468 ■ The Sustainable Jobs Fund (SJF)
400 W. Main St., Ste. 604
Durham, NC 27701
Ph:(919)530-1177
Fax: (919)530-1178
URL: http://www.sjfund.com
Contact: Dan Hoversten, Managing Director
Preferred Investment Size: $250,000 to $1,000,000.
Investment Types: Early, first and second stage, expansion, and private placement. **Industry Preferences:** Computer software, semiconductors and other electronics, medical and health, consumer related, industrial and energy, business service, manufacturing, and utilities. **Geographic Preferences:** Mid Atlantic, Northeast, and Southeast.

63469 ■ Truepilot, LLC
2530 Meridian Pky., 3rd Fl.
Durham, NC 27713
Ph:(919)806-4930
Fax: (919)806-4845
URL: http://www.truepilot.com
Contact: Michael Brader-Araje, Chief Executive Officer
Preferred Investment Size: $50,000 to $500,000. **Investment Types:** Early stage. **Industry Preferences:** Internet specific. **Geographic Preferences:** North Carolina.

63470 ■ Wakefield Group
1110 E. Morehead St.
Charlotte, NC 28204
Ph:(704)372-0355
Fax: (704)372-8216
URL: http://www.wakefieldgroup.com
Contact: Anna Nelson, Partner
Preferred Investment Size: $1,000,000 to $5,000,000. **Investment Types:** Early stage. **Industry Preferences:** Internet specific, computer software

and services, computer hardware, medical and health, semiconductors and other electronics, bio-technology, other products, communications and media, consumer related, and industrial and energy. **Geographic Preferences:** Southeast.

PROCUREMENT ASSISTANCE PROGRAMS

63471 ■ National Institute of Enviromental Heath Sciences–Small Business Administation
c/o NIEHS Contracting Office
PO Box 12874
Durham, NC 27709
Ph:(919)541-7895
Fax: (919)541-2712
Co. E-mail: mallory1@niehs.nih.gov
URL: http://www.niehs.nih.gov
Contact: Larry Mallory, Small Bus Liaison
Description: Covers activities for DHHS, National Institute of Environmental Health (Research Triangle Park, NC), Environmental Protection Agency (Research Triangle Park, NC), Pope Air Force Base (Fayetteville, NC), Seymour Johnson Air Force Base (Goldsboro, NC), Army Corps of Engineers (Wilmington, NC), Fort Bragg (Fayetteville, NC), and Fort Jackson (Columbia, SC).

63472 ■ North Carolina Department of Administration–Purchase and Contract Division–State Purchasing Office (1305)
1305 Mail Service Center
Raleigh, NC 27699-1305
Ph:(919)807-4500
Fax: (919)807-4502
URL: http://www.state.nc.us/pandc/
Contact: Mike Mangum, Dir

63473 ■ University of North Carolina/ SBTDC–Small Buisness Technical Development Center
5 W Hargett St., Ste. 600
Raleigh, NC 27601-1742
Ph:(919)715-7272
Fax: (919)715-7777
Co. E-mail: info@sbtdc.org
URL: http://www.sbtdc.org
Contact: Office Ass.
E-mail: rtruex@sbtdc.org

INCUBATORS/RESEARCH AND TECHNOLOGY PARKS

63474 ■ MCNC Research and Development
3021 Cornwallis Rd.
Durham, NC 27709
Ph:(919)248-1900
Fax: (919)248-1101
URL: http://www.mcnc.org
Contact: John Crites, Pres & CEO
Description: Scope: Promotes the use and development of electronic and information technologies by providing advanced research facilities in North Carolina's universities.

63475 ■ North Carolina A&T State University–Division of Research
1601 E Market St.
Greensboro, NC 27411
Ph:(336)334-7995
Fax: (336)334-7086
Co. E-mail: radha@ncat.edu
URL: http://dor.ncat.edu
Contact: Dr. N. Radhakrishnan, Vice Chancellor
E-mail: radha@ncat.edu
Scope: Administers and coordinates extramurally supported research in various departments of the University, including studies in nutrition, human resources, engineering, manpower, and urban mass transportation.

63476 ■ North Carolina Technological Development Authority–First Flight Venture Center
2 Davis Dr.
PO Box 13169
Research Triangle Park, NC 27709
Ph:(919)990-8558
Fax: (919)558-0156
Co. E-mail: jdraper@nctda.org
URL: http://www.nctda.org
Contact: John Draper, Pres & CEO
Description: Scope: Provides grants to establish incubator facilities for small firms and stimulates the development of new and existing small businesses. Also oversees the Innovation Research Fund and the First Flight Center, an incubator operated specifically to encourage and support technology-based small businesses in the Research Triangle Park region.

63477 ■ Research Triangle Foundation of North Carolina–Research Triangle Park
2 Hanes Dr.
PO Box 12255
Research Triangle Park, NC 27709
Ph:(919)549-8181
Fax: (919)549-8246
Co. E-mail: parkinfo@rtp.org
URL: http://www.rtp.org
Contact: Rick Weddle, Pres./CEO
E-mail: parkinfo@rtp.org
Scope: Telecommunications, microelectronics, environmental research, materials science, biotechnology, pharmaceuticals, chemistry, nanotechnology, and software and hardware development. Facilitates interaction between industrial and governmental research and development organizations with the research communities of the three universities. **Publications:** Viewpoints (quarterly).

63478 ■ University of North Carolina at Charlotte–University Research Park
2 First Union Center, Ste. 1980
Charlotte, NC 28282
Ph:(704)375-6220
Fax: (704)338-9539
Contact: Seddon Goode Jr., Pres.
Scope: 3,200-acre site providing companies located in the park with research and educational interaction with University of North Carolina at Charlotte.

EDUCATIONAL PROGRAMS

63479 ■ Caldwell Community College and Technical Institute–Small Business Center
2855 Hickory Blvd.
Hudson, NC 28638
Ph:(828)726-2200
Fax: (828)726-2472
URL: http://www.cccti.edu
Description: Seminars, workshops, and management consultation are available for small business owners.

63480 ■ Sandhills Community College
3395 Airport Rd.
Pinehurst, NC 28374
Ph:(910)692-6185
Free: 800-338-3944
Fax: (910)695-1823
Co. E-mail: neelym@sandhills.edu
URL: http://www.sandhills.edu
Description: Offers many business-related and personal enrichment classes, both at the college and at various off-campus sites. A Small Business Center has been established to attract, train, counsel, and provide educational services to small business owners or individuals interested in establishing small businesses in the area.

63481 ■ South College
1567 Patton Ave.
Asheville, NC 28806
Ph:(828)252-2486
Fax: (828)252-8558

Co. E-mail: ecue@cecilscollege.com
URL: http://www.southcollegenc.com
Description: Offers a program in small business administration.

63482 ■ Wilson Technical Community College–Small Business Center
PO Box 4305
902 Herring Ave.
Wilson, NC 27893
Ph:(252)291-1195
Fax: (252)243-7148
URL: http://www.wilsontech.cc.nc.us
Description: Provides consultative services, resource information, and a variety of seminars, workshops, and courses to assist in the development of new businesses and the success of existing businesses.

PUBLICATIONS

63483 ■ Smart Start your North Carolina Business
PSI Research
300 N. Valley Dr.
Grants Pass, OR 97526
Ph:(503)479-9464
Free: 800-228-2275
Fax: (503)476-1479
Co. E-mail: info@psi-research.com
URL: http://www.psi-research.com
Ed: Michael D. Jenkins. **Released:** Revised edition, 1992. **Price:** $29.95 (looseleaf binder); $24.95 (paper). **Description:** Part of the Successful Business Library series.

PUBLISHERS

63484 ■ The Accounting Guild Inc.
8713 Short Putt Dr.
Las Vegas, NV 89134-8417
Ph:(702)242-8725
Fax: (702)639-6766
Co. E-mail: info@accountingguild.com
URL: http://www.accountingguild.com
Contact: Jack Fox, Publisher
E-mail: jackfox@accountingguild.com
Description: Publishes on business, self-employment, and finance. Accepts unsolicited manuscripts. Reaches market through Internet, trade sales, and Ingram Books. **Founded:** 1988.

63485 ■ International Puzzle Features
4507 Panther Pl.
Charlotte, NC 28269
Ph:(704)921-1818
Fax: (704)597-1331
Co. E-mail: drfun@cleverpuzzles.com
URL: http://www.cleverpuzzles.com
Contact: Pat Battaglin, Publisher
E-mail: publisher@cleverpuzzles.com
Description: Publishes books of clever word games with surprising answers and amusing features for readers of all ages. Also provides a weekly variety puzzle/game column to newspapers. Accepts submissions of individual puzzles/games, not columns. Send for Writers Guidelines with SASE. Refer to web site for samples. Reaches market through reviews, listings, and distributors and wholesalers. **Founded:** 1990.

63486 ■ NewRoad Publishing
3650 Rogers Rd., Ste. 328
Wake Forest, NC 27587
Ph:(919)453-2850
Fax: (919)453-2851
Co. E-mail: ron@newroadpublishing.com
URL: http://www.newroadpublishing.com/
Description: Publishes books on business how-to and spirituality. Offers newsletter titled *The Triangle Times*.

North Dakota

SMALL BUSINESS DEVELOPMENT CENTER LEAD OFFICE

63487 ■ North Dakota SBDC–University of North Carolina
1600 E. Century Ave., Ste. 2
Bismarck, ND 58503
Ph:(701)328-5375
Fax: (701)328-5320
URL: http://www.ndsbdc.org
Contact: Christine Martin-Goldman, State Dir.
E-mail: christine.martin@und.nodak.edu

63488 ■ University of North Dakota–North Dakota Small Business Development Center
118 Gamble Hall, UND
P O Box 7308
Grand Forks, ND 58202-7308
Ph:(701)777-3700
Free: 800-445-7232
Fax: (701)777-3225
URL: http://bpa.und.nodak.edu/sbdc/
Contact: Walter "Wally" Kearns, State Director

SMALL BUSINESS DEVELOPMENT CENTERS

63489 ■ Belcourt Satellite Center–SBDC
Highway 5, W.
Box 900
Belcourt, ND 58316
Ph:(701)477-2688
Fax: (701)477-6836
Contact: Betty Hamley
E-mail: bhamley@utma.com

63490 ■ Bismarck Regional Small Business Development Center
700 E. Main Ave., 2nd Fl.
Bismarck, ND 58502
Ph:(701)328-5794
Fax: (701)250-4304
Contact: Nancy Krogen-Abel, Business Counselor
E-mail: nancy@ndmep.com

63491 ■ Devils Lake Service Center–SBDC
417 5th St.
Devils Lake, ND 58301
Ph:(701)662-8131
Fax: (701)662-8132
Contact: Barbara Britsch, Business Consultant

63492 ■ Dickinson Service Center–Small Business Development Center
291 Campus Dr.
Dickinson, ND 58601
Ph:(701)483-2470
Fax: (701)483-2470
Contact: Ronald Newman, Regional Dir.

E-mail: ronald.newman@dickinsonstate.edu

63493 ■ Fort Yates Satellite Center–SBDC
1341 92nd St.
Fort Yates, ND 58538
Ph:(701)854-3734
Fax: (701)854-7379
Contact: Jonathan Anderson
E-mail: jonathana@sbci.edu

63494 ■ Grand Forks SBDC Center
1508 28th Ave. S., Ste. 200
Grand Forks, ND 58201
Ph:(701)795-3734
Fax: (701)795-3734
Contact: Andrew Gleich, Business Consultant
E-mail: agleich@state.nd.us/

63495 ■ Jamestown Center–SBDC
120 2nd St., SE
PO Box 903
Jamestown, ND 58402
Ph:(701)952-8060
Fax: (701)252-4930
Contact: Eric Hoberg, Regional Dir.
E-mail: scdrc@daktel.com

63496 ■ Minot Regional Service Center–SBDC
1925 S. Broadway, Ste. 2
Minot, ND 58703
Ph:(701)857-8211
Fax: (701)839-3889
Contact: Mary Beth Votava, Counselor
E-mail: marybethv@ndmep.com

63497 ■ Procurement Assistance Center–SBDC
657 2nd Ave. N., Rm. 219
PO Box 1309
Fargo, ND 58107-1309
Ph:(701)239-9678
Free: 800-698-5726
Fax: (701)237-0986
Contact: Eric Nelson

63498 ■ Red River Regional Planning Council SBDC–SBDC–SBDC (Graft)
Grafton Outreach Ctr.
PO Box 633
Grafton, ND 58237
Free: 800-445-7232
Contact: Gordon Snyder, Regional Dir.

63499 ■ Tri-county Economic Development Corp.–Fargo Regional Small Business Development Center
657 2nd Ave. N, Rm. 219
PO Box 1309
Fargo, ND 58108-1309
Ph:(701)237-0986
Fax: (701)237-9734
Contact: Linda Liebert-Hall, Business Specialist

63500 ■ University of North Dakota–North Dakota SBDC
118 Gamble Hall, UND
Box 7308
Grand Forks, ND 58202-7308
Ph:(701)777-3700
Free: 800-445-7232
Fax: (701)777-3225
URL: http://bpa.und.nodak.edu/sbdc/
Contact: Walter "Wally" Kearns, State Dir.

63501 ■ Williston Service Center–SBDC
Crighton Bldg., WSC
Williston, ND 58802
Ph:(701)774-4279
Fax: (701)774-4229
Contact: Keith Olson, Regional Dir.
E-mail: keith.olson@wsc.nodak.edu

SMALL BUSINESS ASSISTANCE PROGRAMS

63502 ■ North Dakota Department of Commerce–Department of Economic Development and Finance
PO Box 2057
Bismarck, ND 58502-2057
Ph:(701)328-5300
Fax: (701)328-5320
URL: http://www.growingnd.com
Contact: Linda Butts, Dir
Description: Encourages the establishment of new businesses and industries and assists new and expanding businesses with information and location decisions.

63503 ■ University of North Dakota–Center for Innovation
Ina Mae Rude Entrepreneur Center
The Universityof North Dakota
4200 James Ray Dr.
Grand Forks, ND 58203
Ph:(701)777-3132
Fax: (701)777-2339
Co. E-mail: askme@innovators.net
URL: http://www.innovators.net
Contact: Bruce Gjovig, Dir
Description: Provides technical and business support services to entrepreneurs, inventors, and small manufacturers. Assists specifically with the product evaluation process, the patenting process, and technology transfer.

SCORE OFFICES

63504 ■ SCORE Bismarck-Mandan
1925 S Broadway, Ste. 2
Bismarck, ND 58502
Ph:(701)250-4303
Co. E-mail: score365@btinet.net
Description: Provides entrepreneur education for the formation, growth and success of small businesses in the area.

63505 ■ SCORE Fargo
51 Broadway, Ste. 505
Fargo, ND 58108
Ph:(701)239-5677
Fax: (701)237-9734
Co. E-mail: fargoscore@hotmail.com
Description: Provides entrepreneur education for the formation, growth and success of small businesses in the area.

63506 ■ SCORE Minot
1925 S Broadway, Ste. 2
Minot, ND 58701
Ph:(701)852-6883
Fax: (701)852-6905
Co. E-mail: scoreminot@ndak.net
Description: Provides entrepreneur education for the formation, growth and success of small businesses in the area.

63507 ■ SCORE Upper Red River
1501 28th Ave. S
Grand Forks, ND 58201-6727
Ph:(701)746-5851
Fax: (701)746-5748
Co. E-mail: gfscore@qwest.net
Description: Provides entrepreneur education for the formation, growth and success of small businesses in the area.

CHAMBERS OF COMMERCE

63508 ■ Beulah Chamber of Commerce
120 Central Ave. N
PO Box 730
Beulah, ND 58523-0730
Ph:(701)873-4585
Free: 800-441-2649
Fax: (701)873-5361
Co. E-mail: chamber@westriv.com
URL: http://www.beulahnd.org
Contact: Stephanie Boeckel, Exec.Dir.

63509 ■ Bismarck - Mandan Chamber of Commerce
2000 Shafer St.
PO Box 1675
Bismarck, ND 58502-1675
Ph:(701)223-5660
Fax: (701)255-6125
Co. E-mail: info@bismarckmandan.com
URL: http://www.bismarckmandan.com
Contact: Kelvin Hullet, Pres.

63510 ■ Bowman Chamber of Commerce
PO Box 1143
Bowman, ND 58623
Ph:(701)523-5880
Free: (866)752-2691
Fax: (701)523-3322
Co. E-mail: chamber@bowmannd.com
URL: http://www.bowmannd.com
Contact: Kayla Abrahamson-Hansey

63511 ■ Carrington Area Chamber of Commerce
871 Main St.
PO Box 439
Carrington, ND 58421
Ph:(701)652-2524
Free: 800-641-9668
Fax: (701)652-2391
Co. E-mail: cgtncham@daktel.com
URL: http://www.cgtn-nd.com
Contact: Laurie Dietz, Exec.Dir.

63512 ■ Cavalier Area Chamber of Commerce
PO Box 271
Cavalier, ND 58220-0271
Ph:(701)265-8188
Fax: (701)265-8720
Co. E-mail: cacc@polarcomm.com
URL: http://www.cavaliernd.com
Contact: Mary Hines, Exec.Dir.

63513 ■ Chamber of Commerce of Fargo Moorhead
PO Box 2443
Fargo, ND 58108-2443
Ph:(218)233-1100
Fax: (218)233-1200
Co. E-mail: info@fmchamber.com
URL: http://www.fmchamber.com
Contact: David K. Martin, Pres./CEO

63514 ■ Devils Lake Area Chamber of Commerce
Hwy. 2 E
PO Box 879
Devils Lake, ND 58301-0879
Ph:(701)662-4903
Fax: (701)662-2147
Co. E-mail: chamber@stellarnet.com
URL: http://www.devilslakend.com
Contact: Greg Otis, Exec.VP

63515 ■ Dickinson Area Chamber of Commerce
314 3rd Ave. W
PO Box C
Dickinson, ND 58601
Ph:(701)225-5115
Fax: (701)225-5116
Co. E-mail: team@dickinsonchamber.org
URL: http://www.dickinsonchamber.org
Contact: Mr. Richard Wardner, Dir.

63516 ■ Drayton Community Chamber of Commerce
PO Box 265
Drayton, ND 58225
Ph:(701)454-3474
Co. E-mail: chamber@draytonnd.com
URL: http://www.draytonnd.com
Contact: Mr. Rob Boll, Pres.

63517 ■ Garrison Chamber of Commerce
PO Box 459
Garrison, ND 58540
Ph:(701)463-2600
Free: 800-799-4242
Fax: (701)463-7400
Contact: Diane Affeldt, Sec.-Treas.

63518 ■ Geographical Center of North America Chamber of Commerce
224 Hwy. 2 SW
Rugby, ND 58368-2426
Ph:(701)776-5846
Fax: (701)776-6390
Co. E-mail: rugbychamber@gondtc.com
URL: http://www.rugbynorthdakota.com
Contact: Mr. Dondi Sobolik, Exec.Dir.

63519 ■ Grafton Area Chamber of Commerce
432 Hill Ave.
Grafton, ND 58237
Ph:(701)352-0781
Co. E-mail: gracha@polarcomm.com
URL: http://www.graftonchamber.com
Contact: Francis Ricard, Pres.

63520 ■ Grand Forks Chamber of Commerce
202 N 3rd St.
Grand Forks, ND 58203-3733
Ph:(701)772-7271
Fax: (701)772-9238
Co. E-mail: info@gochamber.org
URL: http://www.gfchamber.com
Contact: Dan Schenkein, Pres./CEO

63521 ■ Greater Bottineau Chamber of Commerce
519 Main St.
Bottineau, ND 58318-1202
Ph:(701)228-3849
Free: 800-735-6932
Fax: (701)228-5130
Co. E-mail: bcc@utma.com
URL: http://www.bottineau.com/chamber
Contact: Clint M. Reinoehl, Exec. Dir.

63522 ■ Greater North Dakota Chamber of Commerce
2000 Schafer St.
PO Box 2639
Bismarck, ND 58502-2639
Ph:(701)222-0929
Free: 800-382-1405
Fax: (701)222-1611
Co. E-mail: ndchamber@ndchamber.com
URL: http://www.ndchamber.com
Contact: Dave MacIver, Pres.

63523 ■ Harvey Area Chamber of Commerce
120 W 8th St., Ste. 3
Harvey, ND 58341
Ph:(701)324-2604
Fax: (701)324-2674
Co. E-mail: chamber@harveynd.com
URL: http://www.harveynd.com
Contact: Ms. Sara Balfour, Exec.VP

63524 ■ Hazen Chamber of Commerce
PO Box 423
Hazen, ND 58545
Ph:(701)748-6848
Free: 888-464-2936
Fax: (701)748-2559
Co. E-mail: hazenchamber@westriv.com
URL: http://www.hazennd.org
Contact: Tracee Grosz, Exec.Dir.

63525 ■ Hettinger Area Chamber of Commerce
PO Box 1031
Hettinger, ND 58639-1031
Ph:(701)567-2531
Fax: (701)567-2690
Co. E-mail: adamschmbr@ndsupernet.com
URL: http://www.hettingernd.com
Contact: Earleen Friez, Sec.

63526 ■ Jamestown Area Chamber of Commerce
120 2nd St. SE
PO Box 1530
Jamestown, ND 58401
Ph:(701)252-4830
Fax: (701)252-4837
Co. E-mail: info@jamestownchamber.com
URL: http://www.jamestownchamber.com
Contact: JoDee Rasmusson, Pres.

63527 ■ Kenmare Association of Commerce
PO Box 324
Kenmare, ND 58746
Ph:(701)385-4249
Co. E-mail: leroys@restel.net
URL: http://www.kenmarend.com
Contact: Mr. LeRoy Sandviek, Pres.

63528 ■ Linton Industrial Development Corporation
PO Box 433
Linton, ND 58552
Ph:(701)254-4267
Fax: (701)254-4382
Co. E-mail: lidcbek@bektel.com
URL: http://lintonnd.org
Contact: Sharon Jangula, Coor.

63529 ■ Medora Chamber of Commerce
PO Box 186
Medora, ND 58645-0186
Ph:(701)623-4910
Co. E-mail: medorachamber@midstate.net
Contact: Wally Northrop, Pres.

63530 ■ Minot Area Chamber of Commerce
1020 20th Ave. SW
PO Box 940
Minot, ND 58702-0940
Ph:(701)852-6000
Fax: (701)838-2488
Co. E-mail: chamber@minotchamber.org
Contact: L. John MacMartin, Pres.

63531 ■ Oakes Area Chamber of Commerce
412 Main Ave.
Oakes, ND 58474-1637
Ph:(701)742-3508
Co. E-mail: oakesnd@drtel.net
URL: http://www.oakesnd.com
Contact: Jessica Quandt, Pres.

63532 ■ Rolla Chamber of Commerce
PO Box 712
Rolla, ND 58367
Ph:(701)477-2058
Fax: (701)477-9136
Co. E-mail: dunlap@utma.com
URL: http://rolla.nd.utma.com
Contact: Robin Dunlap, Exec.Dir.

63533 ■ Stanley Commercial Club
PO Box 974
Stanley, ND 58784
Ph:(701)628-1516
Fax: (701)628-2232
Contact: Heather Lee, Sec.

63534 ■ Tioga Chamber of Commerce
PO Box 52
Tioga, ND 58852-0052
Ph:(701)664-2807
Fax: (701)664-2543
Co. E-mail: citytio@nccray.com
Contact: Don Zacharias, Sec.-Treas.

63535 ■ Valley City Area Chamber of Commerce/CVB
PO Box 724
Valley City, ND 58072-0724
Ph:(701)845-1891
Fax: (701)845-1892
Co. E-mail: chamber@hellovalley.com
URL: http://www.hellovalley.com
Contact: Raymond S. Morrell, Exec.VP

63536 ■ Wahpeton Breckenridge Area Chamber of Commerce and Visitors Center
118 6th St. N
Wahpeton, ND 58075-4327
Ph:(701)642-8744
Free: 800-892-6673
Fax: (701)642-8745
Co. E-mail: info@wahpetonbreckenridgechamber.com
URL: http://www.wahpetonbreckenridgechamber.com
Contact: Jim Oliver, Exec. VP

63537 ■ Walhalla Area Chamber of Commerce
PO Box 34
Walhalla, ND 58282
Ph:(701)549-3939
Fax: (701)549-2410
URL: http://www.tradecorridor.com/walhalla
Contact: Melanie Thornberg, Exec. Dir.

63538 ■ Watford City Area Chamber of Commerce
PO Box 458
Watford City, ND 58854-0458
Ph:(701)444-2526
Fax: (701)444-2526
Co. E-mail: aclifton@ruggedwest.com
URL: http://www.watfordcitychamber.com
Contact: Audre A. Clifton, Exec.Sec.

63539 ■ West Fargo Chamber of Commerce
PO Box 753
West Fargo, ND 58078-0753
Ph:(701)282-4444
Fax: (701)282-3665
Co. E-mail: admin3@westfargochamber.com
URL: http://www.westfargochamber.com
Contact: Chris Barton, Pres.

63540 ■ Williston Area Chamber of Commerce
10 Main St.
PO Box G
Williston, ND 58802-0779
Ph:(701)577-6000
Fax: (701)577-8591
Co. E-mail: wchamber@willistonchamber.net
URL: http://www.willistonchamber.net
Contact: Diane Hagen, Exec.Dir.

PROCUREMENT ASSISTANCE PROGRAMS

63541 ■ Fargo Small Business Development Center–University of North Dakota
51 Broadway Ste. 505
Fargo, ND 58102
Ph:(701)235-1495
Free: 800-698-5726
Fax: (701)235-9734
URL: http://www.ndsbdc.org
Contact: Donavon Wadholm, Dir

63542 ■ North Dakota Economic Development and Finance Department–Procurement Division
PO Box 2057
Bismarck, ND 58502-2057
Ph:(701)328-5300
Fax: (701)328-5320
Co. E-mail: lbutts@state.nd.us
URL: http://www.growingnd.com
Contact: Linda Butts, Dir
Description: Helps businesses obtain federal, state, and local government contracts.

INCUBATORS/RESEARCH AND TECHNOLOGY PARKS

63543 ■ North Dakota State University–Transportation Technology Transfer Center
Civil and Industrial Engineering Bldg., Rm. 201H
Fargo, ND 58105
Ph:(701)231-7051
Free: 800-726-4143
Fax: (701)231-5654
Co. E-mail: ndsu.ndltap@ndsu.edu
URL: http://www.ce.ndsu.nodak.edu/ndltap
Contact: Dr. Donald Anderson, Dir
E-mail: theusch@planis.nodak.edu
Description: Enables North Dakota businesses to use the most advanced technologies available.

63544 ■ University of North Dakota–Vice President for Research
Twamley Hall, Rm. 103
PO Box 8367
Grand Forks, ND 58202-8367
Ph:(701)777-6736

Fax: (701)777-6708
Co. E-mail: vpr@mail.und.nodak.edu
URL: http://www.und.edu/dept/research
Contact: Peter Alfonso, VP
E-mail: vpr@mail.und.nodak.edu
Scope: Promotes research and scholarly activity and reviews all proposals for compliance with fiscal and general University policies. Provides information on funding sources for research, fellowships, and other programs sponsored by outside agencies. Also provides assistance to the Senate Scholary Activities Committee and to several institutional compliance committees. Administers and awards internal funds for research and scholarly achievement activities.
Publications: Annual Report.

EDUCATIONAL PROGRAMS

63545 ■ Lake Region State College
1801 N College Dr.
Devils Lake, ND 58301
Ph:(701)662-1600
Free: 800-443-1313
Fax: (701)662-1570
URL: http://www.lrsc.nodak.edu
Description: Two-year college offering a accounting and business management.

63546 ■ University of North Dakota–Workforce Development
PO Box 7131
Grand Forks, ND 58202-7131
Ph:(701)777-2313
Fax: (701)777-2140
Co. E-mail: galen_cariveau@mail.und.nodak.edu
URL: http://www.und.nodak.edu
Contact: Galen Cariveau
Description: Offers a variety of business-related and professional enrichment courses, institutes, seminars, and workshops. The Department of Conferences and Institutes coordinates a large number of business skills and management development seminars and workshops geared for particular audiences, including small business owners/managers.

PUBLISHERS

63547 ■ Center for Innovation
University of North Dakota
Ina Mae Rude Entrepreneur Ctr., 4200 James Ray Dr.
PO Box 8372
Grand Forks, ND 58203
Ph:(701)777-3132
Fax: (701)777-2339
URL: http://www.innovators.net
Contact: Nick Hacker, Entrepreneur Consultant
E-mail: nick@innovators.net
Description: Publishes on business and business history for entrepreneurs and manufacturers. Does not accept unsolicited manuscripts. Reaches market through direct mail and trade sales. **Founded:** 1984.

63548 ■ Gateway Publishing Company Ltd.
276 Cavalier St.
PO Box 559
Pembina, ND 58271-0559
Free: 800-665-4878
Co. E-mail: cookbooks@gatebook.com
URL: http://www.gatebook.com
Description: Publishes books about child safety and also cookbooks. **Founded:** 1966.

SMALL BUSINESS DEVELOPMENT CENTER LEAD OFFICE

63549 ■ Edison Materials Technology Center–Ohio SBDC–Region 4 Lead Center (3155)
3155 Research Park, Ste. 202
Kettering, OH 45420
Ph:(937)259-1331
Co. E-mail: bmcmannon@emtec.org
URL: http://www.emtec.org/SBDC/EMTEC_SBDC.htm
Contact: Harry Bumgarner, Dir.

63550 ■ Ohio Department of Development–Ohio SBDC
77 S. High St.
Box 1001
Columbus, OH 43215
Ph:(614)466-5102
Free: 800-848-1300
Fax: (614)466-0829
URL: http://www.ohiosbdc.org
Contact: Michele Abraham, State Dir.
E-mail: mabraham@odod.state.oh.us

63551 ■ Ohio Department of Development–Small Business Development Center
77 S. High St., 28th Fl.
Columbus, OH 43215-6108
Ph:(614)466-2711
Free: 800-848-1300
Fax: (614)466-0829
Contact: Holly I. Schick, State Director

63552 ■ Toledo Chamber of Commerce–Ohio SBDC–Lead Center (Region 2) (300 M)
300 Madison Ave.
Enterprise Ste. 200
Toledo, OH 43604-1575
Ph:(419)243-8191
Fax: (419)241-8302
URL: http://www.toledochamber.com/chamber/SBdevcenter.asp
Contact: Megan Reichert, Dir.
E-mail: megan.reichert@toledochamber.com

SMALL BUSINESS DEVELOPMENT CENTERS

63553 ■ Akron Regional Development Board–Small Business Development Center
1 Cascade Plz., 8th Fl.
Akron, OH 44308-1192
Ph:(330)379-3170
Fax: (330)379-3164
Contact: Charles Smith, Dir.
E-mail: smith@ardb.org

63554 ■ Clermont County Chamber of Commerce–Ohio SBDC
4440 Glen Este-Withamsville Rd.
Cincinnati, OH 45245
Ph:(513)753-7141
Fax: (513)753-7146
Co. E-mail: ccclink@aol.com
Contact: Russ Cone, Dir.

63555 ■ Dayton Area Chamber of Commerce–Small Business Development Center
Chamber Plz.
5th & Main Sts.
Dayton, OH 45402-2400
Ph:(937)226-1444
Fax: (937)226-8254
Contact: Harry Bumgarner, Dir.
E-mail: harryb@dacc.org

63556 ■ Greater Cleveland Growth Association–Cleveland Small Business Development Center
200 Tower City Center
50 Public Sq.
Cleveland, OH 44113-2291
Ph:(216)696-1294
Fax: (216)621-4617
Contact: Maria Coyne, Dir.
E-mail: mcoyne@clevegrowth.com

63557 ■ Greater Columbus Area Chamber of Commerce–Central Ohio SBDC
37 N. High St., 4th Fl.
Columbus, OH 43215
Ph:(614)225-6910
Fax: (614)469-8250
Contact: Leslie Weilbacher, Dir.
E-mail: leslie_weilbacher@columbus.org

63558 ■ Growth Partnership for Ashtabula County–Small Business Development Center
36 W. Walnut St.
Jefferson, OH 44047
Ph:(216)576-9134
Fax: (216)576-5003
Co. E-mail: ashtabulasbdc@suite224.net
Contact: Stephanie Ward, Dir.
E-mail: stephward@yahoo.com

63559 ■ Jefferson County Chamber of Commerce–Ohio SBDC
630 Market St.
PO Box 278
Steubenville, OH 43952
Ph:(740)282-6226
Fax: (740)282-6285
Co. E-mail: chamber@clover.net
Contact: Tim McFadden, Dir.

63560 ■ Kent State University Portage Campus–SBDC
College of Business Administration, Rm. 300A
Summit and Terrace, Rm. 300A
Kent, OH 44242
Ph:(330)672-2772

Fax: (330)672-9338
Contact: Linda Yost, Dir.
E-mail: lyost@bsa3.kent.edu

63561 ■ Kent State University/Salem Campus–Columbiana County/Salem Small Business Development Center
400 E. 4th St.
East Liverpool, OH 43920
Ph:(330)385-3805
Fax: (330)385-6348
Contact: Doris Davis, Dir.
E-mail: ddavis@e14.kenteliv.kent.edu

63562 ■ Kent State University/Stark Campus–Kent/Stark Small Business Development Center
6000 Frank Ave., NW
Canton, OH 44720
Ph:(330)499-9600
Fax: (330)494-6121
Co. E-mail: achunko@stark.kent.edu
Contact: Connie Collings, Dir.
E-mail: ccollings@stark.kent.edu

63563 ■ Kent State University at Tuscarawas City–Tuscarawas Small Business Development Center
Kent State University
300 University Dr., NE
New Philadelphia, OH 44663-9447
Ph:(330)339-3391
Fax: (330)339-2637
Contact: Patricia Comanitz, Dir.
E-mail: pcomanitz@usc.kent.edu

63564 ■ Lake County Economic Development Center–SBDC
Lake Erie College
391 W. Washington St.
Painesville, OH 44077
Ph:(440)357-2290
Fax: (440)357-2290
Co. E-mail: lcedc@lcedc.org
URL: http://www.lcedc.org
Contact: Catherine C. Haworth, Dir.
E-mail: chaworth@lcedc.org

63565 ■ Lawrence County Chamber of Commerce–Small Business Development Center
216 Collins Ave.
PO Box 488
South Point, OH 45680
Ph:(740)377-4550
Free: 800-408-1334
Fax: (740)377-2091
Co. E-mail: sesbdc@zoomnet.net
Contact: Amber Wilson, Dir.

63566 ■ Lima Technical College–Small Business Development Center
West Central Office
545 W. Market St., Ste. 305
Lima, OH 45801-4717
Ph:(419)229-5320

Fax: (419)229-5424
Co. E-mail: sbdc@worcnet.gen.oh.us
Contact: John Hyter, Dir.

63567 ■ Lorain County Chamber of Commerce–SBDC
6100 S. Broadway, Ste. 201
Lorain, OH 44053
Ph:(216)233-6500
Fax: (440)246-4050
Contact: Dennis Jones, Dir.
E-mail: djones@lorcham.org

63568 ■ Marietta College–SBDC
213 Fourth St., 2nd Fl.
Marietta, OH 45750
Ph:(740)376-4832
Free: 800-789-7232
Fax: (740)376-4901
Contact: Pamela Lankford, Dir.
E-mail: lankforp@marietta.edu

63569 ■ Marion Area Chamber of Commerce–SBDC
206 S. Prospect St.
Marion, OH 43302
Ph:(740)387-0188
Fax: (740)387-7722
Co. E-mail: heartofohio@acc-net.com
Contact: Catherine Gaines, Dir.

63570 ■ Maumee Valley Planning Organization–Northwest Small Business Development Center
197-2-B1 Island Park Avenue
Defiance, OH 43512
Ph:(419)782-6270
Fax: (419)782-6273
Co. E-mail: nwsbdc@bright.net
Contact: Don Wright, Dir.

63571 ■ Maumee Valley Planning Organization–SBDC
197-2-B1 Park Island Ave.
Defiance, OH 43512
Ph:(419)782-6270
Fax: (419)782-6273
Co. E-mail: nwsbdc@msn.com
Contact: Don Wright, Dir.

63572 ■ Mid-Ohio Small Business Development Center–Mansfield-Richland Business Incubator
201 E. 5th St., Ste. 200
PO Box 1208
Mansfield, OH 44901
Ph:(419)521-2655
Free: 800-366-7232
Fax: (419)522-6811
Co. E-mail: mosbdc@rich.net
Contact: Barbara Harmony, Dir.

63573 ■ Ohio Manufacturing SBDC at Central Ohio
1214 Kinnear Rd.
Columbus, OH 43212
Ph:(614)688-4018
Fax: (614)688-4045
URL: http://www.obdosbdc.org/regionc.htm
Contact: Jeff Shick, Dir.
E-mail: jshick@stcc.org

63574 ■ Ohio SBDC at SBDC, Inc.
300 E. Auburn Ave.
Springfield, OH 45505
Ph:(937)322-7821
Fax: (937)322-7874
URL: http://www.smbusdev.org
Contact: Steve Anzur, Exec. Dir.
E-mail: sanzur@smbusdev.org

63575 ■ Ohio State University–Ohio Manufacturing & Technology SBDC
South Centers
1864 Shyville Rd.
Piketon, OH 45661
Ph:(740)289-2071

Free: 800-297-2072
Fax: (740)289-4591
URL: http://southcenters.osu.edu/
Contact: Thomas Worley, Dir.
E-mail: worley.36@osu.edu

63576 ■ Ohio University–Small Business Development Center
Enterprise & Technology Bldg.
20 East Circle Dr., Ste. 174
Athens, OH 45701
Ph:(740)593-1797
Fax: (740)593-1795
Co. E-mail: aa428@seorf.ohiou.edu
Contact: Debra McBride, Dir.
E-mail: mcbride@ohio.edu

63577 ■ Terra Community College–Small Business Development Center
2830 Napoleon Rd.
Fremont, OH 43420-9670
Ph:(419)334-8400
Free: 800-826-2431
URL: http://www.terra.edu/learning/kerndirectory/
   sbdc.asp
Contact: Bill Auxter, Dir.
E-mail: bauxter@terra.cc.oh.us

63578 ■ University of Cincinnati–SBDC
7162 Reading Rd., Ste. 725
Cincinnati, OH 45237-3844
Ph:(513)556-2072
Contact: Bill Fioretti, Dir.
E-mail: bill.fioretti@us.edu

63579 ■ Upper Valley Joint Vocational School–Small Business Development Center
8811 Career Dr. N.
Piqua, OH 45356
Ph:(937)778-8419
Free: 800-589-6963
Fax: (937)778-9237
Contact: Evelyn Shafer, Dir.

63580 ■ Women's Organization for Mentoring, Entrepreneurship & Networking–(WOMEN) & Women's Network Inc.–Small Business Development Center (526 S)
526 S. Main St., Ste. 221
PO Box 544
Akron, OH 44311-1058
Ph:(330)379-9280
Fax: (330)379-9283
URL: http://www.womennet.org
Contact: Julie Sparks, Exec. Dir.

63581 ■ Wood County Small Business Development Center
BGSU Training Ctr.
40 College Park
Bowling Green, OH 43403
Ph:(419)372-9536
Fax: (419)372-8667
Contact: Pat Fligor, Dir.
E-mail: fligor@bgnet.bgsu.edu

63582 ■ Wright State University–SBDC
Raj Soin College of Business
3640 Colonel Glenn Hwy.
Dayton, OH 45435
Ph:(937)775-3487
URL: http://www.sbdcwsu.org/
Contact: Mike Body, Dir.
E-mail: michael.bodey@wright.edu

63583 ■ Wright State University at Lake Campus–Small Business Development Center
7600 State Rte. 703
Celina, OH 45822
Ph:(419)586-0355
Free: 800-237-1477
Fax: (419)586-0358
Contact: Tom Knapke, Dir.
E-mail: tknapke@lake.wright.edu

63584 ■ Youngstown/Warren–Small Business Development Center
Youngstown State University
241 Federal Plaza W.
Youngstown, OH 44503
Ph:(330)746-3350
Fax: (330)746-3324
Co. E-mail: pkveisz@cc.ysu.edu
Contact: Ron Trovellini, Dir.

63585 ■ Youngstown/Warren Satellite–Small Business Development Center
Youngstown/Warren Regional Center
180 E. Market St., Ste. 225
Warren, OH 44482
Ph:(330)393-2565
Fax: (330)392-6040
Co. E-mail: ccsbdc@cc.ysu.edu
Contact: Jim Rowlands, Counselor

63586 ■ Zanesville Mid East–Zanesville Area Chamber of Commerce–Mid-East Small Business Development Center (205 N)
205 N. 5th St.
Zanesville, OH 43701
Ph:(740)452-4868
Fax: (740)454-2963
Contact: Bonnie J. Winnett, Dir.
E-mail: bwinnett@cyberzane.net

SMALL BUSINESS ASSISTANCE PROGRAMS

63587 ■ Ohio Department of Development–Small and Developing Business Division
77 S High St., 28th Fl.
Columbus, OH 43215-6138
Ph:(614)466-2711
Free: 800-848-1300
Fax: (614)466-0829
Co. E-mail: hskick@odod.state.oh.us
URL: http://www.odod.state.oh.us

63588 ■ Ohio Department of Development–Technology Division
77 S High St., 25th Fl.
Columbus, OH 43215-6108
Ph:(614)466-3887
Free: 800-848-1300
Fax: (614)644-5758
Co. E-mail: kwilhelm@odod.state.oh.us
URL: http://www.odod.state.oh.us/tech
Description: Stimulates working partnerships between business and academia in an effort to generate new technological ideas, new products and processes, and new companies. The three major components are: Edison Technology Centers, Edison Seed Development Fund, and Edison Incubators.

SCORE OFFICES

63589 ■ SCORE Akron
Natl. City Bank Bldg.
One Cascade Plz., 18th Fl.
Akron, OH 44308
Ph:(330)379-3163
Free: 877-257-2673
Fax: (330)379-3164
Co. E-mail: akronsscore81@aol.com
URL: http://akronscore.org
Contact: Ron Stallings, Chm.
Description: Provides professional guidance and information to maximize the success of existing and emerging small businesses. Promotes entrepreneur education in Akron area, Ohio.

63590 ■ SCORE Chapter 107
Federal Bldg., Rm. 104
200 W 2nd St.
Dayton, OH 45402
Ph:(937)225-2887

Fax: (937)225-7667
Co. E-mail: score@daytonscore.org
URL: http://www.daytonscore.org
Contact: John Houston, Sec.
Description: Volunteer businessmen and women. Provides free small business management assistance to individuals in Dayton, OH, and surrounding counties.

BETTER BUSINESS BUREAUS

63591 ■ Better Business Bureau of Akron
222 W Market St.
Akron, OH 44303-2111
Ph:(330)253-4590
Free: 800-825-8887
Fax: (330)253-6249
Co. E-mail: vwlaszyn@akronbb.org
URL: http://www.akronbbb.org
Contact: Victor J. Wlaszyn, Pres./CEO

63592 ■ Better Business Bureau of Central Ohio
1335 Dublin Rd., Ste. 30A
Columbus, OH 43215
Ph:(614)486-6336
Free: 800-759-2400
Fax: (614)486-6631
Co. E-mail: info@columbus-ohbbb.org
URL: http://www.centralohiobbb.org
Contact: Kip Morse, Pres.

63593 ■ Better Business Bureau, Cleveland
2217 E 9th St., Ste. 200
Cleveland, OH 44115-1299
Ph:(216)241-7678
Free: 800-233-0361
Fax: (216)861-6365
Co. E-mail: info@cleveland.bbb.org
URL: http://www.cleveland.bbb.org
Contact: David Weiss, Pres.

63594 ■ Better Business Bureau of Dayton/Miami Valley
15 W 4th St., Ste. 300
Dayton, OH 45402
Ph:(937)222-5825
Free: 800-776-5301
Fax: (937)222-3338
Co. E-mail: info@dayton.bbb.org
URL: http://www.dayton.bbb.org
Contact: Donna Childs, Pres.

63595 ■ Better Business Bureau of Mahoning Valley
PO Box 1495
Youngstown, OH 44501-1495
Ph:(330)744-3111
Fax: (330)744-7336
Co. E-mail: info@youngstownbbb.org
URL: http://www.youngstownbbb.org
Contact: Patricia B. Rose, Pres.

63596 ■ Better Business Bureau, Northwest Ohio and Southeastern Michigan
3103 Executive Pkwy., Ste. 200
Toledo, OH 43606-1312
Ph:(419)531-3116
Fax: (419)578-6001
Co. E-mail: info@toledobbb.org
URL: http://www.toledobbb.org
Contact: Richard T. Eppstein, Pres./CEO

63597 ■ Better Business Bureau of West Central Ohio
219 N McDonel St.
Lima, OH 45801
Ph:(419)223-7010
Fax: (419)229-2029
Co. E-mail: info@limabbb.org
URL: http://www.wcohio.bbb.org
Contact: Neil Winget, Pres./CEO

63598 ■ Cincinnati Better Business Bureau
7 W 7th St., Ste. 1600
Cincinnati, OH 45202-2097
Ph:(513)421-3015
Free: 800-471-3015
Fax: (513)621-0907
Co. E-mail: info@cinbbb.org
URL: http://www.cinbbb.org
Contact: Jocile Ehrlich, Pres./CEO

CHAMBERS OF COMMERCE

63599 ■ Adams County Chamber of Commerce
111 W Main St.
PO Box 398
West Union, OH 45693
Ph:(937)544-5454
Free: 888-223-5454
Fax: (937)544-6957
Co. E-mail: acchamber@verizon.net
URL: http://www.adamscountyohchamber.org
Contact: John Holden, Exec. Dir.

63600 ■ Alliance Area Chamber of Commerce
210 E Main St.
Alliance, OH 44601
Ph:(330)823-6260
Fax: (330)823-4434
Co. E-mail: info@allianceohiochamber.org
URL: http://www.allianceohiochamber.org
Contact: R. Mark Locke, Pres.

63601 ■ Anderson Area Chamber of Commerce
8072B Beechmont Ave.
Cincinnati, OH 45255-3177
Ph:(513)474-4802
Fax: (513)474-4857
Co. E-mail: info@andersonareachamber.org
URL: http://andersonareachamber.org
Contact: Carolyn Moseley, Exec. Dir.

63602 ■ Antwerp Chamber of Commerce
PO Box 1111
Antwerp, OH 45813
Ph:(419)258-1722
Contact: Cheryl Lichty, Sec.

63603 ■ Archbold Area Chamber of Commerce
300 N Defiance St.
Archbold, OH 43502
Ph:(419)445-2222
Co. E-mail: archchamber@bnnorth.net
URL: http://www.archbold.com
Contact: Dennis Howell, Village Administrator

63604 ■ Ashland Area Chamber of Commerce
10 W 2nd St., 2nd Fl.
Ashland, OH 44805
Ph:(419)281-4584
Fax: (419)281-4585
Co. E-mail: chamber@ashlandoh.com
URL: http://www.ashlandohio.com
Contact: Marla Akridge, Pres.

63605 ■ Ashtabula Area Chamber of Commerce
4536 Main Ave.
Ashtabula, OH 44004-6925
Ph:(440)998-6998
Fax: (440)992-8216
Co. E-mail: mail@ashtabulachamber.net
URL: http://www.ashtabulachamber.net
Contact: Jim Timonere, Pres./CEO

63606 ■ Aurora Area Chamber of Commerce
549 S Chillicothe Rd.
Aurora, OH 44202
Ph:(330)562-3355
Fax: (330)995-2002
Co. E-mail: jennifer@auroraohiochamber.com

URL: http://www.auroraohiochamber.com
Contact: Jennifer Natale, Exec.Dir.

63607 ■ Baltimore Area Chamber of Commerce
PO Box 193
Baltimore, OH 43105
Ph:(740)438-0837
Co. E-mail: dmaddux@rrohio.com
URL: http://www.baltimoreohiochamber.com
Contact: Dannette Maddux, Pres.

63608 ■ Barnesville Area Chamber of Commerce
130 W Main St.
Barnesville, OH 43713
Ph:(740)425-4300
Fax: (740)425-1048
Co. E-mail: bacc@1st.net
URL: http://www.barnesvilleohio.com
Contact: Sherrie Wharton, Office Mgr.

63609 ■ Beachwood Chamber of Commerce
Three Commerce Park Sq.
23230 Chagrin Blvd., Ste. 835
Beachwood, OH 44122-5424
Ph:(216)831-0003
Fax: (216)360-7333
Co. E-mail: mail@beachwood.org
URL: http://www.beachwood.org
Contact: Tom Sudow, Exec.Dir.

63610 ■ Beavercreek Chamber of Commerce
3299 Kemp Rd.
Beavercreek, OH 45431-2550
Ph:(937)426-2202
Fax: (937)426-2204
Co. E-mail: nancy@beavercreekchamber.org
Contact: Clete Buddelmeyer, Exec.Dir.

63611 ■ Bedford Chamber of Commerce
33 S Park St.
Bedford, OH 44146
Ph:(440)232-0115
Fax: (440)232-0521
Co. E-mail: bedfordchamberoh@sbcglobal.net
URL: http://www.bedfordchamberoh.org
Contact: Judy Groty, Office Mgr.

63612 ■ Bedford Heights Chamber of Commerce
24816 Aurora Rd., Ste. C
Bedford Heights, OH 44146
Ph:(440)232-3369
Fax: (440)232-4862
Co. E-mail: bedfordhtscofc@aol.com
URL: http://www.bedfordheightschamber.com
Contact: Dorothy Pirrung, Pres.

63613 ■ Bellaire Area Chamber of Commerce
PO Box 428
Bellaire, OH 43906
Ph:(740)676-9723
Co. E-mail: information@bellairechamber.com
URL: http://www.bellairechamber.com
Contact: Barb Roman, Pres.

63614 ■ Bellbrook - Sugarcreek Area Chamber of Commerce
64 W Franklin St.
Bellbrook, OH 45305-1903
Ph:(937)848-4930
Fax: (937)848-4930
Co. E-mail: bellbrooksugarcreek@juno.com
URL: http://bellbrooksugarcreekchamber.com
Contact: Chris Ewing, Exec.Dir.

63615 ■ Bellville Chamber of Commerce
142 Park Pl.
Bellville, OH 44813
Ph:(419)886-2245
Fax: (419)886-2297
URL: http://www.bellvilleohio.net
Contact: Larry Rose

63616 ■ Belpre Area Chamber of Commerce
713 Park Dr.
PO Box 8
Belpre, OH 45714

Ph:(740)423-8934
Fax: (740)423-6616
Co. E-mail: chamdir@charter.net
URL: http://www.belprechamber.com
Contact: Joan Knierim, Exec.Dir.

63617 ■ Berea Chamber of Commerce
173 Front St.
PO Box 232
Berea, OH 44017
Ph:(440)243-8415
Fax: (440)243-8470
Co. E-mail: bereachamber@sbcglobal.net
URL: http://www.bereaohio.com/business/
   chamberhome.cfm
Contact: Kathy Kellums, Exec. Dir./Treas.

63618 ■ Bexley Area Chamber of Commerce
2242 E Main St.
Bexley, OH 43209
Ph:(614)470-4500
Co. E-mail: feedback@bexleyareachamber.org
URL: http://www.bexleyareachamber.org
Contact: Mark E. Cooper, Pres.

63619 ■ Blanchester Area Chamber of Commerce
PO Box 274
Blanchester, OH 45107
Ph:(937)783-3601
Co. E-mail: blanchesterareacc@hotmail.com
Contact: Mark Paul, Pres.

63620 ■ Bluffton Area Chamber of Commerce
PO Box 142
Bluffton, OH 45817-0142
Ph:(419)358-5675
Co. E-mail: bacc@sisna.com
Contact: Mrs. Betsy Lee, CEO

63621 ■ Brecksville Chamber of Commerce
4450 Oakes Rd., Rm. 16
Brecksville, OH 44141
Ph:(440)526-7350
Fax: (440)526-7889
Co. E-mail: bccthevoice@att.net
URL: http://www.brecksvillechamber.com
Contact: Michael J. Gorman, Pres.

63622 ■ Bremen Chamber of Commerce
PO Box 127
Bremen, OH 43107
Ph:(740)569-4143
Fax: (740)681-3180
Co. E-mail: blhouse@westermancompanies.com
URL: http://www.bremenvillage.com
Contact: Brian Householder, Pres.

63623 ■ Bridgeport Area Chamber of Commerce
PO Box 86
Bridgeport, OH 43912
Ph:(740)635-3377
Contact: Ann Gallagher, Sec.

63624 ■ Brimfield Area Chamber of Commerce
PO Box 3414
Kent, OH 44240-3414
Ph:(330)348-3573
Co. E-mail: sbennett@landam.com
URL: http://www.brimfieldchamber.com
Contact: Sabrina Christian-Bennett, Pres.

63625 ■ Broadview Heights Chamber of Commerce
1000 E Edgerton Rd.
Broadview Heights, OH 44147-3142
Ph:(440)838-4510
Fax: (440)717-0500
Co. E-mail: bhcc@broadviewhts.org
URL: http://www.broadviewhts.org
Contact: Barb Consiglio, Office Mgr.

63626 ■ Brown County Chamber of Commerce
110 E State St.
Georgetown, OH 45121
Ph:(937)378-4784
Free: 888-BRO-WNOH
Fax: (937)378-1634
Co. E-mail: brchcom@bright.net
Contact: Ray Becraft, Exec.Dir.

63627 ■ Brunswick Area Chamber of Commerce
3511 Center Rd., Ste. AB
Brunswick, OH 44212
Ph:(330)225-8411
Fax: (330)273-8172
Co. E-mail: exec@brunswickareachamber.org
URL: http://www.brunswickareachamber.org
Contact: Murray McDade, Pres.

63628 ■ Bryan Area Chamber of Commerce
138 S Lynn St.
Bryan, OH 43506
Ph:(419)636-2247
Fax: (419)636-5556
Co. E-mail: bryancc@cityofbryan.net
URL: http://www.bryanchamber.org
Contact: Daniel S. Yahraus, Exec.Dir.

63629 ■ Bucyrus Area Chamber of Commerce
122 W Rensselaer St.
Bucyrus, OH 44820-2214
Ph:(419)562-4811
Fax: (419)562-9966
Co. E-mail: bacc@bucyrusohio.com
URL: http://www.bucyrusohio.com
Contact: Deb Pinion, Exec.Dir.

63630 ■ Byesville Board of Trade
PO Box 268
Byesville, OH 43723
Ph:(740)685-8625
Contact: Russ Valentine, Exec.Dir.

63631 ■ Calcutta Area Chamber of Commerce
15442 Pugh Rd.
Calcutta, OH 43920
Ph:(330)386-6060
Fax: (330)386-6060
URL: http://www.calcuttaohiochamber.com
Contact: Marie Boyd, Pres.

63632 ■ Cambridge Area Chamber of Commerce
918 Wheeling Ave.
Cambridge, OH 43725-0488
Ph:(740)439-6688
Fax: (740)439-6689
Co. E-mail: info@cambridgeohiochamber.com
URL: http://www.cambridgeohiochamber.com
Contact: Michael A. Kachilla, Pres.

63633 ■ Camden Area Chamber of Commerce
PO Box 90
Camden, OH 45311
Ph:(937)452-1684
Contact: Karen Feix, Pres.

63634 ■ Canal Winchester Area Chamber of Commerce
58 E Waterloo St.
Canal Winchester, OH 43110
Ph:(614)837-1556
Fax: (614)837-9901
Co. E-mail: chamber@canalwinchester.com
URL: http://www.canalwinchester.com
Contact: Kim Rankin, Exec.Dir.

63635 ■ Canton Regional Chamber of Commerce
222 Market Ave. N
Canton, OH 44702-1418
Ph:(330)456-7253
Free: 800-533-4302

Fax: (330)452-7786
Co. E-mail: info@cantonchamber.org
URL: http://www.cantonchamber.org
Contact: Dennis P. Saunier, Pres.

63636 ■ Carey Area Chamber of Commerce
R119 W Findlay St.
PO Box 94
Carey, OH 43316-0094
Ph:(419)396-7856
Fax: (419)396-7856
Co. E-mail: careychamber@udata.com
URL: http://www.wyandotonline.com/careychamber/
   default.htm
Contact: Nancy Maison, Exec.Dir.

63637 ■ Carroll County Chamber of Commerce and Economic Development
PO Box 277
Carrollton, OH 44615
Ph:(330)627-4811
Fax: (330)627-3647
Co. E-mail: carrollchamber@eohio.net
Contact: Rhonda Cogan, Exec.Dir.

63638 ■ Celina-Mercer County Chamber of Commerce
226 N Main St.
Celina, OH 45822-1663
Ph:(419)586-2219
Fax: (419)586-8645
Co. E-mail: info@celinamercer.com
URL: http://www.celinamercer.com
Contact: Pam Buschur, Exec.Dir.

63639 ■ Chagrin Valley Chamber of Commerce
16 S Main St.
Chagrin Falls, OH 44022-3009
Ph:(440)247-6607
Fax: (440)247-6503
Co. E-mail: info@cvcc.org
URL: http://www.cvcc.org
Contact: Mary Beth Wolfe, Exec.VP

63640 ■ Chamber of Northeast Cincinnati
316 W Main St.
Mason, OH 45040
Ph:(513)336-0125
Fax: (513)398-6371
Co. E-mail: jharris@necchamber.org
URL: http://www.necchamber.org
Contact: John Harris, Pres.

63641 ■ Champaign County Chamber of Commerce
113 Miami St.
Urbana, OH 43078
Ph:(937)653-5764
Free: 877-873-5764
Co. E-mail: info@champaignohio.com
URL: http://www.champaignohio.com/chamber.htm
Contact: Ms. Kelly Evans-Wilson PhD, Exec.Dir.

63642 ■ Chardon Area Chamber of Commerce
111 South St.
Chardon, OH 44024
Ph:(440)285-9050
Fax: (440)286-8964
Co. E-mail: emabel@chardonchamber.com
URL: http://www.chardonchamber.com
Contact: Erna M. Leagan-Mabel, Exec.Sec.

63643 ■ Chesterland Chamber of Commerce
8228 Mayfield Rd., Ste. 4B
Chesterland, OH 44026
Ph:(440)729-7297
Fax: (440)729-2690
Co. E-mail: info@chesterlandchamber.com
URL: http://www.chesterlandchamber.com
Contact: Michelle Krysinski, Office Mgr.

63644 ■ Chillicothe Ross Chamber of Commerce
45 E Main St.
Chillicothe, OH 45601

Ph:(740)702-2722
Fax: (740)702-2727
Co. E-mail: ccinfo@chillicotheohio.com
URL: http://www.chillicotheohio.com
Contact: Marvin E. Jones, Exec.Dir.

63645 ■ Cincinnati USA Regional Chamber
441 Vine St., Ste. 300
Cincinnati, OH 45202-2812
Ph:(513)579-3100
Fax: (513)579-3101
Co. E-mail: info@cincinnatichamber.com
URL: http://www.cincinnatichamber.com
Contact: Ellen van der Horst, Pres.

63646 ■ Circleville - Pickaway Chamber of Commerce
135 W Main St.
PO Box 462
Circleville, OH 43113
Ph:(740)474-4923
Free: 800-897-9424
Fax: (740)477-6800
Co. E-mail: amy_elsea@thepickofohio.com
URL: http://www.pickaway.com
Contact: Amy Elsea, Dir.

63647 ■ Clermont County Chamber of Commerce
553 Chamber Dr.
Milford, OH 45150
Ph:(513)576-5000
Co. E-mail: clermontchamber@clermontchamber.com
URL: http://www.clermontchamber.com
Contact: Matthew Van Sant, Pres./CEO

63648 ■ Coldwater Area Chamber of Commerce
PO Box 57
Coldwater, OH 45828
Ph:(419)678-4881
Co. E-mail: coldwater@bright.net
Contact: Janet Gels

63649 ■ Columbiana Area Chamber of Commerce
328 N Main St.
Columbiana, OH 44408
Ph:(330)482-3822
Fax: (330)482-3960
Co. E-mail: info@columbianachamber.com
URL: http://www.columbianachamber.com
Contact: Chris Davis, Pres.

63650 ■ Columbus Chamber
37 N High St.
Columbus, OH 43215
Ph:(614)221-1321
Fax: (614)221-1408
Co. E-mail: ty_marsh@columbus.org
URL: http://www.columbus-chamber.org
Contact: Ty D. Marsh, Pres./CEO

63651 ■ Conneaut Area Chamber of Commerce
235 Main St.
PO Box 722
Conneaut, OH 44030-0722
Ph:(440)593-2402
Fax: (440)593-2402
Co. E-mail: conneautchamber@suite224.net
URL: http://www.conneautchamber.org
Contact: Geoffrey Klein, Exec. Dir.

63652 ■ Coshocton County Chamber of Commerce
101 N Whitewoman St.
Coshocton, OH 43812
Ph:(740)622-5411
Free: 800-589-2430
Fax: (740)622-9902
Co. E-mail: info@coshoctonchamber.com
URL: http://www.coshoctonchamber.com
Contact: Mr. Scott Thompson, Exec.Dir.

63653 ■ Cuyahoga Falls Chamber of Commerce
2020 Front St., Ste. 103
Cuyahoga Falls, OH 44221-3200
Ph:(330)929-6756
Fax: (330)929-4278
Co. E-mail: info@cfchamber.com
URL: http://www.cuyahogafallschamberofcommerce.com
Contact: Laura Petrella, Exec.Dir.

63654 ■ Dalton Area Chamber of Commerce
PO Box 168
Dalton, OH 44618
Ph:(330)832-9582
Co. E-mail: chamber@leedaservices.com
Contact: Joseph B. Knetzer, Pres.

63655 ■ Darke County Chamber of Commerce
622 S Broadway
PO Box 237
Greenville, OH 45331-0237
Ph:(937)548-2102
Fax: (937)548-5608
Co. E-mail: info@darkecountyohio.com
URL: http://www.darkecountyohio.com
Contact: Louanna Gwinn, Pres.

63656 ■ Dayton Area Chamber of Commerce
1 Chamber Plz.
Dayton, OH 45402-2400
Ph:(937)226-1444
Fax: (937)226-8254
Co. E-mail: info@dacc.org
URL: http://www.daytonchamber.org
Contact: Phillip L. Parker CAE, Pres./CEO

63657 ■ Deerfield Chamber of Commerce
PO Box 193
Deerfield, OH 44411-0193
Ph:(330)584-8440
Fax: (330)686-8880
Co. E-mail: sandie@neorr.com
Contact: Sandie Welch, Pres.

63658 ■ Defiance Area Chamber of Commerce
615 W 3rd St.
Defiance, OH 43512
Ph:(419)782-7946
Fax: (419)782-0111
Co. E-mail: fculver@defiancechamber.com
URL: http://www.defiancechamber.com
Contact: Floyd A. Culver, Pres.

63659 ■ Delaware Area Chamber of Commerce
23 N Union St.
Delaware, OH 43015
Ph:(740)369-6221
Fax: (740)369-4817
Co. E-mail: dachamber@delawareohiochamber.com
URL: http://www.delawareohiochamber.com
Contact: Charlotte Joseph, Pres.

63660 ■ Delphos Area Chamber of Commerce
310 N Main St.
Delphos, OH 45833
Ph:(419)695-1771
Fax: (419)695-1771
Co. E-mail: dchamber1@wcoil.com
URL: http://www.delphos-ohio.com
Contact: Diane Sterling, Exec.Dir.

63661 ■ Delta Chamber of Commerce
PO Box 96
Delta, OH 43515-0096
Ph:(419)822-3089
URL: http://www.deltaohio.com
Contact: Marcy LeFevre, Pres.

63662 ■ Deshler Chamber of Commerce
PO Box 123
Deshler, OH 43516
Ph:(419)278-1826

Co. E-mail: inforequest@deshlerohiochamber.com
URL: http://www.deshlerohiochamber.com
Contact: Jackie Arps, Sec.-Treas.

63663 ■ East Liverpool Area Chamber of Commerce
529 Market St.
East Liverpool, OH 43920-5094
Ph:(330)385-0845
Fax: (330)385-0581
Co. E-mail: office@elchamber.com
URL: http://www.elchamber.com
Contact: Pamela Hoppel, Exec.Dir.

63664 ■ Eastern Maumee Bay Chamber of Commerce
4209 Corduroy Rd.
Oregon, OH 43616
Ph:(419)693-5580
Fax: (419)693-9990
Co. E-mail: director@embchamber.org
URL: http://www.embchamber.org
Contact: Deb Warnke, Exec.Dir.

63665 ■ Eaton - Preble County Chamber of Commerce
Eaton National Bank Bldg.
PO Box 303
Eaton, OH 45320-0303
Ph:(937)456-4949
Fax: (937)456-4949
Co. E-mail: chamberoffices@preblecountyohio.com
URL: http://preblecountyohio.com
Contact: Bonnie Norris, Chair

63666 ■ Edgerton Chamber of Commerce
PO Box 399
Edgerton, OH 43517
Ph:(419)298-2335
Contact: Roger Strup, Sec.

63667 ■ Englewood-Northmont Chamber of Commerce
PO Box 62
Englewood, OH 45322-0062
Ph:(937)836-2550
Fax: (937)836-2485
Co. E-mail: info@englewood-northmontcoc.com
URL: http://www.englewood-northmontcoc.com
Contact: Cathy Hutton, Exec.Dir.

63668 ■ Euclid Chamber of Commerce
21935 Lakeshore Blvd.
Euclid, OH 44123
Ph:(216)731-9322
Fax: (216)731-8354
Co. E-mail: info@euclidchamberofcommerce.com
URL: http://www.euclidchamberofcommerce.com
Contact: Richard Kretschman, Pres.

63669 ■ Fairborn Area Chamber of Commerce
12 N Central Ave.
Fairborn, OH 45324-5097
Ph:(937)878-3191
Fax: (937)878-3197
Co. E-mail: chamber@fairborn.com
URL: http://www.fairborn.com
Contact: John G. Dalton, Exec.Dir.

63670 ■ Fairfield Chamber of Commerce
670 Wessel Dr.
Fairfield, OH 45014
Ph:(513)881-5500
Fax: (513)881-5503
Co. E-mail: deniserawls@hotmail.com
URL: http://www.fairfieldchamber.com
Contact: Ginger Shawver, Pres./CEO

63671 ■ Fayette County Chamber of Commerce
101 E East St.
Washington Court House, OH 43160
Ph:(740)335-0761
Free: 800-479-7797
Fax: (740)335-0762
Co. E-mail: fayettechamber@yahoo.com

URL: http://www.fayettecountyohio.com
Contact: Roger Blackburn, Pres.

63672 ■ Findlay-Hancock County Chamber of Commerce
123 E Main Cross St.
Findlay, OH 45840
Ph:(419)422-3313
Fax: (419)422-9508
Co. E-mail: info@findlayhancockchamber.com
URL: http://www.findlayhancockchamber.com
Contact: Douglas S. Peters, Pres./CEO

63673 ■ Fort Recovery Chamber of Commerce
PO Box 671
Fort Recovery, OH 45846-0671
Ph:(419)375-2530
Fax: (419)375-4709
Co. E-mail: fortrecovery@bright.net
URL: http://www.fortrecovery.org

63674 ■ Fostoria Area Chamber of Commerce
121 N Main St.
Fostoria, OH 44830-2215
Ph:(419)435-0486
Fax: (419)435-0936
Co. E-mail: chamberfost@aol.com
URL: http://www.fostoriachamber.org
Contact: Beverly K. Barber, Admin.Asst.

63675 ■ Franklin Area Chamber of Commerce
201 E 2nd St., Ste. 9
PO Box 721
Franklin, OH 45005-0721
Ph:(937)746-8457
Fax: (937)746-2461
Co. E-mail: franklincc@dayton99.com
URL: http://www.franklinohio.org/chamber/chamber.
    asp
Contact: Cheryl Cooper-Darragh, Exec.Dir.

63676 ■ Gahanna Area Chamber of Commerce
94 N High St.
Gahanna, OH 43230
Ph:(614)471-0451
Fax: (614)471-5122
Co. E-mail: info@gahannaareachamber.com
URL: http://www.gahannaareachamber.com
Contact: Mrs. Leslee Blake, Pres.

63677 ■ Galion Area Chamber of Commerce
106 Harding Way E
Galion, OH 44833-1901
Ph:(419)468-7737
Fax: (419)462-5487
Co. E-mail: galionchamber@galionchamber.org
URL: http://www.galionchamber.org
Contact: Joe Kleinknecht, Pres./CEO

63678 ■ Gallia County Chamber of Commerce
16 State St.
PO Box 465
Gallipolis, OH 45631-0465
Ph:(740)446-0596
Co. E-mail: lneal@galliacounty.org
URL: http://www.galliacounty.org
Contact: Ryan Smith

63679 ■ Garfield Heights Chamber of Commerce
5284 Transportation Blvd.
Garfield Heights, OH 44125
Ph:(216)475-7775
Fax: (216)475-2237
Co. E-mail: mstamler@garfieldchamber.com
URL: http://www.garfieldchamber.com
Contact: Mary Stamler, Exec.Dir.

63680 ■ Garrettsville - Hiram Area Chamber of Commerce
PO Box 1
Garrettsville, OH 44231

Ph:(330)527-5850
Co. E-mail: patrick@apk.net
URL: http://www.garrettsvillehiramarea.com
Contact: Rick Patrick, Pres.

63681 ■ Geneva Area Chamber of Commerce
866 E Main St.
PO Box 84
Geneva, OH 44041-0084
Ph:(440)466-8694
Fax: (440)466-0823
Co. E-mail: info@genevachamber.org
URL: http://www.genevachamber.org
Contact: Sue Ellen Foote, Exec.Dir.

63682 ■ Geneva-on-the-Lake Chamber of Commerce
5536 Lake Rd.
Geneva, OH 44041
Ph:(440)466-8600
Free: 800-862-9948
Fax: (440)466-8911
Co. E-mail: question@visitgenevaonthelake.com
URL: http://www.visitgenevaonthelake.com
Contact: Marge Milliken, Tourism Specialist

63683 ■ Grand Rapids Area Chamber of Commerce
PO Box 309
Grand Rapids, OH 43522
Ph:(419)832-1106
Fax: (419)832-0561
URL: http://www.grandrapidsohio.com

63684 ■ Greater Akron Chamber of Commerce
1 Cascade Plaza, 17th Fl.
Akron, OH 44308-1192
Ph:(330)376-5550
Free: 800-621-8001
Fax: (330)379-3164
Co. E-mail: info@greaterakronchamber.org
URL: http://www.greaterakronchamber.org
Contact: Daniel C. Colantone, CEO & Pres.

63685 ■ Greater Buckeye Lake Chamber of Commerce
PO Box 5
Buckeye Lake, OH 43008
Ph:(740)928-2044
Co. E-mail: info@buckeyelakecc.com
Contact: Jack Holmes, Pres.

63686 ■ Greater Cincinnati Junior Chamber Foundation
PO Box 36444
Cincinnati, OH 45236-0444
Ph:(513)956-7704
Co. E-mail: info@cincinnatijaycees.org
URL: http://www.cincinnatijaycees.org
Contact: Mandi Wise, Pres.

63687 ■ Greater Cincinnati and Northern Kentucky African American Chamber of Commerce
2945 Gilbert Ave.
Cincinnati, OH 45206
Ph:(513)751-9900
Free: 877-810-0245
Fax: (513)751-9100
Co. E-mail: admin@gcaacc.org
URL: http://www.gcaacc.com
Contact: Kory A. Jackson, Chair

63688 ■ Greater Columbus Area Chamber of Commerce
37 N High St.
Columbus, OH 43215
Ph:(614)221-1321
Fax: (614)221-1408
Co. E-mail: ty_marsh@columbus.org
URL: http://www.columbus.org
Contact: Mr. Ty D. Marsh, Pres./CEO

63689 ■ Greater Girard Area Chamber of Commerce
PO Box 457
Girard, OH 44420

Ph:(330)545-8616
Co. E-mail: president@girardchamber.org
URL: http://www.girardchamber.org
Contact: Jeff Kay, Pres.

63690 ■ Greater Hamilton Chamber of Commerce
201 Dayton St.
Hamilton, OH 45011-1633
Ph:(513)844-1500
Fax: (513)844-1999
URL: http://www.hamilton-ohio.com
Contact: Kenny Craig, Pres./CEO

63691 ■ Greater Lawrence County Area Chamber of Commerce
216 Collins Ave.
PO Box 488
South Point, OH 45680-0488
Ph:(740)377-4550
Free: 800-408-1334
Fax: (740)377-2091
Co. E-mail: dingus@ohio.edu
URL: http://www.lawrencecountyohio.org
Contact: Patricia L. Clonch, Exec.Dir.

63692 ■ Green Chamber of Commerce
PO Box 547
Green, OH 44232-0547
Ph:(330)896-3023
Fax: (330)896-3178
Co. E-mail: info@greencoc.org
Contact: Lori Howerton, CEO

63693 ■ Grove City Area Chamber of Commerce
4069 Broadway
Grove City, OH 43123
Ph:(614)875-9762
Free: 877-870-5393
Fax: (614)875-1510
Co. E-mail: info@gcchamber.org
URL: http://www.gcchamber.org
Contact: Lynn A. Smith, Exec.Dir.

63694 ■ Hamilton County Chamber of Commerce
PO Box 42250
Cincinnati, OH 45242
Ph:(513)984-6555
Fax: (513)793-1063
Co. E-mail: hccc@fuse.net
Contact: J. Gruber, Exec.Dir.

63695 ■ Hardin County Chamber of Commerce
United Community Bldg.
225 S Detroit St.
Kenton, OH 43326
Ph:(419)673-4131
Fax: (419)674-4876
Co. E-mail: chamber@hardinohio.org
URL: http://www.hardinohio.org
Contact: Sue Harrison, Pres.

63696 ■ Harrison Regional Chamber of Commerce
3780 Cadiz-Dennison Rd.
Cadiz, OH 43907
Ph:(740)942-3350
Fax: (740)942-0009
Co. E-mail: hrcctour@eohio.net
URL: http://pages.eohio.net/harrisonchamber
Contact: Ed Coultrap, Exec.Dir.

63697 ■ Heights Regional Chamber of Commerce
3109 Mayfield Rd., Ste. 202
Cleveland Heights, OH 44118
Ph:(216)397-7322
Fax: (216)397-7353
Co. E-mail: info@hrcc.org
URL: http://www.hrcc.org
Contact: Angie Pohlman, Dir.

63698 ■ Highland County Chamber of Commerce
1575 N High St., Ste. 400
Hillsboro, OH 45133-0296
Ph:(937)393-1111
Fax: (937)393-2697
Co. E-mail: hccoc@cinci.rr.com
Contact: Melody Johnson, Pres./CEO

63699 ■ Hilliard Area Chamber of Commerce
4081 Main St.
Hilliard, OH 43026-1501
Ph:(614)876-7666
Fax: (614)876-3113
Co. E-mail: info@hilliardchamber.org
URL: http://www.hilliardchamber.org
Contact: Libby Gierach, Pres./CEO

63700 ■ Holland - Springfield Chamber of Commerce
1032 S McCord Rd.
Holland, OH 43528
Ph:(419)865-2110
Fax: (419)865-4888
Co. E-mail: info@hollandspringfieldcoc.org
URL: http://www.hollandspringfieldcoc.org
Contact: Mary Green, Pres.

63701 ■ Holmes County Chamber of Commerce
35 N Monroe St.
Millersburg, OH 44654
Ph:(330)674-3975
Fax: (330)674-3976
Co. E-mail: info@holmescountychamber.com
URL: http://www.holmescountychamber.com
Contact: Shasta Mast, Exec.Dir.

63702 ■ Huber Heights Chamber of Commerce
4756 Fishburg Rd.
Huber Heights, OH 45424-4046
Ph:(937)233-5700
Fax: (937)233-5769
Co. E-mail: hhchamber@sbcglobal.net
URL: http://www.huberheightschamber.com
Contact: Pat Stephens, Exec. Dir.

63703 ■ Hudson Area Chamber of Commerce
156 N Main St.
Hudson, OH 44236-0700
Ph:(330)650-0621
Fax: (330)656-1646
Co. E-mail: info@hudsoncoc.org
URL: http://www.hudsoncoc.org
Contact: Carolyn Konefal, Exec.Dir.

63704 ■ Huron Chamber of Commerce
PO Box 43
Huron, OH 44839
Ph:(419)433-5700
Fax: (419)433-5700
Co. E-mail: chamber@huron.net
URL: http://www.huron.net
Contact: Sheila Ehrhardt, Dir.

63705 ■ Indian Lake Area Chamber of Commerce
126 N Orchard Island Rd.
PO Box 717
Russells Point, OH 43348-0717
Ph:(937)843-5392
Fax: (937)843-9051
Co. E-mail: office@indianlakechamber.org
URL: http://www.indianlakechamber.org
Contact: Frank Dietz, Pres.

63706 ■ Jackson Area Chamber of Commerce
234 Broadway St.
Jackson, OH 45640-1702
Ph:(740)286-2722
Fax: (740)286-8443
Co. E-mail: info@jacksonohio.org
URL: http://www.jacksonohio.org
Contact: Randy R. Heath, Exec.Dir.

63707 ■ Jackson - Beldon Chamber of Commerce
5735 Wales Ave. NW
Massillon, OH 44646-9097
Ph:(330)833-4400
Fax: (330)833-4456
Co. E-mail: info@jbcc.org
URL: http://www.jbcc.org
Contact: Ruthanne Wilkof, Exec.Dir.

63708 ■ Jefferson Area Chamber of Commerce
PO Box 100
Jefferson, OH 44047-0100
Ph:(440)576-3070
Fax: (440)576-4352
Co. E-mail: membership@jeffersonchamber.com
URL: http://www.jeffersonchamber.com
Contact: Peggy Stadler, Corresponding Sec.

63709 ■ Jefferson County Chamber of Commerce
630 Market St.
PO Box 278
Steubenville, OH 43952
Ph:(740)282-6226
Fax: (740)282-6285
Co. E-mail: info@jeffersoncountychamber.com
URL: http://www.jeffersoncountychamber.com
Contact: Domenick Mucci, Pres./CEO

63710 ■ Kelleys Island Chamber of Commerce
PO Box 783-F
Kelleys Island, OH 43438-0783
Ph:(419)746-2360
Fax: (419)746-2360
URL: http://www.kelleysislandchamber.com
Contact: Lisa Klonaris, Pres.

63711 ■ Kent Area Chamber of Commerce
Portage Travel Bldg.
138 E Main St.
Kent, OH 44240
Ph:(330)673-9855
Fax: (330)673-9860
Co. E-mail: dsmith@kentbiz.com
URL: http://www.kentbiz.com
Contact: Daniel D. Smith, Exec.Dir.

63712 ■ Kettering - Moraine - Oakwood Chamber of Commerce
2977 Far Hills Ave.
Kettering, OH 45419
Ph:(937)299-3852
Fax: (937)299-3851
URL: http://www.kmo-coc.org
Contact: Rod J. Sommer, Pres.

63713 ■ Lake Township Chamber of Commerce
PO Box 1207
Hartville, OH 44632
Ph:(330)877-5500
Co. E-mail: president@lakechamber.com
URL: http://www.lakechamber.com
Contact: Paul Tarr, Pres.

63714 ■ Lakewood Chamber of Commerce
14701 Detroit Ave., Ste. 130
Lakewood, OH 44107-4109
Ph:(216)226-2900
Fax: (216)226-1340
Co. E-mail: info@lakewoodchamber.org
URL: http://www.lakewoodchamber.org
Contact: Kathy Berkshire, Exec.Dir.

63715 ■ Lancaster Fairfield County Chamber of Commerce
109 N Broad St.
PO Box 2450
Lancaster, OH 43130-5450
Ph:(740)653-8251
Fax: (740)653-7074
Co. E-mail: info@lancoc.org
URL: http://www.lancoc.org
Contact: Christopher L. Agnitsch, Pres.

63716 ■ Lebanon Area Chamber of Commerce
20 N Broadway
Lebanon, OH 45036
Ph:(513)932-1100
Fax: (513)932-9050
Co. E-mail: info@lebanonchamber.org
URL: http://www.lebanonchamber.org
Contact: Sara Arseneau, Exec. Dir.

63717 ■ Leetonia-Washingtonville Area Chamber of Commerce
300 E Main St.
Leetonia, OH 44431-1197
Ph:(330)427-1600
Fax: (330)427-8080
URL: http://www.leetonia.org
Contact: Heather MacNaughton, Pres.

63718 ■ Leipsic Area Chamber of Commerce
142 E Main St.
Leipsic, OH 45856
Ph:(419)943-2009
Co. E-mail: info@leipsic.com
URL: http://www.leipsic.com
Contact: Greg Warnimont, Pres.

63719 ■ Lima/Allen County Chamber of Commerce
147 N Main St.
Lima, OH 45801-4927
Ph:(419)222-6045
Fax: (419)229-0266
Co. E-mail: chamber@limachamber.com
URL: http://www.limachamber.com
Contact: Jed E. Metzger, Pres./CEO

63720 ■ Lisbon Area Chamber of Commerce
PO Box 282
Lisbon, OH 44432
Ph:(330)424-1803
Fax: (330)424-0717
Co. E-mail: info@lisbonohiochamber.com
URL: http://www.lisbonohiochamber.com/index.html
Contact: Fred Capel, Exec.Dir.

63721 ■ Lodi Area Chamber of Commerce
PO Box 6
Lodi, OH 44254
Ph:(330)948-8047
Co. E-mail: info@lodiohiochamber.com
URL: http://www.lodiohiochamber.com
Contact: Paul Bayus, Pres.

63722 ■ Logan County Area Chamber of Commerce
100 S Main St.
Bellefontaine, OH 43311-2083
Ph:(937)599-5121
Fax: (937)599-2411
Co. E-mail: info@logancountyohio.com
URL: http://www.logancountyohio.com
Contact: Ed Wallace, Pres./CEO

63723 ■ Logan - Hocking Chamber of Commerce
4 E Hunter St.
PO Box 838
Logan, OH 43138
Ph:(740)385-6836
Fax: (740)385-7259
Co. E-mail: contact@logan-hockingchamber.com
URL: http://www.logan-hockingchamber.com
Contact: Bill Rienhart, Exec.Dir.

63724 ■ Lorain County Chamber of Commerce
6100 S Broadway Ave., Ste. 201
Lorain, OH 44053-3875
Ph:(440)233-6500
Fax: (440)246-4050
Co. E-mail: fdetillio@loraincountychamber.com
URL: http://loraincountychamber.com
Contact: Frank P. DeTillio, Pres.

63725 ■ Loudonville - Mohican Area Convention and Visitor's Bureau
249 W Main St.
Loudonville, OH 44842
Ph:(419)994-2519
Fax: (419)994-5950
Co. E-mail: info@loudonville-mohican.com
URL: http://www.loudonville-mohican.com

63726 ■ Louisville Area Chamber of Commerce
229 E Main St.
PO Box 67
Louisville, OH 44641
Ph:(330)875-7371
Fax: (330)875-3839
Co. E-mail: cheryle@louisvilleohchamber.com
URL: http://www.louisvilleohchamber.com
Contact: Cheryle Casar, Pres.

63727 ■ Loveland Area Chamber of Commerce
510 W Loveland Ave.
PO Box 111
Loveland, OH 45140-0111
Ph:(513)683-1544
Fax: (513)683-5449
Co. E-mail: info@lovelandchamber.org
URL: http://www.lovelandchamber.org
Contact: Paulette Leeper, Exec.Dir.

63728 ■ Madison County Chamber of Commerce
730 Keny Blvd.
London, OH 43140-1074
Ph:(740)852-2250
Fax: (740)852-5133
Co. E-mail: nancymorcher@madisoncountychamber.org
URL: http://www.madisoncountychamber.org
Contact: Nancy Morcher, Pres.

63729 ■ Madison - Perry Area Chamber of Commerce
5965 N Ridge Rd.
PO Box 4
Madison, OH 44057
Ph:(440)428-3760
Fax: (440)428-6668
Co. E-mail: exec@mpacc.org
URL: http://www.mpacc.org
Contact: Nancy Currie, Pres.

63730 ■ Mansfield-Richland Area Chamber of Commerce
55 N Mulberry St.
Mansfield, OH 44902
Ph:(419)522-3211
Fax: (419)526-6853
Co. E-mail: info@mrachamber.com
URL: http://www.mrachamber.com
Contact: Kevin Nestor, Pres.

63731 ■ Marblehead Peninsula Chamber of Commerce
210B W Main St.
Marblehead, OH 43440
Ph:(419)798-9777
Fax: (419)798-9777
Co. E-mail: info@marbleheadpeninsula.com
URL: http://www.marbleheadpeninsula.com
Contact: Katrina Webb, Sec.

63732 ■ Marietta Area Chamber of Commerce
316 3rd St.
Marietta, OH 45750
Ph:(740)373-5176
Fax: (740)373-7808
Co. E-mail: info@mariettachamber.com
URL: http://www.mariettachamber.com
Contact: Charlotte Keim, Pres.

63733 ■ Marion Area Chamber of Commerce
205 W Center St.
Marion, OH 43302
Ph:(740)382-2181

Fax: (740)387-7722
Co. E-mail: chamber@marion.net
URL: http://www.marion.net/chamber
Contact: Pamela S. Hall, Pres.

63734 ■ Martins Ferry Area Chamber of Commerce
418 Walnut St.
Martins Ferry, OH 43935
Ph:(740)633-2565
Fax: (740)633-2641
Co. E-mail: mfchamber@aol.com
Contact: Dorothy Powell, Exec.Dir.

63735 ■ Massillon Area Chamber of Commerce
137 Lincoln Way E
Massillon, OH 44646
Ph:(330)833-3146
Fax: (330)833-8944
Co. E-mail: info@massillonohchamber.com
URL: http://massillongateway.com

63736 ■ Maumee Chamber of Commerce
605 Conant St.
Maumee, OH 43537-3356
Ph:(419)893-5805
Fax: (419)893-8699
Co. E-mail: info@maumeechamber.com
URL: http://www.maumeechamber.com
Contact: Brenda Clixby, Exec.Dir.

63737 ■ Medina Area Chamber of Commerce
145 N Court St.
Medina, OH 44256-1927
Ph:(330)723-8773
Fax: (330)722-6844
Co. E-mail: info@medinaohchamber.com
URL: http://www.medinaohchamber.com
Contact: Debra Lynn-Schmitz, Pres./CEO

63738 ■ Meigs County Chamber of Commerce
238 W Main St.
Pomeroy, OH 45769
Ph:(740)992-5005
Fax: (740)992-7942
Co. E-mail: director@meigscountyohio.com
URL: http://www.meigscountychamber.com
Contact: Steve Story, Pres.

63739 ■ Mentor Area Chamber of Commerce
6972 Spinach Dr.
Mentor, OH 44060
Ph:(440)255-1616
Fax: (440)255-1717
Co. E-mail: info@mentorchamber.org
URL: http://www.mentorchamber.org
Contact: Marie S. Pucak, Exec.Dir.

63740 ■ Mid-Miami Valley Chamber of Commerce
1500 Central Ave.
Middletown, OH 45044
Ph:(513)422-4551
Fax: (513)422-6831
Co. E-mail: bill@thechamberofcommerce.org
URL: http://www.mmvchamber.org
Contact: Bill Triick, Pres./CEO

63741 ■ Middlefield Chamber of Commerce
PO Box 801
Middlefield, OH 44062
Ph:(440)632-5705
Fax: (440)632-5705
Co. E-mail: mccinfo@middlefieldcc.com
URL: http://www.geaugalink.com/extlinks/mfdccfrm.html
Contact: Jean Young, Pres.

63742 ■ Milford - Miami Township Chamber of Commerce
983 Lila Ave.
Milford, OH 45150
Ph:(513)831-2411
Fax: (513)831-3547
Co. E-mail: director@milfordmiamitownship.com

URL: http://www.milfordmiamitownship.com
Contact: Karen Huff, Exec. Dir.

63743 ■ Minerva Area Chamber of Commerce
301 Valley St.
Minerva, OH 44657-1853
Ph:(330)868-7979
Fax: (330)868-3347
Co. E-mail: minervachamber@adelphia.net
URL: http://www.minervachamber.com
Contact: W. John Soliday, Exec.Dir.

63744 ■ Monroe County Chamber of Commerce
PO Box 643
Woodsfield, OH 43793
Ph:(740)472-5499
Fax: (740)472-5499
Co. E-mail: monroechamber@gmn4u.com
URL: http://www.monroechamber.com

63745 ■ Montpelier Area Chamber of Commerce
410 W Main
Montpelier, OH 43543
Ph:(419)485-4416
Fax: (419)495-4416
Co. E-mail: macc@bright.net
URL: http://www.montpelieroh.com
Contact: Ms. Terry Buntain, Exec.Dir.

63746 ■ Morrow County Chamber of Commerce and Visitors' Bureau
17-1/2 W High St.
PO Box 174
Mount Gilead, OH 43338
Ph:(419)946-2821
Fax: (419)946-3861
Co. E-mail: chamuway@bright.net
URL: http://www.morrowcochamber.com
Contact: Rosemary Kay Levings, Exec.Dir.

63747 ■ Mount Vernon - Knox County Chamber of Commerce
7 E Ohio Ave.
Mount Vernon, OH 43050
Ph:(740)393-1111
Fax: (740)393-1590
Co. E-mail: chamber@knoxchamber.com
URL: http://www.knoxchamber.com

63748 ■ Muskingum Valley Area Chamber of Commerce
PO Box 837
Beverly, OH 45715
Ph:(740)984-8259
Co. E-mail: jawagner@aep.com
URL: http://www.mvacc.com
Contact: Glen Miller, Chm.

63749 ■ Napoleon - Henry County Chamber of Commerce
611 N Perry St.
Napoleon, OH 43545
Ph:(419)592-1786
Fax: (419)592-4945
Co. E-mail: hcncoc@ohiohenrycounty.com
URL: http://www.naphcchamber.com
Contact: Joel Miller, Dir.

63750 ■ Newcomerstown Chamber of Commerce
PO Box 456
Newcomerstown, OH 43832-0456
Ph:(740)498-7244
Fax: (740)498-6310
Co. E-mail: gjc@sota-oh.com
Contact: Gary Chaney, Treas.

63751 ■ Noble County Chamber of Commerce
PO Box 41
Caldwell, OH 43724-0041
Ph:(740)732-5288
Fax: (740)732-2377
Contact: Barry Parmiter, Pres.

63752 ■ Nordonia Hills Chamber of Commerce
PO Box 34
Northfield, OH 44067-0034
Ph:(330)467-8956
Fax: (330)468-4901
Co. E-mail: laura@nordoniahillschamber.org
URL: http://www.nordoniahillschamber.org
Contact: Laura Sparano, Exec.Dir.

63753 ■ North Baltimore Area Chamber of Commerce
PO Box 284
North Baltimore, OH 45872
Ph:(419)257-3523
Co. E-mail: nboh@wcnet.org
Contact: Bonnie Knaggs, Pres.

63754 ■ North Canton Area Chamber of Commerce
121 S Main St.
North Canton, OH 44720-3021
Ph:(330)499-5100
Fax: (330)499-7181
Co. E-mail: cathy@northcantonchamber.org
URL: http://www.northcantonchamber.org
Contact: Cathy Dunlap, Pres.

63755 ■ North Coast Regional Chamber of Commerce
PO Box 275
Avon Lake, OH 44012-0275
Ph:(440)933-9311
Co. E-mail: contact@northcoastchamber.com
URL: http://www.avonlakeavoncc.com
Contact: John Sobolewski, Exec.Dir.

63756 ■ North Olmsted Chamber of Commerce
25045 Lorain Rd.
North Olmsted, OH 44070-2054
Ph:(440)777-3368
Fax: (440)777-9361
Co. E-mail: dsebri@leeca.org
URL: http://www.nolmstedchamber.org
Contact: John Sobolewski, Exec.Dir.

63757 ■ North Royalton Chamber of Commerce
13737 State Rd.
PO Box 33122
North Royalton, OH 44133
Ph:(440)237-6180
Fax: (440)237-6181
Co. E-mail: rrnews@aol.com
Contact: Ronald Matye, Pres.

63758 ■ Northeast Cincinnati Chamber of Commerce
316 W Main St.
Mason, OH 45040
Ph:(513)336-0125
Fax: (513)398-6371
Co. E-mail: lfergus@necchamber.org
URL: http://www.mlkchamber.org
Contact: John Harris, Pres.

63759 ■ Norwalk Area Chamber of Commerce
10 W Main St.
Norwalk, OH 44857
Ph:(419)668-4155
Fax: (419)663-6173
Co. E-mail: chamber@accnorwalk.com
URL: http://www.norwalkareachamber.com
Contact: Melissa James, Exec.Dir.

63760 ■ Oak Harbor Area Chamber of Commerce
178 W Water St.
Oak Harbor, OH 43449
Ph:(419)898-0479
Fax: (419)898-2429
Co. E-mail: chamber@oakharborohio.net
URL: http://www.oakharborohio.net
Contact: Lisa Hoover, Exec.Dir.

63761 ■ Oberlin Area Chamber of Commerce
20 E College St.
Oberlin, OH 44074
Ph:(440)774-6262
Fax: (440)775-2423
Co. E-mail: oberlinchamber@oberlin.net
URL: http://www.oberlin.org
Contact: Ron Pierre, Pres.

63762 ■ Ohio Chamber of Commerce
230 E Town St.
PO Box 15159
Columbus, OH 43215-0159
Ph:(614)228-4201
Free: 800-622-1893
Fax: (614)228-6403
Co. E-mail: occ@ohiochamber.com
URL: http://www.ohiochamber.com
Contact: Andrew Doehrel, Pres./CEO

63763 ■ Ohio-Israel Chamber of Commerce
PO Box 39007
Cleveland, OH 44139-0007
Ph:(216)965-4474
Fax: (440)248-4888
Co. E-mail: ohioisraelchamber@ameritech.net
URL: http://ohioisraelchamber.com
Contact: Howard Gudell, Pres.

63764 ■ Ottawa Area Chamber of Commerce
129 Court St.
PO Box 68
Ottawa, OH 45875
Ph:(419)523-3141
Fax: (419)523-5860
Co. E-mail: ottawachamber@earthlink.net
URL: http://www.ottawaohiochamber.com
Contact: Mary Bockrath, Exec.Dir.

63765 ■ Over-The-Rhine Chamber of Commerce
222 E 14th St.
Cincinnati, OH 45202-7309
Ph:(513)241-2690
Fax: (513)241-6770
Co. E-mail: otrchamber@zoomtown.com
URL: http://www.otrchamber.com
Contact: Mario San Marco, Chm.

63766 ■ Oxford Chamber of Commerce
30 W Park Pl., 2nd Fl.
Oxford, OH 45056
Ph:(513)523-5200
Fax: (513)523-2308
Co. E-mail: exec@oxfordchamber.org
URL: http://www.oxfordchamber.org
Contact: JoNell Rowan, Exec.Dir.

63767 ■ Painesville Area Chamber of Commerce
391 W Washington St.
Lake Erie College
College Hall
Painesville, OH 44077
Ph:(440)357-7572
Fax: (440)357-8752
Co. E-mail: exec@painesvilleohchamber.org
URL: http://www.painesvilleohchamber.org
Contact: Linda Reed, Exec.Dir.

63768 ■ Parma Area Chamber of Commerce
7908 Day Dr.
Parma, OH 44129
Ph:(440)886-1700
Fax: (440)886-1770
Co. E-mail: chamber@parmaareachamber.org
URL: http://parmaareachamber.org
Contact: Patricia A. Pell, Exec.Dir.

63769 ■ Perry County Chamber of Commerce
103 W Brown St.
New Lexington, OH 43764
Ph:(740)342-3547
Fax: (740)342-3547
Co. E-mail: pccoc@netpluscom.com
Contact: Larry Rentschler, Pres.

63770 ■ Perrysburg Area Chamber of Commerce
105 W Indiana Ave.
Perrysburg, OH 43551
Ph:(419)874-9147
Fax: (419)872-9347
Co. E-mail: director@perrysburgchamber.com
URL: http://www.perrysburgchamber.com
Contact: Sandy Latchem, Exec.Dir.

63771 ■ Pickerington Area Chamber of Commerce
13 W Columbus St.
Pickerington, OH 43147
Ph:(614)837-1958
Fax: (614)837-6420
Co. E-mail: president@pickeringtonchamber.com
URL: http://www.pickeringtonchamber.com
Contact: Helen Mayle, Pres.

63772 ■ Pike County Chamber of Commerce
12455 State Rte. 104
PO Box 107
Waverly, OH 45690
Ph:(740)947-7715
Fax: (740)947-7716
Co. E-mail: mail@pikechamber.org
URL: http://www.pikechamber.org
Contact: Blaine Beekman, Exec.Dir.

63773 ■ Piqua Area Chamber of Commerce
326 N Main St.
PO Box 1142
Piqua, OH 45356
Ph:(937)773-2765
Fax: (937)773-8553
Co. E-mail: ksdyas@piquaareachamber.com
URL: http://www.piquaareachamber.com
Contact: Mr. David E. Vollette, Pres.

63774 ■ Portsmouth Area Chamber of Commerce
324 Chillicothe St.
PO Box 509
Portsmouth, OH 45662
Ph:(740)353-7647
Free: 800-648-2574
Fax: (740)353-5824
Co. E-mail: sogp@portsmouth.org
Contact: Robert Huff, Pres./CEO

63775 ■ Powell Area Chamber of Commerce
30 W Olentangy St.
PO Box 2008
Powell, OH 43065-2008
Ph:(614)888-1090
Fax: (614)888-4803
URL: http://www.powellchamber.com
Contact: Julie Zdanowicz, Pres./CEO

63776 ■ Put-in-Bay Chamber of Commerce
148 Delaware Ave.
PO Box 250
Put In Bay, OH 43456
Ph:(419)285-2832
Fax: (419)285-4702
Co. E-mail: islandinfo@put-in-bay.com
URL: http://www.put-in-bay.com
Contact: Maggie Beckford, Exec.Dir.

63777 ■ Ravenna Area Chamber of Commerce
135 E Main St.
Ravenna, OH 44266
Ph:(330)296-3886
Fax: (330)296-6986
Co. E-mail: director@ravennachamber.com
URL: http://www.ravennachamber.com
Contact: Pat Artz, Exec.Dir.

63778 ■ Reading Chamber of Commerce
PO Box 15164
Reading, OH 45215
Ph:(513)733-5500
Fax: (513)733-5604
Co. E-mail: jims@gentool.com
URL: http://www.readingohiochamber.org

Contact: Jim Stewart, Pres.

63779 ■ Reynoldsburg Area Chamber of Commerce
1580 Brice Rd.
Reynoldsburg, OH 43068
Ph:(614)866-4753
Fax: (614)866-7313
Co. E-mail: jan@reynoldsburgchamber.com
URL: http://www.reynoldsburgchamber.com
Contact: Jan Hills, Exec.Dir.

63780 ■ Rittman Area Chamber of Commerce
12 N Main St., Ste. 2
Rittman, OH 44270
Ph:(330)925-4828
Fax: (330)925-4828
Co. E-mail: rittmanchamber@aol.com
URL: http://www.rittman.com
Contact: John Landers, Exec.Dir.

63781 ■ Rocky River Chamber of Commerce
20160 Detroit Rd.
Rocky River, OH 44116-2444
Ph:(440)331-1140
Fax: (440)331-3485
Co. E-mail: info@rockyriverchamber.com
URL: http://www.rockyriverchamber.com
Contact: Pat Krizansky, Exec.Dir.

63782 ■ Rootstown Area Chamber of Commerce
PO Box 254
Rootstown, OH 44272
Ph:(330)325-2379
Co. E-mail: website@rootstownchamber.org
URL: http://www.rootstownchamber.org
Contact: Ken Cain, Pres.

63783 ■ Salem Area Chamber of Commerce
713 E State St.
Salem, OH 44460-2911
Ph:(330)337-3473
Fax: (330)337-3474
Co. E-mail: chamber@salemohio.com
URL: http://www.salemohio.com/chamber

63784 ■ Sharonville Chamber of Commerce
11006 Reading Rd., Ste. 301
Sharonville, OH 45241
Ph:(513)554-1722
Fax: (513)956-5522
Co. E-mail: info@sharonvillechamber.com
URL: http://www.sharonvillechamber.com
Contact: Pat Madyda, Exec.Dir.

63785 ■ Shelby Chamber of Commerce
142 N Gamble St., Ste. A
Shelby, OH 44875
Ph:(419)342-2426
Free: 888-245-2426
Fax: (419)342-2189
Co. E-mail: carol.knapp@shelbyoh.com
URL: http://www.shelbyoh.com
Contact: Carol A. Knapp, Pres.

63786 ■ Solon Chamber of Commerce
33595 Bainbridge Rd., Ste. 101
Solon, OH 44139-2942
Ph:(440)248-5080
Fax: (440)248-9121
Co. E-mail: staff@solonchamber.com
URL: http://www.solonchamber.com
Contact: Nancy Traum, Pres./CEO

63787 ■ South Metro Regional Chamber of Commerce
7887 Washington Village Dr., Ste. 265
Dayton, OH 45459
Ph:(937)433-2032
Fax: (937)433-6881
Co. E-mail: linda.gibney@smrcoc.org
URL: http://www.smrcoc.org
Contact: Linda Gibney

63788 ■ Southeastern Butler County Chamber of Commerce
8945 Brookside Ave., Ste. 101
West Chester, OH 45069
Ph:(513)777-3600
Fax: (513)777-0188
URL: http://www.sebcchamber.com
Contact: Joseph A. Hinson, Pres./CEO

63789 ■ Southeastern Franklin County Chamber of Commerce
5151 Berger Rd.
Groveport, OH 43125-9722
Ph:(614)836-1138
Fax: (614)836-1138
Co. E-mail: chambersefc@aol.com
URL: http://www.chambersefc.com
Contact: Susan Brobst, Exec.Dir.

63790 ■ Southwestern Auglaize County Chamber of Commerce
PO Box 3
107 W Monroe St., Ste. 2
New Bremen, OH 45869
Ph:(419)629-0313
Fax: (419)629-0411
Co. E-mail: swauglaizechamber@nktelco.net
URL: http://www.swauglaizechamber.com
Contact: Greg Myers, Dir.

63791 ■ Spring Valley Area Chamber of Commerce
PO Box 396
Spring Valley, OH 45370
Ph:(937)862-4110
URL: http://springvalleyoh.com/springvalley/svcc/svcc.htm
Contact: Judy Madden, Pres.

63792 ■ Springboro Chamber of Commerce
325 S Main St.
Springboro, OH 45066
Ph:(937)748-0074
Fax: (937)748-0525
Co. E-mail: chamber@springboroohio.org
URL: http://www.springboroohio.com
Contact: Anne Stremanos, Exec.Dir.

63793 ■ Springfield-Clark County Chamber of Commerce
333 N Limestone St., Ste. 201
Springfield, OH 45503
Ph:(937)325-7621
Free: 800-803-1553
Fax: (937)325-8765
Co. E-mail: chamber@springfieldnet.com
URL: http://www.springfieldnet.com
Contact: Kathy McPommell, VP

63794 ■ Stow-Munroe Falls Chamber of Commerce
4381 Hudson Dr., Ste. K2
Stow, OH 44224
Ph:(330)688-1579
Fax: (330)688-6234
Co. E-mail: smfcc@smfcc.com
URL: http://www.smfcc.com
Contact: Cindy Smith Lewis, Exec.Dir.

63795 ■ Streetsboro Chamber of Commerce
9205 State Rte. 43, Ste. 106
Streetsboro, OH 44241-5323
Ph:(330)626-4769
Fax: (330)422-1118
Co. E-mail: sacc@streetsborochamber.org
URL: http://www.streetsborochamber.org
Contact: Kori Marsinek, Exec. Dir.

63796 ■ Strongsville Chamber of Commerce
18829 Royalton Rd.
Strongsville, OH 44136-5130
Ph:(440)238-3366
Fax: (440)238-7010
Co. E-mail: strongsvillecofc@earthlink.net
URL: http://www.strongsvillecofc.com
Contact: Douglas M. Kawiecki, Pres.

63797 ■ Sunbury - Big Walnut Area Chamber of Commerce
130 Stelzer Ct.
PO Box 451
Sunbury, OH 43074
Ph:(740)965-2860
Fax: (740)965-9969
Co. E-mail: info@sunburybigwalnutchamber.com
URL: http://www.sunburybigwalnutchamber.com
Contact: Chris Quinlan, Pres.

63798 ■ Swanton Area Chamber of Commerce
100 Broadway
Swanton, OH 43558
Ph:(419)826-1941
Fax: (419)826-3242
Co. E-mail: swantoncc@aol.com
URL: http://www.swantonareacoc.com
Contact: Neil Toeppe, Exec.Dir.

63799 ■ Sylvania Area Chamber of Commerce
6616 Monroe St., Ste. 8
Sylvania, OH 43560
Ph:(419)882-2135
Fax: (419)885-7740
Co. E-mail: sylvania.chamber@sev.org
URL: http://www.sylvaniachamber.org
Contact: Ms. Candy Baker, Exec.Dir.

63800 ■ Tallmadge Chamber of Commerce
80 Community Dr.
Tallmadge, OH 44278
Ph:(330)633-5417
Fax: (330)633-5415
Co. E-mail: tallmadgechamber@sbcglobal.net
URL: http://www.tallmadge-chamber.com
Contact: Nikole L. Dack, Exec.Dir.

63801 ■ Tiffin Area Chamber of Commerce
62 S Washington St.
Tiffin, OH 44883
Ph:(419)447-4141
Fax: (419)447-5141
Co. E-mail: tiffinchamber@bpsom.com
URL: http://www.tiffinchamber.com
Contact: Richard Focht Jr., CEO & Pres.

63802 ■ Tipp City Area Chamber of Commerce
12 S 3rd St.
Tipp City, OH 45371-0134
Ph:(937)667-8300
Fax: (937)667-8867
Co. E-mail: tippcham@core.com
Contact: Ms. Vicki Marie Lowery, Pres./C.E.O.

63803 ■ Toledo Area Chamber of Commerce
Enterprise Ste. 200
300 Madison Ave.
Toledo, OH 43604-1575
Ph:(419)243-8191
Fax: (419)241-8302
Co. E-mail: joinus@toledochamber.com
URL: http://www.toledochamber.com
Contact: Mark A. V'Soske CAE, Pres.

63804 ■ Trotwood Chamber of Commerce
400 Lake Ctr. Dr.
Trotwood, OH 45426
Ph:(937)837-1484
Fax: (937)837-1508
Co. E-mail: trotwoodchamber@aol.com
Contact: Marie Battle, Exec.Dir.

63805 ■ Troy Area Chamber of Commerce
405 SW Public Sq., Ste. 330
Troy, OH 45373
Ph:(937)339-8769
Fax: (937)339-4944
Co. E-mail: tacc@troyohiochamber.com
URL: http://www.troyohiochamber.com
Contact: Charles E. Cochran, Pres.

63806 ■ Tuscarawas County Chamber of Commerce
1323 4th St. NW
New Philadelphia, OH 44663
Ph:(330)343-4474
Fax: (330)343-6526
Co. E-mail: info@tuschamber.com
URL: http://www.tuschamber.com
Contact: Lois F. Rembert, Pres.

63807 ■ Twin City Chamber of Commerce
210 E 3rd St.
PO Box 49
Uhrichsville, OH 44683
Ph:(740)922-5623
Fax: (740)922-1371
Co. E-mail: twincityinfo@sbcglobal.net
URL: http://www.twincitychamber.org
Contact: Teri Edwards, Exec.Dir.

63808 ■ Twinsburg Chamber of Commerce
9044 Church St.
Twinsburg, OH 44087
Ph:(330)963-6249
Fax: (330)963-6995
Co. E-mail: djohnson@twinsburgchamber.com
URL: http://www.twinsburgchamber.com
Contact: Mr. Douglas H. Johnson, Exec.Dir.

63809 ■ Union County Chamber of Commerce
227 E 5th St.
Marysville, OH 43040-1297
Ph:(937)642-6279
Free: 800-642-0087
Fax: (937)644-0422
Co. E-mail: chamber@unioncounty.org
URL: http://www.unioncounty.org
Contact: Eric S. Phillips, CEO/Dir.

63810 ■ Upper Arlington Area Chamber of Commerce
2120 Tremont Ctr.
Upper Arlington, OH 43221
Ph:(614)481-5710
Fax: (614)481-5711
Co. E-mail: admin@uachamber.org
URL: http://www.uachamber.org
Contact: Ms. Brenda Schwandt, Pres.

63811 ■ Upper Sandusky Area Chamber of Commerce
108 E Wyandot Ave.
PO Box 223
Upper Sandusky, OH 43351
Ph:(419)294-3349
Fax: (419)294-3531
Co. E-mail: upsancc@bright.net
URL: http://www.uppersanduskychamber.com
Contact: Monica Bess, Exec.Dir.

63812 ■ Valley City Chamber of Commerce
PO Box 304
Valley City, OH 44280-0304
Ph:(330)483-1111
Co. E-mail: webmaster@valleycity.org
URL: http://www.valleycity.org
Contact: Jim Sandor, Pres.

63813 ■ Van Wert Area County Chamber of Commerce
118 W Main St.
Van Wert, OH 45891
Ph:(419)238-4390
Fax: (419)238-4589
Co. E-mail: info@vanwertchamber.com
URL: http://www.vanwertchamber.com
Contact: Jodie A. Perry, Pres./CEO

63814 ■ Vermilion Chamber of Commerce
5495 Liberty Ave.
Vermilion, OH 44089
Ph:(440)967-4477
Fax: (440)967-2877
Co. E-mail: vermilionchamber@centurytel.net
URL: http://vermilionohio.com
Contact: Maureen Coe, Pres.

63815 ■ Vinton County Chamber of Commerce
104 W Main St.
PO Box 307
McArthur, OH 45651
Ph:(740)596-5033
Fax: (740)596-9262
Co. E-mail: dboothe@vintoncounty.com
URL: http://www.vintoncounty.com
Contact: David M. Boothe, Exec.Dir.

63816 ■ Wadsworth Area Chamber of Commerce
125 W Boyer St., Ste. B
Wadsworth, OH 44281
Ph:(330)336-6150
Fax: (330)336-2672
Co. E-mail: business@wadsworthchamber.com
URL: http://www.wadsworthchamber.com
Contact: Beth Workman, CEO

63817 ■ Wapakoneta Area Chamber of Commerce
16 E Auglaize St.
PO Box 208
Wapakoneta, OH 45895
Ph:(419)738-2911
Fax: (419)739-2298
Co. E-mail: wapcofc@bright.net
URL: http://www.wapakoneta.com
Contact: Dan Graf, Dir.

63818 ■ Waterville Area Chamber of Commerce
122 Farnsworth Rd.
Waterville, OH 43566
Ph:(419)878-5188
Fax: (419)878-5199
Co. E-mail: watervillechamber@toast.net
URL: http://www.watervillechamber.com/index.html
Contact: Dawn Bly, Exec.Dir.

63819 ■ Wauseon Chamber of Commerce
115 N Fulton St.
PO Box 217
Wauseon, OH 43567
Ph:(419)335-9966
Fax: (419)335-7693
Co. E-mail: debbie@wauseonchamber.com
URL: http://www.wauseonchamber.com
Contact: Debbie Nelson, Exec.Dir.

63820 ■ Waynesville Area Chamber of Commerce
PO Box 281
10-B N Main St.
Waynesville, OH 45068-0281
Ph:(513)897-8855
Fax: (513)897-9833
Co. E-mail: waynsville@aol.com
URL: http://www.waynesvilleohio.com
Contact: Joseph Coons, Exec.Dir.

63821 ■ Wellington Area Chamber of Commerce
226 Wenner St.
PO Box 42
Wellington, OH 44090
Ph:(440)647-2222
Contact: Virginia Haynes, Pres.

63822 ■ West Shore Chamber of Commerce
24600 Center Ridge Rd., Ste. 480
Westlake, OH 44145-5617
Ph:(440)835-8787
Fax: (440)835-8798
URL: http://www.westshorechamber.org
Contact: John Sobolewski, Exec. Dir.

63823 ■ West Unity Area Chamber of Commerce
PO Box 263
West Unity, OH 43570-0263
Ph:(419)924-2952
Fax: (419)924-2952
Contact: Jean Gerig, Pres.

63824 ■ Westerville Area Chamber of Commerce
99 Commerce Park Dr.
Westerville, OH 43082
Ph:(614)882-8917
Fax: (614)882-2085
Co. E-mail: info@westervillechamber.com
URL: http://www.westervillechamber.com
Contact: Janet Tressler-Davis, Pres./CEO

63825 ■ Whitehall Area Chamber of Commerce
PO Box 13607
Whitehall, OH 43213
Ph:(614)237-7792
Fax: (614)238-3863
Co. E-mail: whitehallchamber@hotmail.com
URL: http://www.whitehallchamber.org
Contact: Leanne Adkins, Pres.

63826 ■ Wickliffe Area Chamber of Commerce
28855 Euclid Ave.
The Provo House
Wickliffe, OH 44092-2538
Ph:(440)943-1134
Fax: (440)943-1114
Co. E-mail: chamber@wickliffechamber.org
URL: http://www.wickliffechamber.org
Contact: Susan E. Peters, Exec.Dir.

63827 ■ Willard Area Chamber of Commerce
PO Box 73
Willard, OH 44890
Ph:(419)935-1888
Co. E-mail: jamesdamon23@hotmail.com
URL: http://www.willardchamber.com
Contact: Todd Shininger, Exec. Dir.

63828 ■ Willoughby Area Chamber of Commerce
28 Public Sq.
Willoughby, OH 44094
Ph:(440)942-1632
Fax: (440)942-0586
Co. E-mail: info@willoughbyareachamber.com
URL: http://www.wacoc.com
Contact: Nikki Matala, Exec.Dir.

63829 ■ Willowick Chamber of Commerce
30435 Lakeshore Blvd.
Willowick, OH 44095
Ph:(440)585-5765
Co. E-mail: info@willowickchamber.org
URL: http://www.willowickchamber.org
Contact: Mary Elyn Bove, Exec.Dir.

63830 ■ Wilmington - Clinton County Chamber of Commerce
40 N South St.
Wilmington, OH 45177
Ph:(937)382-2737
Free: 888-922-2250
Fax: (937)383-2316
Co. E-mail: karenhaley@wccchamber.com
URL: http://www.wccchamber.com
Contact: Karen M. Haley, Pres.

63831 ■ Women's Division of the Lancaster Chamber of Commerce
Lancaster Fairfield County Chamber of Commerce
109 N Broad St.
PO Box 2450
Lancaster, OH 43130
Ph:(740)653-8251
Fax: (740)653-7074
Co. E-mail: info@lancoc.org
URL: http://www.lancoc.org
Contact: Nanciann Rosier, Chair

63832 ■ Wooster Area Chamber of Commerce
377 W Liberty St.
Wooster, OH 44691
Ph:(330)262-5735
Fax: (330)262-5745
Co. E-mail: peeples@neobright.net

URL: http://www.woosterchamber.com
Contact: Sue Peeples, Associate Exec.Dir.

63833 ■ Worthington Area Chamber of Commerce
25 W New England Ave., Ste. 100
PO Box 209
Worthington, OH 43085
Ph:(614)888-3040
Fax: (614)841-4842
Co. E-mail: connect@worthingtonchamber.org
Contact: John Butterfield, Exec.Dir.

63834 ■ Xenia Area Chamber of Commerce
334 W Market St.
Xenia, OH 45385-2843
Ph:(937)372-3591
Fax: (937)372-2192
Co. E-mail: xacc@xacc.com
URL: http://www.xacc.com
Contact: Barbara Zajbel, Pres.

63835 ■ Yellow Springs Chamber of Commerce
101 Dayton St.
Yellow Springs, OH 45387-1817
Ph:(937)767-2686
Fax: (937)767-7876
Co. E-mail: info@yellowspringsohio.com
URL: http://www.yellowspringsohio.org
Contact: Elizabeth Newman, Exec.Dir.

63836 ■ Youngstown/Warren Regional Chamber of Commerce
11 Federal Plz. Central, Ste. 1600
Youngstown, OH 44503
Ph:(330)744-2131
Fax: (330)746-0330
Co. E-mail: kim@regionalchamber.com
URL: http://www.regionalchamber.com
Contact: Thomas M. Humphries, Pres./CEO

63837 ■ Zanesville - Muskingum County Chamber of Commerce
205 N 5th St.
Zanesville, OH 43701
Ph:(740)455-8282
Free: 800-743-2303
Fax: (740)454-2963
Co. E-mail: kashby@zmchamber.com
URL: http://www.zmchamber.com
Contact: Thomas C. Poorman, Pres.

MINORITY BUSINESS ASSISTANCE PROGRAMS

63838 ■ Office Equal Opportunities
City Hall, Rm. 335
601 Lake Side Ave.
Cleveland, OH 44114
Ph:(216)664-4150
Fax: (216)664-3870
URL: http://www.city.cleveland-oh.gov

63839 ■ Ohio Department of Development–Minority Contractors and Business Assistance Program
Division of Minority Business Affairs
77 S High St. 26th Fl.
Columbus, OH -43215
Ph:(614)466-5700
Free: 800-848-1300
Fax: (614)466-4172
URL: http://www.odod.state.oh.us

63840 ■ Ohio Department of Development–Small Business Development
77 S High St., 28th Fl.
Columbus, OH -43216
Ph:(614)466-2718
Free: 800-848-1300
Fax: (614)466-0829
URL: http://www.odod.state.oh.us/
Description: Assists women interested in starting, expanding, or managing a business in Ohio.

63841 ■ Ohio Statewide Minority Business Development Center–Cincinnati Business Development Services, Inc.
7162 Redding Rd., Ste 630
Cincinnati, OH 45237
Ph:(513)631-7666
Fax: (513)631-7613
Co. E-mail: info@osmbdc.org
URL: http://www.ohiostatewidembdc.org
Contact: Anthony Nyame, Project Dir

FINANCING AND LOAN PROGRAMS

63842 ■ Acenet / Appalachian Center for Economic Networks
94 Columbus Rd.
Athens, OH 45701
Ph:(740)592-3854
Fax: (740)593-5451
URL: http://www.acenetworks.com
Contact: June Holley, President and Founder
Investment Policies: Early stage, expansion, and recapitalizations. **Industry Preferences:** Consumer related. **Geographic Preferences:** Mid Atlantic.

63843 ■ Athenian Ventures / Ohio Valley Venture Fund
20 E. Circle Dr., Ste. 190
Athens, OH 45701
Ph:(740)593-9393
Fax: (740)593-9311
URL: http://www.athenianvp.com
Contact: Karl Elderkin, Managing Partner
Preferred Investment Size: $1,000,000 to $10,000,000. **Investment Types:** Early stage. **Industry Preferences:** Communications and media.

63844 ■ Banc One Capital Partners (Columbus)
150 E. Gay St., 24th Fl.
Columbus, OH 43215
Ph:(614)217-1100
Fax: (614)217-1217
Contact: Suzanne B. Kriscunas, Managing Director
E-mail: sbkriscunas@legacyfund.com
Preferred Investment Size: $1,000,000 minimum. **Investment Types:** Second stage, leveraged buyout, mezzanine, industry rollups, and special situation. **Industry Preferences:** Communications and media, computer hardware and software, semiconductors and other electronics, medical and health, consumer related, industrial and energy, financial services, business service, and manufacturing. **Geographic Preferences:** U.S.

63845 ■ Battelle Venture Partners
505 King Ave.
Columbus, OH 43201
Ph:(614)424-7005
Fax: (614)424-4874
Preferred Investment Size: $500,000 to $1,000,000. **Investment Types:** Start-up, first and second stage. **Industry Preferences:** Semiconductors and other electronics, industrial and energy. **Geographic Preferences:** U.S.

63846 ■ Blue Chip Venture Company
1100 Chiquita Ctr.
250 E. Fifth St.
Cincinnati, OH 45202
Ph:(513)723-2300
Fax: (513)723-2306
URL: http://www.bcvp.com
Contact: John Wyant, Managing Director
Preferred Investment Size: $2,000,000 to $10,000,000. **Investment Types:** Start-up, early stage, and expansion. **Industry Preferences:** Internet specific, computer software and services, medical and health, communications and media, semiconductors and other electronics, other products, consumer related, industrial and energy, biotechnology, and computer hardware. **Geographic Preferences:** Midwest, Mid Atlantic, Northeast, and West Coast.

63847 ■ Brantley Partners
3201 Enterprise Pky., Ste. 350
Beachwood, OH 44122
Ph:(216)464-8400
Fax: (216)464-8405
URL: http://www.brantleypartners.com
Contact: Kevin Cook, Principal
Preferred Investment Size: $5,000,000 to $15,000,000. **Investment Types:** Acquisition, expansion, leveraged buyout, management buyouts, generalist PE, mezzanine, private placement, and recapitalizations. **Industry Preferences:** Other products, industrial and energy, medical and health, biotechnology, computer software and services, consumer related, semiconductors and other electronics, communications and media, and Internet specific. **Geographic Preferences:** U.S and Canada.

63848 ■ Capital Technology Group, LLC
400 MetroPlace N., Ste. 300
Dublin, OH 43017
Ph:(614)792-6066
Fax: (614)792-6036
Co. E-mail: info@capitaltech.com
URL: http://www.capitaltech.com
Contact: Lance Schneier, Chairman and Chief Executive Officer
Preferred Investment Size: $250,000 to $1,000,000. **Investment Types:** Seed, early and start-up. **Industry Preferences:** Communications and media, and Internet specific.

63849 ■ Clarion Capital Corp.
1801 E. 9th St., Ste. 1120
Cleveland, OH 44114
Ph:(216)687-1096
Fax: (216)694-3545
URL: http://www.clarioncap.com
Contact: Thomas Niehaus
Investment Types: Early, first and second stage. **Industry Preferences:** Consumer related, biotechnology, other products, medical and health, industrial and energy, computer hardware, software and services, Internet specific, communications and media, semiconductors and other electronics. **Geographic Preferences:** Northeast, Midwest, and West Coast.

63850 ■ Crystal Internet Venture Fund, L.P.
1120 Chester Ave., Ste. 418
Cleveland, OH 44114
Ph:(216)263-5515
Fax: (216)263-5518
URL: http://www.crystalventures.com
Contact: Daniel Kellogg, Managing Director
Preferred Investment Size: $1,000,000 to $6,000,000. **Investment Policies:** Equity. **Investment Types:** Seed, start-up, early and later stage, and expansion. **Industry Preferences:** Internet specific, computer software and services, communications and media, semiconductors and other electronics, and computer hardware. **Geographic Preferences:** U.S and Canada.

63851 ■ Early Stage Partners, L.P.
1801 E. 9th St., Ste., 1700
Cleveland, OH 44144
Ph:(216)781-4600
Fax: (216)781-0158
URL: http://www.esplp.com
Contact: Charles MacMillan, Principal
Investment Policies: Early stage. **Industry Preferences:** Computer software, industrial and energy, and manufacturing. **Geographic Preferences:** Midwest and Ohio.

63852 ■ Key Equity Capital Corp.
127 Public Sq., 28th Fl.
Cleveland, OH 44114
Ph:(216)689-3000
Fax: (216)689-3204
URL: http://www.keybank.com
Contact: Cindy J. Babitt
Preferred Investment Size: $1,000,000 minimum. **Investment Policies:** Willing to make equity investments. **Investment Types:** Expansion, industry rollups, leveraged buyout, second stage, and special situation. **Industry Preferences:** Diversified. **Geographic Preferences:** National.

63853 ■ Morgenthaler Ventures (Cleveland)
Terminal Tower
50 Public Sq., Ste. 2700
Cleveland, OH 44113
Ph:(216)416-7500
Fax: (216)416-7501
URL: http://www.morgenthaler.com
Contact: Robert Belles, Partner
Preferred Investment Size: $500,000 to $25,000,000. **Investment Types:** First and later stage, mezzanine, acquisition, leveraged buyout, management buyouts, recapitalizations, and expansion. **Industry Preferences:** Semiconductors and other electronics, communications and media, medical and health, Internet specific, computer software and services, biotechnology, industrial and energy, other products, computer hardware, and consumer related. **Geographic Preferences:** U.S.

63854 ■ National City Equity Partners, Inc.
1965 E. 6th St., Ste. 1010
Cleveland, OH 44114
Ph:(216)222-2491
Fax: (216)222-9965
URL: http://www.ncequitypartners.com
Contact: Carl Baldassarre, Managing Director
Preferred Investment Size: $1,000,000 to $50,000,000. **Investment Types:** Later stage, mezzanine, turnaround, expansion, acquisition, generalist PE, leveraged buyout, management buyouts, special situation, and recapitalizations. **Industry Preferences:** Semiconductors and other electronics, other products, consumer related, communications and media, industrial and energy, Internet specific, medical and health, and computer hardware. **Geographic Preferences:** U.S.

63855 ■ Northwest Ohio Venture Fund
4159 Holland-Sylvania R., Ste. 202
Toledo, OH 43623
Ph:(419)824-8144
Fax: (419)882-2035
Co. E-mail: bwalsh@novf.com
Contact: Barry P. Walsh, Managing Partner
Preferred Investment Size: $250,000 minimum. **Investment Types:** Seed, start-up, first and second stage, leveraged buyout, mezzanine, research and development. **Industry Preferences:** Biotechnology, medical and health, industrial and energy, semiconductors and other electronics, computer software and services. **Geographic Preferences:** Midwest.

63856 ■ Ohio Partners
62 E. Board St., 3rd Fl.
Columbus, OH 43215
Ph:(614)621-1210
Fax: (614)621-1240
Co. E-mail: mcox@ohiopartners.com
URL: http://www.ohiopartners.com
Contact: Maury Cox, President
Investment Types: Start-up, first and second stage. **Industry Preferences:** Computer software services, Internet specific, and computer hardware. **Geographic Preferences:** Midwest, Northwest, and West Coast.

63857 ■ Primus Venture Partners, Inc.
5900 Landerbrook Dr., Ste. 200
Cleveland, OH 44124-4020
Ph:(440)684-7300
Fax: (440)684-7342
URL: http://www.primusventure.com
Contact: Steven Rothman, Managing Director and Chief Financial Of
Preferred Investment Size: $5,000,000 to $20,000,000. **Investment Types:** Early and later stage, expansion, acquisition, and management buyouts. **Industry Preferences:** Communications and media, other products, Internet specific, consumer related, medical and health, biotechnology, industrial and energy, computer software and services, computer hardware, semiconductors and other electronics. **Geographic Preferences:** Midwest and Northeast.

63858 ■ Reservoir Venture Partners
500 W. Wilson Bridge Rd., Ste. 310
Worthington, OH 43085

Ph:(614)846-7241
Fax: (614)846-7267
URL: http://www.reservoirvp.com
Contact: William Turner, Chief Financial Officer
Preferred Investment Size: $500,000 to $1,000,000. **Investment Policies:** Seed and early stage. **Industry Preferences:** Communications, computer software, biotechnology, medical and health, and industrial and energy. **Geographic Preferences:** Midwest.

63859 ■ Senmed Medical Ventures
4445 Lake Forest Dr., Ste. 600
Cincinnati, OH 45242
Ph:(513)563-3240
Fax: (513)563-3261
URL: http://www.senmed.com
Preferred Investment Size: $500,000 to $1,000,000. **Investment Types:** Seed, start-up, and early stage. **Industry Preferences:** Medical and health, biotechnology, semiconductors and other electronics, communications and media, and Internet specific.

63860 ■ U.S. Medical Resources Corp.
914 Ludlow Ave., Ste. 2
Cincinnati, OH 45220
Ph:(513)751-8926
Fax: (513)751-8926
Preferred Investment Size: $500,000. **Investment Types:** Start-up, first and second stage, leveraged buyout, and special situation. **Industry Preferences:** Medical and health. **Geographic Preferences:** Midwest.

63861 ■ The Walnut Group
312 Walnut St., Ste. 1151
Cincinnati, OH 45202
Ph:(513)651-3300
Fax: (513)929-4441
URL: http://www.thewalnutgroup.com
Contact: James Gould, Managing General Partner
Preferred Investment Size: $2,000,000 to $6,000,000. **Investment Types:** First and second stage, acquisition, expansion, generalist PE, and management buyouts. **Industry Preferences:** Medical and health, consumer related, financial services, business service, and other. **Geographic Preferences:** U.S.

PROCUREMENT ASSISTANCE PROGRAMS

63862 ■ East Gate Regional Council of Government–Mahoning Valley Technical Procurement Center–EDATA (5121)
5121 Mahoning Ave.
Youngstown, OH 44515
Ph:(330)779-3800
Fax: (330)779-3838
Co. E-mail: nwebb@eastgatecog.org
URL: http://www.eastgatecog.org
Contact: Norma Webb
E-mail: npickens@edata.org

63863 ■ Northeast Ohio Procurement Technical Assistance Center–Lake County Economic Development Center
Lake Erie College
391 W Washington St.
Painesville, OH 44077-5198
Ph:(440)357-2292
Fax: (440)357-2296
URL: http://www.lcedc.org
Contact: Bob Fenn, Dir

63864 ■ Ohio Procurement Technical Assistance Center
300 Madison Ave., Ste. 200
Toledo, OH 43403
Ph:(419)243-8191
Fax: (419)241-8302
Co. E-mail: megan.reichart@toledochamber.com
URL: http://www.toledochamber.com
Contact: Megan Reichart, Dir

63865 ■ Ohio Procurement Technical Assistance Center–Cincinnati Procurement Outreach Center
3155 Research Blvd., 2nd Fl.
Dayton, OH 45420
Ph:(937)259-1368
Fax: (937)259-1314
Co. E-mail: brown@techsolve.org
URL: http://www.swcoptac.org
Contact: Chad Hummell, Dir
E-mail: nancy.rogers@uc.edu

63866 ■ Ohio Procurement Technical Assistance Center–Mahoning Valley Technical Procurement Center–MVEDC (4319)
4319 Belmont Ave.
Youngstown, OH 44505
Ph:(330)759-3668
Fax: (330)759-3686
Co. E-mail: steve@mvedc.com
URL: http://www.mvedc.com
Contact: Stephen Danyi, Dir

63867 ■ Ohio Procurement Technical Assistance Center–Ohio University–Procurement Technical Assistance Program (Techn)
Technology & Enterprise Building, Ste. 143
20 E Circle Dr.
Athens, OH 45701
Ph:(740)597-1868
Fax: (740)597-1399
Co. E-mail: ptac@arei.org
URL: http://www.voinovichcenter.ohio.edu/
Contact: Sharon Hopkins, Dir
E-mail: williams@mcnet.marietta.edu

63868 ■ Ohio Procurement Technical Assistance Center–Procurement Technical Assistance Program
77 S High St., 26th Fl.
Columbus, OH -43215
Ph:(614)466-2525
Free: (614)848-1300
Fax: (614)466-4172
Co. E-mail: evanotteren@odod.state.oh.us
URL: http://www.swcoptac.org
Contact: Chad Hummell, Dir
Description: Provides counseling, technical resources, historical contracting data, military specifications, financial guidance, and advocacy for federal procurement opportunities.

63869 ■ Procurement Technical Assistance Center–Lawrence Economic Development Corporation
PO Box 488
South Point, OH 45680-0488
Ph:(740)377-4550
Free: 800-408-1334
Fax: (740)377-2091
Co. E-mail: klawhorn@zoominternet.net
URL: http://www.lawrencecountyohio.org
Contact: Kelly Lawhorn, Dir
E-mail: cfreeman@zoomnet.net

INCUBATORS/RESEARCH AND TECHNOLOGY PARKS

63870 ■ Akron Industrial Incubator
526 S Main St., Ste. 129
Akron, OH 44311
Ph:(330)375-2173
Fax: (330)762-3657
Co. E-mail: akroninc@aol.com
URL: http://www.ci.akron.oh.us/aii/

63871 ■ Allen Economic Development Group
147 N Main St.
Lima, OH 45801
Ph:(419)222-7706
Fax: (419)222-7196
Co. E-mail: info@aedg.org
URL: http://www.aedg.org

Contact: Marcel Wagner, Pres & CEO
Description: A small business incubator dedicated to supporting emerging firms through shared resources and other services.

63872 ■ Appalachian Center for Economic Networks (ACEnet)
94 N Columbus Rd.
Athens, OH 45701
Ph:(740)592-3854
Fax: (740)593-5451
Co. E-mail: info@acenetworks.org
URL: http://www.acenetworks.org/
Contact: June Holley, Pres
Description: The ACEnet is located in rural, southeastern Ohio. This incubator is dedicated to improving the economy of the region.

63873 ■ Barberton Community Development Corp.
542 W Tuscarawas Ave.
Barberton, OH 44203
Ph:(330)745-3070
Fax: (330)745-1070
Co. E-mail: info@bcdc.org
URL: http://www.bcdc.org
Contact: Larry Lallo, Exec Dir

63874 ■ Case Western Reserve University–Office of Research Administration
Adelbert Hall, Rm. 4
10900 Euclid Ave.
Cleveland, OH 44106-7015
Ph:(216)368-4510
Fax: (216)368-4679
Co. E-mail: resadm@po.cwru.edu
Contact: Eric M. Cottington PhD, Dir.
E-mail: resadm@po.cwru.edu
Scope: Administers and coordinates research in all fields of interest at the University. **Publications:** Newsletter.

63875 ■ Cleveland State University–Office of Sponsored Programs and Research
2121 Euclid Ave.
KB 1150
Cleveland, OH 44115-2214
Ph:(216)687-3630
Fax: (216)687-9382
Co. E-mail: k.watkins@csuohio.edu
URL: http://www.csuohio.edu/uored
Contact: Kathryn Watkins, Dir.
E-mail: k.watkins@csuohio.edu
Scope: Promotes and facilitates federal extramurally-supported research conducted at the University in the academic areas of arts and sciences, law, engineering, urban studies, education, business administration, and institutional support. **Publications:** Research News (bimonthly). **Educational Activities:** Grantsmanship workshops, open to faculty, staff, and students.

63876 ■ Edison State Community College–Office of Institutional Research
1973 Edison Dr.
Piqua, OH 45356
Ph:(937)778-8600
Fax: (937)778-4691
Co. E-mail: telford@edisonohio.edu
Contact: Rebecca Telford, Dir.
E-mail: telford@edisonohio.edu
Scope: Conducts institutional studies on enrollment for coordination of shortand long-range planning. Provides computer support for special reports and decision modeling. **Services:** Quality assessment, of program offerings.

63877 ■ Innovation Center & Technology Transfer Office–Ohio University
340 W State St., Unit 7
Athens, OH 45701
Ph:(740)593-1818
Fax: (740)593-0186
URL: http://www.innovationcenter.ohiou.edu
Contact: Linda Clark, Dir

63878 ■ Miami Valley Research Park
3155 Research Blvd.
Dayton, OH 45420
Ph:(937)252-5906
Fax: (937)252-9314
Co. E-mail: mvrf@theresearchpark.com
URL: http://www.theresearchpark.com
Contact: Bruce Pearson, Exec.Dir.
E-mail: mvrf@theresearchpark.com
Scope: Facilitates the transfer of basic and applied scientific technological research from tenants and member institutions to production, manufacture, and marketing of materials and services. Solicits public and private grants for research personnel and facilities of member institutions and recruits tenants for the Park.

63879 ■ Ohio State University–Office of Research
208 Bricker Hall
190 N Oval Mall
Columbus, OH 43210-1321
Ph:(614)292-1582
Fax: (614)292-6602
Co. E-mail: mcgrath.66@osu.edu
URL: http://research.rf.ohio-state.edu
Contact: Dr. Robert T. McGrath, Sr.VP
E-mail: mcgrath.66@osu.edu
Scope: Supports and coordinates research activities conducted by departments and colleges throughout the University. Cooperates with the business and industrial community to improve relations and resources. Serves as a central clearinghouse of information. **Publications:** Annual report; Report to Board of Trustees (monthly). **Educational Activities:** Undergraduate Research Forum (annually). **Awards:** Distinguished Scholar Award; Multidisciplinary awards.

63880 ■ Ohio State University–Science and Technology Campus Corp.
1381 Kinnear Rd., Ste. 218
Columbus, OH 43212
Ph:(614)675-4100
Fax: (614)675-4101
Co. E-mail: vbutland@stcc.org
URL: http://www.stcc.org
Contact: Vicki Butland, Interim Pres.
E-mail: vbutland@stcc.org
Scope: 53-acre park offering research-oriented companies a site for their administrative, research, and development facilities to foster exchange between the University and industry and to encourage economic development of the region. Seeks to enhance the University's teaching and research capabilities through stimulating the exchange of ideas and sharing of resources between University and tenant researchers. Coordinates University and tenant resources in developing commercial applications for new discoveries and technologies.

63881 ■ Ohio State University Research Foundation
1960 Kenny Rd.
Columbus, OH 43210-1063
Ph:(614)292-3815
Fax: (614)292-5913
Co. E-mail: doty7@osu.edu
URL: http://www1.rf.ohio-state.edu
Contact: David Doty, Interim Exec.Dir.
E-mail: doty7@osu.edu
Scope: Administers and coordinates extramurally sponsored faculty and graduate student research conducted in various departments and special research units of the University, including its College of Medicine. **Publications:** Annual Report.

63882 ■ Ohio University–Innovation Center
340 W State St., Unit 7
Athens, OH 45701-3751
Ph:(740)593-1818
Fax: (740)593-0186
Co. E-mail: clark@ohio.edu
URL: http://www.innovation.ohio.edu
Contact: Linda J. Clark, Dir.
E-mail: clark@ohio.edu
Scope: Undertakes analysis to determine patentability of invention disclosures and manages university pa-

tent portfolio. Conducts commercial negotiations with licencees. Fosters entrepreneurial activities and provides technical and business assistance to new and expanding companies. Facilitates consulting, product testing, and technical assistance between business tenants, the university, and the community at large. **Services:** Access to shared office equipment; Business and marketing consultation. **Educational Activities:** Informative business related workshops, for the general public.

63883 ■ Ohio University–Office of Research and Sponsored Programs
105 Research and Technology Center
Athens, OH 45701-2979
Ph:(740)593-2857
Fax: (740)593-0379
Co. E-mail: orsp@ohiou.edu
URL: http://www.ohiou.edu/orsp
Contact: Shane L. Gilkey, Dir.
E-mail: orsp@ohiou.edu
Scope: Promotes and administers sponsored research at the University in physical, social, and biological sciences, engineering, mathematics, humanities, radio and television broadcasting, and international studies. Major research emphases are on avionics engineering, analytical and biochemistry, exercise physiology, polymer and geotechnical engineering, systematic, regulatory, molecular, and neurobiology, nuclear and theoretical physics, coal gasification, utilization, and mining, and human factors engineering. **Publications:** Annual Report.

63884 ■ River East Corp.
615 Front St.
Toledo, OH 43605
Ph:(419)698-2310
Fax: (419)698-3640
Co. E-mail: reerc-rea@kmbs.com
URL: http://www.toledorivereast.com
Contact: Donald Monroe, Exec Dir

63885 ■ Toledo Business and Technology Center
1946 N 13th St.
Toledo, OH 43624
Ph:(419)255-6700
Fax: (419)255-6264
Co. E-mail: toledobtc@aol.com
Contact: Christi Abner, Bldg Mgr

63886 ■ University of Dayton–Research Institute
300 College Park
Dayton, OH 45469-0101
Ph:(937)229-2113
Fax: (937)229-2888
Co. E-mail: mccabe@udri.udayton.edu
URL: http://www.udri.udayton.edu/
Contact: Dr. Michael V. McCabe, Dir.
E-mail: mccabe@udri.udayton.edu
Scope: Administers sponsored research programs of the University in aeronautics and astronautics, biology, chemical engineering, chemistry, civil engineering and engineering mechanics, computer science, electrical engineering, engineering technology, geology, industrial engineering, materials, mathematics, physics, psychology, optical engineering, energy conversion, impact mechanics, human factors, environmental science, aerospace mechanics, electrical and computer engineering, experimental and applied mechanics, materials engineering, metals and ceramics, nonmetallic materials, structural integrity, aging systems technology, electo-optics and photonics, coatings and corrosion control, and nano materials. **Services:** Technical Information Services Office, for reference information. **Publications:** UDRI Informer.

63887 ■ Youngstown Business Incubator
241 Federal Plaza West
Youngstown, OH 44503
Ph:(330)746-5003
Fax: (330)746-6863
Co. E-mail: jcossler@ybi.org
URL: http://www.ybi.org
Contact: James Cossler, Dir

Description: The YBI was established to nurture emerging technology and light manufacturing companies through shared resources, business assistance, and other services.

EDUCATIONAL PROGRAMS

63888 ■ Bryant and Stratton Business Institute–Parma Campus
12955 Snow Rd.
Parma, OH 44130
Ph:(216)265-3151
Fax: (216)265-0325
URL: http://www.bryantstratton.edu
Description: Business college offering programs in business management and business operations.

63889 ■ Cuyahoga Community College
2900 Community College Ave.
BA 200
Cleveland, OH 44115
Ph:(216)987-4462
Free: 800-954-TRIC
Fax: (216)987-4096
URL: http://www.tri-c.cc.oh.us
Description: Two-year college offering a small business management program.

63890 ■ Kent State University–Graduate School of Management
PO Box 5190
Kent State University
Kent, OH 44242
Ph:(330)672-2282
Fax: (330)672-7303
Co. E-mail: gradbus@bsa3.kent.edu
URL: http://www.business.kent.edu

E-mail: carlasle@bsa3.kent.edu
Description: Offers an Executive MBA Program for professional growth. The concentrated seven semester program allows degree candidates to participate in foreign study trips and in elective courses including entrepreneurship and small business financial management.

63891 ■ Southeastern Business College
3879 Rhodes Ave.
New Boston, OH 45662
Ph:(740)456-4124
Fax: (740)456-5163
URL: http://www.careersohio.com
Description: Business college offering classes in small business management.

63892 ■ University of Akron
302 Buchtel Mall
Akron, OH 44325-6501
Ph:(330)972-7111
Fax: (330)972-6952
URL: http://www.uakron.edu
Description: Two-year college offering a small business management program.

LEGISLATIVE ASSISTANCE

63893 ■ Ohio House Economic Development and Small Business Committee
77 South High St. 28th Fl.
Columbus, OH 43216-1001
Ph:(614)466-5420
Free: 800-848-1300
Fax: (614)644-1789
URL: http://www.odod.state.oh.us

TRADE PERIODICALS

63894 ■ *Ohio United Way Legislative Bulletin*
Pub: Ohio United Way
Contact: Judith Bird
E-mail: judith_bird@ouw.org
Released: Weekly. **Price:** $100, individuals includes OUW's Administrative Report; $125, institutions; $375, institutions. **Description:** Reports on human service legislation in Ohio.

PUBLICATIONS

63895 ■ *Business First: The Greater Columbus Business Authority*
471 E. Broad St., Ste. 1500
Columbus, OH 43215
Ph:(614)461-4040
Fax: (614)365-2980
Co. E-mail: businessfirst@amcity.com

63896 ■ *The Clevelander-Growth Association*
200 Tower City Center
50 Public Sq.
Cleveland, OH 44113-2291
Ph:(216)621-3300
Fax: (216)621-6013
URL: http://www.clevelandgrowth.com

63897 ■ *Crain's Cleveland Business*
700 W. St. Clair Ave., Ste 310
Cleveland, OH 44113-1230
Ph:(216)522-1383
Fax: (216)522-0625
Co. E-mail: cle.crains@mail.multiverse.com
URL: http://crainscleveland.com

63898 ■ *How to Form Your Own Ohio Corporation Before the Inc. Dries!: A Step by Step Guide, With Forms*
P. Gaines Publishing Co.
333 S. Taylor Ave.
PO Box 2253
Oak Park, IL 60302
Ph:(708)524-9033
Fax: (708)524-9038
Ed: Phillip Williams. **Released:** Second edition, 1994. **Price:** $24.95. **Description:** Volume 2 of the Small Business Incorporation series. Explains the advantages and disadvantages of incorporation and shows, step-by-step, how the small business owners can incorporate at low cost. Covers Ohio profit and nonprofit corporations, Ohio professional service corporations, subchapter S corporations, and Delaware corporations. Includes forms necessary for incorporation.

63899 ■ *Self Counsil Press*
Business Journal Publishing Co.
1422 Euclid, Ste. 730
Cleveland, OH 44115
Ph:(216)771-2833
Fax: (216)781-6318
Co. E-mail: information@clevelandmagazine.com
Released: Monthly. **Price:** Free to qualified subscribers. **Description:** Regional business journal.

63900 ■ *Smart Start your Ohio Business*
PSI Research
300 N. Valley Dr.
Grants Pass, OR 97526
Ph:(503)479-9464
Free: 800-228-2275
Fax: (503)476-1479
Co. E-mail: info@psi-research.com
URL: http://www.psi-research.com
Ed: Michael D. Jenkins. **Released:** Revised edition, 1992. **Price:** $29.95 (looseleaf binder); $24.95 (paper). **Description:** Part of the Successful Business Library series.

63901 ■ *Toledo Business Journal*
27 Broadway at the River
Toledo, OH 43602
Ph:(419)244-8200
Fax: (419)244-5773
URL: http://www.toledobiz.com

PUBLISHERS

63902 ■ Betterway Books
4700 E Galbraith Rd.
Cincinnati, OH 45236
Ph:(513)531-2690
Free: 800-666-0963
Fax: (513)891-7185
Co. E-mail: sberger@fwpubs.com
URL: http://www.fwpublications.com
Contact: Mark F. Arnett, Exec VP & CFO
Description: Publishes resource guides and handbooks on home building and remodeling, small business and finance, theater, woodworking, home decorating, parenting and genealogy. Accepts unsolicited manuscripts. Reaches market through commission representatives and wholesalers. **Founded:** 1980.

63903 ■ Home Business News
12221 Beaver Pke.
Jackson, OH 45640
Ph:(740)988-2331
Fax: (740)988-2331
URL: http://www.homebiznews.com
Contact: Ed Simpson, Publisher
E-mail: esimpson@zoomnet.net
Description: Publishes books and computer software for home-based business owners. Offers *Home Business News* magazine and mailing lists. Reaches market through direct mail. Does not accept unsolicited manuscripts. **Founded:** 1982.

63904 ■ Life Work Insight L.L.C.
PO Box 750202
Dayton, OH 45475-0202
Ph:(937)439-9967
Fax: (937)439-9968
Co. E-mail: info@lifeworkinsight.com
URL: http://www.lifeworkinsight.com/
Contact: Ann Bizzarro
Description: Publishes a book on succeeding in the workplace and finding happiness in life.

63905 ■ Noguska L.L.C.
741 N Countryline
Fostoria, OH 44830
Ph:(419)435-0404
Fax: (419)435-1844
Co. E-mail: support@noguska.com
URL: http://www.noguska.com
Description: Publishes software on web-based business applications for Linux and Windows. **Founded:** 1973

63906 ■ Opportunity Hot-Line
c/o Business Network
5420 Mayfield Rd., Ste 205
Cleveland, OH 44121
Ph:(440)442-5600
Fax: (440)449-3227
Contact: Irwin Friedman, Vice President
Description: Conducts research and development studies on a negotiated basis. Reports and documents occasionally copyrighted. Also finance, buy, sell, and find businesses. As well as finding investing partners. Reaches market through reviews and listings. **Founded:** 1975.

63907 ■ York Publishing Co.
16781 Chagrin Blvd.
Cleveland, OH 44120-3721
Ph:(216)491-0231
Fax: (216)491-0251
Contact: Rachal Rapoport, President
Description: Publishes books on business with a concentration on business consulting. **Founded:** 1993.

Oklahoma

SMALL BUSINESS DEVELOPMENT CENTER LEAD OFFICE

63908 ■ Southeastern Oklahoma State University–Oklahoma SBDC
1405 N. 4th Ave.
PMB 2584
Durant, OK 74701
Ph:(580)745-7577
Free: 800-522-6154
Fax: (580)745-7471
Co. E-mail: osbdc@sosu.du
URL: http://www.osbdc.org
Contact: Grady Pennington, State Dir.
E-mail: gpennington@sosu.edu

63909 ■ Southeastern Oklahoma State University–Small Business Development Center
517 University
Station A, Box 2584
Durant, OK 74701
Ph:(580)745-7577
Free: 800-522-6154
Fax: (580)745-7471
Contact: Dr. Grady Pennington, State Director
E-mail: gpennington@sosu.edu

SMALL BUSINESS DEVELOPMENT CENTERS

63910 ■ AmQuest Bank, N.A.–Lawton Satellite–Small Business Development Center
601 SW D Ave., Ste. 209
Lawton, OK 73501
Ph:(580)248-4946
Fax: (580)357-4964
Contact: James C. Elliot, Business Specialist
E-mail: elliottjim@usa.net

63911 ■ East Central University–Small Business Development Center
1100 E. 14th St., Ste. 73
Ada, OK 74820-6999
Ph:(580)436-3190
Fax: (580)436-3190
Contact: Ann Ritter, Dir.
E-mail: aritter@mailclerk.ecok.edu

63912 ■ East Central University at Poteau Satellite–Small Business Development Center
1507 S. McKenna
Poteau, OK 74953
Ph:(918)647-1226
URL: http://www.osbdc.org
Contact: Kelly Johnson, Business Consultant
E-mail: kjohnson@carlalbert.edu

63913 ■ Langston University–Small Business Development Center
Minority Assistance Center
4205 N. Lincoln Blvd.
Oklahoma City, OK 73105
Ph:(405)962-1639
URL: http://www.osbdc.org
Contact: Marvin Fisher, Dir.
E-mail: mbfisher@lunet.edu

63914 ■ Northeastern Oklahoma A&M–Miami Satellite–SBDC
215 I St., NE
Miami, OK 74354
Ph:(918)540-0575
Fax: (918)540-0575
Contact: Hugh Simon, Business Development
 Specialist
E-mail: hsimon@neoam.cc.ok.us

63915 ■ Northeastern Oklahoma State University–Small Business Development Center–Tahlequah Satellite Office (Oklah)
Oklahoma Small Business Development Center
309 N. Muskogee
Tahlequah, OK 74464
Ph:(918)449-6280
Fax: (918)449-6281
URL: http://www.nsuok.edu/osbdc/
Contact: Sue Floyd, Specialist
E-mail: floydsm@nsuok.edu

63916 ■ Northeastern State University–Small Business Development Center
3100 E. New Orleans
Broken Arrow, OK 74014
Ph:(918)449-6282
URL: http://www.nsuak.edu/osbdc/
Contact: John Blue, Dir.
E-mail: bluejr@nsuok.edu

63917 ■ Northwestern Oklahoma State University–Small Business Development Center
709 Oklahoma Blvd.
Alva, OK 73717
Ph:(580)327-8608
Fax: (580)327-0560
Contact: Guy Forell, Dir.
E-mail: gvfore@ranger2.nwalva.edu

63918 ■ Phillips University–Small Business Development Center
100 S. University Ave.
Enid, OK 73701
Ph:(580)242-7989
Fax: (580)237-1607
Co. E-mail: b9finger@enid.com
Contact: Bill Gregory, Coordinator

63919 ■ Rose State College–SBDC
Procurement Specialty Center
6420 SE 15th St.
Midwest City, OK 73110
Ph:(405)733-7348
Fax: (405)733-7495

Co. E-mail: sbdc@rose.edu
URL: http://www.rose.edu
Contact: J. Michael Cure, Dir.
E-mail: mcure@rose.edu

63920 ■ Southwestern Oklahoma State University–Small Business Development Center
100 Campus Dr.
Weatherford, OK 73096
Ph:(580)774-7095
Fax: (580)774-7096
Co. E-mail: cebd@swosu.edu
URL: http://www.swosu.edu/cebd/osbdc.htm
Contact: Doug Misak, Business Coord.
E-mail: doug.misak@swosu.edu

63921 ■ Tulsa Satellite Office–Small Business Development Center
Williams Tower II, Ste. 150
2 W. 2nd St.
Tulsa, OK 74119
Ph:(918)583-2676
URL: http://www.nsuak.edu/osbdc/
Contact: Bill Mount, Specialist
E-mail: bilmount@tulsachamber.com

63922 ■ University of Central Oklahoma–Small Business Development Center
115 Park Ave.
Oklahoma City, OK 73102-9005
Ph:(405)232-1968
Fax: (405)232-1967
Co. E-mail: sbdc@aix1.ucok.edu
URL: http://www.osbdc.org/osbdc.htm
Contact: Susan Urbach, Director
E-mail: surbach@aixl.ucok.edu

SMALL BUSINESS ASSISTANCE PROGRAMS

63923 ■ Oklahoma Center for the Advancement of Science Technology–Oklahoma Inventor's Assistance Service
Oklahoma State University
395 Cordell S
Stillwater, OK 74078-8015
Ph:(405)744-8727
Fax: (405)744-8516
Co. E-mail: invent@okstate.edu
URL: http://ias.okstate.edu
Contact: Dr. Tom Bertenshaw, Dir
Description: Helps inventors navigate the invention process with information, educational and referrals.

63924 ■ Oklahoma Department of Agriculture–Market Development Services Division
2800 N Lincoln Blvd.
Oklahoma City, OK 73105-4298
Ph:(405)521-3864

Fax: (405)521-4912
URL: http://oregon.gov/ODA/
Contact: Joanna Ferguson
Description: Develops direct marketing outlets for farmers, including the promotion of direct retail sales, and the promotion of direct wholesaling through commercial systems. Offers the Made in Oklahoma/Grown in Oklahoma marketing program, featuring trademarked logos.

63925 ■ Oklahoma Department of Career and Technology Education–Oklahoma State Department of Vocational and Technical Education–Training for Industry Program (1500)
1500 W 7th Ave.
Stillwater, OK 74074-4364
Ph:(405)377-2000
Fax: (405)743-6809
Co. E-mail: pbowl@okcareertech.org
URL: http://www.okcareertech.org
Description: Provides customized needs assessment, pre-employment training, curriculum development, training facilities, equipment, and instructors at no cost to new or expanding companies. Other services include customized retraining, upgraded training, a bid assistance network, management and business development training programs, and a business development program for small and growing companies.

63926 ■ Oklahoma Department of Commerce–Administration and Central Services
900 N Stiles
Oklahoma City, OK 73104
Ph:800-879-6552
Free: 800-TRY-OKLA
Fax: (405)815-5199
URL: http://okcommerce.gov
Description: Provides assistance in developing business plans, financial packages, industry customized training, domestic and foreign market services, and small and minority business programs.

63927 ■ Oklahoma Department of Commerce–Business Development Division
900 N Stiles
PO Box 26980
Oklahoma City, OK 73104
Ph:(405)815-5146
Free: 800-TRY-OKLA
Fax: (405)815-5142
Co. E-mail: bddinfo@odoc.state.ok.us
URL: http://okcommerce.gov/
Description: Develops industrial prospects and assists local communities in their industrial development efforts. Community profiles provide information to new industries on building and industrial sites, industrial foundations and trusts, local financing, and utility and rail services. Offers one-stop service to businesses on tax information, required permits, and available industrial revenue bonds.

63928 ■ Oklahoma Department of Commerce–Export Assistance Program
301 NW 63rd, Ste. 330
Oklahoma City, OK 73116
Ph:(405)608-5302
Free: 800-879-6552
Fax: (405)608-4211
URL: http://www.export.gov
Description: Specializes in export programs to assist small Oklahoma companies.

63929 ■ Oklahoma Department of Commerce–Global Business Solutions
900 N Stiles Ave.
Oklahoma City, OK 73104
Ph:800-879-6552
Free: 800-879-6552
Fax: (405)815-5245
URL: http://okcommerce.gov/
Description: Encourages foreign investment by working with Oklahoma companies to increase their exports. Works closely with the governor's International and Waterways teams to promote the use and development of the Arkansas River navigation system.

63930 ■ Oklahoma Technology Transfer Center
PO Box 1378
Ada, OK 74820
Ph:(580)332-4100
Fax: (580)332-8716
Co. E-mail: pnorton@okstate.edu
URL: http://www.okstate.edu/osu_ag/ae/
Contact: Phillip Norton
Description: Provides evaluations of new technologies and gives assistance to inventors in applying for patents by providing necessary information.

63931 ■ University of Oklahoma–Not A Working Number
Center for Business and Economic Development
330 W Gray, Ste. 100
Norman, OK 73069
Ph:(405)325-5627
Fax: (405)292-2269
URL: http://www.ou.edu

SCORE OFFICES

63932 ■ SCORE Chapter 194
c/o Jim Solomon, Chm.
Sunoco Bldg.
907 S Detroit St., Ste. 1012
Tulsa, OK 74120
Ph:(918)581-7462
Fax: (918)581-6908
Co. E-mail: consult@tulsascore.org
URL: http://www.tulsascore.org
Contact: Mr. David Layser, Chm.
Description: Volunteer program through which active and retired businesspeople provide free management assistance to people who are considering starting a small business, encountering problems with their business, or expanding their business.

63933 ■ SCORE Lawton
c/o Jack Van Pool, CHR
4500 W. Lee Blvd.
Bldg. 100, Ste. 148
Lawton, OK 73505
Ph:(580)353-8727
Fax: (580)353-8727
Co. E-mail: score304@gpv.org
Description: Business Consulting, workshops and individual counseling.

BETTER BUSINESS BUREAUS

63934 ■ Better Business Bureau of Central Oklahoma
17 S Dewey Ave.
Oklahoma City, OK 73102-2421
Ph:(405)239-6081
Fax: (405)235-5891
Co. E-mail: info@oklahomacity.bbb.org
URL: http://www.oklahomacity.bbb.org
Contact: Bob Manista, Pres.

63935 ■ Tulsa Better Business Bureau
1722 S Carson Ave., Ste. 3200
Tulsa, OK 74119
Ph:(918)492-1266
Fax: (918)492-1276
Co. E-mail: info@tulsabbb.org
URL: http://www.tulsabbb.org
Contact: Rick Brinkley, Pres./CEO

CHAMBERS OF COMMERCE

63936 ■ Ada Area Chamber of Commerce
300 W Main
PO Box 248
Ada, OK 74820-0248
Ph:(580)332-2506

Fax: (580)332-3265
Co. E-mail: jamseyhorton5@hotmail.com
URL: http://www.adachamber.com
Contact: Nancy Carson, Pres.

63937 ■ Aline Chamber of Commerce
33 Heritage Rd.
Aline, OK 73716
Ph:(580)463-2563
Co. E-mail: heritage@pldi.net
URL: http://www.1aj.org
Contact: Carolyn Rexroat, Member

63938 ■ Allen Chamber of Commerce
PO Box 396
Allen, OK 74825
Ph:(580)857-2573
Co. E-mail: allennews@aol.com
Contact: Cindy Davis, Pres.

63939 ■ Altus Chamber of Commerce
123 W Commerce St., 5th Fl.
PO Box 518
Altus, OK 73522-0518
Ph:(580)482-0210
Fax: (580)482-0223
Co. E-mail: altuschamber@altuschamber.com
URL: http://www.altuschamber.com
Contact: Holley Urbanski, Pres.

63940 ■ Alva Area Chamber of Commerce
410 College Ave.
Alva, OK 73717
Ph:(580)327-1647
Free: 888-854-2262
Fax: (580)327-1648
Co. E-mail: chamber@alvaok.net
URL: http://www.alvaok.net
Contact: Alexandra Drenning, Dir.

63941 ■ Anadarko Chamber of Commerce
514 W Kentucky
PO Box 366
Anadarko, OK 73005
Ph:(405)247-6651
Fax: (405)247-6652
Co. E-mail: coc@anadarko.org
URL: http://www.anadarko.org
Contact: Cheryl Weaver, Exec.Dir.

63942 ■ Apache Chamber of Commerce
PO Box 461
Apache, OK 73006-0461
Ph:(580)588-3361
Contact: Roy Young, Pres.

63943 ■ Ardmore Chamber of Commerce
PO Box 1585
Ardmore, OK 73402
Ph:(580)223-7765
Fax: (580)223-7825
Co. E-mail: wstucky@ardmore.org
URL: http://www.ardmore.org
Contact: Wes Stucky, Pres./CEO

63944 ■ Arnett Chamber of Commerce
PO Box 415
Arnett, OK 73832
Ph:(580)885-7535
Co. E-mail: arnettchamber@pldi.net
URL: http://www.arnettchamber.com
Contact: Ms. Terri Shirley, Pres.

63945 ■ Atoka County Chamber of Commerce
PO Box 778
213 E Court St., Ste. 3
Atoka, OK 74525-0778
Ph:(580)889-2410
Fax: (580)889-2410
Co. E-mail: chambermanager@atokachamber.org
URL: http://www.atokachamber.org
Contact: Coby Sherrill, Pres.

63946 ■ Barnsdall Chamber of Commerce
PO Box 443
Barnsdall, OK 74002

Ph:(918)847-2916
Co. E-mail: byevans31@aol.com
Contact: Fred Williams, Pres.

63947 ■ Bartlesville Area Chamber of Commerce
PO Box 2366
Bartlesville, OK 74005
Ph:(918)336-8708
Fax: (918)337-0216
Co. E-mail: generalinfo@bartlesville.com
URL: http://www.bartlesville.com
Contact: Jim Fram, Pres./CEO

63948 ■ Beggs Chamber of Commerce
PO Box 270
Beggs, OK 74421-0270
Ph:(918)267-4329
Contact: Ms. Joy Gullic, Treas.

63949 ■ Billings Community Chamber of Commerce
PO Box 264
Billings, OK 74630
Ph:(580)725-3258
Fax: (580)725-3610
Contact: Mr. Kent Reubell, Pres.

63950 ■ Bixby Chamber of Commerce
113 W Dawes, Ste. 115
Bixby, OK 74008
Ph:(918)366-9445
Fax: (918)366-9443
Co. E-mail: info@bixbychamber.com
URL: http://www.bixbychamber.com
Contact: Deb Marshall, Exec.Dir.

63951 ■ Blackwell Chamber of Commerce
120 S Main
PO Box 230
Blackwell, OK 74631
Ph:(580)363-4195
Fax: (580)363-1704
Co. E-mail: blackwellchamber@4grc.com
URL: http://www.blackwellchamber.org
Contact: Rich Cantillon, Exec.Dir.

63952 ■ Boley Chamber of Commerce
PO Box 31
Boley, OK 74829-0031
Ph:(918)667-9790
Co. E-mail: chamber@boley-ok.com
URL: http://www.boley-ok.com
Contact: Chip Coleman, Pres.

63953 ■ Bristow Chamber of Commerce
One Railroad Place
PO Box 127
Bristow, OK 74010-0127
Ph:(918)367-5151
Fax: (918)367-5151
Co. E-mail: bristcc@galstar.com
Contact: June Hurst, Exec.Dir.

63954 ■ Broken Arrow Chamber of Commerce
123 N Main St.
Broken Arrow, OK 74012
Ph:(918)251-1518
Fax: (918)251-1777
Co. E-mail: info@brokenarrow.org
URL: http://www.brokenarrow.org
Contact: Ted Allison, Pres./CEO

63955 ■ Broken Bow Chamber of Commerce
113 W Martin Luther King Dr.
Broken Bow, OK 74728
Ph:(580)584-3393
Free: 800-528-7337
Fax: (580)584-7698
Co. E-mail: bchamber@pine-net.com
URL: http://www.brokenbowchamber.com
Contact: Charity O'Donnell, Dir.

63956 ■ Buffalo Chamber of Commerce
PO Box 521
Buffalo, OK 73834

Ph:(580)735-6177
Co. E-mail: buffalo@pldi.net
URL: http://www.pldi.net/~buffalo/chamber.html

63957 ■ Burns Flat Chamber of Commerce
500 N Holcomb
PO Box 68
Burns Flat, OK 73624
Ph:(580)562-4871
Fax: (580)562-3113
Co. E-mail: modaok@cottonball.com
URL: http://www.burnsflat-ok.com
Contact: Jerry Seglem, Pres.

63958 ■ Canton Chamber of Commerce
PO Box 307
Canton, OK 73724
Ph:(580)886-2216
Contact: Jenny Chapdelaine, Sec.

63959 ■ Carnegie Chamber of Commerce
PO Box 615
Carnegie, OK 73015
Ph:(580)654-2121
Contact: Kelly Williams, Pres.

63960 ■ Catoosa Chamber of Commerce
750 S Cherokee, Ste. J
PO Box 297
Catoosa, OK 74015-0297
Ph:(918)266-6042
Fax: (918)266-6314
Co. E-mail: catoosa@geotec.net
Contact: JoDawn Nelson, Exec.Dir.

63961 ■ Chandler Chamber of Commerce
804 Manvel
PO Box 561
Chandler, OK 74834
Ph:(405)258-0673
Fax: (405)258-0377
Co. E-mail: chandlerchamber@sbcglobal.net
URL: http://www.chandlerok.com
Contact: George Hicks, Pres.

63962 ■ Checotah Chamber of Commerce
201 N Broadway
Checotah, OK 74426-2431
Ph:(918)473-2070
Fax: (918)473-1453
Co. E-mail: checotahchamber@valornet.com
URL: http://www.checotah.com
Contact: Lloyd Jernigan, Exec.Dir.

63963 ■ Cherokee Chamber of Commerce
111 S Grand Ave.
Cherokee, OK 73728-1515
Ph:(580)596-3053
Fax: (580)596-2376
Co. E-mail: cherokee@akslc.net
URL: http://www.cherokeeoklahoma.net
Contact: Margaret Smith, Exec.Dir.

63964 ■ Cheyenne - Roger Mills Chamber of Commerce and Tourism
PO Box 57
Cheyenne, OK 73628
Ph:(580)497-3318
Free: 877-497-3318
Co. E-mail: cheyennecoc@yahoo.com
URL: http://www.cheyenneokchamber.com
Contact: Becki Seay, Pres.

63965 ■ Chickasha Chamber of Commerce
PO Box 1717
Chickasha, OK 73023-1717
Ph:(405)224-0787
Fax: (405)222-3730
Co. E-mail: mfeaver@chickashachamber.com
URL: http://www.chickashachamber.com
Contact: Marilyn Feaver, Pres.

63966 ■ Choctaw Chamber of Commerce
PO Box 1000
Choctaw, OK 73020
Ph:(405)390-3303
Co. E-mail: chocchamber@tds.net

URL: http://www.choctawcity.org
Contact: Rodney Albee, Pres.

63967 ■ Chouteau Chamber of Commerce
PO Box 332
Chouteau, OK 74337
Ph:(918)476-8222
Co. E-mail: chamber@chouteautel.com
URL: http://www.chouteauok.com
Contact: Mr. Marvis Ashmore, Pres.

63968 ■ Cimarron County Chamber of Commerce
PO Box 1027
Boise City, OK 73933
Ph:(580)544-3344
Fax: (580)544-3344
Co. E-mail: cccc@ptsi.net
URL: http://www.ccccok.org
Contact: Delayne Schwindt, Pres.

63969 ■ City of Oilton Council
PO Box 400
Oilton, OK 74052
Ph:(918)862-3202
Contact: Clyde Humble, Mayor

63970 ■ Claremore Chamber of Commerce
419 W Will Rogers Blvd.
Claremore, OK 74017-6820
Ph:(918)341-2818
Fax: (918)342-0663
Co. E-mail: chamber@claremore.org
URL: http://www.claremore.org
Contact: Tanya Andrews, Exec.Dir.

63971 ■ Cleveland Area Chamber of Commerce
PO Box 240
120 N Broadway St.
Cleveland, OK 74020
Ph:(918)358-2131
Fax: (918)358-5710
Co. E-mail: info@chamberofcleveland.com
URL: http://www.chamberofcleveland.com
Contact: Diana Tilley-Esparza, Exec. Dir.

63972 ■ Clinton Chamber of Commerce
101 S 4th St.
Clinton, OK 73601
Ph:(580)323-2222
Fax: (580)323-2931
Co. E-mail: chamber@clintonok.org
URL: http://www.clintonok.org
Contact: Erin Adams, Pres.

63973 ■ Coal County Chamber of Commerce
PO Box 323
Coalgate, OK 74538
Ph:(580)927-2119
Contact: Ms. Starla Gold, Pres.

63974 ■ Collinsville Chamber of Commerce
PO Box 245
Collinsville, OK 74021
Ph:(918)371-4703
Co. E-mail: info@collinsvillechamber.net
URL: http://www.collinsvillechamber.net
Contact: James Dugger, Pres.

63975 ■ Comanche Chamber of Commerce
PO Box 603
Comanche, OK 73529
Ph:(580)439-6662
Contact: Ron Goetz, Pres.

63976 ■ Cordell Chamber of Commerce
116 S College
Cordell, OK 73632-4823
Ph:(580)832-3538
Free: 888-COR-DELL
Fax: (580)832-5432
Co. E-mail: chamberqueen_2000@yahoo.com
Contact: Claudia "Kristy" Gray, Exec.Sec.

63977 ■ Coweta Chamber of Commerce
117 S Broadway
PO Box 70
Coweta, OK 74429

Ph:(918)486-2513
Fax: (918)279-0829
Co. E-mail: cowetachamber@juno.com
URL: http://www.cowetaok.com/chamber
Contact: Pam Foster, Pres.

63978 ■ Crescent Chamber of Commerce
PO Box 333
Crescent, OK 73028
Ph:(405)969-3773
Contact: Debbie Blades, Pres.

63979 ■ Cushing Chamber of Commerce and Industry
1301 E Main
Cushing, OK 74023
Ph:(918)225-2400
Fax: (918)225-2903
Co. E-mail: psmith@cushingchamber.org
URL: http://www.cushingchamber.org
Contact: Priscilla E. Smith, Exec.Dir.

63980 ■ Davenport Chamber of Commerce
PO Box 66
Davenport, OK 74026
Ph:(918)377-2241
Fax: (918)377-2506
Co. E-mail: davenportcoc@brightok.net
URL: http://www.davenportok.org

63981 ■ Davis Chamber of Commerce
PO Box 5
Davis, OK 73030-0005
Ph:(580)369-2402
Fax: (580)369-3719
Co. E-mail: daviscoc@brightok.net
URL: http://www.davisok.org
Contact: Brad Black, Dir.

63982 ■ Dill City Chamber of Commerce
PO Box 37
Dill City, OK 73641
Ph:(580)674-3376
Contact: Paul Hausbeck, Pres.

63983 ■ Drumright Chamber of Commerce
PO Box 828
Drumright, OK 74030
Ph:(918)352-2204
Fax: (918)352-2065
URL: http://www.drumright.net/chamber.htm
Contact: Michael Davis, Pres.

63984 ■ Duke Chamber of Commerce
PO Box 214
Duke, OK 73532
Ph:(580)679-3345
Co. E-mail: dukechamber@swoi.net
URL: http://www.dukeok.com
Contact: Alan Womack, Pres.

63985 ■ Duncan Chamber of Commerce and Industry
PO Box 699
Duncan, OK 73534
Ph:(580)255-3644
Fax: (580)255-6482
Co. E-mail: duncancc@texhoma.net
URL: http://www.duncanchamber.com
Contact: Carole Scott, Pres.

63986 ■ Edmond Area Chamber of Commerce
825 E 2nd St., Ste. 100
Edmond, OK 73034
Ph:(405)341-2808
Fax: (405)340-5512
Co. E-mail: info@edmondchamber.com
URL: http://www.edmondchamber.com
Contact: Hardy Watkins, Pres.

63987 ■ El Reno Chamber of Commerce and Development Corporation
206 N Bickford
PO Box 67
El Reno, OK 73036
Ph:(405)262-1188

Fax: (405)262-1189
Co. E-mail: elrenochamber@swbell.net
URL: http://www.elrenochamber.com
Contact: Karen Nix, Exec.Dir.

63988 ■ Elk City Chamber of Commerce
PO Box 972
Elk City, OK 73648
Ph:(580)225-0207
Free: 800-280-0207
Co. E-mail: elkcitychamber@itlnet.net
URL: http://www.elkcitychamber.com
Contact: Jeff Waters, Pres.

63989 ■ Erick Chamber of Commerce
PO Box 1232
Erick, OK 73645-1232
Ph:(580)526-3505
Fax: (580)526-3331
URL: http://www.erickchamber.com
Contact: Cindy Tennery, Pres.

63990 ■ Eufaula Area Chamber of Commerce
PO Box 738
Eufaula, OK 74432
Ph:(918)689-2791
Fax: (918)689-3046
Co. E-mail: chamber@eufaulachamberofcommerce.com
URL: http://www.eufaulachamberofcommerce.com
Contact: Sally Ashby, Dir.

63991 ■ Fairview Chamber of Commerce
206 E Broadway
PO Box 180
Fairview, OK 73737-0180
Ph:(580)227-2527
Fax: (580)227-2258
Co. E-mail: fairviewchamber@io2online.com
URL: http://www.fairviewokchamber.com
Contact: Rex Sproul, Exec.Dir.

63992 ■ Fort Cobb Chamber of Commerce
PO Box 100
Fort Cobb, OK 73038
Ph:(405)643-9933
Contact: Mike Sebastian, Pres.

63993 ■ Fort Gibson Chamber of Commerce
PO Box 730
Fort Gibson, OK 74434
Ph:(918)478-4780
Fax: (918)478-2522
Co. E-mail: fortgibson@sbcglobal.net
URL: http://www.fortgibson.com
Contact: Shirley Flaska, Exec.Dir.

63994 ■ Frederick Chamber of Commerce and Industry
105 S Main St.
Frederick, OK 73542
Ph:(580)335-2126
Fax: (580)335-3767
Co. E-mail: frederickcc@pldi.net
URL: http://www.frederickokchamber.org
Contact: Al Allee, Pres.

63995 ■ Freedom Chamber of Commerce
PO Box 125
Freedom, OK 73842-0125
Ph:(580)621-3276
Fax: (580)621-3275
Co. E-mail: freedomchamberofcommerce@yahoo.com
URL: http://www.freedomokla.com/aboutus.htm
Contact: Rocky Hodgson, Pres.

63996 ■ Gage Chamber of Commerce
PO Box 328
Gage, OK 73843
Ph:(580)923-7727
Fax: (580)923-7777
Contact: Ferrall Barnes, Pres.

63997 ■ Garber Area Community Improvement Association
PO Box 574
Garber, OK 73738

Ph:(580)863-2281
Contact: Fred Johnson, Pres.

63998 ■ Geary Chamber of Commerce
PO Box 273
Geary, OK 73040-0273
Ph:(405)884-2765
URL: http://www.gearyok.com
Contact: Melba Nance, Sec.

63999 ■ Glenpool Chamber of Commerce
494 E 141st St.
PO Box 767
Glenpool, OK 74033-0767
Ph:(918)322-3505
Fax: (918)322-3505
Co. E-mail: glenpoolchamber@yahoo.com
Contact: Carol Campbell, Exec.Dir.

64000 ■ Greater Enid Chamber of Commerce
210 Kenwood Blvd.
PO Box 907
Enid, OK 73702
Ph:(580)237-2494
Free: 888-229-2443
Fax: (580)237-2497
Co. E-mail: penny@enidchamber.com
URL: http://www.enidchamber.com
Contact: Jon Blankenship, CEO/Pres.

64001 ■ Greater Muskogee Area Chamber of Commerce
PO Box 797
Muskogee, OK 74402
Ph:(918)682-2401
Fax: (918)682-2403
Co. E-mail: info@muskogeechamber.org
URL: http://www.muskogeechamber.org
Contact: Sue Harris, Pres.

64002 ■ Greater Oklahoma City Chamber of Commerce
123 Park Ave.
Oklahoma City, OK 73102
Ph:(405)297-8900
Fax: (405)297-8916
Co. E-mail: info@okcchamber.com
URL: http://www.okcchamber.com
Contact: Roy Williams, Pres./CEO

64003 ■ Greater Shawnee Area Chamber of Commerce
131 N Bell
PO Box 1613
Shawnee, OK 74802-1613
Ph:(405)273-6092
Fax: (405)275-9851
Co. E-mail: info@shawneechamber.com
URL: http://www.shawneechamber.com
Contact: Nancy Sloan-Keith, Pres./CEO

64004 ■ Grove Area Chamber of Commerce
9630 Hwy. 59 N, Ste. A
Grove, OK 74344
Ph:(918)786-9079
Fax: (918)786-2909
Co. E-mail: gacc@groveok.org
URL: http://www.groveok.org
Contact: Lisa Friden, Pres.

64005 ■ Guthrie Chamber of Commerce
212 W Oklahoma Ave.
Guthrie, OK 73044
Ph:(405)282-1947
Free: 800-299-1889
Fax: (405)282-0061
URL: http://www.guthrieok.com

64006 ■ Guymon Chamber of Commerce
RR 5, Box 120
Guymon, OK 73942
Ph:(580)338-3376
Fax: (580)338-0014
Co. E-mail: chamber@ptsi.net
Contact: Trina Moser, Admin.Asst.

64007 ■ Harmon County Chamber of Commerce
PO Box 566
Hollis, OK 73550-0566
Ph:(580)688-2419
Fax: (580)688-2419
Contact: Michael Moore, Pres.

64008 ■ Hartshorne Chamber of Commerce
PO Box 343
Hartshorne, OK 74547
Ph:(918)297-2131
Co. E-mail: info@cityofhartshorneok.com
URL: http://www.cityofhartshorneok.com
Contact: Nancy Dromgold, Pres.

64009 ■ Haskell Chamber of Commerce
PO Box 252
Haskell, OK 74436
Ph:(918)482-1245
Co. E-mail: info@haskellchamber.com
URL: http://www.haskellchamber.com
Contact: Wayne Stephens, Administrator

64010 ■ Healdton Chamber of Commerce
315 E Main St.
Healdton, OK 73438
Ph:(580)229-0900
Fax: (580)229-0900
URL: http://chamberrocket.com
Contact: Ms. Dana Gossvener, Pres.

64011 ■ Heavener Chamber of Commerce
501 W 1st St.
Heavener, OK 74937
Ph:(918)653-4303
Fax: (918)653-2438
Co. E-mail: heavenercofc@leflorecounty.com
Contact: Vanessa Richie, Exec.Dir.

64012 ■ Henryetta Chamber of Commerce
115 S 4th St.
Henryetta, OK 74437-5272
Ph:(918)652-3331
Fax: (918)652-3332
Co. E-mail: chamber@henryetta.org
URL: http://www.henryetta.org
Contact: Bette Davidson, Exec.Dir.

64013 ■ Hinton Chamber of Commerce
PO Box 519
Hinton, OK 73047
Ph:(405)542-6428
Fax: (405)542-3973
URL: http://www.hintonok.com
Contact: Eldon McComber, Pres.

64014 ■ Hobart Chamber of Commerce
106 W 4th
Hobart, OK 73651
Ph:(580)726-2553
Fax: (580)726-2553
Co. E-mail: hobart_chamber@itlnet.net
URL: http://www.hobartchamberofcommerce.com
Contact: Stephan Boyd, Dir.

64015 ■ Holdenville Chamber of Commerce
PO Box 70
Holdenville, OK 74848
Ph:(405)379-6675
Fax: (405)379-5942
Co. E-mail: holdenvillecofc@okplus.com
URL: http://www.angelfire.com/ok5/
   chamberofcommerce
Contact: Jamie Caudill, Exec.Dir.

64016 ■ Hominy Chamber of Commerce
PO Box 99
Hominy, OK 74035
Ph:(918)885-4939
Co. E-mail: chamber@hominy.lib.ok.us
URL: http://www.hominy.lib.ok.us/commerce/index.
   htm
Contact: Mark Suiter, Pres.

64017 ■ Hooker Chamber of Commerce
PO Box 989
Hooker, OK 73945-0989

Ph:(580)652-2809
Contact: Rowdy McBee, Pres.

64018 ■ Hugo Chamber of Commerce
200 S Broadway
Hugo, OK 74743
Ph:(580)326-7511
Fax: (580)326-7512
Co. E-mail: hugo-chamber@sbcglobal.net
Contact: Judy Wilson, Exec.Dir.

64019 ■ Idabel Chamber of Commerce and Agriculture
7 SW Texas
Idabel, OK 74745
Ph:(580)286-3305
Fax: (580)286-6708
Co. E-mail: jilian@idabelchamber.com
URL: http://www.idabelchamber.com
Contact: Mark Ezell, Mgr.

64020 ■ Jay Chamber of Commerce
PO Box 806
Jay, OK 74346
Ph:(918)253-8698
Contact: Mr. Johnnie Earp, Pres.

64021 ■ Jenks Chamber of Commerce
224 E A St.
PO Box 902
Jenks, OK 74037
Ph:(918)299-5005
Fax: (918)299-5799
Co. E-mail: info@jenkschamber.com
URL: http://www.jenkschamber.com
Contact: Ruth Littlefield, Exec.Dir.

64022 ■ Johnston County Chamber of Commerce
106 W Main
Tishomingo, OK 73460
Ph:(580)371-2175
Fax: (580)371-2175
Co. E-mail: jcchamber@simplynet.net
Contact: W. Sue Robins, Exec.Dir.

64023 ■ Kingfisher Chamber of Commerce
123 W Miles
Kingfisher, OK 73750
Ph:(405)375-4445
Fax: (405)375-5304
Co. E-mail: chamber@pldi.net
URL: http://www.kingfisher.org
Contact: Vicki Rother, Pres.

64024 ■ Konawa Chamber of Commerce
PO Box 112
Konawa, OK 74849
Ph:(580)925-3220
Contact: Daniel Khoury Sr., Treas.

64025 ■ Laverne Area Chamber of Commerce
PO Box 634
Laverne, OK 73848
Ph:(580)921-3612
Co. E-mail: lvrnokcc@ptsi.net
URL: http://www.laverneok.org

64026 ■ Lawton - Fort Sill Chamber of Commerce and Industry
629 SW C Ave.
PO Box 1376
Lawton, OK 73502-1376
Ph:(580)355-3541
Free: 800-872-4540
Fax: (580)357-3642
Co. E-mail: info@lawtonfortsillchamber.com
URL: http://www.lawtonfortsillchamber.com
Contact: Mike Austin, Pres./CEO

64027 ■ Lindsay Chamber of Commerce
107 N Main St.
PO Box 504
Lindsay, OK 73052
Ph:(405)756-4312
Fax: (405)756-8657

Co. E-mail: lchamber@telepath.com
URL: http://www.angelfire.com/biz/lindsayok
Contact: Paula Barker, Mgr.

64028 ■ Love County Chamber of Commerce
PO Box 422
Marietta, OK 73448
Ph:(580)276-3102
Co. E-mail: lovecountychamber@yahoo.com
URL: http://www.lovecountyokla.org
Contact: Brent Hartin, Pres.

64029 ■ Mannford Chamber of Commerce
PO Box 487
Mannford, OK 74044
Ph:(918)865-2000
Fax: (918)865-8272
Contact: Don Engle, Pres.

64030 ■ Marlow Chamber of Commerce
223 W Main
Marlow, OK 73055-2439
Ph:(580)658-2212
Fax: (580)658-6565
Co. E-mail: marlowchamber@starcomm.net
URL: http://www.marlowchamber.org
Contact: Debbe Ridley, Mgr.

64031 ■ Marshall County Chamber of Commerce
PO Box 542
Madill, OK 73446
Ph:(580)795-2431
Fax: (580)795-5870
Co. E-mail: info@mccoconline.org
Contact: Greg Snider, Pres.

64032 ■ Maysville Chamber of Commerce
PO Box 313
Maysville, OK 73057
Ph:(405)867-4457
Contact: Kenneth Wood, Pres.

64033 ■ McAlester Area Chamber of Commerce and Agriculture
10 S 3rd St.
PO Box 759
McAlester, OK 74502
Ph:(918)423-2550
Fax: (918)423-1345
Co. E-mail: info@mcalester.org
URL: http://www.mcalester.org
Contact: Mary Melfenbein, Exec. VP

64034 ■ Mcloud Chamber of Commerce
PO Box 254
Mcloud, OK 74851
Ph:(405)964-6566
Fax: (405)964-6566
Co. E-mail: mcloudchambermenews@aol.com
Contact: Lisa Groff, Pres.

64035 ■ Medford Chamber of Commerce
PO Box 123
Medford, OK 73759
Ph:(580)395-2875
Contact: Wes Christenson, Pres.

64036 ■ Miami Chamber of Commerce
PO Box 760
Miami, OK 74355
Ph:(918)542-4481
Fax: (918)540-1260
Co. E-mail: info@miamiokchamber.com
URL: http://www.miamiokchamber.com
Contact: Jennifer Smalley, Exec.Dir.

64037 ■ Midwest City Chamber of Commerce
PO Box 10980
5905 Trosper Rd.
Midwest City, OK 73110
Ph:(405)733-3801
Fax: (405)733-5633
Co. E-mail: information@midwestcityok.com
URL: http://www.midwestcityok.com
Contact: Bonnie Cheatwood, Exec.Dir.

64038 ■ Midwest City Chamber of Commerce Foundation for Progress
PO Box 10980
Midwest City, OK 73140-1980
Ph:(405)733-3801
Fax: (405)733-5633
Co. E-mail: information@midwestcityok.com
URL: http://www.midwestcityok.com
Contact: Bonnie Cheatwood, Exec.Dir.

64039 ■ Minco Chamber of Commerce
PO Box 451
Minco, OK 73059
Ph:(405)352-4382
Contact: John Hacker, Pres.

64040 ■ Moore Chamber of Commerce
105 Industrial Blvd.
Moore, OK 73160
Ph:(405)794-3400
Fax: (405)794-8555
Co. E-mail: brendar@moorechamber.com
URL: http://www.moorechamber.com
Contact: Brenda Roberts, Exec.Dir.

64041 ■ Mountain View Chamber of Commerce
PO Box 398
Mountain View, OK 73062
Ph:(580)347-2711
Contact: Wayne Askew, Pres.

64042 ■ Mustang Area Chamber of Commerce
PO Box 213
Mustang, OK 73064-0213
Ph:(405)376-2758
Fax: (405)376-4764
Co. E-mail: info@mustangchamber.com
URL: http://www.mustangchamber.com
Contact: Becky Julian, Exec.Dir.

64043 ■ Newcastle Chamber of Commerce
5 N Main
PO Box 1006
Newcastle, OK 73065
Ph:(405)387-3232
Fax: (405)387-3885
Co. E-mail: ncc@oecadvantage.net
Contact: Mona Brite, Exec.Dir.

64044 ■ Newkirk Chamber of Commerce
104 W 7th St.
Newkirk, OK 74647-4012
Ph:(580)362-2155
Fax: (580)362-3774
Co. E-mail: newkirkcofc@hotmail.com
URL: http://cityofnewkirk.com
Contact: Earlene Lane, Sec.

64045 ■ Nicoma Park Chamber of Commerce
PO Box 4520
Nicoma Park, OK 73066-4520
Ph:(405)769-6635
Fax: (405)769-5679
Co. E-mail: npccbud@swbell.net
Contact: Bud Green, Exec.VP

64046 ■ Noble Chamber of Commerce
118 S Main
PO Box 678
Noble, OK 73068
Ph:(405)872-5535
Fax: (405)872-2020
Co. E-mail: ncc@us.inter.net
Contact: Melissa Thompson, Exec.Dir.

64047 ■ Norman Chamber of Commerce
115 E Gray
Norman, OK 73070
Ph:(405)321-7260
Fax: (405)360-4679
Co. E-mail: normanchamber@normanchamber.com
URL: http://www.normanok.org
Contact: Anna-Mary Suggs, Exec. Dir.

64048 ■ Northwest Chamber of Commerce
7440 NW 39th Expy.
Bethany, OK 73008
Ph:(405)789-1256
Fax: (405)789-2478
Co. E-mail: thenorthwestchamber@coxinet.net
URL: http://thenorthwestchamber.com
Contact: Wally Key, Pres./CEO

64049 ■ Nowata Area Chamber of Commerce
PO Box 202
Nowata, OK 74048-0202
Ph:(918)273-2301
Fax: (918)273-0190
Co. E-mail: nowatachamber@sbcglobal.net
URL: http://www.nowatachamber.com
Contact: Mrs. Eunice Stell, Exec.Dir.

64050 ■ Okeene Chamber of Commerce
116 W E St.
PO Box 704
Okeene, OK 73763
Ph:(580)822-3005
Fax: (580)822-3008
Co. E-mail: okchamber@pldi.net
URL: http://www.okeene.com
Contact: Becky Bedwell, Exec.Dir.

64051 ■ Okemah Chamber of Commerce
208 W Broadway
Okemah, OK 74859
Ph:(918)623-2440
URL: http://www.okemah.org
Contact: Maxey Reilly, Pres.

64052 ■ Okmulgee Chamber of Commerce
112 N Morton
Okmulgee, OK 74447
Ph:(918)756-6172
Fax: (918)756-6441
Co. E-mail: okmulgeechamber@ocevnet.org
Contact: Dale Young, Dir.

64053 ■ Oologah Area Chamber of Commerce
PO Box 109
Oologah, OK 74053
Ph:(918)443-2790
Fax: (918)443-2790
Co. E-mail: chamber@oologah.org
URL: http://www.oologah.net
Contact: John Wylie, Pres.

64054 ■ Owasso Chamber of Commerce
315 S Cedar
Owasso, OK 74055
Ph:(918)272-2141
Fax: (918)272-8564
Co. E-mail: fayrene@owassochamber.com
URL: http://www.owassochamber.com
Contact: Fayrene Akin, Office Mgr.

64055 ■ Pauls Valley Chamber of Commerce
112 E Paul St.
Drawer 638
Pauls Valley, OK 73075
Ph:(405)238-6491
Fax: (405)238-2553
Co. E-mail: pvchamber@sbcglobal.net
URL: http://www.paulsvalley.com
Contact: Mr. Karl Burkhardt, Exec.Dir.

64056 ■ Pawhuska Chamber of Commerce
520 Lynn Ave.
Pawhuska, OK 74056
Ph:(918)287-1208
Fax: (918)287-3159
Co. E-mail: pawhuskachamber@sbcglobal.net
URL: http://www.pawhuskachamber.com
Contact: Ms. Dia Doughty, Exec.Dir.

64057 ■ Pawnee Community Chamber of Commerce
608 Harrison St.
Pawnee, OK 74058
Ph:(918)762-2108
Fax: (918)762-2108

Co. E-mail: pawneechamber@cowboy.net
URL: http://www.cityofpawnee.com
Contact: Bill Gosnell, Sec./Mgr.

64058 ■ Perkins Chamber of Commerce
PO Box 502
Perkins, OK 74059
Ph:(405)747-6809
Co. E-mail: info@perkinschamber.com
URL: http://www.perkinscc.com
Contact: Darla Woody, Pres.

64059 ■ Perry Chamber of Commerce
300 6th St.
PO Box 426
Perry, OK 73077
Ph:(580)336-4684
Fax: (580)336-3522
Co. E-mail: chamber@fullnet.net
URL: http://www.perryok.org
Contact: Carolyn Briegge, Exec.Dir.

64060 ■ Piedmont Chamber of Commerce
PO Box 501
Piedmont, OK 73078-0501
Ph:(405)373-2234
Co. E-mail: rogerpugh@sbcglobal.net
URL: http://www.piedmontokchamber.org
Contact: Roger Pugh, Pres.

64061 ■ Ponca City Area Chamber of Commerce
420 E Grand
PO Box 1109
Ponca City, OK 74602-1109
Ph:(580)765-4400
Fax: (580)765-2798
Co. E-mail: staff@poncacitychamber.com
URL: http://www.poncacitychamber.com
Contact: Rich Cantillon, Pres./CEO

64062 ■ Pond Creek Chamber of Commerce
PO Box 88
Pond Creek, OK 73766-0088
Ph:(580)532-6468
Contact: Mike Shaffer, Pres.

64063 ■ Poteau Chamber of Commerce
201 S Broadway
Poteau, OK 74953
Ph:(918)647-9178
Fax: (918)647-4099
Co. E-mail: poteaucofc@clnk.com
URL: http://www.poteau.org
Contact: Bonnie Prigmore, Exec.Dir.

64064 ■ Prague Chamber of Commerce
1023 Jim Thorpe Blvd.
PO Box 111
Prague, OK 74864
Ph:(405)567-2616
Fax: (405)567-2616
Co. E-mail: info@pragueok.org
URL: http://www.pragueok.org
Contact: Vicki Pfeiff, Pres.

64065 ■ Pryor Area Chamber of Commerce
100 E Graham Ave.
PO Box 367
Pryor, OK 74362-0367
Ph:(918)825-0157
Fax: (918)825-0158
Co. E-mail: info@pryorok.com
URL: http://pryorok.com
Contact: Pat Lane, Chair

64066 ■ Purcell Chamber of Commerce
302 W Main, Ste. 106
Purcell, OK 73080
Ph:(405)527-3093
Fax: (405)527-6331
Co. E-mail: purcellchamber@classicnet.net
URL: http://www.purcellchamber.com
Contact: Linda Clark, Exec.Dir.

64067 ■ Pushmataha County Chamber of Commerce
212 N High St.
Antlers, OK 74523
Ph:(580)298-2488
Free: 877-770-4438
Fax: (580)298-3641
Co. E-mail: ccpush@sbcglobal.net
Contact: Lisa Colley, Exec.Dir.

64068 ■ Sallisaw Chamber of Commerce
PO Box 251
Sallisaw, OK 74955-0251
Ph:(918)775-2558
Fax: (918)775-4021
Co. E-mail: sallisawchamber@yahoo.com
URL: http://www.sallisawchamber.com
Contact: Mrs. Judy Martens, Exec.VP

64069 ■ Sand Springs Area Chamber of Commerce
121 N Main St.
Sand Springs, OK 74063
Ph:(918)245-3221
Fax: (918)245-2530
Co. E-mail: info@sandspringschamber.com
URL: http://www.sandspringschamber.com
Contact: Mr. J.C. Kinder Jr., Pres.

64070 ■ Sapulpa Area Chamber of Commerce
101 E Dewey
Sapulpa, OK 74066
Ph:(918)224-0170
Fax: (918)224-0172
Co. E-mail: betty@sapulpachamber.com
URL: http://www.sapulpachamber.com
Contact: Betty Calley, Exec.Dir.

64071 ■ Sayre Chamber of Commerce
PO Box 474
Sayre, OK 73662
Ph:(580)928-3386
Co. E-mail: sayrechamber@itlnet.net
URL: http://www.sayreok.com
Contact: Nancy Sanders, Dir.

64072 ■ Seiling Chamber of Commerce
PO Box 725
Seiling, OK 73663
Ph:(580)922-4922
Contact: Gale Childs, Pres.

64073 ■ Seminole Chamber of Commerce
326 E Evans
PO Box 1190
Seminole, OK 74818-1190
Ph:(405)382-3640
Fax: (405)382-3529
Co. E-mail: info@seminoleokchamber.org
URL: http://seminoleokchamber.org
Contact: Mark Schell, Pres.

64074 ■ Sentinel Chamber of Commerce
PO Box 131
Sentinel, OK 73664-0131
Ph:(580)393-4380
Contact: Barbara Brewer, Pres.

64075 ■ Shattuck Chamber of Commerce
115 S Main
PO Box 400
Shattuck, OK 73858-0400
Ph:(580)938-2818
Fax: (580)938-2852
Co. E-mail: shattuckcc@pldi.net
URL: http://www.shattuckchamber.com
Contact: Tonja Jones, Exec.Dir.

64076 ■ Skiatook Chamber of Commerce
PO Box 272
Skiatook, OK 74070-0272
Ph:(918)396-3702
Fax: (918)396-3577
Co. E-mail: info@skiatookchamber.com
URL: http://www.skiatookchamber.com
Contact: Stephanie Upton, Exec.Dir.

64077 ■ South Grand Lake Area Chamber of Commerce
PO Box 215
Langley, OK 74350
Ph:(918)782-3214
Fax: (918)782-3215
Co. E-mail: director@grandlakechamber.org
URL: http://www.grandlakechamber.org
Contact: Becky Fields, Dir.

64078 ■ South Oklahoma City Chamber of Commerce
701 SW 74th St.
Oklahoma City, OK 73139-4599
Ph:(405)634-1436
Fax: (405)634-1462
Co. E-mail: info@southokc.com
URL: http://www.southokc.com
Contact: Elaine Lyons, Pres./CEO

64079 ■ Spiro Area Chamber of Commerce
210 S Main St.
Spiro, OK 74959
Ph:(918)962-3816
Fax: (918)962-3816
Co. E-mail: spirocc@sbcglobal.net
URL: http://www.myspiro.com
Contact: Dennis Peterson, Pres.

64080 ■ State Chamber - Oklahoma's Association of Business and Industry
330 NE 10th St.
Oklahoma City, OK 73104-3220
Ph:(405)235-3669
Fax: (405)235-3670
Co. E-mail: info@okstatechamber.com
URL: http://www.okstatechamber.com
Contact: Richard P. Rush CCE, CEO/Pres.

64081 ■ Stigler - Haskell County Chamber of Commerce
204 E Main St.
PO Box 482
Stigler, OK 74462
Ph:(918)967-8681
Fax: (918)967-4319
Co. E-mail: chamber@cwis.net
Contact: Margaret Johnson, Exec.Dir.

64082 ■ Stillwater Chamber of Commerce
PO Box 1687
Stillwater, OK 74074-1687
Ph:(405)372-5573
Fax: (405)372-4316
Co. E-mail: info@stillwaterchamber.org
URL: http://stillwaterchamber.org
Contact: John Fowler, CEO

64083 ■ Stilwell Area Chamber of Commerce
1 S Hwy. 59
Stilwell, OK 74960
Ph:(918)696-7845
Co. E-mail: achandga@alltel.com
Contact: Elizabeth Brown, Pres.

64084 ■ Stratford Chamber of Commerce
PO Box 491
Stratford, OK 74872-0491
Ph:(580)759-2977
Contact: Bill Wooten, Pres.

64085 ■ Stroud Chamber of Commerce
216 W Main
Stroud, OK 74079
Ph:(918)968-4043
Fax: (918)968-0599
Co. E-mail: stroudch@brightok.net
URL: http://www.stroudok.com
Contact: Sandy Jones

64086 ■ Sulphur Chamber of Commerce
717 W Broadway
Sulphur, OK 73086
Ph:(580)622-2824
Fax: (580)622-4217
Co. E-mail: sulphur@brightok.net
URL: http://www.sulphurokla.com

Contact: Chance Freeman, Pres.

64087 ■ Tahlequah Area Chamber of Commerce and Tourism Council
123 E Delaware St.
Tahlequah, OK 74464
Ph:(918)456-3742
Fax: (918)456-3751
Co. E-mail: tahlequahchamber@swbell.net
URL: http://tahlequahchamber.com
Contact: David Moore, Exec.Dir.

64088 ■ Talihina Chamber of Commerce
900 2nd St. No. 12
Talihina, OK 74571
Ph:(918)567-3434
Fax: (918)567-3388
Co. E-mail: chamber@talihinacc.com
URL: http://www.talihinacc.com

64089 ■ Tecumseh Chamber of Commerce
114 N Broadway St.
Tecumseh, OK 74873-3226
Ph:(405)598-8666
Fax: (405)598-6760
Co. E-mail: chamber@tecumsehok.com
URL: http://www.tecumsehok.com
Contact: Laureen O. Snyder, Exec.Dir.

64090 ■ Temple Chamber of Commerce
PO Box 618
Temple, OK 73568-0618
Ph:(580)342-6288
Fax: (580)342-6898
Contact: Nina Bruce, Pres.

64091 ■ Thomas Chamber of Commerce
122 W Broadway
PO Box 250
Thomas, OK 73669-0250
Ph:(580)661-3685
Fax: (580)661-3689
Co. E-mail: thomasacoc@pidi.net
Contact: Vicki Litsch, Exec.VP

64092 ■ Tipton Chamber of Commerce
PO Box 403
Tipton, OK 73570
Ph:(580)667-5268
Contact: Patsy Blair, Sec.

64093 ■ Tonkawa Chamber of Commerce
100 E Grand, Ste. A
Tonkawa, OK 74653
Ph:(580)628-2220
Fax: (580)628-2221
Co. E-mail: tonkawacofc@kskc.net
URL: http://www.tonkawa.net
Contact: Cristy Crumrine, Sec.

64094 ■ Tulsa Metro Chamber
Williams Ctr. Tower II
2 W 2nd St., Ste. 150
Tulsa, OK 74103
Ph:(918)585-1201
Fax: (918)585-8016
Co. E-mail: webmaster@tulsachamber.com
URL: http://www.tulsachamber.com
Contact: Jay Clemens, Pres./CEO

64095 ■ Vinita Area Chamber of Commerce
125 S Scraper
PO Box 882
Vinita, OK 74301
Ph:(918)256-7133
Fax: (918)256-8261
Co. E-mail: chamber@vinita.com
URL: http://www.vinita.com
Contact: Ms. Jennifer Shaffer, Exec. Dir.

64096 ■ Wagoner Area Chamber of Commerce
301 S Grant
Wagoner, OK 74467-4908
Ph:(918)485-3414
Fax: (918)485-2523
Co. E-mail: chamber@cityofwagoner.com

URL: http://www.cityofwagoner.com
Contact: Donna McGaha Boyd, Ofc.Mgr.

64097 ■ Walters Chamber of Commerce
116 N Broadway
PO Box 352
Walters, OK 73572
Ph:(580)875-3335
Fax: (580)875-3600
Contact: Levera Thompson, Sec.

64098 ■ Warner Chamber of Commerce
PO Box 190
Warner, OK 74469
Ph:(918)463-6240
Fax: (918)463-2696
Contact: Roger Thomason, Pres.

64099 ■ Watonga Chamber of Commerce
PO Box 537
Watonga, OK 73772-0537
Ph:(580)623-5452
Fax: (580)623-5444
Co. E-mail: cwatonga@pldi.net
URL: http://www.watonga.com/chamber/index.htm
Contact: Meradith Norris, Exec.Dir.

64100 ■ Waurika Chamber of Commerce
120 W Broadway
PO Box 366
Waurika, OK 73573
Ph:(580)228-2081
Co. E-mail: chamber1@waurika.net
Contact: Sandy Dudley, Pres.

64101 ■ Waynoka Chamber of Commerce
PO Box 173
Waynoka, OK 73860
Ph:(580)824-4741
Co. E-mail: jmcole@nwosu.edu
URL: http://www.waynokachamber.com
Contact: Doug Haltom, Pres.

64102 ■ Weatherford Area Chamber of Commerce
PO Box 857
Weatherford, OK 73096
Ph:(580)772-7744
Free: 800-725-7744
Fax: (580)772-7751
Co. E-mail: welcome@weatherfordchamber.com
URL: http://www.weatherfordchamber.com
Contact: Mike Stokes, Exec.Dir.

64103 ■ Wellston Chamber of Commerce
PO Box 188
Wellston, OK 74881
Ph:(405)356-2477
Contact: Jerry Key, Pres.

64104 ■ Wetumka Chamber of Commerce
202 N Main St.
Wetumka, OK 74883
Ph:(405)452-3237
Contact: Vernon Stout, Mgr.

64105 ■ Wewoka Chamber of Commerce
101 W Park
PO Box 719
Wewoka, OK 74884
Ph:(405)257-5485
Fax: (405)257-2662
Co. E-mail: wewokachamber@sbcglobal.net
URL: http://www.wewoka.com
Contact: Dusti Parks, Dir.

64106 ■ Wilburton Chamber of Commerce
302 W Main St.
Wilburton, OK 74578
Ph:(918)465-2759
Co. E-mail: info@wilburton.ok.us
URL: http://www.wilburton.ok.us
Contact: Robert O. Bain, Chm.

64107 ■ Woodward Chamber of Commerce
PO Box 1026
1006 Oklahoma Ave.
Woodward, OK 73802

Ph:(580)256-7411
Free: 800-364-5352
Fax: (580)254-3585
Co. E-mail: wwchamber@sbcglobal.net
URL: http://www.woodwardchamber.com
Contact: C.J. Montgomery, Pres.

64108 ■ Wynnewood Chamber of Commerce
PO Box 616
Wynnewood, OK 73098-0616
Ph:(405)665-4466
Fax: (405)665-4466
Co. E-mail: wynnewoodokla@sbcglobal.net
URL: http://www.wynnewoodokla.com
Contact: Chris Rudiger, Pres.

64109 ■ Yale Chamber of Commerce
209 N Main
PO Box 132
Yale, OK 74085
Ph:(918)387-2406
Contact: Boice Birggs, Pres.

64110 ■ Yukon Chamber of Commerce
510 Elm St.
Yukon, OK 73099
Ph:(405)354-3567
Fax: (405)350-0724
Co. E-mail: chamber@yukoncc.com
URL: http://www.yukoncc.com
Contact: Frank Greer, Exec.Dir.

MINORITY BUSINESS ASSISTANCE PROGRAMS

64111 ■ Oklahoma City Minority Business Enterprise Center
4205 Lincoln Blvd., RM. 109
Oklahoma City, OK 73105
Ph:(405)962-1623
Fax: (405)962-1639
URL: http://www.okcommerce.gov
Contact: Business Development

64112 ■ Oklahoma Department of Commerce–Business Development Division–Minority Business Office (900 N)
900 N Stiles
PO Box 26980
Oklahoma City, OK 73126
Ph:(405)815-6552
Free: 800-879-6552
Fax: (405)815-5199
Co. E-mail: bddinfo@odoc.state.ok.us
URL: http://www.okcommerce.gov
Description: Specializes in finance export programs to assist small Oklahoma companies.

64113 ■ Oklahoma Native American Business Development Center
5840 S Memorial, Ste. 105
Tulsa, OK 74145
Ph:(918)592-1113
Fax: (918)592-1217
Co. E-mail: dadowell@indiansbusiness.org
URL: http://www.onabdc.com

FINANCING AND LOAN PROGRAMS

64114 ■ Chisholm Private Capital Partners
211 N. Robinson, Ste. 1910
Oklahoma City, OK 73102
Ph:(405)605-1111
Fax: (405)605-1115
URL: http://www.chisholmvc.com
Contact: Jeff Williams, General Partner
Preferred Investment Size: $1,000,000 to $4,000,000. **Investment Types:** Early stage, expansion, and generalist PE. **Industry Preferences:** Computer software and services, semiconductors and other electronics, Internet specific, communications and media, medical and health, industrial and energy, other products, and computer hardware. **Geographic Preferences:** Oklahoma.

64115 ■ Davis, Tuttle Venture Partners, L.P. / DTVP (Tulsa)
320 S. Boston, Ste. 1000
Tulsa, OK 74106-3703
Ph:(918)584-7272
Fax: (918)582-3404
URL: http://www.davistuttle.com
Contact: Barry Davis, Managing General Partner
Preferred Investment Size: $1,000,000 to $4,500,000. **Investment Types:** First, second and early stage, mezzanine, balanced, acquisition, and leveraged buyout. **Industry Preferences:** Other products, consumer related, medical and health, industrial and energy, computer software and services, semiconductors and other electronics, Internet specific, and communications and media. **Geographic Preferences:** Southwest.

64116 ■ Moore & Associates
1000 W. Wilshire Blvd., Ste. 370
Oklahoma City, OK 73116
Ph:(405)842-3660
Fax: (405)842-3763
Preferred Investment Size: $500,000 minimum. **Investment Types:** Start-up, first and second stage, mezzanine, and leveraged buyout. **Industry Preferences:** Semiconductors and other electronics, medical and health, consumer related, industrial and energy, transportation, financial services, business service, and manufacturing. **Geographic Preferences:** U.S.

64117 ■ RBC Ventures, Inc.
2627 E. 21st St.
Tulsa, OK 74114
Ph:(918)744-5607
Fax: (918)743-8630
Preferred Investment Size: $2,000,000 minimum. **Investment Types:** Control-block purchases, leveraged buyout, mezzanine, second stage, and special situation. **Industry Preferences:** Transportation. **Geographic Preferences:** Southwest.

PROCUREMENT ASSISTANCE PROGRAMS

64118 ■ Department of Central Services–Purchasing Division
2401 N Lincoln Blvd., Ste. 116
Oklahoma City, OK 73105
Ph:(405)521-2115
Fax: (405)521-4475
URL: http://www.dcs.ok.gov
Contact: Betty Cairns

64119 ■ Oklahoma Department of Career and Technology Education–Bid Assistance Centers
1500 W 7th Ave.
Stillwater, OK 74074-4364
Ph:(405)377-2000
Fax: (405)743-5541
URL: http://www.okcareertech.org
Contact: Shelly Dawson, Prgm Mgr
Description: Provides federal contracting at 21 offices, located at vo-tech schools statewide.

64120 ■ Oklahoma Procurement Technical Assistance Center–Tribal Government Institute
421 E Comanche, Ste. B
Norman, OK 73071
Ph:(405)329-5542
Fax: (405)329-5543
Co. E-mail: tgi@coxnet.net
Contact: Bob Gann

64121 ■ Rose State College–Oklahoma Small Business Development Center–Procurement Center (6420)
6420 SE 15th St. Fl.2 Rm.200
Midwest City, OK 73110-2799
Ph:(405)733-7348
Fax: (405)733-7495
Co. E-mail: mcure@rose.edu

URL: http://www.rose.edu/commfriend/bizdev/index.
htm
Contact: Mike Cure, Dir
Description: Procurement center for all area small
business development centers.

INCUBATORS/RESEARCH AND TECHNOLOGY PARKS

**64122 ■ Atoka Industrial Incubator–Atoka
Kiamichi Area Vo-Tech/Atoka Campus**
1301 W Liberty Rd.
PO Box 240
Atoka, OK 74525
Ph:(580)889-7321
Fax: (580)889-5642
URL: http://www.kavts.tec.ok.us/atoka

**64123 ■ Central Oklahoma Business and Job
Development Corp.–Incubator**
201 N Settle Dr.
Drumright, OK 74030
Ph:(918)352-4517
Fax: (918)352-9545
Co. E-mail: bis.drum@ctechok.org
URL: http://www.ctechok.org

**64124 ■ McAlester Economic Development
Service Inc.–Incubator**
PO Box 3190
McAlester, OK 74502
Ph:(918)423-5735
Free: 888-828-9901
Fax: (918)426-0207
Co. E-mail: jmills@onenet.net
Contact: Jim Mills, Exec Dir

**64125 ■ McAlester Industrial
Incubator–Kiamichi Technology Center—
McAlester**
301 Kiamichi Dr.
McAlester, OK 74501
Ph:(918)426-0940
Fax: (918)426-1626
URL: http://www.kiamichi-mcalester.tec.ok.us
Contact: Sondra Scifres, Administrative Ass.

**64126 ■ Meridian Technology Center for
Business Development Center**
1312 S Sangre Rd.
Stillwater, OK 74074-1899
Ph:(405)377-3333
Fax: (405)377-9604
Co. E-mail: info@meridian-technology.com
URL: http://www.meridian-technology.com
Contact: Kay Wade
Description: A business incubator that fosters the de-
velopment of new and emerging businesses. The
Center offers office and manufacturing space, confer-
ence rooms, and other resources.

**64127 ■ Pioneer Technology
Center–Incubator**
2101 N Ash St.
Ponca City, OK 74601
Ph:(580)762-8336
Fax: (580)765-5101
URL: http://www.pioneertech.org
Contact: Receptionist

**64128 ■ Poteau Kiamichi Technology
Center–Incubator**
PO Box 825
Poteau, OK 74953
Ph:(918)647-4525
Fax: (918)647-4527
Co. E-mail: shosler@okktc.org
URL: http://www.kiamichi-poteau.tec.ok.us
Contact: Joe Carrick, Dir

64129 ■ Rural Enterprises, Inc.
PO Box 1335
Durant, OK 74702
Ph:(580)924-5094
Free: 800-658-2823

Fax: (580)920-2745
URL: http://www.ruralenterprises.com
Contact: Kenny Simpson, Exec VP
Description: Provides technology data searches to
Oklahoma businesses, utilizing over 400 databases.
Makes available a library of world technology informa-
tion with assistance from the Rural Innovation and Fi-
nance Center.

**64130 ■ Stigler Kiamichi Technology
Center–Incubator**
1410 Old Military Rd.
Stigler, OK 74462
Ph:(918)967-2801
Fax: (918)967-2804
URL: http://www.kiamichi-stigler.tec.ok.us
Contact: Jimmy Eakle, Dir

**64131 ■ Tri-County Economic Development
Center–Incubator**
6105 Nowata Rd.
Bartlesville, OK 74006
Ph:(918)333-3422
Fax: (918)335-3795
URL: http://www.tctc.org
Contact: Elaine Dettle

**64132 ■ University of Oklahoma–Office of
Research Services**
731 Elm Ave., Rm. 134
Norman, OK 73019
Ph:(405)325-4757
Fax: (405)325-6029
Co. E-mail: sedwick@ou.edu
URL: http://www.research.ou.edu
Contact: Susan Wyatt Sedwick PhD, Assoc.VP
E-mail: sedwick@ou.edu
Scope: Administers sponsored research, training,
and other projects at the University in physical, life, so-
cial, behavioral, and biomedical sciences and engi-
neering. Performs development and liaison services
for the University for interdisciplinary and interinstitu-
tional projects, negotiates contract and grant awards
for the University and provides post-award financial
support. **Publications:** Annual Report of Sponsored
Programs; Research News (monthly).

**64133 ■ University of Oklahoma–University
Airpark**
1700 Lexington Ave.
Norman, OK 73069
Ph:(405)325-7233
Fax: (405)325-7339
Co. E-mail: wstrong@ou.edu
Contact: Walter Strong, Admin.
E-mail: wstrong@ou.edu
Scope: Provides on a 1,500-acre tract facilities and
services for research administered by the University's
Office of Research Administration, as well as U.S. and
state government, industry, and University of Oklaho-
ma laboratories located in the Park.

**64134 ■ Wes Watkins Technology
Center–Incubator**
7892 Hwy. 9
Wetumka, OK 74883
Ph:(405)452-5500
Fax: (405)452-3561
URL: http://www.wwtech.org
Contact: Frank Alexander, Dir

EDUCATIONAL PROGRAMS

64135 ■ Canadian Valley Technology Center
6505 E Hwy. 66
El Reno, OK 73036
Ph:(405)262-2629
Fax: (405)422-2292
URL: http://www.cvvt.org
Description: Trade and technical college offering a
small business management program.

**64136 ■ Center for Business Technology,
Research and Development**
201 N Settle Dr.
Drumright, OK 74030

Ph:(918)352-4517
Fax: (918)352-9545
Co. E-mail: bis.drum@ctechok.org
URL: http://www.ctechok.org
Description: Trade and technical college offering a
small business management program.

**64137 ■ Central Oklahoma Technology
Center**
1720 S Main St.
Sapulpa, OK 74066
Ph:(918)224-9300
Fax: (918)224-0744
URL: http://www.ctechok.org
Description: Trade and technical college offering a
small business management program.

64138 ■ EOC Technology Center
4601 N Choctaw Rd.
Choctaw, OK 73020
Ph:(405)390-9591
Fax: (405)390-9598
URL: http://www.eoctech.org
Description: Business college offering a small busi-
ness management program.

**64139 ■ Francis Tuttle Technology
Center–Rockwell Campus**
12777 N Rockwell Ave.
Oklahoma City, OK 73142
Ph:(405)717-7799
Fax: (405)717-4771
URL: http://www.francistuttle.com
Description: Business college offering a small busi-
ness management program.

64140 ■ Gordon Cooper Technology Center
1 John C Bruton Blvd.
Shawnee, OK 74804
Ph:(405)273-7493
Fax: (405)273-6354
URL: http://www.gctech.org
Description: Business college offering a small busi-
ness management program.

64141 ■ Great Plains Technology Center
4500 W Lee Blvd.
Lawton, OK 73505
Ph:(580)355-6371
Free: 800-244-1024
Fax: (580)355-6371
Co. E-mail: info@gptech.org
URL: http://www.gptech.org
Description: Business college offering a small busi-
ness management program.

64142 ■ High Plains Technology Center
3921 34th St.
Woodward, OK 73801
Ph:(580)256-6618
Free: 800-725-1492
Fax: (580)571-6190
URL: http://www.hptc.net
Description: Business college offering a small busi-
ness management program.

64143 ■ Kiamichi Area Vo-Tech—Atoka
PO Box 240
Atoka, OK 74525
Ph:(580)889-7321
Fax: (580)889-5642
URL: http://www.kavts.tec.ok.us
Description: Business college offering a small busi-
ness management program.

64144 ■ Kiamichi Technology Center
301 Kiamichi Dr.
McAlester, OK 74501
Ph:(918)426-0940
Free: 888-567-6630
Fax: (918)426-1626
Co. E-mail: fprobis@kavts.tec.ok.us
URL: http://www.kavts.tec.ok.us
Description: Business college offering a small busi-
ness management program.

64145 ■ Kiamichi Technology Center—Stigler
1410 Old Military Rd.
Stigler, OK 74462
Ph:(918)967-2801
Free: 888-567-6805
Fax: (918)967-2804
URL: http://www.kiamichi-stigler.tec.ok.us
Description: Business college offering a small business management program.

64146 ■ Meridian Technology Center
1312 S Sangre Rd.
Stillwater, OK 74074-1899
Ph:(405)377-3333
Fax: (405)377-9604
Co. E-mail: info@meridian-technology.com
URL: http://www.meridian-technology.com
Description: Business college offering a small business management program.

64147 ■ Metro Vocational Technical School
1900 Springlake Dr.
Oklahoma City, OK 73111
Ph:(405)424-8324
Fax: (405)424-8555
Co. E-mail: info@metrotech.org
URL: http://www.metrotech.org
Description: Business college offering a small business management program.

64148 ■ Mid-America Technology Center
PO Box 278
Wayne, OK 73095
Ph:(405)449-3391
Free: 800-232-5580
Fax: (405)449-7321
URL: http://www.matech.org
Description: Business college offering a small business management program.

64149 ■ Moore Norman Technology Center
4701 12th Ave. NW
Norman, OK 73069
Ph:(405)364-5763
Fax: (405)360-9989
URL: http://www.mntechnology.com
Description: Trade and technical college offering a small business management program.

64150 ■ Northeast Technology Center
PO Box 825
Pryor, OK 74362

Ph:(918)825-5555
Fax: (918)825-6281
URL: http://www.netechcenters.com
Description: Business college offering a small business management program.

64151 ■ Pioneer Technology Center
2101 N Ash
Ponca City, OK 74601
Ph:(580)762-8336
Fax: (580)762-3107
URL: http://www.pioneertech.org
Description: Business college offering a small business management program.

64152 ■ Red River Area Technology Center
PO Box 1807
3300 W BOIS D ARC
Duncan, OK 73534
Ph:(580)255-2903
Free: 888-607-2446
Fax: (580)255-0491
Co. E-mail: mmorris@redriver.tec.ok.us
URL: http://www.redriver.tec.ok.us
Description: Business college offering a small business management program.

64153 ■ Tri-County Area Vo-Tech
6101 SE Nowata Rd.
Bartlesville, OK 74006
Ph:(918)333-2422
Free: 888-567-4610
Fax: (918)333-6797
URL: http://www.tctc.org
Description: Business college offering a small business management program.

64154 ■ Tulsa Community College
6111 E Skelly Dr.
Tulsa, OK 74135
Ph:(918)595-7000
Fax: (918)595-7910
URL: http://www.tulsacc.edu
Description: Two-year college offering a small business management program.

64155 ■ Western Oklahoma Technology Center–Burnes Flat Campus
621 Sooner Dr.
Burns Flat, OK 73624
Ph:(580)562-3181

Fax: (580)562-4476
URL: http://www.wtc.tec.ok.us
Description: Business college offering a small business management program.

LEGISLATIVE ASSISTANCE

64156 ■ Oklahoma Department of Commerce–Oklahoma Small Business Conference
PO Box 26980
900 N Stiles Ave.
Oklahoma City, OK 73126-0980
Ph:(405)815-6552
Free: 800-879-6552
Fax: (405)815-5142
URL: http://www.okcommerce.gov
Description: Annual conference in which small business owners study legislative issues affecting their businesses, learn techniques to start or operate their businesses, and network with state, federal, and nonprofit entities offering small business assistance.

TRADE PERIODICALS

64157 ■ Folio (Oklahoma City)
Pub: Department of Commerce
Contact: Tracy Alford
Ed: Tracy Alford, Editor, Tracy_Alford@odoc.state.ok.us. **Released:** Bimonthly. **Description:** Provides information on business and commerce in Oklahoma City.

PUBLISHERS

64158 ■ PrintWorthy Publishing Co.
5972 S Yale Ave.
Tulsa, OK 74135
Ph:(918)499-0331
Fax: (918)493-9408
Co. E-mail: info@printworthypub.com
URL: http://www.printworthypub.com
Contact: Janice Airhart
Description: Publishes books for self-publishing writers. Offers newsletter titled Self-Publishing Partner.

Oregon

SMALL BUSINESS DEVELOPMENT CENTER LEAD OFFICE

64159 ■ Lane Community College–Oregon SBDC
44 W. Broadway St., Ste. 203
Eugene, OR 97401-3021
Ph:(541)726-2250
Fax: (541)345-6006
URL: http://www.bizcenter.org
Contact: Dr. Edward "Sandy" Cutler, State Director
E-mail: cutlers@lanecc.edu

64160 ■ Lane Community College–Oregon SBDC–State Network Office (99 W.)
99 W. 10th Ave., Ste. 390
Eugene, OR 97401
Ph:(541)463-5250
Fax: (541)345-6006
URL: http://www.bizcenter.org
Contact: William Carter, State Dir.
E-mail: carterb@lanecc.edu

SMALL BUSINESS DEVELOPMENT CENTERS

64161 ■ Blue Mountain Community College–Small Business Development Center
Morrow Hall, Rm. M-11
2411 NW, Carden Ave.
PO Box 100
Pendleton, OR 97801
Ph:(541)276-6233
Fax: (541)276-6819
Co. E-mail: Pendleton@bizcenter.org
URL: http://www.bizcenter.org/pendleton
Contact: Art Hill, Dir.
E-mail: ahill@bmcc.cc.or.us

64162 ■ Central Oregon Community College–Small Business Development Center
2600 NW College Way
Bend, OR 97701
Ph:(541)383-7290
Fax: (541)318-3445
Co. E-mail: bend@bizcenter.org
URL: http://www.bizcenter.org/bend
Contact: Beth Wickham, Dir.
E-mail: bwickham@cocc.edu

64163 ■ Chemeketa Community College–Small Business Development Center
TED Center
365 Ferry St. SE
Salem, OR 97301
Ph:(503)399-5088
Fax: (503)581-6017
Co. E-mail: Salem@bizcenter.org
URL: http://www.bizcenter.org/salem
Contact: Jimmie Wilkins, Dir.

E-mail: jimmiew@chemeketa.edu

64164 ■ Clackamas Community College–Small Business Development Center
OIT Bldg., Rm. 172
7736 SE Harmony Rd.
Milwaukie, OR 97222
Ph:(503)656-4447
Fax: (503)650-7358
Co. E-mail: Milwaukie@bizcenter.org
URL: http://www.bizcenter.org/milwaukie
Contact: Tim Shea, Dir.
E-mail: shea@europa.com

64165 ■ Clatsop Community College–Small Business Development Center
1455 N. Roosevelt
Seaside, OR 97138
Ph:(503)738-3346
Fax: (503)738-7843
Co. E-mail: Seaside@bizcenter.org
URL: http://www.bizcenter.org/seaside
Contact: Greg Panichello, Dir.
E-mail: panic@bizcenter.org

64166 ■ Columbia Gorge Community College–SBDC
400 E. Scenic Dr., Ste. 259
The Dalles, OR 97058
Ph:(541)506-6121
Fax: (541)506-6122
Co. E-mail: TheDalles@bizcenter.org
URL: http://www.bizcenter.org/thedalles
Contact: Mr. Bob Cole, Dir.
E-mail: bcole@cgcc.cc.or.us

64167 ■ Eastern Oregon College–Small Business Development Center
1 University Blvd.
La Grande, OR 97850
Ph:(541)962-1532
Fax: (541)962-1532
Co. E-mail: LaGrande@bizcenter.org
URL: http://www.bizcenter.org/lagrande
Contact: Steve Turner, Dir.
E-mail: sturner@eou.edu

64168 ■ Linn-Benton Community College–Small Business Development Center
6500 SW Pacific Blvd.
Albany, OR 97321
Ph:(541)979-6444
Fax: (541)917-4831
Co. E-mail: Albany@bizcenter.org
URL: http://www.bizcenter.org/albany
Contact: Dennis Sargent, Dir.

64169 ■ Mount Hood Community College–Small Business Development Center
323 NE Roberts Ave.
Gresham, OR 97030
Ph:(503)491-7658
Fax: (503)666-1140
Co. E-mail: Gresham@bizcenter.org
URL: http://www.bizcenter.org/gresham
Contact: Don King, Dir.

E-mail: donking@teleport.com

64170 ■ Oregon Coast Community College–Small Business Development Center
1206 SE, 48th St.
Lincoln City, OR 97367
Ph:(541)994-4166
Fax: (541)996-4958
Co. E-mail: LincolnCity@bizcenter.org
URL: http://www.bizcenter.org/lincolncity
Contact: Guy Faust, Dir.
E-mail: guyfaust@hotmail.com

64171 ■ Oregon Institute of Technology–Small Business Development Center
Boivin Hall, Rm. 119
3201 Campus Dr.
Klamath Falls, OR 97601-8801
Ph:(541)885-1760
Fax: (541)885-1761
Co. E-mail: KlamathFalls@bizcenter.org
URL: http://www.bizcenter.org/klamathfalls
Contact: Jamie Albert, Dir.
E-mail: albertj@oit.edu

64172 ■ Portland Community College–Small Business Development Center
2025 Lloyd Center Mall, 3rd Level Offices
Portland, OR 97232
Ph:(503)978-5080
Fax: (503)288-1366
Co. E-mail: Portland@bizcenter.org
URL: http://www.bizcenter.org/portland
Contact: Tom Lowles, Dir.
E-mail: tlowles@pcc.edu

64173 ■ Portland Community College–Small Business International Trade Program
121 SW Salmon St., Ste. 205
Portland, OR 97204
Ph:(503)229-6051
Fax: (503)222-5050
Contact: Bob Repine, Dir.

64174 ■ Rogue Community College–Small Business Development Center
214 SW 4th St.
Grants Pass, OR 97526
Ph:(541)956-7494
Fax: (541)471-3589
Co. E-mail: GrantsPass@bizcenter.org
URL: http://www.bizcenter.org/grantspass
Contact: Ted Risser, Dir.

64175 ■ Southern Oregon University–Small Business Development Center
673 Market St.
Medford, OR 97504
Ph:(541)772-3478
Fax: (541)734-4813
Co. E-mail: Medford@bizcenter.org
URL: http://www.sou.edu/business/sbdc.htm
Contact: Jack Vitacco, Interim Dir.
E-mail: vitaccoja@sou.edu

64176 ■ Southwestern Oregon Community College–Small Business Development Center
2455 Maple Leaf
Coos Bay/North Bend, OR 97459
Ph:(541)756-6866
Fax: (541)756-5735
Co. E-mail: CoosBay/BorthBend@bizcenter.org
URL: http://www.bizcenter.org/coosbay
Contact: Jon Richards, Dir.
E-mail: jrichard@southwestern.cc.or.us

64177 ■ Tillamook Bay Community College–Small Business Development Center
2510 1st St.
Tillamook, OR 97141
Ph:(503)842-8222
Fax: (503)842-2214
Co. E-mail: Tillamook@bizcenter.org
URL: http://www.bizcenter.org/tillamook
Contact: Barb Bush, Dir.
E-mail: bbush@tbcc.cc.or.us

64178 ■ Treasure Valley Community College–Small Business Development Center
650 College Blvd.
Ontario, OR 97914
Ph:(541)881-8822
Fax: (541)881-2743
Co. E-mail: Ontario@bizcenter.org
URL: http://www.bizcenter.org/ontario
Contact: Andrea Testi, Dir.
E-mail: testi@bizcenter.org

64179 ■ Umpqua Community College–Small Business Development Center
2555 NE Diamond Lake Blvd.
Roseburg, OR 97470
Ph:(541)440-4669
Fax: (541)440-4607
Co. E-mail: Roseburg@bizcenter.org
URL: http://www.bizcenter.org/roseburg
Contact: Terry Swagerty, Dir.
E-mail: swagert@rosenet.net

SMALL BUSINESS ASSISTANCE PROGRAMS

64180 ■ Oregon Department of Agriculture–Trade and Marketing Office
1207 NW Naito Pky., Ste. 104
Portland, OR 97209-2832
Ph:(503)872-6600
Fax: (503)872-6601
Co. E-mail: cid-expert@oda.state.or.us
URL: http://oregon.gov/ODA/
Description: Operates a marketing program that assists in the development of new markets or in the expansion of existing markets for agricultural commodities produced or processed in the state.

64181 ■ Oregon Economic and Community Development Department
775 Summer St. NE, Ste. 200
Salem, OR 97301-1280
Ph:(503)986-0155
Fax: (503)581-5115
URL: http://www.econ.state.or.us
Description: Coordinates business, financial, job training, and community development resources for individuals, businesses, and local jurisdictions.

64182 ■ Oregon Economic and Community Development Department–Business Development Division
775 Summer St. NE, Ste. 200
Salem, OR 97301-1280
Ph:(503)986-0123
Fax: (503)581-5115
URL: http://www.econ.state.or.us
Description: Helps to coordinate state programs with local community efforts in business expansion, recruitment, retention, and start-up efforts.

64183 ■ Oregon Economic and Community Development Department–Business Development Division–Eastern Regional Business Development Office (775 S)
775 Summer St. NE, Ste. 200
Salem, OR 97301-1280
Ph:(503)986-0198
Free: 800-233-3306
Fax: (503)581-5115
URL: http://www.econ.state.or.us
Description: Helps to coordinate state programs with local community efforts in business expansion, recruitment, retention, and start-up efforts.

64184 ■ Oregon Economic and Community Development Department–Business Development Division–Southern Oregon Regional Economic Development, Inc. (673 M)
673 Market St.
Medford, OR 97504
Ph:(541)773-8946
Free: 800-805-8740
Fax: (541)779-0953
URL: http://www.soredi.org
Description: Helps to coordinate state programs with local community efforts in business expansion, recruitment, retention, and start-up efforts.

64185 ■ Oregon Economic and Community Development Department–International Trade Division
121 SW Salmon St., Ste. 205
Portland, OR 97209
Ph:(503)229-5625
Fax: (503)222-5050
URL: http://www.econ.state.or.us/oregontrade
Description: Provides assistance through one-to-one consultation, trade shows and exhibitions, export seminars, a Personalized Export Panel session, participation in an overseas trade mission, and student international market research program.

64186 ■ Oregon Economic and Community Development Department–Small Business Program
775 Summer St. NE, Ste. 200
Salem, OR 97301-1280
Ph:(503)986-0123
Fax: (503)581-5115
URL: http://www.oregon-smallbiz.com
Description: Helps small businesses resolve regulatory problems with state agencies.

SCORE OFFICES

64187 ■ SCORE Portland
c/o Bill Klammer, Chm.
601 SW Second Ave.
Ste. 950
Portland, OR 97204-3192
Ph:(503)326-3441
Fax: (503)326-2808
Co. E-mail: scorepdx@wa-net.com
URL: http://www.scorepdx.org
Contact: Bill Klammer, Chm.
Description: Strives to support small business through resource center, workshops and counseling.

BETTER BUSINESS BUREAUS

64188 ■ Better Business Bureau of Oregon and Western Washington
4004 SW Kruse Way Pl., Ste. 375
Lake Oswego, OR 97035
Ph:(503)212-3022
Fax: (503)212-3099
Co. E-mail: info@thebbb.org
URL: http://orwwa.bbb.org
Contact: Bob Andrew, Pres.

CHAMBERS OF COMMERCE

64189 ■ African American Chamber of Commerce of Oregon
PO Box 5488
Portland, OR 97228-5488
Ph:(503)343-5117
Free: 800-909-2882
Fax: (503)345-9535
Co. E-mail: blackchamber@usa.net
URL: http://www.blackchamber.info
Contact: Roy Jay, Pres./CEO

64190 ■ Albany Area Chamber of Commerce
435 W 1st Ave.
PO Box 548
Albany, OR 97321-0161
Ph:(503)926-1517
Fax: (503)926-7064
Co. E-mail: info@albanychamber.com
URL: http://www.albanychamber.com
Contact: Janet Steele, Pres.

64191 ■ Ashland Chamber of Commerce
110 E Main St.
PO Box 1360
Ashland, OR 97520-0046
Ph:(541)482-3486
Fax: (541)482-2350
Co. E-mail: sandra@ashlandchamber.com
URL: http://ashlandchamber.com
Contact: Sandra Slattery, Exec.Dir.

64192 ■ Astoria-Warrenton Area Chamber of Commerce
111 W Marine Dr.
PO Box 176
Astoria, OR 97103-0176
Ph:(503)325-6311
Free: 800-875-6807
Fax: (503)325-9767
Co. E-mail: oldoregon@charterinternet.com
URL: http://www.oldoregon.com
Contact: Steve Nurding, Pres.

64193 ■ Aurora Chamber of Commerce
PO Box 86
Aurora, OR 97002-0086
Ph:(503)939-0312
Co. E-mail: info@auroracolony.com
URL: http://www.auroracolony.com
Contact: Barbara Johnson, Treas.

64194 ■ Baker County Unlimited Chamber of Commerce
490 Campbell St.
Baker City, OR 97814
Ph:(541)523-5855
Free: 800-523-1235
Fax: (541)523-9187
Co. E-mail: stopby@baker-chamber.com
URL: http://www.bakercity.com
Contact: Dave Noble, Exec.Dir.

64195 ■ Bandon Chamber of Commerce
PO Box 1515
Bandon, OR 97411
Ph:(541)347-9616
Fax: (541)347-7006
Co. E-mail: inforequest@bandon.com
URL: http://www.bandon.com
Contact: Julie Miller, Exec.Dir.

64196 ■ Bay Area Chamber of Commerce Visitors Center
145 Central Ave.
Coos Bay, OR 97420
Ph:(541)266-0868
Free: 800-824-8486
Fax: (541)267-6704
Co. E-mail: liberant@uci.net
URL: http://www.oregonsbayareachamber.com
Contact: Shirley Liberante, Exec.Dir.

64197 ■ Beaverton Area Chamber of Commerce
12655 SW Center St., Ste. 140
Beaverton, OR 97005
Ph:(503)644-0123
Fax: (503)526-0349
Co. E-mail: info@beaverton.org
URL: http://www.beaverton.org
Contact: Lorraine Clarno, Pres.

64198 ■ Bend Chamber of Commerce
777 NW Wall St., Ste. 200
Bend, OR 97701
Ph:(541)382-3221
Free: 800-905-BEND
Fax: (541)385-9929
Co. E-mail: info@bendchamber.org
URL: http://www.bendchamber.org
Contact: Mr. Mike Schmidt, Pres./CEO

64199 ■ Brookings-Harbor Chamber of Commerce
PO Box 940
16330 Lower Harbor Rd.
Brookings, OR 97415
Ph:(541)469-3181
Free: 800-535-9469
Fax: (541)469-4094
Co. E-mail: chamber@brookingsor.com
URL: http://www.brookingsor.com
Contact: Les Cohen, Exec.Dir.

64200 ■ Canby Area Chamber of Commerce
PO Box 35
191 SE 2nd Ave.
Canby, OR 97013
Ph:(503)266-4600
Fax: (503)266-4338
Co. E-mail: chamber@canbyareachamber.org
URL: http://www.canbyareachamber.org
Contact: Bev Doolittle, Exec.Dir.

64201 ■ Cannon Beach Chamber of Commerce
PO Box 64
Cannon Beach, OR 97110
Ph:(503)436-2623
Fax: (503)436-0910
Co. E-mail: chamber@cannonbeach.org
URL: http://www.cannonbeach.org
Contact: Kim Bosse, Dir.

64202 ■ Canyonville Chamber of Commerce
PO Box 1028
Canyonville, OR 97417
Ph:(541)839-4125
Fax: (541)839-4680
Co. E-mail: cville@mcsi.net
Contact: Jake Young, Pres.

64203 ■ Central Point Area Chamber of Commerce
27 S 6th St.
PO Box 5046
Central Point, OR 97502
Ph:(541)664-5301
Fax: (541)664-5301
Co. E-mail: cpchamber@qwest.net
URL: http://www.centralpointchamber.org

64204 ■ Chamber of Medford - Jackson County
101 E 8th St.
Medford, OR 97501-7293
Ph:(541)779-4847
Fax: (541)776-4808
Co. E-mail: business@medfordchamber.com
URL: http://www.medfordchamber.com
Contact: Brad S. Hicks, Pres./CEO

64205 ■ Chehalem Valley Chamber of Commerce
415 E Sheridan
Newberg, OR 97132-2811
Ph:(503)538-2014
Fax: (503)538-2463
Co. E-mail: info@newberg.org

URL: http://www.chehalemvalley.org
Contact: Paul Lipscomb, Exec. Dir.

64206 ■ Clatskanie Chamber of Commerce
PO Box 635
Clatskanie, OR 97016-0635
Ph:(503)728-2502
Co. E-mail: chief@clatskanie.com
URL: http://www.clatskanie.com/chamber
Contact: Debi Hazen, Pres.

64207 ■ Condon Chamber of Commerce
PO Box 315
Condon, OR 97823
Ph:(541)384-7777
Fax: (541)384-3215
Co. E-mail: condonchamber@hotmail.com
Contact: Mac Stinchfield, Pres.

64208 ■ Coquille Chamber of Commerce and Visitor Information Center
119 N Birch St.
Coquille, OR 97423
Ph:(541)396-3414
Co. E-mail: coquillechamber@verizon.net
URL: http://www.coquillechamber.org
Contact: Louise Pace, Dir.

64209 ■ Cornelius Chamber of Commerce
PO Box 681
120 N 13th Ave.
Cornelius, OR 97113
Ph:(503)359-4037
Fax: (503)992-1997
Co. E-mail: corneliuschamber@verizon.net
URL: http://www.corneliuschamber.com
Contact: Ms. Jenny Garner, Exec.Dir.

64210 ■ Corvallis Area Chamber of Commerce
420 NW Second St.
Corvallis, OR 97330-6442
Ph:(541)757-1505
Fax: (541)766-2996
Co. E-mail: info@corvallischamber.com
URL: http://www.corvallischamber.com
Contact: Patricia Mulder, Pres.

64211 ■ Cottage Grove Area Chamber of Commerce
PO Box 587
700 E Gibbs, Ste. C
Cottage Grove, OR 97424
Ph:(541)942-2411
Fax: (541)767-0783
Co. E-mail: cgchamber@oip.net
URL: http://www.cgchamber.com
Contact: Tim Flowerday, Exec.Dir.

64212 ■ Creswell Chamber of Commerce
99 S 1st St.
PO Box 577
Creswell, OR 97426
Ph:(541)895-5161
Fax: (541)895-5161
Co. E-mail: creswell-cc@centurytel.net
URL: http://www.creswellchamber.com
Contact: Annette Whittington, Office Administrator

64213 ■ Crooked River Ranch Chamber of Commerce
PO Box 1502
Crooked River, OR 97760
Ph:(541)923-2679
Fax: (541)923-2755
Co. E-mail: info@crrchamber.com
URL: http://www.crookedriverranchchamber.com
Contact: John Bowler, Exec.Dir.

64214 ■ Dallas Area Chamber of Commerce
580 Main St., Ste. C
PO Box 377
Dallas, OR 97338-0377
Ph:(503)623-2564
Fax: (503)623-8936
Co. E-mail: chamber@dallasoregon.org
URL: http://www.dallasoregon.org

Contact: Chelsea Pope, Mgr.

64215 ■ Estacada - Clackamas River Area Chamber of Commerce
475 SE Main
PO Box 298
Estacada, OR 97023-0298
Ph:(503)630-3483
Fax: (503)630-4843
Co. E-mail: estacadacc@cascadeaccess.com
URL: http://www.estacadachamber.org
Contact: Mrs. Jeanette Larson, Chamber Dir.

64216 ■ Eugene Area Chamber of Commerce
1401 Willamette St.
PO Box 1107
Eugene, OR 97401
Ph:(541)484-1314
Fax: (541)484-4942
Co. E-mail: admin@eugenechamber.com
URL: http://www.eugenechamber.com
Contact: David Hauser CCE, Pres.

64217 ■ Florence Area Chamber of Commerce
290 Hwy. 101
Florence, OR 97439
Ph:(541)997-3128
Free: 800-524-4864
Fax: (541)997-4101
Co. E-mail: florence@oregonfast.net
URL: http://www.florencechamber.com
Contact: Julie Knox, Dir.

64218 ■ Forest Grove Chamber of Commerce
2417 Pacific Ave.
Forest Grove, OR 97116-2498
Ph:(503)357-3006
Fax: (503)357-2367
Co. E-mail: fgchamber@groveweb.net
URL: http://www.fgchamber.org
Contact: Lois Hornberger, Exec. Dir.

64219 ■ Garibaldi Chamber of Commerce
PO Box 915
Garibaldi, OR 97118
Ph:(503)322-0301
Fax: (503)322-0334
Co. E-mail: info@garibaldichamber.com
URL: http://www.garibaldichamber.com
Contact: Gunnar Monson, Pres.

64220 ■ Gold Beach Chamber of Commerce
PO Box 489
Gold Beach, OR 97444
Ph:(541)247-0923
Fax: (541)247-4394
Co. E-mail: info@goldbeachchamber.com
URL: http://www.goldbeachchamber.com
Contact: Chip Weinert, Exec.Dir.

64221 ■ Grant County Chamber of Commerce
281 W Main St.
John Day, OR 97845-1026
Ph:(541)575-0547
Free: 800-769-5664
Fax: (541)575-1947
Co. E-mail: grant@grantcounty.cc
URL: http://www.grantcounty.cc
Contact: Arlene McGetrick, Mgr.

64222 ■ Grants Pass - Josephine County Chamber of Commerce
1995 NW Vine St.
PO Box 970
Grants Pass, OR 97528
Ph:(541)476-7717
Free: 800-547-5927
Fax: (541)476-9574
Co. E-mail: gpcoc@grantspasschamber.org
URL: http://www.grantspasschamber.org
Contact: Jon Jordan, Exec. Dir.

64223 ■ Greater Hermiston Chamber of Commerce
415 S Hwy. 395
PO Box 185
Hermiston, OR 97838-0185

Ph:(541)567-6151
Fax: (541)564-9109
Co. E-mail: coyla@eotnet.net
URL: http://www.hermistonchamber.com
Contact: Debbie Pedro, Exec. Dir.

64224 ■ Greater Newport Chamber of Commerce
555 SW Coast Hwy.
Newport, OR 97365-4934
Ph:(541)265-8801
Free: 800-262-7844
Fax: (541)265-5589
Co. E-mail: sh@actionnet.net
URL: http://www.newportchamber.org
Contact: Susan Huntington, Exec. Dir.

64225 ■ Gresham Area Chamber of Commerce
701 NE Hood Ave.
Gresham, OR 97030
Ph:(503)665-1131
Fax: (503)666-1041
Co. E-mail: gacc@greshamchamber.org
URL: http://www.greshamchamber.org
Contact: Carol Nielsen-Hood, Exec.Dir.

64226 ■ Harney County Chamber of Commerce
76 E Washington St.
Burns, OR 97720
Ph:(541)573-2636
Fax: (541)573-3408
Co. E-mail: info@harneycounty.com
URL: http://www.harneycounty.com
Contact: Linda Johnson, Exec.Dir.

64227 ■ Heppner Chamber of Commerce
PO Box 1232
Heppner, OR 97836
Ph:(541)676-5536
Fax: (541)676-9650
Co. E-mail: dir@heppnerchamber.com
URL: http://www.heppnerchamber.com
Contact: Claudia Hughes, Exec.Dir.

64228 ■ Hillsboro Chamber of Commerce
5193 NE Elam Young Pkwy., Ste. A
Hillsboro, OR 97124
Ph:(503)648-1102
Fax: (503)681-0535
Co. E-mail: info@hillchamber.org
URL: http://www.hillchamber.org
Contact: Deanna Palm, Pres.

64229 ■ Hispanic Metropolitan Chamber of Commerce
PO Box 1837
Portland, OR 97207
Ph:(503)222-0280
Fax: (503)243-5597
Co. E-mail: hmcc@qwest.net
URL: http://www.hmccoregon.com
Contact: Gale Castillo, Exec.Dir.

64230 ■ Hood River County Chamber of Commerce
405 Portway Ave.
Hood River, OR 97031
Ph:(541)386-2000
Free: 800-366-3530
Fax: (541)386-2057
Co. E-mail: hrccc@hoodriver.org
URL: http://www.hoodriver.org
Contact: Craig Schmidt, Exec. Dir.

64231 ■ Jacksonville Chamber of Commerce and Visitors' Information
PO Box 33
Jacksonville, OR 97530
Ph:(541)899-8118
Fax: (541)899-4462
Co. E-mail: chamber@jacksonvilleoregon.org
URL: http://www.jacksonvilleoregon.org
Contact: Sandi Torrey, Visitor Center Dir.

64232 ■ Joseph Chamber of Commerce
PO Box 13
Joseph, OR 97846
Ph:(541)432-1015
Fax: (541)432-4205
Co. E-mail: cjdays@oregontrail.net
URL: http://www.chiefjosephdays.com
Contact: Debbie Short, Office Mgr.

64233 ■ Junction City-Harrisburg Chamber of Commerce
235 W 6th Ave.
Junction City, OR 97448-1235
Ph:(541)998-6154
Fax: (541)998-1037
Co. E-mail: jcchamber@unwiredonline.net
URL: http://www.jch-chamber.org
Contact: Ms. Taryl Perry, Exec.Dir.

64234 ■ Keizer Chamber of Commerce and Visitor Center
980 Chemawa Rd. NE
Keizer, OR 97303
Ph:(503)393-9111
Free: 888-218-4747
Fax: (503)393-1003
Co. E-mail: info@keizerchamber.com
URL: http://www.keizerchamber.com
Contact: Christine Dieker, Exec. Dir.

64235 ■ Klamath County Chamber of Commerce
706 Main St.
Klamath Falls, OR 97601
Ph:(541)884-5193
Free: 877-KLA-MATH
Fax: (541)884-5195
Co. E-mail: inquiry@klamath.org
URL: http://www.klamath.org
Contact: Stephanie Bailey, Exec.Dir.

64236 ■ La Pine Chamber of Commerce
51425 Hwy. 97, Ste. A
La Pine, OR 97739-9868
Ph:(541)536-9771
Fax: (541)536-8410
Co. E-mail: info@lapine.org
URL: http://www.lapine.org
Contact: Rose Alsbury, Exec.Dir.

64237 ■ Lake County Chamber of Commerce
126 N St. E
Lakeview, OR 97630-1526
Ph:(541)947-6040
Free: 877-947-6040
Fax: (541)947-4892
Co. E-mail: information@lakecountychamber.org
URL: http://www.lakecountychamber.org
Contact: Caro Johnson, Exec. Dir.

64238 ■ Lake Oswego Chamber of Commerce
242 B Ave.
PO Box 368
Lake Oswego, OR 97034
Ph:(503)636-3634
Fax: (503)636-7427
Co. E-mail: lakeoswego@lake-oswego.com
URL: http://www.lake-oswego.com
Contact: Jerry Wheeler, Exec.Dir.

64239 ■ Lakeside Chamber of Commerce
PO Box 333
Lakeside, OR 97449
Ph:(541)759-3981
Co. E-mail: lkchamber@presys.com
URL: http://lksdchamber.presys.com
Contact: Angelika Burles

64240 ■ Lincoln City Chamber of Commerce
4039 NW Logan Rd. & Hwy. 101
PO Box 787
Lincoln City, OR 97367
Ph:(541)994-3070
Fax: (541)994-8339
Co. E-mail: info@lcchamber.com
URL: http://www.lcchamber.com

Contact: Allyson Longueira, Exec. Dir.

64241 ■ Madras-Jefferson County Chamber of Commerce
274 SW 4th St.
PO Box 770
Madras, OR 97741
Ph:(541)475-2350
Free: 800-967-3564
Fax: (541)475-4341
Co. E-mail: office@madraschamber.com
URL: http://www.madraschamber.com
Contact: Parrish VanWert, Exec.Dir.

64242 ■ McKenzie River Chamber of Commerce and Information Center
PO Box 1117
Leaburg, OR 97489
Ph:(541)896-3330
Fax: (541)822-3358
Co. E-mail: mcrvcofc@aol.com
URL: http://members.aol.com/mcrvcofc
Contact: Louise Engelman, Exec.Dir.

64243 ■ McMinnville Area Chamber of Commerce
417 NW Adams St.
McMinnville, OR 97128
Ph:(503)472-6196
Fax: (503)472-6198
Co. E-mail: chamberinfo@mcminnville.org
URL: http://www.mcminnville.org
Contact: Celia Wheeler, Pres./CEO

64244 ■ Molalla Area Chamber of Commerce
101 N Molalla Ave.
PO Box 578
Molalla, OR 97038-0578
Ph:(503)829-6941
Fax: (503)829-7949
Co. E-mail: macc@molalla.net
URL: http://www.molallachamber.com
Contact: Sheri Kelly, Exec.Dir.

64245 ■ Monmouth-Independence Chamber of Commerce
355 N Pacific Ave., Ste. A
Monmouth, OR 97361
Ph:(503)838-4268
Free: 800-772-2806
Fax: (503)838-6658
Co. E-mail: micc@open.org
URL: http://www.open.org/~micc/index_2.html
Contact: Amberly Van Winkle, Exec. Dir.

64246 ■ Mount Angel Chamber of Commerce
PO Box 221
Mount Angel, OR 97362-0221
Ph:(503)845-9440
Fax: (503)845-6190
Co. E-mail: jerry@oktoberfest.org
URL: http://www.mtangel.org
Contact: Paul Brakeman, Pres.

64247 ■ Mount Hood Area Chamber of Commerce
PO Box 819
Welches, OR 97067
Ph:(503)622-3017
Fax: (503)622-3163
Co. E-mail: chamber@mthood.org
URL: http://www.mthood.org
Contact: Karen Norton, Pres.

64248 ■ North Clackamas County Chamber of Commerce
7740 SE Harmony Rd.
Milwaukie, OR 97222-1269
Ph:(503)654-7777
Fax: (503)653-9515
Co. E-mail: info@yourchamber.com
Contact: Wilda Parks, Pres./CEO

64249 ■ North Santiam Chamber of Commerce
PO Box 222
Mill City, OR 97360

Ph:(503)897-2865
Co. E-mail: stephen_nielsen@santiam.k12.or.us
URL: http://www.northsantiamchamber.org
Contact: Steve Nielsen, Pres.

64250 ■ Nyssa Chamber of Commerce and Agriculture
112 Main St.
Nyssa, OR 97913
Ph:(541)372-3091
Fax: (541)372-2377
Co. E-mail: cleta@nyssachamber.com
URL: http://www.nyssachamber.com
Contact: Kim Braniff, Pres.

64251 ■ Oakridge - Westfir Chamber of Commerce
PO Box 217
Oakridge, OR 97463-0217
Ph:(541)782-4146
Fax: (541)782-1081
Co. E-mail: info@oakridgechamber.com
URL: http://www.oakridgechamber.com
Contact: Kevin Urban, Pres.

64252 ■ Ontario Chamber of Commerce
676 SW 5th Ave.
Ontario, OR 97914
Ph:(541)889-8012
Free: (866)989-8012
Co. E-mail: ontvcb@fmtc.com
URL: http://www.ontariochamber.com
Contact: John Breidenbach, Exec. Dir.

64253 ■ Oregon City Chamber of Commerce
PO Box 226
1810 Washington St.
Oregon City, OR 97045
Ph:(503)656-1619
Fax: (503)656-2274
Co. E-mail: chamberinfo@oregoncity.org
URL: http://www.oregoncity.org
Contact: Amber Holveck, Pres./CEO

64254 ■ Pendleton Chamber of Commerce
501 S Main
Pendleton, OR 97801
Ph:(541)276-7411
Free: 800-547-8911
Fax: (541)276-8849
Co. E-mail: pendleton@pendleton-oregon.org
URL: http://www.pendletonchamber.com
Contact: Leslie Carnes, Exec.Dir.

64255 ■ Philomath Area Chamber of Commerce
2395 Main St.
PO Box 606
Philomath, OR 97370-0606
Ph:(541)929-2454
Fax: (541)929-4420
Co. E-mail: director@philomathchamber.org
URL: http://www.philomathchamber.org
Contact: F. Charles Redfern, Exec. Dir.

64256 ■ Port Orford and North Curry Chamber of Commerce
PO Box 637
Port Orford, OR 97465
Ph:(541)332-8055
Fax: (541)332-8055
Co. E-mail: chamber@discoverportorford.com
URL: http://www.portorfordchamber.com
Contact: Jay Stoler, Pres.

64257 ■ Portland Business Alliance
200 SW Market, Ste. 1770
Portland, OR 97201
Ph:(503)224-8684
Fax: (503)323-9186
Co. E-mail: info@portlandalliance.com
URL: http://www.portlandalliance.com
Contact: Sandra McDonough, Pres./CEO

64258 ■ Prineville-Crook County Chamber of Commerce
390 NE Fairview
Prineville, OR 97754-2307

Ph:(541)447-6304
Fax: (541)447-6537
Co. E-mail: pchamber@prineville.org
URL: http://www.prineville-crookcounty.org
Contact: Diane Williams Bohle PhD, Exec. Dir.

64259 ■ Redmond Chamber of Commerce
446 SW 7th St.
Redmond, OR 97756
Ph:(541)923-5191
Fax: (541)923-6442
Co. E-mail: info@visitredmondoregon.com
URL: http://www.redmondcofc.com
Contact: Eric Sande, Exec. Dir.

64260 ■ Reedsport - Winchester Bay Chamber of Commerce
855 Highway Ave.
PO Box 11
Reedsport, OR 97467-0011
Ph:(541)271-3495
Free: 800-247-2155
Fax: (541)271-3496
Co. E-mail: info@reedsportcc.com
URL: http://www.reedsportcc.org
Contact: Mark Bedard, Pres.

64261 ■ Rogue River Area Chamber of Commerce
PO Box 457
Rogue River, OR 97537
Ph:(541)582-0242
Co. E-mail: info@rrchamber.cc
URL: http://www.rrchamber.cc
Contact: Dean Stirm, Pres.

64262 ■ Roseburg Area Chamber of Commerce
410 SE Spruce St.
PO Box 1026
Roseburg, OR 97470-0239
Ph:(541)672-2648
Free: 800-444-9584
Fax: (541)673-7868
Co. E-mail: info@roseburgareachamber.org
URL: http://www.roseburgareachamber.org
Contact: Debbie Fromdahl, Exec. Dir.

64263 ■ Salem Area Chamber of Commerce
1110 Commercial St. NE
Salem, OR 97301-1020
Ph:(503)581-1466
Fax: (503)581-0972
Co. E-mail: info@salemchamber.org
URL: http://www.salemchamber.org
Contact: Michael T. McLaran, Exec. Dir.

64264 ■ Sandy Area Chamber of Commerce
38775 Pioneer Blvd.
PO Box 536
Sandy, OR 97055
Ph:(503)668-4006
Fax: (503)668-3459
Co. E-mail: chamber@sandyoregonchamber.org
URL: http://www.sandyoregonchamber.org
Contact: Lynn Cabe, Exec. Dir.

64265 ■ Sherwood Chamber of Commerce
16091 SW Railroad St.
PO Box 805
Sherwood, OR 97140-0805
Ph:(503)625-7800
Fax: (503)625-7550
Co. E-mail: chamber@sherwoodchamber.org
URL: http://www.sherwoodchamber.org
Contact: Holli Robinson, Exec. Dir.

64266 ■ Silverton Area Chamber of Commerce
PO Box 257
Silverton, OR 97381
Ph:(503)873-5615
Fax: (503)873-7144
Co. E-mail: info@silvertonchamber.org
URL: http://www.silvertonchamber.org
Contact: Stacy Palmer, Mgr.

64267 ■ Sisters Area Chamber of Commerce
PO Box 430
Sisters, OR 97759
Ph:(541)549-0251
Free: (866)549-0252
Fax: (541)549-4253
Co. E-mail: info@sisterschamber.com
URL: http://www.sisterschamber.com
Contact: Cheryl Mills

64268 ■ South Columbia County Chamber of Commerce
2194 Columbia Blvd.
PO Box 1036
St. Helens, OR 97051-8001
Ph:(503)397-0685
Fax: (503)397-7196
Co. E-mail: info@sccchamber.org
URL: http://www.sccchamber.org
Contact: Marna D. Gatlin, Exec. Dir.

64269 ■ Springfield Area Chamber of Commerce
101 S A St.
PO Box 155
Springfield, OR 97477
Ph:(541)746-1651
Fax: (541)726-4727
Co. E-mail: general@springfield-chamber.org
URL: http://www.springfield-chamber.org
Contact: Dan Egan, Exec. Dir.

64270 ■ Stayton - Sublimity Chamber of Commerce
175 E High St.
PO Box 121
Stayton, OR 97383
Ph:(503)769-3464
Fax: (503)769-3463
Co. E-mail: sscoc@wvi.com
URL: http://www.staytonsublimitychamber.org
Contact: Sue Nichols, Exec. Dir.

64271 ■ Sunriver Area Chamber of Commerce
PO Box 3246
Sunriver, OR 97707
Ph:(541)593-8149
Fax: (541)593-3581
Co. E-mail: info@sunriverchamber.com
URL: http://www.sunriverchamber.com
Contact: Deanna Elliott, Exec.Dir.

64272 ■ Sutherlin Chamber of Commerce and Visitors' Information Center
1310 W Central Ave.
PO Box 327
Sutherlin, OR 97479
Ph:(541)459-5829
Free: 800-371-5829
Fax: (541)459-9363
Co. E-mail: suthvic@mcsi.net
URL: http://www.visitsutherlin.com
Contact: Theresa Jones, Dir.

64273 ■ Sweet Home Chamber of Commerce
1575 Main St.
Sweet Home, OR 97386
Ph:(541)367-6186
Fax: (541)367-6150
Co. E-mail: info@sweethomechamber.org
URL: http://www.sweethomechamber.org
Contact: Carla Claasen, Exec. Dir.

64274 ■ Tigard Area Chamber of Commerce
12345 SW Main St.
Tigard, OR 97223
Ph:(503)639-1656
Fax: (503)639-6302
Co. E-mail: info@tigardchamber.org
URL: http://www.tigardchamber.org
Contact: Jeremy Monlux, Exec. Dir.

64275 ■ Tillamook Chamber of Commerce
3705 Hwy. 101 N
Tillamook, OR 97141
Ph:(503)842-7525

Fax: (503)842-7526
Co. E-mail: tillchamber@oregoncoast.com
URL: http://www.tillamookchamber.org
Contact: Sandy Hemenway, Mgr.

64276 ■ Troutdale Area Chamber of Commerce
PO Box 245
Troutdale, OR 97060
Ph:(503)669-7473
Fax: (503)492-3613
Co. E-mail: troutdale@stateoforegon.com
URL: http://www.troutdalechamber.org
Contact: Diane McKeel, Exec. Dir.

64277 ■ Tualatin Chamber of Commerce
18791 SW Martinazzi Ave., Ste. C
PO Box 701
Tualatin, OR 97062
Ph:(503)692-0780
Fax: (503)692-6955
Co. E-mail: hope@tualatinchamber.com
URL: http://www.tualatinchamber.com
Contact: Hope Howard, Exec. Dir.

64278 ■ Umatilla Chamber of Commerce
1530 6th St.
PO Box 67
Umatilla, OR 97882
Ph:(541)922-4825
Fax: (541)922-4825
Co. E-mail: umatillachamber@eoni.com
URL: http://www.umatilla.org
Contact: Yesenia Rangel, Coor.

64279 ■ Union County Chamber of Commerce
102 Elm St.
La Grande, OR 97850-2514
Ph:(541)963-8588
Free: 800-848-9969
Fax: (541)963-3936
Co. E-mail: info@unioncountychamber.org
URL: http://www.unioncountychamber.org/indexf.cfm
Contact: Judy Loudermilk, Exec. Dir.

64280 ■ Vale Chamber of Commerce
PO Box 661
Vale, OR 97918
Ph:(541)473-3800
Co. E-mail: info@valeoregon.org
URL: http://www.valeoregon.org
Contact: David De Mayo, Pres.

64281 ■ Waldport Chamber of Commerce
PO Box 669
620 NW Spring St.
Waldport, OR 97394
Ph:(541)563-2133
Co. E-mail: chamber@peak.org
URL: http://www.waldport-chamber.com
Contact: Pat Tyron, Pres.

64282 ■ Wallowa County Chamber of Commerce
PO Box 427
Enterprise, OR 97828-0427
Ph:(541)426-4622
Free: 800-585-4121
Fax: (541)426-2032
Co. E-mail: info@wallowacounty.org
URL: http://www.wallowacountychamber.com
Contact: Vicki Searles, Exec. Dir.

64283 ■ Wilsonville Chamber of Commerce
29600 SW Park Pl.
PO Box 3737
Wilsonville, OR 97070
Ph:(503)682-0411
Free: 800-647-3843
Fax: (503)682-4189
Co. E-mail: info@wilsonvillechamber.com
URL: http://www.wils-chamber.org
Contact: Mark Ottenad, Exec.Dir.

64284 ■ Winston Dillard Area Chamber of Commerce
PO Box 68
Winston, OR 97496
Ph:(541)679-0118
Fax: (541)679-4270
Co. E-mail: winstonvic@charter.net
URL: http://www.winstonoregon.net/chamber.html
Contact: Joanne Hayes, Pres.

64285 ■ Woodburn Area Chamber of Commerce
2241 Country Club Rd.
PO Box 194
Woodburn, OR 97071
Ph:(503)982-8221
Fax: (503)982-8410
Co. E-mail: welcome@woodburnchamber.org
URL: http://www.woodburnchamber.org
Contact: Nick Harville, Exec. Dir./Sec.

64286 ■ Yachats Area Chamber of Commerce
PO Box 728
Yachats, OR 97498
Ph:(541)547-3530
Free: 800-929-0477
Co. E-mail: info@yachats.org
URL: http://www.yachats.org
Contact: Larry Spivack, Pres.

MINORITY BUSINESS ASSISTANCE PROGRAMS

64287 ■ Oregon Office of Minority, Women, and Emerging Small Businesses
350 Winter St., NE, Rm. 300
Salem, OR 97310
Ph:(503)947-7976
Fax: (503)373-7041
Co. E-mail: web.omwesb.state.or.us
URL: http://www.cbs.state.or.us
Description: Certifies disadvantaged and emerging small businesses, allowing their participation in the state's targeted purchasing programs. Also identifies and seeks to remove barriers that prevent these businesses from entering the mainstream of commercial activity.

64288 ■ Portland Minority Business Development Center
IMPACT Business Consultants, Inc.
8959 SW Barbour Blvd., Ste. 102
Portland, OR 97219
Ph:(503)245-9253
Fax: (503)246-3841
Co. E-mail: impact1@teleport.com

FINANCING AND LOAN PROGRAMS

64289 ■ Oregon Resource and Technology Development Fund
4370 NE Halsey St., Ste. 233
Portland, OR 97213-1566
Ph:(503)282-4462
Fax: (503)282-2976
Preferred Investment Size: $100,000 to $300,000. **Investment Types:** Seed, start-up, research and development. **Industry Preferences:** Biotechnology, computer hardware, software and services, medical and health, consumer related, industrial and energy. **Geographic Preferences:** West Coast.

64290 ■ Orien Ventures
14523 SW Westlake Dr.
Lake Oswego, OR 97035
Ph:(503)699-1680
Fax: (503)699-1681
Contact: Anthony Miadich, Managing General Partner
Preferred Investment Size: $500,000 minimum. **Investment Types:** Start-up, seed, early and first stage. **Industry Preferences:** Communications, computer software, Internet specific, semiconductors and other electronics, medical and health.

64291 ■ OVP Venture Partners / Olympic Venture Partners (Portland)
6550 SW Macadam Ave., Ste. 300
Portland, OR 97239
Ph:(503)697-8766
Fax: (503)697-8863
URL: http://www.ovp.com
Contact: Bill Funcannon, Chief Financial Officer
Preferred Investment Size: $1,000,000 to $10,000,000. **Investment Types:** Seed, start-up, early and first stage. **Industry Preferences:** Computer software and services, Internet specific, medical and health, biotechnology, communications and media, consumer related, semiconductors and other electronics, computer hardware, industrial and energy, and other products. **Geographic Preferences:** Northwest and West Coast.

64292 ■ Shaw Venture Partners / Shaw Glasgow Partners
9755 SW Barnes Rd., Ste. 670
Portland, OR 97225
Ph:(503)228-4884
Fax: (503)352-1815
URL: http://www.shawventures.com
Contact: Ralph Shaw, General Partner
Preferred Investment Size: $250,000 to $3,000,000. **Investment Types:** Seed, start-up, first, second and early stage, balanced, leveraged buyout, and special situation. **Industry Preferences:** Communications and media, computer software and services, industrial and energy, consumer related, biotechnology, semiconductors and other electronics, computer hardware, medical and health, Internet specific, and other products. **Geographic Preferences:** Northwest and West Coast.

64293 ■ Utah Ventures II LP
10700 SW Beaverton-Hillsdale Hwy., Ste. 548
Beaverton, OR 97005
Ph:(503)574-4125
Co. E-mail: adishlip@uven.com
URL: http://www.uven.com
Preferred Investment Size: $1,000,000 to $7,000,000. **Investment Types:** Early stages. **Industry Preferences:** Diversified technology. **Geographic Preferences:** Northwest and Rocky Mountains.

PROCUREMENT ASSISTANCE PROGRAMS

64294 ■ Oregon Procurement Technical Assistance Center–The Organization for Economic Initiatives
1144 Gateway Loop, Ste. 203
Springfield, OR 97477
Ph:(541)736-1088
Free: 800-497-7551
Fax: (541)736-1090
URL: http://www.gcap.org/
Contact: Jan Hurt, Prgm Mgr
E-mail: jhurt@orednet.org

INCUBATORS/RESEARCH AND TECHNOLOGY PARKS

64295 ■ Agricultural Research Foundation
Strand Agricultural Hall, Ste. 100
Corvallis, OR 97331-2219
Ph:(541)737-3228
Fax: (541)737-4067
Co. E-mail: dorothy.beaton@orst.edu
URL: http://agresearchfoundation.oregonstate.edu
Contact: Dorothy Beaton, Exec.Dir.
E-mail: dorothy.beaton@orst.edu
Scope: Main function is to obtain funds from extramural sources for research in agriculture, fisheries, and wildlife, designed to benefit the state of Oregon.

64296 ■ The Oregon Innovation Center (OIC)
500 SW Bond Ste. 200
Bend, OR 97702

Ph:(541)312-5785
Fax: (541)312-5787
Co. E-mail: info@innovationcenter.org
URL: http://www.innovationcenter.org
Contact: CEO
Description: The OiC is a small business incubator for emerging technology firms and entrepreneurs. In addition to affordable space, the Center offers tenants capital sourcing, economic facilities and other services.

64297 ■ Oregon State University–Office of Vice Provost for Research
312 Kerr Administration Bldg.
Corvallis, OR 97331
Ph:(541)737-3437
Fax: (541)737-3093
Co. E-mail: John.Cassady@oregonstate.edu
URL: http://oregonstate.edu/research
Contact: Dr. John M. Cassady, VP,Res.
E-mail: John.Cassady@oregonstate.edu
Scope: Coordinates University research activities, including individual projects in various academic schools and special research centers and institutes. Also administers University's Technology Transfer Program. **Publications:** Report (annually). **Educational Activities:** Biology Colloquium; Condon Lectures; Workshops. **Awards:** General research fund; URISC research equipment reserves fund.

64298 ■ Riverfront Research Park
1276 University of Oregon
Eugene, OR 97403-1276
Ph:(541)346-5164
Fax: (541)346-6197
Co. E-mail: dwiley@oregon.uoregon.edu
URL: http://researchpark.uoregon.edu
Contact: Diane Wiley, Dir.
E-mail: dwiley@oregon.uoregon.edu
Scope: 67-acre site adjacent to Willamette River and the University. Provides opportunities for research interaction between the University and park tenants engaged in biotechnology, neuroscience, artificial intelligence and behavioral science. Seeks to assist in the diversification of the economic base of the state, particularly the Eugene-Springfield metropolitan area, and provide additional financial opportunities for the University and its community.

64299 ■ University of Oregon–Office of Research Services and Administration
5219 University of Oregon
Eugene, OR 97403-5219
Ph:(541)346-5131
Fax: (541)346-5138
Co. E-mail: gary_chaffins@orsa.uoregon.edu
URL: http://orsa.uoregon.edu/
Contact: Gary Chaffins, Dir.
E-mail: gary_chaffins@orsa.uoregon.edu
Scope: Promotes and encourages scientific and scholarly research at the University through contracts with outside agencies and research grants to faculty members from private and governmental sources. **Publications:** Annual Report; Inquiry Magazine (annually); ORSP Research Report Newsletter (monthly); Research Activity Brochure.

EDUCATIONAL PROGRAMS

64300 ■ Chemeketa Community College–Training and Economic Development Center
4000 Lancaster Dr. NE
PO Box 14007
Salem, OR 97307
Ph:(503)399-5000
Free: 800-398-6262
Fax: (503)581-6017
URL: http://www.chemeketa.edu
Description: Provides noncredit courses, workshops, and short-term in-house and on-site programs to help business owners, managers, and employees learn and improve business knowledge and skills. The Small Business Management Program is a one-year

course of study renewable up to three years offered to small business operators. It includes weekly classes and visits to businesses by instructors for assistance in recordkeeping, cost analysis, and effective operations. State, Targeted Training Funds are coordinated by this area.

64301 ■ Mount Hood Community College
26000 SE Stark St.
Gresham, OR 97030
Ph:(503)491-6422
Fax: (503)491-7388
URL: http://www.mhcc.cc.or.us
Description: Two-year college offering a small business management program.

64302 ■ Southwestern Oregon Community College
1988 Newmark Ave.
Coos Bay, OR 97420
Ph:(541)888-2525
Free: 800-962-2838
Fax: (541)888-7247
URL: http://www.socc.edu
Description: Two-year college offering a small business management program.

64303 ■ Umpqua Community College
PO Box 967
Roseburg, OR 97470
Ph:(541)440-4600
Fax: (541)440-4637
URL: http://www.umpqua.cc.or.us
Description: Two-year college offering a small business management program.

PUBLICATIONS

64304 ■ *Incorporation and Business Guide for Oregon*
Self-Counsel Press, Inc.
1704 N. State St.
Bellingham, WA 98225
Ph:(360)676-4530
Free: 800-663-3007
Fax: (360)676-4549
Ed: C. Thomas Davis. **Released:** Fourth edition, 1992. **Price:** $14.95. **Description:** Includes forms to help entrepreneurs incorporate in Oregon.

64305 ■ *Incorporation Forms*
Self-Counsel Press
1704 N State St.
Bellingham, WA 98225
Ph:(360)676-4530
Free: 800-663-3007
Fax: (360)676-4549
Released: 1993. **Price:** $12.95 (paper). **Description:** Includes forms necessary to form your own corporation in Oregon.

64306 ■ *Media Publications*
3610 Goodpasture Loop
Eugene, OR 97401
Ph:(541)484-1342
Fax: (541)688-0832
Co. E-mail: builders@rio.com

64307 ■ *Oregon Business*
610 SW Broadway, Ste. 200
Portland, OR 97205
Ph:(503)223-0304
Fax: (503)221-6544
URL: http://www.oregonbusiness.com

64308 ■ *Smart Start your Oregon Business*
PSI Research
300 N. Valley Dr.
Grants Pass, OR 97526
Ph:(503)479-9464
Free: 800-228-2275
Fax: (503)476-1479
Co. E-mail: info@psi-research.com
URL: http://www.psi-research.com
Ed: Michael D. Jenkins. **Released:** Revised edition, 1992. **Price:** $29.95 (looseleaf binder); $24.95 (paper). **Description:** Part of the Successful Business Library series.

64309 ■ *Your Business Plan*
Oregon Small Business Development Center Network
44 W. Broadway, Ste. 501
Eugene, OR 97401-3021
Ph:(541)726-2250
Fax: (541)345-6006
URL: http://www.efru.org/~osbdcn
Price: $16.45. **Description:** Spanish version also available.

64310 ■ *Your International Business Plan*
Oregon Small Business Development Center Network
44 W. Broadway, Ste. 501
Eugene, OR 97401
Ph:(541)726-2250
Fax: (541)345-6006
URL: http://culterslanecc.edu
Ed: James L. Otis. **Released:** Revised edition, 1990. **Price:** $16.95 (paper).

64311 ■ *Your Marketing Plan*
Oregon Small Business Development Center Network
44 W. Broadway, Ste. 507
Eugene, OR 97401
Ph:(503)726-2250
Fax: (503)345-6006
URL: http://www.efru.org/~osbdcn
Price: $16.45. **Description:** Helps the small business manager identify and target the potential and actual markets for their goods and services. Also discusses fundamental marketing concepts.

PUBLISHERS

64312 ■ Carolina Pacific Publishing
16350 SE Bel Air Dr.
Clackamas, OR 97015-7836
Contact: John R. Ross, Mgr
Description: Publishes books on company histories, management, corporate culture, entrepreneurs and job enrichment. Accepts unsolicited manuscripts; query first with description. Reaches market through direct mail and Baker & Taylor.

64313 ■ North American Bookdealers Exchange
PO Box 606
Cottage Grove, OR 97424
Ph:(541)942-7455
Fax: (541)942-7455
Co. E-mail: nabe@bookmarketingprofits.com
URL: http://www.bookmarketingprofits.com
Contact: Al Galasso, Dir.
Description: Distributes books related to nonfiction, business, how-to. A national book marketing organization for independent presses and self-publishers, currently with 1000 members. Reaches market through direct mail. **Founded:** 1980.

64314 ■ Opal Creek Press L.L.C.
1675 Fir St. S
Salem, OR 97302
Ph:(503)375-9015
Free: (866)375-9015
Fax: (503)363-6228
Co. E-mail: info@opalcreekpress.com
URL: http://www.opalcreekpress.com
Contact: Kristi Negri, Secretary
E-mail: kristi@opalcreekpress.com
Description: Publishes memoir, including military memoir, business, spirituality, and self-help books. Does not accept unsolicited manuscripts. Reaches market through direct mail, wholesalers, and standard publicity activities. **Founded:** 2000.

64315 ■ Plain and Simple Books
95376 Kentuck Way Ln.
North Bend, OR 97459
Ph:(541)751-1939
Fax: (541)751-1203
URL: http://www.plainandsimplebooks.com
Contact: Carol Denbow

E-mail: cdenbow@plainandsimplebooks.com
Description: Publishes hardcover and paperback start-up business books, particularly about stress relief on the job. Reaches market through direct mail, telephone sales, and the Internet. **Founded:** 2006

64316 ■ PSI Research Inc./Oasis Press/ Hellgate Press
PO Box 3727
Central Point, OR 97502
Ph:(541)855-5566
Free: 800-795-4059
Fax: (541)855-1360
Co. E-mail: information@psi-research.com
URL: http://www.psi-research.com
Description: Publishes books on all aspects of business, including finance, marketing, law, human resources, communications, franchising, military, adventure, and travel. Accepts unsolicited manuscripts. Reaches market through Distributor Midpoint Books. **Founded:** 1975.

64317 ■ Spirit Press/Little Stars Little Moon Publishing
c/o Tim Dickey, 5138 W Las Palmaritas
Glendale, AZ 85302

Free: (866)284-0217
Co. E-mail: spiritpress@hotmail.com
URL: http://papatim.11orless.com/spiritpress
Contact: Suzanne Deakins
Description: Publishes books on spirit in all aspects of life, including business and self-help. Written for children and adults. Accepts unsolicited manuscripts. Reaches market through commission representatives, direct mail, telephone sales, wholesalers, and distributors. **Founded:** 1997.

64318 ■ Thin Book Publishing
86 SW Century Dr., PMB 446
Bend, OR 97702
Ph:(541)390-7893
Free: 888-316-9544
Fax: (541)317-8606
Co. E-mail: info@thinbook.com
URL: http://www.thinbook.com
Description: Publishes books on promoting successful business working relationships within organizations.

64319 ■ Uncommon Technology Inc.
PO Box 2230
Clackamas, OR 97015-2230

Free: 800-910-9000
Fax: 800-910-9505
Co. E-mail: uti_info@uncommon.com
URL: http://uncommontechnology.com
Description: Publishes books and CD-ROMs on resolution of business-related issues.

64320 ■ Wyatt-MacKenzie Publishing Inc.
15115 Hwy. 36
Deadwood, OR 97430
Ph:(541)964-3314
Fax: (541)964-3315
Co. E-mail: info@wymacpublishing.com
URL: http://www.wymacpublishing.com
Contact: Nancy Cleary
E-mail: nancy@wymacpublishing.com
Description: Publishes books and material for and by moms on raising children and managing at-home businesses. **Founded:** 1998

Pennsylvania

SMALL BUSINESS DEVELOPMENT CENTER LEAD OFFICE

64321 ■ University of Pennsylvania–Pennsylvania SBDC
The Wharton School
409 Vance Hall
3733 Spruce St.
Philadelphia, PA 19104-6374
Ph:(215)898-1219
Fax: (215)573-2135
URL: http://pasbdc.org
Contact: Gregory Higgins, State Dir.
E-mail: ghiggins@wharton.upenn.edu

64322 ■ University of Pennsylvania–Small Business Development Center
The Wharton School
Vance Hall, 4th Flr.
3733 Spruce St.
Philadelphia, PA 19104-6374
Ph:(215)898-1219
Fax: (215)573-2135
Co. E-mail: pasbdc@atwharton.upenn.edu
URL: http://www.pasbdc.org
Contact: Gregory L. Higgins Jr., State Director

SMALL BUSINESS DEVELOPMENT CENTERS

64323 ■ Bucknell University–Small Business Development Center
126 Dana Engineering Bldg.
Lewisburg, PA 17837
Ph:(570)577-1249
Free: (866)375-6010
Fax: (570)577-1768
Co. E-mail: sbdc@bucknell.edu
URL: http://www.bucknell.edu/sbdc/
Contact: Jon R. Vernam, Dir.
E-mail: jvernam@bucknell.edu

64324 ■ Bucks County Economic Development Corporation–SBDC Outreach Center
2 E. Court St.
Doylestown, PA 18901
Ph:(215)348-9031
Fax: (215)204-4554
Contact: Bruce Love, Dir.

64325 ■ Clarion University of Pennsylvania–Small Business Development Center
102 Dana Still Business Administration Bldg.
Clarion, PA 16214-1232
Ph:(814)393-2060
Free: 877-292-1843
Fax: (814)393-2636
Co. E-mail: sbdc@clarion.edu

URL: http://www.clarion.edu/sbdc/
Contact: Dr. Woodrow W. Yeaney, Dir.
E-mail: yeaney@clarion.edu

64326 ■ Duquesne University–Chrysler Corporation Small Business Development Center
108 Rockwell Hall
600 Forbes Ave.
Pittsburgh, PA 15282
Ph:(412)396-6233
Fax: (412)396-5884
Co. E-mail: duqsbdc@duq.edu
URL: http://www.duq.edu/sbdc
Contact: Dr. Mary T. McKinney, Dir.

64327 ■ Environmental Management Assistance Program (Central/Western Region)–Pennsylvania State University–SBDC (117 T)
117 Technology Ctr.
University Park, PA 16802-7000
Ph:(814)863-6233
Co. E-mail: sbdc@psu.edu
Contact: Denise F. Bechdel, Consultant
E-mail: dlf14@psu.edu

64328 ■ Gannon University–Small Business Development Center
A.J. Palumbo Bldg.
120 W. 9th St.
Erie, PA 16501
Ph:(814)871-7232
Fax: (814)871-7383
Co. E-mail: gusbdc@gannon.edu
URL: http://www.sbdcgannon.org
Contact: Steve Overholt, Business Consultant

64329 ■ Indiana University of Pennsylvania–Small Business Development Center
208 Eberly College of Business & Information Technology
Indiana, PA 15705
Ph:(724)357-7915
Fax: (724)357-5985
URL: http://www.eberly.iup.edu/sbitemp/SBDC.htm
Contact: Tony Palamone, Dir.
E-mail: tpalamon@iup.edu

64330 ■ Indiana University of Pennsylvania–Small Business Incubator–SBDC (322A)
322A Eberly College of Business
Indiana, PA 15705
Ph:(724)357-2465
URL: http://www.eberly.iup.edu/sbitemp/SBDC.htm
Contact: Dr. Robert Boldin
E-mail: rboldin@iup.edu

64331 ■ International Trade Assistance–Clarion University–Small Business Development Center (102 S)
102 Still Hay
Clarion, PA 16214
Ph:(814)393-2060

Free: 877-292-1843
Co. E-mail: info@clarion.edu
URL: http://www.clarion.edu/sbdc/services/international.shtml
Contact: Kate Curtis Consul

64332 ■ Kutztown University–Small Business Development Center
DeFrancesco Bldg., Rm. 2
PO Box 730
Kutztown, PA 19530
Ph:(610)683-4706
Fax: (610)683-4644
URL: http://www.kutztownsbdc.org
Contact: Ernie Post, Dir.
E-mail: post@kutztown.edu

64333 ■ Lehigh University–Small Business Development Center
Rauch Business Ctr., Rm. 390
621 Taylor St.
Bethlehem, PA 18015-3117
Ph:(610)758-3980
Fax: (610)758-5205
Co. E-mail: insbdc@lehigh.edu
URL: http://lehigh.edu/~insbdc
Contact: Sandra Holsonback, Dir.

64334 ■ Lock Haven University of Pennsylvania–SBDC Outreach Center
McDade Trade & Transit Centre
100 W. Third St.
Williamsport, PA 17701
Ph:(570)326-1971
URL: http://www.lhup.edu/sbdc/

64335 ■ Lock Haven University of Pennsylvania–Small Business Development Center
East Campus
301 W. Church St.
Lock Haven, PA 17745
Ph:(570)893-2589
URL: http://www.lhup.edu/sbdc/
Contact: Timothy J. Keohane, Dir.
E-mail: tkeohane@lhup.edu

64336 ■ Saint Francis College–Small Business Development Center
117 Evergreen Dr.
PO Box 600
Loretto, PA 15940-0600
Ph:(814)472-3200
Fax: (814)472-3202
Co. E-mail: sbdc@francis.edu
URL: http://www.francis.edu/sbdc/
Contact: Ed Huttenhower, Dir.
E-mail: ehuttenhower@francis.edu

64337 ■ Saint Vincent College–Small Business Development Center–Center for Global Competitiveness (Bened)
Benedict Hall, 1st Fl.
300 Fraser Purchase Rd.
Latrobe, PA 15650
Ph:(724)537-4572

Free: (866)723-2242
Fax: (724)537-0919
Co. E-mail: sbdc@stvincent.edu
URL: http://www.stvincent.edu/sbdc/
Contact: James H. Kunkel, Exec. Dir.
E-mail: james.kunkel@mail.stvincent.edu

64338 ■ Satellite Office at Corry–Erie County Redevelopment Authority
1524 Enterprise Rd.
Corry, PA
Ph:(814)871-7232
URL: http://www.sbdcgannon.org
Contact: 877258-6648

64339 ■ Temple University–Small Business Development Center
Beech Bldg., Ste. 200
1510 Cecil B. Moore Ave.
Philadelphia, PA 19121
Ph:(215)204-7282
Fax: (215)204-4554
Co. E-mail: sbdc@sbm.temple.edu
URL: http://sbm.temple.edu/sbdc
Contact: Eustace Kangaju, Dir.

64340 ■ University of Pittsburgh–Small Business Development Center
Wesley W. Posvar Hall, 1st Fl.
Pittsburgh, PA 15260
Ph:(412)648-1542
Fax: (412)648-1636
Co. E-mail: ieeinfo@pitt.edu
URL: http://pasbdc.org
Contact: Christine Kush, Dir.
E-mail: cakush@katz.pitt.edu

64341 ■ University of Scranton–Small Business Development Center
Estate Bldg., 2nd Fl.
800 Monroe Ave.
Scranton, PA 18510
Ph:(570)941-7588
Free: 800-829-7232
Fax: (570)941-4053
URL: http://sbdc.scranton.edu
Contact: Elaine M. Tweedy, Dir.
E-mail: elaine.tweedy@scranton.edu

64342 ■ West Chester University–SBDC
211 Carter Dr.
West Chester, PA 19383
Ph:(610)436-1000
Fax: (610)436-2577
URL: http://www.wcupa.edu
Contact: Bob Scanlon, Dir.

64343 ■ Wharton Small Business Development Center
Vance Hall
3733 Spruce St., 4th Fl.
Philadelphia, PA 19104
Ph:(215)898-4861
Fax: (215)898-1063
URL: http://whartonsbdc.wharton.upenn.edu

64344 ■ Wilkes University–Small Business Development Center
Innovation Center, Ste. 200
7 S. Main St.
Wilkes Barre, PA 18701-1706
Ph:(570)408-4340
Fax: (570)408-7889
Co. E-mail: sbdc@wilkes.edu
URL: http://sbdc.wilkes.edu
Contact: Ruth C. Hughes, Dir.
E-mail: hughes@wilkes.edu

SMALL BUSINESS ASSISTANCE PROGRAMS

64345 ■ Mid-Atlantic Technology Applications Center
University of Pittsburgh
3400 Forbes Ave., 5th Fl.
Pittsburgh, PA 15260

Ph:(412)383-2500
Fax: (412)383-2595
URL: http://www.mtac.pitt.edu
Description: Provides access to over 450 databases worldwide and provides information on such topics as marketing data, patents and licensing, and federal procurement contract opportunities.

64346 ■ Pennsylvania Department of Community and Economic Development–Center for Business Financing–Site Development Division (Commo)
Commonwealth Keystone Bldg.
400 North St., 4th Fl.
Harrisburg, PA 17120-0225
Ph:(717)787-7120
Free: 800-379-7448
Fax: (717)772-2890
URL: http://www.newpa.com
Description: Provides financing for infrastructure improvements such as sewer and water systems, waste disposal facilities, transportation facilities, and fire and safety facilities.

64347 ■ Pennsylvania Department of Community and Economic Development–Center Entrepreneurial Assistance
Commonwealth Keystone Bldg.
400 North St., 4th Fl.
Harrisburg, PA 17120-0225
Ph:(717)783-8950
Free: 800-280-3801
Fax: (717)787-4088
URL: http://www.newpa.com
Description: Pennsylvania's advocate for small business; provides prompt information on licenses and permits needed to start and operate a business.

64348 ■ Pennsylvania Department of Community and Economic Development–Loans Division
Commonwealth Keystone Bldg.
400 North St., 4th Fl.
Harrisburg, PA 17120-0225
Ph:(717)787-6245
Fax: (717)772-2890
URL: http://www.newpa.com
Description: Provides funds to train employees in specific skills to meet an individual employer's needs.

64349 ■ Pennsylvania Department of Community and Economic Development–Office of International Business Development
Commonwealth Keystone Bldg.
400 North St., 4th Fl.
Harrisburg, PA 17120-0225
Ph:(717)787-6245
Fax: (717)772-2890
URL: http://www.newpa.com
Description: Provides assistance to companies seeking the latest information on potential foreign markets for their products, and regional economic development organizations and companies with information about all facets of international trade. Responds to inquiries from foreign importers in search of new suppliers.

64350 ■ Pennsylvania Department of Community and Economic Development–Pennsylvania Industrial Development Authority
Commonwealth Keystone Bldg.
400 North St., 4th Fl.
Harrisburg, PA 17120-0225
Ph:(717)787-6245
Fax: (717)772-2890
URL: http://www.newpa.com
Description: Established in 1956 to make long-term, low-interest business loans to firms engaged in manufacturing or industrial enterprises.

64351 ■ Pennsylvania Department of Community and Economic Development–Technology Innovation–Ben Franklin Partnership (Commo)
Commonwealth Keystone Bldg.
400 North St., 4th Fl.
Harrisburg, PA 17120-0225
Ph:(717)787-6245
Fax: (717)772-2890
URL: http://www.newpa.com
Description: Programs promote advanced technology in an effort to make traditional industry more competitive in the international marketplace. BFP's Advanced Technology Centers represent consortia of businesses that provide joint applied research and development efforts, assistance to higher education institutions and entrepreneurial assistance services.

64352 ■ Pennsylvania State University–Technical Assistance Program
Pennsylvania Technical Asistance Program
118 Kellar Bldg
University Park, PA 16802
Ph:(814)865-0427
Fax: (814)865-3589
Co. E-mail: penntap@psu.edu
URL: http://www.penntap.psu.edu
Description: Provides technical information and assistance in problem-solving, business start-up, and increasing productivity.

SCORE OFFICES

64353 ■ Pottstown SCORE No. 594
c/o Jim Jeffries, Chm.
New York Plz. Bldg.
244 High St., Ste. 302
Pottstown, PA 19464
Ph:(610)327-2673
Fax: (610)327-0150
Co. E-mail: info@pottstownscore.org
URL: http://www.pottstownscore.org
Contact: Jim Jeffries, Chm.
Description: Provides professional guidance and information to maximize the success of existing and emerging small businesses. Offers business counseling and workshops.

64354 ■ SCORE Bucks County
c/o Frank Keating, Co-Chm.
409 Hood Blvd.
Fairless Hills, PA 19030
Ph:(215)943-8850
Fax: (215)943-7404
Contact: Mr. Wendelin Stahl
Description: Works to provide business counseling.

64355 ■ SCORE Central PA
Industry & Technology Ctr.
2820 E College Ave., Ste. E
State College, PA 16801
Ph:(814)234-9415
Fax: (814)234-9415
Co. E-mail: scorecpa@trip.net
URL: http://www.scorecpa.org
Contact: Edward R. Book, Chm.
Description: Provides professional guidance and information to maximize the success of existing and emerging small businesses. Offers business counseling and workshops.

64356 ■ SCORE Chester County
Chester County Government Service Center
601 Westtown Rd., Ste. 281
West Chester, PA 19382-4538
Ph:(610)344-6910
Fax: (610)344-6919
Co. E-mail: info@scorechesco.org
URL: http://www.scorechesco.org
Contact: Mrs. Ellen Ryckman, Office Mgr.
Description: Serves as volunteer program in which working and retired business management professionals provide free business counseling to men and women who are considering starting a small business, encountering problems with their business, or expanding their business. Offers free one-on-one counseling, online counseling and low cost workshops on a variety of business topics.

64357 ■ SCORE Cumberland Valley
District 3
100 Lincoln Way E
Chambersburg, PA 17201
Ph:(717)264-7101
Co. E-mail: chamber@chambersburg.org
Contact: Arlene Long, Chair
Description: Provides professional guidance and information to maximize the success of existing and emerging small businesses. Offers business counseling and workshops.

64358 ■ SCORE East Montgomery County
Baederwood Office Plz.
1653 The Fairway, Ste. 204
Jenkintown, PA 19046
Ph:(215)885-3027
Fax: (215)885-3029
Co. E-mail: counselor@score513.org
URL: http://www.score513.org
Contact: Steve Lember, Chm.
Description: Provides professional guidance and information to maximize the success of existing and emerging small businesses. Offers business counseling and workshops.

64359 ■ SCORE Erie
120 W 9th St.
Erie, PA 16501
Ph:(814)871-5650
Fax: (814)871-7530
Co. E-mail: score193@juno.com
URL: http://www.score193eriepa.com
Contact: Keith Farnham, Chm.
Description: Strives for the formation, growth, and success of small businesses. Promotes entrepreneur education in Erie area, Pennsylvania.

64360 ■ SCORE Harrisburg
HACC Entrepreneurial Program
349 Wiconisco St., Ste. No. 237
Harrisburg, PA 17110
Ph:(717)213-0435
Fax: (717)761-4315
Co. E-mail: score@panetwork.com
URL: http://www.panetwork.com/score
Contact: Archie J. Sybrandt, Chm.
Description: Strives for the formation, growth, and success of small businesses. Promotes entrepreneur education in Harrisburg area, Pennsylvania.

64361 ■ SCORE Lancaster
Liberty Pl., Ste. 231
313 W Liberty St.
Lancaster, PA 17603-2798
Ph:(717)397-3092
Fax: (717)481-7637
Co. E-mail: scorelancaster@verizon.net
URL: http://www.scorelancaster.org
Contact: Louis Davenport, Chm.
Description: Strives for the formation, growth, and success of small businesses. Promotes entrepreneur education throughout Lancaster County.

64362 ■ SCORE Lehigh Valley
Lehigh University
Rauch Business Center, Rm. 390
Bethlehem, PA 18015
Ph:(610)758-4496
Co. E-mail: jmrscore@aol.com
URL: http://www.lehighvalleyscore.org
Description: Strives for the formation, growth, and success of small businesses. Promotes entrepreneur education in Bethlehem area, Pennsylvania.

64363 ■ SCORE Mon-Valley
c/o Herman Meade, Chair
435 Donner Ave.
Monessen, PA 15062
Ph:(724)684-4277
Fax: (724)684-0190
Co. E-mail: score486@monvalleyscore.com
URL: http://www.score.org

64364 ■ SCORE North Central PA
Executive Plz.
330 Pine St., Ste. 305
Williamsport, PA 17701

Ph:(570)322-3720
Fax: (570)322-3720
Co. E-mail: score234@verizon.net
URL: http://www.lycoming.org/score
Description: Provides professional guidance and information to maximize the success of existing and emerging small businesses. Offers business counseling and workshops.

64365 ■ SCORE Philadelphia
Robert N.C. Nix Federal Bldg.
900 Market St., 5th Fl.
Philadelphia, PA 19107
Ph:(215)580-2722
Contact: Harry Anderson, Chm.
Description: Serves as volunteer program in which working and retired business management professionals provide free business counseling to men and women who are considering starting a small business, encountering problems with their business, or expanding their business. Offers free one-on-one counseling, online counseling and low cost workshops on a variety of business topics.

64366 ■ SCORE Pittsburgh
411 7th Ave., Ste. 1450
Pittsburgh, PA 15219
Ph:(412)395-6560
Fax: (412)395-6562
Co. E-mail: info@scorepittsburgh.com
URL: http://www.scorepittsburgh.com
Contact: Lee O'Nan, Chm.
Description: Aims to help small businesses in Southwestern Pennsylvania to grow and prosper by providing workshops and one-on-one counseling by members that have many years of experience in managing businesses.

64367 ■ SCORE Uniontown
140 N Beeson Ave., Rm. 404
Uniontown, PA 15401
Ph:(724)437-4222
Co. E-mail: uniontownscore@lcsys.net
URL: http://www.fayettecountypa.org/score
Contact: John Buchanan, Chm.
Description: Provides professional guidance and information to maximize the success of existing and emerging small businesses. Offers business counseling and workshops.

64368 ■ SCORE Westmoreland County
St. Vincent College
Aurelius Hall
300 Fraser Purchase Rd.
Latrobe, PA 15650-2690
Ph:(724)539-7505
Fax: (724)539-1850
Co. E-mail: score@email.stvincent.edu
URL: http://www.scorewestco555.org
Contact: Ronald Mckenzie, Chm.
Description: Provides professional guidance and information to maximize the success of existing and emerging small businesses. Offers business counseling and workshops.

64369 ■ SCORE Wilkes-Barre
Stegmaier Bldg.
7 Wilkes-Barre Blvd., Ste. 273M
Wilkes-Barre, PA 18702-5241
Ph:(570)826-6502
Fax: (570)826-6498
Co. E-mail: wbscore@epix.net
Contact: John Reddy, Chm.
Description: Provides professional guidance and information to maximize the success of existing and emerging small businesses. Offers business counseling and workshops.

64370 ■ SCORE York
c/o J. Joseph Danyo, MD
Cyber Center
2101 Pennsylvania Ave.
York, PA 17404
Ph:(717)845-8830
Co. E-mail: score441@yorkscore.org
URL: http://www.yorkscore.org
Contact: Dr. J. Joseph Danyo MD, Chm.

Description: Offers mentoring to existing businesses that are experiencing difficulties. Workshops are also given periodically throughout the year in conjunction with Kutztown University's Small Business Development Center to help people start a business, write a business plan, and market their business.

BETTER BUSINESS BUREAUS

64371 ■ Better Business Bureau of Metro Washington and Eastern Pennsylvania-South Central Division
1337 N Front St.
Harrisburg, PA 17102
Ph:(717)364-3250
Fax: (717)364-3251
Co. E-mail: info@mybbb.org
URL: http://www.easternpa.bbb.org
Contact: Chet Amend, Branch Dir.

64372 ■ Better Business Bureau Serving Metropolitan Washington, DC and Eastern Pennsylvania
1608 Walnut St., Ste.402
Philadelphia, PA 19103
Ph:(215)985-9313
Fax: (215)893-9312
Co. E-mail: info@mybbb.org
URL: http://www.mybbb.org
Contact: Andrew P. Goode, Reg.VP

64373 ■ Better Business Bureau of Western Pennsylvania
300 6th Ave., Ste. 100-UL
Pittsburgh, PA 15222-2511
Ph:(412)456-2700
Fax: (412)456-2739
Co. E-mail: info@pittsburgh.bbb.org
URL: http://www.pittsburgh.bbb.org
Contact: Warren King Jr., Pres.

CHAMBERS OF COMMERCE

64374 ■ African-American Chamber of Commerce of Philadelphia
701 Market St., Ste. 6500
Philadelphia, PA 19106
Ph:(215)351-5201
Fax: (215)351-5209
Co. E-mail: info@aachamber.org
URL: http://www.aachamber.org
Contact: John T. Childress, Exec.Dir.

64375 ■ Allegheny Valley Chamber of Commerce
1030 Broadview Blvd.
Brackenridge, PA 15014-1118
Ph:(724)224-3400
Fax: (724)224-3442
Co. E-mail: staff@alleghenyvalleychamber.com
URL: http://www.alleghenyvalleychamber.com
Contact: Mary Bowlin, Pres.

64376 ■ Ambridge Area Chamber of Commerce
422 Merchant St.
Ambridge, PA 15003-2405
Ph:(724)266-3040
Fax: (724)266-3096
Contact: Bea Patterson, Pres.

64377 ■ America-Israel Chamber of Commerce, Central Atlantic Region
200 S Broad St., Ste. 700
Philadelphia, PA 19102
Ph:(215)790-3722
Fax: (215)790-3600
Co. E-mail: aicc@gpcc.com
URL: http://www.AmericaIsraelChamber.com
Contact: David Gitlin, Pres.

64378 ■ Armstrong County Chamber of Commerce
124 Market St.
Kittanning, PA 16201
Ph:(724)543-1305
Fax: (724)548-2951
Co. E-mail: accc1@alltel.net
URL: http://www.armstrongchamber.org
Contact: Patti Miller, Admin.Asst.

64379 ■ Beaver County Chamber of Commerce
300 S Walnut Ln., Ste. 202
Beaver, PA 15009
Ph:(724)775-3944
Fax: (724)728-9737
Co. E-mail: pgeho@bcchamber.com
URL: http://www.beavercountychamber.com
Contact: Patrick J. Geho, Pres.

64380 ■ Bedford County Chamber of Commerce
137 E Pitt St.
Bedford, PA 15522-1318
Ph:(814)623-2233
Fax: (814)623-6089
Co. E-mail: info@bedfordcountychamber.org
URL: http://www.bedfordcountychamber.org
Contact: Carol H. Snyder, Exec.Dir.

64381 ■ Bellefonte Intervalley Area Chamber of Commerce
320 W High St., Train Sta.
Bellefonte, PA 16823
Ph:(814)355-2917
Fax: (814)355-2761
Co. E-mail: bellefontecoc@aol.com
URL: http://www.bellefontechamber.org
Contact: Chip Aikens, Exec.Dir.

64382 ■ Berks County Chamber of Commerce
601 Penn St.
Reading, PA 19601
Ph:(610)376-6766
Fax: (610)376-4135
Co. E-mail: agrimm@berkschamber.org
URL: http://www.berkschamber.org
Contact: Anthony F. Grimm, Pres.

64383 ■ Berwick Area Chamber of Commerce
206 Mulberry St.
Berwick, PA 18603
Ph:(570)752-3601
Fax: (570)752-3602
Co. E-mail: info@berwickpa.org
URL: http://www.berwickpa.org
Contact: Valarie Anderson, Exec.Dir.

64384 ■ Bethlehem Area Chamber of Commerce
509 Main St.
Bethlehem, PA 18018-5810
Ph:(610)867-3788
Fax: (610)758-9533
Co. E-mail: staff@bethlehamchamber.org
Contact: Dale Kochard, Pres./CEO

64385 ■ Blair County Chamber of Commerce
3900 Industrial Park Dr., Ste. 12
Altoona, PA 16602
Ph:(814)943-8151
Fax: (814)943-5239
Co. E-mail: chamber@blairchamber.com
URL: http://www.blairchamber.com
Contact: Joe Hurd, Exec.Dir.

64386 ■ Borough of Dravosburg Chamber of Commerce
226 Maple Ave.
Dravosburg, PA 15034
Ph:(412)466-5200
Fax: (412)466-6027
Co. E-mail: dravoadmin@libcom.com
Contact: Ms. Brenda Honick, Sec.

64387 ■ Borough of Shiremanstown Chamber of Commerce
1 Park Ln.
Shiremanstown, PA 17011
Ph:(717)761-4169

64388 ■ Bradford Area Chamber of Commerce
2 Marilyn Horne Way, 1st Fl., Seneca Bldg.
Bradford, PA 16701
Ph:(814)368-7115
Fax: (814)368-6233
Co. E-mail: info@bradfordchamber.com
URL: http://www.bradfordchamber.com
Contact: Diane L. Sheeley, Exec. Dir.

64389 ■ Brentwood-Baldwin-Whitehall Chamber of Commerce
3501 Brownsville Rd.
Pittsburgh, PA 15227-3115
Ph:(412)884-1233
Fax: (412)884-1233
Co. E-mail: secretary@bbwchamber.com
URL: http://www.bbwchamber.com
Contact: Mac McIlrath, Pres.

64390 ■ British-American Business Council Serving Eastern Pennsylvania, Southern New Jersey and Delaware
200 S Broad St., Ste. 700
Philadelphia, PA 19102-3896
Ph:(215)790-3690
Fax: (215)790-3600
Co. E-mail: babc@philachamber.com

64391 ■ Brookville Area Chamber of Commerce
175 Main St.
Brookville, PA 15825
Ph:(814)849-8448
Fax: (814)849-8455
Co. E-mail: brookville@alltel.net
URL: http://www.brookvillechamber.com
Contact: Tracy Bullers, Exec.Dir.

64392 ■ Brush Valley Regional Chamber of Commerce
415 E Sunbury St.
Shamokin, PA 17872-5622
Ph:(570)648-4675
Fax: (570)648-0679
Co. E-mail: bvrc@minesurfer.com
URL: http://simplesite.hermon.net/bvrchamber
Contact: Sandra N. Hutchinson, CEO

64393 ■ Butler County Chamber of Commerce and Tourism
PO Box 1082
Butler, PA 16003-1082
Ph:(724)283-2222
Fax: (724)283-0224
Co. E-mail: info@butlercountychamber.com
URL: http://www.butlercountychamber.com
Contact: Stan M. Kosciuszko, Pres.

64394 ■ Central Bradford County Chamber of Commerce
PO Box 146
Towanda, PA 18848-0146
Ph:(570)268-2732
Fax: (570)265-4558
Co. E-mail: info@cbradchamber.org
URL: http://www.cbradchamber.org
Contact: Sharon Kaminsky, Administrator

64395 ■ Central Bucks Chamber of Commerce
Bailiwick, Ste. 23
252 W Swamp Rd. (Rt. 313)
Doylestown, PA 18901
Ph:(215)348-3913
Fax: (215)348-7154
Co. E-mail: info@centralbuckschamber.com
URL: http://www.centralbuckschamber.com
Contact: Dr. Vail P. Garvin, Exec.Dir.

64396 ■ Central Pennsylvania Chamber of Commerce
700 Hepburn St.
Milton, PA 17847
Ph:(570)742-7341
Free: 800-326-9211
Fax: (570)742-2008
Co. E-mail: chamber@centpa.com
URL: http://www.centpa.com
Contact: Robert B. Hickox Jr., Pres./CEO

64397 ■ Chamber of Business and Industry of Centre County
200 Innovation Blvd., Ste. 150
State College, PA 16803
Ph:(814)234-1829
Fax: (814)234-5869
Co. E-mail: cbicc@cbicc.org
URL: http://www.cbicc.org
Contact: John F. Coleman Jr., Pres./CEO

64398 ■ Chamber of Commerce of Greater West Chester
2 W Gay St., Ste. 200
West Chester, PA 19380-3145
Ph:(610)696-4046
Fax: (610)696-9110
Co. E-mail: info@gwcc.org
URL: http://www.greaterwestchester.com
Contact: Ms. Katie Walker, Pres.

64399 ■ Chester County Chamber of Business and Industry
1600 Paoli Pike
Malvern, PA 19355
Ph:(610)725-9100
Fax: (610)725-8479
Co. E-mail: info@cccbi.org
URL: http://www.cccbi.org
Contact: Robert Powelson, Pres.

64400 ■ Chilean American Chamber of Commerce
200 S Broad St., Ste. 700
Philadelphia, PA 19102-3896
Ph:(215)790-3690
Fax: (215)790-3600
Co. E-mail: srothberg@philachamber.com
URL: http://www.caccgp.com
Contact: Sheryl K. Rothberg, Dir.

64401 ■ Clarion Area Chamber of Business and Industry
41 S 5th Ave.
Clarion, PA 16214
Ph:(814)226-9161
Fax: (814)226-4903
Co. E-mail: info@clarionpa.com
URL: http://www.clarionpa.com
Contact: Tracy J. Becker, Exec.Dir.

64402 ■ Clearfield Chamber of Commerce
125 E Market St.
Clearfield, PA 16830
Ph:(814)765-7567
Fax: (814)765-6948
Co. E-mail: info@clearfieldchamber.com
URL: http://www.clearfieldchamber.com
Contact: Janice Aleksivich, Dir.

64403 ■ Clinton County Economic Partnership
212 N Jay St.
Lock Haven, PA 17745
Ph:(570)748-5782
Free: 888-388-6991
Fax: (570)893-0433
Co. E-mail: ccep@kcnet.org
URL: http://www.clintoncountyinfo.com
Contact: Wesley P. Grand, Pres./CEO

64404 ■ Columbia Montour Chamber of Commerce
238 Market St.
Bloomsburg, PA 17815
Ph:(570)784-2522
Fax: (570)784-2661

Co. E-mail: chamber@columbiamontourchamber.
com
URL: http://www.bloomsburg.org
Contact: Ed Edwards, Pres.

64405 ■ Corry Area Chamber of Commerce
221 N Center St.
Corry, PA 16407
Ph:(814)665-9925
Fax: (814)665-9925
Co. E-mail: cacc@velocity.net
URL: http://www.corrychamber.com
Contact: Nicole Lambert, Mgr.

64406 ■ Coudersport Chamber of Commerce
PO Box 261
Coudersport, PA 16915
Ph:(814)274-8165
Fax: (814)274-8165
Co. E-mail: cacoc@coudersport.org
URL: http://www.coudersport.org
Contact: Doug Morley, Pres.

64407 ■ Cranberry Area Chamber of Commerce
2525 Rochester Rd., Ste. 200
Cranberry Township, PA 16066-6422
Ph:(724)776-4949
Fax: (724)776-5344
Co. E-mail: chamber@nauticom.net
URL: http://cranberrychamber.com
Contact: Kari A. Geyer, Pres.

64408 ■ Cresson Area Chamber of Commerce
PO Box 113
Cresson, PA 16630
Ph:(814)886-8100
Co. E-mail: info@cressonarea.com
URL: http://www.cressonarea.com
Contact: Veronica Harkins, Sec.

64409 ■ Danville Area Chamber of Commerce
316 Mill St., Ste. B
Danville, PA 17821
Ph:(570)275-5200
Fax: (570)275-1662
Co. E-mail: info@danvillepa.org
URL: http://www.danvillepa.org
Contact: Robert Burns, Pres./CEO

64410 ■ DELCO Chamber of Commerce
602 E Baltimore Pike
Media, PA 19063-1796
Ph:(610)565-3677
Fax: (610)565-1606
Co. E-mail: info@delcochamber.org
URL: http://www.delcochamber.org
Contact: Jack Holefelder, Pres.

64411 ■ Downingtown Area Chamber of Commerce
38 W Lancaster Ave.
Downingtown, PA 19335
Ph:(610)269-1523
Fax: (610)269-8713
Co. E-mail: info@downingtownchamber.org
URL: http://www.downingtownchamber.org
Contact: Michele Hundley, Exec.Dir.

64412 ■ East Liberty Quarter Chamber of Commerce
5907 Penn Ave., Ste. 305
Pittsburgh, PA 15206
Ph:(412)661-9660
Fax: (412)661-9661
Co. E-mail: pbrecht@eastlibertychamber.org
URL: http://www.eastlibertychamber.org
Contact: Paul G. Brecht, Exec.Dir.

64413 ■ Eastern Montgomery County Chamber of Commerce
436 Old York Rd.
Jenkintown, PA 19046
Ph:(215)887-5122
Fax: (215)887-3220

Co. E-mail: info@emccc.org
URL: http://www.emccc.org
Contact: Wendy Klinghoffer, Exec.VP

64414 ■ Ellwood City Area Chamber of Commerce
314 5th St.
Ellwood City, PA 16117
Ph:(724)758-5501
Co. E-mail: info@ellwoodchamber.org
URL: http://www.ellwoodchamber.org
Contact: Marian Owens, Pres.

64415 ■ Ephrata Area Chamber of Commerce
16 E Main St., Ste. 1
Ephrata, PA 17522
Ph:(717)738-9010
Fax: (717)738-9012
Co. E-mail: info@ephrata-area.org
URL: http://www.ephrata-area.org
Contact: Deb Hall, Exec.Dir.

64416 ■ Erie Regional Chamber and Growth Partnership
208 E Bayfront Pkwy., Ste. 100
Erie, PA 16507
Ph:(814)454-7191
Fax: (814)459-0241
Co. E-mail: arobinson@eriepa.com
URL: http://www.eriechamber.com
Contact: Jacob A. Rouch, Pres./CEO

64417 ■ Exton Region Chamber of Commerce
PO Box 314
Exton, PA 19341-0314
Ph:(610)363-7746
Fax: (610)363-2374
Co. E-mail: chamber@ercc.net
URL: http://www.ercc.net
Contact: Larry Bowman, Pres.

64418 ■ Fayette Chamber of Commerce
65 W Main St.
Uniontown, PA 15401-2124
Ph:(724)437-4571
Free: 800-916-9365
Fax: (724)438-3304
Co. E-mail: faycham@faycham.org
URL: http://www.faycham.org
Contact: Muriel J. Nuttall, Exec.Dir.

64419 ■ Franklin Area Chamber of Commerce
1259 Liberty St.
Franklin, PA 16323-1329
Ph:(814)432-5823
Free: 888-547-2377
Fax: (814)437-2453
Co. E-mail: chamber@franklin-pa.org
URL: http://www.franklin-pa.org
Contact: Jerri Gent, Exec.Dir.

64420 ■ Freeland Chamber of Commerce
PO Box 31
Freeland, PA 18224
Ph:(570)636-0670
Contact: Charles Reczkowski, Pres.

64421 ■ French-American Chamber of Commerce
2000 Market St., Ste. 2850
Philadelphia, PA 19103
Ph:(215)419-5559
Fax: (215)419-5533
Co. E-mail: faccphl@aol.com
URL: http://www.faccphila.org
Contact: Judith L. Ujobai, Exec.Dir.

64422 ■ Fulton County Chamber of Commerce and Tourism
PO Box 141
McConnellsburg, PA 17233
Ph:(717)485-4064
Fax: (717)485-0322
Co. E-mail: fultoncountypa@earthlink.net
URL: http://www.fultoncountypa.com

Contact: Anita Mellott, Admin.Asst.

64423 ■ German American Chamber of Commerce - Philadelphia
4 Penn Ctr., Ste. 200
1600 John F. Kennedy Blvd.
Philadelphia, PA 19103-2808
Ph:(215)665-1585
Fax: (215)665-0375
Co. E-mail: admin@gaccphiladelphia.com
URL: http://www.gaccphiladelphia.com
Contact: Stephen E. Stambaugh, Chm.

64424 ■ Gettysburg-Adams County Area Chamber of Commerce
18 Carlisle St., Ste. 203
Gettysburg, PA 17325
Ph:(717)334-8151
Fax: (717)334-3368
Co. E-mail: info@gettysburg-chamber.org
URL: http://www.gettysburg-chamber.org
Contact: Margaret M. Weaver, Pres.

64425 ■ Great Valley Regional Chamber of Commerce
7 Great Valley Pkwy.
Malvern, PA 19355
Ph:(610)889-2069
Fax: (610)889-2063
Co. E-mail: greatchamber@gvrcc.org
URL: http://www.gvrcc.org
Contact: Marie Moughan, Chair

64426 ■ Greater Bridgeville Area Chamber of Commerce
990 Washington Pike
Bridgeville, PA 15017-2711
Ph:(412)221-4100
Fax: (412)257-1210
Co. E-mail: gbacoc@worldnet.att.net
Contact: Emerald VanBuskirk, Exec.Dir.

64427 ■ Greater Brownsville Area Chamber of Commerce
325 Market St.
Brownsville, PA 15417
Ph:(724)785-4160
Contact: W. Scott Bowman, Exec. Sec.

64428 ■ Greater Carbondale Chamber of Commerce
27 N Main St.
Carbondale, PA 18407
Ph:(570)282-1690
Fax: (570)282-1206
Co. E-mail: info@carbondale-pa-coc.com
URL: http://www.carbondale-pa-coc.com
Contact: Cindy Klenk, Pres.

64429 ■ Greater Carlisle Area Chamber of Commerce
212 N Hanover St.
PO Box 572
Carlisle, PA 17013
Ph:(717)243-4515
Fax: (717)243-4446
Co. E-mail: info@carlislechamber.org
URL: http://www.carlislechamber.org
Contact: Ms. Michelle Hornick Crowley, Pres.

64430 ■ Greater Chambersburg Chamber of Commerce
100 Lincoln Way E, Ste. A
Chambersburg, PA 17201
Ph:(717)264-7101
Fax: (717)267-0399
Co. E-mail: chamber@chambersburg.org
URL: http://www.chambersburg.org
Contact: David G. Sciamanna, Pres.

64431 ■ Greater Connellsville Chamber of Commerce
923 W Crawford Ave.
Connellsville, PA 15425
Ph:(724)628-5500
Fax: (724)628-5676
Co. E-mail: info@greaterconnellsville.org

URL: http://www.greaterconnellsville.org
Contact: Christine Wagner, Exec.Dir.

64432 ■ Greater Du Bois Chamber of Commerce - Economic Development
3 S Brady St., Ste. 205
Du Bois, PA 15801
Ph:(814)371-5010
Fax: (814)371-5005
Co. E-mail: dacc@duboispachamber.com
URL: http://www.duboispachamber.com
Contact: Nancy J. Micks, Exec.Dir.

64433 ■ Greater Glenside Chamber of Commerce
452 N Easton Rd.
Glenside, PA 19038
Ph:(215)887-3110
Fax: (215)887-7399
Co. E-mail: info@glensidechamber.org
URL: http://www.glensidechamber.org
Contact: Cathleen Breslin, Exec.Dir.

64434 ■ Greater Hatboro Chamber of Commerce
Red Barn Mall
120 S York Rd.
Hatboro, PA 19040
Ph:(215)956-9540
Fax: (215)956-9635
Co. E-mail: office@hatborochamber.org
URL: http://www.hatboro-pa.com
Contact: Barbara Davis, COO

64435 ■ Greater Hazleton Chamber of Commerce
1 S Church St., Ste. 200
Hazleton, PA 18201-6288
Ph:(570)455-1508
Fax: (570)454-7787
Co. E-mail: dpalermo@hazletonchamber.org
URL: http://www.hazletonchamber.org
Contact: Donna Palermo, Pres.

64436 ■ Greater Johnstown/Cambria County Chamber of Commerce
111 Market St.
Johnstown, PA 15901-1608
Ph:(814)536-5107
Free: 800-790-4522
Fax: (814)539-5800
Co. E-mail: chamber@johnstownchamber.com
URL: http://www.johnstownchamber.com
Contact: Mr. Robert Layo, Pres.

64437 ■ Greater Lehigh County Chamber of Commerce
462 Walnut St.
Allentown, PA 18102
Ph:(610)841-5860
Fax: (610)437-4907
Co. E-mail: info@lehighvalleychamber.org
URL: http://www.lehighvalleychamber.org
Contact: T. Anthony Iannelli, Pres./CEO

64438 ■ Greater Mansfield Area Chamber of Commerce
51-B S Main St.
Mansfield, PA 16933
Ph:(570)662-3442
Fax: (570)662-0259
Co. E-mail: info@mansfield.org
URL: http://www.mansfield.org
Contact: Betsy Tokarz, Pres.

64439 ■ Greater Northeast Philadelphia Chamber of Commerce
8601 E Roosevelt Blvd.
Philadelphia, PA 19152-2001
Ph:(215)332-3400
Fax: (215)332-6050
Co. E-mail: gnpccoffice@aol.com
URL: http://www.gnpcc.org
Contact: Al Taubenberger, Pres.

64440 ■ Greater Philadelphia Chamber of Commerce
200 S Broad St., Ste. 700
Philadelphia, PA 19102
Ph:(215)545-1234
Fax: (215)790-3720
Co. E-mail: memberrelations@philachamber.com
URL: http://www.gpcc.com
Contact: Maureen Glassman, VP

64441 ■ Greater Pittsburgh Chamber of Commerce
Regional Enterprise Tower
425 6th Ave., Ste. 1100
Pittsburgh, PA 15219-1811
Ph:(412)392-1000
Free: 877-392-1300
Fax: (412)281-1896
Co. E-mail: info@alleghenyconference.org
URL: http://www.pittsburghchamber.com
Contact: Barbara McNees, Pres.

64442 ■ Greater Pittston Chamber of Commerce
Kennedy Blvd. and William St.
PO Box 704
Pittston, PA 18640-0704
Ph:(570)655-1424
Fax: (570)655-0336
Co. E-mail: info@pittstonchamber.org
URL: http://pittstonchamber.org
Contact: Rosemary Dessoye, Exec.VP

64443 ■ Greater Scranton Chamber of Commerce
222 Mulberry St.
PO Box 431
Scranton, PA 18501-0431
Ph:(570)342-7711
Fax: (570)347-6262
Co. E-mail: sweiland@scrantonchamber.com
URL: http://www.scrantonchamber.com
Contact: Austin J. Burke, Pres.

64444 ■ Greater Shenandoah Area Chamber of Commerce
PO Box 187
Shenandoah, PA 17976
Ph:(570)622-1942
Fax: (570)622-1638
Contact: Ms. Valerie Mcdonald, Pres.

64445 ■ Greater Susquehanna Valley Chamber of Commerce
PO Box 10
Shamokin Dam, PA 17876-0010
Ph:(570)743-4100
Free: 800-410-2880
Fax: (570)743-1221
Co. E-mail: info@gsvcc.org
URL: http://www.gsvcc.org
Contact: Kurt Kissinger, Pres./CEO

64446 ■ Greater Warminster Chamber of Commerce
1158 York Rd.
Warminster, PA 18974-0513
Ph:(215)672-6633
Fax: (215)672-7637
Contact: Beverly M. Miller, VP

64447 ■ Greater Waynesboro Chamber of Commerce
323 E Main St.
Waynesboro, PA 17268-1694
Ph:(717)762-7123
Fax: (717)762-7124
Co. E-mail: wchamber1@earthlink.net
URL: http://www.waynesboro.org
Contact: Ms. Marybeth Hockenberry, Exec.Dir.

64448 ■ Greater White Haven Chamber of Commerce
PO Box 363
White Haven, PA 18661
Ph:(570)443-0302
Co. E-mail: info@whitehaven.org

URL: http://www.whitehaven.org
Contact: Henry Straub, Pres.

64449 ■ Greencastle-Antrim Chamber of Commerce
217 E Baltimore St.
Greencastle, PA 17225
Ph:(717)597-4610
Fax: (717)597-0709
Co. E-mail: info@greencastlepachamber.org
URL: http://www.greencastlepachamber.org
Contact: Bill Gour, Dir.

64450 ■ Grove City Area Chamber of Commerce
119 S Broad St.
Grove City, PA 16127
Ph:(724)458-6410
Fax: (724)458-6841
Co. E-mail: gcchamber@grovecity-pa.com
URL: http://www.grovecity-pa.com
Contact: Leann Smith, Exec.Dir.

64451 ■ Hanover Area Chamber of Commerce
146 Carlisle St.
Hanover, PA 17331
Ph:(717)637-6130
Fax: (717)637-9127
Co. E-mail: office@hanoverchamber.com
URL: http://www.hanoverchamber.com
Contact: Gary Laird, Pres.

64452 ■ Harrisburg Regional Chamber of Commerce
3211 N Front St., Ste. 201
Harrisburg, PA 17110-1342
Ph:(717)213-5020
Fax: (717)232-5184
Co. E-mail: dblack@hbgrc.org
URL: http://www.harrisburgregionalchamber.org
Contact: David E. Black, Pres./CEO

64453 ■ Hatfield Chamber of Commerce
PO Box 445
Hatfield, PA 19440-0445
Ph:(215)855-3335
Fax: (215)855-3335
Co. E-mail: admin@hatfieldchamber.com
URL: http://www.hatfieldchamber.com
Contact: Deborah Stevens, Sec.

64454 ■ Hawley - Lake Wallenpaupack Chamber of Commerce
PO Box 150
Rte. 6
Hawley, PA 18428
Ph:(570)226-3191
Fax: (570)226-9387
Co. E-mail: hlwchmbr@ptd.net
URL: http://www.hawleywallenpaupackcc.com
Contact: Nancy Barnes De Young, Exec.Dir.

64455 ■ Indian Valley Chamber of Commerce
PO Box 64077
Souderton, PA 18964
Ph:(215)723-9472
Fax: (215)723-2490
Co. E-mail: ivchamber@indianvalleychamber.com
URL: http://www.indianvalleychamber.com
Contact: Sharon Minninger, Exec.Dir.

64456 ■ Indiana County Chamber of Commerce
1019 Philadelphia St.
Indiana, PA 15701-1689
Ph:(724)465-2511
Fax: (724)465-3706
Co. E-mail: dphenry@wpia.net
URL: http://www.indianapa.com/chamber
Contact: Dana P. Henry, Pres.

64457 ■ Ireland Chamber of Commerce
1420 Walnut St., Ste. 924
Philadelphia, PA 19102
Ph:(215)574-3100
Fax: (215)772-3109

Contact: William McLaughlin, Pres.

64458 ■ Jim Thorpe Chamber of Commerce
PO Box 164
Jim Thorpe, PA 18229-0164
Ph:(570)325-5810
Free: 888-JIMTHORPE
Co. E-mail: info@jimthorpe.org
URL: http://jimthorpe.org

64459 ■ Johnsonburg Chamber of Commerce
501 High St.
Johnsonburg, PA 15845-1235
Ph:(814)965-4793
Fax: (814)965-3215
Contact: Bill Simon, Exec. Dir.

64460 ■ Juniata Valley Area Chamber of Commerce
Historic Courthouse
1 W Market St., Ste. 119
Lewistown, PA 17044
Ph:(717)248-6713
Fax: (717)248-6714
Co. E-mail: jvacc@juniatavalleychamber.org
URL: http://www.juniatavalleychamber.org
Contact: Jim Tunall, Pres.

64461 ■ Kane Chamber of Commerce
54 Fraley St.
Kane, PA 16735-1313
Ph:(814)837-6565
Fax: (814)837-6565
Co. E-mail: kanepa.chamber@verizon.net
URL: http://kanepa.com
Contact: Nadeen Steffey, Exec. Dir.

64462 ■ King of Prussia Chamber of Commerce at Valley Forge
King of Prussia Inn
101 Bill Smith Blvd.
King of Prussia, PA 19406
Ph:(610)265-1776
Fax: (610)265-0473
Co. E-mail: chamber@kingofprussia.com
Contact: Albert Paschall, CEO/Pres.

64463 ■ Lancaster Chamber of Commerce and Industry
PO Box 1558
Lancaster, PA 17608-1558
Ph:(717)397-3531
Fax: (717)293-3159
Co. E-mail: info@lcci.com
URL: http://www.lcci.com
Contact: Thomas Baldrige, Pres.

64464 ■ Latrobe Area Chamber of Commerce
326 McKinley Ave., Ste. 102
Latrobe, PA 15650
Ph:(724)537-2671
Fax: (724)537-2690
Co. E-mail: info@latrobearea.com
URL: http://www.latrobearea.com
Contact: Andrew M. Stofan, Pres.

64465 ■ Laurel Highlands Chamber of Commerce
537 W Main St.
Mount Pleasant, PA 15666
Ph:(724)547-7521
Fax: (724)547-5530
Co. E-mail: pattylhcc@zoominternet.net
URL: http://www.laurelhighlandschamber.com
Contact: Patty McGuire, Sec.-Treas.

64466 ■ Lawrence County Chamber of Commerce
138 W Washington St.
New Castle, PA 16101-3910
Ph:(724)654-5593
Fax: (724)654-3330
Co. E-mail: info@lawrencecountychamber.com
URL: http://www.lawrencecountychamber.com
Contact: Robert L. McCracken, Exec.VP

64467 ■ Lebanon Valley Chamber of Commerce
PO Box 899
Lebanon, PA 17042-0899
Ph:(717)273-3727
Fax: (717)273-7940
Co. E-mail: info@lvchamber.org
URL: http://www.lvchamber.org
Contact: Harriet A. Faren, Pres.

64468 ■ Littlestown Area Chamber of Commerce
PO Box 384
Littlestown, PA 17340
Ph:(717)359-7006
Co. E-mail: littlestownchamber@yahoo.com
Contact: Carl Goulden, Pres.

64469 ■ Lower Bucks County Chamber of Commerce
409 Hood Blvd.
Fairless Hills, PA 19030
Ph:(215)943-7400
Fax: (215)943-7404
Co. E-mail: cshuster@lbccc.org
URL: http://www.lbccc.org
Contact: Clark L. Shuster, Pres.

64470 ■ Main Line Chamber of Commerce
175 Strafford Ave., Ste. 130
Wayne, PA 19087-3331
Ph:(610)687-6232
Fax: (610)687-8085
Co. E-mail: info@mlcc.org
URL: http://www.mlcc.org
Contact: Robert A. Pucci, Pres./CEO

64471 ■ Manheim Area Chamber of Commerce
13 E High St.
Manheim, PA 17545-2002
Ph:(717)665-6330
Fax: (717)665-7656
Co. E-mail: info@manheimchamber.com
URL: http://manheimchamber.com
Contact: Sandra Blauch, Sec.

64472 ■ Meadville - Western Crawford County Chamber of Commerce
211 Chestnut St.
Meadville, PA 16335
Ph:(814)337-8030
Fax: (814)337-8022
Co. E-mail: info@meadvillechamber.com
URL: http://www.meadvillechamber.com
Contact: Charlie Anderson, Pres./CEO

64473 ■ Mercersburg Area Chamber of Commerce
21C N Main St.
Mercersburg, PA 17236-0161
Ph:(717)328-5827
Fax: (717)328-4814
Co. E-mail: mercersburgchamber@earthlink.net
URL: http://www.mercersburg.org
Contact: Mrs. Liza Main, Exec.Dir.

64474 ■ Mon Valley Regional Chamber of Commerce
1 Chamber Plz.
Charleroi, PA 15022
Ph:(724)483-3507
Fax: (724)489-1045
Co. E-mail: info@mvrchamber.org
URL: http://www.mvrchamber.org
Contact: Debra Keefer, Exec.Dir.

64475 ■ Monroeville Area Chamber of Commerce
Chamber of Commerce Bldg.
4268 Northern Pike
Monroeville, PA 15146
Ph:(412)856-0622
Free: 888-753-5522
Fax: (412)856-1030
Co. E-mail: macoc@monroevillechamber.com
URL: http://www.monroevillechamber.com

Contact: Chad M. Amond, Pres.

64476 ■ Montco Chamber of Commerce
1341 Sandy Hill Rd.
Norristown, PA 19401-4155
Ph:(610)277-9500
Fax: (610)277-2659
Co. E-mail: info@montcocc.org
URL: http://www.montcocc.org
Contact: Kathleen Brandon, Pres./CEO

64477 ■ Mount Lebanon Dormont Area Chamber of Commerce
733 Washington Rd., Ste. 301
Pittsburgh, PA 15228-2022
Ph:(412)531-1133
Fax: (412)531-1134
Co. E-mail: chamber@mlacc.com
Contact: Eleanor Carpenter, Exec.Dir.

64478 ■ Nazareth Area Chamber of Commerce
201 N Main St.
Nazareth, PA 18064-0173
Ph:(610)759-9188
Fax: (610)759-5262
Co. E-mail: tina@nazarethchamber.com
URL: http://www.nazarethchamber.com
Contact: Tina A. Smith, Pres.

64479 ■ New Bethlehem Area Chamber of Commerce
400 Broad St.
Broadwood Towers, Box 107
New Bethlehem, PA 16242-1098
Ph:(814)275-3929
Fax: (814)275-3929
Co. E-mail: nbchamber@usachoice.net
Contact: Mary Harmon, Sec.

64480 ■ North East Area Chamber of Commerce
21 S Lake St.
North East, PA 16428
Ph:(814)725-4262
Fax: (814)725-3994
Co. E-mail: info@nechamber.org
URL: http://www.nechamber.org
Contact: Diana Hatfield, Community Coor.

64481 ■ North Penn Chamber of Commerce
229 S Broad St.
Lansdale, PA 19446
Ph:(215)362-9200
Fax: (215)362-0393
Co. E-mail: info@northpenn.org
URL: http://www.northpenn.org
Contact: R. Michael Owens, Pres./CEO

64482 ■ Northampton Area Chamber of Commerce
PO Box 355
Northampton, PA 18067
Ph:(610)262-6780
Fax: (610)262-6250
Contact: Lee Lerch, Sec.

64483 ■ Northern Allegheny County Chamber of Commerce
5000 Brooktree Rd.
Wexford, PA 15090
Ph:(724)934-9700
Fax: (724)934-9710
Co. E-mail: naccc@naccc.com
URL: http://www.naccc.com
Contact: Mary Margaret Fisher, Exec.Dir.

64484 ■ Northern Westmoreland Chamber of Commerce
858 4th Ave.
New Kensington, PA 15068-6403
Ph:(724)339-6616
Fax: (724)339-3346
Co. E-mail: admin@newkenchamber.org
Contact: Mr. John Ciesielski, Exec.Dir.

64485 ■ Norwin Chamber of Commerce
321 Main St.
Irwin, PA 15642-3437
Ph:(724)863-0888
Fax: (724)863-5133
Co. E-mail: info@norwinchamber.com
URL: http://www.norwinchamber.com
Contact: Margaree Pertle, Pres.

64486 ■ Oil City Area Chamber of Commerce
41 Main St.
PO Box 376
Oil City, PA 16301-1440
Ph:(814)676-8521
Fax: (814)676-8185
Co. E-mail: chamber@oilcitychamber.org
URL: http://www.oilcitychamber.org
Contact: Ronald E. Shoup, Exec.Dir.

64487 ■ Oxford Area Chamber of Commerce
PO Box 4
Oxford, PA 19363
Ph:(610)932-0740
Fax: (610)932-0827
Co. E-mail: oxfordchamber@zoominternet.net
URL: http://www.oxfordpa.org
Contact: Sheree Aufiero, Pres.

64488 ■ Palmerton Chamber of Commerce
PO Box 214
Palmerton, PA 18071-0214
Ph:(610)824-5100
URL: http://www.palmertonpa.com/chamber
Contact: Peter L. Kern, Pres.

64489 ■ Penn Hills Chamber of Commerce
13049 Frankstown Rd.
Penn Hills, PA 15235-1952
Ph:(412)795-8741
Fax: (412)795-7993
Co. E-mail: phcoc@worldnet.att.net
URL: http://www.pennhillschamber.org
Contact: Sara Werner, Exec.Dir.

64490 ■ Pennridge Chamber of Commerce
538 W Market St.
Perkasie, PA 18944
Ph:(215)257-5390
Fax: (215)257-6840
Co. E-mail: pennridgecc@pennridge.com
URL: http://www.pennridge.com
Contact: Betty Graver, Exec.Dir.

64491 ■ Pennsylvania Chamber of Business and Industry
417 Walnut St.
Harrisburg, PA 17101-1918
Ph:(717)255-3252
Free: 800-225-7224
Fax: (717)255-3298
Co. E-mail: info@pachamber.org
URL: http://www.pachamber.org
Contact: Ms. Laurel Belding, Dir. of Business Development

64492 ■ Perkiomen Valley Chamber of Commerce
351 E Main St.
Collegeville, PA 19426
Ph:(610)489-6660
Fax: (610)454-1270
Co. E-mail: info@pvchamber.net
URL: http://www.pvchamber.net
Contact: Arlene Magargal, Dir. of Operations

64493 ■ Peters Township Chamber of Commerce
PO Box 991
McMurray, PA 15317-0991
Ph:(724)941-6345
Fax: (724)942-2345
Co. E-mail: peterscc@cobweb.net
URL: http://www.peterstownshipchamber.com
Contact: Carol A. Foley, Exec.Dir.

64494 ■ Phoenixville Area Chamber of Commerce
171 E Bridge St.
Phoenixville, PA 19460
Ph:(610)933-3070
Fax: (610)917-0503
Co. E-mail: info@phoenixvillechamber.org
URL: http://www.phoenixvillechamber.org
Contact: Kim Cooley, Exec.Dir.

64495 ■ Pike County Chamber of Commerce
209 E Hartford St.
Milford, PA 18337-0883
Ph:(570)296-8700
Fax: (570)296-3921
Co. E-mail: info@pikechamber.com
URL: http://www.pikechamber.com
Contact: Amy Gruzesky, Exec.Dir.

64496 ■ Pittsburgh Airport Area Chamber of Commerce
850 Beaver Grade Rd.
Moon Township, PA 15108
Ph:(412)264-6270
Fax: (412)264-1575
Co. E-mail: info@paacc.com
URL: http://www.paacc.com
Contact: Sally Haas, Pres./Sec.

64497 ■ Pocono Mountains Chamber of Commerce
556 Main St.
Stroudsburg, PA 18360-2093
Ph:(570)421-4433
Fax: (570)424-7281
Co. E-mail: info@poconochamber.net
URL: http://www.poconochamber.net
Contact: Robert Phillips, Pres./CEO

64498 ■ Pocono Mountains Chamber of Commerce/Women in Business
556 Main St.
Stroudsburg, PA 18360
Ph:(570)421-4433
Fax: (570)424-7281
Co. E-mail: info@poconochamber.net
URL: http://www.poconochamber.net
Contact: Miriam Conway

64499 ■ Port Allegany Chamber of Commerce
63 N Main, Ste. 3
Port Allegany, PA 16743
Ph:(814)642-9555
Free: 800-232-8449
Fax: (814)642-7789
Contact: Mary M. Mensch, Sec.

64500 ■ Punxsutawney Area Chamber of Commerce
102 W Mahoning St.
Punxsutawney, PA 15767-2017
Ph:(814)938-7700
Free: 800-752-PHIL
Fax: (814)938-4303
Co. E-mail: chamber@punxsutawneychamber.com
Contact: Marlene Lelock, Exec.Dir.

64501 ■ Regional Business Alliance
3001 Jacks Run Rd.
White Oak, PA 15131-7426
Ph:(412)678-2450
Fax: (412)678-2451
Co. E-mail: rba@regionalbusinessalliance.com
URL: http://www.regionalbusinessalliance.com
Contact: Constance Yarris, Exec.Dir.

64502 ■ Reynoldsville Area Chamber of Commerce
PO Box 157
Reynoldsville, PA 15851
Ph:(814)653-8270
Fax: (814)653-8200
URL: http://www.penn.com/reynoldsville
Contact: Gary Basinger, Pres.

64503 ■ Ridgway-Elk County Chamber of Commerce
PO Box 357
Ridgway, PA 15853-0357
Ph:(814)776-1424
Fax: (814)772-9150
Co. E-mail: ridgwaychamber@ncentral.com
URL: http://www.ridgwaychamber.com

64504 ■ St. Marys Area Chamber of Commerce
4 Franklin Ctr.
St. Marys, PA 15857
Ph:(814)781-3804
Fax: (814)781-7302
Co. E-mail: swilson@stmaryschamber.org
URL: http://www.stmaryschamber.org
Contact: Sally J. Wilson, Sec./Exec.Dir.

64505 ■ Schuylkill Chamber of Commerce
91 S Progress Ave.
Pottsville, PA 17901
Ph:(570)622-1942
Free: 800-755-1942
Fax: (570)622-1638
Co. E-mail: info@schuylkillchamber.com
URL: http://www.schuylkillchamber.com
Contact: Lori Kane, Exec.Dir.

64506 ■ Scottdale Area Chamber of Commerce
PO Box 531
Scottdale, PA 15683
Ph:(724)887-3611
URL: http://www.scottdale.com
Contact: Frank Kapr, Acting Pres.

64507 ■ Shenango Valley Chamber of Commerce
41 Chestnut St.
Sharon, PA 16146-2713
Ph:(724)981-5880
Fax: (724)981-5480
Co. E-mail: george@svchamber.com
URL: http://www.svchamber.com
Contact: Mr. George Gerhart, Exec.Dir.

64508 ■ Shippensburg Area Chamber of Commerce
29 E King St.
Shippensburg, PA 17257
Ph:(717)532-5509
Fax: (717)532-7501
Co. E-mail: chamber@shippensburg.org
URL: http://www.shippensburg.org
Contact: Lindsay Renninger, Admin.Asst.

64509 ■ Somerset County Chamber of Commerce
601 N Center Ave.
Somerset, PA 15501-1025
Ph:(814)445-6431
Fax: (814)443-4313
Co. E-mail: info@somersetcountychamber.com
URL: http://www.somersetcountychamber.com
Contact: Mr. Ron Aldom, Exec.Dir.

64510 ■ South Hills Chamber of Commerce
Manor Oak One - Ste. 140
1910 Cochan Rd.
Pittsburgh, PA 15220
Ph:(412)306-8090
Fax: (412)306-8093
Co. E-mail: office@shchamber.org
URL: http://www.shchamber.org
Contact: David W. Roof, Pres.

64511 ■ Southern Chester County Chamber of Commerce
PO Box 395
Kennett Square, PA 19348-0395
Ph:(610)444-0774
Fax: (610)444-5105
Co. E-mail: info@scccc.com
URL: http://www.scccc.com
Contact: Tina Altman, Exec.Sec.

64512 ■ Southern Wayne Regional Chamber of Commerce
PO Box 296
Hamlin, PA 18427
Ph:(570)689-4199
Fax: (570)689-4391
Co. E-mail: swrchamber@swrchamber.org
URL: http://www.swrchamber.org
Contact: Patty Blaum, Exec.Dir.

64513 ■ Steel Valley Chamber of Commerce
3905 Main St.
Munhall, PA 15120
Ph:(412)461-4141
URL: http://www.steelvalleychamber.com
Contact: Denise Weidman, Exec. Dir.

64514 ■ Strongland Chamber of Commerce
1129 Industrial Park Rd., Ste. 108
Box 10
Vandergrift, PA 15690-9646
Ph:(724)845-5426
Fax: (724)845-5428
Co. E-mail: strongland@alltel.net
URL: http://www.strongland.org
Contact: A. Allan Walzak, Pres.

64515 ■ Suburban Horsham Willow Grove Chamber of Commerce
PO Box 100
Willow Grove, PA 19090
Ph:(215)657-2227
Fax: (215)657-8564
Co. E-mail: info@suburbanchamber.org
URL: http://www.suburbanchamber.org
Contact: Jean K. Dilley, Pres.

64516 ■ Sullivan County Chamber of Commerce
PO Box 269
Laporte, PA 18626-0269
Ph:(570)946-4160
Fax: (570)946-4421
Co. E-mail: sulchamc@epix.net
URL: http://www.sullivanpachamber.com
Contact: Kathi Keefer, Pres.

64517 ■ Susquehanna Valley Chamber of Commerce and Visitors' Bureau
445 Linden St.
Columbia, PA 17512
Ph:(717)684-5249
Fax: (717)684-5142
Co. E-mail: svcc@parivertowns.com
URL: http://www.parivertowns.com
Contact: Melissa A. Glenn, Dir.

64518 ■ Tamaqua Area Chamber of Commerce
204 E Broad St.
Tamaqua, PA 18252
Ph:(570)668-1880
Fax: (570)668-0826
Co. E-mail: chamber@tamaqua.net
Contact: Beverly Bennett, Sec.

64519 ■ Titusville Area Chamber of Commerce
202 W Central Ave.
Titusville, PA 16354
Ph:(814)827-2941
Fax: (814)827-2914
Co. E-mail: info@titusvillechamber.com
URL: http://www.titusvillechamber.com
Contact: Lynn Cochran, Exec.Dir.

64520 ■ Township of Richland Chamber of Commerce
4011 Dickey Rd.
Gibsonia, PA 15044
Ph:(724)443-5921
Fax: (724)443-8860
Contact: Mr. Dean E. Bastianini, Sec.

64521 ■ Tri-County Area Chamber of Commerce
152 High St., Ste. 360
Pottstown, PA 19464-5555

Ph:(610)326-2900
Fax: (610)970-9705
Co. E-mail: dale@tricountyareachamber.com
URL: http://www.tricountyareachamber.com
Contact: Mrs. Dale P. Mahle, Pres.

64522 ■ Two Rivers Area Chamber of Commerce
1 S 3rd St., 8th Fl.
PO Box 637
Easton, PA 18044-0637
Ph:(610)253-4211
Fax: (610)253-6114
Co. E-mail: tracc@eastonareachamber.org
URL: http://www.eastonareachamber.org
Contact: Michael Moorehead, Pres.

64523 ■ Tyrone Area Chamber of Commerce
1004 Logan Ave.
Tyrone, PA 16686-9510
Ph:(814)684-0736
Fax: (814)684-6070
Co. E-mail: info@tyronechamber.com
URL: http://www.tyronechamber.com
Contact: Ms. Rose Black, Exec.Dir.

64524 ■ Upper Bucks Chamber of Commerce
2170 Portzer Rd.
Quakertown, PA 18951
Ph:(215)536-3211
Fax: (215)536-7767
Co. E-mail: info@ubcc.org
URL: http://ubcc.org
Contact: Deanna Mindler, Exec.Dir.

64525 ■ Upper St. Clair Chamber of Commerce
71 McMurray Rd., Ste. 201
Upper St. Clair, PA 15241
Ph:(412)833-9111
Contact: Rosemary Siddall, Exec. Dir.

64526 ■ Warren County Chamber of Business and Industry
308 Market St.
PO Box 942
Warren, PA 16365-0942
Ph:(814)723-3050
Fax: (814)723-6024
Co. E-mail: info@wccbi.org
URL: http://www.wccbi.org
Contact: James L. Decker, Pres./CEO

64527 ■ Washington County Chamber of Commerce
20 E Beau St.
Washington, PA 15301
Ph:(724)225-3010
Fax: (724)228-7337
Co. E-mail: debbie@washcochamber.com
URL: http://www.washcochamber.com
Contact: Jeff M. Kotula, Exec.Dir.

64528 ■ Wayne County Chamber of Commerce
303 Commercial St.
Honesdale, PA 18431
Ph:(570)253-1960
Fax: (570)253-1517
Co. E-mail: exec@waynecountycc.com
URL: http://www.waynecountycc.com
Contact: Annetta DeYoung, Exec.Dir.

64529 ■ Waynesburg Chamber of Commerce
60 W High St., Ste. No. 4
Waynesburg, PA 15370-2053
Ph:(724)627-5926
Fax: (724)627-8017
Co. E-mail: wbgchamb@greenepa.net
URL: http://www.waynesburgchamber.com
Contact: Melody R. Longstreth, Exec. Dir.

64530 ■ Wellsboro Area Chamber of Commerce
114 Main St.
PO Box 733
Wellsboro, PA 16901

Ph:(570)724-1926
Fax: (570)724-5084
Co. E-mail: info@wellsboropa.com
URL: http://www.wellsboropa.com
Contact: Ms. Micki Millar, Exec.Dir.

64531 ■ West Shore Chamber of Commerce
4211 Trindle Rd.
Camp Hill, PA 17011
Ph:(717)761-0702
Fax: (717)761-4315
Co. E-mail: wschamber@wschamber.org
URL: http://www.wschamber.org
Contact: Edward M. Messner, Pres./CEO

64532 ■ Western Chester County Chamber of Commerce
Lukens Executive Bldg.
50 S 1st Ave.
Coatesville, PA 19320
Ph:(610)384-9550
Fax: (610)380-7215
Co. E-mail: info@westernchestercounty.com
URL: http://www.westernchestercounty.com
Contact: Dawn Stoltzfus, Pres.

64533 ■ Westmoreland Chamber of Commerce
RR 1, PO Box 240
Greensburg, PA 15601
Ph:(724)834-2900
Fax: (724)837-7635
Co. E-mail: info@westmorelandchamber.com
URL: http://www.westmorelandchamber.com
Contact: Thomas L. Sochacki, Pres.

64534 ■ Wilkinsburg Chamber of Commerce
730 Penn Ave.
Standard Bank Bldg.
Wilkinsburg, PA 15221
Ph:(412)242-0234
Fax: (412)243-1404
URL: http://www.wilkinsburgchamber.org
Contact: Owen McAfee, Pres.

64535 ■ Williamsport-Lycoming Chamber of Commerce
100 W Third St.
Williamsport, PA 17701
Ph:(570)326-1971
Fax: (570)321-1208
Co. E-mail: chamber@williamsport.org
URL: http://www.williamsport.org
Contact: Vincent J. Matteo DPA, Pres.

64536 ■ York County Chamber of Commerce
96 S George St., 3rd Fl.
York, PA 17401-1611
Ph:(717)848-4000
Free: 888-878-9675
Fax: (717)843-6737
Co. E-mail: fran@yorkchamber.com
URL: http://www.yorkchamber.com
Contact: Thomas E. Donley, Pres.

64537 ■ Zelienople-Harmony Area Chamber of Commerce
111 W Newcastle St.
PO Box 464
Zelienople, PA 16063
Ph:(724)452-5232
Fax: (724)452-5712
Co. E-mail: zhcc@zoominternet.net
Contact: Marnie Repasky, Exec.Dir.

MINORITY BUSINESS ASSISTANCE PROGRAMS

64538 ■ Pennsylvania Department of General Services–Bureau of Minority and Women's Business Opportunities (BMWBO)
Rm 611, North Office Bldg.
Harrisburg, PA 17125
Ph:(717)787-6708

Fax: (717)787-7052
Co. E-mail: gs-bmwbo@state.pa.us
URL: http://www.dgs.state.pa.us
Description: Actively pursues contracting and subcontracting opportunities in state government and the private sector for minority and women business enterprises.

64539 ■ Pennsylvania Minority Business Development Authority
Pennsylvania Department of Community and Economic Developmen
Keystone Bldg. 4th Floor
Harrisburg, PA 17120
Ph:(717)783-1127
Fax: (717)782-2890
Co. E-mail: dwaters@state.pa.us
URL: http://www.inventpa.com
Contact: David Waters
Description: Provides low-interest, long-term loans and equity guarantees to assist in the start-up or expansion of minority-owned businesses.

64540 ■ Philadelphia Minority Business Development Center
600 Arch St., Ste 10128
Philadelphia, PA 19106
Ph:(215)861-3597
Fax: (215)861-3595
Co. E-mail: pmbdc@aol.com
URL: http://www.philanet.com/pmbdc

FINANCING AND LOAN PROGRAMS

64541 ■ Adams Capital Management, Inc.
500 Blackburn Ave.
Sewickley, PA 15143
Ph:(412)749-9454
Fax: (412)749-9459
URL: http://www.acm.com
Contact: Joel Adams, Managing Partner
Preferred Investment Size: $5,000,000 to $30,000,000. **Investment Types:** Early, first and second stage. **Industry Preferences:** Internet specific, semiconductors and other electronics, computer software and services, medical and health, biotechnology, computer hardware, communications and media. **Geographic Preferences:** U.S.

64542 ■ Alpha Capital Corporation, L.L.C.
529 Favette St.
Conshohocken, PA 19428
Ph:(610)828-8301
Fax: (610)828-1995

64543 ■ Ben Franklin Technology Partners
11 Penn Ctr.
1835 Market St. Ste., 1100
Philadelphia, PA 19103
Ph:(215)972-6700
Fax: (215)972-5588
URL: http://www.benfranklin.org
Contact: Terry Hicks, Vice President
Investment Types: Seed and early stage. **Industry Preferences:** Biotechnology, Internet specific, medical and health, computer software and services, other products, industrial and energy, computer hardware, consumer related, semiconductors and other electronics, communications and media. **Geographic Preferences:** Pennsylvania.

64544 ■ Bioadvance
3701 Market St.
Philadelphia, PA 19104
Ph:(215)966-6214
Fax: (215)966-6215
URL: http://www.bioadvance.com
Contact: Barbara Schilberg, Chief Executive Officer and Managing Dir
Investment Policies: Seed and early stage. **Industry Preferences:** Biotechnology, and medical and health. **Geographic Preferences:** Pennsylvania.

64545 ■ Birchmere Ventures
1 North Shore Ctr.
12 Federal St., Ste. 201
Pittsburgh, PA 15212
Ph:(412)322-3300
Fax: (412)322-3226
URL: http://www.birchmerevc.com
Contact: Bernard Cambou, Partner
Preferred Investment Size: $1,000,000 to $2,500,000. **Investment Types:** Start-up, early, first, second and later stage, and expansion. **Industry Preferences:** Computer software and services, biotechnology, Internet specific, computer hardware, industrial and energy, medical and health, semiconductors and other electronics. **Geographic Preferences:** Mid Atlantic.

64546 ■ Blue Hill Partners LLC
40 W. Evergreen Ave.
Philadelphia, PA 19118
Ph:(215)247-2400
Fax: (215)248-2381
URL: http://www.bluehillpartners.com
Contact: Alan Grant, Managing Partner
Investment Policies: Early stage and expansion. **Industry Preferences:** Industrial an energy, agriculture, forestry and fishing. **Geographic Preferences:** Pennsylvania.

64547 ■ CEO Venture Fund
1 North Shore Ctr.
12 federal St., Ste. 201
Pittsburgh, PA 15212
Ph:(412)322-2572
Fax: (412)322-3226
URL: http://www.ceoventurefund.com
Contact: James Colker, Managing Partner
Preferred Investment Size: $1,000,000 to $2,000,000. **Investment Types:** Start-up, first and second stage, leveraged buyout, and special situation. **Industry Preferences:** Computer software and services, biotechnology, semiconductors and other electronics, Internet specific, computer hardware, other products, industrial and energy, medical and health, communications and media, and consumer related. **Geographic Preferences:** Mid Atlantic.

64548 ■ Cross Atlantic Capital Partners
5 Radnor Corporate Ctr., Ste. 555
Radnor, PA 19087
Ph:(610)995-2650
Fax: (610)971-2062
URL: http://www.xacp.com
Preferred Investment Size: $2,000,000 to $7,000,000. **Investment Types:** Early stage. **Industry Preferences:** Internet specific, computer software and services, communications and media, computer hardware, other products, semiconductors and other electronics, industrial and energy, and biotechnology. **Geographic Preferences:** Mid Atlantic.

64549 ■ Draper Triangle Ventures
2 Gateway Ctr., 20th Fl.
Pittsburgh, PA 15222
Ph:(412)288-9800
Fax: (412)288-9799
URL: http://www.dtvc.com
Contact: Donald Jones, Managing Director
Preferred Investment Size: $500,000 to $3,000,000. **Investment Types:** Early and first stage. **Industry Preferences:** Communications, Internet specific, semiconductors and other electronics, medical and health, computer software, industrial and energy, and consumer related. **Geographic Preferences:** Midwest and Northeast.

64550 ■ Enertech Capital /Enertech Capital Partners, L.P.
435 Devon Park Dr., Bldg. 700
Wayne, PA 19087
Ph:(610)254-4141
Fax: (610)254-4188
URL: http://www.enertechcapital.com
Contact: David Lincoln, Managing Director
Preferred Investment Size: $1,000,000 to $7,000,000. **Investment Types:** Seed, early stage, and expansion. **Industry Preferences:** Internet specific, computer software and services, industrial and energy, semiconductors and other electronics, consumer related, computer hardware, other products, communications and media. **Geographic Preferences:** U.S.

64551 ■ G4 Partners, LLC.
409Broad St., Ste. 101B
Sewickley, PA 15143
Ph:(412)749-4110
Fax: (412)749-4104
URL: http://www.g4partners.com
Contact: Thomas Gill, managing Partner
Investment Policies: First, second, early, and later stage, expansion, and balanced. **Industry Preferences:** Communications, industrial and energy, and manufacturing.

64552 ■ Gamma Investors LLC
555 Croton Rd., Ste. 111
King of Prussia, PA 19406
Ph:(610)265-8116
Fax: (610)265-7245
URL: http://www.gammainvestors.com
Contact: Alec Petro, Managing Director
Preferred Investment Size: $500,000 to $2,000,000. **Investment Types:** Early, first and second stage. **Industry Preferences:** Internet specific. **Geographic Preferences:** U.S.

64553 ■ Greater Philadelphia Venture Capital Corp.
351 East Conestoga Rd.
Wayne, PA 19087
Ph:(610)688-6829
Fax: (610)254-8958
Preferred Investment Size: $100,000 to $300,000. **Investment Types:** First and second stage, leveraged buyout, mezzanine, and special situation. **Industry Preferences:** Communications, computer hardware and software, medical and health, and consumer related. **Geographic Preferences:** Mid Atlantic.

64554 ■ Innovation Works, Inc.
2000 Technology Dr., Ste. 250
Pittsburgh, PA 15219
Ph:(412)681-1520
Fax: (412)681-2625
URL: http://www.innovationworks.org
Preferred Investment Size: $100,000 to $500,000. **Investment Types:** Early and first stage, seed, and start-up. **Industry Preferences:** Communications and media, computer hardware and software, Internet specific, semiconductors and other electronics, biotechnology, medical and health, industrial and energy. **Geographic Preferences:** Pennsylvania.

64555 ■ Innovest Group, Inc.
1528 Walnut St., Ste. 1701
Philadelphia, PA 19102
Ph:(215)545-5505
Fax: (215)545-6065
Preferred Investment Size: $100,000 to $1,000,000. **Investment Types:** Start-up, first and early stage, expansion, generalist PE, private placement, and special situation. **Industry Preferences:** Consumer related, financial services, and business service. **Geographic Preferences:** Mid Atlantic, Midwest, and Northeast.

64556 ■ Katalyst Venture Partners
1200 River Rd., Ste. 1302
Conshohocken, PA 19428
Ph:(484)530-1750
Fax: (484)530-1799
URL: http://www.katalyst.com
Contact: Johnathan Fitzgerald, Managing Director
Investment Types: Early stage and expansion. **Industry Preferences:** Communications and media, computer software, and Internet specific. **Geographic Preferences:** Canada.

64557 ■ Keystone Minority Capital Fund, L.P.
1801 Centre Ave., Ste. 201
Williams Sq.
Pittsburgh, PA 15219

Ph:(412)856-6900
Fax: (412)338-2224
Contact: Earl Hord, General Partner
Preferred Investment Size: $500,000 minimum. **Investment Types:** Start-up, first stage, second stage, mezzanine, and leveraged buyout. **Industry Preferences:** Communications and media, computer related, semiconductors and other electronics, biotechnology, medical and health, consumer related, industrial and energy, business service, and manufacturing. **Geographic Preferences:** Mid Atlantic.

64558 ■ **Keystone Venture Capital Management Co.**
1601 Market St., Ste. 2500
Philadelphia, PA 19103
Ph:(215)241-1200
Fax: (215)241-1211
URL: http://www.keystonevc.com
Contact: Peter Ligeti, General Partner
E-mail: pligeti@keystnevc.com
Preferred Investment Size: $1,000,000 to $4,000,000. **Investment Types:** Start-up, early, first and second stage, private placement, and expansion. **Industry Preferences:** Internet specific, consumer related, computer software and services, communications and media, industrial and energy, medical and health, other products, computer hardware, semiconductors and other electronics. **Geographic Preferences:** Mid Atlantic and Northeast.

64559 ■ **Lancet Capital / Caduceus Capital Partners**
100 technology Dr., Ste. 200
Pittsburgh, PA 15219
Ph:(412)471-7101
Fax: (412)471-7102
URL: http://www.lancetcapital.com
Contact: George Sing, Managing Director
Preferred Investment Size: $100,00 to $4,000,000.
Investment Types: Seed and start-up. **Industry Preferences:** Biotechnology, medical and health.
Geographic Preferences: U.S.

64560 ■ **Launchcyte LLC**
5001 Centre Ave.
Pittsburgh, PA 15213
Ph:(412)697-2900
Fax: (412)697-2951
URL: http://www.launchcyte.com
Contact: Babs Carryer, President
Investment Policies: Start-up. **Industry Preferences:** Biotechnology.

64561 ■ **Liberty Venture Partners, Inc.**
1 Commerce Sq.
2005 Market St., Ste. 2040
Philadelphia, PA 19103
Ph:(215)282-4484
Fax: (215)282-4485
URL: http://www.libertyvp.com
Contact: Thomas Morse, Principal
E-mail: tmorse@liberyvp.com
Preferred Investment Size: $1,000,000 to $5,000,000. **Investment Types:** Expansion. **Industry Preferences:** Medical and health, computer software and services, communications and media, and Internet specific, medical and health, industrial and energy, and biotechnology. **Geographic Preferences:** Mid Atlantic.

64562 ■ **Loyalhanna Venture Fund**
527 Cedar Way, Ste. 104
Oakmont, PA 15139
Ph:(412)820-7035
Fax: (412)820-7036
Preferred Investment Size: $300,000 to $1,000,000.
Investment Types: First and second stage, and leveraged buyout.

64563 ■ **Lycos Ventures**
2 Gateway Ctr., 20th Fl.
Pittsburgh, PA 15222
Ph:(412)338-8600
Fax: (412)338-8699
URL: http://www.lycosventures.com
Contact: Dennis Ciccone, Managing Director

Preferred Investment Size: $1,000,000 to $5,000,000. **Investment Types:** Start-up, first, early and second stage. **Industry Preferences:** Internet specific, computer software and services, computer hardware, communications and media. **Geographic Preferences:** U.S.

64564 ■ **Mellon Ventures, Inc.**
1 Mellon Ctr., Rm. 5210
Pittsburgh, PA 15258-0001
Ph:(412)236-3594
Fax: (412)236-3593
URL: http://www.mellonventures.com
Contact: John Richardson, Senior Managing Director
Preferred Investment Size: $2,000,000 to $15,000,000. **Investment Types:** Start-up, first, second, and early stage, acquisition, expansion, industry rollups, joint ventures, mezzanine, leveraged buyout, recapitalizations, strategic alliances, turnaround, and management buyouts. **Industry Preferences:** Other products, Internet specific, computer software and services, communications and media, computer hardware, consumer related, industrial and energy, semiconductors and other electronics, medical and health.
Geographic Preferences: U.S.

64565 ■ **Meridian Venture Partners (MVP)**
201 King of Prussia Rd., Ste. 240
Radnor, PA 19087
Ph:(610)254-2999
Fax: (610)254-2996
URL: http://www.meridan-venture.com
Contact: Robert Brown, Managing General Partner
Preferred Investment Size: $2,000,000 to $8,000,000. **Investment Types:** Acquisition, expansion, later stage, management buyouts, and recapitalizations. **Industry Preferences:** Consumer related, Internet specific, computer software and services, medical and health, industrial and energy, other products, communications and media, biotechnology, and computer hardware. **Geographic Preferences:** Mid Atlantic, Midwest, Northeast, and Northwest.

64566 ■ **Mid-Atlantic Venture Funds / Nepa Management Corp.**
Ben Franklin Technology Ctr.
125 Goodman Dr.
Bethlehem, PA 18015
Ph:(610)865-6550
Fax: (610)865-6427
URL: http://www.mavf.com
Contact: Thomas Smith, Partner
Preferred Investment Size: $500,000 to $8,000,000.
Investment Types: Seed, start-up, early stage, fund of funds, turnaround, and leveraged buyout. **Industry Preferences:** Internet specific, computer software and services, medical and health, industrial and energy, other products, computer hardware, semiconductors and other electronics, communications and media, consumer related, and biotechnology. **Geographic Preferences:** Mid Atlantic Massachusetts, North Carolina, and Northeast.

64567 ■ **Newspring Ventures**
500 N. Gulph Rd., Ste. 500
King of Prussia, PA 19406
Ph:(610)567-2380
Fax: (610)567-2388
URL: http://www.newsprintventures.com
Contact: Esther Chang, Principal
Preferred Investment Size: $2,000,000 to $6,000,000. **Investment Types:** Second and later stage, acquisition, management buyouts, mezzanine, recapitalizations, and expansion. **Industry Preferences:** Communications and media, computer software, computer related, semiconductors and other electronics, Internet specific, medical and health, financial services, business service, and manufacturing. **Geographic Preferences:** Mid Atlantic.

64568 ■ **PA Early Stage / Pennsylvania Stage Partners**
1200 Liberty Ridge Dr., Ste. 310
Wayne, PA 19087
Ph:(610)293-4075
Fax: (610)254-4240

URL: http://www.paearlystage.com
Contact: Michael Bolton, Managing Director
Preferred Investment Size: $100,000 to $5,000,000.
Investment Types: Start-up, seed, first and early stage. **Industry Preferences:** Internet specific, computer software and services, biotechnology, other products, semiconductors and other electronics, medical and health, consumer related, industrial and energy, communications and media. **Geographic Preferences:** Mid Atlantic.

64569 ■ **Patricof & Co. Ventures, Inc.**
455 S. Gulph Rd., Ste. 410
King of Prussia, PA 19406
Ph:(610)265-0286
Fax: (610)265-4959
URL: http://www.patricof.com
Preferred Investment Size: $500,000 minimum. **Investment Types:** Seed, start-up, first and second stage, mezzanine, and leveraged buyout. **Industry Preferences:** Diversified. **Geographic Preferences:** No preference.

64570 ■ **The Penn-Janney Fund, Inc.**
1801 Market St., 11th Fl.
Philadelphia, PA 19103
Ph:(215)665-4447
Fax: (215)557-0820
Contact: William Rulon-Miller
Preferred Investment Size: $1,000,000 minimum.
Investment Types: Second stage, mezzanine, leveraged buyout, and special situation. **Industry Preferences:** Communications and media, computer hardware and software, semiconductors and other electronics, biotechnology, medical and health, consumer related, industrial and energy, business service, and manufacturing. **Geographic Preferences:** Northeast, West Coast, and Mid Atlantic.

64571 ■ **Pennsylvania Growth Fund**
5850 Ellsworth Ave., Ste. 303
Pittsburgh, PA 15232
Ph:(412)661-1000
Fax: (412)361-0676
Preferred Investment Size: $500,000 minimum. **Investment Types:** Leveraged buyout, mezzanine, second stage, and special situation. **Industry Preferences:** Consumer software, semiconductors and other electronics, medical and health, consumer related, industrial and energy, and financial services. **Geographic Preferences:** Mid Atlantic, Midwest, Northeast, and Southeast.

64572 ■ **Philadelphia Ventures, Inc.**
The Bellevue
200 S. Broad St.
Philadelphia, PA 19102
Ph:(215)732-4445
Fax: (215)732-4644
Contact: Charles Burton, Managing Director
Investment Types: Start-up, first and second stage, mezzanine, and leveraged buyout. **Industry Preferences:** Computer hardware, computer software and services, communications and media, medical and health, biotechnology, industrial and energy, semiconductors and other electronics, other products, Internet specific, and consumer related. **Geographic Preferences:** Pennsylvania.

64573 ■ **Point Venture Partners**
The Century Bldg.
130 Seventh St., 4th Fl.
Pittsburgh, PA 15222
Ph:(412)261-1966
Fax: (412)261-1718
Preferred Investment Size: $2,000,000. **Investment Types:** Start-up, first and second stage, mezzanine, recapitalizations, and leveraged buyout. **Industry Preferences:** Communications and media, computer hardware and software, semiconductors and other electronics, biotechnology, medical and health, consumer related, industrial and energy, transportation, financial services, business service, and manufacturing. **Geographic Preferences:** Mid Atlantic, Midwest, Northeast, and Southeast.

64574 ■ RAF Netventures / RAF Ventures
165 Township Line Rd., Ste. 2100
Jenkintown, PA 19046
Ph:(215)572-0738
Fax: (215)576-1640
URL: http://www.rafnetventures.com
Contact: Richard Horowitz
Preferred Investment Size: $37,000,000 minimum.
Investment Types: Seed, start-up, first and second stage, and leveraged buyout. **Industry Preferences:** Internet specific, medical and health, computer software and services, and biotechnology. **Geographic Preferences:** Northeast.

64575 ■ The Reinvestment Fund (TRF)
718 Arch St., Ste. 300 N.
Philadelphia, PA 19106
Ph:(215)925-1130
Fax: (215)923-4764
URL: http://www.trfund.com
Contact: John Schaefer, Managing Director
Preferred Investment Size: $1,000,000 to $5,000,000. **Investment Types:** Later stage and mezzanine. **Industry Preferences:** Other products, medical and health, Internet specific, industrial and energy, consumer related, computer software and services. **Geographic Preferences:** Mid Atlantic.

64576 ■ Rock Hill Ventures, Inc. / Hillman Medical Ventures, Inc.
100 Front St., Ste. 1350
West Conshohocken, PA 19428
Ph:(610)940-0300
Fax: (610)940-0301
Preferred Investment Size: $1,000,000 to $2,000,000. **Investment Types:** Seed, research and development, start-up, first and second stage, leveraged buyout, and recapitalizations. **Industry Preferences:** Medical and health, and biotechnology. **Geographic Preferences:** Mid Atlantic, Northeast, and Southeast.

64577 ■ The Sandhurst Venture Fund, L.P.
351 E. Constoga Rd.
Wayne, PA 19087
Ph:(610)254-8900
Fax: (610)254-8958
Preferred Investment Size: $500,000 to $1,000,000.
Investment Types: Leveraged buyout, recapitalizations, and second stage. **Industry Preferences:** Semiconductors and other electronics, medical and health, consumer related, industrial and energy. **Geographic Preferences:** Mid Atlantic.

64578 ■ Schoffstall Ventures
5790 Devnonshire Rd.
Harrisburg, PA 17112
Ph:(717)671-3208
Fax: (717)671-3221
URL: http://www.schoffstallventures.com
Contact: Martin Schoffstall, Managing Partner
Investment Types: Early stage and expansion. **Industry Preferences:** Communications and media, and Internet specific. **Geographic Preferences:** U.S.

64579 ■ S.R. One, Limited
Four Tower Bridge
200 Barr Harbor Dr., Ste. 250
W. Conshohocken, PA 19428
Ph:(610)567-1000
Fax: (610)567-1039
Contact: Brenda Gavin, President
Preferred Investment Size: $500,000 to $5,000,000.
Investment Types: Start-up, first and second stage, and seed. **Industry Preferences:** Biotechnology, medical and health, computer software and services, Internet specific, and consumer related. **Geographic Preferences:** U.S.

64580 ■ TDH
259 Radnor-Chester Rd., Ste. 301
Rosemont, PA 19087
Ph:(610)687-8580
Fax: (610)971-2154
Contact: J.B. Doherty, Partner
Preferred Investment Size: $1,000,000 to $2,500,000. **Investment Types:** Second and later

stage, acquisition, expansion, joint ventures, and leveraged buyout. **Industry Preferences:** Communications and media, medical and health, consumer related, industrial and energy, financial services, business service, and manufacturing. **Geographic Preferences:** Mid Atlantic.

64581 ■ TL Ventures / Radnor Venture Partners
435 Devon Park Dr.
700 Bldg.
Wayne, PA 19087-1990
Ph:(610)971-1515
Fax: (610)975-9330
URL: http://www.tlventures.com
Contact: Amir Goldman, Principal
Preferred Investment Size: $3,000,000 to $20,000,000. **Investment Types:** Early stage. **Industry Preferences:** Internet specific, computer software and services, communications and media, biotechnology, semiconductors and other electronics, medical and health, other products, computer hardware, and consumer related. **Geographic Preferences:** Northeast, Northwest, Southwest, and West Coast.

PROCUREMENT ASSISTANCE PROGRAMS

64582 ■ Defense Supply Center Philadelphia
700 Robbins Ave.
Bldg. 36-2
Philadelphia, PA 19111
Ph:(215)737-2321
Free: 800-831-1110
Fax: (215)737-7116
URL: http://www.dscp.dla.mil
Contact: Michael McCall
Description: Covers activities for GSA, Public Building Services (Philadelphia, PA), Army Corps of Engineers (Philadelphia, PA), Defense Personnel Support Center-Clothing & Textile (Philadelphia, PA), Defense Personnel Support Center-Medical (Philadelphia, PA), Defense Personnel Support Center-Subsistence (Philadelphia, PA).

64583 ■ Navy Inventory Control Point
700 Robbins Ave.
Bldg. 1, Rm.3209 (SBS)
Philadelphia, PA 19111
Ph:(215)697-4950
Fax: (215)697-2616
Co. E-mail: Joseph.giordano@sba.gov
URL: http://www.navicp.navy.mil
Contact: Porcurement Spec.
E-mail: joseph.giordano@icpphil.navy.mil
Description: Covers activities for Navy Inventory Control Point (Philadelphia, PA).

64584 ■ Pennsylvania & Maryland Procurement Center
Fleet & Industrial Supply
Center Detachment Philadelphia
700 Robbins Ave., Bldg. 2B
Philadelphia, PA 19111
Ph:(215)697-9555
Fax: (215)697-9554
Co. E-mail: b_j_koehler@phil.fisc.navy.mil
URL: http://www.nor.fisc.navy.mil
Contact: Gerald Furey, SBS Representative
Description: Covers activities for Navy, Fleet & Industrial Support, Center Detachment Philadelphia (Philadelphia, PA), NAVFAC (Philadelphia, PA), Naval Surface Weapons Center (Bethesda, MD), Army Chemical & Biological Defense Command (Edgewood, MD), and Army, Aberdeen Proving Ground (Aberdeen, MD).

64585 ■ Pennsylvania Procurement Center
Navy Inventory Control Point
PO Box 2020
Mechanicsburg, PA 17055
Ph:(717)605-7325
Fax: (717)605-1926
URL: http://www.nicp.navy.mil
Contact: Helen SBS Representative, SBS
    Representative

E-mail: ed_bloss@icpmmech.navy.mil

64586 ■ Pennsylvania Procurement Center–2155802771
Defense Philadelphia Supply Center
700 Robbins Ave., Bldg. 36
Philadelphia, PA 19111
Ph:(215)737-5912
Fax: (215)737-7116
Co. E-mail: rsacidor@dscp.dal.mil
URL: http://www.sba.gov
Contact: Ricardo Sacidor, SBA Representative
Description: Covers activities for Defense Industrial Supply Center (Philadelphia, PA). Purchases food, clothing, medical supplies and general industrial supplies.

64587 ■ Pennsylvania Procurement Technical Assistance Center
University of Pennsylvania, Wharton
3733 Spruce St.
4th Floor-Vance Hall
Philadelphia, PA 19104-6374
Ph:(215)898-1219
Fax: (215)573-2135
Co. E-mail: pasbdc@wharton.upenn.edu
URL: http://www.pasbdc.org
Contact: Clyde Stoltzfus, Dir

64588 ■ Pennsylvania Procurement Technical Assistance Center–Government Agency Coordination Office–California University of Pennsylvania (250 U)
250 University Ave., Box 20
California, PA 15419
Ph:(724)938-5881
Fax: (724)938-4575
Co. E-mail: wojcik@cup.edu
Contact: Deborah Wojcik
E-mail: wojcik@cup.edu

64589 ■ Pennsylvania Procurement Technical Assistance Center–Indiana University of Pennsylvania–Government Contracting Assistance Program (10 Ro)
10 Robertshaw Main Bldg.
650 S 13th St.
Indiana, PA 15705-1087
Ph:(724)357-7824
Fax: (724)357-3082
Co. E-mail: rfmoreau@iup.edu
URL: http://www.eberly.iup.edu/gcap
Contact: Ron Moreau, Prgm Mgr
E-mail: rfmoreau@grove.iup.edu

64590 ■ Pennsylvania Procurement Technical Assistance Center–Johnstown Area Regional Industries
111 Market St.
Johnstown, PA 15901
Ph:(814)539-4951
Fax: (814)535-8677
Co. E-mail: pchirillo@jari.com
URL: http://www.jari.com
Contact: Peter Chirillo

64591 ■ Pennsylvania Procurement Technical Assistance Center–North Central Pennsylvania Regional Planning & Development Commission
651 Montmorenci Ave.
Ridgeway, PA 15853
Ph:(814)773-3162
Fax: (814)772-7045
Co. E-mail: bimof@ncentral.com
URL: http://www.ncentral.com
Contact: Bob Imhof, Receptionist
E-mail: bimhof@ncentral.com

64592 ■ Pennsylvania Procurement Technical Assistance Center–Northeastern Pennsylvania Alliance
1151 Oak St.
Pittston, PA 18640
Ph:(570)655-5581
Fax: (570)654-5137
Co. E-mail: info@nepa.alliance.org
URL: http://www.nepa-alliance.org

Contact: David Kern, Mgr
E-mail: dkk@microserve.net

64593 ■ Pennsylvania Procurement Technical Assistance Center–Northern Tier Regional Planning & Development Commission
312 Main St.
Towanda, PA 18848-1697
Ph:(570)265-9103
Free: 888-868-8800
Fax: (570)265-7585
Co. E-mail: meehan@northerntier.org
URL: http://www.northerntier.org
Contact: Kerry Meehan, Mgr
E-mail: sabatura@northerntier.org

64594 ■ Pennsylvania Procurement Technical Assistance Center–SEDA Council of Governments
201 Furnace Rd.
Lewisburg, PA 17837
Ph:(570)524-4491
Free: 800-332-6701
Fax: (570)524-9190
Co. E-mail: admin@seda-cog.org
URL: http://www.seda-cog.org
Contact: Robert Brown

64595 ■ Pennsylvania Procurement Technical Assistance Center–Southwestern Pennsylvania Commission
Regional Enterprise Tower
425 6th Ave., Ste. 2500
Pittsburgh, PA 15219
Ph:(412)391-5590
Fax: (412)391-9160
Co. E-mail: comments@spcregion.org
URL: http://www.spcregion.org
Contact: Jamie Colecchi, Dev.Spec.

64596 ■ Private Industry Council–Procurement Information Center of Westmoreland/Fay
RR 12, Box 213
Greensburg, PA 15601
Ph:(724)836-2600
Fax: (724)836-8058
Co. E-mail: info.privateindustrycouncil.com
URL: http://www.privateindustrycouncil.com
Contact: Tim Yurcisin, Pres & CEO

64597 ■ Southern Alleghenies Planning and Development Commission
541 58th St.
Altoona, PA 16602-1193
Ph:(814)949-6528
Fax: (814)949-6505
Co. E-mail: shade@sapdc.org
URL: http://www.sapdc.org
Contact: Daniel Shade
E-mail: shade@ssapdc.org

64598 ■ Temple University Small Business Development Center–Temple University
1510 Cecil B. Moore Ave.
Philadelphia, PA 19121
Ph:(215)204-7282
Fax: (215)204-4554
Co. E-mail: sbdc@sbm.temple.edu
URL: http://www.temple.edu/sbdc
Contact: Eustace Kangaju, Dir

INCUBATORS/RESEARCH AND TECHNOLOGY PARKS

64599 ■ Altoona Blair County Development Corporations
3900 Industrial Park Dr.
Altoona, PA 16602
Ph:(814)944-6113
Fax: (814)946-0157
Co. E-mail: abcd@abcdcorp.org
URL: http://www.abcdcorp.org

64600 ■ Ben Franklin Technology Partners
125 Goodman Dr.
Bethlehem, PA 18015-3715
Ph:(610)758-5200
Fax: (610)861-5918
Co. E-mail: info@nep.benfranklin.org
URL: http://www.nep.benfranklin.org
Contact: Bob Thomson, Reg Mgr
Description: The Northeast Tier is one of four BFTCs that operate in Pennsylvania. They are dedicated to nurturing the development of emerging technology firms.

64601 ■ California University of Pennsylvania–Mon Valley Renaissance
250 University Ave., Box 101
California, PA 15419-1394
Ph:(724)938-5885
Fax: (724)938-5888
Co. E-mail: brna@cup.edu
Contact: Michael J. Brna Jr., Exec.Dir.
E-mail: brna@cup.edu
Scope: Multiprogram consortium with a focus on applied research and economic development services to business and industry. Services: Technical assistance, in government procurement, robotics, international procurement technology, technical training, numerical control programming, and graphic communications. Educational Activities: Seminars; Training workshops.

64602 ■ Carnegie Mellon University–Associate Provost for Research and Academic Administration
5000 Forbes Ave., WH405
Pittsburgh, PA 15213
Ph:(412)268-8746
Fax: (412)268-6279
Co. E-mail: osr@andrew.cmu.edu
URL: http://www.cmu.edu/provost/spon-res/osr.html
Contact: Susan Burkett, Assoc. Provost
E-mail: osr@andrew.cmu.edu
Scope: Administers and coordinates extramurally supported faculty and graduate student research in sciences, engineering, business management, urban planning, and related fields.

64603 ■ Catalyst Connections
2000 Technology Dr.
Pittsburgh, PA 15219
Ph:(412)687-2700
Free: 888-88-SPIRC
Fax: (412)687-2791
Co. E-mail: info@spirc.org
URL: http://www.catalystconnection.org/

64604 ■ Chamber Business and Industry
200 Innovation Blvd., Ste 150
State College, PA 16803
Ph:(814)234-1829
Fax: (814)234-5869
Co. E-mail: cbicc@cbicc.org
URL: http://www.cbicc.org
Contact: John Coleman, Pres & CEO

64605 ■ Donald H. Jones Center for Entrepreneurship
Tepper School Of Business
Carnegie Mellon University
Pittsburgh, PA 15213-3890
Ph:(412)268-2269
Fax: (412)268-4804
Co. E-mail: thornet@andrew.cmu.edu
URL: http://business.tepper.cmu.edu

64606 ■ Duquesne University–Office of Research
600 Forbes Ave.
Pittsburgh, PA 15282
Ph:(412)396-6000
Free: 800—456-0590
Fax: (412)396-5176
Co. E-mail: phillips@duq.edu
URL: http://www2.duq.edu/research
Contact: James Phillips PhD, Dir.
E-mail: phillips@duq.edu
Scope: Responsible for locating potential sources of financial support (particularly governmental support)

for faculty research interests, assisting faculty members in preparing proposals, and monitoring the administration of all governmental research grant and contract activities.

64607 ■ Executive Office Link
7 Great Valley Pky., Ste. 210
Malvern, PA 19355
Ph:(610)251-6850
Fax: (610)889-9726
Co. E-mail: info@execofficelink.com
URL: http://www.execofficelink.com
Contact: Sharon Nothnagle, Receptionist

64608 ■ Girard Area Industrial Development Corp.–Model Works Industrial Commons
227 Hathaway St. E
Girard, PA 16417
Ph:(814)774-9339
Fax: (814)774-9235

64609 ■ Lehigh University–Office of Research and Sponsored Programs
526 Brodhead Ave.
Bethlehem, PA 18015
Ph:(610)758-3021
Fax: (610)758-5994
Co. E-mail: tjm5@lehigh.edu
URL: http://www.lehigh.edu/~inors/inors.html
Contact: Thomas J. Meischeid, Dir.
E-mail: tjm5@lehigh.edu
Scope: Administers and coordinates, as administrative agency of the University, sponsored and cooperative research supported by government agencies, industry, and technical associations, including studies in physical, natural, social, and engineering sciences, and the humanities. Assists faculty and students in unsponsored research and scholarly efforts. Services: Consulting; Industrial liaison programs. Publications: Research Notes.

64610 ■ McNeilly Business Center
12 N Diamond St.
Greenville, PA 16125
Ph:(724)588-1161
Fax: (724)588-9881
Co. E-mail: mcneilly@nauticom.net
URL: http://www.gaedc.org
Contact: Jim Lowry, Exec Dir

64611 ■ North Central Pennsylvania Regional Planning and Devolvement Commission
651 Montmorency Ave.
Ridgeway, PA 15853
Ph:(814)773-3162
Free: 800-242-5872
Fax: (814)772-7045
Co. E-mail: ncprpdc@ncentral.com
URL: http://www.ncentral.com

64612 ■ Pennsylvania State University–Research and Graduate Studies Office
College of the Liberal Arts
111 Sparks Bldg.
University Park, PA 16802
Ph:(814)865-9555
Fax: (814)863-2603
Co. E-mail: swelch@psu.edu
Contact: Susan Welch, Dean
E-mail: swelch@psu.edu
Scope: Coordinates research activities of faculty members of the College in crime, law and justice; American studies; African-American studies; anthropology; classics; comparative literature; economics; English; French; German; history; Italian; labor studies and industrial relations; linguistics; philosophy; political science; Portuguese; psychology; religious studies; Slavic languages; sociology; Spanish; speech communication; and women's studies. Publications: RGSO News.

64613 ■ Pennsylvania State University–Research and Technology Transfer Organization
113 Technology Center
University Park, PA 16802

Ph:(814)865-6277
Fax: (814)865-3591
Co. E-mail: rjh22@psu.edu
URL: http://www.techtransfer.psu.edu/home.html
Contact: Ronald J. Huss, Dir.
E-mail: rjh22@psu.edu
Scope: Electronics, nano devices and materials, mems, polymers, pharmaceuticals, medical devices, biotechnology, molecular electronics, and agriculture.

64614 ■ Redevelopment Authority of the City of Meadville
984 Waters St.
Meadville, PA 16335
Ph:(814)337-8200
Fax: (814)337-7257
Co. E-mail: ccdc@gremlan.org
URL: http://www.ccdcgremlan.org
Contact: , Admin. Asst.

64615 ■ The Science Center
3701 Market St., 3rd Fl.
Philadelphia, PA 19104
Ph:(215)966-6000
Fax: (215)382-0057
Co. E-mail: info@sciencecenter.org
URL: http://www.sciencecenter.org
Description: The UCSC is dedicated to fostering science and technology-based economic development. The incubator offers tenants office and laboratory space, business services, and research management assistance.

64616 ■ Temple University–Office of the Vice President for Research and Graduate Studies
406 University Services Bldg. 083-45
1601 N Broad St.
Philadelphia, PA 19122-6099
Ph:(215)204-8691
Fax: (215)204-7486
Co. E-mail: ovpr@temple.edu
URL: http://www.research.temple.edu
Contact: Dr. Kenneth J. Soprano, VP
E-mail: ovpr@temple.edu
Scope: Responsible for promotion of externally funded research, training, and service programs and for academic program planning and development on all of the University's campuses, including its Health Sciences Center. Research development activities include biological, physical, and social sciences, humanities, and the creative arts. **Publications:** Research FLASH (biweekly).

64617 ■ University City Science Center
3701 Market St., 3rd Fl.
Philadelphia, PA 19104
Ph:(215)966-6000
Fax: (215)966-6260
Co. E-mail: info@sciencecenter.org
URL: http://www.sciencecenter.org
Contact: Pradip K. Banerjee PhD, Pres./CEO
E-mail: info@sciencecenter.org
Scope: Accelerates development of information technology and life science business ventures through the Port of Technology. Manages research and development programs and provides facilities and service to support Research Park tenants. Activities are carried out through the Research Park Group and the Programs Group. The park houses 140 organizations in a 15 building complex. The Programs Group includes three Centers of Excellence in indoor environments and energy management. **Services:** Industrial Technology and Energy Management Group, which provides consulting to manufacturers of energy conservation and waste production products; Science Center International, providing international consultation and technical assistance.

64618 ■ University of Pennsylvania–Center for Technology Transfer
3160 Chestnut St., Ste. 200
Philadelphia, PA 19104-6283
Ph:(215)573-4500
Fax: (215)898-9519
Co. E-mail: zawad@ctt.upenn.edu
URL: http://www.ctt.upenn.edu
Contact: Dr. John S. Zawad, Mng.Dir.

E-mail: zawad@ctt.upenn.edu
Scope: Transfers technology from the University to business and industry in the fields of biotechnology, chemistry and chemical engineering, dental medicine, diagnostics, electrical engineering, laboratory devices and reagents, medical devices, mechanical engineering, materials science, pharmaceuticals, nanotechnology, robotics factory automation, software, veterinary medicine, physics and optics. **Publications:** Penntech Connection (quarterly).

64619 ■ University of Pennsylvania–Office of Research Services
3451 Walnut St., Rm. P-221
Philadelphia, PA 19104-6205
Ph:(215)898-7293
Fax: (215)898-9708
Co. E-mail: abrud@pobox.upenn.edu
URL: http://www.upenn.edu/researchservices
Contact: Dr. Andrew B. Rudczynski, Exec.Dir.
E-mail: abrud@pobox.upenn.edu
Scope: Administers extramurally sponsored research for all departments and research units of the University and handles processing of research applications, financial reporting, and indirect cost proposal preparation.

64620 ■ Villanova University–Office of Research and Sponsored Projects
101 Tolentine Hall
800 Lancaster Ave.
Villanova, PA 19085-1699
Ph:(610)519-4220
Fax: (610)519-7839
Co. E-mail: milton.cole@villanova.edu
URL: http://www.orsp.villanova.edu
Contact: Dr. Milton T. Cole, Asst.VP
E-mail: milton.cole@villanova.edu
Scope: Promotes and coordinates theoretical and applied research at the University, primarily in fields of science and technology, including astronomy, biology, chemistry, chemical, civil, electrical, and mechanical engineering, geology, the humanities, social sciences, physics, and education. **Publications:** Research Office Newsletter. **Educational Activities:** Workshops, for faculty and staff.

64621 ■ Warren/Forest Counties Economic Opportunity Council
1209 Pennsylvania Ave.
Warren, PA 16365
Ph:(814)726-2400
Free: 800-231-1797
Fax: (814)723-0510
Co. E-mail: eoc@fcaa.org
URL: http://www.wfcaa.org

64622 ■ Wilkes University–Foundations and Grants Management
PO Box 111
Wilkes-Barre, PA 18766
Ph:(570)408-4307
Free: 800—945-5378
Fax: (570)408-7830
Co. E-mail: pelaka@wilkes.edu
Contact: Ann Pelak, Dir., Grants Support
E-mail: pelaka@wilkes.edu
Scope: Administers grant and foundation monies for research in a wide-range of fields, including physical and biological sciences, atmospheric sciences, social sciences, water chemistry, thermochemistry, organicphosphorous chemistry, ecology, morphology, bacteriology, mathematical analysis, humanities, and elementary, secondary, and general education.

EDUCATIONAL PROGRAMS

64623 ■ Central Pennsylvania College
College Hill Rd.
Summerdale, PA 17093
Ph:(717)732-0702
Free: 800-759-2727
Fax: (717)732-5254
Co. E-mail: admissions@centralpenn.edu
URL: http://www.centralpenn.edu

Description: Two-year college offering a program in small business management.

64624 ■ Community College of Allegheny County, North Campus
8701 Perry Hwy.
Pittsburgh, PA 15237
Ph:(412)366-7000
Fax: (412)369-3624
URL: http://www.ccac.edu
Description: Two-year college offering a small business management program.

64625 ■ Delaware County Community College
901 S Media Line Rd.
Media, PA 19063-1094
Ph:(610)359-5000
Free: 800-543-0146
Fax: (610)359-5343
URL: http://www.dccc.edu
Description: Conducts small business courses, including financial management for small business; choosing microcomputer software; how to cash in on your crafts; how to start a consulting business; marketing for your small business; develop your own typing/word processing business; how to develop a business plan; fundamentals of small business management; start-up financing; record keeping and taxes for small business; and microcomputer awareness. Also offers consulting and technical assistance. Works with Community Accountants of Media to provide free accounting and financial assistance to eligible small business owners.

64626 ■ Northampton Community College
3835 Green Pond Rd.
Bethlehem, PA 18020-7599
Ph:(610)861-5300
Free: 877-543-0998
Fax: (610)861-4560
URL: http://www.northampton.edu
Description: Two-year college offering a small business management program, covering start-up, administration and management, and bookkeeping.

64627 ■ Penn Foster Career School
925 Oak St.
Scranton, PA 18515
Ph:(570)342-7701
Free: 800-233-4191
Fax: (570)343-0560
Co. E-mail: info@pennfoster.com
URL: http://www.educationdirect.com
Description: Home-study school offering a small business management program.

PUBLICATIONS

64628 ■ *Smart Start your Pennsylvania Business*
PSI Research
300 N. Valley Dr.
Grants Pass, OR 97526
Ph:(503)479-9464
Free: 800-228-2275
Fax: (503)476-1479
Co. E-mail: info@psi-research.com
URL: http://www.psi-research.com
Ed: Michael D. Jenkins. **Released:** Revised edition, 1992. **Price:** $29.95 (looseleaf binder); $24.95 (paper). **Description:** Part of the Successful Business Library series.

PUBLISHERS

64629 ■ Bookhaven Press L.L.C.
PO Box 1243
Moon Township, PA 15108-2601
Ph:(412)494-6926
Fax: (412)494-5749
Co. E-mail: bookhaven@aol.com
URL: http://members.aol.com/bookhaven

Contact: Dennis V. Damp, Owner
E-mail: ddamp@aol.com
Description: Publishes trade books for general audience on business and employment. Reaches market through direct mail, internet sales, trade sales and wholesalers. Does not accept unsolicited manuscripts. **Founded:** 1985.

64630 ■ Dalton Directory
24 North Bryn Mawr Ave., No. 278
Bryn Mawr, PA 19010
Ph:(518)583-4545
Free: 800-221-1050
Co. E-mail: info@daltondirectory.com
URL: http://www.daltondirectory.com
Contact: Patrick Dalton, President
Description: Publishes business directories for the New York and Philadelphia metropolitan areas. Offers information in a variety of formats including diskettes, C.D. and via internet, and mailing labels. Reaches market through direct mail and telephone sales. Does not accept unsolicited manuscripts. **Founded:** 1960.

64631 ■ The Danielle Adams Publishing Co.
PO Box 100
Merion Station, PA 19066
Ph:(610)642-1000
Free: 800-234-4332
Fax: (610)642-6832
Co. E-mail: Jeff@Dobkin.com
URL: http://www.dobkin.com
Contact: Jeffrey Dobkin, President
E-mail: jeff@dobkin.com
Description: Publishes books of interest to small business owners, investors, marketers and entrepreneurs. Does not accept unsolicited manuscripts.

Reaches market through commission representatives, direct mail and wholesalers. **Founded:** 1986.

64632 ■ Deltiologists of America
PO Box 8
Norwood, PA 19074-0008
Ph:(610)485-8572
Co. E-mail: postcardclassics@juno.com
URL: http://www.deltiologists-america.com
Contact: Dr. James Lewis Lowe, Director
E-mail: jlewislowe@juno.com
Description: Distributes books, magazines to promote the hobby of collecting and researching picture postcards of all types and from all places around the world with an emphasis on so-called antique postcards, those published prior to 1930. **Founded:** 1960.

64633 ■ Strategic Press
774 Morwood Rd.
Telford, PA 18969
Ph:(215)723-8422
Free: 800-974-4393
Fax: (215)703-0467
Co. E-mail: strategic4@aol.com
URL: http://www.icatmall.com/strategicpress
Contact: Rick Alderfer, Publisher & Owner
Description: Publishes business and marketing books and special reports for small business owners and entrepreneurs. Also offers audio cassettes, posters, and prints. Does not accept unsolicited manuscripts. Reaches market through direct mail. **Founded:** 1998.

64634 ■ Via Media Publishing Co.
821 West 24th St.
Erie, PA 16502
URL: http://www.goviamedia.com

Contact: Michael A. DeMarco, Publisher
E-mail: md@goviamedia.com
Description: Publishes fiction and nonfiction about martial arts. Accepts unsolicited manuscripts. Reaches market through direct mail, reviews, listings, and distributors including Biblio. **Founded:** 1991.

64635 ■ The Windsor Press Inc.
6 North 3rd St.
Hamburg, PA 19526
Ph:(610)562-2267
Free: 800-562-5521
Fax: (610)562-2770
Co. E-mail: george@windsorpress.com
URL: http://www.windsorpress.com
Description: Publishes annual reports, manuals and a variety of books, including employer, ad, and program books. Also offers post cards, brochures, and newsletters.

64636 ■ Xlibris Corp.
2 International Plz., Ste. 340
Philadelphia, PA 19113
Ph:(610)915-5214
Free: 888-795-4274
Fax: (610)915-0294
Co. E-mail: info@xlibris.com
URL: http://www2.xlibris.com
Contact: Mr. John Feldcamp, CEO
Description: Offers publishing kits to help authors become published. New titles include *The World Coup* about global terrorism. Accepts unsolicited manuscripts. Reaches market through commision reps, direct mail, reviews, listings, telephone sales, and wholesalers and distributors, including Amazon, BFN, Borders, Ingram, Books in Print and Lightning Source. **Founded:** 1997.

SMALL BUSINESS DEVELOPMENT CENTER LEAD OFFICE

64637 ■ Bryant College–Rhode Island Small Business Development Center
1150 Douglas Pike
Smithfield, RI 02917-1284
Ph:(401)232-6111
Fax: (401)232-6933
Contact: Robert Hamlin, State Director
E-mail: rhamlin@bryant.edu

64638 ■ Johnson and Wales University–Rhode Island SBDC
Richmond Bldg., 4th Fl.
270 Weybosset St.
Providence, RI 02903
Ph:(401)598-2702
Fax: (401)598-2722
URL: http://www.risbdc.org
Contact: John Cronin, State Dir.
E-mail: john.cronin@jwu.edu

SMALL BUSINESS DEVELOPMENT CENTERS

64639 ■ Bristol County Chamber of Commerce–SBDC
PO Box 250
Warren, RI 02885-0250
Ph:(401)245-0750
Fax: (401)245-0110
Contact: Samuel Carr, Case Mgr.

64640 ■ Bryant College–Export Assistance Center–SBDC (John)
John H. Chafee Center for International Business
1150 Douglas Pike
Smithfield, RI 02917
Ph:(401)232-6407
Fax: (401)232-6416
Co. E-mail: info@chafeecenter.org
URL: http://www.chafeecenter.org
Contact: Raymond Fogarty, Dir.

64641 ■ Bryant College–Rhode Island SBDC
1150 Douglas Pike
Smithfield, RI 02917
Ph:(401)232-6000
URL: http://www.bryant.edu
Contact: Robert Hamlin, State Dir.
E-mail: rhamlin@bryant.edu

64642 ■ Central Rhode Island Chamber of Commerce–Bryant College–Small Business Development Center (3288)
3288 Post Rd.
Warwick, RI 02886
Ph:(401)732-1100
Fax: (401)732-1107

Co. E-mail: info@centralrichamber.com
URL: http://www.centralrichamber.com
Contact: Karen H. Sechio, Program Coord.
E-mail: karen@centralrichamber.com

64643 ■ Central Rhode Island Chamber of Commerce–Central and Southern Rhode Island–SBDC (3288)
3288 Post Rd.
Warwick, RI 02886
Ph:(401)263-5128
Fax: (401)732-1107
URL: http://www.risbdc.org
Contact: Ardena Lee-Fleming, Dir.
E-mail: ardena.lee-fleming@jwu.edu

64644 ■ Enterprise Community SBDC/BIC
550 Broad St.
Providence, RI 02905-1445
Ph:(401)272-1083
Fax: (401)272-1186
URL: http://www.bryant.edu
Contact: Tomas Avila, Program Mgr.
E-mail: tavila@bryant.edu

64645 ■ Entrepreneurship Training Program–Bryant College–SBDC (1150)
1150 Douglas Pike
Smithfield, RI 02917
Ph:(401)232-6000
Contact: Dennis McCarthy, Program Mgr.

64646 ■ Greater Providence Chamber of Commerce–Bryant College–Small Business Development Center (30 Ex)
30 Exchange Terrace
Providence, RI 02903-1793
Ph:(401)521-5000
Fax: (401)751-2434
Co. E-mail: chamber@provchamber.com
URL: http://www.providencechamber.com
Contact: Paula Hopkins, Dir.
E-mail: phopkins@provchamber.com

64647 ■ Institute for Family Enterprise–Bryant University–Small Business Development Center (1150)
1150 Douglas Pike
Smithfield, RI 02917-1284
Ph:(401)232-6477
Fax: (401)232-6416
Co. E-mail: ife@bryant.edu
URL: http://www.bryant.edu

64648 ■ JWU Larry Friedman International Center for Entrepreneurship–Providence Metro SBDC
Taco Ctr.
8 Abbott Park Pl.
Providence, RI 02903
Ph:(401)598-2705
URL: http://www.risbdc.org
Contact: Sixcia Devine, Dir.
E-mail: sixcia.devine@jwu.edu

64649 ■ Newport County Chamber of Commerce–E. Bay Small Business Development Center
45 Valley Rd.
Middletown, RI 02842-6377
Ph:(401)263-5124
Fax: (401)841-0570
URL: http://risbdc.org
Contact: Larry Gadsby, Dir.
E-mail: larry.gadsby@jwu.edu

64650 ■ Northern Rhode Island Chamber of Commerce–SBDC
6 Blackstone Valley Pl.
Lincoln, RI 02865
Ph:(401)263-5124
Fax: (401)598-2722
URL: http://www.risbdc.org
Contact: Doug Jobling, Dir.
E-mail: doug.jobling@jwu.edu

64651 ■ NYNEX Telecommunications Center
Bryant College Koffler
1150 Douglas Pke.
Smithfield, RI 02917-1284
Ph:(401)232-0220
Fax: (401)232-0242
Contact: Kate Dolan, Managing Dir.

64652 ■ Pawtucket Business Resource Center–Pawtucket and Central Falls SBDC
268 Main St.
Pawtucket, RI 02860
Ph:(401)263-5127
Fax: (401)598-2722
URL: http://www.risbdc.org
Contact: Adriana Dawson, Dir.
E-mail: adriana.dawson@jwu.edu

64653 ■ South County SBDC
QP/D Industrial Park
35 Belver Ave., Rm. 212
North Kingstown, RI 02852-7556
Ph:(401)294-1227
Fax: (401)294-6897
Contact: Diane Fournaris, Case Mgr.

64654 ■ Verizon Bryant Center–Bryant University–Small Business Development Center (1150)
1150 Douglas Pike
Smithfield, RI
Ph:(401)232-0220
Co. E-mail: info@verizonbryant.org
URL: http://www.verizonbryant.org

SMALL BUSINESS ASSISTANCE PROGRAMS

64655 ■ Brown Forum for Enterprise
Brown Fourm For Enterprise
PO Box 1949
Providence, RI 02912

Ph:(401)863-3528
Fax: (401)863-1836
Co. E-mail: charles_kingdon@brown.edu
URL: http://www.brownenterpriseforum.org
Contact: Charles Kingdom, Dir
Description: Brings together entrepreneurs, venture capitalists, executives, and others to discuss the problems of starting and expanding a business. Sponsors start-up workshops.

64656 ■ Rhode Island Department of Environmental Management–Division of Agriculture–Division of Agriculture and Resource Marketing (235 P)
235 Promenade St., Rm. 370
Providence, RI 02908
Ph:(401)222-6800
Fax: (401)222-6047
URL: http://www.state.ri.us/dem
Contact: Kenneth Ayers, Chief
Description: Provides information on markets for agriculture, seafood, and aquaculture products.

64657 ■ Rhode Island Economic Development Corporation
1 W Exchange St.
Providence, RI 02903
Ph:(401)222-2601
Fax: (401)222-2102
Co. E-mail: info@riedc.com
URL: http://www.riedc.com
Contact: Michael McMahon, Dir & CEO
Description: Provides site and building information to businesses expanding or relocating within the state. Also provides employee relocation assistance for out-of-state companies moving to Rhode Island.

64658 ■ Rhode Island Economic Development Corporation–Business Services
1 W Exchange St.
Providence, RI 02903
Ph:(401)222-2601
Fax: (401)222-2102
Co. E-mail: info@riedc.com
URL: http://www.riedc.com
Contact: Michael McMahon, Dir & CEO
Description: Provides assistance in finance packaging and information on finance programs, such as the Revolving Loan Fund, insured mortgage financing, and bond programs. The Procurement Program provides federal procurement information. The Office of Minority Business Affairs assists in business planning and loan packaging, and certifies minority-owned, women-owned, and disadvantaged businesses for participation in state procurement and set-aside programs. The Business Retention Program offers advice to owners who are having problems with state agencies.

SCORE OFFICES

64659 ■ SCORE JGE Knight
380 Westminster St.
Providence, RI 02903
Ph:(401)528-4571
Fax: (401)528-4539
Co. E-mail: scoreri@cox.net
URL: http://www.riscore.org
Contact: Frederick Mathews, Chm.
Description: Provides professional guidance and information to maximize the success of existing and emerging small businesses. Offers business counseling and workshops.

BETTER BUSINESS BUREAUS

64660 ■ Better Business Bureau of Rhode Island
120 Lavan St.
Warwick, RI 02888-1025
Ph:(401)785-1212
Fax: (401)785-3061

Co. E-mail: ammarino@rhodeisland.bbb.org
URL: http://www.rhodeisland.bbb.org
Contact: A. Michael Marino, Pres.

CHAMBERS OF COMMERCE

64661 ■ Central Rhode Island Chamber of Commerce
3288 Post Rd.
Warwick, RI 02886
Ph:(401)732-1100
Fax: (401)732-1107
Co. E-mail: info@centralrichamber.com
URL: http://www.centralrichamber.com
Contact: Lauren Slocum, Pres./CEO

64662 ■ Charlestown Chamber of Commerce
4945 Old Post Rd.
PO Box 633
Charlestown, RI 02813
Ph:(401)364-3878
Fax: (401)364-8794
Co. E-mail: charlestowncoc@earthlink.net
URL: http://www.charlestownrichamber.com
Contact: Paula Anderson, Exec.Dir.

64663 ■ East Bay Chamber of Commerce
16 Cutler St.
Warren, RI 02885
Ph:(401)245-0750
Free: 888-278-9948
Fax: (401)245-0110
Co. E-mail: info@eastbaychamberri.org
URL: http://www.eastbaychamberri.org
Contact: Betty J. Pleacher, Pres.

64664 ■ East Greenwich Chamber of Commerce
591 Main St.
East Greenwich, RI 02818
Ph:(401)885-0020
Fax: (401)885-0048
Co. E-mail: jerry@eastgreenwichchamber.com
URL: http://www.eastgreenwichchamber.com
Contact: Jerry Meyer, Exec.Dir.

64665 ■ East Providence Area Chamber of Commerce
850 Waterman Ave.
East Providence, RI 02914
Ph:(401)438-1212
Fax: (401)435-4581
Co. E-mail: office@eastprovchamber.com
URL: http://www.eastprovchamber.com
Contact: Ms. Laura A. McNamara, Exec.Dir.

64666 ■ Greater Cranston Chamber of Commerce
48A Rolfe Sq.
Cranston, RI 02910
Ph:(401)785-3780
Fax: (401)785-3782
Co. E-mail: susan@cranstonchamber.com
URL: http://www.cranstonchamber.com
Contact: Susan Pagnozzi, Pres.

64667 ■ Greater Providence Chamber of Commerce
30 Exchange Terr.
Providence, RI 02903
Ph:(401)521-5000
Fax: (401)751-2434
Co. E-mail: chamber@provchamber.com
URL: http://www.providencechamber.com
Contact: Laurie White, Pres.

64668 ■ Greater Westerly-Pawcatuck Area Chamber of Commerce
1 Chamber Way
Westerly, RI 02891
Ph:(401)596-7761
Free: 800-732-7636
Fax: (401)596-2190
Co. E-mail: info@westerlychamber.org
URL: http://www.westerlychamber.org

Contact: Lisa Konicki, Exec.Dir.

64669 ■ Narragansett Chamber of Commerce
PO Box 742
Narragansett, RI 02882
Ph:(401)783-7121
Fax: (401)789-0220
Co. E-mail: coc@narragansettri.com
URL: http://www.narragansettri.com/chamber
Contact: Jim Hurton, Exec. Dir.

64670 ■ Newport County Chamber of Commerce
45 Valley Rd.
Middletown, RI 02842-6377
Ph:(401)847-1600
Fax: (401)849-5848
Co. E-mail: info@newportchamber.com
URL: http://www.newportchamber.com
Contact: Keith W. Stokes, Exec.Dir.

64671 ■ North Central Chamber of Commerce
1126 Hartford Ave., Ste. 201A
Johnston, RI 02919
Ph:(401)273-1310
Fax: (401)273-2570
Co. E-mail: ncentchamb@aol.com
Contact: Kenneth G. Boehm, Exec.Dir.

64672 ■ North Kingstown Chamber of Commerce
8045 Post Rd.
North Kingstown, RI 02852
Ph:(401)295-5566
Fax: (401)295-5582
Co. E-mail: info@northkingstown.com
URL: http://www.northkingstown.com
Contact: Karla P. Driscoll, Exec.Dir.

64673 ■ Northern Rhode Island Chamber of Commerce
6 Blackstone Valley Pl., Ste. 301
Lincoln, RI 02865
Ph:(401)334-1000
Fax: (401)334-1009
Co. E-mail: general@nrichamber.com
URL: http://www.nrichamber.com
Contact: John C. Gregory, Pres./CEO

64674 ■ Pawtuxet Valley Chamber of Commerce
1192 Main St.
West Warwick, RI 02893
Ph:(401)823-3349
Fax: (401)823-8162
Contact: Diane Boschetti, Exec. Dir.

64675 ■ South Kingstown Chamber of Commerce
PO Box 289
Wakefield, RI 02880
Ph:(401)783-2801
Fax: (401)789-3120
URL: http://www.skchamber.com
Contact: Darlene Towne Evans, Pres./CEO

FINANCING AND LOAN PROGRAMS

64676 ■ Manchester Humphreys, Inc.
40 Westminster St., Ste. 900
Providence, RI 02903
Ph:(401)454-0400
Fax: (401)454-0403
URL: http://www.manchesterhumphreys.com
Contact: Robert Manchester, President
Preferred Investment Size: $500,000 minimum. **Investment Types:** Leveraged and management buyouts. **Industry Preferences:** Computer hardware and software, Internet specific, semiconductors and other electronics, medical and health, consumer related, industrial and energy, business service, and manufacturing. **Geographic Preferences:** Mid Atlantic, Midwest, Northeast, Southeast, and Southwest.

64677 ■ Navis Partners
50 Kennedy Plz., 12th Fl.
Providence, RI 02903
Ph:(401)278-6770
Fax: (401)278-6387
URL: http://www.navispartners.com
Contact: Riordon Smith, General Partner
Preferred Investment Size: $20,000,000 to 120,000,000. **Investment Types:** Acquisition, early, second and later stage, leveraged and management buyouts, recapitalizations, and expansion. **Industry Preferences:** Communications and media, Internet specific, medical and health, semiconductors and other electronics, consumer related, industrial and energy, computer software, hardware and services. **Geographic Preferences:** U.S. and Canada.

64678 ■ Providence Equity Partners, Inc. /Providence Ventures
50 Kennedy Plz., 18th Fl.
Providence, RI 02903
Ph:(401)751-1700
Fax: (401)751-1790
URL: http://www.provequity.com
Contact: Glenn Creamer, Senior Managing Director
Preferred Investment Size: $10,000,000 to $600,000,000. **Investment Types:** Start-up, seed first, second, early and later stage, expansion, leveraged buyout, acquisition, distressed debt, industry rollups, management buyouts, public companies, recapitalizations, special situation, and turnaround. **Industry Preferences:** Communications and media, Internet specific, semiconductors and other electronics, other products, computer hardware, computer software and services, and consumer related. **Geographic Preferences:** U.S. and Canada.

64679 ■ Rex Capital
5784 Post Rd., Ste. 5
East Greenwich, RI 02818
Ph:(401)398-0260
Fax: (401)885-4686
URL: http://www.rexcapital.com
Contact: David Mixer, Partner
Preferred Investment Size: $500,000 to $5,000,000. **Investment Policies:** Sees, early and first stage. **Geographic Preferences:** Northeast.

PROCUREMENT ASSISTANCE PROGRAMS

64680 ■ Rhode Island Procurement Technical Assistance Center–Rhode Island Economic Development Corporation
1 W Exchange St.
Providence, RI 2903
Ph:(401)222-2601
Fax: (401)222-2102
Co. E-mail: info@riedc.com
URL: http://www.federaldollars.com
Contact: Dorothy Reynolds, Prgm Mgr
E-mail: dilly@riedc.com

INCUBATORS/RESEARCH AND TECHNOLOGY PARKS

64681 ■ Brown University–Office of Sponsored Projects
164 Angell St., Box 1929
Providence, RI 02912
Ph:(401)863-2777
Fax: (401)863-7292
Co. E-mail: resadmin@brown.edu
URL: http://www.brown.edu/Administration/
    Research_Administration/
Contact: Norman Hebert, Dir.
E-mail: resadmin@brown.edu
Scope: Administers and coordinates externally sponsored projects at the University, processes proposals, receives awards, and performs accounting function and fiscal control.

EDUCATIONAL PROGRAMS

64682 ■ Johnson and Wales University
8 Abbott Park Pl.
Providence, RI 02903
Ph:(401)598-1000

Free: 800-343-2565
Fax: (401)598-4641
Co. E-mail: admissions@jwu.edu
URL: http://www.jwu.edu
Description: Business college offering classes in small business management.

PUBLICATIONS

64683 ■ *Providence Business News*
300 Richmond St., Ste. 202
Providence, RI 02903
Ph:(401)273-2201
Fax: (401)274-0670
URL: http://www.pbn.com

64684 ■ *Providence Journal Bulletin*
75 Fountain St.
Providence, RI 02902
Ph:(401)277-7000
Fax: (401)277-7346
Co. E-mail: projo@projo.com
URL: http://www.projo.com

PUBLISHERS

64685 ■ Smokin' Donut Books
381 Seaside Dr.
PO Box 37
Jamestown, RI 02835
Ph:(401)423-2400
Free: 877-474-8738
Fax: (401)423-2700
Co. E-mail: info@smokindonut.com
URL: http://www.smokindonut.com
Contact: Kristin Zhivago, Publisher
E-mail: kz@smokindonut.com
Description: Publishes business and how-to books. **Founded:** 2004.

SMALL BUSINESS DEVELOPMENT CENTER LEAD OFFICE

64686 ■ Small Business Development Center–University of South Carolina
College of Business Administration
Hipp Bldg.
1710 College St.
Columbia, SC 29208
Ph:(803)777-4907
Fax: (803)777-4403
URL: http://sbdcweb.badm.sc.edu
Contact: John Lenti, State Director
E-mail: lenti@darla.badm.sc.edu

64687 ■ University of South Carolina–Small Business Development Center
Moore School of Business
1705 College St.
Columbia, SC 29208
Ph:(803)777-4907
Fax: (803)777-4403
Co. E-mail: sbdc@moore.sc.edu
URL: http://scsbdc.moore.sc.edu
Contact: John Lenti, State Dir.
E-mail: lenti@moore.sc.edu

64688 ■ Women's Network for Entrepreneurial Training (WNET)–University of South Carolina–Small Business Development Center (State)
State Director's Office
Moore School of Business
Columbia, SC 29208
Ph:(803)777-4907
Co. E-mail: sbdc@moore.sc.edu
URL: http://scsbdc.moore.sc.edu

SMALL BUSINESS DEVELOPMENT CENTERS

64689 ■ Charleston SBDC
5900 Core Dr., Ste. 104
North Charleston, SC 29406
Ph:(843)740-6160
Fax: (843)740-1607
Co. E-mail: sbdc@moore.sc.edu
URL: http://scsbdc.moore.sc.edu
Contact: Leonard Rubinstein, Area Mgr.
E-mail: lenr@infoave.net

64690 ■ Clemson University–Small Business Development Center
College of Business and Public Affairs
425 Sirrine Hall
Clemson, SC 29634-1392
Ph:(864)656-3227
Fax: (864)656-4869
Co. E-mail: sbdc@moore.sc.edu
URL: http://scsbdc.moore.sc.edu

Contact: Jill Burroughs, Regional Dir.
E-mail: jillb@clemson.edu

64691 ■ Coastal Carolina University–Conway Small Business Development Center
School of Business Administration
Wall Bldg., Ste. 111
PO Box 261954
Conway, SC 29528-6054
Ph:(843)349-2170
Fax: (843)349-2455
Co. E-mail: Robinson@coastal.edu
Contact: Nancy Niles, Area Mgr.

64692 ■ Florence-Darlington Technical College–Small Business Development Center
PO Box 100548
Florence, SC 29501-0548
Ph:(843)661-8256
Fax: (843)661-8041
Co. E-mail: sbdc@moore.sc.edu
URL: http://scsbdc.moore.sc.edu
Contact: Tim Lowder, Area Mgr.
E-mail: lowdert@flo.tec.sc.us

64693 ■ Greenville Area SBDC
Merovan Center
1200 Woodruff Rd., Ste. C-38
Greenville, SC 29607
Ph:(864)297-1016
Co. E-mail: sbdc@moore.sc.edu
URL: http://scsbdc.moore.sc.edu

64694 ■ Greenwood Area SBDC
Upper Savannah Area Office
600 Monument St., Ste. 106
PO Box 246
Greenwood, SC 29648
Ph:(864)943-8028
Co. E-mail: sbdc@moore.sc.edu
URL: http://scsbdc.moore.sc.edu

64695 ■ Myrtle Beach Area–Small Business Development Center
Myrtle Square Mall, No. 11
2501 North Kings Hwy.
Myrtle Beach, SC 29577
Ph:(843)913-7883
Co. E-mail: sbdc@moore.sc.edu
URL: http://scsbdc.moore.sc.edu

64696 ■ National Export Assistance Center–University of South Carolina–Small Business Development Center (Moore)
Moore School of Business
Columbia, SC 29208
Ph:800-243-7232
Co. E-mail: exporthot@darla.badm.sc.edu
URL: http://scsbdc.moore.sc.edu

64697 ■ South Carolina Export Consortium–University of South Carolina–Small Business Development Center (Moore)
Moore School of Business
Columbia, SC 29208

Ph:(803)777-5118
Co. E-mail: sbdc@moore.sc.edu
URL: http://scsbdc.moore.sc.edu

64698 ■ South Carolina Procurement Technical Assistance Program–Small Business Development Center
Moore School of Business
Columbia, SC 29208
Ph:(803)777-4907
Co. E-mail: sbdc@moore.sc.edu
URL: http://scsbdc.moore.sc.edu

64699 ■ South Carolina State University–Small Business Development Center
School of Business
Algernon S. Belcher Hall
300 College Ave.
Campus Box 7176
Orangeburg, SC 29117
Ph:(803)536-8445
Fax: (803)536-8066
Co. E-mail: sbdc@moore.sc.edu
URL: http://scsbdc.moore.sc.edu
Contact: John Gadson, Regional Dir.
E-mail: jgadson@scsu.edu

64700 ■ Spartanburg Area SBDC–Spartanburg Human Resources Center
142 S. Dean St., Ste. 216
Spartanburg, SC 29302
Ph:(864)316-9162
Fax: (864)596-3602
Co. E-mail: sbdc@moore.sc.edu
URL: http://scsbdc.moore.sc.edu

64701 ■ Spartanburg Chamber of Commerce–Small Business Development Center
105 Pine St.
PO Box 1636
Spartanburg, SC 29304
Ph:(864)594-5000
Fax: (864)594-5055
Co. E-mail: info@spartanburg.com
URL: http://spartanburgsc.org
Contact: John Keagle, Area Mgr.

64702 ■ Spartanburg Small Business Development Center
University Center
216 S. Pleasantburg Dr., Rm. 140
Greenville, SC 29607
Ph:(864)316-0170
Fax: (864)250-8897
Contact: David Tinsley, Area Mgr.
E-mail: Dtinsle@clemson.edu

64703 ■ University of South Carolina at Aiken–Small Business Development Center
471 University Pkwy.
Box 9
Aiken, SC 29801
Ph:(803)641-3646

Fax: (803)641-3647
Co. E-mail: sbdc@moore.sc.edu
URL: http://scsbdc.moore.sc.edu
Contact: Reka Mosteller, Area Mgr.
E-mail: rekam@aiken.sc.edu

64704 ■ University of South Carolina at Beaufort–Small Business Development Center
801 Carteret St.
Beaufort, SC 29902
Ph:(843)521-4143
Fax: (843)521-4142
Co. E-mail: sbdc@moore.sc.edu
URL: http://scsbdc.moore.sc.edu
Contact: Martin Goodman, Area Mgr.
E-mail: goodman@gwm.sc.edu

64705 ■ University of South Carolina at Hilton Head–Small Business Development Center
1 College Center Dr.
Hilton Head Island, SC 29928
Ph:(843)842-3552
Co. E-mail: sbdc@moore.sc.edu
URL: http://scsbdc.moore.sc.edu
Contact: Pat Cameron, Consultant

64706 ■ University of South Carolina at Sumter–Small Business Development Center
200 Miller Rd.
Sumter, SC 29150-2498
Ph:(803)938-3833
Co. E-mail: sbdc@moore.sc.edu
URL: http://scsbdc.moore.sc.edu

64707 ■ Upper Savannah Council of Government–Small Business Development Center
SBDC Exchange Bldg.
222 Phoenix St.
PO Box 1366
Greenwood, SC 29648
Ph:(864)941-8071
Fax: (864)941-8090
Contact: Ben Smith, Area Mgr.
E-mail: bensmith@emeraldis.com

64708 ■ Winthrop University–Small Business Development Center
School of Business Administration
118 Thurmond Bldg.
Rock Hill, SC 29733
Ph:(803)323-2283
Fax: (864)323-4281
Co. E-mail: sbdc@moore.sc.edu
URL: http://scsbdc.moore.sc.edu
Contact: Nate Barber, Regional Dir.
E-mail: barbern@winthrop.edu

SMALL BUSINESS ASSISTANCE PROGRAMS

64709 ■ South Carolina Department of Commerce
1201 Main St., Ste. 1600
Columbia, SC 29201
Ph:(803)737-0400
Free: 800-868-7232
Fax: (803)737-0418
URL: http://www.sccommerce.com
Description: Offers a range of innovative services to assist entrepreneurs and expanding industries. Services include: Buyer/Supplier Match; Financing Assistance; International Trade Opportunities; Research Park System; Location, Training, and Labor Assistance; Market Research; and Entrepreneurial Support Services.

64710 ■ South Carolina Jobs-Economic Development Authority
1441 Main St., Ste. 905
PO Box 8327
Columbia, SC 29201
Ph:(803)461-3800

Fax: (803)461-3830
Co. E-mail: generalinfo@scjeda.net
URL: http://www.scjeda.net
Description: Raises capital and provides technical assistance to small businesses in creating jobs; sells general and industrial revenue bonds.

64711 ■ South Carolina Office of Small and Minority Business Assistance
Edgar A. Brown Bldg.
1205 Pendleton St., Rm. 440-A
Columbia, SC 29201
Ph:(803)734-0657
Fax: (803)734-2498
Co. E-mail: mward@govoepp.state.sc.us
URL: http://www.govoepp.state.sc.us/osmba
Description: Provides advocacy and referral services, training and other educational activities for small and minority businesses.

SCORE OFFICES

64712 ■ SCORE Coastal
2750 Speissegger Dr., Ste. 100
North Charleston, SC 29405-8229
Ph:(843)727-4778
Fax: (843)723-4853
Co. E-mail: info@score285.org
URL: http://www.score285.org
Contact: Ross Ahntholz, Chm.
Description: Provides professional guidance and information to maximize the success of existing and emerging small businesses. Offers business counseling and workshops.

64713 ■ SCORE Grand Strand
c/o Robert Goroski, Chm.
605 10th Ave. N
Myrtle Beach, SC 29578
Ph:(843)918-1079
Fax: (843)918-1080
Co. E-mail: info@mbscore.org
URL: http://www.mbscore.org
Contact: Robert Goroski, Chm.
Description: Provides business counseling to small business, both existing businesses and startups.

64714 ■ SCORE Midlands
Strom Thurmond Bldg.
1835 Assembly St., Rm. 1425
Columbia, SC 29201
Ph:(803)765-5131
Fax: (803)765-5962
Co. E-mail: info@scoremidlands.org
URL: http://www.scoremidlands.org
Contact: Aubrey Powell, Chair
Description: Provides professional guidance and information to maximize the success of existing and emerging small businesses. Offers business counseling and workshops.

64715 ■ SCORE Piedmont
Federal Bldg., Rm. B-02
300 E Washington St.
Greenville, SC 29601
Ph:(864)271-3638
Fax: (864)271-3638
Co. E-mail: info@piedmontscore.org
URL: http://www.piedmontscore.org
Contact: Uwe H. Diestel, Chm.
Description: Provides professional guidance and information to maximize the success of existing and emerging small businesses. Offers business counseling and workshops.

BETTER BUSINESS BUREAUS

64716 ■ Better Business Bureau of Central South Carolina and Charleston
PO Box 8326
Columbia, SC 29202

Ph:(803)254-2525
Fax: (803)779-3117
Co. E-mail: info@columbia.bbb.org
URL: http://www.columbia.bbb.org
Contact: Mr. Eric Davis, Pres./CEO

64717 ■ Better Business Bureau of Coastal Carolina
PO Box 379
Conway, SC 29528
Ph:(843)488-2227
Fax: (843)488-0998
Co. E-mail: bbbinfo@sc.rr.com
URL: http://www.carolina.bbb.org
Contact: John W. Trudeau, Pres./CEO

64718 ■ Better Business Bureau Serving Upstate South Carolina
408 N Church St., Ste. C
Greenville, SC 29601
Ph:(864)242-5052
Fax: (864)271-9802
Co. E-mail: info@greenville.bbb.org
URL: http://www.greenville.bbb.org
Contact: Kathy W. Barrett, Pres.

CHAMBERS OF COMMERCE

64719 ■ Abbeville Chamber of Commerce
107 Court Sq.
Abbeville, SC 29620-2418
Ph:(864)366-4600
Fax: (864)366-4068
Co. E-mail: abvchamber@wctel.net
URL: http://www.abbevillescchamber.com
Contact: Victoria Burtt, Exec. Dir.

64720 ■ Anderson Area Chamber of Commerce
907 N Main St., Ste. 200
Anderson, SC 29621
Ph:(864)226-3454
Fax: (864)226-3300
Co. E-mail: info@andersonscchamber.com
URL: http://www.andersonscchamber.com
Contact: Mr. Lee R. Luff CAE, Pres.

64721 ■ Aynor Chamber of Commerce
PO Box 10
Aynor, SC 29511
Ph:(843)358-4808
Contact: Bill Altman, Pres.

64722 ■ Barnwell County Chamber of Commerce
PO Box 898
Barnwell, SC 29812-0898
Ph:(803)259-7446
Fax: (803)259-0030
Co. E-mail: chamber@barnwellsc.com
Contact: Cathie C. Lynn, Exec.Dir.

64723 ■ Batesburg-Leesville Chamber of Commerce
112 E Columbia Ave.
PO Box 2178
Batesburg-Leesville, SC 29070
Ph:(803)532-4339
Fax: (803)532-3978
Co. E-mail: blchamber@bellsouth.net
Contact: Gloria A. Brockman, Exec.Sec.

64724 ■ Beaufort Regional Chamber of Commerce
1106 Carteret St.
PO Box 910
Beaufort, SC 29901-0910
Ph:(843)986-5400
Fax: (843)986-5405
Co. E-mail: president@beaufortsc.org
URL: http://www.beaufortsc.org
Contact: Ms. Carlotta Ungaro, Pres./CEO

64725 ■ Berkeley Chamber of Commerce
PO Box 968
Moncks Corner, SC 29461-0968

Ph:(843)577-9549
Free: 800-882-0337
Fax: (843)899-6491
Co. E-mail: lpeck@bcoc.com
URL: http://www.bcoc.com
Contact: Elaine M. Morgan, CEO

64726 ■ Calhoun County Chamber of Commerce
Courthouse Annex, Ste. 114
St. Matthews, SC 29135
Ph:(803)655-5650
Fax: (803)655-6110
Co. E-mail: calhounchamber@sc.rr.com
URL: http://www.calhouncountychamber.org
Contact: Jane Dyches, Exec. Dir.

64727 ■ Carolinas Association of Chamber of Commerce Executives
930 Richland St.
PO Box 1360
Columbia, SC 29202
Ph:(803)733-1153
Fax: (803)748-0354
Co. E-mail: rstokes@columbiachamber.com
URL: http://www.cacce.org
Contact: Bill E. Russell Jr., Pres.

64728 ■ Charleston Metro Chamber of Commerce
2750 Speissegger Dr., Suite 100
PO Box 975
Charleston, SC 29402-0975
Ph:(843)577-2510
Fax: (843)723-4853
Co. E-mail: mail@charlestonchamber.org
URL: http://www.charlestonchamber.net
Contact: Charles H. Van Rysselberge, Pres./CEO

64729 ■ Cherokee County Chamber of Commerce
225 S Limestone St.
Gaffney, SC 29340
Ph:(864)489-5721
Fax: (864)487-3399
Co. E-mail: info@cherokeechamber.org
URL: http://www.cherokeechamber.org
Contact: James R. Cook III, Exec. Dir.

64730 ■ Chester County Chamber of Commerce
109 Gadsden St.
PO Box 489
Chester, SC 29706-0489
Ph:(803)581-4142
Fax: (803)581-2431
Co. E-mail: ccchamber@infoave.net
URL: http://www.chesterchamber.com
Contact: Sharon B. Blackburn, Pres.

64731 ■ Clarendon County Chamber of Commerce
19 N Brooks St.
Manning, SC 29102
Ph:(803)435-4405
Free: 800-731-LAKE
Fax: (803)435-4406
Co. E-mail: chamber@clarendoncounty.com
URL: http://www.clarendoncounty.com
Contact: Jane Powell, Exec.Dir.

64732 ■ Clemson Area Chamber of Commerce
PO Box 1622
Clemson, SC 29633-1622
Ph:(864)654-1200
Free: 800-542-0746
Fax: (864)654-5096
Co. E-mail: info@clemsonchamber.org
URL: http://www.clemsonchamber.org
Contact: Eddie W. Nail Jr., Pres.

64733 ■ Conway Area Chamber of Commerce
PO Box 831
Conway, SC 29528
Ph:(843)248-2273

Fax: (843)248-0003
Co. E-mail: info@conwayscchamber.com
URL: http://www.conwayscchamber.com
Contact: Kelli S. James, VP of Administration

64734 ■ Fairfield County Chamber of Commerce
Offices in the Town Clock
PO Box 297
Winnsboro, SC 29180
Ph:(803)635-4242
Co. E-mail: fchamber@chestertel.com
URL: http://www.fairfieldchamber.org
Contact: Sean Schaeffner, Chm.

64735 ■ Fountain Inn Chamber of Commerce
400 N Main St.
Fountain Inn, SC 29644
Ph:(864)862-2586
Fax: (864)862-1086
Co. E-mail: fichamber@aol.com
Contact: Maria Bentley, Dir.

64736 ■ Georgetown County Chamber of Commerce
PO Box 1776
Georgetown, SC 29442
Ph:(843)546-8436
Free: 800-777-7705
Fax: (843)520-4876
Co. E-mail: info@georgetownchamber.com
URL: http://www.georgetownchamber.com
Contact: Annette Fisher, Pres.

64737 ■ Greater Aiken Chamber of Commerce
121 Richland Ave. E
PO Box 892
Aiken, SC 29802
Ph:(803)641-1111
Fax: (803)641-4174
Co. E-mail: chamber@aikenchamber.net
URL: http://www.aikenchamber.net
Contact: Mr. J. David Jameson, Pres./CEO

64738 ■ Greater Area Walhalla Chamber of Commerce
214 E Main St.
Walhalla, SC 29691
Ph:(864)638-2727
Fax: (864)638-6451
Co. E-mail: wchamber@nuvox.net
URL: http://walhallasc.com
Contact: Barbara Justus, Exec.Sec.

64739 ■ Greater Cheraw Chamber of Commerce
221 Market St.
Cheraw, SC 29520
Ph:(843)537-7681
Fax: (843)537-5886
Co. E-mail: cherawchamber@bellsouth.net
URL: http://www.cheraw.com
Contact: Mrs. Patsy J. Hendley, Pres.

64740 ■ Greater Chesterfield Chamber of Commerce
Olde Towne Ctre.
100 E Main St.
Chesterfield, SC 29709
Ph:(843)623-2343
Fax: (843)623-2132
Co. E-mail: info@chesterfieldscchamber.com
URL: http://www.chesterfieldscchamber.com
Contact: Donna Curtis, Exec. Dir.

64741 ■ Greater Clover Chamber of Commerce
118 Bethel St.
PO Box 162
Clover, SC 29710
Ph:(803)222-3312
Fax: (803)222-8396
Co. E-mail: sccloverchamber@aol.com
URL: http://www.cloverchamber.com/
Contact: Barbara A. Desser, Exec.Dir.

64742 ■ Greater Columbia Chamber of Commerce
930 Richland St.
Columbia, SC 29201
Ph:(803)733-1110
Fax: (803)733-1149
Co. E-mail: info@columbiachamber.com
URL: http://www.columbiachamber.com
Contact: Donald G. McLeese, Pres./CEO

64743 ■ Greater Darlington Chamber of Commerce
38 Public Sq.
Darlington, SC 29532
Ph:(843)393-2213
Fax: (843)393-8059
Co. E-mail: darlcoc@bellsouth.net
Contact: Tori Kea, Exec.Dir.

64744 ■ Greater Easley Chamber of Commerce
PO Box 241
Easley, SC 29641-0241
Ph:(864)859-2693
Fax: (864)859-1941
Co. E-mail: kent@easleychamber.org
URL: http://www.easleychamber.org
Contact: Kent Dykes, Exec.Dir.

64745 ■ Greater Florence Chamber of Commerce
610 W Palmetto St.
Florence, SC 29503
Ph:(843)665-0515
Fax: (843)662-2010
Co. E-mail: tmarschel@flochamber.com
URL: http://www.flochamber.com
Contact: Mr. Tom Marschel, Pres.

64746 ■ Greater Greenville Chamber of Commerce
24 Cleveland St.
Greenville, SC 29601
Ph:(864)242-1050
Fax: (864)282-8509
Co. E-mail: bhaskew@greenvillechamber.org
URL: http://www.greenvillechamber.org
Contact: Ben Haskew, Pres./CEO

64747 ■ Greater Greer Chamber of Commerce
111 Trade St.
PO Box 507
Greer, SC 29652
Ph:(864)877-3131
Fax: (864)877-0961
Co. E-mail: info@greerchamber.com
URL: http://www.greerchamber.com
Contact: Patty Cornelius, Office Mgr.

64748 ■ Greater Hardeeville Chamber of Commerce
12A Ulmer St.
PO Box 307
Hardeeville, SC 29927
Ph:(843)784-3606
Fax: (843)784-2781
Co. E-mail: bill@billtamiso.com
Contact: Ms. June Smith, Exec.Dir.

64749 ■ Greater Hartsville Chamber of Commerce
PO Box 578
Hartsville, SC 29551
Ph:(843)332-6401
Free: 888-427-8720
Fax: (843)332-8017
Co. E-mail: president@hartsvillechamber.org
URL: http://www.hartsvillechamber.org
Contact: Sharman Poplava, Pres.

64750 ■ Greater Lake City Chamber of Commerce
144 S Acline St.
PO Box 669
Lake City, SC 29560
Ph:(843)374-8611

Fax: (843)374-7938
Co. E-mail: lccoc1@ftc-i.net
URL: http://www.lakecitysc.org

64751 ■ Greater Mullins Chamber of Commerce
1 N Main St.
PO Box 595
Mullins, SC 29574-0595
Ph:(843)464-6651
Fax: (843)464-6651
Co. E-mail: mcofc@bellsouth.net
Contact: Patricia C. Garrett, Exec.Dir.

64752 ■ Greater Pickens Chamber of Commerce
222 W Main St.
PO Box 153
Pickens, SC 29671
Ph:(864)878-3258
Fax: (864)878-5725
Co. E-mail: info@pickenschamber.org
URL: http://www.pickenschamber.org
Contact: Renee R. Watson, Exec.Dir.

64753 ■ Greater Seneca Chamber of Commerce
PO Box 855
Seneca, SC 29679
Ph:(864)882-2097
Fax: (864)882-2881
Co. E-mail: chamber@carol.net
URL: http://www.senecachamber.com
Contact: Christine M. McPhail, Dir. of Administration and Tourism

64754 ■ Greater Summerville/Dorchester County Chamber of Commerce
402 N Main St.
Summerville, SC 29483
Ph:(843)873-2931
Co. E-mail: jbrooks@greatersummerville.org
URL: http://www.gsdcchamber.org
Contact: Quince E. Cody, Pres./CEO

64755 ■ Greater Sumter Chamber of Commerce
32 E Calhoun St.
Sumter, SC 29150
Ph:(803)775-1231
Fax: (803)775-0915
Co. E-mail: grier@sumterchamber.com
URL: http://www.sumterchamber.com
Contact: Grier U. Blackwelder, Pres.

64756 ■ Greater York Chamber of Commerce
23 E Liberty St.
PO Box 97
York, SC 29745
Ph:(803)684-2590
Free: 877-684-2590
Fax: (803)684-2575
Co. E-mail: info@greateryorkchamber.com
URL: http://www.greateryorkchamber.com
Contact: Paul D. Boger Jr.

64757 ■ Greenwood Area Chamber of Commerce
110 Phoenix St.
Greenwood, SC 29646-2727
Ph:(864)223-8431
Fax: (864)229-9785
Co. E-mail: info@greenwoodscchamber.org
URL: http://greenwoodscchamber.org
Contact: Angelle LaBorde, Exec.Dir.

64758 ■ Hampton County Chamber of Commerce
PO Box 122
Hampton, SC 29924
Ph:(803)943-3784
Fax: (803)943-7538
Co. E-mail: dbenton@clarendonmemorial.com
URL: http://hamptoncountychamber.com
Contact: Denise Benton, Pres.

64759 ■ Hilton Head Island Bluffton Chamber of Commerce
PO Box 5647
Hilton Head Island, SC 29938
Ph:(843)785-3673
Free: 800-523-3373
Fax: (843)785-7110
Co. E-mail: info@hiltonheadisland.org
URL: http://www.hiltonheadisland.org
Contact: Bill Miles, Pres./CEO

64760 ■ Jasper County Chamber of Commerce
451B E Wilson St.
PO Box 1267
Ridgeland, SC 29936
Ph:(843)726-8126
Fax: (843)726-6290
Co. E-mail: jaspersccoc@earthlink.net
URL: http://www.jaspersc.org
Contact: Kendall Malphrus, Exec. Dir.

64761 ■ Kershaw County Chamber of Commerce and Visitors' Center
607 S Broad St.
Camden, SC 29020
Ph:(803)432-2525
Free: 800-968-4037
Fax: (803)432-4181
Co. E-mail: camden@camden.net
URL: http://www.camden-sc.org
Contact: Walter B. Clark, Exec. Dir.

64762 ■ Lake Wylie Chamber of Commerce
PO Box 5233
1 Executive Ct.
Lake Wylie, SC 29710
Ph:(803)831-2827
Fax: (803)831-2460
Co. E-mail: info@lakewyliesc.com
URL: http://www.lakewyliesc.com
Contact: Susan Bromfield, Pres.

64763 ■ Lancaster County Chamber of Commerce
604 N Main St.
PO Box 430
Lancaster, SC 29720
Ph:(803)283-4105
Co. E-mail: lanchamber@infoave.net
Contact: Thomas B. White, Pres.

64764 ■ Lee County Chamber of Commerce and Visitors Center
PO Box 548
Bishopville, SC 29010
Ph:(803)484-5145
Fax: (803)484-4270
Co. E-mail: kingcotton@ftc-i.net
URL: http://www.ebishopville.net
Contact: Todd Shifflet, Pres.

64765 ■ Lexington Chamber of Commerce
321 S Lake Dr.
Lexington, SC 29072
Ph:(803)359-6113
Fax: (803)359-0634
Co. E-mail: chamber@lexingtonsc.org
URL: http://www.lexingtonsc.org
Contact: Pandra Lemrow, CEO/Pres.

64766 ■ Little River Chamber of Commerce
1569 Hwy. 17
PO Box 400
Little River, SC 29566
Ph:(843)249-6604
Free: 800-936-2322
Fax: (843)249-9788
Co. E-mail: info@littleriverchamber.org
URL: http://www.littleriverchamber.org
Contact: Ms. Mary Martin, Exec.Dir.

64767 ■ Loris Chamber and Visitors and Convention Bureau
4242 Main St.
PO Box 356
Loris, SC 29569

Ph:(843)756-6030
Free: (866)664-6030
Fax: (843)756-5661
Co. E-mail: loriscoc@sccoast.net
URL: http://www.lorischambersc.com
Contact: Karen Williams

64768 ■ Marion Chamber of Commerce
PO Box 35
Marion, SC 29571-0035
Ph:(843)423-3561
Fax: (843)423-0963
Co. E-mail: marionsc@bellsouth.net
URL: http://www.marionscchamber.com
Contact: Judy J. Johnson, Exec.VP

64769 ■ Mauldin Area Chamber of Commerce
PO Box 881
Mauldin, SC 29662
Ph:(864)297-1323
Fax: (864)297-5645
Co. E-mail: pat.pomeroy@mauldinchamber.org
URL: http://www.mauldinchamber.org
Contact: Pat Pomeroy, Dir.

64770 ■ McCormick County Chamber of Commerce
100 S Main St.
PO Box 938
McCormick, SC 29835
Ph:(864)852-2835
Fax: (864)852-2382
Co. E-mail: mcchamber@wctel.net
URL: http://www.mccormickcountysc.gov
Contact: Martha Hughes, Office Mgr.

64771 ■ Myrtle Beach Area Chamber of Commerce
PO Box 2115
Myrtle Beach, SC 29578
Ph:(843)626-7444
Free: 800-356-3016
Fax: (843)448-3010
Co. E-mail: info@mbchamber.org
URL: http://www.myrtlebeachinfo.com/chamber/default.html
Contact: Brad Dean, Pres./CEO

64772 ■ Newberry County Chamber of Commerce
1109 Main St.
PO Box 396
Newberry, SC 29108
Ph:(803)276-4274
Fax: (803)276-4373
Co. E-mail: chamber@newberrycounty.org
Contact: Cheryl Starnes, Exec.Dir.

64773 ■ Ninety Six Chamber of Commerce
PO Box 8
Ninety Six, SC 29666
Ph:(864)543-2900
Fax: (864)543-3436
Contact: Jennifer Wertz, Sec.

64774 ■ North Augusta Chamber of Commerce
PO Box 6246
North Augusta, SC 29860
Ph:(803)279-2323
Fax: (803)279-0003
Co. E-mail: chamber@northaugusta.net
URL: http://www.northaugusta.net/chamber
Contact: Victoria Hann, Pres.

64775 ■ North Myrtle Beach Chamber of Commerce
270 Hwy. 17 N
North Myrtle Beach, SC 29582
Ph:(843)281-2662
Free: 877-332-2662
Fax: (843)280-2930
Co. E-mail: info@northmyrtlebeachchamber.com
URL: http://www.northmyrtlebeachchamber.com
Contact: Paul C. Williams, Pres.

64776 ■ Orangeburg County Chamber of Commerce
PO Box 328
Orangeburg, SC 29116
Ph:(803)534-6821
Free: 800-545-6153
Fax: (803)531-9435
Co. E-mail: chamber@orangeburgsc.net
URL: http://www.orangeburgchamber.com
Contact: David Coleman, Pres.

64777 ■ Pageland Chamber of Commerce
128 North Pearl St.
PO Box 56
Pageland, SC 29728
Ph:(843)672-6400
Fax: (843)672-6401
Co. E-mail: dkirkley@pagelandchamber.com
Contact: Mr. Darron Kirkley, Admin.Asst.

64778 ■ Partnership for Tomorrow
PO Box 507
Greer, SC 29652
Ph:(864)877-0330
Fax: (864)877-6489
URL: http://www.fcdusa.com/campaigns/
partnr4tomrw.htm
Contact: Mr. Lawrence E. Wilson, Campaign Gen.
  Chm.

64779 ■ Saluda County Chamber of Commerce
111 N Main St.
Saluda, SC 29138
Ph:(864)445-4100
Fax: (864)445-4100
Co. E-mail: chamber@saludasc.com
Contact: Joan Perkins, Dir.

64780 ■ Simpsonville Area Chamber of Commerce
PO Box 605
Simpsonville, SC 29681
Ph:(864)963-3781
Fax: (864)228-0003
Co. E-mail: dhardwick@simpsonvillechamber.com
URL: http://www.simpsonvillechamber.com
Contact: Deborah Hardwick, Exec.Dir.

64781 ■ South Carolina Chamber of Commerce
1201 Main St., Ste. 1700
Columbia, SC 29201
Ph:(803)799-4601
Free: 800-799-4601
Fax: (803)779-6043
Co. E-mail: chamber@sccc.net
URL: http://www.scchamber.net
Contact: S. Hunter Howard Jr., Pres./CEO

64782 ■ Spartanburg Area Chamber of Commerce
105 N Pine St.
PO Box 1636
Spartanburg, SC 29304-1636
Ph:(864)594-5000
Fax: (864)594-5055
Co. E-mail: jpoole@spartanburgchamber.com
URL: http://www.spartanburgchamber.com
Contact: Mr. John Poole, Pres./CEO

64783 ■ Tri-County Regional Chamber of Commerce
5588 Memorial Blvd.
St. George, SC 29477
Ph:(843)563-9091
Free: 800-788-JOIN
Fax: (843)563-9091
Co. E-mail: tcrcc@tri-countyelectric.net
URL: http://www.tri-crcc.com
Contact: Teresa M. Hatchell, Interim Dir.

64784 ■ Union County Chamber of Commerce
135 W Main St.
Union, SC 29379
Ph:(864)427-9039

Free: 877-202-8755
Co. E-mail: torance@unionsc.com
URL: http://www.unionsc.com
Contact: Torance Inman, Exec.Dir.

64785 ■ Walterboro-Colleton Chamber of Commerce
PO Box 426
109 Benson St.
Walterboro, SC 29488-0426
Ph:(843)549-9595
Fax: (843)549-5775
Co. E-mail: info@walterboro.org
URL: http://www.walterboro.org
Contact: David M. Smalls, Pres./CEO

64786 ■ West Metro Chamber of Commerce
1006 12th St.
Cayce, SC 29033
Ph:(803)794-6504
Free: (866)720-5400
Fax: (803)794-6505
Co. E-mail: westmetrochamber@aol.com
URL: http://www.westmetrochamber.com
Contact: Gregg Pinner, Exec. Dir.

64787 ■ Westminster Chamber of Commerce
PO Box 155
Westminster, SC 29693
Ph:(864)647-5316
Co. E-mail: info@westminstersc.com
URL: http://www.westminstersc.com
Contact: Jimmy Powell

64788 ■ Williamsburg HomeTown Chamber of Commerce
130 E Main St.
PO Box 696
Kingstree, SC 29556
Ph:(843)355-6431
Fax: (843)355-3343
Co. E-mail: whtc@ftc-i.net
URL: http://www.williamsburgsc.org
Contact: Stephanie Evans, Exec. Dir.

64789 ■ York County Regional Chamber of Commerce
PO Box 590
Rock Hill, SC 29731
Ph:(803)324-7500
Fax: (803)324-1889
Co. E-mail: info@yorkcountychamber.com
URL: http://www.yorkcountychamber.com
Contact: Rob Youngblood, Pres.

MINORITY BUSINESS ASSISTANCE PROGRAMS

64790 ■ South Carolina Statewide Minority Business Development Center
1515 Richland St.
Columbia, SC 29201
Ph:(803)779-5905
Fax: (803)779-5915
Co. E-mail: busdev@scmbdc.com
URL: http://www.scmbdc.com
Contact: Anthony Washington

FINANCING AND LOAN PROGRAMS

64791 ■ Capital Insights LLC
PO Box 27162
Greenville, SC 29616
Ph:(864)963-6640
Fax: (864)242-6755
URL: http://www.capitalinsights.com
Contact: John Warner, President
Preferred Investment Size: $130,000 to $2,800,000.
Investment Policies: First and second stage. **Industry Preferences:** Communications and media, other products, semiconductors and other electronics, consumer related, and industrial and energy. **Geographic Preferences:** Southeast.

64792 ■ Transamerica Mezzanine Financing
220 N. Main St., Ste. 301
Greenville, SC 29601
Ph:(864)232-6198
Fax: (864)241-4444
Contact: Roger Brook, Vice President
Investment Types: Seed, start-up, first and second stage, and mezzanine. **Industry Preferences:** Communications and media, computer software, semiconductors and other electronics, medical and health, industrial and energy. **Geographic Preferences:** Mid Atlantic, Northeast, Southeast, and Southwest.

PROCUREMENT ASSISTANCE PROGRAMS

64793 ■ South Carolina Procurement Technical Assistance Center–University of South Carolina Procurement Center
Merovan Center
College of Business Administration
1200 Woodruff, Ste. C-38
Greenview, SC 29607
Ph:(864)297-1016
Fax: (864)329-0453
URL: http://www.business.clemson.edu/sbdc
Contact: Virginia Sheppard
E-mail: sheppav@clemson.edu

INCUBATORS/RESEARCH AND TECHNOLOGY PARKS

64794 ■ Clemson University–Office for Sponsored Programs
301A Brackett Hall
Clemson, SC 29634-5702
Ph:(864)656-5266
Fax: (864)656-0881
Co. E-mail: billg@clemson.edu
URL: http://virtual.clemson.edu/groups/SPONPROG/
Contact: William F. Geer Jr., Dir.
E-mail: billg@clemson.edu
Scope: Provides information and assistance concerning all aspects of the University's research effort to faculty members, departments, colleges, and other administrative units. Aids in the preparation and submission of applications for sponsored research, instruction, and public service programs. Provides University liaison between the institution and all public and private, nation and local organizations and/or entities concerned with any aspect of research support, regulation, or administration.

64795 ■ Florence Business and Technology Center
181 E Evans St.
Florence, SC 29506
Ph:(843)664-2800
Fax: (843)664-2803

64796 ■ South Carolina Research Authority–Charleston Research Park
Trident Research Center
5300 International Blvd.
North Charleston, SC 29418
Ph:(843)760-3200
Co. E-mail: info@scra.org
URL: http://www.scra.org
Contact: Dr. Bill Mahoney, Pres./Dir.
E-mail: info@scra.org
Scope: Critical technologies, including information technology, information system security, public safety, flexible computer integrated manufacturing, and the development of international standards for the exchange of engineering drawings.

64797 ■ University of South Carolina at Columbia–Office of Sponsored Programs and Research
Byrnes Bldg., 5th Fl.
901 Sumter St.
Columbia, SC 29208

Ph:(803)777-7093
Fax: (803)777-4136
Co. E-mail: waltone@gwm.su.edu
URL: http://spar.research.sc.edu/
Contact: Ed Walton PhD, Dir.
E-mail: waltone@gwm.su.edu
Scope: Acts as a catalyst and coordinator in all the University's research activities, serves as a information resource for University research capabilities, and provides assistance to scientists from industry and government in using University resources.

EDUCATIONAL PROGRAMS

64798 ■ Florence-Darlington Technical College
PO Box 100548
Florence, SC 29501-0548
Ph:(843)661-8324
Free: 800-228-5745
Fax: (843)661-8041
URL: http://www.fdtc.edu
Description: Two-year college offering a small business management program.

64799 ■ Greenville Technical College–Northwest Campus
PO Box 5616
Greenville, SC 29606
Ph:(864)250-8000
Free: 800-723-0673
Fax: (864)250-8507
URL: http://www.greenvilletech.com
Description: Offers a variety of business-oriented courses, seminars, workshops, and weekend courses for credit or noncredit status. Some courses offer continuing education units. Special emphasis is placed on small business start up, management, and computer and employee training.

64800 ■ Piedmont Technical College–Continuing Education
620 N Emerald Rd.
Greenwood, SC 29648
Ph:(864)941-8324
Fax: (864)941-8555
URL: http://www.ptc.edu
Description: Offer program/classes in small business/small business management.

64801 ■ Spartanburg Technical College–Industry and Business Training
PO Box 4386
Spartanburg, SC 29305-4386

Ph:(864)591-3600
Fax: (864)591-3609
Co. E-mail: compt@spt.tec.sc.us
URL: http://www.stcsc.edu
Description: Acts as an educational and technical resource center for the small businessperson and for those interested in starting their own businesses.

PUBLICATIONS

64802 ■ *Smart Start your South Carolina Business*
PSI Research
300 N. Valley Dr.
Grants Pass, OR 97526
Ph:(503)479-9464
Free: 800-228-2275
Fax: (503)476-1479
Co. E-mail: info@psi-research.com
URL: http://www.psi-research.com
Ed: Michael D. Jenkins. **Released:** Revised edition, 1992. **Price:** $29.95 (looseleaf binder); $24.95 (paper). **Description:** Part of the Successful Business Library series.

SMALL BUSINESS DEVELOPMENT CENTER LEAD OFFICE

64803 ■ University of South Dakota–Small Business Development Center
414 E. Clark St.
Vermillion, SD 57069
Ph:(605)677-5287
Fax: (605)677-5427
Contact: Wade Druin, Acting State Director
E-mail: wdruin@usd.edu

64804 ■ University of South Dakota–Vermillion Lead Office
USD School of Business
Vermillion, SD 57069
Ph:(605)677-6287
Fax: (605)677-5427
URL: http://www.usd.edu/sbdc/regional.cfm
Contact: John S. Hemmingstad, State Dir.
E-mail: jshemmin@usd.edu

SMALL BUSINESS DEVELOPMENT CENTERS

64805 ■ Aberdeen Small Business Development Center (Region III)
416 Production St., N.
Aberdeen, SD 57401
Ph:(605)626-2565
Fax: (605)626-2667
URL: http://www.usd.edu/sbdc/regional.cfm
Contact: Kelly Weaver, Regional Dir.
E-mail: kweaver@midco.net

64806 ■ Mitchell Office (Region V)–Small Business Development Center
601 N. Main
PO Box 1087
Mitchell, SD 57301
Ph:(605)996-1140
Fax: (605)996-8273
URL: http://www.usd.edu/sbdc/regional.cfm
Contact: Teka Gunkel, Business Consultant
E-mail: tekamadc@santel.net

64807 ■ Pierre Small Business Development Center (Region II)
1205 N. Harrison Ave., Ste. 3
Pierre, SD 57501
Ph:(605)773-2783
Fax: (605)773-2784
URL: http://www.usd.edu/sbdc/regional.cfm
Contact: Marcella Hurley, Regional Dir.
E-mail: marcella.hurley@usd.edu

64808 ■ Rapid City Small Business Development Center (Region I)
525 University Loop, Ste. 102
Rapid City, SD 57701

Ph:(605)394-5311
Fax: (605)394-6140
URL: http://www.usd.edu/sbdc/regional.cfm
Contact: Dona Leavens, Regional Dir.
E-mail: dleavens@tie.net

64809 ■ Sioux Falls (Region VI)–SBDC
2329 N. Career Ave.
Sioux Falls, SD 57107
Ph:(605)367-5757
Fax: (605)367-5755
Contact: Mark Slade, Regional Dir.
E-mail: mslade@usd.edu

64810 ■ Watertown Small Business Development Center (Region IV)
124 1st. Ave., NW
PO Box 1207
Watertown, SD 57201
Ph:(605)882-5115
Fax: (605)882-5049
URL: http://www.usd.edu/sbdc/regional.cfm
Contact: Belinda Engelhart, Regional Dir.
E-mail: bengelha@usd.edu

64811 ■ Yankton Small Business Development Center (Region V)
1808 Summit Ave.
PO Box 687
Yankton, SD 57078
Ph:(605)665-0751
Fax: (605)665-0303
URL: http://www.usd.edu/sbdc/regional.cfm
Contact: Sue Stoll, Regional Dir.
E-mail: suesbdc@districtiii.org

SMALL BUSINESS ASSISTANCE PROGRAMS

64812 ■ South Dakota Governor's Office of Economic Development
711 E Wells Ave.
Pierre, SD 57501-3369
Ph:(605)773-3301
Free: 800-872-6190
Fax: (605)773-3256
Co. E-mail: goedinfo@state.sd.us
URL: http://www.sdreadytowork.com
Description: Advocates on behalf of South Dakota's small business community regarding policy determinations and questions concerning other state agencies.

64813 ■ South Dakota Governor's Office of Economic Development–Export, Trade, and Marketing Division
711 E Wells Ave.
Pierre, SD 57501-3369
Ph:(605)773-5032
Free: 800-872-6190
Fax: (605)773-3256
URL: http://www.sdreadytowork.com
Contact: Joop Bollen

Description: Promotes South Dakota's manufactured and processed products to domestic and international markets; fields international direct investment opportunities. Services include the South Dakota Made logotype; foreign buyers list; Trade Show Assistance Program; export services; and computerized trade leads.

CHAMBERS OF COMMERCE

64814 ■ Aberdeen Area Chamber of Commerce
516 S Main St.
Aberdeen, SD 57401
Ph:(605)225-2860
Fax: (605)225-2437
Co. E-mail: info@aberdeen-chamber.com
URL: http://www.aberdeen-chamber.com
Contact: Gail L. Ogdahl, Pres.

64815 ■ Beresford Chamber of Commerce
PO Box 167
Beresford, SD 57004
Ph:(605)763-2021
Fax: (605)763-2021
Co. E-mail: chamber@bmtc.net
Contact: Junelle Hansen, Exec.Dir.

64816 ■ Brookings Area Chamber of Commerce and Convention Bureau
2308 6th St.
PO Box 431
Brookings, SD 57006
Ph:(605)692-6125
Fax: (605)697-8109
Co. E-mail: chamber@brookings.net
URL: http://www.brookingschamber.org
Contact: Richard Olsen, Exec.VP

64817 ■ Canton Chamber of Commerce
PO Box 34
Canton, SD 57013-0034
Ph:(605)764-7864
Free: 800-445-9603
Co. E-mail: lisa.canton@iw.net
URL: http://www.cantonarea.com
Contact: Ms. Lisa Alden, Coor.

64818 ■ Centerville Chamber of Commerce
PO Box 266
Centerville, SD 57014
Ph:(605)563-2291
Fax: (605)563-2615
Co. E-mail: doug.voss@k12.sd.us
Contact: Mr. Doug Voss, Pres.

64819 ■ Chamberlain-Oacoma Area Chamber of Commerce
115 W Lawler
Chamberlain, SD 57325
Ph:(605)734-4416
Fax: (605)734-4416
Co. E-mail: chamber@chamberlainsd.org
URL: http://www.chamberlainsd.org

Contact: Jessica Schoenhard, Exec.Dir.

64820 ■ Custer Arca Chamber of Commerce and Visitors Bureau
615 Washington St.
Custer, SD 57730
Ph:(605)673-2244
Free: 800-992-9818
Fax: (605)673-3726
Co. E-mail: dressler@custersd.com
URL: http://www.custersd.com
Contact: Mr. David Ressler, Exec.Dir.

64821 ■ Deadwood Chamber of Commerce and Visitors' Bureau
767 Main St.
Deadwood, SD 57732
Ph:(605)578-1876
Free: 800-999-1876
Fax: (605)578-2429
Co. E-mail: philysr@deadwood.org
URL: http://www.deadwood.org
Contact: George Milos, Exec. Dir.

64822 ■ Eureka Chamber of Commerce
PO Box 101
Eureka, SD 57437
Ph:(605)284-2639
Contact: Ms. Barb Billotto, Pres.

64823 ■ Faith Chamber of Commerce
PO Box 246
Faith, SD 57626-0246
Ph:(605)967-2001
Co. E-mail: faithcha@gwtc.net
URL: http://www.gwtc.net/~faithcha
Contact: Bill Hibner, Pres.

64824 ■ Greater Madison Area Chamber of Commerce
315 S Egan Ave.
Madison, SD 57042
Ph:(605)256-2454
Fax: (605)256-9606
URL: http://www.chamberofmadisonsd.com
Contact: Sascha Albrecht, Dir.

64825 ■ Gregory Commercial Club
PO Box 191
Gregory, SD 57533
Ph:(605)835-9616
Contact: David Bruns

64826 ■ Hot Springs Area Chamber of Commerce
801 S 6th St.
Hot Springs, SD 57747
Ph:(605)745-4140
Free: 800-325-6991
Fax: (605)745-5849
Co. E-mail: hschamber@gwtc.net
URL: http://www.hotsprings-sd.com

64827 ■ Lead Area Chamber of Commerce
309 W Main St., Ste. A
Lead, SD 57754
Ph:(605)584-1100
Fax: (605)584-2209
Co. E-mail: leadcoc@leadmethere.org
URL: http://www.leadmethere.org
Contact: Melissa Johnson, Exec.Dir.

64828 ■ Lemmon Area Chamber of Commerce
100 3rd St. W
Lemmon, SD 57638
Ph:(605)374-5716
Fax: (605)374-5789
Co. E-mail: lchamber@sdplains.com
URL: http://www.lemmonsd.com
Contact: Ms. Stacy Daley, Coor.

64829 ■ Milbank Area Chamber of Commerce
1001 E 4th Ave., Ste. 101
Milbank, SD 57252
Ph:(605)432-6656
Free: 800-675-6656

Fax: (605)432-9507
Co. E-mail: chamber@milbanksd.com
URL: http://www.milbanksd.com
Contact: Miriah Hicks, Exec. Dir.

64830 ■ Miller Civic and Commerce Association
PO Box 152
Miller, SD 57362
Ph:(605)853-3098
Fax: (605)853-3276
Co. E-mail: onhandtc@turtlecreek.net
Contact: Barb Johnson, Pres.

64831 ■ Mitchell Area Chamber of Commerce
601 N Main St.
PO Box 1026
Mitchell, SD 57301
Ph:(605)996-5567
Fax: (605)996-8273
Co. E-mail: bhiselmadc@santel.net
URL: http://www.mitchellchamber.com
Contact: Bryan Hisel, Exec.Dir.

64832 ■ Mobridge Chamber of Commerce
212 Main St.
Mobridge, SD 57601
Ph:(605)845-2387
Free: 888-614-3474
Fax: (605)845-2500
Co. E-mail: mobridge@mobridge.org
URL: http://www.mobridge.org
Contact: Mike Haas, Exec.Dir.

64833 ■ Pierre Area Chamber of Commerce
800 W Dakota
PO Box 548
Pierre, SD 57501
Ph:(605)224-7361
Free: 800-962-2034
Fax: (605)224-6485
Co. E-mail: contactchamber@pierrechamber.com
URL: http://www.pierrechamber.com
Contact: Ms. Maggie Sobieski, CEO

64834 ■ Rapid City Area Chamber of Commerce
444 Mt. Rushmore Rd. N
PO Box 747
Rapid City, SD 57709-0747
Ph:(605)343-1744
Co. E-mail: info@rapidcitychamber.com
URL: http://www.rapidcitychamber.com
Contact: Jim McKeon IOM, Pres.

64835 ■ Redfield Area Chamber of Commerce
626 Main St.
Redfield, SD 57469
Ph:(605)472-0965
Fax: (605)472-4553
Co. E-mail: redfieldchamber@redfield-sd.com
URL: http://www.redfield-sd.com
Contact: Cathy Fink, Coor.

64836 ■ Sioux Falls Area Chamber of Commerce
200 N Phillips Ave., Ste. 102
PO Box 1425
Sioux Falls, SD 57104
Ph:(605)336-1620
Fax: (605)336-6499
Co. E-mail: sfacc@siouxfalls.com
URL: http://www.siouxfallschamber.com
Contact: Evan C. Nolte, Pres.

64837 ■ Spearfish Area Chamber of Commerce
106 W Kansas
PO Box 550
Spearfish, SD 57783-0550
Ph:(605)642-2626
Free: 800-626-8013
Fax: (605)642-7310
Co. E-mail: spfcoc@spearfish.sd.us
URL: http://www.spearfish.sd.us
Contact: Lisa Langer, Exec.Dir.

64838 ■ Sturgis Area Chamber of Commerce
2040 Junction Ave.
PO Box 504
Sturgis, SD 57785
Ph:(605)347-2556
Fax: (605)347-6682
Co. E-mail: info@sturgis-sd.org
URL: http://www.sturgis-sd.org
Contact: Jennifer Gabriel, Exec.Dir.

64839 ■ Vermillion Area Chamber of Commerce and Development Company
906 E Cherry St.
Vermillion, SD 57069-1602
Ph:(605)624-5571
Free: 800-809-2071
Fax: (605)624-0094
Co. E-mail: vacc@vermillionchamber.com
URL: http://www.vermillionchamber.com
Contact: Lisa Ketcham, Exec.Dir.

64840 ■ Watertown Area Chamber of Commerce
1200 33rd St. SE, No. 309
PO Box 1113
Watertown, SD 57201
Ph:(605)886-5814
Fax: (605)886-5957
Co. E-mail: chamber@watertownsd.com
URL: http://www.watertownsd.com
Contact: Karen Witt, Dir.

64841 ■ Winner Area Chamber of Commerce
PO Box 268
Winner, SD 57580
Ph:(605)842-1533
Fax: (605)842-1512
Co. E-mail: thechamber@gwtc.net
URL: http://www.winnersd.org
Contact: Lindy Harkin

64842 ■ Yankton Area Chamber of Commerce
PO Box 588
Yankton, SD 57078
Ph:(605)665-3636
Free: 800-888-1460
Co. E-mail: visityankton@yanktonsd.com
URL: http://www.yanktonsd.com
Contact: Kurt Hauser, Exec.Dir.

MINORITY BUSINESS ASSISTANCE PROGRAMS

64843 ■ Native American Economic Development Project–Yankton Sioux Tribe
PO Box 248
Marty, SD 57361
Ph:(605)384-3641
Fax: (605)384-5687
Co. E-mail: ysteppwr@charles-mix.com
Description: Provides individual counseling and technical assistance to entrepreneurs from the Yankton Sioux tribe. Also works to increase circulation of monies with the borders of the reservation.

PROCUREMENT ASSISTANCE PROGRAMS

64844 ■ South Dakota Procurement Technical Assistance Center
2329 N Career Pl., Ste. 106
Sioux Falls, SD 57107
Ph:(605)367-5252
Fax: (605)367-5755
Co. E-mail: kdougherty
URL: http://www.usd.edu/sdptac/
Contact: Kareen Dougherty
Description: Helps businesses develop a marketing plan to sell their goods and services to the government. Also serves as a guide through the procurement process.

EDUCATIONAL PROGRAMS

64845 ■ Mitchell Technical Institute
821 N Capital St.
Mitchell, SD 57301
Ph:(605)995-3024
Free: 800-952-0042
Fax: (605)996-3299
Co. E-mail: questions@mti.tec.sd.us
URL: http://www.mitchelltech.edu

Description: School offers programs in small business management.

PUBLICATIONS

64846 ■ *Smart Start Your South Dakota Business*
PSI Research
300 N. Valley Dr.
Grants Pass, OR 97526

Ph:(541)479-9464
Free: 800-228-2275
Fax: (541)476-1479
Co. E-mail: info@psi-research.com
URL: http://www.psi-research.com
Ed: Michael D. Jenkins. **Released:** Revised edition, 1992. **Price:** $29.95 (looseleaf binder); $24.95 (paper). **Description:** Part of the Successful Business Library series.

SMALL BUSINESS DEVELOPMENT CENTER LEAD OFFICE

64847 ■ Tennessee Board of Regents–Tennessee Small Business Development Center
1415 Murfreesboro Rd.
Ste. 350
Nashville, TN 37217
Ph:(615)366-3900
Fax: (615)366-3939
URL: http://www.tsbdc.org
Contact: Dr. Albert Laabs, State Director

64848 ■ Tennessee SBDC–Middle Tennessee State University
PO Box 98
Murfreesboro, TN 37123
Ph:(615)849-9999
Fax: (615)217-8548
URL: http://www.tsbdc.org
Contact: Patrick Geho, State Dir.
E-mail: pgeho@mail.tsbdc.org

SMALL BUSINESS DEVELOPMENT CENTERS

64849 ■ Austin Peay State University–Small Business Development Center
PO Box 4775
106 Public Sq.
Clarksville, TN 37040
Ph:(931)221-1370
Fax: (931)221-7748
URL: http://www.tsdbc.org
Contact: Heather Penney, Dir.
E-mail: hpenney@mail.tsbdc.org

64850 ■ Blount County Chamber–Satellite Office of Pellissippi State Technological Community–SBDC (201 S)
201 S. Washington St.
Maryville, TN 37084
Ph:(865)983-2241
URL: http://www.tsdbc.org

64851 ■ Business Information Center–Tennessee State University–SBDC (Avon)
Avon Williams Campus
330 10th Ave. N., Rm. 314
Nashville, TN 37203-3401
Ph:(615)963-7253
Fax: (615)963-7160
URL: http://www.tsdbc.org

64852 ■ Chattanooga State Technical Community College–SBDC
100 Cherokee Blvd., Ste. 202
Chattanooga, TN 37405-0880

Ph:(423)756-8668
Fax: (423)756-6195
URL: http://www.tsdbc.org
Contact: Kevin Maxfield, Specialist
E-mail: kmaxfield@mail.tsbdc.org

64853 ■ Cleveland State Community College–Small Business Development Center
PO Box 3570
Cleveland, TN 37320-3570
Ph:(423)478-6247
Fax: (423)478-6251
Contact: Don Geren, Dir.

64854 ■ Dyersburg State Community College–Small Business Development Center
1510 Lake Rd.
Dyersburg, TN 38024-2411
Ph:(731)286-3201
Fax: (731)286-3271
URL: http://www.tsdbc.org
Contact: James T. Frakes, Dir.
E-mail: jfrakes@mail.tsbdc.org

64855 ■ East Tennessee State University–College of Business–SBDC (2109)
2109 W. Market St.
PO Box 70698
Johnson City, TN 37614-0698
Ph:(423)439-8505
Fax: (423)439-8506
URL: http://www.tsdbc.org
Contact: Bob Justice, Dir.
E-mail: bjustice@mail.tsbdc.org

64856 ■ East Tennessee State University College of Business–Satellite Office of ETSU–SBDC (2109)
2109 W. Market St.
Johnson City, TN 37614
Ph:(423)439-8505
Fax: (423)439-8506
Co. E-mail: rgraham@mail.tsbdc.org
URL: http://www.tsdbc.org

64857 ■ Four Lakes Regional Development Authority–Satellite Office of Tennessee Technological University–SBDC (PO Bo)
PO Box 63
Hartsville, TN 37074-0063
Ph:(615)374-4607
Fax: (615)374-4608
Co. E-mail: tsbdc@tntech.edu
URL: http://www.tsdbc.org
Contact: Dorothy Vaden, Dir.

64858 ■ International Trade Center for East Tennessee–SBDC
601 W. Summit Hill Dr., Ste. 300
Knoxville, TN 37902-2011
Ph:(615)743-3058
Fax: (615)743-3042
URL: http://www.tsdbc.org
Contact: Patrick Spence, Dir.
E-mail: pspence@mail.tsbdc.org

64859 ■ International Trade Center for Middle Tennessee–SBDC
Commerce Center Bldg.
211 Commerce St., 3rd Fl.
Nashville, TN 37201
Ph:(615)743-3058
Fax: (615)743-3042
URL: http://www.tsdbc.org
Contact: Patrick Spence, Dir.
E-mail: pspence@mail.tsbdc.org

64860 ■ International Trade Center for West Tennessee–SBDC
Commerce Center Bldg.
211 Commerce St., 3rd Fl.
Nashville, TN 37201
Ph:(615)743-3058
Fax: (615)743-3042
URL: http://www.tsdbc.org
Contact: Patrick Spence, Dir.
E-mail: pspence@mail.tsbdc.org

64861 ■ Jackson State Community College–Small Business Development Center
197 Auditorium St.
Jackson, TN 38301
Ph:(731)424-5389
Fax: (731)427-3942
URL: http://www.tsdbc.org
Contact: Charles N. Roth, Dir.
E-mail: croth@mail.tsbdc.org

64862 ■ Labanon/Wilson County Chamber of Commerce–Satellite Office of Memphis Tennessee State University–SBDC (149 P)
149 Public Sq.
Lebanon, TN 37087
Ph:(615)444-5503
Fax: (615)443-0596
URL: http://www.tsdbc.org

64863 ■ Maury County Alliance–Satellite Office of Middle Tennessee State University–SBDC (106 W)
106 W. 6th St.
Columbia, TN 38401
Ph:(931)388-5674
Fax: (931)867-3344
URL: http://www.tsdbc.org

64864 ■ Memphis Renaissance Center–Satellite Office of University of Memphis–SBDC (Busin)
Business Information Center
555 Beale St.
Memphis, TN 38103
Ph:(901)526-9300
Fax: (901)525-2357
URL: http://www.tsdbc.org

64865 ■ Middle Tennessee State University–Small Business Development Center
Rutherford County Chamber of Commerce Bldg.
501 Memorial Blvd.
Murfreesboro, TN 37129

Ph:(615)898-2745
Fax: (615)893-7089
URL: http://www.tsdbc.org
Contact: Patrick Geho, Dir.
E-mail: prgeho@mail.tsbdc.org

64866 ■ Pellissippi State Technical Community College–Knoxville Area Chamber Partnership–SBDC (17 Ma)
17 Market Sq., No. 201
Knoxville, TN 37902-1402
Ph:(865)246-2663
Fax: (865)971-4439
URL: http://www.tsdbc.org
Contact: Larry Rossini, Dir.
E-mail: lrossini@mail.tsbdc.org

64867 ■ Pellissippi State Technical Community College–Tennessee Small Business Development Center–Knoxville Area Chamber Partnership
601 W. Summit Hill Dr.
Knoxville, TN 37902-2011
Ph:(423)632-2990
Fax: (423)521-6367
Co. E-mail: knoxville@memphis.edu
Contact: John David Headrick, IT Specialist

64868 ■ Small Business Development Center (Columbia)
Maury County Chamber of Commerce Bldg.
106 W. 6th St.
PO Box 8069
Columbia, TN 38402-8069
Ph:(615)898-2745
Fax: (615)893-7089
Contact: Eugene Osekowsky, Business Specialist
E-mail: gosekows@mtsu.edu

64869 ■ Southeast Tennessee Development District–Small Business Development Center
25 Cherokee Blvd.
PO Box 4757
Chattanooga, TN 37405-0757
Ph:(423)266-5781
Fax: (423)267-7705
Contact: Sherri E. Bishop, Business Specialist

64870 ■ Technology 2020 Office–Affiliate Office of Pellissippi State Technological Community College–SBDC (1020)
1020 Commerce Park Dr.
Oak Ridge, TN 37830-8026
Ph:(865)483-2668
Fax: (865)220-2030
Co. E-mail: dcollier@mail.tsbdc.org

64871 ■ Tennessee State University–Small Business Development Center
College of Business
330 10th Ave. N.
Nashville, TN 37203-3401
Ph:(615)963-7158
Fax: (615)963-7160
URL: http://www.tsdbc.org
Contact: John Ordung, Dir.
E-mail: jordung@mail.tsbdc.org

64872 ■ Tennessee Technological University–SBDC
College of Business Administration
1105 N. Peachtree St.
PO Box 5023
Cookeville, TN 38505-0001
Ph:(931)372-3638
Fax: (931)372-6534
Co. E-mail: tsbdc@tntech.edu
URL: http://www.tsdbc.org
Contact: Marcia Reel, Dir.
E-mail: mreel@mail.tsbdc.org

64873 ■ University of Memphis–Tennessee SBDC
320 S. Dudley St.
Memphis, TN 38104-3206
Ph:(901)527-1041
Contact: Don Grimsley, Senior Business Specialist

E-mail: dgrimsl@cc.memphis.edu

SMALL BUSINESS ASSISTANCE PROGRAMS

64874 ■ Tennessee Department of Agriculture–Market Development
PO Box 40627
Nashville, TN 37204
Ph:(615)837-5160
Fax: (615)837-5194
URL: http://www.state.tn.us/agriculture
Description: Develops domestic and international markets for farmers and agribusinesses.

64875 ■ Tennessee Department of Economic and Community Development–Business Enterprise Resource Office
Tennessee Tower Bldg., 10th Fl.
312 8th Ave., N
Nashville, TN 37243-0405
Ph:(615)741-2626
Free: 800-872-7201
Fax: (615)532-8715
URL: http://www.state.tn.us/ecd
Description: Serves as a first-stop office for businesses in the state, conducts programs aimed at increasing the success of small businesses.

64876 ■ Tennessee Department of Economic and Community Development–International Development Group
Tennessee Tower Bldg., 11th Fl.
312 8th Ave., N
Nashville, TN 37243-0405
Ph:(615)741-3282
Free: 877-768-6374
Fax: (615)741-5829
URL: http://www.state.tn.us/ecd
Description: Represents state manufacturers at foreign trade shows and missions International Development and co-sponsors seminars and workshops.

BETTER BUSINESS BUREAUS

64877 ■ Better Business Bureau, Chattanooga
1010 Market St., Ste. 200
Chattanooga, TN 37402-2614
Ph:(423)266-6144
Free: 800-548-4456
Fax: (423)267-1924
Co. E-mail: tngabbb@bellsouth.net
URL: http://www.chattanooga.bbb.org
Contact: Jim Winsett, Pres./CEO

64878 ■ Better Business Bureau of Greater East Tennessee
PO Box 31377
Knoxville, TN 37930-0377
Ph:(865)692-1600
Fax: (865)692-1590
Co. E-mail: info@knoxville.bbb.org
URL: http://www.knoxville.bbb.org

64879 ■ Better Business Bureau of the Mid-South
PO Box 17036
Memphis, TN 38187-0036
Ph:(901)759-1300
Free: 800-BBB-8754
Fax: (901)757-2997
Co. E-mail: info@bbbmidsouth.org
URL: http://www.midsouth.bbb.org
Contact: Randall L. Hutchinson, Pres.

64880 ■ Better Business Bureau of Middle Tennessee
PO Box 198436
Nashville, TN 37219
Ph:(615)242-4222

Free: 800-989-4222
Fax: (615)250-4245
Co. E-mail: bbbnash@aol.com
URL: http://www.nashville.bbb.org
Contact: Kathleen Calligan, Pres./CEO

CHAMBERS OF COMMERCE

64881 ■ Anderson County Chamber of Commerce
245 N Main St., Ste. 200
Clinton, TN 37716
Ph:(865)457-2559
Fax: (865)463-7480
Co. E-mail: accc@andersoncountychamber.org
URL: http://www.andersoncountychamber.org
Contact: Jackie L. Nichols, Pres.

64882 ■ Athens Area Chamber of Commerce
13 N Jackson St.
Athens, TN 37303
Ph:(423)745-0334
Fax: (423)745-0335
Co. E-mail: peggy@athenschamber.org
URL: http://www.athenschamber.org
Contact: Peggy Arterburn, CEO/Pres.

64883 ■ Bartlett Area Chamber of Commerce
2969 Elmore Park Rd.
Bartlett, TN 38134-8309
Ph:(901)372-9457
Fax: (901)372-9488
Co. E-mail: info@bartlettchamber.org
URL: http://www.bartlettchamber.org
Contact: Suzanne M. Griffith, Pres.

64884 ■ Bellevue Chamber of Commerce
177 A Belle Forest Cir.
Nashville, TN 37221
Ph:(615)662-2737
Fax: (615)662-0197
Co. E-mail: info@thebellevuechamber.com
URL: http://www.thebellevuechamber.com
Contact: Gayla Pugh, Exec. Dir.

64885 ■ Benton County/Camden Chamber of Commerce
202 W Main St.
Camden, TN 38320
Ph:(731)584-8395
Free: 877-584-8395
Fax: (731)584-5544
Co. E-mail: chamber1@usit.net
URL: http://www.bentoncountycamden.com
Contact: Bill Randall Kee, Exec. Dir.

64886 ■ Blount County Chamber of Commerce
201 S Washington St.
Maryville, TN 37804
Ph:(865)983-2241
Fax: (865)984-1386
Co. E-mail: info@blountchamber.com
URL: http://www.blountchamber.com
Contact: Fred H. Forster, Pres./CEO

64887 ■ Brentwood Cool Springs Chamber of Commerce
5211 Maryland Way, Ste. 1080
Brentwood, TN 37027
Ph:(615)373-1595
Fax: (615)373-8810
Co. E-mail: kim@brentwood.org
URL: http://www.brentwood.org
Contact: Curt Masters, Chm.

64888 ■ Bristol Tennessee/Virginia Chamber of Commerce
20 Volunteer Pkwy.
Bristol, TN 37620
Ph:(423)989-4850
Co. E-mail: lmeadows@bristolchamber.org
URL: http://www.bristolchamber.org
Contact: Lisa Meadows CTTP, Pres./CEO

64889 ■ Brownsville - Haywood County Chamber of Commerce
121 W Main St.
Brownsville, TN 38012
Ph:(731)772-2193
Fax: (731)772-2195
Co. E-mail: brownsvillebrownsvillechamber@pchnet.com
Contact: Sandra Silverstein, Exec.Dir.

64890 ■ Campbell County Chamber of Commerce
PO Box 305
Jacksboro, TN 37757
Ph:(423)566-0329
Fax: (423)562-0535
Co. E-mail: chamber@campbellcountygov.com
URL: http://co.campbell.tn.us
Contact: Betty Snodderly, Administrator

64891 ■ Carroll County Chamber of Commerce
PO Box 726
20740 E Main St.
Huntingdon, TN 38344
Ph:(731)986-4664
Fax: (731)986-2029
Co. E-mail: cchamber@earthlink.net
URL: http://carrollcounty-tn-chamber.com
Contact: Brad Hurley, Pres.

64892 ■ Chamber of Commerce of the Twin Cities
PO Box 5077
Village Plz. Shopping Ctr.
509 Broadway, Ste. 102
South Fulton, TN 38257-5077
Ph:(731)479-7029
Fax: (731)479-7026
Co. E-mail: cofctwin@bellsouth.net
URL: http://www.twincitieschamberofcommerce.com
Contact: Lois Birk, Exec.Dir.

64893 ■ Chattanooga Area Chamber of Commerce
811 Broad St.
Chattanooga, TN 37402
Ph:(423)756-2121
Fax: (423)267-7242
Co. E-mail: frontdesk@chattanooga-chamber.com
URL: http://www.chattanoogachamber.com
Contact: Tom Edd Wilson, Pres./CEO

64894 ■ Cheatham County Chamber of Commerce
165 S Main St., Ste. 107
PO Box 354
Ashland City, TN 37015-0354
Ph:(615)792-6722
Fax: (615)792-5001
Co. E-mail: info@cheathamchamber.org
URL: http://www.cheathamchamber.org
Contact: Ms. Stacey Luna, Exec.Asst.

64895 ■ Chester County Chamber of Commerce
PO Box 1976
Henderson, TN 38340
Ph:(731)989-5222
Fax: (731)983-5518
Co. E-mail: dltacker@charter.net
URL: http://www.chestercountychamber.com
Contact: Lynda Tacker, Exec.Dir.

64896 ■ Claiborne County Chamber of Commerce
3222 Hwy. 25-E, Ste. 1
Tazewell, TN 37879
Ph:(423)626-4149
Co. E-mail: claibornetourism@communicomm.com
URL: http://www.claibornecounty.com
Contact: Dennis Shipley, Exec.Dir./VP

64897 ■ Clarksville Area Chamber of Commerce
312 Madison St.
Clarksville, TN 37040
Ph:(931)647-2331
Free: 800-530-2487
Fax: (931)645-1574
Co. E-mail: cacc@clarksville.tn.us
URL: http://www.clarksville.tn.us
Contact: Sammy Stuard, Chm.

64898 ■ Clay County Partnership Chamber of Commerce
424 Brown St.
PO Box 769
Celina, TN 38551
Ph:(931)243-3338
Fax: (931)243-6809
Co. E-mail: claychamber@twlakes.net
URL: http://www.dalehollowlake.org
Contact: Randall Killman, Exec.Dir.

64899 ■ Cleveland/Bradley Chamber of Commerce
PO Box 2275
Cleveland, TN 37320-2275
Ph:(423)472-6587
Fax: (423)472-2019
Co. E-mail: info@clevelandchamber.com
URL: http://www.clevelandchamber.com
Contact: Jerry Bohannon, Pres./CEO

64900 ■ Collierville Area Chamber of Commerce
485 Halle Park Dr.
Collierville, TN 38017
Ph:(901)853-1949
Free: 888-853-1949
Fax: (901)853-2399
Co. E-mail: info@colliervillechamber.com
URL: http://www.colliervillechamber.com
Contact: Fran Persechini, Pres.

64901 ■ Cookeville Area-Putnam County Chamber of Commerce
1 W First St.
Cookeville, TN 38501
Ph:(931)526-2211
Free: 800-264-5541
Fax: (931)526-4023
Co. E-mail: info@cookevillechamber.com
URL: http://www.cookevillechamber.com
Contact: George Halford, Pres./CEO

64902 ■ Covington - Tipton County Chamber of Commerce
PO Box 683
Covington, TN 38019
Ph:(901)476-9727
Fax: (901)476-0056
Co. E-mail: ljohnston@covingtones.com
Contact: Lee Johnston, Exec.Dir.

64903 ■ Crockett County Chamber of Commerce
320 S Bells St.
Alamo, TN 38001
Ph:(731)696-5120
Fax: (731)696-4855
Co. E-mail: cktchmbr@crockettnet.com
URL: http://www.crockettchamber.org
Contact: Frankie McCord, Exec.Dir.

64904 ■ Crossville-Cumberland County Chamber of Commerce
34 S Main St.
PO Box 453
Crossville, TN 38555-4518
Ph:(931)484-8444
Free: 877-465-3861
Fax: (931)484-7511
Co. E-mail: thechamber@crossville.com
URL: http://www.crossville-chamber.com
Contact: Beth Alexander, Pres./CEO

64905 ■ Dayton Chamber of Commerce
107 Main St.
Dayton, TN 37321
Ph:(423)775-0361
Fax: (423)570-0105
Co. E-mail: chamber@volstate.net
URL: http://www.rheacountyetc.com
Contact: Margie Legg, Pres.

64906 ■ Decatur County Chamber of Commerce
139 Tennessee Ave. N
Parsons, TN 38363
Ph:(731)847-4202
Fax: (731)847-4222
Co. E-mail: dccc@netease.net
URL: http://www.decaturcountytennessee.org
Contact: Janice Strawn, Exec.Dir.

64907 ■ Dickson County Chamber of Commerce
119 Hwy. 70 E
Dickson, TN 37055
Ph:(615)446-2349
Fax: (615)441-3112
Co. E-mail: contactus@dicksoncountychamber.com
URL: http://www.dicksoncountychamber.com
Contact: David Hamilton, CEO/Pres.

64908 ■ Dyersburg-Dyer County Chamber of Commerce
2000 Commerce Ave.
Dyersburg, TN 38024
Ph:(731)285-3433
Fax: (731)286-4926
Co. E-mail: chamber@ecsis.net
URL: http://www.dyerchamber.com
Contact: Allen Hester CCE, Pres./CEO

64909 ■ Elizabethton - Carter County Chamber of Commerce
500 Veteran's Memorial Pkwy.
PO Box 190
Elizabethton, TN 37644
Ph:(423)547-3850
Fax: (423)547-3854
Co. E-mail: eccchamber@earthlink.com
URL: http://www.tourelizabethton.com
Contact: Barbara Treadway, Exec.Dir.

64910 ■ Etowah Area Chamber of Commerce
PO Box 458
Etowah, TN 37331-0458
Ph:(423)263-2228
Fax: (423)263-1670
Co. E-mail: info@etowahcoc.org
URL: http://www.etowahcoc.org
Contact: Durant Tullock, Exec.Dir.

64911 ■ Fairview Area Chamber of Commerce
PO Box 711
Fairview, TN 37062
Ph:(615)799-9290
Fax: (615)799-8459
Co. E-mail: chamber@fairview-tn.com
URL: http://www.fairview-tn.com
Contact: Dianne Ellis, Pres.

64912 ■ Fayette County Chamber of Commerce
PO Box 411
Somerville, TN 38068
Ph:(901)465-8690
Fax: (901)465-6497
Co. E-mail: info@fayettecountychamber.com
URL: http://www.fayettecountychamber.com
Contact: Mike Border, Exec.Dir.

64913 ■ Fayetteville - Lincoln County Chamber of Commerce
208 S Elk Ave.
PO Box 515
Fayetteville, TN 37334
Ph:(931)433-1234
Free: 888-433-1238
Fax: (931)433-9087
Co. E-mail: cofc@vallnet.com
URL: http://www.vallnet.com/chamberofcommerce
Contact: Carolyn Denton, Exec.Dir.

64914 ■ Fentress County Chamber of Commerce
114 Central Ave. W
PO Box 1294
Jamestown, TN 38556
Ph:(931)879-9948
Free: 800-327-3945
Fax: (931)879-6767
Co. E-mail: tourism@bigsouthfork.org
URL: http://www.jamestowntn.org
Contact: Scott S. Sandman, Exec. Dir.

64915 ■ Franklin County Chamber of Commerce
44 Chamber Way
PO Box 280
Winchester, TN 37398
Ph:(931)967-6788
Fax: (931)967-9418
Co. E-mail: info@franklincountychamber.com
URL: http://www.franklincountychamber.com
Contact: Judy DeWeese Taylor, Exec.Dir.

64916 ■ Gallatin Chamber of Commerce
118 W Main St.
PO Box 26
Gallatin, TN 37066
Ph:(615)452-4000
Fax: (615)452-4021
Co. E-mail: info@gallatintn.org
URL: http://www.gallatintn.org
Contact: Tracy L. Carman, Exec.Dir.

64917 ■ Gatlinburg Chamber of Commerce
PO Box 527
811 E Parkway
Gatlinburg, TN 37738
Ph:(865)436-4178
Free: 800-588-1817
Fax: (865)430-3876
Co. E-mail: info@gatlinburg.com
URL: http://www.gatlinburg.com
Contact: Vicki Simms, Exec.Dir.

64918 ■ Germantown Area Chamber of Commerce
2195 Germantown Rd. S
Germantown, TN 38138
Ph:(901)755-1200
Fax: (901)755-9168
Co. E-mail: info@germantownchamber.com
URL: http://www.germantownchamber.com
Contact: Ms. Pat Scroggs, Exec.Dir.

64919 ■ Giles County Chamber of Commerce
110 N 2nd St.
Pulaski, TN 38478
Ph:(931)363-3789
Fax: (931)363-7279
Co. E-mail: gilesdirector@bellsouth.net
URL: http://www.gilescountychamber.com
Contact: D. Anne Story, Exec.Dir.

64920 ■ Goodlettsville Area Chamber of Commerce
117 N Main St.
Goodlettsville, TN 37072
Ph:(615)859-7979
Fax: (615)859-1480
Co. E-mail: debcoc@bellsouth.net
URL: http://www.goodlettsvillechamber.com
Contact: Debbie G. Robinson, Pres.

64921 ■ Greater Gibson County Area Chamber of Commerce
103 S Court Sq.
PO Box 464
Trenton, TN 38382
Ph:(731)855-0973
Fax: (731)855-0979
Co. E-mail: gibsonco@iswt.com
URL: http://www.gibsoncountytn.com/chamber

64922 ■ Greene County Partnership
115 Academy St.
Greeneville, TN 37743-5601
Ph:(423)638-4111

Fax: (423)638-5345
Co. E-mail: gcp@xtn.net
URL: http://greenecountypartnership.com
Contact: Bryan Quinsey, Pres.

64923 ■ Hardeman County Chamber of Commerce
500 W Market St.
PO Box 313
Bolivar, TN 38008
Ph:(731)658-6554
Fax: (731)658-6874
Co. E-mail: infohccc@bellsouth.net
URL: http://www.hardemancotn.org/chamber.html
Contact: Rob Jensik, Exec. Dir.

64924 ■ Hardin County Chamber of Commerce
PO Box 996
Savannah, TN 38372
Ph:(731)925-2363
Free: (866)750-2363
Fax: (731)925-8069
Co. E-mail: hardincochamber@centurytel.net
URL: http://www.hardincountytn.com
Contact: Beth Pippin, Exec.Dir.

64925 ■ Hartsville - Trousdale County Chamber of Commerce
240 Broadway
Hartsville, TN 37074-1336
Ph:(615)374-9243
Fax: (615)374-0068
Co. E-mail: eford@hartsvilletrousdale.com
URL: http://www.hartsvilletrousdale.com
Contact: Eleanor W. Ford, Exec.Dir.

64926 ■ Henderson County Chamber of Commerce
149 Eastern Shores Dr.
Lexington, TN 38351
Ph:(731)968-2126
Co. E-mail: hccc@netease.net
URL: http://www.hendersoncountychamber.com/default.asp
Contact: Lisa Sullivan, Exec.Dir.

64927 ■ Hendersonville Area Chamber of Commerce
101 Wessington Pl.
PO Box 377
Hendersonville, TN 37075
Ph:(615)824-2818
Fax: (615)822-7498
Co. E-mail: wendy@hendersonvillechamber.com
URL: http://www.hendersonvillechamber.com
Contact: Wendy Hughes, Office Mgr.

64928 ■ Hickman County Chamber of Commerce
PO Box 126
Centerville, TN 37033
Ph:(931)729-5774
Fax: (931)729-0874
Co. E-mail: hccocv21@mlec.net
URL: http://www.hickmanco.com/chamber
Contact: Nancy Roland, Exec.Dir.

64929 ■ Humboldt Chamber of Commerce
1200 Main St.
Humboldt, TN 38343
Ph:(731)784-1842
Fax: (731)784-1573
Co. E-mail: jim@humboldttnchamber.org
URL: http://www.humboldttnchamber.org
Contact: Jim Blankenship, Dir.

64930 ■ Humphreys County Area Chamber of Commerce
124 E Main St.
PO Box 733
Waverly, TN 37185
Ph:(931)296-4865
Fax: (931)296-2285
Co. E-mail: hcchamber@bellsouth.net
URL: http://www.waverly.net/hcchamber
Contact: Brenda Palk, Exec.Sec.

64931 ■ Jackson Area Chamber of Commerce
197 Auditorium St.
PO Box 1904
Jackson, TN 38302-1904
Ph:(731)423-2200
Fax: (731)424-4860
Co. E-mail: chamber@jacksontn.com
URL: http://jacksontn.com
Contact: Paul Latture III, Pres./CEO

64932 ■ Jackson - Madison County African American Chamber of Commerce
351 N Royal St.
Jackson, TN 38301-5456
Ph:(731)424-2030
Co. E-mail: aacc@bellsouth.net
Contact: Nell Hunston, Founder

64933 ■ Jefferson County Chamber of Commerce
PO Box 890
Dandridge, TN 37725
Ph:(865)397-9642
Fax: (865)397-0164
Co. E-mail: jeffinfo@jefferson-tn-chamber.org
URL: http://www.jefferson-tn-chamber.org
Contact: Daryl L. Brady, Pres./CEO

64934 ■ Johnson City - Jonesboro - Washington County Chamber of Commerce
PO Box 180
Johnson City, TN 37605
Ph:(423)461-8000
Free: 800-852-3392
Fax: (423)461-8047
Co. E-mail: mentgen@johnsoncitytnchamber.com
URL: http://www.johnsoncitytnchamber.com
Contact: Gary Mabrey, Pres./CEO

64935 ■ Johnson County Chamber of Commerce
PO Box 66
Mountain City, TN 37683
Ph:(423)727-1700
Fax: (423)727-4943
Co. E-mail: info@johnsoncountychamber.org
URL: http://www.johnsoncountychamber.org
Contact: Rudy Lucas, Pres.

64936 ■ Kingsport Area Chamber of Commerce
151 E Main St.
PO Box 1403
Kingsport, TN 37662
Ph:(423)392-8800
Fax: (423)246-7234
Co. E-mail: info@kingsportchamber.org
URL: http://www.kingsportchamber.org/portal/chamberhome.htm
Contact: Miles A. Burdine, Exec.VP/CEO

64937 ■ Knoxville Area Chamber Partnership
17 Market Sq., No. 201
Knoxville, TN 37902
Ph:(865)637-4550
Fax: (865)523-2071
Co. E-mail: partnership@kacp.com
URL: http://www.knoxvillechamber.com
Contact: Ms. Pam Fansler, Chair

64938 ■ Lauderdale County Chamber of Commerce
123 S Jefferson Ave.
Ripley, TN 38063
Ph:(731)635-9541
Fax: (731)635-9064
Co. E-mail: info@lauderdalecountytn.org
URL: http://www.lauderdalecountytn.org
Contact: Lisa Hankins, Exec. Dir.

64939 ■ Lawrence County Chamber of Commerce
1609 N Locust Ave.
PO Box 86
Lawrenceburg, TN 38464
Ph:(931)762-4911

Free: 877-388-4911
Fax: (931)762-3153
Co. E-mail: info@chamberofcommerce.lawrence.tn.
us
URL: http://www.chamberofcommerce.lawrence.tn.
us
Contact: Daphene Cope, Dir. of Operations

64940 ■ Lebanon/Wilson County Chamber of Commerce
149 Public Sq.
Lebanon, TN 37087-2736
Ph:(615)444-5503
Free: (866)264-1249
Fax: (615)443-0596
Co. E-mail: lebchamb@bellsouth.net
URL: http://www.lebanonwilsontnchamber.org
Contact: Sue Vanatta, Pres./CEO

64941 ■ Lewis County Chamber of Commerce
106 N Court St.
Hohenwald, TN 38462
Ph:(931)796-4084
Co. E-mail: president@lewiscountychamber.com
URL: http://www.lewiscountychamber.com

64942 ■ Livingston - Overton County Chamber of Commerce
222 E Main St.
PO Box 354A
Livingston, TN 38570
Ph:(931)823-6421
Free: 800-876-7393
Fax: (931)823-6422
Co. E-mail: chamber@twlakes.net
URL: http://www.overtonco.com
Contact: John Roberts, Exec.Dir.

64943 ■ Loudon County Chamber of Commerce
318 Angel Row
PO Box 87
Loudon, TN 37774
Ph:(865)458-2067
Fax: (865)458-1206
Co. E-mail: lccc@loundcountychamber.com
URL: http://www.loudoncountychamber.com
Contact: Teresa Ward-Keenan, Pres.

64944 ■ Lynchburg - Moore County Chamber of Commerce
PO Box 421
Lynchburg, TN 37352
Ph:(931)759-4111
Co. E-mail: info@lynchburgtenn.com
URL: http://www.lynchburgtenn.com
Contact: Paulette Jennings, Pres.

64945 ■ Macon County Chamber of Commerce
208 Church St.
Lafayette, TN 37083
Ph:(615)666-5885
Fax: (615)666-6969
Co. E-mail: mchamber@nctc.com
URL: http://www.maconcountychamber.com
Contact: Lona Vinson, Exec.Sec.

64946 ■ Madison Chamber of Commerce
PO Box 97
Madison, TN 37116
Ph:(615)865-5400
Fax: (615)865-0448
Co. E-mail: info@madisonrivergatechamber.com
Contact: Susan Williams, Exec.Dir.

64947 ■ Manchester Area Chamber of Commerce
110 E Main St.
Manchester, TN 37355
Ph:(931)728-7635
Fax: (423)728-0736
Co. E-mail: manchestercoc@bellsouth.net
URL: http://www.macoc.org
Contact: Susie McEacharn, Exec.Dir.

64948 ■ Marion County Chamber of Commerce
302 Betsy Pack Dr.
PO Box 789
Jasper, TN 37347
Ph:(423)942-5103
Fax: (423)942-0098
Co. E-mail: marioncoc@bellsouth.net
URL: http://www.marioncountychamber.com
Contact: Brad Carter, Exec.Dir.

64949 ■ Marshall County Chamber of Commerce
227 2nd Ave. N
Lewisburg, TN 37091
Ph:(931)359-3863
Fax: (931)359-8411
Co. E-mail: director@marshallchamber.org
URL: http://www.marshallchamber.org
Contact: Ms. Ritaanne Weaver, Exec.Dir.

64950 ■ Maury Alliance
106 W 6th St.
PO Box 1076
Columbia, TN 38402
Ph:(931)388-2155
Fax: (931)380-0335
Co. E-mail: jearwood@mauryalliance.com
URL: http://www.mauryalliance.com
Contact: Janet Earwood, VP

64951 ■ McMinnville - Warren County Chamber of Commerce
110 S Court Sq.
PO Box 574
McMinnville, TN 37111
Ph:(931)473-6611
Fax: (931)473-4741
Co. E-mail: warrencotn@blomand.net
URL: http://www.warrentn.com
Contact: Lea G. Chrisawn, Pres.

64952 ■ McNairy County Chamber of Commerce
144 Cypress Ave.
Selmer, TN 38375
Ph:(731)645-6360
Fax: (731)645-7663
Co. E-mail: mcnairy@charterinternet.com
URL: http://www.mcnairy.com
Contact: Mr. Thomas Cauley, Exec.Dir.

64953 ■ Memphis Regional Chamber of Commerce
22 N Front St., Ste. 200
PO Box 224
Memphis, TN 38101-0224
Ph:(901)543-3500
Fax: (901)543-3510
Co. E-mail: info@memphischamber.com
URL: http://www.memphischamber.com
Contact: John W. Moore, Pres./CEO

64954 ■ Milan Chamber of Commerce
1061 S Main St.
Milan, TN 38358-2748
Ph:(731)686-7494
Co. E-mail: chamber@cityofmilantn.com
Contact: Tara Bradford, Exec.VP

64955 ■ Millington Chamber of Commerce
7743 Church St.
Millington, TN 38053
Ph:(901)872-1486
Fax: (901)872-0727
Co. E-mail: info@millingtonchamber.com
URL: http://www.millingtonchamber.com
Contact: Ordis D. Copeland, Pres.

64956 ■ Monroe County Chamber of Commerce
PO Box 68
Madisonville, TN 37354
Ph:(423)442-4588
Fax: (423)442-9016
Co. E-mail: info@monroecountychamber.org
URL: http://www.monroecountychamber.org

Contact: Robert Preston, Pres./CEO

64957 ■ Monteagle Mountain Chamber of Commerce
PO Box 353
Monteagle, TN 37356-0353
Ph:(931)924-5353
Fax: (931)924-2264
Co. E-mail: info@monteaglechamber.com
URL: http://www.monteaglechamber.com
Contact: Maxine Partin Wade, Exec.Dir.

64958 ■ Morristown Area Chamber of Commerce
825 W 1st N St.
PO Box 9
Morristown, TN 37815
Ph:(423)586-6382
Fax: (423)586-6576
Co. E-mail: macc@charter.net
URL: http://www.morristownchamber.com
Contact: C. Thomas Robinson CCE, Pres./CEO

64959 ■ Mount Juliet - West Wilson County Chamber of Commerce
46 W Caldwell St.
Mount Juliet, TN 37122
Ph:(615)758-3478
Fax: (615)754-8595
Co. E-mail: aspicer@tds.net
URL: http://www.mtjulietchamber.com
Contact: Mark Hinesley, Pres.

64960 ■ Nashville Area Chamber of Commerce
211 Commerce St., Ste. 100
Nashville, TN 37201-1806
Ph:(615)743-3000
Fax: (615)256-3074
Co. E-mail: info@nashvillechamber.com
URL: http://www.nashvillechamber.com
Contact: Michael Neal, Pres./CEO

64961 ■ Newport/Cocke County Chamber of Commerce
433-B Prospect Ave.
Newport, TN 37821
Ph:(423)623-7201
Fax: (423)623-7216
Co. E-mail: ccpchamber@bellsouth.net
URL: http://www.cockecounty.org
Contact: Kandee Veridal

64962 ■ Oak Ridge Chamber of Commerce
1400 Oak Ridge Tpke.
Oak Ridge, TN 37830
Ph:(865)483-1321
Fax: (865)483-1678
Co. E-mail: hardy@orcc.org
URL: http://www.orcc.org
Contact: Parker Hardy, Pres./CEO

64963 ■ Obion County Chamber of Commerce
214 E Church St.
Union City, TN 38261
Ph:(731)885-0211
Fax: (731)885-7155
Co. E-mail: jbagwell@charterinternet.com
Contact: Jennifer Bagwell, Office Mgr.

64964 ■ Paris/Henry County Chamber of Commerce
2508 E Wood St.
PO Box 8
Paris, TN 38242
Ph:(731)642-3431
Fax: (731)642-3454
Co. E-mail: pariscoc@charterbn.com
URL: http://www.paris.tn.org
Contact: Jennifer Wheatley, Exec.Dir.

64965 ■ Pigeon Forge Chamber of Commerce
2713 Pkwy.
Pigeon Forge, TN 37868-1278
Ph:(865)453-5700

Free: 800-221-9858
Co. E-mail: pifchamber@kmsfia.com
URL: http://www.pigeonforgechamber.com
Contact: Tia Burkett, Exec.Dir.

64966 ■ Pikeville - Bledsoe County Chamber of Commerce
PO Box 205
Pikeville, TN 37367
Ph:(423)447-2791
Co. E-mail: directors@pikeville-bledsoe.com
URL: http://www.pikeville-bledsoe.com
Contact: John Eason, Exec.Chm.

64967 ■ Portland Chamber of Commerce
106 Main St.
PO Box 387
Portland, TN 37148-0387
Ph:(615)325-9032
Fax: (615)325-8399
Co. E-mail: portcofc@bellsouth.net
URL: http://www.portlandtn.com/chamber_of_
commerce.htm
Contact: Gary Driskill, Dir.

64968 ■ Reelfoot Area Chamber of Commerce
130 S Court St.
Tiptonville, TN 38079
Ph:(731)253-8144
Fax: (731)253-9923
Co. E-mail: reelfoot@reelfootareachamber.com
Contact: Marcia Perkins Mills, Exec.Dir.

64969 ■ Roane County Chamber of Commerce
1209 N Kentucky St.
Kingston, TN 37763
Ph:(865)376-5572
Free: 800-386-4686
Fax: (865)376-4978
Co. E-mail: info@roanealliance.org
URL: http://www.roanealliance.org
Contact: Beth W. Sams, VP Community
Development & Tourism

64970 ■ Rutherford County Chamber of Commerce
315 S Lowry St.
Smyrna, TN 37167
Ph:(615)355-6565
Co. E-mail: cjoy.galyon@townofsmyrna.org
URL: http://www.rutherfordchamber.org
Contact: Joy Galyon, Admin. Asst.

64971 ■ Scott County Chamber of Commerce
PO Box 766
Helenwood, TN 37755-0766
Ph:(423)663-6900
Free: 800-645-6905
Fax: (423)663-6906
Co. E-mail: inquiry@scottcountychamber.com
URL: http://www.scottcountychamber.com
Contact: Almeda Peavyhouse, Exec.Dir.

64972 ■ Sevierville Chamber of Commerce
110 Gary Wade Blvd.
Sevierville, TN 37862
Ph:(865)453-6411
Free: 888-738-4378
Fax: (865)453-9649
Co. E-mail: info@seviervillechamber.com
URL: http://www.seviervillechamber.com
Contact: Brenda McCroskey, Exec.Dir.

64973 ■ Shelbyville-Bedford County Chamber of Commerce
100 N Cannon Blvd.
Shelbyville, TN 37160
Ph:(931)684-3482
Free: 888-662-2525
Fax: (931)684-3483
Co. E-mail: bedfordchamber@bellsouth.net
URL: http://www.shelbyvilletn.com
Contact: Walter W. Wood CEcD, CEO

64974 ■ Smith County Chamber of Commerce
PO Box 70
Carthage, TN 37030
Ph:(615)735-2093
Fax: (615)735-2093
Co. E-mail: info@smithcountychamber.org
URL: http://www.smithcountychamber.org
Contact: Mrs. Regina Brooks, Admin.Dir.

64975 ■ Smithville - DeKalb County Chamber of Commerce
PO Box 64
Smithville, TN 37166
Ph:(615)597-4163
Fax: (615)597-4164
Co. E-mail: dekalbtn@dtccom.net
URL: http://www.smithvilletn.com
Contact: Suzanne Williams, Exec.Dir.

64976 ■ South Tipton County Chamber of Commerce
PO Box 1198
Munford, TN 38058
Ph:(901)837-4600
Fax: (901)837-4602
Co. E-mail: chamber@southtipton.com
URL: http://southtipton.com
Contact: Rosemary Bridges, Exec.Dir.

64977 ■ Sparta - White County Chamber of Commerce
16 W Bockman Way
Sparta, TN 38583
Ph:(931)836-3552
Fax: (931)836-2216
Co. E-mail: sparta-chamber@charter.net
URL: http://www.sparta-chamber.net
Contact: Wallace G. Austin, Pres.

64978 ■ Spring City Chamber of Commerce
384 Front St.
PO Box 355
Spring City, TN 37381-0355
Ph:(423)365-5210
Fax: (423)365-9790
Co. E-mail: springcitychamber_1@juno.com
URL: http://springcityonline.com
Contact: Mr. Steve Orender, Office Mgr.

64979 ■ Springfield - Robertson County Chamber of Commerce
100 5th Ave. W
Springfield, TN 37172
Ph:(615)384-3800
Co. E-mail: info@spchamber.org
URL: http://www.springfieldtennchamber.org
Contact: J. Mark Lowe, Exec.Dir.

64980 ■ Stewart County Chamber of Commerce
1008 Moore Rd.
PO Box 147
Dover, TN 37058-0147
Ph:(931)232-8290
Fax: (931)232-4973
Co. E-mail: sccoc@clarksville.com
URL: http://www.stewartcountyvacation.com
Contact: Tracy Keel, Pres.

64981 ■ Tennessee Chamber of Commerce and Industry
611 Commerce St., Ste. 3030
Nashville, TN 37203-3742
Ph:(615)256-5141
Fax: (615)256-6726
Co. E-mail: info@tnchamber.org
URL: http://www.tnchamber.org
Contact: Deborah K. Woolley, Pres.

64982 ■ Tullahoma Area Chamber of Commerce
PO Box 1205
Tullahoma, TN 37388
Ph:(931)455-5497
Fax: (931)455-5350
Co. E-mail: tullahomachamber@tullahoma.org

URL: http://www.tullahoma.org
Contact: Diane Bryant, Exec.Dir.

64983 ■ Unicoi County Chamber of Commerce
100 S Main Ave.
PO Box 713
Erwin, TN 37650
Ph:(423)743-3000
Fax: (423)743-0942
Co. E-mail: info@unicoicounty.org
URL: http://www.unicoicounty.org
Contact: Amanda Bennett-Hensley, Exec.Dir.

64984 ■ Wayne County Chamber of Commerce
Courthouse, Rm. 303
PO Box 675
Waynesboro, TN 38485-0675
Ph:(931)722-9022
Fax: (931)722-5994
Co. E-mail: chamber@netease.net
URL: http://www.waynecountychamber.org
Contact: Karen Baker, Exec.Dir.

64985 ■ Weakley County Chamber of Commerce
PO Box 67
Dresden, TN 38225
Ph:(731)364-3787
Fax: (731)364-2099
Co. E-mail: wccc@crunet.com
Contact: Suzanne German, Dir.

64986 ■ White House Area Chamber of Commerce
414 Hwy. 76
PO Box 521
White House, TN 37188-0521
Ph:(615)672-3937
Fax: (615)672-2828
Co. E-mail: whcoc@bellsouth.net
URL: http://www.whitehousechamber.org
Contact: Ms. Julie Bolton, Exec.Dir.

64987 ■ Williamson County - Franklin Chamber of Commerce
City Hall
PO Box 156
Franklin, TN 37065-0156
Ph:(615)794-1225
Free: 800-356-3445
Co. E-mail: info@wcfchamber.com
URL: http://www.williamson-franklinchamber.com
Contact: Nancy P. Conway, CEO/Pres.

MINORITY BUSINESS ASSISTANCE PROGRAMS

64988 ■ Memphis Minority Business Development Corp.
283 N Bellevue
Memphis, TN 38105
Ph:(901)726-5353
Fax: (901)726-5355

64989 ■ Nashville Minority Business Development Center
223 8th Ave., North No. 205
Nashville, TN 37203
Ph:(615)255-0432
Fax: (615)255-2377
Co. E-mail: nmbdlf@bellsouth.net
URL: http://www.minoritybusinesscenter.com
Contact: Marilyn Robinson, Exec Dir

64990 ■ Tennessee Department of Economic and Community Development Center–Business Enterprise Resource Office (BERO)
312 8th Ave. N, Eleventh Fl.
Nashville, TN 37243-0405
Ph:(615)741-2626
Free: 800-251-8594
Fax: (615)532-8715

Co. E-mail: rick.merideth@state.tn.us
URL: http://www.state.tn.us/ecd/res_guide.htm
Contact: Rick Merideth, Asst Comm
Description: Provides services to minority entrepreneurs through offices located in Nashville, Chattanooga, Knoxville, and Memphis.

FINANCING AND LOAN PROGRAMS

64991 ■ Capital Across America, L.P.
501 Union St., Ste. 201
Nashville, TN 37219
Ph:(615)254-1414
Fax: (615)254-1856
URL: http://www.capitalacrossamerica.com
Contact: Chris Brown, President
Investment Types: Balanced. **Industry Preferences:** Women/minority-owned businesses. **Geographic Preferences:** Mid Atlantic, Midwest, and Southeast.

64992 ■ Capital Services & Resources, Inc.
5159 Wheelis Dr., Ste. 106
Memphis, TN 38117
Ph:(901)761-2156
Fax: (907)767-0060
Contact: Charles Bancroft, Principal
Preferred Investment Size: $10,000,000 to $15,000,000. **Investment Types:** Second stage, leveraged buyout, expansion, public companies, recapitalizations, research and development, strategic alliances, and special situation. **Industry Preferences:** Communications, computer software and hardware, semiconductors and other electronics, biotechnology, medical and health, consumer related, industrial and energy, transportation, financial services, business service, manufacturing, agriculture, forestry and fishing. **Geographic Preferences:** U.S and Canada. and Canada.

64993 ■ Coleman Swenson Booth Inc. / Coleman Swenson Hoffman Booth
237 2nd Ave. S.
Franklin, TN 37064-2649
Ph:(615)791-9462
Fax: (615)791-9636
URL: http://www.colemanswenson.com
Contact: Larry H. Coleman, Managing General Partner
Preferred Investment Size: $1,000,000 to $7,000,000. **Investment Types:** Seed, start-up, first and second stage, mezzanine, and special situation. **Industry Preferences:** Medical and health, Internet specific, other products, computer software and services, consumer related, biotechnology, computer hardware, communications and media. **Geographic Preferences:** U.S.

64994 ■ Eastman Ventures
100 N. Eastman Rd.
PO Box 511
Kingsport, TN 37662
Ph:(423)229-2000
Fax: (423)224-0314
URL: http://www.eastmanventures.com
Contact: Mark Klopp, Managing Director
Preferred Investment Size: $500,000 to $2,000,000. **Investment Policies:** Early, second, and later stage, and expansion. **Industry Preferences:** Computer software, Internet specific, semiconductors and other electronics, biotechnology, medical and health, industrial and energy, manufacturing, and environmental. **Geographic Preferences:** National.

64995 ■ Equitas L.P.
2000 Glen Echo Rd., Ste. 100
PO Box 158838
Nashville, TN 37215-8838
Ph:(615)383-8673
Fax: (615)383-8693
URL: http://www.rodgerscapital.com
Contact: D. Shannon LeRoy, President
Investment Types: Second stage, leveraged buyout, mezzanine, recapitalizations, and special situation.

Industry Preferences: Communications, medical and health, consumer related, industrial and energy. **Geographic Preferences:** Southeast and Midwest.

64996 ■ First Avenue Partners
138 2nd Ave. N.
Nashville, TN 37201
Ph:(615)370-0056
Fax: (615)376-6310
URL: http://www.1stpartners.com
Preferred Investment Size: $3,000,000 to $4,000,000.

64997 ■ Massey Burch Capital Corp.
1 Burton Hills Blvd., Ste. 350
Nashville, TN 37215
Ph:(615)665-3221
Fax: (615)665-3240
URL: http://www.masseyburch.com
Preferred Investment Size: $1,000,000 to $5,000,000. **Investment Types:** Seed, start-up, early and first stage. **Industry Preferences:** Other products, medical and health, Internet specific, communications and media, computer software and services, industrial and energy, biotechnology, consumer related, computer hardware, semiconductors and other electronics. **Geographic Preferences:** Southeast.

64998 ■ MB Venture Partners, LLC
930 Madison Ave., Ste. 100
Memphis, TN 38103
Ph:(901)448-8600
Fax: (901)448-8850
URL: http://www.mbventures.com
Contact: Gary Stevenson, President
Investment Policies: Seed, early and later stage. **Industry Preferences:** Biotechnology, and medical and health. **Geographic Preferences:** Southeast and Tennessee.

64999 ■ Nelson Capital Corp.
3401 W. End Ave., Ste. 300
Nashville, TN 37203
Ph:(615)292-8787
Fax: (615)385-3150
Contact: Jack Harrington, Vice President
Preferred Investment Size: $500,000 minimum. **Investment Types:** First and second stage, leveraged buyout, and mezzanine. **Industry Preferences:** Communications, computer related, medical and health, consumer related, industrial and energy, financial services, and manufacturing. **Geographic Preferences:** Southeast.

65000 ■ Paradigm Capital Partners, LLC
6410 Poplar Ave., Ste. 395
Memphis, TN 38119
Ph:(901)682-6060
Fax: (901)763-3230
URL: http://www.paradigmcp.com
Preferred Investment Size: $500,000 to $6,000,000. **Investment Types:** First and second stage, and seed. **Industry Preferences:** Communications, computer software, Internet specific, semiconductors and other electronics, consumer related, industrial and energy, business service, manufacturing, agriculture, forestry and fishing. **Geographic Preferences:** Southeast.

65001 ■ Salix Ventures
30 Burton Hills Blvd., Ste. 370
Nashville, TN 37215
Ph:(615)665-1409
Fax: (615)665-2912
URL: http://www.salixventures.com
Contact: Mark Donovan, Principal
Preferred Investment Size: $3,000,000 to $8,000,000. **Investment Types:** Early and later stage, and expansion. **Industry Preferences:** Medical and health, computer software and services, Internet specific, biotechnology, other products, and consumer related. **Geographic Preferences:** U.S.

65002 ■ SSM Ventures
6075 Poplar Ave., Ste. 335
Memphis, TN 38119
Ph:(901)767-1131

Fax: (901)767-1135
URL: http://www.ssmventures.com
Contact: James Witherington, Managing General Partner
Preferred Investment Size: $3,000,000 to $10,000,000. **Investment Types:** First, second, early and later stage, and expansion. **Industry Preferences:** Internet specific, computer software and services, communications and media, computer hardware, other products, medical and health, consumer related, semiconductors and other electronics. **Geographic Preferences:** Southeast and Texas.

65003 ■ Valley Capital Corp.
Krystal Bldg.
100 W. Martin Luther King Blvd., Ste. 212
Chattanooga, TN 37402
Ph:(423)265-1557
Fax: (423)265-1588
Contact: Faye Robinson
Preferred Investment Size: $200,000 minimum. **Investment Types:** Second stage, mezzanine, and leveraged buyout. **Industry Preferences:** Diversified. **Geographic Preferences:** Southeast.

PROCUREMENT ASSISTANCE PROGRAMS

65004 ■ Department General Services
Purchasing Division
312 8th Ave. N
Tennessee Towers, 3rd Fl.
Nashville, TN 37243-0557
Ph:(615)741-1035
Fax: (615)741-0684
URL: http://www.state.tn.us/generalserv/purchasing

65005 ■ Tennessee Procurement Technical Assistance Center–Center for Industrial Services
193 Polk Ave., Ste. C
Nashville, TN 37210
Ph:(615)532-8885
Fax: (615)532-4937
URL: http://www.cis.utk.edu
Contact: Bob Matheny
E-mail: matheny@utk.edu

INCUBATORS/RESEARCH AND TECHNOLOGY PARKS

65006 ■ Chattanooga/Hamilton County Business Development Center
100 Cherokee Blvd.
Chattanooga, TN 37405
Ph:(423)752-4301
Fax: (423)752-1700
URL: http://www.chattanoogachamber.com
Contact: Admin. Ass.

65007 ■ The Development Corporation of Knox County
17 Market Square 201
Knoxville, TN 37902
Ph:(865)546-5887
Fax: (865)546-6170
URL: http://www.knoxdevelopment.org/

65008 ■ Technology 2020 Information Technology Incubator
1020 Commerce Park Dr.
Oak Ridge, TN 37830
Ph:(865)220-2020
Fax: (865)220-2030
Co. E-mail: info@tech2020.org
URL: http://www.tech2020.org/
Contact: Tom Rogers, Pres & CEO
Description: This small business incubator emphasizes the development of information technology and internet firms.

65009 ■ University of Tennessee Health Science Center–Research Administration
910 Madison, Ste. 82 J
Memphis, TN 38163
Ph:(901)448-4823
Fax: (901)448-7600
Co. E-mail: research@utmem.edu
URL: http://www.utmem.edu/research/research_admin/
Contact: Deborah L. Smith EdD, Dir.
E-mail: research@utmem.edu
Scope: Administers and coordinates research activities concerning extramurally supported projects conducted in the various colleges, departments, and research units at the University. Research is primarily focused on health science, biomedical, and basic and clinical sciences.

65010 ■ University of Tennessee, Knoxville–Office of Research
404 Andy Holt Tower
Knoxville, TN 37996-0140
Ph:(865)974-3466
Fax: (865)974-2805
Co. E-mail: bcollier@utk.edu
Contact: Dr. Billie J. Collier, Assoc.Vice Chancellor
E-mail: bcollier@utk.edu
Scope: Advocates, administers, and coordinates research, especially extramurally sponsored projects conducted in all colleges, departments, and research units of the Knoxville, Memphis, and Tullahoma campuses. Overseas economic development activities designed and conducted between the University and the public. **Services:** Individual and multidisciplinary proposal development assistance. **Publications:** Annual Reports; Gradsources (monthly); Resources (monthly); Videotex (daily). **Educational Activities:** Seminars, both on proposal and contract development; Workshops.

65011 ■ Vanderbilt University–Division of Sponsored Research
110 21st Ave. S
PO Box 7749, Station B
Nashville, TN 37235-7749
Ph:(615)322-2631
Fax: (615)322-3827
Co. E-mail: sponsored_research@vanderbilt.edu
URL: http://www.vanderbilt.edu/SponsoredResearch/homepg.html

Contact: John Childress, Dir.
E-mail: sponsored_research@vanderbilt.edu
Scope: Coordinates and administers extramurally sponsored research projects and research activities in diverse fields at Vanderbilt University. **Publications:** Newsletter. **Educational Activities:** Research seminars.

EDUCATIONAL PROGRAMS

65012 ■ Chattanooga State Technical Community College
4501 Amnicola Hwy.
Chattanooga, TN 37406
Ph:(423)697-4400
Fax: (423)697-3115
URL: http://www.chattanoogastate.edu
Description: Two-year college offering a small business management program.

TRADE PERIODICALS

65013 ■ *Tennessee Economic Development Quarterly*
Pub: Department of Economic and Community Development
Contact: Caroline Ragsdale
Ed: Caroline Ragsdale, Editor, cragsdale@mail.state.m.us. **Released:** Bimonthly. **Description:** Highlights Tennessee's economic growth and business climate.

PUBLICATIONS

65014 ■ *Business Journal of Upper East Tennessee and Southwest Virginia*
P.O. Box 643
Blountville, TN 37617-0643
Ph:(423)323-7111
Fax: (423)323-1479
Co. E-mail: news@bjournal.com
URL: http://www.bjournal.com

65015 ■ *Memphis Business Journal*
88 Union, Ste. 102
Memphis, TN 38103-5195
Ph:(901)523-1000
Fax: (901)526-5240
Co. E-mail: mbj@mem.net
URL: http://www.amcity.com

65016 ■ *Nashville Business Journal*
PO Box 23229
Nashville, TN 37202-3229
Ph:(615)248-2222
Fax: (615)248-6246
URL: http://www.amcity.com/nashville

65017 ■ *Smart Start your Tennessee Business*
PSI Research
300 N. Valley Dr.
Grants Pass, OR 97526
Ph:(503)479-9464
Free: 800-228-2275
Fax: (503)476-1479
Co. E-mail: info@psi-research.com
URL: http://www.psi-research.com
Ed: Michael D. Jenkins. **Released:** Revised edition, 1992. **Price:** $29.95 (looseleaf binder); $24.95 (paper). **Description:** Part of the Successful Business Library series.

PUBLISHERS

65018 ■ Doing Business in Memphis
1910 Madison Ave., Ste. 120
Memphis, TN 38104-2620
Ph:(901)525-0552
Fax: (901)525-0748
Co. E-mail: bizinfo@memphisbusiness.com
URL: http://www.memphisbusiness.com
Contact: Deborah L. Camp, President
E-mail: dcamp@memphisbusiness.com
Description: Publishes business-to-business directories. Does not accept unsolicited manuscripts. Reaches market through commission representatives, direct mail, reviews and listings, and telephone sales. **Founded:** 1990.

SMALL BUSINESS DEVELOPMENT CENTER LEAD OFFICE

65019 ■ University of Houston–Southeastern Texas Small Business Development Center
2302 Fannin, Ste. 200
Houston, TX 77002
Ph:(713)752-8425
Fax: (713)756-1500
URL: http://smbizsolutions.uh.edu
Contact: Mike Young, Director
E-mail: myoung@uh.edu

SMALL BUSINESS DEVELOPMENT CENTERS

65020 ■ Angelina College–Small Business Development Center
3500 S. First St.
PO Box 1768
Lufkin, TX 75902-1768
Ph:(936)633-5400
Fax: (936)633-5478
URL: http://www.angelina.cc.tx.us
Contact: Brian McClain, Dir.
E-mail: bmcclain@angelina.edu

65021 ■ Angelo State University–Small Business Development Center
2610 West Ave. N.
Campus Box 10910
San Angelo, TX 76909-0910
Ph:(325)942-2098
Fax: (325)942-2096
Contact: Dave Erickson, Dir.
E-mail: david.erickson@angelo.edu

65022 ■ Best Southwest Small Business Development Center–SBDC
207 N. Cannady Dr.
Cedar Hill, TX 75104
Ph:(972)860-7894
Free: 800-317-7232
Fax: (972)291-1320
Co. E-mail: bswcvcc@airmail.net
URL: http://www.ntsbdc.org/bsw.html
Contact: Herb Kamm, Dir.

65023 ■ Blinn College–Small Business Development Center
902 College Ave.
Brenham, TX 77833
Ph:(979)830-4137
Fax: (979)830-4135
Co. E-mail: sbdc@blinn.edu
URL: http://www.blinncol.edu/sbdc
Contact: Matthew Wehring, Dir.
E-mail: matthew.wehring@blinn.edu

65024 ■ Bonham Satellite–Small Business Development Center–SBDC
1201 E. 9th St.
Bldg. 2, No. 401
Bonham, TX 75418
Ph:(903)583-7232
Fax: (903)583-6706
Contact: Karen Stidham, Dir.
E-mail: stidhamk@grayson.edu

65025 ■ Brazos Valley Small Business Development Center–Bryan College Station
4001 E. 29th St., Ste. 175
Bryan, TX 77802
Ph:(979)260-5222
Fax: (979)260-5229
URL: http://www.bvsbdc.org
Contact: Jim Pillans, Dir.
E-mail: jimp@bvsbdc.org

65026 ■ Brazosport College–Small Business Development Center
500 College Dr.
Lake Jackson, TX 77566
Ph:(979)230-3380
Fax: (409)230-3482
URL: http://www.brazosport.cc.tx.us/~sbdc
Contact: Janice Goines, Dir.
E-mail: janice.goines@brazosport.edu

65027 ■ College of the Mainland–Small Business Development Center
1200 Amburn Rd.
Texas City, TX 77591
Ph:(409)938-1211
Fax: (409)938-7578
Contact: Elizabeth Boudreau, Dir.

65028 ■ Collin County Community College–Small Business Development Center
Courtyard Center for Professional & Economic Development
4800 Preston Park Blvd., Ste. A126
Box 15
Plano, TX 75093
Ph:(972)985-3770
Fax: (972)985-3775
Co. E-mail: sbdc@ccccd.edu
URL: http://www.collinsbdc.com
Contact: Lynn Ellis, Dir.

65029 ■ Dallas County Community College–North Texas Small Business Development Center
1402 Corinth St.
Dallas, TX 75215
Ph:(214)860-5831
Free: 800-350-7232
Fax: (214)860-5813
URL: http://www.bizcoach.org/region
Contact: Liz Klimback, Regional Dir.

65030 ■ Dallas County Community College District's Cedar Valley College–Small Business Development Center
207 N. Cannady Dr.
Cedar Hill, TX 75104

Ph:(972)860-7894
Fax: (972)291-1320
Co. E-mail: bswcvcc@airmail.net
URL: http://www.ntsbdc.org/bsw.html
Contact: Obie Greenleaf, Dir.

65031 ■ Del Mar College–Small Business Development Center
101 Baldwin
Corpus Christi, TX 78404
Ph:(361)698-1021
Fax: (361)698-1024
Contact: Ann Fierova, Dir.
E-mail: afierova@delmar.edu

65032 ■ Denton Satellite SBDC
414 Parkway
Denton, TX 76201-9046
Ph:(940)380-1849
Fax: (940)382-0040
Contact: Pam Livingston, Coordinator
E-mail: ckeeler@nctc.edu

65033 ■ El Paso Community College–Small Business Development Center
1359 Lomaland Dr., Ste. 535
El Paso, TX 79935
Ph:(915)831-7743
Fax: (915)831-7734
URL: http://www.elpasosbdc.biz/
Contact: Roque R. Segura, Dir.
E-mail: rsegur12@epcc.edu

65034 ■ Galveston College–Small Business Development Center
4015 Avenue Q
Galveston, TX 77550
Ph:(409)944-4242
Fax: (409)944-1500
Co. E-mail: hrmail@gc.edu
URL: http://www.gc.edu/gc/Default.asp
Contact: Mary Jan Lantz, Dir.

65035 ■ Galveston County–Small Business Development Center
8419 Emmett F. Lowry Expressway
Texas City, TX 77591-2249
Ph:(409)933-1414
URL: http://www.qcsbdc.com/

65036 ■ Grayson County College–Small Business Development Center
6101 Grayson Dr.
Denison, TX 75020
Ph:(903)463-8787
Free: 800-316-7232
Fax: (903)463-5437
URL: http://www.ntsbdc.org/grayson.html
Contact: Karen Stidham, Dir.
E-mail: stidhamk@grayson.edu

65037 ■ Greater Corpus Christi Business Alliance–Small Business Development Center
1201 N. Shoreline
Corpus Christi, TX 78401

Ph:(512)881-1847
Fax: (512)882-4256
Contact: Rudy Ortiz, Dir.

65038 ■ Houston International Trade Center–Small Business Development Center
University of Houston
2302 Fannin, Ste. 300
Houston, TX 77002
Ph:(713)752-8404
Fax: (713)756-1515
Contact: Carlos J. Lopez, Dir.

65039 ■ International Assistance Center–SBDC
World Trade Center, Ste. 156A
2050 Stemmons Fwy.
PO Box 420451
Dallas, TX 75342
Ph:(214)747-1300
Free: 800-337-7232
Fax: (214)748-7937
Contact: Lorraine McCord, Dir.
E-mail: lxm9830@dcccd

65040 ■ Kilgore College–SBDC
911 Loop 281, Ste. 209
Longview, TX 75601
Ph:(903)757-5857
Free: 800-338-7232
Fax: (903)753-7920
URL: http://www.kilgore.edu/sbdc.asp
Contact: Brad Bunt, Dir.
E-mail: bradbunt@aol.com

65041 ■ Kingsville Chamber of Commerce–Small Business Development Center
635 E. King Ave.
PO Box 1030
Kingsville, TX 78363
Ph:(361)592-6438
Fax: (361)592-0866
Co. E-mail: chamber@kingsville.org
Contact: Kathy A. Martinez, Exec. Dir.

65042 ■ Lamar State College at Port Arthur–Small Business Development Center
1401 Procter
Port Arthur, TX 77641
Ph:(409)984-6531
Fax: (409)984-6063
URL: http://www.portarthur.com/sbdc
Contact: Linda Tait, Dir.
E-mail: linda.tait@lamarpa.edu

65043 ■ Lamar University–Small Business Development Center
850 Georgia
Beaumont, TX 77705
Ph:(409)880-2367
Free: 800-722-3443
Fax: (409)880-2201
URL: http://www.lamar.edu/sbdc?
Contact: Gene Arnold, Dir.

65044 ■ Laredo Development Foundation–Small Business Development Center
616 Leal St.
Laredo, TX 78041
Ph:(956)722-0563
Fax: (956)722-6247
Contact: Aracelia Lozano, Acting Dir.
E-mail: lozano@laredo-ldf.com

65045 ■ Lee College–Small Business Development Center
312 W. Sterling St.
Baytown, TX 77522
Ph:(281)425-6309
Fax: (713)425-6307
Co. E-mail: thathawa@lee.edu
Contact: Tommy Hathaway, Dir.

65046 ■ McLennan Community College–Small Business Development Center
1400 College Dr.
Waco, TX 76708
Ph:(254)299-8141
Free: 800-349-7232
Fax: (254)299-8054
URL: http://www.mclennan.edu/sbdc/sbdc.html
Contact: Belinda Pillow, Dir.

65047 ■ Middle Rio Grande Development Council–Small Business Development Center
209 N. Getty St.
Uvalde, TX 78801
Ph:(830)278-2527
Fax: (830)278-2929
Contact: Sheri Rutledge, Dir.

65048 ■ Midlothian SBDC
330 N. 8th St., Ste. 203
Midlothian, TX 76065-0609
Ph:(214)775-4336
Fax:(214)775-4337

65049 ■ Midwestern State University–Small Business Development Center
3410 Taft Blvd.
Wichita Falls, TX 76308
Ph:(940)397-4373
Fax: (940)397-4374
Co. E-mail: msusbdc@mwsu.edu
URL: http://www.msusbdc.org/
Contact: Vanda Wright, Dir.

65050 ■ Navarro College–Small Business Development Center
120 N. 12th St.
Corsicana, TX 75110
Ph:(903)874-0658
Fax: (254)874-4187
URL: http://www.ntsbdc.org/navarro.html
Contact: Antonio Ortega, Dir.
E-mail: tony.ortega@navarrocollege.edu

65051 ■ North Central Texas College–Small Business Development Center
1525 W. California
Gainesville, TX 76240
Ph:(940)668-4220
Free: 800-351-7232
Fax: (940)668-6049
Co. E-mail: nctc_sbdc@lists.nctc.edu
URL: http://www.nctc.edu/sbdc/sbdc.html
Contact: Cathy Keeler, Dir.

65052 ■ North Harris Montgomery–Community College District SBDC
5000 Research Forest Dr.
The Woodlands, TX 77381
Ph:(832)813-6674
Co. E-mail: info@nhmccd.edu
URL: http://www.dstc.nhmccd.edu
Contact: Betsy McKernan, Dir.

65053 ■ North Harris Montgomery Community College District–Small Business Development Center
250 N. Sam Houston Pkwy. E.
Houston, TX 77060
Ph:(281)260-3500
Fax: (281)260-3162
URL: http://www.northhoustonbusiness.com
Contact: Kay Hamilton, Dir.

65054 ■ Northeast Texarkana–Small Business Development Center
PO Box 1307
Mt. Pleasant, TX 75455
Ph:(903)897-2956
Free: 800-357-7232
Fax: (903)897-1106
Co. E-mail: sbdcnetcc@aol.com
Contact: Bob Wall, Dir.

65055 ■ Paris Junior College–Small Business Development Center
2400 Clarksville St.
Paris, TX 75460
Ph:(903)782-0224
Fax: (903)782-0219
URL: http://sbdcparis.org
Contact: Patricia Bell Dir., Dir.
E-mail: pbell@parisjc.edu

65056 ■ Prairie View A&M University–Small Business Development Center
Prairie View A&M University
Hobart Taylor Bldg., Rm. 1B117
Prairie View, TX 77081
Ph:(936)857-4060
Fax: (936)857-2628
Co. E-mail: SBDC@pvamu.edu
URL: http://cob.pvamu.edu/sbdc
Contact: Dan T. Rhodes, Dir.
E-mail: DTRodes@pvamu.edu

65057 ■ Bill J. Priest Institute for Economic Development–Dallas SBDC
1402 Corinth St.
Dallas, TX 75215
Ph:(214)860-5900
Free: 800-348-7232
Fax: (214)860-5881
Contact: Pamela Speraw, Dir.

65058 ■ Sam Houston State University–Small Business Development Center
2424 Sam Houston Ave., Bldg. A
Box 2058
Huntsville, TX 77341-2058
Ph:(936)294-3737
Fax: (936)294-3738
URL: http://www.shsu.edu/~sbd
Contact: Robert A. Barragan, Dir.

65059 ■ San Jacinto College–Small Business Development Center
2006 E. Broadway, Ste. 101
Pearland, TX 77581
Ph:(281)485-5214
URL: http://www.sicd.cc.tx.us/sbdc
Contact: Michael L. Moore, Dir.
E-mail: michael.moore@sicd.edu

65060 ■ Small Business Development Center for Enterprise Excellence–SBDC
7300 Jack Newell Blvd., S.
Fort Worth, TX 76118-7115
Ph:(817)272-5930
Fax: (817)272-5998
Contact: Jo An Weddle, Dir.
E-mail: jweddle@arri.uta.edu

65061 ■ South West Texas Border Region SBDC–University of Texas at San Antonio
San Antonio, TX 78207-4415
Ph:(210)458-2742
Fax: (210)458-2464
URL: http://501 W. Durango Blvd.
Contact: Alberto Salgado, Region Dir.
E-mail: albert.salgado@utsa.edu

65062 ■ Sul Ross State University–Big Bend SBDC Satellite
PO Box C-47, Rm. 319
Alpine, TX 79832
Ph:(915)837-8694
Fax: (915)837-8104
Contact: Dave Wilson, Dir.
E-mail: dwilson@sulross.edu

65063 ■ Tarleton State University–Small Business Development Center
College of Business Administration
Box T-0650
Stephenville, TX 76402
Ph:(254)968-9330
Fax: (254)968-9329
Co. E-mail: burch@tarleton.edu
URL: http://www.tsusbdc.org/
Contact: Ron Beck, Dir.

E-mail: beck@tarleton.edu

65064 ■ Tarrant County College–Small Business Development Center
1150 South Fwy., Ste. 229
Ft. Worth, TX 76104
Ph:(817)871-6028
Fax: (817)332-6417
URL: http://web.tccd.net/ce/ce_sbdc.asp
Contact: David Edmonds, Dir.
E-mail: david.edmonds@tccd.net

65065 ■ Technology Assistance Center–Texas-North SBDC
1402 Corinth St.
Dallas, TX 75215
Ph:(214)860-5835
Fax: (214)860-5813
URL: http://www.ntsbdc.org
Contact: Liz Kimback, Region Dir.
E-mail: emk9402@dcccd.edu

65066 ■ Texas Center for Government Contracting and Technology Assistance–Small Business Development Center
1402 Corinth St.
Dallas, TX 75215
Ph:(214)860-5889
Free: 800-348-7232
Fax: (214)860-5881
Contact: Chuck Waldrop, Dir.

65067 ■ Texas-Houston SBDC–University of Houston
2302 Fannin, Ste. 200
Houston, TX 77002
Ph:(713)752-8425
Fax: (713)756-1500
URL: http://sbdcnetwork.uh.edu
Contact: Mike Young, Exec. Dir.
E-mail: fyoung@uh.edu

65068 ■ Texas State University at San Marcos–Small Business Development Center
1250 Highway 123, No. 104
San Marcos, TX 78666
Ph:(512)558-7050
Fax: (512)558-7053
Contact: Larry Lucero, Dir.
E-mail: 1126@txstate.edu

65069 ■ Texas Tech University–Northwestern Texas SBDC
2579 S. Loop 289, Ste. 210
Lubbock, TX 79423
Ph:(806)745-3973
Free: 800-992-7232
Fax: (806)745-6207
URL: http://www.ttusbdc.org/lubbock/
Contact: Steve Anderson, Dir.

65070 ■ Texas Tech University–Small Business Development Center
500 Chestnut, Ste. 601
Abilene, TX 79602
Ph:(325)670-0300
Fax: (325)670-0311
URL: http://www.ttusbdc.org/abilene
Contact: Judy Wilhelm, Dir.

65071 ■ Trinity Valley Community College–Small Business Development Center
100 Cardinal Dr.
Athens, TX 75751
Ph:(903)675-7403
Fax: (903)675-5199
URL: http://www.ntsbdc.org/trinity.html
Contact: Judy Loden Dir., Dir.
E-mail: jloden@tvcc.edu

65072 ■ Tyler Junior College–Small Business Development Center
1530 South SW Loop 323, Ste. 100
Tyler, TX 75701-2556
Ph:(903)510-2975
Fax: (903)510-2972

Contact: Donald Proudfoot Dir., Dir.
E-mail: dpro@tjc.edu

65073 ■ University of Houston–Fort Bend County SBDC
2440 Texas Pkwy., Ste. 220
Missouri City, TX 77489
Ph:(281)499-9787

65074 ■ University of Houston–Texas Information Procurement Service–Small Business Development Center (2302)
2302 Fannin, Ste. 200
Houston, TX 77002
Ph:(713)752-8477
Free: 800-252-7232
Fax: (713)756-1515
URL: http://www.business.txstate.edu/sbdc/local.htm
Contact: Larry Lucero, Dir.

65075 ■ University of Houston–Texas Manufacturing Assistance Center–TMAC Gulf Coast (815 T)–SBDC (MAC Bldg.)
815 TMAC Bldg.
Houston, TX 77204-6023
Ph:(832)842-7043
Free: 800-625-4876
Fax: (713)747-7509
Co. E-mail: TMACGC@uh.edu
URL: http://tech.uh.edu/tmac

65076 ■ University of Houston Coastal Plains–Small Business Development Center
2200 7th St., Ste. 300
Bay City, TX 77414
Ph:(979)244-8466

65077 ■ University of Houston–Victoria–Small Business Development Center
700 Main Center, Ste. 101
Victoria, TX 77901
Ph:(361)575-8944
Fax: (361)570-8931
Contact: Carole Parks, Dir.
E-mail: parksc@viptx.net

65078 ■ University of Texas (Downtown San Antonio)–South Texas Border SBDC
501 W. Durango
San Antonio, TX 78207-4415
Ph:(210)458-2020
Fax: (210)458-2464
Co. E-mail: rmckinle@utsadt.utsa.edu
URL: http://www.iedtexas.org
Contact: Robert McKinley, Regional Dir.
E-mail: mckinley@utsa.edu

65079 ■ University of Texas–Pan American–Small Business Development Center–Rio Grande Valley Empowerment Zone (2412)
2412 S. Closner
Edinburg, TX 78539
Ph:(956)316-2610
Fax: (956)316-2612
Contact: Pedro Salazar, Dir.

65080 ■ University of Texas–Permian Basin–Small Business Development Center
4901 E. University Blvd.
Odessa, TX 79762
Ph:(915)552-2455
Free: 800-992-7232
Fax: (915)552-3455
URL: http://www.utpbsbdc.org
Contact: Dana Mondragon, Interim Dir.

65081 ■ West Texas A&M University–Small Business Development Center
701 S. Taylor, Ste. 118
1800 S. Washington, Ste. 209
Amarillo, TX 79101
Ph:(806)372-5151
Fax: (806)372-5261
Contact: P.J. Pronger, Dir.

SMALL BUSINESS ASSISTANCE PROGRAMS

65082 ■ Texas Department of Economic Development and Tourism–Business Development Division
1700 N Congress Ave.
PO Box 12728
Austin, TX 78711-2728
Ph:(512)936-0100
Free: 800-888-0511
Fax: (512)936-0093
URL: http://www.tded.state.tx.us
Description: Provides assistance to small businesses across the state in obtaining permits and in business development.

65083 ■ Texas Department of Economic Development and Tourism–Business Development Division–Advisory Council on Small Business Issues (221 E)
221 E 11Th St.
PO Box 12428
Austin, TX 78711-2728
Ph:(512)936-0101
Free: 800-888-0511
Fax: (512)936-0440
URL: http://www.governor.state.tx.us/ecodevo/
Description: Proposes long-range plans for small business activities.

BETTER BUSINESS BUREAUS

65084 ■ Better Business Bureau of Abilene
3300 S 14th St., Ste. 307
Abilene, TX 79605-5052
Ph:(325)691-1533
Fax: (325)691-0309
Co. E-mail: info@abilene.bbb.org
URL: http://www.abilene.bbb.org
Contact: Steve Abel, Pres.

65085 ■ Better Business Bureau of Amarillo, Texas
720 S Tyler St., Ste. 112B
Amarillo, TX 79101-2354
Ph:(806)379-6222
Fax: (806)379-8206
Co. E-mail: info@amarillobbb.org
URL: http://www.amarillobbb.org
Contact: Janna Kiehl, Pres.

65086 ■ Better Business Bureau, Austin
1005 La Posada Dr.
Austin, TX 78752
Ph:(512)445-2911
Fax: (512)445-2096
Co. E-mail: info@austin.bbb.org
URL: http://www.centraltx.bbb.org

65087 ■ Better Business Bureau of Brazos Valley
418 Tarrow
College Station, TX 77840-1822
Ph:(979)260-2222
Fax: (979)846-0276
Co. E-mail: info@bbbbryan.org
URL: http://www.bbbbryan.org
Contact: Larry Lightfoot, Pres.

65088 ■ Better Business Bureau of Central East Texas
PO Box 6652
Tyler, TX 75711-6652
Ph:(903)581-5704
Free: 800-443-0131
Fax: (903)534-8644
Co. E-mail: contactus@easttexasbbb.org
URL: http://www.tyler.bbb.org
Contact: Kay Robinson, Pres.

65089 ■ Better Business Bureau of Central and South Central Texas
2210 Washington Ave.
Waco, TX 76701
Ph:(254)755-7772
Fax: (254)755-7774
Co. E-mail: info@waco.bbb.org
URL: http://www.waco.bbb.org
Contact: Susan Morton, Exec.Dir.

65090 ■ Better Business Bureau of the Coastal Bend
101 N Shoreline, Ste. 216
Corpus Christi, TX 78401
Ph:(361)852-4949
Free: 800-379-4222
Fax: (361)885-0628
Co. E-mail: info@corpuschristi.bbb.org
URL: http://www.caller.com/bbb
Contact: Alan Bligh, Pres./CEO

65091 ■ Better Business Bureau of Metropolitan Dallas
1601 Elm St., Ste. 3838
Dallas, TX 75201-4744
Ph:(214)220-2000
Fax: (214)740-0321
Co. E-mail: info@dallas.bbb.org
URL: http://www.dallas.bbb.org
Contact: Jay Newman, Pres./CEO

65092 ■ Better Business Bureau of Metropolitan Houston
1333 West Loop S, Ste. 1200
Houston, TX 77027
Ph:(713)868-9500
Free: 800-275-3626
Fax: (713)867-4947
Co. E-mail: bbbinfo@bbbhou.org
URL: http://www.bbbhou.org
Contact: Dan Parsons, Pres./CEO

65093 ■ Better Business Bureau of North Central Texas
4245 Kemp Blvd., Ste. 900
Wichita Falls, TX 76308-2830
Ph:(940)691-1172
Fax: (940)691-1175
Co. E-mail: bbbnt@bbbnorcentx.org
URL: http://www.wichitafalls.bbb.org
Contact: Monica Horton, Pres.

65094 ■ Better Business Bureau of San Angelo
3134 Executive Dr., Ste. A
San Angelo, TX 76904
Ph:(325)949-2989
Fax: (325)949-3514
Co. E-mail: gfriedrich@wcc.net
URL: http://www.sanangelo.bbb.org
Contact: Ms. Glenna Friedrich, Pres.

65095 ■ Better Business Bureau, San Antonio
1800 NE Loop 410, Ste. 400
San Antonio, TX 78217-5296
Ph:(210)828-9441
Fax: (210)828-3101
Co. E-mail: info@sanantonio.bbb.org
URL: http://www.sanantonio.bbb.org

65096 ■ Better Business Bureau Serving the Heart of Texas
2210 Washington Ave.
Waco, TX 76701-1019
Ph:(254)755-7772
Fax: (254)755-7774
Co. E-mail: info@waco.bbb.org
URL: http://www.waco.bbb.org
Contact: Carie A. Hurt, Pres./CEO

65097 ■ Better Business Bureau of the South Plains
3333 66th St.
Lubbock, TX 79413
Ph:(806)763-0459
Free: 800-687-7890

Fax: (806)744-9748
Co. E-mail: info@bbbsouthplains.org
URL: http://www.bbbsouthplains.org
Contact: Nan Campbell, Pres./CEO

65098 ■ Better Business Bureau of South Texas
2110 W 6th St.
Weslaco, TX 78596
Ph:(956)968-3678
Fax: (956)968-7638
Co. E-mail: info@weslaco.bbb.org
URL: http://www.weslaco.bbb.org

65099 ■ Better Business Bureau of Southeast Texas
PO Box 2988
Beaumont, TX 77704-2988
Ph:(409)835-5348
Fax: (409)838-6858
Co. E-mail: bureau@bbbsetexas.org
URL: http://www.beaumont.bbb.org
Contact: Michael Clayton, Pres.

CHAMBERS OF COMMERCE

65100 ■ Abilene Chamber of Commerce
174 Cypress St., Ste. 200
Abilene, TX 79601
Ph:(325)677-7241
Fax: (325)677-0622
Co. E-mail: info@abilenechamber.com
URL: http://www.abilenechamber.com
Contact: Mike McMahan, Pres.

65101 ■ African American Chamber of Commerce
1717 N. Loop 1604 E, Ste. 220
San Antonio, TX 78232
Ph:(210)490-1624
Fax: (210)490-5294
Co. E-mail: blackchamber@aol.com
Contact: Lou Miller, Pres.

65102 ■ Alamo Chamber of Commerce
130 S 8th St.
Alamo, TX 78516
Ph:(956)787-2117
Fax: (956)782-1172
Co. E-mail: alamocc@hiline.net
URL: http://www.alamochamber.com
Contact: Janice Prickett, Mgr.

65103 ■ Alamo City Chamber of Commerce
600 Hemisfair Plz. Way, Bldg. 406-10
San Antonio, TX 78205
Ph:(210)226-9055
Fax: (210)226-0524
Co. E-mail: newsjournal@alamocitychamber.org
URL: http://www.alamocitychamber.org

65104 ■ Albany Chamber of Commerce
PO Box 185
Albany, TX 76430-0185
Ph:(325)762-2525
Fax: (325)762-3125
Co. E-mail: chamberc@bitstreet.com
URL: http://www.albanytexas.com
Contact: Chuck Senter, Exec. Dir.

65105 ■ Alice Chamber of Commerce
612 E Main St.
PO Box 1609
Alice, TX 78333
Ph:(361)664-3454
Fax: (361)664-2291
Co. E-mail: msmith@alicetx.org
URL: http://www.alicetx.org/Chamberhome.html
Contact: Mike Smith, Exec.VP

65106 ■ Allen Chamber of Commerce
210 W McDermott Dr.
Allen, TX 75013
Ph:(972)727-5585
Fax: (972)727-9000

Co. E-mail: info@allenchamber.com
URL: http://www.allenchamber.com
Contact: Sharon Mayer, Pres./CEO

65107 ■ Alpine Chamber of Commerce
106 N 3rd St.
Alpine, TX 79830
Ph:(432)837-2326
Free: 800-561-3735
Fax: (432)837-1259
Co. E-mail: chamber@alpinetexas.com
URL: http://www.alpinetexas.com
Contact: John Johnson, Exec.Dir.

65108 ■ Alvin-Manvel Area Chamber of Commerce
105 W Willis
PO Box 2028
Alvin, TX 77512-2028
Ph:(281)331-3944
Free: 800-331-4063
Co. E-mail: amcc@alvintexas.org
URL: http://www.alvinmanvelchamber.org
Contact: Connie Elies, Pres.

65109 ■ Amarillo Chamber of Commerce
1000 S Polk St.
Amarillo, TX 79105-9480
Ph:(806)373-7800
Fax: (806)373-3909
Co. E-mail: chamber@amarillo-chamber.org
URL: http://www.amarillo-chamber.org
Contact: Ken Hargrove, Chm.

65110 ■ Anahuac Area Chamber of Commerce
PO Box R
Anahuac, TX 77514
Ph:(409)267-4190
Co. E-mail: info@anahuacchamber.com
URL: http://www.anahuacchamber.com
Contact: Diane Bertrand, Mgr.

65111 ■ Angleton Chamber of Commerce
445 E Mulberry
Angleton, TX 77515
Ph:(979)849-6443
Fax: (979)849-4520
Co. E-mail: beth@angletonchamber.org
URL: http://www.angletonchamber.org
Contact: Beth Journeay, CEO/Pres.

65112 ■ Aransas Pass Chamber of Commerce
130 W Goodnight
Aransas Pass, TX 78336
Ph:(361)758-2750
Free: 800-633-3028
Fax: (361)758-8320
Co. E-mail: info@cableone.net
URL: http://www.aransaspass.org
Contact: Pam Martin, Acting CEO

65113 ■ Arlington Chamber of Commerce
505 E Border St.
Arlington, TX 76010
Ph:(817)275-2613
Fax: (817)261-7589
Co. E-mail: wjurey@arlingtontx.com
URL: http://www.arlingtontx.com
Contact: Wes Jurey, Pres./CEO

65114 ■ Arlington Hispanic Chamber of Commerce
301 S Center St., Ste. 400
Arlington, TX 76010
Ph:(817)461-8815
Fax: (817)795-9499
Co. E-mail: office@hispanic-chamber.org
URL: http://www.hispanic-chamber.org/default.asp
Contact: Art Robles, Chm.

65115 ■ Athens Chamber of Commerce
1206 S Palestine St.
Athens, TX 75751
Ph:(903)675-5181
Free: 800-755-7878

Fax: (903)675-5183
URL: http://www.athenscc.org

65116 ■ Atlanta Area Chamber of Commerce
101 NE St.
PO Box 29
Atlanta, TX 75551
Ph:(903)796-3296
Fax: (903)796-5711
Co. E-mail: atlantaareacoc@aol.com
URL: http://www.atlantatexas.org
Contact: Bob Embry, Pres.

65117 ■ Azle Area Chamber of Commerce
252 W Main St., Ste. A
Azle, TX 76020
Ph:(817)444-1112
Fax: (817)444-1143
Co. E-mail: director@azlechamber.com
URL: http://www.azlechamber.com
Contact: Barbara Jett, Exec.Dir.

65118 ■ Baird Chamber of Commerce
328 Market St.
Baird, TX 79504
Ph:(325)854-2003
Fax: (325)854-1413
Co. E-mail: baird@bairdtexas.com
URL: http://www.bairdtexas.com
Contact: Trish Duque, Pres.

65119 ■ Balch Springs Chamber of Commerce
PO Box 800095
Balch Springs, TX 75180
Ph:(972)557-0988
Fax: (972)286-2681
Co. E-mail: info@balchspringschamber.org
URL: http://www.balchspringschamber.org
Contact: Sandra Wood, Pres.

65120 ■ Ballinger Chamber of Commerce
PO Box 577
Ballinger, TX 76821
Ph:(325)365-2333
Fax: (325)365-3445
Co. E-mail: coc@balingertx.org
URL: http://www.ballingertx.org
Contact: Betty Irby, Pres.

65121 ■ Bandera County Texas Chamber of Commerce
PO Box 2445
Bandera, TX 78003
Ph:(830)796-3280
Free: 800-364-3833
Fax: (830)796-4121
Co. E-mail: cowboy@banderatex.com
URL: http://www.banderatex.com
Contact: Deana Lara, Exec. Administrator

65122 ■ Bastrop Chamber of Commerce
927 Main St.
Bastrop, TX 78602-3809
Ph:(512)303-0558
Fax: (512)303-0305
Co. E-mail: info@bastropchamber.us
URL: http://www.bastropchamber.com
Contact: Susan Weems Wendel, Pres./CEO

65123 ■ Baytown Chamber of Commerce
Amegy Bank Bldg.
1300 Rollingbrook Dr., Ste. 400
Baytown, TX 77521
Ph:(281)422-8359
Fax: (281)428-1758
Co. E-mail: info@baytownchamber.com
URL: http://www.baytownchamber.com
Contact: Tracey S. Wheeler-Martinez, Pres./CEO

65124 ■ Beaumont Chamber of Commerce
1110 Park St.
PO Box 3150
Beaumont, TX 77704-3150
Ph:(409)838-6581
Fax: (409)833-6718
Co. E-mail: chamber@bmtcoc.org

URL: http://www.bmtcoc.org
Contact: Jim Rich, Pres.

65125 ■ Bee County Chamber of Commerce
1705 N St. Mary's
PO Box 4099
Beeville, TX 78102
Ph:(361)358-3267
Fax: (361)358-3966
Co. E-mail: chamber@beeville.net
Contact: Teresa Holland, Office Mgr.

65126 ■ Belton Area Chamber of Commerce
412 E Central Ave.
Belton, TX 76513
Ph:(254)939-3551
Fax: (254)939-1061
Co. E-mail: info@beltonchamber.com
URL: http://www.seebelton.com
Contact: Stephanie O'Banion, Pres./CEO

65127 ■ Big Lake Chamber of Commerce
403A E 2nd St.
Big Lake, TX 76932
Ph:(915)884-2980
Fax: (915)884-1017
Co. E-mail: blcoc@verizon.net
URL: http://www.biglaketx.com
Contact: Debbie Rockwell, Mgr./Dir.

65128 ■ Big Spring Area Chamber of Commerce
PO Box 1391
Big Spring, TX 79721-1391
Ph:(432)263-7641
Free: 800-734-7641
Fax: (432)264-9111
Co. E-mail: nnewell@bigspringchamber.com
URL: http://www.bigspringchamber.com
Contact: Debbye Valverde, Exec.Dir.

65129 ■ Bishop Chamber of Commerce
213 E Main St.
PO Box 426
Bishop, TX 78343-0426
Ph:(361)584-2214
Fax: (361)584-2214
Co. E-mail: bishopcc@intcomm.net
URL: http://www.bishoptx.com
Contact: Betty Paschal, Sec./Mgr.

65130 ■ Blanco Chamber of Commerce
PO Box 626
Blanco, TX 78606-0626
Ph:(830)833-5101
Fax: (830)833-5101
Co. E-mail: blancotx@moment.net
URL: http://www.blancochamber.com
Contact: Sue McFarlin, Pres.

65131 ■ Bolivar Peninsula Chamber of Commerce
PO Box 1170
Crystal Beach, TX 77650
Ph:(409)684-5940
Free: 800-386-7863
Fax: (409)684-3123
Co. E-mail: bolivarchamber@earthlink.net
URL: http://www.bolivarchamber.org
Contact: Ann Willis, Pres.

65132 ■ Bonham Area Chamber of Commerce and Economic Development
327 N Main St.
Bonham, TX 75418-4342
Ph:(903)583-4811
Fax: (903)583-7972
Co. E-mail: bonhamchamber@cableone.net
URL: http://www.bonhamchamber.com
Contact: Deloris Clemons, Chm.

65133 ■ Borger Chamber of Commerce
613 N Main St.
PO Box 490
Borger, TX 79008-0490
Ph:(806)274-2211
Fax: (806)273-3488

Co. E-mail: borgerchamber@amaonline.com
URL: http://www.borgerchamber.org
Contact: Beverly Benton, Pres./CEO

65134 ■ Bovina Chamber of Commerce
PO Box 550
Bovina, TX 79009
Ph:(806)251-1116
Contact: Toya De Leon, Pres.

65135 ■ Bowie Chamber of Commerce
309 N Smythe St.
Bowie, TX 76230
Ph:(940)872-1173
Free: (866)872-1173
Fax: (940)872-3291
Co. E-mail: bowiechamber@morgan.net
Contact: Bonnie Julius Knouse, Exec.VP

65136 ■ Brady - McCulloch County Chamber of Commerce
101 E 1st St.
Brady, TX 76825-4999
Ph:(325)597-3491
Fax: (325)792-9181
Co. E-mail: chamber@bradytx.us
URL: http://www.bradytx.com
Contact: Mrs. Wendy Ellis, Community Development Dir.

65137 ■ Brazoria Chamber of Commerce
PO Box 992
Brazoria, TX 77422-0992
Ph:(979)798-6100
Fax: (979)798-6101
Co. E-mail: brazoriachamber@sat.net
Contact: Mickey Jones, Exec.Dir.

65138 ■ Breckenridge Chamber of Commerce
2410 W Walker St.
PO Box 1466
Breckenridge, TX 76424
Ph:(254)559-2301
Fax: (254)559-7104
Co. E-mail: brkcofc@texasisp.com
URL: http://www.breckenridgetexas.com
Contact: Patsy Hagler, VP of Operations

65139 ■ Bridge City Chamber of Commerce
150 W Roundbunch
Bridge City, TX 77611-2522
Ph:(409)735-5671
Fax: (409)735-7017
Co. E-mail: chamber@exp.net
URL: http://www.cityofbridgecity.org
Contact: Julia E. Myers, Exec.VP

65140 ■ Bridgeport Area Chamber of Commerce
1107 8th St.
PO Box 1104
Bridgeport, TX 76426
Ph:(940)683-2076
Fax: (940)683-3969
Co. E-mail: chamber@wccs.net
URL: http://www.bport.com
Contact: Susan Miller, Exec. Dir.

65141 ■ Brownsville Chamber of Commerce
1600 University Blvd.
Brownsville, TX 78520
Ph:(956)542-4341
Fax: (956)504-3348
Co. E-mail: info@brownsvillechamber.com
URL: http://www.brownsvillechamber.com
Contact: Angela R. Burton, Pres./CEO

65142 ■ Brownwood Area Chamber of Commerce
PO Box 880
Brownwood, TX 76801-0880
Ph:(915)646-9535
Fax: (915)643-6686
Co. E-mail: info@brownwoodchamber.org
URL: http://www.brownwoodchamber.org
Contact: LaNita Richmond, Exec.VP

65143 ■ Buda Area Chamber of Commerce
PO Box 904
Buda, TX 78610
Ph:(512)295-9999
Fax: (512)295-9999
Co. E-mail: forinfo@budachamber.com
URL: http://www.budachamber.com
Contact: Richard Schneider, Pres.

65144 ■ Buffalo Chamber of Commerce
PO Box 207
Buffalo, TX 75831
Ph:(903)322-5810
Fax: (903)322-3849
URL: http://www.buffalotex.com
Contact: DeAnna Ezell, Pres.

65145 ■ Bulverde/Spring Branch Area Chamber of Commerce
PO Box 1132
Spring Branch, TX 78070
Ph:(830)438-4285
Free: (866)BUL-VERDE
Fax: (830)438-8572
Co. E-mail: bsbacoc@gvtc.com
URL: http://www.bulverdechamber.com
Contact: Dale Wilken, Pres.

65146 ■ Burkburnett Chamber of Commerce
104 W 3rd St.
Burkburnett, TX 76354
Ph:(940)569-3304
Free: 800-460-BURK
Fax: (940)569-3306
Co. E-mail: burk@burkburnett.org
URL: http://burkburnett.org
Contact: Dick Vallon, Exec.Dir.

65147 ■ Burleson Area Chamber of Commerce
PO Box 9
Burleson, TX 76028
Ph:(817)295-6121
Fax: (817)295-6192
Co. E-mail: goodlife@burleson.org
URL: http://www.burleson.org
Contact: Greg Solomon, Pres.

65148 ■ Burleson County Chamber of Commerce - Caldwell Office
212A W Buck St.
PO Box 87
Caldwell, TX 77836
Ph:(979)567-0000
Fax: (979)567-0818
Co. E-mail: pamwood@bc-chamber.com
URL: http://www.rtis.com/reg/somerville
Contact: Pam Wood, Mgr.

65149 ■ Burnet Chamber of Commerce
229 S Pierce
Burnet, TX 78611
Ph:(512)756-4297
Fax: (512)754-2548
Co. E-mail: info@burnetchamber.org
URL: http://www.burnetchamber.org
Contact: Patti Alford, Mgr.

65150 ■ Calvert Chamber of Commerce
PO Box 132
Calvert, TX 77837-0132
Ph:(979)364-2559
Co. E-mail: calverttx@calverttx.com
URL: http://www.calverttx.com
Contact: Walter Qualls, Pres.

65151 ■ Cameron Area Chamber of Commerce
102 E 1st St.
PO Box 432
Cameron, TX 76520
Ph:(254)697-4979
Fax: (254)697-2345
Co. E-mail: chamber@tlab.net
URL: http://www.cameron-tx.com
Contact: Brandy McLerran, Mgr.

65152 ■ Camp County Chamber of Commerce
202 Jefferson St.
Pittsburg, TX 75686
Ph:(903)856-3442
Fax: (903)856-2570
Co. E-mail: thobbs@pittsburgchamber.com
URL: http://www.campchamber.com
Contact: Michele Ragsdale, Pres.

65153 ■ Canadian-Hemphill County Chamber of Commerce
216 S 2nd St.
Canadian, TX 79014
Ph:(806)323-6234
Fax: (806)323-9243
Co. E-mail: canadiantx@cebridge.net
URL: http://www.canadiantx.com
Contact: Jessica Russell, Exec.Asst.

65154 ■ Canton Chamber of Commerce
119 N Buffalo St.
Canton, TX 75103
Ph:(903)567-2991
Fax: (903)567-5708
Co. E-mail: canton@chambercantontx.com
URL: http://www.chambercantontx.com
Contact: Rona Watson, Pres.

65155 ■ Canyon Chamber of Commerce
1518 5th Ave.
Canyon, TX 79015
Ph:(806)655-7815
Free: 800-999-9481
Fax: (806)655-4608
Co. E-mail: info@canyonchamber.org
URL: http://www.canyonchamber.org
Contact: Kelly Hamilton, Exec.Dir.

65156 ■ Cedar Hill Chamber of Commerce
300 W Houston St.
PO Box 355
Cedar Hill, TX 75104
Ph:(972)291-7817
Fax: (972)291-8101
Co. E-mail: info@cedarhillchamber.org
URL: http://cedarhillchamber.org
Contact: Matt McCormick, Pres.

65157 ■ Cedar Park Chamber of Commerce and Tourism
1490 E Whitestone Blvd., Bldg. 2, Ste. 180
PO Box 805
Cedar Park, TX 78613
Ph:(512)260-7800
Fax: (512)260-9269
Co. E-mail: info@cedarparkchamber.org
URL: http://www.cedarparkchamber.org
Contact: Harold Dean, Pres.

65158 ■ Cen-Tex Hispanic Chamber of Commerce
915 La Salle Ave.
Waco, TX 76701
Ph:(254)754-7111
Fax: (254)754-3456
Co. E-mail: info@wacohispanicchamber.com
URL: http://www.wacohispanicchamber.com
Contact: Fidencio Marquez, Pres.

65159 ■ Centerville Chamber of Commerce
PO Box 422
Centerville, TX 75833
Ph:(903)536-7261
Co. E-mail: centerville75833@yahoo.com
URL: http://www.centervilletexas.com
Contact: Tim Coffey, Pres.

65160 ■ Chamber of Commerce for Individuals with DisABILITIES
PO Box 222008
Dallas, TX 75222-2008
Ph:(214)533-3773
Fax: (775)243-4877
Co. E-mail: chamber4@airmail.net
URL: http://Chamber4US.org
Contact: Mr. Dan Howell, Acting Dir.

65161 ■ Childress Chamber of Commerce
237 Commerce St.
PO Box 35
Childress, TX 79201
Ph:(940)937-2567
Fax: (940)937-8836
Co. E-mail: chamber@childresstexas.net
URL: http://biz.childresstexas.net/chamberofcommerce
Contact: Peggy Teague, Pres.

65162 ■ Cisco Chamber of Commerce
309 Conrad Hilton Ave.
Cisco, TX 76437
Ph:(254)442-2537
Fax: (254)442-2553
Co. E-mail: ciscoinfo@ciscotx.com
URL: http://ciscotx.com
Contact: Mr. John Waggoner, Mgr.

65163 ■ City of South Houston Chamber of Commerce
58 Spencer Hwy.
PO Box 75
South Houston, TX 77587
Ph:(713)943-0244
Fax: (713)943-3978
Co. E-mail: sohochamber@sbcglobal.net
URL: http://www.southhoustonchamber.org
Contact: JoAnn Parish, Exec. Admin.

65164 ■ Clarendon - Donley County Chamber of Commerce
318 S Kearney
Clarendon, TX 79226
Ph:(806)874-2421
Free: 800-579-4023
Co. E-mail: clarendon@arn.net
URL: http://www.donleytx.com
Contact: Judith P. Burlin, Exec.Dir.

65165 ■ Clear Lake Area Chamber of Commerce
1201 E NASA Pkwy.
Houston, TX 77058-3391
Ph:(281)488-7676
Fax: (281)488-8981
Co. E-mail: chamber@clearlakearea.com
URL: http://www.clearlakearea.com
Contact: Claudette Alderman, Pres./CEO

65166 ■ Cleburne Chamber of Commerce
1511 W Henderson St.
PO Box 701
Cleburne, TX 76033-0701
Ph:(817)645-2455
Fax: (817)641-3069
Co. E-mail: info@cleburnechamber.com
URL: http://www.cleburnechamber.com
Contact: Ms. Cathy Marchel, Pres.

65167 ■ Clifton Chamber of Commerce
115 N Ave. D
Clifton, TX 76634
Ph:(254)675-3720
Free: 800-344-3720
Co. E-mail: clifton.chamber@htcomp.net
URL: http://www.cliftontexas.org
Contact: Trudy Sheffield, Exec.VP

65168 ■ Coldspring/San Jacinto County Chamber of Commerce
31 N Butler
PO Box 980
Coldspring, TX 77331-0980
Ph:(936)653-2184
Fax: (936)653-2184
Co. E-mail: ccc@coldspringtexas.org
URL: http://www.coldspringtexas.org
Contact: Betty Russo, Exec.Dir.

65169 ■ Coleman County Chamber of Commerce, Agriculture and Tourist Bureau
218 Commercial Ave.
PO Box 796
Coleman, TX 76834
Ph:(325)625-2163

Fax: (325)625-2163
Co. E-mail: coleman@web-access.net
URL: http://www.colemantexas.org
Contact: Mary Griffis, Exec.Dir.

65170 ■ Colleyville Area Chamber of Commerce
6700 Colleyville Blvd.
Colleyville, TX 76034
Ph:(817)488-7148
Fax: (817)488-4242
Co. E-mail: info@colleyvillechamber.org
URL: http://www.colleyvillechamber.org
Contact: Ret Stansberger, Pres.

65171 ■ Collingsworth Chamber of Commerce
PO Box 267
Wellington, TX 79095-0267
Ph:(806)447-5848
Contact: Cheryl Tarver, Exec. Sec.

65172 ■ Colony Chamber of Commerce
6900 Main St.
PO Box 560006
The Colony, TX 75056
Ph:(972)625-4916
Fax: (972)625-8027
Co. E-mail: info@thecolonychamber.org
URL: http://www.thecolonychamber.org
Contact: Allison Mihavics, Pres.

65173 ■ Colorado City Area Chamber of Commerce
157 W 2nd St.
PO Box 242
Colorado City, TX 79512
Ph:(325)728-3403
Fax: (325)728-2911
Co. E-mail: cccham@netwest.com
URL: http://coloradocitychamberofcommerce.com
Contact: Sue Lowrance, Exec.Dir.

65174 ■ Columbus Area Chamber of Commerce
PO Box 20241
Columbus, TX 78934
Ph:(979)732-8385
Fax: (979)732-5881
Co. E-mail: contactus@columbuscofc.org
URL: http://www.columbuscofc.org
Contact: George Fox, Exec.Dir.

65175 ■ Comanche Chamber of Commerce and Agriculture
PO Box 65
100 Indian Creek Dr.
Comanche, TX 76442
Ph:(325)356-3233
Free: 877-356-3233
Fax: (325)356-2940
Co. E-mail: info@comanchechamber.org
URL: http://www.comanchechamber.org
Contact: Darlene Causey, Exec.Dir.

65176 ■ Comfort Chamber of Commerce
PO Box 777
Comfort, TX 78013
Ph:(830)995-3131
Fax: (830)995-5252
Co. E-mail: info@comfort-texas.com
URL: http://www.comfort-texas.com

65177 ■ Commerce Chamber of Commerce
1114 Main St.
PO Box 290
Commerce, TX 75429
Ph:(903)886-3950
Fax: (903)886-8012
Co. E-mail: cchambr@koyote.com
URL: http://www.commerce-chamber.com
Contact: Barbara Kersey, Mgr.

65178 ■ Coppell Chamber of Commerce
PO Box 452
200 E Beltline Rd., Ste. 102
Coppell, TX 75019-0452

Ph:(972)393-2829
Fax: (972)393-7485
Co. E-mail: info@coppellchamber.org
URL: http://www.coppellchamber.org
Contact: Beverly Widner, Pres.

65179 ■ Copperas Cove Chamber of Commerce and Visitors Bureau
204 E Robertson Ave.
Copperas Cove, TX 76522
Ph:(254)547-7571
Fax: (254)547-5015
Co. E-mail: chamber@copperascove.com
URL: http://www.copperascove.com
Contact: David Landmann, Exec.Dir.

65180 ■ Corpus Christi Area Hispanic Chamber of Commerce
PO Box 5523
Corpus Christi, TX 78465-5523
Ph:(361)887-7408
Fax: (361)888-9473
Co. E-mail: jcisneros@cchispanicchamber.org
URL: http://www.cchispanicchamber.org
Contact: Joe C. Cisneros III, Pres./CEO

65181 ■ Corsicana/Navarro County Chamber of Commerce
120 N 12th St.
Corsicana, TX 75110
Ph:(903)874-4731
Free: 877-376-7477
Fax: (903)874-4187
Co. E-mail: chamber@corsicana.org
URL: http://www.corsicana.org
Contact: Daryl W. Schliem, Exec.Dir./CEO

65182 ■ Crane County Chamber of Commerce
409 S Gaston
Crane, TX 79731
Ph:(432)558-2311
Fax: (432)558-7375
Co. E-mail: craneccc@apex2000.net
Contact: Betty Desper, Mgr.

65183 ■ Crockett Area Chamber of Commerce
1100 Edmiston Dr.
Crockett, TX 75835
Ph:(936)544-2359
Fax: (936)544-4355
Co. E-mail: chamber@crockettareachamber.org
URL: http://crockettareachamber.org

65184 ■ Crosby/Huffman Chamber of Commerce
PO Box 452
Crosby, TX 77532
Ph:(281)328-6984
Co. E-mail: info@crosbyhuffmancc.org
URL: http://www.crosbyhuffmancc.org

65185 ■ Crosbyton Chamber of Commerce
114 W Aspen
Crosbyton, TX 79322-2501
Ph:(806)675-2261
Fax: (806)675-2261
Co. E-mail: crosbyton@door.net
Contact: Peggy Ellison, Mgr.

65186 ■ Crowell Chamber of Commerce
PO Box 79
Crowell, TX 79227-0079
Ph:(940)684-1670
Fax: (940)684-1310
Co. E-mail: crowell@chipshot.net
URL: http://www.crowelltex.com
Contact: Larry Smith, Exec.Dir.

65187 ■ Crowley Area Chamber of Commerce
200 E Main St., Ste. D
Crowley, TX 76036
Ph:(817)297-4211
Fax: (817)297-7334
Co. E-mail: info@crowleyareachamber.org

Contact: Jim Wilkinson, Pres.

65188 ■ Cuero Chamber of Commerce and Agriculture
124 E Church St.
Cuero, TX 77954
Ph:(361)275-2112
Co. E-mail: cuerocc@cuero.org
URL: http://www.cuero.org
Contact: Sara Post, Exec.Dir.

65189 ■ Cy-Fair Houston Chamber of Commerce
11050 FM 1960 W, Ste. 100
Houston, TX 77065-3612
Ph:(281)955-1100
Fax: (281)955-0138
Co. E-mail: darcy@cyfairchamber.com
URL: http://www.cyfairchamber.com
Contact: Darcy Mingoia, Pres.

65190 ■ Daingerfield Chamber of Commerce
305 Scurry
Daingerfield, TX 75638
Ph:(903)645-2646
Fax: (903)645-7847
URL: http://www.daingerfield.com
Contact: Janice D. Sullivan, Mgr.

65191 ■ Dalhart Area Chamber of Commerce
PO Box 967
Dalhart, TX 79022
Ph:(806)244-5646
Co. E-mail: chamber@dalhart.org
URL: http://www.dalhart.org
Contact: Kristine Olsen, Pres.

65192 ■ Dallas Black Chamber of Commerce
2838 Martin Luther King, Jr. Blvd.
Dallas, TX 75215
Ph:(214)421-5200
Fax: (214)421-5510
Co. E-mail: rgates@dbcc.org
URL: http://www.dbcc.org
Contact: Reginald Gates, Pres.

65193 ■ Dallas Northeast Chamber of Commerce
6260 E Mockingbird Ln., Ste. 250
Dallas, TX 75214
Ph:(214)828-1400
Fax: (214)828-9994
Co. E-mail: don@dallasnortheastchamber.net
URL: http://www.dallasnortheastchamber.net
Contact: Donald H. Wilson, Pres.

65194 ■ Deaf Smith County Chamber of Commerce
701 N Main
Hereford, TX 79045
Ph:(806)364-3333
Fax: (806)364-3342
Co. E-mail: deafs@wtrt.net
URL: http://www.herefordtx.org/DeafSmithCo/index.htm
Contact: Sid C. Shaw, Exec.VP

65195 ■ Decatur Chamber of Commerce
PO Box 474
Decatur, TX 76234
Ph:(940)627-3107
Fax: (940)627-3771
Co. E-mail: chamber@decaturtx.com
URL: http://www.decaturtx.com
Contact: Misty Hudson, Exec.Dir.

65196 ■ Deer Park Chamber of Commerce
110 Center St.
Deer Park, TX 77536-2734
Ph:(281)479-1559
Fax: (281)476-4041
Co. E-mail: sharonmcl@sbcglobal.net
URL: http://www.deerpark.org
Contact: Sharon McLean, Pres.

65197 ■ DeKalb Chamber of Commerce
PO Box 219
DeKalb, TX 75559

Ph:(903)667-3706
Co. E-mail: smc5058@aol.com
URL: http://dktcoc.home.att.net
Contact: Carolyn McCrary

65198 ■ Del Rio Chamber of Commerce
1915 Veterans Blvd.
Del Rio, TX 78840
Ph:(830)775-3551
Free: 800-889-8149
Fax: (830)774-1813
Co. E-mail: info@drchamber.com
URL: http://www.drchamber.com
Contact: Linda Henderson, Exec.Dir.

65199 ■ DeLeon Chamber of Commerce and Agriculture
133 S Texas St.
DeLeon, TX 76444
Ph:(254)893-2083
Co. E-mail: chamber@deleontexas.com
URL: http://www.deleontexas.com
Contact: Barbara Helberg, Exec.Dir.

65200 ■ Dell Valley Chamber of Commerce
PO Box 709
Dell City, TX 79837
Ph:(915)964-2424
URL: http://www.dellcity.com
Contact: Tracie Kelley, Pres.

65201 ■ Delta County Chamber of Commerce
PO Box 457
Cooper, TX 75432
Ph:(903)395-4314
Fax: (903)395-4318
Co. E-mail: deltacounty@koyote.com
URL: http://www.deltacounty.org
Contact: Gracie Young, Off.Mgr.

65202 ■ Denison Area Chamber of Commerce
313 W Woodard St.
PO Box 325
Denison, TX 75020-0325
Ph:(903)465-1551
Fax: (903)465-8443
Co. E-mail: information@denisontexas.com
URL: http://www.denisontexas.com
Contact: Anna H. McKinney, Pres./COO

65203 ■ Denton Chamber of Commerce
PO Box 1719
Denton, TX 76202-1719
Ph:(940)382-9693
Free: 888-381-1818
Fax: (940)382-0040
Co. E-mail: info@denton-chamber.org
URL: http://www.denton-chamber.org
Contact: Charles W. Carpenter, Pres./Gen.Mgr.

65204 ■ Denver City Chamber of Commerce and CVB
120 N Main St.
Denver City, TX 79323
Ph:(806)592-5424
Free: 888-249-4241
Fax: (806)592-7613
Co. E-mail: dccoc@hiplains.net
Contact: Melissa Howell, Exec.VP

65205 ■ DeSoto Chamber of Commerce
205 E Pleasant Run Rd.
PO Box 220
DeSoto, TX 75123-0220
Ph:(972)224-3565
Fax: (972)224-7228
Co. E-mail: chenderson@desotochamber.org
URL: http://www.desotochamber.org
Contact: Cammy Henderson, Exec. Dir.

65206 ■ Dimmit County Chamber of Commerce
310 W Nopal St.
PO Box 699
Carrizo Springs, TX 78834-6699
Ph:(830)876-5205

Fax: (830)876-5206
Co. E-mail: chambermanager@dimmitcountytx.com
URL: http://www.dimmitcountytx.com
Contact: Bonnie Cervenka, Mgr.

65207 ■ Dimmitt Chamber of Commerce
115 W Bedford St.
Dimmitt, TX 79027
Ph:(806)647-2524
Fax: (806)647-2469
Contact: Roger Malone, Pres.

65208 ■ Dublin Chamber of Commerce
PO Box 309
Dublin, TX 76446
Ph:(254)445-3422
Free: 800-9-DUBLIN
Fax: (254)445-0394
Co. E-mail: info@dublintexas.com
Contact: Jeanette Ward, Mgr.

65209 ■ Dumas - Moore County Chamber of Commerce and Visitors Center
PO Box 735
Dumas, TX 79029-0735
Ph:(806)935-2123
Fax: (806)935-2124
Co. E-mail: samc@xit.net
URL: http://www.dumaschamber.com
Contact: Sam Cartwright, Pres./CEO

65210 ■ Duncanville Chamber of Commerce
300 E Wheatland Rd.
Duncanville, TX 75116
Ph:(972)780-4990
Fax: (972)298-9370
Co. E-mail: info@duncanvillechamber.org
URL: http://www.duncanvillechamber.org
Contact: Lynn McGinley, Pres.

65211 ■ Eagle Lake Chamber of Commerce
121 N McCarty
Eagle Lake, TX 77434
Ph:(979)234-2780
Fax: (979)234-2780
Co. E-mail: chamber@elc.net
Contact: Lana Dulany, Sec.-Treas.

65212 ■ Eagle Pass Chamber of Commerce
400 Garrison St.
PO Box 1188
Eagle Pass, TX 78853-1188
Ph:(830)773-3224
Free: 888-355-3224
Fax: (830)773-8844
Co. E-mail: chamber@eaglepasstexas.com
URL: http://eaglepasstexas.com
Contact: Sandra Martinez, Exec. Dir.

65213 ■ Early Chamber of Commerce and Convention and Tourism Bureau
104 E Industrial Dr.
Early, TX 76802
Ph:(325)649-9317
Free: 800-646-8161
Fax: (325)643-4746
Co. E-mail: ecoc@earlychamber.com
URL: http://www.earlytx.com
Contact: Tammy Means, Sec.

65214 ■ Eastland Chamber of Commerce
102 S Seaman St.
Eastland, TX 76448
Ph:(254)629-2332
Free: 877-265-3747
Co. E-mail: ecofc@eastland.net
URL: http://www.eastlandchamber.com
Contact: Sandra Stevens, Pres.

65215 ■ Eden Chamber of Commerce
PO Box 367
Eden, TX 76837-0367
Fax: (325)869-5075
URL: http://edentexas.com

65216 ■ Edinburg Chamber of Commerce
PO Box 85
602 W University Dr.
Edinburg, TX 78540-0085

Ph:(956)383-4974
Free: 800-800-7214
Fax: (956)383-6942
Co. E-mail: chamber@edinburg.com
URL: http://www.edinburg.com
Contact: Letty Martinez, Interim Pres.

65217 ■ Edwards County Chamber of Commerce
PO Box 267
Rocksprings, TX 78880
Ph:(830)683-6466
Fax: (830)683-3182
Co. E-mail: eccoc@riccnet.com
Contact: Staci Eckhart, Sec.

65218 ■ El Campo Chamber of Commerce and Agriculture
201 E Jackson St.
PO Box 1400
El Campo, TX 77437
Ph:(979)543-2713
Fax: (979)543-5495
Co. E-mail: ecc@elcampochamber.com
URL: http://www.elcampochamber.com
Contact: Becca Socha, Pres.

65219 ■ El Paso Hispanic Chamber of Commerce
201 E Main, Ste. 100
El Paso, TX 79901
Ph:(915)566-4066
Fax: (915)566-9714
Co. E-mail: cindyramosdavidson@ephcc.org
URL: http://www.ephcc.org
Contact: Cindy Ramos-Davidson, CEO

65220 ■ Electra Chamber of Commerce
112 W Cleveland
Electra, TX 76360-2604
Ph:(940)495-3577
Fax: (940)495-3022
Co. E-mail: electracoc@electratexas.org
URL: http://www.electratexas.org
Contact: Sherry Strange, Exec. Dir.

65221 ■ Ennis Chamber of Commerce
108 Chamber of Commerce Dr.
PO Box 1177
Ennis, TX 75119
Ph:(972)878-2625
Fax: (972)875-1473
Co. E-mail: manager@ennis-chamber.com
URL: http://www.ennis-chamber.com
Contact: Patsy Grider, Pres./CEO

65222 ■ Fairfield Chamber of Commerce
PO Box 899
Fairfield, TX 75840
Ph:(903)389-5792
Fax: (903)389-8382
Co. E-mail: chamber@fairfieldtx.com
URL: http://www.fairfieldtxchamber.com
Contact: Kevin Moller, Pres.

65223 ■ Falfurrias Chamber of Commerce
PO Box 476
Falfurrias, TX 78355
Ph:(361)325-3333
Fax: (361)325-2956
Contact: Gustavo Barrera, Exec. Dir.

65224 ■ Farmers Branch Chamber of Commerce
12875 Josey Ln., Ste. 150
Farmers Branch, TX 75234
Ph:(972)243-8966
Fax: (972)243-8968
Co. E-mail: mhall@fbchamber.com
URL: http://www.fbchamber.com
Contact: Melissa Hall, Dir. of Chamber Relations

65225 ■ Farmersville Chamber of Commerce
201 S Main
Farmersville, TX 75442
Ph:(972)782-6533
Fax: (972)782-6603

Co. E-mail: chamber@farmersvilletx.com
URL: http://www.farmersvilletx.com/chamber.htm
Contact: Joe Helmberger, Pres.

65226 ■ Farwell Chamber of Commerce
PO Box 1005
Farwell, TX 79325-1005
Ph:(806)481-3846
Contact: Ronald Byrd, Pres.

65227 ■ Flatonia Chamber of Commerce
208 E Main St.
PO Box 610
Flatonia, TX 78941-0610
Ph:(361)865-3920
Fax: (361)865-2451
Co. E-mail: chamber@flatoniachamber.com
URL: http://flatoniachamber.com
Contact: Ms. Tanya Conner, Exec.Dir.

65228 ■ Floresville Chamber of Commerce
910 10th St.
Floresville, TX 78114
Ph:(830)393-0074
Free: (866)279-6778
Fax: (830)393-9224
Co. E-mail: visitors@felpsis.net
URL: http://www.floresvillechamber.org
Contact: Traci Jaskinia, Exec.Dir.

65229 ■ Flower Mound Chamber of Commerce
700 Parker Sq., Ste. 100
Flower Mound, TX 75028
Ph:(972)539-0500
Fax: (972)539-4307
Co. E-mail: info@flowermoundchamber.com
URL: http://www.flowermoundchamber.com
Contact: Lori Moseley-Fickling, Pres.

65230 ■ Floydada Chamber of Commerce and Floyd County Board of Development
114 W Virginia
PO Box 147
Floydada, TX 79235-0147
Ph:(806)983-3434
Fax: (806)983-5542
Co. E-mail: contact@floydadachamber.com
URL: http://www.floydadachamber.com
Contact: Rachael Castillo, Mgr.

65231 ■ Forney Area Chamber of Commerce
PO Box 570
Forney, TX 75126
Ph:(972)564-2233
Fax: (972)564-3677
Co. E-mail: chamber1@birch.net
URL: http://www.forneytexas.com/chamber
Contact: Laurie Barkham, Pres.

65232 ■ Fort Bend Chamber of Commerce
445 Commerce Green Blvd.
Sugar Land, TX 77478
Ph:(281)491-0800
Fax: (281)491-0112
Co. E-mail: chamber@fortbendcc.org
URL: http://www.fortbendchamber.com
Contact: Louis Garvin, Pres./CEO

65233 ■ Fort Davis Chamber of Commerce
PO Box 378
Fort Davis, TX 79734-0378
Ph:(432)426-3015
Free: 800-524-3015
Fax: (432)426-3978
Co. E-mail: ftdavis@overland.net
URL: http://www.fortdavis.com
Contact: Ms. Lisa Nugent, Exec.Dir.

65234 ■ Fort Stockton Chamber of Commerce
1000 Railroad Ave.
PO Box C
Fort Stockton, TX 79735
Ph:(432)336-2264
Free: 800-336-2166
Fax: (432)336-6114

Co. E-mail: jjackson@ftstockton.net
URL: http://www.fortstockton.org
Contact: Jeri Sue Jackson, Exec.VP

65235 ■ Fort Worth Chamber of Commerce
777 Taylor St., Ste. 900
Fort Worth, TX 76102-4997
Ph:(817)336-2491
Fax: (817)877-4034
Co. E-mail: dbecker@fortworthchamber.com
URL: http://www.fortworthchamber.com
Contact: William J. Thornton Jr., Pres./CEO

65236 ■ Fort Worth Hispanic Chamber of Commerce
1327 N Main St.
Fort Worth, TX 76106
Ph:(817)625-5411
Fax: (817)625-1405
Co. E-mail: rosa.navejar@fwhcc.org
URL: http://www.fwhcc.org
Contact: Rosa Navejar, Pres./CEO

65237 ■ Franklin Chamber of Commerce
PO Box 126
Franklin, TX 77856
Ph:(979)828-3276
Fax: (979)828-1816
Co. E-mail: franklincc@txcyber.com
Contact: Peggy Baxter, Office Mgr.

65238 ■ Franklin County Chamber of Commerce
109 S Kaufman St.
PO Box 554
Mount Vernon, TX 75457
Ph:(903)537-4365
Free: 800-256-3195
Fax: (903)537-4160
Co. E-mail: chamber@mt-vernon.com
URL: http://www.mt-vernon.com/~chamber
Contact: Brenda Hammond, Chamber Mgr.

65239 ■ Fredericksburg Chamber of Commerce
302 E Austin
Fredericksburg, TX 78624
Ph:(830)997-6523
Fax: (830)997-8588
Co. E-mail: evp@fredericksburg-texas.com
URL: http://www.fredericksburg-texas.com
Contact: Joe Kammlah, Pres.

65240 ■ Freer Chamber of Commerce
PO Box 717
Freer, TX 78357
Ph:(361)394-6891
Fax: (361)394-6891
Co. E-mail: freercofc@sbcglobal.net
URL: http://www.freerrattlesnake.com
Contact: Tina Holbein, Chamber Mgr.

65241 ■ Friendswood Chamber of Commerce
PO Box 11
1100 S Friendswood Dr.
Friendswood, TX 77549-0011
Ph:(281)482-3329
Fax: (281)482-3911
Co. E-mail: fwdchmbr@swbell.net
URL: http://www.friendswood-chamber.com
Contact: Carol Jones, Pres.

65242 ■ Frio Canyon Chamber of Commerce
PO Box 743
Leakey, TX 78873-0743
Ph:(830)232-5222
Co. E-mail: friochmbr@hctc.net
URL: http://www.friocanyonchamber.com
Contact: Linda Hassell, Sec.

65243 ■ Friona Chamber of Commerce and Agriculture
621 Main St.
Friona, TX 79035-0905
Ph:(806)250-3491
Fax: (806)250-2348
Co. E-mail: fedc@wtrt.net

URL: http://www.frionachamber.com
Contact: Chris Alexander, Exec. VP

65244 ■ Frisco Chamber of Commerce
6843 Main St.
Frisco, TX 75034
Ph:(972)335-9522
Fax: (972)335-6654
Co. E-mail: aadkins@friscochamber.com
URL: http://www.friscochamber.com
Contact: Audie Adkins, Pres.

65245 ■ Gainesville Area Chamber of Commerce
101 S Culberson St.
PO Box 518
Gainesville, TX 76241
Ph:(940)665-2831
Free: 888-585-4468
URL: http://www.gainesvilletexas.org
Contact: Dana Herr, Pres.

65246 ■ Galleria Chamber of Commerce
5075 Westheimer, Ste. 660
Houston, TX 77056
Ph:(713)629-5555
Fax: (713)629-6403
Co. E-mail: yclayton@galleriachamber.com
URL: http://www.galleriachamber.com
Contact: Yvonne Clayton, Office Mgr.

65247 ■ Galveston Chamber of Commerce
519-25th St.
Galveston, TX 77550
Ph:(409)763-5326
Fax: (409)763-8271
Co. E-mail: gspagnola@galvestonchamber.com
URL: http://www.galvestonchamber.com
Contact: Gina Spagnola, Pres.

65248 ■ Garland Chamber of Commerce
914 S Garland Ave.
Garland, TX 75040
Ph:(972)272-7551
Fax: (972)276-9261
Co. E-mail: paul@garlandchamber.com
URL: http://www.garlandchamber.com
Contact: Paul Mayer, Pres.

65249 ■ Gatesville Area Chamber of Commerce and Agribusiness
2307 S Hwy. 36
Gatesville, TX 76528
Ph:(254)865-2617
Fax: (254)865-5581
URL: http://www.gatesvilletx.info
Contact: Jodie Gaylor, Pres.

65250 ■ George West Chamber of Commerce
PO Box 359
George West, TX 78022
Ph:(361)449-2033
Free: 888-909-3514
Fax: (361)449-1871
Co. E-mail: chamber@fnbnet.net
URL: http://www.georgewest.org
Contact: Becky Allen, Exec. Dir.

65251 ■ Georgetown Chamber of Commerce
100 Stadium Dr.
PO Box 346
Georgetown, TX 78627-0346
Ph:(512)930-3535
Fax: (512)930-3587
Co. E-mail: info@georgetownchamber.org
URL: http://www.georgetownchamber.org
Contact: Mel Pendland, Pres.

65252 ■ Giddings Area Chamber of Commerce
171 E Hempstead
Giddings, TX 78942
Ph:(979)542-3455
Fax: (979)542-7060
Co. E-mail: giddingscofc@verizon.net
URL: http://www.giddingstx.com
Contact: Kathryn Roberts, Pres.

65253 ■ Gilmer Area Chamber of Commerce
106 Buffalo St.
PO Box 854
Gilmer, TX 75644
Ph:(903)843-2413
Co. E-mail: small@etex.net
URL: http://www.gilmerareachamber.com
Contact: Joan Small, Exec.Dir.

65254 ■ Gladewater Chamber of Commerce
215 N Main St.
Gladewater, TX 75647
Ph:(903)845-5501
Free: 800-627-0315
Fax: (903)845-6326
Co. E-mail: info@gladewaterchamber.com
URL: http://www.gladewaterchamber.com

65255 ■ Glen Rose/Somervell County Chamber of Commerce
PO Box 605
Glen Rose, TX 76043
Ph:(254)897-2286
Fax: (254)897-7670
Co. E-mail: grcc@glenrosechamber.com
URL: http://www.glenrosechamber.com

65256 ■ Goliad County Chamber of Commerce
231 S Market St.
PO Box 606
Goliad, TX 77963-0606
Ph:(361)645-3563
Free: 800-848-8674
Fax: (361)645-3579
Co. E-mail: info@goliadcc.org
URL: http://www.goliadcc.org
Contact: Claire Barnhart, Managing Dir.

65257 ■ Gonzales Chamber of Commerce
414 St. Lawrence
PO Box 134
Gonzales, TX 78629-0134
Ph:(830)672-6532
Fax: (830)672-6533
Co. E-mail: info@gonzalestexas.com
URL: http://www.gonzalestexas.com
Contact: Barbara Hand, Exec.Dir.

65258 ■ Graham Chamber of Commerce
608 Elm St.
PO Box 299
Graham, TX 76450
Ph:(940)549-3355
Free: 800-256-4844
Fax: (940)549-6391
Co. E-mail: grahamcc@visitgraham.com
Contact: Lisa McCool, Pres.

65259 ■ Grand Prairie Chamber of Commerce
900 Conover Dr.
Grand Prairie, TX 75051
Ph:(972)264-1558
Fax: (972)264-3419
Co. E-mail: radonna@grandprairiechamber.org
URL: http://www.grandprairiechamber.org
Contact: RaDonna Hessel, Pres.

65260 ■ Grand Saline Chamber of Commerce
PO Box 125
Grand Saline, TX 75140
Ph:(903)962-7147
Fax: (903)962-6291
Co. E-mail: chamber@grandsalinetexas.com
URL: http://www.grandsaline.com
Contact: Donnie Latham, Pres.

65261 ■ Grapevine Chamber of Commerce
200 E Vine St.
PO Box 368
Grapevine, TX 76099-0368
Ph:(817)481-1522
Fax: (817)424-5208
Co. E-mail: info@grapevinechamber.org
URL: http://www.grapevinechamber.org
Contact: Jerry Herrin, Pres./CEO

65262 ■ Greater Austin Chamber of Commerce
210 Barton Springs Rd., Ste. 400
Austin, TX 78704
Ph:(512)478-9383
Fax: (512)478-6389
Co. E-mail: mrollins@austinchamber.org
URL: http://www.austinchamber.org
Contact: Michael W. Rollins, Pres./CEO

65263 ■ Greater Austin Hispanic Chamber of Commerce
2800 S IH 35, Ste. 260
Austin, TX 78704
Ph:(512)476-7502
Fax: (512)476-6417
Co. E-mail: lcge@hispanicaustin.com
URL: http://www.hispanicaustin.com
Contact: Linda Escamilla, Interim Pres.

65264 ■ Greater Boerne Chamber of Commerce
126 Rosewood Ave.
PO Box 2328
Boerne, TX 78006
Ph:(830)249-8000
Free: 888-842-8080
Fax: (830)249-9639
Co. E-mail: info@boerne.org
URL: http://www.boerne.org
Contact: Paula White, Pres./CEO

65265 ■ Greater Cedar Creek Lake Area Chamber of Commerce
1907 W Main
Gun Barrel City, TX 75156
Ph:(903)887-3152
Fax: (903)887-3695
Co. E-mail: info@cclake.net
URL: http://www.cedarcreeklakechamber.com
Contact: Jo Ann Hanstrom, Pres.

65266 ■ Greater Cleveland Chamber of Commerce
222 S Bonham Ave.
PO Box 1733
Cleveland, TX 77328
Ph:(281)592-8786
Fax: (281)592-6949
Co. E-mail: chamber@clevelandtexas.com
URL: http://www.greaterclevelandchamber.com
Contact: Joan Meadows, Exec.VP

65267 ■ Greater Conroe - Lake Conroe Area Chamber of Commerce
505 W Davis
PO Box 2347
Conroe, TX 77305
Ph:(936)756-6644
Fax: (936)756-6462
Co. E-mail: chamber@conroe.org
URL: http://conroe.org
Contact: E.S. Darsey, Pres.

65268 ■ Greater Dallas Asian American Chamber of Commerce
11171 Harry Hines Blvd., Ste. 115
Dallas, TX 75229
Ph:(972)241-8250
Fax: (972)241-8270
Co. E-mail: info@gdaacc.com
URL: http://www.gdaacc.com
Contact: Les Tanaka, Exec.Dir.

65269 ■ Greater Dallas Chamber of Commerce
700 N Pearl St., Ste. 1200
Dallas, TX 75201
Ph:(214)746-6600
Fax: (214)746-6799
Co. E-mail: information@dallaschamber.org
URL: http://www.dallaschamber.org
Contact: Jan Hart Black, Pres.

65270 ■ Greater El Paso Chamber of Commerce
10 Civic Center Plz.
El Paso, TX 79901

Ph:(915)534-0500
Fax: (915)534-0510
Co. E-mail: gepccreceptionist@elpaso.org
URL: http://www.elpaso.org
Contact: Richard E. Dayoub, Pres.

65271 ■ Greater Elgin Chamber of Commerce
114 Central Ave.
PO Box 408
Elgin, TX 78621
Ph:(512)285-4515
Fax: (512)281-3393
Co. E-mail: chamber@elgintx.com
URL: http://www.elgintx.com
Contact: Gena Carter, Pres.

65272 ■ Greater Heights Area Chamber of Commerce
545 W 19th St.
Houston, TX 77008
Ph:(713)861-6735
Fax: (713)861-9310
Co. E-mail: info@heightschamber.com
URL: http://www.heightschamber.com
Contact: Darlene Moody, Pres.

65273 ■ Greater Hewitt Chamber of Commerce
201 Hewitt Dr., Ste. 111
PO Box 661
Hewitt, TX 76643
Ph:(254)666-1200
Fax: (254)666-3181
Co. E-mail: info@hewitt-texas.com
URL: http://www.hewitt-texas.com
Contact: Steve Lundquist, Exec.Dir.

65274 ■ Greater Highlands Chamber of Commerce
127 San Jacinto
Highlands, TX 77562
Ph:(281)426-7227
Co. E-mail: chamber@higlandstxchamber.org
URL: http://www.highlandstxchamber.org
Contact: Ramona Jones, Office Mgr.

65275 ■ Greater Houston Partnership
1200 Smith, Ste. 700
Houston, TX 77002-4400
Ph:(713)844-3600
Fax: (713)844-0200
Co. E-mail: ghp@houston.org
URL: http://www.houston.org
Contact: Jeff Moseley, Pres./CEO

65276 ■ Greater Irving - Las Colinas Chamber of Commerce
5221 N O'Connor Blvd., Ste. 100
Irving, TX 75039
Ph:(214)217-8484
Fax: (214)389-2513
Co. E-mail: chamber@irvingchamber.com
URL: http://www.irvingchamber.com
Contact: Chris Wallace, Pres./CEO

65277 ■ Greater Kaufman Chamber of Commerce and Visitors Bureau
2100 S Washington
PO Box 146
Kaufman, TX 75142
Ph:(972)932-3118
Fax: (972)932-8373
URL: http://www.kaufmantx.com/chamber.html
Contact: Lee Ayres

65278 ■ Greater Keller Chamber of Commerce
200 S Main St.
PO Box 761
Keller, TX 76244
Ph:(817)431-2169
Co. E-mail: keller@kellerchamber.com
URL: http://www.kellerchamber.com
Contact: Ashleah Boykin, Chamber Administrator

65279 ■ Greater Killeen Chamber of Commerce
1 Sante Fe Plz.
Killeen, TX 76541
Ph:(254)526-9551
Fax: (254)526-6090
Co. E-mail: chamber@gkcc.com
URL: http://www.gkcc.com
Contact: John Crutchfield, Pres./CEO

65280 ■ Greater Lavernia Chamber of Commerce
PO Box 1055
Lavernia, TX 78121
Free: (866)352-2462
Co. E-mail: info@lavernia.org
URL: http://www.lavernia.org/html/chamber_of_commerce.html

65281 ■ Greater Lytle Chamber of Commerce
PO Box 148
Lytle, TX 78052-0640
Ph:(830)709-3515
Fax: (830)709-0067
Contact: Reagan Clamon, Pres.

65282 ■ Greater Mission Chamber of Commerce
220 E 9th St.
Mission, TX 78572
Ph:(956)585-2727
Free: 800-580-2700
Fax: (956)585-3044
Co. E-mail: mission@missionchamber.com
URL: http://www.missionchamber.com
Contact: Aida Lerma, Pres./CEO

65283 ■ Greater New Braunfels Chamber of Commerce
PO Box 311417
New Braunfels, TX 78131-1417
Ph:(830)625-2385
Free: 800-572-2626
Fax: (830)625-7918
Co. E-mail: meek@nbcham.org
URL: http://www.nbcham.org
Contact: Michael Meek, Pres.

65284 ■ Greater Orange Area Chamber of Commerce
1012 Green Ave.
Orange, TX 77630
Ph:(409)883-3536
Fax: (409)866-3247
Co. E-mail: thechamber@sbcglobal.net
URL: http://www.goacc.org
Contact: Vicki Scott, Pres./CEO

65285 ■ Greater Pampa Area Chamber of Commerce
PO Box 1942
Pampa, TX 79065
Ph:(806)669-3241
Fax: (806)669-3244
Co. E-mail: pamcoc@pampa.com
URL: http://www.coc.pampa.com
Contact: Clay Rice, Exec.Dir.

65286 ■ Greater Pflugerville Chamber of Commerce
PO Box 483
Pflugerville, TX 78691-0483
Ph:(512)251-7799
Fax: (512)251-7802
Co. E-mail: gpcc@sbcglobal.net
URL: http://www.gpcc.pflugerville.tx.us
Contact: Patricia A. Gervan-Brown, Pres./CEO

65287 ■ Greater Quitman Area Chamber of Commerce
101 E Goode
PO Box 426
Quitman, TX 75783-0426
Ph:(903)763-4411
Free: (866)302-3884
Fax: (903)763-4913
Co. E-mail: qtmncoc@peoplescom.net

URL: http://www.quitman.com
Contact: Ms. Sue Edge, Administrator

65288 ■ Greater San Antonio Chamber of Commerce
602 E Commerce St.
San Antonio, TX 78295
Ph:(210)229-2100
Fax: (210)229-1600
Co. E-mail: skolitz@sachamber.org
URL: http://www.sachamber.org
Contact: Sue Kolitz, Exec. Asst.

65289 ■ Greater Southwest Houston Chamber of Commerce
6900 S Rice Ave.
PO Box 788
Bellaire, TX 77402-0788
Ph:(713)666-1521
Fax: (713)666-1523
Co. E-mail: trishw@gswhcc.org
URL: http://www.southwesthoustonchamber.com
Contact: Trish Wise, Pres./CEO

65290 ■ Greater Waco Chamber of Commerce
PO Box 1220
Waco, TX 76703-1220
Ph:(254)752-6551
Fax: (254)752-6618
Co. E-mail: info@wacochamber.com
URL: http://www.wacochamber.com
Contact: James G. Vaughan Jr., Pres./CEO

65291 ■ Greenville Chamber of Commerce
2713 Stonewall St.
PO Box 1055
Greenville, TX 75403-1055
Ph:(903)455-1510
Fax: (903)455-1736
Co. E-mail: chamber@greenvillechamber.com
URL: http://www.greenville-chamber.org
Contact: Sally Bird, Pres./CEO

65292 ■ Grimes County Chamber of Commerce
117 S LaSalle
PO Box 530
Navasota, TX 77868
Ph:(936)825-6600
Fax: (936)825-3699
Co. E-mail: grimescounty@earthlink.net
URL: http://www.grimescounty.com
Contact: Mary Cunningham, Exec.Dir.

65293 ■ Gruver Chamber of Commerce
PO Box 947
Gruver, TX 79040-0309
Ph:(806)733-5114
Fax: (806)733-5038
Co. E-mail: ajratliff@gruver.net
URL: http://www.gruver.net
Contact: A.J. Ratliff, Mgr.

65294 ■ Hale Center Chamber of Commerce
PO Box 487
Hale Center, TX 79041-0487
Ph:(806)839-2642
Fax: (806)839-9970
Contact: Harley Peoples, Mgr.

65295 ■ Hallettsville Chamber of Commerce
1614 N Texana
PO Box 313
Hallettsville, TX 77964
Ph:(361)798-2662
Fax: (361)798-2662
Co. E-mail: visit@hallettsville.com
URL: http://www.hallettsville.com
Contact: Cheryl Renken, Admin.Dir.

65296 ■ Hallsville Area Chamber of Commerce
PO Box 535
Hallsville, TX 75650
Ph:(903)668-2592
URL: http://www.hallsville.com

Contact: Linda Caver, Pres.

65297 ■ Hamilton Chamber of Commerce
204 E Main St.
Hamilton, TX 76531
Ph:(254)386-3216
Co. E-mail: chamber@hamiltontexas.com
URL: http://www.hamiltontexas.com
Contact: Diana Queen Koether, Mgr.

65298 ■ Harker Heights Chamber of Commerce
552 E FM 2410, Ste. B
Harker Heights, TX 76548
Ph:(254)699-4999
Fax: (254)699-5194
Co. E-mail: bill@hhchamber.org
URL: http://www.harkerheights.com
Contact: Bill Kozlik, Pres.

65299 ■ Harlingen Area Chamber of Commerce
311 E Tyler St.
Harlingen, TX 78550-9121
Ph:(956)423-5440
Free: 800-531-7346
Co. E-mail: info@harlingen.com
URL: http://www.harlingen.com
Contact: Marie McDermott, Pres./CEO

65300 ■ Harlingen Hispanic Chamber of Commerce
2309 N Ed Carey
Harlingen, TX 78550
Ph:(956)421-2400
Fax: (956)364-1879
Co. E-mail: hhcoc@sbcglobal.net
URL: http://www.harlingenchamber.com
Contact: Luis F. Perez, Sec.

65301 ■ Haskell Chamber of Commerce
510 S 2nd St.
Haskell, TX 79521-6504
Ph:(940)864-2477
Fax: (940)864-2477
URL: http://www.haskellchamber.com
Contact: Abe Turner, Gen. Mgr.

65302 ■ Hawkins Area Chamber of Commerce
109 Beaulah
Hawkins, TX 75765
Ph:(903)769-4482
Fax: (903)769-4320
Co. E-mail: chamber@hawkinschamberofcommerce.com
URL: http://www.hawkinschamberofcommerce.com
Contact: Dr. H.L. Peace, Mgr.

65303 ■ Hearne Chamber of Commerce
304 S Market St.
Hearne, TX 77859
Ph:(979)279-2351
Fax: (979)279-2559
Co. E-mail: chamber@hearnetexas.info
URL: http://www.rtis.com/reg/hearne/HearneCofC.htm
Contact: Kent Brunette, Exec.Dir.

65304 ■ Henderson Area Chamber of Commerce
201 N Main St.
Henderson, TX 75652
Ph:(903)657-5528
Fax: (903)657-9454
Co. E-mail: info@hendersontx.com
URL: http://www.hendersontx.com
Contact: Judy Sewell, Exec.Dir.

65305 ■ Henrietta - Clay County Chamber of Commerce
PO Box 75
202 W Omega
Henrietta, TX 76365
Ph:(940)538-5261
Co. E-mail: claycountychambers@sbcglobal.net
URL: http://hccchamber.com

Contact: Linda R. Burleson, Pres.

65306 ■ Hidalgo Chamber of Commerce
611 E Coma Ave.
Hidalgo, TX 78557
Ph:(956)843-2734
Fax: (956)843-2722
Contact: Joe Vera III, Pres./CEO

65307 ■ Hillsboro Chamber of Commerce
115 N Covington St.
PO Box 358
Hillsboro, TX 76645
Ph:(254)582-2481
Free: 800-445-5726
Fax: (254)582-0465
Co. E-mail: chamber@hillsborochamber.org
URL: http://www.hillsborochamber.org
Contact: Diann Bayes, Exec.Dir.

65308 ■ Hitchcock Chamber of Commerce
PO Box 389
Hitchcock, TX 77563
Ph:(409)986-9224
Fax: (409)986-6317
Co. E-mail: hcofc662@msn.com
Contact: Teresa Weishuhn, Exec.Sec.

65309 ■ Holistic Chamber of Commerce
13237 Montfort, No. 672
Dallas, TX 75240
Ph:(972)764-9111
Co. E-mail: president@holisticchamber.org
URL: http://www.holisticchamber.com
Contact: Dr. John McCormick, Pres.

65310 ■ Hondo Area Chamber of Commerce
1607 Ave. K
Hondo, TX 78861
Ph:(830)426-3037
Co. E-mail: hondochamber@ev1.net
URL: http://www.hondochamber.com
Contact: Evelyne Barbutti, Exec.Dir./Mgr.

65311 ■ Honey Grove Chamber of Commerce
PO Box 92
Honey Grove, TX 75446
Ph:(903)378-7211
Fax: (903)378-3217
Co. E-mail: hgchamber@yahoo.com
URL: http://www.honeygrovechamber.com
Contact: Linda Goss, Pres.

65312 ■ Hopkins County Chamber of Commerce
PO Box 347
1200 Houston St.
Sulphur Springs, TX 75483-0347
Ph:(903)885-6515
Free: 888-300-6623
Fax: (903)885-6516
Co. E-mail: chamber@sulphursprings-tx.com
URL: http://www.sulphursprings-tx.com
Contact: Bill Elliott, CEO & Pres.

65313 ■ Houston North Forest Chamber of Commerce
5506 N Wayside Dr.
Houston, TX 77028-5266
Ph:(713)670-7500
Fax: (713)676-2917
Contact: Tobie B. Ross Jr.

65314 ■ Houston Northwest Chamber of Commerce
14511 Falling Creek, Ste. 205
Houston, TX 77014-1280
Ph:(281)440-4160
Fax: (281)440-5229
Co. E-mail: hnwcc@swbell.net
URL: http://www.hnwcc.org
Contact: Ms. Nancy Kennedy, Dir. of Finance

65315 ■ Houston West Chamber of Commerce
10777 Westheimer, Ste. 916
Houston, TX 77042

Ph:(713)785-4922
Fax: (713)785-4944
Co. E-mail: info@hwcoc.org
URL: http://www.hwcoc.org
Contact: Jeannie M. Bollinger, Pres./CEO

65316 ■ Howe Chamber of Commerce
PO Box 250
Howe, TX 75459-0250
Ph:(903)532-HOWE
Co. E-mail: contact@howetx.org
URL: http://www.howetx.org
Contact: Les Bennett, Pres.

65317 ■ Hughes Springs Chamber of Commerce
PO Box 218
Hughes Springs, TX 75656
Ph:(903)639-2351
Fax: (903)639-3769
Co. E-mail: jjdhowell@aol.com
Contact: Ms. Judi Howell, Exec. Dir.

65318 ■ Humble Area Chamber of Commerce
110 W Main St.
Humble, TX 77338
Ph:(281)446-2128
Fax: (281)446-7483
Co. E-mail: mbyers@humblearechamber.org
URL: http://www.humbleareachamber.org
Contact: Mike Byers, Pres.

65319 ■ Hurst - Euless - Bedford Chamber of Commerce
PO Box 969
Bedford, TX 76021
Ph:(817)283-1521
Fax: (817)267-5111
Co. E-mail: chamber@heb.org
URL: http://www.heb.org
Contact: Ms. Mary Martin Frazior, Pres./CEO

65320 ■ Hutto Chamber of Commerce
PO Box 99
Hutto, TX 78634-0099
Ph:(512)759-4400
Fax: (512)846-1618
Co. E-mail: info@hutto.org
URL: http://www.hutto.org
Contact: Elizabeth Page, Pres.

65321 ■ Ingleside Chamber of Commerce
2665 San Angelo St.
PO Box 686
Ingleside, TX 78362
Ph:(361)776-2906
Free: 888-899-2906
Fax: (361)776-0678
Co. E-mail: ingchamber1@cableone.net
URL: http://www.inglesidetxchamber.org
Contact: Sandi Ridgley, Exec.Dir.

65322 ■ Iowa Park Chamber of Commerce
102 N Wall St.
Iowa Park, TX 76367
Ph:(940)592-5441
Fax: (940)592-4793
Co. E-mail: admin@iowaparkchamber.com
URL: http://www.iowapark.com
Contact: Susan Dillard, Sec./Mgr.

65323 ■ Jacksboro Chamber of Commerce
PO Box 606
Jacksboro, TX 76458-0606
Ph:(940)567-2602
Fax: (940)567-2602
URL: http://www.jacksboro-tx.com
Contact: Darlene Maxwell, Sec.

65324 ■ Jacksonville Chamber of Commerce
526 E Commerce
Jacksonville, TX 75766
Ph:(903)586-2217
Free: 800-376-2217
Fax: (903)586-6944
Co. E-mail: chamber@jacksonvilletexas.com
URL: http://www.jacksonvilletexas.com

Contact: Roy Wolfe, Pres.

65325 ■ Jasper Lake Sam Rayburn Area Chamber of Commerce
246 E Milam
Jasper, TX 75951
Ph:(409)384-2762
Fax: (409)384-4733
Co. E-mail: jaspercc@jaspercoc.org
URL: http://www.jaspercoc.org
Contact: Ms. Susan Stover, Exec.Dir.

65326 ■ Jewett Area Chamber of Commerce
PO Box 220
Jewett, TX 75846-0220
Ph:(903)626-4202
Fax: (903)626-6599
Co. E-mail: jacc@glade.net
Contact: David Walton, Pres.

65327 ■ Johnson City Chamber of Commerce
PO Box 485
Johnson City, TX 78636
Ph:(830)868-7684
Fax: (830)868-7803
Co. E-mail: txinfo@lbjcountry.com
URL: http://www.lbjcountry.com
Contact: Denisa Odiorne, Exec.Dir.

65328 ■ Joshua Area Chamber of Commerce
104 N Main St.
PO Box 1292
Joshua, TX 76058-1292
Ph:(817)558-2821
Fax: (817)645-7824
Co. E-mail: joshchamber@usapathway.com
URL: http://www.joshuachamber.org
Contact: Otis Gillaspie, Chair

65329 ■ Jourdanton Community Chamber of Commerce
PO Box 747
Jourdanton, TX 78026
Ph:(830)769-2866
URL: http://www.jourdanton.net
Contact: Larry Pryor, Pres.

65330 ■ Karnes City Community Chamber of Commerce
210 E Calvert St.
Karnes City, TX 78118
Ph:(830)780-3112
Fax: (830)780-3112
Co. E-mail: kccoc@karnesec.net
Contact: Clare Kauffman, Exec.Dir.

65331 ■ Katy Area Chamber of Commerce
2501 S Mason Rd., Ste. 230
Katy, TX 77450
Ph:(281)828-1100
Fax: (281)828-1150
Co. E-mail: info@katychamber.com
URL: http://www.katychamber.com
Contact: Ann Hodge, Pres./CEO

65332 ■ Kerens Chamber of Commerce
PO Box 117
Kerens, TX 75144-0117
Ph:(903)396-2391
Co. E-mail: kerenschamber@txun.net
URL: http://www.ci.kerens.tx.us
Contact: Bobby Bain, Pres.

65333 ■ Kermit Chamber of Commerce
112 N Poplar
Kermit, TX 79745
Ph:(915)586-2507
Fax: (915)586-2508
Co. E-mail: kcoc@metglobal.com
Contact: Ed Simmons, Exec.Dir.

65334 ■ Kerrville Area Chamber of Commerce
1700 Sidney Baker St., Ste. 100
Kerrville, TX 78028
Ph:(830)896-1155

Fax: (830)896-1175
Co. E-mail: info@kerrvilletx.com
URL: http://www.kerrvilletx.com
Contact: Brian Bondy, Pres.

65335 ■ Kilgore Chamber of Commerce
813 N Kilgore St.
Kilgore, TX 75662
Ph:(903)984-5022
Free: (866)984-0400
Fax: (903)984-4975
Co. E-mail: info@kilgorechamber.com
URL: http://www.kilgorechamber.com
Contact: Michael Coston, Exec.VP

65336 ■ Kimble County Chamber of Commerce
402 E Main
Junction, TX 76849
Ph:(325)446-3190
Fax: (325)446-2871
Co. E-mail: chamber@junctiontexas.net
URL: http://www.junctiontexas.net
Contact: Connie Booth, Exec.Dir.

65337 ■ Kingsland - Lake LBJ Chamber of Commerce
PO Box 465
Kingsland, TX 78639
Ph:(915)388-6211
Fax: (325)388-5391
URL: http://www.kingslandchamber.org
Contact: Joyce Morris

65338 ■ Kingsville Chamber of Commerce
PO Box 1030
Kingsville, TX 78363
Ph:(361)592-6438
Fax: (361)592-0866
Co. E-mail: chamber@kingsville.org
URL: http://www.kingsville.org
Contact: Kathy A. Martinez, Exec.Dir.

65339 ■ Kinney County Chamber of Commerce
PO Box 386
Brackettville, TX 78832-0386
Ph:(830)563-2466
Contact: Mrs. Mary Martin, Sec.

65340 ■ Kirbyville Chamber of Commerce
PO Box 417
Kirbyville, TX 75956
Ph:(409)423-5827
Fax: (409)423-3353
URL: http://www.kirbyville.org/main

65341 ■ Knox City Chamber of Commerce
123 Central Ave.
PO Box 91
Knox City, TX 79529
Ph:(940)658-3442
Fax: (940)658-1247
Co. E-mail: kcchamber@knoxcity.net
Contact: Mrs Daveine Clark, Exec.Dir.

65342 ■ Kountze Chamber of Commerce
PO Box 878
Kountze, TX 77625
Ph:(409)246-3413
Free: (866)456-8689
Fax: (409)246-4659
Co. E-mail: mailman@kountzecoc.org
URL: http://www.kountzecoc.com
Contact: Ronnie Stockholm, Pres.

65343 ■ Kyle Area Chamber of Commerce and Visitors' Bureau
PO Box 900
Kyle, TX 78640-0900
Ph:(512)268-4220
Fax: (512)268-4220
Co. E-mail: kacc@austin.rr.com
URL: http://www.cityofkyle.com/chamber-commerce.
   php
Contact: Mr. Tim DeLano, Exec. Dir./VP

65344 ■ La Grange Area Chamber of Commerce
171 S Main
La Grange, TX 78945
Ph:(979)968-5756
Free: 800-524-7264
Fax: (979)968-8000
Co. E-mail: chamber@lagrangetx.org
URL: http://www.lagrangetx.org
Contact: Liz Dujka, Pres.

65345 ■ La Porte-Bayshore Chamber of Commerce
712 W Fairmont Pkwy.
PO Box 996
La Porte, TX 77572-0996
Ph:(281)471-1123
Fax: (281)471-1710
Co. E-mail: info-lpcc@laportechamber.org
URL: http://www.laportechamber.org
Contact: Colleen Hicks, Pres.

65346 ■ Ladonia Chamber of Commerce
PO Box 44
Ladonia, TX 75449
Ph:(903)367-7216
Fax: (903)367-7339
Contact: Alisha Green, Pres.

65347 ■ Lago Vista Area Chamber of Commerce
PO Box 4946
Lago Vista, TX 78645
Ph:(512)267-7952
Free: 888-328-5846
Fax: (512)267-2338
Co. E-mail: info@lagovista.org
URL: http://www.lagovista.org
Contact: Sandra E. Boatright, Coor.

65348 ■ Lake Buchanan - Inks Lake Chamber of Commerce and Tourist Center
PO Box 282
Buchanan Dam, TX 78609-0282
Ph:(512)793-2803
Fax: (512)793-2112
Co. E-mail: info@buchanan-inks.com
URL: http://www.buchanan-inks.org
Contact: Mary Koenning, Mgr.

65349 ■ Lake Cities Chamber of Commerce
PO Box 1028
Lake Dallas, TX 75065
Ph:(940)497-3097
Co. E-mail: lccc@lakecitieschamber.com
URL: http://www.lakecitieschamber.com
Contact: Fon Laughlin, Pres./Chair

65350 ■ Lake Granbury Area Chamber of Commerce
3408 E Hwy. 377
Granbury, TX 76049
Ph:(817)573-1622
Fax: (817)573-0805
Co. E-mail: chamberinfo@granburychamber.com
URL: http://www.granburychamber.com
Contact: Mike Scott, Pres.

65351 ■ Lake Tawakoni Area Chamber of Commerce and CVB
605 E Hwy. 276
West Tawakoni, TX 75474
Ph:(903)447-3020
Fax: (903)447-3820
Co. E-mail: tawakonichamber@argontech.net
Contact: Jim Johnson, Pres.

65352 ■ Lake Whitney Chamber of Commerce
PO Box 604
Whitney, TX 76692
Ph:(254)694-2540
Fax: (254)694-3005
Co. E-mail: bluewater@lakewhitneychamber.com
URL: http://www.lakewhitneychamber.com
Contact: Horace Findley, Exec.Sec.

65353 ■ Lamar County Chamber of Commerce
1125 Bonham St.
Paris, TX 75460
Ph:(903)784-2501
Fax: (903)784-2503
Co. E-mail: chamber@paristexas.com
URL: http://www.paristexas.com
Contact: Gary Vest, Pres.

65354 ■ Lamesa Area Chamber of Commerce
PO Box 880
Lamesa, TX 79331
Ph:(806)872-2181
Fax: (806)872-5700
Co. E-mail: lacoc@pics.net
Contact: Wayne Smith, Exec.VP

65355 ■ Lampasas County Chamber of Commerce
PO Box 627
Lampasas, TX 76550
Ph:(512)556-5172
Free: (866)556-5172
Fax: (512)556-2195
Co. E-mail: info@lampasaschamber.org
URL: http://www.lampasaschamber.org
Contact: Jill Jones, Exec.Dir.

65356 ■ Lancaster Chamber of Commerce
100 N Dallas Ave.
PO Box 1100
Lancaster, TX 75146
Ph:(972)227-2579
Fax: (972)227-9555
Co. E-mail: chamber@lancastertx.org
URL: http://www.lancastertx.org
Contact: Joe Johnson, Pres.

65357 ■ Laredo - Webb County Chamber of Commerce
PO Box 790
Laredo, TX 78042
Ph:(956)722-9895
Free: 800-292-2122
Fax: (956)791-4503
Co. E-mail: chamber@laredochamber.com
URL: http://www.laredochamber.com
Contact: Miguel A. Conchas, Pres./CEO

65358 ■ Leonard Chamber of Commerce
PO Box 117
Leonard, TX 75452
Ph:(903)587-0174
Fax: (903)587-2580
Co. E-mail: cityhall@leonardonline.net
Contact: Mr. Charles M. Vibbert, Pres.

65359 ■ Levelland Area Chamber of Commerce
1101 Ave. H
Levelland, TX 79336
Ph:(806)894-3157
Fax: (806)894-4284
URL: http://levelland.com/CMS/index.php
Contact: Mary Siders, Pres.

65360 ■ Lewisville Area Chamber of Commerce
551 N Valley Pkwy.
Lewisville, TX 75067
Ph:(972)436-9571
Fax: (972)436-5949
Co. E-mail: info@lewisvillechamber.org
URL: http://www.lewisville-chamber.org
Contact: Ronnie Morrison, Pres.

65361 ■ Liberty-Dayton Area Chamber of Commerce
1801 Trinity St.
PO Box 1270
Liberty, TX 77575
Ph:(936)336-5736
Fax: (936)336-1159
Co. E-mail: chamber@imsday.com
URL: http://www.libertydaytonchamber.com
Contact: Mary Anne Campbell, Pres.

65362 ■ Lindale Area Chamber of Commerce
110 E Hubbard St.
PO Box 670
Lindale, TX 75771
Ph:(903)882-7181
Fax: (903)882-1790
Co. E-mail: info@lindalechamber.com
URL: http://www.lindalechamber.com
Contact: John Williams, Pres.

65363 ■ Linden Area Chamber of Commerce
104 S Main St.
Linden, TX 75563
Ph:(903)756-3106
Fax: (903)756-5884
URL: http://www.visitlinden.com
Contact: Sterling Corbett, Pres.

65364 ■ Littlefield Chamber of Commerce
PO Box 507
Littlefield, TX 79339-0507
Ph:(806)385-5331
Fax: (806)385-0108
Contact: Gini Coffman, Exec.VP

65365 ■ Livingston-Polk County Chamber of Commerce
PO Box 600
Livingston, TX 77351
Ph:(936)327-4929
Fax: (936)327-2660
Co. E-mail: chamberadmin@livingston.net
URL: http://www.lpcchamber.com
Contact: Jay Dickson, Exec.Dir.

65366 ■ Llano County Chamber of Commerce
700 Bessemer
Llano, TX 78643
Ph:(325)247-5354
Fax: (325)247-1844
Co. E-mail: info@llanochamber.org
URL: http://www.llanochamber.org
Contact: Elisa Dalrymple, Exec.Dir.

65367 ■ Lockhart Chamber of Commerce
205 S Main St.
PO Box 840
Lockhart, TX 78644
Ph:(512)398-2818
Free: 877-519-7057
Co. E-mail: abrown@lockhart-tx.org
URL: http://www.lockhartchamber.com
Contact: Sam Balkum, Pres./CEO

65368 ■ Lockney Chamber of Commerce
PO Box 477
Lockney, TX 79241
Ph:(806)652-3561
Contact: Bobby Hall, Pres.

65369 ■ Lone Star Chamber of Commerce
PO Box 0505
Lone Star, TX 75668-0505
Ph:(903)656-2184
Contact: Gilbert Alcorn, Pres.

65370 ■ Longview Partnership
410 N Center St.
Longview, TX 75601
Ph:(903)237-4000
Fax: (903)237-4049
Co. E-mail: carolejudy@longviewpartnership.org
URL: http://www.longviewchamber.com
Contact: Carole Judy, VP

65371 ■ Los Fresnos Chamber of Commerce
203 N Arroyo Blvd.
Los Fresnos, TX 78566
Ph:(956)233-4448
Fax: (956)233-9740
Co. E-mail: chamberoffice@losfresnoschamber.com
URL: http://www.losfresnoschamber.com
Contact: Debra Badeaux, Exec. Dir.

65372 ■ Louise-Hillje Chamber of Commerce
PO Box 156
Louise, TX 77455

Ph:(979)648-2615
Fax: (979)648-2646
Co. E-mail: webmaster@louisehilljechamber.org
URL: http://www.louisehilljechamber.org
Contact: Kinnan Stockton, Pres.

65373 ■ Lubbock Chamber of Commerce
1301 Broadway, Ste. 101
Lubbock, TX 79401
Ph:(806)761-7000
Fax: (806)761-7013
Co. E-mail: info@lubbockbiz.org
URL: http://www.lubbockchamber.com
Contact: Eddie McBride, Pres.

65374 ■ Lufkin - Angelina County Chamber of Commerce
1615 S Chestnut
Lufkin, TX 75901
Ph:(936)634-6644
Fax: (936)634-8726
Co. E-mail: chamber@lufkintexas.org
URL: http://www.lufkintexas.org
Contact: Jerry Huffman CCE, Pres./CEO

65375 ■ Luling Area Chamber of Commerce
PO Box 710
Luling, TX 78648
Ph:(830)875-3214
Fax: (830)875-2082
Co. E-mail: lulingcc@bcsnet.net
URL: http://www.lulingcc.org
Contact: Shelly Cox, Exec.Dir.

65376 ■ Lumberton Chamber of Commerce
PO Box 8574
Lumberton, TX 77657
Ph:(409)755-0554
Fax: (409)755-2516
Co. E-mail: lcoc@lumbertoncoc.com
Contact: Diana Worry, Sec.

65377 ■ Madison County Chamber of Commerce
113 W Trinity
Madisonville, TX 77864
Ph:(936)348-3591
Fax: (936)348-2212
Co. E-mail: chamber@rodzoo.com
URL: http://www.madisonvillechamber.com
Contact: June Bevers, Exec.Dir.

65378 ■ Malakoff Chamber of Commerce
PO Box 1042
Community Ctr.
N Terry St.
Malakoff, TX 75148
Ph:(903)489-1518
Fax: (903)489-1518
Co. E-mail: malakoffcc@aol.com
URL: http://cityofmalakoff.com/index.htm
Contact: Pat Isaacson, Sec.-Treas.

65379 ■ Mansfield Area Chamber of Commerce
116 N Main St.
Mansfield, TX 76063
Ph:(817)473-0507
Fax: (817)473-8687
Co. E-mail: becca@mansfieldchamber.org
URL: http://www.mansfieldchamber.org
Contact: Becca Hancock, Pres.

65380 ■ Marble Falls - Lake LBJ Chamber of Commerce
916 Second St.
Marble Falls, TX 78654
Ph:(830)693-4449
Free: 800-759-8178
Fax: (830)693-7594
Co. E-mail: info@marblefalls.org
URL: http://www.marblefalls.org
Contact: Doug Morris, Exec. Dir.

65381 ■ Marfa Chamber of Commerce
PO Box 635
Marfa, TX 79843

Ph:(432)729-4942
Free: 800-650-9696
Co. E-mail: info@marfacc.com
URL: http://www.marfacc.com
Contact: Sondra DeZamberano

65382 ■ Marion County Chamber of Commerce
118 N Vale St.
Jefferson, TX 75657
Ph:(903)665-2672
Free: 888-GO-RELAX
Fax: (903)665-8233
Co. E-mail: thechamber@sbcglobal.net
URL: http://www.jefferson-texas.com

65383 ■ Marlin Chamber of Commerce
245 Coleman St.
Marlin, TX 76661
Ph:(254)803-3301
Fax: (254)883-2171
Co. E-mail: marlintxchamber@aol.com
URL: http://www.marlintexas.com
Contact: Cynthia Dees, Chamber Sec.

65384 ■ Marshall Texas Chamber of Commerce
213 W Austin St.
Marshall, TX 75671
Ph:(903)935-7868
Free: 800-953-7868
Fax: (903)935-9982
Co. E-mail: cware@gower.net
URL: http://www.marshalltxchamber.com
Contact: Connie Ware, Pres./CEO

65385 ■ Mason County Chamber of Commerce
PO Box 187
Mason, TX 76856
Ph:(325)347-5758
Fax: (325)347-5259
Co. E-mail: masontexas@verizon.net
URL: http://www.masontxcoc.com
Contact: Gail Coldiron

65386 ■ Mathis Area Chamber of Commerce
111 E San Patricio Ave.
Mathis, TX 78368
Ph:(361)547-6112
Fax: (361)547-6112
Contact: Nancy Crouch, VP

65387 ■ McAllen Chamber of Commerce
1200 Ash Ave.
McAllen, TX 78501
Ph:(956)682-2871
Fax: (956)687-2917
Co. E-mail: steve@mcallenchamber.com
URL: http://www.mcallenchamber.com
Contact: Steve Ahlenius, Pres./CEO

65388 ■ McCamey Chamber of Commerce
201 E 6th St.
PO Box 906
McCamey, TX 79752
Ph:(432)652-8202
Co. E-mail: info@mccameychamber.com
URL: http://www.mccameychamber.com
Contact: Dollie Lynch, Sec.

65389 ■ McGregor Chamber of Commerce
303 S Main St.
McGregor, TX 76657
Ph:(254)840-2292
Fax: (254)840-4703
Co. E-mail: mcgregorchamber@mcgregor-texas.com
URL: http://mcgregor-texas.com
Contact: Ms. Jennifer Taylor, Exec. VP

65390 ■ McKinney Chamber of Commerce
1650 W Virginia, Ste. 110
McKinney, TX 75069
Ph:(972)542-0163
Fax: (972)548-0876
Co. E-mail: info@mckinneytx.org

URL: http://www.mckinneytx.org
Contact: Terri Ricketts, Pres.

65391 ■ Memphis Chamber of Commerce
113 S Sixth St.
Memphis, TX 79245
Ph:(806)259-3144
Fax: (806)259-3144
Co. E-mail: memphistexaschamber@valornet.com
URL: http://www.memphistexas.org

65392 ■ Menard County Chamber of Commerce
100 E San Saba
PO Box 64
Menard, TX 76859-0064
Ph:(915)396-2365
Co. E-mail: menardcc@airmail.net
Contact: Audrey Owen, Off.Mgr.

65393 ■ Mercedes Chamber of Commerce
PO Box 37
Mercedes, TX 78570-0037
Ph:(956)565-2221
Fax: (956)565-2221
Co. E-mail: macocrrs@hiline.net
URL: http://www.mercedeschamber.com
Contact: Bob Price, Pres.

65394 ■ Merkel Chamber of Commerce
PO Box 536
Merkel, TX 79536
Ph:(325)928-5722
Co. E-mail: coc@merkeltx.com
URL: http://merkeltx.com
Contact: Michael Adkins, Pres.

65395 ■ Mesquite Chamber of Commerce and Convention and Visitors Bureau
617 N Ebrite
Mesquite, TX 75149-3453
Ph:(972)285-0211
Co. E-mail: info@mesquitechamber.com
URL: http://www.mesquitechamber.com
Contact: Todd Price, Chm.-Elect

65396 ■ Metrocrest Chamber of Commerce
1204 Metrocrest Dr.
Carrollton, TX 75006
Ph:(972)416-6600
Fax: (972)416-7874
Co. E-mail: ed@metrocrestchamber.com
URL: http://metrocrestchamber.com
Contact: Ed Brady, CEO/Pres.

65397 ■ Mexia Area Chamber of Commerce
405 E Milam, Ste. 2
Mexia, TX 76667
Ph:(254)562-5569
Free: 888-535-5476
Fax: (254)562-7138
Co. E-mail: linda@mexiachamber.com
URL: http://www.mexiachamber.com
Contact: Linda Archibald, Exec.Dir.

65398 ■ Midland Chamber of Commerce
109 N Main St.
Midland, TX 79701
Ph:(432)683-3381
Free: 800-624-6435
Fax: (432)682-9205
Co. E-mail: info@midlandtxchamber.com
URL: http://www.midlandtxchamber.com/index2.htm
Contact: John A. Breier, Pres./CEO

65399 ■ Midlothian Chamber of Commerce
310 N 9th St., Ste. A
Midlothian, TX 76065-0609
Ph:(972)723-8600
Fax: (972)723-9300
Co. E-mail: info@midlothianchamber.org
URL: http://www.midlothianchamber.org
Contact: Ms. Amanda Miller, Exec.Dir.

65400 ■ Mills County, Goldthwaite Area Chamber of Commerce
1119 Fisher St.
PO Box 308
Goldthwaite, TX 76844

Ph:(325)648-3619
Fax: (325)648-3619
Co. E-mail: gcc@centex.net
URL: http://www.goldthwaite.biz

65401 ■ Mineral Wells Area Chamber of Commerce
511 E Hubbard
PO Box 1408
Mineral Wells, TX 76068
Ph:(940)325-2557
Free: 800-252-6989
Fax: (940)328-0850
Co. E-mail: info@mineralwellstx.com
URL: http://www.mineralwellstx.com
Contact: Shannon McGary, Exec. Dir.

65402 ■ Monahans Chamber of Commerce
401 S Dwight
Monahans, TX 79756
Ph:(432)943-2187
Fax: (432)943-6868
Co. E-mail: chamber@monahans.org
URL: http://www.monahans.org
Contact: Teresa Burnett, Dir.

65403 ■ Morton Area Chamber of Commerce
201 E Wilson St.
Morton, TX 79346
Ph:(806)266-5200
Co. E-mail: mortonareacoc@yahoo.com
Contact: Joey Perez, Pres.

65404 ■ Moulton Chamber of Commerce and Agriculture
PO Box 482
Moulton, TX 77975
Ph:(361)596-7205
Fax: (361)596-4384
Co. E-mail: moultontexas@gvec.net
URL: http://www.moultontexas.com
Contact: Don McIntosh, Pres.

65405 ■ Mount Pleasant/Titus County Chamber of Commerce and Convention and Visitors' Bureau
1604 N Jefferson
Mount Pleasant, TX 75455
Ph:(903)572-8567
Fax: (903)572-0613
Co. E-mail: info@mtpleasanttx.com
URL: http://www.mtpleasanttx.com
Contact: Pat Adams, Exec.VP

65406 ■ Muenster Chamber of Commerce
202 E Division
PO Box 714
Muenster, TX 76252-0714
Ph:(940)759-2227
Fax: (940)759-2228
Co. E-mail: chamber@ntin.net
Contact: Margie Starke, Exec.Dir.

65407 ■ Muleshoe Chamber of Commerce and Agriculture
115 E American Blvd.
PO Box 356
Muleshoe, TX 79347
Ph:(806)272-4248
Fax: (806)272-4614
Co. E-mail: chamber@fivearea.com
URL: http://www.muleshoe.org
Contact: Martha Hunnicutt, Mgr.

65408 ■ Munday Chamber of Commerce and Agriculture
PO Drawer L
Munday, TX 76371
Ph:(940)422-4540
Fax: (940)422-4540
Co. E-mail: mundaychamberofcommerce@dtnspeed.net
Contact: Amanda Bibb, Exec.VP

65409 ■ Nacogdoches County Chamber of Commerce
2516 North St.
Nacogdoches, TX 75965

Ph:(936)560-5533
Fax: (936)560-3920
Co. E-mail: chamber@nactx.com
URL: http://www.nacogdoches.org
Contact: Bruce Partain IOM, Pres.

65410 ■ Nederland Chamber of Commerce and Tourist Bureau
1515 Boston Ave.
PO Box 891
Nederland, TX 77627
Ph:(409)722-0279
Fax: (409)722-0615
Co. E-mail: nedcofc@nederlandtx.com
Contact: Cindy Clifton, Exec.Dir.

65411 ■ New Boston Chamber of Commerce
100 N Center St.
New Boston, TX 75570-2935
Ph:(903)628-2581
Fax: (903)628-2581
Co. E-mail: chamber@newbostontx.org
URL: http://www.newbostontx.org
Contact: Deborah Cook, Exec. Dir.

65412 ■ Newton County Chamber of Commerce
PO Box 66/313 Rusk
Newton, TX 75966
Ph:(409)379-5527
Co. E-mail: chamber@newton-texas.com
URL: http://www.newton-texas.com
Contact: Susan Karpel, Sec.

65413 ■ Nocona Area Chamber of Commerce
PO Box 27
Nocona, TX 76255
Ph:(940)825-3526
Co. E-mail: noconachamber@dtnspeed.net
URL: http://noconachamber.netfirms.com
Contact: Jackie Goldsmith, Sec.

65414 ■ North Channel Area Chamber of Commerce
13301 I-10 E Fwy., No. 100
Houston, TX 77015
Ph:(713)450-3600
Fax: (713)450-0700
Co. E-mail: wayneoq@flash.net
URL: http://www.northchannelarea.com
Contact: June Harris, Chm.

65415 ■ North Dallas Chamber of Commerce
10707 Preston Rd.
Dallas, TX 75230
Ph:(214)368-6485
Fax: (214)691-5584
Co. E-mail: mailbox@ndcc.org
URL: http://www.ndcc.org
Contact: Corey Hill, Dir. of Communications

65416 ■ North Galveston County Chamber of Commerce
2718 FM 517 E
Dickinson, TX 77539
Ph:(281)337-3434
Fax: (281)337-0641
Co. E-mail: contract@northgalvestoncountychamber.com
URL: http://www.northgalvestoncountychamber.com
Contact: Clair Herring, Acting Pres.

65417 ■ North Houston-Greenspoint Chamber of Commerce
15600 JFK Blvd., Ste. 150
Houston, TX 77032
Ph:(281)442-8701
Fax: (281)442-8713
Co. E-mail: mbayless@nhgcc.org
URL: http://www.nhgcc.org
Contact: Marilyn Bayless, Pres.

65418 ■ North San Antonio Chamber of Commerce
12930 Country Pkwy.
San Antonio, TX 78216
Ph:(210)344-4848

Fax: (210)525-8207
Co. E-mail: dwilson@northsachamber.com
URL: http://www.northsachamber.com
Contact: Mr. Duane Wilson, Pres.

65419 ■ Northeast Tarrant Chamber of Commerce
5001 Denton Hwy.
Haltom City, TX 76117-1439
Ph:(817)281-9376
Fax: (817)281-9379
Co. E-mail: tnaini@netarrant.org
URL: http://www.netarrant.org
Contact: Robert G. Hamilton, Pres./CEO

65420 ■ Northwest Tarrant Chamber of Commerce
PO Box 136333
Lake Worth, TX 76136-6333
Ph:(817)237-0060
Fax: (817)237-2365
Co. E-mail: info@nwtarrantchamber.org
Contact: Mattie Millican, Exec.Dir.

65421 ■ Nueces Canyon Chamber of Commerce
PO Box 369
Camp Wood, TX 78833
Ph:(830)597-6241
URL: http://www.campwood.com
Contact: Ben Cox, Pres.

65422 ■ Oak Cliff Chamber of Commerce
400 S Zang Blvd., Ste. 110
Dallas, TX 75208
Ph:(214)943-4567
Fax: (214)943-4582
Co. E-mail: occ@oakcliffchamber.org
URL: http://www.oakcliffchamber.org
Contact: Joel Sontag, Pres.

65423 ■ Olney Chamber of Commerce
108 E Main St.
Olney, TX 76374
Ph:(940)564-5445
Fax: (940)564-3610
Co. E-mail: chamber@brazosnet.com
URL: http://www.olneychamberofcommerce.com
Contact: Jan Williams, Coor.

65424 ■ Olton Chamber of Commerce and Agriculture
PO Box 487
Olton, TX 79064-0487
Ph:(806)285-2292
Fax: (806)285-2292
Co. E-mail: kimberlydeberry@fivearea.com
Contact: Kimberly DeBerry, Exec.Sec.

65425 ■ Omaha Chamber of Commerce
PO Box 816
Omaha, TX 75571
Ph:(903)884-2302
Fax: (903)884-2746
URL: http://www.cityofomahatx.com
Contact: Joan Cook, Pres.

65426 ■ Overton-New London Area Chamber of Commerce
121 E Henderson
PO Box 6
Overton, TX 75684
Ph:(903)834-3542
Fax: (903)834-3063
URL: http://www.ci.overton.tx.us
Contact: Don Gwynn, Pres.

65427 ■ Ozona Chamber of Commerce
PO Box 1135
Ozona, TX 76943-1135
Ph:(325)392-3737
Fax: (325)392-3485
Co. E-mail: oztxcoc@aol.com
URL: http://www.ozona.com/chamber-of-commerce.
htm
Contact: Shanon Biggerstaff, Exec. Dir.

65428 ■ Paducah Chamber of Commerce
PO Box 863
Paducah, TX 79248
Ph:(806)492-2044
Contact: Frieda Brooks, Pres.

65429 ■ Palacios Chamber of Commerce
420 Main St.
Palacios, TX 77465
Ph:(361)972-2615
Free: 800-611-4567
Co. E-mail: palcoc@wcnet.net
URL: http://www.palacioschamber.com
Contact: Melanie Longoria, Office Mgr.

65430 ■ Palestine Area Chamber of Commerce
PO Box 1177
Palestine, TX 75802
Ph:(903)729-6066
Fax: (903)729-2083
Co. E-mail: palcoc@palestinechamber.org
URL: http://www.palestinechamber.org
Contact: Gay Cox, Exec.Dir.

65431 ■ Panhandle Chamber of Commerce
PO Box 1021
Panhandle, TX 79068
Ph:(806)537-4325
Fax: (806)537-5234
Co. E-mail: chamber@panhandletx.com
URL: http://www.panhandletx.com
Contact: Clint Walker, Chm.

65432 ■ Panola County Chamber of Commerce
300 W Panola St.
Carthage, TX 75633
Ph:(903)693-6634
Fax: (903)693-8578
Co. E-mail: chamber@carthagetexas.com
URL: http://www.carthagetexas.com
Contact: Tommie Ritter Smith, Pres.

65433 ■ Pasadena Chamber of Commerce
4334 Fairmont Pkwy.
Pasadena, TX 77504-3306
Ph:(281)487-7871
Fax: (281)487-5530
Co. E-mail: info@pasadenachamber.org
URL: http://www.pasadenachamber.org
Contact: William B. McCoy, Pres./CEO

65434 ■ Pearland Area Chamber of Commerce
3501 Liberty Dr.
Pearland, TX 77581
Ph:(281)485-3634
Fax: (281)485-2420
Co. E-mail: chamber@pearlandchamber.org
URL: http://www.pearlandchamber.com
Contact: Carol R. Artz, Pres.

65435 ■ Pecos Area Chamber of Commerce
111 S Cedar, Hwy. 285
PO Box 27
Pecos, TX 79772-0027
Ph:(432)445-2406
Fax: (432)445-2407
URL: http://www.pecostx.com
Contact: Linda Gholson, Exec. Dir.

65436 ■ Perryton-Ochiltree Chamber of Commerce
2000 S Main
PO Box 789
Perryton, TX 79070
Ph:(806)435-6575
Free: 800-490-6575
Fax: (806)435-9821
Co. E-mail: pococ@ptsi.net
URL: http://www.perryton.org
Contact: Dana Donahue, Pres.

65437 ■ Petersburg Area Chamber of Commerce
PO Box 31
Petersburg, TX 79250-0031

65438 ■ Pharr Chamber of Commerce
307 W Park
Pharr, TX 78577
Ph:(956)787-1481
Fax: (956)787-7972
Co. E-mail: info@pharrchamberofcommerce.com
URL: http://www.pharrchamberofcommerce.com
Contact: Marisol Pena, Exec. Dir.

65439 ■ Pilot Point Chamber of Commerce
300 S Washington
PO Box 497
Pilot Point, TX 76258-0497
Ph:(940)686-5385
Fax: (940)686-9392
Co. E-mail: chamber.ofcommerce@cebridge.net
URL: http://www.pilotpoint.org
Contact: Holly Cox, Dir.

65440 ■ Plainview Chamber of Commerce
710 W 5th St.
Plainview, TX 79072
Ph:(806)296-7431
Free: 800-658-2685
Co. E-mail: plainviewchamber@texasonline.net
URL: http://www.plainviewtex.com
Contact: Jim Ferrell, Exec.VP

65441 ■ Plano Chamber of Commerce
1200 E 15th St.
Plano, TX 75074
Ph:(972)424-7547
Fax: (972)422-5182
Co. E-mail: info@planochamber.org
URL: http://www.planochamber.org
Contact: Mr. Brad Shanklin, Pres./CEO

65442 ■ Pleasanton Chamber of Commerce
777 Peters Ave.
Pleasanton, TX 94566
Ph:(925)846-5858
Fax: (925)846-9697
Co. E-mail: david@pleasanton.org
URL: http://www.pleasanton.org
Contact: David Bouchard, Pres./CEO

65443 ■ Port Aransas Chamber of Commerce
403 W Cotter
Port Aransas, TX 78373
Ph:(361)749-5919
Free: 800-452-6278
Fax: (361)749-4672
Co. E-mail: info@portaransas.org
URL: http://www.portaransas.org
Contact: Ms. Ann B. Vaughan, Exec. Dir.

65444 ■ Port Arthur Chamber of Commerce
4749 Twin City Hwy., Ste. 300
Port Arthur, TX 77642
Ph:(409)963-1107
Fax: (409)962-1997
Co. E-mail: pacc@portarthurtexas.com
URL: http://www.portarthurtexas.com
Contact: Verna Rutherford, Pres.

65445 ■ Port Isabel Chamber of Commerce
421 Queen Isabella Blvd.
Port Isabel, TX 78578
Ph:(956)943-2262
Free: 800-527-6102
Fax: (956)943-4001
Co. E-mail: info@portisabel.org
URL: http://www.portisabel.org
Contact: Deborah Moore, Exec.Dir.

65446 ■ Port Lavaca-Calhoun County Chamber of Commerce and Agriculture
2300 Hwy. 35
Port Lavaca, TX 77979
Ph:(361)552-2959
Free: 800-556-PORT
Fax: (361)552-1288
Co. E-mail: ptlcofc@tisd.net
Contact: Shelby Stockton, Pres.

65447 ■ Port Mansfield Chamber of Commerce
PO Box 75
Port Mansfield, TX 78598
Ph:(956)944-2354
Fax: (956)244-2354
Co. E-mail: pmft@granderiver.net
URL: http://www.port-mansfield.com/chamber.htm
Contact: Berneice Jones, Pres.

65448 ■ Port Neches Chamber of Commerce
PO Box 445
Port Neches, TX 77651
Ph:(409)722-9154
Fax: (409)722-7380
Co. E-mail: pncoc@swbell.net
URL: http://www.portnecheschamber.com
Contact: Debbie Plaia, Exec.Dir.

65449 ■ Port O'Connor Chamber of Commerce
Third and Main
PO Box 701
Port O'Connor, TX 77982-0701
Ph:(361)983-2898
Fax: (361)983-2898
Co. E-mail: poccc@tisd.net
Contact: Henry Pongratz, Pres.

65450 ■ Portland Chamber of Commerce
PO Box 388
Portland, TX 78374
Ph:(361)643-2475
Free: 877-643-2475
Fax: (361)643-7377
Co. E-mail: chamber@portlandtx.org
URL: http://www.portlandtx.org
Contact: Laura Miller, Exec.Dir.

65451 ■ Poteet Chamber of Commerce
PO Box 577
Poteet, TX 78065-0577
Ph:(830)742-8144
Fax: (830)742-3608
Co. E-mail: nidaharvey@scglobal.net
Contact: Diana Martinez, Pres.

65452 ■ Prairie View Chamber of Commerce
PO Box 847
Prairie View, TX 77446-0847
Ph:(936)857-5817
Fax: (936)857-5806
URL: http://www.pvcoc.com
Contact: George E. Higgs, Pres.

65453 ■ Premont Chamber of Commerce
PO Box 1107
Premont, TX 78375
Ph:(361)348-3933
Contact: Epi Vargas, Pres.

65454 ■ Presidio Chamber of Commerce
PO Box 2497
Presidio, TX 79845
Ph:(915)229-3199
Fax: (915)229-4008
Co. E-mail: presidiochamber@bmsol.com
URL: http://www.presidiotx.org

65455 ■ Princeton Area Chamber of Commerce
275 W Princeton Dr., Ste. 105
Princeton, TX 75407
Ph:(972)736-6462
Fax: (972)736-3309
Co. E-mail: chamber@princetontxchamber.com
URL: http://www.princetontxchamber.com
Contact: Jayson Bull, Pres.

65456 ■ Prosper Area Chamber of Commerce
PO Box 432
Prosper, TX 75078
Ph:(972)508-4200
Fax: (866)877-7965
Co. E-mail: prosperareachamber@prospertx.com
URL: http://www.prosperchamber.org

Contact: Bob Luckock, Pres.

65457 ■ Quanah Chamber of Commerce
220 S Main
PO Box 158
Quanah, TX 79252
Ph:(940)663-2222
Fax: (940)663-2620
Co. E-mail: quanahcc@chipshot.net
Contact: Bertha Woods, Exec.Sec.

65458 ■ Ralls Chamber of Commerce
PO Box 807
Ralls, TX 79357
Ph:(806)253-2342
URL: http://www.rootsweb.com/~txcrosby/
       community/ralls.htm

65459 ■ Randolph Metrocom Chamber of Commerce
1001 Pat Booker Rd., Ste. 206
Universal City, TX 78148
Ph:(210)658-8322
Fax: (210)658-1817
Co. E-mail: jwilliams.rmcc@sbcglobal.net
URL: http://www.randolphmetrocomchamber.org
Contact: John Williams, Pres.

65460 ■ Ranger Chamber of Commerce
PO Box 57
Ranger, TX 76470
Ph:(254)647-3091
Fax: (254)647-3091
Contact: Joe Oliver, Pres.

65461 ■ Red River County Chamber of Commerce
101 N Locust St.
Clarksville, TX 75426
Ph:(903)427-2645
Fax: (903)427-5454
Co. E-mail: redrivercc@lstarnet.com
URL: http://www.red-river.net
Contact: Mac Varley, Pres.

65462 ■ Richardson Chamber of Commerce
411 Belle Grove Dr.
Richardson, TX 75080-5297
Ph:(972)792-2800
Fax: (972)792-2825
Co. E-mail: bill@telecomcorridor.com
URL: http://www.telecomcorridor.com
Contact: Bill Sproull, Pres./CEO

65463 ■ Rio Grande Valley Chamber of Commerce
PO Box 1499
Weslaco, TX 78599-1499
Ph:(956)968-3141
Fax: (956)968-0210
Co. E-mail: mail@valleychamber.com
URL: http://www.valleychamber.com
Contact: Bill Summers, Pres./CEO

65464 ■ River Oaks - Sansom Park Area Chamber of Commerce
5136 Jacksboro Hwy.
Fort Worth, TX 76114
Ph:(817)626-3377
URL: http://www.riveroakstx.com
Contact: Sherry Parnell, Pres.

65465 ■ Rockdale Chamber of Commerce
1203 W Cameron Ave.
Rockdale, TX 76567
Ph:(512)446-2030
Fax: (512)446-5969
Co. E-mail: sjenkins@rockdalechamber.com
URL: http://www.rockdalechamber.com
Contact: Denice Doss, Pres.

65466 ■ Rockport-Fulton Area Chamber of Commerce
404 Broadway
Rockport, TX 78382
Ph:(361)729-6445
Free: 800-826-6441

Fax: (361)729-7681
Co. E-mail: visitor@1rockport.org
URL: http://www.1rockport.org
Contact: Laura Denham, Chair

65467 ■ Rockwall County Chamber of Commerce
697 E I-30
PO Box 92
Rockwall, TX 75087-0092
Ph:(972)771-5733
Fax: (972)772-3642
Co. E-mail: admin@rockwallchamber.org
URL: http://www.rockwallchamber.org
Contact: Ms. Cher Bullard, Office Mgr.

65468 ■ Rosebud Chamber of Commerce and Agriculture
PO Box 369
Rosebud, TX 76570
Ph:(254)583-7979
Fax: (254)583-2157
Co. E-mail: mayorrosebudtexas@yahoo.com
Contact: Ken Hensel, Sec.

65469 ■ Rosenberg - Richmond Area Chamber of Commerce
4120 Ave. H
Rosenberg, TX 77471
Ph:(281)342-5464
Fax: (281)342-2990
Co. E-mail: gparker@roserichchamber.org
URL: http://www.roserichchamber.com
Contact: Gail Parker, Pres./CEO

65470 ■ Round Rock Chamber of Commerce
212 E Main St.
Round Rock, TX 78664
Ph:(512)255-5805
Fax: (512)255-3345
Co. E-mail: cdromgoole@roundrockchamber.org
URL: http://www.roundrockchamber.org
Contact: Charlie Dromgoole, Pres.

65471 ■ Rowlett Chamber of Commerce
3910 Main St.
PO Box 610
Rowlett, TX 75030-0610
Ph:(972)475-3200
Fax: (972)463-1699
Co. E-mail: rowlett_chamber@rowlettchamber.com
URL: http://www.rowlettchamber.com
Contact: Ms. Mary Alice Ethridge, Exec.Dir./Advisor

65472 ■ Royse City Chamber of Commerce
118 E Main St.
Royse City, TX 75189
Ph:(972)636-5000
Fax: (972)636-0051
Co. E-mail: info@roysecitychamber.com
URL: http://www.roysecitychamber.com
Contact: Shayna Levine, Exec.Dir.

65473 ■ Rule Chamber of Commerce
PO Box 58
Rule, TX 79547-0058
Ph:(940)997-2141
Contact: Orheana Greeson, Sec.

65474 ■ Runaway Bay Chamber of Commerce
51 Runaway Bay Dr.
Runaway Bay, TX 76426
Ph:(940)575-4525
Fax: (940)575-4308
Contact: Norma Coble, Sec./Mgr.

65475 ■ Rusk Chamber of Commerce
415 N Main St.
PO Box 67
Rusk, TX 75785
Ph:(903)683-4242
Free: 800-933-2381
Fax: (903)683-1054
Co. E-mail: chamber@rusktx.com
URL: http://www.rusktexascoc.org
Contact: Louise Morris, Sec.

65476 ■ Sabinal Chamber of Commerce
PO Box 55
Sabinal, TX 78881
Ph:(830)988-2010
Co. E-mail: sab@sabinalchamber.com
URL: http://www.sabinalchamber.com
Contact: Danny Dean, Pres.

65477 ■ Sabine County Chamber of Commerce
717 Sabine St.
PO Box 717
Hemphill, TX 75948-0717
Ph:(409)787-2732
Fax: (409)787-2158
Co. E-mail: sabinetx@sabinenet.com
URL: http://www.sabinecountytexas.com
Contact: Faye Broadway, Exec. VP

65478 ■ Saginaw Area Chamber of Commerce
301 S Saginaw Blvd.
Saginaw, TX 76179
Ph:(817)232-0500
Fax: (817)232-2311
Co. E-mail: info@saginawtxchamber.org
URL: http://www.saginawtxchamber.org
Contact: Joyce Erwin, Chair

65479 ■ Salado Chamber of Commerce
PO Box 849
Salado, TX 76571
Ph:(254)947-5040
Fax: (254)947-3126
Co. E-mail: saladochamber@vvm.com
URL: http://www.salado.com
Contact: Dawn Orange, Admin.Dir.

65480 ■ San Angelo Chamber of Commerce
418 W Ave. B
San Angelo, TX 76903-6027
Ph:(325)655-4136
Fax: (325)658-1110
Co. E-mail: chamber@sanangelo.org
URL: http://www.sanangelo.org
Contact: Mr. Michael Dalby, Pres.

65481 ■ San Antonio Hispanic Chamber of Commerce
318 W Houston St., Ste. 300
San Antonio, TX 78205
Ph:(210)225-0462
Fax: (210)225-2485
Co. E-mail: ajrodriguez@sahcc.org
URL: http://www.sahcc.org
Contact: A.J. Rodriguez, Pres.

65482 ■ San Antonio Women's Chamber of Commerce of Texas
600 Hemisfair Plz. Way, Bldg. 217
San Antonio, TX 78205
Ph:(210)299-2636
Fax: (210)299-4169
Co. E-mail: sawcc@dcci.com
URL: http://www.sawomenschamber.org
Contact: Denise Powers, Chair

65483 ■ San Augustine County Chamber of Commerce
611 W Columbia St.
San Augustine, TX 75972
Ph:(936)275-3610
Fax: (936)275-0054
Co. E-mail: info@sanaugustinetx.com
URL: http://www.sanaugustinetx.com
Contact: Samye Johnson, Exec.Dir.

65484 ■ San Benito Chamber of Commerce
210 E Heywood St.
San Benito, TX 78586
Ph:(956)399-5321
Co. E-mail: lzamora@cityofsanbenito.com
URL: http://www.sbida.com

65485 ■ San Juan Chamber of Commerce
709 S Nebraska
San Juan, TX 78589

Ph:(956)783-9957
Fax: (956)783-5413
Contact: Estella Salazar, Dir.

65486 ■ San Marcos Area Chamber of Commerce
PO Box 2310
San Marcos, TX 78667
Ph:(512)393-5900
Fax: (512)393-5912
Co. E-mail: chamber@sanmarcostexas.com
URL: http://www.sanmarcostexas.com
Contact: Phil Neighbors, Pres.

65487 ■ San Saba County Chamber of Commerce
302 E Wallace St.
San Saba, TX 76877
Ph:(325)372-5440
Co. E-mail: civicntr@centex.net
URL: http://www.sansabachamber.com
Contact: Ms. Lynda Pack, CEO

65488 ■ Sanger Area Chamber of Commerce
300 Bolivar St.
Sanger, TX 76266
Ph:(940)458-7702
Fax: (940)458-7823
Co. E-mail: chamber@sangertexas.com
URL: http://www.sangertexas.com
Contact: Bret Chance, Pres.

65489 ■ Santa Fe Chamber of Commerce
12406 Hwy. 6
Santa Fe, TX 77510
Ph:(409)925-8558
Fax: (409)925-8551
Co. E-mail: info@santafetexaschamber.com
URL: http://www.santafetexaschamber.com
Contact: Fay Picard, Exec.Dir.

65490 ■ Schulenburg Chamber of Commerce
618 N Main St.
Schulenburg, TX 78956
Ph:(979)743-4514
Free: (866)504-5294
Fax: (979)743-9155
Co. E-mail: info@schulenburgchamber.org
URL: http://www.schulenburgchamber.org
Contact: Vicki Woodard, Pres./CEO

65491 ■ Seagoville Chamber of Commerce
107 Hall St.
Seagoville, TX 75159
Ph:(972)287-5184
Fax: (972)287-5815
Co. E-mail: secretary@
   seagovillechamberofcommerce.org
URL: http://www.seagovillechamberofcommerce.org
Contact: Debra McClellan, Pres.

65492 ■ Seagraves Area Chamber of Commerce
PO Box 1257
Seagraves, TX 79359-1257
Ph:(806)546-2609
Fax: (806)546-0441
Contact: Diann Hill, Sec.

65493 ■ Sealy Chamber of Commerce
309 Main St.
PO Box 586
Sealy, TX 77474
Ph:(979)885-3222
Free: 877-558-7245
Fax: (979)885-7184
Co. E-mail: sealycoc@industryinet.com
URL: http://www.sealy-tx.com
Contact: Charley Burchfield, Pres.

65494 ■ Seguin Area Chamber of Commerce
427 N Austin St.
Seguin, TX 78155
Ph:(830)379-6382
Fax: (830)379-6971
Co. E-mail: rob@seguinchamber.com
URL: http://www.seguintx.org

Contact: Robert Cunningham, Pres.

65495 ■ Seminole Area Chamber of Commerce
119 SE Ave. B
PO Box 1198
Seminole, TX 79360
Ph:(915)758-2352
Fax: (915)758-6698
Co. E-mail: semcoc@midtech.net
Contact: Shelly Concotelli, Exec.VP

65496 ■ Seymour Chamber of Commerce
301 N Washington St.
PO Box 1379
Seymour, TX 76380
Ph:(940)889-2921
Fax: (940)889-8882
Co. E-mail: scoc@nts-online.net
URL: http://www.seymourtxchamber.org
Contact: Myra Busby, Managing Dir.

65497 ■ Shamrock Chamber of Commerce
105 E 12th St.
Shamrock, TX 79079
Ph:(806)256-2501
Fax: (806)256-3739
Co. E-mail: irishedb@hotmail.com
URL: http://www.shamrocktx.net
Contact: David Rushing, Dir.

65498 ■ Shelby County Chamber of Commerce
100 Courthouse Sq., A-101
Center, TX 75935
Ph:(936)598-3682
Fax: (936)598-8163
Co. E-mail: info@shelbycountychamber.com
URL: http://www.shelbycountychamber.com
Contact: Pam Phelps, Exec.Dir.

65499 ■ Sherman Chamber of Commerce
307 W Washington, Ste. 100
Sherman, TX 75090
Ph:(903)893-1184
Free: 888-893-1188
Fax: (903)893-4266
Co. E-mail: chamber@shermantexas.com
URL: http://www.shermantexas.com
Contact: Rad Richardson, Pres.

65500 ■ Shiner Chamber of Commerce
PO Box 221
Shiner, TX 77984
Ph:(361)594-4180
Co. E-mail: shinercc@shinertx.com
URL: http://www.shinertx.com
Contact: Billy Petru, Pres.

65501 ■ Silsbee Chamber of Commerce
835 Hwy. 96 S
Silsbee, TX 77656
Ph:(409)385-5562
Fax: (409)385-5695
Co. E-mail: scc@ih2000.net
Contact: Regina Lindsey, Exec.VP

65502 ■ Sinton Chamber of Commerce
218 W Sinton St.
Sinton, TX 78387
Ph:(361)364-2307
Fax: (361)364-3538
Co. E-mail: sintonchamber@sbcglobal.net
URL: http://www.sintontexas.org

65503 ■ Slaton Chamber of Commerce
PO Box 400
Slaton, TX 79364-0400
Ph:(806)828-6238
Fax: (806)828-5115
Co. E-mail: slatoncoc@nts-online.net
URL: http://www.slatonchamberofcommerce.org
Contact: Lesley Robinson, Mgr.

65504 ■ Smithville Area Chamber of Commerce
100 1st St.
PO Box 716
Smithville, TX 78957

Ph:(512)237-2313
Co. E-mail: chamber@smithvilletx.org
URL: http://www.smithvilletx.org
Contact: Adena Lewis, Exec.Dir.

65505 ■ Snyder Chamber of Commerce
PO Box 840
Snyder, TX 79550
Ph:(325)573-3558
Fax: (325)573-9721
Co. E-mail: snychcom@snydertex.com
URL: http://www.snyderchamber.org
Contact: Vicki Shroyer, Exec.Dir.

65506 ■ Sonora Chamber of Commerce
205 Hwy. 277 N
Sonora, TX 76950-1172
Ph:(325)387-2880
Fax: (325)387-5357
Co. E-mail: soncoc@sonoratx.net
URL: http://www.sonoratx-chamber.com
Contact: Ruth Bounds, Exec.Dir.

65507 ■ South Belt - Ellington Chamber of Commerce
10500 Scarsdale
Houston, TX 77089-2375
Ph:(281)481-5516
Fax: (281)922-7045
URL: http://southbeltchamber.com
Contact: Kathy Valtasaros, Pres.

65508 ■ South Montgomery County - Woodlands Chamber of Commerce
1400 Woodloch Forest Dr., Ste. 300
The Woodlands, TX 77380
Ph:(281)367-5777
Fax: (281)292-1655
Co. E-mail: karen.hoylman@woodlandschamber.org
URL: http://www.smcwcc.org
Contact: Karen Hoylman, Pres./CEO

65509 ■ South Padre Island Chamber of Commerce
600 Padre Blvd.
South Padre Island, TX 78597
Ph:(956)761-4412
Fax: (956)761-2739
Co. E-mail: info@spichamber.com
URL: http://www.spichamber.com
Contact: Roxanne Harris Guenzel, Pres.

65510 ■ South San Antonio Chamber of Commerce
3319 Sidney Brooks, Bldg. 510
Brooks City-Base
San Antonio, TX 78235
Ph:(210)533-1600
Fax: (210)533-1611
Co. E-mail: ctaylor@southsachamber.org
URL: http://www.southsachamber.org
Contact: Cindy Taylor, Pres.

65511 ■ South Tarrant County Chamber of Commerce
PO Box 1338
Kennedale, TX 76060
Ph:(817)568-2685
Fax: (817)568-8490
Co. E-mail: info@southtarrantchamber.org
Contact: Jennifer Meeker, Pres.

65512 ■ Southeast Dallas Chamber of Commerce
PO Box 170132
Dallas, TX 75217
Ph:(214)398-9590
Fax: (214)398-9591
Co. E-mail: info@sedcc.org
URL: http://www.sedcc.org
Contact: Carl Raines, Chm.

65513 ■ Southlake Chamber of Commerce
1501 Corporate Cir., Ste. 100
Southlake, TX 76092
Ph:(817)481-8200
Fax: (817)749-8202

Co. E-mail: info@southlakechamber.com
URL: http://www.southlakechamber.com
Contact: Giovanna Phillips, Pres.

65514 ■ Spearman Chamber of Commerce
211 Main St.
PO Box 161
Spearman, TX 79081
Ph:(806)659-5555
Co. E-mail: spearman@triangleinc.net
URL: http://www.spearman.org
Contact: Keith Hight, Exec.VP

65515 ■ Springtown Area Chamber of Commerce
112 S Main
PO Box 296
Springtown, TX 76082-0296
Ph:(817)220-7828
Fax: (817)523-3268
Co. E-mail: chamber@springtowntexas.com
URL: http://www.springtowntexas.com
Contact: Rachel Gafford, Exec.Dir.

65516 ■ Stamford Chamber of Commerce
113 S Weatherbee
Stamford, TX 79553
Ph:(915)773-2411
Fax: (915)773-5594
Co. E-mail: scoc@sunsetpass.com
Contact: Joe McMeans

65517 ■ Stephenville Chamber of Commerce
187 W Washington St.
PO Box 306
Stephenville, TX 76401
Ph:(254)965-5313
Fax: (254)965-3814
Co. E-mail: chamber@our-town.com
URL: http://www.stephenvilletexas.org
Contact: Jeff Sandford, Pres./CEO

65518 ■ Stonewall Chamber of Commerce
115 St. Francis St.
Stonewall, TX 78671
Ph:(830)644-2735
Fax: (830)644-2165
Co. E-mail: chamber@stonewall.com
URL: http://www.stonewalltexas.com
Contact: Elizabeth Nielsen, Pres.

65519 ■ Stratford Chamber of Commerce
PO Box 570
520 N Third
Stratford, TX 79084-0570
Ph:(806)366-2260
Fax: (806)366-2254
Co. E-mail: stratford@xit.net
Contact: Paula Nusz, Dir.

65520 ■ Sweeny Chamber of Commerce
112 N Main
Sweeny, TX 77480
Ph:(409)548-3249
Fax: (409)548-3251
Co. E-mail: sweenych@fbtc.net
Contact: Amy Dunham, Exec.Dir.

65521 ■ Sweetwater Chamber of Commerce and Convention and Visitors' Bureau
810 E Broadway
PO Box 1148
Sweetwater, TX 79556
Ph:(325)235-5488
Free: 800-658-6757
Fax: (325)235-1026
Co. E-mail: chamber@sweetwatertexas.org
URL: http://sweetwatertexas.org
Contact: Mr. Lynn Adams, Exec.VP/Dir.

65522 ■ Taft Chamber of Commerce
503 Green Ave.
PO Box 123
Taft, TX 78390
Ph:(361)528-3230
Fax: (361)528-3515
Contact: Mary M. Griffin, Sec.

65523 ■ Taylor Chamber of Commerce
1519 N Main St.
Taylor, TX 76574
Ph:(512)352-6364
Fax: (512)365-8485
Co. E-mail: info@taylorchamber.org
URL: http://www.taylorchamber.org
Contact: Shanta Kuhl, Pres.

65524 ■ Teague Chamber of Commerce
PO Box 484
Teague, TX 75860-0484
Ph:(254)739-2061
Fax: (254)739-2670
Contact: Marilyn Michaud, Office Mgr.

65525 ■ Temple Chamber of Commerce
2 N 5th St.
PO Box 158
Temple, TX 76503
Ph:(254)773-2105
Fax: (254)773-0661
Co. E-mail: temple@templetx.org
Contact: Ken Higdon, Pres.

65526 ■ Terrell Chamber of Commerce
1314 W Moore Ave.
Terrell, TX 75160
Ph:(972)563-5703
Free: 877-TER-RELL
Fax: (972)563-2363
Co. E-mail: info@terrelltexas.com
URL: http://www.terrelltexas.com
Contact: Danny R. Booth, Pres.

65527 ■ Texarkana Chamber of Commerce
PO Box 1468
Texarkana, TX 75504
Ph:(903)792-7191
Free: 877-275-5289
Fax: (903)793-4304
Co. E-mail: chamber@texarkana.org
URL: http://www.texarkana.org
Contact: Linda Crawford, Pres.

65528 ■ Texas Association of Business and Chamber of Commerce
1209 Nueces St.
Austin, TX 78701-1719
Ph:(512)477-6721
Fax: (512)477-0836
Co. E-mail: info@txbiz.org
URL: http://www.txbiz.org
Contact: Bill Hammond, Pres./CEO

65529 ■ Texas Association of Mexican American Chambers of Commerce
3000 S IH-35, Ste. 305
Austin, TX 78704
Ph:(512)444-5727
Fax: (512)444-4929
Co. E-mail: info@tamacc.org
URL: http://www.tamacc.org
Contact: Carlos T. Mendoza, Pres./CEO

65530 ■ Texas City - La Marque Chamber of Commerce
8419 E.F. Lowry Expy.
PO Box 1717
Texas City, TX 77591
Ph:(409)935-1408
Free: 888-860-1408
Co. E-mail: jimmy@texascitychamber.com
URL: http://www.texascitychamber.com
Contact: Jimmy Hayley, Pres.

65531 ■ Thorndale Area Chamber of Commerce
PO Box 668
Thorndale, TX 76577
Ph:(512)898-0053
Fax: (512)898-2502
Contact: Mike Richardson, Pres.

65532 ■ Three Rivers Chamber of Commerce
PO Box 1648
Three Rivers, TX 78071

Ph:(361)786-4330
Free: 888-600-3115
Fax: (361)786-2423
Co. E-mail: citytrex@fnbnet.net
URL: http://www.threeriverstx.org

65533 ■ Tomball Area Chamber of Commerce
14011 Park Dr., Ste. 111
PO Box 516
Tomball, TX 77377-0516
Ph:(281)351-7222
Free: (866)670-7222
Fax: (281)351-7223
Co. E-mail: admin@tomballchamber.org
URL: http://dismbr04.nhmccd.edu/tomball
Contact: Bruce E. Hillegeist, Pres.

65534 ■ Trinity County Chamber of Commerce
PO Box 366
Groveton, TX 75845-0366
Ph:(936)642-1715
Fax: (936)642-2144
Co. E-mail: tccoc@consolidated.net
URL: http://www.trinitycountychamber.org

65535 ■ Trinity Peninsula Chamber of Commerce
PO Box 549
Trinity, TX 75862
Ph:(936)594-3856
Fax: (936)594-0558
Co. E-mail: info@trinitychamber.org
URL: http://www.trinitychamber.org
Contact: Julia McMichael, Exec. Dir.

65536 ■ Troup Chamber of Commerce
PO Box 336
Troup, TX 75789
Ph:(903)842-4113
URL: http://www.trouptexas.org

65537 ■ Tulia Chamber of Commerce
PO Box 267
Tulia, TX 79088
Ph:(806)995-2296
Fax: (806)995-4426
Co. E-mail: tuliatexas@amaonline.com
URL: http://www.tuliachamberofcommerce.com
Contact: Lana Barnett, Pres.

65538 ■ Tyler Area Chamber of Commerce
315 N Broadway
PO Box 390
Tyler, TX 75702
Ph:(903)592-1661
Free: 800-235-5712
Fax: (903)593-2746
Co. E-mail: hbell@tylertexas.com
URL: http://www.tylertexas.com/index2.htm
Contact: Henry Bell III, Exec.VP

65539 ■ Tyler County Chamber of Commerce
717 W Bluff
Woodville, TX 75979
Ph:(409)283-2632
Fax: (409)283-6884
Co. E-mail: info@woodvilletx.com
URL: http://www.woodvilletx.com
Contact: Audrey Pelly, Pres.

65540 ■ Uvalde Chamber of Commerce
300 E Main St.
Uvalde, TX 78801
Ph:(830)278-3361
Fax: (830)278-3363
Co. E-mail: director@uvalde.org
URL: http://www.uvalde.org
Contact: Teri Koerner, Exec.Dir.

65541 ■ Van Alstyne Chamber of Commerce
PO Box 698
Van Alstyne, TX 75495-0698
Ph:(903)482-6066
Co. E-mail: vachamber@gcecisp.com

65542 ■ Van Area Chamber of Commerce
PO Box 55
Van, TX 75790
Ph:(903)963-5051
Co. E-mail: vanchamber@vantexas.com
URL: http://www.vantexas.com
Contact: Linda Mastaglio, Pres.

65543 ■ Van Horn Chamber of Commerce
PO Box 762
Van Horn, TX 79855
Ph:(432)283-2043
Fax: (432)283-1413
URL: http://www.vanhorntexas.org
Contact: Larry Simpson, Pres.

65544 ■ Vernon Chamber of Commerce
PO Box 1538
Vernon, TX 76385-1538
Ph:(940)552-2564
Free: 800-687-3137
Fax: (940)552-0654
Co. E-mail: chamber@vernontx.com
URL: http://www.vernontx.com
Contact: Jessica Holton, Asst.Dir.

65545 ■ Victoria Chamber of Commerce
PO Box 2465
Victoria, TX 77902
Ph:(361)573-5277
Fax: (361)573-5911
Co. E-mail: oliviabarrera@victoriachamber.org
URL: http://www.victoriachamber.org
Contact: Phyllis Hunt, Pres./CEO

65546 ■ Vidor Chamber of Commerce
510 N Main St., Ste. 1
PO Box 413
Vidor, TX 77662
Ph:(409)769-6339
Fax: (409)769-0227
Co. E-mail: vidorchamber@netzero.net
Contact: Dena Rambo, Exec.Sec.

65547 ■ Waller Area Chamber of Commerce
Wells Fargo Bank Bldg.
2313 Main St., No. 175
Waller, TX 77484
Ph:(936)372-5300
Co. E-mail: info@wallerchamber.com
URL: http://www.wallerchamber.com
Contact: Mark Dandy, Pres.

65548 ■ Washington County Chamber of Commerce
314 S Austin St.
Brenham, TX 77833
Ph:(979)836-3695
Free: 888-BRE-NHAM
Fax: (979)836-2540
Co. E-mail: info@brenhamtexas.com
URL: http://www.brenhamtexas.com
Contact: John Holchin, Pres./CEO

65549 ■ Waxahachie Chamber of Commerce
102 YMCA Dr.
Waxahachie, TX 75165
Ph:(972)937-2390
Fax: (972)938-9827
Co. E-mail: dwakeland@waxahachiechamber.com
URL: http://www.waxacofc.com
Contact: Debra Wakeland, Pres./CEO

65550 ■ Weatherford Chamber of Commerce
401 Ft. Worth Hwy.
PO Box 310
Weatherford, TX 76086
Ph:(817)596-3801
Free: 888-594-3801
Fax: (817)613-9216
Co. E-mail: info@weatherford-chamber.com
URL: http://www.weatherford-chamber.com
Contact: Andrea Sutten, Pres.

65551 ■ Weimar Area Chamber of Commerce
109 E Main
PO Box 90
Weimar, TX 78962-0090

Ph:(979)725-9511
Free: 888-393-4627
Fax: (979)725-6890
Co. E-mail: weimarcc@cvtv.net
Contact: Pat Davis, Sec.

65552 ■ Weslaco Area Chamber of Commerce
PO Box 8398
Weslaco, TX 78599-8398
Ph:(956)968-2102
Free: 888-968-2102
Fax: (956)968-6451
Co. E-mail: martha@weslaco.com
URL: http://www.weslaco.com
Contact: Martha Noell, Pres./CEO

65553 ■ West Chamber of Commerce
PO Box 123
West, TX 76691
Ph:(254)826-3188
Free: (866)826-3189
Fax: (254)826-3630
Co. E-mail: westcofc8263188@aol.com
Contact: Jennifer Moore, Coor.

65554 ■ West Chambers County Chamber of Commerce
PO Box 750
11340 Eagle Dr., Ste. 4
Mont Belvieu, TX 77580
Ph:(281)576-5440
Fax: (281)576-2135
Co. E-mail: wcccc@teleshare.net
URL: http://www.westchamberscoc.com
Contact: Melissa G. Malechek, Pres.

65555 ■ West Columbia Chamber of Commerce
PO Box 837
West Columbia, TX 77486
Ph:(979)345-3921
Fax: (979)345-6526
Co. E-mail: chamber@westcolumbia.org
URL: http://www.westcolumbia.org
Contact: Rita Terrell

65556 ■ West I-10 Chamber of Commerce
PO Box 100
Pattison, TX 77466
Ph:(281)375-8100
Fax: (281)934-2012
Co. E-mail: chamber@westi10chamber.org
URL: http://www.westi10chamber.org
Contact: Wallace Everitt, Pres.

65557 ■ Wharton Chamber of Commerce
225 N Richmond Rd.
PO Box 868
Wharton, TX 77488
Ph:(979)532-1862
Fax: (979)532-0102
Co. E-mail: torieblakely@sbcglobal.net
URL: http://www.whartontexas.com
Contact: Billie H. Jones, Exec.Dir.

65558 ■ Wheeler Chamber of Commerce and Economic Development Corporation
PO Box 221
Wheeler, TX 79096-0221
Ph:(806)826-3408
Fax: (806)826-3219
Contact: Marla Ford, Pres.

65559 ■ White Settlement Area Chamber of Commerce
601 S Cherry Ln., Ste. C
White Settlement, TX 76108-2565
Ph:(817)246-1121
Fax: (817)246-1121
Co. E-mail: wsacc@whitesettlement-tx.com
URL: http://www.whitesettlement-tx.com
Contact: Roger Chambers, Office Mgr.

65560 ■ Whitehouse Area Chamber of Commerce
PO Box 1041
Whitehouse, TX 75791

Ph:(903)839-6884
Co. E-mail: info@whitehousetx.com
URL: http://www.whitehousetx.com
Contact: Brent Conaway, Pres.

65561 ■ Whitesboro Area Chamber of Commerce
2535 Hwy. 82E, Ste. C
PO Box 522
Whitesboro, TX 76273
Ph:(903)564-3331
Fax: (903)564-3397
Co. E-mail: info@whitesborotx.com
URL: http://www.whitesborotx.com
Contact: Janis Crawley, Pres.

65562 ■ Wichita Falls Board of Commerce and Industry
900 Eighth St., Ste. 218
PO Box 1860
Wichita Falls, TX 76307
Ph:(940)723-2741
Fax: (940)723-8773
Co. E-mail: wfbci@wf.net
URL: http://www.wichitafallscommerce.com
Contact: Tim Chase, Pres./CEO

65563 ■ Wills Point Chamber of Commerce
307 N 4th St.
PO Box 217
Wills Point, TX 75169
Ph:(903)873-3111
Fax: (903)873-2199
Co. E-mail: karen@willspoint.org
URL: http://www.willspoint.org
Contact: Karen Samples, Pres.

65564 ■ Wimberley Chamber of Commerce
PO Box 12
Wimberley, TX 78676
Ph:(512)847-2201
Fax: (512)847-3189
Co. E-mail: info@wimberley.org
URL: http://www.wimberley.org
Contact: Gail Blachly, Pres.

65565 ■ Wink Chamber of Commerce
PO Box 397
Wink, TX 79789
Ph:(915)527-3441
Fax: (915)527-3303
Co. E-mail: kdmaddux@nwol.net
Contact: Bill Beckham, Pres.

65566 ■ Winnsboro Area Chamber of Commerce
101 N Main
Winnsboro, TX 75494-2624
Ph:(903)342-3666
Fax: (903)342-3667
Co. E-mail: info@winnsboro.com
URL: http://www.winnsboro.com
Contact: Debbie Lyn Foster, Administrator

65567 ■ Winters Area Chamber of Commerce
118 W Dale St.
Winters, TX 79567
Ph:(915)754-5210
Fax: (325)754-5826
Co. E-mail: wacc@wcc.net
Contact: Carolyn Scarborough, Sec.

65568 ■ Wolfe City Chamber of Commerce
PO Box 8
Wolfe City, TX 75496
Ph:(903)496-2323
URL: http://www.wolfecitytexas.com
Contact: W. Kelly Wood, Pres.

65569 ■ Wolfforth Area Chamber of Commerce and Agriculture
PO Box 36
Wolfforth, TX 79382
Ph:(806)866-4215
Fax: (806)866-4217
Co. E-mail: wolfweb@wolfforthtx.us
URL: http://wolfforthtx.us/chamber_of_commerce.htm

Contact: Terry Hale, Pres.

65570 ■ Women's Chamber of Commerce of Texas in Austin
PO Box 26051
Austin, TX 78755-0051
Ph:(512)338-0839
Fax: (512)338-1614
Co. E-mail: womenschamber@austin.rr.com
URL: http://www.womenschambertexas.com
Contact: Rose Batson, Pres.

65571 ■ Wylie Chamber of Commerce
108A W Marble St.
Wylie, TX 75098
Ph:(972)442-2804
Fax: (972)429-0139
Co. E-mail: wyliechamber@digitakes.com
URL: http://www.wyliechamber.org
Contact: Steve Reid, Chm.

65572 ■ Yoakum Area Chamber of Commerce
105 Huck St.
PO Box 591
Yoakum, TX 77995
Ph:(361)293-2309
Fax: (361)741-6739
Co. E-mail: info@yoakumareachamber.com
URL: http://www.yoakumusa.com
Contact: Dori Wyatt, Dir.

65573 ■ Yorktown Chamber of Commerce
130 N Riedel St.
PO Box 488
Yorktown, TX 78164
Ph:(361)564-2661
Fax: (361)564-2518
Co. E-mail: yorktowncofc@gvec.net
URL: http://www.yorktowntx.com
Contact: Melissa Armstrong

65574 ■ Zapata Chamber of Commerce
PO Box 1028
Zapata, TX 78076-1028
Ph:(956)765-4871
Free: 800-292-LAKE
Fax: (956)765-5434
Co. E-mail: chamber@zapata.border.net
Contact: Julie Ivey, Dir.

MINORITY BUSINESS ASSISTANCE PROGRAMS

65575 ■ Brownsville Minority Business Development Center–Management Assistance Services
3505 Boca Chica Blvd., Ste. 174
International Plaza Bldg.
Brownsville, TX 78521-2265
Ph:(956)546-3400
Co. E-mail: mector@xanadu2.net

65576 ■ City of Corpus Christi Business Resource Center
400 S.P.I.D., Ste 100
1616 Martin Luther King Dr., 1st Fl.
Corpus Christi, TX 78405
Ph:(361)883-9917
Fax: (361)883-9918
Co. E-mail: ktrevino@davlin.net
URL: http://www.cctexas.com

65577 ■ Corpus Christi Minority Business Development Center
226 Enterprise Pkwy, No. 112
Corpus Christi, TX 78405
Ph:(361)883-1809
Fax: (361)888-9473
Co. E-mail: corpusnbdc@attglobal.net
URL: http://www.mbda.gov

65578 ■ Dallas/Fort Worth Minority Business Development Center
545 E John Carpenter Fwy., Ste. 100
Irving, TX 75062
Ph:(214)688-1612
Fax: (214)688-1753
URL: http://www.dallasfwmbdc.com
Contact: Antonio Grijalva, Pres

65579 ■ El Paso Minority Business Development Center–NEDA Business Consultants, Inc.
5959 Gateway W, Ste. 425
El Paso, TX 79925
Ph:(915)774-0626
Fax: (915)774-0680
Co. E-mail: epneda@aol.com
URL: http://www.nedainc.net
Contact: Jose Rocha, Project Mgr

65580 ■ Houston Minority Business Council
6671 Southwest Fwy., Ste. 110
Houston, TX 77074
Ph:(713)271-7805
Fax: (713)271-9770
Co. E-mail: info@hmbc.org
URL: http://www.hmbc.org/

65581 ■ San Antonio Minority Business Development Enterprise–University of Texas at San Antonio, Downtown
University of Texas at San Antonio, Downtown
501 W Durango Blvd.
San Antonio, TX 78207-4415
Ph:(210)458-2480
Fax: (210)458-2481
Co. E-mail: fparks@utsa.edu
URL: http://www.sa-mbec.org
Contact: Fletcher Parks, Dir

65582 ■ South Texas Minority Business Opportunity Committee
2412 S Closner, Rm. 134
2412 S. Closner
Edinburg, TX 78539
Ph:(956)292-7555
Fax: (956)292-7521
Co. E-mail: mboc@panam.edu
URL: http://www.mboc-occ.org

65583 ■ Texas Department of Economic Development and Tourism–Business Development Division
PO Box 12428
Austin, TX 78711
Ph:(512)936-0100
Free: 800-888-8TEX
Fax: (512)936-0440
URL: http://www.txed.state.tx.us
Description: Promotes and supports small, minority-owned, and women-owned businesses in the areas of government contracting, capital resource identification, and general business counseling.

FINANCING AND LOAN PROGRAMS

65584 ■ Abacus Ventures
5910 N. Central Expy., Ste. 760
Dallas, TX 75206
Ph:(214)346-2560
Fax: (214)346-2563
URL: http://www.abacusventures.com
Contact: Dave Kennedy, Managing Director
Investment Policies: Acquisition.

65585 ■ Akin Gump Investment Partners 2000, LP
1700 Pacific Ave., Ste. 4100
Dallas, TX 75201
Ph:(214)969-2800
Fax: (214)969-4343
URL: http://www.akingump.com
Contact: William Dennis, Partner
Investment Types: Early stage. **Industry Preferences:** Computer software, Internet specific, and biotechnology.

65586 ■ Alliance Financial of Houston
218 Heather Ln.
Conroe, TX 77385-9013
Ph:(936)447-3300
Fax: (936)447-4222
Preferred Investment Size: $300,000 to $500,000.
Investment Types: First and second stage, mezzanine, leveraged buyout, and special situation.

65587 ■ Amerimark Capital Group
511 E. John Carpenter Fwy., Ste. 220
Irving, TX 75062
Ph:(214)638-7878
Fax: (214)638-7612
URL: http://www.amcapital.com
Contact: Charles Martin, Chief Executive Officer
Preferred Investment Size: $500,000 minimum. **Investment Types:** Second stage, mezzanine, and leveraged buyout. **Industry Preferences:** Communications, Internet specific, computer hardware, consumer related, industrial and energy, financial services, and business service. **Geographic Preferences:** U.S.

65588 ■ AMT Capital Ltd. / AMT Venture Partners, Ltd.
5220 Spring Valley Rd., Ste. 600
Dallas, TX 75240
Ph:(214)905-9757
Fax: (214)905-9761
URL: http://www.amtcapital.com
Contact: Peter Walmsley, General Partner
Preferred Investment Size: $100,000 to $500,000.
Investment Policies: Early, first and second stage, and expansion. **Industry Preferences:** Semiconductors and other electronics, industrial and energy. **Geographic Preferences:** U.S.

65589 ■ AMT Venture Partners, Ltd. / AMT Capital Ltd.
5220 Spring Valley Rd., Ste. 600
Dallas, TX 75240
Ph:(214)905-9757
Fax: (214)905-9761
URL: http://www.amtcapital.com
Contact: Peter Walmsley, General Partner
Preferred Investment Size: $100,000 to $500,000.
Investment Types: Early, first and second stage, and expansion. **Industry Preferences:** Semiconductors and other electronics, industrial and energy. **Geographic Preferences:** U.S.

65590 ■ Arkoma Venture Partners
5950 Berkshire Ln., Ste. 1400
Dallas, TX 75225
Ph:(214)739-3515
Fax: (214)739-3572
Contact: Joel Fontenot, Managing Director
E-mail: joelf@arkomavp.com
Preferred Investment Size: $250,000 to $2,500,000.
Investment Types: Seed, start-up, early, first and second stage, and expansion. **Industry Preferences:** Communications and media, computer hardware, semiconductors and other electronics. **Geographic Preferences:** Southwest and Texas.

65591 ■ Austin Ventures, L.P.
300 W. 6th St., Ste. 2300
Austin, TX 78701
Ph:(512)485-1900
Fax: (512)476-3952
URL: http://www.austinventures.com
Contact: Joseph C. Aragona, General Partner
E-mail: joea@ausven.com
Preferred Investment Size: $100,000 to $50,000,000. **Investment Types:** Seed, start-up, first, early, second and later stage, leveraged buyout, management buyouts, expansion, balanced, and special situation. **Industry Preferences:** Internet specific, communications and media, computer software and services, computer hardware, other products, semiconductors and other electronics, consumer related, medical and health, industrial and energy, and biotechnology. **Geographic Preferences:** Southwest and Texas.

65592 ■ AV Labs
300 W. 6th St., Ste. 2300
Austin, TX 78701
Ph:(512)485-1900
Fax: (813)281-6147
URL: http://www.avlabs.com
Contact: Kevin Kunz, Chief Financial Officer
Preferred Investment Size: $500,000 to $5,000,000.
Investment Types: Seed, early and first stage. **Industry Preferences:** Computer software and services, communications and media, Internet specific, other products, and computer hardware. **Geographic Preferences:** Texas.

65593 ■ BCM Technologies, Inc.
11 Greenway Plz., Ste. 2900
Houston, TX
Ph:(713)795-0105
Fax: (713)795-4602
URL: http://www.bcmtechnologies.com
Contact: Alfred Brown, President
Preferred Investment Size: $100,000 minimum. **Investment Types:** Seed and early stage. **Industry Preferences:** Biotechnology, medical and health. **Geographic Preferences:** Southwest.

65594 ■ Bionexus Ventures
1225 N. Loop W., Ste. 850
Houston, TX 77008
Ph:(713)862-8005
Fax: (713)862-9393
URL: http://www.bionexusventures.com
Contact: Norman Newton, Chief Executive Officer
Investment Policies: Seed and early stage. **Industry Preferences:** Medical and health. **Geographic Preferences:** Texas.

65595 ■ Buena Venture Associates
201 Main St., 32nd Fl.
Fort Worth, TX 76102
Ph:(817)339-7400
Fax: (817)390-8408
URL: http://www.buenaventure.com
Contact: John Pergande, Partner
Preferred Investment Size: $1,000,000 to $50,000,000. **Investment Types:** Seed, start-up, early, first and second stage. **Industry Preferences:** Communications, computer software, Internet specific, medical and health. **Geographic Preferences:** U.S.

65596 ■ The Capital Network / Texas Capital Network
2700 Via Fortuna, Ste. 450
Austin, TX 78746
Ph:(512)314-0711
Fax: (512)306-1651
Contact: Michael McAllister, Managing Director
Preferred Investment Size: $100,000 to $500,000.
Investment Types: Seed, start-up, first and second stage, leveraged buyout, mezzanine, research and development, and special situation. **Industry Preferences:** Communications, computer related, semiconductors and other electronics, biotechnology, medical and health, consumer related, industrial and energy, financial services, business service, manufacturing, agriculture, forestry and fishing. **Geographic Preferences:** U.S. and Canada.

65597 ■ Capital Southwest Corp.
12900 Preston Rd., Ste. 700
Dallas, TX 75230
Ph:(972)233-8242
Fax: (972)233-7362
URL: http://www.capitalsouthwest.com
Contact: William Thomas, Chairman and President
Preferred Investment Size: $1,000,000 to $6,000,000. **Investment Types:** Start-up, early, first, second, and later stage, leveraged buyout, management buyouts, acquisition, expansion, generalist PE, and recapitalizations. **Industry Preferences:** Consumer related, industrial and energy, communications and media, computer hardware, computer software and services, other products, Internet specific, medical and health, biotechnology, semiconductors and other electronics. **Geographic Preferences:** U.S.

65598 ■ The Catalyst Group
2 Riverway, Ste. 1710
Houston, TX 77056
Ph:(713)623-8133
Fax: (713)623-0473
Co. E-mail: herman@thecatalystgroup.net
URL: http://www.thecatalystgroup.net
Contact: Rick Herman, Partner
Preferred Investment Size: $1,000,000 to $5,000,000. **Investment Types:** Mezzanine. **Industry Preferences:** Medical and health, business service and manufacturing. **Geographic Preferences:** Southeast.

65599 ■ Centerpoint Venture Partners
13455 Noel Rd.
2 Galleria Tower, Ste. 1670
Dallas, TX 75240
Ph:(972)702-1101
Fax: (972)702-1103
URL: http://www.cpventures.com
Contact: Robert Paluck, Managing General Partner
Preferred Investment Size: $60,000 to $10,000,000.
Investment Types: Early, first and second stage. **Industry Preferences:** Communications and media, Internet specific, computer software and services, computer hardware, other products, semiconductors and other electronics, medical and health. **Geographic Preferences:** Southwest and Texas.

65600 ■ Cureton & Co., Inc.
1100 Louisiana, Ste. 3250
Houston, TX 77002
Ph:(713)658-9806
Fax: (713)658-0476
Contact: Stewart Cureton, President
E-mail: chipcur@aol.com
Preferred Investment Size: $10,000,000 minimum.
Investment Types: First and second stage, leveraged buyout, and special situation. **Industry Preferences:** Communications and media, computer hardware and software, Internet specific, semiconductors and other electronics, medical and health, consumer related, industrial and energy, and financial services. **Geographic Preferences:** Southwest.

65601 ■ Dali, Hook Partners (Dallas)
1 Lincoln Ctr., Ste. 1550
5400 LBJ Fwy.
Dallas, TX 75240
Ph:(972)991-5457
Fax: (972)991-5458
Co. E-mail: dhook@hookpartners.com
URL: http://www.hookpartners.com
Contact: David J. Hook, General Partner
Investment Types: Early stage. **Industry Preferences:** Communications, computer software, semiconductors and other electronics.

65602 ■ Denota Ventures
PO Box 132166
The Woodlands, TX 77393
Ph:(281)296-2424
Contact: Bill Wilson, President
Investment Policies: Early stage.

65603 ■ DFJ Mercury Venture Partners
410 Pierce St.
Houston, TX 77002
Ph:(832)476-9320
Fax: (832)553-1086
Investment Policies: Early stage. **Industry Preferences:** Industrial and energy. **Geographic Preferences:** Texas.

65604 ■ Essex Woodlands Health Ventures / Woodlands Venture (The Woodlands)
10001 Woodlock Forest Dr.
Waterway Plz., Ste. 175
The Woodlands, TX 77380
Ph:(281)364-1555
Fax: (281)364-9755
URL: http://www.essexwoodlands.com
Contact: Richard Kolodziejcyk, Chief Financial Officer
Preferred Investment Size: $2,000,000 to $10,000,000. **Investment Types:** First, early, and

later stage, expansion, and private placement. **Industry Preferences:** Medical and health, biotechnology, computer software and services, Internet specific, consumer related, communications and media, other products, industrial and energy. **Geographic Preferences:** U.S.

65605 ■ First Capital Management Co. LLC / FCG
750 East Mulberry St., Ste. 305
PO Box 15616
San Antonio, TX 78212
Ph:(210)736-4233
Fax: (210)736-5449
URL: http://www.firstcapitalgroup.com
Contact: Jeffrey P. Blanchard, Managing Partner
Preferred Investment Size: $1,000,000 to $6,000,000. **Investment Types:** Early, expansion, first, second and later stage, mezzanine, leveraged buyout, management buyouts, and special situation. **Industry Preferences:** Communications and media, medical and health, consumer related, and business service. **Geographic Preferences:** Southwest.

65606 ■ G-51 Capital LLC
804 Las Cimas Pky., Ste. 140 B
Austin, TX 78746
Ph:(512)929-5151
Fax: (512)732-0886
URL: http://www.g51.com
Contact: N. Rudy Garza, President
Preferred Investment Size: $50,000 to $1,250,000. **Investment Types:** Early and later stage. **Industry Preferences:** Computer software and services, computer hardware, Internet specific, and consumer related. **Geographic Preferences:** U.S.

65607 ■ Gefinor Ventures / Inman Ventures
301 Congress, Ste. 1350
Austin, TX 78701
Ph:(512)346-7111
Fax: (512)346-2111
URL: http://www.gefinorventures.com
Contact: William Bexkett, Chief Financial Officer
Preferred Investment Size: $500,000 to $2,000,000. **Investment Policies:** Early stage. **Industry Preferences:** Communications, computer software, Internet specific, semiconductors and other electronics, and medical and health. **Geographic Preferences:** California, Colorado, District of Columbia, New York, and Texas.

65608 ■ Genesis Park Ventures
2001 Hermann Dr.
Houston, TX 77004
Ph:(713)285-2900
Fax: (713)285-2911
URL: http://www.genesis-park.com
Contact: Blair Garrou, Principal
Preferred Investment Size: $500,000 to $2,000,000. **Investment Policies:** Start-up, early and first stage. **Industry Preferences:** Communications, computer software, industrial and energy. **Geographic Preferences:** Texas.

65609 ■ HO2 Partners
2 Galleria Tower
13455 Noel Rd., Ste. 1670
Dallas, TX 75240
Ph:(972)702-1144
Fax: (972)702-8234
URL: http://www.ho2.com
Contact: Diane Gross, Chief Financial Officer
Preferred Investment Size: $750,000 to $3,000,000. **Investment Types:** Seed, start-up and early stage. **Industry Preferences:** Communications and computer software. **Geographic Preferences:** Texas.

65610 ■ Houston Partners / Houston Venture Partners
PO Box 2023
Houston, TX 77252
Ph:(713)222-8600
Fax: (713)222-8932
URL: http://www.houstonpartners.com
Contact: Harvard Hill, Managing General Partner
Preferred Investment Size: $500,000 to $1,000,000. **Investment Types:** Start-up, first and second stage,

and expansion. **Industry Preferences:** Computer hardware and software, semiconductors and other electronics, biotechnology, medical and health. **Geographic Preferences:** Southeast, Southwest, and West Coast.

65611 ■ Interfase Capital Partners LP
1301 Capital of Texas Hwy., Ste. A300
Austin, TX 78746
Ph:(512)328-8113
Fax: (512)328-9662
URL: http://www.interfasecapital.com
Contact: Scott Hyten, Managing Partner
Investment Types: Early stage. **Industry Preferences:** Internet specific. **Geographic Preferences:** U.S.

65612 ■ Interwest Partners (Dallas)
2 Galleria Tower
13455 Noel Rd., 16th Fl.
Dallas, TX 75240-6615
Ph:(972)392-7279
Fax: (972)490-6348
URL: http://www.interwest.com
Contact: Doug Pepper, Principal
Preferred Investment Size: $2,000,000 to $25,000,000. **Investment Types:** Seed, start-up, early, first, second and later stage, balanced, and expansion. **Industry Preferences:** Medical and health, Internet specific, consumer related, biotechnology, communications and media, computer hardware, computer software and services, semiconductors and other electronics, industrial and energy, and other products. **Geographic Preferences:** U.S.

65613 ■ Jatotech Management LLC
301 Congress, Ste. 2050
Austin, TX 78701
Ph:(512)236-6950
Fax: (512)236-6959
URL: http://www.jatotech.com
Contact: Daniel Ray, Venture Partner
Preferred Investment Size: $500,000 to $5,000,000. **Investment Policies:** Seed and early stage. **Industry Preferences:** Communications, and semiconductors and other electronics. **Geographic Preferences:** Northern California and Southwest.

65614 ■ Jump.Net Ventures
7218 McNeil Dr., Ste. 303
Austin, TX 78729
Ph:(512)532-2235
URL: http://www.jumpnetventures.com
Investment Types: Seed and start-up. **Industry Preferences:** Internet specific. **Geographic Preferences:** Southwest.

65615 ■ Kahala Investments, Inc.
5950 Berkshire Ln.
Ste. 825, LB 28
Dallas, TX 75225
Ph:(214)987-0077
Fax: (214)987-2332
Preferred Investment Size: $10,000,000 minimum. **Investment Types:** Mezzanine, leveraged buyout, special situation, control-block purchases, and industry rollups. **Industry Preferences:** Consumer related, industrial and energy. **Geographic Preferences:** Southeast and Southwest.

65616 ■ MBA Venture Group
1004 Olde Town Rd., Ste. 102
Irving, TX 75061
Ph:(972)986-6703
Contact: John Mason
Preferred Investment Size: $1,000,000 minimum. **Investment Types:** Seed, start-up, first stage and second stage, leveraged buyout, mezzanine, research and development. **Industry Preferences:** Communications and media, computer related, semiconductors and other electronics, medical and health, consumer related, industrial and energy, transportation, business service, and manufacturing. **Geographic Preferences:** U.S.

65617 ■ Medtech International Inc.
1742 Carriageway
Sugarland, TX 77478

Ph:(713)980-8474
Fax: (713)980-6343
Contact: Dave Banker
Preferred Investment Size: $100,000 to $500,000. **Investment Types:** First stage, leveraged buyout, mezzanine, research and development, second stage, seed, special situation, and start-up. **Industry Preferences:** Communications and media, computer hardware and software, semiconductors and other electronics, biotechnology, medical and health, consumer related, industrial and energy, financial services, and manufacturing.

65618 ■ MESBIC Ventures Holding Co.
2435 N. Central Expy., Ste. 200
Richardson, TX 75080
Ph:(972)991-1597
Fax: (972)991-4770
URL: http://www.pacesettercapital.com
Contact: Divaker Kamath, Managing Director
Preferred Investment Size: $1,000,000 minimum. **Investment Types:** Leveraged buyout, mezzanine, and second stage. **Industry Preferences:** Communications and media, computer software, hardware and services, consumer related, semiconductors and other electronics, medical and health, Internet specific, industrial and energy. **Geographic Preferences:** Southeast and Southwest.

65619 ■ Murphree Venture Partners
1100 Louisiana, Ste. 5005
Houston, TX 77002
Ph:(713)655-8500
Fax: (713)655-8503
URL: http://www.murphreeventures.com
Contact: Dennis Murphree, Managing General Partner
Preferred Investment Size: $250,000 to $8,000,000. **Investment Types:** Seed, start-up, early and first stage. **Industry Preferences:** Computer software and services, Internet specific, medical and health, industrial and energy, consumer related, semiconductors and other electronics, computer hardware, communications and media. **Geographic Preferences:** Southwest and Southeast.

65620 ■ Natural Gas Partners (NGP)
125 E. John Carpenter Fwy., Ste., 600
Irving, TX 75062
Ph:(972)432-1440
Fax: (972)432-1441
URL: http://www.naturalgaspartners.com
Contact: William Quinn, Managing Director
Preferred Investment Size: $5,000,000 to $60,000,000. **Investment Types:** Start-up, first and second stage, leveraged buyout, and special situation. **Industry Preferences:** Industrial and energy, Internet specific, other products, communications and media. **Geographic Preferences:** U.S. and Central and Western, Canada.

65621 ■ North Texas MESBIC, Inc.
9500 Forest Ln., Ste. 430
Dallas, TX 75243
Ph:(214)221-3565
Fax: (214)221-3566
Contact: Allan Lee, President
Preferred Investment Size: $300,000 minimum. **Investment Types:** Second stage, mezzanine, and leveraged buyout. **Industry Preferences:** Consumer related. **Geographic Preferences:** Southwest and Texas.

65622 ■ Omnimed Corp.
4611 Montrose Blvd., Ste. 201
Houston, TX 77006
Ph:(713)524-7373
Fax: (713)524-0987
Preferred Investment Size: $500,000 to $1,000,000. **Investment Types:** Start-up, first and second stage. **Industry Preferences:** Biotechnology, medical and health. **Geographic Preferences:** Southwest.

65623 ■ Phillips-Smith Specialty Retail Group
5080 Spectrum Dr., Ste. 805 W.
Addison, TX 75001

Ph:(972)387-0725
Fax: (972)458-2560
URL: http://www.phillips-smith.com
Contact: G. Michael Machens, General Partner
Preferred Investment Size: $1,000,000 to $5,000,000. **Investment Types:** Start-up, first and second stage, and balanced. **Industry Preferences:** Consumer related, Internet specific, computer software and services, and other products. **Geographic Preferences:** U.S.

65624 ■ Q Ventures
301 Commerce St., Ste. 2975
Fort Worth, TX 76102
Ph:(817)332-5572
URL: http://www.qventures.com
Contact: Russ Miron, Managing Director
Investment Types: Early stage. **Industry Preferences:** Internet specific.

65625 ■ Richard Jaffe & Co., Inc.
7318 Royal Cir.
Dallas, TX 75230
Ph:(214)265-9397
Fax: (214)739-1845
Co. E-mail: rjaffe@pssi.net
Contact: Richard R. Jaffe, President
Preferred Investment Size: $100,000 to $300,000. **Investment Types:** Start-up, first stage, leveraged buyout, and special situation. **Industry Preferences:** Communications, computer hardware and software, semiconductors and other electronics, medical and health, consumer related, industrial and energy, financial services, business service, and manufacturing. **Geographic Preferences:** Southwest.

65626 ■ Sagebrook Technology
3401 Armstrong Ave.
Dallas, TX 75205
Ph:(214)443-1991
Fax: (214)443-1980
URL: http://www.sagebrook.com
Contact: Jack Baum, President
Investment Types: Early stage and expansion. **Industry Preferences:** Computer software. **Geographic Preferences:** U.S.

65627 ■ SBC Ventures
2735 Villa Creek, Ste. 140
Dallas, TX 75234
Ph:(972)243-4033
Fax: (972)243-0925
Contact: Viviana Cloninger, General Partner
Preferred Investment Size: $300,000 to $3,000,000. **Investment Types:** Seed, research and development, start-up, and first stage. **Industry Preferences:** Communications and media, computer related, semiconductors and other electronics, biotechnology, medical and health, consumer related, industrial and energy, transportation, financial services, manufacturing, agriculture, forestry and fishing. **Geographic Preferences:** U.S. and Canada.

65628 ■ Seed Company Partners
3008 Taylor St.
Dallas, TX 75226
Ph:(972)354-4350
Fax: (214)651-1862
URL: http://www.seedco.com
Contact: Allen Fleener, General Partner
Preferred Investment Size: $500,000 to $1,000,000. **Investment Types:** Seed, start-up, and first stage. **Industry Preferences:** Computer software, and Internet specific. **Geographic Preferences:** U.S.

65629 ■ Sevin Rosen Management Co. / Sevin Rosen Funds
2 Galleria Tower
Dallas, TX 75240
Ph:(972)702-1100
Fax: (972)702-1103
URL: http://www.srfunds.com
Contact: John V. Jaggers, Partner
Preferred Investment Size: $100,000 to $10,000,000. **Investment Types:** Start-up, early, first and second stage. **Industry Preferences:** Communi-

cations and media, computer software and services, semiconductors and other electronics, consumer related, medical and health, computer hardware, Internet specific, and other products. **Geographic Preferences:** U.S.

65630 ■ Southwest Venture Group
10878 Westheimer, Ste. 178
Houston, TX 77042
Ph:(713)827-8947
Free: (713)461-1470
Preferred Investment Size: $50,000,000 minimum. **Investment Types:** Seed, start-up, first and second stage, control-block purchases, leveraged buyout, mezzanine, research and development, and special situation. **Industry Preferences:** Communications, computer computer hardware and software, Internet specific, semiconductors and other electronics, biotechnology, medical and health, consumer related, industrial and energy, financial services, agriculture, forestry and fishing. **Geographic Preferences:** U.S. and Canada.

65631 ■ The Southwest Venture Partnerships
16414 San Pedro, Ste. 345
San Antonio, TX 78232
Ph:(210)402-1200
Fax: (210)402-1221
Co. E-mail: swvp@aol.com
Contact: C.R. Tucker, General Partner
Investment Types: Start-up, first and second stage, and leveraged buyout. **Industry Preferences:** Communications and media, computer hardware and software, medical and health, industrial and energy. **Geographic Preferences:** Southwest.

65632 ■ Startech
1302 E. Collins, Blvd.
PO Box 832047
Richardson, TX 75083-2047
Ph:(214)576-9800
Fax: (214)576-9849
URL: http://www.startech.org
Contact: Vinson Davidson, Chief Financial Officer
Preferred Investment Size: $500,000 to $900,000. **Investment Types:** Seed, start-up, and early stage. **Industry Preferences:** Computer software, and Internet specific. **Geographic Preferences:** Texas.

65633 ■ Sternhill Partners
777 Post Oak Blvd., Ste 250
Houston, TX 77056
Ph:(713)622-2727
Fax: (713)622-3529
URL: http://www.sternhillpartners.com
Contact: Marc Geller, Managing Director
Preferred Investment Size: $500,000 to $6,000,000. **Investment Types:** Seed, start-up, early, first and second stage. **Industry Preferences:** Internet specific, communications and media, computer software and services, semiconductors and other electronics. **Geographic Preferences:** Southwest and West Coast.

65634 ■ Stratford Capital Partners, L.P. / Stratford Equity Partners
300 Crescent Ct., Ste. 500
Dallas, TX 75201
Ph:(214)740-7377
Fax: (214)720-7393
URL: http://www.stratfordcapital.com
Contact: Michael Brown, Managing Partner
E-mail: mbrown@hmtf.com
Preferred Investment Size: $3,000,000 to $9,000,000. **Investment Types:** Later stage, acquisition, leveraged buyout, management buyouts, mezzanine, and recapitalizations. **Industry Preferences:** Consumer related, computer software and services, medical and health, other products, computer hardware, communications and media, Internet specific, industrial and energy. **Geographic Preferences:** U.S.

65635 ■ Sunwestern Investment Group
12221 Merit Dr., Ste. 1300
Dallas, TX 75251
Ph:(972)239-5650

Fax: (972)701-0024
Preferred Investment Size: $500,000 to $1,000,000. **Investment Types:** Second stage, leveraged buyout, and special situation. **Industry Preferences:** Communications, computer hardware and software, semiconductors and other electronics, medical and health. **Geographic Preferences:** Southwest and West Coast.

65636 ■ Techxas Ventures LLC
5000 Plaza on the Lake
Austin, TX 78746
Ph:(512)343-0118
Fax: (512)343-1879
Co. E-mail: bruce@techxas.com
URL: http://www.techxas.com
Contact: Bruce Ezell, General Partner
Preferred Investment Size: $100,000 to $3,000,000. **Investment Types:** Seed, start-up, early, first and second stage, balanced, and joint ventures. **Industry Preferences:** Computer software and services, computer hardware, semiconductors and other electronics, Internet specific, communications and media, industrial and energy, other products. **Geographic Preferences:** Texas.

65637 ■ Triad Ventures, LTD–AM Fund
4600 Post Oak Pl., Ste. 100
Houston, TX 77027
Ph:(713)627-9111
Fax: (713)627-9119
Contact: Kathy Mattina, Chief Financial Officer
Preferred Investment Size: $300,000 to $800,000. **Investment Types:** First and second stage, and mezzanine. **Industry Preferences:** Semiconductors and other electronics, medical and health, Internet specific, computer software and services, industrial and energy, communications and media, biotechnology, and consumer related. **Geographic Preferences:** Southwest.

65638 ■ Triton Ventures
6801 N. Capital of Texas Hwy.
Bldg. 2, Ste. 225
Austin, TX 78731
Ph:(512)795-5820
Fax: (512)795-5828
URL: http://www.tritonventures.com
Contact: D. Scott Collier, Managing Director
Preferred Investment Size: $500,000 to $6,000,000. **Investment Types:** Seed, start-up, and early stage. **Industry Preferences:** Communications and media, computer software, Internet specific, semiconductors and other electronics, industrial and energy. **Geographic Preferences:** U.S.

65639 ■ Ventex Management, Inc.
3417 Milam St.
Houston, TX 77002-9531
Ph:(713)522-4239
Fax: (713)659-7855
Preferred Investment Size: $2,000,000 minimum. **Investment Types:** Second stage, mezzanine, leveraged buyout, and special situation. **Industry Preferences:** Communications, computer hardware and software, semiconductors and other electronics, biotechnology, medical and health, consumer related, industrial and energy, transportation, manufacturing, agriculture, forestry and fishing. **Geographic Preferences:** Southwest.

65640 ■ Ventures Medical Associates
7 Switchbud Pl., Ste. 192
Spring, TX 77380
Ph:(281)364-1003
Fax: (281)364-1082
Contact: William Mullaney, Managing Partner
Preferred Investment Size: $500,000 to $2,000,000. **Investment Types:** Start-up and early stage. **Industry Preferences:** Medical and health, biotechnology, computer software and services. **Geographic Preferences:** Southwest and West Coast.

65641 ■ Wingate Partners, L.P.
750 N. St. Paul, Ste. 1200
Dallas, TX 75201
Ph:(214)720-1313

Fax: (214)871-8799
URL: http://www.wingatepartners.com
Contact: Frederick Hegi, Principal
Preferred Investment Size: $20,000,000 minimum.
Investment Types: Leveraged buyout and control-block purchases. **Industry Preferences:** Semiconductors and other electronics, medical and health, consumer related, industrial and energy, business service, and manufacturing. **Geographic Preferences:** U.S. and Canada.

PROCUREMENT ASSISTANCE PROGRAMS

65642 ■ Texas Procurement Technical Assistance Center–Angelina College
PO Box 1768
Lufkin, TX 75902-1768
Ph:(936)633-5424
Fax: (936)633-5478
Co. E-mail: acpac@txucom.net
URL: http://www.acpactx.org
Contact: James R. Rollins, Dir

65643 ■ Texas Procurement Technical Assistance Center–Cross Timbers Procurement Center
University of Texas at Arlington
7300 Jack Newell Blvd. S
Ft. Worth, TX 76118
Ph:(817)272-5978
Fax: (817)272-5952
Co. E-mail: jhicks@arri.uta.edu
URL: http://arri.uta.edu/crosstimbers/
Contact: Jim Hicks, Dir

65644 ■ Texas Procurement Technical Assistance Center–Pan Handle Regional Planning Commission
PO Box 9257
Amarillo, TX 79101
Ph:(806)372-3381
Fax: (806)372-3268
Co. E-mail: eesparza@theprpc.org
URL: http://www.prpc.cog.tx.us
Contact: Edmund Esparza

65645 ■ Texas Procurement Technical Assistance Center–San Antonio Procurement Outreach Program
PO Box 839966
San Antonio, TX 78283-3966
Ph:(210)207-3910
Fax: (210)207-3909
Co. E-mail: cmcclure@sanantonio.gov
URL: http://www.sanantonio.gov/edd
Contact: Courtney McClure, Sectretary

65646 ■ Texas Procurement Technical Assistance Center–Texas Information Procurement Service
University of Houston
2302 Fanning, Ste. 200
Houston, TX 77002
Ph:(713)752-8477
Fax: (713)756-1515
Co. E-mail: jtaylor@uh.edu
URL: http://www.sbdc.uh.edu
Contact: Jacqueline Taylor
E-mail: jtaylor@uh.edu

65647 ■ Texas Procurement Technical Assistance Center–Texas Tech University
2579 S Loop 289, Ste. 210
Lubbock, TX 79423
Ph:(806)745-3973
Free: 800-992-7232
Fax: (806)745-6717
Co. E-mail: o.castellano@nwtsbdc.org
URL: http://www.nwtsbdc.org
Contact: Otilo Castellano, Dir
E-mail: o.castellano@ttu.edu

65648 ■ Texas Procurement Technical Assistance Center–Valley Procurement Technical Assistance Center
1600 E Elizabeth St.
Brownsville, TX 78520
Ph:(956)548-8741
Fax: (956)548-8750
Co. E-mail: rosalie@utb.edu
URL: http://wtce.utb.edu/vptac/
Contact: Rosalie Manzano
E-mail: rosalie@utb1.edu

INCUBATORS/RESEARCH AND TECHNOLOGY PARKS

65649 ■ Austin Technology Incubator (IC2-ATI)
The University of Texas at Austin
3925 W Braker Ln., Ste. 400
Austin, TX 78759-5321
Ph:(512)305-0000
Fax: (512)305-0009
Co. E-mail: edefosse@ati.utexas.edu
URL: http://www.ati.utexas.edu
Contact: Eric Defosse, Dir
Description: Located at the University of Texas at Austin, this incubator specializes in supporting emerging high-risk technology firms.

65650 ■ Baylor University–Office of Sponsored Programs and Contracts
1 Bear Pl., No. 97360
Waco, TX 76798-7360
Ph:(254)710-3817
Fax: (254)710-3534
Co. E-mail: charles_e_patterson@baylor.edu
URL: http://www.baylor.edu/osp/
Contact: Charles E. Patterson, Interim Actg.Dir.
E-mail: charles_e_patterson@baylor.edu
Scope: Responsible for development and administration grants, contracts, and other sponsored program activities.

65651 ■ The Business Resource Center
801 Elm St.
Waco, TX 76704
Ph:(254)754-8898
Fax: (254)756-0776
Co. E-mail: brc@brc-waco.com
URL: http://www.brc-waco.com
Contact: Toni Herbert, Exec Dir
Description: This small business incubator supports the development of emerging firms through a variety of business assistance services.

65652 ■ Rice University–Office of Sponsored Research
6100 Main St., MS-16
Houston, TX 77005
Ph:(713)348-4820
Fax: (713)348-5425
Co. E-mail: nnisbett@rice.edu
URL: http://osr.rice.edu/
Contact: Nancy Nisbett, Dir.
E-mail: nnisbett@rice.edu
Scope: Responsible for research development and administration of all sponsored research at the University. **Publications:** Scholarly Interests and Activities of the Faculty (annually).

65653 ■ Southern Methodist University–Office of Research Administration
PO Box 750302
Dallas, TX 75275-0302
Ph:(214)768-4306
Fax: (214)768-1079
Co. E-mail: lsmith@mail.smu.edu
URL: http://www.smu.edu/research/
Contact: Larry Smith, Dir.
E-mail: lsmith@mail.smu.edu
Scope: Provides coordination for research and development activities and serves as administrator of grants and contracts for the University in natural, mathematical, engineering, and social sciences, law, business, and economics. **Publications:** Annual Summary; Monthly Opportunities and Deadlines; Newsletter (quarterly).

65654 ■ Stephen F. Austin State University–Office of Research and Sponsored Programs
PO Box 13024, SFA Sta.
Nacogdoches, TX 75962
Ph:(936)468-6606
Fax: (936)468-1251
Co. E-mail: orsp@sfasu.edu
URL: http://www.sfasu.edu/orsp/
Contact: Carrie Brown, Dir.
E-mail: orsp@sfasu.edu
Scope: Coordinates all extramural grants from outside the University in support of research and sponsored projects conducted in various colleges of the University, including its Colleges of Forestry and Agriculture, Liberal Arts, Sciences and Mathematics, Fine Arts, Business, Education, and Applied Arts and Sciences. **Services:** Technical assistance, in locating sources for external support for research and sponsored programs; Workshops, on proposal writing and post-award grant management. **Publications:** ORSP Report. **Educational Activities:** University Research Council, an advisory council determining ways of enhancing the research environment.

65655 ■ Texas A&M Research Foundation
3578 TAMU
College Station, TX 77843
Ph:(979)845-8600
Fax: (979)862-3250
Co. E-mail: webmaster@rf-mail.tamu.edu
URL: http://rf-web.tamu.edu
Contact: Mark Smock, Pres./CEO
E-mail: webmaster@rf-mail.tamu.edu
Scope: Serves as contracting agency on extramurally sponsored research conceived and performed in various divisions of the University and other system components, particularly in oceanography, transportation, meteorology, engineering, physics, chemistry, agriculture, and biology. Advises researchers of potential sponsors for research, assists in the preparation of proposals to sponsors, provides travel assistance to researchers, provides an administrative link between the University system and sponsors, and provides expertise in the administration of the research project, including accounting, purchasing, travel and insurance details, equipment inventory and control, and report preparation. Manages operation of seagoing vessel.

65656 ■ Texas A&M University–Office of Sponsored Projects
Administration, Rm. 315
College Station, TX 77843-3121
Ph:(979)845-1811
Fax: (979)845-1855
Co. E-mail: g-foxworth@tamu.edu
Contact: Gregory L. Foxworth, Dir.
E-mail: g-foxworth@tamu.edu
Scope: Responsible for coordination of all research conducted within the University in fields of life, physical, and social sciences, business administration, education, and the humanities. Assists in administration of research projects and serves as a data collection unit which gathers information about research activities throughout the University for review, analysis, and various reporting requirements of the University's research managers. **Publications:** Research Information (monthly).

65657 ■ Texas A&M University—Commerce–Graduate Studies and Research
PO Box 3011
Commerce, TX 75429-3011
Ph:(903)886-5163
Fax: (903)886-5165
Co. E-mail: graduate_school@tamu-commerce.edu
URL: http://www7.tamu-commerce.edu/gradschool/research/
Contact: Dr. Mathew Kanjirathinkal, Dean
E-mail: graduate_school@tamu-commerce.edu
Scope: Administers and coordinates extramurally and intramurally supported research activities conducted at the University in the humanities, biological, earth, physical, and social sciences and in professional education, including studies on teacher preparation, teacher-preparing institutions, and related areas involving both professional and academic disciplines. **Educational Activities:** Grant writing workshops.

65658 ■ Texas A&M University Research Park
1500 Research Pky., Ste. A200
College Station, TX 77845
Ph:(979)862-1769
Fax: (979)845-9262
Co. E-mail: harold.strong@tamu.edu
URL: http://researchpark.tamu.edu/
Contact: Harold E. Strong, Dir.
E-mail: harold.strong@tamu.edu
Scope: Located on 324 acres west of main campus, the Park serves to assist private utilization of University resources, to promote closer ties between industry engaged in research and the University, to improve the quality and productivity of University research activities, and to accelerate the dissemination of new knowledge and the transfer of new technologies. **Publications:** Parkview Newsletter.

65659 ■ Texas Tech University–Office of the Vice President for Research
103 Holden Hall
Lubbock, TX 79409-1075
Ph:(806)742-3905
Fax: (806)742-3947
Co. E-mail: dean.smith@ttu.edu
URL: http://www.ttu.edu/administration/vpr/
Contact: Dr. Dean Smith, VP,Res.
E-mail: dean.smith@ttu.edu
Scope: Encourages and coordinates faculty and graduate student research at the University, assists in preparation of proposals for grant or contract research, and participates in administration and allocation of funds appropriated for research support. **Publications:** Research and Graduate Education Annual Report; VISTAS (semiannually).

65660 ■ University of Houston–Division of Research
4800 Calhoun Rd.
Houston, TX 77204
Ph:(713)743-2255
Fax: (713)743-0646
Co. E-mail: rgrimmet@uh.edu
URL: http://www.research.uh.edu
Contact: Rosemary Grimmet, Exec.Dir.
E-mail: rgrimmet@uh.edu
Scope: Serves as focal point for faculty research and other sponsored activities at the University. Assists faculty members in preparing and submitting proposals for both federally and privately supported projects and administers awards for funded projects. Programs in the fields of energy, engineering, superconductivity, chemistry, virtual reality, and molecular design.

65661 ■ University of North Texas–Office for Research Services
PO Box 305250
Denton, TX 76203-5250
Ph:(940)565-3940
Fax: (940)565-4277
Co. E-mail: rbusby@unt.edu
URL: http://www.unt.edu/ospa/vp/index.html
Contact: Reata Houlditch Busby, Assoc.VP
E-mail: rbusby@unt.edu
Scope: Promotes and administers sponsored research with core competencies in materials science, simulation modeling, and life sciences. **Publications:** UNT Research (annually).

65662 ■ University of Texas
301 S Frio
San Antonio, TX 78207
Ph:(210)270-4500
Fax: (210)270-4501
Co. E-mail: myoung3578@aol.com
URL: http://www.utsa.edu

65663 ■ University of Texas at Arlington–Office of Research
PO Box 19145
Arlington, TX 76019-0145
Ph:(817)272-2105
Fax: (817)272-5808
Co. E-mail: elsenbaumer@uta.edu
URL: http://www2.uta.edu/ogcs/

Contact: Dr. Ronald L. Elsenbaumer, VP,Res.
E-mail: elsenbaumer@uta.edu
Scope: Responsible for all sponsored research activities of the University. Provides assistance and administrative guidance for the preparation and processing of research grant and contract proposals. Develops, recommends, and implements institutional policies relative to research and sponsored activities. Matches faculty research interests with funding agencies and interested parties outside the University. Disseminates information on funding sources and provides assistance in fiscal management of all grants and contracts. Responsible for all post-award and grant/contract accounting issues including but not limited to regulatory compliance, account set-up, subcontracting, and financial reporting. **Publications:** Newsletter (monthly). **Educational Activities:** Workshops, on the grant and contract application process.

65664 ■ University of Texas at Austin–Faculty Development Program
Office of the Dean of Graduate Studies
1 University Station, Mail Stop G0400
Austin, TX 78712-0531
Ph:(512)471-4511
Fax: (512)471-7620
Co. E-mail: mhackert@mail.utexas.edu
URL: http://www.utexas.edu/ogs/fdp/
Contact: Marvin L. Hackert, Dir.
E-mail: mhackert@mail.utexas.edu
Scope: Supports individual UT-Austin faculty research in all areas. **Awards:** Faculty Research Assignments; Summer Research Assignments.

EDUCATIONAL PROGRAMS

65665 ■ El Paso Community College
PO Box 20500
El Paso, TX 79998
Ph:(915)831-2000
Fax: (915)831-2161
URL: http://www.epcc.edu
Description: Two-year college offering small business management courses.

65666 ■ Kilgore College
1100 Broadway
Kilgore, TX 75662
Ph:(903)984-8531
Fax: (903)983-8600
URL: http://www.kilgore.edu
Description: Two-year college offering a program in small business management.

LEGISLATIVE ASSISTANCE

65667 ■ Texas Department of Economic Development
PO Box 12428
Austin, TX 78711-2728
Ph:(512)936-0100
Free: 800-888-0511
Fax: (512)936-0303
URL: http://www.txed.state.tx.us
Description: Brings together government efforts to support economic growth through world trade development, domestic business development, and small business assistance.

TRADE PERIODICALS

65668 ■ *Houston Business*
Pub: Federal Reserve Bank of Dallas
Released: 8/year. **Price:** Free. **Description:** Provides a perspective on the Houston, Texas economy.

65669 ■ *Perspectives*
Pub: Federal Reserve Bank of Dallas
Ed: Kay Champagne, Editor. **Released:** Quarterly. **Description:** Discusses various banking and community topics.

65670 ■ *Vista*
Pub: Federal Reserve Bank of Dallas
Contact: Jennifer Afflerbach, Copy Editor
Ed: Keith Phillips, Editor, keith.r.phillips@dal.frb.org. **Released:** Semiannual. **Description:** Studies economic issues and trends in South Texas.

PUBLICATIONS

65671 ■ *How to Form Your Own Texas Corporation*
Nolo Press
950 Parker St.
Berkeley, CA 94710
Ph:(510)549-1976
Free: 800-992-6656
URL: http://www.nolo.com
Ed: Anthony Mancuso. **Released:** Fourth edition, 1988. **Price:** $29.95 (paper).

65672 ■ *Smart Start your Texas Business Guide*
PSI Research
300 N. Valley Dr.
Grants Pass, OR 97526
Ph:(503)479-9464
Free: 800-228-2275
Fax: (503)476-1479
Co. E-mail: info@psi-research.com
URL: http://www.psi-research.com
Ed: Michael D. Jenkins. **Released:** Revised edition, 1992. **Price:** $29.95 (looseleaf binder); $24.95 (paper). **Description:** Part of the Successful Business Library series.

PUBLISHERS

65673 ■ Dockery House Publishing Inc.
1720 Regal Row, Ste. 112
Dallas, TX 75235
Ph:(214)630-4300
Free: 800-520-2665
Fax: (214)638-4049
Co. E-mail: questions@dockerypublishing.com
URL: http://www.dockerypublishing.com
Contact: Rob Dockery, CEO & Pres
E-mail: rdockery@dockerypublishing.com
Description: Publishes customized books for new business development. Publishes magazines and books for chain stores. Does not accept unsolicited manuscripts. Reaches market through commission representatives. Doing business as: Heritage Publishing, Inc. **Founded:** 1980.

65674 ■ Mesa House Publishing
3228 College Ave.
Fort Worth, TX 76110-4045
Ph:(817)920-0114
Free: 888-306-0060
Fax: (817)920-0419
Co. E-mail: books@mesahouse.com
URL: http://www.mesahouse.com
Contact: Karee Galloway, Publisher
E-mail: kgalloway@mesahouse.com
Description: Publishes and distributes books and software for commercial real estate, site selection, site evaluation, market analysis and related fields. Reaches market through direct mail, web site, wholesalers and distributors. **Founded:** 1999.

65675 ■ MLM Consultants
2410 Cinco Woods Plaza
San Antonio, TX 78259
Ph:(210)494-3884
Fax: (210)494-9909
URL: http://www.mlmconsultant.com
Contact: Rod Cook, Consultant
Description: Publishes books, software and resources on business topics.

65676 ■ Mullaney Publishing Group
PO Box 833383
Richardson, TX 75083-3383

Ph:(972)234-5310
Fax: (972)234-3255
Description: Publishes on retail business and ecommerce.

65677 ■ Principle Publications Inc.
4101 W Green Oaks Blvd., Ste. 305-585
Arlington, TX 76016
Ph:(817)887-2397
Co. E-mail: info@principlepublications.com
URL: http://www.principlepublications.com
Description: Publishes books on nonfiction, pharmaceutical sales, job interview guides. Accepts unsolicited manuscripts; see website for guidelines. Reaches market through Amazon, Barnes & Noble, Borders, and Books-A-Million. **Founded:** 1998

65678 ■ Probabilistic Press
1634 Overland Pass Dr.
Sugar Land, TX 77478
Ph:(281)277-4006
Fax: (281)277-4006
URL: http://www.decisions-books.com
Contact: Dave Charlesworth
E-mail: dave@decisions-books.com
Description: Publishes books and CD-ROMs on decision analysis for business students and professionals. Reaches market through website.

65679 ■ Shopkeeper Software
1005 Lakewood Ln.
Round Rock, TX 78681
Ph:(512)388-3290
Fax: (512)310-9855
Co. E-mail: sales@shopkeeper.com

URL: http://www.shopkeeper.com
Contact: Michael F. Nudd, President
E-mail: mike@shopkeeper.com
Description: Publishes small business software for Macintosh computers. Does not accept unsolicited manuscripts. Reaches market through direct mail, trade sales, and wholesalers and distributors. **Founded:** 1985.

65680 ■ World Gumbo Publishing
7801 Alma St. 105-323
Plano, TX 75025-3483
Free: 888-318-2911
Co. E-mail: dbarkley@worldgumbo.com
URL: http://www.worldgumbo.com
Contact: Douglas Barkley
Description: Publishes business and personal growth books. **Founded:** 2004

SMALL BUSINESS DEVELOPMENT CENTER LEAD OFFICE

65681 ■ Salt Lake City Small Business Development Center–Salt Lake Community College
1623 S State St.
Salt Lake City, UT 84115
Ph:(801)957-3480
Fax: (801)957-3489
Contact: Mike Finnerty, State Director
E-mail: FinnerMi@slcc.edu

65682 ■ Salt Lake Community College–Small Business Development Center
115 S. Main St., Ste. 503
Salt Lake City, UT 84111
Ph:(801)957-3493
URL: http://www.utahsbdc.org
Contact: Breg Panichello, State Dir.
E-mail: greg.panichello@slcc.edu

65683 ■ Utah SBDC–Salt Lake Community College
9750 S. 300 W.
Sandy, UT 84070
Ph:(801)957-3493
Fax: (801)957-3488
URL: http://www.slcc.edu/sbdc
Contact: Greg Panichello, State Dir.
E-mail: greg.panichello@slcc.edu

SMALL BUSINESS DEVELOPMENT CENTERS

65684 ■ College of Eastern Utah at San Juan Campus–Small Business Development Center
639 W. 100 S.
Blanding, UT 84511
Ph:(435)678-2201
URL: http://www.utahsbdc.org
Contact: Bill Olderog, Dir.
E-mail: billolderog@sjc.ceu.edu

65685 ■ Dixie College–Small Business Development Center
225 South 700 East
St. George, UT 84770
Ph:(435)652-7741
URL: http://www.utahsbdc.org
Contact: Jill Elliss, Dir.
E-mail: ellis_i@dixie.edu

65686 ■ Salt Lake Community College–Sandy SBDC
9750 South 300 West
Sandy, UT 84070
Ph:(801)255-5259
URL: http://www.utahsbdc.org

Contact: Randy Schouten, Dir.
E-mail: randy.schouten@slcc.edu

65687 ■ Snow College–Small Business Development Center
150 E. College Ave.
Ephraim, UT 84627
Ph:(435)283-7376
URL: http://www.utahsbdc.org
Contact: Alan Christensen, Dir.
E-mail: alan.christensen@snow.edu

65688 ■ Southeastern Applied Technology College–Small Business Development Center
375 South Carbon Ave.
Price, UT 84501
Ph:(435)613-1438
URL: http://www.utahsbdc.org
Contact: Ethan Migliori, Dir.
E-mail: emigliori@seatc.org

65689 ■ Southern Utah University–Small Business Development Center
351 W. Center St.
Cedar City, UT 84720
Ph:(435)586-5497
URL: http://www.utahsbdc.org
Contact: Craig Isom, Dir.
E-mail: isom@suu.edu

65690 ■ Utah State University
1680 W. Hwy. 40
Vernal, UT 84078
Ph:(435)789-6100
URL: http://www.utahsbdc.org
Contact: Mark Holmes, Dir.
E-mail: markh@ext.usu.edu

65691 ■ Utah State University–Small Business Development Center
1330 E. 700 N., No. 124
Logan, UT 84322-8330
Ph:(435)797-2277
Fax: (435)797-3317
URL: http://www.utahsbdc.org
Contact: Frank Prante, Dir.
E-mail: fprante@ext.usu.edu

65692 ■ Utah Valley State College–Utah Small Business Development Center
800 West University Pkwy.
Orem, UT 84058
Ph:(801)863-8230
Fax: (801)577-3344
URL: http://www.utahsbdc.org
Contact: Stephen Clark, Dir.
E-mail: clarkse@uvsc.edu

65693 ■ Weber State University–Small Business Development Center
3806 University Cir.
Ogden, UT 84408-3806
Ph:(435)626-7232
URL: http://www.utahsbdc.org
Contact: Beverly King, Dir.
E-mail: bking1@weber.edu

SMALL BUSINESS ASSISTANCE PROGRAMS

65694 ■ Utah Community and Economic Development Department–International Development Office
324 S State St., Ste. 500
Salt Lake City, UT 84111
Ph:(801)538-8737
Fax: (801)538-8889
Co. E-mail: intlmail@utah.gov
URL: http://international.utah.gov/
Description: Assists businesses by developing marketing efforts, providing technical assistance in exporting, and matching foreign market opportunities with Utah sources.

BETTER BUSINESS BUREAUS

65695 ■ Better Business Bureau of Utah
5673 S Redwood Rd., No. 22
Salt Lake City, UT 84123
Ph:(801)892-6009
Fax: (801)892-6002
Co. E-mail: info@utah.bbb.org
URL: http://www.utah.bbb.org
Contact: Ms. Jane Driggs, Pres./CEO

CHAMBERS OF COMMERCE

65696 ■ American Fork Chamber of Commerce
51 E Main St.
PO Box 162
American Fork, UT 84003-0162
Ph:(801)756-5110
Fax: (801)763-3004
Co. E-mail: chamber@afcity.net
Contact: D. Jessica Wilson, Exec.Dir.

65697 ■ Bear Lake Rendezvous Chamber of Commerce
PO Box 55
Garden City, UT 84028
Free: 800-448-2327
Co. E-mail: swww@mac.com
URL: http://www.bearlakechamber.com
Contact: Suzy Wright, Pres.

65698 ■ Bear River Valley Chamber of Commerce
PO Box 311
Tremonton, UT 84337
Ph:(435)257-7585
Fax: (435)257-7585
Co. E-mail: nikkijdr@yahoo.com
URL: http://www.bearriverchamber.com
Contact: Bill Hull, Pres.

65699 ■ Beaver Chamber of Commerce and Travel Council
PO Box 760
Beaver, UT 84713
Ph:(435)438-5081
Free: 888-848-5081
Co. E-mail: chamber@beaverutchamber.com
URL: http://www.beaverutchamber.com
Contact: Brent Stapley, Chm.

65700 ■ Blanding Chamber of Commerce
PO Box 792
Blanding, UT 84511
Ph:(435)678-3662
Co. E-mail: info@blandingutah.org
URL: http://www.blandingutah.org
Contact: K. Perkins, Pres.

65701 ■ Brigham City Area Chamber of Commerce
6 N Main
PO Box 458
Brigham City, UT 84302
Ph:(435)723-3931
Fax: (435)723-5761
Co. E-mail: chamber@brighamchamber.com
URL: http://www.bcareachamber.com
Contact: Kelly Driscoll, Chair

65702 ■ Brigham City Chamber of Commerce Women in Business
PO Box 458
6 N Main St.
Brigham City, UT 84302
Ph:(435)723-3931
Fax: (435)723-5761
Co. E-mail: chamber@brighamchamber.com
URL: http://bcareachamber.com
Contact: Kelly Driscoll, Chm.

65703 ■ Cache Chamber of Commerce
160 N Main
Logan, UT 84321
Ph:(435)752-2161
Free: 800-882-4433
Fax: (435)753-5825
URL: http://www.cachechamber.com
Contact: Sandra Emile, Pres./CEO

65704 ■ Carbon County Chamber of Commerce
90 N 100 E, No. 3
Price, UT 84501
Ph:(435)637-2788
Fax: (435)637-8182
Co. E-mail: cccc@priceutah.com
URL: http://www.carboncountychamber.com
Contact: Shane Baggs, Pres.

65705 ■ Cedar City Area Chamber of Commerce
581 N Main St.
Cedar City, UT 84720
Ph:(435)586-4484
Fax: (435)586-4022
Co. E-mail: chamber@cedarcity.org
URL: http://www.chambercedarcity.org
Contact: Donna Brown, Dir.

65706 ■ ChamberWest
1241 W Village Main Dr., Ste. B
West Valley City, UT 84119
Ph:(801)969-8755
Fax: (801)977-8329
URL: http://www.chamberwest.com
Contact: Alan Anderson, Pres./CEO

65707 ■ Davis Chamber of Commerce
PO Box 457
Centerville, UT 84014
Ph:(801)295-6944
Fax: (801)298-1114
Co. E-mail: daviscc@davischamberofcommerce.com
URL: http://www.davischamberofcommerce.com
Contact: Chris L. Dallin, Pres./CEO

65708 ■ Delta Area Chamber of Commerce
76 N 200 W
Delta, UT 84624-9440
Ph:(435)864-4316
Free: 800-864-0345
Fax: (435)864-4313
Co. E-mail: chamber@deltautah.com
URL: http://www.chamber.deltautah.com
Contact: Camille DeLoach, Pres.

65709 ■ Duchesne County Area Chamber of Commerce
50 E 200 S
PO Box 1417
Roosevelt, UT 84066-1417
Ph:(435)722-4598
Fax: (435)722-4579
Co. E-mail: dcac2@ubtanet.com
URL: http://www.duchesne.net
Contact: Irene Hansen, Exec. Dir.

65710 ■ Emery County Chamber of Commerce
25 N Ctr. St.
PO Box 327
Castle Dale, UT 84513
Ph:(435)381-2547
Fax: (435)381-5102
Co. E-mail: echamber@etv.net
Contact: Linda Jewkes, Pres.

65711 ■ Fillmore Area Chamber of Commerce
460 N Main St.
PO Box 1214
Fillmore, UT 84631
Ph:(435)743-6121
Free: 800-441-4288
Fax: (435)743-7803
URL: http://www.fillmoreutah.com
Contact: Mark Huntsman, Pres.

65712 ■ Flaming Gorge Corporation
PO Box 10
Manila, UT 84046
Ph:(435)784-3483
Co. E-mail: flaming@gorge.net

65713 ■ Heber Valley Chamber of Commerce and Visitor Center
475 N Main St.
PO Box 427
Heber City, UT 84032
Ph:(435)654-3666
Fax: (435)654-3667
Co. E-mail: info@hebervalleycc.org
URL: http://www.hebervalleycc.org
Contact: Jennifer Kohler, Exec.Dir.

65714 ■ Hurricane Valley Chamber of Commerce
PO Box 101
Hurricane, UT 84737
Ph:(435)635-3402
Fax: (435)635-5733
Co. E-mail: hurricanechamber@hotmail.com
URL: http://www.hvchamber.com

65715 ■ Kanab Chamber of Commerce
78 S 100 E
Kanab, UT 84741
Ph:(435)644-5033
Free: 800-733-5263
Fax: (435)644-5923
Co. E-mail: kanetrav@kanab.net
URL: http://www.visitsouthernutah.com
Contact: Cyrus Majia, Pres.

65716 ■ Midvale Area Chamber of Commerce
7349 S 900 E, No. 7
Midvale, UT 84047
Ph:(801)561-3880
Co. E-mail: info@midvalechambers.com
URL: http://www.midvalechamber.com
Contact: Marie Marshall, Pres./CEO

65717 ■ Moab Area Chamber of Commerce
217 W Center St., Ste. 250
Moab, UT 84532
Ph:(435)259-7814
Fax: (435)259-8519
Co. E-mail: info@moabchamber.com
URL: http://www.moabchamber.com
Contact: Teresa Wyatt, Administrator

65718 ■ Monticello Chamber of Commerce
PO Box 217
Monticello, UT 84535
Ph:(435)587-2992
Free: 800-574-4386
Contact: Douglas Harkey

65719 ■ Mount Pleasant Main Street Comm.
City Hall
115 W Main St.
Mount Pleasant, UT 84647
Ph:(435)462-2456
Fax: (435)462-2581
Contact: Monte Bona, Dir.

65720 ■ Murray Area Chamber of Commerce
5250 S Commerce Dr., Ste. 180
Murray, UT 84107
Ph:(801)263-2632
Fax: (801)263-8262
Co. E-mail: anne@spackmanrealtors.com
URL: http://www.murraychamber.net
Contact: R. Scott Baker, Pres./CEO

65721 ■ Ogden/Weber Chamber of Commerce
2484 Washington Blvd., Ste. 400
Ogden, UT 84401
Ph:(801)621-8300
Free: (801)621-8306
Fax: (801)392-7609
Co. E-mail: ron@echamber.cc
Contact: Mr. Dave Hardman, Pres./CEO

65722 ■ Panguitch Chamber of Commerce
PO Box 400
Panguitch, UT 84759
Ph:(435)676-8585
URL: http://www.panguitch.com
Contact: Janet Oldham, Pres.

65723 ■ Park City Chamber of Commerce
PO Box 1630
Park City, UT 84060
Ph:(435)649-6100
Free: 800-453-1360
Fax: (435)649-4132
Co. E-mail: info@parkcityinfo.com
URL: http://www.parkcityinfo.com
Contact: Bill Malone, Exec.Dir.

65724 ■ Payson Chamber of Commerce
439 W Utah Ave.
Payson, UT 84651
Ph:(801)465-2634
URL: http://www.payson.org/chamber.shtml
Contact: Brian Hulet, Pres.

65725 ■ Provo-Orem Chamber of Commerce
51 S University Ave., Ste. 215
Provo, UT 84601
Ph:(801)851-2555
Fax: (801)851-2557
Co. E-mail: info@thechamber.org
URL: http://www.thechamber.org
Contact: Steven T. Densley, Pres./CEO

65726 ■ St. George Area Chamber of Commerce
97 E St. George Blvd.
St. George, UT 84770-2853
Ph:(435)628-1658
Fax: (435)673-1587
Co. E-mail: hotspot@stgeorgechamber.com
URL: http://www.stgeorgechamber.com
Contact: Lorri Kocinski-Puchlik, Exec.Dir.

65727 ■ Salt Lake Chamber
175 E 400 S, Ste. 600
Salt Lake City, UT 84111-2329
Ph:(801)364-3631
Fax: (801)328-5098
Co. E-mail: info@saltlakechamber.org
URL: http://www.saltlakechamber.org
Contact: Craig E. Peterson, COO

65728 ■ Sandy Area Chamber of Commerce
8807 S 700 E
Sandy, UT 84070
Ph:(801)566-0344
Fax: (801)566-0346
URL: http://www.sandychamber.com
Contact: Tim Bricker, Chm. Elect

65729 ■ South Salt Lake Chamber of Commerce
PO Box 65001
South Salt Lake, UT 84165
Ph:(801)466-3377
Fax: (801)467-3322
Co. E-mail: info@sslchamber.com
URL: http://www.sslchamber.com
Contact: Stacey Liddiard, Pres./CEO

65730 ■ Southwest Valley Chamber of Commerce
PO Box 95848
South Jordan, UT 84095
Ph:(801)280-0595
Fax: (801)280-3674
Co. E-mail: suez@mail.burgoyne.com
URL: http://www.swvchamber.org
Contact: Donna Rentmeister, Chair

65731 ■ Spanish Fork Area Chamber of Commerce
40 S Main St.
PO Box 576
Spanish Fork, UT 84660
Ph:(801)798-8352
Fax: (801)798-6594
Co. E-mail: sfchamber@spanishfork.org

65732 ■ Tooele County Chamber of Commerce
201 N Main St.
PO Box 460
Tooele, UT 84074-0460
Ph:(435)882-0690
Free: 800-378-0690
Fax: (435)833-0946
Co. E-mail: chamber@trilobyte.net
URL: http://www.tooelechamber.com
Contact: Mark Taylor, Board Chm.

65733 ■ Vernal Area Chamber of Commerce
134 W Main
Vernal, UT 84078-2504
Ph:(435)789-1352
Fax: (435)789-1355
Co. E-mail: info@vernalchamber.com
URL: http://www.vernalchamber.com
Contact: Richard Harrington, Exec.Dir.

65734 ■ West Jordan Chamber of Commerce
8000 S Redwood Rd.
West Jordan, UT 84088
Ph:(801)569-5151
Fax: (801)569-5153
Co. E-mail: info@westjordanchamber.com
URL: http://www.westjordanchamber.com
Contact: N. Craig Dearing, Pres./CEO

MINORITY BUSINESS ASSISTANCE PROGRAMS

65735 ■ Utah Community and Economic Development Department–Office of Asian Affairs
324 S State, Ste. 500
Salt Lake City, UT 84111

Ph:(801)538-8883
Fax: (801)538-8678
Co. E-mail: emitko@utah.gov
URL: http://www.dced.utah.gov/asian
Description: Works to improve the educational, employment, and economic status of minorities in the state.

65736 ■ Utah Community and Economic Development Department–Office of BL Affairs
324 S State, Ste. 500
Salt Lake City, UT 84111
Ph:(801)538-8815
Fax: (801)538-8678
URL: http://dced.utah.gov/
Description: Works to improve the educational, employment, and economic status of minorities in the state.

65737 ■ Utah Community and Economic Development Department–Office of Hispanic Affairs
324 S State, Ste. 500
Salt Lake City, UT 84111
Ph:(801)538-8755
Fax: (801)538-8678
URL: http://dced.utah.gov/
Description: Works to improve the educational, employment, and economic status of minorities in the state.

65738 ■ Utah Community and Economic Development Department–Office of Indian Affairs
324 S State, Ste. 500
Salt Lake City, UT 84114
Ph:(801)538-8808
Fax: (801)538-8803
URL: http://dced.utah.gov/
Description: Works to improve the educational, employment, and economic status of minorities in the state.

FINANCING AND LOAN PROGRAMS

65739 ■ First Security Business Investment Corp.
15 E. 100 S., Ste. 100
Salt Lake City, UT 84111
Ph:(801)246-5737
Fax: (801)246-5740
Preferred Investment Size: $300,000 to $800,000.
Investment Types: Leveraged buyout, mezzanine, and second stage. **Industry Preferences:** Communications and media, computer hardware, semiconductors and other electronics, medical and health, consumer related, industrial and energy. **Geographic Preferences:** West Coast and Rocky Mountains.

65740 ■ Utah Ventures II, L.P.
423 Wakara Way, Ste. 206
Salt Lake City, UT 84108
Ph:(801)583-5922
Fax: (801)583-4105
URL: http://www.uven.com
Contact: James C. Dreyfous, Managing General Partner
Preferred Investment Size: $1,000,000 to $7,000,000. **Investment Types:** Early stage. **Industry Preferences:** Diversified technology. **Geographic Preferences:** Northwest and Rocky Mountain region.

65741 ■ Wasatch Venture Corporation / Wasatch Venture Fund
15 W. South Temple St., Ste. 520
Salt Lake City, UT 84101
Ph:(801)524-8939
Fax: (801)524-8941
URL: http://www.wasatchvc.com
Contact: Todd Stevens, Managing Director
Preferred Investment Size: $500,000 to $3,000,000.
Investment Types: Seed, first and second stage. **In-**

dustry Preferences: Internet specific, computer software and services, computer hardware, communications and media, semiconductors and other electronics, consumer related, biotechnology, medical and health, and other products. **Geographic Preferences:** Rocky Mountains, Southwest, and West Coast.

PROCUREMENT ASSISTANCE PROGRAMS

65742 ■ Utah Department of Community and Economic Development Department–Procurement Technical Assistance Center
324 S State, Ste. 500
Salt Lake City, UT 84111
Ph:(801)538-8775
Fax: (801)538-8888
Co. E-mail: fglange@utah.gov
URL: http://goed.utah.gov/PTAC/
Contact: Fred Lange, Dir
Description: Assists businesses in competing for government and commercial contracts.

INCUBATORS/RESEARCH AND TECHNOLOGY PARKS

65743 ■ Brigham Young University–Office of Research and Creative Activities
A-285 ASB
Provo, UT 84602
Ph:(801)422-3841
Fax: (801)422-0620
Co. E-mail: gary_reynolds@byu.edu
URL: http://orca.byu.edu/orca2.htm
Contact: Gary R. Reynolds, Dir.
E-mail: gary_reynolds@byu.edu
Scope: Coordinates and handles institutional and extramurally sponsored research projects, grants, and contracts in life, physical, and social sciences, the humanities and arts, and engineering throughout the University. Assists faculty members of the University. **Publications:** Annual Reports. **Awards:** Faculty mentoring awards.

65744 ■ University of Utah–Technology Commercialization Office
615 Arapeen Dr., Ste. 310
Salt Lake City, UT 84108
Ph:(801)581-7792
Fax: (801)581-7538
Co. E-mail: bcummings@tco.utah.edu
URL: http://www.tco.utah.edu
Contact: Brian Cummings, Dir.
E-mail: bcummings@tco.utah.edu
Scope: Technology transfer and licensing; new business start-ups based on university-developed technologies; and intellectual property management. **Publications:** Innovations (semiannually).

65745 ■ University of Utah–University of Utah Research Park
505 Wakara Way
Salt Lake City, UT 84108
Ph:(801)581-8133
Fax: (801)581-7195
Co. E-mail: charles.evans@admin.utah.edu
Contact: Charles A. Evans, Dir.
E-mail: charles.evans@admin.utah.edu
Scope: 300-acre tract designed to facilitate scientific research projects between government agencies, industrial organizations, and the University. Facilities include general and technical libraries, scientific and research equipment, and computer center.

65746 ■ Utah State University–Office of Research Services
2800 Old Main Hill
Logan, UT 84322-2800
Ph:(435)797-1469
Fax: (435)797-0200

Co. E-mail: jim.dorward@usu.edu
URL: http://www.coe.usu.edu/brs/home.htm
Contact: Jim Dorward, Assoc. Dean
E-mail: jim.dorward@usu.edu
Scope: Facilitates research funding activities at the College, represents the College in University, state, and nationwide educational research projects, and provides guidance and research source materials to faculty members and graduate students of the College. **Publications:** Publication and Grants Report (annually); Research Newsletter (quarterly). **Educational Activities:** Research symposia.

65747 ■ Utah State University–Utah State University Innovation Campus
1770 N Research Pky., Ste. 120
North Logan, UT 84341
Ph:(435)797-9610
Fax: (435)797-9605
Co. E-mail: mcknight@cc.usu.edu
URL: http://www.usu.edu/innovationcampus
Contact: Teresa McKnight, Interim Dir.
E-mail: mcknight@cc.usu.edu
Scope: Research and technology-based enterprises.

EDUCATIONAL PROGRAMS

65748 ■ Salt Lake Community College–Redwood Road Campus
PO Box 30808
Salt Lake City, UT 84130-0808
Ph:(801)957-4111
Fax: (801)957-4444
URL: http://www.slcc.edu
Description: Provides courses and workshops on topics relevant to entrepreneurs and small business owners.

PUBLICATIONS

65749 ■ *Smart Start Your Utah Business*
PSI Research
300 N. Valley Dr.
Grants Pass, OR 97526
Ph:(541)479-9464
Free: 800-228-2275
Fax: (541)476-1479
Co. E-mail: info@psi-research.com
URL: http://www.psi-research.com
Ed: Michael D. Jenkins. **Released:** Revised edition, 1992. **Price:** $29.95 (looseleaf binder); $24.95 (paper). **Description:** Part of the Successful Business Library series.

PUBLISHERS

65750 ■ Creating Keepsakes Books
14850 Pony Express Rd.
Bluffdale, UT 84065
Ph:(801)984-2070
Free: 888-247-5282
Fax: (801)984-2080
Co. E-mail: creatingkeepsakes@palmcoastd.com
URL: http://www.creatingkeepsakes.com
Contact: Lisa Bearnson, President
Description: Publishes books and CD-ROMs on photography, paper crafts, and scrapbooking.

65751 ■ Executive Excellence Publishing
1366 E 1120 S
Provo, UT 84606-6379
Ph:(801)375-4060
Free: 800-304-9782
Fax: (801)377-5960
Co. E-mail: info@eep.com
URL: http://www.eep.com
Contact: Mr. Ken Shelton, President
E-mail: kens@eep.com
Description: Publishes business books and a newsletter. Accepts unsolicited manuscripts. Reaches market through commission representatives, direct mail, reviews and listings, telephone sales, Ingram, Baker & Taylor and National Book Network. **Founded:** 1984.

SMALL BUSINESS DEVELOPMENT CENTER LEAD OFFICE

65752 ■ Vermont Small Business Development Center–Vermont Technical College
PO Box 188
Randolph Center, VT 05060-0422
Ph:(802)728-9101
Free: 800-464-SBDC
Fax: (802)728-3026
Contact: Donald L. Kelpinski, State Director
E-mail: dkelpins@vtc.vsc.edu

65753 ■ Vermont Technical College–Small Business Development Center
PO Box 188
Randolph Center, VT 05061-0188
Ph:(802)728-9101
Free: 800-464-7232
Fax: (802)728-3026
URL: http://www.vtsbdc.org
Contact: Lenae Quillen-Blume, State Dir.
E-mail: lquillen@vtc.edu

SMALL BUSINESS DEVELOPMENT CENTERS

65754 ■ Addison County Chamber of Commerce–SBDC
2 Court St.
Middlebury, VT 05753
Ph:(802)388-7951
Fax: (802)388-8066
Co. E-mail: info@midvermont.com
URL: http://www.midvermont.com

65755 ■ Addison County Economic Development Corp.–SBDC
RD4, Box 1309A
Middlebury, VT 05753
Ph:(802)388-7953
URL: http://www.vtsbdc.org
Contact: Steve Paddock, Program Dir.
E-mail: spaddock@vtsbdc.ort

65756 ■ Bennington Area Chamber of Commerce
Veterans Memorial Dr.
Bennington, VT 05201
Ph:(802)447-3311
Fax: (802)447-1163
Co. E-mail: chamber@bennington.com

65757 ■ Bennington County Industrial Corp. –SBDC
PO Box 357
North Bennington, VT 05257-0357
Ph:(802)442-8975
Free: 800-464-7232

URL: http://www.vtsbdc.org
Contact: Heather M. Gonyaw, Office Mgr.
E-mail: hgonyaw@vtsbdc.org

65758 ■ Brattleboro Development Credit Corp.–SBDC
76 Cotton Mill Hill
Brattleboro, VT 05301
Ph:(802)257-7731
Fax: (802)257-0294
Co. E-mail: BDCC@sover.net
URL: http://www.brattleborodevelopment.com
Contact: Jeff Lewis, Executive V.P.
E-mail: bdccjl@sover.net

65759 ■ Central Vermont Economic Development Center–SBDC
PO Box 1439
Montpelier, VT 05601-1439
Ph:(802)223-4654
Fax: (802)223-4655
URL: http://www.vtsbdc.org
Contact: John Brennan, Business Advisor
E-mail: jbrennan@vtsbdc.org

65760 ■ Franklin County Industrial Development Corp.–SBDC
PO Box 1099
St. Albans, VT 05478-1099
Ph:(802)524-2194
Fax: (802)524-6793
URL: http://www.vtsbdc.org
Contact: Pat Travers, Business Advisor
E-mail: ptravers@vtsbdc.org

65761 ■ Greater Burlington Industrial Corp. –Northwestern Vermont Small Business Development Center
PO Box 786
Burlington, VT 05402-0786
Ph:(802)658-9228
Fax: (802)860-1899
Contact: Derek Cohen, Business Advisor
E-mail: dcohen@vtsbdc.org

65762 ■ Green Mountain Economic Development Corporation–SBDC
171 Bridge St.
PO Box 246
White River Jct., VT 05001-0246
Ph:(802)295-3710
Fax: (802)295-3779
URL: http://www.gmedc.com
Contact: Neal Fox, Exec. Dir.
E-mail: nfox@gmedc.com

65763 ■ Irasville Incubator & Storage LLC–Irasville Business Park–SBDC (151 M)
151 Mad River Canoe Rd.
PO Box 658
Waitsfield, VT 05673
Ph:(802)496-3100
Fax: (802)329-2050
Co. E-mail: ibp@cimark.com
Contact: Robin Morris, Incubator Mgr.

65764 ■ Lake Champlain Islands Chamber of Commerce–SBDC
PO Box 213
North Hero, VT 05474-0213
Ph:(802)372-5683
Fax: (802)372-3205
URL: http://www.champlainislands.com
Contact: Ruth Wallman, Exec. Dir.
E-mail: ruth@champlainislands.com

65765 ■ Lamoille Economic Development Corp.–SBDC
PO Box 455
Morrisville, VT 05661-0455
Ph:(802)888-4542
Fax: (802)888-7612
URL: http://www.vtsbdc.org
Contact: John Brennan, Business Advisor
E-mail: jbrennan@vtsbdc.org

65766 ■ Northeastern Vermont Development Association–Small Business Development Center
PO Box 630
St. Johnsbury, VT 05819-0630
Ph:(802)748-1014
Fax: (802)748-1223
URL: http://www.vtsbdc.org
Contact: John Mandeville
E-mail: jmandeville@vtsbdc.org

65767 ■ Rutland Economic Development Corp.–Southwest Vermont Small Business Development Center
112 Quality Ln.
Rutland, VT 05701
Ph:(802)773-9147
Fax: (802)773-8009
URL: http://www.vtsbdc.org
Contact: Wendy Wilton, SBDC Specialist
E-mail: wwilton@vtsbdc.org

65768 ■ Southern Windsor County Incubator–SBDC
14 Clinton St.
Springfield, VT 05156
Ph:(802)885-3061
Fax: (802)885-3027
URL: http://www.SpringfieldDevelopment.org
Contact: Bob Flint, Exec. Dir.
E-mail: BobF@SpringfieldDevelopment.org

65769 ■ Springfield Regional Development Corp.–Southeastern Vermont Small Business Development Center
14 Clinton St.
Springfield, VT 05156
Ph:(802)885-2071
Fax: (802)885-3027
Co. E-mail: info@springfielddevelopment.org
URL: http://ww.springfielddevelopment.org
Contact: Pat Flint, Exec. Dir.
E-mail: bobf@springfielddevelopment.org

65770 ■ Vermont Tech Enterprise Center Incubator–SBDC
PO Box 500
Randolph Center, VT 05061-0500
Ph:(802)728-9101
Contact: Laura Kent
E-mail: LauraKent@aol.com

65771 ■ VT Center for Emerging Technologies Incubator–SBDC
Farrell Hall
210 Colchester Ave.
Burlington, VT 05405-1757
Ph:(802)656-3880
Free: 800-639-3188
Fax: (802)656-3881
URL: http://www.VermontTechnologies.com
Contact: Thomas Rainey, President
E-mail: thomas.rainey@uvm.edu

SMALL BUSINESS ASSISTANCE PROGRAMS

65772 ■ Agency of Commerce and Community Development–Economic Development Department
National Life Bldg.
Drawer 20
Montpelier, VT 05620-0501
Ph:(802)828-3211
Free: 800-622-4553
Fax: (802)828-3258
URL: http://www.thinkvermont.com
Description: A full-service business consulting and referral network, coordinating the efforts of the state's regional development corporations, the Vermont Industrial Development Authority, and federal employment training and financing agencies.

65773 ■ Agency of Commerce and Community Development–Economic Development Department–Site Selection Office (Natio)
National Life Bldg.
Drawer 20
Montpelier, VT 05620-0501
Ph:(802)828-3211
Free: 800-622-4553
Fax: (802)828-3258
URL: http://www.thinkvermont.com
Description: Maintains a computerized inventory of industrial parks, sites, commercial and industrial buildings.

65774 ■ Agency of Commerce and Community Development–Economic Development Department–Vermont Business Expansion Program (Natio)
National Life Bldg.
Drawer 20
Montpelier, VT 05620-0501
Ph:(802)828-3211
Free: 800-622-4553
Fax: (802)828-3258
URL: http://www.thinkvermont.com
Description: Helps companies take advantage of international research and development in traditional manufacturing, high technology, and information applications.

65775 ■ Vermont Small Business Development Center–Economic Development Department–Vermont Small Business Development Center (PO Bo)
PO Box 188
Randolph Center, VT 05061
Ph:(802)728-9101
Free: 800-622-4553
Fax: (802)728-3026
URL: http://www.vtsbdc.org/
Contact: Lenae Quillen-Blume, State Dir
Description: Directly assists small businesses, and offers referrals when necessary.

65776 ■ Vermont World Trade Office, Inc. –Economic Development Department–Export Development Program (Natio)
National Life Bldg.
Drawer 20
Montpelier, VT 05620
Ph:(802)828-1175
Free: 800-622-4553
Fax: (802)828-3258
Co. E-mail: brad@thinkvermont.com
URL: http://www.vwto.org
Description: Help is given to develop overseas markets for products and services by conducting export seminars, organizing trade missions and putting firms in touch with specialists in exporting and foreign trade.

CHAMBERS OF COMMERCE

65777 ■ Addison County Chamber of Commerce
2 Court St.
Middlebury, VT 05753
Ph:(802)388-7951
Free: 800-733-8376
Fax: (802)388-8066
Co. E-mail: info@midvermont.com
URL: http://www.midvermont.com
Contact: Ted Shambo, Membership Dir.

65778 ■ Barton Area Chamber of Commerce
PO Box 343
Barton, VT 05822
Ph:(802)525-1137
Co. E-mail: info@bartonareachamber.com
URL: http://www.bartonareachamber.com
Contact: Nancy Rodgers

65779 ■ Bennington Area Chamber of Commerce
100 Veterans Memorial Dr.
Bennington, VT 05201
Ph:(802)447-3311
Free: 800-229-0252
Co. E-mail: chamber@bennington.com
URL: http://www.bennington.com
Contact: Joann Erenhouse, Exec. Dir.

65780 ■ Brandon Area Chamber of Commerce
PO Box 267
Brandon, VT 05733
Ph:(802)247-6401
Co. E-mail: info@brandon.org
URL: http://www.brandon.org
Contact: Janet Mondlak, Exec.Dir.

65781 ■ Brattleboro Area Chamber of Commerce
180 Main St.
Brattleboro, VT 05301
Ph:(802)254-4565
Free: 877-254-4565
Fax: (802)254-5675
Co. E-mail: info@brattleborochamber.org
URL: http://www.brattleborochamber.org
Contact: Jerry Goldberg, Exec.Dir.

65782 ■ Central Vermont Chamber of Commerce
PO Box 336
Barre, VT 05641-0336
Ph:(802)229-5711
Fax: (802)229-5713
Co. E-mail: cvchamber@aol.com
URL: http://www.central-vt.com
Contact: George Malek, Exec.VP

65783 ■ Franklin County Regional Chamber of Commerce
2 N Main St., Ste. 101
St. Albans, VT 05478
Ph:(802)524-2444
Fax: (802)527-2256
Co. E-mail: fcrcc@verizon.net
URL: http://www.stalbanschamber.com

Contact: Alisha Sawyer, Exec.Dir.

65784 ■ Great Falls Regional Chamber of Commerce
PO Box 554
Bellows Falls, VT 05101-0554
Ph:(802)463-4280
Co. E-mail: info@gfrcc.org
URL: http://www.gfrcc.org
Contact: Roger Riccio, Exec.Dir.

65785 ■ Hardwick Area Chamber of Commerce
PO Box 111
Hardwick, VT 05843
Ph:(802)472-5906
Fax: (802)472-6865
Co. E-mail: hdwkarea@vtlink.net
URL: http://www.hardwickvtarea.com
Contact: Ron Sanville, Pres.

65786 ■ Hartford Area Chamber of Commerce
100 Railroad Row
White River Junction, VT 05001
Ph:(802)295-7900
Free: 800-295-5451
Co. E-mail: info@hartfordvtchamber.com
URL: http://www.hartfordvtchamber.com
Contact: Gayle C. Ottmann, Exec.Dir.

65787 ■ Island Pond Chamber of Commerce
PO Box 255
Island Pond, VT 05846
Co. E-mail: chamber@islandpondchamber.org
URL: http://www.islandpondchamber.org
Contact: Mrs. Patricia Whitney, Sec.

65788 ■ Killington Chamber of Commerce
PO Box 114
Killington, VT 05751
Ph:(802)773-4181
Free: 800-337-1928
Fax: (802)775-7070
Co. E-mail: info@killingtonchamber.com
URL: http://www.killingtonchamber.com
Contact: Jane Costello, Business Mgr.

65789 ■ Lake Champlain Islands Chamber of Commerce
PO Box 213
North Hero, VT 05474
Ph:(802)372-8400
Free: 800-262-5226
Fax: (802)372-5107
Co. E-mail: info@champlainislands.com
URL: http://www.champlainislands.com
Contact: Ruth Wallman, Exec.Dir.

65790 ■ Lake Champlain Region Chamber of Commerce
60 Main St., Ste. 100
Burlington, VT 05401-8418
Ph:(802)863-3489
Free: 877-686-5253
Fax: (802)863-1538
Co. E-mail: vermont@vermont.org
URL: http://www.vermont.org
Contact: A. Wayne Roberts, Pres.

65791 ■ Lyndon Area Chamber of Commerce
PO Box 886
Lyndonville, VT 05851
Ph:(802)626-9696
Fax: (802)626-1234
Co. E-mail: info@lyndonvermont.com
URL: http://www.lyndonvermont.com
Contact: Mindy Wren, Pres.

65792 ■ Manchester and the Mountains Regional Chamber of Commerce
5046 Main St., Ste. 1
Manchester Center, VT 05255-9787
Ph:(802)362-2100
Free: 800-362-4144
Fax: (802)362-3451
Co. E-mail: manager@manchesterchamber.net

URL: http://www.manchestervermont.net
Contact: Jay Hathaway, Exec.Dir.

65793 ■ Mount Snow Valley Chamber of Commerce
PO Box 3
Wilmington, VT 05363
Ph:(802)464-8092
Free: 877-887-6884
Fax: (802)464-0287
Co. E-mail: info@visitvermont.com
URL: http://www.visitvermont.com
Contact: Joanne Fiore, Exec.Dir.

65794 ■ Northeast Kingdom Chamber of Commerce
51 Depot Sq., Ste. 3
St. Johnsbury, VT 05819
Ph:(802)748-3678
Free: 800-639-6379
Fax: (802)748-0731
Co. E-mail: nekinfo@nekchamber.com
URL: http://www.nekchamber.com
Contact: Darcie McCann, Exec. Dir.

65795 ■ Randolph Chamber of Commerce
PO Box 9
Randolph, VT 05060
Ph:(802)728-9027
Co. E-mail: chamber@randolphvt.com
URL: http://www.randolphvt.com
Contact: Marty Strange, Pres.

65796 ■ Rutland Region Chamber of Commerce
256 N Main St.
Rutland, VT 05701
Ph:(802)773-2747
Free: 800-756-8880
Fax: (802)773-2772
Co. E-mail: info@rutlandvermont.com
URL: http://www.rutlandvermont.com
Contact: Thomas L. Donahue, Exec.VP/CEO

65797 ■ Smugglers' Notch Area Chamber of Commerce
PO Box 364
Jeffersonville, VT 05464-0364
Ph:(802)644-8232
Co. E-mail: snacc15@hotmail.com
URL: http://www.smugnotch.com
Contact: Ray Saloomey

65798 ■ Springfield Regional Chamber of Commerce
14 Clinton St., Ste. 6
Springfield, VT 05156
Ph:(802)885-2779
Fax: (802)885-6826
Co. E-mail: chamber@springfieldvt.com
URL: http://www.springfieldvt.com
Contact: Patricia Chaffee, Exec.VP

65799 ■ Stowe Area Association
51 Main St.
PO Box 1320
Stowe, VT 05672
Ph:(802)253-7321
Free: 800-247-8693
Fax: (802)253-2159
Co. E-mail: askus@gostowe.com
URL: http://www.gostowe.com
Contact: Valerie Rochon, Exec.Dir.

65800 ■ Sugarbush Chamber of Commerce
PO Box 173
Waitsfield, VT 05673
Ph:(802)496-3409
Free: 800-828-4748
Fax: (802)496-5420
Co. E-mail: info@madrivervalley.com
URL: http://www.madrivervalley.com
Contact: Susan Roy, Exec. Dir.

65801 ■ Swanton Chamber of Commerce
PO Box 237
Swanton, VT 05488

Ph:(802)868-7200
URL: http://www.swantonchamber.com
Contact: David Chevalier, Pres.

65802 ■ Upper Valley Bi-State Regional Chamber of Commerce
PO Box 697
White River Junction, VT 05001
Ph:(802)295-6200
Fax: (802)295-3779
Co. E-mail: director@uppervalleychamber.com
URL: http://uppervalleychamber.com
Contact: Catherine Carter, Pres.

65803 ■ Vermont Chamber of Commerce
PO Box 37
Montpelier, VT 05601
Ph:(802)223-3443
Fax: (802)223-4257
Co. E-mail: info@vtchamber.com
URL: http://www.vtchamber.com
Contact: Duane Marsh, Pres.

65804 ■ Woodstock Area Chamber of Commerce
PO Box 486
Woodstock, VT 05091
Ph:(802)457-3555
Free: 888-496-6378
Fax: (802)457-1601
Co. E-mail: info@woodstockvt.com
URL: http://www.woodstockvt.com
Contact: Annette Compton, Marketing Dir.

FINANCING AND LOAN PROGRAMS

65805 ■ Aggregate Capital LLC
2463 Stowe Hollow Rd.
Stowe, VT 05672
Ph:(802)253-6843
Fax: (617)812-6040
URL: http://www.aggregatecapital.com
Contact: David Bradbury, Managing Partner
Preferred Investment Size: $25,000 to $500,000. **Investment Policies:** Start-up, seed, early and first stage, and expansion. **Industry Preferences:** Internet specific. **Geographic Preferences:** Mid Atlantic, Northeast, and Southeast U.S.; Ontario and Quebec Canada.

65806 ■ Green Mountain Advisors, Inc.
694 Main St.
Quechee, VT 05059
Ph:(802)296-7800
Fax: (802)296-6012
URL: http://www.gmtcap.com
Contact: Guy Roberts, President
Preferred Investment Size: $4,000,000 to $40,000,000. **Investment Types:** Mezzanine. **Industry Preferences:** Industrial and energy, computer software and services, computer hardware, consumer related, other products, medical and health, communications and media. **Geographic Preferences:** U.S.

PROCUREMENT ASSISTANCE PROGRAMS

65807 ■ Agency of Commerce and Community Development Center–Department of Economic Development–Government Marketing Assistance Program (Natio)
National Life Bldg.
Drawer 20
Montpelier, VT 05620-0501
Ph:(802)828-3080
Free: 800-341-2211
Fax: (802)828-3258
URL: http://www.thinkvermont.com
Contact: Greg Maguire, Dir

INCUBATORS/RESEARCH AND TECHNOLOGY PARKS

65808 ■ Bennington County Industrial Corp.
PO Box 357
North Bennington, VT 5257
Ph:(802)442-8975
Fax: (802)447-1101
Co. E-mail: peter@bcic.org
URL: http://www.bcic.org

65809 ■ Precision Valley Development Corp.
100 River St.
Springfield, VT 5156
Ph:(802)885-2138
Fax: (802)885-3745
Co. E-mail: twparker@vermontel.net
URL: http://www.springfieldvt.com/pvdc/home.htm

65810 ■ University of Vermont–Office of Sponsored Programs
340 Waterman Bldg.
Burlington, VT 05405-0160
Ph:(802)656-3360
Fax: (802)656-1326
Co. E-mail: ruth.farrell@uvm.edu
URL: http://www.uvm.edu/osp1
Contact: Ruth Farrell, Assoc.VP, Res.
E-mail: ruth.farrell@uvm.edu
Scope: Provides support services to faculty and staff members of the University, processes proposals for, and awards of, external funding of research projects, and administers Institutional Review Board activities. **Services:** Funding searches, for nonprofit organizations, city government, and state government. **Publications:** Funding Highlights (biweekly). **Educational Activities:** Training workshops, on proposal development.

EDUCATIONAL PROGRAMS

65811 ■ Lyndon State College–Continuing Education Department
PO Box 919
Lyndonville, VT 05851
Ph:(802)626-6200
Fax: (802)626-9770
URL: http://www.lsc.vsc.edu
Description: Offers courses for professional, personal, and academic enrichment. Conducts business and management courses on a credit or noncredit basis. Presents institutes, seminars, and workshops. Offers degree programs in small business management, management training, and personnel management.

PUBLICATIONS

65812 ■ *Smart Start Your Vermont Business*
PSI Research
300 N. Valley Dr.
Grants Pass, OR 97526
Ph:(541)479-9464
Free: 800-228-2275
Fax: (541)476-1479
Co. E-mail: info@psi-research.com
URL: http://www.psi-research.com
Ed: Michael D. Jenkins. **Released:** Revised edition, 1992. **Price:** $29.95 (looseleaf binder); $24.95 (paper). **Description:** Part of the Successful Business Library series.

PUBLISHERS

65813 ■ Velocity Business Publishing Inc.
10 Seymour St., Ste. A
Middlebury, VT 05753-1109
Ph:(802)388-6250
Free: 888-805-8600
Fax: (802)453-2164

Co. E-mail: action@velocityagency.com
URL: http://www.velocityagency.com
Contact: Jeff Olson, President
Description: Publishes business products in a variety of formats. **Founded:** 1997.

SMALL BUSINESS DEVELOPMENT CENTER LEAD OFFICE

65814 ■ Department of Business Assistance–Small Business Development Center
707 East Main St. Ste. 300
Richmond, VA 23219
Ph:(804)371-8253
Fax: (804)225-3384
Contact: Dr. Robert C. Wilburn, Dir.
E-mail: rwilburn@dba.state.va.us

65815 ■ Virginia SBDC Network–George Mason University
4031 University Dr., Ste. 200
Fairfax, VA 22030-3409
Ph:(703)277-7727
Fax: (703)352-8515
URL: http://www.virginiasbdc.org
Contact: Jody Keenan, Director
E-mail: jkeenan@gmu.edu

65816 ■ Virginia Small Business Development Center–Commonwealth of Virginia–Department of Economic Development (901 E)
901 E Byrd St., Ste. 1400
Richmond, VA 23219
Ph:(804)371-8253
Fax: (804)225-3384
Contact: Robert D. Wilburn, State Director
E-mail: rwilburn@dba.state.va.us

SMALL BUSINESS DEVELOPMENT CENTERS

65817 ■ Alexandria SBDC–Alexandria Chamber of Commerce
801 N. Fairfax St., Ste. 402
Alexandria, VA 22314
Ph:(703)778-1295
Fax: (703)778-1293
URL: http://www.alexandriasbdc.org
Contact: Bill Reagan, Dir.
E-mail: billr@alexandriasbdc.org

65818 ■ Arlington Small Business Development Center–George Mason University
3401 N. Fairfax Dr.
Arlington, VA 22201
Ph:(703)993-8129
Fax: (703)430-7293
URL: http://www.arlingtonsbdc.org
Contact: Nalin Jain, Dir.
E-mail: njain@gmu.edu

65819 ■ Central Virginia Small Business Development Center
210 Ridge/McIntire Rd., Ste. 500
Charlottesville, VA 22902
Ph:(434)295-8198
Co. E-mail: sbdc@cstone.net
URL: http://www.avenue.org/sbdc
Contact: Nora Gillespie, Dir.

65820 ■ Fairfax SBDC–George Mason University
4031 University Dr., Ste. 200
Fairfax, VA 22030
Ph:(703)277-7700
Fax: (703)277-7722
URL: http://www.sbdc.org
Contact: John Casey, Dir.
E-mail: jcasey1@gmu.edu

65821 ■ Flory Small Business Center, Inc. –Small Business Development Center
10311 Sudley Manor Dr.
Manassas, VA 20109-2962
Ph:(703)335-2500
Co. E-mail: FloryCenter@attglobal.net
Contact: Linda Decker, Dir.

65822 ■ Greater Richmond Small Business Development Center–Greater Richmond Chamber of Commerce
600 E. Main St., Ste. 700
Richmond, VA 23219-2118
Ph:(804)648-7838
Free: 800-646-SBDC
Fax: (804)648-7849
URL: http://www.grsbdc.com
Contact: Mike Leonard, Dir.
E-mail: mike.leonard@grcc.com

65823 ■ James Madison University–Shenandoah Valley SBDC
1598 S. Main St.
MSC 5502
Harrisonburg, VA 22807
Ph:(540)568-3227
Fax: (540)801-8469
URL: http://www.jmu.edu/sbdcenter
Contact: Henry Reeves, Dir.
E-mail: reevesha@jmu.edu

65824 ■ Longwood University - Crater SBDC
PO Box 1808
Petersburg, VA 23805
Ph:(804)518-2003
Fax: (804)518-2004
URL: http://www.longwood.edu/sbdc
Contact: Diane Howerton, Dir.
E-mail: dhowerton@cpd.state.va.us

65825 ■ Longwood University at Farmville–Small Business Development Center
515 Main St.
Farmville, VA 23909
Ph:(434)395-2086
Fax: (434)395-2359

URL: http://www.longwood.edu/sbdc
Contact: Sheri McGuire, Dir.
E-mail: mcguiresr@longwood.edu

65826 ■ Longwood University SBDC at Martinsville
115 Broad St.
PO Box 709
Martinsville, VA 24114
Ph:(276)632-4462
Fax: (276)632-5059
URL: http://www.longwood.edu/sbdc
Contact: Richard G. Ephgrave Sr., Dir.
E-mail: ephgraverg@longwood.edu

65827 ■ Longwood University SBDC at South Boston
820 Bruce St.
South Boston, VA 24592
Ph:(434)572-5484
Fax: (434)572-5462
URL: http://www.longwood.edu/sbdc
Contact: Larry Harris, Dir.
E-mail: harrislb@longwood.edu

65828 ■ Lord Fairfax Community College–Lord Fairfax SBDC at Middletown
7718 Valley Ave.
Middletown, VA 22645
Ph:(540)868-7093
Fax: (540)868-7095
URL: http://www.lfsbdc.org
Contact: Bill Sirbaugh, Dir.
E-mail: bsirbaugh@lfsbdc.org

65829 ■ Lord Fairfax SBDC at Fauquier–Lord Fairfax Community College–Lord Fairfax SBDC (6480)
6480 College St.
Warrenton, VA 20187
Ph:(540)351-1595
Fax: (540)351-1597
URL: http://www.lfsbdc.org
Contact: Bill Sirbaugh, Dir.
E-mail: bsirbaugh@lfsbdc.org

65830 ■ Loudoun County SBDC
21145 Whitfield Pl., Ste. 104
Sterling, VA 20165
Ph:(703)430-7222
Fax: (703)430-7258
Co. E-mail: sbdc@loudounsbdc.org
URL: http://www.loudounsbdc.org
Contact: Giovanni Cozzarelli, Dir.
E-mail: gcozzarelli@loudounsbdc.org

65831 ■ Mountain Empire Community College–Mountain Empire SBDC
3441 Mountain Empire Rd.
Big Stone Gap, VA 24219
Ph:(276)523-6529
Fax: (276)523-8139
URL: http://www.me.cc.va.us/sbdc
Contact: Tim Blankenbecler, Dir.
E-mail: tblankenbecler@me.vccs.edu

65832 ■ New River Valley SBDC–Radford University–SBDC (Busin)
Business Assistance Center
7516 Lee Hwy., Ste. A2
PO Box 6953
Radford, VA 24141
Ph:(540)831-6056
Fax: (540)831-6735
URL: http://btp.radford.edu/ba
Contact: David Shanks, Dir.
E-mail: dshanks@radford.edu

65833 ■ Rappahannock Region SBDC at Fredericksburg
James Monroe Center
121 University Blvd.
Fredericksburg, VA 22406
Ph:(540)654-1060
Fax: (540)654-1070
URL: http://cgps.umw.edu/sbdc
Contact: Brian Baker, Dir.
E-mail: bbaker@radford.edu

65834 ■ Rappahannock Region SBDC at Warsaw–University of Mary Washington
479 Main St.
PO Box 490
Warsaw, VA 22572
Ph:(804)333-0286
Free: 800-524-8915
Fax: (804)333-0187
URL: http://cgps.umw.edu/sbdc
Contact: Joy Corprew, Dir.
E-mail: jcorprew@umw.edu

65835 ■ Region 2000 SBDC
Business Development Center
147 Mill Ridge Rd.
Lynchburg, VA 24502
Ph:(434)582-6170
Fax: (434)582-6106
Co. E-mail: sbdcdir@lbdc.com
URL: http://www.lbdc.com
Contact: Niro Rasanayagam, Dir.

65836 ■ Roanoke Regional Small Business Development Center
212 S. Jefferson St.
Roanoke, VA 24011
Ph:(540)983-0717
Fax: (540)983-0723
URL: http://www.rrsbdc.org
Contact: Roy Baldwin, Dir.
E-mail: rbaldwin@roanokechamber.org

65837 ■ SBDC of Hampton Roads, Inc. –Hampton Roads Chamber of Commerce
PO Box 133
Melfa, VA 23410
Ph:(757)789-3418
Fax: (757)787-7579
Co. E-mail: sbdc@esva.net
URL: http://www.hrsbdc.org
Contact: Nial Finnegan, Dir.

65838 ■ SBDC of Hampton Roads Inc. –Thomas Nelson Community College
600 Butler Farm Rd.
Ste. A, Rm. 1105
Hampton, VA 23666
Ph:(757)825-2957
Fax: (757)825-2960
URL: http://www.hrsbdc.org
Contact: Debra Farley, Dir.
E-mail: dfarley@tncc.edu

65839 ■ Shenandoah Valley SBDC–Blue Ridge Community College
50 Lodge Ln.
Verona, VA 24482
Ph:(540)248-0600
Fax: (540)234-8102
URL: http://www.jmu.edu/sbdcenter
Contact: Sandy Showalter, Dir.
E-mail: brshows@brcc.edu

65840 ■ South Boston Satellite Office of Longwood–Small Business Development Center
515 Broad St.
PO Box 1116
South Boston, VA 24592
Ph:(804)575-0044
Fax: (804)572-1762
Contact: Vince Decker, Dir.
E-mail: ddecker@halifax.com

65841 ■ South Fairfax SBDC of the Community Business Partnership
7001 Loisdale Rd., 2nd Fl.
Springfield, VA 22150
Ph:(703)768-1440
Fax: (703)768-0547
URL: http://www.cbponline.org
Contact: Patricia Peacock, Dir.
E-mail: ppeacock@gmu.edu

65842 ■ Southwest Virginia Community College–Southwest Small Business Development Center
PO Box SVCC, Rte. 19
Richlands, VA 24641
Ph:(276)964-7345
Fax: (276)964-7575
URL: http://www.sw.edu
Contact: Jim Boyd, Dir.
E-mail: jim.boyd@sw.edu

65843 ■ Virginia Highlands SBDC–Virginia Highlands Community College
851 French Moore Jr. Blvd., Ste. 178
Abingdon, VA 24210
Ph:(540)676-5615
Fax: (540)676-5591
URL: http://www.vhcc.edu/sbdc
Contact: Jim Tilley, Dir.
E-mail: jtilley@vhcc.edu

65844 ■ Virginia Small Business Development Center
707 E. Main St., Ste. 300
PO Box 446
Richmond, VA 23218-0446
Ph:(804)371-8253
Fax: (804)225-3384
Contact: Robert C. Wilburn, State Dir.
E-mail: rwilburn@dba.state.va.us

65845 ■ Williamsburg SBDC/Hampton Roads SBDC–Thomas Nelson Community College/Hampton Roads Chamber of Commerce
Historic Triangle Office
161-C John Jefferson Rd.
Williamsburg, VA 23185
Ph:(757)253-4322
Fax: (757)253-5335
Co. E-mail: vogte@tncc.edu
URL: http://www.hrsbdc.org
Contact: Erica Gledhill, Dir.

65846 ■ Wytheville Community College–Wytheville Small Business Development Center
1000 E. Main St.
Wytheville, VA 24382
Ph:(540)223-4798
Free: 800-467-1195
Fax: (540)223-4716
URL: http://www.wc.cc.va.us/SBDC/
Contact: Rob Edwards, Dir.
E-mail: redwards@naxs.com

65847 ■ Wytheville SBDC–Wytheville Community College
Smyth County Education Center
300 Gordondale Rd.
Atkins, VA 24311
Ph:(276)783-1777
Fax: (276)783-8335
URL: http://www.wcc.vccs.edu/sbdc
Contact: Rob Edwards, Dir.
E-mail: redwards1956@aol.com

SMALL BUSINESS ASSISTANCE PROGRAMS

65848 ■ Virginia Department of Agriculture and Consumer Services–Office of International Marketing
1100 Bank St.
Richmond, VA 23219
Ph:(804)786-3953
Fax: (804)225-4434
URL: http://www.vdacs.virginia.gov/international/index.html
Description: Works to maximize the export of Virginia's agricultural products; provides market, exporter, and sales development assistance.

65849 ■ Virginia Department of Business Assistance–Small Business Development Division
PO Box 446
Richmond, VA 23218-0446
Ph:(804)371-8200
Fax: (804)225-3384
Co. E-mail: csurface@dba.state.va.us
URL: http://www.dba.virginia.gov
Description: Small business persons appointed by the governor to advise the Department of Economic Development on small business programs and concerns.

65850 ■ Virginia Department of Business Assistance–Small Business and Financing Authority
PO Box 446
Richmond, VA 23218-0446
Ph:(804)371-8200
Fax: (804)225-3384
Co. E-mail: scott.parsons@dba.virginia.gov
URL: http://www.dba.virginia.gov
Contact: Scott Parsons, Exec Dir
Description: Assists small businesses by providing information on sources of technical, management, and financial assistance programs. Serves as an ombudsman, helping small businesses to resolve state regulatory problems.

65851 ■ Virginia Economic Development Partnership–Trade Division
901 E Byrd St.
PO Box 798
Richmond, VA 23218
Ph:(804)371-8100
Fax: (804)371-8860
URL: http://www.yesvirginia.org
Description: Consulting program designed to assist Virginia firms in identifying and developing foreign markets for their goods and services.

BETTER BUSINESS BUREAUS

65852 ■ Better Business Bureau of Central Virginia
701 E Franklin, Ste. 712
Richmond, VA 23219-2332
Ph:(804)648-0016
Fax: (804)648-3115
Co. E-mail: info@richmond.bbb.org
URL: http://www.richmond.bbb.org
Contact: Thomas J. Gallagher, Pres./CEO

65853 ■ Better Business Bureau of Greater Hampton Roads
586 Virginian Dr.
Norfolk, VA 23505
Ph:(757)531-1300
Fax: (757)531-1388
Co. E-mail: info@hamptonroadsbbb.org
URL: http://www.hamptonroadsbbb.org
Contact: C.C. Shelton, Pres./CEO

65854 ■ Better Business Bureau of Western Virginia
31 W Campbell Ave.
Roanoke, VA 24011-1301
Ph:(540)342-3455
Free: 800-533-5501
Fax: (540)345-2289
Co. E-mail: info@roanoke.bbb.org
URL: http://www.vabbb.org
Contact: Julie Wheeler, Pres./CEO

CHAMBERS OF COMMERCE

65855 ■ Alexandria Chamber of Commerce
801 N Fairfax St., Ste. 402
Alexandria, VA 22314
Ph:(703)549-1000
Fax: (703)739-3805
Co. E-mail: info@alexchamber.com
URL: http://www.alexchamber.com
Contact: Ken Moore CCE, Pres./CEO

65856 ■ Alleghany Highlands Chamber of Commerce
241 W Main St.
Covington, VA 24426
Ph:(540)962-2178
Free: 888-430-5786
Fax: (540)962-2179
Co. E-mail: info@ahchamber.com
URL: http://www.ahchamber.com
Contact: Karen Knuckles, Exec.Dir.

65857 ■ Altavista Area Chamber of Commerce
PO Box 606
Altavista, VA 24517
Ph:(434)369-6665
Fax: (434)369-6665
Co. E-mail: info@altavistachamber.org
URL: http://www.altavistachamber.org
Contact: Bill Smith, Pres.

65858 ■ Amherst County Chamber of Commerce
154 S Main St.
PO Box 560
Amherst, VA 24521
Ph:(434)946-0990
URL: http://www.amherstvachamber.com
Contact: Carrie Weeks, Pres.

65859 ■ Annandale Chamber of Commerce
7263 Maple Pl., Ste. 207
Annandale, VA 22003-3004
Ph:(703)256-7232
Fax: (703)256-7233
Co. E-mail: info@annandalechamber.com
URL: http://www.annandalechamber.com
Contact: Ms. Linda Bufano, Administrator

65860 ■ Appomattox County Chamber of Commerce
PO Box 704
Appomattox, VA 24522
Ph:(434)352-2621
Fax: (434)352-2621
Co. E-mail: appomattoxcc@earthlink.net
URL: http://www.appomattoxchamber.org
Contact: Patricia D'Amario, Exec.Sec.

65861 ■ Arlington Chamber of Commerce
2009 14th St. N, Ste. 111
Arlington, VA 22201
Ph:(703)525-2400
Fax: (703)522-5273
Co. E-mail: chamber@arlingtonchamber.org
URL: http://www.arlingtonchamber.org
Contact: Richard V. Doud Jr., Pres.

65862 ■ Bath County Chamber of Commerce
PO Box 718
Hot Springs, VA 24445
Ph:(540)839-5409
Free: 800-628-8092

Fax: (540)839-5409
Co. E-mail: bathco@va.tds.net
URL: http://www.bathcountyva.org/clubs_
    organizations/Chamber%20of%20Commerce.
    htm
Contact: Patrick Sheridan, Pres.

65863 ■ Bedford Area Chamber of Commerce
305 E Main St.
Bedford, VA 24523
Ph:(540)586-9401
Free: 800-933-9535
Fax: (540)587-6650
Co. E-mail: dshilling@fnbonline.com
URL: http://www.bedfordareachamber.com
Contact: Lee Ann Carr, Pres.

65864 ■ Berryville-Clarke County Chamber of Commerce
PO Box 365
Berryville, VA 22611
Co. E-mail: info@clarkechamber.com
URL: http://www.clarkechamber.com
Contact: Roberta J. Kerns, Exec.Dir.

65865 ■ Blackstone Chamber of Commerce
PO Box 295
Blackstone, VA 23824
Ph:(434)292-1677
Fax: (434)292-1588
Co. E-mail: chamber@blackstoneva.com
URL: http://blackstoneva.com
Contact: Mrs. Field W. Green, Pres.

65866 ■ Botetourt County Chamber of Commerce
PO Box 81
Fincastle, VA 24090-0081
Ph:(540)473-8280
Fax: (540)473-8365
Co. E-mail: bccoc@rbnet.com
URL: http://www.bot-co-chamber.com
Contact: Dan Naff, Sec.-Treas.

65867 ■ Broadway-Timberville Chamber of Commerce
233 McCauley Dr.
Timberville, VA 22853
Ph:(540)896-7413
Fax: (540)896-2825
Co. E-mail: secretary@btchamber.org
URL: http://www.btchamber.org
Contact: Crystal Collins, Exec.Sec.

65868 ■ Brunswick Chamber of Commerce
400 N Main St.
Lawrenceville, VA 23868-1818
Ph:(434)848-3154
Fax: (434)848-9356
Co. E-mail: brunschamber@meckcom.net
Contact: Elaine Clary, Exec.Dir.

65869 ■ Buchanan County Chamber of Commerce
PO Box 2818
Grundy, VA 24614-2818
Ph:(276)935-4147
Fax: (276)935-5458
Co. E-mail: chamber@buchanancounty.org
Contact: Mary M. Belcher, Exec.Dir.

65870 ■ Buckingham Chamber of Commerce
PO Box 951
Dillwyn, VA 23936
Ph:(434)983-2372
Fax: (434)983-4891
Co. E-mail: info@buckinghamchamber.org
URL: http://www.buckinghamchamber.org
Contact: Tony Martin, Pres.

65871 ■ Buena Vista Chamber of Commerce
PO Box 207
Buena Vista, VA 24416
Ph:(540)261-2880
Fax: (540)261-1810
Contact: Sarah Decon, Dir.

65872 ■ Caroline County Chamber of Commerce
PO Box 384
Bowling Green, VA 22427
Ph:(804)633-5264
Fax: (804)633-5264
Co. E-mail: chamber@bealenet.com
Contact: Jeff Sili, Pres.

65873 ■ Carroll County Chamber of Commerce
515 N Main St.
PO Box 1184
Hillsville, VA 24343
Ph:(276)728-5397
Co. E-mail: carrollchamber@aisva.net
Contact: Katie Dalton, Exec.Dir.

65874 ■ Central Fairfax Chamber of Commerce
11166 Main St., 1st Fl.
Fairfax, VA 22030
Ph:(703)591-2450
Fax: (703)591-2820
Co. E-mail: melissa@cfcc.org
URL: http://www.cfcc.org
Contact: Melissa Choate, Pres./CEO

65875 ■ Chamber of Commerce of Smyth County
214 W Main St.
Marion, VA 24354
Ph:(276)783-3161
Fax: (276)783-8003
Co. E-mail: info@smythchamber.org
URL: http://www.smythchamber.org
Contact: Barbara DeBord, Exec.Dir.

65876 ■ Charlottesville Regional Chamber of Commerce
PO Box 1564
Charlottesville, VA 22902-1564
Ph:(434)295-3141
Fax: (434)295-3144
Co. E-mail: chamber@cvillechamber.com
URL: http://www.cvillechamber.com
Contact: Timothy Hulbert, Pres./CEO

65877 ■ Chase City Chamber of Commerce
316 N Main St.
Chase City, VA 23924
Ph:(434)372-0379
Fax: (434)372-4699
Co. E-mail: chasecityva@meckcom.net
URL: http://www.chasecitychamberofcomm.com
Contact: Janet Flynn, Exec.Dir.

65878 ■ Chesterfield County Chamber of Commerce
9330 Iron Bridge Rd., Ste. B
Chesterfield, VA 23832
Ph:(804)748-6364
Fax: (804)425-5669
URL: http://www.chesterfieldchamber.com
Contact: Lenita Gilreath, Exec. Dir.

65879 ■ Chincoteague Chamber of Commerce
PO Box 258
Chincoteague, VA 23336
Ph:(757)336-6161
URL: http://www.chincoteaguechamber.com
Contact: Suzanne Taylor, Exec. Dir. of Marketing
    and Tourism

65880 ■ Clarkesville Lake Country Chamber of Commerce
105 2nd St.
PO Box 1017
Clarksville, VA 23927-1017
Ph:(434)374-2436
Free: 800-557-5582
Fax: (434)374-8174
Co. E-mail: clarksville@kerrlake.com
URL: http://www.clarksvilleva.com
Contact: Mrs. Linda Williams, Exec. Dir.

65881 ■ Colonial Beach Chamber of Commerce
PO Box 475
Colonial Beach, VA 22443
Ph:(804)224-8145
Fax: (804)224-8145
Co. E-mail: info@colonialbeach.org
Contact: Phil Bolin, Pres.

65882 ■ Colonial Heights Chamber of Commerce
201 Temple Ave., Ste. E
Colonial Heights, VA 23834
Ph:(804)526-5872
Fax: (804)526-9637
Co. E-mail: chchamber@colonialheights.cc
URL: http://www.colonial-heights.com
Contact: Lamese Essey, Exec.Dir.

65883 ■ Crewe - Burkeville Chamber of Commerce
PO Box 305
Crewe, VA 23930
Ph:(434)645-7222
Fax: (434)645-7232
Co. E-mail: chamber@creweburkeville.org
URL: http://www.creweburkeville.org
Contact: Beth Robertson, Pres.

65884 ■ Culpeper County Chamber of Commerce
109 S Commerce St.
Culpeper, VA 22701
Ph:(540)825-8628
Fax: (540)825-1449
Co. E-mail: info@culpepervachamber.com
URL: http://www.culpepervachamber.com

65885 ■ Danville - Pittsylvania County Chamber of Commerce
PO Box 99
Blairs, VA 24527
Ph:(434)836-6990
Fax: (434)836-6955
Co. E-mail: chamber@dpchamber.org
URL: http://www.dpchamber.org
Contact: Laurie S. Moran CCE, Pres.

65886 ■ Dickenson County Chamber of Commerce
PO Box 1989
Clintwood, VA 24228
Ph:(276)926-6074
Free: 800-665-1260
Co. E-mail: chamber@dcwin.org
URL: http://www.dickensonchamber.net
Contact: Rita Surratt, Pres./CEO

65887 ■ Eastern Shore of Virginia Chamber of Commerce
19056 Industrial Pkwy.
PO Box 460
Melfa, VA 23410-0460
Ph:(757)787-2460
Fax: (757)787-8687
Co. E-mail: info@esvachamber.org
URL: http://www.esvachamber.org
Contact: Rose Rulon, CEO

65888 ■ Edinburg Area Chamber of Commerce
PO Box 511
Edinburg, VA 22824
Ph:(540)984-8318
Co. E-mail: chamcom@shentel.net
URL: http://www.edinburgchamber.com
Contact: Matt Burgwald, Pres.

65889 ■ Emporia - Greensville Chamber of Commerce
Emporia Train Depot
400 Halifax St.
Emporia, VA 23847
Ph:(434)634-9441
Fax: (434)634-3485
Co. E-mail: ontrack@telpage.net
URL: http://www.emporia-greensvillechamber.com

Contact: Amanda Dianis, Exec.Dir.

65890 ■ Fairfax County Chamber of Commerce
8230 Old Courthouse Rd., Ste. 350
Vienna, VA 22182-3853
Ph:(703)749-0400
Fax: (703)749-9075
Co. E-mail: blecos@fccc.org
URL: http://www.fccc.org
Contact: William D. Lecos, Pres./CEO

65891 ■ Falls Church Chamber of Commerce
417 W Broad St.
Falls Church, VA 22046
Ph:(703)532-1050
Fax: (703)237-7904
Co. E-mail: info@fallschurchchamber.org
URL: http://www.fallschurchchamber.org

65892 ■ Farmville Chamber of Commerce
PO Box 361
Farmville, VA 23901
Ph:(434)392-3939
Co. E-mail: webmaster@chamber.farmville.net
URL: http://www.chamber.farmville.net
Contact: Wanda Whitus, Exec.Dir.

65893 ■ Fauquier County Chamber of Commerce
183A Keith St.
Warrenton, VA 20186
Ph:(540)347-4414
Fax: (540)347-7510
Co. E-mail: mailbox@fauquierchamber.org
URL: http://www.fauquierchamber.org
Contact: Karen Henderson, Pres.

65894 ■ Floyd County Chamber of Commerce
PO Box 510
Floyd, VA 24091
Ph:(540)745-4407
Co. E-mail: chamber@swva.net
URL: http://www.visitfloyd.org

65895 ■ Fluvanna County Chamber of Commerce
PO Box 93
Palmyra, VA 22963-0093
Ph:(434)589-3262
Fax: (434)589-6212
Co. E-mail: fluvannacountycoc@earthlink.net
URL: http://www.fluvannachamber.org
Contact: Mr. Robert Mayfield, Pres.

65896 ■ Franklin County Chamber of Commerce
261 Franklin St.
PO Box 158
Rocky Mount, VA 24151
Ph:(540)483-9542
Fax: (540)483-0653
Co. E-mail: info@franklincounty.org
URL: http://www.franklincounty.org
Contact: Ms. Janie Hopkins, Exec.Dir.

65897 ■ Franklin-Southampton Area Chamber of Commerce
PO Box 531
Franklin, VA 23851
Ph:(757)562-4900
Fax: (757)562-6138
Co. E-mail: join@fsachamber.com
URL: http://www.fsachamber.com
Contact: Teresa B. Beale, Exec.Dir.

65898 ■ Fredericksburg Regional Chamber of Commerce
PO Box 7476
Fredericksburg, VA 22404-7476
Ph:(540)373-9400
Fax: (540)373-9570
Co. E-mail: linda@fredericksburgchamber.org
URL: http://www.fredericksburgchamber.org
Contact: Ms. Linda Worrell, Pres.

65899 ■ Front Royal - Warren County Chamber of Commerce
104 E Main St.
Front Royal, VA 22630
Ph:(540)635-3185
Fax: (540)635-9758
Co. E-mail: info@frontroyalchamber.com
URL: http://www.frontroyalchamber.com
Contact: Sharon Baroncelli, Pres.

65900 ■ Galax - Carroll - Grayson Chamber of Commerce
608 W Stuart Dr.
Galax, VA 24333
Ph:(276)236-2184
Fax: (276)236-1338
Co. E-mail: info@gcgchamber.com
URL: http://www.gcgchamber.com
Contact: Brian Funk, Pres.

65901 ■ Gloucester Chamber of Commerce
PO Box 296
Gloucester, VA 23061
Ph:(804)693-2425
Fax: (804)693-7193
Co. E-mail: information@gloucestervacc.com
URL: http://www.gloucestervacc.com
Contact: Jim Allison, Pres.

65902 ■ Goochland County Chamber of Commerce
2941 River Rd. W
PO Box 123
Goochland, VA 23063
Ph:(804)556-3811
Fax: (804)556-2131
Co. E-mail: info@goochlandchamber.org
URL: http://www.goochlandchamber.us
Contact: Doris Elderman, Exec.Dir.

65903 ■ Greater Augusta Regional Chamber of Commerce
PO Box 1107
Fishersville, VA 22939
Ph:(540)324-1133
Fax: (540)324-1136
Co. E-mail: chamber@ntelos.net
URL: http://www.augustachamber.org
Contact: Benjamin E. Carter MEd, Pres./CEO

65904 ■ Greater Reston Chamber of Commerce, Business Visitors Center
1763 Fountain Dr.
Spectrum II Shopping Ctr.
Reston, VA 20190
Ph:(703)707-9045
Fax: (703)707-9049
Co. E-mail: restonbiz@restonchamber.org
URL: http://www.restonchamber.org
Contact: Tracey White, Pres./CEO

65905 ■ Greater Richmond Chamber of Commerce
201 E Franklin St.
PO Box 12280
Richmond, VA 23219
Ph:(804)648-1234
Fax: (804)783-9366
Co. E-mail: chamber@grcc.com
URL: http://www.grcc.com
Contact: James Dunn, Pres.

65906 ■ Greater Springfield Chamber of Commerce
6434 Brandon Ave., Ste. 3A
Springfield, VA 22150
Ph:(703)866-3500
Fax: (703)866-3501
Co. E-mail: manney@springfieldchamber.org
URL: http://www.springfieldchamber.org
Contact: Nancy-jo Manney, Exec.Dir.

65907 ■ Greater Williamsburg Chamber and Tourism Alliance
421 N Boundary St.
PO Box 3495
Williamsburg, VA 23187-3495

Ph:(757)229-6511
Fax: (757)229-2047
Co. E-mail: wacc@williamsburgcc.com
URL: http://www.williamsburgcc.com

65908 ■ Halifax County Chamber of Commerce
515 Broad St.
PO Box 399
South Boston, VA 24592
Ph:(434)572-3085
Fax: (434)572-1733
Co. E-mail: info@halifaxchamber.net
URL: http://www.halifaxchamber.net
Contact: Nancy L. Pool, Pres.

65909 ■ Hampton Roads Chamber of Commerce
PO Box 327
Norfolk, VA 23501-0327
Ph:(757)622-2312
Fax: (757)622-5563
Co. E-mail: jhornbeck@hrccva.com
URL: http://www.hamptonroadschamber.com
Contact: John A. Hornbeck Jr., CEO/Pres.

65910 ■ Hanover Association of Businesses and Chamber of Commerce
PO Box 16
Ashland, VA 23005
Ph:(804)798-8130
Fax: (804)798-0014
Co. E-mail: admin@habcc.com
URL: http://www.habcc.com
Contact: Mrs. Kristine L. Holt, Office Administrator

65911 ■ Harrisonburg-Rockingham Chamber of Commerce
800 Country Club Rd.
Harrisonburg, VA 22802
Ph:(540)434-3862
Fax: (540)434-4508
Co. E-mail: information@hrchamber.org
URL: http://www.hrchamber.org
Contact: Katey Steward, Admin.Asst.

65912 ■ Herndon Dulles Chamber of Commerce
PO Box 327
Herndon, VA 20172
Ph:(703)437-5556
Fax: (703)787-8859
Co. E-mail: info@herndondulleschamber.org
URL: http://www.herndondulleschamber.org
Contact: Eileen Curtis, Pres./CEO

65913 ■ Highland County Chamber of Commerce
PO Box 223
Monterey, VA 24465-0223
Ph:(540)468-2550
Fax: (540)468-2551
Co. E-mail: info@highlandcounty.org
URL: http://www.highlandcounty.org
Contact: Carolyn H. Pohowsky, Exec.Dir.

65914 ■ Hopewell-Prince George Chamber of Commerce
PO Box 1297
Hopewell, VA 23860-1297
Ph:(804)458-5536
Fax: (804)458-0041
Co. E-mail: becky@hpgchamber.org
URL: http://www.hpgchamber.org
Contact: Becky McDonough, Exec.VP

65915 ■ Irvington Chamber of Commerce
PO Box 282
Irvington, VA 22480
Ph:(804)438-9324
Fax: (804)438-6865
URL: http://www.irvington.org
Contact: David Raffetto, Pres.

65916 ■ Isle of Wight - Smithfield - Windsor Chamber of Commerce
100 Main St.
PO Box 38
Smithfield, VA 23431

Ph:(757)357-3502
Fax: (757)357-6884
Co. E-mail: chamber@theisle.org
URL: http://www.theisle.org

65917 ■ King George County Chamber of Commerce
PO Box 409
King George, VA 22485
Ph:(540)775-2024
Fax: (540)775-4099
Contact: Larry Leonhartt, Pres.

65918 ■ Lancaster County Chamber of Commerce
PO Box 1868
Kilmarnock, VA 22482
Ph:(804)435-6092
Fax: (804)435-3092
Co. E-mail: info@lancasterva.com
URL: http://www.lancasterva.com
Contact: Ed Fuehrer, Pres.

65919 ■ Lee County Area Chamber of Commerce
PO Box 417
Pennington Gap, VA 24277
Ph:(276)546-2233
Co. E-mail: info@leecountyvachamber.org
URL: http://www.leecountyvachamber.org

65920 ■ Lexington-Rockbridge County Chamber of Commerce
100 E Washington St.
Lexington, VA 24450
Ph:(540)463-5375
Fax: (540)463-3567
Co. E-mail: chamber@lexrockchamber.com
URL: http://www.lexrockchamber.com
Contact: James Samuel Moore, Exec.Dir.

65921 ■ Loudoun County Chamber of Commerce
101 Blue Seal Dr., Ste. 100
PO Box 1298
Leesburg, VA 20177
Ph:(703)777-2176
Fax: (703)777-1392
Co. E-mail: rcollins@loudounchamber.org
URL: http://www.loudounchamber.org
Contact: Randy Collins, Pres./CEO

65922 ■ Louisa County Chamber of Commerce
PO Box 955
Louisa, VA 23093
Ph:(540)967-0944
Fax: (540)854-7827
Co. E-mail: pam@louisatitle.com
URL: http://www.louisacountychamber.org
Contact: Pamela Brooks, Pres.

65923 ■ Luray-Page County Chamber of Commerce
46 E Main St.
Luray, VA 22835
Ph:(540)743-3915
Free: 888-743-3915
Fax: (540)743-3944
Co. E-mail: info@luraypage.com
URL: http://www.luraypage.com
Contact: Karen Culpepper, Exec.Dir.

65924 ■ Lynchburg Regional Chamber of Commerce
2015 Memorial Ave.
Lynchburg, VA 24501
Ph:(434)845-5966
Fax: (434)522-9592
Co. E-mail: info@lynchburgchamber.org
URL: http://www.lynchburgchamber.org
Contact: Rex K. Hammond, Pres./CEO

65925 ■ Madison Chamber of Commerce
110A N Main St.
PO Box 373
Madison, VA 22727-0373

Ph:(540)948-4455
Fax: (540)948-3174
Co. E-mail: tourism@madison-va.com
URL: http://www.madison-va.com
Contact: Marge Berry, Dir.

65926 ■ Martinsville - Henry County Chamber of Commerce
115 Broad St.
PO Box 709
Martinsville, VA 24114
Ph:(276)632-6401
Fax: (276)632-5059
Co. E-mail: mhccoc@mhcchamber.com
URL: http://www.martinsville.com
Contact: Kim Adkins, Pres.

65927 ■ Mathews County Chamber of Commerce
PO Box 1126
Mathews, VA 23109-1126
Ph:(804)725-9029
Fax: (804)725-9009
Co. E-mail: mchamber@crosslink.net
Contact: Bruce Shomaker, Pres.

65928 ■ Montgomery County Chamber of Commerce
612 New River Rd.
Christiansburg, VA 24073
Ph:(540)382-4010
Fax: (540)382-4390
Co. E-mail: chamber@montgomerycc.org
URL: http://www.montgomerycc.org
Contact: Shane Adams IOM, Pres./CEO

65929 ■ Mount Vernon - Lee Chamber of Commerce
8804D Pear Tree Village Ct.
Alexandria, VA 22309
Ph:(703)360-6925
Fax: (703)360-6928
Co. E-mail: info@mtvernon-leechamber.org
URL: http://mtvernon-leechamber.org
Contact: Holly Hicks Dougherty, Exec.Dir.

65930 ■ New Kent Chamber of Commerce
PO Box 119
Providence Forge, VA 23140
Ph:(804)966-1983
Co. E-mail: president@newkentchamber.org
URL: http://www.newkent.net/chamber.html
Contact: Wayne Hayden, Pres.

65931 ■ New Market Area Chamber of Commerce
9386 S Congress St.
New Market, VA 22844
Ph:(540)740-3212
Free: 877-740-3212
Fax: (540)740-3212
Co. E-mail: nmchambr@shentel.net
Contact: Mary Alice Burch, Pres.

65932 ■ Northampton County Chamber of Commerce
109 Mason Ave., Ste. A
Cape Charles, VA 23310
Ph:(757)331-2304
Co. E-mail: info@northamptoncountychamber.com

65933 ■ Orange County Chamber of Commerce
PO Box 146
Orange, VA 22960
Ph:(540)672-5216
Fax: (540)672-2304
Co. E-mail: occc@ns.gemlink.com
URL: http://orangevachamber.com
Contact: Barbara Bannar, Exec.Dir.

65934 ■ Patrick County Chamber of Commerce
PO Box 577
Stuart, VA 24171-0577
Ph:(276)694-6012
Co. E-mail: pchamber@sitestar.net

URL: http://www.patrickchamber.com
Contact: Harold Dean Goad, Pres.

65935 ■ Petersburg Chamber of Commerce
PO Box 928
Petersburg, VA 23804-0928
Ph:(804)733-8131
Fax: (804)733-9891
Co. E-mail: pcocva@verizon.net
URL: http://www.petersburg-va.org/chamber
Contact: Cynthia Raitt Devereaux, Exec.VP

65936 ■ Powhatan Chamber of Commerce
3829 Old Buckingham Rd.
PO Box 643
Powhatan, VA 23139
Ph:(804)598-2636
Fax: (804)598-2636
Co. E-mail: info@powhatanchamberofcommerce.org
URL: http://www.powhatanchamberofcommerce.org
Contact: Kathleen Budner, Exec.Dir.

65937 ■ Prince William County - Greater Manassas Chamber of Commerce
8963 Center St.
Manassas, VA 20110
Ph:(703)368-6600
Fax: (703)368-4733
Co. E-mail: djones@pwcgmcc.org
URL: http://www.pwcgmcc.org
Contact: Deborah L. Jones, Pres.

65938 ■ Prince William Regional Chamber of Commerce
4320 Ridgewood Center Dr.
Prince William, VA 22192-5307
Ph:(703)590-5000
Fax: (703)590-9815
Co. E-mail: pwrcc@regionalchamber.org
URL: http://www.regionalchamber.org
Contact: Laurie C. Wieder, Pres.

65939 ■ Pulaski County Chamber of Commerce
4440 Cleburne Blvd.
Dublin, VA 24084
Ph:(540)674-1991
Co. E-mail: pcchamber2@swva.net
URL: http://www.pulaskichamber.info
Contact: Judy Ison, Pres.

65940 ■ Radford Chamber of Commerce
27 W Main St.
Radford, VA 24141
Ph:(540)639-2202
Fax: (540)639-2228
Co. E-mail: radford@i-plus.net
URL: http://radfordchamber.com
Contact: Jennifer Collins, Pres.

65941 ■ Richlands Area Tazewell County Chamber of Commerce
1413 Front St.
Richlands, VA 24641-2491
Ph:(276)963-3385
Fax: (276)963-1413
Co. E-mail: ccrichldva@inetone.net
Contact: Ginger H. Branton, Exec.Dir.

65942 ■ Roanoke Regional Chamber of Commerce
210 S Jefferson St.
Roanoke, VA 24011
Ph:(540)983-0700
Fax: (540)983-0723
Co. E-mail: business@roanokechamber.org
URL: http://www.roanokechamber.org
Contact: Beth Doughty, Pres.

65943 ■ Salem-Roanoke County Chamber of Commerce
611 E Main St.
PO Box 832
Salem, VA 24153
Ph:(540)387-0267
Fax: (540)387-4110
Co. E-mail: chamber@salemva.org

Contact: Debbie Kavitz, Exec.Dir.

65944 ■ Scott County Chamber of Commerce
PO Box 609
Gate City, VA 24251
Ph:(540)386-6665
Fax: (540)386-9198
URL: http://www.mounet.com/~scottcc

65945 ■ Scottsville Community Chamber of Commerce
PO Box 11
Scottsville, VA 24590-0011
Ph:(434)286-6000
Fax: (434)286-2301
Co. E-mail: sccc@bnsi.net
URL: http://www.scottsvilleva.com
Contact: Brian LaFontaine, Pres.

65946 ■ Smith Mountain Lake Chamber of Commerce/Partnership
16430 Booker T. Washington Hwy., No. 2
Bridgewater Plz.
Moneta, VA 24121
Ph:(540)721-1203
Free: 800-676-8203
Fax: (540)721-7796
Co. E-mail: vgardner@visitsmithmountainlake.com
URL: http://www.visitsmithmountainlake.com
Contact: Vicki Gardner, Exec.Dir.

65947 ■ South Hill Chamber of Commerce
201 S Mecklenburg Ave.
South Hill, VA 23970
Ph:(434)447-4547
Free: 800-524-4347
Fax: (434)447-4461
Co. E-mail: frank@southhillchamber.com
URL: http://www.southhillchamber.com
Contact: Frank Malone, Exec.Dir.

65948 ■ Strasburg Chamber of Commerce
132 W King St.
PO Box 42
Strasburg, VA 22657
Ph:(540)465-3187
Fax: (540)465-2812
Co. E-mail: schamber@shentel.net
URL: http://www.strasburgva.com
Contact: Kate Sowers, Admin.Asst.

65949 ■ Surry County Chamber of Commerce
PO Box 353
Surry, VA 23883
Ph:(757)294-0066
Free: 877-290-0066
URL: http://www.surrychamber.org
Contact: David Coggin, Pres.

65950 ■ Tappahannock-Essex County Chamber of Commerce
PO Box 481
Tappahannock, VA 22560
Ph:(804)443-5241
Fax: (804)443-4157
Co. E-mail: llumpkin@crosslink.net
URL: http://www.essex-virginia.org
Contact: Linda E. Lumpkin, Exec.Sec.

65951 ■ Tazewell Area Chamber of Commerce
Tazewell Mall Box 6
Tazewell, VA 24651-9998
Ph:(276)988-5091
Co. E-mail: info@tazewellchamber.org
URL: http://www.tazewellchamber.org
Contact: Anita J. Short, Exec.Dir.

65952 ■ Vienna-Tysons Regional Chamber of Commerce
513 Maple Ave. W, 2nd Fl.
Vienna, VA 22180-4229
Ph:(703)281-1333
Fax: (703)242-1482
Co. E-mail: info@vtrcc.org
URL: http://www.vtrcc.org

Contact: Diane Poldy, Pres.

65953 ■ Vinton Area Chamber of Commerce
PO Box 83
Vinton, VA 24179
Ph:(540)343-1364
Co. E-mail: vintonchamber1@aol.com
URL: http://www.vintonchamber.com
Contact: Anthony Conner, Pres.

65954 ■ Virginia Association of Chamber of Commerce Executives
9 S Fifth St.
Richmond, VA 23219-3890
Ph:(804)644-1607
Free: 800-477-7682
Fax: (804)783-6112
Co. E-mail: m.crowder@vachamber.com
URL: http://www.vachamber.com
Contact: Maryann Crowder, Exec. Dir.

65955 ■ Virginia Chamber of Commerce
9 S 5th St.
Richmond, VA 23219
Ph:(804)644-1607
Fax: (804)783-6112
Co. E-mail: c.miracle@vachamber.com
URL: http://www.vachamber.com
Contact: Cyndi Miracle, VP, Marketing and Communications

65956 ■ Virginia Peninsula Chamber of Commerce
21 Enterprise Pkwy., Ste. 100
Hampton, VA 23666
Ph:(757)262-2000
Free: 800-556-1822
Fax: (757)262-2009
Co. E-mail: vpcc@vpcc.org
URL: http://www.vpcc.org
Contact: Clyde R. Hoey II, Pres./CEO

65957 ■ Warsaw-Richmond County Chamber of Commerce
PO Box 1141
Warsaw, VA 22572
Ph:(804)313-2252
Co. E-mail: warsaw_rcchamber@hotmail.com
URL: http://www.warsaw-rcchamber.com
Contact: Myles Gaythwaite, Pres.

65958 ■ Washington County Chamber of Commerce
179 E Main St.
Abingdon, VA 24210
Ph:(276)628-8141
Fax: (276)628-3984
URL: http://www.washingtonvachamber.org
Contact: Tim McVey, Pres.

65959 ■ West Point - Tri-Rivers Chamber of Commerce
618 Main St.
PO Box 1035
West Point, VA 23181
Ph:(804)843-4620
Fax: (804)843-4396
Co. E-mail: wptrcc@oasisonline.com
Contact: Gene Jenkins, Pres.

65960 ■ Winchester-Frederick County Chamber of Commerce
2 N Cameron St., Ste. 200
Winchester, VA 22601
Ph:(540)662-4118
Co. E-mail: cocinfo@winchesterva.org
URL: http://www.winchesterva.org
Contact: Charles H. Weiss, Pres./CEO

65961 ■ Wise County Chamber of Commerce
PO Box 226
Norton, VA 24273
Ph:(276)679-0961
Fax: (276)679-2655
Co. E-mail: wisecountycoc@verizon.net
URL: http://www.wisecountychamber.org
Contact: Joyce M. Payne, Exec.VP/CEO

65962 ■ Woodstock Chamber of Commerce
N Main St.
PO Box 605
Woodstock, VA 22664
Ph:(540)459-2542
Fax: (540)459-3085
Co. E-mail: commerce@shentel.net
URL: http://www.woodstockva.com
Contact: Alma F. Hottle, Exec. Sec.

65963 ■ Wytheville-Wythe-Bland Chamber of Commerce
PO Box 563
Wytheville, VA 24382
Ph:(276)223-3365
Fax: (276)223-3315
Co. E-mail: chamber@wytheville.org
URL: http://chamber.wytheville.com
Contact: Jennifer W. Jones, Exec.Dir.

MINORITY BUSINESS ASSISTANCE PROGRAMS

65964 ■ Virginia Department of Minority Business Enterprise
200-202 N 9th St., 11th Fl.
Richmond, VA 23219
Ph:(804)786-6585
Fax: (804)371-7359
Co. E-mail: dmbe@dmbe.state.va.us
URL: http://www.dmbe.state.va.us/
Contact: Stacey Burrs, Dir
Description: Assists minority firms in identifying and targeting state agencies, as well as other public and private sector entities; sponsors seminars and workshops; provides a support program and one-on-one consultations.

FINANCING AND LOAN PROGRAMS

65965 ■ Albemarle Capital Management
308 E. Market St.
Charlottesville, VA 22902
Ph:(804)293-6660
Fax: (804)293-6640
URL: http://www.albemarlecapitalmgmt.com
Contact: Harold Taylor, Managing Partner
Preferred Investment Size: $25,000 to $100,000. Investment Policies: Seed and early stage. Industry Preferences: Medical and health. Geographic Preferences: Virginia.

65966 ■ AOL Time Warner Ventures
22000 AOL Way
Dulles, VA 20166
Ph:(703)265-1000
Fax: (703)265-3925
URL: http://www.aolwventures.com
Contact: Lennert Leader, President
Preferred Investment Size: $2,000,000 to $10,000,000. Investment Policies: Early stage. Industry Preferences: Women/Minority-owned business. Geographic Preferences: U.S.

65967 ■ Calvert Social Venture Partners, L.P.
402 Maple Ave., W.
Vienna, VA 22180
Ph:(703)255-4930
Fax: (703)255-4931
URL: http://www.calvertventures.com
Contact: John May, Managing Director
Preferred Investment Size: $250,000 to $1,000,000. Investment Types: Start-up, first and second stage. Industry Preferences: Environment. Geographic Preferences: U.S.

65968 ■ Continental S.B.I.C.
4141 N. Henderson Rd., Ste. 8
Arlington, VA 22203
Ph:(703)527-5200
Fax: (703)527-3700

Contact: Arthur Williams, President
Preferred Investment Size: $250,000 to $5,100,000. Investment Types: Acquisition, distressed debt, expansion, fund of funds, generalist PE, joint ventures, later stage, leveraged buyout, management buyouts, mezzanine, private placement, and special situation. Industry Preferences: Communications and media, semiconductors and other electronics, biotechnology, medical and health, consumer related, industrial and energy, financial services, utilities, and other. Geographic Preferences: Mid Atlantic, Midwest, Northeast, Southeast, and Southwest U.S.; Ontario and Quebec, Canada.

65969 ■ The Dinner Club, LLC
402 Maple Ave. W.
Vienna, VA 22180
Ph:(703)255-4930
Fax: (703)255-4931
URL: http://www.thedinnerclub.com
Preferred Investment Size: $250,000 to $1,000,000. Investment Types: Early, first and second stage. Industry Preferences: Communications and media, computer software, Internet specific, semiconductors and other electronics, biotechnology, medical and health, consumer related, and financial services. Geographic Preferences: Mid Atlantic.

65970 ■ Dome Capital, LLC
5440 Cherokee Ave.
Alexandria, VA 22312
Ph:(703)642-2933
Fax: (703)642-3139
URL: http://www.domecapital.com
Contact: Bruce Waldack, Managing Director
Preferred Investment Size: $500,000 to $6,000,000. Investment Policies: Seed and early stage. Industry Preferences: Communications and media, computer software, and Internet specific. Geographic Preferences: U.S.

65971 ■ ECentury Capital Partners, L.P.
8180 Greensboro Dr., Ste. 1150
McLean, VA 22102
Ph:(703)442-4480
Fax: (703)448-1816
URL: http://www.ecenturycapital.com
Contact: Hank Tuten, Managing Director
Preferred Investment Size: $126,000 to $4,000,000. Investment Policies: Seed, early, first, and second stage, and expansion. Industry Preferences: Communications, computer software, semiconductors and other electronics, and industrial and energy. Geographic Preferences: East Coast.

65972 ■ Fairfax Partners
8000 Towers Crescent Dr., Ste. 940
Vienna, VA 22182
Ph:(703)847-9486
Fax: (703)847-0911
Contact: Robert Carlin, Managing Director
Preferred Investment Size: $1,000,000 to $5,000,000. Investment Types: Early stage. Industry Preferences: Communications, Internet specific, medical and health, and business service. Geographic Preferences: Mid Atlantic.

65973 ■ Global Internet Ventures / GIV Venture Partners
8150 Leesburg Pike, Ste. 1210
Vienna, VA 22182
Ph:(703)442-3300
Fax: (703)442-3388
URL: http://www.givinc.com
Contact: Jim McGregor, Managing Director
Preferred Investment Size: $2,000,000 to $4,000,000. Investment Types: Early stage. Industry Preferences: Communications, computer software, Internet specific, medical and health. Geographic Preferences: Mid Atlantic.

65974 ■ Harbert Venture Partners
1210 E. Cary St., Ste. 400
Richmond, VA 23219
Ph:(804)782-3800
Fax: (804)782-3810
URL: http://www.harbert.net

Contact: Thomas Roberts, Principal
Preferred Investment Size: $500,000 to $2,500,000. Investment Policies: Start-up, seed, and early stage. Industry Preferences: Communications, computer related, biotechnology, medical and health, and industrial and energy. Geographic Preferences: Mid Atlantic and Southeast.

65975 ■ HFS Capital, LLC
7918 Jones Branch Dr., Ste. 600
McLean, VA 22102
Ph:(703)817-1160
Fax: (703)817-1794
URL: http://www.hfscpa.com
Contact: Larry Hoffman, Managing Director
Preferred Investment Size: $100,000 to $5,000,000. Investment Types: Start-up, early stage, expansion, joint ventures, leveraged buyout, management buyouts, and recapitalizations. Industry Preferences: Medical and health, consumer related, and business service. Geographic Preferences: Mid Atlantic.

65976 ■ Neuroventures Capital
Zero Court Sq.
Charlottesville, VA 22902
Ph:(434)297-1000
Fax: (434)297-1001
URL: http://www.neuroventures.com
Contact: Mark Cochran, Partner
Preferred Investment Size: $250,000 to $2,000,000. Investment Policies: Start-up, early and first stage, and expansion. Industry Preferences: Biotechnology, and medical and health. Geographic Preferences: U.S.

65977 ■ New Horizons Venture Capital
1000 Wilson Blvd., Ste. 2700
Arlington, VA 22209
Ph:(703)807-1900
Fax: (703)807-1950
URL: http://www.newhorizonsvc.com
Preferred Investment Size: $500,000 to $5,000,000. Investment Policies: Early, first and second stage. Industry Preferences: Internet specific, and computer software and services. Geographic Preferences: Mid Atlantic.

65978 ■ Oxford Financial Services Corp.
Alexandria, VA 22314
Ph:(703)519-4900
Fax: (703)519-4910
Co. E-mail: oxford133@aol.com
URL: http://133 N. Fairfax St.
Contact: J. Alden Philbrick
Preferred Investment Size: $1,000,000. Investment Types: Seed, research and development, start-up, first stage, second stage, and mezzanine. Industry Preferences: Diversified technology. Geographic Preferences: National.

65979 ■ Renaissance Ventures
33 S. 13th St., 3rd Fl.
PO Box 2157
Richmond, VA 23219
Ph:(804)643-5500
Fax: (804)643-5322
URL: http://www.renventures.com
Contact: Herbert Jackson, General Partner
Investment Policies: Early stage. Industry Preferences: Biotechnology. Geographic Preferences: National.

65980 ■ Spacevest
11911 Freedom Dr., Ste. 500
Reston, VA 20190
Ph:(703)904-9800
Fax: (703)904-0571
URL: http://www.spacevest.com
Contact: Roger Widing, Managing Director
Preferred Investment Size: $1,000,000 to $8,000,000. Investment Types: Second stage and expansion. Industry Preferences: Communications and media, computer software and services, Internet specific, semiconductors and other electronics, industrial and energy, and other products. Geographic Preferences: U.S.

65981 ■ Taylor Corporation
209 Madison St., Ste. 300
Alexandria, VA 22314
Ph:(703)739-1000
Fax: (703)997-2392
URL: http://www.taylorventure.com
Contact: Ken Snyder, President
Investment Policies: Start-up, early stage, and balanced. **Industry Preferences:** Business service, and manufacturing. **Geographic Preferences:** U.S. and Canada.

65982 ■ Virginia Capital
1801 Libbie Ave., Ste. 201
Richmond, VA 23226
Ph:(804)648-4802
Fax: (804)648-4809
URL: http://www.vacapital.com
Contact: Justin Marriott, Principal
Preferred Investment Size: $1,000,000 to $5,000,000. **Investment Types:** Acquisition, control-block purchases, expansion, later stage, leveraged buyout, special situation, private placement, recapitalizations, balanced, expansion, management buyouts. **Industry Preferences:** Communications and media, medical and health, consumer related, and transportation, financial services, and business service. **Geographic Preferences:** Mid Atlantic.

65983 ■ Walnut Capital Corp. (Vienna)
8000 Towers Crescent Dr., Ste. 1070
Vienna, VA 22182
Ph:(703)448-3771
Fax: (703)448-7751
Contact: Joel Kanter, General Partner
Preferred Investment Size: $300,000 to $500,000. **Investment Types:** Start-up, first and second stage, mezzanine, and leveraged buyout. **Industry Preferences:** Consumer related, biotechnology, medical and health, computer software, hardware and services, Internet specific, semiconductors and other electronics.

PROCUREMENT ASSISTANCE PROGRAMS

65984 ■ Virginia Department of General Services–Division of Purchases and Supply–Procurement Assistance (1111)
1111 E Broad St., 6th Fl.
PO Box 1199
Richmond, VA 23218-1199
Ph:(804)786-3842
Fax: (804)225-3707
URL: http://www.dgs.state.va.us/dps
Contact: Eugene Anderson

65985 ■ Virginia Procurement Center–Defense Supply Center-Richmond
8000 Jefferson Davis Hwy.
Richmond, VA 23297-5124
Ph:(804)279-5242
Fax: (804)279-6615
URL: http://www.dla.mil
Contact: Mrs. Mcneill, Small Business Sp.
Description: Covers activities for Defense Supply Center Richmond (Richmond, VA), Army Training & Doctrine Command, Army Corps of Engineers (Norfolk, VA), Navy FISC (Norfolk, VA), NAVFAC (Norfolk, VA), NASA, Langley Research Center (Hampton, VA).

65986 ■ Virginia Procurement Technical Assistance Center–Crater Planning District Commission
PO Box 1808
Petersburg, VA 23805
Ph:(804)861-1667
Fax: (804)732-8972
Co. E-mail: jfedkenheuer@cpd.state.va.us
URL: http://www.craterpdc.state.va.us
Contact: John Fedkenheuer

65987 ■ Virginia Procurement Technical Assistance Program–George Mason University
4031 University Dr., Ste. 200
Fairfax, VA 22030-3409
Ph:(703)277-7750
Fax: (703)352-8195
Co. E-mail: ptap@gmu.edu
URL: http://www.gmu.edu/gmu/PTAP
Contact: James Regan

INCUBATORS/RESEARCH AND TECHNOLOGY PARKS

65988 ■ The New Century Venture Center
1354 Eighth St.
Roanoke, VA 24015-1812
Ph:(540)344-6402
Fax: (540)345-0262
Co. E-mail: lison@ncvc.com
URL: http://www.ncvc.com
Description: The Center is a small business incubator that serves emerging firms through shared resources and a variety of financial services.

65989 ■ New River Valley Development Corporation
6580 Valley Center Dr.
Radford, VA 24141
Ph:(540)633-6730
Fax: (540)633-6768
Co. E-mail: wayne@nrvdc.org
URL: http://www.nrvdc.org/nrvcc.html
Contact: Wayne Carpenter, Mgr
Description: This incubator serves as a seeding location for emerging businesses hoping to expand operations. These include entrepreneurs and manufacturing/industrial companies.

65990 ■ University of Virginia–Office of Sponsored Programs
PO Box 400195
Charlottesville, VA 22904-4195
Ph:(434)924-4270
Fax: (434)982-3096
Co. E-mail: mgg5E@virginia.edu
URL: http://www.virginia.edu/sponooredprograms/
Contact: Michael G. Glasgow Jr., Asst.VP
E-mail: mgg5E@virginia.edu
Scope: Responsible for administration and accounting control of grants and contracts with U.S. government, foundations, and industry for research performed at the University.

65991 ■ University of Virginia–Office of Vice President for Research and Graduate Studies
Madison Hall 314
PO Box 400301
Charlottesville, VA 22904
Ph:(434)924-3606
Fax: (434)924-3667
Co. E-mail: rg@virginia.edu
URL: http://www.virginia.edu/vprgs/
Contact: R. Ariel Gomez MD, VP, Res. & Grad. Stud.
E-mail: rg@virginia.edu
Scope: Responsible for University policy and program development for research and administration of institutional research funds and the University's patents program, including activities of the Environmental Health and Safety Department. Supports Office of Sponsored Programs in negotiation and administration of grants and contracts for research and other sponsored programs. Administers university-industry relations and contracts. **Publications:** Research Highlights; Research News (monthly).

65992 ■ University of Virginia–Shannon Center for Advanced Studies
PO Box 400308
Charlottesville, VA 22904-4308
Ph:(434)924-3728
Fax: (434)982-2920
Co. E-mail: gdb@virginia.edu
Contact: Dr. Gene D. Block, VP/Provost

E-mail: gdb@virginia.edu
Scope: Assists research activities at the University by providing funds to support members, research associates, and fellows. Works to establish a faculty of excellence at the University. Coordinates function of research centers and institutes at the University and manages visiting committees.

65993 ■ Virginia Biotechnology Research Park
800 E Leigh St.
Richmond, VA 23219
Ph:(804)828-5390
Free: 888-822-4675
Fax: (804)828-8566
Co. E-mail: vbrp@vabiotech.com
URL: http://www.vabiotech.com
Contact: Robert Skunda, Pres & Ceo
Description: This incubator offers tenants a variety of services including a biotechnology library, talent bank, fiber optic telecommunications, conference and office space, and more.

65994 ■ Virginia Polytechnic Institute and State University–Virginia Tech Corporate Research Center
1872 Pratt Dr., Ste. 1000
Blacksburg, VA 24060
Ph:(540)961-3600
Fax: (540)961-2304
Co. E-mail: joe.meredith@vtcrc.com
URL: http://www.vtcrc.com
Contact: Joe W. Meredith PhD, Pres.
E-mail: joe.meredith@vtcrc.com
Scope: 120-acre research park. the main campus and university airport providing building sites and buildings for lease to companies interested in developing or expanding a research relationship with the University. Houses an innovation center and other buildings to provide facilities for emerging companies.

65995 ■ VMI Research Laboratories
Virginia Military Institute
Lexington, VA 24450-0304
Ph:(540)464-7434
Fax: (540)464-7761
Co. E-mail: rowera@vmi.edu
Contact: Dr. Richard A. Rowe, Dir.
E-mail: rowera@vmi.edu
Scope: Administers and coordinates extramurally supported faculty research at the Institute in sciences, engineering, and humanities, including chemistry; English; physics; history; civil, mechanical, and electrical engineering; modern languages; economics; mathematics; biology; and computer and information science. Sample projects have studied water quality and distribution, stream navigability, engineering management, optical properties of glasses, lunar basalts, nuclear waste immobilization, applications of microcomputers, expert systems and robotics, room temperature liquid phosphorescence, physiological mechanisms (hunger and stress), physics of X-rays and ultrasonic interferometry, and fuel alcohol synthesis. **Publications:** Annual report. **Educational Activities:** Commonwealth and Virginia Information Technology Symposium; Virginia Transportation Conference. **Awards:** Maury and Hinman research awards, to VMI faculty and students; Research performance awards, to VMI faculty and students.

EDUCATIONAL PROGRAMS

65996 ■ Bryant and Stratton College–Virginia Beach Campus
301 Center Pointe Dr.
Virginia Beach, VA 23462
Ph:(757)499-7900
Fax: (757)499-9977
URL: http://www.bryantstratton.edu
Description: Business college offering a course in small business management.

65997 ■ John Tyler Community College
13101 Jefferson Davis Hwy.
Chester, VA 23831-5316

Ph:(804)796-4000
Fax: (804)796-4362
URL: http://www.jt.cc.va.us
Description: Two-year college offering a small business management program.

65998 ■ Mountain Empire Community College
3441 Mountain Empire Rd.
Big Stone Gap, VA 24219
Ph:(276)523-2400
Fax: (276)523-8297
URL: http://www.me.cc.va.us
Description: Two-year college offering programs in business management.

65999 ■ Northern Virginia Community College
8333 Little River Tpke.
Annandale, VA 22003
Ph:(703)323-3000
Fax: (703)323-3767
URL: http://www.nvcc.edu/
Description: Two-year college offering a small business management course.

LEGISLATIVE ASSISTANCE

66000 ■ Virginia Senate Committee on Commerce and Labor
Senate Committee Operations
PO Box 396
Richmond, VA 23218
Ph:(804)698-7450
Fax: (804)698-7672
Co. E-mail: jlance@sov.state.virginia.us
URL: http://www.senate.state.va.us
Description: Handles small business legislation.

PUBLICATIONS

66001 ■ *Smart Start your Virginia Business*
PSI Research
300 N. Valley Dr.
Grants Pass, OR 97526
Ph:(503)479-9464
Free: 800-228-2275
Fax: (503)476-1479
Co. E-mail: info@psi-research.com
URL: http://www.psi-research.com
Ed: Michael D. Jenkins. **Released:** Revised edition, 1992. **Price:** $29.95 (looseleaf binder); $24.95 (paper). **Description:** Part of the Successful Business Library series.

66002 ■ *Virginia Business*
411 E. Franklin St., Ste. 105
Richmond, VA 23219

Ph:(804)649-6999
Fax: (804)649-6311
Co. E-mail: lugincius@va-business.com
URL: http://www.virginiabusiness.com

PUBLISHERS

66003 ■ Capital Books Inc.
22841 Quicksilver Dr.
Sterling, VA 20166
Ph:(703)661-1571
Free: 800-758-3756
Fax: (703)661-1547
Co. E-mail: newcaplital@aol.com
URL: http://www.capital-books.com/Books/
    EventReview.aspx
Contact: Azad Ajamian, President
Description: Publishes historical fiction, cookbooks, how-to, travel, home and garden, business, and lifestyles. **Founded:** 1998.

66004 ■ The GOALS Institute
1893 Preston White Dr.
PO Box 3736
Reston, VA 20191
Ph:(703)264-2000
Fax: (703)264-2408
Co. E-mail: info@goalsinstitute.com
URL: http://www.goalsinstitute.com
Contact: Jennifer Kuchta, Vice President
Description: Publishes self-help, business and personal development books. Does not accept unsolicited manuscripts. Reaches market through direct mail, telephone and trade sales. **Founded:** 1993.

66005 ■ GTM Co.
6729 Glenmont St.
Falls Church, VA 22042
Ph:(703)241-4915
Fax: (703)241-9586
Contact: William F. Penoyar, President
Description: Publishes a book on how to do business with the U.S. government. **Founded:** 1984.

66006 ■ Information International
10814 Fawn Dr.
PO Box 579
Great Falls, VA 22066
Ph:(703)450-7049
Fax: (925)226-4865
Co. E-mail: robert@isquare.com
URL: http://www.isquare.com
Contact: Robert A. Sullivan, Owner
E-mail: robert@isquare.com
Description: Publishes business publications and software, especially start-up and entrepreneurial related. Does not accept unsolicited manuscripts. Reaches market through direct mail, and the internet. **Founded:** 1986.

66007 ■ Ivy Software Inc.
1146 Richmond-Tappahannock Hwy.
Manquin, VA 23106
Ph:(804)769-7193
Free: 800-342-5489
Fax: (804)769-7019
Co. E-mail: ivyinfo@ivysoftware.com
URL: http://www.ivysoftware.com
Contact: Robert N. Holt, President
Description: Publishes on business management, accounting and finance. Offers seminars, microcomputer training and stand-up instruction. Reaches market through telephone sales, trade sales and in-office contact. Does not accept unsolicited manuscripts. **Founded:** 1986.

66008 ■ Management Concepts Inc.
8230 Leesburg Pke., Ste. 800
Vienna, VA 22182-2641
Ph:(703)790-9595
Free: 800-506-4450
Fax: (703)790-1371
Co. E-mail: info@managementconcepts.com
URL: http://www.managementconcepts.com
Contact: Catherine A. Kreyche, Man. Ed.
E-mail: ckreyche@managementconcepts.com
Description: Publishes books on federal government contracting, including marketing and proposal development and small business resources. Also publishes newsletters. Accepts unsolicited manuscripts. Reaches market through direct mail and the National Contract Management Association. **Founded:** 1973.

66009 ■ Stylus Publishing L.L.C.
22883 Quicksilver Dr.
PO Box 605
Sterling, VA 20166-2012
Ph:(703)661-1504
Free: 800-232-0223
Fax: (703)661-1547
Co. E-mail: stylusinfo@styluspub.com
URL: http://www.styluspub.com
Contact: John Von Knorring, President
E-mail: hjvk@aol.com
Description: Publishes books on higher education, corporate training, business and management and third world development. **Founded:** 1996.

66010 ■ Visibooks
47 E 5th St.
Frederick, MD 21701
Ph:(301)560-4611
Free: 877-597-5672
Fax: (208)279-5336
Co. E-mail: info@visibooks.com
URL: http://www.visibooks.com
Contact: Chris Charuhas, President
E-mail: chris@visibooks.com
Description: Publishes computer how-to books for visual learners. Does not accept unsolicited manuscripts. **Founded:** 2001.

SMALL BUSINESS DEVELOPMENT CENTER LEAD OFFICE

66011 ■ Washington SBDC–Washington State University
534 E. Trent Ave.
PO Box 1495
Spokane, WA 99210-1495
Ph:(509)358-7765
Fax: (509)358-7764
URL: http://www.wsbdc.org
Contact: Brett Rogers, State Dir.
E-mail: barogers@wsu.edu

66012 ■ Washington State University–Small Business Development Center
College of Business & Economics
501 Johnson Tower
Pullman, WA 99164-4851
Ph:(509)335-1576
Fax: (509)335-0949
URL: http://www.sbdc.wsu.edu
Contact: Carol Riesenberg, Acting State Director

SMALL BUSINESS DEVELOPMENT CENTERS

66013 ■ Bellevue Community College–Small Business Development Center
3000 Landerholm Circle, SE
Bellevue, WA 98007-6484
Ph:(425)643-2888
Fax: (425)649-3113
Contact: Bill Huenefeld, Business Development Specialist
E-mail: bhuenefe@bcc.ctc.edu

66014 ■ Bellingham Western Washington University–Small Business Development Center
College of Business and Economics
308 Parks Hall
Bellingham, WA 98225-9073
Ph:(360)650-3899
Fax: (360)650-4844
Contact: Tom Dorr, Business Development Specialist
E-mail: tom.dorr@wwu.edu

66015 ■ Big Bend Community College–Small Business Development Center
7662 Chanute St. NE
Moses Lake, WA 98837
Ph:(509)793-2222
Free: 877-745-1212
Contact: Dr. Bill Bonaudi, Pres.
E-mail: billb@bigbend.edu

66016 ■ Centralia Community College–Small Business Development Center
600 W. Locust St.
Centralia, WA 98036
Ph:(360)736-9391
Fax: (360)753-3404
Contact: Ann Tuning, Business Development Specialist

66017 ■ Columbia River Economic Development Council–Small Business Development Center
100 E. Columbia Way
Vancouver, WA 98660-3156
Ph:(360)693-2555
Fax: (360)694-9927
Contact: Janet Harte, Business Dev. Specialist
E-mail: harte@vancouver.wsu.edu

66018 ■ Edmonds Community College–Small Business Development Center
20000 68th Ave. W.
Lynnwood, WA 98036
Ph:(425)640-1435
Fax: (425)640-1371
Co. E-mail: info@edcc.edu
URL: http://www.edcc.edu/
Contact: Jennifer Shelton, Business Development Specialist
E-mail: jennifer.shelton@edcc.edu

66019 ■ Mt. Vernon Skagit Valley College–Small Business Development Center
2405 College Way
Mount Vernon, WA 98273
Ph:(360)428-1282
Fax: (360)336-6116
Contact: Peter Stroosma, Business Development Specialist

66020 ■ Quest Small Business Development Center
327 E. Penny Rd.
Industrial Bldg. 2, Ste. D.
Wenatchee, WA 98801-2443
Ph:(509)662-8016
Fax: (509)663-0455
Contact: Rich Reim, Business Dev. Specialist

66021 ■ South Puget Sound Community College–Small Business Development Center
721 Columbia St. SW
Olympia, WA 98501
Ph:(360)753-5616
Fax: (360)586-5493
Contact: Douglas Hammel, Business Dev. Specialist
E-mail: douglashammel@olywa.net

66022 ■ South Seattle Community College–Duwamish Industrial Education Center–Small Business Development Center (6000)
6000 16th Ave. SW
Seattle, WA 98106
Ph:(206)764-5300
Fax: (206)764-7945

Co. E-mail: ssccsbdc@hotmail.com
URL: http://www.southseattle.edu
Contact: Corey Hansen, Business Development Specialist

66023 ■ Tacoma Business Assistance Center–Small Business Development Center
KeyBank Bldg.
101 Pacific Ave.
Corner of 11th & Pacific
Tacoma, WA 98410
Ph:(253)274-1288
Contact: Neil Delisanti, Business Dev. Specialist

66024 ■ Tri-Cities Industrial Development Council (TRIDEC)–Small Business Development Center
901 N. Colorado St.
Kennewick, WA 99336
Ph:(509)735-1000
Fax: (509)735-6609
Co. E-mail: tridec@tridec.org
URL: http://www.tridec.org/
Contact: Deanna Smith, Dir.
E-mail: dsmith@tridec.org

66025 ■ U.S. Export Assistance–North Seattle Community College–Small Business Development Center (2001)
2001 6th Ave., Ste. 650
Seattle, WA 98121
Ph:(206)553-0052
Fax: (206)553-7253
Contact: Ann Tamura, IT Specialist

66026 ■ Walla Walla Community College–SBDC
500 Tausick Way
Walla Walla, WA 99362
Ph:(509)522-2500
Free: 877-992-9922
Fax: (509)525-3101

66027 ■ Washington Small Business Development Center at Seattle
3600 15th Ave. W., Ste. 303
Seattle, WA 98119
Ph:(206)464-5450
Contact: Warner Wong, Business Dev. Specialist
E-mail: wwong@wolfenet.com

66028 ■ Washington State University at Pullman–Small Business Development Center
501 Johnson Tower
PO Box 644851
Pullman, WA 99164-4851
Ph:(509)335-1576
Fax: (509)335-0949
Contact: Carol Clark, State Dir.
E-mail: clrk@wsu.edu

66029 ■ Washington State University at Spokane–Small Business Development Center
SIRTI Bldg.
665 North Riverpoint Blvd.

PO Box 1495
Spokane, WA 99210-1495
Ph:(509)358-7890
Fax: (509)358-7896
Contact: Terry Chambers, Business Development
Specialist
E-mail: tchambers@iel.spokane.edu

**66030 ■ Yakima Valley Community
College–Small Business Development Center**
PO Box 1647
Yakima, WA 98907
Ph:(509)454-3608
Fax: (509)454-4155
URL: http://www.uwec.edu/Academic/COB/
programs/traindev/frametraindevhome.htm

SMALL BUSINESS ASSISTANCE PROGRAMS

66031 ■ Washington Department of Revenue
1025 Union Ave. SE, Ste. 500
PO Box 47454
Olympia, WA 98501
Ph:(360)753-5574
Free: 800-647-7706
Fax: (360)586-5543
Co. E-mail: communication@dor.wa.gov
URL: http://www.dor.wa.gov
Description: Provides information about Washington
taxes for prospective businesses.

**66032 ■ Washington Department of Trade
and Economic Development–International
Trade Division**
2001 6th Ave., Ste. 2600
Seattle, WA 98121
Ph:(206)256-6100
Fax: (206)956-3151
Co. E-mail: trade@cted.wa.gov
URL: http://www.cted.wa.gov
Contact: Larry Williams, Dir

**66033 ■ Washington State Department of
Community, Trade, and Economic
Development–Business Development
Division**
2001 6th Ave., Ste. 2600
Seattle, WA 98121
Ph:(206)256-6100
Fax: (206)956-6158
URL: http://www.cted.wa.gov
Description: Intercedes with government agencies
on behalf of businesses experiencing licensing, taxa-
tion, and regulation difficulties.

**66034 ■ Washington State Department of
Community, Trade, and Economic
Development–Product Export Development
Division**
2001 6th Ave., Ste. 2600
Seattle, WA 98121
Ph:(206)464-7143
Fax: (206)956-6158
URL: http://www.cted.wa.gov

BETTER BUSINESS BUREAUS

66035 ■ Better Business Bureau
PO Box 1000
DuPont, WA 98327
Ph:(206)431-2222
Fax: (206)431-2200
Co. E-mail: info@thebbb.org
URL: http://www.thebbb.org
Contact: Robert W.G. Andrew, Pres./CEO

**66036 ■ Better Business Bureau of the
Inland Northwest**
508 W 6th Ave., Ste. 401
Spokane, WA 99204-2356

Ph:(509)455-4200
Free: 800-356-1007
Fax: (509)838-1079
Co. E-mail: info@thelocalbbb.com
URL: http://www.spokane.bbb.org
Contact: Jan Quintrall, Pres.

**66037 ■ Better Business Bureau, Oregon/
Western Washington**
1000 Station Dr., Ste. 222
DuPont, WA 98327
Ph:(206)431-2222
Fax: (206)431-2211
Co. E-mail: info@thebbb.org
URL: http://thebbb.org
Contact: Bob Andrew, Pres.

**66038 ■ Better Business Bureau Serving
Eastern Washington, North Idaho and
Montana**
152 S Jefferson, Ste. 200
Spokane, WA 99201-4532
Ph:(509)455-4200
Free: 800-356-1007
Fax: (509)838-1079
Co. E-mail: info@thelocalbbb.com
URL: http://www.thelocalbbb.com
Contact: Jan Quintrall, Pres.

66039 ■ Tri-City Better Business Bureau
101 N. Union, No. 105
Kennewick, WA 99336-3819
Ph:(509)783-0892
Fax: (509)783-2893

CHAMBERS OF COMMERCE

66040 ■ Anacortes Chamber of Commerce
819 Commercial Ave.
Anacortes, WA 98221
Ph:(360)293-3832
Fax: (360)293-1595
Co. E-mail: info@anacortes.org
URL: http://www.anacortes.org
Contact: Bill Berry, Exec.Dir.

66041 ■ Asotin Chamber of Commerce
PO Box 574
Asotin, WA 99402
Ph:(509)243-4242
Fax: (509)243-4123
URL: http://www.rootsweb.com/~wasgs/asotin.htm

66042 ■ Auburn Area Chamber of Commerce
108 S Division St., Ste. B
Auburn, WA 98001-5305
Ph:(253)833-0700
Fax: (253)735-4091
Co. E-mail: auburncc@auburnareawa.org
URL: http://www.auburnareawa.org
Contact: Jamelle Garcia, Chm.

**66043 ■ Bainbridge Island Chamber of
Commerce**
590 Winslow Way E
Bainbridge Island, WA 98110
Ph:(206)842-3700
Fax: (206)842-3713
Co. E-mail: info@bainbridgechamber.com
URL: http://www.bainbridgechamber.com
Contact: Kevin Dwyer, Exec.Dir.

66044 ■ Ballard Chamber of Commerce
2208 NW Market St., Ste. 100
Seattle, WA 98107
Ph:(206)784-9705
Fax: (206)783-8154
Co. E-mail: info@ballardchamber.com
URL: http://www.ballardchamber.com
Contact: Beth Williamson Miller, Exec.Dir.

**66045 ■ Battle Ground Chamber of
Commerce**
2903 W Main St.
Battle Ground, WA 98604

Ph:(360)687-1510
Fax: (360)687-4505
Co. E-mail: ttweedell@battlegroundchamber.org
URL: http://www.battlegroundchamber.org
Contact: Terri Tweedell, Pres.

66046 ■ Beacon Hill Chamber of Commerce
2821 Beacon Ave. S
Seattle, WA 98144
Ph:(206)264-1996
Co. E-mail: info@beaconhillchamber.com
URL: http://beaconhillchamber.com/index.php
Contact: Jackie Lum, Pres.

66047 ■ Bellevue Chamber of Commerce
10500 NE 8th St., Ste. 212
Bellevue, WA 98004
Ph:(425)454-2464
Fax: (425)462-4660
Co. E-mail: staffteam@bellevuechamber.org
URL: http://www.bellevuechamber.org
Contact: Betty Nokes, Pres./CEO

**66048 ■ Bellingham/Whatcom Chamber of
Commerce and Industry**
PO Box 958
Bellingham, WA 98227-0958
Ph:(360)734-1330
Fax: (360)734-1332
Co. E-mail: chamber@bellingham.com
URL: http://www.bellingham.com
Contact: Ken Oplinger, Pres./CEO

66049 ■ Benton City Chamber of Commerce
PO Box 401
Benton City, WA 99320
Ph:(509)588-5848
Fax: (509)588-3216
Co. E-mail: bcbulletin@earthlink.net
Contact: Bea Baker, Pres.

66050 ■ Birch Bay Chamber of Commerce
4550 Birch Bay Lynden Rd.
Birch Bay, WA 98230
Ph:(360)371-5004
Co. E-mail: info@birchbaychamber.com
URL: http://www.birchbaychamber.com
Contact: Genee Haws Kay, Pres.

**66051 ■ Blaine Community Chamber of
Commerce**
728 Peace Portal Dr.
Blaine, WA 98230
Ph:(360)332-6484
Fax: (360)332-4544
Co. E-mail: info@blainechamber.com
URL: http://www.blainechamber.com
Contact: Ms. Carroll Solomon, Sec.

66052 ■ Bonney Lake Chamber of Commerce
PO Box 7171
Bonney Lake, WA 98390
Ph:(253)840-9683
Fax: (253)891-9412
Co. E-mail: blchamber@bonneylake.com
URL: http://www.bonneylake.com
Contact: Katrina Minton, Pres.

**66053 ■ Bremerton Area Chamber of
Commerce**
301 Pacific Ave.
PO Box 229
Bremerton, WA 98337-0229
Ph:(360)479-3579
Fax: (360)479-1033
Co. E-mail: chamber@bremertonchamber.org
URL: http://www.bremertonchamber.org
Contact: Silvia Klatman, Exec.Dir.

66054 ■ Brewster Chamber of Commerce
PO Box 1087
Brewster, WA 98812
Ph:(509)689-0189
Co. E-mail: info@brewsterchamber.org

66055 ■ Bridgeport Area Chamber of Commerce
Box 1060
Bridgeport, WA 98813-1060
Ph:(509)686-9501
Fax: (509)686-4052
Co. E-mail: gschmidt@bridgeport.wednet.edu
URL: http://www.bridgeportwashington.com
Contact: Gene Schmidt, Pres.

66056 ■ Buckley Chamber of Commerce
177 S River Rd.
Buckley, WA 98321
Ph:(360)829-0975
Fax: (360)829-1599
Co. E-mail: pres@buckleychamber.org
URL: http://www.buckleychamber.org/chamber.htm
Contact: Rebecca Esser, Pres.

66057 ■ Burlington Chamber of Commerce
600 E Victoria Ave.
Burlington, WA 98233-1244
Ph:(360)757-0994
Co. E-mail: info@burlington-chamber.com
URL: http://www.burlington-chamber.com
Contact: Dick Irwin, Exec.Dir.

66058 ■ Camas-Washougal Chamber of Commerce
422 NE Fourth Ave.
PO Box 919
Camas, WA 98607-0919
Ph:(360)834-2472
Fax: (360)834-9171
Co. E-mail: brent@cwchamber.com
URL: http://www.cwchamber.com
Contact: Brent Erickson, Exec. Dir.

66059 ■ Cashmere Chamber of Commerce
PO Box 834
Cashmere, WA 98815
Ph:(509)782-7404
Fax: (509)782-1265
Co. E-mail: info@cashmerechamber.com
URL: http://www.cashmerechamber.com
Contact: Bob Wright, Pres.

66060 ■ Central Washington SCORE
300 S Columbia St., 3rd Fl.
Wenatchee, WA 98801
Ph:(509)662-2116
Fax: (509)662-2022
Co. E-mail: inquiries@wenatcheescore.org
URL: http://www.wenatcheescore.org

66061 ■ Central Whidbey Chamber of Commerce
PO Box 152
107 S Main St., Bldg. E
Coupeville, WA 98239
Ph:(360)678-5434
Co. E-mail: cwcc@centralwhidbeychamber.com
URL: http://www.centralwhidbeychamber.com
Contact: Carol Moliter, Pres.

66062 ■ Centralia-Chehalis Chamber of Commerce
500 NW Chamber of Commerce Way
Chehalis, WA 98532
Ph:(360)748-8885
Fax: (360)748-8763
Co. E-mail: thechamber@chamberway.com
URL: http://www.chamberway.com
Contact: Todd Christensen, Pres./CEO

66063 ■ Chamber of Eastern Pierce County
417 E Pioneer
PO Box 1298
Puyallup, WA 98371
Ph:(253)845-6755
Fax: (253)848-6164
Co. E-mail: info@eastpiercechamber.com
URL: http://www.eastpiercechamber.com
Contact: George Chappell, Exec.Dir.

66064 ■ Chewelah Chamber of Commerce
PO Box 94
Chewelah, WA 99109

Ph:(509)935-8991
Co. E-mail: info@chewelah.org
URL: http://www.chewelah.org
Contact: Gloria Davidson, Treas.

66065 ■ Clallam Bay - Sekiu Chamber of Commerce
PO Box 355
Clallam Bay, WA 98326-0355
Ph:(360)963-2339
Free: 877-812-4933
Co. E-mail: chamber@clallambay.com
URL: http://www.clallambay.com
Contact: Mr. Bill Drath, Pres.

66066 ■ Clarkston Chamber of Commerce
502 Bridge St.
Clarkston, WA 99403
Ph:(509)758-7712
Free: 800-933-2128
Fax: (509)751-8767
Co. E-mail: info@clarkstonchamber.org
URL: http://www.clarkstonchamber.org
Contact: Renee Olsen, Exec.Dir.

66067 ■ Cle Elum-Roslyn Chamber of Commerce
401 W 1st St.
PO Box 43
Cle Elum, WA 98922
Ph:(509)674-5958
Fax: (509)674-1674
Co. E-mail: cle_elum@cleelum.com
URL: http://cleelumroslyn.org
Contact: Judy Moen, Office Mgr.

66068 ■ Colfax Chamber of Commerce
117 S Main
Colfax, WA 99111
Ph:(509)397-3712
Fax: (509)397-4458
Co. E-mail: chamber@colfax.com
Contact: Judy Liddle, Sec.

66069 ■ Colville Chamber of Commerce
121 E Astor
Colville, WA 99114-0267
Ph:(509)684-5973
Fax: (509)684-1344
Co. E-mail: colvillecoc@plix.com
URL: http://www.colville.com
Contact: Bill Danekas Jr., Pres.

66070 ■ Concrete Chamber of Commerce
PO Box 743
Concrete, WA 98237
Ph:(360)853-7042
Co. E-mail: ccofc@concrete-wa.com
URL: http://www.concrete-wa.com
Contact: Valerie Stafford, Pres.

66071 ■ Coulee City Chamber of Commerce
PO Box 896
Coulee City, WA 99115-0896
Ph:(509)632-5043
URL: http://www.couleecity.com
Contact: Alan Fox

66072 ■ Cranberry Coast Chamber of Commerce
PO Box 305
Grayland, WA 98547
Ph:(360)267-2003
Free: 800-473-6018
Fax: (360)267-2003
Co. E-mail: info@2thebeach.org
URL: http://www.cranberrycoastcoc.com
Contact: Beverly Ripley, Events Coor.

66073 ■ Davenport Chamber of Commerce
PO Box 869
Davenport, WA 99122
Ph:(509)725-8330
URL: http://www.davenportwa.org
Contact: Karen Wilson

66074 ■ Dayton Chamber of Commerce and Visitor Information Center
166 E Main
PO Box 22
Dayton, WA 99328
Ph:(509)382-4825
Free: 800-882-6299
Co. E-mail: chamber@historicdayton.com
URL: http://www.historicdayton.com
Contact: Jennie Dickinson, Exec.Dir.

66075 ■ Deer Park Chamber of Commerce
316 E Crawford, Lower Level, Ste. A
PO Box 518
Deer Park, WA 99006
Ph:(509)276-5900
Fax: (509)276-5900
Co. E-mail: info@deerparkchamber.com
URL: http://www.deerparkchamber.com
Contact: Cordelia Jeffery, Office Mgr.

66076 ■ East County Coalition of Grays Harbor County
PO Box 53
McCleary, WA 98557-0053
Ph:(360)495-4659
Co. E-mail: infocus@techline.com
URL: http://users.techline.com/infocus/ecc.htm
Contact: Janis Aaron Moore, Systems Analyst/ Consultant

66077 ■ Ellensburg Chamber of Commerce
609 N Main St.
Ellensburg, WA 98926
Ph:(509)925-3138
Free: 888-925-2204
Co. E-mail: info@ellensburg-chamber.com
URL: http://www.ellensburg-chamber.com
Contact: Ron Cridlebaugh, Exec.Dir.

66078 ■ Elma Chamber of Commerce
PO Box 798
Elma, WA 98541
Ph:(360)482-3055
Co. E-mail: elmap@ghpud.org
URL: http://www.elmachamber.org
Contact: Stephanie Aho, Pres.

66079 ■ Enumclaw Area Chamber of Commerce
1421 Cole St.
Enumclaw, WA 98022
Ph:(360)825-7666
Fax: (360)825-8369
Co. E-mail: info@enumclawchamber.com
URL: http://www.enumclawchamber.com
Contact: Cathy Rigg, Exec.Dir.

66080 ■ Ephrata Chamber of Commerce
90 Alder St. NW
PO Box 275
Ephrata, WA 98823-0275
Ph:(509)754-4656
Fax: (509)754-5788
Co. E-mail: echamber@sagensun.com
URL: http://www.ephratawachamber.com
Contact: Rita Tuller, Exec.Dir.

66081 ■ Everett Area Chamber of Commerce
2000 Hewitt Ave., Ste. 205
Everett, WA 98201
Ph:(425)257-3222
Fax: (425)257-2074
Co. E-mail: info@everettchamber.com
URL: http://www.everettchamber.com
Contact: Louise Stanton-Masten, Pres./CEO

66082 ■ Federal Way Chamber of Commerce
PO Box 3440
Federal Way, WA 98063
Ph:(253)838-2605
Fax: (253)661-9050
Co. E-mail: federalway@federalwaychamber.com
URL: http://www.federalwaychamber.com
Contact: Tom Pierson, CEO

66083 ■ Ferndale Chamber of Commerce
PO Box 1264
Ferndale, WA 98248
Ph:(360)384-3042
Free: 888-722-2062
Fax: (360)384-3042
Co. E-mail: ferndalecc@ferndale-chamber.com
URL: http://ferndale-chamber.com
Contact: Brenda Rinesmith, Pres.

66084 ■ Fife Area Chamber of Commerce
5303 Pacific Hwy. E
PMB 272
Fife, WA 98424
Ph:(253)922-9320
Free: 800-305-9926
Fax: (253)922-1638
Co. E-mail: p.k.macdonald@fifechamber.org
URL: http://www.fifechamber.org
Contact: P.K. MacDonald, Exec.Dir.

66085 ■ Forks Chamber of Commerce
PO Box 1249
Forks, WA 98331-0249
Ph:(360)374-2531
Free: 800-443-6757
Fax: (360)374-9253
Co. E-mail: chamber@forkswa.com
URL: http://www.forkswa.com
Contact: Diane Schostak, Exec.Dir.

66086 ■ Garfield Chamber of Business
PO Box 454
Garfield, WA 99130-0454
Ph:(509)635-1604
Contact: Maureen Byrne, Treas.

66087 ■ Gig Harbor Peninsula Area Chamber of Commerce
3311 Harborview Dr., Ste. 201
Gig Harbor, WA 98332
Ph:(253)851-6865
Free: 800-359-8804
Fax: (253)851-6881
Co. E-mail: info@gigharborchamber.com
URL: http://www.gigharborchamber.com
Contact: Kim D.E.D. Hails, Exec.Dir.

66088 ■ Grand Coulee Dam Area Chamber of Commerce
PO Box 760
Grand Coulee, WA 99133-0760
Ph:(509)633-3074
Free: 800-268-5332
Fax: (509)633-2366
Co. E-mail: chamber@grandcouleedam.org
URL: http://www.grandcouleedam.org
Contact: Susan Miller, Mgr.

66089 ■ Grandview Chamber of Commerce
107 Division St.
Grandview, WA 98930
Ph:(509)882-2100
Fax: (509)882-5014
Co. E-mail: grancofc@grandviewchamber.com
URL: http://www.grandviewchamber.com
Contact: Gaylene Tucker, Pres.

66090 ■ Granger Chamber of Commerce
PO Box 250
Granger, WA 98932
Ph:(509)854-7304
Co. E-mail: webmaster@bentonrea.com
URL: http://www.grangerchamber.org
Contact: Bruce Hall

66091 ■ Grays Harbor Chamber of Commerce
506 Duffy St.
Aberdeen, WA 98520-3531
Ph:(360)532-1924
Free: 800-321-1924
Fax: (360)533-7945
Co. E-mail: info@graysharbor.org
URL: http://www.graysharbor.org
Contact: LeRoy Tipton, Pres.

66092 ■ Greater Arlington Area Chamber of Commerce
PO Box 102
Arlington, WA 98223-0102
Ph:(360)435-3708
Fax: (360)435-3708
Co. E-mail: info@arlington-chamber.com
URL: http://www.arlington-chamber.com
Contact: Patti Duncan, Sec.

66093 ■ Greater Connell Area Chamber of Commerce
600 S Columbia
PO Box 401
Connell, WA 99326
Ph:(509)234-8731
Fax: (509)234-8722
Contact: Monica Pruett

66094 ■ Greater Des Moines Chamber of Commerce
22030 7th Ave. S, Ste. 104
Des Moines, WA 98198
Ph:(206)878-7000
Fax: (206)824-8779
Co. E-mail: admin@desmoineswa.org
URL: http://www.desmoineswa.org
Contact: Vickie Bergquist, Pres.

66095 ■ Greater Eatonville Chamber of Commerce
PO Box 845
Eatonville, WA 98328
Ph:(360)832-4000
Co. E-mail: info@eatonvillechamber.com
URL: http://www.eatonvillechamber.com
Contact: Tanya Dow, Sec.

66096 ■ Greater Edmonds Chamber of Commerce
121 5th Ave. N
PO Box 146
Edmonds, WA 98020
Ph:(425)670-1496
Fax: (425)712-1808
Co. E-mail: chamberofcommerce@edmondswa.com
URL: http://www.edmondswa.com
Contact: Chris Guitton, Exec.Dir.

66097 ■ Greater Goldendale Chamber of Commerce
903 E Broadway
Goldendale, WA 98620
Ph:(509)773-3400
Fax: (509)773-3411
Co. E-mail: ggcc@gorge.net
URL: http://www.goldendalechamber.org
Contact: Tom Ireland, Pres.

66098 ■ Greater Issaquah Chamber of Commerce
155 NW Gilman Blvd.
Issaquah, WA 98027
Ph:(425)392-7024
Fax: (425)392-8101
Co. E-mail: info@issaquahchamber.com
URL: http://www.issaquahchamber.com
Contact: Suzanne Suther, Exec.Dir.

66099 ■ Greater Kingston Community Chamber of Commerce
11212 State Hwy. 104
PO Box 78
Kingston, WA 98346
Ph:(360)297-3813
URL: http://kingstonchamber.com
Contact: Sally Christy, Exec. Dir.

66100 ■ Greater Kirkland Chamber of Commerce
401 Parkplace, Ste. 102
Kirkland, WA 98033
Ph:(425)822-7066
Fax: (425)827-4878
Co. E-mail: info@kirklandchamber.org
URL: http://www.kirklandchamber.org
Contact: Bill Vadino, Exec.Dir.

66101 ■ Greater Lake City Chamber of Commerce
12345 30th Ave. NE, Ste. F-G
Seattle, WA 98125-5436
Ph:(206)363-3287
Fax: (206)363-6456
Co. E-mail: chamber@lakecitychamber.org
URL: http://www.lakecitychamber.org
Contact: Jo Ellen McNeal, Exec.Dir.

66102 ■ Greater Lake Stevens Chamber of Commerce
PO Box 439
Lake Stevens, WA 98258-0439
Ph:(425)334-0433
Co. E-mail: info@lschamber.org
URL: http://www.lschamber.org
Contact: Mrs. Donna Foster, Office Mgr.

66103 ■ Greater Maple Valley - Black Diamond Chamber of Commerce
PO Box 302
Maple Valley, WA 98038
Ph:(425)432-0222
Fax: (425)413-8017
Co. E-mail: mvbd@vircom.net
URL: http://www.maplevalley.com
Contact: Roxanne Michelson, Office Mgr.

66104 ■ Greater Marysville - Tulalip Chamber of Commerce
8825 34th Ave. NE, Ste. C
Tulalip, WA 98271
Ph:(360)659-7700
Fax: (360)653-7539
Co. E-mail: caldie@marysvilletulalipchamber.com
URL: http://www.marysvilletulalipchamber.com
Contact: Caldie Rogers, Pres./CEO

66105 ■ Greater Oak Harbor Chamber of Commerce
32630 State Rd. 20
PO Box 883
Oak Harbor, WA 98277
Ph:(360)675-3755
Fax: (360)679-1624
Co. E-mail: info@oakharborchamber.org
URL: http://www.oakharborchamber.org
Contact: Priscilla Heidecker

66106 ■ Greater Othello Chamber of Commerce
PO Box 2813
Othello, WA 99344
Ph:(509)488-2683
Free: (866)OTH-ELLO
Fax: (509)488-3123
Co. E-mail: manager@othellochamber.com
URL: http://www.othellochamber.com
Contact: Grace Shelby, Mgr.

66107 ■ Greater Pasco Area Chamber of Commerce
2705 St. Andrews Loop, Ste. C
Pasco, WA 99301
Ph:(509)547-9755
Fax: (509)547-9756
Co. E-mail: info@pascochamber.org
URL: http://www.pascochamber.org
Contact: Ms. Wendi Hendricks, Exec.Asst.

66108 ■ Greater Poulsbo Chamber of Commerce
PO Box 1063
Poulsbo, WA 98370
Ph:(360)779-4999
Fax: (360)779-3115
Co. E-mail: admin@poulsbochamber.com
URL: http://www.poulsbochamber.com
Contact: Stuart Leidner, Exec.Dir.

66109 ■ Greater Redmond Chamber of Commerce
PO Box 628
Redmond, WA 98073-0628
Ph:(425)885-4014
Fax: (425)882-0996

Co. E-mail: chrish@redmondchamber.org
URL: http://www.redmondchamber.org
Contact: Christine Hoffmann, Pres./CEO

66110 ■ Greater Renton Chamber of Commerce
300 Rainier Ave. N
Renton, WA 98055-1390
Ph:(425)226-4560
Fax: (425)226-4287
Co. E-mail: info@renton-chamber.com
URL: http://www.renton-chamber.com
Contact: Sara Garner, Interim Pres./CEO

66111 ■ Greater Seattle Chamber of Commerce
1301 5th Ave., Ste. 2500
Seattle, WA 98101-2611
Ph:(206)389-7200
Fax: (206)389-7288
Co. E-mail: info@seattlechamber.com
URL: http://www.seattlechamber.com
Contact: Steve Leahy, Pres./CEO

66112 ■ Greater University Chamber of Commerce
4710 University Way NE, Ste. 212
Seattle, WA 98105
Ph:(206)527-4417
Fax: (206)547-5266
Co. E-mail: director@udistrictchamber.org
URL: http://www.udistrictchamber.org
Contact: Teresa Lord Hugel, Exec.Dir.

66113 ■ Greater Vancouver Chamber of Commerce
1101 Broadway, Ste. 120
Vancouver, WA 98660
Ph:(360)694-2588
Fax: (360)693-8279
Co. E-mail: yourchamber@vancouverusa.com
URL: http://www.vancouverusa.com
Contact: John McKibbin, Pres./CEO

66114 ■ Greater Woodinville Chamber of Commerce
17401 133rd Ave. NE, Ste. A-02
Woodinville, WA 98072
Ph:(425)481-8300
Fax: (425)481-9743
Co. E-mail: info@woodinvillechamber.org
URL: http://www.woodinvillechamber.org
Contact: Mr. John C. Erdman, Exec. Dir.

66115 ■ Greater Yakima Chamber of Commerce
PO Box 1490
Yakima, WA 98907-1490
Ph:(509)248-2021
Fax: (509)248-0601
Co. E-mail: chamber@yakima.org
URL: http://www.yakima.org
Contact: Mike Morrisette, Pres./CEO

66116 ■ Hispanic Chamber of Commerce Yakima County
PO Box 11146
8 E Washington Ave.
Yakima, WA 98909
Ph:(509)453-2050
Fax: (509)453-5165
Contact: Ernesto Gonzalez, Pres.

66117 ■ Kalama Chamber of Commerce
PO Box 824
Kalama, WA 98625
Ph:(360)673-6299
Co. E-mail: kalamachamber@kalama.com
URL: http://www.cityofkalama.com/chamber/index.
   htm
Contact: Shanara Schmidt, Pres.

66118 ■ Kelso Longview Chamber of Commerce
1563 Olympia Way
Longview, WA 98632
Ph:(360)423-8400

Fax: (360)423-0432
Co. E-mail: info@kelsolongviewchamber.org
URL: http://www.kelsolongviewchamber.org

66119 ■ Kent Chamber of Commerce
524 W Meeker St., Ste. 1
PO Box 128
Kent, WA 98035-0128
Ph:(253)854-1770
Fax: (253)854-8567
Co. E-mail: info@kentchamber.com
URL: http://www.kentchamber.com
Contact: Marcelle Pechler, Exec.Dir.

66120 ■ Kettle Falls Area Chamber of Commerce
265 W 3rd St.
PO Box 119
Kettle Falls, WA 99141
Ph:(509)738-2300
Co. E-mail: manager@kettlefalls.org
URL: http://www.kettlefalls.org
Contact: David Keeley, Pres.

66121 ■ La Conner Chamber of Commerce
606 Morris St.
PO Box 1610
La Conner, WA 98257
Ph:(360)466-4778
Free: 888-642-9284
Fax: (360)466-0204
Co. E-mail: info@laconnerchamber.com
URL: http://www.laconnerchamber.com
Contact: David Bricka, Exec.Dir.

66122 ■ Lacey Thurston County Chamber of Commerce
4804-A Lacey Blvd.
Lacey, WA 98503
Ph:(360)491-4141
Fax: (360)491-9403
Co. E-mail: info@laceychamber.com
URL: http://www.laceychamber.com
Contact: Jenny Thorsell, Exec.Dir.

66123 ■ Lake Chelan Chamber of Commerce
PO Box 216
Chelan, WA 98816-0216
Ph:(509)682-3503
Free: 800-4CH-ELAN
Fax: (509)682-3538
Co. E-mail: info2@lakechelan.com
URL: http://www.lakechelan.com
Contact: Mr. Dan Hodge, Exec.Dir.

66124 ■ Lakewood Chamber of Commerce
6122 Motor Ave. SW
Lakewood, WA 98499-1599
Ph:(253)582-9400
Fax: (253)581-5241
Co. E-mail: chamber@lakewood-wa.com
URL: http://www.lakewood-wa.com
Contact: Linda K. Smith, Exec.Dir.

66125 ■ Langley South Whidbey Chamber of Commerce
PO Box 403
Langley, WA 98260
Ph:(360)221-6765
Co. E-mail: langley@whidbey.com
URL: http://www.whidbey.com/langley
Contact: Nancy Rowan, Exec. Dir.

66126 ■ Leavenworth Chamber of Commerce
PO Box 327
Leavenworth, WA 98826
Ph:(509)548-5807
Fax: (509)548-1014
Co. E-mail: info@leavenworth.org
URL: http://www.leavenworth.org

66127 ■ Lopez Island Chamber of Commerce
PO Box 102
Lopez Island, WA 98261
Ph:(360)468-4664
Free: 877-433-2789
Co. E-mail: lopezchamber@lopezisland.com

URL: http://www.lopezisland.com
Contact: David Schwartz, Pres.

66128 ■ Lynden Chamber of Commerce
PO Box 647
Lynden, WA 98264
Ph:(360)354-5995
Fax: (360)354-0401
Co. E-mail: lynden@lynden.org
URL: http://www.lynden.org

66129 ■ Magnolia Chamber of Commerce
3300 W McGraw St., Ste. 222
Seattle, WA 98199
Ph:(206)284-5836
Fax: (206)352-7494
Co. E-mail: info@magnoliachamber.org
URL: http://www.magnoliachamber.org
Contact: Jennifer Kroeger

66130 ■ McCleary Community Chamber of Commerce
PO Box 53
McCleary, WA 98557-0053
Ph:(360)495-3667
Fax: (360)495-7857
Co. E-mail: chrisr@cityofmccleary.com
URL: http://www.cityofmccleary.com/chamber.htm
Contact: Don Hays, Pres.

66131 ■ Mercer Island Chamber of Commerce
7613 SE 27th
PO Box 108
Mercer Island, WA 98040-0108
Ph:(206)232-3404
Fax: (206)232-8903
Co. E-mail: mi_chamber@msn.com
URL: http://www.mercerislandchamber.org
Contact: Judy Clibborn, Exec.Dir.

66132 ■ Metalines Chamber of Commerce
PO Box 388
Metaline Falls, WA 99153
Ph:(509)446-3683
URL: http://www.povn.com/byway/towns/metafls.
   html

66133 ■ Monroe Chamber of Commerce
118 N Lewis St., Ste. 112
Monroe, WA 98272
Ph:(360)794-5488
Fax: (360)794-2044
Co. E-mail: vic@chamber-monroe.org
URL: http://www.chamber-monroe.org
Contact: Neil Watkins, Exec.Dir.

66134 ■ Montesano Chamber of Commerce and Visitor Information Center
Monte Sq.
PO Box 688
Montesano, WA 98563
Ph:(360)249-5522
Co. E-mail: montechamber@techline.com
Contact: Charli Luensman, Dir.

66135 ■ Morton Chamber of Commerce
PO Box 10
Morton, WA 98356
Ph:(360)496-6086
Fax: (360)496-6210
Co. E-mail: chamber@lewiscounty.com
URL: http://www.lewiscounty.com/morton
Contact: Ellie Worsham

66136 ■ Moses Lake Area Chamber of Commerce
324 S Pioneer Way
Moses Lake, WA 98837-1737
Ph:(509)765-7888
Free: 800-992-6234
Fax: (509)765-7891
Co. E-mail: information@moseslake.com
URL: http://www.moseslakechamber.org
Contact: Jacie Daschel, Pres.

66137 ■ Mount Adams Chamber of Commerce
PO Box 449
White Salmon, WA 98672
Ph:(509)493-3630
Free: (866)493-3630
Fax: (509)493-3670
Co. E-mail: mtadamschamber@gorge.net
URL: http://www.mtadamschamber.com
Contact: Debra Reed, Mgr.

66138 ■ Mount St. Helens Chamber of Commerce
5304 Spirit Lake Hwy.
Toutle, WA 98649
Ph:(360)274-8920
Fax: (360)274-7737
Contact: Greg Drew, Pres.

66139 ■ Mount Vernon Chamber of Commerce
PO Box 1007
Mount Vernon, WA 98273
Ph:(360)428-8547
Fax: (360)424-6237
Co. E-mail: info@mountvernonchamber.com
URL: http://www.mountvernonchamber.com
Contact: Kristen Whitener, Pres./CEO

66140 ■ Newport - Oldtown Chamber of Commerce
325 W 4th
Newport, WA 99156
Ph:(509)447-5812
Free: 877-818-1008
Fax: (509)447-7737
Co. E-mail: chamber@povn.com
URL: http://www.newportoldtownchamber.org
Contact: Mr. Cliff Martin, Pres.

66141 ■ North Mason Chamber of Commerce
PO Box 416
Belfair, WA 98528
Ph:(360)275-4267
Fax: (360)275-0853
Co. E-mail: communications@northmasonchamber.com
URL: http://www.northmasonchamber.com
Contact: Debby Baker, Exec.Dir.

66142 ■ Oakesdale Chamber of Commerce
PO Box 84
Oakesdale, WA 99158
Ph:(509)285-4771
Fax: (509)285-4771
Contact: Mike Crossett, Pres.

66143 ■ Oakville Chamber of Commerce
PO Box 331
Oakville, WA 98568-0331
Ph:(360)273-2702
Co. E-mail: fernfarms@aol.com
URL: http://www.oakville-wa.org
Contact: Janice Howell, Pres.

66144 ■ Ocean Park Area Chamber of Commerce
1715 Bay Ave.
PO Box 403
Ocean Park, WA 98640
Ph:(360)665-4448
Free: 888-751-9354
Fax: (360)665-2938
Co. E-mail: info@opwa.com
URL: http://www.opwa.com
Contact: Susan Madsen

66145 ■ Ocean Shores Chamber of Commerce
PO Box 382
Ocean Shores, WA 98569
Ph:(360)289-2451
Free: 800-762-3224
URL: http://www.oceanshores.org

66146 ■ Odessa Chamber of Commerce
PO Box 355
Odessa, WA 99159

Ph:(509)982-0049
Co. E-mail: chamber@odessachamber.net
URL: http://www.odessachamber.net
Contact: Carol Bell, Treas.

66147 ■ Okanogan Chamber of Commerce
PO Box 1125
Okanogan, WA 98840-1125
Ph:(509)422-3658
Co. E-mail: okchamber@ncidata.com
URL: http://www.okanoganwash.com/chamber.htm
Contact: Dede Beck, Sec.

66148 ■ Omak Chamber of Commerce
401 Omak Ave.
Omak, WA 98841
Ph:(509)826-1880
Free: 800-225-6625
Fax: (509)826-6201
Co. E-mail: chamber@omakchamber.com
URL: http://www.omakchamber.com
Contact: Linda Lewis, Dir.

66149 ■ Oroville Chamber of Commerce
PO Box 2140
Oroville, WA 98844
Ph:(509)476-2739
Fax: (509)476-2739
Co. E-mail: orovillechamber@gdicom.net
URL: http://www.orovillewashington.com
Contact: Mr. Raleigh Chinn, Pres.

66150 ■ Palouse Chamber of Commerce
PO Box 174
Palouse, WA 99161-0174
Ph:(509)878-1300
Co. E-mail: palousechamber@visitpalouse.com
URL: http://VisitPalouse.com
Contact: Patti Green-Kent, Pres.

66151 ■ Point Roberts Chamber of Commerce
PO Box 128
Point Roberts, WA 98281
Ph:(360)945-2313
Fax: (360)945-2855
Co. E-mail: triplem@pointroberts.net
URL: http://www.pointrobertschamber.com
Contact: Heather McPhee, Sec.

66152 ■ Port Ludlow Chamber of Commerce
PO Box 65305
Port Ludlow, WA 98365
Ph:(360)437-9798
Fax: (360)437-7684
Co. E-mail: info@portludlowchamber.org
URL: http://www.portludlowchamber.org
Contact: Dana Petrick, Pres.

66153 ■ Port Orchard Chamber of Commerce
1014 Bay St., No. 8
Port Orchard, WA 98366-5205
Ph:(360)876-3505
Free: 800-982-8139
Fax: (360)895-1920
Co. E-mail: pochamber@wavecable.com
URL: http://www.portorchard.com
Contact: Billi J. Gurnsey, Pres.

66154 ■ Port Townsend Chamber of Commerce
2437 E Sims Way
Port Townsend, WA 98368
Ph:(360)385-7869
Free: 888-ENJ-OYPT
Fax: (360)379-3804
Co. E-mail: info@ptchamber.org
URL: http://www.ptchamber.org
Contact: Tim Caldwell, Gen.Mgr.

66155 ■ Prosser Chamber of Commerce
1230 Bennett Ave.
Prosser, WA 99350
Ph:(509)786-3177
Free: 800-408-3177
Fax: (509)786-2399
Co. E-mail: prchmb@bentonrea.com

URL: http://www.prosserchamber.org
Contact: Jim Milne, Exec.Dir.

66156 ■ Pullman Chamber of Commerce
415 N Grand Ave.
Pullman, WA 99163
Ph:(509)334-3565
Free: 800-365-6948
Fax: (509)332-3232
Co. E-mail: chamber@pullmanchamber.com
URL: http://www.pullmanchamber.com
Contact: Fritz Hughes, Exec.Dir.

66157 ■ Quincy Valley Chamber of Commerce
PO Box 668
Quincy, WA 98848-0668
Ph:(509)787-2140
Fax: (509)787-4500
Co. E-mail: qvcc@quincyvalley.org
URL: http://www.quincyvalley.org
Contact: Lisa Karstetter, Exec.Dir.

66158 ■ Richland Chamber of Commerce
710-A George Washington Way
PO Box 637
Richland, WA 99352
Ph:(509)946-1651
Fax: (509)943-6187
Co. E-mail: rccadmin@owt.com
Contact: Maureen Frix, Exec.Dir.

66159 ■ Ritzville Area Chamber of Commerce
111 W Main
PO Box 122
Ritzville, WA 99169-0122
Ph:(509)659-1936
Fax: (509)659-0142
Co. E-mail: chamber@ritzville.com
URL: http://www.ritzville.com/chamber

66160 ■ Rosalia Chamber of Commerce
208 W 3rd St.
PO Box 132
Rosalia, WA 99170-0132
Ph:(509)523-2323
Fax: (509)523-4402
Contact: Nan Konishi, Pres.

66161 ■ San Juan Island Chamber of Commerce
PO Box 98
Friday Harbor, WA 98250
Ph:(360)378-5240
Fax: (360)370-5055
Co. E-mail: chamberinfo@sanjuanisland.com
URL: http://www.sanjuanisland.org
Contact: Paul Hopkins, Pres.

66162 ■ Sedro Woolley Chamber of Commerce
714-B Metcalf St.
Sedro Woolley, WA 98284
Ph:(360)855-1841
Free: 888-225-8365
Fax: (360)855-1582
Co. E-mail: swchamber@tricoisp.com
URL: http://www.sedro-woolley.com
Contact: Pola Kelly, Pres.

66163 ■ Selah Chamber of Commerce
216 S 1st St.
PO Box 415
Selah, WA 98942
Ph:(509)698-7303
Co. E-mail: selahchamber@elltel.net
URL: http://www.selahchamber.com
Contact: Bruce Sears, Pres.

66164 ■ Sequim-Dungeness Valley Chamber of Commerce
1192 E Washington
PO Box 907
Sequim, WA 98382
Ph:(360)683-6197
Free: 800-737-8462

Fax: (360)683-6349
Co. E-mail: info@cityofsequim.com
URL: http://www.cityofsequim.com
Contact: Marny Hannan, Exec. Dir.

66165 ■ Shelton-Mason County Chamber of Commerce
PO Box 2389
Shelton, WA 98584
Ph:(360)426-2021
Free: 800-576-2021
Fax: (360)426-8678
Co. E-mail: info@sheltonchamber.org
URL: http://sheltonchamber.org
Contact: Kasey Cronquist, Exec.Dir.

66166 ■ Shoreline Chamber of Commerce
18560 1st Ave. NE
Shoreline, WA 98155-2148
Ph:(206)361-2260
Fax: (206)361-2268
Co. E-mail: chamber@shorelinechamber.com
URL: http://www.shorelinechamber.com

66167 ■ Silverdale Chamber of Commerce
PO Box 1218
Silverdale, WA 98383
Ph:(360)692-6800
Fax: (360)692-1379
Co. E-mail: communications@silverdalechamber.com
URL: http://www.silverdalechamber.com
Contact: Gene Straw, Pres.

66168 ■ Skamania County Chamber of Commerce
PO Box 1037
Stevenson, WA 98648
Ph:(509)427-8911
Free: 800-989-9178
Co. E-mail: info@skamania.org
URL: http://www.skamania.org

66169 ■ Sky Valley Chamber of Commerce
PO Box 46
Sultan, WA 98294-0046
Ph:(360)793-0983
Fax: (360)793-0841
Contact: Ramona Quesinberry, Dir.

66170 ■ Snohomish Chamber of Commerce
127 Ave. A
PO Box 135
Snohomish, WA 98291-0135
Ph:(360)568-2526
Fax: (360)568-3869
Co. E-mail: manager@cityofsnohomish.com
URL: http://www.cityofsnohomish.com
Contact: Pam Osborne, Office Mgr.

66171 ■ Snoqualmie Valley Chamber of Commerce
PO Box 357
North Bend, WA 98045-0357
Ph:(425)888-4440
Fax: (425)888-4665
Co. E-mail: info@snovalley.org
URL: http://www.snovalley.org
Contact: Lisa S. Schaffer, Exec.Dir.

66172 ■ Soap Lake Chamber of Commerce
PO Box 433
Soap Lake, WA 98851
Ph:(509)246-1821
Fax: (509)246-1821
Co. E-mail: slcoc@2fast.net
URL: http://www.soaplakecoc.org

66173 ■ South Snohomish County Chamber of Commerce
3815 196th St. SW, Ste. 136
Lynnwood, WA 98036
Ph:(425)774-0507
Fax: (425)774-4636
Co. E-mail: info@s2c3.com
URL: http://www.s2c3.com
Contact: Jean Hales, Pres./CEO

66174 ■ Southwest King County Chamber of Commerce
PO Box 58591
Seattle, WA 98138
Ph:(206)575-1633
Fax: (206)575-2007
Co. E-mail: staff@swkcc.org
URL: http://www.swkcc.org
Contact: Paul Barden, Chm.

66175 ■ Spokane Regional Chamber of Commerce
801 W Riverside, Ste. 100
Spokane, WA 99201
Ph:(509)624-1393
Fax: (509)747-0077
Co. E-mail: info@chamber.spokane.net
URL: http://www.spokanechamber.org
Contact: Richard Hadley, Pres./CEO

66176 ■ Sprague Chamber of Commerce
PO Box 17
Sprague, WA 99032-0017
Ph:(509)257-2444
Co. E-mail: treasurer@spraguechamber.org
URL: http://www.spraguechamber.org
Contact: Kriss McLaughlin, Treas.

66177 ■ Stanwood Chamber of Commerce
PO Box 641
Stanwood, WA 98292-0641
Ph:(360)629-0562
Co. E-mail: stacykj3@hotmail.com
URL: http://www.stanwoodchamber.org
Contact: Stacy Johnson, Adm.Asst.

66178 ■ Steilacoom Chamber of Commerce
PO Box 88584
Steilacoom, WA 98388
Ph:(253)582-4204
Fax: (253)582-4204
Co. E-mail: rehburg@aol.com
URL: http://www.steilacoom.org
Contact: Don Rehburg, Pres.

66179 ■ Sunnyside Chamber of Commerce
520 S 7th St.
PO Box 329
Sunnyside, WA 98944
Ph:(509)837-5939
Free: 800-457-8089
URL: http://sunnysidechamber.com

66180 ■ Tacoma-Pierce County Chamber of Commerce
950 Pacific Ave., Ste. 300
PO Box 1933
Tacoma, WA 98401-1933
Ph:(253)627-2175
Fax: (253)597-7305
Co. E-mail: info@tacomachamber.org
URL: http://www.tacomachamber.org
Contact: David W. Graybill CCE, Pres./CEO

66181 ■ Tenino Chamber of Commerce and Economic Development Commission
PO Box 506
Tenino, WA 98589
Ph:(360)264-5075
Contact: Robin Rudy, Pres.

66182 ■ Thurston County Chamber of Commerce
PO Box 1427
Olympia, WA 98507
Ph:(360)357-3362
Fax: (360)357-3376
Co. E-mail: info@thurstonchamber.com
URL: http://www.thurstonchamber.com
Contact: David Schaffert, Pres./CEO

66183 ■ Tonasket Chamber of Commerce
215 S Whitcomb Ave.
Tonasket, WA 98855
Ph:(509)486-4543
Free: (866)440-8828
Fax: (509)486-4969
Co. E-mail: info@tonasket.org

URL: http://www.tonasketwa.org
Contact: Bill Kauffold, Pres.

66184 ■ Toppenish Chamber of Commerce
5A S Toppenish Ave.
Toppenish, WA 98948-0028
Ph:(509)865-3262
Free: 800-569-3982
Fax: (509)865-3549
Co. E-mail: chamber@toppenish.net
URL: http://www.toppenish.net
Contact: Shelley Bjornson, Dir.

66185 ■ Town of Conconully Chamber of Commerce
PO Box 309
Conconully, WA 98819-0309
Ph:(509)826-9050
Free: 877-826-9050
Fax: (509)826-3374
Co. E-mail: conconully@nvinet.com
URL: http://www.conconully.com
Contact: Nihla Lowden, Sec.

66186 ■ Tri-City Regional Chamber of Commerce
3180 W Clearwater Ave., Ste. F
PO Box 6986
Kennewick, WA 99336
Ph:(509)736-0510
Fax: (509)783-1733
Co. E-mail: info@tricityregionalchamber.com
URL: http://www.tcacc.com
Contact: Kristofer T. Johnson IOM, Pres./CEO

66187 ■ Tumwater Area Chamber of Commerce
5304 Littlerock Rd. SW
Tumwater, WA 98512
Ph:(360)357-5153
Fax: (360)786-1685
Co. E-mail: office@tumwaterchamber.com
URL: http://www.tumwaterchamber.com
Contact: Corinne M. Tobeck, Exec.Dir.

66188 ■ Twisp Chamber of Commerce
PO Box 686
Twisp, WA 98856
Ph:(509)997-2926
Fax: (509)997-2164
Co. E-mail: info@twispinfo.com
URL: http://www.twispinfo.com
Contact: Bill Simons, Pres.

66189 ■ Waitsburg Commercial Club
PO Box 451
Waitsburg, WA 99361
Ph:(509)337-6145
Contact: Don Helgeson, Pres.

66190 ■ Walla Walla Valley Chamber of Commerce
29 E Sumach St.
PO Box 644
Walla Walla, WA 99362
Ph:(509)525-0850
Free: 877-998-4748
Fax: (509)522-2038
Co. E-mail: info@wwvchamber.com
URL: http://www.wwchamber.com
Contact: Dave Warkentin, Exec.Dir.

66191 ■ Wallingford Chamber of Commerce
2100-A N 45th St.
Seattle, WA 98103
Ph:(206)632-3165
Fax: (206)632-4759
Co. E-mail: chamber@wallingford.org
URL: http://www.wallingford.org
Contact: Karen Buschow, Treas.

66192 ■ Washington Coast Chamber of Commerce
2616-A State Rte. 109
Ocean City, WA 98569
Ph:(360)289-4552
Free: 800-286-4552

Co. E-mail: info@washingtoncoastchamber.org
URL: http://www.washingtoncoastchamber.org

66193 ■ Waterville Chamber of Commerce
PO Box 628
Waterville, WA 98858
Ph:(509)745-8871

66194 ■ Wenatchee Valley Chamber of Commerce
PO Box 850
Wenatchee, WA 98807-0850
Ph:(509)662-2116
Fax: (509)663-2022
Co. E-mail: info@wenatchee.org
URL: http://www.wenatchee.org
Contact: Craig Larsen, Exec.Dir.

66195 ■ West Plains Chamber of Commerce
201 1st St.
Cheney, WA 99004
Ph:(509)235-8480
Fax: (509)235-9338
Co. E-mail: info@westplainschamber.org
URL: http://www.westplainschamber.org
Contact: Ms. Joelean Copeland, Exec.Dir.

66196 ■ West Seattle Chamber of Commerce
PO Box 16487
3614-A California Ave. SW
Seattle, WA 98116-4413
Ph:(206)932-5685
Fax: (206)932-5753
Co. E-mail: info@wschamber.com
URL: http://www.wschamber.com
Contact: Amy Bovenkamp, Pres.

66197 ■ Westport-Grayland Chamber of Commerce
2985 S Montesano Ave.
PO Box 306
Westport, WA 98595
Ph:(360)268-9422
Free: 800-345-6223
Fax: (360)268-1990
Co. E-mail: info@westportgrayland-chamber.org
URL: http://www.westportgrayland-chamber.org
Contact: Leslie Eichner, Office Mgr.

66198 ■ White Center Chamber of Commerce
1612 SW 114th St., Ste. 108
Seattle, WA 98146-3562
Ph:(206)763-4196
Fax: (206)763-1042
Co. E-mail: wcchamber@hotmail.com
Contact: Sigrid A. Wilson, Mgr.

66199 ■ Wilbur Chamber of Commerce
PO Box 111
Wilbur, WA 99185
Ph:(509)647-5551
URL: http://www.wilburwa.com
Contact: Sharon Farmer, Pres.

66200 ■ Willapa Harbor Chamber of Commerce
PO Box 1249
South Bend, WA 98586
Ph:(360)942-5419
Co. E-mail: visitorinfo@willapabay.org
URL: http://visit.willapabay.org
Contact: Ms. Anne Steele, Dir.

66201 ■ Winthrop Chamber of Commerce
PO Box 39
Winthrop, WA 98862
Ph:(509)996-2125
Free: 888-463-8469
Co. E-mail: info@winthropwashington.com
URL: http://winthropwashington.com

66202 ■ Woodland Chamber of Commerce
PO Box 1012
Woodland, WA 98674
Ph:(360)225-9552
Fax: (360)225-3490
Co. E-mail: debbie.kennell.lye8@statefarm.com

URL: http://www.lewisriver.com/woodlandchamber
Contact: Debbie Kennell, Pres.

66203 ■ Yakima County Hispanic Chamber of Commerce
PO Box 11146
Yakima, WA 98909
Ph:(509)453-2050
Fax: (509)453-5165
Contact: Velma Perez, Pres.

66204 ■ Yelm Area Chamber of Commerce
PO Box 444
Yelm, WA 98597
Ph:(360)458-6608
Fax: (360)458-6383
Co. E-mail: info@yelmchamber.com
URL: http://www.yelmchamber.com
Contact: Cecelia Jenkins, Activities Committee Chair

MINORITY BUSINESS ASSISTANCE PROGRAMS

66205 ■ Washington State Office of Minority and Women's Business Enterprises
PO Box 41160
Olympia, WA 98504-1160
Ph:(360)753-9693
Fax: (360)586-7079
Co. E-mail: carolync@omwbe.wa.gov
URL: http://www.omwbe.wa.gov
Contact: Carolyn Crowson, Dir
Description: Created to increase opportunities for minorities and women wishing to obtain state contracts.

FINANCING AND LOAN PROGRAMS

66206 ■ Bear Creek Venture Partners
1000 2nd Ave., Ste. 1200
Seattle, WA 98104
Ph:(206)332-1217
Fax: (206)322-1201
URL: http://www.bearcreekvp.com
Contact: Jay Powers, General Partner
Investment Policies: Early stage. **Industry Preferences:** Communications, computer software, and Internet specific. **Geographic Preferences:** Northwest.

66207 ■ Benaroya Capital Compaby
1001 4th Ave., Ste. 4700
Seattle, WA 98154
Ph:(206)343-4750
Fax: (206)447-9384
URL: http://www.benaroya.com
Preferred Investment Size: $500,000 to $3,000,000. **Investment Policies:** Seed, first and second stage. **Industry Preferences:** Communications, and semiconductors and other electronics. **Geographic Preferences:** Northwest.

66208 ■ Digital Partners
401 Parkplace Ctr., Ste. 311
Kirkland, WA 98033
Ph:(425)468-3950
Fax: (425)468-3901
URL: http://www.digitalpartners.com
Contact: Bill Tenneson, Managing Director
Preferred Investment Size: $100,000 to $3,000,000. **Investment Types:** Seed, start-up, early, first and second stage. **Industry Preferences:** Communications, computer software, Internet specific, medical and health. **Geographic Preferences:** West Coast.

66209 ■ EFund, LLC
5350 NE Carillon Point
Kirkland, WA 98033
Ph:(206)389-4901
Fax: (206)389-4901
URL: http://www.efundllc.com
Contact: Dan Kranzler, Managing Partner
Investment Policies: Early stage. **Industry Preferences:** Communications and media, and Internet specific. **Geographic Preferences:** U.S.

66210 ■ Encompass Ventures Management Company
401 Parkplace Ctr., Ste. 311
Kirkland, WA 98033
Ph:(425)486-3900
Fax: (425)486-3901
URL: http://www.encompassventures.com
Contact: Scot Land, Managing Partner
Preferred Investment Size: $1,000,000 to $5,000,000. **Investment Types:** Seed, start-up, early, first and second stage, expansion, and balanced. **Industry Preferences:** Internet specific, computer software and services, computer hardware, consumer related, communications and media, biotechnology, medical and health. **Geographic Preferences:** West Coast.

66211 ■ FBR Comotion Venture Capital
1111 Third Ave., Ste. 2400
Seattle, WA 98101
Ph:(206)382-9191
Fax: (206)342-9047
URL: http://www.comotionvc.com
Contact: David Billstrom, Managing Partner
Preferred Investment Size: $100,000 to $5,000,000. **Investment Types:** Seed, start-up, early and first stage. **Industry Preferences:** Internet specific, computer software and services. **Geographic Preferences:** Northwest.

66212 ■ Fluke Venture Partners
11400 SE Sixth St., Ste. 230
Bellevue, WA 98004
Ph:(425)453-4590
Fax: (425)453-4675
URL: http://www.flukeventures.com
Contact: Dennis Weston, Senior Managing Director
E-mail: weston@flukeventures.com
Preferred Investment Size: $500,000 to $4,000,000. **Investment Types:** Seed, early and second stage, and balanced. **Industry Preferences:** Computer software and services, computer hardware, Internet specific, medical and health, communications and media, consumer related, industrial and energy, biotechnology, semiconductors and other electronics, and other products. **Geographic Preferences:** Northwest.

66213 ■ Frazier & Company / Frazier Healthcare and Technology Ventures
601 Union St., Ste. 3300
Seattle, WA 98101
Ph:(206)621-7200
Fax: (206)621-1848
URL: http://www.frazierco.com
Contact: Alan Frazier, Managing Partner
Preferred Investment Size: $500,000 to $15,000,000. **Investment Types:** Early and later stage, and balanced. **Industry Preferences:** Computer software and services, Internet specific, medical and health, communications and media, computer hardware, other products, consumer related, industrial and energy, biotechnology, semiconductors and other electronics. **Geographic Preferences:** Midwest and Northwest.

66214 ■ Jaguar Ventures
601 W. 1st Ave.
Dept. 12000
Spokane, WA 99201
Ph:(509)835-3111
Fax: (509)624-8582
URL: http://www.jaguarventures.com
Preferred Investment Size: $250,000 to $1,000,000. **Investment Policies:** Early stage. **Industry Preferences:** Biotechnology and consumer related. **Geographic Preferences:** Idaho, Northwest, and Washington.

66215 ■ Kellett Investment Group
2415 Carillon Point
Kirkland, WA 98033
Ph:(425)828-8106
Fax: (425)828-8101
Contact: John Cunningham, President
Investment Policies: Seed and early stage. **Industry Preferences:** Communications and Internet specific. **Geographic Preferences:** U.S. .

66216 ■ Kirlan Venture Capital, Inc.
221 First Ave. W., Ste. 108
Seattle, WA 98119-4223
Ph:(206)281-8610
Fax: (206)285-3451
URL: http://www.kirlanventure.com
Contact: Kirk Lanterman, Chairman and Chief
    Executive Officer
Preferred Investment Size: $200,000 to
$200,000,000. **Investment Types:** Early, first and
later stage, mezzanine, balanced, and expansion. **In-
dustry Preferences:** Communications and media,
medical and health, computer software and services,
Internet specific, industrial and energy, and computer
hardware. **Geographic Preferences:** Northwest,
Washington, and West Coast U.S.; Western Canada.

66217 ■ Maristeth Ventures, LLC
4820 Foxhall Dr., NE
Olympia, WA 98516
Ph:(360)459-6546
Fax: (360)459-6541
URL: http://www.carlsongroup.com
Contact: Tariq Ali, Venture Partner
Preferred Investment Size: $250,000 to
$10,000,000. **Investment Types:** Seed, start-up,
early, first and second stage, expansion, balanced,
and special situation. **Industry Preferences:** Com-
munications, computer hardware and software, Inter-
net specific, semiconductors and other electronics,
industrial and energy, financial services, and utilities.
Geographic Preferences: Midwest, Northwest,
Rocky Mountains, and West Coast.

66218 ■ Materia Venture Associates, L.P.
3435 Carillon Pointe
Kirkland, WA 98033-7354
Ph:(425)822-4100
Fax: (425)827-4086
Preferred Investment Size: $500,000 to $1,000,000.
Investment Types: Start-up, first and second stage,
and mezzanine. **Geographic Preferences:** U.S.

**66219 ■ Northwest Venture Associates, Inc. /
Spokane Capital MGMT**
221 N. Wall St., Ste. 628
Spokane, WA 99201
Ph:(509)747-0728
Fax: (509)747-0758
URL: http://www.nwva.com
Contact: Robert Wolfe, Managing Partner
Preferred Investment Size: $500,000 to $5,000,000.
Investment Types: Start-up, first, second, early and
later stage, leveraged buyout, and expansion. **Indus-
try Preferences:** Internet specific, computer software
and services, communications and media, consumer
related, medical and health, industrial and energy,
semiconductors and other electronics. **Geographic
Preferences:** Idaho, Montana, Oregon, and Washington.

**66220 ■ OVP Venture Partners / Olympic
Venture Partners (Kirkland)**
1010 Market St.
Kirkland, WA 98033
Ph:(425)889-9192
Fax: (425)889-0152
URL: http://www.ovp.com
Contact: Bill Funcannon, Chief Financial Officer
Preferred Investment Size: $1,000,000 to
$10,000,000. **Investment Types:** Seed, start-up, first
and early stage. **Industry Preferences:** Computer
software and services, Internet specific, medical and
health, biotechnology, communications and media,
consumer related, semiconductors and other electronics, computer hardware, and other products. **Geographic Preferences:** Northwest and West Coast.

**66221 ■ Pacific Northwest Partners SBIC,
L.P.**
15352 SE 53rd St.
Bellevue, WA 98006
Ph:(425)747-5558
Fax: (425)455-9404
URL: http://www.pnwp.com
Contact: Louis General Partner, Vice President
Preferred Investment Size: $500,000 minimum. **In-
vestment Types:** Seed, start-up, early and first stage,

and expansion. **Industry Preferences:** Internet specific, medical and health, consumer related, computer
software and services, and other products. **Geographic Preferences:** Northwest and West Coast.

66222 ■ Paladin Partners
1644 10th St., W.
Kirkland, WA 98033
Ph:(425)739-0978
Fax: (425)739-0980
URL: http://www.paladinpartners.com
Contact: Janis Machala, Managing Partner
Investment Types: Seed, start-up, early and first
stage. **Industry Preferences:** Communications, com-
puter software, Internet specific, and business ser-
vice. **Geographic Preferences:** West Coast.

**66223 ■ Perennial Ventures / Tredegar
Investments**
9039 SE 59th St.
Mercer Island, WA 98040
Ph:(206)652-9240
Fax: (206)652-9250
URL: http://www.perennialventures.com
Contact: Michael Beblo, Chief Financial Officer
Investment Policies: Seed, early, first and second
stage. **Industry Preferences:** Medical and health,
computer software and services, biotechnology, Internet specific, communications and media, computer
hardware, semiconductors and other electronics,
other products, and industrial and energy. **Geographic Preferences:** U.S. and Western, Canada.

66224 ■ The Phoenix Partners
1000 2nd Ave., Ste. 3600
Seattle, WA 98104
Ph:(206)624-8968
Fax: (206)624-1907
Contact: Will Horne, Chief Financial Officer
Preferred Investment Size: $2,000,000 to
$3,000,000. **Investment Types:** Seed, research and
development, start-up, first and second stage, and
mezzanine. **Industry Preferences:** Biotechnology,
Internet specific, computer software and services,
computer hardware, consumer related, medical and
health, semiconductors and other electronics, communications and media, and other products.

66225 ■ Seapoint Ventures
777 108th Ave., NE, Ste. 1895
Bellevue, WA 98004
Ph:(425)455-0879
Fax: (425)455-1093
URL: http://www.seapointventures.com
Contact: Thomas Huseby, Managing Partner
Preferred Investment Size: $300,000 to $4,000,000.
Investment Types: Seed, start-up, early, first and
second stage. **Industry Preferences:** Internet specif-
ic, computer software and services, computer hard-
ware, communications and media, and biotechnology.
Geographic Preferences: Northwest and West
Coast.

66226 ■ Timberline Venture Partners
203 SE Park Plz. Dr., Ste. 205
Vancouver, WA 98684
Ph:(360)882-9577
Fax: (360)882-9590
URL: http://www.timberlinevc.com
Contact: Jeffrey Tung, Managing Partner
Preferred Investment Size: $500,000 to $5,000,000.
Investment Types: Seed, start-up, early, first and
second stage. **Industry Preferences:** Communica-
tions, computer software, Internet specific, semicon-
ductors and other electronics. **Geographic
Preferences:** California and Northwest.

66227 ■ Voyager Capital
719 2nd Ave., Ste. 1400
Seattle, WA 98104
Ph:(206)438-1800
Fax: (206)438-1900
URL: http://www.voyagercap.com
Contact: Erik Benson, Managing Director
Preferred Investment Size: $3,000,000 to
$12,000,000. **Investment Types:** Early stage. **Indus-

try Preferences:** Internet specific, computer software
and services, semiconductors and other electronics,
communications and media, computer hardware, and
other products. **Geographic Preferences:** West
Coast.

PROCUREMENT
ASSISTANCE PROGRAMS

**66228 ■ Washington Procurement Technical
Assistance Center–Bellingham Whatcom
Economic Development Council**
105 E Holly St.
PO Box 2803
Bellingham, WA 98227
Ph:(360)676-4255
Fax: (360)647-9413
Co. E-mail: info@bwedc.org
URL: http://www.bwedc.org
Contact: Nancy Jordan, Exec Dir

**66229 ■ Washington Procurement Technical
Assistance Center–Metropolitan
Development Center**
15 North Broadway Ste. B
Tacoma, WA 98403
Ph:(253)591-7026
Fax: (253)572-5583
Co. E-mail: twesterlund@mdc-tacoma.org
URL: http://www.mdc-tacoma.org
Contact: Teresa Lemmons, Dir
E-mail: tlemmons_ceo@compuserve.com

**66230 ■ Washington Procurement Technical
Assistance Center–Snohomish Counuty
Economic Development Council–PTAC (728
1)**
728 134th St. SW, Ste. 128
Everett, WA 98204
Ph:(425)743-4567
Fax: (425)745-5563
Co. E-mail: info@snoedc.org
URL: http://www.snoedc.org
Contact: Erin Nelson, Prgm Mgr

**66231 ■ Washington Procurement Technical
Assistance Center–Washington State
University Tri-City Business LINK**
2710 University Dr.
Richland, WA 99354
Ph:(509)372-7142
Fax: (509)372-7512
Co. E-mail: links@tricity.wsu.edu
URL: http://www.tricity.wsu.edu/links
Contact: Johan Curtiss

INCUBATORS/RESEARCH
AND TECHNOLOGY PARKS

**66232 ■ Central Washington
University–Office of Graduate Studies and
Research**
400 E University Way
Ellensburg, WA 98926-7510
Ph:(509)963-3101
Fax: (509)963-1799
Co. E-mail: quirkw@cwu.edu
URL: http://www.cwu.edu/~masters
Contact: Wayne Quirk, Assoc.VP
E-mail: quirkw@cwu.edu
Scope: Coordinates and administers institutional and
extramurally supported research at the University, in-
cluding current studies conducted by faculty members
at departmental level and through interdisciplinary
groups.

66233 ■ Tri-Cities Enterprise Center
2000 Logston Blvd.
Richland, WA 99352
Ph:(509)375-3268
Fax: (509)375-4838
Co. E-mail: info@enterprisecenter.net

URL: http://www.enterprisecenter.net
Contact: Stanley Stave, Pres & Gen. Mgr
Description: A non-profit incubator dedicated to ensuring the survival of emerging firms in Benton and Franklin counties of Washington state.

66234 ■ University of Washington–UW TechTransfer
4311 11th Ave. NE, Ste. 500
Seattle, WA 98105-4608
Ph:(206)543-0905
Fax: (206)543-0586
Co. E-mail: techtran@u.washington.edu
URL: http://depts.washington.edu/techtran/
Contact: Dr. James A. Severson, Vice Provost
E-mail: techtran@u.washington.edu
Scope: Transfers technology from the University to business and industry, particularly in the areas of bioengineering, biotechnology, engineering, medicine, and software technologies. **Publications:** Annual Report; Listing of Available Technologies and Information Pieces. **Educational Activities:** Conferences; Symposia, to educate faculty inventors and entrepreneurs about technology transfer issues and processes; Workshops, on staff development.

66235 ■ Washington State University–Research and Technology Park
1610 NE Eastgate Blvd.
Pullman, WA 99163
Ph:(509)335-1216
Fax: (509)335-7237
Co. E-mail: jonesk@wsu.edu
URL: http://www.wsu.edu/~rtp/
Contact: Dr. Keith Jones, Dir.
E-mail: jonesk@wsu.edu
Scope: Encourages research interaction between Washington State University and industry. Seeks to promote economic development in southeastern Washington. The Park leases land to industries engaged in research, development, and light manufacturing. Industrial tenants share University research facilities and services, use faculty as consultants, and utilize graduate students as a part-time work force. Major research areas include agriculture, forestry, veterinary medicine, plant and animal biotechnology, and engineering.

66236 ■ Washington Technology Center
300 Fluke Hall
University of Washington Campus
PO Box 352140
Seattle, WA 98195-2140
Ph:(206)685-1920
Fax: (206)543-3059
Co. E-mail: info@watechcenter.org
URL: http://www.watechcenter.org
Contact: R. Lee Cheatham, Exec Dir
Description: A joint industry/state/university enterprise engaged in commercially promising research and technology development.

EDUCATIONAL PROGRAMS

66237 ■ Big Bend Community College
7662 Chanute St. NE
Moses Lake, WA 98837-3299
Ph:(509)762-5351
Fax: (509)762-6329
URL: http://www.bigbend.edu
Description: Two-year college offering a small business management program.

66238 ■ Olympic College
1600 Chester Ave.
Bremerton, WA 98337-1699
Ph:(360)792-6050
Free: 800-259-6718
Fax: (360)475-7150
URL: http://www.olympic.edu
Description: Provides a variety of certificate programs and courses specifically designed to assist small businesses.

66239 ■ South Seattle Community College
6000 16th Ave. SW
Seattle, WA 98106-1499
Ph:(206)764-5300
Fax: (206)764-7947
URL: http://www.southseattle.org
Description: Two-year college offering a program in small business management.

66240 ■ Spokane Falls Community College
3410 W Fort George Wright Dr.
Spokane, WA 99224-5288
Ph:(509)533-3500
Free: 888-509-7944
Fax: (509)533-3237
Co. E-mail: donnam@spokanefalls.edu
URL: http://www.spokanefalls.edu
Description: Two-year college offering a small business management program.

66241 ■ Tacoma Community College–Business and Industry Resource Center
6501 S 19th St.
Tacoma, WA 98466
Ph:(253)566-5000
Fax: (253)272-7968
URL: http://www.tacoma.ctc.edu
Description: Offers day and evening small business courses, for credit or noncredit, at the main campus and at the downtown center. Selected courses also are held on Saturdays to meet the scheduling needs of working students. Classes are co-sponsored by the Tacoma-Pierce County Chamber of Commerce as part of its Small Business Profit Center. Customized training for business and organizations is designed to meet the needs of employees and managers. Training workshops are held on site for the convenience of the participants.

PUBLICATIONS

66242 ■ *Incorporation and Business Guide for Wahsington*
Self-Counsel Press, Inc.
1704 N. State St.
Bellingham, WA 98225
Ph:(360)676-4530
Free: 800-663-3007
Fax: (360)676-4549
Ed: Victoria Van Hof. **Released:** Sixth edition, 1993. **Price:** $12.95. **Description:** Includes forms to help entrepreneurs incorporate in Washington.

66243 ■ *Incorporation Forms For Washington*
Self-Counsel Press
1704 N State St.
Bellingham, WA 98225
Ph:(360)676-4530
Free: 800-663-3007
Fax: (360)676-4549
Released: 1993. **Price:** $12.95 (paper). **Description:** Provides forms for forming your own corporation in the state of Washington.

66244 ■ *Smart Start your Washington Business*
PSI Research
300 N. Valley Dr.
Grants Pass, OR 97526
Ph:(503)479-9464
Free: 800-228-2275
Fax: (503)476-1479
Co. E-mail: info@psi-research.com
URL: http://www.psi-research.com
Ed: Michael D. Jenkins. **Released:** Revised edition, 1992. **Price:** $29.95 (looseleaf binder); $24.95 (paper). **Description:** Part of the Successful Business Library series.

PUBLISHERS

66245 ■ Cleaning Consultant Services Inc.
3693 E Marginal Way S
PO Box 1273
Seattle, WA 98111
Ph:(206)682-9748
Fax: (206)622-6876
Co. E-mail: ccs@cleaningconsultants.com
URL: http://www.cleaningconsultants.com
Contact: William R. Griffin, President
E-mail: wgriffin@cleaningconsultants.com
Description: Accepts unsolicited manuscripts (books, reports, games, software), related to cleaning and small business. Reaches market through direct mail, reviews and listings, telephone sales, ads, catalogs, and trade shows. **Founded:** 1975.

66246 ■ Learning Edge Publishing
PO Box 97041-P
Tacoma, WA 98497-0041
Ph:(253)588-5174
Fax: (253)588-1594
URL: http://www.lepublishing.com/
Description: Publishes business-related guidebooks such as writing training courses and project planning along with establishing individual goals.

66247 ■ Lotus Bloom Publishing Pte. Ltd.
323 Strait View Dr.
Friday Harbor, WA 98250
Ph:(360)378-5036
Co. E-mail: info@lotusbloom.com
URL: http://www.lotusbloom.com/
Contact: Steve Morris
Description: Publishes books on business covering topics such as inspirational, self-development, and leadership. Reaches market through distributor Biblio Distribution (NBN Books) **Founded:** 2001

66248 ■ Online Training Solutions Inc.
PO Box 951
Bellevue, WA 98009-0951
Ph:(425)671-0640
Free: 800-854-3344
Fax: (425)671-0640
Co. E-mail: CustomerService@otsi.com
URL: http://www.otsi.com
Contact: Steve Lambert, President
Description: Publishes training books. **Founded:** 1999.

66249 ■ Patron Saint Productions Inc.
1240 W Sims Way, No. 68
Port Townsend, WA 98368
Ph:(504)342-4806
Fax: (504)342-4157
Co. E-mail: info@patronsaintpr.com
URL: http://www.patronsaintpr.com
Contact: Steve O'Keefe, Exec. Dir.
E-mail: steve.okeefe@patronsaintpr.com
Description: Publishes on online marketing strategies, campaigns, and training. **Founded:** 2001

66250 ■ Rec Room Publishing Inc.
PO Box 404
Richland, WA 99352
Ph:(509)946-7315
Free: 888-325-4263
Fax: (509)943-7629
Co. E-mail: info@gamesforgroups.com
URL: http://www.gamesforgroups.com
Contact: Alanna Jones
Description: Publishes books on team-building and therapeutic games for both children and adults that can be used by professionals and also by therapists. **Founded:** 1998

66251 ■ Redmond Technology Press
15365 NE 90th St.
Redmond, WA 98052
Ph:(425)885-9499
Fax: (425)882-0160
Co. E-mail: steve@stephenlnelson.com
URL: http://www.redtechpress.com
Contact: Stephen L. Nelson

Description: Publishes computer books for business people, including MBA's Guides, Effective Executive's Guides and New Webmaster's Guides.

66252 ■ Stat Communications Ltd.
PMB 803, 250 H St.
PO Box 803
Blaine, WA 98230

Ph:(604)535-8505
Fax: (604)531-8818
Co. E-mail: publisher@statpub.com
URL: http://www.statpub.com
Contact: Brian Clancey, Publisher
Description: Publishes on international trade and agriculture. Accepts unsolicited manuscripts, should be business-related and include a self-addressed, stamped envelope. Reaches market through direct mail. **Founded:** 1988.

SMALL BUSINESS DEVELOPMENT CENTER LEAD OFFICE

66253 ■ West Virginia Development Office–Small Business Development Center
950 Kanawha Blvd. E., Ste. 200
Charleston, WV 25301
Ph:(304)558-2960
Free: 888-WVA-SBDC
Fax: (304)558-0127
Contact: Joe Cicarello, Acting State Director
E-mail: jciccarello@wvsbdc.org

66254 ■ West Virginia Development Office–West Virginia SBDC
Capital Complex
Bldg. 6, Rm. 652
Charleston, WV 25301
Ph:(304)558-2960
Fax: (304)558-0127
URL: http://www.wvsbdc.org
Contact: Conley Sayler, State Dir.
E-mail: csalyer@wvsbdc.org

SMALL BUSINESS DEVELOPMENT CENTERS

66255 ■ College of West Virginia (Beckley Area)–SBDC
200 Value City Ctr., Ste. 601
Beckley, WV 25801
Ph:(304)252-4022
Free: 800-766-4556
Fax: (304)252-9584
URL: http://www.sbdcwv.org
Contact: Tara Elder, Business Analyst
E-mail: telder@r1workforcewv.org

66256 ■ Fairmont State College–Small Business Development Center
1000 Technology Dr., Ste. 1120
Fairmont, WV 26554
Ph:(304)367-2712
Fax: (304)367-2717
Co. E-mail: sbdc@westvirginia.com
URL: http://www.sbdcwv.org
Contact: Jack Kirby, Program Mgr.
E-mail: jrkl@fscvax.wvnet.edu

66257 ■ Fairmont State College (Elkins Satellite)–SBDC
10 Eleventh St., Ste. 1
Elkins, WV 26241
Ph:(304)637-7205
Fax: (304)637-4902
Contact: James Martin, Business Analyst
E-mail: jrjm@access.mountain.net

66258 ■ Marshall Community & Technical College–Small Business Development Center
2000 7th Ave.
Cabell Hall, Ste. 304
Huntington, WV 25703
Ph:(304)696-6789
Fax: (304)696-4835
Contact: Amber Wilson, Center Mgr.
E-mail: wilsona@marshall.edu

66259 ■ Shepherd College–Small Business Development Center
Gardiner Hall
PO Box 3210
Shepherdstown, WV 25443-3210
Ph:(304)876-5000
Free: 800-344-5231
Fax: (304)876-3101
Co. E-mail: pgroen@shephrd.edu
URL: http://www.shepherd.edu/
Contact: Fred Baer, Program Mgr.
E-mail: fbaer@hepherd.wvnet.edu

66260 ■ West Virginia Development Office at Logan–Small Business Development Center
300 Main St.
Logan, WV 25601
Ph:(304)792-7234
Fax: (304)792-7239
Contact: Harold Patterson, Business Analyst
E-mail: hpatterson@frontiernet.net

66261 ■ West Virginia Flatwoods Area–Small Business Development Center
The Braxton County Ctr.
200 Jerry Burton Dr.
Sutton, WV 26601
Ph:(304)368-7235
Fax: (304)368-7240
Contact: Paul Cook, Center Mgr.
E-mail: ecook@fairmontstate.edu

66262 ■ West Virginia Institute of Technology–Small Business Development Center
912 E. Main St.
Oak Hill, WV 25901
Ph:(304)465-1434
Fax: (304)465-8680
Contact: James Epling, Program Mgr.
E-mail: jeepli@wvit.wvnet.edu

66263 ■ West Virginia Northern Community College–Small Business Development Center
College Square
Wheeling, WV 26003
Ph:(304)233-5900
Fax: (304)232-3819
Contact: Donna Schramm, Center Mgr.
E-mail: dschramm@northern.wvnet.edu

66264 ■ West Virginia SBDC at Pineville - Welch Area
PO Box 85
Northfork, WV 24868
Ph:(304)862-3144

Fax: (304)862-3071
URL: http://www.sbdcwv.org
Contact: Harold Patterson, Business Analyst
E-mail: hpatterson@frontiernet.net

66265 ■ West Virginia SBDC at Summersville
812 Northside Dr., Ste. 7J
Summersville, WV 26651
Ph:(304)872-0020
URL: http://www.sbdcwv.org
Contact: Jim Epling, Center Mgr.
E-mail: jepling@r1workforcewv.org

66266 ■ West Virginia University–Small Business Development Center (886 C)
886 Chestnut Ridge Rd.
PO Box 6884
Morgantown, WV 26506-6684
Ph:(304)293-5839
Fax: (304)225-2210
Contact: Sharon Stratton, Center Mgr.
E-mail: sharon.stratton@mail.wvu.edu

66267 ■ West Virginia University (Parkersburg)–Small Business Development Center
300 Campus Dr.
Parkersburg, WV 26104
Ph:(304)424-8391
Fax: (304)424-8266
URL: http://www.sbdcwv.org
Contact: Greg Hill, Center Mgr.
E-mail: ghill@alpha.wvup.wvnet.edu

SMALL BUSINESS ASSISTANCE PROGRAMS

66268 ■ West Virginia Development Office–Business and Industrial Development Division
State Capitol Complex, Bldg. 6, Rm. 553
1900 Kanawha Blvd. E
Charleston, WV 25305-0311
Ph:(304)558-2234
Free: 800-982-3386
Fax: (304)558-0449
URL: http://www.wvdo.org
Contact: Steve Spence, Exec Dir
Description: Offers assistance to small business.

CHAMBERS OF COMMERCE

66269 ■ Beckley - Raleigh County Chamber of Commerce
245 N Kanawha St.
Beckley, WV 25801
Ph:(304)252-7328
Free: 877-987-3847
Fax: (304)252-7373
Co. E-mail: chamber@charterbn.com
URL: http://www.brccc.com

Contact: Ellen Taylor, Exec.Dir.

66270 ■ Berkeley Springs - Morgan County Chamber of Commerce
127 Fairfax St.
Berkeley Springs, WV 25411
Ph:(304)258-3738
Co. E-mail: chamber@berkeleysprings.com
URL: http://www.berkeleyspringschamber.com
Contact: Andrea Curtin, Exec.Dir.

66271 ■ Chamber of Commerce of the Mid-Ohio Valley
214 8th St.
Parkersburg, WV 26101-4615
Ph:(304)422-3588
Fax: (304)422-3580
Co. E-mail: pksbgchamber@eurekanet.com
Contact: George Kellenberger, Pres.

66272 ■ Charleston Regional Chamber of Commerce and Development
1116 Smith St.
Charleston, WV 25301
Ph:(304)340-4253
Fax: (304)340-4275
Co. E-mail: rak@charlestonwvchamber.org
URL: http://www.charlestonareaalliance.org
Contact: Richard A. Kennedy Jr., Pres./CEO

66273 ■ Fayette County Chamber of Commerce
310 Oyler Ave.
Oak Hill, WV 25901
Ph:(304)465-5617
Fax: (304)465-5618
Co. E-mail: cindy@fayettecounty.com
URL: http://www.fayettecounty.com
Contact: Sharon Cruikshank, Dir.

66274 ■ Follansbee Chamber of Commerce
1334 Main St.
Follansbee, WV 26037
Ph:(304)527-1330
Contact: Tony Paesano, Pres.

66275 ■ Grant County Chamber of Commerce
105 Virginia Ave., Ste. 1
Petersburg, WV 26847
Ph:(304)257-2722
Co. E-mail: mkimble@gowv.com
URL: http://www.gowv.com
Contact: Mernie Kimble, Dir.

66276 ■ Greater Bluefield Chamber of Commerce
PO Box 4098
Bluefield, WV 24701
Ph:(304)327-7184
Fax: (304)325-3085
Co. E-mail: bluefieldchamber@citlink.net
URL: http://www.bluefieldchamber.com
Contact: Marc Meachum, Pres./CEO

66277 ■ Greenbrier County Convention and Visitors Bureau
540 N Jefferson St., Ste. N
Box 17
Lewisburg, WV 24901-1303
Ph:(304)645-1000
Free: 800-833-2068
Fax: (304)647-3001
Co. E-mail: info@greenbrierwv.com
URL: http://www.greenbrierwv.com
Contact: Kim Cooper, Exec.Dir.

66278 ■ Hampshire County Chamber of Commerce
91 S High St.
Romney, WV 26757
Ph:(304)822-7221
Fax: (304)822-7221
Co. E-mail: hampshirechamberofcommerce@citlink.net
URL: http://www.hampshirecountychamber.com
Contact: Louise Blauvelt, Pres.

66279 ■ Harrison County Chamber of Commerce
168 W Main St., Ste. 100
Clarksburg, WV 26301-2964
Ph:(304)624-6331
Fax: (304)624-5190
Co. E-mail: info@harrisoncountychamber.com
URL: http://www.harrisoncountychamber.com
Contact: Katherine D. Wagner IOM, Pres.

66280 ■ Huntington Regional Chamber of Commerce
720 4th Ave.
PO Box 1509
Huntington, WV 25716-1509
Ph:(304)525-5131
Fax: (304)525-5158
Co. E-mail: info@huntingtonchamber.org
URL: http://www.huntingtonchamber.org
Contact: Mark B. Bugher, Pres./CEO

66281 ■ Jefferson County Chamber of Commerce
201 Frontage Rd.
PO Box 426
Charles Town, WV 25414-0426
Ph:(304)725-2055
Free: 800-624-0577
Fax: (304)728-8307
Co. E-mail: chamber@jeffersoncounty.com
URL: http://www.jeffersoncounty.com
Contact: Mary M. Via, Exec.Dir.

66282 ■ Lewis County Chamber of Commerce
345 Center Ave.
Weston, WV 26452
Ph:(304)269-2608
Fax: (304)269-3271
Co. E-mail: lcinfo@lcchamber.org
URL: http://www.lcchamber.org
Contact: Ms. Susan Church, Exec.Dir.

66283 ■ Logan County Chamber of Commerce
214 Stratton St.
PO Box 218
Logan, WV 25601-0218
Ph:(304)752-1324
Fax: (304)752-5988
Co. E-mail: logancountychamber@verizon.net
URL: http://www.logancountychamberofcommerce.com
Contact: Debrina J. Williams, Mgr.Dir.

66284 ■ Marion County Chamber of Commerce
110 Adams St.
Fairmont, WV 26554
Ph:(304)363-0442
Fax: (304)363-0480
Co. E-mail: mccc@marionchamber.com
URL: http://www.marionchamber.com
Contact: Tina Shaw, Pres.

66285 ■ Marshall County Chamber of Commerce
604 Jefferson Ave.
Moundsville, WV 26041
Ph:(304)845-2773
Co. E-mail: chamber@marshallcountychamber.com
URL: http://www.marshallcountychamber.com
Contact: David W. Knuth, Exec.Dir.

66286 ■ Martinsburg-Berkeley County Chamber of Commerce
198 Viking Way
Martinsburg, WV 25401-5338
Ph:(304)267-4841
Free: 800-322-9007
Fax: (304)263-4695
Co. E-mail: chamber@berkeleycounty.org
URL: http://www.berkeleycounty.org
Contact: Tina H. Combs, Exec.Dir.

66287 ■ Mason County Area Chamber of Commerce
305 Main St.
Point Pleasant, WV 25550
Ph:(304)675-1050
Fax: (304)675-2838
URL: http://www.masoncountychamber.org
Contact: Hilda Austin, Exec. Dir.

66288 ■ Mineral County Chamber of Commerce
1 Grand Central Park
Keyser, WV 26726
Ph:(304)788-2513
Fax: (304)788-3887
Co. E-mail: office@mineralchamber.com
URL: http://www.mineralchamber.com
Contact: Anne Palmer, Sec.

66289 ■ Morgantown Area Chamber of Commerce
1009 University Ave.
Morgantown, WV 26507-0658
Ph:(304)292-3311
Free: 800-618-2525
Fax: (304)296-6619
Co. E-mail: info@morgantownchamber.org
URL: http://www.mgnchamber.org
Contact: Brad Allamong, Pres.

66290 ■ Mullens Area Chamber of Commerce
PO Box 235
Mullens, WV 25882-0235
Ph:(304)294-5497
Co. E-mail: kayk@mail.drs.state.wv.us
Contact: Sue Wade, Pres.

66291 ■ Preston County Chamber of Commerce
200 1/2 W Main St.
Kingwood, WV 26537
Ph:(304)329-0576
Fax: (304)329-1407
Co. E-mail: prestoncoc@labyrinth.net
URL: http://www.prestonchamber.com
Contact: Kathy Casseday, Exec.Dir.

66292 ■ Princeton-Mercer County Chamber of Commerce
1522 N Walker St.
Princeton, WV 24740
Ph:(304)487-1502
Fax: (304)425-0227
Co. E-mail: pmccc@frontiernet.net
URL: http://www.pmccc.com
Contact: Mr. Robert Farley, Pres. /CEO

66293 ■ Putnam County Chamber of Commerce
PO Box 553
Teays, WV 25569
Ph:(304)757-6510
Fax: (304)757-6562
Co. E-mail: chamber@putnamcounty.org
URL: http://www.putnamcounty.org
Contact: Mr. Marty Chapman, Pres.

66294 ■ Randolph County Convention and Visitors Bureau
1035 N Randolph Ave.
Elkins, WV 26241
Ph:(304)636-2780
Free: 800-422-3304
Fax: (304)636-2780
Co. E-mail: bpritt@randolphcountycvb.com
URL: http://www.randolphcountywv.com
Contact: Brenda Pritt, Exec.Dir.

66295 ■ Richwood Chamber of Commerce
PO Box 267
Richwood, WV 26261
Ph:(304)846-6790
Co. E-mail: rwdchamber@richwoodwv.com
URL: http://www.richwoodwv.com
Contact: Maxine Corbett, Exec.Dir.

66296 ■ Roane County Chamber of Commerce
PO Box 1
Spencer, WV 25276-0001
Ph:(304)927-1780
Fax: (304)927-5953
Co. E-mail: roanechamberwv@zzzip.net
URL: http://www.roanechamberwv.org
Contact: Paul Taylor, Pres.

66297 ■ St. Albans Area Chamber of Commerce
PO Box 675
St. Albans, WV 25177-0675
Ph:(304)727-7251
Fax: (304)727-7251
Co. E-mail: stacoc@netzero.net
URL: http://www.stalbanswv.com/about.shtml
Contact: Janet Painter, Pres.

66298 ■ South Charleston Chamber of Commerce
PO Box 8595
South Charleston, WV 25303
Ph:(304)744-0051
Fax: (304)746-5554
Co. E-mail: soccoc@wv-dsl.net
Contact: Bonnie Brown, Exec.Dir.

66299 ■ Summers County Chamber of Commerce
200 Ballengee St.
PO Box 231
Hinton, WV 25951
Ph:(304)466-5332
Fax: (304)466-5301
URL: http://www.summerscounty.net
Contact: Mary Lou Haley, Pres.

66300 ■ Summersville Area Chamber of Commerce
One Old Wilderness Rd.
Summersville, WV 26651
Ph:(304)872-1588
Free: 800-760-6158
Fax: (304)872-0506
Co. E-mail: info@summersvillechamber.com
URL: http://www.summersvillechamber.com
Contact: Lisa Hess, Dir.

66301 ■ Taylor County Chamber of Commerce
214 W Main St., Rm. 100
Grafton, WV 26354
Ph:(304)265-3938
Fax: (304)265-3962
Co. E-mail: tcda1@yahoo.com
Contact: Paul Elder, Pres.

66302 ■ Tug Valley Chamber of Commerce
PO Box 376
Williamson, WV 25661
Ph:(304)235-5240
Fax: (304)235-4509
Co. E-mail: tvcoc@charter.net
URL: http://www.tugvalleychamberofcommerce.com
Contact: Cecil E. Hatfield, Exec. Dir.

66303 ■ Upper Kanawha Valley Chamber of Commerce and Economic Development Corporation
PO Box 831
Montgomery, WV 25136-0831
Ph:(304)442-5756
Fax: (304)442-5763
Contact: Tina Williams, Sec.

66304 ■ Weirton Area Chamber of Commerce
3200 Main St.
Weirton, WV 26062
Ph:(304)748-7212
Fax: (304)748-0241
Co. E-mail: info@weirtonchamber.com
URL: http://www.weirtonchamber.com
Contact: Brenda Mull, Pres.

66305 ■ Welch Area Chamber of Commerce
92 McDonald St., Ste. 100
Welch, WV 24801
Ph:(304)436-4260
Fax: (304)436-6041
URL: http://www.welchchamberofcommerce.com
Contact: Ron Wyatt, Pres.

66306 ■ Wellsburg Chamber of Commerce
PO Box 487
Wellsburg, WV 26070-0487
Ph:(304)479-2115
Fax: (304)748-1832
Co. E-mail: kjroberts@comcast.net
URL: http://www.wellsburgchamber.com
Contact: Kristine Roberts, Exec.Dir.

66307 ■ West Virginia Chamber of Commerce
PO Box 2789
Charleston, WV 25330
Ph:(304)342-1115
Fax: (304)342-1130
Co. E-mail: forjobs@wvchamber.com
URL: http://www.wvchamber.com
Contact: Stephen G. Roberts, Pres.

66308 ■ Wheeling Area Chamber of Commerce
1310 Market St.
Wheeling, WV 26003
Ph:(304)233-2575
Fax: (304)233-1320
Co. E-mail: terrysterling@wheelingchamber.com
URL: http://www.wheelingchamber.com
Contact: Terry A. Sterling, Pres.

PROCUREMENT ASSISTANCE PROGRAMS

66309 ■ Mid-Ohio Valley Regional Council
531 Market St.
Parkersburg, WV 26102
Ph:(304)422-4993
Free: 800-924-7047
Fax: (304)422-4998
Co. E-mail: dberkey@mountain.net
URL: http://www.movrc.org
Contact: David Berkey
Description: Provides advice, assistance, and technical support to businesses and industries interested in becoming involved in the government procurement process.

66310 ■ Regional Contracting Assistance Center
1116 Smith St., Ste. 202
Charleston, WV 25301
Ph:(304)344-2546
Fax: (304)344-2574
Co. E-mail: rcac@rcacwv.com
URL: http://www.rcacwv.com
Contact: Bridgette Venanzi, Pres
Description: Nonprofit organization that provides advice, assistance, and support to businesses and industries interested in becoming involved in the government procurement process.

66311 ■ Regional Contracting Assistance Center–Robert C. Byrd Institute–Huntington (1050)
1050 4th Ave.
Huntington, WV 25701
Ph:(304)696-6275
Free: 800-469-RCBI
Fax: (304)696-4834
Co. E-mail: ebrown@rcbi.org
URL: http://www.rcacwv.com
Contact: Erin Brown
Description: Serves as a clearinghouse for information on contracting/subcontracting opportunities, and as a source for technical resources, information, and training. Offers an electronic bid match, access to government and industry regulations and standards, past

procurement histories, technical assistance in understanding bid and contract requirements, assistance in bid proposal preparation, training in various aspects of contracting, and assistance in understanding contract pricing, packaging, and administration.

66312 ■ Regional Contracting Assistant Center–Princeton
195 Davis St., Ste. 103
Princeton, WV 24740
Ph:(304)425-9438
Fax: (425)648-4751
Co. E-mail: dbailey@rcacwv.com
URL: http://www.rcacwv.com
Contact: Donna Bailey, Dir of Marketing

66313 ■ West Virginia Procurement Technical Assistance Center
PO Box 5528
Vienna, WV 26105
Ph:(304)428-6889
Free: 800-868-3924
Fax: (304)428-6891
Co. E-mail: belinda@cssiwv.com
URL: http://www.wvptac.org
Contact: Belinda Sheridan, Director
E-mail: snyder@access.mountain.net

INCUBATORS/RESEARCH AND TECHNOLOGY PARKS

66314 ■ Marshall University–Research Committee
Graduate Sch.
Huntington, WV 25755
Ph:(304)696-4748
Fax: (304)697-3662
Co. E-mail: aulick@marshall.edu
URL: http://www.marshall.edu/research
Contact: Dr. Howard Aulick, VP
E-mail: aulick@marshall.edu
Scope: Administers and coordinates research at the University with the exception of medical research. **Educational Activities:** Business meetings (monthly). **Awards:** Travel awards.

66315 ■ Unlimited Future, Inc.
1650 8th Ave.
Huntington, WV 25703
Ph:(304)697-3007
Fax: (304)522-0367
Co. E-mail: ufi@unlimitedfuture.org
URL: http://www.unlimitedfuture.org
Description: This incubator is dedicated to eliminated barriers to the creation of successful businesses. The non-profit center specializes in assisting minority-owned businesses through the reduction of overhead and other services.

EDUCATIONAL PROGRAMS

66316 ■ Southern West Virginia Community and Technical College
Wyoming/McDowell Campus
PO Box 638
Pineville, WV 24874
Ph:(304)294-8346
Fax: (304)294-8534
Co. E-mail: tomn@southern.wvnet.edu
URL: http://www.southern.wvnet.edu
Description: Two-year college offering a program in small business management.

66317 ■ West Virginia Northern Community College (Wheeling)
1704 Market St.
Wheeling, WV 26003
Ph:(304)233-5900
Fax: (304)232-8187
Co. E-mail: info@northern.wvnet.edu
URL: http://www.northern.wvnet.edu
Description: Two-year college offering a small business management program.

**66318 ■ West Virginia University
(Parkersburg)**
300 Campus Dr.
Parkersburg, WV 26101-9577
Ph:(304)424-8000
Fax: (304)424-8315
Co. E-mail: info@mail.wvup.edu
URL: http://www.wvup.edu
Description: Conducts management and supervisory
training courses. Also offers training programs and
free consultation for small business owners.

PUBLICATIONS

**66319 ■ *Smart Start Your West Virginia
Business***
PSI Research
300 N. Valley Dr.
Grants Pass, OR 97526
Ph:(541)479-9464
Free: 800-228-2275
Fax: (541)476-1479

Co. E-mail: info@psi-research.com
URL: http://www.psi-research.com
Ed: Michael D. Jenkins. **Released:** Revised edition,
1992. **Price:** $29.95 (looseleaf binder); $24.95
(paper). **Description:** Part of the Successful Business
Library series.

Wisconsin

SMALL BUSINESS DEVELOPMENT CENTER LEAD OFFICE

66320 ■ University of Wisconsin–Wisconsin SBDC
432 N. Lake St., Rm. 423
Madison, WI 53706
Ph:(608)263-7794
Fax: (608)263-7830
URL: http://www.wisconsinsbdc.org/
Contact: Erica Kauten, State Dir.
E-mail: erica.kauten@uwex.edu

66321 ■ University of Wisconsin—Extension–Small Business Development Center
432 N. Lake St., Rm. 423
Madison, WI 53706-1498
Ph:(608)263-7794
Fax: (608)262-7830
URL: http://www.uwsbdc.org/
Contact: Erica Kauten, State Director

SMALL BUSINESS DEVELOPMENT CENTERS

66322 ■ University of Wisconsin at Green Bay–Small Business Development Center
Wood Hall, Ste. 460
Green Bay, WI 54311-7001
Ph:(920)465-2089
Fax: (920)465-2552
URL: http://www.uwgb.edu/outreach/sbdc/
Contact: Jan Thornton, Dir.

66323 ■ University of Wisconsin—La Crosse–Small Business Development Center
120 North Hall
La Crosse, WI 54601
Ph:(608)785-8782
Fax: (608)785-6919
URL: http://www.uwlax.edu/bdc/
Contact: Jan Gallagher, Dir.

66324 ■ University of Wisconsin—Madison–Small Business Development Center
975 University Ave.
Madison, WI 53706
Ph:(608)263-2221
Fax: (608)263-0818
URL: http://www.uwsbdc.org/
Contact: Neil Lerner, Dir.

66325 ■ University of Wisconsin at Milwaukee–Small Business Development Center
161 W. Wisconsin Ave., Ste. 6752
Milwaukee, WI 53203
Ph:(414)227-3240

Fax: (414)227-3142
URL: http://www.uwm.edu/UniversityOutreach/
catalog/DBM_SBDC/index.shtml
Contact: Tim Peterson, Interim Dir.
E-mail: timp@uwm.edu

66326 ■ University of Wisconsin—Oshkosh–Small Business Development Center
201 Clow Faculty
800 Algoma Blvd.
Oshkosh, WI 54901-4825
Ph:(920)424-1453
Fax: (920)424-7413
URL: http://www.ccp.uwosh.edu/services/services_
smallbusiness.html
Contact: John Mozingo, Dir.

66327 ■ University of Wisconsin - Parkside–Kenosha Area Business Association–Small Business Development Center (600 5)
600 52nd St., Ste. 120
Kenosha, WI 53140
Ph:(414)605-1100
URL: http://www.uwp.edu/admin/community.
partnerships/kenosha_sbdc.htm
Contact: David Schachtner, Dir.

66328 ■ University of Wisconsin at Stevens Point–Small Business Development Center
103 Old Main Bldg.
2100 Main St.
Stevens Point, WI 54481-3871
Ph:(715)346-3838
Free: 800-898-9472
Fax: (715)346-4045
URL: http://www.uwsp.edu/extension/NonCredit/
SBDC/index.html
Contact: Vicki Lobermeier, Dir.
E-mail: vloberme@uwsp.edu

66329 ■ University of Wisconsin—Superior–Small Business Development Center
Sundquist Hall
1800 Grand Ave.
Superior, WI 54880
Ph:(715)394-8351
Fax: (715)394-8454
Contact: Lauren Erickson, Dir.
E-mail: nhensrud@wpo.uwsuper.edu

66330 ■ University of Wisconsin—Whitewater–Small Business Development Center
800 W. Main St.
Carlson Bldg., Rm. 2000
Whitewater, WI 53190
Ph:(414)472-3217
Fax: (414)472-4863
URL: http://www.sbdc.uww.edu/
Contact: Carla Lenk, Dir.

66331 ■ University of Wisconsin at Whitewater–Wisconsin Innovation Service Center–SBDC (402 M)
402 McCutchen Hall
Whitewater, WI 53190
Ph:(414)472-1365
Fax: (414)472-1600
URL: http://www.sbdc.uww.edu/
Contact: Debra Malewicki, Dir.

SMALL BUSINESS ASSISTANCE PROGRAMS

66332 ■ Wisconsin Department of Agriculture, Trade, and Consumer Protection–Marketing Division
2811 Agriculture Dr.
PO Box 8911
Madison, WI 53718-8911
Ph:(608)224-5012
Fax: (608)224-5111
URL: http://www.datcp.state.wi.us
Description: Provides marketing services to promote the interests of agriculture and agricultural products domestically and in international markets.

66333 ■ Wisconsin Department of Commerce
201 W Washington Ave.
PO Box 7970
Madison, WI 53707-7970
Ph:(608)266-1018
Fax: (608)267-0436
URL: http://www.commerce.state.wi.us
Description: Develops resources, programs, and policies to strengthen Wisconsin's entrepreneurial network. Cosponsors business development and training workshops and conferences.

66334 ■ Wisconsin Department of Commerce–International
201 W Washington Ave.
PO Box 7970
Madison, WI 53707-7970
Ph:(608)267-9227
Fax: (608)266-5551
URL: http://www.commerce.state.wi.us
Description: Assists Wisconsin manufacturers in exploring international sales opportunities, joint ventures and licensing, and encouraging foreign manufacturers to establish companies in Wisconsin.

BETTER BUSINESS BUREAUS

66335 ■ Better Business Bureau of Wisconsin
10101 W Greenfield Ave., No. 125
Milwaukee, WI 53214
Ph:(414)847-6000
Free: 800-273-1002

Fax: (414)302-0355
Co. E-mail: info@wisconsin.bbb.org
URL: http://www.wisconsin.bbb.org
Contact: Randall Hoth, Pres.

CHAMBERS OF COMMERCE

66336 ■ Adams County Chamber of Commerce and Tourism
252 S Main St.
PO Box 576
Adams, WI 53910
Ph:(608)339-6997
Free: 888-339-6997
Fax: (608)339-8079
Co. E-mail: chamber@adamscountywi.com
URL: http://www.adamscountywi.com
Contact: Alice Parr, Exec.Dir.

66337 ■ Algoma Area Chamber of Commerce
1226 Lake St.
Algoma, WI 54201
Ph:(920)487-2041
Free: 800-498-4888
Fax: (920)487-5519
Co. E-mail: chamber@algoma.org
URL: http://www.algoma.org

66338 ■ Almena Commercial Club
PO Box 175
Almena, WI 54805
Ph:(715)357-6103
Contact: Kay Rundhaug, Pres.

66339 ■ Antigo Area Chamber of Commerce
329 Superior St.
PO Box 339
Antigo, WI 54409
Ph:(715)623-4134
Free: 888-526-4523
Fax: (715)623-4135
Co. E-mail: antigocc@newnorth.net
Contact: Denise Wendt, Exec.Dir.

66340 ■ Arcadia Chamber of Commerce
PO Box 81
Arcadia, WI 54612-0081
Ph:(608)323-2319
Co. E-mail: arcadia@triwest.net
URL: http://arcadiawi.org
Contact: Noreen Haines, Exec.Sec.

66341 ■ Ashland Area Chamber of Commerce
PO Box 746
Ashland, WI 54806
Ph:(715)682-2500
Free: 800-284-9484
Fax: (715)682-9404
Co. E-mail: ashchamb@centurytel.net
URL: http://www.visitashland.com
Contact: Mary McPhetridge, Exec.Dir.

66342 ■ Baileys Harbor Community Association
PO Box 31
Baileys Harbor, WI 54202
Ph:(920)839-2366
Fax: (920)839-2366
Co. E-mail: bhinfo@dcwis.com
URL: http://www.baileysharbor.com
Contact: Stephanie Heald-Fisher, Pres.

66343 ■ Baldwin Area Chamber of Commerce
PO Box 813
Baldwin, WI 11510
Ph:(715)684-2221
URL: http://www.baldwinchamber.com
Contact: Kathleen Healy Englehart, Sec.

66344 ■ Bangor Business Club
PO Box 2
Bangor, WI 54614
Ph:(608)486-4060

66345 ■ Baraboo Area Chamber of Commerce
PO Box 442
Baraboo, WI 53913
Ph:(608)356-8333
Free: 800-BAR-ABOO
Fax: (608)356-8422
Co. E-mail: chamber@baraboo.com
URL: http://www.baraboo.com/chamber
Contact: Gene Dalhoff, Exec.Dir.

66346 ■ Bayfield Chamber of Commerce
42 S Broad St.
PO Box 138
Bayfield, WI 54814
Ph:(715)779-3335
Free: 800-447-4094
Fax: (715)779-5080
Co. E-mail: chamber@bayfield.org
URL: http://www.bayfield.org
Contact: Cari Obst, Exec.Dir.

66347 ■ Beaver Dam Area Chamber of Commerce
127 S Spring St.
Beaver Dam, WI 53916
Ph:(920)887-8879
Fax: (920)887-9750
Co. E-mail: info@beaverdamchamber.com
URL: http://www.beaverdamchamber.com
Contact: Philip Fritsche, Exec.Dir.

66348 ■ Belleville Community Club
Box 16
Belleville, WI 53508
Ph:(608)424-3747
Contact: Mr. Dan Edge, Pres.

66349 ■ Berlin Chamber of Commerce
161 W Hurin St.
Berlin, WI 54923
Ph:(920)361-3636
Free: 800-979-9334
Fax: (920)361-5439
Co. E-mail: berlinchamber@dotnet.com
Contact: Lisa Schilling, Exec.Dir.

66350 ■ Blair Chamber of Commerce
PO Box 413
Blair, WI 54616
Ph:(608)989-2517
Contact: Dale Olson, Pres.

66351 ■ Bloomer Chamber of Commerce
PO Box 273
Bloomer, WI 54724
Ph:(715)568-3339
Fax: (715)568-3345
Co. E-mail: bchamber@bloomer.net
URL: http://www.bloomer.net/~bchamber
Contact: Rod Turner, Exec.Dir.

66352 ■ Boscobel Chamber of Commerce
800 Wisconsin Ave.
Boscobel, WI 53805
Ph:(608)375-2672
Co. E-mail: bchamber@centurytel.net
URL: http://www.boscobelwisconsin.com
Contact: Corey Grassel, Pres.

66353 ■ Boulder Junction Chamber of Commerce
PO Box 286
Boulder Junction, WI 54512-0286
Ph:(715)385-2400
Free: 800-466-8759
Fax: (715)385-2379
Co. E-mail: boulderjct@boulderjct.org
URL: http://www.boulderjct.org

66354 ■ Brillion Area Chamber of Commerce
PO Box 123
Brillion, WI 54110
Ph:(920)756-3175
Co. E-mail: kgolaw@charter.net
URL: http://www.brillionchamber.com
Contact: Keith G. Ondrasek, Pres.

66355 ■ Brodhead Chamber of Commerce
PO Box 16
Brodhead, WI 53520-0016
Ph:(608)897-8411
Co. E-mail: nancy@brodheadchamber.org
URL: http://www.brodheadchamber.org
Contact: Nancy Sutherland, Sec.

66356 ■ Brooklyn Area Chamber of Commerce
PO Box 33
108 Hotel St.
Brooklyn, WI 53521
Ph:(608)455-1627
Fax: (608)455-1627
Co. E-mail: brooklyn@quicksitemaker.com
URL: http://www.brooklynwisconsin.com
Contact: LaVorn Dvorak, Pres.

66357 ■ Brown Deer Chamber of Commerce
3900 W Brown Deer Rd.
Brown Deer, WI 53209
Ph:(414)371-3055
Fax: (414)355-7879
Co. E-mail: dausavich@ckrueger.net
URL: http://www.browndeerchamber.org
Contact: Diane Ausavich, Pres.

66358 ■ Burlington Area Chamber of Commerce
113 E Chestnut St.
Burlington, WI 53105
Ph:(262)763-6044
Co. E-mail: eherter@burlingtonchamber.org
URL: http://www.burlingtonchamber.org
Contact: Janice Ludtke, Exec.Dir.

66359 ■ Butler Area Chamber of Commerce
12810 W Hampton Ave.
Butler, WI 53007-1606
Ph:(262)781-5195
Fax: (262)781-7870
Co. E-mail: info@butlerchamber.org
URL: http://www.butlerchamber.org
Contact: Linda C. Ryfinski, Exec.Dir.

66360 ■ Cable Area Chamber of Commerce
PO Box 217
Cable, WI 54821
Ph:(715)798-3833
Free: 800-533-7454
Fax: (715)798-4456
Co. E-mail: info@cable4fun.com
URL: http://www.cable4fun.com
Contact: Holly Henry, Exec.Dir.

66361 ■ Cadott Area Chamber of Commerce
PO Box 84
Cadott, WI 54727
Ph:(715)289-3338
Contact: Jim Buetow, Sec.-Treas.

66362 ■ Cambridge Chamber of Commerce
PO Box 572
Cambridge, WI 53523-0572
Ph:(608)423-3780
Fax: (608)423-7558
Co. E-mail: chamber@smallbytes.net
URL: http://www.cambridgewi.com
Contact: Craig Carpenter, Pres.

66363 ■ Cedarburg Chamber of Commerce
PO Box 104
Cedarburg, WI 53012
Ph:(262)377-5856
Free: 800-237-2874
Fax: (262)377-6470
Co. E-mail: info@cedarburg.org
URL: http://www.cedarburg.org
Contact: Kristine Hage, Exec.Dir.

66364 ■ Center for Commerce Tourism
PO Box 700227
Oostburg, WI 53070-0227
Ph:(920)564-2336
Fax: (920)564-3596
Co. E-mail: oostburg@wi.rr.com

URL: http://www.oostburg.org
Contact: Terry Katsma, Sec.-Treas.

66365 ■ Chetek Area Chamber of Commerce
PO Box 747
Chetek, WI 54728
Free: 800-317-1720
Fax: (715)924-4496
Co. E-mail: info@chetekwi.net
URL: http://www.chetekwi.net

66366 ■ Chilton Chamber of Commerce
PO Box 351
Chilton, WI 53014
Ph:(920)849-1585
Co. E-mail: info@chiltonchamber.com
URL: http://www.chiltonchamber.com
Contact: Tammy Pethan, Sec.

66367 ■ Chippewa Falls Area Chamber of Commerce
10 S Bridge St.
Chippewa Falls, WI 54729
Ph:(715)723-0331
Free: (866)723-0340
Fax: (715)723-0332
Co. E-mail: info@chippewachamber.org
URL: http://www.chippewachamber.org
Contact: Mike D. Jordan, Pres.

66368 ■ Clear Lake Community Club
PO Box 266
Clear Lake, WI 54005
Ph:(715)263-2755
Fax: (715)263-2267
Contact: Matt Anderson, Pres.

66369 ■ Cleveland Chamber of Commerce
PO Box 56
Cleveland, WI 53015-0056
Ph:(920)693-8256
Co. E-mail: information@chamberofcleveland.com
URL: http://www.chamberofcleveland.com
Contact: Tim Schueler, Sec.-Treas.

66370 ■ Clintonville Area Chamber of Commerce
18 S Main St.
PO Box 56
Clintonville, WI 54929
Ph:(715)823-4606
Fax: (715)823-7318
Co. E-mail: cvlchmbr@frontiernet.net
URL: http://www.clintonvillewi.org/chamber
Contact: Joanne Doornink, Exec.Dir.

66371 ■ Colby Chamber of Commerce
Box 444
Colby, WI 54421-0444
Ph:(715)223-2342
Co. E-mail: colbych@charter.net
Contact: Tod Smith, Pres.

66372 ■ Columbus Area Chamber of Commerce
PO Box 362
Columbus, WI 53925
Ph:(920)623-3699
Fax: (920)623-0171
Contact: Beverly Hartl, Pres.

66373 ■ Crandon Area Chamber of Commerce
PO Box 88
Crandon, WI 54520
Ph:(715)478-3450
Free: 800-334-3387
Fax: (715)478-4650
Co. E-mail: info@crandonwi.com
URL: http://www.crandonwi.com

66374 ■ Cuba City Chamber of Commerce
PO Box 706
Cuba City, WI 53807
Ph:(608)744-3456
Contact: Tim Gile, Pres.

66375 ■ Cumberland Chamber of Commerce
PO Box 665
Cumberland, WI 54829
Ph:(715)822-3378
Co. E-mail: bagafest@chibardun.net
URL: http://www.cumberland-wisconsin.com
Contact: Starr Avery, Exec.Sec.

66376 ■ Darlington Chamber of Commerce
439 Main St., Ste. B
Darlington, WI 53530
Ph:(608)776-3067
Free: 888-506-6553
Fax: (608)776-3067
Co. E-mail: dtonmain@mhtc.net
URL: http://www.darlingtonwi.org

66377 ■ De Forest Area Chamber of Commerce
201 De Forest St.
De Forest, WI 53532
Ph:(608)846-2922
Co. E-mail: info@deforestchamber.com
URL: http://www.deforestchamber.com
Contact: Rhonda Gilbertson, Exec.Dir.

66378 ■ Delafield Chamber of Commerce
PO Box 180171
Delafield, WI 53018
Ph:(262)646-8100
Free: 888-294-1082
Fax: (262)646-8237
Co. E-mail: info@delafieldchamber.org
URL: http://www.delafieldchamber.org
Contact: Debra Smith, Chamber Rep.

66379 ■ Delavan - Delavan Lake Area Chamber of Commerce
53 E Walworth Ave.
Delavan, WI 53115
Ph:(262)728-5095
Free: 800-624-0052
Fax: (262)728-9199
Co. E-mail: info@delavanwi.org
URL: http://www.delavanwi.org
Contact: Jackie Baar, Exec.Dir.

66380 ■ Denmark Community Business Association
PO Box 97
Denmark, WI 54208-0097
Ph:(920)863-6400
Fax: (920)863-3237
Co. E-mail: markl@denmarkstate.com
Contact: Mark Looker, VP

66381 ■ Dodgeville Area Chamber of Commerce
338 N Iowa
Dodgeville, WI 53533
Ph:(608)935-9200
Free: 877-863-6343
Fax: (608)930-5324
Co. E-mail: info@dodgeville.com
URL: http://www.dodgeville.com
Contact: Ron Dentinger, Exec.Dir.

66382 ■ Door County Chamber of Commerce
1015 Green Bay Rd.
PO Box 406
Sturgeon Bay, WI 54235-0406
Ph:(920)743-4456
Free: 800-52R-ELAX
Fax: (920)743-7873
Co. E-mail: info@doorcounty.com
URL: http://www.doorcountyvacations.com
Contact: Karen Raymore, CEO

66383 ■ East Troy Area Chamber of Commerce
PO Box 312
East Troy, WI 53120
Ph:(262)642-3770
Fax: (262)642-8769
Co. E-mail: info@easttroywi.org
URL: http://www.easttroywi.org
Contact: Linda Kaplan, Pres.

66384 ■ Eau Claire Area Chamber of Commerce
101 N Farwell St., Ste. 101
Eau Claire, WI 54702
Ph:(715)834-1204
Fax: (715)834-1956
Co. E-mail: information@eauclairechamber.org
URL: http://www.eauclairechamber.org
Contact: Robert S. McCoy, Pres.

66385 ■ Eau Claire Lakes Business Association of Barnes and Gordon
13702 S Crystal Beach Rd.
Gordon, WI 54838
Ph:(715)376-2322
Free: 800-299-7506
Co. E-mail: vacation@eauclairelakes.com
URL: http://www.eauclairelakes.com
Contact: Andrea Babcock, Sec.

66386 ■ Edgerton Area Chamber of Commerce
20 S Main St.
Edgerton, WI 53534
Ph:(608)884-4408
Free: 888-298-4408
Fax: (608)884-4408
Co. E-mail: info@edgertonwisconsin.com
URL: http://www.edgertonwisconsin.com
Contact: Diane Everson, Pres.

66387 ■ Elkhart Lake Area Chamber of Commerce
41 E Rhine St.
Elkhart Lake, WI 53020
Ph:(920)876-2922
Free: 877-ELK-HART
Co. E-mail: elcoc@bizwi.rr.com
URL: http://www.elkhartlake.com

66388 ■ Elkhorn Area Chamber of Commerce
114 W Court St.
PO Box 41
Elkhorn, WI 53121
Ph:(262)723-5788
Fax: (262)723-5784
Co. E-mail: elkchamber@elkhorn-wi.org
URL: http://www.elkhorn-wi.org
Contact: Diane Riese, Exec.Dir.

66389 ■ Ellsworth Chamber of Commerce
PO Box 927
Ellsworth, WI 54011
Ph:(715)273-6442
Co. E-mail: ellsworthchamber@sbcglobal.net
URL: http://www.ellsworthchamber.com
Contact: Joanne Hines, Pres.

66390 ■ Elroy Area Advancement Corporation
PO Box 52
Elroy, WI 53929
Ph:(608)462-5872
Co. E-mail: elroywi@mwt.net
URL: http://www.elroywi.com
Contact: Joan Sartori, Pres.

66391 ■ Evansville Chamber of Commerce
PO Box 51
Evansville, WI 53536
Ph:(608)882-5131
Co. E-mail: chamber-info@evansville-wi.com
URL: http://www.evansville-wi.com
Contact: Trish Graves, Admin. Asst.

66392 ■ Fennimore Area Chamber of Commerce
850 Lincoln Ave.
Fennimore, WI 53809
Ph:(608)822-3599
Fax: (608)822-6007
Co. E-mail: promo@fennimore.com
URL: http://fennimore.com
Contact: Linda Parrish, Promotions Coor.

66393 ■ Fond du Lac Area Association of Commerce
207 N Main St.
Fond du Lac, WI 54935
Ph:(920)921-9500
Fax: (920)921-9559
Co. E-mail: info@fdlac.com
URL: http://www.fdlac.com
Contact: Joe Reitemeier, Pres./CEO

66394 ■ Fort Atkinson Area Chamber of Commerce
244 N Main St.
Fort Atkinson, WI 53538
Ph:(920)563-3210
Free: 888-SEE-FORT
Fax: (920)563-8946
Co. E-mail: evp@fortchamber.com
URL: http://www.fortchamber.com
Contact: Dianne A. Hrobsky, Exec.VP

66395 ■ Forward Janesville
51 S Jackson St.
Janesville, WI 53548
Ph:(608)757-3160
Fax: (608)757-3170
Co. E-mail: forward@forwardjanesville.com
URL: http://www.forwardjanesville.com
Contact: Mr. John Beckord, Pres.

66396 ■ Fox Cities Chamber of Commerce and Industry
PO Box 1855
Appleton, WI 54912-1855
Ph:(920)734-7101
Fax: (920)734-7161
Co. E-mail: information@foxcitieschamber.com
URL: http://www.foxcitieschamber.com
Contact: William J. Welch, Pres./CEO

66397 ■ Fox Lake Area Chamber of Commerce
PO Box 94
Fox Lake, WI 53933-0094
Ph:(920)928-3777
Free: 800-858-4904
Fax: (920)928-2033
Co. E-mail: foxlake@powercom.net
URL: http://www.foxlake.com
Contact: Lorraine Mund, Administrator

66398 ■ Frederic Area Community Association
PO Box 250
Frederic, WI 54837-0250
Ph:(715)327-4836
Contact: Rebecca Harlander, Sec.-Treas.

66399 ■ Fremont Area Chamber of Commerce
PO Box 114
Fremont, WI 54940
Ph:(920)446-3838
Co. E-mail: uberfrau9@centurytel.net
URL: http://www.fremontwis.com
Contact: Debby Gramer, Pres.

66400 ■ Friesland Chamber of Commerce
PO Box 127
Friesland, WI 53935-0127
Ph:(920)348-5267
Contact: Don DeYoung, Pres.

66401 ■ Galesville Area Chamber of Commerce
PO Box 196
Galesville, WI 54630
Ph:(608)582-2868
Co. E-mail: info@galesvillewi.com
URL: http://www.galesvillewi.com
Contact: Einar Daffinson, Pres.

66402 ■ Geneva Lake Area Chamber of Commerce
201 Wrigley Dr.
Lake Geneva, WI 53147-2004
Ph:(262)248-4416

Free: 800-345-1020
Fax: (262)248-1000
Co. E-mail: lgcc@lakegenevawi.com
URL: http://www.lakegenevawi.com
Contact: George F. Hennerley, Exec.VP

66403 ■ German-American Chamber of Commerce of the Midwest - Wisconsin Chapter
PO Box 1099
Milwaukee, WI 53201
Ph:(262)695-3856
Contact: Dr. John Gatto

66404 ■ Germantown Area Chamber of Commerce
PO Box 12
Germantown, WI 53022
Ph:(262)255-1812
Fax: (262)255-9033
Co. E-mail: lgrgich@germantownchamber.org
URL: http://germantownchamber.org
Contact: Lynn Grgich, Admin.Asst.

66405 ■ Glendale Association of Commerce
5909 N Milwaukee River Pkwy.
Glendale, WI 53209-3815
Ph:(414)228-1716
Fax: (414)332-6182
URL: http://www.shopcpn.com/webpage/display.cfm?ID=42962
Contact: Bob Porsche, Pres.

66406 ■ Grafton Area Chamber of Commerce
1634 Wisconsin Ave.
PO Box 132
Grafton, WI 53024
Ph:(262)377-1650
Fax: (262)375-7087
Co. E-mail: info@grafton-wi.org
URL: http://grafton-wi.org
Contact: Nancy Hundt, Exec.Dir.

66407 ■ Grantsburg Chamber of Commerce
PO Box 451
Grantsburg, WI 54840
Ph:(715)463-2587
URL: http://www.grantsburgwi.com
Contact: Greg Peer, Pres.

66408 ■ Greater Beloit Chamber of Commerce
520 E Grand Ave.
Beloit, WI 53511
Ph:(608)365-8835
Fax: (608)365-9345
Co. E-mail: info@greaterbeloitchamber.com
URL: http://www.greaterbeloitchamber.com
Contact: Nancy Forbeck, Pres.

66409 ■ Greater Brookfield Chamber of Commerce
1305 N Barker Rd., Ste. 5
Brookfield, WI 53045
Ph:(262)786-1886
Fax: (262)786-1959
Co. E-mail: carol@brookfieldchamber.com
URL: http://www.brookfieldchamber.com
Contact: Carol White, Exec.Dir.

66410 ■ Greater Madison Chamber of Commerce
PO Box 71
615 E Washington Ave., 2nd Fl.
Madison, WI 53701-0071
Ph:(608)256-8348
Fax: (608)256-0333
Co. E-mail: info@greatermadisonchamber.com
URL: http://www.greatermadisonchamber.com
Contact: Mrs. Jennifer Alexander, Pres.

66411 ■ Greater Mauston Area Chamber of Commerce
PO Box 171
Mauston, WI 53948
Ph:(608)847-4142
Fax: (608)847-4142

Co. E-mail: chamber@mauston.com
URL: http://www.mauston.com
Contact: Stacy Havill, Office Administrator

66412 ■ Greater Menomonie Area Chamber of Commerce
342 E Main St.
Menomonie, WI 54751
Ph:(715)235-9087
Free: 800-283-1862
Fax: (715)235-2824
Co. E-mail: info@menomoniechamber.org
URL: http://www.menomoniechamber.org
Contact: Linda McIntyre, Exec.Dir.

66413 ■ Greater Princeton Area Chamber of Commerce
PO Box 45
Princeton, WI 54968
Ph:(920)295-3877
Fax: (920)295-4375
Co. E-mail: chamber@princetonwi.com
URL: http://www.princetonwi.com
Contact: Paul Metcalf, Pres.

66414 ■ Greater Tomah Area Chamber of Commerce
805 Superior Ave.
Tomah, WI 54660-0625
Ph:(608)372-2166
Free: 800-94-TOMAH
Fax: (608)372-2167
Co. E-mail: tchamber@mwt.net
URL: http://www.tomahwisconsin.com
Contact: Christopher Hanson, Exec.Dir.

66415 ■ Greater Union Grove Area Chamber of Commerce
PO Box 44
Union Grove, WI 53182-0044
Ph:(262)878-4606
Fax: (262)878-9125
Co. E-mail: ugchambr@wi.net
URL: http://www.uniongrovechamber.org
Contact: Carol Knight, Exec.Dir.

66416 ■ Green Bay Area Chamber of Commerce
400 S Washington St.
PO Box 1660
Green Bay, WI 54305-1660
Ph:(920)437-8704
Fax: (920)437-1024
Co. E-mail: info@titletown.org
URL: http://www.titletown.org
Contact: Paul Jadin, Pres.

66417 ■ Green Lake Area Chamber of Commerce
550 Mill St.
PO Box 337
Green Lake, WI 54941-0337
Ph:(920)294-3231
Free: 800-253-7354
Fax: (920)294-3415
Co. E-mail: info@visitgreenlake.com
URL: http://www.visitgreenlake.com
Contact: Dusty Walker, Exec. Dir.

66418 ■ Greendale Chamber of Commerce
PO Box 467
Greendale, WI 53129
Ph:(414)423-3900
Co. E-mail: info@greendalechamber.com
URL: http://www.greendalechamber.com
Contact: Lynn M. Magner, Pres.

66419 ■ Greenfield Chamber of Commerce
4818 S 76th St., Ste. 129
PO Box 20786
Greenfield, WI 53220
Ph:(414)327-8500
Co. E-mail: support@greenfieldchamber.org
URL: http://www.greenfieldchamber.org
Contact: Cindy M. Leranth, Pres.

66420 ■ Greenwood Chamber of Commerce
PO Box 86
Greenwood, WI 54437
Ph:(715)267-6205
Contact: Patricia Lindner, Pres.

66421 ■ Hartford Area Chamber of Commerce
225 N Main St.
Hartford, WI 53027
Ph:(262)673-7002
Free: (866)222-5401
Fax: (262)673-7057
Co. E-mail: info@hartfordchamber.org
URL: http://www.hartfordwi.net
Contact: Doreen Buntrock, Exec.Dir.

66422 ■ Hartland Area Chamber of Commerce
140 E Capitol Dr.
Hartland, WI 53029-2104
Ph:(262)367-7059
Fax: (262)367-2980
Co. E-mail: admin@hartland-wi.org
URL: http://www.hartland-wi.org
Contact: Ms. Lynn Minturn, Exec.Dir.

66423 ■ Hayward Area Chamber of Commerce
PO Box 726
Hayward, WI 54843
Ph:(715)634-8662
Free: 800-724-2992
Fax: (715)634-8498
Co. E-mail: info@haywardareachamber.com
URL: http://www.haywardareachamber.com
Contact: Kevin Ruetten, Exec.Dir.

66424 ■ Heart of the Valley Chamber of Commerce
101 E Wisconsin Ave.
Kaukauna, WI 54130-2153
Ph:(920)766-1616
Fax: (920)766-5504
Co. E-mail: bbeckman@heartofthevalleychamber.
    com
URL: http://www.heartofthevalleychamber.com
Contact: Bobbie Beckman, Exec.Dir.

66425 ■ Horicon Chamber of Commerce
PO Box 23
Horicon, WI 53032-0023
Ph:(920)485-3200
Co. E-mail: writeus@horiconchamber.com
URL: http://www.horiconchamber.com

66426 ■ Hudson Area Chamber of Commerce and Tourism Bureau
502 Second St.
Hudson, WI 54016
Ph:(715)386-8411
Free: 800-657-6775
Fax: (715)386-8432
Co. E-mail: info@hudsonwi.org
URL: http://www.hudsonwi.org
Contact: Kim Heinemann, Pres.

66427 ■ Hurley Area Chamber of Commerce
316 Silver St.
Hurley, WI 54534
Ph:(715)561-4334
Free: (866)340-4334
Fax: (715)561-3742
Co. E-mail: hurley@hurleywi.com
URL: http://www.hurleywi.com
Contact: Tina Paruolo, Exec.Dir.

66428 ■ Iola - Scandinavia Area Chamber of Commerce
PO Box 167
Iola, WI 54945
Ph:(715)445-4000
Co. E-mail: mike@iolaoldcarshow.com
URL: http://www.ischamber.org
Contact: Terry Murphy, Pres.

66429 ■ Jefferson Chamber of Commerce
122 W Garland St.
Jefferson, WI 53549-1717
Ph:(920)674-4511
Fax: (920)674-1499
Co. E-mail: coc@jefnet.com
URL: http://www.jeffersonchamberwi.com
Contact: Janet Werner, Exec. Dir.

66430 ■ Johnson Creek Area Chamber of Commerce
PO Box 527
Johnson Creek, WI 53038-0527
Ph:(920)699-4949
Co. E-mail: joellen@johnsoncreekchamber.com
URL: http://www.johnsoncreekchamber.com
Contact: Jim Luedtke, Pres.

66431 ■ Juneau Chamber of Commerce
PO Box 4
Juneau, WI 53039
Ph:(920)386-3359
Co. E-mail: juneau@juneauwi.org
URL: http://www.juneauwi.org
Contact: Gretchen Last, Pres.

66432 ■ Kenosha Area Chamber of Commerce
PO Box 518
715 56th St.
Kenosha, WI 53140
Ph:(262)654-1234
Fax: (262)654-4655
Co. E-mail: info@kenoshaareachamber.com
URL: http://www.kenoshaareachamber.com
Contact: Cory Ann St. Marie-Carls, Exec. Dir.

66433 ■ Kewaunee Area Chamber of Commerce
PO Box 243
Kewaunee, WI 54216
Ph:(920)388-4822
Free: 800-666-8214
Fax: (920)388-4901
Co. E-mail: kewchamber@itol.com
URL: http://www.kewaunee.org
Contact: April Dahl, Pres.

66434 ■ Kiel Area Association of Commerce
PO Box 44
Kiel, WI 53042-0044
Ph:(920)894-4638
Co. E-mail: secretary@kielwi.org
URL: http://www.kielwi.org
Contact: Linda Bauman, Sec.

66435 ■ La Crosse Area Chamber of Commerce
712 Main St.
La Crosse, WI 54601
Ph:(608)784-4880
Fax: (608)784-4919
Co. E-mail: lse_chamber@centurytel.net
URL: http://www.lacrossechamber.com
Contact: Dick Granchalek, Pres.

66436 ■ Lac Du Flambeau Chamber of Commerce
602 Peace Pipe Rd.
Lac Du Flambeau, WI 54538
Ph:(715)588-3346
Free: 877-588-3346
Fax: (715)588-9408
Co. E-mail: info@lacduflambeauchamber.com
Contact: Randy Soulier, Pres.

66437 ■ Lake Mills Area Chamber of Commerce
200C Water St.
Lake Mills, WI 53551
Ph:(920)648-3585
Fax: (920)648-6751
Co. E-mail: chamber@lakemills.org
URL: http://www.lakemills.org
Contact: Teri Nelson, Pres.

66438 ■ Lake Wisconsin Chamber of Commerce
PO Box 441
Poynette, WI 53955
Ph:(608)635-8070
Co. E-mail: info@lakewisconsin.org
URL: http://www.lakewisconsin.org
Contact: Denise Miller, Sec.

66439 ■ Lakewood Area Chamber of Commerce
PO Box 87
Lakewood, WI 54138
Ph:(715)276-6500
Fax: (715)276-6458
Co. E-mail: lkwd@ez-net.com
URL: http://www.lakewoodareachamber.com
Contact: Ruth Benoit, Exec. Sec.

66440 ■ Lancaster Area Chamber of Commerce
206 S Madison St.
PO Box 292
Lancaster, WI 53813
Ph:(608)723-2820
Fax: (608)723-7409
Co. E-mail: lanchamber@pcii.net
URL: http://www.lancasterwisconsin.com
Contact: Marge Sherwin, Exec.Dir.

66441 ■ Land O'Lakes Chamber of Commerce
PO Box 599
Land O' Lakes, WI 54540
Ph:(715)547-3432
Free: 800-236-3432
Fax: (715)547-8010
Co. E-mail: lolinfo@nnex.net
Contact: Sandy Wait, Exec.Sec.

66442 ■ Lena Community Development Corp.
PO Box 59
Lena, WI 54139
Ph:(920)829-5525
Fax: (920)829-5154
Co. E-mail: maplevalleyinf@ez-net.com
Contact: A. H. Schuettpelz, Treas.

66443 ■ Lodi Chamber of Commerce
PO Box 43
Lodi, WI 53555
Ph:(608)592-4412
Fax: (608)712-4414
Co. E-mail: lodichamber@lodicommerce.com
Contact: Sally Pierick, Exec.Sec.

66444 ■ Lomira Area Chamber of Commerce
PO Box 386
Lomira, WI 53048
Ph:(920)269-7229
Co. E-mail: warehousewebs@charter.net
URL: http://www.lomira.com/Servgrop/COC/Index-
    COC.htm
Contact: Jim Bisek, Pres.

66445 ■ Luxemburg Chamber of Commerce
PO Box 141
Luxemburg, WI 54217-0307
Ph:(920)845-2722
Fax: (920)845-2902
Co. E-mail: info@luxemburgusa.com
URL: http://www.luxemburgusa.com
Contact: Bernadine Mathu, Sec.

66446 ■ Madeline Island Chamber of Commerce
PO Box 274
La Pointe, WI 54850
Ph:(715)747-2801
Free: 888-475-3386
Co. E-mail: info@madelineisland.com
URL: http://www.madelineisland.com

66447 ■ Manawa Area Chamber of Commerce
PO Box 221
Manawa, WI 54949

Ph:(920)596-2495
Co. E-mail: manawa@wolfnet.net
URL: http://www.manawachamber.com/
Contact: Lola Bonikowske, Sec.

66448 ■ Manitowish Waters Chamber of Commerce
PO Box 251 4
S US Hwy. 51
Manitowish Waters, WI 54545
Ph:(715)543-8488
Free: 888-626-9877
Fax: (715)543-2519
Co. E-mail: funinfo@manitowishwaters.org
URL: http://www.manitowishwaters.org
Contact: Jodi McMahon, Dir.

66449 ■ Manitowoc/Two Rivers Area Chamber of Commerce
1515 Memorial Dr.
PO Box 903
Manitowoc, WI 54221-0903
Ph:(920)684-5575
Free: 800-262-7892
Fax: (920)684-1915
Co. E-mail: chamber@lakefield.net
URL: http://www.manitowocchamber.com
Contact: Betsy Alles, Exec.Dir.

66450 ■ Marinette Area Chamber of Commerce
601 Marinette Ave.
Marinette, WI 54143
Ph:(715)735-6681
Free: 800-236-6681
Fax: (715)735-6682
Co. E-mail: chamber@centurytel.net
URL: http://www.marinettechamber.com
Contact: Gary A. Nadolny, Exec.Dir./CEO

66451 ■ Marshfield Area Chamber of Commerce and Industry
700 S Central Ave.
PO Box 868
Marshfield, WI 54449
Ph:(715)384-3454
Fax: (715)387-8925
Co. E-mail: info@marshfieldchamber.com
URL: http://www.marshfieldchamber.com
Contact: Barbara Fleisner, Exec.Dir.

66452 ■ Mayville Area Chamber of Commerce
12 S Main St.
PO Box 185
Mayville, WI 53050-0185
Ph:(920)387-5776
Free: 800-256-7670
Co. E-mail: info@mayvillechamber.com
URL: http://www.mayvillechamber.com
Contact: Linda Turk, Chamber Staff

66453 ■ Mazomanie Chamber of Commerce
PO Box 321
Mazomanie, WI 53560
Ph:(608)795-9838
Fax: (608)795-2102
URL: http://www.villageofmazomanie.com
Contact: Dan Viste, Pres.

66454 ■ McFarland Chamber of Commerce
5124 Farwell St.
PO Box 372
McFarland, WI 53558
Ph:(608)838-4011
Fax: (608)838-4011
Co. E-mail: m.mcfarlandchamber@verizon.net
URL: http://www.mcfarlandchamber.com

66455 ■ Medford Area Chamber of Commerce
104 E Perkins St.
PO Box 172
Medford, WI 54451
Ph:(715)748-4729
Free: 888-682-9567
Fax: (715)748-6899

Co. E-mail: chamber@dwave.net
URL: http://www.medfordwis.com
Contact: Susan Emmerich, Exec.Dir.

66456 ■ Mellen Area Chamber of Commerce
PO Box 193
Mellen, WI 54546
Ph:(715)274-2330
Co. E-mail: mellen001@centurytel.net
URL: http://www.mellenwi.org
Contact: Jerry Parker

66457 ■ Menomonee Falls Chamber of Commerce
N88 W16621 Appleton Ave.
PO Box 73
Menomonee Falls, WI 53052-0073
Ph:(262)251-2430
Free: 800-801-6565
Fax: (262)251-0969
Co. E-mail: jan@fallschamber.com
URL: http://www.menomoneefallschamber.com
Contact: Jenny Polachowski, Exec.Dir.

66458 ■ Mequon-Thiensville Area Chamber of Commerce
250 S Main St.
Thiensville, WI 53092
Ph:(262)512-9358
Fax: (262)512-9359
Co. E-mail: info@mtchamber.org
URL: http://www.mtchamber.org
Contact: Linda Oakes, Exec.Dir.

66459 ■ Mercer Area Chamber of Commerce
5150 N Hwy. 51
Mercer, WI 54547
Ph:(715)476-2389
Fax: (715)476-2389
Co. E-mail: info@mercercc.com
URL: http://www.mercercc.com
Contact: Tina Brunell, Office Mgr.

66460 ■ Merrill Area Chamber of Commerce
120 S Mill St.
Merrill, WI 54452
Ph:(715)536-9474
Free: 877-90P-ARKS
Fax: (715)539-2043
Co. E-mail: info@merrillchamber.com
URL: http://www.merrillchamber.com
Contact: Jane Ann Savaske, Exec.Dir.

66461 ■ Metropolitan Milwaukee Association of Commerce
756 N Milwaukee St., Ste. 400
Milwaukee, WI 53202
Ph:(414)287-4100
Fax: (414)271-7753
Co. E-mail: info@mmac.org
URL: http://www.mmac.org
Contact: Timothy Sheehy, Pres.

66462 ■ Middleton Chamber of Commerce
7507 Hubbard Ave.
Middleton, WI 53562
Ph:(608)827-5797
Fax: (608)831-7765
Co. E-mail: chamber@middletonchamber.com
URL: http://www.middletonchamber.com
Contact: Mr. Van Nutt, Exec.Dir.

66463 ■ Milton Area Chamber of Commerce
508 Campus St.
PO Box 222
Milton, WI 53563
Ph:(608)868-6222
Co. E-mail: macc2@charter.net
URL: http://www.miltonareachamber.com
Contact: Mary J. Roehl, Exec.Dir.

66464 ■ Milwaukee Minority Chamber of Commerce
PO Box 1662
Milwaukee, WI 53201-1662
Ph:(414)226-4105
Fax: (414)277-4152

Contact: J. Paul Jordan, Pres.

66465 ■ Mineral Point Chamber of Commerce
225 High St.
Mineral Point, WI 53565
Ph:(608)987-3201
Free: 888-POI-NTWI
Fax: (608)987-4425
Co. E-mail: info@mineralpoint.com
URL: http://www.mineralpoint.com
Contact: Joy Gieseke, Dir.

66466 ■ Minocqua - Arbor Vitae - Woodruff Chamber of Commerce
PO Box 1006
Minocqua, WI 54548
Ph:(715)356-5266
Free: 800-446-6784
Fax: (715)358-2446
Co. E-mail: mavwacc@minocqua.org
URL: http://www.minocqua.org
Contact: Cambria Mares, Exec.Dir.

66467 ■ Mishicot Area Growth and Improvement Committee
PO Box 237
Mishicot, WI 54228
Ph:(920)755-3411
Fax: (920)755-2525
Co. E-mail: mishicot@milwpc.com
URL: http://mishicot.org
Contact: Kathy Lindsey, Mgr.

66468 ■ Monona Chamber of Commerce
6320 Monona Dr.
Monona, WI 53716-3952
Ph:(608)222-8565
Fax: (608)222-8596
Co. E-mail: chamber@monona.com
URL: http://monona.com
Contact: Terri Groves, Exec. Dir.

66469 ■ Monroe Chamber of Commerce and Industry
1505 9th St.
Monroe, WI 53566
Ph:(608)325-7648
Fax: (608)325-7710
Co. E-mail: contactus@monroechamber.org
URL: http://www.monroechamber.org
Contact: Matthew Urban, Exec.Dir.

66470 ■ Montello Area Chamber of Commerce
PO Box 325
Montello, WI 53949
Ph:(608)297-7420
Free: 800-684-7199
Co. E-mail: montellochamber@hotmail.com
URL: http://www.montellowi.com
Contact: Susanne Kufahl, Exec.Sec.

66471 ■ Mosinee Area Chamber of Commerce
301 Main St., Ste. 102
Mosinee, WI 54455
Ph:(715)693-4330
Fax: (715)693-9555
Co. E-mail: macoc@mtc.net
URL: http://www.mosineechamber.org
Contact: Michelle Ringhoffer, Exec. Dir.

66472 ■ Mount Horeb Area Chamber of Commerce
100 S 1st St.
PO Box 84
Mount Horeb, WI 53572
Ph:(608)437-5914
Free: 888-765-5929
Fax: (608)437-1427
Co. E-mail: info@trollway.com
URL: http://www.trollway.com
Contact: Melissa Theisen, Exec.Dir.

66473 ■ Mukwonago Area Chamber of Commerce and Tourism Center
121 Wolf Run, Ste. 4
Mukwonago, WI 53149
Ph:(262)363-7758
Fax: (262)363-7357
Co. E-mail: director@mukwonagochamber.org
URL: http://www.mukwonagochamber.org
Contact: Barbara Cowsert, Exec. Dir.

66474 ■ Muskego Area Chamber of Commerce
W182 S8200 Racine Ave.
Muskego, WI 53150
Ph:(262)679-2550
Fax: (262)679-5592
Co. E-mail: info@muskego.org
URL: http://www.muskego.org
Contact: Kathy Chiaverotti, Exec.Dir.

66475 ■ Nebagamon Community Association
11507 E Waterfront Dr.
Lake Nebagamon, WI 54849
Ph:(715)374-2283
Fax: (715)374-3766
Co. E-mail: nca@pressenter.com
URL: http://www.lakenebagamonwi.com
Contact: Catherine Coletta, Prog. Chair

66476 ■ Neillsville Area Chamber of Commerce
PO Box 52
Neillsville, WI 54456-0052
Ph:(715)743-6444
Fax: (715)743-8262
Co. E-mail: nacc@tds.net
URL: http://www.neillsville.org
Contact: Cindy Schwanz

66477 ■ New Berlin Chamber of Commerce and Visitors Bureau
2140 S Calhoun Rd.
New Berlin, WI 53151
Ph:(262)786-5280
Fax: (262)786-9165
Co. E-mail: nbcadmin@nb-chamber.org
URL: http://www.nb-chamber.org
Contact: Jeff Seidl, Pres.

66478 ■ New Glarus Chamber of Commerce
418 Railroad St.
PO Box 713
New Glarus, WI 53574-0713
Ph:(608)527-2095
Free: 800-527-6838
Fax: (608)527-4991
Co. E-mail: info@swisstown.com
URL: http://www.swisstown.com
Contact: Susie Weiss, Office Mgr.

66479 ■ New Holstein Area Chamber of Commerce
PO Box 17
New Holstein, WI 53061
Ph:(920)898-9095
Co. E-mail: nhsecretary@newholstein.org
URL: http://www.newholstein.org
Contact: Samantha Ploor, Sec.

66480 ■ New Lisbon Area Chamber of Commerce
PO Box 79
New Lisbon, WI 53950
Ph:(608)562-3555
Fax: (608)562-5625
Co. E-mail: nlchambr@mwt.net
URL: http://www.homestead.com/newlisbonchamber
Contact: Tina Brounacker, Exec.Sec.

66481 ■ New London Area Chamber of Commerce
301 E Beacon Ave.
New London, WI 54961
Ph:(920)982-5822
Fax: (920)982-6344
Co. E-mail: chamber@newlondonwi.org
URL: http://www.newlondonchamber.com

Contact: Deborah Lederhaus, Exec.Dir.

66482 ■ New Richmond Area Chamber of Commerce and Visitors Bureau
235 S Knowles Ave.
New Richmond, WI 54017
Ph:(715)246-2900
Free: 800-654-6380
Fax: (715)246-7100
Co. E-mail: info@newrichmondchamber.com
URL: http://www.newrichmondchamber.com
Contact: Russ Korpela, Exec.Dir.

66483 ■ Oconomowoc Area Chamber of Commerce
152 E Wisconsin Ave.
Oconomowoc, WI 53066
Ph:(262)567-2666
Fax: (262)567-3477
Co. E-mail: chamber@oconomowoc.org
URL: http://www.oconomowoc.org
Contact: Stephanie Phillips, Exec.Dir.

66484 ■ Oconto Area Chamber of Commerce
PO Box 174
110 Brazeau Ave.
Oconto, WI 54153
Ph:(920)834-6254
Fax: (920)834-6254
Co. E-mail: ocontocmbr@aol.com
Contact: Nancy Rhode, Sec.

66485 ■ Oconto Falls Area Chamber of Commerce
PO Box 24
Oconto Falls, WI 54154
Ph:(920)846-8306
URL: http://www.ocontofallschamber.com
Contact: Pam Langlay, Pres.

66486 ■ Omro Area Chamber of Commerce
PO Box 91
Omro, WI 54963
Ph:(920)685-6960
Fax: (920)685-6942
Co. E-mail: omrochamber@charterinternet.net
URL: http://www.omro-wi.com
Contact: Ms. Jamie Kiesling, Dir.

66487 ■ Osceola Area Chamber of Commerce
310 Chieftain St.
Osceola, WI 54020
Ph:(715)755-3300
Co. E-mail: chamber@vil.osceola.wi.us
URL: http://www.osceolachamber.org
Contact: Aaron Mork, Pres.

66488 ■ Oshkosh Chamber of Commerce
120 Jackson St.
Oshkosh, WI 54901
Ph:(920)303-2266
Fax: (920)303-2263
Co. E-mail: john@oshkoshchamber.com
URL: http://www.oshkoshchamber.com
Contact: John A. Casper, Pres./CEO

66489 ■ Palmyra Area Chamber of Commerce
PO Box 139
Palmyra, WI 53156-0139
Ph:(262)495-2611
Fax: (262)495-8775
Co. E-mail: cleanmats@hotmail.com
URL: http://www.palmyrawi.com
Contact: Rick Ball, Acting Pres.

66490 ■ Pardeeville Area Business Association
PO Box 337
Pardeeville, WI 53954
Ph:(608)429-3121
Contact: Sue Schlapman, Sec.

66491 ■ Park Falls Area Chamber of Commerce
400 4th Ave. S
Park Falls, WI 54552

Ph:(715)762-2703
Free: 800-762-2709
Co. E-mail: chamber@parkfalls.com
URL: http://www.parkfalls.com
Contact: Jane Bentz, Exec.Dir.

66492 ■ Pelican Lake Chamber of Commerce
PO Box 45
Pelican Lake, WI 54463
Ph:(715)487-5222
Co. E-mail: pelicanlakecc@frontiernet.net
URL: http://www.pelicanlakewi.org
Contact: Susan Welch, Sec.

66493 ■ Pewaukee Chamber of Commerce
214 Oakton Ave.
Pewaukee, WI 53072-3430
Ph:(262)691-8851
Fax: (262)691-0922
Co. E-mail: info@pewaukeechamber.org
URL: http://www.pewaukeechamber.org
Contact: Amy Kommer, Exec. Dir.

66494 ■ Phelps Chamber of Commerce
PO Box 217
Phelps, WI 54554
Ph:(715)545-3800
Free: 877-669-7077
Co. E-mail: pcoc@nnex.net
URL: http://www.phelpswi.org
Contact: Debbie Vold, Pres.

66495 ■ Phillips Area Chamber of Commerce
305 S Lake Ave.
Phillips, WI 54555
Ph:(715)339-4100
Free: 888-408-4800
Fax: (715)339-4190
Co. E-mail: pacc@pctcnet.net
Contact: Angela Hahn, Exec.Dir.

66496 ■ Platteville Chamber of Commerce
PO Box 16
Platteville, WI 53818
Ph:(608)348-8888
Fax: (608)348-8890
Co. E-mail: chamber@platteville.com
URL: http://www.platteville.com
Contact: Kathy Kopp, Exec.Dir.

66497 ■ Plymouth Chamber of Commerce
PO Box 584
Plymouth, WI 53073
Ph:(920)893-0079
Free: 888-693-8263
Fax: (920)893-8473
Co. E-mail: plymouthchamber@excel.net
URL: http://www.plymouthwisconsin.com
Contact: Lisa Hurley, Exec.Dir.

66498 ■ Port Washington Chamber of Commerce
PO Box 514
126 E Grand Ave.
Port Washington, WI 53074-0514
Ph:(262)284-0900
Free: 800-719-4881
Fax: (262)284-0591
Co. E-mail: mary@portwashingtonchamber.com
URL: http://www.portwashingtonchamber.com
Contact: Mary Monday, Exec.Dir.

66499 ■ Portage Area Chamber of Commerce
132 W Cook St.
Portage, WI 53901
Ph:(608)742-6242
Free: 800-474-2525
Fax: (608)742-3799
Co. E-mail: pacc@portagewi.com
URL: http://www.portagewi.com
Contact: Marian Hanson, Exec. Dir.

66500 ■ Portage County Business Council
5501 Vern Holmes Dr.
Stevens Point, WI 54481
Ph:(715)344-1940
Fax: (715)344-4473

Co. E-mail: info@portagecountybiz.com
URL: http://www.portagecountybiz.com
Contact: Jeff Landin, Exec.Dir.

66501 ■ Potosi - Tennyson Area Chamber of Commerce
PO Box 11
Potosi, WI 53820
Ph:(608)763-2261
Fax: (608)763-2537
URL: http://www.potosiwisconsin.com
Contact: Marilyn Hauth, Pres.

66502 ■ Poynette Chamber of Commerce
PO Box 625
Poynette, WI 53955
Ph:(608)635-2425
Co. E-mail: humblehost@tds.net
URL: http://www.poynettechamber.com/index.html
Contact: Garry Gill, Pres.

66503 ■ Prairie Du Chien Area Chamber of Commerce
211 S Main
PO Box 326
Prairie Du Chien, WI 53821
Ph:(608)326-8555
Free: 800-732-1673
Fax: (608)326-7744
Co. E-mail: info@prairieduchien.org
URL: http://www.prairieduchien.org
Contact: Sharon Dearborn, Exec.Dir.

66504 ■ Prescott Area Chamber of Commerce
237 Broad St.
Prescott, WI 54021
Ph:(715)262-3284
Fax: (715)262-5943
Co. E-mail: info@prescottwi.com
URL: http://www.prescottwi.com
Contact: Trisha Huber, Coor.

66505 ■ Presque Isle Chamber of Commerce
PO Box 135
Presque Isle, WI 54557
Ph:(715)686-2910
Free: 888-835-6508
Fax: (715)686-2913
Co. E-mail: info@presqueislewi.org
URL: http://www.presqueislewi.org
Contact: George Nelson, Dir.

66506 ■ Pulaski Area Chamber of Commerce
159 W Pulaski St.
PO Box 401
Pulaski, WI 54162-0401
Ph:(920)822-4400
Fax: (920)822-4455
Co. E-mail: pacc@netnet.net
URL: http://www.pulaskichamber.org
Contact: Mr. Doug Prentice, Chamber Board Pres.

66507 ■ Racine Area Manufacturers and Commerce
300 5th St.
Racine, WI 53403
Ph:(262)634-1931
Fax: (262)634-7422
Co. E-mail: ramac@racinechamber.com
URL: http://www.racinechamber.com
Contact: Roger Caron, Pres.

66508 ■ Randolph Chamber of Commerce
349 Stark St.
Randolph, WI 53956
Ph:(920)326-4769
Fax: (920)326-4129
Co. E-mail: ken.hillman@centurytel.com
URL: http://www.randolphwi.net
Contact: Harold De Vries, Sec.-Treas.

66509 ■ Reedsburg Area Chamber of Commerce
PO Box 142
Reedsburg, WI 53959
Ph:(608)524-2850

Free: 800-844-3507
Fax: (608)524-5392
Co. E-mail: webmaster@reedsburg.org
URL: http://www.reedsburg.org/
Contact: Jan Wirth, Exec.Dir.

66510 ■ Rhinelander Area Chamber of Commerce
PO Box 795
Rhinelander, WI 54501
Ph:(715)365-7464
Free: 800-236-4386
Fax: (715)365-7467
Co. E-mail: info@rhinelanderchamber.com
URL: http://www.rhinelanderchamber.com
Contact: Crystal Lake Johnson, Exec. Dir.

66511 ■ Rice Lake Area Chamber of Commerce
37 S Main St.
Rice Lake, WI 54868-2299
Ph:(715)234-2126
Free: 800-523-6318
Fax: (715)234-2085
Co. E-mail: chamber@rice-lake.com
URL: http://www.rice-lake.com
Contact: Roger Rivard, Pres.

66512 ■ Richland Area Chamber of Commerce/Main Street Partnership
397 W Seminary St.
PO Box 128
Richland Center, WI 53581-0128
Ph:(608)647-6205
Free: 800-422-1318
Fax: (608)647-5449
Co. E-mail: info@richlandchamber.com
URL: http://www.richlandchamber.com
Contact: Susan Price, Dir.

66513 ■ Ripon Area Chamber of Commerce
127 Jefferson St.
PO Box 305
Ripon, WI 54971-0305
Ph:(920)748-6764
Fax: (920)748-6784
Co. E-mail: chamber@ripon-wi.com
URL: http://www.ripon-wi.com
Contact: Paula Price, Exec. Dir.

66514 ■ River Falls Area Chamber of Commerce and Tourism Bureau
214 N Main St.
River Falls, WI 54022
Ph:(715)425-2533
Fax: (715)425-2305
Co. E-mail: info@rfchamber.com
URL: http://www.rfchamber.com
Contact: Rossane Bump, CEO

66515 ■ St. Croix Falls Chamber of Commerce
106 S Washington St.
St. Croix Falls, WI 54024
Ph:(715)483-3580
Fax: (715)483-0022
Co. E-mail: ann@scfwi.com
URL: http://www.scfwi.com
Contact: Ann Perszyk, Exec.Dir.

66516 ■ St. Germain Chamber of Commerce
PO Box 155
St. Germain, WI 54558-0155
Ph:(715)477-2205
Free: 800-727-7203
Fax: (715)542-3423
Co. E-mail: info@st-germain.com
Contact: Jim Anderson, Pres.

66517 ■ Sauk Prairie Area Chamber of Commerce
421 Water St., Ste. 105
Prairie Du Sac, WI 53578
Ph:(608)643-4168
Free: 800-68-EAGLE
Fax: (608)643-3544
Co. E-mail: saukprairie@verizon.net

URL: http://www.saukprairie.com
Contact: Leslie McFarlane, Exec. Dir.

66518 ■ Saukville Chamber of Commerce
PO Box 80238
Saukville, WI 53080
Ph:(262)268-1970
Co. E-mail: saukvillechamber@earthlink.net
URL: http://www.village.saukville.wi.us
Contact: Stacey Frey, Exec. Dir.

66519 ■ Sayner-Starlake Chamber of Commerce
PO Box 191
Sayner, WI 54560
Ph:(715)542-3789
Free: 888-722-3789
Fax: (715)542-4363
Co. E-mail: bonbehling@nnex.net
URL: http://www.sayner-starlake.org
Contact: Marcia Kittleson, Pres.

66520 ■ Shawano Area Chamber of Commerce
PO Box 38
Shawano, WI 54166-0038
Ph:(715)524-2139
Free: 800-235-8528
Fax: (715)524-3127
Co. E-mail: nsmith@shawano.com
URL: http://www.shawanocountry.com
Contact: Nancy J. Smith, Exec. Dir.

66521 ■ Sheboygan County Chamber of Commerce and Convention and Visitors Bureau
712 Riverfront Dr., Ste. 101
Sheboygan, WI 53081
Ph:(920)457-9491
Free: 800-457-9497
Fax: (920)457-6269
Co. E-mail: chamber@sheboygan.org
URL: http://www.sheboygan.org
Contact: Delores Olsen, Exce.Dir.

66522 ■ Sheboygan Falls Chamber Main Street
504 Broadway
Sheboygan Falls, WI 53085
Ph:(920)467-6206
Fax: (920)467-9571
Co. E-mail: chambermnst@sheboyganfalls.org
URL: http://www.sheboyganfalls.org
Contact: Nancy L. Verstrate, Exec. Dir.

66523 ■ Shell Lake Chamber of Commerce
PO Box 121
Shell Lake, WI 54871
Ph:(715)468-4340
Co. E-mail: shelllake_chamberofcommerce@yahoo.com
URL: http://www.shelllakeonline.com/contacts.htm
Contact: Louis Steele, Pres.

66524 ■ Somerset Area Chamber of Commerce
PO Box 357
Somerset, WI 54025-0357
Ph:(715)247-3366
Fax: (715)247-2408
Co. E-mail: schamber@somtel.net

66525 ■ South Eastern Chamber United in Business
8580 S Howell Ave.
Oak Creek, WI 53154
Ph:(414)768-5845
Fax: (414)570-0461
Co. E-mail: jenny@secub.com
Contact: Jenny Polachowski, Exec.Dir.

66526 ■ Sparta Area Chamber of Commerce
111 Milwaukee Ave.
Sparta, WI 54656
Ph:(608)269-4123
Fax: (608)269-3350
Co. E-mail: spartachamber@centurytel.net

URL: http://www.spartachamber.org
Contact: Todd Hammond, Pres.

66527 ■ Spencer Area Chamber of Commerce
105 Park St.
Spencer, WI 54479
Ph:(715)659-4133
Contact: Mike Endreas, Pres.

66528 ■ Spooner Area Chamber of Commerce
122 N River St.
Spooner, WI 54801
Ph:(715)635-2168
Free: 800-367-3306
Fax: (715)635-5170
Co. E-mail: chamber@spooneronline.com
URL: http://chamber.spooneronline.com
Contact: Brooke Fairbanks, Pres.

66529 ■ Spring Green Area Chamber of Commerce
PO Box 3
Spring Green, WI 53588
Ph:(608)588-2054
Free: 800-588-2042
Fax: (608)588-2054
Co. E-mail: info@springgreen.com
URL: http://www.springgreen.com
Contact: Jon Wiebe, VP

66530 ■ Stoughton Chamber of Commerce
532 E Main St.
Stoughton, WI 53589
Ph:(608)873-7912
Free: 888-873-7912
Fax: (608)873-7743
Co. E-mail: info@stoughtonwi.com
URL: http://www.stoughtonwi.com
Contact: Mickey McCormick, Asst.

66531 ■ Stratford Area Chamber of Commerce
PO Box 312
Stratford, WI 54484-0312
Ph:(715)687-4466
Contact: Jill Mielke, Sec.

66532 ■ Superior - Douglas County Chamber of Commerce
205 Belknap St.
Superior, WI 54880
Ph:(715)394-7716
Free: 800-942-5313
Fax: (715)394-3810
Co. E-mail: dm@superiorchamber.org
URL: http://www.superiorchamber.org
Contact: David W. Minor, Pres./CEO

66533 ■ Sussex Area Chamber of Commerce
N64 W24050 Main St., Ste. 201
PO Box 24
Sussex, WI 53089-0024
Ph:(262)246-4940
Fax: (262)246-7350
Co. E-mail: info@sussexareachamber.org
URL: http://www.sussexareachamber.org
Contact: Denise Schwid, Admin.

66534 ■ Tomahawk Regional Chamber of Commerce
PO Box 412
Tomahawk, WI 54487-0412
Ph:(715)453-5334
Free: 800-569-2160
Fax: (715)453-1178
Co. E-mail: chambert@gototomahawk.com
URL: http://www.gototomahawk.com
Contact: Christine S. Brown, Exec.VP

66535 ■ Verona Area Chamber of Commerce
205 S Main St.
PO Box 930003
Verona, WI 53593-0003
Ph:(608)845-5777
Fax: (608)845-2519

Co. E-mail: info@veronawi.com
URL: http://veronawi.com
Contact: David Phillips, Exec.Dir.

66536 ■ Vilas County Chamber of Commerce
330 Court St.
Eagle River, WI 54521
Ph:(715)479-3649
Fax: (715)479-1978
Contact: Cindy Burzinski, Sec.

66537 ■ Washburn Area Chamber of Commerce
PO Box 74
Washburn, WI 54891-0074
Ph:(715)373-5017
Free: 800-253-4495
Fax: (715)373-0240
Co. E-mail: washburn@cheqnet.net
URL: http://www.washburnchamber.com
Contact: Bruce M. Hanson, Exec. Dir.

66538 ■ Washington Island Chamber of Commerce
Rte. 1, Box 222
Washington Island, WI 54246-9768
Ph:(920)847-2179
Co. E-mail: info@washingtonislandwi.org
URL: http://www.washingtonislandchamber.com
Contact: Marianna Gibson, Sec.-Treas.

66539 ■ Waterford Area Chamber of Commerce
102 E Main St.
Waterford, WI 53185
Ph:(262)534-5911
Fax: (262)534-6507
Co. E-mail: chamber@waterford-wi.org
URL: http://www.waterford-wi.org
Contact: Raegan Dexter, Exec.Dir.

66540 ■ Waterloo Chamber of Commerce
PO Box 1
Waterloo, WI 53594
Ph:(920)478-2500
Co. E-mail: wchamber@hurleycomputers.com
URL: http://www.waterloowis.com
Contact: Kristen Klein, Sec.

66541 ■ Watertown Area Chamber of Commerce
519 E Main St.
Watertown, WI 53094
Ph:(920)261-6320
Fax: (920)261-6434
Co. E-mail: watncofc@powercom.net
URL: http://www.watertownchamber.com
Contact: Randy Roeseler, Exec.Dir.

66542 ■ Waukesha County Chamber of Commerce
223 Wisconsin Ave.
Waukesha, WI 53186
Ph:(262)542-4249
Fax: (262)542-8068
Co. E-mail: pwallner@waukesha.org
URL: http://www.waukesha.org
Contact: Patti Wallner, Pres.

66543 ■ Waunakee/Westport Chamber of Commerce
100 E Main St.
PO Box 41
Waunakee, WI 53597
Ph:(608)849-5977
Fax: (608)849-9825
Co. E-mail: wchamber@tds.net
URL: http://www.waunakee.com
Contact: Lisa Pertzborn-Whiting, Exec. Dir.

66544 ■ Waupaca Area Chamber of Commerce
221 S Main St.
Waupaca, WI 54981-1522
Ph:(715)258-7343
Free: 888-417-4040
Fax: (715)258-7868

Co. E-mail: discoverwaupaca@
  waupacaareachamber.com
URL: http://www.waupacaareachamber.com
Contact: Terri Schulz, Pres.

66545 ■ Waupun Area Chamber of Commerce
16 S Mill St.
Waupun, WI 53963
Ph:(920)324-3491
Fax: (920)324-4357
Co. E-mail: info@waupunchamber.com
URL: http://www.waupunchamber.com
Contact: Ginger Kieltyka, Exec.Dir./Exec.VP

66546 ■ Wausau/Marathon County Chamber of Commerce
PO Box 6190
Wausau, WI 54402-6190
Ph:(715)845-6231
Fax: (715)845-6235
Co. E-mail: info@wausauchamber.com
URL: http://www.wausauchamber.com
Contact: Roger A. Luce, Exec. Dir.

66547 ■ Wausaukee Area Business Association
502 Main St.
PO Box 254
Wausaukee, WI 54177-0254
Ph:(715)856-5627
Free: 888-856-5164
Fax: (715)856-6209
Co. E-mail: waba@wausaukee.com
URL: http://www.wausaukee.com
Contact: Brian Hartnell, Pres.

66548 ■ Waushara Area Chamber of Commerce
440 W Main St.
PO Box 65
Wautoma, WI 54982-0065
Ph:(920)787-3488
Free: 877-WAU-TOMA
Fax: (920)787-3788
Co. E-mail: wacc@centurytel.net
URL: http://www.wausharachamber.com
Contact: Lisa Larson, Co-Pres.

66549 ■ Webster Area Chamber of Commerce
PO Box 48
Webster, WI 54893
Ph:(715)866-4856
Co. E-mail: websterfacts@websterwisconsin.com
URL: http://www.websterwisconsin.com
Contact: Angie Gibbs, Pres.

66550 ■ West Allis/West Milwaukee Chamber of Commerce
7149 W Greenfield Ave.
West Allis, WI 53214
Ph:(414)302-9901
Fax: (414)302-9918
Co. E-mail: contact@wawmchamber.com
URL: http://www.wawmchamber.com
Contact: Gerise LaSpisa, Pres.

66551 ■ West Bend Area Chamber of Commerce
548 S Main St.
West Bend, WI 53095
Ph:(262)338-2666
Free: 888-338-8666
Fax: (262)338-1771
Co. E-mail: info@wbachamber.org
URL: http://www.wbchamber.org
Contact: Craig Farrell, Exec. Dir.

66552 ■ West Suburban Chamber of Commerce
2300 N Mayfair Rd., Ste. 380
Wauwatosa, WI 53226
Ph:(414)453-2330
Fax: (414)453-2336
Co. E-mail: info@westsuburbanchamber.com
URL: http://www.westsuburbanchamber.com

Contact: Sharon Scaccia, Exec. Dir.

66553 ■ Westfield Chamber of Commerce
PO Box 393
Westfield, WI 53964
Ph:(608)296-2363
Co. E-mail: michelle@westfieldwi.com
URL: http://www.westfieldwi.com
Contact: Michelle Fenske, Pres.

66554 ■ Weyauwega Area Chamber of Commerce
PO Box 531
Weyauwega, WI 54983
Ph:(920)867-2500
Co. E-mail: bruce.ulbrich@centurytel.net
URL: http://www.weyauwegachamber.com
Contact: Eunice Kempf, Pres.

66555 ■ Whitehall Area Chamber of Commerce
PO Box 281
Whitehall, WI 54773
Ph:(715)538-4353
Fax: (715)538-2301
Co. E-mail: kwitte@wppisys.org
URL: http://whitehall-chamber.com
Contact: Bernard Ziegeweid, Pres.

66556 ■ Whitewater Area Chamber of Commerce
171 W Main St.
PO Box 34
Whitewater, WI 53190-0034
Ph:(262)473-4005
Free: (866)4WW-TOUR
Fax: (262)473-0529
Co. E-mail: wacc@idcnet.com
URL: http://www.whitewaterchamber.com
Contact: Betsy Gasper, Exec. Dir.

66557 ■ Wisconsin Manufacturers and Commerce
PO Box 352
501 E Washington Ave.
Madison, WI 53701-0352
Ph:(608)258-3400
Fax: (608)258-3413
Co. E-mail: jhaney@wmc.org
URL: http://www.wmc.org
Contact: James S. Haney, Pres.

66558 ■ Wittenberg Area Chamber of Commerce
PO Box 284
Wittenberg, WI 54499
Ph:(715)253-3525
Co. E-mail: wittcham@wittenbergchamber.org
URL: http://wittenbergchamber.org
Contact: Benell Thomas, Pres.

MINORITY BUSINESS ASSISTANCE PROGRAMS

66559 ■ Small Business Development Center–UWSP Continuing Education–University of Wisconsin-Stevens Point (Unive)
University of Wisconsin at Stevens Point
Main Bldg., Rm. 103
Stevens Point, WI 54481
Ph:(715)346-3838
Free: 800-898-9472
Fax: (715)346-4045
Co. E-mail: vloberme@uwsp.edu
URL: http://www.uwsp.edu/conted/sbdc
Contact: Vicki Lobermeier
Description: Provides counseling, in-depth studies, workshops, seminars, and communication development to American Indian tribes and individuals in Wisconsin.

66560 ■ Wisconsin Department of Commerce–Bureau of Minority Business Development
201 W Washington Ave.
PO Box 7970
Madison, WI 53707-7970
Ph:(608)266-1018
Fax: (608)267-2829
URL: http://www.commerce.state.wi.us
Description: Provides assistance to existing and potential minority businesses in market assessment, access to credit, capital formation, and coordination of public and private resources. Also certifies minority vendors.

66561 ■ Wisconsin Department of Commerce–Women's Business Ventures
201 W Washington Ave.
PO Box 7970
Madison, WI 53707-7970
Ph:(608)266-1018
Free: 800-HELP-BUS
Description: Helps women entrepreneurs start or expand their businesses. Identifies accessible sources of financing; assists in business planning, financial projections, and cash-flow statement preparations.

FINANCING AND LOAN PROGRAMS

66562 ■ Capital Investments, Inc.
1009 W. Glen Oaks Ln., Ste. 103
Mequon, WI 53092
Ph:(262)241-0303
Fax: (262)241-8451
URL: http://www.capitalinvestmentsinc.com
Preferred Investment Size: $500,000 to $5,000,000.
Investment Types: Acquisition, expansion, later stage, leveraged buyout, management buyouts, mezzanine, and recapitalizations. **Industry Preferences:** Industrial and energy, computer software and services, computer hardware, other products, medical and health, consumer related, communications and media. **Geographic Preferences:** U.S.

66563 ■ Future Value Ventures, Inc.
330 E. Kibourn Ave., Ste. 771
Milwaukee, WI 53203
Ph:(414)278-0377
Fax: (414)278-7321
Contact: William Beckett, President
Preferred Investment Size: $100,000 to $300,000.
Investment Types: First and second stage, start-up, and mezzanine. **Geographic Preferences:** U.S.

66564 ■ GCI
20875 Crossroads Cir., Ste. 100
Waukesha, WI 53186
Ph:(262)798-5080
Fax: (262)798-5087
Preferred Investment Size: $2,000,000 minimum.
Investment Types: First and second stage, and leveraged buyout. **Industry Preferences:** Communications, computer hardware and software, semiconductors and other electronics, consumer related, industrial and energy, and business service. **Geographic Preferences:** U.S.

66565 ■ Lubar & Co.
700 N. Water St., Ste. 1200
Milwaukee, WI 53202
Ph:(414)291-9000
Fax: (414)291-9061
URL: http://www.lubar.com
Contact: David J. Lubar, Partner
Preferred Investment Size: $10,000,000 minimum.
Investment Types: Second stage, leveraged buyout, special situation, and control-lock purchases. **Industry Preferences:** Communications, computer hardware and software, semiconductors and other electronics, medical and health, consumer related, industrial and energy, transportation, financial services, manufacturing, agriculture, forestry and fishing. **Geographic Preferences:** Midwest.

66566 ■ Mason Wells Private Equity / M&I Ventures
411 E. Wisconsin Ave., Ste. 1280
Milwaukee, WI 53202
Ph:(414)727-6400
Fax: (414)727-6410
URL: http://www.masonwells.com
Contact: John Byrnes, Chairman and Chief Executive Officer
Preferred Investment Size: $500,000 to $8,000,000.
Investment Policies: Start-up, seed, management buyouts, leveraged buyout, and early stage. **Industry Preferences:** Computer software, biotechnology, financial services, and business service. **Geographic Preferences:** Midwest.

66567 ■ Venture Investors LLC
University Research Park
505 S. Rosa Rd.
Madison, WI 53719
Ph:(608)441-2700
Fax: (608)441-2727
Co. E-mail: roger@ventureinvestors.com
URL: http://www.ventureinvesters.com
Contact: Roger Ganser, Managing Partner
Preferred Investment Size: $300,000 to $2,000,000.
Investment Types: Seed and early stage. **Industry Preferences:** Biotechnology, medical and health, computer software and services, semiconductors and other electronics, consumer related, Internet specific, industrial and energy, communications and media, and computer hardware. **Geographic Preferences:** Midwest and Wisconsin.

PROCUREMENT ASSISTANCE PROGRAMS

66568 ■ Wisconsin Department of Administration–Minority Business Programs
101 E Wilson, Rm. 621
PO Box 7867
Madison, WI 53707
Ph:(608)267-7806
Fax: (608)267-0600
Co. E-mail: godwin.amegashie@wisconsin.gov
URL: http://www.doa.state.wi.us/deo/mbe
Contact: Godwin Amegashie, Dir
Description: Reviews small business purchasing by the state and advises and submits to the Department of Administration and the governor reports and recommendations concerning small and minority businesses opportunities.

66569 ■ Wisconsin Procurement Technical Assistance Center–Wisconsin Procurement Institute, Inc.
756 N Milwaukee St.
Milwaukee, WI 53202
Ph:(414)270-3600
Fax: (414)270-3610
Co. E-mail: info@wispro.org
URL: http://www.wispro.org
Contact: Joseph Endres

INCUBATORS/RESEARCH AND TECHNOLOGY PARKS

66570 ■ ADVOCAP, Inc.
19 W 1st St.
PO Box 1108
Fond du Lac, WI 54936
Ph:(920)922-7760
Fax: (920)922-7214
Co. E-mail: mikeb@advocap.org
URL: http://www.advocap.org
Contact: Michael Bonertz, Exec Dir

66571 ■ Madison Enterprise Center
100 South Baldwin St.
Madison, WI 53703
Ph:(608)256-6565
Fax: (608)256-6561

Co. E-mail: sich@cwd.org
URL: http://www.cwd.org/mec/index.html
Description: A small business incubator for emerging light industrial companies.

66572 ■ Medical College of Wisconsin–MCW Research Foundation
8701 Watertown Plank Rd.
PO Box 26509
Milwaukee, WI 53226-0509
Ph:(414)456-4362
Fax: (414)456-6555
Co. E-mail: whendee@mcw.edu
URL: http://www.mcw.edu/research/foundation/foundation.html
Contact: William R. Hendee PhD, Exec.VP
E-mail: whendee@mcw.edu
Scope: Creates intellectual property from ideas and processes of College researchers for licensing of products and services to the marketplace primarily in the areas of biophysics, biomedical engineering, biochemistry, microbiology, neuroscience and vision, pharmacology, medical instrumentation and medical imaging, cardiovascular physiology, genomics, and bioinformatics.

66573 ■ Milwaukee School of Engineering–Applied Technology Center
1025 N Broadway
Milwaukee, WI 53202-3109
Ph:(414)277-7416
Free: 800—332-6763
Fax: (414)277-7470
Co. E-mail: bray@msoe.edu
URL: http://www.msoe.edu
Contact: Thomas E. Bray, Dean
E-mail: bray@msoe.edu
Scope: Coordinates the School's resources to assist in the solution of technological problems confronting business and industry, including services required in product development, testing, and research of new applications of engineering science. Serves as an experimental station for extramurally sponsored industrial research investigations in applied engineering and as a clearinghouse on specific scientific information for the public. Areas of expertise include: aerodynamics and wind tunnel testing, agile manufacturing, artificial intelligence and expert systems, biomedical engineering, computer systems performance, creative thinking, energy management, fluid jet cutting, fluid power and electrohydraulic interfaces, fuzzy logic, hazardous waste, human factors/ergonomics, internal combustion engines, information systems, manufacturing systems and robotics, material sciences, photonics and sensors, quality assurance, rapid prototyping stereolithography, laminated object manufacturing, fused deposition modelling, selective laser sintering, rehabilitation equipment design, statistical process control, and technical communication. **Publications:** MSOE Dimensions (quarterly). **Educational Activities:** Rapid Prototyping Consortium seminars (monthly), for members only.

66574 ■ The Superior Business Center Inc.
1423 N 8th St.
Superior, WI 54880
Ph:(715)392-4749
Co. E-mail: johnsenm@developmentassociation.com
URL: http://www.superbus.com
Description: The SBC serves emerging businesses through a variety of resources including affordable office space. The Center also assists home-based businesses with telecommunications support.

66575 ■ University of Wisconsin–Madison–University Research Park
510 Charmany Dr., Ste. 250
Madison, WI 53719-1235
Ph:(608)441-8000
Fax: (608)441-8010
Co. E-mail: mdbugher@wisc.edu
URL: http://www.universityresearchpark.org
Contact: Mark D. Bugher, Dir.
E-mail: mdbugher@wisc.edu
Scope: The 321-acre Park facilitates technology transfer between the research produced on the Uni-

versity campus and applied research of industry and provides a long-term endowment income to the University. Leases land to private companies and agencies and offers laboratory and office services to start-up companies.

66576 ■ University of Wisconsin–Stout–Research Services
152 Voc. Rehab. Bldg.
Menomonie, WI 54751
Ph:(715)232-1126
Fax: (715)232-1749
Co. E-mail: foxwells@uwstout.edu
URL: http://www.uwstout.edu/rs
Contact: Sue Foxwell, Admin.
E-mail: foxwells@uwstout.edu
Scope: Provides preparation and submission of all proposals and contracts requesting extramural funds, including assistance in budget preparation, proposal and contract development, extramural funding options and patent policies. Also reviews all proposals and contracts prior to submission to ensure compliance with system and university policies, and verifies budgets, resource needs, and clearance for the protection of human subjects, intellectual property, patents, and copyrights. **Educational Activities:** Information dissemination, on new technologies and program emphases; In-service training; Seminars; Workshops.

66577 ■ Wisconsin Alumni Research Foundation
614 Walnut St., 13th Fl.
Madison, WI 53726
Ph:(608)263-2500
Fax: (608)263-1064
Co. E-mail: info@warf.org
URL: http://www.warf.org
Contact: Carl E. Gulbrandsen PhD, Mng.Dir.
E-mail: info@warf.org
Scope: Supports research at the University through grants-in-aid, establishment of special professorships and fellowships, and contributions for buildings and special projects.

LEGISLATIVE ASSISTANCE

66578 ■ Representative Jeff Mursau
State Capitol, Rm 18 N
PO Box 8953
Madison, WI 53708
Ph:(608)266-3780
Fax: (608)282-3636
Co. E-mail: rep.mursau@legis.state.wi.us

66579 ■ Wisconsin Department of Commerce
201 W Washington Ave.
PO Box 7970
Madison, WI 53707-7970
Ph:(608)266-1018
Fax: (608)267-0436
URL: http://www.commerce.state.wi.us
Description: Works with state agencies, individual businesses, and business organizations to advance the concerns of businesses at the policy level.

TRADE PERIODICALS

66580 ■ *Focus*
Pub: Wisconsin Taxpayers Alliance
Contact: Todd A. Berry
Released: 28/year. **Price:** $49, individuals. **Description:** Contains analysis of Wisconsin's government and policy.

PUBLICATIONS

66581 ■ *Corporate Report-Wisconsin*
PO Box 878
Menomonee Falls, WI 53052
Ph:(414)255-9077
Fax: (414)255-3388

66582 ■ *Entrepreneurial Assistance in Wisconsin: Sources of Management and Technical Support*
Wisconsin Department of Development
Bureau of Information Services
201 W. Washington Ave.
PO Box 7970
Madison, WI 53707
Ph:(608)267-6876
Free: 800-HELP-BUS
Fax: (608)267-0436
URL: http://www.badger.state.wi.us/agency/commerce
Released: 1990. **Price:** $5.00. **Description:** Lists programs offering small business assistance. Includes alphabetical, geographical, and subject indexes.

66583 ■ *Going Into Business in Wisconsin: An Entrepreneur's Guide*
Wisconsin Department of Development
Bureau of Information Services
201 W. Washington Ave.
PO Box 7970
Madison, WI 53707
Ph:(608)267-6876
Free: 800-HELP-BUS
Fax: (608)267-0436
URL: http://www.badger.state.wi.us/agency/commerce
Released: Second editon, 1992. **Price:** Free. **Description:** Topics covered include going into business, business planning, legal forms of organization, financing, taxation/regulation/permits, marketing, finding personnel, legal assistance, accounting, location decisions, technology, international trade, and assistance for women and minority entrepreneurs. Includes worksheets and a bibliography.

66584 ■ *Smart Start your Wisconsin Business*
PSI Research
300 N. Valley Dr.
Grants Pass, OR 97526
Ph:(541)479-9464
Free: 800-228-2275
Fax: (541)476-1479
Co. E-mail: info@psi-research.com
URL: http://www.psi-research.com
Ed: Michael D. Jenkins. **Released:** Revised edition, 1992. **Price:** $29.95 (looseleaf binder); $24.95 (paper). **Description:** Part of the Successful Business Library series.

66585 ■ *Technology Resources for Business in Wisconsin*
Wisconsin Department of Development
Bureau of Information Services
201 W. Washington Ave.
PO Box 7970
Madison, WI 53707
Ph:(608)267-6876
Free: 800-HELP-BUS
Fax: (608)267-0436
URL: http://www.badger.state.wi.us/agency/commerce
Released: 1990. **Price:** $3.50. **Description:** Lists and describes university, public, and private resources for technology-driven firms; includes sources of assistance for research and development, technology transfer, testing, patenting, start-up, product introduction, and marketing.

66586 ■ *Venture Financing: Raising Capital in Wisconsin*
Wisconsin Department of Development
Bureau of Information Services
201 W. Washington Ave.
PO Box 7970
Madison, WI 53707
Ph:(608)267-6876
Fax: (608)267-0436
URL: http://www.badger.state.wi.us/agency/commerce
Released: 1990. **Price:** Free. **Description:** Topics covered include equity financing, "mezzanine" financing, strategic partnering, government financing, debt financing, leasing, and other sources of financing.

66587 ■ Wisconsin Financing Alternatives
Wisconsin Department of Commerce
Bureau of Information Services
201 West Washington Ave.
PO Box 7970
Madison, WI 53707
Ph:(608)267-6876
Fax: (608)267-0436
URL: http://www.badger.state.wi.us/agency/
   commerce
Released: Reprinted October 1991. **Price:** $2.00. **Description:** Listing and description of programs with financing, finance labor training support, and incubator facilities for businesses in Wisconsin.

66588 ■ Wisconsin Minority Business Resource Directory
Wisconsin Department of Development
Bureau of Information Services
201 W. Washington Ave.
PO Box 7970
Madison, WI 53707
Ph:(608)266-5381

Fax: (608)267-0436
URL: http://www.badger.state.wi.us/agency/
   commerce
Released: Second edition. **Price:** $5.00. **Description:** Listing and description of general business assistance and financial resources for minority-owned and -run businesses in Wisconsin.

PUBLISHERS

66589 ■ American Society for Quality Press
600 N Plankinton Ave.
PO Box 3005
Milwaukee, WI 53201-3005
Ph:(414)272-8575
Free: 800-248-1946
Fax: (414)272-1734
Co. E-mail: help@asq.org
URL: http://www.asq.org
Contact: Roger Holloway, Mgr
Description: Publishes technical books on quality control, ISO900, and management books on TQM, human resources, teamwork, and benchmarking. **Founded:** 1983.

66590 ■ Guild Publishing
931 E Main St., Ste. 9
Madison, WI 53703-2955
Ph:(608)257-2590
Free: 800-930-1856
Fax: (608)257-2690
Co. E-mail: art-info@guild.com
URL: http://www.guild.com
Contact: Toni F. Sikes, CEO
Description: Publishes artists sourcebooks and books on contemporary art for architects and interior designers. **Founded:** 1985.

66591 ■ Upwrite Press
PO Box 460
Burlington, WI 53105
Ph:(262)763-8258
Free: 800-261-0637
Fax: (262)763-8023
URL: http://www.upwritepress.com
Contact: Thomas Spicuzza
Description: Publishes books on improving business communication skills (writing and speaking). Offers free newsletter via email titled *eTips*.

Wyoming

SMALL BUSINESS DEVELOPMENT CENTER LEAD OFFICE

66592 ■ Wyoming Small Business Development Center–State Office
100 E. University
Dept. 3922
Laramie, WY 82071
Ph:(307)766-3505
Free: 800-348-5194
Fax: (307)766-3406
URL: http://uwadmnweb.uwyo.edu/SBDC/
Contact: Debbie Popp, Actg. State Dir.
E-mail: debk@uwyo.edu

SMALL BUSINESS DEVELOPMENT CENTERS

66593 ■ Casper SBDC–Region III
300 S. Wolcott, Ste. 300
Casper, WY 82601
Ph:(307)234-6683
Free: 800-348-5207
Fax: (307)577-7014
Co. E-mail: sbdc@trib.com
URL: http://uwadmnweb.uwyo.edu/SBDC/
Contact: Leonard Holler, Dir.

66594 ■ Cheyenne SBDC–Region IV
1400 E. College Dr.
Cheyenne, WY 82007-3298
Ph:(307)632-6141
Free: 800-348-5208
Fax: (307)632-6061
Co. E-mail: sewsbdc@wyoming.com
URL: http://uwadmnweb.uwyo.edu/SBDC/
Contact: Arlene Soto, Regional Dir.

66595 ■ Fremont County Office–SBDC
213 W. Main, Ste. C
Riverton, WY 82501
Ph:(307)857-1174
Free: 800-969-8639
Fax: (307)857-0873
Co. E-mail: wsbdc@wyoming.com
URL: http://uwadmnweb.uwyo.edu/SBDC/
Contact: Margie Rowell, Dir.

66596 ■ Gillette SBDC–Region V
201 W. Lakeway Rd., Ste. 1004
Gillette, WY 82718
Ph:(307)682-5232
Free: 888-956-6060
Fax: (307)686-5792
Co. E-mail: sbdc@vcn.com
URL: http://uwadmnweb.uwyo.edu/SBDC/
Contact: Jill Kline, Dir.

66597 ■ GRO-Biz SBDC
LCCC
1400 E. College Dr.
Cheyenne, WY 82007
Ph:(307)637-4990
Free: (866)253-3300
Fax: (307)632-6061
URL: http://uwadmnweb.uwyo.edu/SBDC/
Contact: Rudy Nesvik, Dir.
E-mail: nesvik@wyoming.com

66598 ■ Laramie SBDC–Region IV Satellite Office
1000 E. University Dr.
Dept. 3922
Laramie, WY 82071
Ph:(307)766-3515
Co. E-mail: WTSchep@uwyo.edu
URL: http://uwadmnweb.uwyo.edu/SBDC/
Contact: Bill Schepeler, Dir.

66599 ■ Powell SBDC–Region II
143 South Bent St., Ste. A
Powell, WY 82435
Ph:(307)754-2139
Free: 800-383-0371
Fax: (307)754-0368
Co. E-mail: directon@wir.net
URL: http://uwadmnweb.uwyo.edu/SBDC/
Contact: Dwane Heintz, Dir.

66600 ■ Rock Springs SBDC–Region I
1400 Dewar Dr., Ste. 205
Rock Springs, WY 82901
Ph:(307)352-6894
Free: 800-348-5205
Fax: (307)352-6876
URL: http://uwadmnweb.uwyo.edu/SBDC/
Contact: Bill Ellis, Regional Dir.
E-mail: bellis@uwyo.edu

SMALL BUSINESS ASSISTANCE PROGRAMS

66601 ■ Wyoming Department of Commerce–Wyoming Business Council
214 W 15th St.
Cheyenne, WY 82002
Ph:(307)777-2800
Fax: (307)777-2837
Co. E-mail: info@wyomingbusiness.org
URL: http://www.wyomingbusiness.org
Description: Works to attract new businesses; provides technical assistance.

CHAMBERS OF COMMERCE

66602 ■ Buffalo, Wyoming Chamber of Commerce
55 N Main St.
Buffalo, WY 82834
Ph:(307)684-5544
Free: 800-227-5122
Fax: (307)684-0291
Co. E-mail: buffalochamber@wyoming.com
URL: http://www.buffalowyo.com
Contact: Ms. Dee Woodall, Exec.Dir.

66603 ■ Campbell County Chamber of Commerce
314 S Gillette Ave.
Gillette, WY 82716
Ph:(307)682-3673
Fax: (307)682-0538
Co. E-mail: frontoffice@gillettechamber.com
URL: http://www.gillettechamber.com
Contact: Brenda Boss, Pres.

66604 ■ Casper Area Chamber of Commerce
PO Box 399
Casper, WY 82602-0399
Ph:(307)234-5311
Free: (866)234-5311
Fax: (307)263-2643
Co. E-mail: chamber@casperwyoming.org
URL: http://www.casperwyoming.org
Contact: Lori Becker, Exec.Dir.

66605 ■ Cody Country Chamber of Commerce
836 Sheridan Ave.
Cody, WY 82414
Ph:(307)587-2777
Fax: (307)527-6228
Co. E-mail: info@codychamber.org
URL: http://www.codychamber.org
Contact: Christine Houze, Membership Dir.

66606 ■ Douglas Area Chamber of Commerce
121 Brownfield Rd.
Douglas, WY 82633
Ph:(307)358-2950
Fax: (307)358-2972
Co. E-mail: chamber@jackalope.org
URL: http://www.jackalope.org
Contact: Gary Hirt, Exec.Dir.

66607 ■ Dubois Chamber of Commerce
616 W Ramshorn St.
PO Box 632
Dubois, WY 82513-0632
Ph:(307)455-2556
Fax: (307)455-3168
Co. E-mail: duboiscc@wyoming.com
URL: http://duboiswyoming.org
Contact: Dorothea Stewart, Exec.Dir.

66608 ■ Evanston Chamber of Commerce
PO Box 365
Evanston, WY 82931-0365
Ph:(307)783-0370
Free: 800-328-9708
Fax: (307)789-4807
Co. E-mail: chamber@etownchamber.com
URL: http://www.etownchamber.com
Contact: Peggy Rounds, Dir.

66609 ■ Glenrock Chamber of Commerce
W Birch St.
Glenrock, WY 82637
Ph:(307)436-5652
Fax: (307)436-5477
Co. E-mail: glenrockchamber@sundancewireless.com
URL: http://www.glenrockchamber.com
Contact: Mary Kay Kindt, Dir.

66610 ■ Goshen County Chamber of Commerce
350 W 21st Ave.
Torrington, WY 82240
Ph:(307)532-3879
Free: 800-577-3555
Fax: (307)534-2360
Co. E-mail: goshenco@communicomm.com
URL: http://www.wyomingchambers.com/local_chambers.html
Contact: Dick Fullmer, Exec.Dir.

66611 ■ Greater Cheyenne Chamber of Commerce
One Depot Sq.
121 W 15th St. Ste. 204
Cheyenne, WY 82003-1147
Ph:(307)638-3388
Fax: (307)778-1407
Co. E-mail: info@cheyennechamber.org
URL: http://www.cheyennechamber.org
Contact: Mr. Larry Atwell CCE, Pres.

66612 ■ Green River Chamber of Commerce
541 E Flaming Gorge Way, Ste. E
Green River, WY 82935
Ph:(307)875-5711
Free: 800-354-6743
Fax: (307)875-8993
Co. E-mail: grchamber@sweetwaterhsa.com
URL: http://www.grchamber.com
Contact: Janet L. Hartford, Exec.Dir.

66613 ■ Greybull Area Chamber of Commerce
521 Greybull Ave.
Greybull, WY 82426
Ph:(307)765-2100
Free: 877-765-2100
Fax: (307)765-2100
Co. E-mail: chamber@greybull.com
URL: http://www.greybull.com
Contact: Ms. SC Anderson, Exec.Dir.

66614 ■ Jackson Hole Chamber of Commerce
PO Box 550
Jackson, WY 83001-0550
Ph:(307)733-3316
Co. E-mail: info@jacksonholechamber.com
URL: http://www.jacksonholechamber.com
Contact: Steve Duerr, Exec.Dir.

66615 ■ Kemmerer/Diamondville Area Chamber of Commerce
800 Pine Ave.
Kemmerer, WY 83101
Ph:(307)877-9761
Free: 888-300-3413
Fax: (307)877-9762
Co. E-mail: chamber@kemmererchamber.com
URL: http://www.kemmererchamber.com
Contact: Teri Picerno, Exec.Dir.

66616 ■ La Barge Chamber of Commerce
PO Box 327
La Barge, WY 83123-0327
Ph:(307)386-2676
Fax: (307)386-2221

66617 ■ Lander Area Chamber of Commerce
160 N 1st St.
Lander, WY 82520
Ph:(307)332-3892
Free: 800-433-0662
Co. E-mail: info@landerchamber.org
URL: http://www.landerchamber.org

Contact: Mr. Scott Goetz, Exec.Dir.

66618 ■ Laramie Area Chamber of Commerce
800 S 3rd St.
Laramie, WY 82070
Ph:(307)745-7339
Free: (866)876-1012
Fax: (307)745-4624
Co. E-mail: chamberofcommerce@laramie.org
URL: http://www.laramie.org
Contact: P.J. Burns, Exec.Dir.

66619 ■ Lovell Area Chamber of Commerce
287 E Main
Lovell, WY 82431
Ph:(307)548-7552
Fax: (307)548-7582
Co. E-mail: lovell@tctwest.net
URL: http://www.lovellchamber.com
Contact: Suzanne Winterholler, Sec.

66620 ■ Newcastle Area Chamber of Commerce
1323 Washington Blvd.
Newcastle, WY 82701
Ph:(307)746-2739
Free: 800-835-0157
Fax: (307)746-2739
Co. E-mail: chamber@newcastlewyo.com
URL: http://www.newcastlewyo.com
Contact: Norman Shelton, Dir.

66621 ■ Niobrara Chamber of Commerce
PO Box 457
Lusk, WY 82225-0457
Ph:(307)334-2950
Free: 800-223-5875
Fax: (307)334-2950
Co. E-mail: luskwy@coffey.com
URL: http://www.luskwyoming.com
Contact: Jackie Bredthauer, Exec.Dir.

66622 ■ Pine Bluffs Area Chamber of Commerce
PO Box 563
Pine Bluffs, WY 82082-0486
Ph:(307)245-3746
Fax: (307)245-3883
Co. E-mail: rmfusez@email.msn.com
Contact: Scott Zimmerman, Pres.

66623 ■ Platte County Chamber of Commerce
65 16th St.
PO Box 427
Wheatland, WY 82201-0427
Ph:(307)322-2322
Fax: (307)322-3419
Co. E-mail: services@plattechamber.com
URL: http://www.plattechamber.com
Contact: Julie Minear, Exec.Dir.

66624 ■ Powell Valley Chamber of Commerce
111 S Day St.
PO Box 814
Powell, WY 82435-0814
Ph:(307)754-3494
Free: 800-325-4278
Fax: (307)754-3483
Co. E-mail: info@powellchamber.org
URL: http://www.powellchamber.org
Contact: Sharon Earhart, Exec.Dir.

66625 ■ Rawlins-Carbon County Chamber of Commerce
519 W Cedar St.
PO Box 1331
Rawlins, WY 82301-1331
Ph:(307)324-4111
Free: 800-935-4821
Fax: (307)324-5078
Co. E-mail: rcchamberdirector@yahoo.com
URL: http://www.rawlinscarboncountychamber.com
Contact: Mr. Ed Vandenburg, Dir.

66626 ■ Riverton Chamber of Commerce
213 W Main St.
Riverton, WY 82501
Ph:(307)856-4801
Free: 800-325-2732
Fax: (307)857-0873
Co. E-mail: info@rivertonchamber.org
URL: http://www.rivertonchamber.org
Contact: William Maxwell, Exec.Dir.

66627 ■ Rock Springs Chamber of Commerce
1897 Dewar Dr.
PO Box 398
Rock Springs, WY 82902-0398
Ph:(307)362-3771
Free: 800-46D-UNES
Fax: (307)362-3838
Co. E-mail: rschamber@sweetwaterhsa.com
URL: http://www.rockspringswyoming.net
Contact: Dave Hanks, CEO

66628 ■ Saratoga/Platte Valley Chamber of Commerce
106 N First St.
PO Box 1095
Saratoga, WY 82331-1095
Ph:(307)326-8855
Free: (866)828-8855
Fax: (307)326-8850
Co. E-mail: info@saratogachamber.info
URL: http://www.saratogachamber.info
Contact: Elizabeth Wood, Admin.Asst.

66629 ■ Sheridan County Chamber of Commerce
PO Box 707
Sheridan, WY 82801-0707
Ph:(307)672-2485
Free: 800-453-3650
Fax: (307)672-7321
Co. E-mail: info@sheridanwyomingchamber.org
URL: http://sheridanwyomingchamber.org
Contact: Ms. Melissa Butcher, Exec.Dir.

66630 ■ Star Valley Chamber of Commerce
PO Box 1097
Afton, WY 83110-1097
Ph:(307)883-2759
Free: 800-426-8833
Co. E-mail: svccom@silverstar.com
URL: http://www.starvalleychamber.com
Contact: Karen Haderlie, Exec.Dir.

66631 ■ Sublette County Chamber of Commerce
PO Box 176
Pinedale, WY 82941-0176
Ph:(307)367-2242
Free: 888-285-7282
Fax: (307)367-2248
Co. E-mail: sublettechamber@wyoming.com
URL: http://www.pinedalechamber.com

66632 ■ Sundance Area Chamber of Commerce
PO Box 1004
Sundance, WY 82729
Ph:(307)283-1000
Free: 800-477-9340
Fax: (307)437-6689
Co. E-mail: chamber@sundancewyoming.com
URL: http://www.sundancewyoming.com
Contact: Pat Goodson, Pres.

66633 ■ Thermopolis - Hot Springs Chamber of Commerce
PO Box 768
Thermopolis, WY 82443
Ph:(307)864-3192
Free: 800-SUN-NSPA
Fax: (307)864-3192
Co. E-mail: thercc@rtconnect.net
URL: http://www.thermopolis.com
Contact: Lorraine Quarberg, Dir.

66634 ■ Worland Area Chamber of Commerce
120 N 10th St.
Worland, WY 82401
Ph:(307)347-3226
Fax: (307)347-3025
Co. E-mail: wtschamber@rtconnect.net
URL: http://www.worlandchamber.com
Contact: Mike Willard, Exec. Dir.

66635 ■ Wright Area Chamber of Commerce
PO Box 430
Wright, WY 82732-0430
Ph:(307)464-1312
Fax: (307)464-6115
Co. E-mail: wacc@intrq.com
Contact: Colleen Long, Exec.Dir.

PROCUREMENT ASSISTANCE PROGRAMS

66636 ■ Wyoming Administration and Information Department–Procurement Services
Herschler Bldg.
122 W 25th Ave
Cheyenne, WY 82002
Ph:(307)777-7253
Fax: (307)757-5852
Co. E-mail: mlande@state.wy.us
URL: http://ai.state.wy.us/generalservices/
    Procurement/index.asp

Contact: Mac Lande, Dir

INCUBATORS/RESEARCH AND TECHNOLOGY PARKS

66637 ■ University of Wyoming–Division of Research Support
College of Arts Sciences, Dept. 3391
1000 E University Ave.
Laramie, WY 82071-3391
Ph:(307)766-2120
Fax: (307)766-2128
Co. E-mail: shops@uwyo.edu
URL: http://uwadmnweb.uwyo.edu/resup/default.htm
Contact: Tom Denton, Dir.
E-mail: shops@uwyo.edu
Scope: The humanities, fine arts, mathematics, and biological, physical, and social sciences.

66638 ■ University of Wyoming–Office of Research
1000 E University Ave., Dept. 3355
Laramie, WY 82071
Ph:(307)766-5353
Fax: (307)766-5320
Co. E-mail: osterman@uwyo.edu
URL: http://uwacadweb.uwyo.edu/research
Contact: William Gern, VP
E-mail: osterman@uwyo.edu
Scope: Coordinates research conducted in the seven accredited colleges of the University: Agriculture, Arts

and Sciences, Commerce and Industry, Education, Engineering, Law, and Health Sciences. Interdisciplinary research programs and numerous teaching and research facilities are operated by the University.

PUBLICATIONS

66639 ■ *Guide to Business Permitting and Licensing in Wyoming*
Wyoming Department of Commerce
Barrett Bldg.
6101 N. Yellowstone Rd., 4th Fl.
Cheyenne, WY 82002
Ph:(307)777-7696
Fax: (307)777-6005
Ed: Paul Howard. **Description:** Includes general and specific permit requirements, permits listed by business type, a listing of state agencies administering professional licenses, a checklist and worksheet, and two appendices.

66640 ■ *Smart Start Your Wyoming Business*
PSI Research
300 N. Valley Dr.
Grants Pass, OR 97526
Ph:(541)479-9464
Free: 800-228-2275
Fax: (541)476-1479
URL: http://www.psi-research.com
Ed: Michael D. Jenkins and Daniel J. Herron. **Released:** Revised edition, 1992. **Price:** $29.95 (looseleaf binder); $24.95 (paper). **Description:** Part of the Successful Business Library series.

SMALL BUSINESS DEVELOPMENT CENTER LEAD OFFICE

66641 ■ Pacific Islands Small Business Development Center–University of Guam
UOG Station
Mangilao, GU 96923
Ph:(671)735-2590
Fax: (671)734-2002
Contact: Mr. Jack Peters, Director

SMALL BUSINESS DEVELOPMENT CENTERS

66642 ■ University of Guam–Guam Small Business Development Center
UOG Station
PO Box 5014
Mangilao, GU 96923
Ph:(671)735-2590
Fax: (671)734-2002
URL: http://www.pacificsbdc.com
Contact: Casey Jeszenka, Dir.
E-mail: casey@pacificsbdc.com

CHAMBERS OF COMMERCE

66643 ■ Guam Chamber of Commerce
PO Box 283
Hagatna, GU 96932
Ph:(671)472-6311
Fax: (671)472-6202
Co. E-mail: gchamber@guamchamber.com.gu
URL: http://www.guamchamber.com.gu
Contact: Eloise R. Baza, Pres.

SMALL BUSINESS DEVELOPMENT CENTER LEAD OFFICE

66644 ■ Inter-American University of Puerto Rico–Puerto Rico SBDC
Union Plaza, 7th Fl.
416 Ponce de Leon Ave.
Hato Rey, PR 00918
Ph:(787)763-6811
Fax: (787)763-4629
URL: http://www.prsbdc.org
Contact: Carmen Marti, State Dir.
E-mail: cmarti@prsbdc.org

66645 ■ Puerto Rico Small Business Development Center
Edificio Union Plaza, Ste. 701
416 Ponce de Leon Ave.
Hato Rey, PR 00918
Ph:(787)763-6811
Fax: (787)763-4629
Contact: Carmen Marti, Exec. Dir.
E-mail: cmarti@prsbdc.org

66646 ■ University of Puerto Rico at Mayaguez–Small Business Development Center
Mayaguez Campus
Box 5253, College Station
Mayaguez, PR 00681
Ph:(809)834-3790
Fax: (809)834-3790
Contact: Carmen Marti, Executive Director
E-mail: cmarti@ns.inter.edu

SCORE OFFICES

66647 ■ SCORE Puerto Rico and Virgin Islands
c/o Luis felipe Amador, Chair
252 Ponce De Leon Ave.
Citibank Tower, Ste. 20
San Juan, PR 00918
Ph:(787)766-5572
Fax: (787)766-5309
Co. E-mail: sjscore200@hotmail.com
URL: http://www.score.org

CHAMBERS OF COMMERCE

66648 ■ Chamber of Commerce of the West of Puerto Rico
PO Box 9
Mayaguez, PR 00681
Ph:(787)832-3749
Fax: (787)832-4287
Co. E-mail: ccopr@coqui.net
Contact: Wanda Gonzalez, Pres.

66649 ■ Ponce and Southern Puerto Rico Chamber of Commerce
PO Box 7455
Ponce, PR 00732-7455
Ph:(787)844-4400
Fax: (787)844-7705
Co. E-mail: info@camarasur.org
URL: http://camarasur.org
Contact: Hector E. Lopez Palermo, Admin.

66650 ■ Puerto Rico Chamber of Commerce
PO Box 9024033
San Juan, PR 00902-4033
Ph:(787)721-6060
Fax: (787)723-1891
Co. E-mail: camarapr@camarapr.net
URL: http://www.camarapr.org
Contact: Edgardo Bigas Valladares, Exec. VP

MINORITY BUSINESS ASSISTANCE PROGRAMS

66651 ■ Ponce Minority Business Development Center
M. L. Prats & Associates, Inc.
Edificio El Pardo, 19 Salud St.
Ponce, PR 731
Ph:(787)840-8100
Fax: (787)840-8115

66652 ■ Puerto Rico Minority Business Development Center
PO Box 363631
San Juan, PR 00936
Ph:(787)753-8484
Fax: (787)753-0855
Co. E-mail: mbdcsj@mbdcpr.com
Contact: Teresa Berrios, Dir

FINANCING AND LOAN PROGRAMS

66653 ■ Advent-Morro Equity Partners
Banco Popular Bldg.
206 Tetuan St., Ste. 903
San Juan, PR 00901
Ph:(787)725-5285
Fax: (787)721-1735
Contact: Cyril Meduna, President
E-mail: cmeduna@adventmorro.com
Preferred Investment Size: $500,000 to $3,000,000.
Investment Types: Early, first, second and later stage, acquisition, expansion, generalist PE, leveraged buyout, management buyouts, recapitalizations, and turnaround. **Industry Preferences:** Communications, computer hardware and software, Internet specific, medical and health, consumer related, financial services, business service, and manufacturing. **Geographic Preferences:** Puerto Rico.

66654 ■ North America Investment Corp.
Mercantil Plaza, Ste. 813
PO Box 1831
Hato Rey Sta.
San Juan, PR 00919
Ph:(787)754-6178
Fax: (787)754-6181
Contact: Marcelino Torres, President
Preferred Investment Size: $25,000 to $250,000. **Investment Types:** Early stage and expansion. **Industry Preferences:** Communications, consumer related, financial services, and business service. **Geographic Preferences:** Puerto Rico.

PROCUREMENT ASSISTANCE PROGRAMS

66655 ■ Puerto Rico Procurement Technical Assistance Center–Commonwealth of Puerto Rico
355 Roosevelt Ave.
Hato Rey, PR 918
Ph:(787)753-6861
Fax: (787)751-6239
Co. E-mail: juliesantana@pridco.com

LEGISLATIVE ASSISTANCE

66656 ■ Puerto Rico House Standing Committee on Industry and Commerce
PO Box 2228
San Juan, PR 901
Ph:(787)722-0704
Fax: (787)722-1567

PUBLISHERS

66657 ■ Book Service of Puerto Rico Inc.
102 De Diego Ave.
San Juan, PR 00907-2345
Ph:(787)728-5000
Fax: (787)726-6131
Co. E-mail: bellbook@caribe.net
Contact: William Irizarry Sr., President
Description: Distributor. **Founded:** 1970.

SMALL BUSINESS DEVELOPMENT CENTER LEAD OFFICE

66658 ■ University of the Virgin Islands–Small Business Development Center
8000 Nisky Center, Ste. 202
Charlotte Amalie
St. Thomas, VI 00802-5804
Ph:(340)776-3206
Fax: (340)775-3756
Contact: Warren T. Bush, State Director
E-mail: wbush@webmail.uvi.edu

66659 ■ Virgin Islands SBDC–University of the Virgin Islands
8000 Nisky Center, Ste. 720
St. Thomas, VI 00802-5804
Ph:(340)776-3206
Fax: (340)775-3756
URL: http://rps.uvi.edu/sbdc
Contact: Warren Bush, State Dir.
E-mail: wbush@webmail.uvi.edu

SMALL BUSINESS DEVELOPMENT CENTERS

66660 ■ University of the Virgin Islands–USVI Small Business Development Center
Sunshine Mall
No.1 Estate Cane, Ste. 104
Frederiksted, St. Croix, VI 00840
Ph:(340)692-5470
Fax: (340)692-5629
Contact: Daniel Hogue, Assoc. State Dir.

66661 ■ University of the Virgin Islands at Charlotte Amalie–Small Business Development Center
Nisky Center, Ste. 202
St. Thomas, VI 00802-5804
Ph:(809)776-3206
Fax: (809)775-3756
Contact: Warren Bush, State Dir.

CHAMBERS OF COMMERCE

66662 ■ St. Croix Chamber of Commerce
3009 Orange Grove, Ste. 12
Christiansted, VI 00820

Ph:(340)773-1435
Fax: (340)773-8172
Co. E-mail: stcroixchamber@viaccess.net
Contact: Frank Fox, Pres.

66663 ■ St. Thomas - St. John Chamber of Commerce
PO Box 324
Charlotte Amalie, VI 00804
Ph:(340)776-0100
Fax: (340)776-0588
Co. E-mail: chamber@islands.vi
URL: http://www.usvichamber.com
Contact: Joe S. Aubain, Exec. Dir.

LEGISLATIVE ASSISTANCE

66664 ■ Legislature Of the Virgin Islands–Virgin Islands Senate Standing Committee on Economic Development Center
1 Lagoon St Complex
St. Croix, VI 840
Ph:(340)712-2258
Fax: (340)712-2380
URL: http://www.senate.gov.vi
Contact: Johnathan Chief of Resources, Chief of Resources

FINANCING AND LOAN PROGRAMS

66665 ■ Launchworks Inc.
1902J 11th St., SE
Calgary, AB, Canada T2G 3G2
Ph:(403)269-1119
Fax: (403)269-1141
URL: http://www.launchworks.com
Contact: Byron Osing, Chief Executive Officer
Investment Types: Start-up. **Geographic Preferences:** Canada.

66666 ■ Miralta Capital, Inc.
475 Dumont Ave., Ste. 300
Dorval, QC, Canada H9S 5W2
Ph:(514)631-2682
Fax: (514)631-1257
Contact: Robert Mee
Preferred Investment Size: $1,000,000 minimum.
Investment Types: First and second stage, and leveraged buyout. **Industry Preferences:** Communications and media, computer hardware and software, semiconductors and other electronics, consumer related, industrial and energy, and manufacturing. **Geographic Preferences:** Canada.

66667 ■ Native Venture Capital Co., Ltd.
21 Artist View Point, Box 7
Site 25, RR 12
Calgary, AB, Canada T3E 6W3
Ph:(903)208-5380
Contact: Milt Pahl
Preferred Investment Size: $300,000 minimum. **Investment Types:** Seed, start-up, first and second stage, and leveraged buyout. **Geographic Preferences:** Western Canada.

66668 ■ Vencap Equities Alberta, Ltd.
10180-101st St., Ste. 1980
Edmonton, AB, Canada T5J 3S4
Ph:(403)420-1171
Fax: (403)429-2451
Preferred Investment Size: $1,000,000 minimum.
Investment Types: Start-up, first and second stage, control-block purchases, leveraged buyout, and mezzanine. **Industry Preferences:** Communications and media, computer related, semiconductors and other electronics, medical and health, consumer related, industrial and energy, transportation, manufacturing, and agriculture, forestry and fishing. **Geographic Preferences:** Northwest, Rocky Mountains, and Western Canada.

INCUBATORS/RESEARCH AND TECHNOLOGY PARKS

66669 ■ Edmonton Research Park
203 Advanced Technology Centre
9650 20 Ave. NW
Edmonton, AB, Canada T6N 1G1

Ph:(780)462-2121
Fax: (780)436-2762
Co. E-mail: csawatsky@edmonton.com
URL: http://www.edmonton.com/researchpark
Contact: Carrie Sawatsky, Admin.
E-mail: csawatsky@edmonton.com
Scope: Serves as a link between University research resources and tenants involved in basic, applied, and developmental research, product development, light production, advanced technology activities, and related support services. **Services:** Biotechnology Land Lease Program. **Publications:** Newsletter.

66670 ■ University of Calgary–Office of the Vice President, Research
2500 University Dr. NW
Administration 110
Calgary, AB, Canada T2N 1N4
Ph:(403)220-7833
Fax: (403)289-6800
Co. E-mail: dennis.salahub@ucalgary.ca
URL: http://www.ucalgary.ca/UofC/research/html/res_admin/off_vpr.html
Contact: Dr. Dennis R. Salahub, VP,Res.
E-mail: dennis.salahub@ucalgary.ca
Scope: Responsible for administration and coordination of research activities at the University. **Publications:** Annual Report; OnCampus (weekly); U magazine (quarterly).

PUBLISHERS

66671 ■ Platypus Publisher
2323E 3rd Ave. NW
Calgary, AB, Canada T2N 0K9
Ph:(403)283-0498
Fax: (403)270-3023
Co. E-mail: platypus@cadvision.com
Contact: Nattalia Lea, President
E-mail: nattalia@shaw.ca
Description: Publishes how-to on entrepreneurs and small business for individuals. Offers T-shirts and cartoons. Does not accept unsolicited manuscripts. Reaches market through commission representatives, One-On-One, and Temeron Books. **Founded:** 1996.

66672 ■ Sextant Publishing
Empire Bldg., Ste. 208
10080 Jasper Ave.
Edmonton, AB, Canada T5J 1V9
Ph:(780)420-0505
Fax: (780)420-1256
Co. E-mail: sextant@cambridgestrategies.com
URL: http://www.cambridgestrategies.com/sextant/sextant.htm
Contact: Ken Chapman
E-mail: ken@cambridgestrategies.com
Description: Publishes books, articles, pamphlets, and monographs on public policy, society, business, and culture relating to Alberta, Canada. **Founded:** 2002

66673 ■ The Soap Box
424 3 St. W
Cochrane, AB, Canada T4C 1Z6
Ph:(403)932-4530
Fax: (403)851-0363
Co. E-mail: customde@cadvision.com
URL: http://www.thesoapbox.org
Contact: Donna Ramsey
Description: Publishes books on natural cosmetics and soaps. Does not accept unsolicited manuscripts. Reaches market through direct mail, telephone sales, demos, and classes. **Founded:** 1998.

66674 ■ United Library Services Inc.
7140 Fairmount Dr. SE
Calgary, AB, Canada T2H 0X4
Ph:(403)252-4426
Free: 888-342-5857
Fax: (403)252-3426
Co. E-mail: info@uls.com
URL: http://www.uls.com
Contact: Robin Hoogwerf, Gen Mgr
E-mail: robin@uls.com
Description: Wholesaler. **Founded:** 1939.

66675 ■ Unlimited Learning Publications
123-28342 Township Rd., Ste. 384
Red Deer County, AB, Canada T4S 2B6
Ph:(403)347-0008
Free: 888-535-5059
Fax: (403)343-6688
Co. E-mail: dunning1@telusplanet.net
Contact: Paul Dunning, Owner
Description: Publishes books on learning, career development, and work performance. Does not accept unsolicited manuscripts. Reaches market through distributors. **Founded:** 1992.

66676 ■ Visions International Publishing
PO Box 4072
Edmonton, AB, Canada T6E 4S8
Ph:(780)434-9202
Fax: (780)436-1798
Co. E-mail: vip-books@telus.net
URL: http://www.thejoyofnotworking.com
Contact: Ernie Zelinski, President
E-mail: ernie@attcanada.net
Description: Publishes on personal growth in business. Reaches market through direct mail and Sandhill Book Marketing in Canada and Ten Speed Press in the U.S. **Founded:** 1989.

66677 ■ Word Engines Press Inc.
2125 Summerfield Blvd.
Airdrie, AB, Canada T4B 1X2
Ph:(403)948-7774
Free: (866)467-4550
Fax: (403)912-0199
Co. E-mail: abbottr@managersguide.com
URL: http://www.managersguide.com
Contact: Robert F. Abbott, Publisher
E-mail: abbottr@managersguide.com
Description: Publishes books for managers and professionals. Does not accept unsolicited manuscripts. Reaches market through direct mail and their website. **Founded:** 1998.

FINANCING AND LOAN PROGRAMS

66678 ■ Discovery Capital
5th Fl., 1199 West Hastings
Vancouver, BC, Canada V6E 3T5
Ph:(604)683-3000
Fax: (604)662-3457
Co. E-mail: info@discoverycapital.com
URL: http://www.discoverycapital.com
Investment Types: Start-up, early stage, and balanced. **Industry Preferences:** Communications and media, and Internet specific. **Geographic Preferences:** British Columbia and Canada.

66679 ■ Greenstone Venture Partners
1177 West Hastings St., Ste. 400
Vancouver, BC, Canada V6E 2K3
Ph:(604)717-1977
Fax: (604)717-1976
URL: http://www.greenstonevc.com
Contact: Brent Holliday, General Partner
Preferred Investment Size: $300,000 to $300,000,000. **Investment Types:** Seed, start-up, first and second stage. **Industry Preferences:** Communications and media, computer software, Internet specific, semiconductors and other electronics. **Geographic Preferences:** Northern California, Northwest U.S., and Western Canada.

66680 ■ Growthworks
2600-1055 West Georgia St.
Box 11170 Royal Centre
Vancouver, BC, Canada V6E 3R5
Ph:(604)633-1418
Fax: (604)669-7605
URL: http://www.wofund.com
Contact: Mike Philips
Preferred Investment Size: $330,000 to $3,300,000. **Investment Types:** Seed, start-up, first and second stage, balanced, joint ventures, mezzanine, private placement, research and development, and management buyout. **Industry Preferences:** Communications and media, Internet specific, computer related, semiconductors and other electronics, biotechnology, medical and health, consumer related, industrial and energy, transportation, manufacturing, agriculture, forestry and fishing, and environment. **Geographic Preferences:** British Columbia, Canada.

66681 ■ MDS Discovery Venture Management, Inc.
555 W. Eighth Ave., Ste. 305
Vancouver, BC, Canada V5Z 1C6
Ph:(604)872-8464
Fax: (604)872-2977
Co. E-mail: info@mds-ventures.com
Contact: David Scott, President
Preferred Investment Size: $500,000 to $1,000,000. **Investment Types:** Seed, research and development, start-up, first and second stage. **Industry Preferences:** Biotechnology, communications and media, and Internet specific. **Geographic Preferences:** Western Canada and Northwest U.S.

66682 ■ Ventures West Management, Inc.
1285 West Pender St., Ste. 280
Vancouver, BC, Canada V6E 4B1
Ph:(604)688-9495
Fax: (604)687-2145
URL: http://www.ventureswest.com
Contact: Robin Louis, President
Preferred Investment Size: $1,000,000 minimum to $9,999,000. **Investment Types:** Seed, research and development, start-up, early, first and second stage, and balanced. **Industry Preferences:** Communications and media, computer software and services, computer hardware, biotechnology, Internet specific, medical and health, semiconductors and other electronics, industrial and energy related. **Geographic Preferences:** Canada.

INCUBATORS/RESEARCH AND TECHNOLOGY PARKS

66683 ■ Discovery Parks Incorporated
1333 W. Broadway, Ste. 750
Vancouver, BC, Canada V6H 4C1
Ph:(604)734-7275
Fax: (604)734-7278
Co. E-mail: information@discoveryparks.com
URL: http://www.discoveryparks.com
Contact: Mark Betteridge, Exec.Dir./CEO
E-mail: information@discoveryparks.com
Scope: Manages a park at University of British Columbia, 75-acre park at Simon Fraser University, and 80-acre park adjacent to British Columbia Institute of Technology that link university research resources with technological and research companies in the parks.

PUBLISHERS

66684 ■ J.A. Hall Publications
2401-9304 Salish Ct.
Burnaby, BC, Canada V3J 7C5
Ph:(604)738-9688
Free: 888-993-6133
Fax: (604)738-9425
Co. E-mail: info@hallpublications.com
URL: http://www.hallpublications.com
Contact: Joan Ruddell, Mgr
Description: Publishes health science books and manuals. Does not accept unsolicited manuscripts. Reaches market through direct mail, distributors and their website. **Founded:** 1997.

66685 ■ John Markham & Associates
11210 Elderberry Way
Sidney, BC, Canada V8L 5J6
Ph:(250)655-1823
Free: (866)562-8247
Fax: (250)655-1826
Co. E-mail: jma@mercuriustags.com
URL: http://www.johnmarkham.com/home
Contact: John Markham, Owner
Description: Distributor. **Founded:** 1991.

66686 ■ Self-Counsel Press Ltd.
1481 Charlotte Rd.
North Vancouver, BC, Canada V7J 1H1
Ph:(604)986-3366
Free: 800-663-3007
Fax: (604)986-3947
Co. E-mail: service@self-counsel.com
URL: http://www.self-counsel.com
Contact: Diana Douglas, President
Description: Publishes legal, business, and reference books. **Founded:** 1977.

66687 ■ Sound Current Music & Books
RR 1
PO Box 251
Bowen Island, BC, Canada V0N 1G0
Ph:(604)222-0060
Free: 877-777-6863
Fax: (604)947-0975
Co. E-mail: soundcurrent@sprint.ca
URL: http://www.soundcurrent.homestead.com
Contact: Deborah Van Dyke, President
E-mail: soundcurrent@sprint.ca
Description: Publishes sound healing resources in print and audio. Does not accept unsolicited manuscripts. Reaches market through direct mail, wholesalers and distributors. **Founded:** 1998.

66688 ■ Total Design
12975 Degraff Rd.
Mission, BC, Canada V2V 4J1
Ph:(604)826-5681
Co. E-mail: ducks@uniserve.com
Contact: Rita A. Boehler
Description: Publishes books on entrepreneurial activity. They are meant to awaken the the entrepreneurial ability in everyone. Does not accept unsolicited manuscripts. Reaches market through direct mail, wholesalers, and distributors. **Founded:** 1990.

66689 ■ Turnagain Enterprises Ltd.
1401 West Broadway, Ste. 601
Vancouver, BC, Canada V6H 1H6
Ph:(604)757-1312
Fax: (604)737-1317
Co. E-mail: info@albertgivton.com
URL: http://www.albertgivton.com
Contact: Albert Givton, Owner
Description: Publishes book on wines. Does not accept unsolicited manuscripts. Reaches market through direct mail, distributors, print ads, and the Web. **Founded:** 1974.

SMALL BUSINESS ASSISTANCE PROGRAMS

66690 ■ Canada Manitoba Business Service Centre
240 Graham Ave., Rm. 250
PO Box 2609
Winnipeg, MB, Canada R3C 4B3
Ph:(204)984-2272
Fax: (204)983-3852
Co. E-mail: manitoba@cbsc.ic.gc.ca
URL: http://www.cbsc.org/manitoba
Description: Offers assistance, training, and expertise to business and entrepreneurs. Offers a variety of programs.

66691 ■ Canada Manitoba Business Service Centre–Business Information Programs (240 G)
240 Graham Ave., Rm. 250
PO Box 2609
Winnipeg, MB, Canada R3C 4B3
Ph:(204)984-2272
Fax: (204)983-3852
Co. E-mail: manitoba@cbsc.ic.gc.ca
URL: http://www.cbsc.org/manitoba
Description: Provides business information such as self-help management guides, information books, reference-use materials, and contacts with other provincial government departments.

66692 ■ Canada Manitoba Business Service Centre–Business Library (240 G)
240 Graham Ave., Rm. 250
PO Box 2609
Winnipeg, MB, Canada R3C 4B3
Ph:(204)984-2272
Fax: (204)983-3852
Co. E-mail: manitoba@cbsc.ic.gc.ca
URL: http://www.cbsc.org/manitoba
Description: Maintains hard copy, database, and video resources for use by government agencies and the public.

66693 ■ Canada Manitoba Business Service Centre–General Business Counselling (240 G)
240 Graham Ave., Rm. 250
PO Box 2609
Winnipeg, MB, Canada R3C 4B3
Ph:(204)984-2272
Fax: (204)983-3852
Co. E-mail: manitoba@cbsc.ic.gc.ca
URL: http://www.cbsc.org/manitoba
Description: Provides telephone and in-person counseling to entrepreneurs and refers inquiries to other Department of Industry, Trade and Tourism branches.

66694 ■ Canada Manitoba Business Service Centre–Manitoba Marketing Network, Inc. (240 G)
240 Graham Ave., Rm. 250
PO Box 2609
Winnipeg, MB, Canada R3C 4B3

Ph:(204)984-2272
Fax: (204)983-3852
Co. E-mail: manitoba@cbsc.ic.gc.ca
URL: http://www.cbsc.org/manitoba
Description: A public/private partnership between the Department of Industry, Trade and Tourism and members of Manitoba's business community that provides consultative assistance in marketing and product promotion to business clients, via its private sector advisory board.

66695 ■ Canada/Manitoba Business Services Centre
240 Graham Ave., Rm. 250
PO Box 2609
Winnipeg, MB, Canada R3C 4B3
Ph:(204)984-2272
Fax: (204)983-3852
Co. E-mail: manitoba@cbsc.ic.gc.ca
URL: http://www.cbsc.org/manitoba/
Description: Provides information on import/export permits.

66696 ■ Industry Economic Development–Western Regional Office
131 9th St., Rm. 107
Brandon, MB, Canada R7A 6C2
Ph:(204)726-6250
Fax: (204)726-6403
Co. E-mail: keglemie@gov.mb.ca
Description: Provides program assistance to small businesses.

66697 ■ Industry Economic Development and Mines–Technology Commercialization Program
The Paris Bldg.
1040-259 Portage Ave
Winnipeg, MB, Canada R3B 3P4
Ph:(204)945-2475
Fax: (204)945-3977
URL: http://www.gov.mb.ca/iedm
Description: Negotiates individual agreements with private sector firms whereby, in return for certain provincial incentives, a firm will establish new operations or expand existing operations in Manitoba, undertaking specific capital investment as well as creating long-term jobs.

66698 ■ Manitoba Intergovernmental Affairs and Trade–Community Economic Development Branch
648-155 Carlton
Winnipeg, MB, Canada R3C-3H8
Ph:(204)945-8221
Fax: (204)945-5059
Co. E-mail: apenston@gov.mb.ca
URL: http://www.gov.mb.ca/ia

66699 ■ Manitoba Intergovernmental Affairs and Trade–Rural Economic Development Initiative
648-155 Carlton
Winnipeg, MB, Canada R3C-3H8
Ph:(204)945-2157
Fax: (204)945-5059

URL: http://www.gov.mb.ca/ia
Description: Trained students offer consulting to owners/managers of small and medium-sized Manitoba businesses in the areas of marketing, accounting, and production.

66700 ■ Manitoba Tax Assistance Office
809-368 Broadway
Winnipeg, MB, Canada R3C 3R6
Ph:(204)948-2115
Fax: (204)948-2263
Co. E-mail: toa@gov.mb.ca
URL: http://www.gov.mb.ca/finance/tao
Description: Administers the Small Business Tax Reduction program.

MINORITY BUSINESS ASSISTANCE PROGRAMS

66701 ■ Manitoba Industry, Trade and Tourism–Canada Manitoba Business Service Center–Women's Entrepreneurial Programs (240 G)
240 Graham Ave., 2nd Fl. Rm. 250
PO Box 2609
Winnipeg, MB, Canada R3C 4B3
Ph:(204)945-6942
Fax: (204)983-3852
Co. E-mail: mgault@tt.gov.mb.ca
URL: http://www.gov.mb.ca
Description: Promotes entrepreneurship as an economic alternative for women. Liaison is provided between women business owners and provincial programs and services. Business information, seminars, and counseling are also provided to individuals and community organizations.

INCUBATORS/RESEARCH AND TECHNOLOGY PARKS

66702 ■ University of Manitoba–Technology Transfer Office
Drake Centre, Rm. 631
181 Freedman Cres.
Winnipeg, MB, Canada R3T 5V4
Ph:(204)474-6200
Fax: (204)261-3475
Co. E-mail: Garold_Breit@umanitoba.ca
URL: http://www.umanitoba.ca/research
Contact: Garold Breit, Exec.Dir.
E-mail: Garold_Breit@umanitoba.ca
Scope: Serves as the Technology Transfer Office; identifying and protecting intellectual property resulting from academic-based research and preparing such intellectual property for commercialization. **Services:** Start-up business development; Technology assessments. **Publications:** Connections; Interface. **Educational Activities:** Certificate program in intellectual property and technology commercialization management; Intellectual Property Management; Special interest workshops and seminars.

PUBLISHERS

66703 ■ Gateway Publishing Company Ltd.
385 DeBaets St.
Winnipeg, MB, Canada R2J 4J8

Ph:(204)222-4294
Free: 800-665-4878
Fax: (204)224-4410
Co. E-mail: cookbooks@gatebook.com
URL: http://www.gatebook.com

Description: Publishes books about child safety. Also publishes cookbooks. **Founded:** 1965.

SMALL BUSINESS ASSISTANCE PROGRAMS

66704 ■ Business New Brunswick–Finance and Support
PO Box 6000
Fredericton, NB, Canada E3B 5H1
Ph:(506)444-5228
Free: 800-561-0123
Fax: (506)444-4586

Co. E-mail: alda.descosta@gnb.ca
URL: http://www.gnb.ca

INCUBATORS/RESEARCH AND TECHNOLOGY PARKS

66705 ■ Enterprise UNB
2 Garland Ct.
PO Box 69000
Fredericton, NB, Canada E3B 6C2

Ph:(506)453-4500
Fax: (506)453-3541
Co. E-mail: bmoxon@unb.ca
Contact: Brenda Moxon
Description: Jointly sponsored by the University of New Brunswick and the Research and Productivity Council, this incubator supports emerging technology firms.

INCUBATORS/RESEARCH AND TECHNOLOGY PARKS

66706 ■ Memorial University of Newfoundland–Office of Research
Inco Innovation Centre, 2nd Fl., Rm. IIC 2015
230 Elizaberh Ave.
St. John's, NL, Canada A1C 5S7
Ph:(709)737-8251
Fax: (709)737-4612

Co. E-mail: bcox@mun.ca
URL: http://www.mun.ca/research
Contact: Barbara Cox, Dir.
E-mail: bcox@mun.ca
Scope: Administers individual and faculty research funding (approximately $30,000,000) in science, medicine, engineering, social sciences, humanities, education, business administration, nursing, physical education and athletics, social work, music, fine arts, and pharmacy. Also assists specialized research units at the University, including the Centre for Earth Re-

sources Research, Centre for Offshore and Remote Medicine, Institute for Social and Economic Research, Labrador Institute of Northern Studies, Ocean Sciences Centre, Aquaculture Research and Development Facility, Ocean Engineering Research Centre, Maritime Studies Research Unit, Telemedicine and Educational Technology Resources Agency, and Fisheries and Marine Institu. **Publications:** Annual Inventory of Sponsored Projects; Research Directory of Faculty Expertise and Current Research Projects; Research Matters Newsletter.

SMALL BUSINESS ASSISTANCE PROGRAMS

66707 ■ Nova Scotia Business, Inc. –Business Services Center
1800 Argyle St., Ste 701
Halifax, NS, Canada B3J 3E4
Ph:(902)424-6650
Free: 800-668-1010
Fax: (902)424-5739
Co. E-mail: nsbi@gov.ns.ca
URL: http://www.novascotiabusiness.com/
Description: Provides counseling to Nova Scotia businesses on such areas as start-up, finance, management, marketing, and technical assessment to enhance overall effectiveness and growth. Services include review of business plans, financial statements, and projections.

66708 ■ Nova Scotia Economic Development
14th Fl. S, Maritime Centre
1505 Barrington St.
Halifax, NS, Canada B3J 3K5
Ph:(902)424-0377
Free: 800-565-2009
Fax: (902)424-7008
URL: http://www.gov.ns.ca/

FINANCING AND LOAN PROGRAMS

66709 ■ ACF Equity Atlantic, Inc.
Purdy's Wharf Tower II, Ste. 2106
Halifax, NS, Canada B3J 3R7
Ph:(902)421-1965
Fax: (902)421-1808
URL: http://www.acf.ca
Contact: David Wilson
Investment Types: Seed, start-up, first and second stage, balanced, mezzanine, and leveraged buyout. **Industry Preferences:** Communications and media, computer hardware and software, Internet specific, semiconductors and other electronics, biotechnology, medical and health, consumer related, industrial and energy related, agriculture, forestry and fishing. **Geographic Preferences:** Canada.

66710 ■ Montgomerie, Huck & Co.
146 Bluenose Dr.
PO Box 538
Lunenburg, NS, Canada B0J 2C0
Ph:(902)634-7125
Fax: (902)634-7130
Contact: Christopher Huck
Preferred Investment Size: $300,000 to $500,000. **Investment Types:** First and second stage, leveraged buyout, mezzanine, and special situation. **Industry Preferences:** Communications and media, computer software, industrial and energy. **Geographic Preferences:** Northeast U.S. and Canada.

INCUBATORS/RESEARCH AND TECHNOLOGY PARKS

66711 ■ Agritech Park Incorporated
90 Research Dr.
Truro, NS, Canada B2N 6Z4
Ph:(902)896-7275
Fax: (902)896-7276
Co. E-mail: admin@agritechpark.com
URL: http://www.agritechpark.com
Contact: Sharron MacKenzie, Admin. Ass.
Description: This incubator assists emerging firms in the agriculture and biotechnology industries.

PUBLISHERS

66712 ■ Time-Use Research Program
St. Mary's University, 5670 Spring Garden Rd., Ste. 601
Halifax, NS, Canada B3J 1H6
Ph:(902)420-5676
Fax: (902)422-7039
Co. E-mail: timeuse@stmarys.ca
URL: http://www.stmarys.ca/partners/turp/main.html
Contact: Dr. Andrew S. Harvey, Director
E-mail: andrew.harvey@stmarys.ca
Description: Publishes research findings, time-use literature and newsletters. Aimed towards academic audiences. Does not accept unsolicited manuscripts. **Founded:** 1992.

PUBLISHERS

66713 ■ Nortext Multimedia Inc. (Iqaluit)
Bldg. 157
PO Box 8
Iqaluit, NT, Canada X0A 0H0

Ph:(867)979-4376
Fax: (867)979-7841
Co. E-mail: ads@nortext.com
URL: http://www.nortext.com
Contact: Roberta Roberts, Director
E-mail: rroberts@nortext.com

Description: Publishes school books, aboriginal language, business, Nunavut and travel books.
Founded: 1990.

FINANCING AND LOAN PROGRAMS

66714 ■ Bailey & Company Inc.
594 Spadina Ave.
Toronto, ON, Canada M5S 2H4
Ph:(416)921-6930
Fax: (416)925-4670
Preferred Investment Size: $500,000 to $1,000,000.
Investment Types: Research and development, first stage, mezzanine, and special situation. **Industry Preferences:** Communications and media, semiconductors and other electronics, biotechnology, medical and health, industrial and energy.

66715 ■ BCE Capital
250 Yonge St., 9th Fl.
Toronto, ON, Canada M5B 2L7
Ph:(416)408-0100
Fax: (416)585-9749
URL: http://www.bcecapital.com
Contact: Gary Rubinoff, President
Preferred Investment Size: $2,000,000 to $10,000,000. **Investment Types:** Seed, early stage, and expansion. **Industry Preferences:** Communications and media, Internet specific, semiconductors and other electronics, computer software and services. **Geographic Preferences:** Canada.

66716 ■ Betwin Investments Inc.
Box 23110
Sault Ste. Marie, ON, Canada P6A 6W6
Ph:(705)253-0744
Fax: (705)253-0744
Contact: D.B. Stinson
Preferred Investment Size: $500,000 to $1,000,000.
Investment Types: Second stage. **Industry Preferences:** Computer related, semiconductors and other electronics, medical and health, consumer related, industrial and energy. **Geographic Preferences:** U.S. and Canada.

66717 ■ Castlehill Ventures
11 King St. W., Ste. 600
Toronto, ON, Canada M5H 4C7
Ph:(416)862-8574
Fax: (416)862-8875
URL: http://www.castlehillventures.com
Investment Types: Start-up. **Industry Preferences:** Telecommunications, and computer related. **Geographic Preferences:** Ontario, Canada.

66718 ■ CCFL Mezzanine Partners of Canada
70 University Ave., Ste. 1450
Toronto, ON, Canada M5J 2M4
Ph:(416)977-1450
Fax: (416)977-6764
Co. E-mail: info@ccfl.com
URL: http://www.ccfl.com
Contact: Robert Olsen, President
Preferred Investment Size: $10,000,000 minimum.
Investment Types: Generalist PE, and mezzanine.
Geographic Preferences: Canada.

66719 ■ Celtic House International
555 Legget Dr.
Tower B, Ste. 530
Kanata, ON, Canada K2K 2X3
Ph:(613)271-2020
Fax: (613)271-2025
URL: http://www.celtic-house.com
Contact: Terry Matthews, Principal
Investment Types: Early stage. **Industry Preferences:** Computer software and services, semiconductors and other electronics, communications and media, Internet specific, medical and health, and computer hardware. **Geographic Preferences:** U.S. and Canada.

66720 ■ Clairvest Group Inc.
22 St. Clair Ave. E., Ste. 1700
Toronto, ON, Canada M4T 2S3
Ph:(416)925-9270
Fax: (416)925-5753
URL: http://www.clairvest.com
Contact: Jeffrey Parr, Chief Executive Officer
Preferred Investment Size: $5,000,000 minimum.
Investment Types: Balanced, control-block purchases, later stage, leveraged buyout, public companies, and special situation. **Geographic Preferences:** Canada.

66721 ■ Crosbie & Co. Inc.
One First Canadian Pl., 9th Fl.
PO Box 116
Toronto, ON, Canada M5X 1A4
Ph:(416)362-7726
Fax: (416)362-3447
Co. E-mail: info@crosbieco.com
URL: http://www.crosbieco.com
Contact: Allan Crosbie, Managing Partner
Investment Types: Acquisition, distressed debt, expansion, management buyouts, mezzanine, recapitalizations, special situation, and turnarounds. **Industry Preferences:** Communications and media, computer software, semiconductors and other electronics, medical and health, consumer related, industrial and energy, business service, manufacturing, agriculture, forestry and fishing. **Geographic Preferences:** Ontario, Canada.

66722 ■ Drug Royalty Corp., Inc.
Eight King St. E.
Ste. 202
Toronto, ON, Canada M5C 1B5
Ph:(416)863-1865
Fax: (416)863-5161
Preferred Investment Size: $3,000,000 to $4,000,000. **Investment Types:** Research and development, and special situation. **Industry Preferences:** Biotechnology, medical and health.

66723 ■ Grieve, Horner, Brown & ASCULAI
8 King St. E., Ste. 1704
Toronto, ON, Canada M5C 1B5
Ph:(416)362-7668
Fax: (416)362-7660
Preferred Investment Size: $300,000 to $500,000.
Investment Types: Start-up, first and second stage.

Industry Preferences: Communications and media, computer software, Internet specific, medical and health, consumer related, and manufacturing. **Geographic Preferences:** U.S. and Canada.

66724 ■ IPS Industrial Promotion Services, Ltd.
60 Columbia Way, Ste. 720
Markham, ON, Canada L3R 0C9
Ph:(905)475-9400
Fax: (905)475-5003
Contact: Nizar Alibhai
Preferred Investment Size: $500,000 minimum. **Investment Types:** Control-block purchases, leveraged buyout, second stage, and special situation. **Industry Preferences:** Communication and media, computer hardware, semiconductors and other electronics, biotechnology, medical and health, consumer related, industrial and energy, and transportation. **Geographic Preferences:** U.S. and Canada.

66725 ■ Jefferson Partners
260 Queen St. W., 4th Fl.
Toronto, ON, Canada M5V 1Z8
Ph:(416)367-1533
Fax: (416)367-5827
URL: http://www.jefferson.com
Contact: David Folk, Managing General Partner
Preferred Investment Size: $3,000,000 to $10,000,000. **Investment Types:** Seed, expansion, early and later stage. **Industry Preferences:** Communications and media, computer software, and Internet specific. **Geographic Preferences:** Northeast U.S. and Canada.

66726 ■ J.L. Albright Venture Partners
Canada Trust Tower
161 Bay St., Ste. 4440
PO Box 215
Toronto, ON, Canada M5J 2S1
Ph:(416)367-2440
Fax: (416)367-4604
URL: http://www.jlaventures.com
Contact: Gary Rubinoff, Partner
Preferred Investment Size: $2,000,000 to $20,000,000. **Investment Types:** Early, first stage, and private placement. **Industry Preferences:** Internet specific, other products, computer software and services, and computer hardware. **Geographic Preferences:** Ontario and Quebec.

66727 ■ McLean Watson Capital Inc.
One First Canadian Pl., Ste. 1410
PO Box 129
Toronto, ON, Canada M5X 1A4
Ph:(416)363-2000
Fax: (416)363-2010
URL: http://www.mcleanwatson.com
Contact: John Eckert, Partner
Investment Types: First and second stage, early and later stage, expansion, and balanced. **Industry Preferences:** Communications and media, computer software, computer related, semiconductors and other electronics. **Geographic Preferences:** U.S. and Canada.

66728 ■ Middlefield Capital Fund
One First Canadian Pl., 58th Fl.
PO Box 192
Toronto, ON, Canada M5X 1A6
Ph:(416)362-0714
Fax: (416)362-7925
URL: http://www.middlefield.com
Contact: Garth Jestley, President and Chief
Operating Officer
Preferred Investment Size: $3,000,000 minimum.
Investment Types: Second stage, control-block purchases, industry rollups, leveraged buyout, and mezzanine. **Industry Preferences:** Communications and media, computer hardware, semiconductors and other electronics, medical and health, consumer related, industrial and energy, transportation, financial services, agriculture, forestry and fishing. **Geographic Preferences:** U.S. and Canada.

66729 ■ Mosaic Venture Partners
49 Wellington St. E., 3rd Fl.
Toronto, ON, Canada M5E 1C9
Ph:(416)367-2888
Fax: (416)597-2345
Investment Types: Early stage. **Industry Preferences:** Internet specific. **Geographic Preferences:** Canada.

66730 ■ Onex Corp.
161 Bay St., 49th Fl.
PO Box 700
Toronto, ON, Canada M5J 2S1
Ph:(416)362-7711
Fax: (416)362-5765
URL: http://www.onex.com
Preferred Investment Size: $10,000,000 minimum.
Investment Types: Control-block purchases, leveraged buyout, and special situation. **Geographic Preferences:** U.S. and Canada.

66731 ■ Penfund Partners, Inc.
Munich Re Center
300 Bay St., Ste. 1720
Toronto, ON, Canada M5H 2Y2
Ph:(416)865-0707
Fax: (416)364-4149
URL: http://www.penfund.com
Preferred Investment Size: $667,000 to $4,670,000.
Investment Types: Generalist PE, leveraged and management buyouts, and mezzanine. **Geographic Preferences:** Canada.

66732 ■ Primaxis Technology Ventures Inc.
1 Richmond St. W., 8th Fl.
Toronto, ON, Canada M5H 3W4
Ph:(416)313-5210
Fax: (416)313-5218
URL: http://www.primaxis.com
Contact: Joel Liederman, Vice President
Investment Types: Seed and early stage. **Industry Preferences:** Communications and media, semiconductors and other electronics, and manufacturing. **Geographic Preferences:** Canada.

66733 ■ Priveq Capital Funds
240 Duncan Mill Rd., Ste. 602
Toronto, ON, Canada M3B 3P1
Ph:(416)447-3330
Fax: (416)447-3331
Co. E-mail: priveq@sympatico.ca
URL: http://www.priveq.ca
Contact: Brad Ashley, Managing Partner
Preferred Investment Size: $1,611,000 to $8,307,000. **Investment Types:** Acquisition, expansion, later stage, management and leveraged buyout, and special situation. **Industry Preferences:** Semiconductors and other electronics, consumer related, industrial and energy, transportation, business services, and manufacturing. **Geographic Preferences:** Midwest, Northeast, Southwest U.S., and Canada.

66734 ■ Roynat Ventures / Roynat Capital Corp.
40 King St. W., 26th Fl.
Toronto, ON, Canada M5H 1H1
Ph:(416)933-2730
Fax: (416)933-2783

URL: http://www.roynatcapital.com
Preferred Investment Size: $3,000,000 minimum.
Investment Types: Early stage, expansion, and balanced. **Geographic Preferences:** Canada.

66735 ■ Tera Capital Corp.
366 Adelaide St. E., Ste. 337
Toronto, ON, Canada M5A 3X9
Ph:(416)368-8372
Fax: (416)368-1427
Contact: Duncan Stewart, Partner
Preferred Investment Size: $250,000 to $1,000,000.
Investment Types: Early stage, first and second stage, later stage, and mezzanine. **Industry Preferences:** Computer hardware, semiconductors and other electronics, biotechnology, and consumer related. **Geographic Preferences:** Canada.

66736 ■ Working Ventures Canadian Fund Inc.
250 Bloor St., Ste. 1600
Toronto, ON, Canada M4W 1E6
Ph:(416)934-7777
Fax: (416)463-1652
URL: http://www.workingventures.ca
Preferred Investment Size: $334,000 to $10,008,000. **Investment Types:** No preference. **Industry Preferences:** Consumer related, communications and media, other products, computer software and services, computer hardware, Internet specific, industrial and energy, semiconductors and other electronics, biotechnology, and medical and health. **Geographic Preferences:** Ontario and Western Canada.

INCUBATORS/RESEARCH AND TECHNOLOGY PARKS

66737 ■ McMaster University–Office of Research Services
1280 Main St. W
Hamilton, ON, Canada L8S 4L8
Ph:(905)525-9140
Fax: (905)540-8019
Co. E-mail: morwald@mcmaster.ca
URL: http://www.mcmaster.ca/ors/
Contact: Emmi Morwald, Exec.Dir.
E-mail: morwald@mcmaster.ca
Scope: Responsible for administration of government infrastructure, government and not-for profit research funding programs; financial administration and management of research funds; ethics of non-medical research involving human subjects and research policies and procedures. **Services:** Institutional Expertise Database (quarterly); Resource for research funding opportunities (weekly). **Publications:** Annual Summary Statistical Reports of Externally Supported Research at the University (annually). **Educational Activities:** Workshops for research community on ethics of research involving human subjects (annually); Workshops on Competing for Research Funding (annually).

66738 ■ National Research Council Canada–Social Sciences and Humanities Research Council of Canada–Conseil de recherches en sciences humaines du Canada
350 Albert St.
PO Box 1610
Ottawa, ON, Canada K1P 6G4
Ph:(613)992-0691
Fax: (613)992-1787
Co. E-mail: janet.halliwell@sshrc.ca
URL: http://www.crsh.ca
Contact: Dr. Stan M. Shapson, Interim Pres.
E-mail: janet.halliwell@sshrc.ca
Scope: Promotes and assists Canadian research and scholarship in the social sciences and the humanities by administering funding programs for basic and applied research, doctoral and postdoctoral studies, research communication, and international relations. Administers the Jules and Gabrielle Leger Fellowship for studies on the history, role, and functions of the Crown and its representatives (federal and provincial)

in a parliamentary democracy; the Therese F. Casgrain Fellowship for studies on women and social change in Canada; the Bora Laskin National Fellowship in Human Rights Research for multidisciplinary studies in the field of human rights, focusing on Canadian Human rights issues; the Queens' Fellowship for Canadian studies at the doctoral level; the William E. Taylor Fellowship awarded annually to the most outstanding SSHRC doctoral award candidate; SSHRC Gold Medal awarded annually to an eminent Canadian researcher. Most research training programs are open to Canadian citizens and permanent residents only; other programs are open to researchers affiliated with a Canadian postsecondary institution. **Publications:** Annual report; Committee reports; Announcements of competition results; Program guide.

66739 ■ Ryerson University–Office of Research Services
350 Victoria St.
Toronto, ON, Canada M5B 2K3
Ph:(416)979-5042
Fax: (416)979-5336
Co. E-mail: dirstein@ryerson.ca
URL: http://www.ryerson.ca/org/
Contact: Robert Dirstein, Dir.
E-mail: dirstein@ryerson.ca
Scope: Provides administrative support and services for faculty research activities in the areas of research grants and contracts. Offers a full range of pre- and post-awards services as required by the University. Seeks to expand and promote research in engineering, applied science, community services, business administration, arts, communication and design and graduate studies. **Services:** Research services for Ryerson faculty..

66740 ■ University of Toronto Innovation Foundation
101 College St., Ste. 320
Toronto, ON, Canada M5G 1L7
Ph:(416)978-5117
Fax: (416)978-6052
Co. E-mail: innovations.foundation@utoronto.ca
Contact: Dr. Richard Owens, Interim Exec.Dir.
E-mail: innovations.foundation@utoronto.ca
Scope: Technology licensing and business creation, company acts as a catalyst and promoter between University researchers and industry, in all areas. **Publications:** The Better Mousetrap Newsletter (quarterly). **Awards:** Innovations Challenge (annually), a business plan competition.

66741 ■ University of Waterloo–Office of Research–Contract Section
200 University Ave. W
Waterloo, ON, Canada N2L 3G1
Ph:(519)888-4567
Fax: (519)746-7151
Co. E-mail: bscott@uwaterloo.ca
URL: http://www.research.uwaterloo.ca/craig/
Contact: Barry Scott, Dir.
E-mail: bscott@uwaterloo.ca
Scope: Acts as the contract arm of the Office of Research, bringing together faculty and resources of the University to undertake joint research activities through contracts with industry, government, and public and private institutions, particularly in the areas of engineering, the chemical and earth sciences, biotechnology, computer science, and health and environmental studies. Collaborates with the Technology Transfer and Licensing Office to facilitate technology transfer and licensing of University inventions and discoveries to the private sector.

66742 ■ University of Waterloo–Technology Transfer and Licensing Office
200 University Ave. W.
Waterloo, ON, Canada N2L 3G1
Ph:(519)888-4058
Fax: (519)746-3575
Co. E-mail: gghgray@uwaterloo.ca
URL: http://www.research.uwaterloo.ca/ttlo/

E-mail: gghgray@uwaterloo.ca
Scope: Identification, management, and deployment of intellectual property. **Educational Activities:** Lunchtime forums and conferences; Workshops.

66743 ■ York University–Office of Research Service
214 York Ln.
4700 Keele St.
Toronto, ON, Canada M3J 1P3
Ph:(416)736-5055
Fax: (416)736-5512
Co. E-mail: dphipps@york.ca
URL: http://www.research.yorku.ca
Contact: David Phipps PhD
E-mail: dphipps@york.ca
Scope: Assists faculty members in obtaining research funding; ensures that University policies on research are honored; acts as official liaison and negotiator between funding agencies and University researchers; signs research proposals and agreements on behalf of the University; and handles internal competition for Social Sciences and Humanities Research Council (SSHRC) small grants, SSHRC travel grants, and other awards. **Educational Activities:** Seminars.

TRADE PERIODICALS

66744 ■ *In Touch*
Pub: The City Centre Business Association of Windsor
Contact: Fran Funaro, Managing Editor
Released: Quarterly. **Description:** Acts as the publication of The City Centre Business Association of Windsor. Recurring features include news of members and a calendar of events.

PUBLISHERS

66745 ■ Canadian Small Business Institute
4936 Yonge St., Ste. 250
Toronto, ON, Canada M6K 1V5
Ph:(905)886-4674
Free: 800-481-2721
Fax: (905)886-4672
Co. E-mail: info@bsma.ca
Contact: Richard J. Stacey, President
Description: Publishes materials to help people start their own business. Offers home study courses and distributes books and magazines on related topics. Also offers audio cassettes, seminars, and consulting and business services. Accepts unsolicited manuscripts. Distributes for Prentice Hall, Stoddart, John Wiley, Wade World Trade, Made in Europe, Trade Winds, and Business Opportunities Monthly. Reaches market through direct mail. **Founded:** 1982.

66746 ■ CDG Books Canada Inc.
99 Yorkville Ave., Ste. 400
Toronto, ON, Canada M5R 3K5
Ph:(416)963-8830
Free: 800-263-1686
Fax: (416)923-4821
Co. E-mail: info@cdgbooks.com
URL: http://www.cdgbooks.com
Contact: Tom Best, President
E-mail: tbest@cdgbooks.com
Description: Publishes adult nonfiction. The subject areas include business, consumer technology, health and nutrition, personal finance, reference, and self-help. Accepts unsolicited manuscripts. Reaches market through distributors.

66747 ■ Digital Leisure Inc.
33 Cedar Ridge Rd.
Gormley, ON, Canada L0H 1G0
Ph:(905)888-9550
Free: 888-836-4383
Fax: (905)888-9440
Co. E-mail: info@digitalleisure.com
URL: http://www.digitalleisure.com
Contact: Elizabeth Foster, President
E-mail: elizabethf@digitalleisure.com
Description: Publishes video games. **Founded:** 1997.

66748 ■ DreamCatcher, The Adventure Co.
5000 Dufferin St., Bldg. R
Toronto, ON, Canada M3H 5T5

Ph:(416)638-5000
Fax: (416)398-4476
Co. E-mail: info@dreamcatchergames.com
URL: http://www.dreamcatchergames.com
Contact: Richard Wah Kan, President
E-mail: rwahkan@dreamcatchergames.com
Description: Publishes games and software. **Founded:** 1996.

66749 ■ Dun & Bradstreet Canada
5770 Hurontario St.
Mississauga, ON, Canada L5R 3G5
Ph:(905)568-6000
Free: 800-668-7800
Fax: (905)568-6197
Co. E-mail: cic@dnb.com
URL: http://www.dnb.ca
Contact: Lawrence Franco, President
Description: Publishes business information reports and directories. Reaches market through sales and service representatives, telephone sales, and direct mail. **Founded:** 1841.

66750 ■ Frasers Trade Directories Company Ltd.
777 Bay St.
Toronto, ON, Canada M5W 1A7
Ph:(416)596-5086
Fax: (416)593-3201
Contact: Maclean Hunter, Owner
Description: Publishes directories on Canadian industry, manufacturing and trade.

66751 ■ The G7 Report Inc.-G7 Books
PO Box 824, Postal Sta. Q
Toronto, ON, Canada M4T 2N7
Ph:(416)699-3530
Fax: (416)699-5683
Co. E-mail: g7report@passport.ca
Contact: William B.Z. Vukson, Publisher
Description: Publishes books on business and economic reference, currency, globalized markets, investing, organized crime, financial crises, and laundering. Does not accept unsolicited manuscripts. Reaches market through commission representatives, wholesalers, and distributors, including Lavis Marketing/Femma. **Founded:** 1991.

66752 ■ Innovation Canada Inc.
1447 Royal York Rd.
Etobicoke, ON, Canada M9P 3V8
Ph:(416)240-9003
Fax: (416)240-9008
Co. E-mail: innovation_canada@sympatico.ca
Contact: William O. Munns, CEO & Chm Bd
Description: A Canadian charity that promotes interest in and the study of innovation management, new product and service development, and entrepreneurship. Offers seminars on innovation, globalization of business development, and starting up an international business especially in Asia, South America, the Caribbean, Africa, and the South Pacific. Reaches market through direct mail. Distributed by John Coutts Library Services, Ltd. and Curran Associates, Inc. Accepts unsolicited manuscripts. **Founded:** 1977.

66753 ■ Ivey Publishing
Richard Ivey School of Business
The University of Western Ontario
London, ON, Canada N6A 3K7
Ph:(519)661-3208
Free: 800-649-6355
Fax: (519)661-3882
Co. E-mail: cases@ivey.uwo.ca
URL: http://www.ivey.uwo.ca/cases
Contact: Sheryl Gregson, Mgr
E-mail: sgregson@ivey.uwo.ca
Description: Publishes business case studies. Publishes CD-ROMs. Reaches market through direct mail and telephone sales. Accepts unsolicited manuscripts. **Founded:** 1922.

66754 ■ The Laurier Institute
75 University Ave. W
Waterloo, ON, Canada N2L 3C5
Ph:(519)884-1970
Free: 888-646-8338

Fax: (519)884-9408
Co. E-mail: laurinst@wlu.ca
URL: http://www.wlu.ca
Contact: Jan Varner, Director
E-mail: jvarner@wlu.ca
Description: Publishes management case studies in all areas of business and economics in English and French. **Founded:** 1983.

66755 ■ Life Untangled Publishing
77 Howard St., Ste. 801
Toronto, ON, Canada M4X 1J9
URL: http://www.lifeuntangled.com
Contact: Polina Skibinskaya
Description: Online book publisher that publishes on Canada's "multinational, multicultural, and multidimensional life." **Founded:** 2005

66756 ■ maranGraphics Inc.
5755 Coopers Ave.
Mississauga, ON, Canada L4Z 1R9
Ph:(905)890-3300
Free: 800-469-6616
Fax: (905)890-9434
Co. E-mail: family@maran.com
URL: http://www.maran.com
Contact: Rob Maran, President
E-mail: rob@maran.com
Description: Publishes computer books and manuals. **Founded:** 1975.

66757 ■ Multi-Media Publications Inc.
PO Box 58043, Rosslynn RPO
Oshawa, ON, Canada L1J 8L6
Ph:(905)721-1540
Fax: (905)721-1540
Co. E-mail: info@mmpubs.com
URL: http://www.mmpubs.com
Description: Publishes nonfiction books on a variety of business topics. **Founded:** 1988.

66758 ■ Munsey Music
PO Box 511
Richmond Hill, ON, Canada L4C 4Y8
Ph:(905)737-0208
Fax: (905)737-0208
Co. E-mail: info@munseymusic.com
URL: http://www.munseymusic.com
Contact: J. P. Munsey, VP of Sales
Description: Wholesaler. **Founded:** 1969.

66759 ■ Nortext Multimedia Inc. (Ottawa)
52 Antares Dr., Ste. 9
Ottawa, ON, Canada K2E 7Z1
Ph:(613)727-5466
Free: 800-263-1452
Fax: (613)727-6910
Co. E-mail: ads@nortext.com
URL: http://www.nortext.com
Contact: Roberta Roberts, Director
E-mail: rroberts@nortext.com
Description: Publishes school books, aboriginal language, business, Nunavut and travel books. **Founded:** 1990.

66760 ■ Ocapt Business Books
27 Donna Marie Dr.
Welland, ON, Canada L3C 2X7
Ph:(905)735-2967
Free: 888-579-3013
Fax: (905)788-0839
Co. E-mail: ocapt@iaw.on.ca
URL: http://www.ocapt.com
Contact: Gail Grinaldi, Owner
Description: Distributes finance and management books. **Founded:** 1989.

66761 ■ Okhai - Diagnostics L.L.C.
287 Wycliffe Ave.
Woodbridge, ON, Canada L4L 3N7
Ph:(905)851-2299
Fax: (905)264-2580
Co. E-mail: adamo@WondrousMinds.com
Contact: Adam Okhai, President
E-mail: adamo@wondrousminds.com
Description: Distributor. Reaches market through direct mail. **Founded:** 1884.

66762 ■ Pearson Canada
26 Prince Andre Pl.
Toronto, ON, Canada M3C 2T8
Ph:(416)447-5101
Free: 800-263-9965
Fax: (416)443-0948
Co. E-mail: pubcanada@pearsoned.ca
URL: http://www.pearsoned.ca
Contact: Allan T. Reynolds, CEO & Pres
Description: Publishes fiction, nonfiction, textbooks, reference books and trade books. **Founded:** 1966.

66763 ■ Productive Publications
1930 Yonge St., Ste. 1210
Toronto, ON, Canada M4S 1Z4
Ph:(416)483-0634
Fax: (416)322-7434
Co. E-mail: productivepublications@rogers.com
URL: http://www.productivepublications.ca
Contact: Iain Williamson, President
Description: Publishes books relating to small business companies on self help, business management, personal finance and personal computers. Audience includes entrepreneurs, individuals, computer users and business managers. Reaches market through direct mail and wholesalers. Accepts unsolicited manuscripts. **Founded:** 1985.

66764 ■ Summit Group
263 Holmwood Ave., Ste. 100
Ottawa, ON, Canada K1S 2P8
Ph:(613)688-0760
Free: 800-575-1146
Fax: (613)688-0767
Co. E-mail: info@summitconnects.com
URL: http://www.summitconnects.com
Description: Publishes business and trade publications for Canadian government and businesses. Also publishes a professional journal for public sector procurement managers and a magazine for Canadians with chronic illness. Offers CD-ROMS, diskettes, and online service. Does not accept unsolicited manuscripts. Reaches market through direct mail, telephone sales and government distribution. **Founded:** 1998.

66765 ■ Treehouse Publishing
403-10 Preston St.
Ottawa, ON, Canada K1R 7W4
Ph:(613)231-7601
Fax: (613)231-5873
Contact: John R. Trinnell, Publisher
Description: Publishes books on forestry and lumbering. Published *J.R. Booth: The Life and Times of an Ottawa Lumberking*. Does not accept unsolicited

manuscripts. Reaches market through personal visits. **Founded:** 1998.

66766 ■ VCR Active Media Ltd.
3055 Lenworth Dr.
Mississauga, ON, Canada L4X 2G3
Ph:(905)629-2553
Fax: (905)629-3437
URL: http://www.vcractive.com
Description: Publishes business-related materials for Canadian marketers and advertisers. **Founded:** 1985

66767 ■ White Mountain Publications
PO Box 1178
New Liskeard, ON, Canada P0J 1P0
Ph:(705)647-5424
Free: 800-258-5451
Fax: (705)647-8366
Co. E-mail: wmpub@wmpub.ca
URL: http://www.wmpub.ca
Contact: Deborah Ranchuk, President
Description: Publishes books about the Baha'i faith, children's literature, poetry, nonfiction and how-to books. Accepts unsolicited manuscripts. Reaches market through direct mail, telephone sales, wholesalers, the Internet, Amazon, bookstores, John Coutts, Library Bound and Ontario Library Services. **Founded:** 1982.

Quebec

FINANCING AND LOAN PROGRAMS

66768 ■ Altamira Capital Corp.
202 University
Niveau de Maisoneuve, Bur. 201
Montreal, QC, Canada H3A 2A5
Ph:(514)499-1656
Fax: (514)499-9570
Preferred Investment Size: $1,000,000 minimum.
Investment Types: First stage.

66769 ■ Federal Business Development Bank
Venture Capital Division
Five Place Ville Marie, Ste. 600
Montreal, QC, Canada H3B 5E7
Ph:(514)283-1896
Fax: (514)283-5455
Preferred Investment Size: $1,000,000. **Investment Types:** Seed, start-up, first and second stage, mezzanine, research and development, and leveraged buyout. **Industry Preferences:** Biotechnology, Internet specific, computer software, hardware, and services. **Geographic Preferences:** Canada.

66770 ■ Hydro-Quebec Capitech Inc.
75 Boul, Rene Levesque Quest
22e etage
Montreal, QC, Canada H2Z 1A4
Ph:(514)289-4783
Fax: (514)289-5420
URL: http://www.hqcapitech.com
Contact: Jean-Claude Sinard, Vice President
Investment Types: Seed, start-up, early, first and second stage, balanced, expansion, and mezzanine. **Industry Preferences:** Communications and media, Internet specific, semiconductors and other electronics, industrial and energy, and utilities. **Geographic Preferences:** Canada.

66771 ■ Investissement Desjardins
2 complexe Desjardins
C.P. 760
Montreal, QC, Canada H5B 1B8
Ph:(514)281-7131
Fax: (514)281-7808
URL: http://www.desjardins.com/id
Preferred Investment Size: $5,000,000 minimum.
Investment Types: Start-up, first, second, and later stage, control-block purchases, mezzanine, and leveraged buyout. **Industry Preferences:** Computer software and services, Internet specific, communications and media, biotechnology, other products, medical and health, and industrial and energy. **Geographic Preferences:** Quebec, Canada.

66772 ■ Marleau Lemire, Inc.
One Place Ville-Marie, Ste. 3601
Montreal, QC, Canada H3B 3P2
Ph:(514)877-3800
Fax: (514)875-6415
Preferred Investment Size: $3,000,000 minimum.
Investment Types: Second stage, mezzanine, leveraged buyout, and special situation. **Industry Preferences:** Communications and media, computer software and hardware, Internet specific, semiconductors and other electronics, medical and health, consumer related, industrial and energy, business service, manufacturing, agriculture, forestry and fishing. **Geographic Preferences:** Canada.

66773 ■ Speirs Consultants, Inc.
365 Stanstead
Montreal, QC, Canada H3R 1X5
Ph:(514)342-3858
Fax: (514)342-1977
Preferred Investment Size: $1,000,000 minimum.
Investment Types: Seed, start-up, first and second stage, control-block purchases, industry rollups, leveraged buyout, mezzanine, research and development, and special situation. **Geographic Preferences:** Canada.

66774 ■ Technocap, Inc.
1250 Rene Levesque
Montreal, QC, Canada H3B 2G4
Ph:(514)205-5203
Fax: (514)205-5694
URL: http://www.technocap.com
Contact: Richard Prytula, President
Preferred Investment Size: $1,000,000 to $10,000,000. **Investment Types:** Start-up, early stage and expansion. **Industry Preferences:** Communications and media, computer software, computer related, Internet specific, semiconductors and other electronics, medical and health, industrial and energy. **Geographic Preferences:** Canada.

66775 ■ Telsoft Ventures
1000, Rue de la Gauchetiere
Quest, 25eme Etage
Montreal, QC, Canada H3B 4W5
Ph:(514)397-8450
Fax: (514)397-8451
Investment Types: First and second stage, and mezzanine. **Industry Preferences:** Computer related. **Geographic Preferences:** West Coast and Western Canada.

INCUBATORS/RESEARCH AND TECHNOLOGY PARKS

66776 ■ McGill University–Office of Technology Transfer
Cours Mon-Royal
1555 Peel St., 11th Fl.
Montreal, QC, Canada H3A 3L8
Ph:(514)398-4200
Fax: (514)398-1482
Co. E-mail: casual.ott@mcgill.ca
URL: http://www.mcgill.ca/ott/
Contact: Michael Avedesian, Interim Dir.
E-mail: casual.ott@mcgill.ca
Scope: Promote and facilitate the transfer of technology between McGill University researchers and outside sponsors, including the negociation and management of research contracts and the commercialization of Intellectual Property.

PUBLISHERS

66777 ■ Diffusion Dimedia Inc.
539 Lebeau Blvd.
Ville Saint Laurent, QC, Canada H4N 1S2
Ph:(514)536-3941
Fax: (514)331-3916
Co. E-mail: general@dimedia.qc.ca
URL: http://www.dimedia.qc.ca
Contact: Pascal Assathiany, President
Description: Wholesaler of French titles of fiction and nonfiction. **Founded:** 1974.

66778 ■ Modus Vivendi Inc.
55, rue Jean-Talon ouest
Montreal, QC, Canada H2R 2W8
Ph:(514)272-0433
Fax: (514)272-7234
Co. E-mail: info@modusaventure.com
URL: http://www.modusaventure.com
Contact: Marc Alain, President
Description: Publishes books in French. **Founded:** 1991.

66779 ■ White Rock Publishing
2700 Mont-Joli St.
Sainte Foy, QC, Canada G1V 1C8
Ph:(418)580-9019
Fax: (418)658-7177
Co. E-mail: info@whiterockpub.com
URL: http://www.whiterockpub.com
Contact: Luc Dupont, President
E-mail: dupontluc@videotron.ca
Description: Publishes advertising and marketing books. Accepts unsolicited manuscripts. Reaches market through direct mail and wholesalers. **Founded:** 1996.

SMALL BUSINESS ASSISTANCE PROGRAMS

66780 ■ Regina Economic Development Authority
1919 Rose St., Ste. 255
Regina, SK, Canada S4P 3P1
Ph:(306)522-0227
Free: 800-866-5644
Fax: (306)352-1630
Co. E-mail: rreda@rreda.com
URL: http://www.rreda.com
Description: Provides business information as well as counseling and consulting services to the business community, with emphasis on management information. Acts as facilitators in accessing a variety of program initiatives provided by other departments, the federal government, Crown corporations, and financial institutions.

66781 ■ Tourism Saskatchewan
1922 Park St.
Regina, SK, Canada S4N 7M4

Ph:(306)787-9600
Fax: (306)787-6293
URL: http://www.sasktourism.com
Description: Strives to enhance the growth of the tourism industry in Saskatchewan. Subprograms include Tourism Product Development, Tourism Market Development, Industry Organization Support, and Research and Planning Support.

FINANCING AND LOAN PROGRAMS

66782 ■ Saskatchewan Government Growth Fund
1801 Hamilton St., Ste. 1210
Canada Trust Tower
Regina, SK, Canada S4P 4B4
Ph:(306)787-2994
Fax: (306)787-2994
Contact: Rob M. Duguid, Vice President

Investment Types: Start-up, first and second stage, and mezzanine. **Geographic Preferences:** Saskatchewan and Western Canada.

INCUBATORS/RESEARCH AND TECHNOLOGY PARKS

66783 ■ Innovation Place
114-15 Innovation Blvd.
Saskatoon, SK, Canada S7N 2X8
Ph:(306)933-6295
Fax: (306)933-8200
Co. E-mail: tastad@innovationplace.com
URL: http://www.innovationplace.com
Contact: Doug Tastad, Pres./CEO
E-mail: tastad@innovationplace.com
Scope: 120-acre research and development park providing office, industrial, and research space for lease to tenants interested in accessing research resources at the University. **Publications:** Innovation Place Newsletter (monthly).

SMALL BUSINESS ASSISTANCE PROGRAMS

**66784 ■ Yukon Department of Economic
Development**
PO Box 2703
Whitehorse, YT, Canada Y1A 2C6
Ph:(867)393-7191
Fax: (867)393-6944
Co. E-mail: ecdev@gov.yk.ca
URL: http://www.economicdevelopment.gov.yk.ca

Federal Government Assistance

AGENCY FOR INTERNATIONAL DEVELOPMENT

66785 ■ International Franchise Association–Office of Small and Disadvantaged Business Utilization–Minority/Women Diversity Services (1350)
1350 New York Ave., NW, Ste. 900
Washington, DC
Ph:(202)662-0784
Fax: (202)628-0812
URL: http://www.franchise.org

66786 ■ U.S. Agency for International Development–Freedom of Information Act Request–Bureau for Management/Information and Records Division (Ronal)
Ronald Reagan Bldg.
Washington, DC 20523
Ph:(202)712-5027
Fax: (202)216-3070
URL: http://www.usaid.gov

66787 ■ U.S. Agency for International Development–Office of the Inspector General
PO Box 657
Washington, DC 20044-0657
Ph:(202)712-1023
Free: 800-230-6539
Co. E-mail: ig.hotline@usaid.gov
URL: http://www.usaid.gov

66788 ■ U.S. Agency for International Development–USAID Library
Ronald Reagan Bldg.
Mezzanine Level
Washington, DC 20523
Ph:(202)712-0569

66789 ■ U.S. Agency for International Development–USAID Office of Procurement
Ronald Reagan Bldg.
Washington, DC 20523
Ph:(202)712-5130
Fax: (202)712-5130
Co. E-mail: aandaombudsman@usaid.gov
URL: http://www.usaid.gov

66790 ■ Agency for International Development–Office of Small and Disadvantaged Business Utilization/Minority Resource Center
Ronald Reagan Bldg.
1300 Pennsylvania Ave., NW
Washington, DC 20523
Ph:(202)712-0000
Fax: (202)216-3524
URL: http://www.info.usaid.gov/business/small_business
Description: An advocate for U.S. small businesses and disadvantaged enterprises, (including women-owned businesses), OSDBU/MRU ensures their consideration as sources for the procurement of goods and services financed through USAID development assistance activities. The office maintains the USAID Consultant Registry Information System (ACRIS) and publishes *The Guide to Doing Business with the Agency for International Development.*

BUREAU OF THE CENSUS

66791 ■ Alaska Department of Commerce, Community and Economic Development
550 W. 7th St., Ste. 1790
Anchorage, AK 99501-3510
Ph:(907)465-4752
Fax: (907)465-5086
Co. E-mail: indra_arriaga@commerce.state.ak.us
URL: http://www.commerce.state.ak.us

66792 ■ Alaska State Library–Government Publications/Technical Services
PO Box 110571
Juneau, AK 99811-0571
Ph:(907)465-2927
Fax: (907)465-2665
Co. E-mail: dan_cornwall@educ.state.ak.us
URL: http://www.educ.state.ak.us

66793 ■ Arizona Department of Economic Security–DES 045Z
1789 W. Jefferson St.
1st Fl., NE Wing
Phoenix, AZ 85007
Ph:(602)542-5746
Fax: (602)542-7425
Co. E-mail: abarnes@azdes.gov
URL: http://www.azdes.gov

66794 ■ Association of Bay Area Governments
Metro Ctr.
101 8th St.
PO Box 2050
Oakland, CA 94604-2050
Ph:(510)464-7900
Fax: (510)464-7970
Co. E-mail: patriciap@abag.ca.gov
URL: http://www.abag.ca.gov

66795 ■ Capital Region Council of Governments
241 Main St.
Hartford, CT 06106
Ph:(860)522-2217
Fax: (860)724-1274
Co. E-mail: crcog@ct1.nai.net
URL: http://www.crcog.us

66796 ■ Center for Business and Economic Research–University of Alabama
149 Bidgood Hall
Tuscaloosa, AL 35487-0221
Ph:(205)348-6191
Fax: (205)348-2951
Co. E-mail: awatters@cba.ua.edu
URL: http://www.cba.ua.edu

66797 ■ Center for Neighborhood Information Services
1155 15th St. NW, Ste. 900
Washington, DC 20005-2706
Ph:(202)223-2598
Fax: (202)223-2604

66798 ■ Connecticut Department of Economic and Community Development, Research, Planning, and Information Systems
505 Hudson St.
Hartford, CT 06106
Ph:(860)270-8166
Fax: (860)270-8174
Co. E-mail: mark.prisloe@po.state.ct.us
URL: http://www.po.state.ct.us

66799 ■ EDECA
401 Adams Ave., Ste. 410
PO Box 5690
Montgomery, AL 36104-5690
Ph:(334)242-5525
Fax: (334)242-5515
Co. E-mail: lchilders@edeca.state.al.us
URL: http://www.adeca.state.al.us

66800 ■ Metropolitan Washington Council of Governments
777 N. Capitol St. NE, Ste. 300
Washington, DC 20002-4201
Ph:(202)962-3200
Co. E-mail: pdesjardin@mwcog.org

66801 ■ Office of Financial Management–Forecasting Division
450 Insurance Bldg., 4th fl.
Olympia, WA 98504-3113
Ph:(360)902-0592
Fax: (360)664-8941
Co. E-mail: yi_zhao@ofm.wa.gov
URL: http://www.census.gov/sdc/www/wasdc.html

66802 ■ State Census Data Center - Department of Finance
915 L St., 8th Fl.
Sacramento, CA 95814-3706
Ph:(916)323-4086
Fax: (916)327-0222
Co. E-mail: julie.hoang@dof.ca.gov
URL: http://www.dof.ca.gov

66803 ■ University of Alaska - Anchorage
3211 Providence Dr.
Anchorage, AK 99508
Ph:(907)786-7706
Fax: (907)786-1377
Co. E-mail: anslm!@uaa.alaska.edu
URL: http://ww.uaa.alaska.edu

66804 ■ Bureau of the Census
4700 Silver Hill Rd.
Washington, DC 20233-1922

Ph:(301)763-4748
Co. E-mail: charles.louis.kincannon@census.gov
URL: http://www.census.gov/
Description: The Census Bureau gathers and disseminates a wide variety of statistics about the people and economy of the United States. It is the principal source in the federal government for business information relating to manufacturers, retail trade, wholesale trade, construction trade, and services. These data are generated both from the regular five-year census programs and from annual, quarterly, and monthly survey programs. Data concerning the number of establishments, production, value added by manufacture, shipments, receipts, employees, payrolls—as well as other general and specific business statistics—are compiled and published periodically. Small business owners interested in learning more about the statistics available from the Census Bureau and how to use them may obtain a set of introductory materials and order forms by contacting Customer Services. Other information may be obtained from Census Bureau regional. In addition, the Census Bureau sponsors a state data center program, which provides (for a fee) local access to the bureau's computer products in all states, the District of Columbia, Puerto Rico, Guam, and the U.S. Virgin Islands.

The following is a list of the Census Bureau's regional offices, arranged alphabetically by city.

66805 ■ **Bureau of the Census–Atlanta Regional Office**
101 Marietta St. NW, Ste. 3200
Atlanta, GA 30303-2700
Ph:(404)730-3832
Free: 800-424-6974
Fax: (404)730-3835
Co. E-mail: Atlanta.regional.office@census.gov

66806 ■ **Bureau of the Census–Boston Regional Office**
4 Copley Pl., Ste. 301
PO Box 9108
Boston, MA 02117-9108
Ph:(617)424-4501
Free: 800-562-5721
Fax: (617)424-0547
Co. E-mail: boston.regional.office@census.gov

66807 ■ **Bureau of the Census–Charlotte Regional Office**
901 Center Park Dr., Ste. 106
Charlotte, NC 28217-2935
Ph:(704)424-6400
Free: 800-331-7360
Fax: (704)344-6444
Co. E-mail: charlotte.regional.office@census.gov

66808 ■ **Bureau of the Census–Chicago Regional Office**
2255 Enterprise Dr., Ste. 5501
Westchester, IL 60154
Ph:(708)562-1350
Free: 800-865-6384
Fax: (708)562-1788
Co. E-mail: Chicago.regional.office@census.gov

66809 ■ **Bureau of the Census–Dallas Regional Office**
8585 N. Stemmons Fwy., Ste. S
Dallas, TX 75247-3836
Ph:(214)653-4400
Free: 800-835-9752
Fax: (214)655-5362
Co. E-mail: dallas.regional.office@census.gov

66810 ■ **Bureau of the Census–Denver Regional Office**
6900 W. Jefferson Ave., Ste. 100
PO Box 272020
Denver, CO 80235-2032
Ph:(303)264-0202
Free: 800-852-6159
Fax: (303)969-6777
Co. E-mail: Denver.regional.office@census.gov

66811 ■ **Bureau of the Census–Detroit Regional Office**
1395 Brewery Park Blvd.
PO Box 35405
Detroit, MI 48207
Ph:(313)259-1158
Free: 800-432-1495
Fax: (313)259-5045
Co. E-mail: Detroit.regional.office.census.gov

66812 ■ **Bureau of the Census–Kansas City Regional Office**
1211 N. 8th St.
400 State Ave.
Kansas City, KS 66101-2129
Ph:(913)551-6728
Free: 800-728-4748
Fax: (913)551-6789
Co. E-mail: kc.regional.office.census.gov

66813 ■ **Bureau of the Census–Los Angeles Regional Office**
15350 Sherman Way, Ste. 300
Van Nuys, CA 91406-4224
Ph:(818)904-6393
Free: 800-992-3530
Fax: (818)904-6427
Co. E-mail: la.regional.office@census.gov

66814 ■ **Bureau of the Census–New York City Regional Office**
395 Hudson St., Ste. 800
New York, NY 10014
Ph:(212)584-3400
Free: 800-991-2520
Fax: (212)478-4800
Co. E-mail: new.york.regional.office@census.gov

66815 ■ **Bureau of the Census–Philadelphia Regional Office**
833 Chestnut St., Ste. 504
Philadelphia, PA 19107
Ph:(215)597-4920
Free: 800-262-4236
Fax: (215)717-0755
Co. E-mail: Philadelphia.regional.office@census.tov

66816 ■ **Bureau of the Census–Seattle Regional Office**
700 5th Ave., Ste. 5100
Seattle, WA 98104-5018
Ph:(206)553-5837
Free: 800-233-3308
Fax: (206)553-5859
Co. E-mail: seattle.regional.office@census.gov

The following is a list of the state coordinating organizations in the Census Bureau's State Data Center Program and Business and Industry Data Center Program, arranged alphabetically by state.

66817 ■ **Alabama Public Library Service**
6030 Monticello Dr.
Montgomery, AL 36130-6000
Ph:(334)213-3900
Fax: (334)213-3993
Co. E-mail: aplref01@asnmail.asc.edu

66818 ■ **University of Alabama–Center for Business and Economic Research**
Box 870221
149 Bidgood Hall
Tuscaloosa, AL 35487-0221
Ph:(205)348-6191
Fax: (205)348-2951
Co. E-mail: awatters@cba.ua.edu
URL: http://www.cba.ua.edu
Contact: Ms. Annette Watters
E-mail: awatters@ua1vm.ua.edu

66819 ■ **Alaska Department of Labor–Census and Geographic Information Network–Research and Analysis (PO Bo)**
PO Box 25504
Juneau, AK 99802-5504
Ph:(907)465-2437
Fax: (907)465-4506

66820 ■ **Arizona State Department of Economic Security–DES**
1717 W. Jefferson St.
Phoenix, AZ 85007
Ph:(602)542-4791
Free: (866)362-2837
Fax: (602)542-5339
URL: http://www.azdes.gov

66821 ■ **Arizona State Department of Library, Archives, and Public Records–Research Library**
1700 W. Washington, Ste. 200
Phoenix, AZ 85007
Ph:(602)542-4035
Fax: (602)542-4972
Co. E-mail: services@lib.az.us
URL: http://www.dlapr.lib.az.us

66822 ■ **Arizona State University–College of Business Administration–Center for Business Research (PO Bo)**
PO Box 873801
Tempe, AZ 85287-3801
Ph:(480)965-3097
Fax: (480)965-1091

66823 ■ **Northern Arizona University–College of Business Administration**
Box 15066
Flagstaff, AZ 86011
Ph:(502)523-7313
Fax: (502)523-7331
Co. E-mail: jerry.conover@nau.edu
URL: http://www.census.gov/sdc/www/azsdc.html

66824 ■ **The University of Arizona–Economic and Business Research Program–College of Business and Public Administration (McCle)**
McClelland Hall 204
PO Box 210108
Tucson, AZ 85721-0108
Ph:(520)621-2155
Fax: (520)621-2150
Co. E-mail: ebrlib@bpa.arizona.edu
URL: http://www.bpa.arizona.edu

66825 ■ **Arkansas Employment Security Department–Research and Analysis Section–Department of Workforce Service (1 Per)**
1 Pershing Cir.
North Little Rock, AR 72114
Ph:(501)683-4300
Co. E-mail: artee.williams.aesd@mail.state.ar.us
URL: http://www.state.ar.us/esd

66826 ■ **Arkansas State Library**
1 Capitol Mall
Little Rock, AR 72201
Ph:(501)682-2053
Fax: (501)682-1529
Co. E-mail: aslref@asl.lib.ar.us
URL: http://www.asl.lib.ar.us/index.html

66827 ■ **University of Arkansas - Little Rock–State Data Center**
2801 S. University
Little Rock, AR 72204
Ph:(501)569-8530
Fax: (501)569-8538
Co. E-mail: sgbreshears@ualr.edu
URL: http://www.ualr.edu

66828 ■ **Association of Bay Area Governments**
Joseph P. Bort MetroCenter
101 8th & Oak Sts.
PO Box 2050
Oakland, CA 94604-2050
Ph:(510)464-7900
Fax: (510)464-7970
Co. E-mail: info@abag.ca.gov
URL: http://www.abag.ca.gov

66829 ■ Association of Monterey Bay Area Governments
445 Reservation Rd., Ste. G
PO Box 809
Marina, CA 93933
Ph:(831)883-3750
Fax: (831)883-3755
Co. E-mail: info@ambag.org
URL: http://www.ambag.org

66830 ■ California Department of Finance–State Census Data Center
915 L St.
Sacramento, CA 95814
Ph:(916)445-3878
URL: http://www.dof.ca.gov
Contact: Linda Gage, Director

66831 ■ Sacramento Area COG
1415 L St., Ste. 300
Sacramento, CA 95814
Ph:(916)321-9000
Fax: (916)321-9551
Co. E-mail: gbiedler@sacog.org

66832 ■ San Diego Association of Governments
Wells Fargo Plz.
401 B St., Ste. 800
San Diego, CA 92101-3585
Ph:(619)699-1905
Fax: (619)699-1905
Co. E-mail: kla@sandag.org

66833 ■ Southern California Association of Governments
818 W. 7th St., 12th Fl.
Los Angeles, CA 90017
Ph:(213)236-1893
Fax: (213)236-1862
Co. E-mail: minjares@scag.ca.gov
URL: http://www.scag.ca.gov

66834 ■ University of California, Berkeley–UC Data Archive and Technical Assistance
2538 Channing Way
Berkeley, CA 94720-5100
Ph:(510)642-6571
Fax: (510)643-8292
Co. E-mail: ucdata@berkeley.edu
URL: http://www.ucdata.berkeley.edu

66835 ■ Colorado Department of Local Affairs–Division of Local Government
1313 Sherman St., Rm. 521
Denver, CO 80203
Ph:(303)866-2156
Fax: (303)866-4819
URL: http://www.dola.state.co.us

66836 ■ Colorado State University–Agricultural and Resources Economics
B-320 Clark Bldg.
Ft. Collins, CO 80523
Ph:(303)491-6325
Fax: (303)491-2067
URL: http://dare.agsci.colostate.edu

66837 ■ Colorado State University Libraries–Morgan Library
501 University Ave.
Ft. Collins, CO 80523
Ph:(303)491-1880
URL: http://lib.colostate.edu

66838 ■ University of Colorado at Boulder–Business Research Division–Graduate School of Business Administration
Boulder, CO 80309
Ph:(303)492-8227
Co. E-mail: gin.hayden@colorado.edu
URL: http://www.colorado.edu

66839 ■ University of Northern Colorado–Library Government Publics
Greeley, CO 80639
Ph:(970)351-2987
Co. E-mail: maanders@bentley.univ
URL: http://www.bentley.univ
Contact: Mark Anderson
E-mail: maanders@bentley.univ

66840 ■ Capital Region Council of Governments
241 Main St.
Hartford, CT 06106-5310
Ph:(860)522-2217
Free: 800-522-2217
Fax: (860)724-1274
Co. E-mail: info@crcog.org
URL: http://www.crcog.org

66841 ■ Connecticut Department of Economic Census and Community Development–Research, Planning, and Information Systems
505 Hudson St.
Hartford, CT 06106-7107
Ph:(860)270-8000
Co. E-mail: decd@po.state.ct.us

66842 ■ Connecticut Office of Policy and Management–Policy Development and Planning Division–Budget and Financial Management Division (450 C)–Office of Finance (apitol Ave)
450 Capitol Ave.
Hartford, CT 06106-1308
Ph:(860)418-6200
Fax: (860)418-6487
Co. E-mail: OPMwebmaster@po.state.ct.us
URL: http://opm.state.ct.us

66843 ■ Connecticut State Library–Government Documents
231 Capitol Ave.
Hartford, CT 06106
Ph:(203)566-4971
Fax: (203)566-3322
URL: http://www.cslib.org

66844 ■ Delaware Economic Development Office (DEDO)
99 Kings Hwy.
PO Box 1401
Dover, DE 19903
Ph:(302)739-4271
Fax: (302)739-5749
URL: http://www.state.de.us/dedo/default.shtml

66845 ■ University of Delaware–College of Urban Affairs and Public Policy
Graham Hall, Rm. 286
Academy St.
Newark, DE 19716
Ph:(302)831-8406
Fax: (302)831-6434
Co. E-mail: ratledge@udel.edu
URL: http://www.udel.edu

66846 ■ Mayor's Office of Planning–Data Services Division
Presidential Bldg., Rm. 570
415 12th St. NW
Washington, DC 20004
Ph:(202)727-6533
Fax: (202)727-6964
Co. E-mail: op@dc.gov
URL: http://planning.dc.gov

66847 ■ Metropolitan Washington Council of Governments
Metropolitan Washington COG, Ste. 300
777 N. Capitol St., NE
Washington, DC 20002
Ph:(202)962-3200
Fax: (202)962-3201
URL: http://www.mwcog.org

66848 ■ Bureau of Economic Analysis–Florida Department of Commerce
107 E. Gaines St.
315 Collins Bldg.
Tallahassee, FL 32399-2000
Ph:(904)487-2971
Fax: (904)487-3014

66849 ■ Florida Department of Labor and Employment Security (DLES)–Bureau of Labor Market Information
Hartman Bldg., Ste. 303
2012 Capital Cir., SE
Tallahassee, FL 32399-2152
Ph:(850)922-7021
Contact: Pam Schenker

66850 ■ Florida State University–Center for the Study of Population–Institute for Social Research (654 B)
654 Bellemy Bldg., R-93
Tallahassee, FL 32306-4063
Ph:(850)644-7101
Fax: (850)644-8818

66851 ■ REA/OPB–Executive Office of the Governor–Florida State Data Center (107 E)
107 E. Madison St.
MSC G-020
Tallahassee, FL 32399-6545
Ph:(850)488-1048
Fax: (850)921-1048

66852 ■ State Library of Florida
R. A. Gray Bldg.
500 S. Bronough St.
Tallahassee, FL 32399-0250
Ph:(850)487-2651
Fax: (850)487-6242
Co. E-mail: info@mail.dos.state.fl.us
URL: http://www.dos.state.fl.us

66853 ■ Albany State College–State Data Center Program–Documents Librarian (504 C)
504 College Dr.
Albany, GA 31705-2797
Ph:(229)430-4600
Fax: (229)430-3936

66854 ■ Georgia Department of Community Affairs–Office of Planning and Quality Growth
60 Executive Park South, NE
Atlanta, GA 30329
Ph:(404)679-4940
Free: 800-359-4663
Fax: (404)679-0589
URL: http://www.dca.state.ga.us

66855 ■ Georgia Institute of Technology–Georgia Tech Library–Government Information Department (704 C)
704 Cherry St.
Atlanta, GA 30332-0900
Ph:(404)894-4529
Free: 888-225-7804
Fax: (404)894-3005
URL: http://www.library.gatech.edu
Contact: Barbara Walker
E-mail: barbara.walker@library.gatech.edu

66856 ■ Georgia Office of Planning and Budget–Division of Operational Support and Development
270 Washington St. SW, 8th Fl.
Atlanta, GA 30334
Ph:(404)656-3820
Fax: (404)656-3828
URL: http://www.opb.state.ga.us

66857 ■ University of Georgia Libraries–Government Documents Department
2nd Fl.
Athens, GA 30602
Ph:(706)542-3472

Co. E-mail: prechtel@libris.libs.uga.edu
URL: http://www.libris.libs.uga.edu

66858 ■ Guam Department of Commerce
102 M St.
Tiyan, GU 96931
Ph:(671)475-0321
Fax: (671)646-9031

66859 ■ Hawaii Department of Budget and Finance–Information and Communication Services Division
Kalanimoku Bldg.
1151 Punchbowl St.
Honolulu, HI 96813
Ph:(808)568-1800
Fax: (808)586-2337
Co. E-mail: Richard_h_niide@exec.state.hi.us
URL: http://www.census.gov/sdc/www/hisdc.html

66860 ■ Hawaii Department of Business, Economic Development, and Tourism–Hawaii State Data Center
220 S. Hotel St., 4th Fl.
PO Box 2359
Honolulu, HI 96804
Ph:(808)586-2493
Fax: (808)586-8449
Co. E-mail: jnakamot@dbedt.hawaii.gov
URL: http://www.census.gov/sdc/www/hisdc.html

66861 ■ Boise State University–Institutional Research–Office of Research Administration (Alber)
Albertson Library L153
1910 University Dr.
Boise, ID 83725
Ph:(208)426-1574
Fax: (208)426-1048
Co. E-mail: bmcdiarm@boisestate.edu
URL: http://www.boisestate.edu/research

66862 ■ Idaho Department of Commerce
700 W. State St.
Boise, ID 83720-0093
Ph:(208)334-2470
Free: 800-842-5858
Fax: (208)334-2631
URL: http://cl.idaho.gov

66863 ■ Idaho State Library
325 W. State St.
Boise, ID 83702
Ph:(208)334-2150
Co. E-mail: lili@isl.state.id.us
URL: http://www.lili.org

66864 ■ Idaho State University–Center for Business Research and Services
Campus Box 8044
Pocatello, ID 83209
Ph:(208)236-3050
Co. E-mail: zelupaul@isu.edu
URL: http://www.isu.edu

66865 ■ Chicago Area Geographic Information Study–University of Illinois at Chicago
Department of Anthropology, Mail Code 027
1007 W. Harrison St., Rm. 2102
Chicago, IL 60607-7138
Ph:(312)996-5274
Fax: (312)996-3254
URL: http://www.cagis.uic.edu

66866 ■ Department of Commerce and Community Affairs
620 E. Adams St.
Springfield, IL 62701
Ph:(217)785-7545
Fax: (217)524-3701
URL: http://www.commerce.state.il.us
Contact: Edwin R. Taft
E-mail: etaft@mhd084r1.state.il.us

66867 ■ Illinois Bureau of the Budget–Office of Management and Budget
108 Statehouse
Springfield, IL 62706
Ph:(217)782-4520
Fax: (217)524-1514
Co. E-mail: BureauBudget.OMB@illinois.gov
URL: http://www.state.il.us/budget

66868 ■ Illinois State University–Census and Data User Services
Department 4950
Research Services Bldg., Ste. A
Normal, IL 61790-4950
Ph:(309)438-5946
Fax: (309)438-2898
Co. E-mail: cadus@rs6000.cmp.ilstu.edu
URL: http://www.cadus.ilstu.edu

66869 ■ Northeastern Illinois Planning Commission–Data Research and Forcasting
222 S. Riverside Plaza, Ste. 1800
Chicago, IL 60606-6097
Ph:(312)454-0400
Fax: (312)454-0411
Co. E-mail: tomasso@nipc.org
URL: http://www.census.gov/sdc/www/ilsdc.html

66870 ■ Northern Illinois University–The Regional Development Institute (RDI)–Center for Governmental Studies (148 N)
148 N. 3rd St.
De Kalb, IL 60115-2854
Ph:(815)753-1907
Fax: (815)753-2305
Co. E-mail: info@rdiniu.org
URL: http://www.cgsniu.org

66871 ■ Regional Research and Development Services–Southern Illinois University at Edwardsville
PO Box 1456
Edwardsville, IL 62026-1456
Ph:(618)650-2000

66872 ■ Indiana Business Research Center (IBRC)–Research at Indiana University
801 W. Michigan St. BS 4015
Indianapolis, IN 46202-5151
Ph:(317)274-2205
Fax: (317)274-3312
Co. E-mail: ibrc@indiana.edu
URL: http://www.research.iu.edu/centers/ibrc.html

66873 ■ Indiana Department of Commerce–Research Division and Technology
1 N. Capitol, Ste. 700
Indianapolis, IN 46204
Ph:(317)232-8959
Fax: (317)232-4146
Co. E-mail: tjockel@commerce.state.in.us
URL: http://www.census.gov/sdc/www/insdc.html

66874 ■ Indiana State Data Center–Indiana State Library
140 N. Senate Ave.
Indianapolis, IN 46204
Ph:(317)232-3733
Fax: (317)232-3728
Co. E-mail: fwilmot@statelib.lib.in.us
URL: http://www.census.gov/sdc/www/insdc.html

66875 ■ Indiana University–Indiana Business Research Center
801 W. Michigan St., BS 4015
1275 E. 10th St.
Indianapolis, IN 46202-5151
Ph:(317)274-2205
Fax: (317)274-3312
Co. E-mail: nelson@indiana.edu
URL: http://www.census.gov/sdc/www/insdc.html

66876 ■ Iowa Department of Education–Census Data Center
Grimes State Office Bldg.
Des Moines, IA 50319-0147

Ph:(515)281-4730
Co. E-mail: steve.boal@edu.state.ia.us

66877 ■ Iowa State University–Census Services
320 East Hall
Ames, IA 50011-0001
Ph:(515)294-8337
Co. E-mail: wgoudy@iastate.edu

66878 ■ State Library of Iowa
1112 E. Grand
Des Moines, IA 50319-0232
Ph:(515)281-4350
Fax: (515)242-6543
Co. E-mail: beth.henning@lib.state.ia.us
URL: http://www.lib.state.ia.us

66879 ■ University of Iowa–Iowa Social Science Institute
123 N. Linn
Iowa City, IA 52242-1409
Ph:(319)335-2371
Co. E-mail: joyce-baker@uiowa.edu
URL: http://www.uiowa.edu

66880 ■ University of Northern Iowa–Center for Social and Behavioral Research
Cedar Falls, IA 50614-0402
Ph:(319)273-2105
Co. E-mail: Kramer@uni.edu
URL: http://www.uni.edu

66881 ■ Kansas Division of the Budget
State Capitol Bldg., Rm. 152-E
Topeka, KS 66612
Ph:(785)296-2436
Fax: (785)296-0231
Co. E-mail: budget.info@da.state.ks.us
URL: http://da.state.ks.us/budget

66882 ■ Kansas State University–Department of Sociology–Population and Research Laboratory
Manhattan, KS 66506
Ph:(913)532-6865
Co. E-mail: bloomqui@ksuvm.ksu.edu

66883 ■ State Library of Kansas
State Capitol Bldg.
300 SW 10th Ave., Rm. 343-N
Topeka, KS 66612
Ph:(785)296-3296
Free: 800-432-3919
Fax: (785)296-6650
Co. E-mail: infolib@kslib.info
URL: http://skyways.lib.ks.us/Kansas/KSL

66884 ■ The University of Kansas–Institute for Public Policy and Business Research
607 Blake Hall
Lawrence, KS 66044-3177
Ph:(785)864-3701
Fax: (785)864-3683

66885 ■ Wichita State University–Center for Economic Development and Business Research
1845 Fairmount
Box 121
Wichita, KS 67260-0121
Ph:(316)978-3225
Fax: (316)978-3950
Co. E-mail: nickel@twsuvm.uc.twsu.edu
URL: http://www.wichita.edu

66886 ■ Governor's Office of Policy and Management
702 Capitol Ave.
Capitol Annex, Rm. 284
Frankfort, KY 40601
Ph:(502)564-7300
Fax: (502)564-6684
URL: http://www.osbd.ky.gov

66887 ■ Kentucky Department for Libraries and Archives–State Library Division
300 Coffee Tree Rd.
PO Box 537
Frankfort, KY 40601-0537
Ph:(502)564-8300
URL: http://www.kdla.ky.gov

66888 ■ University of Louisville–College of Business and Public Administration–Urban Studies Institute (426 W)
426 W. Bloom St.
Louisville, KY 40208
Ph:(502)852-7990
Fax: (502)852-7386
Co. E-mail: ron.crouch@louisville.edu
URL: http://www.louisville.edu

66889 ■ Maine Department of Labor–Division of Economic Analysis and Research
20 Union St.
PO Box 259
Augusta, ME 04332-0259
Ph:(207)624-6400
Fax: (207)289-5292
Co. E-mail: mdol@maine.gov
URL: http://www.maine.gov/labor

66890 ■ Maine State Library
State House
Station 64
Augusta, ME 04333-0064
Ph:(207)287-5600
Fax: (207)287-5615
Co. E-mail: gary.nichols@maine.gov
URL: http://www.state.me.us/msl

66891 ■ University of Southern Maine–Maine State Data Center–Center for Business and Economic Research (96 Fa)
96 Falmouth St.
PO Box 9300
Portland, ME 04104-9300
Ph:(207)780-4308
Fax: (207)780-4046
Co. E-mail: mcmahon@usm.maine.edu
URL: http://www.usm.maine.edu
Contact: Robert McMahon
E-mail: mcmahon@usm.maine.edu

66892 ■ Enoch Pratt Free Library–State Library Resource Center
400 Cathedral St.
Baltimore, MD 21201-4484
Ph:(410)396-5430
Fax: (410)396-1441
URL: http://www.epfl.net/index.html

66893 ■ Maryland Office of Planning
301 W. Preston St., Ste. 1101
Baltimore, MD 21201-2305
Ph:(410)767-4450
Free: 877-767-6272
Fax: (410)767-4480
URL: http://www.mdp.state.md.us

66894 ■ Maryland Small Business Development Center (SBDC)
7100 Baltimore Ave., Ste. 401
College Park, MD 20740
Ph:(301)403-8300
Co. E-mail: jgraham@mbs.umd.edu

66895 ■ University of Maryland–Department of Computer Science
A.V. Williams Bldg.
College Park, MD 20742
Ph:(301)405-2662
Fax: (301)405-6707
URL: http://www.cs.umd.edu

66896 ■ Massachusetts Institute for Social and Economic Research (MISER)
The State House
1 Ashburton Pl., Rm. 1004
PO Box 219
Boston, MA 02133-0219

Ph:(617)727-4537
Fax: (617)727-4660
Co. E-mail: wmurray@miser.umass.edu
URL: http://www.umass.edu/miser

66897 ■ University of Massachusetts–Massachusetts Institute for Social and Economic Research
128 Thompson Hall
Amherst, MA 01003-7515
Ph:(413)545-3460
Fax: (413)545-3686
URL: http://www.umass.edu/miser

66898 ■ The Library of Michigan–Government Documents Service
717 W. Allegan St.
PO Box 30007
Lansing, MI 48909
Ph:(517)373-9489
Co. E-mail: asanders@libofmich.lib.mi.us
URL: http://www.michigan.gov

66899 ■ Michigan Department of Management and Budget–Demographic Research and Statistics–Michigan Information Center (PO Bo)
PO Box 30026
Lansing, MI 48909
Ph:(517)373-7910
Fax: (517)373-2939
Co. E-mail: eric_swanson@state.mi.us
URL: http://www.michigan.gov/dmb

66900 ■ Wayne State University–MIMIC/Center for Urban Studies
Faculty/Administration Bldg.
656 W. Kirby St.
Detroit, MI 48202
Ph:(313)577-8996
Co. E-mail: kurt.metzger@wayne.edu
URL: http://www.wayne.edu

66901 ■ Headwaters Regional Development Commission
403 4th St. NW, Ste. 310
PO Box 906
Bemidji, MN 56619-0906
Ph:(218)444-4732
Fax: (218)444-4722
Co. E-mail: hrdc@hrdc.org
URL: http://www.hrdc.org
Contact: Tim Flathers
E-mail: tflathers@vax1.bemidji.msus.edu

66902 ■ Metropolitan Council Research–Metropolitan Council Data Center
230 E. 5th St.
St. Paul, MN 55101
Ph:(651)602-1140
Fax: (651)602-1464
Co. E-mail: data.center@metc.state.mn.us
URL: http://www.metrocouncil.org

66903 ■ Minnesota Department of Education–Education Resource Center
501 Capitol Square Bldg.
St. Paul, MN 55101
Ph:(612)296-6684
Fax: (612)296-6684
Co. E-mail: education@state.mn.us
URL: http://www.education.state.mn.us

66904 ■ Minnesota Planning–State Demographic Center
300 Centennial Office
Bldg. 658
Cedar St.
St. Paul, MN 55155
Ph:(612)296-2557
Fax: (612)296-3698
Co. E-mail: Barbara.Ronningen@state.mn.us
URL: http://www.census.gov/sdc/www/mnsdc.html

66905 ■ Mississippi Department of Economic and Community Development–Industry Resource Bureau–Mississippi Development Authority (1200)
1200 Walter Sillas Bldg.
PO Box 849
Jackson, MS 39205
Ph:(601)359-3593
Fax: (601)359-3454
Co. E-mail: dtate@mississippi.org
URL: http://www.mississippi.org

66906 ■ The University of Mississippi–Center for Population Studies
310 Leavell Hall, Rm. 302
University, MS 38677
Ph:(662)915-7288
Fax: (662)915-7736
Co. E-mail: dswanson@olemiss.edu
URL: http://www.olemiss.edu

66907 ■ Geographic Resources Center–University of Missouri—Columbia
Rm. 104, Stewart Hall
Columbia, MO 65211-0001
Ph:(573)882-1404
URL: http://www.grc.missouri.edu

66908 ■ Missouri Small Business Development Centers
300 University Pl.
Columbia, MO 65211
Ph:(573)882-0344
Fax: (314)884-4297
Co. E-mail: summersm@missouri.edu
URL: http://www.missouribusiness

66909 ■ Missouri State Library–Library Development
600 W. Main St.
PO Box 387
Jefferson City, MO 65102
Ph:(573)526-7648
Fax: (573)751-3612
URL: http://www.sos.mo.gov/library

66910 ■ Missouri State Office of Administration
124 Capitol Bldg.
PO Box 809
Jefferson City, MO 65102
Ph:(573)751-2345
Fax: (573)526-4811
Co. E-mail: bursor@mail.oa.state.mo.us
URL: http://www.census.gov/sdc/www/mosdc.html

66911 ■ Missouri State Office of Social and Economic Data Analysis–University of Missouri—Columbia
224 Lewis Hall
Columbia, MO 65211
Ph:(573)882-7396
Fax: (573)884-2727
Co. E-mail: blodgettj@umsystem.edu
URL: http://www.census.gov/sdc/www/mosdc.html

66912 ■ University of Missouri-Kansas City–Center for Economic Information
207 Haag Hall
Kansas City, MO 64131
Ph:(816)235-2832
Co. E-mail: peaton@cctr.umkc.edu
URL: http://www.cctr.umkc.edu

66913 ■ Urban Information Center–University of Missouri—St. Louis
8001 Natural Bridge Rd.
St. Louis, MO 63121-4499
Ph:(314)516-6014
Fax: (314)516-6274
Co. E-mail: john@oseda.missouri.edu
URL: http://www.oseda.missouri.edu

66914 ■ Montana Department of Commerce–Census and Economic Information Center
1424 9th Ave.
PO Box 200501
Helena, MT 59620-0501

Ph:(406)841-2700
Fax: (406)444-1518
URL: http://www.commerce.mt.gov

66915 ■ Montana State Library–Digital Library Division
Capitol Station
1515 E. 6th Ave.
Helena, MT 59620
Ph:(406)444-3004
Fax: (406)444-5612
Co. E-mail: jkammerer@mt.gov
URL: http://www.census.gov/sdc/www/mtsdc.html

66916 ■ Research and Analysis Bureau–Employment Policy Division–Montana Department of Labor and Industry (PO Bo)
PO Box 1728
Helena, MT 59624
Ph:(406)444-2430
Fax: (406)444-2638
Co. E-mail: bliffring@mt.gov
URL: http://www.census.gov/sdc/www/mtsdc.html

66917 ■ University of Montana–Bureau of Business and Economic Research
Missoula, MT 59812
Ph:(406)243-5113
Fax: (406)243-2086
Co. E-mail: jim.sylvester@business.umt.edu
URL: http://www.business.umt.edu

66918 ■ Center for Public Affairs Research–Nebraska State Data Center
University of Nebraska at Omaha
Peter Kiewit Conference Center, No. 232
Omaha, NE 68182-0001
Ph:(402)554-2134
Fax: (402)595-2366

66919 ■ Natural Resources Commission
301 Centennial Mall S.
PO Box 94876
Lincoln, NE 68509-4876
Ph:(402)471-2081
Fax: (402)471-2900
Co. E-mail: mbansal@dnr.state.ne.us
URL: http://www.census.gov/sdc/www/nesdc.html

66920 ■ Nebraska Department of Administration Services–The Central Data Processing Division
301 Centennial Mall S.
PO Box 94876
Lincoln, NE 68509-4876
Ph:(402)471-2081
Co. E-mail: aicjerry@vmhost.cdp.state.ne.us
URL: http://www.census.gov/sdc/www/nesdc.html

66921 ■ Nebraska Department of Labor
550 S. 16th St.
PO Box 94600
Lincoln, NE 68509-2006
Ph:(402)471-2600
Co. E-mail: pbaker@dol.state.ne.us
URL: http://www.census.gov/sdc/www/nesdc.html

66922 ■ Nebraska Library Commission–Federal Document Librarian
The Atrium
1200 North St., Ste. 120
Lincoln, NE 68508-2006
Ph:(402)471-2045
Co. E-mail: lsailors@neon.nlc.state.ne.us
URL: http://www.census.gov/sdc/www/nesdc.html

66923 ■ Nebraska Policy Research Office
State Capitol, Rm. 1319
PO Box 94601
Lincoln, NE 68509-4601
Ph:(402)471-2414
Co. E-mail: lhill@pro.state.ne.us
URL: http://www.census.gov/sdc/www/nesdc.html

66924 ■ Nevada State Library–Department of Cultural Affairs
Capitol Complex
100 Stewart St.
Carson City, NV 89701
Ph:(702)687-8326
Fax: (775)687-8330
Co. E-mail: sfjones@clan.lib.nv.us/docs/nsla
URL: http://dmla.clan.lib.nv.us

66925 ■ New Hampshire Office of Energy and Planning
57 Regional Dr., Ste. 3
Concord, NH 03301-8519
Ph:(603)271-2155
Fax: (603)271-2615
Co. E-mail: OEPinfo@nh.gov
URL: http://nh.gov/oep/index.htm

66926 ■ New Hampshire State Library
20 Park St.
Concord, NH 03301
Ph:(603)271-2392
Free: 800-462-1726
Fax: (603)271-6826
URL: http://www.state.nh.us/nhsl

66927 ■ University of New Hampshire–Office of Biometrics
Pettee Hall
Durham, NH 03824
Ph:(603)862-3930

66928 ■ New Jersey Data Center–New Jersey Department of Labor–Division of Labor Market and Demographic Research (PO Bo)
PO Box 388
Trenton, NJ 08625-0388
Ph:(609)984-2595
Fax: (609)984-6833
Co. E-mail: Leonard.Preston@dol.state.nj.us
URL: http://www.census.gov/sdc/www/njsdc.html

66929 ■ New Jersey State Library–U.S. Documents Office
185 W. State St.
PO Box 520
Trenton, NJ 08625-0520
Ph:(609)292-6529
Fax: (609)984-7900
Co. E-mail: dmercer@njstatelib.org
URL: http://www.census.gov/sdc/www/njsdc.html

66930 ■ Princeton University–Firestone Library–Social Science Reference Center (1 Was)–Data and Statistical Services (hington Rd)
1 Washington Rd.
Princeton, NJ 08544
Ph:(609)258-6051
Fax: (609)258-4105
Co. E-mail: daniele@princeton.edu
URL: http://www.census.gov/sdc/www/njsdc.html

66931 ■ Rutgers University–Rutgers Regional Report
33 Livingston Ave., Ste. 300
New Brunswick, NJ 08901-1981
Ph:(732)932-5475
Fax: (732)932-1771
Co. E-mail: jwhughes@rci.rutger.edu
URL: http://rucs.camden.rutgers.edu

66932 ■ Rutgers University Computing Services
CCIS—Hill Center, Busch Campus
258A Hill Center
Busch Campus, Box 879
Piscataway, NJ 08854-0879
Ph:(732)445-3137
Fax: (732)445-5539
Co. E-mail: bilder@nbcs.rutgers.edu
URL: http://rucs.camden.rutgers.edu

66933 ■ New Mexico Economic Development Department–New Mexico State Data Center
1100 St. Francis Dr.
PO Box 20003
Santa Fe, NM 87504-5003

Ph:(505)827-0264
Fax: (505)827-0407
Co. E-mail: Elizabeth.davis@edd.state.nm.us
URL: http://www.census.gov/sdc/www/nmsdc.html

66934 ■ New Mexico State Library
1209 Camino Carlos Rey
Santa Fe, NM 87505-9860
Ph:(505)476-9717
Fax: (505)476-9703
Co. E-mail: laurie.canepa@state.nm.us
URL: http://www.census.gov/sdc/www/nmsdc.html

66935 ■ New Mexico State University–Department of Economics/3CQ
Box 30001
Las Cruces, NM 88003-0001
Ph:(505)646-2112
Co. E-mail: kbrook@nmsu.edu
URL: http://www.census.gov/sdc/www/nmsdc.html

66936 ■ University of New Mexico–Bureau of Business and Economic Research–Business and Industrial Data Center (1920)
1920 Lomas NE
Albuquerque, NM 87131-6021
Ph:(505)277-6626
Fax: (505)277-2773
Co. E-mail: kshore@unm.edu
URL: http://www.unm.edu

66937 ■ Cornell University–Cornell Institute for Social and Economic Research (CISER) Data Archive
391 Pine Tree Rd.
Ithaca, NY 14850-2820
Ph:(607)255-4801
Fax: (607)255-9353
Co. E-mail: ciser@cornell.edu
URL: http://www.ciser.cornell.edu

66938 ■ New York Department of Economic Development–Division of Policy and Research
1 Commerce Plz., Rm. 905
99 Washington Ave.
Albany, NY 12245
Ph:(518)474-1141
Fax: (518)473-9748

66939 ■ New York State Library–Cultural Education Center
Empire State Plz., 6th Fl.
Albany, NY 12245
Ph:(518)474-3940
Co. E-mail: mrredmond@unix2.nysed.gov
URL: http://www.census.gov/sdc/www/nysdc.html

66940 ■ Office of Real Property Services
16 Sheridan Ave.
Albany, NY 12210
Ph:(518)474-6742
Co. E-mail: mary.goldblatt@orps.state.ny.us
URL: http://www.census.gov/sdc/www/nysdc.html

66941 ■ Nelson A. Rockefeller Institute of Government
411 State St.
Albany, NY 12203
Ph:(518)443-5258
Co. E-mail: cooperm@rockinst.org

66942 ■ Center for Geographic Information and Analysis–Office of State Planning
301 N. Wilmington St., Ste. 700
115 Hillsborough St.
Raleigh, NC 27601-2825
Ph:(919)733-2090
Fax: (919)715-0725
Co. E-mail: dataq@ncmail.net
URL: http://www.cgia.state.nc.us

66943 ■ North Carolina Office of State Budget and Management
116 W. Jones St.
Raleigh, NC 27603-8005
Ph:(919)807-4700

Fax: (919)733-0640
URL: http://www.osbm.state.nc.us/osbm

66944 ■ State Library of North Carolina Division of State Library
State Library Bldg.
109 E. Jones St.
Raleigh, NC 27601-2807
Ph:(919)807-7450
Fax: (919)733-5679
URL: http://statelibrary.dcr.state.nc.us

66945 ■ University of North Carolina–Odum Institute for Research in Social Science
Manning Hall
Campus Box 3355
Chapel Hill, NC 27599-3355
Ph:(919)962-0512
Co. E-mail: ed_bachmann@unc.edu
URL: http://www.unc.edu

66946 ■ North Dakota State Library
Liberty Memorial Bldg.
Capitol Grounds
Bismarck, ND 58505-0800
Ph:(701)328-4622
Co. E-mail: msmail.spahlmey@ranch.state.nd.us
URL: http://www.censud.gov/sdc/www/ndsdc.html

66947 ■ North Dakota State University–North Dakota State Data Center
IACC 424
PO Box 5636
Fargo, ND 58105
Ph:(701)231-8621
Fax: (701)231-7400
Co. E-mail: Richard.rathge@ndsu.edu
URL: http://www.cenus.gov/sdc/www/ndsdc.html

66948 ■ Office of Intergovernmental Assistance
State Capitol, 14th Fl.
600 E. Blvd. Ave.
Bismarck, ND 58505-0170
Ph:(701)328-2094
Co. E-mail: ccmail.jboyd@ranch.state.nd.us
URL: http://www.census.gov/sdc/www/ndsdc.html

66949 ■ University of North Dakota–Department of Geography
PO Box 9020
Grand Forks, ND 58202-9020
Ph:(701)777-4246
Fax: (701)777-4592
Co. E-mail: devon_hansen@und.nodak.edu
URL: http://www.und.nodak.edu

66950 ■ Buckeye Hills Hocking Valley–Regional Development District
Route 1, County Rd. 9
Box 299D
Marietta, OH 45750
Ph:(614)374-9436
Co. E-mail: bhhvrddmarietta@ee.net

66951 ■ Cleveland State University–Northern Ohio Data and Information Service–Maxine Goodman Levin College of Urban Affairs (1737)
1737 E. Euclid Ave.
Cleveland, OH 44115
Ph:(216)687-2135
Co. E-mail: ustweb@urban.csuohio.edu
URL: http://www.urban.csuohio.edu

66952 ■ Ohio Department of Development–Office of Strategic Research
77 High St., 27th Fl.
PO Box 1001
Columbus, OH 43266-0101
Ph:(614)466-2116
Fax: (614)466-9697
Co. E-mail: skelly@odod.state.oh.us
URL: http://www.census.gov/sdc/www/ohsdc.html

66953 ■ Ohio Occupational Information Coordinating Commission–Ohio Bureau of Employment Services–Division of Labor Market Information (145 S)
145 S. Front St.
Columbus, OH 43215
Ph:(614)752-9494
Co. E-mail: khewald@obes01.a1.ohio.gov
URL: http://www.census.gov/clo/www/dc/sdclist.asc

66954 ■ Ohio State University Library–Census Data Center
126 Main Library
1858 Neil Avenue Mall
Columbus, OH 43210
Ph:(614)292-6175
Fax: (614)292-7859
URL: http://www.osu.edu

66955 ■ State Library of Ohio
274 E. 1st Ave.
Columbus, OH 43201
Ph:(614)995-0033
Fax: (614)752-0178
Co. E-mail: govinfo@sloma.state.oh.us
URL: http://www.loma.state.oh.us

66956 ■ University of Cincinnati–Southwest Ohio Regional Data Center–Institute for Policy Research (3110)
3110 1 Edwards Ctr.
PO Box 210132
Cincinnati, OH 45221-0132
Ph:(513)556-5028
Fax: (513)556-9023
URL: http://www.ipr.uc.edu

66957 ■ Center for Economic and Management Research–University of Oklahoma–Michael F. Prince College of Business (Adams)
Adams Hall
307 W. Brooks, Rm. 4
Norman, OK 73019-0450
Ph:(405)325-2931
Fax: (405)325-7688

66958 ■ Oklahoma Department of Commerce–Oklahoma State Data Center
900 N. S. Stiles Ave.
PO Box 26980
Oklahoma City, OK 73126-0980
Ph:(405)815-5184
Fax: (405)815-5163
Co. E-mail: jeff_wallace@odoc.state.ok.us
URL: http://www.census.gov/sdc/www/oksdc.html

66959 ■ Oklahoma Department of Libraries–U.S. Government Information Division
200 NE 18th St.
Oklahoma City, OK 73105-3205
Ph:(405)521-2502
Fax: (405)525-7804
Co. E-mail: sbeleu@oltn.odl.state.ok.us
URL: http://www.census.gov/sdc/www/oksd.html

66960 ■ Office of Economic Analysis
155 Cottage St. NE
Salem, OR 97310-0310
Ph:(503)378-4967
Fax: (503)378-7643
Co. E-mail: kanhaiya.l.vaidya@state.or.us
URL: http://www.census.gov/sdc/www/orsdc.html

66961 ■ Oregon Geographic Information Systems
Department of Energy Bldg.
625 Marion St., NE
Salem, OR 97301-3737
Ph:(503)378-4040
Free: 800-221-8035
Fax: (503)373-7806
Co. E-mail: energy.in.internet@.state.or.us
URL: http://www.oregon.gov

66962 ■ Oregon Housing and Community Services Department
725 Summer St. NE, Ste. B
PO Box 14508
Salem, OR 97309-0409
Ph:(503)986-2000
Fax: (503)986-2100
Co. E-mail: info@hcs.state.or.us
URL: http://www.ohcs.oregon.gov

66963 ■ Oregon State Library
State Library Bldg.
Salem, OR 97310
Ph:(503)378-4277
Co. E-mail: susan.b.westin@state.or.us
URL: http://www.census.gov/sdc/www/orsdc.html

66964 ■ Portland State University–Center for Population Research and Census
PO Box 751
Portland, OR 97207-0751
Ph:(503)725-5159
Free: 800-547-8887
Fax: (503)725-5162
Co. E-mail: houghg@pdx.edu
URL: http://www.census.gov/sdc/www/orsdc.html

66965 ■ University of Oregon Library–Documents and Microforms Department
Eugene, OR 97403-1299
Ph:(503)346-3070
Fax: (503)346-3094
Co. E-mail: tstave@oregon.uoregon.edu
URL: http://www.oregon.uoregon.edu

66966 ■ Penn State University at Harrisburg–Pennsylvania State Data Center–Institute of State and Regional Affairs (777 W)
777 W. Harrisburg Pke.
Middletown, PA 17057-4898
Ph:(717)948-6336
Fax: (717)948-6754
Co. E-mail: sdc3@psu.edu
URL: http://www.census.gov/sdc/www/pasdc.html

66967 ■ Pennsylvania State Library
Forum Bldg., Rm. 219
Harrisburg, PA 17105
Ph:(717)787-2327
Co. E-mail: khale@state.pa.us
URL: http://www.census.gov/sdc/www/pasdc.html

66968 ■ State Capital Office
Forum Bldg., Rm. 357
Harrisburg, PA 17120
Ph:(717)772-2683
Fax: (717)772-2683
Co. E-mail: PASDC-SCO@psu.edu
URL: http://www.pasdc.edu

66969 ■ Departmento de Educacion
PO Box 190759
San Juan, PR 00919-0759
Ph:(787)759-2000
Fax: (787)250-0275
URL: http://www.de.gobierno.pr

66970 ■ Janta de Planificacion–Oficina del Censo
Centro Gubernamental Minillas
PO Box 41119
San Juan, PR 00940-1119
Ph:(787)728-4430
Fax: (787)268-0506
URL: http://www.censo.gobierno.pr

66971 ■ Recinto Universitario De Mayaguez–Universidad de Puerto Rico
Apartado 5000
Mayaguez, PR 00681-5000
Ph:(787)832-4040
Co. E-mail: Arlene@rumac.upr.clu.edu
URL: http://www.census.gov/sdc/www/outsdc.html

66972 ■ Brown University–Social Science Data Center
University Library, Box A
Rockefeller Library
Providence, RI 02912
Ph:(401)863-2522
Fax: (401)863-1272
Co. E-mail: yvonne_federowicz@brown.edu
URL: http://www.brown.edu

66973 ■ Rhode Island Department of Education
3 Shepard Bldg.
255 Westminster St.
Providence, RI 02903
Ph:(401)222-6667
Co. E-mail: ride1560@ride.ro.net

66974 ■ Rhode Island Department of Health–Office of Health Statistics
3 Capitol Hill
Providence, RI 02908
Ph:(401)222-2550
Co. E-mail: jbuechner@doh.state.ri.us
URL: http://www.census.gov/sdc/www/risdc.html

66975 ■ Rhode Island Department of State Library Services
300 Richmond St.
Providence, RI 02903
Ph:(401)277-2728
Fax: (401)831-1131
Co. E-mail: frankio@rhilinet.gov

66976 ■ Rhode Island Economic Development Corporation
1 W. Exchange St.
Providence, RI 02903
Ph:(401)222-2601
Co. E-mail: mdoherty@riedc.com

66977 ■ Rhode Island State Department of Administration–Office of Municipal Affairs
1 Capitol Hill, 3rd Fl.
Providence, RI 02908-5873
Ph:(401)222-2726
Fax: (401)222-4195
Co. E-mail: mtondra@doa.state.ri.us
URL: http://www.muni-info.ri.gov

66978 ■ United Way of Rhode Island
229 Waterman St.
Providence, RI 02906
Ph:(401)444-0629
Co. E-mail: jane_nugent@unitedwayri.org
URL: http://www.unitedwayre.org

66979 ■ South Carolina State Budget and Control Board–Office of Research and Statistical Services
Rembert Dennis Bldg., Rm. 425
Columbia, SC 29201
Ph:(803)734-3780
Fax: (803)734-3619
Co. E-mail: mmacfarl@drss.state.sc.us

66980 ■ South Carolina State Library
PO Box 11469
Columbia, SC 29211
Ph:(803)734-7625
Co. E-mail: Elaine@leo.scsl.state.sc.us

66981 ■ South Dakota Department of Health–Director of Administration
600 E. Capitol Ave.
Pierre, SD 57501-2436
Ph:(605)773-4958
Fax: (605)773-5683

66982 ■ South Dakota Department of Labor–Labor Market Information Center
420 S. Roosevelt
PO Box 4730
Aberdeen, SD 57402-4730
Ph:(605)626-2314
Fax: (605)626-2322
Co. E-mail: phil.george@state.sd.us

66983 ■ South Dakota State Library–Documents Department
800 Governors Dr.
Pierre, SD 57501-2294
Ph:(605)773-5241
Fax: (605)773-4950
Co. E-mail: ann.eichinger@state.sd.us

66984 ■ South Dakota State University–Rural Sociology Department
Scobey Hall, Rm. 226
Box 504
Brookings, SD 57007-1296
Ph:(605)688-4132
Fax: (605)688-6354
Co. E-mail: sdsu_censusdata@sdstate.edu

66985 ■ University of South Dakota–School of Business–Business Research Bureau (414 E)
414 E. Clark
Vermillion, SD 57069
Ph:(605)677-5287
Fax: (605)677-5427
Co. E-mail: tbendert@charlie.usd.edu
URL: http://www.usd.edu

66986 ■ Tennessee Department of Economic and Community Development–Research Division
Rachel Jackson Bldg., 10th Fl.
312 8th Ave. N.
Nashville, TN 37243-0405
Ph:(615)741-2373
Fax: (615)741-0607
URL: http://www.state.tn.us/ecd

66987 ■ University of Tennessee–College of Business Administration–Center for Business and Economic Research (Rm. 1)
Rm. 100, Glocker Hall
Knoxville, TN 37996-4170
Ph:(423)974-5441
Co. E-mail: bvickers@utk.edu
URL: http://www.utkk.edu

66988 ■ Texas A&M University System–Department of Rural Sociology
Special Services Bldg.
College Station, TX 77843-2125
Ph:(409)845-5115
Fax: (409)845-8529
Co. E-mail: texassdc@txsdcsun.tamu.edu
URL: http://www.txsdcsun.tamu.edu

66989 ■ Texas Department of Commerce–State Data Center
9th and Congress Sts.
PO Box 12728, Capitol Sta.
Austin, TX 78701
Ph:(512)936-0223
Co. E-mail: donna@mail.tdoc.tex.gov
URL: http://www.tdoc.tex.gov

66990 ■ Texas Natural Resources Information System (TNRIS)
PO Box 13231
Austin, TX 78711
Ph:(512)463-8399
Fax: (512)463-7274
Co. E-mail: wbrown@tnris.state.tx.us
URL: http://www.tnris.state.tx.us

66991 ■ Texas State Library and Archive Commission
Lorenzode Zavala Bldg.
PO Box 12927
Austin, TX 78711-2927
Ph:(512)463-5426
Fax: (512)463-5436
Co. E-mail: dhouston@tsl.state.tx.us
URL: http://www.tsl.state.tx.us

66992 ■ University of the Virgin Islands–Eastern Caribbean Center
John Brewer's Bay, No. 2
Charlotte Amalie
St. Thomas, VI 00802

Ph:(340)693-1027
Fax: (340)693-1025
Co. E-mail: fmills@uvi.edu
URL: http://www.uvi.edu

66993 ■ Virgin Islands Department of Economic Development
Charlotte Amalie
PO Box 6400
St. Thomas, VI 00803
Ph:(340)774-8784
Co. E-mail: ab782@virgin.usvi.ne
URL: http://www.virgin.usvi.ne

66994 ■ Department of Community and Economic Development–Department of Employment Security
140 East 300 South
PO Box 11249
Salt Lake City, UT 84147-0249
Ph:(801)536-7813
Co. E-mail: eslmid.kjensen@email.state.ut.us
URL: http://www.state.ut.us

66995 ■ University of Utah–Bureau of Economic and Business Research
401 KDGB
Salt Lake City, UT 84112
Ph:(801)581-3353
Co. E-mail: bebrfch@business.utah.edu
URL: http://www.business.utah.edu

66996 ■ Utah Department of Community and Economic Development
324 S. State St., Ste. 500
Salt Lake City, UT 84111
Ph:(801)538-8826
Fax: (801)538-8888
Co. E-mail: djex@utah.gov
URL: http://www.utah.gov

66997 ■ Utah Office of Planning and Budget
Utah State Capital Complex, Ste. E120
PO Box 142210
Salt Lake City, UT 84114
Ph:(801)538-1038
Fax: (801)538-1547

66998 ■ University of Vermont–Center for Rural Studies
207 Morrill Hall
Burlington, VT 05405-0106
Ph:(802)656-3021
Co. E-mail: jcruise@moose.uvm.edu

66999 ■ Vermont Department of Libraries
109 State St.
Montpelier, VT 05609-0601
Ph:(802)828-3265
Fax: (802)828-2199
Co. E-mail: sybil.mcshane@.dol.state.vt.us
URL: http://www.dol.state.vt.us

67000 ■ Vermont Office of Policy Research and Coordination
Pavilion Office Bldg.
109 State St.
Montpelier, VT 05609
Ph:(802)828-3261
Co. E-mail: sybil@dol.state.vt.us
URL: http://www.dol.state.vt.us

67001 ■ Vermont Travel Department
134 State St.
Montpelier, VT 05602
Ph:(802)828-3676
Free: 800-837-6668

67002 ■ Library of Virginia–Collection Management Division
800 E. Broad St.
Richmond, VA 23219-8000
Ph:(804)692-3663
Fax: (804)692-3603
Co. E-mail: recman@lva.lib.va.us
URL: http://www.lva.lib.va.us

67003 ■ University of Virginia–Center for Public Service
918 Emmet St. N., Ste. 300
Charlottesville, VA 22903-4823
Ph:(804)982-5585
Co. E-mail: mas6g@virgina.edu
URL: http://www.virgina.edu

67004 ■ Virginia Employment Commission
703 E. Main St.
Richmond, VA 23219
Ph:(804)786-8026
Fax: (804)371-0412
Co. E-mail: dlillywhite@vec.state.va.us
URL: http://www.vec.state.va.us

67005 ■ Central Washington University–Department of Sociology–Applied Social Data Center (400 E)
400 E. University Way
Ellensburg, WA 98926-7545
Ph:(509)963-1111
Fax: (509)963-1308
URL: http://www.cwu.edu

67006 ■ Department of Employment Security–LMEA
PO Box 46000
Olympia, WA 98504-6000
Ph:(360)438-4804

67007 ■ Puget Sound Council of Governments
1011 Western Ave., Ste. 500
Seattle, WA 98104-1035
Ph:(206)464-7964
Co. E-mail: nkilgren@psrc.org
URL: http://www.census.gov/sdc/www/wasdc.html

67008 ■ University of Washington–CSSCR
145 Savery Hall, DK 45
PO Box 353345
Seattle, WA 98195
Ph:(206)543-8110
Co. E-mail: fred@u.washington.edu
URL: http://www.washington.edu

67009 ■ Washington State Library–Government Publics Division
PO Box 42475
Olympia, WA 98504-2460
Ph:(360)753-4027
Fax: (360)586-7575
Co. E-mail: abregent@wln.com
URL: http://www.wln.com

67010 ■ Washington State Office of Financial Management–Forecasting Division
450 Insurance Bldg., 4th Fl.
Box 43113
Olympia, WA 98504-3113
Ph:(360)902-0592
Fax: (360)664-8941
Co. E-mail: zi.zhao@ofm.wa.gov
URL: http://www.ofm.wa.gov

67011 ■ Washington State University–Extension Economist
203 Hubert Hall
Pullman, WA 99164-0001
Ph:(509)335-2811
Fax: (509)335-1173
Co. E-mail: gsmith@nsu.edu
URL: http://www.nsu.edu

67012 ■ Washington State University–Social Research Center–Department of Rural Sociology (PO Bo)
PO Box 464006
Pullman, WA 99164-4006
Ph:(509)335-4519
Co. E-mail: kirschner@wsu.edu
URL: http://www.wsa.edu

67013 ■ Western Washington University–Demographic Research Laboratory–Department of Sociology
Bellingham, WA 98225
Ph:(360)650-3176
Co. E-mail: tedrow@ss.wwu.edu
URL: http://www.cc.wwu.edu

67014 ■ Bureau of Business and Economic Research–West Virginia University–College of Business and Economics (5 Bus)
5 Business and Economic Bldg.
PO Box 6025
Morgantown, WV 26506-6025
Ph:(304)293-4092
Fax: (304)293-5652
URL: http://www.bber.wvu.edu

67015 ■ West Virginia Development Office–Research and Strategic Planning Division
Capitol Complex
Bldg. 6, Rm. 553
Charleston, WV 25305
Ph:(304)558-2045
Fax: (304)558-2044
Co. E-mail: calvertd@wvlc.wvnet.edu
URL: http://www.wvlc.wvnet.edu

67016 ■ West Virginia State Library Commission–Reference Library
Science and Cultural Center
Capitol Complex
Charleston, WV 25305
Ph:(304)558-2045
Fax: (304)293-7061
Co. E-mail: calvertd@wvlc.wvnet.edu
URL: http://www.wvlc.wvnet.edu

67017 ■ West Virginia University Health Science Center–Office of Health Services Research
Medical Center Dr.
PO Box 9145
Morgantown, WV 26506-9145
Ph:(304)293-1086
Fax: (304)293-6685
Co. E-mail: alex@wvuohsr.hsc.wvu.edu
URL: http://www.wvuohsr.hsc.wvu.edu

67018 ■ Department of Administration–Demographic Services Center
101 E. Wilson St., 6th Fl.
PO Box 7868
Madison, WI 53702-7868
Ph:(608)266-1927
Fax: (608)267-6931
URL: http://www.doa.state.wi.us

67019 ■ University of Wisconsin - Madison–Applied Population Laboratory–Department of Rural Sociology (1450)
1450 Linden Dr., Rm. 316
Madison, WI 53706
Ph:(608)262-3097
Fax: (608)262-6022
Co. E-mail: dmohn@ssc.wisc.edu
URL: http://www.wisc.edu

67020 ■ Department of Administration and Information–Economic Analysis Division
1807 Capitol Ave., Ste. 206
Cheyenne, WY 82002-0060
Ph:(307)777-7504
Fax: (307)632-1819
Co. E-mail: ead@state.wy.us
URL: http://eadiv.state.wy.us

67021 ■ University of Wyoming–Survey Research Center
PO Box 3925
Laramie, WY 82071-3925
Ph:(307)766-2010
Co. E-mail: wliu@missc.state.wy.us
URL: http://www.missc.state.wy.us

CORPORATION FOR NATIONAL SERVICE

67022 ■ Corporation for National and Community Service–Department of AmeriCorps
1201 New York Avenue., NW, Rm. 9601
Washington, DC 20525-0001
Ph:(202)606-5000
Fax: (202)565-2791
URL: http://www.nationalservice.org

67023 ■ Corporation for National and Community Service–Field Liaison
1201 New York Ave., NW
Washington, DC 20525-0001
Ph:(202)606-6924
Fax: (202)565-2789
URL: http://www.cns.gov

67024 ■ Corporation for National and Community Service–Office of Learn and Serve
1201 New York Ave., NW, Rm. 9606
Washington, DC 20525-0001
Ph:(202)606-6927
Fax: (202)565-2781
URL: http://www.nationalservice.org

67025 ■ Corporation for National and Community Service–Office of Public Affairs
1201 New York Ave., NW, Rm. 8609
Washington, DC 20525-0001
Ph:(202)606-6927
Fax: (202)565-2782
URL: http://www.nationalservice.org

67026 ■ Corporation for National and Community Service (CNCS)–Office of Procurement
1201 New York Ave., NW
Washington, DC 20525-0001
Ph:(202)606-5000
Fax: (202)606-2784
URL: http://www.nationalservice.org

ENVIRONMENTAL PROTECTION AGENCY

67027 ■ Environmental Protection Agency–Office of Small and Disadvantaged Business Utilization
1200 Pennsylvania Ave. NW
Mail Code 1230A
Washington, DC 20460
Ph:(202)272-0167
URL: http://www.epa.gov/osdbu
Description: The Environmental Protection Agency's Office of Small and Disadvantaged Business Utilization performs the following duties: provides a convenient way for small businesses to access the EPA; facilitates communication between small businesses and the EPA; helps small businesses understand and comply with environmental regulations; investigates and resolves individual small business disputes with the EPA; and works with EPA personnel to increase their understanding of small businesses in the development and enforcement of environmental regulations. Provides procurement information as it regards to small businesses, small and disadvantaged businesses, minority-owned businesses, and women-owned businesses.

The following EPA offices are arranged by region.

67028 ■ Environmental Protection Agency (Region 1)
1 Congress St., Ste. 1100
Boston, MA 02114-2023
Ph:(617)918-1111
Fax: (617)918-0101
URL: http://www.epa.gov/region01
Description: Serves Connecticut, Massachusetts, Maine, New Hampshire, Rhode Island, and Vermont.

67029 ■ Environmental Protection Agency (Region 2)
290 Broadway
New York, NY 10007-1866
Ph:(212)637-3000
Fax: (212)637-3526
Co. E-mail: R2_Web_Inquiry@epa.gov
URL: http://www.epa.gov/region02
Description: Serves New Jersey, New York, Puerto Rico, and the Virgin Islands.

67030 ■ Environmental Protection Agency (Region 3)
1650 Arch St.
Philadelphia, PA 19103-2029
Ph:(215)814-5000
Free: 800-438-2474
Fax: (215)814-5103
URL: http://www.epa.gov/region03
Description: Serves Delaware, Maryland, Pennsylvania, Virginia, West Virginia, and the District of Columbia.

67031 ■ Environmental Protection Agency (Region 4)
61 Forsyth St., SW
Atlanta, GA 30303-3104
Ph:(404)562-9900
Free: 800-241-1754
Fax: (404)562-8174
URL: http://www.epa.gov/region04
Description: Serves Alabama, Florida, Georgia, Kentucky, Mississippi, North Carolina, South Carolina, and Tennessee.

67032 ■ Environmental Protection Agency (Region 5)
77 W. Jackson Blvd.
Chicago, IL 60604-3507
Ph:(312)353-2000
Free: 800-621-8431
Fax: (312)353-4135
URL: http://www.epa.gov/region05
Description: Serves Illinois, Indiana, Michigan, Minnesota, Ohio, and Wisconsin.

67033 ■ Environmental Protection Agency (Region 6)
Fountain Pl., 12th Fl.
1445 Ross Ave., Ste. 1200
Dallas, TX 75202-2733
Ph:(214)655-2200
Free: 800-887-6063
Fax: (214)665-7113
URL: http://www.epa.gov/region06
Description: Serves Arkansas, Louisiana, New Mexico, Oklahoma, and Texas.

67034 ■ Environmental Protection Agency (Region 7)
901 N. 5th St.
Kansas City, KS 66101
Ph:(913)551-7003
Free: 800-223-0425
URL: http://www.epa.gov/region07
Description: Serves Iowa, Kansas, Missouri, and Nebraska.

67035 ■ Environmental Protection Agency (Region 8)
999 18th St., Ste. 500
Denver, CO 80202-2466
Ph:(303)312-6312
Free: 800-227-8917
Fax: (303)312-6339
Co. E-mail: r8eisc@epa.gov
URL: http://www.epa.gov/region08
Description: Serves Colorado, Montana, North Dakota, South Dakota, Utah, and Wyoming.

67036 ■ Environmental Protection Agency (Region 9)
75 Hawthorne St.
San Francisco, CA 94105
Ph:(415)947-8000
Fax: (415)947-3553
Co. E-mail: r9.info@epa.gov

URL: http://www.epa.gov/region09
Description: Serves Arizona, California, Hawaii, Nevada, American Samoa, Guam, and the Trust Territory of the Pacific Islands.

67037 ■ Environmental Protection Agency (Region 10)
1200 6th Ave.
Seattle, WA 98101
Ph:(206)553-1200
Free: 800-424-4372
Fax: (206)553-0149
URL: http://www.epa.gov/region10
Description: Serves Alaska, Idaho, Oregon, and Washington.

The following are State Superfund Offices for EPA Region One.

67038 ■ Environmental Protection Agency State Superfund Office (Connecticut)–Department of Environmental Protection–Small Business Assistance (79 El)
79 Elm St.
Hartford, CT 06106-5127
Ph:(860)424-3000
Fax: (860)424-4051
Co. E-mail: dep.webmaster@po.state.ct.us

67039 ■ Environmental Protection Agency State Superfund Office (Maine)–Department of Environmental Protection–Office of the Commissioner (17 St)
17 State House Station
Augusta, ME 04333-0017
Ph:(207)287-7688
Free: 800-452-1942
URL: http://www.maine.gov/dep/index.shtml

67040 ■ Environmental Protection Agency State Superfund Office (Massachusetts)–Department of Environmental Protection–Bureau of Waste Prevention (1 Win)–Recycle (ter St.)
1 Winter St.
Boston, MA 02108
Ph:(617)292-5500
Fax: (617)556-1049
Co. E-mail: depwww@state.ma.us
URL: http://www.mass.gov/dep

67041 ■ Environmental Protection Agency State Superfund Office (New Hampshire)–Department of Environmental Services–Commissioners Office (29 Ha)
29 Hazen Dr.
PO Box 95
Concord, NH 03302-0095
Ph:(603)271-3503
Fax: (603)271-2867
URL: http://www.des.state.nh.us

67042 ■ Environmental Protection Agency State Superfund Office (Rhode Island)–Department of Environmental Management–Waste Management (235 P)
235 Promenade St.
Providence, RI 02908-5767
Ph:(401)222-6800
Fax: (401)222-3812
URL: http://www.dem.ri.gov

The following are State Superfund offices for EPA Region Two.

67043 ■ Environmental Protection Agency State Superfund Office (New Jersey)–Department of Environmental Protection–Hazardous Waste Management Division (401 E)
401 E. State St.
PO Box 414
Trenton, NJ 08625
Ph:(609)984-6800
Fax: (609)984-6874
Co. E-mail: askDEP@dep.state.nj.us
URL: http://www.state.nj.us/dep

67044 ■ Environmental Protection Agency State Superfund Office (New York)–Department of Environmental Conservation–Hazardous Waste Remediation Division (625 B)
625 Broadway
Albany, NY 12233-1011
Ph:(518)402-8540
Fax: (518)402-9016
Co. E-mail: dpaeweb@gw.dec.state.ny.us
URL: http://www.dec.state.ny.us

The following are State Superfund Offices for EPA Region Three.

67045 ■ Environmental Protection Agency State Superfund Office (Delaware)–Department of Natural Resources and Environmental Control–Air and Waste Management Section (89 Ki)
89 Kings Hwy.
Dover, DE 19901
Ph:(302)739-9002
URL: http://www.dnrec.delaware.gov

67046 ■ Environmental Protection Agency State Superfund Office (District of Columbia)–Environmental Health Administration–Hazardous Materials, Pesticides and Underground Strorage Tank Management (51 N.)
51 N. St., NE
Washington, DC 20020
Ph:(202)532-2500
URL: http://www.doh.dc.gov

67047 ■ Environmental Protection Agency State Superfund Office (Maryland)–Department of the Environment–Recycling in Maryland (1800)
1800 Washington Blvd.
Baltimore, MD 21230
Ph:(410)537-3000
Free: 800-633-6101
URL: http://www.mde.state.md.us

67048 ■ Environmental Protection Agency State Superfund Office (Pennsylvania)–Department of Environmental Resources–Bureau of Land Recycling and Waste Management (PO Bo)
PO Box 8471
Harrisburg, PA 17105-8471
Ph:(717)787-9871
Fax: (717)787-1904
URL: http://www.depweb.state.pa.us

67049 ■ Environmental Protection Agency State Superfund Office (Virginia)–Department of Environmental Quality
Center Bldg.
103 S. Main St.
Waterbury, VA 05671-0301
Ph:(802)241-3600
Free: 800-592-5482
Fax: (802)974-9559
URL: http://www.anr.state.vt.us

67050 ■ Environmental Protection Agency State Superfund Office (West Virginia)–Division of Environmental Protection–Office of Waste Management (601 5)
601 57th St.
Charleston, WV 25304
Ph:(304)926-0477
Fax: (304)368-3959
URL: http://www.dep.state.wv.us

The following are State Superfund Offices for EPA Region Four.

67051 ■ Environmental Protection Agency State Superfund Office (Alabama)–Department of Environmental Management–Land Division (PO Bo)
PO Box 301463
Montgomery, AL 36130-1463

Ph:(334)271-7700
Fax: (334)271-7950
Co. E-mail: webmaster@adem.state.us
URL: http://www.adem.state.al.us

67052 ■ Environmental Protection Agency State Superfund Office (Florida)–Department of Environmental Protection–Division of Waste Management (2600)
2600 Blair Stone Rd.
Mail Stop 4500
Tallahassee, FL 32399-2400
Ph:(850)245-8705
URL: http://www.dep.state.fl.us/waste

67053 ■ Environmental Protection Agency State Superfund Office (Georgia)–Department of Natural Resources–Land Protection Branch (East)–Solid Waste Management Program (Tower)
East Tower
2 Martin Luther King Jr. Dr. SE, Ste. 1152
Atlanta, GA 30334
Ph:(404)656-3500
URL: http://www.gadnr.org

67054 ■ Environmental Protection Agency State Superfund Office (Kentucky)–Department for Environmental Protection–Division of Waste Management (14 Re)
14 Reilly Rd.
Frankfort, KY 40601
Ph:(502)564-6716
Fax: (502)564-4049
Co. E-mail: waste@ky.gov
URL: http://www.waste.ky.gov

67055 ■ Environmental Protection Agency State Superfund Office (Mississippi)–Department of Environmental Quality
PO Box 20305
Jackson, MS 39289-1305
Ph:(601)961-5171
Fax: (601)354-6612
URL: http://www.deq.state.ms.us

67056 ■ Environmental Protection Agency State Superfund Office (North Carolina)–Department of Environment and Natural Resources
Mail Service Center 1617
512 N. Salisbury St.
Raleigh, NC 27699-1617
Ph:(919)733-7015
Fax: (919)733-2496
URL: http://www.enr.state.nc.us

67057 ■ Environmental Protection Agency State Superfund Office (South Carolina)–Department of Health and Environmental Control
2600 Bull St.
Columbia, SC 29201
Ph:(803)898-4000
Fax: (803)896-4001

67058 ■ Environmental Protection Agency State Superfund Office (Tennessee)–Department of Environment and Conservation–Division of Solid and Hazardous Waste Management (401 C)
401 Church St., L & C Annex, 1st Fl.
Nashville, TN 37243-0435
Ph:(615)532-0109
Free: 888-891-8332
Co. E-mail: ask.tdec@state.tn.us
URL: http://www.state.tn.us/environment/index.htm

The following are State Superfund Offices for EPA Region Five.

67059 ■ Environmental Protection Agency State Superfund Office (Illinois)–Environmental Protection Agency–Bureau of Land (1021)–Pollution Prevention (N. Grand A)
1021 N. Grand Ave., E.
PO Box 19276
Springfield, IL 62794-9276
Ph:(217)782-3397
URL: http://www.epa.state.il.us

67060 ■ Environmental Protection Agency State Superfund Office (Indiana)–State Department of Environmental Management–Office of Environmental Response (India)–Office of Land Quality (na Governm)
Indiana Government Center-North
100 N. Senate Ave.
Indianapolis, IN 46204
Ph:(317)234-0338
Free: 800-451-6027
Fax: (317)308-3063
URL: http://www.in.gov/idem/land

67061 ■ Environmental Protection Agency State Superfund Office (Michigan)–Michigan Department of Environmental Quality–Waste Management Division (525 W)
525 W. Allegan St.
PO Box 30473
Lansing, MI 48909-7973
Ph:(517)373-7917
Free: 800-292-4706
Fax: (517)373-2637
Co. E-mail: deq-officeofcommunications@michigan.
gov
URL: http://www.michigan.gov/deq

67062 ■ Environmental Protection Agency State Superfund Office (Minnesota)–Pollution Control Agency–Groundwater & Solid Waste Division (520 L)
520 Lafayette Rd.
St. Paul, MN 55155-4194
Ph:(612)296-6300
Free: 800-657-3864
URL: http://www.pca.state.mn.us/index.cfm

67063 ■ Environmental Protection Agency State Superfund Office (Ohio)–Environmental Protection Agency–Division of Emergency and Remedial Response (122 S)
122 S. Front St.
PO Box 1049
Columbus, OH 43216-1049
Ph:(614)644-2160
Free: 800-686-2330
Fax: (614)644-2737
URL: http://www.epa.state.oh.us

67064 ■ Environmental Protection Agency State Superfund Office (Wisconsin)–Department of Natural Resources–Bureau of Waste Management (101 S)
101 S. Webster St.
Madison, WI 53703
Ph:(608)266-2621
Fax: (608)261-4380
URL: http://www.dnr.state.wi.us

The following are State Superfund Offices for EPA Region Six.

67065 ■ Environmental Protection Agency State Superfund Office (Arkansas)–Department of Environmental Quality–Waste Programs Division (8001)
8001 National Dr.
PO Box 8913
Little Rock, AR 72219
Ph:(501)682-0744
URL: http://www.adeq.stste.ar.us

67066 ■ Environmental Protection Agency State Superfund Office (New Mexico)–Environmental Improvement Division–Hazardous and Radioactive Waste Bureau (Harol)
Harold Reynolds Bldg., 2nd Fl., Rm. N2250
1900 St. Francis Dr. N4050
PO Box 26110
Santa Fe, NM 87502-0110
Ph:(505)827-2855
Free: 800-219-6157
URL: http://www.nmenv.state.nm.us

67067 ■ Environmental Protection Agency State Superfund Office (Oklahoma)–Department of Environmental Quality–Land Protection Division (PO Bo)
PO Box 1677
Oklahoma City, OK 73101-1677
Ph:(405)702-5100
Fax: (405)702-5101
URL: http://www.deq.state.ok.us/LPDnew/index.htm

67068 ■ Environmental Protection Agency State Superfund Office (Texas)–Water Commission–Hazardous and Solid Waste Division (PO Bo)–Superfund and Emergency Response Section (x 13087)
PO Box 13087
Austin, TX 78711-3087
Ph:(512)239-5500
Fax: (512)239-5533
Co. E-mail: ac@tceq.state.tx.us
URL: http://www.tceq.state.tx.us

The following are State Superfund Offices for EPA Region Seven.

67069 ■ Environmental Protection Agency State Superfund Office (Iowa)–Department of Natural Resources Waste Management–Air Quality Bureau (Walla)–Water Supply Section (ce Bldg.)
Wallace Bldg.
502 E. 9th St.
Des Moines, IA 50319-0034
Ph:(515)281-5918
Fax: (515)281-8895
URL: http://www.iowadnr.com/waste/index.html

67070 ■ Environmental Protection Agency State Superfund Office (Kansas)–Department of Health and Environment–Bureau of Waste Management (Curti)–Storage Tank Section (s State Of)
Curtis State Office Bldg.
1000 SW Jackson
Topeka, KS 66612
Ph:(785)296-1500
Fax: (785)368-6368
Co. E-mail: info@kdhe.state.ks.us
URL: http://www.kdheks.gov

67071 ■ Environmental Protection Agency State Superfund Office (Missouri)–Department of Natural Resources–Hazardous Waste Management Program (PO Bo)
PO Box 176
Jefferson City, MO 65102
Ph:(573)751-3443
Free: 800-361-4827
Fax: (573)571-7569
Co. E-mail: contact@dnr.mo.gov
URL: http://www.dnr.state.mo.us/env/hwp/index.html

67072 ■ Environmental Protection Agency State Superfund Office (Nebraska)–Department of Environmental Quality–Air and Waste Management Division (1200)
1200 North St., Ste. 400
PO Box 98922
Lincoln, NE 68509
Ph:(402)471-2186
Fax: (402)471-2909
URL: http://www.deq.state.ne.us

The following are State Superfund Offices for EPA Region Eight.

67073 ■ Environmental Protection Agency State Superfund Office (Colorado)–Department of Public Health and Environment–Hazardous Materials and Waste Management Division (4300)
4300 Cherry Creek Dr., S.
Denver, CO 80246-1530
Ph:(303)692-2000
Co. E-mail: cdphe.information@state.co.us
URL: http://www.cdphe.state.co.us

67074 ■ Environmental Protection Agency State Superfund Office (Montana)–Department of Environmental Quality
Lee Metcalf Bldg.
1520 E. 6th Ave.
PO Box 200901
Helena, MT 59620-0901
Ph:(406)444-2544
Fax: (406)444-4384
URL: http://deq.mt.gov

67075 ■ Environmental Protection Agency State Superfund Office (North Dakota)–Department of Health–Waste Management Division (918 E)
918 E. Divide Ave.
Bismarck, ND 58501-1947
Ph:(701)328-5150
Fax: (701)328-5200
URL: http://www.health.state.nd.us

67076 ■ Environmental Protection Agency State Superfund Office (South Dakota)–Department of Environment and Natural Resources–Waste Management Program (Joe F)
Joe Foss Bldg.
523 E. Capitol Ave.
Pierre, SD 57501-3181
Ph:(605)773-3151
Fax: (605)773-6035
Co. E-mail: denrinternetet@state.sd.us
URL: http://www.state.sd.us/denr/denr.html

67077 ■ Environmental Protection Agency State Superfund Office (Utah)–Department of Environmental Quality–Division of Air Quality (150 N)
150 North 1950 West
PO Box 144810
Salt Lake City, UT 84114-4810
Ph:(801)536-4402
Free: 800-270-4440
Fax: (801)536-0061
Co. E-mail: dnielson@utah.gov
URL: http://www.deq.utah.gov

67078 ■ Environmental Protection Agency State Superfund Office (Wyoming)–Department of Environmental Quality–Water Quality Division (Hersc)
Herscler Bldg.
122 W. 25th St.
Cheyenne, WY 82002
Ph:(307)777-7937
Fax: (307)777-7937
Co. E-mail: deqwyo@missc.state.wy.us
URL: http://deq.state.wy.us

The following are State Superfund Offices for EPA Region Nine.

67079 ■ Environmental Protection Agency State Superfund Office (Arizona)–Department of Environmental Quality–Office of Waste and Water Quality (1110)
1110 W. Washington St.
Phoenix, AZ 85007
Ph:(602)771-2300
Free: 800-234-5677
URL: http://www.azdeq.gov

67080 ■ Environmental Protection Agency State Superfund Office (California)–Department of Toxic Substances Control
PO Box 806
Sacramento, CA 95812-0806
Ph:(916)255-3545
Fax: (916)255-3785
URL: http://www.dtsc.ca.gov

67081 ■ Environmental Protection Agency State Superfund Office (Guam)–Environmental Protection Agency
PO Box 22439
GMF
Barrigada, GU 96921
Ph:(671)475-1658
Fax: (671)477-9402
URL: http://www.guamepa.govguam.net

67082 ■ Environmental Protection Agency State Superfund Office (Hawaii)–Department of Health–Environmental Management Division (PO Bo)
PO Box 3378
Honolulu, HI 96801
Ph:(808)586-4400
Fax: (808)586-4444
URL: http://www.hawaii.gov

67083 ■ Environmental Protection Agency State Superfund Office (Nevada)–Division of Environmental Protection–Department of Conservation and Natural Resources (901 S)
901 S. Stewart St., Ste. 4001
Carson City, NV 89701-5249
Ph:(775)687-4670
Fax: (775)687-5856
URL: http://www.ndep.nv.gov

The following are State Superfund Offices for EPA Region Ten.

67084 ■ Environmental Protection Agency State Superfund Office (Alaska)–Department of Environmental Conservation–Division of Environmental Quality (410 W)
410 Willoughby Ave., Ste. 303
Juneau, AK 99801-1795
Ph:(907)465-5066
Fax: (907)465-5070
Co. E-mail: commissioner@dec.state.ak.us
URL: http://www.state.ak.us/local/akpages/ENV.
   CONSERV

67085 ■ Environmental Protection Agency State Superfund Office (Idaho)–Department of Health–Environmental Health (1410)–Solid and Hazardous Waste Branch (N. Hilton)
1410 N. Hilton
Boise, ID 83706
Ph:(208)373-0502
Fax: (208)373-0417
URL: http://www.deq.state.id.us

67086 ■ Environmental Protection Agency State Superfund Office (Oregon)–Department of Environmental Quality–Environmental Cleanup Division (811 S)
811 SW 6th Ave.
Portland, OR 97204-1390
Ph:(503)229-5696
Free: 800-452-4011
Fax: (503)229-6124
Co. E-mail: DEQInfo@deq.state.or.us
URL: http://www.deq.state.or.us

67087 ■ Environmental Protection Agency State Superfund Office (Washington)–Department of Ecology–Waste Management Program (PO Bo)–Investigations and Cleanup Program (x 47600)
PO Box 47600
Olympia, WA 98504-7600
Ph:(206)407-6700
Free: 800-258-5990
URL: http://www.ecy.wa.gov/programs/hwtr/index.
   html

EXECUTIVE OFFICE OF THE PRESIDENT

67088 ■ Executive Office of the President–Office of Management and Budget–Office of Federal Procurement Policy (725 1)
725 17th St. NW
Washington, DC 20503
Ph:(202)395-3080
Fax: (202)395-3888
URL: http://www.whitehouse.gov/omb/
The Office of Federal Procurement Policy of the Executive Office of the President establishes the rules and guidelines on how to do business with the federal government, specifically for small and disadvantaged, minority-owned, and women-owned businesses. The Office of Federal Procurement Policy is strictly a policy setting office. Within the Executive Offices of the President, the Office of Administration is the procuring office for all of the various offices within the EOP.

67089 ■ Executive Office of the President–Office of Management and Budget–Small Business Administration (725 1)
725 17th St. NW
Washington, DC 20503
Ph:(202)395-1096
Fax: (202)395-3888
URL: http://www.whitehouse.gov/omb/

EXPORT-IMPORT BANK OF THE UNITED STATES

67090 ■ Export-Import Bank of the United States–Domestic Business development
811 Vermont Ave., NW, Rm. 919
Washington, DC 20571-0002
Ph:(202)565-3900
Fax: (202)565-7731
Co. E-mail: info@exim.gov
URL: http://www.exim.gov

67091 ■ Export-Import Bank of the United States–International Business Development
811 Vermont Ave., NW, Rm. 1123
Washington, DC 20571-0002
Ph:(202)565-3939
Fax: (202)565-3961
Co. E-mail: info@exim.gov
URL: http://www.exim.gov

67092 ■ Export-Import Bank of the United States–Midwest Regional Office–Chicago Regional Office & U.S. Export Assistance Center (200 W)
200 W. Adams St., Ste. 2450
Chicago, IL 60606
Ph:(312)353-8081
Fax: (312)353-8098
URL: http://www.exim.gov

67093 ■ Export-Import Bank of the United States–Northeast and Mid-Atlantic Regional Office–New York City Regional Office (20 Ex)
20 Exchange Pl., 40/F
New York, NY 10005
Ph:(212)809-2650
Fax: (212)809-2646
URL: http://www.exim.gov

67094 ■ Export-Import Bank of the United States–Office of Administration and Security
811 Vermont Ave., NW, Rm. 1023
Washington, DC 20571-0002
Ph:(202)565-3312
Co. E-mail: jt.mcmullen@.emim.gov
URL: http://www.exim.gov

67095 ■ Export-Import Bank of the United States–Office of Contracting Services
811 Vermont Ave., NW, Rm. 1023
Washington, DC 20571-0002

Ph:(202)565-3330
Fax: (202)565-3528
Co. E-mail: mark.pitra@exim.gov
URL: http://www.exim.gov

67096 ■ Export-Import Bank of the United States–Office of Operations
811 Vermont Ave., NW, Rm. 907
Washington, DC 20571-0002
Ph:(202)565-3674
Fax: (202)565-3961
Co. E-mail: ray.ellis@exim.gov
URL: http://www.exim.gov

67097 ■ Export-Import Bank of the United States–Southeast Regional Office–Miami Regional Office (5835)
5835 Blue Lagoon Dr., Ste. 203
Miami, FL 33126
Ph:(305)526-7436
Fax: (305)526-7435
URL: http://www.exim.gov

67098 ■ Export-Import Bank of the United States–Southwest Regional Office–Houston Regional Office (1880)
1880 S. Dairy Ashford II, Ste. 585
Houston, TX 77077
Ph:(281)721-0465
Fax: (281)679-0156
URL: http://www.exim.gov

67099 ■ Export-Import Bank of the United States–Western Regional Office–Long Beach Regional Office (1 Wor)
1 World Trade Center, St. 1670
Long Beach, CA 90831
Ph:(562)980-4580
Fax: (562)980-4590
URL: http://www.exim.gov

67100 ■ Export-Import Bank of the United States–Western Regional Office–Northern California Office (250 M)
250 Montgomery St., 14th Fl.
San Francisco, CA 94104
Ph:(415)705-2285
Fax: (415)705-1156
URL: http://www.exim.gov

67101 ■ Export-Import Bank of the United States–Western Regional Office–San Diego Office (6363)
6363 Greenwich Dr., Ste. 230
San Diego, CA 92122
Ph:(619)557-7091
Fax: (619)557-6176
URL: http://www.exim.gov

67102 ■ Export-Import Bank of the United States
811 Vermont Ave. NW
Washington, DC 20571
Ph:(202)565-3946
Free: 800-565-3946
URL: http://www.exim.gov/
Description: The Export-Import Bank of the United States assists in financing and in facilitating the export sales of U.S. goods and services. Programs directed at small businesses include pre-export guarantees to assist small and medium-sized businesses in obtaining working capital from financial entities for export-related activities such as inventory purchases or the manufacture of goods; a small business insurance policy, that assists in providing risk protection on export receivables for companies just beginning to export or with limited export volumes; and loan and guarantee programs that enable U.S. banks to offer medium-term, fixed-rate export loans to finance the sales of products and services produced or performed by small businesses. Nonfinancial assistance includes the operation of the Eximbank Hotline (800-565-EXIM). Through this service, Eximbank International Business Development Division is available to assist more business owners in developing competitive export financing plans, answer questions regard-

ing Eximbank financing programs, and explain how to apply for Eximbank assistance, where to locate credit insurance, or how to make maximum use of complementary export programs offered by other U.S. government agencies. In addition, Eximbank offers monthly seminars in Washington, D.C., to help firms new to exporting understand the programs available from the federal government.

FARM CREDIT ADMINISTRATION

67103 ■ Farm Credit Administration–Office of Equal Employment Opportunity and Ombudsman
1501 Farm Credit Dr., Rm. 4301
McLean, VA 22102-5090
Ph:(703)883-4481
Co. E-mail: howarde@fca.gov
URL: http://www.fca.gov

67104 ■ Farm Credit Administration–Office of Inspector General
1501 Farm Credit Dr., Rm. 2328
McLean, VA 22102-5090
Ph:(703)883-4030
URL: http://www.fca.gov/oig/oig.htm

67105 ■ Farm Credit Administration–Office of Support
1501 Farm Credit Dr.,
McLean, VA 22102-5090
Ph:(703)883-4275
Co. E-mail: smiths@fca.gov
URL: http://www.fca.gov

67106 ■ Farm Credit Administration (FCA)–Office of Procurement
1501 Farm Credit Dr.
McLean, VA 22102-5090
Ph:(703)883-4056
Co. E-mail: info-line@fca.gov
URL: http://www.fca.gov

FEDERAL COMMUNICATIONS COMMISSION

67107 ■ Federal Communications Commission–Administrative Law Division
445 - 12th St., SW, Rm. 8-B616
Washington, DC 20554
Ph:(202)418-1720
Fax: (202)418-7540
URL: http://www.fcc.gov/ogc/admin.html

67108 ■ Federal Communications Commission–Consumer Inquiries and Complaints Division
445 - 12th St., SW, Rm. 4C763
Washington, DC 20554
Ph:(202)418-0263
Co. E-mail: Martha.contee@fcc.gov

67109 ■ Federal Communications Commission–Enforcement Bureau
445 - 12th St., SW, Rm. 7-C485
Washington, DC 20554
Ph:(202)418-7450
Fax: (202)418-0232
Co. E-mail: kris.monteith@fcc.gov
URL: http://www.fcc.gov/eb

67110 ■ Federal Communications Commission–Office of Media Relations
445 - 12th St., Rm. CY-C314
Washington, DC 20554-0001
Ph:(202)418-0513
Fax: (202)418-7286
Co. E-mail: david.fiske@fcc.gov

67111 ■ Federal Communications Commission–Office of Workplace Diversity
445 - 12th St., SW, Rm. 5-C750
Washington, DC 20554
Ph:(202)418-1799
Fax: (202)418-0379
Co. E-mail: june.taylor@fcc.gov

67112 ■ Federal Communications Commission–Wireless Telecommunications Bureau
445 - 12th St., SW
Washington, DC 20554
Ph:(202)418-0600
Fax: (202)418-0787
Co. E-mail: fccinfo@fcc.gov
URL: http://www.fcc.gov/wtb

67113 ■ Federal Communications Commission–Office of Communications Business Opportunities
445 12th St. SW
Washington, DC 20554
Ph:(202)418-0990
Free: 888-225-5322
Fax: (866)418-0232
Co. E-mail: fccinfo@fcc.gov
URL: http://www.fcc.gov/ocbo

E-mail: kbeverly@fcc.gov
The OCBO's mission is to promote opportunities for ownership and employment in the communications industry for small businesses in order to increase competition, encourage innovation, improve service to all communities and increase diversity of voices and viewpoints over the public airwaves. OCBO is the principal advisor to the Chairman and Commissioners regarding the formulation of policy and rules that enhance opportunities for small businesses to compete. It is the industry's primary contact for small businesses and individuals seeking ownership, investment, and employment opportunities in burgeoning communications services. OCBO also provides information to the public, industry trade organizations, and public interest organizations on the participation of small businesses, minorities, and women in various communications services. OCBO is a primary resource for research material on small businesses, minority and female ownership, and employment in the communications industry. OCBO has published and compiled various studies, including an overview of the communications market and the opportunities it provides for small businesses. OCBO's outreach efforts enable small businesses to participate in the rulemaking process by disseminating information about Commission proceedings and publicizing the opportunity for comment through mass mailings. OCBO monthly mailings also provide notification of upcoming FCC activities.

FEDERAL DEPOSIT INSURANCE CORPORATION

67114 ■ Federal Deposit Insurance Corporation–Boston Area Office (New York Region)
15 Braintree Hill Office Park
Braintree, MA 02184-8701
Ph:(781)794-5500
URL: http://www.fdic.gov
Description: Serves Connecticut, Maine, Massachusetts, New Hampshire, Rhode Island, and Vermont.

67115 ■ Federal Deposit Insurance Corporation–Chicago Regional Office
500 W. Monroe St., Ste. 3300
Chicago, IL 60661-3697
Ph:(312)382-7500
Free: 800-944-5343
Fax: (312)382-6901
URL: http://www.fdic.gov
Description: Serves Illinois, Indiana, Kentucky, Michigan, Ohio, and Wisconsin.

67116 ■ Federal Deposit Insurance Corporation–Kansas City Regional Office
2345 Grand Blvd., Ste. 1200
Kansas City, MO 64108-2638
Free: 800-209-7459
URL: http://www.fdic.gov
Description: Serves Iowa, Kansas, Minnesota, Missouri, Nebraska, North Dakota, and South Dakota.

67117 ■ Federal Deposit Insurance Corporation–New York Regional Office
20 Exchange Pl., Rm. 6014
New York, NY 10005
Free: 800-334-9593
URL: http://www.fdic.gov
Description: Serves Delaware, District of Columbia, Maryland, New Jersey, New York, Pennsylvania, Puerto Rico, and Virgin Islands.

67118 ■ Federal Deposit Insurance Corporation–San Francisco Regional Office
25 Jessie St. at Ecker Sq., Ste. 2300
San Francisco, CA 94105-2760
Ph:(415)546-0160
Free: 800-756-3558
URL: http://www.fdic.gov
Description: Serves Alaska, Arizona, California, Guam, Hawaii, Idaho, Montana, Nevada, Oregon, Utah, Washington, and Wyoming.

The following FDIC service centers are arranged alphabetically by region.

67119 ■ Federal Deposit Insurance Corporation–Office of Diversity and Economic Opportunity–Minority and Women Outreach Program (500 W)–Midwest Service Center (. Monroe,)
500 W. Monroe, Ste. 3300
Chicago, IL 60661-3697
Ph:(312)382-7500
Free: 800-944-5343
Fax: (312)382-6901
Contact: Judith M. Wood, MWOP Field Operations
Description: Serves Illinois, Indiana, Kentucky, Michigan, Ohio, and Wisconsin.

67120 ■ Federal Deposit Insurance Corporation–Office of Diversity and Economic Opportunity–Minority and Women Outreach Program (North)–Northeast Service Center (Connecticut) (Tower, Rm)
North Tower, Rm. 3026
101 East River Dr.
East Hartford, CT 06108
Ph:(860)520-2612
Fax: (860)541-5170
Contact: Herbert Chin, MWOP Field Operations

67121 ■ Federal Deposit Insurance Corporation–Office of Diversity and Economic Opportunity–Minority and Women Outreach Program (124 G)–Northeast Service Center (Massachusetts) (rove St.)
124 Grove St.
PO Box 9104
Franklin, MA 02038
Ph:(508)520-2612
Fax: (508)541-5170
Contact: Herbert Chin, MWOP Field Operations

67122 ■ Federal Deposit Insurance Corporation–Office of Diversity and Economic Opportunity–Minority and Women Outreach Program (10th)–Southeast Service Center (St. NE, St)
10th St. NE, Ste. 800
Atlanta, GA 30309-3849
Ph:(678)916-2249
Fax: (404)817-8817
Contact: Angelisa M. Harris, MWOP Field Operations
Description: Serves Alabama, Florida, Georgia, North Carolina, South Carolina, Virginia, and West Virginia

67123 ■ Federal Deposit Insurance Corporation–Office of Diversity and Economic Opportunity–Minority and Women Outreach Program (1910)–Southwest Service Center (Pacific Av)
1910 Pacific Ave., 20th Fl.
Dallas, TX 75201
Ph:(972)761-8010
Contact: Robert Elcan, MWOP Field Operations
Description: Serves Colorado, New Mexico, Oklahoma, and Texas.

67124 ■ Federal Deposit Insurance Corp.–Office of Diversity and Economic Opportunity–Minority and Women Outreach Program (4 Par)–Western Service Center (k Plaza, R)
4 Park Plaza, Rm. J-1014
Irvine, CA 92714
Ph:(714)263-7669
Fax: (714)263-7202
URL: http://www.fdic.gov
Contact: Otis Felton, MWOP Field Operations

FEDERAL EMERGENCY MANAGEMENT AGENCY

67125 ■ Department of Homeland Security–Office of Small and Disadvantaged Business Utilization
7th and D Sts., SW, Rm. 3514
Washington, DC 20528
Ph:(202)205-0129
Co. E-mail: Kevin.boeshears@dhs.gov
URL: http://www.dhs.gov

67126 ■ Federal Communications Commission (FCC)–Homeland Security Policy Council
445 - 12th St., SW, Rm. 7-C751
Washington, DC 20554
Ph:(202)418-7450
URL: http://www.fcc.gov/hspc

67127 ■ Federal Emergency Management Agency
500 C St., SW
Washington, DC 20472
Ph:(202)566-1600
Co. E-mail: femaopa@dhs.gov
URL: http://www.fema.gov

67128 ■ Federal Emergency Management Agency (Region 1)–Boston Regional Office
99 High St., 6th Fl.
Boston, MA 02110
Ph:(617)956-7506
URL: http://www.fema.gov/regions
Description: Serves New Hampshire, Vermont, Rhode Island, Connecticut, and Massachusetts.

67129 ■ Federal Emergency Management Agency (Region 2)–New York Regional Office
26 Federal Plz.
New York, NY 10278
Ph:(212)680-3609
URL: http://www.fema.gov/regions
Description: Serves New York, New Jersey, Puerto Rico, and the Virgin Islands.

67130 ■ Federal Emergency Management Agency (Region 3)–Philadelphia Regional Office
615 Chestnut St.
Philadelphia, PA 19106
Ph:(215)931-5608
URL: http://www.fema.gov/regions
Description: Serves Delaware, District of Columbia, Maryland, Pennsylvania, Virginia, and West Virginia.

67131 ■ Federal Emergency Management Agency (Region 4)–Atlanta Regional Office
3003 Chamblee-Tucker Rd.
Atlanta, GA 30341
Ph:(770)220-5200

URL: http://www.fema.gov/regions
Description: Serves Georgia, Florida, Kentucky, Mississippi, North Carolina, South Carolina, and Tennessee.

67132 ■ Federal Emergency Management Agency (Region 5)–Chicago Regional Office
536 S. Clark St.
Chicago, IL 60605
Ph:(312)408-5500
URL: http://www.fema.gov/regions
Description: Serves Illinois, Indiana, Michigan, Ohio, Minnesota, and Wisconsin.

67133 ■ Federal Emergency Management Agency (Region 6)–Denton Regional Office
Federal Regional Ctr.
800 N. Loop 288
Denton, TX 76209
Ph:(940)898-5399
URL: http://www.fema.gov/regions
Description: Serves Arkansas, Louisiana, New Mexico, Oklahoma, and Texas.

67134 ■ Federal Emergency Management Agency (Region 7)–Kansas City Regional Office
9221 Ward Pkwy., Ste. 300
Kansas City, MO 64114
Ph:(816)283-7061
URL: http://www.fema.gov/regions
Description: Serves Iowa, Kansas, Missouri, and Nebraska.

67135 ■ Federal Emergency Management Agency (Region 8)–Denver Regional Office
Bldg. 710
PO Box 25267
Denver, CO 80225-0267
Ph:(303)235-4800
Fax: (303)235-4976
URL: http://www.fema.gov/regions
Description: Serves Colorado, Montana, North Dakota, South Dakota, Utah, and Wyoming.

67136 ■ Federal Emergency Management Agency (Region 9)–Oakland Regional Office
1111 Broadway, Ste. 1200
Oakland, CA 94607
Ph:(510)627-7100
URL: http://www.fema.gov/regions
Description: Serves Arizona, California, Hawaii, and Nevada.

67137 ■ Federal Emergency Management Agency (Region 10)–Bothell Regional Office
130 - 228th St., SW
Bothell, WA 98021
Ph:(425)487-4600
URL: http://www.fema.gov/regions
Description: Serves Alaska, Idaho, Washington, and Oregon.

67138 ■ U.S. Department of Homeland Security–Office for Domestic Preparedness (ODP)
810 7th St., NW
Washington, DC 20531
Free: 800-368-6498
Fax: (202)786-9920
Co. E-mail: askcsid@dhs.gov
URL: http://www.ojp.usdoj.gov

67139 ■ U.S. Department of Homeland Security–Office of Procurement Operations
245 Murray Dr., SW, Bldg. 410
Washington, DC 20528
Ph:(202)401-2622
Co. E-mail: patricia.wyatt@hq.dhs.gov
URL: http://www.dhs.gov

67140 ■ U.S. Department of Homeland Security–Office of Small and Disadvantaged Business Utilization
Rm. 3514
Washington, DC 20528
Ph:(202)692-4343

Fax: (202)777-8467

67141 ■ U.S. Department of Homeland Security–U.S. Citizenship and Immigration Services–Procurement Division (70 Ki)
70 Kimball Ave.
South Burlington, VT 05403
Ph:(802)872-4102
Fax: (802)951-6455
Co. E-mail: ne.ross@dhs.gov

FEDERAL HOME LOAN MORTGAGE CORPORATION

67142 ■ Federal Home Loan Mortgage Corporation–Northeast Region
1410 Springhill Rd., 600
PO Box 50122
McLean, VA 22102-8922
Ph:(703)902-7700
URL: http://www.freddiemac.com

67143 ■ Federal Home Loan Mortgage Corporation–Southeast Region
North Tower, Ste. 200
2300 Windy Ridge Pkwy., SE
Atlanta, GA 30339-5665
Ph:(770)857-8800
URL: http://www.freddiemac.com

67144 ■ Federal Home Loan Mortgage Corporation–Southwest Region
5000 Plano Pkwy.
Carrollton, TX 75010-4902
Ph:(972)395-4000
URL: http://www.freddiemac.com

67145 ■ Federal Home Loan Mortgage Corporation–Western Region
21700 Oxnard St., Ste. 1900
Woodland Hills, CA 91367-3642
Ph:(818)-710-3000
URL: http://www.freddiemac.com

67146 ■ Federal Home Loan Mortgage Corporation (Freddie Mac)
401 9th St., NW, Ste. 600 S.
Washington, DC 20004
Ph:(202)434-8600
URL: http://www.freddiemac.gov

FEDERAL HOUSING FINANCE BOARD

67147 ■ Federal Housing Finance Board
1625 Eye St., NW
Washington, DC 20006-4001
Ph:(202)408-2500
Fax: (202)408-1435
URL: http://www.fhfb.gov

67148 ■ Federal Housing Finance Board–Office of Supervision
1777 F St., NW, Rm. 317
Washington, DC 20006-4001
Ph:(202)408-2980
Co. E-mail: cross@fhfb.gov
URL: http://www.fhfb.gov

FEDERAL MEDIATION AND CONCILIATION SERVICE

67149 ■ Federal Mediation and Conciliation Service–Office of Public Affairs
2100 K St., NW, Rm. 900
Washington, DC 20427
Ph:(202)606-3661
Fax: (202)606-3433
Co. E-mail: fleonard@fmcs.gov

URL: http://www.fmcs.gov

67150 ■ Federal Mediation and Conciliation Service (FMCS)–Office of Procurement
2100 K St., NW
Washington, DC 20427
Ph:(202)606-3664
Fax: (202)606-4216
URL: http://www.fmcs.gov

FEDERAL NATIONAL MORTGAGE ASSOCIATION

67151 ■ Government National Mortgage Association (Ginnie Mae)–Procurement Management Division
Potomac Ctr. S.
550 - 12th St., SW, 3rd Fl., Rm. 6286
Washington, DC 20024
Ph:(202)708-2648
Fax: (202)485-0208
URL: http://www.ginniemae.gov

FEDERAL TRADE COMMISSION

67152 ■ Federal Trade Commission–Bureau of Consumer Protection
600 Pennsylvania Ave., NW, Rm. 470
Washington, DC 20580
Ph:(202)326-2676
Fax: (202)326-3799
Co. E-mail: lparnes@ftc.gov
URL: http://www.ftc.gov/bcp/bcp.htm

67153 ■ Federal Trade Commission–Office of Inspector General
601 New Jersey Ave., Rm. 1119
Washington, DC 20001
Ph:(202)326-2743
Fax: (202)326-2034
Co. E-mail: hsribnick@ftc.gov
URL: http://www.ftc.gov/oig/oighome.htm

67154 ■ Federal Trade Commission–Procurement and General Service Division
600 Pennsylvania Ave. NW
Washington, DC 20580
Ph:(202)326-2258
Fax: (202)326-2502
URL: http://www.ftc.gov/
Description: The Federal Trade Commission works to preserve a free marketplace by acting as the advocate of consumers and by resisting efforts of any one group to profit at the expense of the general public. The FTC maintains three bureaus and ten regional offices through which to carry out its responsibilities: the Bureau of Competition seeks to prevent business practices that restrain competition by investigating alleged violations, by recommending enforcement action when appropriate, and by participating in an advocacy program; the Bureau of Consumer Protection helps to preserve competition by prohibiting deceptive claims or practices that interfere with the public's ability to make informed purchasing decisions; and the Bureau of Economics offers support to these activities by ensuring that the FTC's actions are based on sound economic principles. FTC regional offices conduct investigations and litigations, offer advice, recommend cases, provide outreach services, sponsor conferences, and coordinate activities with local, state, and regional authorities.

The following regional offices are arranged alphabetically by city.

67155 ■ Federal Trade Commission–Atlanta Regional Office–Southeast Region (225 P)
225 Peachtree St., NE
Ste. 1500
Atlanta, GA 30303

URL: http://www.ftc.gov/
Description: Serves Alabama, Florida, Georgia, Mississippi, North Carolina, South Carolina, Tennessee, and Virginia (except Metropolitan DC area).

67156 ■ Federal Trade Commission–Boston Regional Office–Northeast Region (1 Bow)
1 Bowling Green
New York, NY 10004
URL: http://www.ftc.gov/ro/northeast.htm
Description: Serves Connecticut, Maine, Massachusetts, New Hampshire, Rhode Island, and Vermont.

67157 ■ Federal Trade Commission–Chicago Regional Office–Midwest Region (55 E.)
55 E. Monroe St., Ste. 1860
Chicago, IL 60603-5701
Ph:(312)353-4423
Fax: (312)960-5600
URL: http://www.ftc.gov/ro/midwest.htm
Description: Serves Illinois, Indiana, Iowa, Kentucky, Minnesota, Missouri, and Wisconsin.

67158 ■ Federal Trade Commission–Cleveland Regional Office–East Central Region (1111)
1111 Superior Ave., Ste. 200
Cleveland, OH 44114-2507
Ph:(216)522-4207
Fax: (216)263-3426
URL: http://www.ftc.gov/ro/eastcentral.htm
Description: Serves Delaware, Maryland (excluding metropolitan Washington, DC area), Michigan, Ohio, Pennsylvania, and West Virginia.

67159 ■ Federal Trade Commission–Dallas Regional Office–Southwest Region (1999)
1999 Bryan St., Ste. 2150
Dallas, TX 75201-6808
Ph:(214)767-5501
Fax: (214)767-5519
URL: http://www.ftc.gov/to/southwest.htm
Description: Serves Arkansas, Louisiana, New Mexico, Oklahoma, and Texas.

67160 ■ Federal Trade Commission–Denver Regional Office
1405 Curtis St., Ste. 2900
Denver, CO 80202-2393
Description: Serves Colorado, Kansas, Montana, Nebraska, North Dakota, South Dakota, Utah, and Wyoming.

67161 ■ Federal Trade Commission–Los Angeles Regional Office
11000 Wilshire Blvd., Ste. 13209
Los Angeles, CA 90024
Ph:(310)235-7890
Fax: (310)235-7976
URL: http://www.ftc.gov
Description: Serves Arizona and southern California.

67162 ■ Federal Trade Commission–New York Regional Office
150 William St., Ste. 1300
New York, NY 10038
Ph:(212)264-1207
Fax: (212)264-0459
URL: http://www.ftc.gov
Description: Serves New Jersey and New York.

67163 ■ Federal Trade Commission–San Francisco Regional Office
901 Market St., Ste. 570
San Francisco, CA 94103
Ph:(415)356-5270
Fax: (415)356-5284
URL: http://www.ftc.gov/ro/western.htm
Description: Serves northern California, Hawaii, and Nevada.

67164 ■ Federal Trade Commission–Seattle Regional Office
2806 Federal Bldg.
915 2nd Ave.
Seattle, WA 98174
Ph:(206)220-6350

Fax: (206)220-6366
URL: http://www.ftc.gov/ro/northwest.htm
Description: Serves Alaska, Idaho, Oregon, and Washington.

GENERAL SERVICES ADMINISTRATION

67165 ■ General Services Administration–Federal Technology Service (FTS)–Office of Regional Services (10304)
10304 Eaton Pl., 3rd Fl.
Fairfax, VA 22030
Ph:(703)306-6500
Co. E-mail: margaret.binns@gsa.gov
URL: http://www.fts.gsa.gov

67166 ■ General Services Administration–Office of Electronic Government and Technology
18th & F Sts., NW, Rm. 2239
Washington, DC 20405
Ph:(202)501-0202
Fax: (202)219-2310
Co. E-mail: mary.mitchell@gsa.gov
URL: http://www.egov.gov

67167 ■ General Services Administration–Office of Global Supply–Logistics Operations Ctr. (Cryst)
Crystal Mall Bldg. 4
1901 S. Bell St., Rm. 1005
Arlington, VA 20406
Ph:(703)605-5514
Co. E-mail: ken.latta@gsa.gov

67168 ■ General Services Administration (GSA)–Office of Enterprise Development
Regional Office Bldg.
7th and D. Sts. SW
Washington, DC 20407-0002
Ph:(202)501-1021
Free: 800-OED-IGSA
Fax: (202)208-5938
URL: http://www.gsa.gov/
Description: The General Services Administration (GSA), the Federal government's purchasing agent, real estate developer, telecommunications manager, and computer overseer, contracts for over $10 billion worth of commodities and services each year. The GSA's Office of Enterprise Development (OED) develops and oversees GSA procurement preference programs for small, disadvantaged and women-owned businesses. In addition to other pamphlets, the OED publishes four major publications to assist businesses in their marketing efforts: *Doing Business with GSA*, *GSA Small Purchases*, *GSA Subcontracting Directory* (published semiannually), and *Forecast of GSA Contracting Opportunities* (published annually). Information about upcoming contracting opportunities is placed on GSA's Electronic Bulletin Board. GSA operates Business Service Centers (BSCs) in 11 major metropolitan areas throughout the country. The BSCs implement GSA procurement preference programs by providing assistance, information and counseling to small businesses interested in pursuing Federal Government contracts. Counselors at the BSCs help small businesses understand GSA contracting procedures and locate GSA buyers for their products or services. The BSCs are also involved in monitoring local GSA contracting programs to insure that small, disadvantaged and women-owned businesses are given access to contracts and subcontracts and to find ways to expand their participation. As part of GSA's program, the BSCs sponsor breakfasts and networking seminars to give small businesses an opportunity to meet contracting personnel and each other.

The following business service centers are arranged alphabetically by city.

67169 ■ General Services Administration–Atlanta Business Service Center
401 Peachtree St., Rm. 2900
Atlanta, GA 30365-2550

Ph:(404)331-5103
Fax: (404)331-1813
Description: Serves Alabama, Florida, Georgia, Kentucky, Mississippi, North Carolina, South Carolina, and Tennessee.

67170 ■ General Services Administration–Auburn Business Service Center
15th C St., SW
Rm. 9AB-10
Auburn, WA 98001
Ph:(206)931-7956
Description: Serves Alaska, Idaho, Oregon, and Washington.

67171 ■ General Services Administration–Boston Business Service Center
Thomas P. O'Neill Federal Bldg.
10 Causeway St., Rm. 290
Boston, MA 02222
Ph:(617)565-8100
Fax: (617)565-8101
Description: Serves Connecticut, Maine, Massachusetts, New Hampshire, Rhode Island, and Vermont.

67172 ■ General Services Administration–Chicago Business Service Center
230 S. Dearborn St., Ste. 3714
Chicago, IL 60604
Ph:(312)353-5383
Fax: (312)353-5385
Description: Serves Illinois, Indiana, Michigan, Minnesota, Ohio, and Wisconsin.

67173 ■ General Services Administration–Denver Business Service Center
Denver Federal Center, Bldg. 41, Rm. 2530
PO Box 25006
Denver, CO 80225-0506
Ph:(303)236-7408
Fax: (303)236-7403
Description: Serves Colorado, Montana, North Dakota, South Dakota, Utah, and Wyoming.

67174 ■ General Services Administration–Ft. Worth Business Service Center
819 Taylor St., Rm. 11A05
Ft. Worth, TX 76102
Ph:(817)334-3284
Fax: (817)334-4867
Description: Serves Arkansas, Louisiana, New Mexico, Oklahoma, and Texas.

67175 ■ General Services Administration–Kansas City Business Service Center
1500 E. Bannister Rd., Ste. 1137
Kansas City, MO 64131-3088
Ph:(816)926-7203
Fax: (816)823-1167
Description: Serves Iowa, Kansas, Missouri, and Nebraska.

67176 ■ General Services Administration–New York Business Service Center
26 Federal Plz.
New York, NY 10278
Ph:(212)264-1234
Fax: (212)264-2760
Description: Serves New Jersey, New York, Puerto Rico, and the Virgin Islands.

67177 ■ General Services Administration–Philadelphia Business Service Center–Office of Business and Public Affairs (John)
John Wanamaker Bldg., Rm. 808
100 Penn Sq. E
Philadelphia, PA 19107
Ph:(215)656-5525
Fax: (215)656-6404
Description: Serves Delaware, Maryland, Pennsylvania, Virginia, and West Virginia.

67178 ■ General Services Administration–San Francisco Business Service Center
450 Golden Gate Ave., Rm. 0405
San Francisco, CA 94102
Ph:(415)522-2700
Fax: (415)522-2705
URL: http://www.gsa.gov
Description: Serves California, Hawaii, Nevada, and Arizona.

67179 ■ General Services Administration–Washington, DC, Business Services Center
7th & D Sts. SW
Washington, DC 20407
Ph:(202)708-5804
Fax: (202)205-2872
Description: Serves the metropolitan Washington, D.C., area.

INTERNATIONAL TRADE ADMINISTRATION

67180 ■ International Trade Administration–Office of Public Affairs
Herbert Clark Hoover Bldg., Rm. 3414
14th St. & Constitution Ave., NW
Washington, DC 20230
Ph:(202)482-2867
Free: 800-872-8723
Fax: (202)482-4821
Co. E-mail: TIC@ita.doc.gov
URL: http://www.ita.doc.gov
Description: The International Trade Administration's domestic and overseas programs are designed to stimulate the expansion of U.S. exports. Major programs include export counseling and assistance; promotion of U.S. products abroad; coordination and conduct of overseas trade missions; support for the Export Trading Company formation; and management of federal participation in international expositions held in the United States. The ITA gathers, analyzes, and disseminates commercially usable trade and marketing information, including advice on marketing opportunities abroad; information about government assistance available for expanding trade with other nations; location of needed materials and resources; and advice on international trade policy and tariff questions. The ITA operates a network of 48 U.S. and foreign Commercial Service district offices through which to carry out its programs. The ITA's information services, market research, and overseas promotion programs provide opportunities to introduce products abroad at small costs. The ITA, with its variety of low-cost marketing aids, also may assist small firms in locating overseas outlets for their products, namely agents, distributors, licensees, buyers, and suppliers.

The following is a list of ITA Export Assistance Centers, arranged alphabetically by state.

67181 ■ International Trade Administration–U.S. and Foreign Commercial Service–Export Assistance Center (Birmingham) (950 2)
950 22nd St. N, Rm. 707
Birmingham, AL 35203-5309
Ph:(205)731-1331
Fax: (205)731-0076
Co. E-mail: Office.Birmingham@mail.doc.gov
URL: http://www.usatrade.gov

67182 ■ International Trade Administration–U.S. and Foreign Commercial Service–Export Assistance Center (Anchorage) (World)
World Trade Center Alaska
431 W. 7th Ave., Ste. 108
Anchorage, AK 99501
Ph:(907)278-7233
Fax: (907)278-2982
Co. E-mail: info@wtcak.org
URL: http://www.wtcak.org

67183 ■ International Trade Administration–U.S. and Foreign Commercial Service–Export Assistance Center (Phoenix) (2901)
2901 N. Central Ave., Ste. 970
Phoenix, AZ 85012
Ph:(602)640-2513
Fax: (602)640-2518
Co. E-mail: Phoenix.Office.Box@mail.doc.gov
URL: http://azexport.com

67184 ■ International Trade Administration–U.S. and Foreign Commercial Service–Export Assistance Center (Little Rock) (425 W)
425 W. Capitol Ave., Ste. 700
Little Rock, AR 72201
Ph:(501)324-5794
Fax: (501)324-7380
Co. E-mail: little.rock.office.box@mail.doc.gov
URL: http://www.usatrade.gov

67185 ■ International Trade Administration–U.S. and Foreign Commercial Service–Export Assistance Center (Long Beach) (One W)
One World Trade Center, Ste. 1670
Long Beach, CA 90831
Ph:(310)980-4550
Fax: (310)980-4561

67186 ■ International Trade Administration–U.S. and Foreign Commercial Service–Export Assistance Center (Los Angeles) (11150)
11150 West Olympic Blvd., Ste. 975
Los Angeles, CA 90064
Ph:(310)235-7204
Fax: (310)235-7220
Co. E-mail: los.angeles.office.box@mail.doc.gov
URL: http://www.usatrade.gov

67187 ■ International Trade Administration–U.S. and Foreign Commercial Service–Export Assistance Center (Monterey) (c/o C)
c/o Center for Trade and Commercial Diplomacy
411 Pacific St., Ste. 316A
Monterey, CA 93940
Ph:(831)641-9850
Fax: (831)641-9849
Co. E-mail: montereyca.office.box@mail.doc.gov

67188 ■ International Trade Administration–U.S. and Foreign Commercial Service–Export Assistance Center (Newport Beach) (3300)
3300 Irvine Ave., Ste. 307
Newport Beach, CA 92660
Ph:(949)660-1688
Fax: (949)660-1338
Co. E-mail: Newport.beach.office.box@mail.doc.gov
URL: http://www.buyusa.gov/newportbeach/

67189 ■ International Trade Administration–U.S. and Foreign Commercial Service–Export Assistance Center (Novato) (4040)
4040 Civic Center Dr., Ste. 200
San Rafael, CA 94903
Ph:(415)492-4548
Fax: (415)492-4549
Co. E-mail: north.bay.office.box@mail.doc.gov

67190 ■ International Trade Administration–U.S. and Foreign Commercial Service–Export Assistance Center (Oakland) (1301)
1301 Clay St., Ste. 630 N
Oakland, CA 94612
Ph:(510)273-7350
Fax: (510)273-7352
Co. E-mail: oakland.office.box@mail.doc.gov
URL: http://www.usatrade.gov

67191 ■ International Trade Administration–U.S. and Foreign Commercial Service–Export Assistance Center (Sacramento) (917 7)
917 7th St., 2nd Fl.
Sacramento, CA 95814
Ph:(916)498-5155
Fax: (916)498-5923
Co. E-mail: sacramento.office.box@mail.doc.gov
URL: http://www.usatrade.gov

67192 ■ International Trade Administration–U.S. and Foreign Commercial Service–Export Assistance Center (San Diego) (6363)
6363 Greenwich Dr., Ste. 230
San Diego, CA 92122
Ph:(619)557-6119
Fax: (619)557-6176
Co. E-mail: matt.andersen@mail.doc.gov
URL: http://www.usatrade.gov

67193 ■ International Trade Administration–U.S. and Foreign Commercial Service–Export Assistance Center (San Francisco) (250 M)
250 Montgomery St., 14th Fl.
San Francisco, CA 94104
Ph:(415)705-2301
Fax: (415)705-2299
Co. E-mail: san.francisco.office.box@mail.doc.gov
URL: http://www.usatrade.gov

67194 ■ International Trade Administration–U.S. and Foreign Commercial Service–Export Assistance Center (San Jose) (152 N)
152 N. 3rd St., Ste. 550
San Jose, CA 95112-5591
Ph:(408)271-7300
Fax: (408)271-7306
Co. E-mail: san.joseca.office.box@mail.doc.gov
URL: http://www.buyusa.gov/norcal

67195 ■ International Trade Administration–U.S. and Foreign Commercial Service–Export Assistance Center (Santa Clara) (5201)
5201 Great American Pkwy., Ste. 456
Santa Clara, CA 95054
Ph:(408)970-4610
Fax: (408)970-4618
Co. E-mail: santa.clara.office.box@mail.doc.gov

67196 ■ International Trade Administration–U.S. and Foreign Commercial Service–Export Assistance Center (Denver) (World)
World Trade Center
1625 Broadway, Ste. 680
Denver, CO 80202
Ph:(303)844-6001
Fax: (303)844-5651
Co. E-mail: Denver.office.box@mail.doc.gov
URL: http://www.ita.doc.gov/denver
Description: Denver office also services the states of Montana and Wyoming.

67197 ■ International Trade Administration–U.S. and Foreign Commercial Service–Export Assistance Center (Middletown) (213 C)
213 Court St., Ste. 903
Middletown, CT 06457-3382
Ph:(860)638-6950
Fax: (860)638-6970
Co. E-mail: office.middletown@mail.doc.gov
URL: http://www.buyusa.gov/newengland
Description: Affiliated with the Providence district office.

67198 ■ International Trade Administration–U.S. and Foreign Commercial Service–Export Assistance Center (Clearwater) (13805)
13805 58 St. N., Ste. 1-200
Clearwater, FL 33760
Ph:(727)893-3738

Fax: (727)893-3839
Co. E-mail: office.clearwater@mail.doc.gov
URL: http://www.usatrade.gov

67199 ■ International Trade Administration–U.S. and Foreign Commercial Service–Export Assistance Center (Miami) (5835)
5835 Blue Lagoon Dr., Ste. 203
Miami, FL 33126-3009
Ph:(305)526-7429
Fax: (305)526-7434
Co. E-mail: office.miami@mail.doc.gov
URL: http://www.usatrade.gov/us/sunshine/

67200 ■ International Trade Administration–U.S. and Foreign Commercial Service–Export Assistance Center (Orlando) (200 E)
200 E. Robinson St., Ste. 1270
Orlando, FL 32801
Ph:(407)648-6235
Fax: (407)648-6756
Co. E-mail: orlando@mail.doc.gov
URL: http://www.ita.doc.gov/miamiuseac

67201 ■ International Trade Administration–U.S. and Foreign Commercial Service–Export Assistance Center (Tallahassee) (The A)
The Atrium Bldg.
325 John Knox Rd., Ste. 201
Tallahassee, FL 32303
Ph:(850)942-9635
Fax: (850)922-9595
Co. E-mail: office.tallahassee@mail.doc.gov
URL: http://www.usatrade.gov

67202 ■ International Trade Administration–U.S. and Foreign Commercial Service–Export Assistance Center (Savannah) (111 E)
111 E. Liberty St., Ste. 202
Savannah, GA 31401
Ph:(912)652-4204
Fax: (912)652-4241
Co. E-mail: joseph.kramer@mail.doc.gov
URL: http://www.export.gov

67203 ■ International Trade Administration–U.S. and Foreign Commercial Service–Export Assistance Center (Honolulu) (521 A)
521 Ala Moana Blvd., Rm. 214
PO Box 50026
Honolulu, HI 96813
Ph:(808)522-8041
Fax: (808)356-0320
Co. E-mail: honolulu.office.box@mail.doc.gov
URL: http://www.usatrade.gov

67204 ■ International Trade Administration–U.S. and Foreign Commercial Service–Export Assistance Center (Boise) (700 W)
700 W. State St., 2nd Fl.
Boise, ID 83720
Ph:(208)364-7791
Fax: (208)334-2783
Co. E-mail: boise.office.box@mail.doc.gov
URL: http://www.buyusa.gov/boise

67205 ■ International Trade Administration–U.S. and Foreign Commercial Service–Export Assistance Center (Chicago) (55 W.)
55 W. Adams St., Rm. 2450
Chicago, IL 60603
Ph:(312)353-8490
Fax: (312)353-8120
Co. E-mail: juli.carducci@mail.doc.gov
URL: http://www.export.gov

67206 ■ International Trade Administration–U.S. and Foreign Commercial Service–Export Assistance Center (Highland Park) (610 C)
610 Central Ave., Ste. 150
Highland Park, IL 60035

Ph:(847)681-8010
Fax: (847)681-8012

**67207 ■ International Trade
Administration–U.S. and Foreign Commercial
Service–Export Assistance Center (Rockford)
(515 N)**
515 N. Court St.
Rockford, IL 61103
Ph:(815)987-8123
Fax: (815)963-7943
Co. E-mail: rockford.office.box@mail.doc.gov
URL: http://www.export.gov

**67208 ■ International Trade
Administration–U.S. and Foreign Commercial
Service–Export Assistance Center (Wheaton)
(Illin)**
Illinois Institute of Technology
201 E. Loop Dr.
Wheaton, IL 60187
Ph:(708)353-4332
Fax: (708)353-4336

**67209 ■ International Trade
Administration–U.S. and Foreign Commercial
Service–Export Assistance Center (Carmel)
(11405)**
11405 N. Pennsylvania St., Ste. 106
Carmel, IN 46032
Ph:(317)582-2300
Fax: (317)582-2301
Co. E-mail: office.indianapolis@mail.doc.gov
URL: http://www.export.gov/cs

**67210 ■ International Trade
Administration–U.S. and Foreign Commercial
Service–Export Assistance Center (Des
Moines) (Partn)**
Partnership Bldg.
700 Locust St., Ste. 100
Des Moines, IA 50309
Ph:(515)288-8614
Fax: (515)288-1437
Co. E-mail: des.moines.office.box@mail.doc.gov
URL: http://www.usatrade.gov

**67211 ■ International Trade
Administration–U.S. and Foreign Commercial
Service–Export Assistance Center (Wichita)
(209 E)**
209 E. William St., Ste. 300
Wichita, KS 67202-4012
Ph:(316)263-4067
Fax: (316)263-8306
Co. E-mail: george.lavid@mail.doc.gov
URL: http://www.usatrade.gov
Description: Affiliated with the Kansas City, Missouri,
district office.

**67212 ■ International Trade
Administration–U.S. and Foreign Commercial
Service–Export Assistance Center
(Louisville) (Gene)**
Gene Snyder Courthouse Bldg.
601 W. Broadway, Rm. 6348
Louisville, KY 40202
Ph:(502)582-5066
Fax: (502)582-6573
Co. E-mail: office.louisville@mail.doc.gov
URL: http://www.usatrade.gov

**67213 ■ International Trade
Administration–U.S. and Foreign Commercial
Service–Export Assistance Center
(Somerset) (2292)**
2292 S. Hwy. 27, Ste. 320
Somerset, KY 42501
Ph:(606)677-6160
Fax: (606)677-6161

**67214 ■ International Trade
Administration–U.S. and Foreign Commercial
Service–Export Assistance Center (Portland,
ME) (511 C)**
511 Congress St.
Portland, ME 04101
Ph:(207)541-7430

Fax: (207)541-7420
Co. E-mail: jeffrey.porter@mail.doc.gov
URL: http://www.buyusa.gov/newengland
Description: Affiliated with the Boston, Massachu-
setts, district office.

**67215 ■ International Trade
Administration–U.S. and Foreign Commercial
Service–Export Assistance Center
(Baltimore) (U.S.)**
U.S. Export Assistance Center
World Trade Center
401 E. Pratt St., Ste. 300
Baltimore, MD 21202-6504
Ph:(410)962-4539
Fax: (410)962-4529
Co. E-mail: office.baltimoreusec@mail.doc.gov
URL: http://www.export.gov/comm_svc
Description: Serves as both the Baltimore and Wash-
ington, D.C., district office.

**67216 ■ International Trade
Administration–U.S. and Foreign Commercial
Service–Export Assistance Center
(Gaithersburg) (c/o N)**
c/o National Institute of Standards and Technology
100 Bureau Dr.
Stop 2160
Gaithersburg, MD 20899-2160
Ph:(301)975-4040
Fax: (301)926-1559

**67217 ■ International Trade
Administration–U.S. and Foreign Commercial
Service–Export Assistance Center (Boston)
(World)**
World Trade Center
164 Northern Ave., Ste. 307
Boston, MA 02210
Ph:(617)424-5990
Fax: (617)424-5992
Co. E-mail: Office.Boston@mail.doc.gov
URL: http://www.buyusa.gov/newengland
Description: Boston office also services the states of
New Hampshire and Vermont.

**67218 ■ International Trade
Administration–U.S. and Foreign Commercial
Service–Export Assistance Center (Detroit)
(211 W)**
211 W. Fort St., Ste. 1104
Detroit, MI 48226
Ph:(313)226-3650
Fax: (313)226-3657
Co. E-mail: office.detroit@mail.doc.gov
URL: http://www.usatrade.gov

**67219 ■ International Trade
Administration–U.S. and Foreign Commercial
Service–Export Assistance Center (Grand
Rapids) (301 W)**
301 W. Fulton St., Ste. 309C
Grand Rapids, MI 49504-6495
Ph:(616)458-3564
Fax: (616)458-3872
Co. E-mail: office.grandrapids@mail.doc.gov
URL: http://www.usatrade.gov

**67220 ■ International Trade
Administration–U.S. and Foreign Commercial
Service–Export Assistance Center (Pontiac)
(Oakla)**
Oakland Pointe Office Bldg.
250 Elizabeth Lake Rd.
Pontiac, MI 48341
Ph:(248)975-9600
Fax: (248)975-9606
Co. E-mail: Richard.corson@mail.doc.gov
URL: http://www.ita.doc.gov/uscs/mi/eacs.htm

**67221 ■ International Trade
Administration–U.S. and Foreign Commercial
Service–Export Assistance Center (Ypsilanti)
(c/o E)**
c/o Eastern Michigan University
300 W. Michigan Ave., Room 306
Ypsilanti, MI 48197
Ph:(734)487-0259

Fax: (734)485-2396
Co. E-mail: ypsilanti.office.box@mail.doc.gov
URL: http://www.usatrade.gov

**67222 ■ International Trade
Administration–U.S. and Foreign Commercial
Service–Export Assistance Center
(Minneapolis) (Minne)**
Minnesota Export Assistance Ctr.
45 S. 7th St.
Plaza VII, Ste. 2240
Minneapolis, MN 55402
Ph:(612)348-1638
Fax: (612)348-1650
Co. E-mail: minneapolis.office.box@mail.doc.gov
URL: http://www.buyusa.gov/uppermidwest

**67223 ■ International Trade
Administration–U.S. and Foreign Commercial
Service–Export Assistance Center (Jackson)
(175 E)**
175 E. Capitol St., Ste. 255
Jackson, MS 39201
Ph:(601)965-4130
Fax: (601)965-4132
Co. E-mail: Dominique.crouch@mail.doc.gov
URL: http://www.export.gov/comm_svc/

**67224 ■ International Trade
Administration–U.S. and Foreign Commercial
Service–Export Assistance Center (Kansas
City) (2345)**
2345 Grand Blvd., Ste. 650
Kansas City, MO 64108
Ph:(816)426-6285
Fax: (816)426-6292
Co. E-mail: Kansas.city.office.box@mail.doc.gov
URL: http://www.buyusa.gov/kansascity
Description: Affiliated with the Wichita district office.

**67225 ■ International Trade
Administration–U.S. and Foreign Commercial
Service–Export Assistance Center (St. Louis)
(8235)**
8235 Forsyth Blvd., Ste. 520
St. Louis, MO 63105
Ph:(314)425-3302
Fax: (314)425-3381
Co. E-mail: st.louis.office.box@mail.doc.gov
URL: http://www.buyusa.gov/stlouis

**67226 ■ International Trade
Administration–U.S. and Foreign Commercial
Service–Export Assistance Center (Omaha)
(11133)**
11133 "O" St.
Omaha, NE 68137
Ph:(402)597-0193
Fax: (402)597-0194
Co. E-mail: omaha.office.box@mail.doc.gov
URL: http://www.usatrade.gov
Description: Omaha office also services the states of
North Dakota and South Dakota.

**67227 ■ International Trade
Administration–U.S. and Foreign Commercial
Service–Export Assistance Center (Reno) (1
E.)**
1 E. 1st St., 16th Fl.
Reno, NV 89501
Ph:(775)784-5203
Fax: (775)784-5343
Co. E-mail: reno.office.box@mail.doc.gov
URL: http://www.usatrade.gov

**67228 ■ International Trade
Administration–U.S. and Foreign Commercial
Service–Export Assistance Center
(Portsmouth) (17th)**
17th New Hampshire Ave.
Portsmouth, NH 03801-2838
Ph:(603)334-6074
Fax: (603)334-6110
Co. E-mail: office.portsmouth@mail.doc.gov
URL: http://www.buyusa.gov/newengland

67229 ■ International Trade Administration–U.S. and Foreign Commercial Service–Export Assistance Center (Newark) (744 B)
744 Broad St., Ste. 1505
Newark, NJ 07102
Ph:(973)645-4682
Fax: (973)645-4783
Co. E-mail: office.newark@mail.doc.gov
URL: http://www.buyusa.gov/nynj

67230 ■ International Trade Administration–U.S. and Foreign Commercial Service–Export Assistance Center (Trenton) (20 W.)
20 W. State St.
PO Box 820
Trenton, NJ 08625-0820
Ph:(609)989-2100
Fax: (856)722-0716
Co. E-mail: office.trenton@mail.doc.gov
URL: http://www.usatrade.gov

67231 ■ International Trade Administration–U.S. and Foreign Commercial Service–Export Assistance Center (Santa Fe) (c/o N)
c/o New Mexico Dept. of Economic Development
1100 St. Francis Dr.
Santa Fe, NM 87505-4147
Ph:(505)827-0350
Fax: (505)827-0263
Co. E-mail: santa.fe.office.box@mail.doc.gov
URL: http://www.usatrade.gov

67232 ■ International Trade Administration–U.S. and Foreign Commercial Service–Export Assistance Center (Buffalo) (Feder)
Federal Bldg.
111 W. Huron St., Rm. 1304
Buffalo, NY 14202
Ph:(585)551-4191
Fax: (585)551-5290
Co. E-mail: Office.Buffalo@mail.doc.gov
URL: http://www.usatrade.gov

67233 ■ International Trade Administration–U.S. and Foreign Commercial Service–Export Assistance Center (Long Island) (1550)
1550 Franklin Ave., Rm. 207
Mineola, NY 11501
Ph:(516)738-1765
Fax: (516)738-3310

67234 ■ International Trade Administration–U.S. and Foreign Commercial Service–Export Assistance Center (Rochester) (400 A)
400 Andrews St., Ste. 710
Rochester, NY 14604
Ph:(585)263-6480
Fax: (585)325-6505
Co. E-mail: erin.cole@mail.doc.gov

67235 ■ International Trade Administration–U.S. and Foreign Commercial Service–Export Assistance Center (Westchester) (707 W)
707 Westchester Ave., Ste. 209
White Plains, NY 10604
Ph:(914)682-6712
Fax: (914)682-6698
Co. E-mail: office.westchester@mail.doc.gov

67236 ■ International Trade Administration–U.S. and Foreign Commercial Service–Export Assistance Center (Charlotte) (521 E)
521 E. Morehead St., Ste. 435
Charlotte, NC 28202
Ph:(704)333-4886
Fax: (704)332-2681
Co. E-mail: office.charlotte@mail.doc.gov
URL: http://www.buyusa.gov/northcarolinas

67237 ■ International Trade Administration–U.S. and Foreign Commercial Service–Export Assistance Center (Greensboro) (342 N)
342 N. Elm St.
Greensboro, NC 27401
Ph:(336)333-5345
Fax: (336)333-5158
Co. E-mail: office.greensboro@mail.doc.gov
URL: http://www.buyusa.gov/northcarolina

67238 ■ International Trade Administration–U.S. and Foreign Commercial Service–Export Assistance Center (Cincinnati) (36 E.)
36 E. 7th St., Ste. 2650
Cincinnati, OH 45202
Ph:(513)684-2944
Fax: (513)684-3227
Co. E-mail: office.cincinnati@mail.doc.gov
URL: http://www.usatrade.gov

67239 ■ International Trade Administration–U.S. and Foreign Commercial Service–Export Assistance Center (Cleveland) (600 S)
600 Superior Ave. E, Ste. 700
Cleveland, OH 44114
Ph:(216)522-4750
Fax: (216)522-2235
Co. E-mail: office.cleveland@mail.doc.gov
URL: http://www.usatrade.gov

67240 ■ International Trade Administration–U.S. and Foreign Commercial Service–Export Assistance Center (Columbus) (37 N.)
37 N. High St., 4th Fl., Ste. 1400
Columbus, OH 43215
Ph:(614)365-9510
Fax: (614)365-9598
Co. E-mail: office.columbus@mail.doc.gov
URL: http://www.usatrade.gov

67241 ■ International Trade Administration–U.S. and Foreign Commercial Service–Export Assistance Center (Toledo) (300 M)
300 Madison Ave., Ste. 270
Toledo, OH 43604
Ph:(419)241-0683
Fax: (419)241-0684
Co. E-mail: office.toledo@mail.doc.gov
URL: http://www.usatrade.gov

67242 ■ International Trade Administration–U.S. and Foreign Commercial Service–Export Assistance Center (Oklahoma City) (301 N)
301 NW 63rd St., Ste. 330
Oklahoma City, OK 73116
Ph:(405)608-5302
Fax: (405)608-4211
Co. E-mail: oklahomacity.office.box@mail.doc.gov
URL: http://www.mail.doc.gov

67243 ■ International Trade Administration–U.S. and Foreign Commercial Service–Export Assistance Center (Tulsa) (700 N)
700 N. Greenwood Ave., Ste. 1400
Tulsa, OK 74106
Ph:(918)581-7650
Fax: (918)581-6263
Co. E-mail: office.tulsa@mail.doc.gov
URL: http://www.usatrade.gov

67244 ■ International Trade Administration–U.S. and Foreign Commercial Service–Export Assistance Center (Eugene) (1401)
1401 Willamette St.
Eugene, OR 97401-4003
Ph:(541)484-6575
Fax: (541)484-6704

67245 ■ International Trade Administration–U.S. and Foreign Commercial Service–Export Assistance Center (Portland, OR) (1 Wor)
1 World Trade Center
121 SW Salmon St., Ste. 250
Portland, OR 97204
Ph:(503)326-3001
Fax: (503)464-8880
Co. E-mail: scott.goddin@mail.doc.gov
URL: http://www.export.gov/cs

67246 ■ International Trade Administration–U.S. and Foreign Commercial Service–Export Assistance Center (Harrisburg) (228 W)
228 Walnut St., No. 850
PO Box 11698
Harrisburg, PA 17108-1698
Ph:(717)221-4510
Fax: (717)221-4505
Co. E-mail: office.harrisburg@mail.doc.gov
URL: http://www.usatrade.gov

67247 ■ International Trade Administration–U.S. and Foreign Commercial Service–Export Assistance Center (Philadelphia) (The C)
The Curtis Ctr., Suite 580 W.
Independence Sq. W.
Philadelphia, PA 19106
Ph:(215)597-6101
Fax: (215)597-6123
Co. E-mail: office.philadelphia@mail.doc.gov
URL: http://www.usatrade.gov
Description: Philadelphia office also services the state of Delaware.

67248 ■ International Trade Administration–U.S. and Foreign Commercial Service–Export Assistance Center (Pittsburgh) (425 6)
425 6th Ave., Ste. 2950
Pittsburgh, PA 15219
Ph:(412)644-2800
Fax: (412)644-2803
Co. E-mail: office.pittsburgh@mail.doc.gov
URL: http://www.usatrade.gov

67249 ■ International Trade Administration–U.S. and Foreign Commercial Service–Export Assistance Center (Scranton) (One M)
One Montage Mountain Rd., Ste. B
Moosic, PA 18507
Ph:(717)969-2530
Fax: (717)969-2539

67250 ■ International Trade Administration–U.S. and Foreign Commercial Service–Export Assistance Center (San Juan) (Centr)
Centro Internacional de Mercadeo Torre II, Ste. 702
Carr. 165
Guaynabo, PR 00968-8058
Ph:(787)775-1992
Fax: (809)766-5692
Co. E-mail: office.sanjuanpr@mail.doc.gov

67251 ■ International Trade Administration–U.S. and Foreign Commercial Service–Export Assistance Center (Providence) (1 W.)
1 W. Exchange St.
Providence, RI 02903
Ph:(401)528-5104
Fax: (401)528-5067
Co. E-mail: office.providence@mail.doc.gov
URL: http://www.buyusa.gov/newengland
Description: Affiliated with the Hartford district office.

67252 ■ International Trade Administration–U.S. and Foreign Commercial Service–Export Assistance Center (Charleston) (5300)
5300 International Blvd., Ste. 201-C
North Charleston, SC 29418
Ph:(843)760-3794

Fax: (843)760-3798
Co. E-mail: phil.minard@mail.doc.gov
URL: http://www.buyusa.gov/southeast/charelston_
sc.html

**67253 ■ International Trade
Administration–U.S. and Foreign Commercial
Service–Export Assistance Center
(Columbia) (1201)**
1201 main St., Ste. 1720
Columbia, SC 29201
Ph:(803)765-5345
Fax: (803)253-3614
Co. E-mail: office.columbia@mail.doc.gov
URL: http://www.usatrade.gov

**67254 ■ International Trade
Administration–U.S. and Foreign Commercial
Service–Export Assistance Center (Sioux
Falls) (Augus)**
Augustana College
2001 S. Summit Ave., Rm. 122
Sioux Falls, SD 57197
Ph:(605)330-4265
Fax: (605)330-4266
Co. E-mail: cinnamon.king@mail.doc.gov
URL: http://www.usatrade.gov

**67255 ■ International Trade
Administration–U.S. and Foreign Commercial
Service–Export Assistance Center (Knoxville)
(Histo)**
Historic City
17 Market Sq., No. 201
Knoxville, TN 37902-1405
Ph:(865)-545-4637
Fax: (865)545-4435
Co. E-mail: Knoxville.office.box@mail.doc.gov
URL: http://www.usatrade.gov

**67256 ■ International Trade
Administration–U.S. and Foreign Commercial
Service–Export Assistance Center (Memphis)
(Buckm)**
Buckman Hall
650 E. Pkwy. S., Ste. 328
Memphis, TN 38104
Ph:(901)544-0930
Fax: (901)320-9128
URL: http://www.memphisexports.com

**67257 ■ International Trade
Administration–U.S. and Foreign Commercial
Service–Export Assistance Center (Nashville)
(211 C)**
211 Commerce St., 3rd Fl.
Ste. 100
Nashville, TN 37201
Ph:(615)259-6060
Fax: (615)259-6064
Co. E-mail: office.nashville@mail.doc.gov
URL: http://www.usatrade.gov

**67258 ■ International Trade
Administration–U.S. and Foreign Commercial
Service–Export Assistance Center (Austin)
(221 E)**
221 E. 11th St., 4th Fl.
PO Box 12428
Austin, TX 78711
Ph:(512)916-5939
Fax: (512)916-5940
Co. E-mail: Austin.office.box@mail.doc.gov
URL: http://www.export.gov.cs

**67259 ■ International Trade
Administration–U.S. and Foreign Commercial
Service–Export Assistance Center (Dallas)
(2050)**
2050 N. Stammons Fwy., Ste. 170
PO Box 420069
Dallas, TX 75258
Ph:(214)767-0542
Fax: (214)767-8240

**67260 ■ International Trade
Administration–U.S. and Foreign Commercial
Service–Export Assistance Center (Ft. Worth)
(808 T)**
808 Throckmorton St.
Ft. Worth, TX 76102
Ph:(817)392-2673
Fax: (817)392-2668
Co. E-mail: fort.worth.office.box@mail.doc.gov
URL: http://www.usatrade.gov

**67261 ■ International Trade
Administration–U.S. and Foreign Commercial
Service–Export Assistance Center (Houston)
(15600)**
15600 John F. Kennedy Blvd., Ste. 530
Houston, TX 77032
Ph:(281)449-9402
Fax: (281)449-9437
Co. E-mail: Houston.office.box@mail.doc.gov
URL: http://www.usatrade.gov

**67262 ■ International Trade
Administration–U.S. and Foreign Commercial
Service–Export Assistance Center (San
Antonio) (203 S)**
203 S. Saint Mary St., Ste. 360
San Antonio, TX 78212
Ph:(210)228-9878
Fax: (210)228-9874
Co. E-mail: daniel.rodriguez@mail.doc.gov
URL: http://www.export.gov

**67263 ■ International Trade
Administration–U.S. and Foreign Commercial
Service–Export Assistance Center (Salt Lake
City) (324 S)**
324 S. State St., Ste. 221
Salt Lake City, UT 84111
Ph:(801)524-5116
Fax: (801)524-5886
Co. E-mail: salt.lake.city.office.box@mail.doc.gov
URL: http://www.buyusa.gov/utah

**67264 ■ International Trade
Administration–U.S. and Foreign Commercial
Service–Export Assistance Center
(Montpelier) (Natio)**
National Life Bldg., 6th Fl.
Montpelier, VT 05620-0501
Ph:(802)828-4508
Fax: (802)828-3258
Co. E-mail: office.montpelier@mail.doc.gov
URL: http://www.buyusa.gov/newengland

**67265 ■ International Trade
Administration–U.S. and Foreign Commercial
Service–Export Assistance Center
(Richmond) (400 N)**
400 N. 8th St., No. 412
PO Box 10026
Richmond, VA 23240-0026
Ph:(804)771-2246
Fax: (804)771-2390
Co. E-mail: eric.mcdonald@mail.doc.gov

**67266 ■ International Trade
Administration–U.S. and Foreign Commercial
Service–Export Assistance Center (Seattle)
(2601)**
2601 4th Ave., Ste. 320
Seattle, WA 98121
Ph:(206)553-5615
Fax: (206)553-7253
Co. E-mail: seattle.office.box@mail.doc.gov
URL: http://www.buyusa.gov/seattle

**67267 ■ International Trade
Administration–U.S. and Foreign Commercial
Service–Export Assistance Center (Spokane)
(801 W)**
801 W. Riverside Ave., Ste. 100
Spokane, WA 99201
Ph:(509)353-2625
Fax: (509)353-2449
Co. E-mail: spokane.office.box@mail.doc.gov
URL: http://www.usatrade.gov

**67268 ■ International Trade
Administration–U.S. and Foreign Commercial
Service–Export Assistance Center (Wheeling)
(c/o W)**
c/o Wheeling Jesuit University/NTTC
316 Washington Ave.
Wheeling, WV 26003
Ph:(304)243-5493
Fax: (304)243-5494
Co. E-mail: office.wheeling@mail.doc.gov
URL: http://www.usatrade.gov

**67269 ■ International Trade
Administration–U.S. and Foreign Commercial
Service–Export Assistance Center
(Milwaukee) (Feder)**
Federal Bldg.
517 E. Wisconsin Ave., Rm. 596
Milwaukee, WI 53202
Ph:(414)297-3473
Fax: (414)297-3470
Co. E-mail: milwaukee.office.box@mail.doc.gov
URL: http://www.usatrade.gov

INTERNATIONAL TRADE COMMISSION

**67270 ■ International Trade
Commission–Office of Economics**
500 E St., SW, Rm. 602F
Washington, DC 20436
Ph:(202)205-3216
Fax: (202)205-2340
Co. E-mail: robert.koopman@usitc.gov
URL: http://www.usitc.gov

**67271 ■ International Trade
Commission–Office of Industries**
500 E St., SW, Rm. 504A
Washington, DC 20436
Ph:(202)205-3296
Fax: (202)205-3161
Co. E-mail: karen.laney-cummings@usitc.gov
URL: http://www.usitc.gov

**67272 ■ International Trade
Commission–Office of Operations**
500 E St., SW, Rm. 715A
Washington, DC 20436
Ph:(202)205-2230
Fax: (202)205-1893
Co. E-mail: robert.rogowsky@usitc.gov
URL: http://www.usitc.gov

**67273 ■ International Trade
Commission–Office of Tariff Affairs and
Trade Agreements**
500 E St., SW, Rm. 404B
Washington, DC 20436
Ph:(202)205-2603
Fax: (202)205-2616
Co. E-mail: davis.beck@usitc.gov
URL: http://www.usitc.gov

**67274 ■ International Trade
Commission–Office of Unfair Import
Investigations**
500 E St., SW, Rm. 401G
Washington, DC 20436
Ph:(202)205-2560
Fax: (202)205-2158
Co. E-mail: lynn.levine@usitc.gov
URL: http://www.usitc.gov

LIBRARY OF CONGRESS

67275 ■ Library of Congress
101 Independence Ave, SE
Washington, DC 20540
Ph:(202)707-5000

MINORITY BUSINESS DEVELOPMENT AGENCY

67276 ■ Minority Business Development Agency
Department of Commerce
Herbert Clark Hoover Bldg., Rm. 5053
14th St. & Constitution Ave. NW
Washington, DC 20230
Ph:(202)482-5061
Free: 888-324-1551
Co. E-mail: rlangston@mbda.gov
URL: http://www.mbda.gov
Description: The Minority Business Development Agency is the only federal agency specifically created to establish policies and programs to develop the U.S. minority business community. The agency's goal is to increase opportunities for racial and ethnic minorities to participate in the free enterprise system through the formation and development of competitive minority-owned and managed firms, with emphasis on private sector involvement and entrepreneurial self-reliance. To accomplish this goal, the agency coordinates the federal government's plans, programs, and operations that affect or may contribute to the establishment, preservation, and strengthening of minority business enterprise. The MBDA also promotes the mobilization of activities and resources of state and local governments, business and trade associations, universities, foundations, professional organizations, and other groups towards the growth of minority business enterprise, as well as facilitates the coordination of the efforts of these groups with those of federal departments and agencies. In addition, the MBDA acts as a center for the development, collection, summarization, and dissemination of information that will be helpful to persons and organizations throughout the United States in undertaking or promoting the establishment and successful operation of minority business enterprises. The agency also provides financial assistance to public and private organizations so that they may render technical and management assistance to minority business enterprises and defray all or part of the costs of pilot or demonstration projects conducted by public or private agencies or organizations that are designed to overcome the special problems of minority business enterprises. The MBDA sponsors a network of approximately 100 Minority Business Development Centers, located throughout the country in areas with the largest minority populations. The mission of the centers is to increase the formation of minority-owned firms, to expand existing minority-owned enterprises, and to minimize minority business failures. Counselors at each center provide management, marketing, and technical assistance to minority individuals wishing to start, expand, or improve their businesses. Socially or economically disadvantaged individuals eligible for assistance include, but are not limited to, Blacks, Hispanics, Native Americans, Eskimos, Aleuts, Asian Pacific Americans, Asian Indians, and Hasidic Jews. General referral assistance is provided free of charge to minority entrepreneurs seeking management, marketing, procurement, and financial assistance from federal, state, and local agencies, private institutions, and other sources. For a nominal fee counselors provide assistance to eligible individuals and firms in such areas as accounting, inventory control, bid estimating, bonding, personnel management, contract negotiations, and marketing. Each minority business development center develops and maintains a listing of existing minority-owned firms for inclusion in the agency's PROFILE National Minority Data Base. The PROFILE system is used by government and private industry purchasing officials to identify minority vendors qualified to supply the goods and services they need. Minority business owners wishing to register their firms in the PROFILE system may do so at no charge at any minority business development center. Counselors at the centers also identify both private and public sector sources of financing for minority-owned firms. They assist minority entrepreneurs with the preparation of financial packages and plans for submission to lenders for the purpose of financing business ventures. The centers cannot make or underwrite loans because the MBDA has no loan-making authority. In addition, center personnel match minority-owned firms with new business opportunities in domestic and foreign markets. They maintain contact with major corporations to identify business opportunities for minority-owned enterprises, and they utilize other federal, state, and local government agencies to identify contract opportunities and sources of financing to expand the minority business community. Center personnel also determine constraints to minority business development at the federal, state, and local levels and make recommendations for improvement. The centers are funded on a competitive basis. Applicants for the operation of these centers may be individuals, nonprofit organizations, private firms, state and local governments, Native American tribes, or educational institutions. The maximum federal funding of each center represents not more than 85 percent of the total cost of the project. Each center is expected to provide the other 15 percent.

The following MBDA regional offices are arranged alphabetically by city. (See appropriate state listings for individual minority business development centers.)

67277 ■ Minority Business Development Agency–Atlanta Regional Office
Peachtree Summit Federal Bldg., Ste. 1715
401 W. Peachtree St., NW
Atlanta, GA 30308-3516
Ph:(404)730-3300
Fax: (404)730-3313
Co. E-mail: aro-info@mbda.gov
URL: http://www.mbda.gov
Description: Serves Alabama, Florida, Georgia, Kentucky, Mississippi, North Carolina, South Carolina, and Tennessee.

67278 ■ Minority Business Development Agency–Chicago Regional Office
Xerox Center, Ste. 1406
55 E. Monroe St.
Chicago, IL 60603
Ph:(312)353-0182
Fax: (312)353-0191
Co. E-mail: cro-info@mbda.gov
URL: http://www.mbda.gov
Description: Serves Illinois, Indiana, Iowa, Kansas, Michigan, Minnesota, Missouri, Nebraska, Ohio, and Wisconsin.

67279 ■ Minority Business Development Agency–Dallas Regional Office
Earl Cabell Federal Bldg., Rm. 7B23
1100 Commerce St.
Dallas, TX 75242
Ph:(214)767-8001
Fax: (214)767-0613
Co. E-mail: dro-info@mbda.gov
URL: http://www.mbda.gov
Description: Serves Arkansas, Colorado, Louisiana, Montana, New Mexico, North Dakota, Oklahoma, South Dakota, Texas, Utah, and Wyoming.

67280 ■ Minority Business Development Agency–New York Regional Office
Javits Federal Bldg., Rm. 37-20
26 Federal Plaza
New York, NY 10278
Ph:(212)264-3262
Fax: (212)264-0725
Co. E-mail: nyro-info@mbda.gov
URL: http://www.mbda.gov
Description: Serves Connecticut, Maine, Massachusetts, New Hampshire, New Jersey, New York, Puerto Rico, Rhode Island, Vermont, and the Virgin Islands.

67281 ■ Minority Business Development Agency–San Francisco Regional Office
221 Main St., Rm. 1280
San Francisco, CA 94105
Ph:(415)744-3001
Fax: (415)744-3061
Co. E-mail: sfro-info@mbda.gov
URL: http://www.mbda.gov
Description: Serves Alaska, American Samoa, Arizona, California, Hawaii, Idaho, Nevada, Oregon, and Washington.

67282 ■ Minority Business Development Agency–Washington, DC, Regional Office
64 New York Ave., NE
Washington, DC 20005
Ph:(202)671-1552
Fax: (202)671-3073
Co. E-mail: rtaylor@ncrc.org
Description: Serves Delaware, the District of Columbia, Maryland, Pennsylvania, Virginia, and West Virginia.

The following MBDA district offices are arranged alphabetically by state.

67283 ■ Minority Business Development Agency District Office (Los Angeles)
11138 Valley Mall, Ste. 200
El Monte, CA 91731
Ph:(626)442-3701
Fax: (626)442-7115
Co. E-mail: schambers@ncaied.org

67284 ■ Minority Business Development Agency District Office (Miami)
Claude Plaza Federal Bldg., Ste. 1314
51 SW 1st Ave.
PO Box 25
Miami, FL 33130
Ph:(305)536-5054
Fax: (305)530-7068
Co. E-mail: aguzman@mbda.gov

67285 ■ Minority Business Development Agency District Office (Boston)
10 Causeway St., Ste. 418
Boston, MA 02222
Ph:(617)565-6850
Fax: (617)565-8897

67286 ■ Minority Business Development Agency District Office (Philadelphia)
William J. Green, Jr. Federal Bldg.
600 Arch St., Ste. 10128
Philadelphia, PA 19106
Ph:(215)861-3597
Fax: (215)861-3595

NATIONAL AERONAUTICS AND SPACE ADMINISTRATION

67287 ■ National Aeronautics and Space Administration–Office of Small and Disadvantaged Business Utilization
Headquarters Code K, Rm. 9K70
300 E. St., SW
Washington, DC 20546
Ph:(202)358-2088
Fax: (202)358-3261
Co. E-mail: rthomas@hq.nasa.gov
URL: http://osdbu.nasa.gov
Description: The development and management of the National Aeronautics and Space Administration's programs to assist small businesses are administered by its Office of Small and Disadvantaged Business Utilization. Services include individual counseling sessions for business owners seeking advice on how to best pursue contracting opportunities at NASA. NASA's procurement program is decentralized, with procurements planned and accomplished by field installations that also maintain small and minority business specialists. NASA's Technology Utilization Program provides information and other assistance to small business owners seeking to apply the results of NASA research and development projects to new commercial products or processes.

The following field installations are arranged alphabetically by center name.

67288 ■ National Aeronautics and Space Administration–Ames Research Center–Small Business Specialist (Mail)
Mail Stop 241-1
Moffett Field, CA 94035-1000
Ph:(650)604-6888
Fax: (650)604-3020

67289 ■ National Aeronautics and Space Administration–Goddard Space Flight Center–Small Business Specialist (Mail)
Mail Code 210
Greenbelt, MD 20771
Ph:(301)286-8400
Fax: (301)286-0257

67290 ■ National Aeronautics and Space Administration–Jet Propulsion Laboratory–Contractor Capabilities Office (4800)
4800 Oak Grove Dr.
Mail Code 249-104
Pasadena, CA 91109
Ph:(818)354-5722
Fax: (818)393-1978

67291 ■ National Aeronautics and Space Administration–Johnson Space Center–Small Business Specialist (Mail)
Mail Code BD3
Houston, TX 77058
Ph:(281)483-4157
Fax: (281)483-5100

67292 ■ National Aeronautics and Space Administration–Kennedy Space Center–Small Business Specialist (Mail)
Mail Code OP
Kennedy Space Center
NASA
Orlando, FL 32899
Ph:(321)867-7346
Fax: (321)867-8599

67293 ■ National Aeronautics and Space Administration–Langley Research Center–Small Business Specialist (Mail)
Mail Stop 134
Hampton, VA 23681
Ph:(757)864-2456
Fax: (757)864-9299

67294 ■ National Aeronautics and Space Administration–Marshall Space Flight Center–Small Business Specialist (Mail)
Mail Code PS01
Huntsville, AL 35812
Ph:(256)544-0254
Fax: (256)544-5851

67295 ■ National Aeronautics and Space Administration–Resident Office—JPL–Small Business Specialist (4800)
4800 Oak Grove Dr.
Mail Code 180-802K
Pasadena, CA 91109
Ph:(818)354-6315
Fax: (818)354-6015

67296 ■ National Aeronautics and Space Administration–Small Business Innovation Research Office
300 E. St., SW
Washington, DC 20546
Ph:(202)358-4652
Co. E-mail: carl.g.ray@nasa.gov

67297 ■ National Aeronautics and Space Administration–John C. Stennis Space Center–Small Business Specialist (Mail)–Procurement Office (Code BA30)
Mail Code BA30
Stennis Space Center, MS 39529-6000
Ph:(228)688-1720
Fax: (228)688-1141

67298 ■ National Aeronautics and Space Administration (NASA)–John H. Glenn Research Center at Lewis Field–Small Business Specialist (21000)
21000 Brookpark Rd.
Cleveland, OH 44135
Ph:(216)433-4000

The following NASA Industrial Applications Centers are arranged alphabetically by state.

67299 ■ NASA Industrial Applications Center (Los Angeles)
University of Southern California
3716 S. Hope St.
Research Annex, Rm. 200
Los Angeles, CA 90007-4344
Ph:(213)743-6132
Free: 800-872-7477
Fax: (213)746-9043

67300 ■ NERAC, Inc.
1 Technology Dr.
Tolland, CT 06084
Ph:(860)872-7000
Fax: (860)875-1749

67301 ■ Southern Technology Applications Center
13709 Progress Blvd., Box 24
1 Progress Blvd.
Alachua, FL 32615
Ph:(904)462-3913
Free: 800-225-0308
Fax: (904)462-3898

67302 ■ Aerospace Research Applications Center
611 N. Capitol Ave.
Indianapolis, IN 46204
Ph:(317)262-5036
Fax: (317)262-5044
URL: http://www.hq.nasa.gov/HQ.homepage.html

67303 ■ Technology Applications Center
University of Kentucky
109 Kinkhead Hall
Lexington, KY 40506
Ph:(606)257-6322

67304 ■ Earth Data Analysis Center
1 University of New Mexico
MSC01 1110
Albuquerque, NM 87131-0001
Ph:(505)277-3622
Fax: (505)277-3614

67305 ■ Central Industrial Applications Center
Rural Enterprises, Inc.
PO Box 1335
Durant, OK 74702
Ph:(580)924-5094
Free: 800-658-2823
Fax: (580)920-2745

67306 ■ NASA Industrial Applications Center (Pittsburgh)
823 William Pitt Union
Pittsburgh, PA 15260
Ph:(412)648-7000
Fax: (412)648-7003

NATIONAL CREDIT UNION ADMINISTRATION

67307 ■ National Credit Union Administration (Region 1)–Albany Regional Office
9 Washington Sq.
Washington Ave. Extension
Albany, NY 12205
Ph:(518)862-7400
Fax: (518)862-7420
Co. E-mail: region1@ncua.gov

URL: http://www.ncua.gov

67308 ■ National Credit Union Administration (Region 2)–Alexandria Regional Office
1775 Duke St., Ste. 4206
Alexandria, VA 22314-3437
Ph:(703)519-4600
Fax: (703)518-6674
Co. E-mail: region2@ncua.gov
URL: http://www.ncua.gov

67309 ■ National Credit Union Administration (Region 3)–Atlanta Regional Office
7000 Central Pkwy., Ste. 1600
Atlanta, GA 30328
Ph:(678)443-3000
Fax: (678)443-3020
Co. E-mail: region3@ncua.gov
URL: http://www.ncua.gov

67310 ■ National Credit Union Administration (Region 4)–Austin Regional Office
4807 Spicewood Springs Rd., Ste. 5200
Austin, TX 78759-8490
Ph:(512)342-5600
Fax: (512)342-5620
Co. E-mail: region4@ncua.gov
URL: http://www.ncua.gov

67311 ■ National Credit Union Administration (Region 5)–Tempe Regional Office
1230 W. Washington St., Ste. 301
Tempe, AZ 85281
Ph:(602)302-6000
Fax: (602)302-6024
Co. E-mail: region5@ncua.gov
URL: http://www.ncua.gov

67312 ■ National Credit Union Administration–Office of Small and Disadvantaged Business Utilization
1775 Duke St.
Alexandria, VA 22314-3428
Ph:(703)518-6300
Fax: (703)518-6661
Description: The National Credit Union Administration's Office of Small and Disadvantaged Business Utilization offers small businesses information and guidance on procurement procedures, how to be placed on a bidder's mailing list, and identification of both prime and subcontracting opportunities.

NATIONAL LABOR RELATIONS BOARD

67313 ■ National Labor Relation Board (Region 30)–Milwaukee Regional Office
310 W. Wisconsin Ave., Ste. 700
Milwaukee, WI 53203-2211
Ph:(414)297-3861
Fax: (414)297-3880
URL: http://www.nlrb.gov

67314 ■ National Labor Relations Board
1099 14th St., NW
Washington, DC 20570-0001
Ph:(202)273-1000
URL: http://www.nlrb.gov

67315 ■ National Labor Relations Board–Office of Small and Disadvantaged Business Utilization
1099 14th St., NW, Ste. 7108
Washington, DC 20570
Ph:(202)273-3890
Fax: (202)273-2928
Co. E-mail: gloria.joseph@nlrb.gov
URL: http://www.nlrb.gov

67316 ■ National Labor Relations Board (Region 1)–Boston Regional Office
10 Causeway St., 6th Fl.
Boston, MA 02222-1072
Ph:(617)565-6700
Fax: (617)565-6725

URL: http://www.nlrb.gov

**67317 ■ National Labor Relations Board
(Region 2)–New York Regional Office**
26 Federal Plz., Rm. 3614
New York, NY 10278-0104
Ph:(212)264-0300
Fax: (212)264-2450
URL: http://www.nlrb.gov

**67318 ■ National Labor Relations Board
(Region 3)–Buffalo Regional Office**
Niagara Center Bldg.
130 S. Elmwood Ave.
Buffalo, NY 14202-2387
Ph:(716)551-4931
Fax: (716)551-4972
URL: http://www.nlrb.gov

**67319 ■ National Labor Relations Board
(Region 4)–Philadelphia Regional Office**
615 Chestnut St., 7th Fl.
Philadelphia, PA 19106-4404
Ph:(215)597-7601
Fax: (215)597-7658
URL: http://www.nlrb.gov

**67320 ■ National Labor Relations Board
(Region 6)–Pittsburgh Regional Office**
2 Chatham Ctr.
112 Washington Pl.
Pittsburgh, PA 15219
Ph:(412)395-4400
Fax: (412)395-5986
URL: http://www.nlrb.gov

**67321 ■ National Labor Relations Board
(Region 7)–Detroit Regional Office**
477 Michigan Ave., Rm. 300
Detroit, MI 48226-2569
Ph:(313)226-3200
Fax: (313)226-2569
URL: http://www.nlrb.gov

**67322 ■ National Labor Relations Board
(Region 8)–Cleveland Regional Office**
1240 E. 9th St., Rm. 1695
Cleveland, OH 44199-2086
Ph:(216)522-3716
Fax: (216)522-2418
URL: http://www.nlrb.gov

**67323 ■ National Labor Relations Board
(Region 9)–Cincinnati Regional Office**
John Weld Peck Federal Bldg.
550 Main St., Rm. 3003
Cincinnati, OH 45202-3271
Ph:(513)684-3686
Fax: (513)684-3946
URL: http://www.nlrb.gov

**67324 ■ National Labor Relations Board
(Region 10)–Atlanta Regional Office**
Harris Tower, Ste. 1000
233 Peachtree St., NE
Atlanta, GA 30303-1531
Ph:(404)331-2896
Fax: (404)331-2858
URL: http://www.nlrb.gov

**67325 ■ National Labor Relations Board
(Region 11)–Winston-Salem Regional Office**
Republic Sq.
4035 University Pkwy., Ste. 200
Winston-Salem, NC 27106-3325
Ph:(336)631-5201
Fax: (336)631-5210
URL: http://www.nlrb.gov

**67326 ■ National Labor Relations Board
(Region 12)–Tampa Regional Office**
South Trust Plz., Ste. 550
201 E. Kennedy Blvd.
Tampa, FL 33602-5824
Ph:(813)228-2641
Fax:(813)228-2874
URL: http://www.nlrb.gov

**67327 ■ National Labor Relations Board
(Region 13)–Chicago Regional Office**
The Rookery Bldg.
209 S. LaSalle St., Ste. 900
Chicago, IL 60604-5208
Ph:(312)353-7570
Fax: (312)886-1341
URL: http://www.nlrb.gov

**67328 ■ National Labor Relations Board
(Region 14)–St. Louis Regional Office**
1222 Spruce St., Rm. 8.302
St. Louis, MO 63103-2829
Ph:(314)539-7770
Fax: (314)539-7794
URL: http://www.nlrb.gov

**67329 ■ National Labor Relations Board
(Region 16)–Ft. Worth Regional Office**
819 Taylor St., Rm. 8A24
Ft. Worth, TX 76102-6178
Ph:(817)978-2921
Fax: (817)978-2928
URL: http://www.nlrb.gov

**67330 ■ National Labor Relations Board
(Region 17)–Overland Park Regional Office**
8600 farley St., Ste. 100
Overland Park, KS 66212-4677
Ph:(913)967-3000
Fax: (913)967-3010
URL: http://www.nlrb.gov

**67331 ■ National Labor Relations Board
(Region 18)–Minneapolis Regional Office**
Towle Bldg., Ste. 790
330 2nd Ave., S.
Minneapolis, MN 55401-2221
Ph:(612)348-1757
Fax: (612)348-1785
URL: http://www.nlrb.gov

**67332 ■ National Labor Relations Board
(Region 19)–Seattle Regional Office**
210 Walnut St., Rm. 439
Seattle, WA 98174-1078
Ph:(206)220-6300
Fax: (206)220-6305
URL: http://www.nlrb.gov

**67333 ■ National Labor Relations Board
(Region 20)–San Francisco Regional Office**
901 Market St., Ste. 400
San Francisco, CA 94103-1735
Ph:(415)356-5130
Fax: (415)356-5156
URL: http://www.nlrb.gov

**67334 ■ National Labor Relations Board
(Region 21)–Los Angeles Regional Office**
888 S. Figueroa St. 9th Fl.
Los Angeles, CA 90017-5449
Ph:(213)894-5200
Fax: (213)894-2778
URL: http://www.nlrb.gov

**67335 ■ National Labor Relations Board
(Region 22)–Newark Regional Office**
20 Washington Pl., 5th Fl.
Newark, NJ 07102-3110
Ph:(973)645-2100
Fax: (973)645-3852
URL: http://www.nlrb.gov

**67336 ■ National Labor Relations Board
(Region 24)–Hato Rey Regional Office**
La Torre de Plz., Ste. 1002
525 F.D. Roosevelt Ave.
San Juan, PR 00918-1002
Ph:(787)766-5347
Fax: (787)766-5478
URL: http://www.nlrb.gov

**67337 ■ National Labor Relations Board
(Region 25)–Indianapolis Regional Office**
575 N. Pennsylvania St., Rm. 238
Indianapolis, IN 46204-1577

Ph:(317)226-7381
Fax: (317)226-5103
URL: http://www.nlrb.gov

**67338 ■ National Labor Relations Board
(Region 26)–Memphis Regional Office**
Brinkley Plz. Bldg., Ste. 350
Memphis, TN 38103-2481
Ph:(901)544-0018
Fax: (901)544-0008
URL: http://www.nlrb.gov

**67339 ■ National Labor Relations Board
(Region 27)–Denver Regional Office**
600 17th St.
7th Fl., North Tower
Denver, CO 80202-5433
Ph:(303)844-3551
Fax: (303)844-6249
URL: http://www.nlrb.gov

**67340 ■ National Labor Relations Board
(Region 28)–Phoenix Regional Office**
2600 N. Central Ave., Ste. 1800
Phoenix, AZ 85004-3099
Ph:(602)640-2160
Fax: (602)640-2178
URL: http://www.nlrb.gov

**67341 ■ National Labor Relations Board
(Region 29)–Brooklyn Regional Office**
1 Metro Tech Ctr., N.
J St. & Myrtle Ave., 10th Fl.
Brooklyn, NY 11201-4201
Ph:(718)330-7713
Fax: (718)330-7579
URL: http://www.nlrb.gov

**67342 ■ National Labor Relations Board
(Region 31)–Los Angeles Regional Office**
11150 W. Olympic Blvd., Ste. 700
Los Angeles, CA 90064-1824
Ph:(310)235-7352
Fax: (310)235-7420
URL: http://www.nlrb.gov

**67343 ■ National Labor Relations Board
(Region 32)–Oakland Regional Office**
Oakland Federal Bldg.
1301 Clay St., Rm. 300-N
Oakland, CA 94612-5211
Ph:(510)637-3300
Fax: (510)637-3315
URL: http://www.nlrb.gov

**67344 ■ National Labor Relations Board
(Region 34)–Hartford Regional Office**
280 Trumbull St., 21st Fl.
Hartford, CT 06103-3503
Ph:(860)240-3522
Fax: (860)240-3564
URL: http://www.nlrb.gov

**67345 ■ National Labor Relations (Region
5)–Baltimore Regional Office**
The Appraisers Store Bldg.
103 S. Gay St., 8th Fl.
Baltimore, MD 21202-4061
Ph:(410)962-2822
Fax: (410)962-2198
URL: http://www.nlrb.gov

NATIONAL SCIENCE
FOUNDATION

**67346 ■ National Science Foundation–Office
of Small and Disadvantaged Business
Utilization**
4201 Wilson Blvd., Rm. 527
Arlington, VA 22203
Ph:(703)292-7082
Fax: (703)306-0301
Co. E-mail: dsenich@nsf.gov
URL: http://www.nsf.gov/
Description: The National Science Foundation's Office of Small and Disadvantaged Business Utilization

offers small businesses information and guidance on procurement procedures, how to be placed on a bidder's mailing list, and identification of both prime and subcontracting opportunities.

67347 ■ National Science Foundation–Small Business Innovation Research Programs
4201 Wilson Blvd., Rm. 590
Arlington, VA 22230
Ph:(703)306-1390
Fax: (703)306-0337

67348 ■ National Science Foundation–Small Business Technology Transfer Program
4201 Wilson Blvd., Rm. 590
Arlington, VA 22230
Ph:(703)306-1390
Fax: (703)306-0337

OCCUPATIONAL SAFETY AND HEALTH ADMINISTRATION

67349 ■ Occupational Safety and Health Administration–Office of Communications
200 Constitution Ave., NW, Rm. N3647
Washington, DC 20210
Ph:(202)693-1999
URL: http://www.osha.gov

67350 ■ Occupational Safety and Health Administration–Office of Small Business Assistance–Directorate of Cooperative and State Programs (200 C)
200 Constitution Ave., NW, Rm. N3660
Washington, DC 20210
Ph:(202)693-2220
URL: http://www.osha.gov

67351 ■ Occupational Safety and Health Administration (OSHA)
200 Constitution Ave., NW, Rm. S2315
Washington, DC 20210
Ph:(202)693-2000
Fax: (202)693-1659
URL: http://www.osha.gov

OFFICE OF PERSONNEL MANAGEMENT

67352 ■ Office of Personnel Management–Center for National Security–Office of Operations (Theod)
Theodore Roosevelt Bldg., Rm. 7653
1900 E St., NW
Washington, DC 20415-0001
Ph:(202)606-1868
Fax: (202)606-2663
Co. E-mail: michael.carmichael@opm.gov
URL: http://www.opm.gov

67353 ■ Office of Personnel Management–Division for Human Capital Leadership and Merit System Accountability
Theodore Roosevelt Bldg., Rm. 7470
1900 E. St., NW
Washington, DC 20415-0001
Ph:(202)606-1575
Fax: (202)606-1798
URL: http://www.opm.gov

67354 ■ Office of Personnel Management–Office of Communications and Public Liaison
Theodore Roosevelt Federal Bldg., Rm. 5347
1900 E Street, NW
Washington, DC 20415-0001
Ph:(202)606-2402
Fax: (202)606-2264
URL: http://www.opm.gov

67355 ■ Office of Personnel Management–Office of Small and Disadvantaged Business Utilization–Contracting Division (Theod)
Theodore Roosevelt Federal Bldg.
1900 E. St., NW
Washington, DC 20415-1000
Ph:(202)606-1800
Fax: (202)606-1464
Description: The Office of Personnel Management's Office of Small and Disadvantaged Business Utilization offers small businesses information and guidance on procurement procedures, how to be placed on a bidder's mailing list, and identification of both prime and subcontracting opportunities.

ONE STOP CAPITAL SHOP

The following is a list of One Stop Capital Shops, arranged alphabetically by state.

67356 ■ One Stop Capital Shop (Glendale)
330 N. Brand, Ste. 1200
Glendale, CA 91203-2304
Ph:(818)552-3308
Fax: (818)552-3286
Contact: Cyndi Jones, Facilitator
E-mail: cyndi.jones@sba.gov

67357 ■ One Stop Capital Shop (Oakland)
519 17th St., Ste. 600
519 17th St.
Oakland, CA 94612
Ph:(510)238-3703
Fax: (510)238-7999
URL: http://www.oakland1stop.org
Contact: Michael Elkin, Facilitator
E-mail: michael.elkin@sba.gov

67358 ■ One Stop Capital Shop (Atlanta)
675 Ponce de Leon Ave. N., 1st Fl.
Atlanta, GA 30308
Ph:(404)853-7675
Fax: (404)853-7677
URL: http://www.apps.atlantage.gov/resserv/atlonestop.html
Contact: David W. Perry, Facilitator
E-mail: dwperry1@sba.gov

67359 ■ One Stop Capital Shop (Kansas City)
UMB Bank Bldg.
601 Minnesota Ave., 3rd Fl.
Kansas City, KS 66101
Ph:(913)371-6007
Fax: (913)371-3207
Co. E-mail: debra.ramsey@sba.gov
URL: http://www.sba.gov/mo/kansas/kc-oscs.html
Contact: Ray Williams, Facilitator
E-mail: ray.williams@sba.gov

67360 ■ One Stop Capital Shop (Somerset)
Small Business Development Center
2292 S. Hwy. 27, Ste. 260
Somerset, KY 42501
Ph:(606)677-6120
Fax: (606)622-1413
Contact: Kay Stucker, Facilitator
E-mail: kstucker@centertech.com

67361 ■ One Stop Capital Shop (Baltimore)
34 Market Pl., Ste. 800
34 Market Place, 8th Fl.
Baltimore, MD 21202
Ph:(410)783-4222
Fax: (410)783-4637
Contact: Hallot Watkins, Facilitator
E-mail: Hallot.Watkins@sba.gov

67362 ■ One Stop Capital Shop (Roxbury)
20 Hampden St.
Roxbury, MA 02119
Ph:(617)445-3413
Fax: (617)445-5675
Contact: Armando Fernandez, Facilitator

E-mail: armando.fernandez@sba.gov

67363 ■ One Stop Capital Shop (Detroit)
2051 Rosa Parks Blvd.
Detroit, MI 48216
Ph:(313)965-1100
Fax: (313)965-1101
Contact: Connie Logan, Facilitator
E-mail: connie.logan@sba.gov

67364 ■ One Stop Capital Shop (Mississippi Mid-Delta)
L.S. Rogers Bldg.
14000 Hwy. 82 W.
Itta Bena, MS 38941
Ph:(601)254-3730
Fax: (601)254-3734
Contact: John Greer, Facilitator
E-mail: john.greer@sba.gov

67365 ■ One Stop Capital Shop (Jamaica)
90-33 160th St.
Jamaica, NY 11432-6125
Ph:(718)206-2255
Fax: (718)206-3693
Co. E-mail: JBRCenter@aol.com
URL: http://www.jbrc.org

67366 ■ One Stop Capital Shop (New York)
290 Lenox Ave., 2nd Fl.
New York, NY 10027
Ph:(212)876-2246
Fax: (212)876-4236
URL: http://www.brisc.umez.org
Contact: Norman Hunt, Facilitator

67367 ■ One Stop Capital Shop (Bismarck)
700 E. Main Ave., 2nd Fl.
P.O. Box 5509
Bismarck, ND 58506
Ph:(701)328-5850
Free: 800-544-4674
Fax: (701)250-4304
Contact: Mike Gallagher, Facilitator
E-mail: michael.gallagher@aba.gov

67368 ■ One Stop Capital Shop (Hugo)
Little Dixie Community Action Agency
502 W. Duke St.
Hugo, OK 74743
Ph:(580)326-3351
Fax: (580)326-2305
Contact: Jerry Reese, Facilitator
E-mail: jerry.reese@sba.gov

67369 ■ One Stop Capital Shop (Philadelphia/Camden)
The Small Business Support Center
1315 Walnut St.
Philadelphia, PA 19107
Ph:(215)790-5000
Fax: (215)790-2222
Contact: Joseph McDevitt, Facilitator
E-mail: Joseph.McDevitt@sba.gov

67370 ■ One Stop Capital Shop (Edinburg)
2412 S. Closner
Edinburg, TX 78539
Ph:(956)316-2610
Fax: (956)316-2612
Contact: Alonzo Gracia, Facilitator
E-mail: alonzo.gracia@sba.gov

67371 ■ One Stop Capital Shop (Houston)–U.S. General Store
5330 Griggs Rd.
Houston, TX 77021
Ph:(713)643-8000
Fax: (713)643-8193
Co. E-mail: james.blanton@sba.gov
Contact: Neal Blanton, Facilitator

67372 ■ One Stop Capital Shop (Tacoma)
KeyBank Bldg.
1101 Pacific Ave.
Tacoma, WA 98402
Ph:(253)274-1288

Fax: (253)274-1289
Contact: Bill Bell, Facilitator
E-mail: bill.bell@sba.gov

PATENT AND TRADEMARK OFFICE

67373 ■ Patent and Trademark Office–Board of Patent Appeals and Inferences
Madison Bldg., E.
600 Dulany St., Ste. ME-A974-A
Alexandria, VA 22313
Ph:(571)272-9797
Fax: (571)273-0053
Co. E-mail: gary.harkcom@uspto.gov
URL: http://www.uspto.gov/web/offices/dcom/bpai/index.html

67374 ■ Patent and Trademark Office–Office of Enforcement
Madison Bldg., 10th Fl. W.
600 Dulany St.
Alexandria, VA 22313-1450
Ph:(571)272-9300
Co. E-mail: Robert.stoll@uspto.gov
URL: http://www.uspto.gov

67375 ■ Patent and Trademark Office–Office of Enrollment and Discipline
Madison W. Bldg.
600 Dulany St., 8th Fl., D Corridor
Alexandria, VA 22313
Ph:(571)272-4097
Fax: (571)273-0074
Co. E-mail: harry.moatz@uspto.gov
URL: http://www.uspto.gov/web/offices/dcom/gcounsel/oed.htm

67376 ■ Patent and Trademark Office–Office of Initial Patent Examination
PO Box 1450
Alexandria, VA 22313-1450
Ph:(703)308-9210
Fax: (703)746-9195
Co. E-mail: tom.koontz@uspto.gov
URL: http://www.uspto.gov

67377 ■ Patent and Trademark Office–Office of International Relations
Madison Bldg.
600 Dulany St., 10th Fl. W.
Alexandria, VA 22313-1450
Ph:(571)272-9300
Co. E-mail: lois.boland@uspto.gov
URL: http://www.uspto.gov

67378 ■ Patent and Trademark Office–Office of Patent and Cooperation Operations (PCT)
PO Box 1450
Alexandria, VA 22313-1450
Ph:(703)308-9290
Fax: (703)305-3230
Co. E-mail: don.levin@uspto.gov
URL: http://www.uspto.gov

67379 ■ Patent and Trademark Office–Office of Patent Publication
PO Box 1450
Alexandria, VA 22313-1450
Ph:(703)308-6789
Fax: (703)308-5065
Co. E-mail: dick.bawcombe@uspto.gov
URL: http://www.uspto.gov

67380 ■ Patent and Trademark Office–Office of Petitions
PO Box 1450
Alexandria, VA 22313-1450
Ph:(571)272-3282
Fax: (571)273-0025
Co. E-mail: cpearson@uspto.gov
URL: http://www.uspto.gov/web/offices/pac/dapp/petitionsmain.html

67381 ■ Patent and Trademark Office–Office of Procurement
Madison W. Bldg.
600 Dulany St.
PO Box 1450
Alexandria, VA 22313-1450
Ph:(703)305-8014
Fax: (571)273-0464
URL: http://www.uspto.gov

67382 ■ Patent and Trademark Office–Office of Public Affairs
Madison W. Bldg.
600 Dulany St.
Alexandria, VA 22313-1450
Ph:(517)272-8400
Free: 800-786-9199
Fax: (517)272-0340
URL: http://www.uspto.gov/web/offices/ac/ahrpa/opa/index.html
Description: The Patent and Trademark Office examines applications for patents and trademarks to determine whether an invention is patentable or if a trademark may be registered. Patents and trademarks, because of the legal rights they represent, are important to small businesses competing against larger or more established businesses. The Patent and Trademark Office maintains the Public Search Room for use by individuals wishing to identify new products, find solutions to problems, or check patents in a field of technology. The Patent and Trademark Office's Trademark Search Room is also open to the public. In addition, the office sponsors a system of Patent Depository Libraries, which brings collections of U.S. patents to within one hour commuting time of 45 percent of the U.S. population. An automated system known as CASSIS (Classification and Search Support Information System) is available in most of the libraries. CASSIS provides free, online access to the Patent and Trademark Office's classification databases to assist users in their patent searches.

SECURITIES AND EXCHANGE COMMISSION

67383 ■ Securities and Exchange Commission–Office of Small Business Policy–Small Business Ombudsman (100 F)
100 F St., NE
Washington, DC 20549-0310
Ph:(202)551-3460
Co. E-mail: smallbusiness@sec.gov
URL: http://www.sec.gov/info/smallbus/reachsec.htm
Contact: William E. Toomey, Deputy Chief
Description: The Security and Exchange Commission's responsibilities under the securities laws are to protect investors and to ensure that capital markets operate in a fair and orderly manner. Nevertheless, the SEC believes that its regulations should not have the effect of inadvertently impairing capital formation by small businesses. Therefore the SEC has taken a number of steps to facilitate capital-raising by small businesses and to reduce undue regulatory burdens arising from the federal securities laws. The SEC is in a continuous process of examining other ways to further aid in accomplishing these goals. The SEC's Office of Small Business Policy, for example, directs the commission's small business rulemaking initiatives. It also reviews and comments on the impact of SEC rule proposals on smaller issuers and serves as a liaison with Congressional committees, government agencies, and other groups concerned with small business.

The following district and regional offices are arranged alphabetically by organization name.

67384 ■ Securities and Exchange Commission–Atlanta District Office
3475 Lenox Rd. NE, Ste. 1000
Atlanta, GA 30326-1232
Ph:(404)842-7600
Fax: (404)842-7666
Co. E-mail: Atlanta@sec.gov
URL: http://www.sec.gov
Description: Serves Alabama, Florida, Georgia, Louisiana (eastern portion), Mississippi, North Carolina,

Puerto Rico, South Carolina, Tennessee, and the Virgin Islands.

67385 ■ Securities and Exchange Commission–Boston District Office
73 Tremont St., Ste. 600
Boston, MA 02108-3912
Ph:(617)424-5900
Fax: (617)573-8900
Co. E-mail: boston@sec.gov
URL: http://www.sec.gov
Description: Serves Connecticut, Maine, Massachusetts, New Hampshire, Rhode Island, and Vermont.

67386 ■ Securities and Exchange Commission–Central Regional Office (Denver)
1801 California St., Ste. 1500
Denver, CO 80202-2656
Ph:(303)844-1000
Fax: (303)391-6868
Co. E-mail: Denver@sec.gov
URL: http://www.sec.gov
Description: Serves Colorado, Nebraska, New Mexico, North Dakota, South Dakota, Utah, and Wyoming.

67387 ■ Securities and Exchange Commission–Fort Worth District Office
801 Cherry St., 19th Fl.
Ft. Worth, TX 76102
Ph:(817)978-3821
Fax: (817)334-2700
Co. E-mail: dfw@sec.gov
URL: http://www.sec.gov
Description: Serves Arkansas, Kansas, Louisiana (western portion), Oklahoma, and Texas.

67388 ■ Securities and Exchange Commission–Midwest Regional Office (Chicago)
175 W. Jackson Blvd., Ste. 900
Chicago, IL 60604
Ph:(312)353-7390
Fax: (312)353-7398
Co. E-mail: Chicago@sec.gov
URL: http://www.sec.gov
Description: Serves Illinois, Indiana, Iowa, Kentucky, Michigan, Minnesota, Missouri, Ohio, and Wisconsin.

67389 ■ Securities and Exchange Commission–Northeast Regional Office (New York)
3 World Financial Ctr., Rm. 4300
New York, NY 10281
Ph:(212)336-1100
Co. E-mail: newyork@sec.gov
URL: http://www.sec.gov
Description: Serves New Jersey and New York.

67390 ■ Securities and Exchange Commission–Pacific Regional Office (Los Angeles)
5670 Wilshire Blvd., 11th Fl.
Los Angeles, CA 90036-3648
Ph:(323)965-3998
Fax: (323)965-3815
Co. E-mail: losangeles@sec.gov
URL: http://www.sec.gov
Description: Serves Arizona, California, Guam, Hawaii, Nevada, Alaska, Idaho, Montana, Oregon, and Washington.

67391 ■ Securities and Exchange Commission–Philadelphia District Office
The Mellon Independence Center
700 Market St.
Philadelphia, PA 19106-1532
Ph:(215)597-3100
Fax: (215)597-5885
Co. E-mail: philadelphia@sec.gov
URL: http://www.sec.gov
Description: Serves Delaware, the District of Columbia, Maryland, Pennsylvania, Virginia, and West Virginia.

The following branch and district offices are arranged alphabetically by city.

67392 ■ Securities and Exchange Commission–Salt Lake District Office
15 W. South Temple St., Ste. 1800
Salt Lake City, UT 84101
Ph:(801)524-5796
Fax: (801)524-3558
Co. E-mail: saltlake@sec.gov
URL: http://www.sec.gov
Description: Administered by the Denver regional office.

67393 ■ Securities and Exchange Commission–San Francisco District Office
44 Montgomery St., Ste. 1100
San Francisco, CA 94104
Ph:(415)705-2500
Fax: (415)705-2501
Co. E-mail: sanfrancisco@sec.gov
URL: http://www.sec.gov
Description: Administered by the Los Angeles regional office.

67394 ■ Securities and Exchange Commission–Southeast Regional Office
801 Brickell Ave., Ste. 1800
Miami, FL 33131
Ph:(305)982-6300
Co. E-mail: miami@sec.gov
URL: http://www.sec.gov
Description: Administered by the Atlanta regional office.

SMITHSONIAN INSTITUTION

67395 ■ Smithsonian Institute–Office of Small and Disadvantaged Business Utilization
759 9th St., NW, Ste. 8100
Washington, DC 20013
Ph:(202)275-0157
Fax: (202)326-2050
Co. E-mail: marsher@si.edu
URL: http://www.si.edu

TENNESSEE VALLEY AUTHORITY

67396 ■ Tennessee Valley Authority
400 W. Summit Hill Dr.
Knoxville, TN 37902-1499
Ph:(865)632-2101
Co. E-mail: tvainfo@tva.com
URL: http://www.tva.gov

67397 ■ Tennessee Valley Authority–Minority Economic and Small Business Development
PO Box 292409
Nashville, TN 37229-2409
Ph:(423)632-2101
Co. E-mail: tvainfo.@.gov
URL: http://www.tva.gov
Description: The Tennessee Valley Authority maintains agency-wide Minority Economic Development initiatives that assist small minority and women-owned businesses (SMWOBs) that seek TVA business opportunities, as well as, the entire business community of the Valley. TVA's Economic Development organization provides capital, technical, and managerial assistance for SMWOBs, start-ups, retention and expansions. Assistance takes the form of revolving loan funds, pulic/private partnerships that administer training programs, and in-house technical assistance. Through its Procurement organizations, TVA encourages minority participation in prime and subcontracting opportunities. Its policy is to promote the full participation of SMWOBs in all of its procurement and contracting activities. Further, priority shall be given to fostering the economic development of the Valley through use of products and services of such firms located in the Valley region. TVA's commitment is to maximize participation through the development of mutually beneficial business relationships with these firms consistent with achieving the best value to TVA.

U.S. DEPARTMENT OF AGRICULTURE

67398 ■ U.S. Department of Agriculture–Office of Small and Disadvantaged Business Utilization
1400 Independence Ave., SW
South Bldg., Rm. 1085
Washington, DC 20250
Ph:(202)720-7117
Fax: (202)720-3001
URL: http://www.usda.gov/osdbu
Description: The USDA's Office of Small and Disadvantaged Business Utilization offers information and other services to minority-owned, women-owned, and small and disadvantaged businesses to assist them in increasing and maintaining their participation in the department's procurement and other program opportunities. The department has 18 major procurement offices, and an additional 260 offices across the country that offer procurement assistance to the small business community. These services are provided to increase the overall viability and competitiveness of businesses as part of maintaining an economically strong national industrial and commercial base. Emphasis is given to assisting firms that can contribute to revitalizing the nation's rural communities, improving the private agricultural sector's foreign trade competitiveness, and/or increasing the federal government's productivity. The department procures approximately $2 billion in products and services each year, $1 billion of which is awarded to minority-owned, women-owned, and small and disadvantaged businesses.

The following USDA agencies are arranged alphabetically.

67399 ■ U.S. Department of Agriculture–Administrative Services Division–Farmers Home Administration (1400)–Office of Small and Disadvantaged Business Utilization Coordinator (Independen)
1400 Independence Ave. SW
AG Stop 9501, Rm. 1566 S.
Washington, DC 20250
Ph:(202)720-7117
Fax: (202)720-3001
Co. E-mail: jamese.house@usda.gov
URL: http://www.usda.gov/osdbu

67400 ■ U.S. Department of Agriculture–Administrative Services Division–Food and Nutrition Service (3101)–Office of Small and Disadvantaged Business Utilization Coordinator (Park Cente)
3101 Park Center Dr., Rm. 914
Alexandria, VA 22302
Ph:(703)305-2250
Co. E-mail: patsy_palmer@FNS.udsa.gov

67401 ■ U.S. Department of Agriculture–Administrative Services Division–Rural Electrification Administration (1400)–Office of Small and Disadvantaged Business Utilization Coordinator (Independen)
1400 Independence Ave., SW
AG Stop 9501, Rm. 1566 S.
Washington, DC 20250
Ph:(202)720-7117
Fax: (202)720-3001
Co. E-mail: jamese.house@usda.gov
URL: http://www.usda.gov/osdbu

67402 ■ U.S. Department of Agriculture–Administrative Services Division–U.S. Forest Service (Rossl)–Office of Small and Disadvantaged Business Utilization Coordinator (yn Plz.-E,)
Rosslyn Plz.-E, Rm. 706
PO Box 96090
Washington, DC 20090-6090
Ph:(703)605-4744

67403 ■ U.S. Department of Agriculture–Agricultural Research Service–Office of Small and Disadvantaged Business Utilization (6303)
6303 Ivy Ln., Ste. 838
Greenbelt, MD 20770-1433
Ph:(301)344-2878

67404 ■ U.S. Department of Agriculture–Contracting and Acquisition Management Division–Agricultural Stabilization and Conservation Service (14th)–Office of Small and Disadvantaged Business Utilization Coordinator (St. & Inde)
14th St. & Independence Ave., SW
South Bldg., Rm. 6958
Washington, DC 20250
Ph:(202)690-0689

67405 ■ U.S. Department of Agriculture–Contracts and Procurement Branch–Office of the Inspector General (1400)–Office of Small and Disadvantaged Business Utilization Coordinator (Independen)
1400 Independence Ave., SW
Administration Bldg., Rm. 40-E
Washington, DC 20250
Ph:(202)720-5931

67406 ■ U.S. Department of Agriculture–Cooperative State Research, Education, and Extension Service (CSREES)–Small Business Innovation Research Representative (Water)
Waterfront Centre
1400 Independence Ave., SW
Mail Stop 2201
Washington, DC 20250-2201
Ph:(202)720-7441
Fax: (202)720-8987

67407 ■ U.S. Department of Agriculture–Management Services Branch–Extension Service (South)–Office of Small and Disadvantaged Business Utilization Coordinator (Agricultu)
South Agriculture Bldg.
1400 Independence Ave., SW, Rm. 1566 S.
Washington, DC 20250
Ph:(202)720-7117
Fax: (202)720-3001
URL: http://www.usda.gov/da/smallbus

67408 ■ U.S. Department of Agriculture–Management Services Division–Animal and Plant Health Inspection Service (4700)–Office of Small and Disadvantaged Business Utilization Coordinator (River Rd.)
4700 River Rd.
Riverdale, MD 20737
Ph:(301)734-5684

67409 ■ U.S. Department of Agriculture–Management Services Division–Farm Service Agency (1400)–Office of Small and Disadvantaged Business Utilization Coordinator (Independen)
1400 Independence Ave., SW
Mail Stop 0567
Washington, DC 20250-0567
Ph:(202)720-7335
URL: http://www.fsa.usda.gov/amb

67410 ■ U.S. Department of Agriculture–Management Services Division–Natural Resources Conservation Service (1400)–Office of Small and Disadvantaged Business Utilization Coordinator (Independen)
1400 Independence Ave., SW
South Bldg., Rm. 0106
Washington, DC 20250
Ph:(202)720-8758
Co. E-mail: terry.kirby@usda.gov

67411 ■ U.S. Department of Agriculture–Procurement Division–Office of Operations (USDA)–Office of Small and Disadvantaged Business Utilization Coordinator (Reporters)
USDA Reporters Bldg.
300 7th St. SW, Ste. 377
Washington, DC 20250
Ph:(202)720-2649

67412 ■ U.S. Department of Agriculture–Procurement and Property Branch–Food Safety and Inspection Service (14th)
14th St. & Independence Ave. SW
South Bldg., Rm. 2128
Washington, DC 20250
Ph:(202)720-8215

67413 ■ U.S. Department of Agriculture–Procurement, Property and Space–Economics Management Staff (14th)
14th St. & Independence Ave. SW
South Bldg., Rm. 1310
Washington, DC 20250
Ph:(202)720-3998

67414 ■ U.S. Department of Agriculture–Resources Management Staff–Office of Communications (1400)
1400 Independence Ave., SW
James L. Whitten Bldg., Rm. 535-A
Washington, DC 20250
Ph:(202)720-3118
Co. E-mail: tlogan@usda.gov
URL: http://www.usda.gov/da/smallbus/sbcoord.htm

U.S. DEPARTMENT OF COMMERCE

67415 ■ U.S. Department of Commerce–Office of Small and Disadvantaged Business Utilization
Herbert Clark Hoover Bldg., Rm. 6411
14th St. & Constitution Ave. NW
Washington, DC 20230
Ph:(202)482-1472
Fax: (202)482-0501
Co. E-mail: ldesmukes@doc.gov
URL: http://www.commerce.gov

67416 ■ U.S. Department of Commerce–Economic Development Administration
Herbert Clark Hoover Bldg.
1401 Constitution Ave., NW
Washington, DC 20230
Ph:(202)482-5081
URL: http://www.eda.gov

67417 ■ U.S. Department of Commerce–Office of Business Liaison
Herbert Clark Hoover Bldg., Rm. 5062
1401 Constitution Ave., NW
Washington, DC 20230
Ph:(202)482-1360
Fax: (202)482-4054
URL: http://www.osec.doc.gov/obl
Description: The Department of Commerce's Office of Business Liaison seeks to develop and promote a cooperative working relationship and to assure effective communication between the department and the business community, including small businesses. The office serves as the focal point for all of the department's agencies to contact the business community. It informs the business community of department and administration resources, policies, and programs, as well as informs department and administration officials about business community interests and issues. In addition, the office promotes business involvement in departmental policymaking and program development. The office also provides business assistance to individuals and firms that need help dealing with the federal government. The Business Assistance Pro-

gram provides professional staff members to give guidance on the many federal programs; to answer inquiries concerning government policies, programs, and services; and to provide information and published materials on a variety of business topics.

U.S. DEPARTMENT OF DEFENSE

67418 ■ Defense Information Systems Agency (DISA)–Office of Small and Disadvantaged Business Utilization
701 S. Courthouse Rd., D04 RM. 1108B
Arlington, VA 22204-2199
Ph:(703)607-6436
Fax: (703)607-4173
Co. E-mail: disasmallbusinessoffice@disa.mil

67419 ■ Defense Threat Reduction Agency–Office of Small and Disadvantaged Business Utilization
6801 Telegraph Rd.
Alexandria, VA 22310-3398
Ph:(703)767-7889
Co. E-mail: edward.archer@dtra.mil

67420 ■ Office of Civil Rights–Office of Small and Disadvantaged Business Utilization
400 7th St., SW, Rm. 5414A
Washington, DC 20590
Ph:(202)366-1732
Fax: (202)366-7717
Co. E-mail: beatrice.pacheco@ost.dot.gov

67421 ■ U.S. Department of Defense–Office of Small and Disadvantaged Business Utilization
The Pentagon, Rm. 3B514
Washington, DC 20301-0106
Ph:(703)697-2868
Fax: (703)693-2898
URL: http://www.acq.osd.mil/sadbu
Description: One of the primary objectives of the Department of Defense (DOD) is to acquire weapons and materials that fully meet qualitative, quantitative, and delivery requirements at the lowest overall cost. Maximum emphasis is placed on full and free competition to achieve this objective, with equal opportunity to all interested, qualified suppliers to compete for defense contracts. The Department of Defense's military departments and defense agencies have contracting offices located throughout the United States. Each department and agency has an office of the director of small and disadvantaged business utilization. They also have small business specialists at each of their procurement and contract administration offices to assist small and disadvantaged businesses, women-owned businesses, minority-owned businesses, and firms to market their products and services with the DOD. These specialists can provide information and guidance on defense procurement procedures, placement on the solicitation mailing lists, and identification of both prime and subcontract opportunities.

The following offices, arranged alphabetically, provide information and guidance about federal procurement programs.

67422 ■ Ballistic Missile Defense Organization
7100 Defense Pentagon
Washington, DC 20301-7100
Ph:(703)693-6634
Co. E-mail: mda.info@mda.mil
URL: http://www.mda.mil

67423 ■ Defense Information Systems Agency
PO Box 4502
Arlington, VA 22204-4502
Ph:(703)607-6515
Fax: (703)607-4344
URL: http://www.disa.mil

67424 ■ Office of the Secretary of the Army–Office of Small and Disadvantaged Business Utilization
106 Defense Pentagon
Washington, DC 20310-0106
Ph:(703)697-2868
Fax: (703)693-3898
URL: http://www.sellingtoarmy.info

67425 ■ Office of the Under Secretary of the Navy–Director of Small and Disadvantaged Business Utilization
Washington Navy Yard, Bldg. 36, Rm. 207
720 Kennon St., NE
Washington, DC 20374-5015
Ph:(202)685-6485
Fax: (202)685-6865
URL: http://www.hq.navy.mil/sadbu

The following defense plant representative offices are arranged alphabetically by state.

67426 ■ Defense Plant Representative Office (Tucson)
Hughes Aircraft Co.
Missile Systems Group
PO Box 11337
Tucson, AZ 85734-1337
Ph:(602)794-2575
Fax: (602)794-3275

67427 ■ Defense Plant Representative Office (Los Angeles)
Hughes Aircraft Co.
PO Box 92463
Los Angeles, CA 90009-2463
Ph:(310)364-8097

67428 ■ Defense Plant Representative Office (West Palm Beach)
Pratt & Whitney Aircraft Group
Government Engine and Space Propulsion Division
PO Box 109600
West Palm Beach, FL 33410-9600
Ph:(561)96—7319

67429 ■ Defense Plant Representative Office (Marietta)
c/o Lockheed Georgia Co.
86 S. Cobb Dr.
Marietta, GA 30063-0260
Ph:(404)494-2016

67430 ■ Naval Technical Representative Office (Laurel)
Johns Hopkins Rd.
Laurel, MD 20723-6090
Ph:(301)953-5230
Fax: (301)953-6370

67431 ■ Defense Plant Representative Office (Great Neck)
Defense Logistics Agency
Northeast DPRO
c/o Unisys Corp.
365 Lakerville Rd.
Great Neck, NY 11020-1696
Ph:(516)574-2987
Fax: (516)228-5938

The following area operations are arranged alphabetically by state.

67432 ■ Defense Contract Management Center
1910 Third Ave. N., Ste. 201
Birmingham, AL 35203-3502
Ph:(205)716-7402
Fax: (205)716-7836

67433 ■ Defense Contract Administration, Services, and Management Area Operations (Phoenix)
The Monroe School Bldg.
215 N. 7th St.
Phoenix, AZ 85034-1012
Ph:(602)379-6170

Fax: (602)379-6409
URL: http://www.dtic.dla.mil/defenselink/

**67434 ■ Defense Contract Management Area
Operations (San Diego)**
7675 Dagget St., Ste. 200
San Diego, CA 92111-2241
Ph:(858)495-7401
Fax: (858)-495-7660

**67435 ■ Defense Contract Management Area
Operations (San Francisco)**
1265 Borregas Ave.
Sunnyvale, CA 94089
Ph:(408)541-7042
Fax: (408)541-7084
Co. E-mail: jfosbery@dcmdw.dla.mil

**67436 ■ Defense Contract Management Area
Operations (Van Nuys)**
6230 Van Nuys Blvd.
Van Nuys, CA 91401-2713
Ph:(818)756-4444
Fax: (818)904-6532
Co. E-mail: romeo_allas@vnyao.dcmdw.dla.mil

**67437 ■ Defense Contract Management
Command (Santa Ana)**
34 Civic Center Plz.
PO Box C-12700
Santa Ana, CA 92712-2700
Ph:(714)836-2912
Fax: (714)836-2358
URL: http://ga.dcmdw.dla.mil/

**67438 ■ Defense Contract Management
Center (Denver)**
Orchard Pl. 2
5975 Greenwood Plaza Blvd., Ste. 200
Englewood, CO 80111-4751
Ph:(303)220-4005
Fax: (303)220-4125
Co. E-mail: dcmadenverseniorstaff@dcma.mil
URL: http://gd.dcmdw.dla.mil/

**67439 ■ Defense Contract Management
Center (East Hartford)**
130 Darlin St.
East Hartford, CT 06108-3234
Ph:(860)291-7702
Fax: (860)291-7905
Co. E-mail: dcmahartfordseniorleaders@dcma.mil

**67440 ■ Defense Contract Management
Center (Stratford)**
550 Main St.
Stratford, CT 06497-7574
Ph:(203)385-4418
Fax: (203)385-4418

**67441 ■ Defense Contract Management
Center (Orlando)**
3555 Maguire Blvd.
Orlando, FL 32803-3726
Ph:(407)228-5115
Fax: (407)228-5312
Co. E-mail: dcmaorlando@dcma.mil

**67442 ■ Defense Contract Management
Command (Clearwater)**
Gasden Bldg., Ste. 200
9549 Kroger Blvd.
St. Petersburg, FL 33702-2455
Ph:(813)579-3100
Fax: (813)579-3106

**67443 ■ Defense Contract Management
Command (Orlando)**
1425 Troutman Blvd., NE
Palm Bay, FL 32905-4102
Ph:(407)727-4367
Fax: (407)729-3334

**67444 ■ Defense Contract Management
Center - Aircraft Program–Management
Office**
805 Walker St.
Marietta, GA 30060-2789

Ph:(770)590-6197
Fax: (770)590-6551

**67445 ■ Defense Contract Management
Command (Atlanta)**
805 Walker St.
Marietta, GA 30060-2789
Ph:(770)590-6197
Fax: (770)590-6551

**67446 ■ Defense Contract Management
Command (Chicago)**
10601 W. Higgins Rd., Bldg. 4
PO Box 66911
Chicago, IL 60666-0911
Ph:(773)825-6800
Free: 800-637-3848
Fax: (773)825-5424
URL: http://www.dcmdc.hq.dla.mil

**67447 ■ Defense Contract Management
Center (Indianapolis)**
8899 E. 56th St.
Indianapolis, IN 46249-5701
Ph:(317)510-2016
Fax: (317)510-2348
Co. E-mail: indygid@dcma.mil
URL: http://www.indy.dcmde.dla.mil/

**67448 ■ Defense Contract Management
Command (Indianapolis-South Bend)**
244 S. Olive St.
South Bend, IN 46619-7726
Ph:(219)429-7726
Fax: (219)236-8118

**67449 ■ Defense Contract Management
Command (Wichita)**
271 W. 3rd St., N., Ste. 6000
401 N. Market, Ste. B-34
Wichita, KS 67202-1212
Ph:(316)299-7219
Fax: (316)299-7302
Co. E-mail: gluckman@mwest.dcmdw.dla.mil
URL: http://www.gk.dcmdw.dla.mil/

**67450 ■ Defense Contract Management
Command (Dayton-Louisville)**
120 Rochester Dr.
Louisville, KY 40214-2681
Ph:(502)364-6492

**67451 ■ Defense Contract Management
Center (Baltimore)**
217 E. Redwood St., Ste. 1800
Baltimore, MD 21202-5299
Ph:(410)962-9800
Fax: (410)962-3299
Co. E-mail: gtd@dcma.mil
URL: http://www.baltimore.dcmde.dla.mil/

**67452 ■ Defense Contract Management
Command (Boston)**
495 Summer St.
Boston, MA 02210-2138
Ph:(617)753-4006
Fax: (617)753-4005
Co. E-mail: casboston@dcma.mil

**67453 ■ Defense Contract Management
District Headquarters (Boston)**
495 Summer St., 8th Fl.
Boston, MA 02210-2184
Ph:(617)753-4317
Free: 800-321-1861
Fax: (617)753-3174

**67454 ■ Defense Contract Management Area
Operations (Detroit)**
905 McNamara Federal Bldg.
477 Michigan Ave., Rm. 515
Detroit, MI 48226
Ph:(313)226-6075
Fax: (313)226-4769

**67455 ■ Defense Contract Management Area
Operations (Grand Rapids)**
Riverview Center Bldg.
678 Front St. NW
Grand Rapids, MI 49504-5352
Ph:(616)233-4601
Fax: (616)233-4630
Co. E-mail: dcm_detroit@dcma.mil

**67456 ■ Defense Contract Management Area
Operations (Twin Cities)**
3001 Metro Dr., Ste. 200
Bloomington, MN 55425-1573
Ph:(612)814-4103
Fax: (612)814-4154
Co. E-mail: omurry@gt-link.dcmdc.dla.mil

**67457 ■ Defense Contract Management
Command (St. Louis)**
1222 Spruce St.
St. Louis, MO 63103-2812
Ph:(314)331-5431
Free: 800-797-8375
Fax: (314)331-5800
URL: http://www.gl.dcmdw.dla.mil/

**67458 ■ Defense Contract Management
Command (Boston-Manchester)**
2 Wall St.
Manchester, NH 03101-1518
Ph:(603)621-0413
Fax: (603)621-4835
Co. E-mail: casboston@dcma.mil

**67459 ■ Defense Contract Management Area
Operations (Springfield)**
955 S. Springfield Ave.
Springfield, NJ 07081-3170
Ph:(201)564-7204
Fax: (201)467-5387

**67460 ■ Defense Contract Management Area
Operations (Garden City)**
605 Stewart Ave.
Garden City, NY 11530-4761
Ph:(516)228-5722
Fax: (516)228-5938
Co. E-mail: dvc2251@dcrb.dla.mil

**67461 ■ Defense Contract Management Area
Operations (Syracuse)**
615 Erie Blvd. W., Ste. 300
Syracuse, NY 13204-2408
Ph:(315)423-8594
Fax: (315)423-8960
Co. E-mail: Syracuse_cas_poc@dcma.mil

**67462 ■ Defense Contract Management
Command (New York City)**
Ft. Wadsworth
Staten Island, NY 10305
Ph:(718)390-1016
Fax: (718)390-1020
URL: http://131.69.25.189/

**67463 ■ Defense Contract Management
Command (Syracuse-Buffalo)**
Thaddeus J. Dulski Federal Bldg., Rm. 1103
111 W. Huron St.
Buffalo, NY 14202-2392
Ph:(716)551-4761
Fax: (716)551-4531

**67464 ■ Defense Contract Management
Command (Cleveland)**
555 E. 88th St.
Bratenahl, OH 44108-1068
URL: http://www.dcro.dla.mil/

**67465 ■ Defense Contract Management
Command (Dayton)**
Area C, Bldg. 30
1725 Van Patton Dr.
Wright Patterson AFB, OH 45433-5302
Ph:(937)656-3104
Fax: (937)656-3228
URL: http://www.gcfeb.com/dcmcdayton/

67466 ■ Defense Contract Management Area Operations (Philadelphia)
2800 S. 20th St.
PO Box 7699
Philadelphia, PA 19101-7478
Ph:(215)737-5818
Fax: (215)737-7046

67467 ■ Defense Contract Management Area Operations (Pittsburgh)
1612 William S. Moorehead Federal Bldg.
1000 Liberty Ave.
Pittsburgh, PA 15222-4190
Ph:(412)644-5926
Fax: (412)644-5907

67468 ■ Defense Contract Management Area Operations (Reading)
1125 Berkshire Blvd., Ste. 160
Wyomissing, PA 19610-1249
Ph:(610)320-5012
Fax: (610)320-5075

67469 ■ Defense Contract Management Area Operations (San Antonio)
615 E. Houston St.
PO Box 1040
San Antonio, TX 78294-1040
Ph:(210)472-4667
Fax: (210)472-4667
Co. E-mail: contract@dcma.mil

67470 ■ Defense Contract Management Command (Dallas)
1200 Main St., Rm. 640
PO Box 50500
Dallas, TX 75202-4399
Ph:(214)670-9205
Free: 800-255-8574
Fax: (214)573-2185
URL: http://gb.dcmdw.dla.mil/

67471 ■ Defense Contract Management Command (Seattle)
3009 112th Ave., NE, Ste. 200
Bellevue, WA 98004-8019
Ph:(206)889-7317
Fax: (206)889-7252
URL: http://dcmc-seattle.dcmdw.dla.mil/

The following list of supply centers is arranged alphabetically.

67472 ■ Department of Defense–Defense Logistics Agency–Defense Construction Supply Center (3990)
3990 E. Broad St.
PO Box 3990
Columbus, OH 43218-3990
Ph:(614)692-3131
Co. E-mail: dlacontactcenter@dla.mil
URL: http://www.dscc.dla.mil

67473 ■ Department of Defense–Defense Logistics Agency–Defense Electronics Supply Center (1507)
1507 Wilmington Pke.
Dayton, OH 45444-5000
Ph:(513)296-5321
Fax: (513)296-5038

67474 ■ Department of Defense–Defense Logistics Agency–Defense General Supply Center (8000)
8000 Jefferson Davis Hwy.
Richmond, VA 23297-5764
Ph:(804)279-3617
Fax: (804)279-6615
URL: http://www.dscr.dla.mil

67475 ■ Department of Defense–Defense Logistics Agency–Defense Industrial Supply Center (700 R)
700 Robbins Ave.
Philadelphia, PA 19111-5092
Ph:(215)697-2747
Fax: (215)697-3465

Co. E-mail: discdu@disc.dla.mil
URL: http://www.dscp.dla/mil

67476 ■ Department of Defense–Defense Logistics Agency–Defense Personnel Support Center (2800)
2800 S. 20th St.
Philadelphia, PA 19101-8419
Ph:(215)737-2321
Free: 800-523-0705
Fax: (215)737-7116

U.S. DEPARTMENT OF EDUCATION

67477 ■ University of Delaware
33 Smith Hall
Newark, DE 19716-4311
Ph:(302)831-1466
Fax: (302)831-4205
Co. E-mail: dsacher@udel.edu
URL: http://www.udel.edu

67478 ■ U.S. Department of Education–Office of Small and Disadvantaged Business Utilization
400 Maryland Ave. SW, Rm. 7049, PCP
Washington, DC 20202-0521
Ph:(202)245-6300
Fax: (202)245-7304
URL: http://www.ed.gov/offices/ods
Description: The Department of Education solicits proposals for the following services and materials: management consulting; program evaluation or surveys; computer-based projects; student testing materials; plus other professional services. In addition, federal funds may be used by schools, state agencies, and other recipients for the purchase of audiovisual and other types of equipment. Inquiries should be made to the applicable organization. The department also provides various publications to aid small businesses in their dealings. These publications include *A Guide to U.S. Department of Education Programs.* This annual guide provides the information necessary to begin the process of applying for funding from individual federal education programs. Another publication is *Doing Business With the Department of Education.* This guide is designed to provide business firms, small businesses, small disadvantaged businesses, and small disadvantaged subcontractors with basic information on contracting opportunities with the Department of Education. A "Forecast of Contract Opportunities" is also available listing upcoming contracts, which is distributed by the OSDBU office.

67479 ■ U.S. Department of Education–Assistant Secretary for Educational Research and Improvement–Small Business Innovation Research Program Coordinator (Capit)
Capitol Pl.
555 New Jersey Ave., NW
Washington, DC 20208-5644
Ph:(202)219-2004
Co. E-mail: lee.eiden@ed.gov

U.S. DEPARTMENT OF ENERGY

67480 ■ U.S. Department of Energy–Argonne National Laboratory (West)–Idaho Operations Office (1955)
1955 N. Freemont Ave.
PO Box 1625
Idaho Falls, ID 83415
Ph:(208)533-7341
URL: http://www.inl.gov

67481 ■ U.S. Department of Energy–Bettis Atomic Power Laboratory
c/o Bechtel Bettis, Inc.
814 Pittsburgh McKeesport Blvd.
West Mifflin, PA 15122-0079

Ph:(412)476-5000
URL: http://www.bettislab.com
Description:

67482 ■ U.S. Department of Energy–National Energy Technology Laboratory (NETL-MGN)
3610 Collins Ferry Rd.
PO Box 880
Morgantown, WV 26507-0880
Ph:(304)285-4764
Free: 800-553-7681
Co. E-mail: anna@netl.doe.gov
URL: http://www.netl.doe.gov

67483 ■ U.S. Department of Energy–Pittsburgh Naval Reactors (PNR)
814 Pittsburgh McKeesport Blvd.
West Mifflin, PA 15122-0109
Ph:(412)476-5000

67484 ■ U.S. Department of Energy–Schenectady Navel Reactors Office
Knolls Atomic Power Lab
U.S. DOE Bldg., MS Warehouse
2401 River Rd.
Schenectady, NY 12309
Ph:(518)395-4000

67485 ■ Waste Isolation Pilot Plant
Carlsbad Field Office
4021 National Parks Hwy.
Carlsbad, NM 88221
Free: 800-336-9477

67486 ■ U.S. Department of Energy, Headquarters–Office of Small and Disadvantaged Business Utilization
1000 Independence Ave. SW, Rm. 5B-148
1000 Independence Ave. SW
Washington, DC 20585
Ph:(202)586-7377
Fax: (202)586-5488
URL: http://www.osdbu.gov
Description: The Department of Energy purchases a wide variety of materials, equipment, supplies, and support services at each DOE buying office. Small business/disadvantaged business specialists are located at DOE offices throughout the United States to assist small business owners in procurement matters. DOE also administers—together with the National Bureau of Standards—the Energy-Related Inventions Program, a comprehensive program for research and development of all potentially beneficial energy sources and utilization technologies. The program calls for particular attention to be paid to individual inventors and small companies seeking direct grants (for information on this program call (301)975-5500).

The following is a list of DOE procurement operations offices arranged alphabetically.

67487 ■ U.S. Department of Energy–Albuquerque Operations Office
PO Box 5400
Albuquerque, NM 87185-5400
Ph:(505)845-0011
Fax: (505)845-4420

67488 ■ U.S. Department of Energy–Chicago Operations Office
9800 S. Cass Ave.
Argonne, IL 60439
Ph:(630)252-2000
Fax: (630)252-2527
URL: http://www.anl.gov

67489 ■ U.S. Department of Energy–Idaho Operations Office
850 Energy Dr.
Idaho Falls, ID 83401-1563
Ph:(208)526-1322
Fax: (208)526-5406

67490 ■ U.S. Department of Energy–Nevada Operations Office
PO Box 98518
Las Vegas, NV 89193-8518

Ph:(702)295-3521

67491 ■ U.S. Department of Energy–Oak Ridge Operations Office
200 Administration Rd.
PO Box 2001
Oak Ridge, TN 37831
Ph:(865)576-0885
Free: 800-382-6938
Fax: (865)576-1665
URL: http://www.oakridge.doe.gov

67492 ■ U.S. Department of Energy–Oakland Operations Office
Federal Bldg., Ste. 700N
1301 Clay St.
Oakland, CA 94612-5208
Ph:(510)637-1762
Co. E-mail: judy.weisse@oak.doe.gov
URL: http://www.oak.doe.gov

67493 ■ U.S. Department of Energy–Richland Operations Office
PO Box 550, A7-75
Richland, WA 99352
Ph:(509)376-7501
Fax: (509)376-1563

67494 ■ U.S. Department of Energy–Savannah River Operations Office
PO Box A
Aiken, SC 29802
Ph:(803)952-7697
Co. E-mail: james-r.qiusti@srs.gov
URL: http://sro.srs.gov/index.html

The following support offices, arranged alphabetically, are administered by the Albuquerque Operations Office.

67495 ■ U.S. Department of Energy–Amarillo Field Office
801 S. Fillmore St., Ste. 500
Amarillo, TX 79101-3545
Ph:(806)356-1000
Fax: (806)356-1041

67496 ■ U.S. Department of Energy–Carlsbad Field Office
620 E. Greene St.
Carlsbad, NM 88220-6292
Ph:(505)887-6544
Fax: (505)885-9264

67497 ■ U.S. Department of Energy–Kirtland Area Office
PO Box 5400
Albuquerque, NM 87185-5400
Ph:(505)845-4094
Fax: (505)845-6867

67498 ■ U.S. Department of Energy–Los Alamos Area Office
528 35th St.
Los Alamos, NM 87544
Ph:(505)667-5491
Fax: (505)665-1718

67499 ■ U.S. Department of Energy–Office of Kansas City Site Operations
2000 E. 9th St.
PO Box 410202
Kansas City, MO 64131-3202
Ph:(816)997-2000
Fax: (816)997-5059

67500 ■ U.S. Department of Energy–Pinellas Area Office
PO Box 2900
Largo, FL 33779
Ph:(813)541-8196
Fax: (813)545-6287

The following support offices, arranged alphabetically, are administered by the Chicago Operations Office.

67501 ■ U.S. Department of Energy–Argonne Area Office
9700 S. Cass Ave.
Argonne, IL 60439
Ph:(630)252-2200
Fax: (630)252-5274

67502 ■ U.S. Department of Energy–Boston Regional Office
John F. Kennedy Federal Bldg., Rm. 675
Boston, MA 02203-0002
Ph:(617)565-9700
Fax: (617)565-9723

67503 ■ U.S. Department of Energy–Brookhaven Area Office
53 Bell Ave., Bldg. 464
53 Bell Ave.
Upton, NY 11973
Ph:(631)344-3427

67504 ■ U.S. Department of Energy–Chicago Regional Office
1 S. Wacker Dr., Ste. 2380
Chicago, IL 60606-4616
Ph:(312)353-6749
Fax: (312)886-8561

67505 ■ U.S. Department of Energy–Energy Efficiency and Renewable Energy–Golden Field Office (1617)
1617 Cole Blvd.
Mail Stop 1501
Golden, CO 80401
Ph:(303)275-4700
Fax: (303)275-4788
URL: http://www.eere.energy.gov

67506 ■ U.S. Department of Energy–Firmi Site Office
PO Box 2000
Mail Stop 118
Kirk Rd. & Pine St.
Batavia, IL 60510-0500
Ph:(630)840-3000

67507 ■ U.S. Department of Energy–Philadelphia Regional Support Office
1880 John F. Kennedy Blvd., Ste. 501
Philadelphia, PA 19103-7483
Ph:(215)656-6950
Fax: (215)656-6981

67508 ■ U.S. Department of Energy–Princeton Area Office
PO Box 102
Princeton, NJ 08542
Ph:(609)243-3700
Fax: (609)243-2032

67509 ■ U.S. Department of Energy–U.S. Department of Homeland Security–Environmental Measurements Lab (201 V)
201 Varick Street - 5th Floor
New York, NY 10014-7447
Ph:(212)620-3619
Fax: (212)620-3651
Co. E-mail: mitchell.erickson@dhs.gov
URL: http://www.eml.doe.gov

The following support offices, arranged alphabetically, are administered by the Idaho Operations Office.

67510 ■ U.S. Department of Energy–Denver Regional Office
1617 Cole Blvd.
Mail Stop 1521
Golden, CO 80401
Ph:(303)275-4826

The following support office is administered by the Savannah River Operations Office.

67511 ■ U.S. Department of Energy–Atlanta Support Office
730 Peachtree St. NE, Ste. 876
Atlanta, GA 30308-1212

Ph:(404)347-2837
Fax: (404)347-3098

The following energy technology centers are arranged alphabetically.

67512 ■ U.S. Department of Energy–Bartlesville Project Office
PO Box 1398
Bartlesville, OK 74005
Ph:(918)337-4405
Fax: (918)337-4418

67513 ■ U.S. Department of Energy–Morgantown Energy Technology Center
3610 Collins Ferry Rd.
PO Box 880
Morgantown, WV 26507-0880
Ph:(304)285-4764
Fax: (304)285-4292
URL: http://www.netl.doe.gov

67514 ■ U.S. Department of Energy–Pittsburgh Energy Technology Center
626 Cochran Mill Rd.
PO Box 10940
Pittsburgh, PA 15236-0940
Ph:(412)386-4687
URL: http://www.netl.doe.gov

The following power administration offices are arranged alphabetically.

67515 ■ U.S. Department of Energy–Alaska Power Administration
2770 Sherwood Ln., Ste. 2B
Juneau, AK 99801
Ph:(907)586-7405
Fax: (907)586-7270

67516 ■ U.S. Department of Energy–Bonneville Power Administration
905 NE 11th Ave.
PO Box 3621
Portland, OR 97208-3621
Ph:(503)230-3000
Free: 800-282-3713
Fax: (501)230-3285
URL: http://www.bpa.gov

67517 ■ U.S. Department of Energy–Southeastern Power Administration
1166 Athens Tech Rd.
Elberton, GA 30635-6711
Ph:(708)213-3800
Fax: (706)213-3884
Co. E-mail: info@sepa.doe.gov
URL: http://www.sepa.doe.gov

67518 ■ U.S. Department of Energy–Southwestern Power Administration
1 W. 3rd St.
Tulsa, OK 74103-3519
Ph:(918)595-6600
Fax: (918)595-6656
Co. E-mail: info@swpa.gov
URL: http://www.swpa.gov

67519 ■ U.S. Department of Energy–Western Area Power Administration
12155 W. Alameda Pkwy.
PO Box 281213
Lakewood, CO 80228-8213
Ph:(720)962-7000
Free: 800-982-4523
Fax: (720)962-7200
Co. E-mail: corpcomm@wapa.gov
URL: http://www.wapa.gov

U.S. DEPARTMENT OF HEALTH AND HUMAN SERVICES

67520 ■ Health Resources and Services Administration (HRSA)–Office of Equal Opportunity and Civil Rights
Parklawn Building, Room 14A-27
5600 Fishers Ln.
Rockville, MD 20857
Ph:(301)443-5636
Fax: (301)443-7898
Co. E-mail: alinkins@hrsa.gov

67521 ■ U.S. Department of Health and Human Services–Office of Small and Disadvantaged Business Utilization
Humphrey Bldg., Rm. 517D
200 Independence Ave. SW
Washington, DC 20201
Ph:(202)690-7300
Fax: (202)690-8772
URL: http://www.os.dhhs.gov/
Description: The procurement policy of the Department of Health and Human Services seeks to stimulate competition among potential contractors and to make awards on a competitive basis to the fullest degree consistent with quality, efficiency, and economy. It is the department's policy that small businesses, disadvantaged businesses, women-owned businesses, and labor-surplus area concerns receive a fair and equitable share of the contracts awarded. Procurement assistance is available from the HHS's Office of Small and Disadvantaged Business Utilization and from the small business specialists at each HHS regional office.

The following operating components of the Department of Health and Human Services are arranged alphabetically.

67522 ■ U.S. Department of Health and Human Services–Office for Civil Rights–Equal Employment Opportunity/ Affirmation Action Coordinator (HHH B)
HHH Bldg., Rm. 509F
200 Independence Ave., SW
Washington, DC 20201
Ph:(202)619-0257
Free: 800-368-1019
Co. E-mail: ocrmail@hhs.gov
URL: http://www.hhs.gov/ocr/

67523 ■ U.S. Health Care Financing Administration–Equal Employment Opportunity Office
Professional Bldg., Rm. 100
6325 Security Blvd.
Baltimore, MD 21207
Ph:(410)966-5352
Fax: (410)966-9549

67524 ■ U.S. Public Health Service–Division of Grants and Contracts–PHS Small Business Specialist (Parkl)
Parklawn Bldg.
5600 Fishers Ln., Rm. 13A-03
Rockville, MD 20857
Ph:(301)443-1443
Fax: (301)443-8254

67525 ■ U.S. Social Security Administration–Office of Acquisitions and Grants–Small and Disadvantaged Business Utilization Specialist (1st F)
1st Fl., Rear Entrance
7111 Security Blvd.
Baltimore, MD 21244
Ph:(410)965-7467
Fax: (410)965-2965

The following HHS offices are arranged by region.

67526 ■ U.S. Department of Health and Human Services (Region 1)
John F. Kennedy Federal Bldg., Rm. 2100
Government Center
Boston, MA 02203
Ph:(617)565-1500
Fax: (617)565-1491
URL: http://www.hhs.gov/region1
Description: Serves Connecticut, Maine, Massachusetts, New Hampshire, Rhode Island, and Vermont.

67527 ■ U.S. Department of Health and Human Services (Region 2)
Jacob K. Javits Federal Bldg.
26 Federal Plaza
New York, NY 10278
Ph:(212)264-4600
Fax: (212)264-3620
URL: http://www.hhs.gov/region2
Description: Serves New Jersey, New York, Puerto Rico, and the Virgin Islands.

67528 ■ U.S. Department of Health and Human Services (Region 3)
Public Ledger Bldg., Ste. 436
150 S. independence Mall W.
PO Box 13716
Philadelphia, PA 19106-3499
Ph:(215)861-4633
Fax: (215)861-4625
URL: http://www.hhs.gov/region3
Description: Serves Delaware, the District of Columbia, Maryland, Pennsylvania, Virginia, and West Virginia.

67529 ■ U.S. Department of Health and Human Services (Region 4)
Sam Nunn Atlanta Federal Ctr.
61 Forsyth St., SW
Atlanta, GA 30303-8909
Ph:(404)562-7888
Fax: (404)562-7899
URL: http://www.hhs.gov/region4
Description: Serves Alabama, Florida, Georgia, Kentucky, Mississippi, North Carolina, South Carolina, and Tennessee.

67530 ■ U.S. Department of Health and Human Services (Region 5)
233 N. Michigan Ave., Ste. 1300
Chicago, IL 60601
Ph:(312)353-5160
Fax: (312)353-4144
URL: http://www.hhs.gov/region5
Description: Serves Illinois, Indiana, Michigan, Minnesota, Ohio, and Wisconsin.

67531 ■ U.S. Department of Health and Human Services (Region 6)
1301 Young St., Ste. 1124
Dallas, TX 75202
Ph:(214)767-3301
Fax: (214)767-3617
URL: http://www.hhs.gov/region6
Description: Serves Arkansas, Louisiana, New Mexico, Oklahoma, and Texas.

67532 ■ U.S. Department of Health and Human Services (Region 7)
Bowlling Federal Bldg., Rm. 210
601 E. 12th St.
Kansas City, MO 64106
Ph:(816)426-2821
Fax: (816)426-3535
URL: http://www.hhs.gov/region7
Description: Serves Iowa, Kansas, Missouri, and Nebraska.

67533 ■ U.S. Department of Health and Human Services (Region 8)
Rogers Federal Office Bldg.
1961 Stout St., No. 1076
Denver, CO 80294-3538
Ph:(303)844-3372
Fax: (303)844-4545
URL: http://www.hhs.gov/region8
Description: Serves Colorado, Montana, North Dakota, South Dakota, Utah, and Wyoming.

67534 ■ U.S. Department of Health and Human Services (Region 9)
Federal Office Bldg., Rm. 431
50 United Nations Plz.
San Francisco, CA 94102
Ph:(415)437-8500
Fax: (415)536-1023
Co. E-mail: www.hhs.gov/region9
Description: Serves Arizona, California, Guam, Hawaii, Nevada, and the Trust Territory of the Pacific Islands.

67535 ■ U.S. Department of Health and Human Services (Region 10)
Blanchard Plaza Bldg.
2201 6th Ave.
Seattle, WA 98121
Ph:(206)615-2010
Fax: (206)615-2087
URL: http://www.hhs.gov/region10/
Description: Serves Alaska, Idaho, Oregon, and Washington.

The following HHS agencies are arranged alphabetically.

67536 ■ National Institutes of Health–Division of Contracts and Grants–Small and Disadvantaged Business Utilization Specialist (9000)
9000 Rockville Pke.
Bethesda, MD 20892
Ph:(301)496-4000
Co. E-mail: nihinfo@od.nih.gov
URL: http://www.nih.gov

67537 ■ U.S. Food and Drug Administration–Division of Contracts and Grants Management–Office of Management (5600)
5600 Fishers Ln., Rm. 2129
5600 Fishers Ln.
Rockville, MD 20857
Ph:(301)827-7180
Free: 800-216-7331
Co. E-mail: rspringe@oc.fda.gov
URL: http://www.fda.gov

67538 ■ U.S. Food and Drug Administration–Division of Contracts and Grants Management–Small and Disadvantaged Business Utilization Specialist (12420)
12420 Parklawn Dr., Ste. 3-30
Rockville, MD 20857
Ph:(301)443-6890

67539 ■ U.S. Food and Drug Administration–Office of Small Business, Scientific, and Trade Affairs
5600 Fishers Ln., HF-40
Rockville, MD 20857
Ph:(301)827-4450
Fax: (301)443-1863

67540 ■ U.S. Health Resources Services Administration–Grants and Procurement Management Division–Contracts Policies and Operations (Parkl)
Parklawn Bldg., Rm. 13A-03
5600 Fishers Ln.
Rockville, MD 20857-0001
Ph:(301)443-1433

67541 ■ U.S. Public Health Service–Administrative Services Center–Small and Disadvantaged Business Utilization Specialist (Parkl)–Division of Acquisitions Management, PSC (awn Bldg.,)
Parklawn Bldg., Rm. 5C-26
5600 Fishers Ln.
Rockville, MD 20857
Ph:(301)443-1715
Fax: (301)443-7593
Co. E-mail: ldanley@psc.dhhs.gov

U.S. DEPARTMENT OF HOUSING AND URBAN DEVELOPMENT

67542 ■ U.S. Department of Housing and Urban Development–Deputy Assistant Secretary for Economic Development–Grants Management Division (451 7)
451 7th Ave., SW, Rm. 7149
Mail Stop DEC
Washington, DC 20410
Ph:(202)708-2035
Fax: (202)401-2231
Co. E-mail: mark_a._horwath@hud.gov

67543 ■ U.S. Department of Housing and Urban Development–Office of the Chief Procurement Officer
451 7th St., SW, Rm. 5280
Washington, DC 20410
Ph:(202)708-0600
Fax: (202)708-5607

67544 ■ U.S. Department of Housing and Urban Development–Office of Departmental Operations and Coordination
451 7th St., SW, Rm. 2124
Mail Stop I
Washington, DC 20410
Ph:(202)708-2806
Fax: (202)401-8848

67545 ■ U.S. Department of Housing and Urban Development–Office of Healthy Homes and Lead Hazard
490 L'Enfant Plz., SW, Rm. P3206
Washington, DC 20410
Ph:(202)708-0310
Fax: (202)755-1000
Co. E-mail: michael_f._hill@hud.gov
URL: http://www.hud.gov/offices/lead

67546 ■ U.S. Department of Housing and Urban Development–Office of Security and Emergency Planning
431 7th St., SW, Rm. 6186
Mail Stop AG
Washington, DC 20410
Ph:(202)708-4022
Fax: (202)401-8354
Co. E-mail: robert_e.langston@hud.gov

67547 ■ U.S. Department of Housing and Urban Development–Office of Small and Disadvantaged Business Utilization
Ph:(202)708-1428
Fax: (202)708-7642
Co. E-mail: valerie_t._hayes@hud.gov
URL: http://www.hud.gov/offices/osdbu/index.cfm

67548 ■ U.S. Department of Housing and Urban Development–Office of Small and Disadvantaged Business Utilization
451 7th St. SW, Rm. 10156
Washington, DC 20410-1000
Ph:(202)708-1428
Fax: (202)708-7642
URL: http://www.hud.gov/
Description: The Department of Housing and Urban Development purchases supplies and services to repair and provide housing management services for the properties it acquires, as well as to fulfill its logistical, administrative, and programmatic requirements. Private contractors, including small and disadvantaged firms, are awarded contracts based on bids that they submit to appropriate HUD offices or area managers. HUD encourages and facilitates the participation of small business firms, minority business firms, and firms located in labor-surplus areas. Activities are carried out through a network of field offices. HUD also encourages small business firms to participate in its research and demonstration programs, as the majority of competitively awarded contracts and assistance agreements have been granted to small businesses.

The following HUD offices are arranged by region.

67549 ■ U.S. Department of Housing and Urban Development (Region 1)
10 Causeway Sy., Rm. 301
10 Causeway St.
Boston, MA 02222-1092
Ph:(617)994-8223
Fax: (617)565-5257
Description: Administers field offices in Connecticut, Maine, Massachusetts, New Hampshire, Rhode Island, and Vermont.

67550 ■ U.S. Department of Housing and Urban Development (Region 2)
26 Federal Plz., Ste. 3541
26 Federal Plz.
New York, NY 10278-0068
Ph:(212)264-8000
Fax: (212)264-3068
Description: Administers field offices in New Jersey and New York.

67551 ■ U.S. Department of Housing and Urban Development (Region 3)
The Wanamaker Bldg.
100 Penn Square E.
Philadelphia, PA 19107-3380
Ph:(215)656-0500
Fax: (215)656-3445
Description: Administers field offices in Delaware, the District of Columbia, Maryland, Pennsylvania, Virginia, and West Virginia.

67552 ■ U.S. Department of Housing and Urban Development (Region 4)
40 Marietta St.
5 Points Plz.
Atlanta, GA 30303-2806
Ph:(404)331-4111
Fax: (404)331-2392
Description: Administers field offices in Alabama, Florida, Georgia, Kentucky, Mississippi, North Carolina, Puerto Rico, South Carolina, Tennessee, and the Virgin Islands.

67553 ■ U.S. Department of Housing and Urban Development (Region 5)
Ralph Metcalfe Federal Bldg.
77 W. Jackson Blvd.
Chicago, IL 60604-3507
Ph:(312)353-5680
Fax: (312)886-2729
Description: Administers field offices in Illinois, Indiana, Michigan, Minnesota, Ohio, and Wisconsin.

67554 ■ U.S. Department of Housing and Urban Development (Region 6)
801 Cherry St.
PO Box 2905
Ft. Worth, TX 76102-2905
Ph:(817)978-5965
Fax: (817)978-5567
Description: Administers field offices in Arkansas, Louisiana, New Mexico, Oklahoma, and Texas.

67555 ■ U.S. Department of Housing and Urban Development (Region 7)
400 State Ave., Rm. 200
Kansas City, KS 66101-2406
Ph:(913)551-5462
Fax: (913)551-5469
Description: Administers field offices in Iowa, Kansas, Missouri, and Nebraska.

67556 ■ U.S. Department of Housing and Urban Development (Region 8)
1670 Broadway, 23rd Fl.
Denver, CO 80202
Ph:(303)672-5440
Fax: (303)672-5004
Description: Administers field offices in Colorado, Montana, North Dakota, South Dakota, Utah, and Wyoming.

67557 ■ U.S. Department of Housing and Urban Development (Region 9)
600 Harrison St., 3rd Fl.
San Francisco, CA 94107-1300
Ph:(415)489-6400
Fax: (415)489-6419
Description: Administers field offices in the American Samoa, Arizona, California, Guam, Hawaii, and Nevada.

67558 ■ U.S. Department of Housing and Urban Development (Region 10)
909 1st Ave., Ste. 200
Seattle, WA 98104-1000
Ph:(206)220-5101
Fax: (206)220-5108
Description: Administers field offices in Alaska, Idaho, Oregon, and Washington.

U.S. DEPARTMENT OF THE INTERIOR

67559 ■ U.S. Department of the Interior–Office of Small and Disadvantaged Business Utilization
1849 C St., NW, Rm. 2252
Washington, DC 20240
Ph:(202)208-1829
Co. E-mail: robert_faithful@ios.doi.gov
URL: http://www.doi.gov/osdbu/index.html

67560 ■ U.S. Department of the Interior–Office of the Solicitor
1849 C St., NW, Rm. 6352
Washington, DC 20240
Ph:(202)208-4423
Fax: (202)208-5584

67561 ■ U.S. Department of the Interior–Office of Small and Disadvantaged Business Utilization
1849 C St. NW
Washington, DC 20240
Ph:(202)208-3100
Co. E-mail: webteam@ios.doi.gov
URL: http://www.doi.gov
Description: The Department of the Interior's Small and Disadvantaged Business Program provides counseling and advice to small, women-owned, and minority-owned businesses on opportunities in the department. The program helps the bureaus and offices of the department in their efforts to increase contracting opportunities for such businesses. (This applies to direct contracting and subcontracting opportunities as well as to the Small Business Administration's programs.) For instance, the department's Bureau of Land Management sets aside certain commodities and services for procurement from small businesses. This bureau also conducts a lottery to allow the public the opportunity to purchase land. The Bureau of Indian Affairs provides technical assistance to Native American and tribal businesses on reservations for the establishment of enterprises, the preparation of economic development plans, the development of educational and residential facilities, and related undertakings. Furthermore, the department provides various publications that assist small business and small and disadvantaged business concerns with contracting opportunities. The Department of the Interior also hosts an annual Small Business Procurement Fair, which provides contact between the department's acquisition officials and small businesses.

The area offices for the Bureau of Indian Affair are arranged alphabetically by state.

67562 ■ Bureau of Indian Affairs–Business Utilization and Development Specialist–Juneau Area Office (709 W)
709 W. 9th St.
PO Box 25520
Juneau, AK 99802-5520
Ph:(907)586-7171
Free: 800-645-8397
Fax: (907)586-7252

URL: http://www.doi.gov/bureau-indian-affairs.html

67563 ■ Bureau of Indian Affairs–Business Utilization and Development Specialist–Phoenix Area Office (1 N.)
1 N. 1st St.
PO Box 10
Phoenix, AZ 85001
Ph:(602)379-6600
Fax: (602)379-4413
URL: http://www.doi.gov/bureau-indian-affairs.html

67564 ■ Bureau of Indian Affairs–Business Utilization and Development Specialist–Sacramento Area Office (2800)
2800 Cottage Way
Sacramento, CA 95825
Ph:(916)978-6000
Fax: (916)978-6099

67565 ■ Bureau of Indian Affairs–Business Utilization and Development Specialist–Minneapolis Area Office (1 Fed)
1 Federal Dr., Rm. 550
Minneapolis, MN 55111-4007
Ph:(612)713-4400
Fax: (612)713-4401

67566 ■ Bureau of Indian Affairs–Business Utilization and Development Specialist–Billings Area Office (316 N)
316 N. 26th St.

Billings, MT 59101-1362
Ph:(406)247-7943
Fax: (406)247-7976

67567 ■ Bureau of Indian Affairs–Business Utilization and Development Specialist–Albuquerque Area Office (615 F)
615 First St.
PO Box 25567
Albuquerque, NM 87125-6567
Ph:(505)346-7590
Fax: (505)346-7517

67568 ■ Bureau of Indian Affairs–Business Utilization and Development Specialist–Navajo Area Office (PO Bo)
PO Box 1060
Gallup, NM 87305
Ph:(505)863-8314
Fax: (505)863-8324

67569 ■ Bureau of Indian Affairs–Business Utilization and Development Specialist–Anadarko Area Office (W.C.D)
W.C.D. Office Complex
PO Box 368
Anadarko, OK 73005-0368
Ph:(405)247-6673
Fax: (405)247-2242

67570 ■ Bureau of Indian Affairs–Business Utilization and Development Specialist–Muskogee Area Office (101 N)
101 N. 5th St.
Muskogee, OK 74401-6206
Ph:(918)687-2296
Fax: (918)687-2571

67571 ■ Bureau of Indian Affairs–Business Utilization and Development Specialist–Portland Area Office (911 N)
911 NE, 11th Ave.
Portland, OR 97232
Ph:(503)231-6702
Fax: (503)231-2201

67572 ■ Bureau of Indian Affairs–Business Utilization and Development Specialist–Aberdeen Area Office (115 4)
115 4th Ave. SE
Aberdeen, SD 57401
Ph:(605)226-7343
Fax: (605)228-7448

67573 ■ Bureau of Indian Affairs–Business Utilization and Development Specialist–Eastern Area Office (711 S)
711 Stewarts Ferry Pke.
Nashville, TN 37214
Ph:(615)467-1700
Fax: (615)467-1701

The following Bureau of Land Management offices are arranged alphabetically by state.

67574 ■ Bureau of Land Management–Alaska State Office
222 W. 7th Ave., No. 13
Anchorage, AK 99513
Ph:(907)271-5076
Fax: (907)271-4596
URL: http://www.ak.blm.gov

67575 ■ Bureau of Land Management–Arizona State Office
222 N. Central Ave.
Phoenix, AZ 85004-2203
Ph:(602)417-9200
Fax: (602)417-9556
URL: http://azwww.az.blm.gov/

67576 ■ Bureau of Land Management–California State Office
2800 Cottage Way, Rm. W-1834
Sacramento, CA 95825
Ph:(916)978-4400
URL: http://www.ca.blm.gov/caso/

67577 ■ Bureau of Land Management–Colorado State Office
2850 Youngfield St.
Lakewood, CO 80215
Ph:(303)239-3634
URL: http://www.co.blm.gov/

67578 ■ Bureau of Land Management–Business Utilization and Development Specialist–Branch of Procurement Management (1620)
1620 L St. NW, Rm. 1075
Washington, DC 20240
Ph:(202)785-6586
Contact: Milton Hill

67579 ■ Bureau of Land Management–Idaho State Office
1387 S. Vinnell Way
Boise, ID 83709-1657
Ph:(208)373-4000
Fax: (208)373-3904
URL: http://www.id.blm.gov/

67580 ■ Bureau of Land Management–Montana State Office
5001 Southgate Dr.
PO Box 36800
Billings, MT 59107-6800
Ph:(406)896-5012
URL: http://www.mt.blm.gov/

67581 ■ Bureau of Land Management–Neveda State Office
1340 Financial Blvd.
PO Box 12000
Reno, NV 89502-0006
Ph:(705)861-6400
URL: http://www.nv.blm.gov

67582 ■ Bureau of Land Management–New Mexico State Office
1474 E. Rodeo Rd.
Santa Fe, NM 87505
Ph:(505)438-7400
Fax: (505)438-7435
URL: http://www.nm.blm.gov
Serves Kansas, New Mexico, Oklahoma, and Texas.

67583 ■ Bureau of Land Management–Business Utilization and Development Specialist–Division of Procurement Management (333 S)
333 SW 1st St.
PO Box 2965
Portland, OR 97208-2965
Ph:(503)808-6026
Contact: Roger Sharp

67584 ■ Bureau of Land Management–Oregon State Office
333 SW 1st St.
PO Box 2965
Portland, OR 97208-2965
Ph:(503)808-6026
Fax: (503)952-6308
URL: http://www.or.blm.gov
Serves Oregon and Washington.

67585 ■ Bureau of Land Management–Utah State Office
324 S. State St., Ste. 301
Salt Lake City, UT 84111
Ph:(801)539-4001
Fax: (801)539-4103
URL: http://www.blm.gov/uta

67586 ■ Bureau of Land Management–Eastern States Office
7450 Boston Blvd.
Springfield, VA 22153
Ph:(703)440-1600
URL: http://www-a.blm.gov/eso
Serves Arkansas, Iowa, Louisiana, Minnesota, Mississippi, and all states east of the Mississippi River.

67587 ■ Bureau of Land Management–Wyoming State Office
5353 Yellowstone Rd.
PO Box 1828
Cheyenne, WY 82003
Ph:(307)775-6256
Fax: (307)775-6082
Serves Nebraska and Wyoming.

The following Bureau of Reclamation offices are arranged alphabetically by state.

67588 ■ Bureau of Reclamation–Business Utilization and Development Specialist–Phoenix Area Office (2222)
2222 W. Dunlap Ave., Ste. 100
PO Box 81169
Phoenix, AZ 85021-1169
Ph:(602)216-3999
Fax: (602)216-4003

67589 ■ Bureau of Reclamation–Business Utilization and Development Specialist–Mid-Pacific Region (Feder)
Federal Office Bldg.
2800 Cottage Way
Sacramento, CA 95825-1898
Ph:(916)978-5000
Fax: (916)978-5599
URL: http://www.usbr.gov/mp/

67590 ■ Bureau of Reclamation–Business Utilization and Development Specialist–Acquisition and Assistance Management Services (6th &)
6th & Kipling, Bldg. 67
PO Box 25007
Denver, CO 80225-0007
Ph:(303)236-3750
URL: http://www.usbr.gov
Contact: Ron Simonich

67591 ■ Bureau of Reclamation–Business Utilization and Development Specialist–Administrative Service Center (PO Bo)
PO Box 25007
Denver, CO 80225
Ph:(303)969-7235
Contact: Jackie Saxon

67592 ■ Bureau of Reclamation–Business Utilization and Development Specialist–Denver Office (Denve)
Denver Federal Center
PO Box 25007
Denver, CO 80225-0007
Ph:(303)445-2670
Fax: (303)236-6763

67593 ■ Bureau of Reclamation–Business Utilization and Development Specialist–Pacific Northwest Region (1150)
1150 N. Curtis Rd., Ste. 100
Boise, ID 83706-1234
Ph:(208)378-5012
Fax: (208)378-5019
URL: http://www.usbr.gov/pn/

67594 ■ Bureau of Reclamation–Business Utilization and Development Specialist–Great Plains Region (PO Bo)
PO Box 36900
Billings, MT 59107-6900
Ph:(406)247-7600
Fax: (406)247-7793
URL: http://www.usbr.gov/gp/

67595 ■ Bureau of Reclamation–Business Utilization and Development Specialist–Lower Colorado Region (PO Bo)
PO Box 61470
Boulder City, NV 89006-1470
Ph:(702)293-8411
Fax: (702)293-8414
URL: http://www.usbr.gov/lc/

67596 ■ Bureau of Reclamation–Business Utilization and Development Specialist–Upper Colorado Region (125 S)
125 S. State St., Rm. 6107
Salt Lake City, UT 84138-1102
Ph:(801)524-3600
Fax: (801)524-5499
URL: http://www.usbr.gov/uc/

The following Surface Mining Reclamation and Enforcement offices are arranged alphabetically by region.

67597 ■ Office of Surface Mining Reclamation and Enforcement–Appalachian Regional Office
3 Parkway Center
Pittsburgh, PA 15220
Ph:(412)937-2828
URL: http://www.arcc.osmre.gov

67598 ■ Office of Surface Mining Reclamation and Enforcement–Mid-Continent Regional Office
Alton Federal Bldg.
501 Belle St., Rm. 216
Alton, IL 62002
Ph:(618)463-6460
Co. E-mail: sandber@osmre.gov
URL: http://www.mcrcc.osmre.gov

67599 ■ Office of Surface Mining Reclamation and Enforcement–Western Regional Office
1999 Broadway, Ste. 3320
Denver, CO 80201-6667
Ph:(303)844-1401
Co. E-mail: aklein@osmre.gov
URL: http://www.wrcc.osmre.gov

The offices following the main office of the U.S. Fish and Wildlife Service (Washington, DC) are arranged by region.

67600 ■ U.S. Fish and Wildlife Service–Budget and Administration Division–Region 5 (300 W)–Northeast Regional Office (estgate Ce)
300 Westgate Center Dr.
Hadley, MA 01035-9589
Ph:(413)253-8200
Fax: (413)253-8308

Co. E-mail: northeast@fws.gov
URL: http://www.fws.gov/northeast
Serves Connecticut, Delaware, Maine, Maryland, Massachusetts, New Hampshire, New Jersey, New York, Pennsylvania, Rhode Island, Vermont, Virginia, and West Virginia.

67601 ■ U.S. Fish and Wildlife Service–Business Utilization and Development Specialist–Branch of Construction Contracting (Denve)
Denver Federal Center
PO Box 25486
Denver, CO 80225-0046
Ph:(303)275-2371
Fax: (303)275-2371
URL: http://www.fws.gov
Contact: Diana Ostenson

67602 ■ U.S. Fish and Wildlife Service–Business Utilization and Development Specialist–Division of Contracting and General Services (4401)
4401 N. Fairfax Dr., Rm. 212B
Arlington, VA 22203
Ph:(703)358-2225
Co. E-mail: southeast@fws.gov
URL: http://www.fws.gov/southeast
Contact: James W. McKoy

67603 ■ U.S. Fish and Wildlife Service–Contracting & General Services Chief–Region 4 (1875)
1875 Century Blvd., Ste. 240
Atlanta, GA 30345
Ph:(404)679-4157
Fax: (404)679-4141
URL: http://www.fws.gov
Serves Alabama, Arkansas, Florida, Georgia, Kentucky, Louisana, Mississippi, North Carolina, South Carolina, Tennesse, and the Virgin Islands.

67604 ■ U.S. Fish and Wildlife Service–Contracting & General Services Chief–Region 7 (1011)
1011 E. Tudor Rd.
Anchorage, AK 99503
Ph:(907)786-3309
Fax: (907)786-3495
Co. E-mail: ak_admin@fws.gov
URL: http://www.fws.gov
Serves Alaska.

67605 ■ U.S. Fish and Wildlife Service–Contracting & General Services Officer–Region 2 (500 G)
500 Gold Ave. SW
PO Box 1306
Albuquerque, NM 87102-1306
Ph:(505)248-6911
Co. E-mail: rdhall@fws.gov
URL: http://www.fws.gov
Serves Arizona, New Mexico, Oklahoma, and Texas.

67606 ■ U.S. Fish and Wildlife Service–Contracting Officer–Region 6 (134 U)
134 Union Blvd.
Lakewood, CO 80228
Ph:(303)236-7905
Co. E-mail: mountainprairie@fws.gov
URL: http://www.fws.gov
Serves Colorado, Kansas, Montana, Nebraska, North Dakota, South Dakota, Utah, and Wyoming.

67607 ■ U.S. Fish and Wildlife Service–Contracting & Procurement Officer–Region 3 (Bisho)
Bishop Henry Whipple Federal Bldg.
1 Federal Dr.
Ft. Snelling, MN 55111
Ph:(612)713-5360
Co. E-mail: midwestnews@fws.gov
URL: http://www.fws.gov/midwest
Serves Illinois, Indiana, Iowa, Michigan, Minnesota, Missouri, Ohio, and Wisconsin.

67608 ■ U.S. Fish and Wildlife Service–Procurement Assistant–Region 1 (911 N)
911 NE 11th Ave.
Portland, OR 97232-4181
Ph:(503)872-2763
Fax: (503)231-2062
Serves California, Hawaii, Idaho, Nevada, Oregon, Washington, and the Pacific Islands.

The following Policy, Management and Budget offices are arranged alphabetically by region.

67609 ■ U.S. Fish and Wildlife Service–Policy, Management and Budget–Alaska Region (1011)
1011 Tudor Rd.
Anchorage, AK 99503
Ph:(907)786-3309
Fax: (907)786-3495
URL: http://www.fws.gov/alaska
Serves Alaska.

67610 ■ U.S. Fish and Wildlife Service–Policy, Management and Budget–Great Lakes, Big Rivers Region (1 Fed)
1 Federal Dr.
BHW Federal Bldg.
Ft. Snelling, MN 55111
Ph:(612)713-5360
Co. E-mail: r3_pao@mail.fws.gov
URL: http://www.fws.gov/r3pao
Serves Illinois, Indiana, Iowa, Michigan, Minnesota, Missouri, Ohio, and Wisconsin.

67611 ■ U.S. Fish and Wildlife Service–Policy, Management and Budget–Mountain Prairie Region (134 U)
134 Union Blvd.
Lakewood, CO 80228
Ph:(303)236-7905
Co. E-mail: jim_renne@fws.gov
Serves Colorado, Iowa, Kansas, Montana, Missouri, Nebraska, North Dakota, South Dakota, Utah, and Wyoming.

67612 ■ U.S. Fish and Wildlife Service–Policy, Management and Budget–Northeast Regional Office (300 W)
300 Westgate Center Dr.
Hadley, MA 01035-9589
Ph:(413)253-8200
Fax: (413)253-8308
Co. E-mail: northeast@fws.gov
Serves Connecticut, Maine, Massachusetts, New Hampshire, New Jersey, New York, Pennsylvania, Rhode Island, and Vermont, Virginia, West Virginia.

67613 ■ U.S. Fish and Wildlife Service–Policy, Management and Budget–Pacific Region (Easts)
Eastside Federal Complex
911 NE 11th Ave.
Portland, OR 97232-4181
Ph:(503)231-6118
URL: http://www.r1.fws.gov/
Serves California, Hawaii, Idaho, Nevada, Oregon, the Pacific Islands, and Washington.

67614 ■ U.S. Fish and Wildlife Service–Policy, Management and Budget–Southeast Region (1875)
1875 Century Blvd., Ste. 380
Atlanta, GA 30345
Ph:(404)679-7057
Fax: (404)679-7065
URL: http://www.fws.gov/southeast
Serves Alabama, Arkansas, Florida, Georgia, Kentucky, Mississippi, North Carolina, Puerto Rico, South Carolina, Tennesse, and the Virgin Islands.

67615 ■ U.S. Fish and Wildlife Service–Policy, Management and Budget–Southwest Region (PO Bo)
PO Box 1306
Albuquerque, NM 87103-1306
Ph:(505)248-6865

Fax: (505)248-6845
Serves Arizona, New Mexico, Oklahoma, and Texas.

The following U.S. Geological Survey offices are arranged alphabetically by state.

67616 ■ U.S. Geological Survey–Business Utilization and Development Specialist
345 Middlefield Rd.
MS 285
Menlo Park, CA 94025
Ph:(650)853-8300
URL: http://www.usgs.gov
Contact: Rita Leach

67617 ■ U.S. Geological Survey–Business Utilization and Development Specialist–Central Region (Denve)
Denver Federal Center
PO Box 25046
Denver, CO 80225-0046
Ph:(303)202-4274
URL: http://www.usgs.gov
Contact: Jeanie Foster
E-mail: jfoster@usgs.gov

67618 ■ U.S. Geological Survey–Business Utilization and Development Specialist
12201 Sunrise Valley Dr.
MS 205P
Reston, VA 22092
Ph:(703)648-7347
Co. E-mail: ask@usgs.gov
URL: http://www.usgs.gov
Contact: Lisa E. Zukowski
E-mail: lukows@usgs.gov

The following Minerals Management Service offices are arranged alphabetically by state.

67619 ■ Minerals Management Service–Alaska OCS
949 E. 36th Ave., Rm. 300
Anchorage, AK 99508-4363
Ph:(907)334-5209
Free: 800-764-2627
URL: http://www.mms.gov/alaska

67620 ■ Minerals Management Service–Pacific Region OCS
770 Paseo Camarillo
Camarillo, CA 93010
Ph:(805)389-7520
Fax: (805)389-7526
URL: http://www.mms.gov

67621 ■ Minerals Management Service–Business Utilization and Development Specialist–Western ASC Procurement and Contracts (12600)
12600 W. Colfax Ave., Ste. C-200
PO Box 25165, Mail Stop 2700
Lakewood, CO 80215-3736
Ph:(303)231-3900
URL: http://www.mms.gov
Contact: Mary Jo Patrick

67622 ■ Minerals Management Service–Business Utilization and Development Specialist–Division of Procurement and Contracts (381 E)
381 Elden St.
Herndon, VA 2070-4817
Ph:(703)787-1370
Fax: (703)787-1009

The offices of the National Park Service are arranged alphabetically by state.

67623 ■ National Park Service–Business Utilization and Development Specialist–Alaska Region (240 W)
240 W. 5th Ave.
Anchorage, AK 99501
Ph:(907)644-3501

67624 ■ National Park Service–Business Utilization and Development Specialist–Pacific West Region (Natio)
National Jackson Center
1111 Jackson St., Ste. 700
Oakland, CA 94607
Ph:(510)817-1300

67625 ■ National Park Service–Business Utilization and Development Specialist–Intermountain Region (12795)
12795 Alameda Pkwy.
PO Box 25287
Denver, CO 80225-0287
Ph:(303)969-2500
Fax: (303)969-2785

67626 ■ National Park Service–Business Utilization and Development Specialist–Business and Economic Development Program (1849)
1849 C St., NW
Washington, DC 20240
Ph:(202)208-4747
Fax: (202)219-0910
Co. E-mail: waso_public_affairs@npa.gov
URL: http://www.npa.gov
Contact: Ben Saji

67627 ■ National Park Service–Business Utilization and Development Specialist–National Capitol Region (1100)
1100 Ohio Dr., SW
Washington, DC 20242
Ph:(202)619-7000
Fax: (202)619-7220

67628 ■ National Park Service–Business Utilization and Development Specialist–Southeast Region (100 A)
100 Alabama St., SW
1924 Bldg.
Atlanta, GA 30303
Ph:(404)562-3100
Fax: (404)562-3263

67629 ■ National Park Service–Business Utilization and Development Specialist–Midwest Region (601 R)
601 Riverfront Dr.
Omaha, NE 68102
Ph:(402)661-1736

67630 ■ National Park Service–Business Utilization and Development Specialist–Northeast Region (U.S.)
U.S. Custom House
200 Chestnut St., 5th Fl.
Philadelphia, PA 19106
Ph:(215)597-7013
Fax: (215)597-0815

67631 ■ National Park Service–Business Utilization and Development Specialist–Pacific Northwest Region (909 F)
909 First Ave.
Seattle, WA 98104-1060
Ph:(206)220-4013

The following Interior Service Center Offices are arranged alphabetically by state.

67632 ■ Interior Service Center–Business Utilization and Development Specialist–Branch of Acquisitions, Fiscal and Property Services (1849)
1849 C St. NW
Washington, DC 20240
Ph:(202)208-3100

The following Office of Aircraft Services offices are arranged alphabetically by state.

67633 ■ Office of Aircraft Services–Business Utilization and Development Specialist–Division of Contracting (4405)
4405 Lear Ct.
Anchorage, AK 99502-1032

Ph:(907)271-6061
Fax: (907)271-4788
URL: http://www.oas.gov
Contact: Alf Aanensen

67634 ■ Office of Aircraft Services–Business Utilization and Development Specialist–Division of Contracting (300 E)–Aviation Management Directorate (. Mallard)
300 E. Mallard Dr., Ste. 200
Boise, ID 83706-3991
Ph:(208)433-5000
Fax: (208)433-5007
URL: http://www.oas.gov
Contact: Edith Stansbury

U.S. DEPARTMENT OF JUSTICE

67635 ■ U.S. Department of Justice–Federal Bureau of Investigation–Seattle Field Office (1110)
1110 3rd Ave.
Seattle, WA 98101-2904
Ph:(206)622-0460
URL: http://www.seattle.fbi.gov

67636 ■ U.S. Department of Justice–Office of Small and Disadvantaged Business Utilization
National Place Bldg., Rm. 1010
1331 Pennsylvania Ave. NW
Washington, DC 20530
Ph:(202)616-0521
Free: 800-345-3712
Fax: (202)616-1717
Description: The Department of Justice's Office of Small and Disadvantaged Business Utilization develops and implements appropriate outreach programs aimed at heightening the awareness of the small business community to the contracting opportunities available within the department. Outreach efforts include activities such as sponsoring small business fairs and procurement conferences, and participating in trade group seminars, conventions, and other forums that promote the utilization of small businesses as contractors. The office also provides counseling and advice to inquiring small businesses regarding their possible eligibility for special consideration under preferential purchasing programs that the department employs.

The following Department of Justice divisions are arranged alphabetically by office or agency name.

67637 ■ Federal Bureau of Prisons–National Contracts and Policy Section
320 1st St. NW, 6th Fl.
320 1st St. NW, Rm. 600
Washington, DC 20534
Ph:(202)307-3067
Fax: (202)514-4418
URL: http://www.usdoj.gov

67638 ■ Justice Management Division–Procurement Services Staff
1331 Pennsylvania Ave. NW, Rm. 1000
1331 Pennsylvania Ave. NW
Washington, DC 20530
Ph:(202)307-2000
Fax: (202)307-1931
Co. E-mail: askdoj@usdoj.gov
URL: http://www.usdoj.gov

67639 ■ Office of Justice Programs–Information Systems Division
810 7th St., NW
Washington, DC 20531
Ph:(202)307-0703
Fax: (202)307-0086

67640 ■ U.S. Drug Enforcement Administration–Office of Procurement
700 Army Navy Dr., Rm. W5140
Arlington, VA 22202

Ph:(202)307-4921
Fax: (202)307-4877
URL: http://www.dea.gov

67641 ■ U.S. Federal Bureau of Investigation–Administrative Services Division–Property Procurement and Management (935 P)
935 Pennsylvania Ave. NW, Rm. 1B015
Washington, DC 20525-0001
Ph:(202)324-0569
Fax: (202)324-0570

67642 ■ U.S. Federal Prisons Industries/ UNICOR–Procurement Division
400 1st St. NW, 7th Fl.
Washington, DC 20534
Ph:(202)305-7333
Fax: (202)305-7363

67643 ■ U.S. Immigration and Naturalization Service–Human Resources and Administrative Services Division–Procurement Policy and Evaluation (425 E)
425 Eye St. NW, Rm. 2208
Washington, DC 20536
Ph:(202)305-1270
Fax: (202)616-2414

67644 ■ U.S. Marshals Service–Procurement Policy and Oversight Team
600 Army Navy Dr., Ste. 1118, CS3
Arlington, VA 22202-4210
Ph:(202)307-9349
Fax: (202)307-9695

U.S. DEPARTMENT OF LABOR

67645 ■ Florida Agency for Workforce Innovation–Labor Market Statistics–State Census Data Center (107 E)
107 E. Madison St.
MSC G-020
Tallahassee, FL 32399-4111
Ph:(850)488-1048
Fax: (850)921-0776
Co. E-mail: pamela.schenker@awi.state.fl.us
URL: http://www.awi.state.fl.us

67646 ■ U.S. Department of Labor–Office of Small Business and Minority Affairs
Frances Perkins Bldg.
200 Constitution Ave. NW
Washington, DC 20210
Ph:(202)693-6000
Fax: (202)693-6485
URL: http://www.dol.gov/
Description: The Department of Labor's Office of Small Business and Minority Affairs (OSBMA), formerly the Office of Small and Disadvantaged Business Utilization (OSDBU), emphasizes development of small and disadvantaged business utilization in contract and grant activities, promotes interaction with Historically Black Colleges and Universities and Hispanic and other minority colleges and universities, and has management oversight responsibility for Department of Labor advisory committees. The department fully supports the federal government's Small and Disadvantaged Business Utilization Program created to give small, disadvantaged, and women-owned businesses maximum opportunity to participate in government contracting and grant activities for supplies and services (including research, evaluation, maintenance, repairs, and construction).

U.S. DEPARTMENT OF STATE

67647 ■ U.S. Department of State–Bureau of Diplomatic Security–Office of Foreign Missions (Harry)
Harry S. Truman Bldg., Rm. 6316
2201 C St.
Washington, DC 20520
Ph:(202)647-6290
URL: http://www.state.gov/m/ds

67648 ■ U.S. Department of State–Office of Civil Rights
Harry S. Truman Bldg., Rm. 7428
2201 C St., NW
Washington, DC 20520
Ph:(202)647-9294

67649 ■ U.S. Department of State–Office of the Inspector General
Harry S. Truman Bldg., Rm. 7720
2201 C St., NW
Washington, DC 20520
Ph:(202)647-9641
Fax: (202)647-6047

67650 ■ U.S. Department of State–Office of Small and Disadvantaged Business Utilization
2201 C St., NW
Washington, DC 20520
Ph:(202)647-4000
URL: http://www.state.gov/index.html
Description: The Department of State actively seeks qualified small businesses, minority-owned businesses, and women-owned businesses for participation in contract work generated in the course of day-to-day operations. The mission of the State Department—the making and conduct of foreign policy—does not require a large procurement support program on the magnitude of many federal agencies. However in 1995, the Department spent approximately $1 billion in goods and services in support of that mission. Of that amount, the fifteen domestic procurement offices spent $750 million. The contract spectrum of the domestic procurement pattern includes some minor research and development; office and household furniture and furnishings; transportation, warehousing and packing/shipping services; information technology supplies and services; training; translation and interpreting services (personal services contracts only); building construction, renovation/rehabilitation and architect/engineer services; and security support services, among other things. The Department of State embassies, consulates and Regional Procurement & Support Offices worldwide spent the remaining $400 million.

U.S. DEPARTMENT OF TRANSPORTATION

67651 ■ U.S. Department of Transportation–Federal Highway Administration–Central Federal Lands Highway Division (12300)
12300 W. Dakota Ave.
Lakewood, CO 80228-2583
Ph:(720)963-3448
URL: http://www.cflhd.gov

67652 ■ U.S. Department of Transportation–Federal Highway Administration–Federal Lands Highway Division (400 7)
400 7th St., SW, Rm. 631, HFL-1
Washington, DC 20590
Ph:(202)366-9494
URL: http://www.fhwa.dot.gov

67653 ■ U.S. Department of Transportation–Federal Highway Administration–Western Federal Lands Highway Division (610 E)
610 E. 5th St.
Vancouver, WA 98661-3801
Ph:(360)619-7710
URL: http://www.wfl.fha.dot.gov

67654 ■ U.S. Department of Transportation–John A. Volpe National Transportation Center–Office of Management Services (55 Br)–Contracts and Small Business Programs Branch (oadway, Bl)
55 Broadway, Bldg. 4, Rm. 2100
DTS-1
Cambridge, MA 02142-1093
Ph:(617)494-3661
Fax: (617)494-2497
URL: http://www.volpe.dot.gov

67655 ■ U.S. Department of Transportation–Pipeline and Hazardous Materials Safety Administration
400 7th St., SW, Rm. 8410
Washington, DC 20590
Ph:(202)366-4433
Co. E-mail: publicaffairs@dot.gov
URL: http://www.phmsa.dot.gov

67656 ■ U.S. Department of Transportation–Research and Innovative Technology Administration (RITA)
400 7th Ave., SW, Rm. 3103
Washington, DC 20590
Ph:(202)366-4180
Co. E-mail: rita.administrator@dot.gov
URL: http://www.rita.dot.gov

67657 ■ U.S. Department of Transportation–Transportation Safety Institute–Operations Support Division (6500)
6500 S. MacArthur Blvd.
PO Box 25082
Oklahoma City, OK 73125-5050
Ph:(405)954-3159
Fax: (405)954-3521
Co. E-mail: operationssupport@tsi.jccbi.gov
URL: http://www.tsi.dot.gov

67658 ■ U.S. Department of Transportation–Office of Small and Disadvantaged Business Utilization
400 7th St. SW, Rm. 9410
Washington, DC 20590
Ph:(202)366-1930
Free: 800-532-1169
Fax: (202)366-7228
URL: http://www.dot.gov/
Description: The DOT's Office of Small and Disadvantaged Business Utilization provides policy direction for minority, women-owned, and small and disadvantaged business enterprise participation in direct procurement and federal financial assistance activities. It also is responsible for conducting programs directed at encouraging, promoting, and assisting disadvantaged business enterprises in securing contracts, subcontracts, and projects generated by these activities. The office schedules presentations for firms to present their capabilities to the procurement and program staff and monitors all procurement activities for disadvantaged business enterprises by the department, its grantees, and recipients nationwide. All proposed procurements are reviewed for the participation of small business. When possible, specific procurements are set aside exclusively for small business competition.

The following Department of Transportation offices are arranged alphabetically by agency name.

67659 ■ U.S. Department of Transportation–Coast Guard–Procurement Management Division (2100)–Minority Business Program (2nd St., S)
2100 2nd St., SW
Washington, DC 20593
Ph:(202)267-2499

Fax: (202)267-4158

**67660 ■ U.S. Department of
Transportation–Federal Aviation
Administration–Small Business Utilization
Office (800 I)**
800 Independence Ave. SW, Rm. 715
Washington, DC 20591
Ph:(202)267-8881

**67661 ■ U.S. Department of
Transportation–Federal Highway
Administration–Eastern Federal Lands
Highway Division (Loudo)–Small and
Disadvantaged Business Utilization Liaison
(un Technic)**
Loudoun Technical Center
21400 Ridge Top Cir.
Sterling, VA 20166-6511
Ph:(703)404-6201
Free: 800-892-8776
Fax: (703)285-0011
URL: http://www.efl.fhwa.dot.gov

**67662 ■ U.S. Department of
Transportation–Federal Highway
Administration–Small and Disadvantaged
Business Utilization Liaison (400 7)**
400 7th St. SW, Rm. 9414
Washington, DC 20590
Ph:(202)366-1930
Free: 800-532-1169
Fax: (202)366-7538

**67663 ■ U.S. Department of
Transportation–Federal Railroad
Administration–Small and Disadvantaged
Business Utilization Liaison (400 7)**
400 7th St. SW, Rm. 9414
Washington, DC 20590
Ph:(202)366-1930
Free: 800-532-1169
Fax: (202)366-7538
Co. E-mail: Stephanie.curtis@fhwa.dot.gov

**67664 ■ U.S. Department of
Transportation–Federal Transit
Administration–Small and Disadvantaged
Business Utilization Liaison (400 7)**
400 7th St. SW, Rm. 9101
Washington, DC 20590
Ph:(202)366-8922
Fax: (202)366-3475
Co. E-mail: darren.brown@fta.dot.gov

**67665 ■ U.S. Department of
Transportation–Maritime
Administration–Small and Disadvantaged
Business Utilization Liaison (400 7)–Office of
Acquisition (th St. SW,)**
400 7th St. SW, Rm. 7310
Washington, DC 20590
Ph:(202)366-2802
Fax: (202)366-3889
Co. E-mail: rita.thomas@marad.dot.gov

**67666 ■ U.S. Department of
Transportation–National Highway Traffic
Safety Administration–Small and Minority
Business Utilization Liaison (400 7)–Office of
Contracts and Procurement (th St. SW,)**
400 7th St. SW, Rm. 5301
Washington, DC 20590
Ph:(202)366-8573
Fax: (202)366-9555
Co. E-mail: darren.brown@fta.dot.gov

**67667 ■ U.S. Department of
Transportation–Research and Special
Programs Administration–Office of Contracts
and Administration (400 7)**
400 7th St. SW, Rm. 8321
Washington, DC 20590
Ph:(202)366-5513
Fax: (202)366-7974

**67668 ■ U.S. Department of
Transportation–St. Lawrence Seaway
Development Corporation–Office of the
Associate Administrator (180 A)**
180 Andrews St.
PO Box 520
Massena, NY 13662-0520
Ph:(315)764-3236
Fax: (315)764-3235

U.S. DEPARTMENT OF THE TREASURY

**67669 ■ U.S. Department of the
Treasury–Office of Small and Disadvantaged
Business Utilization**
1500 Pennsylvania Ave. NW
655 15th St., Rm. 6099
Washington, DC 20220
Ph:(202)622-2826
Fax: (202)622-4963
Co. E-mail: graham@do.treas.gov
URL: http://www.ustreas.gov/sba
Description: The mission of the Department of the
Treasury includes formulating and recommending financial, tax, and fiscal policies; serving as the financial agent for the U.S. government; enforcing various
federal laws; protecting the President & Vice President of the United States; and manufacturing coins
and currency. The accomplishment of this mission requires the procurement of a wide variety of commercial goods and services at an annual expenditure of
approximately two billion dollars. Contracting authority
has been delegated to the various bureaus of the department, and each conducts the procurement transactions necessary to carry out its respective program.
The department's procurement efforts include a commitment to increase contract awards to small, minority, and women-owned business firms.

*The following are arranged alphabetically by bureau
name.*

**67670 ■ U.S. Department of the
Treasury–Bureau of Alcohol, Tobacco Tax
and Trade (TTB)**
1310 G St. NW, Ste. 300 E
Washington, DC 20220
Ph:(202)927-5611
Fax: (202)927-7311
URL: http://www.ttb.gov
Contact: Jackie Barber, Small Business Specialist

**67671 ■ U.S. Department of the
Treasury–Bureau of Engraving and Printing**
14th & C Sts., SW
Washington, DC 20228
Ph:(202)874-3019
Fax: (202)874-3135
Contact: Dennis Milsten, Small Business Specialist

**67672 ■ U.S. Department of the
Treasury–Bureau of the Public Debt**
PO Box 1328
Parkersburg, WV 26106-1328
Ph:(304)480-6639
Fax: (304)480-6632
Contact: Jeff Stephenson, Small Business Specialist

**67673 ■ U.S. Department of the
Treasury–Comptroller of the Currency**
Independence Square
250 E. St., SW
Washington, DC 20219-0001
Ph:(202)874-5000
Free: 800-613-6743
Fax: (202)874-4950
URL: http://www.occ.treas.gov
Contact: Karen Waters, Small Business Specialist

**67674 ■ U.S. Department of the
Treasury–Departmental Offices–Procurement
Services Division (1500)**
1500 Pennsylvania Ave. NW
1310 G St., Ste. 200 E.
Washington, DC 20220

Ph:(202)927-8210
Fax: (202)622-2243
Contact: Renee Fitzgerald, Small Business
  Specialist

**67675 ■ U.S. Department of the
Treasury–Federal Law Enforcement Training
Center**
Glynco Facility
1131 Chapel Crossing Rd.
Glynco, GA 31524
Ph:(912)267-2070
Fax: (912)267-2071
URL: http://www.fletc.gov
Contact: Susan Smallwood, Small Business
  Specialist

**67676 ■ U.S. Department of the
Treasury–Financial Management Service**
Liberty Center
401 - 14th St. SW, Rm. 548
Washington, DC 20227
Ph:(202)874-7000
Fax: (202)874-6743
Co. E-mail: Richard.gregg@fma.treas.gov
Contact: Wendi Smith, Small Business Specialist

**67677 ■ U.S. Department of the
Treasury–Office of Thrift Supervision**
1700 G St. NW, 3rd Fl.
Washington, DC 20552
Ph:(202)906-6900
Fax: (202)906-5748
Contact: Doug Mason, Small Business Specialist

**67678 ■ U.S. Department of the
Treasury–U.S. Customs Service**
1300 Pennsylvania Ave. NW, Ste. 4.4B
Washington, DC 20229
Ph:(202)344-2990
Fax: (202)344-2950
Contact: William Bickelman, Small Business
  Specialist

**67679 ■ U.S. Department of the
Treasury–U.S. Customs Service–Field
Procurement Services (6026)**
6026 Lakeside Blvd.
PO Box 68905
Indianapolis, IN 46278
Ph:(317)298-1180
Fax: (317)298-1344
Contact: Lee Sullivan, Small Business Specialist

**67680 ■ U.S. Department of the
Treasury–U.S. Mint**
801 9th St., NW
Washington, DC 20220
Ph:(202)354-7821
Fax: (202)354-6299
Contact: Caroline Bennington, Small Business
  Specialist

**67681 ■ U.S. Department of the
Treasury–U.S. Secret Service**
Procurement Division
950 H St., NW
Washington, DC 20373-5802
Ph:(202)406-6940
Contact: Andy Anderson, Small Business Specialist

*The following Internal Revenue Service (IRS) offices
are arranged by region.*

**67682 ■ U.S. Department of the
Treasury–Internal Revenue Service**
Constellation Centre, MPP
6009 Oxon Hill Rd.
Oxon Hill, MD 20745
Ph:(202)283-1416
Fax: (202)283-1437
URL: http://procurement.irs.gov
Contact: Jodie Paustian, Small Business Specialist

67683 ■ **U.S. Department of the Treasury–Internal Revenue Service–Mid-States Region (4050)**
4050 Alpha Rd.
MSRO1800
Dallas, TX 75244-4203
Ph:(972)308-1637
Fax: (972)308-1928
Contact: Marguerite Overs, Small Business Specialist
Description: Serves Oklahoma, Texas, Arkansas, Kansas, Missouri, Illinois, Nebraska, Iowa, Wisconsin, Minnesota, North Dakota, and South Dakota. This office also supports the IRS Service Centers in Austin, TX, Kansas City, MO, and Ogden, UT.

67684 ■ **U.S. Department of the Treasury–Internal Revenue Service–Northeast Region (290 B)**
290 Broadway
New York, NY 10007-1867
Ph:(212)436-1481
Fax: (212)436-1849
Contact: Deborah Foster, Small Business Specialist
Description: Serves Maine, Massachusetts, New Hampshire, Vermont, Rhode Island, Connecticut, New York, New Jersey, Pennsylvania, Ohio, and Michigan. This office also supports the IRS Service Centers in Andover, MA, Brookhaven, NY, and Philadelphia, PA.

67685 ■ **U.S. Department of the Treasury–Internal Revenue Service–Southeast Region (2888)**
2888 Woodcock Blvd., Ste. 300
Atlanta, GA 30341
Ph:(404)338-9204
Fax: (404)338-9203
Contact: Peggie Lynch, Small Business Specialist
Description: Serves Delaware, District of Columbia, Maryland, Virginia, West Virginia, Indiana, Kentucky, Tennessee, South Carolina, Georgia, Alabama, Louisiana, Mississippi, North Carolina, and Florida. This office also supports the IRS Service Centers in Atlanta, GA, Memphis, TN, and Covington, KY (Cincinnati).

67686 ■ **U.S. Department of the Treasury–Internal Revenue Service–Western Region (333 M)**
333 Market St.
San Francisco, CA 94105
Ph:(415)848-4716
Fax: (415)848-4711
Contact: Jan Janson, Small Business Specialist
Description: Serves Montana, Idaho, Washington, Oregon, Wyoming, Colorado, Utah, Nevada, California, Arizona, New Mexico, Alaska, and Hawaii. This office also supports the IRS Service Center in Fresno, CA.

The following IRS computing centers are arranged alphabetically by state.

67687 ■ **U.S. Department of the Treasury–Internal Revenue Service–Detroit Computing Center (477 M)**
477 Michigan Ave.
Procurement
Detroit, MI 48226
Ph:(313)628-3722
Fax: (313)234-2180
Contact: Wenda Hollenbeck, Small Business Specialist

67688 ■ **U.S. Department of the Treasury–Internal Revenue Service–Martinsburg Computing Center (55 Me)**
55 Meridian Pkwy.
PO Box 1208
Martinsburg, WV 25401
Ph:(304)263-4901
Fax: (304)264-7008
Contact: Linda Miller, Small Business Specialist

The following Treasury Department Regional Financial Centers are arranged alphabetically by city.

67689 ■ **U.S. Department of the Treasury–Austin Financial Center**
PO Box 149058
Austin, TX 78714-9058
Ph:(512)342-7300
Fax: (512)342-7225

67690 ■ **U.S. Department of the Treasury–Birmingham Financial Center**
190 Vulcan Rd.
PO Box 2451
Birmingham, AL 35201-2451
Ph:(205)912-6207
Fax: (205)912-6114

67691 ■ **U.S. Department of the Treasury–Chicago Financial Center**
PO Box 8670
Chicago, IL 60680-8670
Ph:(312)353-5622
Fax: (312)353-3183

67692 ■ **U.S. Department of the Treasury–Kansas City Financial Center**
PO Box 12599-0599
Kansas City, KS 64116-0599
Ph:(816)414-2100
Fax: (816)414-2111

67693 ■ **U.S. Department of the Treasury–Philadelphia Financial Center**
PO Box 51317
Philadelphia, PA 19115-6317
Ph:(215)516-8021
Fax: (215)516-8010

67694 ■ **U.S. Department of the Treasury–San Francisco Financial Center**
PO Box 24700
Oakland, CA 94623-1700
Ph:(510)594-7182

U.S. DEPARTMENT OF VETERANS AFFAIRS

67695 ■ **U.S. Department of Veterans Affairs–Office of Small and Disadvantaged Business Utilization**
Tech World Plz.
810 Vermont Ave., NW
Washington, DC 20420
Free: 800-949-8387
Fax: (202)565-8156
URL: http://www.osdbu@mail.va.gov

67696 ■ **U.S. Department of Veterans Affairs–Public Health and Environmental Hazards**
810 Vermont Ave., NW, Rm. 870
Washington, DC 20420
Ph:(202)273-8575
Fax: (202)273-9079

U.S. INFORMATION AGENCY

67697 ■ **U.S. Printing Office–General Procurement Division–Office of Small and Disadvantaged Business Utilization (732 N)**
732 N. Capitol St., NW, Rm. A332
Stop MMG
Washington, DC 20401
Ph:(202)512-0916
Fax: (202)512-0975

U.S. NUCLEAR REGULATORY COMMISSION

67698 ■ **U.S. Nuclear Regulatory Commission (Region 1)–King of Prussia Regional Office**
475 Allendale Rd.
King of Prussia, PA 19406-1415
Ph:(610)337-5000
Free: 800-432-1156
URL: http://www.nrc.gov
Description: Serves Connecticut, Delaware, Maine, Maryland, Massachusetts, New Hampshire, New Jersey, New York, Pennsylvania, Rhode Island, Vermont, and Washington.

67699 ■ **U.S. Nuclear Regulatory Commission (Region 2)–Atlanta Regional Office**
Sam Nunn Atlanta Federal Ctr., 23 T85
61 Forsyth St., SW
Atlanta, GA 30303-8931
Ph:(404)562-4400
Free: 800-577-8510
URL: http://www.nrc.gov
Description: Serves Alabama, Florida, Georgia, Kentucky, Mississippi, North Carolina, Puerto Rico, South Carolina, Tennessee, Virginia, Virgin Islands, and West Virginia.

67700 ■ **U.S. Nuclear Regulatory Commission (Region 3)–Lisle Regional Office**
2443 Warrenville Rd., St. 210
Lisle, IL 30532-4352
Ph:(630)829-9500
Free: 800-522-3025
Fax: (630)515-1078
URL: http://www.nrc.gov
Description: Serves Illinois, Indiana, Iowa, Michigan, Minnesota, Missouri, Ohio, and Wisconsin.

67701 ■ **U.S. Nuclear Regulatory Commission (Region 4)–Arlington Regional Office**
Texas Health Resources Tower
611 Ryan Plz., Ste. 400
Arlington, TX 76011-4005
Ph:(817)860-8100
Free: 800-952-9677
URL: http://www.nrc.gov
Description: Serves Alaska, Arizona, Arkansas, California, Colorado, Hawaii, Idaho, Kansas, Louisiana, Montana, Nebraska, Nevada, New Mexico, North Dakota, Oklahoma, Oregon, South Dakota, Texas, Utah, Washington, and Wyoming.

67702 ■ **U.S. Nuclear Regulatory Commission–Office of Small and Disadvantaged Business Utilization/Civil Rights**
11555 Rockville Pike
Rockville, MD 20852-2738
Ph:(301)415-7380
Free: 800-368-5642
Fax: (301)415-5953
URL: http://www.nrc.gov/
Description: The Nuclear Regulatory Commission's Office of Small and Disadvantaged Business Utilization offers small businesses information and guidance on procurement procedures, how to be placed on a bidder's mailing list, and identification of both prime and subcontracting opportunities.

U.S. POSTAL SERVICE

67703 ■ **U.S. Postal Service–Administrative Operations–Information Technology Division (2111)**
2111 Wilson Blvd., Ste. 500
Arlington, VA 22201
Ph:(703)248-3701
URL: http://www.usps.gov

67704 ■ U.S. Postal Service–Chicago Service Center
150 S. Wacker Dr., Ste. 200
Chicago, IL 60606-4100
Ph:(312)424-3488
Fax: (312)424-3170
URL: http://www.usps.gov

67705 ■ U.S. Postal Service–Environmental and MRO Category Management Center
PO Box 667190
Dallas, TX 75266-7190
Ph:(214)819-7100
Fax: (214)819-7125
Co. E-mail: don.i.jones@usps.gov
URL: http://www.usps.gov
Description: Serves Arizona, Louisiana, Oklahoma, and Texas.

67706 ■ U.S. Postal Service–Field Operations - East
2 Gateway Ctr., 9th Fl., Rm. 3100
Newark, NJ 07173-0001
Ph:(610)668-4544
URL: http://www.usps.gov

67707 ■ U.S. Postal Service–Field Operations - South
1 Church Cir., Rm. 208
Annapolis, MD 21404-0426
Ph:(410)267-1081
URL: http://www.usps.gov

67708 ■ U.S. Postal Service–Field Operations - West
1 Church Cir., Rm. 208
Annapolis, MD 21404-0426
Free: 800-275-8777
URL: http://www.usps.gov

67709 ■ U.S. Postal Service–General Counsel–Business Services (475 L)
475 L'Enfant Plz. W., SW, Rm. 6015
Washington, DC 20260-0010
Ph:(202)268-2802
Co. E-mail: james.g.schlett@usps.gov
URL: http://www.usps.gov

67710 ■ U.S. Postal Service–Intelligent Mail and Address Quality
475 L'Enfant Plz., SW, Rm. 2100
Washington, DC 20260-0010
Ph:(202)268-6200
Fax: (202)268-4492
Co. E-mail: cbravo@mail.usps.gov
URL: http://www.usps.gov

67711 ■ U.S. Postal Service–Investigations and Security–Dangerous Mail Investigations and Homeland Security (475 L)
475 L'Enfant Plz. W., SW, Rm. 3301
Washington, DC 20260-0010
Ph:(202)268-4432

67712 ■ U.S. Postal Service–Memphis Purchasing Service Center
225 N. Humphreys Blvd.
Memphis, TN 38166-6260
Ph:(901)747-7530
Fax: (901)747-7492
URL: http://www.usps.gov

67713 ■ U.S. Postal Service–Office of the Inspector General
1735 N. Lynn Street, Rm. 12011
Arlington, VA 22209-2020
Ph:(703)248-2300
Fax: (703)248-2291
Co. E-mail: dave.williams@uspsoig.gov
URL: http://www.uspsoig.gov

67714 ■ U.S. Postal Service–Office of Operations
475 L'Enfant Plz. W., SW, Rm. 3010
Washington, DC 20260-0010
Ph:(202)268-5425
URL: http://www.usps.gov

67715 ■ U.S. Postal Service–San Francisco Purchasing Service Center
395 Oyster Point Blvd., Ste. 205
San Francisco, CA 94080-1996
Ph:(650)615-7260
Fax: (650)615-7293
URL: http://www.usps.gov
Description: Serves California and Hawaii.

67716 ■ U.S. Postal Service–United States Postal Inspection Service
475 L'Enfant Plz., SW, Rm. 3100
Washington, DC 20260-0010
Ph:(202)268-4264
Fax: (202)268-4563
URL: http://www.usps.gov

67717 ■ U.S. Postal Service–Windsor Purchasing Service Center E
8 Griffin Rd., N.
Windsor, CT 06095-1572
Ph:(860)285-7126
Fax: (860)285-7272
Co. E-mail: Robert.a.bress@usps.gov
URL: http://www.usps.gov

67718 ■ U.S. Postal Service–Office of Small and Disadvantaged Business Utilization
475 L'Enfant Plz. SW, Rm. 4320
Washington, DC 20260-4320
Ph:(202)268-4633
Fax: (202)268-7288
URL: http://www.usps.gov/
Description: The Postal Service's Office of Small and Disadvantaged Business Utilization offers small businesses information and guidance on procurement procedures, how to be placed on a bidder's mailing list, and identification of both prime and subcontracting opportunities.

U.S. SMALL BUSINESS ADMINISTRATION

67719 ■ U.S. Small Business Administration–Office of Small Business Development Centers
2600 6th St. NW, Rm. 128
Washington, DC 20416
Ph:(202)806-1550
Fax: (202)806-1777
URL: http://www.dcsbdc.com
Description: Although other federal agencies also provide some services to small business, the SBA's primary duties are to aid, counsel, assist, and protect the interests of small business. It ensures that small business concerns receive a fair portion of government purchases, contracts, and subcontracts, as well as fair portions of the sales of government property. The SBA grants loans to small business concerns, to state and local development companies, and to the victims of floods, other catastrophes, or certain types of economic injuries. The administration also licenses, regulates, and grants loans to small business investment companies (SBICs). A small business must meet SBA size standards to be eligible for its loans, procurement assistance, and other services. Interested small business owners should contact the nearest SBA field offices for current standards since they vary by industry and are subject to change. The SBA administers a variety of loan programs for eligible small business concerns that cannot borrow money on reasonable terms from conventional lenders without government assistance. Most of the SBA's loans are made by private lenders and then guaranteed by the SBA, which can guarantee loans up to 90 percent for a maximum of $500,000. In addition to these regular business loans, the SBA offers a variety of special loan programs, including local development company loans that are offered to groups of local citizens. The SBA licenses and regulates small business investment companies (SBICs) which provide venture capital to small businesses. SBA field officers provide counseling and other services to small business owners seeking to do business with the federal govern-

ment. Procurement specialists at district offices assist in identifying the government agencies that are prospective customers, in instructing small businesses about inclusion on bidders' lists, and in obtaining drawings and specifications for specific contracts. The SBA seeks to increase small business' share of procurement through the activities of its network of procurement center representatives (PCRs), stationed at or in liaison with all federal military and civilian installations with major buying programs. The SBA's procurement assistance program sets aside suitable government purchases for competitive award to small business concerns and provides an appeal procedure when the ability of a low-bidding small firm to perform a contract is questioned. The SBA also develops subcontracting opportunities, designating the amounts to be subcontracted to small business concerns by prime contractors undertaking major federal projects. The SBA administers the Small Business Innovation Research Program, which fosters participation by small businesses in federal research and development; and provides counseling and information to small businesses through a network of resource programs. The SBA also sponsors the Small Business Development Center (SBDC) Program in conjunction with the educational community, state and local governments, the federal government, and the private sector. In each state there is one "lead" organization that sponsors each SBDC and from which a statewide director manages the program. SBDCs seek to further economic development by providing management and technical assistance to existing and prospective small businesses. The lead organizations coordinate the activities performed on behalf of small business through the participation and establishment of SBDC subcenters and satellite locations. The SBA also offers export counseling and training through its Office of International Trade or small businesses wishing to export products and materials. The SBA is authorized, under Section 8 (a) of the Small Business Act, to enter into contracts with other federal agencies for goods and services and then to subcontract the work to firms owned by socially and economically disadvantaged persons. The firms must be approved to participate in the 8(a) program by the SBA. In addition, the SBA also is authorized, under Section 7(j) of the act, to provide management and technical assistance to SBA clients and small businesses in areas of high unemployment. This program allows the SBA to contract with qualified individuals, state and local governments, educational institutions, Native American tribes, and other nonprofit institutions. The SBA seeks to increase the strength, profitability, and visibility of women-owned businesses by enhancing their access to existing government and private sector resources. Specific efforts include assisting women business owners in surviving business crises; providing SBA personnel with the appropriate skills to respond to the needs of women business owners; increasing federal marketing opportunities; negotiating an annual goal for procurement from women business owners for each federal department and agency; and collecting and analyzing data about women-owned businesses. The SBA's Office of Advocacy attempts to evaluate the impact of legislative proposals and other public policy issues on small business and represents its views before Congress, federal agencies, and state and local governments. The chief counsel also coordinates and conducts applied economic research on a wide range of small business issues, as well as serves as a source of information about the federal government for small business. The office's activities are supported by advocates located at each of the ten SBA regional offices. The SBA also publishes a variety of pamphlets and booklets about its programs and services.

The following offices are arranged by region.

67720 ■ U.S. Small Business Administration (Region 1)
10 Causeway St., Rm. 812
Boston, MA 02222-1093
Ph:(617)565-8415
Fax: (617)565-8420
Description: Serves Connecticut, Maine, Massachusetts, New Hampshire, Rhode Island, and Vermont.

67721 ■ U.S. Small Business Administration (Region 2)
26 Federal Plz., Rm. 3108
New York, NY 10278
Ph:(212)264-1450
Fax: (212)264-0038
Description: Serves New Jersey, New York, Puerto Rico, and the Virgin Islands.

67722 ■ U.S. Small Business Administration (Region 3)
Robert N.C. Nix Federal Bldg.
900 Market St. 5th Fl.
Philadelphia, PA 19107
Ph:(215)580-2807
Fax: (215)580-2746
Description: Serves Delaware, the District of Columbia, Maryland, Pennsylvania, Virginia, and West Virginia.

67723 ■ U.S. Small Business Administration (Region 4)
233 Peachtree St. NE, Ste. 1800
Atlanta, GA 30303
Ph:(404)331-4999
Fax: (404)331-2354
Description: Serves Alabama, Florida, Georgia, Kentucky, Mississippi, North Carolina, South Carolina, and Tennessee.

67724 ■ U.S. Small Business Administration (Region 5)
Citicorp Center
500 W. Madison St., Ste. 1240
Chicago, IL 60606-2511
Ph:(312)353-0357
Fax: (312)353-3426
Description: Serves Illinois, Indiana, Michigan, Minnesota, Ohio, and Wisconsin.

67725 ■ U.S. Small Business Administration (Region 6)
Dallas Regional Office
4300 Amon Carter Blvd., Ste. 108
Ft. Worth, TX 76155
Ph:(817)684-5581
Fax: (817)684-5588
Description: Serves Arkansas, Louisiana, New Mexico, Oklahoma, and Texas.

67726 ■ U.S. Small Business Administration (Region 7)
Kansas City Regional Office
323 W. 8th St., Ste. 307
Kansas City, MO 64105-1500
Ph:(816)374-6380
Fax: (816)374-6339
Description: Serves Iowa, Kansas, Missouri, and Nebraska.

67727 ■ U.S. Small Business Administration (Region 8)
Denver regional Office
721 19th St., Ste. 400
Denver, CO 80202-2599
Ph:(303)844-0500
Fax: (303)844-0506
Description: Serves Colorado, Montana, North Dakota, South Dakota, Utah, and Wyoming.

67728 ■ U.S. Small Business Administration (Region 9)
Los Angeles Regional Office
330 N. Brand Blvd., Ste. 1270
Glendale, CA 91203-2304
Ph:(818)552-3434
Fax: (818)552-3440
Description: Serves American Samoa, Arizona, California, Guam, Hawaii, Nevada, and the Trust Territory of the Pacific Islands.

67729 ■ U.S. Small Business Administration (Region 10)
Seattle Regional Office
2401 4th Ave., Ste. 400
Seattle, WA 98121
Ph:(206)553-5676

Fax: (206)553-4155
Description: Serves Alaska, Idaho, Oregon, and Washington.

The following field offices are arranged alphabetically by state.

67730 ■ U.S. Small Business Administration–Birmingham District Office
801 Tom Martin Dr., Ste. 201
Birmingham, AL 35211
Ph:(205)290-7101
Fax: (205)290-7404
URL: http://www.sba.gov

67731 ■ U.S. Small Business Administration–Anchorage District Office
510 L St., Ste. 310
Anchorage, AK 99501
Ph:(907)271-4842
Fax: (907)271-4545
Co. E-mail: martin.carlton@sba.gov

67732 ■ U.S. Small Business Administration–Phoenix District Office
2828 N. Central Ave., Ste. 800
Phoenix, AZ 85004-1093
Ph:(602)745-7200
Fax: (602)745-7210

67733 ■ U.S. Small Business Administration–Little Rock District Office
2120 Riverfront Dr., Ste. 250
Little Rock, AR 72202-1796
Ph:(501)324-7379
Fax: (501)324-7394

67734 ■ U.S. Small Business Administration–Fresno District Office
2719 N. Air Fresno Dr., Ste. 200
Fresno, CA 93727
Ph:(559)487-5791
Fax: (559)487-5636

67735 ■ U.S. Small Business Administration–Los Angeles District Office
330 N. Brand Blvd., Ste. 1200
Glendale, CA 91203
Ph:(818)552-3215

67736 ■ U.S. Small Business Administration–Sacramento Branch Office
660 J St., Ste. 215
Sacramento, CA 95814
Ph:(916)498-6410
Fax: (916)498-6422
Co. E-mail: sac-needhelp@sba.gov
URL: http://www.sba.gov/regions/states/ca/sacr.html

67737 ■ U.S. Small Business Administration–San Diego District Office
550 W. C St., Ste. 550
San Diego, CA 92101-3500
Ph:(619)557-7250
Fax: (619)557-5894

67738 ■ U.S. Small Business Administration–San Francisco District Office
455 Market St., 6th Fl.
San Francisco, CA 94105-2420
Ph:(415)744-6820
Fax: (415)744-6812

67739 ■ U.S. Small Business Administration–Santa Ana District Office
200 W. Santa Ana Blvd., Ste. 700
Santa Ana, CA 92701
Ph:(714)550-7420
Fax: (714)550-0191

67740 ■ U.S. Small Business Administration–Denver District Office
721 19th St., Ste. 426
Denver, CO 80202-2517
Ph:(303)844-2607
Fax: (303)844-6468
Co. E-mail: joseph.edwards@sba.gov

URL: http://www.sba.gov/cp/index.html

67741 ■ U.S. Small Business Administration–Hartford District Office
330 Main St., 2nd Fl.
Hartford, CT 06106
Ph:(860)240-4700
Fax: (860)240-4659

67742 ■ U.S. Small Business Administration–Wilmington Branch Office
824 N. Market St., Ste. 610
Wilmington, DE 19801-3011
Ph:(302)573-6294
Fax: (302)573-6060

67743 ■ U.S. Small Business Administration–Associate Deputy Administrator for Economic Development
409 3rd St. SW, Rm. 7000
Washington, DC 20416
Ph:(202)205-6657

67744 ■ U.S. Small Business Administration–Associate Deputy Administrator for Government Contracting and Minority Enterprise Development
409 3rd St. SW, Rm. 8000
Washington, DC 20416
Ph:(202)205-6459

67745 ■ U.S. Small Business Administration–Office of Business and Community Initiatives–Office of Entrepreneurial Development (409 3)
409 3rd St. SW, Ste. 7000
Washington, DC 20416
Ph:(202)205-6605
Free: 800-877-8339
Fax: (202)205-6802
URL: http://www.sba.gov/bi

67746 ■ U.S. Small Business Administration–Office of Communications and Public Liaison
409 3rd St., SW
Washington, DC 20416
Ph:(202)205-6740

67747 ■ U.S. Small Business Administration–Office of Financial Assistance–Office of Loan Programs (740 1)
740 15th St. NW, 3rd Fl.
Washington, DC 20005-3544
Ph:(202)272-0345
Fax: (202)272-0344
URL: http://www.sba.gov/dc

67748 ■ U.S. Small Business Administration–Office of Government Contracting
409 3rd St., SW
Washington, DC 20416
Ph:(202)205-6618
Fax: (202)205-6390
Co. E-mail: sizestandards@sba.gov
URL: http://www.sba.gov/gc

67749 ■ U.S. Small Business Administration–Office of Minority Enterprise Development
409 3rd St. SW
Washington, DC 20416
Ph:(202)205-6412
Fax: (202)205-7064

67750 ■ U.S. Small Business Administration–Office of Minority Enterprise Development–Division of 8(a) Program Certification and Eligibility (409 3)
409 3rd St. SW
Washington, DC 20416
Ph:(202)619-0628
Free: 800-827-5722

67751 ■ U.S. Small Business Administration–Office of Women's Business Ownership
409 3rd St. SW, 6th Fl.
Washington, DC 20416
Ph:(202)205-6673
Fax: (202)205-7287
Co. E-mail: owbo@sba.gov
URL: http://www.sba.gov/womeninbusiness

67752 ■ U.S. Small Business Administration–Washington, DC, District Office
740 15th St. NW, 3rd Fl.
PO Box 34500
Washington, DC 20005-3544
Ph:(202)272-0345
Fax: (202)272-0344
URL: http://www.sba.gov

67753 ■ U.S. Small Business Administration–Jacksonville District Office
North Florida District Office
7825 Baymeadows Way, Ste. 100B
Jacksonville, FL 32256-7504
Ph:(904)443-1900
Fax: (904)443-1980

67754 ■ U.S. Small Business Administration–Miami District Office
100 S. Biscayne Blvd., 7th Fl.
Miami, FL 33131
Ph:(305)536-5521
Fax: (305)536-5058

67755 ■ U.S. Small Business Administration–West Palm Beach Post of Duty
1320 S. Dixie Hwy., 501
Coral Gables, FL 33146-2911
Ph:(305)536-5521
Fax: (305)536-5058

67756 ■ U.S. Small Business Administration–Atlanta District Office
233 Peachtree St., Ste. 1900
Atlanta, GA 30303
Ph:(404)331-0100
Fax: (404)331-0101

67757 ■ U.S. Small Business Administration–Honolulu District Office
300 Ala Moana Blvd., Rm. 2-235
PO Box 50207
Honolulu, HI 96850
Ph:(808)541-2990
Fax: (808)541-2976

67758 ■ U.S. Small Business Administration–Boise District Office
380 E. Parkcenter Blvd., Ste. 330
Boise, ID 83702-5745
Ph:(208)334-1696
Fax: (208)334-9353
URL: http://www.sba.gov

67759 ■ U.S. Small Business Administration–Chicago Regional Office
Illinois District Office
500 W. Madison, Ste. 1250
Chicago, IL 60661-2511
Ph:(312)353-4528
Fax: (312)886-5688

67760 ■ U.S. Small Business Administration–Springfield, IL, Branch Office
511 W. Capitol St., Ste. 302
Springfield, IL 62704
Ph:(217)492-4416
Fax: (217)492-4867

67761 ■ U.S. Small Business Administration–Indianapolis District Office
Indiana District Office
8500 Keystone Crossing, Ste. 400
Indianapolis, IN 46240
Ph:(317)226-7272

Fax: (317)226-7259

67762 ■ U.S. Small Business Administration–Cedar Rapids District Office
2750 1st Ave. NE, Ste. 350
215 4th Ave. SE
Cedar Rapids, IA 52402-4831
Ph:(319)362-6405
Fax: (319)362-7861

67763 ■ U.S. Small Business Administration–Des Moines Office
210 Walnut St., Rm. 749
Des Moines, IA 50309-4106
Ph:(515)284-4422
Fax: (515)284-4572

67764 ■ U.S. Small Business Administration–Wichita District Office
271 W. 3rd St. N., Ste. 2500
Wichita, KS 67202-1212
Ph:(316)269-6616
Fax: (316)269-6499

67765 ■ U.S. Small Business Administration–Louisville District Office
600 Dr. Martin Luther King Jr. Pl., Rm. 188
Louisville, KY 40202
Ph:(502)582-5971
Fax: (502)582-5009

67766 ■ U.S. Small Business Administration–Augusta District Office
Edmund S. Muskie Federal Bldg.
68 Sewall St., Rm. 512
Augusta, ME 04330
Ph:(207)622-8274
URL: http://www.sba.gov

67767 ■ U.S. Small Business Administration–Baltimore District Office
City Crescent Bldg., 6th Fl.
10 S. Howard St.
Baltimore, MD 21201-2525
Ph:(410)962-4392
Fax: (410)962-1805
URL: http://www.sba.gov

67768 ■ U.S. Small Business Administration–Boston District Office
Federal Bldg.
10 Causeway St., Rm. 265
Boston, MA 02222-1093
Ph:(617)565-5590
Fax: (617)565-5598
URL: http://www.sba.gov

67769 ■ U.S. Small Business Administration–Springfield, MA, Branch Office
1441 Main St., Ste. 410
Springfield, MA 01103
Ph:(413)785-0268
Fax: (413)785-0267

67770 ■ U.S. Small Business Administration–Detroit District Office
McNamara Federal Bldg.
477 Michigan Ave., Ste. 515
Detroit, MI 48226
Ph:(313)226-6075
Fax: (313)226-4769
Co. E-mail: michigan@sba.gov

67771 ■ U.S. Small Business Administration–Minneapolis District Office
610-C Butler Sq.
100 N. 6th St.
Minneapolis, MN 55403
Ph:(612)370-2324
Fax: (612)370-2303
URL: http://www.sba.gov

67772 ■ U.S. Small Business Administration–Gulfport Branch Office
Gulf Coast Business Technology Center
1636 Popps Ferry Rd., Ste. 203
Biloxi, MS 39532

Ph:(228)863-4449
Fax: (228)864-0179

67773 ■ U.S. Small Business Administration–Jackson District Office
Amsouth Bank Plaza
210 E. Capitol St., Ste. 900
Jackson, MS 39201
Ph:(601)965-4378
Fax: (601)965-5629

67774 ■ U.S. Small Business Administration–Kansas City District Office
Lucas Pl., Ste. 501
323 W. 8th St.
Kansas City, MO 64105
Ph:(816)374-6708
Fax: (816)374-6759

67775 ■ U.S. Small Business Administration–St. Louis District Office
200 N. Broadway, Ste. 1500
St. Louis, MO 63102
Ph:(314)539-6600
Fax: (314)539-3785

67776 ■ U.S. Small Business Administration–Springfield, MO, Branch Office
Cherrystone Center
620 S. Glenstone St., Ste. 110
Springfield, MO 65802-3200
Ph:(417)864-7670
Fax: (417)864-4108

67777 ■ U.S. Small Business Administration–Helena District Office
Montana District Office
10 W. 15th St., Ste. 1100
Helena, MT 59626
Ph:(406)441-1081
Fax: (406)441-1090

67778 ■ U.S. Small Business Administration–Omaha District Office
11145 Mill Valley Rd.
Omaha, NE 68154-3949
Ph:(402)221-4691
Fax: (402)221-3680

67779 ■ U.S. Small Business Administration–Las Vegas District Office
Nevada District Office
400 S. 4th St., Ste. 250
Las Vegas, NV 89101
Ph:(702)388-6611
Fax: (702)388-6469

67780 ■ U.S. Small Business Administration–Concord District Office
New Hampshire District Office
JV Cleveland Federal Bldg.
55 Pleasant St., Ste. 3101
Concord, NH 03301
Ph:(603)225-1400
Fax: (603)225-1409

67781 ■ U.S. Small Business Administration–Newark District Office
New Jersey District Office
2 Gateway Center, 15th Fl.
Newark, NJ 07102
Ph:(973)645-2434
Fax: (973)645-6265

67782 ■ U.S. Small Business Administration–Albuquerque District Office
625 Silver Ave. SW, Ste. 320
Albuquerque, NM 87102
Ph:(505)346-7909
Fax: (505)346-6711

67783 ■ U.S. Small Business Administration–Buffalo District Office
Niagara Center
130 S. Elmwood Ave., Ste 540
Buffalo, NY 14202

Ph:(716)551-4301
Fax: (716)551-4418
Co. E-mail: sba@buffalo.com
URL: http://www.sba.gov

67784 ■ **U.S. Small Business Administration–Elmira Branch Office**
333 E. Water St., 4th Fl.
Elmira, NY 14901
Ph:(607)734-8130
Fax: (607)733-4656

67785 ■ **U.S. Small Business Administration–Melville Branch Office**
35 Pinelawn Rd.
Melville, NY 11747
Ph:(631)454-0764
Fax: (631)454-0769

67786 ■ **U.S. Small Business Administration–New York District Office**
Jacob K. Javits Federal Bldg.
26 Federal Plz., Rm. 3100
New York, NY 10278
Ph:(212)264-4354
Fax: (212)264-4963

67787 ■ **U.S. Small Business Administration–Rochester Office**
Federal Bldg., Rm. 410
100 State St.
Rochester, NY 14614
Ph:(585)263-6700
Fax: (585)263-3146

67788 ■ **U.S. Small Business Administration–Syracuse District Office**
401 S. Salina St., 5th Fl.
Syracuse, NY 13202-2415
Ph:(315)471-9393
Fax: (315)471-9288

67789 ■ **U.S. Small Business Administration–Charlotte District Office**
North Carolina District Office
6302 Fairview Rd., Ste. 300
Charlotte, NC 28210-2227
Ph:(704)344-6563
Free: 800-827-5722
Fax: (704)344-6769

67790 ■ **U.S. Small Business Administration–Fargo District Office**
657 2nd Ave. N., Rm. 218
Fargo, ND 58102
Ph:(701)239-5131
Fax: (701)239-5645
Co. E-mail: north.dakota@sba.gov

67791 ■ **U.S. Small Business Administration–Cleveland District Office**
Ohio District Office
1350 Euclid Ave., Ste. 211
Cleveland, OH 44115
Ph:(216)522-4180
Fax: (216)522-2038

67792 ■ **U.S. Small Business Administration–Columbus District Office**
Ohio District Office
401 N. Front St., Ste. 200
Columbus, OH 43215
Ph:(614)469-6860
Fax: (614)469-2391

67793 ■ **U.S. Small Business Administration–Oklahoma City District Office**
Federal Bldg.
301 NW 6th St.
Oklahoma City, OK 73102
Ph:(405)609-8000

67794 ■ **U.S. Small Business Administration–Portland District Office**
601 SW 2nd Ave., Ste. 950
Portland, OR 97204-3192
Ph:(503)326-2682

Fax: (503)326-2808
Co. E-mail: por-needheld@sba.gov

67795 ■ **U.S. Small Business Administration–Philadelphia District Office**
Robert N.C. Nix Federal Bldg.
900 Market St., 5th Fl.
Philadelphia, PA 19107
Ph:(215)580-2722
Fax: (215)580-2746

67796 ■ **U.S. Small Business Administration–Pittsburgh District Office**
411 7th Ave., Ste. 1450
1000 Liberty Ave., Rm. 1128
Pittsburgh, PA 15219
Ph:(412)395-6560
Fax: (412)395-6562
URL: http://www.sba.com

67797 ■ **U.S. Small Business Administration–Wilkes-Barre Branch Office**
Stegmaier Bldg., Rm. 403
7 N. Wilkes-Barre Blvd.
Wilkes Barre, PA 18702
Ph:(570)826-6502
Fax: (570)826-6287

67798 ■ **U.S. Small Business Administration–Puerto Rico and U.S. Virgin Islands District Office**
Citibank Tower, Ste. 200
252 Ponce de Leon Ave.
San Juan, PR 00918
Ph:(787)766-5572
Free: 800-669-8049
Fax: (787)766-5309

67799 ■ **U.S. Small Business Administration–Providence District Office**
380 Westminster St., Ste. 511
Providence, RI 02903
Ph:(401)528-4561
Fax: (401)528-4539

67800 ■ **U.S. Small Business Administration–Columbia District Office**
South Carolina District Office
1835 Assembly St., Rm. 1425
Columbia, SC 29201
Ph:(803)765-5377
Fax: (803)765-5962

67801 ■ **U.S. Small Business Administration–Sioux Falls District Office**
South Dakota District Office
2329 N. Career Ave., Ste. 105
Sioux Falls, SD 57107
Ph:(605)330-4243
Fax: (605)330-4215

67802 ■ **U.S. Small Business Administration–Nashville District Office**
Tennessee District Office
50 Vantage Way, Ste. 201
Nashville, TN 37228-1500
Ph:(615)736-5881
Fax: (615)736-7232

67803 ■ **U.S. Small Business Administration–Corpus Christi Branch Office**
3649 Leopard St., Ste. 411
Corpus Christi, TX 78408
Ph:(361)879-0017

67804 ■ **U.S. Small Business Administration–Dallas District Office**
4300 Amon Carter Blvd., Ste. 114
Ft. Worth, TX 76155
Ph:(817)684-5500
Fax: (817)684-5516

67805 ■ **U.S. Small Business Administration–El Paso District Office**
10737 Gateway W.
El Paso, TX 79935
Ph:(915)633-7001

Fax: (915)633-7005

67806 ■ **U.S. Small Business Administration–Harlingen District Office**
222 E. Van Buren, Ste. 500
Harlingen, TX 78550
Ph:(956)427-8533
Fax: (956)427-8537

67807 ■ **U.S. Small Business Administration–Houston District Office**
9301 Southwest Fwy., Ste. 550
Houston, TX 77074-1591
Ph:(713)773-6500
Fax: (713)773-6550

67808 ■ **U.S. Small Business Administration–Lubbock District Office**
1205 Texas Ave., Rm. 408
Lubbock, TX 79401-2693
Ph:(806)472-7462
Fax: (806)472-7487

67809 ■ **U.S. Small Business Administration–Marshall Post of Duty**
505 E. Travis, Rm. 103
Marshall, TX 75670
Ph:(903)935-5257
Fax: (903)935-1248

67810 ■ **U.S. Small Business Administration–San Antonio District Office**
17319 San Pedro, Ste. 200
San Antonio, TX 78232-1411
Ph:(210)403-5900
Fax: (210)403-5936
Co. E-mail: sado.email@sba.gov

67811 ■ **U.S. Small Business Administration–St. Croix Post of Duty**
Sunny Isle Professional Bldg.
Ste. 5 and 6
St. Croix, VI 00830
Ph:(340)778-5380
Free: 800-669-8049
Fax: (340)778-5380

67812 ■ **U.S. Small Business Administration–St. Thomas Post of Duty**
3800 Crown Bay
Virgin Islands Maritime Bldg.
St. Thomas, VI 00802
Ph:(809)774-8530
Fax: (809)776-2312

67813 ■ **U.S. Small Business Administration–Salt Lake City District Office**
2235 Federal Bldg.
125 S. State St., Rm. 2227
Salt Lake City, UT 84138-1195
Ph:(801)524-3209
Fax: (801)524-4160

67814 ■ **U.S. Small Business Administration–Montpelier District Office**
Vermont District Office
87 State St., Rm. 205
PO Box 605
Montpelier, VT 05601-0605
Ph:(802)828-4422
Fax: (802)828-4485

67815 ■ **U.S. Small Business Administration–Richmond District Office**
Federal Bldg.
400 N. 8th St., Ste. 1150
PO Box 10126
Richmond, VA 23240-0126
Ph:(804)771-2400
Fax: (804)771-2764

67816 ■ **U.S. Small Business Administration–Seattle Regional Office**
2401 4th Ave., Ste. 400
1200 6th Ave.
Seattle, WA 98121
Ph:(206)553-5676

Fax: (206)553-4155

67817 ■ U.S. Small Business Administration–Spokane, WA Branch Office
Spokane Sub Office
801 W. Riverside Ave., Ste. 200
Spokane, WA 99201
Ph:(509)353-2811
Fax: (509)353-2829
Description: Serving Eastern Washington and Northern Idaho.

67818 ■ U.S. Small Business Administration–Charleston Branch Office
405 Capitol St., Ste. 412
Charleston, WV 26301
Ph:(304)347-5220
Fax: (304)347-5350

67819 ■ U.S. Small Business Administration–Clarksburg District Office
320 W. Pike St., Ste. 330
Clarksburg, WV 26301
Ph:(304)623-5631
Fax: (304)623-0023

67820 ■ U.S. Small Business Administration–Madison District Office
Wisconsin District Office
740 Regent St., Ste. 100
Madison, WI 53715
Ph:(608)441-5263
Fax: (608)441-5541

67821 ■ U.S. Small Business Administration–Casper District Office
Federal Bldg.
100 E. B St.
PO Box 44001
Casper, WY 82602-5013
Ph:(307)261-6500
Fax: (307)261-6535

The following Business Information Centers are arranged alphabetically by state.

67822 ■ U.S. Small Business Administration–Business Information Center (Los Angeles, CA)
Los Angeles District Office
330 N. Brand, Ste. 1200
Glendale, CA 91203
Ph:(818)552-3215
Contact: Mr. Ken Davis

67823 ■ U.S. Small Business Administration–Business Information Center (San Diego, CA)
San Diego District Office
550 W. C St., Ste. 550
San Diego, CA 92101
Ph:(619)557-7250
Fax: (619)557-5894
Contact: Mr. Bob Nelson

67824 ■ U.S. Small Business Administration–Business Information Center (Denver, CO)
721 19th St., Ste. 426
Denver, CO 80202-2599
Ph:(303)844-2607
Fax: (303)844-6490
URL: http://www.sba.gov
Contact: Ms. Cyndi Jones

67825 ■ U.S. Small Business Administration–SBA/Bell Atlantic–Business Information Center (Washington, DC) (Washi)
Washington District Office
1110 Vermont Ave. NW, 9th Fl.
Washington, DC 20005
Ph:(202)606-4000
URL: http://www.sba.gov/dc
Contact: Hy Gardner

67826 ■ U.S. Small Business Administration–Business Information Center (Atlanta, GA)
Georgia District Office
Harris Tower
270 Peachtree St., Ste. 1900
Atlanta, GA 30303
Ph:(404)331-0100
Fax: (404)331-0101
URL: http://www.sba.gov/ga/
Contact: Mr. Fred Brandt

67827 ■ U.S. Small Business Administration–Business Information Center (Boise, ID)
Boise District Office
1020 Main St., Ste. 290
Boise, ID 83702
Ph:(208)334-1696
Fax: (208)334-9353
URL: http://www.sba.gov/id/
Contact: Mr. Rod Grzadzieleski

67828 ■ U.S. Small Business Administration–Business Information Center (Chicago, IL)
Chicago District Office
500 W. Madison St., Ste. 1250
Chicago, IL 60661-2511
Ph:(312)353-4528
Fax: (312)886-5688
URL: http://www.sba.gov
Contact: Ms. Phyllis Scott

67829 ■ U.S. Small Business Administration–Business Information Center (Boston, MA)
Massachusetts District Office
Thomas P. I'Neill Federal Bldg.
10 Causeway St., Rm. 265
Boston, MA 02222-1093
Ph:(617)565-5590
Fax: (617)565-5598
URL: http://www.sba.gov/ma/
Contact: Ms. Andrea Ross

67830 ■ U.S. Small Business Administration–Business Information Center (Kansas City, MO)
Kansas City District Office
323 W. 8th St., Ste. 501
Kansas City, MO 64105
Ph:(816)374-6701
Fax: (816)374-6692
Contact: Ms. Kim Malcolm

67831 ■ U.S. Small Business Administration–Business Information Center (St. Louis, MO)
200 N. Broadway, Ste. 1500
St. Louis, MO 63102
Ph:(314)539-6600
Fax: (314)539-3785
Contact: Sydney Shrage

67832 ■ U.S. Small Business Administration–Business Information Center (Omaha, NE)
11145 Mill Valley Rd.
Omaha, NE 68154
Ph:(402)221-4691
Fax: (402)221-3680
Contact: Ms. Kathy Marlow

67833 ■ U.S. Small Business Administration–Business Information Center (Warm Springs, OR)
Portland District Office
1134 Paiute St.
PO Box 849
Warm Springs, OR 97761
Ph:(541)553-3592
Fax: (541)553-3593
Co. E-mail: trudytho@bendnet.com
URL: http://www.sba.gov/or/orbicws.html
Contact: Mr. David Dona

67834 ■ U.S. Small Business Administration–Confederated Tribes of the Grand Ronde Community–Business Information Center (9615)
9615 Grand Ronde Rd.
Grand Ronde, OR 97347
Ph:(503)879-5211
Free: 800-422-0232
Fax: (503)879-2117
URL: http://www.grandronde.org
Contact: Ms. Elaine Moore

67835 ■ U.S. Small Business Administration–The Klamath Tribes–Business Information Center (501 C)
501 Chiloquin Blvd.
PO Box 436
Chiloquin, OR 97624
Ph:(541)783-2219
Free: 800-524-9787
Fax: (541)783-2029
URL: http://www.klamathtribes.org
Contact: Mr. Gordon Thompson

67836 ■ U.S. Small Business Administration–Business Information Center (Providence, RI)
380 Westminister Mall, Rm. 511
Providence, RI 02903
Ph:(401)528-4561
Fax: (401)528-4539
Contact: Ms. Patricia O'Rouke

67837 ■ U.S. Small Business Administration–SBA/NationsBank/MBDA/BellSouth/College of Charleston–Business Information Center (Small)
Small Business Resource Center
284 King St.
Charleston, SC 29401
Ph:(843)853-3900
Fax: (843)853-2529
Contact: Kit Rogers

67838 ■ U.S. Small Business Administration–SBA/NationsBank/MBDA–Business Information Center (Nashville, TN) (Small)
Small Business Resource Center
3401 W. End Ave., Ste. 110
Nashville, TN 37203-1609
Ph:(615)749-4088
Free: 800-342-8217
Fax: (615)749-3685
Contact: Ms. Lillie Taylor

67839 ■ U.S. Small Business Administration–Business Information Center (Fort Worth, TX)
4300 Amon Carter Blvd., Ste. 114
1150 South Fwy., Ste. 134
Ft. Worth, TX 76155
Ph:(817)684-5500
Fax: (817)684-5516
Contact: Mr. Joe E. Reyes

67840 ■ U.S. Small Business Administration–Business Information Center (Houston, TX)
Houston District Office
8701 S. Gessner Dr., Ste. 1200
Houston, TX 77074
Ph:(713)773-6500
Fax: (713)773-6550
Contact: Mr. Neil Blanton

67841 ■ U.S. Small Business Administration–SBA/Greater El Paso Chamber of Commerce–Business Information Center (10 Ci)
10 Civic Center Plaza
El Paso, TX 79901
Ph:(915)534-0500
Fax: (915)534-0510
Contact: Ms. Cindy Ramos Davidson

67842 ■ U.S. Small Business Administration–Business Information Center (East Randolph, VT)
Vermont Technical College
Hartness Library
PO Box 500
Randolph Center, VT 05061-0500
Ph:(802)728-1000
Free: 800-442-8821
Fax: (802)728-1390
URL: http://www.vtc.edu
Contact: Ms. Jane U. Bartlett, Director

67843 ■ U.S. Small Business Administration–Business Information Center (Seattle, WA)
Seattle District Office
1201 4th Ave., Ste. 450
Seattle, WA 98121
Ph:(206)553-7310
Contact: Ms. Darlene Robbins

67844 ■ U.S. Small Business Administration–Spokane Regional Chamber of Commerce–Business Information Center (801 W)
801 W. Riverside, Ste. 100
Spokane, WA 99201
Ph:(509)624-1393
Fax: (509)747-0077
Co. E-mail: info@chamber.spokane.net
Contact: Ms. Coralie Myers

67845 ■ U.S. Small Business Administration–WVHTC Foundation–Business Information Center (1000)
1000 Technology Dr., Ste. 1000
Fairmont, WV 26554
Ph:(304)366-2577
Fax: (304)366-2699
Co. E-mail: info@wvhtc.org
URL: http://www.wvhtc.org
Contact: Mr. Nick Lambernedis

The following branches are Disaster Area offices. The SBA offers two types of loans to disaster areas. Physical disaster loans can be used to repair or replace damaged or destroyed homes, personal property, and businesses within the disaster area. Economic injury disaster loans are offered to small businesses that suffer substantial economic losses because of the disaster.

67846 ■ U.S. Small Business Administration (Area 1)
360 Rainbow Blvd. S, 3rd Fl.
Niagara Falls, NY 14303-1192
Ph:(716)282-4612
Free: 800-659-2955
Fax: (716)282-1472
Description: Covers regions one and two.

67847 ■ U.S. Small Business Administration (Area 2)
1 Baltimore Pl., Ste. 300
Atlanta, GA 30308
Ph:(404)347-3771
Free: 800-359-2227
Fax: (404)347-3882
Description: Covers regions three, four, and five.

67848 ■ U.S. Small Business Administration (Area 3)
4400 Amon Carter Blvd., Ste. 102
Ft. Worth, TX 76155
Ph:(817)885-7600
Free: 800-366-6303
Fax: (817)885-7621
Description: Covers regions six and seven.

67849 ■ U.S. Small Business Administration (Area 4)
1825 Bell St., Ste. 208
PO Box 13795
Sacramento, CA 95853-4795
Ph:(916)566-7240

Free: 800-488-5323
Description: Covers regions eight, nine, and ten.

The following U.S. Export Assistance Centers are arranged alphabetically by state.

67850 ■ U.S. Small Business Administration–U.S. Export Assistance Center (California)
3300 Irvine Ave., No. 307
Newport Beach, CA 92660-3198
Ph:(949)660-1688
Fax: (949)660-1338
Co. E-mail: martin.selander@sba.gov
URL: http://www.sba.gov/oit/export/useac.html
Contact: Joseph Sachs
E-mail: jsachs@doc.gov
Description: Serves Southern California, Nevada, Arizona, and Hawaii.

67851 ■ U.S. Small Business Administration–U.S. Export Assistance Center (Colorado)
1625 Broadway Ave., Ste. 680
Denver, CO 80202
Ph:(303)844-6622
Fax: (303)844-5651
Co. E-mail: dennis.chrisbaum@.sba.gov
URL: http://www.sba.gov/oit/export/useac.html
Contact: Dennis Chrisbaum
E-mail: dchrisba@doc.gov
Description: Serves Wyoming, Utah, Colorado, and New Mexico.

67852 ■ U.S. Small Business Administration–Sunbelt U.S. Export Assistance Center (Florida)
5835 Blue Lagoon Dr., Ste. 203
Miami, FL 33126
Ph:(305)526-7425
Fax: (305)526-7434
Co. E-mail: mary.hernandez@sba.gov
URL: http://www.sba.gov/oit/export/useac.html
Contact: Kurt Fabian
E-mail: kfabian@doc.gov
Description: Serves Florida.

67853 ■ U.S. Small Business Administration–U.S. Export Assistance Center (Georgia)
75 5th St., NW Ste. 1055
Atlanta, GA 30303
Ph:(404)897-6089
Fax: (404)897-6085
Co. E-mail: Raymond.gibeau@sba.gov
URL: http://www.
Contact: Ray Gibeau
E-mail: rgibeau@doc.gov
Description: Serves Georgia, Alabama, Kentucky, Tennessee, Mississippi.

67854 ■ U.S. Small Business Administration–U.S. Export Assistance Center (Illinois)
200 Adams St., Ste. 2450
55 W. Monroe St., Ste. 2440
Chicago, IL 60606
Ph:(312)353-8065
Fax: (312)353-8098
Co. E-mail: john.nevell@.sba.gov
URL: http://www.sba.gov/oit/export/useac.html
Contact: Mary Joyce
E-mail: mjoyce@doc.gov
Description: Serves Wisconsin, Illinois, and Indiana.

67855 ■ U.S. Small Business Administration–U.S. Export Assistance Center (Maryland)
300 W. Pratt St., Ste. 300
Baltimore, MD 21201'
Ph:(410)962-4539
Fax: (410)962-4529
Co. E-mail: Deborah.conrad@sba.gov
URL: http://www.sba.gov/oit/export/useac.html
Contact: Marsha McPhee
E-mail: mmcphee@doc.gov
Description: Serves Maryland, Virginia, West Virginia, and District of Columbia.

67856 ■ U.S. Small Business Administration–U.S. Export Assistance Center (Massachusetts)
SBA
World Trade Center, Ste. 307
Boston, MA 02210
Ph:(617)424-5953
Fax: (617)424-5992
Co. E-mail: john.joyce@sba.gov
URL: http://www.sba.gov/oit/export/useac.html
Contact: John Joyce
E-mail: jjoyce@doc.gov
Description: Serves Maine, Vermont, New Hampshire, Massachusetts, Connecticut, and Rhode Island.

67857 ■ U.S. Small Business Administration–U.S. Export Assistance Center (Michigan)
SBA
211 W. Fort St., Ste. 1104
Detroit, MI 48226
Ph:(313)226-3670
Fax: (313)226-3657
Co. E-mail: john.ogara@sba.gov
URL: http://www.sba.gov/oit/export/useac.html
Contact: John O'Gara
E-mail: jro@det.sba.gov
Description: Serves Michigan.

67858 ■ U.S. Small Business Administration–U.S. Export Assistance Center (Missouri)
8235 Forsyth Blvd., Ste. 520
St. Louis, MO 63105
Ph:(314)425-3304
Fax: (314)425-3381
Co. E-mail: john.blum@mail.doc.gov
URL: http://www.sba.gov/oit/export/useac.html
Contact: John Blum
E-mail: jblum@doc.gov
Description: Serves South Dakota, Nebraska, Iowa, Kansas, and Missouri.

67859 ■ U.S. Small Business Administration–U.S. Export Assistance Center (New York)
20 Exchange Pl., 40th Fl.
New York, NY 10005
Ph:(212)809-2642
Fax: (212)809-2687
Co. E-mail: Office.NewYork@mail.doc.gov
Contact: Herbert Austin
E-mail: haustin@doc.gov

67860 ■ U.S. Small Business Administration–U.S. Export Assistance Center (Ohio)
600 Superior Ave. E., Ste. 700
Cleveland, OH 44114-2650
Ph:(216)522-4750
Fax: (216)522-2235
Contact: Inge McNeese
E-mail: imcneese@doc.gov

67861 ■ U.S. Small Business Administration–U.S. Export Assistance Center (Pennsylvania)
The Curtis Center, Ste. 580 W.
Independence Square W.
Philadelphia, PA 19106
Ph:(215)597-6101
Fax: (215)597-6123
URL: http://www.buyusa.gov/philadelphia
Contact: Ken Olson
E-mail: kolson@doc.gov

67862 ■ U.S. Small Business Administration–North Texas U.S. Export Assistance Center (Texas)
North Texas USEAC
1450 Hughes Rd., Ste. 220
Grapevine, TX 76051
Ph:(817)310-3749
Fax: (817)-310-3757
Co. E-mail: richard.schulze@sba.gov
Contact: Rick Schulze
E-mail: rschulze@doc.gov
Description: Serves Oklahoma, Texas, Louisiana, and Arkansas.

67863 ■ U.S. Small Business Administration–U.S. Export Assistance Center (Washington)
2601 4th Ave., Ste. 320
2001 6th Ave., Ste. 650
Seattle, WA 98121

Ph:(206)553-5615
Fax: (206)553-7253
Co. E-mail: seattle.office.box@mail.doc.gov
Contact: Sandra Edwards
E-mail: sedwards@doc.gov

This index provides an alphabetical listing of all organizations, products, services, and other activities covered in the Descriptive Listings section of this directory. Citations include organization, product, or service name, followed by book entry number(s). Entry numbers appear in boldface type if the reference is to the organization for which information is provided and in lightface type if the reference is to a former or alternate name included within the text of a cited entry. Organizations or services that have appeared in earlier editions and have already been described in a previous edition as defunct, inactive, or unable to be contacted receive an annotated citation to that effect.

NUMERIC

"$1 Billion Outreach" in *Hispanic Business* (April 2005, pp. 14) **[12511]**, **[48013]**, **[48518]**, **[56107]**

"$1 Million Grant Program Aims to Boost Renewable Energy" in *Milwaukee Journal Sentinel* (December 13, 2005) **[21213]**, **[39976]**, **[41492]**, **[50800]**, **[52028]**

1st Source Capital Corp. **[60027]**

1st Step, Inc.–Michigan Small Business and Technology Development Center **[61168]**

"2 Companies' Scrap Equals 392,649 Tons of Cargo for Port of Tampa" in *Tampa Tribune* (November 22, 2005) **[12942]**, **[21214]**

2 Formula' For Success" in *Inc.* (August 1, 2003); "The '4 **[29781]**, **[30500]**, **[35745]**

"2 Lawsuits Challenge State's Canker Policy" in *Tampa Tribune* (December 22, 2005) **[26467]**, **[40136]**

2 M Invest Inc. **[57895]**

2 Scoops Cafe **[12799]**

"3 Companies Dip Into Swim" in *WWD* (November 20, 2003, pp. 12) **[5640]**

"3-D Negotiation: Playing the Whole Game" in *Harvard Business Review* (Vol. 81, No. 11, November 2003, pp. 64) **[29779]**, **[39125]**, **[44861]**

"3Q a good one for local firms, if you ignore auto industry" in *Crain's Detroit Business* (Vol. 22, November 13, 2006, No. 46, pp. 3) **[27740]**, **[32230]**, **[48857]**

"3rd Annual LP Survey & Report Card" in *Venture Capital Journal* (October 1, 2005) **[49777]**, **[55474]**

"'04 Was Good Year for Show Managers" in *Tradeshow Week* (Vol. 34) **[22460]**, **[24872]**, **[27741]**, **[55054]**

4C Ventures / Olivetti Holding, N.V. **[63051]**

"4Smartphone's Mobility Solution for Small and Medium Size Businesses" in *Small Business Opportunities* (Vol. 17, May 2005, No. 3) **[4903]**, **[48935]**

"The 5 Keys to Value Investing" in *Black Enterprise* (Vol. 36, December 2005, No. 5, pp. 52) **[9799]**, **[14713]**, **[37861]**

"5 Moves to Make Before the New Year" in *My Business* (December/January 2004, pp. 14) **[17959]**, **[48936]**, **[54127]**, **[54415]**

"5 Steps to Audit-Free Returns" in *My Business* (February/March 2004, pp. 38) **[53]**, **[2859]**, **[23871]**, **[54416]**

"5 Tips to Make Your Web Site Work" in *My Business* (December/January 2004, pp. 45) **[25782]**, **[33504]**, **[46644]**

5AM Ventures / 5AM Partners **[57896]**

5S for Manufacturers (Canada) **[46175]**

"6 Secrets of eBay Sales Success" in *My Business* (December/January 2004, pp. 46) **[1770]**, **[18635]**, **[33505]**, **[51540]**

The 7 Irrefutable Rules of Small Business Growth **[27742]**, **[29780]**, **[39126]**, **[41493]**, **[42162]**

"7 Mesh Networking Startups Snag Funding" in *Venture Capital Journal* (September 1, 2005) **[41439]**, **[55475]**

"7(a) Program Restored" in *Black Enterprise* (Vol. 35, October 2004, No. 3, pp. 36) **[39784]**, **[44457]**

"The $7B Question" in *Venture Capital Journal* (October 1, 2005) **[13792]**, **[14714]**, **[49778]**, **[55476]**

"8 Detroit Projects Get More Than $170M in Tax Breaks" in *Crain's Detroit Business* (Vol. 23, January 8, 2007, No. 2, pp. 10) **[32231]**, **[54417]**

"10 Hottest Deals in Franchising" in *Black Enterprise* (Vol. 35, September 2004, No. 2, pp. 77) **[38704]**, **[47937]**

"10 Local Companies Make Inc. List of Fastest-Growing" in *Crain's Detroit Business* (Vol. 21, October 31, 2005, No. 44, pp. 32) **[4588]**, **[4904]**, **[13793]**, **[22158]**, **[22904]**, **[27743]**, **[32136]**, **[53196]**

10 Tools for Resilience and Wellness in the Workplace (Canada) **[44720]**

"12 Steps to Preventing Identity Theft" in *Home Business* (Vol. 12, March/April 2005, No. 2, pp. 92) **[22159]**

"18th Street Deli Breaks Ground on $2M Production Center" in *Crain's Detroit Business* (Vol. 21, October 3, 2005, No. 43, pp. 47) **[4532]**, **[7087]**, **[25573]**

"19th Annual Entrepreneurial Woman's Conference" in *Entrepreneur* (Vol. 33, August 2005, No. 8, pp. 4) **[24543]**, **[24873]**, **[34618]**, **[35743]**, **[39977]**, **[44555]**, **[46645]**, **[55055]**, **[56108]**

"20 Keys to Leadership" in *Small Business Opportunities* (Vol. 16, No. 1, January 2004, pp. 12, 20) **[35744]**, **[44862]**

"20 Steps for Pricing a Patent: To Value an Invention You Have to Understand It" in *Journal of Accountancy* (Vol. 198, November 2004) **[54]**, **[2860]**, **[23872]**, **[26137]**, **[27074]**, **[43981]**

"20 Words That Sell" in *Small Business Opportunities* (Vol. 16, November 2004, No. 6, pp. 12, 20) **[27288]**, **[51541]**

21st Century Adventures **[2456]**, **[24750]**, **[25278]**, **[30458]**

21st Century Health Ventures **[56903]**

21st Century Internet Venture Partners **[57897]**

24x7 **[17112]**

"25 Biz for Kids" in *Small Business Opportunities* (Fall 2005) **[1676]**, **[5311]**, **[8121]**, **[8430]**, **[9668]**, **[18721]**, **[19216]**, **[19283]**, **[19812]**, **[22110]**

"The $2.6 Billion Men" in *Inc.* (Volume 27, December 2005, No. 12, pp. 104) **[4905]**, **[13794]**

"30 of 32 Condos Offered at Solitude Auction Sale" in *Salt Lake Tribune* (March 5, 2005) **[1771]**, **[12512]**, **[20414]**, **[20787]**

"33 Tool-and-Die Firms Get State Tax Breaks in 'Recovery' Zones" in *Crain's Detroit Business* (Vol. 21, January 10, 2005, No. 2, pp. 10) **[16358]**, **[54418]**

35-Year Old Downtown Shop is Expanding" in *Bellingham Business Journal* (December 2006, pp. A5); "A **[5822]**, **[7156]**, **[27748]**

"40-Year Plan" in *Entrepreneur* (Vol. 33, September 2005, No. 9, pp. 62) **[17356]**, **[36469]**, **[37862]**

"The '4-2 Formula' For Success" in *Inc.* (August 1, 2003) **[29781]**, **[30500]**, **[35745]**

"The $50 Million Giveaway" in *Business 2.0* (Vol. 6, September 2005, No. 8, pp. 76) **[34218]**, **[35306]**, **[42411]**, **[44384]**, **[52598]**, **[55350]**

"50 Most Powerful Black Women in Business" in *Black Enterprise* (Vol. 36, February 2006, No. 7, pp. 124) **[44863]**, **[56109]**

"60 Seconds On Doing the Impossible" in *Fast Company* (March 2005, No. 92, pp. 32) **[35746]**, **[41494]**, **[50801]**, **[52029]**

"The 75 Most Powerful African Americans in Corporate America" in *Black Enterprise* (Vol. 35, February 2005, No. 7, pp. 104) **[35747]**, **[48014]**

"75 Most Powerful Blacks on Wall Street" in *Black Enterprise* (Vol. 37, October 2006, No. 3, pp. 136) **[9800]**, **[14715]**, **[35748]**, **[55477]**

"75 Reasons to Be Glad You're an American Entrepreneur Right Now" in *Inc.* (October 2005, pp. 88-95) **[27744]**, **[35749]**, **[39127]**

"88-Year-Old Printing Company in Ch. 11, Hopes to Rebound" in *Crain's Detroit Business* (Vol. 21, January 3, 2005, No. 1, pp. 20) **[19865]**, **[48015]**

"The 90-Day Difference" in *Inc.* (October 1, 2003) **[44864]**

The 100 Best Businesses to Start When You Don't Want to Work Hard Anymore **[35307]**, **[39021]**

"The 100 Best Companies To Work For" in *Fortune* (Vol. 151, January 24, 2005, No. 2, pp. 72) **[34804]**, **[44865]**, **[52811]**

"$100 Bottles of Beer on the Wall" in *Business 2.0* (Vol. 7, January/February 2006, No. 1, pp. 26) **[3121]**

100 X **[61023]**

"100th Bank" in *San Fernando Valley Business Journal* (Vol. 12, January 2007, No. 2, pp. 37) **[9801]**, **[14716]**, **[27745]**

101 Businesses You Can Satrt at with Less Thank One Thousand Dollars: For Retirees **[35308]**, **[39022]**, **[42496]**

101 Businesses You Can Start at with Less Than One Thousand Dollars: For Stay-At-Home Moms and Dads **[35309]**, **[39023]**, **[42497]**

"101 Dumbest Moments in Business" in *Business 2.0* (Vol. 7, January/February 2006, No. 1, pp. 98-102, 104-106, 108, 110, 136) **[39128]**

101 Internet Businesses You Can Start from Home: How to Choose and Build Your Own Successful E-Business **[13735]**, **[29782]**, **[33412]**, **[42498]**, **[46646]**

101 Small Business Ideas for Under $5000 **[35310]**, **[39024]**

101 Ways to Really Satisfy Your Customers: How to Keep Your Customers and Attract New Ones **[31633]**, **[46647]**

"112 Million Handsets Can't Be Wrong" in *Inc.* (July 1, 2004) **[4906]**, **[46648]**, **[53573]**

"12.1 Inch SVGA Modules From Toshiba..." in *PR Newswire* (Dec. 9, 2003) **[7712]**, **[15914]**, **[41495]**

201 Great Tips for Your Small Business: Increase Your Profit and Joy in Your Work **[35750]**, **[39129]**, **[42570]**

202 Things You Can Make and Sell for Big Profits **[7993]**, **[8148]**, **[33506]**

"250 Unleash the Entrepreneur Within You!" in *Home Business* (Vol. 12, March/April 2005, No. 2, pp. 16, 20-23, 26-29, 100-101, 104-105) **[35311]**, **[38599]**, **[42499]**

365 Answers about Human Resources for the Small Business Owner: What Every Manager Needs to Know about Work Place Law **[29087]**, **[42825]**, **[44866]**

401 Questions Every Entrepreneur Should Ask **[35751]**, **[39130]**

The 510 (k) Register **[17262]**

550 Digital Media Ventures **[63052]**

1000 Islands - Clayton Region Chamber of Commerce **[62811]**

1394 Newsletter **[5198]**

1953-54 Buick Skylark Club **[17948]**

"The 2003 Tax Relief Act: What Does It Mean for You?" in *My Business* (October/November 2003, pp. 26) **[39131]**, **[54419]**

"The 2003 Teenpreneur Money Guide" in *Black Enterprise* (Vol. 34, No. 2, September 2003, pp. S10) **[9802]**, **[14717]**, **[37863]**, **[44458]**, **[56733]**

"2004 Corporate Elite Directory" in *Hispanic Business* (January/February 2004, pp. 36, 38, 40, 42, 44, 46) **[35752]**, **[44867]**, **[48016]**

"2005-2006 Meetings, Conventions and Trade Shows" in *Crain's Detroit Business* (Vol. 21, October 10, 2005, No. 43, pp. 17) **[22461]**, **[24658]**, **[24874]**, **[25142]**, **[55056]**

"2005: A Quiet, But Critical Year for Venture Capital" in *Venture Capital Journal* (January 1, 2005) **[27746]**, **[35312]**, **[44385]**, **[55351]**

"2005 Corporate Elite Directory" in *Hispanic Business* (January/February 2005, pp. 22) **[44868]**, **[48017]**, **[53574]**

"2005 Elite Women" in *Hispanic Business* (April 2005, pp. 54) **[44869]**, **[53335]**, **[56110]**

"2005 Housing and Mortgage Markets: A Personal Perspective" in *Mortgage Banking* (Vol. 65, November 2004, No. 2, pp. 18) **[17357]**, **[20415]**

"2005 National Minority Supplier Development Council Conference and Business Opportunity Fair" in *Entrepreneur* (Vol. 33, Aug. 2005) **[24545]**, **[24875]**, **[48018]**, **[49915]**, **[55057]**, **[57445]**

"2005 Outlook: Low Growth Is OK" in *Tradeshow Week* (Vol. 34, December 20, 2004, No. 51, pp. 8) **[22462]**, **[24876]**, **[27747]**, **[55058]**

"2005 Standard Mileage Rates" in *Home Business* (Vol. 12, March/April 2005, No. 2, pp. 78) **[55]**, **[2861]**, **[23873]**, **[42571]**, **[54420]**

"2006 Hispanic Business Diversity Report: Employment" in *Hispanic Business* (September 2006, pp. 40, 42, 44, 48, 50) **[42163]**, **[48019]**

"2007 Conference Calendar" in *Journal of Business Communication* (Vol. 44, January 2007, No. 1, pp. 103) **[39132]**, **[55059]**

"2007's Trends in Travel and Tourism" in *Bellingham Business Journal* (January 2007, pp. C15) **[24659]**, **[25143]**, **[30280]**

2010 Fund 5 **[31263]**, **[38508]**, **[43917]**, **[48817]**, **[53068]**

5280 Partners **[58442]**

"145,000 Americans' Identity Data Stolen" in *San Jose Mercury News* (February 17, 2005) **[22160]**

A

A-1 Concrete Leveling Inc. **[7651]**, **[16978]**

"A 35-Year Old Downtown Shop is Expanding" in *Bellingham Business Journal* (December 2006, pp. A5) **[5822]**, **[7156]**, **[27748]**

A & A Research **[20362]**, **[24487]**

A Friend of the Family **[26996]**

A; LD **[9118]**

A-Lighting Equipment Accessories Directory Issue; LD **[9112]**

"A Little Lost? Get Directions at Your Fingertips" in *Entrepreneur* (Vol. 31, No. 10, October 2003, pp. 46) **[13795]**, **[30281]**, **[48937]**

"A Market for Ideas" in *The Economist* (Vol. 377, October 22-28, 2005, No. 8449, pp. 3-6, 8-10, 12-18) **[29783]**, **[41496]**, **[43982]**, **[44269]**, **[48692]**, **[52030]**

"A North Carolina Entrepreneur Sets His Sights On Creating the H&R Block of Public Relations" in *Inc.* (May 1, 2005) **[12783]**, **[12865]**, **[19885]**, **[20098]**, **[37248]**, **[38705]**

A-Plus-One Paralegal **[3997]**

A/R/C Associates Inc. **[7594]**, **[22075]**

A-Real-Check Inspection Services **[3266]**

"A Sobering Vacation" in *Wall Street Journal* (Vol. 248, December 2006, No. 142, pp. P1-P5) **[52812]**, **[53575]**, **[54330]**

"The "A" team" in *WorkingWoman* (Vol. 25, No. 5, May 2000, pp. 24) **[40137]**, **[48020]**, **[56111]**

A & W **[21732]**

A2LA News **[17197]**

"A9.COM" in *Entrepreneur* (Vol. 33, October 2005, No. 10, pp. 6) **[13703]**, **[13796]**, **[32508]**, **[33507]**

AA Antivirus **[49396]**, **[49573]**

"AAA celebrates 75 years" in *Dispute Resolution Journal* (Vol. 56, No. 1, February-April 2001, pp. 45) **[17041]**, **[27289]**

AAA Employment **[9265]**

AAA Franchise Legal Help Hotline **[4450]**, **[29612]**

"AAA Imaging & Supplies Has Become the Exclusive U.S. Distributor of Oblo Multimedial Kiosk" in *Photo Marketing Newsline* (Aug. 13, 03) **[15915]**

AAB Bulletin **[17198]**

AACE Bonus Briefs **[4406]**, **[9244]**, **[33290]**

AACE Distinguished Member Series **[4407]**, **[9245]**, **[33291]**

AACSB International - Association to Advance Collegiate Schools of Business **[32886]**

AACSB Newsline **[33292]**

AAF Government Report **[851]**

AAHA Dialogue **[11863]**

AAHPERD Update **[8456]**

AAIS Viewpoint **[13532]**

AAMCO Transmissions, Inc. **[22655]**

AAMI News **[17113]**

AAMPlifier **[4062]**

A&W Food Services of Canada Inc. - CFA **[21733]**

AAO News **[25652]**

AAP Monthly Report **[2759]**

AAPEX **[2040]**

AAPEX Export Interest Directory **[12937]**

Aarbor Industries, Inc. **[59715]**

Aarons Sales & Leasing **[51445]**

The AARP Pharmacy Service Enjoying Good Health Newsletter **[41145]**

"Aastrom Gets $22M Financing Boost; Stem-Cell Trials Pique Wall Street's Interest" in *Crain's Detroit Business* (January 17, 2005) **[14718]**, **[40138]**, **[50802]**, **[52031]**

Aatrix Top Pay **[18798]**, **[26441]**, **[27222]**

Aavin Equity Advisors, LLC **[60234]**

AB Associates **[50282]**

ABA Banking Journal **[10359]**, **[15739]**, **[17469]**

ABA/BMA National Conference for Community Bankers **[10325]**, **[38502]**, **[55191]**

ABA/BNA Lawyers' Manual on Professional Conduct **[29645]**

ABA Inc. **[45949]**

ABA Sales Management Workshop **[10326]**, **[38503]**, **[55192]**

Abacus Benefit Consultants Inc. **[26997]**

Abacus Ventures **[65584]**

"Abandoned by Your Accountants" in *Inc.* (August 2005, pp. 19-21) **[56]**, **[2862]**, **[23874]**, **[26138]**, **[53576]**

Abbaye Saint-Benoit–Bibliotheque **[1643]**

Abbeville Chamber of Commerce **[64719]**

Abbey of Regina Laudis, Order of St. Benedict–Our Lady of the Rock Monastery–Priory Library **[12157]**

Abbeyfield Houses Society of Canada Newsletter **[12381]**, **[18346]**, **[41146]**

Abbott's Frozen Custard **[12800]**

ABC Country Restaurants Inc. **[21734]**

ABC Dialogue **[3203]**

a.b.c. Reports **[12110]**, **[41147]**

ABC Seamless Siding **[7652]**

ABC Today-Associated Builders and Contractors National Membership Directory Issue **[7235]**

ABC Tutors In Home Tutoring **[25473]**

"ABCS of E-Learning" in *Training* (Vol. 40, No. 1, January 2003, pp. 61) **[9128]**, **[32987]**

"The ABCs of setting up a home office" in *Women in Business* (Vol. 54, No. 5, September-October 2002, pp. 23) **[42500]**, **[44459]**, **[49481]**

Abell Venture Fund **[58202]**, **[60860]**

Aberdare Ventures **[57898]**

Aberdeen Area Chamber of Commerce **[64814]**

Aberdeen Chamber of Commerce **[60812]**

Aberdeen Small Business Development Center (Region III) **[64805]**

Aberlyn Capital Management Co., Inc. **[62580]**

ABI Designs Inc. **[49574]**

ABI/INFORM **[3457]**, **[3930]**, **[10360]**, **[20084]**, **[27053]**, **[32831]**, **[42495]**, **[50729]**

Abilene Area Chamber of Commerce **[60283]**

Abilene Chamber of Commerce **[65100]**

Abilities Expo Chicago Metro **[17135]**, **[17270]**

Abingdon Chamber of Commerce **[59413]**

Abington's Collectibles **[5934]**

ABLE Energy Franchising L.L.C. **[22656]**

ABLEDATA **[19585]**

Ablesoft **[62581]**

ABN AMRO Private Equity **[59716]**

"ABN Amro To Cut 900 Positions In North America" in *Wall Street Journal* (Vol. 248, December 2006, No. 152, pp. A7) **[30501]**, **[30776]**

About Books, Inc. **[2641]**, **[2789]**

"About His Life: Bob Dallmeyer" in *Tradeshow Week* (Vol. 34, December 20, 2004, No. 51, pp. S4) **[22463]**, **[24877]**, **[35753]**, **[44870]**, **[55060]**

"About this index" in *Crain's Detroit Business* (Vol. 18, No. 23, June 10, 2002, pp. E-14) **[13797]**, **[25783]**, **[33508]**

"About My Raise...How To Ask For and Get More Money" in *Black Enterprise* (Vol. 34, July 2004, No. 12, pp. 65) **[27075]**, **[44871]**

"About Penny Stocks" in *Black Enterprise* (Vol. 34, No. 4, November 2003, pp. 40) **[9803]**, **[14719]**, **[33509]**, **[37864]**

"About the Power Breakfast series" in *Crain's Detroit Business* (Vol. 19, No. 1, January 6, 2003, pp. 3) **[37383]**, **[39133]**, **[40139]**, **[44872]**

"About this report" in *Crain's Detroit Business* (Vol. 19, No. 17, April 28, 2003, pp. 14) **[27749]**, **[32232]**

ABP Acquisition Corporation **[58578]**

"Abraham Lincoln and the Global Economy" in *Harvard Business Review* (Vol. 81, No. 8, August 2003, pp. 58) **[32233]**, **[43537]**

Abrakadoodle Remarkable Art Education **[21373]**

Sol Abrams Public Relations Counsel & Marketing Consultants **[20175]**, **[47821]**, **[50488]**, **[50722]**

Abry Partners, LLC **[61024]**

ABS Consulting Training Services **[60896]**

ABS Payroll System **[18799]**

ABS Ventures **[60861]**, **[61123]**

"The ABSc of ESOPs" in *My Business* (February/March 2003, pp. 36-38) **[40140]**, **[52403]**

Absolute Best Care **[17870]**

Absolute Franchising **[3834]**

Abstracts in Social Gerontology **[18347]**

"Abuse-awareness initiative lets employers help parents" in *Business First Columbus* (Vol. 18, No. 26, February 15, 2002, pp. B7) **[26734]**, **[40141]**, **[54128]**

"ABWA entrepreneurs are making fun their business!" in *Women in Business* (Vol. 54, No. 5, September-October 2002, pp. 18) **[2327]**, **[2422]**, **[5877]**, **[56112]**

ABX-Associates Business Xchange **[3835]**, **[31475]**

ACA International **[8366]**

ACA International-Membership Roster **[8374]**

ACACIA Venture Partners **[57899]**, **[60585]**

Academic Emergency Medicine **[41148]**

Academic and Workplace Sexual Harassment: A Resource Manual **[31998]**

Academy of Art College–Library **[5601]**

Academy of Dispensing Audiologists **[12099]**

Academy of Dispensing Audiologists-Membership Directory **[12105]**

Academy for Educational Development–National Institute for Work and Learning **[15904]**

Academy Funds / Longleaf Venture Fund LLC **[63451]**, **[63752]**

Academy of Legal Studies in Business **[53570]**

Academy for Mathematics & Science **[25474]**

Academy of Motion Picture Arts and Sciences–Margaret Herrick Library **[17547]**

Academy of Pharmaceutical Research and Science **[8886]**

AcademyHealth **[40908]**

Accel-kkr, LLC **[57900]**

Accel Partners **[57901]**, **[62582]**

Accent on Design - A Division of the New York International Gift Fair **[11119]**, **[11183]**, **[12238]**, **[13703]**

Accent on Design - A Division of the San Francisco International Gift Fair **[12239]**, **[13704]**

"Accentuating the accent" in *The New York Times* (September 3, 2000, pp. BU10) **[42164]**, **[44873]**

Accenture–Consulting Information Center **[6538]**, **[16688]**

Accenture Technology Ventures **[57902]**

"Access to Capital: Closing the 'Gap'" in *Hispanic Business* (September 2004, pp. 46) **[44460]**, **[48021]**

"Access to Capital: Government Financiers" in *Hispanic Business* (September 2004, pp. 44) **[9804]**, **[14720]**, **[44461]**, **[48022]**

"Access to Capital: Money to Grow" in *Hispanic Business* (October 2004, pp. 98-100) **[9805]**, **[44462]**, **[48023]**

"Access to Capital and Terms of Credit: A Comparison of Men- and Women-Owned Small Businesses" in *Journal of Small Business Management* **[31510]**, **[55478]**, **[56113]**

"Access Corporate Data on Your Wireless Phone" in *E-business Advisor* (Vol. 18, No. 3, March 2000, pp. 16) **[4907]**, **[33510]**

Access to Finance **[9806]**, **[37865]**, **[40142]**

Access Management Corp. **[50283]**

"Access Now...Or Lawsuit Later" in *Birmingham Business Journal* (Vol. 20, No. 40, October 3, 2003, pp. 1) **[29088]**, **[31999]**

ACCESS Payroll–Warren Computer Center **[18800]**

Access Venture Partners **[55713]**, **[57903]**, **[58443]**

Accessible Web Design: Complying with Section 508 **[53154]**

Accessing the Financial Markets: Creating Strategies to Boost Corporate Profitability **[37843]**

"Accessing Minority Markets" in *Hispanic Business* (Vol. 24, No. 5, May 2002, pp. 14) **[27750]**, **[46649]**, **[48024]**

Accessories **[9649]**

Accessory Allure **[9650]**, **[11919]**

Accident Investigation: A Tool for Effective Prevention **[56609]**

Accident Prevention **[56595]**

The Accidental Entrepreneur: Practical Wisdom for People Who Never Expected to Work for Themselves **[35313]**, **[39025]**

Accordionists and Teachers Guild-Bulletin **[17608]**

"Account Balances Indicate That 401(k) Participants Have Heard The Long-Term Investor Message" in *Employee Benefit Plan Review* (Vol. 55) **[14721]**, **[26735]**, **[31108]**, **[32234]**, **[37866]**, **[40953]**, **[43066]**

Account for Your Own Success: Everything You Need to Manage Your Own Business and Personal Finances **[37867]**

"Accountability key factor in family business success" in *Business First Columbus* (Vol. 18, No. 25, February 8, 2002, pp. B3) **[37583]**, **[44874]**

The Accountant as a Business Advisor **[348]**

Accountants Global Network **[11]**, **[26107]**

Accountants, Inc. **[379]**, **[24120]**

"Accountants on the Move" in *Rough Notes* (Vol. 146, No. 3, March 2003, pp. 30) **[57]**, **[13175]**, **[26139]**, **[43067]**

Accountant's Relief **[404]**, **[24158]**

Accountant's Tax Letter **[310]**, **[2978]**, **[24080]**

"Accounting for intangible assets" in *Rough Notes* (Vol. 146, No. 3, March 2003, pp. 128) **[58]**, **[13176]**, **[40143]**

Accounting & Auditing Update: Implementation of Recent Developments **[349]**

"Accounting for the Budget" in *Law Firm Inc.* (December 2004) **[59]**, **[26140]**, **[27076]**

Accounting the Business Environment **[26141]**

The Accounting Cycle **[26142]**

"Accounting Education; Response to Corporate Scandals: Helping the Profession Find Opportunity in Crisis" in *Journal of Accountancy* **[60]**, **[2863]**, **[23875]**, **[26143]**, **[27077]**, **[32988]**

Accounting and Finance Benchmarking Consortium **[12]**, **[9781]**

Accounting and Finance for Non-Financial Managers **[38495]**

Accounting and Finance for Your Small Business **[61]**, **[26144]**, **[37868]**

"Accounting Firms" in *San Diego Business Journal* (Vol. 28, January 15, 2007, No. 3, pp. 20) **[62]**, **[26145]**

"The Accounting Fraud Squads" in *Atlanta Business Chronicle* (Vol. 25, November 15, 2002, No. 23 pp. SS1) **[63]**, **[26146]**, **[37384]**

"Accounting Group Gets a New Name" in *Hispanic Business* (Vol. 24, No. 1/2, January/February 2002, pp. 60) **[64]**, **[23876]**

The Accounting Guild Inc. **[63484]**

"Accounting Has Record of Trustworthiness" in *Crain's Detroit Business* (Vol. 18, No. 15, April 15, 2002, pp. 9) **[65]**, **[23877]**, **[26147]**, **[37385]**

Accounting Library **[350]**

"Accounting Moves to the Web" in *Home Office Computing* (Vol. 18, No. 8, August 2000, pp. 36) **[66]**, **[53197]**

Accounting Review **[311]**

Accounting Service Center 54110

Accounting & Tax Database **[387]**, **[24136]**

Accounting Technology (Vol. 19, No. 1, January-February 2003, pp. 16); "Crafting a Web presence" in **[116]**, **[23920]**, **[25822]**, **[26200]**, **[30832]**, **[33711]**

Accounting Today (Vol. 14, No. 8, May 1, 2000, pp. 3); "Congress Moves to Repeal Business Sale Lump-Sum Rule" in **[40277]**, **[54500]**

Accounting Today (Vol. 14, No. 16, September 4, 2000, pp. 3); "GAO blames IRS, Congress for small business tax woes" in **[40402]**, **[54566]**

Accounting Today (Vol. 14, No. 12, July 10, 2000, pp. 41); "Reaching the Small Business Accounting Market" in **[23146]**, **[26338]**, **[34399]**, **[53432]**

Accounting Today (Vol. 14, No. 13, July 24, 2000, pp. 29); "Sage unveils big plans for small business" in **[23158]**, **[26342]**, **[34427]**, **[48786]**, **[53444]**

Accounting Today (Vol. 14, No. 16, September 4, 2000, pp. 10); "Small Business and the Use of Accrual Accounting" in **[26360]**

Accounting Today (Vol. 14, No. 14, August 7, 2000, pp. 27); "Small Firms Slow to Board E-com Boat" in **[34498]**, **[53976]**

Accounting Today (Vol. 14, No. 7, April 17, 2000, pp. 26); "Successful IT practices know their clients well" in **[269]**, **[26373]**, **[31224]**, **[54781]**

Accounting Today (Vol. 14, No. 6, April 3, 2000, pp. 1); "SWARM Online services seek small biz through CPAs" in **[272]**, **[26377]**, **[37193]**, **[54783]**

Accounting Today (Vol. 14, No. 11, June 26, 2000, pp. 20); "VEBAs and 412(i)s: Maximize client deductions" in **[26395]**, **[54854]**

ACCPAC BPI Accounting **[18801]**

ACCPAC Plus Accounting **[18802]**

ACCRA Research in Review **[32812]**

Accreditation Council on Optometric Education **[25617]**

Accredited Gemologists Association **[15813]**

Accredited Pet Cemetery Society **[19101]**

Accredited Review Appraisers Council **[1426]**

Accuitive Medical Ventures LLC / AMV Partners **[59182]**

"Accumulated Earnings Tax: Deductibility of Paid But Contested Liabilities" in *Journal of Accountancy* (January 2005) **[67]**, **[2864]**, **[23878]**, **[26148]**, **[27078]**, **[54421]**

"Accumulations of Real, Virtual Stuff Inspire Innovations in Storage" in *Boston Globe* (July 26, 2004) **[20010]**, **[20214]**

Accurate Solutions Franchising Inc. **[3998]**

Accutips **[47780]**, **[50712]**

AccuTrak Inventory Specialists **[44262]**

ACDI/VOCA **[26449]**

ACE America's Cash Express **[5255]**

Ace DuraFlo Systems LLC **[19774]**

Ace Hardware Fall Convention and Exhibit **[11905]**

ACEI Exchange **[5350]**

Acenet / Appalachian Center for Economic Networks **[63842]**

Acer Technology Ventures **[57904]**

ACF Equity Atlantic, Inc. **[66709]**

ACFA Bulletin **[1194]**

ACFN - The ATM Franchise Business **[52616]**

Achieve Success by Prospecting with Phillip Wexler **[51936]**

The Achievement Challenge **[37021]**

"Achieving High Reliability" in *PC Magazine* (March 7, 2000, pp. 142) **[13798]**, **[48938]**

Achieving Planned Innovation: A Proven System for Success with New Products & Services **[46650]**, **[48693]**

K.B. Ackerman Co. **[20243]**

ACM Transactions on Computer Systems (TOCS) **[6494]**

ACM Transactions on Programming Languages and Systems **[6495]**

Glenn Acomb Associates Inc. **[1544]**

Acordia Employers Service Marketing Inc. **[26998]**

Acorn Campus **[57905]**

Acorn Ventures, Inc. **[57906]**

Acoustic Guitar Magazine **[17609]**, **[17784]**, **[17846]**

"Acquire and Rewire" in *Memphis Business Journal* (Vol. 25, No. 16, August 15, 2003, pp. 31) **[44875]**, **[54129]**

"An Acquired Taste" in *Entrepreneur* (Vol. 32, October 2004, No. 10, pp. 62) **[22754]**, **[30661]**, **[44463]**, **[46184]**, **[48897]**, **[52404]**

"Acquisitions Likely to Pick Up, But Pressure Remains" in *Crain's Detroit Business* (Vol. 19, No. 45, November 10, 2003, pp. 14) **[14722]**, **[15267]**, **[49779]**, **[50879]**

"Acquisitions helped increase offerings" in *Crain's Detroit Business* (Vol. 19, No. 13, March 31, 2003, pp. 12) **[14723]**, **[27751]**, **[41497]**, **[49780]**

Action for Enterprise **[32190]**, **[52792]**

Action International **[3836]**

Action International Canada Inc. **[3837]**

Action Plans for Implementing Quality and Productivity **[30635]**

Action Plans for the Small Business: Growth Strategies for Businesses Wondering Where to Go Next **[27752]**

"Action Sacked" in *Entrepreneur* (Vol. 33, August 2005, No. 8, pp. 18) **[28458]**, **[29089]**, **[38499]**, **[40144]**

Action Sports Photos **[19324]**

Action Sports Retailer - ASR Trade Expo, Atlantic City **[23667]**, **[55193]**

Action Sports Retailer - ASR Trade Expo, Long Beach **[23668]**, **[55194]**

Action Sports Retailer - ASR Trade Expo, San Diego **[23669]**, **[55195]**

Action Van & Truck World **[2010]**

"Action Yet in Need of Affirming" in *Hispanic Business* (Vol. 23, No. 7/8, July/August 2001, pp. 29) **[39978]**, **[40145]**, **[48025]**

ActionCoach **[3838]**

"Actioncoaching.com" in *Entrepreneur.com* (Vol. 34, January 2006, No. 1, pp. 6) **[31086]**, **[38600]**, **[46651]**, **[51542]**

Activant **[7677]**

Active Asset Allocation: State-of-the-Art Portfolio Policies, Strategies & Tactics **[14724]**

Active Green + Ross **[2091]**

Active Server Pages (ASP) **[25769]**

Active Training: A Handbook of Techniques, Designs, Case Examples, and Tips **[32989]**

"Active.com Helps You Just Do It" in *Business Week Online* (April 22, 2002) **[19370]**, **[23711]**, **[33511]**

"The Activist Ingredient" in *Inc.* (July 1, 2003) **[27753]**, **[34805]**, **[44876]**

"Activists, pragmatists, technophiles, and tree-huggers?" in *Journal of Business Ethics* (Vol. 28, No. 3, December 1, 2000, pp. 211) **[37243]**

Activities of Daily Living **[18363]**

Activities Unlimited **[18740]**

Activity-Based Costing for Small and Mid-sized Businesses: An Implementation Guide **[26149]**

Activity Experiments & Programming within Long-Term Care **[18315]**

Acton Chamber of Commerce **[57315]**

Actor's Garage **[17544]**

Acu-Yoga for Flexibility **[19462]**

Warren Acuff **[49397]**

Acuity Ventures **[57907]**

Acupressure Massage (Shiatsu) **[17016]**

Acupuncture Foundation of Canada Institute **[17876]**

"AcutionASAP: Another eBay But Without All the Hassles" in *Long Island Business News* (April 2, 2004) **[1772]**, **[7157]**, **[18636]**, **[33512]**

"ACVB member hotels, resorts" in *Atlanta Business Chronicle* (Vol. 24, No. 14, September 7, 2001, pp. S23) **[12513]**, **[24878]**

A.D. Banker & Company - Training Centers **[33359]**

Ad Campaigns That Work **[861]**, **[50717]**

"Ad Companies Probe Potential of Blog World" in *Chicago Tribune* (February 22, 2005) **[529]**, **[13799]**, **[33513]**, **[46652]**

"Ad firm monkeys around with its old office design" in *Washington Business Journal* (Vol. 21, No. 50, April 11, 2003, pp. 60) **[530]**, **[46653]**

"Ad Sales Growth to Slow in 2001" in *Folio: the Magazine for Magazine Management* (Vol. 30, No. 1, January 2001, pp. 15) **[27754]**, **[46654]**

Ad Source **[47778]**

"Ad Spending Heats Up" in *Hispanic Business* (December 2002, pp. 30, 32-34, 36, 38) **[531]**, **[46655]**

"Ad Time Firm Expands" in *San Fernando Valley Business Journal* (Vol. 11, December 2006, No. 25, pp. 28) **[532]**, **[13800]**, **[27755]**, **[43983]**, **[46656]**

Ada Area Chamber of Commerce **[63936]**

Ada Chamber of Commerce **[61550]**

ADA: Commonsense Compliance **[32078]**

ADA Handbook: Employment and Construction Issues Affecting Your Business **[32000]**

"Ada Liquor Store Growing Through a Lighthearted Approach to Sales" in *Journal Record* (June 24, 2003) **[533]**, **[542]**, **[15998]**, **[16227]**, **[46657]**, **[48547]**, **[49042]**, **[51543]**

The ADA Maze: What You Can Do **[32079]**

ADA: Understanding the Law **[32080]**

AdAgeGlobal **[47924]**

Adairville - South Logan Chamber of Commerce **[60479]**

Adam & Eve Stores **[51446]**

Adam Market Research Inc. **[16849]**

Adams and Associates Inc. **[1050]**, **[9092]**, **[19768]**

Adams-Blake Company Inc. **[58247]**

Adams Capital Management, Inc. **[64541]**

Adams County Chamber of Commerce **[63599]**

Adams County Chamber of Commerce and Tourism **[66336]**

Adams County Genealogical Society–Library **[10996]**

Adams Executive Recruiters Almanac **[9549]**

Adams, Harkness & Hill, Inc. **[61025]**

Adams Jobs Almanac **[9189]**

Adams State College–Alamosa Small Business Development Center **[58291]**

Adams Streetwise Complete Business Plan: Create a Business Plan to Finance & Run a New or Existing Business **[29784]**

"Adapt or die: surviving the government's digital push" in *Black Enterprise* (Vol. 33, No. 6, January 2003, pp. 42) **[13801]**, **[33514]**, **[48026]**, **[48939]**, **[53577]**

Adapting to Change: Making It Work for You **[44877]**

"Adapting to a multicultural workforce" in *Safety & Health* (Vol. 163, No. 3, March 2001, pp. 282) **[48519]**, **[56552]**

Adara Healthcare Staffing **[23418]**

"Adcomparator" in *Entrepreneur.com* (Vol. 34, January 2006, No. 1, pp. 6) **[534]**, **[33515]**, **[46658]**

"Add An 'Inc' And Get Some Respect" in *Home Office Computing* (Vol. 19, No. 1, January 2001, pp. 24) **[33516]**, **[35754]**, **[42572]**, **[53578]**

"Add Some Magic to Your Marketing" in *Home Business* (Vol. 12, March/April 2005, No. 2, pp. 46, 94) **[42573]**, **[46659]**

"Add fudge factor to cost to equal business success" in *Crain's Detroit Business* (Vol. 18, No. 49, December 9, 2002, pp. 12) **[37869]**, **[39134]**

"Added Security" in *Entrepreneur* (Vol. 33, January 2005, No. 1, pp. 43) **[4589]**, **[22161]**, **[22905]**, **[53198]**

"Addicted to Success" in *Success* (Vol. 47, No. 2, June 2000, pp. 50) **[35755]**

Addictions Foundation of Manitoba–William Potoroka Memorial Library **[54375]**

Addison Chamber of Commerce and Industry **[59414]**

Addison County Chamber of Commerce **[65777]** SBDC **[65754]**

Addison County Economic Development Corp.–SBDC **[65755]**

Addo Laboratories **[25693]**

Address Book for Germanic Genealogy **[10923]**

"Addressing the Inhibitors" in *Washington Business Journal* (Vol. 21, No. 50, April 11, 2003, pp. 28) **[40146]**, **[43984]**, **[50803]**, **[52032]**

Addressing Sexual Harassment in the Workplace: Trainer's Package **[32001]**

Adel-Cook County Chamber of Commerce **[59052]**

Adel Partners Chamber of Commerce **[60086]**

Adelanto Chamber of Commerce **[57316]**

Adelphi University–Human Performance Laboratory **[19592]**

ADG Group **[31264]**, **[38509]**

Adirondack Regional Chamber of Commerce **[62812]**

Adirondacks-Speculator Region Chamber of Commerce **[62813]**

Adjust Your Set: The Static Is Real **[32081]**

ADL Ventures / Arthur D. Little Enterprises, Inc. **[61026]**

Adler & Co. **[63053]**

Adler Pollock & Sheehan, P.C.–Law Library **[9525]**

Charles Adler & Son Inc. **[20071]**, **[21069]**

ADM Flash **[16833]**, **[47781]**

Administrative Management Group Inc. **[26999]**

Adobe Acrobat Capture **[53155]**

Adobe Acrobat eFormsI **[32901]**

Adobe Acrobat I **[32902]**

Adobe Acrobat II **[53156]**

Adobe Acrobat Section 508 Accessibility **[40134]**, **[53157]**

Adobe After Effects **[32903]**

Adobe After Effects II **[53158]**

Adobe FrameMaker I **[32904]**

Adobe FrameMaker II **[32905]**

Adobe FrameMaker III: Structured **[53159]**

Adobe GoLive **[25770]**

Adobe Illustrator I **[32906]**

Adobe Illustrator II **[32907]**

Adobe Illustrator III: Classic Art Techniques **[32908]**

Adobe InDesign I **[32909]**

Adobe InDesign II **[32910]**

Adobe InDesign III **[53160]**

Adobe PageMaker I **[32911]**

Adobe PageMaker II **[32912]**

Adobe PageMaker III **[32913]**

Adobe Photoshop Camera Raw **[53161]**

Adobe Photoshop Digital Mastery **[53162]**

Adobe Photoshop: Digital Scanning for Production **[32914]**

Adobe Photoshop I **[32915]**

Adobe Photoshop II **[32916]**

Adobe Photoshop III: Tips and Tricks **[32917]**

Adobe Photoshop for Photography **[32918]**

Adobe Premiere **[32919]**

"Adobe Systems upgrades FrameMaker to version 7.0" in *Electronic Publishing* (Vol. 26, No. 5, May 2002, pp. 10) **[2674]**, **[8602]**, **[8986]**, **[9129]**, **[18221]**, **[18847]**

Adoption Resource Book **[40954]**, **[48858]**

Adoption Searchbook **[10924]**

ADP Parts Exchange New (PXN) **[2019]**, **[22710]**

"ADR: new challenges, new roles and new opportunities" in *Dispute Resolution Journal* (Vol. 56, No. 1, February-April 2001, pp. 20) **[17042]**, **[27290]**, **[29090]**

ADR Institute of Canada **[17029]**

"Adriane Brown: Driven To Succeed At Honeywell" in *Business Week* (February 14, 2005, No. 3920, pp. 10) **[1890]**, **[17960]**, **[44878]**

Ads" in *Entrepreneur* (Vol. 31, No. 9, September 2003, pp. 88); "Just Teasing: A **[683]**, **[47166]**

ADT Authorized Dealer Program **[22441]**

Adult Day Care in America: Summary of a National Survey **[461]**

Adult Day Care: Findings From a National Survey **[462]**

Adult Day Services Letter **[463]**, **[12382]**

Adult Learning? You've Got to Be Kidding! **[6351]**, **[33307]**

Adult Money Maker **[14667]**

"Adults Fueling Back To School Movement" in *Crain's Detroit Business* (Vol. 23, January 15, 2007, No. 3, pp. 9) **[32990]**, **[42826]**

Advance Coordination Manual **[24879]**

Advance Directives and the Elderly: Making Decisions about Treatment Limitations **[18364]**

Advance Grower Solutions–Nursery / Greenhouse Accounting Software **[11504]**, **[16085]**

Advance Realty **[20740]**

"Advanced Accessory looks to acquire with new owner" in *Crain's Detroit Business* (Vol. 19, No. 16, April 21, 2003, pp. 1) **[1891]**, **[14725]**, **[49781]**

Advanced Benefits & Human Resources **[16557]**, **[27000]**, **[31265]**, **[42938]**, **[45950]**

Advanced Benefits Planning **[26736]**

Advanced Computer Consulting Inc. **[6997]**

Advanced Cost Accounting **[26118]**

Advanced Editing **[27228]**

Advanced Fixed Income Portfolio Management **[14726]**

Advanced Interest Rate and Currency Swaps: State-of-the-Art Products, Strategies & Risk Management Applications **[14727]**

Advanced Manufacturing Technology **[41498]**, **[52232]**

Advanced Materials & Composites News **[52233]**

Advanced Materials Partners, Inc. **[58579]**

Advanced Medical Technology Association **[17084]**, **[17251]**

Advanced Medical Technology Association-Directory **[17092]**

Advanced Negotiating Skills: Beyond Win-Win Results (Canada) **[27229]**

Advanced Network Consulting **[49398]**, **[49575]**

Advanced Options Trading: The Analysis and Evaluation of Trading Strategies, Hedging Tactics and Pricing Models **[14728]**

Advanced Progressions for Across the Floor **[8462]**

Advanced Sales Management Level 2 **[51515]**, **[53753]**

Advanced Sales Management-Level 2 (Canada) **[51516]**

Advanced Shiatsu Massage **[17017]**

Advanced Skills for the EMT **[1091]**

Advanced Strategies for Controllers (Canada) **[37844]**

Advanced Strategies for Marketing Management Success **[46618]**

Advanced Systems Development Inc. **[4873]**

Advanced Technology Development Center **[59213]**

Advanced Technology Development Fund **[59183]**

Advanced Technology Park **[62212]**

Advanced Technology Ventures (ATV) **[61027]**

Advanced Technology Ventures (Palo Alto) **[57908]**

Advanced Training for Your Retriever **[19119]**

Advanced Walleye Systems I **[2182]**

Advanced Walleye Systems II **[2183]**

Advanced Walleye Systems III **[2184]**

Advanced Walleye Trolling Tactics **[2185]**

"Age Rage: Younger Employees are Crying Age Discrimination" in *Entrepreneur* (Vol. 32, No. 4, April 2004, pp. 24) [26737], [32003], [40150], [40956]

Age Small Business Show [39735]

AgeLine [481]

The Agencies [23831]

Agency Accounting [13589]

Agency of Commerce and Community Development Economic Development Department [65772]

    Economic Development Department–Site Selection Office [65773]

    Economic Development Department–Vermont Business Expansion Program [65774]

Agency of Commerce and Community Development Center–Department of Economic Development–Government Marketing Assistance Program [65807]

Agency Information Management System [13590]

Agency for International Development–Office of Small and Disadvantaged Business Utilization/Minority Resource Center [66790]

Agency Sales Magazine [16705]

"Agency with a Small Focus" in *Hispanic Business* (September 2003, pp. 24, 26, 28) [39136], [39786]

"Agenda Items" in *Fast Company* (June 2001, pp. 147) [39137], [43985]

"Agendas Cross in SHCC Boardroom" in *Hispanic Business* (March 2002, pp. 56-58) [32238], [35757]

"Agent of Change" in *Rough Notes* (Vol. 145, No. 9, September 2002, pp. 38) [6328], [13179], [32994], [35758], [43069]

"An agent for change" in *BlackEnterprise* (Vol. 31, No. 6, January 2001, pp. 99) [3475], [31087], [35314], [47938]

"Agent flips over high-flying sport" in *Atlanta Business Chronicle* (Vol. 25, January 10, 2003, No. 31, pp. 28A) [20417], [20789], [35759], [44880]

Agents and Buyer's Guide Marketing Service [43070]

Agent's Guide to Real Estate: Power Your Career to Financial Success & Personal Happiness [20418]

"Agents Urged to Answer the Call" in *Rough Notes* (Vol. 145, No. 12, December 2002, pp. 127) [13180], [43071], [51544]

Ages of Infancy: Caring for Young, Mobile, and Older Infants [5365]

Aggregate Capital LLC [65805]

The Agile Manager's Guide to Hiring Excellence [42166]

Agile Manufacturing Benchmarking Consortium [30497]

Agilent Technologies–Santa Clara Site Library [7015], [7764]

Agilent Ventures [57910]

Agility Computer Network Services L.L.C. [49399], [49576]

Aging Excellence [474]

Aging News Alert [1700]

Aging Population: Caring for the Family [468]

Agitation, Aggression and Violence [18365]

Agland Investment Services Inc. [26609]

AGN International - North America [13]

Agnes Press [61505]

The Agony and the Ecstasy-The Special Problems of Running a Closely-Held or Family Business [37823]

Lino J. Agosti & Associates [49577]

Agoura - Oak Park - Las Virgenes Chamber of Commerce [57317]

Agpro Inc. [26610]

Persephone C. Agrafiotis [30641]

"AgraQuest Fumigant OK'd" in *Sacramento Bee* (November 18, 2005) [26469], [50805], [52033]

"Agreement on Internet taxes eludes deeply divided commission" in *The New York Times* (March 21, 2000, pp. C1) [13807], [33522], [54423]

Agri-Business Consultants Inc. [26611]

Agri Business Group Inc. [26612]

Agri-Energy Roundtable [26450]

Agri Marketing [26565]

Agri Marketing-Farm Show Issue [26470]

Agri Marketing-Marketing Services Guide Issue [26471]

Agri Marketing-The Top 50 [26472]

Agri-Personnel [26613], [50284]

Agribusiness [26473], [26566]

Agribusiness: An Entrepreneurial Approach [26474]

Agribusiness Council [26451]

AgriCapital Corp. [26614], [50285]

AGRICOLA Database [26648]

"Agricultural firm aiming to grow software clients" in *Atlanta Business Chronicle* (Vol. 24, No. 8, July 27, 2001, pp. 19A) [10656], [22877]

Agricultural Consulting Services Inc. [26615]

Agricultural Engineering Associates [26616]

Agricultural Groups Concerned About Resources and the Environment [26452]

Agricultural & Industrial Manufacturers Representatives Association-Membership Directory [26475]

Agricultural Investment Associates Inc. [26617]

The Agricultural Marketplace [26602]

Agricultural Producers Union [55258]

Agricultural Products Marketing Board [26453]

Agricultural Relations Council [20091]

Agricultural Research Foundation [64295]

Agricultural Utilization Research Institute [26677]

Agriculture and Agri-Food Canada Atlantic Cool Climate Crop Research Centre [26678]

    Brandon Research Centre [26679]

    Lethbridge Research Centre [26680]

AgriSolutions Inc. [26618]

AgriTech Inc. [26619]

Agritech Park Incorporated [66711]

Agritech Publishing Group Inc. [57105]

AGRR [11224]

AGSA News [12226]

AGVISE Laboratories Inc. [26620]

"Ah! Spa: An Eastern European Approach to Wellness" in *Black Enterprise* (Vol. 35, September 2004, No. 2, pp. 192) [12515], [19371]

AHA News [41152]

"AHAA: Computer Manufacturers Missing the Boat" in *Hispanic Business* (January/February 2003, pp. 14) [4591], [6575], [22908]

AHCA Notes [1701], [18348]

"Ahead of the Curve" in *Ingram's* (Vol. 28, No. 9, September 2002, pp. 19) [37870], [54424]

"Ahead of Her Time" in *Success* (Vol. 47, No. 3, July 2000, pp. 84) [35760], [56114]

AHEAD Human Resources - Staffing [9266], [24543]

"Ahead of the Law" in *Adweek* (Vol. 46, January 17, 2005, No. 3, pp. 16) [542], [24373], [29093], [40151], [46669]

AHFS Drug Information [8773]

Ahh-Some Gourmet Coffee [11363]

AHI Newsletter [1241]

AHR Expo - International Air-Conditioning, Heating, Refrigerating Exposition [1045]

Ahwatukee Foothills Chamber of Commerce [57007]

"AIA Georgia announces awards of excellence" in *Atlanta Business Chronicle* (Vol. 25, December 6, 2002, No. 26, pp. 16C) [1494], [7236]

AIA Today! [42135]

AIADA News [18169]

AIAS, Inc.–Library [27060]

AICHE Journal [52234]

AICPA Online [388]

Aid to Artisans [7978]

"Aid package" in *Entrepreneur* (Vol. 30, No. 12, December 2002, pp. 27) [26738], [37871]

AIDS/Hepatitis B: Handling and Processing Infectious Waste [11951], [17216]

AIDS, Hepatitis and the Emergency Responder [1092]

AIDS Litigation Reporter [17199]

AIDS Partnership Michigan [32105]

AIDS Policy and Law [17200]

AIDS Reference Guide [41153]

AIDS Research and Human Retroviruses [17201]

AIDS: The Workplace and the Law [17217]

AIDS: What You Need to Know [17218]

"AIG Plans to Cut 27 Jobs at Neptune, N.J., Offices" in *The Record* (November 8, 2005) [13181], [26739], [27759], [32239], [43072]

Aikido in Training: A Manual of Traditional Aikido Practice and Principles [16912]

"Ailing Wellness Plan considers job cuts" in *Crain's Detroit Business* (Vol. 19, No. 9, March 3, 2003, pp. 3) [13182], [40957], [43073]

AIM Associates [49578]

AIM Mail Centers [17316]

Aims Community College [58475]

Ainsworth Area Chamber of Commerce and North Central Development Center [62239]

"AIP's OJPS to Host ASME International's Journals" in *Information Today* (Vol. 17, No. 7, July 2000, pp. 53) [2675], [9130], [18848]

Air Bag Technology, 1999 [918]

"Air Campaign: Think Wireless Devices and Air Travel Don't Mix?" in *Entrepreneur* (Vol. 32, November 2004, No. 11, pp. 60) [4909], [30283], [41502]

Air Cargo World-Freight Forwarders Directory Issue [10666]

Air Communication Corp. [50286]

Air Conditioning Contractors of America [993]

Air Conditioning Contractors of America-Membership Directory [1012]

Air Conditioning, Heating and Refrigeration News [1033]

Air Conditioning, Heating & Refrigeration News (Vol. 219, No. 17, August 25, 2003, pp. 23); "Buying Online-Who Needs Contractors?" in [1016], [1789], [33638]

Air Conditioning, Heating & Refrigeration News-Directory Issue [1013]

Air-Conditioning and Refrigeration Institute [994], [23329]

Air-conditioning & Refrigeration Wholesalers International-Membership Directory [1014]

Air Filtration: An Integrated Approach to the Theory and Applications of Fibrous Filters [1070]

Air Line Pilots Association International - Canada [932]

Air Medical Journal [958], [41154]

The Air Pollution Consultant [1072]

Air Pollution: Indoor [1074]

Air Pollution Monitoring and Sampling Newsletter [1073]

Air Raid [23656]

"Air Raid" in *Entrepreneur* (Vol. 32, No. 4, April 2004, pp. 39) [13808], [22164], [33523]

Air Services Development Office of New Jersey [62611]

"Air-Tight Technology For the Business Traveler" in *My Business* (April/May 2004, pp. 20) [16271], [30284]

Air Transport Association of America [933] Library [10723]

Air Transport Association of Canada [934]

Air & Waste Management Association Collection [11972]

"Airborne intelligence" in *Entrepreneur* (Vol. 30, No. 10, October 2002, pp. 114) [35315], [38601]

Aircraft Owners and Pilots Association [935]

Aircraft Technical Publishers [983]

Aire-Master of America, Inc. [3341]

Aire Serv Heating and Air Conditioning [1063]

"Airfares Increase Amid High Demand" in *Tampa Tribune* (November 30, 2005) [30285]

"Airline Kiosks Save Time at Las Vegas Center" in *Tradeshow Week* (Vol. 33, No. 48, December 1, 2003, pp. 3) [15916]

"Airline Slump Hurts Houston-Based Maker of Tow Tractors" in *Houston Chronicle* (April 11, 2003) [32240], [46188]

"Airlines to match United offer" in *Wall Street Journal* (June 9, 2003, pp. A6) [30286]

Airport Area Chamber of Commerce [59053]

"Airport Industrial Sites in Demand" in *Milwaukee Journal Sentinel* (December 19, 2005) [7237], [20215], [27760], [32138], [32241], [46189]

Airport Minority Advisory Council [936]

Airport Operations [959]

AIS Media [3839], [42785]

Aitkin Area Chamber of Commerce [61551]

AJIC (American Journal of Infection Control) [41155]

Ajo District Chamber of Commerce [57008]

"AK Steel Goes Ahead with Bid for National" in Pittsburgh Post-Gazette (April 11, 2003) [14733], [46190], [49784]

AKC Gazette-List of Clubs Issue [1184]

Akeela Inc.–Library [54376]

Akers Capital LLC [59337]

Akin Gump Investment Partners 2000, LP [65585]

Akron Industrial Incubator [63870]

Akron Regional Development Board–Small Business Development Center [63553]

Al Shugart International (ASI) [57911]

Alabama A & M University–J.F. Drake Memorial Learning Resources Center [4042], [18674]

Alabama Department of Economic and Community Affairs–Planning and Economic Development [56791]

Alabama Department of Finance–Division of Purchasing [56915]

Alabama Gulf Coast Area Chamber of Commerce [56805]

Alabama Law Institute [54104]

Alabama Procurement Center Representatives [54106], [56916]

Alabama Public Library Service [66817]

Alabama SBDC–University of Alabama [56779]

Alabama Small Business Development Consortium [56917]

Office of the State Director–University of Alabama at Birmingham [56780]

Alabama (State) Department of Transportation–Research & Development Bureau–Research Library [2108], [8734], [16194], [24252]

Alabama State House of Representatives Bill Status Office [56928]

House Commerce Committee [56929]

Alachua Chamber of Commerce [58749]

Alamance County Area Chamber of Commerce [63316]

Alameda Chamber of Commerce [57318]

Alameda County Library–Business Library [3935], [4043]

"Alameda high-tech incubator is expanding" in Kiplinger California Letter (Vol. 38, No. 17, September 4, 2002) [39760], [41440], [43034], [55484]

Alamo Chamber of Commerce [65102]

Alamo City Chamber of Commerce [65103]

Alamogordo Chamber of Commerce [62670]

Alamosa County Chamber of Commerce [58324]

Alan I. Goldman & Associates [62583]

"Alarcon Backs McCain Bill" in Hispanic Business (March 2003, pp. 18) [20299], [40152], [48031]

Alarm Clock [6140], [17610], [17785]

Alarm Set, Anti-Intrusion, Restricted Areas [22165]

Alaska AVHRR Data [11501]

Alaska Business Monthly [56985]

Alaska Business Monthly (Vol. 18, No. 10, Oct. 2002, pp. 82); "Cottage industry pays off for Eskimo women" in [8155], [26497], [50851], [54163]

Alaska Department of Commerce, Community, and Economic Development [56942], [66791]

Alaska Department of Labor–Census and Geographic Information Network–Research and Analysis [66819]

Alaska Industrial Directory [46191]

Alaska Marine Safety Education Association–Library [16784]

Alaska Minority Business Development Center–Tanana Chief Conference, Inc. [56980]

Alaska SBDC–University of Alaska - Anchorage [56936]

Alaska State Chamber of Commerce [56945]

Alaska State Library–Government Publications/Technical Services [66792]

Albanian-American Trade and Development Association [43467]

Albany Area Chamber of Commerce [59054], [64190]

Albany Chamber of Commerce [57319], [61552], [65104]

Albany-Colonie Regional Chamber of Commerce [62815]

"Albany Eyes Real Estate Transfer Tax" in Long Island Business News (May 7, 2004) [20419], [20790], [54425]

Albany Historical Society, Inc.–Library/Special Collections [26652]

Albany Medical College–Schaffer Library of Health Sciences [1711]

Albany Park Chamber of Commerce [59415]

Albany State College–State Data Center Program–Documents Librarian [66853]

"Albany's High-Tech Park Already Creating Jobs" in Tampa Tribune (November 28, 2005) [6576], [41503], [50806], [52034]

Albee-Campbell L.L.C. [46533]

Albemarle Capital Management [65965]

Albert Lea Business Development Center–Small Business Development Center [61514]

Albert Lea - Freeborn County Chamber of Commerce [61553]

Alberta - Agriculture, Food and Rural Development Business Management Innovations Branch–Library [26653]

Crop Diversification Centre South [12169]

Crop Diversification Centre - South–Branch Library [26654]

Alberta Band Association–Music Lending Library [17811]

Alberta Land Surveyor's Association–Library [23783]

Alberta Securities Commission–Resource Centre [15788], [29694], [39018]

Albert's Family Restaurant [21735]

Albertville Chamber of Commerce [56806]

Albion Chamber of Commerce [62240]

Albion Economic Development Corp. [61474]

Albuquerque Journal (January 24, 2003); "Pottery from Albuquerque, N.M., Designer Puts Area Color on Clay" in [8178], [8275]

Albuquerque SBDC [62642]

Albuquerque Technical-Vocational Institute [62734]

Small Business Development Center [62643]

Albuquerque Technology Incubator [62726]

"Alcatel Draws Contract" in San Fernando Valley Business Journal (Vol. 11, December 2006, No. 25, pp. 28) [6922], [27291], [41504]

Alcatel Network Systems, Inc.–Library [25689]

Alcatel Ventures [57912]

"Alchemist Among the Vines" in Hispanic Business (Vol. 24, No. 4, April 2002, pp. 20-21) [23453], [35761], [37584], [48032]

ALCO Capital Group Inc. [50287]

"Alcoa's Results Could Hint at Manufacturers' Outlook" in Wall Street Journal (Vol. 249, January 2007, No. 5, pp. B4) [14734], [43539], [46192]

Alcohol, Health and Research World [41156]

Alcohol Research Group–Library [54377]

Alcohol, Tobacco, & Other Drugs: Prevention in the Workplace: A Resource Guide [54331]

Alcoholics Anonymous World Services [54320]

Alcorn State University–SBDC [61741]

Alden and Associates Marketing Research [47823]

Aldrich & Cox Inc. [27001]

Ale Street News [3145]

Aledo Area Chamber of Commerce [59416]

Alert! [16834]

Alexander Associates [49400]

Alexander City Chamber of Commerce [56807]

Alexander County Chamber of Commerce [63317]

Alexander Technique International [17877]

Alexandria Bay Chamber of Commerce [62816]

Alexandria Chamber of Commerce [65855]

Alexandria Lakes Area Chamber of Commerce [61554]

Alexandria - Monroe Chamber of Commerce [59871]

Alexandria SBDC–Alexandria Chamber of Commerce [65817]

Alexandria Technical College [61723]

Alfalfa Processors Council Membership Directory [26476]

Alfred University–Center for Glass Research [11239]

Alger Chamber of Commerce [61244]

Algoma Area Chamber of Commerce [66337]

Algona Area Chamber of Commerce [60087]

Algonquin - Lake in the Hills Chamber of Commerce [59417]

Alhambra Chamber of Commerce [57320]

Alice Chamber of Commerce [65105]

Aliceville Area Chamber of Commerce [56808]

Aligning IT with Corporate Strategy [30498]

Alimansky Capital Group Inc. [55967], [63054]

Aline Chamber of Commerce [63937]

Alive [41157]

"Alive with Sound of Music Selling" in Chicago Tribune (March 6, 2005) [4910], [17729], [46193]

AlixPartners L.L.C. [35290]

All About Credit [8298], [8345], [31511]

All About Herbs [12140]

All About Honeymoons [25330]

"All About Me" in My Business (February/March 2004, pp. 41) [68], [23880], [26740], [35762], [54426]

All American Ice Cream & Frozen Yogurt Shops [12801]

A All Animal Control [3342]

"All in a day's work" in Harvard Business Review (Vol. 79, No. 11, December 2001, pp. 54) [30502], [34807], [44881]

"All in the Delivery" in Entrepreneur (Vol. 31, No. 10, October 2003, pp. 112) [8891], [37554], [38602]

"All Eyes on Univision" in Hispanic Business (December 2006, pp. 46-47, 49) [4084], [24374]

"All Fired Up: With the Right Marketing Plan, Your Product Will Blaze Trails Across the Globe" in Entrepreneur (Vol. 32, July 2004) [35763], [46670], [51545]

"All Funds Aren't Created Equal: When Is It Wise To Get Into a Late-Stage Fund?" in Venture Capital Journal (July 1, 2003) [14735], [55485]

All Handwriting Services L.L.C. [11866]

"The All-in-One Market" in Harvard Business Review (Vol. 78, No. 3, May 2000, pp. 19) [13809], [33524]

"All-inclusive trips" in Black Enterprise (Vol. 31, No. 5, December 2000, pp. 172) [24661]

All Nations Flag Co., Inc. [5935]

"All new: be the first on the block with one of these 66 fresh opportunities" in Entrepreneur (Vol. 30, No. 12, Dec. 2002, pp. 118) [35316], [38603]

All Night Auto [22657]

"All Offices Are Not Created Equal" in Rough Notes (Vol. 146, No. 3, March 2003, pp. 54) [13183], [43074]

"All in One" in Entrepreneur (Vol. 32, No. 2, February 2004, pp. 44) [6577], [33525], [48942]

"All the Rage: Wondering What Everyone Will Be Crazy About in the Coming Year?" in Entrepreneur (Vol. 33, January 2005, No. 1, pp. 84) [432], [1757], [6147], [10657], [18291], [19340], [25461], [31088], [38604], [53557]

All Seasons Tree Service Inc. [16138]

"All-star performance" in Incentive (Vol. 174, No. 10, October 2000, pp. 126) [46671], [52814]

All State Home Inspection and Environmental Testing, Ltd [3267]

"All Systems Go" in Entrepreneur (Vol. 32, December 2004, No. 12, pp. 52) [25787], [33526], [51048]

"All Systems Grow: You Don't Have to be a Rocket Scientist to Grow Your Business." in Entrepreneur (Vol. 33, March 2005, No. 3) [27761], [29785]

"All That Glitters: Dreaming of Starting Your Own Jewelry Business? " in Entrepreneur (Vol. 33, March 2005, No. 3) [15833]

All Tune and Lube [20264], [22658]

All Tune Transmission [22659]

"All the Web's a Stage" in Business Week (December 11, 2000, pp. 16) [13810], [33527]

"All work, All play" in Entrepreneur (Vol. 30, No. 3, March 2002, pp.) [37585], [38707]

All You Need to Know About Cigars! [24627]

All You Need to Know about the Music Business [17585], [17730]

ALLDATA Online [928]

Allegan Area Chamber of Commerce [61245]
Allegan County Economic Alliance–SBDC [61170]
Alleghany County Chamber of Commerce [60813]
Alleghany County Chamber of Commerce [63318]
Alleghany Highlands Chamber of Commerce [65856]
Allegheny Valley Chamber of Commerce [64375]
"Allegiant Files Statement for IPO of Common Stock" in *Bellingham Business Journal* (December 2006, pp. A3) [24662], [25146], [27762], [30503]
"Allegis Capital Markets New Fund" in *Venture Capital Journal* (Vol. 40, No. 10, November 2000, pp. 20, 22) [55486]
Allegis Capital / Media Technology Ventures [57913]
Allegra Partners / Lawrence, Smith & Horey [63055]
Allegra Print & Imaging [27602]
Allen; Anshen [49579]
Charles J. Allen and Associates [45952], [47824]
D.E.M. Allen & Associates Ltd. [20363], [24488]
Allen Business Investments [3441], [3632]
Allen Chamber of Commerce [63938], [65106]
Allen County Public Library–Business and Technology Department [51017]
Allen Economic Development Group [63871]
Allen Sapp Gallery–Archives [1644]
"Allen Tate Expanding to Research Triangle Park: Firm Expects Raleigh Market to Grow Faster" in *Charlotte Observer* (January 31, 2007) [20420], [20791], [27763], [52645]
Allendale Chamber of Commerce [61246]
Allergy/Asthma Information Association [1069]
Alleviating Stress Associated with Nursing Home Admission [18366]
Alley Ventures LLC [61692]
Alliance [10808]
Alliance Against Fraud in Telemarketing and Electronic Commerce Focus on Fraud [30269]
Alliance for Amesbury [60924]
Alliance of Area Business Publications [18817]
Alliance Area Chamber of Commerce [62241], [63600]
Alliance of Canadian Cinema, Television and Radio Artists [20281], [24350]
Alliance for Children and Television–Resource Library [24505]
Alliance for Community Media–Library [4153]
Alliance Cost Containment LLC [3840]
Alliance Financial of Houston [65586]
The Alliance Management Group Inc. [3633], [16560], [31269], [45953]
Alliance Management International Ltd. [3634], [16561], [27703], [31270], [45954]
Alliance of Minority Women for Business and Political Development [47988], [56086]
Alliance of Practicing Certified Public Accountants [14]
Alliance of Professionals & Consultants Inc. [9588]
Alliance Security Systems, Inc. [22442]
Alliance Small Business Development Center–Merced Satellite [57248]
Alliance Technology Ventures [59184]
Alliance Texas [27571], [40116], [45948]
Alliance Venture Management, LLC [57914]
Allied Beauty Association [11769]
Allied Board of Trade [12492]
Allied Capital Corporation [58669]
Allied Distribution, Inc. [20203], [32128]
Allied Distribution, Inc.-Membership Directory [20216]
Allied Purchasing Company [12759]
Allin Corp. [3635]
AllOver Media [871]
Alloy Digest [52235]
Alloy Ventures [57915]
"All's Fair: In Love and Business, So You May Need a Prenup to Protect Your Company's Assets" in *Entrepreneur* (Vol. 31, Sept. 2003) [37872], [39138]
"Allsbrook Predicts Economic Pickup in Months Ahead" in *Birmingham Business Journal* (Vol. 20, No. 33, August 15, 2003, pp. 6) [9808], [27764], [32242]
Allsop Venture Partners [60235]
Allstate Private Equity [59717]

Allsup Inc. [45955]
Alltel Ventures [57233]
Allworth Press [63240]
Allyson Management Services [42939]
Alma Area Chamber of Commerce [57127]
Alma-Bacon County Chamber of Commerce [59055]
Alma Chamber of Commerce [60284], [62242]
"Almanac: Analysis" in *Inc.* (October 17, 2000, pp. 67) [53580]
Almanac of Business and Industrial Financial Ratios [308], [848], [955], [1031], [1118], [1741], [2363], [2754], [3141], [5194], [5732], [7518], [8809], [9078], [9752], [10465], [11446], [11572], [11680], [11896], [12317], [12657], [13529], [16236], [16387], [16751], [16965], [17107], [17195], [17535], [18166], [18342], [18687], [18948], [19646], [19759], [19897], [20239], [20710], [21672], [22622], [23529], [24244], [25416], [25468], [26564]
Almanac, Tour Finder, and Ride Guide [2497]
Almena Commercial Club [66338]
"Almost 26 residential acres bought for nearly $8M by development firm" in *Daily Business Review* (Vol. 77, No. 146, Jan. 7, 2003) [7238]
"Almost Famous: Market Yourself as an Expert" in *My Business* (October/November 2003, pp. 45) [30779], [46672], [50548], [51546]
"Almost office" in *Entrepreneur* (Vol. 30, No. 12, December 2002, pp. 64) [4592], [22909], [48943], [53202]
ALOA Security Expo [16266]
Aloette Cosmetics, Inc. [11818], [23840]
Aloha Hotels [12700]
"Alone in Your Time Zone: Are You Plagued by Chronic Lateness?" in *Black Enterprise* (Vol. 35, December 2004, No. 5, pp. 155) [35764], [54934]
"Along For the Ride: Losing Touch With Your Reps?" in *Entrepreneur* (Vol. 31, No. 10, October 2003, pp. 87) [44882], [51547]
Alpaca Breeders of the Rockies [1156]
Alpena Community College [61493]
　　Huron Shores Campus–SBDC [61171]
　　SBTDC [61172]
Alpha Capital Corporation, L.L.C. [64542]
Alpha Capital Partners Ltd. [55968], [59718]
Alpha Dogs: How Your Small Business Can Become a Leader of the Pack [30779], [30780], [31635], [34637], [34808], [35765], [37634], [39139], [41505], [51548]
Alpha Forum [6338]
Alpha Legal Forms & More, Inc. [3841], [3999]
The Alphabet Jungle Game [5366]
AlphaGraphics, Inc. [19928]
Alpine Chamber of Commerce [57009], [57321], [65107]
Alpine County Chamber of Commerce [57322]
Alpine Technology Ventures [57916]
ALSA [1545]
Alsip Chamber of Commerce and Economic Development [59418]
Alta Chamber of Commerce [60088]
Alta Mere Window Tinting and Auto Alarm [4348]
Alta Partners [57917]
Altadena Chamber of Commerce [57323]
Altamira Capital Corp. [66768]
Altamont Chamber of Commerce [59419]
Altanta Journal-Constitution (January 24, 2007); "Alternative Energy Attracts Big Money" in [9809], [14736], [26477], [50807], [52035], [55487]
Altanta Journal-Constitution (February 3, 2007); "Annual Computer Security Conference Focuses on Growing Threats to PCs" in [6580], [22168]
Altanta Journal-Constitution (February 2, 2007); "Bill Will Allow Consumers to Order Wine Shipped Directly from Maker" in [16424], [23459], [40188]
Altanta Journal-Constitution (January 20, 2007); "Biotech Crops Turn into Growing Field" in [26485], [27848]
Altanta Journal-Constitution (January 18, 2007); "Cable TV Firm Announces Hundreds of Job Openings in Atlanta" in [4095], [24389], [42189]

Altanta Journal-Constitution (January 24, 2007); "Chrysler to Introduce Cleaner Diesel Engines" in [17995], [37256], [46239]
Altanta Journal-Constitution (February 2, 2007); "Coke Dives Into 'Enhanced' Beverage Market with Fuze Beverage Purchase" in [11599], [14871], [49866]
Altanta Journal-Constitution (January 31, 2007); "Comcast to Raise Cable TV Rates" in [4100], [24395]
Altanta Journal-Constitution (February 3, 2007); "Companies Increasingly Turn to Perks to Retain, Lure Quality Employees" in [26773], [42206]
Altanta Journal-Constitution (February 7, 2007); "Delta Agrees to Settle Potential Allegations of Employee-Fund Misuse" in [29192], [37420]
Altanta Journal-Constitution (February 7, 2007); "Delta Apparel Earnings Drop" in [5533], [5651], [51126]
Altanta Journal-Constitution (February 7, 2007); "EarthLink Posts Loss for Fourth Quarter" in [14002], [14944], [28075]
Altanta Journal-Constitution (February 3, 2007); "Economy Expands Modestly, but Unemployment Rate Rises" in [28089], [32391], [42223]
Altanta Journal-Constitution (February 1, 2007); "Economy Refuses to Fall" in [20503], [20871], [28090], [32392]
Altanta Journal-Constitution (February 4, 2007); "Ethanol Push Has Roots from Early 1990s, Support from Farmers" in [26503], [37274]
Altanta Journal-Constitution (February 2, 2007); "Flowers Foods Profits Rise" in [2247], [28167]
Altanta Journal-Constitution (February 1, 2007); "Foreclosures: Troubled Owners Offered Free Help" in [9968], [17384], [39824], [49945]
Altanta Journal-Constitution (January 28, 2007); "Fresh-Produce Prices Set to Rise in Wake of Crop Freeze" in [11621], [26511]
Altanta Journal-Constitution (January 18, 2007); "Globalized Economy a Double-Edged Sword for Americans" in [32451], [43676]
Altanta Journal-Constitution (January 20, 2007); "Hank Aaron Moves Closer to Benching Himself with Sale of Dealerships" in [18054], [52427]
Altanta Journal-Constitution (January 30, 2007); "Home Depot Swings into Spring Hiring Season" in [11887], [42289], [51184]
Altanta Journal-Constitution (February 4, 2007); "India Set to Enter U.S. Auto Market" in [12986], [18061], [43705]
Altanta Journal-Constitution (January 23, 2007); "Making Fast Food Faster" in [14221], [21556], [34164], [38851]
Altanta Journal-Constitution (February 7, 2007); "Meet the New Taurus" in [18089], [46371]
Altanta Journal-Constitution (January 28, 2007); "Microsoft Lawyer Makes Living Hunting Down Pirates" in [4726], [6724], [19000], [22293], [23079], [29385], [53366]
Altanta Journal-Constitution (January 20, 2007); "New Entrepreneurs Arise from Bad Breaks" in [10568], [36537], [56341]
Altanta Journal-Constitution (January 29, 2007); "Newton Gets Whiff of Success in Bottles: Glass Factory Makes Vials for Perfumes" in [2599], [7899], [46391]
Altanta Journal-Constitution (January 31, 2007); "Restaurant King, Hotel Developer to Hook Up" in [12626], [21598], [50163]
Altanta Journal-Constitution (February 2, 2007); "State OKs Minimum Wage Boost" in [40725], [42426], [42894]
Altanta Journal-Constitution (January 18, 2007); "Two Franchisees Buy Buffalo's Wings Chain" in [21655], [38937]
Altanta Journal-Constitution (February 6, 2007); "UPS to Buy 27 Boeing Craft" in [6103], [10705], [43867]
Altanta Journal-Constitution (February 7, 2007); "Venerable Financial Firms to Join" in [15574], [38439], [48468], [50244]
Altarum [61475]
Altavista Area Chamber of Commerce [65857]

Alterlayer Venture Services [57918]

Alternate Work Sites: At Home, at Work [42780]

Alternative Aquaculture Network [10466]

The Alternative Board Tab [3842]

"Alternative Capital Sourcing" in *My Business* (September/October 2001, pp. 42) [44465], [48898]

"Alternative Energy Attracts Big Money" in *Altanta Journal-Constitution* (January 24, 2007) [9809], [14736], [26477], [50807], [52035], [55487]

"Alternative Energy Companies" in *Crain's Detroit Business* (Vol. 22, February 6, 2006, No. 6, pp. 14) [21215], [41506]

"Alternative Energy Powers Up In Michigan - Part 1 of 2" in *Crain's Detroit Business* (Vol. 22, February 6, 2006, No. 6, pp. 10) [22464], [26478], [27765], [41507], [50808], [52036]

"Alternative Energy Powers Up In Michigan - Part 2 of 2" in *Crain's Detroit Business* (Vol. 22, February 6, 2006, No. 6, pp. 10) [21216], [21436], [26479], [27766], [41508], [50809], [52037]

Alternative Energy Resources Organization [23330]

Alternative Energy Resources Organization (AERO)–Library [23342]

Alternative Health Professionals Association [19549]

Alternative Ideas in Real Estate Investment [20792]

"Alternative Market Grows As Rates Harden" in *Rough Notes* (Vol. 146, No. 3, March 2003, pp. 38) [13184], [43075]

"Alternative Markets and Risk Financing" in *Rough Notes* (Vol. 145, No. 9, September 2002, pp. 82) [13185], [43076]

"Alternative Minimum Tax has Expanded Annually to Include More and More Taxpayers" in *Long Island Business News* (March 5, 2004) [53581], [54427]

Alternative Services Inc. [3636], [31271], [41323]

Alternative Travel Directory [23367]

Alticor Inc.–Corporate Library [48684]

Altira Group LLC [58444]

Altoona Area Chamber of Commerce [60089]

Altoona Blair County Development Corporations [64599]

Altos Ventures [57919]

Altotech Ventures [57920]

Altracolor Systems [2044], [48506]

Alturas Chamber of Commerce [57324]

Altus Chamber of Commerce [63939]

Aluminum Extruders Council [16347]

Aluminum Extrusion Press Directory [16385]

Alva Area Chamber of Commerce [63940]

Alvin-Manvel Area Chamber of Commerce [65108]

"The 'Always On' Economy" in *Inc.* (Volume 27, June 2005, No. 6, pp. 59-60) [4911], [32243], [33528], [41509]

"Always Say Thank You" in *Incentive* (Vol. 175, No. 10, October 2001, pp. S14) [34809]

Alzheimer's Disease: Effects on Communication [469], [18367]

"Am. Axle Plans China, Europe Plants" in *Crain's Detroit Business* (Vol. 21, October 31, 2005, No. 44, pp. 4) [1894], [27767], [43540], [46194]

A.M. Pappas & Associates LLC [63452]

Am/Pm Convenience Stores- Entrepreneur.com [7791]

AMA Customer Satisfaction Research [31636]

The AMA Handbook for Employee Recruitment and Retention [42827]

Amador County Chamber of Commerce and Visitors Bureau [57325]

Amador County Outreach - Satellite SBDC [57249]

Amalgamated Printers' Association [19839]

Amarillo Chamber of Commerce [65109]

AMA's 5-Day MBA Program [44721]

AMA's 5-day "MBA" Workshop [39123]

AMA's Advanced Course in Strategic Marketing [46619]

AMA's Advanced Executive Leadership Program [34788]

AMA's Course on Direct Marketing [46620]

AMA's Course on Financial Analysis [26119]

AMA's Course on Financial Forecasting for Dynamic Business Results [26120]

AMA's Course on Mergers and Acquisitions [47437], [49776]

AMA's Course for Presidents and CEOs [44722], [49904], [52481]

AMA's Course for Senior Executives [52482]

AMA's Course on Supply Chain Management [44723]

AMA's Employment Law Course: Avoiding the Legal Pitfalls of EEO, FMLA and ADA [42816]

AMA's Finance Workshop for Nonfinancial Executives [37845]

AMA's Leading with Emotional Intelligence [44724]

Amato's [21736]

"The Amazing, Real-Life Adventures of Microfly" in *Venture Capital Journal* (Vol. 42, No. 8, August 2002, pp. 30-31) [41441], [50790], [52016], [55352]

Amazon Cafe [8539]

"Ambitious business women search for mentors during challenging times" in *San Francisco Business Times* (Vol. 16, No. 42, May 24, 2002) [35317], [54130], [56115]

Ambler Growth Strategy Consultants Inc. [3637], [31272], [50777]

Amboy Area Chamber of Commerce [59420]

Ambridge Area Chamber of Commerce [64376]

"Ambulance Chasing, Web-Style" in *Forbes* (Vol. 174, December 27, 2004, No. 13, pp. 56) [543], [29094], [33529], [40958], [46673]

AMC International Inc. [27213], [30642], [33332], [45956], [47825], [50288]

AMCinstitute [1724]

"Amendment to Thwart Scavengers Could Hurt Scrap Dealers" in *Crain's Detroit Business* (Vol. 22, December 4, 2006, No. 49, pp. 27) [21217], [30131], [40153]

Ameren Corporation–Library [56677]

"Ameribank Plans Branch in Palm Beach Gardens" in *South Florida Business Journal* (Vol. 23, No. 47, June 27, 2003, pp. 2) [9810], [27768], [37873]

America-Israel Chamber of Commerce, Central Atlantic Region [64377]

America-Israel Chamber of Commerce and Industry [43468]

American Academy of Advertising [511], [50518]

American Academy of Implant Dentistry Annual Meeting [17136], [17271]

American Academy of Optometry [25618]
    Library [25667]

American Academy of Physical Medicine and Rehabilitation Annual Meeting [19576]

American Academy of Professional Coders [46605], [56087]

American Accounting Association [15]

American Accounting Association Annual Meeting [355]

American Advertising Federation [512], [50519]

American Agents Association [13139]

"American Airlines' Future Hangs Union Votes" in *Dallas Morning News* (April 11, 2003) [30287], [55280]

American Alliance for Health, Physical Education, Recreation and Dance [19353]

American Alliance for Health, Physical Education, Recreation, and Dance - National Conference and Exposition [23670]

American Alternative Medical Association [19550]

American Amateur Karate Federation [16901]

American Ambulance Association [1086]

American Amusement Machine Association [1097]

American Animal Hospital Association [1230]

American Apparel and Footwear Association [5266], [16207]

American Apparel Producers' Network-Directory for Sourcing Apparel [5283], [5580], [16216]

American Appraisal Associates Inc. [50289]

American Arbitration Association [17030]
    Library and Information Center on the Resolution of Disputes [17072]

American Association of Advertising Agencies [513], [50520]

American Association of Attorney-Certified Public Accountants [16]

American Association of Attorney-Certified Public Accountants Annual Conference [356]

American Association of Bioanalysts [17168]

American Association for Budget and Program Analysis [27072]

American Association of Candy Technologists [4268]

American Association of Colleges of Pharmacy [8751]

American Association for Continuity of Care [12356]

American Association of Cosmetology Schools Annual Conference-AACS Annual Convention & Expo [2409], [7923]

American Association of Cosmetology Schools/Cosmetology Educators of America [11770]

American Association of Exporters and Importers [12926], [43469]

American Association of Franchisees and Dealers [3843], [4000], [38696]

American Association of Fund-Raising Counsel Membership Directory [10730]

American Association of Fundraising Counsel [10724]

American Association of Handwriting Analysts [11851]
    Library [11868]

American Association of Hispanic CPAs [357]

American Association of Home Based Businesses [42563]

American Association for Homecare [12357], [17252]

American Association of Homes and Services for the Aging [18294]

American Association of Homes and Services for the Aging Convention [18374]

American Association of Insurance Management Consultants [13140]

American Association of Insurance Services [13141]

American Association for Laboratory Accreditation [17169], [17242]

American Association for Laboratory Animal Science Conference & Exhibits [17222]

American Association of Language Specialists [25073]

American Association of Managing General Agents [13142]

American Association of Meat Processors [4054]

American Association for Medical Transcription [17294]

American Association of Minority Businesses [47989]

American Association of Nutritional Consultants [18424]

American Association of Occupational Health Nurses–Library [1712]

American Association of Pharmacy Technicians [8752]

American Association of Radon Scientists and Technologists [20390]

American Association of Teachers of Italian [32887]

American Auditory Society [12100]

American Automobile Association–Research Library [8735], [18213]

American Automotive Leasing Association [2065], [17949]

"American Axle hopes new 4WD unit can shift it into high gear" in *Crain's Detroit Business* (Vol. 18, No. 51, Dec. 23, 2002, pp. 17) [1895], [17961], [48694]

"American Axle's Dauch rewarded handsomely for company success" in *Crain's Detroit Business* (Vol. 19, No. 16, April 21, 2003, pp. 4) [1896], [17962], [35766]

American Bakers Association [2146], [2228]

American Ballet Competition [8432]

American Banker (Vol. 170, February 4, 2005, No. 24, pp. 10); "A Business Real Estate Appraisal Problem" in [3103], [7770], [12528], [18316], [20448], [21458], [22610], [39201], [40218]

American Banker (Vol. 170, February 4, 2005, No. 24, pp. 5); "Amex Says MBNA Card Spending is 7 Percent Above Plan" in [8299], [32244]

American Banker (Vol. 171, November 27, 2006, No. 226, pp. 2); "Banks Try to Make Tele-Touch Satisfy Small Businesses" in [9837], [14775], [33562], [39161], [41535], [53601]

Master Index

American Banker (Vol. 170, February 2, 2005, No. 22, pp. 5); "Broker In a Rival's Branch? Your Bank Can Do It Too" in [9857], [31649]

American Banker (Vol. 171, November 20, 2006, No. 223, pp. 1); "Card Firms Try Two-Pronged Approach to Small Business" in [8302], [46778]

American Banker (Vol. 170, February 4, 2005, No. 24, pp. 17); "CarsDirect.com Buys 2 Web Sites" in [576], [13886], [14832], [17367], [17991], [33650], [46779]

American Banker (Vol. 169, December 28, 2004, No. 247, pp. 1); "Casting Wider Net in Realty Rehab Market" in [9866], [17368], [20458], [20826], [52650]

American Banker (Vol. 170, February 4, 2005, No. 24, pp. 11); "Chief Risk Officer No Solution" in [35944], [44998]

American Banker (Vol. 170, February 4, 2005, No. 24, pp. 12); "Credit Unions Win A Door-Opener For PassMark?" in [9902], [13938], [22205], [40291]

American Banker (Vol. 170, February 1, 2005, No. 270, pp. 9); "E-Loan Exec Chides Lenders" in [9926], [17377], [44510]

American Banker Financial Publications [3459], [10361], [15741], [17470]

American Banker (Vol. 172, January 17, 2006, No. 11, pp. 17); "First Data: New Terminal POS Lift for Small Outfits" in [4662], [22999], [41689], [44231], [49937], [51158], [53285]

American Banker (Vol. 170, February 4, 2005, No. 24, pp. 1); "For Biggest, No Brakes On This Trend" in [9966], [15008], [49943], [53738]

American Banker (Vol. 170, February 2, 2005, No. 22, pp. 1); "How Fee Drop Would Alter Servicing" in [10008], [17398]

American Banker (Vol. 170, February 4, 2005, No. 24, pp. 4); "In Brief: 1st California to Pay $36M for South Coast" in [10015], [15115]

American Banker (Vol. 171, September 15, 2006, No. 178, pp. 9); "In Brief: Amex Targets Midsize Corporate Market" in [10016], [15116]

American Banker (Vol. 172, January 31, 2007, No. 21, pp. 16); "In Brief: Discover Touting Gas Rewards" in [8309], [31558], [47123], [53804]

American Banker (Vol. 171, November 2, 2006, No. 211, pp. 17); "In Brief: Firms Eager to Avoid Illegal Workers" in [29302], [40455]

American Banker (Vol. 170, February 4, 2005, No. 24, pp. 3); "In Brief: Grassley Offers a Bankruptcy Bill" in [8310], [8385], [26516], [27138], [29303], [40456]

American Banker (Vol. 171, November 17, 2006, No. 222, pp. 8); "In Brief: SBA Assesses Role Of Scores in Lending" in [8352], [8386], [10017], [39842], [44552]

American Banker (Vol. 170, September 5, 2006, No. 170, pp. 9); "In Brief: Small-Business Poll: Economy Worsening" in [28319], [32505]

American Banker (Vol. 170, February 4, 2005, No. 24, pp. 4); "Indiana Bill Would Multiply U.S. Development Tax Credit" in [10022], [15122], [40463], [54610]

American Banker (Vol. 170, September 30, 2005, No. 189, pp. 11); "Lessons From Katrina on Prepaid Cards" in [8312], [8387], [10059], [18781], [31562]

American Banker (Vol. 172, January 18, 2007, No. 12, pp. 1); "Maine Thing: Camden Tries New Approach" in [10078], [15244], [28448], [38208], [44582]

American Banker (Vol. 170, February 3, 2005, No. 23, pp. 1); "Michigan Bank Finally Gets Georgia Toehold" in [10087], [15263], [28482], [50079]

American Banker Newsletter (Vol. 168, No. 208, October 29, 2003, pp. 9); "In Brief: MBNA Issuing eBay Product in Canada" in [31559], [34056]

American Banker (Vol. 170, February 3, 2005, No. 23, pp. 2); "Northern Trust Close To an Outsourcing Foothold in Britain" in [10114], [15310], [43768], [49719]

American Banker (Vol. 171, November 30, 2006, No. 229, pp. 1); "Panel Chief Set To Reopen SBA Budget Debate" in [10129], [15340], [39883], [44617]

American Banker (Vol. 170, February 3, 2005, No. 23, pp. 17); "Pipeline" in [10134], [17427]

American Banker (Vol. 170, February 4, 2005, No. 24, pp. 1); "Publix Alliances Upend Payment-Fee Models" in [10145], [11654]

American Banker (Vol. 170, February 3, 2005, No. 23, pp. 3); "Reg Complexity Fuels Demand for ABA Institute" in [10157], [33220]

American Banker (Vol. 170, February 2, 2005, No. 22, pp. 5); "Renewed Effort for Reintroduced Rural Credit Bill" in [10160], [40638], [54720]

American Banker (Vol. 170, February 2, 2005, No. 22, pp. 4); "Revenue-Raising Ideas Could Hit Financial Services" in [10167], [54725]

American Banker (Vol. 172, February 2, 2007, No. 23, pp. 3); "SBA Chief: Storm Relief Advances" in [39907], [44641]

American Banker (Vol. 170, February 1, 2005, No. 270, pp. 6); "SBA Loan Lenders Ranked by Value of 7(a) Loans" in [39914], [44645]

American Banker (Vol. 171, December 14, 2006, No. 239, pp. 3); "SEC Offers Small Banks Internal Controls Leeway" in [10176], [15438], [39566], [40678]

American Banker (Vol. 170, Feb. 4, 2005, No. 24) "Simplify CRA? Not So Fast: Citi, GE Say Keep As Is; JPM Offers Alternative" in [10183], [40694]

American Banker (Vol. 172, January 16, 2006, No. 10, pp. 6A); "Small Firms Flock to Remote Deposit Service" in [10186], [15459], [26361]

American Banker (Vol. 170, September 5, 2006, No. 170, pp. 4A); "The Laziness Factor in Loyalty" in [10058], [15209], [30904]

American Banker (Vol. 170, February 4, 2005, No. 24, pp. 11); "To Sell or Not to Sell? Here's How to Decide" in [10210], [15529], [50217], [52462]

American Banker (Vol. 170, February 4, 2005, No. 24, pp. 12); "Verifiers Try New Tactics To Counter Check Decline" in [8404], [10230], [54061]

American Banker (Vol. 171, December 15, 2006, No. 240, pp. 11); "Viewpoint: Rule on Race, Gender Data Has Outlived Its Intent" in [828], [10231], [15577], [40805], [47692], [48605]

American Banker (Vol. 171, September 27, 2006, No. 186, pp. 7); "Visa Rolls Out Business Card" in [8324], [31600]

American Banker (Vol. 170, February 2, 2005, No. 22, pp. 17); "Will Presentment Growth Enliven Online Bill Pay?" in [7032], [10253], [34728]

American Bar Association Small Business [29095]

American Bee Journal [2470]

American Beekeeping Federation [2464]

American Beekeeping Federation Convention [2477]

American Beekeeping Federation-News Letter [2471]

American Beverage Institute [3114]

American Beverage Licensees [16223]

American Big Businesses Directory [46195]

American Board of Alternative Medicine [17878]

American Board of Bioanalysis [17170]

American Board of Funeral Service Education [10784]

American Board of Opticianry [25619]

American Boarding Kennels Association [19066], [19189]

American Boarding Kennels Association Annual Convention and Trade Show [19090], [19172]

American Boat Builders and Repairers Association [16712]

American Boat and Yacht Council [16713]

American Boat and Yacht Council-Membership List [16727]

American Book Producers Association [2642], [8944]

American Booksellers Association [2643], [3012], [63241]

American Booksellers Association (ABA)–Information Center [2810], [3074]

American Border Leicester Association [1157]

American Brahmousin Council [1158], [26454]

American Breweriana Association [3115]

American Bus Association's Motorcoach Marketer [24663], [25147]

American Business Connections [3414]

American Business Management Series [45912]

American Business Media [18818]

American Business Sales Series [51937]

American Business Women's Association [56088]

American Businesspersons Association [52793]

American Camp Association [4220]

American Camping Association–Library [4264]

American Camping Association Conference & Exhibits [4258]

American-Canadian Genealogical Society, Inc.–Library [10997]

"The American Cancer Society's Next Crusade" in *Fast Company* (November 2001, pp. 58) [39140], [44883]

American Casino Guide [10893]

American Cat Association [1159]

American Cat Fanciers Association [1160]

American Ceramic Society Bulletin [8025]

American Chain of Warehouses [20204]

American Chain of Warehouses-Membership Directory [20217]

American Chambers of Commerce Abroad [43541]

American Cheese Society [23447]

American Choral Directors Association National Convention [17648], [17801]

American Christmas Tree Journal [5481]

American City and County [50358]

American Clinical Laboratory Association [17171]

American Coin-Op [8912]

American Coin-Op-Buyers Guide Issue [8899]

American Coin-Op (Vol. 44, No. 11, November 2003, pp. 8); "Drop-Off Kiosk Accepts Customer Orders So You Don't Have To" in [7776], [8903], [15919]

American College of Apothecaries [8753]
    Research and Education Resource Center [41357]

American College and Career Counseling Center [4382]

American College of Health Care Administrators [1697], [18295]
    ACHCA Information Center [485], [18394]

American College of Veterinary Pathologists Newsletter [1242]

American Congress on Surveying and Mapping [23758]

American Conservatory of Music–Robert R. McCormick Memorial Library [17659]

American Convention of Meat Processors [4072]

American Council on Alcoholism [54321]

American Council for Construction Education [7200]

American Council on Consumer Awareness, Inc. [41358]

American Council on Exercise [19354]

American Council of Life Insurers [13143]

American Counseling Association [4383]

American Court and Commercial Newspapers [18819]

American Craft [8191]

American Craft Council [7979], [8138]

American Craft Council Library [8111], [8254]

American Craft-News Section [7994]

American Culinary Federation [7804]

American Custom Gunmakers Guild [11720]

American Cut Crystal Corp. [16850]

American Dance Guild [8433]

American Dance Therapy Association [8434]

American Defense Institute [52347]

The American Demand for Office Furniture and Anticipated Trends–Aktrin [18618]

American Demographics (October 1, 2001, pp. 24); "Trend Central: What's new with candy?" in [4318], [48805]

American Diamond Industry Association [15814]

American Dietetic Association [18425]
    Knowledge Center [12040], [12092], [18490], [26066]

American Disc Jockey Association [8675]

"American Dreamers Nominations Due Thursday" in *Crain's Detroit Business* (Vol. 22, December 11, 2006, No. 50, pp. 9) [34810], [35767], [50426]

American Driver and Traffic Safety Education Association [8725]

American Driving Society [12436]

American Drop-Shippers Directory [16423]

American Drycleaner [8913]

American Edged Products Manufacturers Association-Annual Membership Directory [12180]

American Electrology Association [11754]

American Engine Installations [2092]

American English Academy [3638], [27574], [27704], [31273], [33333]

American Enterprise Institute [40902]

The American Entrepreneur Today [37022]

American Falls Chamber of Commerce [59285]

American Family Records Association [10911]

American Federation for Medical Research [17243]

American Federation of Teachers-Library [25488]

American Federation of Violin and Bow Makers [17831]

American Film Institute-Louis B. Mayer Library [4154], [17548], [25613]

American Financial Services Association [8340]

American Fisheries Society [10437]

American Fisheries Society Annual Meeting [10471]

American Fisheries Society-Membership Directory and Handbook [10456]

American Fitness [19454]

American Floorcovering Alliance [10499], [13621]

American Floral Art School-Floral Library [10604], [22829]

American Forensic Engineers [3249], [56652]

American Fork Chamber of Commerce [65696]

American Foundation for Pharmaceutical Education [8754]

American Franchise Consultants [3844], [31476]

American Franchisee Association [38697]

American-French Genealogical Society-Library [10998]

American Gaming Association [10851]

The American Gardener [11450]

American Gear Manufacturers Association-News Digest [46496]

American Gem Trade Association [15815]

The American Genealogist [10955]

American Gladiators Fitness Franchise [19493]

The American Grocery Store: The Business Evolution of an Architectural Space [11590]

American Hair Loss Council [11755]

American Handwriting Analysis Foundation [11852]

American Hardware Manufacturers Association [11871]

American Harp Society National Conference [17649]

American Hatpin Society [1294], [5785], [15816]

American Health and Beauty Aids Institute [2385], [11771]

American Health Care Association [18296], [40909]

American Health Care Association Annual Convention and Exposition [18375]

American Health Information Management Association [17154]
    FORE Library [17304]

American Hellenic Institute [43470]

American Herb Association [12134]
    Library [12158]

American Herbal Products Association [12135]

American Hockey Magazine [22836]

American Home Business Association [42564]

American Home Furnishings Alliance [12259]

American Horse Council [12437]

American Horse Publications [12438]

American Horticultural Society [11404]
    Library [10605], [11505], [16086]

American Hospital Association [12358], [18297]

American Hospital Association-Ambulatory Outreach [12383]

The American Hospital Directory [17229], [17282]

American Hotel and Lodging Association [12493]
    Information Center [12739], [25347]

American Hotel and Lodging Educational Foundation [12494]

American Housing Survey [1394]

American Hydrangea Society [11405]

"An American Icon" in *Entrepreneur* (Vol. 33, January 2005, No. 1, pp. 76) [38708], [39141]

American Indian and Alaska Native Arts and Crafts-Source Directory [1594]

American Indonesian Chamber of Commerce [43471]

American Institute of Baking [2229], [2322]
    Information Services Department-Ruth Emerson Library [2318]

American Institute of Baking Technical Bulletin [2262]

American Institute for Biosocial and Medical Research, Inc.-Library [18491]

American Institute for Cancer Research [18521]

American Institute of Certified Public Accountants [17]

American Institute for Chartered Property Casualty Underwriters-Insurance Institute of America-Nancy W. Spellman Memorial Library [13591]

American Institute of Commemorative Art [10785]

American Institute of Constructors [7201]

American Institute for CPCU [13144]

American Institute for Economic Research [24194]

American Institute for Economic Research-Research Reports [32813]

American Institute of Fishery Research Biologists [10438]

American Institute of Floral Designers [10547]

American Institute of Food Distribution [11579]

American Institute of Food Distribution, Inc.-Information and Research Center [2319], [4571], [7104], [8587], [10649], [11717], [22030], [23582]

American Institute of Graphic Arts [5951], [19840]

American Institute of the History of Pharmacy [8755]

American Institute of Inspectors [3226]

American Institute of Musical Studies [17717]

American Institute of Organbuilders [17832]

American Institute of Small Business [3845], [61734]

American Institute of Small Business: Setting Up a Home-Based Business [42781], [53049]

American Institute of Small Business: Starting a Business-Advice from Experts [53050]

American Institute of Small Business: Women in Business [56533]

American Institute of Small Business: Your Personal Financial Guide to Success, Power & Security [38496]

American Insurance Association [13145]
    Law Library [13592]

American Intercontinental University-Library [5602], [13720]

American International Automobile Dealers Association [17950]

American Islamic Chamber of Commerce [47990]

American Israel Chamber of Commerce - Southeast Region [43472], [59056]

American Journal of Agricultural Economics [26567]

American Journal of Bariatric Medicine [26042]

American Journal of Clinical Nutrition [18445]

American Journal of Electroneurodiagnostic Technology [41158]

American Journal of Hospice and Palliative Care [41159]

American Journal on Mental Retardation [41160]

American Journal of Veterinary Research [1243]

American Journey: The African-American Experience [10989]

American Journey: The Constitution and Supreme Court [29646], [40893]

American Judo Association [16902]

American Junior Golf Association [11242]

The American Keiretsu: A Strategic Weapon for Global Competitiveness [12943], [43542]

American Kennel Club [1161]
    Library [1219], [19134]

American Kennel Club Museum of the Dogs [62113]

American Kenpo Karate International [16903]

American Land Title Association [20397]

American Law Institute [24195]

American Leak Detection- Entrepreneur.com [19775]

American Library Association [13056]

American Life Foundation-Prang-Mark Society-Library [11575]

American Lighting Association [9103]

American Lighting Association-Membership Directory [9107]

American Lock Collectors Association Newsletter [16263]

American Lumber Standard Committee [16283]

American Lutheran Publicity Bureau [50521]

American Machine Tool Distributors' Association [16348]

American Machinist [16389]

American Mailorder Association [16419]

American Managed Behavioral Healthcare Association [40910]

American Management Association [16492], [44706]

American Marketing Association [16795], [46606]

American Marketing Association-The M Guide Directory [16801], [46674]

American Massage Therapy Association [16994]

American Matchcover Collecting Club-Library [5937]

American Meat Institute [4055]

American Medical Directors Association [18298]

American Medical Equestrian Association/Safe Riders Foundation [12439]

American Medical News (Vol. 41, No. 4, January 26, 1998, pp. 11); "Conquering Clutter" in [20016], [52521]

American Medical Publishers' Association [2644]

American Medical Technologists [17172]

American Medical Technologists Convention [17223]

"American Megatrends vets start a new company" in *Atlanta Business Chronicle* (Vol. 24, No. 11, August 17, 2001, pp. 2A) [6228], [35318], [48685], [55353]

American Montessori Society [5319]

American Motor Carrier Directory [10667], [25375]

American Motorcyclist [17494]

American Motorcyclist Association [17480]

American Moving and Storage Association [17554]

American Museum of Magic-Lund Memorial Library [8255]

American Music [17786]

American Music Center Collection at the New York Public Library for the Performing Arts [17660]

American Music Conference [17724]

American Music Teacher [17611]

American Musical Instrument Society [17833]

American Musicological Society-Directory [17586]

American Mustang and Burro Association, Inc.-Library [12469]

American Mutual Life Association [26722]

American Needlepoint Guild [22721]

American Numismatic Association [5786]

American Numismatic Society [5787], [5876]
    Library [5863]

American Nursery and Landscape Association [11406], [15960]

American Nurseryman [11451]

American Nurses Association-Library Information Center [1713]

American Optometric Association [25620]

American Optometric Foundation [25621]

American Optometric Student Association [25622]

American Organization for Bodywork Therapies of Asia [16995]

"American Outcast" in *Entrepreneur.com* (Vol. 34, February 2006, No. 2, pp. 81) [27769], [29786], [43543]

American Outdoor Adventures [18741], [24776], [25331]

American Outreach Association [54322]

American Painting Contractor-Buyers' Guide [18705]

American Payroll Association [18768]

American Pet Products Manufacturers Association [19142]

American Pharmacists Association-Foundation Library [8858]

American Philatelic Congress [5788]

American Philatelic Research Library [5864]

American Philatelic Society [5789]

American Philatelic Society CAC Newsletter [5829]

American Photographic Artists Guild [19218]

American Physical Therapy Association [19551]
    Information Resources [19586]

American Physical Therapy Association Annual Conference [19577]

"America's Labor Federation" in *The Economist* (Vol. 376, July 30-August 5, 2005, No. 8437, pp. 25-26) **[39143]**, **[55281]**

"America's Newest Entrepreneurial Patron" in *Inc.* (October 1, 2003) **[35768]**, **[39144]**

America's Pharmacist **[8812]**

"America's Top Black Lawyers" in *Black Enterprise* (Vol. 34, No. 4, November 2003, pp. 120) **[29096]**

America's Wash-N-Stor **[4376]**, **[8924]**, **[20252]**

Americinn **[12701]**

Americus Chamber of Commerce **[60285]**

Americus-Sumter County Chamber of Commerce **[59057]**

Americuts Family Barber Shops **[11819]**

AmeriFlex Financial Services **[27002]**

"Amerigon, BorgWarner Fare Better Among Suppliers" in *Crain's Detroit Business* (Vol. 21, October 31, 2005, No. 44, pp. 4) **[1897]**, **[17963]**, **[46196]**

AmeriHost Franchise Systems **[12702]**

Amerimark Capital Group **[65587]**

AmeriSpec Home Inspection Service **[3268]**, **[3376]**

AmeriSuites **[12703]**

Ameritech Development Corp. **[59719]**

Ameritek Painting **[18716]**

Ameriwest Business Consultants Inc. **[30060]**, **[30643]**

Ames Chamber of Commerce **[60090]**

"Amex Says MBNA Card Spending is 7 Percent Above Plan" in *American Banker* (Vol. 170, February 4, 2005, No. 24, pp. 5) **[8299]**, **[32244]**

Amgen, Inc. **[57922]**

    Amgen Libraries **[8859]**

"Amgen Looking to Develop Medicines with Competitors" in *Providence Business News* (Vol. 18, No. 20, September 1, 2003, pp. 2) **[8774]**, **[14737]**, **[48695]**, **[49785]**, **[50810]**, **[52038]**

"Amgen's Profit Up 58 Percent in 2nd Quarter" in *Providence Business News* (Vol. 18, No. 15, July 28, 2003, pp. 1) **[27770]**, **[46676]**

Amherst Area Chamber of Commerce **[60925]**

Amherst Chamber of Commerce **[62817]**

Amherst County Chamber of Commerce **[65858]**

"Amherst, N.Y., Firm Feel Good Greetings Creates Board Game for Children" in *Buffalo News* (February 17, 2004) **[11556]**, **[24800]**

AMI Insider **[1867]**

"Amid Customer Backlash, eBay Reduces Some Fees" in *eWeek* (February 7, 2005) **[1773]**, **[13812]**, **[31008]**, **[31637]**, **[33530]**

Amidzad, LLC **[57923]**

Amite Chamber of Commerce **[60615]**

"Amityville-Based Napco Security Systems Back in Good With Nasdaq" in *Long Island Business News* (February 27, 2004) **[14738]**, **[22167]**

"Amortization of Certain Intangible Assets" in *Journal of Accountacncy* **[70]**, **[2865]**, **[23881]**, **[26150]**, **[27079]**, **[38709]**, **[43986]**, **[54428]**

"Amount raised by venture funds plunged to $6.9 billion in 2002" in *Wall Street Journal* (February 11, 2003, pp. C5) **[27771]**, **[55488]**

Ampersand Ventures **[61030]**

Amphion Capital Management, LLC / Wolfensohn Associates **[63056]**

Amphora **[4170]**

AmQuest Bank, N.A.–Lawton Satellite–Small Business Development Center **[63910]**

AMS–Knowledge Center–Library **[7016]**

AMS Newsletter **[17613]**

AMT Capital Ltd. / AMT Venture Partners, Ltd. **[65588]**

AMT-Member Product Directory **[16359]**

AMT Venture Partners, Ltd. / AMT Capital Ltd. **[65589]**

"AMTDA members can self-update info online" in *Tooling & Production* (Vol. 69, No. 1, January 2003, pp. 10) **[6234]**, **[16360]**, **[33531]**

Amusement Business **[1142]**, **[7094]**

Amusement Industry Manufacturers and Suppliers International **[1125]**

Amusement and Music Operators Association Convention **[1120]**

Amusement Parks **[1130]**

The Amusement and Theme Parks Industry Market **[1140]**

L'amyx Tea Bar **[11364]**

"An Attractive Site" in *Black Enterprise* (Vol. 36, November 2005, No. 4, pp. 74) **[544]**, **[25788]**, **[33532]**, **[46677]**, **[48033]**

"An Oasis of Luxury" in *Hispanic Business* (Vol. 23, No. 5, May 2001, pp. 74) **[30288]**

"An Older Sibling In Your Corner Eases Entry Into The Real World" in *Wall Street Journal* (Vol. 248, December 2006, No. 149, pp. B6) **[32995]**, **[35769]**, **[39145]**

"An Option to Do Nothing" in *Forbes* (Vol. 170, No. 4, September 2, 2002, pp. 45) **[71]**, **[23882]**, **[26151]**

Anaconda Chamber of Commerce **[62144]**

Anacortes Chamber of Commerce **[66040]**

Anadarko Chamber of Commerce **[63941]**

"Anadarko Laying Off 400 Workers to Cut Costs" in *Houston Business Journal* (Vol. 34, No. 13, August 8, 2003, pp. 3) **[26152]**, **[32245]**

"Anadarko Seeks Bidders for Possible Buyout" in *Houston Business Journal* (Vol. 34, No. 14, August 15, 2003, pp. 3) **[14739]**, **[26153]**, **[32246]**, **[49786]**

Anago Franchising, Inc. **[3344]**

Anaheim Chamber of Commerce **[57326]**

Anahuac Area Chamber of Commerce **[65110]**

"Analog TV" in *Business Week* (January 23, 2006, No. 3968, pp. 22) **[4085]**, **[24375]**, **[40154]**, **[41511]**

Analysis for Financial Management **[37874]**

"Analysts Mixed on WNY Economy" in *Business First Buffalo* (Vol. 19, No. 44, July 25, 2003, pp. 1) **[31387]**, **[32247]**, **[44466]**, **[45158]**

"Analysts: Pricing, Material Costs to Spur Supplier Mergers" in *Crain's Detroit Business* (Vol. 21, January 10, 2005, No. 2, pp. 19) **[1898]**, **[17964]**, **[31009]**, **[46197]**, **[49787]**

Analytical Consulting Services **[11960]**

Analytical Engineering Services Corp. **[13572]**

Analytical Solutions **[49401]**

"Analyze this: from "automation" to "effectiveness"" in *E-business Advisor* (Vol. 18, No. 10, October 2000, pp. 10) **[33533]**, **[53583]**

"Analyze This" in *Black Enterprise* (Vol. 34, No. 6, January 2004, pp. 41) **[41512]**, **[44884]**, **[53203]**

"Analyze This: Charles Phillips Makes Bold Career Move to Oracle as Executive Vice President" in *Black Enterprise* (Vol. 34, No. 6) **[41513]**, **[44885]**, **[53204]**

"Analyze This" in *Entrepreneur.com* (Vol. 34, February 2006, No. 2, pp. 42) **[13813]**, **[25789]**, **[33534]**

"Analyze This" in *Forbes* (April 1, 2002, p. 96) **[44270]**, **[53205]**

Analyzing Our Time Usage **[55009]**

Analyzing Sales Promotions **[46678]**

Anamosa Chamber of Commerce **[60091]**

The Anatomical Record **[52236]**

Anatomy of a Business Plan: A Step-by-Step Guide to Starting Smart, Building the Business, & Securing Your Companies Future **[29787]**

Anatomy of a Leveraged Buyout **[3439]**

"Anatomy of a Merger" in *Rough Notes* (Vol. 145, No. 2, February 2003, pp. 66) **[13186]**, **[29788]**, **[43077]**, **[49788]**

Anatomy of a Merger: The Causes & Effects of Mergers & Acquisitions **[49789]**

"The Anatomy of a Sale" in *Inc.* (September 2005, pp. 116-123, 160, 162, 164, 168) **[18849]**, **[52405]**

Anatomy of a Start-Up: Why Some New Businesses Succeed and Others Fail **[53584]**

"Anatomy of a Startup" in *Black Enterprise* (Vol. 35, November 2004, No. 4, pp. 112) **[4593]**, **[22910]**, **[41442]**, **[53206]**

Ancestry **[10956]**

Ancestry's Redbook: State, County & Town Sources **[10925]**

Anchor Bay Chamber of Commerce **[61247]**

Anchor Point Chamber of Commerce **[56946]**

Anchorage Chamber of Commerce **[56947]**

Anchorage Daily News (November 20, 2003); "Tax Possible for Anchorage, Alaska-Area Bed and Breakfast Businesses" in **[2454]**, **[54809]**

"And on your Left" in *Entrepreneur* (Vol. 28, No. 9, September 2000, pp. 48) **[29704]**, **[55354]**

"And Now, the Handheld Trainer" in *Business Week* (January 9, 2006, No. 3966, pp. 92) **[4594]**, **[6579]**, **[19373]**, **[22911]**, **[48944]**, **[53207]**

"And Now a Syllable From Our Sponsor" in *Inc.* (August 2005, pp. 22) **[545]**, **[46679]**, **[53585]**

"And Now, a Word From Our Sponsor" in *Harvard Business Review* (Vol. 81, No. 10, October 2003, pp. 31) **[546]**, **[46680]**

Andalusia Area Chamber of Commerce **[56809]**

Andersen European Community Sourcebook; Arthur **[43547]**

Andersen Horticultural Library's Source List of Plants and Seeds **[11419]**

Anderson Area Chamber of Commerce **[63601]**, **[64720]**

Anderson Area Medical Center Library **[8860]**, **[18395]**

Anderson Chamber of Commerce **[57327]**

Anderson County Chamber of Commerce **[60480]**, **[64881]**

Anderson, Kill & Olick, LLP–Library **[43455]**

Larry J. Anderson **[26417]**, **[27214]**

Richard I. Anderson **[6209]**

Anderson/Roethle Inc. **[16562]**, **[31274]**, **[45958]**, **[46534]**, **[47826]**

Anderson Valley Chamber of Commerce **[57328]**

Anderson's Campground & RV Park Travel Directory **[4231]**

Andover Area Chamber of Commerce and Convention and Visitors' Bureau **[60286]**

Andover Chamber of Commerce **[62818]**

"Andrea Electronics Completes Stage 1 of Restructuring" in *Long Island Business News* (February 27, 2004) **[7714]**, **[44886]**

Andrew Harper's Hideaway Report **[25281]**

"Andrew Lo" in *Business Week* (February 20, 2006, No. 3972, pp. 22) **[14740]**, **[32248]**, **[37875]**

Andrew Seybold's Outlook **[6496]**

Andrew Smash **[12802]**, **[21737]**

Andrews Chamber of Commerce **[63319]**

"Andrews & Kurth goes high-tech with ex-Brobeck attorneys" in *Houston Business Journal* (Vol. 33, No. 49, April 18, 2003, pp. 2A) **[29097]**, **[41514]**

Andrews & Kurth L.L.P.–Library **[9424]**

Andrews University–Office of Scholarly Research **[61476]**

Androscoggin County Chamber of Commerce **[60729]**

Androscoggin Valley Council of Governments–Small Business Development Center **[60686]**

Andy Oncall **[7653]**

"Andy Pearson Finds Love" in *Fast Company* (August 2001, pp. 78) **[35770]**, **[44887]**

Andy Warhol Museum–Archives Study Center **[1645]**, **[17661]**, **[17812]**

Andy's Parties **[18742]**

Anesthesia Malpractice Prevention **[41161]**

Angel Associates Inc. **[12416]**

Angel Crafts Video Vol. 1 **[8224]**

Angel Fire Chamber of Commerce **[62671]**

"Angel Flight" in *Ingram's* (Vol. 27, No. 12, December 2001, pp. 70) **[54131]**

"Angel Investing Still Alive, Barely, in Chicago Area" in *Chicago Tribune* (November 10, 2002) **[16175]**, **[24221]**, **[24643]**, **[35319]**, **[44386]**, **[55355]**

Angel Investors, LP **[57924]**

"Angel Investors Take a Plunge" in *Milwaukee Journal Sentinel* (December 20, 2005) **[44467]**, **[55489]**

"Angel on you Side" in *Entrepreneur* (Vol. 28, No. 10, October 2000, pp. 171) **[48872]**, **[55356]**

Angelina College–Small Business Development Center **[65020]**

Angelo State University–Small Business Development Center **[65021]**

Angels Forum & the Halo Fund **[57925]**

Angels Ice Cream and Hot Dog Franchise **[12803]**

"Apex Property Management Moves" in *Bellingham Business Journal* (January 2007, pp. A6) [20048], [27776], [30132]

Apex Venture Partners [59720]

"Apex Venture Partners Preps for Fifth Vehicle" in *Venture Capital Journal* (Vol. 40, No. 10, November 2000, pp. 16) [22913], [27777], [41520], [55493]

Apiary Inspectors of America [2465]

"Apocalypse Net" in *Red Herring* (No. 102, August 15, 2001, pp. 54-56) [13818], [27778]

Apollo Beach Chamber of Commerce [58752]

Apopka Area Chamber of Commerce [58753]

Appalachia-Science in the Public Interest Library [9425]

Appalachian Center for Economic Networks (ACEnet) [63872]

Appalachian State University
   Appalachian Regional Development Institute [39759]
   Small Business and Technology Development Center (Northwestern Region) [63273]

Appalachian State University at Hickory Office–SBTDC [63274]

Apparel News South [5287], [5735]

"Appearances Count" in *Small Business Opportunities* (Vol. 12, No. 2, March 2000, pp. 12) [27615], [51550]

"The Appellation Trail" in *Forbes* (Vol. 170, No. 5, September 16, 2002, pp. 103) [23455], [27779]

Appendx [1537], [7522]

"Appetite for Destruction" in *Washington Business Journal* (Vol. 22, No. 14, August 8, 2003, pp. 29) [13188], [22172], [40961], [52507]

Appian Ventures [58445]

Apple Auto Glass Limited [11231]

Apple DVD Studio Pro I [53163]

Apple Electrical Services Inc. [49581]

Apple Final Cut Pro I [53164]

"Apple, Goodyear Each Climb 4.9 Percent" in *Wall Street Journal* (Vol. 248, December 2006, No. 153, pp. B3) [14742], [27780], [32251]

Apple II Repair, Maintenance and Expansion [6425]

Apple Motion I [53165]

"Apple Squares Off Against Resellers" in *Inc.* (September 1, 2004) [6581], [29098], [40157], [51050]

Apple Valley Chamber of Commerce [57335], [61556]

"Apple Wanted Cornice To Supply Tiny Hard Drives for a New Device, the iPod Mini" in *Inc.* (October 2005, pp. 59-60) [6582], [41521], [49791]

"Apple of Your Eye?" in *Entrepreneur* (Vol. 31, No. 8, August 2003, pp. 40) [4596], [22914], [48947], [53210]

"Applebee Int'l Sets Up Loans for Remodeling by Franchises" in *Long Island Business News* (March 12, 2004) [21439], [22178], [37253], [38710], [44470]

"Applebee's to open in Lancaster" in *Business First of Buffalo* (Vol. 18, No. 46, August 12, 2002, pp. 15) [21440], [27781]

Applebee's Neighborhood Grill & Bar [21738]

"Appleseed's distribution center expands" in *Boston Business Journal* (Vol. 22, No. 12, April 26, 2002, pp. 5) [27782], [32140], [51051]

"Appleton, Wis.-Based Construction Company Settles Racial Harassment Suit" in *Milwaukee Journal Sentinel* (December 1, 2005) [7244], [29099], [32006]

Appliance [1421]

Appliance-Appliance Industry Purchasing Section Issue [1029], [1408], [7715]

Appliance Design [1422]

Appliance Parts Distributors Association [1402]

The Application of Good Design [6025]

"Application Integration for Real-Time B2B" in *E-business Advisor* (Vol. 18, No. 9, September 2000, pp. 20) [33537], [49792]

"Application Servers: BEA battles for platform dominance" in *Red Herring* (No. 105, October 1, 2001, pp. 76-77) [13819], [22915]

"Application Service Providers on the Move" in *E-business Advisor* (Vol. 17, No. 12, December 1999, pp. 18) [4914], [13820], [33538]

Applied Arts Magazine [6012], [19235]

Applied Bioengineering Multidisciplinary Research Center 61151

Applied Engineering in Agriculture [52237]

The Applied Management Series [37023]

Applied Materials Ventures [57928]

Applied Personnel Research [32106]

Applied Technology [57929], [61031]

"Apply Yourself" in *Entrepreneur* (Vol. 32, October 2004, No. 10, pp. 98) [13821], [33539], [40158], [42167]

"Applying Old Ideals to Crain's New Tasks" in *Crain's New York Business* (Vol. 23, January 8, 2007, No. 2, pp. 11) [547], [13822], [18851], [25790], [27783], [30504], [46682]

Appomattox County Chamber of Commerce [65860]

Appraisal Institute [1428]
   Y.T. and Louise Lee Lum Library [1462]

Appraisal Institute Conference [1454]

The Appraiser [1448]

Appraisers Association of America [1296], [1429]

Appraisers Association of America-Membership Directory [1314], [1438]

The Appraisers Standard [1449], [3245]

"Appraising The Agency" in *Rough Notes* (Vol. 145, No. 2, February 2002, pp. 50) [3497], [13189], [43079]

APQC [54921]

Apricot Lane [9659]

APRO - Association of Progressive Rental Organizations Annual Convention and Trade Show [21371]

Aptos Chamber of Commerce [57336]

APV Technology Partners [57930]

AQUA-Buyers' Guide Issue [23794]

AQUA Magazine [23796]

"Aquaculture Becoming Big Business in Rhode Island" in *Providence Business News* (Vol. 18, No. 16, August 4, 2003, pp. 3) [10424], [10457], [26480], [50813], [52041]

Aquaculture Magazine [10467]

Aquaculture Magazine Buyer's Guide & Industry Directory [10464], [46494], [47779]

Aquarian Alternatives [17927]

Aquatic Biology, Aquaculture & Fisheries Resources [1466], [10475]

Aquatic Control Inc. [10472]

Aquatic Exercise Association [19358]

Aquatic Research Institute [10439], [10483]

Aquinas Group [50290]

Arab Chamber of Commerce [56810]

Arabian Horse Historians Association [1162]

Arabian Horse Owners Foundation–W.R. Brown Memorial Library [12472]

Arabian Horse Trust–Library [12473]

Arabica Coffeehouse [11365]

"Aramark executive joins VIPdesk.com" in *Washington Business Journal* (Vol. 19, No. 17, September 1, 2000, pp. 22) [7119], [44890]

Aransas Pass Chamber of Commerce [65112]

Arapahoe Chamber of Commerce [62243]

"Arbitration in public sector labor disputes" in *Dispute Resolution Journal* (Vol. 56, No. 1, February-April 2001, pp. 64) [17043], [27292]

The Arbitration of Rights Disputes in the Public Sector [17044]

Arbor Age [11452]

Arbor Partners LLC [61453], [61716]

"Arbor Realty Provides $35M in Financing" in *Long Island Business News* (February 27, 2004) [20424], [20797], [27784], [51052]

The Arboretum at Flagstaff–Transition Zone Horticultural Institute–Library [16088]

Arboretum Ventures [61454]

Arboriculture Consultant [16033]

"Arbortext's bread and butter" in *Crain's Detroit Business* (Vol. 19, No. 11, March 17, 2003, pp. 25) [6462], [22916], [53211]

"Arbortext's windfall" in *Crain's Detroit Business* (Vol. 19, No. 11, March 17, 2003, pp. 3) [4597], [22917], [53212], [55494]

Arby's [21739]

The Arc News [41162]

Arcade Area Chamber of Commerce [62819]

Arcadia Academy of Music [17656]

Arcadia Chamber of Commerce [57337], [66340]

Arcadia Valley Chamber of Commerce [61910]

Arcata Chamber of Commerce [57338]

Arch Venture Partners [59721]

Archadeck [4496]

Archbold Area Chamber of Commerce [63603]

Archdale-Trinity Chamber of Commerce [63323]

Archer's Digest [1472]

Archery [1473]

Archery Range and Retailers Organization [1468]

Architects' Guide to Glass, Metal & Glazing [7523], [11225]

"Architects study safety, build security into design" in *Atlanta Business Chronicle* (Vol. 25, No. 21, November 1, 2002, pp. 14C) [1495], [7245], [22173]

"Architects reframe strategy to suit slow year" in *Atlanta Business Chronicle* (Vol. 25, No. 21, November 1, 2002, pp. 20C) [1496], [7246], [37244]

Architectural Alliance [49582]

Architectural Arts & Sculpture [5968], [7995]

Architectural Consultants Ltd. [3251]

Architectural Designs [4482], [7524]

Architectural Digest [13682]

Architectural Glass and Metal Contractors Association [7204]

Architectural Lighting [9116]

Architectural Research Consultants Inc. [52763]

Architectural Woodwork Institute [4472]

Architecture, Building Codes & Inspection [3252]

Architerra [1546]

Archives of Environmental Health [41163]

Archives of Pathology & Laboratory Medicine [17202]

Arcola Chamber of Commerce [59422]

ardea consulting [9403]

ARDITO Information & Research Inc. [31003], [40877], [50291]

Ardmore Chamber of Commerce [63943]

"Are American workers vacation deprived?" in *Incentive* (Vol. 174, No. 9, September 2000, pp. 7) [26741], [34812]

"Are CIOs Obsolete?" in *Harvard Business Review* (Vol. 78, No. 2, March 2000, pp. 55) [44891], [53587]

"Are Customers Selling For You?" in *Sales and Marketing.com* (Vol. 156, No. 3, March 2004, pp. 22) [46683], [51551]

Are Government Purchasing Policies Failing Small Business?: Congressional Hearing [29100], [39148], [39981], [40159]

"Are Green Funds True To Their Colors?" in *Fortune* (Vol. 151, February 7, 2005, No. 3, pp. 106) [9811], [14743], [37245], [54132]

"Are you picking the right leaders?" in *Harvard Business Review* (Vol. 80, No. 2, February 2002, pp. 58) [42168], [44892]

"Are you the weak link?" in *Harvard Business Review* (Vol. 81, No. 4, April 2003, pp. 18) [6158], [22174]

"Are Portals Just Another Integration Problem?" in *E-business Advisor* (Vol. 18, No. 7, July 2000, pp. 40) [33540], [43544]

"Are Race-Specific Drugs Unethical?" in *Black Enterprise* (Vol. 36, November 2005, No. 4, pp. 37) [37387], [40962]

"Are sec. 529 plans a better choice than education IRAs?" in *The Tax Adviser* (Vol. 32, No. 10, October 2001, pp. 668) [23883], [32997], [39787], [54429]

"Are Some Stocks Too Cool: Wall Street Keeps Falling in Love With Growth Stocks. Why the Magic Fades" in *Barron's* (August 18, 2003) [9812], [14744], [37877]

"Are the Tax-Free Net's Days Numbered?" in *Home Office Computing* (Vol. 18, No. 7, July 2000, pp. 16) [33541], [40160], [51053], [53588], [54430]

"Are We There Yet?" in *Entrepreneur* (Vol. 28, No. 1, January 2000, pp. 328) [11141], [35774]

"Are You In With the In Crowd?" in *Harvard Business Review* (Vol. 81, No. 7, July 2003, pp. 86) [44893]

"Are You Ready for Some Football Cliches?" in *Inc.* (October 1, 2003) **[35775]**, **[44894]**

"Are You Ready for Your Accounts?" in *Home Business* (Vol. 12, October 2005, No. 5, pp. 74) **[73]**, **[2866]**, **[23884]**

"Are Your Employees Job Hunting?" in *Women In Business* (Vol. 52, No. 3, May 2000, pp. 42) **[44895]**

"Are Your Staffers Stealing" in *Inc.* (November 2006, pp. 33-35) **[35277]**, **[42828]**, **[44896]**

"Area Arab-Americans can help rebuild Iraq" in *Crain's Detroit Business* (Vol. 19, No. 15, April 14, 2003, pp. 8) **[39982]**, **[43545]**

Area Development Partnership **[61771]**

"Area HMOs get the point about acupuncture" in *San Francisco Business Times* (Vol. 15, No. 2, August 18, 2000, pp. 29) **[17888]**, **[43080]**

Arenac County Extension Service–SBDC **[61173]**

Arete Corporation **[62441]**

Arete Ventures Administration L.L.C. **[35213]**

ARF - Advertising Research Foundation **[50522]**

ARG & Associates **[47827]**

The Argentum Group **[63057]**

Argo Global Capital **[61032]**

Argonne National Laboratory–Office of Technology Transfer **[59770]**

Argos Software–ABECAS Insight **[26442]**, **[27223]**

The Argus Group **[50292]**

ARICP Directory of Certified Riding Instructors **[12458]**

ARIDO **[13683]**

Arizona Canine Academy **[19106]**

Arizona Chamber of Commerce **[57011]**

Arizona City Chamber of Commerce **[57012]**

Arizona Daily Star (January 28, 2005); "Business Picks Up at Tucson, Ariz., eBay Consignment Shop" in **[1788]**, **[7158]**, **[13870]**

Arizona Daily Star (October 7, 2002); "Tucson, Ariz., Senior Citizen Keeps Moving with Dance Studio" in **[8454]**, **[52486]**

Arizona Department of Commerce **[56999]**

Arizona Department of Economic Security–DES 045Z **[66793]**

Arizona Farm Bureau News **[26568]**

Arizona Hispanic Chamber of Commerce **[57013]**

Arizona Hospitality Expo **[2460]**, **[12677]**, **[21701]**

Arizona Minority Business Development Center **[57085]**

Arizona Native American Business Development Center–National Center for American Indian Enterprise Development Center **[57086]**

Arizona Procurement Technical Assistance Center–The National Center for AIED **[57095]**

Arizona Small Business Development Center Network

    Maricopa County Community College–SBDC **[56987]**

    Maricopa County Community Colleges **[56988]**

Arizona State Department of Economic Security–DES **[66820]**

Arizona (State) Department of Environmental Quality–Library **[25727]**

Arizona State Department of Library, Archives, and Public Records–Research Library **[66821]**

Arizona State University

    Architectural and Environmental Design Library **[2570]**, **[23343]**

    Architectural and Environmental Design Library–Solar Energy Collection **[23344]**

    Bank One Economic Outlook Center **[32840]**

    Biomedical Engineering Laboratories **[17148]**

    CAPS Research **[50774]**

    Child Development Laboratory **[5457]**

    Child Study Laboratory **[5458]**

    College of Business Administration–Center for Business Research **[66822]**

    Exercise and Sport Research Institute **[19593]**

    Sustainable Technologies, Agribusiness Resource Center **[26682]**

Arizona State University Research Park **[57097]**

Arizona USA International Trade Directory **[43546]**

Arizona Western College–Small Business Development Center **[56990]**

ARK Services Corp. **[44197]**

Arkadelphia Area Chamber of Commerce **[57128]**

Arkansas Aging Foundation–Information Center **[486]**, **[1714]**, **[18396]**

Arkansas Agribusiness Directory **[26481]**

Arkansas Biotechnology Incubator–Biomedical Biotechnology Center **[57236]**

Arkansas Business **[57241]**

Arkansas Capital Corp. **[57234]**

Arkansas City Area Chamber of Commerce **[60288]**

Arkansas Department Of Economic Development–Small and Minority Business Division **[57232]**

Arkansas Employment Security Department–Research and Analysis Section–Department of Workforce Service **[66825]**

Arkansas Hospitality Association Convention & Exhibition **[12678]**

Arkansas House and Senate Committees on Insurance and Commerce **[57240]**

Arkansas Procurement Assistance Center (APAC) **[57235]**

Arkansas SBDC–University of Arkansas **[57112]**

Arkansas State Chamber of Commerce **[57129]**

Arkansas State Library **[66826]**

Arkansas State University, Jonesboro Center–Small Business Development Center **[57114]**

Arkoma Venture Partners **[65590]**

Arlington Area Chamber of Commerce **[61557]**

Arlington Chamber of Commerce **[60926]**, **[65113]**, **[65861]**

Arlington Heights Chamber of Commerce **[59423]**

Arlington Hispanic Chamber of Commerce **[65114]**

"Arlington the Site of HD Career Expo" in *Hispanic Business* (Vol. 23, No. 10, October, 2001, pp. 104) **[39149]**, **[42169]**, **[48036]**

Arlington Small Business Development Center–George Mason University **[65818]**

"Arlington, Texas, High-Tech Incubator Gets $2.85 Million Boost" in *Dallas Morning News* (October 27, 2002) **[41522]**, **[43048]**, **[55495]**

"Arm yourself for the coming battle over social security" in *Harvard Business Review* (Vol. 80, No. 11, November 2002, pp. 52) **[29101]**, **[40161]**, **[53589]**

ARMA International Annual Conference and Expo **[4872]**

ARMA International - Canadian Region **[13058]**

"Armed for Profit-Taking" in *Small Business Opportunities* (Vol. 16, November 2004, No. 6, pp. 90) **[1098]**, **[35776]**, **[43987]**

Armor Fueling **[22661]**

ARMS Supermarket Promotion Show **[51054]**

Armstrong County Chamber of Commerce **[64378]**

"Army Extends Contract With Maine Company to Improve Armor On Humvees" in *Portland Press Herald* (December 3, 2005) **[39983]**, **[46198]**

Army High Performance Computing Research Center **[6557]**

"An Army of Moms and Pops" in *Business Week* (No. 3799, Sept. 16, 2002, pp.18) **[27785]**

"Army's Tech Needs Boost General Dynamics' Role" in *Crain's Detroit Business* (Vol. 21, January 17, 2005, No. 3, pp. 14) **[39984]**, **[41523]**

Arnett Chamber of Commerce **[63944]**

Arnheim & Neely Inc. **[21070]**

Arnold Chamber of Commerce **[61911]**

Arnold Consulting Group **[42940]**

Arnold & Porter–Library **[29695]**, **[54915]**

Around Town Community Magazine Inc. **[18975]**

"Around Town: Paris" in *Black Enterprise* (Vol. 35, January 2005, No. 6, pp. 104) **[2329]**, **[12516]**, **[21441]**, **[30289]**

"Around ground zero, an effort to rescue mom-and-pop shops" in *Wall Street Journal* (February 8, 2002, pp. A1) **[27786]**, **[39788]**

"Arranged Marriages: We present our media-merger dream team" in *Red Herring* (No. 102, August 15, 2001, pp. 90-91, 93) **[13823]**, **[14745]**, **[49793]**

Array Healthcare Facilities Solutions **[49583]**

"Arrested Development?" in *Entrepreneur* (Vol. 32, November 2004, No. 11, pp. 75) **[39789]**, **[44471]**

"Arris trades road shows for online presentations" in *Atlanta Business Chronicle* (Vol. 25, No. 19, October 18, 2002, pp. 8B) **[13190]**, **[22466]**, **[24884]**, **[26742]**, **[33542]**, **[43081]**

"Arrow Electronics Moves to Cut Costs, Reports 4Q Income" in *Long Island Business News* (February 20, 2004) **[7716]**, **[14746]**

Arrow Neighborhood Pub **[23555]**

Arrow Pharmacy and Nutrition Centers **[8844]**

Arrow's Complete Guide to Mail Order Sporting Goods **[23606]**

Arroyo Grande Chamber of Commerce **[57339]**

"Arson Charges Spotlight Downtown Bergenfield, N.J., Business Slump" in *The Record* (February 17, 2004) **[2520]**, **[11312]**, **[27787]**

Art and Antique Dealers League of America **[1297]**

Art & Antiques **[1343]**

"The Art Auctioneer" in *Home Business* (Vol. 12, March/April 2005, No. 2, pp. 71) **[1595]**, **[1774]**

"Art of Business" in *Entrepreneur.com* (Vol. 34, February 2006, No. 2, pp. 46) **[29790]**, **[35777]**, **[39150]**

"The Art of Business Judo" in *Fast Company* (August 2001, pp. 116) **[27788]**, **[30781]**

Art Business News (Vol. 28, No. 4, April 2001, pp. 1); "Collectors Still Flock to Classic Vintage Posters" in **[1603]**, **[5899]**

Art Center College of Design–James Lemont Fogg Memorial Library **[6058]**

Art of the Cocktail, Part 1 **[2370]**

Art of the Cocktail, Part 2 **[2371]**

"Art Collectors Get Patriotic" in *Business Week* (No. 3764, December 31, 2001, pp. 110) **[1596]**

The Art of Communicating: Achieving Interpersonal Impact in Business **[27293]**

Art and Creative Materials Institute **[1679]**

Art Dealers Association of America **[1590]**

Art Dealers Association of America-Directory **[1597]**

The Art of Dress Modelling: Shape Within Shape **[23812]**

The Art of Eating **[23532]**

Art with the Elders in Long-Term Care **[470]**

Art Gallery of Greater Victoria–Library **[1646]**

Art Index **[6053]**, **[18586]**

Art Institute of Boston at Lesley University–Library **[6059]**

Art Institute of Philadelphia–Library **[2142]**, **[5603]**, **[6060]**, **[19271]**, **[26088]**

Art Institute of Portland–Library **[5604]**, **[10845]**

The Art of Interior Decorating **[13701]**

"Art Lover Plays Fair Game" in *Crain's New York Business* (Vol. 23, January 29, 2007, No. 5, pp. F19) **[1598]**, **[7996]**, **[35778]**, **[46684]**, **[55065]**, **[56117]**

The Art of Magic **[18737]**

The Art of Negotiating **[45914]**

ART/New York, Vol. 11 **[19252]**

"Art Noir" in *Black Enterprise* (Vol. 35, December 2004, No. 5, pp. 62) **[1599]**, **[1681]**, **[48037]**

Art Now Gallery Guides **[1600]**

"The art of making a plan and making it happen" in *The New York Times* (December 18, 2000, pp. C16) **[29705]**, **[35320]**, **[52768]**

"The art of Web selling: company finds a smart way to boost sales" in *Black Enterprise* (Vol. 33, No. 6, January 2003, pp. 41) **[1775]**, **[25791]**, **[33543]**, **[35779]**, **[48038]**, **[51552]**

"The Art of the Perfect Business Gift" in *Crain's Detroit Business* (Vol. 21, October 3, 2005, No. 43, pp. 14) **[11142]**, **[39151]**

"The Art of the Real" in *Inc.* (September 1, 2003) **[24376]**, **[35780]**, **[44897]**

The Art of Riding **[12459]**

"The Art of the Sale" in *Entrepreneur* (Vol. 31, No. 8, August 2003, pp. 58) **[51055]**, **[51553]**

"The Art and Science of Networking" in *Sales and Marketing.com* (Vol. 153, No. 3, March 2004, pp. 49) **[39152]**, **[42170]**

Art on Screen Database **[1638]**, **[6054]**, **[8108]**

Art Source & Design **[1695]**, **[19829]**

The Art of the Start: The Time-Tested, Battle-Hardened Guide for Anyone Starting Anything **[30773]**, **[35321]**, **[39026]**, **[42151]**, **[44387]**

Art Surprises [5367]

The Art of Telecommunication [27562], [49390]

"Art Van Shoots to Score with Yzerman, Ireland Furniture Lines" in *Crain's Detroit Business* (Vol. 19, No. 40, October 13, 2003, pp. 1) [12273], [46685], [48579]

"The Art of the Woman Warrior" in *Inc.* (August 2005, pp. 26) [35781], [44898], [56118]

ARTAFAX [25282]

"Artascope Carves Out Niche In Arts and Crafts" in *Portland Press Herald* (June 17, 2005) [7997], [8149], [8271], [56119]

Artemis Inc. [1457]

Artemis Ventures [57931]

Artesia Historical Museum and Art Center–Research Facility [11089]

Artesian Capital [61693]

Artful Mediation: Constructive Conflict at Work [17045]

Artful Negotiating [37024]

Arthur Andersen European Community Sourcebook [43547]

Arthur Andersen LLP
　　Business Information Center [2988]
　　Knowledge Management Center [18810]

"Arthur Andersen announces YoungIT Entrepreneur Award" in *Crain's Detroit Business* (Vol. 26, No. 12, March 20, 2000, pp. 37) [37100], [56735]

Arthur Association of Commerce [59424]

Arthur P. Gould & Co. [63058]

Arthur Treacher's Fish & Chips [21740]

Artificial Cells, Blood Substitutes and Immobilization Biotechnology [52238]

Artistamp News [5831]

"Artists Can Help Draw Tourists to Detroit" in *Crain's Detroit Business* (Vol. 19, No. 49, December 8, 2003, pp. 9) [25148], [25992], [27330], [27789]

ARTnews Magazine [1617]

The ARTnewsletter [1618]

Arts and Business Council [7981]

"Arts and Crafts are Big with Women" in *Marketing to Women* (Vol. 19, October 2006, No. 10, pp. 1) [1682], [8150], [46686]

"Arts Group Adopts New Name, Look, Enhanced Agenda" in *Mississippi Business Journal* (Vol. 28, September 2006, No. 36, pp. 28) [20099], [27294], [39153]

Artsfocus [1619]

ARTWEEK [1620]

ARTWEEK-Gallery Calendar Section [1601]

Arvada Chamber of Commerce [58326]

Arvin Chamber of Commerce [57340]

"Arvin Meritor Says It's Done Selling" in *Crain's Detroit Business* (Vol. 23, February 5, 2007, No. 6, pp. 29) [29791], [30505], [52406]

"ArvinMeritor wins patent case" in *Crain's Detroit Business* (Vol. 19, No. 14, April 7, 2003, pp. 40) [1901], [25376], [43988]

"ArvinMeritor Rival Files New Patent Suit" in *Crain's Detroit Business* (Vol. 19, No. 49, December 8, 2003, pp. 4) [1902], [1915], [29102], [30029], [43989], [45663]

"As virtual teaming arrives, discipline still an essential" in *Atlanta Business Chronicle* (Vol. 24, No. 13, August 31, 2001, pp. 42A) [7120], [34813]

"As Clock Ticks on 2006, Tax Debate Continues" in *Crain's Detroit Business* (Vol. 22, December 11, 2006, No. 50, pp. 7) [29792], [54431]

"As Home Prices Soar, People Renovate To Move Up But Not Out" in *Tampa Tribune* (November 9, 2005) [4477], [7247], [9108], [10506], [23792]

"As economy softens, firms trimming travel budgets" in *Atlanta Business Chronicle* (Vol. 24, No. 8, July 27, 2001, pp. NA) [27080], [30290], [32252]

"As seen on TV" in *Entrepreneur* (Vol. 30, No. 2, Fe) [548], [46687], [51554]

"As seen on TV: Mark Burnett knows a little something about survival" in *Entrepreneur* (Vol. 30, No. 3, March 2002, pp.) [9691], [24377], [35782]

"As Web sites seek an attractive mix of content, a new type of business is providing the right stuff"in *The New York Times*(Sept25,2000) [13824], [25792], [33544]

As-You-Like-It Library [17941]

As You Sow Foundation [54121]

AS3 - Aviation Services and Suppliers Supershow [969]

ASA Artisan [7998]

ASAE Membership Developments [1743]

ASAI Architecture [49584]

ASBC Newsletter [3146]

ASC Bulletin [1196]

"ASC Pushes Niche Vehicles as Industry Cure" in *Crain's Detroit Business* (Vol. 22, January 16, 2006, No. 3, pp. 22) [17965], [46199]

ASC Retail Consulting. [2009], [18199]

"ASC Specialty Cars to Get Sony Multimedia Products Under Deal" in *Crain's Detroit Business* (Vol. 21, January 17, 2005, No. 3, pp. 29) [1903], [17966], [20301], [49794]

Ascension Chamber of Commerce [60616]

Ascent Venture Partners [61033]

Ascheman Associates Inc. [26621]

Asgat Agency, Inc. [3846], [4001]

Ashar Press [58249]

Ashburn - Turner County Chamber of Commerce [59058]

Scott Ashby Teleselling Inc. [3640], [16564], [31277], [45960]

Ashe County Chamber of Commerce and Visitors Center [63324]

Asheboro/Randolph Chamber of Commerce [63325]

Asheville Area Chamber of Commerce [63326]

Asheville Branch of Cherokee Native American Indian Business Development [63450]

"Asheville, N.C., Bed & Breakfast Owner Finds Business Requires Total Immersion" in *Charlotte Observer* (October 20, 2003) [2423]

Asheville Note Brokers [10350], [42786]

Asheville SBTDC [63275]

Ashford Area Chamber of Commerce [56811]

Ashland Alliance [60481]

Ashland Area Chamber of Commerce [62244], [63604], [64341]

Ashland Chamber of Commerce [60289], [64191]

Ashland Group L.P. [10758], [20176]

"Ashley Capital branches out into new kind of development" in *Crain's Detroit Business* (Vol. 19, No. 17, April 28, 2003, pp. 3) [20425], [20798], [27790], [32141]

ASHRAE Journal [1034]

Ashtabula Area Chamber of Commerce [63605]

ASI Sign Systems Inc [22808]

Asia Pacific Foundation of Canada [32192]

"Asia Rising" in *Black Enterprise* (Vol. 35, October 2004, No. 3, pp. 46) [14747], [27791], [37878], [43548], [46200], [49676]

"Asia: The VC sum rises in the East" in *Red Herring* (No. 99, June 15 & July 1, 2001, pp. 35-36) [43549], [55496]

Asiafit [23674]

Asian American Alliance–SBDC [59361]

Asian American Hotel Owners Association [12496], [47991]

Asian American Writers' Workshop [8946]

Asian Chamber of Commerce [57014]

Asian, Inc. [57887]

Asian Markets: A Guide to Company and Industry Sources [43550]

"Asian Persuasion" in *Entrepreneur* [5525], [56120]

Asian Women in Business [47992], [56090]

"Aside from taking M-commerce requests, Quixi wouldn't do anything on the Web" in *Inc.* (November 15, 2000, pp. 33) [48948]

ASIS International [22145]

"Ask the Attorney" in *Red Herring* (No. 99, June 15 & July 1, 2001, pp. 148) [858], [1781], [4598], [9813], [22918], [27295], [27616], [28961], [29103], [37879], [37951], [40162], [42171], [42497], [43551], [43990], [44271], [44472], [44975], [50814], [52407], [52741], [54432], [55497]

Ask Dr. Jim about Cats [19165]

Ask Dr. Jim about Dogs [19120], [19166]

"Ask the Etiquette Doctor" in *Sales and Marketing.com* (Vol. 153, No. 3, March 2004, pp. 52) [27296], [51555]

"Ask Inc: Dividing the Corporate Pie" in *Inc.* (July 1, 2003) [29793], [49795]

"Ask Inc, Marketing" in *Inc.* (November 2006, pp. 53) [24281], [40163], [46688]

"Ask Inc.: Do I Have to Go to School?" in *Inc.* (October 1, 2003) [32998], [35783], [51556]

"Ask Inc. Education" in *Inc.* (November 2006, pp. 51-52) [32999], [35784], [52815]

"Ask Inc. Importing" in *Inc.* (September 2006, pp. 53-54) [43552], [43991]

"Ask Inc." in *Inc.* (Volume 28, January 2006, No. 1, pp. 51-52) [74], [2577], [7877], [9551], [11143], [11557], [14748], [17358], [19148], [26156], [29104], [29819], [31110], [31512], [33000], [40963], [42172], [42829], [42906], [44899], [45868], [49796], [51557]

"Ask Inc. Partnerships" in *Inc.* (November 2006, pp. 57) [30662], [31111], [37880], [49797]

"Ask Inc. Profit Sharing" in *Inc.* (September 2006, pp. 53) [26743], [34814], [44900]

Ask NELMA Newsletter [16326]

Ask for the Order. . .and Get It! [10295], [15692], [51938]

Ask for the Order...and Get It! (Revised) [51939]

"Ask yourself this" in *Entrepreneur* (Vol.) [27297], [35785]

"Ask Yourself What the Hell Really Works Here?" in *Fast Company* (May 2001, pp. 82) [31619], [35322]

"Asking For It: You Can't Always Get What You Want, But Chances are Better If You Learn How To Ask" in *Entrepreneur* (August 2004) [35786], [44901]

"Asking Too Much? Not a Chance. Questions Are One of the Best Tools for Unlocking Creativity" in *Entrepreneur* (Vol. 31, October 2003) [35787], [44902]

ASMP Bulletin [19308]

Asotin Chamber of Commerce [66041]

ASP Pool & Spa Co. [23805]

"ASPA President Shares Regulatory Outlook, Plans New Association Initiatives" in *Employee Benefit Plan Review* (Vol. 55, No. 7, Jan.2001) [26744], [40164]

ASPCA Animal Watch Magazine [1245]

ASPCA Complete Dog Training Manual [19109]

"Aspects of dealing with digital information" in *Library Trends* (Vol. 51, No. 2, Fall 2002, pp. 199) [13067]

Aspen Chamber Resort Association [58327]

Aspen Publishers Inc. [58630]

Aspen Ventures [57932]

The Asphalt Contractor [2547]

Asphalt Emulsion Manufacturers Association-Membership Directory [2541]

Asphalt Institute [2538]
　　Research Library [2549]

Asphalt Paving Technologists [2542]

Asphalt Recycling & Reclaiming Association-Membership Directory [2543]

Asphalt Roofing Manufacturers Association [22055]

"Aspirations for '05" in *Inc.* (January 1, 2005) [35788], [44903]

ASP.NET with VB.NET and C I [53166]

ASP.NET with VB.NET and C II [53167]

ASP.NET with VB.NET and C III [53168]

Assabet Valley Chamber of Commerce [60927]

"Assemble Your E-Business Team" in *E-business Advisor* (Vol. 17, No. 12, December 1999, pp. 30) [33545], [34815], [44904]

"Assembling a Crack Sales Team" in *Hispanic Business* (October 2003, pp. 92, 94, 96) [44905], [51558]

Assertiveness for Managers: Learning Effective Skills for Managing People [44906]

Assertiveness Training for Managers (Canada) [27230]

Assertiveness Training for Women in Business [27231]

Assertiveness Training for Women in Business (Canada) [27232]

Assessing Your Team: 7 Measures of Team Success [34816]

Assessment & Intervention: The Confused Elderly [471]

Assessment Strategies [42941]

Asset Development Group [31956]

Asset Management Company Venture Capital [57933]

"Asset managers become psychologists in recession" in *Atlanta Business Chronicle* (Vol. 25, No. 20, October 25, 2002, pp. 4C) [9814], [14749], [37881]

Asset Verification Franchise Corp. [10351]

Assets Protection Inc. [35291]

Assets Protection Systems Associates Inc. [35292]

Assist-2-Sell [20743]

Assist 2 Auction LLC [1870]

"Assist2Sell Expands to Service Home Buyers" in *Bellingham Business Journal* (January 2007, pp. 3) [17359], [20426], [20799], [27792], [33001]

"Assist.com www.assist.com/assist.htm" in *Entrepreneur* (Vol. 32, No. 1, January 2004, pp. 10) [39154], [50815]

Assisted Living Federation of America [436], [1698], [18300]

Associated Bodywork and Massage Professionals [16997]

Associated Builders and Contractors [7205]

Associated Corset and Brassiere Manufacturers [16208]

Associated Designers of Canada [5952]

Associated Enterprises Ltd. [16565]

Associated Equipment Distributors-Membership Directory [32142]

Associated Funeral Directors International [10786]
   James L. Allhands Memorial Library [7678]

Associated General Contractors of America-National Profile Directory [2544], [7248]

Associated Glass and Pottery Manufacturers [12174]

Associated Locksmiths of America [16258]

Associated Luxury Hotels International [12497]

Associated Management Services Inc. [16566]

Associated Management Systems Inc. [3442], [50293]

Associated Marketers [3443], [50294]

Associated Medical Services [40911]

Associated Pipe Organ Builders of America [17834]

Associated Plumbing Heating & Cooling [1035]

Associated Press Broadcasters [20282], [24351]

Associated Schools of Construction [7207]

Associated Specialty Contractors [996], [7208]

Associated Title, Inc. [3449]

Associated Warehouses-Directory of Services [20218]

Association for Accounting Administration [21]

Association to Advance Collegiate Schools of Business [32889]

Association for the Advancement of Medical Instrumentation [17085]

Association for the Advancement of Medical Instrumentation Annual Conference and Expo [17137]

Association for the Advancement of Medical Instrumentation-Membership Directory [17094]

Association des Aides Familiales du Quebec [55259]

Association of Alternate Postal Systems [6091]

Association of Alternative Newsweeklies [18822]

Association of American Publishers [2645]

Association of American University Presses [2646]

Association of American University Presses-Directory [2676]

Association of America's Public Television Stations [24352]

Association of Applied IPM Ecologists [19014]

Association of Area Business Publications [58250]

Association of Authors' Representatives [16247]

Association of Automotive Aftermarket Distributors/Parts Plus [1881]

Association of Bay Area Governments [66794], [66828]

Association of Bridal Consultants [3170]

Association for Business Communication [27225], [27603]

Association for Business Communication Annual Convention [27572]

Association for the Calligraphic Arts [4162]

Association of Canadian Publishers [2647]

Association of Canadian Search, Employment and Staffing Services [4384]

Association of Canadian Travel Agencies [24649], [25122]

Association of Career Management Consulting Firms International [9181]

Association of Chartered Accountants in the United States [22]

Association for Childhood Education International [5320]

Association for Childhood Education International Annual International Conference & Exhibition [5415]

"Association is adjusting image of chiropractors" in *Washington Business Journal* (Vol. 18, No. 47, March 24, 2000, pp. 53) [17871], [29706]

Association of Commerce and Industry–SBDC [61174]

Association for Computing Machinery [6194], [6421], [14645]

Association for Conflict Resolution [17031]

Association of Consulting Engineers of Canada [3489]

Association for Convention Operations Management [24859]

Association for Corporate Growth - Toronto Chapter [3490], [27738], [44707]

Association of Destination Management Executives [25123]

Association of Directory Marketing [46607]

Association for Enterprise Integration [39112]

Association of Executive Search Consultants [9182]

Association for the Export of Canadian Books [2648]

Association of Food Industries [21418]

Association of Forensic Document Examiners [11853]

Association of Free Community Papers [50523]

Association of Fund-Raising Distributors and Suppliers [10725]

Association of Fundraising Professionals [10726]

Association of Golf Merchandisers [11244], [23593]

Association of Gospel Rescue Missions–Library [41353]

Association for Graphic Arts Training [5953]

Association of Graphic Communication-Buyers Guide of Members [8631]

Association of Home Appliance Manufacturers [1403]

Association of Home-Based Women Entrepreneurs [3641], [16567], [31278], [37047], [56541]

Association of Image Consultants International [12863]

Association of Independent Commercial Producers [50524]

Association of Independent Consultants [3491], [31102]

Association of Independent Manufacturers'/Representatives [19738]

Association of Information and Dissemination Centers [13059]

Association for Information Media and Equipment [9672]

Association of Insolvency and Restructuring Advisors [358]

Association for Interactive Marketing [24353]

Association for International Business [39113], [43475]

Association of International Photography Art Dealers [1591]

Association for Investment Management & Research-Membership Directory [14750]

Association of Jewish Aging Services [18301]

Association of Jewish Sponsored Camps [4221]

Association of Knitwear Designers [5516]

Association Law and Policy [29593]

Association of Legal Court Interpreters and Translators [25075]

"Association Listing" in *Black Enterprise* (Vol. 34, No. 5, December 2003, pp. 6) [50549]

Association of Machinery and Equipment Appraisers [1430]

Association of Management Consulting Firms [16493], [31103]

Association Management-Convention Center & Convention Bureau Directory [1730], [24885]

Association of Manpower Franchise Owners [24515]

Association of Marina Industries [16714]

Association for Maximum Service Television [24354]

Association Meeting Trends [1742]

Association Meetings [1744], [25054]

Association of Millwork Distributors [4473]

Association of Monterey Bay Area Governments [66829]

Association of Moving Image Archivists [9673]

Association for Multicultural Counseling and Development [4385], [48510]

Association of Municipal Recycling Coordinators [9310], [21201], [37223]

Association of National Advertisers [514], [50525]

Association News [1745]

Association of Pool and Spa Professionals [23788]

Association of Professional Computer Consultants [6151], [31104]

Association of Professional Landscape Designers [15962], [15990]

Association of Professional Recruiters of Canada [9547]

Association of Professional Researchers for Advancement [10727]

Association of Progressive Rental Organizations [21304]

Association of Proposal Management Professionals [8593], [31105]

Association of Regulatory Boards of Optometry [25623]

Association for Research on Nonprofit Organizations and Voluntary Action Conference (ACNOVA) [41320], [55203]

Association of Retail Marketing Services [51506]

Association of Retail Travel Agents [25124]

Association of Sales Administration Managers [51507]

Association of Schools and Colleges of Optometry [25624]

Association for Services Management International [3941]

Association of Small Business Development Centers [52794]

Association of Specialists in Cleaning and Restoration Annual Convention and Exhibition [8426]

Association of Talent Agents [16248], [23819]

Association of Teachers of Technical Writing [8947]

Association for Technology in Music Instruction [17570]

Association of TeleServices International [24319], [25680]

Association of Tongue Depressors–Library [17287]

Association of Travel Marketing Executives [25125]

Association Trends [1746]

Association of University Interior Designers [13622]

Association of University Research Parks [57098]

Association of Vision Science Librarians [25625]

Association of Visual Language Interpreters of Canada [25076]

Association of the Wall and Ceiling Industries - International [16925]

Association of the Wall and Ceiling Industries International-Buyer's Guide [16942]

Association for Wedding Professionals International [3171]

Association for Women in Computing [6452]

Association of Writers and Writing Programs [8948]

Associations Canada [1755]

Associations Plus [55038]

Assumption Area Chamber of Commerce [60617]

Assurent Secure Technologies [14663]

ASTD [6321], [32890], [42808]

Astoria-Warrenton Area Chamber of Commerce [64192]

AstraZeneca Pharamaceuticals LP–Library and Information Services [8861]

The Astro Investor [3423], [15626]

Astrological Research Library of Canada [17942]

AT Associates [6033]

"At Deadline" in *Crain's New York Business* (Vol. 20, No. 12, March 22, 2004, pp. 1) [1776], [27793], [33546], [38711]

Atlanta Business Chronicle (Vol. 25, No. 22, November 8, 2002, pp. 18C); "Atlanta's 25 Largest Hotels" in **[12518]**, **[22467]**, **[24889]**, **[25151]**

Atlanta Business Chronicle (Vol. 25, No. 19, Oct. 18, 2002, pp. 3A); "Auto insurer files for $350 million initial public offering" in **[13193]**, **[14758]**, **[43084]**, **[49801]**

Atlanta Business Chronicle (Vol. 24, No. 11, August 17, 2001, pp. 40A); "Axion CEO heads in new, profitable direction" in **[22920]**, **[27804]**, **[37105]**

Atlanta Business Chronicle (Vol. 26, No. 10, August 15, 2003, pp. 1); "Back to Business as Usual" in **[20428]**, **[32257]**

Atlanta Business Chronicle (Vol. 25, January 10, 2003, No. 31, pp. 9A); "Bank acquisitions likely to pick up in 2003" in **[14768]**, **[49804]**

Atlanta Business Chronicle (Vol. 26, No. 9, August 8, 2003, pp. 1A); "Bankruptcy Could Cost Firm $310M" in **[27813]**, **[52508]**

Atlanta Business Chronicle (Vol. 24, No. 8, July 27, 2001, pp. 4A); "Bankruptcy Reform Trying to Scale Final Hurdle" in **[29115]**, **[40170]**

Atlanta Business Chronicle (Vol. 25, No. 20, October 25, 2002, pp. 38A); "Bankruptcy Reform Will Punish Debtors" in **[29116]**, **[37906]**, **[40171]**

Atlanta Business Chronicle (Vol. 25, No. 22, November 8, 2002, pp. 6C); "Banks: 'Atlanta's Quiet Ambassador of Good Will'" in **[24665]**, **[25152]**, **[35806]**

Atlanta Business Chronicle (Vol. 24, No. 9, August 3, 2001, pp. 3A); "Banks' distressed loans are on the rise" in **[32265]**, **[44479]**

Atlanta Business Chronicle (Vol. 25, Dec. 13, 2002, No. 27, pp. A1); "Battle brews against tort reform" in **[13199]**, **[29119]**, **[40175]**, **[43087]**

Atlanta Business Chronicle (Vol. 25, December 20, 2002, No. 28, pp. 3A); "Beaming in on safety business" in **[22180]**, **[41537]**

Atlanta Business Chronicle (Vol. 25, December 6, 2002, No. 26, pp. 1); "Bells want to raise rates of competitors" in **[4923]**, **[30793]**, **[31011]**

Atlanta Business Chronicle (Vol. 25, Jan. 10, 2003, No. 31, pp. 27A); "BellSouth drops hike in deposits" in **[4924]**, **[13841]**, **[33570]**, **[40178]**

Atlanta Business Chronicle (Vol. 25, January 3, 2003, No. 30, pp. 22A); "BEO role growin on Geisel" in **[4605]**, **[22926]**

Atlanta Business Chronicle (Vol. 25, No. 21, November 1, 2002, pp. 18C); "Beyond blueprints: Bring building plans to life" in **[1498]**, **[7252]**

Atlanta Business Chronicle (Vol. 25, December 6, 2002, No. 26, pp. 3C); "Billy Mitchell outstanding in industry and community" in **[20434]**, **[20805]**, **[35846]**, **[44939]**

Atlanta Business Chronicle (Vol. 24, No. 11, August 17, 2001, pp. 4B); "Biotech sector seeks advanced degrees" in **[33013]**, **[37109]**

Atlanta Business Chronicle (Vol. 25, No. 20, October 25, 2002, pp. 8); "Blueprint setting the tone for development" in **[7260]**, **[16213]**

Atlanta Business Chronicle (Vol. 24, No. 14, September 7, 2001, pp. 5C); "Bob Mathews sees reduced activity, but steady demand" in **[20436]**, **[27855]**

Atlanta Business Chronicle (Vol. 25, No. 22, November 8, 2002, pp. 20A); "Born in an infertility clinic, nursed in a dish" in **[41562]**, **[50834]**, **[52061]**

Atlanta Business Chronicle (Vol. 25, December 6, 2002, No. 26, pp. 8C); "Brasfield & Gorrie captures award" in **[1499]**, **[7263]**, **[18540]**, **[40203]**

Atlanta Business Chronicle (Vol. 25, No. 22, November 8, 2002, pp. 5A); "Bread-and-butter deals dominate office leases" in **[20438]**, **[20808]**, **[21311]**

Atlanta Business Chronicle (Vol. 25, November 8, 2002, No. 22 pp. 1A); "BresaGen moves slowly to grow stem cell work" in **[39991]**, **[44006]**, **[50836]**, **[52064]**

Atlanta Business Chronicle (Vol. 23, No. 30, December 29, 2000, pp. 27A); "Buckle up" in **[27880]**, **[32284]**

Atlanta Business Chronicle (Vol. 25, January 10, 2003, No. 31, pp. 4B); "Business gurus talk about practicing basics" in **[39190]**, **[53627]**

Atlanta Business Chronicle (Vol. 25, November 15, 2002, No. 23 pp. 2B); "Business, Employee Short-Term Focus Is on Survival" in **[34839]**, **[44967]**

Atlanta Business Chronicle (Vol. 24, No. 13, August 31, 2001, pp. 2C); "Business schools vying for professors with Ph.D.s" in **[33026]**, **[39196]**

Atlanta Business Chronicle (Vol. 24, No. 7, July 20, 2001, pp. 3A); "Businesses Hope to Limit Lawsuits, Expand Health-Care Access" in **[13219]**, **[26761]**, **[40221]**

Atlanta Business Chronicle (Vol. 25, December 6, 2002, No. 26, pp. 32C); "Calif. Company snaps up Texas Winn-Dixie center" in **[11595]**, **[14825]**, **[20820]**, **[32146]**, **[49835]**

Atlanta Business Chronicle (Vol. 25, January 10, 2003, No. 31, pp. 17A); "Canada Rx offers access to Canadian pharmacies" in **[8776]**, **[31017]**, **[33646]**, **[43573]**

Atlanta Business Chronicle (Vol. 24, No. 8, July 27, 2001, pp. 16A); "Capital City Bank & Trust Co. expands to Albany" in **[27926]**, **[48083]**

Atlanta Business Chronicle (Vol. 25, No. 19, October 18, 2002, pp. 4B); "Careful planning can ease stress of layoffs" in **[32308]**, **[42194]**

Atlanta Business Chronicle (Vol. 26, No. 11, August 22, 2003, pp. 5A); "Celecast Selling Sports Broadcasts" in **[20308]**, **[33656]**

Atlanta Business Chronicle (Vol. 25, No. 20, October 25, 2002, pp. 14C); "CFOs under pressure to disclose all transactions" in **[103]**, **[23908]**, **[37952]**

Atlanta Business Chronicle (Vol. 24, No. 9, August 3, 2001, pp. 4C); "Choosy tenants are finding bargains, flexibility" in **[20463]**, **[37118]**, **[52653]**

Atlanta Business Chronicle (Vol. 24, No. 14, September 7, 2001, pp. 3C); "CID businesses self-tax to fund improvements" in **[53646]**, **[54493]**

Atlanta Business Chronicle (Vol. 25, November 15, 2002, No. 23 pp. 3A); "Circulation losses continue at most state newspapers" in **[18859]**, **[27950]**

Atlanta Business Chronicle (Vol. 25, December 20, 2002, No. 28, pp. 14A); "Clarion Partners buys 36 buildings in Atlanta" in **[20467]**, **[20834]**, **[27952]**, **[46240]**

Atlanta Business Chronicle (Vol. 25, November 15, 2002, No. 23 pp. 7C); "Climbing tech stocks can't match Nasdaq" in **[9887]**, **[14867]**, **[37119]**

Atlanta Business Chronicle (Vol. 25, No. 21, Nov. 1, 2002, pp. 3A); "Coming out of hibernation" in **[4101]**, **[24396]**

Atlanta Business Chronicle (Vol. 25, November 15, 2002, No. 23 pp. S10); "Commercials are music to recording artists' ears" in **[588]**, **[17733]**, **[46821]**

Atlanta Business Chronicle (Vol. 24, No. 14, September 7, 2001, pp. 4B); "Communications initiatives vital for small business" in **[27324]**, **[46822]**

Atlanta Business Chronicle (Vol. 25, No. 19, October 18, 2002, pp. 4C); "Companies spiff up dress codes in recession" in **[32325]**, **[45016]**

Atlanta Business Chronicle (Vol. 25, November 15, 2002, No. 23 pp. 5C); "Companies struggle to define technology ROI" in **[37121]**, **[48994]**

Atlanta Business Chronicle (Vol. 26, No. 11, August 22, 2003, pp. 3A); "Competition Forces Malls to Redefine Marketing" in **[30821]**, **[46826]**, **[51108]**

Atlanta Business Chronicle (Vol. 25, No. 22, November 8, 2002, pp. 16C); "Concierge service is key despite low occupancy" in **[7125]**, **[12537]**

Atlanta Business Chronicle (Vol. 24, No. 10, August 10, 2001, pp. 40A); "Congress Looking at Proposed Tax Deferral Program" in **[40276]**, **[54499]**

Atlanta Business Chronicle (Vol. 24, No. 7, July 20, 2001, pp. 5A); "Congress rejects plan to raise SBA loan fees" in **[39802]**, **[44498]**

Atlanta Business Chronicle (Vol. 24, No. 8, July 27, 2001, pp. 3B); "Consolidation can mean a lot to small business" in **[14884]**, **[49872]**

Atlanta Business Chronicle (Vol. 24, No. 10, August 10, 2001, pp. 3A); "Consultants on their own" in **[13921]**, **[31130]**, **[46831]**

Atlanta Business Chronicle (Vol. 25, Nov. 8, 2002, No. 22 pp. S1); "Corporate Governance" in **[35978]**, **[45028]**

Atlanta Business Chronicle (Vol. 25, No. 20, October 25, 2002, pp. A3); "Courses going green with gray water" in **[11255]**, **[16008]**

Atlanta Business Chronicle (Vol. 26, No. 10, August 15, 2003, pp. 1); "Court Battle Pits Fridge Pack vs. FridgeMaster" in **[29172]**, **[44019]**, **[46846]**

Atlanta Business Chronicle (Vol. 26, No. 9, August 8, 2003, pp. 1A); "Cousins Mulls $100 Million Dividend" in **[14892]**, **[20475]**, **[20846]**

Atlanta Business Chronicle (Vol. 25, November 15, 2002, No. 23 pp. SS9); "CPA exam changes to be implemented in 2004" in **[114]**, **[23918]**

Atlanta Business Chronicle (Vol. 24, No. 13, August 31, 2001, pp. 3A); "Creaming up the competition" in **[12770]**, **[27987]**, **[38748]**

Atlanta Business Chronicle (Vol. 25, No. 20, October 25, 2002, pp. 6); "Creation of tech corridor to spur Midtown's growth" in **[7303]**, **[41621]**

Atlanta Business Chronicle (Vol. 24, No. 8, July 27, 2001, pp. 24A); "Creative Loafing: new editor to set city 'on fire'" in **[18862]**

Atlanta Business Chronicle (Vol. 23, No. 51, May 25, 2001, pp. 8A); "Credit crunch unlikely for most small businesses" in **[39263]**, **[44501]**

Atlanta Business Chronicle (Vol. 25, November 15, 2002, No. 23 pp. 13C); "CRM providers fighting for market share" in **[4630]**, **[22956]**, **[31682]**

Atlanta Business Chronicle (Vol. 24, No. 14, September 7, 2001, pp. S5); "Cutbacks manifesting as lower hotel occupancy" in **[12540]**, **[30315]**

Atlanta Business Chronicle (Vol. 24, No. 11, August 17, 2001, pp. 5A); "CyberStarts backs new benefits administrator" in **[13137]**, **[22879]**, **[26781]**

Atlanta Business Chronicle (Vol. 25, November 15, 2002, No. 23 pp. 3A); "Daimler deal: You can see state's offer - for $11,538" in **[18005]**, **[46257]**, **[52662]**

Atlanta Business Chronicle (Vol. 24, No. 13, August 31, 2001, pp. 3A); "Dartfish swimming in bigger pool" in **[22958]**, **[24401]**, **[44024]**

Atlanta Business Chronicle (Vol. 25, December 13, 2002, No. 27, pp. A3); "Datatrac trucks in $3 million in venture capital funding" in **[6243]**, **[6933]**, **[13952]**, **[25381]**, **[33739]**, **[55561]**

Atlanta Business Chronicle (Vol. 23, No. 15, September 15, 2000, pp. 1B); "Death and Taxes" in **[54508]**

Atlanta Business Chronicle (Vol. 24, No. 8, July 27, 2001, pp. 1B); "Defusing disasters" in **[39275]**, **[56555]**

Atlanta Business Chronicle (Vol. 24, No. 14, September 7, 2001, pp. 3A); "Dekor faces challenges" in **[12277]**, **[28013]**

Atlanta Business Chronicle (Vol. 25, January 10, 2003, No. 31, pp. 3A); "Delta may lose $1 billion again" in **[28014]**, **[30318]**

Atlanta Business Chronicle (Vol. 25, No. 22, November 8, 2002, pp. 7A); "Delta compromises on new $100 standby fee" in **[30319]**

Atlanta Business Chronicle (Vol. 24, No. 8, July 27, 2001, pp. 14A); "Delta to promote Atlanta's Latin tourism drive" in **[24682]**, **[25175]**

Atlanta Business Chronicle (Vol. 25, November 15, 2002, No. 23 pp. SS2); "Detecting accounting fraud can be tricky" in **[129]**, **[23928]**, **[26214]**

Atlanta Business Chronicle (Vol. 23, No. 26, December 1, 2000, pp. 1B); "Determining your deductions" in **[54515]**

Atlanta Business Chronicle (Vol. 25, December 6, 2002, No. 26, pp. 3A); "Developer raises $200 million to buy buildings" in **[1511]**, **[7317]**, **[20486]**, **[20855]**, **[46265]**, **[55570]**

Atlanta Business Chronicle (Vol. 25, January 10, 2003, No. 31, pp. 3B); "Don't subject those around you to cell hell" in **[4979]**, **[27350]**, **[34875]**

Atlanta Business Chronicle (Vol. 23, No. 46, April 20, 2001, pp. 66A); "Don't get bogged down with futile procedures" in **[29726]**, **[35396]**

Atlanta Business Chronicle (Vol. 25, January 10, 2003, No. 31, pp. 33A); "Double taxation is double wrong" in **[40322]**, **[54523]**

Atlanta Business Chronicle (Vol. 23, No. 49, May 11, 2001, pp. 3B); "Downturn brings opportunities along with risks" in **[27114]**, **[46915]**

Atlanta Business Chronicle (Vol. 24, No. 13, August 31, 2001, pp. 9B); "Duty on Canadian lumber may raise home prices" in **[7337]**, **[16303]**, **[40327]**

Atlanta Business Chronicle (Vol. 25, December 13, 2002, No. 27, pp. A3); "E-mail Marketer Looks for More Clout" in **[28066]**, **[33811]**, **[46922]**, **[49907]**, **[50585]**

Atlanta Business Chronicle (Vol. 24, No. 13, August 24, 2001, pp. 5A); "E-mail Security Firm is Chaudry's Last Start-up" in **[13745]**, **[22137]**, **[22880]**, **[27629]**, **[35403]**

Atlanta Business Chronicle (Vol. 25, No. 19, October 18, 2002, pp. 31A); "EarthLink Inc. to purchase customers of Orlando ISP" in **[14001]**, **[33828]**, **[49909]**

Atlanta Business Chronicle (Vol. 24, No. 9, August 3, 2001, pp. 19A); "Ebank gains altitude after midflight change" in **[28082]**, **[33831]**, **[49911]**

Atlanta Business Chronicle (Vol. 25, December 6, 2002, No. 26, pp. 8A); "Economic Developers Expect a Busier Year in '03" in **[7339]**, **[20870]**, **[28083]**, **[32375]**, **[46271]**, **[52667]**

Atlanta Business Chronicle (Vol. 25, January 10, 2003, No. 31, pp. 24A); "Electricity, natural gas facing uncertain future" in **[28094]**, **[32399]**, **[40339]**

Atlanta Business Chronicle (Vol. 25, No. 19, October 18, 2002, pp. 13C); "Employees still rate health care No. 1 benefit" in **[13275]**, **[26794]**, **[43166]**

Atlanta Business Chronicle (Vol. 25, November 15, 2002, No. 23 pp. 37A); "Employers important in shaping health care" in **[13276]**, **[43167]**, **[51626]**

Atlanta Business Chronicle (Vol. 25, No. 19, October 18, 2002, pp. 3C); "Employers alter investment advice post-Enron" in **[9931]**, **[14952]**

Atlanta Business Chronicle (Vol. 26, No. 14, September 12, 2003, pp. 4A); "Energy Firm Surges with High-Tech Utility Meters" in **[41663]**

Atlanta Business Chronicle (Vol. 24, No. 14, September 7, 2001, pp. S4); "Entertaining speakers can reinforce your message" in **[24926]**

Atlanta Business Chronicle (Vol. 25, December 20, 2002, No. 28, pp. 8A); "Environmental technology firm files bankruptcy" in **[28121]**, **[46275]**, **[52093]**

Atlanta Business Chronicle (Vol. 24, No. 3, June 22, 2001, pp. 54A); "Ex-Im Bank cuts effect on small business unclear" in **[39320]**, **[39817]**, **[40355]**

Atlanta Business Chronicle (Vol. 24, No. 14, September 7, 2001, pp. 9B); "Excellent leadership is all in the people leading" in **[36128]**, **[45117]**

Atlanta Business Chronicle (Vol. 23, No. 36, February 9, 2001, pp. 52A); "Exchange may improve small-business lending" in **[39321]**, **[44514]**

Atlanta Business Chronicle (Vol. 25, No. 19, October 18, 2002, pp. 21A); "Extreme Pizza eying Atlanta for expansion" in **[19630]**, **[21502]**, **[28136]**, **[38770]**

Atlanta Business Chronicle (Vol. 25, November 29, 2002, No. 25, pp. 1A); "Facing new pressure" in **[54175]**, **[56211]**

Atlanta Business Chronicle (Vol. 25, January 3, 2003, No. 30, pp. 2B); "Fat-free selling expands wallets, not waistlines" in **[17379]**, **[20507]**, **[20875]**

Atlanta Business Chronicle (Vol. 25, January 10, 2003, No. 31, pp. 32A); "Federal stimulus can ensure recovery" in **[28155]**, **[32426]**, **[40374]**, **[54549]**

Atlanta Business Chronicle (Vol. 25, No. 19, October 18, 2002, pp. 1B); "Fellowship of the rings" in **[34900]**, **[45137]**

Atlanta Business Chronicle (Vol. 25, January 10, 2003, No. 31, pp. 18A); "Financial services firms foresee mixed results" in **[9953]**, **[32431]**, **[38061]**, **[55608]**

Atlanta Business Chronicle (Vol. 24, No. 9, August 3, 2001, pp. 3A); "Firms playing dot-name game" in **[14045]**, **[25851]**, **[53729]**

Atlanta Business Chronicle (Vol. 25, November 15, 2002, No. 23 pp. SS10); "Firms maintain strong pro bono presence" in **[29242]**, **[54180]**

Atlanta Business Chronicle (Vol. 24, No. 11, August 17, 2001, pp. 3B); "Firms shape students into future workers" in **[33098]**, **[37135]**, **[49936]**

Atlanta Business Chronicle (Vol. 24, No. 11, August 17, 2001, pp. 49A); "Focus on fundamentals to get back in sales groove" in **[51643]**

Atlanta Business Chronicle (Vol. 24, No. 14, September 7, 2001, pp. 1A); "Food may become next public enemy" in **[21510]**, **[40392]**

Atlanta Business Chronicle (V. 25, No. 19, Oct. 18, 2002, pp. 9C); "401(k) Loans: Borrowing against the Future" in **[26812]**

Atlanta Business Chronicle (Vol. 25, November 8, 2002, No. 22 pp. 1A); "Franklin pitches Atlanta to free-trade delegates" in **[43663]**, **[52674]**

Atlanta Business Chronicle (Vol. 24, No. 10, August 10, 2001, pp. 39A); "Freedom of Speech: The legacy you leave yourself" in **[50592]**, **[51646]**

Atlanta Business Chronicle (Vol. 25, November 29, 2002, No. 25 pp. 28A); "Ga. Chamber seeking 'civil justice' reform" in **[29257]**, **[39348]**, **[40401]**

Atlanta Business Chronicle (Vol. 24, No. 10, August 10, 2001, pp. 1B); "Gad Zeus!" in **[37139]**, **[50877]**

Atlanta Business Chronicle (Vol. 24, No. 13, August 31, 2001, pp. 8B); "Galt's heritage and history led to design career" in **[13645]**

Atlanta Business Chronicle (Vol. 25, November 15, 2002, No. 23 pp. 10C); "Georgia CEOs debate global leadership issues" in **[36197]**, **[37140]**

Atlanta Business Chronicle (Vol. 25, November 8, 2002, No. 22 pp. 3A); "Georgia ringing up new telecom contract" in **[4995]**, **[28199]**

Atlanta Business Chronicle (Vol. 25, No. 19, October 18, 2002, pp. 3A); "Georgia medical device business growing" in **[28200]**, **[41708]**, **[50880]**, **[52110]**

Atlanta Business Chronicle (Vol. 25, December 13, 2002, No. 27, pp. A2); "Georgia has ad revenue on its mind" in **[635]**, **[18877]**, **[24689]**, **[25187]**, **[47005]**

Atlanta Business Chronicle (Vol. 24, No. 14, September 7, 2001, pp. 5B); "Georgia ranks so-so in business 'survival index'" in **[52676]**, **[54570]**

Atlanta Business Chronicle (Vol. 24, No. 13, August 24, 2001, pp. 30A); "Grandma inspires woman to create online kid's books" in **[2636]**, **[13752]**

Atlanta Business Chronicle (Vol. 25, No. 20, October 25, 2002, pp. 1C); "Greener pastures" in **[17386]**, **[29276]**

Atlanta Business Chronicle (Vol. 25, January 10, 2003, No. 31, pp. 10A); "Greensboro firm buys Sembler retail center" in **[12188]**, **[12287]**, **[51173]**

Atlanta Business Chronicle (Vol. 24, No. 14, September 7, 2001, pp. S9); "Group connects out-of-towners, worthy cause" in **[24942]**, **[54196]**

Atlanta Business Chronicle (Vol. 24, No. 8, July 27, 2001, pp. 1C); "Guarding gizmos" in **[30341]**, **[39377]**

Atlanta Business Chronicle (Vol. 25, December 6, 2002, No. 26, pp. 10C); "Hardin overcomes intown construction challenges" in **[1515]**, **[7352]**, **[18546]**

Atlanta Business Chronicle (Vol. 25, No. 22, November 8, 2002, pp. 7C); "Hardman helped develop thriving tourism industry" in **[24692]**, **[24945]**, **[25192]**

Atlanta Business Chronicle (Vol. 24, No. 14, September 7, 2001, pp. 1A); "Harris Teeter sued by black employees" in **[29284]**, **[32030]**, **[40431]**

Atlanta Business Chronicle (Vol. 25, January 3, 2003, No. 30, pp. 1A); "Hartsfield bracing for choppy '03" in **[14103]**, **[28266]**, **[30343]**

Atlanta Business Chronicle (Vol. 25, January 10, 2003, No. 31, pp. 7A); "Health-care foundation awards its first grants" in **[13312]**, **[26824]**, **[43205]**, **[52117]**

Atlanta Business Chronicle (Vol. 25, December 20, 2002, No. 28, pp. 4B); "Healthy ways to handle rivalry in the workplace" in **[34928]**, **[45227]**

Atlanta Business Chronicle (Vol. 25, No. 22, November 8, 2002, pp. 21C); "Heartbreak hotels: Westin Charlotte in weak market" in **[12561]**, **[22510]**, **[24946]**, **[25194]**

Atlanta Business Chronicle (Vol. 25, December 6, 2002, No. 26, pp. 3A); "High-end home sales falter in North Fulton" in **[7359]**, **[20523]**, **[20892]**, **[28275]**

Atlanta Business Chronicle (Vol. 25, December 6, 2002, No. 26, pp. 5C); "Hines blends architecture, environmental awareness" in **[1517]**, **[13647]**, **[18547]**, **[20524]**, **[37295]**

Atlanta Business Chronicle (Vol. 25, November 29, 2002, No. 25, pp. 1C); "HIPAA hysteria" in **[6253]**, **[13322]**, **[14115]**, **[22250]**, **[40439]**, **[43215]**

Atlanta Business Chronicle (Vol. 25, No. 21, Nov. 1, 2002, pp. 10B); "Hollywood, Silicon Valley at odds over digital piracy bills" in **[9719]**, **[17745]**, **[25592]**, **[34017]**, **[41745]**, **[44057]**

Atlanta Business Chronicle (Vol. 25, January 10, 2003, No. 31, pp. 16A); "Hospitality Industry Continues Rough Ride in 2003" in **[12565]**, **[30348]**

Atlanta Business Chronicle (Vol. 25, No. 22, November 8, 2002, pp. 8C); "Hospitality, tourism up, but not in Atlanta market" in **[22511]**, **[24694]**, **[24949]**, **[25195]**

Atlanta Business Chronicle (Vol. 25, No. 21, Nov. 1, 2002) "Hot housing areas start to cool: Sales slow; prices keep rising" in **[20538]**, **[20899]**

Atlanta Business Chronicle (Vol. 24, No. 14, September 7, 2001, pp. S6); "Hotels skip surcharges, focus on conservation" in **[12575]**, **[37296]**, **[53785]**

Atlanta Business Chronicle (Vol. 23, No. 51, May 25, 2001, pp. 7A); "House Exempts Small Businesses From Superfund" in **[37297]**, **[40442]**

Atlanta Business Chronicle (Vol. 25, January 10, 2003, No. 31, pp. 1A); "Housing market at high risk" in **[7378]**, **[17396]**, **[20545]**, **[20902]**, **[28298]**, **[32492]**

Atlanta Business Chronicle (Vol. 24, No. 14, September 7, 2001, pp. 6B); "How can you find the elusive prospect hot button" in **[51679]**

Atlanta Business Chronicle (Vol. 25, December 6, 2002, No. 26, pp. 35A); "How to Improve Georgia's Economy" in **[25198]**, **[28305]**, **[32497]**, **[40445]**, **[43698]**

Atlanta Business Chronicle (Vol. 24, No. 14, September 7, 2001, pp. 3A); "Howle turns to new tech start-up" in **[6916]**, **[37062]**, **[49768]**

Atlanta Business Chronicle (Vol. 25, January 3, 2003, No. 30, pp. 3A); "Humana battles for growth" in **[13331]**, **[26832]**, **[28315]**, **[30886]**, **[43226]**

Atlanta Business Chronicle (Vol. 25, January 10, 2003, No. 31, pp. 23A); "In retail, discounters beat out high-end stores" in **[31039]**, **[51200]**

Atlanta Business Chronicle (Vol. 25, November 15, 2002, No. 23 pp. 4C); "Incremental upgrades boosts smaller firms" in **[22262]**, **[49095]**

Atlanta Business Chronicle (Vol. 24, No. 13, August 24, 2001, pp. 3A); "Small banks may draw buyers' interest" in **[15456]**, **[50180]**

Atlanta Business Chronicle (Vol. 23, No. 35, February 2, 2001, pp. 53A); "Small business tax cuts 'complement' Bush plan" in **[54764]**

Atlanta Business Chronicle (Vol. 24, No. 13, August 31, 2001, pp. 5B); "Smaller, greener jobs dominate remodeling" in **[7480]**, **[28792]**, **[53980]**

Atlanta Business Chronicle (Vol. 24, No. 14, September 7, 2001, pp. 10C); "Smart growth advocates push for change" in **[28793]**, **[39600]**

Atlanta Business Chronicle (Vol. 25, January 10, 2003, No. 31, pp. 3A); "Software firms end duel with an acquisition" in **[4810]**, **[15462]**, **[24324]**, **[50182]**

Atlanta Business Chronicle (Vol. 25, November 15, 2002, No. 23 pp. 8C); "Software Firms Predict M&A Increase for 2003" in **[4813]**, **[15463]**, **[23195]**, **[50183]**

Atlanta Business Chronicle (Vol. 25, No. 21, November 1, 2002, pp. 3A); "Software-Maker Bulks up with $20 Million VC Deal" in **[3586]**, **[4816]**, **[23200]**, **[31859]**, **[55837]**

Atlanta Business Chronicle (Vol. 25, No. 21, November 1, 2002, pp. 11B); "Some prison program deals not using inmates" in **[40099]**, **[40706]**

Atlanta Business Chronicle (Vol. 25, November 15, 2002, No. 23 pp. 11C); "Some Local Firms Find Opportunity in Telecom" in **[5114]**, **[14460]**, **[28795]**

Atlanta Business Chronicle (Vol. 25, January 10, 2003, No. 31, pp. 21A); "Some Service-Related Businesses Surge Ahead" in **[28796]**, **[52592]**

Atlanta Business Chronicle (Vol. 25, November 15, 2002, No. 23 pp. S10); "Some Wichita listeners misled by radio spots" in **[790]**, **[20337]**, **[47557]**

Atlanta Business Chronicle (Vol. 24, No. 8, July 27, 2001, pp. 6B); "Someone switching careers could be the perfect match" in **[42421]**

Atlanta Business Chronicle (Vol. 25, No. 21, November 1, 2002, pp. 8A); "Something's fishy: More Captain D's coming" in **[21628]**, **[38912]**

Atlanta Business Chronicle (Vol. 25, No. 22, November 8, 2002, pp. 5C); "Southern gentleman sparks downtown growth" in **[24728]**, **[25245]**, **[28801]**

Atlanta Business Chronicle (Vol. 24, No. 3, June 22, 2001, pp. 62A); "Speak employees' language to build their loyalty" in **[48598]**, **[53987]**

Atlanta Business Chronicle (Vol. 23, No. 49, May 11, 2001, pp. 12B); "Spring cleaning: tips to get fiscal house in order" in **[26367]**, **[30005]**, **[54771]**

Atlanta Business Chronicle (Vol. 25, December 13, 2002, No. 27, pp. A3); "State Coughs as Firms Seek Millions" in **[4353]**, **[29513]**, **[37327]**, **[40719]**

Atlanta Business Chronicle (Vol. 23, No. 48, May 4, 2001, pp. 70A); "Staying within their niche yields success for winners" in **[9179]**, **[35670]**, **[39096]**

Atlanta Business Chronicle (Vol. 25, December 6, 2002, No. 26, pp. 15C); "Steven Clem heads two TVS winning projects" in **[1532]**, **[13672]**, **[18561]**

Atlanta Business Chronicle (Vol. 24, No. 9, August 3, 2001, pp. 3B); "Stick-to-itiveness will always lead you to success" in **[30606]**, **[36794]**

Atlanta Business Chronicle (Vol. 25, No. 22, November 8, 2002, pp. 17C); "Strong demand for fine wine but oenophiles seek value" in **[21637]**, **[23510]**

Atlanta Business Chronicle (Vol. 25, No. 21, November 1, 2002, pp. 22C); "Studies keep coming in response to down market" in **[20680]**, **[21017]**

Atlanta Business Chronicle (Vol. 25, No. 20, October 25, 2002, pp. 16A); "Study focuses on improving Dallas' taxi system" in **[24241]**, **[25024]**, **[25250]**

Atlanta Business Chronicle (Vol. 25, December 6, 2002, No. 26, pp. 31C); "Sublease steals kick-starting leasing in Portland" in **[20681]**, **[21018]**, **[21353]**, **[52734]**

Atlanta Business Chronicle (Vol. 24, No. 13, August 24, 2001, pp. 7B); "Successful firms keep sales teams highly motivated" in **[51855]**

Atlanta Business Chronicle (Vol. 25, November 15, 2002, No. 23 pp. SS12); "Survey: economy will continue to affect growth" in **[28847]**, **[29529]**, **[32731]**

Atlanta Business Chronicle (Vol. 24, No. 14, Sept. 7, 2001); "Survey Says: Hospitality executives offer views on changes, challenges" in **[12641]**, **[25028]**

Atlanta Business Chronicle (Vol. 24, No. 14, September 7, 2001, pp. 26A); "Sweetwoods' a man with a brand" in **[12642]**, **[47594]**, **[50685]**

Atlanta Business Chronicle (Vol. 25, November 8, 2002, No. 22 pp. 1B); "Take a bow" in **[18733]**, **[37514]**, **[38920]**

Atlanta Business Chronicle (Vol. 25, December 6, 2002, No. 26); "Taking stock in Atlanta public companies" in **[15502]**

Atlanta Business Chronicle (Vol. 26, No. 13, September 5, 2003, pp. 1A); "Taking a Chance" in **[4834]**, **[10887]**, **[23221]**

Atlanta Business Chronicle (Vol. 24, No. 1, June 8, 2001, pp. 5A); "Tax Bill Doesn't Repeal Estate Tax Uncertainty" in **[37795]**, **[54792]**

Atlanta Business Chronicle (Vol. 25, January 10, 2003, No. 31, pp. 33A); "Tax Lien Sales: Money and Politics" in **[40754]**, **[54807]**

Atlanta Business Chronicle (Vol. 24, No. 14, September 7, 2001, pp. S11); "Team-Building Remains Essential in Downturn" in **[31227]**, **[35095]**

Atlanta Business Chronicle (Vol. 25, November 15, 2002, No. 23 pp. 2C); "Tech firms uncertain about tech forecast" in **[28867]**, **[37199]**, **[49299]**

Atlanta Business Chronicle (Vol. 25, January 3, 2003, No. 30, pp. 3A); "Telecom recession may have hit bottom" in **[5139]**, **[14520]**, **[28874]**, **[34579]**, **[42057]**

Atlanta Business Chronicle (Vol. 25, January 10, 2003, No. 31, pp. 17A); "Telecom's transformation continues in Georgia" in **[5143]**, **[14523]**, **[28875]**, **[34581]**, **[42059]**

Atlanta Business Chronicle (Vol. 25, December 6, 2002, No. 26, pp. 14C); "Teton wins construction award with speed, safety" in **[1533]**, **[7494]**, **[18563]**

Atlanta Business Chronicle (Vol. 25, December 6, 2002, No. 26, pp. 30C); "Texas considers outsourcing real estate needs" in **[20684]**, **[21021]**, **[21355]**, **[40103]**, **[49745]**

Atlanta Business Chronicle (Vol. 25, November 15, 2002, No. 23 pp. SS1); "The Accounting Fraud Squads" in **[63]**, **[26146]**, **[37384]**

Atlanta Business Chronicle (Vol. 23, No. 51, May 25, 2001, pp. 1B); "The Challenges of Equal Access" in **[35931]**, **[48096]**

Atlanta Business Chronicle (Vol. 23, No. 35, February 2, 2001, pp. 51A); "The economics of ergonomics" in **[40337]**, **[56557]**

Atlanta Business Chronicle (Vol. 24, No. 11, August 17, 2001, pp. 48A); "The franchising industry continues to heighten" in **[1936]**, **[2028]**, **[3947]**, **[7347]**, **[12554]**, **[21519]**, **[38806]**, **[51168]**, **[52535]**

Atlanta Business Chronicle (Vol. 24, No. 9, August 3, 2001, pp. 6B); "The How-Tos of Writing a Strong Business Plan" in **[29907]**

Atlanta Business Chronicle (Vol. 25, November 15, 2002, No. 23 pp. 4B); "The isolation process: a powerful path to more sales" in **[51700]**

Atlanta Business Chronicle (Vol. 25, No. 21, November 1, 2002, pp. 1B); "The Show Must Go On" in **[22561]**, **[25017]**

Atlanta Business Chronicle (Vol. 25, Jan. 10, 2003, No. 31, pp. 1B); "The bargaining table: check your ego at the door." in **[27301]**, **[35809]**, **[44919]**

Atlanta Business Chronicle (Vol. 25, No. 20, October 25, 2002, pp. 12B); "The workplace: learn to do more with less" in **[33285]**, **[35166]**, **[42472]**, **[45873]**, **[55006]**

Atlanta Business Chronicle (Vol. 24, No. 13, August 31, 2001, pp. 1B); "To lend or not to lend" in **[39945]**, **[44674]**

Atlanta Business Chronicle (Vol. 24, No. 8, July 27, 2001, pp. 2B); "Top 10 characteristics of Cintas' top salesperson" in **[51875]**

Atlanta Business Chronicle (Vol. 25, No. 22, November 8, 2002, pp. 16A); "Travel agents regroup as consumer advocates" in **[24738]**, **[25260]**

Atlanta Business Chronicle (Vol. 25, January 3, 2003, No. 30, pp. 2A); "Travel Web sites reaching out to business" in **[14550]**, **[25265]**, **[30431]**, **[34624]**

Atlanta Business Chronicle (Vol. 25, No. 19, October 18, 2002, pp. 1C); "Tripped up" in **[13503]**, **[26943]**, **[43406]**

Atlanta Business Chronicle (Vol. 26, No. 12, August 29, 2003, pp. 1); "UPS Drives Changes to Postal Service" in **[10706]**, **[40798]**

Atlanta Business Chronicle (Vol. 25, December 13, 2002, No. 27, pp. A5); "Vacancies up but investors still high on retail" in **[20697]**, **[21034]**, **[21361]**, **[44682]**, **[51399]**, **[52748]**, **[54057]**

Atlanta Business Chronicle (Vol. 24, No. 10, August 10, 2001, pp. 3A); "VCs Get Back to Basics" in **[55899]**

Atlanta Business Chronicle (Vol. 26, No. 14, September 12, 2003, pp. 3A); "VCs Investing Their Money in Nontech Firms" in **[54058]**, **[55900]**

Atlanta Business Chronicle (Vol. 25, November 15, 2002, No. 23 pp. 3C); "Vendors tweak strategies to help clients buy" in **[38438]**, **[49753]**, **[51892]**

Atlanta Business Chronicle (Vol. 24, No. 11, August 17, 2001, pp. 11B); "Venture funding down sharply from June" in **[37083]**, **[55450]**

Atlanta Business Chronicle (Vol. 25, November 15, 2002, No. 23 pp. 47A); "Viruses, not snooping, top companies' worries" in **[6188]**, **[22416]**

Atlanta Business Chronicle (Vol. 25, January 10, 2003, No. 31, pp. 4A); "Voters will be asked to expand industrial park" in **[7509]**, **[28969]**, **[54856]**

Atlanta Business Chronicle (Vol. 25, No. 20, October 25, 2002, pp. 11C); "Wall Street wooing wary investors with reforms" in **[10232]**, **[15585]**, **[37525]**, **[38444]**

Atlanta Business Chronicle (Vol. 25, December 6, 2002, No. 26, pp. 9C); "Walz wants to extend NAIOP's reach" in **[1534]**, **[7510]**, **[18566]**, **[40809]**

Atlanta Business Chronicle (Vol. 24, No. 13, August 24, 2001, pp. 3B); "When your good sales go bad: Ask, don't whine" in **[51905]**

Atlanta Business Chronicle (Vol. 24, No. 10, August 10, 2001, pp. 46A); "When Does Bending Rules Become Breaking Rules?" in **[37532]**, **[45826]**

Atlanta Business Chronicle (Vol. 25, November 15, 2002, No. 23 pp. 6B); "Why business ethics is worthy of discussion" in **[30266]**, **[37533]**

Atlanta Business Chronicle (Vol. 25, November 29, 2002, No. 25, pp. 1B); "Why Haven't You Called" in **[31080]**, **[32796]**, **[51913]**

Atlanta Business Chronicle (Vol. 25, Nov. 8, 2002, No. 22 pp. 4B); "Winning at Work: What doesn't kill you will make you stronger" in **[35155]**, **[45857]**

Atlanta Business Chronicle (Vol. 25, November 15, 2002, No. 23 pp. 3A); "Witness Systems adopts anti-takeover plan" in **[15609]**, **[37212]**, **[50268]**

Atlanta Business Chronicle (Vol. 24, No. 8, July 27, 2001, pp. 3A); "Yamacraw fund broadens its focus" in **[4078]**, **[37088]**, **[55459]**

Atlanta Business Chronicle (Vol. 25, December 13, 2002, No. 27, pp. A3); "Year's biggest industrial deal months in making" in **[7516]**, **[32168]**, **[52757]**

Atlanta Business Chronicle (Vol. 23, No. 46, April 20, 2001, pp. 65A); "You better shop around" in **[21417]**, **[39782]**, **[44453]**

Auburn University
    Alabama Agricultural Experiment
        Station–Department of Fisheries and
        Allied Aquacultures [10484]
    Alabama Agricultural Experiment
        Station–Ornamental Horticulture
        Substation [11550]
    Center for Governmental Services [24196]
    Charles Allen Cary Veterinary Medical
        Library [1276]
    Economic Development Institute [56918]
    International Center for Aquaculture and
        Aquatic Environments [1467]
    International Center for Aquaculture and
        Aquatic Environments–Library [10476]
    National Center for Asphalt Technology
        [2555]
    Office of Vice President for Research
        [56919]
    Small Business Development Center
        [56781]
Auburn University at Montgomery–Center for
    Business [3938]
Auburndale-Mainstreet Chamber of Commerce
    [58754]
Auction Mojo [1871]
Auction it Today Inc. [14668]
The Auctioneer [1868]
Auctioneer-Directory Issue [1778]
Audatex [22711]
Audio Engineering Society [21130]
Audio in Media: The Recording Studio [21140]
Audio/Video Handyman [7654]
Audiotex News [8668]
Audiotex Update [25685]
AudioVideo International [7751], [25601]
Audit Bureau of Circulations [18823]
Auditing [312]
Audrain County Extension Center–SBDC [61857]
Audubon Chamber of Commerce [60094]
Audubon House: Building the Environmentally
    Responsible, Energy-Efficient Office [37246]
August Capital Management [57935]
"August, Ga., Lacks Demographics to Draw Upscale
    Retailers" in Augusta Chronicle (February 17,
    2004) [7717], [27800], [51060]
Augusta Chronicle (February 17, 2004); "August,
    Ga., Lacks Demographics to Draw Upscale
    Retailers" in [7717], [27800], [51060]
Augusta Chronicle (February 17, 2004); "New
    Clothing Store in Augusta, Ga., Features High-
    End Brands" in [5562], [5696]
Augusta Metro Chamber of Commerce [59060]
Augusta Nutrition Consultants [18477]
Auntie Anne's Inc. [23556]
Auntie Fanny's [12339]
Aurora Administrative Solutions Ltd. [27003]
Aurora Area Chamber of Commerce [63606]
Aurora Area Chamber and Development [62246]
Aurora Chamber of Commerce [58328], [61912],
    [64193]
Aurora Funds, Inc. [63453]
Aurora Management Partners Inc. [3642], [16568],
    [31279], [38510], [45961], [48818], [53069]
Aussie Pet Mobile [19093]
Austin Area Chamber of Commerce [61558]
Austin Business Journal (Vol. 21, No. 25,
    September 7, 2001, pp. 17); "How to Calm
    Workers' Fears" in [32494], [34933]
Austin Business Journal (Vol. 22, No. 28,
    September 27, 2002, pp. 1); "Papermaster in
    startup mode" in [4758], [23119], [41895],
    [43058], [55770]
Austin Business Journal (Vol. 21, No. 25,
    September 7, 2001, pp. 21); "Surveys:
    Unhappiness growing in workforce" in [32734],
    [35084]
Austin Peay State University–Small Business
    Development Center [64849]
The Austin/San Antonio JobBank [9286]
Austin Technology Incubator (IC2-ATI) [65649]
Austin Ventures, L.P. [65591]
Australian/American Chamber of Commerce -
    Hawaii [59240]
Australian-American Chamber of Commerce,
    Orange County [57344]

"Australian Computer Emergency Response Team:
    www.auscert.org.au" in Entrepreneur (Vol. 31,
    No. 10, October 2003, pp. 6) [6585], [22176],
    [33551]
Australian Homemade [12804]
Australian Trade Commission [43476]
Austrian Information [25283]
Austrian Trade Commission [43477]
Austrian Trade Commissions in the United States
    [43478]
"Authentic Bavarian Beer Hall to Open" in
    Milwaukee Journal Sentinel (December 1, 2005)
    [2330], [21443]
"Author, Expert to Discuss Socially Responsible
    Business Methods" in Portland Press Herald
    (April 20, 2005) [39156], [54135]
"The Authority of Ideas" in Harvard Business
    Review (Vol. 81, No. 8, August 2003, pp. 144)
    [29794], [35793]
"Authors Defend Study on Great Lakes Shipping
    Value" in Milwaukee Journal Sentinel
    (December 1, 2005) [10668], [12944], [43553]
Authors and Publishers Association [2649]
Authorship [9021]
Authorware 7–Macro Media [9771]
Authosis [57936]
"Auto insurer files for $350 million initial public
    offering" in Atlanta Business Chronicle (Vol. 25,
    No. 19, Oct. 18, 2002, pp. 3A) [13193], [14758],
    [43084], [49801]
Auto Accents [2011]
"Auto Aftermarket Targets Tech Savvy Shoppers" in
    Retail Merchandiser (Vol. 43, No. 10, October,
    2003, pp. 38) [1905]
Auto Buyer Alert [18188]
"Auto Consolidation Likely to Speed Up" in Crain's
    Detroit Business (Vol. 23, January 8, 2007, No.
    2, pp. 15) [1906], [29795], [46201], [49802]
Auto Detailing [2062]
Auto Detailing for Show and Profit [2025]
Auto International Association [1882]
Auto Laundry News [4372]
Auto Merchandising News [1993], [18170]
"Auto News Digest" in Automotive News (Vol. 78,
    No. 6059, September 29, 2003, pp. 36) [1779],
    [17967], [37104]
The Auto Parts Report [920]
"Auto Review" in Hispanic Business (March 2005,
    pp. 42, 44, 46, 48) [17968], [53592]
"Auto Sector Leads in Investment; Michigan No. 2
    State" in Crain's Detroit Business (Vol. 21,
    October 17, 2005, No. 43, pp. 1) [14759],
    [17969], [46202]
"Auto show also an engine for small-business
    growth" in Crain's Detroit Business (Vol. 19, No.
    2, January 20, 2003, pp. 1) [17970], [27801]
Auto Suppliers Benchmarking Association [1883],
    [29778]
"Auto suppliers: Steel tariffs kill U.S. jobs
    permanently" in Crain's Detroit Business (Vol.
    19, No. 14, April 7, 2003, pp. 34) [1907],
    [43554], [46203]
Auto and Truck Rental and Leasing [2081]
Autofinders USA [4002]
AutoGlass [22624]
AutoInc [921]
"Automaker pullback blamed for Detroit stamper's
    closing" in Crain's Detroit Business (Vol. 19,
    No. 8, February 24, 2003, pp. 6) [17971],
    [31010], [46204], [53593]
"Automaker-Union Talks Critical to State" in Crain's
    Detroit Business (Vol. 22, November 27, 2006,
    No. 48, pp. 8) [17972], [32256], [46205],
    [55282]
"Automate Excel Functions: Easy-to-Create Macros
    Can Take Over Many Manual Processes" in
    Journal of Accountancy (January 2005) [76],
    [2867], [23886], [26158], [27081], [53594]
Automate Your Business Plan 12.0 [30126]
Automated Accounting [363], [3643], [3956],
    [10333], [16569], [27215], [31280], [38511],
    [45962]
"The Automated Agent" in Rough Notes (Vol. 146,
    No. 9, September 2003, pp. 92) [6586],
    [13194], [33552], [48951], [49484]

Automated Manufacturing Exposition and
    Conference [46529]
"Automated advice sites turning up the heat on
    planners" in The New York Times (September
    20, 2000, pp. D44, H44) [9819], [33553]
Automated Sciences Group, Inc.–Library [4886]
Automated Storage/Retrieval Systems [6230]
Automatic Merchandiser [5773], [25583]
Automatic Merchandiser-Blue Book Buyer's Guide
    Issue [5769], [25574]
"Automatic Riches" in Small Business Opportunities
    (Vol. 13, No. 6, November 2001, pp. 66, 68)
    [17946], [33413], [35324], [37058]
Automatic Transmission Rebuilders Association
    Annual Meeting [2002], [2041]
"Automatic Turn-Off" in My Business (April/May
    2002, pp. 47) [37885], [49485]
Automating the Office [49572]
"Automation Accountability" in Rough Notes (Vol.
    145, No. 1, January 2003, pp. 82) [3499],
    [13195], [48952], [49486]
"Automation Alley Awards" in Crain's Detroit
    Business (Vol. 22, September 25-October 1,
    2006, No. 39, pp. E1-E7) [41526]
Automotive Aftermarket Industry Association [1884]
"The Automotive Aftermarket Industry Association
    has Launched a New Online Feature for Its
    Members" in Aftermarket Business (Jul. 03)
    [1908], [53595]
"Automotive Aftermarket Products Show in Las
    Vegas Is Gaining in Popularity" in Las Vegas
    Review-Journal (November 6, 2003) [1909],
    [24890]
"Automotive Aftermarket Suppliers Association
    (AASA)" in Motor Age (Vol. 122, No. 9,
    September 2003, pp. 100) [1910]
Automotive Body Repair; "Con Artists Target
    Collision Industry" in [11215], [22611], [30208]
Automotive Body Repair News; "Medical Lessons:
    What Can Collision Repair Shops Learn About
    Insurance From the Health Care Industry?" in
    [11218], [13384], [22616], [43276]
Automotive Cooling Journal [22625]
"Automotive Dealers Move Wheels" in Hispanic
    Business (Vol. 22, No. 6, June 2000, pp. 100)
    [17973], [27802], [35794], [48043]
Automotive Design and Production [16391], [46497]
"Automotive" in Entrepreneur (Vol. 32, No. 1,
    January 2004, pp. 162) [1911], [2026], [20256],
    [22607]
Automotive Fleet [2083]
Automotive Fleet and Leasing Association [2066]
Automotive Fleet and Leasing Association-Forum
    [2084]
Automotive Industries [18171]
Automotive Litigation Reporter [922]
Automotive Maintenance Solutions [22663]
Automotive Market Report [18172]
Automotive Market Research Council [2121]
Automotive News [18173], [18207]
Automotive News (Vol. 78, No. 6059, September
    29, 2003, pp. 36); "Auto News Digest" in
    [1779], [17967], [37104]
Automotive News (Vol. 79, January 31, 2005, No.
    6132, pp. 12); "Despite Flaws, Franchise
    System is Solid" in [18009], [38752], [43618]
Automotive News (Vol. 79, February 28, 2005, No.
    6136, pp. 12); "Is a Minority Share Really Worth
    It?" in [18064], [46325]
Automotive News (Vol. 79, February 7, 2005, No.
    6133, pp. 42); "Low-Volume Chevy Dealers
    Criticize Incentive Program" in [18082], [38849],
    [46348]
Automotive News (Vol. 79, February 7, 2005, No.
    6133, pp. 12); "NADA Was a Success and
    Then Some" in [18095], [46381]
Automotive News (Vol. 79, February 21, 2005, No.
    6135, pp. 12); "No Wonder Market Shares are
    Falling" in [18102], [28568], [46394]
Automotive News (Vol. 9, January 31, 2005, No. 3,
    pp. 24); "Pontiac-GMC Dealers are Excited
    About New Products" in [18112], [48776]
Automotive News (Vol. 79, January 24, 2005, No.
    6131, pp. 38); "Reducing Turnover" in [18116],
    [51789], [53936]

"Bank on Real Estate" in *Black Enterprise* (Vol. 34, No. 6, January 2004, pp. 51) [17166], [17360], [20430], [20802], [21563], [21713]

"Bank Reform: Should You Be Celebrating?" in *Business Week* (No. 3658, December 6, 1999, pp. F8) [40168], [44476]

"Bank Stock Binge" in *Black Enterprise* (Vol. 35, January 2005, No. 6, pp. 34) [9828], [14769], [32261], [37898], [49805]

"Bank and Thrift Stocks Report Solid 4th Quarter" in *Long Island Business News* (February 20, 2004) [9829], [14770]

"Bank Wants Doubletree Novi Placed in Receivership" in *Crain's Detroit Business* (Vol. 22, January 30, 2006, No. 5, pp. 41) [12519], [37899]

"Bankable Skills" in *Hispanic Business* (October 2004, pp. 126) [9830], [44914]

BankAmerica Ventures / BA Venture Partners [57941]

Bankcard Barometer [8328]

Bankcard Holders of America-Low Interest Rate List [8296], [9794]

Bankcard Update [8329]

"Banker Boosts Community" in *Crain's New York Business* (Vol. 23, January 29, 2007, No. 5, pp. F14) [14771], [32262], [35805], [37900], [46704], [54136]

"Banker Right on the Money with Financial Powerhouse" in *Houston Business Journal* (Vol. 34, No. 13, August 8, 2003, pp. 2) [9831], [14772], [29798], [37901], [44915], [46705]

Bankers Capital Corp. [62076]

"Bankers' Gaze Turns Northward" in *South Florida Business Journal* (Vol. 23, No. 53, August 8, 2003, pp. 1A) [27810], [37902]

"Banking on California" in *San Francisco Business Times* (Vol. 18, No. 6, September 19, 2003, pp. 19) [9832], [14773], [27811], [30787], [49806]

"Banking on Culture" in *Boston Business Journal* (Vol. 23, No. 31, September 5, 2003, pp. 3) [9833], [37903], [46706], [48051]

"Banking on Diversity" in *Hispanic Business* (November 2006, pp. 74, 76) [42177], [48523]

Banking & Financial Services Policy Report [10267], [15628]

Banking & Financial Services Policy Report (Vol. 23, August 2004); "Servicing Pitfalls: How To Avoid Having Your REMIC Disqualified" in [17439], [21003], [54746]

Banking Information Source [10362], [15742], [21104]

Banking Law Journal [10268], [15629]

"Banking on Tomorrow" in *Fast Company* (November 2001, pp. 50) [9834], [14774], [30506]

"Bankruptcies" in *Crain's Detroit Business* (Vol. 18, No. 24, 2002, pp. 6) [27812], [32263]

Bankruptcy Basics for Small Business [29113]

"Bankruptcy Could Cost Firm $310M" in *Atlanta Business Chronicle* (Vol. 26, No. 9, August 8, 2003, pp. 1A) [27813], [52508]

"Bankruptcy Court Streamlines Rules - to Drum Up Business" in *Crain's Detroit Business* (Vol. 21, January 3, 2005, No. 1, pp. 18) [37904], [40169]

"Bankruptcy filings grow. Ohio stats among leaders" in *Business First Columbus* (Vol. 18, No. 40, May 24, 2002, pp. A1) [27814], [32264]

Bankruptcy Law Reporter [29648]

"Bankruptcy Law Would Mean Tougher Consequences for Consumers" in *Chicago Tribune* (March 11, 2005) [29114], [37905]

"Bankruptcy Reform Trying to Scale Final Hurdle" in *Atlanta Business Chronicle* (Vol. 24, No. 8, July 27, 2001, pp. 4A) [29115], [40170]

"Bankruptcy Reform Will Punish Debtors" in *Atlanta Business Chronicle* (Vol. 25, No. 20, October 25, 2002, pp. 38A) [29116], [37906], [40171]

"Banks: 'Atlanta's Quiet Ambassador of Good Will'" in *Atlanta Business Chronicle* (Vol. 25, No. 22, November 8, 2002, pp. 6C) [24665], [25152], [35806]

"Banks: Big vs. Small" in *Hispanic Business* (October 2002, pp. 36, 38) [35807], [44477]

"Bank's branch-a-year strategy gets trimmed back by circumstances" in *Crain's Detroit Business* (Vol. 16, No. 49, Dec. 4, 2000, pp. 32) [27815]

Banks County Chamber of Commerce [59062]

"Banks, Groups Use Program to Improve Money Smarts" in *Memphis Business Journal* (Vol. 25, No. 16, August 15, 2003, pp. 38) [37907]

"Banks May Sell Off Your Loans" in *Inc.* (September 1, 2003) [9835], [44478]

"Banks Reaching Out to New Communities" in *San Francisco Business Times* (Vol. 18, No. 6, September 19, 2003, pp. 22) [9836], [37908], [46707]

"Banks' distressed loans are on the rise" in *Atlanta Business Chronicle* (Vol. 24, No. 9, August 3, 2001, pp. 3A) [32265], [44479]

"Banks Try to Make Tele-Touch Satisfy Small Businesses" in *American Banker* (Vol. 171, November 27, 2006, No. 226, pp. 2) [9837], [14775], [33562], [39161], [41535], [53601]

BANKSCOPE [10363]

Bannastrow's Crepes [2162]

"Banner Year" in *Entrepreneur* (Vol. 32, September 2004, No. 9, pp. 34) [554], [27816], [33563], [46708]

Banners Restaurants Canada Ltd [21744]

"Banners Tout Development" in *Mississippi Business Journal* (Vol. 29, January 2007, No. 4, pp. 11) [12868], [20103], [30507], [32266], [46709], [50553]

Banning Chamber of Commerce [57347]

Bar-B-Cutie [21745]

"Bar the door; New threats from viruses" in *Crain's Detroit Business* (Vol. 19, No. 3, Jan. 20, 2003, pp. 11) [4600], [6237], [6464], [22178], [22921], [30206], [44275]

Bar Harbor Chamber of Commerce [60731]

"Bar None" in *Entrepreneur* (Vol. 32, December 2004, No. 12, pp. 24) [40172], [43556], [48955], [51064]

"Bar None" in *My Business* (December/January 2004, pp. 11) [40173], [43557], [51065]

The Bar Register of Preeminent Lawyers [29649]

Baraboo Area Chamber of Commerce [66345]

Barada Associates Inc. [42492]

Barber-Osophy: Shear Success for Your Cutting Edge [11759], [11782]

Barberton Community Development Corp. [63873]

Barclay Consulting Associates [31957]

Bardstown-Nelson County Chamber of Commerce [60482]

"Barduous journey" in *Entrepreneur* (Vol. 30, No. 1, Januar) [35808], [44916]

Bare-Bones Guide to Starting a Successful Small Business [52819]

"Bare Essentials" in *Entrepreneur* (Vol. 31, No. 11, November 2003, pp. 180) [5526], [5641], [9612], [56129]

"Bargain Season Begins" in *Hispanic Business* (Vol. 24, No. 4, April 2002, pp. 62) [30291], [32267]

"Bargaining a good-bye" in *BlackEnterprise* (Vol. 32, No. 2, September 2001, pp. 61) [39162], [44917]

"Bargaining Power" in *Sales & Marketing Management* (Vol. 157, February 2005, No. 2, pp. 20) [44918], [51562]

"The bargaining table: check your ego at the door." in *Atlanta Business Chronicle* (Vol. 25, Jan. 10, 2003, No. 31, pp. 1B) [27301], [35809], [44919]

"The Bargaining Table" in *Small Business Opportunities* (Vol. 17, November 2005, No. 6, pp. 12, 20) [27302], [51563]

Barger & Wolen Newsletter [13533]

Bark Busters Home Dog Training [19132]

Barker & Associates [31958], [42942], [47829]

Jess Barker, Document Research/Retrieval [17808], [21156]

"The Barker Portfolio" in *Business Week* (January 16, 2006, No. 3967, pp. 22) [14776], [37909]

Barks [1198]

The Barksdale Group [57942]

Barmetrix Canada [3847]

Barnard's Retail Trend Report [51426]

"Barnes & Noble unit is dropped by 2 big chains" in *Wall Street Journal* (February 5, 2003, pp. B4) [2679], [3026], [51066], [56008]

"Barnes-Pettey Financial Advisors, LLC" in *Mississippi Business Journal* (Vol. 29, January 2007, No. 4, pp. 6) [9838], [14777], [37910], [39163]

Barnesville Area Chamber of Commerce [63608]

Barnesville-Lamar County Chamber of Commerce [59063]

Melvin E. Barnette & Associates Inc. [3644], [45965]

Barnie's Coffee & Tea Co., Inc. [11366]

Barnsdall Chamber of Commerce [63946]

Barnwell County Chamber of Commerce [64722]

Baroli Caffe [11367]

Barrington Area Chamber of Commerce [59426]

Barrington Partners [57943]

Barron's [3424], [15630]

Barron's (Vol. 82, No. 58, February 17, 2003, pp. T8); "A grim adventure: Amphion Capital's venture fund loses all" in [9991], [15057], [28234], [41720], [55650]

Barron's (Vol. 82, No. 58, February 17, 2003, pp. 28); "A clarion call: the tech and telecom sectors are finally on the mend" in [4618], [4951], [14863], [16806], [22940], [24393], [33671], [37970], [41604], [50849]

Barron's (July 7, 2003, pp. 24); "A Corrupt Calculus: The Line Between 'Making the Numbers' and Making Them Up Remains Blurry" in [112], [2887], [23916], [26197], [29171], [37413]

Barron's (July 7, 2003, pp. T1); "A Graphic Shoot-Em Up" in [4679], [9989], [15052], [23020], [41718]

Barron's (July 28, 2003, pp. 17); "A Rough Round: Why Golf's Prospects are Dimming" in [11271], [53948]

Barron's (July 21, 2003, pp. 15); "Adventures in the Paper Trade: Boise Buys OfficeMax" in [14729], [18597], [46185], [49782]

Barron's (Vol. 82, No. 58, February 17, 2003, pp. 31); "An old-fashioned fate: it takes the tax collector to really ruin somebody" in [213], [24007], [26310], [37484], [54687]

Barron's (August 18, 2003); "Are Some Stocks Too Cool: Wall Street Keeps Falling in Love With Growth Stocks. Why the Magic Fades" in [9812], [14744], [37877]

Barron's (August 25, 2003, pp. T3); "At Last, Stirrings in the PC Market" in [6584], [27795], [48950]

Barron's (August 18, 2003, pp. T1); "ATI's Moment of Glory" in [4599], [9816], [14753], [22919], [41525]

Barron's (August 18, 2003, pp. 27); "Back to the Future: Are Payouts Becoming a Top Priority Again?" in [9820], [14761], [37888]

Barron's (Vol. 82, No. 59, Feb. 24, 2003, pp. T8); "Back to business with Staples: new chief works to reclaim the chain's roots" in [9822], [14762], [18598], [27807], [37889], [51062]

Barron's (July 28, 2003, pp. T2); "BEA's Next Act" in [4602], [9840], [13839], [14781], [22923], [33567], [53213]

Barron's (August 25, 2003); "Biggest and Best of the Internet? That's Diller's Goal" in [9847], [13849], [14795], [33587]

Barron's (September 8, 2003, pp. 9); "Bird Dog" in [9850], [14799], [37391], [37922], [40194]

Barron's (August 25, 2003, pp. MW17); "Booting the Bear: E-Trade is Poised for the Bull's Return" in [9853], [14806], [33601], [41561]

Barron's (Vol. 82, No. 58, February 17, 2003, pp. 23); "Breaking out" in [9854], [12183], [12276], [14807], [27871], [41566]

Barron's (September 8, 2003); "Car's Star Turn: August Sales Zoom-For Foreign Models. At Least U.S. Makers' Bonds are Thriving" in [17990], [46226]

Barron's (Vol. 82, No. 57, February 10, 2003, pp. 21); "Chop, chop: Bush's plan changes all: tax planning" in [105], [23909], [26187], [37966], [54490]

Barron's (Vol. 82, No. 58, February 17, 2003, pp. T8); "E-bug exterminator: NetScreen nabs viruses and market share" in [4642], [9925], [13987], [14940], [22218], [22971], [33792], [38023]

Barron's (Vol. 82, No. 58, February 17, 2003, pp. T1); "Elephants on a chip" in **[28095]**, **[30844]**, **[41660]**

Barron's (July 7, 2003); "Enjoy It While It Lasts: Charts Suggest the Market Will Resume a Long-Term Decline at Summer's End" in **[9933]**, **[14954]**, **[38031]**

Barron's (August 25, 2003, pp. T6); "Every Picture Tells a Story: New Web Displays Provide Market Data at a Glance" in **[9940]**, **[14023]**, **[14965]**, **[25847]**, **[33864]**, **[38040]**

Barron's (August 11, 2003, pp. T2); "Extract, Transform and Load" in **[4654]**, **[14971]**, **[22990]**, **[49923]**, **[53275]**

Barron's (July 21, 2003, pp. MW11); "Fallen and Can't Get Up: Even Greenspan Can't Hold Off the Bond Bears" in **[9946]**, **[14974]**, **[32421]**, **[38047]**

Barron's (August 18, 2003, pp. 15); "Fed Model is Pointing to Some Upside for Stocks" in **[9947]**, **[14979]**, **[38049]**, **[40368]**

Barron's (September 8, 2003, pp. 18); "French Fried: GE Wins in Vivendi Deal" in **[1132]**, **[4105]**, **[9716]**, **[15017]**, **[24410]**, **[49951]**

Barron's (August 18, 2003, pp. 17); "Going for Brokers: Recent Enthusiasm for Shares of Street Firms Appears Premature" in **[9984]**, **[15040]**, **[38097]**

Barron's (July 7, 2003, pp. 19); "Good Calls: Gains, Losses and Straddles" in **[9986]**, **[15043]**, **[38099]**, **[54579]**

Barron's (July 7, 2003, pp. L3); "Good Vibes: Socially Responsible Investing is Gaining Fans...and Clout" in **[9987]**, **[15045]**, **[29269]**, **[37450]**, **[38100]**, **[54190]**

Barron's (July 21, 2003, pp. F2); "Greener Pastures: Exodus from Fidelity Continues as Another Hot Manager Heads to a Hedge Fund" in **[9990]**, **[15055]**, **[29277]**, **[38105]**, **[40422]**

Barron's (Vol. 82, No. 59, Feb. 24, 2003, pp. T4); "Growing apart: investment Websites keep advancing, even as the market retreats" in **[9992]**, **[14095]**, **[15060]**, **[25862]**, **[33982]**, **[38106]**

Barron's Guide to Graduate Business Schools **[33007]**

Barron's (July 28, 2003); "Hurricane Watch:Whether the Market's Boisterous or Becalmed, the Web's the Place to Vent and Pontificate" in **[10013]**, **[14137]**, **[15108]**, **[34040]**, **[38133]**

Barron's (Vol. 82, No. 58, February 17, 2003, pp. 26); "In Houston, a spreading sea of empty offices" in **[20551]**, **[20905]**, **[21326]**

Barron's (August 18, 2003, pp. T3); "In Texas a 'transformative' merger" in **[4695]**, **[23042]**, **[49999]**, **[53330]**

Barron's (July 7, 2003, pp. L12); "Independents' Day: Would Giving More Power to Outside Directors Boost Funds' Performance?" in **[10021]**, **[15121]**, **[38139]**, **[40462]**

Barron's (August 25, 2003, pp. T1); "Intel Inside: The Chips Get Hot" in **[6693]**, **[28335]**, **[41772]**, **[49098]**

Barron's (Vol. 82, Feb. 24, 2003, pp.17); "Intuitively clear: the king of personal-finance software sets sights on small business" in **[4701]**, **[10029]**, **[15139]**, **[23050]**, **[28339]**, **[38148]**, **[53338]**

Barron's (August 18, 2003, pp. 14); "Is It Time for the Fed to Take a Good, Long Vacation?" in **[10041]**, **[15181]**, **[40479]**

Barron's (August 11, 2003, pp. 26); "Job Flight: Is it Real: Evidence is Scant, but a Shift Would be Welcome" in **[42314]**, **[43726]**, **[53819]**

Barron's (Vol. 82, No. 54, January 20, 2003, pp. T1); "Jump-starting broadband" in **[5038]**, **[14180]**, **[30896]**, **[40488]**

Barron's (July 7, 2003, pp. MW11); "Knock on Wood: Lumber Prices Uncertain after 'inventory rally'" in **[7396]**, **[16307]**, **[44233]**

Barron's (July 7, 2003, pp. 30); "Let Freedom Ring: The Internet is a Powerful Force for Telephone Deregulation" in **[5042]**, **[14202]**, **[34134]**, **[40513]**

Barron's (September 8, 2003); "Local Hero: Ken Enright of MFS Bets on Underdogs-and Usually Wins" in **[10067]**, **[15224]**, **[38193]**

Barron's (July 28, 2003, pp. 30); "Manufacturing History: Tales of Turning Points in Factory Jobs are Just That" in **[32562]**, **[42335]**, **[46360]**

Barron's (August 11, 2003, pp. MW3); "Market Drifts While Tech Stocks Wilt" in **[10084]**, **[15251]**, **[32564]**, **[41828]**

Barron's (July 7, 2003, pp. 22); "Mixed Grill: A Quarter's Menu: Good-and Some Bad-News" in **[10090]**, **[15268]**, **[32576]**, **[38228]**, **[53857]**, **[54661]**

Barron's (July 21, 2003, pp. 16); "Mobile Situation UT Starcom Soars" in **[5058]**, **[14248]**, **[41840]**, **[43755]**

Barron's (August 25, 2003, pp. 10); "More Shrinkage: Digest Readers Cut and Run" in **[15277]**, **[18911]**, **[28508]**

Barron's (July 28, 2003, pp. 15); "Needs Toner: Facing Rivals, Lexmark Shares Could Go Lower" in **[6733]**, **[10100]**, **[15290]**, **[30919]**, **[46384]**

Barron's (July 28, 2003, pp. T1); "On the Internet, a Second Act" in **[14306]**, **[29425]**, **[37485]**, **[40592]**

Barron's (July 7, 2003, pp. 22); "On the March: War and Peace Aid General Dynamics" in **[32610]**, **[40070]**

Barron's Online **[10364]**, **[15743]**, **[17471]**

Barron's (July 7, 2003, pp. L7); "Other People's Money: A Pension Fund Learns About Soft Dollars-the Hard Way" in **[10126]**, **[15331]**, **[26868]**, **[38268]**, **[53902]**

Barron's (July 7, 2003); "Overplayed Hand: Portfolio Recovery Associates, a Credit-Card Debt Collector, May be Flying too High" in **[8316]**, **[8357]**, **[8392]**, **[31573]**

Barron's (July 21, 2003, pp. 17); "Pill Pusher: Drug Maker Biovail Sparks Controversy by Paying Doctors to Write Prescriptions" in **[8799]**, **[37488]**, **[40613]**

Barron's (August 18, 2003, pp. 28); "Policy Follies: Fiscal and Monetary Levers Lose their Power" in **[32631]**

Barron's (July 21, 2003, pp. 15); "Retail Rut: Sears Holders Might Get a $10 Payout. But Don't Expect Much More from the Stock" in **[8395]**, **[10162]**, **[15413]**, **[38317]**, **[50164]**, **[51315]**

Barron's (August 11, 2003, pp. 17); "Searching for Signs of Intelligent Life" in **[7069]**, **[10175]**, **[14416]**, **[15435]**, **[25954]**, **[28747]**, **[30944]**, **[34442]**

Barron's (August 11, 2003, pp. 16); "Secret Weapon: Synopsys is Thriving Behind the Scenes in the Semiconductor Business" in **[4791]**, **[23163]**, **[41966]**, **[53451]**

Barron's (Vol. 82, No. 59, February 24, 2003, pp. 23); "Smart inventory: start electing superior filing options now" in **[260]**, **[15460]**, **[24043]**, **[26365]**, **[29506]**, **[54310]**, **[54769]**

Barron's (July 21, 2003, pp. 7); "Street Talk" in **[13782]**, **[41484]**

Barron's (July 21, 2003); "Taking a Dive: A Federally Chartered Insurer of Pensions has Fallen on Hard Times. Taxpayers, Beware" in **[13484]**, **[26923]**, **[40751]**, **[43387]**, **[54786]**

Barron's (Vol. 82, No. 57, February 10, 2003, pp. T4); "Tastes great? Less taxing?" in **[275]**, **[4836]**, **[24050]**, **[38401]**, **[54880]**

Barron's (Vol. 82, No. 59, February 24, 2003, pp. T1); "The Big Disconnect" in **[27839]**, **[41544]**, **[44000]**

Barron's (Vol. 82, No. 57, February, 10, 2003, pp. 39); "The 80-20 Rule: It's Not Just a Glib Remark" in **[36051]**, **[45095]**

Barron's (July 28, 2003, pp. 31); "The Good Deflation: Falling Prices Can be Sign of Economic Strength" in **[32453]**

Barron's (July 28, 2003, pp. 7); "The Prevaricator" in **[10138]**, **[15366]**, **[37493]**

Barron's (August 25, 2003, pp. F2); "The Producers: Fixed Payouts Mimic Yield. But Will the Hit Keep Playing?" in **[10143]**, **[15377]**, **[38294]**, **[54711]**

Barron's (September 8, 2003, pp. F2); "The Unlevel Playing Field: At Some Mutual Funds, Big Investors Got Big Breaks" in **[10224]**, **[15558]**, **[38432]**

Barron's (Vol. 82, No. 59, February 24, 2003, pp. T6); "Thrifts adrift? Mortgage slowdown would hurt the industry" in **[7496]**, **[17447]**, **[20686]**, **[28900]**

Barron's (Vol.82, Feb.17, 2003, pp.T7); "Top-drawer advice: new software tells you how much your charitable contributions are worth" in **[285]**, **[4847]**, **[23238]**, **[24064]**, **[26390]**, **[38420]**, **[54266]**, **[54839]**

Barron's (August 11, 2003, pp. 17); "Warren Buffet's Still-Golden Touch: The Wizard of Omaha's Magic is Alive and Well" in **[10234]**, **[13513]**, **[15590]**, **[43417]**

Barron's (August 11, 2003, pp. 26); "Winning and Losing Lotteries: the Right to Future Income Isn't a Capital Gain" in **[54874]**

Barron's (Vol. 82, Sept. 9, 2002, pp. 26); "Witness to history...and tragedy: a Wall Street veteran reflects on his 9/11 loss" in **[10255]**, **[15608]**, **[36978]**, **[37816]**

Barrow County Chamber of Commerce **[59064]**

Barry County Area Chamber of Commerce **[61253]**

Barson Marketing Inc. **[47830]**

Barstow Area Chamber of Commerce **[57348]**

"Bartech and Nucon Win Staffing Deals" in *Black Enterprise* (Vol. 35, November 2004, No. 4, pp. 32) **[9194]**, **[24518]**, **[30788]**

"Barter systems put the 'trade' in trade group" in *Crain's Detroit Business* (Vol. 19, No. 16, April 21, 2003, pp. 16) **[26707]**, **[49807]**

Bartercard USA Inc. **[4003]**

"Barter's latest comeback" in *The Economist* (Vol. 357, No. 8, October 21, 2000, pp. 78) **[13736]**, **[26700]**, **[35325]**, **[53558]**

Bartlesville Area Chamber of Commerce **[63947]**

Bartlett Arboretum and Gardens–Library **[11507]**

Bartlett Area Chamber of Commerce **[64883]**

Bartlett Chamber of Commerce **[59427]**

Barton Area Chamber of Commerce **[65778]**

Barton County Chamber of Commerce **[61914]**

Barton County Historical Society **[11001]**

Baruch College–Mid-town Manhattan SBDC–SBDC **[62174]**

Basalt Chamber of Commerce **[58329]**

Baseball Card Collector **[5928]**

Basecamp Ventures **[62584]**

BASELINE In Production **[9770]**, **[24504]**, **[25609]**

Basement Finishing Systems **[7655]**

Basic Accounting Video Series **[351]**

Basic Business Statistics **[27817]**

Basic Electricity for Auto Mechanics **[22647]**

Basic Homebrewing **[3122]**

Basic Legal Forms for Business **[29117]**

Basic Masonry **[16972]**

Basic Medical Laboratory Techniques **[17182]**

Basic Plumbing Techniques **[19744]**

Basic Real Estate Investing **[21064]**

Basic Screen Printing **[22126]**

Basic Shooting **[9762]**

Basic Steps for Better Business Writing **[27697]**

Basic Techniques in Practical Chemistry **[33308]**

"Basic Training" in *Crain's Detroit Business* (Vol. 21, October 10, 2005, No. 43, pp. 12) **[12869]**, **[20104]**, **[33008]**

Basics of Budgeting, Purchasing & Financial Statements **[27085]**, **[50753]**

The Basics of Business Writing **[27618]**

Basics of Successful Investing **[10296]**

"Basis of Corporate Average Fuel Economy Could Change" in *Detroit Free Press* (April 11, 2003) **[17975]**, **[37247]**

"Basket Case: A Lesson in Eggs, Baskets and Diversification" in *Entrepreneur* (Vol. 33, January 2005, No. 1, pp. 49) **[14778]**, **[37911]**

Baskin-Robbins Ice Cream **[12806]**

Bass & Co. **[7037]**

Bass Lake Chamber of Commerce **[57349]**

Bass Tackle: How to Buy & Save **[2186]**

Bastion Capital Corp. **[57944]**

Bastrop Chamber of Commerce **[65122]**

Bastyr University–Library **[17943]**, **[18492]**

Batavia Chamber of Commerce **[59428]**

Bates International Motor Home Rental Systems, Inc. **[2093]**

Batesburg-Leesville Chamber of Commerce **[64723]**

Batesville Area Chamber of Commerce [57131], [59874]

Bath County Chamber of Commerce [65862]

Bath Fitter [12340]

"Bath Iron Works Wins Contract for Tri-Hulled Navy Warship" in *Portland Press Herald* (October 15, 2005) [16361], [39987]

Bathcrest, Inc. [19784]

Battelle Venture Partners [63845]

"Battenberg is riding along with Segway" in *Crain's Detroit Business* (Vol. 18, No. 24, June 17, 2002, pp. 8) [41536], [48699]

Batter Up Kids Culinary Center [7824]

Batteries Plus - America's Battery Experts [2012]

Batterson Venture Partners (BVP) [59723]

"Battery Tests" in *Entrepreneur* (Vol. 33, September 2005, No. 9, pp. 46) [4922], [48956], [50944]

Battery Ventures, L.P. (Wellesley) [61038]

"Battle of the Business Plans: a new march madness" in *Fortune* (Vol. 141, No. 2, January 24, 2000, pp. 128) [29707], [55358]

"Battle over restaurant smoking still smolders in state Capitol" in *Crain's Detroit Business* (Vol. 18, No. 22, June 3, 2002, pp. 41) [21445], [40174]

"Battle between Compuware, IBM escalates in counterclaim" in *Crain's Detroit Business* (Vol. 19, No. 14, April 7, 2003, pp. 4) [4601], [6589], [22922], [29118], [30789]

Battle Creek Area Chamber of Commerce [61254]
   SBDC [61175]

Battle Ground Chamber of Commerce [66045]

Battle Mountain Chamber of Commerce [62340]

"The Battle of the Portals" in *The Economist* (Vol. 377, October 22-28, 2005, No. 8449, pp. 65-66) [13836], [25796], [33564]

"Battle brews against tort reform" in *Atlanta Business Chronicle* (Vol. 25, Dec. 13, 2002, No. 27, pp. A1) [13199], [29119], [40175], [43087]

"Battle of the Sexes" in *Kiplinger's Personal Finance Magazine* (Vol. 55, No. 1, January, 2001, pp. 24) [43088]

"Battle of the Wily Worms" in *Hispanic Business* (March 2004, pp. 42) [6160], [13837], [22179], [33565]

Bauder College–Library [2143], [5605]

Baudette-Lake of the Woods Chamber of Commerce [61559]

Baum Fallenbaum, Attorneys [4451], [29613]

Bavier, Bulger & Goodyear Inc. [32176]

Baxley-Appling County Chamber of Commerce [59065]

Baxter Associates, Inc. [58581]

Baxter Springs Chamber of Commerce [60293]

Baxter & Woodman Inc. [11961]

Bay Area Chamber of Commerce [61255]
   SBDC [61176]

Bay Area Chamber of Commerce Visitors Center [64196]

Bay Area Independent Publishers Association [2650], [8949]

Bay County Chamber of Commerce [58757]

Bay Meadows Racetrack–William P. Kyne Memorial Thoroughbred Racing Library [12474]

Bay Partners [57945]

"Bay State VC pace falls to 1999 level" in *Boston Business Journal* (Vol. 22, No. 16, May 24, 2002, pp. 1) [27818], [55359]

Bay Tree Publishing [58251]

Bayard Taylor Memorial Library [1354]

BayerDiag, a Bayer Company–Library [16888], [17288]

Bayfield Chamber of Commerce [66346]

"Bayla's Plea: Put Your Money Where Your Mouth Is" in *Fortune* (Vol. 142, No. 4, August 14, 2000, pp. 276+) [12274], [35810], [55500]

Baylor College of Medicine
   Center for Medical Ethics and Health Policy [41359]
   Jerry Lewis Neuromuscular Disease Research Center [19595]

Baylor University
   Center for Business and Economic Research [32844]
   Center for Private Enterprise [37052]
   Crouch Fine Arts Library [17663]

Office of Sponsored Programs and Contracts [65650]

Baymont Inns & Suites [12704]

Bayonne Chamber of Commerce [62474]

"Bayou Boycott Spurs Buying" in *Inc.* (July 1, 2003) [27819]

Bayou La Batre Chamber of Commerce [56815]

Baytown Chamber of Commerce [65123]

Bayview Chamber of Commerce [59286]

BBB Wise Giving Alliance [30203]

BBIA enews [2524], [3106]

BBLM Architects [49585]

"BBoC and FSB to merge: more deals within banking community are possible" in *Black Enterprise* (Vol. 33, No. 3, October 2002, pp. 31) [14779], [15727], [49808], [50902]

BC Innovation Council [39114]

BCE Capital [66715]

BCI Partners [62585]

BCM Technologies, Inc. [65593]

BD Ventures / Becton, Dickinson and Co. [62586]

"B.E. teams up with CNNfn" in *Black Enterprise* (Vol. 33, No. 6, January 2003, pp. 10) [32268], [48052], [49809]

Be an Even Better Manager: Improve Performance, Profits, and Productivity [44920]

"Be a complete lawyer" in *Daily Business Review* (Vol. 77, No. 198, March 24, 2003, pp. A6) [29120], [54137]

"Be a Loan Shark" in *Success* (Vol. 47, No. 3, July 2000, pp. 59) [35326], [55360]

"Be Prepared" in *Harvard Business Review* (Vol. 81, No. 11, November 2003, pp. 20) [29799], [44276], [44921]

"Be Prepared" in *Inc.* (Volume 28, January 2006, No. 1, pp. 53-54) [30790], [39164]

Be Prepared to Speak [22586], [27563]

"Be Reasonable" in *Entrepreneur* (Vol. 32, November 2004, No. 11, pp. 24) [17976], [27086]

Be Safe, Not Sorry [8525]

"Be a Savvy Franchise Sleuth" in *My Business* (December/January 2004, pp. 49) [38606]

"B.E. Successpert Speaks" in *Black Enterprise* (Vol. 34, No. 5, December 2003, pp. 139) [34677], [35811], [44922], [45501]

"B.E. Wall St. All-Stars" in *Black Enterprise* (Vol. 33, No. 3, October 2002, pp. 88) [9839], [10690], [14780], [15728], [37912], [38665], [48053], [49954]

Be Your Own Boss [35327], [39027]

"Be Your Own Boss" in *Small Business Opportunities* (July 2005) [496], [1758], [1876], [4265], [11300], [17721], [19061], [19137], [19186], [21197], [23435], [23588], [25616], [35328], [39028], [55999]

Be Your Own Boss: Start a Business [54315]

Be Your Own Dick: Private Investigating Made Easy [19961]

"BEA Ships Platform for Deploying Advanced Telecom Services" in *eWeek* (February 7, 2005) [13838], [27303], [33566]

Franklin F. Beach & Co. [27004]

"The Beach Less Traveled" in *Business Week* (January 9, 2006, No. 3966, pp. 89-90) [12520], [24666], [25153]

Beachcomber Body & Soul [23807], [51447]

Beachwood Chamber of Commerce [63609]

Beacon Hill Chamber of Commerce [66046]

Beacon Management Group Inc. [3645], [16571], [30061], [31282], [37048], [38512], [45966]

Beacon Partners Inc. [58582]

Beacon Technology Ventures [61039]

"Beacon Telco Aims To Jumpstart Optics" in *Venture Capital Journal* (Vol. 40, No. 10, November 2000, pp. 6, 8) [41443], [43035], [55361]

Beacon Venture Capital [60864]

Bead and Button [8194]

"Bead It! For Johnna Snell, Her Hobby's a Charm" in *Black Enterprise* (Vol. 34, No. 4, November 2003, pp. 171) [7999], [15834], [56130]

"Bead Store Blends Ancient and Modern to Find Success Downtown" in *San Jose Mercury News* (March 1, 2005) [15835], [56131]

Beall Investigation Bureau Inc. [35293]

"Beall's Push to Expand Existing Florida Stores Reaps Dividends On Grand Scale" in *Bradenton Herald* (January 20, 2005) [3027], [5642], [27820], [51067]

"Beaming in on safety business" in *Atlanta Business Chronicle* (Vol. 25, December 20, 2002, No. 28, pp. 3A) [22180], [41537]

BeamPines Inc. [42943]

"Bean Counter" in *Forbes* (Vol. 175, February 14, 2005, No. 3, pp. 78) [11313], [51068]

"Bean Counter" in *San Francisco Business Times* (Vol. 17, No. 53, August 8, 2003, pp. 27) [11314], [27821], [37592]

"Bean Enjoys Expanding Eat With Us Restaurants, Franchises" in *Mississippi Business Journal* (Vol. 28, January 2007, No. 36, pp. 34) [21446], [27822], [37593]

Beaner's Coffee [11368]

Beaners Fun Cuts for Kids [11820]

Beans: Four Principles for Running a Business in Good Times or Bad [11315], [27823], [39165]

"Beantown Flavor: Columnist Adrian Walker Gives Us a Taste of Boston" in *Black Enterprise* (Vol. 34, No. 5, December 2003, pp. 152) [24667], [25154], [26797], [30292], [30970]

Bear Creek Venture Partners [66206]

Bear Lake Rendezvous Chamber of Commerce [65697]

"Bear market: how one company repositioned itself for a plush success story" in *Entrepreneur* (Vol. 30, No. 9, September 2002, pp. 30) [5894], [24801]

Bear River Valley Chamber of Commerce [65698]

Bear Rock Cafe [8542]

The Bearclaw Coffee Company [11369]

Bearcom Building Services [8697]

Beard Papa's Sweets Cafe [2288]

Beardstown Chamber of Commerce [59429]

Bearly Used Auto Rental [2094]

"BEA's Next Act" in *Barron's* (July 28, 2003, pp. T2) [4602], [9840], [13839], [14781], [22923], [33567], [53213]

Beat the Taxman 2006: Easy Ways to Save Tax in Your Small Business [23891], [54440]

Beat the Taxman 2007: Easy Ways to Save Tax in Your Small Business, 2007 Edition For the 2006 Tax Year [23892], [54441]

Beat the Taxman: Easy Ways to Tax Save in Your Small Business [2872], [23893], [26164], [54442]

"Beat Those Bouncing Checks" in *Hispanic Business* (December 2003, pp. 58) [8375], [31513], [33568]

"Beating Burnout" in *Sales and Marketing.com* (Vol. 153, No. 3, March 2004, pp. 47) [32269]

"Beating the Cash Flow Blues" in *Home Business* (Vol. 12, October 2005, No. 5, pp. 76) [82], [27087]

Beating the Competition: A Practical Guide to Benchmarking [30791]

Beating the Competition: 150 Ways to Win New Customers for Your Small Business [30792], [46710]

"Beating the Dream-Busters: Don't Let Loved Ones Keep You From Living Your Dream" in *Black Enterprise* (Vol. 34, No. 5, December 2003) [30508], [31490], [34678], [35812]

"Beating the Odds" in *Entrepreneur* (Vol. 27, No. 12, December 1999, pp. 154) [35813], [55501]

"Beating the odds: remembering the basics of business can help" in *Black Enterprise* (Vol. 32, No. 6, January 2002, pp. 35) [29708], [30474], [35329], [47939], [52769]

Beating the Odds in Small Business [52820]

"Beating the Odds" in *Success* (Vol. 47, No. 3, July 2000, pp. 28) [32270], [40176]

"Beating Strong" in *Houston Business Journal* (Vol. 34, No. 14, August 15, 2003, pp. 17) [17254], [29800], [30135], [44923]

"Beating Travel Stress" in *Small Business Opportunities* (Vol. 16, November 2004, No. 6, pp. 100, 104) [25155], [30293]

Beatrice Area Chamber of Commerce [62247]

Beatty Chamber of Commerce [62341]

"Beau Restoration Complete" in *Mississippi Business Journal* (Vol. 29, January 2007, No. 2, pp. 7) **[10860]**, **[17510]**

"Beau Rivage Resort And Casino" in *Mississippi Business Journal* (Vol. 29, January 2007, No. 2, pp. 6) **[555]**, **[5969]**, **[46711]**, **[50554]**

Beaufort Regional Chamber of Commerce **[64724]**

"Beaumont Aims to Commercialize Research" in *Crain's Detroit Business* (Vol. 22, January 16, 2006, No. 3, pp. 3) **[50817]**, **[52042]**

Beaumont Chamber of Commerce **[57350]**, **[65124]**

Beaumont Enterprise (January 24, 2005); "Houston-Based Restaurant Chain Uses Mystery Shoppers to Ensure Quality" in **[10006]**, **[12577]**, **[17521]**, **[21324]**, **[21531]**, **[29291]**, **[31035]**, **[31735]**, **[51187]**

Beaumont Enterprise (November 6, 2003); "Sour Lake, Texas, Looks to Bed and Breakfast to Help Revive Downtown" in **[2453]**

"Beauty and the Beast" in *Hispanic Business* (Vol. 23, No. 11, November 2001, pp. 62-64) **[17977]**, **[48054]**

Beauty Brands Salon - Spa - Superstore **[11821]**

"Beauty and the Bugs" in *Home Business* (Vol. 12, March/April 2005, No. 2, pp. 81) **[19019]**, **[35814]**, **[42576]**, **[56132]**

Beauty Fair **[2618]**, **[5597]**, **[7924]**, **[9652]**, **[11816]**

Beauty First **[11822]**

The Beauty Industry Report **[11807]**

Beauty Prague **[7925]**, **[17859]**

The Beauty Supply Outlet **[2410]**

"Beauty's new age" in *WWD* (Vol. 184, No. 59, September 20, 2002, pp. S1) **[2580]**, **[7880]**, **[17890]**, **[27824]**

Beaver Chamber of Commerce and Travel Council **[65699]**

Beaver County Chamber of Commerce **[64379]**

Beaver Dam Area Chamber of Commerce **[66347]**

Beaverbrook Art Gallery–Library **[1647]**

Beavercreek Chamber of Commerce **[63610]**

Beaverhead Chamber of Commerce **[62146]**

Beaverton Area Chamber of Commerce **[64197]**

Don L. Beck Associates Inc. **[45967]**

Beck Powell & Parsons Inc. **[49586]**

Becker College **[61152]**

Beckett and Raeder Inc. **[1547]**

Beckley - Raleigh County Chamber of Commerce **[66269]**

"Become Famous for What You Do" in *Journal of Accountancy* (Vol. 198, December 2004, No. 6, pp. 30) **[83]**, **[2873]**, **[9841]**, **[14782]**, **[23894]**, **[27088]**

"Becoming a Great Agency: Part One" in *Rough Notes* (Vol. 145, No. 9, September 2002, pp. 62) **[13200]**, **[43089]**

Becoming a Personal Trainer for Dummies **[16993]**, **[18422]**, **[19341]**, **[26035]**, **[29060]**, **[29709]**

Becoming a Publications Manager **[8597]**

Bed & Breakfast Encyclopedia **[2421]**

"Bed & Breakfast" in *Home Accents Today* (Vol. 18, No. 9, August 2003, pp. 26) **[2425]**

"Bed, Breakfast House in Arcadia, Miss., Reopens with New Owner" in *Sun Herald* (January 11, 2004) **[2426]**, **[42577]**, **[56133]**

"Bed, Breakfast Owner Banks on Lure of Downtown Grapevine, Texas" in *Fort Worth Star-Telegram* (July 20, 2003) **[2427]**

Bedford Area Chamber of Commerce **[59875]**, **[65863]**

Bedford Associates Inc. **[10334]**, **[15724]**

Bedford Capital Corp. **[63063]**

Bedford Chamber of Commerce **[60095]**, **[60928]**, **[63611]**

   SBDC **[59819]**

Bedford County Chamber of Commerce **[64380]**

Bedford Heights Chamber of Commerce **[63612]**

Bedford Hills Chamber of Commerce **[62822]**

Bedrock Capital Partners **[61040]**

Bee Biology and Systematics Laboratory–Library **[2478]**

Bee Breeding: The Search for the Perfect Honeybee **[2476]**

Bee County Chamber of Commerce **[65125]**

Bee Culture-Who's Who in Apiculture Issue **[2468]**

Beech Mountain Area Chamber of Commerce **[63328]**

Beech-Nut Nutrition Corporation–Library **[18493]**

Brian A. Beecher and Associates **[18571]**

Beecher Chamber of Commerce **[59430]**

Beecken, Petty & Company LLC (Lisle) **[59724]**

Beef O'Bradys Family Sports Pubs **[21746]**

"Been there, done that: growing an entrepreneurial empire?" in *Entrepreneur* (Vol. 30, No. 9, September 2002, pp. 25) **[35815]**, **[44480]**, **[55502]**

Beer Associates **[21713]**

Beer Cans and Brewery Collectibles **[5922]**

Beer Institute **[3116]**

Beer Marketer's Insights Newsletter **[3147]**

Beer Statistics News **[3148]**

Beer-Wells Real Estate Services Inc. **[20072]**

Bees of the World **[2469]**

Before & After **[6013]**

"Before he could set up a business, the founder of Portable Church Industries faced a more daunting task: inventing an industry" in *Inc.* **[35330]**

"Before You Do That 'Amazing' Biotech Deal, Read This Story" in *Venture Capital Journal* (Vol. 42, No. 8, August 2002, pp. 36-37) **[41538]**, **[50818]**, **[52043]**, **[55503]**

"Before You Sign on the Dotted Line..." in *Black Enterprise* (Vol. 35, October 2004, No. 3, pp. 200) **[29121]**, **[40177]**

"Before You Try To Sell, Make Sure You Know What Buyers Want" in *Inc.* (April 1, 2005) **[14783]**, **[30663]**, **[49810]**

Beggs Chamber of Commerce **[63948]**

Beginning Bodybuilding **[19464]**

The Beginning Filmmaker's Business Guide: Financial, Legal, Marketing and Distribution Basics of Making Movies **[9694]**

Beginning in the Nursery Business **[11420]**

Beginning Training for Your Retriever **[19121]**

"The Beginning of a Whole New Friendship" in *Black Enterprise* (Vol. 34, No. 5, December 2003, pp. S5) **[35331]**, **[36174]**, **[49764]**, **[51917]**

Samuel D. Begola Associates Inc. **[50297]**

"Behave yourself" in *Harvard Business Review* (Vol. 80, No. 10, October 2002, pp. 22) **[16499]**, **[44924]**

Behavioral Research in Accounting **[314]**

Behavioural Interviewing (Canada) **[42817]**

"Behind the Boards" in *Forbes* (Vol. 170, No. 9, October 28, 2002, pp. 252) **[9842]**, **[14784]**, **[44925]**

"Behind the Curve" in *Hispanic Business* (Vol. 24, No. 5, May 2002, pp. 40-41) **[33569]**, **[41539]**, **[48055]**, **[53214]**, **[53602]**

"Behind the Deals" in *Entrepreneur* (Vol. 28, No. 6, June 2000, pp. 38) **[13840]**, **[48899]**, **[55504]**

"Behind the looking glass" in *Red Herring* (March 2003, pp. 58) **[41540]**, **[46206]**, **[50819]**, **[52044]**

"Behind the Numbers" in *Forbes* (October 30,2000, pp. 222) **[27825]**

"Behind the Scenes" in *Washington Business Journal* (Vol. 22, No. 12, July 25, 2003, pp. 18) **[4603]**, **[13201]**, **[22924]**, **[43090]**, **[49811]**, **[53215]**

"Behind the Veil" in *Entrepreneur* (Vol. 30, No. 2, Februa) **[3175]**, **[35816]**

BEI Polar Clips **[51448]**

Beijing International Jewellery Fair **[15872]**

"Being Big Brother: Shh...Spy Tool Helps You Snoop Undetected" in *Black Enterprise* (Vol. 35, October 2004, No. 3, pp. 72) **[4604]**, **[22181]**, **[22925]**, **[53216]**

"Being strong comes at high cost" in *Women In Business* (Vol. 52, No. 5, September-October 2000, pp. 18) **[35817]**, **[56134]**

Being an Entrepreneur in Illinois **[59802]**

Being a Homemaker-Home Health Aide **[12367]**

Being Self-Employed: How to Run a Business Out of Your Home, Claim Travel and Depreciation and Earn a Good Income Well into Your 70s or 80s **[30294]**, **[39166]**, **[42578]**, **[54443]**

"Being Small, Looking Big" in *Boston Business Journal* (Vol. 23, No. 21, June 27, 2003, pp. 24) **[30509]**, **[46712]**, **[48660]**, **[50555]**

The Belbin Team-Roles Package **[34822]**

Belcourt Satellite Center–SBDC **[63489]**

Belen Chamber of Commerce **[62673]**

Belfast Area Chamber of Commerce **[60732]**

Belgrade Chamber of Commerce **[62147]**

"Belhaven College" in *Mississippi Business Journal* (Vol. 28, September 2006, No. 36, pp. 6) **[33009]**, **[35818]**

Belhaven Community Chamber of Commerce **[63329]**

Bell Chamber of Commerce **[57351]**

Bell County Chamber of Commerce **[60483]**

Bell Gardens Association of Merchants and Commerce **[57352]**

Bell Industries Tech.logix Group **[49402]**, **[49587]**

Bell Springs Publishing **[58252]**

Bell World **[51449]**

Bellacino's Pizza & Grinders Inc. **[19652]**

Bellaire Area Chamber of Commerce **[61256]**, **[63613]**

Bellavia & Kassel, PC **[4452]**, **[29614]**

Bellbrook - Sugarcreek Area Chamber of Commerce **[63614]**

Belle Glade Chamber of Commerce **[58758]**

Belle Plaine Area Chamber of Commerce **[60294]**

Belle Plaine Chamber of Commerce **[60096]**

Bellefonte Intervalley Area Chamber of Commerce **[64381]**

Belleview-South Marion Chamber of Commerce **[58759]**

Belleville Area Chamber of Commerce **[61257]**

Belleville Chamber of Commerce **[60295]**

Belleville Community Club **[66348]**

Belleville News-Democrat (December 22, 2003); "Fairview Heights, Ill., Mall Kiosk Vendors Say Holiday Sales Brisk" in **[15920]**

Belleville News-Democrat (September 27, 2004); "Pet Sitters in St. Louis Area Will Sit With Fido When the Master is Out" in **[19079]**, **[36623]**

Bellevue Area Chamber of Commerce **[60097]**

Bellevue Chamber of Commerce **[62248]**, **[64884]**, **[66047]**

Bellevue Community College–Small Business Development Center **[66013]**

Bellflower Chamber of Commerce **[57353]**

"" in *Bellingham Business Journal* (January 2007, pp.) **[17482]**, **[27826]**-**[27826]**, **[35819]**

Bellingham Business Journal (January 2007, pp. C15); "2007's Trends in Travel and Tourism" in **[24659]**, **[25143]**, **[30280]**

Bellingham Business Journal (December 2006, pp. A5); "A 35-Year Old Downtown Shop is Expanding" in **[5822]**, **[7156]**, **[27748]**

Bellingham Business Journal (December 2006, pp. A3); "Allegiant Files Statement for IPO of Common Stock" in **[24662]**, **[25146]**, **[27762]**, **[30503]**

Bellingham Business Journal (January 2007, pp. A6); "Apex Property Management Moves" in **[20048]**, **[27776]**, **[30132]**

Bellingham Business Journal (January 2007, pp. 3); "Assist2Sell Expands to Service Home Buyers" in **[17359]**, **[20426]**, **[20799]**, **[27792]**, **[33001]**

Bellingham Business Journal (December 2006, pp. A6); "Bottle Shoppe Owner Looking to Sell" in **[16230]**, **[23462]**, **[52409]**

Bellingham Business Journal (January 2007, pp. A17); "Bystrom Providing In-Room Massages at Lakeway Inn & Convention Center" in **[17004]**, **[30306]**, **[42187]**

Bellingham Business Journal (December 2006, pp. A6); "Catering Company Expands Operations" in **[4536]**, **[27934]**, **[30137]**, **[35923]**, **[37608]**

Bellingham Business Journal (December 2006, pp. 4); "Chamber Kicks Off Weekly Member-Appreciation Program" in **[35932]**, **[39228]**, **[50432]**, **[56158]**

Bellingham Business Journal (December 2006, pp. A1); "Construction Delayed on Tower Project" in **[7297]**, **[29832]**, **[32329]**

Bellingham Business Journal (December 2006, pp. A4); "Electrical-Wiring Company is Moving to Ferndale" in **[7726]**, **[9073]**, **[28093]**, **[30144]**

Bellingham Business Journal (December 2006, pp. A6); "Fairhaven Business Owners Open Pottery Production Facility" in **[8007]**, **[28141]**, **[37639]**

Berryville-Clarke County Chamber of Commerce [65864]

Bert Dohmen's Wellington Letter [15632]

Berthel Fisher & Company Planning, Inc. [60236]

Berthoud Area Chamber of Commerce [58330]

Berwick Area Chamber of Commerce [64383]

Ken Berwitz Marketing Research [16851]

Bessemer Area Chamber of Commerce [56816]

Bessemer Venture Partners (Larchmont) [63064]

Bessemer Venture Partners (Menlo Park) [57948]

Bessemer Venture Partners (Wellesley Hills) [61042]

"The Best of 2000: PCs" in *PC Magazine* (January 2, 2001, pp. 145) [48940], [48957]

"Best of 2005" in *Business Week* (December 19, 2005, No. 3964, pp. 58-64, 66, 68, 72) [35821], [39168], [44926]

Best Bagels in Town [2289]

"Best of the best" in *Entrepreneur* (Vol. 31, No. 4, April 2003, pp. 88) [35332], [38607]

"Best of the Best" in *Hispanic Business* (June 2002, pp. 32, 34, 36) [35822], [44927], [48056]

"Best of Both Worlds" in *Entrepreneur* (Vol. 31, No. 9, July 2003, pp. 100) [556], [9695], [35823], [46713]

Best of Both Worlds: Winning Government Funding for Commercial Product Development under the Small Business Innovation Research Program [32271]

"Best Business Books" in *Black Enterprise* (Vol. 36, February 2006, No. 7, pp. 165) [35824], [39169]

"The Best CEO in Silicon Valley" in *Black Enterprise* (Vol. 35, September 2004, No. 2, pp. 108) [4606], [14785], [22182], [22927], [49812], [53217]

Best Coupon Book [874]

The Best Directory of Recruiters, Agencies & Consultants [9552]

BEST Employers Association [52795]

"The best facility managers strive to be one-stop shops" in *Boston Business Journal* (Vol. 22, No. 3, February 22, 2002, pp. S11) [20049]

"The Best" in *Forbes* (May 13, 2002, p. 104) [39170], [44928]

The Best of Golf in Paradise [23657]

Best Holiday Trav-L-Park Association [4222]

Best Home-Based Franchises [38714], [42579]

Best Home Businesses for the 90's [42580]

"Best Ideas" in *Business Week* (December 19, 2005, No. 3964, pp. 74-78, 80-82) [39171], [43995]

The Best Internet Businesses You Can Start [18627], [33415], [37059]

"Best national Internet sites" in *Crain's Detroit Business* (Vol. 18, No. 23, June 10, 2002, pp. E-15) [13842], [25797], [33571]

"The Best Jobs That Nobody Wants" in *Inc.* (September 2005, pp. 30, 32) [33010], [35825]

"The best-laid incentive plans" in *Harvard Business Review* (Vol. 81, No. 1, January 2003, pp. 27) [31645], [34824], [35826], [44929], [46209]

The Best Nonfranchise Business Opportunities: The Smart Entrepreneur's Guide to Dealerships, License Agreements, Distributors, and More [38715]

"Best places to put your money now" in *Black Enterprise* (Vol. 33, No. 6, Jan. 2003, pp. 72) [9843], [14786], [37913]

Best Places to Stay in New England [2428]

Best Practice in Business Advisory, Counseling and Information Services [35827], [39172], [43558]

Best Practice in Development of Entrepreneurship and SMEs in Countries in Transition: The Belarusian Experience [32272], [35828], [43559]

Best Practices for Effective Operations, Production and Plant Management [44725]

Best Practices for Effective Operations, Production and Plant Management (Canada) [44726]

"Best Practices" in *Entrepreneur* (Vol. 32, October 2004, No. 10, pp. 84) [27830], [29122], [33011], [35829], [40968]

Best Practices for the Multi-project Manager [44727]

Best Practices for the Multi-Project Manager (Canada) [44728]

Best Practices in Strategic Outsourcing: It's Not Just for manufacturing Anymore [49675]

"Best Products" *Business Week* (December 19, 2005, No. 3964, pp. 84-88, 90-92) [4925], [39173], [43996]

"Best in Shoe" in *Entrepreneur* (Vol. 31, No. 9, September 2003, pp. 164) [22756], [35830]

Best Southwest Small Business Development Center–SBDC [65022]

"The Best Sunset Provision Ever" in *Inc.* (October 2005, pp. 34) [14787], [32273], [37248], [40182]

"The Best of Technology Q&A: Answers to Readers' Most-Asked Questions" in *Journal of Accountancy* (Vol. 198, December 2004, No. 6) [84], [2874], [23896], [26165], [27089], [53218]

"Best of Times" in *Entrepreneur* (Vol. 31, No. 12, December 2003, pp. 14) [35333]

"Best Travel Web Site: Hotwire.com" in *Entrepreneur* (Vol. 32, No. 4, April 2004, pp. 47) [30295], [33572]

"Best of the Web" in *Inc.* (June 2000, pp. 137) [25753], [25798], [35373], [35831]

"The Best of the Web" in *Inc.* (December 1999, pp. 92) [13843], [42581]

Best's Key Rating Guide [13203]

Best's Review [13534]

Best's Statement File-Life/Health - United States [3460]

Best's Statement File-Property/Casualty - United States [3461], [13583], [15744]

BestWeek Life/Health Edition [13535]

BestWeek Property/Casualty Editions [13536]

BETA (Bulletin of Experimental Treatments for AIDS) [17203], [41164]

"Beth Blake and Sophie Simmons: 34 and 32, Founders of Thread in New York City" in *Entrepreneur* (Vol. 32, July 2004, No. 7, pp. 25) [3176], [37595], [56135]

Bethany Area Chamber of Commerce [61916]

Bethany-Fenwick Area Chamber of Commerce [58645]

Bethel Area Chamber of Commerce [60733]

Bethel Chamber of Commerce [56948], [58512]

Bethel Island Chamber of Commerce [57357]

Bethlehem Area Chamber of Commerce [64384]

Bethlehem Chamber of Commerce [62401], [62823]

"Bethpage-based Cablevision Systems to Complete an Internal Accounting Review" in *Long Island Business News* (March 5, 2004) [85], [86], [4076], [4086], [25793], [26166]

"Bets are off at state racetracks" in *Crain's Detroit Business* (Vol. 18, No. 21, May 27, 2002, pp. 18) [10861], [27831]

"Bette LaPlante & Diane Cuvelier" in *Entrepreneur* (Vol. 31, No. 4, April 2003, pp. 17) [2238], [46210], [56136]

Bettendorf Chamber of Commerce [60099]

Better Bottom Lines [45969], [47831]

Better Business Bureau [57306], [63311], [66035]

Better Business Bureau of Abilene [65084]

Better Business Bureau of Acadiana [60609]

Better Business Bureau of Akron [63591]

Better Business Bureau of Alaska [56944]

Better Business Bureau of Amarillo, Texas [65085]

Better Business Bureau of Arkansas [57126]

Better Business Bureau of Asheville/Western North Carolina [63312]

Better Business Bureau, Augusta [59046]

Better Business Bureau, Austin [65086]

Better Business Bureau, Birmingham [56801]

Better Business Bureau of Brazos Valley [65087]

Better Business Bureau, Buffalo [62806]

Better Business Bureau of Central California [57307]

Better Business Bureau of Central East Texas [65088]

Better Business Bureau of Central and Eastern Iowa [60084]

Better Business Bureau of Central and Eastern Kentucky [60477]

Better Business Bureau of Central Florida [58744]

Better Business Bureau of Central Georgia [59047]

Better Business Bureau of Central Illinois [59411]

Better Business Bureau of Central Indiana [59865]

Better Business Bureau of Central Louisiana [60610]

Better Business Bureau of Central New England [60921]

Better Business Bureau of Central New Jersey [62467]

Better Business Bureau, Central/Northern Arizona [57005]

Better Business Bureau of Central Ohio [63592]

Better Business Bureau of Central Oklahoma [63934]

Better Business Bureau of Central South Carolina and Charleston [64716]

Better Business Bureau of Central and South Central Texas [65089]

Better Business Bureau of Central Virginia [65852]

Better Business Bureau, Chattanooga [64877]

Better Business Bureau of Chicago and Northern Illinois [59412]

Better Business Bureau, Cleveland [63593]

Better Business Bureau of the Coastal Bend [65090]

Better Business Bureau of Coastal Carolina [64717]

Better Business Bureau, Connecticut [58509]

Better Business Bureau of Dayton/Miami Valley [63594]

Better Business Bureau of Delaware [58644]

Better Business Bureau of Denver [58321]

Better Business Bureau of Detroit and Eastern Michigan [61242]

Better Business Bureau of Eastern Idaho and Western Wyoming [59283]

Better Business Bureau of Eastern Missouri and Southern Illinois [61906]

Better Business Bureau of Eastern North Carolina [63313]

Better Business Bureau of Elkhart County [59866]

Better Business Bureau, Encino [57308]

Better Business Bureau of Greater East Tennessee [64878]

Better Business Bureau of Greater Hampton Roads [65853]

Better Business Bureau of Greater Kansas City [61907]

Better Business Bureau of Greater Maryland [60811]

Better Business Bureau of the Greater Sioux Region [60085]

Better Business Bureau of Hawaii [59239]

Better Business Bureau of the Inland Northwest [66036]

Better Business Bureau - Louisville, Southern Indiana and Western Kentucky [60478]

Better Business Bureau of Mahoning Valley [63595]

Better Business Bureau of Metro Atlanta, Athens and Northeast Georgia [59048]

Better Business Bureau of Metro Washington and Eastern Pennsylvania-South Central Division [64371]

Better Business Bureau of Metropolitan Dallas [65091]

Better Business Bureau of Metropolitan Houston [65092]

Better Business Bureau of Metropolitan New York [62807]

Better Business Bureau of Metropolitan Washington [58666]

Better Business Bureau of the Mid-South [64879]

Better Business Bureau of Middle Tennessee [64880]

Better Business Bureau of Mississippi [61770]

Better Business Bureau, Montgomery [56802]

Better Business Bureau of the Mountain States [58322]

Better Business Bureau of New Hampshire [62400]

Better Business Bureau of New Jersey [62468]

Better Business Bureau of New Mexico [62668]

Better Business Bureau of North Alabama [56803]

Better Business Bureau of North Central Texas [65093]

Better Business Bureau of Northeast California [57309]

Better Business Bureau of Northeast Florida [58745]

Better Business Bureau of Northeast Kansas [60281]

Better Business Bureau of Northeast Louisiana [60611]

Better Business Bureau of Northeastern Indiana [59867]

Better Business Bureau of Northern New Jersey [62469]

Better Business Bureau of Northwest Florida [58746]

Better Business Bureau of Northwest Indiana [59868]

Better Business Bureau of Northwest North Carolina [63314]

Better Business Bureau, Northwest Ohio and Southeastern Michigan [63596]

Better Business Bureau of Oregon and Western Washington [64188], [66037]

Better Business Bureau of Port St. Lucie [58747]

Better Business Bureau of Rhode Island [64660]

Better Business Bureau, Rochester [62808]

Better Business Bureau of San Angelo [65094]

Better Business Bureau, San Antonio [65095]

Better Business Bureau of San Diego [57310]

Better Business Bureau of San Mateo County [57311]

Better Business Bureau Serving Eastern Massachusetts, Maine and Vermont [60922]

Better Business Bureau Serving Eastern Washington, North Idaho and Montana [66038]

Better Business Bureau Serving Four Corners and Western Slope [62669]

Better Business Bureau Serving the Heart of Texas [65096]

Better Business Bureau Serving Metropolitan Washington, DC and Eastern Pennsylvania [64372]

Better Business Bureau Serving Minnesota and North Dakota [61549]

Better Business Bureau Serving Ocean County [62470]

Better Business Bureau Serving Upstate South Carolina [64718]

Better Business Bureau, Shreveport [60612]

Better Business Bureau of Silicon Valley [57312]

Better Business Bureau of South Alabama [56804]

Better Business Bureau of South Central Louisiana [60613]

Better Business Bureau of the South Plains [65097]

Better Business Bureau of South Texas [65098]

Better Business Bureau Southeast Atlantic [59049]

Better Business Bureau of Southeast Texas [65099]

Better Business Bureau of Southern Colorado [58323]

Better Business Bureau of Southern Nevada [62339]

Better Business Bureau of Southern Piedmont [63315]

Better Business Bureau of the Southland [57313]

Better Business Bureau of Southwest Georgia [59050]

Better Business Bureau of Southwest Idaho and Eastern Oregon [59284]

Better Business Bureau of Southwest Louisiana [60614]

Better Business Bureau of Southwest Missouri [61908]

Better Business Bureau of Tri-Counties [57314]

Better Business Bureau of Tucson [57006]

Better Business Bureau of Utah [65695]

Better Business Bureau of West Central Ohio [63597]

Better Business Bureau of West Florida [58748]

Better Business Bureau of West Georgia - East Alabama [59051]

Better Business Bureau of Western Michigan [61243]

Better Business Bureau of Western Pennsylvania [64373]

Better Business Bureau of Western Virginia [65854]

Better Business Bureau, Wichita [60282]

Better Business Bureau of Wisconsin [66335]

Better Business Grammar [27698]

Better Business Traveling [30459]

Better Business Writing [27619]
   Crisp Learning [27711]

Better Homes and Gardens Complete Cooking Suite [7825], [22026]

Better Homes and Gardens Complete Guide to Gardening [11502], [16084]

Better Homes Realty, Inc. [20744]

"Better Ingredients for Better Ads" in *Tampa Tribune* (December 3, 2005) [557], [16802], [19624], [46714]

Better Investing [3425]

"Better Luck Next Year?" in *Black Enterprise* (Vol. 32, No. 8, March 2002, pp. 33) [27832], [32274]

"Better Methods" in *Inc.* (September 1, 2003) [558], [46715]

"The Better Mousetrap: Detroit holds its own nationally in gaining new patents" in *Crain's Detroit Business* (Vol.16, Mar. 20, 2000) [27833], [43997]

Better Nutrition Magazine [18446]

"Better Off Red" in *Entrepreneur.com* (Vol. 34, February 2006, No. 2, pp. 74) [559], [46716], [51069], [53603]

Better Productivity Is Not By Chance-Dr. Robert Lorher [35172]

"Better Rivals" in *My Business* (June/July 2004, pp. 47) [30794], [31646]

Better Roads-Annual Winter Maintenance Equipment & Materials Issue [2545]

"Better Safe: Does Your Product Need a Warning Label?" in *Entrepreneur* (Vol. 31, No. 9, July 2003, pp. 76) [13204], [21310], [29123], [32144], [43093], [46211]

"Better Searching with Win 2000 Indexing-A valuable feature enables fast, detailed content searches" in *PC Magazine* (Dec. 5, 2000) [4], [48958]

A Better Solution, Inc. [12417]

Better Vision Institute [25626]

"Better Way for Better Made?" in *Crain's Detroit Business* (Vol. 21, October 3, 2005, No. 43, pp. 3) [11592], [46717], [48700], [55283]

"A Better Way to Innovate" in *Harvard Business Review* (Vol. 81, No. 7, July 2003, pp. 12) [43998], [49813]

"A better way to deliver bad news" in *Harvard Business Review* (Vol. 80, No. 9, Sept. 2002, pp. 114) [34825], [44930]

"Better Ways to Buy: Educate Yourself with a Consumer Handbook" in *Black Enterprise* (Vol. 35, December 2004, No. 5, pp. 160) [50754], [51070]

Betterway Books [63902]

"Betting on Business" in *Hispanic Business* (December 2002, pp. 57) [12521], [22470], [24668], [24893], [25156], [30296]

"Betting the Farm" in *Business 2.0* (Vol. 6, September 2005, No. 8, pp. 108) [26097], [26483], [39824], [41542], [50822], [52046]

"Betting on Growth" in *Hispanic Business* (June 2005, pp. 98) [14788], [27834], [37914]

"Betting on the Net" in *Hispanic Business* (Vol. 22, No. 6, June 2000, pp. 14) [33574], [37107]

Betty Boop International Collectible Club [5880]

"Betty Crocker: can she cook in cyberspace?" in *The New York Times* (December 13, 2000, pp. D13, H13) [33575]

Between the Lines: Understanding Yourself and Others Through Handwriting Analysis [11856]

"Between Right And Right" in *Fortunet* (Vol. 146, No. 9, November 11, 2002, pp. 66) [37389], [44931]

Between Rounds Bakery Sandwich Cafe [2164]

Between Worlds: Interpreters, Guides, and Survivors [25082]

Betwin Investments Inc. [66716]

Beulah Chamber of Commerce [63508]

Bev Capital / Brand Equity Ventures [58583]

Beverage Alcohol Market Report [16239]

Beverage Dynamics [16240]

Beverage Industry-Annual Manual Issue [2331], [16228], [23526]

Beverage Marketing Directory [2362], [16229], [23457]

Beverage Network [2324], [21419]

Beverage World [16241]

Beverage World-Buyers Guide Issue [2332], [16235]

The Beveridge Consulting Group Inc. [51996]

Beveridge & Diamond, P.C.-Library [9426]

Beverly Chamber of Commerce [60931]

Beverly Foundation [18302]

Beverly Hills Chamber of Commerce [57358]

Beverly Hills Chamber of Commerce and Civic Association [57359]

Beverly Hills Public Library–Fine and Performing Arts Division [8491]

Bevill Manufacturing Technology Center [46547]

Bevinco [2378], [16244], [44263]

The Bevmax Wine & Liquor Superstore! [23557]

"Beware Blowhards" in *Forbes* (Vol. 175, February 14, 2005, No. 3, pp. 16) [9844], [14789]

"Beware the Dotted Line" in *Hispanic Business* (December 2002, pp. 55) [29124], [37390]

"Beware of Love at First Byte" in *Success* (Vol. 47, No. 6, November 2000, pp. 42) [13844], [25799], [33576]

"Beware the busy manager" in *Harvard Business Review* (Vol. 80, No. 2, February 2002, pp. 62) [44932], [54937]

Beware the Naked Man Who Offers You His Shirt [48675], [51434], [51942]

"Beware of credit card offers ($s and sense)" in *Black Enterprise* (Vol. 33, No. 3, October 2002, pp. S4) [31514], [33050], [37915], [38668]

"Beware the Venture Catalyst" in *Inc.* (August 2000, pp. 127) [40183], [55506]

Bexley Area Chamber of Commerce [63618]

"Beyond the Banner Ad" in *Business Week* (December 11, 2000, pp. 16) [13845], [33577], [46713]

"Beyond the Big Idea: You've Got a Million-Dollar Idea; Now All You Need is a Strategy To Make It Marketable" in *Entrepreneur* (Vol. 32) [43999], [48701]

"Beyond Big Macs" in *Hispanic Business* (December 2002, pp. 50-52) [21447], [35832], [48057]

"Beyond blueprints: Bring building plans to life" in *Atlanta Business Chronicle* (Vol. 25, No. 21, November 1, 2002, pp. 18C) [1498], [7252]

"Beyond Burgers" in *My Business* (December/January 2004, pp. 49) [2521], [7718], [7769], [19149], [19375], [19625], [21448], [38716]

Beyond Close to the Customer [31918]

Beyond Customer Service [31647]

"Beyond dot.com" in *PC Computing* (April 2000, pp. 112) [13846], [33578]

"Beyond empowerment: Building a company of citizens" in *Harvard Business Review* (Vol. 81, No. 1, January 2003, pp. 48) [35833], [39174], [44933]

Beyond Entrepreneurship: Turning Your Business into an Enduring Great Company [44934], [52821]

"Beyond the exchange: the future of B2B" in *Harvard Business Review* (Vol. 78, No. 6, November-December 2000, pp. 86) [13847], [30511], [33579], [53604]

Beyond Protection [19465]

"Beyond the resume" in *Women In Business* (Vol. 52, No. 4, July 2000, pp. 36) [42179], [44277], [44935], [56137]

"Beyond ROI: Taking Advantage of PR" in *Tradeshow Week* (Vol. 34, November 29, 2004, No. 48, pp. 72) [22471], [24894], [55069]

Beyond Routine [8466]

"Beyond Sales" in *My Business* (June/July 2002, pp. 42) [2239], [33580]

Beyond Start-Up: Management Lessons for Growing Companies [45915], [53051]

"Beyond Their Years: These Entrepreneurs Have It All" in *Entrepreneur* (Vol. 31, No. 11, November 2003, pp. 74) [35834]

Bias-Free Communications [27233]

BIA's Radio Yearbook [20351]

BIA's Television Yearbook [24464]

Bibliographical Center for Research, Inc.–Rocky Mountain Region [14691]

Bibliography of the History of Art [1639]

"A Bicultural Bias" in *Hispanic Business* (December 2003, pp. 24, 26) [48058], [48524]

Bicycle Network [2490]

Bicycle Product Suppliers Association [2491]

Bicycle Stamps Club [5792]

Bicycling [2508]

"Biddeford, Maine, Cord Business Weathers Trials of Domestic Textile Industry" in *Portland Press Herald* (November 18, 2005) [27835], [35835], [46212]

"Biddeford, Maine, Partners Highlight Weirdest eBay 'Auctions on New Web Site" in *Portland Press Herald* (July 8, 2005) [1781], [33581], [49814]

Biddeford-Saco Chamber of Commerce and Industry [60734]

"Bidding war" in *Entrepreneur* (Vol. 30, No. 12, December 2002, pp. 32) [1782], [33582], [52408]

Big Apple Bagels [2165], [21751]

"The Big, Bad Wolf Meets His Match" in *Kiplinger's Personal Finance Magazine* (Vol. 54, No. 12, December 2000, pp. 32) [7253], [16298]

"The Big Bang: How Franchising Became an Economic Powerhouse the World Over" in *Entrepreneur* (Vol. 32, No. 1, January 2004, pp. 86) [32275], [35836], [38717], [53605]

Big Bear Chamber of Commerce [57360]

Big Bend Community College [66237]
    Small Business Development Center [66015]

"Big Biz on Campus: Class Is Now In Session For College Entrepreneurs." in *Entrepreneur* (Vol. 32, December 2004, No. 12, pp. 130) [33012], [35837]

Big Bob's Flooring Outlets of America, Inc. [10532]

"Big Bonus" in *Entrepreneur* (Vol. 30, No. 3, March 2002, pp. 77) [40184], [53606]

The Big Book of Small Business: You Don't Have to Run Your Business by the Seat of Your Pants [35838], [39175]

"Big Box vs. Online" in *Hispanic Business* (March 2003, pp. 25) [31012], [33583], [48959], [51071]

"Big Boxes of the Road" in *Hispanic Business* (March 2002, pp. 5052) [17978], [39176]

Big Boy Family Restaurant [21752]

"Big Boy Plans Big Growth in Franchises; Deals Signed for 23 Diners, One for 60 in Works" in *Crain's Detroit Business* (Vol. 21) [21449], [27836], [38718]

"Big Breaks" in *Inc.* (November 2000, pp. 90) [35334], [38608]

"Big Bucks in Big Mouth" in *Small Business Opportunities* (Vol. 14, No. 1, January 2002, pp. 96, 103) [21393], [46558], [47940], [50509]

"Big Bucks in Boats" in *Small Business Opportunities* (Vol. 17, September 2005, No. 5, pp. 126-127) [16729], [37596]

"Big Bucks in Bojangles" in *Small Business Opportunities* (Vol. 16, No. 2, March 2004, pp. 76-79) [21450], [38609]

"Big Bucks" in *Entrepreneur* (Vol. 28, No. 2, February 2000, pp. 28) [27620], [33584]

"Big Bucks in Little Gym" in *Small Business Opportunities* (Winter 2005) [19376], [38610]

The Big Catfish Connection [2187]

The Big Catfish Connection II [2188]

"The Big Cheese" in *Entrepreneur* (Vol. 32, November 2004, No. 11, pp. 164) [24802], [35839]

"Big Clients Push Construction Boom" in *Hispanic Business* (Vol. 22, No. 6, June 2000, pp. 102) [7254], [27837], [48059]

"The Big Comeback. How do you get a faltering team back on track?" in *Harvard Business Review* (Vol. 80, No. 1, January 2002, pp. 20) [34826], [44936]

The Big Comfy Couch: Are You Ready for School? [5370]

The Big Comfy Couch: Be Nice, Snicklefritz! [5371]

The Big Comfy Couch: Dustbunny Dreams [5372]

"Big Communications Deals Keep On Coming" in *Venture Capital Journal* (Vol. 40, No. 10, October 2000, pp. 10, 12) [41543], [55507]

"Big Deal" in *Entrepreneur* (Vol. 33, January 2005, No. 1, pp. 63) [30795], [49815]

"Big Deal: Landing a Large Account Doesn't Have to Be Out of Your Reach" in *Entrepreneur* [27838], [51565]

"The Big Deals" in *PC Computing* (April 2000, pp. 114) [13848], [33585]

"The Big Disconnect" in *Barron's* (Vol. 82, No. 59, February 24, 2003, pp. T1) [27839], [41544], [44000]

Big Fish Ontario [2189]

"Big Generic Pharma" in *The Economist* (Vol. 376, July 30-August 5, 2005, No. 8437, pp. 58) [14790], [49816], [52047]

"Big Goals, Small Steps" in *Hispanic Business* (January/February 2003, pp. 46, 48) [39988], [48060]

"Big Gulp" in *Forbes* (Vol. 175, January 10, 2005, No. 1, pp. 68) [23458], [27840]

"The Big Guns" in *Entrepreneur* (Vol. 31, No. 11, November 2003, pp. 68) [49817], [55508]

"The Big Guns' Next Target: eBay" in *Business 2.0* (Vol. 7, January/February 2006, No. 1, pp. 21-22) [560], [1783], [18638], [30796], [33586]

"Big Ideas for Small Biz" in *Small Business Opportunities* (Vol. 16, No. 1, January 2004, pp. 92) [27841], [31648], [34827], [35840], [39177]

The Big Instruction Book of Small Business (New Mexico Edition) [52822]

"The Big Issues for Small Concerns: Listen up, candidates" in *Time Inc.* (Vol. 156, No. 3, July 17, 2000, pp. B7) [40185], [54445]

Big Kids Baseball Cards [5929]

Big Lake Chamber of Commerce [56949], [65127]

"Big-League R&D Gets Its Own eBay" in *Fortune* (Vol. 149, No. 9, May 3, 2004, pp. 74) [50823], [52048]

"Big Mac Attack? A Wake-Up Call for OS X Users" in *Black Enterprise* (Vol. 35, September 2004, No. 2, pp. 58) [6590], [6924], [22183]

"Big Mistake: How to Avoid Common Tax Mistakes" in *My Business* (February/March 2003, pp. 46) [86], [23897], [26167], [54446]

Big O Tires [22664], [24594]

"Big Pharma Eyeing Startups" in *Venture Capital Journal* (October 1, 2204) [44001], [52049], [55509]

"Big Pharm's Favorite Gadfly" in *Business Week* (December 19, 2005, No. 3964, pp. 50-51) [40969], [50824], [52050]

"The Big Picture" in *Entrepreneur* (Vol. 31, No. 10, October 2003, pp. 144) [5269], [44002]

"The Big Picture" in *Fast Company* (November 2001, pp. 134) [27842], [37108], [53607]

Big Picture Framing [19830]

"Big Plans on the Drawing Board" in *Boston Business Journal* (Vol. 22, No. 16, May 24, 200) [27843], [43560]

"Big Plans" in *Entrepreneur* (Vol. 30, No. 2, February 2002, p) [27844], [35841], [56138]

"Big Problem for Small Businesses: A Poor Work Ethic" in *Wall Street Journal* (February 8, 2000, pp. A1) [34828]

"Big Profits In Small Packages" in *Black Enterprise* (Vol. 36, November 2005, No. 4, pp. 52) [14791], [37916]

The Big Project: Not So Great Moments in Time Management [55011]

"Big Projects Give Some Life to Sluggish Real Estate Sector" in *Crain's Detroit Business* (Vol. 19, No. 45, November 10, 2003, pp. 15) [20217], [20431], [20803], [21548], [39827], [41545], [46213], [48047]

"Big Religious Meetings Hold Promise of Big Payoffs for Local Economy" in *Crain's Detroit Business* (Vol. 22, February 13, 2006, No. 7) [24895], [32276], [55070]

"Big Retailers Discover Metro Milwaukee" in *Business Journal-Milwaukee* (Vol. 20, No. 46, August 1, 2003, pp. A27) [12182], [12275], [51072]

"Big Returns in the Smallest Packages" in *Black Enterprise* (Vol. 35, August 2004, No. 1, pp. 42) [9845], [14792], [37917]

Big Sky Business Journal [62215]

Big Sky Economic Development Authority [62127]
    Small Business Development Center [62118]

Big Spring Area Chamber of Commerce [65128]

"The Big Squeeze Part II: How VC Firms Are Coping" in *Venture Capital Journal* (Vol. 42, No. 5, May 2002, pp. 27, 29-31) [27845], [55510]

"The Big Squeeze" in *Venture Capital Journal* (Vol. 42, No. 5, May 2002, pp. 20-26) [9846], [14793], [27846], [49818], [55511]

Big Stone Lake Area Chamber of Commerce [61561]

"Big pay for directors of small companies comes to light in a new study" in *Wall Street Journal* (March 9, 2000, pp. A1) [44937]

"Big Success Can Start With a Few Steps" in *Mississippi Business Journal* (Vol. 29, January 2007, No. 4, pp. 5) [2581], [32277], [35842], [39178]

"Big Switch: Walk a Mile In Your Employees' Shoes-You Could Learn a Lot" in *Entrepreneur* (Vol. 32, August 2004, No. 8, pp. 32) [34829], [35843], [44938]

Big and Tall Men's Apparel Needs Show [5742]

"Big Taxes Top Lansing Agenda, Will Granholm Proposal Shift?" in *Crain's Detroit Business* (Vol. 23, January 8, 2007, No. 2, pp. 1) [37918], [40186], [54447]

"Big Tenants Buy Space at Bradenton, Fla. Office Park" in *Bradenton Herald* (January 6, 2005) [20432], [20804]

"Big Time on the Small Screen" in *Black Enterprise* (Vol. 34, No. 5, December 2003, pp. 92) [24381]

Big Town Hero [2166], [8543]

"Big five win little respect from small U.S. companies" in *Wall Street Journal* (February 13, 2002, pp. A12) [87], [53608]

Big Walleye Presentations [2190]

Big Water Catfish [2191]

"A Big Windfall for Small Biz" in *Business Week* (No. 3843, July 28, 2003, pp. 14) [53609], [54448]

"Big Winners Help State Stocks Top S&P; Housing, Finance Companies Boost Returns" in *Crain's Detroit Business* (Vol. 21, Jan. 3, 2005) [7255], [14794], [20433], [37919]

Big Yellow: Yellow Pages on the Web [903], [24314]

Biga & Associates, Inc. [31478]

Jean M. Bigaouette [18478]

"Bigcat Systems leaves little to chance in Internet Marketing" in *Crain's Detroit Business* (Vol. , No. , pp.) [13737], [35335], [46559]

"Bigfooting the Winter" in *Business Week* (January 16, 2006, No. 3967, pp. 91) [23608], [53610]

Bigfork Area Chamber of Commerce [62148]

Bigger Isn't Always Better [27847], [39179]

"Bigger Office, Bigger Breaks" in *Home Office Computing* (Vol. 18, No. 10, October 2000, pp. 19) [42582], [54449]

"Biggest and Best of the Internet? That's Diller's Goal" in *Barron's* (August 25, 2003) [9847], [13849], [14795], [33587]

"The Biggest TV Network You've Never Heard Of" in *Inc.* (Volume 27, June 2005, No. 6, pp. 110-113, 116, 117) [561], [4087], [24382], [46719]

"Bill Proposes Tax for Maine's Bottled Water Industry" in *Portland Press Herald* (October 14, 2005) [3079], [54450]

"Bill Requiring State Copy of Tax Form on Way to Granholm" in *Crain's Detroit Business* (Vol. 19, No. 45, November 10, 2003, pp. 6) [40187], [41245], [54421], [54451]

"Bill Will Allow Consumers to Order Wine Shipped Directly from Maker" in *Altanta Journal-Constitution* (February 2, 2007) [16424], [23459], [40188]

"Bill Woodward: the Hollywood VC with staying power" in *Red Herring* (No. 87, December 18, 2000, pp. 56, 58) [35844], [55512]

"Bill Would Boost Small Businesses" in *Bradenton Herald* (February 13, 2007) [39790], [40970], [43094], [53611], [54452]

"Bill Would Ease Rules on Store Price Tags" in *Crain's Detroit Business* (Vol. 22, December 4, 2006, No. 49, pp. 6) [31013], [40189], [51073]

"Bill Would Let Biz Keep Unclaimed $100 Paychecks" in *Crain's Detroit Business* (Vol. 18, No. 18, May 6, 2002, pp. 24) [26168], [40190]

Billboard Connection [875]

Billboard's International Talent and Touring Directory [23822]

James E. Biller, Aboricultural Consultant [16067], [16140]

Alan D. Biller & Associates Inc. [10335]

Billerica Chamber of Commerce [60932]

Billet Forming [46499]

Billiard Basics [2526]

Billiard and Bowling Institute of America [2518], [3093]

Billiard Congress of America [2519]

Billiard Congress of America Trade Expo [2531]

Billiards for All Age Groups [2527]

Billiards and Bowling Institute of America Annual Conference [2532], [3109], [23675]

Billiards Digest [2525]

"Billing Bad Debt" in *Hispanic Business* (October 2003, pp. 102) [88], [8376], [9848], [14796], [26169], [31515]

Billings Area Chamber of Commerce [62149]

"Billings Bonanza" in *Hispanic Business* (December 2001, pp. 41, 44, 46, 48) [89], [46720]

Billings Community Chamber of Commerce [63949]

Billings Gazette (August 23, 2003); "Investors Sue Montana-Based Coffee Kiosk Businesses Alleging Financial Fraud" in [5767], [11332], [15923]

"A Billion in Baskets" in *Small Business Opportunities* (Vol. 13, No. 6, November 2001, pp. 38, 40) [35845], [37597], [46214], [56139]

"Billion-Dollar Plan in Limbo" in *Pacific Business News* (Vol. 41, No. 20, July 25, 2003, pp. 1) [7256], [29125], [40191]

"Bills would allow government land banks" in *Crain's Detroit Business* (Vol. 18, No. 21, May 27, 2002, pp. 6) [39180], [40192]

"The Bill's In the Mail"Bill Me Later" Payment Option" in *Entrepreneur.com* (Vol. 34, February 2006, No. 2, pp. 36) [31516], [33588], [51566]

"Bills Would Restart SBT Rollback, Add New Tax Credits" in *Crain's Detroit Business* (Vol. 19, No. 40, October 13, 2003, pp. 6) [54422], [54453]

"Billy Mitchell outstanding in industry and community" in *Atlanta Business Chronicle* (Vol. 25, December 6, 2002, No. 26, pp. 3C) [20434], [20805], [35846], [44939]

Biloxi Bay Chamber of Commerce [61774]

Biloxi Chamber of Commerce [61775]

"Biloxi, Miss.-Area Pet Sitting Services Offer Alternative to Kennel Boarding" in *Sun Herald* (November 12, 2004) [19072], [56140]

"Biloxi, Miss., Bed, Breakfast Law Upheld" in *Sun Herald* (January 7, 2004) [2429], [3177], [29126], [40193]

"Biloxi, Miss., Historic Bed and Breakfast Up For Sale" in *Sun Herald* (August 15, 2003) [2430]

Irene Bilyeu [12408], [18377]

BIN Number Directory of All Visa/Mastercard Issuing Banks [8300]

Binders Bulletin [2839]

Binders' Guild [2825]

Binding Industries Association International [2826]

Binghamton University–Small Business Development Center [62745]

The Bingo Bugle Newspaper [18976]

Bio-Integral Resource Center [19052]

"Bio-Layoffs Cool Once-Booking Job Market" in *Boston Business Journal* (Vol. 23, No. 21, June 27, 2003, pp. 1) [32278], [41546], [42180]

"Bio-Pharmaceutical Emphasis" in *San Diego Business Journal* (Vol. 28, January 15, 2007, No. 3, pp. 11) [50825], [52051]

Bio-Solutions [9412], [9493]

"Bio Solutions Acquisition" in *Mississippi Business Journal* (Vol. 29, January 2007, No. 2, pp. 9) [26484], [48702], [49819]

Bio-Technical Resources [3156], [3647], [31284], [52338]

Bioadvance [64544]

"Biocentric Security" in *PC Magazine* (February 6, 2001, pp. 26) [22184], [41547]

BioChem Technology Inc. [3648], [31285], [52339]

Biochemistry and Cell Biology (Biochimie et Biologie Cellulaire) [52239]

"BioGift Goes After Cancer Tissue Niche" in *Business Journal-Portland* (Vol. 20, No. 25, August 22, 2003, pp. 1) [49502], [50826], [52052], [53019]

"Biographies" in *Venture Capital Journal* (February 1, 2006) [50827], [52053], [55513]

Biography and Genealogy Master Index [10927], [10991]

"Bioigen Unchained" in *Harvard Business Review* (Vol. 78, No. 3, May 2000, pp. 28) [33589], [46215]

Biological Control [19029]

Biologix [1076], [37369]

Biomedical Equipment: Use, Maintenance and Management [17095]

Biomedical Instrumentation & Technology [17115]

Biomedical Management Resources [30062], [45970], [50299], [53070]

"Biomedical, Marine Research Funds Could Grow If Voters Approve Seed Money" in *Portland Press Herald* (November 2, 2005) [39791], [41548], [50828], [52054]

Biomedical Products [17116], [52240]

Biomedical Safety & Standards [17117]

"Biometric conversion" in *Red Herring* (January 2003, pp. 63) [22185], [41549], [52055]

Bionexus Ventures [65594]

BioPed Footcare Centres [17140]

Biopolymers [52241]

BioQUEST Library IV [9413]

Bioremediation of Hazardous Wastes, Wastewater, and Municipal Waste [11941]

Biosafety in Microbiological and Biomedical Laboratories [17183]

BioScan: The Worldwide Biotech Industry Reporting Service [52056]

BioSciCon Inc. [3649], [3957], [16573], [31286], [41324]

"Biotech Balance: Mutual Fund Diversification Lets Investors Temper Biotech's Risk" in *Black Enterprise* (Vol. 34, No. 4, Nov. 2003) [9849], [14797], [37920], [41550], [50829]

"Biotech Believer" in *Fortune* (Vol. 151, February 21, 2005, No. 4, pp. 128) [14798], [37921], [41551]

"Biotech" in *Business Week* (January 23, 2006, No. 3968, pp. 38, 40) [50830], [52057]

"Biotech Crops Turn into Growing Field" in *Altanta Journal-Constitution* (January 20, 2007) [26485], [27848]

"Biotech sector seeks advanced degrees" in *Atlanta Business Chronicle* (Vol. 24, No. 11, August 17, 2001, pp. 4B) [33013], [37109]

"Biotech: Frankenforests cropping up" in *Red Herring* (No. 105, October 1, 2001, pp. 25-26) [16299], [50831]

"Biotech Hotbeds: Where Are They, and How Do You Get One?" in *Venture Capital Journal* (October 1, 2004) [41552], [52058], [55514]

"Biotech II Alan Frazier" in *Venture Capital Journal* (January 1, 2005) [41553], [52059], [55515]

"Biotech Takes Heart in Potential New Drug" in *Pacific Business News* (Vol. 41, No. 23, August 15, 2003, pp. 1) [8775], [41554], [50832], [52060]

BioTechniques [52242]

Biotechnology Advances [52243]

Biotechnology & Bioengineering [52244]

Bioventures Investors [61043]

Birch Bay Chamber of Commerce [66050]

Birch Run Area Chamber of Commerce [61259]

Birchfield Jacobs Foodsystems Inc. [3650], [12082], [31287]

Birchmere Ventures [64545]

"Bird Biz Takes Off" in *Small Business Opportunities* (Vol. 12, No. 2, March 2000, pp. 64, 66) [35336], [37556], [51021]

Bird City Community Club [60297]

"Bird Dog" in *Barron's* (September 8, 2003, pp. 9) [9850], [14799], [37391], [37922], [40194]

Birders Nature Store [18287], [19176]

Birenbaum & Associates [54360]

Birmingham-Bloomfield Chamber of Commerce [61260]

Birmingham Botanical Gardens–Library [11509], [16089]

Birmingham Business Journal (Vol. 20, No. 40, October 3, 2003, pp. 1); "Access Now...Or Lawsuit Later" in [29088], [31999]

Birmingham Business Journal (Vol. 20, No. 33, August 15, 2003, pp. 6); "Allsbrook Predicts Economic Pickup in Months Ahead" in [9808], [27764], [32242]

Birmingham Business Journal (Vol. 20, No. 28, July 11, 2003, pp. 1); "Bluff Park Gym Has a Knockout Program" in [19377]

Birmingham Business Journal (Vol. 20, No. 33, August 15, 2003, pp. 13); "Delicate Deliveries" in [600], [10559], [45053], [46876]

Birmingham Business Journal (Vol. 20, No. 39, September 26, 2003, pp. 1); "Emageon Vies With Big Guns" in [4648], [22978], [41004], [53270]

Birmingham Business Journal (Vol. 20, No. 20, July 4, 2003, pp. 15); "Fill-In Physicians" in [9204], [9559], [24523], [41009]

Birmingham Business Journal (Vol. 20, No. 31, August 1, 2003, pp. 15); "Grand Slam" in [1442], [3233], [7349], [20517], [28224]

Birmingham Business Journal (Vol. 20, October 3, 2003) "He's Boss of the Blues; Phillip Pope Stays a Fiscally Prudent Course" in [13321], [41029], [43214], [45234]

Birmingham Business Journal (Vol. 20, No. 29, July 18, 2003, pp. 1); "Homewood Gets a $7M Hilton" in [12563], [28292]

Birmingham Business Journal (Vol. 17, No. 22, June 2, 2000, pp. 10); "IRS to aid businesses, but tax code is a problem" in [40478], [54616]

Birmingham Business Journal (Vol. 20, No. 29, July 18, 2003, pp. 11); "Keeping Art Alive" in [1687], [20916]

Birmingham Business Journal (Vol. 20, No. 37, September 12, 2003, pp. 1); "Kenworth Dealership in Works" in [18073], [25395]

Birmingham Business Journal (Vol. 20, No. 28, July 11, 2003, pp. 15); "Local Truckers Cheer an Upsurge in Business" in [25397], [28427]

Birmingham Business Journal (Vol. 17, No. 36, September 8, 2000, pp. 14); "Many firms don't know they can deduct premiums" in [43270]

Birmingham Business Journal (Vol. 20, No. 28, July 11, 2003, pp. 11); "On A Shoestring" in [1327], [1415], [5912], [15856]

Birmingham Business Journal (Vol. 20, No. 28, July 11, 2003, pp. 11); "Patio Appeal" in [12204], [12307]

Birmingham Business Journal (Vol. 20, No. 27, July 4, 2003, pp. 1); "Rehashing Fashion: Consignment Shops Do It All" in [5630], [7153], [9605]

Birmingham Business Journal (Vol. 20, No. 35, August 29, 2003, pp. 1); "Renewed Biotech Interest Boosts BioCryst" in [8800], [15409], [38315], [41942], [50954], [52185]

Birmingham Business Journal (Vol. 20, No. 31, August 1, 2003, pp. 1); "Summerford, Dixon Odom Cite Sarbanes in Breakup" in [271], [2966], [24048], [26376], [40743]

Birmingham Business Journal (Vol. 20, No. 31, August 1, 2003, pp. 11); "The Business of Fitness" in [19383], [27899], [38729]

Birmingham Business Journal (Vol. 20, No. 30, July 25, 2003, pp. 11); "The Time Machine" in [5917], [36862]

Birmingham Business Journal (Vol. 20, No. 20, July 4, 2003, pp. 1); "VitalMed Absorbs Doctors' Paperwork" in [16537], [41131]

Birmingham Business Resource Center [56902]

Birmingham Home and Garden Show [11485]

Birmingham Regional Chamber of Commerce [56817]

"The birth of a web site" in *Women in Business* (Vol. 54, No. 2, March-April 2002, pp. 26) [13850], [25800], [56141]

The Birthday Party Business [18751]

Birthflowers.com [16073]

Bisbee Chamber of Commerce and Visitor Center [57016]

Bishop Area Chamber of Commerce and Visitors Bureau [57361]

Bishop Chamber of Commerce [65129]

Bismarck - Mandan Chamber of Commerce [63509]

Bismarck Regional Small Business Development Center [63490]

"The Bite of the ASP" in *Forbes* (November 27, 2000, pp. 296) [13851], [33590]

Bitner Goodman [47832], [50489]

Bits, Bytes, & Bots Computer Adventures [6369]

"Bits and Bytes" in *Kansas City Star* (February 1, 2005) [4926], [30297], [52509]

Bitter Root Valley Chamber of Commerce [62150]

Bixby Chamber of Commerce [63950]

Bixler Consulting Group [12923]

"Biz By the Book" in *Small Business Opportunities* (Vol. 17, September 2005, No. 5, pp. 58, 60) [3010], [46560], [49820], [56142]

"Biz assembles new approach to flexible design" in *Crain's Detroit Business* (Vol. 18, No. 19, May 13, 2002, pp. 15) [18534], [18589]

Biz Kids Guide to Success: Money-Making Ideas for Young Entrepreneurs [56736]

"Biz Leaders Want Quick Action on SBT replacement" in *Crain's Detroit Business* (Vol. 22, November 13, 2006, No. 46, pp. 1) [29801], [54454]

"Biz Paved With Gold" in *Small Business Opportunities* (Vol. 14, No. 1, January 2002, pp. 50-51, 54) [7188], [38611]

"Biz Plan Competition" in *Black Enterprise* (Vol. 34, No. 2, September 2003, pp. 12) [29802], [35847]

"Biz has an interest in keeping Prop A" in *Crain's Detroit Business* (Vol. 18, No. 18, May 6, 2002, pp. 8) [40195], [54455]

"Biz Schools Find 'Flat is the New Up' for MBA Enrollment" in *Crain's Detroit Business* (Vol. 21, October 17, 2005, No. 43, pp. 17) [30797], [33014]

"Biz Travelers Adapting To Ever-Changing Security Measures" in *Mississippi Business Journal* (Vol. 28, September 2006, No. 36, pp. 12) [22186], [40196]

BizBest Media Corp. [58253]

"Bizdom U. Set to Teach Next Gen of Startups" in *Crain's Detroit Business* (Vol. 22, November 13, 2006, No. 46, pp. 1) [29710], [32876], [35337]

Bizsupplies [3849], [4005]

"BizWare" in *Hispanic Business* (Vol. 23, No. 11, November 2001, pp. 70) [4607], [13852], [22928], [25801], [35338], [48061], [53219]

BKR International [23]

Black American Income Tax Service [24121]

Black Belt Magazine [16916]

"Black Board Directors Form Network" in *Black Enterprise* (Vol. 35, December 2004, No. 5, pp. 38) [35848], [41555], [44940], [48062]

Black Book, Inc. [2107], [18211]

Black Book Photography [5970]

Black Business Association of Los Angeles [57362]

Black Chamber of Commerce of Greater Kansas City [61917]

Black Chamber of Commerce of Orange County [57363]

Black Data Processing Associates [6453]

Black Diamond Golf [52617]

"Black Diamonds in Our Backyard" in *Crain's Detroit Business* (Vol. 22, January 2, 2006, No. 1, pp. 11) [12522], [22855]

"Black Dotcom Shake-Up" in *Black Enterprise* (Vol. 31, No. 5, December 2000, pp. 134) [25754], [47941], [55362]

Black Enterprise (Vol. 36, December 2005, No. 5, pp.); "" in [8301]

Black Enterprise (Vol. 35, October 2004, No. 3, pp. 36); "7(a) Program Restored" in [39784], [44457]

Black Enterprise (Vol. 35, September 2004, No. 2, pp. 77); "10 Hottest Deals in Franchising" in [38704], [47937]

Black Enterprise (Vol. 36, February 2006, No. 7, pp. 124); "50 Most Powerful Black Women in Business" in [44863], [56109]

Black Enterprise (Vol. 37, October 2006, No. 3, pp. 136); "75 Most Powerful Blacks on Wall Street" in [9800], [14715], [35748], [55477]

Black Enterprise (Vol. 33, No. 3, October 2002, pp. 154); "A family affair" in [29180], [29449], [29871], [30539], [36141], [37374], [37641], [38980], [50906], [54545]

Black Enterprise (Vol. 33, No. 6, January 2003, pp. 38); "A less taxing bite on small business" in [185], [23983], [54644]

Black Enterprise (Vol. 34, No. 5, December 2003); "A Car is Born: Wydens Gabriel Transforms Ordinary Model Cars into Masterpieces" in [8152], [8712], [56739], [57920]

Black Enterprise (Vol. 35, January 2005, No. 6, pp. 50); "A Close Call: Cell Phone Offers Good Mix of Price and Performance" in [4954], [48989]

Black Enterprise (Vol. 34, No. 4, Nov. 2003, pp. 65); "A Comfortable Retirement" in [14875], [37975]

Black Enterprise (Vol. 35, November 2004, No. 4, pp. 141); "A Cure for Health Concerns" in [13253], [40992], [43143]

Black Enterprise (Vol. 35, August 2004, No. 1, pp. 40); "A Focus on Firm Profits" in [9964], [15002], [28168]

Black Enterprise (Vol. 37, October 2006, No. 3, pp. 89); "A Gambling Man: Career Transitions that Put a Vegas Hotshot on Top" in [12556], [36195], [45171], [48861]

Black Enterprise (Vol. 34, No. 7, February 2004, pp. 40); "A Happy Return on Equities" in [9993], [15068], [38110]

Black Enterprise (Vol. 34, No. 2, September 2003); "A High-Flying Time: Ronald Mays Zips Through the Air with Jets of His Own" in [950], [36284], [52543]

Black Enterprise (Vol. 34, No. 6, January 2004); "A Home is the Foundation for Wealth" in [20529], [20894], [38120]

Black Enterprise (Vol. 35, December 2004, No. 5, pp. 48); "A Less Taxing Way to Invest" in [15214], [38188], [54645]

Black Enterprise (Vol. 34, No. 2, September 2003, pp. S2); "A Lesson Learned" in [36438], [56753]

Black Enterprise (Vol. 34, July 2004, No. 12, pp. 140); "A Market of One" in [2638], [18816]

Black Enterprise (Vol. 37, November 2006, No. 4, pp. 16); "A New Breed of Entrepreneurs" in [36534], [42356], [48324], [48586]

Black Enterprise (Vol. 34, December 2003); "A New Deal for SBK-Brooks: B.E. Investment Bank Completes $233 Million Bond Offering" in [10101], [10892], [15294], [15824]

Black Enterprise (Vol. 33, No. 7, Feb. 2003, pp. 19); "A New Game for Johnson: BET Founder Looking to Acquire Baseball Franchise" in [36540], [48332]

Black Enterprise (Vol. 34, No. 2, September 2003, pp. 38); "A Rally Deferred" in [10148], [15392], [38301]

Black Enterprise (Vol. 34, No. 5, December 2003, pp. 66); "A Rap for Manners: Angelo Ellerbee Refines the Rough on Urban Artist" in [12908], [13375], [20154], [21424], [48224], [50466], [50660]

Black Enterprise (Vol. 36, November 2005, No. 4, pp. 161); "A Reason for Ranting" in [27483], [36675]

Black Enterprise (Vol. 34, No. 2, September 2003, pp. 62); "A Reason to Smile" in [36676], [41085], [56380]

Black Enterprise (Vol. 36, February 2006, No. 7, pp. 165); "A Recipe for Success" in [21594], [54243]

Black Enterprise (Vol. 32, No. 10, May 2002, pp. 107); "A tough review" in [35122], [45759]

Black Enterprise (Vol. 32, No. 9, April 2002); "A matter of safety" in [35560], [43965], [48688]

Black Enterprise (Vol. 34, No. 3, October 2003, pp. 142); "A San Francisco Chronicle: George Dewey's View of the Bay" in [30172], [52722]

Black Enterprise (Vol. 37, February 2007, No. 7, pp. 52); "A Self-Serving Opportunity" in [25568]

Black Enterprise (Vol. 34, No. 6, January 2004, pp. 91); "A Soldier's Story" in [2729], [2745], [40098], [41544]

Black Enterprise (Vol. 35, September 2004, No. 2, pp. 37); "A Step Toward Independence" in [15473], [21015]

Black Enterprise (Vol. 37, January 2007, No. 6, pp. 6); "A Taxing Proposition" in [14511], [25981], [54830]

Black Enterprise (Vol. 35, September 2004, No. 2, pp. 95); "A Time to Sell?" in [10209], [15527], [38414]

Black Enterprise (Vol. 34, No. 4, November 2003); "A Time to Shine: Awards Celebration Spotlights Today's Successful Entrepreneurs" in [36863], [37397], [45743], [47544], [48440], [49166]

Black Enterprise (Vol. 33, No. 6, January 2003, pp. 43); "A clearer view" in [6608], [48988]

Black Enterprise (Vol. 34, July 2004, No. 12, pp. 65); "About My Raise...How To Ask For and Get More Money" in [27075], [44871]

Black Enterprise (Vol. 34, No. 4, November 2003, pp. 40); "About Penny Stocks" in [9803], [14719], [33509], [37864]

Black Enterprise (Vol. 33, No. 6, January 2003, pp. 42); "Adapt or die: surviving the government's digital push" in [13801], [33514], [48026], [48939], [53577]

Black Enterprise (Vol. 34, No. 2, September 2003, pp. S9); "Aerobatic Ace: Young Pilot Flies Plane That's Smaller Than a Car" in [540], [52505], [56734]

Black Enterprise (Vol. 34, No. 2, September 2003, pp. 23); "Affirmative Action Upheld" in [29091], [32002], [32993]

Black Enterprise (Vol. 36, February 2006, No. 7, pp. 74); "Age On Your Side" in [29092], [40149], [42165]

Black Enterprise (Vol. 35, September 2004, No. 2, pp. 192); "Ah! Spa: An Eastern European Approach to Wellness" in [12515], [19371]

Black Enterprise (Vol. 31, No. 5, December 2000, pp. 172); "All-inclusive trips" in [24661]

Black Enterprise (Vol. 35, December 2004, No. 5, pp. 155); "Alone in Your Time Zone: Are You Plagued by Chronic Lateness?" in [35764], [54934]

Black Enterprise (Vol. 34, No. 7, February 2004, pp. 64); "American Urban Radio Networks" in [20090], [20300], [46675]

Black Enterprise (Vol. 34, No. 4, November 2003, pp. 120); "America's Top Black Lawyers" in [29096]

Black Enterprise (Vol. 35, January 2005, No. 6); "An African American in Paris: Ricki Stevenson's Entree to the City of Light" in [30282], [35756], [43538], [52644]

Black Enterprise (Vol. 36, November 2005, No. 4, pp. 74); "An Attractive Site" in [544], [25788], [33532], [46677], [48033]

Black Enterprise (Vol. 34, No. 6, January 2004, pp. 41); "Analyze This" in [41512], [44884], [53203]

Black Enterprise (Vol. 34, No. 6); "Analyze This: Charles Phillips Makes Bold Career Move to Oracle as Executive Vice President" in [41513], [44885], [53204]

Black Enterprise (Vol. 35, November 2004, No. 4, pp. 112); "Anatomy of a Startup" in [4593], [22910], [41442], [53206]

Black Enterprise (Vol. 32, No. 8, March 2002, pp. 52); "Answering the call: security firm is expanding as demand increases" in [22169], [27774], [48034]

Black Enterprise (Vol. 36, November 2005, No. 4, pp. 37); "Are Race-Specific Drugs Unethical?" in [37387], [40962]

Black Enterprise (Vol. 35, January 2005, No. 6, pp. 104); "Around Town: Paris" in [2329], [12516], [21441], [30289]

Black Enterprise (Vol. 35, December 2004, No. 5, pp. 62); "Art Noir" in [1599], [1681], [48037]

Black Enterprise (Vol. 35, October 2004, No. 3, pp. 46); "Asia Rising" in [14747], [27791], [37878], [43548], [46200], [49676]

Black Enterprise (Vol. 34, No. 5, December 2003, pp. 6); "Association Listing" in [50549]

Black Enterprise (Vol. 35, November 2004, No. 4, pp. 32); "Atlanta Life to Manage MetLife Assets" in [13192], [14755], [43082], [48041], [49800]

Black Enterprise (Vol. 37, November 2006, No. 4, pp. 66); "Attract More Online Customers: Make Your Website Work Harder for You" in [13830], [18637], [25794], [33550], [53591]

Black Enterprise (Vol. 32, No. 8, March 2002, pp. 49); "Avoid litigation" in [29108], [35795], [52816]

Black Enterprise (Vol. 34, July 2004); "Avoiding a Cash Flow Crunch: Accurate Projections Are Key To Your Business' Survival" in [80], [2870], [26162], [27084], [37886]

Black Enterprise (Vol. 34, September 2003); "Avoiding a Communication Breakdown: Keeping Employees Informed Benefits Business" in [14760], [27300], [34819], [44909]

Black Enterprise (Vol. 37, January 2007, No. 6, pp. 46); "Avoiding Invention Scams" in [30204], [43993], [46696], [48698], [50816], [52368]

Black Enterprise (Vol. 34, No. 5, December 2003, pp. 85); "Avoiding Year-End Tax Traps" in [37887], [54437]

Black Enterprise (Vol. 34, July 2004, No. 12, pp. 26); "B-School Gets Stamp of Approval" in [33002], [44910], [48044]

Black Enterprise (Vol. 35, October 2004, No. 3, pp. 72); "Back It Up" in [6236], [6588], [13834], [48953]

Black Enterprise (Vol. 37, January 2007, No. 6, pp. 112); "Back Talk with Chris Gardner" in [2678], [14763], [35800], [37890], [48049]

Black Enterprise (Vol. 35, January 2005, No. 6, pp. 112); "Back Talk: With Billionaire & BET CEO Robert L. Johnson" in [24379], [35801], [48050]

Black Enterprise (Vol. 34, No. 7, February 2004, pp. 54); "Back on the Tech Block" in [13739], [13835], [33560]

Black Enterprise (Vol. 34, No. 6, January 2004); "Back to Technology" in [9823], [14764], [32258], [37891], [41532]

Black Enterprise (Vol. 34, January 2004); "Back to Technology: Patrick Lyons of NCM Capital Management Says a Tech Binge is Likely" in [9824], [14765], [32259], [37892], [41533]

Black Enterprise (Vol. 31, No. 5, December 2000, pp. 172); "Bad credit and employment" in [29109], [40166], [42176], [42830]

Black Enterprise (Vol. 36, November 2005, No. 4, pp. 88); "Balancing Act" in [14766], [22725], [37591], [37893]

Black Enterprise (Vol. 34, No. 6, January 2004, pp. 51); "Bank on Real Estate" in [17166], [17360], [20430], [20802], [21563], [21713]

Black Enterprise (Vol. 35, January 2005, No. 6, pp. 34); "Bank Stock Binge" in [9828], [14769], [32261], [37898], [49805]

Black Enterprise (Vol. 35, November 2004, No. 4, pp. 32); "Bartech and Nucon Win Staffing Deals" in [9194], [24518], [30788]

Black Enterprise (Vol. 33, No. 3, October 2002, pp. 31); "BBoC and FSB to merge: more deals within banking community are possible" in [14779], [15727], [49808], [50902]

Black Enterprise (Vol. 33, No. 6, January 2003, pp. 10); "B.E. teams up with CNNfn" in [32268], [48052], [49809]

Black Enterprise (Vol. 34, No. 5, December 2003, pp. 139); "B.E. Successpert Speaks" in [34677], [35811], [44922], [45501]

Black Enterprise (Vol. 33, No. 3, October 2002, pp. 88); "B.E. Wall St. All-Stars" in [9839], [10690], [14780], [15728], [37912], [38665], [48053], [49954]

Black Enterprise (Vol. 34, No. 4, November 2003, pp. 171); "Bead It! For Johnna Snell, Her Hobby's a Charm" in [7999], [15834], [56130]

Black Enterprise (Vol. 34, No. 5, December 2003, pp. 152); "Beantown Flavor: Columnist Adrian Walker Gives Us a Taste of Boston" in [24667], [25154], [26797], [30292], [30970]

Black Enterprise (Vol. 34, No. 5, December 2003); "Beating the Dream-Busters: Don't Let Loved Ones Keep You From Living Your Dream" in [30508], [31490], [34678], [35812]

Black Enterprise (Vol. 32, No. 6, January 2002, pp. 35); "Beating the odds: remembering the basics of business can help" in [29708], [30474], [35329], [47939], [52769]

Black Enterprise (Vol. 35, October 2004, No. 3, pp. 200); "Before You Sign on the Dotted Line..." in [29121], [40177]

Black Enterprise (Vol. 35, October 2004, No. 3, pp. 72); "Being Big Brother: Shh...Spy Tool Helps You Snoop Undetected" in [4604], [22181], [22925], [53216]

Black Enterprise (Vol. 36, February 2006, No. 7, pp. 165); "Best Business Books" in [35824], [39169]

Black Enterprise (Vol. 33, No. 6, Jan. 2003, pp. 72); "Best places to put your money now" in [9843], [14786], [37913]

Black Enterprise (Vol. 32, No. 8, March 2002, pp. 33); "Better Luck Next Year?" in [27832], [32274]

Black Enterprise (Vol. 35, December 2004, No. 5, pp. 160); "Better Ways to Buy: Educate Yourself with a Consumer Handbook" in [50754], [51070]

Black Enterprise (Vol. 33, No. 3, October 2002, pp. S4); "Beware of credit card offers ($s and sense)" in [31514], [33050], [37915], [38668]

Black Enterprise (Vol. 35, September 2004, No. 2, pp. 58); "Big Mac Attack? A Wake-Up Call for OS X Users" in [6590], [6924], [22183]

Black Enterprise (Vol. 36, November 2005, No. 4, pp. 52); "Big Profits In Small Packages" in [14791], [37916]

Black Enterprise (Vol. 35, August 2004, No. 1, pp. 42); "Big Returns in the Smallest Packages" in [9845], [14792], [37917]

Black Enterprise (Vol. 34, No. 5, December 2003, pp. 92); "Big Time on the Small Screen" in [24381]

Black Enterprise (Vol. 34, No. 4, Nov. 2003); "Biotech Balance: Mutual Fund Diversification Lets Investors Temper Biotech's Risk" in [9849], [14797], [37920], [41550], [50829]

Black Enterprise (Vol. 34, No. 2, September 2003, pp. 12); "Biz Plan Competition" in [29802], [35847]

Black Enterprise (Vol. 35, December 2004, No. 5, pp. 38); "Black Board Directors Form Network" in [35848], [41555], [44940], [48062]

Black Enterprise (Vol. 31, No. 5, December 2000, pp. 134); "Black Dotcom Shake-Up" in [25754], [47941], [55362]

Black Enterprise (Vol. 31, No. 5, December 2000, pp. 12); "Black Enterprise.com" in [9696], [33591], [48063]

Black Enterprise (Vol. 31, No. 5, December 2000, pp. 153); "Black Enterprise's 2000 Business Entertaining Guide" in [27304], [48064], [53612]

Black Enterprise (Vol. 35, December 2004, No. 5, pp. 36); "Black Farmers Sue USDA for $20.5 Billion" in [26486], [29127], [48065]

Black Enterprise (Vol. 35, October 2004, No. 3, pp. 40); "Black Investment Trends: Report Ranks What Buyers Care Most About" in [14801], [37924]

Black Enterprise (Vol. 34, No. 2, September 2003, pp. S4); "Blackgirl Rules!" in [18852], [56143], [56737]

Black Enterprise (Vol. 35, October 2004, No. 3, pp. 145); "Blazing New Trails" in [27849], [35850], [48068]

Black Enterprise (Vol. 34, No. 3, October 2003); "Blind Ambition: Robert Jones Lost His Eyesight, But His Vision Is Crystal Clear" in [17587], [17731], [22472], [35852]

Black Enterprise (Vol. 36, November 2005, No. 4, pp. 148); "Blown Away By Katrina" in [7258], [32280], [48069]

Black Enterprise (Vol. 33, No. 6, Jan. 2003, pp. 45); "Board certified" in [35855], [44944]

Black Enterprise (Vol. 36, February 2006, No. 7, pp. 40); "Bob Johnson Makes Hotel History" in [12524], [20435], [20806], [48070]

Black Enterprise (Vol. 31, No. 5, December 2000, pp. 43); "Bond Bonus" in [37925]

Black Enterprise (Vol. 32, No. 9, April 2002, pp. 43); "Boosting moral" in [34832], [44950]

Black Enterprise (Vol. 35, January 2005, No. 6); "Borrowing From Dad: Financing From Relatives and Friends Has Risks and Rewards" in [35340], [44389]

Black Enterprise (Vol. 34, No. 5, December 2003, pp. 153); "Boston Around Town" in [24670], [25158], [30300]

Black Enterprise (Vol. 35, December 2004, No. 5, pp. 78); "Brand Me: Marketing Techniques to Make You Stand Out" in [46737], [50559]

Black Enterprise (Vol. 34, July 2004, No. 12, pp. 58); "Brave New Tech World" in [6594], [41565]

Black Enterprise (Vol. 35, January 2005, No. 6, pp. 28); "Bridgewater Interiors Closes $400 Million Deal" in [17982], [48073], [49823]

Black Enterprise (Vol. 34, No. 5, December 2003, pp. 66); "Bridging the Gap" in [9753], [9855], [37928], [39330], [40389], [42183]

Black Enterprise (Vol. 35, November 2004, No. 4, pp. 68); "Broadband Deluxe: High-Speed Firms Take the Stress Out of Networking" in [4089], [13859], [33611], [41570]

Black Enterprise (Vol. 34, No. 5, December 2003, pp. 159); "Broadcast News: B.E. Breaks Ground With New TV Program" in [18653], [18855], [24384], [34734], [35876], [45798], [48074]

Black Enterprise (Vol. 34, No. 3, October 2003, pp. 144); "Buenas Vistas and Other Good Things: It's the Splendor of Las Casitas" in [11783], [12526], [24672], [25162]

Black Enterprise (Vol. 35, October 2004, No. 3, pp. 136); "Build a Better Business" in [4934], [27882], [31651], [41573], [48966], [49488], [52825]

Black Enterprise (Vol. 36, November 2005, No. 4, pp. 47); "Build a Relationship With Your Lender" in [9858], [17362], [20444]

Black Enterprise (Vol. 35, January 2005, No. 6, pp. 41); "Building Character" in [22474], [33022], [35879], [44961]

Black Enterprise (Vol. 33, No. 6, Jan. 2003, pp. 39); "Building on experience" in [7190], [35348], [44391], [48873]

Black Enterprise (Vol. 32, No. 7, February 2002, pp.); "Building for the future" in [7191], [35349], [47945]

Black Enterprise (Vol. 36, December 2005, No. 5, pp. 136); "Building a Good Rep" in [17363], [35880], [44962]

Black Enterprise (Vol. 32, No. 9, April 2002, pp. 70); "Building on success" in [1602], [19228], [19294], [33418], [37557], [37930], [47946]

Black Enterprise (Vol. 34, No. 5, December 2003, pp. 50); "Built For Speed: Baba Garba Looks to Take His Broadband Business Abroad" in [3505], [30279], [31117], [34741], [35884], [41576], [43100], [43566], [45243]

Black Enterprise (Vol. 32, No. 8, March 2002, pp. 28); "Bullish on minority business: MBDA director sees better days ahead" in [27889], [48077]

Black Enterprise (Vol. 34, No. 6, January 2004, pp. 51); "Burger King Corp" in [21165], [21454], [38727]

Black Enterprise (Vol. 31, No. 5, December 2000, pp. 165); "Burned down to the wick" in [35888]

Black Enterprise (Vol. 35, August 2004, No. 1, pp. 23); "Burrell CEO Steps Down" in [569], [29133], [35889], [48078]

Black Enterprise (Vol. 35, August 2004, No. 1); "Business Dining Etiquette: Beat Your Competition With Winning Table Manners" in [12873], [20108], [27314], [30807]

Black Enterprise (Vol. 35, Jan. 2005, No. 6); "Business Integrator Entrepreneur Marries Technology and Advertising to Grow Business" in [571], [5972], [6598], [24674], [25166], [27901], [41578], [46763], [48661], [48969]

Black Enterprise (Vol. 35, August 2004, No. 1, pp. 57); "Business On Her Own Terms" in **[16502]**, **[22477]**, **[31120]**, **[39969]**, **[40975]**, **[41445]**, **[56032]**

Black Enterprise (Vol. 35, September 2004, No. 2, pp. 46); "Business and Pleasure" in **[5527]**, **[22757]**, **[34840]**

Black Enterprise (Vol. 33, No. 6, January 2003, pp. 10; "Business plan pro" in **[25811]**, **[29717]**, **[35353]**, **[39033]**

Black Enterprise (Vol. 34, July 2004, No. 12, pp. 116); "Buy, Sell & Rent" in **[20817]**, **[21314]**, **[29138]**, **[40225]**

Black Enterprise (Vol. 31, No. 5, December 2000, pp. 117); "Buying Stocks in a Slowing Economy" in **[37936]**

Black Enterprise (Vol. 37, January 2007, No. 6., pp. 101); "By Land, Air, and Sea: New Passport Rules in Effect" in **[30304]**, **[40227]**

Black Enterprise (Vol. 34, No. 6, January 2004, pp. 36); "Calculating Profits" in **[97]**, **[25807]**, **[26180]**, **[37939]**

Black Enterprise (Vol. 35, January 2005, No. 6, pp. 38); "Calculating Savings Bonds Values" in **[9861]**, **[14823]**, **[37940]**

Black Enterprise (Vol. 33, No. 3, Oct. 2002, pp. 71); "Can everyone contribute?" in **[31433]**, **[32302]**, **[44978]**, **[44998]**

Black Enterprise (Vol. 31, No. 3, October 2000, pp. 59); "Can I get into IT?" in **[41587]**, **[42191]**

Black Enterprise (Vol. 35, August 2004, No. 1, pp. 61); "Can You Hear Me Yet?" in **[4943]**, **[13884]**, **[48980]**

Black Enterprise (Vol. 35, October 2004, No. 3, pp. 188); "Can You Help Me?" in **[22479]**, **[34845]**, **[35909]**

Black Enterprise (Vol. 31, No. 5, December 2000, pp. 34); "Can't Save the Farm" in **[26490]**, **[39795]**, **[40236]**, **[48081]**

Black Enterprise (Vol. 31, No. 5, December 2000, pp. 66); "Capital expansion" in **[5645]**, **[11147]**, **[48084]**, **[55532]**, **[56154]**

Black Enterprise (Vol. 34, No. 3, October 2003, pp. 34); "Capital Gains Pains" in **[20453]**, **[23903]**, **[54475]**

Black Enterprise (Vol. 30, No. 11, July 2000, pp. 235); "Capital Ventures" in **[47948]**, **[55364]**

Black Enterprise (Vol. 33, No. 7, February 2003, pp. 6); "Career Guide" in **[39222]**, **[44986]**

Black Enterprise (Vol. 34, No. 6, January 2004, pp. 36); "Caribbean Connection: Mortgage Firm Looking to Tap Into the Latino Market" in **[17366]**, **[17999]**, **[20455]**, **[20824]**

Black Enterprise (Vol. 34, July 2004, No. 12); "Caribbean Connection: This Shipping Professional is Taking His Company Overseas" in **[10670]**, **[27929]**, **[43575]**, **[48087]**

Black Enterprise (Vol. 35, December 2004, No. 5, pp. 96); "Carver vs. OneUnited" in **[9864]**, **[30812]**, **[48089]**, **[56155]**

Black Enterprise (Vol. 37, November 2006, No. 4, pp. 156); "Cash in Your Attic: Is Your Junk Someone Else's Treasure?" in **[1790]**, **[7159]**, **[51580]**

Black Enterprise (Vol. 37, October 2006, No. 3, pp. 90); "Cashing in Before You Join: Negotiating a Signing Bonus" in **[39225]**, **[42196]**, **[54479]**

Black Enterprise (Vol. 36, November 2005, No. 4, pp. 180); "Caviar Dreams" in **[23463]**, **[35924]**, **[48091]**

Black Enterprise (Vol. 37, December 2006, No. 5, pp. 36); "CBC and Chrysler Strike Deal" in **[32311]**, **[33036]**, **[49847]**, **[54151]**

Black Enterprise (Vol. 37, February 2007, No. 7, pp. 145); "Celebrate Success. Embrace Innovation" in **[24903]**, **[32312]**, **[34850]**, **[35926]**, **[48092]**, **[52833]**, **[55074]**, **[56156]**

Black Enterprise (Vol. 37, October 2006, No. 3, pp. 86); "Cell Tower Potential" in **[40247]**, **[41595]**

Black Enterprise (Vol. 34, July 2004, No. 12, pp. 138); "Champagne Toasts: Brian Nembhard Schools Us On the Best of the Bubbly" in **[12533]**, **[21466]**, **[23464]**, **[32148]**, **[43578]**

Black Enterprise (Vol. 33, No. 6, Jan. 2003); "Changing gears: Gregory Blache pilots against the tide on the Mississippi River" in **[16733]**, **[35937]**, **[52513]**

Black Enterprise (Vol. 31, No. 5, December 2000, pp. 71); "Changing hats" in **[33663]**, **[35938]**, **[48100]**

Black Enterprise (Vol. 34, No. 2, September 2003, pp. 26); "Chapman Charged with Fraud" in **[9874]**, **[14846]**, **[29150]**, **[37403]**, **[37955]**

Black Enterprise (Vol. 35, February 2005, No. 7, 159); "Chapter 7 or Chapter 13? What Filing for Bankruptcy Really Means" in **[8347]**, **[8378]**, **[37956]**

Black Enterprise (Vol. 35, February 2005, No. 7, pp. 64); "Charmed, I'm Sure: Proper Business Etiquette Goes Beyond the Salad Fork" in **[35940]**, **[39231]**, **[44994]**

Black Enterprise (Vol. 33, No. 6, Jan. 2003, pp. 30); "Charting a course" in **[9877]**, **[14849]**, **[37958]**

Black Enterprise (Vol. 34, July 2004, No. 12, pp. 65); "Charting Your Course" in **[44699]**

Black Enterprise (Vol. 34, No. 6, January 2004, pp. 29); "Charts Show the Way" in **[9878]**, **[14850]**, **[37959]**

Black Enterprise (Vol. 34); "Charts Show the Way: Money Manager Terry Bedford's Stock Selections Are Going in the Right Direction" in **[9879]**, **[14851]**, **[37960]**

Black Enterprise (Vol. 34, July 2004, No. 12, pp. 150); "Checking In: Chicago: Cheryl Burton Whirls Through the Windy City" in **[12534]**, **[21468]**, **[25170]**, **[30310]**, **[52652]**

Black Enterprise (Vol. 34, No. 5, December 2003, pp. 38); "Chemical Balance" in **[9882]**, **[14853]**, **[37962]**, **[46231]**

Black Enterprise (Vol. 35, December 2004, No. 5, pp. 86); "Chicago Defender" in **[18858]**, **[44996]**

Black Enterprise (Vol. 35, February 2005, No. 7, pp. 75); "Choosing the Right Investment Properties" in **[14858]**, **[20830]**

Black Enterprise (Vol. 32, No. 5, December 2001, pp. 21); "Citizens expands through tough times" in **[48104]**, **[49857]**

Black Enterprise (Vol. 35, November 2004, No. 4, pp. 28); "Clarence Otis Named CEO of Darden Restaurants" in **[21473]**, **[45000]**

Black Enterprise (Vol. 31, No. 2, September 2000, pp. 56); "Coaching Companies" in **[33420]**, **[35368]**, **[46564]**

Black Enterprise (Vol. 37, December 2006, No. 5, pp. 31); "Coca-Cola Bottler Up for Sale: CEO J. Bruce Llewellyn Seeks Retirement" in **[11598]**, **[30819]**, **[43014]**, **[46243]**, **[48106]**, **[52414]**

Black Enterprise (Vol. 34, July 2004, No. 12, pp. 21); "Cochran Firm Wins Record $1.62 Billion Insurance Fraud Case" in **[13238]**, **[29155]**, **[33044]**, **[42204]**, **[43129]**

Black Enterprise (Vol. 35, September 2004, No. 2, pp. 54); "Come Fly With Me" in **[13909]**, **[25172]**, **[30313]**, **[33687]**

Black Enterprise (Vol. 35, September 2004, No. 2, pp. 67); "Community Crusader" in **[20843]**, **[56168]**

Black Enterprise (Vol. 31, No. 5, December 2000, pp. 52); "Community Investing Online" in **[37979]**

Black Enterprise (Vol. 33, No. 6, Jan. 2003); "Confidence is key: economist cites the importance of business outlook to recovery" in **[27968]**, **[32327]**

Black Enterprise (Vol. 35, November 2004, No. 4, pp. 81); "Connections for Business" in **[27970]**, **[35968]**, **[48108]**

Black Enterprise (Vol. 35, September 2004, No. 2, pp. 64); "Convention Calendar" in **[11254]**, **[22488]**, **[23204]**, **[23218]**, **[24913]**, **[25757]**, **[26119]**, **[33052]**, **[35971]**, **[39253]**, **[45021]**, **[45832]**, **[48111]**, **[54974]**, **[55080]**, **[56022]**, **[56174]**

Black Enterprise (Vol. 34, No. 3, October 2003, pp. 140); "Copy This: An Authenticity Check of High-End Handbags" in **[5530]**, **[9615]**

Black Enterprise (Vol. 34, July 2004, No. 12, pp. 41); "Corporate Ties" in **[16508]**, **[31673]**, **[33056]**, **[35979]**, **[56178]**

Black Enterprise (Vol. 34, No. 5, December 2003, pp. 22; "Crackdown on Mutual Fund Abuse" in **[9897]**, **[14893]**, **[29180]**, **[37415]**, **[40289]**

Black Enterprise (Vol. 34, No. 4, November 2003, pp. 28); "Cracker Barrel Faces More Racial Bias Charges" in **[21188]**, **[21481]**, **[32012]**, **[33103]**

Black Enterprise (Vol. 35, December 2004, No. 5, pp. 38); "Cracker Barrel Pays $8.7M to Settle Race Case" in **[21482]**, **[29181]**, **[32013]**

Black Enterprise (Vol. 35, January 2005, No. 6, pp. 10); "Creating An Effective Website" in **[13936]**, **[25824]**, **[46851]**

Black Enterprise (Vol. 33, No. 6, Jan. 2003, pp. 49); "Creating a strong foundation" in **[9899]**, **[14896]**, **[37986]**, **[54165]**

Black Enterprise (Vol. 33, No. 3, October 2002, pp. 66); "Creating human links" in **[6329]**, **[6585]**, **[33060]**, **[48116]**, **[48733]**, **[56167]**, **[56180]**

Black Enterprise (Vol. 36, February 2006, No. 7, pp. 169); "Credit Checkup" in **[31531]**, **[37987]**

Black Enterprise (Vol. 35, November 2004, No. 4, pp. 38); "Credit Use Strangles Wealth" in **[31534]**, **[32340]**

Black Enterprise (Vol. 35, August 2004, No. 1, pp. 63); "Cruise Control: Yacht Captain Charts Luxury Liners" in **[5243]**, **[24678]**, **[48118]**

Black Enterprise (Vol. 35, November 2004, No. 4, pp. 30); "CSFB Repositions Top Exec" in **[9904]**, **[31684]**, **[45038]**

Black Enterprise (Vol. 34, No. 5, December 2003, pp. 159); "Customer Officer: Haberdasher Frank Pena Dresses Clients to Suit" in **[5532]**, **[5650]**, **[5717]**, **[5840]**, **[9616]**, **[10031]**

Black Enterprise (Vol. 32, No. 5, December 2001, pp. 22); "Cutting the layoff line" in **[24400]**, **[28001]**, **[48121]**

Black Enterprise (Vol. 36, December 2005, No. 5, pp. 54); "Damage Control" in **[52522]**

Black Enterprise (Vol. 35, December 2004, No. 5, pp. 120); "Daytime's Other Drama" in **[9702]**, **[24402]**

Black Enterprise (Vol. 34, October 2003); "Debit or Credit? Knowing the Benefits of Each Card Can Help You Manage Money Better" in **[9907]**, **[37996]**

Black Enterprise (Vol. 34, No. 3, October 2003, pp. 136); "Debt Collection" in **[8351]**, **[8382]**, **[31539]**, **[37997]**

Black Enterprise (Vol. 34, No. 5, December 2003); "Deduct Now, Pay Later: New Provisions Provide a Tax Break for Business Owners" in **[9908]**, **[10307]**, **[14709]**, **[14909]**, **[51807]**, **[54511]**

Black Enterprise (Vol. 35, November 2004, No. 4, pp. 46); "Delightful Dividends" in **[9909]**, **[14910]**, **[38001]**

Black Enterprise (Vol. 33, No. 6, January 2003, pp. 23); "Democrats fall short: McCall, Kirk lose major elections" in **[40306]**

Black Enterprise (Vol. 34, No. 5, December 2003); "Demolition Man: This Entrepreneur Builds His Business by Tearing Things Down" in **[1468]**, **[1508]**, **[3299]**, **[3310]**, **[36007]**, **[52524]**, **[54775]**

Black Enterprise (Vol. 34, No. 3, October 2003); "Desktop Roundup: Here's How To Find the Perfect PC For Your Small Business Buck" in **[6628]**, **[49009]**

Black Enterprise (Vol. 35, January 2005, No. 6, pp. 53); "Devalued by Diversity" in **[42218]**, **[45059]**

Black Enterprise (Vol. 32, No. 10, May 2002, pp. 47); "Developing a brand" in **[13965]**, **[25831]**, **[33752]**, **[46885]**

Black Enterprise (Vol. 32, No. 10, May 2002, pp. 109); "Dial again" in **[4970]**, **[49010]**

Black Enterprise (Vol. 35, January 2005, No. 6, pp. 97); "Don't Just Dream-Plan" in **[29852]**, **[30531]**

Black Enterprise (Vol. 30, No. 8, March 2000, pp. 82); "Dot Com Fever Black-Oriented" in **[33429]**, **[55373]**

Black Enterprise (Vol. 33, No. 3, Oct. 2002, pp. 52); "Down payment help" in **[17374]**, **[18008]**, **[53696]**, **[54787]**

Black Enterprise (Vol. 32, No. 7, February 2002, pp. 184); "Down, not out" in [28061], [41647]

Black Enterprise (Vol. 33, No. 6, January 2003, pp. 84); "Dream Your Way to Success: Think Visualization Is Easier Said than Done?" in [30532], [36034]

Black Enterprise (Vol. 34, No. 4, Nov. 2003, pp. 108); "Drive Time Live" in [1929], [18016]

Black Enterprise (Vol. 33, No. 198, March 24, 2003, pp. A1); "Dutch fund pays nearly $14M for Sunrise retail center" in [20501], [20867], [51137]

Black Enterprise (Vol. 32, No. 9, April 2002, pp. 48); "E-biz baffled" in [13743], [25756], [33431]

Black Enterprise (Vol. 32, No. 8, March 2002, pp.); "Early warning" in [14000], [25838], [28071], [33827]

Black Enterprise (Vol. 35, January 2005, No. 6, pp. 30); "Earnings Gain, Wealth Loss" in [14943], [32370], [38025]

Black Enterprise (Vol. 31, No. 5, December 2000, pp. 170); "Eateries team up for clout" in [21493], [28080], [48139]

Black Enterprise (Vol. 35, Dec. 2004); "Eight Black Physicians Partnered to Open an International House of Pancakes in Harlem..." in [21496], [38763], [48140], [49915]

Black Enterprise (Vol. 35, October 2004, No. 3, pp. 98); "Eight Moves for Your Money" in [9929], [14948], [38027]

Black Enterprise (Vol. 34, No. 7, February 2004, pp. 14); "Embracing Diversity, Not Division" in [32020], [48544]

Black Enterprise (Vol. 34, No. 3, October 2003, pp. 139); "En Garde! Herby Raynaud's Fencing Fancy" in [4649], [22979], [36057], [53271]

Black Enterprise (Vol. 33, No. 3, October 2002, pp. 102); "Enjoy your income today while saving for your future" in [9932], [10327], [14953], [35992], [38030]

Black Enterprise (Vol. 36, November 2005, No. 4, pp. 162); "Enjoy the Silence" in [27359], [45103]

Black Enterprise (Vol. 35, February 2005, No. 7, pp. 58); "Entering a Hot Zone" in [14013], [41665]

Black Enterprise (Vol. 34, No. 7, February 2004, pp. 32); "Entrepreneurial Enthusiasm" in [36075], [48145], [56741]

Black Enterprise (Vol. 31, No. 4, November 2000, pp. 50); "Entrepreneurial Spirit" in [8994], [36083], [38034], [56207]

Black Enterprise (Vol.33, No.3, Oct. 2002, pp. 40); "Equality through equities: African Americans turning to stocks to build wealth" in [9936], [10298], [14956], [38036]

Black Enterprise (December 2004); "Excusez moi, parlez-vous francais? Learn Another Language to Increase Your Marketability" in [25084], [33093]

Black Enterprise (Vol. 37, December 2006, No. 5, pp. 70); "Executive Training" in [29868], [33094]

Black Enterprise (Vol. 35, January 2005, No. 6, pp. 111); "Expanding Your Network of Contacts" in [22496], [24931], [30851], [36132], [55091]

Black Enterprise (Vol. 35, February 2005, No. 7, pp. 92); "Fabric of Success" in [5509], [5626], [9604]

Black Enterprise (Vol. 31, No. 5, December 2000, pp. 107); "Fade to Black" in [9707], [48154]

Black Enterprise (Vol. 35, November 2004, No. 4, pp. 56); "Family Ties: Father and Sons Create Flooring Enterprise" in [10509], [37651]

Black Enterprise (Vol. 33, No. 3, October 2002, pp. S8); "Fashion's phat cats" in [5510], [5627], [5728], [53898], [56722]

Black Enterprise (Vol. 35, November 2004, No. 4, pp. 60); "Feast or Famine" in [22114], [36148], [46954]

Black Enterprise (Vol. 34, No. 4, November 2003, pp. 62); "Federated Department Stores Inc." in [45879], [48159], [48680], [51154]

Black Enterprise (Vol. 34, No. 7, February 2004, pp. 12); "Filing for Bankruptcy" in [38051], [53725]

Black Enterprise (Vol. 35, October 2004, No. 3, pp. 44); "Financially Sound" in [9957], [14988], [38065]

Black Enterprise (Vol. 34, No. 6, January 2004, pp. 10); "Find a Job" in [40431], [42233]

Black Enterprise (Vol. 31, No. 5, December 2000, pp. 79); "Find your working way" in [32880], [35450]

Black Enterprise (Vol. 35, February 2005, No. 7, pp. 82); "Finding Cash for Your Business" in [44407], [48881]

Black Enterprise (Vol. 32, No. 6, January 2002, pp. 8); "Finding financing" in [35452], [39767], [44408], [47955], [48882], [55382]

Black Enterprise (Vol. 34, No. 7, February 2004, pp. 48); "Finding Funding" in [38146], [39768], [42435], [44409], [47956], [49848]

Black Enterprise (Vol. 34, No. 6, January 2004); "Finding the Middle Ground" in [9959], [14990], [32432], [38068]

Black Enterprise (Vol. 31, No. 5, December 2000, pp. 56); "Finding More Funds for Retirement" in [38069]

Black Enterprise (Vol. 36, February 2006, No. 7, pp. 93); "Finding a Niche Within a Niche" in [29879], [30856], [46958]

Black Enterprise (Vol. 35, January 2005, No. 6, pp. 48); "Finding Your Way: Navigation Systems Move Beyond High-End Cars" in [6649], [18032], [41683], [53728]

Black Enterprise (Vol. 37, January 2007, No. 6, pp. 106); "Finishing Touches: the Fashion Statement is in the Detail" in [5660], [9621], [36153], [39333], [51157]

Black Enterprise (Vol. 36, February 2006, No. 7, pp. 35); "Firms Skid on Rising Oil and Gas Prices" in [32433], [53731]

Black Enterprise (Vol. 36, December 2005, No. 5, pp. 62); "First Impressions" in [27375], [39336], [45145], [46963]

Black Enterprise (Vol. 36, December 2005, No. 5, pp. 32); "First to the Starting Line" in [44524], [56221]

Black Enterprise (Vol. 35, November 2004, No. 4); "First-Time Investor: Where Should You Put Your Money Straight Out of College?" in [9960], [14993], [38070]

Black Enterprise (Vol. 35, September 2004, No. 2, pp. 194); "Fit To Be Tied: New York Designer Directs Neckwear Fashions" in [5544], [36158]

Black Enterprise (Vol. 34, No. 5, December 2003, pp. S11); "Five Checking Account Mistakes to Avoid" in [142], [147], [26236], [27155], [38073], [39479]

Black Enterprise (Vol. 31, No. 3, October 2000, pp. 43); "Five Ways to Finance Your Business" in [26703], [35455], [44412], [55384]

Black Enterprise (Vol. 36, February 2006, No. 7, pp. 74); "Fixing Diversity-Challenged Companies" in [48548], [53733]

Black Enterprise (Vol. 30, No. 6, January 2000, pp. 72); "Fly Solo: How to Build a Profitable Enterprise" in [29733], [30479], [35457]

Black Enterprise (Vol. 35, September 2004, No. 2, pp. 63); "Focus on Fundraising" in [36165], [48164], [54182], [56224]

Black Enterprise (Vol. 32, No. April 2002, 9, pp. 30); "Focus on emerging markets" in [15003], [28169], [48165], [53736]

Black Enterprise (Vol. 34, July 2004, No. 12, pp. 35); "Follow the Banker" in [9965], [15004], [44528]

Black Enterprise (Vol. 36, November 2005, No. 4, pp. 50); "Follow the Corporate Insiders" in [15005], [38076]

Black Enterprise (Vol. 34, No. 3, October 2003, pp. 20); "Food For Thought" in [11614], [23479], [37655], [48166]

Black Enterprise (Vol. 35, February 2005, No. 7, pp. 36); "Food Industry Veteran Has It His Way" in [28172], [38781], [48167]

Black Enterprise (Vol. 32, No. 5, December 2001, pp. 46); "Food resources" in [11577], [47957], [51027]

Black Enterprise (Vol. 32, No. 9, Ma rch 2002, pp. 102); "Food for thought" in [15007], [23480], [32439], [38077], [46291], [46973], [48733]

Black Enterprise (Vol. 35, August 2004); "For the Love of the Game: How One Woman Scores in the Sports Entertainment Industry" in [23721], [31153], [46975], [50441], [56226]

Black Enterprise (Vol. 34, No. 7, February 2004); "Ford Motor Company Is Sponsoring the Ford BEST Business Plan Contest..." in [29882], [36173]

Black Enterprise (Vol. 34, July 2004, No. 12, pp. 143); "Forgive Us Our Debts...The Creditor May, But the IRS Won't" in [31549], [54560]

Black Enterprise (Vol. 37, October 2006, No. 3, pp. 36); "Former Apprentice Candidate Launches Jewelry Line" in [9622], [15844], [36175]

Black Enterprise (Vol. 35, October 2004, No. 3, pp. 33); "Former B.E. 100s CEO Convicted" in [9969], [29247], [40396]

Black Enterprise (Vol. 35, September 2004, No. 2, pp. 30); "Former B.E. 100s Clerk Faces Prison Time" in [26241], [29248], [41695]

Black Enterprise (Vol. 34, No. 4, November 2003, pp. 46); "Fostering Urban Entrepreneurship" in [35465], [48883], [55386]

Black Enterprise (Vol. 35, September 2004, No. 2, pp. 50); "Franchise Financing" in [38786], [44530]

Black Enterprise (Vol. 35, January 2005, No. 6, pp. 10); "Franchise Finder" in [35467], [38638]

Black Enterprise (Vol. 32, No. 9, April 2002, pp. 46); "Franchise to go: despite a recession some of these businesses are hot" in [28183], [38787], [48168]

Black Enterprise (Vol. 33, No. 7, February 2003, pp. 6); "Franchise solutions" in [35468], [38641]

Black Enterprise (Vol. 32, No. 10, May 2002, pp. 101); "Franchising" in [3292], [12353], [21399], [27721], [35469], [38642], [47958], [52774]

Black Enterprise (Vol. 34, No. 3, October 2003, pp. 136); "Free Art! Gallery Loans Visual Art to the Public" in [1608], [39344]

Black Enterprise (Vol. 36, November 2005, No. 4, pp. 124); "From Concept to Customer" in [46990], [48734]

Black Enterprise (Vol. 36, November 2005, No. 4, pp. 59); "From Drab to Fab" in [12187], [12281], [13644], [18682]

Black Enterprise (Vol. 33, No. 6, Jan. 2003, pp. 32); "From the Firehouse to the Schoolhouse" in [33100], [35473]

Black Enterprise (Vol. 36, November 2005, No. 4, pp. 85); "From Football to Financial Plan" in [15019], [38082]

Black Enterprise (Vol. 34, No. 5, December 2003, pp. S4); "From Landscaper to Landowner" in [16014], [16538], [20290], [20515], [20627], [20881], [36186], [53919], [56744]

Black Enterprise (Vol. 34, No. 3, October 2003, pp. 29); "From Real Estate to Retirement Plan" in [15020], [20516], [20882], [36188], [48174]

Black Enterprise (Vol. 35, January 2005, No. 6, pp. 97); "From Wish to Goal" in [29883], [30544], [36189]

Black Enterprise (Vol. 35, December 2004, No. 5, pp. 70); "Fujitsu Biometric Notebook PC" in [6654], [22235], [49039]

Black Enterprise (Vol. 36, February 2006, No. 7, pp. 64); "Fulfilling Audiovisual Dreams" in [4186], [7165], [7727], [24341]

Black Enterprise (Vol. 36, December 2005, No. 5, pp. 71); "Funny Business" in [5878], [36194]

Black Enterprise (Vol. 34, No. 3, October 2003, pp. 135); "Funny Money: Counterfeit Money Scams Persist" in [30226]

Black Enterprise (Vol. 34, No. 3, October 2003); "Gearing Up for the Golden Years" in [9976], [15027], [38085]

Black Enterprise (Vol. 34, No. 7, February 2004, pp. 38); "Georgia's a Peach for Profits" in [9977], [15029], [38086]

Black Enterprise (Vol. 37, October 2006, No. 3, pp. 119); "Get Hired Now! A 28-Day Program for Landing the Job You Want" in [42245], [48552]

Black Enterprise (Vol. 34, No. 2, September 2003, pp. 62); "Get It Straight" in **[4397]**, **[31156]**

Black Enterprise (Vol. 33, No. 6, January 2003, pp. 10); "Get organized" in **[45179]**, **[54947]**

Black Enterprise (Vol. 34, No. 4, November 2003, pp. 91); "Getting Back on the Bull" in **[9978]**, **[15031]**, **[38088]**

Black Enterprise (Vol. 35, August 2004, No. 1, pp. 78); "Getting the Corner Office" in **[45185]**, **[48179]**, **[56238]**

Black Enterprise (Vol. 34, No. 6, January 2004); "Getting More Bang for Your Buck" in **[9979]**, **[15032]**, **[38089]**

Black Enterprise (Vol. 37, December 2006, No. 5, pp. 53); "Getting Out of an IRS Mess" in **[9980]**, **[29262]**, **[38090]**, **[40028]**, **[40409]**, **[54572]**

Black Enterprise (Vol. 35, December 2004, No. 5, pp. 65); "Getting Paid: Collection Tips for Handling Slow- or Non-Paying Clients" in **[8384]**, **[31552]**

Black Enterprise (Vol. 36, February 2006, No. 7, pp. 58); "Getting Paid Faster" in **[28204]**, **[31553]**, **[40029]**

Black Enterprise (Vol. 35, October 2004, No. 3, pp. 125); "Getting on the Road Toward Financial Freedom" in **[15033]**, **[32449]**, **[38091]**

Black Enterprise (Vol. 34, No. 4, Nov. 2003, pp. 43); "Getting Stars to Shine: Dawn To Dusk Image Agency has an A-List Clientele" in **[12885]**, **[20121]**, **[47014]**, **[50598]**

Black Enterprise (Vol. 34, No. 5, December 2003, pp. S10); "Getting To Know the Bull and the Bear" in **[9981]**, **[15035]**, **[33104]**

Black Enterprise (Vol. 34, No. 6, January 2004); "Getting the Word Out-Inexpensively" in **[638]**, **[5983]**, **[47015]**

Black Enterprise (Vol. 34, No. 6); "Getting the Word Out-Inexpensively: How to Get the Most Bang Out of Your Marketing Dollars" in **[639]**, **[5984]**, **[47016]**

Black Enterprise (Vol. 36, February 2006, No. 7, pp. 155); "Girl Franchising Power" in **[38815]**, **[56240]**

Black Enterprise (Vol. 36, February 2006, No. 7, pp. 40); "Give Me a Tax Break" in **[2908]**, **[17385]**, **[23952]**, **[38093]**, **[40410]**, **[54577]**

Black Enterprise (Vol. 34, July 2004, No. 12); "Giving Where It Counts: Blackgiving.com Lets Consumers Choose Their Charities" in **[36213]**, **[48182]**, **[54188]**

Black Enterprise (Vol. 36, November 2005, No. 4, pp. 54; "Go Where the Money Is" in **[9983]**, **[15039]**, **[38095]**

Black Enterprise (Vol. 33, No. 3, October 2002, pp. 145); "Going digital for dollars" in **[33958]**, **[34357]**, **[35404]**, **[36220]**, **[47025]**, **[48184]**, **[48915]**, **[50119]**

Black Enterprise (Vol. 35, November 2004, No. 4, pp. 58); "Going the Extra Mile" in **[5668]**, **[16215]**, **[31726]**

Black Enterprise (Vol. 35, January 2005, No. 6, pp. 103); "Going For a Whirl: Jamail Larkin Soars, Dips, and Shows Off a Few Stunts" in **[949]**, **[36221]**, **[47026]**

Black Enterprise (Vol. 34, No. 7, February 2004, pp. 140); "Going Once, Going Twice: Online Auctions Offer Great Deals" in **[1780]**, **[1817]**, **[33963]**, **[34917]**

Black Enterprise (Vol. 34, No. 5, December 2003, pp. S6); "Goldmining for Internships" in **[33106]**, **[34191]**, **[40445]**, **[42248]**

Black Enterprise (Vol. 37, October 2006, No. 3, pp. 216); "Good for Business: Houston is a Hot Spot for Economic Growth" in **[30148]**, **[32452]**, **[41016]**, **[52112]**, **[52677]**

Black Enterprise (Vol. 35, December 2004, No. 5, pp. 86); "Granite Broadcasting Corp." in **[4106]**, **[24413]**

Black Enterprise (Vol. 33, No. 3, October 2002, pp. 176); "Great Expectations" in **[9136]**, **[9208]**, **[24100]**, **[24526]**

Black Enterprise (Vol. 33, No. 3, October 2002, pp. 56); "Guarding your turf: how the small guy can fend off big biz encroachment" in **[30872]**, **[31922]**, **[33983]**, **[34931]**

The Black Enterprise Guide to Starting Your Own Business **[47942]**

Black Enterprise (Vol. 31, No. 5, December 2000, pp. 72); "Hand-to-hand combat" in **[53310]**

Black Enterprise (Vol. 32, No. 8, March 2002, pp. 50); "Handing it over: businesses need a plan for passing the torch" in **[29894]**, **[37674]**, **[48200]**, **[54302]**

Black Enterprise (Vol. 33, No. 7, February 2003, pp. 14); "Handling conflict" in **[34923]**, **[45216]**

Black Enterprise (Vol. 35, November 2004, No. 4); "Hands-On Experience: Tech Exec Rolls Up Sleeves to Tackle Homeland Security" in **[22245]**, **[41728]**

Black Enterprise (Oct. 2002, pp. 55); "Hanging tough: Wilhelmina Bell-Taylor overcame cancer to launch a successful business" in **[3481]**, **[16490]**, **[17567]**, **[35499]**, **[36897]**, **[39708]**, **[42517]**, **[47960]**, **[48544]**, **[56049]**, **[58583]**

Black Enterprise (Vol. 37, February 2007, No. 7, pp. 1); "Harding Brews Success at Anheuser-Busch" in **[3127]**, **[45222]**

Black Enterprise (Vol. 36, November 2005, No. 4, pp. 62); "Harlem Haven" in **[3042]**, **[11328]**

Black Enterprise (Vol. 36, November 2005, No. 4, pp. 60); "Have a Talent for Sales?" in **[7891]**, **[31164]**, **[48201]**, **[51661]**, **[56257]**

Black Enterprise (Vol. 32, No. 10, May 2002); "Head of the class" in **[36268]**, **[48203]**

Black Enterprise (Vol. 35, November 2004, No. 4, pp. 68); "Head of the Class: Multitasking Made Easy" in **[6672]**, **[49067]**

Black Enterprise (Vol. 34, No. 2, September 2003, pp. 48); "Healthcare Insurance" in **[13319]**, **[40435]**, **[41025]**, **[42629]**, **[43212]**

Black Enterprise (Vol. 32, No. 9, April 2002, pp.); "Healthy prospects" in **[19406]**, **[39835]**, **[44542]**, **[48207]**, **[56259]**

Black Enterprise (Vol. 34, No. 7, February 2004, pp. 48); "Herbal Remedies: Couple Looks to Make Bad Hair Days a Thing of the Past" in **[2394]**, **[11704]**, **[11792]**, **[12145]**, **[12583]**, **[37680]**, **[39030]**

Black Enterprise (Vol. 35, January 2005, No. 6, pp. 61); "Here's to 5 Years of DOFE" in **[15077]**, **[38115]**

Black Enterprise (Vol. 34, No. 3, October 2003, pp. 19); "Heritage Networks Wins Showdown" in **[24414]**, **[49977]**

Black Enterprise (Vol. 36, December 2005, No. 5, pp. 28); "Herman J. Russell" in **[7356]**, **[36278]**

Black Enterprise (Vol. 34, No. 6, January 2004, pp. 19); "Herman J. Russell Passes Torch" in **[7357]**, **[37681]**, **[48210]**

Black Enterprise (Vol. 34, No. 2, September 2003, pp. 43); "He's Still Standing" in **[4684]**, **[6169]**, **[6673]**, **[23027]**, **[36280]**, **[44545]**, **[53315]**

Black Enterprise (Vol. 33, No. 6, January 2003, pp. 47); "Hibernia Southcoast Capital Corp." in **[9998]**, **[15078]**, **[45236]**

Black Enterprise (Vol. 32, No. 7, February 2002, pp. 56); "Hidden messages" in **[4685]**, **[6473]**, **[22248]**, **[23028]**, **[53316]**

Black Enterprise (Vol. 34, No. 7, February 2004, pp. 54); "Hide and Click: Optio S4 is Small but Powerful" in **[4188]**, **[49070]**

Black Enterprise (Vol. 33, No. 3, October 2002, pp. 74); "High designs: the architect's career is taking flight" in **[1516]**, **[1519]**, **[3433]**, **[3539]**, **[34386]**, **[36283]**, **[48212]**, **[48862]**

Black Enterprise (Vol. 37, February 2007, No. 7, pp. 42); "High Hopes: Ralph Mitchell's Picks Have Growth Potential" in **[7360]**, **[11883]**, **[15080]**, **[28276]**, **[38117]**

Black Enterprise (Vol. 35, February 2005, No. 7, pp. 162); "High-Speed Web Access" in **[6675]**, **[14112]**, **[34007]**, **[49071]**

Black Enterprise (Vol. 35, November 2004, No. 4, pp. 54); "Hiring the Right People to Rep Your Products" in **[32157]**, **[42278]**, **[51671]**

Black Enterprise (Vol. 37, December 2006, No. 5, pp. 69); "His Brother's Keeper: a Mentor Learns the True Meaning of Leadership" in **[33116]**, **[36286]**, **[45243]**

Black Enterprise (Vol. 33, No. 6, January 2003, pp. 89); "His stand on football: Reginald Rutledge creates a stadium rush" in **[5908]**, **[36287]**, **[48214]**

Black Enterprise (Vol. 34, No. 4, November 2003, pp. 28); "Hit Discriminators Where it Hurts" in **[32031]**, **[32480]**, **[48236]**

Black Enterprise (Vol. 34, No. 3, October 2003, pp. 54); "Hold Your Tongue" in **[42286]**, **[45246]**

Black Enterprise (Vol. 35, November 2004, No. 4, pp. 34); "Home Improvement: Black Homeownership Is Up, But at What Cost?" in **[7368]**, **[20530]**

Black Enterprise (Vol. 37, October 2006, No. 3, pp. 78); "Home Work" in **[22041]**, **[42524]**, **[52775]**

Black Enterprise (Vol. 35, February 2005, No. 7, pp. 156); "Honor Thy Self" in **[35511]**, **[56052]**

Black Enterprise (Vol. 37, December 2006, No. 5, pp. 34); "Hot Kicks, Cool Price" in **[5670]**, **[9625]**, **[22763]**, **[44232]**, **[48744]**, **[51185]**

Black Enterprise (Vol. 36, December 2005, No. 5, pp. 102); "Hotlist 05" in **[36297]**, **[56268]**

Black Enterprise (Vol. 35, December 2004, No. 5, pp. 38); "Houston-Based ChaseCom L.P." in **[5015]**, **[14128]**, **[28299]**, **[31733]**, **[41751]**, **[52546]**

Black Enterprise (Vol. 34, No. 6, January 2004, pp. 51); "Houston Super Bowl XXXVIII Host Committee" in **[23725]**

Black Enterprise (Vol. 34, No. 4, November 2003); "How to Boost Your Portfolio's Performance" in **[10007]**, **[15096]**, **[38123]**

Black Enterprise (Vol. 35, February 2005, No. 7, pp. 98); "How Networking Really Works" in **[36308]**, **[45263]**

Black Enterprise (Vol. 36, February 2006, No. 7, pp. 60); "How to Open a Successful Coffee House" in **[11302]**, **[21403]**

Black Enterprise (Vol. 34, July 2004, No. 12, pp. 104); "How To Choose an Annuity" in **[15103]**, **[38129]**

Black Enterprise (Vol. 34, No. 6, January 2004); "Howard University's School of Communications has Been Named After John H. Johnson" in **[18886]**, **[20076]**, **[45961]**, **[48243]**

Black Enterprise (Vol. 35, December 2004, No. 5, pp. 71); "HP iPAQ h6315 Pocket PC Phone Edition" in **[5022]**, **[49080]**

Black Enterprise (Vol. 34, No. 7, February 2004, pp. 137); "Hungry for Success" in **[10508]**, **[10622]**, **[45962]**, **[48244]**

Black Enterprise (Vol. 34, No. 4, Nov. 2003, pp. 48); "If at First You Don't Succeed..." in **[5316]**, **[35523]**, **[49769]**, **[56055]**

Black Enterprise (Vol. 33, No. 6, January 2003, pp. 43); "I'll Trade You" in **[14141]**, **[34051]**

Black Enterprise (Vol. 35, December 2004, No. 5, pp. 84); "In Retail Fashion" in **[5673]**, **[51199]**

Black Enterprise (Vol. 35, November 2004, No. 4, pp. 64); "In a Snap! Fuji Offers New Photo Options" in **[49093]**

Black Enterprise (Vol. 33, No. 6, January 2003, pp. 85); "In search of great soup" in **[2716]**, **[8999]**

Black Enterprise (Vol. 33, No. 3, October 2002, pp. 60); "In business with the U.S." in **[39843]**, **[40042]**, **[40192]**

Black Enterprise (Vol. 33, No. 6, Jan. 2003); "Income for life: Dawn Greene needs a plan to help her live beyond her injuries" in **[10020]**, **[38138]**

Black Enterprise (Vol. 37, January 2007, No. 6, pp. 40); "Inflation Woes: Secure Your Portfolio Against Rising Prices" in **[10024]**, **[15124]**, **[20907]**, **[38140]**

Black Enterprise (Vol. 35, November 2004, No. 4, pp. 124); "Inn Vogue" in **[2442]**, **[12581]**, **[37702]**

Black Enterprise (Vol. 35, October 2004, No. 3, pp. 60); "Inside or Out?" in **[42155]**, **[49674]**

Black Enterprise (Vol. 36, December 2005, No. 5, pp. 138); "Inspirational Notes" in **[5549]**, **[22116]**, **[51207]**, **[56280]**

Black Enterprise (Vol. 35, January 2005, No. 6, pp. 58); "Inspiring Black Investors" in **[15128]**, **[36351]**, **[38141]**, **[48251]**

Black Enterprise (Vol. 34, No. 5, December 2003); "Market Upswing" in **[10085]**, **[15253]**, **[38217]**

Black Enterprise (Vol. 30, No. 5, December 1999, pp. 42); "Marketing Know-How" in **[27726]**, **[46580]**, **[52780]**

Black Enterprise (Vol. 35, February 2005, No. 7); "Maximizing Employee Performance: Grow Your Business by Empowering Your Workforce" in **[34987]**, **[36494]**, **[45424]**

Black Enterprise (Vol. 34, No. 5); "Measuring Progress: A Look at the Economic Strides of African Americans in Recent Decades" in **[31659]**, **[32568]**, **[38219]**, **[39640]**

Black Enterprise (Vol. 34, July 2004, No. 12); "Membership Privileges: How To Benefit From Joining a Professional Organization" in **[36500]**, **[45432]**

Black Enterprise (Vol. 35, January 2005, No. 6, pp. 97); "Mentor Wanted" in **[5512]**, **[5629]**, **[35563]**, **[46165]**, **[46582]**, **[47966]**

Black Enterprise (Vol. 35, February 2005, No. 7, pp. 38); "Miami's Royal Palm Sells for $127.5 M" in **[12597]**, **[15262]**, **[25215]**, **[48293]**

Black Enterprise (Vol. 35, November 2004, No. 4, pp. 60); "Microloans Face Budgetary Ax" in **[39869]**, **[44587]**

Black Enterprise (Vol. 31, No. 5, December 2000, pp. 44); "Middle of the Road" in **[38221]**

Black Enterprise (Vol. 32, No. 7, February 2002,); "Mining venture capital" in **[35568]**, **[44428]**, **[55404]**

Black Enterprise (Vol. 34, No. 4, November 2003, pp. 27); "Mixed Fate for Black Law Firms" in **[28493]**, **[29387]**, **[48312]**

Black Enterprise (Vol. 34, No. 2, September 2003, pp. S1); "Mixing Books with Business" in **[18910]**, **[56755]**

Black Enterprise (Vol. 32, No. 9, April 2002, pp. 52); "Money talks" in **[41842]**, **[54227]**

Black Enterprise (Vol. 32, No. 5, December 2001, pp. 46); "More than a green thumb" in **[15984]**, **[35573]**, **[47970]**

Black Enterprise (Vol. 33, No. 3, October 2002, pp. 179); "Mortgage Arm Wrestle" in **[17408]**

Black Enterprise (Vol. 35, January 2005, No. 6, pp. 33); "Mortgage Help for Black College Students" in **[7427]**, **[17413]**, **[20597]**

Black Enterprise (Vol. 33, No. 3, October 2002, pp. 179); "Mortgage arm wrestle" in **[17420]**

Black Enterprise (Vol. 33, No. 3, October 2002, pp. S9); "Mrs. D & I are cool (handle your business)" in **[33176]**, **[34258]**

Black Enterprise (Vol. 32, No. 9, April 2); "Mrs., Mom, and CEO" in **[24235]**, **[36514]**, **[37737]**, **[42682]**, **[48316]**, **[52565]**, **[56327]**

Black Enterprise (Vol. 34, July 2004, No. 12, pp. 61); "Much Higher Learning: Exploring the Benefits Of an Academic Career" in **[33178]**, **[45449]**

Black Enterprise (Vol. 34, No. 4, November 2003, pp. 52); "Music-Go-Round: Webcasters Reach Tentative Agreement with RIAA, DiMA" in **[14261]**, **[17753]**, **[20328]**, **[34219]**, **[44097]**

Black Enterprise (Vol. 34, No. 3, October 2003); "Music To Her Ears: Lamonica Thomas Taps Into the Digital Greeting Card Market" in **[11159]**, **[11569]**

Black Enterprise (Vol. 35, January 2005, No. 6); "My First Home" in **[17421]**, **[20603]**

Black Enterprise (Vol. 34, No. 5, December 2003, pp. 55); "Naked at Work: Psst! The Boss is Watching" in **[22305]**, **[23034]**, **[41852]**, **[42883]**, **[49155]**, **[51176]**

Black Enterprise (Vol. 32, No. 10, May 2002, pp. 26); "Narrowing the divide" in **[14269]**, **[34231]**

Black Enterprise (Vol. 30, No. 10, May 2000, pp. 52); "NASA Training Program" in **[30918]**, **[33180]**, **[48319]**

Black Enterprise (Vol. 35, December 2004, No. 5, pp. 86); "National Association of Black Accountants" in **[200]**, **[12601]**, **[26298]**, **[48320]**

Black Enterprise (Vol. 34, July 2004, No. 12, pp. 28); "National Urban League: State of Black America" in **[7433]**, **[28527]**, **[32584]**, **[33182]**

Black Enterprise (Vol. 34, No. 4, November 2003, pp. 62); "National Womens Business Council" in **[53534]**, **[56334]**

Black Enterprise (Vol. 34, No. 3, October 2003, pp. 58); "NEC Solutions (America) Inc." in **[45455]**

Black Enterprise (Vol. 37, December 2006, No. 5, pp. 70); "Negotiating Tips" in **[2726]**, **[3044]**, **[33183]**, **[35001]**, **[45460]**

Black Enterprise (Vol. 35, November 2004, No. 4, pp. 102); "Network Marketing or Pyramid Scheme?" in **[29397]**, **[30241]**, **[47318]**

Black Enterprise (Vol. 34, No. 6, January 2004, pp. 101); "Networking is a Click Away" in **[24984]**, **[36527]**, **[48322]**, **[55131]**

Black Enterprise (Vol. 34, No. 2, September 2003) "Networking Made Easy; Three Quick Tips for Setting Up a Wired Connection" in **[6735]**, **[6953]**, **[49158]**

Black Enterprise (Vol. 34, No. 4, Nov. 2003, pp. 72); "Networking for Success: It Takes More Than Just Handling Out Business Cards" in **[36530]**

Black Enterprise (Vol. 37, November 2006, No. 4, pp. 34); "New Beginnings for VIBE" in **[18913]**, **[28531]**, **[30572]**, **[36532]**, **[50757]**

Black Enterprise (Vol. 35, November 2004, No. 4, pp. 188); "New Me" in **[5949]**, **[35586]**

Black Enterprise (Vol. 33, No. 7, February 2003, pp. 20); "New Urban Entertainment shuts doors" in **[24438]**, **[48335]**

Black Enterprise (Vol. 34, No. 6, January 2004, pp. 10); "New Year's Resolutions" in **[10107]**, **[10460]**, **[36804]**, **[38245]**

Black Enterprise (Oct. 2002, pp. 175); "No Bad Days: Sherry Williams excels as a Mary Kay sales pro while battling breast cancer" in **[2600]**, **[2635]**, **[7900]**, **[7955]**, **[40840]**, **[42689]**, **[56349]**

Black Enterprise (Vol. 32, No. 9, April 2002, pp. 54); "No more boxes" in **[4741]**, **[23100]**

Black Enterprise (Vol. 35, February 2005, No. 7); "No Credit? No Problem! Here's How to Get Good Credit If You Don't Have Any" in **[8315]**, **[8356]**, **[8390]**, **[31569]**

Black Enterprise (Vol. 37, December 2006, No. 5, pp. 72); "No Fast Cash Class" in **[10109]**, **[33191]**, **[38247]**

Black Enterprise (Vol. 37, November 2006, No. 4, pp. 159); "No More Debt" in **[31570]**, **[38249]**

Black Enterprise (Vol. 32, No. 6, January 2002, pp. 39); "No More Free Rides: It's the End of the Free Lunch on the Web" in **[14298]**, **[25915]**, **[28565]**, **[34267]**

Black Enterprise (Vol. 35, January 2005, No. 6); "No More Postdating: New Bill Allows Banks to Process Your Checks at Warp Speed" in **[207]**, **[2937]**, **[10111]**, **[26303]**

Black Enterprise (Vol. 32, No. 8, March 2002, pp. 64); "No Small Change" in **[14300]**, **[25916]**, **[34269]**, **[48343]**, **[56352]**

Black Enterprise (Vol. 31, No. 4, November 2000, pp. 62); "No Ticket to Easy Street" in **[35590]**, **[38666]**

Black Enterprise (Vol. 36, December 2005, No. 5, pp. 62); "No Vacancies" in **[20612]**, **[20952]**

Black Enterprise (Vol. 35, December 2004, No. 5, pp. 70); "Nokia 9300 SmartPhone" in **[5072]**, **[49172]**

Black Enterprise (Vol. 36, December 2005, No. 5, pp. 45); "Northern Bounty" in **[10113]**, **[15309]**

Black Enterprise (Vol. 33, No. 6, Jan. 2003, pp. 87); "Not just for a rainy day" in **[10115]**, **[15311]**, **[38252]**

Black Enterprise (Vol. 34, No. 3, October 2003, pp. 51); "Not In My Inbox: Moving Large Files Is As Easy AS FTP" in **[25524]**, **[26095]**, **[49175]**

Black Enterprise (Vol. 35, February 2005, No. 7, pp. 170); "Not Just Window Dressing: the Art of Hanging a Great Curtain" in **[12201]**, **[12304]**

Black Enterprise (Vol. 33, No. 6, January 2003, pp. 43); "Now, ear this" in **[5073]**, **[49178]**

Black Enterprise (Vol. 37, February 2007, No. 7, pp. 138); "Off the Wall: Keith Collins' Larger-Than-Life Designs" in **[8016]**, **[36567]**

Black Enterprise (Vol. 34, No. 5, December 2003, pp. 60); "Old Cell Phones" in **[5076]**, **[5464]**, **[21247]**, **[21962]**, **[37312]**, **[38616]**

Black Enterprise (Vol. 37, December 2006, No. 5, pp. 38); "Omniplex on the Case" in **[30922]**, **[39511]**, **[40590]**, **[52571]**, **[56579]**

Black Enterprise (Vol. 33, No. 6, Jan. 2003, pp. 31); "On a Bank Roll" in **[10118]**, **[15318]**, **[38255]**

Black Enterprise (Vol. 33, No. 3, Oct. 2002, pp. 79); "On the road to financial fitness" in **[10120]**, **[15320]**, **[38257]**

Black Enterprise (Vol. 34, No. 5, December 2003, pp. 50); "On a Mission" in **[29238]**, **[29946]**, **[30577]**, **[31675]**

Black Enterprise (Vol. 33, No. 3, Oct. 2002, pp. 79); "On the Road to Financial Fitness" in **[10121]**, **[15322]**, **[38260]**

Black Enterprise (Vol. 32, No. 9, Ap); "On the fast track" in **[9777]**, **[14695]**, **[47972]**, **[49773]**

Black Enterprise (Vol. 34, No. 4, November 2003, pp. 55); "One-Button Backups: Creating a Batch File is as Easy as...(Tech 1-2-3)" in **[49187]**

Black Enterprise (Vol. 35, November 2004, No. 4, pp. 76); "One Final Note: Why Your Last Impression Is As Important As Your First" in **[28591]**, **[36579]**

Black Enterprise (Vol. 37, November 2006, No. 4, pp. 90); "Online Self-Publishing Services" in **[2730]**, **[8622]**, **[14321]**, **[25925]**, **[36585]**, **[52382]**

Black Enterprise (Vol. 34, No. 5, December 2003, pp. S5); "Organizations" in **[35599]**, **[53903]**, **[56727]**

Black Enterprise (Vol. 37, February 2007, No. 7, pp. 145); "Our World with Black Enterprise" in **[750]**, **[14330]**, **[24442]**, **[25928]**, **[47381]**

Black Enterprise (Vol. 31, No. 5, December 2000, pp. 79); "Over their heads" in **[27467]**

Black Enterprise (Vol. 36, December 2005, No. 5, pp. 38); "Overreaching for the Roof" in **[17426]**, **[38272]**

Black Enterprise (Vol. 34, No. 6, January 2004, pp. 44); "Own or Rent? Revisiting the Pros and Cons of Leasing vs. Purchasing" in **[21341]**, **[36828]**, **[38273]**, **[47191]**, **[49189]**, **[49194]**, **[49533]**

Black Enterprise (Vol. 35, December 2004, No. 5, pp. 77); "Paint Hustle: New Orleans Artist Went from the Streets to Mainstream" in **[8017]**, **[36600]**, **[48351]**

Black Enterprise (Vol. 34, No. 5, December 2003, pp. 147); "Paper Jam: Curtis Sherrod's Hip-Hop History Session" in **[9229]**, **[10008]**, **[36601]**, **[37818]**

Black Enterprise (Vol. 35, October 2004, No. 3); "Parlez-vous e-Commerce? Here's How To Give Your Website International Appeal" in **[25090]**, **[34327]**, **[43779]**

Black Enterprise (Vol. 37, December 2006, No. 5, pp. 70); "Part-Time Assignments" in **[42376]**, **[45514]**, **[53909]**

Black Enterprise (Vol. 35, February 2005, No. 7, pp. 46); "Peach State Slow to Ripen" in **[10131]**, **[15345]**

Black Enterprise (Vol. 32, No. 10, May 2002, pp. 44); "Penny wise, pound foolish" in **[26322]**, **[36613]**, **[48357]**

Black Enterprise (Vol. 34, No. 3, October 2003, pp. 30); "Pick of the Pack" in **[10133]**, **[15353]**, **[38281]**

Black Enterprise (Vol. 36, November 2005, No. 4, pp. 74); "Pick Your Startup Tool" in **[1189]**, **[22856]**, **[26326]**, **[29754]**, **[31055]**, **[39073]**, **[47401]**, **[53410]**

Black Enterprise (Vol. 37, February 2007, No. 7, pp. 46); "Picking a 529 College Savings Plan" in **[15354]**, **[26880]**

Black Enterprise (Vol. 32, No. 9, April 2002, pp. 44); "Picking Up the Pieces" in **[41904]**, **[45536]**, **[48362]**

Black Enterprise (Vol. 32, No. 6, January 2002, pp. 37); "Pilot program to assist young entrepreneurs" in **[44433]**, **[48888]**, **[52782]**, **[56728]**

Black Enterprise (Vol. 35, August 2004, No. 1, pp. 28); "Pioneering Black Ad Agency Closes Doors Forever" in **[756]**, **[48363]**

Black Enterprise (Vol. 32, No. 9, April 2002, pp. 54); "Smart Business Tools" in [4805], [23182], [29760], [35652]

Black Enterprise (Vol. 35, August 2004, No. 1, pp. 61); "Smart Tech Solutions For Small Businesses" in [6802], [14450], [27179], [49270], [53472]

Black Enterprise (Vol. 34, No. 6, January 2004, pp. 46); "Snare and Share Alike: Here's a Quick and Easy Way to Capture Video" in [4807], [9742], [10153], [23184], [49273], [50820], [53473]

Black Enterprise (Vol. 37, October 2006, No. 3, pp. 38); "SoBran Partners with U.S. Navy" in [43032], [50181], [52590]

Black Enterprise (Vol. 34, No. 2, September 2003, pp. 51); "Soft Landing: James Garrett Took a Leap of Faith and Found Security" in [4809], [22381], [23186], [36770], [52591], [53474]

Black Enterprise (Vol. 31, No. 5, December 2000, pp. 30); "Sold for $20 Million" in [34511], [37192], [52458]

Black Enterprise (Vol. 35, December 2004, No. 5, pp. 70); "SoniqCast Element" in [6804], [49276]

Black Enterprise (Vol. 34, No. 5, December 2003, pp. S6); "Sony Ericsson's T310/T316 Mobile Phone" in [5080], [5115], [49277], [50131]

Black Enterprise (Vol. 35, August 2004, No. 1, pp. 30); "Spam Could Be a Scam: Internet Tricks Are Becoming High Crimes" in [14465], [22383], [29510], [30253], [34515], [40709]

Black Enterprise (Vol. 34, No. 7, February 2004, pp. 54); "Speak and Slide: Siemens' Small Phone Packs in Big Features" in [5082], [5117], [49278], [50132]

Black Enterprise (Vol. 32, No. 9, April 2002, pp. 28); "Spirited leadership: Carl Horton named President & CEO of Absolut" in [36781], [45660], [48417]

Black Enterprise (Vol. 35, December 2004, No. 5, pp. 84); "Springboard to Success" in [52987], [56414]

Black Enterprise (Vol. 34, No. 4, November 2003, pp. 60); "Star Attorney" in [29512], [33240]

Black Enterprise (Vol. 34, July 2004, No. 12, pp. 53); "Starting From Zero: Entrepreneur Reaps Success During Rocky Tech Times" in [28814], [31221], [34536], [42007], [48418]

Black Enterprise (Vol. 33, No. 6, January 2003, pp. 39); "Starting in Style" in [5515], [35668]

Black Enterprise (Vol. 36, December 2005, No. 5, pp. 166); "State Farm Signs On As Host" in [13474], [25022], [43378], [45665], [55159], [56417]

Black Enterprise (Vol. 35, February 2005, No. 7); "Stay Out of Foreclosure: Here's What to Do If You Miss a Mortgage Payment" in [17443], [38372]

Black Enterprise (Vol. 30, No. 10, May 2000, pp. 50); "Staying Afloat" in [38373]

Black Enterprise (Vol. 32, No. 9, April 2002, pp. 108); "Staying power" in [39606], [45667]

Black Enterprise (Vol. 36, February 2006, No. 7, pp. 48); "Stick with the Trends" in [10188], [15474], [38376]

Black Enterprise (Vol. 32, No. 9, April 2002, pp. 59); "Stiff upper lips: are your employees happy or just biding their time?" in [35078], [45669]

Black Enterprise (Vol. 34, September 2003); "Stimulus or Bust? Although Bush Touts Tax Cut, the B.E. 100s Have Mixed Feelings" in [32718], [54776]

Black Enterprise (Vol. 34, July 2004, No. 12, pp. 152); "Stone Perfect: Leslie Rinehardt and Marvin Miller Are In the Cut" in [13673], [16963]

Black Enterprise (Vol. 35, September 2004, No. 2, pp. 58); "Storage on the Go" in [6288], [49281]

Black Enterprise (Vol. 31, No. 5, December 2000, pp. 54); "Strategic Mission" in [38380]

Black Enterprise (Vol. 34, July 2004, No. 12, pp. 48); "Strong Structure" in [29768], [35678], [49775], [51480], [52790]

Black Enterprise (Vol. 32); "Study shows businesses are slow to embrace e-commerce" in [14492], [25975], [28839], [34548], [42015], [48426], [49284]

Black Enterprise (Vol. 37, February 2007, No. 7, pp. 135); "Success Products" in [14494], [25025], [25976], [36815], [47585], [48794], [53002], [55161]

Black Enterprise (Vol. 32, No. 7, February 2002, pp. 66); "Surviving a corporate marriage" in [48430], [50197]

Black Enterprise (Vol. 35, October 2004, No. 3, pp. 84); "Surviving Self-Employment" in [9743], [21019], [36821], [56423]

Black Enterprise (Vol. 35, November 2004, No. 4); "Suspended Animation: New Technology Lets You Take Your PC Anywhere-Virtually" in [6818], [42022]

Black Enterprise (Vol. 35, December 2004, No. 5); "Sweet Expectations: A Recipe for Success: In the Darkest Period of Her Life" in [11669], [56426]

Black Enterprise (Vol. 33, No. 3, October 2002, pp. S6); "Sweet success" in [2199], [2226], [35682], [53905], [56729]

Black Enterprise (Vol. 34, July 2004, No. 12, pp. 124); "Switching Tracks" in [14500], [22390], [24242], [25978], [34557], [37794], [50686]

Black Enterprise (Vol. 34, No. 4, November 2003, pp. 55); "Take One Tablet" in [6822], [49290]

Black Enterprise (Vol. 36, December 2005, No. 5, pp. 72); "Take the Work Home" in [45702], [54017]

Black Enterprise (Vol. 32, No. 10, May 2002, pp. 58); "Takes the cake" in [45704], [47600], [48797], [50688]

Black Enterprise (Vol. 31, No. 4, November 2000, pp. 57); "Taking Advantage of Technology" in [34562], [54018], [54991]

Black Enterprise (Vol. 34, July 2004, No. 12, pp. 145); "Taking Care of Business: Downloadable Programs For Your Enterprise" in [274], [4833], [15504], [22391], [23220], [26379], [38397], [49293], [53500]

Black Enterprise (Vol. 32, No. 9, March 2002, pp. 102); "Taking the 'dis' out of disability" in [35687], [46594], [47980], [56081]

Black Enterprise (Vol. 34, No. 5, December 2003); "Taking It Outside: Outsourcing Can Be a Great Time Saver-But Mind the Costs" in [38921], [49741]

Black Enterprise (Vol. 34, No. 5, December 2003); "Taking It Outside: Outsourcing Can Be a Great Time Saver-But Mind the Costs" in [38922], [49742]

Black Enterprise (Vol. 34, No. 3, October 2003, pp. 12); "Taking Our Affluence For Granted" in [32736], [47601]

Black Enterprise (Vol. 35, October 2004, No. 3, pp. 63); "Taking Technology Curbside and Beyond" in [6825], [12644], [14505], [42029]

Black Enterprise (Vol. 32, No. 9, April 2002, pp. 123); "Talking the talk" in [22454], [35688]

Black Enterprise (Vol. 30, No. 12, July 2000, pp. 47); "Tap into Expert Input" in [30019], [30949], [38262], [43388], [45709]

Black Enterprise (Vol. 33, No. 7, February 2003, pp. 6); "Tax time is approaching" in [277], [26382], [54790]

Black Enterprise (Vol. 34, No. 7, February 2004, pp. 42); "Taxes on Roth IRAs" in [10203], [15510], [16155], [38403], [38813], [54824], [57206]

Black Enterprise (Vol. 34, No. 5, December 2003); "Tech the Halls" in [4207], [5135], [6828], [42040]

Black Enterprise (Vol. 35, November 2004, No. 4, pp. 42); "Tech Stock Knockout" in [10204], [15514], [42042]

Black Enterprise (Vol. 32, No. 8, March 2002, pp. 87); "Technology makes a comeback: fizzling dotcoms were last year's news" in [35690], [41486], [44444], [47981], [55439]

Black Enterprise (Vol. 35, January 2005, No. 6, pp. 36); "Technology Stocks Show Some Life" in [15516], [38405], [42053]

Black Enterprise (Vol. 37, January 2007, No. 6, pp. 52); "Tee Off Online" in [14519], [18632], [25984], [30021], [34578], [53008]

Black Enterprise (Vol. 34, No. 5, December 2003, pp. S2); "Teen Biz? Piece of Cake!" in [2256], [56764], [56765]

Black Enterprise (Vol. 34, No. 2, September 2003); "Teen Decorating Diva: A Designer Turns Cluttered Corners Into Dream Spaces" in [13674], [56766]

Black Enterprise (Vol. 33, No. 7, February 2003, pp. 16); "Temp help" in [9237], [24536]

Black Enterprise (Vol. 36, December 2005, No. 5, pp. 52); "The 5 Keys to Value Investing" in [9799], [14713], [37861]

Black Enterprise (Vol. 35, February 2005, No. 7, pp. 104); "The 75 Most Powerful African Americans in Corporate America" in [35747], [48014]

Black Enterprise (Vol. 34, No. 2, September 2003, pp. S10); "The 2003 Teenpreneur Money Guide" in [9802], [14717], [37863], [44458], [56733]

Black Enterprise (Vol. 37, February 2007, No. 7, pp. 118); "The Balancing Act: How Busy Executives Make Their Lives Work" in [27808], [33006], [54935]

Black Enterprise (Vol. 34, No. 5, December 2003, pp. S5); "The Beginning of a Whole New Friendship" in [35331], [36174], [49764], [51917]

Black Enterprise (Vol. 35, September 2004, No. 2, pp. 108); "The Best CEO in Silicon Valley" in [4606], [14785], [22182], [22927], [49812], [53217]

Black Enterprise (Vol. 35, August 2004, No. 1, pp. 47); "The Buddy System: These Longtime Friends Formed a Growing CPA Firm" in [92], [2877], [3504], [23899], [26175], [31115], [49827]

Black Enterprise (Vol. 35, November 2004, No. 4, pp. 191); "The Business Traveler: Taking Advantage of Bargains on the Road" in [25167], [30303]

Black Enterprise (Vol. 37, February 2007, No. 7, pp. 58); "The Buzz About HD Radio" in [20306], [41582]

Black Enterprise (Vol. 32, No. 5, December 2001, pp. 126); "The inn crowd" in [2441], [48250]

Black Enterprise (Vol. 34, No. 6, January 2004, pp. 69); "The Cure for What Ails You" in [7306], [32342]

Black Enterprise (Vol. 32, No. 8, March 2002, pp. 63); "The case against disorganization: how to arrest this time bandit" in [4396], [54938]

Black Enterprise (Vol. 36, February 2006, No. 7, pp. 168); "The Doctor Will E-Mail You Now" in [33771], [41001], [43159]

Black Enterprise (Vol. 35, October 2004, No. 3, pp. 203); "The Doll Maker: Cozbi Cabrera Breaks the Mold" in [5903], [8005], [8164], [42603], [56192]

Black Enterprise (Vol. 33, Oct. 2002, pp. 134); "The investors next door: trying to figure out the best moves in today's market?" in [10036], [15162], [38161]

Black Enterprise (Vol. 34, No. 2, September 2003, pp. 60); "The Dress Code: How Business Style is Communicated" in [39287], [45080], [56198]

Black Enterprise (Vol. 37, January 2007, No. 6, pp. 111); "The Early Bird Gets the Worm" in [24924], [33079], [36040], [52846], [55086]

Black Enterprise (Vol. 32, No. 6, January 2002, pp. 53); "The domino effect: ripples from September 11 spread FAR and WIDE" in [28050], [39285]

Black Enterprise (Vol. 35, September 2004, No. 2, pp. 118); "The Fashion Elite" in [5542], [5657], [12882], [20118]

Black Enterprise (Vol. 32, No. 2); "The Future of Franchising: Taking Advantage of the Changing Complexion of the American Economy" in [28195], [38813], [48178]

Black Enterprise (Vol. 34, No. 5, December 2003); "The Hot List" in [36295], [41749]

Black Enterprise (Vol. 34, No. 4, Nov. 2003); "What's In a Name? Often Overlooked, Choosing the Right Business Moniker is Key" in [29775], [46600]

Black Enterprise (Vol. 36, November 2005, No. 4); "What's In Your Wallet? The Smartcard Is Emerging as a Major E-Commerce Tool" in [8325], [34700], [54072]

Black Enterprise (Vol. 34, No. 5, December 2003, pp. S9; "Wheels in Motion: Ian Hardman Takes Rims to the Next Level" in [1986]

Black Enterprise (Vol. 31, No. 5, December 2000, pp. 169); "When diamonds aren't forever" in [1866]

Black Enterprise (Vol. 34, July 2004, No. 12, pp. 42); "When Is the Price Right?" in [31078], [44256]

Black Enterprise (Vol. 35, January 2005, No. 6, pp. 54); "When the Love is Gone: How to Reignite Passion for the Job" in [35141], [36951], [45828]

Black Enterprise (Vol. 37, November 2006, No. 4, pp. 50); "When to Roll Over" in [10248], [15601], [38459]

Black Enterprise (Vol. 34, No. 6, January 2004, pp. 12); "When Will 'Content of Character' Count?" in [32070], [33167], [42462], [44116]

Black Enterprise (Vol. 34, No. 5, December 2003, pp. 63); "When Your Job Really Makes You Sick" in [3610], [16539], [31248], [42759], [56478]

Black Enterprise (Vol. 34, December 2003); "When Your Job Really Makes You Sick: Why You Need to Develop a High Adversity Quotient" in [3611], [16540], [31249], [42760], [56479]

Black Enterprise (Vol. 34, No. 5, December 2003, pp. 40); "Where Are the 529 Plans?" in [32292], [33279], [38460], [54871]

Black Enterprise (Vol. 31, No. 5, December 2000, pp. 61); "Where Do I E-Sign?" in [34710]

Black Enterprise (Vol. 31, No. 5, December 2000, pp. 87); "Where Do You Go From Here" in [38461], [48480]

Black Enterprise (Vol. 32, No. 7, February 2002, pp. 95); "Where the Jobs Are" in [29002], [32794]

Black Enterprise (Vol. 35, September 2004, No. 2); "While I'm Gone: Transitioning Into-and Back From-Family and Medical Leave" in [26960], [41135]

Black Enterprise (Vol. 31, No. 5, December 2000, pp. 82); "Whipping up a great meeting" in [27537], [45836]

Black Enterprise (Vol. 33, No. 3, October 2002, pp. S12); "Whose moves ya doin'" in [8455], [9066], [9750], [10602]

Black Enterprise (Vol. 34, No. 3, October 2003, pp. 51); "Windows 98 Lives" in [6867], [25528], [26100], [31908]

Black Enterprise (Vol. 34, July 2004, No. 12, pp. 54); "Wireless Freedom: Installing an AirPort Network Can Be a Breeze" in [6868], [6981], [49368]

Black Enterprise (Vol. 34, July 2004, No. 12, pp. 145); "Work At Home" in [14632], [34744], [42561]

Black Enterprise (Vol. 35, October 2004, No. 3, pp. 200); "Work-At-Home Scheme" in [30268], [42767]

Black Enterprise (Vol. 36, February 2006, No. 7, pp. 44); "Working Hard for the Money" in [45869], [48609], [54089]

Black Enterprise (Vol. 32, No. 7, February 2002, pp. 51); "Working virtually works for her" in [3618], [6295], [14635], [34748], [48485], [52613], [56514]

Black Enterprise (Vol. 34, January 2004); "Working on the Highway: This Entrepreneur Minds Her Cash Flow and the Traffic Flow" in [3244], [3459], [7514], [7743], [56515], [59086]

Black Enterprise (Vol. 37, January 2007, No. 6, pp. 55); "Working It Out! How a Young Executive Overcomes Obstacles on the Job" in [20704], [21039], [35163], [36987], [39693]

Black Enterprise (Vol. 37, December 2006, No. 5, pp. 34); "World Wide Technology Expands" in [29032], [42129], [43033]

Black Enterprise (Vol. 33, No. 3, Oct. 2002, pp. 46); "Wrestling with the bear" in [10257], [10315], [15114], [15612], [37008], [38474], [48486]

Black Enterprise (Vol. 31, No. 5, December 2000, pp. 125); "Year-End Tax Tips" in [54878]

Black Enterprise (Vol. 31, No. 5, December 2000, pp. 64); "Yes, you can" in [29776], [30495], [35733], [47987], [52791]

Black Enterprise (Vol. 33, Oct. 2002, pp. 43); "You Can Take It with You: Clubs that Let the Stocks Travel with Individual Owners" in [10260], [15619], [38476]

Black Enterprise (Vol. 33, Oct. 2002, pp. 43); "You can take it with you: clubs that let the stocks travel with individual owners" in [10261], [15621], [38478]

Black Enterprise (Vol. 33, No. 3, October 2002, pp. 163); "Your career can still thrive in an age of flux" in [29038], [29760], [42477], [43530]

Black Enterprise (Vol. 34, No. 7, February 2004, pp. 140); "Your Kind of News: Free Personalized Information for the Public" in [37012], [38480], [39784], [47039], [49383]

Black Enterprise (Vol. 34, No. 6, January 2004, pp. 59); "Your Safety Is What Drives Us: Auto Safety Tips from Allstate" in [13435], [13526], [41518], [43431]

Black Enterprise (Vol. 36, February 2006, No. 7, pp. 57); "Your Story Here" in [20350], [24463], [34767], [47775], [50484], [50710]

Black Enterprise (Vol. 31, No. 2, September 2000, pp. 215); "Yourshop@Black Enterprise.com" in [31913], [34768], [47776], [51921]

Black Enterprise (Vol. 31, No. 5, December 2000, pp. 166); "You've got the power!" in [37015], [48488], [56525]

Black Enterprise (Vol. 37, October 2006, No. 3, pp. 36); "Z-Tech Lands Contract with CMS" in [6297], [6491]

"Black Enterprise.com" in *Black Enterprise* (Vol. 31, No. 5, December 2000, pp. 12) [9696], [33591], [48063]

"Black Enterprise's 2000 Business Entertaining Guide" in *Black Enterprise* (Vol. 31, No. 5, December 2000, pp. 153) [27304], [48064], [53612]

"Black Farmers Sue USDA for $20.5 Billion" in *Black Enterprise* (Vol. 35, December 2004, No. 5, pp. 36) [26486], [29127], [48065]

"Black Firm Sues SBA, Alleges Funding Bias" in *Boston Business Journal* (Vol. 23, No. 30, August 29, 2003, pp. 18) [29128], [39989], [40197], [44481], [48066]

Black Genealogy [10928]

"Black Gold: Oil is Key to the Success of this Russian Fund" in *Entrepreneur* (Vol. 32, December 2004, No. 12, pp. 61) [14800], [37923]

Black Hawk College
    Quad-Cities Campus [59796]
    Small Business Development Center [59363]

"Black Hawk down at work" in *Harvard Business Review* (Vol. 81, No. 1, January 2003, pp. 16) [34830], [35849], [44941]

"Black Ink brings dollars into the data-flow equation" in *Boston Business Journal* (Vol. 22, No. 16, May 24, 2002, pp. 17) [3500], [26170], [33592]

"Black Investment Trends: Report Ranks What Buyers Care Most About" in *Black Enterprise* (Vol. 35, October 2004, No. 3, pp. 40) [14801], [37924]

Black Mountain-Swannanoa Chamber of Commerce [63331]

"Black Technology Pioneers Credit Family Support for Success" in *San Jose Mercury News* (February 26, 2005) [6591], [37598], [48067]

Black Tennis Magazine [24573]

"BlackBerry Harvest" in *Entrepreneur* (Vol. 32, September 2004, No. 9, pp. 40) [4927], [48960]

BlackEnterprise (Vol. 32, No. 3, October 2001, pp. 56); "A new venue for seeking capital" in [37170], [44602], [48336], [55752]

BlackEnterprise (Vol. 32, No. 3, October 2001, pp. 54); "A different kind of service" in [32151], [35389], [48131]

BlackEnterprise (Vol. 32, No. 2, September 2001, pp. 88); "Affordable Franchises" in [2235], [7030], [21435], [22606], [22786], [38706], [52506]

BlackEnterprise (Vol. 31, No. 6, January 2001, pp. 99); "An agent for change" in [3475], [31087], [35314], [47938]

BlackEnterprise (Vol. 32, No. 2, September 2001, pp. 22); "Atlanta Life to manage investments" in [13191], [14754], [27797], [48040]

BlackEnterprise (Vol. 31, No. 8, March 2001, pp. 47); "Back from the Brink" in [35798], [39157], [48047], [52818]

BlackEnterprise (Vol. 32, No. 2, September 2001, pp. 61); "Bargaining a good-bye" in [39162], [44917]

BlackEnterprise (Vol. 31, No. 7, February 2001, pp. 134); "Brainy Is As Brainy Does" in [29806], [35868], [48071]

BlackEnterprise (Vol. 32, No. 2, September 2001, pp. 21); "Breakthroughs for black-owned agencies" in [568], [27872], [48072]

BlackEnterprise (Vol. 32, No. 3, October 2001, pp. 68); "Bringing home the dough" in [4534], [7811], [35344], [47944]

BlackEnterprise (Vol. 32, No. 3, October 2001, pp. 161); "Bringing the dead back to life" in [17555], [35874]

BlackEnterprise (Vol. 31, No. 6, January 2001, pp. 39); "Building vs. buying" in [29715], [30652], [35350], [47947]

BlackEnterprise (Vol. 32, No. 1, August 2001, pp. 28); "Bush may trim SBA budget" in [39793], [40212]

BlackEnterprise (Vol. 31, No. 12, July 2001, pp. 48); "Business information centers" in [29716], [39031], [39761], [52770]

BlackEnterprise (Vol. 32, No. 2, September 2001, pp. 50); "Careful planning" in [24644], [25116], [29718], [47949]

BlackEnterprise (Vol. 32, No. 3, October 2001, pp. 56); "Children's stories" in [2634], [8590], [46563]

BlackEnterprise (Vol. 32, No. 3, October 2001, pp. 52); "Connecting businesses through technology's window" in [13919], [48107]

BlackEnterprise (Vol. 32, No. 3, October 2001, pp. 26); "Construction workers charge bias" in [7293], [32011]

BlackEnterprise (Vol. 32, No. 3, October 2001, pp. 59); "Copy this" in [13930], [19870]

BlackEnterprise (Vol. 31, No. 10, May 2001, pp. 47); "Cream of the crop" in [27986], [35985], [39262], [48115]

BlackEnterprise (Vol. 32, No. 3, October 2001, pp. 32); "Department of Justice grounds DC air" in [14913], [49893]

BlackEnterprise (Vol. 32, No. 3, October 2001, pp. 62); "Equal access for all" in [14020], [54172]

BlackEnterprise (Vol. 31, No. 6, January 2001, pp. 102); "Get fiscally fit" in [27128], [38087]

BlackEnterprise (Vol. 32, No. 2, September 2001, pp. 114); "Give good presence" in [36211], [39357]

BlackEnterprise (Vol. 31, No. 8, March 2001, pp. 48); "Global financing options" in [43186], [44536], [48183], [56246]

BlackEnterprise (Vol. 31, No. 12, July 2001, pp. 53); "Going legit" in [35484], [41458], [47959]

BlackEnterprise (Vol. 32, No. 3, October 2001, pp. 168); "Got milked?" in [29271]

BlackEnterprise (Vol. 31, No. 7, February 2001, pp. 57); "Hey, you can't do that!" in [29286], [44308], [48211]

BlackEnterprise (Vol. 31, No. 12, July 2001, pp. 50); "It's in the card" in [39066], [44422], [47963], [52777]

BlackEnterprise (Vol. 32, No. 2, September 2001, pp. 50); "It's a 'go' in Detroit" in [21539], [38841], [39844]

BlackEnterprise (Vol. 31, No. 11, June 2001, pp. 74); "Keep them flying" in [39771], [47964], [52494]

BlackEnterprise (Vol. 31, No. 6, January 2001, pp. 40); "Keeping it all in the family" in [3318], [37710], [48261], [52553]

Boston Business Journal (Vol. 22, No. 14, May 10, 2002, pp. 22); "Marketing and sales" in **[28462]**, **[47250]**, **[51727]**

Boston Business Journal (Vol. 22, No. 14, May 10, 2002, pp. 1); "More tech firms feed off federal defense, IT spending growth" in **[22301]**, **[40059]**, **[41843]**, **[44340]**

Boston Business Journal (Vol. 23, No. 30, August 29, 2003, pp. 1); "Mortgage Lenders Brace for Layoffs" in **[17415]**, **[20598]**, **[22821]**, **[32581]**

Boston Business Journal (Vol. 23, No. 21, June 27, 2003, pp. 1); "New 'Heads in Beds' in Suburban Hotels" in **[12602]**, **[25219]**, **[30384]**

Boston Business Journal (Vol. 22, No. 16, May 24, 2002, pp. 7); "90 percent of laid-off hotel workers back on the job" in **[12604]**, **[32600]**, **[42362]**

Boston Business Journal (Vol. 23, No. 31, September 5, 2003, pp. 1); "Nonprofits Eye New Revenue Ideas as Gifts, Grants Dwindle" in **[10745]**, **[32602]**, **[38251]**

Boston Business Journal (Vol. 22, No. 3, February 22, 2002, pp. S7); "On the paper trail" in **[6269]**, **[52381]**

Boston Business Journal (Vol. 22, No. 15, May 17, 2002); "Paper Mountain" in **[6271]**, **[28611]**

Boston Business Journal (Vol. 23, July 11, 2003); "Peter Falvey: Whiz Kid: Peter Falvey is Betting the Company on Tech Investment" in **[36624]**, **[41900]**, **[46403]**, **[55776]**

Boston Business Journal (Vol. 22, No. 16, Ma); "Premium pain" in **[13422]**, **[41081]**, **[43318]**

Boston Business Journal (Vol. 22, No. 14, May 10, 2002, pp. 42); "Read fine print yearly to avoid costly contractual obligations" in **[29462]**

Boston Business Journal (Vol. 23, No. 30, August 29, 2003, pp. 5); "Report: Brokers See Tough Going Rest of Year" in **[20652]**, **[20990]**

Boston Business Journal (Vol. 23, No. 25, July 25, 2003, pp. 24); "Rescue Squad" in **[3577]**, **[16529]**

Boston Business Journal (Vol. 23, No. 27, August 8, 2003); "Restart: Network Engines Finds Profits After the Tech Bubble Burst" in **[14398]**, **[28699]**, **[41947]**

Boston Business Journal (Vol. 22, No. 15, May 17, 2002, pp. 13); "Restaurants stay hot commodities despite downturn" in **[21606]**, **[32666]**

Boston Business Journal (Vol. 23, Aug. 22, 2003); "Ring It Up. Way Systems Helps Convert Cell Phones into Portable Cash Registers" in **[5097]**, **[41953]**, **[48782]**

Boston Business Journal (Vol. 23, No. 30, August 29, 2003, pp. 3); "Rivaling a Giant" in **[6963]**, **[30938]**, **[41955]**, **[47481]**, **[48784]**

Boston Business Journal (Vol. 22, No. 14, May 10, 2002, pp. 21); "Room at the table" in **[3578]**, **[16531]**, **[45608]**

Boston Business Journal (Vol. 22, No. 3, February 22, 2002, pp. 22); "SBA adjusts revenue standards for inflation" in **[32680]**, **[40667]**

Boston Business Journal (Vol. 22, No. 15, May 17, 2002); "Seeing the light" in **[3135]**, **[30947]**, **[47508]**, **[48789]**

Boston Business Journal (Vol. 23, No. 25, July 25, 2003, pp. 20); "Seizing the Sun" in **[41971]**, **[46427]**

Boston Business Journal (Vol. 22, No. 16, May 24, 2002, pp. 10); "Several restaurants to be added to Boston's menu" in **[21623]**, **[28756]**

Boston Business Journal (Vol. 23, No. 25, July 25, 2003, pp. 3); "Sizing Up the Market" in **[11662]**, **[29992]**, **[30951]**, **[47536]**

Boston Business Journal (Vol. 23, No. 27, August 8, 2003, pp. 21); "SmaL Camera Technologies Snaps Up $13.5M in V.C." in **[4204]**, **[55826]**

Boston Business Journal (Vol. 22, No. 15, May 17, 2002, p); "Smith & Nephew's local spark" in **[17105]**, **[36765]**

Boston Business Journal (Vol. 22, No. 14, May 10, 2002, pp. 38); "Some outplacement firms benefit in down economy" in **[32705]**, **[49735]**, **[53984]**

Boston Business Journal (Vol. 22, No. 16, May 24, 2002, pp. 38); "SpeechWorks International" in **[4822]**, **[5120]**, **[23208]**, **[53488]**

Boston Business Journal (Vol. 22, No. 11, April 19, 2002, pp. 27); "Spirit of business" in **[36779]**, **[45659]**

Boston Business Journal (Vol. 23, Aug. 22, 2003); "Taking the Leap. Minority Staffing Services Owner Proves He Can Make It in MA" in **[9235]**, **[24535]**, **[48433]**

Boston Business Journal (Vol. 23, No. 21, June 27, 2003, pp. 16); "Tech Biz. Tough Crowd" in **[42032]**, **[55856]**

Boston Business Journal (Vol. 22, No. 3, February 22, 2002, pp. S11); "The best facility managers strive to be one-stop shops" in **[20049]**

Boston Business Journal (Vol. 22, No. 15, May 17, 2002, pp. 11); "Tiny Chelsea grows as home to big, active food companies" in **[11671]**

Boston Business Journal (Vol. 23, No. 29, August 22, 2003, pp. 1); "To Stay Afloat, Travel Agents Alter Course" in **[24736]**, **[25257]**

Boston Business Journal (Vol. 22, No. 3, February 22, 2002, pp. S4); "Toxic mold" in **[9374]**, **[20061]**, **[37331]**

Boston Business Journal (Vol. 23, No. 33, September 19, 2003, pp. 40); "Venturing Forward?" in **[28966]**, **[54060]**, **[55926]**

Boston Business Journal (Vol. 22, No. 3, February 22, 2002, pp. S6); "When small firms work from big-name locations" in **[20063]**, **[52751]**

Boston Business Journal (Vol.); "When planning to landscape a property, earlier is better" in **[16031]**, **[20064]**

Boston Capital Ventures **[61045]**

Boston College
 Center for Corporate Citizenship **[50743]**
 Center on Wealth and Philanthropy **[50387]**
 Office for Sponsored Programs **[61138]**

Boston Consulting Group–Chicago Information and Research Group **[4046]**

Boston Financial Consulting Group **[21071]**

Boston Financial & Equity Corp. **[61046]**

Boston Gift Show **[11120]**, **[11184]**, **[18284]**

Boston Globe (July 26, 2004); "Accumulations of Real, Virtual Stuff Inspire Innovations in Storage" in **[20010]**, **[20214]**

Boston Globe (February 2, 2005); "Boston Scientific Looks To Expand Its Products Beyond Stents" in **[48703]**, **[52062]**, **[55521]**

Boston Globe (February 4, 2005); "Caritas Seeking Cambridge Lab Space" in **[41592]**, **[50844]**, **[52071]**

Boston Globe (February 4, 2005); "Citizens Bank To Lend Low-Interest Loans to Firms Relocating to Massachusetts" in **[30139]**, **[44493]**, **[52656]**

Boston Globe (February 8, 2005); "Consumers Hit Harder by Medicine Copayments" in **[13244]**, **[40988]**, **[43135]**

Boston Globe (March 8, 2005); "Dean of Boston College Business School Wants to Emphasize Ethics and Values" in **[33065]**, **[37419]**, **[39274]**

"The Boston Globe Downtown Column" in *Boston Globe* (April 11, 2003) **[7262]**, **[24896]**, **[27863]**

Boston Globe (February 9, 2005); "Eco-Products In Demand, But Labels Can Be Murky" in **[37266]**, **[40336]**

Boston Globe (March 5, 2005); "Economy Adds 262,000 Jobs" in **[28088]**, **[32390]**

Boston Globe (February 2, 2005); "Eyeing Rivals, Foxwoods Set To Expand" in **[10864]**, **[28137]**

Boston Globe (February 3, 2005); "Federal Reserve Raises Key Interest Rate by Quarter Point" in **[40375]**, **[44517]**, **[54550]**

Boston Globe (February 4, 2005); "For Advertisers, Super Bowl Still Holds Promise of Super Payoffs" in **[629]**, **[23720]**, **[46974]**

Boston Globe (January 25, 2005); "Genzyme Battles An Old Adversary" in **[41706]**, **[44300]**, **[49956]**, **[50879]**, **[52109]**

Boston Globe (March 8, 2005); "Harvard Pilgrim Purchases Medical Benefits Company" in **[13308]**, **[15069]**, **[26822]**, **[43199]**, **[49974]**

Boston Globe (February 2, 2005); "Higher Revenue Boosts Call for Tax Cut" in **[28280]**, **[40438]**, **[54590]**

Boston Globe (January 31, 2005); "Housing, Immigration Called Keys to the Future" in **[7374]**, **[20542]**, **[48559]**

Boston Globe (March 7, 2005); "Hybrid Phones Hold Promise of Cellular, VoIP" in **[5023]**, **[49081]**

Boston Globe (January 27, 2005); "Insurance System Changes Would Raise Rates of Bad Drivers" in **[13345]**, **[43237]**

Boston Globe (February 3, 2005); "Jetblue Outlines Massive Logan Expansion" in **[28356]**, **[30359]**, **[42312]**

Boston Globe (February 2, 2005); "Judge Halts Initial Step in Auto-Insurance Revamp" in **[13358]**, **[43251]**

Boston Globe (April 11, 2003); "Judge Rejects Effort to Keep Billing Records for Boston's Big Dig a Secret" in **[29324]**, **[37468]**, **[40486]**

Boston Globe (February 2, 2005); "Judge Stays Implementation of Massachusetts Governor's Auto Insurance Plan" in **[13359]**, **[40487]**, **[43252]**

Boston Globe (April 11, 2003); "Massachusetts House Plan Seeks More Excise Tax for Newer Cars" in **[18085]**, **[54658]**

Boston Globe (April 11, 2003); "Massachusetts Jobless Insurance Trust Fund May Need Federal Help" in **[28467]**, **[32565]**, **[39865]**

Boston Globe (March 5, 2005); "Massport Drops Metal Recycling Facility Plan" in **[21243]**

Boston Globe (January 14, 2003); "Merger to Join Cambridge, Mass., Rivals in Anti-Aging Work" in **[17872]**, **[49772]**, **[55726]**

Boston Globe (February 11, 2005); "Microsoft, Pfizer Target Fake Viagra Spammers" in **[14243]**, **[22295]**, **[34195]**

Boston Globe (March 7, 2005); "Microsoft to Unveil Product to Manage Net Communications" in **[4730]**, **[5056]**, **[14244]**, **[23083]**, **[27437]**, **[53371]**

Boston Globe (April 11, 2003); "Murdoch's Bid for DirecTV Parent May Lead to Launch of New Networks" in **[4113]**, **[15283]**, **[24436]**, **[50090]**

Boston Globe (March 3, 2005); "New Group Plan Offers 'Free-Agent' Workers Affordable Health Benefits" in **[13397]**, **[26858]**, **[43289]**

Boston Globe (January 27, 2005); "New RCN Service Offers Net-Connected Surveillance" in **[4115]**, **[4192]**, **[14288]**, **[19969]**, **[22306]**, **[34255]**

Boston Globe (March 7, 2005); "Plugging Into the Future with New Wave of Communication Services" in **[5089]**, **[14354]**

Boston Globe (January 28, 2005); "Popular Lance Armstrong Wristbands Spawn Counterfits" in **[30245]**, **[54238]**

Boston Globe (February 10, 2005); "Reebok Rolls Out Marketing Device" in **[770]**, **[22765]**, **[47458]**

Boston Globe (January 31, 2005); "Romney, Businesses Wrangle On 'Loopholes'" in **[40656]**, **[54729]**

Boston Globe (February 3, 2005); "Romney Set To Unveil Jobs Program" in **[39902]**, **[40657]**, **[42402]**

Boston Globe (December 5, 2004); "Seasoned Professional Offers Holiday Gift of Stress-Free Shopping" in **[19007]**

Boston Globe (February 13, 2005); "Second Bank Set To Offer Small-Business Job Incentives" in **[10177]**, **[44652]**

Boston Globe (January 28, 2005); "Sports Merchandisers Tap Into Feminine Side" in **[5573]**, **[5716]**, **[23638]**, **[23737]**

Boston Globe (January 26, 2005); "State, U.S. Housing Sales Hit New Highs in 2004" in **[7486]**, **[17442]**, **[20675]**, **[28819]**

Boston Globe (July 11, 2004); "Stresses of Elder Care Hitting the Workplace" in **[459]**, **[18339]**, **[54005]**

Boston Globe (March 7, 2005); "Tewksbury Firm Cashes in as Internet Calling Grows" in **[5145]**, **[14526]**, **[28879]**

Boston Globe (February 11, 2005); "The Blush Is Off As Consumers Pick Variety in Flowers for Valentine's Day" in **[10557]**, **[27853]**, **[43562]**

Boston Globe (April 11, 2003); "The Boston Globe Downtown Column" in [7262], [24896], [27863]

Boston Globe (February 13, 2005); "The Endangered Department Store" in [30845], [49916], [51145], [53711]

Boston Globe (January 31, 2005); "The Life Sciences Building Boom" in [7403], [28413], [50909], [52139]

Boston Globe (February 7, 2005); "The Lure of Bay State Technology" in [15242], [41820], [43739], [50064], [52145], [55717]

Boston Globe (April 11, 2003); "Wal-Mart Said to Be Weighing Bid for Massachusetts-Based BJ's Wholesale Club" in [15583], [28971], [50249], [51403], [56018]

Boston JobBank [23381]

Boston Millennia Partners [61047]

Boston Pizza International Inc. [21758]

Boston Public Library–Kirstein Business Branch [47927], [53125]

"Boston Scientific Looks To Expand Its Products Beyond Stents" in *Boston Globe* (February 2, 2005) [48703], [52062], [55521]

Boston University
Center for Law and Technology [29703]
Corporate Education Center Library [6539], [23315]
Entrepreneurial Management Institute [37053]
Frederick S. Pardee Management Library [46147]
Morin Center for Banking and Financial Law [10408]
Multimedia Communications Laboratory [6317]
Neuromuscular Research Center [19597]
NeuroMuscular Research Center–Muscle Fatigue Laboratory [19598]
Office of Sponsored Programs [61139]

Boston University Community Technology Fund [61048]

The Boston's Gourmet Pizza [19654], [21759]

Botetourt County Chamber of Commerce [65866]

"Botox Tax Could Throw Wrinkle Into Tax Code" in *Sacramento Bee* (December 19, 2005) [2393], [2583], [7882], [54458]

Bottin Touristique du Quebec [25159]

"Bottle Perfection" in *Entrepreneur* (Vol. 33, February 2005, No. 2, pp. 83) [23461], [38722]

"Bottle Shoppe Owner Looking to Sell" in *Bellingham Business Journal* (December 2006, pp. A6) [16230], [23462], [52409]

The Bottled Water Market [3082]

Bottled Water Reporter [3083]

"Bottom feeding for blockbuster businesses" in *Harvard Business Review* (Vol. 81, No. 3, March 2003, pp. 52) [27864], [35865], [44953]

Bottom Line Service System [22027]

"Boudin Rises, Again; Bakery Restaurant Set for Suburban Return" in *Crain's Chicago Business* (Vol. 30, January 2007, No. 4, pp. 13) [2240], [21451], [27865], [30513]

Boulder Chamber of Commerce [58331]

Boulder City Chamber of Commerce [62342]

Boulder Junction Chamber of Commerce [66353]

Boulder Small Business Development Center–Boulder Chamber of Commerce [58292]

Boulder Ventures, Ltd. [60865]

"Bouncing back" in *Entrepreneur* (Vol. 30, No. 3, March 2002, pp. 134) [29712], [31090], [35341]

Bound Brook Area Chamber of Commerce [62476]

"Bound by the Long View" in *Business Journal-Milwaukee* (Vol. 20, No. 48, August 15, 2003, pp. A25) [2684], [2833], [20219], [27866], [46218]

"BountyQuest Introduces New Service to Help Strengthen U.S. Patent System" in *Information Today* (Vol. 17, No. 11, December 2000, pp. 6) [33605], [44003]

Bourget Research Group [47835]

Bouse Chamber of Commerce [57017]

Bovina Chamber of Commerce [65134]

"Bovine Blues?" in *Entrepreneur* (Vol. 31, No. 8, August 2003, page 25) [12870], [20105], [30802], [46729], [50557]

Bow and Arrow Hunting [1477]

Law Offices of David Bow Woo [29607]

Bowdens International Directory [4088]

Bowes & Co. [21072]

Bowie Chamber of Commerce [65135]

Bowker's Annual Library and Book Trade Almanac [2685], [3032], [18853]

Bowker's Complete Video Directory [25590], [25610]

Bowlers Journal [3107]

"Bowling for dollars" in *Crain's Detroit Business* (Vol. 19, No. 9, March 3, 2003, pp. 1) [3102]

Bowling-Golfing News [3108]

Bowling Green Area Chamber of Commerce [60484]

Bowling Green Chamber of Commerce [61921]

Bowling Green Community College of Western Kentucky University [60591]

Bowling Green State University–Music Library and Sound Recordings Archives [21162]

Bowling Inc. [3094]

Bowling Proprietors' Association of America [3095]

Bowling Proprietors' Association of Canada [3096]

"Bowling for drug research: families take entrepreneurial tack in signing up biotech firms" in *Wall Street Journal* (Feb. 27, 2003) [41564], [48900], [50835], [52063]

Bowling Writers Association of America [8951]

Bowman Capital [57951]

Bowman Chamber of Commerce [63510]

Bowman R&C Projects [16852]

The Bowser Directory of Small Stocks [15633]

"Box Office" in *Entrepreneur* (Vol. 32, December 2004, No. 12, pp. 54) [4930], [48963]

"Boxing Match" in *Entrepreneur* (Vol. 33, September 2005, No. 9, pp. 32) [17788], [17981], [47148], [49487]

Boxoffice-Buyers Directory Issue [17512]

BOXOFFICE Magazine [17537]

Boyd Company Inc. [30192]

Boyne Area City Chamber of Commerce [61262]

Bozeman Area Chamber of Commerce [62151]

Bozeman Small Business Development Center–Gallatin Development Corporation [62119]

"BP Amoco wants to sell much more than gas at its new stations" in *The New York Times* (July 25, 2000, pp. C6) [22609], [33606], [50558], [51075]

BPT Consulting Associates Ltd. [3652], [3958], [16576], [29047], [30063], [30713], [31290], [45974], [53071]

Brace Your Space: Earthquake Safety in the Work Environment [56611]

Bracewell & Patterson–Library [9427]

Bracken County Chamber of Commerce [60485]

Brad Peery Capital, Inc. [57952]

"Bradenton Central CRA To Launch New Business Development Center" in *Bradenton Herald* (January 29, 2005) [27867], [29129], [40202], [44483], [46730]

"Bradenton Firm Capitalizes On Restroom 'Downtime' With 'Captive Audience' Ads" in *Bradenton Herald* (February 14, 2005) [566], [46731]

"Bradenton, Fla., Sees More Beach Weddings, Sells More Informal Bridal Wear" in *Bradenton Herald* (March 22, 2004) [3178], [53616]

Bradenton Herald (February 12, 2005); "Bakery Wishes, Cake-Decorating Dreams" in [2236], [8509], [37590], [56127]

Bradenton Herald (January 20, 2005); "Beall's Push to Expand Existing Florida Stores Reaps Dividends On Grand Scale" in [3027], [5642], [27820], [51067]

Bradenton Herald (February 2, 2005); "Bennett Pursues Public Input On Growth Issues" in [27828], [40181]

Bradenton Herald (January 6, 2005); "Big Tenants Buy Space at Bradenton, Fla. Office Park" in [20432], [20804]

Bradenton Herald (February 13, 2007); "Bill Would Boost Small Businesses" in [39790], [40970], [43094], [53611], [54452]

Bradenton Herald (January 29, 2005); "Bradenton Central CRA To Launch New Business Development Center" in [27867], [29129], [40202], [44483], [46730]

Bradenton Herald (February 14, 2005); "Bradenton Firm Capitalizes On Restroom 'Downtime' With 'Captive Audience' Ads" in [566], [46731]

Bradenton Herald (March 22, 2004); "Bradenton, Fla., Sees More Beach Weddings, Sells More Informal Bridal Wear" in [3178], [53616]

Bradenton Herald (December 24, 2004); "Builder Outlines Plans for Affordable Housing in Palmetto, Fla" in [1500], [7273]

Bradenton Herald (January 25, 2005); "Charter Service Gets OK To Build Hangar At SRQ" in [947], [27943]

Bradenton Herald (January 6, 2005); "Coagulating-Powder Firm Seeks Site To Build New Factory In Florida" in [46242], [52657]

Bradenton Herald (January 22, 2005); "Condos Coming To U.S. 301 Property" in [7292], [20844], [51109]

Bradenton Herald (April 11 2003); "Dentist Office to Anchor New Sarasota County, Fla., Office Park" in [128], [13263], [28015], [29193]

Bradenton Herald (February 12, 2005); "Developer Buys Moores Farm for $8.66 Million" in [20856], [26501]

Bradenton Herald (January 27, 2005); "Developer Eyes North County" in [7318]

Bradenton Herald (January 13, 2005); "Economist Offers 2005 Outlook For 2 Florida Counties" in [7340], [25180], [28086], [32385]

Bradenton Herald (January 5, 2005); "Fantastic Sams To Open Manatee County, Fla. Hair Salon" in [11789], [28144], [38771], [52671]

Bradenton Herald (January 25, 2005) "Fisherman Joe's Reopens; Owner Hopes To Hook Customers With Late Hours" in [21507], [36157]

"The Bradenton Herald, Fla., Dana Sanchez Column" in *Bradenton Herald* (January 5, 2005) [24671], [25160], [46732]

Bradenton Herald (February 14, 2005); "For Beall's, Bigger Is Always Better" in [28173], [51164]

Bradenton Herald (); "Former Airline Workers Navigate Into Florida Liquor Business" in [16222], [52638], [54561]

Bradenton Herald (January 29, 2005); "Got 20 Minutes? Gym Champions Quick, Occasional Workouts" in [19404], [37670], [38820]

Bradenton Herald (January 5, 2005); "Group Buys Bradenton, Fla.-Area Retail Center" in [20521], [20887], [51174], [52678], [53766], [54584]

Bradenton Herald (January 22, 2005); "Kirkland's, Gap Will Close At Leases' End" in [28381], [51219]

Bradenton Herald (February 3, 2005); "Lakewood Hotel Draws Lofty Rating From Chain" in [12588], [25205], [30366]

Bradenton Herald (February 7, 2005); "Local Businesses Discover There's No Place Like Home" in [28419], [36451], [52693]

Bradenton Herald (January 28, 2005); "Local Realty Firm's Owner Confident In Strength of Real Estate Market" in [20576], [28425]

Bradenton Herald (February 3, 2005); "Maintenance-Free Condos Offer Stunning Views" in [20581], [28449]

Bradenton Herald (February 4, 2005); "Manatee Boat Makers Are Hiring, But Workers Aren't Plentiful" in [16737], [28454], [42334], [46356]

Bradenton Herald (January 5, 2005); "Manatee County, Fla. New Home Permits Up 13 Percent in 2004" in [7418], [28455]

Bradenton Herald (February 11, 2005); "Michigan Firm Buys Signs Now" in [15264], [19885], [22792], [28483], [38855], [50080]

Bradenton Herald (January 20, 2005); "Parrish, Fla. Farmland Sells for $6.5 Million" in [7449], [20962], [26527]

Bradenton Herald (January 27, 2005); "Potential Landfill Study Raises Radiation Concerns" in [37317]

Brentwood-Baldwin-Whitehall Chamber of Commerce [64389]

Brentwood Chamber of Commerce [57371], [61924]

Brentwood Cool Springs Chamber of Commerce [64887]

Brentwood Venture Capital [57953]

"Brentwood's Blue Light Special" in *Washington Business Journal* (Vol. 22, No. 15, August 15, 2003, pp. 1) [30136], [51076], [52410]

"BresaGen moves slowly to grow stem cell work" in *Atlanta Business Chronicle* (Vol. 25, November 8, 2002, No. 22 pp. 1A) [39991], [44006], [50836], [52064]

Brevard Community College (Melbourne)–Small Business Development Center [58699]

Brevard - Transylvania Chamber of Commerce [63334]

Brewers Association of Canada [3117]
Library [3160]

The Brewer's Companion [3123]

Brewery Adventures in the Wild West [3124]

Brewing and Malting Barley Research Institute [3118]

Brewing Up a Business: Adventures in Entrepreneurship from the Founder of Dogfish Head Craft [3112], [35342], [39029]

Brewster Chamber of Commerce [62827], [66054]

"Brick by brick" in *Crain's Detroit Business* (Vol. 19, No. 12, March 24, 2003, pp. 3) [7265], [27873]

Brick Industry Association [16926]
Library [16986]

Brick Industry Association-Membership Directory [16943]

Brick Township Chamber of Commerce [62477]

"Brickell is Crown Jewel Setting for Emerald" in *South Florida Business Journal* (Vol. 23, No. 47, June 27, 2003, pp. 6) [20440], [20810]

The BrickKicker [3269], [7656], [20745]

"Bricks-and-Clicks World Needs Commercial Space" in *The New York Times* (October 30, 2000, pp. C1) [13856], [20220], [33607]

"Bricks & Clicks" in *Entrepreneur* (Vol. 33, October 2005, No. 10, pp. 64) [1785], [32605], [33608], [48608], [51077]

Bridal Association of America [3172]

Bridal Crafts [8026]

"A Bridal Planner: Tips, Trends and Ideas for the Perfect Wedding Day" in *Sarasota Magazine* (Vol. 26, No. 5, February 2004, pp. 321) [3179]

Bride and Groom Planner [876]

Bridge Business & Property Brokers, Inc. [2380]

Bridge City Chamber of Commerce [65139]

Bridge Partners, LLC [60866]

Bridgeport Area Chamber of Commerce [63623], [65140], [66055]

Bridgeport Chamber of Commerce [57372]

Bridgeport Economic Resource Center–Small Business Development Center [58492]

Bridgeport Innovation Center [58623]

Bridgeport Regional Business Council [58515]

Bridges: Skills to Manage a Diverse Workforce [32083], [48617]

Bridgeton Area Chamber of Commerce [62478]

Bridgeview Chamber of Commerce [59441]

"Bridgewater Interiors Closes $400 Million Deal" in *Black Enterprise* (Vol. 35, January 2005, No. 6, pp. 28) [17982], [48073], [49823]

Bridgewater State College–Human Performance Lab [19599]

Bridging the Age Gap [32007]

"Bridging the Gap" in *Black Enterprise* (Vol. 34, No. 5, December 2003, pp. 66) [9753], [9855], [37928], [39330], [40389], [42183]

"Bridging the Gap: Networking Can Be Key to Creating Sales Opportunities." in *Entrepreneur* (Vol. 32, November 2004, No. 11, pp. 89) [35872], [51571]

"Bridging the Gap" in *Sales & Marketing Management* [46219], [46746], [49824], [51078], [53619]

"Bridging the On-the-Road Blues" in *Business Journal-Milwaukee* (Vol. 20, No. 50, August 29, 2003, pp. A30) [20441], [20811], [30804], [52510]

Brief Encounters [42483]

"Briefing Book: E-Procurement" in *Internet Week* (August 9, 2002) [33609]

"Briefing: Internet Infrastructure" in *Red Herring* (No. 102, August 15, 2001, pp. 66-67) [13857], [27305]

"Briefing: Semiconductors" in *Red Herring* (No. 99, June 15 & July 1, 2001, pp. 100-101) [27874], [41567], [50837]

Briefings on Assisted Living (BAL) [464], [12384], [41166]

Briefings on JCAHO: Home Health, Hospice, and HME [18349]

Briefings on Laboratory Safety and Accreditation [17204]

"Briefly" in *Crain's Detroit Business* (Vol. 21, December 19, 2005, No. 51, pp. 14) [1786], [9856], [11253], [14808], [18854], [29130], [33019], [37601], [38724], [39992], [40204], [55522]

Brigantine Beach Chamber of Commerce [62479]

Brigham City Area Chamber of Commerce [65701]

Brigham City Chamber of Commerce Women in Business [65702]

Brigham Young University
    Human Performance Research Center [19600]
    Office of Research and Creative Activities [65743]
    University Computing Services [6393]
    Utah Valley Regional Family History Center and Microforms Department [11003]

"Bright Biz Idea" in *Small Business Opportunities* (Vol. 16, No. 1, January 2004, pp. 58, 110) [5464], [9056], [15975]

"Bright Idea" in *My Business* (February/March 2004, pp. 48) [3476], [29713], [35343]

"Bright Idea Takes Off" in *Small Business Opportunities* (Vol. 16, No. 3, May 2004, pp. 70) [9102], [33417]

"Bright ideas" in *Entrepreneur* (Vol. 31, No. 6, June 2003, pp. 48) [6595], [22473], [35873], [44007], [48964], [51572], [56030]

"Bright lights" in *Entrepreneur* (Vol. 30, No. 2, Feb) [27306], [44958], [48965]

"Bright Lights" in *Red Herring* (No. 99, June 15 & July 1, 2001, pp. 55-56, 58) [6926], [41568], [50838]

"Bright Signs for 2004" in *My Business* (February/March 2004, pp. 44) [27875], [32282]

"Brighton, Howell Hope Plans Boost Retail" in *Crain's Detroit Business* (Vol. 21, January 17, 2005, No. 3, pp. 28) [27876], [51079], [52647]

Brightscape Investment Centers, Inc. [10352], [38987]

BrightStar Healthcare [12418]

Brillion Area Chamber of Commerce [66354]

Brimfield Area Chamber of Commerce [63624]

"Bring Back Old Territories" in *Sales & Marketing Management* (Vol. 158, November-December 2006, No. 11, pp. 13) [46747], [51573]

"Bring the New Economy Home" in *Home Office Computing* (Vol. 18, No. 12, December 2000, pp. 66) [32283], [42583], [49677], [53620]

"Bringing Back a Classic" in *Inc.* (August 1, 2003) [24803], [44008], [46748], [48707], [56144]

"Bringing home the dough" in *BlackEnterprise* (Vol. 32, No. 3, October 2001, pp. 68) [4534], [7811], [35344], [47944]

"Bringing the dead back to life" in *BlackEnterprise* (Vol. 32, No. 3, October 2001, pp. 161) [17555], [35874]

"Bringing the Noise" in *Hispanic Business* (December 2001, pp. 54, 56) [91], [46749]

Brink Associates Ltd. [16853]

Brinkley Chamber of Commerce [57138]

Brisbane Chamber of Commerce [57373]

Ben Briskin Associates Inc. [1051]

Bristol Capital Management [63068]

Bristol County Chamber of Commerce–SBDC [64639]

"Bristol Firm Focuses on Innovative Sailboat Masts" in *Providence Business News* (Vol. 18, No. 11, June 30, 2003, pp. 4) [16731]

Bristol Investment Trust [61049]

Bristol Tennessee/Virginia Chamber of Commerce [64888]

"Bristow Car Dealership Owner Receives Education Award" in *Journal Record* (February 4, 2004) [17983], [18583], [33020]

Bristow Chamber of Commerce [63953]

Brite Site, Inc. [3347]

British-American Business Council [52796]

British-American Business Council Serving Eastern Pennsylvania, Southern New Jersey and Delaware [64390]

British Canadian Chamber of Trade and Commerce [32194]

British Columbia Genealogical Society–Resource Centre [11004]

British Columbia Genealogist-Quarterly [10957]

British Columbia Institute of Technology–Aerospace and Technology Campus–Library [985]

British Columbia Land Surveyors Foundation–Anna Papove Memorial Library [23784]

British Columbia Technology Industries Association [6152], [6455], [6920]

British Journal of Music Education [17615]

British Trade Office at Consulate-General [43481]

"British Virgin Islands firm finances Miami apartments" in *Daily Business Review* (Vol. 77, No. 146, January 7, 2003, pp. A4) [7266], [20442], [20812], [44484]

BritishAmerican Business Inc. of New York and London [43482]

Britt Chamber of Commerce [60101]

Kay Britten Communications Inc. [27576]

"Britt's Grit: Why He Left the Safety of JPMorgan in a Down Market" in *Venture Capital Journal* (Vol. 42, No. 10, Oct. 2002, pp. 22) [14809], [35875], [55523]

BRM Capital [16725]

Broad Universe [8952]

"Broadband Access" in *Hispanic Business* (March 2005, pp. 14) [13858], [27877], [33610], [41569]

"Broadband Deluxe: High-Speed Firms Take the Stress Out of Networking" in *Black Enterprise* (Vol. 35, November 2004, No. 4, pp. 68) [4089], [13859], [33611], [41570]

Broadband Fixed Wireless [4133]

"Broadband Internet access" in *Red Herring* (No. 105, October 1, 2001, pp. 34) [4931], [13860], [27878], [33612]

Broadband Investment Group (BIG) [62078]

"Broadband agency makes its first loan" in *Crain's Detroit Business* (Vol. 19, No. 12, March 24, 2003, pp. 6) [4932], [6596], [39792], [41571], [44485]

"Broadband Wagon: Greater Connectivity is Coming to a Neighborhood Near You." in *Entrepreneur* (Vol. 32, November 2004, No. 11, pp. 59) [4933], [6597], [41572]

Broadcast Cable Credit Association [20283], [24355]

Broadcast Cable Financial Management Association [20284], [24356]

Broadcast Cable Financial Management Association Conference [4151], [55207]

Broadcast Education Association [24357]

Broadcast Engineering [24466]

Broadcast Engineering-Equipment Reference Manual [20303], [21148], [24383]

"Broadcast News: B.E. Breaks Ground With New TV Program" in *Black Enterprise* (Vol. 34, No. 5, December 2003, pp. 159) [18653], [18855], [24384], [34734], [35876], [45798], [48074]

Broadcaster [24467]

Broadcasting & Cable Yearbook [4090], [20304], [22082], [24385]

Broadcasting and Cable's TV International [4134]

"Broaddus Opens Office" in *Mississippi Business Journal* (Vol. 28, September 2006, No. 36, pp. 23) [3503], [7267], [9347], [31114], [44959]

"Broader Wheelchair Access Rules Proposed" in *Inc.* (September 2005, pp. 32) [40205], [40973], [54140]

"Broad's eye view" in *WorkingWoman* (Vol. 25, No. 8, September 2000, pp. 64) [37110], [56145]

Broadview Heights Chamber of Commerce [63625]

Broadview International [50300]

BroadVision Inc. [30644], [45977]

Broadway-Timberville Chamber of Commerce [65867]

Brodhead Chamber of Commerce [66355]

Irwin Broh & Associates Inc. [16854]

Broken Arrow Chamber of Commerce [63954]

Broken Bow Chamber of Commerce [62250], [63955]

"Broken plan" in *Crain's Detroit Business* (Vol. 18, No. 19, May 13, 2002, pp. 1) [37602]

Broker Dealer Operations Under Securities & Commodities Law: Financial Responsibility, Credit Regulation, & Consumer Protection [14810]

"Broker In a Rival's Branch? Your Bank Can Do It Too" in *American Banker* (Vol. 170, February 2, 2005, No. 22, pp. 5) [9857], [31649]

Broker Magazine (Vol. 7); "Virtual Assistants A Reality: Now You Can Outsource an Assistant's Job to A Remote Provider" in [7146], [17449], [49754], [52604]

Broker Management Council [3410], [21420]

"Brokerage to be acquired by Phoenix Company" in *Crain's Detroit Business* (Vol. 18, No. 51, December 23, 2002, pp. 3) [14811], [20443], [20813], [49825]

"Bromley, AHAA shine at Confab" in *Hispanic Business* (Vol. 22, No. 11, November 2000, pp. 12) [46750], [55071]

"Bronto Email Marketing Toolkit" in *Entrepreneur.com* (Vol. 34, February 2006, No. 2, pp. 6) [13861], [27307], [27621], [33613], [46751], [53223]

Bronx Chamber of Commerce [62828]

Bronx Community College–Small Business Development Center [62747]

Bronx Outreach Center–Con Edison–SBDC [62748]

Bronxville Chamber of Commerce [62829]

Brook Venture Partners, L.L.C. [61050]

Brookdale Community College [62626]
    Small Business Development Center [62454]

Brooke Franchise Corp. [10353], [13579]

Brooke Insurance & Financial Services [10354], [13580], [38588]

Brookfield Area Chamber of Commerce [61925]

Brookfield Chamber of Commerce [59442]

"Brookfield, Wis., Staffing Firm to Get $3 Million Venture-Capital Infusion" in *Milwaukee Journal Sentinel* (December 7, 2005) [9195], [9553], [24519], [55524]

Brookgreen Gardens–Library [11510]

Brookhaven - Lincoln County Chamber of Commerce [61777]

"Brookhaven Revising Commercial Development Codes After Developer Backlash" in *Long Island Business News* (March 12, 2004) [7268], [7536], [38554], [40206]

Brookings Area Chamber of Commerce and Convention Bureau [64816]

Brookings-Harbor Chamber of Commerce [64199]

Brookline Chamber of Commerce [60934]

Brooklyn Area Chamber of Commerce [66356]

Brooklyn Botanic Garden–Library [11511]

Brooklyn Chamber of Commerce [62830]

Brooklyn Historical Society–Library [11005]

Brooklyn - Irish Hills Chamber of Commerce [61264]

Brooklyn Minority Business Development Center–Opportunity Development Association (ODA) [63046]

Brooklyn Museum of Art–Art Reference Library [5606]

Brooklyn Public Library–Business Library [412], [24168]

Brooks Institute of Photography–Library [19272], [19336]

Brookville Area Chamber of Commerce [64391]

Brookville-Franklin County Chamber of Commerce [59880]

Broome County Industrial Development Agency [63187]

Broomfield Chamber of Commerce [58333]

"Brothers Rev Up Roostertail" in *Crain's Detroit Business* (Vol. 22, February 6, 2006, No. 6, pp. 22) [4535], [21453], [37603]

"Broward Commission moves to take control of redevelopment" in *Daily Business Review* (Vol. 77, No. 146, January 7, 2003, pp. A1) [7269], [40207]

Brown Associates Inc. [42947]

Brown & Caldwell–Library [11973]

Brown, Chudleigh, Schuler Donaldson & Associates [21073]

Brown County Chamber of Commerce [59881], [63626]
    SBDC [59820]

Brown County Genealogy Society–Library [11006]

Brown Deer Chamber of Commerce [66357]

"Brown Delivers..." in *Ingram's* (Vol. 29, No. 1, January 2003, pp. 31) [6094], [54141]

Brown Forum for Enterprise [64655]

Brown Koff & Fried Inc. [16855]

Brown University
    Center for Environmental Studies [21294]
    Center for Environmental Studies–Library [11974]
    Center for Gerontology and Health Care Research [494]
    Office of Sponsored Projects [64681]
    Orwig Music Library [17665]
    Social Science Data Center [66972]
    Watson Institute for International Studies [41363]

The Browning Group [16856]

Brownsburg Chamber of Commerce [59882]

Brownsville Chamber of Commerce [65141]

Brownsville - Haywood County Chamber of Commerce [64889]

Brownsville Herald (January 8, 2003); "Brownsville, Texas, Center Gives Women Variety of Fitness Options" in [19379]

Brownsville Minority Business Development Center–Management Assistance Services [65575]

"Brownsville, Texas, Center Gives Women Variety of Fitness Options" in *Brownsville Herald* (January 8, 2003) [19379]

Brownwood Area Chamber of Commerce [65142]

Bruce Chamber of Commerce [61778]

Bruce F. Glaspell & Associates [62720]

"Bruce Sunstein: Inventor Defender" in *Boston Business Journal* (Vol. 23, No. 27, August 8, 2003, pp. 1) [29131], [44009], [44278]

Bruegger's [2170]

"Bruised but Unbowed" in *Hispanic Business* (December 2001, pp. 66) [35877], [39184]

Brunswick Area Chamber of Commerce [63627]

Brunswick Chamber of Commerce [65868]

Brunswick County Chamber of Commerce [63335]

Brunswick-Golden Isles Chamber of Commerce [59068]

Brush Chamber of Commerce [58334]

Brush Valley Regional Chamber of Commerce [64392]

Bruster's Real Ice Cream [12810]

Bryan Area Chamber of Commerce [63628]

Bryan Cave LLP–Law Library [9428], [29696], [40901]

Bryant Chamber of Commerce [57139]

Bryant College
    Export Assistance Center–SBDC [64640]
    Rhode Island SBDC [64641]
    Rhode Island Small Business Development Center [64637]

Bryant and Stratton Business Institute
    Henrietta Campus [63217]
    Parma Campus [63888]
    Syracuse Campus [63218]

Bryant and Stratton College
    Buffalo Campus [63219]
    Virginia Beach Campus [65996]

"Bryson Buys Two Agencies" in *Mississippi Business Journal* (Vol. 29, January 2007, No. 2, pp. 8) [27879], [37929], [43105], [49826]

BtoB [34786], [39739], [47925]

BUC Used Boat Price Guide [16732]

Buchanan Area Chamber of Commerce [61265]

Buchanan Chamber of Commerce–SBDC [61178]

Buchanan County Chamber of Commerce [65869]

Bucher, Willis & Ratliff Corp. [23801]

Larry W. Buck & Associates Inc. [27010]

Buck or Two [51451]

Buck or Two Extreme Retail Inc. [51452]

Buckeye Hills Hocking Valley–Regional Development District [66950]

Buckeye Valley Chamber of Commerce [57018]

"Bucking Convention" in *Entrepreneur* (Vol. 33, January 2005, No. 1, pp. 268) [2584], [7883], [54142]

"Bucking the Odds at Amylin" in *Business Week* (January 9, 2006, No. 3966, pp. 64, 66) [44960], [48708], [50839], [52065]

Buckingham Chamber of Commerce [65870]

"Buckle up" in *Atlanta Business Chronicle* (Vol. 23, No. 30, December 29, 2000, pp. 27A) [27880], [32284]

Buckler Software Consulting [6034]

Buckley Chamber of Commerce [66056]

Bucknell University–Small Business Development Center [64323]

Buckner Chamber of Commerce [61926]

"Buck's Annual 401(k) Survey Shows Dramatic Growth In Web Administration" in *Employee Benefit Plan Review* (Vol. 55, No. 7, Jan. 2001) [13862], [26756], [33614], [43106], [53621]

Bucks County Economic Development Corporation–SBDC Outreach Center [64324]

Buck's Pizza [19656]

"The Bucks Start Here" in *Business Week* (No. 3658, December 6, 1999, pp. F10) [27881], [44486], [53622]

Bucksport Bay Area Chamber of Commerce [60737]

Bucyrus Area Chamber of Commerce [63629]

Buda Area Chamber of Commerce [65143]

"Buddy System" in *Entrepreneur* (Vol. 33, October 2005, No. 10, pp. 118) [35345], [47426], [49765]

"The buddy system" in *WorkingWoman* (Vol. 25, No. 5, May 2000, pp. 84) [30301], [56146]

"The Buddy System: These Longtime Friends Formed a Growing CPA Firm" in *Black Enterprise* (Vol. 35, August 2004, No. 1, pp. 47) [92], [2877], [3504], [23899], [26175], [31115], [49827]

Budget Blinds [2567]

Budget Brake & Muffler Distributors Ltd [2095]

Budget Car and Truck Rental [1872], [2096], [18201]

Budget Framer [19831]

"Budget cuts target cities with living-wage laws" in *Crain's Detroit Business* (Vol. 18, No. 24,) [27093], [40208]

"Budget Sportswear Store Coming to Tampa, Fla." in *Tampa Tribune* (November 22, 2005) [5643], [23609], [51080]

"Budget hole brings tax-hike whispers" in *Crain's Detroit Business* (Vol. 19, No. 4, January 27, 2003, pp. 6) [39185], [54459]

Budgetel Inn [12705], [25332]

Budgeting [27210]

Budgeting for Publications [26121]

Budgeting for a Small Business [27094], [31116]

Buena Park Chamber of Commerce [57374]

Buena Venture Associates [65595]

Buena Vista Area Chamber of Commerce [58335]

Buena Vista Chamber of Commerce [65871]

"Buenas Vistas and Other Good Things: It's the Splendor of Las Casitas" in *Black Enterprise* (Vol. 34, No. 3, October 2003, pp. 144) [11783], [12526], [24672], [25162]

Buffalo Area Chamber of Commerce [61565], [61927]

Buffalo Chamber of Commerce [63956], [65144]

Buffalo Chips [10958]

Buffalo & Erie County Public Library–Business, Science & Technology [26443], [29055], [43456]

Buffalo Grove Area Chamber of Commerce [59443]

Buffalo Home and Garden Show [11486]

Buffalo News (February 17, 2004); "Amherst, N.Y., Firm Feel Good Greetings Creates Board Game for Children" in [11556], [24800]

Buffalo News (February 17, 2004); "Fisher-Price Takes Top Honors at Annual Toy Fair" in [24811]

Buffalo News (February 17, 2004) "Insurer State Farm Closes Buffalo, N.Y.-Area Claims Offices; 30 Jobs to Be Cut" in **[13346]**, **[28334]**, **[43238]**

The Buffalo News (April 11, 2203); "Lockport, N.Y.-Based First Niagara Financial to Open More Branches, Buy Bank" in **[10068]**, **[38194]**, **[44577]**, **[50056]**

Buffalo News (April 11, 2003); "New York State Officials May Allow Wine Sales in Supermarkets" in **[11647]**, **[16234]**, **[23500]**, **[40570]**

Buffalo News (March 29, 2004); "Ugly Salt and Pepper Shakers Spur Buffalo, N.Y., Woman's eBay Business" in **[1863]**, **[7177]**, **[18667]**, **[34632]**, **[56454]**

Buffalo Niagara Partnership **[62831]**

Buffalo Philly's - Wings, Cheesesteaks N' More **[21760]**

Buffalo State College–Small Business Development Center **[62749]**

Buffalo Wild Wings Grill & Bar **[21761]**

Buffalo Wings & Rings **[21762]**

Buffalo, Wyoming Chamber of Commerce **[66602]**

Buffalo's Cafe **[21763]**

"Bug Control" in *Entrepreneur* (Vol. 32, No. 4, April 2004, pp. 34) **[4608]**, **[13863]**, **[22187]**, **[22929]**, **[33615]**, **[53224]**

"Bugged out" in *Entrepreneur* (Vol. 31, No. 5, May 2003, pp. 38) **[31650]**, **[33616]**, **[46752]**

Buhl Chamber of Commerce **[59288]**

W.A. Buie Consulting Services **[49405]**

"Build a Better Business" in *Black Enterprise* (Vol. 35, October 2004, No. 3, pp. 136) **[4934]**, **[27882]**, **[31651]**, **[41573]**, **[48966]**, **[49488]**, **[52825]**

"Build a Better Virus" in *Inc.* (September 1, 2003) **[4351]**, **[22188]**, **[22930]**, **[33021]**, **[53225]**

"Build Fault Reporting Into Your System" in *E-business Advisor* (Vol. 18, No. 6, June 2000, pp. 41) **[25805]**, **[33617]**

"Build a Relationship With Your Lender" in *Black Enterprise* (Vol. 36, November 2005, No. 4, pp. 47) **[9858]**, **[17362]**, **[20444]**

"Build a Strong Customer-Brand Relationship" in *E-business Advisor* (Vol. 18, No. 4, April 2000, pp. 34) **[31015]**, **[33618]**, **[46753]**, **[51574]**

"Build a Successful Business Partner Network" in *E-business Advisor* (Vol. 18, No. 5, May 2000, pp. 36) **[14812]**, **[33619]**, **[49828]**, **[53623]**

"The "Build-the-Box" Lesson" in *Business Communication Quarterly* (Vol. 63, No. 3, September 2000, pp. 60) **[27308]**

"Build Your Business with eBay" in *Home Business* (Vol. 13, January/February 2006, No. 1, pp. 58, 60) **[1787]**, **[13864]**, **[27883]**, **[46754]**

"Build Your Dream Home Business" in *Home Business* (Vol. 12, October 2005, No. 5, pp. 16, 18-22, 102, 104) **[29714]**, **[35346]**, **[39030]**, **[42503]**, **[44390]**, **[46561]**

Build Your Own American Dream Home, Ltd. **[3850]**

"Build Your Own Web Site" in *Home Business* (Vol. 12, October 2005, No. 5, pp. 88, 90-91) **[13865]**, **[25806]**, **[46755]**

"Build Your Web Identity" in *E-business Advisor* (Vol. 18, No. 5, May 2000, pp. 30) **[25807]**, **[33621]**, **[46756]**, **[50565]**

Builder **[7525]**

"Builder plans $80M in homes; Majority are proposed for Macomb County" in *Crain's Detroit Business* (Vol. 19, Jan. 13, 2003, pp. 3) **[7270]**, **[20445]**, **[27884]**

"Builder Bandits" in *Tampa Tribune* (December 12, 2005) **[7271]**, **[30805]**, **[32285]**, **[42184]**

Builder-Buyer's Guide Issue **[7272]**

Builder Insider **[7526]**

"Builder Outlines Plans for Affordable Housing in Palmetto, Fla" in *Bradenton Herald* (December 24, 2004) **[1500]**, **[7273]**

Builders Hardware Manufacturers Association **[11872]**

Builders Home and Garden Show **[11487]**, **[16135]**

Builders Industry Association Southern California-Baldy View Chapter **[57375]**

"Builders Land Rutenberg Deal" in *Charlotte Observer* (February 2, 2007) **[7274]**, **[37604]**, **[38725]**

"Builders Risk Options" in *Rough Notes* (Vol. 146, No. 3, March 2003, pp. 106) **[7275]**, **[13215]**

The Builders' Show **[7589]**

Building an Association Management Company **[1731]**

"Building a Better Skunk Works" in *Fast Company* (March 2005, No. 92, pp. 68) **[6566]**, **[7840]**, **[27714]**

Building Better Work Relationships: New Techniques for Results-Oriented Communication (Canada) **[27234]**

The Building Blocks of Business Writing **[27622]**

Building Blocks for Team Performance **[35173]**

"Building Boom Hits Homestead" in *South Florida Business Journal* (Vol. 23, No. 48, July 4, 2003, pp. 1) **[7276]**, **[27885]**

Building Bridges to Customers **[31652]**

Building Business & Apartment Management **[1382]**

Building a Business the Buddhist Way **[30515]**, **[35878]**, **[39186]**

"Building Business Leaders" in *Hispanic Business* (December 2002, pp. 64) **[35347]**

"Building Character" in *Black Enterprise* (Vol. 35, January 2005, No. 6, pp. 41) **[22474]**, **[33022]**, **[35879]**, **[44961]**

Building Code Requirements for Masonry Structures **[16944]**

Building Code Requirements for Masonry Structures and Specifications for Masonry Structures, and Related Commentaries **[16945]**

"Building a collection" in *Crain's Detroit Business* (Vol. 19, No. 6, February 10, 2003, pp. 1) **[17984]**, **[27886]**

Building Community: The Human Side of Work **[34835]**

Building Conservation Associates Inc. **[1548]**

Building and Construction Trades Department - Canadian Office **[55260]**

Building Contractor **[7277]**

Building Cost Analysis **[1460]**

"Building Design" in *Inc.* (Volume 27, June 2005, No. 6, pp. 65-66) **[1501]**, **[18541]**, **[37249]**

"Building Downline...Online" in *Success* (Vol. 47, No. 2, June 2000, pp. 80) **[33622]**, **[46757]**

Building Dreams **[4493]**

Building a Dynamic Team: Maximizing Team Performance **[34836]**

"Building on experience" in *Black Enterprise* (Vol. 33, No. 6, Jan. 2003, pp. 39) **[7190]**, **[35348]**, **[44391]**, **[48873]**

"Building your own foundation" in *Ingram's* (Vol. 27, No. 12, December 2001, pp. 28) **[14813]**, **[54143]**, **[54460]**

"Building for the future" in *Black Enterprise* (Vol. 32, No. 7, February 2002, pp.) **[7191]**, **[35349]**, **[47945]**

"Building a Good Rep" in *Black Enterprise* (Vol. 36, December 2005, No. 5, pp. 136) **[17363]**, **[35880]**, **[44962]**

Building High Performing Teams **[35174]**

"Building on History" in *Philadelphia Inquirer* (October 16, 2006) **[26072]**, **[34837]**, **[35881]**, **[46220]**

"Building Hope" in *Ingram's* (Vol. 28, No. 6, June 2002, pp. 29) **[7278]**, **[54144]**

Building an Import/Export Business **[12947]**

"Building an Innovation Factory" in *Harvard Business Review* (Vol. 78, No. 3, May 2000, pp. 157) **[29807]**, **[30516]**

Building an Internet Based Mail Order Business First Class: Your Complete Step-by-Step Manual for Success **[16425]**

Building a Mail Order Business: A Complete Manual for Success **[16426]**

Building Maintenance Contractors Association of Canada **[3300]**

"Building the Minority High-Tech Work Force" in *Hispanic Business* (Vol. 23, No. 7/8, July/August 2001, pp. 116) **[41574]**, **[42185]**, **[48075]**, **[56147]**

"Building the Mommy Track" in *Inc.* (September 1, 2003) **[21312]**, **[26757]**, **[49829]**

"Building strength in New Mexico" in *New Mexico Business Journal* (Vol. 26, No. 8, September 2002, pp. 30) **[19380]**, **[53624]**

Building Officials and Code Administrators International-Membership Directory **[3231]**, **[7279]**

Building an Online Store **[18639]**

Building Owners and Managers Association International–Library **[21109]**

Building Owners and Managers Association International Annual Convention and The Office Building Show **[20068]**

"Building the Perfect Tech CEO" in *Hispanic Business* (Vol. 23, No. 5, May 2001, pp. 28, 30) **[6927]**, **[35882]**, **[41575]**, **[48076]**

"Building Permitted" in *Entrepreneur.com* (Vol. 34, February 2006, No. 2, pp. 104) **[7192]**, **[20395]**, **[38613]**

"Building a Portfolio" in *Crain's Detroit Business* (Vol. 21, October 3, 2005, No. 43) **[16300]**, **[20814]**, **[35883]**, **[54145]**

Building Products **[7527]**

Building Products Digest **[11900]**, **[16327]**

"Building a Professional Pipeline" in *Hispanic Business* (March 2004, pp. 44-45) **[33023]**, **[39187]**, **[44963]**

Building a Profitable Business: A Proven Step-by-Step Guide to Starting and Running Your Own Business **[52826]**

Building a Profitable Consulting Practice Series **[3628]**, **[12921]**, **[16554]**, **[20174]**

Building Profits with Group Travel **[25163]**

Building Service Contractors Association International **[3301]**

Building Services of America, Inc. **[3270]**, **[3348]**

Building Standards **[7528]**

Building Stone Institute **[16927]**

Building Strategic Relationships **[30998]**

"Building on success" in *Black Enterprise* (Vol. 32, No. 9, April 2002, pp. 70) **[1602]**, **[19228]**, **[19294]**, **[33418]**, **[37557]**, **[37930]**, **[47946]**

Building a Successful Business: What Every New Business Must Know Before Even Thinking about Making That Million Bucks! **[52827]**

Building a Successful Medical Transcription Business **[17295]**

Building Team Power: How to Unleash the Collaborative Genius of Work Teams **[34838]**

"Building vital region requires teamwork" in *Crain's Detroit Business* (Vol. 19, No. 17, April 28, 2003, pp. 9) **[27887]**, **[32286]**, **[40209]**

Building the Trans-National Team **[43915]**

"Building visibility" in *Women in Business* (Vol. 54, No. 2, March-April 2002, pp. 32) **[27309]**, **[44964]**

"Building owners look to build voice" in *Crain's Detroit Business* (Vol. 18, No. 23, June 10, 2002, pp. 16) **[20050]**

"Building vs. buying" in *BlackEnterprise* (Vol. 31, No. 6, January 2001, pp. 39) **[29715]**, **[30652]**, **[35350]**, **[47947]**

"Building on the Web" in *Pittsburgh Business Times* (Vol. 23, No. 7, September 5, 2003, pp. 19) **[13866]**, **[33623]**

"Building Your Business" in *Small Business Opportunities* (Vol. 17, May 2005, No. 3, pp. 12) **[27888]**, **[38726]**, **[40210]**, **[46758]**, **[54146]**, **[56009]**

Building Your Own High-Tech Small Office **[48967]**

BuildingStars Inc. **[3349]**

"Built For Speed: Baba Garba Looks to Take His Broadband Business Abroad" in *Black Enterprise* (Vol. 34, No. 5, December 2003, pp. 50) **[3505]**, **[30279]**, **[31117]**, **[34741]**, **[35884]**, **[41576]**, **[43100]**, **[43566]**, **[45243]**

Built to Last: Successful Habits of Visionary Companies **[35885]**, **[39188]**

Bulk Barn Foods Limited **[23560]**

"Bulk chocolate" in *Prepared Foods* (Vol. 171, No. 5, May 2002, pp. 83) **[4276]**, **[48709]**

Bulk Liquid Terminals Directory **[10665]**

"Bulk Mail Through the Internet" in *PC Magazine* (April 4, 2000, pp. 115) **[13867]**, **[16427]**, **[53226]**

"Bulking up; Dollar Castle's ruler plans retailing, distribution kingdom" in *Crain's Detroit Business* (Dec. 9, 2002, pp. 3) **[32145]**, **[44965]**, **[51081]**

"Bull in a China Shop? If That's How Parents Feel Bringing Kids Into Your Store, They'll Pass You By" in *Entrepreneur* (Vol. 32) **[31653]**, **[51082]**

Bull Shoals Lake - White River Chamber of Commerce **[57140]**

Bulldog Reporter Business Media **[20165]**

Bullets Black Angus Burgers **[21764]**

Bullhead Area Chamber of Commerce **[57019]**

"Bullied by the Big Guys? Try Fighting Back!" in *Fortune* (Vol. 142, No. 2, July 10, 2000, pp. 200T) **[25808]**, **[44966]**

"Bullish on minority business: MBDA director sees better days ahead" in *Black Enterprise* (Vol. 32, No. 8, March 2002, pp. 28) **[27889]**, **[48077]**

Bullitt County Chamber of Commerce **[60486]**

Bullitt-Hutchins **[3445]**

Jack J. Bulloff Consulting and Expert Witness Services **[6035]**

"The Bulls are Back" in *My Business* (June/July 2004, pp. 13) **[14814]**, **[32287]**, **[37931]**

Bulverde/Spring Branch Area Chamber of Commerce **[65145]**

"A Bumper Crop of Worries" in *Tampa Tribune* (November 30, 2005) **[26488]**, **[30806]**, **[53625]**

"Bumpy Ride" in *Hispanic Business* (October 2006, pp. 24, 26) **[20446]**, **[32288]**

"The Bumpy Road to Success" in *Home Business* (Vol. 12, October 2005, No. 5, pp. 56) **[22475]**, **[35886]**

Bundy & Morrill **[4453]**, **[29615]**

Bunker Hill Community College **[61153]**

Bunkie Chamber of Commerce **[60622]**

"Bunny Money" in *Entrepreneur* (Vol. 30, No. 3, March 2002) **[11104]**, **[11145]**, **[27890]**, **[35887]**, **[51083]**

"Buoyed by Biotech" in *Venture Capital Journal* (February 1, 2006) **[50840]**, **[52066]**, **[55525]**

Burbank Chamber of Commerce **[57376]**, **[59444]**

"The burden of borrowing" in *Entrepreneur* (Vol. 31, No. 4, April 2003, pp. 53) **[37932]**, **[44487]**

Bureau of Business and Economic Research–West Virginia University–College of Business and Economics **[67014]**

Bureau of the Census **[66804]**
    Atlanta Regional Office **[66805]**
    Boston Regional Office **[66806]**
    Charlotte Regional Office **[66807]**
    Chicago Regional Office **[66808]**
    Dallas Regional Office **[66809]**
    Denver Regional Office **[66810]**
    Detroit Regional Office **[66811]**
    Kansas City Regional Office **[66812]**
    Los Angeles Regional Office **[66813]**
    New York City Regional Office **[66814]**
    Philadelphia Regional Office **[66815]**
    Seattle Regional Office **[66816]**

Bureau of Economic Analysis–Florida Department of Commerce **[66848]**

Bureau of Indian Affairs
    Business Utilization and Development Specialist–Aberdeen Area Office **[67572]**
    Business Utilization and Development Specialist–Albuquerque Area Office **[67567]**
    Business Utilization and Development Specialist–Anadarko Area Office **[67569]**
    Business Utilization and Development Specialist–Billings Area Office **[67566]**
    Business Utilization and Development Specialist–Eastern Area Office **[67573]**
    Business Utilization and Development Specialist–Juneau Area Office **[67562]**
    Business Utilization and Development Specialist–Minneapolis Area Office **[67565]**
    Business Utilization and Development Specialist–Muskogee Area Office **[67570]**
    Business Utilization and Development Specialist–Navajo Area Office **[67568]**
    Business Utilization and Development Specialist–Phoenix Area Office **[67563]**
    Business Utilization and Development Specialist–Portland Area Office **[67571]**

Business Utilization and Development Specialist–Sacramento Area Office **[67564]**

Bureau of Land Management
    Alaska State Office **[67574]**
    Arizona State Office **[67575]**
    Business Utilization and Development Specialist–Branch of Procurement Management **[67578]**
    Business Utilization and Development Specialist–Division of Procurement Management **[67583]**
    California State Office **[67576]**
    Colorado State Office **[67577]**
    Eastern States Office **[67586]**
    Idaho State Office **[67579]**
    Montana State Office **[67580]**
    Neveda State Office **[67581]**
    New Mexico State Office **[67582]**
    Oregon State Office **[67584]**
    Utah State Office **[67585]**
    Wyoming State Office **[67587]**

Bureau of National Affairs, Inc.–Library **[56678]**

"Bureau begins PR campaign to change images of Detroit" in *Crain's Detroit Business* (Vol. 19, No. 6, February 10, 2003, pp. 16) **[24897]**, **[25164]**, **[50430]**

Bureau of Reclamation
    Business Utilization and Development Specialist–Acquisition and Assistance Management Services **[67590]**
    Business Utilization and Development Specialist–Administrative Service Center **[67591]**
    Business Utilization and Development Specialist–Denver Office **[67592]**
    Business Utilization and Development Specialist–Great Plains Region **[67594]**
    Business Utilization and Development Specialist–Lower Colorado Region **[67595]**
    Business Utilization and Development Specialist–Mid-Pacific Region **[67589]**
    Business Utilization and Development Specialist–Pacific Northwest Region **[67593]**
    Business Utilization and Development Specialist–Phoenix Area Office **[67588]**
    Business Utilization and Development Specialist–Upper Colorado Region **[67596]**

"Burger King Corp" in *Black Enterprise* (Vol. 34, No. 6, January 2004, pp. 51) **[21165]**, **[21454]**, **[38727]**

Burger King Corp. **[21765]**

"Burger King Franchisees, Parent Squabble Over Firm's Declining Fortunes" in *Portland Press Herald* (November 8, 2005) **[21455]**, **[29132]**, **[38728]**

Sarah G. Burger **[18378]**

"Buried Alive-There's no such thing as a paperless office" in *PC Computing* (March 2000, pp. 104) **[48968]**, **[53227]**

Burkburnett Chamber of Commerce **[65146]**

M.W. Burke & Associates Inc. **[20244]**

Burke County Chamber of Commerce **[63336]**

Burkesville Cumberland County Chamber of Commerce **[60487]**

Burleson Area Chamber of Commerce **[65147]**

Burleson County Chamber of Commerce - Caldwell Office **[65148]**

Burlingame Chamber of Commerce **[57377]**

Burlington Area Chamber of Commerce **[66358]**

Burlington Chamber of Commerce **[66057]**

Burlington County Chamber of Commerce **[62480]**

Burlington County College **[62627]**

Burlington/West Burlington Area Chamber of Commerce **[60102]**

"Burn, babay, Burn" in *Entrepreneur* (Vol. 28, No. 6, June 2000, pp. 76) **[27715]**, **[35351]**

Burn Rate: How I Survived the Gold Rush Years on the Internet **[37111]**

"Burned down to the wick" in *Black Enterprise* (Vol. 31, No. 5, December 2000, pp. 165) **[35888]**

Burnet Chamber of Commerce **[65149]**

Burney Chamber of Commerce **[57378]**

"Burning Cash, MannKind is Raising More Money" in *San Fernando Valley Business Journal* (Vol. 11, December 2006, No. 25, pp. 11) **[48710]**, **[52067]**, **[55526]**

Burns Flat Chamber of Commerce **[63957]**

Burns Public Relations Services Inc. **[50490]**

Burnsville Chamber of Commerce **[61566]**

Burr, Egan, Deleage, and Co. (Boston) **[61051]**

Burr, Egan, Deleage, and Co. (San Francisco) **[57954]**

"Burrell CEO Steps Down" in *Black Enterprise* (Vol. 35, August 2004, No. 1, pp. 23) **[569]**, **[29133]**, **[35889]**, **[48078]**

Burrelle's Media Directory **[50566]**

Burrelle's New Jersey Media Directory **[4091]**

Burrill & Company **[57955]**

Burson-Marsteller–Knowledge Center **[20198]**, **[50732]**

"Burst of Energy" in *Entrepreneur.com* (Vol. 34, February 2006, No. 2, pp. 46) **[21219]**, **[27891]**, **[37250]**, **[53626]**

Burt Hill **[49588]**

Burt Hill Kosar Rittelmann Associates–Library **[23347]**

Burwell Chamber of Commerce **[62251]**

"Burying the Hatchet" in *Hispanic Business* (March 2003, pp. 18) **[17985]**, **[48079]**, **[49830]**

"Bus or bust" in *Women in Business* (Vol. 54, No. 5, September-October 2002, pp. 11) **[16180]**, **[22476]**, **[24898]**, **[56148]**

"Bus deal stalls as Oakland's council fumes" in *San Francisco Business Times* (Vol. 16, No. 43, May 31, 2002, pp. 3) **[15917]**, **[22787]**

Bus Ride **[24246]**

"Busch Gardens Sees 2005 Attendance Grow" in *Tampa Tribune* (December 28, 2005) **[1131]**, **[27892]**

Buses International Association **[24224]**

Buset & Partners–Library **[13593]**, **[20766]**, **[21110]**

"Bush Backs Contracting Program" in *Hispanic Business* (Vol. 23, No. 10, October, 2001, pp. 22) **[39993]**, **[40211]**, **[48080]**

"Bush Growth Package Boost for Main Street" in *My Business* (April/May 2003, pp. 19) **[27893]**, **[54461]**

"Bush talks up small business tax relief" in *Tax Notes* (Vol. 97, No. 9, December 2, 2002, pp. 1135-1136) **[93]**, **[23900]**, **[26176]**, **[27894]**, **[32289]**, **[54462]**

"Bush may trim SBA budget" in *BlackEnterprise* (Vol. 32, No. 1, August 2001, pp. 28) **[39793]**, **[40212]**

"Bush Signs HSAs Into Law" in *Tax Notes* (Vol. 101, No. 11, December 15, 2003, pp. 1250-1251) **[26758]**, **[40974]**

Bushnell Chamber of Commerce **[59445]**

Business 2.0 **[34772]**

Business 2.0 (Vol. 7, January/February 2006, No. 1, pp. 26); "$100 Bottles of Beer on the Wall" in **[3121]**

Business 2.0 (Vol. 7, January/February 2006, No. 1, pp. 98-102, 104-106, 108, 110, 136); "101 Dumbest Moments in Business" in **[39128]**

Business 2.0 (Vol. 6, July 2005, No. 6, pp. 34); "A Hearing Aid for Cell Phones" in **[4579]**, **[4890]**, **[22884]**, **[53147]**

Business 2.0 (Vol. 7, January/February 2006, No. 1, pp. 24); "A Match Made in Hormones" in **[7061]**, **[34180]**

Business 2.0 (Vol. 6, May 2005, No. 4, pp. 66); "A More Profitable Harvest" in **[10567]**, **[11568]**, **[34212]**, **[51737]**

Business 2.0 (Vol. 6, September 2005, No. 8, pp. 90); "A Sales Channel They Can't Resist" in **[4108]**, **[4121]**, **[28735]**, **[48854]**, **[51341]**

Business 2.0 (Vol. 6, May 2005, No. 4, pp. 56-57); "Bagging the Right Customers" in **[9611]**, **[46700]**, **[51063]**

Business 2.0 (Vol. 6, September 2005, No. 8, pp. 108); "Betting the Farm" in **[26097]**, **[26483]**, **[39824]**, **[41542]**, **[50822]**, **[52046]**

Business 2.0 (Vol. 6, May 2005, No. 4, pp. 76); "Breaking Through Excuses" in **[35871]**, **[44957]**

Business 2.0 (Vol. 6, September 2005, No. 8, pp. 132); "B.Y.O. GPS" in **[29561]**, **[30305]**, **[46639]**, **[48973]**, **[49489]**

Business 2.0 (Vol. 6, September 2005, No. 8, pp. 119); "Cashing In On Cash Flow" in **[9865]**, **[14837]**, **[37948]**

Business 2.0 (Vol. 6, September 2005, No. 8, pp. 36); "Consumer Research" in **[4611]**, **[4625]**, **[22950]**, **[33699]**, **[44709]**, **[46833]**, **[53241]**

Business 2.0 (Vol. 6, July 2005, No. 6, pp. 62); "Dialing for Dollars" in **[1100]**, **[4971]**, **[24806]**

Business 2.0 (Vol. 6, September 2005, No. 8, pp. 30); "Digital Entertainment" in **[4945]**, **[4973]**, **[17538]**, **[17736]**, **[28038]**

Business 2.0 (Vol. 6, May 2005, No. 4, pp. 78-86); "Do This, Get Rich" in **[500]**, **[2123]**, **[6567]**, **[9174]**, **[12489]**, **[13617]**, **[16711]**, **[33427]**, **[37220]**, **[40904]**, **[41449]**, **[44226]**, **[53145]**

Business 2.0 (Vol. 6, July 2005, No. 6, pp. 32); "Economic Outlook" in **[28085]**, **[32379]**

Business 2.0 (Vol. 6, September 2005, No. 8, pp. 42); "Ending Advertising's Spiral" in **[583]**, **[612]**, **[55591]**, **[58032]**

Business 2.0 (Vol. 7, January/February 2006, No. 1, pp. 113-115); "Free! (With Purchase)" in **[4669]**, **[6653]**, **[23008]**, **[41700]**, **[46987]**, **[53293]**

Business 2.0 (Vol. 7, January/February 2006, No. 1, pp. 24); "From Cow Pies to Clean Power" in **[41702]**, **[50875]**, **[52104]**

Business 2.0 (Vol. 6, May 2005, No. 4, pp. 90-95); "Going Nuclear" in **[28215]**, **[41716]**

Business 2.0 (Vol. 6, July 2005, No. 6, pp. 112); "Guerrilla Marketing via Wi-Fi" in **[5008]**, **[49060]**, **[52861]**

Business 2.0 (Vol. 6, July 2005, No. 6, pp. 54-55); "Helping Doctors Go Digital" in **[658]**, **[41027]**, **[41733]**, **[47064]**

Business 2.0 (Vol. 6, July 2005, No. 6, pp. 56); "Hipper Than Thou" in **[2713]**, **[2836]**

Business 2.0 (Vol. 6, September 2005, No. 8, pp. 56); "How Adobe is Pushing Quark Off the Page" in **[4689]**, **[8615]**, **[18231]**, **[18884]**, **[23031]**, **[50674]**, **[53318]**

Business 2.0 (Vol. 6, May 2005, No. 4, pp. 28); "How MMetrics Is Making Mobile Content Count" in **[1108]**, **[4691]**, **[5019]**, **[23034]**, **[24817]**, **[53321]**

Business 2.0 (Vol. 6, July 2005, No. 6, pp. 78-83, 85); "How to Ride the Fifth Wave" in **[5020]**, **[6679]**, **[14136]**, **[41755]**, **[53787]**

Business 2.0 (Vol. 6, May 2005, No. 4, pp. 108-114); "How To Beat WalMart" in **[30884]**, **[51191]**

Business 2.0 (Vol. 6, September 2005, No. 8, pp. 130); "How To Love Your Layover" in **[30350]**, **[52225]**, **[54957]**

Business 2.0 (Vol. 7, January/February 2006, No. 1, pp. 78-80); "Imagining the Google Future" in **[14144]**, **[34054]**

Business 2.0 (Vol. 6, July 2005, No. 6, pp. 28); "Instant Phone Companies" in **[4891]**, **[13761]**, **[35535]**

Business 2.0 (Vol. 7, January/February 2006, No. 1, pp. 32); "Luring MP3ers Back to the Mall" in **[17751]**, **[51234]**

Business 2.0 (Vol. 6, July 2005, No. 6, pp. 50); "New Muscle for Old Strip Malls" in **[11646]**, **[19422]**, **[28548]**, **[53879]**

Business 2.0 (Vol. 7, January/February 2006, No. 1, pp. 30); "On the Launch Pad: Spot Runner" in **[502]**, **[46584]**

Business 2.0 (Vol. 6, July 2005, No. 6, pp. 110-111); "One Site Does Not Fit All" in **[12610]**, **[24718]**, **[25230]**, **[30398]**, **[35012]**

Business 2.0 (Vol. 6, May 2005, No. 4, pp. 25-26); "Online Video Ads Get Ready to Grab You" in **[747]**, **[34305]**, **[47374]**

Business 2.0 (Vol. 6, May 2005, No. 4, pp. 121-122, 126-127); "Playbook" in **[28631]**, **[36632]**, **[45543]**

Business 2.0 (Vol. 7, January/February 2006, No. 1, pp. 69); "Rabbit on a Run" in **[30935]**, **[46413]**

Business 2.0 (Vol. 6, July 2005, No. 6, pp. 30); "Retail" in **[5708]**, **[9636]**, **[51310]**, **[53942]**

Business 2.0 (Vol. 6, May 2005, No. 4, pp. 34); "Rolling the Dice on Hedge Funds" in **[15424]**, **[38328]**

Business 2.0 (Vol. 7, January/February 2006, No. 1, pp. 30); "Safekeeping for Software" in **[4785]**, **[23155]**, **[44141]**, **[53441]**

Business 2.0 (Vol. 6, May 2005, No. 4, pp. 38, 41); "Shawn Fanning's New Tune" in **[17769]**, **[34464]**

Business 2.0 (Vol. 6, September 2005, No. 8, pp. 62); "Showing Products In a Better Light" in **[48868]**, **[51357]**

Business 2.0 (Vol. 6, July 2005, No. 6, pp. 40, 42); "Start Spreading the News" in **[794]**, **[13780]**, **[15470]**, **[34533]**, **[47572]**, **[55841]**

Business 2.0 (Vol. 6, May 2005, No. 4, pp. 116-118); "Surfing the Virtual Wave" in **[5126]**, **[42020]**

Business 2.0 (Vol. 7, January/February 2006, No. 1, pp. 34, 37); "Tag Sale" in **[25979]**, **[34560]**

Business 2.0 (Vol. 6, September 2005, No. 8, pp. 76); "The $50 Million Giveaway" in **[34218]**, **[35306]**, **[42411]**, **[44384]**, **[52598]**, **[55350]**

Business 2.0 (Vol. 7, January/February 2006, No. 1, pp. 21-22); "The Big Guns' Next Target: eBay" in **[560]**, **[1783]**, **[18638]**, **[30796]**, **[33586]**

Business 2.0 (Vol. 6, July 2005, No. 6, pp. 68-74); "The CEO's Secret Handbook" in **[27318]**, **[35930]**, **[37402]**, **[44988]**

Business 2.0 (Vol. 6, July 2005, No. 6, pp. 30); "The Film Biz Goes Filmless" in **[9710]**, **[17517]**, **[32154]**, **[53726]**

Business 2.0 (Vol. 7, January/February 2006, No. 1, pp. 116-118, 120, 122, 124); "The Malaria Fighter" in **[36474]**, **[50918]**, **[52147]**

Business 2.0 (Vol. 6, July 2005, No. 6, pp. 60-61); "The Mother of Stunt Marketers" in **[12899]**, **[20139]**, **[47298]**, **[50457]**, **[50634]**, **[51738]**

Business 2.0 (Vol. 7, January/February 2006, No. 1, pp. 48, 50, 52); "The New Skin Trade" in **[2598]**, **[7898]**, **[28552]**

Business 2.0 (Vol. 6, May 2005, No. 4, pp. 58, 60); "The New Sounds of Selling" in **[734]**, **[47333]**, **[51271]**, **[53882]**

Business 2.0 (Vol. 7, January/February 2006, No. 1, pp. 22); "The New Way to Make Babies" in **[50935]**, **[52159]**

Business 2.0 (Vol. 6, September 2005, No. 8, pp. 50); "The Only Question That Matters" in **[23768]**, **[31808]**, **[45165]**, **[47375]**

Business 2.0 (Vol. 6, July 2005, No. 6, pp. 64); "The Pay-for-Performance Fallacy" in **[26871]**, **[35015]**, **[45520]**

Business 2.0 (Vol. 6, September 2005, No. 8, pp. 99); "The ROI On Your MBA" in **[33223]**, **[45605]**

Business 2.0 (Vol. 6, July 2005, No. 6, pp. 102-107); "The Sales Force that Rocks" in **[17766]**, **[51812]**

Business 2.0 (Vol. 6, May 2005, No. 4, pp. 30); "The Super-Cheap Supercomputer" in **[6817]**, **[6969]**, **[49285]**

Business 2.0 (Vol. 6, May 2005, No. 4, pp. 88); "The World According to Clark" in **[22818]**, **[36991]**

Business 2.0 (Vol. 6, July 2005, No. 6, pp. 58); "Thinking Out of the Clamshell" in **[44166]**, **[46459]**, **[51388]**

Business 2.0 (Vol. 7, January/February 2006, No. 1, pp. 28); "Through a Wall, Clearly" in **[42067]**

Business 2.0 (Vol. 6, May 2005, No. 4, pp. 54); "Top of the Heap" in **[1978]**, **[34614]**

Business 2.0 (Vol. 6, July 2005, No. 6, pp. 98-100); "Turing the Page" in **[7846]**, **[42079]**, **[45771]**

Business 2.0 (Vol. 6, May 2005, No. 4, pp. 49-51); "What Works" in **[6859]**, **[42109]**

Business 2.0 (Vol. 7, January/February 2006, No. 1, pp. 41-43); "What Works: Start Last, Finish First" in **[35724]**, **[39108]**

Business 2.0 (Vol. 6, July 2005, No. 6, pp. 27-28); "What's Next" in **[5173]**, **[24462]**, **[42110]**

Business 2.0 (Vol. 6, July 2005, No. 6, pp. 36); "Why 'Buy' Buttons Are Booming" in **[34717]**, **[51415]**, **[51911]**

Business 2.0 (Vol. 7, January/February 2006, No. 1, pp. 76); "Why Employees Should Lead Themselves" in **[35149]**, **[45848]**

Business 2.0 (Vol. 6, July 2005, No. 6, pp. 109); "Workplace" in **[23644]**, **[35164]**, **[45872]**

"Business 101" in *Inc.* (November 2000, pp. 129) **[26708]**

The Business Advisor **[365]**, **[24116]**

"Business After Divorce" in *Entrepreneur* (Vol. 28, No. 4, April 2000, pp. 132) **[37605]**

Business Alabama Monthly **[56931]**

Business Alliance Inc. **[23419]**, **[38988]**, **[42788]**

Business America **[1458]**, **[3450]**

Business Asia **[39707]**

"Business dodges budget ax; But fee hikes, tax moves raise concerns" in *Crain's Detroit Business* (Vol. 19, No. 10, March 10, 2003) **[40213]**, **[54463]**

"The Business of Base Closures" in *Inc.* (September 2005, pp. 34) **[32290]**, **[39189]**

Business Basics: A Microbusiness Start-Up Guide **[52828]**

"Business gurus talk about practicing basics" in *Atlanta Business Chronicle* (Vol. 25, January 10, 2003, No. 31, pp. 4B) **[39190]**, **[53627]**

Business Basics in Hawaii: Secrets of Starting Your Own Business in Our State **[59267]**

"Business by the Book" in *Home Office Computing* (Vol. 18, No. 12, December 2000, pp. 99) **[40214]**, **[42584]**, **[44010]**

Business Books International **[58631]**

"Business Bookshelf" in *Small Business Opportunities* (Vol. 16, No. 2, March 2004, pp. 180) **[9859]**, **[13868]**, **[14815]**, **[15976]**, **[20447]**, **[20815]**, **[30233]**, **[32291]**, **[33024]**, **[33624]**, **[34779]**, **[35890]**, **[37394]**, **[39191]**, **[40681]**, **[54464]**, **[56149]**

Business Borrowers Complete Success Kit **[55527]**

"Business is Bouncin'" in *Home Business* (Vol. 12, October 2005, No. 5, pp. 71) **[21313]**, **[42585]**, **[56150]**

"Business ethics issues cross all boundaries" in *Colorado Springs Business Journal* (March 7, 2003) **[94]**, **[23901]**, **[26177]**, **[37395]**

The Business of Bridal Beauty **[3180]**

"Business Briefs" in *News Tribune* (March 2, 2005) **[7280]**, **[13216]**, **[29134]**, **[43107]**

"Business Briefs" in *St. Louis Post-Dispatch* (December 8, 2004) **[26489]**, **[50841]**, **[52068]**

"Business Briefs" in *Salt Lake Tribune* (February 24, 2005) **[2687]**, **[20221]**, **[20816]**, **[21456]**, **[39994]**, **[41577]**, **[46221]**

"Business Briefs" in *The Record* (December 23, 2002) **[95]**, **[8451]**, **[10799]**, **[11784]**, **[19381]**, **[24230]**

Business Brokers Hawaii L.L.C. **[50301]**, **[52470]**

Business in Broward **[59005]**

Business Browser U.S. **[43932]**

"Business Budgeting Basics" in *Home Business* (Vol. 12, October 2005, No. 5, pp. 72) **[7]**, **[27071]**

Business Bulletin **[60595]**

Business Buying Basics **[30664]**, **[39192]**

"Business Buzz" in *Tribune* (February 3, 2004) **[570]**, **[2333]**, **[24673]**, **[25165]**, **[27895]**, **[30302]**, **[46759]**, **[54147]**

Business Cards Tomorrow & Business Cards Tomorrow Satellite **[4006]**, **[56025]**

Business, Careers, and Lifestyle Series **[37025]**

The Business of Caring **[12401]**, **[18368]**

Business Center of Decatur **[59772]**

"Business information centers" in *BlackEnterprise* (Vol. 31, No. 12, July 2001, pp. 48) **[29716]**, **[39031]**, **[39761]**, **[52770]**

"Business Challenge: Rex Bird Noticed Some Online Customers" in *My Business* (October/November 2003, pp. 42) **[19382]**, **[25809]**, **[33625]**, **[46760]**

"Business groups urge caution on pension law changes" in *Business First Columbus* (Vol. 18, No. 25, February 8, 2002, pp. A5) **[26759]**, **[29135]**, **[40215]**

Business China **[39708]**

Business Coaching Practice Builder **[3622]**, **[16544]**

Business Communication **[27310]**

Business Journal-Portland (Vol. 20, No. 22, August 1, 2003, pp. 7); "Pizza Schmizza Ready to Take on Puget Sound" in **[19638]**, **[20360]**, **[28628]**, **[29798]**, **[30262]**, **[30582]**, **[30932]**, **[31943]**, **[43489]**, **[45537]**

Business Journal-Portland (Vol. 20, No. 22, August 1, 2003, pp. 3); "Ranks of Banker-Brokers Growing at Local Banks" in **[10033]**, **[10150]**, **[15168]**, **[15394]**, **[38302]**, **[39084]**

Business Journal-Portland (Vol. 20, No. 26, August 29, 2003, pp. 18); "Rate Increases Nail Homebuilding Sector" in **[7398]**, **[7458]**, **[13435]**, **[13917]**, **[29459]**, **[30385]**, **[43330]**, **[43467]**

Business Journal-Portland (Vol. 20, No. 22, August 1, 2003, pp. 11); "Retail Experts Laud Costco's Shopping Strategy" in **[31747]**, **[32667]**, **[45598]**, **[46210]**, **[47465]**, **[48050]**, **[51312]**, **[53540]**

Business Journal-Portland (Vol. 20, No. 23, August 8, 2003, pp. 8); "Some Relief Over End of Pixelworks Merger" in **[15464]**, **[41998]**, **[43606]**, **[47784]**, **[50184]**

Business Journal-Portland (Vol. 20, No. 24, August 15, 2003, pp. 14); "Washington a Leader in Organic Cereal Market" in **[11674]**, **[26558]**

Business Journal-Portland (Vol. 20, No. 29, September 19, 2003, pp. 1); "What Will Remain of PGE" in **[296]**, **[39128]**, **[40827]**

Business Journal-Portland (Vol. 20, No. 24, August 15, 2003, pp. 17); "Who's Got the Power?" in **[46488]**, **[48340]**

The Business Journal Serving Greater Milwaukee **[26569]**

The Business Journal Serving San Jose and Silicon Valley **[58239]**

The Business Journal (Vol. 18, No. 10, June 30, 2000, pp. 41); "Strategize your e-mail newsletter to realize more grins than groans" in **[9162]**, **[14491]**, **[34546]**

Business Journal of Upper East Tennessee and Southwest Virginia **[65014]**

Business Journal's Directory of Manufacturing **[46181]**

Business Know-How: An Operational Guide for Home-Based and Micro-Sized Businesses with Limited Budgets **[39194]**, **[42587]**

Business Law Made Simple **[29136]**

Business Learning Center **[26419]**

Business Library Series: Sales and Motivation **[51943]**

Business Litigation **[29606]**

Business Logic Inc. **[49406]**

Business Mailers Review **[16479]**

Business Management Consultants Directory **[16501]**

Business Management for the Hairdresser, Beauty & Holistic **[11760]**, **[11785]**

Business Management Newsletter **[16119]**

Business & Management Practices **[4039]**, **[16687]**

Business Marketing Association-Membership & Resource Directory **[847]**, **[16804]**, **[46764]**

Business Matters **[316]**

Business Methods Corp. **[27216]**

Business Middle East **[39711]**

Business Modeling and Integration Domain Task Force **[44708]**

"Business Models: SSPs adapt to market change" in *Red Herring* (No. 105, October 1, 2001, pp. 84) **[6238]**, **[27903]**

A Business of My Own? 21 Steps to Successfully Starting and Running a Small Business **[29810]**, **[30475]**, **[39032]**

"The Business of Nanotech" in *Business Week* (February 14, 2005, No. 3920, pp. 64) **[27904]**, **[41579]**, **[52069]**, **[53629]**

"Business Near You: Beverly Hills Franchise Offers Directors for Smaller Firms" in *Detroit Free Press* (January 21, 2007) **[3507]**, **[31119]**, **[38730]**

Business New Brunswick–Finance and Support **[66704]**

Business NewsBank **[3931]**

"Business On Her Own Terms" in *Black Enterprise* (Vol. 35, August 2004, No. 1, pp. 57) **[16502]**, **[22477]**, **[31120]**, **[39969]**, **[40975]**, **[41445]**, **[56032]**

Business Opportunities Journal(online) **[3427]**, **[21042]**, **[38952]**, **[53041]**

Business Opportunities in the United States: The Complete Reference Guide to Practices and Procedures **[52830]**

Business Organizations, Agencies, and Publications Directory **[39195]**

"Business Owners: Are You Getting Your Share of Investment Capital?" in *Women in Business* (Vol. 54, No. 5, Sept.-Oct. 2002, pp. 28) **[35893]**, **[44488]**, **[55528]**, **[56151]**

"Business Owners Frown on Economic Ills" in *Pittsburgh Business Times* (Vol. 22, No. 4, August 16, 2002, pp. 3) **[27905]**, **[32293]**

Business Owner's Guide to Accounting & Bookkeeping **[2879]**, **[26179]**

Business Periodicals Index **[5504]**, **[5505]**, **[39712]**, **[39740]**

"Business schools vying for professors with Ph.D.s" in *Atlanta Business Chronicle* (Vol. 24, No. 13, August 31, 2001, pp. 2C) **[33026]**, **[39196]**

"Business Picks Up at Tucson, Ariz., eBay Consignment Shop" in *Arizona Daily Star* (January 28, 2005) **[1788]**, **[7158]**, **[13870]**

"Business Plan Basics" in *Crain's Detroit Business* (Vol. 19, No. 49, December 8, 2003, pp. 12) **[29811]**, **[30479]**

Business Plan Handbook **[29812]**

"Business Plan Helps Set Goals, Draw Investors" in *Crain's Detroit Business* (Vol. 22, November 20, 2006, No. 47, pp. 18) **[29813]**, **[30517]**, **[37934]**, **[46765]**

The Business Planner: A Complete Guide to Raising Finances for Your Business **[29814]**, **[55529]**

Business Planning in Four Steps & a Leap **[29815]**

The Business Planning Guide: Creating a Plan for Success in Your Own Business **[29816]**

Business Plans Handbook **[29817]**

Business Plans Kit for Dummies, 2nd Edition **[29818]**, **[39197]**

Business Plans to Manage Day-to-Day Operations: Real-life Results for Small Business Owners and Operators **[29819]**

Business Plans That Work: A Guide for Small Business **[29820]**, **[39198]**

Business Plans That Work for Your Small Business **[29821]**

"Business and Pleasure" in *Black Enterprise* (Vol. 35, September 2004, No. 2, pp. 46) **[5527]**, **[22757]**, **[34840]**

Business Press (September 3, 2003); "Pomona, Calif., Aftermarket Auto Firm Goes After Markets in Midwest" in **[1961]**, **[28635]**

"Business Primer for Legislators" in *Hispanic Business* (November 2002, pp. 32) **[35894]**, **[39199]**, **[40217]**

"Business plan pro" in *Black Enterprise* (Vol. 33, No. 6, January 2003, pp. 10) **[25811]**, **[29717]**, **[35353]**, **[39033]**

"Business Products" in *Ingram's* (Vol. 29, No. 8, August 2003, pp. 43) **[3033]**, **[10558]**, **[11316]**, **[15836]**, **[17986]**, **[39200]**

"Business Prophet" in *Business Week* (January 23, 2006, No. 3968, pp. 68-73) **[35895]**, **[44968]**

The Business Publisher **[2763]**

"A Business Real Estate Appraisal Problem" in *American Banker* (Vol. 170, February 4, 2005, No. 24, pp. 10) **[3103]**, **[7770]**, **[12528]**, **[18316]**, **[20448]**, **[21458]**, **[22610]**, **[39201]**, **[40218]**

Business Record **[60249]**

Business Record (Vol. 22, August 30, 2004, No. 35, pp. 1); "Mystery Shoppers Take a Second Glance at Customer Service" in **[19420]**, **[31793]**, **[47310]**, **[51261]**

Business Research: An Informal Guide **[50842]**

Business Research Law Clinic 54110

Business Research Library–Maui Research and Technology Park–SBDC **[59230]**

The Business Resource Center **[65651]**

Business Resource Network Inc. **[63243]**

Business Resource Services Inc. **[42948]**

Business Resource Software Inc. **[30066]**, **[53547]**

Business Russia **[39713]**

"Business for Sale Update" in *Inc.* (September 2000, pp. 82) **[52411]**

"Business Services" in *Entrepreneur* (Vol. 32, No. 1, January 2004, pp. 168) **[3508]**, **[4610]**, **[20305]**, **[22932]**, **[29137]**, **[33629]**, **[35896]**, **[36620]**, **[38731]**, **[42588]**, **[52511]**

"Business Services" in *Ingram's* (Vol. 29, No. 8, August 2003, pp. 33) **[52369]**

"Business Services" in *PC Computing* (March 2000, pp. 159) **[7109]**, **[13871]**, **[33419]**, **[33630]**

The "Business" of Sewing: How to Start, Maintain & Achieve Success **[22726]**

Business Simulator **[53124]**

The Business of Small Business: Succeeding and Prospering in Business for Reasonably Intelligent Entrepreneurs **[35897]**, **[39202]**

Business for Social Responsibility **[54122]**

Business Software Alliance **[22895]**, **[53152]**

Business Start-Up Guide: How to Create, Grow & Manage Your Own Successful Enterprise **[52831]**

Business Statistics **[27906]**

Business Statistics of the United States **[27907]**

Business Systems Analysis and Design **[41490]**

Business Systems Analysis and Design (Canada) **[44730]**

Business Systems Development Process (Canada) **[32921]**

Business Team **[3446]**, **[30714]**, **[50302]**, **[52471]**

Business and Technical Assistance Programs **[55989]**

Business Technology Association **[18592]**, **[26089]**

Business and Technology Center (Champaign) **[59773]**

Business Technology Center of Los Angeles County **[58196]**

Business and Technology Centre (Omaha) **[62313]**

Business and Technology Institute–Department of Economic Development **[60268]**

Business & Technology Solutions Show **[359]**, **[2981]**, **[7035]**

"Business-to-Consumer E-Commerce: What is(n't) the Problem?" in *E-business Advisor* (Vol. 18, No. 8, August 2000, pp. 6) **[22933]**, **[33631]**, **[49678]**, **[53229]**

The Business Torts Reporter **[29595]**

Business Travel News **[30460]**

"The Business Traveler: Taking Advantage of Bargains on the Road" in *Black Enterprise* (Vol. 35, November 2004, No. 4, pp. 191) **[25167]**, **[30303]**

Business Trend Analysts–Library **[4047]**, **[16889]**

Business Trends **[54097]**

Business Unusual **[35898]**, **[39203]**

Business Upgrade: 21 Days to Reignite the Entrepreneurial Spirit in You and Your Team **[34841]**, **[35899]**

Business Ventures Inc. **[31960]**, **[45980]**

Business Warrior: Strategy for Entrepreneurs **[30808]**, **[35900]**, **[39204]**, **[42832]**, **[44969]**, **[46766]**, **[51575]**

"Business first Web site gets updated design, new URL" in *Business First Columbus* (Vol. 18, No. 25, February 8, 2002, pp. A6) **[13872]**, **[25812]**, **[33632]**

Business Week **[39714]**, **[39741]**

Business Week-1,000 Issue **[39205]**

Business Week (No. 3843, July 28, 2003, pp. 14); "A Big Windfall for Small Biz" in **[53609]**, **[54448]**

Business Week (January 31, 2005, pp. 14); "A Corporate Peace Corps Catches On" in **[53665]**, **[54162]**

Business Week (December 19, 2005, No. 3964, pp. 108); "A Corporate Science Project" in **[30830]**, **[33055]**, **[39260]**

Business Week (No. 3762, December 17, 2001, pp. 10); "A Family Affair-In Advertising" in **[621]**, **[46944]**, **[50588]**

Business Week (No. 3699, September 18, 2000, pp. 104); "A Galaxy of Knowledge" in **[44299]**

Business Week Online (February 17, 2006); "The First Task" in [51636]

Business Week Online (September 25, 2003); "The High Cost of Penny-Ante Scams" in [30229]

Business Week Online (Sept. 5, 2002); "The importance of being multilingual" in [48562], [53802]

Business Week Online (April 25, 2002); "The Not-So-Golden state? Economic optimism is gathering steam across most of the country" in [28573], [32603]

Business Week Online (Oct. 8, 2002); "The Return of the Black Entrepreneur" in [28708], [36696], [48388]

Business Week Online (Dec. 24, 2002); "The Switch from a SEP-IRA" in [10197], [38390], [54785]

Business Week Online (February 3, 2005); "Ticket Resellers Aim to Be Top Draws" in [14537], [30974], [34601]

Business Week Online (February 16, 2006); "Tips for Tough Transitions" in [30025], [37802]

Business Week Online (February 9, 2005); "Trucking Stocks: Downshifting Soon?" in [15545], [25414]

Business Week Online (February 9, 2005); "Wal-Mart's Clean Bill of Health?" in [50477], [51404]

Business Week Online (April 29, 2002); "Want New Customers? Go Guerrilla: Ad campaigns can be expensive" in [4895], [42557], [46598]

Business Week Online (November 18, 2002) "Weathering the Storm; True, things have been better for the nation's entrepreneurs" in [28978], [32787], [36925], [39660]

Business Week Online (November 15, 2002); "When the Going Gets Tough...many turn to financial counselors" in [10246], [32791], [38458]

Business Week Online (); "When an Incubator Goes Cold" in [15599], [32792], [43061], [55944]

Business Week Online (February 10, 2005) "Where Fiorina Went Wrong; A Charismatic Leader, She Helped Make HP a Powerful Marketer" in [6862], [45832]

Business Week Online (January 22, 2002); "Who Gets Disaster Aid? Who Doesn't?" in [39679], [39956]

Business Week (March 27, 2000, pp. F6); "OSHA Ushers Itself Out" in [42702], [56581]

Business Week (January 9, 2006, No. 3966, pp. 82, 84); "Penney" in [28619], [45525], [51286]

Business Week (January 9, 2006, No. 3966, pp. 94); "Personal Business" in [10132], [10574], [10688], [13003], [14348], [15351], [18111], [21582], [28622], [31577], [38279], [39521], [41899], [43782], [44123], [49204], [50129], [51287], [52174], [53409]

Business Week (February 7, 2005, No. 3919, pp. 81); "Picking Up the Pace of the Space Tourism Race" in [24719], [25232], [41903]

Business Week (No. 3670, February 28, 2000, pp. f32); "Pipe Dreams" in [49210], [49536]

Business Week (June 12, 2000, pp. F14); "Premium Pain Relief" in [43319]

Business Week (January 9, 2006, No. 3966, pp. 29-30); "Publishing" in [764], [18925], [34379], [47437], [53927]

Business Week (January 23, 2006, No. 3968, pp. 24); "Putting the Screws to Google" in [766], [14379], [34387], [47441]

Business Week (No. 3698, September 11, 2000, pp. F6); "Quicker SBA Loans" in [48378], [52937], [55792]

Business Week (December 19, 2005, No. 3964, pp. 30-32); "Real Estate" in [20638], [20978]

Business Week (No. 3779, April 22, 2002, pp. 16); "Repaying the Loan Isn't Enough" in [26340], [44633]

Business Week (No. 3678, April 24, 2000, pp. F10); "Riding the Greenback" in [36700], [44636]

Business Week (No. 3761, December 10, 2001, pp. SB4); "Right at Home with Telecommuting" in [35052], [42718], [45603], [51806]

Business Week (No. 3853, Oct. 13, 2003, pp. 82) "Right Place, Right Time; Small Businesses Aren't Just Surviving." in [28715], [54726]

Business Week (No. 3666, January 31,, 2000 pp. 6); "Rollups Redux" in [52448]

Business Week (January 16, 2006, No. 3967, pp. 87); "SciTech Developments to Watch" in [7743], [26537], [41093], [41965], [50963], [52199]

Business Week (February 14, 2005, No. 3920, pp. 45); "Seeing Red Over Big Blue's China Deal" in [15444], [22375], [29483], [40682]

Business Week (January 16, 2006, No. 3967); "Sexy Or Sensible? What You Buy To Drive May Not Be What You're Driven To Buy" in [18122], [47519]

Business Week (February 20, 2006, No. 3972, pp. 63); "Should Doctors Own Hospitals?" in [41099], [53962]

Business Week (No. 3666, January 31, 2000, pp. F30); "Site Seeing" in [14438], [34481]

Business Week (May 22, 2000, pp. 126); "Small is Bountiful" in [44655]

Business Week (January 8, 2007); "Small Business: Just When Hopes Were High" in [32690], [52952]

Business Week (No. 3853, October 13, 2003, pp. 86); "Small, Yes-But With A Big Back Office" in [4804], [23181], [28791], [30957], [53470]

Business Week (No. 3694, August 14, 2000, pp. F14); "Smart Answers" in [25244], [29998], [37782], [49269]

Business Week (No. 3772, March 4, 2002, pp.73); "Smoother Ice Cream From Winter Wheat" in [12789], [48793]

Business Week (January 9, 2006, No. 3966, pp. 79-80); "So Many Lenders, So Few Takers" in [17440], [20671], [21010], [32698]

Business Week (No. 3702, October 9, 2000, pp. F24); "Soaring Salaries: It's Payback Time" in [26915], [27180], [36767], [42420]

Business Week (June 12, 2000, pp. F24); "Spies Like Us" in [44367], [53990]

Business Week (No. 3689, July 10, 2000, pp. F8); "Starts Slow, Jobs Grow" in [35669], [52787], [55434]

Business Week (No. 3761, December 10, 2001, pp. SB9); "Stats of the Month" in [28821], [52999]

Business Week (No. 3702, October 9, 2000, pp. F16); "Staying Out of Court" in [29518], [40732], [54002]

Business Week (December 19, 2005, No. 3964, pp. 34, 36); "Stock Options" in [15479], [38377]

Business Week (January 9, 2006, No. 3966, pp. 92); "Stocks" in [15482], [18133], [31863]

Business Week (January 16, 2006, No. 3967, pp. 28-31); "Storms" in [13475], [43379]

Business Week (No. 3691, July 24, 2000, pp. EB47); "Story of E" in [9161]

Business Week (December 19, 2005, No. 3964, pp. 44-45); "Strategies" in [7744], [29519], [44153]

Business Week (January 31, 2005, pp. 23); "Strong Demand Is Firing Up U.S. Factories" in [28836], [44248], [46447]

Business Week (February 20, 2006, No. 3972, pp. 65); "Studying Molecules to Build a Better Grape" in [23511], [50974], [52211]

Business Week (December 11, 2000, pp. 18); "Surfing the Tongues" in [14496], [34551]

Business Week (January 9, 2006, No. 3966, pp. 26-28); "Talent" in [35086], [45707]

Business Week (May 22, 2000, pp. F30); "Taming the Techno Beast" in [49296]

Business Week (No. 3666, January 31, 2000, pp. 124E4); "Tax Breaks: Don't Forget Your Home Office" in [42732], [54795]

Business Week (No. 3702, October 9, 2000, pp. F4); "Tax Experts Are Standing By" in [33249], [54026], [54802]

Business Week (January 31, 2005, pp. 30); "That Trade Deficit Is No Debacle" in [28882], [43839]

Business Week (January 16, 2006, No. 3967, pp. 22); "The Barker Portfolio" in [14776], [37909]

Business Week (January 9, 2006, No. 3966, pp. 89-90); "The Beach Less Traveled" in [12520], [24666], [25153]

Business Week (No. 3658, December 6, 1999, pp. F10); "The Bucks Start Here" in [27881], [44486], [53622]

Business Week (February 14, 2005, No. 3920, pp. 64); "The Business of Nanotech" in [27904], [41579], [52069], [53629]

Business Week (January 16, 2006, No. 3967, pp. 26-27); "The Business Week" in [12529], [14818], [32294], [39206], [40219], [43567], [54466]

Business Week (January 23, 2006, No. 3968, pp. 30-31); "The Business Week News You Need to Know" in [13873], [17987], [27908], [33633], [39208], [44970], [46223], [51084]

Business Week (January 9, 2006, No. 3966, pp. 24-25); "The Business Week News You Need To Know" in [4092], [11594], [24386], [39209], [40220], [43568], [51085]

Business Week (February 14, 2005, No. 3920, pp. 45); "The Chamber Steps Up Its War On the SEC" in [29147], [40249]

Business Week (February 7, 2005, pp. 96) "The Counterfeit Catastrophe; Curbing Piracy Is As Urgent As Taking Down Trade Barriers" in [13931], [22203], [33710], [43599]

Business Week (January 9, 2006, No. 3966, pp. 20); "The Daily Paper of Tomorrow" in [599], [18864], [33736], [46868], [53678]

Business Week (January 16, 2006, No. 3967, pp. 92-93); "The Digital Schusser" in [4974], [23613], [41637]

Business Week (January 23, 2006, No. 3968, pp. 74-75); "The Dirty Little Secret About Buybacks" in [14920], [38008]

Business Week (January 23, 2006, No. 3968, pp. 78-82); "The Easy Way to Find the Best" in [14945], [38026]

Business Week (No. 3658, December 6, 1999, pp. F46); "The Entrepreneurial Elite" in [35421], [56041]

Business Week (January 16, 2006, No. 3967, pp. 23-24); "The Export Engine Is Shifting Into High Gear" in [12960], [28135], [32420], [43651]

Business Week (February 14, 2005, No. 3920) "The Fog of the Budget; How Bush Will Mask the Biggest National Debt in History" in [32437]

Business Week (No. 3689, July 10, 2000, pp. F18); "The Health Care Crisis" in [43204]

Business Week (February 7, 2007); "The Impact of Immigrant Entrepreneurs" in [32504], [36338], [48247]

Business Week (March 27, 2000, pp. F28); "The Ire Next Time" in [42311], [42870]

Business Week (February 7, 2005, No. 3919, pp. 10); "The Lid On Spam Is Still Loose" in [14204], [22283], [27420], [39368], [34136]

Business Week (December 11, 2000, pp. 5); "The Limo Jet: Its Time is Coming" in [30370]

Business Week (No. 3691, July 24, 2000, pp. 26); "The Little Guys Spy a Slowdown" in [28415], [42328], [53837]

Business Week (January 23, 2006, No. 3968, pp. 62); "The NSA" in [22315], [42366]

Business Week (January 9, 2006, No. 3966, pp. 60-62); "The Patent Epidemic" in [29433], [40606], [44113]

Business Week (January 9, 2006, No. 3966, pp. 62-63); "The Peterman Principle" in [15352], [38280]

Business Week (June 12, 2000, pp. F26); "The Spies Have It" in [44366], [53989]

Business Week (January 23, 2006, No. 3968, pp. 43); "The Struggle to Sell the Economy's Sizzle" in [32724]

Business Week (December 19, 2005, No. 3964, pp. 42); "The Supreme Court" in [15520], [29545], [40763]

Business Week (February 20, 2006, No. 3972, pp. 18); "The Upside and Downside of Outsourcing" in [26556], [32769], [46471], [49750], [52603], [54056]

Business Week (No. 3853, October 13, 2003, pp. 88); "Throwing a Line to Uninsured Workers" in [26936]

Business Week (January 23, 2006, No. 3968, pp. 25); "Too High a Price for Black Ink" in **[15530]**, **[51392]**

Business Week (January 16, 2006, No. 3967, pp. 18); "Treo" in **[4848]**, **[6847]**, **[23240]**, **[42074]**, **[49327]**, **[53521]**

Business Week (No. 3761, December 10, 2001, pp. 60EU1); "Turning Designers Into Managers" in **[1615]**, **[33270]**, **[36893]**

Business Week (January 9, 2006, No. 3966, pp. 44); "Ukraine" in **[15553]**, **[43859]**

Business Week (No. 3689, July 10, 2000, pp. F10); "Uncle Sam Wants YOU!" in **[35576]**, **[36899]**, **[40105]**

Business Week (March 27, 2000, pp. F6); "Uncle Same Eases Up on Barter" in **[26719]**, **[34635]**, **[40789]**, **[54849]**

Business Week (January 16, 2006, No. 3967, pp. 11-12, 14); "Up Front" in **[7507]**, **[14558]**, **[18154]**, **[30981]**, **[34639]**, **[51397]**

Business Week (February 20, 2006, No. 3972, pp. 29); "U.S." in **[15564]**, **[28951]**, **[32771]**, **[40799]**

Business Week (February 7, 2005, No. 3919, pp. 25); "U.S.: Signs That Inflation Is Losing Its Fangs" in **[30982]**, **[32772]**, **[43868]**

Business Week (February 14, 2005, No. 3920, pp. 23); "U.S.: The Fed: Trying To Shift Into Neutral" in **[15565]**, **[28952]**, **[32773]**

Business Week (January 23, 2006, No. 3968, pp. 20); "Voices of Innovation" in **[4853]**, **[23251]**, **[48524]**, **[49662]**, **[50989]**, **[52226]**, **[53529]**

Business Week (December 11, 2000, pp. 14); "Wanted: A Few Good Hackers" in **[14574]**, **[34654]**

Business Week (No. 3675, April 3, 2000, pp. EB22); "Weblining" in **[14588]**, **[31602]**, **[34682]**, **[44380]**

Business Week (No. 3666, January 31, 2000, pp. 4); "We've Got To Get Our Hands on Some Workers" in **[42458]**, **[54066]**

Business Week (No. 3658, December 6, 1999, pp. F30); "What Comes Next" in **[40820]**, **[43418]**, **[54067]**

Business Week (No. 3658, December 6, 1999, pp. F9); "What Rate Hike?" in **[38453]**

Business Week (January 16, 2006, No. 3967, pp. 70-71); "What's That Ringing in iPod's Ears?" in **[5176]**, **[17778]**, **[49357]**

Business Week (January 31, 2005, pp. 20); "When a BlackBerry Is Overkill: The Phones Are Fine for Reading, But Not Writing e-Mails" in **[4857]**, **[5177]**, **[14610]**, **[23259]**, **[49359]**, **[53535]**

Business Week (January 16, 2006, No. 3967, pp. 42-43); "Where the Jobs Are" in **[42465]**, **[49757]**, **[54075]**

Business Week (February 14, 2005, No. 3920, pp. 68); "Why the Old Rules Don't Apply" in **[42116]**, **[52229]**, **[55953]**

Business Week (February 10, 2005); "Why S&P Is Standing Pat on HP" in **[6864]**, **[10251]**, **[15604]**, **[38469]**

Business Week (May 6, 2002, pp. 36); "Williams-Sonoma Tries a New Recipe: Pottery Barn Kids is a hit" in **[29013]**, **[51416]**

Business Week (January 23, 2006, No. 3968, pp. 84-85); "Wish You Were Here. Oh-You Are" in **[24746]**, **[25272]**

Business Week (No. 3699, September 18, 2000, pp. 112); "Work at Home? First, Get Real" in **[42769]**

Business Week (February 20, 2006, No. 3972) "You Data, Naked On the Net; What's Jeopardizing Your Privacy?" in **[6296]**, **[14640]**, **[22427]**, **[34762]**

Business Week (December 28, 2006); "Your Annual Business Tune-Up" in **[14641]**, **[26023]**, **[30634]**, **[37010]**

Business Wire **[6307]**, **[6384]**, **[7006]**, **[10369]**, **[15749]**, **[17473]**

Business World Exhibition/Quebec City **[53066]**

Business World's Guide to Computers **[49391]**

Business Writing for Administrative Professionals (Canada) **[25514]**

Business Writing the Modular Way **[27623]**

Business Writing: Quick, Clear, Concise **[27699]**

Business Writing Skills Series **[27700]**

"The Business Year That Was" in *Inc.* (December 1, 2003) **[35901]**, **[39210]**

"Business.com Pushes Portal Envelope" in *Information Today* (Vol. 17, No. 11, December 2000, pp. 14) **[13874]**, **[33634]**

"Businesses Assessing Granholm's Plans for SBT Overhaul" in *Crain's Detroit Business* (Vol. 21, January 31, 2005, No. 5, pp. 6) **[27909]**, **[39794]**, **[54467]**

"Businesses Balk at Required Art" in *San Jose Mercury News* (March 4, 2005) **[5973]**, **[7281]**, **[8000]**

"Businesses' Cost From Flu Are Nothing To Sneeze At" in *Tampa Tribune* (November 3, 2005) **[39211]**, **[40976]**

"Businesses hope comments don't mean a tense border" in *Crain's Detroit Business* (Vol. 19, No. 14, April 7, 2003, pp. 39) **[39212]**, **[43569]**

"Businesses Get Creative in Wake of Storm" in *Memphis Business Journal* (Vol. 25, No. 14, August 1, 2003, pp. 3) **[39213]**

"Businesses Have Faith in the Economy's Resiliency" in *Kiplinger Letter* (Vol. 78, January 5, 2007, No. 1) **[27910]**, **[32295]**

"Businesses Hope to Limit Lawsuits, Expand Health-Care Access" in *Atlanta Business Chronicle* (Vol. 24, No. 7, July 20, 2001, pp. 3A) **[13219]**, **[26761]**, **[40221]**

"Businesses work to offer wireless Internet access" in *Crain's Detroit Business* (Vol. 18, No. 20, May 20, 2002, pp. 14) **[13875]**, **[33635]**

"Businesses Must Now Notify of Possible ID Theft" in *Crain's Detroit Business* (Vol. 23, January 8, 2007, No. 2, pp. 6) **[33636]**, **[40222]**, **[48971]**

"Businesses Oppose Family Leave Change" in *Crain's Detroit Business* (Vol. 16, No. 4, January 24, 2000, pp. 4) **[26762]**, **[40223]**

"Businesses push better public transit" in *Crain's Detroit Business* (Vol. 19, No. 17, April 28, 2003, pp. 18) **[27911]**, **[32296]**

"Businesses Use Wireless Access to Draw Customers" in *Crain's Detroit Business* (Vol. 19, No. 42, October 20, 2003, pp. 14) **[3034]**, **[3121]**, **[13876]**, **[18599]**, **[21459]**, **[22196]**, **[33637]**, **[41580]**, **[43106]**

"Businesses Warn State: Don't Hurt Economy to Fix Budget" in *Crain's Detroit Business* (Vol. 19, No. 42, October 20, 2003, pp. 29) **[31429]**, **[32297]**, **[38571]**, **[40224]**, **[54434]**, **[54468]**

BusinessPlanWorld.com **[30067]**

BusinessWeek Guide to the Best Business Schools **[32984]**

BusinessWoman Magazine **[56526]**

"Busy Out-of-Towners Find Everett B&Bs the Way To Go" in *Everett Business Journal* (Vol. 6, No. 7, July 2003, pp. B1) **[2431]**

But a Good Cigar Is a Smoke! **[24628]**

But I Don't Have Customers **[54287]**

"But Wait, There's More" in *Entrepreneur* (Vol. 31, No. 11, November 2003, pp. 98) **[46767]**, **[51086]**, **[51576]**

Butler Area Chamber of Commerce **[61928]**, **[66359]**

Butler County Chamber of Commerce and Tourism **[64393]**

Butler Tri-Boro Area Chamber of Commerce **[62481]**

"Butler, Wis., Printing Plant Expands Operations" in *Milwaukee Journal Sentinel* (December 17, 2005) **[19868]**, **[27912]**, **[37607]**

Butte College–Small Business Development Center **[57250]**

Butte County Chamber of Commerce **[59289]**

"Butte, Montana, Luxury Home Turned into European-Style Bed and Breakfast" in *Montana Standard* (July 20, 2003) **[2432]**

Butte-Silver Bow Chamber of Commerce **[62152]**

Butte Small Business Development Center–Southwest Montana Service Center **[62120]**

Butterfly Life **[19500]**

Buttonwillow Chamber of Commerce **[57379]**

Butts County Chamber of Commerce **[59069]**

"The Buy-A-Wish Foundation Catalog" in *Fast Company* (August 2001, pp. 148) **[35902]**, **[39214]**

"Buy, buy biotech?" in *Entrepreneur* (Vol. 30, No. 3, March 2002, pp. 72) **[27913]**, **[37935]**, **[41581]**

"Buy Now, Pay More Later: Paying Premiums Over Time Can Cost You" in *Entrepreneur* (Vol. 32, November 2004, No. 11, pp. 70) **[13220]**, **[43110]**

Buy the Right Business-At the Right Price: The Guide to Small Business Acquisition **[30665]**

"Buy, Sell & Rent" in *Black Enterprise* (Vol. 34, July 2004, No. 12, pp. 116) **[20817]**, **[21314]**, **[29138]**, **[40225]**

Buy Your Own Business: The Definitive Guide to Identifying & Purchasing a Business You Can Make **[30666]**

"Buyers Check Out Telecom Hotel" in *Houston Business Journal* (Vol. 34, No. 18, September 12, 2003, pp. 1) **[12530]**, **[20449]**, **[20818]**

"Buyers Gain Upper Hand as House Sales Decline" in *Sacramento Bee* (November 18, 2005) **[20450]**, **[20819]**, **[27914]**

The Buyer's Guide to Affordable Antique Jewelry: How to Find, Buy, and Care for Fabulous Antique Jewelry **[15837]**

Buyer's Guide & Membership Directory **[9063]**

"Buyer's Mentality" in *Sales & Marketing Management* (Vol. 159, January-February 2007, No. 1, pp. 45) **[42186]**, **[44971]**

Buying a Business **[30667]**

"Buying Guide" in *My Business* (April/May 2004, pp. 18-19) **[6599]**, **[48972]**

"Buying Guide: Software" in *My Business* (June/July 2004, pp. 18-19) **[4611]**, **[22189]**, **[22934]**, **[53230]**

Buying In: A Complete Guide to Acquiring a Business or Professional Practice **[30668]**

"Buying Long-Term-Care Insurance: A Security Blanket for Old Age" in *Journal of Accountancy* (Vol. 199, January 2005, No. 1, pp. 78) **[96]**, **[2880]**, **[12531]**, **[23902]**, **[43111]**

"Buying Online-Who Needs Contractors?" in *Air Conditioning, Heating & Refrigeration News* (Vol. 219, No. 17, August 25, 2003, pp. 23) **[1016]**, **[1789]**, **[33638]**

Buying & Selling Small Business **[30669]**, **[52412]**

"Buying a Small Business? Beware!" in *Business Week Online* (December 4, 2002) **[29061]**, **[35354]**

"Buying Stocks in a Slowing Economy" in *Black Enterprise* (Vol. 31, No. 5, December 2000, pp. 117) **[37936]**

"Buying Tunes Online" in *Kiplinger's Personal Finance Magazine* (Vol. 54, No. 12, December 2000, pp. 28) **[6136]**, **[17732]**, **[33639]**, **[40226]**, **[44011]**

Buying Your First Franchise **[38732]**, **[42589]**

Buying Your Own Business **[30670]**

Buyouts (October 3, 2005); "Private Equity Firms Help Hurricane Victims" in **[15371]**, **[54241]**, **[55782]**

"The Buzz About HD Radio" in *Black Enterprise* (Vol. 37, February 2007, No. 7, pp. 58) **[20306]**, **[41582]**

"The buzz on buzz" in *Harvard Business Review* (Vol. 78, No. 6, November-December 2000, pp. 139) **[46768]**

"Buzz Skill" in *Entrepreneur* (Vol. 33, October 2005, No. 10, pp. 81) **[46769]**, **[48145]**, **[50568]**

"Buzzwords: Plog" in *Inc.* (September 1, 2004) **[13877]**, **[33640]**, **[34842]**, **[53231]**

BV Capital / Bertelsmann Ventures, LP (Santa Barbara) **[57956]**

"By the Book" in *Entrepreneur.com* (Vol. 34, February 2006, No. 2, pp. 77) **[44972]**, **[51577]**

"By Degrees" in *Entrepreneur* (Vol. 32, December 2004, No. 12, pp. 98) **[33027]**, **[44973]**

"By Gum!...It Is Possible to Beat Everyone-Even Big Companies-To Market..." in *Entrepreneur* (Vol. 32, November 2004, No. 11, pp. 26) **[30809]**, **[35903]**, **[43570]**

"By Land, Air, and Sea: New Passport Rules in Effect" in *Black Enterprise* (Vol. 37, January 2007, No. 6., pp. 101) **[30304]**, **[40227]**

"By the Numbers: Hopes are pinned on a second-half recovery" in *Red Herring* (No. 99, June 15 & July 1, 2001, pp. 136) **[14819]**, **[32298]**

"By Special Request: Pleasing One Client Pays Off in the Long Run" in *Entrepreneur* (Vol. 31, No. 8, August 2003, pp. 73) **[9698]**, **[31655]**

"By Special Request: Upscale Concierge Business Give New Meaning to the Phrase 'Service With a Smile'" in *Entrepreneur* (July 2004) **[7110]**

"Bye-Bye, Tax Break" in *Business Week* (No. 3666, January 31, 2000, pp. 6) **[54469]**

Byesville Board of Trade **[63630]**

"B.Y.O. GPS" in *Business 2.0* (Vol. 6, September 2005, No. 8, pp. 132) **[29561]**, **[30305]**, **[46639]**, **[48973]**, **[49489]**

Willard C. Byrd Landscape Architect **[12690]**

ByrneMRG **[3656]**, **[16579]**, **[31295]**, **[45981]**, **[48821]**

Byron Area Chamber of Commerce **[59446]**

"Bystrom Providing In-Room Massages at Lakeway Inn & Convention Center" in *Bellingham Business Journal* (January 2007, pp. A17) **[17004]**, **[30306]**, **[42187]**

BYTE **[6308]**, **[6385]**, **[6536]**, **[7007]**

BYU Idaho **[59349]**

C

"C & A Says Company Will Be Sold" in *Crain's Detroit Business* (Vol. 22, November 20, 2006, No. 47, pp. 4) **[30518]**, **[37937]**, **[46224]**

"C-DHP: Where Is The Movement Headed" in *Rough Notes* (Vol. 145, No. 1, January 2003, pp. 108) **[13221]**, **[27316]**, **[33028]**, **[43112]**

C-E-O & M-O-M, Same Time, Same Place **[56152]**

C F Services Group Inc. **[27011]**

C. W Post Campus of Long Island University–Long Island University **[63220]**

"C2G-Network" in *Entrepreneur.com* (Vol. 34, January 2006, No. 1, pp. 6) **[9860]**, **[14820]**, **[41583]**, **[42188]**, **[42833]**, **[44974]**, **[46770]**

CAA News **[1622]**

CABDA Cycling Expo **[2514]**

"Cabela's reels in local developer to Dundee" in *Crain's Detroit Business* (Vol. 19, No. 15, April 14, 2003, pp. 1) **[7282]**, **[12532]**, **[17988]**, **[21460]**, **[23610]**, **[27915]**

Cabin Crew Safety **[964]**

"CABIR Phone Virus is Bad, But Not That Bad" in *St. Louis Post-Dispatch* (February 23, 2005) **[4935]**, **[13878]**, **[22190]**

Cable Ad Ventures Corp. **[24491]**

Cable Area Chamber of Commerce **[66360]**

"Cable-Free USB" in *Entrepreneur* (Vol. 33, October 2005, No. 10, pp. 41) **[6239]**, **[13782]**, **[13879]**, **[48974]**, **[50963]**

"Cable Networks Help Boost First-Quarter Profit for E.W. Scripps Co." in *Denver Post* (April 11, 2003) **[4093]**, **[18856]**, **[27916]**

"Cable cuts out slice of the broadband pie" in *InfoWorld* (Vol. 23, No. 5, January 29, 2001, pp. 40) **[4936]**, **[14821]**, **[33641]**, **[48975]**, **[49833]**

"Cable ready" in *WorkingWoman* (Vol. 25, No. 4, April 2000, pp. 38) **[24387]**, **[37938]**

Cable & Station Coverage Atlas, 1995 **[24388]**

Cable TV Facts **[4094]**

"Cable TV Firm Announces Hundreds of Job Openings in Atlanta" in *Atlanta Journal-Constitution* (January 18, 2007) **[4095]**, **[24389]**, **[42189]**

Cable TV, Video, and Imaging **[4150]**

Cable Yellow Pages **[4135]**, **[24468]**

Cablecaster **[4136]**, **[24469]**

Cabletelevision Advertising Bureau **[24358]**

Cabletelevision Advertising Bureau - Cable Advertising Conference **[4152]**, **[55208]**

Cabletter **[24470]**

"Cablevision Plans Faster Internet Service Without Raising Price" in *The Record* (November 8, 2005) **[4096]**, **[13880]**, **[31016]**

"Cablevision Systems Corp. Tops 1M Interactive Optimum Customers" in *Long Island Business News* (March 12, 2004) **[4086]**, **[4097]**, **[27917]**

"Cablevision in Talks to Sell Fox Sports Stake to Comcast" in *Long Island Business News* (February 27, 2004) **[14822]**, **[24390]**, **[49834]**

Caboodle Cartridge **[4007]**

Cabool Area Chamber of Commerce **[61929]**

Cabot Chamber of Commerce **[57141]**

Cache Chamber of Commerce **[65703]**

Cactus Car Wash **[4377]**

"Cadence Bank" in *Mississippi Business Journal* (Vol. 29, January 2007, No. 3, pp. A6) **[39215]**, **[44975]**

Cadillac Area Chamber of Commerce **[61266]**

Cadiz-Trigg County Chamber of Commerce **[60488]**

Cadott Area Chamber of Commerce **[66361]**

Cadwalader, Wickersham & Taft–Library **[1080]**, **[9429]**

Cafe Ala Carte **[5779]**, **[11370]**

Cafe Depot/Coffee Depot **[11371]**

"CAFTA Action" in *Hispanic Business* (September 2006, pp. 14) **[12948]**, **[40228]**, **[43571]**

Cahokia Area Chamber of Commerce **[59447]**

Cairo Chamber of Commerce **[59448]**, **[62833]**

Caixa Geral do Depositos SA (CGD)–Mediateca e Centro de Informacao Europeia **[413]**, **[24169]**

Cake Decorating for All Occasions **[2275]**

Calabasas Chamber of Commerce **[57380]**

Calaveras County Chamber of Commerce **[57381]**

"Calculate This" in *My Business* (April/May 2002, pp. 45) **[52648]**

"Calculating clicks" in *Entrepreneur* (Vol. 30, No. 2, February 2002, pp. 72) **[572]**, **[13881]**, **[33642]**, **[46771]**

"Calculating Profits" in *Black Enterprise* (Vol. 34, No. 6, January 2004, pp. 36) **[97]**, **[25807]**, **[26180]**, **[37939]**

"Calculating Savings Bonds Values" in *Black Enterprise* (Vol. 35, January 2005, No. 6, pp. 38) **[9861]**, **[14823]**, **[37940]**

Calcutta Area Chamber of Commerce **[63631]**

Caldwell Area Chamber of Commerce **[60299]**

Caldwell Chamber of Commerce **[59290]**

Caldwell Community College and Technical Institute–Small Business Center **[63479]**

Caldwell County Chamber of Commerce **[63337]**

"Calendar" in *San Fernando Valley Business Journal* (Vol. 12, January 2007, No. 2, pp. 40) **[24899]**, **[33029]**, **[35904]**

"Calendar" in *Venture Capital Journal* (Vol. 42, No. 10, October 2002, pp. 51-52) **[14824]**, **[15377]**, **[51873]**, **[55530]**

Calexico Chamber of Commerce **[57382]**

Calhoun City Chamber of Commerce **[61779]**

Calhoun County Chamber of Commerce **[58762]**, **[64726]**

Caliche Ltd. **[56653]**

Caliente Chamber of Commerce **[62343]**

"Calif. Company snaps up Texas Winn-Dixie center" in *Atlanta Business Chronicle* (Vol. 25, December 6, 2002, No. 26, pp. 32C) **[11595]**, **[14825]**, **[20820]**, **[32146]**, **[49835]**

California Apparel News **[5288]**

California Association of Homes and Services for the Aging Annual Meeting and Exhibition **[1710]**

"California Auto Dealers Attack Government Vehicle Plan" in *Sacramento Bee* (November 19, 2005) **[17989]**, **[39995]**

California Builder & Engineer **[7529]**

California Business Law Practitioner **[29596]**

The California Capitol Restoration Series **[1543]**

California Chamber of Commerce **[57383]**, **[61930]**

California Chamber of Commerce, Southern California Office **[57384]**

California City Chamber of Commerce **[57385]**

California Closet Company **[18584]**, **[18621]**, **[20030]**, **[49667]**

California Closet Co. Inc. (Canada) **[20031]**

California College of the Arts Libraries–Meyer Library **[6062]**, **[8113]**, **[8257]**

"California Commissioner Plans Hearings to Lower Title Insurance Premiums" in *Sacramento Bee* (December 16, 2005) **[13222]**, **[17364]**, **[43113]**

"California Commissioner Proposes Overhaul to Auto Insurance Premiums" in *Sacramento Bee* (December 23, 2005) **[13223]**, **[40229]**, **[43114]**

California Corporation Formation Package and Minute Book **[58240]**

California Culinary Academy–Library **[7827]**, **[12093]**, **[12740]**, **[18494]**, **[22031]**

California Department of Conservation–Division of Recycling–Resource Center **[11975]**, **[21288]**

California Department of Finance–State Census Data Center **[66830]**

California Department of Pesticide Regulation–Library **[19047]**

California Dietetic Association Meeting **[18475]**, **[26047]**

"California Dreamin'" in *Entrepreneur* (Vol. 31, No. 9, September 2003, pp. 22) **[51087]**, **[52649]**

California Employer Advisor **[58236]**

California Environmental Protection Agency–Library **[1081]**

California Federal Bank–Technical Library **[7017]**

California Garden **[10579]**, **[11455]**, **[16034]**

California Gift Show **[11121]**, **[11185]**

California Indian Business Development Center–National Center for American Indian Enterprise **[57888]**

California Institute for Rural Studies **[26683]**

California Institute of Technology–Office of Sponsored Research **[58197]**

California Integrated Waste Management Board–Library **[21289]**

California Israel Chamber of Commerce **[57386]**

"California Job Growth Slows" in *Sacramento Bee* (November 19, 2005) **[32299]**, **[51578]**, **[53630]**

California Job Journal **[23382]**

California Labor and Employment ALERT Newsletter **[29597]**, **[58237]**

California Labor and Employment Law Quarterly **[58238]**

California Land Surveyors Association Conference **[23778]**

"California Lost Jobs in September" in *Sacramento Bee* (October 22, 2005) **[27918]**, **[32300]**, **[42190]**

"California Offers Paid Leave for All Workers" in *Inc.* (October 1, 2004) **[26763]**, **[40230]**

California Optometric Association OPTOWEST **[25662]**

California Polytechnic State University–Robert F. Kennedy Library - Government Documents and Map Department–Diablo Canyon Power Plant Depository Library **[4048]**

California Procurement Technical Assistance Center

    Federal Technology Center Procurement Technical Assistance Center **[58193]**

    Riverside Community College District **[58194]**

    San Diego Contracting Opportunities Center **[58195]**

California Quivers **[15953]**

California Real Estate Journal **[21043]**

(California) Real Estate Services Division–Library **[7680]**

"California Regulator Seeks Cut in Lawn-Mower Emissions" in *Daily News* (April 11, 2003) **[16005]**, **[16112]**, **[37254]**, **[40231]**

"California Regulators Approve SBC, AT&T Merger" in *Sacramento Bee* (November 19, 2005) **[4937]**, **[14826]**, **[41584]**, **[49836]**

"California based Robeks Fruit Smoothies Sets Expansion in NY Metro..." in *Long Island Business News* (Feb.27,2004) **[12051]**, **[21461]**, **[27919]**, **[38733]**

California Small Business Development Center–California Trade and Commerce Agency **[57243]**

California Society of Printmakers **[5954]**

California Special Education Alert **[31259]**, **[33293]**

California (State) Department of Housing and Community Development–Housing Resource Center **[20085]**

California State Department of Motor Vehicles–Licensing Operations Division - Research and Development Branch–Traffic Safety Research Library **[2109]**, **[8736]**, **[16195]**, **[24253]**

California (State) Film Commission–Location Resource Center–Library **[9772]**

California State Polytechnic University–W.K. Kellogg Arabian Horse Library **[12476]**

California State Polytechnic University, Pomona Apparel Technology and Research Center **[46548]**

John T. Lyle Center for Regenerative Studies **[23353]**
California State University, Fresno
    Center for Agricultural Business **[26684]**
    Office of Research and Sponsored Programs **[58198]**
California State University Fresno Foundation **[58199]**
California State University, Hayward–California Urban Environmental Research and Education Center **[37373]**
California State University, Long Beach
    Graduate Center for Public Policy and Administration **[50388]**
    Graduate Center for Public Policy and Administration–Bureau of Governmental Research and Services **[50389]**
    Office of University Research **[58200]**
California State University, Long Beach Foundation **[58201]**
California State University, Los Angeles–Edmund G. "Pat" Brown Institute of Public Affairs **[41364]**
California State University, Northridge–Office of Research and Sponsored Projects **[58202]**
California State University Press **[58256]**
"California Teaming" in *Fast Company* (November 2001, pp. 30) **[39216]**, **[53631]**
California Technology Ventures LLC **[57957]**
California Trade and Commerce Agency
    Office of Business Development **[57280]**
    Office of Economic Research **[57281]**
    Office of Small Business **[57282]**
California Travel Parks Association Convention and Trade Show **[4259]**
"California takes a tumble" in *Red Herring* (March 2003, pp. 65) **[14827]**, **[49837]**
California University of Pennsylvania
    Louis L. Manderino Library–Special Collections **[1355]**, **[1648]**, **[17666]**, **[17814]**
    Mon Valley Renaissance **[64601]**
"California bill on Web sales tax" in *The New York Times* (September 1, 2000, pp. C2) **[33643]**, **[40232]**, **[54470]**
Calimesa Chamber of Commerce **[57387]**
Calistoga Chamber of Commerce **[57388]**
Call Center Conference & Exposition **[24312]**
"Call Centers In the Rec Room" in *Business Week* (January 23, 2006, No. 3968, pp. 76-77) **[42590]**, **[49679]**, **[53632]**
"Call Forward: No Question About It" in *Entrepreneur* (Vol. 32, November 2004, No. 11, pp. 17) **[4938]**, **[48976]**
"Call Waiting?" in *Entrepreneur* (Vol. 31, No. 7, July 2003, pp. 37) **[4939]**, **[6600]**, **[48977]**
Call and Whistle Collectors Association **[1299]**, **[5793]**
"Call of the Wi-Fi: Digital Edge" in *Entrepreneur* (Vol. 31, No. 9, September 2003, pp. 39) **[4940]**, **[40233]**
"Calling All VoIP Adopters: Tech Shows" in *Tradeshow Week* (Vol. 34, November 29, 2004, No. 48, pp. 54) **[4941]**, **[22478]**, **[24900]**, **[41585]**, **[48978]**, **[55072]**
"Calling security" in *Entrepreneur* (Vol. 30, No. 9, September 2002, pp. 23) **[22191]**, **[41586]**, **[53633]**
"Calling the Shots: Is a VoIP Telephone System in Your Company's Future?" in *Entrepreneur* (Vol. 32, October 2004, No. 10, pp. 57) **[4942]**, **[13882]**, **[48979]**
"Calling in Sick" in *Fortune* (Vol. 152, August 8, 2005, No. 3, pp. 96H) **[29822]**, **[42977]**, **[44976]**
"Callon Adds Inventory" in *Mississippi Business Journal* (Vol. 28, September 2006, No. 36, pp. 24) **[39217]**, **[49838]**
"Calm After the Storm" in *Hispanic Business* (December 2001, pp. 64) **[573]**, **[20307]**, **[46772]**
Calmac Manufacturing Corp. **[1052]**
Calmas Associates **[37824]**
Calorie Control Commentary **[26043]**
CALTRUX **[25431]**
Calumet City Chamber of Commerce **[59449]**
Calvert Chamber of Commerce **[65150]**
Calvert County Chamber of Commerce **[60818]**

Calvert Social Venture Partners, L.P. **[65967]**
Camara de Comercio Hispana de Hialeah **[58763]**
Camarillo Chamber of Commerce **[57389]**
Camarro Research **[47838]**
"Camas, Vancouver advance toward boundary compromise" in *Vancouver, WA Business Journal* (February 28, 2003) **[27920]**
Camas-Washougal Chamber of Commerce **[66058]**
Camayd Architects; Hemmler **[1556]**
Cambria Chamber of Commerce **[57390]**
The Cambria Group **[57958]**
Cambrian Ventures **[57959]**
Cambridge Area Chamber of Commerce **[61567]**, **[63632]**
Cambridge Chamber of Commerce **[60935]**, **[62252]**, **[66362]**
    Small Business Development Center **[61516]**
Cambridge Public Library–Audio-Visual Department **[17667]**
Cambridge Quarterly of Healthcare Ethics **[41169]**
Cambridge Samsung Partners **[61052]**
Cambridge Seven Associates Inc. **[49589]**
Cambridge Venture Partners **[60028]**
Cambridgelight Partners **[61053]**
Camden Area Chamber of Commerce **[57142]**, **[62834]**, **[63633]**
Camden-Kings Bay Area Chamber of Commerce **[59070]**
Camdenton Area Chamber of Commerce **[61931]**
"Cameco Reports Record Revenue, Earnings and Cash Flows for 2006" in *Canadian Corporate News* (February 7, 2007) **[14828]**, **[32301]**
Camelot Therapeutic Horsemanship–Camelot Library **[12477]**
Camelot Ventures **[61455]**
Cameron Area Chamber of Commerce **[65151]**
Cameron Chamber of Commerce **[61932]**
Camilla Chamber of Commerce **[59071]**
Camille's Sidewalk Cafe **[7098]**, **[8545]**
CAMM News **[46500]**
Camp Bow Wow **[19094]**
Camp County Chamber of Commerce **[65152]**
Camp Directors Purchasing Guide **[4232]**
Camp Verde Chamber of Commerce **[57020]**
"Campaign Close-Up: Cargill" in *Sales & Marketing Management* (Vol. 158, November-December 2006, No. 11, pp. 15) **[44977]**, **[46773]**, **[51579]**
Campaign Solutions **[20177]**
"Campaigns allow chapters and networks to share ABWA" in *Women In Business* (Vol. 52, No. 1, January-February 2000, pp. 42) **[56153]**
"Campaigns for several products are shifting their focus from 'women only' to include 'real men'" in *New York Times* (August 31, 2001) **[2585]**, **[7884]**, **[12765]**, **[46774]**
Campbell Chamber of Commerce **[57391]**
Campbell County Chamber of Commerce **[64890]**, **[66603]**
Campbell Mithun–Library & Information Services **[50733]**
Campbell Soup Company–Research Information Center **[18495]**
Campbellsville - Taylor County Chamber of Commerce **[60489]**
Campgroundata **[4253]**
Camping Magazine **[4254]**
Camping Magazine-Buyer's Guide Issue **[4233]**
Campsix **[57960]**
The Campus CEO: The Student Entrepreneur's Guide to Launching a Multi-Million Dollar Business **[33030]**, **[35355]**
Campventures **[57961]**
CAMUS International **[46167]**
"Can Brand Management Help You Succeed?" in *Success* (Vol. 47, No. 6, November 2000, pp. 58) **[46775]**
"Can C.K. Prahalad Pass the Test?" in *Fast Company* (August 2001, pp. 108) **[31121]**, **[35356]**
Can Clean **[8427]**
"Can everyone contribute?" in *Black Enterprise* (Vol. 33, No. 3, Oct. 2002, pp. 71) **[31433]**, **[32302]**, **[44978]**, **[44998]**

"Can Entrepreneurship Be Taught? You Bet It Can" in *Entrepreneur* (Vol. 31, No. 4, April 2003, pp. 62) **[33031]**, **[35905]**
"Can the Fed Keep Things Cooking At a Low Boil?" in *Business Week* (January 9, 2006, No. 3966, pp. 21) **[32303]**, **[40234]**
"Can you trust your law firm?" in *Harvard Business Review* (Vol. 80, No. 11, November 2002, pp. 22) **[29139]**, **[37400]**
"Can Firms Ban Weapons?" in *St. Louis Post-Dispatch* (December 6, 2004) **[29140]**, **[40235]**, **[44979]**
"CAN Forms In Capital City" in *Mississippi Business Journal* (Vol. 29, January 2007, No. 3, pp. A10) **[15890]**, **[40977]**
"Can Gates Remember Being Small?" in *Fortune* (Vol. 148, No. 12, December 8, 2003, pp. 204H) **[35906]**, **[53232]**
"Can Harry Potter Carry the Day for the Book and Film Industries?" in *Kiplinger Letter* (Vol. 78, January 19, 2007, No. 2) **[2688]**, **[9699]**
"Can I get into IT?" in *Black Enterprise* (Vol. 31, No. 3, October 2000, pp. 59) **[41587]**, **[42191]**
"Can I Use My Retirement Savings To Start a Business?" in *Fortune* (Vol. 151, February 21, 2005, No. 4, pp. 134) **[48874]**, **[52771]**
"Can Loyalty Be Leased?" in *Harvard Business Review* (Vol. 80, No. 9, Sept. 2002, pp. 24) **[33032]**, **[34843]**, **[44980]**
"Can a Nice Guy Finish First?" in *Washington Business Journal* (Vol. 22, No. 3, May 23, 2003, pp. 28) **[20451]**, **[20821]**, **[35907]**, **[44981]**
"Can Productivity Keep Up the Good Work?" in *Business Week* (December 19, 2005, No. 3964, pp. 25-26) **[27921]**, **[32304]**
"Can the Profit Boom Last? Businesses Have Been Churning Out Earnings" in *Fortune* (Vol. 152, October 17, 2005, No. 8, pp. 215) **[27922]**, **[31436]**, **[32305]**
"Can you keep a secret?" in *Fast Company* (June 2001, pp. 186) **[13883]**, **[33644]**, **[46776]**
"Can Spending A Day Stuck To A Velcro Wall Help Build A Team" in *Wall Street Journal* (Vol. 248, December 2006, No. 149, pp. B1) **[34844]**, **[35908]**, **[42834]**, **[44982]**, **[54471]**
"Can This Duo be Saved? Renovating 2 Tallest Edifices Downtown Will Be Costly, Owner Says" in *Charlotte Observer* (February 4, 2007) **[1502]**, **[27923]**
"Can This Off-Site Be Saved?" in *Fast Company* (November 2001, pp. 119) **[24901]**, **[39218]**
"Can This Really Be Hewlett-Packard?" in *Business Week* (December 19, 2005, No. 3964, pp. 49-50) **[6601]**, **[27924]**, **[30810]**
"Can you be a merchant vendor?" in *Home Office Computing* (Vol. 18, No. 11, November 2000, pp. 20) **[31517]**, **[33645]**
"Can You Hear Me Yet?" in *Black Enterprise* (Vol. 35, August 2004, No. 1, pp. 61) **[4943]**, **[13884]**, **[48980]**
"Can You Help Me?" in *Black Enterprise* (Vol. 35, October 2004, No. 3, pp. 188) **[22479]**, **[34845]**, **[35909]**
"Can You Judge a Biz by Its Color?" in *Inc.* (August 1, 2004) **[29141]**, **[32008]**
"Can You Manage? Should the Office Hotshot Be Your Next Manager?" in *Entrepreneur* (Vol. 31, No. 7, July 2003) **[19385]**, **[35910]**, **[44983]**
"Can You 'Pass' on Passion?" in *Women in Business* (Vol. 53, No. 5, September-October, 2001, pp. 12) **[34846]**, **[35911]**, **[44984]**
"Can You Patent Your Business Model?" in *Harvard Business Review* (Vol. 78, No. 4, July 2000, pp. 16) **[44012]**
"Can Your Company Get VC Funding?" in *Success* (Vol. 47, No. 2, June 2000, pp. 25) **[55531]**
"Can Your Product Make It In Mail Order?" in *Home Business* (Vol. 12, March/April 2005, No. 2, pp. 68) **[16408]**
Canaan Partners **[58584]**
Canaan Partners (Menlo Park) **[57962]**
Canada
    Canadian Grain Commission–Library **[26656]**
    Industry Canada–Journal Towers Library **[4155]**, **[22106]**

National Research Council–CISTI - Institute for Research in Construction Branch [7681]

Canada - Agriculture and Agri-Food Canada–Dairy and Swine Research and Development Centre Lennoxville–Library [26657]

Canada Bread Company, Limited [2171]

Canada-Czech Republic Chamber of Commerce [32195]

Canada - Department of Foreign Affairs and International Trade–Main Library [43941]

Canada-Finland Chamber of Commerce [32196]

Canada - Forest Alliance of British Columbia–Library [9430]

Canada-India Business Council [32197]

Canada Manitoba Business Service Centre [66690]
Business Information Programs [66691]
Business Library [66692]
General Business Counselling [66693]
Manitoba Marketing Network, Inc. [66694]

Canada/Manitoba Business Services Centre [66695]

Canada - Office of the Auditor General–Knowledge Centre–Library [414]

Canada-Pakistan Business Council [32198]

"Canada mum on funding for border projects" in Crain's Detroit Business (Vol. 18, No. 50, December 16, 2002, pp. 5) [25378], [43572]

Canada - Public Works & Government Services Canada–Consulting and Audit Canada–Information Centre [4049]

"Canada Rx offers access to Canadian pharmacies" in Atlanta Business Chronicle (Vol. 25, January 10, 2003, No. 31, pp. 17A) [8776], [31017], [33646], [43573]

Canada School of Public Service–Library [46149]

Canada Taiwan Trade Association [32199]

Canada - Telesat Canada–Information Resource Centre [5229], [22107]

Canada - Transport Canada
Aircraft Services Directorate–Technical Library, AAFBAA [986]
Technical Reference Centre (PAHQ) [987]

Canada-United States Business Association [43483]

Canada's Venture Capital and Private Equity Association [55463]

Canadian Academic Accounting Association [24]

Canadian Academy of Periodontology [40912]

Canadian Academy of Recording Arts and Sciences [21131]

Canadian Academy of Sport Medicine [19552]

Canadian Advertising Research Foundation [515]

Canadian Aerophilatelic Society [5794]

Canadian Agri-Food Research Council [26456]

Canadian Alliance Against Software Theft [4587], [22896]

Canadian Alliance of Franchise Operators [38698]

Canadian-American Business Council [43484]

Canadian Apparel Directory [5644], [16217]

The Canadian Appraiser [1450]

Canadian Association of Aquarium Clubs [1463]

Canadian Association of Broadcasters [20285], [24359]

Canadian Association of Chemical Distributors [32129]

Canadian Association for Community Care [12359]

Canadian Association for Distance Education [32891]

Canadian Association Environmental Management [3302], [8683]

Canadian Association of Ethnic Radio Broadcasters [20286]

Canadian Association of Fairs and Exhibitions [1126]

Canadian Association of Family Enterprise [35737], [37578], [52797]

Canadian Association of Gerontology [40913]

Canadian Association for Health, Physical Education, Recreation and Dance [19359]

Canadian Association of Home and Property Inspectors [3227]

Canadian Association of Importers and Exporters [32200]

Canadian Association of Independent Schools [32892]

Canadian Association for Information Science [13060]

Canadian Association of Insolvency and Restructuring Professionals [9783]

Canadian Association of Insurance Women [13147], [56091]

Canadian Association of International Development Consultants [3492], [31106]

Canadian Association of Journalists [8953], [18825]

Canadian Association of Labour Media [55261]

Canadian Association of Mutual Insurance Companies [13148]

Canadian Association of Numismatic Dealers [5795]

Canadian Association of Nurses in Oncology [12360]

Canadian Association of Optometrists [25627]

Canadian Association of Photographers and Illustrators in Communications [5955], [19221]

Canadian Association of Physical Medicine and Rehabilitation [19553]

Canadian Association of Professional Employees [55262]

Canadian Association of Recycling Industries [21202]

Canadian Association of Regulated Importers [32201]

Canadian Association of Rehabilitation Professionals [19554]

Canadian Association for School Health [40914]

Canadian Association of Token Collectors [5881]

Canadian Association on Water Quality [37224]

Canadian Association of Women Executives and Entrepreneurs [56092]

Canadian Athletic Therapists Association [19555]

Canadian Auto Workers [55263]

Canadian Auto World [18175]

Canadian Automatic Merchandising Association [25570]

Canadian Automobile Dealers Association [17951]

Canadian Automobile Dealers Association Annual Convention and Trade Show [18192]

Canadian Automotive Repair and Service Council [22592]

The Canadian Badge Maker Ltd. [4008]

Canadian Board of Marine Underwriters [13149]

The Canadian Book of Charities [9795]

Canadian Bookbinders & Book Artists Guild–Library [2846]

Canadian Booksellers Association [3017]

Canadian Broadcasting Corporation–Reference Library/Design Library [20378]

Canadian Business Aviation Association [937]

Canadian Business Press [18826]

Canadian Business Resource Centre [3657]

Canadian Call Management Association [2482], [24320], [25681]

Canadian Camping Association [4223]

Canadian Cancer Society [40915]

Canadian Cardiovascular Society [40916]

Canadian Carpet Institute [25532]

Canadian Carwash Association [4368]

Canadian Cat Association [1164]

Canadian Centre for Architecture [1490]

Canadian Centre for Fisheries Innovation [10485]

Canadian Chamber of Commerce [32202]

Canadian Children's Book Centre [2654]

Canadian Circulation Management Association [18827]

Canadian Coast Guard–Library [16786]

Canadian Coin News [5832]

Canadian College of Health Service Executives [40917]

Canadian Committee for Pacific Economic Cooperation [32203]

Canadian Community Newspapers Association [18828]

Canadian Construction Association [7209]

Canadian Consulting Agrologists Association [26457]

Canadian Cooperative Wool Growers Magazine [10823]

Canadian Copyright Institute [2655], [8954], [18829]

Canadian Corporate News (February 7, 2007); "Cameco Reports Record Revenue, Earnings and Cash Flows for 2006" in [14828], [32301]

Canadian Corporate News (February 7, 2007); "Cineplex Galaxy Income Fund Reports Fourth Quarter and Year End Results" in [14859], [27949], [37967]

Canadian Corporate News (February 7, 2007); "Nurun Transforms Loews Hotels Website Into a More User-Friendly Experience" in [12606], [34274], [47358]

Canadian Cosmetic, Toiletry and Fragrance Association [7865]

Canadian Council for Aboriginal Business [32204]

Canadian Council of Chief Executives [32205]

Canadian Council of Grocery Distributors [11580]

Canadian Council on Health Services Accreditation [40918]

Canadian Council for International Business [32206]

Canadian Council of Land Surveyors [23759]

Canadian Courier and Logistics Association [17309]

Canadian Craft and Hobby Association [8140]

Canadian Crafts Federation [8268]

Canadian Credit Institute Educational Foundation [9784]

Canadian Culinary Federation [4523], [7805]

Canadian Dermatology Association [40919]

The Canadian Direct Marketing Association-Communicator [47783]

Canadian Direct Marketing Notes [16480]

Canadian Disc Jockey Association [8676], [20287]

"Canadian companies ponder best options for e-waste" in Computing Canada (Vol. 28, No. 21, October 25, 2002, pp. 1) [6602], [21220], [41588]

Canadian Entrepreneurship and Small Business Management [35912], [43574], [44985]

Canadian Environmental Law Association [9311]

Canadian Environmental Network [9312], [21203], [37225]

Canadian Family Camping Federation [4224]

Canadian Federation of Business and Professional Women's Clubs [56093]

Canadian Federation of Independent Business [32207], [39115], [42565], [52798]
Research Library [37051]

Canadian Federation of Independent Grocers [11581]

Canadian Federation of Music Teachers' Associations [17571]

Canadian Federation of University Women [32893]

Canadian Film and Television Production Association [9674]

Canadian Fine Food Show [11704], [23550]

Canadian Fire Alarm Association [22146]

Canadian Fishery Consultants Ltd. [10473]

Canadian Fitness and Lifestyle Research Institute [19360], [19545]

Canadian Foundation for Dietetic Research [18426]

Canadian Foundry Association [16349]

Canadian Franchise Association [38699]

Canadian Gemmological Association [15818]

Canadian German Chamber of Industry and Commerce [32208]

Canadian Golf Hall of Fame–Library and Archives [11297]

Canadian Grocer [11686]

Canadian Health Coalition [40920]

Canadian Health Food Association [11998], [12048], [18427]

Canadian Healthcare Association [40921]

Canadian Hearing Society–Grace Harris Library [12122]

Canadian-Hemphill County Chamber of Commerce [65153]

Canadian Home Builders' Association [7210]

Canadian Home Care Association [12361]

Canadian Home Inspection Services Inc. [3271]

Canadian Image Processing and Pattern Recognition Society [6153], [6456]

Canadian Independent Adjusters' Association [13150]

Canadian Independent Record Production Association [21132]

Canadian Industrial Relations Association [55264]

Canadian Innovation Centre [35738], [48845]

Canadian Institute of Chartered Accountants [25], [2855], [23862]

Canadian Institute for Environmental Law and Policy [9313]
Canadian Institute of Financial Planning [9785]
Canadian Institute of Gemmology [15819]
Canadian Institute of Management [44709]
Canadian Institute of Plumbing and Heating [11873]
Canadian Institute of Professional Home Inspectors [3228]
Canadian Institute of Public and Private Real Estate Companies [20399], [20778]
Canadian Institute of Quantity Surveyors [26], [2856]
Canadian Institute of Resources Law [9314]
Canadian Institute of Steel Construction [7211]
Canadian Institute of Travel Counsellors [25126]
Canadian Insurance Accountants Association [27]
Canadian International Trade Tribunal–Library [43942]
Canadian Investor Relations Institute [9786]
Canadian Jewellers Association [15820]
Canadian Journal of Chemistry (Revue Canadienne de Chimie) [52246]
Canadian Journal of Dietetic Practice and Research [41170]
Canadian Journal of Public Health [41171]
Canadian Journal of Respiratory Therapy [41172]
Canadian Journal of Rural Medicine [41173]
Canadian Kendo Federation [16904]
Canadian Kennel Club [1165]
Canadian Labour and Business Centre [55265]
Canadian Labour Congress [32209], [55266]
        Library [55341]
Canadian Law List [29650]
Canadian Life and Health Insurance Association [13151]
Canadian Long Distance Riding Association [12441]
Canadian Luggage, Leathergoods, Handbags and Accessories Show [16280]
Canadian Management Centre [44710]
Canadian Management Centre's 5-Day "MBA"(Canada) [44731]
Canadian Management Centre's Advanced Course in Strategic Marketing (Canada) [46621]
Canadian Management Centre's Course in Supply Chain Management (Canada) [44732]
Canadian Marketing Association [516]
Canadian Massage Therapist Alliance [16998]
Canadian Meat Council [4056]
        Technical Library [4075]
Canadian Media Guild [55267]
Canadian Medical Association [40922]
Canadian Medical Protective Association [40923]
Canadian Mental Health Association [40924]
Canadian MoneySaver [24081]
Canadian Motion Picture Distribution Association [9675]
Canadian Museum of Contemporary Photography–Research Centre [19273]
Canadian National Exhibition [24860]
Canadian Natural Health Association [17881]
Canadian Netherlands Business and Professional Association [32210]
Canadian Network of Toxicology Centres [9315]
Canadian Newspaper Association [18830]
Canadian Numismatic Association [5796]
        Library [5865]
Canadian Numismatic Association Convention [5860]
Canadian Numismatic Research Society [5797]
Canadian Nursery Landscape Association [11409], [15991]
Canadian Nurses Foundation [12362]
Canadian Occupational Safety [56596]
Canadian Ophthalmological Society [25628]
Canadian Ornamental Plant Foundation [10549]
Canadian Paediatric Society [40925]
Canadian Pain Society [40926]
Canadian Parks and Wilderness Society [9316]
Canadian Patent Reporter Plus [44208]
Canadian Payroll Association [18769], [26108]
Canadian Pharmacists Association [8759]
Canadian Pizza Magazine [10627], [19647], [38953]
Canadian Plastics Industry Association [46168]
Canadian Pool Players Association [19777]

Canadian Professional Sales Association [51508]
        Sales Resource Centre [52013]
Canadian Psychiatric Association [40927]
Canadian Public Administration (Administration publique du Canada) [50360]
Canadian Public Health Association [40928]
Canadian Public Relations Society [20092]
Canadian Publishers' Council [2656]
Canadian Real Estate Association [20400]
Canadian Real Estate Association Annual Conference and Trade Show [1388], [55209]
Canadian Recording Industry Association [21133]
Canadian Recreational Vehicle Association [21166]
Canadian Recycling Handbook and Directory [21221]
Canadian Residential Inspection Services, Ltd. [3272]
Canadian Resort Development Association [12498]
Canadian Respiratory Journal [41174]
Canadian Restaurant and Foodservices Association [4524], [7082], [8505], [10613], [12049], [21421]
        Resource Centre [7828], [22032]
Canadian Retreat Guide [2433]
Canadian Roofing Contractors Association [22056]
Canadian Rose Society [10550]
Canadian Satellite Users Association [22080]
Canadian School of Natural Nutrition [33360]
Canadian Securities Institute [14698]
Canadian Security Association [22147]
Canadian ShareOwners Association [14699]
Canadian Ski Museum–Archives [22875]
Canadian Small Business Institute [66745]
Canadian Small Business Kit for Dummies [29142], [35357], [35913], [39034], [39219], [43460], [54472]
The Canadian Small Business Survival Guide: How to Start and Operate Your Own Successful Business [38614], [39035], [39762], [43461], [44392], [46562], [52637]
Canadian Society of Association Executives [1726]
Canadian Society for Bioengineering [26458]
Canadian Society of Cinematographers-Directory [9700]
Canadian Society for Clinical Investigation [40929]
Canadian Society of Environmental Biologists [9317]
Canadian Society of Gastroenterology Nurses and Associates [12363]
Canadian Society for International Health [40930]
Canadian Society of Landscape Architects [15992]
Canadian Society for Medical Laboratory Science [17175]
        Library [17241]
Canadian Society for Nutritional Sciences [18428]
Canadian Society of Scientific Photography–Library [19274]
Canadian Society for Training and Development [42809]
Canadian Sporting Goods Association [23596]
"Canadian online pharmacy to open Springs storefront" in *Colorado Springs Business Journal* (March 7, 2003) [8777], [33647]
The Canadian Stamp News [5833]
Canadian Tax Foundation [28], [23863], [24197]
Canadian Tax Journal (Revue fiscale canadienne) [24082]
Canadian Teachers' Federation [55268]
Canadian Telecommunications Employees' Association [55269]
Canadian Therapeutic Riding Association [12442]
Canadian Thoroughbred Horse Society [1166]
Canadian Tire Corp., Ltd [24595]
Canadian Tooling and Machining Association [46169]
Canadian Tourism Research Institute [24650], [25127]
Canadian Toy and Hobby Fair [24846]
Canadian Translators, Terminologists and Interpreters Council [25077]
Canadian Trucking Alliance [25358]
Canadian Union of Public Employees [55270]
Canadian University Music Society [17572]
Canadian University Press [18831]
Canadian Valley Technology Center [64135]
Canadian Veterinary Journal [1247]

Canadian Veterinary Medical Association [1233]
Canadian Water Resources Association [37226]
Canadian Web Consultants Ltd. [6036]
Canadian Welding Bureau [16350]
Canadian Wireless Telecommunications Association [4897]
Canadian Work/Family Directions Co. [27012]
Canadian Writers Foundation [8955]
Canal Winchester Area Chamber of Commerce [63634]
Canam Franchise Development Group [3851]
Canandaigua Chamber of Commerce [62835]
Canastota Bee-Journal [18950]
Canastota Chamber of Commerce [62836]
Canby Area Chamber of Commerce [61568], [64200]
"Cancer Drug May Hold Key to Company's Survival" in *Crain's Detroit Business* (Vol. 18, No. 21, May 27, 2002, pp. 3) [41589], [44013]
"Cancer Scans a Lifesaver for Crystal Maker" in *Orlando Business Journal* (Vol. 20, No. 8, August 8, 2003, pp. 2) [39870], [41590], [48394], [50843], [52045], [52070]
"Candidates' Take on Premiums" in *Inc.* (October 1, 2003) [13224], [40978], [43115]
Candleman [11199]
Candles As a Business: A Report [11146], [18278]
Candlewick Homes [7657]
"C&S Marketing to be CoreLogic" in *Sacramento Bee* (October 25, 2005) [12874], [17365], [20109], [27925], [50569], [53233]
Candy Bouquet International [4331]
Candy Buyers' Directory [4277]
Candy Express Franchising, Inc. [4332]
Candy Industry [4323]
Candy Industry (Vol. 167, April 2002, pp. 29); "A 50-Year Legacy" in [4289], [28160], [37654]
Candy Industry Buying Guide [4278]
Candy Industry (Vol. 167, No. 4, April 2002, pp. 88); "Chocolate temperers" in [4284], [46237], [48713]
Candy Industry (Vol. 167, No. 4, April 2002, pp. 24); "Full circle" in [4293], [28191], [37660]
Candy Industry (Vol. 167, No. 3, March 2002, pp. 34); "In Helen's good graces" in [4294], [28321], [30559]
Candy Industry (Vol. 167, No. 2, February 2002, pp. 18); "Updates on sugar, peanut reform" in [4320], [40796]
Candy, Nuts & Snacks As a Business - A Report [4279]
Caney Chamber of Commerce [60300]
Canis Dog Owner's Database [1218]
"Canned Profits" in *Forbes* (Vol. 175, January 10, 2005, No. 1, pp. 152) [14829], [46225]
CANNEX [10370], [15750], [17474]
Cannon Beach Chamber of Commerce [64201]
Cannon Falls Area Chamber of Commerce [61569]
"Canoga Park Purchase" in *San Fernando Valley Business Journal* (Vol. 12, January 2007, No. 2, pp. 32) [20452], [20822], [21222], [54149]
Canoga Park - West Hills Chamber of Commerce [57392]
Canola Digest [26570]
Canon City Chamber of Commerce [58336]
Canon City Small Business Development Center [58293]
"Can't Pay Like the Big Guys? Think Creatively." in *Crain's Detroit Business* (Vol. 23, January 15, 2007, No. 3, pp. 18) [30729], [34847]
"Can't Save the Farm" in *Black Enterprise* (Vol. 31, No. 5, December 2000, pp. 34) [26490], [39795], [40236], [48081]
"Can't We All Get Along?" in *Inc.* (Volume 27, June 2005, No. 6, pp. 34, 36) [3125], [29143]
"Can't Win For Losing: A Mutual Fund Tax Quirk Limits Your Capital Losses" in *Entrepreneur* (Vol. 31, No. 7, July 2003, pp. 52) [9862], [14830], [37941], [54473]
Cantey & Company Inc. [21074]
Canton Area Chamber of Commerce [59450]
Canton Chamber of Commerce [58516], [61267], [61780], [62837], [63958], [64817], [65154]
Canton Regional Chamber of Commerce [63635]
Cantrell, Harris & Associates [21075]
Canusa (Brant) Pet Products [19177]

"Careful planning can ease stress of layoffs" in *Atlanta Business Chronicle* (Vol. 25, No. 19, October 18, 2002, pp. 4B) **[32308]**, **[42194]**

"Careful planning" in *BlackEnterprise* (Vol. 32, No. 2, September 2001, pp. 50) **[24644]**, **[25116]**, **[29718]**, **[47949]**

Carelli & Associates **[3959]**, **[9050]**, **[16580]**, **[42949]**, **[45983]**

CARES Directory **[40979]**

The Caretakers Inc. **[16141]**

Carey Area Chamber of Commerce **[63636]**

Cargill, Incorporated–Information Center **[26658]**

Caribbean American Chamber of Commerce and Industry **[47993]**

Caribbean-Central American Action **[30276]**

"Caribbean Charisma" in *Hispanic Business* (October 2003, pp. 104, 106) **[24675]**, **[25168]**, **[30307]**

"Caribbean Connection: Mortgage Firm Looking to Tap Into the Latino Market" in *Black Enterprise* (Vol. 34, No. 6, January 2004, pp. 36) **[17366]**, **[17999]**, **[20455]**, **[20824]**

"Caribbean Connection: This Shipping Professional is Taking His Company Overseas" in *Black Enterprise* (Vol. 34, July 2004, No. 12) **[10670]**, **[27929]**, **[43575]**, **[48087]**

Caribbean Society of Hotel Association Executives **[12499]**

"Caribbean-type savings helps build businesses" in *Wall Street Journal* (October 27, 2000, pp. B1) **[37945]**

Caribou Chamber of Commerce and Industry **[60738]**

Caring **[12386]**

Caring for Lawns **[16007]**

Caring People **[12387]**, **[41176]**

Caring Senior Service **[475]**

Caring for Someone in Your Home **[12368]**

Caring Transitions **[9546]**

Caring for Your Dog **[19122]**

"Caritas Seeking Cambridge Lab Space" in *Boston Globe* (February 4, 2005) **[41592]**, **[50844]**, **[52071]**

Carl Gunnard Johnson Powder Metallurgy Research Center 61151

Carl Rogers: Communication and Management **[45916]**

"Carle-Based Pliskin Realty & Dev. Brokers Space for All State and Carvel" in *Long Island Business News* (February 27, 2004) **[20456]**, **[20825]**

Carleton University
    Carleton Research Unit on Innovation, Science, and Environment **[50390]**
    Centre for Policy and Program Assessment **[50391]**

Carlin Ventures LLC **[63069]**

Carlinville Community Chamber of Commerce **[59452]**

Carlisle - Nicholas County Chamber of Commerce **[60490]**

Carl's Jr. **[21768]**

Carlsbad Chamber of Commerce **[57395]**

"Carlsbad: SkinMedica Has New Treatment for Acne" in *San Diego Business Journal* (Vol. 28, January 15, 2007, No. 3, pp. 16) **[2586]**, **[7885]**

"Carlsbad: Weevil Bugs $900M Nursery Industry" in *San Diego Business Journal* (Vol. 28, January 8, 2007, No. 2, pp. 27) **[11422]**, **[26491]**

Carlson Communications **[19262]**

Carlson Wagonlit Travel Associates, Inc. **[877]**, **[25333]**, **[47920]**

"Carlyle looking for more acquisitions after buying Breed" in *Crain's Detroit Business* (Vol. 19, No. 11, March 17, 2003, pp. 20) **[1916]**, **[49840]**

Carlyle Lake Chamber of Commerce **[59453]**

Carmel Chamber of Commerce **[57396]**

Carmel Clay Chamber of Commerce **[59883]**

Carmel - Kent Chamber of Commerce **[62839]**

Carmel Valley Chamber of Commerce **[57397]**

Carmi Chamber of Commerce **[59454]**

Carmichael/Associates **[18572]**, **[49590]**

Carmichael Chamber of Commerce **[57398]**

Carnegie Chamber of Commerce **[63959]**

Carnegie Library of Pittsburgh
    Library Center **[26444]**, **[38594]**, **[46150]**, **[47928]**, **[53127]**
    Music and Art Department **[1649]**, **[7959]**

Carnegie Mellon University
    Associate Provost for Research and Academic Administration **[64602]**
    Hunt Institute for Botanical Documentation–Library **[12159]**
    Software Engineering Institute **[23322]**
    University Libraries–Special Collections **[19943]**, **[25503]**

Caro Chamber of Commerce **[61269]**

Carol R. Johnson & Associates, Inc.–Library **[16090]**

Carol Stream Chamber of Commerce **[59455]**

The Carolina Craftsmen's Classic Arts & Crafts Festival-Columbia **[8072]**

Carolina JobBank **[23384]**

Carolina Pacific Publishing **[64312]**

Carolinas Association of Chamber of Commerce Executives **[64727]**

Carolinas Capital Investment Corp. **[63454]**

Caroline County Chamber of Commerce **[60819]**, **[65872]**

Caroline Myss' The Energetics of Healing **[17938]**

CAROPAM Corp. **[973]**

The Carpenter **[4483]**

Carpet Cleaners Institute of the Northwest-Membership Roster **[25535]**

Carpet Directory **[10507]**

Carpet Gang **[3350]**, **[25548]**

Carpet Network **[10534]**

Carpet and Rug Institute **[10500]**

Carpets and Rugs Market U.S.A. **[10515]**

Carpinteria Valley Chamber of Commerce **[57399]**

"Carrier Services Centers" in *Rough Notes* (Vol. 146, No. 3, March 2003, pp. 98) **[13229]**, **[43121]**

Carrington Area Chamber of Commerce **[63511]**

Carrizozo Chamber of Commerce **[62676]**

Carrol County Economic Development Office–SBDC **[60795]**

Carroll Chamber of Commerce **[60103]**

Carroll County Chamber of Commerce **[59072]**, **[60491]**, **[60820]**, **[64891]**, **[65873]**

Carroll Chamber of Commerce and Economic Development **[63637]**

Carrollton Chamber of Commerce **[59456]**, **[61934]**

Carrot Capital LLC **[63070]**

CARRS The Traditional Barber **[11823]**

"Carry a Tune" in *Fast Company* (August 2001, pp. 38) **[37112]**, **[48981]**

"Carry Your Memory" in *Tampa Tribune* (November 28, 2005) **[6603]**, **[48982]**

"Carrying Coffee to Seattle" in *The Economist* (Vol. 377, October 1-7, 2005, No. 8446, pp. 37) **[11317]**, **[30811]**

"Carrying Off the Gold" in *San Francisco Business Times* (Vol. 17, No. 48, July 4, 2003, pp. 3) **[20457]**, **[35921]**

"Car's Star Turn: August Sales Zoom-For Foreign Models. At Least U.S. Makers' Bonds are Thriving" in *Barron's* (September 8, 2003) **[17990]**, **[46226]**

"CarsDirect.com Buys 2 Web Sites" in *American Banker* (Vol. 170, February 4, 2005, No. 24, pp. 17) **[576]**, **[13886]**, **[14832]**, **[17367]**, **[17991]**, **[33650]**, **[46779]**

Carson Chamber of Commerce **[57400]**

Carson City Area Chamber of Commerce **[62344]**

Carson City Chamber of Commerce–Small Business Development Center **[62321]**

Christopher N. Carson CRE **[20073]**, **[30193]**

Carson Research Center **[55039]**

Carson Valley Chamber of Commerce and Visitors Authority **[62345]**
    SBDC **[62322]**

"Cart Blanche: Think Retailing is Strictly Brick-and-Mortar Opportunity? Not So." in *Entrepreneur* (Vol. 31, No. 8, Aug. 2003, pp. 78) **[15908]**, **[35360]**, **[51022]**

"Cartel Creativo wins army contract" in *Hispanic Business* (Vol. 22, No. 10, October 2000, pp. 24) **[577]**, **[39996]**, **[48088]**

Carter County Chamber of Commerce **[62153]**

Carter & Tani **[4454]**, **[29616]**

Carteret County Chamber of Commerce **[63338]**

Carteret Mortgage Corp. **[17466]**

Cartersville-Bartow County Chamber of Commerce **[59073]**

Carterville Chamber of Commerce **[59457]**

Carthage Area Chamber of Commerce **[59458]**, **[62840]**

Carthage Chamber of Commerce **[61935]**

Cartoon Cuts **[2381]**, **[11824]**

Cartoonists Northwest **[5882]**

Cartridge World **[18622]**, **[19931]**

Carvel Ice Cream **[7099]**, **[12811]**

"Carver vs. OneUnited" in *Black Enterprise* (Vol. 35, December 2004, No. 5, pp. 96) **[9864]**, **[30812]**, **[48089]**, **[56155]**

Cary Chamber of Commerce **[63339]**

Cary/Grove Area Chamber of Commerce **[59459]**

Caryl Baker Visage **[7928]**

Cascade Chamber of Commerce **[59291]**

Cascade Communications Ventures, LLC **[57964]**

Cascade Policy Institute **[24198]**

Cascade Small Business Development Center **[57251]**

Cascading Style Sheets (CSS) I **[25771]**

Cascading Style Sheets II **[53169]**

"The Case of A Lifetime" in *Hispanic Business* (April 2005, pp. 22, 24-25) **[29145]**, **[33033]**, **[40244]**

"The case against disorganization: how to arrest this time bandit" in *Black Enterprise* (Vol. 32, No. 8, March 2002, pp. 63) **[4396]**, **[54938]**

The Case Center **[63188]**

"A case for clinical informatics" in *Ingram's* (Vol. 28, No. 6, June 2002, pp. 61) **[41593]**, **[52072]**

Case Handyman & Remodeling **[7658]**, **[16979]**

Case In Point **[19993]**

"Case In Point" in *Entrepreneur* (Vol. 31, No. 8, August 2003, pp. 66) **[33034]**, **[35922]**

Case Management Advisor **[17158]**

Case Management Resource Guide **[12369]**, **[40980]**, **[54332]**

The Case Manager **[41177]**

CASE Matching Gifts Clearinghouse **[10728]**

"The case of the obsolete inventory" in *Red Herring* (March 2003, pp. 34) **[100]**, **[23906]**, **[26183]**, **[37401]**, **[44228]**

"Case Study. Anatomy of a Business Decision" in *Inc.* (September 2006, pp. 47-48, 50) **[27930]**, **[29823]**, **[46780]**

"Case Study" in *Inc.* (August 1, 2004) **[578]**, **[579]**, **[4613]**, **[4944]**, **[12875]**, **[20111]**, **[22936]**, **[24804]**, **[26451]**, **[30813]**, **[33035]**, **[39997]**, **[42195]**, **[46227]**, **[46781]**, **[49680]**, **[50431]**, **[51090]**, **[53235]**, **[53635]**

Case Western Reserve University
    Center for Regional Economic Issues **[32845]**
    Elderly Care Research Center **[495]**
    Office of Research Administration **[63874]**
    Skeletal Research Center **[19601]**

Cases in Corporate Acquisitions, Buyouts, Mergers & Takeovers **[43576]**, **[49841]**

Cases in Online Search Strategy **[13068]**

Caseyville Chamber of Commerce **[59460]**

Cash Converters **[20005]**

Cash Copy: How to Offer Your Products and Services So Your Prospects Buy Them... Now! **[46782]**

"Cash crunch" in *Entrepreneur* (Vol. 30, No.2 February 2002, pp. 53) **[14833]**, **[44491]**, **[55533]**

Cash Flow, Credit and Collection: Over 100 Proven Techniques for Protecting and Strengthening Your Balance Sheet **[31518]**

"The Cash Flow Crunch" in *Home Office Computing* (Vol. 19, No. 1, January 2001, pp. 88) **[27096]**, **[33651]**

"Cash From Trash: 1-800-Got-Junk?" in *Fortune* (Vol. 148, No. 9, October 27, 2003, pp. 196) **[3288]**, **[8679]**, **[38615]**, **[52489]**

"Cash In At Home" in *Small Business Opportunities* (Vol. 16, No. 2, March 2004, pp. 22) **[38616]**, **[42504]**

Cash In On Cash Flow **[35361]**, **[39037]**, **[44393]**

"Cash In On Coupons" in *Small Business Opportunities* (Vol. 13, No. 5, September 2001, pp. 44) **[497]**, **[46783]**

"Cash in, cash out" in *Entrepreneur* (Vol. 31, No. 6, June 2003, pp. 53) **[101]**, **[2883]**, **[26184]**, **[37946]**

"Cash in: Tax talk: Cash accounting is about to get more use" in *Entrepreneur* (Vol. 30, No. 3, March 2002, pp. 74) **[40245]**, **[54478]**

"Cash is King" in *Fast Company* (May 2001, pp. 80) **[27931]**, **[32309]**, **[46784]**

Cash Now - USA **[5258]**

Cash Plus **[5259]**, **[24122]**, **[54895]**

Cash Traps: Small Business Secrets for Reducing Costs and Improving Cash Flow **[27097]**, **[37947]**

Cash-X Inc. **[44695]**

"Cash in Your Attic: Is Your Junk Someone Else's Treasure?" in *Black Enterprise* (Vol. 37, November 2006, No. 4, pp. 156) **[1790]**, **[7159]**, **[51580]**

"Cashflow: August 1-15, 2001" in *Red Herring* (No. 105, October 1, 2001, pp. 32) **[37113]**, **[50845]**, **[55534]**

"Cashflow: August 15-31, 2001" in *Red Herring* (No. 105, October 1, 2001, pp. 36) **[37114]**, **[55535]**

"Cashflow: July 1-15, 2001" in *Red Herring* (No. 102, August 15, 2001, pp. 28) **[14834]**, **[41594]**, **[49842]**

"Cashflow: July 15-31, 2001" in *Red Herring* (No. 103, September 1, 2001, pp. 30) **[14835]**, **[49843]**

"Cashflow: September 1-15, 2001" in *Red Herring* (No. 106, October 15, 2001, pp. 32) **[14836]**, **[49844]**, **[55536]**

Cashiers Area Chamber of Commerce **[63340]**

"Cashing in Before You Join: Negotiating a Signing Bonus" in *Black Enterprise* (Vol. 37, October 2006, No. 3, pp. 90) **[39225]**, **[42196]**, **[54479]**

"Cashing In on Bad Debts" in *Hispanic Business* (Vol. 24, No. 5, May 2002, pp. 52) **[31519]**, **[54480]**

"Cashing In On Cash Flow" in *Business 2.0* (Vol. 6, September 2005, No. 8, pp. 119) **[9865]**, **[14837]**, **[37948]**

"Cashless customers" in *WorkingWoman* (Vol. 25, No. 2, February 2000, pp. 69) **[26709]**, **[53636]**

Cashmere Chamber of Commerce **[66059]**

CASI News **[20262]**, **[22628]**

"Casino Case Hits Legal Jackpot" in *Inc.* (August 1, 2003) **[29146]**, **[40246]**, **[42197]**, **[44987]**

Casino Chip and Gaming Token Collectors Club **[10852]**

Casino Chronicle **[10895]**

Casino Gaming in the United States **[10863]**

Casino, Hotel & Resort Consultants L.L.C. **[3659]**, **[10904]**, **[27577]**, **[31297]**, **[45984]**, **[48822]**

Casino Journal's National Gaming Summary **[10896]**

Casino Tony Goes Restaurant **[21769]**

Casket and Funeral Supply Association of America **[10787]**

Casket & Funeral Supply Association of America Newsletter **[10809]**

Casper Area Chamber of Commerce **[66604]**

Casper SBDC–Region III **[66593]**

Cass City Chamber of Commerce **[61270]**

Cassville Area Chamber of Commerce **[61936]**

Cassway/Albert Ltd. **[18573]**, **[49591]**

CAST Management Consultants Inc. **[30069]**

Cast Polymer Connection **[7530]**

The Caster **[23823]**

Castile Ventures **[61054]**

Casting News **[23832]**

"Casting Wider Net in Realty Rehab Market" in *American Banker* (Vol. 169, December 28, 2004, No. 247, pp. 1) **[9866]**, **[17368]**, **[20458]**, **[20826]**, **[52650]**

Castle Rock Chamber of Commerce **[58338]**

Castlehill Ventures **[66717]**

Castles Unlimited **[20746]**, **[21101]**

Castro Valley Chamber of Commerce **[57401]**

Castroville Chamber of Commerce **[57402]**

Casual Furniture Retailers **[12260]**

Casual Living **[10834]**, **[12227]**, **[12321]**

Casual Living-Casual Outdoor Furniture and Accessory Directory Issue **[12217]**

"Casual rules" in *Incentive* (Vol. 174, No. 9, September 2000, pp. 54) **[34848]**, **[53637]**

Caswell County Chamber of Commerce **[63341]**

Cat Fanciers' Association **[1167]**

Cat Fanciers' Association-Yearbook **[1186]**

Cat Fanciers' Federation **[1168]**

Catalina Island Chamber of Commerce and Visitors' Bureau **[57403]**

The Catalog of Catalogs IV: The Complete Mail-Order Directory **[16428]**

Catalog of Funeral Home & Cemetery Supplies **[10800]**

"Catalog companies show the upstarts that they know a thing or two about Internet retailing" in *The New York Times* (May 15,2000, pp.C16) **[33652]**, **[46785]**, **[51581]**

Catalog and Multichannel Marketing Council **[16420]**

Catalog of Products of Coldset/Non-heatset Printers **[19869]**

Catalog Success Magazine **[39715]**, **[51427]**

"Cataloging the web" in *Incentive* (Vol. 174, No. 10, October 2000, pp. 99) **[13887]**, **[26766]**, **[33653]**, **[53638]**

Catalyst **[6339]**

Catalyst Connections **[64603]**

The Catalyst Group **[65598]**

"A Catalyst for Innovation" in *Fortune* (Vol. 142, No. 6, September 18, 2000, pp. 248) **[52832]**, **[54481]**

Catalyst Ventures **[60867]**

Catalysta Partners **[63455]**

Catawba County Chamber of Commerce **[63342]**

"Catch-22: Are Small Companies that Buy from Giant Retailers Sleeping with the Enemy" in *Entrepreneur* (Vol. 31, No. 9, September 2003) **[30814]**, **[51091]**

"Catch the Carrot" in *Entrepreneur.com* (Vol. 34, February 2006, No. 2, pp. 74) **[34849]**, **[51582]**

"Catch of the Day: Next up: distributed networks" in *Red Herring* (No. 103, September 1, 2001, pp. 18) **[6928]**, **[13888]**, **[27932]**, **[53639]**

"Catch 'Em If You Can" in *Entrepreneur.com* (Vol. 34, February 2006, No. 2, pp. 90) **[27933]**, **[38617]**

Catching the Wave of Workforce Diversity: Powerful New Skills for Managers **[48527]**

"Catering Company Expands Operations" in *Bellingham Business Journal* (December 2006, pp. A6) **[4536]**, **[27934]**, **[30137]**, **[35923]**, **[37608]**

"Catering to Fickle Customers" in *Hispanic Business* (June 2005, pp. 90) **[52512]**

Catering Industry Employee **[4558]**

Catering Like a Pro: From Planning to Profit **[4537]**

Catering: Start and Run a Money Making Business **[4538]**

"Catering to Those Who Want Their Gun TV" in *Inc.* (July 1, 2003) **[11724]**, **[24392]**

"Caterpillar" in *Sales & Marketing Management* (Vol. 158, October 2006, No. 10, pp. 17) **[46786]**, **[51583]**

Catfish Farmers of America **[10441]**

Catfish Fever **[2192]**

Cathedral City Chamber of Commerce **[57404]**

Catholic Book Publishers Association **[2657]**

Catholic Health Association of Canada **[40931]**

Catholic University of America–Music Library **[17668]**

Catoosa Chamber of Commerce **[63960]**

Catoosa County Chamber of Commerce **[59074]**

Cats and Dogs **[19123]**

The Cat's Inn **[19095]**

"The cat's meow" in *Entrepreneur* (Vol. 31, No. 5, May 2003, pp. 80) **[579]**, **[46787]**

CATTAN Services Group Inc. **[6037]**

Catterton Partners **[58585]**

"Catuity starts reaping loyalty-card rewards" in *Crain's Detroit Business* (Vol. 19, No. 10, March 10, 2003, pp. 32) **[4614]**, **[22937]**, **[53236]**

"Caucus Decries Bush Plan" in *Hispanic Business* (Vol. 23, No. 5, May 2001, pp. 20) **[48090]**, **[54482]**

"Caught In the Crossfire" in *Inc.* (August 1, 2003) **[4615]**, **[22938]**, **[33654]**, **[46788]**, **[53237]**

"Caught in the 'Net" in *Journal of Business Strategies* (Vol. 21, No. 5, September 2000, pp. 4) **[29824]**, **[33655]**

"Caught in 'Tween" in *Entrepreneur* (Vol. 32, October 2004, No. 10, pp. 40) **[5270]**, **[46789]**

CAUS News **[13685]**

"Causes and Effects" in *Harvard Business Review* (Vol. 81, No. 7, July 2003, pp. 95) **[39226]**, **[54150]**

"Caution: Merger Ahead" in *Ingram's* (Vol. 28, No. 9, September 2002, pp. 20) **[14838]**, **[27935]**, **[31018]**, **[49845]**

"Cautious Hiring in January Report" in *Charlotte Observer* (February 3, 2007) **[42198]**, **[42835]**

"A Cautious Optimism" in *Forbes* (Vol. 175, February 14, 2005, No. 3, pp. 132) **[9867]**, **[14839]**, **[32310]**, **[37949]**

Cavalier Area Chamber of Commerce **[63512]**

Cave City Chamber of Commerce **[57143]**, **[60492]**

Caveat Emptor **[50762]**

"Caveats to Selling Financial Services" in *Journal of Accountancy* (Vol. 199, January 2005, No. 1, pp. 29) **[102]**, **[2884]**, **[9868]**, **[14840]**, **[23907]**, **[26185]**, **[27098]**, **[51584]**

"Caviar Dreams" in *Black Enterprise* (Vol. 36, November 2005, No. 4, pp. 180) **[23463]**, **[35924]**, **[48091]**

Cayucos Chamber of Commerce **[57405]**

Cayuga County Chamber of Commerce **[62841]**

"CB Acquisition" in *San Fernando Valley Business Journal* (Vol. 11, December 2006, No. 25, pp. 23) **[20459]**, **[49846]**

CB Capital Investors, L.P. **[59186]**

CB Richard Ellis **[20074]**

"CB Richard Ellis Nabs Leasing Contract of 175 Fulton Ave. in Hempstead" in *Long Island Business News* (February 27, 2004) **[20460]**, **[20827]**, **[21315]**, **[52651]**

CBA **[3018]**

CBA Marketplace **[3055]**

"CBC and Chrysler Strike Deal" in *Black Enterprise* (Vol. 37, December 2006, No. 5, pp. 36) **[32311]**, **[33036]**, **[49847]**, **[54151]**

CBC/Radio Canada Atlantic–Broadcast Materials, Halifax **[24506]**

CBIZ Inc. **[366]**, **[3660]**, **[16581]**, **[26420]**, **[31298]**, **[38516]**, **[45985]**

CBS News Reference Library **[20379]**

CBS Television–Law Library **[4156]**

C.C. Canada Forestry Co. **[26622]**

CCA Strategies L.L.C. **[27013]**

CCFL Mezzanine Partners of Canada **[66718]**

CCH Business Owner's Toolkit Tax Guide **[54483]**

CCH PROTOS **[29651]**, **[40894]**, **[54897]**

CCH Toolkit Tax Guide 2007 **[39227]**, **[54484]**

CCI/USA Membership Directory **[4234]**

CCIM Institute **[20779]**

CD Computing News **[4866]**

CD Research, Ltd.–Library Services **[13122]**

CD-ROM Databases **[4867]**

CD-ROMs in Print **[4616]**, **[13069]**

CD Tradepost **[6144]**

CD Warehouse Inc. **[6145]**

CDG Books Canada Inc. **[66746]**

CDM–Herman G. Dresser Library **[25728]**

C.D.S. Building Movers **[30194]**

CDS International **[12500]**

"CDs Unlocked" in *Business Week* (February 7, 2205, pp. 91) **[9869]**, **[14841]**, **[37950]**

CE News **[7531]**, **[23773]**

CEA Investments Corp. **[30070]**, **[45986]**

"CEA Makes Leaving Las Vegas Easier" in *Tradeshow Week* (Vol. 34, November 29, 2004, No. 48, pp. 6) **[22192]**, **[22480]**, **[24902]**, **[55073]**

Cecchetti Council of America **[8436]**

Cecil County Chamber of Commerce **[60821]**

Cecil's Texas Style Bar-B-Q **[21770]**

Cedar City Area Chamber of Commerce **[65705]**

Cedar Falls Chamber of Commerce **[60104]**

Cedar Hill Chamber of Commerce **[65156]**

Cedar Key Chamber of Commerce **[58764]**

Cedar Lake Chamber of Commerce **[59884]**

Cedar Park Chamber of Commerce and Tourism **[65157]**

Cedar Rapids Area Chamber of Commerce **[60105]**

Cedar Vale Chamber of Commerce [60301]
Cedarburg Chamber of Commerce [66363]
Cedaredge Area Chamber of Commerce [58339]
Ceebraid Signal [58624]
CEI Ventures, Inc. / CVI [60783]
Ceilings and Interior Systems Construction Association [7212], [16928]
Ceilings & Interior Systems Construction Association-Industry Resource Guide [7284]
"Celeb-Savvy Publisher" in *Crain's New York Business* (Vol. 23, January 29, 2007, No. 5, pp. F24) [580], [18857], [35925], [46790], [50570]
"Celebrate Good Times" in *Entrepreneur* (Vol. 33, October 2005, No. 10, pp. 110) [18752]
"Celebrate Success. Embrace Innovation" in *Black Enterprise* (Vol. 37, February 2007, No. 7, pp. 145) [24903], [32312], [34850], [35926], [48092], [52833], [55074], [56156]
Celebrating 25 Years in the Canadian Craft Industry [8073], [8238], [19827], [22826], [51436]
"Celebrating Business Heroes" in *Hispanic Business* (December 2002, pp. 58-60) [35927], [46791], [48093]
"Celebration of Culture and Commerce" in *Hispanic Business* (September 2003, pp. 34, 36, 38) [46792], [48094]
"Celebs are sweet on Hawkins' new eatery" in *Crain's Detroit Business* (Vol. 19, No. 2, January 13, 2003, pp. 10) [19626], [21465]
"Celecast Selling Sports Broadcasts" in *Atlanta Business Chronicle* (Vol. 26, No. 11, August 22, 2003, pp. 5A) [20308], [33656]
Celina-Mercer County Chamber of Commerce [63638]
Cell Motility and the Cytoskeleton [52247]
"Cell Tower Potential" in *Black Enterprise* (Vol. 37, October 2006, No. 3, pp. 86) [40247], [41595]
"CELLIT Technologies Empowers CB Richard Ellis to Deliver Superior Customer Service" in *PR Newswire* (October 29, 2001, pp. NA) [20461], [20828], [31657]
Cello for Beginners [17631]
Cellular Immunology [52248]
Cellular Sales & Marketing Newsletter [5199]
CELOTEX Technical Center–Library [56679]
Celsius Tannery [23841], [42789]
Celtic House International [66719]
"Cement Shortage Has Builders In a Bind" in *Inc.* (October 2005, pp. 32, 34) [7285], [16946]
Cen-Tex Hispanic Chamber of Commerce [65158]
Monica A. Cengia [18479]
"Censorship" in *Business Week* (January 23, 2006, No. 3968, pp. 32-34) [13889], [22193], [33657]
The Centech Group Inc. [6998]
Centennial College of Applied Arts & Technology–Warden Woods Campus Learning & Resource Centre [5607]
Centennial Rehabilitation Associates [4447]
Centennial Ventures [58448]
Center for Advanced Manufacturing and Packaging of Microwave, Optical and Digital Electronics [6134]
Center for Auto Safety [930]
Center for Auto Safety-Impact [923]
Center for Autonomous Control Engineering [46549]
Center for the Book [2658]
Center for Book Arts [2828]
"Center Braces for New Wave of Business" in *Orlando Business Journal* (Vol. 20, No. 13, September 12, 2003, pp. 3) [22166], [22481], [24904], [25749]
Center for Business and Economic Research–University of Alabama [66796]
Center for Business Research/AZB [57106]
Center for Business Technology, Research and Development [64136]
Center for the Child Care Workforce, A Project of the American Federation of Teachers Educational Foundation [5321], [17863]
Center for Commerce Tourism [66364]
Center for Creative Leadership [54922]
Center for Dispute Settlement [17032], [17076]
Center for Drug Abuse Policy Analysis 41362
Center for Economic and Management Research–University of Oklahoma–Michael F. Prince College of Business [66957]

Center for Economic Options [47994], [56094]
Center for Economic Policy Analysis [24199]
Center on Education and Training for Employment [15888]
Center for Entrepreneurial Management Inc. [63244]
Center for Entrepreneurial Studies and Development [33388]
Center for Entrepreneurship and Outreach–University of Missouri at Rolla–Small Business Development Center [61860]
Center for Environmental Information [9476]
Center for Environmental Information, Inc.–CEI Library [9498]
Center for Environmental Research [9465]
Center for Environmental Sciences and Technology Management [63189]
Center for Environmental Study [9513]
Center for Exhibition Industry Research [24861], [46608]
"Center for Exhibition Industry Research (CEIR)" in *Entrepreneur* (Vol. 32, No. 1, January 2004, pp. 10) [16805], [22482], [24905], [33658]
Center for Family Business [37579], [37825]
Center for Geographic Information and Analysis–Office of State Planning [66942]
Center for Health Care Strategies [18414]
Center for Health, Environment and Justice–Library [11976]
Center for the History of American Needlework–Library [22743]
Center for Holographic Studies and Laser Technology 61151
Center for Innovation [48846], [63547]
Center for International Private Enterprise [39968]
"Center Is One-Stop Shop for Brides" in *Indianapolis Business Journal* (Vol. 25, December 27, 2004, No. 43, pp. 21) [3165], [7152]
Center for Lifestyle Enhancement - Columbia Medical Center of Plano [3661], [18480], [26048], [31299], [41325]
Center for Managing Diversity Inc. [48633]
Center for Medical Consumers [18522]
Center for Neighborhood Information Services [64360], [66797]
Center for the New West [37216]
The Center for Organizational Excellence [3662], [16582], [31300], [42950], [45987]
Center for Personal Empowerment [3663], [16583], [31301], [33339]
Center Point Area Chamber of Commerce [56820]
Center for Policy Research [17077]
Center to Prevent Handgun Violence–Library [11743]
Center on Profit [8526], [45917]
Center for Public Affairs Research–Nebraska State Data Center [66918]
Center for Public Policy Research 41398
Center for Self-Sufficiency–Publishing Div. [58484]
Center for the Study of Aging of Albany [18303]
Center for the Study of Aging, Inc. [18415]
Center for the Study of Economics [32846]
Center for the Study of Social Policy [41365]
Center for Substance Abuse Services Research 41362
Center for Sutton Movement Writing [8437]
The Center for Technical Communication [865], [9051]
Center for Thanatology Research & Education, Inc.–Library [10816]
Center for Venture Research [55464]
Center on Vulnerable Populations 41362
Center for Wireless Information Network Studies 61151
Center for Women Policy Studies [32127]
Center for Women's Business Research [56095]
"Centerpoint is sidelined" in *Red Herring* (March 2003, pp. 67) [4945], [27936], [41596], [52073]
Centerpoint Venture Partners [65599]
"CenterPoint Ventures: 'Hunting Elephants'" in *Venture Capital Journal* (Vol. 41, No. 8, August 2000, pp. 39-40) [55537]
Centers for Prevention and Intervention–Library [54378]
Centerville Area Chamber of Commerce [60106]
Centerville Chamber of Commerce [64818], [65159]

Centrac Inc. [16857]
Central Arizona College–Pinal County Small Business Development Center [56991]
Central Bakery Portuguese Muffins Cafe [2293]
Central Baldwin Chamber of Commerce [56821]
Central Bark Doggy Day Care [19198]
Central Bradford County Chamber of Commerce [64394]
Central Bucks Chamber of Commerce [64395]
Central California–Small Business Development Center [57252]
Central California Hispanic Chamber of Commerce [57406]
Central California /Visalia Satellite–SBDC [57253]
Central City Area Chamber of Commerce [62253]
Central City Chamber of Commerce [60493]
Central Coast Small Business Development Center–Cabrillo College [57254]
"Central command" in *Crain's Detroit Business* (Vol. 19, No. 14, April 7, 2003, pp. 38) [1917], [17992], [43577]
Central Delaware Chamber of Commerce [58646]
Central Fairfax Chamber of Commerce [65874]
Central Florida Career Guide [23369]
Central Florida Research Park [58984]
Central Indiana Better Business Bureau [59869]
Central Indiana SBDC [59821]
"Central Indiana's High-Tech Incubator Lands First Tenant" in *Indianapolis Star* (September 24, 2002) [41597], [43049], [52074]
Central Industrial Applications Center [67305]
Central Institute for the Deaf [12126]
    Speech, Hearing and Education Library [12123]
Central Islipislandia Chamber of Commerce [62842]
Central Jersey Chamber of Commerce [62483]
Central Lake Chamber of Commerce [61271]
Central Lakes College [61724]
    Small Business Development Center [61517]
Central Louisiana Chamber of Commerce [60623]
Central Macomb County Chamber of Commerce [61272]
Central Michigan University–Small Business Development Center [61179]
Central Missouri State University
    Center for Technology and Small Business Development [61893]
    Office of Sponsored Programs [62094]
Central Missouri State University SBTDC–Center for Technology and Small Business Development [61861]
Central Oklahoma Business and Job Development Corp.–Incubator [64123]
Central Oklahoma Technology Center [64137]
Central Oregon Community College–Small Business Development Center [64162]
Central Park Restaurants [21771]
Central Pasco Chamber of Commerce [58765]
Central Pennsylvania Chamber of Commerce [64396]
Central Pennsylvania College [64623]
"Central Perks" in *Entrepreneur* (Vol. 33, September 2005, No. 9, pp. 34) [26371], [26767], [34851], [56157]
Central Point Area Chamber of Commerce [64203]
Central Rhode Island Chamber of Commerce [64661]
    Bryant College–Small Business Development Center [64642]
    Central and Southern Rhode Island–SBDC [64643]
Central State University–International Center for Water Resources Management [25739]
Central Valley Minority Business Development Center [57889]
Central Vermont Chamber of Commerce [65782]
Central Vermont Economic Development Center–SBDC [65759]
Central Virginia Small Business Development Center [65819]
Central Washington SCORE [66060]
Central Washington University
    Department of Sociology–Applied Social Data Center [67005]

Office of Graduate Studies and Research [66232]

Central Whidbey Chamber of Commerce [66061]

Centralia Area Chamber of Commerce [61937]

Centralia-Chehalis Chamber of Commerce [66062]

Centralia Community College–Small Business Development Center [66016]

Centre for Addiction and Mental Health Library [54379]
Social, Prevention, and Health Policy Research [54398]

Centre for Bioethics [37379]

Centre Daily Times (January 30, 2005); "For Centre Region Concierge, It's All in the Details" in [7131], [18996], [52533]

Centre for the Study of Living Standards [32847]

CENTREX Hotel & Restaurant Tradeshow [12679]

Century 21 Canada Limited Partnership [20747]

Century City Chamber of Commerce [57407]

Century Small Business Solutions [4874], [23300]

CEO Advisors [3664], [31302], [53072], [58966]

"CEO Buyer's Guide: Computers" in *Hispanic Business* (November 2002, pp. BG4) [48983]

"CEO Buyer's Guide: Office" in *Hispanic Business* (November 2002, pp. BG18-BG19) [48984]

"CEO Buyer's Guide: Telecom" in *Hispanic Business* (November 2002, pp. BG8, BG10) [4946]

"CEO Buyer's Guide: Travel" in *Hispanic Business* (November 2002, pp. BG14) [30308]

"CEO Buyers's Guide: Financial" in *Hispanic Business* (November 2002, pp. BG12-13) [9870], [14842], [37951]

"CEO Confidence on the Rise" in *Hispanic Business* (November 2003, pp. 22) [27937], [32313]

"CEO of Fort Lauderdale, Fla., Women's Fitness Chain Creates Smaller Outlets" in *Miami Herald* (November 11, 2002) [19386], [27938], [38735]

"CEO Incentives and Corporate Social Performance" in *Journal of Business Ethics* (Vol. 45, No. 4, July 15, 2003, pp. 341) [35928], [54152]

"CEO sells IT company to help it grow" in *Crain's Detroit Business* (Vol. 18, No.) [6161], [27939], [41598], [49848]

"CEO Runs a Site with Bite" in *Crain's New York Business* (Vol. 23, January 29, 2007, No. 5, pp. F17) [13890], [20462], [20829], [25813], [30671], [35929], [52413]

CEO Venture Fund [64547]

"The CEO's Secret Handbook" in *Business 2.0* (Vol. 6, July 2005, No. 6, pp. 68-74) [27318], [35930], [37402], [44988]

Cequis International [21376]

Ceramics Monthly [8027], [8195]

Cereal Chemistry [52249]

Ceres Chamber of Commerce [57408]

Ceridian Corp. [61716]

Cerritos Chamber of Commerce [57409]

Certa Propainters Ltd. [18693]

Certa Propainters, US Ltd. [3351], [18717]

Certified Coin Dealer Newsletter [5834]

Certified Housekeeping Consultants [12691]

The Certified Property Manager: Profile & Compensation Study [20051]

Certigard (Petro Canada) [1873]

Certirestore Certified Furniture Restoration [10838]

Cerulean Fund / WGC Enterprises [59727]

The CF Apartment Reporter [20713], [21044]

CF Child Care Bulletin [5351]

CFA Digest [15634]

CFA Institute [14700]

CFI Group USA L.L.C. [31303], [35217], [42951], [45988]

C.F.M.A. Building Profits [7532]

CFO & Controller Alert [317], [38482]

CFO Service [367], [2984], [3960], [16584], [30071], [30645], [31304], [45989]

CFO Today [380], [2987], [24123]

"CFO's Exit Returns CPI Aerostructures Inc. to Recruiting Market" in *Long Island Business News* (February 6, 2004) [42199], [44989]

"CFOs under pressure to disclose all transactions" in *Atlanta Business Chronicle* (Vol. 25, No. 20, October 25, 2002, pp. 14C) [103], [23908], [37952]

CGW Southeast Partners / Cravey, Green, & Wahlen [59187]

CH2M Hill [11962]

CH2M Hill, Inc.–Technical Library [11977]

CHA - Certified Horsemanship Association [12443]

CHA Show [8074]

Chabot College [58227]

Chadron - Dawes County Area Chamber of Commerce [62254]

Chadron State College
Nebraska Business Development Center [30127]
SBDC [62220]

Chaffee Chamber of Commerce [61938]

Chagrin Valley Chamber of Commerce [63639]

Chain Drug Marketing Association [8760]

"Chain Lightening" in *Hispanic Business* (May 2005, pp. 72, 74) [38736], [48095], [53640]

"Chairman Sees T. Rowe Price Group Positioned for Economic Rebound" in *Baltimore Sun* (April 11, 2003) [9871], [14843], [27940]

"The Challenges of Equal Access" in *Atlanta Business Chronicle* (Vol. 23, No. 51, May 25, 2001, pp. 1B) [35931], [48096]

Chama Valley Chamber of Commerce [62677]

"Chamber, Blues team up for expo" in *Crain's Detroit Business* (Vol. 18, No. 44, November 4, 2002, pp. 39) [13230], [43122]

Chamber Business and Industry [64604]

Chamber of Business and Industry of Centre County [64397]

"Chamber prepares for fight over tax changes" in *Crain's Detroit Business* (Vol. 19, No. 13, March 31, 2003, pp. 5) [40248], [54485]

Chamber of Commerce–SBDC–Seacoast Regional Office [62386]

Chamber of Commerce for Anderson and Madison County [59885]

Chamber of Commerce of the Attleboro Area [60938]

Chamber of Commerce of the Bellmores [62843]

Chamber of Commerce-Bessemer Area [56822]

Chamber of Commerce of the Borough of Queens [62844]

Chamber of Commerce of Cape Coral [58766]

Chamber of Commerce for the City of Loganville [59075]

Chamber of Commerce of Corydon and Allerton [60107]

Chamber of Commerce of Dana Point [57410]

Chamber of Commerce for Decatur and Macon County [59461]

Chamber of Commerce of Eastern Connecticut [58517]

Chamber of Commerce of Fargo Moorhead [61570], [63513]

Chamber of Commerce of Frederick County [60822]

Chamber of Commerce of Greater Bay Shore [62845]

Chamber of Commerce of Greater Cape May [62484]

Chamber of Commerce for Greater Milford [58647]

Chamber of Commerce of the Greater Ronkonkoma [62846]

Chamber of Commerce of Greater West Chester [64398]

Chamber of Commerce of Harrison County [59886]

Chamber of Commerce of Hawaii [59241]
Small Business Council [59235]

Chamber of Commerce of Highlands Ranch [58340]

Chamber of Commerce of Huntington Beach, Women of Action [57411]

Chamber of Commerce of Huntsville/Madison County [56823]

Chamber of Commerce for Individuals with DisABILITIES [65160]

Chamber of Commerce of La Habra [57412]

Chamber of Commerce of Lafourche and the Bayou Region [60624]

Chamber of Commerce of the Massapequas [62847]

Chamber of Commerce of the Mastics and Shirley [62848]

Chamber of Commerce of the Mid-Ohio Valley [66271]

Chamber of Commerce Mountain View [57413]

Chamber of Commerce of Newtown [58518]

Chamber of Commerce of Northwest Connecticut [58519]

Chamber of Commerce of the Nyacks [62849]

Chamber of Commerce of Olean and Vicinity [62850]

Chamber of Commerce of the Palm Beaches [58767]

Chamber of Commerce in Pendleton [59887]

Chamber of Commerce of the Rockaways [62851]

Chamber of Commerce of St. Joseph County [59888]

Chamber of Commerce Serving Old Bridge, Sayerville and South Amboy [62485]

Chamber of Commerce of Smyth County [65875]

Chamber of Commerce of Southeastern Connecticut [58520]

Chamber of Commerce Southern New Jersey [62486]

Chamber of Commerce of the Tonawandas [62852]

Chamber of Commerce of the Twin Cities [64892]

Chamber of Commerce of Ulster County [62853]

Chamber of Commerce of Walker County [56824]

Chamber of Commerce of West Alabama [56825]

Chamber of Commerce of the West of Puerto Rico [66648]

Chamber of Commerce of West Volusia [58768]

Chamber of Commerce of the Willistons [62854]

Chamber of Commerce, Windham Region [58521]

Chamber of Eastern Pierce County [66063]

Chamber - Grand Haven, Spring Lake, Ferrysburg [61273]

"Chamber Kicks Off Weekly Member-Appreciation Program" in *Bellingham Business Journal* (December 2006, pp. 4) [35932], [39228], [50432], [56158]

Chamber-Main Street Sac City [60108]

Chamber of Medford - Jackson County [64204]

Chamber of Northeast Cincinnati [63640]

"Chamber Offers Seminar on Web Design" in *Charlotte Observer* (February 6, 2007) [22483], [25814]

"Chamber Puts Spotlight on Small-Business Issues" in *Crain's Detroit Business* (Vol. 19, No. 42, October 20, 2003, pp. 31) [26768], [27651], [39229], [40707]

"Chamber Revisits Business-Tax Proposal" in *Crain's Detroit Business* (Vol. 22, January 23, 2006, No. 4, pp. 19) [54486]

Chamber South [58769]

Chamber - Southwest Louisiana [60625]

"The Chamber Steps Up Its War On the SEC" in *Business Week* (February 14, 2005, No. 3920, pp. 45) [29147], [40249]

"Chamber trouble: organizations in California and Texas suffer high-profile resignations" in *Hispanic Business* (Vol.22, July-Aug. 2000) [48097], [53641]

Chamberlain & Cansler Inc. [3665], [16585], [30072], [31305], [45990], [53073]

Chamberlain-Oacoma Area Chamber of Commerce [64819]

Chambers Ltd. [13713]

ChamberWest [65706]

Champagne Group Launches 'Manager Makeover' Program" in *Bellingham Business Journal* (January 2007, pp. 4); "The [3595], [27514], [28884], [35110], [45723], [53010]

"Champagne Toasts: Brian Nembhard Schools Us On the Best of the Bubbly" in *Black Enterprise* (Vol. 34, July 2004, No. 12, pp. 138) [12533], [21466], [23464], [32148], [43578]

Champaign County Chamber of Commerce [59462], [63641]

Champion Cleaners Franchise Inc. [8925]

Champion Networks L.L.C. [49407], [49592]

"Champion Sells Five Retail Centers, Closes 12 Others" in *Crain's Detroit Business* (Vol. 21, January 10, 2005, No. 2, pp. 22) [46228], [51092]

"A Chance at a Second Career" in *Home Business* (Vol. 13, January/February 2006, No. 1, pp. 81) **[3309]**, **[35933]**, **[37609]**

"Chandler, Ariz., PostNet Among Chain's Stores that has eBay-Selling Service" in *The Tribune* (November 25, 2003) **[1791]**, **[10671]**, **[33659]**, **[37115]**

Chandler Chamber of Commerce **[57021]**, **[63961]**

Chandler, Franklin & O'Bryan **[29617]**

Change **[5352]**

"Change of Address: There's a New Internet Protocol in Town. Is it Time to Upgrade?" in *Entrepreneur* (Vol. 32, No. 1, January 2004) **[13891]**, **[33660]**

The Change Agents **[50304]**, **[52472]**

"Change, of Course" in *Entrepreneur.com* (Vol. 34, February 2006, No. 2, pp. 79) **[581]**, **[24676]**, **[25169]**, **[33661]**, **[35934]**, **[46793]**

"Change of Face: Tactics: Is Your Logo Losing Its Luster?" in *Entrepreneur* (Vol. 31, No. 9, September 2003, pp. 87) **[46794]**, **[50571]**

"Change is Good" in *Success* (Vol. 47, No. 5, October 2000, pp. 6) **[38737]**

"The Change Makers" in *Harvard Business Review* (Vol. 81, No. 7, July 2003, pp. 20) **[35935]**, **[39230]**

"Change Of Face" in *Entrepreneur* (Vol. 28, No. 4, April 2000, pp. 125) **[35362]**, **[53642]**

"Change the way you persuade" in *Harvard Business Review* (Vol. 80, No. 5, May 2002, pp. 65) **[35936]**, **[44990]**

"Change is Sweet" in *Fast Company* (June 2001, pp. 169) **[13892]**, **[25815]**, **[33662]**

"The Change Up: Find New Uses for Your Products" in *My Business* (February/March 2003, pp. 15) **[46795]**, **[48711]**, **[50572]**, **[50846]**, **[51585]**

"Change Without Pain" in *Harvard Business Review* (Vol. 78, No. 4, July 2000, pp. 75) **[27941]**, **[29148]**

Change Your Mind: Inner Training for Women in Business **[37026]**, **[56534]**

"Changes in Care" in *Pittsburgh Business Times* (Vol. 23, No. 1, July 25, 2003, pp. 1s) **[40981]**, **[53643]**

"Changes at issue" in *Crain's Detroit Business* (Vol. 19, No. 15, April 14, 2003, pp. 33) **[40250]**, **[54487]**

"Changing for the better through conferences and conventions" in *Women in Business* (Vol. 54, No. 2, March-April 2002, pp. 24) **[24906]**, **[44991]**, **[56159]**

Changing Course **[4413]**

"Changing Course" in *Pittsburgh Business Times* (Vol. 23, No. 5, August 22, 2003, pp. 13) **[9872]**, **[14844]**, **[29149]**, **[37953]**

"Changing Economic Factors Put Nursing Homes at Risk" in *Crain's Detroit Business* (Vol. 16, No. 49, December 4, 2000, pp. 28) **[18317]**, **[40251]**

"The changing face of technology" in *Hispanic Business* (Vol. 22, No. 10, October 2000, pp. 26) **[41599]**, **[48098]**

"Changing gears: Gregory Blache pilots against the tide on the Mississippi River" in *Black Enterprise* (Vol. 33, No. 6, Jan. 2003) **[16733]**, **[35937]**, **[52513]**

"Changing of the Guard" in *Hispanic Business* (Vol. 24, No. 1/2, January/February 2002, pp. 57) **[40252]**, **[48099]**

"Changing hands" in *WorkingWoman* (Vol. 25, No. 2, February 2000, pp. 38) **[42836]**, **[49849]**

"Changing hats" in *Black Enterprise* (Vol. 31, No. 5, December 2000, pp. 71) **[33663]**, **[35938]**, **[48100]**

"Changing Lanes; Retirements Spur Wave of Sales of Ford Dealerships" in *Crain's Detroit Business* (Vol. 20, December 20, 2004, No. 51) **[17993]**, **[38738]**

"Changing Spaces" in *My Business* (June/July 2004, pp. 12-13) **[49490]**

"Changing times: tax relief for women business owners" in *Women in Business* (Vol. 54, No. 5, September-October 2002, pp. 12) **[37954]**, **[40253]**, **[54488]**, **[56160]**

"Changing Times Require Changes in Recruiting Styles" in *Rough Notes* (Vol. 145, No. 2, February 2003, pp. 65) **[9873]**, **[13231]**, **[31658]**, **[42200]**, **[44992]**

Changing Values: Moving Toward the Future - Trends That Will Affect Your Business **[53052]**

"The Changing World of Crisis Management" in *Rough Notes* (Vol. 145, No. 12, December 2002, pp. 74) **[13232]**, **[43123]**, **[53644]**

"Channel Surfing" in *Sales and Marketing.com* (Vol. 156, No. 3, March 2004, pp. 7) **[44993]**, **[51586]**

Chanute Area Chamber of Commerce and Office of Tourism **[60302]**

"Chaos, Inc." in *Red Herring* (January 2003, pp. 38) **[44229]**, **[50847]**, **[52075]**

Chaos Theory in the Financial Markets **[14845]**

Chapel Hill - Carrboro Chamber of Commerce **[63343]**

"Chapman Charged with Fraud" in *Black Enterprise* (Vol. 34, No. 2, September 2003, pp. 26) **[9874]**, **[14846]**, **[29150]**, **[37403]**, **[37955]**

Chapman University
    A. Gary Anderson Center for Economic Research **[32848]**
    Albert Schweitzer Institute–Library **[17669]**

Chappell Chamber of Commerce **[62255]**

"Chapter 7 or Chapter 13? What Filing for Bankruptcy Really Means" in *Black Enterprise* (Vol. 35, February 2005, No. 7, pp. 159) **[8347]**, **[8378]**, **[37956]**

Chardon Area Chamber of Commerce **[63642]**

"Charged Up" in *Entrepreneur* (Vol. 33, October 2005, No. 10, pp. 98) **[7719]**, **[35939]**, **[38739]**

"Charging Ahead" in *Inc.* (January 1, 2004) **[44394]**, **[48875]**

"Charging an Arm and a Leg?" in *Orlando Business Journal* (Vol. 20, No. 2, June 27, 2003, pp. 1) **[39281]**, **[40982]**

Charioteer **[1623]**

Charismedia **[3666]**, **[3961]**, **[27578]**, **[31306]**, **[35218]**

"Charities find auto-show parties an ideal vehicle" in *Crain's Detroit Business* (Vol. 19, No. 2, January 13, 2003, pp. 18) **[17994]**, **[54153]**

Chariton Chamber and Development Corp. **[60109]**

"Charity Pays" in *My Business* (February/March 2004, pp. 41) **[54154]**, **[54489]**

Charles County Chamber of Commerce **[60823]**

The Charles J. Givens Financial Library **[10297]**

Charles River Media **[60897]**

Charles River Ventures **[61055]**

Charleston Area Chamber of Commerce **[59463]**

Charleston Chamber of Commerce **[57144]**, **[61939]**

Charleston Metro Chamber of Commerce **[64728]**

Charleston Regional Chamber of Commerce and Development **[66272]**

Charleston SBDC **[64689]**

Charlestown Chamber of Commerce **[64662]**

Charlevoix Area Chamber of Commerce **[61274]**

Charley Chapters: Contraction Action **[33309]**

Charley Chapters: Root Words, Prefixes, and Suffixes **[33310]**

Charley Chapters: Suffixes and Their Rule Changes **[33311]**

Charley Chapters: Writing with Synonyms, Antonyms, and the Thesaurus **[33312]**

Charley's Grilled Subs **[21772]**

Charlotte Business Journal (Vol. 16, No. 17, July 27, 2001, pp. 48); "Knit One, Stitch Too" in **[8130]**

Charlotte Business Journal (Vol. 18, No. 1, April 4, 2003, pp. 7); "Triad venture firms invest in Charlotte companies" in **[55875]**

Charlotte Chamber of Commerce **[61275]**, **[63344]**

Charlotte County Chamber of Commerce **[58770]**

Charlotte Gift and Jewelry Show **[8075]**, **[11186]**, **[12240]**, **[22827]**

"Charlotte, N.C., Jeweler Offers to Sell Stuff for You on eBay" in *Charlotte Observer* (April 2, 2004) **[1792]**, **[7160]**, **[15838]**, **[18640]**, **[33664]**, **[52514]**

"Charlotte, N.C., Private Business Club Rates First in Culinary Operations" in *Charlotte Observer* (November 9, 2002) **[2334]**, **[19387]**

Charlotte Observer (January 31, 2007); "Allen Tate Expanding to Research Triangle Park: Firm Expects Raleigh Market to Grow Faster" in **[20420]**, **[20791]**, **[27763]**, **[52645]**

Charlotte Observer (October 20, 2003); "Asheville, N.C., Bed & Breakfast Owner Finds Business Requires Total Immersion" in **[2423]**

Charlotte Observer (February 7, 2007); "Belmont Annexation Approved" in **[7251]**, **[40179]**

Charlotte Observer (January 31, 2007); "BofA Cutting 70 Charlotte Tech Jobs" in **[9851]**, **[27856]**, **[41559]**, **[42831]**

Charlotte Observer (February 2, 2007); "Builders Land Rutenberg Deal" in **[7274]**, **[37604]**, **[38725]**

Charlotte Observer (February 4, 2007); "Can This Duo be Saved? Renovating 2 Tallest Edifices Downtown Will Be Costly, Owner Says" in **[1502]**, **[27923]**

Charlotte Observer (February 3, 2007); "Cautious Hiring in January Report" in **[42198]**, **[42835]**

Charlotte Observer (February 6, 2007); "Chamber Offers Seminar on Web Design" in **[22483]**, **[25814]**

Charlotte Observer (April 2, 2004); "Charlotte, N.C., Jeweler Offers to Sell Stuff for You on eBay" in **[1792]**, **[7160]**, **[15838]**, **[18640]**, **[33664]**, **[52514]**

Charlotte Observer (November 9, 2002); "Charlotte, N.C., Private Business Club Rates First in Culinary Operations" in **[2334]**, **[19387]**

Charlotte Observer (February 6, 2007); "Check Provider Says It Plans to Close Call Center in Charlotte" in **[9880]**, **[52516]**

Charlotte Observer (February 4, 2007); "Customer Service Center Will Rise in Indian Land" in **[7307]**, **[16362]**, **[31693]**

Charlotte Observer (February 5, 2007); "Designer is Walking Ad for TIBI Line" in **[601]**, **[5534]**, **[5652]**, **[46879]**

Charlotte Observer (February 8, 2007); "Designers' Hats Foretell a Big Comeback Next Fall" in **[5535]**, **[9617]**

Charlotte Observer (February 4, 2007); "Drawn to York County: Less-Expensive Homes, Good Schools Attract Charlotteans" in **[7335]**, **[20497]**, **[20864]**, **[52666]**

Charlotte Observer (April 11, 2003); "Dueling North Carolina Bills Would Revive Payday Lending" in **[38022]**, **[40326]**

Charlotte Observer (February 8, 2007); "Eastland Future Unclear: Local Merchants Say They're OK Amid Closings of 4 More Stores" in **[28078]**, **[51141]**

Charlotte Observer (February 8, 2007); "Ed Otto, Director of Biotechnology at RCCC" in **[36048]**, **[50864]**, **[52089]**

Charlotte Observer (February 7, 2007); "EEOC Sues Charlotte-Based Lebo's" in **[22760]**, **[29215]**, **[32019]**

Charlotte Observer (February 7, 2007); "Fashionistas Weigh in on the Super-Thin" in **[5543]**, **[5659]**, **[17337]**

Charlotte Observer (February 4, 2007); "Goodyear Extends Exclusive Deal to Supply NASCAR's Tires" in **[23724]**, **[24584]**

Charlotte Observer (February 7, 2007); "Green Business Push Blooms" in **[37285]**, **[53762]**

Charlotte Observer (February 4, 2007); "He Has a Sky-High Outlook on His Business" in **[7354]**, **[36267]**

Charlotte Observer (February 2, 2007); "Hickory Unemployment Stays Steady" in **[42260]**, **[42861]**

Charlotte Observer (February 5, 2007); "Invasion of the New York Pizza" in **[19633]**, **[21537]**

Charlotte Observer (February 8, 2007); "Let Your Stuff Tell a Story: How to Edit Your Accessories to Showcase Your Personality" in **[12895]**, **[13660]**, **[18550]**

Charlotte Observer (January 31, 2007); "Mann to Lead Builders" in **[7419]**, **[20584]**, **[20935]**

Charlotte Observer (February 1, 2007); "Modular Home Center Opens in Arcadia" in **[7424]**, **[20593]**, **[40539]**, **[46377]**

Charlotte Observer (January 31, 2007); "Murdock Carrousel Sold" in [30689], [51255], [52440]

Charlotte Observer (February 1, 2007); "New Career Center Opens at Right Time: Laid-Off Freightliner Workers Will Need Help" in [33185], [42876]

Charlotte Observer (February 2, 2007) "Orders Up; Jobs Below Forecast" in [32619], [42372], [42879]

Charlotte Observer (February 1, 2007); "Punta Gorda Interested in Wi-Fi Internet" in [14376], [34381], [41925]

Charlotte Observer (February 6, 2007); "Rules Will Tighten, Bankers are Told: House Panel Chairman Expects More Regulation" in [10170], [17436]

Charlotte Observer (October 10, 2004); "Shopping Spies Help Retail Businesses Keep Eye on Service" in [31069], [31853], [51356]

Charlotte Observer (February 5, 2007); "Skinny Jeans Sticking Around for Fall" in [5570], [5715], [53965]

Charlotte Observer (January 31, 2007); "Stone to Run Hickory Farmer's Market" in [11666], [26543], [45670]

Charlotte Observer (February 7, 2007); "Success a Big Seller: N. Carolina, Duke Coaches Cash in as Marketers' Dreams" in [798], [47583]

Charlotte Observer (February 7, 2007); "Top Coffee Has Concord Ties" in [11355], [21653]

Charlotte Observer (February 1, 2007); "US Airways Stock Up 5 Percent on Day Merger Try Ends" in [15563], [50240]

Charlotte Observer (February 5, 2007); "Want a Facial With That Steak?" in [2610], [7908], [17011], [21660], [56468]

Charlottesville Regional Chamber of Commerce [65876]

"Charm City" in *Forbes* (Vol. 174, December 27, 2004, No. 13, pp. 190) [9875], [14847], [37957]

"Charmed, I'm Sure: Proper Business Etiquette Goes Beyond the Salad Fork" in *Black Enterprise* (Vol. 35, February 2005, No. 7, pp. 64) [35940], [39231], [44994]

"Charms Linked to Girl's Lead Poisoning" in *San Jose Mercury News* (March 4, 2005) [8153], [15839]

Charo Chicken Systems, Inc. [21773]

Charolais Journal [1200]

Charp Associates Inc. [56654]

"Chart-toppers" in *Entrepreneur* (Vol. 30, No. 3, March 2002, pp. 88) [46796], [50573]

"Chart-Toppers; Largest M&A Deals in U.S. History" in *Crain's Chicago Business* (Vol. 30, January 2007, No. 4, pp.30) [14848], [39232], [49850]

Chartcraft Weekly Service [15635]

"Charted Territory: Candy Crosses the Border to Open New Doors" in *Entrepreneur* (Vol. 31, No. 9, September 2003, pp. 85) [4280], [27942]

Charter Life Sciences [57965]

"Charter One Leads State Banks in Small-Biz Loans" in *Crain's Detroit Business* (Vol. 21, October 24, 2005, No. 43, pp. 24) [9876], [44492]

"Charter Service Gets OK To Build Hangar At SRQ" in *Bradenton Herald* (January 25, 2005) [947], [27943]

"Charter Service Suspends Use of Plane After Crash" in *San Fernando Valley Business Journal* (Vol. 12, January 2007, No. 2, pp. 6) [948], [30309]

Charter Venture Capital / Charter Ventures [57966]

Charter Ventures /Charter Venture Capital [57967]

Chartered Institute of Logistics and Transport in North America [24225]

Chartered Management Co. [3667], [16586], [31307], [38517], [45991], [53074]

"Charting a course" in *Black Enterprise* (Vol. 33, No. 6, Jan. 2003, pp. 30) [9877], [14849], [37958]

"Charting Your Course" in *Black Enterprise* (Vol. 34, July 2004, No. 12, pp. 65) [44699]

"Charts Show the Way" in *Black Enterprise* (Vol. 34, No. 6, January 2004, pp. 29) [9878], [14850], [37959]

"Charts Show the Way: Money Manager Terry Bedford's Stock Selections Are Going in the Right Direction" in *Black Enterprise* (Vol. 34) [9879], [14851], [37960]

Chartwell Capital Management Co., Inc. [58967]

Chase City Chamber of Commerce [65877]

Chase County Chamber of Commerce [60303]

Chase County Historical Society–Museum and Library [11007]

"Chase Reshapes PE Investments" in *Venture Capital Journal* (Vol. 40, No. 10, November 2000, pp. 28) [14852], [49851], [55538]

"Chasing the bottleneck" in *Red Herring* (No. 106, October 15, 2001, pp. 18) [4617], [4947], [6929], [13893], [22939], [37116]

Chatham Area Chamber of Commerce [62487]

Chatham Chamber of Commerce [60939]

Chatham County United Chamber of Commerce [63345]

The Chatham Group Inc. [16858]

"Chatom Offers Wines With Cause Tie-Ins" in *Marketing to Women* (Vol. 19, November 2006, No. 11, pp. 5) [23465], [46797], [48712], [54155], [56161]

Chatsworth-Murray County Chamber of Commerce [59076]

Chatsworth - Porter Ranch Chamber of Commerce [57414]

Chattanooga Area Chamber of Commerce [64893]

Chattanooga/Hamilton County Business Development Center [65006]

Chattanooga State Technical Community College [65012]

    SBDC [64852]

Chattanooga Times/Free Press (June 24, 2004); "Owner of Adult Day Services Firm Picked to Lead Tennessee Industry Group" in [454], [18331]

"Chatting With the Enemy" in *My Business* (April/May 2004, pp. 49) [30815], [44279]

Chattooga County Chamber of Commerce [59077]

Chatty Cathy Collectors Club [1300], [5798], [24795]

Chautauqua County Chamber of Commerce [62855]

"Cheap frills" in *Boston Business Journal* (Vol. 22, No. 22, May 10, 2002, pp. 36) [7122], [52515]

"Cheap Jet Update" in *Forbes* (Vol. 175, January 10, 2005, No. 1, pp. 31) [35941], [46229]

"Cheap labor: Insurance: How to get a lower workers' comp premium" in *Entrepreneur* (Vol. 30, No. 3, March 2002, pp. 84) [13233], [43124]

"Cheap Tricks" in *The Economist* (Vol. 377, October 1-7, 2005, No. 8446, pp. 62) [6604], [46230], [54156]

Cheatham County Chamber of Commerce [64894]

Cheboygan Area Chamber of Commerce [61276]

"Check out our new book-What E-sourcing Means to You" in *Publishers Weekly* (Vol. 249, No. 19, November 21, 2002, pp. 3) [13894], [33665]

"Check 'Em Out" in *Entrepreneur* (Vol. 28, No. 11, November 2000, pp. 40) [13895], [33666]

"Check It Out" in *Entrepreneur* (Vol. 32, November 2004, No. 11, pp. 14) [35942], [46798], [51587]

"Check Provider Says It Plans to Close Call Center in Charlotte" in *Charlotte Observer* (February 6, 2007) [9880], [52516]

"Checkers to Grow After Eliminating Rally's Name Locally" in *Crain's Detroit Business* (Vol. 23, January 22-28, 2007, No. 4, pp. 10) [21467], [49852]

Checkers / Ralley's [21774]

"Checking In: Chicago: Cheryl Burton Whirls Through the Windy City" in *Black Enterprise* (Vol. 34, July 2004, No. 12, pp. 150) [12534], [21468], [25170], [30310], [52652]

"Checking In? First Pass the Picket Line" in *Business Week* (February 20, 2006, No. 3972, pp. 39) [12535], [55284]

"Checking Inn at the Office" in *Home Office Computing* (Vol. 18, No. 10, October 2000, pp. 92) [44995], [49491]

"Checking with Interest" in *Business Week* (No. 3678, April 24, 2000, pp. F10) [37961], [40254]

"Checking Out" in *Harvard Business Review* (Vol. 78, No. 2, March 2000, pp. 22) [33667], [51093]

Checkmark Software Inc. [368], [4875], [23301], [26421], [53548]

"The Check's in the E-Mail" in *Entrepreneur* (Vol. 32, October 2004, No. 10, pp. 66) [9881], [31520], [33668]

"The Check's in the Mail" in *Home Office Computing* (Vol. 18, No. 11, November 2000, pp. 98) [31521]

"Check's in the Mail" in *Small Business Opportunities* (Vol. 12, No. 5, September 2000, pp. 58-59) [16429], [52517]

Checotah Chamber of Commerce [63962]

Cheeburger Cheeburger Restaurants, Inc. [21775]

Cheektowaga Chamber of Commerce [62856]

Cheekwood Botanical Gardens–Library [11512]

Cheers [2365]

Cheese 101 [23546]

Cheese Classics of America [23547]

The Cheese Market [23530]

The Cheese Reporter [23534]

Chef [12060]

Chefs de Cuisine Association of America [7806]

"Chefs Show Off at Schoolcraft College Fundraiser" in *Crain's Detroit Business* (Vol. 21, October 3, 2005, No. 43, pp. 20) [1793], [7812], [21469], [23466], [33037], [54157]

Chehalem Valley Chamber of Commerce [64205]

Chelsea Area Chamber of Commerce [61277]

Chelsea Chamber of Commerce [60940]

Chem-Dry Carpet Drapery & Upholstery Cleaning [25549]

Chem-Dry Carpet and Upholstery Cleaning [25550]

"Chem-dry, a Franchise Rated No. 1 in its Category for 15 Years Straight..." in *Entrepreneur* (Vol. 32, No. 5, May 2004, pp. 131) [25530], [38618]

Chemeketa Community College
    Small Business Development Center [64163]
    Training and Economic Development Center [64300]

"Chemical Balance" in *Black Enterprise* (Vol. 34, No. 5, December 2003, pp. 38) [9882], [14853], [37962], [46231]

The Chemical Educator [33294]

Chemical Engineering Research and Design (ChERD) [52250]

Chemical Monographs Review [52251]

Chemical and Petroleum Engineering [52252]

Chemical Process Alert [50995]

Chemical Week Price Report [11943]

Chemistri–Information Center [906]

"The chemistry of super-growth" in *Hispanic Business* (Vol. 21, No. 12, December 1999, pp. 26) [27944], [48101]

CHEMSAFE [56612]

Chemstation International Inc. [3352]

Chemung County Chamber of Commerce [62857]

Cheney Chamber of Commerce [60304]

Chernoff Diamond & Company L.L.C. [27014]

Cherokee Chamber of Commerce [60110], [63346], [63963]

Cherokee County Chamber of Commerce [56826], [59078], [63347], [64729]

Cherokee County Genealogical-Historical Society–Library [11008]

Cherry County Historical Society [11009]

Cherry Creek Chamber of Commerce [58341]

Cherry Hill Regional Chamber of Commerce [62488]

"Cherry to Move 100 Jobs to Mexico" in *Milwaukee Journal Sentinel* (December 21, 2005) [7720], [43579], [46232]

Cherry Tree Investments, Inc. [61695]

Cherryvale Chamber of Commerce [60305]

Cherryville Chamber of Commerce EDC [63348]

Chesaning Chamber of Commerce [61278]

Chesapeake Bay Maritime Museum–Howard I. Chapelle Memorial Library [16787]

Cheshire Chamber of Commerce [58522]

Cheskin [16859]

Chester Chamber of Commerce [59464]

Chester College of New England [62444]

Chester County Chamber of Business and Industry [64399]

Chester County Chamber of Commerce [64730], [64895]

Chester/Lake Almanor Chamber of Commerce [57415]

Chesterfield Chamber of Commerce [61940]

Chesterfield County Chamber of Commerce [65878]

Chesterland Chamber of Commerce [63643]

Chester's International, LLC [21776]

Chesterton and Duneland Chamber of Commerce [59889]

Chestnut Street Partners, Inc. [61056]

Chetek Area Chamber of Commerce [66365]

Chetopa Chamber of Commerce [60306]

Diego Chevere & Co. [50305]

Chevys Fresh Mex [21777]

Chewelah Chamber of Commerce [66064]

Cheyenne County Chamber of Commerce [62256]

Cheyenne - Roger Mills Chamber of Commerce and Tourism [63964]

Cheyenne SBDC–Region IV [66594]

Chi Kung the Healing Workout [19466]

Chicago Apparel News [5289]

Chicago Area Gay and Lesbian Chamber of Commerce [59465]

Chicago Area Geographic Information Study–University of Illinois at Chicago [66865]

Chicago Bicycle & Fitness Show [2515]

"Chicago Can Be Greener" in *Crain's Chicago Business* (Vol. 30, January 2007, No. 1, pp. 15) [37255], [40255]

Chicago Chinatown Chamber of Commerce [59466]

"Chicago Defender" in *Black Enterprise* (Vol. 35, December 2004, No. 5, pp. 86) [18858], [44996]

Chicago Design Show [10527], [13705]

Chicago-Edison Electrical & Lighting [49593]

"Chicago" in *Entrepreneur* (Vol. 28, No. 17, July 2000, pp. 142) [3510], [29825]

Chicago Home and Garden [11456], [13686]

Chicago JobBank [23385]

"Chicago Mercantile Exchange" in *Sales & Marketing Management* (Vol. 159, January-February 2007, No. 1, pp. 10) [582], [14854], [46799], [51588]

Chicago Minority Business Development Center [59713]

"Chicago Observer: Owners Hope to Keep Plumbing Problems from Leaking" in *Crains Chicago Business* (Vol. 26, No. 50, December 15, 2003) [19746], [20471], [38599], [40256]

Chicago Park District–Garfield Park Conservatory [10606], [11513], [16091]

Chicago Public Library–Visual & Performing Arts Division–Music Information Center [6146], [17670], [17815]

Chicago Public Library Central Library–Business/Science/Technology Division [4457], [44218], [46151], [47929], [49469], [53128]

Chicago Ridge - Worth Business Association [59467]

Chicago Southland Enterprise Center [59774]

Chicago State University
 Institutional Research and Academic Evaluation [59775]
 Office of Continuing Education [59797]

Chicago Technology Park [59776]

Chicago Tribune (February 22, 2005); "Ad Companies Probe Potential of Blog World" in [529], [13799], [33513], [46652]

Chicago Tribune (March 6, 2005); "Alive with Sound of Music Selling" in [4910], [17729], [46193]

Chicago Tribune (November 10, 2002); "Angel Investing Still Alive, Barely, in Chicago Area" in [16175], [24221], [24643], [35319], [44386], [55355]

Chicago Tribune (March 11, 2005); "Bankruptcy Law Would Mean Tougher Consequences for Consumers" in [29114], [37905]

Chicago Tribune (February 17, 2005); "Blue Bag Site Faces Scrutiny" in [21218], [26487], [40198]

"Chicago Tribune Business Agenda" in *Chicago Tribune* (February 28, 2005) [32314], [42201], [46233], [53645]

Chicago Tribune (February 28, 2005); "Chicago Tribune Business Agenda" in [32314], [42201], [46233], [53645]

Chicago Tribune (March 3, 2005); "Chicago Tribune Inside Health Care" in [13234], [40983], [43125]

Chicago Tribune (April 11, 2003); "Chicago Tribune Market Report Column" in [9883], [14855], [37963]

Chicago Tribune (February 24, 2005); "Coalition Aims to End 'Disrespect' of Taxi Drivers" in [24231]

Chicago Tribune (October 27, 2002); "Curves for Women Fitness Centers Power Up by Going Lean, Not Mean" in [19391], [27994]

Chicago Tribune (March 6, 2005); "Designs Changing as New Generation of Buyers Emerges" in [1510], [7310], [53687]

Chicago Tribune (April 11, 2003); "Elk Grove Village, Ill. Officials Wary of O'Hare Airport Expansion" in [28097]

Chicago Tribune (March 9, 2005); "Family Delivers on Father's Dream" in [19620], [35442], [37564]

Chicago Tribune (March 4, 2005); "Greenspan Floats Sales Tax" in [32458], [40425], [54582]

Chicago Tribune (February 23, 2005); "High Court Hears Case Pitting Property Rights Against Redevelopment" in [7358], [29287]

Chicago Tribune (March 6, 2005); "Home Designers Have Women in Mind" in [1519], [7367], [13649]

Chicago Tribune (April 11, 2003); "Illinois Businesses Anxious about Governor's Plans on Fees, Taxes" in [40450], [54606]

Chicago Tribune (February 23, 2005); "Illinois Regulators Investigate Possible Title Insurance Kickbacks" in [7383], [13333], [17400], [40452], [43228]

Chicago Tribune (March 2, 2005); "Illinois Tax Scofflaws Land on New Internet List" in [14142], [54607]

"Chicago Tribune Inside Health Care" in *Chicago Tribune* (March 3, 2005) [13234], [40983], [43125]

Chicago Tribune (February 27, 2005); "Investors Fueling Home-Sales Heat" in [7389], [20557], [20910]

Chicago Tribune (February 16, 2005); "Knitting a Close Bond with Dogs" in [8013], [8170]

Chicago Tribune (February 17, 2005); "Like Hair, Barbers' Ranks Thinning" in [11794], [53835]

"Chicago Tribune Market Report Column" in *Chicago Tribune* (April 11, 2003) [9883], [14855], [37963]

Chicago Tribune (March 1, 2005); "Merger to Form Nation's Largest Freight Consolidator" in [10681], [15259], [50077]

Chicago Tribune (March 4, 2005); "More Cell Phone Providers Using Stealthy Approach to Erecting Towers" in [5060], [28504]

Chicago Tribune (July 4, 2004); "Mystery Shoppers Help Provide Certainty for Several Major Companies" in [31791], [51259]

Chicago Tribune (February 17, 2005); "New Home Construction Reaches 21-Year-High Pace in January" in [7435], [20607], [28542]

Chicago Tribune (March 3, 2005); "New Jersey Builder Hovnanian Enters Chicago Home Market" in [7437], [15299], [50097]

Chicago Tribune (February 25, 2005); "New Lenox Drawing Up Plans for a Big Mall" in [7439], [17526], [21572], [51268]

Chicago Tribune (March 3, 2005); "Panel Seeks to Put Organic Loophole Out to Pasture" in [12016], [26526], [40604]

Chicago Tribune (March 11, 2005); "Pollution Rules to Cost Illinois Firms" in [11937], [40618]

Chicago Tribune (February 21, 2005); "Sales of Scooters Get in the Fast Lane" in [2503], [17490], [53951]

Chicago Tribune (February 16, 2005); "Senator Urges 'Measurable Standard' for Awarding Farm Subsidies" in [26539], [40092], [40687]

Chicago Tribune (February 22, 2005); "Serving Fine Fare, Cafe Alters the Course of At-Risk Youth" in [12634], [21620], [54253]

Chicago Tribune (March 9, 2005); "Skokie Taxed by School-Business Rift" in [28767], [54749]

Chicago Tribune (February 18, 2005); "Trainers of Racing Horses Face New Drug Fine" in [10890], [26550], [29554], [40781]

Chicago Tribune (March 2, 2005); "Union, Nursing Home Owners in Tense Negotiations" in [460], [18341], [41127], [55315]

Chicago Tribune (October 3, 2004); "Virtual Assistants Become Real Help as more U.S. Firms Use Outsourced Aides" in [7147], [31242]

Chicago Tribune (February 3, 2003); "Women Find 'Grass Ceiling' of Men-Only Clubs Impediment to Business" in [2358], [11275], [39691], [56499]

Chicagoland Chamber of Commerce [59468]

"Chicago's Top Brands" in *Crain's Chicago Business* (Vol. 30, January 2007, No. 3, pp. 15) [583], [46800], [50433]

"Chick magnet: How can you attract women to your business?" in *Entrepreneur* (Vol. 30, No. 3, March 2002, pp. 93) [46801], [51589], [56162]

Chickasha Chamber of Commerce [63965]

Chicken Connection Franchise Corp. [21778]

Chicken Delight [19657], [21779]

Chico Chamber of Commerce [57416]

Chicopee Chamber of Commerce [60941]

"Chief concern" in *Entrepreneur* (Vol. 31, No. 4, April 2003, pp. 51) [104], [26186], [35943], [37964], [44997]

Chief Executive Officers Club [37090], [44711]

Chief Executive Officer's Newsletter [37017], [45887]

"Chief Risk Officer No Solution" in *American Banker* (Vol. 170, February 4, 2005, No. 24, pp. 11) [35944], [44998]

Child Care ActioNews [5353]

Child Care Bridges [5354]

; *Child Care Plus* [5355]

Child Health Investment Company, LLC [60439]

John S. Child Jr. [44198]

Child Safety [5375]

Child Welfare [5356]

Child Welfare League of America [5322]

Child and Youth Services [41178]

Childersburg Chamber of Commerce [56827]

Children's Advertising Review Unit [50526]

Children's Book Insider [9023]

Children's Books in Print [2689], [3035]

Children's Business [2130], [5290]

Children's Defense Fund [5323]

Children's Lighthouse Franchise Co. [2138], [5418], [12342]

Children's Orchard [5303], [5750]

"Children's Products and Services" in *Entrepreneur* (Vol. 32, No. 1, January 2004, pp. 178) [5271], [5335], [33038], [38740]

The Children's Psychological Trauma Center [3668], [31308], [41326]

"Children's stories" in *BlackEnterprise* (Vol. 32, No. 3, October 2001, pp. 56) [2634], [8590], [46563]

Children's Technology Workshop [42790]

Children's Voice [41179]

Childrensbooksinprint.com [3070]

Childress Chamber of Commerce [65161]

Child's Play [24842]

"Child's Play" in *Entrepreneur* (Vol. 31, No. 9, September 2003, pp. 119) [5336], [19388], [56163]

Child's Play: The World of Learning [5376]

Chilean American Chamber of Commerce [64400]

"Chili Shack Draws Interest" in *Kansas City Star* (February 15, 2005) [19627], [21470], [38741], [44014]

Chillicothe Area Chamber of Commerce [61941]

Chillicothe Chamber of Commerce [59469]

Chillicothe Ross Chamber of Commerce [63644]

Chillicothe Satellite Center–SBDC [61862]

"Chilling Out" in *Forbes* (Vol. 174, December 27, 2004, No. 13, pp. 64) [6605], [48985]

Chilson's Management Controls Inc. [26623]

Chilton Chamber of Commerce [66366]

Chilton County Chamber of Commerce [56828]

Frederick Chin [47841]

China Area Chamber of Commerce [60739]

"China" in *Business Week* (January 23, 2006, No. 3968, pp. 44-45) **[9884]**, **[27945]**, **[30816]**, **[43580]**, **[55539]**

China International Footwear Fair **[22772]**

The China List **[52076]**

The China Painter **[8028]**

"China Presents Opportunities, Risks for Investors" in *Sacramento Bee* (December 27, 2005) **[14856]**, **[37965]**, **[43581]**

"China Route Hinges on Biz vs Politics" in *Crain's Detroit Business* (Vol. 22, September 25-October 1, 2006, No. 39, pp. 1, 40) **[27946]**, **[30311]**

"China Syndrome" in *Boston Business Journal* (V) **[41600]**, **[43582]**

China Telecom **[13024]**, **[22091]**, **[40858]**, **[43893]**

China Weekly Fax Bulletin **[27547]**, **[29040]**

China's Rational Entrepreneurs: The Development of the New Private Business Sector **[35945]**, **[39233]**, **[43583]**

"China's cheap labor is next threat to suppliers" in *Crain's Detroit Business* (Vol. 19, No. 2, January 13, 2003, pp. 13) **[1918]**, **[30817]**, **[43584]**, **[46234]**

Chincoteague Chamber of Commerce **[65879]**

Chinese for Affirmative Action **[42484]**

Chinese American Association of Commerce **[43485]**

"The Chinese Are Coming" in *Inc.* (Volume 27, July 2005, No. 7, pp. 32) **[1410]**, **[1919]**, **[7721]**, **[14857]**, **[43585]**, **[46235]**, **[52077]**

Chinese Chamber of Commerce **[57417]**

Chinese Chamber of Commerce of Hawaii **[59242]**

Chinese Ethnic Business **[43586]**, **[48102]**, **[48528]**

Chinese Music Society of North America–Library **[17671]**

"The Chinese Negotiation" in *Harvard Business Review* (Vol. 81, No. 10, October 2003, pp. 82) **[27319]**, **[43587]**

"Chinese Supplier Plans R&D Center in Canton Twp." in *Crain's Detroit Business* (Vol. 21, October 31, 2005, No. 44, pp. 15) **[1920]**, **[50848]**, **[52077]**

Chino Valley Area Chamber of Commerce **[57022]**

Chino Valley Chamber of Commerce **[57418]**

"Chip legend Carver Mead mixes analog and digital" in *Red Herring* (No. 106, October 15, 2001, pp. 26) **[4948]**, **[13896]**, **[37117]**, **[44015]**

Chip Chats **[8029]**

"Chip Demand Worldwide Drives Up 1Q Earnings for Intel" in *San Jose Mercury News* (March 11, 2005) **[6606]**, **[41601]**, **[43588]**

"Chip Shot. Teradyne's New President is Crafting a Comeback after an Industry Slump" in *Boston Business Journal* (Vol. 23, Jul. 4, 03) **[41602]**, **[44999]**, **[46236]**

CHIP - The Child ID Program **[5419]**

Chippewa Falls Area Chamber of Commerce **[66367]**

Chisholm Area Chamber of Commerce **[61571]**

Chisholm Private Capital Partners **[64114]**

Chloride Chamber of Commerce **[57023]**

"Chocolat flick on tap for Valentine's Day special" in *Business First Columbus* (Vol. 18, No. 25, February 8, 2002, pp. A12) **[21471]**, **[46802]**

Chocolate Chocolate Chocolate Co. **[12812]** (Vol. 16, No. 2, February, 2002, pp. B6); "Chocolate Factory is a sweet deal" in **[4281]**

"Chocolate Maker Plans New Plant in Pauls Valley, Okla" in *Knight-Ridder/Tribune Business News* (April 11, 2002, pp. ITEM02101008) **[4282]**, **[30519]**, **[48103]**

"Chocolate Makes a Success Story for Boca Raton Fla. Shop" in *South Florida Sun-Sentinel* (December 23, 2002) **[4283]**, **[16430]**, **[42592]**

Chocolate Manufacturers Association of the U.S.A. **[4270]**

"Chocolate temperers" in *Candy Industry* (Vol. 167, No. 4, April 2002, pp. 88) **[4284]**, **[46237]**, **[48713]**

Choctaw Chamber of Commerce **[63966]**

Choice Hotels International **[12706]**

"ChoicePoint's Actions Could be Damaging, Experts Say" in *Atlanta Journal-Constitution* (March 5, 2005) **[22194]**, **[29151]**, **[40257]**

Choices **[32084]**, **[48618]**

Choices: How to Control Internal Shrink **[35288]**

Choose Home **[52618]**

"Choose Leasing: www.chooseleasing.org" in *Entrepreneur* (Vol. 32, November 2004, No. 11, pp. 6) **[13897]**, **[21316]**

"Choose the Right Application Server" in *E-business Advisor* (Vol. 18, No. 1, January 2000, pp. 32) **[13898]**, **[25816]**, **[33669]**

"Choose Your Path" in *Entrepreneur* (Vol. 33, March 2005, No. 3, pp. 114) **[51094]**

Choose Your Weapon **[11739]**

"Choosing a Business Entity" in *Crain's Detroit Business* (Vol. 18, No. 49, December 9, 2002, pp. 15) **[35363]**, **[39038]**

Choosing Careers **[4426]**

"Choosing an Incubator for your Business Baby" in *Ingram's* (Vol. 28, No. 6, June 2002, pp. 49) **[35364]**, **[39763]**, **[43036]**

Choosing a Job **[4427]**

"Choosing the Right Investment Properties" in *Black Enterprise* (Vol. 35, February 2005, No. 7, pp. 75) **[14858]**, **[20830]**

Choosing and Working with Your Advertising Agency **[46803]**

"Choosy tenants are finding bargains, flexibility" in *Atlanta Business Chronicle* (Vol. 24, No. 9, August 3, 2001, pp. 4C) **[20463]**, **[37118]**, **[52653]**

"Chop, chop: Bush's plan changes all: tax planning" in *Barron's* (Vol. 82, No. 57, February 10, 2003, pp. 21) **[105]**, **[23909]**, **[26187]**, **[37966]**, **[54490]**

Chouteau Chamber of Commerce **[63967]**

Chow! A Nutrition Curriculum **[18458]**

Chowchilla District Chamber of Commerce **[57419]**

"Chris Brown Takes Helm: IAEM Chairman" in *Tradeshow Week* (Vol. 34, November 29, 2004, No. 48, pp. 22) **[22484]**, **[24907]**, **[55075]**

Christian Booksellers Association International Convention **[3063]**

Christian Camping International/U.S.A. **[4225]**

Christmas Craft Fair by Loris **[8076]**

Christmas Craft Fair USA **[5470]**, **[8077]**, **[8239]**

Christmas Crafts **[5466]**

Christmas Decor **[5476]**, **[5488]**

Christmas Entertaining **[8225]**

Christmas Gift and Hobby Show **[5471]**, **[8078]**, **[8240]**

Christmas Trees **[5482]**

The Chronicle of Philanthropy **[10752]**

Chrysalis Ventures **[60580]**

"Chrysler Deal Has SET Looking at Opening New Plant In Ohio" in *Crain's Detroit Business* (Vol. 21, October 10, 2005, No. 43, pp. 42) **[1921]**, **[27947]**, **[46238]**, **[52654]**

"Chrysler to Introduce Cleaner Diesel Engines" in *Atlanta Journal-Constitution* (January 24, 2007) **[17995]**, **[37256]**, **[46239]**

Chugiak-Eagle River Chamber of Commerce **[56950]**

Chula Vista Chamber of Commerce **[57420]**

"Chula Vista: Dobson's Has Designs on Eastlake" in *San Diego Business Journal* (Vol. 28, January 8, 2007, No. 2, pp. 27) **[21472]**, **[27948]**

"Chunk of Change: Navigating Employment Taxes" in *My Business* (June/July 2004, pp. 14) **[18771]**, **[23910]**, **[49681]**, **[54491]**

Kelley Chunn & Associates **[47842]**, **[50491]**

"Church Case May Impact Land Use" in *Crain's Detroit Business* (Vol. 23, January 8, 2007, No. 2, pp. 18) **[40258]**, **[52655]**, **[54492]**

Church of Jesus Christ of Latter-Day Saints
Cleveland, Ohio Stake–Family History Center **[11010]**
Valley Forge, Pennsylvania Stake–Family History Center **[11011]**

Church Point Area Chamber of Commerce **[60626]**

Church World Service–Film & Video Library **[9431]**

Churchill County Economic Development Authority (CEDA)–SBDC **[62323]**

Church's Chicken **[21780]**

"Churn Plagues Wal-Mart Labor Effort" in *Tampa Tribune* (December 23, 2005) **[51095]**, **[55285]**

John Chute & Associates **[27015]**

Chyten Educational Services **[25475]**

Ciba Vision–Corporate Library **[25668]**

Cicero Area Chamber of Commerce **[59890]**

Cicero Chamber of Commerce and Industry **[59470]**

CiCi's Pizza **[19658]**, **[21781]**

CICS Update **[6497]**

CID Equity Partners **[60029]**

"CID businesses self-tax to fund improvements" in *Atlanta Business Chronicle* (Vol. 24, No. 14, September 7, 2001, pp. 3C) **[53646]**, **[54493]**

CID Service **[26649]**

Cigar Aficionado **[24613]**

Cigar Association of America **[24602]**

"Cigar Company Promoting Hand-Rolled Products, Delta Blues" in *Mississippi Business Journal* (Vol. 29, January 2007, No. 2, pp. 3) **[5478]**, **[24608]**, **[48714]**

Cigars 101 **[24629]**

CIGNA Corporation–Philadelphia Research Library **[56680]**

Cimarron Chamber of Commerce **[60307]**, **[62678]**

Cimarron County Chamber of Commerce **[63968]**

Cincinnati Better Business Bureau **[63598]**

Cincinnati Business Expo/Fall **[49394]**, **[53067]**

Cincinnati Golf Show **[11284]**

Cincinnati Home and Garden Show **[11488]**

Cincinnati Travel, Sports, and Boat Show **[2207]**, **[16771]**, **[23676]**

Cincinnati USA Regional Chamber **[63645]**

Cincinnati Wedding **[3204]**

Cincy Business Magazine **[39716]**

"Cindy Kauanui: 45, Founder of Jet Set Management in La Jolla, California" in *Entrepreneur* (Vol. 32, October 2004, No. 10, pp. 26) **[17335]**, **[23824]**

Cindy's Cinnamon Rolls **[2214]**, **[2294]**

Cinema Grill **[17545]**, **[21782]**

"Cineplex Galaxy Income Fund Reports Fourth Quarter and Year End Results" in *Canadian Corporate News* (February 7, 2007) **[14859]**, **[27949]**, **[37967]**

"Cingular Increases Bid for AT&T Wireless" in *Atlanta Journal-Constitution* (February 17, 2004) **[4949]**, **[14860]**, **[49854]**

Cini-Little International Inc. **[4568]**, **[12692]**, **[21715]**

Cinnamon Street Bakery & Coffee Company **[11372]**

CinnaMonster **[2172]**, **[2215]**

Cinnzeo **[2216]**, **[2295]**

Circle Chamber of Commerce and Agriculture **[62154]**

Circleville - Pickaway Chamber of Commerce **[63646]**

"Circulation losses continue at most state newspapers" in *Atlanta Business Chronicle* (Vol. 25, November 15, 2002, No. 23 pp. 3A) **[18859]**, **[27950]**

Cisco Chamber of Commerce **[65162]**

"Cisco rolls out small business DSL router" in *InfoWorld* (Vol. 22, No. 17, April 24, 2000, pp. 65) **[13899]**, **[48986]**

Cisco Network Design Solutions for Small-Medium Businesses **[4950]**, **[6408]**, **[6466]**, **[6607]**, **[6930]**, **[13900]**, **[31659]**, **[48987]**

"Cisco, SBA announce online learning program" in *Network World* (July 24, 2000, pp. NA) **[33039]**, **[33670]**, **[39798]**

The CIT Group/Venture Capital, Inc. **[62589]**

"Citgo Mulls Relocation to Houston" in *Houston Business Journal* (Vol. 34, No. 14, August 15, 2003, pp. 1) **[30138]**, **[32315]**, **[54494]**

"Citibank announces credit card targeted to small businesses" in *Wall Street Journal* (May 22, 2000, pp. C24, C15) **[9885]**, **[37968]**

Citicorp Venture Capital Ltd. (New York City) **[63071]**

"Cities Talk Taxes; Mt. Clemens, Ann Arbor Look at Adding Income Levels to Help Fix Budgets" in *Crain's Detroit Business* (Vol. 21) **[40259]**, **[54495]**

"Citigroup Names President Of GDB" in *Wall Street Journal* (Vol. 248, December 2006, No. 145, pp. B10) **[37969]**, **[40984]**, **[49855]**

"Citigroup, NCLR Announce $105 million Revitalization Pact" in *Hispanic Business* (March 2003, pp. 16) **[17369]**, **[20464]**, **[20831]**, **[49856]**

"Citizens Bank To Lend Low-Interest Loans to Firms Relocating to Massachusetts" in *Boston Globe* (February 4, 2005) **[30139]**, **[44493]**, **[52656]**

Citizens Budget Commission **[50392]**

Citizens League Research Institute **[50393]**

"Citizens Rates Set to Rise Yet Again" in *Tampa Tribune* (December 15, 2005) **[13235]**, **[43126]**

Citizens for Tax Justice **[24200]**

"Citizens expands through tough times" in *Black Enterprise* (Vol. 32, No. 5, December 2001, pp. 21) **[48104]**, **[49857]**

Citronelle Area Chamber of Commerce **[56829]**

Citrus County Chamber of Commerce **[58771]**

Citrus County Chamber of Commerce - Crystal River Office **[58772]**

Citrus Heights Chamber of Commerce **[57421]**

"City of Angels" in *Hispanic Business* (Vol. 23, No. 10, October, 2001, pp. 96) **[30312]**

"City Bank Expands as Merger Bid Threatens Branches" in *Pacific Business News* (Vol. 41, No. 16, June 27, 2003, pp. 12) **[9886]**, **[14861]**, **[27951]**, **[49858]**

City of Barrow Chamber of Commerce **[56951]**

City College of City University of New York–Art Visual Resources Library **[1575]**, **[13721]**

City College of San Francisco–Culinary Arts and Hospitality Studies Department–Alice Statler Library **[4572]**, **[7829]**, **[12094]**, **[12741]**, **[22033]**

City of Corpus Christi Business Resource Center **[65576]**

City Government Economic Program Administration Directory **[32228]**

"City Guide for Moms Launched" in *Marketing to Women* (Vol. 20, January 2007, No. 1, pp. 3) **[584]**, **[3943]**, **[13901]**, **[41603]**, **[46804]**, **[52370]**

City of Jackson–Economic Development Division **[61842]**

City Kitchen **[4569]**

"The City Market" in *Ingram's* (Vol. 28, No. 5, May 2002, pp. 25) **[20465]**, **[20832]**

City of Oilton Council **[63969]**

"City Policy Slows Efforts to Rehab Homes" in *Crain's Detroit Business* (Vol. 19, No. 10, March 10, 2003, pp. 9) **[20466]**, **[20833]**, **[40260]**

City Publications **[878]**

City and Regional Magazine Association **[18832]**

City of Ridgeland Chamber of Commerce **[61781]**

"City building department slow, costly, audit says" in *Crain's Detroit Business* (Vol. 16, No. 49, December 4, 2000, pp. 1) **[7286]**, **[40261]**

City of South Houston Chamber of Commerce **[65163]**

City of Tulelake Chamber of Commerce **[57422]**

City University of New York–Sponsored Research **[63190]**

City Wide Maintenance Franchise Co. **[3353]**

City Wok **[21783]**

CITYART MAGAZINE **[1624]**, **[1689]**, **[8030]**

Civil Engineering-ASCE **[3246]**

"CIWMB wants e-waste law signed, looks at zero waste, landfills" in *Solid Waste Report* (Vol. 34, No. 1, January 10, 2003) **[21223]**, **[40262]**

CLA Member Journal **[8914]**

Clackamas Community College–Small Business Development Center **[64164]**

Claflin Capital Management, Inc. **[61057]**

Claiborne Chamber of Commerce **[60627]**

Claiborne County Chamber of Commerce **[64896]**

CLAIMS /CITATION (1947-1970) **[44209]**

Clairborne Chamber of Commerce **[60628]**

"Claire's Baubles, Bangles, and Profits" in *Business Week Online* (February 8, 2005) **[9613]**, **[14862]**, **[51096]**

Clairol, Inc.–Research Library **[2625]**, **[7943]**, **[11850]**

Clairvest Group Inc. **[66720]**

Clallam Bay - Sekiu Chamber of Commerce **[66065]**

Clapp and Mayne, Inc.–Library **[16890]**

Clare Area Chamber of Commerce **[61279]**

Claremont Chamber of Commerce **[57423]**

Claremont Consulting Group **[3669]**, **[16587]**, **[31309]**, **[45992]**, **[53549]**

Claremont McKenna College–Reed Institute for Applied Statistics **[50394]**

Claremore Chamber of Commerce **[63970]**

Clarence Chamber of Commerce **[62858]**

"Clarence Otis Named CEO of Darden Restaurants" in *Black Enterprise* (Vol. 35, November 2004, No. 4, pp. 28) **[21473]**, **[45000]**

Clarendon Chamber of Commerce **[57145]**

Clarendon County Chamber of Commerce **[64731]**

Clarendon - Donley County Chamber of Commerce **[65164]**

Clarinda Chamber of Commerce **[60111]**

Clarinet for Beginners **[17632]**

Clarion Area Chamber of Business and Industry **[64401]**

Clarion Area Chamber of Commerce **[60112]**

"A clarion call: the tech and telecom sectors are finally on the mend" in *Barron's* (Vol. 82, No. 58, February 17, 2003, pp. 28) **[4618]**, **[4951]**, **[14863]**, **[16806]**, **[22940]**, **[24393]**, **[33671]**, **[37970]**, **[41604]**, **[50849]**

Clarion Capital Corp. **[63849]**

Clarion Inns, Hotels, Suites & Resorts **[12707]**, **[21784]**

"Clarion Partners buys 36 buildings in Atlanta" in *Atlanta Business Chronicle* (Vol. 25, December 20, 2002, No. 28, pp. 14A) **[20467]**, **[20834]**, **[27952]**, **[46240]**

Clarion University of Pennsylvania–Small Business Development Center **[64325]**

Claritas Demographics - Annual Update **[1395]**, **[32832]**

Clarity Capital **[61058]**

Clark Consulting International Inc. **[26624]**

Clark University

    George Perkins Marsh Institute–Center for Technology, Environment, and Development **[9514]**

    Small Business Development Center **[60905]**

Clarkdale Chamber of Commerce **[57024]**

Clarke County Chamber of Commerce **[61782]**

Clarkesville-Habersham County Library **[11012]**

Clarkesville Lake Country Chamber of Commerce **[65860]**

Clarksdale - Coahoma County Chamber of Commerce and Industry Foundation **[61783]**

Clarkston Area Chamber of Commerce **[61280]**

Clarkston Chamber of Commerce **[66066]**

Clarksville Area Chamber of Commerce **[64897]**

Clarksville Chamber of Commerce **[61942]**

Clarksville-Johnson County Chamber of Commerce **[57146]**

"A Class Act" in *Entrepreneur* (Vol. 32, December 2004, No. 12, pp. 61) **[26188]**, **[32316]**, **[33040]**, **[35946]**, **[45001]**

Class Action Litigation Report **[29652]**

"Class-Based Pensions: A Cost-Saving Alternative for Companies of All Sizes" in *Journal of Accountancy* (Vol. 199, January 2005) **[106]**, **[2885]**, **[23911]**, **[26189]**, **[26769]**, **[27099]**

"Class distinction" in *Entrepreneur* (Vol. 30, No. 1, January 2) **[13902]**, **[33672]**

"Class of their Own" in *Entrepreneur* (Vol. 31, No. 11, November 2003, pp. 126) **[5312]**, **[37558]**

"Class Reunion: Corporate Alumni Groups Keep Business Connections Going" in *Sales & Marketing Management* (Vol. 157, January 2005) **[42202]**, **[53647]**

A Classic Guide to Custom Deli Trays **[8527]**

Classic Handyman **[7659]**, **[20032]**

"A classical gas" in *Rough Notes* (Vol. 146, No. 4, April 2003, pp. 58) **[13236]**, **[16734]**, **[17996]**, **[43127]**

The Classroom Collection, Vol. 2: Basic Daylight Exposure and Equivalent Exposures **[19253]**

The Classroom Collection, Vol. 3: Metering and Exposure Controls **[19254]**

The Classroom Collection, Vol. 4: Advanced Camera Techniques **[19255]**

The Classroom Collection, Vol. 5: Black and White Techniques **[19256]**

The Classroom Collection, Vol. 6: Careers in Photography **[19257]**

Classy Maids **[8698]**

Clatskanie Chamber of Commerce **[64206]**

Clatstop Community College–Small Business Development Center **[64165]**

Clavier **[17616]**

Claxton-Evans County Chamber of Commerce - Welcome Center **[59079]**

Clay Center Area Chamber of Commerce **[60308]**

Clay County Chamber of Commerce **[56830]**, **[58773]**, **[59891]**, **[63349]**

Clay County Partnership Chamber of Commerce **[64898]**

Clay For Kids **[8106]**, **[33361]**

Claymore Engineering **[56655]**

Clayton Chamber of Commerce **[61943]**, **[63350]**

Clayton County Chamber of Commerce **[59080]**

Clayton/Curtis/Cottrell **[3670]**, **[30073]**, **[31310]**, **[38518]**, **[47843]**, **[53075]**

Clayton State University–Small Business Development Center **[59026]**

Clayton-Union County Chamber of Commerce **[62679]**

Cle Elum-Roslyn Chamber of Commerce **[66067]**

Clean Air News **[9376]**, **[37338]**

Clean Air Report **[9377]**

Clean & Clean USA LLC **[8926]**

Clean First Time, Inc. **[16681]**

Clean, Fresh & Friendly **[8528]**, **[51944]**

"Clean and Green" in *Entrepreneur* (Vol. 33, October 2005, No. 10, pp. 20) **[8900]**

Clean & Happy Windows **[3354]**

Clean Living Specialists **[3355]**

Clean Show - World Educational Congress for Laundering and Drycleaning **[8921]**

"A Clean Slate" in *Entrepreneur* (Vol. 31, No. 11, November 2003, pp. 94) **[35947]**, **[45002]**

"Clean Sweep" in *Entrepreneur* (Vol. 24, No. 7, July 1996, pp. 59) **[20012]**, **[52518]**

"A Clean Sweep: Take Your Work Environment from Cluttered to Clear with these Steps" in *Entrepreneur* (Vol. 32, July 2004, No. 7) **[20013]**, **[49492]**

"Clean-Water Company Begins a Growth Spurt" in *Portland Press Herald* (April 22, 2005) **[14864]**, **[25698]**, **[27953]**, **[49859]**

Clean Water Council **[25694]**

Clean Water Report **[25713]**

The Cleaning Authority **[3356]**, **[8699]**

Cleaning Consultant Services Inc. **[3338]**, **[3357]**, **[8696]**, **[8700]**, **[16682]**, **[25545]**, **[66245]**

Cleaning Management Conference and Exposition **[3336]**

Cleaning Management Institute **[3303]**

Cleaning & Restoration **[8422]**, **[25540]**

The Cleaning Supplier **[3273]**, **[11913]**

"Cleaning Up At Newsstands" in *Inc.* (August 1, 2003) **[18222]**, **[18860]**

"Cleaning Up in Health Care" in *Boston Business Journal* (Vol. 23, No. 27, August 8, 2003, pp. 16) **[17255]**, **[40985]**

"Cleaning Up" in *Small Business Opportunities* (Vol. 12, No. 3, May 2000, pp. 60) **[3289]**, **[35365]**, **[38619]**

Cleaning Up Toxics **[37351]**

Cleannet USA, Inc. **[3358]**

"Cleantech Becomes Catalyst" in *Crain's Detroit Business* (Vol. 22, November 20, 2006, No. 47, pp. 13) **[14865]**, **[35948]**, **[37257]**, **[55540]**

"Cleanup Delays Lessens Katrina's Economic Toll, Economist Says" in *Milwaukee Journal Sentinel* (December 21, 2005) **[7287]**, **[27954]**, **[32317]**

Clear Lake Area Chamber of Commerce **[60113]**, **[65165]**

Clear Lake Chamber of Commerce **[57424]**

Clear Lake Community Club **[66368]**

"The Clear Leader: Marcus Buckingham Has Spent a Lot of Time Watching Leadership At Its Best" in *Fast Company* (March 2005, No. 92) **[35949]**, **[45003]**

"Clear leadership" in *Women in Business* (Vol. 54, No. 5, September-October 2002, pp. 41) **[30520]**, **[35950]**, **[45004]**

Clear Light Books **[32178]**

"Clear as mud" in *Rough Notes* (Vol. 146, No. 4, April 2003, pp. 104) **[13237]**, **[43128]**

"Clear Sailing" in *Refrigerated & Frozen Foods* (Vol. 14, No. 7, July 2003, pp. 19) **[11597]**, **[23467]**, **[27955]**

ClearBra **[22668]**

"Clearer Regs on Wellness Programs in the Workplace" in *Kiplinger Letter* (Vol. 78, January 19, 2007, No. 2) [26770], [40263], [42837]

"A clearer view" in *Black Enterprise* (Vol. 33, No. 6, January 2003, pp. 43) [6608], [48988]

Clearfield Chamber of Commerce [64402]

Clearinghouse for Volunteer Accounting Services [26109]

Clearstone Venture Partners / Idealab! Capital Partners [57968]

"Clearwater Man Puts Technology To Work" in *Tampa Tribune* (November 27, 2005) [41605], [50850], [52078]

Clearwater Regional Chamber of Commerce [58774]

Cleburne Chamber of Commerce [65166]

Cleburne County Chamber of Commerce [56831]

"A CLEC Clicks" in *Boston Business Journal* (Vol. 23, No. 27, August 8, 2003, pp. 19) [4952], [41606]

Clements Lockeford Chamber of Commerce [57425]

Mark Clements Research Inc. [16860]

Clemson Area Chamber of Commerce [64732]

Clemson University
  College of Health, Education & Human Development–Learning Resource Center [18397]
  Office for Sponsored Programs [64794]
  Small Business Development Center [64690]

Clermont County Chamber of Commerce [63647]
  Ohio SBDC [63554]

Cleveland Area Chamber of Commerce [63971]

Cleveland-Bolivar County Chamber of Commerce [61784]

Cleveland Botanical Garden–Eleanor Squire Library [11514], [12160], [16092]

Cleveland/Bradley Chamber of Commerce [64899]

Cleveland Chamber of Commerce [66369]

Cleveland County Chamber of Commerce [63351]

Cleveland FES Center [19602]

Cleveland Health Sciences Library [18496]

Cleveland Institute of Art–Jessica R. Gund Memorial Library [6063], [8114]

Cleveland Institute of Music–Library [17672]

Cleveland Public Library
  Cleveland Research Center [47933]
  Literature Department [2811], [9054], [25504]
  Science and Technology Department [1221]

Cleveland Sport, Travel & Outdoor Show [2208], [5250]

Cleveland State Community College–Small Business Development Center [64853]

Cleveland State University
  Northern Ohio Data and Information Service–Maxine Goodman Levin College of Urban Affairs [66951]
  Office of Sponsored Programs and Research [63875]
  Research and Public Service Initiative [50395]

The Clevelander-Growth Association [63896]

Clevenger Associates [12693], [21716]

Clewiston Chamber of Commerce [58775]

"A Click Away: Automotive Web Sites are Revved Up and Ready to Help You Buy" in *Entrepreneur* (Vol. 31, No. 8, August 2003, pp. 22) [17997], [33673]

"Click on a Fortune" in *Small Business Opportunities* (Vol. 17, May 2005, No. 3, pp. 22-24, 26-28, 30, 32, 34, 36, 38, 40, 42, 44) [441], [1794], [3036], [4953], [7123], [17322], [18318], [18993], [20835], [24855], [33674], [38620], [38743], [39039], [41607], [52519], [55050]

"Click Here For Credit Info" in *Business Week* (No. 3761, December 10, 2001, pp.SB4) [4619], [22941], [31522], [53238]

"Clickalyzer www.clickalyzer.com" in *Entrepreneur* (Vol. 32, No. 1, January 2004, pp. 10) [585], [16807], [33675], [46805]

"Clicking for Cash" in *Business Week* (No. 3698, September 11, 2000, pp. F37) [27956], [33676], [37971]

"Clicking against the Current" in *Crain's Detroit Business* (Vol. 19, No. 9, March 3, 2003, pp. 3) [6609], [27100], [41608]

"Clicking with Hispanics" in *Hispanic Business* (March 2004, pp. 54, 56) [6610], [46806], [54158]

"Clicking online: mergers, consolidations predicted for Hispanic targeted Web sites in 2000" in *Hispanic Business* (Dec. 1999, pp. 60) [13903], [14866], [33677], [48105], [49860]

Clicking Through: A Survival Guide for Bringing Your Company Online [13904], [25817], [29152], [33678], [44016]

"Clicks to Bricks" in *Entrepreneur* (Vol. 33, August 2005, No. 8, pp. 44) [27478], [27957], [32675], [33679], [44686], [46807], [50574], [51097]

"Clicks, not licks, as Green Stamps go digital" in *The New York Times* (March 9, 2000, pp. D1, G1) [31660], [33680], [46808]

Clicktown International [14669], [26029]

Client-Centered Consulting: A Practical Guide for Internal Advisers and Trainers [16503], [31122]

ClieNT Server News [6983]

"Client Surveys Slow to Catch on as a Legal Marketing Tool" in *Journal Record (Oklahoma City, OK)* (February 8, 2007) [29153], [46809]

"Clients breathe easy thanks to outsourced tech support" in *Colorado Springs Business Journal* (March 7, 2003) [4620], [6148], [22136], [22942], [35366], [49682]

Clifton Chamber of Commerce [60309], [65167]

Clifton Springs Area Chamber of Commerce [62859]

"Climbing tech stocks can't match Nasdaq" in *Atlanta Business Chronicle* (Vol. 25, November 15; 2002, No. 23 pp. 7C) [9887], [14867], [37119]

"Clinic shut down as union vote neared" in *Crain's Detroit Business* (Vol. 19, No. 15, April 14, 2003, pp. 30) [17184], [55286]

Clinical Gerontologist [465], [18351]

Clinical Immunology [52253]

Clinical Laboratory Management Association [17176]

Clinical Laboratory News [41180]

Clinical and Laboratory Standards Institute [17177]

Clinical Leadership and Management Review [41181]

Clinical Ligand Assay Society [17178]

Clinical Pharmacology [8850]

Clinical Techniques in Small Animal Practice [1248]

Clinics in Laboratory Medicine [17205]

Clintar Groundskeeping Services [3359], [16074], [16151]

Clinton Area Chamber of Commerce [59471], [60114], [61944]

Clinton Chamber of Commerce [57147], [58523], [61785], [63972]

Clinton Community College–SBDC [62750]

Clinton County Chamber of Commerce [59892]

Clinton County Economic Partnership [64403]

Clinton - Oneida County Chamber of Commerce [62860]

Clinton-Sampson Chamber of Commerce [63352]

Clintonville Area Chamber of Commerce [66370]

Clipping Service Business Guide [5493]

CLIX [5420]

CLMA/ASCP Annual Conference and Exhibition (ThinkLab) [17224]

"Clocking In: For Low-Wage Workers, Overtime May Get More Lucrative" in *Entrepreneur* (Vol. 31, No. 7, July 2003, pp. 22) [40264], [42838]

"Clone yourself" in *WorkingWoman* (Vol. 25, No. 5, May 2000, pp. 79) [33041], [45005], [56164]

"Cloning Around" in *Entrepreneur* (Vol. 32, No. 1, January 2004, pp. 130) [35951], [38744]

"Cloning: Venture capitalists decline a visit to the animal farm" in *Red Herring* (No. 103, September 1, 2001, pp. 34) [41609], [55541]

Cloquet Carlton Area Chamber of Commerce [61572]

"A Close Call: Cell Phone Offers Good Mix of Price and Performance" in *Black Enterprise* (Vol. 35, January 2005, No. 6, pp. 50) [4954], [48989]

"Close to Finding RedZone's Niche" in *Pittsburgh Business Times* (Vol. 4, August 15, 2003, pp. 14) [30521], [41610], [45006], [46810]

"Close to Home" in *Entrepreneur* (Vol. 33, February 2005, No. 2, pp. 69) [586], [13905], [33681], [46811]

"Close-Knit" in *Forbes* (December 25, 2000, pp. 134) [37610], [49861]

"Close the Loop" in *Entrepreneur* (Vol. 31, No. 10, October 2003, pp. 82) [27958], [49683], [53648]

"Close Shave" in *Portland Press Herald* (September 28, 2005) [11786], [37611], [53649]

"Close Up: Teen Sensations" in *Entrepreneur* (Vol. 28, No. 11, November 2000, pp. 24) [35367], [56718]

"Closer Call" in *Entrepreneur* (Vol. 33, October 2005, No. 10, pp. 85) [40404], [42203], [51590]

"Closet Capers; There Are Closets, Then There Are Closets. Step Inside Three Designer Closets That Are Much More" in *Sarasota Herald-Tribune* [20014]

The Closet Factory [20033]

Closets by Design Franchising [20034]

Closets & Storage Concepts [20035]

"Closing Bell: TiVo" in *Business Week* (February 14, 2005, No. 3920, pp. 42) [4098], [9888], [14868], [24394]

"Closing the Book on Public Records" in *Kiplinger's Personal Finance Magazine* (Vol. 55, No. 1, January, 2001, pp. 26) [13906], [29154], [33682]

"Closing Raises Loan Questions" in *Pittsburgh Business Times* (Vol. 23, No. 3, August 8, 2003, pp. 1) [27959], [51098]

Closing the Sale: A Process Not a Problem [51591]

Cloth by the Yard [5589]

Clothes Mentor [9660]

"Clothes-Minded" in *Entrepreneur* (Vol. 31, No. 8, August 2003, pp. 102) [2122], [5265]

Clothes That Fit [5590]

Clothing Around the World [5591]

Clothing and Fashion: A History [5592]

Clothing Manufacturers Association-News Bulletin [5581]

Clothing Manufacturers Association of the U.S.A. [5267]

Clothing Sewing Techniques Series [5593]

Cloud County Community College–Small Business Development Center [60257]

Cloudcroft Chamber of Commerce [62680]

"Clouds Pass and Tourism Forecast is Sunny as Ever" in *Miami Herald* (March 10, 2005) [12536], [24677], [25171]

Cloverdale Area Chamber of Commerce [59893]

Cloverdale Chamber of Commerce [57426]

Clovis Community College–Small Business Development Center [62644]

Clovis - Curry County Chamber of Commerce [62681]
  Small Business Development Center [62645]

Clovis District Chamber of Commerce [57427]

Clowns of America, International [18723]

Club 50 Fitness [19501]

"Club Meds: Could Drug-Buying Clubs Cure High Prescription Costs?" in *Entrepreneur* (Vol. 32, November 2004, No. 11, pp. 24) [40986], [53650]

"Club Planet Takes Off" in *Small Business Opportunities* (Vol. 17, May 2005, No. 3, pp. 72) [2335], [33683], [46812]

Club Z! In-Home Tutoring [25476]

"Clubs merge" in *Des Moines Business Record* (Vol. 18, No. 41, October 14, 2002, pp. 16) [2336], [49862]

"Clueing in customers." in *Harvard Business Review* (Vol. 81, No. 2, February 2003, pp. 100) [31661], [46813], [50575]

"The clumsy multinational" in *Harvard Business Review* (Vol. 80, No. 9, September 2002, pp. 128) [39234], [48529]

Clutch Doctors [22669]

"Collecting Pesky Past Due Debts" in *My Business* (September/October 2001, pp. 39) **[31525]**

Collection-Master **[8414]**

Collection Resource System **[8415]**

Collection Techniques for Small Business **[31526]**

Collections & Credit Risk **[8409]**, **[31611]**

Collective Bargaining Contract Library **[55336]**

Collective Bargaining Contract Settlements **[55337]**

Collective Bargaining Negotiations and Contracts **[55324]**

"CollectiveGood and eBay Team Up to Recycle Cell Phones for Charity" in *PR Newswire* (March 25, 2004) **[1796]**, **[4955]**, **[33686]**, **[54159]**

Collector **[8410]**

Collector Car Appraisers Association **[1431]**

Collectors Club–Library **[5866]**

Collectors Club of Chicago–Library **[5867]**

The Collectors Club Philatelist **[5841]**

Collectors Mart Magazine Resource Guide **[1316]**, **[5898]**

Collectors News **[1344]**, **[5923]**

"Collectors Still Flock to Classic Vintage Posters" in *Art Business News* (Vol. 28, No. 4, April 2001, pp. 1) **[1603]**, **[5899]**

College Accounting: A Small Business Approach **[26190]**

College & Career Guide News for College Students **[56775]**

College of DuPage–Small Business Development Center **[59365]**

College of Eastern Utah at San Juan Campus–Small Business Development Center **[65684]**

College of Family Physicians of Canada - Ontario Chapter **[40932]**

College of Forestry and Conservation–Institute for Tourism and Recreation Research **[24787]**, **[25354]**, **[62213]**

College of Lake County–Small Business Development Center **[59366]**

"A College Lockout?" in *Hispanic Business* (October 2002, pp. 30-32, 34) **[33045]**, **[45012]**

College of the Mainland–Small Business Development Center **[65027]**

College Music Society Annual Meeting **[17651]**, **[17803]**

College Nannies **[5421]**

College of Optometrists in Vision Development **[25629]**

College of Southern Idaho
    Business Incubator **[59341]**
    School of Vo-Tech Education **[59350]**

College of Southern Idaho (Region IV)–Small Business Development Center **[59275]**

College of Southern Maryland
    Southern Maryland SBDC–SBDC **[60796]**
    Southern Maryland Studies Center **[11090]**

College of Staten Island–SBDC **[62752]**

College Store Executive **[3056]**

The College Student's Resume Guide **[22043]**

"College Students Take on eBay: CollegeJunktion.com, Where Your Junk Becomes Treasure" in *PR Newswire* (February 14, 2005) **[1797]**, **[13908]**

College of West Virginia (Beckley Area)–SBDC **[66255]**

College of William and Mary
    Center for Archaeological Research **[1579]**
    Mason School of Business–Professional Resource Center **[39745]**

Collegiate Reformed Dutch Church–Library **[11013]**

Colleyville Area Chamber of Commerce **[65170]**

Colliers International **[21077]**

Collierville Area Chamber of Commerce **[64900]**

Collin County Community College–Small Business Development Center **[65028]**

Collin County Genealogical Society–Library **[11014]**

Collingsworth Chamber of Commerce **[65171]**

"Collins & Aikman Corp. (NYSE: CKC)" in *Crain's Detroit Business* (Vol. 16, No. 49, December 4, 2000, pp. 4) **[14873]**

"Collins & Aikman Faces Risk with Futura" in *Crain's Detroit Business* (Vol. 19, No. 45, November 10, 2003, pp. 29) **[1922]**, **[46244]**, **[48073]**

Collins Publications **[58258]**

Collinson, Howe, and Lennox **[58586]**

Collinsville Chamber of Commerce **[59472]**, **[63974]**

The Collision Shop **[2045]**

David Collison **[23302]**

Coloma-Watervliet Area Chamber of Commerce **[61281]**

Colombian American Association **[43486]**

Colonial Beach Chamber of Commerce **[65881]**

Colonial Heights Chamber of Commerce **[65882]**

Colonial Heritage Consultants Ltd. **[49409]**

Colonial Life & Accident Insurance Company–Archives and Library **[13594]**

The Colonial Newsletter **[5842]**

Colonie Chamber of Commerce **[62862]**

Colony Chamber of Commerce **[65172]**

Color and Black and White Television Theory and Servicing **[24335]**

"Color-Blind?" in *Entrepreneur* (Vol. 32, December 2004, No. 12, pp. 49) **[6611]**, **[48990]**

Color-Glo International **[22740]**

Color Management for Digital Publishing **[53170]**

Color Me Mine Franchising, Inc. **[8285]**

"Color Me Successful" in *Inc.* (September 1, 2004) **[12876]**, **[20112]**

Color Q Connection **[47784]**

The Color Resource Digital Design Source **[19941]**

"Color Scheme" in *Entrepreneur* (Vol. 32, No. 1, January 2004, pp. 39) **[6612]**, **[48991]**

Color Seal Inc. **[2046]**

Color Your World **[18694]**

Colorado Calligraphers' Guild Newsletter **[4171]**

Colorado City Area Chamber of Commerce **[65173]**

Colorado Department of Local Affairs–Division of Local Government **[66835]**

Colorado Economic and Demographic Information System **[1396]**

Colorado Job Finder **[58480]**

"Colorado Man Helped Contribute to Overseas Tech Development" in *Colorado Springs Business Journal* (February 28, 2003) **[16231]**, **[35952]**, **[41612]**, **[43589]**

Colorado Mountain College–Alpine Campus Library **[12742]**, **[54100]**

Colorado Northwestern Community College (Craig) **[58476]**

Colorado Office of Business Development–Minority Business Office **[58439]**

Colorado Office of Economic Development–Small Business Development Center **[58289]**

Colorado Office of Economic Development International Trade
    Minority Business Office **[58440]**
    Small Business Development Center **[58313]**

Colorado Procurement Technical Assistance Center–Denver Small Business Development Procurement Center **[58465]**

Colorado RV Adventure Travel Show **[24770]**

Colorado SBDC–Office of Economic Development **[58290]**

Colorado Senate Committee on Business Affairs and Labor **[58479]**

Colorado Springs Business Journal (March 7, 2003); "Business ethics issues cross all boundaries" in **[94]**, **[23901]**, **[26177]**, **[37395]**

Colorado Springs Business Journal (March 7, 2003); "Canadian online pharmacy to open Springs storefront" in **[8777]**, **[33647]**

Colorado Springs Business Journal (March 7, 2003); "Clients breathe easy thanks to outsourced tech support" in **[4620]**, **[6148]**, **[22136]**, **[22942]**, **[35366]**, **[49682]**

Colorado Springs Business Journal (February 28, 2003); "Colorado Man Helped Contribute to Overseas Tech Development" in **[16231]**, **[35952]**, **[41612]**, **[43589]**

Colorado Springs Business Journal (March 7, 2003); "Commentary: Good customer service-a ghost of retail's past?" in **[31663]**, **[51105]**

Colorado Springs Business Journal (March 7, 2003); "Green industry finding ways to thrive, despite restrictions" in **[16015]**

Colorado Springs Business Journal (February 28, 2003); "KILO still rockin' after 25 years in the business" in **[20321]**, **[36408]**

Colorado Springs Business Journal (February 28, 2003); "Licensed massage therapist helps high performers" in **[17005]**, **[17903]**

Colorado Springs Business Journal (March 7, 2003); "Major food company backs trendy sandwich shop" in **[8515]**, **[12057]**, **[21555]**

Colorado Springs Business Journal (December 10, 2004); "Personal Shoppers Give Clients a Stress-Free Alternative to Shopping" in **[19004]**, **[51288]**

Colorado Springs Business Journal (March 7, 2003); "Rocky Mountain Steel Mill, a decade and counting" in **[46420]**

Colorado Springs Business Journal (July 23, 2004); "Senior In-Home Care a Burgeoning Business" in **[458]**, **[18336]**, **[38903]**

Colorado Springs Small Business Development Center–University of Colorado at Colorado Springs **[58294]**

Colorado (State) Department of Labor & Employment–Labor Market Information Library **[23430]**

Colorado State University
    Agricultural and Resources Economics **[66836]**
    Center for Research on Communication and Technologies **[27712]**
    Human Performance Laboratory **[19603]**
    Industrial Assessment Center **[37374]**
    Office of Vice President for Research **[58466]**
    Solar Energy Applications Laboratory **[23354]**

Colorado State University Libraries–Morgan Library **[66837]**

Colorado State University Research Foundation **[58467]**

Colorado Technical University–Library **[6222]**

Colorado Technology Incubator **[58468]**

Colorado University Business Advancement Centers **[58314]**

Colorado Venture Management / CVM Equity Funds **[58449]**

ColoradoBiz (Vol. 30, No. 1, January 2003, pp. 61); "Van Briggle Art Pottery" in **[8186]**, **[8279]**, **[37808]**

ColorChef Custom Painters **[18718]**

Colored Stone-Tucson Show Guide Issue **[15862]**

Colors on Parade **[2047]**

Colors and Shapes Circus **[5377]**

Colortyme **[21377]**

Colquitt - Miller County Chamber of Commerce **[59082]**

Colter's Bar-B-Q **[21785]**

Colton Chamber of Commerce **[57429]**

Colucci, Blendow & Johnson **[17138]**, **[17274]**

Columbia-Adair County Chamber of Commerce **[60494]**

Columbia Capital Group, Inc. **[58673]**

Columbia Chamber of Commerce **[61945]**

Columbia City Area Chamber of Commerce **[59894]**

Columbia Consultants **[3671]**, **[23415]**, **[31311]**

Columbia County Chamber of Commerce **[62863]**

"Columbia Credit Union branch targets 21st-century crowd" in *Vancouver, WA Business Journal* (February 28, 2003) **[37973]**, **[44494]**

Columbia Falls Area Chamber of Commerce **[62155]**

Columbia Falls Area Chamber Foundation **[62156]**

Columbia Gorge Community College–SBDC **[64166]**

Columbia Montour Chamber of Commerce **[64404]**

Columbia River Economic Development Council–Small Business Development Center **[66017]**

Columbia River Inter-Tribal Fish Commission–StreamNet Library **[10477]**

Columbia University
    Center for Social Policy and Practice in the Workplace **[54399]**
    Columbia Institute for Tele-Information **[24317]**
    Institute of Human Nutrition **[18523]**
    New York Obesity Research Center **[26068]**
    Office of Projects and Grants **[63192]**
    Science and Technology Ventures **[63193]**

Complementary Alternative Medical Association [19556]

Complete Body Massage [17019]

Complete Book of Business Forms [27624]

The Complete Book of Business Forms and Agreements [27625], [29161]

The Complete Book of Business Plans: Simple Steps to Writing a Powerful Business Plan [29828]

Complete Book of Business Schools [32985]

The Complete Book of Collection Letters, Telephone Collection Scripts, and Faxes [31527]

The Complete Book of Raising Capital [55547]

The Complete Business Guide for a Profitable Internet, BBS, or Online Service [3396], [13916]

Complete Business Management Guide for Kitchen & Bathroom Professionals: Starting & Staying in Business [7193], [29719]

The Complete Credits and Collection Starter Success Kit [8348], [8379], [31528]

The Complete Customer Service Letter Book [31666]

The Complete Demographic Reference Guide [27967]

The Complete Direct Marketing Sourcebook: A Step-by-Step Guide to Organizing and Managing a Successful Direct Marketing Program [16431]

Complete Employee Handbook: A Step-by-Step Guide to Create a Custom Handbook That Protects Both the Employer and the Employee [29162], [42840]

The Complete Games Trainers Play [33048]

The Complete Garage [20037]

The Complete Gift Basket Industry Reference Directory [11106]

Complete Guide to Building & Outfitting an Office in Your Home [49493]

The Complete Guide to Consulting Success [3512], [31125]

The Complete Guide to Food Service Success: What You Need to Know to Plan a Profitable Operation [8510], [21475]

The Complete Guide to Greeting Card Design and Illustration [11560]

The Complete Guide to Home Roofing Installation and Maintenance [22062]

Complete Guide for Horse Business Success [12460]

The Complete Guide to Making Money at Home: Everything You Need to Know to Earn Riches at Home [42505]

Complete Guide to Public Employment [23370]

The Complete Guide to Publicity: Maximize Visibility for Your Products, Services & Organizations [46827], [50579]

The Complete Guide to Selling Your Business [52393], [52415]

The Complete Guide to Telemarketing Management [24282]

The Complete Handbook of Dog Training [19110]

The Complete Handbook of Profitable Trade Show Exhibiting [24909]

Complete Home Taxidermy [24268]

Complete Idiot's Guide to Buying & Selling a Business [30672], [52416]

The Complete Idiot's Guide to Finance for Small Business [35964], [37980], [39244]

Complete Idiot's Guide to Starting an Ebay Business [1759], [8380], [18628], [31019], [31529], [33422], [39042]

Complete Idiot's Guide to Starting Your Own Business [52834]

The Complete Illustrated Guide to Everything Sold in Hardware Stores [11879]

The Complete Information Bank for Entrepreneurs & Small Business Managers [52835]

Complete Music [18743]

The Complete Scholarship Book [7052]

Complete Secretary's Handbook [25520]

The Complete Small Business Guide: A Sourcebook for New and Small Businesses [35965], [39245]

The Complete Small-Business Sourcebook: Information, Services & Experts Every Small & Home-Based Business Needs [42594]

The Complete Small Business Start-up Guide [498], [13738], [29720], [33423], [39043], [42153], [44397], [46565], [52366]

Complete Speakers' and Toastmasters' Library [22486]

The Complete Startup Guide for the Black Entrepreneur [35373], [39044], [47950]

Complex Derivatives: Understanding and Managing the Risks of Exotic Options, Complex Swaps, Warrants, and Other Synthetic Derivatives [14879]

Compliance Action [40859]

Compliance Consultants [40881]

Compliance Consulting Corp. [27017]

Compliance Guide for Plan Administrators [27055]

Compliance Systems Inc. [32179]

"Compliments to Piropos" in *Ingram's* (Vol. 28, No. 5, May 2002, pp. 52) [21476], [35966], [37612]

Complying with the ADA: A Small Business Guide to Hiring and Employing the Disabled [32009], [42207]

Complying with the Americans with Disabilities Act: A Guidebook for Management and People with Disabilities [32010]

"Composing a Conference; Motor City Music Festival Racing to Find Paying Sponsors" in *Crain's Detroit Business* (January 17, 2005) [17734], [20309], [22487], [24397], [24910], [55077]

"Composite forecasting: combining forecasts for improved accuracy" in *Journal of Business Forecasting* (Vol.19,No. 2,Summer 2000, pp. 2) [30523]

Composites eNews 52233

Composites in Manufacturing [46501]

Composting Council of Canada [37227]

Composting News [9378], [21270], [26571], [37339]

Compoundings [46502]

Comprehensive Care of Elderly [18369]

The Comprehensive Financial Planning System [10355]

Comprehensive Integrated Payroll System: CHIPS–Donald R. Frey and Company, Inc. [18803]

Comprehensive Planning Services [30075], [38521]

Comprehensive Professional Management Inc. [26422], [27018], [29608], [38522]

Comprehensive Proofreading [27240]

Compton Chamber of Commerce [57431]

Compucentre/CompuSmart/CompuSmart Express [6895]

Compuchild Services of America [5751], [6372], [24850]

"Compulsory ethics education and the cognitive moral development of salespeople" in *Journal of Business Ethics* (Vol. 28, No. 3) [20474], [33049], [37405], [51593]

CompuMath Citation Index [6220], [6386], [7008]

CompuSystems, Inc. [18804]

Computer-Aided Software Engineering: Issues and Trends for the 1990s and Beyond [22944]

Computer Applications for Business Planning: A Practical Hands-On Text [29829]

Computer Applications: Lifestyle [6352]

"Computer-Assisted Consulting" in *Hispanic Business* (Vol. 24, No. 5, May 2002, pp. 50) [3513], [4622], [22945], [29830], [46828], [51594], [53240]

Computer Assisted Language Instruction Consortium [6323]

Computer and Automated Systems Association of Society of Manufacturing Engineers [6921]

Computer Builders Warehouse [6896]

Computer Communication Networks [14659]

Computer Connections Inc. [49410], [49596]

Computer Consulting on Your Home-Based PC [6467], [42595]

Computer Database [6309], [6387], [6537], [6905], [7009]

Computer Ethics [6468], [22946]

"A Computer on Every Desk: Online Learning Takes Off" in *Long Island Business News* (February 27, 2004) [4623], [6613], [13917], [22947], [33050], [33696]

Computer Fest [6207]

The Computer Game Company Directory [4624], [22948]

Computer Game Developers' Conference [6892], [23298], [55210]

The Computer Glossary: The Complete Illustrated Desk Reference [48995]

Computer Industry Almanac [3397]

Computer and Information Systems Abstracts [6310], [6388], [7010]

Computer Integrations Inc. [6999]

Computer Link Magazine [6195], [6882]

Computer Link Professional Services and Software Training Center [59214]

Computer Literacy Series [6353]

The Computer Literacy Training Series [6354], [6526]

Computer Medics of America, Inc. [6430]

Computer Network Software Functions (82-1XX) [6989]

"Computer Recycling Bill Sent to California Governor" in *San Jose Mercury News* (September 1, 2002) [6614], [21224], [24336], [40271]

"Computer Recycling Clicks in San Jose, Calif." in *San Jose Mercury News* (September 15, 2002) [6615], [21225]

Computer Renaissance [6897]

Computer Science Education [6340]

Computer Science Index [6341]

Computer Sciences Corporation–Corporate Library [6541], [7018]

Computer Software [22949]

Computer Technology Law Report [29653]

The Computer Training Library [6355]

Computer Troubleshooters [6431]

Computer Troubleshooters Ltd. [6432]

Computer U Learning Centers [6373]

Computerized Investing [3428]

Computers: From Pebbles to Programs [6356]

ComputerTalk for the Pharmacist-Buyers Guide Issue [8779]

Computertots/Computer Explorers [6374]

Computerworld [6311], [6389], [6498], [7011]

Computerworld (Vol. 39, August 22, 2005, No. 34, pp. 33); "Awaiting the PC Killers" in [6587], [22177]

Computing Canada (Vol. 28, No. 21, October 25, 2002, pp. 1); "Canadian companies ponder best options for e-waste" in [6602], [21220], [41588]

Computing Canada (September 13, 2002, pp. 22); "Hewlett-Packard leading the assault on e-waste" in [6674], [21236], [41734]

Computing Reviews (CR) [6499]

"Computing Riches" in *Small Business Opportunities* (Vol. 12, No. 3, May 2000, pp. 108, 130) [35374]

Computing Surveys (CSUR) [6500]

Computing Technology Industry Association-Membership Directory [6193], [6616]

Computists' Weekly [23275]

"Compuware to Buy Back up to 34 Million Shares" in *Crain's Detroit Business* (Vol. 22, December 18, 2006, No. 51 pp. 4) [6617], [14880], [29831], [41616]

COMsciences Inc. [27580], [50723]

Comtex (April 1, 2004); "Sell2All Launches DropShop Services for Selling on eBay" in [1850], [6100], [7173], [16466], [18662], [34454], [52584]

Comtronic Debtmaster: Software for Debt Collection [8416]

"Con Artists Target Collision Industry" in *Automotive Body Repair* [11215], [22611], [30208]

"Con Fusion" in *Entrepreneur* (Vol. 33, February 2005, No. 2, pp. 53) [14881], [37981]

ConAgra Grocery Products–R&D Technical Library [10651]

Concept Development Associates Inc. [55972]

ConcepTrac [8523], [12061], [21676]

"A conceptual mistake in the calculation of social security taxes" in *Tax Notes* (Vol. 97, No. 2, October 14, 2002, pp. 283-285) [108], [23914], [26192], [54498]

Concerned Children's Advertisers [518]

Convenience Caterers and Food Manufacturers Association [4525]

"Convenience pushes pendulum back to PPO coverage" in *Crain's Detroit Business* (Vol. 18, No. 16, April 22) [13246], [26776], [37617], [43137], [53662]

Convenience Stores Directory [7773]

"Convention Calendar" in *Black Enterprise* (Vol. 35, September 2004, No. 2, pp. 64) [11254], [22488], [23204], [23218], [24913], [25757], [26119], [33052], [35971], [39253], [45021], [45832], [48111], [54974], [55080], [56022], [56174]

"Conventions" in *Crain's Chicago Business* (Vol. 30, January 2007, No. 5, pp. 15) [24914], [33053], [39254]

"ConventionSouth Honors Jackson CVB" in *Mississippi Business Journal* (Vol. 29, January 2007, No. 2, pp. 28) [7126], [7774], [24915], [30674]

"Convergence" in *Inc.* (November 15, 2000, pp. 88) [13925], [33704]

Convergence Partners [57975]

"Convergent Fund VI Hits $64M Mark" in *Venture Capital Journal* (Vol. 40, No. 10, November 2000, pp. 26) [55552]

Converging Communications Technologies 6471, 6647

"A Conversation with George Jackson, Detroit Economic Growth Corp." in *Crain's Detroit Business* (Vol. 21, January 3, 2005, No. 1) [23715], [32331]

"Conversation with Martha Rogers" in *Inc.* (November 15, 2000, pp. 69) [31670]

"Conversation with Randy Hinrichs" in *Inc.* (November 15, 2000, pp. 83) [33424], [43949]

"A Conversation With Duane Tarnacki, Clark Hill PLC" in *Crain's Detroit Business* (Vol. 21, November 7, 2005, No. 45, pp. 25) [10732], [54502]

"A Conversation With Michael Beauregard, Huron Capital Partners" in *Crain's Detroit Business* (Vol. 21, January 31, 2005, No. 5) [14886], [32332], [49875]

"A Conversation With Robin Asher, Clark Hill, LLC" in *Crain's Detroit Business* (Vol. 23, February 5, 2007, No. 6, pp. 11) [29166], [35972], [40283], [44017]

"A Conversation With Steve Cassin, Macomb County Director of Planning and Economic Development" in *Crain's Detroit Business* (Vol. 21) [27978], [32333], [52660]

Conversion Watch [15638]

"ConversionCenter.com Specializes in Customer Service and Conversion Van Sales on Website" in *PR Newswire* (January 12, 2005) [7127], [18001]

"Convicts Stealing Small Business Jobs" in *My Business* (September/October 2001, pp. 19) [40002], [53663]

Conway Area Chamber of Commerce [57148], [64733]

Conway Village Area Chamber of Commerce [62402]

Conyers-Rockdale Chamber of Commerce [59083]

Cook Area Chamber of Commerce [61575]

Martin Cook Associates Ltd. [2790]

Cook County Chamber of Commerce [59473]

Cook International Inc. [54362]

Peter Cooke Associates [21717]

Cookeville Area-Putnam County Chamber of Commerce [64901]

Cookie Cutters Haircuts for Kids [11826]

"Cooking Again" in *Hispanic Business* (June 2005, pp. 78) [10619], [37618]

Cooking for Profit [4559], [7818], [12062], [21677]

"Cooking Up a Winner in Manny Garcia's Kitchen" in *Orlando Business Journal* (Vol. 20, No. 2, June 27, 2003, pp. 26) [21186], [21478], [45022], [45610]

Cookware Manufacturers Association [12175]

"A Cool $2 Billion" in *Hispanic Business* (June 2005, pp. 32, 34, 36, 38) [7302], [20845], [35973]

"Cool New Software, Free of Charge" in *Inc.* (November 2006, pp. 42-43) [3944], [4626], [22951], [33705], [53242]

"Cool Novelty Cups" in *Dairy Foods* (Vol. 102, No. 10, October 2001, pp. 50) [12768], [46838]

"Cool Pics" in *Entrepreneur.com* (Vol. 34, February 2006, No. 2, pp. 47) [4182], [4961], [13926], [48997]

"Cool Tools" in *Inc.* (November 15, 2000, pp. 145) [13927], [25821], [33706], [46839]

"Cool Tools" in *My Business* (October/November 2003, pp. 25) [4183], [4962], [5116], [6587], [6618], [6867], [7219], [7722], [18600], [20310], [22201], [22820], [26195], [27334], [32701], [33707], [48998], [50991]

"Cool Tools: Take Adobe Acrobat to the next level with Compose 4.1" in *Entrepreneur* (Vol. 30, No. 2, February 2002, pp. 34) [4627], [22952], [53243]

Coolidge Chamber of Commerce [57025]

Cooling Technology Institute [25740]

Cooper Institute for Aerobics Research [19546]

Cooper Union Research Foundation [63194]

"Cooperation Needed for Budget Priorities" in *Crain's Detroit Business* (Vol. 21, January 31, 2005, No. 5, pp. 8) [27105], [32334]

"Cooperation vs. conflict" in *Incentive* (Vol. 174, No. 7, July 2000, pp. 78) [31671], [51598]

Cooperstown Chamber of Commerce [62865]

Coopersville Area Chamber of Commerce [61282]

"Coordinating Staff With IT Technology" in *Ingram's* (Vol. 27, No. 8, August 2001, pp. 23) [13928], [22953], [33054], [45023], [53244]

"Coordination of Overseas Efforts is Sought" in *Detroit Free Press* (October 23, 2006) [12951], [43596]

Coors Brewing Company–Technical Library [3161]

"COOs: Less Room At the Top" in *Business Week* (January 31, 2005, pp. 11) [13929], [45024], [53664]

Copiah-Lincoln Community College–Small Business Development Center [61742]

"Coping with change" in *Women In Business* (Vol. 52, No. 3, May 2000, pp. 22) [35974], [56175]

Coping and Home Safety Tips for Caregivers of the Elderly [18370]

"Coping secrets for new stay-at-home Moms" in *Women In Business* (Vol. 52, No. 4, July 2000, pp. 18) [56176]

Copley Venture Partners [61061]

Coppell Chamber of Commerce [65178]

Copper Basin Chamber of Commerce [57026]

"Copper Prices Hover Near Record Highs" in *Milwaukee Journal Sentinel* (December 17, 2005) [46249]

Copperas Cove Chamber of Commerce and Visitors Bureau [65179]

"Copy Cop Fights Back, Takes the Digital Plunge" in *Boston Business Journal* (Vol. 23, No. 30, August 29, 2003, pp. 4) [30828], [41618], [44499], [46840]

Copy Editor [27694]

"Copy Talk" in *Entrepreneur* (Vol. 32, October 2004, No. 10, pp. 54) [6619], [48999]

"Copy That" in *Entrepreneur* (Vol. 31, Oct. 2003) [7843], [49000]

"Copy This: An Authenticity Check of High-End Handbags" in *Black Enterprise* (Vol. 34, No. 3, October 2003, pp. 140) [5530], [9615]

"Copy this" in *BlackEnterprise* (Vol. 32, No. 3, October 2001, pp. 59) [13930], [19870]

Copyright Clearance Center [7841]

Copyrights, Patents and Trademarks [44018]

Copywriting I [8976]

Copywriting II [8977]

Coquille Chamber of Commerce and Visitor Information Center [64208]

COR Healthcare Market Strategist [12388]

Coral Gables Chamber of Commerce [58778]

Coral Springs Chamber of Commerce [58779]

Coral Ventures [61696]

Cora's Breakfast and Lunch [21786]

Corbeil Electromenagers [1424]

Corcoran Chamber of Commerce [57432]

CORD [33389]

Cordele-Crisp Chamber of Commerce [59084]

Cordell Chamber of Commerce [63976]

CorDev Financial Inc. [50309]

Cordova Capital (Montgomery) [56905]

Cordova Chamber of Commerce [56952]

Cordova Ventures / Cordova Capital (Alpharetta) [59188]

Core Capital Partners [58674]

The Corlund Group L.L.C. [3677], [16590], [31319], [35221], [45998], [53077]

Corn Dog Factory [21787]

Cornelius Chamber of Commerce [64209]

Donna Cornell Enterprises Inc. [16591], [20179], [31320], [33342], [37049], [50492], [56542]

Cornell Feline Health Center [1234]

The Cornell Hotel and Restaurant Administration Quarterly [12660], [21678]

Cornell University

    Bailey Hortorium Library [11515]

    Baker Institute for Animal Health [1283]

    Cornell BioRobotics and Locomotion Laboratory [2517]

    Cornell Business and Technology Park [63195]

    Cornell Center for Technology, Enterprise and Commercialization [63196]

    Cornell Cooperative Extension–New York State Integrated Pest Management Program [19053]

    Cornell Feline Health Center [1284]

    Cornell Institute for Social and Economic Research (CISER) Data Archive [66937]

    Cornell Waste Management Institute [21296]

    Department of City Regional Planning–Program in International Studies in Planning [1580], [50396]

    Johnson Graduate School of Management–Library [51498]

    The Nestle Library [12743], [22034]

    Office of Sponsored Programs [63197]

    School of Industrial and Labor Relations–Martin P. Catherwood Library [56683]

    Schwardt Laboratory [19054]

Cornerstone Equity Investors, LLC [63075]

Cornhusker Better Business Bureau [62238]

Corning Area Chamber of Commerce [57149]

Corning Capital / Corning Technology Ventures [61062], [61313]

Corning Community College–Small Business Development Center [62753]

Corning District Chamber of Commerce [57433]

"Cornucopia" in *Forbes* (Vol. 175, January 10, 2005, No. 1, pp. 145) [14887], [26496]

Corona Chamber of Commerce [57434]

Corona Del Mar Chamber of Commerce [57435]

Coronado Chamber of Commerce [57436]

"Coronado: Program Looks to Empower Restaurateurs" in *San Diego Business Journal* (Vol. 28, January 15, 2007, No. 3, pp. 17) [21479], [49876]

Coronado Venture Fund [57088]

Coronary Artery Disease [41310]

A Corporate A'Fair, Inc. [2534]

Corporate Affiliations Library [39255]

The Corporate Body Franchise, L.L.C. [41339]

Corporate Business Services of America Inc. [50310], [52473]

Corporate Business Taxation Monthly [24083]

"Corporate Cases" in *Business Week* (January 23, 2006, No. 3968, pp. 37-38) [14888], [29167]

Corporate Caterers [4570]

"Corporate Coffers Full of Cash" in *Kansas City Star* (March 8, 2005) [14889], [27979], [32335], [37983]

"Corporate Collateral" in *Entrepreneur* (Vol. 28, No. 7, July 2000, pp. 38) [44500], [48901], [55553]

Corporate Consulting Inc. [3678], [16592], [31321], [38524], [45999], [53078]

Corporate Crisis and Risk Management: Modeling, Strategies and SME Application [35975], [39256], [45025]

Corporate Directions [54881]

"Courses going green with gray water" in *Atlanta Business Chronicle* (Vol. 25, No. 20, October 25, 2002, pp. A3) **[11255]**, **[16008]**

"Court Battle Pits Fridge Pack vs. FridgeMaster" in *Atlanta Business Chronicle* (Vol. 26, No. 10, August 15, 2003, pp. 1) **[29172]**, **[44019]**, **[46846]**

"Court Battles" in *Business Week* (December 19, 2005, No. 3964, pp. 33-34) **[29173]**, **[41620]**, **[44020]**

"Court Decisions - Privacy coverage differs from patent infringement" in *Rough Notes* (Vol. 145, No. 1, January 2003, pp. 10) **[13247]**, **[29174]**, **[43138]**, **[44021]**

"Court Expands Accommodation Obligations in Retail Stores" in *Employment Relations Today* (Vol. 26, No. 4, Winter 2000, pp. 119) **[51116]**

"Court OKs Meridian Ch. 11 Plan" in *Crain's Detroit Business* (Vol. 22, December 11, 2006, No. 50, pp. 6) **[29175]**, **[37985]**, **[46251]**

"Court Review of IRS Abuse of Discretion" in *Journal of Accountancy* (Vol. 198, December 2004, No. 6, pp. 93) **[113]**, **[2888]**, **[23917]**, **[26198]**, **[27106]**, **[54504]**

"Court Sides With Biz on Disability" in *Inc.* (August 1, 2003) **[26777]**, **[29176]**, **[39261]**, **[40286]**

"Courting the future" in *Crain's Detroit Business* (Vol. 19, No. 14, April 7, 2003, pp. 1) **[29177]**, **[40287]**

"Courting Trouble" in *Inc.* (October 1, 2003) **[29178]**, **[37414]**, **[40003]**, **[40288]**, **[48113]**, **[56179]**

Coushatta-Red River Chamber of Commerce **[60629]**

"Cousins Mulls $100 Million Dividend" in *Atlanta Business Chronicle* (Vol. 26, No. 9, August 8, 2003, pp. 1A) **[14892]**, **[20475]**, **[20846]**

Cousins Subs **[8549]**, **[21790]**

Coustic-Glo **[3360]**

"Cover Me: How to Spread the Risk of a Deal Around" in *Entrepreneur* (Vol. 33, February 2005, No. 2, pp. 73) **[29179]**, **[35981]**

"Cover Story" in *Inc.* (September 2000, pp. 70) **[29721]**, **[55366]**

"Cover Story: The mean streets" in *Crain's Chicago Business* (Vol.23, September 11, 2000) **[35982]**, **[54164]**

"Cover Your Assets" in *Success* (Vol. 47, No. 6, November 2000, pp. 62) **[13932]**, **[53245]**

Coverall Cleaning Concepts **[3361]**

"Covering Contractors" in *Rough Notes* (Vol. 145, No. 9, September 2002, pp. 52) **[13248]**, **[43139]**

"Covering Home Base: Insuring Your Homebased Business is Easier than Ever" in *Entrepreneur* (Vol. 33, March 2005, No. 3, pp. 64) **[13249]**, **[42596]**, **[43140]**

"Covert Operations" in *Entrepreneur* (Vol. 31, No. 8, August 2003, pp. 51) **[4628]**, **[22204]**, **[22954]**, **[49001]**, **[53246]**

Covina Chamber of Commerce **[57441]**

Covington County Chamber of Commerce **[61789]**

Covington - Tipton County Chamber of Commerce **[64902]**

T.L. Coward **[19580]**

Coweta Chamber of Commerce **[63977]**

Cox Graae Spack Architects **[1550]**

The Coxe Group Inc. **[16863]**

Coyne Associates **[3679]**, **[20180]**, **[31323]**, **[47848]**, **[50493]**, **[51999]**

Coyote Canyon - A Steak Buffet **[11378]**

Coyote Enterprises Inc. **[52619]**

"CPA exam changes to be implemented in 2004" in *Atlanta Business Chronicle* (Vol. 25, November 15, 2002, No. 23 pp. SS9) **[114]**, **[23918]**

CPA Associates International **[31]**

CPA Auto Dealer Consultants Association **[32]**, **[26112]**

CPA Client Bulletin **[318]**

CPA Client Master **[408]**

CPA Client Tax Letter **[319]**, **[24084]**

The CPA Journal **[320]**

The CPA Letter **[321]**

CPA Manufacturing Services Association **[33]**, **[26113]**

CPA Personnel Report **[322]**

CPA Technology & Internet Advisor **[323]**

CPB Public Broadcasting Directory **[20311]**, **[24399]**

CPCU Conferment Ceremony **[13570]**

CPCU Society **[13155]**

CPE Network: Accounting and Auditing Report **[352]**, **[26414]**

CPE Network: Tax & Accounting Report **[353]**, **[24113]**, **[54886]**

"CPI Aerostructures Wins $3M Contract for Assemblies" in *Long Island Business News* (March 12, 2004) **[27981]**, **[28949]**, **[44186]**, **[46252]**

CPR Services **[41340]**

CQ Monitor **[50361]**

"Crackdown on Mutual Fund Abuse" in *Black Enterprise* (Vol. 34, No. 5, December 2003, pp. 22) **[9897]**, **[14893]**, **[29180]**, **[37415]**, **[40289]**

"Cracker Barrel Faces More Racial Bias Charges" in *Black Enterprise* (Vol. 34, No. 4, November 2003, pp. 28) **[21188]**, **[21481]**, **[32012]**, **[33103]**

"Cracker Barrel Pays $8.7M to Settle Race Case" in *Black Enterprise* (Vol. 35, December 2004, No. 5, pp. 38) **[21482]**, **[29181]**, **[32013]**

Cracker Jack Collectors Association **[1301]**, **[5799]**

"Cracking the Code of Change" in *Harvard Business Review* (Vol. 78, No. 3, May 2000, pp. 133) **[27982]**, **[53667]**

"Cracking the Code" in *Entrepreneur* (Vol. 32, August 2004, No. 8, pp. 48) **[115]**, **[23919]**, **[26199]**, **[33057]**, **[54505]**

"Cracking the Code" in *My Business* (October/November 2003, pp. 49) **[1877]**, **[3290]**, **[3940]**, **[7194]**, **[12488]**, **[21394]**, **[30653]**, **[38622]**, **[51023]**

"Cracking Down On Copycats" in *Milwaukee Journal Sentinel* (December 6, 2005) **[16735]**, **[29182]**, **[46253]**

"Cracking Jones Soda's Secret Formula" in *Fast Company* (March 2005, No. 92, pp. 74) **[12879]**, **[20115]**, **[46847]**, **[50435]**

"Cracking Wise" in *Entrepreneur* (Vol. 28, No. 4, April 2000, pp. 150) **[27337]**, **[31133]**

"Cracks in the Melting Pot" in *Inc.* (Volume 27, December 2005, No. 12, pp. 27-29) **[35983]**, **[40290]**, **[43601]**, **[48531]**

The Cradlerock Group **[35222]**

The Craft Business Answer Book: Starting, Managing, and Marketing a Home-Based Art, Crafts, Design Business **[8001]**, **[8123]**, **[42507]**, **[46848]**

Craft Council of Newfoundland and Labrador–Library **[8259]**

Craft and Hobby Association **[5800]**, **[8141]**

Craft Related Newsletters, Periodicals, and Publications, Etc.-An Updating Reference **[8156]**

Roy C. Craft **[56657]**

Craft Train News **[8198]**

Crafting As a Business **[8002]**

"Crafting the most productive and efficient work force" in *Fairfield County Business Journal* (Vol. 42, No. 3, Jan. 20, 2003, pp. 4) **[34858]**, **[42209]**, **[45031]**

"Crafting a specialty: how to target a pleasant and profitable niche" in *Meetings & Conventions* (Vol. 37, No. 10, Sept. 2002, pp. 49) **[16794]**, **[22452]**, **[24856]**, **[46566]**, **[56035]**

Crafting the Successful Business Plan **[29836]**

"Crafting a Web presence" in *Accounting Technology* (Vol. 19, No. 1, January-February 2003, pp. 16) **[116]**, **[23920]**, **[25822]**, **[26200]**, **[30832]**, **[33711]**

The Craftmen's Christmas Classic Arts & Crafts Festival **[8079]**

"Crafts Americana Group to Expand Presence in Vancouver, Wash." in *The Columbian* (February 22, 2003) **[8157]**, **[13933]**, **[16432]**, **[27983]**, **[33712]**, **[53668]**

The Crafts Fair Guide **[8034]**

Crafts in Less Than 10 Minutes Video Vol. 1 **[8226]**

Crafts 'N Things **[8035]**, **[8199]**

Crafts News **[8036]**

Crafts-Newsletter **[8037]**

The Crafts Report-"Shows & Fairs" Column **[8003]**, **[8158]**

The Crafts Supply Sourcebook **[8024]**

Craftsmen **[8065]**

The Craftsmen's Classic Arts and Crafts Festival-Chantilly **[5472]**, **[8080]**

The Craftsmen's Classic Arts & Crafts Festival-Greensboro **[8081]**

The Craftsmen's Classic Arts & Crafts Festival-Myrtle Beach **[8082]**

"A crafty Christmas: with people cutting spending, more gifts are homemade" in *Wall Street Journal* (Dec. 20, 2002, pp. W14) **[8159]**, **[32338]**, **[53669]**

Craig Chamber of Commerce **[58345]**

"Craig Rosebraugh's War" in *Inc.* (October 2005, pp. 136-139, 141-142) **[21483]**, **[29837]**, **[35984]**

Craig-Satellite Glenwood Springs Small Business Development Center–Colorado Mountain College and Northwestern Community College **[58296]**

Craigdarroch Castle–Archives **[1651]**, **[13723]**

"Craigslist Founder has a Hands-On Style" in *San Jose Mercury News* (March 4, 2005) **[591]**, **[33713]**, **[42210]**

Crain Communications, Inc.–Information Center **[18214]**

"Crain's seeks benefits vendors for buyer's guide" in *Crain's Detroit Business* (Vol. 19, No. 15, April 14, 2003, pp. 12) **[3519]**, **[9898]**, **[13250]**, **[14894]**, **[26778]**, **[43141]**

Crain's Chicago Business (Vol. 26, No. 50, December 15, 2003, pp. 13); "After the Gold Rush" in **[9807]**, **[14731]**, **[44464]**, **[55481]**

Crain's Chicago Business (Vol. 26, No. 50, December 15, 2003, pp. 8); "An Urban Survivor Poised for Better Times" in **[28948]**, **[29887]**, **[31838]**, **[32770]**

Crain's Chicago Business (Vol. 26, No. 50, December 15, 2003, pp. 1); "Another Wave of HQ Job Cuts at Sears" in **[27316]**, **[27772]**, **[32249]**, **[32942]**, **[48582]**, **[51049]**

Crain's Chicago Business (Vol. 30, January 2007, No. 3, pp. 6); "Bank CEO Aims to Compound Marketshare" in **[9826]**, **[27809]**, **[37895]**

Crain's Chicago Business (Vol. 26, No. 51, December 22, 2003, pp. 22); "Blow-Ho-Ho! Inflatables Sales On Rise" in **[48605]**, **[51074]**, **[53613]**, **[55971]**

Crain's Chicago Business (Vol. 23, October 23, 2000, pp. FB5); "Book Reviews" in **[37600]**

Crain's Chicago Business (Vol. 30, January 2007, No. 4, pp. 13) "Boudin Rises, Again; Bakery Restaurant Set for Suburban Return" in **[2240]**, **[21451]**, **[27865]**, **[30513]**

Crain's Chicago Business (Vol. 30, January 2007, No. 3, pp. 16) "Branding in a Chicken Suit; The Marketing Game had Changed" in **[567]**, **[13855]**, **[25804]**, **[46741]**

Crain's Chicago Business (Vol. 30, January 2007, No. 4, pp.30) "Chart-Toppers; Largest M&A Deals in U.S. History" in **[14848]**, **[39232]**, **[49850]**

Crain's Chicago Business (Vol. 30, January 2007, No. 1, pp. 15); "Chicago Can Be Greener" in **[37255]**, **[40255]**

Crains Chicago Business (Vol. 26, No. 50, December 15, 2003); "Chicago Observer: Owners Hope to Keep Plumbing Problems from Leaking" in **[19746]**, **[20471]**, **[38599]**, **[40256]**

Crain's Chicago Business (Vol. 30, January 2007, No. 3, pp. 15); "Chicago's Top Brands" in **[583]**, **[46800]**, **[50433]**

Crain's Chicago Business (Vol. 30, January 2007, No. 1, pp. 8); "Clybourn Ave.'s PMD Corridor Leads Nowhere" in **[20468]**, **[20836]**, **[30140]**, **[32318]**, **[40265]**, **[46241]**

Crain's Chicago Business (Vol. 26, No. 51, December 22, 2003, pp. 9); "Coke Out to Woo Mall Rats Here With Lounge" in **[46814]**, **[47805]**, **[48630]**, **[51099]**, **[53652]**, **[56015]**

Crain's Chicago Business (Vol. 30, January 2007, No. 4, pp. 36); "Compass Group PLC" in **[4539]**, **[21474]**, **[49869]**

Crain's Chicago Business (Vol. 26, No. 51, December 22, 2003, pp. 1); "Condo Builder Doubles Down" in **[7291]**, **[7801]**, **[38612]**, **[40272]**

Crain's Chicago Business (Vol. 30, January 2007, No. 5, pp. 15); "Conventions" in **[24914]**, **[33053]**, **[39254]**

Crain's Chicago Business (Vol.23, September 11, 2000); "Cover Story: The mean streets" in **[35982]**, **[54164]**

Crain's Chicago Business; "Death and taxes" in **[26782]**, **[54509]**

Crain's Chicago Business (Vol. 26, No. 51, December 22, 2003, pp. 16); "Downtown Cafes Build on Lunchtime Basics" in **[11322]**, **[21198]**, **[21491]**, **[53697]**, **[56063]**

Crain's Chicago Business (Vol. 30, January 2007, No. 3, pp. 12); "El Commuters Brace for Cuts" in **[7342]**, **[30322]**

Crain's Chicago Business (Vol. 23, October 9, 2000, pp. SB2); "Execs getting more political: Efforts to influence policy growing" in **[32418]**, **[40357]**

Crain's Chicago Business (Vol. 26, No. 50, December 15, 2003, pp. 6); "Factory Card Gets Back in Party Mood" in **[11149]**, **[11562]**, **[28138]**, **[51148]**

Crains Chicago Business (Vol. 26) "Factory Card Gets Back in Party Mood; Judicious Growth, Curtailed Costs Restore Firms Health" in **[11150]**, **[11563]**, **[28139]**, **[51149]**

Crain's Chicago Business (Vol. 23, September 11, 2000, pp. 4); "Firms Seek Tonic for Labor-Pool Headaches" in **[17893]**, **[26805]**, **[53730]**

Crain's Chicago Business; "Flip Taking Control of Online Auction House" in **[1814]**, **[5907]**, **[23618]**, **[36163]**

Crain's Chicago Business (December 8, 2003) "Foreclosures Rise; Yuppie Belt Hit Hard as Defaults Climb 10% City wide" in **[17382]**, **[32442]**

Crains Chicago Business (Vol. 26, No. 49) "Foreclosures Rise; Yuppie Belt Hit Hard as Defaults Climb 10 Percent Citywide" in **[17383]**, **[32443]**

Crain's Chicago Business (Vol. 26, No. 50, December 15, 2003, pp. 12); "From Fifth Hire to Top Exec, New CEO to Lead SurePayroll" in **[154]**, **[18774]**, **[19457]**, **[25867]**, **[26244]**, **[30197]**, **[31032]**, **[43146]**

Crain's Chicago Business (Vol.23,Nov.13,2000); "Going outside for expert help: Family businesses have options to get objective advice" in **[31159]**, **[37668]**

Crain's Chicago Business (Vol. 26, No. 50, December 15, 2003, pp. 22); "Group Casts Another Line Into Seafood" in **[21234]**, **[21528]**, **[36239]**, **[36944]**

Crain's Chicago Business (Vol. 30, January 2007, No. 3, pp. 16); "Guerrillas in our Midst" in **[651]**, **[47050]**, **[50602]**

Crain's Chicago Business (Vol. 30, January 2007, No. 1, pp. 15); "Here's What You Can Do" in **[7355]**, **[9361]**, **[20891]**, **[31166]**, **[37293]**

Crain's Chicago Business (Vol. 26, No. 50, December 15, 2003, pp. 1); "Hollinger Contacts VC Giant" in **[15086]**, **[18882]**, **[49981]**, **[55665]**

Crains Chicago Business (Vol. 26, No. 50) "Hollinger Contacts VC Giant; Hicks Muse Could See Synergies with Radio Here" in **[15087]**, **[18883]**, **[49982]**, **[55666]**

Crain's Chicago Business (Vol. 26, No. 51, December 22, 2003, pp. 3); "Hollinger VC Unit has Family Ties" in **[15089]**, **[37687]**, **[49984]**, **[55668]**

Crains Chicago Business (Vol. 26, No. 51) "Hollinger VC Unit has Family Ties; Black's Nephew has Few Hits, Many Misses With Fund" in **[15088]**, **[37686]**, **[49983]**, **[55667]**

Crain's Chicago Business (Vol. 30, January 2007, No. 3, pp. 13); "Home Depot Offers Expensive Lesson in Curbing Execs' Pay" in **[11885]**, **[12288]**, **[30556]**, **[31171]**, **[45248]**

Crain's Chicago Business (Vol. 26, No. 50, December 15, 2003, pp. 1); "Housing to Rise on CSX Yard" in **[7376]**, **[17394]**

Crains Chicago Business (Vol. 26, No. 50) "Housing to Rise on CSX Yard; South Loop Boom Goes on With Plans for 1,500 Units" in **[7377]**, **[17395]**

Crain's Chicago Business (Vol. 30, January 2007, No. 5, pp. 12); "Indiana Electric Utility for Sale" in **[39411]**, **[48862]**, **[52431]**

Crain's Chicago Business (Vol. 26, No. 51, December 22, 2003, pp. 3); "Inspection Indigestion" in **[21536]**, **[40468]**

Crains Chicago Business "Inspection Indigestion; Chicago Restaurant Owners Deal with a Dizzying Array of Bureaucrats and Licensing Fees" in **[21535]**, **[40467]**

Crain's Chicago Business (Vol. 30, January 2007, No. 1, pp. 8); "Investment in Transit System the First Step in Pursuit of Games" in **[15152]**, **[20909]**, **[30355]**, **[30893]**, **[32512]**

Crain's Chicago Business (Vol. 30, February 2007, No. 6, pp. 8); "Kraft Not Alone" in **[37470]**, **[47178]**, **[50452]**, **[50617]**

Crain's Chicago Business (Vol. 26, No. 50, December 15, 2003, pp. 1); "Lights, Camera, Trauma!" in **[24426]**, **[41045]**, **[50620]**

Crain's Chicago Business (Vol. 30, January 2007, No. 3, pp. 18); "Many Eggs, Many Baskets" in **[707]**, **[14228]**, **[24430]**, **[25894]**, **[47230]**

Crain's Chicago Business (Vol. 30, February 2007, No. 6, pp. 40); "Meet the Gatekeepers" in **[15256]**, **[42340]**

Crain's Chicago Business (Vol. 30, January 2007, No. 1, pp. 12); "Money Is Out There, But Where?" in **[14250]**, **[25898]**, **[33175]**, **[48917]**, **[52564]**, **[52918]**, **[55733]**

Crain's Chicago Business (Vol. 23, Nov. 27, 2000); "Money Talks to New Economy Firms: More Startups Choose Chicago for Home Base" in **[52640]**, **[55735]**

Crain's Chicago Business (Vol. 26, No. 51, December 22, 2003, pp. 6); "More Retail Chains Heading this Way" in **[5688]**, **[12197]**, **[12300]**, **[18602]**, **[23625]**, **[30157]**, **[30916]**, **[51252]**

Crains Chicago Business (Vol. 26, No. 51) "More Retail Chains Heading this Way; Drawn by Vacant Sites, Competitive Considerations" in **[5689]**, **[12198]**, **[12301]**, **[18603]**, **[23626]**, **[30158]**, **[30917]**, **[51253]**

Crain's Chicago Business (Vol. 30, January 2007, No. 4, pp. 12); "Motorola to Cut 3,500 Jobs" in **[39482]**, **[41847]**

Crain's Chicago Business (Vol. 26, No. 50, December 15, 2003, pp. 3); "Motorola's Cell Slide Resumes" in **[5063]**, **[28513]**

Crains Chicago Business (Vol. 26, No. 50) "Motorola's Cell Slide Resumes; Rivals with Camera Phones Steal Marketshare" in **[5064]**, **[28514]**

Crain's Chicago Business (Vol. 30, January 2007, No. 4, pp. 36); "Navteq Corp." in **[14271]**, **[50091]**

Crain's Chicago Business (Vol. 26, No. 51, December 22, 2003, pp. 20); "New CEO: So What is Moto, Anyway?" in **[5066]**, **[5240]**, **[12816]**, **[12900]**, **[19925]**, **[20140]**, **[40103]**, **[41859]**, **[43419]**, **[45126]**, **[45464]**, **[47323]**, **[50641]**, **[52812]**

Crain's Chicago Business (Vol. 26, No. 50, December 15, 2003); "New Computer Sellers Bite Into Market..." in **[6736]**, **[49159]**, **[51265]**

Crains Chicago Business (Vol. 26) "New Computer Sellers Bite Into Market; MDG, Fry's Set to Debut, While CompUSA Grows Again" in **[6737]**, **[49160]**, **[51266]**

Crain's Chicago Business (Vol. 26, No. 50, December 15, 2003, pp. 4); "Oreo Woes Bringing Kraft Down" in **[11648]**, **[30926]**, **[31051]**

Crains Chicago Business (Vol. 26, No. 50) "Oreo Woes Bringing Kraft Down; Fat Fears, Price Hikes, Private-Label Brands Sap Sales" in **[11649]**, **[30927]**, **[31052]**

Crain's Chicago Business (Vol. 26, No. 51, December 22, 2003, pp. 12); "Pace Exec Taking Creative Route to Expand Bus Service" in **[15955]**, **[16185]**, **[23909]**, **[24238]**

Crain's Chicago Business (November 29) "Personal Shoppers Save Your Lunchtime; Put Them To Work-Then Head for the Restaurant" in **[19005]**

Crain's Chicago Business (Vol. 26, No. 50, December 15, 2003); "Profile: Chicago Native on the Front Lines of WaMu's Local Push" in **[10027]**, **[10144]**, **[30168]**, **[30832]**

Crain's Chicago Business (December 22, 2003); "Profile: Local Web Developer Plays a Starring Role in NASA's Mission to Mars" in **[4771]**, **[4922]**, **[23134]**, **[23945]**, **[25938]**, **[27684]**, **[40077]**, **[41522]**, **[50142]**, **[51174]**, **[53419]**, **[55752]**

Crains Chicago Business (Vol. 26, No. 51) "Recovery for Some; Chicago's Economy Will Lag the State and Nation Next Year" in **[10037]**, **[10155]**, **[12622]**, **[13080]**, **[15174]**, **[15401]**, **[20020]**, **[20236]**, **[25237]**, **[26070]**, **[28683]**, **[29656]**, **[30314]**, **[30408]**, **[31298]**, **[31737]**, **[32161]**, **[32657]**, **[38310]**, **[39734]**

Crain's Chicago Business (Vol. 26, No. 50, December 15, 2003, pp. 4); "Sara Lee's Apparel Biz Bind" in **[5714]**, **[30942]**, **[31065]**

Crain's Chicago Business (Vol. 30, January 2007, No. 2, pp. 19); "Seen & Noted: Fitness-Minded Bare Motivations in Stores" in **[19436]**, **[51349]**, **[51828]**

Crain's Chicago Business (Vol. 25, No. 42, October 21, 2002, pp. SR11); "Skip the links and head to the gym or the spa" in **[2349]**, **[11802]**, **[19440]**, **[56407]**

Crain's Chicago Business (Vol. 23, October 9, 2000, pp. 23); "Small Business Adviser: Aim resources at biggest accounts" in **[19822]**, **[19894]**, **[52455]**

Crain's Chicago Business (Vol. 23, November 13, 2000, pp. SB17); "Small Business Advisor: Choose kids' or collectors' market" in **[28772]**, **[52948]**, **[55827]**

Crain's Chicago Business (Vol. 23, December 11, 2000, pp. SB16); "Small Business Advisor: Dialing for dollars" in **[24291]**, **[31218]**, **[31856]**, **[33237]**

Crain's Chicago Business (Vol. 23, December 11, 2000, pp. SB17); "Small Business Advisor: Focus effort on receptive audience" in **[42414]**

Crain's Chicago Business (Vol. 23, October 9, 2000, pp. SB15); "Small Business Advisor: Identify and protect your niches" in **[19824]**, **[19838]**, **[28773]**, **[52949]**

Crain's Chicago Business (Vol. 23); "Small Business Advisor: Toy Story: Sharon P. John's Toy Company is Relaunching the Dawn Doll" in **[24829]**, **[36751]**, **[46432]**

Crain's Chicago Business (Vol.23, Dec. 11); "Small Firms Still Strain for Space: Outlook Brighter for Companies in Need of More Room" in **[28788]**, **[53977]**

Crain's Chicago Business (Vol. 30, February 2007, No. 6, pp. 30); "Smart Businesses See Value, and Profit, in Promoting Women" in **[39599]**, **[50357]**, **[50468]**

Crain's Chicago Business (Vol. 26, No. 51, December 22, 2003, pp. 14); "Spanish Firm Hopes U.S. Is In the Bag" in **[9641]**, **[10458]**, **[30178]**, **[30840]**, **[43823]**, **[45482]**, **[51364]**, **[53594]**

Crain's Chicago Business (Vol. 30, February 2007, No. 6, pp. 58); "Speed Reader" in **[18127]**, **[36777]**

Crain's Chicago Business (Vol. 30, January 2007, No. 2, pp. 5) "Spotlight Rick Chesley; Chairman Builds Law Office From Ground Up" in **[28807]**, **[29511]**, **[30605]**, **[36782]**

Crain's Chicago Business (Vol. 30, January 2007, No. 3, pp. 18); "Spreading Viruses Can be a Good Thing" in **[14474]**, **[27679]**, **[34527]**, **[47567]**, **[50680]**

Crain's Chicago Business (Vol. 30, February 2007, No. 6, pp. 39) "Suiting Up; Yes, You're Smart, But Can You Look the Part" in **[5720]**, **[15493]**, **[50759]**

Crain's Chicago Business (Vol. 30, January 2007, No. 3, pp. 23); "Team-Building Outings Heat Up" in **[7816]**, **[31226]**, **[35094]**

Crain's Chicago Business (Vol. 30, January 2007, No. 5, pp. 6); "Tech Firm CEO's Solution: Unify Segments" in **[30613]**, **[35107]**, **[36837]**, **[42035]**

Crain's Chicago Business (Vol. 23, December 11, 2000, pp. SB1); "The State of Small Business: Confident, yet cautious, in 2001" in **[28818]**, **[32711]**, **[54000]**

Crain's Chicago Business (Vol. 30, February 2007, No. 6, pp. 1); "This Week: McD's Eyes Ad Plan, Shifts Breakfast Biz" in **[810]**, **[21651]**, **[47636]**

Crain's Chicago Business (Vol. 29, December 2006, No. 50, pp. 1); "This Week: McD's Tests Trans-Free Oil in 1,200 Locations" in **[21652]**, **[30972]**, **[40766]**, **[47637]**, **[50981]**

Crain's Chicago Business (Vol. 29, December 2006, No. 51, pp. 1); "This Week: Raising the Roof at North Pier?" in **[21023]**, **[28895]**

Crain's Chicago Business (Vol. 26, No. 51, December 22, 2003, pp. 3); "Unions Buying Amalgamated" in **[10223]**, **[15556]**, **[50236]**, **[55318]**

Crains Chicago Business (Vol. 26, No. 51) "Unions Buying Amalgamated; CFL, Other Groups Take Stake in Bank Long Tied to Labor" in **[10222]**, **[15555]**, **[50235]**, **[55317]**

Crain's Chicago Business (Vol. 29, December 2006, No. 51, pp.); "Union's Job is to Protect Due Process, Not Bad Teachers" in **[40792]**, **[55319]**

Crain's Chicago Business (Vol. 30, January 2007, No. 1, pp. 12); "When in Doubt Grab a Mouse, or a Phone" in **[14612]**, **[26018]**, **[36948]**, **[39955]**, **[52609]**, **[53028]**

Crain's Chicago Business (Vol. 30, January 2007, No. 3, pp. 18); "Who's Talking Behind Your Back?" in **[840]**, **[27538]**, **[47744]**, **[50707]**

Crain's Chicago Business (Vol. 25, No. 49, Dec. 9, 2002, pp. SB1); "Yielding to Yoga" in **[17922]**, **[19449]**, **[29035]**

Crain's Chicago Business (Vol. 26, No. 51, December 22, 2003) "Zander's Chip Shot; New CEO Faces Tough Call on Semiconductor Unit" in **[15624]**, **[16272]**, **[42133]**, **[43764]**, **[45885]**, **[47701]**, **[50276]**, **[51274]**

Crain's Chicago Businesss; "Small Business Advisor: A pressing matter" in **[19823]**, **[19895]**, **[28771]**, **[52947]**

Crain's Cleveland Business **[63897]**

Crain's Cleveland Business (Vol. 22, No. 43, October 22, 2001, pp. 11); "Adviser: Temporary tax act makes planning tough" in **[23879]**, **[39785]**, **[54422]**

Crain's Cleveland Business (Vol. 22, No. 42, October 15, 2001, pp. 11); "Malley's Chocolates opens first Summit County store" in **[4296]**, **[37724]**

Crain's Cleveland Business (Vol. 26, January 10, 2005, No. 2, pp. 7); "O-Web Design Firm Makes Case for Student Startups" in **[25920]**, **[56757]**

Crain's Cleveland Business (Vol. 23, No. 42, October 21, 2002, pp. 14); "Pottery school expansion to put more behind the wheel" in **[8180]**, **[8277]**

Crain's Cleveland Business (Vol. 24, No. 41, October 13, 2003, pp. 21); "Short Takes" in **[2452]**

"Crain's Co-Sponsoring Sales-Training Seminar" in *Crain's Detroit Business* (Vol. 22, January 2, 2006, No. 1, pp. 17) **[22489]**, **[33058]**, **[51599]**

Crain's Detroit Business (Vol. 22, November 13, 2006, No. 46, pp. 3); "3Q a good one for local firms, if you ignore auto industry" in **[27740]**, **[32230]**, **[48857]**

Crain's Detroit Business (Vol. 23, January 8, 2007, No. 2, pp. 10); "8 Detroit Projects Get More Than $170M in Tax Breaks" in **[32231]**, **[54417]**

Crain's Detroit Business (Vol. 21, October 31, 2005, No. 44, pp. 32); "10 Local Companies Make Inc. List of Fastest-Growing" in **[4588]**, **[4904]**, **[13793]**, **[22158]**, **[22904]**, **[27743]**, **[32136]**, **[53196]**

Crain's Detroit Business (Vol. 21, October 3, 2005, No. 43, pp. 47); "18th Street Deli Breaks Ground on $2M Production Center" in **[4532]**, **[7087]**, **[25573]**

Crain's Detroit Business (Vol. 21, January 10, 2005, No. 2, pp. 10); "33 Tool-and-Die Firms Get State Tax Breaks in 'Recovery' Zones" in **[16358]**, **[54418]**

Crain's Detroit Business (Vol. 21, January 3, 2005, No. 1, pp. 20); "88-Year-Old Printing Company in Ch. 11, Hopes to Rebound" in **[19865]**, **[48015]**

Crain's Detroit Business (Vol. 21, October 10, 2005, No. 43, pp. 17); "2005-2006 Meetings, Conventions and Trade Shows" in **[22461]**, **[24658]**, **[24874]**, **[25142]**, **[55056]**

Crain's Detroit Business (Vol. 18, No. 18, May 6, 2002, pp. 11); "A perilous chopping block" in **[26878]**

Crain's Detroit Business (Vol. 21, January 3, 2005, No. 1) ; "A Conversation with George Jackson, Detroit Economic Growth Corp." in **[23715]**, **[32331]**

Crain's Detroit Business (Vol. 21, November 7, 2005, No. 45, pp. 25); "A Conversation With Duane Tarnacki, Clark Hill PLC" in **[10732]**, **[54502]**

Crain's Detroit Business (Vol. 21, January 31, 2005, No. 5); "A Conversation With Michael Beauregard, Huron Capital Partners" in **[14886]**, **[32332]**, **[49875]**

Crain's Detroit Business (Vol. 23, February 5, 2007, No. 6, pp. 11); "A Conversation With Robin Asher, Clark Hill, LLC" in **[29166]**, **[35972]**, **[40283]**, **[44017]**

Crain's Detroit Business (Vol. 21); "A Conversation With Steve Cassin, Macomb County Director of Planning and Economic Development" in **[27978]**, **[32333]**, **[52660]**

Crain's Detroit Business (Vol. 16, No. 50, December 11, 2000, pp. E-5); "A day of pondering leads to a life-altering change" in **[19837]**, **[35380]**

Crain's Detroit Business (Vol. 19, No. 10, March 10, 2003, pp. 34); "A Lucky journey" in **[17599]**, **[17750]**, **[36457]**, **[37717]**

Crain's Detroit Business (Vol. 19, No. 5, Feb. 3, 2003, pp. 11); "A storm offshore" in **[15484]**, **[38379]**, **[54778]**

Crain's Detroit Business (Vol. 19, No. 7, February 17, 2003, pp. 25); "A rosy sales picture" in **[10572]**, **[51336]**

Crain's Detroit Business (Vol. 19, No. 14, April 7, 2003, pp. 20); "A touch of the Pointes" in **[20689]**, **[21025]**

Crain's Detroit Business (Vol. 19, No. 42, October 20, 2003, pp. 1) "A Quickened Pace; Lender Powers through Rapid Growth" in **[17429]**, **[28666]**

Crain's Detroit Business (Vol. 19) "A Quickened Pace; Lender Powers through Rapid Growth, Prepares for Interest Rates to Rise" in **[17430]**, **[28667]**

Crain's Detroit Business (Vol. 22, February 13, 2006, No. 7, pp. 11); "A Super Selling Point" in **[12640]**, **[21640]**, **[25027]**, **[55164]**

Crain's Detroit Business "A Web Wake-Up; Posting of OU Student's Paper Turns Into Lesson That Helps Define Defamation in a New Medium" in **[14586]**, **[29573]**, **[34679]**, **[39661]**, **[40819]**

Crain's Detroit Business (Vol. 21, December 12, 2005, No. 50, pp. 2); "A Year of Advice is Prize in Woman-Owned Program" in **[46492]**, **[51419]**, **[52615]**, **[56521]**

Crain's Detroit Business (January 17, 2005) "Aastrom Gets $22M Financing Boost; Stem-Cell Trials Pique Wall Street's Interest" in **[14718]**, **[40138]**, **[50802]**, **[52031]**

Crain's Detroit Business (Vol. 18, No. 23, June 10, 2002, pp. E-14); "About this index" in **[13797]**, **[25783]**, **[33508]**

Crain's Detroit Business (Vol. 19, No. 1, January 6, 2003, pp. 3); "About the Power Breakfast series" in **[37383]**, **[39133]**, **[40139]**, **[44872]**

Crain's Detroit Business (Vol. 19, No. 17, April 28, 2003, pp. 14); "About this report" in **[27749]**, **[32232]**

Crain's Detroit Business (Vol. 18, No. 15, April 15, 2002, pp. 9); "Accounting Has Record of Trustworthiness" in **[65]**, **[23877]**, **[26147]**, **[37385]**

Crain's Detroit Business (Vol. 19, No. 45, November 10, 2003, pp. 14); "Acquisitions Likely to Pick Up, But Pressure Remains" in **[14722]**, **[15267]**, **[49779]**, **[50879]**

Crain's Detroit Business (Vol. 19, No. 13, March 31, 2003, pp. 12); "Acquisitions helped increase offerings" in **[14723]**, **[27751]**, **[41497]**, **[49780]**

Crain's Detroit Business (Vol. 18, No. 49, December 9, 2002, pp. 12); "Add fudge factor to cost to equal business success" in **[37869]**, **[39134]**

Crain's Detroit Business (Vol. 23, January 15, 2007, No. 3, pp. 9); "Adults Fueling Back To School Movement" in **[32990]**, **[42826]**

Crain's Detroit Business (Vol. 19, No. 16, April 21, 2003, pp. 1); "Advanced Accessory looks to acquire with new owner" in **[1891]**, **[14725]**, **[49781]**

Crain's Detroit Business (Vol. 23, January 15, 2007, No. 3, pp. 13); "Advertisers Want to Leave Their Message on Your Cell Phone" in **[535]**, **[4908]**, **[41499]**, **[46661]**

Crain's Detroit Business (Vol. 19, No. 9, March 3, 2003, pp. 3); "Ailing Wellness Plan considers job cuts" in **[13182]**, **[40957]**, **[43073]**

Crain's Detroit Business (Vol. 22, February 6, 2006, No. 6, pp. 14); "Alternative Energy Companies" in **[21215]**, **[41506]**

Crain's Detroit Business (Vol. 22, February 6, 2006, No. 6, pp. 10); "Alternative Energy Powers Up In Michigan - Part 1 of 2" in **[22464]**, **[26478]**, **[27765]**, **[41507]**, **[50808]**, **[52036]**

Crain's Detroit Business (Vol. 22, February 6, 2006, No. 6, pp. 10); "Alternative Energy Powers Up In Michigan - Part 2 of 2" in **[21216]**, **[21436]**, **[26479]**, **[27766]**, **[41508]**, **[50809]**, **[52037]**

Crain's Detroit Business (Vol. 21, October 31, 2005, No. 44, pp. 4); "Am. Axle Plans China, Europe Plants" in **[1894]**, **[27767]**, **[43540]**, **[46194]**

Crain's Detroit Business (Vol. 22, December 4, 2006, No. 49, pp. 27); "Amendment to Thwart Scavengers Could Hurt Scrap Dealers" in **[21217]**, **[30131]**, **[40153]**

Crain's Detroit Business (Vol. 18, No. 51, Dec. 23, 2002, pp. 17); "American Axle hopes new 4WD unit can shift it into high gear" in **[1895]**, **[17961]**, **[48694]**

Crain's Detroit Business (Vol. 19, No. 16, April 21, 2003, pp. 4); "American Axle's Dauch rewarded handsomely for company success" in **[1896]**, **[17962]**, **[35766]**

Crain's Detroit Business (Vol. 22, December 11, 2006, No. 50, pp. 9); "American Dreamers Nominations Due Thursday" in **[34810]**, **[35767]**, **[50426]**

Crain's Detroit Business (Vol. 21, October 31, 2005, No. 44, pp. 4); "Amerigon, BorgWarner Fare Better Among Suppliers" in **[1897]**, **[17963]**, **[46196]**

Crain's Detroit Business (Vol. 21, January 10, 2005, No. 2, pp. 19); "Analysts: Pricing, Material Costs to Spur Supplier Mergers" in **[1898]**, **[17964]**, **[31009]**, **[46197]**, **[49787]**

Crain's Detroit Business (Vol. 22, February 13, 2006, No. 7, pp. 25); "Ann Arbor's QuatRx Pharmaceuticals Files for Stock Offering" in **[14741]**, **[49790]**, **[50812]**, **[52040]**, **[55491]**

Crain's Detroit Business (Vol. 19, No. 11, March 17, 2003, pp. 13); "Answering the call" in **[24321]**, **[27773]**, **[37587]**

Crain's Detroit Business (Vol. 19, No. 40, October 13, 2003, pp. 3); "Anything but Boring" in **[1900]**, **[41519]**

Crain's Detroit Business (Vol. 19, No. 40) "Anything but Boring; CBS Boring Draws Big Attention with New Robotic System" in **[1899]**, **[41518]**

Crain's Detroit Business (Vol. 18, No. 17, April 29, 2002, pp.); "Apartment, office sales slow down" in **[20047]**, **[20794]**

Crain's Detroit Business (Vol. 19, No. 11, March 17, 2003, pp. 25); "Arbortext's bread and butter" in **[6462]**, **[22916]**, **[53211]**

Crain's Detroit Business (Vol. 19, No. 11, March 17, 2003, pp. 3); "Arbortext's windfall" in **[4597]**, **[22917]**, **[53212]**, **[55494]**

Crain's Detroit Business (Vol. 19, No. 15, April 14, 2003, pp. 8); "Area Arab-Americans can help rebuild Iraq" in **[39982]**, **[43545]**

Crain's Detroit Business (Vol. 21, January 17, 2005, No. 3, pp. 14); "Army's Tech Needs Boost General Dynamics' Role" in **[39984]**, **[41523]**

Crain's Detroit Business (Vol. 19, No. 40, October 13, 2003, pp. 1); "Art Van Shoots to Score with Yzerman, Ireland Furniture Lines" in **[12273]**, **[46685]**, **[48579]**

Crain's Detroit Business (Vol. 26, No. 12, March 20, 2000, pp. 37); "Arthur Andersen announces YoungIT Entrepreneur Award" in **[37100]**, **[56735]**

Crain's Detroit Business (Vol. 19, No. 49, December 8, 2003, pp. 9); "Artists Can Help Draw Tourists to Detroit" in **[25148]**, **[25992]**, **[27330]**, **[27789]**

Crain's Detroit Business (Vol. 23, February 5, 2007, No. 6, pp. 29); "Arvin Meritor Says It's Done Selling" in **[29791]**, **[30505]**, **[52406]**

Crain's Detroit Business (Vol. 19, No. 14, April 7, 2003, pp. 40); "ArvinMeritor wins patent case" in **[1901]**, **[25376]**, **[43988]**

Crain's Detroit Business (Vol. 19, No. 49, December 8, 2003, pp. 4); "ArvinMeritor Rival Files New Patent Suit" in **[1902]**, **[1915]**, **[29102]**, **[30029]**, **[43989]**, **[45663]**

Crain's Detroit Business (Vol. 22, December 11, 2006, No. 50, pp. 7); "As Clock Ticks on 2006, Tax Debate Continues" in **[29792]**, **[54431]**

Crain's Detroit Business (Vol. 22, January 16, 2006, No. 3, pp. 22); "ASC Pushes Niche Vehicles as Industry Cure" in **[17965]**, **[46199]**

Crain's Detroit Business (Vol. 21, January 17, 2005, No. 3, pp. 29); "ASC Specialty Cars to Get Sony Multimedia Products Under Deal" in **[1903]**, **[17966]**, **[20301]**, **[49794]**

Crain's Detroit Business (Vol. 19, No. 17, April 28, 2003, pp. 3); "Ashley Capital branches out into new kind of development" in **[20425]**, **[20798]**, **[27790]**, **[32141]**

Crain's Detroit Business (Vol. 22, December 18, 2006, No. 51, pp. 5); "AT & T Heads Into TV Fray With Passage of Video Bill" in **[4915]**, **[30782]**, **[38712]**, **[41524]**

Crain's Detroit Business (Vol. 19, No. 10, March 10, 2003, pp. 17); "Atwater exec parlays experience into success" in **[18724]**, **[56125]**

Crain's Detroit Business (Vol. 23, January 8, 2007, No. 2, pp. 15); "Auto Consolidation Likely to Speed Up" in **[1906]**, **[29795]**, **[46201]**, **[49802]**

Crain's Detroit Business (Vol. 21, October 17, 2005, No. 43, pp. 1) "Auto Sector Leads in Investment; Michigan No. 2 State" in **[14759]**, **[17969]**, **[46202]**

Crain's Detroit Business (Vol. 19, No. 2, January 20, 2003, pp. 1); "Auto show also an engine for small-business growth" in **[17970]**, **[27801]**

Crain's Detroit Business (Vol. 19, No. 14, April 7, 2003, pp. 34); "Auto suppliers: Steel tariffs kill U.S. jobs permanently" in **[1907]**, **[43554]**, **[46203]**

Crain's Detroit Business (Vol. 19, No. 8, February 24, 2003, pp. 6); "Automaker pullback blamed for Detroit stamper's closing" in **[17971]**, **[31010]**, **[46204]**, **[53593]**

Crain's Detroit Business (Vol. 22, November 27, 2006, No. 48, pp. 8); "Automaker-Union Talks Critical to State" in **[17972]**, **[32256]**, **[46205]**, **[55282]**

Crain's Detroit Business (Vol. 22, September 25-October 1, 2006, No. 39, pp. E1-E7); "Automation Alley Awards" in **[41526]**

Crain's Detroit Business (Vol. 22, December 18, 2006, No. pp. 16); "Aven Hopes Portable Microscope Drives Growth" in **[41527]**, **[46695]**, **[48697]**

Crain's Detroit Business (Vol. 21, January 24, 2005, No. 4, pp. 19); "Avis Ford Owner Passes Reins of Dealerships to Sons" in **[17974]**, **[29796]**, **[37589]**

Crain's Detroit Business (Vol. 19, No. 49, December 8, 2003); "Away Game: Right Messages Will Help Exhibit Booth Bring in Business" in **[22468]**, **[23199]**, **[24561]**, **[24891]**, **[55067]**, **[56092]**

Crain's Detroit Business (Vol. 19, No. 42, October 20, 2003, pp. 11) "Back to Basics; Single Portal for Business" in **[13832]**, **[33558]**, **[39986]**, **[41530]**

Crain's Detroit Business (Vol. 19, No. 7, Feb. 17, 2003); "Back in bloom: Thrifty Florist owner buys back chain, plans to expand" in **[10556]**, **[35797]**

Crain's Detroit Business (Vol. 19, No. 1, January 6, 2003, pp. 19); "Backers of border projects press on despite split decision" in **[25377]**, **[43555]**

Crain's Detroit Business (Vol. 16, No. 12, March 20, 2000, pp. 53); "Bad image may keep patent board away" in **[43994]**, **[44273]**, **[50550]**

Crain's Detroit Business (Vol. 22, January 30, 2006, No. 5, pp. 3); "Balancing Act" in **[44912]**, **[53598]**

Crain's Detroit Business (Vol. 16, No. 49, December 4, 2000, pp. 7); "Bank merger aims for 2002 wrap" in **[14767]**, **[49803]**

Crain's Detroit Business (Vol. 22, January 30, 2006, No. 5, pp. 41); "Bank Wants Doubletree Novi Placed in Receivership" in **[12519]**, **[37899]**

Crain's Detroit Business (Vol. 18, No. 24, 2002, pp. 6); "Bankruptcies" in **[27812]**, **[32263]**

Crain's Detroit Business (Vol. 21, January 3, 2005, No. 1, pp. 18); "Bankruptcy Court Streamlines Rules - to Drum Up Business" in **[37904]**, **[40169]**

Crain's Detroit Business (Vol. 16, No. 49, Dec. 4, 2000, pp. 32); "Bank's branch-a-year strategy gets trimmed back by circumstances" in **[27815]**

Crain's Detroit Business (Vol. 19, No. 3, Jan. 20, 2003, pp. 11) "Bar the door; New threats from viruses" in **[4600]**, **[6237]**, **[6464]**, **[22178]**, **[22921]**, **[30206]**, **[44275]**

Crain's Detroit Business (Vol. 19, No. 16, April 21, 2003, pp. 16); "Barter systems put the 'trade' in trade group" in **[26707]**, **[49807]**

Crain's Detroit Business (Vol. 21, October 10, 2005, No. 43, pp. 12); "Basic Training" in **[12869]**, **[20104]**, **[33008]**

Crain's Detroit Business (Vol. 18, No. 24, June 17, 2002, pp. 8); "Battenberg is riding along with Segway" in **[41536]**, **[48699]**

Crain's Detroit Business (Vol. 18, No. 22, June 3, 2002, pp. 41); "Battle over restaurant smoking still smolders in state Capitol" in **[21445]**, **[40174]**

Crain's Detroit Business (Vol. 19, No. 14, April 7, 2003, pp. 4); "Battle between Compuware, IBM escalates in counterclaim" in **[4601]**, **[6589]**, **[22922]**, **[29118]**, **[30789]**

Crain's Detroit Business (Vol. 22, January 16, 2006, No. 3, pp. 3); "Beaumont Aims to Commercialize Research" in **[50817]**, **[52042]**

Crain's Detroit Business (Vol. 23, February 5, 2007, No. 6, pp. 25); "Bereinga Starts $150M Fund, Opens China Office" in **[1913]**, **[27829]**, **[46208]**, **[55505]**

Crain's Detroit Business (Vol. 18, No. 23, June 10, 2002, pp. E-15); "Best national Internet sites" in **[13842]**, **[25797]**, **[33571]**

Crain's Detroit Business (Vol. 18, No. 21, May 27, 2002, pp. 18); "Bets are off at state racetracks" in **[10861]**, **[27831]**

Crain's Detroit Business (Vol. 21, October 3, 2005, No. 43, pp. 3); "Better Way for Better Made?" in **[11592]**, **[46717]**, **[48700]**, **[55283]**

Crain's Detroit Business (Vol. 21) "Big Boy Plans Big Growth in Franchises; Deals Signed for 23 Diners, One for 60 in Works" in **[21449]**, **[27836]**, **[38718]**

Crain's Detroit Business (Vol. 19, No. 45, November 10, 2003, pp. 15); "Big Projects Give Some Life to Sluggish Real Estate Sector" in **[20217]**, **[20431]**, **[20803]**, **[21548]**, **[39827]**, **[41545]**, **[46213]**, **[48047]**

Crain's Detroit Business (Vol. 22, February 13, 2006, No. 7); "Big Religious Meetings Hold Promise of Big Payoffs for Local Economy" in **[24895]**, **[32276]**, **[55070]**

Crain's Detroit Business (Vol. 23, January 8, 2007, No. 2, pp. 1); "Big Taxes Top Lansing Agenda, Will Granholm Proposal Shift?" in **[37918]**, **[40186]**, **[54447]**

Crain's Detroit Business (Vol. 21, Jan. 3, 2005) "Big Winners Help State Stocks Top S&P; Housing, Finance Companies Boost Returns" in **[7255]**, **[14794]**, **[20433]**, **[37919]**

Crain's Detroit Business (Vol. , No. , pp.); "Bigcat Systems leaves little to chance in Internet Marketing" in **[13737]**, **[35335]**, **[46559]**

Crain's Detroit Business (Vol. 19, No. 45, November 10, 2003, pp. 6); "Bill Requiring State Copy of Tax Form on Way to Granholm" in **[40187]**, **[41245]**, **[54421]**, **[54451]**

Crain's Detroit Business (Vol. 22, December 4, 2006, No. 49, pp. 6); "Bill Would Ease Rules on Store Price Tags" in **[31013]**, **[40189]**, **[51073]**

Crain's Detroit Business (Vol. 18, No. 18, May 6, 2002, pp. 24); "Bill Would Let Biz Keep Unclaimed $100 Paychecks" in **[26168]**, **[40190]**

Crain's Detroit Business (Vol. 18, No. 21, May 27, 2002, pp. 6); "Bills would allow government land banks" in **[39180]**, **[40192]**

Crain's Detroit Business (Vol. 19, No. 40, October 13, 2003, pp. 6); "Bills Would Restart SBT Rollback, Add New Tax Credits" in **[54422]**, **[54453]**

Crain's Detroit Business (Vol. 18, No. 19, May 13, 2002, pp. 15); "Biz assembles new approach to flexible design" in **[18534]**, **[18589]**

Crain's Detroit Business (Vol. 22, November 13, 2006, No. 46, pp. 1); "Biz Leaders Want Quick Action on SBT replacement" in **[29801]**, **[54454]**

Crain's Detroit Business (Vol. 18, No. 18, May 6, 2002, pp. 8); "Biz has an interest in keeping Prop A" in **[40195]**, **[54455]**

Crain's Detroit Business (Vol. 21, October 17, 2005, No. 43, pp. 17); "Biz Schools Find 'Flat is the New Up' for MBA Enrollment" in **[30797]**, **[33014]**

Crain's Detroit Business (Vol. 22, November 13, 2006, No. 46, pp. 1); "Bizdom U. Set to Teach Next Gen of Startups" in **[29710]**, **[32876]**, **[35337]**

Crain's Detroit Business (Vol. 22, January 2, 2006, No. 1, pp. 11); "Black Diamonds in Our Backyard" in **[12522]**, **[22855]**

Crain's Detroit Business (Vol. 19, No. 6, February 10, 2003, pp. 25); "Blight Busters puts $1.6M into theater plan" in **[7257]**, **[17511]**, **[27851]**

Crain's Detroit Business (Vol. 19, No. 3, January 20, 2003, pp. 1); "Blip in auto sales could spell doom for suppliers" in **[1914]**, **[17979]**, **[27852]**, **[32279]**

Crain's Detroit Business (Vol. 19, No. 16, April 21, 2003, pp. 1); "Blue Cross to cut benefits for its workers" in **[13206]**, **[26751]**, **[43096]**

Crain's Detroit Business (Vol. 18, No. 44, Nov. 4, 2002, pp. 1); "Blues' exclusive deals under fire" in **[13207]**, **[43097]**

Crain's Detroit Business (Vol. 19, No. 15, April 14, 2003, pp. 14); "Blues offer grant to study nurse shortage" in **[13208]**, **[33016]**, **[43098]**, **[50833]**

Crain's Detroit Business (Vol. 19, No. 40, October 13, 2003, pp. 1); "Blues' Small-Biz Rates to Rise 10% in 2004" in **[13209]**, **[43099]**

Crain's Detroit Business (Vol. 19, No. 40) "Blues' Small-Biz Rates to Rise 10% in 2004; Insurer Cuts Costs with Lower Commissions" in **[13210]**, **[43100]**

Crain's Detroit Business (Vol. 18, No. 17, April 29, 2002, pp. 22); "Blues losses decline for small-group business coverage" in **[13211]**, **[26752]**, **[40971]**, **[43101]**

Crain's Detroit Business (Vol. 18, No. 19, May 13, 2002,); "Blues reforms raise cost worries" in **[13212]**, **[27090]**, **[43102]**

Crain's Detroit Business (Vol. 19, No. 40, October 13, 2003, pp. 10); "Border-Crossing Backers Could Lose Own Plans" in **[7261]**, **[7532]**, **[43564]**

Crain's Detroit Business (Vol.22, December 18, 2006, No. 51, pp. 1); "Borders of Life" in **[40972]**, **[48859]**

Crain's Detroit Business (Vol. 19, No. 11, March 17, 2003); "Borders: New stores, efficiencies help improve financial picture" in **[3031]**, **[27860]**

Crain's Detroit Business (Vol. 19, No. 12, March 24, 2003, pp. 14); "Bosch posts sales spike but expects tighter 2003" in **[1915]**, **[17980]**, **[27862]**

Crain's Detroit Business (Vol. 19, No. 9, March 3, 2003, pp. 1); "Bowling for dollars" in **[3102]**

Crain's Detroit Business (Vol. 19, No. 12, March 24, 2003, pp. 3); "Brick by brick" in **[7265]**, **[27873]**

Crain's Detroit Business (Vol. 21, December 19, 2005, No. 51, pp. 14); "Briefly" in **[1786]**, **[9856]**, **[11253]**, **[14808]**, **[18854]**, **[29130]**, **[33019]**, **[37601]**, **[38724]**, **[39992]**, **[40204]**, **[55522]**

Crain's Detroit Business (Vol. 21, January 17, 2005, No. 3, pp. 28); "Brighton, Howell Hope Plans Boost Retail" in **[27876]**, **[51079]**, **[52647]**

Crain's Detroit Business (Vol. 19, No. 12, March 24, 2003, pp. 6); "Broadband agency makes its first loan" in **[4932]**, **[6596]**, **[39792]**, **[41571]**, **[44485]**

Crain's Detroit Business (Vol. 18, No. 19, May 13, 2002, pp. 1); "Broken plan" in **[37602]**

Crain's Detroit Business (Vol. 18, No. 51, December 23, 2002, pp. 3); "Brokerage to be acquired by Phoenix Company" in **[14811]**, **[20443]**, **[20813]**, **[49825]**

Crain's Detroit Business (Vol. 22, February 6, 2006, No. 6, pp. 22); "Brothers Rev Up Roostertail" in **[4535]**, **[21453]**, **[37603]**

Crain's Detroit Business (Vol. 18, No. 24,); "Budget cuts target cities with living-wage laws" in **[27093]**, **[40208]**

Crain's Detroit Business (Vol. 19, No. 4, January 27, 2003, pp. 6); "Budget hole brings tax-hike whispers" in **[39185]**, **[54459]**

Crain's Detroit Business (Vol. 19, Jan. 13, 2003, pp. 3) "Builder plans $80M in homes; Majority are proposed for Macomb County" in **[7270]**, **[20445]**, **[27884]**

Crain's Detroit Business (Vol. 19, No. 6, February 10, 2003, pp. 1); "Building a collection" in **[17984]**, **[27886]**

Crain's Detroit Business (Vol. 21, October 3, 2005, No. 43); "Building a Portfolio" in **[16300]**, **[20814]**, **[35883]**, **[54145]**

Crain's Detroit Business (Vol. 19, No. 17, April 28, 2003, pp. 9); "Building vital region requires teamwork" in **[27887]**, **[32286]**, **[40209]**

Crain's Detroit Business (Vol. 18, No. 23, June 10, 2002, pp. 16); "Building owners look to build voice" in **[20050]**

Crain's Detroit Business (Dec. 9, 2002, pp. 3) "Bulking up; Dollar Castle's ruler plans retailing, distribution kingdom" in **[32145]**, **[44965]**, **[51081]**

Crain's Detroit Business (Vol. 19, No. 6, February 10, 2003, pp. 16); "Bureau begins PR campaign to change images of Detroit" in **[24897]**, **[25164]**, **[50430]**

Crain's Detroit Business (Vol. 19, No. 10, March 10, 2003) "Business dodges budget ax; But fee hikes, tax moves raise concerns" in **[40213]**, **[54463]**

Crain's Detroit Business (Vol. 19, No. 15, April 14, 2003, pp. 20); "Business Diary" in **[14817]**, **[27358]**, **[27897]**, **[49831]**, **[49911]**

Crain's Detroit Business (Vol. 19, No. 17, April 28, 2003, pp. 6); "Business Groups Divided Over Cuts to MEDC Funding" in **[27900]**, **[32292]**, **[40216]**, **[54465]**

Crain's Detroit Business (Vol. 19, No. 49, December 8, 2003, pp. 12); "Business Plan Basics" in **[29811]**, **[30479]**

Crain's Detroit Business (Vol. 22, November 20, 2006, No. 47, pp. 18); "Business Plan Helps Set Goals, Draw Investors" in **[29813]**, **[30517]**, **[37934]**, **[46765]**

Crain's Detroit Business (Vol. 21, January 31, 2005, No. 5, pp. 6); "Businesses Assessing Granholm's Plans for SBT Overhaul" in **[27909]**, **[39794]**, **[54467]**

Crain's Detroit Business (Vol. 19, No. 14, April 7, 2003, pp. 39); "Businesses hope comments don't mean a tense border" in **[39212]**, **[43569]**

Crain's Detroit Business (Vol. 18, No. 20, May 20, 2002, pp. 14); "Businesses work to offer wireless Internet access" in **[13875]**, **[33635]**

Crain's Detroit Business (Vol. 23, January 8, 2007, No. 2, pp. 6); "Businesses Must Now Notify of Possible ID Theft" in **[33636]**, **[40222]**, **[48971]**

Crain's Detroit Business (Vol. 16, No. 4, January 24, 2000, pp. 4); "Businesses Oppose Family Leave Change" in **[26762]**, **[40223]**

Crain's Detroit Business (Vol. 19, No. 17, April 28, 2003, pp. 18); "Businesses push better public transit" in **[27911]**, **[32296]**

Crain's Detroit Business (Vol. 19, No. 42, October 20, 2003, pp. 14); "Businesses Use Wireless Access to Draw Customers" in **[3034]**, **[3121]**, **[13876]**, **[18599]**, **[21459]**, **[22196]**, **[33637]**, **[41580]**, **[43106]**

Crain's Detroit Business (Vol. 19, No. 42, October 20, 2003, pp. 29); "Businesses Warn State: Don't Hurt Economy to Fix Budget" in **[31429]**, **[32297]**, **[38571]**, **[40224]**, **[54434]**, **[54468]**

Crain's Detroit Business (Vol. 22, November 20, 2006, No. 47, pp. 4); "C & A Says Company Will Be Sold" in **[30518]**, **[37937]**, **[46224]**

Crain's Detroit Business (Vol. 19, No. 15, April 14, 2003, pp. 1); "Cabela's reels in local developer to Dundee" in **[7282]**, **[12532]**, **[17988]**, **[21460]**, **[23610]**, **[27915]**

Crain's Detroit Business (Vol. 18, No. 50, December 16, 2002, pp. 5); "Canada mum on funding for border projects" in **[25378]**, **[43572]**

Crain's Detroit Business (Vol. 18, No. 21, May 27, 2002, pp. 3); "Cancer Drug May Hold Key to Company's Survival" in **[41589]**, **[44013]**

Crain's Detroit Business (Vol. 23, January 15, 2007, No. 3, pp. 18); "Can't Pay Like the Big Guys? Think Creatively." in **[30729]**, **[34847]**

Crain's Detroit Business (Vol. 16, No. 49, December 4, 2000, pp. 7); "Capitol Briefings" in **[40240]**, **[43116]**

Crain's Detroit Business (Vol. 19, No. 15, April 14, 2003, pp. 3); "Capitol hits brakes on tax plan" in **[40243]**, **[54477]**

Crain's Detroit Business (Vol. 19, No. 11, March 17, 2003, pp. 20); "Carlyle looking for more acquisitions after buying Breed" in **[1916]**, **[49840]**

Crain's Detroit Business (Vol. 19, No. 10, March 10, 2003, pp. 32); "Catuity starts reaping loyalty-card rewards" in **[4614]**, **[22937]**, **[53236]**

Crain's Detroit Business (Vol. 19, No. 2, January 13, 2003, pp. 10); "Celebs are sweet on Hawkins' new eatery" in **[19626]**, **[21465]**

Crain's Detroit Business (Vol. 19, No. 14, April 7, 2003, pp. 38); "Central command" in **[1917]**, **[17992]**, **[43577]**

Crain's Detroit Business (Vol. 18, No.); "CEO sells IT company to help it grow" in **[6161]**, **[27939]**, **[41598]**, **[49848]**

Crain's Detroit Business (Vol. 18, No. 44, November 4, 2002, pp. 39); "Chamber, Blues team up for expo" in **[13230]**, **[43122]**

Crain's Detroit Business (Vol. 19, No. 13, March 31, 2003, pp. 5); "Chamber prepares for fight over tax changes" in **[40248]**, **[54485]**

Crain's Detroit Business (Vol. 19, No. 42, October 20, 2003, pp. 31); "Chamber Puts Spotlight on Small-Business Issues" in **[26768]**, **[27651]**, **[39229]**, **[40707]**

Crain's Detroit Business (Vol. 22, January 23, 2006, No. 4, pp. 19); "Chamber Revisits Business-Tax Proposal" in **[54486]**

Crain's Detroit Business (Vol. 21, January 10, 2005, No. 2, pp. 22); "Champion Sells Five Retail Centers, Closes 12 Others" in **[46228]**, **[51092]**

Crain's Detroit Business (Vol. 19, No. 15, April 14, 2003, pp. 33); "Changes at issue" in **[40250]**, **[54487]**

Crain's Detroit Business (Vol. 16, No. 49, December 4, 2000, pp. 28); "Changing Economic Factors Put Nursing Homes at Risk" in **[18317]**, **[40251]**

Crain's Detroit Business (Vol. 20, December 20, 2004, No. 51) "Changing Lanes; Retirements Spur Wave of Sales of Ford Dealerships" in **[17993]**, **[38738]**

Crain's Detroit Business (Vol. 19, No. 2, January 13, 2003, pp. 18); "Charities find auto-show parties an ideal vehicle" in **[17994]**, **[54153]**

Crain's Detroit Business (Vol. 21, October 24, 2005, No. 43, pp. 24); "Charter One Leads State Banks in Small-Biz Loans" in **[9876]**, **[44492]**

Crain's Detroit Business (Vol. 23, January 22-28, 2007, No. 4, pp. 10); "Checkers to Grow After Eliminating Rally's Name Locally" in **[21467]**, **[49852]**

Crain's Detroit Business (Vol. 21, October 3, 2005, No. 43, pp. 20); "Chefs Show Off at Schoolcraft College Fundraiser" in **[1793]**, **[7812]**, **[21469]**, **[23466]**, **[33037]**, **[54157]**

Crain's Detroit Business (Vol. 22, September 25-October 1, 2006, No. 39, pp. 1, 40); "China Route Hinges on Biz vs Politics" in **[27946]**, **[30311]**

Crain's Detroit Business (Vol. 19, No. 2, January 13, 2003, pp. 13); "China's cheap labor is next threat to suppliers" in **[1918]**, **[30817]**, **[43584]**, **[46234]**

Crain's Detroit Business (Vol. 21, October 31, 2005, No. 44, pp. 15); "Chinese Supplier Plans R&D Center in Canton Twp." in **[1920]**, **[50848]**, **[52077]**

Crain's Detroit Business (Vol. 18, No. 49, December 9, 2002, pp. 15); "Choosing a Business Entity" in **[35363]**, **[39038]**

Crain's Detroit Business (Vol. 21, October 10, 2005, No. 43, pp. 42); "Chrysler Deal Has SET Looking at Opening New Plant In Ohio" in **[1921]**, **[27947]**, **[46238]**, **[52654]**

Crain's Detroit Business (Vol. 23, January 8, 2007, No. 2, pp. 18); "Church Case May Impact Land Use" in **[40258]**, **[52655]**, **[54492]**

Crain's Detroit Business (Vol. 21) "Cities Talk Taxes; Mt. Clemens, Ann Arbor Look at Adding Income Levels to Help Fix Budgets" in **[40259]**, **[54495]**

Crain's Detroit Business (Vol. 19, No. 10, March 10, 2003, pp. 9); "City Policy Slows Efforts to Rehab Homes" in **[20466]**, **[20833]**, **[40260]**

Crain's Detroit Business (Vol. 16, No. 49, December 4, 2000, pp. 1); "City building department slow, costly, audit says" in **[7286]**, **[40261]**

Crain's Detroit Business (Vol. 22, November 20, 2006, No. 47, pp. 13); "Cleantech Becomes Catalyst" in **[14865]**, **[35948]**, **[37257]**, **[55540]**

Crain's Detroit Business (Vol. 19, No. 9, March 3, 2003, pp. 3); "Clicking against the Current" in **[6609]**, **[27100]**, **[41608]**

Crain's Detroit Business (Vol. 19, No. 15, April 14, 2003, pp. 30); "Clinic shut down as union vote neared" in **[17184]**, **[55286]**

Crain's Detroit Business (Vol. 20, December 20, 2004, No. 51) "Cobasys Powers Up for Possible IPO; New Deal, HQ Spur Optimism" in **[14870]**, **[17998]**, **[41611]**, **[48715]**, **[49865]**

Crain's Detroit Business (Vol. 19, No. 6, February 10, 2003, pp. 11); "Cobo Center: Grow or go" in **[22485]**, **[24908]**

Crain's Detroit Business (Vol. 16, No. 49, December 4, 2000, pp. 4); "Collins & Aikman Corp. (NYSE: CKC)" in **[14873]**

Crain's Detroit Business (Vol. 19, No. 45, November 10, 2003, pp. 29); "Collins & Aikman Faces Risk with Futura" in **[1922]**, **[46244]**, **[48073]**

Crain's Detroit Business (Vol. 19, No. 1, January 6, 2003, pp. 16); "Commercialization gets attention in life-science funding" in **[44396]**, **[48716]**, **[52017]**

Crain's Detroit Business (Vol. 16, No. 46, November 13, 2000, pp. 42); "Communities push ambitious SmartZone plans" in **[32324]**

Crain's Detroit Business (Vol. 22, September 25-October 1, 2006, No. 39, pp. 1, 38-39); "Medstat Acquisition May Bring More Jobs" in [41060], [50073]

Crain's Detroit Business (Vol. 21) "Memo: Lift 1, Curl 2; Make No Excuses, Bassett & Bassett Employees Get Fit While They Work" in [19418], [34989]

Crain's Detroit Business (Vol. 18,); "Memo to Web shops" in [14238], [25895], [34190]

Crain's Detroit Business (Vol. 15, No. 49, December 6, 1999, pp. 45); "Mental health software company gets boost" in [22885], [33461]

Crain's Detroit Business (Vol. 232, January 8, 2007, No. 2, pp. 4); "Merger with Advo May Mean Shift in Business for Valassis" in [28476], [47280], [50074]

Crain's Detroit Business (Vol. 16, No. 37, Sept. 11, 2000, pp. 55); "Merit Networks offshoot draws $5M in venture capital funding" in [41467], [55403]

Crain's Detroit Business (Vol. 19, No. 14, April 7, 2003, pp. 1); "Metro firms maintain pay for called-up reservists" in [26852], [39468], [53853], [54223]

Crain's Detroit Business (Vol. 21, February 7, 2005, No. 6, pp. 3); "MGM Taking Bids for Two Casinos in Detroit" in [10879], [29384], [40534], [52439]

Crain's Detroit Business (Vol. 18, Dec. 9, 2002, pp. 14); "Michigan Department of Consumer and Industry Services: What it does" in [39469], [39866]

Crain's Detroit Business (Vol. 19, No. 4, January 27, 2003, pp. 20); "Midsize suppliers will buy others or be bought" in [1948], [50083]

Crain's Detroit Business (Vol. 21, November 7, 2005, No. 45, pp. 36); "Milford DDA to Redevelop Former TRW Plant" in [7423], [12598], [28486]

Crain's Detroit Business (Vol.16, No.31,July 31,2000, pp.35); "Minority Architects Say Reaching Out to Youth Will Help Add Diversity" in [48299], [54226], [56323]

Crain's Detroit Business (Vol. 19, No. 40, October 13, 2003); "Minority Business Group Looks to Cement Ties with Foreign Automakers" in [1950], [1963], [17891], [18091], [41816], [43753], [46016], [46375], [47143], [48304]

Crain's Detroit Business (Vol. 21, October 10, 2005, No. 43); "Minority Businesses Look For a Boost From Super Bowl and Beyond" in [28488], [48305], [56324]

Crain's Detroit Business (Vol. 18, No. 20, May 20, 2002, pp. 8); "Minority Certification Needs Examination" in [28489], [48306], [50085]

Crain's Detroit Business (Vol. 19, No. 16, April 21, 2003, pp. 6); "Minority-certified paper company sets up shop in Canton Twp." in [46166], [47968]

Crain's Detroit Business (Vol. 16, No. 49, December 4, 2000, pp. 8); "Mixed-use development deserves a good look" in [52917]

Crain's Detroit Business (Vol. 16, No. 34, August 21, 2000, pp. E-6); "Molly Maid franchise owners have own site" in [8691], [34202], [38857]

Crain's Detroit Business (Vol. 22, November 20, 2006, No. 47, pp. 9) "Money Talks; Here's Message to Michigan" in [28501], [30569], [43757]

Crain's Detroit Business (Vol. 19, No. 9, March 3, 2003, pp. 18); "More fly charter, wing it themselves" in [30379], [53868]

Crain's Detroit Business (Vol. 19, No. 10, March 10, 2003, pp. 37); "More condos, lofts in pipeline for Detroit" in [20595], [20943]

Crain's Detroit Business (Vol. 19, No. 4, January 27, 2003, pp. 1); "More deals, smaller portions" in [15274], [50088]

Crain's Detroit Business (Vol. 19, No. 49, December 8, 2003) "More Fun for the Money; ASC Lures 'Car Nuts' to Reshape the Company" in [1951], [1964], [40540], [42349]

Crain's Detroit Business (Vol. 18, No. 49, December 9, 2002, pp. 25); "More dealers may signal end of mobile-phone boom" in [5061], [28506], [30570]

Crain's Detroit Business (Vol. 22, January 2, 2006, No. 1, pp. 20); "More Tool-and-Die Firms to Get Tax Relief" in [16375], [46378], [54665]

Crain's Detroit Business (Vol. 19, No. pp. 11); "Movin' on up" in [2344], [7428], [11337], [20599], [20945], [21564]

Crain's Detroit Business (Vol. 19, No. 13, March 31, 2003, pp. 13); "Moving from one product was their prize" in [14256], [25901], [28517], [34215], [41848]

Crain's Detroit Business (Vol. 18, No. 24, June 17, 2002, pp. 22); "Mr. Pita legal woes haven't put a wrap on expansion" in [21566], [28518], [29390], [38859]

Crain's Detroit Business (Vol. 22, February 6, 2006, No. 6, pp. 21); "Mr. Pita Wagons Rolling Along" in [21567], [28519], [38860]

Crain's Detroit Business (Vol. 21, January 24, 2005, No. 4, pp. 1); "MSU Enlists Biz Help On $1B Isotope Project Bid" in [40060], [50928], [52155]

Crain's Detroit Business (Vol. 19, No. 10, March 10, 2003, pp. 34); "Musical cases" in [17601], [17758], [29391], [44100]

Crain's Detroit Business (Vol. 23, January 1, 2007, No. 1, pp. 1); "NAIAS Spotlight Shines on Design" in [28523], [29939], [55129]

Crain's Detroit Business (Vol. 16, No. 46, November 13, 2000, pp. 15); "National trends in Webcast advertising" in [14270], [34232], [47314]

Crain's Detroit Business (Vol. 18, No. 19, May 13, 2002, pp); "Nature's Way" in [13663], [18553], [18604], [49520]

Crain's Detroit Business (Vol. 16, No. 10, March 6, 2000, pp. 21); "NAWBO honors top business women" in [56335]

Crain's Detroit Business (Vol. 19, No. 44, November 3, 2003, pp. 1); "Nemes Allen Merges with Wisconsin Firm" in [203], [2934], [23995], [50094]

Crain's Detroit Business (Vol. 19, No. 44) "Nemes Allen Merges with Wisconsin Firm; Accountants to Pursue Middle-Market Clients" in [202], [2933], [23994], [50093]

Crain's Detroit Business (Vol. 19, No. 14, April 7, 2003, pp. 46); "New disease has businesses cautious, but few effects seen" in [41068], [43758]

Crain's Detroit Business (Vol. 16, No. 7, February 14, 2000, pp. 37); "New Detroit survey targets metro area minority business" in [48326], [52922]

Crain's Detroit Business (Vol. 19, No. 16, April 21, 2003, pp. 25); "New Group Weighs Solutions" in [32590]

Crain's Detroit Business (Vol. 19, No. 9, March 3, 2003, pp. 7); "New Land-Use Council Set to Tackle Urban Sprawl" in [20609], [20950], [40551]

Crain's Detroit Business (Vol. 19, No. 1, Jan. 6, 2003, pp. 16); "New Law Likely to Save Businesses Money on Terrorism Insurance" in [13398], [40552], [43290]

Crain's Detroit Business (Vol. 21, January 10, 2005, No. 2, pp. 22); "New Law Reduced Liability for Architects, Engineers" in [1523], [7438], [29402], [40066], [40553]

Crain's Detroit Business (Vol. 22, January 16, 2006, No. 3, pp. 23); "New Laws Tighten Rules, Penalties for Accountants" in [206], [2936], [24000], [26302]

Crain's Detroit Business (Vol. 22, December 18, 2006, No. 51,pp. 19); "New Office Created to Market Michigan for Films" in [9733], [47328], [50644]

Crain's Detroit Business (Vol. 22, December 4, 2006, No. 29, pp. 24); "New Owners Cook Up Redo of Clarkston Cafe" in [21408], [27729], [30490]

Crain's Detroit Business (Vol. 22, January 2, 2006, No. 1); "New Shopping Centers on Tap in Fast-Growing Livingston County" in [28550], [51270]

Crain's Detroit Business (Vol. 23, January 8, 2007, No. 2, pp. 10); "New Site Gives Lipari Foods Room to Continue Growth" in [10623], [28551], [29942], [30163], [56014]

Crain's Detroit Business (Vol. 21, February 7, 2005, No. 6, pp. 14); "New Space in an Old Place" in [18097], [36544], [37741]

Crain's Detroit Business (Vol. 16, No. 50, December 11, 2000, pp. 21); "New Team Joins Raymond James Investment Office" in [10106], [15302], [50099]

Crain's Detroit Business (Vol. 19, No. 49, December 8, 2003, pp. 22); "New Tenants Reverse Birmingham Center's Decline" in [11892], [12328], [17423], [18056], [19423], [20139]

Crain's Detroit Business (Vol. 18, No. 2, June 3, 2002, pp. 43); "New Venture-Capital Group Wants to Keep Entrepreneurs in State" in [35588], [44431], [55409]

Crain's Detroit Business (Vol. 21, October 10, 2005, No. 43, pp. 1); "New Wireless Service to Debut in 2006" in [5069], [41867], [55753]

Crain's Detroit Business (Vol. 21, October 10, 2005, No. 43, pp. 8); "New Work Rules Will Help Cobo, Auto Show" in [18098], [46390], [55301]

Crain's Detroit Business (Vol. 22, December 11, 2006, No. 50, pp. 13); "New Wright Museum CEO: Increase Role in Schools" in [33190], [48338], [50100]

Crain's Detroit Business (Vol. 21, October 31, 2005, No. 44, pp. 30); "Newton Furniture Shutters Stores" in [12200], [12303]

Crain's Detroit Business (Vol. 19, No. 10, March 10, 2003, pp. 11); "Next step: Bricks and mortar" in [41869], [44104], [50102], [52160]

Crain's Detroit Business (Vol. 19, No. 10, March 10, 2003, pp. 29); "NextEnergy gets $2M from feds" in [40573], [41870], [44605], [50936], [52161]

Crain's Detroit Business (Vol. 22, February 6, 2006, No. 6, pp. 11); "NextEnergy May Get HQ" in [41871], [52704]

Crain's Detroit Business (Vol. 21, January 3, 2005, No. 1, pp. 12); "NFL Reaches Out" in [36552], [48339], [56347]

Crain's Detroit Business (V. 19, No. 7, 2/17/03, pp. 22); "$ 93M in Development Planned for South Lyon" in [7441], [20610], [20951], [28564]

Crain's Detroit Business (January 17, 2005) No "Lodi Twp. Development Homes To Start at $1 M; Project Would Be First in County" in [7406]

Crain's Detroit Business (Vol. 22, November 27, 2006, No. 48, pp. 21); "No Slowdown Likely for Rising Health Costs" in [29944], [39878], [41069]

Crain's Detroit Business (January 26, 2004, pp. 20); "Noble International to Buy Laser Welding International" in [15306], [18103], [46395]

Crain's Detroit Business (Vol. 22, November 27, 2006, No. 48, pp. 20); "Nonprofit Consolidation to Increase" in [38250], [48920], [50107]

Crain's Detroit Business (Vol. 22, February 13, 2006, No. 7, pp. 26); "Nonprofit Seminar is March 13" in [10744], [24987], [55135]

Crain's Detroit Business (Vol. 19, No. 7, Feb. 17, 2003); "Northwest seeks to cut $1.5B, but little impact felt at Metro for now" in [28570], [30389]

Crain's Detroit Business (Vol. 19, No. 6, February 10, 2003, pp. 1); "Northwest may be next with low-cost subsidiary" in [28571], [30391]

Crain's Detroit Business (Vol. 16, No. 50, December 11, 2000, pp. 21); "Northwest worries labor could harm on-time record" in [55304]

Crain's Detroit Business (Vol. 19, No. 1, Jan. 6, 2003, pp. 18) "Northwest sees friendlier skies; Detroit called key to strategy" in [28572]

Crain's Detroit Business (Vol. 19, No. 45, November 10, 2003, pp. 28); "Number-Portability Change to Increase Wireless Competition" in [5225], [40581], [42047]

Crain's Detroit Business (Vol. 19, No. 1, Jan. 6, 2003, pp. 7); "Oakland cities try to reinvigorate neglected areas" in [7443], [28580]

Crain's Detroit Business (Vol. 21, October 10, 2005, No. 43, pp. 23); "Objectivity, Consensus Key For Survival of Family Biz" in [37747], [45480]

Crain's Detroit Business (Vol. 18, No. 51, Dec. 23, 2002, pp. 1); "Research's reward" in **[40643]**, **[44133]**, **[48781]**, **[52191]**

Crain's Detroit Business (Vol. 18, No. 19, May 13, 2002, pp. 1); "Restaurant chains look for bite of local market" in **[21599]**, **[38897]**

Crain's Detroit Business (Vol. 19, No. 45, November 10, 2003, pp. 44); "Restaurateur Inks Subway Deal for Eastern Wayne County" in **[8521]**, **[21610]**, **[23039]**, **[38898]**

Crain's Detroit Business (Vol. 19, No. 42, October 20, 2003, pp. 1); "Retailers Beginning to Get Holiday Spirit" in **[28704]**, **[51318]**

Crain's Detroit Business (Vol. 19) "Retailers Beginning to Get Holiday Spirit; Many Boost Inventory in Hopes of Strong Sales" in **[28705]**, **[51319]**

Crain's Detroit Business (Vol. 21, October 31, 2005, No. 44, pp. 3); "Retailers Optimistic They Can Compete for Slice of Macomb" in **[30937]**, **[51324]**, **[52718]**

Crain's Detroit Business (Vol. 19, No. 1, January 6, 2003, pp. 12); "Richard Whitmer" in **[13449]**, **[40651]**, **[43344]**

Crain's Detroit Business (Vol. 19, No. 8, February 24, 2003, pp. 3) "Riding a buzz; Local shop hopes Tomahawk limelight pays off" in **[1965]**, **[18118]**

Crain's Detroit Business (Vol. 20) "Riding the Rebates; Wixom Company Grows by Hitching Itself to National Retail Trend" in **[47476]**, **[51332]**

Crain's Detroit Business (Vol. 21, October 10, 2005, No. 43, pp. 16); "Right Message, Right Time Key for Hospitality Marketing" in **[12627]**, **[22555]**, **[24726]**, **[25010]**, **[25240]**, **[47478]**, **[55151]**

Crain's Detroit Business (Vol. 21, October 10, 2005, No. 43); "Ritz-Carlton Offers Henry Ford Patients a Place to Recuperate" in **[12628]**, **[41091]**

Crain's Detroit Business (Vol. 16, No. 49, December 4, 2000, pp. 41); "Riverview, Trenton try to salvage riverfront dreams" in **[25409]**, **[52940]**

Crain's Detroit Business (Vol. 19, No. 17, April 28, 2003, pp. 1); "Road-money halt slows $172.5M Oakland plan" in **[28716]**, **[32673]**

Crain's Detroit Business (Vol. 16, No. 16, April 17, 2000, pp. 34); "Roberts' Internet venture to set up shop in Detroit" in **[13775]**, **[33483]**, **[47975]**, **[52641]**

Crain's Detroit Business (Vol. 18, No. 51, December 23, 2002, pp. 1); "Rochester OKs plans for $30M, 140-room hotel" in **[12629]**

Crain's Detroit Business (Vol. 16, No. 46, November 13, 2000, pp. 4); "Rofin-Sinar sales rise 61 percent" in **[16380]**, **[28717]**

Crain's Detroit Business (Vol. 19, No. 43, October 27, 2003, pp. 17); "Rouge Industries' Russian Suitor Promises New Furnace" in **[46422]**, **[47769]**, **[48260]**, **[50167]**

Crain's Detroit Business (Vol. 23, January 8, 2007, No. 2, pp. 1); "Round Two: Microsoft Appeals $140M Judgment For Local Inventor" in **[29471]**, **[44139]**

Crain's Detroit Business (Vol. 21, October 3, 2005, No. 43, pp. 18); "Rugby Grille Walks Tightrope in Redoing Menu" in **[21613]**

Crain's Detroit Business (Vol. 21, January 31, 2005, No. 5, pp. 33); "Ruling on Tax Incentives May Head to High Court" in **[29473]**, **[40658]**, **[54731]**

Crain's Detroit Business (Vol. 19, No. 1, January 6, 2003, pp. 22); "Rumblings" in **[15427]**, **[19434]**, **[29474]**, **[40659]**, **[43351]**, **[50168]**

Crain's Detroit Business (Vol. 21, October 24, 2005, No. 43, pp. 24); "Salvation Army Picks Center Site" in **[7474]**, **[52720]**, **[54250]**

Crain's Detroit Business (Vol. 18, No. 49, December 9, 2002, pp. 17); "Sample business plans" in **[29985]**, **[30594]**

Crain's Detroit Business (Vol. 18, No. 49, December 9, 2002, pp. 16); "SBA can be a boon, but it doesn't make loans" in **[39906]**, **[40665]**

Crain's Detroit Business (Vol. 18, No. 49, December 9, 2002, pp. 16); "SBA info" in **[39912]**, **[40668]**

Crain's Detroit Business (Vol. 19, No. 42, October 20, 2003, pp. 18); "SBA Preferred Lenders" in **[38279]**, **[39915]**, **[44647]**

Crain's Detroit Business (Vol. 18, No. 40, October 7, 2002, pp. 43); "SBA limits program's loan amounts to $500,000" in **[39917]**, **[44648]**

Crain's Detroit Business (Vol. 21, October 3, 2005, No. 43, pp. 6); "SBC, Other Providers Spar on Phone Rules" in **[5100]**, **[30943]**, **[40674]**

Crain's Detroit Business (Vol. 19, No. 16, April 21, 2003, pp. 8); "SBC's withdrawal speaks volumes" in **[5101]**

Crain's Detroit Business (Vol. 19, No. 49, December 8, 2003); "Second Base: Getting the Right Accountant Can Pay Big Dividends" in **[235]**, **[242]**, **[25961]**, **[26345]**

Crain's Detroit Business (Jan. 13, 2003, pp. 3) "Secure access; Carriersnet building Web-based system to track worldwide cargo" in **[10696]**, **[14419]**, **[22360]**, **[34447]**

Crain's Detroit Business (Vol. 19, No. 12, March 24, 2003, pp. 24); "Security Companies Expect War to Increase Business" in **[22365]**, **[28750]**, **[41967]**

Crain's Detroit Business (Vol. 22, February 6, 2006, No. 6, pp. 3); "SEE Change" in **[25649]**, **[50174]**

Crain's Detroit Business (Vol. 19, No. 8, February 24, 2003, pp. 11); "Seeking outside help" in **[41095]**, **[49733]**

Crain's Detroit Business (Vol. 23, February 5, 2007, No. 6, pp. 26); "Seeking Up-and-Comers Under 30." in **[35064]**, **[36733]**, **[50672]**

Crain's Detroit Business (Vol. 18, No. 49, December 9, 2002, pp. 6); "Senate votes to ease effect of high SBT bills" in **[40685]**, **[54743]**

Crain's Detroit Business (Vol. 16, No. 50, December 11, 2000, pp. E-13); "Service Providers" in **[29989]**, **[36737]**, **[37495]**, **[39924]**

Crain's Detroit Business (Vol. 16, No. 26, June 26, 2000, pp. E-15); "Services finalists" in **[45635]**, **[52586]**

Crain's Detroit Business (Dec. 16, 2002, pp. 17); "Several buildings may change hands in coming months" in **[20668]**, **[21005]**, **[30174]**, **[52726]**

Crain's Detroit Business (Vol. 21, January 31, 2005, No. 5, pp. 35); "Shelby Supervisor Hopes Township Plan Can Spur More Growth" in **[7477]**, **[17530]**, **[28759]**, **[51352]**

Crain's Detroit Business (Vol. 21, October 10, 2005, No. 43, pp. 36); "Shift to Military Contracts Could Help Excel Stay Afloat" in **[1967]**, **[40093]**

Crain's Detroit Business (Vol. 18, No. 16, April 22, 2002, pp. 3); "Shifting gears: Suit and tie gone, passion becomes his business" in **[17479]**, **[35640]**

Crain's Detroit Business (Vol. 21, January 31, 2005) "Shopping Spree; Ramco-Gershenson Rings Up $500M in Acquisitions in 2004" in **[15451]**, **[21006]**, **[50177]**

Crain's Detroit Business (Vol. 19, No. 49, December 8, 2003, pp. 3); "Sibleys Shores Inc. History" in **[22767]**

Crain's Detroit Business (Vol. 21, January 24, 2005) "Sides Vie to Regulate Internet-Based Service; Michigan Wants to Play Role" in **[5106]**, **[14430]**, **[34472]**, **[40692]**, **[41982]**

Crain's Detroit Business; "Silicon Peninsula?" in **[41482]**, **[55428]**

Crain's Detroit Business (Vol. 22, January 30, 2006, No. 5, pp. 6); "Small-Biz Leaders Mixed on Retirement Proposal" in **[26913]**, **[40696]**

Crain's Detroit Business (Vol. 19, No. 9, March 3, 2003, pp. 29); "Small Biz Tentative about Testing Web Waters" in **[14441]**, **[34487]**, **[53969]**

Crain's Detroit Business (Vol. 18, No. 45, November 11, 2002, pp. 23); "Small business" in **[28775]**, **[31071]**, **[47541]**

Crain's Detroit Business (Vol. 16, May 29, 2000, pp. 54); "Small Business: Crunching numbers via the Internet" in **[23176]**, **[26356]**, **[34491]**

Crain's Detroit Business (Vol. 15, No. 50, Dec. 13, 1999, pp. E-11); "Small Business Resource Guide: Service Providers: Part 1 of 2" in **[28780]**, **[39929]**, **[55831]**

Crain's Detroit Business (Vol. 15, No. 50, Dec. 13, 1999, pp. E-13); "Small Business Resource Guide: Service Providers: Part 2 of 2" in **[28781]**, **[39930]**, **[55832]**

Crain's Detroit Business (Vol. 18, No. 49, December 9, 2002, pp. 18); "Small Businesses Don't Have to Spend Big for Web Sites" in **[14445]**, **[25964]**, **[34497]**

Crain's Detroit Business (Vol. 21, February 7, 2005, No. 6, pp. 24); "Small Firms Emphasize Trade-Show Marketing" in **[25019]**, **[30955]**, **[36762]**, **[47549]**, **[50675]**, **[51843]**, **[55157]**

Crain's Detroit Business (Vol. 18, No. 50, December 16, 2002, pp. 6); "Small-Group Reform, Blue Changes on Hold" in **[13465]**, **[40703]**, **[43366]**

Crain's Detroit Business (Vol. 19, No. 16, April 21, 2003, pp. 7); "Small-group insurance reforms are in works" in **[13466]**, **[40704]**, **[43367]**

Crain's Detroit Business (Vol. 16, No. 16, April 17, 2000, pp. 32); "Small businesses fight to repeal tax-law change" in **[52456]**, **[54766]**

Crain's Detroit Business (Vol. 22, December 4, 2006, No. 49, pp. 33); "Smaller Shopping Centers Adopt Larger Style" in **[29997]**, **[47550]**

Crain's Detroit Business (Vol. 16, No. 46, November 13, 2000, pp. 16); "Software, computer leasing providers jockey to survive" in **[49275]**, **[53485]**

Crain's Detroit Business (Vol. 19, No. 17, April 28, 2003, pp. 1); "Solving the regional puzzle" in **[32704]**, **[39603]**

Crain's Detroit Business (Vol. 22, January 16, 2006, No. 3, pp. 3); "Some Suppliers Expanding Biz" in **[1969]**, **[28797]**, **[43822]**

Crain's Detroit Business (Vol. 22, January 2, 2006, No. 1, pp. 8); "Something to Prove" in **[14462]**

Crain's Detroit Business (Vol. 19, No. 17, April 28, 2003, pp. 30); "Sorting out Enron mess pumps up Plante & Moran" in **[262]**, **[24044]**, **[26366]**

Crain's Detroit Business (Vol. 16, No. 47) "Sour forecasts reach fruition; Local companies' 3Q profits fall 26.8 percent from '99" in **[28798]**

Crain's Detroit Business (Vol. 18, No. 22, June 3, 2002, pp. 37); "Spectacular growth forces Accident Fund to limit new biz" in **[13470]**, **[28803]**, **[43373]**

Crain's Detroit Business (Vol. 22, January 16, 2006, No. 3, pp. 16); "Spend, Target Ad Dollars Wisely" in **[792]**, **[47561]**

Crain's Detroit Business (Vol. 18, No. 21, May 27, 2002, pp. 40); "Spot-condemnation law better for neighborhoods, leaders say" in **[28806]**, **[40714]**

Crain's Detroit Business (Vol. 21, October 17, 2005, No. 43, pp. 24); "Spotlight On" in **[9233]**, **[9578]**, **[15469]**, **[22564]**, **[24533]**, **[24729]**, **[25021]**, **[25247]**, **[38369]**, **[55158]**

Crain's Detroit Business (Vol. 21, February 7, 2005, No. 6, pp. 28); "Spotlight On: Detroit Marriott at the Renaissance Center" in **[12637]**, **[21633]**, **[25248]**

Crain's Detroit Business (Vol. 19, No. 11, March 17, 2003, pp. 11); "Spy tech" in **[22387]**, **[42003]**, **[52208]**

Crain's Detroit Business (Vol. 21, January 3, 2005, No. 1, pp. 5); "Squeezing Suppliers Can Cost Automakers, Study Says" in **[1970]**, **[18128]**, **[23770]**, **[46436]**

Crain's Detroit Business (Vol. 23, January 1, 2007, No. 1, pp. 3); "Stakes High For Region as Big Three, UAW Sit Down to Talk." in **[18129]**, **[30006]**, **[46437]**, **[55313]**

Crain's Detroit Business (Vol. 19, No. 9, March 3, 2003, pp. 1); "Standing pat. Most employers not changing size of work force" in **[42425]**, **[53996]**

Crain's Detroit Business (Vol. 18, No. 49, December 9, 2002, pp. 17); "Starting a business? Then get with the plan" in **[29765]**, **[30493]**, **[35667]**, **[44705]**

Master Index

"Dairy Queen phasing out frozen yogurt" in (Vol. 14, No. 9, August 29, 2001, pp. 1) **[12772]**, **[27344]**

Daito-Ryu Revelations **[16920]**

Daito-Ryu Secrets **[16921]**

Dakota County Technical College
    St. Thomas College of Business–Small Business Development Center **[61518]**
    SBDC **[61181]**

The Dakota Group **[57978]**

Dale Carnegie Training **[33362]**

Dale System Inc. **[35295]**

Daleville Chamber of Commerce **[56835]**

Dalhart Area Chamber of Commerce **[65191]**

Dalhousie University–Population Health Research Unit **[41366]**

Dali, Hook Partners (Dallas) **[65601]**

Dallas Apparel News **[5291]**, **[5582]**

Dallas Area Chamber of Commerce **[64214]**

Dallas Black Chamber of Commerce **[65192]**

Dallas County Community College–North Texas Small Business Development Center **[65029]**

Dallas County Community College District's Cedar Valley College–Small Business Development Center **[65030]**

Dallas/Ft. Worth JobBank **[23386]**

Dallas/Fort Worth Minority Business Development Center **[65578]**

Dallas Market Center-Permanent Directory **[12218]**

Dallas Men's and Boys' Apparel Market **[5295]**

Dallas Morning News (April 11, 2003); "American Airlines' Future Hangs Union Votes" in **[30287]**, **[55280]**

Dallas Morning News (October 27, 2002); "Arlington, Texas, High-Tech Incubator Gets $2.85 Million Boost" in **[41522]**, **[43048]**, **[55495]**

Dallas Morning News (August 7, 2003); "Dell Plugs in First Airport Retail Kiosk at Dallas/Fort Worth" in **[6625]**, **[15918]**

Dallas Northeast Chamber of Commerce **[65193]**

Dalton Area Chamber of Commerce **[63654]**

Dalton Directory **[64630]**

Dalton-Whitfield Chamber of Commerce **[59088]**

Daly City - Colma Chamber of Commerce **[57450]**

"Damage Control" in *Black Enterprise* (Vol. 36, December 2005, No. 5, pp. 54) **[52522]**

"Damages Aren't Always Patently Obvious" in *Journal of Accountancy* **[119]**, **[2889]**, **[23923]**, **[26205]**, **[27109]**, **[44023]**, **[44286]**

"Damariscotta, Maine, Merchants Worry About Wal-Mart" in *Portland Press Herald* (December 1, 2005) **[30834]**, **[51121]**

Damariscotta Region Chamber of Commerce **[60741]**

Damas & Associates **[38963]**

"Damm Dotcoms!" in *Entrepreneur* (Vol. 28, No. 8, August 2000, pp. 78) **[33737]**, **[53679]**

Damon's International, Inc. **[21793]**

"Dan Case's Next Great IPO" in *Fast Company* (May 2001, pp. 175) **[14902]**, **[36000]**, **[49886]**

"Dana Has Cash, Looks for Ways to Spend It" in *Crain's Detroit Business* (Vol. 21, January 31, 2005, No. 5, pp. 12) **[14903]**, **[46258]**, **[49887]**

Dance Educators of America **[8440]**

Dance Films Association, Inc. **[8492]**

Dance International **[8459]**

Dance Magazine **[8460]**

Dance Magazine College Guide **[8452]**

Dance Notation Bureau **[8441]**

Dances for Drill and Dance Teams **[8471]**

Dancing in Hollywood: A Guide for the Professional Dancer **[8472]**

Dancing a Miracle **[19467]**

Dandini Research Park **[62378]**

"D&O: Hard and Getting Harder" in *Rough Notes* (Vol. 145, No. 9, September 2002, pp. 71) **[13257]**, **[37417]**, **[43146]**

"D&PL Reports Loss" in *Mississippi Business Journal* (Vol. 29, January 2007, No. 2, pp. 8) **[26500]**, **[28007]**, **[39271]**

Dangerous Goods Advisory Council **[11926]**

Dangerous Goods Council Inc. **[11964]**

"The Dangers of a Lack of Accountability" in *Automotive News* (Vol. 20, October 4, 2004, No. 40, pp. 8) **[120]**, **[26206]**, **[29189]**, **[32014]**, **[40298]**, **[48123]**

"Dangle Carrots: How To Keep Your Sales Force Hopping" in *My Business* (October/November 2003, pp. 45) **[45042]**, **[51607]**

The Danielle Adams Publishing Co. **[64631]**

Daniels County Chamber of Commerce and Agriculture **[62160]**

Danish American Chamber of Commerce **[43491]**

Dansville Chamber of Commerce **[62870]**

DANTH Inc. **[1552]**

Danville Area Chamber of Commerce **[57451]**, **[64409]**

Danville Area Community College–Small Business Development Center **[59367]**

Danville-Boyle County Chamber of Commerce **[60497]**

Danville - Pittsylvania County Chamber of Commerce **[65885]**

D'Arcy Masius Benton & Bowles–Information Center **[50734]**

"Dare to Compare." in *Entrepreneur* (Vol. 33, January 2005, No. 1, pp. 43) **[30835]**, **[31022]**, **[33738]**, **[46869]**, **[51122]**

"Dare to Disconnect" in *Home Office Computing* (Vol. 19, No. 1, January 2001, pp. 92) **[30316]**, **[42600]**

Darien Chamber of Commerce **[58525]**, **[59477]**

"The Dark Art of Letting People Go" in *Business Week Online* () **[42845]**, **[45043]**

"Dark Dollar Signs" in *Hispanic Business* (June 2005, pp. 22, 24) **[14904]**, **[32345]**

"Dark Horse Wins Verizon Space Race" in *Washington Business Journal* (Vol. 22, No. 14, August 8, 2003, pp. 1) **[4967]**, **[20481]**, **[20852]**

Darke County Chamber of Commerce **[63655]**

Darke County Historical Society–Library **[11018]**

Darlington Chamber of Commerce **[66376]**

DART: British Columbia Labour Decisions **[29656]**

DART: British Columbia Statute Service **[29657]**

DART: Western Decisions **[29658]**

"Dartfish swimming in bigger pool" in *Atlanta Business Chronicle* (Vol. 24, No. 13, August 31, 2001, pp. 3A) **[22958]**, **[24401]**, **[44024]**

Dartmouth College–Center for Evaluative Clinical Sciences **[41367]**

Data Analysis in Hotel & Catering Management **[4541]**, **[12541]**

The DATA BASE for Advances in Information Systems **[13094]**

Data Base Alert **[13095]**, **[14646]**

Data Base and Organizational Structure **[6990]**

"Data Centers: Infrastructure upgrades ahead" in *Red Herring* (No. 102, August 15, 2001, pp. 74-75) **[6242]**, **[6932]**, **[13951]**, **[49689]**

"Data key to Centerstone's resource-tracking software" in *Boston Business Journal* (Vol. 22, No. 11, April 19, 2002, pp. 19) **[1507]**, **[4631]**, **[13639]**, **[16511]**, **[20052]**, **[22211]**, **[22959]**, **[53248]**

Data Concepts **[49413]**

Data Conversion Laboratory Inc. **[4878]**

"Data Discovery" in *Entrepreneur* (Vol. 31, No. 7, July 2003, pp. 40) **[4632]**, **[22212]**, **[22960]**, **[53249]**

"Data Disposal Questions" in *Hispanic Business* (Vol. 23, No. 7/8, July/August 2001, pp. 112, 114) **[39272]**, **[49495]**

Data Doctors **[6435]**, **[6898]**

"Data to Go: When You're on the Move, Stay Connected for Less" in *Entrepreneur* (Vol. 33, February 2005, No. 2, pp. 38) **[4968]**, **[49005]**

Data Resources in Gerontology **[1699]**

"Database Dollars" in *Small Business Opportunities* (Vol. 12, No. 5, September 2000, pp. 44) **[46870]**, **[52841]**, **[53250]**

Database Marketing: The Ultimate Marketing Tool **[46871]**

Datamation **[6502]**, **[23277]**

"Datatrac trucks in $3 million in venture capital funding" in *Atlanta Business Chronicle* (Vol. 25, December 13, 2002, No. 27, pp. A3) **[6243]**, **[6933]**, **[13952]**, **[25381]**, **[33739]**, **[55561]**

"Dating Service: Don't Call Anymore" in *United Press International* (December 5, 2003) **[7053]**

Dat@Line **[13096]**

Dauphin Capital Partners **[63078]**

Davenport Chamber of Commerce **[63980]**, **[66073]**

Davenport University–Thomas F. Reed, Jr. Memorial Library **[17305]**, **[24781]**, **[25348]**

DavenportOne **[60120]**

David Armstrong Paints **[1632]**

David City Area Chamber of Commerce **[62259]**

David Hall's Inside View **[5844]**

"David Nicklaus Column" in *St. Louis Post-Dispatch* (September 24, 2004) **[9905]**, **[14905]**, **[17370]**, **[20482]**, **[32346]**, **[37993]**, **[40299]**, **[44398]**, **[49888]**, **[51123]**, **[55368]**

"David Wetherell" in *Internet World* (Vol. 7, No. 2, January 15, 2001, pp. 30) **[13953]**, **[33740]**

James W. Davidson Company Inc. **[50312]**, **[52474]**

Davie-Cooper City Chamber of Commerce **[58781]**

Davie County Chamber of Commerce **[63353]**

Daviess County Chamber of Commerce **[59900]**

Davis Chamber of Commerce **[57452]**, **[63981]**, **[65707]**

W. F. Davis Consultants **[2844]**, **[6039]**

Davis Database **[32169]**

Davis Group **[57979]**

Davis, Tuttle Venture Partners, L.P. / DTVP (Tulsa) **[64115]**

Davison Area Chamber of Commerce **[61283]**

The Davlin Report **[26572]**, **[37340]**

Dawes Arboretum–Library **[11517]**

Dawntreader Ventures **[63079]**

"Dawson on Board at Melville-based Fala Direct Marketing" in *Long Island Business News* (March 12, 2004) **[44744]**, **[45044]**, **[46777]**, **[46872]**

Dawson County Chamber of Commerce **[59089]**

Dawson Springs Chamber of Commerce **[60498]**

"Day Care for Dot-Coms: Warmer, Fuzzier Venture Capitalism" in *Fortune* (Vol. 140, No. 11, pp. 72+) **[13739]**, **[55369]**

Day Care Grows Up **[5379]**, **[17869]**

The Day Care Providers Tax Survival Manual:...A Complete Tax Guide & Recordkeeping System **[5337]**, **[54507]**

Day in the Career Series **[9258]**

A Day to Cherish Wedding Videos **[4009]**, **[19265]**

"Day of E-tonement" in *Forbes* (December 25, 2000, pp. 262) **[13954]**, **[33741]**

"A day of pondering leads to a life-altering change" in *Crain's Detroit Business* (Vol. 16, No. 50, December 11, 2000, pp. E-5) **[19837]**, **[35380]**

"Daydream Believer" in *My Business* (February/March 2003, pp. 52) **[33426]**, **[35381]**

Days Inn-Canada **[3856]**

Days Inns Worldwide, Inc. **[12711]**

"Day's 'lean' philosophy to face new test at Venture Holdings" in *Crain's Detroit Business* (Vol. 19, No. 14, April 7, 2003, pp. 41) **[45045]**, **[46259]**

Days of Reckoning **[45919]**

"Daytime's Other Drama" in *Black Enterprise* (Vol. 35, December 2004, No. 5, pp. 120) **[9702]**, **[24402]**

Dayton Area Chamber of Commerce **[62346]**, **[63656]**
    Small Business Development Center **[63555]**

Dayton Auto Show **[925]**

Dayton Chamber of Commerce **[64905]**

Dayton Chamber of Commerce and Visitor Information Center **[66074]**

Dayton Daily News (July 29, 2004); "Dayton, Ohio, Inventor of Garden Tool Organizer Looks to Expand Business" in **[20017]**, **[37624]**, **[44025]**

"Dayton, Ohio, Inventor of Garden Tool Organizer Looks to Expand Business" in *Dayton Daily News* (July 29, 2004) **[20017]**, **[37624]**, **[44025]**

Daytona Beach Community College–Small Business Development Center **[58700]**

Daytona Beach - Halifax Area Chamber of Commerce **[58782]**

Daytona Beach Shores Chamber of Commerce **[58783]**

DB2 Update **[6503]**

DBA Books **[61163]**

The DBS Report **[22092]**

Defense Contract Management Area Operations (Twin Cities) [67456]

Defense Contract Management Area Operations (Van Nuys) [67436]

Defense Contract Management Center [67432]

Defense Contract Management Center - Aircraft Program–Management Office [67444]

Defense Contract Management Center (Baltimore) [67451]

Defense Contract Management Center (Denver) [67438]

Defense Contract Management Center (East Hartford) [67439]

Defense Contract Management Center (Indianapolis) [67447]

Defense Contract Management Center (Orlando) [67441]

Defense Contract Management Center (Stratford) [67440]

Defense Contract Management Command (Atlanta) [67445]

Defense Contract Management Command (Boston) [67452]

Defense Contract Management Command (Boston-Manchester) [67458]

Defense Contract Management Command (Chicago) [67446]

Defense Contract Management Command (Clearwater) [67442]

Defense Contract Management Command (Cleveland) [67464]

Defense Contract Management Command (Dallas) [67470]

Defense Contract Management Command (Dayton) [67465]

Defense Contract Management Command (Dayton-Louisville) [67450]

Defense Contract Management Command (Indianapolis-South Bend) [67448]

Defense Contract Management Command (New York City) [67462]

Defense Contract Management Command (Orlando) [67443]

Defense Contract Management Command (St. Louis) [67457]

Defense Contract Management Command (Santa Ana) [67437]

Defense Contract Management Command (Seattle) [67471]

Defense Contract Management Command (Syracuse-Buffalo) [67463]

Defense Contract Management Command (Wichita) [67449]

Defense Contract Management District Headquarters (Boston) [67453]

Defense Environment Alert [9379], [11944], [37341], [37536], [40860], [50996]

Defense Finance & Accounting Service–Denver Center–Learning Center [2989]

Defense Information and Electronics Report [40111]

Defense Information Systems Agency [67423]

Defense Information Systems Agency (DISA)–Office of Small and Disadvantaged Business Utilization [67418]

Defense Plant Representative Office (Great Neck) [67431]

Defense Plant Representative Office (Los Angeles) [67427]

Defense Plant Representative Office (Marietta) [67429]

Defense Plant Representative Office (Tucson) [67426]

Defense Plant Representative Office (West Palm Beach) [67428]

Defense Procurement Technical Assistance Center–New Jersey Institute of Technology [62612]

Defense Supply Center Philadelphia [64582]

Defense Threat Reduction Agency–Office of Small and Disadvantaged Business Utilization [67419]

Defensive Driving Techniques [8731]

Defiance Area Chamber of Commerce [63658]

"Deficits" in *Business Week* (February 20, 2006, No. 3972, pp. 30) [28012], [32349]

The Definitive Drucker: The Final Word from the Father of Modern Management [36005], [45052]

Defta Partners [57981]

"Defusing disasters" in *Atlanta Business Chronicle* (Vol. 24, No. 8, July 27, 2001, pp. 1B) [39275], [56555]

DEI Franchising Systems [42792], [52010]

D.E.I. Sales Training Systems, Inc. [52011]

Aaron Deitsch, F.S.A. [27021]

DeKalb Chamber of Commerce [59090], [59479], [65197]

"Dekor faces challenges" in *Atlanta Business Chronicle* (Vol. 24, No. 14, September 7, 2001, pp. 3A) [12277], [28013]

Del Mar College–Small Business Development Center [65031]

Del Mar Regional Chamber of Commerce [57454]

Del Norte Chamber of Commerce [58351]

Del Rio Chamber of Commerce [65198]

Del Technology Inc. [46004], [49414]

Delafield Chamber of Commerce [66378]

"Delagardelle Joins Sprout Group" in *Venture Capital Journal* (Vol. 40, No. 10, November 2000, pp. 36) [41630], [55566]

DeLand Area Chamber of Commerce [58784]

Delano Area Chamber of Commerce [61578]

Delano Chamber of Commerce [57455]

Delavan - Delavan Lake Area Chamber of Commerce [66379]

Delaware Area Chamber of Commerce [63659]

Delaware County Chamber of Commerce [62871]

Delaware County Community College [64625]

Delaware Economic Development Office Business Finance Section [58641] International Section–Exporter Assistance Program [58642]

Delaware Economic Development Office (DEDO) [66844]

Delaware House Committee on Small Business [58657]

Delaware SBDC–Small Business Development Center [58636]

Delaware Senate Committee on Small Business [58658]

Delaware State Chamber of Commerce [58648]

Delaware State Museums–Johnson Victrola Museum [21163]

Delaware State University–Small Business Resource and Information Center–SBDC [58638]

Delaware Valley College of Science and Agriculture–Joseph Krauskopf Memorial Library [26659]

"Delayed Obsolescence" in *Hispanic Business* (March 2005, pp. 64) [4633], [22961], [53251], [53682]

Delbe Home Services [7660]

DELCO Chamber of Commerce [64410]

Delegating Responsibility [45921]

"Delegating the dirty work of cleaning up" in *The New York Times* (February 17, 2000, pp. D4, G4) [13958], [33744], [42215]

DeLeon Chamber of Commerce and Agriculture [65199]

Deli Meats 101 [8529]

Deli Meats & Poultry: Classic Tastes for Today's Consumer [8530]

"A delicate balance" in *Red Herring* (March 2003, pp. 44) [30528], [39276]

"Delicate Deliveries" in *Birmingham Business Journal* (Vol. 20, No. 33, August 15, 2003, pp. 13) [600], [10559], [45053], [46876]

Delight Area Chamber of Commerce [57154]

"Delightful Dividends" in *Black Enterprise* (Vol. 35, November 2004, No. 4, pp. 46) [9909], [14910], [38001]

"Delivering At Domino's Pizza" in *Fortune* (Vol. 151, February 7, 2005, No. 3, pp. 28) [14911], [19628], [21485], [38751], [43616], [49891]

Delivering Customer Value: It's Everyone's Job [31698]

Delivering Effective Training Sessions [33067]

Delivering Knock Your Socks Off Service, 4th Edition [39277], [52523]

Delivering Knock Your Socks off Service [31699]

"Delivering a New (Business) Life" in *Ingram's* (Vol. 28, No. 5, May 2002, pp. 32) [17307], [31007], [35382]

"Delivering the Right Technology at the Right Time" in *Rough Notes* (Vol. 146, No. 9, September 2003, pp. 62) [4634], [13261], [22962], [53252]

Delivering Successful Presentations [22587]

Delivering Superior Customer Service (for Front Line Staff) (Canada) [31631]

Delivering Superior Customer Service for Supervisors and Managers (Canada) [31632]

"Dell and NetObjects make small business play" in *Network World* (October 24, 2000, pp. NA) [33745], [49006], [53253], [53683]

"Dell NFIB The Voice of Small Business" in *My Business* (June/July 2004, pp. 26-27) [31700], [36006], [39278]

"Dell, Other Corporations Shut Venture Units" in *Venture Capital Journal* (February 1, 2005) [6624], [53684], [55567]

"Dell Plugs in First Airport Retail Kiosk at Dallas/Fort Worth" in *Dallas Morning News* (August 7, 2003) [6625], [15918]

"Dell Rolls Out New Models, Upgrade Program" in *eWeek* (February 1, 2005) [6626], [49007]

Dell Valley Chamber of Commerce [65200]

"Dell to offer hosting of small business Web sites" in *Wall Street Journal* (February 22, 2000, pp. B23) [13959], [33746], [46877]

"Dell's High-End Home Run" in *Business Week Online* (February 17, 2006) [6627], [49008]

Delmag Ventures [60868]

Delohery Associates [46005]

"Deloitte unit gets 1st woman" in *Crain's Detroit Business* (Vol. 19, No. 17, April 28, 2003, pp. 3) [127], [26213], [53685]

Deloitte Services LLP–Research Center [2990]

Deloitte & Touche
Library and Information Center [2991]
Research Center [2992]
Toronto North Library [24172]

Deloitte & Touche LLP–Library [416], [24173]

"Delphi engineers hoping carbon dioxide puts a chill in the air" in *Business First of Buffalo* (Vol. 18, No. 46, Aug. 12, 2002, pp. 1) [1017], [18008], [48720]

"Delphi looks to fund pension plan by spinning off real estate holdings" in *Crain's Detroit Business* (Vol. 19, No. 17, Apr. 28, 2003) [1926], [9910], [14912], [20483], [20853], [26783]

Delphi Ventures [57982]

Delphos Area Chamber of Commerce [63660]

"Delphos Gets OK to Take $3.4B Cerberus-led offer" in *Crain's Detroit Business* (Vol. 23, January 15, 2007, No. 3, pp. 1) [38002], [46261], [55288]

"Delta may lose $1 billion again" in *Atlanta Business Chronicle* (Vol. 25, January 10, 2003, No. 31, pp. 3A) [28014], [30318]

"Delta compromises on new $100 standby fee" in *Atlanta Business Chronicle* (Vol. 25, No. 22, November 8, 2002, pp. 7A) [30319]

"Delta Agrees to Settle Potential Allegations of Employee-Fund Misuse" in *Altanta Journal-Constitution* (February 7, 2007) [29192], [37420]

Delta Alpha Publishing Ltd. [61506]

"Delta Apparel Earnings Drop" in *Atlanta Journal-Constitution* (February 3, 2007) [5533], [5651], [51126]

Delta Area Chamber of Commerce [58352], [65708]

"Delta to promote Atlanta's Latin tourism drive" in *Atlanta Business Chronicle* (Vol. 24, No. 8, July 27, 2001, pp. 14A) [24682], [25175]

Delta Chamber of Commerce [56953], [63661]

Delta College Corporate Services–Small Business Technology Development Center [61182]

Delta County Area Chamber of Commerce [61285]

Delta County Chamber of Commerce [65201]

"Delta Industries Inc" in *Mississippi Business Journal* (Vol. 29, January 2007, No. 4, pp. 6) [39279], [45054]

Delta Properties [61478]

Delta SBDC–Region 10 [58297]

Delta Small Business Development Center [58298]

Delta State University
SBDC Business Assistance
Center–Greenville Higher Education
Center [61743]
Small Business Development Center
[61744]
Delta State University Business Assistance
Center–Coahoma Co. Higher Education Center
[61745]
Delta Systems [35223]
Deltiologists of America [64632]
"Delusions of Success: How Optimism Undermines
Executives' Decisions" in *Harvard Business
Review* (Vol. 81, No. 7, July 2003, pp. 56)
[30529], [45055]
"Demand For Flood Insurance Swells Locally" in
Sacramento Bee (December 31, 2005) [13262],
[43150]
"Demand surges in manufacturing" in *Hispanic
Business* (Vol. 22, No. 6, June 2000, pp. 106)
[46262], [48127]
DeMers Programming Media Consultants [20367],
[24493]
Deming-Luna County Chamber of Commerce
[62683]
"Demo 2002 Cuts the Fluff" in *Business Week
Online* (Februa) [41631], [55083]
Democracy Data & Communications L.L.C. [10760],
[20182]
*Democratization Without Representation: The
Politics of Small Industry in Mexico* [40305],
[43617]
"Democrats fall short: McCall, Kirk lose major
elections" in *Black Enterprise* (Vol. 33, No. 6,
January 2003, pp. 23) [40306]
Demokratizatsiya [50362]
"Demolition derby: two guys, plus slurs, lies and
videotape" in *Wall Street Journal* (July 21,
2000, pp. A1) [30837]
"Demolition Man: This Entrepreneur Builds His
Business by Tearing Things Down" in *Black
Enterprise* (Vol. 34, No. 5, December 2003)
[1468], [1508], [3299], [3310], [36007],
[52524], [54775]
Demopolis Area Chamber of Commerce [56837]
Demotte Chamber of Commerce [59903]
Denali Venture Capital [57983]
"Denbury Selects Digital Oilfield" in *Mississippi
Business Journal* (Vol. 29, January 2007, No. 2,
pp. 13) [6469], [43015], [49892]
Dennis M. Dengel [26424], [49415]
Denison Area Chamber of Commerce [65202]
Denison Chamber of Commerce [60123]
Denmark Community Business Association [66380]
Dennis Township Chamber of Commerce [62490]
Denny's, Inc. [21795]
Denota Ventures [65602]
Dent Clinic Canada 2000, Inc. [22672]
Dent Doctor [22673]
Dental Dealers of America [17086], [17253]
Dental Economics [17118]
Dental Trade Alliance [17087]
"Dental, vision plan vendors use the Web to
administer, communicate, market benefits" in
Employee Benefit Plan Review (Vol. 55, No. 6)
[13960], [17156], [26784], [40995], [43151],
[46878]
Dentaletter [17119], [41186], [50997]
Dentalpeople [23420]
DentalWare [1272]
The Dentist Choice, Inc. [18486], [41341]
"Dentist Office to Anchor New Sarasota County,
Fla., Office Park" in *Bradenton Herald* (April 11
2003) [128], [13263], [28015], [29193]
Denton Chamber of Commerce [65203]
Denton Satellite SBDC [65032]
Denver Apparel and Accessory Market [2132],
[5296], [5743], [16219]
Denver Botanic Gardens–Helen Fowler Library
[11518]
Denver Business Associates [58441]
The Denver Business Journal [58481]
Denver Business Journal (Vol. 52, No. 1, August 18,
2000, pp. 15A); "Ranks are thinning in
concierge industry" in [7144]

Denver City Chamber of Commerce and CVB
[65204]
The Denver Enterprise Center [58469]
Denver Hispanic Chamber of Commerce [58353]
Denver JobBank [23387]
Denver Merchandise Mart Directory [5284]
Denver Metro Chamber of Commerce [58354]
Small Business Development Center
[58315]
Denver Post (April 11, 2003); "Cable Networks Help
Boost First-Quarter Profit for E.W. Scripps Co."
in [4093], [18856], [27916]
Denver Post (April 11, 2003); "Effects of SARS Hit
Colorado Firms' Dealings with Asia" in [30321],
[43635]
Denver Post (April 11, 2003); "Homeless Group
Seeks to Buy Denver Hotel Property" in
[20535], [20896], [54205]
Denver Post (January 26, 2005); "Interest Rate
Speculation May Be Fueling Home Buying in
Denver Area" in [20553], [32511]
Denver Post (April 11, 2003); "Low Rates Drive 25
Percent Increase in Denver-Area Home
Construction" in [7410], [20578], [20932]
Denver Post (October 24, 2003); "Parking Kiosk
Failure Gives Denver Shoppers Break" in
[15932]
Denver Small Business Development
Center–Community College of Denver–Denver
Metro Chamber of Commerce [58299]
Denver Strikers Matchcover Club [1303], [5802]
Denville Chamber of Commerce [62491]
dEpagnier Furniture [49599]
Department of Administration–Demographic
Services Center [67018]
Department of Administration and
Information–Economic Analysis Division [67020]
Department of Administrative Services–Office of
Small and Minority Business Division [59210]
Department of Business Assistance–Small Business
Development Center [65814]
Department of Central Services–Purchasing Division
[64118]
Department of Commerce and Community Affairs
[66866]
Department of Commerce and Economic
Opportunity–Illinois SBDC [59359]
Department of Community and Economic
Development–Department of Employment
Security [66994]
Department of Defense
Defense Logistics Agency–Defense
Construction Supply Center [67472]
Defense Logistics Agency–Defense
Electronics Supply Center [67473]
Defense Logistics Agency–Defense General
Supply Center [67474]
Defense Logistics Agency–Defense
Industrial Supply Center [67475]
Defense Logistics Agency–Defense
Personnel Support Center [67476]
Department of Economic Development &
Community Development–Small Business
Assistance [58502]
Department of Employment Security–LMEA [67006]
Department of Energy–National Renewable Energy
Laboratory [23355]
Department General Services [65004]
Department of Homeland Security–Office of Small
and Disadvantaged Business Utilization [67125]
"Department of Justice grounds DC air" in
BlackEnterprise (Vol. 32, No. 3, October 2001,
pp. 32) [14913], [49893]
*The Department of Labor's Overtime Regulations
Effect on Small Business: Congressional
Hearing* [40307], [42846]
"Department-Store Chain Boosts N.J. Index" in *The
Record* (November 13, 2005) [14914], [28016],
[51127]
Department of Trade and Economic
Development–Minnesota SBDC [61519]
Departmento de Educacion [66969]
"Departures Raise Questions About Loss of
Women" in *Crain's Detroit Business* (Vol. 22,
November 27, 2006, No. 48, pp. 12) [1927],
[34862], [45056], [46263], [56185]

Deposit Chamber of Commerce [62872]
Deposit Growth Strategies [10269], [38484]
"Deposit-Rich Boca Raton has Few Banks of its
Own" in *South Florida Business Journal* (Vol.
23, No. 47, June 27, 2003, pp. 1) [9911]
Derby Chamber of Commerce [60317]
Dermacare Laser & Skin Care Clinics [7930]
Dermott Area Chamber of Commerce [57155]
Derwent–Patent Agency [44219]
Des Moines Area Community College–Urban
Campus [60245]
Des Moines Art Center–Library [6064]
Des Moines Business Record (Vol. 18, No. 41,
October 14, 2002, pp. 16); "Clubs merge" in
[2336], [49862]
Des Moines Sportshow [23678]
Des Plaines Chamber of Commerce and Industry
[59480]
Desert Hot Springs Chamber of Commerce [57456]
*Desert Landscaping: How to Start and Maintain a
Healthy Landscape in the Southwest* [16009]
Desert Moon Fresh Mexican Grill [2217], [23561]
Deshler Chamber of Commerce [63662]
Design Collective Inc. [49600]
Design & Construction Expo [7591]
Design Cost Data [7548]
"The Design of an Ideal Business" in *Home
Business* (Vol. 12, October 2005, No. 5, pp. 58,
60) [29722], [35383], [39046]
"Design Innovation Brings Communications
Challenges" in *Employee Benefit Plan Review*
(Vol. 55, No. 7, January 2001, pp. 27) [13961],
[26785], [27346], [33747], [53686]
Design Line [7549]
Design Management Institute [26034]
Design News (Vol.58, No.10, July 7, 2003); "eBay
Revs Up Its Industrial Sales: It's Now Easier for
Engineers to Go Shopping Online" in [33837]
Design for Presentations [22459]
"Design Principal" in *Fast Company* (September
2001, pp. 48) [50856], [54940]
Design for Print [8598]
"Design Turns Theater-Going Into a Grand Night
Out" in *Houston Business Journal* (Vol. 34, No.
19, September 19, 2003, pp. 1B) [1509],
[17514]
*Design Your Own Effective Employee Handbook:
How to Make the Most of Your Staff with
Companion CD-ROM* [34863], [45057]
Design Your Own Home [13718]
DesigNation [5598], [6028], [13706], [48497]
"Designer Babies" in *Entrepreneur* (Vol. 33,
September 2005, No. 9, pp. 24) [5240], [5272],
[27532], [28017]
"Designer is Walking Ad for TIBI Line" in *Charlotte
Observer* (February 5, 2007) [601], [5534],
[5652], [46879]
"Designers' Hats Foretell a Big Comeback Next
Fall" in *Charlotte Observer* (February 8, 2007)
[5535], [9617]
DesignFest [10528], [13707]
Designing Competence-Based Training [34864]
The Designing Editor [8978]
Designing Websites for Every Audience [13962],
[25828], [33748]
"Designing Woman" in *Hispanic Business*
(January/February 2003, pp. 54-55) [5536],
[36008]
"Designing Women" in *Success* (Vol. 47, No. 3,
July 2000, pp. 52) [4889], [35384], [41446]
Designing Women's Weight Loss, Inc. [19504]
"Designing web sites that work" in *Women in
Business* (Vol. 53, No. 3, May-June, 2001, pp.
26) [13963], [25829], [46880]
"Designs Changing as New Generation of Buyers
Emerges" in *Chicago Tribune* (March 6, 2005)
[1510], [7310], [53687]
"Designs on Success" in *Small Business
Opportunities* (Vol. 17, November 2005, No. 6,
pp. 72, 106) [3521], [5507], [12880], [20116],
[31138], [35385], [42508]
"Desire-more than need-builds a business" in *Wall
Street Journal* (May 21, 2002, pp. B4) [28018],
[36009]
Desi's Famous Pizza, Inc. [19660]
Desktop Design [8606]

Digital Photography Techniques [32924]

Digital Prepress [6015], [8632]

Digital Printing and Imaging Association [5956], [19841]

"Digital Rules" in *Forbes* (February 19, 2001, pp. 51) [35390], [41448], [44700], [51502]

"Digital Rx" in *Fast Company* (May 2001, pp. 183) [26215], [28039], [37123]

"Digital Scammer" in *Entrepreneur* (Vol. 30, No. 2, February 2002, pp. 28) [13972], [30213], [33758]

Digital Scanning for Production [53171]

"The Digital Schusser" in *Business Week* (January 16, 2006, No. 3967, pp. 92-93) [4974], [23613], [41637]

"Digital Signatures vs. Electronic Signatures" in *E-business Advisor* (Vol. 18, No. 4, April 2000, pp. 48) [29198], [33759], [40312]

Digital Television [24471]

Digital United [4879]

"Digital Video Editing" in *Home Office Computing* (Vol. 19, No. 1, January 2001, pp. 77) [53256]

Digital Video Production for Streaming and DVD [53172]

"DigitalLife Tries New Approach: Reaching Consumers" in *Tradeshow Week* (Vol. 34, November 29, 2004, No. 48, pp. 56) [4975], [6631], [17737], [22492], [24920], [41638], [55084]

"Digitally speaking, builders remain on the ground floor" in *The New York Times* (December 13, 2000, pp. D4, H4) [7331], [33760]

DigitalTV [24472]

Digitas Inc. [34775]

"The Dilemma of CNET's Success; It Gets Top Dollar For Online Ads, Most Tech-Oriented" in *Business Week Online* (February 9, 2005) [602], [33761], [46889]

Dill City Chamber of Commerce [63982]

Dillingham Chamber of Commerce [56954]

Dimension Data [49416], [49601]

"The Dimensions of Ping Fu" in *Inc.* (Volume 27, December 2005, No. 12, pp. 90-97, 132, 134-135) [4637], [22966], [46266], [53257], [56188]

Dimmit County Chamber of Commerce [65206]

Dimmitt Chamber of Commerce [65207]

Dimond Hospitality Consulting Group Inc. [3686], [31329], [35224], [53081]

Ding King [2048]

Dinner By Design [8286]

The Dinner Club, LLC [65969]

Dinsmore Tree & Landscape Service [16142]

Dinuba Chamber of Commerce [57458]

"Diplomat Sells Trade with China at Tacoma, Wash., Symposium" in *News Tribune* (April 11, 2003) [24921], [43624]

Dippin' Dots Franchising Inc. [12817]

Dippin' Dots "Ice Cream of the Future" [12818]

Direct Car Rentals Limited [18202], [43445]

"Direct Effect: Make the Most of Your Direct-Mail Campaign" in *Entrepreneur* (Vol. 32, November 2004, No. 11, pp. 91) [603], [46890]

"Direct Hit: Can Direct Marketing Survive a Consumer Backlash?" in *Entrepreneur* (Vol. 31, No. 9, September 2003, pp. 23) [24286], [33762], [40313], [46891]

Direct Information Access Corp. [44199]

Direct Mail Magic [46892]

Direct Marketing Association [16421], [46610]

Direct Marketing Association Annual Conference & Exhibition [16485]

Direct Marketing Association, Inc.–Library & Resource Center [16488]

"The direct marketing industry hopes to get Internet retailers to see things in an old light"in *The New York Times*(Jul.12,2000, pp.C6) [33763], [46893]

Direct Marketing and the Law: What Managers Need to Know [16434]

Direct Marketing List Source [16435]

Direct Marketing Magazine [16481]

Direct Marketing: Strategy, Planning, Execution [46894]

Direct Marketing Survival Guide for the Small Business Owner on a Budget [46895]

Direct Selling Association [51509]

Direct Selling Education Foundation [51510]

"Direct Success" in *Small Business Opportunities* (Vol. 13, No. 6, November 2001, pp. 58, 60) [499], [35391], [46567]

DirectBuy [51453]

Direction [17561]

Directions Ltd. [46007]

The Director [10810]

Directors Guild of America-Directory of Members [9705]

Directors Guild of Canada [9676]

"Directors of High-Tech Incubator in Tampa, Fla., Vote to Shut Down" in *Tampa Tribune* (October 4, 2002) [41639], [43050]

Directorship [10270], [38485]

Directory of Accredited Cosmetology Schools [7876], [11788]

"Directory of AICPA Selected Services" in *Journal of Accountancy* (Vol. 199, February 2005, No. 2, pp. 89) [131], [2894], [23930], [26216], [27113]

Directory of American Agriculture [26502]

Directory of American Firms Operating in Foreign Countries [43625]

Directory of American Professional Artists & Craftspeople [8004], [8162]

Directory of Animal Care and Control Agencies [1237]

Directory of Apparel Specialty Stores [5273], [5653]

Directory of the Association of Machinery and Equipment Appraisers [1440]

Directory of Automotive Aftermarket Suppliers [1928]

Directory of Better Business Bureaus [30214]

Directory of Bond Agents [9796]

The Directory of Business Information Resources: Associations, Newsletters, Magazines & Trade Shows [24922]

Directory of Canadian Media [3037], [18867]

The Directory of Canadian Recruiters [4392]

Directory of Cartoonists/Gagwriters/Short Humor Markets [8990]

Directory of Catholic Charities USA Directories [40997]

Directory of Certified Applied Air-Conditioning Products [1018]

Directory of Certified Unitary Air-Conditioners, Unitary Air-Source Heat Pumps and Sound-Rated Outdoor Unitary Equipment [1019]

Directory of Chain Restaurant Operators [10620], [21488]

Directory of College Stores [2693], [3038]

Directory of Community Care Facilities [40998], [48860]

Directory of Community Resources [41142]

The Directory of Computer Assisted Assessment Products and Producers [32986]

Directory of Computer & Consumer Electronics Retailers [22084]

Directory of Contract Staffing Firms [23371]

Directory of Department Stores [51134]

Directory of Drug Store & HBC Chains [8781]

Directory of Electrical Wholesale Distributors [9065]

Directory of Executive Recruiters [9555]

Directory of Family Associations [10929]

Directory of Federal Laboratory and Technology Resources [17230], [51009]

Directory of Festivals and Workshops [17589]

Directory of Food and Nutrition Information for Professionals and Consumers [18437]

Directory of Foodservice Distributors [4542], [11606], [21671]

Directory of Freight Forwarders and Custom House Brokers [10672]

Directory of High-Discount Merchandise and Product Sources for Distributors and Mail-Order Wealth Builders [16436], [18279]

Directory of High Volume Independent Restaurants [12053]

Directory of Home Center Operators & Hardware Chains [11880], [16302], [18680]

Directory of Home Furnishings Retailers [12279]

Directory of Human Services [41143]

Directory of Human Services for Delaware [41144]

Directory of Human Services and Self Help Support Groups-Maricopa County [40999]

Directory of Incentives for Business Investment and Development in the United States [3415], [32356]

Directory of International and Regional Organizations Conducting Standards-Related Activities [17185]

Directory of International Suppliers of Printing, Publishing, and Converting Technologies [5979]

Directory of Jewish Homes and Housing for the Aged in the United States and Canada [18321]

Directory of Libraries in Canada [13073]

Directory of Listed Plumbing Products [19747]

The Directory of Mail Order Catalogs [16437]

Directory of Major Mailers [6095]

Directory of Management Consultants [16512], [45064]

Directory Marketplace [2764], [18669]

Directory of Municipal Bond Dealers of the United States [9797]

A Directory of Music Collections in the Midwestern United States [17590], [17738]

Directory of Nationally Certified Teachers [17591]

Directory of New Age & Alternative Publications [17892]

Directory of Nontraditional Training and Employment Programs [9200]

Directory of North American International Trade Associations [1732], [43626]

Directory of Nursing Homes [18391]

Directory of Operating Small Business Investment Companies [13047], [43051], [55575]

Directory of Outplacement and Career Management Firms [9201], [23372]

Directory of Private Accredited Career Schools and Colleges of Technology [51], [946], [1011], [2832], [3308], [4476], [5334], [5966], [6407], [6461], [6573], [7234], [9062], [9300], [9688], [10555], [11418], [11723], [11758], [11781], [12457], [12510], [12938], [13637], [15832], [16261], [16357], [16726], [16941], [17181], [17333], [17839], [17854], [17865], [18220], [18704], [19071], [19108], [19293], [19743], [19863], [19959], [20413], [21139], [21433], [22157], [22605], [23762], [23811], [24267], [24334], [24372], [24657], [25141], [25373], [25518], [25534], [25643], [26091], [51047]

Directory of Professional Appraisers [1441]

Directory of Professional Genealogists [10930]

Directory of Real Estate Development & Related Education Programs [20786]

Directory of Small Magazine-Press Editors and Publishers [2694], [18868]

Directory of SRCC Certified Collectors and Solar Water Heating Systems Ratings [23335]

Directory of Supermarket, Grocery & Convenience Store Chains [7775], [11607]

The Directory of Toronto Recruiters [9202], [9556], [24522]

Directory of United Nations Databases and Information Systems [13064]

Directory of Venture Capital [55576]

Directory of Venture Capital and Private Equity Firms [52844]

Directory of Window Manufacturers [11216]

Directory of Worker's Compensation [30734]

"The Dirty Dozen" in *Forbes* (Vol. 175, January 31, 2005, No. 2, pp. 108) [9915], [14919], [38007]

"Dirty laundry.com" in *Incentive* (Vol. 174, No. 9, September 2000, pp. 17) [13973], [33764], [34869]

"The Dirty Little Secret About Buybacks" in *Business Week* (January 23, 2006, No. 3968, pp. 74-75) [14920], [38008]

Disa Conas [59767]

Disabled Businesspersons Association [47996]

Disabled Collectors' Correspondence Club [5803]

"Disabled Rise Up As Entrepreneurs" in *Pacific Business News* (Vol. 41, No. 16, June 27, 2003, pp. 1) [36017], [39807]

"Disappearing Ink" in *Kiplinger's Personal Finance Magazine* (Vol. 54, No. 10, October 2000, pp. 118) [33765], [40314]

Disaster Recovery Planning: Insuring Business Continuity [44746]

"Drawn to York County: Less-Expensive Homes, Good Schools Attract Charlotteans" in *Charlotte Observer* (February 4, 2007) **[7335]**, **[20497]**, **[20864]**, **[52666]**

Drayton Community Chamber of Commerce **[63516]**

"The Dream Achievers" in *Women in Business* (Vol. 54, No. 2, March-April 2002, pp. 7) **[36032]**, **[56197]**

Dream Dinners Inc. **[8287]**

"The Dream of Homeownership" in *Tribune* (March 11, 2005) **[17375]**, **[20498]**

"Dream Machines" in *Business Week* (January 16, 2006, No. 3967, pp. 52-56, 58) **[18015]**, **[30841]**, **[46267]**

"Dream Team or Nightmare Relationship" in *My Business* (April/May 2003, pp. 34-37) **[36033]**, **[49900]**

"Dream Your Way to Success: Think Visualization Is Easier Said than Done?" in *Black Enterprise* (Vol. 33, No. 6, January 2003, pp. 84) **[30532]**, **[36034]**

"Dream of Zinfandel, delivered to the door" in *The New York Times* (September 27, 2000, pp. B14, F7) **[23474]**, **[33786]**

DreamCatcher, The Adventure Co. **[66748]**

DreamMaker Bath and Kitchen by Worldwide **[4499]**

Dreams with a Deadline: How to Turn a Strategy for Tomorrow Into a Plan for Today **[29853]**, **[36035]**

Drennan Communications **[47854]**

Dresdner Kleinwort Capital (New York) **[63081]**

Dresdner RCM Global Investors–Research Library **[15795]**

Dresner Capital Resources, Inc. **[59730]**

"The Dress Code: How Business Style is Communicated" in *Black Enterprise* (Vol. 34, No. 2, September 2003, pp. 60) **[39287]**, **[45080]**, **[56198]**

"Dressed for Success" in *Small Business Opportunities* (Vol. 12, No. 3, May 2000, pp. 86, 130) **[5508]**, **[5625]**, **[35401]**, **[37560]**, **[38759]**, **[42511]**

"Dresser to Close Plant Eliminate 244 Jobs" in *Houston Business Journal* (Vol. 34, No. 14, August 15, 2003, pp. 3) **[32366]**, **[46268]**

Drexel University–Center for Research in Technology and Strategy **[50347]**

DRI Consulting **[3965]**, **[16596]**, **[30077]**, **[31331]**, **[46010]**

Dried Flower Arranging and Silk Flower Making **[22825]**

Jordan Driks **[44200]**

"Drink tank" in *Entrepreneur* (Vol. 30, No. 1, January 20) **[25701]**, **[28062]**

Drinking Water & Backflow Prevention **[25714]**

Drive a Modest Car: And 16 Other Keys to Small Business Success **[36036]**, **[39288]**

"Drive Time Live" in *Black Enterprise* (Vol. 34, No. 4, Nov. 2003, pp. 108) **[1929]**, **[18016]**

"Drives Provide New Electronics Avenue" in *Inc.* (September 1, 2003) **[7723]**, **[41648]**

"Driving Change on the Car Lot" in *Hispanic Business* (Vol. 24, No. 4, April 2002, pp. 24) **[18017]**, **[48137]**

"Driving Force" in *Hispanic Business* (April 2005, pp. 56, 58) **[18018]**, **[42222]**, **[48542]**, **[51621]**

"Driving a Hard Bargain" in *Business Week* (January 16, 2006, No. 3967, pp. 66) **[610]**, **[18019]**, **[46917]**

Driving School Association of America Convention **[8733]**

"Drop-Off Kiosk Accepts Customer Orders So You Don't Have To" in *American Coin-Op* (Vol. 44, No. 11, November 2003, pp. 8) **[7776]**, **[8903]**, **[15919]**

Drop Shipping Marketing Methods **[32172]**

Dropkin & Co. **[3688]**, **[16597]**, **[31332]**, **[35225]**, **[46011]**, **[53083]**

Drug & Alcohol Treatment Association of Rhode Island–In-Rhodes Resource Center–Library **[54380]**

Drug Detection Report **[54340]**

Drug Discovery/Technology News **[8816]**

The Drug-Free Workplace **[54349]**

"Drug Importation and the Capital Markets" in *Venture Capital Journal* (November 1, 2004) **[14935]**, **[40324]**, **[41003]**, **[43629]**, **[55581]**

Drug Royalty Corp., Inc. **[66722]**

Drug Store News (Vol. 25, No. 9, July 21, 2003, pp. 6); "Stop & Shop Offers Health Kiosk" in **[8802]**, **[15941]**, **[17194]**

The Drug Test Consultant **[42794]**, **[52622]**

Drug Testing Consultants Inc. **[54363]**

Drug Testing in the Workplace **[54350]**

Drug Topics **[8817]**

"Drugmaker Ups Dosage; Acquisition Expected to Double Revenue" in *Crain's New York Business* (Vol. 23, January 22, 2007, No. 4, pp. 4) **[8782]**, **[28063]**, **[30533]**, **[38021]**, **[49901]**

Drugs for Abuse Digest: A Prevention Guide for the Family, School & Workplace **[54333]**

Drugs in the Workplace **[54351]**

Drugs in the Workplace 2: What Every Manager and Supervisor Must Know **[54352]**

Drum Business **[17788]**

"Drumming Up Business For the Democrats" in *Business Week* (January 9, 2006, No. 3966, pp. 39) **[45081]**, **[53698]**

Drumright Chamber of Commerce **[63983]**

Drury University–F.W. Olin Library–Art & Architecture Slide Library **[1652]**, **[19275]**

DRY-B-LO International, Inc. **[4500]**

"Dry Cleaning Dons a Corporate Veneer" in *Tampa Tribune* (December 9, 2005) **[8904]**, **[30842]**, **[38760]**

Dry Cleaning Station **[8930]**

Dry Cleaning To-Your-Door **[8931]**

Dry Eye and Tear Research Center **[25674]**

Dry-King **[25553]**

"Dry Powder Dilemma" in *Venture Capital Journal* (Vol. 42, No. 5, May 2002, pp. 32-35) **[14936]**, **[49902]**, **[55582]**

Drycleaners News **[8916]**

"Drypers Co-Founder Gets Fresh Start" in *Houston Business Journal* (Vol. 34, No. 9, July 11, pp. 1) **[7336]**, **[20499]**, **[20865]**

Drysdale Enterprises **[57999]**

"DSL Users Brace for Bumpy Ride" in *Home Office Computing* (Vol. 18, No. 11, November 2000, pp. 19) **[33787]**, **[42605]**, **[49016]**

DSN Retail Fax (Vol. 10, No. 26, June 30, 2003); "eBay" in **[1803]**, **[10673]**, **[32152]**, **[33833]**, **[49912]**

DSN Retailing Today (Vol. 42, No. 21, November 10, 2003, pp. 37); "Career Looks Pump Up Plus" in **[5646]**

DSN Retailing Today (Vol. 42, No. 18, September 22, 2003, pp. 16); "Expanding Plus-Size Range Grows Sales" in **[5655]**

DSN Retailing Today (Vol. 41, No. 19, October 7, 2002, pp. 23); "Newly revived yoga, Pilates show promise over long stretch" in **[17710]**, **[17905]**, **[19424]**, **[20140]**

DSSCourse **[6298]**

DST International **[10337]**, **[15726]**

"DTE aims to spark growth beyond electricity" in *Crain's Detroit Business* (Vol. 19, No. 15, April 14, 2003, pp. 3) **[28064]**, **[32367]**

DTS Language Services Inc. **[25100]**

Du Quoin Chamber of Commerce **[59484]**

Roger du Toit Architects Ltd. **[1553]**

Dual News **[8727]**

Duarte Chamber of Commerce **[57461]**

"The Dubious Dole" in *Entrepreneur* (Vol. 28, No. 10, October 2000, pp. 123) **[39289]**, **[40325]**, **[45082]**

"The Dubious Logic of Global Megamergers" in *Harvard Business Review* (Vol. 78, No. 4, July 2000, pp. 65) **[14937]**, **[49903]**

Dublin Chamber of Commerce **[57462]**, **[65208]**

Dublin - Laurens County Chamber of Commerce **[59095]**

Dubois Chamber of Commerce **[66607]**

Dubuc Lucke & Co. **[3689]**, **[16598]**, **[31333]**, **[38526]**, **[43921]**, **[46012]**, **[53084]**

Dubuque Area Chamber of Commerce **[60124]**

Duchesne County Area Chamber of Commerce **[65709]**

Duchossois Technology Partners LLC (DTEC) **[59731]**

"Duck Season" in *Entrepreneur* (Vol. 33, January 2005, No. 1, pp. 67) **[611]**, **[46918]**

"Duckworth Realty Inc." in *Mississippi Business Journal* (Vol. 28, September 2006, No. 36, pp. 6) **[20500]**, **[20866]**, **[36037]**

Duct Tape Marketing: The World's Most Practical Small Business Marketing Guide **[46919]**

Dude, Guest & Vacation Ranches **[24756]**, **[25290]**

"Dueling North Carolina Bills Would Revive Payday Lending" in *Charlotte Observer* (April 11, 2003) **[38022]**, **[40326]**

Duff & Phelps L.L.C. **[50315]**, **[52476]**

Duke Chamber of Commerce **[63984]**

Duke University–Eye Center **[25675]**

"Dulling the Tax Bite" *Fortune* (Vol.141, No. 9, May 1, 2000) **[42606]**, **[54524]**

Duluth Area Chamber of Commerce **[61580]**

"Duly noted; Sheet-music company doesn't rest in copyright fight" in *Crain's Detroit Business* (Vol. 19, No. 10, March 10, 2003) **[17592]**, **[17739]**, **[37630]**, **[44032]**

"Dumars company diversifies with deal for Troy tech firm" in *Crain's Detroit Business* (Vol. 19, No. 4, January 27, 2003, pp. 26) **[1930]**, **[4640]**, **[6635]**, **[14938]**, **[22969]**, **[41649]**, **[49904]**, **[53260]**

Dumas Chamber of Commerce **[57159]**

Dumas - Moore County Chamber of Commerce and Visitors Center **[65209]**

The DuMond Group **[3690]**, **[16599]**, **[31334]**, **[35226]**, **[46013]**, **[53085]**

Dun & Bradstreet Canada **[66749]**

Dun and Bradstreet's Industrial Guide **[16366]**

Duncan Chamber of Commerce and Industry **[63985]**

Duncan Direct Associates **[47855]**

"Duncan Manufacturing Firm to Receive Exemption from OSHA" in *Journal Record* (February 4, 2004) **[16145]**, **[16367]**, **[46269]**, **[47062]**, **[56556]**, **[59130]**

Duncanville Chamber of Commerce **[65210]**

Dundee Area Chamber of Commerce **[58788]**

Dunedin Chamber of Commerce **[58789]**

Dunelm International **[3691]**, **[16600]**, **[31335]**, **[46014]**, **[53086]**

Dunham Tavern Museum–Library **[1356]**

Dunhill Staffing Systems, Inc. **[9270]**, **[24546]**

"Dunkin' Donuts" in *Hispanic Business* (March 2002, pp. 66) **[2244]**, **[38761]**

Dunkin' Donuts, Inc. **[2298]**

Dunkirk Area Chamber of Commerce **[59904]**

"Dunkirk, N.Y.-Based Ice Cream Manufacturer Files for Bankruptcy" in *Knight-Ridder/Tribune Business News* (September 25,2001) **[12774]**

Dunkirk Satellite–Jamestown Community College–SBDC **[62755]**

Dunn Area Chamber of Commerce **[63354]**

Dunn Bros. Coffee **[11381]**

Dunnellon Area Chamber of Commerce **[58790]**

Dun's Marketing Services **[62634]**

Dunsmuir Chamber of Commerce **[57463]**

Duo" in *Success* (Vol. 47, No. 3, July 2000, pp. 36); "Dynamic **[35402]**

The duPont Registry **[12228]**, **[12322]**, **[16756]**, **[20716]**

Duquesne University
　Chrysler Corporation Small Business Development Center **[64326]**
　Office of Research **[64606]**

"Dura buys German maker of steering column parts" in *Crain's Detroit Business* (Vol. 16, No. 49, December 4, 2000, pp. 5) **[14939]**, **[49905]**

Duraclean International, Inc. **[25554]**

Durand Area Chamber of Commerce **[61288]**

Durango Chamber of Commerce **[58356]**

Durango Small Business Development Center–Fort Lewis College **[58300]**

Durango Steakhouse **[21800]**

"Dutch fund pays nearly \$14M for Sunrise retail center" in *Black Enterprise* (Vol. 33, No. 198, March 24, 2003, pp. A1) **[20501]**, **[20867]**, **[51137]**

Dutch Genealogical Research **[10931]**

"Duty on Canadian lumber may raise home prices" in *Atlanta Business Chronicle* (Vol. 24, No. 13, August 31, 2001, pp. 9B) [7337], [16303], [40327]

DVD Now Kiosks Inc. [15955]

DVD Report (Vol. 8, No. 16, August 18, 2003); "SwiftCD Taps PayPal as On-Demand Payment Engine" in [18792], [34555], [51377]

DVM Newsmagazine [1251]

DW Smothers and Associates [54364]

Dwight Area Chamber of Commerce [59485]

Dyer Chamber of Commerce [59905]

Dyersburg-Dyer County Chamber of Commerce [64908]

Dyersburg State Community College–Small Business Development Center [64854]

Dyersville Area Chamber of Commerce [60125]

Dyna-Gym [19468]

Dynafund Ventures LLC [58000]

Dynamic Dance: Principles of Choreography [8473]

Dynamic Development [31966]

Dynamic Firm Management [35227], [46015]

The Dynamic Small Business Manager [39290], [45083]

"Dynamic capabilities and new product development in high technology ventures" in *Journal of Business Venturing* (Vol.15, No.3, May2000) [41650]

"Dynamic-Duo" in *Success* (Vol. 47, No. 3, July 2000, pp. 36) [35402]

Dynamics of Diversity: Strategic Programs for Your Organization [48543]

"The dynamics of team interaction" in *Women in Business* (Vol. 53, No. 2, March-April, 2001, pp. 42) [34876], [45084]

The Dynamics of Service: Reflections on the Changing Nature of Customer-Provider Interactions [31704]

Dynamotive Engineering Inc. [4356]

E

E [9381]

"E-biz baffled" in *Black Enterprise* (Vol. 32, No. 9, April 2002, pp. 48) [13743], [25756], [33431]

"e-Biz Buzz" in *E-business Advisor* (Vol. 18, No. 3, March 2000, pp. 50) [31705], [32780], [33788], [46920], [53699]

"E-book report from the field" in *Online* (Vol. 26, No. 5, September-October 2002, pp. 6) [2695], [9133]

"E-Book vendors look to libraries for growth" in *Publishers Weekly* (Vol. 249, No. 40, October 7, 2002, pp. 12) [2696], [4641], [9134], [13986], [22970], [33789]

"E-book users surveyed online, in college" in *Publishers Weekly* (Vol. 249, No. 36, September 9, 2002, pp. 12) [9135]

"E-book poll, results" in *Online* (Vol. 26, No. 5, September-October 2002, pp. 6) [2697], [9136]

"E-book writer for print" in *Publishers Weekly* (Vol. 249, No. 50, December 16, 2002, pp. 14) [2698], [9137]

"E-Brand Lessons" in *Small Business Opportunities* (Vol. 12, No. 5, September 2000, pp. 18) [33790], [51138]

"E-Brands: Building an Internet Business at Breakneck Speed" in *Harvard Business Review* (Vol. 78, No. 4, July 2000, pp. 152) [33791], [36038]

"E-bug exterminator: NetScreen nabs viruses and market share" in *Barron's* (Vol. 82, No. 58, February 17, 2003, pp. T8) [4642], [9925], [13987], [14940], [22218], [22971], [33792], [38023]

E-business Advisor (Vol. 18, No. 3, March 2000, pp. 16); "Access Corporate Data on Your Wireless Phone" in [4907], [33510]

E-business Advisor (Vol. 18, No. 8, August 2000, pp. 46); "Advisor Answers" in [13802], [20278], [22162], [22906], [25784], [27561], [30688], [33517], [45167], [53199]

E-business Advisor (Vol. 18, No. 3, March 2000, pp. 44); "Advisor Tips" in [13709], [13803], [22163], [25465], [25785], [26739], [30230], [32263], [33518], [34665], [48940], [53200]

E-business Advisor (Vol. 18, No. 10, October 2000, pp. 12); "Affordable branding 101" in [33520], [46667]

E-business Advisor (Vol. 18, No. 10, October 2000, pp. 10); "Analyze this: from "automation" to "effectiveness"" in [33533], [53583]

E-business Advisor (Vol. 18, No. 9, September 2000, pp. 20); "Application Integration for Real-Time B2B" in [33537], [49792]

E-business Advisor (Vol. 17, No. 12, December 1999, pp. 18); "Application Service Providers on the Move" in [4914], [13820], [33538]

E-business Advisor (Vol. 18, No. 7, July 2000, pp. 40); "Are Portals Just Another Integration Problem?" in [33540], [43544]

E-business Advisor (Vol. 17, No. 12, December 1999, pp. 30); "Assemble Your E-Business Team" in [33545], [34815], [44904]

E-business Advisor (Vol. 18, No. 7, July 2000, pp. 18); "Avoid the Supply Chain Squeeze" in [2677], [9693], [21141], [27803], [33554]

E-business Advisor (Vol. 18, No. 10, October 2000, pp. 14); "Bluetooth: Get Wired Without the Wires" in [4929], [33598], [48961]

E-business Advisor (Vol. 18, No. 6, June 2000, pp. 41); "Build Fault Reporting Into Your System" in [25805], [33617]

E-business Advisor (Vol. 18, No. 4, April 2000, pp. 34); "Build a Strong Customer-Brand Relationship" in [31015], [33618], [46753], [51574]

E-business Advisor (Vol. 18, No. 5, May 2000, pp. 36); "Build a Successful Business Partner Network" in [14812], [33619], [49828], [53623]

E-business Advisor (Vol. 18, No. 5, May 2000, pp. 30); "Build Your Web Identity" in [25807], [33621], [46756], [50565]

E-business Advisor (Vol. 18, No. 8, August 2000, pp. 22); "Business Intelligence" in [29809], [33627], [48970]

E-business Advisor (Vol. 18, No. 8, August 2000, pp. 6); "Business-to-Consumer E-Commerce: What is(n't) the Problem?" in [22933], [33631], [49678], [53229]

E-business Advisor (Vol. 18, No. 1, January 2000, pp. 32); "Choose the Right Application Server" in [13898], [25816], [33669]

E-business Advisor (Vol. 18, No. 10, October 2000, pp. 42); "Control Your Content" in [27977], [29834], [33703]

E-business Advisor (Vol. 18, No. 2, February 2000, pp. 24); "Create Compelling Web Content" in [25823], [31676], [33717]

E-business Advisor (Vol. 18, No. 12, December 2000, pp. 26); "Create Customer-Effective E-Services" in [31677], [33718]

E-business Advisor (Vol. 18, No. 9, September 2000, pp. 10); "CyberStaking: Why Partnerships Matter" in [14901], [33735], [49885]

E-business Advisor (Vol. 18, No. 1, January 2000, pp. 22); "Develop a Solid E-Commerce Architecture" in [25830], [33751]

E-business Advisor (Vol. 18, No. 4, April 2000, pp. 48); "Digital Signatures vs. Electronic Signatures" in [29198], [33759], [40312]

E-business Advisor (Vol. 18, No. 9, September 2000, pp. 28); "Do You Need E-Business Insurance" in [33768], [43157]

E-business Advisor (Vol. 18, No. 12, December 2000, pp. 16); "Do You Need Web Services?" in [33769], [53694]

E-business Advisor (Vol. 18, No. 10, October 2000, pp. 48); "Dot-Com for Sale" in [14932], [30675], [33780], [49899]

E-business Advisor (Vol. 18, No. 3, March 2000, pp. 50); "e-Biz Buzz" in [31705], [32780], [33788], [46920], [53699]

E-business Advisor (Vol. 18, No. 7, July 2000, pp. 32); "E-Marketplaces: Opportunity or Threat?" in [28067], [33816], [49908], [51622]

E-business Advisor (Vol. 18, No. 10, October 2000, pp. 34); "EAI Meets B2B" in [33826]

E-business Advisor (Vol. 18, No. 3, March 2000, pp. 28); "Eliminate Fulfillment Problems" in [25841], [28096], [31708], [33846], [49693]

E-business Advisor (Vol. 18, No. 3, March 2000, pp. 34); "Establish and Effective Privacy Policy" in [22223], [33861]

E-business Advisor (Vol. 18, No. 3, March 2000, pp. 8); "Even "E-Active" Organizations Have a Lot to Learn" in [25846], [33863], [53715]

E-business Advisor (Vol. 18, No. 12, December 2000, pp. 6); "For Want of a Nail...The War Was Lost" in [4988], [30329], [33915]

E-business Advisor (Vol. 18, No. 7, July 2000, pp. 26); "Fulfill the Promise of Electronic Billing" in [26245], [31550], [33930]

E-business Advisor (Vol. 18, No. 6, June 2000, pp. 24); "Get the Best Domain Name" in [25854], [33934]

E-business Advisor (Vol. 18, No. 7, July 2000, pp. 36); "Get the Best Usability Expertise" in [25855], [33935]

E-business Advisor (Vol. 18, No. 12, December 2000, pp. 42); "Get the Current View of Your Customers" in [31722], [33938]

E-business Advisor (Vol. 18, No. 9, September 2000, pp. 36); "Get Ready for the Wireless Web" in [4998], [33941]

E-business Advisor (Vol. 18, No. 2, February 2000, pp. 30); "Handle Web Transactions with the BEA WebLogic Server" in [14100], [23024], [33991], [53311]

E-business Advisor (Vol. 18, No. 3, March 2000, pp. 20); "How ASPs Can Accelerate Your E-Business" in [23032], [34026], [44311], [53319]

E-business Advisor (Vol. 18, No. 9, September 2000, pp. 16); "How to Create an E-Culture" in [34030], [34934], [47099]

E-business Advisor (Vol. 18, No. 8, August 2000, pp. 30); "How to Pick the Best Portal" in [14135], [25869], [34037]

E-business Advisor (Vol. 18, No. 10, October 2000, pp. 22); "How a Virtual Supply Chain Can Help Your Business" in [34038]

E-business Advisor (Vol. 18, No. 8, August 2000, pp. 12); "Humanize Your Web Customer Service" in [25870], [31741], [34039]

E-business Advisor (Vol. 18, No. 5, May 2000, pp. 16); "Integrate Enterprise Applications with XML" in [23047], [34070], [53334]

E-business Advisor (Vol. 18, No. 10, October 2000, pp. 28); "International E-Commerce: The Time is Now" in [29312], [34072], [40471], [43713]

E-business Advisor (Vol. 18, No. 3, March 2000, pp. 10); "Make Small Devices A Corporate Asset" in [5048], [7138], [34160]

E-business Advisor (Vol. 18, No. 5, May 2000, pp. 10); "Making B2B Better" in [34162], [50067]

E-business Advisor (Vol. 18, No. 8, August 2000, pp. 18); "Meet Your Customers' Needs Through Cultural Marketing" in [34185], [43749], [47276]

E-business Advisor (Vol. 18, No. 1, January 2000, pp. 38); "Monitor and Manage Your Web Server" in [23091], [34204], [53379]

E-business Advisor (Vol. 17, No. 12, December 1999, pp. 22); "Monitor Your E-Business Systems' Health" in [23092], [34205], [53380]

E-business Advisor (Vol. 18, No. 1, January 2000, pp. 16); "Navigate the Application Framework Terrain" in [23096], [25906], [34233], [53383]

E-business Advisor (Vol. 18, No. 7, July 2000, pp. 8); "On the Radar" in [23109], [25500], [25921], [28588], [29947], [32785], [33243], [34280], [34808], [35175], [43774], [47362], [53395]

E-business Advisor (Vol. 18, No. 6, June 2000, pp. 10); "Open Source Solutions: Good Enough for E-Business?" in [34309], [49192]

E-business Advisor (Vol. 18, No. 1, January 2000, pp. 10); "Overcome E-Business Barriers" in [28606], [34320], [45508], [47383]

E-business Advisor (Vol. 18, No. 4, April 2000, pp. 22); "Overcome Your B2B Challenge" in [25929], [34321], [52931]

E-business Advisor (Vol. 18, No. 2, February 2000, pp. 10); "Power to the Buyer With Group Buying Sites" in [31821], [34361], [47411], [53923]

E-business Advisor (Vol. 17, No. 12, December 1999, pp. 36); "Prepare for Y2K Litigation" in [29448], [34364], [40624]

E-business Advisor (Vol. 18, No. 6, June 2000, pp. 34); "Process Online Payments Quickly and Effectively" in **[228]**, **[26330]**, **[31580]**, **[34369]**, **[53418]**

E-business Advisor (Vol. 18, No. 4, April 2000, pp. 28); "Protect Customer's Web Privacy" in **[22334]**, **[34374]**

E-business Advisor (Vol. 18, No. 7, July 2000, pp. 44); "Put Your Web Applications to the Test" in **[34383]**, **[49222]**, **[53425]**

E-business Advisor (Vol. 17, No. 12, December 1999, pp. 16); "RosettaNet: The Key to Supply Chain Efficiency?" in **[23153]**, **[28723]**, **[34421]**, **[53439]**

E-business Advisor (Vol. 18, No. 12, December 2000, pp. 34); "Secure Your Database" in **[22362]**, **[34448]**

E-business Advisor (Vol. 18, No. 2, February 2000, pp. 16); "Set Up Shop in Europe" in **[34458]**, **[43810]**

E-business Advisor (Vol. 18, No. 10, October 2000, pp. 18); "Should You Get Incubated?" in **[43042]**, **[53566]**

E-business Advisor (Vol. 17, No. 12, December 1999, pp. 38); "Simplify Web Development with Java Server Pages" in **[23172]**, **[25960]**, **[34478]**, **[53464]**

E-business Advisor (Vol. 18, No. 6, June 2000, pp. 28); "Smart Content Management" in **[25966]**, **[34500]**

E-business Advisor (Vol. 18, No. 12, December 2000, pp. 22); "Tackle Your International Logistics Obstacles" in **[34559]**, **[43834]**

E-business Advisor (Vol. 18, No. 5, May 2000, pp. 12); "Tap WAP for Enterprise Mobile Solutions?" in **[5134]**, **[34568]**

E-business Advisor (Vol. 17, No. 12, December 1999, pp. 10); "The Customer Loyalty Puzzle" in **[27996]**, **[31691]**, **[33724]**

E-business Advisor (Vol. 18, No. 5, May 2000, pp. 26); "The Evolution of XML Schemes" in **[22987]**, **[33867]**, **[53274]**

E-business Advisor (Vol. 18, No. 10, October 2000, pp. 11); "The next best thing to being there?" in **[9734]**, **[34264]**, **[48771]**

E-business Advisor (Vol. 18, No. 10, October 2000, pp. 8); "Thinking Outside the Box" in **[30615]**, **[34590]**

E-business Advisor (Vol. 18, No. 10, October 2000, pp. 10); "This will keep you up at night" in **[34594]**, **[47635]**

E-business Advisor (Vol. 18, No. 7, July 2000, pp. 12); "3G Wireless Networks: Worth the Wait?" in **[5150]**, **[34599]**, **[48802]**

E-business Advisor (Vol. 17, No. 12, December 1999, pp. 44); "Tip of the Month" in **[34605]**, **[47644]**

E-business Advisor (Vol. 18, No. 4, April 2000, pp. 14); "Transform Your Business Into a B2B Portal" in **[25989]**, **[34620]**, **[54045]**

E-business Advisor (Vol. 17, No. 12, December 1999, pp. 8); "Trends" in **[28916]**, **[34626]**, **[47666]**, **[54048]**

E-business Advisor (Vol. 18, No. 9, September 2000, pp. 40); "Use XML to Speed Application Development" in **[23243]**, **[25994]**, **[34643]**

E-business Advisor (Vol. 17, No. 12, December 1999, pp. 6); "Wanted: E-Business Professionals" in **[34655]**, **[35134]**, **[45798]**

E-business Advisor (Vol. 18, No. 8, August 2000, pp. 41); "What's the Secret to Successful CRM?" in **[26017]**, **[31903]**, **[34704]**

E-business Advisor (Vol. 18, No. 6, June 2000, pp. 16); "Win Consumers with Better Usability" in **[26019]**, **[34729]**

E-business Advisor (Vol. 18, No. 12, December 2000, pp. 10); "Wireless Devices: The New Marketing Frontier" in **[5183]**, **[7148]**, **[34734]**

E-business Advisor (Vol. 18, No. 4, April 2000, pp. 10); "XML: The Only Chance for a Worldwide Standard" in **[34756]**, **[43887]**, **[53035]**

E-business Advisor (Vol. 18, No. 5, May 2000, pp. 44); "XML: What's Still Needed for B2B?" in **[22426]**, **[26022]**, **[34757]**, **[49380]**

E-business Advisor (Vol. 18, No. 10, Oct. 2000, pp. 12); "You hire them to do the tough work, but how easy is it to work with them?" in **[31257]**, **[49382]**

"E-Business Busters" in *Entrepreneur* (Vol. 28, No. 1, January 2000, pp. 46) **[13988]**, **[33793]**

"E-Business Cards" in *Hispanic Business* (Vol. 23, No. 10, October, 2001, pp. 100) **[22972]**, **[33794]**, **[53261]**

e-Business, e-Government and Small and Medium-Size Enterprises: Opportunities and Challenges **[33795]**, **[39291]**, **[40011]**

"E-business firm spreads Influence to Ann Arbor" in *Crain's Detroit Business* (Vol. 16, No. 33, August 14, 2000, pp. 30) **[33796]**, **[41651]**

"E-Business for Tourism" in *Business Information Alert* (Vol. 14, No. 9, Oct. 2002, pp. 8) **[24685]**, **[25179]**, **[33797]**

"The e-changes are just beginning" in *Hispanic Business* (Vol. 22, No. 6, June 2000, pp. 30) **[13744]**, **[33432]**, **[37060]**, **[47953]**

"E-Cognita founders to lead group at Miller, Canfield" in *Crain's Detroit Business* (Vol. 19, No. 15, April 14, 2003, pp. 25) **[4643]**, **[17376]**, **[22973]**, **[29207]**, **[44508]**, **[49906]**

"E-Cognita plots Web software for commercial real estate loans" in *Crain's Detroit Business* (Vol. 16, No. 46, Nov. 13, 2000, pp. 32) **[20868]**, **[44509]**, **[53262]**

"E-commerce can pose legal risks for businesses" in *Crain's Detroit Business* (Vol. 16, No. 16, April 17, 2000, pp. 17) **[29208]**, **[33798]**, **[40328]**

"E-Commerce Complaints" in *Small Business Opportunities* (Vol. 14, No. 1, January 2002, pp. 16) **[31706]**, **[33799]**

"E-Commerce Market Heats Up" in *Hispanic Business* (October 2003, pp. 98, 100) **[13989]**, **[28065]**, **[33800]**, **[46921]**

"E-Commerce: Risky Business" in *Working Woman* (Vol. 25, No. 2, February 2000, pp. S20) **[18641]**, **[33801]**

"E-commerce: Too Valuable to Tax" in *Success* (Vol. 47, No. 2, June 2000, pp. 22) **[33802]**, **[54525]**

"E-Commerce: When You Put Your 'John Hancock' on the Web Form!" in *Ingram's* (Vol. 27, No. 5, May 2001, pp. 33) **[29209]**, **[33803]**, **[40329]**, **[53700]**

"E-conomic Publishing" in *The Economist* (Vol. 356, No. 8182, August 5, 2000, pp. 69) **[2699]**, **[9138]**

"E-Degree" in *Entrepreneur* (Vol. 28, No. 1, January 2000, pp. 36) **[33433]**

E is for Ethics: Essentials for Entrepreneurs **[37424]**

"E-Government Catching On" in *Hispanic Business* (Vol. 23, No. 5, May 2001, pp. 22, 24) **[32368]**, **[33804]**, **[39809]**, **[40012]**

"E-Hubs: The New B2B Marketplaces" in *Harvard Business Review* (Vol. 78, No. 3, May 2000, pp. 97) **[33805]**, **[37127]**

e-JEP **[390]**, **[10375]**, **[24138]**, **[26440]**, **[38589]**, **[54898]**

"E-Learning Takes Off!" in *Small Business Opportunities* (Vol. 13, No. 6, November 2001, pp. 92, 94) **[13990]**, **[33076]**, **[33806]**

"E-Loan Exec Chides Lenders" in *American Banker* (Vol. 170, February 1, 2005, No. 270, pp. 9) **[9926]**, **[17377]**, **[44510]**

"E-Loyalty" in *Harvard Business Review* (Vol. 78, No. 4, July 2000, pp. 105) **[13991]**, **[31707]**, **[33807]**

"E-Mail Alternative" in *Entrepreneur* (Vol. 32, No. 1, January 2004, pp. 47) **[27351]**, **[33808]**, **[53263]**

"E-Mail and Communications" in *PC Computing* (April, 2000, pp. 74) **[4980]**, **[7129]**, **[13992]**, **[33809]**

"An E-Mail from the IRS? Don't Believe It" in *Long Island Business News* (May 7, 2004) **[13993]**, **[27352]**, **[27627]**, **[30217]**, **[33810]**, **[54526]**

"E-mail Marketer Looks for More Clout" in *Atlanta Business Chronicle* (Vol. 25, December 13, 2002, No. 27, pp. A3) **[28066]**, **[33811]**, **[46922]**, **[49907]**, **[50585]**

E-mail Marketing **[46624]**

E-mail Marketing, RSS Feeds, and Blogs **[32925]**, **[46625]**

"E-Mail Marketing" in *Small Business Opportunities* (Vol. 13, No. 5, September 2001, pp. 100, 102) **[13994]**, **[33812]**, **[46923]**

"E-mail Offers a Little Wit with Your News" in *Crain's Detroit Business* (Vol. 19, No. 6, February 10, 2003, pp. 9) **[13995]**, **[27353]**, **[27628]**, **[33813]**

"E-Mail Secrets Revealed" in *Home Office Computing* (Vol. 18, No. 12, December 2000, pp. 48) **[33814]**, **[53264]**

"E-mail Security Firm is Chaudry's Last Start-up" in *Atlanta Business Chronicle* (Vol. 24, No. 13, August 24, 2001, pp. 5A) **[13745]**, **[22137]**, **[22880]**, **[27629]**, **[35403]**

"E-Mail the Way it Should Be" in *PC Computing* (April 2000, pp. 117) **[33815]**, **[49690]**

"E-Marketplaces: Opportunity or Threat?" in *E-business Advisor* (Vol. 18, No. 7, July 2000, pp. 32) **[28067]**, **[33816]**, **[49908]**, **[51622]**

E-Myth Mastery: The Seven Essential Disciplines for Building a World Class Company **[28068]**, **[36039]**, **[45085]**

The E-Myth Revisited: Why Most Small Businesses Don't Work and What to Do About It **[28069]**, **[39292]**

E-netegrations Inc. **[49418]**, **[49602]**

"E-Procurement Catching On" in *Hispanic Business* (October 2002, pp. 88) **[13996]**, **[33817]**, **[53701]**

"E-Procurement at Schlumberger" in *Harvard Business Review* (Vol. 78, No. 3, May 2000, pp. 21) **[33818]**

"E-retailers turn to the printed page to put their wares before consumers" in *The New York Times* (July 10, 2000, pp. C12) **[33819]**, **[46924]**, **[51139]**

"E-Scarcity" in *Entrepreneur* (Vol. 28, No. 8, August 2000, pp. 18) **[13997]**, **[25837]**, **[37128]**

E Securities **[30272]**

"E-signing law seen as a boon to e-business" in *The New York Times* (July 4, 2000, pp. C1) **[28070]**, **[29210]**, **[33820]**

"E-Strategies" in *Inc.* (November 15, 2000, pp. 98) **[2245]**, **[13998]**, **[33821]**

E-Tactics Letter **[16835]**, **[20167]**, **[47786]**, **[50714]**

"E-Tail Therapy" in *Entrepreneur* (Vol. 33, January 2005, No. 1, pp. 35) **[33822]**, **[51140]**

"E-Tailers Pay a High Price for Free Shipping" in *Business Week Online* (December 6, 2001) **[31025]**, **[33823]**

"E-Ticket in the Caribbean" in *Hispanic Business* (Vol. 23, No. 7/8, July/August 2001, pp. 68) **[13999]**, **[48138]**

"E-Trade Financial Cuts Prices of Many Online Transactions" in *Kansas City Star* (February 16, 2005) **[14941]**, **[33824]**, **[38024]**

"E-Train" in *Sales & Marketing Management* (Vol. 157, February 2005, No. 2, pp. 20) **[4644]**, **[22974]**, **[33077]**, **[51623]**, **[53265]**

"E-Train" in *Sales and Marketing.com* (Vol. 156, No. 3, March 2004, pp. 18) **[4645]**, **[16513]**, **[22975]**, **[33078]**, **[33825]**, **[45086]**, **[53266]**

"E-waste Bill in Oregon" in *Solid Waste Report* (Vol. 33, No. 39, December 27, 2002) **[6636]**, **[21226]**, **[24337]**, **[40330]**

"E-waste Management Muddled as Agencies Grope for Solutions" in *Solid Waste Report* (Vol. 33, No. 32, September 20, 2002) **[6637]**, **[21227]**, **[40331]**

"E-waste Reuse" in *Industry Week* (Vol. 252, No. 1, January 2003, pp. 19) **[4981]**, **[6638]**, **[7724]**, **[21228]**, **[24338]**

E4E, Inc. **[58001]**

EA Capital LLC **[63082]**

"EAC Goes Beyond the Call of Duty" in *Tradeshow Week* (Vol. 34, December 6, 2004, No. 49, pp. S11) **[22493]**, **[24923]**, **[55085]**

Eads Chamber of Commerce **[58357]**

The Eagle **[19902]**

Eagle Cleaners **[8932]**

Eagle Grove Area Chamber of Commerce **[60126]**

Eagle Lake Chamber of Commerce **[65211]**

Eagle Nest Chamber of Commerce **[62684]**

Eagle Pass Chamber of Commerce **[65212]**

Eagle Rock Chamber of Commerce [57464]

Eagle Times (August 3, 2003); "Newport, N.H., Couple Soon to Open Bed and Breakfast" in [2448]

Eagle Valley Chamber of Commerce [58358]

Eaglerider Motorcycle Rental [2098]

Eaglestone Investment Partners [58002]

"EAI Meets B2B" in *E-business Advisor* (Vol. 18, No. 10, October 2000, pp. 34) [33826]

EAP Digest [26971]

Earle Palmer Brown–Information Center [50735]

"Early Adopters' Paradise: What Else Is Popping In Tech? Plenty" in *Fortune* (Vol. 151, January 10, 2005, No. 1, pp. 52) [6639], [24339], [41652]

"The Early Bird Gets the Worm" in *Black Enterprise* (Vol. 37, January 2007, No. 6, pp. 111) [24924], [33079], [36040], [52846], [55086]

"Early-Bird Special" in *Success* (Vol. 47, No. 1, January 2000, pp. 58) [38762]

Early Chamber of Commerce and Convention and Tourism Bureau [65213]

Early Music America [17726]

"Early Stage Deals Could Come Back" in *Venture Capital Journal* (October 1, 2204) [14942], [41653], [52088], [55583]

Early Stage Enterprises, L.P. [62593]

"Early-Stage Loans With A Venture Capital Twist" in *FSB* (Vol. 10, No. 9, December 1, 2000, pp. 38) [55584]

Early Stage Partners, L.P. [63851]

"Early warning" in *Black Enterprise* (Vol. 32, No. 8, March 2002, pp.) [14000], [25838], [28071], [33827]

EarlyBirdCapital.com Inc. [63083]

Earn Cash Crafting at Home: An MBA At-Home Mom Explains Step-by-Step Her Fun, Proven, Money-Making, Own-Your-Own Business Formula [8006], [8124], [42512]

"The earned income tax credit and the child tax credit under the Tax Act of 2001" in *Tax Notes* (Vol. 92, No. 4, July 23, 2001) [23933], [39810], [54527]

Earned Value Management Systems (EVMS) for Project Managers [44747]

"Earning Your Wings" in *Inc.* (January 1, 2005) [44511], [55585]

"Earnings up 18 Percent for '02; 4Q Totals Rise 141 Percent from '01" in *Crain's Detroit Business* (V. 19, No. 8, 2/24/03) [18020], [28072], [32369]

"Earnings Gain, Wealth Loss" in *Black Enterprise* (Vol. 35, January 2005, No. 6, pp. 30) [14943], [32370], [38025]

"Earnings Improve, but Overall Picture Isn't Exactly Rosy" in *Crain's Detroit Business* (Vol. 18, No. 21, May 27, 2002, pp. 1) [28073], [32371]

"Earnings Rise Is 3rd Straight; Analysts See a Recovery" in *Crain's Detroit Business* (Vol. 18, No. 50, December 16, 2002, pp. 1) [28074], [32372]

Earnshaw's Infants, Girls, Boys Wear Review-Children's Wear Directory Issue [2125], [5274]

Earth Data Analysis Center [67304]

Earth Day Canada [9318]

Earth Energy Society of Canada [9319]

Earth Island Journal [9382]

Earth and Mineral Sciences [52259]

Earth View Inc. [4880]

"EarthLink Inc. to purchase customers of Orlando ISP" in *Atlanta Business Chronicle* (Vol. 25, No. 19, October 18, 2002, pp. 31A) [14001], [33828], [49909]

"EarthLink Posts Loss for Fourth Quarter" in *Altanta Journal-Constitution* (February 7, 2007) [14002], [14944], [28075]

Earthquake Intensity Database Search 1638-1985 [9414]

EarthSave Canada [9320], [21204]

EarthSave International [9477]

Earthshots [19269], [19335]

Earthworm, Inc. [21297]

"Ease up on us, one industry that finances small firms asks the U.S." in *Wall Street Journal* (July 18, 2000, pp. B2) [29211], [40332]

East Bay Chamber of Commerce [64663]

East Bay Small Business Development Center [57256]

East Boston Chamber of Commerce [60945]

East Brunswick Regional Chamber of Commerce [62493]

East Carolina University
Center for Applied Technology [63289]
Small Business and Technology Development Center (Eastern Region)–SBDC [63276]

East Central Community College–SBDC [61746]

East Central Idaho Planning Development Association–Upper Snake River Valley Incubator [59342]

East Central Indiana SBDC [59822]

East Central Missouri/St. Louis County–Extension Center [61864]

East Central Regional Development Commission–Small Business Development Center [61520]

East Central University–Small Business Development Center [63911]

East Central University at Poteau Satellite–Small Business Development Center [63912]

East of Chicago Pizza Co. [19665]

East County Coalition of Grays Harbor County [66076]

"East End PR Firm Helps Give Webshots One More Shot" in *Long Island Business News* (February 27, 2004) [4184], [19229], [19297], [46925], [48664]

East Gate Regional Council of Government–Mahoning Valley Technical Procurement Center–EDATA [63862]

East Georgia College [59220]

East Glacier Chamber of Commerce [62161]

East Granby Chamber of Commerce [58526]

East Grand Forks Chamber of Commerce [61581]

East Greenwich Chamber of Commerce [64664]

East Hampton Chamber of Commerce [62873]

East Harlem Outreach Center–SBDC [62756]

East Hartford Chamber of Commerce [58527]

East Haven Chamber of Commerce [58528]

East Jordan Area Chamber of Commerce [61289]

East Lake County Chamber of Commerce [58791], [61582]

East Liberty Quarter Chamber of Commerce [64412]

East Liverpool Area Chamber of Commerce [63663]

East Los Angeles Chamber of Commerce [57465]

East Los Angeles Minority Business Development Center [57890]

"East Meets West" in *Entrepreneur* (Vol. 32, December 2004, No. 12, pp. 24) [36041], [39293]

East Orange Chamber of Commerce [62494]

East Orlando Chamber of Commerce [58792]

East Peoria Chamber of Commerce and Tourism [59486]

East Prairie Chamber of Commerce [61952]

East Providence Area Chamber of Commerce [64665]

East River Ventures, L.P. [63084]

East Side Chamber of Commerce [59487]

East Side Dogs - Shakes - More [21801]

East Side Mario's [21802]

East Tennessee State University
Bureau of Business and Economic Research [32849]
College of Business–SBDC [64855]
Tennessee Small Business Development Center [54106]

East Tennessee State University College of Business–Satellite Office of ETSU–SBDC [64856]

East Troy Area Chamber of Commerce [66383]

Eastchester - Tuckahoe Chamber of Commerce [62874]

"Easter Is Big Business for Pennsylvania Candy Companies" in *Knight-Ridder/Tribune Business News* (March 30, 2002, pp. ITEM02089101) [4287], [28076]

Eastern Aftermarket Journal-Directory and Buyers Guide Issue [1931]

Eastern Annual Meeting [16335]

Eastern Apicultural Society of North America [2466]

Eastern Arizona College [57102]
Small Business Development Center [56994]

Eastern Connecticut State University–Small Business Development Center [58495]

The Eastern Europe Business Database CD-ROM [43933]

Eastern Fishing and Outdoor Exposition [2210], [5251], [23680]

Eastern Idaho Technical College [59351]

Eastern Iowa Community College–Small Business Development Center [60054]

Eastern Kentucky University–Small Business Development Center [60455]

Eastern Laboratory Service Associates [26627]

Eastern Maine Development Corp.–Maine SBDC Service Center at Bangor [60688]

Eastern Maumee Bay Chamber of Commerce [63664]

Eastern Michigan University
Office of Research Development [61479]
Small Business Technology Development Center [61184]

Eastern Monmouth Area Chamber of Commerce [62495]

Eastern Montgomery County Chamber of Commerce [64413]

Eastern New Mexico University–Office of Grant and Contract Management [62727]

Eastern New Mexico University-Roswell [62735]
Small Business Development Center [62646]

Eastern Oregon College–Small Business Development Center [64167]

Eastern Perishable Products Association-Membership Directory [8511]

Eastern Perishable Products Association Trade Show [8534]

Eastern Plumas Chamber of Commerce [57466]

Eastern Point Consulting Group Inc. [3692], [31336], [32112], [35228], [42960], [48682]

Eastern Shore Chamber of Commerce [56839]

Eastern Shore of Virginia Chamber of Commerce [65887]

Eastern Sports & Outdoor Show [16773], [21189], [23681], [24771], [25321]

Eastern Winter Sports Representatives Association [22844]

"EastGroup Buys Buildings" in *Mississippi Business Journal* (Vol. 29, January 2007, No. 4, pp. 9) [20502], [20869], [28077], [32373], [49910]

Eastham Chamber of Commerce [60946]

Easthampton Chamber of Commerce [60947]

Eastland Chamber of Commerce [65214]

"Eastland Future Unclear: Local Merchants Say They're OK Amid Closings of 4 More Stores" in *Charlotte Observer* (February 8, 2007) [28078], [51141]

Eastman - Dodge County Chamber of Commerce [59096]

Eastman Ventures [64994]

Easton Hunt Capital Partners [63085]

Eastpointe Chamber of Commerce [61290]

Eastport Area Chamber of Commerce [60743]

Eastport Partners [63086]

Eastwest Venture Group / Eastwest Capital Associates [58003]

"Easy Does It" in *Entrepreneur* (Vol. 33, October 2005, No. 10, pp. 122) [28079], [29765], [30534], [36042], [45087], [52210], [52526], [54941]

"Easy e-commerce" in *WorkingWoman* (Vol. 25, No. 6, June 2000, pp. 107) [33829], [53702], [56199]

Easy Financials for Your Home-Based Business: The Friendly Guide to Successful Management Systems for Busy Home Entrepreneurs [42607]

"Easy Math" in *Entrepreneur* (Vol. 31, No. 5, May 2003, pp. 38) [133], [4646], [22976], [26218], [53267]

"Easy Read: Build Business Relationships with a Company Blog" in *Entrepreneur* (Vol. 31, No. 12, December 2003, pp. 25) [25839], [33830], [39294]

"Easy Router" in *Entrepreneur* (Vol. 32, No. 2, February 2004, pp. 45) [6640], [41654], [49017]

Easy to Start, Fun to Run, & Highly Profitable Home Businesses [42608]

"Easy Target? Budget-Cutters in Congress Have Set Their Sights on the SBA" in *Entrepreneur.com* (Vol. 34, January 2006, No. 1, pp. 18) [39811], [40333]

"The Easy Way to Find the Best" in *Business Week* (January 23, 2006, No. 3968, pp. 78-82) [14945], [38026]

EasyChair Media LLC [18977]

Easyinternetcafe [14670]

"Eat the upper crust" in *Entrepreneur* (Vol. 30, No. 3, March 2002, pp. 28) [21492], [53703]

"Eat, Drink and Be Merry, Trans Fats or No" in *San Diego Business Journal* (Vol. 28, January 8, 2007, No. 2, pp. 31) [11323], [53704]

"Eat Our Dust: Broadband infrastructure has made Redpoint the hottest VC firm you've never heard of" in *Fortune* (Oct. 9, 2000, pp. 200) [35404], [55374]

"Eat Your Heart Out" in *Entrepreneur* (Vol. 33, February 2005, pp. 106) [2246], [36043]

"Eateries team up for clout" in *Black Enterprise* (Vol. 31, No. 5, December 2000, pp. 170) [21493], [28080], [48139]

"Eateries Fend Off Nutrition Labels" in *Tampa Tribune* (November 8, 2005) [21494], [40334]

"Eateries Shut In Raids Over Labor Laws" in *Sacramento Bee* (November 15, 2005) [21495], [29212], [40335]

Eating for Life: The Nutrition Pyramid [18461]

"Eating Up Profits" in *Hispanic Business* (June 2005, pp. 94) [28081], [32374], [46270]

Eating Well Magazine [18447]

Eaton Design Group Inc. [49603]

Eaton - Preble County Chamber of Commerce [63665]

Eatonton-Putnam County Chamber of Commerce [59097]

Eau Claire Area Chamber of Commerce [66384]

Eau Claire Lakes Business Association of Barnes and Gordon [66385]

"Ebank gains altitude after midflight change" in *Atlanta Business Chronicle* (Vol. 24, No. 9, August 3, 2001, pp. 19A) [28082], [33831], [49911]

"EBay Acknowledges Changes That Have Alienated Some Users" in *San Jose Mercury News* (February 8, 2005) [1801], [14003]

"eBay Auction Integration Will Be a Major Player with Irun's Website Builder Tools" in *PR Newswire* (December 2, 2003) [1802], [1846], [25840], [33832], [53268]

"eBay" in *DSN Retail Fax* (Vol. 10, No. 26, June 30, 2003) [1803], [10673], [32152], [33833], [49912]

"eBay Enters Electrical Market" in *Electrical Wholesaling* (Vol. 84, No. 9, September 1, 2003) [9066], [33834]

"EBay Ex-Operating Chief Webb Joins LiveOps As Chief Executive" in *Wall Street Journal* (Vol. 248, December 2006, No. 145, pp. B10) [14004], [33835], [41655]

"eBay Fees Cause Vendor to Bid Adieu" in *Post and Courier* (January 20, 2005) [1804], [5905], [8166], [14005]

"eBay Fever" in *Entrepreneur.com* (Vol. 34, February 2006, No. 2, pp. 114) [1760], [33434]

"eBay Motors the Smart Way" in *Small Business Opportunities* (Vol. 16, November 2004, No. 6, pp. 134) [1805], [18021]

"eBay Phenomenon Embraced by Online Piano Company" in *PR Newswire* (November 13, 2003) [1806], [17740], [17840], [33836]

"eBay Revs Up Its Industrial Sales: It's Now Easier for Engineers to Go Shopping Online" in *Design News* (Vol.58, No.10, July 7, 2003) [33837]

"EBay Shippers Receive Special Service at Virginia Beach, Va., Post Office" in *Virginian-Pilot* (September 9, 2004) [1807], [14006], [39812]

"EBay Springs a Price Increase on eBay Store Owners" in *Inc.* (April 1, 2005) [1808], [18442], [18642], [33838]

"EBay Tackles E-Waste" in *Waste News* (Vol. 10, January 17, 2005, No. 21, pp. 1) [1809], [21229]

"eBay" in *Travel Weekly* (Vol. 38, No. 13, December 2003, pp. 32) [37129]

"EBay's Bid To Go Beyond Auctions Isn't Selling Well" in *Wall Street Journal* (Vol. 248, December 2006, No. 145, pp. B1) [1810], [18643], [33839], [51624]

Eblast Ventures LLC [59732]

Ebony/Jet Guide to Black Excellence: The Entrepreneurs [48496]

"Eboys: The First Inside Account of Venture Capitalists at Work" in *Harvard Business Review* (Vol. 78, No. 4, July 2000, pp. 152) [14946], [55586]

"ebrary Snags Key Investors for Pay-Per-Use Service" in *Information Today* (Vol. 17, No. 11, December 2000, pp. 41) [33840], [49913]

EBRI Issue Brief [26972], [30748]

EBRI Pension Investment Report [26973]

E.B.'s Express [21803]

"EBSCO Expands Book Services, Creates E-Journal Licensing Web Site" in *Information Today* (Vol. 17, No. 10, November 2000, pp. 39) [3039], [33841]

"EC Outlook returns from Ohio." in *Houston Business Journal* (Vol. 33, No. 51, May 2, 2003, pp. 1A) [4647], [22977], [53269]

"eC-T spins localized Web" in *InfoWorld* (Vol. 22, No. 5, January 31, 2000, pp. 8) [14007], [33842]

ECA Magazine [7550]

E*Capital Corporation [58004]

"ECD short of cash at critical time as partners pull out of ventures" in *Crain's Detroit Business* (Vol. 19, No. 8, Feb. 24, 2003) [49914], [50863], [55087], [55587]

ECentury Capital Partners, L.P. [65971]

Echelon Ventures LLC [61067]

"Eclipse gum: Paul Chibe" in *Advertising Age* (Vol. 72, October 8, 2001, pp. S10) [4288], [46926]

"Eco-Preneuring" in *Small Business Opportunities* (Vol. 17, September 2005, No. 5, pp. 100, 104) [2590], [2657], [3478], [7890], [8141], [8905], [9481], [10611], [11994], [12172], [12254], [15811], [16282], [21198], [31092], [31622], [34308], [35405], [36633], [37221], [37265], [37922], [53705], [54115], [54154], [54168], [56721]

"Eco-Products In Demand, But Labels Can Be Murky" in *Boston Globe* (February 9, 2005) [37266], [40336]

"Eco-Radicals Target Growth in Sierra Hills" in *San Jose Mercury News* (March 9, 2005) [7338], [29213], [37267]

Eco-Rating International Inc. [37357]

Ecole des Hautes Etudes Commerciales–Information Systems Research Group [7021]

Ecology Action Centre [9321], [21298], [37228]

Ecompanies [58005]

Econo Lodge [12712]

Econo Lube N' Tune [20265], [22675]

"Economic Developers Expect a Busier Year in '03" in *Atlanta Business Chronicle* (Vol. 25, December 6, 2002, No. 26, pp. 8A) [7339], [20870], [28083], [32375], [46271], [52667]

Economic Development [32815]

Economic Development Administration-Annual Report [32376]

Economic Development Alliance of St. Clair County [61185]

Economic Development Assistance Programs in State Government [39813]

Economic Development Commission–DEAL WITH VARIOUS ISSUES OF SMALL BUSINESSES [62335]

Economic Development Research Focus [32816]

Economic Edge [6016], [8633], [19903]

"Economic and Financial Indicators" in *The Economist* (Vol. 376, July 16-22, 2005, No. 8435, pp. 96-97) [9927], [14947], [28084], [30843], [31502], [32377], [54528]

"The Economic Ground War" in *Hispanic Business* (March 2003, pp. 18) [32378], [36044], [45088]

"Economic Outlook" in *Business 2.0* (Vol. 6, July 2005, No. 6, pp. 32) [28085], [32379]

Economic and Social Research Institute [41368]

The Economics of Entrepreneurship [32380], [36045]

"Economics Focus" in *The Economist* (Vol. 376, July 30-August 5, 2005, No. 8437, pp. 70) [32381], [39295], [43630]

"The Economics" in *Law Firm Inc.* (August 2004) [29214], [49691]

The Economics and Management of Small Business: An International Perspective [32382], [43631], [45089]

"The economics of ergonomics" in *Atlanta Business Chronicle* (Vol. 23, No. 35, February 2, 2001, pp. 51A) [40337], [56557]

The Economics of Self-Employment and Entrepreneurship [32383], [36046]

The Economics of Small Firms [32384], [39296]

The Economist (Vol. 377, October 22-28, 2005, No. 8449, pp. 3-6, 8-10, 12-18); "A Market for Ideas" in [29783], [41496], [43982], [44269], [48692], [52030]

The Economist (Vol. 376, July 30-August 5, 2005, No. 8437, pp. 25-26); "America's Labor Federation" in [39143], [55281]

The Economist (Vol. 357, No. 8, October 21, 2000, pp. 78); "Barter's latest comeback" in [13736], [26700], [35325], [53558]

The Economist (Vol. 376, July 30-August 5, 2005, No. 8437, pp. 58); "Big Generic Pharma" in [14790], [49816], [52047]

The Economist (Vol. 377, October 1-7, 2005, No. 8446, pp. 37); "Carrying Coffee to Seattle" in [11317], [30811]

The Economist (Vol. 377, October 1-7, 2005, No. 8446, pp. 62); "Cheap Tricks" in [6604], [46230], [54156]

The Economist (Vol. 376, July 30-August 5, 2005, No. 8437, pp. 14); "Crooks and Books" in [118], [26203], [40293]

The Economist (Vol. 376, July 30-August 5, 2005, No. 8437, pp. 67); "Cross-Border Property Deals" in [20849], [43605], [53672]

The Economist (Vol. 377, October 22-28, 2005, No. 8449, pp. 66, 68); "Death By Red Ink" in [18006], [46260]

The Economist (Vol. 356, No. 8182, August 5, 2000, pp. 69); "E-conomic Publishing" in [2699], [9138]

The Economist (Vol. 376, July 16-22, 2005, No. 8435, pp. 96-97); "Economic and Financial Indicators" in [9927], [14947], [28084], [30843], [31502], [32377], [54528]

The Economist (Vol. 376, July 30-August 5, 2005, No. 8437, pp. 70); "Economics Focus" in [32381], [39295], [43630]

The Economist (Vol. 376, July 16-22, 2005, No. 8435, pp. 98); "Emerging-Market Indicators" in [14950], [31521], [32403]

The Economist (Vol. 376, July 30-August 5, 2005, No. 8437, pp. 60); "Face Value" in [11608], [12004], [20873], [21319]

The Economist (Vol. 377, October 1-7, 2005, No. 8446, pp. 65-67); "Flying From the Computer" in [24687], [25183], [30327], [30661], [33909]

The Economist (Vol. 376, July 16-22, 2005, No. 8435, pp. 29); "Greyhound Racing" in [10868], [54195]

The Economist (Vol. 376, July 30-August 5, 2005, No. 8437, pp. 11); "How China Runs the World Economy" in [15097], [32495]

The Economist (Vol. 376, July 16-22, 2005, No. 8435, pp. 59); "Identity Theft" in [22259], [44317]

The Economist (Vol. 376, July 16-22, 2005, No. 8435, pp. 39-40); "Indian Retail Reform" in [12987], [28325], [43706], [51202]

The Economist (Vol. 377, October 1-7, 2005, No. 8446, pp. 69-70); "Industrial Metamorphosis" in [28326], [46318], [53808]

The Economist Intelligence Unit–Information Center [13042]

The Economist (Vol. 356, No. 8189, September 23, 2000, pp. NA); "Knowledge is power" in [44330]

The Economist (Vol. 377, October 1-7, 2005, No. 8446, pp. 72); "Natural Hedge" in [15288], [38237]

"Economist Offers 2005 Outlook For 2 Florida Counties" in *Bradenton Herald* (January 13, 2005) **[7340]**, **[25180]**, **[28086]**, **[32385]**

The Economist (Vol. 377, October 1-7, 2005, No. 8446, pp. 62); "Pay Per Sale" in **[755]**, **[1844]**, **[34331]**, **[47391]**

"Economist Says Focus on Emerging Markets to Boost Foreign Trade" in *Portland Press Herald* (June 17, 2005) **[12957]**, **[32386]**, **[43632]**

The Economist (Vol. 376, July 16-22, 2005, No. 8435, pp. 75-76); "Space and Technology" in **[42000]**, **[52207]**

The Economist (Vol. 376, July 16-22, 2005, No. 8435, pp. 65-67); "Special Report" in **[4820]**, **[6413]**, **[15467]**, **[23206]**, **[32706]**, **[42001]**, **[43825]**, **[53486]**

The Economist (Vol. 376, July 16-22, 2005, No. 8435, pp. 71); "Terrorism Insurance" in **[13487]**, **[39940]**, **[43391]**

The Economist (Vol. 377, October 22-28, 2005, No. 8449, pp. 65-66); "The Battle of the Portals" in **[13836]**, **[25796]**, **[33564]**

The Economist (Vol. 377, October 1-7, 2005, No. 8446, pp. 13, 16); "The Great Jobs Switch" in **[32455]**, **[46306]**

The Economist (Vol. 377, October 22-28, 2005, No. 8449, pp. 35); "The Greens Bite Back" in **[29278]**, **[40424]**

The Economist (Vol. 377, October 1-7, 2005, No. 8446, pp. 60); "The Merry Go-Round" in **[40533]**, **[41061]**, **[50924]**, **[52150]**

The Economist (Vol. 376, July 30-August 5, 2005, No. 8437, pp. 65-66); "The Ones That Get Away" in **[214]**, **[26311]**

The Economist (Vol. 377, October 1-7, 2005, No. 8446, pp. 76-77); "The Power of Spin" in **[37318]**, **[44125]**, **[48777]**, **[50946]**, **[52178]**

The Economist (Vol. 376, July 16-22, 2005, No. 8435, pp. 60); "The Restaurant Business" in **[21596]**, **[32665]**, **[38896]**

The Economist (Vol. 376, July 30-August 5, 2005, No. 8437, pp. 53-54); "The War of the Wires" in **[4126]**, **[5169]**, **[14575]**, **[24460]**, **[30987]**

The Economist (Vol. 377, October 22-28, 2005, No. 8449, pp. 33-34); "Too Sensible to Survive" in **[40775]**, **[54837]**

The Economist (Vol. 376, July 30-August 5, 2005, No. 8437, pp. 66); "Trade Policy" in **[13013]**, **[40779]**, **[43847]**

"Economist Upbeat About Macomb in 2005 Despite Lagging Recovery" in *Crain's Detroit Business* (Vol. 21, January 24, 2005, No. 4, pp. 5) **[18022]**, **[32387]**, **[46272]**

The Economist (Vol. 377, October 1-7, 2005, No. 8446, pp. 37); "Use It Or Lose It" in **[24457]**, **[55321]**

The Economist (Vol. 376, July 16-22, 2005, No. 8435, pp. 30); "Watch That Bird's Rear" in **[26560]**, **[29572]**, **[37333]**

The Economist (Vol. 355, No. 8170, May 13, 2000, pp. 81); "Will journal publishers perish?" in **[2751]**, **[9168]**, **[18946]**

"Economists Divided Over Downturn" in *Hispanic Business* (Vol. 23, No. 11, November 2001, pp. 16) **[28087]**, **[32388]**

"Economists Raise Concerns about South Carolina Governor's Tax Cut Proposal" in *The State* (February 17, 2004) **[32389]**, **[54529]**

"Economy Adds 262,000 Jobs" in *Boston Globe* (March 5, 2005) **[28088]**, **[32390]**

"Economy Expands Modestly, but Unemployment Rate Rises" in *Altanta Journal-Constitution* (February 3, 2007) **[28089]**, **[32391]**, **[42223]**

"Economy Refuses to Fall" in *Altanta Journal-Constitution* (February 1, 2007) **[20503]**, **[20871]**, **[28090]**, **[32392]**

"Economy: So much for technology's third-quarter save" in *Red Herring* (No. 103, September 1, 2001, pp. 24) **[28091]**, **[32393]**, **[41656]**

"Economy Stephen Levy" in *Venture Capital Journal* (January 1, 2005) **[32394]**, **[55588]**

"Economy's Pain Reaches Office Landlords" in *Wall Street Journal* (May 22, 2002, pp. B8) **[32395]**

"Economy.sup.2" in *Entrepreneur* (Vol. 30, No. 2, February 2002,) **[9928]**, **[32396]**, **[36047]**

Econotax **[24125]**

Ecopreneuring: The Complete Guide to Small Business Opportunities from the Environmental Revolution **[9475]**, **[21199]**, **[37268]**

"ECOWORKS Leeding The Way" in *Ingram's* (Vol. 28, No. 1, January 2002, pp. 32) **[7341]**, **[9352]**, **[37269]**

ECRI **[17149]**
        Library **[17289]**

Ed-Expo **[24277]**

"Ed Otto, Director of Biotechnology at RCCC" in *Charlotte Observer* (February 8, 2007) **[36048]**, **[50864]**, **[52089]**

EDECA **[66799]**

Edelson Technology Partners **[62594]**

Edelweiss Deli Express **[21804]**

Eden Chamber of Commerce **[63355]**, **[65215]**

Eden Prairie Chamber of Commerce **[61583]**

Edenton-Chowan Chamber of Commerce **[63356]**

EDF Ventures / Enterprise Development Fund **[61456]**

The Edge **[324]**

Edge Capital Investment Co., LLC (Las Vegas) **[62373]**

Edgebrook Chamber of Commerce **[59488]**

Edgerton Area Chamber of Commerce **[66386]**

Edgerton Chamber of Commerce **[63666]**

Edgewalkers: People and Organizations That Take Risks, Build Bridges, and Break New Ground **[36049]**, **[39297]**

"Edgy Bistro Mixes Fancy and Casual" in *Kansas City Star* (February 8, 2005) **[21395]**, **[37561]**

"The EDI revolution" in *Hispanic Business* (Vol. 22, No. 4, April 2000, pp. 20) **[33843]**, **[40013]**

Edinboro University–Baron-Forness Library–Special Collections **[1653]**, **[17676]**, **[17817]**

Edinburg Area Chamber of Commerce **[65888]**

Edinburg Chamber of Commerce **[65216]**

Edison Chamber of Commerce **[62496]**

Edison Materials Technology Center–Ohio SBDC–Region 4 Lead Center **[63549]**

Edison State Community College–Office of Institutional Research **[63876]**

Edison Venture Fund **[62595]**

Editing Stronger Magazines **[32926]**

Editorial Code and Data Inc. **[2791]**, **[8651]**, **[18264]**

The Editorial Eye **[9025]**

Editorial Freelancers Association **[8956]**

Editorial Freelancers Association-Membership Directory **[8992]**

Editorial Skills for Non-Editors **[27244]**

Editors' Association of Canada **[8957]**, **[55273]**

Edmond Area Chamber of Commerce **[63986]**

Edmonds Community College–Small Business Development Center **[66018]**

Edmonton Chamber of Commerce/World Trade Center Edmonton **[32215]**

Edmonton - Metcalfe County Chamber of Commerce **[60499]**

Edmonton Research Park **[66669]**

Edo Japan **[21805]**

EDR Sanborn Maps **[10376]**, **[15756]**

Educate Our Kids **[5425]**

"Education" in *Business Week* (January 9, 2006, No. 3966, pp. 40-43) **[33080]**, **[43633]**, **[45090]**

Education Development Center **[3693]**, **[31337]**, **[52340]**

"Education, Economy Key for Voters" in *Hispanic Business* (September 2004, pp. 16) **[32397]**, **[33081]**

Education Index **[25464]**

Education Network **[33295]**

"The education of Clint Reilly" in *San Francisco Business Times* (Vol. 16, No. 43, May 21, 2002, pp. 3) **[20872]**, **[31143]**

Education Today **[24273]**, **[33296]**

Education Update **[33297]**

Educational Dealer **[24274]**

Educational Dealer-Buyers' Guide Issue **[24272]**

Educational Foundation for Women in Accounting **[34]**, **[56097]**

Educational Outfitters **[5304]**

"Educational-software concern is cutting work force by 20 percent" in *Wall Street Journal* (May 20, 2002, pp. C9) **[28092]**, **[45091]**

Educational Technology Magazine **[6343]**

Edward-Dean Museum & Gardens–Art Reference Library **[10846]**

Edwards County Chamber of Commerce **[60321]**, **[65217]**

Edwardsburg Area Chamber of Commerce **[61291]**

Edwardsville - Glen Carbon Chamber of Commerce **[59489]**

EE Product News **[9080]**

EEO Bi-monthly **[23373]**

"EEOC Sues Charlotte-Based Lebo's" in *Charlotte Observer* (February 7, 2007) **[22760]**, **[29215]**, **[32019]**

Effect of the Overvalued Dollar on Small Exporters: Congressional Hearing **[12958]**, **[29216]**, **[32398]**, **[40338]**, **[43634]**

"The Effect of Social Style on Peer Evaluation Ratings in Project Teams" in *Journal of Business Communications* (Vol. 43, January 2006) **[34877]**, **[45092]**

Effective Business Communications **[27630]**

Effective Business Writing **[27245]**

Effective Compensation Inc. **[3694]**, **[31338]**, **[38527]**, **[42961]**

Effective E-Mail Marketing **[46626]**, **[47232]**

Effective Executive Speaking (Canada) **[27246]**

The Effective Facilitator: Maximizing Involvement and Results **[34790]**

The Effective Facilitator: Maximizing Involvement and Results (Canada) **[34791]**

Effective Hiring & ADA Compliance **[42224]**

Effective Internal Auditing **[37848]**

Effective Mailers **[880]**

The Effective Manager **[42486]**, **[51950]**, **[55014]**

Effective Meeting Skills **[27354]**

Effective Presentation Skills **[27355]**

Effective Presentation Techniques **[27247]**

Effective Presentations: How to Make Powerhouse Presentations That Get the Results You Want **[27566]**

Effective Project Leadership: Building High Commitment Through Superior Communication **[44748]**

Effective Project Leadership: Building High Commitment Through Superior Communication (Canada) **[34792]**, **[44749]**

Effective Purchasing Negotiations Workshop: Techniques and Tools for Today's Competitive Environment **[44750]**

Effective Recruiting, Selecting and Behavioral Interviewing: A Practical Techniques Workshop (Canada) **[42161]**

Effective Resources Inc. **[31339]**, **[35229]**, **[42962]**, **[46016]**

Effective Resumes & Job Applications **[4428]**

Effective Security Screening **[22219]**

Effective Small Business Management **[43079]**, **[45093]**

Effective Technical Writing **[27248]**, **[27607]**

Effective Telephone Calling **[31930]**

Effective Telephone Techniques **[24298]**

Effectively Marketing to Women: Tapping into Hidden Profits **[46627]**

Effectiveness Resource Group Inc. **[3695]**, **[31340]**, **[50778]**

"Effects of SARS Hit Colorado Firms' Dealings with Asia" in *Denver Post* (April 11, 2003) **[30321]**, **[43635]**

Effectuation **[36050]**, **[39298]**

"Efficiency Creates Opportunity" in *Hispanic Business* (June 2002, pp. 74) **[45094]**, **[54942]**

Effingham County Chamber of Commerce **[59098]**

"eFindOutTheTruth.com: www.efindoutthetruth.com" in *Entrepreneur* (Vol. 32, November 2004, No. 11, pp. 6) **[14008]**, **[33844]**, **[42225]**

EFO Collector **[5845]**

"Efulfillment Service" in *Entrepreneur.com* (Vol. 34, February 2006, No. 2, pp. 6) **[49692]**

EFund, LLC **[66209]**

TRECI/Thomas R. Egan Consulting Inc. **[49419]**, **[49604]**

Egan-Managed Capital **[61068]**

Egg Harbor City Chamber of Commerce **[62497]**

Egismoz **[7756]**

EGL Holdings **[46017]**

EGL Ventures **[59190]**

"EGTRRA lowers rates and expands credits, education benefits" in *The Tax Adviser* (Vol. 32, No. 10, October 2001, pp. 677) **[23934]**, **[39814]**, **[54530]**

EHatchery, LLC **[59191]**

Ehousing **[21379]**

EI Environmental Services Directory **[11930]**

EIFS Industry Members Association **[13130]**

"Eight Black Physicians Partnered to Open an International House of Pancakes in Harlem..." in *Black Enterprise* (Vol. 35, Dec. 2004) **[21496]**, **[38763]**, **[48140]**, **[49915]**

Eight at Eight Dinner Club **[7076]**

Eight Great Steps to Choreography **[8474]**

"Eight Moves for Your Money" in *Black Enterprise* (Vol. 35, October 2004, No. 3, pp. 98) **[9929]**, **[14948]**, **[38027]**

"8 Secrets of a Winning E-Mail Newsletter" in *PC Magazine* (February 22, 2000, pp. 135) **[18226]**, **[33845]**

Eight Sheet Outdoor Advertising Association **[50527]**

"Eight Tips to Spot Bad Checks" in *My Business* (February/March 2003, pp. 15) **[30218]**, **[31542]**, **[51142]**

8 Weeks to Optimum Health **[18462]**

"8(a) Advantage or Disadvantage?" in *Hispanic Business* (March 2003, pp. 60) **[40014]**, **[48141]**

Eighteenth Street Development Corp.–Small Business Development Center **[59368]**

"80 Elite Hispanic Women Directory" in *Hispanic Business* (Vol. 24, No. 4, Apr. 2002, pp. 32) **[48142]**, **[56200]**

Eighty-Plus Great Ideas for Making Money at Home: A Guide for the First-Time Entrepreneur **[42609]**

80% Preventable (Burn Injury Prevention) **[56615]**

"The 80-20 Rule: It's Not Just a Glib Remark" in *Barron's* (Vol. 82, No. 57, February, 10, 2003, pp. 39) **[36051]**, **[45095]**

EIMCO Baker Process Equipment Company–Technical Library **[25729]**

"EISC partners start-up with unique technology" in *Toledo Business Journal* (Vol. 19, No. 2, February 2003, pp. 23) **[39765]**, **[41450]**, **[50791]**, **[52018]**

The Eisenhower Era, 1940-1960 **[33315]**

EIU ViewsWire **[3464]**, **[15757]**, **[29659]**, **[43934]**

"El Cajon: Bookseller Still Shining From the Sunbelt" in *San Diego Business Journal* (Vol. 28, January 15, 2007, No. 3, pp. 16) **[3040]**, **[51143]**

El Camino Hospital–Health Library and Resource Center **[1716]**, **[12434]**

El Campo Chamber of Commerce and Agriculture **[65218]**

El Centro Chamber of Commerce and Visitors Bureau **[57467]**

El Centro SBDC Service Center **[57257]**

El Cerrito Chamber of Commerce **[57468]**

"El Commuters Brace for Cuts" in *Crain's Chicago Business* (Vol. 30, January 2007, No. 3, pp. 12) **[7342]**, **[30322]**

El Dorado Chamber of Commerce **[57160]**, **[60322]**

El Dorado County Chamber of Commerce **[57469]**

El Dorado Hills Chamber of Commerce **[57470]**

El Dorado Springs Chamber of Commerce **[61953]**

El Dorado Ventures **[58006]**

El Monte-South El Monte Chamber of Commerce **[57471]**

El Paso Chamber of Commerce **[59490]**

El Paso Community College **[65665]**
    Small Business Development Center **[65033]**

El Paso Hispanic Chamber of Commerce **[65219]**

El Paso Minority Business Development Center–NEDA Business Consultants, Inc. **[65579]**

El Planeta Platica **[25291]**

El Pollo Loco **[21806]**

"El Pollo Loco" in *Hispanic Business* (March 2002, pp. 64) **[21497]**, **[38764]**

El Reno Chamber of Commerce and Development Corporation **[63987]**

El Segundo Chamber of Commerce **[57472]**

El Sobrante Chamber of Commerce **[57473]**

"Elan Frozen Yogurt returns to New York" in *Ice Cream Reporter* (Vol. 14, No. 2, January 20, 2001, pp. 2) **[12775]**, **[46927]**

Elba Chamber of Commerce **[56840]**

Elbert County Chamber of Commerce **[59099]**

"Elbows Off the Table" in *My Business* (February/March 2004, pp. 14) **[27356]**, **[36052]**, **[39299]**, **[45096]**

Elder Engineering Inc. **[20368]**, **[24494]**

ElderCare at Home **[12420]**

Elderly Health Services Letter **[18355]**

ELDirect Homecare **[477]**, **[41342]**

Eldon Chamber of Commerce **[61954]**

Eldora Area Chamber and Development Council **[60127]**

Electra Chamber of Commerce **[65220]**

"Electric Avenue" in *Entrepreneur* (Vol. 32, December 2004, No. 12, pp. 46) **[7725]**, **[18023]**, **[41657]**

"Electric Avenue" in *Small Business Opportunities* (Vol. 13, No. 6, November 2001, pp. 108) **[7708]**, **[35406]**, **[56000]**, **[56038]**

Electric Machines Components and Systems **[52260]**

Electric Pages **[4869]**

"Electric Shoes and 'Breadcrumbs' for the Troops" in *Venture Capital Journal* (Vol. 42, No. 9, September 2002, pp. 26-27) **[37130]**, **[40015]**, **[52090]**, **[55589]**

"Electric Slide: Sign Up for Electric Filing, and You Could Get a Tax-Penalty Refund" in *Entrepreneur* (Vol. 32, November 2004, No. 11) **[14009]**, **[54531]**

Electrical Appliance and Utilization Equipment Directory **[1413]**

Electrical Case Histories **[9085]**, **[56616]**

Electrical Construction Equipment Directory **[9067]**

Electrical Contractor **[9081]**

Electrical Contractor: Start and Run a Money-Making Business **[9068]**

Electrical Engineering in Japan **[52261]**

Electrical News-Distributor Directory for the Pacific Northwest Edition **[9069]**

Electrical News-Distributor Directory for the Pacific Southwest Edition **[9070]**

Electrical News-Fax Directory for the Pacific Northwest Edition **[9071]**

Electrical News-Fax Directory for the Pacific Southwest Edition **[9072]**

Electrical Principles **[9086]**

Electrical Product News **[46505]**

Electrical Safety in the Lab **[56617]**

Electrical Safety Related Work Practices **[56618]**

Electrical Showcase **[9088]**

Electrical Wholesaling **[9082]**

Electrical Wholesaling (Vol. 84, No. 9, September 1, 2003); "eBay Enters Electrical Market" in **[9066]**, **[33834]**

"Electrical-Wiring Company is Moving to Ferndale" in *Bellingham Business Journal* (December 2006, pp. A4) **[7726]**, **[9073]**, **[28093]**, **[30144]**

"Electricity, natural gas facing uncertain future" in *Atlanta Business Chronicle* (Vol. 25, January 10, 2003, No. 31, pp. 24A) **[28094]**, **[32399]**, **[40339]**

"Electronic Arts to Convert Some of Its Salaried Employees to Hourly Pay" in *San Jose Mercury News* (March 10, 2005) **[1101]**, **[6641]**, **[41658]**, **[45097]**

Electronic Clipper **[6055]**

Electronic Commerce & Law Report **[29660]**

Electronic Editing I **[32927]**

Electronic Editing II **[32928]**

Electronic Industries Alliance **[7709]**, **[24331]**

Electronic Information Report **[6299]**

Electronic Literature Organization **[9127]**

"The Electronic Negotiator" in *Harvard Business Review* (Vol. 78, No. 1, January 2000, pp. 16) **[27357]**, **[27631]**

Electronic News (Vol. 48, No. 11, March 11, 2002, pp); "A growing problem" in **[21235]**, **[37292]**

"The Electronic Personal Touch" in *Fortune* (Vol. 141, No. 6, March 20, 2000, pp. 214) **[7112]**, **[35407]**

"The electronic personality and digital self" in *Dispute Resolution Journal* (Vol. 56, No. 1, February-April 2001, pp. 8) **[14010]**, **[17050]**, **[27358]**

Electronic Print Media Service **[8664]**

Electronic Privacy Information Center **[22148]**

Electronic Products **[6422]**

Electronic Publishing (Vol. 26, No. 5, May 2002, pp. 10); "Adobe Systems upgrades FrameMaker to version 7.0" in **[2674]**, **[8602]**, **[8986]**, **[9129]**, **[18221]**, **[18847]**

Electronic Publishing (Vol. 26, No. 5, May 2002, pp. 51); "H.C. Turk" in **[5987]**, **[8009]**, **[9144]**

Electronic Publishing (Vol. 27, No. 7, July 2003, pp. 4); "No More Waiting" in **[15931]**, **[18242]**

Electronic Retailing Association **[46611]**, **[51043]**

Electronic Solutions Co. **[49420]**

Electronic Tax Filers (ETF) **[24126]**

"Electronics recycling firm looks to power up $8M plant in Oakland County" in *Crain's Detroit Business* (Vol. 19, Feb. 10, 2003) **[21230]**, **[41659]**

Electronics for Imaging / EFI **[58007]**

Electronics Representatives Association **[7710]**

Elegant Bride **[3205]**

Element of Risk: The Politics of Radon **[20391]**

The Elements of Business Writing: A Guide to Writing Clear, Concise Letters, Memos, Reports, Proposals, and Other Business Documents **[27632]**

Elements of Information Management **[13074]**

Elements of Mediation **[17051]**

"Elements of a business plan" in *Crain's Detroit Business* (Vol. 16, No. 50, December 11, 2000, pp. E-2) **[29854]**

The Elements of Small Business **[29727]**, **[39048]**

The Elements of Technical Writing **[27633]**

Elephant Butte Chamber of Commerce **[62685]**

"Elephants on a chip" in *Barron's* (Vol. 82, No. 58, February 17, 2003, pp. T1) **[28095]**, **[30844]**, **[41660]**

"11th Hour" in *Entrepreneur* (Vol. 27, No. 12, December 1999, pp. 20) **[26219]**, **[29217]**, **[38028]**, **[40340]**

Elgin Area Chamber of Commerce **[59491]**

Elgin Community College–Small Business Development Center **[59369]**

J. S. Eliezer Associates Inc. **[2792]**, **[18968]**, **[19927]**

"Eliminate Fulfillment Problems" in *E-business Advisor* (Vol. 18, No. 3, March 2000, pp. 28) **[25841]**, **[28096]**, **[31708]**, **[33846]**, **[49693]**

Charlotte Eliopoulos Considine, Ph.D. **[18380]**

"Elite Company" in *Hispanic Business* (December 2002, pp. 54) **[14011]**, **[18024]**, **[36053]**, **[48143]**, **[52091]**

Elite Med Spa **[7931]**

Elizabeth Area Chamber of Commerce **[58359]**

Elizabeth Chamber of Commerce **[59492]**

Elizabeth City Area Chamber of Commerce **[63357]**

Elizabeth City State University–Small Business and Technology Development Center (Northeastern Region) **[63277]**

Elizabethton - Carter County Chamber of Commerce **[64909]**

Elizabethtown-Hardin County Chamber of Commerce **[60500]**

Elizabethtown-White Lake Area Chamber of Commerce **[63358]**

Elk Associates Funding Corp. **[63087]**

Elk City Chamber of Commerce **[63988]**

Elk Grove Chamber of Commerce **[57474]**

"Elk Grove Village, Ill. Officials Wary of O'Hare Airport Expansion" in *Chicago Tribune* (April 11, 2003) **[28097]**

Elk Rapids Area Chamber of Commerce **[61292]**

Elk River Area Chamber of Commerce **[61584]**

Elkader Area Chamber of Commerce **[60128]**

Elkhart Area Chamber of Commerce **[60323]**

Elkhart Lake Area Chamber of Commerce **[66387]**

Elkhorn Area Chamber of Commerce **[66388]**

Elko Chamber of Commerce **[62347]**

Elkton Chamber and Alliance **[60826]**

Ellaville - Schley County Chamber of Commerce **[59100]**

Ellensburg Chamber of Commerce **[66077]**

Ellenville - Wawarsing Chamber of Commerce **[62875]**

Ellianos Coffee Co. **[11382]**

Ellicottville Chamber of Commerce **[62876]**

Ellington Chamber of Commerce **[61955]**

Ellinwood Area Chamber of Commerce **[60324]**

Ellis Chamber of Commerce **[60325]**

"Ellman: Building a VC Empire in the Empire State" in *Venture Capital Journal* (Vol. 40, No. 10, October 2000, pp. 48-49) **[35408]**, **[55375]**

Ellsworth Area Chamber of Commerce **[60744]**

Ellsworth Chamber of Commerce **[66389]**

Ellsworth-Kanopolis Area Chamber of Commerce **[60326]**

Ellwood City Area Chamber of Commerce **[64414]**

Elma Chamber of Commerce **[66078]**

Elmhurst Chamber of Commerce and Industry **[59493]**

Eloy Chamber of Commerce **[57029]**

Elrick and Lavidge–Library **[16891]**

Elroy Area Advancement Corporation **[66390]**

ELS Language Centers **[25109]**

Elsberry Chamber of Commerce **[61956]**

"Elsevier launches e-Book program" in *Information Today* (Vol. 20, No. 3, March 2003, pp. 26) **[2700]**, **[3041]**, **[9139]**

Elwood Chamber of Commerce **[59906]**

Ely Chamber of Commerce **[61585]**

EM Microelectronic-US Inc. **[49421]**

EMA Reporter **[9247]**, **[42905]**

Emack & Bolio's Ice Cream **[12819]**

"Emageon Vies With Big Guns" in *Birmingham Business Journal* (Vol. 20, No. 39, September 26, 2003, pp. 1) **[4648]**, **[22978]**, **[41004]**, **[53270]**

Email Marketing by the Numbers: How to Use the World's Greatest Marketing Tool to Take Any Organization to the Next Level **[28098]**, **[33847]**, **[46928]**

"The emancipates organization. Insights on gender, leadership, and power" in *Harvard Business Review* (Vol. 80, Sept. 2002, pp. 20) **[45098]**, **[56201]**

"An Embarrassment of riches" in *WorkingWoman* (Vol. 25, No. 5, May 2000, pp. 66) **[38029]**, **[56202]**

EMBASE: Pharmacy **[8852]**

Embedded Systems Programming **[6505]**

Embers America Restaurants **[21807]**

"Embrace the Deficit" in *Wall Street Journal* (Vol. 248, January 2007, No. 146, pp. B1-B3) **[14949]**, **[32400]**, **[43636]**

"Embracing Diversity, Not Division" in *Black Enterprise* (Vol. 34, No. 7, February 2004, pp. 14) **[32020]**, **[48544]**

Embroiderers' Guild of America **[8143]**

Embroidme **[5753]**

Embryon Capital **[60869]**

EMediaLive **[4870]**

Emerald Venture Group **[58008]**

Emergence Capital Partners, L.L.C. **[58009]**

Emergency **[41188]**

"Emergency services gets a breath of fresh air" in *Red Herring* (January 2003, pp. 56) **[22220]**, **[50865]**, **[52092]**

"Emergency care for Detroit's health system" in *Crain's Detroit Business* (Vol. 19, No. 15, April 14, 2003, pp. 11) **[32401]**, **[40341]**

Emergency Evacuation Training: Preparing for the Future **[56619]**

Emergency Management Today **[8423]**

Emergency Medical Services Magazine-Buyers Guide Issue **[1088]**, **[17256]**

Emergency Medicine Alert **[1089]**

Emergency Planning and Crisis Management Series **[56620]**

Emergency Preparedness News **[8424]**

Emergency Procedures for the Small Business & Shop: A Guide & Disaster Plan Framework **[29855]**

The Emerging Digital Economy: Entrepreneurship, Clusters, and Policy **[32402]**, **[36054]**, **[52668]**, **[53706]**

"Emerging-Market Indicators" in *The Economist* (Vol. 376, July 16-22, 2005, No. 8435, pp. 98) **[14950]**, **[31521]**, **[32403]**

"Emerging Market Investing Means More Than Just India or China" in *Venture Capital Journal* (November 1, 2004) **[14951]**, **[55590]**

"Emerging Opportunities from the Evolving Book" in *Information Today* (Vol. 17, No. 7, July 2000, pp. 7) **[2701]**, **[9140]**

Emerging Stock Markets Factbook **[9930]**

Emerging Technologies in Hazardous Waste Management IV **[11931]**

"Emerging Threat: Human Rights Claims" in *Harvard Business Review* (Vol. 81, No. 8, August 2003, pp. 16) **[29218]**, **[48545]**

Steve Emerine Strategic Public Relations **[50496]**, **[50724]**

Emery County Chamber of Commerce **[65710]**

Emeryville Chamber of Commerce **[57475]**

Emily Griffith Opportunity School **[58477]**

"Eminem" in *Crain's Detroit Business* (Vol. 19, No. 1, January 6, 2003, pp. 11) **[9706]**, **[28099]**

Eminence Chamber of Commerce **[61957]**

"Eminent Danger" in *Entrepreneur* (Vol. 33, January 2005, No. 1, pp. 19) **[1102]**, **[37631]**, **[40342]**

Emmanuel College–Cardinal Cushing Library **[1654]**, **[8863]**

Emmetsburg Chamber of Commerce **[60129]**

Emory University–Center for Lifelong Learning **[59221]**

Empire Bldg. Diagnostics Inc. **[7603]**

"Empire Blossoms" in *Small Business Opportunities* (Vol. 12, No. 2, March 2000, pp. 86, 88) **[15977]**, **[35409]**

Empire Business Brokers **[3451]**

Empire College–School of Business **[58230]**

Empire State Development–Division for Small Business–Procurement Assistance Program **[60572]**, **[63180]**

Empire State Tattoo Club of America **[23851]**

"The empire strikes back; Counterrevolutionary strategies for industry leaders" in *Harvard Business Review* (Vol. 80, Nov. 2002, pp. 66) **[30535]**, **[36055]**, **[39300]**, **[45099]**, **[53707]**

Employability Skills Video Series **[9259]**

Employee Benefit Notes **[26974]**, **[30749]**

Employee Benefit Plan Review **[26975]**, **[42906]**

Employee Benefit Plan Review (Vol. 55); "Account Balances Indicate That 401(k) Participants Have Heard The Long-Term Investor Message" in **[14721]**, **[26735]**, **[31108]**, **[32234]**, **[37866]**, **[40953]**, **[43066]**

Employee Benefit Plan Review (Vol. 55, No. 7, Jan.2001); "ASPA President Shares Regulatory Outlook, Plans New Association Initiatives" in **[26744]**, **[40164]**

Employee Benefit Plan Review (Vol. 55); "Attention to Nonmedical Factors Can Facilitate Return-To-Work For Workers' Comp Claimants" in **[26745]**, **[40964]**, **[43083]**

Employee Benefit Plan Review (Vol. 55, No. 10, April 2001 pp. 14); "Benefits Costs Averaged 36.8 Percent Of Payroll In 1999" in **[26749]**, **[40967]**, **[43092]**

Employee Benefit Plan Review (Vol. 55, No. 7, Jan. 2001); "Buck's Annual 401(k) Survey Shows Dramatic Growth In Web Administration" in **[13862]**, **[26756]**, **[33614]**, **[43106]**, **[53621]**

Employee Benefit Plan Review (Vol. 55, No. 12); "Consultant Outlines Steps For Measuring Effectiveness Of Communications Program" in **[16504]**, **[26775]**, **[27330]**, **[31126]**, **[34856]**

Employee Benefit Plan Review (Vol. 55, No. 6); "Dental, vision plan vendors use the Web to administer, communicate, market benefits" in **[13960]**, **[17156]**, **[26784]**, **[40995]**, **[43151]**, **[46878]**

Employee Benefit Plan Review (Vol. 55, No. 7, January 2001, pp. 27); "Design Innovation Brings Communications Challenges" in **[13961]**, **[26785]**, **[27346]**, **[33747]**, **[53686]**

Employee Benefit Plan Review (Vol. 55, No. 10, April 2001); "Employee Need, Distribution Strategies, Drive Growth in Group Legal" in **[26793]**

Employee Benefit Plan Review (Vol. 55, No. 6); "Employers Can Use State Programs to Help Employees Save for College Education" in **[26796]**, **[39815]**, **[54533]**

Employee Benefit Plan Review (Vol. 56, No. 1, July 2001, pp. 42); "ESOPs largely a positive tool, survey finds" in **[26800]**, **[34892]**

Employee Benefit Plan Review (Vol. 55, No.12); "Internet Facilities Defined Contribution Model For Employer-Sponsored Health Benefits" in **[14153]**, **[26834]**, **[41035]**, **[43240]**

Employee Benefit Plan Review (Vol. 55, No. 8, February 2001, pp. 13); "IRS changes and finalizes 2000 cafeteria plan rules" in **[40476]**, **[41037]**, **[43242]**

Employee Benefit Plan Review (Vol. 55, No. 12, June 2001, pp. 8); "MSA Withdrawals: Rules on Tax Exclusion" in **[26856]**, **[41063]**, **[43283]**, **[54666]**

Employee Benefit Plan Review (Vol. 56, No. 1, July 2001, pp. 10); "President signs tax cut bill with pension reform" in **[24017]**, **[26888]**, **[39889]**, **[54709]**

Employee Benefit Plan Review (Vol. 56, No. 1, July 2001, pp. 46); "Report recommends path to foster equity ownership" in **[26898]**

Employee Benefit Plan Review (Vol. 55, No. 8, February 2001, pp. 40); "Small Firms, Consumers Have PWBA Health Care Benefit Tools" in **[26914]**, **[40702]**, **[41104]**, **[43365]**

Employee Benefit Plan Review (Vol. 56, No. 1, July 2001, pp. 36) "Stock option communications evolve; challenges remain" in **[26918]**, **[35079]**

Employee Benefit Plan Review (Vol. 55, No. 12); "Tax Cut Bill Includes Pension Reform, Other Provisions Affecting Employee Benefits" in **[24052]**, **[26925]**, **[39938]**, **[54798]**

Employee Benefit Plan Review (Vol. 55); "The Perfect Storm? Employers Need Navigation Tools For The Newest Set of Health Cost Waves" in **[26324]**, **[26877]**, **[41078]**, **[43310]**

Employee Benefit Plan Review (Vol. 56, No. 1, July 2001, pp. 18); "TPA business for self-funded plans balanced in 2000" in **[26942]**, **[41120]**, **[43403]**

Employee Benefit Plan Review (Vol.55, No. 6); "Web-based services provide easy access to no-cost employer-sponsored discount programs" in **[14581]**, **[26950]**, **[34666]**, **[35135]**

Employee Benefit Research Institute **[24202]**, **[26725]**, **[27023]**, **[30723]**

Employee Benefits **[30735]**

Employee Benefits Cases **[26976]**, **[27056]**, **[30750]**

Employee Benefits with Cost Control **[26791]**

Employee Benefits Digest **[30751]**

Employee Benefits Infosource **[27057]**

Employee Benefits Management Directions **[26977]**

Employee Benefits Of St Cloud Inc. **[27024]**

Employee Benefits Review **[30752]**

Employee Compensation **[26978]**, **[30753]**

Employee Development Systems Inc. **[35230]**

"Employee theft on the rise - Fidelity coverage is crucial" in *Rough Notes* (Vol. 146, No. 4, April 2003, pp. 30) **[13274]**, **[22221]**, **[43165]**, **[45100]**

"Employee Health Costs Rose 6.1 Percent" in *Tampa Tribune* (November 22, 2005) **[26792]**, **[41005]**

Employee Incentive Contests: For Improved Marketing, Customer Service, and Morale **[31709]**, **[34878]**

Employee Management for Small Business **[36056]**, **[42847]**, **[45101]**

Employee Matters: A Legal Guide to Hiring, Firing & Setting Employee Policies **[42226]**

"Employee Matters" in *Home Business* (Vol. 12, March/April 2005, No. 2, pp. 90) **[42227]**, **[42610]**

Employee Motivation: What to Do When What You Say Isn't Working **[34879]**

"Employee Need, Distribution Strategies, Drive Growth in Group Legal" in *Employee Benefit Plan Review* (Vol. 55, No. 10, April 2001) **[26793]**

"Employee Organizations: Tomorrow's Possibilities" in *Employment Relations Today* (Vol. 26, No. 4, Winter 2000, pp. 53) **[32404]**, **[42848]**, **[53708]**

Employee Recognition Program **[19842]**

Employee Relations Law Journal **[26979]**

Employee Services Management **[26980]**

Employee Services Management Association [27025]
  Information Center [27062]
"The employee strikes back" in *Wall Street Journal* (April 16, 2002, pp. B1) [34880], [42228], [53709]
Employee Terminations Law Bulletin [42907]
Employee Theft Control [35279]
Employee Theft: How to Spot It, How to Stop It! [35280]
"Employees still rate health care No. 1 benefit" in *Atlanta Business Chronicle* (Vol. 25, No. 19, October 18, 2002, pp. 13C) [13275], [26794], [43166]
"Employees Sue Best Buy for Race, Gender Discrimination" in *Sacramento Bee* (December 9, 2005) [29219], [32021], [51144], [51625]
"Employer-Provided Education Benefits: Section 132(d) is Worth a Second Look" in *Journal of Accountancy* (Vol. 198, September 2004) [134], [2896], [23935], [26220], [26795], [27115], [54532]
Employers of America [52799]
"Employers Can Expect More Legal Challenges from Workers" in *Kiplinger Letter* (Vol. 84, January 26, 2007, No. 4) [29220], [42849]
"Employers Can Use State Programs to Help Employees Save for College Education" in *Employee Benefit Plan Review* (Vol. 55, No. 6) [26796], [39815], [54533]
"Employers important in shaping health care" in *Atlanta Business Chronicle* (Vol. 25, November 15, 2002, No. 23 pp.\37A) [13276], [43167], [51626]
Employers Council on Flexible Compensation [26726], [30724]
"Employers' extra credit" in *Hispanic Business* (Vol. 22, No. 6, June 2000, pp. 156) [39816], [54534]
"Employers Finding Low-Cost Ways to Motivate, Reward Staff" in *San Diego Business Journal* (Vol. 22, No. 41, October 8, 2001, pp. 13) [26797], [34881]
"Employers Get Personal with Doctors in Push for More Generic Use" in *Crain's Detroit Business* (Vol. 19, No. 15, April 14, 2003) [13277], [26798], [43168]
Employers Group [54924]
"Employers alter investment advice post-Enron" in *Atlanta Business Chronicle* (Vol. 25, No. 19, October 18, 2002, pp. 3C) [9931], [14952]
"Employers Won't Give Big Pay Raises in 2006, Survey Finds" in *Sacramento Bee* (December 3, 2005) [32405], [53710]
"Employing Her Literary Skills" in *San Diego Business Journal* (Vol. 28, January 8, 2007, No. 2, pp. 10) [8993], [29221], [42850], [43637], [56203]
Employing People with Capabilities: Responding to the Americans with Disabilities Act [32022]
Employment Discrimination Report [32124]
Employment Law: A Guide to the Workplace Rights of Managers and Workers [32023]
"Employment Law at the Dawn of the New Millennium" in *Employment Relations Today* (Vol. 26, No. 4, Winter 2000, pp. 109) [29222], [32024], [40343]
Employment Law Strategist [29598]
Employment Opportunities, USA [23389]
Employment Relations Today [26981]
Employment Relations Today (Vol. 27, No. 1, Spring 2000, pp. 117); "A Guide through the Garnishment Jungle" in [29280], [40429]
Employment Relations Today (Vol. 26, No. 4, Winter 2000, pp. 73); "A Leadership Evolution" in [45348]
Employment Relations Today (Vol.26, No. 4, Winter 2000); "Consequences of Information Technology on Work in the Twenty-First Century" in [27104], [33051], [42841]
Employment Relations Today (Vol. 26, No. 4, Winter 2000, pp. 119); "Court Expands Accommodation Obligations in Retail Stores" in [51116]
Employment Relations Today (Vol. 26, No. 4, Winter 2000, pp. 95); "Digging Deeper and Keeping Up" in [28036], [53690], [55289]

Employment Relations Today (Vol. 26, No. 4, Winter 2000, pp. 53); "Employee Organizations: Tomorrow's Possibilities" in [32404], [42848], [53708]
Employment Relations Today (Vol. 26, No. 4, Winter 2000, pp. 109); "Employment Law at the Dawn of the New Millennium" in [29222], [32024], [40343]
Employment Relations Today (Vol. 26, No. 4, Winter 2000, pp. 17); "Families and Work: Some Future Probabilities" in [40364], [54176]
Employment Relations Today (Vol. 27, No. 2, Summer 2000, pp. 29); "Holding a Job, Having a Life: The Next Level in Work" in [34931], [53776]
Employment Relations Today (Vol. 27, No. 1); "Interviews with Part-Time MBAs Point the Way for Retaining Executive Track Managers" in [44321], [45308]
Employment Relations Today (Vol. 27, No. 2, Summer 2000, pp. 43); "Like It or Not...Culture Matters" in [34972], [45374]
Employment Relations Today (Vol. 27, No. 2, Summer 2000, pp. 15); "Measurement of Human Potential" in [33169]
Employment Relations Today (Vol. 27, No. 1, Spring 2000, pp. 83); "Minimizing the Risk of Violence in the Workplace" in [56572]
Employment Relations Today (Vol. 26, No. 4, Winter 2000, pp. 99); "New EEOC and OFCCP Issues for the Year 2000 and Beyond" in [29399], [32047], [40549]
Employment Relations Today (Vol. 27, No. 2, Summer 2000, pp. 81) "OFCCP Contractor Survey; New Worker Economic Opportunity Law" in [32051], [40585]
Employment Relations Today (Vol. 27, No. 1, Spring 2000) ; "OSHA's Proposed Ergonomic Standard and Clarification on Home Work Policy" in [40599], [42703]
Employment Relations Today (Summer 2000, pp. 89); "Recent State Legislative Developments Concerning Employment Discrimination..." in [32056], [40633]
Employment Relations Today (Vol. 27,No. 2, Summer 2000, pp. 1); "Six Sigma: New Opportunites for HR, New Career Growth for Employees" in [31854], [42891]
Employment Relations Today (Vol. 27, No. 2, Summer 2000, pp. 53) "Succession Management for the Entire Organization" in [45689], [54008]
Employment Relations Today (Vol. 26, No. 4, pp. 61); "The Future of Cyberwork" in [14060], [42855], [45169], [53744]
Employment Relations Today (Vol. 27, No. 1, Spring 2000, pp. 61); "The Need for Speed in New Millennium Leadership Styles" in [34235], [45457], [53875]
Employment Relations Today (Vol. 26, No. 4, Winter 2000); "The Postmodern Shift in Values and Jobs and the Implications for HR" in [37489], [42882]
Employment Relations Today (Vol.27, No.1); "The Problem of Perceptions: Reasons for Outsourcing the Sexual Harassment Investigation" in [32053], [42884], [49729]
Employment Relations Today (Vol. 27, No. 1, Spring 2000, pp. 19); "The Regenerative Organization" in [42887], [43794]
Employment Relations Today (Vol. 27, No. 2, Summer 2000, pp. 101); "The Right to Regulate Off-Duty Conduct" in [40652], [53945], [54247]
Employment Relations Today (Vol.27, No.1, Spring 2000, pp. 47); "Traditional vs. On-Line Learning: It's Not an Either/or Proposition" in [33264], [34619], [45763]
Employment Relations Today (Vol. 27, No. 1, Spring 2000, pp. 73); "Training Managers to be Better Communicators" in [27519], [45764]
Employment Relations Today (Vol. 26, No. 4, Winter 2000, pp. 5); "Transforming Business Structures to Hyborg" in [30977], [32752], [42899], [43851]

Employment Relations Today (Vol. 27, No. 2, Summer 2000, pp. 63); "Unlocking the Hidden Value in Organizations" in [54054]
Employment Relations Today (Vol.27, No.1, Spring2000); "US Supreme Court Rules on Punitive Damages in Title VII Discrimination Cases" in [32068], [40800]
Employment Relations Today (Vol. 27, No. 2, Summer 2000, pp. 7); "Using a Reverse RFP Process to Assess Your Outsourcing Options" in [44377], [49752]
Employment Relations Today (Vol. 27, No. 1, Spring 2000, pp. 1); "Workers as Assets: A Good Start But..." in [54086], [54283]
Employment Safety and Health Guide-Summary [56597]
Employment Support Center–Library [9296], [35271], [53129]
"Employment Will Be Stable, Survey Says" in *Milwaukee Journal Sentinel* (December 13, 2005) [28100], [32406], [42229]
Emporia Chamber of Commerce and Convention and Visitors Bureau [60327]
Emporia - Greensville Chamber of Commerce [65889]
Emporia State University–Small Business Development Center [60258]
Empowered Teams: Creating Self-Directed Work Teams That Improve Quality, Productivity, and Participation [34882]
Empowered Women's Golf Shops, Inc. [11290]
Empowering Employees [34883]
Empowering Employees to Claim Their Autonomy [35181]
Empowerment: A Practical Guide for Success [34884]
Empowerment: Communicating with Others [35182]
Empowerment: How to Receive Work Assignments [37030]
Empowerment: It's Your Career [9260]
Empowerment: Managing Your Time [55015]
Empowerment: Meeting Change Creatively [35183]
Empowerment: Moving from Criticism to Feedback [37031]
Empowerment in Organizations: How to Spark Exceptional Performance [34885]
Empowerment: Solving Problems Together [35184]
Empowerment: Team Skills for Meeting Together [35185]
Empowerment: The Attitude Opportunity [45924]
Empowerment: The Employee Development Series [37032], [55016]
Empowerment: Working Effectively with Others [35186]
Empress Chili [21808]
Empress Chinchilla Breeders Cooperative [10820], [10825]
Empress Travel L.P. [25338]
EMS Network International [46018]
"En Garde! Herby Raynaud's Fencing Fancy" in *Black Enterprise* (Vol. 34, No. 3, October 2003, pp. 139) [4649], [22979], [36057], [53271]
Enabling Environments for Jobs and Entrepreneurship: The Role of Policy and Law in Small Enterprise Employment [29223], [40344], [56558]
Enact Expert Systems [49422]
Enchanted Honeymoons [25339]
Encinitas Chamber and Visitors Center [57476]
"Encinitas: Insta-Theatres Finds Home In Old Town" in *San Diego Business Journal* (Vol. 28, January 15, 2007, No. 3, pp. 17) [17515]
Encino Chamber of Commerce [57477]
Encompass Ventures Management Company [66210]
Encore Venture Partners, LP [58010]
Encounters [41189]
"Encourage superior performance from people and teams through coaching" in *Women In Business* (Vol. 52, No. 1, Jan.- Feb. 2000, pp. 38) [34886]
"Encourage General Ledger Efficiency" in *Journal of Accountancy* (Vol. 198, September 2004, No. 3, pp.) [135], [2897], [23936], [26221], [27116]
Encyclopedia of Associations [1733]

The Encyclopedia of Associations and Information Sources for Architects, Designers, and Engineers **[1493]**

Encyclopedia of Deafness and Hearing Disorders **[12106]**

Encyclopedia of Food Science, Food Technology and Nutrition **[18438]**, **[21498]**

The Encyclopedia of Group Activities: 150 Practical Designs for Successful Facilitating **[33082]**

The Encyclopedia of Icebreakers: Structured Activities That Warm-Up, Motivate, Challenge, Acquaint and Energize **[33083]**

Encyclopedia of Perennials: A Gardener's Guide **[11424]**

Encyclopedia of Small Business **[36058]**, **[39301]**

Encyclopedia of Sports Business Contacts **[23709]**

The Encyclopedia of Team-Building Activities **[34887]**

The Encyclopedia of Team-Development Activities **[34888]**

End A Flat Tire Safety Sealant **[2099]**

"The End of Corporate Imperialism" in *Harvard Business Review* (Vol. 81, No. 8, August 2003, pp. 109) **[43638]**

"The End of Detroit: How the Big Three Lost Their Grip on the American Car Market" in *Harvard Business Review* (Vol.81, No.11, Nov. 2003) **[18025]**, **[28101]**

"The End of Entrepreneurship As We Know It" in *Entrepreneur* (Vol. 28, No. 9, September 2000, pp. 18) **[36059]**

The End of the Line **[31931]**

"The end of the PC world as we know it" in *Red Herring* (No. 106, October 15, 2001, pp. 16) **[6642]**, **[28102]**, **[49018]**

"End of the Road" in *Entrepreneur* (Vol. 31, No. 8, August 2003, pp. 24) **[40345]**, **[41661]**, **[46273]**, **[50866]**

"End of the Road? Success Isn't a Destination; It's Simply Undertaking the Journey" in *Entrepreneur* (Vol. 31, No. 9, September 2003) **[36060]**

"End of Some Tariffs a Boon to Suppliers" in *Crain's Detroit Business* (Vol. 22, December 18, 2006, No. 51, pp. 6) **[40346]**, **[43639]**, **[50756]**, **[54535]**

"The Endangered Department Store" in *Boston Globe* (February 13, 2005) **[30845]**, **[49916]**, **[51145]**, **[53711]**

Endeavor Capital Management **[58592]**

"Ending Advertising's Spiral" in *Business 2.0* (Vol. 6, September 2005, No. 8, pp. 42) **[583]**, **[612]**, **[55591]**, **[58032]**

Endrust Auto Appearance Centers **[2050]**

"The enemies of trust" in *Harvard Business Review* (Vol. 81, No. 2, February 2003, pp. 88) **[31710]**, **[34889]**, **[36061]**, **[45102]**

"Enemy Mine: Learning to Live with the Competitors You Love to Hate" in *Entrepreneur* (Vol. 31, No. 10, October 2003, pp. 34) **[136]**, **[18773]**, **[30846]**

"Energy: Coming soon to a roof over you: solar shingles" in *Red Herring* (No. 105, October 1, 2001, pp. 28) **[22063]**, **[48725]**

"Energy Conference in Novi March 23" in *Crain's Detroit Business* (Vol. 22, February 6, 2006, No. 6, pp. 13) **[24925]**, **[41662]**, **[55088]**

Energy Design Update **[23341]**

Energy Detente **[9415]**

Energy and Environmental Building Association **[7218]**

Energy & Environmental Management, Inc. (E2M)–Library **[9433]**

"Energy Firm Surges with High-Tech Utility Meters" in *Atlanta Business Chronicle* (Vol. 26, No. 14, September 12, 2003, pp. 4A) **[41663]**

Energy Kitchen **[12085]**

Energy in the News **[10271]**

Energy Probe Research Foundation **[9322]**

Energy Research Institute **[23356]**

"The energy roller coaster" in *Red Herring* (No. 103, September 1, 2001, pp. 42-43) **[27117]**, **[39302]**

"Energy: The changing balance of power" in *Red Herring* (No. 103, September 1, 2001, pp. 66) **[28103]**, **[37270]**, **[41664]**

Energy Wise, Inc. **[52623]**

Enertech Capital /Enertech Capital Partners, L.P. **[64550]**

"Engaging Before Merger" in *Rough Notes* (Vol. 146, No. 9, September 2003, pp. 68) **[13278]**, **[49917]**

Engine Builder **[22629]**

"Engine of Progress" in *Fast Company* (November 2001, pp. 144) **[44033]**, **[50867]**

"Engineer Turned Winemaker Became Toast of State Industry" in *Milwaukee Journal Sentinel* (December 14, 2005) **[23475]**, **[36062]**

Engineered Lighting Products **[49605]**

Engineering Contractors Association **[7219]**

"Engineering a Culture" in *Crain's Detroit Business* (Vol. 19, No. 45, November 10, 2003, pp. 41) **[28104]**, **[41451]**

Engineering Design and Automation **[6984]**, **[52262]**

"Engineering the Engineer" in *Sales & Marketing Management* (Vol. 157, January 2005, No. 1, pp. 11) **[46929]**, **[51627]**

Engineering Export Promotion Council of India **[43492]**

Engineering Harmonics Inc. **[20369]**, **[21157]**

Engineering Quality Software: Defect Detection and Prevention **[22980]**

"Engineering a Structure that's Lasted Generations" in *San Francisco Business Times* (Vol. 17, No. 48, July 4, 2003, pp. 18) **[29856]**, **[37632]**

Engineering and Technical Consultants Inc. **[7604]**

"Engler and business" in *Crain's Detroit Business* (Vol. 18, No. 50, December 16, 2002, pp. 21) **[39303]**, **[40347]**

"Engler budget would cut small business taxes" in *Crain's Detroit Business* (Vol. 16, No. 5, January 31, 2000, pp. 7) **[54536]**

"Engler's tax web" in *Wall Street Journal* (December 17, 2001, pp. A18) **[14012]**, **[33848]**, **[54537]**

Englewood-Cape Haze Area Chamber of Commerce **[58793]**

Englewood Chamber of Commerce **[62498]**

Englewood-Northmont Chamber of Commerce **[63667]**

English Butler Canada Ltd. **[12248]**

"English-Spanish Made Easy" in *Hispanic Business* (June 2002, pp. 94) **[1187]**, **[22981]**, **[49019]**

Engraved Stationery Manufacturers Association **[11135]**

"Enhance your people skills" in *Women In Business* (Vol. 52, No. 5, September-October 2000, pp. 34) **[43640]**, **[56204]**

Enhancing Your Presentation Skills: A Seminar for Sales Professionals **[51519]**

"Enjoy your income today while saving for your future" in *Black Enterprise* (Vol. 33, No. 3, October 2002, pp. 102) **[9932]**, **[10327]**, **[14953]**, **[35992]**, **[38030]**

"Enjoy It While It Lasts: Charts Suggest the Market Will Resume a Long-Term Decline at Summer's End" in *Barron's* (July 7, 2003) **[9933]**, **[14954]**, **[38031]**

"Enjoy your meal!" in *Entrepreneur* (Vol. 30, No. 12, December 2002, pp. 32) **[21396]**, **[56039]**

"Enjoy the Silence" in *Black Enterprise* (Vol. 36, November 2005, No. 4, pp. 162) **[27359]**, **[45103]**

ENLASO Corp. **[25101]**

"Enlighten Me: One Entrepreneur Brings Business-and Spirituality-to New Heights" in *Entrepreneur* (Vol. 33, March 2005, No. 3, pp. 93) **[11561]**, **[36063]**

Enlightened Leadership: Best Practice Guidelines and Timesaving Tools for Easily Implementing Learning Organizations **[33084]**, **[34890]**, **[36064]**, **[45104]**, **[54943]**

Ennis Area Chamber of Commerce **[62162]**

Ennis Chamber of Commerce **[65221]**

Enoch Pratt Free Library–State Library Resource Center **[66892]**

ENR-Top 600 Specialty Contractors Issue **[22064]**

Enrich! **[4415]**, **[30057]**

"Enrolling online is No. 1 choice among workers, survey finds" in *Crain's Detroit Business* (Vol. 18, No. 18, May 6, 2002, pp. 12) **[13279]**, **[26799]**, **[33849]**, **[43169]**

ENT **[18952]**, **[23280]**

"Enter the Limelight" in *Entrepreneur* (Vol. 28, No. 8, August 2000, pp. 36) **[45105]**

"Enter the Wagon: Station Wagons Aren't Just for Families Anymore." in *Entrepreneur* (Vol. 33, January 2005, No. 1, pp. 24) **[18026]**

"Entering a Hot Zone" in *Black Enterprise* (Vol. 35, February 2005, No. 7, pp. 58) **[14013]**, **[41665]**

Enterprise Chamber of Commerce **[56841]**

Enterprise Communications 6471, 6647

Enterprise Community SBDC/BIC **[64644]**

Enterprise Computing 6471, 6647

Enterprise Consulting Inc. **[31967]**

Enterprise, Entrepreneurship and Innovation: Concepts, Context and Commercialization **[28105]**, **[36065]**, **[39304]**, **[44034]**

Enterprise Florida, Inc.–Marketing And Development Division **[58719]**

Enterprise Merchant Bank **[60440]**

Enterprise Newfoundland and Labrador–Business Resource Centre **[32834]**, **[47930]**, **[53130]**

Enterprise North Florida Corporation, Inc. (ENFC) **[58985]**

Enterprise Partners Venture Capital / EPVC **[58011]**

Enterprise Planning and Development: Small Business and Enterprise Start-Up Survival and Growth **[29063]**, **[35410]**, **[39049]**, **[44035]**, **[44292]**

"Enterprise Risk Management-A Fading Fad?" in *Rough Notes* (Vol. 145, No. 5, May 2002, pp. 53) **[9934]**, **[13280]**, **[22222]**, **[43170]**

Enterprise and Small Business: Principles, Practice and Policy **[36066]**, **[39305]**

"Enterprise Software: An industry finds order in the madness" in *Red Herring* (No. 105, October 1, 2001, pp. 74-75) **[4650]**, **[22982]**, **[31711]**, **[33850]**

"Enterprise Software Sector Analysis" in *Red Herring* (No. 105, October 1, 2001, pp. 86-87) **[4651]**, **[14014]**, **[22983]**, **[33851]**

"Enterprise Solutions" in *Hispanic Business* (October 2004, pp. 120, 122) **[4652]**, **[22984]**, **[53272]**

Enterprise UNB **[66705]**

"Enterprising Moves" in *MEDIAWEEK* (Vol. 11, No. 4, January 22, 2001, pp. 65) **[2702]**, **[28106]**, **[53712]**

"Enterprising Union Creates $100M Bank" in *Houston Business Journal* (Vol. 34, No. 15, August 22, 2003, pp. 1A) **[14955]**, **[49918]**

Enterprising Women **[56535]**

Enterprising Women: Lessons from 100 of the Greatest Entrepreneurs of Our Day **[56205]**

"Entertaining speakers can reinforce your message" in *Atlanta Business Chronicle* (Vol. 24, No. 14, September 7, 2001, pp. S4) **[24926]**

"An entertainment hybrid finds an audience" in *Providence Business News* (Vol. 17, No. 27, October 21, 2002, pp. 18) **[2338]**, **[17516]**, **[21499]**

"Entertainment Properties Trust" in *Ingram's* (Vol. 28, No. 5, May 2002, pp. 39) **[9669]**, **[14694]**, **[35411]**

Entertainment Software Association **[22897]**

Entertainment and Specialty Projects **[21049]**

Entertainment on Wheels **[18726]**

"Entravision Acquires Three L.A. Stations" in *Hispanic Business* (March 2003, pp. 20) **[20315]**, **[28107]**, **[48144]**

Entree **[25292]**

Entrepreneur (Vol. 30, No. 2, February 2002, pp. 46); "9/11 Call: When Crisis Hit, Business Owners Answered" in **[36555]**, **[39500]**

Entrepreneur (Vol. 30, No. 1, January 2002, pp. 39); "9/11 Calls: Wireless Devices in the Post-Attacks Era"in **[5071]**, **[27457]**, **[41873]**

Entrepreneur (Vol. 30, No. 3, March 2002, pp. 109); "Imperial forces" in **[35526]**, **[38653]**

Entrepreneur (Vol. 33, August 2005, No. 8, pp. 4); "19th Annual Entrepreneurial Woman's Conference" in **[24543]**, **[24873]**, **[34618]**, **[35743]**, **[39977]**, **[44555]**, **[46645]**, **[55055]**, **[56108]**

"Entrepreneur plans 31 strip malls for underserved areas" in *Crain's Detroit Business* (Vol. 16, No. 23, June 5, 2000, pp. 54) **[35412]**, **[51025]**

Entrepreneur (Vol. 33, September 2005, No. 9, pp. 62); "40-Year Plan" in [17356], [36469], [37862]

Entrepreneur (Vol. 33, Aug. 2005); "2005 National Minority Supplier Development Council Conference and Business Opportunity Fair" in [24545], [24875], [48018], [49915], [55057], [57445]

Entrepreneur (Vol. 28, No. 10, October 2000, pp. 86); "A tale of 25 Cities" in [30018], [36830]

Entrepreneur (Vol. 33, March 2005, No. 3, pp. 134); "A Brand New Day" in [35869], [44955]

Entrepreneur (Vol. 32, December 2004, No. 12, pp. 61); "A Class Act" in [26188], [32316], [33040], [35946], [45001]

Entrepreneur (Vol. 31, No. 11, November 2003, pp. 94); "A Clean Slate" in [35947], [45002]

Entrepreneur (Vol. 32, July 2004, No. 7); "A Clean Sweep: Take Your Work Environment from Cluttered to Clear with these Steps" in [20013], [49492]

Entrepreneur (Vol. 31, No. 8, August 2003, pp. 22); "A Click Away: Automotive Web Sites are Revved Up and Ready to Help You Buy" in [17997], [33673]

Entrepreneur (Vol. 28, No. 10, October 2000, pp. 156); "A Collect Calling" in [31523]

Entrepreneur (Vol. 32, July 2004, No. 7, pp. 34); "A Fair Case: These Pretty Laptop Cases Are Pretty Functional, Too" in [6643], [49024]

Entrepreneur (Vol. 31, October 2003); "A Fair Trade" in [4985], [26710], [49924]

Entrepreneur (Vol. 32, No. 5, May 2004, pp. 130); "A Fitting Memorial" in [10783], [35454], [43959]

Entrepreneur (Vol. 28, No. 6, June 2000, pp. 163); "A Franchise of Her Own" in [38640], [56047]

Entrepreneur (Vol. 33, March 2005, No. 3, pp. 62); "A Good Time for an IPO Gold Mine?" in [15044], [49964]

Entrepreneur (Vol. 31, No. 9, September 2003, pp. 116); "A Hand in Remarriage" in [3184], [37673]

Entrepreneur (Vol. 31, Sept. 2003); "A Hand Up: Urban, Minority Entrepreneurs are Hotter Than Ever-So Where is Their Funding?" in [44540], [48198], [55656]

Entrepreneur; "A Happy Ending" in [3185], [13305], [43196]

Entrepreneur (Vol. 31, No. 8, August 2003, pp. 76); "A Hard Sell" in [653], [13306], [33995], [43197], [47056]

Entrepreneur (Vol. 31, No. 7, July 2003, pp. 73); "A Head Start: Need Some Help Thinking More Clearly Under Pressure" in [3538], [17895], [31165]

Entrepreneur (Vol. 31, No. 10, October 2003, pp. 56); "A Knack for Macs" in [6701], [49114]

Entrepreneur (Vol. 31, No. 8, August 2003, pp. 46); "A La Modem" in [6702], [14191], [49116]

Entrepreneur (Vol. 32, November 2004, No. 11, pp. 130); "A Labor of Love: Have You Lost That Lovin' Feeling For Your Business?" in [30565], [36415]

Entrepreneur (Vol. 32, July 2004, No. 7, pp. 46); "A Light Touch" in [6710], [49126]

Entrepreneur (Vol. 31, No. 10, October 2003, pp. 46); "A Little Lost? Get Directions at Your Fingertips" in [13795], [30281], [48937]

Entrepreneur (Vol. 32, November 2004, No. 11, pp. 69); "A Loan Time" in [10065], [44573]

Entrepreneur (Vol. 31, No. 8, August 2003, pp. 26); "A Man's World?" in [34167], [36483], [41826], [52560], [56317]

Entrepreneur (Vol. 31, No. 8, August 2003, pp. 72); "A Matter of Opinion" in [31776], [47266], [48667], [51244]

Entrepreneur (Vol. 31, No. 7, July 2003, pp. 68); "A Mixed Blessing" in [38227], [39477]

Entrepreneur (Vol. 30, No); "A New Hope" in [7049], [12758], [21407], [26036], [35585], [38665]

Entrepreneur (Vol. 32, November 2004, No. 11, pp. 95); "A New Leaf" in [3565], [28545], [31195], [35003], [36541], [45467]

Entrepreneur; "A New Twist" in [11339], [23499], [36545], [37742]

Entrepreneur (Vol. 31, No. 4, April 2003, pp. 102); "A model occupation: who says you can't turn business into play?" in [8132], [35570], [37571], [38662]

Entrepreneur (Vol. 31, No. 10, October 2003, pp. 112); "A One-Stop Marketing Shop" in [47369], [48658], [48669], [51033]

Entrepreneur (Vol. 30, No. 3, March 2002, pp. 37); "A perfect pair" in [5084], [34342], [49201]

Entrepreneur (Vol. 33, August 2005, No. 8, pp. 53); "A Penchant for Profits" in [4741], [4762], [22814], [23124], [28048], [28617], [36612], [50760], [53407]

Entrepreneur (Vol. 31, No. 8, August 2003, pp. 30); "A Penny Not Saved" in [38278], [53913]

Entrepreneur (Vol. 31, No. 10, October 2003, pp. 60); "A Perfect Match?" in [11341], [15349], [36616], [37756], [55774]

Entrepreneur (Vol. 28, No. 8, August 2000, pp. 30); "A Question of Character" in [44624]

Entrepreneur (Vol. 31, No. 6, June 2003, pp. 83); "A bad rap: have you been slammed as a spammer? Here's how to fight back" in [33561], [46699]

Entrepreneur (Vol. 33, March 2005, No. 3, pp. 55); "A Run of Luck" in [4784], [23154], [29475], [52450], [53440]

Entrepreneur (Vol. 31, No. 7, July 2003, pp. 42); "A Safe Bet" in [22350], [34425], [49238]

Entrepreneur (Vol. 32, December 2004, No. 12, pp. 18); "A Slice of Life" in [19643], [21626], [37781]

Entrepreneur (Vol. 28, No. 10, October 2000, pp. 38); "A Sore Site for Eyes" in [14463], [34514], [55838]

Entrepreneur (Vol. 30, No. 10, October 2002, pp. 83); "A new standard" in [40564], [46389]

Entrepreneur (Vol. 31, No. 5, May 2003, pp. 45); "A real steal" in [30249], [31581]

Entrepreneur (Vol. 32, July 2004, No. 7, pp. 44); "A Step Beyond" in [6812], [33243], [53494]

Entrepreneur (Vol. 31, No. 8, August 2003, pp. 55); "A Tax Act" in [40752], [54789]

Entrepreneur (Vol. 31, No. 9, September 2003, pp. 27); "A Team Sport" in [42031], [44161], [50204]

Entrepreneur (Vol. 28, No. 11, November 2000, pp. 22); "A Thousand to One" in [25578], [54038]

Entrepreneur (Vol. 28, No. 10, October 2000, pp. 29); "A Touch of Class" in [14546], [34615], [37204], [47658]

Entrepreneur (Vol. 31, No. 9, September 2003, pp. 81); "A Tug of War: Real Deal: You Can't Have It All." in [27520], [45770]

Entrepreneur (Vol. 31, October 2003); "A Wild Ride: The Twists and Turns of Running Your Own Business Can Throw You for a Loop" in [29010], [36972]

Entrepreneur (Vol. 32, December 2004, No. 12, pp. 24); "A Work of Art" in [3617], [36984], [44179]

Entrepreneur (Vol. 32, October 2004, No. 10, pp. 78); "A World of Difference" in [36992], [50481], [54285]

Entrepreneur (Vol. 33, October 2005, No. 10, pp. 6); "A9.COM" in [13703], [13796], [32508], [33507]

Entrepreneur (Vol. 33, August 2005, No. 8, pp. 18); "Action Sacked" in [28458], [29089], [38499], [40144]

Entrepreneur (Vol. 33, January 2005, No. 1, pp. 43); "Added Security" in [4589], [22161], [22905], [53198]

Entrepreneur (Vol. 32, August 2004); "Against the Grain: Forget Big Marketing Budgets-Its Time to Think Outside the (Cereal) Box" in [541], [46668]

Entrepreneur (Vol. 32, No. 4, April 2004, pp. 24); "Age Rage: Younger Employees are Crying Age Discrimination" in [26737], [32003], [40150], [40956]

Entrepreneur (Vol. 30, No. 12, December 2002, pp. 27); "Aid package" in [26738], [37871]

Entrepreneur (Vol. 32, November 2004, No. 11, pp. 60); "Air Campaign: Think Wireless Devices and Air Travel Don't Mix?" in [4909], [30283], [41502]

Entrepreneur (Vol. 32, No. 4, April 2004, pp. 39); "Air Raid" in [13808], [22164], [33523]

Entrepreneur (Vol. 30, No. 10, October 2002, pp. 114); "Airborne intelligence" in [35315], [38601]

Entrepreneur (Vol. 31, No. 10, October 2003, pp. 112); "All in the Delivery" in [8891], [37554], [38602]

Entrepreneur (Vol. 32, July 2004); "All Fired Up: With the Right Marketing Plan, Your Product Will Blaze Trails Across the Globe" in [35763], [46670], [51545]

Entrepreneur (Vol. 30, No. 12, Dec. 2002, pp. 118); "All new: be the first on the block with one of these 66 fresh opportunities" in [35316], [38603]

Entrepreneur (Vol. 32, No. 2, February 2004, pp. 44); "All in One" in [6577], [33525], [48942]

Entrepreneur (Vol. 33, January 2005, No. 1, pp. 84); "All the Rage: Wondering What Everyone Will Be Crazy About in the Coming Year?" in [432], [1757], [6147], [10657], [18291], [19340], [25461], [31088], [38604], [53557]

Entrepreneur (Vol. 32, December 2004, No. 12, pp. 52); "All Systems Go" in [25787], [33526], [51048]

Entrepreneur (Vol. 33, March 2005, No. 3); "All Systems Grow: You Don't Have to be a Rocket Scientist to Grow Your Business." in [27761], [29785]

Entrepreneur (Vol. 33, March 2005, No. 3); "All That Glitters: Dreaming of Starting Your Own Jewelry Business? " in [15833]

Entrepreneur (Vol. 30, No. 3, March 2002, pp.); "All work, All play" in [37585], [38707]

Entrepreneur (Vol. 31, Sept. 2003); "All's Fair: In Love and Business, So You May Need a Prenup to Protect Your Company's Assets" in [37872], [39138]

Entrepreneur (Vol. 30, No. 12, December 2002, pp. 64); "Almost office" in [4592], [22909], [48943], [53202]

Entrepreneur (Vol. 31, No. 10, October 2003, pp. 87); "Along For the Ride: Losing Touch With Your Reps?" in [44882], [51547]

Entrepreneur (Vol. 32, October 2004, No. 10, pp. 62); "An Acquired Taste" in [22754], [30661], [44463], [46184], [48897], [52404]

Entrepreneur (Vol. 33, January 2005, No. 1, pp. 76); "An American Icon" in [38708], [39141]

Entrepreneur (Vol. 31, No. 9, September 2003, pp. 105); "An Office of One's Own" in [42694], [49529]

Entrepreneur (Vol. 31, No. 7, July 2003, pp. 55); "An Unsure Thing: Can't Pay Your Federal Tax Bill?" in [39951], [54851]

Entrepreneur (Vol. 28, No. 9, September 2000, pp. 48); "And on your Left" in [29704], [55354]

Entrepreneur (Vol. 28, No. 10, October 2000, pp. 171); "Angel on you Side" in [48872], [55356]

Entrepreneur (Vol. 31, No. 7, July 2003, pp. 40); "Another Act" in [46681], [51549]

Entrepreneur (Vol. 33, September 2005, No. 9, pp. 32); "Answer the Call" in [4913], [47143], [48945], [49482], [50930]

Entrepreneur (Vol. 31, No. 10, October 2003, pp. 57); "Antivirus Extras" in [4595], [22171], [22912], [53208]

Entrepreneur (Vol. 31, No. 8, August 2003, pp. 40); "Apple of Your Eye?" in [4596], [22914], [48947], [53210]

Entrepreneur (Vol. 32, October 2004, No. 10, pp. 98); "Apply Yourself" in [13821], [33539], [40158], [42167]

Entrepreneur (Vol. 28, No. 1, January 2000, pp. 328); "Are We There Yet?" in [11141], [35774]

Entrepreneur (Vol. 32, November 2004, No. 11, pp. 75); "Arrested Development?" in [39789], [44471]

Entrepreneur (Vol. 30, No. 2, Fe); "As seen on TV" in [548], [46687], [51554]

Entrepreneur (Vol. 30, No. 3, March 2002); "Bunny Money" in [11104], [11145], [27890], [35887], [51083]

Entrepreneur (Vol. 28, No. 6, June 2000, pp. 76); "Burn, babay, Burn" in [27715], [35351]

Entrepreneur (Vol. 28, No. 4, April 2000, pp. 132); "Business After Divorce" in [37605]

Entrepreneur (Vol. 32, July 2004, No. 7, pp. 69); "Business Gone Wild" in [21457], [31654], [46762]

Entrepreneur (Vol. 32, No. 1, January 2004, pp. 168); "Business Services" in [3508], [4610], [20305], [22932], [29137], [33629], [35896], [36620], [38731], [42588], [52511]

Entrepreneur (Vol. 31, No. 11, November 2003, pp. 98); "But Wait, There's More" in [46767], [51086], [51576]

Entrepreneur (Vol. 30, No. 3, March 2002, pp. 72); "Buy, buy biotech?" in [27913], [37935], [41581]

Entrepreneur (Vol. 32, November 2004, No. 11, pp. 70); "Buy Now, Pay More Later: Paying Premiums Over Time Can Cost You" in [13220], [43110]

Entrepreneur (Vol. 33, October 2005, No. 10, pp. 81); "Buzz Skill" in [46769], [48145], [50568]

Entrepreneur (Vol. 32, December 2004, No. 12, pp. 98); "By Degrees" in [33027], [44973]

Entrepreneur (Vol. 32, November 2004, No. 11, pp. 26); "By Gum!...It Is Possible to Beat Everyone-Even Big Companies-To Market..." in [30809], [35903], [43570]

Entrepreneur (Vol. 31, No. 8, August 2003, pp. 73); "By Special Request: Pleasing One Client Pays Off in the Long Run" in [9698], [31655]

Entrepreneur (July 2004); "By Special Request: Upscale Concierge Business Give New Meaning to the Phrase 'Service With a Smile'" in [7110]

Entrepreneur (Vol. 33, October 2005, No. 10, pp. 41); "Cable-Free USB" in [6239], [13782], [13879], [48974], [50963]

Entrepreneur (Vol. 30, No. 2, February 2002, pp. 72); "Calculating clicks" in [572], [13881], [33642], [46771]

Entrepreneur (Vol. 31, No. 9, September 2003, pp. 22); "California Dreamin'" in [51087], [52649]

Entrepreneur (Vol. 32, November 2004, No. 11, pp. 17); "Call Forward: No Question About It" in [4938], [48976]

Entrepreneur (Vol. 31, No. 7, July 2003, pp. 37); "Call Waiting?" in [4939], [6600], [48977]

Entrepreneur (Vol. 31, No. 9, September 2003, pp. 39); "Call of the Wi-Fi: Digital Edge" in [4940], [40233]

Entrepreneur (Vol. 30, No. 9, September 2002, pp. 23); "Calling security" in [22191], [41586], [53633]

Entrepreneur (Vol. 32, October 2004, No. 10, pp. 57); "Calling the Shots: Is a VoIP Telephone System in Your Company's Future?" in [4942], [13882], [48979]

Entrepreneur (Vol. 31, No. 4, April 2003, pp. 62); "Can Entrepreneurship Be Taught? You Bet It Can" in [33031], [35905]

Entrepreneur (Vol. 31, No. 7, July 2003); "Can You Manage? Should the Office Hotshot Be Your Next Manager?" in [19385], [35910], [44983]

Entrepreneur (Vol. 31, No. 7, July 2003, pp. 52); "Can't Win For Losing: A Mutual Fund Tax Quirk Limits Your Capital Losses" in [9862], [14830], [37941], [54473]

Entrepreneur (Vol. 30, No. 10, October 2002, pp. 60); "Capital infusion" in [39796], [40239]

Entrepreneur (Vol. 31, No. 6, June 2003, pp. 51); "Caps off to you!" in [39797], [44489]

Entrepreneur (Vol. 33, February 2005, No. 2, pp. 66); "Capture the Tag: Are RFID Tags in Danger of Being Hacked?" in [4612], [22935], [51088], [53234]

Entrepreneur (Vol. 32, October 2004, No. 10, pp. 42); "Carb Games" in [2241], [12002], [12766], [21462], [46777]

Entrepreneur (Vol. 32, No. 4, April 2004); "Carb Your Enthusiasm: Here's the Skinny on How to Tap Into the Hot Low-Carb Market" in [11596], [12767], [21463]

Entrepreneur (Vol. 33, October 2005, No. 10, pp. 99); "Card Shark" in [11148], [38734]

Entrepreneur (Vol. 30, No. 2, February 2002, pp); "Card Tricks" in [13885], [30207], [31656], [33648]

Entrepreneur (Vol. 31, No. 8, Aug. 2003, pp. 78); "Cart Blanche: Think Retailing is Strictly Brick-and-Mortar Opportunity? Not So." in [15908], [35360], [51022]

Entrepreneur (Vol. 31, No. 8, August 2003, pp. 66); "Case In Point" in [33034], [35922]

Entrepreneur (Vol. 30, No.2 February 2002, pp. 53); "Cash crunch" in [14833], [44491], [55533]

Entrepreneur (Vol. 31, No. 6, June 2003, pp. 53); "Cash in, cash out" in [101], [2883], [26184], [37946]

Entrepreneur (Vol. 30, No. 3, March 2002, pp. 74); "Cash in: Tax talk: Cash accounting is about to get more use" in [40245], [54478]

Entrepreneur (Vol. 31, No. 9, September 2003); "Catch-22: Are Small Companies that Buy from Giant Retailers Sleeping with the Enemy" in [30814], [51091]

Entrepreneur (Vol. 32, October 2004, No. 10, pp. 40); "Caught in 'Tween" in [5270], [46789]

Entrepreneur (Vol. 33, October 2005, No. 10, pp. 110); "Celebrate Good Times" in [18752]

Entrepreneur (Vol. 32, No. 1, January 2004, pp. 10); "Center for Exhibition Industry Research (CEIR)" in [16805], [22482], [24905], [33658]

Entrepreneur (Vol. 33, September 2005, No. 9, pp. 34); "Central Perks" in [26371], [26767], [34851], [56157]

Entrepreneur (Vol. 32, No. 1, January 2004); "Change of Address: There's a New Internet Protocol in Town. Is it Time to Upgrade?" in [13891], [33660]

Entrepreneur (Vol. 31, No. 9, September 2003, pp. 87); "Change of Face: Tactics: Is Your Logo Losing Its Luster?" in [46794], [50571]

Entrepreneur (Vol. 28, No. 4, April 2000, pp. 125); "Change Of Face" in [35362], [53642]

Entrepreneur (Vol. 33, October 2005, No. 10, pp. 98); "Charged Up" in [7719], [35939], [38739]

Entrepreneur (Vol. 30, No. 3, March 2002, pp. 88); "Chart-toppers" in [46796], [50573]

Entrepreneur (Vol. 31, No. 9, September 2003, pp. 85); "Charted Territory: Candy Crosses the Border to Open New Doors" in [4280], [27942]

Entrepreneur (Vol. 30, No. 3, March 2002, pp. 84); "Cheap labor: Insurance: How to get a lower workers' comp premium" in [13233], [43124]

Entrepreneur (Vol. 28, No. 11, November 2000, pp. 40); "Check 'Em Out" in [13895], [33666]

Entrepreneur (Vol. 32, November 2004, No. 11, pp. 14); "Check It Out" in [35942], [46798], [51587]

Entrepreneur (Vol. 32, No. 5, May 2004, pp. 131); "Chem-dry, a Franchise Rated No. 1 in its Category for 15 Years Straight..." in [25530], [38618]

Entrepreneur (Vol. 28, No. 17, July 2000, pp. 142); "Chicago" in [3510], [29825]

Entrepreneur (Vol. 30, No. 3, March 2002, pp. 93); "Chick magnet: How can you attract women to your business?" in [46801], [51589], [56162]

Entrepreneur (Vol. 31, No. 4, April 2003, pp. 51); "Chief concern" in [104], [26186], [35943], [37964], [44997]

Entrepreneur (Vol. 32, No. 1, January 2004, pp. 178); "Children's Products and Services" in [5271], [5335], [33038], [38740]

Entrepreneur (Vol. 31, No. 9, September 2003, pp. 119); "Child's Play" in [5336], [19388], [56163]

Entrepreneur (Vol. 32, November 2004, No. 11, pp. 6); "Choose Leasing: www.chooseleasing.org" in [13897], [21316]

Entrepreneur (Vol. 33, March 2005, No. 3, pp. 114); "Choose Your Path" in [51094]

Entrepreneur (Vol. 32, October 2004, No. 10, pp. 26); "Cindy Kauanui: 45, Founder of Jet Set Management in La Jolla, California" in [17335], [23824]

Entrepreneur (Vol. 30, No. 1, January 2); "Class distinction" in [13902], [33672]

Entrepreneur (Vol. 31, No. 11, November 2003, pp. 126); "Class of their Own" in [5312], [37558]

Entrepreneur (Vol. 33, October 2005, No. 10, pp. 20); "Clean and Green" in [8900]

Entrepreneur (Vol. 24, No. 7, July 1996, pp. 59); "Clean Sweep" in [20012], [52518]

Entrepreneur (Vol. 32, No. 1, January 2004, pp. 10); "Clickalyzer www.clickalyzer.com" in [585], [16807], [33675], [46805]

Entrepreneur (Vol. 33, August 2005, No. 8, pp. 44); "Clicks to Bricks" in [27478], [27957], [32675], [33679], [44686], [46807], [50574], [51097]

Entrepreneur (Vol. 31, No. 7, July 2003, pp. 22); "Clocking In: For Low-Wage Workers, Overtime May Get More Lucrative" in [40264], [42838]

Entrepreneur (Vol. 32, No. 1, January 2004, pp. 130); "Cloning Around" in [35951], [38744]

Entrepreneur (Vol. 33, February 2005, No. 2, pp. 69); "Close to Home" in [586], [13905], [33681], [46811]

Entrepreneur (Vol. 31, No. 10, October 2003, pp. 82); "Close the Loop" in [27958], [49683], [53648]

Entrepreneur (Vol. 28, No. 11, November 2000, pp. 24); "Close Up: Teen Sensations" in [35367], [56718]

Entrepreneur (Vol. 33, October 2005, No. 10, pp. 85); "Closer Call" in [40404], [42203], [51590]

Entrepreneur (Vol. 31, No. 8, August 2003, pp. 102); "Clothes-Minded" in [2122], [5265]

Entrepreneur (Vol. 32, November 2004, No. 11, pp. 24); "Club Meds: Could Drug-Buying Clubs Cure High Prescription Costs?" in [40986], [53650]

Entrepreneur; "Clutter Busters: From Closets to Cabinets to Garages, Americans' Clutter is Piling Up Like Never Before" in [20015], [31123], [53651]

Entrepreneur (Vol. 28, No. 2, February 2000, pp. 34); "Co-Ed Management" in [14869], [45007], [49863]

Entrepreneur (Vol. 31, No. 11, November 2003, pp. 128); "Cold Feet?" in [20257], [35370], [38621]

Entrepreneur (Vol. 30, No. 3, March 2002, pp. 92); "Cold gold" in [587], [1411], [46815], [50576]

Entrepreneur (Vol. 32, December 2004, No. 12, pp. 49); "Color-Blind?" in [6611], [48990]

Entrepreneur (Vol. 32, No. 1, January 2004, pp. 39); "Color Scheme" in [6612], [48991]

"Entrepreneur Column" in *Entrepreneur* (August 18, 2005) [26941], [27193], [27360], [27634], [29857], [30029], [30192], [30847], [31026], [32841], [33852], [37757], [38684], [39306], [40348], [42851], [45106], [46930], [51628]

"Entrepreneur Column" in *Entrepreneur Column* (April 11, 2003) [36067]

"Entrepreneur Column" in *Entrepreneur.com* (December 21, 2007) [137], [613], [14015], [25842], [26222], [26942], [27361], [28108], [29728], [29858], [30477], [30536], [31712], [32407], [33822], [34891], [35413], [36068], [37633], [38765], [41666], [42513], [42611], [44036], [44512], [45107], [46274], [46931], [48726], [50586], [51629], [52669], [53713], [55592], [56206], [58033]

Entrepreneur (Vol. 32); "Come Together" in [4957], [13910], [41613]

Entrepreneur (Vol. 33, January 2005, No. 1, pp. 44); "Come Together. Is It Time to Combine Your Voice and Data Networks?" in [4958], [13911], [48993]

Entrepreneur (Vol. 30, No. 2, February 2002, pp. 81); "Comic genius" in [5901], [13912], [33688]

Entrepreneur; "Coming of Age: Americans Are Hitting 50 and Finding They're Anything But Over the Hill" in [35953], [38745]

Entrepreneur (Vol. 32, December 2004, No. 12, pp. 64); "Coming Up Short" in [9891], [27102], [37976]

Entrepreneur (Vol.32); "Commercial Break" in [8902], [9894], [44495]

Entrepreneur (Vol. 32, November 2004, No. 11, pp. 72); "Common Cents" in [44496], [55543]

Entrepreneur (Vol. 31, Oct. 2003); "For Better Or. How Women Entrepreneurs Strike a Balance Between Business and Marriage" in **[36171]**, **[56225]**

Entrepreneur (Vol. 33, October 2005, No. 10, pp. 104); "For Better or Worse" in **[37656]**, **[47580]**, **[49942]**

Entrepreneur (Vol. 30, No. 10, October 2002, pp. 100); "For the low, low price" in **[35462]**, **[38635]**

Entrepreneur (Vol. 33, March 2005, No. 3, pp. 56); "Foreign Affairs" in **[12972]**, **[43658]**

Entrepreneur (Vol. 30, No. 10, October 2002, pp. 58); "Foreign currency" in **[39825]**, **[43659]**, **[46294]**

Entrepreneur (Vol. 28, No. 1, January 2000, pp. 42); "Forget Diamonds" in **[55622]**

Entrepreneur (Vol. 30, No. 3, March 2002, pp. 40); "Form finder" in **[4668]**, **[23006]**, **[29246]**, **[49034]**, **[53289]**

Entrepreneur (Vol. 28, No. 8, August 2000, pp. 23); "Fortune Teller" in **[9970]**

Entrepreneur (Vol. 28, No. 10, October 2000, pp. 60); "Found in Cyberspace" in **[14054]**, **[49036]**

"Entrepreneur Foundation Retools Its Teaching Model" in *Business First Columbus* (Vol. 18, No. 40, March 24, 2002, pp. A11) **[33085]**, **[36069]**

Entrepreneur (Vol. 30, N pp. 81); "401 Ok?" in **[9971]**, **[15015]**, **[26810]**, **[38081]**

Entrepreneur (Vol. 31, No. 4, April 2003); "Fraction action: can't afford an entire jet? Try winging it with a piece of one" in **[30331]**, **[49950]**

Entrepreneur (Vol. 31, No. 6, June 2003, pp. 86); "Franchise country" in **[38785]**

Entrepreneur (Vol. 33, October 2005, No. 10, pp. 49); "Free At Last!" in **[4960]**, **[4990]**, **[49037]**, **[51041]**

Entrepreneur (Vol. 31, No. 5, May 2003, pp. 23); "Free rein" in **[39827]**, **[44531]**

Entrepreneur (Vol. 32, September 2004, No. 9, pp. 42); "Free to Roam" in **[4991]**, **[49038]**

Entrepreneur (Vol. 31, No. 9, July 2003, pp. 80); "Free Speech" in **[22503]**, **[46985]**

Entrepreneur (Vol. 32, December 2004, No. 12, pp. 91); "Fresh Ideas" in **[4292]**, **[46988]**, **[50593]**

Entrepreneur (Vol. 31, No. 6, June 2003, pp. 77); "Friends forever?" in **[36181]**, **[49952]**

Entrepreneur (Vol. 30, No. 3, March 2002, pp. 29); "From idea to inspiration" in **[29736]**, **[30480]**, **[48736]**

Entrepreneur (Vol. 32, No. 1, January 2004, pp. 148); "From Zero to Hero: Even the Best Franchisor has to Start Somewhere" in **[8512]**, **[21520]**, **[36190]**, **[38811]**

Entrepreneur (Vol. 31, No. 6, June 2003, pp. 114); "Frozen assets" in **[36191]**, **[46297]**

Entrepreneur (Vol. 31, No. 9, September 2003, pp. 104); "Full Esteem Ahead: Act Like an Executive-And Get the Respect You Deserve" in **[27377]**, **[36192]**, **[45168]**

Entrepreneur (Vol. 31, No. 4, April 2003, pp. 94); "Fun money" in **[8125]**, **[35476]**

Entrepreneur (Vol. 32, August 2004, No. 8, pp. 48); "Fun Money: Mixing Business and Pleasure Can Pay Off" in **[30333]**, **[54563]**

Entrepreneur (Vol. 31, No. 8, August 2003, pp. 54); "Fund Sharks" in **[9974]**, **[15024]**, **[38083]**, **[40399]**

Entrepreneur (Vol. 32, October 2004, No. 10, pp. 93); "Funny Business: No Ifs, Ands or Buts" in **[632]**, **[30863]**, **[46998]**

Entrepreneur (Vol. 33, February 2005, No. 2, pp. 78); "Funny Stuff: Laughter is the Best Marketing, so Find Your Sense of Humor" in **[2126]**, **[5276]**, **[46999]**

Entrepreneur (Vol. 33, January 2005, No. 1, pp. 46); "G Whiz!" in **[6655]**, **[49040]**

Entrepreneur (Vol. 33, September 2005, No. 9, pp. 22); "Gadget Gurus" in **[47002]**, **[48024]**, **[50443]**

Entrepreneur (Vol. 28, No. 9, September 2000, pp. 132); "Gag Order" in **[37663]**

Entrepreneur (Vol. 32, November 2004, No. 11, pp. 28); "Game On!" in **[24814]**, **[27378]**

Entrepreneur (Vol. 32, No. 4, April 2004, pp. 22); "Game On! Game-Makers are Definitely not Sleeping in Seattle" in **[24815]**, **[44050]**, **[55642]**

Entrepreneur (Vol. 28, No. 1, January 2000, pp. 32); "GE Whiz!" in **[52536]**, **[53745]**

Entrepreneur (Vol. 28, No. 4, April 2000, pp. 66); "Get Bizzed" in **[33936]**, **[36198]**

Entrepreneur (Vol. 30, No. 2, February 2002, pp. 61); "Get carded" in **[27127]**, **[39353]**

Entrepreneur (Vol. 30, No. 12, December 2002, pp. 85); "Get 'em while they're hot" in **[1761]**, **[5628]**, **[12755]**, **[19139]**, **[19342]**, **[22882]**, **[27722]**, **[33440]**, **[35477]**, **[39059]**

Entrepreneur (Vol. 31, No. 4, April 2003, pp. 75); "Get your fix: had enough of auctions?" in **[1815]**, **[31033]**, **[33939]**

Entrepreneur (Vol. 33, January 2005, No. 1, pp. 106); "Get in the Game" in **[35478]**, **[38649]**

Entrepreneur (Vol. 28, No. 7, July 2000, pp. 90); "Get outta here" in **[54571]**

Entrepreneur (Vol. 31, No. 10, October 2003, pp. 38); "Get In Sync: To Spark Business Growth, Follow the Leader In Your Industry" in **[28201]**, **[29886]**, **[45176]**

Entrepreneur (Vol. 32, October 2004, No. 10, pp. 49); "Get Lost! While You Still Can, That Is." in **[4996]**, **[41709]**

Entrepreneur (Vol. 32, October 2004, No. 10); "Get the Message? SMS Technology Could Bring Mobile Commerce Within Your Reach" in **[4997]**, **[41710]**, **[53747]**

Entrepreneur (Vol. 33, October 2005, No. 10, pp. 14); "Get On The Plan" in **[29065]**, **[29723]**, **[29737]**, **[30481]**

Entrepreneur (Vol. 30, No. 2, February 2002, pp. 56); "Get a second opinion" in **[52372]**

Entrepreneur (Vol. 32, November 2004, No. 11, pp. 62); "Get Organized" in **[6249]**, **[6657]**, **[49044]**

Entrepreneur (Vol. 31, No. 10, October 2003, pp. 88); "Get Over It!" in **[51648]**

Entrepreneur (Vol. 32, August 2004); "Get Physical! Former Couch Potatoes are Jumping on a New Trend: Interactive Video Games" in **[1107]**, **[6658]**, **[19400]**, **[53748]**

Entrepreneur (Vol. 31, No. 11, November 2003, pp. 91); "Get the Picture?" in **[4672]**, **[23011]**, **[25387]**, **[52537]**, **[53294]**

Entrepreneur (Vol. 31, No. 5, May 2003, pp. 58); "Get with the program!" in **[4673]**, **[23012]**, **[49045]**, **[53295]**

Entrepreneur (Vol. 28, No. 2, February 2000, pp. 142); "Get the Scoop" in **[30867]**, **[31723]**, **[47009]**

Entrepreneur (Vol. 32, July 2004, No. 7, pp. 34); "Get Smart" in **[30547]**, **[36200]**

Entrepreneur (Vol. 32, July 2004, No. 7, pp. 45); "Get Smart! When Using Wi-Fi Hot Spots, Don't Throw Caution to the Wind" in **[14069]**, **[22236]**, **[30334]**

Entrepreneur (Vol. 32, October 2004, No. 10, pp. 92); "Get Smarty" in **[637]**, **[4999]**, **[5546]**, **[5666]**, **[13296]**, **[18044]**, **[47010]**

Entrepreneur (Vol. 30, No. 3, March 2002, pp. 40); "Get it together" in **[4674]**, **[23013]**, **[49046]**, **[53296]**

Entrepreneur (Vol. 33, January 2005, No. 1, pp. 28); "Get Tough: No More Mr. Nice Guy." in **[30868]**, **[45181]**

Entrepreneur (Vol. 31, No. 5, May 2003, pp. 79); "Get in tune: keep your site visitors dialed in and buying" in **[14071]**, **[25856]**, **[33944]**, **[47011]**, **[51649]**

Entrepreneur (Vol. 31, No. 7, July 2003); "Get With the Program! Save Money with a New Approach to Managing Disability Benefits" in **[13297]**, **[43184]**

Entrepreneur (Vol. 33, October 2005, No. 10, pp. 88); "Getting Clocked" in **[26417]**, **[26816]**, **[40407]**

Entrepreneur (Vol. 33, February 2005, No. 2); "Getting Ink: Need Exposure?" in **[12884]**, **[20120]**, **[47013]**, **[50444]**, **[50595]**

Entrepreneur (Vol. 31, No. 6, June 2003); "Getting past 'No': how do you turn that 'no' into a 'yes'?" in **[51650]**

Entrepreneur (Vol. 33, February 2005, pp. 110); "Getting No Respect?" in **[36205]**, **[56745]**

Entrepreneur (Vol. 31, No. 10, October 2003, pp. 114); "Getting Noticed" in **[20258]**, **[38814]**

Entrepreneur (Vol. 33, October 2005, No. 10, pp. 44); "Getting Personal" in **[30199]**, **[31034]**

Entrepreneur (Vol. 33, February 2005, No. 2); "Getting Personal: Take a Closer Look at the Up-And-Coming Personalized Search Engine" in **[14074]**, **[33951]**

Entrepreneur (Vol. 33, March 2005, No. 3, pp. 38); "Getting Props: Awards Can Boost Your Self-Esteem-And Your Business" in **[36206]**, **[56239]**

Entrepreneur (Vol. 32, September 2004); "Getting Their Slice: Save Money, and Keep Employees Happy With Stock Ownership Plans" in **[15034]**, **[26817]**, **[34911]**, **[54573]**

Entrepreneur (Vol. 31, No. 5, May 2003, pp. 28); "Girl power" in **[36209]**, **[54186]**, **[56241]**

Entrepreneur (Vol. 28, No. 3, March 2000, pp. 38); "Girls Just Wanna Have Funds" in **[55644]**, **[56243]**

Entrepreneur (Vol. 31, No. 8, August 2003, pp. 55); "Give 'Em Credit" in **[44535]**, **[48906]**

Entrepreneur (Vol. 33, September 2005, No. 9, pp. 85); "Give 'Em Liberty" in **[605]**, **[640]**, **[47019]**

Entrepreneur (Vol. 31, No. 9, July 2003, pp. 112); "Give 'Em the Sack" in **[11153]**, **[56245]**

Entrepreneur (Vol. 32, No. 1, January 2004, pp. 77); "Give 'Em Space: A Well-Designed Work Space, that is" in **[18545]**, **[34914]**, **[49503]**, **[51653]**

Entrepreneur (Vol. 32); "Give It a Go: A 'Hands-On' Approach to Marketing Your Product Could Be Just the Thing to Win Customers" in **[641]**, **[47020]**

Entrepreneur (Vol. 30, No. 12, December 2002, pp. 38); "Glad that's over" in **[3534]**, **[36214]**

Entrepreneur (Vol. 31, No. 9, September 2003, pp. 42); "Global Appeal: Connecting the World With the Push of a Button" in **[5002]**, **[14080]**

Entrepreneur (Vol. 32, October 2004, No. 10, pp. 68); "Go For the Gold" in **[28210]**, **[29888]**, **[36216]**, **[52423]**

Entrepreneur (Vol. 31, No. 4, April 2003, pp. 81); "Go major league" in **[34916]**, **[47023]**, **[51655]**

Entrepreneur (Vol. 33, March 2005, No. 3, pp. 90); "Go Live: They've Got Questions, You've Got Answers." in **[14081]**, **[25859]**, **[27382]**, **[33957]**, **[51656]**

Entrepreneur (Vol. 31, No. 4, April 2003, pp. 41); "Go retro! Budget tight?" in **[49051]**, **[49504]**

Entrepreneur (Vol. 28, No. 6, June 2000, pp. 38); "Go Small" in **[55645]**

Entrepreneur (Vol. 33, October 2005, No. 10, pp. 26); "Go South" in **[12975]**, **[41747]**, **[43677]**

Entrepreneur (Vol. 32, November 2004, No. 11, pp. 22); "Go West: Want a Few Business Pointers? Mosey on Over to Deadwood" in **[24412]**, **[28211]**, **[29265]**, **[36217]**, **[47024]**

Entrepreneur (Vol. 32, August 2004, No. 8, pp. 32); "Go With the Flow" in **[36218]**, **[45193]**

Entrepreneur (Vol. 32, December 2004, No. 12, pp. 34); "Going Global: International Business Tips Make a World of Difference" in **[28212]**, **[43679]**, **[56247]**

Entrepreneur (Vol. 31, No. 11, November 2003, pp. 65); "Going Public" in **[15042]**, **[28216]**, **[49962]**

Entrepreneur (Vol. 32, July 2004, No. 7, pp. 54); "Going Public: A Public Insurance Adjuster Could Help You Get What You Deserve" in **[13298]**, **[43187]**

Entrepreneur (Vol. 32, August 2004); "Going Separate Ways: In a Law Suit, You and an Employee Could Be Sent Down Different Paths" in **[13299]**, **[43188]**

Entrepreneur (Vol. 28, No. 11, November 2000, pp. 34); "Going solo" in **[49052]**

Entrepreneur (Vol. 31, No. 9, September 2003, pp. 50); "Going Somewhere?" in **[6660]**, **[49053]**

Entrepreneur (Vol. 33, March 2005, No. 3); "Gold Standard: Get the Best in IP Phone Bennies Without a PBX or Even a VoIP Provider" in **[5003]**, **[14083]**

Entrepreneur MASTER INDEX

Entrepreneur (Vol. 28, No. 3, March 2000, pp. 86); "Gone Fishin'" in **[26818]**, **[39362]**, **[42249]**, **[53755]**

Entrepreneur (Vol. 33, September 2005, No. 9, pp. 84); "Good Company" in **[51657]**

Entrepreneur (Vol. 32, No. 1, January 2004, pp. 106); "Good as Gold" in **[445]**, **[3535]**, **[5277]**, **[5338]**, **[7348]**, **[8273]**, **[11327]**, **[12778]**, **[15845]**, **[18322]**, **[19403]**, **[23954]**, **[33108]**, **[38817]**, **[53756]**, **[56248]**

Entrepreneur (Vol. 32, December 2004, No. 12, pp. 100); "Good Libations?" in **[29268]**, **[36228]**

Entrepreneur (Vol. 30, No. 10, October 2002, pp. 98); "Good question! Ask, and the people will read" in **[642]**, **[47030]**

Entrepreneur (Vol. 32, September 2004, No. 9, pp. 104); "Good Sports" in **[23621]**, **[23723]**, **[37669]**, **[49963]**

Entrepreneur (Vol. 32, August 2004, No. 8, pp. 65); "Good Timing" in **[643]**, **[23018]**, **[47031]**, **[50600]**, **[53303]**

Entrepreneur (Vol. 31, No. 9, September 2003, pp. 108); "Goodwill Hunting?" in **[38819]**, **[54192]**

Entrepreneur (Vol. 31, No. 10, October 2003, pp. 6); "Google World: http://google.indicateur.com" in **[28223]**, **[33972]**

Entrepreneur (Vol. 32, October 2004, No. 10, pp. 95); "Got Game?" in **[29890]**, **[30551]**, **[36230]**, **[53757]**

Entrepreneur (Vol. 32, December 2004, No. 12, pp. 47); "Got It Covered?" in **[13300]**, **[18050]**, **[43190]**

Entrepreneur (Vol. 31, No. 9, September 2003); "Got Leverage? Dollar Signs: If You're Ready to Sell, You've Got the Upper Hand" in **[15049]**, **[49966]**, **[52424]**, **[53758]**

Entrepreneur (Vol. 30, No. 10, October 2002, pp. 83); "Got anything smaller?" in **[42251]**, **[45201]**, **[53759]**

Entrepreneur (Vol. 33, October 2005, No. 10, pp. 6); "GoWholesale" in **[1782]**, **[1819]**, **[32955]**, **[33977]**, **[37804]**, **[39370]**, **[53239]**, **[56011]**

Entrepreneur (Vol. 31, No. 10, October 2003, pp. 106); "Grape Expectations: Are You Thinking About Getting Into the Wine Business?" in **[23440]**, **[28225]**, **[35489]**

Entrepreneur (Vol. 33, February 2005, No. 2, pp. 72); "Great Expectation" in **[42252]**, **[45202]**

Entrepreneur; "Great Expectations: Think Your Business Technology Is All That and a Bag of Microchips? Well, It's Not" in **[5004]**, **[6663]**, **[41719]**, **[49054]**

Entrepreneur (Vol. 31, No. 7, July 2003, pp. 34); "Green Machines" in **[36235]**, **[37286]**, **[37451]**

Entrepreneur (Vol. 32, December 2004, No. 12); "Groom to Grow: Animal Grooming is More Than a Pet Project for a Former HR Executive" in **[19074]**, **[38821]**, **[52540]**

Entrepreneur (Vol. 32, August 2004, No. 8, pp. 34); "Ground Control" in **[5005]**, **[6665]**, **[7350]**, **[7728]**, **[14094]**, **[27384]**, **[41721]**

Entrepreneur (Vol. 30, No. 12, December 2002, pp. 101); "Group dynamics" in **[36240]**, **[39372]**

Entrepreneur (Vol. 32, November 2004, No. 11, pp. 64); "Group Effort" in **[6667]**, **[49057]**

Entrepreneur (Vol. 31, No. 7, July 2003, pp. 27); "Growth Guru: How to Turn Your Business Into a Hot Commodity" in **[28250]**, **[36250]**, **[45212]**

Entrepreneur (Vol. 32); "Growth Spurt: Thanks to the Spread of Bluetooth, Now Your Business Can Be As Wireless As You Want It To Be" in **[4187]**, **[5006]**, **[6668]**, **[41724]**

Entrepreneur (Vol. 33, March 2005, No. 3, pp. 87); "Guaranteed Results" in **[51175]**, **[52541]**

Entrepreneur (Vol. 33, March 2005, No. 3, pp. 58); "Guardian Angel" in **[39834]**, **[44539]**, **[55652]**

Entrepreneur (Vol. 33, August 2005, No. 8, pp. 16); "Guiding Light" in **[11155]**, **[44235]**, **[46308]**, **[49061]**, **[56561]**

Entrepreneur (Vol. 31, No. 8, August 2003, pp. 84) "Guiding Light; Feeling a Little Lost at the Helm of Your Business?" in **[32884]**, **[35493]**

Entrepreneur (Vol. 31, No. 6, June 2003, pp. 39); "gWHIZ!: swimming through the alphabet soup of today's wireless standards" in **[5009]**, **[6669]**, **[14096]**, **[41726]**, **[49062]**

Entrepreneur (Vol. 31, No. 10, October 2003, pp. 32); "Hack Attack:...And Other Threats From the Politically Offended" in **[22240]**, **[33987]**

Entrepreneur (Vol. 30, No. 3, March); "Hack away" in **[6166]**, **[22241]**, **[42255]**, **[53769]**

Entrepreneur (Vol. 32, No. 4, April 2004, pp. 38); "Hacked!" in **[14097]**, **[22242]**, **[33988]**

Entrepreneur (Vol. 33, January 2005, No. 1, pp. 42); "Half Pints: Wireless Routers Have the Size Advantage" in **[30342]**, **[41727]**, **[49063]**

Entrepreneur (Vol. 31, No. 8, August 2003, pp. 68); "Hand In Hand" in **[45215]**, **[48740]**, **[49972]**

Entrepreneur (Vol. 32, No. 4, April 2004, pp. 38); "Hands Down" in **[6670]**, **[22244]**, **[49064]**

Entrepreneur (Vol. 32, August 2004, No. 8, pp. 72); "Hangin' Tough: How to Beef Up Your Negotiating Game" in **[27392]**, **[36259]**, **[45219]**

Entrepreneur (Vol. 32, No. 1, January 2004, pp. 39); "Happy Returns" in **[31728]**, **[33993]**, **[51177]**

Entrepreneur (Vol. 28, No. 11, November 2000, pp. 34); "Hard copy" in **[49065]**

Entrepreneur (Vol. 28, No. 11, November 2000, pp. 40); "Hard Sell" in **[29895]**

Entrepreneur (Vol. 30, No. 3, March 2002, pp. 78); "Head Games" in **[13309]**, **[43200]**

Entrepreneur (Vol. 32, October 2004, No. 10, pp. 96); "Head to Head: How to Deal With Difficult Opponents" in **[27393]**, **[45226]**

Entrepreneur (Vol. 31, No. 9, July 2003, pp. 84); "Head Long" in **[655]**, **[47062]**

Entrepreneur (Vol. 30, No. 3, March 2002, pp. 40); "Heading for new domains" in **[14107]**, **[25863]**, **[34001]**

Entrepreneur (Vol. 32, No. 1, January 2004, pp. 208); "Health Businesses" in **[38823]**, **[41018]**

Entrepreneur (Vol. 33, March 2005, No. 3, pp. 70); "Health of a Nation" in **[13317]**, **[41731]**, **[43210]**

Entrepreneur (Vol. 28, No. 11, November 2000, pp. 16); "Healthy Choice" in **[36270]**

Entrepreneur (Vol. 32, December 2004, No. 12, pp. 58); "Heard the News?" in **[34002]**, **[36272]**

Entrepreneur (Vol. 32, September 2004, No. 9); "Heart of Gold: Nonprofits Are Reaping the Rewards of Starting For-Profit Ventures" in **[36273]**, **[53772]**

Entrepreneur (Vol. 33, February 2005, No. 2, pp. 82); "Heir Raising" in **[22614]**, **[29898]**, **[37678]**, **[38824]**

Entrepreneur (Vol. 30, No. 10, October 2002, pp. 40); "Help me out, here" in **[36274]**, **[56261]**

Entrepreneur (Vol. 31, Sept.2003); "Help Wanted: Net Profits: Want to Hand a Project to a Freelancer But Don't Know Where to Start?" in **[14108]**, **[49702]**

Entrepreneur (Vol. 32, December 2004, No. 12, pp. 16); "Here Comes the Sun" in **[15846]**, **[30346]**, **[36276]**, **[49069]**

Entrepreneur (Vol. 33, February 2005, No. 2, pp. 50); "Here Comes Trouble: Avoid Independent Contractor Snags" in **[23958]**, **[49704]**, **[54587]**

Entrepreneur (Vol. 32, July 2004); "Here to Stay: When You're Looking for New Hires, Temps May Not be as Temporary as You Might Think" in **[9210]**, **[24527]**, **[42258]**, **[53773]**

Entrepreneur (Vol. 30, No. 10, Oct. 2002); "Here's what I'm thinking: you'll get your best deal if prospects see things your way" in **[27394]**, **[36277]**, **[45231]**

Entrepreneur (Vol. 30, No. 10, October 2002, pp. 116); "Here's the keys: looking for a new business idea?" in **[17947]**, **[35503]**

Entrepreneur (Vol. 30, No. 10, October 2002, pp. 58); "Here's a tip" in **[21529]**, **[54588]**

Entrepreneur (Vol. 28, No. 9, September 2000, pp. 228); "He's Giving It Away!" in **[14110]**, **[37146]**

Entrepreneur (Vol. 30, No. 3, March 2002, pp. 22); "Hey, entrepreneurs! What's in your briefcase?" in **[36281]**

Entrepreneur (Vol. 32, No. 1, January 2004, pp. 112); "Hey, Get a Clue!" in **[38827]**, **[47067]**

Entrepreneur (Vol. 31, No. 9, July 2003, pp. 124); "Hey, Listen Up!" in **[28273]**, **[36282]**

Entrepreneur (Vol. 30, No. 2, February 2002, pp. 56); "Hidden treasure" in **[32472]**, **[44546]**, **[48909]**, **[55662]**

Entrepreneur (Vol. 32, No. 4, April 2004, pp. 20); "High and Dry? A New Federal Contract Program May Not Be an Oasis After All" in **[22249]**, **[40040]**, **[53774]**

Entrepreneur (Vol. 30, No. 2, February 2002, pp. 35); "High resolution" in **[3541]**, **[27396]**, **[29288]**, **[34006]**

Entrepreneur (Vol. 31, No. 12, December 2003, pp. 8); "HighRankings.com: www.highrankings.com" in **[14114]**, **[25864]**, **[34009]**

Entrepreneur (Vol. 31, No. 10, October 2003, pp. 26); "Highway Robbery? You Can Make Renting a Car Easier on the Company Budget" in **[2077]**, **[27135]**

Entrepreneur (Vol. 33, March 2005, No. 3, pp. 28); "Hire Ground" in **[18775]**, **[42265]**, **[45241]**

Entrepreneur (Vol. 32, November 2004, No. 11, pp. 100); "Hire Learning" in **[33115]**, **[42266]**

Entrepreneur (Vol. 33, March 2005, No. 3, pp. 128); "Hire Power" in **[14116]**, **[42267]**

Entrepreneur (Vol. 31, No. 4, April 2003, pp. 56); "Hire purpose" in **[42268]**, **[54591]**

Entrepreneur (Vol. 31, No. 9, September 2003, pp. 30); "Hired Guns: Is Enlisting Bloggers the Wave of the Future in Marketing?" in **[660]**, **[14117]**, **[34010]**, **[47075]**

Entrepreneur (Vol. 33, September 2005, No. 9, pp. 19); "History Lesson" in **[1320]**, **[37685]**, **[51182]**

Entrepreneur (Vol. 31, No. 10, October 2003, pp. 87); "Hit the Road" in **[47080]**, **[50607]**, **[54203]**

Entrepreneur (Vol. 32, December 2004, No. 12, pp. 37); "Hit the Road: Itching to Throw Your Business Into High Gear?" in **[18058]**, **[27136]**

Entrepreneur (Vol. 28, No. 8, August 2000, pp. 48); "Hogan's Inferno" in **[6170]**, **[49075]**

Entrepreneur (Vol. 31, No. 8, August 2003, pp. 66); "Hold On Tight" in **[36290]**, **[42863]**, **[45245]**

Entrepreneur (Vol. 28, No. 7, July 2000, pp. 78); "Hold'Em" in **[35505]**, **[37837]**, **[44417]**, **[55392]**

Entrepreneur (Vol. 33, September 2005, No. 9, pp. 26); "Holding Pattern" in **[31582]**, **[32481]**, **[40482]**, **[42287]**, **[53777]**

Entrepreneur (Vol. 30, No. 2, February 2002, pp. 31); "Holding pattern: It's not time to go 3G quite yet" in **[5013]**, **[41744]**, **[49076]**

Entrepreneur (Vol. 33, September 2005, No. 9, pp. 48); "Holiday Bonus" in **[32994]**, **[34016]**, **[47081]**, **[51674]**

Entrepreneur (Vol. 30, No. 9, September 2002, pp. 32); "Home, cheap home" in **[663]**, **[47083]**

Entrepreneur (Vol. 32, No. 1, January 2004, pp. 210); "Home Improvements" in **[3314]**, **[7369]**, **[11217]**, **[13650]**, **[26073]**, **[38828]**

Entrepreneur (Vol. 33, October 2005, No. 10, pp. 39); "Home Smart Home" in **[7731]**, **[13560]**, **[13651]**

Entrepreneur (Vol. 31, No. 11, November 2003, pp. 72); "Home, Sweet Office" in **[162]**, **[23960]**, **[26253]**, **[42647]**, **[54594]**

Entrepreneur (Vol. 30, No. 1, January 2002, pp. 43); "Hook up" in **[6676]**, **[6942]**, **[41747]**, **[49077]**

Entrepreneur (Vol. 31, No. 6, June 2003, pp. 64); "Hot 100" in **[501]**, **[10659]**, **[25356]**, **[27725]**, **[32487]**, **[35512]**, **[46573]**, **[48656]**, **[52492]**

Entrepreneur (Vol. 32, September 2004, No. 9, pp. 46); "Hot Disks" in **[4688]**, **[4924]**, **[5014]**, **[6171]**, **[6254]**, **[6644]**, **[6677]**, **[14126]**, **[15257]**, **[22252]**, **[22981]**, **[23030]**, **[23826]**, **[23833]**, **[25774]**, **[26254]**, **[34020]**, **[46741]**, **[47088]**, **[49073]**, **[49078]**, **[50673]**, **[53317]**, **[54953]**

Entrepreneur (Vol. 31, No. 8, August 2003, pp. 57); "Hot Property" in **[13326]**, **[43218]**

Entrepreneur (Vol. 33, October 2005, No. 10, pp. 68); "Hot Spots" in **[28296]**, **[29420]**, **[30150]**, **[52682]**

Entrepreneur (Vol. 32, No. 2, February 2004, pp. 43); "Hot Stuff" in **[2592]**, **[7892]**, **[10564]**, **[11628]**, **[11888]**, **[12009]**, **[23484]**, **[34022]**, **[51186]**

Entrepreneur (Vol. 32, December 2004, No. 12, pp. 94); "Hot on Their Trail: How to Use the Net to Track Offline Customers" in **[664]**, **[25867]**, **[34023]**, **[47089]**

3538 Small Business Sourcebook ■ 22nd Edition

Entrepreneur (Vol. 32, No. 1, January 2004, pp. 216); "Hotels & Motels" in **[12574]**, **[24696]**, **[25197]**

Entrepreneur (Vol. 31, October 2003); "House of Cards? Home-Equity Borrowing Could be Risky Business as Interest Rates Rise" in **[17392]**, **[32488]**

Entrepreneur (Vol. 32); "House Rules: Before You Let Your People Work at Home, Find Out What You're Liable For-And Cover Your Bases" in **[13327]**, **[40443]**, **[43219]**

Entrepreneur (Vol. 31, No. 7, July 2003, pp. 50); "Housing Project" in **[34932]**, **[42292]**

Entrepreneur (Vol. 30, No. 1, January 2002, pp. 18); "Hover craft" in **[22791]**, **[47091]**

Entrepreneur (Vol. 28, No. 9, September 2000, pp. 33); "How Much Of A Good Thing?" in **[43222]**

Entrepreneur (Vol. 28, No. 10, October 2000, pp. 44); "How to Net Vets" in **[42297]**

Entrepreneur (Vol. 32, October 2004, No. 10, pp. 104); "Howdy, Partner" in **[13758]**, **[33450]**, **[35519]**, **[49767]**

Entrepreneur (Vol. 32, December 2004, No. 12, pp. 67); "HSAs-A Growing Trend In Health Benefits for Businesses and Individuals" in **[13329]**, **[26831]**, **[43224]**, **[53788]**, **[54603]**

Entrepreneur (Vol. 27, No. 12, December 1999, pp. 131); "Huddle Up" in **[34946]**, **[45279]**

Entrepreneur (Vol. 33, March 2005, No. 3, pp. 131); "Humble Beginning" in **[1376]**, **[21325]**, **[37695]**

Entrepreneur (August 2004); "Hungry for More: With Four Food Franchises on His Plate, This Owner Reveals His Recipe for Success" in **[21534]**, **[38835]**

Entrepreneur (Vol. 32, September 2004, No. 9); "Hunting Season: Feds Try to Protect the Little Guy From Payroll Tax Predators" in **[165]**, **[18777]**, **[23962]**, **[26257]**, **[29295]**, **[40447]**, **[54604]**

Entrepreneur (Vol. 31, No. 8, August 2003, pp. 112); "I Did It My Way" in **[29747]**, **[35521]**

Entrepreneur (Vol. 32, No. 1, January 2004, pp. 38); "I Spy With My Little Wi-Fi: Wireless Video Cameras can Mean More Security" in **[4189]**, **[22254]**

Entrepreneur (Vol. 31, No. 8, August 2003, pp. 20); "I Spy...: Workplace Surveillance is Coming to Small and Midsize Businesses" in **[22255]**, **[53792]**, **[56566]**

Entrepreneur (Vol. 32, October 2004, No. 10, pp. 44); "I Think I'll Pass: Do Women Have a Tougher Time Delegating Tasks?" in **[36332]**, **[45281]**, **[56275]**

Entrepreneur (Vol. 32, No. 1, January 2004, pp. 22); "I Want my WTV" in **[7733]**, **[15109]**, **[49083]**

Entrepreneur (Vol. 31, No. 4, April 2003, pp. 78); "Ideas on demand: you don't have to wait for inspiration" in **[36333]**, **[45282]**

Entrepreneur (Vol. 31, No. 4, April 2003, pp. 24); "Identity crisis" in **[22257]**, **[39406]**, **[44316]**

Entrepreneur (Vol. 31, No. 8, August 2003, pp. 30); "If You Build It" in **[25872]**, **[34049]**, **[51195]**

Entrepreneur (Vol. 31, Oct. 2003); "If You Built It" in **[7382]**, **[54605]**

Entrepreneur (Vol. 32); "Illicit Affairs?" in **[29300]**, **[31038]**, **[40449]**, **[43701]**

Entrepreneur (Vol. 31, No. 11, November 2003, pp. 132); "I'm with the Band" in **[17595]**, **[24420]**, **[52547]**

Entrepreneur (Vol. 32, September 2004); "I'm Game: What Hot, New Pastime is Inspiring Entrepreneurs to Launch Businesses?" in **[15111]**, **[24794]**, **[26261]**, **[35525]**, **[53563]**

Entrepreneur (Vol. 32, September 2004, No. 9, pp. 106); "Image is Everything" in **[12888]**, **[20126]**, **[22521]**, **[24959]**, **[47122]**, **[50610]**, **[55105]**, **[56277]**

Entrepreneur (Vol. 32, October 2004, No. 10, pp. 59); "In the Balance: A Good Blend Scales Down This Fund's Risk" in **[15513]**, **[38134]**

Entrepreneur (Vol. 31, No. 7, July 2003, pp. 30); "In the Balance: Learn the Factors Banks Really Weight When Setting Loan Terms" in **[38135]**, **[44551]**

Entrepreneur (Vol. 32, September 2004, No. 9, pp. 39); "In the Book? A 'White Pages' for Mobile Phone Users Is On Its Way" in **[5026]**, **[6256]**

Entrepreneur (Vol. 30, No. 2, February 2002, pp. 34); "In control: Organize your work-and your workers-with Wintility Pro" in **[4694]**, **[23039]**, **[53327]**

Entrepreneur (Vol. 31, No. 5, May 2003, pp. 39); "In this corner" in **[6685]**, **[45287]**, **[49090]**, **[51685]**

Entrepreneur (Vol. 28, No. 9, September 2000, pp. 60); "In for the Count" in **[35528]**, **[44421]**, **[55397]**, **[56056]**

Entrepreneur (Vol. 32, November 2004, No. 11, pp. 89); "In Demand" in **[9217]**, **[9720]**, **[24528]**, **[25873]**, **[30151]**, **[34057]**, **[47125]**

Entrepreneur (Vol. 33, September 2005, No. 9, pp. 18); "In-Depth View" in **[1109]**, **[5965]**, **[5992]**, **[49091]**, **[51104]**

Entrepreneur (Vol. 33, September 2005, No. 9, pp. 10); "In the Driver's Seat" in **[36340]**, **[37567]**

Entrepreneur (Vol. 31, No. 4, April 2003, pp. 58); "In care of emergency" in **[16182]**, **[22260]**, **[24234]**, **[29916]**

Entrepreneur (Vol. 28, No. 7, July 2000, pp. 97); "In Good Forum" in **[55398]**

Entrepreneur (Vol. 31, No. 7, July 2003, pp. 40); "In the Groove" in **[23040]**, **[25522]**, **[26093]**, **[53328]**

Entrepreneur (Vol. 31, No. 4, April 2003); "In High Spirits: How to Get Yourself and Your Business Fired up from the Inside out" in **[34950]**, **[47127]**, **[51686]**

Entrepreneur (Vol. 28, No. 8, August 2000, pp. 100); "In the Hood" in **[32506]**

Entrepreneur (Vol. 32, September 2004); "In Hot Water? Take a Closer Look at Your Marketing Materials, Or You May Get Burned" in **[674]**, **[14146]**, **[25874]**, **[29305]**, **[34058]**, **[40458]**, **[44065]**, **[47128]**

Entrepreneur (Vol. 33, January 2005, No. 1, pp. 20); "In the Jeans" in **[5548]**, **[5672]**

Entrepreneur (Vol. 33, January 2005, No. 1, pp. 30); "In the Lap of Luxury: The Luxury RV Market is Revved Up and Rarin' to Go." in **[21171]**

Entrepreneur (Vol. 33, October 2005, No. 10, pp. 130); "In the Mood" in **[47130]**, **[48750]**, **[50723]**, **[51197]**

Entrepreneur (Vol. 28, No. 10, October 2000, pp. 102); "In with the New" in **[28322]**, **[31744]**, **[47132]**, **[51688]**

Entrepreneur (Vol. 32, September 2004, No. 9); "In the 'No': Pessimistic Employees May Not Be So Bad For Your Business After All" in **[34952]**, **[45291]**

Entrepreneur; "In a Nutshell: Something as Unexpected as a Talking Almond Could be Just What You Need to Catch the Reader's Eye" in **[675]**, **[47133]**

Entrepreneur (Vol. 32, November 2004, No. 11); "In Search of...Can Customers Search Your Website-And Actually Find What They Need?" in **[14148]**, **[25875]**, **[30888]**, **[34061]**, **[51201]**

Entrepreneur (Vol. 32, November 2004, No. 11, pp. 28); "In Strictist Confidence" in **[34953]**, **[36344]**

Entrepreneur (Vol. 31, No. 9, September 2003, pp. 83); "In Times of Crisis" in **[22261]**, **[51690]**

Entrepreneur (Vol. 32, July 2004, No. 7, pp. 24); "In Vain: What Does the Future Hold for the Once-Hot Metrosexual?" in **[676]**, **[47135]**

Entrepreneur (Vol. 31, No. 5, May 2003); "In With the New: Get Your Customers to Get Rid of Your Products-So They Can Buy More" in **[47136]**, **[48751]**, **[51691]**

Entrepreneur (Vol. 30, No. 2, Feb); "In Your Eyes" in **[677]**, **[47137]**

Entrepreneur (Vol. 31, October 2003); "In Your Face: Cross Your Fingers, Hold Your Breath...And Put Out Ads With No Holds Barred" in **[678]**, **[47138]**, **[52126]**

Entrepreneur (Vol. 32, December 2004, No. 12, pp. 62); "Independent's Day" in **[15120]**, **[29309]**

Entrepreneur (Vol. 28, No. 1, January 2000, pp. 132); "Industrial Cleanser" in **[37300]**, **[46317]**

Entrepreneur; "Infectious Agents: A Growing Number of Uninvited Guests Are Pushing Their Way Onto Your PCs. Here Are the Latest Antidotes" in **[6688]**, **[14149]**, **[22263]**, **[34065]**

Entrepreneur (Vol. 31, No. 7, July 2003, pp. 37); "Inking Up: Now Coming to a Printer Near You-Files From a Cell Phone or PDA" in **[5029]**, **[6690]**, **[41768]**, **[49096]**

Entrepreneur (Vol. 28, No. 2, February 2000, pp. 136); "Inner-City Innovation" in **[35533]**, **[39770]**, **[40124]**

Entrepreneur (Vol. 30, No. 1, January 2002, pp. 44); "Inside the box: Buyer's guide: New software slowing you down?" in **[4698]**, **[6691]**, **[23045]**, **[49097]**, **[53332]**

Entrepreneur (Vol. 33, March 2005, No. 3, pp. 132); "Inside Job" in **[12291]**, **[13653]**, **[51205]**

Entrepreneur (Vol. 31, No. 6, June 2003, pp. 74); "Intern affairs: more and more companies are hiring virtual interns." in **[34071]**, **[42307]**

Entrepreneur (Vol. 32, November 2004, No. 11, pp. 96); "Intern Burn: Hired the Ultimate Intern from Hell?" in **[42308]**, **[45307]**

Entrepreneur (Vol. 31, No. 8, August 2003, pp. 6); "International Association of Virtual Office Assistants" in **[173]**, **[2920]**, **[3949]**, **[18778]**, **[23968]**, **[25523]**, **[26094]**

Entrepreneur (Vol. 30, No. 12, December 2002, pp. 75); "IRS informants: everything you ever wanted to know about taxes" in **[23973]**, **[54621]**

Entrepreneur (Vol. 32, No. 2, February 2004, pp. 27); "Is that Kosher? Here's a Food Niche You May Not Have Considered" in **[2249]**, **[8514]**, **[11630]**, **[23488]**, **[37703]**

Entrepreneur (Vol. 31, No. 5, May 2003, pp. 32); "It figures" in **[14169]**, **[28348]**, **[32516]**, **[34096]**, **[35272]**, **[36365]**, **[39418]**, **[56286]**

Entrepreneur (Vol. 32, July 2004, No. 7, pp. 76); "It'll Cost Ya: Know How Your Lawyer Tallies Up Your Legal Tab" in **[27145]**, **[29317]**

Entrepreneur (Vol. 32, October 2004, No. 10, pp. 92); "It's All About Results" in **[682]**, **[34098]**, **[47155]**

Entrepreneur (Vol. 32, No. 2, February 2004, pp. 38); "It's All Coming Together: A Hybrid Cradle Saves You Wireless Phone Minutes" in **[5035]**, **[27146]**

Entrepreneur (Vol. 33, January 2005, No. 1, pp. 58); "It's All In Your Head" in **[28350]**, **[32518]**

Entrepreneur (Vol. 33, March 2005, No. 3, pp. 74); "It's All Relative" in **[36367]**, **[37707]**

Entrepreneur (Vol. 33, September 2005, No. 9, pp. 44); "It's All Talk" in **[5004]**, **[5036]**, **[29318]**, **[49105]**, **[51119]**

Entrepreneur (Vol. 32, September 2004); "It's a Chic Thing: Boutique Hotel Chains Are Going Strong With Cheap, Stylish Offerings" in **[12584]**, **[38840]**

Entrepreneur (Vol. 28, No. 9, September 2000, pp. 142); "It's a Given" in **[45314]**

Entrepreneur (Vol. 30, No. 3, March 2002, pp. 42); "It's the Law" in **[29319]**, **[34099]**, **[40481]**

Entrepreneur (Vol. 28, No. 8, August 2000, pp. 30); "It's Not Enough" in **[44556]**

Entrepreneur (Vol. 30, No. 2, February 2002, pp. 53); "It's Not the First Time" in **[35537]**, **[44423]**, **[55399]**

Entrepreneur (Vol. 33, September 2005, No. 9, pp. 94); "It's Not Personal" in **[40482]**, **[42872]**

Entrepreneur (Vol. 31, No. 8, August 2003, pp. 20); "It's On Us: On Your Next Trip, Let Your Hotel Pick Up the Tab For Extras" in **[12585]**, **[30356]**

Entrepreneur (Vol. 31, No. 7, July 2003, pp. 26); "It's Optional: What Do You Really Need, and What Can You Live Without?" in **[18065]**, **[38167]**

Entrepreneur (Vol. 33, February 2005, No. 2, pp. 74); "It's Settled: A New Law Makes it Easier to Reach Settlements" in **[29320]**, **[32037]**, **[39421]**

Entrepreneur (Vol. 30, No. 1, January 2002, pp. 48); "It's a Stretch" in **[28352]**, **[44557]**, **[52134]**, **[55697]**

Entrepreneur (Vol. 31, No. 8, August 2003, pp. 75); "It's That Time of Season" in [18998], [34102], [51213], [51703]

Entrepreneur (Vol. 33, August 2005, No. 8, pp. 40); "It's a Trap! Watch Your Step-Pharming Scams Are Lurking Around Every Corner" in [6152], [6174], [21956], [22268], [27650], [29321], [34103], [36093], [37467]

Entrepreneur (Vol. 30, No. 12, December 2002, pp. 61); "It's got wings!" in [4706], [23055], [49107]

Entrepreneur (Vol. 31, No. 10, October 2003, pp. 30); "James L. McNeil" in [2718], [3546], [22269], [25088], [36383], [44323]

Entrepreneur (Vol. 32, December 2004, No. 12, pp. 164); "Java Enabled" in [11334], [36384], [51215]

Entrepreneur (Vol. 32, July 2004, No. 7, pp. 75); "Jeepers, Creepers" in [8365], [22270], [52686]

Entrepreneur (Vol. 32, September 2004, No. 9, pp. 24); "Jeff Jonas" in [4707], [22271], [23057], [40045], [44081], [53344]

Entrepreneur (Vol. 31, No. 5, May 2003, pp. 132); "Join the club: launching your first product" in [43962], [46576], [48686]

Entrepreneur (Vol. 33, September 2005, No. 9, pp. 138); "Join Hands" in [18477], [18683], [18708], [44082], [47160], [48758], [50731]

Entrepreneur (Vol. 33, October 2005, No. 10, pp. 89); "Joining the Ranks" in [42322], [43294], [45327]

Entrepreneur (Vol. 30, No. 1, January 2002, pp. 18); "Just down the block" in [4709], [23059], [34112], [47164], [53345]

Entrepreneur (Vol. 32, November 2004, No. 11, pp. 66); "Just Browsing" in [14183], [22275], [34113]

Entrepreneur (Vol. 28, No. 11, November 2000, pp. 30); "Just Can't Hack It" in [14184], [34114]

Entrepreneur (Vol. 30, No. 1, January 2002, pp. 26); "Just for shows with a new design, these booths are gonna walk all over you" in [24963], [47165]

Entrepreneur (Vol. 28, No. 17, July 2000, pp. 162); "Just Do It" in [43963], [55400]

Entrepreneur (Vol. 30, No. 1, January 2002, pp. 20); "Just for kicks: Every car you buy doesn't have to go to work with you" in [18070], [45331]

Entrepreneur (Vol. 31, No. 8, August 2003, pp. 24); "Just a Mirage? Proposed Legislation May Expand SBIC Financing-Someday" in [39848], [40490], [44559]

Entrepreneur (Vol. 32, December 2004, No. 12, pp. 39); "Just the Tax" in [23978], [54633]

Entrepreneur (Vol. 31, No. 9, September 2003, pp. 88); "Just Teasing: A Ads" in [683], [47166]

Entrepreneur (August 2004); "Just 'To-Do' It: Having Trouble Getting Organized? Start by Getting a Grip on Your To-Do List" in [36393], [54960]

Entrepreneur (Vol. 32, No. 4, April 2004, pp. 29; "Just Woo It: It's Possible to Flirt with Success After All" in [44084], [47167]

Entrepreneur (Vol. 32, November 2004, No. 11, pp. 96); "Just Zip It: A Confidentiality Agreement Can Give You the Upper Hand" in [39424], [44325]

Entrepreneur (Vol. 32, August 2004); "Ka-Boom! Looks Like the Economy is Finally Growing-And Guess What's Leading the Way?" in [28372], [32530], [41792]

Entrepreneur (Vol. 31, No. 8, August 2003, pp. 6); "Karaoke Nation" in [36394]

Entrepreneur (Vol. 30, No. 3, March); "Keep it coming" in [40493], [44560]

Entrepreneur (Vol. 32, No. 1, January 2004, pp. 79); "Keep in Touch: Be Sure to Reconnect with Your Key Clients" in [27412], [27653]

Entrepreneur (Vol. 32, December 2004, No. 12); "Keep in Touch...Even in the Air. These New Tech Features Are Ready for Takeoff" in [5040], [14186], [24424], [30361]

Entrepreneur (Vol. 32, October 2004, No. 10, pp. 42); "Keep on Truckin': These Powerful Trucks Help Keep Your Business Going" in [18072], [25394]

Entrepreneur (Vol. 30, No. 10, October 2002, pp. 39); "Keeping the Balls Rolling" in [4295], [36399]

Entrepreneur (Vol. 28, No. 8, August 2000, pp. 94); "Keeping It Simple" in [27148], [45335]

Entrepreneur (Vol. 33, February 2005, No. 2, pp. 71; "Keeping Mums" in [685], [34965], [45336], [47169], [50450]

Entrepreneur (Vol. 31, No. 12, December 2003, pp. 8); "KeepMedia Inc.: www.keepmedia.com" in [18891], [34119]

Entrepreneur (Vol. 31, No. 9, September 2003); "Ken & Jennifer Miller: 43, 40, Co-Founders of Thousand Mile, in Vista, California" in [5553], [5676]

Entrepreneur (Vol. 33, January 2005, No. 1, pp. 27); "Key Bored? Innovative Alternatives to the Old QWERTY Keyboard" in [6700], [49112]

Entrepreneur; "Kick Back and Relax" in [35540], [54920]

Entrepreneur (Vol. 31, No. 5, May 2003, pp. 24); "Kid stuff: want to light your child's entrepreneurial fire?" in [36406], [56749]

Entrepreneur (Vol. 31, No. 6, June 2003, pp. 73); "Know your limits" in [29331], [40496], [53824]

Entrepreneur (Vol. 31, No. 9, September 2003, pp. 110); "Labor of Love" in [20259], [23765], [31756], [36414], [38843]

Entrepreneur (Vol. 31, No. 5, May 2003); "Labor pains: if immigration laws tighten, all entrepreneurs could feel the squeeze" in [29334], [40500], [42324]

Entrepreneur (Vol. 30, No. 3, March 2002, pp. 66); "Lack o' tax: the return from these funds all yours" in [15200], [38177], [54637]

Entrepreneur (Vol. 31, No. 6, June 2003, pp. 24); "Lagging behind? Get ahead of jet lag before it gets the best of you" in [30364]

Entrepreneur (Vol. 33, September 2005, No. 9, pp. 48); "Lapping It Up" in [6669], [6703], [49117], [51133]

Entrepreneur (Vol. 30, No. 2, February 2002, pp. 36); "Laser pointers" in [6704], [49118]

Entrepreneur (Vol. 27, No. 12, December 1999, pp. 144); "Last But Not Least" in [51709]

Entrepreneur (Vol. 30, No. 2, February 2002); "Laugh track" in [3550], [17901], [36418], [45343]

Entrepreneur (Vol. 30, No. 2, February 2002, pp. 18); "Laurel Touby" in [14193], [35545], [50908]

Entrepreneur (Vol. 31, No. 8, August 2003, pp. 53); "Law Away" in [10055], [15207], [38182]

Entrepreneur (Vol. 33, October 2005, No. 10, pp. 89); "Law of the Land" in [25899], [26277], [38183]

Entrepreneur (Vol. 32, October 2004, No. 10, pp. 98); "Law Talent" in [29345], [45345]

Entrepreneur (Vol. 31, No. 9, September 2003, pp. 39); "Lead the Way: New Gadgets Blaze Trails for Mobile Workers" in [6707], [10680], [14196], [49120]

Entrepreneur (Vol. 32, November 2004, No. 11, pp. 106); "Leader of the Pack" in [6097], [36419], [38845], [56295]

Entrepreneur (Vol. 32, October 2004, No. 10, pp. 21); "Leap of Faith" in [15211], [50044]

Entrepreneur; "Learn Your Lines" in [27418], [47189], [51712]

Entrepreneur (Vol. 33, September 2005, No. 9, pp. 126); "Learning Curve" in [32189], [33152], [36429], [37648]

Entrepreneur (Vol. 33, October 2005, No. 10, pp. 99); "Learning the Ropes" in [1], [13138], [21827], [22139], [23538], [23859], [28440], [29068], [37199], [38656], [41164], [43063]

Entrepreneur (Vol. 32, December 2004, No. 12, pp. 106); "Lease Lessons" in [20925], [21332], [52689]

Entrepreneur (Vol. 32, November 2004, No. 11, pp. 98); "Lease on Life?" in [9224], [18780], [24530], [26280], [29354], [40508]

Entrepreneur (Vol. 30, No. 12, December 2002, pp. 43); "Leasing 101: need a new fleet but low on dough? Leasing may be the key" in [18076], [49515], [49710]

Entrepreneur (Vol. 31, No. 8, August 2003, pp. 6); "Leasingsecrets.com" in [21334], [49121]

Entrepreneur; "Leave It To Them: Make Sure Your Family Gets What It Needs by Including a Disclaimer Provision in Your Estate Plan" in [29355], [54641]

Entrepreneur (Vol. 32, August 2004, No. 8, pp. 31); "Leave Me Alone!" in [690], [31757], [47190]

Entrepreneur (Vol. 32, December 2004, No. 12, pp. 8); "Leaving their Mark" in [36431], [39437]

Entrepreneur (Vol. 30, No. 1, January 2002, pp. 18); "Led poisoning" in [36432], [45366]

Entrepreneur (Vol. 32, October 2004, No. 10, pp. 89); "Legal Eagle?" in [691], [4715], [22280], [23065], [24290], [29359], [40510], [47191], [53351]

Entrepreneur (Vol. 32, No. 4, April 2004, pp. 22); "Leo Rivera" in [11793], [36437]

Entrepreneur (Vol. 33, October 2005, No. 10, pp. 100); "Less Is More" in [29857], [30656], [37200], [38657]

Entrepreneur (Vol. 31, No. 8, August 2003, pp. 114); "Less Is More: Believe It Or Not" in [8171], [46578], [48687]

Entrepreneur (Vol. 32, November 2004); "Let Them Eat Cake: When It Comes to Small Business, a New Tax-Cut Bill is Half-Baked" in [186], [23984], [26281], [46340], [54647]

Entrepreneur (Vol. 30, No. 10, Oct. 2002, pp. 42); "Lets get creative: creativity is what makes the world go round." in [36441]

Entrepreneur (Vol. 32, No. 4, April 2004, pp. 26); "Let's Do Launch" in [18077], [39441]

Entrepreneur (Vol. 32, November 2004, No. 11, pp. 34); "Let's Do Lunch: Giving New Meaning to the Term 'Power Lunch'" in [27419], [36442], [39442]

Entrepreneur (Vol. 32, July 2004); "Let's Have Some Funds!" in [55707], [56300]

Entrepreneur (Vol. 32, November 2004, No. 11, pp. 70); "Let's Make a Dual" in [15218], [50049]

Entrepreneur (Vol. 32, No. 4, April 2004); "Let's Talk About Sexism: Do Sexist Attitudes Still Exist in Business? Women Sound Off" in [32039], [45370], [56301]

Entrepreneur (Vol. 32, No. 2, February 2004, pp. 28); "Level Playing Field" in [30905], [40049]

Entrepreneur (Vol. 31, Oct. 2003); "Liar, Liar: In the Race to Make Money, Some American Businesses Have Been Lying Their Pants Off" in [29367], [37471]

Entrepreneur (Vol. 33, October 2005, No. 10, pp. 22); "License to Thrive" in [44085], [48762], [50734], [53833]

Entrepreneur (Vol. 32, September 2004, No. 9, pp. 44); "License to Upgrade" in [4717], [23068], [44087], [53353]

Entrepreneur (Vol. 30, No. 3, March 2002,); "Life in the slow lane" in [17314], [30906], [53834]

Entrepreneur (Vol. 31, October. 2003); "Lighten Up! Weighed Down By Your Portable PC?" in [6711], [49127]

Entrepreneur (Vol. 28, No. 3, March 2000, pp. 26); "Lightning Speed" in [14206], [41808], [52556]

Entrepreneur (Vol. 31, No. 4, April 2003, pp. 126); "Lights, camera, action" in [24425], [47196], [50619], [51231], [51716]

Entrepreneur; "Lights, Camera, Action! Do You Dream of Promoting Your Business On Oprah Or the Today Show, But Don't Know Where To Start?" in [695], [13661], [24343], [47195], [50618]

Entrepreneur (Vol. 32, November 2004, No. 11); "Listen Up! If You're Not Advertising on Internet Radio, You Could Be Missing Out" in [696], [14208], [20322], [34140], [47197]

Entrepreneur (Vol. 31, No. 10, October 2003, pp. 120); "Listen While You Work" in [17748], [20323], [34141]

Entrepreneur (Vol. 33, January 2005, No. 1, pp. 52); "Little Extras: Get More From Your Insurance Company than Just Coverage" in [13368], [43261]

Entrepreneur (Vol. 31, No. 9, September 2003, pp. 68); "Movin' On Up" in **[6729]**, **[49151]**

Entrepreneur (Vol. 32, October 2004, No. 10, pp. 28); "Moving On: Ex-Apprentices Find Life After 'The Donald' is All Business" in **[1835]**, **[5560]**, **[15281]**, **[20601]**, **[20946]**, **[31566]**, **[36512]**

Entrepreneur (Vol. 28, No. 8, August 2000, pp. 192); "Mr. Fix-It" in **[3561]**, **[14257]**

Entrepreneur (Vol. 32, July 2004, No. 7, pp. 32); "Mutual Attraction: Despite the Headlines, Mutual Funds are Still a Good Thing" in **[15284]**, **[38236]**

Entrepreneur (Vol. 33, March 2005, No. 3, pp. 94); "My Bad! Playing the Blame Game is Out." in **[39483]**, **[45452]**

Entrepreneur (Vol. 33, January 2005, No. 1, pp. 27); "My Kind of Town" in **[44101]**, **[52702]**

Entrepreneur (Vol. 30, No. 2, February 2002, pp. 20); "My, Oh, Miami" in **[25217]**, **[30380]**

Entrepreneur (Vol. 31, No. 6, June 2003, pp. 100); "Nab your Niche" in **[7431]**, **[47311]**, **[50638]**

Entrepreneur (Vol. 33, March 2005, No. 3, pp. 86); "Nail the Sale: Need Some Surefire Ways to Seal the Deal with Customers?" in **[51741]**

Entrepreneur (Vol. 33, March 2005, No. 3, pp. 53); "Name that Domain" in **[14267]**, **[24709]**, **[25218]**, **[25905]**

Entrepreneur (Vol. 33, September 2005, No. 9, pp. 108); "Name Your Price" in **[30214]**, **[31049]**

Entrepreneur (Vol. 28, No. 10, October 2000, pp. 138); "National" in **[35580]**, **[46583]**

Entrepreneur (Vol. 33, August 2005, No. 8, pp. 4); "National Association for the Exchange of Industrial Resources" in **[39485]**, **[40904]**, **[42271]**, **[44235]**, **[46383]**, **[54667]**

Entrepreneur (Vol. 33, October 2005, No. 10, pp. 26); "National Treasure" in **[36522]**, **[37743]**, **[39486]**

Entrepreneur (Vol. 31, No. 8, August 2003, pp. 90); "Natural Instinct" in **[4053]**, **[11303]**, **[12151]**, **[12757]**, **[26447]**, **[35581]**

Entrepreneur (Vol. 32, No. 1, January 2004, pp. 134); "Neck and Neck" in **[36523]**, **[38862]**

Entrepreneur (Vol. 30, No. 12, December 2002, pp. 109); "Needful things?" in **[36524]**, **[47315]**, **[51742]**

Entrepreneur (Vol. 33, October 2005, No. 10, pp. 54); "Net Deposits" in **[34241]**, **[38239]**

Entrepreneur (Vol. 27, No. 12, December 1999, pp. 48); "Net Profits" in **[14276]**, **[30240]**, **[34243]**

Entrepreneur (Vol. 31, No. 12, December 2003, pp. 8); "NetNose: www.netnose.com" in **[14277]**, **[25907]**, **[34244]**

The Entrepreneur Network **[44183]**

Entrepreneur (Vol. 33, March 2005, No. 3, pp. 48); "Network It" in **[6734]**, **[14280]**, **[49156]**

Entrepreneur (Vol. 30, No. 12, Dec. 2002); "Never say die: how a family beat the odds (and the weather) to improve a franchise" in **[37739]**, **[38863]**

Entrepreneur (Vol. 31, No. 6, June 2003, pp. 34); "New frontiers" in **[3564]**, **[9990]**, **[10102]**, **[15079]**, **[15296]**, **[36538]**, **[38241]**, **[43760]**

Entrepreneur (Vol. 32, August 2004, No. 8, pp. 67); "New Territory: To Get New Customers, Widen Your Ad Campaign" in **[735]**, **[24711]**, **[25223]**, **[47335]**

Entrepreneur (Vol. 33, February 2005, No. 2, pp. 49); "New Way to 7(a)" in **[39876]**, **[44603]**

Entrepreneur (Vol. 32, No. 4, April 2004, pp. 19); "New World Order: the European Union Will Soon be a Bigger Cash Cow" in **[28559]**, **[43764]**

Entrepreneur (Vol. 28, No. 9, September 2000, pp. 50); "New to You?" in **[39877]**, **[40571]**, **[44604]**

Entrepreneur (Vol. 28, No. 8, August 2000, pp. 34); "Newbie Rules" in **[42360]**

The Entrepreneur Next Door: Discover the Secrets to Financial Independence **[36070]**, **[39307]**

Entrepreneur (Vol. 30, No. 12, December 2002, pp. 111); "Nice meeting you!" in **[27456]**, **[36553]**, **[39499]**

Entrepreneur (Vol. 32, November 2004, No. 11, pp. 95); "Nip It In the Bud" in **[29417]**, **[45474]**

Entrepreneur (Vol. 31, No. 4, April 2003, pp. 17); "No Escape? Even the Internet May Not Be Able to Avoid Taxes" in **[14296]**, **[34266]**, **[54678]**

Entrepreneur (Vol. 32, October 2004, No. 10, pp. 107); "No Free Lunch" in **[12785]**, **[37745]**, **[38866]**

Entrepreneur (Vol. 31, No. 10, October 2003, pp. 60); "No Guts, Some Glory" in **[10110]**, **[15303]**, **[38248]**

Entrepreneur (Vol. 28, No. 11, November 2000, pp. 40); "No Husband, No Loan" in **[44606]**

Entrepreneur (Vol. 30, No. 12, December 2002, pp. 79); "No mercy: are VCs sucking the life out of your business?" in **[32601]**, **[55755]**

Entrepreneur (Vol. 33, February 2005, No. 2, pp. 34); "No More Ms. NiceGuy: Do Nice Girls Really Finish Last in the Business World" in **[45475]**, **[56351]**

Entrepreneur (Vol. 30, No. 12, December 2002, pp. 109); "No experience necessary" in **[42363]**, **[51745]**

Entrepreneur (Vol. 28, No. 4, April 2000, pp. 42); "No Pain, No Gain" in **[14299]**, **[34268]**

Entrepreneur (Vol. 32, December 2004, No. 12, pp. 108); "No Place Like Home" in **[453]**, **[19002]**, **[37746]**, **[52569]**

Entrepreneur (Vol. 33, October 2005, No. 10, pp. 56); "No Refuge" in **[51965]**, **[54679]**

Entrepreneur (Vol. 33, January 2005, No. 1, pp. 63); "No Surrender" in **[45476]**, **[51746]**

Entrepreneur (Vol. 32, December 2004, No. 12, pp. 126); "No Sweat" in **[5563]**, **[9633]**, **[23628]**

Entrepreneur (Vol. 32, October 2004, No. 10, pp. 96); "No Train, No Gain?" in **[27156]**, **[33192]**

Entrepreneur (Vol. 32, August 2004, No. 8, pp. 21); "Nobody's Fool? Health Insurance Scams Target Entrepreneurs" in **[13404]**, **[26862]**, **[30243]**, **[41070]**, **[43296]**

Entrepreneur (Vol. 31, August 2003); "Northern Exposure: American Entrepreneurs are Finding Success by Heading for the Border" in **[36560]**, **[55756]**

Entrepreneur (Vol. 31, No. 6, June 2003, pp. 30); "Not so fast!: Studies show many of you aren't looking before you leap" in **[30575]**, **[36562]**, **[39502]**

Entrepreneur (Vol. 30, No. 12, December 2002, pp. 103); "Not hiring" in **[29420]**, **[42365]**

Entrepreneur (Vol. 32, December 2004, No. 12, pp. 16); "Not Lost in Translation" in **[741]**, **[47353]**

Entrepreneur (Vol. 31, No. 9, September 2003, pp. 55); "Not So Fast! Raising Money: Seeking an Investor?" in **[20614]**, **[20954]**, **[44609]**, **[55757]**

Entrepreneur (Vol. 31, No. 8, August 2003, pp. 22); "Not Your Arena?" in **[23728]**, **[36563]**

Entrepreneur (Vol. 31, No. 10, October 2003, pp. 85); "Nothing Personal" in **[27458]**, **[39503]**

Entrepreneur (Vol. 32); "Novel Ideas: Two Entrepreneurs Write Books About Their Experiences-And Learn Something in the Process" in **[2601]**, **[2728]**, **[7901]**, **[11161]**, **[16461]**, **[46396]**, **[51275]**, **[56353]**

Entrepreneur (Vol. 33, October 2005, No. 10, pp. 18); "Now in 3-D" in **[25571]**, **[25918]**, **[34272]**

Entrepreneur (Vol. 33, March 2005, No. 3, pp. 87); "Now Playing" in **[742]**, **[17527]**, **[47355]**

Entrepreneur (Vol. 32, No. 1, January 2004, pp. 46); "Now Presenting..." in **[4194]**, **[6743]**, **[22535]**, **[49177]**, **[53389]**

Entrepreneur (Vol. 31, No. 9, September 2003); "Now Showing: Win Partners by Letting Them See What You're Made Of" in **[44106]**, **[50112]**

Entrepreneur (Vol. 31, Aug.2003); "Now You See It: Payroll Tax is Likely the Tax You Most Want to Have Cut, But Will It Ever Happen?" in **[210]**, **[2940]**, **[24004]**, **[26306]**, **[54682]**

Entrepreneur (Vol. 30, No. 3, March 2002, pp.); "Now you've done it! Real deal" in **[27459]**, **[47357]**

Entrepreneur (Vol. 32, December 2004, No. 12, pp. 46); "Numbers Game" in **[18104]**, **[39505]**, **[40582]**, **[41881]**, **[48589]**

Entrepreneur (Vol. 31, No. 8, August 2003, pp. 23); "Of One Mind: Keep Employees by Getting on the Same Page From the Get-Go" in **[42368]**, **[45482]**

Entrepreneur (Vol. 31, No. 11, November 2003, pp. 60); "Office Offers" in **[4747]**, **[23106]**, **[49181]**, **[53392]**

Entrepreneur (Vol. 30, No. 10, October 2002, pp. 91); "Ok, let's review" in **[45485]**, **[51752]**

Entrepreneur (Vol. 31, No. 10, October 2003, pp. 6); "Olddebts.com: www.olddebts.com" in **[31572]**

Entrepreneur (Vol. 30, No. 2, February 2002, pp. 39); "On the Agenda" in **[34277]**, **[40591]**

Entrepreneur (Vol. 32); "On the Disabled List? Save Employees (and Your Business) a World of Hurt With Disability Insurance" in **[13407]**, **[26865]**, **[43299]**

Entrepreneur (Vol. 31, No. 9, September 2003, pp. 46); "On Display" in **[6745]**, **[49183]**

Entrepreneur (Vol. 33, October 2005, No. 10, pp. 40); "On the Edge" in **[6708]**, **[6746]**, **[10005]**, **[10119]**, **[15101]**, **[15319]**, **[38256]**, **[46844]**, **[49184]**

Entrepreneur (Vol. 32, October 2004, No. 10, pp. 28); "On the Fly: Try These Money-Saving Tricks for Last-Minute Travel Plans" in **[25228]**, **[30395]**

Entrepreneur (Vol. 31, No. 11, November 2003); "On Guard: What Does it Take to Keep Your Computers and Intellectual Property Safe?" in **[6748]**, **[22318]**, **[44347]**

Entrepreneur (Vol. 31, No. 8, August 2003, pp. 67); "On the Job" in **[13408]**, **[43300]**

Entrepreneur (Vol. 33, October 2005, No. 10, pp. 82); "On the Lookout" in **[28586]**, **[51277]**

Entrepreneur (Vol. 33, October 2005, No. 10, pp. 87); "On the Merge" in **[15103]**, **[15321]**, **[29886]**, **[30692]**, **[33930]**, **[35009]**, **[47730]**, **[50118]**

Entrepreneur (Vol. 31, No. 11, November 2003, pp. 65); "On the Move?" in **[17425]**, **[34279]**, **[53897]**

Entrepreneur (Vol. 31, No. 4, April 2003, pp. 168); "On the record" in **[6137]**, **[17761]**, **[21143]**, **[36574]**

Entrepreneur (Vol. 32, September 2004, No. 9, pp. 30); "On the Rise: What Will Expected Interest-Rate Hikes Mean To You?" in **[32612]**, **[38259]**

Entrepreneur (Vol. 32, November 2004, No. 11, pp. 39); "On the Road? Then Don't Forget to Pack These Tech Essentials" in **[5078]**, **[41885]**

Entrepreneur (Vol. 28, No. 8, August 2000, pp. 23); "On a Roll" in **[49186]**, **[53396]**

Entrepreneur (Vol. 31, No. 9, September 2003, pp. 118); "On a Shoestring" in **[2396]**, **[2602]**, **[6268]**, **[7740]**, **[14309]**, **[31805]**, **[36576]**, **[37748]**

Entrepreneur (Vol. 31, No. 11, November 2003, pp. 99); "On Target: Get the Specifics on Potential Customers" in **[47364]**, **[51757]**

Entrepreneur (Vol. 32, August 2004, No. 8, pp. 88); "On Target: You Need Market Research to Hit the Mark with Prospects" in **[16821]**, **[47365]**

Entrepreneur (Vol. 28, No. 2, February 2000, pp. 20); "Once Upon A Time" in **[45491]**

Entrepreneur (Vol. 30, No. 12, December 2002, pp. 144); "One of a kind? Make your product conform to break away from the norm" in **[43966]**, **[46585]**, **[48773]**

Entrepreneur (Vol. 31, No. 5, May 2003, pp. 48); "One-stop shop? Brokerage firms make a play for your bank business, too" in **[10122]**, **[15324]**, **[38263]**

Entrepreneur (Vol. 32, No. 1, January 2004, pp. 47); "Online Office" in **[4751]**, **[23111]**, **[27464]**, **[34296]**, **[53398]**

Entrepreneur (Vol. 33, October 2005, No. 10, pp. 6); "Onvia Business Builder" in **[34307]**, **[40071]**

Entrepreneur (Vol. 31, No. 9, September 2003, pp. 72); "Open Doors?" in **[20618]**, **[20958]**, **[36586]**, **[40595]**, **[53900]**

Entrepreneur (Vol. 30, No. 2, Fe); "Opportunities" in **[20619]**, **[36589]**, **[37749]**, **[38870]**

Entrepreneur (Vol. 28, No. 8, August 2000, pp. 40); "Opportunity of the Fly" in **[39971]**, **[56066]**

Entrepreneur (Vol. 31, No. 8, August 2003, pp. 6); "Opt-In News" in [749], [20143], [34311], [47378]

Entrepreneur (Vol. 33, August 2005, No. 8, pp. 4); "Optimost" in [25578], [25927], [33276], [34312]

Entrepreneur (Vol. 33, January 2005, No. 1); "Opting Out? Don't Want to Stick with the Microsoft's Default Browser Applications?" in [14328]

Entrepreneur (Vol. 28, No. 1, January 2000, pp. 26); "Our Kinda Town" in [3484], [13770], [33476], [35600]

Entrepreneur (Vol. 31, No. 9, September 2003, pp. 104); "Out of the Ashes: This Company Faced Sure Disaster-But Came Out Shining" in [46399]

Entrepreneur (Vol. 30, No. 12, December 2002, pp. 83); "Out with the bad, in with the good" in [44236], [54690]

Entrepreneur (Vol. 32, August 2004); "Out in the Cold? If Wi-Fi 'Cold Spots' Are Leaving You in the Lurch, Try These Solutions" in [6750], [41893]

Entrepreneur (Vol. 30, No. 2, February 2002, pp. 22); "Out of control? Has individualized investing come and gone?" in [15332], [38269]

Entrepreneur (Vol. 32, No. 1, January 2004, pp. 24); "Out with the Old?" in [36597], [38667], [39515]

Entrepreneur (Vol. 32, August 2004, No. 8, pp. 31); "Out of Sight: Stock Options Can Stay Off Your Balance Sheet-For Now" in [217], [2943], [15333], [24009], [26314]

Entrepreneur (Vol. 30, No. 3, March 2002, pp. 65); "Out of stock" in [15334], [28603], [45505], [50122]

Entrepreneur (Vol. 31, No. 8, August 2003, pp. 43); "Out With the Old?" in [6751], [21248], [37313], [49193]

Entrepreneur (Vol. 33, October 2005, No. 10, pp. 56); "Over the Limit" in [10013], [10127], [38270]

Entrepreneur (Vol. 31, No. 8, August 2003, pp. 65); "Owning Up" in [36598], [45511], [52713]

Entrepreneur (Vol. 31, No. 11, November 2003, pp. 102); "Pack a Punch" in [751], [6752], [22540], [47385], [49195]

Entrepreneur (Vol. 31, No. 4, April 2003, pp. 22); "Package deal" in [28610], [32623], [38873], [39518], [40602], [54692]

Entrepreneur (Vol. 32, November 2004, No. 11, pp. 62); "Pain-Free Patching" in [4757], [23118], [44110], [53403]

Entrepreneur (Vol. 32, October 2004, No. 10, pp. 60); "Papers Away: Tax Records Weighing You Down? Switch to Electronic Storage" in [219], [22321], [24010], [26316], [54694]

Entrepreneur (Vol. 33, March 2005, No. 3, pp. 96); "Parent Trap?" in [35303], [36602], [37820], [42374], [52239], [54973]

Entrepreneur (Vol. 31, No. 4, April 2003, pp. 76); "Parents for hire" in [36603], [42375], [45513]

Entrepreneur (Vol. 32); "Passing the Buck" in [5082], [14338], [49197]

Entrepreneur (Vol. 31, No. 11, November 2003, pp. 70); "Passing Marks?" in [221], [24012], [26318], [40605], [54695]

Entrepreneur (Vol. 31, No. 11, November 2003, pp. 97); "Passing the Torch" in [45515], [51762]

Entrepreneur (Vol. 32, December 2004, No. 12, pp. 52); "Password Protection" in [4759], [22322], [23120], [53404]

Entrepreneur (Vol. 33, October 2005, No. 10, pp. 28); "Patent Pending" in [28778], [29434], [44115]

Entrepreneur (Vol. 32, October 2004, No. 10, pp. 102); "Paternal Instincts" in [753], [47388]

Entrepreneur (Vol. 32, December 2004, No. 12, pp. 93); "Patriot Acts: Should You Play Up the 'Made in the USA' Angle?" in [754], [47389]

Entrepreneur (Vol. 28, No. 11, November 2000, pp. 22); "Pattern Behavior" in [14339], [29437], [44122]

Entrepreneur (Vol. 32, September 2004, No. 9, pp. 80); "Pay Attention" in [18785], [36607]

Entrepreneur (Vol. 30, No. 10, October 2002, pp. 38); "Pay you back: your employees may be better off driving their own cars" in [26870], [30739]

Entrepreneur (Vol. 31, No. 11, November 2003); "Pay Dirt! Finally Making a Profit? Put It Where It Belongs-Back in Your Business" in [26320], [38276]

Entrepreneur (Vol. 32, August 2004, No. 8); "Payback Time: Mutual Funds are Paying the Price, But Will You Get Your Fair Share?" in [15344], [38277], [40608]

Entrepreneur (Vol. 31, No. 5, May 2003, pp. 70); "Paying your respects" in [35017], [45523]

Entrepreneur (Vol. 32); "Paying Your Dues" in [5083], [41897], [44619]

Entrepreneur (Vol. 31, No. 9, September 2003, pp. 61); "Payroll Piggy Bank?" in [222], [18787], [29438], [54698]

Entrepreneur (Vol. 30, No. 2, February 2002, pp. 28); "Peaks & Silicon Valleys" in [49200], [49534]

Entrepreneur (Vol. 30, No. 1, January 2002, pp. 10); "Peek ahead" in [28616], [32624]

Entrepreneur (Vol. 33, January 2005, No. 1, pp. 70); "Peering In" in [35018], [42377], [45524]

Entrepreneur (Vol. 28, No. 6, June 2000, pp. 155); "Pennsylvania" in [35604], [39774], [40125], [54410]

Entrepreneur (Vol. 31, No. 5, May 2003, pp. 76); "People who need people" in [51763]

Entrepreneur (Vol. 32, No. 1, January 2004, pp. 10); "PeopleProfileUSA" in [16822], [34338], [47393]

Entrepreneur (Vol. 32, No. 4, April 2004, pp. 39); "Performing Triage" in [22140], [34343], [35607]

Entrepreneur (Vol. 32, No. 1, January 2004, pp. 42); "Peripherals Vision" in [6755], [49203]

Entrepreneur (Vol. 31, No. 8, August 2003, pp. 71); "Perk Avenue" in [35019], [47396]

Entrepreneur (Vol. 32, No. 1, January 2004, pp. 228); "Personal Care" in [455], [3323], [8694], [38876]

Entrepreneur (Vol. 31, No. 8, August 2003, pp. 51); "Personal Decision" in [5085], [14349], [34345], [49205]

Entrepreneur (Vol. 30, No. 2, February 2002, pp. 22); "Personal issues" in [13087], [22324], [31816], [34346]

Entrepreneur (Vol. 32, November 2004, No. 11, pp. 30); "Pet Projects: Cats and Dogs and Babies, Oh My!" in [35022], [53916]

Entrepreneur (Vol. 32, No. 1, January 2004, pp. 232); "Pets" in [19081], [19115], [19155], [38877]

Entrepreneur (Vol. 31, No. 8, August 2003, pp. 43); "Phone, Camera, Action!(Wireless)" in [4195], [5087], [49206]

Entrepreneur (Vol. 33, October 2005, No. 10, pp. 40); "Phone on the Range" in [5088], [46866], [49207]

Entrepreneur (Vol. 28, No. 3, March 2000, pp. 220); "Pick A Topic" in [34347]

Entrepreneur (Vol. 31, No. 11, November 2003, pp. 95); "Pick Your Battles" in [36628], [45535]

Entrepreneur (Vol. 32); "Picture Perfect " in [4196], [49208]

Entrepreneur (Vol. 32, July 2004, No. 7, pp. 46); "Picture This" in [4197], [4763], [6000], [6756], [23125], [49209], [53411]

Entrepreneur (Vol. 32, November 2004, No. 11, pp. 112); "Planning for Gold" in [29756], [30933], [35610], [55777]

Entrepreneur (Vol. 28, No. 11, November 2000, pp. 38); "Play Keyboard for Cash" in [11799], [14352], [15359], [34350]

Entrepreneur (Vol. 32, September 2004, No. 9, pp. 32); "Play Nice" in [36631], [54976]

Entrepreneur (September 2004); "Playing Cupid: These Matchmaking Sisters Aim to Give Busy Singles a Fast-and Fun-Way to Date" in [7066], [37760], [38883]

Entrepreneur (Vol. 30, No.); "Playing e-Detective" in [34352], [42379]

Entrepreneur (Vol. 31, No. 4, April 2003, pp. 22); "Playing favorites" in [4581], [22887], [34353], [35611], [36634], [39529], [45544], [55418], [56369]

Entrepreneur (Vol. 32, No. 4, April 2004, pp. 35); "Playing It Safe: What Can You Do to Protect Your E-Commerce Site From Fraud?" in [14353], [22327], [34354]

Entrepreneur (Vol. 30, No. 10, October 2002, pp. 34); "Please stay! You have the hotels rights where you want them" in [12618], [30403]

Entrepreneur (Vol. 30, No. 1, January 2002, pp. 44); "Pocket protector" in [6759], [49211]

Entrepreneur (Vol. 32, November 2004, No. 11, pp. 26); "Point of Sale: Software Giants Focus on Selling to Small Businesses" in [4766], [23129], [53414]

Entrepreneur (Vol. 28, No. 4, April 2000, pp. 114); "Poor Health" in [43315]

Entrepreneur (Vol. 31, No. 5, May 2003, pp. 35); "Portable lite" in [6760], [49212]

Entrepreneur (Vol. 30, No. 12, December 2002, pp. 77); "Postage unpaid" in [24016], [53922], [54706]

Entrepreneur (Vol. 32, No. 1, January 2004, pp. 37); "Power House" in [6761], [7741], [41912]

Entrepreneur (Vol. 32, August 2004, No. 8, pp. 42); "Power Play" in [4198], [6762], [6957], [7026], [30404], [46872], [49213]

Entrepreneur (Vol. 28, No. 4, April 2000, pp. 62); "Power Shopping" in [36639], [51295], [56371]

Entrepreneur (Vol. 31, No. 9, September 2003, pp. 20); "Power Up!" in [28640], [39531]

Entrepreneur (Vol. 32, No. 1, January 2004, pp. 10); "PR Leads www.prleads.com" in [47417], [50460], [50651]

Entrepreneur (Vol. 31, No. 11, November 2003, pp. 97); "PR Power" in [47418], [50461], [50652]

Entrepreneur (Vol. 31, No. 6, June 2003, pp. 124); "Prepare for takeoff" in [30586], [36640]

Entrepreneur; "Press Conference: You've Worked Hard to Land That Media Interview-So Don't Blow Your Opportunity" in [22549], [27475], [47422], [50653]

Entrepreneur (Vol. 33, September 2005, No. 9, pp. 56); "Price Fix" in [30221], [31056], [51296]

Entrepreneur (Vol. 31, No. 10, October 2003, pp. 94); "Price is Right: 114 Franchises You Can Buy for Less than $25,000" in [38887]

Entrepreneur (Vol. 27, No. 12, December 1999, pp. 20); "Prince of Management" in [45563]

Entrepreneur (Vol. 28, No. 1, January 2000, pp. 38); "Priority Mail" in [14364], [31824], [34366]

Entrepreneur (Vol. 32, October 2004, No. 10, pp. 38); "Private Matters: Retail Alert: Keep an Eye on New RFID Privacy Legislation" in [22332], [29449], [40626], [41918], [51299]

Entrepreneur (Vol. 33, September 2005, No. 9, pp. 6); "ProcessLibrary.com" in [6411], [14215], [14367], [22333]

Entrepreneur (Vol. 33, August 2005, No. 8, pp. 26); "Promised Land" in [41921], [43789], [50144]

Entrepreneur (Vol. 32, September 2004); "Proper Care and Feeding: Think Your CDs and DVDs are Indestructible? Guess Again" in [6768], [49219]

Entrepreneur (Vol. 33, February 2005, No. 2, pp. 46); "Protect the Source" in [4772], [6769], [22335], [23136], [53421]

Entrepreneur (Vol. 31, No. 7, July 2003, pp. 64); "Prove Your Worth: Forget the Stock Market." in [29966], [36656]

Entrepreneur (Vol. 33, August 2005, No. 8, pp. 4); "Proxity Electronic Commerce System" in [34376], [35554], [40079]

Entrepreneur (Vol. 30, No. 10, October 2002, pp. 76); "Public opinion" in [15384], [50148], [55787]

Entrepreneur (Vol. 32, No. 2, February 2004, pp. 73); "Pump it Up" in [36659], [51780]

Entrepreneur (Vol. 33, January 2005, No. 1, pp. 20); "Put Your Finger On It" in [6771], [22338], [49221]

Entrepreneur (Vol. 32, No. 4, April 2004, pp. 34); "Putting the Heat on Spam" in [14378], [22339], [34385]

Entrepreneur (Vol. 30, No. 3, March 2002, pp. 106); "Putting signage on shirts is a cinch for sign-a-Rama's founder" in [22728], [22794], [36662], [38888]

Entrepreneur; "Quality Time: Not Getting What You Want Out of Your Sales Meeting? Here are 5 Tips to Point You in the Right Direction" in [27480], [35035], [45575], [51782]

Entrepreneur (Vol. 32, No. 4, April 2004, pp. 27; "Quick Fix: Do SBA Express Loans Really Shortchange Entrepreneurs?" in [36665], [39892], [44625], [46412], [51302], [56016]

Entrepreneur (Vol. 30, No. 2, February 2002, pp. 34); "Quick fix: Help your IT staff save time and energy with PC Pinpoint" in [6412], [34393]

Entrepreneur (Vol. 32, No. 1, January 2004, pp. 79); "Quick Pick" in [767], [3574], [8625], [18244], [18930], [20329], [24445], [29970], [47378], [47444], [48369], [50659], [53426]

Entrepreneur (Vol. 33, September 2005, No. 9, pp. 6); "QuickSeek" in [708], [768], [28668], [34394], [35572], [45226], [47446]

Entrepreneur (Vol. 31, No. 9, July 2003, pp. 79); "Radical Rendezvous: Bye-Bye Boring" in [22551], [25006], [51784]

Entrepreneur (Vol. 30, No. 2, February 2002, pp. 96); "Rah-Rah rides" in [1880], [35617]

Entrepreneur; "Raise Your Voice: A New Committee Promises to Give Small Businesses a Say in Accounting Standards. But Will It Help?" in [235], [2950], [26337]

Entrepreneur (Vol. 32, July 2004); "Raising the Woof: Make No Bones About It-This Bakery Takes Dog Food to a Whole New Level" in [2224], [19141], [37573], [38672], [56071]

Entrepreneur (Vol. 31, No. 5, May 2003, pp. 45); "Ray of hope?" in [44628], [55798]

Entrepreneur (Vol. 32, December 2004, No. 12); "Reaching Out: Finding Good Leads Takes More Than Just Making a Few Phone Calls." in [51785]

Entrepreneur (Vol. 33, August 2005, No. 8, pp. 4); "ReachLocal" in [709], [769], [34400], [45231], [47451]

Entrepreneur (Vol. 33, February 2005, No. 2, pp. 8); "Ready Business: www.ready.gov" in [14387], [22342]

Entrepreneur (Vol. 31, No. 9, September 2003, pp. 87); "Ready? Set? Search! Rev Up Your Sales With Comparison-Shopping Engines" in [31061], [34402], [47452], [51786]

Entrepreneur (Vol. 31, No. 8, August 2003, pp. 25); "Reality Check: Even the Best Execs Can Blow It When They Lose Tough" in [29975], [33481]

Entrepreneur (Vol. 30, No. 3, March 2002, pp.); "Recession session" in [28678], [32654], [36678], [38309], [41936], [45580], [47456]

Entrepreneur (Vol. 32, November 2004, No. 11, pp. 75); "Recipe for Disaster?" in [13438], [43333]

Entrepreneur (Vol. 32, September 2004); "Recipe for Success: Smart Partnering Can Transform a Lone Inventor Into a Market Force" in [12205], [44131]

Entrepreneur (Vol. 32, No. 1, January 2004, pp. 234); "Recreation" in [5914], [8908], [12206], [12309], [23631], [38895]

Entrepreneur (Vol. 28, No. 1, January 2000, pp. 138); "Reeling in the Big Ones" in [35622], [51503]

Entrepreneur (Vol. 30, No. 3, March 2002, pp. 87); "Refer madness" in [34403], [47459], [51790]

Entrepreneur (Vol. 31, No. 5, May 2003, pp. 50); "Reforming pro forma" in [236], [2951], [24023], [29466], [38312], [40634]

Entrepreneur (Vol. 32, October 2004, No. 10, pp. 32); "Regulation Nation" in [28694], [29467], [40635]

Entrepreneur (Vol. 31, No. 8, August 2003, pp. 24); "Regulatory Rescue" in [39896], [40636]

Entrepreneur (Vol. 32, No. 1, January 2004, pp. 47); "Relationship Advice" in [31833], [34405], [51792]

Entrepreneur (Vol. 30, No. 3, March 2002, pp. 24); "Relaxed fit: Tailor your travel for less stress and maximum chill" in [3047], [17009], [25595], [30409]

Entrepreneur; "Release the Hounds " in [772], [14392], [34406], [47462]

Entrepreneur; "Relief Valve? Done Right, a Private Investment in Public Equity, Or Pipe, Could Bring Your Business Much-Needed Cash" in [10159], [15408], [38314]

Entrepreneur (Vol. 33, February 2005, No. 2, pp. 56); "Remote Control" in [36686], [45591], [51795]

Entrepreneur (Vol. 31, No. 7, July 2003, pp. 32); "Required Reading" in [29980], [36688], [56383]

Entrepreneur (Vol. 33, August 2005, No. 8, pp. 15); "Rescue Mission" in [41855], [43795], [54245]

Entrepreneur (Vol. 33, October 2005, No. 10, pp. 53); "Rescue Plan" in [9230], [9574], [39898]

Entrepreneur (Vol. 31, No. 5, May 2003, pp. 40); "Research methods" in [14395], [34408], [51308]

"Entrepreneur in Residence" in *Red Herring* (No. 87, December 18, 2000, pp. 212) [30478], [35414]

Entrepreneur (Vol. 32, August 2004, No. 8, pp. 53); "Resource Directory" in [39560]

Entrepreneur (Vol. 32, February 2004, pp. 8); "Resources: Web Sites, Organizations, Events and More to Grow Your Business" in [6779], [12625], [14397], [18246], [20656], [20995], [21595], [22554], [25009], [25946], [28697], [29480], [31208], [34409], [35815], [40082], [40644], [41945], [43796], [44134], [44358], [45102], [47463], [51309], [53437], [55150], [56384]

Entrepreneur (Vol. 32, September 2004, No. 9, pp. 8); "Resources: Web Sites, Organizations, Events and More To Grow Your Business" in [25947], [28698], [34410], [39899], [40645], [41946], [43797], [44634], [51796], [54722], [55806], [56760]

Entrepreneur (Vol. 32, No. 1, January 2004, pp. 238); "Retail" in [10694], [19821], [38899], [51311]

Entrepreneur (Vol. 28, No. 4, April 2000, pp. 58); "Retailers, Beware" in [31836], [51320]

Entrepreneur (Vol. 33, September 2005, No. 9, pp. 68); "Retire Rich" in [15186], [15414], [36694], [38320]

Entrepreneur (Vol. 33, September 2005, No. 9, pp. 28); "Return To Me" in [28710], [47470]

Entrepreneur (Vol. 33, October 2005, No. 10, pp. 60); "Revamping Roth" in [10048], [10166], [15193], [15421], [38324]

Entrepreneur (Vol. 31, No. 8, August 2003, pp. 6); "Reveries" in [47473]

Entrepreneur (Vol. 28, No. 2, February 2000, pp. 125); "Review with Care" in [37768]

Entrepreneur (Vol. 32, December 2004, No. 12, pp. 39); "Reward Me: Rebates and Incentives Make Buying all the More Appealing" in [18117], [44242], [47474], [51801]

Entrepreneur (Vol. 33, October 2005, No. 10, pp. 48); "Rich in Fiber" in [5096], [14245], [14401], [46887], [49230]

Entrepreneur (Vol. 31, No. 8, August, 2003, pp. 19); "Richard Rhodes" in [1531], [7472], [36699]

Entrepreneur (Vol. 33, August 2005, No. 8, pp. 40); "Right in Sight" in [4185], [4199], [22345], [40997], [42888]

Entrepreneur (Vol. 30, No. 1, January 2002, pp. 47); "Right to the source" in [6278], [6481], [14404], [34418]

Entrepreneur (Vol. 33, February 2005, No. 2, pp. 65); "Right on Target" in [51807]

Entrepreneur; "Ring Bearers: Some Would-Be Grooms Need a Little Direction in Finding the Perfect Diamond. Here Comes the Guides" in [3192], [15857], [37769]

Entrepreneur (Vol. 30, No. 1, January 2002, pp. 36); "Rising money" in [35627], [44435], [48889], [55423]

Entrepreneur (Vol. 31, No. 6, June 2003, pp. 73); "Risky business: on the lookout for business insurance?" in [13453], [43348], [53946]

Entrepreneur (Vol. 31, No. 9, September 2003, pp. 78); "Risky Business: Staff Smarts" in [31582], [42401]

Entrepreneur (Vol. 32, August 2004, No. 8, pp. 26); "Risky Business: Wacky Marketing Moves Put These Businesses on the Map" in [47480], [50663]

Entrepreneur (Vol. 33, September 2005, No. 9, pp. 85); "Road Signs" in [775], [47482]

Entrepreneur (Vol. 31, No. 9, September 2003); "Roamin' Holiday: Let a Vacation Put You On the Road to a Great Start-Up Idea" in [9637], [36703]

Entrepreneur (Vol. 33, January 2005, No. 1, pp. 104); "Robert Wagner Hosts The Litigation Explosion" in [22349], [29470], [31209], [38327], [54728]

Entrepreneur (Vol. 31, No. 6, June 2003, pp. 106); "Rolling dough: do you go with original butter and salt or almond crunch?" in [20179], [38900]

Entrepreneur (Vol. 32, November 2004, No. 11, pp. 64); "Room to Grow" in [6279], [49235]

Entrepreneur (Vol. 31, No. 6, June 2003, pp. 28); "Room to Grow: yes, even in the most stagnant economy, it's possible to expand" in [16530], [28720], [32675]

Entrepreneur (Vol. 32, December 2004, No. 12, pp. 54); "Rout and About" in [6781], [14405], [30413], [49236]

Entrepreneur (Vol. 31, No. 10, October 2003, pp. 120); "Ruffing It" in [12631], [19082]

Entrepreneur (Vol. 30, No. 3, March 2002, pp. 123); "Run for the border" in [43803], [44140], [46423], [48785]

Entrepreneur (Vol. 33, August 2005, No. 8, pp. 20); "Running Dry" in [36883], [38269], [38330], [39903], [44638], [55813]

Entrepreneur (Vol. 31, No. 11, November 2003, pp. 93); "Safety Dance: Get Policies in Place Now, and Avoid Liability Later" in [13456], [43352], [56586]

Entrepreneur (Vol. 31, No. 11, November 2003, pp. 60); "Safety First" in [4786], [22355], [23156], [49239], [53442]

Entrepreneur (Vol. 33, September 2005, No. 9, pp. 86); "Sage Advice" in [27059], [27489], [47484]

Entrepreneur (Vol. 28, No. 4, April 2000, pp. 149); "Said The Spider" in [31210], [51810]

Entrepreneur (July 2004); "Sales Report: Once Tainted by Get-Rich-Quick Schemes, the Direct-Sales Industry is Changing its Image" in [51342], [51820], [53950]

Entrepreneur (Vol. 31, No. 10, October 2003, pp. 57); "Save the Date" in [4789], [23160], [49240], [53447]

Entrepreneur (Vol. 32, December 2004, No. 12, pp. 68); "Save It For Later" in [26907], [38333]

Entrepreneur (Vol. 31, No. 9, September 2003, pp. 27); "Saving the Day: Does Your Brand Need Triage? Here's Something to Help" in [47493], [50668]

Entrepreneur (Vol. 33, March 2005, No. 3, pp. 48); "Say Cheese!" in [4200], [49242]

Entrepreneur (Vol. 33, January 2005, No. 1, pp. 66); "Say It Again" in [777], [47495]

Entrepreneur (Vol. 32, December 2004, No. 12, pp. 98); "Say What? Decipher Common Contract Legalese" in [29478], [40664]

Entrepreneur (Vol. 32, August 2004, No. 8, pp. 43); "Say the Word" in [6282], [6783]

Entrepreneur (Vol. 31, No. 10, October 2003, pp. 6); "SBA's Office of Entrepreneurial Development: www.sba.gov/training" in [35631], [39775]

Entrepreneur (Vol. 33, March 2005, No. 3, pp. 50); "Scan Artists" in [6784], [49243]

Entrepreneur (Vol. 32, October 2004, No. 10, pp. 90); "Scare Tactics: Creative Ways to Profit from Halloween" in [47498], [51344]

Entrepreneur (Vol. 30, No. 3, March 2002, pp. 116); "Scenic route" in [10911], [24727], [25242], [36720]

Entrepreneur (Vol. 30, No. 2, February 2002); "Sci-Finance" in [44142], [50962], [52196]

Entrepreneur (Vol. 31, Oct. 2003); "Score Savvy: Business Credit Scores are on the Horizon" in [31583], [38339], [44651]

Entrepreneur (Vol. 33, February 2005, No. 2, pp. 42); "Screen Dream" in [6785], [49244]

Entrepreneur (Vol. 32, October 2004, No. 10, pp. 54); "Screen Test: Time for a Monitor Upgrade?" in **[6786]**, **[49245]**

Entrepreneur (Vol. 31, No. 6, June 2003); "'?Se Habla Espanol? If you don't already, it's time to start. " in **[779]**, **[47504]**

Entrepreneur (Vol. 33, October 2005, No. 10, pp. 6); "SE Tools" in **[25594]**, **[25951]**, **[33396]**, **[34440]**

Entrepreneur (Vol. 33, September 2005, No. 9, pp. 28); "Search Party" in **[33980]**, **[35060]**, **[53955]**

Entrepreneur (Vol. 32, December 2004, No. 12, pp. 42); "Second Act" in **[18119]**, **[38341]**

Entrepreneur (Vol. 33, September 2005, No. 9, pp. 58); "Second Chance" in **[23701]**, **[24030]**, **[38991]**, **[40679]**, **[52019]**, **[54738]**

Entrepreneur (Vol. 31, No. 7, July 2003, pp. 24); "Second Time Around" in **[13777]**, **[33486]**, **[35633]**, **[41480]**

Entrepreneur (Vol. 31, No. 4, April 2003, pp. 18); "Second wind" in **[6788]**, **[49247]**, **[53956]**

Entrepreneur (Vol. 31, No. 9, July 2003, pp. 86); "Secrets to Success: Yes, You Can Be a Successful Franchisee in 2003" in **[35634]**, **[38675]**

Entrepreneur (Vol. 33, March 2005, No. 3, pp. 46); "Security Blanket" in **[1193]**, **[14421]**, **[22363]**, **[23164]**, **[53453]**

Entrepreneur (Vol. 30, No. 3, March 2002, pp. 19); "Security Blanket: Terrorists changed your employees" in **[35062]**, **[45628]**, **[53957]**

Entrepreneur (Vol. 33, October 2005, No. 10, pp. 24); "Security Breach? New Laws Could Change How You Handle Customer Info" in **[6283]**, **[22364]**, **[28821]**, **[29482]**

Entrepreneur (Vol. 31, No. 7, July 2003, pp. 31); "Seeing is Believing" in **[4201]**, **[5102]**

Entrepreneur (Vol. 32, November 2004, No. 11); "Seeing is Believing: Will VoIP Technology Finally Make Videoconferencing a Reality?" in **[5103]**, **[6791]**, **[14423]**, **[27494]**

Entrepreneur (Vol. 33, September 2005, No. 9, pp. 56); "Seeing Green" in **[10057]**, **[10178]**, **[15211]**, **[15443]**, **[36894]**, **[38343]**, **[44653]**, **[55819]**

Entrepreneur (Vol. 32, November 2004, No. 11, pp. 126); "Seeing Greens" in **[781]**, **[11272]**, **[47507]**

Entrepreneur (Vol. 33, September 2005, No. 9, pp. 92); "Seeing the Light" in **[19232]**, **[19435]**, **[21618]**, **[28171]**, **[28752]**, **[37969]**, **[38993]**, **[39568]**, **[40681]**, **[51348]**

Entrepreneur (Vol. 33, September 2005, No. 9, pp. 120); "Seeing the Sites" in **[25597]**, **[25955]**, **[33407]**, **[34451]**, **[47509]**

Entrepreneur (Vol. 33, August 2005, No. 8, pp. 18); "Seeing Stars" in **[12550]**, **[12633]**, **[29663]**, **[30415]**, **[33408]**, **[34452]**

"Entrepreneur Seeks Riches In Pixels-Again" in *Wall Street Journal* (Vol. 248, December 2006, No. 149, pp. B4) **[614]**, **[14016]**, **[25843]**, **[33853]**

Entrepreneur; "Seller's Market: Selling on eBay Can Help You Grow Your Business, But is This Site the Right Marketplace For You?" in **[1851]**, **[51829]**

Entrepreneur (Vol. 31, No. 9, September 2003, pp. 128); "Send in the Clones" in **[30948]**, **[44143]**

Entrepreneur (Vol. 33, January 2005, No. 1, pp. 47); "Send Out the Search Party" in **[6792]**, **[23166]**, **[53457]**

Entrepreneur (Vol. 31, No. 9, July 2003); "Sending Out an SOS: Our Franchisees Just Hit an Iceberg in Negotiating Their Land Deal" in **[20665]**, **[37776]**, **[38902]**

Entrepreneur (Vol. 31, No. 10, October 2003, pp. 88); "Seniority Rules" in **[47511]**, **[51351]**

Entrepreneur (Vol. 28, No. 6, June 2000, pp. 170); "Separation Anxiety" in **[19284]**, **[30129]**, **[42549]**

Entrepreneur (Vol. 31, No. 11, November 2003, pp. 57); "Server it Right" in **[6964]**, **[41977]**, **[49250]**

Entrepreneur (Vol. 30, No. 2, February 2002, pp. 66); "Service with a smile" in **[29485]**, **[39573]**, **[40689]**

Entrepreneur (Vol. 28, No. 4, April 2000, pp. 172); "Service To A Tee" in **[31214]**, **[47512]**

Entrepreneur (Vol. 32, No. 1, January 2004, pp. 242); "Services" in **[3243]**, **[17767]**, **[17845]**, **[21619]**, **[38904]**, **[52585]**

Entrepreneur (Vol. 31, No. 11, November 2003, pp. 86); "Serving Up Success: There's Something to be Said for Doing Things Your Way" in **[11346]**, **[21621]**, **[36738]**, **[47513]**

Entrepreneur (Vol. 30, No. 3, March 2002, pp. 40); "Set up shop" in **[4794]**, **[14427]**, **[23168]**, **[25956]**, **[34457]**, **[53459]**

Entrepreneur (Vol. 33, October 2005, No. 10, pp. 30); "Severed Ties" in **[28826]**, **[29487]**, **[36895]**, **[38344]**

Entrepreneur (Vol. 30, No. 2, February 2002, pp. 22); "Shady Business" in **[41980]**, **[49252]**

Entrepreneur (Vol. 31, No. 10, October 2003, pp. 100); "Shape Up!" in **[29757]**, **[35639]**

Entrepreneur (Vol. 33, September 2005, No. 9, pp. 100); "Shaping Up" in **[19233]**, **[19437]**, **[38905]**

Entrepreneur (Vol. 33, January 2005, No. 1); "Share the Health: When Encouraging Healthy Living, You've Got to Walk the Walk" in **[41097]**, **[50356]**

Entrepreneur (Vol. 32, November 2004, No. 11, pp. 62); "Share Safely" in **[6794]**, **[22377]**, **[49253]**

Entrepreneur (Vol. 32, November 2004, No. 11, pp. 90); "Share the Wealth" in **[51831]**

Entrepreneur (Vol. 31, No. 5, May 2003, pp. 88); "Sharing the wealth: never mind the dismal economy." in **[52498]**

Entrepreneur (Vol. 33, February 2005, No. 2, pp. 40); "Sharing the Wealth: Want to Get a Piece of the eBay Pie?" in **[784]**, **[1853]**, **[34463]**, **[47521]**

Entrepreneur (Vol. 32, October 2004, No. 10, pp. 49); "Sharper Image: Smartphones are the Brainier Mobile Choice" in **[5104]**, **[53960]**

Entrepreneur (Vol. 32, December 2004, No. 12, pp. 15); "Shell Shock?" in **[15448]**, **[40690]**, **[50176]**

Entrepreneur (Vol. 31, No. 6, June 2003, pp. 42); "Shipping out" in **[31067]**, **[34466]**, **[51353]**

Entrepreneur (Vol. 32, Oct. 2004); "Shock Value: A Belief in the Power of Batteries Charged This Couple Up for Franchise Ownership" in **[37777]**, **[38908]**

Entrepreneur (Vol. 31, No. 5, May 2003, pp. 75); "Shooting from the hip" in **[47525]**

Entrepreneur (Vol. 32, July 2004, No. 7, pp. 28); "Shop Around: This Technology Can Help You Comparison Shop for Low Fares" in **[25243]**, **[30416]**, **[31068]**

Entrepreneur (Vol. 32, September 2004, No. 9, pp. 44); "Shopping List" in **[4203]**, **[6795]**, **[6965]**, **[7285]**, **[7341]**, **[41981]**, **[46912]**, **[49256]**, **[50271]**

Entrepreneur (Vol. 32, October 2004, No. 10, pp. 56); "Shopping List: Thin is When It Comes to Monitors. Try These Models for Size" in **[6796]**, **[49257]**

Entrepreneur (Vol. 27, No. 8, August 2000, pp. 20); "Shopping Pals" in **[3583]**, **[34470]**

Entrepreneur (Vol. 32, No. 2, February 2004, pp. 74); "Short and Sweet" in **[28761]**, **[51835]**

Entrepreneur (Vol. 33, September 2005, No. 9, pp. 128); "Shout It Out" in **[36742]**

Entrepreneur (Vol. 33, September 2005, No. 9, pp. 102); "Show Me the Money" in **[12047]**, **[21411]**, **[37220]**, **[38677]**, **[44438]**

Entrepreneur (Vol. 31, No. 6, June 2003, pp. 108); "Show me the money" in **[37778]**, **[38909]**, **[52727]**

Entrepreneur (Vol. 30, No. 12, December 2002, pp. 106); "Shred of evidence: learn a lesson from Arthur Anderson" in **[249]**, **[26350]**, **[29490]**, **[37501]**

Entrepreneur (Vol. 28, No. 10, October 2000, pp. 29); "Sign of the Times" in **[14433]**, **[34475]**, **[40693]**

Entrepreneur (Vol. 33, January 2005, No. 1); "Sign of the Times: Are You Missing Out on This Simple, Inexpensive Marketing Tool?" in **[27677]**, **[34474]**, **[47527]**

Entrepreneur (Vol. 33, March 2005, No. 3, pp. 18); "Signal Strength" in **[31214]**, **[31218]**, **[55824]**

Entrepreneur (Vol. 31, No. 10, October 2003, 28); "Signs of Life? You'll Need Plenty of Patience to Profit from M-Commerce" in **[5107]**, **[28763]**, **[34477]**, **[36744]**, **[41983]**, **[53963]**

Entrepreneur (Vol. 30, No. 3, March 2002, pp. 97); "Silent treatment: Want big buzz? keep your mouth shut" in **[5916]**, **[47529]**, **[48790]**

Entrepreneur (Vol. 33, March 2005, No. 3, pp. 44); "Singin' the Blues: Is It the End for Bluetooth?" in **[5108]**, **[6797]**, **[14436]**, **[49258]**

Entrepreneur (Vol. 31, No. 4, April 2003, pp. 20); "Singing the blues?" in **[17771]**, **[27498]**, **[35069]**

Entrepreneur (Vol. 28, No. 10, October 2000, pp. 146); "Site-isfaction" in **[13778]**, **[37077]**, **[53149]**

Entrepreneur (Vol. 32, No. 1, January 2004, pp. 27); "Six Degrees: Can Who Your Employees Know Make a Difference in Your Sales?" in **[4797]**, **[23173]**, **[51838]**, **[53465]**

Entrepreneur (Vol. 32, July 2004, No. 7, pp. 51); "Sixth Sense: Sometimes Six Heads are Better Than One" in **[15455]**, **[21009]**

Entrepreneur (August 2004); "Size Matters: Does Your Product Jam a Lot of Benefits Into a Small Package? Here's How to Sell It" in **[786]**, **[47535]**, **[51840]**

Entrepreneur (Vol. 33, October 2005, No. 10, pp. 17); "Sizing Things Up" in **[40094]**

Entrepreneur (Vol. 33, January 2005, No. 1, pp. 21); "Skin Deep" in **[2605]**, **[56406]**

Entrepreneur (Vol. 32, No. 4, April 2004, pp. 132); "Sky's the Limit: Think Your Product has Limited Appeal?" in **[12258]**, **[35645]**, **[43969]**

Entrepreneur (Vol. 30, No. 2, February 2002, pp. 20); "Sleep tight" in **[12635]**, **[30417]**

Entrepreneur (Vol. 31, No. 7, July 2003, pp. 73); "Slick Tricks" in **[5110]**, **[14440]**, **[29492]**, **[34486]**, **[37502]**, **[40695]**

Entrepreneur (Vol. 32, July 2004, No. 7); "Slim Down: Sick of Your Bulky PC? A Desktop Replacement Notebook Could Be the Answer" in **[6799]**, **[49260]**

Entrepreneur (Vol. 31, No. 10, October 2003); "Smack Down! Show Those Numbers Who's Boss With a New Accounting Software Program" in **[253]**, **[2959]**, **[4798]**, **[23174]**, **[24038]**, **[26352]**, **[53466]**

The Entrepreneur and Small Business Problem Solver **[36071]**, **[39308]**, **[44401]**, **[48727]**

Entrepreneur (Vol. 28, No. 9, September 2000, 170); "Small But Special" in **[2639]**, **[8592]**, **[33491]**, **[37079]**

Entrepreneur (Vol. 33, January 2005, No. 1, pp. 44); "Small Fry" in **[6801]**, **[49266]**

Entrepreneur (Vol. 30, No. 3, March 2002, pp. 40); "Smart Design" in **[4806]**, **[6007]**, **[23183]**, **[53471]**

Entrepreneur (Vol. 33, January 2005, No. 1); "Smart Money: Where to Spend Your Marketing Dollars When a Product Isn't Selling" in **[47552]**, **[51844]**

Entrepreneur (Vol. 32, August 2004, No. 8, pp. 42); "Smarten Up" in **[5111]**, **[14451]**

Entrepreneur (Vol. 30, No. 3, March 2002, pp. 42); "Smarty pants" in **[6182]**, **[49271]**

Entrepreneur (Vol. 30, No. 9, September 2002, 30); "Smoke screening" in **[45654]**, **[54257]**

Entrepreneur (Vol. 32, November 2004, No. 11, pp. 18); "Snap n' Print" in **[4205]**, **[49272]**

Entrepreneur (Vol. 28, No. 10, October 2000, pp. 38); "So Close...Yet so Far" in **[30657]**, **[44440]**

Entrepreneur (Vol. 33, September 2005, No. 9, 91); "Social Grace" in **[35960]**, **[37326]**, **[46435]**, **[54259]**

Entrepreneur (Vol. 32, November 2004, No. 11, pp. 92); "Sock It To 'Em: Can a Negative Marketing Campaign Have Positive Results?" in **[789]**, **[47555]**

Entrepreneur (Vol. 33, October 2005, No. 10, pp. 156); "Sock It To You" in **[5248]**, **[5280]**, **[5542]**, **[5571]**, **[9640]**

Entrepreneur (Vol. 31, No. 7, July 2003, pp. 22); "Soft Touch" in **[5112]**, **[5202]**, **[6803]**, **[46930]**, **[49274]**

Entrepreneur (Vol. 31, No. 5, May 2003, pp. 27); "Soldiers of fortune" in **[14458]**, **[36771]**, **[41997]**

Entrepreneur (Vol. 30, No. 3, March 2002, pp. 160); "Solo Mission: Paul Stannard used to make software for other companies" in **[4583]**, **[22889]**, **[35653]**, **[53150]**

Entrepreneur (Vol. 28, No. 2, February 2000, pp. 40); "Something Different" in **[29999]**, **[30602]**

Entrepreneur (Vol. 30, No. 12, December 2002, pp. 112); "Soothe operator: word-of-mouth was the cure for discouragement" in **[2572]**, **[50798]**, **[56076]**

Entrepreneur (Vol. 32, November 2004, No. 11, pp. 67); "Space Case" in **[6286]**, **[6805]**

Entrepreneur (Vol. 32, August 2004, No. 8, pp. 23); "Spacing Out: There's Plenty of Elbow Room in these Cargo-Friendly Minivans" in **[18126]**

Entrepreneur (Vol. 32, November 2004, No. 11, pp. 62); "Spam Stopper" in **[14467]**, **[22384]**, **[34518]**

Entrepreneur (Vol. 32, July 2004, No. 7, pp. 72); "Spam Uncanned: Why the Recent Anti-Spam Legislation Isn't Protecting You" in **[14468]**, **[30255]**, **[34519]**, **[40711]**

Entrepreneur (Vol. 31, No. 4, April 2003, pp. 48); "Spam wars" in **[20261]**, **[34520]**

Entrepreneur (Vol. 32, No. 1, January 2004, pp. 10); "SpamCheck http://spamcheck.sitesell.com" in **[27502]**, **[34521]**

Entrepreneur (Vol. 30, No. 1, January 2002, pp. 31); "Speak and spell" in **[5118]**, **[49279]**

Entrepreneur (Vol. 32, September 2004); "Speak Up: Hate to Negotiate? That's Still No Excuse to Avoid Learning This Skill" in **[27503]**, **[36774]**, **[45657]**

Entrepreneur (Vol. 32, No. 2, February 2004, pp. 75); "Speak Up! The Ins and Outs of Hiring a Spokesperson" in **[12911]**, **[20157]**, **[47559]**, **[48671]**, **[50470]**, **[50678]**

Entrepreneur (Vol. 31, No. 6, June 2003, pp. 46); "Speaking up" in **[5119]**, **[6806]**, **[14469]**, **[34522]**, **[53988]**

Entrepreneur (Vol. 32, October 2004, No. 10, pp. 38); "Special Opps" in **[3587]**, **[12209]**, **[12310]**, **[16534]**, **[21351]**, **[31220]**, **[36775]**, **[43824]**

Entrepreneur (Vol. 28, No. 7, July 2000, pp. 150); "Specifically Speaking" in **[36776]**, **[47560]**

Entrepreneur (Vol. 30, No. 2, February 2002, pp. 28); "Spend cycle" in **[28805]**, **[32707]**

Entrepreneur (Vol. 33, September 2005, No. 9, pp. 164); "Spices of Life" in **[21631]**

Entrepreneur (Vol. 33, February 2005, No. 2, pp. 8); "Spider Simulator: http://tools.summitmedia.co.uk/spider" in **[14470]**, **[25970]**, **[34523]**

Entrepreneur (Vol. 31, No. 11, November 2003, pp. 136); "Spilling the Beans?" in **[30003]**, **[30604]**, **[36778]**

Entrepreneur (Vol. 32, November 2004, No. 11, pp. 18); "Spinoff Doctors" in **[42002]**, **[44663]**, **[53991]**, **[55839]**

Entrepreneur (Vol. 33, September 2005, No. 9, pp. 64); "Spitzer's Stand" in **[15235]**, **[15468]**, **[26513]**, **[26916]**, **[36916]**, **[38368]**, **[40712]**

Entrepreneur (Vol. 32); "Split Personalities" in **[5572]**, **[23635]**, **[37783]**

Entrepreneur (Vol. 30, No. 10, October 2002, pp. 55); "Spot a fake" in **[30256]**

Entrepreneur (Vol. 31, No. 4, April 2003, pp. 24); "Spot of tea?" in **[21632]**, **[53992]**

Entrepreneur (Vol. 33, February 2005, No. 2); "Spread the Word: Get Customers Talking and They'll Do Your Advertising For You" in **[793]**, **[31861]**, **[47566]**

Entrepreneur (Vol. 31, No. 4, April 2003, pp. 44); "Spring cleaning" in **[14475]**, **[23209]**, **[25972]**, **[34528]**, **[47568]**, **[51847]**, **[53489]**

Entrepreneur (Vol. 28, No. 11, November 2000, pp. 28); "Sprinkling Data Dust" in **[49280]**

Entrepreneur (Vol. 28, No. 3, March 2000, pp. 98); "Spy Away" in **[44368]**

Entrepreneur (Vol. 33, February 2005, No. 2, pp. 71); "Spy Games" in **[8399]**, **[14476]**, **[15572]**, **[22386]**, **[23505]**, **[34529]**, **[42422]**, **[45663]**, **[53995]**

Entrepreneur (Vol. 31, No. 4, April 2003); "Squeezed out? Is there any room left for small businesses in federal contracting?" in **[40100]**, **[40715]**, **[42004]**, **[49736]**

Entrepreneur (Vol. 28, No. 1, January 2000, pp. 20); "Stake A Claim" in **[14478]**, **[34530]**, **[44151]**

Entrepreneur (Vol. 33, February 2005, No. 2, pp. 52); "Stake a Claim: With Liability Insurance, Timing is Everything" in **[13472]**, **[43376]**

Entrepreneur; "Stake Your Claim: Contrary to Popular Belief, There's No Need to Ante Up a Fortune When You're Playing the Startup Game" in **[12490]**, **[19349]**, **[21302]**, **[29762]**, **[35659]**, **[46590]**

Entrepreneur (Vol. 32, July 2004, No. 7, pp. 28); "Stamp It Out: A New Proposal Aims to Bring Spam Under Control" in **[14479]**, **[30257]**, **[34531]**, **[40716]**

Entrepreneur (Vol. 31, No. 6, June 2003, pp. 28); "Standing Proud" in **[3588]**, **[35076]**, **[36783]**

Entrepreneur (Vol. 31, July 2003); "Standing on Their Own: Couple Decides to Go It Alone With Their Own Woody's Hot Dogs Kiosk" in **[15911]**, **[35660]**, **[51039]**

Entrepreneur (Vol. 30, No. 10, October 2002, pp. 91); "Stars of PR" in **[46592]**, **[50421]**, **[50512]**

Entrepreneur (Vol. 30, No. 12, December 2002, pp. 41); "Start your engines" in **[18130]**, **[49551]**

Entrepreneur (Vol. 32); "Start the Presses: Publishing a Magazine May Seem Like a Dream, But These Entrepreneurs Made It a Reality" in **[18938]**, **[36787]**

Entrepreneur (Vol. 28, No. 10, October 2000, pp. 106); "State Of The Unions" in **[53999]**, **[55314]**

Entrepreneur (Vol. 33, September 2005, No. 9, pp. 23); "Status Quota? Without Trade Quotas, U.S. Textile-Makers Struggle" in **[30129]**, **[30960]**, **[43826]**, **[46440]**

Entrepreneur (Vol. 32, No. 4, April 2004, pp. 23); "Status Woe: Contractors' Illegal Workers Could Put You in a Legal Pickle" in **[7487]**, **[29517]**, **[40731]**, **[48600]**

Entrepreneur (Vol. 33, September 2005, No. 9, pp. 44); "Stay In Touch" in **[266]**, **[2948]**, **[2964]**, **[4825]**, **[23212]**, **[23716]**, **[24046]**, **[25984]**, **[26369]**, **[53492]**

Entrepreneur (Vol. 32, December 2004, No. 12, pp. 52); "Stay in Touch" in **[4826]**, **[5122]**, **[6811]**, **[23213]**, **[53493]**

Entrepreneur (Vol. 30, No. 2, February 2002, pp. 64); "Stepping down" in **[32717]**, **[45668]**, **[54003]**

Entrepreneur (Vol. 32, July 2004, No. 7, pp. 35); "Stepping On It: Will New Measures Really Rev Up U.S. Manufacturers' Engines?" in **[28824]**, **[40733]**, **[46442]**

Entrepreneur (Vol. 30, No. 9, September 2002, pp. 25); "Steve Richardson" in **[24830]**, **[36793]**

Entrepreneur (Vol. 28, No. 11, November 2000, pp. 38); "Sticky Money" in **[34540]**, **[44665]**, **[55849]**

Entrepreneur (Vol. 28, No. 8, August 2000, pp. 102); "Stock of Ages" in **[30008]**, **[37784]**

Entrepreneur (Vol. 30, No. 3, March 2002, pp. 28); "Stock answers: Workers need 401(K) advice? Too bad! You can't give it!" in **[26917]**, **[40735]**

Entrepreneur (Vol. 28, No. 11, November 2000, pp. 30); "Stop, e-Thief!" in **[14489]**, **[30258]**, **[34541]**

Entrepreneur (Vol. 28, No. 9, September 2000, pp. 89); "Stop-gap Measures" in **[45671]**

Entrepreneur (Vol. 31, No. 10, October 2003, pp. 50); "Store More" in **[6813]**, **[6967]**, **[49282]**

Entrepreneur (Vol. 31, No. 9, September 2003, pp. 83); "Straight to the Outsource: Sales Force: Feeling the Crunch?" in **[49738]**, **[51848]**

Entrepreneur (Vol. 30, No. 10, October 2002, pp. 47); "Straight talking: to tell or not to tell?" in **[14490]**, **[25974]**, **[31864]**, **[34542]**, **[51372]**

Entrepreneur (Vol. 30, No. 2, February 2002, pp. 58); "Straight to video" in **[15485]**, **[34543]**

Entrepreneur (Vol. 32); "Stress Case? Is the Pressure to 'Get the Sale' Getting to You? Keep Your Cool With These Stress-Busters" in **[35082]**, **[51850]**

Entrepreneur (Vol. 32, December 2004, No. 12, pp. 108); "Stretch Your Limits" in **[19350]**, **[38684]**, **[54006]**

Entrepreneur (Vol. 28, No. 1, January 2000, pp. 118); "Strictly Business" in **[37787]**, **[45682]**

Entrepreneur (Vol. 30, No. 10, October 2002, pp. 93); "Student teachers" in **[33244]**, **[39612]**

Entrepreneur (Vol. 32, November 2004, No. 11, pp. 108); "Students of Enterprise" in **[8522]**, **[21638]**, **[36810]**, **[38916]**, **[56764]**

Entrepreneur (Vol. 30, No. 2, February 2002, pp. 90); "Stump the slump" in **[29769]**, **[32727]**, **[35679]**, **[44443]**

Entrepreneur (Vol. 32, October 2004, No. 10, pp. 107); "Super Bowl Sundae" in **[12791]**, **[18732]**, **[18762]**, **[38918]**

Entrepreneur (Vol. 32, September 2004, No. 9, pp. 73); "Survey Says...Market Research on the Cheap is Just a Click Away" in **[14498]**, **[16827]**, **[23771]**, **[34552]**, **[47589]**

Entrepreneur (Vol. 32, December 2004, No. 12); "Survival of the Fittest: As Your Business Grows, So Do the Challenges." in **[28849]**, **[36819]**

Entrepreneur (Vol. 32, July 2004, No. 7, pp. 38); "Survival of the Fittest: What Do Entrepreneurs Do to Stay Happy and Healthy?" in **[36820]**

Entrepreneur (Vol. 30, No. 3, Marc); "Sweat rewards" in **[5721]**, **[6334]**, **[7092]**, **[9164]**, **[12913]**, **[15942]**, **[17913]**, **[24832]**, **[26716]**, **[34554]**, **[49740]**, **[54013]**

Entrepreneur (Vol. 31, No. 9, July 2003, pp. 81); "Sweet Reward: Reaching Out to the Media Really Does Pay Off" in **[800]**, **[4314]**, **[47591]**, **[50472]**, **[56427]**

Entrepreneur (Vol. 31, No. 8, August 2003, pp. 75); "Sweet Rewards" in **[31870]**, **[47592]**, **[51375]**

Entrepreneur (Vol. 32, November 2004, No. 11, pp. 69); "Switch Gears: Flexibility is Key Feature of Convertible Funds" in **[15497]**, **[38389]**

Entrepreneur (Vol. 31, No. 10, October 2003, pp. 57); "Tablet Tools" in **[4831]**, **[6821]**, **[23218]**, **[49288]**, **[53498]**

Entrepreneur (Vol. 33, March 2005, No. 3); "Take Cover: No Need to Panic-We've Got Tips to Help You Cut Your Car Insurance Costs" in **[13481]**, **[43384]**

Entrepreneur (Vol. 33, January 2005, No. 1, pp. 50); "Take It For Granted" in **[39935]**, **[42027]**, **[44667]**, **[48796]**, **[50976]**, **[52213]**

Entrepreneur (Vol. 31, No. 4, April 2003, pp. 26); "Take it from me" in **[3592]**, **[28857]**, **[36826]**, **[45701]**, **[56429]**

Entrepreneur (Vol. 31, No. 9, September 2003); "Take Me To Your Leaders: A New Research Tool Helps You Find Leading Mutual Funds" in **[10200]**, **[15499]**, **[38394]**

Entrepreneur (October 2004); "Take No For an Answer: Don't Dismiss Naysayers-Ask For Advice, and Turn It Into a Tool for Success" in **[3593]**, **[31225]**, **[36827]**

Entrepreneur (Vol. 32, October 2004, No. 10, pp. 64); "Take Note: Document Incidents Now, and Avoid Lawsuits Later" in **[13482]**, **[29537]**, **[43385]**

Entrepreneur (Vol. 31, No. 9, September 2003, pp. 46); "Take One Tablet: Buyer's Guide" in **[5128]**, **[6823]**, **[14501]**

Entrepreneur (Vol. 33, January 2005, No. 1, pp. 27); "Take a Peek: What Does Congress Have in Mind for 2005?" in **[39625]**, **[40750]**

Entrepreneur (Vol. 31, No. 5, May 2003, pp. 69); "Take your pick" in **[13483]**, **[26921]**, **[41112]**, **[43386]**

Entrepreneur (Vol. 32, November 2004, No. 11, pp. 93); "Take the Plunge" in **[801]**, **[47599]**, **[50687]**

Entrepreneur (Vol. 31, No. 11, November 2003, pp. 118); "Take the Plunge! Teetering on the Edge of Unemployment?" in **[35685]**, **[53568]**

Entrepreneur (Vol. 33, August 2005, No. 8, pp. 4); "U.S. Postal Service Business Reply Mail" in **[6102]**, **[16472]**, **[17040]**, **[31029]**, **[31893]**, **[47682]**

Entrepreneur (Vol. 30, No. 1, January 2002, pp. 43); "Universal connectivity" in **[6850]**, **[6974]**, **[42084]**, **[49336]**

Entrepreneur (Vol. 31, No. 10, October 2003, pp. 38); "Up in the Air: Dotcom Stocks Could be Poised for a Comeback" in **[10225]**, **[14556]**, **[15559]**, **[28943]**, **[34637]**

Entrepreneur (Vol. 33, January 2005, No. 1, pp. 70); "Up in Arms: Prepare for Litigation With These Weapons of Mass Discussion" in **[27522]**, **[29566]**

Entrepreneur (Vol. 31, August, 2003); "Up to Speed? Wireless Could be Just What the Lagging Tech Market Needs to Get Moving Again" in **[5160]**, **[14559]**, **[34640]**, **[42086]**

Entrepreneur (Vol. 30, No. 2, February 2002, pp. 66); "Ups & downs" in **[13511]**, **[32768]**, **[43414]**

Entrepreneur (Vol. 31, No. 8, Aug., 2003); "Urban Legend: Do 90 Percent of Startups Really Fail to Make It Past Their First Year?" in **[27736]**, **[35710]**, **[53569]**

Entrepreneur (Vol. 30, No. 2, February 2002, pp. 54); "Use the index: The scoop on fully tradable ETFs" in **[15566]**, **[38433]**

Entrepreneur (Vol.32); "Use It or Lose It: Is Your Business Usable-or Disposable? Figure It Out Before Your Competitors Gain an Edge" in **[30983]**, **[41129]**, **[50987]**

Entrepreneur (Vol. 33, March 2005, No. 3, pp. 85); "Use Your Intuition" in **[5726]**, **[56461]**

Entrepreneur (Vol. 31, No. 11, November 2003, pp. 72); "Value Added: Here's a Midcap Fund that's More than Just Middle of the Road" in **[10228]**, **[15569]**

Entrepreneur (Vol. 30, No. 3, March); "Value system" in **[29568]**, **[45787]**, **[54270]**

Entrepreneur (Vol. 31, No. 10, October 2003, pp. 52); "VAT Facts" in **[43870]**, **[54853]**

Entrepreneur (Vol. 28, No. 6, June 2000, pp. 38); "VC Vintage" in **[55889]**

"Entrepreneur. Venturing Out" in *Boston Business Journal* (Vol. 23, No. 21, June 27, 2003, pp. 18) **[6149]**, **[6911]**, **[13746]**, **[35415]**

Entrepreneur (Vol. 31, No. 11, November 2003, pp. 92); "Vets, Your Best Bet?" in **[42451]**

Entrepreneur (Vol. 31, No. 9, September 2003, pp. 32); "Video To Go" in **[27523]**, **[49339]**

Entrepreneur (Vol. 33, January 2005, No. 1); "View from the Top: Subway Takes the Title of the 1 Franchise for the 13th Time." in **[8508]**, **[21434]**, **[38703]**

Entrepreneur (Vol. 30, No. 3, March 2002, pp. 44); "Viewer's Choice" in **[4208]**, **[27524]**, **[36916]**, **[49340]**, **[54062]**

Entrepreneur (Vol. 31, Oct. 2003); "Vintage Vehicles: Manufacturers' Inspection Programs Make It Worth Your While to Buy Used" in **[4354]**, **[18156]**

Entrepreneur (Vol. 31, No. 7, July 2003, pp. 40); "Virus Blockers" in **[4852]**, **[22414]**, **[23249]**, **[53528]**

Entrepreneur (Vol. 31, No. 6, June 2003, pp. 80); "Voices carry" in **[27525]**, **[45792]**, **[49345]**

Entrepreneur (Vol. 33, January 2005, No. 1, pp. 26); "VoIP Lessons: Learn How to Get Around Potential Problems" in **[5165]**, **[14571]**, **[49346]**

Entrepreneur (Vol. 32, No. 1, January 2004, pp. 21); "Waiting in the Wings" in **[15581]**, **[20701]**, **[41132]**, **[42102]**, **[50248]**, **[52227]**, **[52606]**

Entrepreneur (Vol. 32, October 2004, No. 10, pp. 60); "Waive Goodbye" in **[15582]**, **[38443]**

Entrepreneur (Vol. 30, No. 2, February 2002, pp. 35); "Walk 'N' Talk" in **[5167]**, **[49349]**

Entrepreneur (Vol. 33, January 2005, No. 1, pp. 41); "Wall-To-Wall: Wireless Jacks are the 'In' Thing for Networking" in **[6851]**, **[42103]**, **[49350]**

Entrepreneur (Vol. 32, No. 4, April 2004, pp. 34); "Walled In" in **[6852]**, **[14573]**, **[22417]**, **[34653]**, **[49351]**

Entrepreneur (Vol. 30, No. 10, October 2002, pp. 32); "Wanda Wen" in **[11133]**, **[11553]**, **[35716]**, **[56083]**

Entrepreneur (Vol. 30, No. 2, February 2002, pp. 59); "Wanna trade? Tax Talk" in **[54858]**

Entrepreneur (Vol. 28, No. 11, November 2000, pp. 40); "Watch Out!" in **[38447]**

Entrepreneur (Vol. 31, No. 6, June 2003, pp. 55); "Watch your step" in **[290]**, **[24069]**, **[26397]**, **[50252]**, **[51494]**, **[54861]**

Entrepreneur (Vol. 31, No. 9, September 2003, pp. 53); "Way to Give!" in **[14576]**, **[34657]**, **[54274]**

Entrepreneur (Vol. 32, September 2004, No. 9, pp. 49); "Way to Grow: A Computer Model Picks This Fund's Winners" in **[15592]**, **[38448]**

Entrepreneur (Vol. 32, August 2004, No. 8, pp. 22); "Wayne Samiere: 42, Founder of Honolulu Fish Co. in Honolulu" in **[10427]**, **[12651]**, **[21661]**

Entrepreneur (Vol. 30, No. 2, February 2002, pp. 8); "We, the entrepreneurs" in **[28977]**, **[32784]**, **[36922]**

Entrepreneur (Vol. 32, October 2004, No. 10, 104); "We Have Liftoff" in **[9647]**, **[14577]**, **[25996]**, **[34658]**, **[56472]**

Entrepreneur (Vol. 28, No. 2, February 2000, 38); "Web Site" in **[27528]**, **[31897]**

Entrepreneur (Vol. 32, December 2004, No. 12, pp. 52); "Website Builder" in **[4854]**, **[23255]**, **[26006]**, **[53533]**

Entrepreneur (Vol. 33, October 2005, No. 10, pp. 42); "Websites and Beyond" in **[25640]**, **[26009]**, **[28365]**, **[28979]**, **[34685]**

Entrepreneur (Vol. 31, No. 6, June 2003, pp. 160); "Weekend warrior" in **[5578]**, **[56473]**

Entrepreneur (Vol. 30, No. 10, October 2002, pp. 96); "Weigh your opt-ins" in **[27530]**, **[27683]**, **[31899]**, **[47709]**

Entrepreneur (Vol. 31, No. 4, April 2003, pp. 112); "We'll drink to that! " in **[2323]**, **[11997]**, **[35721]**, **[48690]**

Entrepreneur (Vol. 31, No. 6, June 2003, pp. 32); "What dreams may come" in **[3607]**, **[30624]**

Entrepreneur (Vol. 30, No. 2, February 2002, pp. 71); "What a deal!" in **[16831]**, **[47714]**

Entrepreneur (Vol. 33, January 2005, No. 1, pp. 22); "What a Deal! You Can Keep Hotel Costs Down-If You Know What To Look For" in **[12654]**, **[27199]**, **[30444]**

Entrepreneur (Vol. 32, October 2004, No. 10, pp. 22); "What Drives Inspiration?" in **[28985]**, **[30625]**, **[31901]**, **[35586]**, **[36933]**, **[37245]**, **[42107]**, **[45805]**

Entrepreneur (Vol. 28, No. 9, September 2000, pp. 20); "What Gives?" in **[39954]**, **[40822]**, **[48479]**

Entrepreneur (Vol. 32, No. 1, January 2004, pp. 30); "What Goes Up: Now There's a New Way to Track Small Business's Ups and Downs" in **[13018]**, **[28986]**, **[31603]**, **[39666]**, **[43874]**

Entrepreneur (Vol. 31, No. 8, August 2003, pp. 36); "What a Lightweight!" in **[4209]**, **[22577]**, **[49354]**, **[51899]**

Entrepreneur (Vol. 33, October 2005, No. 10, pp. 94); "What Office?" in **[28372]**, **[28989]**, **[34695]**

Entrepreneur (Vol. 31, No. 8, August 2003, pp. 57); "What a Relief!" in **[49355]**, **[54865]**

Entrepreneur (Vol. 30, No. 12, December 2002, pp. 74); "What a relief! New tax laws mean more money stays in your business" in **[24072]**, **[54866]**

Entrepreneur (Vol. 28, No. 10, October 2000, pp. 18); "What Taboo?" in **[54277]**

Entrepreneur (Vol. 32, No. 2, February 2004, pp. 54); "What Women Want" in **[47725]**, **[51903]**

Entrepreneur (Vol. 32, December 2004, No. 12, pp. 30); "What's Cookin'?" in **[29576]**, **[38945]**, **[40828]**

Entrepreneur (Vol. 31, No. 10, October 2003, pp. 34); "What's the Deal?" in **[3608]**, **[27535]**, **[39670]**, **[45817]**

Entrepreneur (Vol. 31, No. 8, August 2003, pp. 148); "What's For Dinner?" in **[4522]**, **[7803]**, **[35725]**, **[56084]**

Entrepreneur (Vol. 32); "What's In a Name?" in **[836]**, **[14606]**, **[26016]**, **[34699]**, **[47729]**

Entrepreneur (Vol. 33, September 2005, No. 9, pp. 84); "What's In Store? Get Ahead of the Game with the Latest Retail Trends" in **[51401]**, **[51408]**, **[54071]**

Entrepreneur (Vol. 32, December 2004, No. 12, pp. 92); "What's It Worth? Get Your Prices Right, Or It'll Cost You" in **[31077]**, **[51409]**

Entrepreneur (Vol. 32, December 2004, No. 12, pp. 49); "What's Next? Hardware that Can Straddle Wireless LANs and Cellular Networks" in **[5174]**, **[6860]**, **[42111]**, **[49356]**

Entrepreneur (Vol. 33, January 2005, No. 1, pp. 24); "What's the Plan? How President Bush's Second-Term Agenda Will Affect You" in **[26954]**, **[39671]**, **[40830]**, **[54868]**

Entrepreneur (Vol. 32, December 2004, No. 12, pp. 94); "What's the Plan? Need a Marketing Plan?" in **[837]**, **[47731]**

Entrepreneur (Vol. 31, No. 5, May 2003, pp. 126); "What's your problem?" in **[9]**, **[838]**, **[1535]**, **[2854]**, **[7511]**, **[18767]**, **[23860]**, **[31508]**, **[35726]**, **[42756]**, **[47732]**

Entrepreneur (Vol. 30, No. 3, March 2002, pp. 142); "What's your problem? People don't open junk mail, so send a postcard" in **[47733]**, **[51904]**

Entrepreneur (Vol. 28, No. 10, October 2000, pp. 132); "What's Up Doc?" in **[13786]**, **[37087]**, **[48894]**

Entrepreneur (Vol. 32, July 2004); "What's Up Doc? They May Not be Old Enough for Medical School, But Now Kids Can Look the Part" in **[5579]**, **[5728]**, **[46487]**, **[56476]**

Entrepreneur (Vol. 30, No. 12, December 2002, pp. 43); "What's the word? (Extra: Commercial Vehicle Guide)" in **[18162]**, **[49564]**

Entrepreneur (Vol. 31, No. 9, September 2003, pp. 81); "What's Your Angle? Get Fresh Ideas When You Change Your Perspective" in **[3609]**, **[36945]**, **[45824]**

Entrepreneur (Vol. 33, October 2005, No. 10, pp. 97); "What's Your Problem?" in **[8327]**, **[8407]**, **[23643]**, **[23740]**, **[30042]**, **[30185]**, **[30751]**, **[31605]**, **[40832]**, **[42757]**, **[54870]**

Entrepreneur (July 2004); "What's Your Problem? A Mobile Photography Business Can Go a Long Way If You Know Where You're Going" in **[19286]**, **[37577]**

Entrepreneur (Vol. 31, No. 10, October 2003, pp. 109); "What's Your Problem? So You Want to Start a Secretarial Service" in **[25527]**, **[26099]**

Entrepreneur (Vol. 32, December 2004, No. 12, pp. 104); "What's Your Problem? When to Tell Customers You Work From Your Home" in **[36946]**, **[42758]**

Entrepreneur (Vol. 31, No. 9, July 2003, pp. 104); "What's Your Problem? Your Store May Not Be a Big, City-Slicker Business" in **[5729]**, **[9648]**, **[11805]**, **[51410]**

Entrepreneur (Vol. 33, March 2005, No. 3, pp. 128); "Wheels of Fortune" in **[2505]**, **[36947]**

Entrepreneur (Vol. 28, No. 3, March 2000, pp. 127); "When Duty Calls" in **[39675]**, **[40833]**

Entrepreneur (Vol. 28, No. 7, July 2000, pp. 113); "When Egos Collide" in **[37810]**

Entrepreneur (Vol. 30, No. 1); "When You Really Lose Customers" in **[14613]**, **[31906]**, **[34707]**, **[47736]**

Entrepreneur (Vol. 32, No. 2, February 2004, pp. 32); "Where There's Smoke...One Entrepreneur Feels the Heat of Anti-Smoking Laws" in **[2357]**, **[21665]**, **[40837]**

Entrepreneur (Vol. 31, No. 10, October 2003, pp. 64); "Wherefore Art Thou Board Member?" in **[10249]**, **[15602]**, **[45834]**

Entrepreneur (Vol. 31, No. 11, November 2003, pp. 92); "Where's the Beef? Has Your Business Lost Momentum?" in **[29004]**, **[36957]**

Entrepreneur (Vol. 31, No. 7, July 2003); "Where's Big Brother? Orwell's Nightmare Won't Be Coming to the Internet Anytime Soon" in **[14614]**, **[34711]**

Entrepreneur (Vol. 31, No. 10, October 2003); "Where's the Love?" in **[30629]**, **[36958]**

Entrepreneur.com (Vol. 34, February 2006, No. 2, pp. 6); "Adwatcher" in **[539]**, **[33519]**, **[46665]**

Entrepreneur.com (Vol. 34, January 2006, No. 1, pp. 17); "Age of the iPod-icame, isaw, I conquered" in **[6574]**, **[48941]**

Entrepreneur.com (Vol. 34, February 2006, No. 2, pp. 81); "American Outcast" in **[27769]**, **[29786]**, **[43543]**

Entrepreneur.com (Vol. 34, February 2006, No. 2, pp. 42); "Analyze This" in **[13813]**, **[25789]**, **[33534]**

Entrepreneur.com (Vol. 34, February 2006, No. 2, pp. 46); "Art of Business" in **[29790]**, **[35777]**, **[39150]**

Entrepreneur.com (Vol. 34, February 2006, No. 2, pp. 74); "Better Off Red" in **[559]**, **[46716]**, **[51069]**, **[53603]**

Entrepreneur.com (Vol. 34, February 2006, No. 2, pp. 112); "Book Meets Girl" in **[2631]**, **[54139]**, **[56029]**

Entrepreneur.com (Vol. 34, February 2006, No. 2, pp. 6); "Bronto Email Marketing Toolkit" in **[13861]**, **[27307]**, **[27621]**, **[33613]**, **[46751]**, **[53223]**

Entrepreneur.com (Vol. 34, February 2006, No. 2, pp. 104); "Building Permitted" in **[7192]**, **[20395]**, **[38613]**

Entrepreneur.com (Vol. 34, February 2006, No. 2, pp. 46); "Burst of Energy" in **[21219]**, **[27891]**, **[37250]**, **[53626]**

Entrepreneur.com (Vol. 34, February 2006, No. 2, pp. 77); "By the Book" in **[44972]**, **[51577]**

Entrepreneur.com (Vol. 34, January 2006, No. 1, pp. 6); "C2G-Network" in **[9860]**, **[14820]**, **[41583]**, **[42188]**, **[42833]**, **[44974]**, **[46770]**

Entrepreneur.com (Vol. 34, February 2006, No. 2, pp. 74); "Catch the Carrot" in **[34849]**, **[51582]**

Entrepreneur.com (Vol. 34, February 2006, No. 2, pp. 90); "Catch 'Em If You Can" in **[27933]**, **[38617]**

Entrepreneur.com (Vol. 34, February 2006, No. 2, pp. 79); "Change, of Course" in **[581]**, **[24676]**, **[25169]**, **[33661]**, **[35934]**, **[46793]**

Entrepreneur.com (Vol. 34, January 2006, No. 1, pp. 6); "Commercial Fraud Insight" in **[6240]**, **[29158]**, **[53239]**

Entrepreneur.com (Vol. 34, February 2006, No. 2, pp. 47); "Cool Pics" in **[4182]**, **[4961]**, **[13926]**, **[48997]**

Entrepreneur.com (Vol. 34, January 2006, No. 1, pp. 25); "Cream of the Crop" in **[12769]**, **[31674]**, **[38623]**

Entrepreneur.com (Vol. 34, February 2006, No. 2, pp. 45); "Different Stripes" in **[5539]**, **[33754]**, **[36015]**

Entrepreneur.com (Vol. 34, January 2006, No. 1, pp. 18); "Easy Target? Budget-Cutters in Congress Have Set Their Sights on the SBA" in **[39811]**, **[40333]**

Entrepreneur.com (Vol. 34, February 2006, No. 2, pp. 114); "eBay Fever" in **[1760]**, **[33434]**

Entrepreneur.com (Vol. 34, February 2006, No. 2, pp. 6); "Efulfillment Service" in **[49692]**

Entrepreneur.com (December 21, 2007); "Entrepreneur Column" in **[137]**, **[613]**, **[14015]**, **[25842]**, **[26222]**, **[26942]**, **[27361]**, **[28108]**, **[29728]**, **[29858]**, **[30477]**, **[30536]**, **[31712]**, **[32407]**, **[33822]**, **[34891]**, **[35413]**, **[36068]**, **[37633]**, **[38765]**, **[41666]**, **[42513]**, **[42611]**, **[44036]**, **[44512]**, **[45107]**, **[46274]**, **[46931]**, **[48726]**, **[50586]**, **[51629]**, **[52669]**, **[53713]**, **[55592]**, **[56206]**, **[58033]**

Entrepreneur.com (Vol. 34, February 2006, No. 2, pp. 6); "Ezsupport Life" in **[14028]**, **[27368]**, **[27638]**, **[31716]**, **[33874]**, **[53277]**

Entrepreneur.com (Vol. 34, January 2006, No. 1, pp. 36); "Fair Share" in **[6645]**, **[49026]**

Entrepreneur.com (Vol. 34, February 2006, No. 2, pp. 144); "Fear Factor" in **[28151]**, **[29875]**, **[36146]**

Entrepreneur.com (Vol. 34, February 2006, No. 2, pp. 77); "Feeding Frenzy" in **[623]**, **[27373]**, **[27639]**, **[33891]**, **[46955]**

Entrepreneur.com (Vol. 34, February 2006, No. 2, pp. 84); "Flip the Switch" in **[35456]**, **[39057]**

Entrepreneur.com (Vol. 34, January 2006, No. 1, pp. 24); "Focus on Finances" in **[40387]**, **[54301]**, **[54557]**

Entrepreneur.com (Vol. 34, February 2006, No. 2, pp. 110); "Focus on the Positive" in **[7047]**, **[54116]**

Entrepreneur.com (Vol. 34, February 2006, No. 2, pp. 49); "Focused Fundraising" in **[22233]**, **[40022]**, **[44527]**, **[55620]**

Entrepreneur.com (Vol. 34, February 2006, No. 2, pp. 68); "For the People" in **[28174]**, **[40023]**, **[49696]**

Entrepreneur.com (Vol. 34, February 2006, No. 2, pp. 52); "Furry Friends" in **[13291]**, **[19151]**, **[43179]**, **[53743]**

Entrepreneur.com (Vol. 34, January 2006, No. 1, pp. 36); "Give Me a Break" in **[4675]**, **[23014]**, **[53299]**, **[54576]**

Entrepreneur.com (Vol. 34, February 2006, No. 2, pp. 120); "Global Trade" in **[25085]**, **[33105]**, **[43673]**, **[54578]**

Entrepreneur.com (Vol. 34, January 2006, No. 1, pp. 6); "Google Smackdown" in **[14085]**, **[33969]**

Entrepreneur.com (Vol. 34, February 2006, No. 2, pp. 51); "Green Machines" in **[18051]**, **[37287]**, **[54581]**

Entrepreneur.com (Vol. 34, January 2006, No. 1, pp. 40); "Happy Returns" in **[31729]**, **[33994]**, **[51178]**

Entrepreneur.com (Vol. 34, February 2006, No. 2, pp. 80); "Help Wanted" in **[30875]**, **[42257]**, **[43690]**, **[45229]**, **[49701]**

Entrepreneur.com (Vol. 34, February 2006, No. 2, pp. 42); "I Want My Cell TV" in **[5024]**, **[6682]**, **[41758]**, **[49082]**

Entrepreneur.com (Vol. 34, January 2006, No. 1, pp. 19); "In the Hot Seat" in **[32035]**, **[45290]**

Entrepreneur.com (Vol. 34, February 2006, No. 2, pp. 110); "It's in the Bag, Baby" in **[2127]**, **[56287]**

Entrepreneur.com (Vol. 34, February 2006, No. 2, pp. 98); "Keep It Up! Need Some Motivation? Someone To Show You the Ropes?" in **[3547]**, **[31181]**

Entrepreneur.com (Vol. 34, February 2006, No. 2, pp. 60); "Keep it Simple" in **[181]**, **[15196]**, **[23979]**, **[28375]**, **[29926]**, **[31561]**, **[38173]**, **[39425]**, **[41793]**, **[45333]**, **[49109]**, **[50033]**, **[54634]**

Entrepreneur.com (Vol. 34, February 2006, No. 2, pp. 50); "Know Thy Worth" in **[31182]**, **[39427]**, **[52375]**

Entrepreneur.com (Vol. 34, January 2006, No. 1, pp. 22); "Know Your Way Around?" in **[18074]**, **[49115]**

Entrepreneur.com (Vol. 34, February 2006, No. 2, pp. 28); "Life Is What You Make It" in **[10062]**, **[36445]**

Entrepreneur.com (Vol. 34, February 2006, No. 2, pp. 34); "Listen Up! Get the Scoop on Bluetooth Headsets With This Guide" in **[5044]**, **[41809]**, **[49128]**

Entrepreneur.com (Vol. 34, February 2006, No. 2, pp. 38); "Maps on Tap" in **[5051]**, **[30374]**, **[34172]**

Entrepreneur.com (Vol. 34, February 2006, No. 2, pp. 113); "Music To Your Ears" in **[17756]**, **[37738]**, **[44099]**

Entrepreneur.com (Vol. 34, January 2006, No. 1, pp. 6); "MyPayNet" in **[199]**, **[2931]**, **[4736]**, **[23094]**, **[26297]**, **[31567]**, **[34225]**, **[53381]**

Entrepreneur.com (Vol. 34, January 2006, No. 1, pp. 35); "Not On His Watch" in **[4743]**, **[6742]**, **[22314]**, **[23102]**, **[53387]**, **[56756]**

Entrepreneur.com (Vol. 34, February 2006, No. 2, pp. 38); "Ode to a Server" in **[6266]**, **[6744]**, **[49179]**

Entrepreneur.com (Vol. 34, February 2006, No. 2, pp. 51); "On Good Terms" in **[38258]**, **[44612]**

Entrepreneur.com (Vol. 34, February 2006, No. 2, pp. 33); "One-Track Mind" in **[4750]**, **[6270]**, **[23110]**, **[53397]**, **[56359]**

Entrepreneur.com (Vol. 34, February 2006, No. 2, pp. 58); "Over the Wall" in **[15337]**, **[38271]**, **[43777]**

Entrepreneur.com (Vol. 34, February 2006, No. 2, pp. 82); "Paying in Kind" in **[31813]**, **[45522]**

Entrepreneur.com (Vol. 34, February 2006, No. 2, pp. 122); "Personality Test" in **[27224]**, **[35608]**, **[39072]**

Entrepreneur.com (Vol. 34, January 2006, No. 1, pp. 40); "Pretty Picture" in **[6765]**, **[49215]**

Entrepreneur.com (Vol. 34, February 2006, No. 2, pp. 100); "Priced to Sell" in **[31059]**, **[47423]**

Entrepreneur.com (Vol. 34, February 2006, No. 2, pp. 20); "Primal Need" in **[51298]**

Entrepreneur.com (Vol. 34, February 2006, No. 2, pp. 34); "Put It In Drive" in **[39544]**, **[49540]**, **[53928]**

Entrepreneur.com (Vol. 34, February 2006, No. 2, pp. 52); "Reap What You Grow" in **[15398]**, **[38305]**

Entrepreneur.com (Vol. 34, January 2006, No. 1, pp. 26); "Requisite Relief" in **[39559]**, **[39897]**

Entrepreneur.com (Vol. 34, January 2006, No. 1, pp. 19); "Return of the Agent" in **[24725]**, **[25239]**, **[30410]**, **[34412]**

Entrepreneur.com (Vol. 34, February 2006, No. 2, pp. 75); "Riding the Airwaves" in **[774]**, **[20334]**, **[47475]**, **[50662]**

Entrepreneur.com (Vol. 34, February 2006, No. 2, pp. 30); "Right of Fashion" in **[5566]**, **[5711]**, **[51333]**, **[56387]**

Entrepreneur.com (Vol. 34, January 2006, No. 1, pp. 32); "Salad Daze" in **[10624]**, **[12058]**, **[21616]**, **[34429]**

Entrepreneur.com (Vol. 34, February 2006, No. 2, pp. 6); "Security Guide for Small Business" in **[6790]**, **[22368]**, **[53454]**

Entrepreneur.com (Vol. 34, February 2006, No. 2, pp. 22); "Sedan Savvy" in **[18120]**, **[53958]**

Entrepreneur.com (Vol. 34, February 2006, No. 2, pp. 6); "Sharebuilder 401(k)" in **[248]**, **[4795]**, **[18791]**, **[23169]**, **[24036]**, **[26909]**, **[53461]**

Entrepreneur.com (Vol. 34, February 2006, No. 2, pp. 82); "Shh...It's a Secret" in **[29488]**, **[30950]**, **[44362]**

Entrepreneur.com (Vol. 34, February 2006, No. 2, pp. 58); "Soaring Angels" in **[44661]**, **[54770]**

Entrepreneur.com (Vol. 34, January 2006, No. 1, pp. 27); "Stop on a Dime" in **[31073]**

Entrepreneur.com (Vol. 34, January 2006, No. 1, pp. 22); "Straight to Video" in **[797]**, **[34544]**, **[47580]**

Entrepreneur.com (Vol. 34, February 2006, No. 2, pp. 104); "Stress Relief" in **[38683]**, **[56079]**

Entrepreneur.com (Vol. 34, February 2006, No. 2, pp. 50); "Strike a Balance" in **[15490]**, **[38383]**

Entrepreneur.com (Vol. 34, February 2006, No. 2, pp. 36); "Sweet Relief" in **[54784]**

Entrepreneur.com (Vol. 34, February 2006, No. 2, pp. 35); "That's the Spot" in **[4840]**, **[5147]**, **[23229]**, **[42061]**, **[49311]**, **[53511]**

Entrepreneur.com (Vol. 34, February 2006, No. 2, pp. 36); "The Bill's In the Mail"Bill Me Later" Payment Option" in **[31516]**, **[33588]**, **[51566]**

Entrepreneur.com (Vol. 34, February 2006, No. 2, pp. 17); "The New China?" in **[43759]**, **[46386]**

Entrepreneur.com (Vol. 34, February 2006, No. 2, pp. 28); "The New School" in **[33188]**, **[41862]**, **[53384]**

Entrepreneur.com (Vol. 34, January 2006, No. 1, pp. 27); "Time to Change" in **[6839]**, **[49319]**

Entrepreneur.com (Vol. 34, February 2006, No. 2); "Time to Collect? Tacking Taxes Onto Internet Sales Could Soon Become Mandatory" in **[24062]**, **[34602]**, **[40769]**, **[51389]**, **[54834]**

Entrepreneur.com (Vol. 34, February 2006, No. 2, pp. 100); "Tough Talk" in **[27518]**, **[45760]**

Entrepreneur.com (Vol. 34, February 2006, No. 2, pp. 64); "Up To the Challenge" in **[28945]**, **[36906]**

Entrepreneur.com (Vol. 34, February 2006, No. 2, pp. 80); "Walk the Line" in **[29569]**, **[46479]**

Entrepreneur.com (Vol. 34, February 2006, No. 2, pp. 57); "Warning Signs" in **[24068]**, **[54859]**

Entrepreneur.com (Vol. 34, February 2006, No. 2, pp. 73); "What Ales You?" in **[2356]**, **[3140]**, **[19645]**, **[21664]**, **[28984]**

Environmental Guide to the Internet [9354], [9483], [37272]

Environmental Hazards Management Institute [11986]
> Library [11978]

Environmental Health Science Inc. [3697], [31341], [41329]

Environmental Industry Associations [11927]

Environmental Law Reporter [9417]

Environmental Management Assistance Program (Central/Western Region)–Pennsylvania State University–SBDC [64327]

Environmental Management Consultants Inc. [40886]

Environmental Management Information Systems Report [9375]

Environmental Monitoring Inc. [40887]

Environmental News Network [9384]

"Environmental and Ownership Characteristics of Small Businesses and their Impact on Development" in *Journal of Small Business Management* [28122], [29864], [30145], [30537], [30677], [32416]

Environmental Plus Inc. [37359]

Environmental Protection Agency–Office of Small and Disadvantaged Business Utilization [67027]

Environmental Protection Agency (Region 1) [67028]

Environmental Protection Agency (Region 2) [67029]

Environmental Protection Agency (Region 3) [67030]

Environmental Protection Agency (Region 4) [67031]

Environmental Protection Agency (Region 5) [67032]

Environmental Protection Agency (Region 6) [67033]

Environmental Protection Agency (Region 7) [67034]

Environmental Protection Agency (Region 8) [67035]

Environmental Protection Agency (Region 9) [67036]

Environmental Protection Agency (Region 10) [67037]

Environmental Protection Agency State Superfund Office (Alabama)–Department of Environmental Management–Land Division [67051]

Environmental Protection Agency State Superfund Office (Alaska)–Department of Environmental Conservation–Division of Environmental Quality [67084]

Environmental Protection Agency State Superfund Office (Arizona)–Department of Environmental Quality–Office of Waste and Water Quality [67079]

Environmental Protection Agency State Superfund Office (Arkansas)–Department of Environmental Quality–Waste Programs Division [67065]

Environmental Protection Agency State Superfund Office (California)–Department of Toxic Substances Control [67080]

Environmental Protection Agency State Superfund Office (Colorado)–Department of Public Health and Environment–Hazardous Materials and Waste Management Division [67073]

Environmental Protection Agency State Superfund Office (Connecticut)–Department of Environmental Protection–Small Business Assistance [67038]

Environmental Protection Agency State Superfund Office (Delaware)–Department of Natural Resources and Environmental Control–Air and Waste Management Section [67045]

Environmental Protection Agency State Superfund Office (District of Columbia)–Environmental Health Administration–Hazardous Materials, Pesticides and Underground Strorage Tank Management [67046]

Environmental Protection Agency State Superfund Office (Florida)–Department of Environmental Protection–Division of Waste Management [67052]

Environmental Protection Agency State Superfund Office (Georgia)–Department of Natural Resources–Land Protection Branch–Solid Waste Management Program [67053]

Environmental Protection Agency State Superfund Office (Guam)–Environmental Protection Agency [67081]

Environmental Protection Agency State Superfund Office (Hawaii)–Department of Health–Environmental Management Division [67082]

Environmental Protection Agency State Superfund Office (Idaho)–Department of Health–Environmental Health–Solid and Hazardous Waste Branch [67085]

Environmental Protection Agency State Superfund Office (Illinois)–Environmental Protection Agency–Bureau of Land–Pollution Prevention [67059]

Environmental Protection Agency State Superfund Office (Indiana)–State Department of Environmental Management–Office of Environmental Response–Office of Land Quality [67060]

Environmental Protection Agency State Superfund Office (Iowa)–Department of Natural Resources Waste Management–Air Quality Bureau–Water Supply Section [67069]

Environmental Protection Agency State Superfund Office (Kansas)–Department of Health and Environment–Bureau of Waste Management–Storage Tank Section [67070]

Environmental Protection Agency State Superfund Office (Kentucky)–Department for Environmental Protection–Division of Waste Management [67054]

Environmental Protection Agency State Superfund Office (Maine)–Department of Environmental Protection–Office of the Commissioner [67039]

Environmental Protection Agency State Superfund Office (Maryland)–Department of the Environment–Recycling in Maryland [67047]

Environmental Protection Agency State Superfund Office (Massachusetts)–Department of Environmental Protection–Bureau of Waste Prevention–Recycle [67040]

Environmental Protection Agency State Superfund Office (Michigan)–Michigan Department of Environmental Quality–Waste Management Division [67061]

Environmental Protection Agency State Superfund Office (Minnesota)–Pollution Control Agency–Groundwater & Solid Waste Division [67062]

Environmental Protection Agency State Superfund Office (Mississippi)–Department of Environmental Quality [67055]

Environmental Protection Agency State Superfund Office (Missouri)–Department of Natural Resources–Hazardous Waste Management Program [67071]

Environmental Protection Agency State Superfund Office (Montana)–Department of Environmental Quality [67074]

Environmental Protection Agency State Superfund Office (Nebraska)–Department of Environmental Quality–Air and Waste Management Division [67072]

Environmental Protection Agency State Superfund Office (Nevada)–Division of Environmental Protection–Department of Conservation and Natural Resources [67083]

Environmental Protection Agency State Superfund Office (New Hampshire)–Department of Environmental Services–Commissioners Office [67041]

Environmental Protection Agency State Superfund Office (New Jersey)–Department of Environmental Protection–Hazardous Waste Management Division [67043]

Environmental Protection Agency State Superfund Office (New Mexico)–Environmental Improvement Division–Hazardous and Radioactive Waste Bureau [67066]

Environmental Protection Agency State Superfund Office (New York)–Department of Environmental Conservation–Hazardous Waste Remediation Division [67044]

Environmental Protection Agency State Superfund Office (North Carolina)–Department of Environment and Natural Resources [67056]

Environmental Protection Agency State Superfund Office (North Dakota)–Department of Health–Waste Management Division [67075]

Environmental Protection Agency State Superfund Office (Ohio)–Environmental Protection Agency–Division of Emergency and Remedial Response [67063]

Environmental Protection Agency State Superfund Office (Oklahoma)–Department of Environmental Quality–Land Protection Division [67067]

Environmental Protection Agency State Superfund Office (Oregon)–Department of Environmental Quality–Environmental Cleanup Division [67086]

Environmental Protection Agency State Superfund Office (Pennsylvania)–Department of Environmental Resources–Bureau of Land Recycling and Waste Management [67048]

Environmental Protection Agency State Superfund Office (Rhode Island)–Department of Environmental Management–Waste Management [67042]

Environmental Protection Agency State Superfund Office (South Carolina)–Department of Health and Environmental Control [67057]

Environmental Protection Agency State Superfund Office (South Dakota)–Department of Environment and Natural Resources–Waste Management Program [67076]

Environmental Protection Agency State Superfund Office (Tennessee)–Department of Environment and Conservation–Division of Solid and Hazardous Waste Management [67058]

Environmental Protection Agency State Superfund Office (Texas)–Water Commission–Hazardous and Solid Waste Division–Superfund and Emergency Response Section [67068]

Environmental Protection Agency State Superfund Office (Utah)–Department of Environmental Quality–Division of Air Quality [67077]

Environmental Protection Agency State Superfund Office (Virginia)–Department of Environmental Quality [67049]

Environmental Protection Agency State Superfund Office (Washington)–Department of Ecology–Waste Management Program–Investigations and Cleanup Program [67087]

Environmental Protection Agency State Superfund Office (West Virginia)–Division of Environmental Protection–Office of Waste Management [67050]

Environmental Protection Agency State Superfund Office (Wisconsin)–Department of Natural Resources–Bureau of Waste Management [67064]

Environmental Protection Agency State Superfund Office (Wyoming)–Department of Environmental Quality–Water Quality Division [67078]

Environmental Quality Management [21271]

Environmental Research Foundation [25741]

Environmental Response Inc. [11965]

Environmental Review [9385]

Environmental Sciences & Pollution Management [9418]

Environmental Software Report [9386], [23281]

Environmental Solutions Inc. [40888]

Environmental Support Network Inc. [40889], [56660]

Environmental Toxicology and Chemistry [52263]

The Environmentalist [9419]

Environmex/Watermex South China - International Environment & Water Management Technology, Equipment & Control Systems Exhibition [25723]

Environnement Jeunesse [9325]

EnviroSpect, Inc. [9495]

EOC Technology Center [64138]

EOS Partners, L.P. [63088]

ePartners Inc. [49423], [49606]

"The Eparty's Over" in *Forbes* (December 11, 2000, pp. 144) [14018], [33855], [43053]

Epcon Communities [7661]

Ephrata Area Chamber of Commerce [64415]

Ephrata Chamber of Commerce [66080]

EPIC Systems (Expert Professional Interior Cleaning) [25555]

Epilepsy Canada [40935]

Epilepsy Wellness Newsletter [41190]

Episcopal Church Annual [41006]

The Epler Co. [27026], [30761]

EPM Entertainment Marketing Sourcebook [23825]

ePostal News [6985]

"EPrize Touts Small Business" in *Detroit Free Press* (January 17, 2007) [615], [14019], [25844], [33856], [46932]

Epstein, Becker, & Green, PC–Law Library [24174]

"Equal access for all" in *BlackEnterprise* (Vol. 32, No. 3, October 2001, pp. 62) [14020], [54172]

Equal Opportunity [42487], [48620]

"Equal Time? Legal" in *Entrepreneur* (Vol. 31, No. 9, September 2003, pp. 80) [27635], [33857], [40350], [55291]

Equal Treatment/Equal Opportunity [42488]

"Equal Work, Unequal Pay?" in *Hispanic Business* (October 2004, pp. 26) [42230]

"Equality through equities: African Americans turning to stocks to build wealth" in *Black Enterprise* (Vol.33, No.3, Oct. 2002, pp. 40) [9936], [10298], [14956], [38036]

"Equation Predicts Returns-Real Math or Wishful Thinking" in *Venture Capital Journal* (Vol. 42, No. 10, October 2002, pp. 8, 10, 12) [9937], [14957], [55595]

Equilibrium [41191]

Equine Canada [12444]

Equipment Leasing Association of America [21305]

"Equipment Maintenance Insurance Coverage" in *Rough Notes* (Vol. 145, No. 1, January 2003, pp. 44) [13281], [43171], [46276]

Equipment World's Top Bid [7344]

Equipro Inc. [20266]

Equitas L.P. [64995]

Equity Partners Of America Ltd. [29610], [30716], [52477], [55974]

Equity Properties [4012]

Equity-South Advisors, LLC / Grubb & Williams Ltd. [59192]

"Equity Strategies: Small caps could be the best bet for big gains" in *Red Herring* (No. 103, September 1, 2001, pp. 90-92) [14958], [38037], [41671]

Equity Swaps: A Self-Study Guide to Mastering and Applying Equity Swaps [14959]

ERA Canada [3857]

"An Era of Downsized Expectations" in *Hispanic Business* (March 2002, pp. 28, 30-31) [9938], [14960], [32417]

"The era of e-taxes" in *Hispanic Business* (Vol. 22, No. 3, March 2000, pp. 62) [33858], [54539]

Erbert & Gerbert's Subs & Clubs [8550]

ERC Directory of Real Estate Appraisers and Brokers [39315]

ErgoKinetics: Safety in Motion [56621]

Ergometrics Inc. [49607]

"Ergonomics & Economics" in *Crain's Detroit Business* (Vol. 21, November 7, 2005, No. 45, pp. 1) [37273], [40351], [49496]

Ergonomics: Low-Cost, Common-Sense Training Solutions [56622]

Ergonomics at Work [56623]

Erick Chamber of Commerce [63989]

Erico Inc.–Information Resources Center [16406]

Erie Chamber of Commerce [58360]

Erie Community College, City Campus [63221]

Erie Insurance Group–Corporate Library [13595]

Erie Regional Chamber and Growth Partnership [64416]

Erie Times-News (March 4, 2002); "New Jersey-Based Arts, Crafts Chain to Open Store in Erie, Pa" in [8175], [28543]

Erin Services Inc. [1123], [1147], [3339], [8536], [16069], [19649], [21718]

ERISA Industry Committee [26727]

"ERM to the rescue" in *Rough Notes* (Vol. 146, No. 3, March 2003, pp. 116) [36119], [45112]

ERM - West, Inc.–Library [9434]

Ernst & Young
Center for Business Knowledge [417], [2994], [24175]
Center for Business Knowledge Libraries [418], [18811]
Library [419], [18812], [24176]

The Ernst and Young Business Plan Guide [29865]

Ernst & Young LLP
Center for Business Knowledge [420], [24177]
Center for Business Knowledge–Library [6543]

"Ernst & Young Seeks Nominations for Southwest Area 2004 Entrepreneur of the Year" in *Journal Record* (February 5, 2004) [34893], [36120]

Error Analysis Inc. [49608], [56661]

Erwin Area Chamber of Commerce [63359]

ESAPP Financial, LLC [3858], [4013]

Escalon District Chamber of Commerce [57478]

Escape [19167]

Escapees Magazine [21181]

Escondido Chamber of Commerce [57479]

"Escondido: Sometimes, the Best Advice is Free" in *San Diego Business Journal* (Vol. 28, January 8, 2007, No. 2, pp. 27) [14961], [36121], [38038], [39316], [46933]

ESOPS: The Ultimate Way to Finance a Company [48929]

"ESOPs largely a positive tool, survey finds" in *Employee Benefit Plan Review* (Vol. 56, No. 1, July 2001, pp. 42) [26800], [34892]

ESP - Psychic Expo and Psychic, Mystics, and Seers Fair [17939]

Espanola Valley Chamber of Commerce [62686]

Esparto District Chamber of Commerce [57480]

ESPICOM Country Health Care Reports [41345]

ESPICOM Pharmaceutical & Medical Company Profiles [17142]

ESPICOM Pharmaceutical & Medical Device News [8853], [17143], [41346]

Espionage Research Institute [46019]

The Espresso Bartenders Guide to Expresso Bartending [11324]

Espresso!: Starting & Succeeding with Your Own Coffee Business [11325]

ESSENCE [7819]

The Essence of Business Ethics [37426]

The Essence of Small Business [52851]

The Essential Administrative Professional: The Skills and Know-How to Make You Invaluable [34793], [44751]

The Essential Administrative Professional: The Skills and Know-How to Make You Invaluable (Canada) [25516]

The Essential Corporation Handbook [29225], [43016]

The Essential Online Solution: The 5-Step Formula for Small Business Success [25845], [33859], [51146]

"The Essential Tech Toolbox" in *Hispanic Business* (Vol. 23, No. 5, May 2001, pp. 38, 40) [4982], [14021], [22986], [41672], [49020]

The Essentials of Budgeting: From Creation through Application [26123]

The Essentials of Budgeting: From Creation Through Application [26124], [37849]

The Essentials of Budgeting: From Creation Through Application (Canada) [37850]

Essentials of Business Communication [27362]

Essentials of Business Ethics [37427]

Essentials of Entrepreneurship and Small Business Management [29866], [33860], [35434], [36122], [38039], [44701], [46934]

Essentials of Labor Relations [55292]

Essentials of Management (Canada) [44752]

Essentials of Pharmacy Management [8783]

Essentials Protective Coatings [16981]

Essentials of Technical Writing and Information Design [27249]

Essex Commercial Club [60130]

Essex - Middle River - White Marsh Chamber of Commerce [60827]

Essex Woodlands Health Ventures / Woodlands Venture (The Woodlands) [65604]

"Establish and Effective Privacy Policy" in *E-business Advisor* (Vol. 18, No. 3, March 2000, pp. 34) [22223], [33861]

"Establish strong team with game plan, feedback" in *Minneapolis-St. Paul City Business* (Vol. 19, No. 15, September 14, 2001, pp. 12) [34893]

Estacada - Clackamas River Area Chamber of Commerce [64215]

"Estate of affairs" in *Entrepreneur* (Vol. 31, No. 4, April 2003, pp. 52) [37635], [40352], [54540]

"Estate tax huge headache for small business owners" in *Indianapolis Business Journal* (Vol. 21, No. 15, June 26, 2000, pp. 33A) [54541]

Estate Planners Alert [9518], [37820]

Estate Planning [9522]

Estate Planning Review [9519]

"Estate tax foes awaiting more shots at a repeal" in *Business First Columbus* (Vol. 18, No. 26, February 15, 2002, pp. A16) [40353], [54542]

Estee Lauder, Inc.–Library [2415], [2627], [7945]

Estero Chamber of Commerce [58794]

Estes Park Chamber of Commerce [58361]

Estherville Area Chamber of Commerce [60131]

Estill County Development Alliance [60501]

Estreetcapital.com [57089]

Estuarine Research Federation Conference [52337], [55211]

ETA International - Electronics Technicians Association, International [22081], [24332]

Eternal Value Review: World Report and Market Monitor [10272], [38486]

"Ethanol Additive Pushes Long Island Gas Prices Up In January" in *Long Island Business News* (January 30, 2004) [22612]

"Ethanol Push Has Roots from Early 1990s, Support from Farmers" in *Altanta Journal-Constitution* (February 4, 2007) [26503], [37274]

"Ethentica Ethenticator MS 3000 PC Card" in *PC Magazine* (February 6, 2001, pp. 26) [22224], [33862], [49021]

"Ethical and fair work behavior" in *Journal of Business Ethics* (Vol. 28, No. 3, December 1, 2000, pp. 187) [37428]

Ethical Conduct and the Professional's Dilemma: Choosing Between Service and Success [37429]

Ethical Issues in Business [37430]

Ethical Issues in Business: A Philosophical Approach [37431]

"The ethical leader's decision tree." in *Harvard Business Review* (Vol. 81, No. 2, February 2003, pp. 18) [36123], [37432], [45113]

"Ethical Problems, Conflicts and Beliefs of Small Business Professionals" in *Journal of Business Ethics* (Vol. 28, No. 1, Nov. 1, 2000) [36124], [37433]

Ethical Workplace [37434]

Ethics in American Business [37543]

Ethics in the Business World [37435]

Ethics Centre CA–Library [37548]

"The Ethics of Consumer Sovereignty in an Age of High Tech" in *Journal of Business Ethics* (Vol. 28, No. 1, November 1, 2000, pp. 1) [30849], [37436], [41673]

"Ethics, Deception and Labor Negotiation" in *Journal of Business Ethics* (Vol. 28, No. 2, November 15, 2000, pp. 145) [37437], [55293]

Ethics in Hospitality Management: A Book of Readings [12546]

Ethics: Is It Profitable in Business? [37544]

"Ethics of Justice and Care in Corporate Crisis Management" in *Journal of Business Ethics* (Vol. 46, No. 4, Sept. 15, 2003, pp. 351) [29226], [36125], [37438], [45114]

"Ethics in negotiation: does getting to yes require candor?" in *Dispute Resolution Journal* (Vol. 56, No. 2, May-July 2001, pp. 8) [27363]

Ethics & Policy [37537]

Ethics Resource Center, Inc. [54290]

Ethics: The Enemy in the Workplace [37439]

Ethics Today [37538]

"Ethnic Enterprises and their Clientele" in *Journal of Small Business Management* (Vol. 38, No. 2, April 2000, pp. 48) [48150]

Ethnic and Multicultural Information Exchange Roundtable [48512]

Ethnic NewsWatch: A History [18985] ·

Ethnicity & Mental Health Associates [48635]

ETOH Database [54374]

Etowah Area Chamber of Commerce [64910]

etracks Newsletter [21149]

"ety8 Bluetooth Earphones: Music to Your Ears" in *Sales & Marketing Management* (Vol. 159, January-February 2007, No. 1, pp. 40) [4983], [41674], [49022]

Euclid Chamber of Commerce [63668]

Euclidsr Partners [63089]

Eudora Chamber of Commerce [57161]

Eufaula Area Chamber of Commerce [63990]

Eufaula - Barbour County Chamber of Commerce [56842]

Eugene Area Chamber of Commerce [64216]

Eugene O'Neill Theater Center–Leibling-Wood Library–Monte Cristo Cottage Collection [7960]

Eunice Chamber of Commerce [60633]

Euphoria Smoothies & Nutritional Supplements, Ltd [11383]

Eureka Area Chamber of Commerce [60328], [62163]

Eureka Chamber of Commerce [61958], [64822]

Eureka Chamber of Commerce and Visitors Center [62348]

"Eureka! I have an idea - how a business is born" in *Women in Business* (Vol. 54, No. 5, September-October 2002, pp. 30) [35435], [56042]

Eureka, The California Career Information System–Library [4458]

Eureka! The Canadian Invention & Innovation Newsletter [44184]

Eurodollar Futures and Options: Controlling Money Market Risk [14962]

European - American Business Council [43493]

European-American Chamber of Commerce in the United States [43494]

European Clinical Laboratory [8041], [41192]

European Marketing: A Strategic Guide to the New Opportunities [43647]

European Research and Development Database (ERDD) [13117]

European Travel Commission [25128], [30277]

Europe's Romantic Inns [25315]

Eustis Area Chamber of Commerce [58795]

Eutaw Area Chamber of Commerce [56843]

"Evaluating and Managing a Potential Clawback Liability, Part 2" in *Venture Capital Journal* (Vol. 42, No. 10, Oct. 2002, pp. 45-46) [14963], [55596]

"Evaluating and Managing a Potential Clawback Liability" in *Venture Capital Journal* (Vol. 42, No. 9, September 2002, pp. 34-35) [53714], [55597]

"Evaluating promotion opportunities" in *Women in Business* (Vol. 53, No. 2, March-April, 2001, pp. 36) [34894], [39317]

Evaluation & the Health Professions [41193]

Evangelical Christian Publishers Association [2659]

Evangelical Lutheran Good Samaritan Society–Library [18398]

Evans Area Chamber of Commerce [58362]

Evanston Business Investment Corp. [59733]

Evanston Business and Technology Innovation Center–Small Business Development Center [59370]

Evanston Chamber of Commerce [59494], [66608]

Evansville Chamber of Commerce [66391]

Evaporative Cooling Institute [997]

Evart Area Chamber of Commerce [61293]

"Even "E-Active" Organizations Have a Lot to Learn" in *E-business Advisor* (Vol. 18, No. 3, March 2000, pp. 8) [25846], [33863], [53715]

"Even as the M&A Market Heats Up, Unloading a Company Gets Trickier" in *Inc.* (May 1, 2005) [9836], [9939], [14760], [14964], [47562], [49920], [53716]

Even More Games Trainers Play [33091]

"Even Privacy Has Its Price" in *Success* (Vol. 47, No. 2, June 2000, pp. 12) [14022], [16811]

"Evenhandedly Political: VCs Back Candidates in Both Camps" in *Venture Capital Journal* (Vol. 40, No. 10, October 2000, pp. 5) [39318], [55598]

"An Evening with the Brain Trust" in *Hispanic Business* (October 2003, pp. 40) [28123], [40354], [48151]

Event Planning Business Guide [18722], [18754]

Event Solutions Expo [18739], [55212]

"Ever-Changing SUVs" in *Business First Buffalo* (Vol. 19, No. 44, July 25, 2003, pp. 17) [17833], [18027], [46277]

Everest Marketing [3698], [31342], [47856]

Everett Area Chamber of Commerce [66081]

Everett Business Journal (Vol. 6, No. 7, July 2003, pp. B1); "Busy Out-of-Towners Find Everett B&Bs the Way To Go" in [2431]

Everett Business Journal (Vol. 6, No. 12, December 2003, pp. A9); "The Wedding Planner" in [3200], [25045], [47708]

Everett Chamber of Commerce [60948]

Everett & Co. [3699], [10338], [16601], [31343], [38528]

Everett L. Gracey [62383]

Everglades Area Chamber of Commerce [58796]

Evergreen Area Chamber of Commerce [58363]

Evergreen Capital Partners Inc. [63090]

Evergreen/Conecuh Chamber of Commerce [56844]

Evergreen Freedom Foundation [41369]

Evergreen Park Chamber of Commerce [59495]

Evergreen Services Corp. [16143]

Everton's Genealogical Helper & Genealogy Online [10959]

Every Business Is a Growth Business: How Your Company Can Prosper Year after Year [28124]

"Every Picture Tells a Story: New Web Displays Provide Market Data at a Glance" in *Barron's* (August 25, 2003, pp. T6) [9940], [14023], [14965], [25847], [33864], [38040]

Everyone's Backyard [9387]

"Everyone's a CFO" in *Inc.* (September 2005, pp. 42, 45) [138], [2898], [26223], [45115]

"Everyone's Doing It" in *Entrepreneur* (Vol. 28, No. 4, pp. 62) [35436]

"Everyone's a Winner at the Chub Charity Challenge" in *Rough Notes* (Vol. 145, No. 2, February 2003, pp. 68) [11257], [54173]

"Everything I know about business I learned from Monopoly" in *Harvard Business Review* (Vol. 80, No. 3, March 2002, pp. 51) [24807], [39319], [46935]

"Everything In Its Place" in *San Fernando Valley Business Journal* (Vol. 8, No. 12, June 9, 2003, pp. 23) [20018], [30538], [52527]

"Everything designed with the customer in mind" in *Rough Notes* (Vol. 146, No. 3, March 2003, pp. 18) [13282], [31713], [43172]

"Everything in its Place: Can the Art of Feng Shui Help You Optimize Your Business?" in *Entrepreneur* (Vol. 32, August 2004, No. 8) [13640], [18542], [49497], [51147]

Everything You Always Wanted to Know about Management [35187], [37033], [45925]

"Everything You Ever Wanted to Know About Email" in *Inc.* (October 2005, pp. 113-117, 119, 122) [27364], [27636], [33865]

Everything You Need to Know to Start a House Cleaning Service [8684]

"The Evolution of E-Mail" in *Ingram's* (Vol. 28, No. 9, September 2002, pp. 62) [14024], [27365], [33866]

"The evolution of corporate diversity" in *Hispanic Business* (Vol. 22, No. 9, September 2000, pp. 36) [28125], [54174]

"The Evolution of XML Schemes" in *E-business Advisor* (Vol. 18, No. 5, May 2000, pp. 26) [22987], [33867], [53274]

eWeek (February 7, 2005); "Amid Customer Backlash, eBay Reduces Some Fees" in [1773], [13812], [31008], [31637], [33530]

eWeek (February 7, 2005); "BEA Ships Platform for Deploying Advanced Telecom Services" in [13838], [27303], [33566]

eWeek (February 1, 2005); "Dell Rolls Out New Models, Upgrade Program" in [6626], [49007]

eWeek (February 7, 2005); "Fake Microsoft Mail Is Sypware Phishing Attack" in [14030], [22227], [30219], [33878]

eWeek (February 2, 2005); "First Was Phishing, Next Is Pharming" in [14046], [22232], [30221], [33903]

eWeek (February 2, 2005); "Hacker 'Mudge' Returns to BBN" in [14098], [22243], [30227]

eWeek (February 3, 2005); "ISPs Need To Keep Moving Against Spam" in [14168], [30234], [34095]

eWeek (February 8, 2005); "Microsoft Buys Enterprise Anti-Virus Firm" in [4725], [6723], [22292], [23078], [50081], [53854]

eWeek (February 3, 2005); "Municipal Wi-Fi: Let's Keep It Local" in [14260], [34217], [41851]

eWeek (February 7, 2005); "OASIS Overhauls Intellectual Property Rights Policy" in [14302], [44107], [44344]

eWeek (February 7, 2005); "Socialtext Update Knots Closer Enterprise Ties" in [4808], [14454], [23185], [27501], [34508], [53981]

eWeek (February 7, 2005); "Sun CTO: New License Protects Developer Rights" in [4828], [23215], [44157], [54009]

eWeek (April 2, 2001, pp. 49); "The fast track to fortitude - Helping harried tech pros confront adversity" in [17052], [27371], [37132]

eWeek (February 3, 2005); "The Software Patent Conundrum" in [4817], [23202], [44150], [53482]

eWeek (February 2, 2005); "Xign's Order-to-Pay Service Aims to Save Time, Money" in [14637], [31609], [34753]

EWF International [21284]

"Ex-BBDO Exec Forms New Agency" in *Crain's Detroit Business* (Vol. 21, January 24, 2005, No. 4, pp. 18) [616], [3524], [19872], [31144], [36126], [46936], [50439]

"Ex-Breed exec sues automakers, suppliers over sensor patent" in *Crain's Detroit Business* (Vol. 19, No. 9, March 3, 2003, pp. 28) [1932], [18028], [29227], [44039]

"Ex-burger king teams with Hawkins; Group may be pursuing KFC deal" in *Crain's Detroit Business* (Vol. 18, No.51, Dec. 23, 2002, pp. 1) [21500], [28126], [38768], [49921]

"Ex-Im Bank cuts effect on small business unclear" in *Atlanta Business Chronicle* (Vol. 24, No. 3, June 22, 2001, pp. 54A) [39320], [39817], [40355]

"Ex-NYC Mayor's Investment Group Opens Office in Troy" in *Crain's Detroit Business* (Vol. 21, January 17, 2005, No. 3, pp. 29) [3525], [9941], [14966]

"Ex-Publisher Wants to Stop Gannett's Purchase of HomeTown" in *Crain's Detroit Business* (Vol. 21, January 31, 2005, No. 5, pp. 34) [14967], [18869], [49922]

"Ex-Tiger adds trucking company to his lineup" in *Crain's Detroit Business* (Vol. 16, No. 9, February 28, 2000, pp. 1) [25383], [28127], [48152]

Ex-Tracts - A Trade Show for Aromatherapy, Fragrance, and Personal Care [2619], [7926]

"Ex-TV Exec Sues Over Lentek Deal" in *Orlando Business Journal* (Vol. 20, No. 2, June 27, 2003, pp. 1) [24405], [25226], [29228]

"Exaggeration Nation" in *Inc.* (Volume 27, July 2005, No. 7, pp. 112) [28128], [37440]

"Exbayer Online Trading Assistant Helps You Sell Items on eBay with New Store" in *PR Newswire* (March 15, 2004) [1811], [7163], [10675], [18644], [33868]

Exceeding Customer Expectations [3629]

Excellence in Business Communication [27366]

"The Excellence Group Helping Good Schools Become Great." in *Mississippi Business Journal* (Vol. 28, September 2006, No. 37, pp. 30) [31145], [33092], [36127]

Excellence in Management [45116]

"Excellent leadership is all in the people leading" in *Atlanta Business Chronicle* (Vol. 24, No. 14, September 7, 2001, pp. 9B) [36128], [45117]

Excelsior Springs Area Chamber of Commerce [61959]

Export SBDC of Southern California **[57258]**

Export Services Center 54110

The Exporter **[13029]**, **[43896]**

Exporters' Encyclopedia **[12967]**

Exporter's Guide to Federal Resources for Small Business **[12968]**, **[39819]**

"The Exporting Advantage" in *Inc.* (August 2005, pp. 40, 42) **[12969]**, **[37636]**, **[43654]**, **[46280]**, **[51631]**

Exporting to Canada **[12970]**

Exportise: An International Trade Sourcebook for the Smaller Company Executive **[12971]**

"Exposed!" in *Red Herring* (Jan. 2003, pp. 42) **[44515]**, **[55599]**

Exposition Services and Contractors Association **[24864]**

Express Delivery and Logistics Association **[10660]**

Express Mart Franchising Corp. **[7793]**

Express Oil Change **[20267]**

Express One **[10720]**

"Express Personnel Exec Named American Staffing Association Committee Chair" in *Journal Record* (June 25, 2003) **[46941]**, **[48830]**, **[53423]**, **[56210]**

Express Personnel Services **[9271]**, **[9590]**, **[24547]**

"Express to Success" in *Small Business Opportunities* (Vol. 17, November 2005, No. 6, pp. 126-128) **[9175]**, **[37637]**, **[38632]**

Expressions Custom Furniture **[12345]**

ExpressTax **[24127]**

Extel Financial Cards **[15758]**

Extending Credit and Collecting Cash **[31543]**

Exton Region Chamber of Commerce **[64417]**

"Extra Credit" in *Entrepreneur* (Vol. 31, No. 5, May 2003, pp. 69) **[40361]**, **[54543]**

"The Extra Mile: Customer Service That's a Step Beyond" in *Sales & Marketing Management* (Vol. 157, February 2005, No. 2, pp. 18) **[14027]**, **[22225]**, **[30856]**, **[31715]**, **[45127]**, **[46942]**, **[51632]**

"The Extra Mile: Going Above and Beyond May Be Your Winning Business Strategy" in *Entrepreneur* (Vol. 32, No. 1, January 2004, pp. 27) **[22498]**, **[29870]**

"Extra scrutiny" in *Crain's Detroit Business* (Vol. 19, No. 11, March 17, 2003, pp. 14) **[36133]**, **[39324]**, **[45128]**

Extra Sense-Assistive Listening Devices for the Hearing Impaired **[12114]**

"Extra Special: Booking Sites Offer More Bang for Your Buck-And Then Some" in *Entrepreneur* (Vol. 32, November 2004, No. 11, pp. 22) **[25181]**, **[30323]**, **[33873]**

The Extra Step **[56625]**

"Extract, Transform and Load" in *Barron's* (August 11, 2003, pp. T2) **[4654]**, **[14971]**, **[22990]**, **[49923]**, **[53275]**

Extraordinary Entrepreneurship: The Professional's Guide to Starting an Exceptional Enterprise **[35439]**, **[39054]**

"Extreme hunter scores big with tiny funds" in *Red Herring* (March 2003, pp. 52) **[41677]**, **[46281]**, **[50868]**, **[52094]**

The Extreme Pita **[21809]**

Extreme Pizza **[19666]**

"Extreme Pizza eying Atlanta for expansion" in *Atlanta Business Chronicle* (Vol. 25, No. 19, October 18, 2002, pp. 21A) **[19630]**, **[21502]**, **[28136]**, **[38770]**

"Exxon Damages for Valdez Spill Are Cut In Half" in *Wall Street Journal* (Vol. 248, December 2006, No. 149, pp. A2) **[40362]**, **[44294]**

Exxon Research and Engineering Company–Information, Computing, and Business Systems **[56684]**

"Eye Candy: Life is Sweet for Two Visionaries Who Mix Sugary Treats with Style" in *Entrepreneur* (Vol. 32, No. 4, April 2004, pp. 168) **[4266]**, **[35440]**, **[51026]**

"Eye to Eye" in *Entrepreneur* (Vol. 32, October 2004, No. 10, pp. 89) **[27367]**, **[36134]**

"Eye to Eye: Sending Photos by Mobile Phone is Getting Easier" in *Entrepreneur* (Vol. 32, August 2004, No. 8, pp. 39) **[4185]**, **[4984]**

"An eye for a dye" in *Red Herring* (March 2003, pp. 60) **[46282]**, **[50869]**, **[52095]**, **[55600]**

"Eye on the Storm" in *Entrepreneur* (Vol. 33, September 2005, No. 9, pp. 43) **[4639]**, **[4655]**, **[6247]**, **[22687]**, **[22991]**, **[52528]**, **[53276]**

An Eye for Winners **[16409]**

Eyecare Business **[25654]**

"Eyeing Rivals, Foxwoods Set To Expand" in *Boston Globe* (February 2, 2005) **[10864]**, **[28137]**

"The eyes have it" in *Entrepreneur* (Vol. 30, No. 1, January 2002, pp. 18) **[25646]**

"Eyes on Iraq; 'I'd rather go with a Michigan company'" in *Crain's Detroit Business* (Vol. 19, No. 16, April 21, 2003, pp. 3) **[9355]**, **[40016]**, **[43655]**

"Eyes Wide Shut? The Inspiration You Need Could Be Right Under Your Nose" in *Entrepreneur* (Vol. 31, No. 9, July 2003, pp. 76) **[36135]**, **[45129]**

Eyewitness **[25655]**

EZ-DOCS : Government Documents for the People **[40895]**

"EZ Does It" in *Entrepreneur* (Vol. 33, January 2005, No. 1, pp. 53) **[23939]**, **[54544]**

"Ezsupport Life" in *Entrepreneur.com* (Vol. 34, February 2006, No. 2, pp. 6) **[14028]**, **[27368]**, **[27638]**, **[31716]**, **[33874]**, **[53277]**

F

F/22 Press **[19263]**

F & I Billing System **[18212]**

F & M Deli Express **[21810]**

F1RSTMARK Diagnostic Imaging Centers and Chains Directory **[17231]**

F1RSTMARK HMO Chains Directory **[17165]**

FA Technology Ventures **[63093]**

Fabled Service: Ordinary Acts, Extraordinary Outcomes **[34895]**

Jose Fabregas **[56662]**

"Fabric Flower Brooches, a 1930s-Era Wooden Crib, Dustpans Made Out of Old License Plates" in *Kansas City Star* (March 4, 2005) **[1513]**, **[5275]**, **[7164]**, **[12186]**, **[12280]**

"The fabric of consumer reality" in *Red Herring* (March 2003, pp. 54) **[31027]**, **[41678]**, **[46283]**, **[50870]**, **[52096]**

"Fabric of Success" in *Black Enterprise* (Vol. 35, February 2005, No. 7, pp. 92) **[5509]**, **[5626]**, **[9604]**

Fabricare **[8917]**

Fabricare Canada **[8918]**

FABRICARE - Great Western Exhibit **[8922]**

"Fabricating Photons" in *Red Herring* (No. 99, June 15 & July 1, 2001, pp. 110, 112-113) **[6935]**, **[41679]**, **[50871]**

The Fabricator **[16394]**

Fabricators and Manufacturers Association, International **[16351]**

Fabrion **[2013]**, **[22676]**

"Face to face" in *Incentive* (Vol. 174, No. 9, September 2000, pp. 102) **[27369]**, **[33875]**, **[51633]**

"Face-Off: Online Postage" in *FSB* (Vol. 10, No. 9, December 1, 2000, pp. 116) **[49023]**

"Face-Off: Survival of the Fittest" in *Folio: the Magazine for Magazine Management* (Vol. 32, No. 1, January 1, 2003) **[620]**, **[18870]**, **[19396]**, **[46943]**

"Face Up" in *Entrepreneur* (Vol. 28, No. 9, September 2000, pp. 56) **[27370]**

"Face Value" in *The Economist* (Vol. 376, July 30-August 5, 2005, No. 8437, pp. 60) **[11608]**, **[12004]**, **[20873]**, **[21319]**

FACES **[7932]**

Faces Cosmetics **[7933]**

Facilitation Skills for Team Leaders **[34896]** Crisp Learning–Thomson Learning **[35269]**

The Facilitator **[27552]**, **[56528]**

Facility Directions Inc. **[3700]**, **[31344]**, **[53087]**

Facility Layout and Location: An Analytical Approach **[52670]**

Facility Manager **[25056]**

"Facing the Cyber Threat" in *Hispanic Business* (Vol. 24, No. 5, May 2002, pp. 30, 32, 34) **[4656]**, **[22226]**, **[22992]**, **[53278]**

"Facing the Online Music" in *Inc.* (July 1, 2003) **[17741]**, **[29229]**, **[33876]**, **[36136]**, **[40363]**, **[44295]**

"Facing new pressure" in *Atlanta Business Chronicle* (Vol. 25, November 29, 2002, No. 25, pp. 1A) **[54175]**, **[56211]**

FACSNET **[8983]**

"Fact and Comment" in *Forbes Global* (Vol. 7, December 20, 2004, No. 22, pp. 9) **[29230]**, **[44296]**

"Factor Hurt by Funding Investments" in *South Florida Business Journal* (Vol. 24, No. 7, September 26, 2003, pp. 1) **[9945]**, **[14972]**, **[38044]**

"The Factoring Factor" in *Inc.* (February 1, 2002) **[31544]**

Factoring Small Receivables: How to Make Money in Little Deals the Big Guys Brush Off **[38045]**

"Factory Card Gets Back in Party Mood" in *Crain's Chicago Business* (Vol. 26, No. 50, December 15, 2003, pp. 6) **[11149]**, **[11562]**, **[28138]**, **[51148]**

"Factory Card Gets Back in Party Mood; Judicious Growth, Curtailed Costs Restore Firms Health" in *Crains Chicago Business* (Vol. 26) **[11150]**, **[11563]**, **[28139]**, **[51149]**

The Facts about Drug Use: Coping with Drugs and Alcohol in Your Family, at Work, in Your Community **[54334]**

"Facts about venture capital firms" in *Crain's Detroit Business* (Vol. 16, No. 19, May 8, 2000, pp. 20) **[55601]**

Facts about OSHA Inspections **[56626]**

"Fade to Black" in *Black Enterprise* (Vol. 31, No. 5, December 2000, pp. 107) **[9707]**, **[48154]**

"Failing to Rise to Women's Size" in *WWD* (September 24, 2003, pp. 14) **[5656]**

"Failure of Genius" in *Inc.* (August 1, 2003) **[26505]**, **[36137]**, **[45130]**

"Failure is Glorious" in *Fast Company* (November 2001, pp. 35) **[36138]**, **[37638]**, **[51150]**

"Failure is not an option" in *Fast Company* (June 2001, pp. 44) **[14029]**, **[31148]**, **[33877]**

"Failure Rates for Female-Controlled Businesses: Are They Any Different?" in *Journal of Small Business Management* (Vol. 41, July 2003) **[28140]**, **[56212]**

"A Fair Case: These Pretty Laptop Cases Are Pretty Functional, Too" in *Entrepreneur* (Vol. 32, July 2004, No. 7, pp. 34) **[6643]**, **[49024]**

Fair & Effective Discipline **[42925]**

"Fair Game" in *Entrepreneur* (Vol. 32, September 2004, No. 9, pp. 55) **[14973]**, **[38046]**

Fair Haven Area Chamber of Commerce **[62877]**

Fair Lawn Chamber of Commerce **[62499]**

Fair Oaks Chamber of Commerce **[57482]**

"Fair process: Managing in the knowledge economy" in *Harvard Business Review* (Vol. 81, No. 1, January 2003) **[34897]**, **[36139]**, **[45131]**

"Fair Share" in *Entrepreneur* (Vol. 33, January 2005, No. 1, pp. 44) **[6644]**, **[49025]**

"Fair Share" in *Entrepreneur.com* (Vol. 34, January 2006, No. 1, pp. 36) **[6645]**, **[49026]**

Fair, Square, & Legal: Safe Hiring, Managing & Firing Practices to Keep You & Your Company Out of Court **[42232]**

"A Fair Trade" in *Entrepreneur* (Vol. 31, October 2003) **[4985]**, **[26710]**, **[49924]**

Fairborn Area Chamber of Commerce **[63669]**

Fairbury Chamber of Commerce **[59496]**, **[62260]**

Fairchild Tropical Garden Views **[16036]**

The Fairer Sex? **[32087]**

Fairfax County Chamber of Commerce **[65890]**

Fairfax Partners **[65972]**

Fairfax SBDC–George Mason University **[65820]**

Fairfield Area Chamber of Commerce **[60132]**

Fairfield Bay Area Chamber of Commerce **[57162]**

Fairfield Chamber of Commerce **[58529]**, **[62164]**, **[63670]**, **[65222]**

Fairfield County Business Journal (Vol. 42, No. 3, Jan. 20, 2003, pp. 4); "Crafting the most productive and efficient work force" in **[34858]**, **[42209]**, **[45031]**

Fairfield County Business Journal (Vol. 43, November 1, 2004, No. 44, pp. 20); "Short of Time? Call a Wedding Planner" in **[3195]**

Fairfield County Chamber of Commerce [64734]

The Fairfield Factor Inc. [16866]

Fairfield University–Office of Grants and Sponsored Programs [58625]

"Fairhaven Business Owners Open Pottery Production Facility" in *Bellingham Business Journal* (December 2006, pp. A6) [8007], [28141], [37639]

Fairmont Area Chamber of Commerce [61586]

"Fairmont Hotels and Resorts Offers Help Asking Life's Most Important Question" in *PR Newswire* (January 20, 2005) [3181], [7130], [12547]

Fairmont State College–Small Business Development Center [66256]

Fairmont State College (Elkins Satellite)–SBDC [66257]

Fairview Area Chamber of Commerce [64911]

Fairview Chamber of Commerce [63991]

Fairview Heights Chamber of Commerce [59497]

"Fairview Heights, Ill., Mall Kiosk Vendors Say Holiday Sales Brisk" in *Belleville News-Democrat* (December 22, 2003) [15920]

Faith Chamber of Commerce [64823]

"Faith, Determination, and a Little Marinara Sauce" in *Success* (Vol. 47, No. 1, January 2000, pp. 80) [19619], [35441]

Faithworks Fitness [19505]

"Fake Microsoft Mail Is Sypware Phishing Attack" in *eWeek* (February 7, 2005) [14030], [22227], [30219], [33878]

Falcon Fund [58012]

Falfurrias Chamber of Commerce [65223]

Edgar Falk Communications [47857]

Fall River Area Chamber of Commerce and Industry [60949]

Fallbrook Chamber of Commerce [57483]

"Fallen and Can't Get Up: Even Greenspan Can't Hold Off the Bond Bears" in *Barron's* (July 21, 2003, pp. MW11) [9946], [14974], [32421], [38047]

"Fallen Idols" in *Fortune* (Vol. 142, No. 10, October 30, 2000, pp. 108+) [13747], [33437], [55378]

"Falling Behind" in *Entrepreneur* (Vol. 31, No. 8, August 2003, pp. 53) [28142], [32422]

"Falling Flat? How Flat is Too Flat When It Comes to Management?" in *Entrepreneur* (Vol. 33, January 2005, No. 1, pp. 69) [36140], [45132]

"Falling in Gov" in *Entrepreneur* (Vol. 30, No. 3, March 200) [6163], [25848], [30146], [33879], [53718]

"Falling for a Scan" in *Entrepreneur* (Vol. 31, No. 8, August 2003, pp. 50) [6646], [49027]

Falls Church Chamber of Commerce [65891]

Falls City Area Chamber of Commerce [62261]

Falmouth Chamber of Commerce [60950]

"False Start" in *Venture Capital Journal* (October 1, 2005) [14975], [49925], [55602]

"FAM Matters: This is Not Your Father's Equity-Income Fund" in *Entrepreneur* (Vol. 33, February 2005, No. 2, pp. 49) [14976], [38048]

Famaco Publishers [59016]

"Families and Work: Some Future Probabilities" in *Employment Relations Today* (Vol. 26, No. 4, Winter 2000, pp. 17) [40364], [54176]

"Family keeps answering calls after 75 years" in *Crain's Detroit Business* (Vol. 19, No. 11, March 17, 2003, pp. 13) [24423], [37640]

"A Family Affair-In Advertising" in *Business Week* (No. 3762, December 17, 2001, pp. 10) [621], [46944], [50588]

"A family affair" in *Black Enterprise* (Vol. 33, No. 3, October 2002, pp. 154) [29180], [29449], [29871], [30539], [36141], [37374], [37641], [38980], [50906], [54545]

"A Family Affair" in *Pittsburgh Business Times* (Vol. 22, No. 52, July 11, 2003, pp. 19) [16368], [18871], [37642], [46284]

"Family-Biz Circle" in *Business Week Online* (February 17, 2006) [29872], [37643], [45133]

Family Business [37644]

Family Business Advisor [37821]

Family Business Institute Inc. [3701], [3966], [16662], [37826], [46020]

"Family-Business Psychology" in *Forbes* (December 25, 2000, pp. 134) [31149], [37645]

Family Business: Text, Readings, & Cases [37646]

Family Campers and RVers [4226]

The Family Child Care Handbook: A Guide on How to Open Your Own Home Day Care [5313]

"Family Delivers on Father's Dream" in *Chicago Tribune* (March 9, 2005) [19620], [35442], [37564]

Family Findings [10960]

"Family Fun Center to Offer Laser Tag, Paintball, Miniature Golf" in *Gazette* (February 2, 2005) [1103], [17323]

Family Golf Centers: Business Profile [11258]

Family History Volume 10935

"Family divisions threaten Jervis B. Webb" in *Crain's Detroit Business* (Vol. 19, No. 11, March 17, 2003, pp. 20) [37647], [46285]

Family Law Reporter [29661]

"Family matters" in *Entrepreneur* (Vol. 31, No. 5, May 2003, pp. 30) [26803], [37648], [39325], [55603]

"Family Partnerships Under Scrutiny" in *Inc.* (Volume 27, July 2005, No. 7, pp. 26) [37649], [49926], [54546]

Family Resource Center on Disabilities [3702], [31345], [41330]

"Family Ties" in *Entrepreneur* (Vol. 31, No. 7, July 2003, pp. 30) [28143], [37650]

"Family Ties: Father and Sons Create Flooring Enterprise" in *Black Enterprise* (Vol. 35, November 2004, No. 4, pp. 56) [10509], [37651]

Family Tree Maker Family Histories [10993]

Family Tree Maker Family Pedigrees [10994]

"Family values: companies are catering to the needs of dad, mom and kids" in *Incentive* (Vol. 174, No. 10, October 2000, pp. 9) [26804], [53719]

Famous Famiglia [19667]

Famous Sam's, Inc. [21811]

Fan-A-Mania Entertainment & Sports [23704]

Fancy Food & Confection Show - Spring [4327], [23552]

Fancy Food & Culinary Products [4325], [21680]

"Fancy Footwork at Skechers and Brown" in *Business Week Online* (February 17, 2006) [9618], [22761]

"Fancy-Sounding Tax Hurts S Corps" in *Inc.* (January 1, 2005) [54547]

"Fandango Events Adds Show Division" in *Tradeshow Week* (Vol. 34, December 6, 2004, No. 49, pp. 2) [22499], [24933], [55093]

Fandom Directory [5906]

Fannin County Chamber of Commerce [59101]

Fanning, Fanning & Associates Inc. [1054], [7606]

"Fantastic Forum" in *Entrepreneur* (Vol. 33, September 2005, No. 9, pp. 92) [4641], [4657], [9708], [22689], [22993], [32865], [33880], [34898], [53279]

"Fantastic Plastic" in *Entrepreneur* (Vol. 33, January 2005, No. 1, pp. 49) [8308], [8383], [31545], [51151], [53720]

Fantastic Sams [11828]

"Fantastic Sams To Open Manatee County, Fla. Hair Salon" in *Bradenton Herald* (January 5, 2005) [11789], [28144], [38771], [52671]

"FAQs of Life in the New Economy" in *Fast Company* (September 2001, pp. 22) [28145], [32423]

Far East Capital Corp. [58013]

Fard Engineers Inc. [7607]

"Fare Cuts Might Signal End to Airlines as We Know Them" in *St. Louis Post-Dispatch* (January 9, 2005) [28146], [30324]

"Fare Game" in *Success* (Vol. 47, No. 1, January 2000, pp. 26) [30325]

Fargo Small Business Development Center–University of North Dakota [63541]

Faribault Area Chamber of Commerce [61587]

Farm Bureau ACRES [26650]

Farm Bureau News [26573]

Farm Credit Administration
    Office of Equal Employment Opportunity and Ombudsman [67103]
    Office of Inspector General [67104]
    Office of Support [67105]

Farm Credit Administration (FCA)–Office of Procurement [67106]

Farm Industry News [26574]

Farm and Ranch News [26575]

Farm and Ranch Tax Letter [26576]

Farm Tax Saver [24087]

Farmer Boys [10640], [21812]

"Farmer Jack plans to add up to 17 stores" in *Crain's Detroit Business* (Vol. 16, No. 50, December 11, 2000, pp. 25) [11609], [28147]

Farmers Branch Chamber of Commerce [65224]

"Farmers Faithful to Their Fields" in *Tampa Tribune* (November 28, 2005) [20505], [20874], [26506]

"Farmers' Livelihood Dried Up by Federal Regs" in *My Business* (September/October 2001, pp. 19) [26507], [40365]

Farmersville Chamber of Commerce [57484], [65225]

"Farming IT Out" in *Home Office Computing* (Vol. 18, No. 10, October 2000, pp. 16) [33881], [42612], [49028], [49694]

Farming Uncle [26577]

"Farmingdale-based THM Scientific Introduces Product Line Based on Sustainable Agriculture" in *Long Island Business News* (Feb.6, 2004) [16012], [26508], [48728], [49927], [50872], [52097]

Farmingdale State University of New York–Small Business Development Center [60178], [62757]

Farmington Area Chamber of Commerce [61588]

Farmington Chamber of Commerce [58530], [61960], [62687], [62878]

Farmington - Farmington Hills Chamber of Commerce [61294]

Farmington River Watershed Association–Environmental Research Center [9435]

Farmville Chamber of Commerce [63360], [65892]

The Farnsworth Group [47858]

Farwell Area Chamber of Commerce [61295]

Farwell Chamber of Commerce [65226]

Farwest Nursery Show [11489]

FAS Property Tax & Fixed Asset Programs–Sage Software SB, Inc. [409], [24161]

FASB 95: Statement of Cash Flows [27212]

Fashion Calendar [5541]

"The Fashion Elite" in *Black Enterprise* (Vol. 35, September 2004, No. 2, pp. 118) [5542], [5657], [12882], [20118]

Fashion Exports New York [5520], [5636], [43495]

Fashion Group International [2388], [5521], [9608], [12176], [12261]

Fashion Institute of Design & Merchandising
    Cyril Magnin Resource and Research Center [2144], [5609], [5760], [11922]
    Resource and Research Center [5610], [7961], [11923]

Fashion Institute of Technology–Gladys Marcus Library [2145], [5611], [5761], [7962], [9662], [11924], [13725]

Fashion International [5584], [5737]

Fashion & Print Directory [5981], [17336], [23826], [46945]

"Fashion Sense Dictates Where Women Shop" in *Marketing to Women* (Vol. 19, October 2006, No. 10, pp. 7) [5658], [9619], [28148], [46946]

"Fashionistas Weigh in on the Super-Thin" in *Charlotte Observer* (February 7, 2007) [5543], [5659], [17337]

"Fashion's phat cats" in *Black Enterprise* (Vol. 33, No. 3, October 2002, pp. S8) [5510], [5627], [5728], [53898], [56722]

Fasken Martineau DuMoulin LLP–Toronto Library [9528]

"The fast & the franchising" in *Entrepreneur* (Vol. 30, No. 3, March 2002, pp. 100) [35443], [38772]

"Fast Change for Lopez Foods" in *Hispanic Business* (January/February 2004, pp. 58, 60) [4059], [21503], [48155]

Fast Company (March 2005, No. 92, pp. 32); "60 Seconds On Doing the Impossible" in [35746], [41494], [50801], [52029]

Fast Company (August 2001, pp. 50); "A Dose of Change" in [36028], [37125]

Fast Company (March 2005, No. 92, pp. 35); "A Matter of Taste" in [48766], [50920], [52148]

Fast Company (August 2001, pp. 38); "A Message About Managing Email" in **[14240]**, **[54968]**

Fast Company (May 2001, pp. 143); "A Tale of Two Cities" in **[14506]**, **[23222]**, **[37196]**, **[52737]**, **[54023]**

Fast Company (May 2001, pp. 155); "A Tale of Two Cities: Livin' La Vida Boca" in **[14507]**, **[23223]**, **[37197]**, **[52738]**

Fast Company (May 2001, pp. 201); "Against the Grain" in **[13806]**, **[27758]**, **[33521]**

Fast Company (June 2001, pp. 147); "Agenda Items" in **[39137]**, **[43985]**

Fast Company (August 2001, pp. 78); "Andy Pearson Finds Love" in **[35770]**, **[44887]**

Fast Company (May 2001, pp. 82); "Ask Yourself What the Hell Really Works Here?" in **[31619]**, **[35322]**

Fast Company (July 2001, pp. 50); "Attention Readers!" in **[39155]**, **[44907]**, **[46692]**

Fast Company (November 2001, pp. 46); "Attitude Adjustment" in **[13828]**, **[37103]**

Fast Company (November 2001, pp. 50); "Banking on Tomorrow" in **[9834]**, **[14774]**, **[30506]**

Fast Company (March 2005, No. 92, pp. 68); "Building a Better Skunk Works" in **[6566]**, **[7840]**, **[27714]**

Fast Company (November 2001, pp. 30); "California Teaming" in **[39216]**, **[53631]**

Fast Company (August 2001, pp. 108); "Can C.K. Prahalad Pass the Test?" in **[31121]**, **[35356]**

Fast Company (June 2001, pp. 186); "Can you keep a secret?" in **[13883]**, **[33644]**, **[46776]**

Fast Company (November 2001, pp. 119); "Can This Off-Site Be Saved?" in **[24901]**, **[39218]**

Fast Company (August 2001, pp. 38); "Carry a Tune" in **[37112]**, **[48981]**

Fast Company (May 2001, pp. 80); "Cash is King" in **[27931]**, **[32309]**, **[46784]**

Fast Company (June 2001, pp. 169); "Change is Sweet" in **[13892]**, **[25815]**, **[33662]**

Fast Company (November 2001, pp. 138); "Code of Conduct" in **[4621]**, **[22943]**

Fast Company (May 2001, pp. 62); "Control Freak" in **[48996]**

Fast Company (March 2005, No. 92, pp. 74); "Cracking Jones Soda's Secret Formula" in **[12879]**, **[20115]**, **[46847]**, **[50435]**

Fast Company (May 2001, pp. 88); "Cycles teach you patience" in **[32344]**, **[35999]**, **[45041]**

Fast Company (May 2001, pp. 175); "Dan Case's Next Great IPO" in **[14902]**, **[36000]**, **[49886]**

Fast Company (September 2001, pp. 48); "Design Principal" in **[50856]**, **[54940]**

Fast Company (May 2001, pp. 183); "Digital Rx" in **[26215]**, **[28039]**, **[37123]**

Fast Company (March 2005, No. 92, pp. 88); "Do You Love What You Do?" in **[31141]**, **[33074]**, **[34872]**, **[45071]**

Fast Company (August 2001, pp. 140); "Don't Just Listen Connect" in **[31142]**, **[31702]**, **[46910]**

Fast Company (November 2001, pp. 144); "Engine of Progress" in **[44033]**, **[50867]**

Fast Company (November 2001, pp. 35); "Failure is Glorious" in **[36138]**, **[37638]**, **[51150]**

Fast Company (June 2001, pp. 44); "Failure is not an option" in **[14029]**, **[31148]**, **[33877]**

Fast Company (September 2001, pp. 22); "FAQs of Life in the New Economy" in **[28145]**, **[32423]**

Fast Company (September 2001, pp. 80); "Fast Talk" in **[31717]**, **[46948]**

Fast Company (October 2001, pp. 46); "FC Shortlist" in **[30852]**, **[37133]**, **[46953]**

Fast Company (June 2001, pp. 46); "Five Ways to Avoid Disaster" in **[31152]**, **[33906]**, **[36160]**, **[37136]**

Fast Company (August 2001, pp. 10); "Flip the Competition" in **[30860]**, **[37137]**

Fast Company (June 2001, pp. 64); "Fred Smith" in **[10677]**, **[36180]**, **[45162]**

Fast Company (May 2001, pp. 136); "Free Agents in the Olde World" in **[28184]**, **[31031]**, **[46982]**

Fast Company (May 2001, pp. 62); "Full-time freelancers" in **[35475]**, **[37565]**

Fast Company (March 2005, No. 92, pp. 90); "Gearing Up For Expansion" in **[4671]**, **[23010]**, **[28197]**, **[45173]**, **[53746]**

Fast Company (May 2001, pp. 196); "Get Your Digital Data Fix" in **[14072]**, **[33946]**, **[36201]**

Fast Company (September 2001, pp. 74); "Give Me Mylanta" in **[30337]**

Fast Company (November 2001, pp. 90); "Good to Great" in **[28218]**

Fast Company (May 2001, pp. 96); "Groove makes it possible to light up the edge" in **[6939]**, **[23023]**, **[53307]**

Fast Company (May 2001, pp. 108); "Hard Cell" in **[5010]**, **[47055]**, **[48741]**

Fast Company (August 2001, pp. 40); "Has Your Company Found Its Voice?" in **[33997]**, **[47057]**, **[50603]**

Fast Company (November 2001, pp. 48); "Have Kid, Won't Travel" in **[30344]**, **[31163]**, **[36264]**, **[41730]**

Fast Company (September 2001, pp. 186); "He drills for knowledge" in **[44306]**

Fast Company (November 2001, pp. 44); "Hey, Got a Qpass Rookie Card?" in **[47068]**, **[50605]**

Fast Company (November 2001, pp. 66); "His Word is Law" in **[36288]**, **[37147]**

Fast Company (November 2001, pp. 106); "How EDS Got Its Groove Back" in **[28302]**, **[36303]**, **[37148]**

Fast Company (September 2001, pp. 134); "How do Fast Companies Work Now?" in **[3543]**, **[35513]**, **[55393]**

Fast Company (March 2005, No. 92, pp. 72); "How IBM Builds New Businesses" in **[6678]**, **[7844]**, **[28304]**

Fast Company (July 2001, pp. 113); "How to Stay on the Move...When the World is Slowing Down" in **[29746]**, **[30484]**, **[35517]**

Fast Company (March 2005, No. 92, pp. 82); "Humanizing Leaders" in **[33126]**, **[36328]**, **[45280]**

Fast Company (November 2001, pp. 140); "If the Gene Fits" in **[50893]**

Fast Company (June 2001, pp. 161); "If I had had more experience, if I was more careful, if I was more competent" in **[15110]**, **[29299]**, **[40448]**

Fast Company (May 2001, pp. 54); "If the spirit moves you" in **[30352]**, **[53798]**

Fast Company (November 2001, pp. 82); "In My Humble Opinion" in **[14147]**, **[18887]**, **[24421]**, **[32507]**

Fast Company (September 2001, pp. 92); "In My Humble Opinion: They gathered this past spring" in **[34059]**, **[47131]**

Fast Company (February 2005, No. 91, pp. 26); "In Tune With the Environment" in **[17842]**, **[37299]**

Fast Company (July 2001, pp. 39); "Innovation To Go" in **[5030]**, **[37152]**

Fast Company (July 2001, pp. 152); "Intel is putting its chips on the Net" in **[39416]**, **[45306]**

Fast Company (June 2001, pp. 52); "Is Anybody in Charge?" in **[36361]**, **[45309]**

Fast Company (July 2001, pp. 145); "Is the Internet Second Nature" in **[14166]**, **[28347]**, **[34092]**

Fast Company (May 2001, pp. 193); "Jazzed About Work" in **[23056]**, **[53343]**

Fast Company (September 2001, pp. 177); "Job Inside" in **[14176]**, **[43951]**, **[49709]**

Fast Company (July 2001, pp. 50); "Job Titles of the Future" in **[5037]**, **[12891]**, **[16523]**, **[20129]**, **[22272]**, **[45323]**, **[50613]**

Fast Company (September 2001, pp. 60); "Job Titles of the Future: Chief Academic Officer" in **[33142]**, **[39422]**

Fast Company (September 2001, pp. 70); "Job Titles of the Future: Project Meanie" in **[4708]**, **[23058]**, **[45324]**

Fast Company (July 2001, pp. 100); "John Chambers after the deluge" in **[14177]**, **[34106]**, **[36387]**

Fast Company (March 2005, No. 92, pp. 44); "Kate and Andy Spade Are That Rare Thing: A Great Husband-and-Wife Business Team" in **[5552]**, **[5675]**, **[9627]**, **[36395]**, **[37708]**

Fast Company (May 2001, pp. 125); "Land of the Free" in **[32537]**, **[39428]**

Fast Company (July 2001, pp. 46); "Lead Softly, but Carry a Big Baton" in **[39430]**, **[47188]**

Fast Company (July 2001, pp. 56); "Leaders for the Long Haul" in **[25396]**, **[39431]**, **[45346]**

Fast Company (June 2001, pp. 179); "Lear won't take a back seat" in **[37159]**, **[46338]**

Fast Company (March 2005, No. 92, pp. 28); "Liquidity Events" in **[14207]**, **[55709]**

Fast Company (June 2001, pp. 70); "Many things matter, and here's what matters most" in **[39459]**

Fast Company (August 2001, pp. 88); "Marcus Buckingham Thinks Your Boss Has an Attitude Problem" in **[31189]**, **[45417]**

Fast Company (November 2001, pp. 46); "Master of Disaster" in **[3558]**, **[31192]**, **[36490]**

Fast Company (May 2001, pp. 72); "Meg Whitman" in **[14237]**, **[34188]**, **[45431]**

Fast Company (November 2001, pp. 156); "Merrill Lynch Phones Ahead" in **[5055]**, **[14239]**, **[15261]**, **[49143]**, **[53851]**

Fast Company (November 2001, pp. 38); "My Favorite Fiascos" in **[36517]**, **[47306]**, **[51256]**

Fast Company (August 2001, pp. 129); "Net Company: Don't Shout, Listen" in **[14272]**, **[31796]**, **[34238]**, **[47316]**, **[50640]**

Fast Company (September 2001, pp. 76); "New Frontiers to Explore" in **[36539]**, **[39490]**

Fast Company (August 2001, pp. 36); "New Growth in the Garden State" in **[27662]**, **[39491]**

Fast Company (September 2001, pp. 160); "No Room for Mediocrity" in **[12605]**, **[31801]**

Fast Company (November 2001, pp. 36); "Nothing but Net" in **[37172]**, **[53890]**

Fast Company (September 2001, pp. 68); "One Smart Customer" in **[31807]**, **[34284]**

Fast Company (September 2001, pp. 60); "Organize Yourself" in **[14329]**, **[36593]**

Fast Company (May 2001, pp. 166); "Past Track to the Future" in **[36605]**, **[45517]**

Fast Company (September 2001, pp. 164); "Present Perfect" in **[30405]**, **[31822]**

Fast Company (May 2001, pp. 50); "Quiet Riot" in **[18558]**, **[49542]**

Fast Company (August 2001, pp. 102); "Rapid Motion" in **[5095]**, **[37183]**

Fast Company (May 2001, pp. 202); "Read Smart, Grow Smart" in **[6276]**, **[13773]**, **[14386]**, **[27732]**, **[33480]**, **[35618]**

Fast Company (November 2001, pp. 40); "Recipe for Growth" in **[1417]**, **[28680]**, **[44130]**

Fast Company (July 2001, pp. 52); "Reproduction Right" in **[39558]**, **[49229]**

Fast Company (June 2001, pp. 48); "Reverence for radicals" in **[45601]**, **[47472]**

Fast Company (May 2001, pp. 42); "Right on the Money?" in **[55810]**

Fast Company (July 2001, pp. 88); "Roger Cass the Last Optimist" in **[36705]**, **[39564]**

Fast Company (March 2005, No. 92, pp. 39); "Screen Gems" in **[9739]**, **[17529]**, **[25596]**, **[35059]**, **[36724]**, **[45623]**

Fast Company (September 2001, pp. 62); "Simplicity by Design" in **[5569]**, **[36745]**

Fast Company (August 2001, pp. 27); "Slack Off" in **[31217]**, **[35072]**, **[37187]**, **[54988]**

Fast Company (August 2001, pp. 44); "Small Package" in **[14448]**, **[37191]**

Fast Company (August 2001, pp. 22); "Soul Progress" in **[5116]**, **[14464]**, **[25969]**, **[35654]**

Fast Company (March 2005, No. 92, pp. 30); "Speak Easy" in **[22562]**, **[36773]**, **[45656]**

Fast Company (August 2001, pp. 145); "Starbucks Brews a New Strategy" in **[11349]**, **[14480]**, **[34532]**, **[47570]**

Fast Company (May 2001, pp. 84); "Succeeding in adversity makes success all the sweeter" in **[36814]**, **[56419]**

Fast Company (July 2001, pp. 52); "Take Your Life for a Spin" in **[15501]**, **[45703]**

Fast Company (May 2001, pp. 44); "Taking Stock" in **[15505]**, **[37195]**, **[38399]**

Fast Company (July 2001, pp. 62); "Taste, Bud" in **[12793]**, **[47612]**, **[48799]**

Fast Company (September 2001, pp. 66); "Teacher in Chief" in **[31876]**, **[35089]**, **[45713]**

Fast Company (September 2001, pp. 18); "The Age of Disruption" in **[32237]**, **[37099]**

Fast Company (November 2001, pp. 58); "The American Cancer Society's Next Crusade" in **[39140]**, **[44883]**

Fast Company (August 2001, pp. 116); "The Art of Business Judo" in **[27788]**, **[30781]**

Fast Company (November 2001, pp. 134); "The Big Picture" in **[27842]**, **[37108]**, **[53607]**

Fast Company (August 2001, pp. 148); "The Buy-A-Wish Foundation Catalog" in **[35902]**, **[39214]**

Fast Company (March 2005, No. 92); "The Clear Leader: Marcus Buckingham Has Spent a Lot of Time Watching Leadership At Its Best" in **[35949]**, **[45003]**

Fast Company (May 2001, pp. 102); "The new culture of criticism is hurting you and your company" in **[47324]**, **[50642]**

Fast Company (November 2001, pp. 62); "The Incredible Shrinking Man" in **[50895]**, **[52127]**

Fast Company (July 2001, pp. 70); "The Innovation Conversation" in **[28329]**, **[39414]**, **[44067]**

Fast Company (November 2001, pp. 70); "The Old Economy Meets the New Economy" in **[28584]**, **[30576]**, **[31803]**, **[37174]**, **[39509]**

Fast Company (May 2001, pp. 90); "The last thing you should do is panic" in **[29927]**, **[32538]**

Fast Company (August 2001, pp. 196); "The Ultimate 12-Step in Business" in **[28934]**, **[32761]**

Fast Company (February 2005, No. 91, pp. 23); "The Urge to Unbundle" in **[12862]**, **[20090]**, **[31101]**

Fast Company (September 2001, pp. 168); "The Wheel Deal" in **[16275]**, **[30445]**

Fast Company (June 2001, pp. 76); "There is no correlation at all between success and hours worked" in **[36849]**, **[54993]**

Fast Company (September 2001, pp. 70); "This Phone Connects" in **[5149]**, **[49316]**

Fast Company (September 2001, pp. 166); "3.5 Trillion Miles...and Counting" in **[30426]**

Fast Company (May 2001, pp. 86); "Tough Times build character" in **[15537]**, **[36882]**, **[39635]**

Fast Company (September 2001, pp. 170); "Travel...More and Less" in **[30433]**, **[54047]**

Fast Company (May 2001, pp. 85); "Trouble on the horizon...isn't going away" in **[36886]**, **[45767]**

Fast Company (September 2001, pp. 36); "Vancouver Vanguard" in **[28956]**, **[30984]**, **[43869]**

Fast Company (September 2001, pp. 72); "View Master" in **[31241]**, **[36915]**

Fast Company (June 2001, pp. 62); "Virus hunter" in **[14569]**, **[23250]**

Fast Company (May 2001, pp. 186); "Web Audio - You Can Take It With You" in **[14580]**, **[25998]**, **[34664]**

Fast Company (May 2001, pp. 66); "What are you complaining about?" in **[35138]**, **[39663]**, **[45803]**

Fast Company (March 2005, No. 92, pp. 96); "What I Know Now" in **[7848]**, **[45809]**

Fast Company (September 2001, pp. 118); "What Is the New Economics?" in **[14601]**, **[32788]**

Fast Company (November 2001, pp. 165); "What Took You So Long To Call?" in **[5172]**, **[14602]**, **[28992]**

Fast Company (June 2001, pp. 85); "What's on Your Agenda?" in **[39672]**, **[45823]**

Fast Company (June 2001, pp. 138); "When a Customer Believes in You...They'll Stick with You Almost No Matter What" in **[31905]**

Fast Company (September 2001, pp. 128); "Where is the new frontier of innovation?" in **[35144]**, **[37210]**, **[44381]**, **[50992]**

Fast Company (September 2001, pp. 108); "Who has the next big idea?" in **[3612]**, **[29005]**, **[31251]**, **[39680]**, **[54076]**

Fast Company (September 2001, pp. 192); "Who Owns Your Intranet?" in **[14616]**, **[43954]**

Fast Company (July 2001, pp. 158); "Why 'Real-Time' Business Takes Real Time" in **[14620]**, **[23260]**, **[34721]**

Fast Company (March 2005, No. 92, pp. 94); "Wingate Inn, the Preferred Hotel of the Company of Friends" in **[12656]**, **[30449]**, **[50266]**

Fast Company (November 2001, pp. 48); "Work and Play" in **[39692]**, **[49374]**

Fast Company (July 2001, pp. 66); "You Can Quote Him" in **[15618]**, **[37001]**

Fast Company (June 2001, pp. 106); "You can't lead without making sacrifices" in **[39700]**, **[45878]**

Fast Company (May 2001, pp. 60); "Your space is the place" in **[20706]**, **[30056]**, **[42478]**, **[52758]**

Fast Company (May 2001, pp. 92); "You've got to keep your nose down and your fanny up" in **[32810]**, **[45884]**

Fast Company's Greatest Hits: Ten Years of the Most Innovative Ideas in Business **[36142]**, **[39326]**, **[44040]**

Fast Eddie's Twin Drive-Thru Restaurants **[21813]**

"Fast Facts" in *Entrepreneur* (Vol. 28, No. 11, November 2000, pp. 30) **[33882]**

"Fast, Faster, and Fastest" in *Fortune* (Vol. 142, No. 11, November 13, 2000, pp. F384FF) **[14031]**, **[53721]**

Fast-Fix Jewelry Repairs **[15882]**

The Fast Food & Multi-Unit Restaurant Business **[21504]**, **[21673]**

"Fast and fun" in *WorkingWoman* (Vol. 25, No. 7, August 2000, pp. 88) **[18030]**, **[18031]**

"The Fast Lane: A New Concept in Retail is Popping Up All Over" in *Entrepreneur* (Vol. 33, January 2005, No. 1, pp. 64) **[15921]**, **[51152]**, **[53722]**

"Fast Learner" in *My Business* (April/May 2004, pp. 48) **[11108]**, **[42613]**, **[56214]**

"Fast times at Pepsi High" in *WorkingWoman* (Vol. 25, No. 2, February 2000, pp. 20) **[46947]**

Fast Start in Real Estate: A Survival Guide for New Agents **[20506]**

"Fast Talk" in *Fast Company* (September 2001, pp. 80) **[31717]**, **[46948]**

Fast-teks On-site Computer Serviced **[6437]**, **[48507]**

"Fast Times" in *Entrepreneur* (Vol. 32, November 2004, No. 11, pp. 28) **[36143]**, **[56742]**

"Fast Track Business" in *Hispanic Business* (March 2002, pp. 60-62) **[36144]**, **[45134]**

Fast-Track Business Start-Up Kit: California **[35444]**, **[37275]**, **[39055]**, **[40366]**, **[42852]**, **[51483]**, **[54300]**, **[54548]**

"The Fast Track to CE Credits" in *Rough Notes* (Vol. 145, No. 2, February 2003, pp. 84) **[6330]**, **[13283]**, **[33095]**, **[33883]**, **[43173]**

Fast-Track Employer's Kit: California **[36145]**, **[39327]**

"Fast Track" in *Entrepreneur* (Vol. 28, No. 1, January 2000, pp. 42) **[7802]**, **[56001]**, **[56044]**

"The Fast Track: How to Jet Through the Airport and Get On Your Way" in *Entrepreneur* (Vol. 31, No. 7, July 2003, pp. 24) **[30326]**

Fast Track Marketing: Implementing Innovative Tactics in the Global Marketplace **[46949]**

"The fast track to fortitude - Helping harried tech pros confront adversity" in *eWeek* (April 2, 2001, pp. 49) **[17052]**, **[27371]**, **[37132]**

FastBucks **[5261]**

Faster Company: Building the World's Nuttiest, Turn-on-a-Dime, Home-Grown, Billion Dollar Business **[28149]**, **[29873]**

"Faster Tech Transfer" in *Inc.* (July 1, 2003) **[29231]**, **[35445]**, **[41680]**, **[44041]**, **[44297]**

"Fastest Growth by Revenue Category" in *San Fernando Valley Business Journal* (Vol. 11, November 2006, No. 24, pp. 21) **[14977]**, **[28150]**, **[39328]**

Fastfit 30 Minute Fitness For Men **[19506]**

Fastframe USA **[19833]**

Fastline-Bluegrass Truck Edition **[6109]**, **[10711]**

Fastline-Florida Truck Edition **[6110]**, **[10712]**

Fastline-Georgia Truck Edition **[6111]**, **[10713]**

Fastline-Illinois Farm Edition **[26578]**

Fastline-Indiana Farm Edition **[26579]**

Fastline-Iowa Farm Edition **[26580]**

Fastline-Kansas Farm Edition **[26581]**

Fastline-Kentucky Farm Edition **[26582]**

Fastline-Mid-Atlantic Farm Edition **[26583]**

Fastline-Mid-South Farm Edition **[26584]**

Fastline-Minnesota Farm Edition **[26585]**

Fastline Missouri Farm Edition **[26586]**

Fastline-Nebraska Farm Edition **[26587]**

Fastline-Northeast Farm Edition **[26588]**

Fastline Ohio Farm Edition **[26589]**

Fastline-Oklahoma Farm Edition **[26590]**

Fastline-Rocky Mountain Farm Edition **[26591]**

Fastline-Southeast Farm Edition **[26592]**

Fastline-Tennessee Farm Edition **[26593]**

Fastline-Tennessee Truck Edition **[6112]**, **[10714]**

Fastline-Texas Farm Edition **[26594]**

Fastline-Tri-State Truck Edition **[6113]**, **[10715]**

Fastline-Wisconsin Farm Edition **[26595]**

Fastrackids International, Ltd. **[33364]**

FastSigns International, Inc. **[22809]**

"Fat-free selling expands wallets, not waistlines" in *Atlanta Business Chronicle* (Vol. 25, January 3, 2003, No. 30, pp. 2B) **[17379]**, **[20507]**, **[20875]**

"Father/Daughter Duo Finds Success in Classic Car Business" in *Macon Telegraph* (January 31, 2005) **[1813]**, **[14032]**, **[18031]**, **[37652]**

"Father Figure" in *Entrepreneur* (Vol. 33, October 2005, No. 10, pp. 36) **[37653]**, **[56215]**

"The Father of Spam: Half of All E-Mail Sent Today is Spam" in *Entrepreneur* (Vol. 31, No. 10, October 2003) **[33884]**, **[46950]**

"Fattah's Plan for Small Business" in *Philadelphia Inquirer* (February 6, 2007) **[39820]**, **[42614]**, **[44516]**

Faulkner Information Services **[6471]**, **[6647]**

John C. Faulkner **[47859]**

Fauquier County Chamber of Commerce **[65893]**

"Faurecia May Buy to Grow, but Only If It Fits Plan" in *Crain's Detroit Business* (Vol.23, January 15, 2007, No.3, pp. 1) **[29874]**, **[46286]**, **[49928]**

"Fax Attack: This Entrepreneur's Fighting Mad About Junk Faxes" in *Entrepreneur* (Vol. 32, No. 1, January 2004, pp. 34) **[622]**, **[27372]**, **[29232]**, **[46951]**

"Fax Regs Rethought" in *Inc.* (December 1, 2004) **[29233]**, **[40367]**, **[46952]**

Fayette Area Chamber of Commerce **[56845]**

Fayette Chamber of Commerce **[60133]**, **[64418]**

Fayette County Chamber of Commerce **[59102]**, **[63671]**, **[64912]**, **[66273]**

Fayetteville Chamber of Commerce **[57163]**, **[63361]**

Fayetteville - Lincoln County Chamber of Commerce **[64913]**

Fayetteville State University–Cape Fear Small Business and Technology Development Center **[63278]**

Fazoli's Systems Inc. **[21814]**

FBR Comotion Venture Capital **[66211]**

"FC Shortlist" in *Fast Company* (October 2001, pp. 46) **[30852]**, **[37133]**, **[46953]**

The FCA Newsletter **[10811]**

FCC Report **[5202]**

FCICA Update **[10518]**

FCP Consulting **[3703]**, **[16603]**, **[30079]**, **[31346]**, **[46021]**

FDA News **[7915]**, **[8818]**, **[40863]**

FDA Newsletter **[18178]**

FDA Week **[8819]**, **[40864]**, **[41194]**

"Fear Factor" in *Entrepreneur.com* (Vol. 34, February 2006, No. 2, pp. 144) **[28151]**, **[29875]**, **[36146]**

"Fear factor: does the idea of starting your own business paralyze you?" in *Entrepreneur* (Vol. 31, No. 6, June 2003, pp. 92) **[35446]**

"Fear of feedback" in *Harvard Business Review* (Vol. 81, No. 4, April 2003, pp. 101) **[30540]**, **[34899]**, **[36147]**, **[45135]**

"Fear of Filing" in *Working Woman* (Vol. 25, No. 2, February 2000, pp. 84) **[20019]**, **[33885]**, **[52529]**

"Fear of Filing" in *WorkingWoman* (Vol. 25, No. 2, February 2000, pp. 84) **[3527]**, **[33886]**, **[37134]**

"Feast or Famine" in *Black Enterprise* (Vol. 35, November 2004, No. 4, pp. 60) **[22114]**, **[36148]**, **[46954]**

"Feasts of Fancy" in *Ingram's* (Vol. 28, No. 2, February 2002, pp. 36) **[4543]**

Featherlite Exhibits **[55253]**

"Feature Filmdom" in *Hispanic Business* (March 2004, pp. 16) **[9709]**, **[48156]**

"February sales at Claire's jump 6 percent" in *Daily Business Review* (Vol. 77, No. 187, March 7, 2003) **[9620]**, **[15843]**, **[28152]**, **[43656]**, **[51153]**

"February Job Gains Boost Stocks, But Pay Scales Show Decline" in *Atlanta Journal-Constitution* (March 5, 2005) **[14978]**, **[28153]**, **[32424]**

"Fed Bumps Rate to 4.25 Percent" in *Milwaukee Journal Sentinel* (December 14, 2005) **[28154]**, **[32425]**

"The Fed Connection: 100 Most Influential Hispanics" in *Hispanic Business* (Vol. 23, No. 10, October, 2001) **[36149]**, **[39329]**

"Fed Model is Pointing to Some Upside for Stocks" in *Barron's* (August 18, 2003, pp. 15) **[9947]**, **[14979]**, **[38049]**, **[40368]**

"FedBizOpps Opens for Biz" in *Hispanic Business* (Vol. 23, No. 10, October, 2001, pp. 24) **[40017]**, **[48157]**

Federal Acquisition Regulation **[40018]**

Federal Bureau of Prisons–National Contracts and Policy Section **[67637]**

Federal Business Development Bank **[66769]**

Federal Career Opportunities **[23390]**

"Federal contractor arms itself with new CEO, scouts workers" in *Washington Business Journal* (Vol. 21, No. 44, Feb. 28, 2003, pp.1,3) **[16514]**

Federal Communications Commission
    Administrative Law Division **[67107]**
    Consumer Inquiries and Complaints Division **[67108]**
    Enforcement Bureau **[67109]**
    Office of Communications Business Opportunities **[67113]**
    Office of Media Relations **[67110]**
    Office of Workplace Diversity **[67111]**
    Wireless Telecommunications Bureau **[67112]**

Federal Communications Commission (FCC)–Homeland Security Policy Council **[67126]**

"Federal Contracts Draw New Scrutiny" in *Inc.* (August 2005, pp. 24) **[29234]**, **[40019]**, **[40369]**

Federal Contracts Report **[40120]**

Federal Deposit Insurance Corporation
    Boston Area Office (New York Region) **[67114]**
    Chicago Regional Office **[67115]**
    Kansas City Regional Office **[67116]**
    New York Regional Office **[67117]**
    Office of Diversity and Economic Opportunity–Minority and Women Outreach Program–Midwest Service Center **[67119]**
    Office of Diversity and Economic Opportunity–Minority and Women Outreach Program–Northeast Service Center (Connecticut) **[67120]**
    Office of Diversity and Economic Opportunity–Minority and Women Outreach Program–Northeast Service Center (Massachusetts) **[67121]**
    Office of Diversity and Economic Opportunity–Minority and Women Outreach Program–Southeast Service Center **[67122]**
    Office of Diversity and Economic Opportunity–Minority and Women Outreach Program–Southwest Service Center **[67123]**
    Office of Diversity and Economic Opportunity–Minority and Women Outreach Program–Western Service Center **[67124]**
    San Francisco Regional Office **[67118]**

"Federal agencies generate most e-waste" in *Waste News* (Vol. 8, No. 10, September 16, 2002, pp. 12) **[21231]**, **[40370]**

Federal Emergency Management Agency **[67127]**

Federal Emergency Management Agency (Region 1)–Boston Regional Office **[67128]**

Federal Emergency Management Agency (Region 2)–New York Regional Office **[67129]**

Federal Emergency Management Agency (Region 3)–Philadelphia Regional Office **[67130]**

Federal Emergency Management Agency (Region 4)–Atlanta Regional Office **[67131]**

Federal Emergency Management Agency (Region 5)–Chicago Regional Office **[67132]**

Federal Emergency Management Agency (Region 6)–Denton Regional Office **[67133]**

Federal Emergency Management Agency (Region 7)–Kansas City Regional Office **[67134]**

Federal Emergency Management Agency (Region 8)–Denver Regional Office **[67135]**

Federal Emergency Management Agency (Region 9)–Oakland Regional Office **[67136]**

Federal Emergency Management Agency (Region 10)–Bothell Regional Office **[67137]**

"Federal File: News & Developments in the Business of Government" in *Hispanic Business* (December 2001, pp. FG4, FG6, FG14, FG16) **[26509]**, **[40020]**, **[40371]**, **[48158]**, **[48546]**

Federal Home Loan Mortgage Corporation
    Northeast Region **[67142]**
    Southeast Region **[67143]**
    Southwest Region **[67144]**
    Western Region **[67145]**

Federal Home Loan Mortgage Corporation (Freddie Mac) **[67146]**

Federal Housing Finance Board **[67147]**
    Office of Supervision **[67148]**

Federal Income Taxation of Corporations and Shareholders **[24139]**, **[54899]**

Federal Income Taxation of S Corporations **[51497]**, **[54900]**

Federal Jobs Digest **[23374]**

Federal Laboratory Research and Technology **[17232]**, **[51010]**

"Federal Legislation Lays Groundwork for Electronic Check Exchange" in *Long Island Business News* (February 13, 2004) **[9948]**, **[31546]**, **[40372]**

"Federal funds may spur Legislature to re-enact transit bill" in *Crain's Detroit Business* (Vol. 19, No. 1, January 6, 2003, pp. 5) **[39766]**, **[40373]**

Federal Licensable Technologies and Patents **[44210]**

Federal Mediation and Conciliation Service–Office of Public Affairs **[67149]**

Federal Mediation and Conciliation Service (FMCS)–Office of Procurement **[67150]**

"Federal-Mogul Reaches Ch. 11 Deal" in *Crain's Detroit Business* (Vol. 19, No. 45, November 10, 2003, pp. 4) **[1934]**, **[1946]**, **[38050]**, **[38476]**

Federal Motor Carrier Safety Regulations: Management Edition **[25384]**

"Federal suit alleges MVM overbilled" in *Washington Business Journal* (Vol. 21, No. 50, April 11, 2003, pp. 1) **[141]**, **[22228]**, **[29235]**, **[37442]**, **[43174]**

Federal Prime Contracts Data Base **[40121]**

"Federal stimulus can ensure recovery" in *Atlanta Business Chronicle* (Vol. 25, January 10, 2003, No. 31, pp. 32A) **[28155]**, **[32426]**, **[40374]**, **[54549]**

Federal Research in Progress (FEDRIP) **[52098]**

Federal Research Report **[52099]**, **[55604]**

"Federal Reserve Raises Key Interest Rate by Quarter Point" in *Boston Globe* (February 3, 2005) **[40375]**, **[44517]**, **[54550]**

"Federal Resource Guide 2002-2003" in *Hispanic Business* (December 2002, pp. FRG1-FRG2) **[39821]**, **[40021]**

Federal Taxation of Partnerships & Partners **[54901]**

Federal Taxes Weekly Alert **[24140]**, **[54902]**

"Federal Trade Comm. Report Says Long Island a Favorite of Scam Artists" in *Long Island Business News* (January 30, 2004) **[29236]**, **[30220]**

Federal Trade Commission
    Atlanta Regional Office–Southeast Region **[67155]**
    Boston Regional Office–Northeast Region **[67156]**
    Bureau of Consumer Protection **[67152]**
    Chicago Regional Office–Midwest Region **[67157]**
    Cleveland Regional Office–East Central Region **[67158]**
    Dallas Regional Office–Southwest Region **[67159]**
    Denver Regional Office **[67160]**
    Los Angeles Regional Office **[67161]**
    New York Regional Office **[67162]**
    Office of Inspector General **[67153]**
    Procurement and General Service Division **[67154]**
    San Francisco Regional Office **[67163]**
    Seattle Regional Office **[67164]**

Federal and University Research and Technology **[17233]**, **[51011]**

Federal Veterinarian **[1252]**

Federal Way Chamber of Commerce **[66082]**

Federated Business Agencies **[3447]**

"Federated Department Stores Inc." in *Black Enterprise* (Vol. 34, No. 4, November 2003, pp. 62) **[45879]**, **[48159]**, **[48680]**, **[51154]**

Federation of American Scientists **[52027]**

Federation of BC Writers **[8958]**

Federation of Genealogical Societies **[10914]**

Federation of International Trade Associations **[43496]**

Federation des Travailleurs et Travailleuses du Quebec–Centre de Documentation **[55342]**

Federer Resources Inc. **[3704]**, **[16604]**, **[31347]**, **[35231]**, **[38529]**, **[46022]**, **[48824]**, **[53088]**

"FedEx Moves to Expand With Purchase of Kinko's" in *New York Times* (December 31, 2003, pp. C1) **[9949]**, **[14980]**, **[17313]**, **[19873]**, **[49929]**

"FedEx to launch service that allows small companies to build online stores" in *Wall Street Journal* (June 12, 2000, pp. A6) **[18645]**, **[33887]**

FEDLINK Technical Notes **[13097]**

"Feds Accuse Sacramento, Calif.-Based Restaurant of Sex Discrimination" in *Sacramento Bee* (September 30, 2005) **[21505]**, **[29237]**, **[32025]**

"The Feds Are Following You" in *PC Computing* (March 2000, pp. 94) **[13075]**, **[33888]**

FedUSA Insurance & Financial Services **[13581]**, **[43447]**

"Fee Bargain: Law Firm Mergers May Give You More Room to Negotiate Legal Fees" in *Entrepreneur* (Vol. 31, No. 7, July 2003, pp. 27) **[14981]**, **[29238]**, **[31028]**, **[49930]**

Feed-Lot **[1201]**

"Feed Me" in *Forbes* (Vol. 175, January 10, 2005, No. 1, pp. 38) **[14033]**, **[33889]**

"Feed the Need" in *Entrepreneur* (Vol. 32, July 2004, No. 7, pp. 47) **[14034]**, **[33890]**

Feedback **[20354]**

"Feedback Needed" in *Sales and Marketing.com* (Vol. 156, No. 3, March 2004, pp. 63) **[45136]**

"Feeding Frenzy" in *Entrepreneur.com* (Vol. 34, February 2006, No. 2, pp. 77) **[623]**, **[27373]**, **[27639]**, **[33891]**, **[46955]**

"Feel the Burn" in *Entrepreneur* (Vol. 32, December 2004, No. 12, pp. 54) **[6648]**, **[38709]**, **[39304]**, **[40376]**, **[41007]**, **[41681]**, **[46694]**, **[49029]**, **[51845]**, **[54551]**

"Feeling Loaded Down? Use Partnerships to Bag New Customers" in *My Business* (October/November 2003, pp. 44) **[32153]**, **[46287]**, **[49030]**, **[49931]**, **[51634]**

"Feeling his oats" in *Entrepreneur* (Vol. 30, No. 2, February 2002, p) **[11610]**, **[35447]**, **[54177]**

"Fees of Danger" in *Entrepreneur* (Vol. 33, February 2005, No. 2, pp. 50) **[9950]**, **[44518]**

Steven S. Feinberg **[38530]**

"FEI's Strategy for Reaching Big Leagues" in *Business Journal-Portland* (Vol. 20, No. 24, August 15, 2003, pp. 1) **[28156]**, **[29104]**, **[29771]**, **[30541]**, **[41682]**, **[43211]**, **[46288]**, **[47030]**

William J. Fejes **[49424]**

Barbara Whyte Felicetti **[37360]**

Feliciana Chamber of Commerce **[60634]**

"Feline Fortunes" in *Small Business Opportunities* (Vol. 12, No. 3, May 2000, pp. 62, 64) **[19138]**, **[35448]**

Feline Health Topics **[1253]**

"Fellowship of the rings" in *Atlanta Business Chronicle* (Vol. 25, No. 19, October 18, 2002, pp. 1B) **[34900]**, **[45137]**

Ben Felt & Associates **[26628]**

"Firms Will Spend Less on Buildings and Equipment This Year" in *Kiplinger Letter* (Vol. 78, January 19, 2007, No. 2) **[32434]**, **[41688]**, **[49031]**, **[49498]**

"Firms shape students into future workers" in *Atlanta Business Chronicle* (Vol. 24, No. 11, August 17, 2001, pp. 3B) **[33098]**, **[37135]**, **[49936]**

The First 90 Days Workshop (Canada) **[44754]**

First Aid on the Job **[56628]**

First Analysis Corp. **[59734]**

First Avenue Partners **[64996]**

"First Base: Finding Ways to Finance Your Venture" in *Crain's Detroit Business* (Vol. 19, No. 49, December 8, 2003, pp. 13) **[44411]**, **[46089]**, **[48905]**, **[49866]**

First, Break All the Rules: What the World's Greatest Managers Do Differently **[39335]**, **[45144]**

First Capital Management Co. LLC / FCG **[65605]**

First Choice Haircutters **[11829]**

First Class Auto - The Custom Shops **[2014]**

"First-Class Delivery" in *Small Business Opportunities* (Vol. 13, No. 5, September 2001, pp. 66, 80) **[6096]**, **[49695]**

First Class Seats Business Services, LLC **[11830]**

"First Data: New Terminal POS Lift for Small Outfits" in *American Banker* (Vol. 172, January 17, 2006, No. 11, pp. 17) **[4662]**, **[22999]**, **[41689]**, **[44231]**, **[49937]**, **[51158]**, **[53285]**

First Editions, a Guide to Identification **[2705]**

"First Finishes" in *Entrepreneur* (Vol. 32, No. 1, January 2004, pp. 84) **[38777]**

First Growth Capital, Inc. **[59194]**

"First-Half Disbursements Continue Venture Capital's Record-Setting Pace" in *Venture Capital Journal* (Vol. 40, No. 10, Oct.2000, pp. 47) **[28161]**, **[55615]**

First Health **[27027]**

"First Impressions" in *Black Enterprise* (Vol. 36, December 2005, No. 5, pp. 62) **[27375]**, **[39336]**, **[45145]**, **[46963]**

"First Impressions" in *Entrepreneur* (Vol. 33, March 2005, No. 3, pp. 90) **[626]**, **[46964]**

First Line Supervisor **[46506]**

First Moves: Welcoming a Child to a New Caregiving Setting **[5381]**

First New England Capital, L.P. **[58593]**

"First Person" in *Entrepreneur* (Vol. 28, No. 3, March 2000, pp. 146) **[31721]**, **[46965]**

First Princeton Capital Corp. **[62596]**

1st Propane **[32183]**

First-Rate Customer Service **[31915]**

First Security Business Investment Corp. **[65739]**

"First Slot Machines To Start Cranking in Maine Today" in *Portland Press Herald* (November 4, 2005) **[10865]**

"First to the Starting Line" in *Black Enterprise* (Vol. 36, December 2005, No. 5, pp. 32) **[44524]**, **[56221]**

First Step, Inc.–Small Business Development Center **[61187]**

First Strike Management Consulting Inc. **[3967]**, **[16605]**, **[31348]**, **[46024]**, **[53089]**

"First, Take a girl scout" in *Ingram's* (Vol. 27, No. 12, December 2001, pp. 30) **[21506]**, **[54181]**

"The First Task" in *Business Week Online* (February 17, 2006) **[51636]**

"First-Time Investor: Where Should You Put Your Money Straight Out of College?" in *Black Enterprise* (Vol. 35, November 2004, No. 4) **[9960]**, **[14993]**, **[38070]**

The First-Time Manager: A Survival Guide **[45146]**

The First-Time Sales Manager: A Survival Guide **[51637]**

First Tuesday **[20717]**, **[21050]**

First Union Capital Partners **[63456]**

"First Was Phishing, Next Is Pharming" in *eWeek* (February 2, 2005) **[14046]**, **[22232]**, **[30221]**, **[33903]**

First Washington Associates Ltd. **[43922]**

"The First Wedding Planning Board Game to Help Lower Divorce" in *PR Newswire* (January 5, 2004) **[3182]**, **[24810]**

"First Women's Sports Talk Show Launches" in *Marketing to Women* (Vol. 19, October 2006, No. 10, pp. 5) **[627]**, **[20316]**, **[23617]**, **[23719]**, **[46966]**

FirstList **[3418]**, **[49938]**

Fiscal Agents–Financial Information Service–Research Department - Library **[10400]**

Fish Window Cleaning Services, Inc. **[3365]**

"Fisher-Price Takes Top Honors at Annual Toy Fair" in *Buffalo News* (February 17, 2004) **[24811]**

Fisheries Museum of the Atlantic–Library **[10479]**

Fisheries of the United States **[10459]**

"Fisherman Joe's Reopens; Owner Hopes To Hook Customers With Late Hours" in *Bradenton Herald* (January 25, 2005) **[21507]**, **[36157]**

"Fishermen's Days Numbered; New Regs Would Cut Time at Sea" in *Providence Business News* (Vol. 18, No. 23, September 22, 2003, pp. 1) **[10426]**, **[10460]**, **[26510]**, **[40384]**

Fishers Chamber of Commerce **[59908]**

Fishery Bulletin **[10468]**

Fishing Tackle Retailer **[2180]**

Fishing Tackle Retailer-Buyer's Guide Issue **[2178]**

"Fishing for trouble" in *Entrepreneur* (Vol. 30, No. 12, December 2002, pp. 112) **[46967]**, **[51638]**

Fishkill SBDC Satellite–Marist College Extension **[62758]**

Fisons Corporation Limited–Information Resources Centre **[8864]**

"A Fistful of Hours" in *Inc.* (October 2000, pp. 58) **[26702]**, **[52773]**

Fit By Five Development Corp. **[5426]**

"Fit to Commit: This Small-Cap Fund Wants Investors for the Long Haul" in *Entrepreneur* (Vol. 31, No. 7, July 2003, pp. 50) **[9961]**, **[14994]**, **[38071]**

"Fit For a Waif" in *Business Week* (February 20, 2006, No. 3972, pp. 14) **[5661]**, **[51159]**

"Fit To Be Tied: New York Designer Directs Neckwear Fashions" in *Black Enterprise* (Vol. 35, September 2004, No. 2, pp. 194) **[5544]**, **[36158]**

"Fit and Trim" in *Entrepreneur* (Vol. 31, No. 7, July 2003, pp. 74) **[26235]**, **[38072]**

Fitch Insights **[15639]**

"Fitness 24 Buys DAC Club" in *Mississippi Business Journal* (Vol. 29, January 2007, No. 2, pp. 8) **[10461]**, **[19397]**, **[30678]**, **[49939]**

"Fitness Chain Curves Makes Boston Push" in *Boston Business Journal* (Vol. 23, No. 30, August 29, 2003, pp. 3) **[19398]**, **[28162]**, **[38778]**, **[46968]**

Fitness and Conditioning: Benefits for a Lifetime **[19470]**

Fitness Management Magazine **[18448]**, **[19455]**, **[26044]**, **[41196]**

"Fitting Home Offices Into Small Spaces" in *Home Business* (Vol. 12, March/April 2005, No. 2, pp. 82, 84-87) **[13642]**, **[18543]**, **[42616]**, **[49499]**

"A Fitting Memorial" in *Entrepreneur* (Vol. 32, No. 5, May 2004, pp. 130) **[10783]**, **[35454]**, **[43959]**

Fitzgerald Valuation Services Inc. **[21080]**

Fitzpatrick & Associates Inc. **[3086]**, **[3157]**

Fitzroy Dearborn Directory of Venture Capital Funds **[55616]**

FIU Hospitality Review **[12661]**

"Five Angels With Angles" in *Inc.* (Volume 27, July 2005, No. 7, pp. 92-99) **[44525]**, **[55617]**

"Five Checking Account Mistakes to Avoid" in *Black Enterprise* (Vol. 34, No. 5, December 2003, pp. S11) **[142]**, **[147]**, **[26236]**, **[27155]**, **[38073]**, **[39479]**

5 & Diner Franchise Corp. **[21817]**

"The Five Don'ts" in *Forbes* (Vol. 175, February 14, 2005, No. 3, pp. 110) **[9962]**, **[14995]**, **[38074]**

The Five Dysfunctions of a Team: A Leadership Fable **[34903]**, **[45147]**

"5 Ergonomic Guidelines for Yourself" in *My Business* (April/May 2002, pp. 44) **[56559]**

Five Guys **[21818]**

"5 Honeymoon Hints" in *My Business* (November/December 2001, pp. 46) **[34904]**, **[42240]**, **[45148]**

"Five Ideas To Watch" in *Inc.* (October 1, 2004) **[7055]**, **[11259]**, **[24408]**, **[52532]**

"Five Ideas to Watch" in *Inc.* (July 1, 2004) **[619]**, **[628]**, **[4663]**, **[6650]**, **[11612]**, **[12005]**, **[12548]**, **[21508]**, **[23000]**, **[24340]**, **[24686]**, **[25182]**, **[33904]**, **[41010]**, **[46408]**, **[46969]**, **[48679]**, **[48731]**

"The Five Minds of a Manager" in *Harvard Business Review* (Vol. 81, No. 11, November 2003, pp. 54) **[45149]**

"Five things to remember when raising money" in *Red Herring* (No. 76, March 2000, pp. 92) **[55383]**

"Five More VCs Slash Funds, Is There Any Room for More?" in *Venture Capital Journal* (Vol. 42, No. 8, August 2002, pp. 6, 8, 10) **[14996]**, **[55618]**

Five Paces Ventures **[59195]**

"The 5 Pitfalls Of CEO Succession" in *Fortuneit* (Vol. 146, No. 10, November 18, 2002, pp. 78) **[36159]**, **[39337]**, **[45150]**

"Five Questions: Diane Primo, Vice President, Chief Marketing Office, CDW" in *Sales & Marketing Management* (Vol. 157, February 2005) **[45151]**, **[46970]**, **[51639]**

"Five Questions" in *Sales & Marketing Management* (Vol. 157, January 2005, No. 1, pp. 15) **[28163]**, **[46971]**, **[50440]**, **[51640]**

"Five Questions" in *Sales and Marketing.com* (Vol. 156, No. 3, March 2004, pp. 11) **[33905]**, **[45152]**, **[46972]**

"5 Steps to Bigger Sales" in *Incentive* (Vol. 174, No. 10, October 2000, pp. 117) **[51641]**

Five Steps to Genealogy Publishing: A Guide to Researching, Preparing, Publishing, and Marketing Your Genealogical Publication **[10932]**

Five Steps to Successful Selling **[51952]**

"Five Ways to Avoid Disaster" in *Fast Company* (June 2001, pp. 46) **[31152]**, **[33906]**, **[36160]**, **[37136]**

"Five Ways to Finance Your Business" in *Black Enterprise* (Vol. 31, No. 3, October 2000, pp. 43) **[26703]**, **[35455]**, **[44412]**, **[55384]**

"Five Ways to Get People to Listen" in *Folio: the Magazine for Magazine Management* (Vol. 30, No. 1, January 2001, pp. 9) **[27376]**

"5 Ways to Get Rid of Clutter: Spring Cleaning" in *My Business* (April/May 2003, pp. 12) **[39338]**, **[54944]**

Fixed Asset Accounting **[26126]**

Fixed Coverage **[18179]**, **[22630]**

Fixed-Income Active Total Return Management: Risk Management and Portfolio Optimization Strategies **[14997]**

Fixed Income Analytics: State-of-the-Art Debt Analysis and Valuation Modeling **[14998]**

Fixed Income Mathematics **[14999]**

"Fixing the Alternative Minimum Tax" in *Kiplinger Letter* (Vol. 82, January 12, 2007, No. 1) **[54556]**

"Fixing Diversity-Challenged Companies" in *Black Enterprise* (Vol. 36, February 2006, No. 7, pp. 74) **[48548]**, **[53733]**

FJC Growth Capital **[56907]**

FJC Growth Capital Corp. **[56908]**

The Flag Shop **[20007]**

Flagler Beach Chamber of Commerce **[58797]**

Flagler County Palm Coast Chamber of Commerce **[58798]**

Flagship Ventures **[61070]**

Flagstaff Chamber of Commerce **[57030]**

"Flagstar splits its stock" in *Crain's Detroit Business* (Vol. 19, No. 17, April 28, 2003, pp. 2) **[9963]**, **[15000]**

The Flame Broiler, Inc. **[21819]**

Flamers Charbroiled **[21820]**

Flaming Gorge Corporation **[65712]**

Flamingo A Friend **[52624]**

Flash Book-on-Demand Publishing: Publishing & Printing Books on Your Laser Printer **[8610]**

"Flash: our outlook on what's new, what's hot and what's happening" in *Entrepreneur* (Vol. 31, No. 5, May 2003, pp. 6) **[4987]**, **[11613]**, **[21509]**, **[23477]**, **[24812]**, **[49032]**, **[53734]**

"Flat Fee Delivers Flexibility" in *Detroit News* (February 17, 2005) **[20508]**, **[53735]**

"A flat road ahead" in *My Business* (September/October 2001, pp. 47) **[28164]**, **[32435]**

Flatfooting Workshop **[8475]**

Flatiron Partners **[63095]**

Flatonia Chamber of Commerce **[65227]**

Flavour and Fragrance Journal **[2614]**

"The Flaw of averages" in *Harvard Business Review* (Vol. 80, No. 11, November 2002, pp. 20) **[148]**, **[4664]**, **[15001]**, **[23001]**, **[26237]**, **[38075]**, **[51642]**

"Flaw and Order: Are You Apt to Make Mistakes? You're Not Alone" in *Entrepreneur* (Vol. 32) **[36161]**, **[45153]**

Flawless Consulting: A Guide to Getting Your Expertise Used **[3532]**, **[9357]**, **[12883]**, **[16516]**, **[20119]**

"Flea-market bill would ban sales of certain items" in *Crain's Detroit Business* (Vol. 16, No. 49, December 4, 2000, pp. 44) **[40385]**, **[51160]**

Fleeced: Telemarketing Rip-offs & How to Avoid Them **[30222]**

Fleet Equipment **[25433]**

Fleet Equipment-Management Resource Directory Issue **[25385]**

Fleet Owner-Maintenance Shop Issue and Buyer's Directory **[2074]**

Fleet Owner-Specs and Buyers' Directory Issue **[2075]**, **[25415]**

"Fleeting Moment" in *Entrepreneur* (Vol. 32, December 2004, No. 12, pp. 39) **[18033]**, **[27123]**, **[46289]**, **[47288]**

Fleming County Chamber of Commerce **[60502]**

Fletcher Rowley Chao Riddle Inc. **[20183]**

Fletcher Spaght Associates **[61071]**

Flett Research Ltd. **[3705]**, **[31349]**, **[52341]**

Flex-Plan Services Inc. **[27028]**

"Flexibility drove new revenue source" in *Crain's Detroit Business* (Vol. 19, No. 13, March 31, 2003, pp. 14) **[14047]**, **[18034]**, **[28165]**, **[33907]**, **[41690]**

Flexible Benefits **[26982]**

Flexible Working Time: More Time to Live **[42926]**

Flexing Your Creative Muscle in the Financial Marketplace **[48930]**

FLEXO **[19905]**

Flexographic Technical Association **[19843]**

"Flight of Fancy? Launching a High-Tech Product Can be a Technical and Financial Challenge" in *Entrepreneur* (Vol. 32, August 2004) **[36162]**, **[41691]**, **[44042]**, **[48732]**, **[49940]**, **[50874]**, **[52102]**

Flight Safety Digest **[965]**

Flight Safety Foundation **[938]**
    Library **[988]**

Flint Area Chamber of Commerce **[61297]**

Flint Ink–Information Resource Center **[19944]**

"Flip the Competition" in *Fast Company* (August 2001, pp. 10) **[30860]**, **[37137]**

"Flip Flipowski" in *Internet World* (Vol. 6, No. 13, July 1, 2000, pp. 60) **[13749]**, **[33439]**, **[55385]**

"Flip the Switch" in *Entrepreneur.com* (Vol. 34, February 2006, No. 2, pp. 84) **[35456]**, **[39057]**

"Flip Taking Control of Online Auction House" in *Crain's Chicago Business* **[1814]**, **[5907]**, **[23618]**, **[36163]**

Flippin Chamber of Commerce **[57164]**

The Floor to Ceiling Store **[12346]**

Floor Covering Installation Contractors Association **[10501]**

Floor Covering News **[10519]**

Floor Covering Weekly **[10520]**

Floor Covering Weekly-Annual Product Source Guide **[10510]**, **[13643]**

Floor Coverings International **[10536]**

Floor Focus **[10521]**

Floortastic **[16982]**

Flor & Associates **[29048]**, **[30646]**, **[47861]**, **[48825]**

Flora Chamber of Commerce **[59498]**

Flora Magazine **[10580]**

FloraCulture International Magazine **[11458]**

Floral Design **[10588]**

Floral Fundamentals **[10589]**

Florence Area Chamber of Commerce **[64217]**

Florence Business and Technology Center **[64795]**

Florence Chamber of Commerce **[58364]**, **[60329]**

Florence-Darlington Technical College **[64798]**
    Small Business Development Center **[64692]**

Floresville Chamber of Commerce **[65228]**

Florida A&M University–Science Research Center Library **[17306]**, **[19588]**

Florida Agency for Workforce Innovation–Labor Market Statistics–State Census Data Center **[67645]**

Florida Agricultural and Mechanical University–Small Business Development Center **[58701]**

Florida Atlantic Research and Development Park **[58986]**

Florida Atlantic University–Small Business Development Center **[55977]**, **[58702]**

Florida Black Business Investment Board **[58960]**

Florida Capital Ventures, Ltd. **[58969]**

Florida Chamber of Commerce **[58799]**

Florida Department of Education–Division of Workforce Development **[59000]**

Florida Department of Labor and Employment Security (DLES)–Bureau of Labor Market Information **[66849]**

Florida Department of Management Services–Division of Purchasing **[58981]**

Florida Fashion Focus Show **[5297]**, **[5744]**, **[9653]**, **[16220]**

"Florida is Fastest-Growing State in U.S." in *Tampa Tribune* (December 22, 2005) **[28166]**, **[32436]**, **[52672]**

Florida Gulf Coast University
    Small Business Development Center **[58703]**
    Small Business Development Center–Center for Leadership & Innovation **[58704]**

Florida Hotel and Motel Association Conference and Trade Show **[12680]**

Florida International Restaurant & Hotel Expo **[12681]**

Florida International University–Small Business Development Center **[58705]**

Florida JobBank **[23391]**

Florida Jurisprudence on Westlaw **[29662]**

Florida Keys Community College **[59001]**

Florida Keys Keynoter (November 22, 2003); "Atlanta Couple Buys Marathon, Fla., Bed and Breakfast Inn" in **[2424]**, **[12517]**

Florida Minority Supplier Development Council **[58961]**

Florida/NASA Business Incubation Center–Technology Research and Development Authority **[58987]**

"Florida Online Dating Service Tries to Find Love Link for Urban Professionals" in *Miami Herald* (March 1, 2004) **[7056]**, **[18727]**, **[18755]**, **[33908]**, **[36164]**, **[56222]**

Florida Ophthalmic Institute–Library **[25669]**

Florida Pest Management Association Convention and Exposition **[19039]**

Florida Pharmacy Association Annual Meeting and Convention **[8837]**

Florida Procurement Center Representatives **[58982]**

Florida Procurement Technical Assistance Center **[58983]**

Florida Regional Minority Business Council **[58962]**

Florida RV Supershow **[2003]**, **[55214]**

Florida Small Business Development Center–University of West Florida **[58697]**

Florida Solar Energy Center–Research Library **[23348]**

Florida (State) Department of Agriculture and Consumer Services–Division of Plant Industry–Library **[2479]**

Florida State University
    Career Center Library **[4459]**
    Center for Arts Administration Program **[58988]**
    Center for Human Resource Management **[15906]**
    Center for Music Research **[17719]**
    Center for the Study of Population–Institute for Social Research **[66850]**

Florida Center for Public Management **[50398]**
    Institute of Science and Public Affairs **[58989]**
    Office of Research **[58990]**
    Special Collections **[12162]**

Florida TaxWatch **[24203]**

Florida Trend **[4040]**, **[59007]**

Florida Tropical Fish Farms Association **[10442]**

Florida Veterinary Medical Association Annual Meeting **[1264]**

Florissant Valley Chamber of Commerce **[61962]**

Florists' Review Magazine **[10581]**

Flory Small Business Center, Inc.–Small Business Development Center **[65821]**

"Flourishing programs give rise to businesses' recycling interest" in *Solid Waste Report* (Vol. 33, No. 37, November 29, 2002) **[6651]**, **[21232]**

"Flourishing in the Windy City" in *Hispanic Business* (January/February 2003, pp. 49) **[14048]**, **[55619]**

Flower Arrangements Made Easy **[10590]**

Flower Mound Chamber of Commerce **[65229]**

Flower and Plant Production in the Greenhouse **[11425]**

"Flower Power: A Nearly Overlooked Opportunity is Blooming Into an Ideal Business" in *Entrepreneur* (Vol. 32, July 2004, No. 7, pp. 87) **[1678]**, **[10545]**, **[38634]**

"Flower power" in *Entrepreneur* (Vol. 31, No. 5, May 2003, pp. 104) **[17593]**, **[17742]**, **[17841]**, **[46290]**, **[56223]**

"Flower Power" in *My Business* (February/March 2004, pp. 45-46) **[10562]**, **[38779]**, **[51161]**

The Flower Shop Series **[10591]**

Flowerama of America **[10602]**

Flowers Canada **[10551]**, **[11410]**

"Flowers Foods Profits Rise" in *Atlanta Journal-Constitution* (February 2, 2007) **[2247]**, **[28167]**

Flowers for Sale: Growing and Marketing Cut Flowers **[10563]**, **[19722]**

Flowers& **[10582]**

"Flowfinity Wireless and Partners Extend Microsoft Business Solutions to BlackBerry" in *Internet Wire* (February 14, 2005) **[6652]**, **[14049]**, **[49033]**

Floyd County Chamber of Commerce **[60503]**, **[65894]**

Floydada Chamber of Commerce and Floyd County Board of Development **[65230]**

Fluke Venture Partners **[66212]**

"Flurry of developments reshaping Ypsilanti area" in *Crain's Detroit Business* (Vol. 19, No. 10, March 10, 2003, pp. 28) **[20509]**, **[20876]**

Flushing Area Chamber of Commerce **[61298]**

Flute for Beginners **[17633]**

Fluvanna County Chamber of Commerce **[65895]**

"Fly By Night? Don't Fall for a Scam-Use These Tips Before You Buy Health Insurance" in *Entrepreneur* (Vol. 31, No. 10, October 2003) **[13288]**, **[30223]**, **[41011]**, **[43177]**

Fly Fishing for Pike **[2194]**

"Fly Solo: How to Build a Profitable Enterprise" in *Black Enterprise* (Vol. 30, No. 6, January 2000, pp. 72) **[29733]**, **[30479]**, **[35457]**

"Flying From the Computer" in *The Economist* (Vol. 377, October 1-7, 2005, No. 8446, pp. 65-67) **[24687]**, **[25183]**, **[30327]**, **[30861]**, **[33909]**

Flying Funeral Directors of America **[10789]**

"Flying solo: pay more for a travel agent? Why not just go online?" in *Entrepreneur* (Vol. 30, No. 9, September 2002, pp. 24) **[25184]**, **[30328]**, **[33910]**

"Flying Solo" in *Small Business Opportunities* (Vol. 12, No. 3, May 2000, pp. 20) **[29734]**, **[35458]**

Flynn Ventures, LLC **[58015]**

Flywheel Ventures **[58016]**

FMedia! **[20355]**

"FMLA Needs to be Fixed to Stop Abuse" in *Crain's Detroit Business* (Vol. 21, January 10, 2005, No. 2, pp. 9) **[26807]**, **[29243]**, **[39339]**, **[40386]**

FMN (Financial Management Network) **[354]**

"FNC, HomeSafe Team Up" in *Mississippi Business Journal* (Vol. 29, January 2007, No. 2, pp. 19) **[12549]**, **[41692]**, **[44526]**, **[49941]**

"For Beall's, Bigger Is Always Better" in *Bradenton Herald* (February 14, 2005) **[28173]**, **[51164]**

"For Better Or. How Women Entrepreneurs Strike a Balance Between Business and Marriage" in *Entrepreneur* (Vol. 31, Oct. 2003) **[36171]**, **[56225]**

"For Better or Worse" in *Entrepreneur* (Vol. 33, October 2005, No. 10, pp. 104) **[37656]**, **[47580]**, **[49942]**

"For Big-Box Retailers, It's Market, Market, Market" in *Long Island Business News* (March 12, 2004) **[48689]**, **[50076]**, **[51165]**, **[52673]**

"For Biggest, No Brakes On This Trend" in *American Banker* (Vol. 170, February 4, 2005, No. 24, pp. 1) **[9966]**, **[15008]**, **[49943]**, **[53738]**

"For Cash-Strapped Cloudveil, It Was a Very Hard Offer to Refuse" in *Inc.* (August 2005, pp. 44-45) **[23619]**, **[52422]**

"For Centre Region Concierge, It's All in the Details" in *Centre Daily Times* (January 30, 2005) **[7131]**, **[18996]**, **[52533]**

"For some companies, it pays to be private" in *Red Herring* (March 2003, pp. 66) **[39340]**, **[51484]**, **[53739]**

For Formulation Chemists Only **[7917]**

"For the Last Time: Stock Options Are an Expense" in *Harvard Business Review* (Vol. 81, No. 3, March 2003, pp. 63) **[151]**, **[26240]**, **[26809]**

"For the Love of the Game: How One Woman Scores in the Sports Entertainment Industry" in *Black Enterprise* (Vol. 35, August 2004) **[23721]**, **[31153]**, **[46975]**, **[50441]**, **[56226]**

"For Love of the Game" in *Success* (Vol. 47, No. 6, November 2000, pp. 46) **[35461]**, **[43960]**

"For the low, low price" in *Entrepreneur* (Vol. 30, No. 10, October 2002, pp. 100) **[35462]**, **[38635]**

"For now, dealers win online battle for fleet buyers" in *Hispanic Business* (Vol. 22, No. 6, June 2000, pp. 132) **[18035]**, **[33913]**

"For Offering Hope and Help to the Parents of Autistic Children" in *Inc.* (April 1, 2005) **[33914]**, **[39309]**, **[41012]**, **[53440]**, **[56227]**

"For the People" in *Entrepreneur.com* (Vol. 34, February 2006, No. 2, pp. 68) **[28174]**, **[40023]**, **[49696]**

"For the Renaissance Driver" in *Hispanic Business* (November 2002, pp. 40, 42, 46, 48) **[18036]**

"For the small retailer, life on the Internet is one big bazaar" in *The New York Times* (March 27, 2000, pp. D9) **[14053]**, **[51166]**

"For Riesterer's Bake Shops, Low-Carb Diets are Just Another Fad" in *Long Island Business News* (March 12, 2004) **[2248]**, **[2291]**, **[11228]**, **[11326]**, **[11920]**, **[12007]**, **[12054]**, **[13073]**

"For Sale by (Home Office) Owner" in *Home Office Computing* (Vol. 18, No. 9, September 2000, pp. 13) **[42617]**

"For Small Businesses, Future of Biz Taxes Will be Crucial" in *Crain's Detroit Business* (Vol. 22, November 27, 2006, No. 48, pp. 15) **[29881]**, **[38078]**, **[40394]**, **[54559]**

"For Some, ITC's Steel Stance a Lose-Lose Deal" in *Pittsburgh Business Times* (Vol. 23, No. 8, September 12, 2003, pp. 1) **[40395]**, **[46292]**

"For Truckers, Insurance Barrels Out of Control" in *Business Journal-Portland* (Vol. 20, No. 26, August 29, 2003, pp. 16) **[13289]**, **[25386]**, **[43178]**

"For U.S. Small Biz, Fertile Soil in Europe" in *Business Week Online* (April 3, 2002) **[32441]**, **[41694]**, **[43657]**, **[53740]**

"For Want of a Nail...The War Was Lost" in *E-business Advisor* (Vol. 18, No. 12, December 2000, pp. 6) **[4988]**, **[30329]**, **[33915]**

"For-Your-Own-Good Innovation" in *Inc.* (September 1, 2003) **[4667]**, **[18037]**, **[23004]**, **[31548]**, **[53287]**

Foragers Cosmetic Industry Associates **[7870]**

Forbes **[39717]**

Forbes (November 27, 2000, pp. 98); "A Career, Not a Job" in **[32877]**, **[35358]**

Forbes (Vol. 175, February 14, 2005, No. 3, pp. 132); "A Cautious Optimism" in **[9867]**, **[14839]**, **[32310]**, **[37949]**

Forbes (Vol. 174, December 27, 2004, No. 13, pp. 51); "A Rose With Another Name" in **[6003]**, **[9301]**, **[10571]**, **[11659]**, **[19893]**, **[44137]**

Forbes (Vol. 170, No. 13, December 23, 2002, pp. 248); "A Virtuous Cycle" in **[36917]**, **[37523]**, **[45791]**

Forbes (Vol. 174, December 27, 2004, No. 13, pp. 56); "Ambulance Chasing, Web-Style" in **[543]**, **[29094]**, **[33529]**, **[40958]**, **[46673]**

Forbes (Vol. 170, No. 4, September 2, 2002, pp. 45); "An Option to Do Nothing" in **[71]**, **[23882]**, **[26151]**

Forbes (April 1, 2002, p. 96); "Analyze This" in **[44270]**, **[53205]**

Forbes (Vol. 175, February 14, 2005, No. 3, pp. 130); "Back Office" in **[9821]**, **[31643]**

Forbes (Vol. 171, No. 1, January 6, 2003, pp. 150); "Bad Policy" in **[13197]**, **[30205]**

Forbes (Vol. 175, February 14, 2005, No. 3, pp. 78; "Bean Counter" in **[11313]**, **[51068]**

Forbes (Vol. 170, No. 9, October 28, 2002, pp. 252); "Behind the Boards" in **[9842]**, **[14784]**, **[44925]**

Forbes (October 30,2000, pp. 222); "Behind the Numbers" in **[27825]**

Forbes (Vol. 175, February 14, 2005, No. 3, pp. 16); "Beware Blowhards" in **[9844]**, **[14789]**

Forbes (Vol. 175, January 10, 2005, No. 1, pp. 68); "Big Gulp" in **[23458]**, **[27840]**

Forbes (Vol. 174, December 27, 2004, No. 13, pp. 90); "Boat Gambling" in **[10669]**, **[14804]**, **[27854]**

Forbes (Vol. 170, No. 12, December 9, 2002, pp. 190); "Booz Allen's Sweet Spot" in **[3502]**, **[25803]**, **[33602]**, **[40200]**, **[54456]**

Forbes (Vol. 175, January 10, 2005, No. 1, pp. 152); "Canned Profits" in **[14829]**, **[46225]**

Forbes (Vol. 174, December 27, 2004, No. 13, pp. 190); "Charm City" in **[9875]**, **[14847]**, **[37957]**

Forbes (Vol. 175, January 10, 2005, No. 1, pp. 31); "Cheap Jet Update" in **[35941]**, **[46229]**

Forbes (Vol. 174, December 27, 2004, No. 13, pp. 64); "Chilling Out" in **[6605]**, **[48985]**

"Forbes Chocolate" in *Dairy Field* (Vol. 185, No. 2, February 2002, pp. 53) **[4291]**, **[12776]**, **[28175]**

Forbes (December 25, 2000, pp. 134); "Close-Knit" in **[37610]**, **[49861]**

Forbes (Vol. 175, January 10, 2005, No. 1, pp. 142); "Comeback Bank" in **[9890]**, **[14874]**, **[37974]**

Forbes (December 25, 2000, pp. 92); "Confessions of a Car Dot-Commer" in **[18000]**, **[33697]**

Forbes (December 25, 2000, pp. 278); "Consider Your Options" in **[52417]**

Forbes (Vol. 175, January 10, 2005, No. 1, pp. 145); "Cornucopia" in **[14887]**, **[26496]**

Forbes (Vol. 174, December 27, 2004, No. 13, pp. 116); "Criminal Outbreak" in **[6621]**, **[13939]**, **[22207]**

Forbes (January 21, 2002, p. 29); "Current Events" in **[29187]**, **[39269]**

Forbes (October 30, 2000, pp. 36); "Daddy Dearest" in **[37621]**

Forbes (December 25, 2000, pp. 262); "Day of E-tonement" in **[13954]**, **[33741]**

Forbes (Vol. 175, February 14, 2005, No. 3, pp. 56); "De-Vine Tragedy" in **[9703]**, **[23471]**, **[28008]**, **[43614]**

Forbes (Vol. 174, December 13, 2004, No. 12, pp. 110); "Digital Fingerprints" in **[6244]**, **[22216]**, **[49012]**

Forbes (February 19, 2001, pp. 51); "Digital Rules" in **[35390]**, **[41448]**, **[44700]**, **[51502]**

Forbes (Vol. 170, No. 8, October 14, 2002, pp. 97); "Don Quixote In Court" in **[29204]**, **[37423]**, **[41645]**

Forbes (Vol. 174, December 27, 2004, No. 13, pp. 25); "Don't Junk Property Rights" in **[29205]**, **[44291]**

Forbes (February 28, 2000, pp. 74); "Entrepreneurs" in **[33435]**, **[35425]**

Forbes (December 25, 2000, pp. 134); "Family-Business Psychology" in **[31149]**, **[37645]**

Forbes (Vol. 175, January 10, 2005, No. 1, pp. 38); "Feed Me" in **[14033]**, **[33889]**

Forbes (Vol. 174, December 27, 2004, No. 13, pp. 186); "Fighting the Borg" in **[11611]**, **[51156]**

Forbes (Vol. 175, February 14, 2005, No. 3, pp. 102); "Food Porn" in **[11615]**, **[12006]**, **[51162]**

Forbes (Vol. 175, February 14, 2005, No. 3, pp. 44); "Fool's Paradise" in **[32440]**

Forbes (Vol. 175, February 14, 2005, No. 3, pp. 46); "Founders Face Off" in **[4103]**, **[15014]**, **[49949]**

Forbes Global (Vol. 7, December 20, 2004, No. 22, pp. 9); "Fact and Comment" in **[29230]**, **[44296]**

Forbes (Vol. 175, January 31, 2005, No. 2, pp. 146); "Go for the Big Ones" in **[9982]**, **[15038]**, **[38094]**

Forbes (Vol. 174, December 13, 2004, No. 12, pp. 110); "Going Vertical" in **[6250]**, **[6661]**

Forbes (March 6, 2000, pp. 102); "Goveernment Nannies: Close to Home" in **[5339]**

Forbes (December 25, 2000, pp. 242); "Grandma's Recipe" in **[23439]**, **[35488]**

Forbes (Vol. 175, January 10, 2005, No. 1, pp. 143); "Gray Winds" in **[15053]**, **[21170]**

Forbes (Vol. 170, No. 9, October 28, 2002, pp. 246); "Greased Lightning" in **[21526]**, **[28228]**

Forbes (April 3, 2000, pp. 138); "Group Therapy" in **[30552]**, **[36241]**

Forbes (December 25, 2000, pp. 270); "Hands Off" in **[6914]**, **[13754]**, **[35497]**

Forbes (Vol. 175, February 14, 2005, No. 3, pp. 78); "Have It Your Way" in **[18055]**, **[47060]**, **[48742]**

Forbes (Vol. 175, January 31, 2005, No. 2, pp. 108); "Hidden Expenses" in **[9999]**, **[15079]**, **[38116]**

Forbes (Vol. 175, January 10, 2005, No. 1, No. 13, pp. 153); "Hoping for a Bad Winter" in **[1938]**, **[15092]**, **[49986]**

Forbes (Vol. 172, No. 9, October 27, 2003, pp. 139); "Hot Shots: 200 Up And Coming Companies" in **[10005]**, **[15095]**, **[28294]**, **[39388]**, **[52866]**

Forbes (Vol. 6, No. 20, October 27, 2003, pp. 53); "Hot Shots: U.S. Top 15" in **[28295]**, **[39389]**, **[52867]**

Forbes (Vol. 174, December 27, 2004, No. 13, pp. 38); "I Feel Your Pain" in **[53791]**

Forbes (Vol. 175, January 31, 2005, No. 2, pp. 60); "I Tune, You Tune" in **[17746]**, **[41757]**

Forbes (April 15, 2002, p. 225); "If Telemarketers Paid For Your Time" in **[47120]**, **[53797]**

Forbes (August 7, 2000, pp. 134); "Insiders' Tax Break" in **[40466]**, **[54611]**

Forbes (October 30, 2000, pp. 282); "Junkyard Blues" in **[44558]**, **[55701]**

Forbes (Vol. 171, No. 2, January 20, 2003, pp. 108); "Keep It Simple" in **[29925]**, **[44561]**

"Forbes Keeps Track In It's Upscale Or Hot on the Lot" in *Sacramento Bee* (November 16, 2005) **[18038]**, **[18872]**, **[36172]**, **[45159]**

Forbes (Vol. 172, No. 13, December 22, 2003, pp. 220); "Large Potential in Small Companies" in **[10054]**, **[15202]**, **[38179]**

Forbes (May 29, 2000, pp. 104); "Look for the Pony" in **[28436]**

Forbes (Vol. 174, December 27, 2004, No. 13, pp. 121); "Macro Money Maker" in **[10077]**, **[15243]**, **[38206]**

Forbes (Vol. 175, February 28, 2005, No. 4, pp. 48); "Matchmaker" in **[42339]**, **[42875]**

Forbes (June 10, 2002, p. 146); "Medicine Man" in **[13385]**, **[41059]**, **[43277]**

Forbes (January 24, 2000, pp. 138); "Moonlighting" in **[37068]**

Forbes (Vol. 175, February 14, 2005, No. 3, pp. 102); "More Organic Than Thou" in **[11643]**, **[12014]**

Forbes (Vol. 175, January 10, 2005, No. 1, pp. 140); "Mr. Clean" in **[3322]**, **[15282]**, **[21565]**

Forbes (Vol. 175, January 31, 2005, No. 2, pp. 42); "Music Like Water" in **[17754]**, **[34220]**, **[44098]**

Forbes (Vol. 175, January 10, 2005, No. 1, pp. 144); "Natural Selection" in **[12015]**, **[15289]**

Forbes (Vol. 10, 2000, pp. 188); "Needbucks.com" in **[29751]**, **[55407]**

Forbes (Vol. 175, January 10, 2005, No. 1, pp. 44); "No Money Down" in **[17424]**, **[20611]**

Forbes (Vol. 175, January 10, 2005, No. 1, pp. 38); "Not So Swift" in **[15312]**, **[25403]**

Forbes (Vol. 175, January 31, 2005, No. 2, pp. 156); "On the Business of Life" in **[27460]**, **[27666]**, **[36572]**

Forbes (February 19, 2001, pp. 34); "On Your Mind" in **[29948]**, **[39514]**

Forbes (October 30, 2000, pp. 280); "Once is Not Enough" in **[15323]**, **[50120]**

Forbes (Vol. 170, No. 9, October 28, 2002, pp. 238); "One Tough Lesson Plan" in **[33199]**, **[36584]**, **[45496]**

Forbes (February 21, 2000, pp. 96); "Only a Few Sea Turtles Survive" in **[35598]**, **[41474]**, **[55414]**

Forbes (Vol. 174, December 27, 2004, No. 13, pp. 192; "Open Bar for Health Costs" in **[10124]**, **[15325]**, **[38266]**, **[41074]**

Forbes (Vol. 170, No. 13, December 23, 2002, pp. 88); "Options vigilantes" in **[10125]**, **[15329]**, **[38267]**

Forbes (Vol. 170, No. 6, September 30, 2002, pp. 36); "Other Comments" in **[5080]**, **[32620]**, **[34315]**, **[41892]**

Forbes (Vol. 170, No. 12, December 9, 2002, pp. 164); "Oxymoron 101" in **[33202]**, **[37487]**

Forbes (November 13, 2000, pp. 58); "Patent Chutzpah" in **[13771]**, **[33477]**, **[35602]**, **[43967]**

Forbes (Vol. 170, No. 4, September 2, 2002, pp. 144); "Pension Pain" in **[224]**, **[24014]**, **[26323]**, **[26874]**, **[40611]**

Forbes-Platinum 400-America's Best Big Companies **[39341]**

Forbes (Vol. 175, January 10, 2005, No. 1, pp. 152); "Population Boom" in **[24444]**, **[53919]**

Forbes (Vol. 174, December 27, 2004, No. 13, pp. 54); "Postcards From The Edge" in **[760]**, **[47410]**

Forbes (November 13, 2000, pp. 252); "Publish or Perish" in **[18924]**, **[34378]**, **[47436]**

Forbes (December 25, 2000, pp. 238); "Raw Deal" in **[19641]**, **[38893]**

Forbes (February 19, 2001, pp. 95); "Reality Checker" in **[31207]**, **[36673]**, **[55799]**

Forbes (February 21, 2000, pp. 118); "Rent-A-Mom" in **[7114]**, **[35624]**

Forbes (December 11, 2000, pp. 206); "Requiem for a Telecom" in **[4893]**, **[13774]**, **[35625]**

Forbes (Vol. 175, February 14, 2005, No. 3, pp. 88); "Return of the Kings" in **[10165]**, **[14399]**, **[15418]**

Forbes (May 13, 2002, p. 64); "Rough-Cut Dimon" in **[28724]**, **[45609]**

Forbes (Vol. 175, February 14, 2005, No. 3, pp. 136); "Saving Grace" in **[10174]**, **[15431]**

Forbes (Vol. 175, February 14, 2005, No. 3, pp. 58); "Shake 'Em Up" in **[41096]**, **[50967]**, **[52203]**

Forbes (April 15, 2002, p. 130); "Shelf-Determination" in **[11661]**, **[47523]**

Forbes (Vol. 175, January 31, 2005, No. 2, pp. 110); "Shopping for Value" in **[10182]**, **[15452]**, **[38348]**

Forbes (Vol. 170, No. 3, August 12, 2002, pp. 22); "Side Lines" in **[40691]**

Forbes (March 25, 2002, p. 60); "Silicon Still Matters" in **[28764]**, **[41986]**

Forbes (May 27, 2002, p. 88); "Small Is Big" in **[26363]**, **[53468]**

Forbes (Vol. 175, February 14, 2005, No. 3, pp. 78); "Snowboarding Secrets" in **[14453]**, **[23634]**, **[34507]**, **[36766]**

Forbes (October 30, 2000, pp. 274); "So What's Your Story?" in **[3585]**, **[15461]**, **[38363]**

Forbes (December 25, 2000, pp. 300); "Soft Landing Strategy" in **[32702]**, **[38365]**

Forbes Special Situation Survey **[15640]**

Forbes (October 30, 2000, pp. 266); "Speculations" in **[28804]**

Forbes (Vol. 175, February 14, 2005, No. 3, pp. 54); "Speech! Speech!" in **[4821]**, **[23207]**, **[53487]**

Forbes (Vol. 174, December 13, 2004, No. 12, pp. 110); "Speed Demon" in **[6287]**, **[6807]**

Forbes (Vol. 170, No. 5, September 16, 2002, pp. 45); "Spies in the Boardroom?" in **[30959]**, **[37509]**

Forbes (May 15, 2000, pp. 324); "Spreading The Wealth" in **[55840]**

Forbes (December 25, 2000, pp. 273); "State of the Banner" in **[34538]**, **[47575]**

Forbes (Vol. 175, January 31, 2005, No. 2, pp. 144); "Strategy for a Weak Market" in **[10192]**, **[15488]**, **[38381]**

Forbes (Vol. 175, February 14, 2005, No. 3, pp. 46); "Super Cell" in **[6816]**, **[24831]**, **[42017]**

Forbes (Vol. 175, February 14, 2005, No. 3, pp. 100); "Technology's Growth Champs" in **[28872]**, **[42055]**

Forbes (Vol. 175, January 10, 2005, No. 1, pp. 150); "Thank You For Spending $300" in **[9644]**, **[15518]**, **[16274]**, **[18142]**

Forbes (Vol. 175, February 14, 2005, No. 3, pp. 82); "The Answer Is Always Yes" in **[24882]**, **[55063]**

Forbes (Vol. 170, No. 5, September 16, 2002, pp. 103); "The Appellation Trail" in **[23455]**, **[27779]**

Forbes (May 13, 2002, p. 104); "The Best" in **[39170]**, **[44928]**

Forbes (November 27, 2000, pp. 296); "The Bite of the ASP" in **[13851]**, **[33590]**

Forbes (Vol. 6, No. 5, March 2003, pp. 46); "The thrifty boss" in **[4843]**, **[23232]**, **[44250]**, **[50760]**

Forbes (Vol. 170, No. 13, December 23, 2002, pp. 234); "The Confidence Game" in **[37406]**, **[45020]**

Forbes (Vol. 174, December 27, 2004, No. 13, pp. 182); "The Crying Game" in **[1798]**, **[33063]**

Forbes (Vol. 174, December 27, 2004, No. 13, pp. 184); "The Deal of the Art" in **[1605]**, **[9906]**, **[14906]**, **[37994]**

Forbes (January 21, 2002, p. 86); "The Death and Life of Buy.com" in **[33743]**, **[51124]**

Forbes (Vol. 175, January 31, 2005, No. 2, pp. 108); "The Dirty Dozen" in **[9915]**, **[14919]**, **[38007]**

Forbes (Vol. 170, No. 12, December 9, 2002, pp. 140); "The Diversity Game" in **[40007]**, **[48134]**, **[56190]**

Forbes (December 11, 2000, pp. 144); "The Eparty's Over" in **[14018]**, **[33855]**, **[43053]**

Forbes (Vol. 175, February 14, 2005, No. 3, pp. 110); "The Five Don'ts" in **[9962]**, **[14995]**, **[38074]**

Forbes (Vol. 175, January 10, 2005, No. 1, pp. 150); "The Innovator" in **[13337]**, **[15127]**, **[43230]**

Forbes (December 11, 2000, pp. 168); "The Killer Ad Machine" in **[34120]**, **[47173]**

Forbes (Vol. 174, December 27, 2004, No. 13, pp. 80); "The Merchant of Bay Ridge" in **[33462]**, **[35564]**, **[51032]**, **[56725]**

Forbes (May 29, 2000, pp. 96); "The Plumtree Software Soap Opera" in **[23128]**, **[45545]**

Forbes (Vol. 175, February 14, 2005, No. 3, pp. 138); "The Price Makes the Stock" in **[10139]**, **[15367]**, **[38287]**

Forbes (Vol. 170, No. 9, October 28, 2002, pp. 228); "The Rat Pack" in **[1191]**, **[28671]**, **[36669]**

Forbes (Vol. 174, November 29, 2004, No. 11, pp. 44); "The Security-Industrial Complex" in **[15442]**, **[22369]**, **[28751]**, **[41968]**

Forbes (December 24, 2001, p. 100); "The Skinflint Goes Shopping" in **[31070]**, **[34484]**, **[51361]**

Forbes (Vol. 175, January 31, 2005, No. 2, pp. 102); "The T. Rowe Small-Cap Gauge" in **[10198]**, **[15498]**, **[38392]**

Forbes (Vol. 175, February 14, 2005, No. 3, pp. 134); "The Year of the Convertible" in **[10259]**, **[15616]**, **[32805]**, **[38475]**

Forbes (Vol. 170, No. 13, December 23, 2002, pp. 217); "They Almost Changed the World" in **[36852]**, **[44164]**

Forbes (August 21, 2000, pp. 70); "This Is Not About Charity" in **[30616]**, **[36856]**, **[56767]**

Forbes (Vol. 170, No. 13, December 23, 2002, pp. 396); "Thoughts On the Business of Life" in **[36858]**, **[45735]**

Forbes (Vol. 175, January 31, 2005, No. 2, pp. 39); "Three Trends for 2005" in **[34598]**, **[35697]**, **[54039]**

Forbes (Vol. 175, January 10, 2005, No. 1, pp. 154); "Top Cop" in **[4846]**, **[15532]**, **[22406]**, **[23237]**, **[38419]**, **[53520]**

Forbes (Vol. 174, December 27, 2004, No. 13, pp. 156); "Top Drawer" in **[1861]**, **[5826]**, **[10214]**, **[15533]**, **[38421]**

Forbes (December 25, 2000, pp. 232); "Tough Mama" in **[15536]**, **[37803]**, **[50221]**

Forbes (Vol. 175, February 14, 2005, No. 3, pp. 86); "Trustbuster" in **[24611]**, **[40784]**

Forbes (Vol. 175, January 31, 2005, No. 2, pp. 98); "Turning Corn Into Clothing" in **[5576]**, **[5725]**, **[15549]**, **[22731]**, **[50230]**

Forbes (Vol. 170, No. 9, October 28, 2002, pp. 227); "200 Best Small Companies" in **[10626]**, **[39645]**

Forbes (Vol. 174, December 27, 2004, No. 13, pp. 54); "Udder Irony" in **[26552]**, **[40788]**

Forbes-Up-and-Comers 200 **[39342]**

Forbes (Vol. 175, January 10, 2005, No. 1, pp. 140); "War Earnings" in **[15589]**, **[28973]**, **[38446]**, **[40106]**

Forbes (Vol. 170, No. 3, August 12, 2002, pp. 62); "Warning: Credit Crunch" in **[289]**, **[7031]**, **[26396]**, **[32782]**

Forbes (Vol. 175, January 31, 2005, No. 2, pp. 58); "Water Wagons" in **[18159]**, **[46482]**

Forbes (November 13, 2000, pp. 332); "We Know Where You Live" in **[14578]**, **[34659]**

Forbes (December 11, 2000, pp. 216); "Who (Gonna) Dunnit" in **[22144]**, **[22894]**, **[35727]**

Forbes (Vol. 170, No. 8, October 14, 2002, pp. 56); "Who Needs The Aggravation?" in **[300]**, **[24074]**, **[26403]**, **[40838]**, **[54077]**

Forbes (Vol. 175, February 28, 2005, No. 4, pp. 34); "Workers' Con" in **[26961]**, **[40854]**

Forbes (Vol. 174, December 13, 2004, No. 12, pp. 89); "You're Fired!" in **[3620]**, **[31258]**, **[32073]**, **[42479]**, **[42903]**

Forbidden Flavours (Canada) Ltd. **[5782]**, **[12820]**

"Ford Backs Off Supporting Expanded Freight Terminal" in *Crain's Detroit Business* (Vol. 19, No. 42, October 20, 2003, pp. 2) **[10561]**, **[10676]**, **[17845]**, **[18039]**, **[46293]**, **[48125]**

Ford Equity Research Data Bases **[10377]**, **[15759]**

"Ford Falls Behind" in *Business Week* (February 14, 2005, No. 3920, pp. 42) **[9967]**, **[15009]**, **[18040]**

"Ford Field scores as site for meetings" in *Crain's Detroit Business* (Vol. 19, No. 6, February 10, 2003, pp. 14) **[22501]**, **[24935]**

Ford Investment Management Report **[15641]**

"Ford to Mark 100th Anniversary This Year" in *San Jose Mercury News* (April 11, 2003) **[630]**, **[18041]**, **[28176]**, **[46976]**, **[50442]**, **[50591]**

"Ford Motor Company Is Sponsoring the Ford BEST Business Plan Contest..." in *Black Enterprise* (Vol. 34, No. 7, February 2004) **[29882]**, **[36173]**

Ford Motor Minority Dealers Association **[17952]**

Fordham University–Office of Research and Sponsored Programs **[63198]**

Fordyce Chamber of Commerce **[57165]**

"Fore Profit Biz" in *Small Business Opportunities* (Vol. 13, No. 6, November 2001, pp. 72) **[11241]**, **[22748]**, **[35463]**

Forecast **[3057]**

"Forecast for IPOs? Wait Till Next Year" in *Venture Capital Journal* (Vol. 41, No. 8, August 2000, pp. 16-17) **[15010]**, **[49944]**, **[55621]**

"Forecasts Call for More Green" in *Hispanic Business* (December 2003, pp. 60) **[12551]**, **[21321]**, **[24688]**, **[25185]**, **[30330]**

"Foreclosure Activity Drops in Valley, State" in *San Jose Mercury News* (February 18, 2005) **[17381]**, **[20510]**

"Foreclosures Rise; Yuppie Belt Hit Hard as Defaults Climb 10% City wide" in *Crain's Chicago Business* (December 8, 2003) **[17382]**, **[32442]**

"Foreclosures Rise; Yuppie Belt Hit Hard as Defaults Climb 10 Percent Citywide" in *Crains Chicago Business* (Vol. 26, No. 49) **[17383]**, **[32443]**

"Foreclosures: Troubled Owners Offered Free Help" in *Altanta Journal-Constitution* (February 1, 2007) **[9968]**, **[17384]**, **[39824]**, **[49945]**

Forefront-Health Investigations **[17929]**

Foreign Activity Report **[15642]**

"Foreign Affairs" in *Entrepreneur* (Vol. 33, March 2005, No. 3, pp. 56) **[12972]**, **[43658]**

"Foreign Aid" in *Meetings & Conventions* (Vol. 32, No. 12, November 1997, pp. 72) **[20020]**, **[22502]**, **[24936]**

Foreign Credit Insurance Association **[12928]**

"Foreign currency" in *Entrepreneur* (Vol. 30, No. 10, October 2002, pp. 58) **[39825]**, **[43659]**, **[46294]**

Foreign Entry Requirements **[24780]**

"Foreign expansion of small firms: the impact of domestic alternatives" in *Journal of Business Venturing* (Vol. 16, No. 6, Nov. 2001) **[28177]**, **[43660]**

Foreign Pharmacy Graduate Examination Committee **[8761]**

"Foreign Targets" in *Hispanic Business* (July/August 2004, pp. 48) **[30862]**, **[43661]**, **[56010]**

Foreign Trade Fairs New Products Newsletter **[13030]**

Foreman's Accident Protection Series **[56629]**

Foremost Liquors **[16245]**

Forensic Accident Investigations Inc. **[13574]**

Forensic Drug Abuse Advisor **[41198]**, **[54341]**

Forest Area Chamber of Commerce **[61792]**

Forest City Tree Protection Company Inc. **[16144]**

Forest Grove Chamber of Commerce **[64218]**

Forest Lake Area Chamber of Commerce **[61590]**

Forest Park Chamber of Commerce **[59499]**

Forest Products Association of Canada **[46170]**

Foresthill Divide Chamber of Commerce **[57492]**

Forestville Chamber of Commerce **[57493]**

Forever Fit **[19471]**

"Forget About Bartering. For Start-Ups, It's All About the Freebies" in *Inc.* (May 1, 2005) **[26704]**, **[33916]**, **[44413]**, **[46977]**

"Forget Diamonds" in *Entrepreneur* (Vol. 28, No. 1, January 2000, pp. 42) **[55622]**

"Forget vive la difference" in *Incentive* (Vol. 174, No. 8, August 2000, pp. 16) **[45160]**

"Forget India, Outsource to Oregon!" in *Venture Capital Journal* (December 1, 2004) **[35464]**, **[41453]**, **[49697]**, **[55623]**

"Forget the Series; St. Louis has Bragging Rights for Job Growth" in *St. Louis Post-Dispatch* (December 19, 2004) **[15011]**, **[28178]**, **[32444]**, **[49946]**

"Forget VC: Successful Entrepreneur Says Good Riddance" in *Venture Capital Journal* (October 1, 2004) **[23005]**, **[36174]**, **[53288]**, **[55624]**

"Forgive Us Our Debts...The Creditor May, But the IRS Won't" in *Black Enterprise* (Vol. 34, July 2004, No. 12, pp. 143) **[31549]**, **[54560]**

"The Forgotten Strategy" in *Harvard Business Review* (Vol. 81, No. 11, November 2003, pp. 76) **[28179]**, **[43662]**, **[53741]**

Forks Chamber of Commerce **[66085]**

"Form finder" in *Entrepreneur* (Vol. 30, No. 3, March 2002, pp. 40) **[4668]**, **[23006]**, **[29246]**, **[49034]**, **[53289]**

"Form Follows Function" in *Small Business Opportunities* (Vol. 12, No. 3, May 2000, pp. 52-53) **[49500]**

Form You 3 International, Inc. **[26051]**

Formalwords **[5738]**

"Former Airline Workers Navigate Into Florida Liquor Business" in *Bradenton Herald* () **[16222]**, **[52638]**, **[54561]**

"Former Apprentice Candidate Launches Jewelry Line" in *Black Enterprise* (Vol. 37, October 2006, No. 3, pp. 36) **[9622]**, **[15844]**, **[36175]**

"Former B.E. 100s CEO Convicted" in *Black Enterprise* (Vol. 35, October 2004, No. 3, pp. 33) **[9969]**, **[29247]**, **[40396]**

"Former B.E. 100s Clerk Faces Prison Time" in *Black Enterprise* (Vol. 35, September 2004, No. 2, pp. 30) **[26241]**, **[29248]**, **[41695]**

"Former Collection Attorney Needs Consultants to Offer Bulletproof Asset Protection" in *Success* (Vol. 47, No. 2, June 2000, pp. 88) **[29249]**, **[31154]**, **[38079]**

"Former Computer Associates Executive Pleads Guilty in U.S. District Court in Brooklyn" in *Long Island Business News* (Jan. 30, 2004) **[152]**, **[2904]**, **[23945]**, **[26242]**, **[29250]**, **[40397]**

"Former Couch Street Figure Heads to Prison" in *Business Journal-Portland* (Vol. 20, No. 24, August 15, 2003, pp. 8) **[21223]**, **[21515]**, **[29251]**, **[37445]**, **[38139]**, **[38728]**, **[40398]**

"Former Execs Go Franchising" in *Boston Business Journal* (Vol. 23, No. 24, July 18, 2003, pp. 1) **[38636]**, **[53560]**

"Former Female Weightlifter Opens Yuba City, Calif., Women-Only Fitness Center" in *Marysville Appeal-Democrat* (January 26, 2003) **[19399]**, **[36176]**, **[56228]**

"Former Flight Attendant Starts Biz & Soars To $1.5 Million" in *Small Business Opportunities* (Vol. 17, May 2005, No. 3, pp. 72) **[17296]**, **[56229]**

"Former Information Warrior D'Amico Now Fighting Cyberwarfare" in *Long Island Business News* (March 12, 2004) **[22234]**, **[22961]**, **[33917]**, **[34477]**, **[42328]**, **[44298]**, **[53290]**, **[55600]**

"Former Manager Files Suit Against OKC-based Hudiburg Auto Group" in *Journal Record (Oklahoma City, OK)* (February 6, 2007) **[18042]**, **[29252]**

"Former Model Opens Hollywood, Fla. Maternity Clothes Boutique" in *South Florida Sun-Sentinel* (November 5, 2003) **[5662]**, **[56230]**

"Former Nortel VP Joins Enterprise" in *Venture Capital Journal* (Vol. 40, No. 10, October 2000, pp. 36) **[41696]**, **[44529]**, **[55625]**

"Former Teacher in Munster, Ind., Makes Transition to Professional Organizer" in *The Times* (November 16, 2002) **[20021]**, **[52534]**

"Former Wrestling Star Body Slams Private Equity" in *Venture Capital Journal* (Vol. 42, No. 9, September 2002, pp. 15-16) **[15012]**, **[36177]**, **[49947]**, **[55626]**

Forming Corporations and Partnerships **[43017]**, **[51485]**

Forney Area Chamber of Commerce **[65231]**

Forrest, Binkley & Brown **[58017]**

Forrest City Area Chamber of Commerce **[57166]**

Forsyth Chamber of Commerce **[61963]**

Forsyth Consulting **[20371]**, **[24496]**

Forsyth-Monroe County Chamber of Commerce **[59103]**

Fort Atkinson Area Chamber of Commerce **[66394]**

Fort Bend Chamber of Commerce **[65232]**

Fort Benton Chamber of Commerce **[62165]**

Fort Bragg - Mendocino Coast Chamber of Commerce **[57494]**

Fort Cobb Chamber of Commerce **[63992]**

Fort Collins Area Chamber of Commerce **[58365]**

Fort Davis Chamber of Commerce **[65233]**

Fort Deposit Chamber of Commerce **[56846]**

Fort Dodge Area Chamber of Commerce **[60134]**

Fort Edward Chamber of Commerce **[62879]**

Fort Fairfield Chamber of Commerce **[60745]**

Fort Gibson Chamber of Commerce **[63993]**

Fort Hayes State University–Kansas Small Business Development Center State Office **[60254]**

Fort Hays State University–Small Business Development Center **[60259]**

Fort Knoxx Copy Jewelry Franchise, Inc. **[15883]**

Fort Lauderdale Furniture and Accessory Market **[12331]**

Fort Lauderdale Home Design & Remodeling Show **[12332]**, **[13708]**

Fort Lauderdale International Boat Show **[16774]**

Fort Lewis College–Office of Economic Analysis and Business Research **[32850]**

Fort Madison Area Chamber of Commerce **[60135]**

Fort Morgan Area Chamber of Commerce **[58366]**

Fort Morgan Small Business Development Center–Morgan Community College **[58301]**

Fort Payne Chamber of Commerce **[56847]**

Fort Recovery Chamber of Commerce **[63673]**

Fort Scott Area Chamber of Commerce **[60330]**

Fort Smith Chamber of Commerce **[57167]**

Fort Smith Regional Office–Small Business Development Center **[57115]**

Fort Stockton Chamber of Commerce **[65234]**

Fort Sumner Chamber of Commerce **[62688]**

Fort Wayne Sports, Vacation, and Boat Show **[16775]**, **[21190]**, **[23682]**, **[24772]**, **[25322]**

Fort Worth Chamber of Commerce **[65235]**

Fort Worth Hispanic Chamber of Commerce **[65236]**

Fort Worth Star-Telegram (July 20, 2003); "Bed, Breakfast Owner Banks on Lure of Downtown Grapevine, Texas" in **[2427]**

Fort Worth Star-Telegram (August 10, 2004); "Wave of Self-Storage Facilities, Organizers Emerges in Dallas-Fort Worth" in **[20028]**, **[20238]**

Fort Yates Satellite Center–SBDC **[63493]**

Fortuna Chamber of Commerce **[57495]**

Fortune **[39718]**

Fortune (Vol. 142, No. 6, September 18, 2000, pp. 248); "A Catalyst for Innovation" in **[52832]**, **[54481]**

Fortune (Vol. 152, October 3, 2005, No. 7, pp. 50); "A Mediation on Risk" in **[39464]**, **[40531]**

Fortune (Vol. 152, October 3, 2005, No. 7, pp. 69); "An Executive Risk Handbook" in **[29177]**, **[29867]**, **[43103]**, **[45121]**

Fortune (Vol. 151, February 7, 2005, No. 3, pp. 106); "Are Green Funds True To Their Colors?" in **[9811]**, **[14743]**, **[37245]**, **[54132]**

Fortune (Vol. 151, February 21, 2005, No. 4, pp. 36); "Avalanche Gear Alert!" in **[23607]**, **[48696]**

Fortune (Vol. 141, No. 2, January 24, 2000, pp. 128); "Battle of the Business Plans: a new march madness" in **[29707]**, **[55358]**

Fortune (Vol. 142, No. 4, August 14, 2000, pp. 276+); "Bayla's Plea: Put Your Money Where Your Mouth Is" in **[12274]**, **[35810]**, **[55500]**

Fortune (Vol. 149, No. 9, May 3, 2004, pp. 74); "Big-League R&D Gets Its Own eBay" in **[50823]**, **[52048]**

Fortune (Vol. 151, February 21, 2005, No. 4, pp. 128); "Biotech Believer" in **[14798]**, **[37921]**, **[41551]**

Fortune (Vol. 142, No. 2, July 10, 2000, pp. 200T); "Bullied by the Big Guys? Try Fighting Back!" in **[25808]**, **[44966]**

Fortune (Vol. 152, August 8, 2005, No. 3, pp. 96H); "Calling in Sick" in **[29822]**, **[42977]**, **[44976]**

Fortune (Vol. 148, No. 12, December 8, 2003, pp. 204H); "Can Gates Remember Being Small?" in **[35906]**, **[53232]**

Fortune (Vol. 151, February 21, 2005, No. 4, pp. 134); "Can I Use My Retirement Savings To Start a Business?" in **[48874]**, **[52771]**

Fortune (Vol. 152, October 17, 2005, No. 8, pp. 215); "Can the Profit Boom Last? Businesses Have Been Churning Out Earnings" in **[27922]**, **[31436]**, **[32305]**

Fortune (Vol. 148, No. 9, October 27, 2003, pp. 196); "Cash From Trash: 1-800-Got-Junk?" in **[3288]**, **[8679]**, **[38615]**, **[52489]**

Fortune (Vol. 152, October 3, 2005, No. 7, pp. 64); "Coming Back to Life" in **[27482]**, **[27961]**, **[31448]**, **[32320]**

Fortune (Vol. 142, No. 3, July 24, 2000, pp. 336+); "Credit Denied: Dot-Coms Feel the Squeeze" in **[31532]**

Fortune (Vol. 140, No. 11, pp. 72+); "Day Care for Dot-Coms: Warmer, Fuzzier Venture Capitalism" in **[13739]**, **[55369]**

Fortune (Vol. 151, February 7, 2005, No. 3, pp. 28); "Delivering At Domino's Pizza" in **[14911]**, **[19628]**, **[21485]**, **[38751]**, **[43616]**, **[49891]**

Fortune (Vol. 142, No. 3, July 24, 2000, pp. 48); "Dot-Com Deathwatch" in **[13741]**, **[33428]**, **[35397]**, **[55372]**

Fortune (Vol.141, No. 9, May 1, 2000); "Dulling the Tax Bite" **[42606]**, **[54524]**

Fortune (Vol. 151, January 10, 2005, No. 1, pp. 52); "Early Adopters' Paradise: What Else Is Popping In Tech? Plenty" in **[6639]**, **[24339]**, **[41652]**

Fortune (Oct. 9, 2000, pp. 200); "Eat Our Dust: Broadband infrastructure has made Redpoint the hottest VC firm you've never heard of" in **[35404]**, **[55374]**

Fortune (Vol. 142, No. 10, October 30, 2000, pp. 108+); "Fallen Idols" in **[13747]**, **[33437]**, **[55378]**

Fortune (Vol. 142, No. 11, November 13, 2000, pp. F384FF); "Fast, Faster, and Fastest" in [14031], [53721]

Fortune (Vol. 151, February 7, 2005, No. 3, pp. 34); "Find Online Training That Pays Off" in [4659], [6331], [14036], [22995], [33097], [33894], [53281]

Fortune (Vol. 142, No. 10, October 30, 2000, pp. 294+); "Finding the Fault Line Where A New Business Can Grow" in [27719], [35451], [55381]

Fortune (Vol. 141, No. 4, April 3, 2000, pp. 264J); "From the Corner Office To Around the Corner" in [3480], [35472]

"A Fortune From Home" in *Small Business Opportunities* (Vol. 13, No. 5, September 2001, pp. 22-24, 26, 28, 30, 32, 34, 36, 40) [16410], [27720], [29735]

Fortune (Vol. 151, January 10, 2005, No. 1, pp. 54); "Genetic Medicine's Next Big Step" in [15028], [41013], [41705], [50878], [52108]

Fortune (Vol. 151, February 7, 2005, No. 3, pp. 87); "Getting Ahead Of the Weather" in [25388], [28203], [52857], [53750]

Fortune (Vol. 149, No. 9, May 3, 2004, pp. 105); "Google's Banker" in [14087], [15047], [33973], [49965], [55647]

Fortune (Vol. 142, No. 11, November 13, 2000, pp. F348B+); "Heroes Of Small Business" in [28272], [36279]

Fortune (Vol. 151, February 21, 2005, No. 4, pp. 125); "Hold That Bid on eBay" in [1823], [15085]

Fortune (Vol. 142, No. 9, October 16, 2000, pp. 312T); "How Do I Value a Small Business?" in [3419], [52430]

Fortune (Vol. 151, February 21, 2005, No. 4, pp. 42); "How To Prevent Violence At Work" in [45273], [56565]

Fortune; "How a Virtuoso Plays the Web: Eclectic, Inquisitive, and Academic, Yahoo's Jerry Yang Reinvents the Role of the Entrepreneur" in [35518]

Fortune (Vol. 142, No. 1, June 26, 2000, pp. 294); "I Want My meVC!: the armchair venture capitalist" in [55396]

Fortune (Vol. 141, No. 4, February 21, 2000, pp. 274+); "Imagining a Web Beyond the Browser: a new kind of dot" in [14145], [34055], [52896]

Fortune (Vol. 141, No. 12, June 12, 2000, pp. 311+); "In the Family Way: Adam's Excellent Venture" in [55677]

Fortune International (Vol. 146, No. 4, March 3, 2003, pp. 41); "Staying Ahead of the Curve" in [35077], [45666]

Fortune International (Vol. 147, No. 6, March 31, 2003, pp. 42); "This Yogi Is Hot-And Bothered" in [17916], [19445]

Fortune (Vol. 142, No. 2, July 10, 2000, pp. 200B+); "Is Anyone Listening?" in [43244], [54625]

Fortune (Vol. , No. 11, December 6, 1999, pp. 156+); "Is Excite@Home The AOL of Broadband?" in [14165], [34091], [50023]

Fortune (Vol. 151, January 10, 2005, No. 1, pp. 55); "It Even Makes Calls!" in [5034], [41780], [49103]

Fortune (Vol. 142, No. 10, October 30, 2000, pp. 208); "It's Fall, And The Shopping Is Easy" in [28351], [49106]

Fortune (Vol. 143, No. 1, January 8, 2001, pp. 54); "It's The Business Model, Stupid!" in [29924], [52899]

Fortune (Vol. 149, No. 9, May 3, 2004, pp. 40) "Jobs Are Back; Too Bad Wages Aren't" in [13357], [26838], [32524], [42320]

Fortune (Vol. 151, January 10, 2005, No. 1, pp. 55); "Kiss Privacy Goodbye" in [22278], [29329], [40495], [41798]

Fortune (Vol. 151, January 24, 2005, No. 2, pp. 42); "Let Your Fingers Do the Locking: Forgotten That Password?" in [4716], [6708], [22282], [23067], [41806], [49122], [53352], [53832]

Fortune (Vol. 151, February 7, 2005, No. 3, pp. 26); "Loehmann's New Owner Keeps the Faith" in [15227], [28430], [36452], [51232], [52557]

Fortune (May 15, 2000, p. 441); "Looking for The Prevailing Wind The bulls and bears are both blowing plenty of hot air these days" in [52910]

Fortune (Vol. 141, No. 12, June 12, 2000, pp. 264N+); "Make Your Company an Idea Factory" in [36469], [55720]

Fortune Management [31480]

Fortune (Vol. 142, No. 14, December 18, 2000, pp. 292B); "My Best Practices: Do you want to sell smarter and don't know how?" in [3563], [14262], [25903], [49153]

Fortune (Vol. 140, No. 11, December 6, 1999, pp. 313+); "My Short, Unhappy Life as an E-Tailer" in [18629], [33464]

Fortune (Vol. 141, No. 6, Mar. 20, 2000, pp. 82); "New Ethics or No Ethics? Questionable behavior is Silicon Valley's next big thing" in [37483], [55748]

Fortune (Vol. 152, October 3, 2005, No. 7, pp. 87); "New Lessons to Learn" in [37902], [39492], [45468]

Fortune (Vol. 140, No. 11, December 6, 1999, pp. 177+); "Nice work If You Can Get It" in [55410]

Fortune (Vol. 151, January 24, 2005, No. 2, pp. 36); "Offshoring Could Boost Your Career" in [41882], [43772], [45483], [49720], [53893]

Fortune (Vol. 151, February 21, 2005, No. 4, pp. 114); "Old King Coal Comes Back: Actually, It Never Really Left" in [15317], [28585], [52926], [53894]

Fortune (Vol. 142, No. 8, October 9, 2000, pp. 180+); "One Life To Live: They say starting up is hard to do" in [55413]

Fortune (Vol. 149, No. 9, May 3, 2004, pp. 33); "Private Sector Soldiers" in [7454], [56583]

Fortune (Vol. 142, No. 7, October 2, 2000, pp. 284); "Protecting Your Idea From Bigmouths, and Calling All CFOs" in [43968]

Fortune (Vol. 141, No. 1, January 10, 2000, pp. 218); "Remember The Nanny Tax? Now It's the Granny Tax" in [12379], [40637], [54719]

Fortune (Vol. 141, No. 3, February 7, 2000, pp. 56); "Report From Las Vegas: Inside the Home Office Of the Future" in [30592], [42715]

Fortune (Vol. 141, No. 12, June 12, 2000, pp. F274Z); "Right off the Shelf or Made-to-Order?" in [49231]

Fortune (Vol. 152, October 3, 2005, No. 7, pp. 61); "Risk is His Business" in [13451], [43346]

Fortune (Aug. 14, 2000, pp. 268); "Sand Hill Road's Networking Guru Plugs Us In: Vinod Khosla on Cisco, Redback, Juniper, and more" in [55424]

Fortune (Vol. 151, February 21, 2005, No. 4, pp. 30); "SBC Can't Resist a Blast From Its Past" in [5099], [14411], [34436]

Fortune (Vol. 141, No. 2, January 24, 2000, pp. 96+); "Scaling a Vertical Learning Curve" in [14412], [36719]

Fortune (Vol. 151, January 10, 2005, No. 1, pp. 60); "Scanning For Dollars" in [41964], [47497], [50961], [52195]

Fortune (Vol. 151, January 24, 2005, No. 2, pp. 140); "Send In the Robots!" in [41976], [46431], [53959]

Fortune (Vol. 141, No. 7, April 3, 2000, pp. 68); "Sex, Drugs, and Career Choices" in [55310]

Fortune (Vol. 141, No. 5, March 6, 2000, pp. 430); "Signing Internet Noncompetes And Working From Home" in [14434], [34476], [37186], [42722]

Fortune (Vol. , No. , pp.); "Software Preserves Knowledge, People Pass It On" in [44365]

Fortune (Vol. 141, No. 11, May 29, 2000, pp. 278); "Startups, Beware: Obey the Law Of Supply and Demand" in [55435]

Fortune (Vol. 152, October 17, 2005, No. 8, pp. 41); "Stuck in a Storm of Controversy" in [35962], [37329], [40739]

Fortune (Vol. 151, February 21, 2005, No. 4, pp. 36); "Taking Boutique Hotels to the Extreme" in [12643], [24733], [25252]

Fortune (Vol. 151, February 7, 2005, No. 3, pp. 97); "Taking On the Energy Crunch" in [21257], [27188], [53005], [54021]

Fortune (Vol. 141, No. 5, March 6, 2000, pp. 432L); "Taxing Unfairly...Brand Mascots...Slotting Wars...The Genetic Jerk" in [36836], [54831]

"Fortune Teller" in *Entrepreneur* (Vol. 28, No. 8, August 2000, pp. 23) [9970]

Fortune (Vol. 151, January 24, 2005, No. 2, pp. 72); "The 100 Best Companies To Work For" in [34804], [44865], [52811]

Fortune (Vol. 141, No. 6, March 20, 2000, pp. 214); "The Electronic Personal Touch" in [7112], [35407]

Fortune (No. 9, Oct. 16, 2000, pp.13); "The 50 Most Powerful Women In Business: Secrets of the Fastest-Rising Stars" in [45138]

Fortune (Vol. 142, No. 7, October 2, 2000, pp. 278+); "The House That Knowledge Built" in [44310]

Fortune (Vol. 141, No. 3, February 7, 2000, pp. 199+); "The Joy of Quitting" in [32526], [52901], [53821]

Fortune (Vol. 142, No. 9, October 16, 2000, pp. 312X); "The Latest and Greatest Disease" in [49119], [53350]

Fortune (Vol. 143, No. 3, February 5, 2001, pp. 180); "The Man Who Launched 4,000 Businesses" in [35558], [38660]

Fortune (Vol. 142, No. 10, October 30, 2000, pp. 56); "The Most Successful VC Isn't Who You Think" in [55738]

Fortune (Vol. 140, December 20, 1999); "The Next Big Things: Nothing is more profitable than an investment idea whose time has come" in [38246], [53885]

Fortune (Vol. 148, No. 8, October 13, 2003, pp. 214); "The Nonprofit Motive" in [6955], [36558], [50937]

Fortune (Vol. 140, No. 12, December 20, 1999 pp. 52); "The Numbers" in [28576], [32605], [52925]

Fortune (Vol. 142, No. 9, October 16, 2000, pp. 139+); "The Power 50" in [45551]

Fortune (Vol.141, No.7, Apr. 3, 2000, pp.302); "The Reverse Greenhouse Effect: Why pay another to gardener to cultivate your stock?" in [43059], [55807]

Fortune (Vol. 142, No. 2, July 10, 2000, pp. 200V+); "The Smart Way to Hire Superstars" in [9577], [42418]

Fortune (Vol. 142, No. 2, July 10, 2000, pp. 200J); "The Spotlight's on Health Care" in [43374]

Fortune (Vol. 151, February 21, 2005, No. 4, pp. 58); "The U.S. Is In Decline-And That's a Good Thing" in [28939], [32764]

Fortune (Vol. 151, February 21, 2005, No. 4, pp. 21); "The Urge to Merge" in [10226], [15562], [28950], [50239]

Fortune (July 10, 2000, pp.154); "The Village Vanguard: Two new-economy entrepreneurs aim to jump-start businesses in college towns" in [29772], [35713], [55451]

Fortune (Vol. 151, January 24, 2005, No. 2, pp. 62); "The Wegman's Way" in [11675], [30989], [35136]

Fortune (Vol. 141, No. 8, April 17, 2000, pp. 532); "These Days, Who Isn't a Venture Capitalist?" in [55862]

Fortune (Vol. 149, No. 9, May 3, 2004, pp. 58); "This Detective has Rediscovered a Lost Art" in [1614], [1858], [19979], [50209]

Fortune (Vol. 151, February 7, 2005, No. 3, pp. 32); "This V-Day, Money Can Buy You Love" in [7070], [14535], [34595]

Fortune (Vol. 142, No. 3, July 24, 2000, pp. 54); "This VC Firm's Motto: Make Money, Not War" in [41488], [43045], [55443]

Fortune (Vol. 152, October 17, 2005, No. 8, pp. 33); "Three Cheers for Bankruptcy" in [36957], [38412], [40767]

Fortune (Vol. 151, January 10, 2005, No. 1, pp. 27); "Tin Whiskers" in [5152], [7745], [14538], [34604], [42069]

Fortune (Vol. 142, No. 9, October 16, 2000, pp. 312); "Tip Clubbing" in [26717], [54040]

Fortune (Vol. 151, February 21, 2005, No. 4, pp. 124); "Trouble Ahead For Stocks" in [10217], [15544], [28918]

"Free Reign" in *Home Office Computing* (Vol. 18, No. 12, December 2000, pp. 45) **[33924]**, **[42619]**, **[46984]**

"Free rein" in *Entrepreneur* (Vol. 31, No. 5, May 2003, pp. 23) **[39827]**, **[44531]**

"Free to Roam" in *Entrepreneur* (Vol. 32, September 2004, No. 9, pp. 42) **[4991]**, **[49038]**

Free Software Foundation **[22898]**

"Free Speech" in *Entrepreneur* (Vol. 31, No. 9, July 2003, pp. 80) **[22503]**, **[46985]**

"Free yourself from taxes" in *Women in Business* (Vol. 53, No. 7, January-February 2002, pp. 27) **[15016]**, **[54562]**

"Free Tuition: Win New Customers With Educational Programs" in *Sales & Marketing Management* (Vol. 157, February 2005, No. 2, pp. 20) **[33099]**, **[46986]**, **[51645]**

"Free! (With Purchase)" in *Business 2.0* (Vol. 7, January/February 2006, No. 1, pp. 113-115) **[4669]**, **[6653]**, **[23008]**, **[41700]**, **[46987]**, **[53293]**

Freeburg Chamber of Commerce **[59503]**

Freedom Chamber of Commerce **[63995]**

"Freedom of Speech: The legacy you leave yourself" in *Atlanta Business Chronicle* (Vol. 24, No. 10, August 10, 2001, pp. 39A) **[50592]**, **[51646]**

Freelance Dee-Jaying: How to Become a Successful Discotheque & Radio Jock **[8677]**

Freelance Self Publishing **[8611]**, **[8995]**, **[18227]**

Freelance Teaching & Tutoring: How to Earn Good Money by Teaching Others What You Know **[25465]**

Freelance Writer's Report **[9028]**

Freelance Writing Business Guide **[8996]**

Freelance Writing for Greeting Card Companies **[11564]**

The Freelancer **[9029]**

Freeland Chamber of Commerce **[64420]**

"The Freeland Conundrum" in *Inc.* (December 1, 2004) **[9206]**, **[24525]**, **[27125]**, **[49698]**

Freeport Area Chamber of Commerce **[59504]**

Freeport Merchants Association **[60747]**

Freer Chamber of Commerce **[65240]**

Freese & Associates Inc. **[3709]**, **[16606]**, **[31351]**, **[46026]**, **[47863]**

Freight Brokerage Business Guide **[10678]**

Freight Carriers Association of Canada **[25360]**

Freight Transportation Consultants Association **[10661]**

Fremont Area Chamber of Commerce **[59911]**, **[61302]**, **[62262]**, **[66399]**

Fremont Chamber of Commerce **[57499]**

Fremont County Business Development Center **[58470]**

Fremont County Office–SBDC **[66595]**

French-American Chamber of Commerce **[43498]**, **[64421]**

French-Canadian Genealogical Society of Connecticut, Inc.–French-Canadian Genealogical Library **[11025]**

French and French-Canadian Family Research **[10933]**

"French Fried: GE Wins in Vivendi Deal" in *Barron's* (September 8, 2003, pp. 18) **[1132]**, **[4105]**, **[9716]**, **[15017]**, **[24410]**, **[49951]**

French Language Press Association **[18833]**

French Lick - West Baden Chamber of Commerce **[59912]**

Fresh City **[21823]**

Fresh Coat **[20268]**

Fresh Facts **[10583]**

Fresh Fruit Bouquet Company **[23562]**, **[56544]**

"Fresh Ideas" in *Entrepreneur* (Vol. 32, December 2004, No. 12, pp. 91) **[4292]**, **[46988]**, **[50593]**

Fresh Ideas in Letterhead and Business Card Design **[5982]**

"A Fresh Look for Northeast Brookfield" in *Business Journal-Milwaukee* (Vol. 20, No. 51, September 5, 2003, pp. A1) **[20222]**, **[20513]**, **[20879]**, **[28185]**, **[51169]**

"Fresh-Produce Prices Set to Rise in Wake of Crop Freeze" in *Atlanta Journal-Constitution* (January 28, 2007) **[11621]**, **[26511]**

Fresh from the Roaster **[11361]**

"Fresh Sets of Eyes on Detroit" in *Crain's Detroit Business* (Vol. 22, January 30, 2006, No. 5, pp. 1) **[28186]**, **[52675]**

"Fresh-Tossed Profits" in *Small Business Opportunities* (Vol. 17, November 2005, No. 6, pp. 48, 50) **[21401]**, **[38647]**

"Freshmen LPs Prep for PE" in *Venture Capital Journal* (Vol. 42, No. 10, October 2002, pp. 6) **[9972]**, **[15018]**, **[55632]**

Freshwater Aquarium Basics **[19168]**

Fresno SBDC–UC Merced Lead Center–University of California at Merced **[57244]**

Leonard R. Friedman Risk Management Inc. **[43440]**, **[56664]**

Friedman, Rosenwasser & Goldbaum, P.A. **[29622]**

"Friend or Faux? Why Big Businesses Want to Look Like You" in *My Business* (February/March 2003, pp. 51) **[39345]**, **[53742]**

"FriendFinder Online Dating Far Outranks the Competition; Multiple Awards Bestowed..." in *PR Newswire* (Jan. 5, 2004) **[7057]**, **[33925]**

Friendly Computers **[6438]**

"Friendly firing" in *WorkingWoman* (Vol. 25, No. 4, April 2000, pp. 36) **[39346]**, **[45163]**

Friendly Persuasion: The Art of Converting Objections into Sales **[51954]**

Friendly's Restaurants **[21824]**

Friends of American Writers **[8959]**

Friends of the Earth **[58690]**

"Friends forever?" in *Entrepreneur* (Vol. 31, No. 6, June 2003, pp. 77) **[36181]**, **[49952]**

"Friends in High Places" in *Hispanic Business* (Vol. 23, No. 7/8, July/August 2001, pp. 62, 64) **[28187]**, **[36182]**, **[41701]**, **[48172]**, **[55633]**

"Friends should never ask friends to spam-even if Big Blue says to do so" in *InfoWorld* (Vol. 22, No. 38, September 18, 2000 pp. 109) **[33926]**, **[37447]**, **[46989]**

Friends and Strangers **[5382]**

Friends of the Western Philatelic Library **[5869]**

Friendswood Chamber of Commerce **[65241]**

Friesland Chamber of Commerce **[66400]**

Chris Frings & Associates **[54365]**

Frio Canyon Chamber of Commerce **[65242]**

Friona Chamber of Commerce and Agriculture **[65243]**

Frisch's Restaurants, Inc. **[21825]**

Frisco Chamber of Commerce **[65244]**

The Frog Chronicles **[8207]**

"From Barracks to Boardroom" in *Hispanic Business* (Vol. 24, No. 1/2, January/February 2002, pp. 59-60) **[42242]**, **[45164]**, **[48173]**

"From big idea to big bust: the wild ride of Boo.com" in *The New York Times* (December 13 2000, pp. D3, H3) **[14058]**, **[33927]**, **[37138]**

"From Concept to Customer" in *Black Enterprise* (Vol. 36, November 2005, No. 4, pp. 124) **[46990]**, **[48734]**

From Concept to Form in Landscape Design **[16013]**

"From the Corner Office To Around the Corner" in *Fortune* (Vol. 141, No. 4, April 3, 2000, pp. 264J) **[3480]**, **[35472]**

"From Cow Pies to Clean Power" in *Business 2.0* (Vol. 7, January/February 2006, No. 1, pp. 24) **[41702]**, **[50875]**, **[52104]**

"From Digital Image to Document" in *Sales & Marketing Management* (Vol. 158, November-December 2006, No. 11, pp. 62) **[4992]**, **[33928]**, **[46991]**, **[51647]**

"From Drab to Fab" in *Black Enterprise* (Vol. 36, November 2005, No. 4, pp. 59) **[12187]**, **[12281]**, **[13644]**, **[18682]**

"From Dream to Reality: Inventor Takes Invention from Prototype to Product" in *Small Business Opportunities* (Vol. 17, May 2005, No. 3) **[24813]**, **[44045]**

From Entrepreneur to Infopreneur: Make Money with Books, E-Books, and Other Information Products **[2706]**, **[8612]**, **[22504]**, **[33929]**, **[36183]**

From Executive to Entrepreneur: Making the Transition **[52854]**

"From Feast to Famine?" in *Hispanic Business* (Vol. 23, No. 11, November 2001, pp. 42, 44, 46, 48-49) **[12973]**, **[28188]**, **[43664]**

"From Fifth Hire to Top Exec, New CEO to Lead SurePayroll" in *Crain's Chicago Business* (Vol. 26, No. 50, December 15, 2003, pp. 12) **[154]**, **[18774]**, **[19457]**, **[25867]**, **[26244]**, **[30197]**, **[31032]**, **[43146]**

"From the Firehouse to the Schoolhouse" in *Black Enterprise* (Vol. 33, No. 6, Jan. 2003, pp. 32) **[33100]**, **[35473]**

"From Football to Financial Plan" in *Black Enterprise* (Vol. 36, November 2005, No. 4, pp. 85) **[15019]**, **[38082]**

"From Golf to Software" in *Crain's Detroit Business* (Vol. 19, No. 42, October 20, 2003, pp. 28) **[9717]**, **[11260]**, **[36184]**

"From Golf to Software; Entrepreneur Nixes Retirement to Build Businesses in Farmington Hills" in *Crain's Detroit Business* (Vol. 19) **[9718]**, **[11261]**, **[36185]**

"From the Ground Floor: From hosted applications to Web services" in *Red Herring* (No. 103, September 1, 2001, pp. 36) **[6913]**, **[13750]**

"From the Ground Floor: The business paths to nanotech" in *Red Herring* (No. 99, June 15 & July 1, 2001, pp. 42, 44) **[41455]**, **[44415]**, **[55387]**

"From the Ground Up" in *Boston Business Journal* (Vol. 23, No. 24, July 18, 2003, pp. 3) **[20514]**, **[20880]**

From Hiring to Firing: The Legal Survival Guide for Employers in the 90's **[42243]**

"From Idea to Marketplace" in *Small Business Opportunities* (May 2005) **[24857]**, **[43961]**, **[44046]**, **[44847]**, **[46296]**, **[46992]**, **[48735]**, **[55051]**

"From idea to inspiration" in *Entrepreneur* (Vol. 30, No. 3, March 2002, pp. 29) **[29736]**, **[30480]**, **[48736]**

"From office catnaps to lunchtime jogs" in *Wall Street Journal* (May 16, 2002, pp. D1) **[34907]**, **[45166]**, **[54945]**

From Kitchen to Market: Selling Your Gourmet Food Specialty **[20000]**

"From Landscaper to Landowner" in *Black Enterprise* (Vol. 34, No. 5, December 2003, pp. S4) **[16014]**, **[16538]**, **[20290]**, **[20515]**, **[20627]**, **[20881]**, **[36186]**, **[53919]**, **[56744]**

From Law School to Law Practice: What Every Associate Needs to Know-The Set **[9173]**, **[9261]**, **[9587]**

"From Managing Pills to Managing Brands" in *Harvard Business Review* (Vol. 78, No. 2, March 2000, pp. 20) **[8785]**, **[46993]**

From Mind to Market: The Patent Process **[44195]**

"From Mushing to Management" in *Inc.* (January 1, 2005) **[36187]**, **[42853]**, **[45167]**, **[56234]**

From the Other Side of the Bed: A Woman Looks at Life in the Family Business **[37658]**

From Patent to Profit **[44047]**

From Patent to Profit: Secrets & Strategies for Success **[44048]**

"From Real Estate to Retirement Plan" in *Black Enterprise* (Vol. 34, No. 3, October 2003, pp. 29) **[15020]**, **[20516]**, **[20882]**, **[36188]**, **[48174]**

"From the Recruiter: Enliven Your Resume" in *Sales & Marketing Management* (Vol. 157, January 2005, No. 1, pp. 51) **[9207]**, **[42244]**, **[42854]**

"From Tee to Green" in *Home Business* (Vol. 12, March/April 2005, No. 2, pp. 96) **[11262]**, **[42620]**, **[44049]**

"From Vacation to Vocation" in *My Business* (September/October 2001, pp. 48) **[4219]**, **[35474]**, **[37659]**

"From Wish to Goal" in *Black Enterprise* (Vol. 35, January 2005, No. 6, pp. 97) **[29883]**, **[30544]**, **[36189]**

"From Zero to Hero: Even the Best Franchisor has to Start Somewhere" in *Entrepreneur* (Vol. 32, No. 1, January 2004, pp. 148) **[8512]**, **[21520]**, **[36190]**, **[38811]**

Front Royal - Warren County Chamber of Commerce **[65899]**

Frontal Lobe **[58259]**

Frontenac Company **[59735]**

Frontier Capital, LLC **[63457]**

"Frontier Could Land Here" in *Pittsburgh Business Times* (Vol. 22, No. 52, July 11, 2003, pp. 1) **[28189]**, **[30332]**

"Frontier Country Marketing Association Gives Out Awards" in *Journal Record* (June 25, 2003) **[46983]**, **[46994]**

"Frontier Online" in *Business Week* (No. 3694, August 14, 2000, pp. F8) **[40025]**, **[48175]**, **[56235]**

Frontiers Benefit Services **[27029]**

Frontiers of Health Services Management **[41199]**

Frontline Capital, Inc. **[59196]**

Frontline Teamwork: One Company's Story of Success **[34908]**

Froots Franchising Companies **[12821]**

Frostproof Chamber of Commerce **[58800]**

"Frozen assets" in *Entrepreneur* (Vol. 31, No. 6, June 2003, pp. 114) **[36191]**, **[46297]**

"Frozen Assets" in *Inc.* (January 1, 2002) **[10621]**, **[21521]**

Frozen Custard Outfitters **[12822]**

Frozen Food Age (Vol. 51, No. 12, July 2003, pp. 40); "Kahiki Launches Frozen Meals, Refrigerated Rice Bowls" in **[11635]**, **[23490]**

Frozen Food Age (Vol. 52, No. 3, October 2003, pp. 36); "Pierogi Power" in **[11651]**, **[23502]**

Frozen Food Age (Vol. 51, No. 12, July 2003, pp. 34); "Southern Expansion" in **[11665]**, **[23508]**

Frozen Food Age (Vol. 50, No. 3, October 2001, pp. 12); "Starbucks Gets A New Look" in **[12790]**, **[47571]**, **[50187]**, **[50681]**

"Frozen yogurt is sweet deal for Planet Sun" in *Wenatchee Business Journal* (Vol. 15, No. 5, May 2001, pp. A9) **[12055]**, **[12777]**, **[23837]**, **[25186]**

Frozen Ropes Training Centers **[33365]**

"Fruit of the Vine" in *Business First Buffalo* (Vol. 19, No. 40, June 27, 2003, pp. 1) **[14816]**, **[15021]**, **[23168]**, **[23482]**, **[47590]**, **[49953]**

Fruita Chamber of Commerce **[58368]**

"The Fruitful Flaws of Strategy Metaphors" in *Harvard Business Review* (Vol. 81, No. 9, September 2003, pp. 86) **[29884]**, **[30545]**

Fruitland Chamber of Commerce **[59295]**

Fruits & Passion **[2620]**

Frullati Cafe & Bakery **[8551]**

FSB (Vol. 10, No. 9, December 1, 2000, pp. 98); "Advice on Advisors: Fed up with bad advise?" in **[31109]**

FSB (Vol. 10, No. 9, December 1, 2000, pp. 38); "Early-Stage Loans With A Venture Capital Twist" in **[55584]**

FSB (Vol. 10, No. 9, December 1, 2000, pp. 116); "Face-Off: Online Postage" in **[49023]**

FSB (Vol. 10, No. 9, December 1, 2000, pp. 79); "How You Can Hire Gray Hairs" in **[42300]**

FSB (Vol. 10, No. 9, December 1, 2000, pp. 48); "In Search Of The Pay Off: What's more confusing than buying tech products?" in **[49092]**

FSB (Vol. 10, No. 4, May 1, 2000, pp. 144); "In a Zen Mindset: Stressed? Try meditating" in **[17897]**

FSB (Vol. 10, No. 9, December 1, 2000, pp. 118); "Marketers, a Lawyer, And a Techie-Cheap" in **[31190]**, **[34175]**

FSB (Vol. 10, No. 9, Dec. 1, 2000, pp. 54); "My Best Practices: Sell smarter. Streamline your office. Work better. Crush competition" in **[30774]**, **[48932]**

Fuchsia Flash **[16037]**

Fuddruckers, Inc. **[2299]**, **[21826]**

Fudge Co. **[4333]**

"Fuel Efficiency Becomes Grail" in *Crain's Detroit Business* (Vol. 23, January 8, 2007, No. 2, pp. 11) **[29885]**, **[30546]**, **[46298]**

"Fueling the Ads" in *Crain's Detroit Business* (Vol. 21, October 31, 2005, No. 44, pp. 3) **[631]**, **[18043]**, **[46995]**

"Fueling tomorrow's growth" in *Harvard Business Review* (Vol. 80, No. 9, September 2002, pp. 51) **[28190]**, **[52105]**

"Fujitsu Biometric Notebook PC" in *Black Enterprise* (Vol. 35, December 2004, No. 5, pp. 70) **[6654]**, **[22235]**, **[49039]**

Fujitsu Microelectronics, Inc.–FMI Library **[6909]**, **[7765]**

Fulbright & Jaworski L.L.P.–Library **[15798]**

"Fulfill the Promise of Electronic Billing" in *E-business Advisor* (Vol. 18, No. 7, July 2000, pp. 26) **[26245]**, **[31550]**, **[33930]**

"Fulfilling Audiovisual Dreams" in *Black Enterprise* (Vol. 36, February 2006, No. 7, pp. 64) **[4186]**, **[7165]**, **[7727]**, **[24341]**

"Full circle" in *Candy Industry* (Vol. 167, No. 4, April 2002, pp. 24) **[4293]**, **[28191]**, **[37660]**

Full Circle Image **[21286]**

"Full-Court Press" in *Hispanic Business* (May 2005, pp. 20, 22) **[18873]**, **[46996]**, **[48176]**

"Full Esteem Ahead: Act Like an Executive-And Get the Respect You Deserve" in *Entrepreneur* (Vol. 31, No. 9, September 2003, pp. 104) **[27377]**, **[36192]**, **[45168]**

"Full-Figured Women are Avid Online Shoppers" in *Marketing to Women* (Vol. 19, November 2006, No. 11, pp. 11) **[5665]**, **[14059]**, **[16214]**, **[41703]**, **[46997]**

"A Full House" in *Home Business* (Vol. 12, October 2005, No. 5, pp. 40) **[5545]**, **[9624]**, **[22762]**, **[36193]**, **[37661]**

"Full-time freelancers" in *Fast Company* (May 2001, pp. 62) **[35475]**, **[37565]**

Full Voice **[3710]**, **[3968]**, **[9768]**, **[27583]**, **[31352]**, **[33345]**

Fullerton Chamber of Commerce **[57500]**

Fulltext Sources Online **[5495]**

Fulton Carroll Center Incubator **[59777]**

Fulton Chamber of Commerce **[59505]**

Fulton County Chamber of Commerce and Tourism **[64422]**

Fulton County Regional Chamber of Commerce and Industry **[62881]**

Fulton Pennysaver **[19009]**

Fun Bus USA, Inc. - 'Fitness Fun on Wheels' **[19507]**

Fun, Creative, & Profitable Salon Marketing: 67 Ways to Grow Your Salon Business **[11761]**, **[11790]**

FUN Expo **[1121]**, **[1144]**, **[3110]**, **[11285]**, **[17330]**, **[22840]**, **[23683]**

Fun & Games for Family Gatherings: With a Focus on Reunions **[18756]**

"Fun money" in *Entrepreneur* (Vol. 31, No. 4, April 2003, pp. 94) **[8125]**, **[35476]**

"Fun Money: Mixing Business and Pleasure Can Pay Off" in *Entrepreneur* (Vol. 32, August 2004, No. 8, pp. 48) **[30333]**, **[54563]**

"Fund gets boost from Masco connection" in *Crain's Detroit Business* (Vol. 16, No. 16, April 17, 2000, pp. 27) **[55634]**

"Fund Profile: Hey, Abbott! FoF Tops Target" in *Venture Capital Journal* (Vol. 42, No. 9, September 2002, pp. 12) **[55635]**

"Fund Profile" in *Venture Capital Journal* (February 1, 2006) **[50876]**, **[52106]**, **[55636]**

"Fund-Raising Falters, VCs Keep Cutting Back" in *Venture Capital Journal* (Vol. 42, No. 10, October 2002, pp. 18-20) **[9973]**, **[15022]**, **[28192]**, **[49954]**, **[55637]**

The Fund-Raising Handbook **[10734]**

"Fund-Raising Soars 78 Percent, Momentum Builds" in *Venture Capital Journal* (December 1, 2004) **[15023]**, **[28193]**, **[55638]**

"Fund Sharks" in *Entrepreneur* (Vol. 31, No. 8, August 2003, pp. 54) **[9974]**, **[15024]**, **[38083]**, **[40399]**

Fundamental Selling Techniques for the New or Prospective Salesperson-Level 1 (Canada) **[51520]**

Fundamentals of Business Strategy **[44755]**

Fundamentals of Business Writing (Canada) **[27608]**

Fundamentals of Cost Accounting **[26127]**

Fundamentals of Cost Accounting (Canada) **[26128]**

Fundamentals of Finance and Accounting for Administrative Professionals **[26129]**

Fundamentals of Finance and Accounting for Administrative Professionals (Canada) **[37853]**

Fundamentals of Finance and Accounting for Non-Financial Executives (Canada) **[37854]**

Fundamentals of Finance and Accounting for Non-Financial Managers (Canada) **[26130]**, **[37855]**

Fundamentals of Finance and Accounting for Nonfinancial Managers **[37856]**

The Fundamentals of Franchising **[38812]**

The Fundamentals of Fundamental Analysis: A Back-to-the-Basics Investment Guide to Selecting Quality Stocks **[15025]**

Fundamentals of Human Resources Management (Canada) **[42818]**

Fundamentals of IT Cost Management **[26131]**, **[32929]**

Fundamentals of Marketing: Your Action Plan for Success **[46628]**

Fundamentals of Marketing: Your Action Plan for Success (Canada) **[46629]**

Fundamentals of Purchasing for the New Buyer **[50749]**

Fundamentals of Purchasing for the New Buyer (Canada) **[50750]**

Fundamentals of Risk Management and Insurance for Non-insurance Executives **[43065]**

Fundamentals of Sales Management (Canada) **[51521]**

Fundamentals of Sales Management-Level 1 (Canada) **[51522]**

Fundamentals of Sales Management for the Newly Appointed Sales Manager **[51523]**

Fundamentals of Selling Techniques for the New or Prospective Salesperson (Canada) **[51524]**

Fundamentals of Successful Newsletters: Everything You Need to Write, Design and Publish More Effective Newsletters **[18228]**

Fundamentals of Total Rewards Management **[40951]**, **[42819]**

"Funding from the Feds: Local interest in Small Business Investment Corporations is growing" in *Crain's Detroit Business* (Vol.16, No.33) **[39828]**, **[55639]**

"Funding a Franchise Startup" in *Hispanic Business* (Vol. 23, No. 5, May 2001, pp. 52, 54) **[38648]**, **[44416]**, **[48884]**, **[55388]**

"Funds Face Unexpected Antitrust Problem" in *Venture Capital Journal* (January 1, 2005) **[15026]**, **[29256]**, **[40400]**, **[55640]**

Funeral Consumers Alliance **[10790]**, **[10802]** Library **[10817]**

Funeral Directors Management System **[10815]**

Funk, Funk & More Funk **[8476]**

"Funny Business" in *Black Enterprise* (Vol. 36, December 2005, No. 5, pp. 71) **[5878]**, **[36194]**

"Funny Business: No Ifs, Ands or Buts" in *Entrepreneur* (Vol. 32, October 2004, No. 10, pp. 93) **[632]**, **[30863]**, **[46998]**

"Funny Money: Counterfeit Money Scams Persist" in *Black Enterprise* (Vol. 34, No. 3, October 2003, pp. 135) **[30226]**

Funny River Chamber of Commerce **[56955]**

"Funny Stuff: Laughter is the Best Marketing, so Find Your Sense of Humor" in *Entrepreneur* (Vol. 33, February 2005, No. 2, pp. 78) **[2126]**, **[5276]**, **[46999]**

Fuqua Ventures LLC **[59197]**

Fuquay-Varina Area Chamber of Commerce **[63364]**

Fur Council of Canada **[10821]**, **[10826]**

Fur Information Council of America **[10822]**, **[10827]**

Furla **[51456]**

"Furnishing an Alternative for Tenants" in *Washington Business Journal* (Vol. 22, No. 14, August 8, 2003, pp. 33) **[21323]**, **[49501]**

The Furniture Executive **[12324]**

Furniture Library Association–Library **[10847]**, **[13726]**

"Furniture Market Adapting Strategy to Combat Competition" in *Mississippi Business Journal* (Vol. 29, January 2007, No. 2, pp. 17) **[10831]**, **[12282]**, **[37662]**

Furniture Medic of Canada **[10839]**

Furniture Medic, L.P. **[10840]**

Furniture Today **[12325]**

Furniture Transporter **[12326]**

Furniture Weekend **[12347]**

Furniture World Magazine **[12327]**

"Furncom.com stages revival, forges ties with non-com allies" in *Boston Business Journal* (Vol. 22, No. 11, April 19, 2002, pp. 1) **[12283]**, **[28194]**, **[33931]**, **[47000]**, **[49955]**, **[51170]**

The Gauge [16836], [20168], [27553], [47787], [50715]

Gavilan College–Small Business Development Center [57259]

Gaylord - Otsego County Chamber of Commerce [61304]

Gazelle Techventures [60030]

Gazette (February 2, 2005); "Family Fun Center to Offer Laser Tag, Paintball, Miniature Golf" in [1103], [17323]

GBA Inc. [47865]

GCI [66564]

GE Energy [37361]

"GE Whiz!" in *Entrepreneur* (Vol. 28, No. 1, January 2000, pp. 32) [52536], [53745]

Gear Technology [52265]

"Gearing Up For Expansion" in *Fast Company* (March 2005, No. 92, pp. 90) [4671], [23010], [28197], [45173], [53746]

"Gearing Up for the Golden Years" in *Black Enterprise* (Vol. 34, No. 3, October 2003) [9976], [15027], [38085]

Geary Chamber of Commerce [63998]

Gebbie Press All-in-One Directory [5497], [18876]

GEC Consultants Inc. [2377], [3711], [12083], [21720], [31353]

Geeks on Call [6440]

The Geek's Guide to Internet Business Success [14064]

Gefinor Ventures / Inman Ventures [65607]

Geibel Marketing & Public Relations [47866]

"GEICO Pays 24.2 Percent In Worker Bonuses" in *Ledger* (February 26, 2005) [12557], [13293], [26813], [43181]

Geisinger Medical Center–Community Health Resource Library [12041], [12095], [17944], [18498]

Gelato Amare/ Jazzy Juices [12824]

Leon Gelfond & Associates [2793], [16486]

J.B. Geller Consulting Inc. [30647]

Gem County Chamber of Commerce [59296]

Gemini Investors / GMN Investors [61073]

Gemini Tub Repair [19786]

Gemological Institute of America–Richard T. Liddicoat Gemological Library and Information Center [15887]

"Gemstar may unload e-book assets (Who will Buy?)" in *Publishers Weekly* (Vol. 249, No. 47, November 25, 2002, pp. 18) [2708], [9143], [14065]

Gen X [39349]

"Gender Inequity at Top" in *Crain's Detroit Business* (Vol. 19, No. 42, October 20, 2003, pp. 8) [39350], [39617], [43154], [45174]

Gender and Racial Inequality at Work: The Sources and Consequences of Employment Segregation [32027]

Gender & Successful Human Resource Decisions in Small Businesses [42856]

Gendered Processes: Korean Small Business Ownership [39351], [48551]

Genealogical Center Library [11026]

Genealogical Computing [10961]

Genealogical Helper-Bureau of Missing Ancestors Section [10934]

Genealogical Journal of Jefferson County, New York [10962]

Genealogical and Local History Books in Print [10935]

Genealogical Periodical Annual Index [10936]

The Genealogist's Address Book [10937]

General Business Consultants Inc. [32180]

General Business Services Corp. [38970], [54888]

General Catalyst Partners / General Catalyst Group LLC [61074]

General Driving Safety [8732]

"General Dynamics will build 2,131 vehicles for Army" in *Crain's Detroit Business* (Vol. 16, No. 49, December 4, 2000, pp. 2) [40027]

General Electric Company–G.E. Asset Management Information Center [15799]

General Engineering Laboratories, Inc.–Library [9436], [9499]

General Merchandise Distributors Council [32132]

General Mills, Inc.
    Betty Crocker Kitchens Library [18499]

Business Information Center [16893]

General Nutrition Centers [18487]

General Reference Volume 10935

General Services Administration
    Atlanta Business Service Center [67169]
    Auburn Business Service Center [67170]
    Boston Business Service Center [67171]
    Chicago Business Service Center [67172]
    Denver Business Service Center [67173]
    Federal Technology Service (FTS)–Office of Regional Services [67165]
    Ft. Worth Business Service Center [67174]
    Kansas City Business Service Center [67175]
    New York Business Service Center [67176]
    Office of Electronic Government and Technology [67166]
    Office of Global Supply–Logistics Operations Ctr. [67167]
    Philadelphia Business Service Center–Office of Business and Public Affairs [67177]
    San Francisco Business Service Center [67178]
    Washington, DC, Business Services Center [67179]

General Services Administration (GSA)–Office of Enterprise Development [67168]

"A Generally Beneficial Law" in *Hispanic Business* (Vol. 23, No. 10, October, 2001, pp. 98) [40404], [54567]

"Generate More Revenue with a Bottom-Up Marketing Plan" in *Home Business* (Vol. 12, March/April 2005, No. 2, pp. 32, 34-35) [28198], [42621], [47004]

Generation Capital Partners [58594]

"Generation Gap at the Office" in *Hispanic Business* (November 2002, pp. 58, 60, 62) [27379], [34909], [37665], [45175]

"Generation next" in *San Francisco Business Times* (Vol. 16, No. 42, May 24, 2002, pp. S4) [26814], [36196], [56236]

"Generation W" in *Success* (Vol. 47, No. 4, September 2000, pp. 62) [55389], [56048]

Generic Pharmaceutical Association [8762]

Genesee County Chamber of Commerce [62883]

Genesee County Metropolitan Planning Commission [61464]

Genesee Funding, Inc. [63098]

Geneseo Chamber of Commerce [59508]

Genesis Business Centers, Ltd. [61717]

Genesis Park Ventures [65608]

The Genesis Society Inc. [63249]

Genesis Technology Incubator [57237]

Genesys Partners [63099]

"Genetic Medicine's Next Big Step" in *Fortune* (Vol. 151, January 10, 2005, No. 1, pp. 54) [15028], [41013], [41705], [50878], [52108]

Geneva Area Chamber of Commerce [62884], [63681]

Geneva Chamber of Commerce [59509]

Geneva Lake Area Chamber of Commerce [66402]

Geneva Merchant Banking Partners [63458]

Geneva-on-the-Lake Chamber of Commerce [63682]

Geneva Pennysaver [19010]

Geneva Roth Advertising LLC [882]

Geneva Venture Partners [58024]

Genoa Chamber of Commerce [59510]

Gentle Fitness [19472]

Gentry Main Street - Chamber of Commerce [57168]

"Genzyme Battles An Old Adversary" in *Boston Globe* (January 25, 2005) [41706], [44300], [49956], [50879], [52109]

Geocapital Partners, LLC [62597]

Geocosmic Magazine [17930]

Geographic Resources Center–University of Missouri-Columbia [66907]

Geographical Center of North America Chamber of Commerce [63518]

"Geography is Destiny" in *Inc.* (September 1, 2004) [20776], [30865]

The Geography of Small Firm Innovation [39352], [41707]

Geologic Controls on Radon [20392]

Geomatica [23774]

Geomicrobiology Journal [52266]

"GeoPhoenix is ready for its close-up" in *Red Herring* (January 2003, pp. 23) [4994], [48737]

George Brown College of Applied Arts & Technology–Archives [5612], [9663]

George Eastman House–International Museum of Photography & Film–Richard and Ronay Menschel Library [19337]

George Mason University–Software Engineering Research Laboratory [7022]

George Morris Centre [26685]

George Washington University–Center for International Science and Technology Policy [50399]

George Washington's First Business: A Guide to Starting New Ventures [52856]

George West Chamber of Commerce [65250]

Georgetown Chamber of Commerce [65251]

Georgetown County Chamber of Commerce [64736]

Georgetown Promotions Committee [58369]

Georgetown-Scott County Chamber of Commerce [60507]

Georgetown University
    Credit Research Center [8419]
    Maternal and Child Health Library [5455]

Georgia Association of Chamber of Commerce Executives [59104]

"Georgia CEOs debate global leadership issues" in *Atlanta Business Chronicle* (Vol. 25, November 15, 2002, No. 23 pp. 10C) [36197], [37140]

Georgia Chamber of Commerce [59105]

"Georgia ringing up new telecom contract" in *Atlanta Business Chronicle* (Vol. 25, November 8, 2002, No. 22 pp. 3A) [4995], [28199]

Georgia Department of Community Affairs
    Department of Economic Development [59041]
    Office of Planning and Quality Growth [66854]

Georgia Department of Economic Development–Entrepreneur and Small Business Development [59042]

Georgia Financial Institutions Directory & Fact Book [44533]

"Georgia medical device business growing" in *Atlanta Business Chronicle* (Vol. 25, No. 19, October 18, 2002, pp. 3A) [28200], [41708], [50880], [52110]

Georgia Highlands College
    Floyd Campus [59222]
    Small Business Development Center [59027]

Georgia Hispanic Chamber of Commerce [59106]

Georgia House of Representatives [59224]

Georgia Institute of Technology
    Advanced Technology Development Center [42144], [59216]
    Center for Assistive Technology and Environmental Access [19604]
    Enterprise Innovation Institute [43945]
    Georgia Tech Library–Government Information Department [66855]

"Georgia Insurer Riles Its Rivals" in *Crain's Detroit Business* (Vol. 19, No. 43, October 27, 2003, pp. 3) [13294], [29259], [43182]

"Georgia Insurer Riles Its Rivals; Palmer & Cay's Moves In Detroit Prompt Marsh USA to Sue" in *Crain's Detroit Business* (Vol. 19) [13295], [29260], [43183]

"Georgia Legislature Passes Business Tax Break" in *Atlanta Journal-Constitution* (March 4, 2005) [23949], [54568]

"Georgia has ad revenue on its mind" in *Atlanta Business Chronicle* (Vol. 25, December 13, 2002, No. 27, pp. A2) [635], [18877], [24689], [25187], [47005]

Georgia Office of Planning and Budget–Division of Operational Support and Development [66856]

Georgia Procurement Technical Assistance Center–Georgia Institute of Technology (ATDC) [59211]

Georgia SBDC Network State Office–University of Georgia Business SBDC–SBDC [59040]

"Getting the Corner Office" in *Black Enterprise* (Vol. 35, August 2004, No. 1, pp. 78) **[45185]**, **[48179]**, **[56238]**

"Getting the Dish; Blogs Allow Everyone to be a Critic" in *Crain's New York Business* (Vol. 23, January 29, 2007, No. 5, pp. 48) **[14073]**, **[21522]**, **[25857]**, **[27640]**, **[30869]**, **[33948]**, **[50594]**

"Getting in on the E-Signature Game" in *Inc.* (November 15, 2000, pp. 26) **[33949]**, **[40408]**

"Getting Girls to the Lab Bench" in *Business Week* (February 7, 2005, No. 3919, pp. 42) **[33103]**, **[52111]**

"Getting Ink: Need Exposure?" in *Entrepreneur* (Vol. 33, February 2005, No. 2) **[12884]**, **[20120]**, **[47013]**, **[50444]**, **[50595]**

Getting Into the Mail Order Business **[16439]**

"Getting It Right the Second Time" in *Harvard Business Review* (Vol. 80, No. 1, January 2002, pp. 62) **[30548]**, **[44301]**, **[45186]**

"Getting a Leg up: Montemayor y Asociados Partners with Web-Hed Technologies" in *Hispanic Business* (Vol. 22, No. 5, May 2000, pp. 18) **[11622]**, **[33950]**, **[48180]**, **[49958]**

"Getting More Bang for Your Buck" in *Black Enterprise* (Vol. 34, No. 6, January 2004) **[9979]**, **[15032]**, **[38089]**

Getting the Most from Change (Canada) **[44756]**

"Getting past 'No': how do you turn that 'no' into a 'yes'?" in *Entrepreneur* (Vol. 31, No. 6, June 2003) **[51650]**

"Getting No Respect?" in *Entrepreneur* (Vol. 33, February 2005, pp. 110) **[36205]**, **[56745]**

"Getting Noticed" in *Entrepreneur* (Vol. 31, No. 10, October 2003, pp. 114) **[20258]**, **[38814]**

"Getting Noticed at Work" in *Women in Business* (Vol. 53, No. 1, January-February, 2001, pp. 22) **[27380]**, **[39354]**

"Getting tough on slow payers can pay off" in *Crain's Detroit Business* (Vol. 19, No. 7, February 17, 2003, pp. 14) **[31551]**

"Getting Organized" in *Small Business Opportunities* (Vol. 16, No. 2, March 2004, pp. 60) **[51651]**, **[54948]**

"Getting Out of an IRS Mess" in *Black Enterprise* (Vol. 37, December 2006, No. 5, pp. 53) **[9980]**, **[29262]**, **[38090]**, **[40028]**, **[40409]**, **[54572]**

"Getting Paid: Collection Tips for Handling Slow- or Non-Paying Clients" in *Black Enterprise* (Vol. 35, December 2004, No. 5, pp. 65) **[8384]**, **[31552]**

"Getting Paid Faster" in *Black Enterprise* (Vol. 36, February 2006, No. 7, pp. 58) **[28204]**, **[31553]**, **[40029]**

"Getting Personal" in *Entrepreneur* (Vol. 33, October 2005, No. 10, pp. 44) **[30199]**, **[31034]**

"Getting Personal" in *Home Office Computing* (Vol. 18, No. 11, November 2000, pp. 88) **[31725]**

"Getting Personal: Hyatt Serves Up a Choice Meal" in *Sales & Marketing Management* (Vol. 159, January-February 2007, No. 1, pp. 41) **[12558]**, **[21523]**, **[22506]**, **[24938]**

"Getting Personal: Take a Closer Look at the Up-And-Coming Personalized Search Engine" in *Entrepreneur* (Vol. 33, February 2005, No. 2) **[14074]**, **[33951]**

"Getting a Piece of the Federal Pie" in *Hispanic Business* (Vol. 23, No. 7/8, July/August 2001, pp. 38) **[40030]**, **[41711]**, **[48181]**

"Getting Props: Awards Can Boost Your Self-Esteem-And Your Business" in *Entrepreneur* (Vol. 33, March 2005, No. 3, pp. 38) **[36206]**, **[56239]**

Getting Publicity: A Do-It-Yourself Guide for Small Business and Non-Profit Groups **[50596]**

Getting Publicity: The Very Best Book for Your Small Business **[50597]**

Getting Ready **[29887]**

Getting Results Without Authority (Canada) **[44757]**

Getting Rich in Mail Order **[16440]**

"Getting off to the Right Start" in *Venture Capital Journal* (Vol. 40, No. 10, November 2000, pp. 40-41) **[29738]**, **[35479]**, **[41456]**, **[44266]**

"Getting on the Road Toward Financial Freedom" in *Black Enterprise* (Vol. 35, October 2004, No. 3, pp. 125) **[15033]**, **[32449]**, **[38091]**

"Getting your bucks in a row" in *WorkingWoman* (Vol. 25, No. 5, May 2000, pp. 34) **[38092]**

Getting to Scale: Growing Your Business Without Selling Out **[28205]**, **[30870]**, **[36207]**

"Getting Set for Success" in *Small Business Opportunities* (Vol. 16, No. 2, March 2004, pp. 162-163) **[35480]**, **[39060]**

"Getting Set for Success with Your Own Small Business" in *Small Business Opportunities* (Vol. 12, No. 3, May 2000, pp. 110) **[29739]**, **[30482]**, **[35481]**

"Getting Stars to Shine: Dawn To Dusk Image Agency has an A-List Clientele" in *Black Enterprise* (Vol. 34, No. 4, Nov. 2003, pp. 43) **[12885]**, **[20121]**, **[47014]**, **[50598]**

Getting Started **[52858]**

Getting Started in Federal Contracting **[40031]**

"Getting Started" in *Inc.* (Volume 27, March 2005, No. 3, pp. 48, 51) **[13646]**, **[18544]**, **[49502]**

"Getting the truth into workplace surveys" in *Harvard Business Review* (Vol. 80, No. 1, January 2002, pp. 111) **[39355]**, **[50881]**

"Getting Their Slice: Save Money, and Keep Employees Happy With Stock Ownership Plans" in *Entrepreneur* (Vol. 32, September 2004) **[15034]**, **[26817]**, **[34911]**, **[54573]**

Getting Things Done: An Achiever's Guide to Better Time-Management **[55018]**

Getting Things Done: The Art of Stress-Free Productivity **[39356]**, **[45187]**, **[54949]**

"Getting To Know the Bull and the Bear" in *Black Enterprise* (Vol. 34, No. 5, December 2003, pp. S10) **[9981]**, **[15035]**, **[33104]**

"Getting To No" in *Inc.* (October 1, 2003) **[45188]**, **[51652]**

"Getting it together" in *Incentive* (Vol. 174, No. 10, October 2000, pp. 138) **[34912]**, **[42246]**, **[53751]**

"Getting Unwired" in *Internet World* (Vol. 7, No. 1, January 15, 2001, pp. 56) **[5001]**, **[14075]**, **[33952]**

"Getting started on the Web" in *Hispanic Business* (Vol. 22, No. 5, May 2000, pp. 98) **[33442]**, **[53298]**

"Getting the Word Out-Inexpensively" in *Black Enterprise* (Vol. 34, No. 6, January 2004) **[638]**, **[5983]**, **[47015]**

"Getting the Word Out-Inexpensively: How to Get the Most Bang Out of Your Marketing Dollars" in *Black Enterprise* (Vol. 34, No. 6) **[639]**, **[5984]**, **[47016]**

Getting to Yes: Negotiating Agreement Without Giving In **[27381]**, **[45189]**

"Getting Your Head Around the Long Tail" in *Venture Capital Journal* (September 1, 2005) **[33953]**

The Getty Conservation Institute **[1582]**

The Getty Provenance Index **[1640]**

Gettysburg-Adams County Area Chamber of Commerce **[64424]**

Geyserville Chamber of Commerce **[57505]**

G.G.W. and Associates **[51440]**

GHC Business Books **[62318]**

"The Ghost in the Family Business" in *Harvard Business Review* (Vol. 78, No. 3, May 2000, pp. 34) **[37667]**

GHT Ltd. **[1055]**, **[7608]**, **[9094]**, **[19769]**

"The Giant that would be King" in *Red Herring* (No. 102, August 15, 2001, pp. 40-45) **[14076]**, **[28206]**, **[53561]**

Giant Tiger/Tigre Geant **[51457]**

Gibson Area Chamber of Commerce **[59511]**

Gibson, Dunn & Crutcher–Law Library **[9438]**, **[15800]**, **[24280]**

Giddings Area Chamber of Commerce **[65252]**

Gideon Hixon Fund **[61700]**

Gideon Hixon Venture **[61701]**

Gift Associates Interchange Network **[11136]**

Gift Association of America **[11137]**

Gift Basket Service Business Guide **[11109]**

Gift Baskets & Beyond-Fabulous Forms, Great Promotions, and Dazzling Ideas for Your Business **[11110]**

Gift and Bazaar Projects, Part 2 **[18283]**

Gift Businesses: Baskets, Balloons, Herbal, Baby & More Telemarketing Scripts Idea Index **[11111]**, **[24288]**

Gift and Collectibles Guild **[5885]**, **[18273]**

Gift and Decorative Accessories Center Association-Directory **[11151]**

Gift, Housewares & Home Textiles Buyers **[11152]**, **[12286]**

"Gift Management: The Business of Charitable Giving" in *My Business* (October/November 2002, pp. 15) **[54185]**, **[54574]**

"A Gift is a Reward is an Incentive" in *Incentive* (Vol. 174, No. 8, August 2000, pp. S8) **[16517]**, **[31157]**, **[34913]**

GifTech Corp. **[58260]**

Gifts & Decorative Accessories **[11118]**, **[11177]**, **[12229]**

Gifts & Decorative Accessories (Jan. 2003, pp.190); "Trinity Potter celebrates 15th anniversary behind strong commitment to quality" in **[8185]**, **[8278]**, **[11170]**, **[31886]**

Gifts & Tablewares **[11178]**, **[12230]**

Gifts & Tablewares-Directory Issue **[12221]**

Giftware Business **[11179]**, **[12231]**

Giftware News **[11180]**

Gig Harbor Peninsula Area Chamber of Commerce **[66087]**

"GigaTrans hopes to get share of wireless market" in *Crain's Detroit Business* (Vol. 19, No. 16, April 21, 2003, pp. 12) **[14077]**, **[33954]**, **[41457]**, **[49047]**

Gilbert Chamber of Commerce **[57032]**

Gilchrist County Chamber of Commerce **[58803]**

Gildea Review **[21272]**

"Gilded and Gelded. Hard-Won Lessons From the PR Wars" in *Harvard Business Review* (Vol. 81, No. 10, October 2003, pp. 44) **[47017]**, **[50445]**, **[50599]**

"Gilded Paper Route" in *Success* (Vol. 47, No. 1, January 2000, pp. 20) **[2709]**, **[19818]**, **[19878]**, **[36208]**

Giles County Chamber of Commerce **[64919]**

Stephen J. Gill Consulting **[42966]**

Gill Solutions Management Inc. **[4023]**

Gillette Company–Technical Information Center **[7946]**

Gillette SBDC–Region V **[66596]**

Gilman Chamber of Commerce **[59512]**

Gilmer Area Chamber of Commerce **[65253]**

Gilmer County Chamber of Commerce **[59107]**

Gilroy Chamber of Commerce **[57506]**

Gimbel Associates **[49427]**

The K.S. Giniger Company Inc. **[866]**, **[2794]**, **[18265]**, **[18969]**, **[20184]**

Giorgio Restaurants **[21828]**

Girard Area Chamber of Commerce **[60336]**

Girard Area Industrial Development Corp.–Model Works Industrial Commons **[64608]**

Girard Chamber of Commerce **[59513]**

"Girl Franchising Power" in *Black Enterprise* (Vol. 36, February 2006, No. 7, pp. 155) **[38815]**, **[56240]**

"Girl power" in *Entrepreneur* (Vol. 31, No. 5, May 2003, pp. 28) **[36209]**, **[54186]**, **[56241]**

Girl Power USA Finishing Center, LLC **[25477]**

The Girl's Guide to Being a Boss (Without Being a Bitch): Valuable Lessons, Smart Suggestions, and True Stories for Succeeding **[36210]**, **[45190]**, **[56242]**

"Girls Just Wanna Have Funds" in *Entrepreneur* (Vol. 28, No. 3, March 2000, pp. 38) **[55644]**, **[56243]**

"Girls Learn to Ride" in *Marketing to Women* (Vol. 19, December 2006, No. 12, pp. 5) **[14078]**, **[23722]**, **[47018]**

Girls & Young Women Entrepreneurs: True Stories about Starting & Running a Business Plus How You Can Do It Yourself **[56244]**

Gisser & Associates **[17275]**

"Give Advice? Get Protected!" in *Small Business Opportunities* (Vol. 13, No. 5, September 2001, pp. 18) **[29263]**, **[43185]**

"Give the BID Plan a Break" in *Crain's Detroit Business* (Vol. 19, No. 45, November 10, 2003, pp. 8) **[51866]**, **[54575]**

"Give 'Em Credit" in *Entrepreneur* (Vol. 31, No. 8, August 2003, pp. 55) **[44535]**, **[48906]**

"Give 'Em Liberty" in *Entrepreneur* (Vol. 33, September 2005, No. 9, pp. 85) **[605]**, **[640]**, **[47019]**

"Give 'Em the Sack" in *Entrepreneur* (Vol. 31, No. 9, July 2003, pp. 112) **[11153]**, **[56245]**

"Give 'Em Space: A Well-Designed Work Space, that is" in *Entrepreneur* (Vol. 32, No. 1, January 2004, pp. 77) **[18545]**, **[34914]**, **[49503]**, **[51653]**

"Give It a Go: A 'Hands-On' Approach to Marketing Your Product Could Be Just the Thing to Win Customers" in *Entrepreneur* (Vol. 32) **[641]**, **[47020]**

"Give Me a Break" in *Entrepreneur.com* (Vol. 34, January 2006, No. 1, pp. 36) **[4675]**, **[23014]**, **[53299]**, **[54576]**

"Give Me Mylanta" in *Fast Company* (September 2001, pp. 74) **[30337]**

"Give Me a Tax Break" in *Black Enterprise* (Vol. 36, February 2006, No. 7, pp. 40) **[2908]**, **[17385]**, **[23952]**, **[38093]**, **[40410]**, **[54577]**

"Give good presence" in *BlackEnterprise* (Vol. 32, No. 2, September 2001, pp. 114) **[36211]**, **[39357]**

Given the Opportunity: Interacting with Individuals with Disabilities **[32089]**

"Giving Back" in *Inc.* (November 1, 2004) **[11112]**, **[36212]**, **[54187]**

"Giving Small Biz Short Shrift" in *Business Week* (No. 3660, December 20, 1999, pp. 32) **[49048]**

"Giving mergers a head start" in *Harvard Business Review* (Vol. 80, No. 10, October 2002, pp. 20) **[15036]**, **[29264]**, **[49959]**

"Giving Where It Counts: Blackgiving.com Lets Consumers Choose Their Charities" in *Black Enterprise* (Vol. 34, July 2004, No. 12) **[36213]**, **[48182]**, **[54188]**

"Glad that's over" in *Entrepreneur* (Vol. 30, No. 12, December 2002, pp. 38) **[3534]**, **[36214]**

Glades County Chamber of Commerce **[58804]**

Glades Crop Care Inc. **[49428]**

Gladewater Chamber of Commerce **[65254]**

Gladstone Equestrian Association **[12445]**

Gladwin County Chamber of Commerce **[61305]**

"Glam Media Launches Fashion Week Site" in *Marketing to Women* (Vol. 19, October 2006, No. 10, pp. 5) **[5547]**, **[5667]**, **[14079]**, **[25858]**, **[41712]**, **[47021]**

Glamour Secrets **[2412]**

Glamour Shots Licensing Inc. **[19325]**

Glasco Chamber Pride **[60337]**

Glaser Associates Inc. **[49611]**

Glasgow Area Chamber of Commerce and Agriculture **[62168]**

Glasgow-Barren County Chamber of Commerce **[60508]**

Glass Art Society Journal **[1627]**

Glass & Associates Inc. **[3713]**, **[16607]**, **[31355]**, **[38535]**, **[46028]**

Glass Canada **[11226]**

"Glass Ceiling Persists in the Board Room" in *Marketing to Women* (Vol. 19, December 2006, No. 2, pp. 8) **[28207]**, **[30549]**, **[34915]**, **[39358]**, **[45191]**, **[47022]**

Glass Craftsman **[8209]**

Glass Doctor **[11234]**

"Glass Foundation: Profession Grew From a Boyhood Love of Stained Glass" in *Pittsburgh Business Times* (Vol. 23, August 29, 2003) **[8008]**, **[8167]**

Glass Magazine **[11227]**

Glass Patterns Quarterly **[8210]**

Glass Show **[11228]**

Glastonbury Chamber of Commerce **[58531]**

GlaxoSmithKline
 Information Services–Library **[8865]**
 U.S. Medical Information Library (FP1045) **[8866]**

Gleams **[25656]**

Glen Cove Chamber of Commerce **[62885]**

Glen Ellyn Chamber of Commerce **[59514]**

Glen Rock Chamber of Commerce **[62501]**

Glen Rose/Somervell County Chamber of Commerce **[65255]**

Glencoe Area Chamber of Commerce **[61591]**

Glencoe Chamber of Commerce **[59515]**

Glendale Association of Commerce **[66405]**

Glendale Chamber of Commerce **[57033]**, **[57507]**

Glendale Public Library–Special Collections Room **[1222]**

Glendive Chamber of Commerce and Agriculture **[62169]**

Glendora Chamber of Commerce **[57508]**

Glenns Ferry Chamber of Commerce **[59297]**

Glenpool Chamber of Commerce **[63999]**

Glenrock Chamber of Commerce **[66609]**

Glenview Chamber of Commerce **[59516]**

Glenwood Area Chamber of Commerce **[61592]**

Glenwood/Mills County Chamber of Commerce and Economic Development **[60137]**

Glenwood Springs Small Business Development Center–Colorado Mountain College **[58302]**

"GlitzyShow, Worry Galore" in *Wall Street Journal* (Vol. 249 January 2007, No. 5, pp. A2) **[30871]**, **[43665]**, **[46300]**

GLMV Area Chamber of Commerce **[59517]**

"Global Appeal: Connecting the World With the Push of a Button" in *Entrepreneur* (Vol. 31, No. 9, September 2003, pp. 42) **[5002]**, **[14080]**

Global Broker Training Systems Inc. **[10356]**, **[42795]**

Global Business Browser **[43935]**

Global Business Consultants **[3714]**, **[16608]**, **[31356]**, **[42967]**, **[43923]**, **[46029]**, **[53552]**

"Global accounting is coming" in *Harvard Business Review* (Vol. 81, No. 4, April 2003, pp. 24) **[157]**, **[23953]**, **[26248]**, **[37448]**, **[40411]**

Global Crossing **[58025]**

Global Custodian **[10276]**

The Global Dumping Ground: International Traffic in Hazardous Waste **[11952]**

Global E-Commerce: Impacts of National Environment and Policy **[33955]**, **[43666]**

"Global Economy Reaches Into Your Wallet" in *Hispanic Business* (March 2005, pp. 6) **[12974]**, **[32450]**, **[43667]**

Global Electronic Business Research: Opportunities and Directions **[33956]**, **[43668]**, **[50882]**

"Global Entrepreneur" in *Inc.* (September 2005, pp. 48, 50) **[6938]**, **[36215]**, **[43669]**

"Global Fitness, Weight-Loss Franchise Opens Sites in Willoughby, Ohio Area" in *Willoughby News-Herald* (December 17, 2002) **[19401]**, **[38816]**

Global Guide To International Business **[43670]**

Global Health Directory **[41015]**

Global Internet Ventures / GIV Venture Partners **[65973]**

Global Investment Magazine **[15644]**

The Global Investor: Opportunities, Risks and Realities for Institutional Investors in the World's Markets **[15037]**

The Global Learning Organization: Gaining Competitive Advantage through Continuous Learning **[43671]**

Global Licensing Handbook: A Guide to Success **[44051]**

Global Mobile **[5203]**

Global Mobile Daily **[5204]**

Global Offset and Countertrade Association **[43499]**

"Global financing options" in *BlackEnterprise* (Vol. 31, No. 8, March 2001, pp. 48) **[43186]**, **[44536]**, **[48183]**, **[56246]**

Global Quality: A Synthesis of the World's Best Management Methods **[43672]**

Global Recruiters Network **[3881]**

Global Ryan's Pet Foods **[19178]**

Global Secure Training **[11966]**

Global Shop - Tradeshow and Seminars for Visual Merchandiser **[26080]**

"Global Spectrum: Making a Difference in the Convention Center Industry" in *Tradeshow Week* (Vol. 34, November 29, 2004, No. 48, pp. S2) **[22507]**, **[24939]**, **[28208]**, **[31158]**, **[55096]**

Global Technology Transfer **[3715]**, **[16609]**, **[31357]**, **[38536]**, **[46030]**, **[48826]**, **[53090]**

"Global Trade" in *Entrepreneur.com* (Vol. 34, February 2006, No. 2, pp. 120) **[25085]**, **[33105]**, **[43673]**, **[54578]**

"Global Trader" in *Hispanic Business* (April 2005, pp. 40, 42) **[40412]**, **[43674]**

Global Training: How to Design a Program for the Multinational Corporation **[43675]**

Global Voice **[43897]**

"Globalized Economy a Double-Edged Sword for Americans" in *Altanta Journal-Constitution* (January 18, 2007) **[32451]**, **[43676]**

GlobalNET Corp. **[49429]**, **[49612]**

Globalnet Management LLC **[63100]**

Globalport.com Inc. **[6213]**

GLOBE - International Environmental Industry Trade Fair and Conference **[9402]**, **[9490]**, **[21283]**

Globe-Miami Regional Chamber of Commerce and Economic Development Corporation **[57034]**

Dennis G. Glore Inc. **[1148]**

Gloria Jean's Gourmet Coffees **[11384]**

Glossbrenner's Guide to Shareware for Small Businesses **[49049]**

Gloucester Chamber of Commerce **[65901]**

"Gluttons for Punishment" in *Success* (Vol. 47, No. 1, January 2000, pp. 30) **[45192]**

Glynn Ventures **[58026]**

"GM Hopes Boosting Mileage Will Slow Big Models' Sales Drain" in *Milwaukee Journal Sentinel* (December 10, 2005) **[18045]**, **[28209]**, **[51654]**

"GM Hoping that Safety Sells" in *Pittsburgh Post-Gazette* (February 6, 2005) **[7134]**, **[18046]**

"GM Set To Unleash $3B In IT Deals" in *Crain's Detroit Business* (Vol. 21, December 19, 2005, No. 51, pp. 1) **[18047]**, **[41713]**, **[46301]**, **[49960]**

"GM Smiles on Local Suppliers; New Contracts Mean Big Growth for Brake Producer" in *Crain's Detroit Business* (December 20, 2004) **[1937]**, **[18048]**, **[46302]**

GMC Philadelphia Home Show **[1389]**, **[55215]**

GMPro-All-Industry Buyers' Guide Product Directory Issue **[11429]**, **[19723]**

GMS Capital Partners **[63101]**

"GM's Way Or the Highway" in *Business Week* (December 19, 2005, No. 3964, pp. 48-49) **[18049]**, **[41714]**, **[46303]**, **[49699]**

Gnossos Software Inc. **[49430]**

"Go For the Big Ones" in *Forbes* (Vol. 175, January 31, 2005, No. 2, pp. 146) **[9982]**, **[15038]**, **[38094]**

"Go For Fir or Spruce Up, But It Could Cost You" in *Tampa Tribune* (December 10, 2005) **[5479]**, **[11430]**

"Go For the Gold" in *Entrepreneur* (Vol. 32, October 2004, No. 10, pp. 68) **[28210]**, **[29888]**, **[36216]**, **[52423]**

"Go major league" in *Entrepreneur* (Vol. 31, No. 4, April 2003, pp. 81) **[34916]**, **[47023]**, **[51655]**

"Go Live: They've Got Questions, You've Got Answers." in *Entrepreneur* (Vol. 33, March 2005, No. 3, pp. 90) **[14081]**, **[25859]**, **[27382]**, **[33957]**, **[51656]**

"Go Pro 2.4 GHZ Gyrotransport Air Mouse Presenter" in *Sales & Marketing Management* (Vol. 159, January-February 2007, No. 1, pp. 42) **[4676]**, **[6659]**, **[23015]**, **[49050]**, **[53300]**

"Go retro! Budget tight?" in *Entrepreneur* (Vol. 31, No. 4, April 2003, pp. 41) **[49051]**, **[49504]**

"Go Small" in *Entrepreneur* (Vol. 28, No. 6, June 2000, pp. 38) **[55645]**

"Go South" in *Entrepreneur* (Vol. 33, October 2005, No. 10, pp. 26) **[12975]**, **[41747]**, **[43677]**

"Go West: Want a Few Business Pointers? Mosey on Over to Deadwood" in *Entrepreneur* (Vol. 32, November 2004, No. 11, pp. 22) **[24412]**, **[28211]**, **[29265]**, **[36217]**, **[47024]**

"Go Where the Money Is" in *Black Enterprise* (Vol. 36, November 2005, No. 4, pp. 54) **[9983]**, **[15039]**, **[38095]**

"Go With the Flow" in *Entrepreneur* (Vol. 32, August 2004, No. 8, pp. 32) **[36218]**, **[45193]**

"Go With the Flow" in *Small Business Opportunities* (Vol. 13, No. 6, November 2001, pp. 114) **[27130]**, **[38096]**

"Goal for Entrepreneurs who have more equipment or employees than business demands" in *Business First Columbus* (Vol. 18, No. 25) **[29740]**, **[35482]**

Goal Setting **[30636]**

"Goal Tending" in *Small Business Opportunities* (Fall 2005) **[29889]**, **[36219]**, **[39359]**

Goals and Goal Setting **[30550]**

The GOALS Institute **[66004]**

Goals and Objectives **[30637]**

Goals: Setting and Achieving Them on Schedule **[30638]**

GoalsGuy Learning Systems **[59018]**

Goddard School **[5427]**

Goddard Systems Inc. **[5428]**

Godfather's Pizza, Inc. **[19672]**

Godfrey Memorial Library **[11028]**

"Godwin Group" in *Mississippi Business Journal* (Vol. 29, January 2007, No. 3, pp. A6) **[30679]**, **[39360]**, **[45194]**

"Going After Nike" in *Inc.* (October 1, 2004) **[22749]**, **[35483]**

Going Bare: Crisis in Insurance **[13567]**, **[43439]**

"Going for Brokers: Recent Enthusiasm for Shares of Street Firms Appears Premature" in *Barron's* (August 18, 2003, pp. 17) **[9984]**, **[15040]**, **[38097]**

"Going Digital" in *Hispanic Business* (July-August 2000, pp. 76) **[33443]**, **[37061]**

"Going digital for dollars" in *Black Enterprise* (Vol. 33, No. 3, October 2002, pp. 145) **[33958]**, **[34357]**, **[35404]**, **[36220]**, **[47025]**, **[48184]**, **[48915]**, **[50119]**

"Going the Extra Mile" in *Black Enterprise* (Vol. 35, November 2004, No. 4, pp. 58) **[5668]**, **[16215]**, **[31726]**

"Going For a Whirl: Jamail Larkin Soars, Dips, and Shows Off a Few Stunts" in *Black Enterprise* (Vol. 35, January 2005, No. 6, pp. 103) **[949]**, **[36221]**, **[47026]**

"Going Global" in *Home Office Computing* (Vol. 18, No. 10, October 2000, pp. 87) **[25860]**, **[33959]**, **[42623]**, **[43678]**, **[53752]**

"Going Global: International Business Tips Make a World of Difference" in *Entrepreneur* (Vol. 32, December 2004, No. 12, pp. 34) **[28212]**, **[43679]**, **[56247]**

"Going Global: Lessons from Late Movers" in *Harvard Business Review* (Vol. 78, No. 2, March 2000, pp. 132) **[28213]**, **[52859]**

"Going, going, gone" in *Harvard Business Review* (Vol. 78, No. 6, November-December 2000, pp. 30) **[33960]**, **[46304]**

"Going for the green? Consultants can dig up all the dirt" in *Boston Business Journal* (Vol. 22, No. 14, May 10, 2002, pp. 43) **[9358]**, **[37279]**

"Going Green?" in *Crain's Detroit Business* (Vol. 22, November 20, 2006, No. 47, pp. 30) **[33961]**, **[37280]**

Going Green: How to Communicate Your Company's Environmental Commitment **[37281]**

"Going by the Handbook" in *Success* (Vol. 47, No. 4, September 2000, pp. 69) **[42857]**, **[45195]**

"Going outside for expert help: Family businesses have options to get objective advice" in *Crain's Chicago Business* (Vol.23,Nov.13,2000) **[31159]**, **[37668]**

Going Into Business in Wisconsin: An Entrepreneur's Guide **[66583]**

Going It Alone: How to Survive & Thrive As an Independent Consultant **[10735]**

"Going legit" in *BlackEnterprise* (Vol. 31, No. 12, July 2001, pp. 53) **[35484]**, **[41458]**, **[47959]**

"Going Local for Travel" in *Ingram's* (Vol. 29, No. 7, July 2003, pp. 41) **[25189]**, **[30338]**

"Going Medium-Tech" in *Inc.* (Volume 27, December 2005, No. 12, pp. 77-78) **[28214]**, **[41715]**

"Going Nuclear" in *Business 2.0* (Vol. 6, May 2005, No. 4, pp. 90-95) **[28215]**, **[41716]**

"Going Once, Going Twice..." in *Home Office Computing* (Vol. 18, No. 11, November 2000, pp. 90) **[1816]**, **[33962]**

"Going Once, Going Twice: Online Auctions Offer Great Deals" in *Black Enterprise* (Vol. 34, No. 7, February 2004, pp. 140) **[1780]**, **[1817]**, **[33963]**, **[34917]**

Going Places **[25316]**

"Going Places" in *Success* (Vol. 47, No. 6, November 2000, pp. 38) **[13751]**, **[25117]**, **[33444]**, **[35485]**

"Going Private: How VCs Can Get in the Game" in *Venture Capital Journal* (Vol. 42, No. 10, October 2002, pp. 49) **[15041]**, **[29266]**, **[48185]**, **[49961]**, **[50883]**, **[53753]**

"Going Public: A Public Insurance Adjuster Could Help You Get What You Deserve" in *Entrepreneur* (Vol. 32, July 2004, No. 7, pp. 54) **[13298]**, **[43187]**

"Going Public" in *Entrepreneur* (Vol. 31, No. 11, November 2003, pp. 65) **[15042]**, **[28216]**, **[49962]**

"Going Separate Ways: In a Law Suit, You and an Employee Could Be Sent Down Different Paths" in *Entrepreneur* (Vol. 32, August 2004) **[13299]**, **[29267]**, **[43188]**

Going Solo: Developing a Home-Based Consulting Business from the Ground Up **[27723]**, **[29741]**, **[31093]**, **[42515]**, **[46569]**

"Going solo" in *Entrepreneur* (Vol. 28, No. 11, November 2000, pp. 34) **[49052]**

"Going Somewhere?" in *Entrepreneur* (Vol. 31, No. 9, September 2003, pp. 50) **[6660]**, **[49053]**

"Going Vertical" in *Forbes* (Vol. 174, December 13, 2004, No. 12, pp. 110) **[6250]**, **[6661]**

Gold Beach Chamber of Commerce **[64220]**

Gold Book **[18686]**

"Gold Diggers" in *PC Magazine* (February 20, 2001, pp. 7a) **[6251]**, **[33964]**, **[44302]**

"Gold Rush" in *Business Week* (January 9, 2006, No. 3966, pp. 68-72, 74, 76) **[9985]**, **[14082]**, **[22237]**, **[31554]**, **[33965]**, **[38098]**

"Gold Standard: Get the Best in IP Phone Bennies Without a PBX or Even a VoIP Provider" in *Entrepreneur* (Vol. 33, March 2005, No. 3) **[5003]**, **[14083]**

Golden Bear Oil Specialties–QC/R & D Library **[2550]**

Golden Chick **[21829]**

Golden Corral Family Restaurants **[21830]**

Golden Eagle Business Services Inc. **[31968]**

Golden Entrepreneuring **[36222]**

Golden Gate University–University Library **[4050]**

Golden Griddle Family Restaurants **[21831]**

The Golden Mailbox: How to Get Rich Direct Marketing Your Product **[47027]**

"Golden opportunities: Older workers bring experience and special needs" in *Crain's Detroit Business* (Vol. 17, No. 44, Oct. 22, 2001) **[39361]**, **[42247]**

Golden Rule Insurance Co.–Library **[13596]**

Golden States Financial Directory **[44537]**

Golden Triangle Chamber of Commerce **[57509]**

The Golden Triangle Enterprise Center **[61847]**

Golden Valley Chamber of Commerce **[57035]**, **[57510]**

Goldenrod Area Chamber of Commerce **[58805]**

Goldey Beacom College–J. Wilbur Hirons Library **[6225]**

Goldhaber Research Associates L.L.C. **[16867]**

Arnold S. Goldin & Associates Inc. **[371]**, **[10341]**, **[16610]**, **[26429]**, **[31358]**, **[46031]**

Goldman Associates Inc. **[21082]**

"Goldmining for Internships" in *Black Enterprise* (Vol. 34, No. 5, December 2003, pp. S6) **[33106]**, **[34191]**, **[40445]**, **[42248]**

Goldore Consulting Inc. **[3716]**, **[31359]**, **[35232]**, **[46032]**, **[50780]**

"Gold's Buys Gym, Converts to Women's Facility in Tallahassee, Fla." in *Tallahassee Democratic* (October 3, 2002) **[19402]**, **[53754]**

Gold's Gym Franchising **[19508]**

N.R. Goldstein & Associates **[3256]**

Joseph Goldsten & Associates **[38537]**

Goleta Valley Chamber of Commerce **[57511]**

Golf Digest **[11276]**

Golf Etc. **[23705]**

Golf for Fun & Profit **[11263]**

Golf Magazine **[11277]**

Golf Magazine-Golf Club Buyers' Guide Issue **[11264]**

Golf Market Today **[11278]**

Golf Range Association of America **[11245]**

Golf Range Magazine **[11279]**

"Golf School Caters to Women" in *Marketing to Women* (Vol. 20, January 2007, No. 1, pp. 8) **[11265]**, **[23620]**, **[33107]**, **[47028]**

Golf USA, Inc. **[11291]**

Golf World Business **[11280]**

Goliad County Chamber of Commerce **[65256]**

Golub Associates **[63102]**

"Gone Fishin'" in *Entrepreneur* (Vol. 28, No. 3, March 2000, pp. 86) **[26818]**, **[39362]**, **[42249]**, **[53755]**

"Gone Fishing" in *Inc.* (July 1, 2004) **[25190]**, **[36223]**

Gonzales Chamber of Commerce **[57512]**, **[65257]**

"Gonzales and Lizarraga Speak Out" in *Hispanic Business* (January/February 2003, pp. 20, 22) **[39363]**, **[48186]**

"Gonzales Names PepsiCo VP" in *Hispanic Business* (Vol. 23, No. 11, November 2001, pp. 20) **[45196]**, **[48187]**

Goochland County Chamber of Commerce **[65902]**

Obie Good & Associates **[46537]**

The Good Business Basics Series: The Basics of Entrepreneuring **[37034]**

"GOOD business and good BUSINESS" in *Harvard Business Review* (Vol. 81, No. 3, March 2003, pp. 10) **[26819]**, **[36224]**, **[45197]**

"Good for Business: Houston is a Hot Spot for Economic Growth" in *Black Enterprise* (Vol. 37, October 2006, No. 3, pp. 216) **[30148]**, **[32452]**, **[41016]**, **[52112]**, **[52677]**

"Good-bye Doesn't Mean Forever" in *Inc.* (January 1, 2002) **[4677]**, **[6252]**, **[23016]**, **[42250]**, **[53301]**

"Good Calls: Gains, Losses and Straddles" in *Barron's* (July 7, 2003, pp. 19) **[9986]**, **[15043]**, **[38099]**, **[54579]**

Good Choices . . . Bad Choices **[5383]**

"Good Company" in *Entrepreneur* (Vol. 33, September 2005, No. 9, pp. 84) **[51657]**

"Good Deeds and Watchful Eyes" in *Business Week Online* (March 8, 2002) **[36225]**, **[39364]**, **[54189]**

"The Good Deflation: Falling Prices Can be Sign of Economic Strength" in *Barron's* (July 28, 2003, pp. 31) **[32453]**

Good Discipline, Good Kids **[5384]**

Good Dog, Bad Dog: Dog Training Made Easy **[19113]**

Good Earth Coffee House & Bakery **[11385]**

Good Fat/Bad Fat: The No-Nonsense Cholesterol Guide **[18463]**

"The Good Fight" in *Entrepreneur* (Vol. 30, No. 3, March 2002, pp. 48) **[28217]**, **[36226]**

"The Good Fire" in *Entrepreneur* (Vol. 28, No. 3, March 2000, pp. 127) **[39365]**, **[45198]**, **[56560]**

Good Food for Good Health **[18464]**

"Good as Gold" in *Entrepreneur* (Vol. 32, No. 1, January 2004, pp. 106) **[445]**, **[3535]**, **[5277]**, **[5338]**, **[7348]**, **[8273]**, **[11327]**, **[12778]**, **[15845]**, **[18322]**, **[19403]**, **[23954]**, **[33108]**, **[38817]**, **[53756]**, **[56248]**

Good to Great **[36227]**, **[39366]**

"Good to Great" in *Fast Company* (November 2001, pp. 90) **[28218]**

Good to Great: Why Some Companies Make the Leap...and Others Don't **[28219]**, **[39367]**, **[45199]**

Good Health Bulletin **[41201]**

"Good Health is Just a Costly Way to Die" in *Red Herring* (No. 103, September 1, 2001, pp. 54-58, 60) **[17186]**, **[52113]**

"Good intentions, bad policy" in *Crain's Detroit Business* (Vol. 16, No. 49, December 4, 2000, pp. 8) **[40413]**, **[43189]**

Good Laboratory Practice Regulations **[17187]**

"Good Libations?" in *Entrepreneur* (Vol. 32, December 2004, No. 12, pp. 100) **[29268]**, **[36228]**

"The Good Life by the Bay" in *Hispanic Business* (Vol. 24, No. 1/2, January/February 2002, pp. 64) **[25191]**, **[30339]**

"Good relationships cement requests for business loans" in *Crain's Detroit Business* (Vol. 16, No. 50, December 11, 2000, pp. E-1) **[44538]**

"The Good Manager-A Moral Manager?" in *Journal of Business Ethics* (Vol. 27, No. 3, October 1, 2000, pp. 247) **[37449]**, **[45200]**

"A Good Man(ager) is Hard to Find" in *My Business* (August/September 2002, pp. 47) **[21524]**, **[36229]**, **[38818]**

"Good Marketing Moves" in *Crain's Detroit Business* (Vol. 22, February 13, 2006, No. 7, pp. 17) **[21525]**, **[47029]**

Good Money Management **[10303]**

"Good News (Almost) Everywhere You Look" in *My Business* (June/July 2004, pp. 42) **[28220]**, **[32454]**

"Good News for News Overload" in *My Business* (October/November 2003, pp. 24) **[4678]**, **[23017]**, **[53302]**

"Good night, sweetheart" in *Red Herring* (No. 106, October 15, 2001, pp. 35) **[28221]**, **[37142]**

The Good Old Days of Quality Service **[31932]**

"Good question! Ask, and the people will read" in *Entrepreneur* (Vol. 30, No. 10, October 2002, pp. 98) **[642]**, **[47030]**

"Good References, Easy to Find" in *Sales and Marketing.com* (Vol. 156, No. 3, March 2004, pp. 20) **[33966]**, **[51658]**

"Good Sports" in *Entrepreneur* (Vol. 32, September 2004, No. 9, pp. 104) **[23621]**, **[23723]**, **[37669]**, **[49963]**

"A Good Time for an IPO Gold Mine?" in *Entrepreneur* (Vol. 33, March 2005, No. 3, pp. 62) **[15044]**, **[49964]**

"Good Timing" in *Entrepreneur* (Vol. 32, August 2004, No. 8, pp. 65) **[643]**, **[23018]**, **[47031]**, **[50600]**, **[53303]**

"Good Vibes: Socially Responsible Investing is Gaining Fans...and Clout" in *Barron's* (July 7, 2003, pp. L3) **[9987]**, **[15045]**, **[29269]**, **[37450]**, **[38100]**, **[54190]**

"Goodbye B-School" in *Harvard Business Review* (Vol. 78, No. 2, March 2000, pp. 16) **[35486]**, **[41459]**

Goodbye Graffiti Inc. **[3366]**

"Goodbye, Retainers" in *Inc.* (November 2006, pp. 35,38) **[38101]**, **[47032]**, **[50446]**

Goodeal Discount Transmissions **[2015]**

Goodland Area Chamber of Commerce **[60338]**

Goodlettsville Area Chamber of Commerce **[64920]**

Goodman and Carr–LLP Library **[9529]**

Goodmans–Library **[9530]**

"Goodwill Gets Back Into Retail Game" in *Crain's Detroit Business* (Vol. 21, January 17, 2005, No. 3, pp. 22) **[33967]**, **[51171]**, **[54191]**

"Goodwill Hunting?" in *Entrepreneur* (Vol. 31, No. 9, September 2003, pp. 108) **[38819]**, **[54192]**

"Goodwill for Your Ex" in *Inc.* (September 1, 2003) **[29270]**, **[39368]**

David Goodwin, PhD **[38971]**

"Goodyear Extends Exclusive Deal to Supply NASCAR's Tires" in *Charlotte Observer* (February 4, 2007) **[23724]**, **[24584]**

"The Google Effect Kicks In" in *Venture Capital Journal* (December 1, 2004) **[14084]**, **[15046]**, **[33968]**, **[55646]**

"Google Smackdown" in *Entrepreneur.com* (Vol. 34, January 2006, No. 1, pp. 6) **[14085]**, **[33969]**

The Google Story: Inside the Hottest Business, Media, and Technology Success of Our Time **[14086]**, **[28222]**, **[33970]**, **[41717]**

"Google Update Draws Criticism from Small Biz" in *Inc.* (January 1, 2004) **[644]**, **[33971]**, **[47033]**

"Google World: http://google.indicateur.com" in *Entrepreneur* (Vol. 31, No. 10, October 2003, pp. 6) **[28223]**, **[33972]**

"Google's Banker" in *Fortune* (Vol. 149, No. 9, May 3, 2004, pp. 105) **[14087]**, **[15047]**, **[33973]**, **[49965]**, **[55647]**

"Google's Boodle" in *Business Week* (February 14, 2005, No. 3920, pp. 42) **[9988]**, **[14088]**, **[15048]**

"Goose Busters" in *Pittsburgh Business Times* (Vol. 23, No. 5, August 5, 2003, pp. 19) **[19022]**, **[52538]**

"GOP tells business owners that effort to finance fights against OSHA is lost" in *Wall Street Journal* (February 16, 2000, pp. A6) **[40414]**

Gordian Concepts & Solutions **[38538]**, **[46033]**, **[48827]**, **[51441]**, **[54889]**

Gordo Area Chamber of Commerce **[56851]**

Barb Gordon **[8652]**

Gordon Chamber of Commerce **[62263]**

Gordon Cooper Technology Center **[64140]**

Gordon County Chamber of Commerce **[59108]**

Gordon's Print Prices CD-ROM **[1641]**

Goren and Associates Inc. **[42968]**

Gorin's Homemade Cafe & Grill **[8552]**

Goshen Chamber of Commerce **[59915]**, **[62886]**

Goshen County Chamber of Commerce **[66610]**

"Got 20 Minutes? Gym Champions Quick, Occasional Workouts" in *Bradenton Herald* (January 29, 2005) **[19404]**, **[37670]**, **[38820]**

"Got Fit?" in *Success* (Vol. 47, No. 6, November 2000, pp. 18) **[9177]**, **[35487]**, **[52490]**

"Got Game?" in *Entrepreneur* (Vol. 32, October 2004, No. 10, pp. 95) **[29890]**, **[30551]**, **[36230]**, **[53757]**

"Got Ideas? Book 'Em" in *Success* (Vol. 47, No. 6, November 2000, pp. 68) **[14089]**, **[33974]**, **[44303]**

"Got It Covered?" in *Entrepreneur* (Vol. 32, December 2004, No. 12, pp. 47) **[13300]**, **[18050]**, **[43190]**

"Got Leverage? Dollar Signs: If You're Ready to Sell, You've Got the Upper Hand" in *Entrepreneur* (Vol. 31, No. 9, September 2003) **[15049]**, **[49966]**, **[52424]**, **[53758]**

"Got milked?" in *BlackEnterprise* (Vol. 32, No. 3, October 2001, pp. 168) **[29271]**

Got a Problem? Solve It! **[33316]**

"Got anything smaller?" in *Entrepreneur* (Vol. 30, No. 10, October 2002, pp. 83) **[42251]**, **[45201]**, **[53759]**

Gotcha Covered **[26082]**

Gothenburg Area Chamber of Commerce **[62264]**

The Gottesman Libraries at Teachers College **[18500]**

Gottscheer Heritage and Genealogy Association **[10916]**

GourMade Franchise **[8288]**

The Gourmet Cup **[11386]**

"Gourmet G-Day" in *San Diego Business Journal* (Vol. 28, January 15, 2007, No. 3, pp. 12) **[23483]**, **[47034]**

Gourmet News **[23536]**

Gove Lumber Co. **[1554]**

Goventure: Live the Life of an Entrepreneur **[36231]**, **[39369]**

"Goverentment Nannies: Close to Home" in *Forbes* (March 6, 2000, pp. 102) **[5339]**

Governing Magazine **[50363]**

Government Contract Negotiations: A Practical Guide for Small Business **[40032]**

Government Contracts & Subcontract Leads Directory **[40033]**

"Government on Demand" in *Microsoft Executive Circle* (Vol. 1, No. 2, Q2 2001, pp. 38-40) **[14090]**, **[33975]**, **[39830]**

Government of the District of Columbia–Department of Small and Local Business Development **[58668]**

Government Employee Relations Report **[17070]**

Government Giveaways for Entrepreneurs III **[48928]**

"Government Hooks Man for Phishing" in *Cardline* (Vol. 4, No. 13, March 26, 2004, pp. 1) **[1818]**, **[18647]**, **[22238]**, **[29272]**, **[33976]**, **[40415]**, **[44304]**, **[52539]**

Government Loans & Assistance Small Business Directory **[39831]**

Government Market Report **[40112]**

Government National Mortgage Association (Ginnie Mae)–Procurement Management Division **[67151]**

Government Prime Contractors Directory **[40034]**

Government Recreation and Fitness **[41202]**

Government Relations **[1749]**

"Governor Backs Solar-Panel Plan" in *San Jose Mercury News* (March 2, 2005) **[37282]**, **[40416]**

Governors Highway Safety Association **[8726]**

Governor's Office of Policy and Management **[66886]**

Governor's Small Business Center **[59181]**

Governors State University–Small Business Development Center **[59371]**

Gowanda Area Chamber of Commerce **[62887]**

"GoWholesale" in *Entrepreneur* (Vol. 33, October 2005, No. 10, pp. 6) **[1782]**, **[1819]**, **[32955]**, **[33977]**, **[37804]**, **[39370]**, **[53239]**, **[56011]**

Gowling Lafleur Henderson LLP **[29623]**

GPD Inc. **[1056]**

"GPs Say Valuation Standard Is 'Important' But Can't Agree on One" in *Venture Capital Journal* (Vol. 42, No. 10, Oct. 2002, pp. 47-48) **[15050]**, **[49967]**, **[55648]**

GPS Solutions **[23282]**

Grace Contrino Abrams Peace Education Foundation **[17034]**

Grace Venture Capital / Grace Internet Capital **[60870]**

Grace Venture Partners **[58970]**

Gradient Corporation–Information Resource Center **[9500]**

"Grading confusion: Computer makers balk at report card's methods" in *Waste News* (Vol. 7, No. 16, December 10, 2001, pp. 1) **[6164]**, **[6409]**, **[6662]**, **[21234]**, **[37283]**, **[53760]**

Graduate Assistantship Directory in Computing **[6472]**, **[23019]**

Graduating Engineer & Computer Careers **[23406]**

"Graduating with Wings" in *Small Business Opportunities* (Vol. 16, No. 3, May 2004, pp. 76, 130) **[21402]**, **[38651]**

Grafton Area Chamber of Commerce **[63519]**, **[66406]**

Graham Chamber of Commerce **[65258]**

Graham County Chamber of Commerce **[57036]**

Joseph Grahame **[5485]**

Grainews **[26596]**

The Grammar Course (Canada) **[27250]**

Granada Hills Chamber of Commerce **[57513]**

Granby Chamber of Commerce **[58370]**, **[58532]**

Grand Blanc Chamber of Commerce **[61306]**

Grand Canyon Chamber of Commerce **[57037]**

Grand Coulee Dam Area Chamber of Commerce **[66088]**

Grand Council of Hispanic Societies in Public Service **[47998]**

Grand Forks Chamber of Commerce **[63520]**

Grand Forks SBDC Center **[63494]**

"Grand Hyatt, others spend millions on makeovers" in *Washington Business Journal* (Vol. 21, No. 50, April 11, 2003, pp. 13) **[12559]**, **[24940]**

Grand Island Area Chamber of Commerce **[62265]**

Grand Island Chamber of Commerce **[62888]**

Grand Junction Area Chamber of Commerce **[58371]**

Grand Junction Small Business Development Center–Western Colorado Business Development Corp. **[58303]**

Grand Lake Area Chamber of Commerce **[58372]**

Grand Ledge Area Chamber of Commerce **[61307]**

Grand Marais Chamber of Commerce **[61593]**

Grand Prairie Chamber of Commerce **[65259]**

Grand Rapids Area Chamber of Commerce **[61308]**, **[61594]**, **[63683]**

Grand Rapids Public Library–Furniture Design Collection **[10848]**

Grand Rental Station **[21380]**

Grand Rivers Tourism Commission **[60509]**

Grand Saline Chamber of Commerce **[65260]**

"Grand Slam" in *Birmingham Business Journal* (Vol. 20, No. 31, August 1, 2003, pp. 15) **[1442]**, **[3233]**, **[7349]**, **[20517]**, **[28224]**

Grand Terrace Area Chamber of Commerce **[57514]**

Grand Valley State University
  Human Performance Laboratory **[19605]**
  Michigan SBTDC **[61230]**
  Michigan Small Business Development Center **[46550]**, **[61169]**
  Robert B. Annis Water Resources Institute **[25742]**
  Small Business Technology Development Center **[61188]**

The Grandich Letter **[15645]**

"Grandma inspires woman to create online kid's books" in *Atlanta Business Chronicle* (Vol. 24, No. 13, August 24, 2001, pp. 30A) **[2636]**, **[13752]**

"Grandma's Recipe" in *Forbes* (December 25, 2000, pp. 242) **[23439]**, **[35488]**

Grandview Area Chamber of Commerce [61966]
Grandview Chamber of Commerce [66089]
Grandville Chamber of Commerce [61309]
Grandy's, Inc.–American Restaurant Group [21832]
Granger Chamber of Commerce [66090]
Grangeville Chamber of Commerce [59298]
"Granholm Criticized for HMO Bill Inaction" in
    Crain's Detroit Business (Vol. 21, January 3,
    2005, No. 1, pp. 20) [13301], [40417], [43191]
"Granholm to Propose New Revenue-Sharing Plan"
    in Crain's Detroit Business (Vol. 23, January 29,
    2007, No. 5, pp. 32) [38102], [40418], [54580]
"Granholm wants to scrap workers' comp appeal
    board" in Crain's Detroit Business (Vol. 19, No.
    11, March 17, 2003, pp. 6) [29273], [40419],
    [46305]
"Granite Broadcasting Corp." in Black Enterprise
    (Vol. 35, December 2004, No. 5, pp. 86) [4106],
    [24413]
Granite Falls Area Chamber of Commerce [61595]
Granite Transformations [4503], [20039]
"Granite Ventures Chisels Out Its Own Identity" in
    Venture Capital Journal (September 1, 2005)
    [55649]
A. Davis Grant & Co. [13115]
Grant County Chamber of Commerce [57169],
    [60339], [60510], [64221], [66275]
"Granting Options Like It's 1999" in Inc. (October
    2005, pp. 34) [158], [2909], [15051], [23955],
    [26249], [26820]
Grants/Cibola County Chamber of Commerce
    [62690]
Grants Pass - Josephine County Chamber of
    Commerce [64222]
"Grants for Rural Biz" in Inc. (September 1, 2003)
    [26512], [39832], [50884], [52114]
Grantsburg Chamber of Commerce [66407]
GrantSelect [41347]
Granville County Chamber of Commerce [63367]
Granville Sentinel [18953]
The Grape [23563]
"Grape Expectations: Are You Thinking About
    Getting Into the Wine Business?" in
    Entrepreneur (Vol. 31, No. 10, October 2003,
    pp. 106) [23440], [28225], [35489]
Grapevine Chamber of Commerce [65261]
Graph Expo and Converting Expo [6029]
Graphic Arts Blue Book [6056]
Graphic Arts - Charlotte Show [6030]
Graphic Arts Education and Research Foundation
    [6089]
Graphic Arts Employers of America [19844]
Graphic Arts Monthly Magazine [6018], [19906]
Graphic Communications Today [6019]
Graphic Communications World [19907]
    Library [6066], [19945]
Graphic Communicator [6020]
The Graphic Monthly [6021]
Graphic Monthly-Estimators' & Buyers' Guide Issue
    [5985]
Graphic News [19908]
"A Graphic Shoot-Em Up" in Barron's (July 7, 2003,
    pp. T1) [4679], [9989], [15052], [23020],
    [41718]
Graphic Trade [6031]
"Graphically Speaking" in Small Business
    Opportunities (Vol. 12, No. 2, March 2000, pp.
    70, 72) [5947], [37566]
Graphics of the Americas [6032], [19922], [25501]
GRAPHICS MASTER 5 [5986], [8614], [18229],
    [18878], [19879]
Graphics Update [19909]
"Graphiti: Eking out e-commerce" in Red Herring
    (No. 103, September 1, 2001, pp. 28) [14091],
    [28226], [33978], [51172]
"Graphiti: Online demographics" in Red Herring
    (No. 102, August 15, 2001, pp. 26) [14092],
    [28227]
"Graphiti: commercial real estate retrenches" in Red
    Herring (No. 99, June 15 & July 1, 2001, pp.
    40-41) [20518], [20883]
Graphology Explained: A Workbook [11858]
"Grassley Offers Discussion Draft on COLI Policies"
    in Tax Notes (Vol. 102, No. 3, January 19,
    2004, pp. 323-325) [13302], [38103], [40420],
    [43192]

"Grassroots Marketing" in Home Business (Vol. 12,
    March/April 2005, No. 2, pp. 58) [645], [35490],
    [42516], [46570]
Grassroots NGOs by Women for Women: The
    Driving Force of Development in India [43680],
    [54193], [56249]
Gratiot Area Chamber of Commerce [61310]
    SBDC [61189]
"Grave Matters" in Crain's Detroit Business (Vol.
    22, January 16, 2006, No. 3, pp. 3) [16950],
    [29274]
Gravure Association of America [19946]
"Gray Might be a Geek, thought DeVeau, but he
    was a Geek with Vision" in Inc. (May 2000, pp.
    94) [13753], [29742], [52639]
Gray Ventures [59198]
"Gray Winds" in Forbes (Vol. 175, January 10,
    2005, No. 1, pp. 143) [15053], [21170]
Grayling Regional Chamber of Commerce [61311]
Grays Harbor Chamber of Commerce [66091]
Grayslake Area Chamber of Commerce [59518]
Grayson Area Chamber of Commerce [60511]
Grayson County Chamber of Commerce [60512]
Grayson County College–Small Business
    Development Center [65036]
Grayson-Jockey Club Research Foundation [12483]
Grayville Chamber of Commerce [59519]
Greacen Consulting Engineers Inc. [1057], [7609],
    [19770]
Grease Monkey International, Inc. [20269]
"Greased Lightning" in Forbes (Vol. 170, No. 9,
    October 28, 2002, pp. 246) [21526], [28228]
Great Ad! Low Cost, Do-It-Yourself Advertising for
    Your Small Business [47035]
The Great American Bagel/ The Great Canadian
    Bagel [2173]
Great American Cookie Co., Inc. [2300]
The Great American Idea Book - Make Money from
    Your Ideas: Movies, Music, Books, Inventions,
    Businesses, & Almost Anything Else! [44052]
Great Basin College–Small Business Development
    Center [62324]
Great Bend Chamber of Commerce [60340]
Great Big Book of Business Lists: All the Info You
    Need to Run a Small Business [36232], [39371]
The Great Blue Beacon [9030]
The Great Canadian Bagel [21833]
Great Canadian Dollar Store (1993) Ltd. [51458]
Great Clips, Inc. [11831]
"The Great Comeback" in My Business (April/May
    2003, pp. 26-28, 30-32) [28229], [36233]
Great Customer Service on the Telephone [24289],
    [31727]
"Great Expectation" in Entrepreneur (Vol. 33,
    February 2005, No. 2, pp. 72) [42252], [45202]
"Great Expectations" in Black Enterprise (Vol. 33,
    No. 3, October 2002, pp. 176) [9136], [9208],
    [24100], [24526]
"Great Expectations: Think Your Business
    Technology Is All That and a Bag of
    Microchips? Well, It's Not" in Entrepreneur
    [5004], [6663], [41719], [49054]
Great Falls Area Chamber of Commerce [62170]
Great Falls Development Authority–Great Falls
    SBDC [62122]
Great Falls Regional Chamber of Commerce
    [65784]
The Great Frame Up, Inc. [19835]
Great Harvest Franchising, Inc. [2301]
Great Hill Equity Partners, LLC [61075]
"The Great Hyped Hope" in Washington Business
    Journal (Vol. 22, No. 17, August 29, 2003, pp.
    20) [646], [47036]
Great Ideas for Gift Baskets, Bags, and Boxes
    [11113]
"The Great Jobs Switch" in The Economist (Vol.
    377, October 1-7, 2005, No. 8446, pp. 13, 16)
    [32455], [46306]
Great Lakes Booksellers Association [3019]
Great Lakes Chemical Corporation–Library [23808]
Great Lakes Consulting Group Inc. [3717], [16611],
    [30083], [31360], [43924], [46034], [53091]
Great Lakes Industrial Show [48871], [55216]
Great Leaders in Business and Administration
    [39731]
The Great Marketing Turnaround [47037]

Great Neck Chamber of Commerce [62889]
The Great Numbers Game [5385]
Great Opportunities, Inc. [3882]
Great Outdoor Sub Shops, Inc. [21834]
"The Great Outdoors" in Entrepreneur (Vol. 31, No.
    4, April 2003, pp. 82) [647], [22790], [47038]
Great Plains RC & D–Environmental
    Education–Library [9439]
Great Plains Technology Center [64141]
"The Great Rebate" in Entrepreneur (Vol. 31, No. 9,
    September 2003, pp. 43) [6664], [37284]
Great San Francisco Crystal Fair [17940]
"The Great Software Equalizer" in Hispanic
    Business (Vol. 24, No. 4, April 2002, pp. 64)
    [4680], [23021], [53304]
The Great Steak & Potato Co. [21835]
"Great Time to Go It Alone" in Kiplinger's Personal
    Finance Magazine (Vol. 58, No. 5, May 2004,
    pp. 20) [28230], [32456], [35491]
"The Great Transition" in Harvard Business Review
    (Vol. 81, No. 10, October 2003, pp. 70) [43681],
    [53761]
"The great unknown" in Entrepreneur (Vol. 31, No.
    6, June 2003, pp. 19) [28231], [32457], [36234]
Great Valley Regional Chamber of Commerce
    [64425]
"The Great Wall" in Entrepreneur (Vol. 32, No. 4,
    April 2004, pp. 38) [14093], [22239], [33979],
    [53305]
A Great Way to Get Wealth: How to Start & Build a
    Network Marketing Business from Your Home
    [48665]
Great Western Association Management Inc.
    [3969], [9052], [16612], [27585], [31361],
    [46035]
Great Wraps! [21836]
Greater Abbeville-Vermilion Chamber of Commerce
    [60635]
Greater Aiken Chamber of Commerce [64737]
Greater Akron Chamber of Commerce [63684]
Greater Albion Chamber of Commerce [61312]
Greater Albuquerque Chamber of Commerce
    [62691]
Greater Algonac Chamber of Commerce [61313]
The Greater Antelope Valley Economic Alliance
    [58204]
Greater Area Walhalla Chamber of Commerce
    [64738]
Greater Arlington Area Chamber of Commerce
    [66092]
Greater Artesia Chamber of Commerce [62692]
Greater Asbury Park Chamber of Commerce
    [62502]
Greater Atlantic City Chamber of Commerce–Small
    Business Development Center [62455]
Greater Augusta Regional Chamber of Commerce
    [65903]
Greater Aurora Chamber of Commerce [59520]
Greater Austin Chamber of Commerce [62350],
    [65262]
Greater Austin Hispanic Chamber of Commerce
    [65263]
Greater Avon Chamber of Commerce [59916]
Greater Bakersfield Chamber of Commerce [57515]
Greater Baldwinsville Chamber of Commerce
    [62890]
Greater Bartow Chamber of Commerce [58806]
Greater Bath Area Chamber of Commerce [62891]
Greater Baton Rouge Chamber of Commerce
    [60636]
Greater Bear Lake Valley Chamber of Commerce
    [59299]
Greater Beauregard Area Chamber of Commerce
    [60637]
Greater Belleville Chamber of Commerce [59521]
Greater Beloit Chamber of Commerce [66408]
Greater Berkley Chamber of Commerce [61314]
Greater Bernalillo Chamber of Commerce [62693]
Greater Bethesda-Chevy Chase Chamber of
    Commerce [60830]
Greater Binghamton Chamber of Commerce
    [62892]
Greater Blackfoot Area Chamber of Commerce
    [59300]
Greater Bloomington Chamber of Commerce
    [59917]

Greater Blouse, Skirt and Undergarment Association [16209]

Greater Bluefield Chamber of Commerce [66276]

Greater Boca Raton Chamber of Commerce [58807]

Greater Boerne Chamber of Commerce [65264]

Greater Bonners Ferry Chamber of Commerce [59301]

Greater Bordentown Chamber of Commerce [62503]

Greater Boston Chamber of Commerce [60952]

Greater Bottineau Chamber of Commerce [63521]

Greater Bowie Chamber of Commerce [60831]

Greater Boynton Beach Chamber of Commerce [58808]

Greater Brandon Chamber of Commerce [58809]

Greater Breckinridge County Chamber of Commerce [60513]

Greater Brewton Area Chamber of Commerce [56852]

Greater Bridgeville Area Chamber of Commerce [64426]

Greater Bridgton-Lakes Region Chamber of Commerce [60748]

Greater Brighton Area Chamber of Commerce [58373], [61315]

Greater Brockport Chamber of Commerce [62893]

Greater Brookfield Chamber of Commerce [66409]

Greater Brownsville Area Chamber of Commerce [64427]

Greater Buckeye Lake Chamber of Commerce [63685]

Greater Burlington Industrial Corp.–Northwestern Vermont Small Business Development Center [65761]

Greater Carbondale Chamber of Commerce [64428]

Greater Carlisle Area Chamber of Commerce [64429]

Greater Casa Grande Chamber of Commerce [57038]

Greater Cazenovia Area Chamber of Commerce [62894]

Greater Cedar Creek Lake Area Chamber of Commerce [65265]

Greater Cedar Valley Chamber of Commerce - Waterloo [60138]

Greater Centralia Chamber of Commerce [59522]

Greater Chadbourn Chamber of Commerce [63368]

Greater Chambersburg Chamber of Commerce [64430]

Greater Channahon-Minooka Area Chamber of Commerce [59523]

Greater Cheraw Chamber of Commerce [64739]

Greater Chesterfield Chamber of Commerce [64740]

Greater Cheyenne Chamber of Commerce [66611]

Greater Chiefland Area Chamber of Commerce [58810]

Greater Cincinnati Junior Chamber Foundation [63686]

Greater Cincinnati and Northern Kentucky African American Chamber of Commerce [63687]

Greater Clairemont Chamber of Commerce [57516]

Greater Claremont Chamber of Commerce [62405]

Greater Cleveland Chamber of Commerce [65266]

Greater Cleveland Growth Association–Cleveland Small Business Development Center [63556]

Greater Clover Chamber of Commerce [64741]

Greater Colorado Springs Chamber of Commerce [58374]

Greater Columbia Chamber of Commerce [64742]

Greater Columbus Area Chamber of Commerce [63688]

Central Ohio SBDC [63557]

Greater Columbus Chamber of Commerce [59109]

Greater Concord Chamber of Commerce [57517]

Greater Connell Area Chamber of Commerce [66093]

Greater Connellsville Chamber of Commerce [64431]

Greater Conroe - Lake Conroe Area Chamber of Commerce [65267]

Greater Copper Valley Chamber of Commerce [56956]

Greater Corbin Chamber of Commerce [60514]

Greater Corning Area Chamber of Commerce [62895]

Greater Corpus Christi Business Alliance–Small Business Development Center [65037]

Greater Cranston Chamber of Commerce [64666]

Greater Crofton Chamber of Commerce [60832]

Greater Croswell - Lexington Chamber of Commerce [61316]

Greater Dade City Chamber of Commerce [58811]

Greater Dallas Asian American Chamber of Commerce [65268]

Greater Dallas Chamber of Commerce [65269]

Greater Danbury Chamber of Commerce [58533]

Greater Dania Beach Chamber of Commerce [58812]

Greater Danville Chamber of Commerce [59918]

Greater Darlington Chamber of Commerce [64743]

Greater Decatur Chamber of Commerce [61317]

Greater Deerfield Beach Chamber of Commerce [58813]

Greater Delray Beach Chamber of Commerce [58814]

Greater Denham Springs Chamber of Commerce [60638]

Greater Derry Chamber of Commerce [62406]

Greater Des Moines Chamber of Commerce [66094]

Greater Des Moines Partnership [60139]

Greater Dover Chamber of Commerce [62407]

Greater Dowagiac Area Chamber of Commerce [61318]

Greater Du Bois Chamber of Commerce - Economic Development [64432]

Greater Durham Chamber of Commerce [63369]

Greater Easley Chamber of Commerce [64744]

Greater East Aurora Chamber of Commerce [62896]

Greater East St. Louis Chamber of Commerce [59524]

Greater Eatonville Chamber of Commerce [66095]

Greater Edinburgh Community Chamber of Commerce [59919]

Greater Edmonds Chamber of Commerce [66096]

Greater Effingham Chamber of Commerce and Industry [59525]

Greater El Paso Chamber of Commerce [65270]

Greater Eldora Chamber of Commerce [60140]

Greater Elgin Chamber of Commerce [65271]

Greater Elizabeth Chamber of Commerce [62504]

Greater Elkhart County Chamber of Commerce [59920]

Greater Englewood Chamber of Commerce [58375]

Greater Enid Chamber of Commerce [64000]

Greater Eureka Chamber of Commerce [57518]

Greater Eureka Springs Chamber of Commerce [57170]

Greater Fairbanks Chamber of Commerce [56957]

Greater Fairfield Area Chamber of Commerce [59526]

Greater Fallon Area Chamber of Commerce [62351]

Greater Florence Chamber of Commerce [57039], [64745]

Greater Fort Kent Area Chamber of Commerce [60749]

Greater Fort Lauderdale Chamber of Commerce [58815]

Greater Fort Lee Chamber of Commerce [62505]

Greater Fort Myers Chamber of Commerce [58816]

Greater Fort Walton Beach Chamber of Commerce [58817]

Greater Fort Wayne Chamber of Commerce [59921]

Greater Franklin Chamber of Commerce [62408]

Greater Fresno Area Chamber of Commerce [57519]

Greater Fulton Chamber of Commerce [62897]

Greater Gardner Chamber of Commerce [60953]

Greater Geneva Area Chamber of Commerce [56853]

Greater Gibson County Area Chamber of Commerce [64921]

Greater Girard Area Chamber of Commerce [63689]

Greater Glassboro Chamber of Commerce [62506]

Greater Glenside Chamber of Commerce [64433]

Greater Golden Chamber of Commerce [58376]

Greater Goldendale Chamber of Commerce [66097]

Greater Gouverneur Chamber of Commerce [62898]

Greater Gratiot Development, Inc.–Small Business Center [61190]

Greater Greencastle Chamber of Commerce [59922]

Greater Greenfield Chamber of Commerce [59923]

Greater Greenville Chamber of Commerce [64746]

Greater Greenwich Chamber of Commerce [62899]

Greater Greenwood Chamber of Commerce [59924]

Greater Greer Chamber of Commerce [64747]

Greater Hackensack Chamber of Commerce [62507]

Greater Hall Chamber of Commerce [59110]

Greater Hamilton Chamber of Commerce [63690]

Greater Hammonton Chamber of Commerce [62508]

Greater Hampstead Chamber of Commerce [63370]

Greater Hardeeville Chamber of Commerce [64748]

Greater Harlem Chamber of Commerce [62900]

Greater Hartsville Chamber of Commerce [64749]

Greater Harvard Area Chamber of Commerce [59527]

Greater Hatboro Chamber of Commerce [64434]

Greater Haverhill Chamber of Commerce [60954]

Greater Hazleton Chamber of Commerce [64435]

Greater Healy-Denali Chamber of Commerce [56958]

Greater Heights Area Chamber of Commerce [65272]

Greater Helen Area Chamber of Commerce [59111]

Greater Hendersonville Chamber of Commerce [63371]

Greater Hermiston Chamber of Commerce [64223]

Greater Hernando County Chamber of Commerce [58818]

Greater Hewitt Chamber of Commerce [65273]

Greater Highlands Chamber of Commerce [65274]

Greater Hollywood Chamber of Commerce [58819]

Greater Holyoke Chamber of Commerce [60955]

Greater Homestead/Florida City Chamber of Commerce [58820]

Greater Hot Springs Chamber of Commerce [57171]

Greater Houlton Chamber of Commerce [60750]

Greater Houston Partnership [65275]

Greater Hudson Chamber of Commerce [62409]

Greater Huntington Park Area Chamber of Commerce [57520]

Greater Iberia Chamber of Commerce [60639]

Greater Indianapolis Chamber of Commerce [59925]

Greater Irondale Chamber of Commerce [56854]

Greater Irving - Las Colinas Chamber of Commerce [65276]

Greater Issaquah Chamber of Commerce [66098]

Greater Jackson Chamber of Commerce [61319]

Greater Jackson County Chamber of Commerce [56855]

Greater Jennings Chamber of Commerce [60640]

Greater Johnstown/Cambria County Chamber of Commerce [64436]

Greater Kansas City Chamber of Commerce [61967]

Greater Kaufman Chamber of Commerce and Visitors Bureau [65277]

Greater Keene Chamber of Commerce [62410]

Greater Keller Chamber of Commerce [65278]

Greater Ketchikan Chamber of Commerce [56959]

Greater Killeen Chamber of Commerce [65279]

Greater Kingston Community Chamber of Commerce [66099]

Greater Kirkland Chamber of Commerce [66100]

Greater La Porte Chamber of Commerce [59926]

Greater LaBelle Chamber of Commerce [58821]

Greater Laconia/Weirs Beach Chamber of Commerce [62411]

Greater Lafayette Area SBDC [59824]

Greater Lafayette Chamber of Commerce [60641]

Greater Lafayette Community Development Corp.–SBDC [59825]

Greater Lake City Chamber of Commerce [64750], [66101]

Greater Lake Stevens Chamber of Commerce [66102]

Greater Lake Worth Chamber of Commerce [58822]

Greater Lantana Chamber of Commerce [58823]
Greater LaPorte Chamber of Commerce–Small Business Development Center [59826]
Greater Las Cruces Chamber of Commerce [62694]
Greater Lavernia Chamber of Commerce [65280]
Greater Lawrence County Area Chamber of Commerce [63691]
Greater Leeds Area Chamber of Commerce [56856]
Greater Lehigh County Chamber of Commerce [64437]
Greater Lexington Chamber of Commerce [60515]
Greater Limestone Chamber of Commerce [60751]
Greater Lincolnshire Chamber of Commerce [59528]
Greater Liverpool Chamber of Commerce [62901]
Greater Long Branch Chamber of Commerce [62509]
Greater Louisville–Small Business Development Center [60456]
Greater Louisville Inc. - The Metro Chamber of Commerce [60516]
Greater Louisville SBDC [60457]
Greater Lowell Chamber of Commerce [60956]
Greater Lytle Chamber of Commerce [65281]
Greater Macon Chamber of Commerce [59112]
Greater Madawaska Chamber of Commerce [60752]
Greater Madison Area Chamber of Commerce [64824]
Greater Madison Chamber of Commerce [66410]
Greater Mahopac-Carmel Chamber of Commerce [62902]
Greater Mahwah Chamber of Commerce [62510]
Greater Manchester Chamber of Commerce [58534], [62412]
Greater Mankato Chamber of Commerce [61596]
Greater Mansfield Area Chamber of Commerce [64438]
Greater Maple Valley - Black Diamond Chamber of Commerce [66103]
Greater Marathon Chamber of Commerce [58824]
Greater Martinsville Chamber of Commerce [59927]
Greater Marysville - Tulalip Chamber of Commerce [66104]
Greater Massena Chamber of Commerce [62903]
Greater Mauston Area Chamber of Commerce [66411]
Greater Menomonie Area Chamber of Commerce [66412]
Greater Merced Chamber of Commerce [57521]
Greater Meriden Chamber of Commerce [58535]
Greater Mexico Chamber of Commerce [62904]
Greater Miami Chamber of Commerce [58825]
Greater Miami Chamber of Commerce, Women in Business Group [58826]
Greater Miami Shores Chamber of Commerce [58827]
Greater Millville Chamber of Commerce [62511]
Greater Mission Chamber of Commerce [65282]
Greater Mitchell Chamber of Commerce [59928]
Greater Monticello Chamber of Commerce and Visitors Bureau [59929]
Greater Mount Airy Chamber of Commerce [63372]
Greater Mulberry Chamber of Commerce [58828]
Greater Mullins Chamber of Commerce [64751]
Greater Muscatine Chamber of Commerce and Industry [60141]
Greater Muskogee Area Chamber of Commerce [64001]
Greater Naples Chamber of Commerce [58829]
Greater Nashua Chamber of Commerce [62413]
Greater Nassau County Chamber of Commerce [58830]
Greater New Braunfels Chamber of Commerce [65283]
Greater New Haven Chamber of Commerce [58536] Small Business Development Center [58496]
Greater New Milford Chamber of Commerce [58537]
Greater New York Chamber of Commerce [62905]
Greater Newburyport Chamber of Commerce [60957]
Greater Newport Chamber of Commerce [64224]
Greater Niles Economic Development Fund–SBDC [61191]

Greater North Dakota Chamber of Commerce [63522]
Greater North Fulton Chamber of Commerce [59113]
Greater North Miami Chamber of Commerce [58831]
Greater North Pulaski Development Corp.–Small Business Development Center [59372]
Greater Northampton Chamber of Commerce [60958]
Greater Northeast Philadelphia Chamber of Commerce [64439]
Greater Norwalk Chamber of Commerce [58538]
Greater Oak Harbor Chamber of Commerce [66105]
Greater Ogdensburg Chamber of Commerce [62906]
Greater Oklahoma City Chamber of Commerce [64002]
Greater Olean Area Chamber of Commerce [62907]
Greater Omaha Chamber of Commerce [62266]
Greater Oneida Chamber of Commerce [62908]
Greater Orange Area Chamber of Commerce [65284]
Greater Ossining Chamber of Commerce [62909]
Greater Ossipee Area Chamber of Commerce [62414]
Greater Oswego Chamber of Commerce [62910]
Greater Othello Chamber of Commerce [66106]
Greater Oviedo Chamber of Commerce [58832] Business Library [53131], [54101]
Greater Palm Bay Chamber of Commerce [58833]
Greater Palm Harbor Area Chamber of Commerce [58834]
Greater Palmer Chamber of Commerce [56960]
Greater Pampa Area Chamber of Commerce [65285]
Greater Panama City Beaches Chamber of Commerce [58835]
Greater Paramus Chamber of Commerce [62512]
Greater Pasco Area Chamber of Commerce [66107]
Greater Patchogue Chamber of Commerce [62911]
Greater Paterson Chamber of Commerce [62513]
Greater Paw Paw Chamber of Commerce [61320]
Greater Peterborough Chamber of Commerce [62415]
Greater Pflugerville Chamber of Commerce [65286]
Greater Philadelphia Chamber of Commerce [64440]
Greater Philadelphia Venture Capital Corp. [64553]
Greater Phoenix Black Chamber of Commerce [57040]
Greater Phoenix Chamber of Commerce [57041]
Greater Phoenix Chamber Membership List-Home-Based Businesses [42624]
Greater Phoenix Chamber Membership List-International Trade Businesses [43682]
Greater Phoenix Chamber Membership List-Minority-Owned or Operated Businesses [48188]
Greater Phoenix Chamber Membership List-Women-Owned or Operated Businesses [56250]
Greater Picayune Area Chamber of Commerce [61793]
Greater Pickens Chamber of Commerce [64752]
Greater Pine Bluff Chamber of Commerce [57172]
Greater Pine Island Chamber of Commerce [58836]
Greater Pittsburgh Chamber of Commerce [64441]
Greater Pittston Chamber of Commerce [64442]
Greater Plant City Chamber of Commerce [58837]
Greater Plantation Chamber of Commerce [58838]
Greater Pocatello Chamber of Commerce [59302]
Greater Pointe Coupee Chamber of Commerce [60642]
Greater Pompano Beach Chamber of Commerce [58839]
Greater Poplar Bluff Area Chamber of Commerce [61968]
Greater Port Huron Area Chamber of Commerce [61321]
Greater Port Jefferson Chamber of Commerce [62912]
Greater Portage Chamber of Commerce [59930]
Greater Portland Chamber of Commerce [60753]
Greater Portsmouth Chamber of Commerce [62416]
Greater Poulsbo Chamber of Commerce [66108]

Greater Princeton Area Chamber of Commerce [66413]
Greater Productivity Through Improved Work Processes: A Guide for Administrative Professionals [34794]
Greater Providence Chamber of Commerce [64667] Bryant College–Small Business Development Center [64646]
Greater Pueblo Chamber of Commerce [58377]
Greater Quitman Area Chamber of Commerce [65287]
Greater Raleigh Chamber of Commerce [63373]
Greater Redding Chamber of Commerce [57522]
Greater Redmond Chamber of Commerce [66109]
Greater Renton Chamber of Commerce [66110]
Greater Reston Chamber of Commerce, Business Visitors Center [65904]
Greater Richmond Chamber of Commerce [65905]
"Greater Richmond Convention Center Richmond, VA" in *Tradeshow Week* (Vol. 34, November 29, 2004, No. 48, pp. S4) [22508], [24941], [55097]
Greater Richmond Small Business Development Center–Greater Richmond Chamber of Commerce [65822]
Greater Riverside Chamber of Commerce [57523]
Greater Riverview Chamber of Commerce [58840]
Greater Rochester Chamber of Commerce [62417]
Greater Rochester Metro Chamber of Commerce, International Business Council [62913]
Greater Rochester Metro Chamber of Commerce, Retail Rochester [62914]
Greater Romulus Chamber of Commerce [61322]
Greater Royal Oak Chamber of Commerce [61323]
Greater Sacramento SBDC [57260]
Greater St. Anthony Chamber of Commerce [59303]
Greater St. Francisville Chamber of Commerce [60643]
Greater Salem Chamber of Commerce [59529], [62418]
Greater San Antonio Chamber of Commerce [65288]
Greater San Diego Chamber of Commerce–Small Business Development Center [57261]
Greater Sandpoint Chamber of Commerce [59304]
Greater Sarasota Chamber of Commerce [58841]
Greater Scott County Chamber of Commerce [59931]
Greater Scranton Chamber of Commerce [64443]
Greater Seaford Chamber of Commerce [58649]
Greater Seattle Chamber of Commerce [66111]
Greater Sebring Chamber of Commerce [58842]
Greater Seffner Area Chamber of Commerce [58843]
Greater Seminole Area Chamber of Commerce [58844]
Greater Seneca Chamber of Commerce [64753]
Greater Severna Park Chamber of Commerce [60833]
Greater Seymour Chamber of Commerce [59932]
Greater Shawnee Area Chamber of Commerce [64003]
Greater Shelby County Chamber of Commerce [56857]
Greater Shenandoah Area Chamber of Commerce [64444]
Greater Sherman Oaks Chamber of Commerce [57524]
Greater Shreveport Chamber of Commerce [60644]
Greater Sierra Vista Area Chamber of Commerce [57042]
Greater Silver Spring Chamber of Commerce [60834]
Greater Sitka Chamber of Commerce [56961]
Greater Slidell Area Chamber of Commerce [60645]
Greater Smithfield-Selma Area Chamber of Commerce [63374]
Greater Soldotna Chamber of Commerce [56962]
Greater Somersworth Chamber of Commerce [62419]
Greater South Haven Area Chamber of Commerce [61324]
Greater South Haven Chamber of Commerce–SBDC [61192]
Greater Southern Dutchess Chamber of Commerce [62915]

Greater Southington Chamber of Commerce [58539]

Greater Southwest Houston Chamber of Commerce [65289]

Greater Springfield Chamber of Commerce [59530], [65906]

Greater Sterling Development Corporation [59779]

Greater Stillwater Chamber of Commerce [61597]

Greater Stillwater County Chamber of Commerce [62171]

Greater Stockton Chamber of Commerce [57525]

Greater Summerville/Dorchester County Chamber of Commerce [64754]

Greater Sumter Chamber of Commerce [64755]

Greater Sunrise Chamber of Commerce [58845]

Greater Susquehanna Valley Chamber of Commerce [64445]

Greater Syracuse Chamber of Commerce [62916]

Greater Tabor City Chamber of Commerce [63375]

Greater Talladega Area Chamber of Commerce [56858]

Greater Tallahassee Chamber of Commerce [58846]

Greater Tallassee Area Chamber of Commerce [56859]

Greater Tampa Chamber of Commerce [58847]

Greater Tattnall Chamber of Commerce [59114]

Greater Tehachapi Chamber of Commerce [57526]

Greater Temple Terrace Chamber of Commerce [58848]

Greater Terre Haute Chamber of Commerce [59933]

Greater Tomah Area Chamber of Commerce [66414]

Greater Topeka Chamber of Commerce [60341]

Greater Topsail Area Chamber of Commerce and Tourism [63376]

Greater Trinidad Chamber of Commerce [57527]

Greater Ukiah Chamber of Commerce [57528]

Greater Union Grove Area Chamber of Commerce [66415]

Greater University Chamber of Commerce [66112]

Greater Valley Area Chamber of Commerce [56860]

Greater Valley Chamber of Commerce [58540]

Greater Valparaiso Chamber of Commerce [59934]

Greater Van Buren Chamber of Commerce [60754]

Greater Vancouver Chamber of Commerce [66113]

Greater Vernon Chamber of Commerce [60646]

Greater Vineland Chamber of Commerce [62514]

Greater Waco Chamber of Commerce [65290]

Greater Warminster Chamber of Commerce [64446]

Greater Warrensburg Area Chamber of Commerce [61969]

Greater Warsaw Chamber of Commerce [62917]

Greater Wasilla Chamber of Commerce [56963]

Greater Watertown - North Country Chamber of Commerce [62918]

Greater Waynesboro Chamber of Commerce [64447]

Greater Wayzata Area Chamber of Commerce [61598]

Greater Weiser Area Chamber of Commerce [59305]

Greater West Bloomfield Chamber of Commerce [61325]

Greater West Plains Area Chamber of Commerce [61970]

Greater Westerly-Pawcatuck Area Chamber of Commerce [64668]

Greater Westhampton Chamber of Commerce [62919]

Greater White Haven Chamber of Commerce [64448]

Greater Whiteville Chamber of Commerce [63377]

Greater Wildwood Chamber of Commerce [62515]

Greater Williamsburg Chamber and Tourism Alliance [65907]

Greater Wilmington Chamber of Commerce [63378]

Greater Winston-Salem Chamber of Commerce [63379]

Greater Winter Haven Chamber of Commerce [58849]

Greater Woodinville Chamber of Commerce [66114]

Greater Woodland Park Chamber of Commerce [58378]

Greater Yakima Chamber of Commerce [66115]

Greater York Area Chamber of Commerce [62267]

Greater York Chamber of Commerce [64756]

Greater Zionsville Chamber of Commerce [59935]

Greco Pizza Donair [19673]

"Greed Is Bad" in *Red Herring* (No. 106, October 15, 2001, pp. 92) [29275], [37143], [44053], [44305]

Greek Food and Wine Institute [23448]

"Greektown Casino cuts back hotel plans" in *Crain's Detroit Business* (Vol. 19, No. 17, April 28, 2003, pp. 30) [2339], [10866], [12560], [21527]

"Greektown Casino Seeks Financial Extension" in *Crain's Detroit Business* (Vol. 22, December 11, 2006, No. 50, pp. 25) [10867], [38104], [40421]

Greeley County Historical Society–Library [11029]

Greeley and Hansen LLC–Library [25730]

Greeley Small Business Development Center–Aims Community College–Greeley and Weld Chamber of Commerce [58304]

Greeley Tribune (November 5, 2002); "Yoga Studio to Open in Greeley, Colo." in [17924], [19451]

Greeley/Weld Chamber of Commerce [58379]

"Green Acres" in *Small Business Opportunities* (Vol. 13, No. 5, September 2001, pp. 60, 64) [15978], [49760]

Green Bay Area Chamber of Commerce [66416]

The Green Business Letter [9388], [37343]

"Green Business Push Blooms" in *Charlotte Observer* (February 7, 2007) [37285], [53762]

Green Chamber of Commerce [63692]

"Green Energy Co. Goes Public" in *Long Island Business News* (May 7, 2004) [15054], [16304], [28232]

"Green Grocer" in *Crain's New York Business* (Vol. 22, December 11, 2006, No. 50, pp. 33) [11623], [54194]

Green Guide to Antiquing in New England [1318]

Green Hotels Association [12501], [37229]

Green Industry Expo [16136]

Green Lake Area Chamber of Commerce [66417]

Green Life Interiors [16077]

"Green Machines" in *Entrepreneur* (Vol. 31, No. 7, July 2003, pp. 34) [36235], [37286], [37451]

"Green Machines" in *Entrepreneur.com* (Vol. 34, February 2006, No. 2, pp. 51) [18051], [37287], [54581]

Green Marketing: Challenges and Opportunities for the New Marketing Age [9484]

Green Mountain Advisors, Inc. [65806]

Green Mountain Economic Development Corporation–SBDC [65762]

The Green PC: Making Choices That Make a Difference [37288]

Green Profit Magazine [10584], [11461]

"Green Reporting" in *Harvard Business Review* (Vol. 78, No. 1, January 2000, pp. 15) [37289]

Green River Chamber of Commerce [66612]

Green Seal [9515]

"Green industry finding ways to thrive, despite restrictions" in *Colorado Springs Business Journal* (March 7, 2003) [16015]

Lynn Greenberg Associates [16868]

GreenBook Worldwide-Directory of Marketing Research Companies and Services [47039]

Greenbrier County Convention and Visitors Bureau [66277]

Greenbucks: The Challenge of Sustainable Development [37353]

Greencastle-Antrim Chamber of Commerce [64449]

Greendale Chamber of Commerce [66418]

Greene County Chamber of Commerce [59115], [62920]

Greene County Extension SBDC [61866]

Greene County Partnership [64922]

Greene Group [35298]

Greene Radovsky Maloney Share–Library [24179], [54917]

"Greener pastures" in *Atlanta Business Chronicle* (Vol. 25, No. 20, October 25, 2002, pp. 1C) [17386], [29276]

"Greener Pastures: Exodus from Fidelity Continues as Another Hot Manager Heads to a Hedge Fund" in *Barron's* (July 21, 2003, pp. F2) [9990], [15055], [29277], [38105], [40422]

Greenfield Chamber of Commerce [57529], [66419]

Greenfield Chamber/Main Street and Community Development Corporation [60142]

Greenhouse Business [11462]

The Greenhouse Gardener's Companion: Growing Food and Flowers in Your Greenhouse or Sunspace [11431]

Greenhouse Gardening: Step by Step to Growing Success [11432]

"Greenhouse Gas Limits are Called Affordable" in *The Record* (November 21, 2005) [37290], [40423]

Greenhouse Management and Production [10585], [11463]

Greenhouse Operation and Management [11433]

The Greening of Business [37291]

Greenland Irrigation [16078]

The GreenMoney Journal & Online Guide [3624], [9389], [37344], [37539]

Greenpeace Magazine [9487]

Greenport Southold Chamber of Commerce [62921]

"The Greens Bite Back" in *The Economist* (Vol. 377, October 22-28, 2005, No. 8449, pp. 35) [29278], [40424]

Greensboro Area Chamber of Commerce [63380]

"Greensboro firm buys Sembler retail center" in *Atlanta Business Chronicle* (Vol. 25, January 10, 2003, No. 31, pp. 10A) [12188], [12287], [51173]

Greensburg Chamber of Commerce [60342]

Greensburg Decatur County Chamber of Commerce [59936]

Greensburg-Green County Chamber of Commerce [60517]

"Greenspan Floats Sales Tax" in *Chicago Tribune* (March 4, 2005) [32458], [40425], [54582]

"Greenspan in Florida warns home prices are likely to fall this year" in *Daily Business Review* (Vol. 77, March 5, 2003) [20519], [20884], [28233]

Greenspan & Greenspan [29624]

Joel Greenstein & Associates [3718], [3970], [16613], [31362], [46036], [48499], [56543]

Greenstone Venture Partners [66679]

Greenvale Chamber of Commerce [62922]

Greenville Area Chamber of Commerce [56861], [61326], [61794]

Greenville Area SBDC [64693]

Greenville Chamber of Commerce [59531], [65291]

Greenville-Muhlenberg County Chamber of Commerce [60518]

Greenville - Pitt County Chamber of Commerce [63381]

Greenville Technical College–Northwest Campus [64799]

Greenwich Chamber of Commerce [58541]

Greenwich Village-Chelsea Chamber of Commerce [62923]

GREENWIRE [37345]

Greenwood Area Chamber of Commerce [64757]

Greenwood Area SBDC [64694]

Greenwood Chamber of Commerce [57173], [66420]

Greenwood-Leflore Chamber of Commerce [61795]

Greers Ferry Area Chamber of Commerce [57174]

Greeting Card Industry Directory [11154], [11565]

Greeting Cards - US [11174], [11573]

Gregory Commercial Club [64825]

Gregory J. Ellis & Associates, Ltd. [29625]

Grenada County Chamber of Commerce [61796]

Gresham Area Chamber of Commerce [64225]

Grey Areas Newsletter [391], [20760], [21105], [25346], [29663]

Grey Worldwide–Information Center [50737]

Greybull Area Chamber of Commerce [66613]

"Greyhound Racing" in *The Economist* (Vol. 376, July 16-22, 2005, No. 8435, pp. 29) [10868], [54195]

Greylock Management Corp. (Boston) [61076]

Greylock (San Mateo) [58027]

The Greystone Group Inc. [3719], [16614], [30084], [31363], [38539], [42969], [46037]

"Grice, Lund & Tarkington Merges with Oregon Firm" in *San Diego Business Journal* (Vol. 28, January 15, 2007, No. 3, pp. 19) [159], [15056], [26250], [49968]

Gridley Area Chamber of Commerce [57530]

"Gridlock Alert; Who is Driving" in *Crain's New York Business* (Vol. 22, December 11, 2006, No. 50, pp. 14) **[32459]**, **[40426]**, **[50447]**

"'Gridlock' Guru Studies Border Crossings; Report May Recharge Political Discussions" in *Crain's Detroit Business* (Vol. 21) **[43683]**

Grief Counseling & Support Services **[3720]**, **[31364]**, **[41331]**

Grieve, Horner, Brown & ASCULAI **[66723]**

Griffin-Spalding Chamber of Commerce **[59116]**

Griffin's Foot Long Hot Dogs **[21837]**

Griffith Chamber of Commerce **[59937]**

"A grim adventure: Amphion Capital's venture fund loses all" in *Barron's* (Vol. 82, No. 58, February 17, 2003, pp. T8) **[9991]**, **[15057]**, **[28234]**, **[41720]**, **[55650]**

Grime Goes Green: Your Business & the Environment **[37354]**

Grimes County Chamber of Commerce **[65292]**

Grimmick Consulting Services **[3721]**, **[16615]**, **[30085]**, **[31365]**, **[35233]**, **[46038]**, **[53092]**

Grinnell Area Chamber of Commerce **[60143]**

Grinnell College–Burling Library–Listening Room **[17677]**, **[17818]**

"Grist: A Passport to America" in *Inc.* (October 1, 2004) **[27383]**, **[28235]**, **[52860]**

"Grist: An Entrepreneurs Resolutions" in *Inc.* (January 1, 2005) **[28236]**, **[36236]**, **[53763]**

"Grist: Beyond the Vale of Smiles" in *Inc.* (July 1, 2004) **[34917]**, **[45203]**

"Grist: Micromanagers, Unite!" in *Inc.* (December 1, 2004) **[36237]**, **[45204]**

"Grist: More Power Than Point" in *Inc.* (August 1, 2003) **[4681]**, **[23022]**, **[49055]**, **[53306]**, **[53764]**

"Grist: The Inevitable Rise of the Entrepreneur" in *Inc.* (October 1, 2003) **[32460]**, **[36238]**

Griswold Special Care **[18488]**

GRO-Biz SBDC **[66597]**

Groberg - Holbrook Genealogical Organization **[10917]**

Grocers Report **[11694]**

Grocery Headquarters **[7787]**, **[11695]**

Grocery Industry Directory of New England & Upstate New York **[11679]**

Grocery Industry Market Share Report **[11681]**

Grocery Manufacturers of America **[11584]**

"Grocery Prices in 2007" in *Kiplinger Letter* (Vol. 78, January 19, 2007, No. 2) **[11624]**, **[32461]**

Grolier **[58632]**

Grolier Club of New York–Library **[2813]**, **[2847]**, **[3075]**, **[25506]**

"Groom to Grow: Animal Grooming is More Than a Pet Project for a Former HR Executive" in *Entrepreneur* (Vol. 32, December 2004, No. 12) **[19074]**, **[38821]**, **[52540]**

"Groom Your Workforce" in *PC Computing* (March 2000, pp. 137) **[33109]**, **[33980]**, **[34918]**, **[53765]**

Groomer On The Go **[19096]**

"Groove makes it possible to light up the edge" in *Fast Company* (May 2001, pp. 96) **[6939]**, **[23023]**, **[53307]**

"A Gross Tax Proposal" in *Inc.* (July 1, 2003) **[160]**, **[2910]**, **[23956]**, **[26251]**, **[54583]**

Lee Grossman Associates **[48636]**

Grosvenor Barber and Associates–Library **[13124]**

The Grosvenor Funds **[58675]**

Grotech Capital Group **[60871]**

"Ground Control" in *Entrepreneur* (Vol. 32, August 2004, No. 8, pp. 34) **[5005]**, **[6665]**, **[7350]**, **[7728]**, **[14094]**, **[27384]**, **[41721]**

"Ground Rules columnist cited for 'intelligence, insight'" in *Daily Business Review* (Vol. 77, No. 146, January 7, 2003, pp. A2) **[18879]**, **[20520]**, **[20885]**

Grounds Maintenance **[16039]**

Groundskeeping Series **[16056]**

"Group wants leasing rights on 53 closed Kmart stores" in *Crain's Detroit Business* (Vol. 18, No. 24, June 17, 2002, pp. 1) **[1820]**, **[15058]**, **[20053]**, **[20886]**

"Group sees beauty in an attempt to revive BeOS operating system" in *Wall Street Journal* (February 5, 2003, pp. B4A) **[6666]**, **[6940]**, **[49056]**

"Group Buys Bradenton, Fla.-Area Retail Center" in *Bradenton Herald* (January 5, 2005) **[20521]**, **[20887]**, **[51174]**, **[52678]**, **[53766]**, **[54584]**

"Group Casts Another Line Into Seafood" in *Crain's Chicago Business* (Vol. 26, No. 50, December 15, 2003, pp. 22) **[21234]**, **[21528]**, **[36239]**, **[36944]**

"Group dynamics" in *Entrepreneur* (Vol. 30, No. 12, December 2002, pp. 101) **[36240]**, **[39372]**

"Group Effort" in *Entrepreneur* (Vol. 32, November 2004, No. 11, pp. 64) **[6667]**, **[49057]**

"Group connects out-of-towners, worthy cause" in *Atlanta Business Chronicle* (Vol. 24, No. 14, September 7, 2001, pp. S9) **[24942]**, **[54196]**

"Group Quietly Pushes for New Bridge to Canada" in *Crain's Detroit Business* (Vol. 19, No. 45, November 10, 2003, pp. 1) **[25389]**, **[26241]**, **[41753]**, **[43684]**

"Group Sees Window of Opportunity" in *Pittsburgh Business Times* (Vol. 23, No. 3, August 8, 2003, pp. 1) **[41722]**, **[48738]**

"Group Therapy" in *Forbes* (April 3, 2000, pp. 138) **[30552]**, **[36241]**

"Group thinking" in *Crain's Detroit Business* (Vol. 19, No. 16, April 21, 2003, pp. 16) **[26711]**, **[49969]**

Groupe DGE International Inc. **[9407]**

Groups in Context: Leadership and Participation in Small Groups **[27385]**, **[36242]**, **[45205]**

"Groups Pick Up Push for Women in Tech World" in *Crain's Detroit Business* (Vol. 22, December 4, 2006, No. 49, pp. 13) **[41723]**, **[56251]**

"Groups Push Forward on Mass Transit Proposals" in *Crain's Detroit Business* (Vol. 23, February 5, 2007, No. 6, pp. 1) **[29891]**, **[30340]**, **[39833]**

"Groups Working on Conflict Resolution for Stock Analysts, Investment Bankers" in *Knight-Ridder/Tribune Business News* (July 29, 2001) **[15059]**, **[17053]**, **[27386]**

Grove Area Chamber of Commerce **[64004]**

Grove City Area Chamber of Commerce **[63693]**, **[64450]**

Grove Hill Area Chamber of Commerce **[56862]**

Grove Recreations, Inc. **[18744]**

Grove Street Advisors LLC **[61077]**

"Grow Up: Teach Employees to Lead" in *My Business* (April/May 2003, pp. 44) **[36243]**, **[45206]**

"Grow Your Client BASE" in *Home Office Computing* (Vol. 18, No. 8, August 2000, pp. 54) **[28237]**, **[42625]**, **[47040]**

"Grow Your Market" in *PC Computing* (April 2000, pp. 100) **[47041]**, **[51659]**, **[53308]**

"Grow Your Own Executive Team" in *Journal of Accountancy* (Vol. 199, January 2005, No. 1, pp. 108) **[33110]**, **[34919]**, **[45207]**

"Grow Your Technology" in *Home Office Computing* (Vol. 18, No. 10, October 2000, pp. 52) **[3536]**, **[25861]**, **[33981]**, **[42626]**, **[49058]**

GrowerExpo **[11490]**

"Growing apart: investment Websites keep advancing, even as the market retreats" in *Barron's* (Vol. 82, No. 59, Feb. 24, 2003, pp. T4) **[9992]**, **[14095]**, **[15060]**, **[25862]**, **[33982]**, **[38106]**

"Growing for broke" in *Harvard Business Review* (Vol. 80, No. 9, September 2002, pp. 27) **[15061]**, **[28238]**, **[49970]**

Growing a Business **[53055]**

Growing Business Handbook: Inspirational Advice from Successful Entrepreneurs and Fast-Growing UK Companies **[28239]**, **[36244]**, **[45208]**

"Growing a Business" in *Small Business Opportunities* (Vol. 16, No. 3, May 2004, pp. 80, 84) **[11434]**, **[28240]**, **[36245]**

"Growing Concern" in *Pittsburgh Business Times* (Vol. 23, No. 4, August 15, 2003, pp. 19) **[19748]**, **[28241]**, **[45209]**, **[47042]**

"Growing From the Middle" in *Hispanic Business* (July/August 2004, pp. 20, 22, 24) **[28242]**, **[32462]**, **[48189]**

Growing Gourmet **[7820]**

"Growing Influence" in *Hispanic Business* (January/February 2005, pp. 18, 20) **[39373]**, **[40427]**, **[48190]**, **[48553]**

Growing Local Value: How to Build Business Partnerships That Strengthen Your Community **[36246]**, **[39374]**, **[49971]**, **[54197]**

Growing and Managing a Small Business: An Entrepreneurial Perspective **[28243]**, **[36247]**, **[39375]**, **[45210]**

"A Growing Market for Talk" in *Hispanic Business* (Vol. 24, No. 4, April 2002, pp. 22) **[12886]**, **[20122]**, **[24943]**, **[27387]**, **[28244]**, **[48191]**

"The Growing Number of Female Managers in VC-backed Firms means that Women are seen as Less Risky" in *Inc.* (September 2000, pp. 60) **[45211]**, **[55651]**, **[56252]**

"The Growing Opportunity in Server Consolidation" in *Venture Capital Journal* (Vol. 42, No. 9, September 2002, pp. 36-37) **[6165]**, **[38107]**, **[49059]**, **[53767]**

"Growing Pains" in *Home Business* (Vol. 13, January/February 2006, No. 1, pp. 88, 90-91) **[28245]**, **[42253]**, **[42627]**

"Growing Pains" in *Inc.* (October 2000, pp. 20) **[28246]**, **[36248]**, **[54950]**

"A growing problem" in *Electronic News* (Vol. 48, No. 11, March 11, 2002, pp) **[21235]**, **[37292]**

"Growing Representation?" in *Hispanic Business* (Vol. 24, No. 1/2, January/February 2002, pp. 28, 30) **[28247]**, **[48192]**

Growing Your Business **[28248]**, **[36249]**

Growing Your Business International **[43685]**

Growing Your Business Using QuickBooks 6.0 **[53309]**

Growing Your Company **[29045]**

Growing Your Home-Based Business: A Complete Guide to Proven Sales and Marketing Communications Strategies **[42628]**

"Growth Amid Uncertainty" in *Hispanic Business* (Vol. 23, No. 11, November 2001, pp. 12) **[28249]**, **[48193]**

The Growth Coach, Inc. **[3883]**

"Growth Guru: How to Turn Your Business Into a Hot Commodity" in *Entrepreneur* (Vol. 31, No. 7, July 2003, pp. 27) **[28250]**, **[36250]**, **[45212]**

"Growth of home health products industry brings liability issues" in *Pittsburgh Business Times* (Vol. 22, No. 39, April 11, 2003) **[29279]**, **[46307]**

Growth/Management of Entrepreneur Businesses **[28251]**, **[45213]**

"The Growth of Minority Car Dealerships" in *Minority Business Journal* (Vol. 17, No. 5, September/October 2001, pp. 3, 6-7) **[18052]**, **[28252]**, **[48194]**

Growth Opportunity Connection–Center for Business Innovation **[62095]**

Growth Oriented Women Entrepreneurs and Their Businesses: A Global Research Perspective **[36251]**, **[43686]**, **[56253]**

"Growth Outside the Core" in *Harvard Business Review* (Vol. 81, No. 12, December 2003, pp. 66) **[11266]**, **[28253]**, **[32155]**, **[48739]**

Growth Partnership for Ashtabula County–Small Business Development Center **[63558]**

"Growth in a streamling sector" in *Hispanic Business* (Vol. 22, No. 4, April 2000, pp. 24) **[40035]**, **[53768]**

"Growth Slow But Sure" in *My Business* (April/May 2003, pp. 48) **[28254]**, **[32463]**

"Growth Spurt: Thanks to the Spread of Bluetooth, Now Your Business Can Be As Wireless As You Want It To Be" in *Entrepreneur* (Vol. 32) **[4187]**, **[5006]**, **[6668]**, **[41724]**

"Growth Strategies" in *Inc.* (November 2000, pp. 78) **[2488]**, **[27724]**, **[35492]**, **[46571]**

The Growth Strategy: How to Build a New Business into a Successful Enterprise **[28255]**

"Growth Tales; Key Strategies Used by Young Firms" in *Crain's New York Business* (Vol. 22, December 11, 2006, No. 50, pp. 27) **[28256]**, **[30553]**, **[36252]**, **[46572]**

Growthworks **[66680]**

GRP Partners / Global Retail Partners **[58028]**

Grundy Center Chamber of Commerce and Development **[60144]**

Gruver Chamber of Commerce **[65293]**

Gryphon Ventures **[61078]**

GSC Associates Inc. **[49431]**

GTCR Golder Rauner LLC [59736]
GTE Telephone Operations Headquarters–Library [5230], [25690]
GTM Co. [66005]
Guadalupe Chamber of Commerce and Visitor Center [57531]
Guam Chamber of Commerce [43500], [66643]
Guam Department of Commerce [66858]
"Guaranteed Results" in *Entrepreneur* (Vol. 33, March 2005, No. 3, pp. 87) [51175], [52541]
Guard-A-Kid [5429]
Guard Force Management [19962]
"Guarded About the Hispanic Economy" in *Hispanic Business* (Vol. 24, No. 5, May 2002, pp. 18, 20, 22, 25) [28257], [32464], [48195]
"Guardian Angel" in *Entrepreneur* (Vol. 33, March 2005, No. 3, pp. 58) [39834], [44539], [55652]
"Guardian of the Past" in *Crain's Detroit Business* (Vol. 21, January 3, 2005, No. 1, pp. 19) [27388], [39376]
"Guarding gizmos" in *Atlanta Business Chronicle* (Vol. 24, No. 8, July 27, 2001, pp. 1C) [30341], [39377]
"Guarding your turf: how the small guy can fend off big biz encroachment" in *Black Enterprise* (Vol. 33, No. 3, October 2002, pp. 56) [30872], [31922], [33983], [34931]
"Guards Unionize" in *San Fernando Valley Business Journal* (Vol. 12, January 2007, No. 2, pp. 37) [19963], [55294]
Guardsman Furniturepro [10841]
Guerilla Marketing Newsletter [47788]
"The 'Guerrilla' Approach" in *Hispanic Business* (July/August 2004, pp. 28) [5007], [41725], [48196]
Guerrilla Financing: Alternative Techniques to Finance Any Small Business [48907], [55653]
Guerrilla Marketing, 4th Edition: Easy and Inexpensive Strategies for Making Big Profits from Your Small Business [28258], [47043]
Guerrilla Marketing During Tough Times [648], [32465], [47044]
Guerrilla Marketing Excellence: The Fifty Golden Rules for Small Business Success [47045]
Guerrilla Marketing for the New Millennium [649], [33984], [47046]
Guerrilla Marketing: Put Your Advertising on Steroids [650], [33985], [47047]
Guerrilla Marketing Weapons: 100 Affordable Marketing Methods for Maximizing Profits from Your Small Business [47048]
"Guerrilla Marketing via Wi-Fi" in *Business 2.0* (Vol. 6, July 2005, No. 6, pp. 112) [5008], [49060], [52861]
"Guerrilla Tactic Targets Golfers" in *Inc.* (October 1, 2004) [11267], [47049], [50601]
"Guerrillas in our Midst" in *Crain's Chicago Business* (Vol. 30, January 2007, No. 3, pp. 16) [651], [47050], [50602]
"Guest Article" in *Venture Capital Journal* (February 1, 2006) [40428], [55654]
"Guest Speaker. The Saltshaker Theory" in *Inc.* (November 2006, pp. 69-70) [34920], [42858], [45214]
Guide to ACA-Accredited Camps [4235]
"Guide Advises Would-Be Entrepreneurs" in *Marketing to Women* (Vol. 20, January 2007, No. 1, pp. 8) [2710], [29892], [30554], [36253], [47051], [56254]
Guide to Affirmative Action [32028]
Guide to Business Information on Central and Eastern Europe [27389]
Guide to Business Information on Russia, the NIS, and the Baltic States [27390]
Guide to Business Permitting and Licensing in Wyoming [66639]
Guide to Buying & Selling a Business, Vol. 2 [30680], [52425]
A Guide to College Programs in Hospitality and Tourism [24691]
The Guide to Cooking Schools [4530], [7813]
Guide to Doing Business in All 50 States for A E P & Environmental Consulting Firms [9359]
A Guide to Doing Business with the Department of State [40036]
Guide to Employee Handbooks [42859]

A Guide to Federal Sector Equal Employment Law and Practice [29664]
"A Guide through the Garnishment Jungle" in *Employment Relations Today* (Vol. 27, No. 1, Spring 2000, pp. 117) [29280], [40429]
The Guide to Graduate Environmental Programs [9345]
Guide to Karate-Do [16922]
Guide to the Management of Hazardous Waste: A Handbook for the Businessman and the Concerned Citizens [11932]
Guide to Marketing and Business Resources [47052]
A Guide to Merit Systems Protection Board Law and Practice [29665]
Guide to the Nursing Home Industry [18343]
Guide to Psychological Practice in Geriatric Long-Term Care [18323]
A Guide to Research in Music Education [17594]
The Guide to Screenprinting [22115]
Guide to Selling Your Business [49853], [52426]
A Guide to Site Planning & Landscape Construction [52679]
Guide to Small Business Consulting Engagements [3537], [31160]
Guide to Summer Camps and Summer Schools [4236]
Guide to Technical, Trade, & Business Schools (TTB) [25374], [25521], [25536]
"Guide To Managing Employees: Forget Cash" in *My Business* (November/December 2001, pp. 41) [34921]
A Guide to Travel Writing & Photography [19298]
The Guide to Understanding Financial Statements [38108]
A Guide to Understanding Land Surveys [23763]
"Guiding Light" in *Entrepreneur* (Vol. 33, August 2005, No. 8, pp. 16) [11155], [44235], [46308], [49061], [56561]
"Guiding Light; Feeling a Little Lost at the Helm of Your Business?" in *Entrepreneur* (Vol. 31, No. 8, August 2003, pp. 84) [32884], [35493]
Guild of American Papercutters [7983]
Guild of Book Workers [2829]
Library [2848]
Guild of Book Workers-Membership List [2834], [4166]
Guild of Book Workers Newsletter [2766], [2840], [4172], [19910]
Guild of Book Workers-Supply List [2711], [2835], [4167]
Guild of Prescription Opticians of America-Guild Reference Directory [25647]
Guild Publishing [66590]
Guilderland Chamber of Commerce [62924]
Guilford Chamber of Commerce [58542]
"Guilford Pharmaceuticals gets dose of health news" in *Washington Business Journal* (Vol. 22, No. 3, May 23, 2003, pp. 25) [44054], [50885], [52115]
The Guinness Book of Stamps: Facts and Feats [5824]
Gulf Breeze Area Chamber of Commerce [58850]
Gulf Coast Community College–Small Business Development Center [58706]
Gulf Coast SBDC [61747]
Gulf County Chamber of Commerce [58851]
"Gulf Team With Corpedia on Ethics Course" in *Rough Notes* (Vol. 146, No. 9, September 2003, pp. 44) [13303], [33986], [34922], [37452], [43193], [47053]
"Gulfport, Miss., Business Club Considers Requesting Removal of Rebel Flag" in *Gulfport Sun Herald* (August 20, 2002) [54198]
Gulfport Sun Herald (August 20, 2002); "Gulfport, Miss., Business Club Considers Requesting Removal of Rebel Flag" in [54198]
Gulliver's Doggie Daycare [19103]
Gun Dealers Guide to Wholesalers [11725]
Gun Digest Book of Firearms Assembly-Disassembly, Part V: Shotguns [11726]
Gun & Knife Show Calendar [11733]
Gun List [11734]
The Gun Report [11735]
Gun Safety [11740]
Gunnison County Chamber of Commerce [58380]

Guns & Ammo [1478]
Guns Illustrated [1474]
Gurdon Chamber of Commerce [57175]
"Gurus in the garage" in *Harvard Business Review* (Vol. 78, No. 6, November-December 2000, pp. 71) [31161], [36254], [42254], [55655]
Gustine Chamber of Commerce [57532]
Gutenberg Festival [19923], [25502]
Guthrie Center Chamber of Commerce [60145]
Guthrie Chamber of Commerce [64005]
Guthrie Theater Foundation–Staff Reference Library [7963]
Guts & Borrowed Money: Straight Talk for Starting & Growing Your Small Business [28259]
Guttenberg Civic and Commerce Club [60146]
The Gutter Guys [46545]
Guymon Chamber of Commerce [64006]
Guysborough Historical Society–Archives [11030]
"Guzman to Head CHCC" in *Hispanic Business* (December 2001, pp. 14) [36255], [48197], [56255]
"gWHIZ!: swimming through the alphabet soup of today's wireless standards" in *Entrepreneur* (Vol. 31, No. 6, June 2003, pp. 39) [5009], [6669], [14096], [41726], [49062]
Gwinnett Chamber of Commerce [59117]
Gymboree Play and Music [5430]

H

H & A International [48637]
H2X Canada Hardware & Home Improvement Expo & Conference [11908], [12241], [23684]
Haagen-Dazs [12825]
Haas Wheat & Partners L.P. [50319]
Habersham County Chamber of Commerce [59118]
Habitats and Ecosystems [9360], [11929]
Habits of Wealth, Volume 1: Achieving in the Futuristic Workplace [37035]
Habits of Wealth, Volume 2: Conquering the Leadership Challenge [37036]
Habitual Entrepreneurs [36256]
"Hack Attack:...And Other Threats From the Politically Offended" in *Entrepreneur* (Vol. 31, No. 10, October 2003, pp. 32) [22240], [33987]
"Hack away" in *Entrepreneur* (Vol. 30, No. 3, March) [6166], [22241], [42255], [53769]
"Hacked!" in *Entrepreneur* (Vol. 32, No. 4, April 2004, pp. 38) [14097], [22242], [33988]
"Hacker 'Mudge' Returns to BBN" in *eWeek* (February 2, 2005) [14098], [22243], [30227]
Haflinger Breeders Organization [1170]
Hagerman Valley Chamber of Commerce [59306]
Hagerstown-Washington County Chamber of Commerce [60835]
"The Hague: Laws without Borders" in *Red Herring* (No. 106, October 15, 2001, pp. 25-26) [14099], [29281], [33989], [37144], [40430], [43687], [44055]
Haight Consulting [32115]
Hailey Chamber of Commerce [59307]
Haines Chamber of Commerce [56964]
Haines City Chamber of Commerce [58852]
Hair Cut and Style [11808]
Hair Cuttery [11832]
Hair International/Associated Master Barbers and Beauticians of America [11772]
Haircutting Basics [11813]
Haircutting with Clippers-Basic Techniques [11814]
Hairshaping [11847]
Hakky Instant Shoe Repair [22746]
Hale Center Chamber of Commerce [65294]
Haleyville Chamber of Commerce [56863]
Half Moon Bay - Coastside Chamber of Commerce and Visitors' Bureau [57533]
"Half Pints: Wireless Routers Have the Size Advantage" in *Entrepreneur* (Vol. 33, January 2005, No. 1, pp. 42) [30342], [41727], [49063]
Halftone Effects [19880]
Halifax County Chamber of Commerce [65908]
"Hall of Mirrors" in *Small Business Opportunities* (Vol. 12, No. 3, May 2000, pp. 44) [30483], [35494]
Hall of Names Marketing [23312]
The Hall Partnership, Architects L.L.P. [3257]
Hallador Venture Partners [58029]

Hardball for Women: Winning at the Game of Business [56256]
Hardee County Chamber of Commerce [58854]
Hardee's [21839]
Hardeman County Chamber of Commerce [64923]
"The Harder They Fall" in *Harvard Business Review* (Vol. 81, No. 10, October 2003, pp. 58) [36261], [45221]
Hardin Area Chamber of Commerce and Agriculture [62172]
"Hardin overcomes intown construction challenges" in *Atlanta Business Chronicle* (Vol. 25, December 6, 2002, No. 26, pp. 10C) [1515], [7352], [18546]
Hardin County Chamber of Commerce [63695], [64924]
Hardin-Simmons University
        Rupert and Pauline Richardson Library [1655]
        Smith Music Library [17678], [17819]
"Harding Brews Success at Anheuser-Busch" in *Black Enterprise* (Vol. 37, February 2007, No. 7, pp. 1) [3127], [45222]
Harding & Co. [31366], [33346], [46039], [52000]
"Hardman helped develop thriving tourism industry" in *Atlanta Business Chronicle* (Vol. 25, No. 22, November 8, 2002, pp. 7C) [24692], [24945], [25192]
Hardware Merchandising [11901]
Hardwick Area Chamber of Commerce [65785]
Hardwood Manufacturers Association [16286]
Hardwood Plywood and Veneer Association [16287], [16346]
        Library [16340]
Hardy Stevenson and Associates Ltd. [3722], [6214]
J.H. Hare & Associates Ltd. [26629]
Harford County Chamber of Commerce [60836]
Harian Creative Enterprises [2795], [9053]
Harker Heights Chamber of Commerce [65298]
"Harlem Haven" in *Black Enterprise* (Vol. 36, November 2005, No. 4, pp. 62) [3042], [11328]
Harlem Outreach Center–SBDC [62759]
"Harley's '06 Models Revving Sales" in *Milwaukee Journal Sentinel* (December 20, 2005) [17484], [28263]
"Harley's Angels" in *Success* (Vol. 47, No. 4, September 2000, pp. 66) [55390]
"Harley's Leadership U-Turn" in *Harvard Business Review* (Vol. 78, No. 4, July 2000, pp. 43) [28264], [45223]
"Harley's New Color Schemes Draw Raves" in *Business Journal-Milwaukee* (Vol. 20, No. 51, September 5, 2003, pp. A3) [17485]
Harlingen Area Chamber of Commerce [65299]
Harlingen Hispanic Chamber of Commerce [65300]
Harmon County Chamber of Commerce [64007]
Donald Harmon [31969]
Harmonica Happenings [17789]
Harmony Foundation [9326]
"Harmony and bottom line: hm..." in *The New York Times* (February 9, 2000, pp. G1) [34925], [45224]
Harness Racing Museum & Hall of Fame–Peter D. Haughton Memorial Library [12478]
Harnessing the Power in the Canadian Marketplace (Canada) [46630]
"Harnessing Rhino Power" in *Hispanic Business* (July/August 2002, pp. 73) [6168], [6915], [35500], [47961]
Harney County Chamber of Commerce [64226]
Harold L. Kestenbaum, Esq. [29626]
Harper Chamber of Commerce [60344]
Harper County Genealogical Society–Library [11032]
HarperBusiness [63250]
Harrington College of Design–Design Library [7684], [10849], [13727]
Harris Advertising [3723], [31367], [50781]
Richard M. Harris Associates [31970]
"Harris Beach Will Move Law Offices to Main Street" in *Business First Buffalo* (Vol. 19, No. 47, August 15, 2003, pp. 1) [29283], [29419], [30149], [30211]
Harris County Chamber of Commerce [59120]
Harris & Harris Group, Inc. [63105]

"Harris Teeter sued by black employees" in *Atlanta Business Chronicle* (Vol. 24, No. 14, September 7, 2001, pp. 1A) [29284], [32030], [40431]
Harrisburg Area Chamber of Commerce [57177]
Harrisburg Regional Chamber of Commerce [64452]
Harrison Chamber of Commerce [57178], [61330], [62927]
Harrison County Chamber of Commerce [66279]
Harrison County Research Center [11091]
"Harrison, Maine, Homeland Security Consultant Telecommutes Around the Globe" in *Portland Press Herald* (May 20, 2005) [22246], [31162], [36262]
Harrison Regional Chamber of Commerce [63696]
Harrisonburg-Rockingham Chamber of Commerce [65911]
Harrisonville Area Chamber of Commerce [61972]
Hart County Chamber of Commerce [59121], [60520]
Hart - Silver Lake Mears Chamber of Commerce [61331]
Hartech Inc. [20373]
Hartford Area Chamber of Commerce [65786], [66421]
Hartford City Chamber of Commerce [59940]
Hartford Conservatory–Carolyn B. Taylor Library [13597], [17679]
Hartford Courant (December 19, 2004); "Mobile Gaming Sector Growing, and Middletown, Conn. Firm Wants to be Player" in [1112], [5057], [17324], [23089]
Hartford Despatch International [30196]
"Hartford Expands Small Commercial Offerings" in *Rough Notes* (Vol. 145, No. 6, June 2002, pp. 50) [13307], [28265], [43198]
The Hartford Financial Services Company–Loss Control Library [56685]
Hartington Area Chamber of Commerce [62268]
Hartland Area Chamber of Commerce [66422]
Hartley Chamber of Commerce [60148]
Hartselle Area Chamber of Commerce [56864]
"Hartsfield bracing for choppy '03" in *Atlanta Business Chronicle* (Vol. 25, January 3, 2003, No. 30, pp. 1A) [14103], [28266], [30343]
Hartshorne Chamber of Commerce [64008]
Hartsville - Trousdale County Chamber of Commerce [64925]
Harvard Business (Vol. 78, No. 1, January 2000, pp. 137); "1999 McKinsey Awards" in [31800], [46392], [52923]
Harvard Business Review (Vol. 81, No. 11, November 2003, pp. 64); "3-D Negotiation: Playing the Whole Game" in [29779], [39125], [44861]
Harvard Business Review (Vol. 81, No. 7, July 2003, pp. 12); "A Better Way to Innovate" in [43998], [49813]
Harvard Business Review (Vol. 81, No. 9, September 2003, pp. 30); "A Blogger in Their Midst" in [33595], [37392], [44942], [46722]
Harvard Business Review (Vol. 80, No. 5, May 2002, pp. 31); "A pain in the supply chain" in [44237], [46400], [51760]
Harvard Business Review (Vol. 80, No. 4, April 2002, pp. 24); "A smarter way to sell commodities" in [30958], [31072], [51845]
Harvard Business Review (Vol. 81, No. 2, February 2003, pp. 26); "A consultant's comeuppance" in [3516], [16505], [31128]
Harvard Business Review (Vol. 80, No. 10, October 2002, pp. 94); "A letter to the chief executive" in [36443], [45371]
Harvard Business Review (Vol. 78, No. 1, January 2000, pp. 103); "A Market-Driven Approach to Retaining Talent" in [26850], [30738], [34986]
Harvard Business Review (Vol. 78, No. 1, January 2000, pp. 127); "A Modest Manifesto for Shattering the Glass Ceiling" in [45441], [53860]
Harvard Business Review (Vol. 78, No. 5, September-October 2000, pp. 18); "A stealthier way to raise money" in [35671], [48892], [55436]
Harvard Business Review (Vol. 81, No. 3, March 2003, pp. 29); "A rose by any other name" in [46421], [51335]

Harvard Business Review (Vol. 80, No. 1, January 2002, pp. 81); "A New Game Plan for C Players" in [35002], [42357], [45465]
Harvard Business Review (Vol. 80, No. 9, Sept. 2002, pp. 114); "A better way to deliver bad news" in [34825], [44930]
Harvard Business Review (Vol. 81, No. 8, August 2003, pp. 58); "Abraham Lincoln and the Global Economy" in [32233], [43537]
Harvard Business Review (Vol. 79, No. 11, December 2001, pp. 54); "All in a day's work" in [30502], [34807], [44881]
Harvard Business Review (Vol. 81, No. 10, October 2003, pp. 31); "And Now, a Word From Our Sponsor" in [546], [46680]
Harvard Business Review (Vol. 78, No. 2, March 2000, pp. 55); "Are CIOs Obsolete?" in [44891], [53587]
Harvard Business Review (Vol. 80, No. 2, February 2002, pp. 58); "Are you picking the right leaders?" in [42168], [44892]
Harvard Business Review (Vol. 81, No. 4, April 2003, pp. 18); "Are you the weak link?" in [6158], [22174]
Harvard Business Review (Vol. 81, No. 7, July 2003, pp. 86); "Are You In With the In Crowd?" in [44893]
Harvard Business Review (Vol. 80, No. 11, November 2002, pp. 52); "Arm yourself for the coming battle over social security" in [29101], [40161], [53589]
Harvard Business Review (Vol. 80, No. 2, February 2002, pp. 101); "Avoid the four perils of CRM" in [31642], [44908]
Harvard Business Review (Vol. 78, No. 3, May 2000, pp. 73); "Balancing Act: How to Capture Knowledge Without Killing It" in [44274]
Harvard Business Review (Vol. 81, No. 11, November 2003, pp. 20); "Be Prepared" in [29799], [44276], [44921]
Harvard Business Review (Vol. 80, No. 10, October 2002, pp. 22); "Behave yourself" in [16499], [44924]
Harvard Business Review (Vol. 80, No. 2, February 2002, pp. 62); "Beware the busy manager" in [44932], [54937]
Harvard Business Review (Vol. 81, No. 1, January 2003, pp. 48); "Beyond empowerment: Building a company of citizens" in [35833], [39174], [44933]
Harvard Business Review (Vol. 78, No. 6, November-December 2000, pp. 86); "Beyond the exchange: the future of B2B" in [13847], [30511], [33579], [53604]
Harvard Business Review (Vol. 78, No. 3, May 2000, pp. 28); "Bioigen Unchained" in [33589], [46215]
Harvard Business Review (Vol. 81, No. 1, January 2003, pp. 16); "Black Hawk down at work" in [34830], [35849], [44941]
Harvard Business Review (Vol. 81, No. 3, March 2003, pp. 52); "Bottom feeding for blockbuster businesses" in [27864], [35865], [44953]
Harvard Business Review (Vol. 78, No. 3, May 2000, pp. 157); "Building an Innovation Factory" in [29807], [30516]
Harvard Business Review (Vol. 80, No. 11, November 2002, pp. 22); "Can you trust your law firm?" in [29139], [37400]
Harvard Business Review (Vol. 80, No. 9, Sept. 2002, pp. 24); "Can Loyalty Be Leased?" in [33032], [34843], [44980]
Harvard Business Review (Vol. 78, No. 4, July 2000, pp. 16); "Can You Patent Your Business Model?" in [44012]
Harvard Business Review (Vol. 81, No. 7, July 2003, pp. 36); "Capital Versus Talent: The Battle That's Reshaping Business" in [98], [2881], [23904], [26181]
Harvard Business Review (Vol. 81, No. 7, July 2003, pp. 95); "Causes and Effects" in [39226], [54150]
Harvard Business Review (Vol. 80, No. 5, May 2002, pp. 65); "Change the way you persuade" in [35936], [44990]

Harvard Business Review (Vol. 78, No. 4, July 2000, pp. 75); "Change Without Pain" in **[27941]**, **[29148]**

Harvard Business Review (Vol. 78, No. 2, March 2000, pp. 22); "Checking Out" in **[33667]**, **[51093]**

Harvard Business Review (Vol. 81, No. 2, February 2003, pp. 100); "Clueing in customers." in **[31661]**, **[46813]**, **[50575]**

Harvard Business Review (Vol. 78, No. 1, January 2000, pp. 79); "Co-opting Customer Competence" in **[29826]**, **[31662]**, **[33684]**

Harvard Business Review (Vol. 78, No. 1, January 2000, pp. 91); "Coevolving At Last, a Way to Make Synergies Work" in **[30522]**, **[45010]**

Harvard Business Review (Vol. 81, No. 11, November 2003, pp. 88; "Coming Up Short on Nonfinancial Performance Measurement" in **[27962]**, **[39236]**

Harvard Business Review (Vol. 78, No. 1, January 2000, pp. 139); "Communities of Practice: The Organizational Frontier" in **[44280]**

Harvard Business Review (Vol. 80, No. 1, January 2002, pp. 21); "Consorting with Competitors" in **[27329]**, **[27973]**, **[30826]**, **[39246]**, **[49873]**

Harvard Business Review (Vol. 78, No. 6, November-December 2000, pp. 119); "Contextual marketing" in **[33702]**, **[46837]**

Harvard Business Review (Vol. 78, No. 6, November-December 2000, pp. 169); "Control your inventory in a world of lean retailing" in **[44230]**, **[51113]**

Harvard Business Review (Vol. 78, No. 2, March 2000, pp. 43); "Cost Transparency: The Net's Real Threat to Prices and Brands" in **[31020]**, **[33708]**, **[46250]**, **[51114]**

Harvard Business Review (Vol. 78, No. 3, May 2000, pp. 133); "Cracking the Code of Change" in **[27982]**, **[53667]**

Harvard Business Review (Vol. 80, No. 9, September 2002, pp. 39); "Crucibles of leadership" in **[35992]**, **[45037]**

Harvard Business Review (Vol. 80, No. 4, April 2002, pp. 74); "Customers as Innovators" in **[31696]**, **[46865]**, **[48718]**, **[50853]**

Harvard Business Review (Vol. 78, No. 5, September-October 2000, pp. 155); "Cutting Costs Without Drawing Blood" in **[27108]**, **[29844]**

Harvard Business Review (Vol. 80, No. 11, November 2002, pp. 76) "Dear white boss; What it's really like to be a black manager" in **[45049]**, **[48126]**

Harvard Business Review (Vol. 81, No. 7, July 2003, pp. 56); "Delusions of Success: How Optimism Undermines Executives' Decisions" in **[30529]**, **[45055]**

Harvard Business Review (Vol. 81, No. 12, December 2003, pp. 76); "Developing Your Leadership Pipeline" in **[27347]**, **[36013]**, **[45062]**

Harvard Business Review (Vol. 78, No. 1, January 2000, pp. 54); "Discovering New Value in Intellectual Property" in **[44290]**

Harvard Business Review (Vol. 81, No. 3, March 2003, pp. 18); "Disintegrated marketing" in **[604]**, **[46896]**

Harvard Business Review (Vol. 80, No. 5, May 2002, pp. 94); "Disruptive change: When trying harder is part of the problem" in **[45066]**, **[46898]**

Harvard Business Review (Vol. 81, No. 7, July 2003, pp. 23); "Do Something - He's About to Snap" in **[45069]**

Harvard Business Review (Vol. 80, No. 3, March 2002, pp. 117); "Do you have a well-designed organization?" in **[28045]**, **[29850]**, **[36021]**, **[45070]**

Harvard Business Review (Vol. 80, No. 4, April 2002, pp. 22); "Doing business in a dangerous world" in **[22217]**, **[32358]**, **[39283]**

Harvard Business Review (Vol. 78, No. 3, May 2000, pp. 170); "Don't Hire the Wrong CEO" in **[45077]**

Harvard Business Review (Vol. 78, No. 4, July 2000, pp. 152); "E-Brands: Building an Internet Business at Breakneck Speed" in **[33791]**, **[36038]**

Harvard Business Review (Vol. 78, No. 3, May 2000, pp. 97); "E-Hubs: The New B2B Marketplaces" in **[33805]**, **[37127]**

Harvard Business Review (Vol. 78, No. 4, July 2000, pp. 105); "E-Loyalty" in **[13991]**, **[31707]**, **[33807]**

Harvard Business Review (Vol. 78, No. 3, May 2000, pp. 21); "E-Procurement at Schlumberger" in **[33818]**

Harvard Business Review (Vol. 78, No. 4, July 2000, pp. 152); "Eboys: The First Inside Account of Venture Capitalists at Work" in **[14946]**, **[55586]**

Harvard Business Review (Vol. 81, No. 8, August 2003, pp. 16); "Emerging Threat: Human Rights Claims" in **[29218]**, **[48545]**

Harvard Business Review (Vol. 80, No. 3, March 2002, pp. 51); "Everything I know about business I learned from Monopoly" in **[24807]**, **[39319]**, **[46935]**

Harvard Business Review (Vol. 80, No. 4, April 2002, pp. 66); "Executive women and the myth of having it all" in **[45119]**, **[56209]**

Harvard Business Review (Vol. 81, No. 12, December 2003, pp. 105); "Expensing Stock Options: A Fair-Value Approach" in **[9943]**, **[14969]**, **[26225]**, **[26802]**, **[38043]**

Harvard Business Review (Vol. 78, No. 4, July 2000, pp. 18); "Explaining XML" in **[14026]**, **[33871]**

Harvard Business Review (Vol. 78, No. 3, May 2000, pp. 26); "Exploding the Self-Service Myth" in **[31714]**, **[33872]**

Harvard Business Review (Vol. 81, No. 1, January 2003); "Fair process: Managing in the knowledge economy" in **[34897]**, **[36139]**, **[45131]**

Harvard Business Review (Vol. 81, No. 4, April 2003, pp. 101); "Fear of feedback" in **[30540]**, **[34899]**, **[36147]**, **[45135]**

Harvard Business Review (Vol. 81, No. 3, March 2003, pp. 20); "Filling big shoes at Adobe" in **[36151]**, **[45139]**

Harvard Business Review (Vol. 81, No. 11, November 2003, pp. 18); "Finding Ideas" in **[39332]**, **[42236]**

Harvard Business Review (Vol. 81, No. 3, March 2003, pp. 120); "Finding your innovation sweet spot" in **[46961]**, **[48730]**

Harvard Business Review (Vol. 80, No. 5, May 2002, pp. 20); "Follow the Market Cues" in **[28171]**, **[45155]**

Harvard Business Review (Vol. 80, No. 10, October 2002, pp. 10); "Folly and fortitude" in **[32438]**, **[37444]**

Harvard Business Review (Vol. 81, No. 3, March 2003, pp. 63); "For the Last Time: Stock Options Are an Expense" in **[151]**, **[26240]**, **[26809]**

Harvard Business Review (Vol. 78, July 2000); "Free for All: How Linus and the Free Software Movement Undercut the High-Tech Titans" in **[23007]**, **[53292]**

Harvard Business Review (Vol. 78, No. 2, March 2000, pp. 20); "From Managing Pills to Managing Brands" in **[8785]**, **[46993]**

Harvard Business Review (Vol. 80, No. 9, September 2002, pp. 51); "Fueling tomorrow's growth" in **[28190]**, **[52105]**

Harvard Business Review (Vol. 78, No. 3, May 2000, pp. 107); "Get the Right Mix of Bricks & Clicks" in **[33942]**, **[37141]**

Harvard Business Review (Vol. 79, No. 1, January 2001, pp. 142); "Getting 360 degree feedback right" in **[45182]**

Harvard Business Review (Vol. 80, No. 1, January 2002, pp. 62); "Getting It Right the Second Time" in **[30548]**, **[44301]**, **[45186]**

Harvard Business Review (Vol. 80, No. 1, January 2002, pp. 111); "Getting the truth into workplace surveys" in **[39355]**, **[50881]**

Harvard Business Review (Vol. 81, No. 10, October 2003, pp. 44); "Gilded and Gelded. Hard-Won Lessons From the PR Wars" in **[47017]**, **[50445]**, **[50599]**

Harvard Business Review (Vol. 80, No. 10, October 2002, pp. 20); "Giving mergers a head start" in **[15036]**, **[29264]**, **[49959]**

Harvard Business Review (Vol. 81, No. 4, April 2003, pp. 24); "Global accounting is coming" in **[157]**, **[23953]**, **[26248]**, **[37448]**, **[40411]**

Harvard Business Review (Vol. 78, No. 2, March 2000, pp. 132); "Going Global: Lessons from Late Movers" in **[28213]**, **[52859]**

Harvard Business Review (Vol. 78, No. 6, November-December 2000, pp. 30); "Going, going, gone" in **[33960]**, **[46304]**

Harvard Business Review (Vol. 81, No. 3, March 2003, pp. 10); "GOOD business and good BUSINESS" in **[26819]**, **[36224]**, **[45197]**

Harvard Business Review (Vol. 78, No. 2, March 2000, pp. 16); "Goodbye B-School" in **[35486]**, **[41459]**

Harvard Business Review (Vol. 78, No. 1, January 2000, pp. 15); "Green Reporting" in **[37289]**

Harvard Business Review (Vol. 80, No. 9, September 2002, pp. 27); "Growing for broke" in **[15061]**, **[28238]**, **[49970]**

Harvard Business Review (Vol. 81, No. 12, December 2003, pp. 66); "Growth Outside the Core" in **[11266]**, **[28253]**, **[32155]**, **[48739]**

Harvard Business Review (Vol. 78, No. 6, November-December 2000, pp. 71); "Gurus in the garage" in **[31161]**, **[36254]**, **[42254]**, **[55655]**

Harvard Business Review (Vol. 78, No. 4, July 2000, pp. 43); "Harley's Leadership U-Turn" in **[28264]**, **[45223]**

Harvard Business Review (Vol. 78, No. 5, September-October 2000, pp. 167); "Having trouble with your strategy? Then map it" in **[29896]**, **[30555]**

Harvard Business Review (Vol. 78, No. 3, May 2000, pp. 179); "How to Acquire Customers on the Web" in **[34025]**, **[47094]**

Harvard Business Review (Vol. 80, No. 10, October 2002, pp. 18); "How to build a blockbuster" in **[47098]**, **[48746]**, **[50609]**

Harvard Business Review (Vol. 78, No. 2, March 2000, pp. 107); "How to Fight a Price War" in **[31036]**

Harvard Business Review (Vol. 81, No. 10, October 2003, pp. 16); "How to Fix Knowledge Management" in **[34936]**, **[44312]**, **[45259]**

Harvard Business Review (Vol. 81, No. 1, January 2003, pp. 57); "How to Motivate Your Problem People" in **[34939]**, **[36307]**, **[45262]**

Harvard Business Review (Vol. 81, No. 11, November 2003, pp. 119); "How Much Cash Does Your Company Need?" in **[38125]**, **[44314]**

Harvard Business Review (Vol. 81, No. 9, September 2003, pp. 117); "How to Pitch a Brilliant Idea" in **[671]**, **[44060]**, **[47110]**, **[48748]**

Harvard Business Review (Vol. 81, No. 1, January 2003, pp. 20); "How Presidents Persuade" in **[3544]**, **[16521]**, **[36309]**, **[37457]**, **[45265]**

Harvard Business Review (Vol. 81, No. 7, July 2003, pp. 76); "How the Quest for Efficiency Corroded the Market" in **[10009]**, **[15101]**, **[32499]**, **[38127]**

Harvard Business Review (Vol. 80, No. 1, January 2002, pp. 47); "How Snapple Got Its Juice Back" in **[45267]**, **[47112]**, **[49990]**

Harvard Business Review (Vol. 80, No. 5, May 2002, pp. 18); "How Surveys Influence Customers" in **[31740]**, **[47113]**, **[50891]**

Harvard Business Review (Vol. 81, No. 12, December 2003, pp. 56); "How (Un)Ethical Are You?" in **[36325]**, **[37458]**, **[45274]**

Harvard Business Review (Vol. 81, No. 12, December 2003, pp. 96); "How We're Fixing Up Tyco" in **[24818]**, **[29909]**, **[45275]**

Harvard Business Review (Vol. 80, No. 5, May 2002, pp. 46); "How resilience works" in **[45276]**, **[52893]**

Harvard Business Review (Vol. 81, No. 12, December 2003, pp. 28); "They Bought In. Now They Want to Bail Out" in **[4841]**, **[23230]**, **[31881]**, **[45726]**, **[53513]**

Harvard Business Review (Vol. 80, No. 2, February 2002, pp. 70); "They're not employees, they're people" in **[35114]**, **[42897]**, **[45728]**, **[49747]**

Harvard Business Review (Vol. 80, No. 9, September 2002, pp. 80); "Three questions you need to ask about your brand" in **[30973]**, **[47638]**, **[50693]**

Harvard Business Review (Vol. 81, No. 8, August 2003, pp. 119); "Thriving Locally in the Global Economy" in **[28901]**, **[32746]**

Harvard Business Review (Vol. 81, No. 4, April 2003, pp. 60); "Tipping point leadership" in **[36865]**, **[45745]**

Harvard Business Review (Vol. 78, No. 6, November-December 2000, pp. 37); "Too old to learn?" in **[13499]**, **[33255]**, **[45747]**

Harvard Business Review (Vol. 78, No. 2, March 2000, pp. 96); "Transforming Life, Transforming Business: The Life-Science Revolution" in **[30030]**, **[30619]**, **[54046]**

Harvard Business Review (Vol. 80, No. 1, January 2002, pp. 91); "Turn Customer Input into Innovation" in **[28924]**, **[31889]**, **[47671]**

Harvard Business Review (Vol. 81, No. 8, August 2003, pp. 129); "Turn Public Problems into Private Account" in **[39643]**, **[54269]**

Harvard Business Review (Vol. 80, No. 5, May 2002, pp. 57); "Turning an industry inside out: a conversation with Robert Redford" in **[9744]**

Harvard Business Review (Vol. 78, No. 4, July 2000, pp. 26); "Venture Philanthropist" in **[14566]**, **[36912]**, **[54271]**

Harvard Business Review (Vol. 78, No. 4, July 2000, pp. 137); "Waking Up IBM: How a Gang of Unlikely Rebels Transformed Big Blue" in **[28970]**, **[53024]**

Harvard Business Review (Vol. 81, No. 11, November 2003, pp. 22); "Wanted: Chief Ignorance Officer" in **[44379]**, **[45797]**

Harvard Business Review (Vol. 80, No. 4, April 2002, pp. 49); "Wealth happens" in **[32786]**

Harvard Business Review (Vol. 78, No. 5, September-October 2000, pp. 20); "Web Attack" in **[25997]**, **[34663]**

Harvard Business Review (Vol. 81, No. 7, July 2003, pp. 16); "Web Surveys' Hidden Hazards" in **[34678]**, **[47703]**

Harvard Business Review (Vol. 78, No. 3, May 2000, pp. S4); "Web Wise" in **[34680]**, **[37208]**

Harvard Business Review (Vol. 78, No. 3, May 2000, pp. 24); "Welcome Back, Mom and Pop" in **[51407]**, **[54065]**

Harvard Business Review (Vol. 80, No. 10, October 2002, pp. 32); "Welcome aboard (but don't change a thing)" in **[36928]**, **[45801]**

Harvard Business Review (Vol. 81, No. 3, March 2003, pp. 43); "What Becomes an Icon Most" in **[47711]**, **[50701]**

Harvard Business Review (Vol. 78, No. 4, July 2000, pp. 129); "What Every Executive Needs to Know About Global Warming" in **[37334]**

Harvard Business Review (Vol. 79, No. 1, January 2001, pp. 159); "What is science good for?" in **[45806]**

Harvard Business Review (Vol. 81, No. 8, August 2003, pp. 101); "What is a Global Manager?" in **[43873]**, **[45807]**

Harvard Business Review (Vol. 80, No. 9, Sept. 2002, pp. 106); "What makes great boards great." in **[27532]**, **[45808]**

Harvard Business Review (Vol. 79, No. 11, December 2001, pp. 85); "What Leaders Really Do" in **[30991]**, **[36936]**, **[45811]**

Harvard Business Review (Vol. 81, No. 7, July 2003, pp. 14); "What Makes Global Firms Resilient?" in **[32789]**, **[43875]**

Harvard Business Review (Vol. 81, No. 7, July 2003, pp. 42); "What Really Works" in **[45813]**, **[53027]**

Harvard Business Review (Vol. 79, No. 11, December 2001, pp. 70); "What the Titans Can Teach Us" in **[28991]**, **[30626]**, **[36941]**, **[45815]**, **[47724]**

Harvard Business Review (Vol. 81, No. 7, July 2003, pp. 18); "What Venture Trends Can Tell You" in **[54070]**, **[55938]**

Harvard Business Review (Vol. 78, No. 2, March 2000, pp. 121); "What You Need to Know About Stock Options" in **[26953]**

Harvard Business Review (Vol. 80, No. 10, October 2002, pp. 114); "What's your real cost of capital?" in **[30039]**, **[39669]**

Harvard Business Review (Vol. 81, No. 1, January 2003, pp. 69); "What's Wrong with Executive Compensation" in **[26955]**, **[36944]**, **[45822]**

Harvard Business Review (Vol. 81, No. 9, September 2003, pp. 20); "What's Your Project's Real Price Tag?" in **[297]**, **[26401]**

Harvard Business Review (Vol. 80, No. 11, November 2002, pp. 18); "When company values backfire" in **[28997]**, **[30627]**, **[37531]**

Harvard Business Review (Vol. 78, No. 1, January 2000, pp. 25); "When the Boss Won't Budge" in **[45825]**

Harvard Business Review (Vol. 78, No. 4, July 2000, pp. 17); "When Bots Collide" in **[14611]**, **[34705]**

Harvard Business Review (Vol. 78, No. 2, March 2000, pp. 28); "When Everything Isn't Half Enough" in **[36949]**

Harvard Business Review (Vol. 81, No. 2, February 2003, pp. 20); "When to Put the Brakes on Learning." in **[33277]**, **[35142]**, **[45829]**

Harvard Business Review (Vol. 80, No. 2, February 2002, pp. 45); "When a turnaround stalls" in **[28998]**, **[30992]**

Harvard Business Review (Vol. 81, No. 12, Dec. 2003); "Who Are the Gurus' Gurus? One Thing is Clear: They're Not the Usual Suspects" in **[36959]**, **[45837]**

Harvard Business Review (Vol. 81, No. 2, February 2003, pp. 108); "Who Needs Budgets?" in **[299]**, **[26402]**, **[36961]**, **[45840]**

Harvard Business Review (Vol. 80, No. 9, September 2002, pp. 22); "Who benefits from price promotions?" in **[31079]**, **[47742]**, **[51413]**, **[51908]**

Harvard Business Review (Vol. 78, No. 4, July 2000, pp. 53); "Who Wants to Manage a Millionaire?" in **[14617]**, **[35147]**

Harvard Business Review (Vol. 81, No. 2, February 2003, pp. 58); "Who's bringing you hot ideas, and how are you responding?" in **[36965]**, **[45842]**

Harvard Business Review (Vol. 80, No. 11, November 2002, pp. 96); "Why good accountants do bad audits" in **[301]**, **[3613]**, **[24075]**, **[26404]**

Harvard Business Review (Vol. 81, No. 2, February 2003, pp. 48); "Why Bad Projects Are So Hard to Kill" in **[36966]**, **[45845]**, **[49364]**

Harvard Business Review (Vol. 81, No. 2, February 2003, pp. 14); "Why Do They Keep Leaving" in **[45847]**, **[50262]**, **[54079]**

Harvard Business Review (Vol. 81, No. 9, September 2003, pp. 109); "Why Good Projects Fail Anyway" in **[30049]**, **[53030]**

Harvard Business Review (Vol. 81, No. 9, September 2003, pp. 66); "Why Hard-Nosed Executives Should Care About Management Theory" in **[30050]**, **[45851]**

Harvard Business Review (Vol. 81, No. 3, March 2003, pp. 96); "Why Hierarchies Thrive" in **[36970]**, **[39683]**, **[45852]**

Harvard Business Review (Vol. 80, No. 5, May 2002, pp. 86); "Why business models matter" in **[30051]**, **[30630]**, **[30993]**

Harvard Business Review (Vol. 81, No. 1, January 2003); "Why We Misread Motives" in **[33282]**, **[35151]**, **[36971]**, **[45854]**

Harvard Business Review (Vol. 78, No. 5, September-October 2000, pp. 102); "Will disruptive innovations cure health care?" in **[29011]**, **[49366]**

Harvard Business Review (Vol. 78, No. 3, May 2000, pp. 189); "Will E-Commerce Erode Liberty?" in **[34727]**, **[40847]**

Harvard Business Review (Vol. 78, No. 5, September-October 2000, pp. 26); "Winning with the big box retailers" in **[34732]**, **[50267]**

Harvard Business Review (Vol. 78, No. 6, Nov.-Dec. 2000); "Winning the talent war for women: sometimes it takes a revolution" in **[35154]**, **[54083]**

Harvard Business Review (Vol. 81, No. 3, March 2003, pp. 16); "Your Best M&A Strategy" in **[15622]**, **[32807]**, **[50274]**

The Harvard Entrepreneurs Club Guide to Starting Your Own Business **[29743]**, **[35501]**

Harvard Graphics 2.3 **[6026]**

Harvard Management Communication Letter **[27554]**

Harvard Management Update **[16546]**, **[45888]**

"Harvard Pilgrim Purchases Medical Benefits Company" in *Boston Globe* (March 8, 2005) **[13308]**, **[15069]**, **[26822]**, **[43199]**, **[49974]**

Harvard University
    A. Alfred Taubman Center for State and Local Government **[50400]**
    Belfer Center for Science and International Affairs–Environment and Natural Resources Program **[9466]**
    Botany Libraries **[11521]**
    Harvard Negotiation Project **[17078]**
    Joint Center for Housing Studies **[1398]**
    Motion Analysis Laboratory **[19606]**
    Office for Sponsored Research **[61140]**
    Office of Technology Development **[61141]**
    School of Medicine–The Libraries of the Massachusetts Eye and Ear Infirmary **[17290]**

Harvest Partners, Inc. **[63106]**

Harvey Area Chamber of Commerce **[63523]**

Harvey's Restaurant Limited **[21840]**

Harwich Chamber of Commerce **[60960]**

The Harwood Institute for Public Innovation **[20185]**

"Has the Divide Closed?" in *Hispanic Business* (July/August 2002, pp. 56-57) **[6671]**, **[14104]**, **[33996]**, **[37145]**

"Has eBay Finally Gone Too Far? EBay's Arrogance Paves the Way for the Competition" in *PR Newswire* (January 20, 2005) **[1821]**, **[30873]**

"Has the Free Software Paradox Been Solved?" in *Venture Capital Journal* (September 1, 2005) **[4683]**, **[23026]**, **[53313]**, **[55657]**

"Has Riverboat Gambling Enhanced Kansas City's River Front?" in *Ingram's* (Vol. 29, No. 1, January 2003, pp. 6) **[28267]**, **[32469]**

"Has Your Company Found Its Voice?" in *Fast Company* (August 2001, pp. 40) **[33997]**, **[47057]**, **[50603]**

Haskell Chamber of Commerce **[64009]**, **[65301]**

Haskell County Historical Society **[11033]**

Hastings Area Chamber of Commerce **[62269]**

Hastings Area Chamber of Commerce and Tourism Bureau **[61599]**

Hastings Co. **[20080]**

Hastings Industrial Incubator–SBDC **[61194]**

Hastings-on-Hudson Chamber of Commerce **[62928]**

Hat Life Directory **[11918]**

Hat Zone Franchising Co., LLC **[11921]**

Hatch Group, LLC **[60872]**

Hatch Valley Chamber of Commerce **[62695]**

"Hatching a Better Incubator" in *Red Herring* (No. 87, December 18, 2000, pp. 88-92, 94) **[43054]**, **[55658]**

"Hate Performance Appraisals? Here's a better way to evaluate employees" in *My Business* (November/December 2001, pp. 43) **[34926]**, **[45225]**

Hatfield Chamber of Commerce **[64453]**

Hatfield House Books **[60598]**

The Hathaway Group Inc. **[10761]**, **[20186]**

"Hatred of Spam Puts Crinkle in Faxing" in *Crain's Detroit Business* (Vol. 19, No. 45, November 10, 2003, pp. 9) **[14105]**, **[14675]**, **[32976]**, **[33998]**, **[38758]**, **[40432]**, **[44901]**, **[47058]**

"Hauppauge-Based Robert Martin Advertising Attracts Customers in the Same Way It Helps Them" in *Long Island Business News* (Mar.5,2004) **[654]**, **[47059]**

"Hauppauge-based Spellman High Voltage Electronics Doubles the Size of Its Bohemia Facility" in *Long Island Business News* (Jan.30,2004) **[7730]**, **[28268]**, **[41729]**, **[46311]**

Havana Area Chamber of Commerce **[59534]**

The Havana: Cigar of Connoisseurs **[24630]**

"Have Faith, Not Fear" in *Venture Capital Journal* (Vol. 42, No. 9, September 2002, pp. 31) **[36263]**, **[55659]**

"Have It Your Way" in *Forbes* (Vol. 175, February 14, 2005, No. 3, pp. 78) **[18055]**, **[47060]**, **[48742]**

"Have Kid, Won't Travel" in *Fast Company* (November 2001, pp. 48) **[30344]**, **[31163]**, **[36264]**, **[41730]**

"Have Kudos, Will Travel" in *Hispanic Business* (July/August 2002, pp. 80) **[24693]**, **[25193]**, **[30345]**, **[34927]**

"Have Ricochet, Will Travel" in *PC Magazine* (February 20, 2001, pp. 35) **[7136]**, **[14106]**, **[33999]**, **[49066]**

"Have a Talent for Sales?" in *Black Enterprise* (Vol. 36, November 2005, No. 4, pp. 60) **[7891]**, **[31164]**, **[48201]**, **[51661]**, **[56257]**

Have You Got What It Takes? **[52862]**

"Have Your Job and Leave It, Too" in *Kiplinger's Personal Finance Magazine* (Vol. 54, No. 10, October 2000, pp. 96) **[26823]**

Havelock Chamber of Commerce **[63382]**

"Haven't Filed Your Taxes Yet?" in *My Business* (April/May 2002, pp. 15) **[54586]**

Haviland Collectors International Foundation **[5886]**

"Having a Black Woman In Charge Shows the Construction Field is Changing" in *Sacramento Bee* (November 27, 2005) **[7353]**, **[48554]**

"Having trouble with your strategy? Then map it" in *Harvard Business Review* (Vol. 78, No. 5, September-October 2000, pp. 167) **[29896]**, **[30555]**

Havre Area Chamber of Commerce **[62173]**

Havre De Grace Chamber of Commerce **[60837]**

Havre Small Business Development Center–Bear Paw Development Corporation **[62123]**

Hawaii Business **[59268]**

Hawaii Business, Economic Development, and Tourism Department–Research and Economic Analysis Division **[32853]**

Hawaii Business (Vol. 47, No. 2, August 2001, pp. 208); "The Tax Act of 2001" in **[24051]**, **[39937]**, **[54788]**

Hawaii Chinese History Center **[11092]**

Hawaii Department of Budget and Finance–Information and Communication Services Division **[66859]**

Hawaii Department of Business, Economic Development, and Tourism
Hawaii State Data Center **[66860]**
Strategic Marketing & Support **[59236]**

Hawaii House Labor and Public Employment Committee **[59263]**

Hawaii Industrial Directory **[46312]**

Hawaii Island Chamber of Commerce **[59244]**

Hawaii Island Portuguese Chamber of Commerce **[59245]**

Hawaii Korean Chamber of Commerce **[59246]**

Hawaii Senate Consumer Protection Committee **[59264]**

Hawaii Senate Water and Land Use Planning Committee **[59265]**

Hawaiian Mainland Pacific Apparel Association **[5745]**, **[9654]**

"Hawaii's Growers Wake Up and Sell the Coffee" in *Pacific Business News* (Vol. 41, No. 19, July 18, 2003, pp. 23) **[11329]**, **[26513]**, **[47061]**

Hawarden Area Partnership for Progress **[60149]**

Hawkeye's Home Sitters **[19199]**

Hawkins Area Chamber of Commerce **[65302]**

George Hawkins & Associates **[21721]**

"Hawkins wins support in his suit against Burger King" in *Crain's Detroit Business* (Vol. 16, No. 46, November 13, 2000, pp. 3) **[38822]**

"Hawkins says Pizza Hut sold to parent firm" in *Crain's Detroit Business* (Vol. 19, No. 11, March 17, 2003, pp. 3) **[15070]**, **[19631]**, **[49975]**

Hawkinsville-Pulaski County Chamber of Commerce **[59122]**

Hawley - Lake Wallenpaupack Chamber of Commerce **[64454]**

Hawthorn Suites and Hawthorn Suites, Ltd. **[12713]**

Hawthorne Area Chamber of Commerce **[58855]**

Hawthorne Chamber of Commerce **[57536]**

Hawthorne Management Consulting Inc. **[46040]**

Haxtun Chamber of Commerce **[58381]**

Claude Hayes & Associates **[30648]**, **[46041]**

Richard Haynes & Associates L.L.C. **[35299]**, **[54366]**

Hays Area Chamber of Commerce **[60345]**

Haystack Mountain School of Crafts–Library **[8116]**, **[8261]**, **[18290]**

Haysville Chamber of Commerce **[60346]**

Hayward Area Chamber of Commerce **[66423]**

Hayward Chamber of Commerce **[57537]**

Haywood County Chamber of Commerce **[63383]**

The Hazard Awareness Training Series **[56631]**

Hazard Management Safety Series **[11954]**

Hazard-Perry County Chamber of Commerce **[60521]**

Hazardous Materials and Hazardous Waste Management: A Technical Guide **[11933]**

Hazardous Waste **[11955]**

Hazardous Waste Consultant-Directory of Commercial Hazardous Waste Management Facilities Issue **[11934]**

Hazardous Waste Management **[11935]**

Hazardous Waste Management Facilities Directory: Treatment, Storage, Disposal and Recycling **[11936]**

Hazardous Waste/Superfund Week **[11947]**

"Hazards of 401(k) debt" in *Hispanic Business* (Vol. 22, No. 11, November 2000, pp. 92) **[38111]**

HAZCOM Case Histories **[56632]**

Hazelden Foundation–Library and Information Resources **[54381]**

Hazelden Voice **[54342]**

Hazen Chamber of Commerce **[57179]**, **[63524]**

Hazlehurst-Jeff Davis County Chamber of Commerce **[59123]**

"Hazlet, N.J., Firm Stays Ahead of Real Estate Trends" in *The Record* (November 18, 2005) **[20223]**, **[20889]**, **[36265]**

HazMat Transport News **[11948]**

HazTECH News **[11949]**

"HB Diversity Stock Index" in *Hispanic Business* (December 2006, pp. 10) **[9994]**, **[15071]**, **[38112]**, **[48202]**

H.B. Zachry Company–Central Records and Library **[7685]**

"H.C. Turk" in *Electronic Publishing* (Vol. 26, No. 5, May 2002, pp. 51) **[5987]**, **[8009]**, **[9144]**

HCX Salons **[11833]**

"He Came. He Saw. He Took On the Whole Power-Tool Industry" in *Inc.* (Volume 27, July 2005, No. 7, pp. 86-91) **[11882]**, **[16369]**, **[36266]**, **[44056]**, **[48743]**

"He Has a Sky-High Outlook on His Business" in *Charlotte Observer* (February 4, 2007) **[7354]**, **[36267]**

"He drills for knowledge" in *Fast Company* (September 2001, pp. 186) **[44306]**

"He knows if you've been naughty, but you can still send him e-mail" in *The New York Times* (December 13, 2000, pp. D10, H10) **[28269]**, **[34000]**

"Head of the class" in *Black Enterprise* (Vol. 32, No. 10, May 2002) **[36268]**, **[48203]**

"Head of the Class: Multitasking Made Easy" in *Black Enterprise* (Vol. 35, November 2004, No. 4, pp. 68) **[6672]**, **[49067]**

"Head Games" in *Entrepreneur* (Vol. 30, No. 3, March 2002, pp. 78) **[13309]**, **[43200]**

"Head to Head: How to Deal With Difficult Opponents" in *Entrepreneur* (Vol. 32, October 2004, No. 10, pp. 96) **[27393]**, **[45226]**

"Head Long" in *Entrepreneur* (Vol. 31, No. 9, July 2003, pp. 84) **[655]**, **[47062]**

"A Head Start: Need Some Help Thinking More Clearly Under Pressure" in *Entrepreneur* (Vol. 31, No. 7, July 2003, pp. 73) **[3538]**, **[17895]**, **[31165]**

Headcutters, Inc. **[7934]**, **[11834]**

"Headed for the Web" in *Hispanic Business* (Vol. 22, No. 6, June 2000, pp. 158) **[656]**, **[48204]**

"Heading for new domains" in *Entrepreneur* (Vol. 30, No. 3, March 2002, pp. 40) **[14107]**, **[25863]**, **[34001]**

"Heading Up in a Down Year" in *Hispanic Business* (June 2002, pp. 38, 40, 42) **[32470]**, **[48205]**

Headland Chamber of Commerce **[56865]**

Headland Ventures, LP / Sterling Payot Capital **[58031]**

Headwaters Regional Development Commission **[66901]**

Healdsburg Chamber of Commerce and Visitors Bureau **[57538]**

Healdton Chamber of Commerce **[64010]**

Health Affairs **[41203]**

"Health Alliance Plan offers discounts on alternative therapies, medicines" in *Crain's Detroit Business* (Vol. 16, No. 49, Dec. 4, 2000) **[43201]**

"Health care guide gets the Army's OK" in *Crain's Detroit Business* (Vol. 19, No. 15, April 14, 2003, pp. 12) **[2712]**, **[40038]**

"Health Businesses" in *Entrepreneur* (Vol. 32, No. 1, January 2004, pp. 208) **[38823]**, **[41018]**

Health Capital Group **[58032]**

Health Care Analysis **[41204]**

"Health Care Battle Heats Up" in *San Francisco Business Times* (Vol. 17, No. 50, July 18, 2003, pp. 1) **[13310]**, **[30874]**, **[41019]**, **[43202]**

"Health care, federal contracts high on Bush's small business agenda" in *Crain's Detroit Business* (Vol. 18, No. 22, June 3, 2002, pp.50) **[40039]**, **[40433]**, **[41020]**

"Health Care: California's Next Freakout?" in *Business Week Online* (September 5, 2003) **[41021]**

"Health Care Coverage Reform Introduced in Congress" in *My Business* (April/May 2003, pp. 18) **[13311]**, **[40434]**, **[43203]**

"The Health Care Crisis" in *Business Week* (No. 3689, July 10, 2000, pp. F18) **[43204]**

Health Care Daily Report **[41348]**

Health Care Directory **[12370]**

"Health-care foundation awards its first grants" in *Atlanta Business Chronicle* (Vol. 25, January 10, 2003, No. 31, pp. 7A) **[13312]**, **[26824]**, **[43205]**, **[52117]**

Health Care for the Homeless **[41312]**

Health Care Management REVIEW (HCMR) **[41205]**

The Health Care Manager (HCM) **[17159]**, **[41206]**

Health Care Policy Report **[41349]**

Health Care for Women International **[41207]**

Health Career Agents **[23421]**, **[42796]**

"Health Crisis Inspires Medesto, Calif. Woman to Open Needlework Store" in *Modesto Bee* (January 22, 2003) **[8126]**, **[19548]**, **[35502]**, **[42518]**, **[56050]**

Health Devices Alerts **[12118]**, **[17121]**, **[17283]**

Health Devices CD-ROM **[17144]**, **[17284]**

Health Devices International Sourcebase **[12119]**, **[17145]**, **[17234]**, **[17285]**

Health Devices Sourcebook **[17097]**, **[17257]**

"Health and Female Self-Employment" in *Journal of Small Business Management* (Vol. 41, No. 3, July 2003, pp. 233) **[36269]**, **[56258]**

Health Fitness Dynamics Inc. **[12694]**, **[19492]**

Health and Fitness Expo **[19491]**, **[41321]**, **[55218]**

Health & Fitness for Fun & Profit **[19405]**

Health Groups in Washington **[41022]**

"Health and Happiness" in *My Business* (April/May 2003, pp. 17) **[13313]**, **[43206]**

Health and Home Senior Care **[12421]**

Health Industry Distributors Association **[17088]**, **[18305]**

Health Industry Distributors Association Trade Show and Education Forum **[12405]**

Health Information Referral System **[3724]**, **[12409]**, **[18381]**, **[31368]**, **[41332]**

Health Information Resource Center **[11999]**, **[40937]**

"Health Insurance Crisis: How Did We Get Here?" in *My Business* (April/May 2003, pp. 15) **[13314]**, **[43207]**

"Health Insurance Rates Still Rising as Hospitals Struggle" in *Crain's Detroit Business* (Vol. 19, No. 45, November 10, 2003, pp. 25) **[13315]**, **[39319]**, **[41023]**, **[43208]**

Health Insurance Specialists Inc. **[27031]**, **[43441]**

Health Management Systems Inc. **[7038]**

Health and Medical Care Archive **[12430]**

"Health care needs some strong medicine" in *Crain's Detroit Business* (Vol. 18, No. 19, May 13, 2002, pp. 9) **[13316]**, **[27132]**, **[43209]**

"Health of a Nation" in *Entrepreneur* (Vol. 33, March 2005, No. 3, pp. 70) **[13317]**, **[41731]**, **[43210]**

Health Occupations Center–Learning Resource Center **[1717]**

Health Products Business **[12025]**

Health Professions Career and Education Directory **[12371]**, **[18324]**, **[18439]**

Health Progress **[41208]**

Health Reference Center **[41350]**

Health Research and Educational Trust **[41372]**

Health Research and Educational Trust of New Jersey **[41373]**

Health Resources and Services Administration (HRSA)–Office of Equal Opportunity and Civil Rights **[67520]**

Health & Safety Guidelines for the Laboratory **[17188]**

Health and Safety Science Abstracts **[41209]**, **[56674]**

"Health Savings Accounts Not Getting Much Attention from Garden City-Area Employers" in *Long Island Business News* (January 30, 2004) **[13318]**, **[41024]**, **[43211]**

Health Science **[41210]**

Health and Slim Center **[19509]**

Health Strategy Group Inc. **[3725]**, **[30086]**, **[31369]**, **[31971]**, **[48828]**, **[50498]**, **[51000]**, **[53093]**

"Health service heats ups" in *Hispanic Business* (Vol. 22, No. 6, June 2000, pp. 108) **[48206]**

Health & Wellness InSite **[483]**, **[18392]**, **[18489]**, **[33384]**, **[41351]**, **[44211]**

Healthcare Advertising Review **[41211]**

Healthcare Capital Partners **[59199]**

HealthCare Concepts Inc. **[12410]**, **[18382]**

Healthcare Convention & Exhibitors Association-AIP Alert **[25057]**

Healthcare Corporate Finance News **[13538]**, **[17122]**, **[41212]**

Healthcare Distribution Management Association **[8763]**

HealthCare Distributor **[8820]**

Healthcare Executive **[41213]**

Healthcare Financial Management (Vol. 56, Sept. 2002, pp. 26); "HFMA identifies financial implications of workforce shortages" in **[39382]**, **[42259]**

Healthcare Fraud and Abuse **[41214]**

"Healthcare: Information Systems Help Patients and Providers Breathe Easier" in *Microsoft Executive Circle* (Vol. 1, No. 2, Q2 2001) **[31730]**, **[41732]**

"Healthcare Insurance" in *Black Enterprise* (Vol. 34, No. 2, September 2003, pp. 48) **[13319]**, **[40435]**, **[41025]**, **[42629]**, **[43212]**

"Healthcare Options" in *Small Business Opportunities* (Vol. 12, No. 3, May 2000, pp. 10, 130) **[26721]**, **[43062]**

Healthcare Purchasing News **[41215]**

Healthcare Purchasing News (Vol. 24, No. 8, August 2000, pp. 13); "HHS lawsuit allowed" in **[17896]**, **[40437]**

Healthcare Standards Directory **[12372]**

Healthcare Ventures LLC / Healthcare Investments **[62598]**

HealthChoice **[27032]**

Healthfinder **[41352]**

Healthscope Inc. **[30087]**

"HealthSouth Corp. Feels Fallout from Corporate Scandal" in *Atlanta Journal-Constitution* (April 11, 2003) **[37453]**

Healthy Bites Grill **[12086]**

"Healthy Choice" in *Entrepreneur* (Vol. 28, No. 11, November 2000, pp. 16) **[36270]**

"Healthy Habits" in *My Business* (June/July 2004, pp. 35) **[13320]**, **[43213]**

Healthy Habits Video Series **[12074]**

"The Healthy Home Office" in *Home Office Computing* (Vol. 18, No. 10, October 2000, pp. 58) **[42630]**, **[56563]**

Healthy Inspirations IFP Inc. **[19510]**, **[26052]**

Healthy Massage Series **[17020]**

"Healthy prospects" in *Black Enterprise* (Vol. 32, No. 9, April 2002, pp.) **[19406]**, **[39835]**, **[44542]**, **[48207]**, **[56259]**

"Healthy Prospects" in *Hispanic Business* (October 2004, pp. 128) **[446]**, **[18325]**

"Healthy Transition" in *Success* (Vol. 47, No. 2, June 2000, pp. 52) **[29897]**, **[37677]**

"Healthy, Wealthy and Wise" in *Home Business* (Vol. 13, January/February 2006, No. 1, pp. 40) **[12008]**, **[19407]**, **[36271]**, **[42631]**, **[51662]**

"Healthy ways to handle rivalry in the workplace" in *Atlanta Business Chronicle* (Vol. 25, December 20, 2002, No. 28, pp. 4B) **[34928]**, **[45227]**

Healy & Associates Inc. **[27033]**, **[54367]**

HEAR Center **[12101]**

Hear Now **[12102]**

"Heard the News?" in *Entrepreneur* (Vol. 32, December 2004, No. 12, pp. 58) **[34002]**, **[36272]**

"A Hearing Aid for Cell Phones" in *Business 2.0* (Vol. 6, July 2005, No. 6, pp. 34) **[4579]**, **[4890]**, **[22884]**, **[53147]**

Hearing Aids in Children and Adults **[12115]**

Hearing Industries Association **[12103]**, **[17089]**

Hearing Journal-Hearing Health Industry World Directory Issue **[12107]**

The Hearing Professional **[12111]**

"Hearing Them Out" in *Sales & Marketing Management* **[9209]**, **[9560]**, **[49700]**, **[51663]**

Hearne Chamber of Commerce **[65303]**

Heart of Catskill Association - Catskill Chamber of Commerce **[62929]**

"Heart of Gold: Nonprofits Are Reaping the Rewards of Starting For-Profit Ventures" in *Entrepreneur* (Vol. 32, September 2004, No. 9) **[36273]**, **[53772]**

Heart and Lung **[41216]**

"Heart of the Matter" in *Hispanic Business* (March 2005, pp. 58, 60) **[41026]**, **[45228]**

Heart of the Rockies Chamber of Commerce **[58382]**

Heart of the Valley Chamber of Commerce **[66424]**

"Heartbreak hotels: Westin Charlotte in weak market" in *Atlanta Business Chronicle* (Vol. 25, No. 22, November 8, 2002, pp. 21C) **[12561]**, **[22510]**, **[24946]**, **[25194]**

Hearth & Home-Buyers' Guide **[1020]**

"Heartland completes $2B purchase of Masco Tech" in *Crain's Detroit Business* (Vol. 16, No. 49, December 4, 2000, pp. 5) **[15072]**, **[49976]**

Heartland Capital Fund, Ltd. **[62310]**

Heartland Ham Co. **[23564]**

Heartland Institute **[9440]**, **[41374]**

Heartlines **[10963]**

Heather's Teddy Bear Organization **[5805]**, **[24796]**

Heating/Piping/Air Conditioning Engineering (HPAC) **[1037]**

Heating, Plumbing, Air Conditioning Buyers' Guide **[1038]**

Heating, Refrigeration and Air Conditioning Institute of Canada **[998]**

Heatset Web Offset Directory **[19864]**

Heavener Chamber of Commerce **[64011]**

Heavenly Gold Card **[10769]**

Heaven's Best Carpet & Upholstery Cleaning **[25556]**

Heavy Duty Representatives Profile Directory **[25390]**

Heavy Duty Trucking **[25434]**

Heavy Duty Trucking-Council of Fleet Specialists Equipment Buyer's Guide & Services Directory **[25391]**

Heavy Equipment Guide **[7553]**, **[21366]**

"Heavy Hoop Dreams: Jackson Women, Partner Market New Fitness Twist" in *Business Journal-Milwaukee* (Vol. 20, No. 42, July 4, 2003) **[19408]**, **[56260]**

Heber - Overgaard Chamber of Commerce **[57043]**

Heber Springs Area Chamber of Commerce **[57180]**

Heber Valley Chamber of Commerce and Visitor Center **[65713]**

Hebron Chamber of Commerce **[62270]**

Hebron State Fish Hatchery **[10486]**

HEC Montreal–Group for Women, Management and Organizations **[56547]**

"Hedge Fund Investing: Current Advice for Financial Advisers and Planners" in *Journal of Accountancy* (Vol. 199, February 2005, No. 2) **[161]**, **[2911]**, **[9995]**, **[15073]**, **[23957]**, **[27133]**

"Hedge Funds Beat S&P 500 Index's Return in January 2004" in *Long Island Business News* (February 20, 2004) **[9996]**, **[15074]**, **[32471]**

"Hedging Its Bets" in *Hispanic Business* (October 2003, pp. 44, 46, 48) **[9997]**, **[15075]**, **[38113]**, **[48208]**

Heel Quik! & Heel/Sew Quik! **[22747]**, **[23818]**

Heidelberg Graphics **[2796]**, **[18266]**, **[18970]**

Heights Regional Chamber of Commerce **[63697]**

"Heir Raising" in *Entrepreneur* (Vol. 33, February 2005, No. 2, pp. 82) **[22614]**, **[29898]**, **[37678]**, **[38824]**

Helen Hecker's Hotline: Marketing Strategies for Publishers & Entrepreneurs **[2767]**, **[25584]**, **[47789]**

Helena Area Chamber of Commerce **[62174]**

Helendale Chamber of Commerce **[57539]**

HELI-EXPO - Helicopter Association International Annual Meeting and Industry Exposition **[970]**

Helicopter Association International **[939]**

Hellenic-American Chamber of Commerce **[43501]**

"Heller Family Pays $4.1M for Warehouse" in *Journal Record (Oklahoma City, OK)* (February 6, 2007) **[15076]**, **[20224]**, **[28270]**, **[38825]**

Hellgate Press 64316

"Hello, please give me $9 million" in *WorkingWoman* (Vol. 25, No. 7, August 2000, pp. 72) **[55391]**, **[56051]**

"Hello, can we take photos of your home office today?" in *Business First Columbus* (Vol. 18, No. 26, February 15, 2002, pp. 48) **[42632]**, **[49505]**

Help Desk Institute **[31624]**

"Help! I Need a Job" in *Crain's New York Business* (Vol. 23, January 8, 2007, No. 2, pp. 23) **[27134]**, **[39380]**, **[42256]**

"Help! My brain's being eaten by a zillion dot-com ads!" in *The New York Times* (March 27, 2000, pp. D18, H18) **[657]**, **[34003]**, **[47063]**

"Help me out, here" in *Entrepreneur* (Vol. 30, No. 10, October 2002, pp. 40) **[36274]**, **[56261]**

Help-U-Sell Real Estate **[20749]**

"Help Wanted" in *Entrepreneur.com* (Vol. 34, February 2006, No. 2, pp. 80) **[30875]**, **[42257]**, **[43690]**, **[45229]**, **[49701]**

"Help Wanted: Net Profits: Want to Hand a Project to a Freelancer But Don't Know Where to Start?" in *Entrepreneur* (Vol. 31, Sept.2003) **[14108]**, **[49702]**

"Help Wanted" in *Small Business Opportunities* (Vol. 12, No. 5, September 2000, pp. 10, 130) **[42860]**, **[49703]**

Help Your Child Succeed in School **[5386]**

"Help for Your Small Business: Office 2000's Small Business Tools can help you manage and run a small business more effectively"in *PCMagazine* **[49068]**, **[53314]**

"Helping Doctors Go Digital" in *Business 2.0* (Vol. 6, July 2005, No. 6, pp. 54-55) **[658]**, **[41027]**, **[41733]**, **[47064]**

"Helping the Economy, One Snip at a Time" in *New York Times* (November 2, 2003, pp. 1) **[11791]**, **[39836]**, **[44543]**, **[48908]**

"Helping Hand" in *Crain's New York Business* (Vol. 23, January 15, 2007, No. 3, pp. 24) **[659]**, **[20522]**, **[20890]**, **[47065]**, **[50604]**, **[52680]**

"Helping Hands Overseas" in *Hispanic Business* (November 2003, pp. 52, 54) **[12976]**, **[39837]**, **[43691]**

"Helping HBO Discover Hispanics" in *Hispanic Business* (Vol. 23, No. 5, May 2001, pp. 16) **[4107]**, **[47066]**, **[54200]**

"Helping each other - one woman at a time" in *Women in Business* (Vol. 53, No. 7, January-February 2002, pp. 9) **[45230]**, **[56262]**

"Helping Victims Unravel Identity Theft" in *Business Journal-Portland* (Vol. 20, No. 29, September 19, 2003, pp. 1) **[22138]**, **[29285]**, **[29981]**, **[31506]**, **[32550]**, **[33111]**

"Helping You Realize Your Potential...on eBay" in *Journal Record (Oklahoma City, OK)* (October 2003) **[1822]**, **[34004]**

Helping Your Child Succeed in School **[33317]**

"HelpStar" in *Sales & Marketing Management* (Vol. 157, February 2005, No. 2, pp. 22) **[31731]**, **[51664]**, **[52542]**

Arthur Helt, Jr. **[46538]**

Hemet San Jacinto Valley Chamber of Commerce **[57540]**

Hemmings Motor News **[18180]**

Hemmler Camayd Architects **[1556]**

Hemophilia Ontario News **[41217]**

Hempstead Chamber of Commerce **[62930]**

Hempstead Outreach Center–SBDC **[62760]**

Henderson Area Chamber of Commerce **[65304]**

Henderson Chamber of Commerce **[62352]**

Henderson County Chamber of Commerce **[64926]**

Henderson - Henderson County Chamber of Commerce **[60522]**

"Henderson, Nev., Boot Camp Teaches How to Combat Hackers" in *Las Vegas Review-Journal* (December 21, 2004) **[14109]**, **[22247]**, **[36275]**

Henderson Nevada SBDC **[62325]**

Henderson State University–Small Business Development Center **[57116]**

Henderson-Vance County Chamber of Commerce **[63384]**

Hendersonville Area Chamber of Commerce **[64927]**

"Hennessey VC company looks for small business" in *Crain's Detroit Business* (Vol. 18, No. 23, June 1) **[16519]**, **[44544]**, **[55660]**

Henrietta - Clay County Chamber of Commerce **[65305]**

Henry Area Chamber of Commerce **[59535]**

Henry & Co. **[58971]**, **[59035]**

Henry County Chamber of Commerce **[59124]**, **[60523]**

"Henry Schein Expands Office Space in Melville" in *Long Island Business News* (February 27, 2004) **[8786]**, **[28271]**, **[41028]**

Henryetta Chamber of Commerce **[64012]**

Henryetta Daily Free-Lance **[18955]**

Edward M. Hepner & Associates **[3726]**, **[3971]**, **[42494]**, **[42970]**

Heppner Chamber of Commerce **[64227]**

"Her Line of Credit Was in Default. Her Partnership With Her Mom Was Faltering" in *Inc.* (Volume 27, December 2005, No. 12, pp. 59-60) **[31555]**, **[37679]**, **[38114]**

Herb Growing and Marketing Network **[12136]**

Herb, Health, Vitamin & Natural Food Catalogs: An International Directory **[12141]**

Herb Research Foundation **[12137]**, **[12170]**

Herb Society of America **[12138]**

Herb Society of America-Membership Directory and By-laws **[12142]**

Herbal Businesses - A Report **[12143]**

Herbal Green Pages **[12144]**

"Herbal Remedies: Couple Looks to Make Bad Hair Days a Thing of the Past" in *Black Enterprise* (Vol. 34, No. 7, February 2004, pp. 48) **[2394]**, **[11704]**, **[11792]**, **[12145]**, **[12583]**, **[37680]**, **[39030]**

The Herbalist **[12146]**

Herbalists Without Borders **[8764]**

Herbert Young Securities, Inc. **[63107]**

Herbs **[12156]**

Herbs for Sale: Growing and Marketing Herbs, Herbal Products and Herbal Knowledge **[12147]**

Hercules Chamber of Commerce **[57541]**

"Here Comes the Sun" in *Entrepreneur* (Vol. 32, December 2004, No. 12, pp. 16) **[15846]**, **[30346]**, **[36276]**, **[49069]**

"Here Comes Trouble: Avoid Independent Contractor Snags" in *Entrepreneur* (Vol. 33, February 2005, No. 2, pp. 50) **[23958]**, **[49704]**, **[54587]**

"Here to Stay: When You're Looking for New Hires, Temps May Not be as Temporary as You Might Think" in *Entrepreneur* (Vol. 32, July 2004) **[9210]**, **[24527]**, **[42258]**, **[53773]**

"Here's to 5 Years of DOFE" in *Black Enterprise* (Vol. 35, January 2005, No. 6, pp. 61) **[15077]**, **[38115]**

"Here's How To Purchase Used Goods Wisely" in *My Business* (October/November 2003, pp. 14) **[49506]**

"Here's what I'm thinking: you'll get your best deal if prospects see things your way" in *Entrepreneur* (Vol. 30, No. 10, Oct. 2002) **[27394]**, **[36277]**, **[45231]**

"Here's the keys: looking for a new business idea?" in *Entrepreneur* (Vol. 30, No. 10, October 2002, pp. 116) **[17947]**, **[35503]**

"Here's a Late Resolution, But One to Be Taken Seriously" in *St. Louis Post-Dispatch* (January 9, 2005) **[27395]**, **[34929]**, **[39381]**, **[45232]**

Here's the Scoop **[12827]**

"Here's the Scoop: Five Sweet Advantages to Owning a Franchise" in *My Business* (October/November 2003, pp. 48) **[12779]**, **[38826]**

"Here's a tip" in *Entrepreneur* (Vol. 30, No. 10, October 2002, pp. 58) **[21529]**, **[54588]**

"Here's What You Can Do" in *Crain's Chicago Business* (Vol. 30, January 2007, No. 1, pp. 15) **[7355]**, **[9361]**, **[20891]**, **[31166]**, **[37293]**

Heritage Commission Corporation–Library **[11034]**

Heritage Foundation–Asian Studies Center **[13045]**

"Heritage Networks Wins Showdown" in *Black Enterprise* (Vol. 34, No. 3, October 2003, pp. 19) **[24414]**, **[49977]**

"A heritage of success" in *Hispanic Business* (Vol. 22, No. 3, March 2000, pp. 18) **[44307]**, **[45233]**, **[48209]**

Heritage Quest Magazine **[10964]**

Heritage Rose Foundation **[10552]**

HeritageQuest–Library **[11035]**

Herkimer County Chamber of Commerce **[62931]**

Herkimer County Community College **[63223]**

"Herman J. Russell" in *Black Enterprise* (Vol. 36, December 2005, No. 5, pp. 28) **[7356]**, **[36278]**

"Herman J. Russell Passes Torch" in *Black Enterprise* (Vol. 34, No. 6, January 2004, pp. 19) **[7357]**, **[37681]**, **[48210]**

Hermann Area Chamber of Commerce **[61973]**

Hermantown Chamber of Commerce **[61600]**

Hermosa Beach Chamber of Commerce and Visitors Bureau **[57542]**

Hernando Area Chamber of Commerce **[61798]**

Herndon Dulles Chamber of Commerce **[65912]**

"Heroes Of Small Business" in *Fortune* (Vol. 142, No. 11, November 13, 2000, pp. F348B+) **[28272]**, **[36279]**

Herpers Gowling L.L.P. **[29049]**, **[38540]**

Herrin Chamber of Commerce **[59536]**

Herscher Chamber of Commerce **[59537]**

David Herson Associates **[31972]**

"He's Boss of the Blues; Phillip Pope Stays a Fiscally Prudent Course" in *Birmingham Business Journal* (Vol. 20, October 3, 2003) **[13321]**, **[41029]**, **[43214]**, **[45234]**

"He's Giving It Away!" in *Entrepreneur* (Vol. 28, No. 9, September 2000, pp. 228) **[14110]**, **[37146]**

"He's Grrrreat!" in *Hispanic Business* (January/February 2004, pp. 26, 28) **[11625]**, **[45235]**

"He's Still Standing" in *Black Enterprise* (Vol. 34, No. 2, September 2003, pp. 43) **[4684]**, **[6169]**, **[6673]**, **[23027]**, **[36280]**, **[44545]**, **[53315]**

Hesser College **[62445]**

Hesston Community Chamber of Commerce **[60347]**

Hettinger Area Chamber of Commerce **[63525]**

Hewitt Architects **[18575]**

Hewitt Associates L.L.C. **[27034]**

Hewitt Development Enterprises **[3727]**, **[16616]**, **[30088]**, **[31370]**, **[38541]**, **[46042]**, **[46539]**, **[48829]**, **[53094]**

Hewlett-Packard Company
Legal/Tax Library **[29697]**
Roseville Research Library **[7019]**

Hewlett Packard / Compaq Computer Corporation **[58033]**

"Hewlett-Packard leading the assault on e-waste" in *Computing Canada* (September 13, 2002, pp. 22) **[6674]**, **[21236]**, **[41734]**

"Hewlett-Packard Was Far From First To Try 'PreTexting'" in *Wall Street Journal* (Vol. 248, December 2006, No. 149, pp. A1) **[30228]**, **[37454]**, **[40436]**, **[51665]**

"Hey, you can't do that!" in *BlackEnterprise* (Vol. 31, No. 7, February 2001, pp. 57) **[29286]**, **[44308]**, **[48211]**

"Hey, entrepreneurs! What's in your briefcase?" in *Entrepreneur* (Vol. 30, No. 3, March 2002, pp. 22) **[36281]**

"Hey, Get a Clue!" in *Entrepreneur* (Vol. 32, No. 1, January 2004, pp. 112) **[38827]**, **[47067]**

"Hey, Got a Qpass Rookie Card?" in *Fast Company* (November 2001, pp. 44) **[47068]**, **[50605]**

"Hey, Listen Up!" in *Entrepreneur* (Vol. 31, No. 9, July 2003, pp. 124) **[28273]**, **[36282]**

The Hezner Corp. **[18576]**

"HFMA identifies financial implications of workforce shortages" in *Healthcare Financial Management* (Vol. 56, Sept. 2002, pp. 26) **[39382]**, **[42259]**

HFN (January 26, 2004, pp. 22); "Online Sites are Registering with Couples" in **[3189]**, **[12202]**, **[18657]**, **[34302]**, **[51282]**

HFN (January 26, 2004) "The Soft Sell; Few Soft-Goods Vendors Have Developed Formal Programs to Tap Into the Bridal Market" in **[3197]**, **[12208]**, **[51363]**

HFN The Weekly Newspaper for the Home Furnishing Network (Jul. 14, 2003); "Mohawk to Introduce Retail Kiosk" in **[12196]**, **[12299]**, **[15928]**

HFS Capital, LLC **[65975]**

"HHS lawsuit allowed" in *Healthcare Purchasing News* (Vol. 24, No. 8, August 2000, pp. 13) **[17896]**, **[40437]**

Hialeah Chamber of Commerce and Industry **[58856]**

Hiawatha Chamber of Commerce and Visitors Bureau **[60348]**

Hibbing Area Chamber of Commerce **[61601]**

Hibbing Community College **[61725]**
Small Business Development Center **[61521]**

Hibel Studio Inc. **[59019]**

"Hibernia Southcoast Capital Corp." in *Black Enterprise* (Vol. 33, No. 6, January 2003, pp. 47) **[9998]**, **[15078]**, **[45236]**

Hickey & Hill Inc. **[3728]**, **[16617]**, **[31371]**, **[38542]**, **[46043]**

Hickman Chamber of Commerce **[60524]**

Hickman County Chamber of Commerce **[64928]**

Hickory Nut Gorge Chamber of Commerce **[63385]**

"Hickory Unemployment Stays Steady" in *Charlotte Observer* (February 2, 2007) **[42260]**, **[42861]**

Hickory Venture Capital Corp. **[56910]**

"Hicksville-Based KeySpan Trains Managers to Take Over Blue-Collar/Clerical Jobs..." in *Long Island Business News* (Feb. 20, 2004) **[45237]**, **[55295]**

Hicksville Chamber of Commerce **[62932]**

Hidalgo Chamber of Commerce **[65306]**

"Hidden Assets" in *Hispanic Business* (June 2002, pp. 68) **[47069]**, **[51666]**

"The hidden challenge of cross-border negotiations" in *Harvard Business Review* (Vol. 80, No. 3, March 2002, pp. 76) **[43692]**, **[48555]**

"The Hidden Dragon" in *Harvard Business Review* (Vol. 81, No. 10, October 2003, pp. 92) **[30876]**, **[43693]**

"Hidden Expenses" in *Forbes* (Vol. 175, January 31, 2005, No. 2, pp. 108) **[9999]**, **[15079]**, **[38116]**

"A Hidden Gem? Quebec Looks To Flex Muscle" in *Venture Capital Journal* (Vol. 42, No. 5, May 2002, pp. 44-45) **[28274]**, **[41735]**, **[43694]**, **[52118]**, **[55661]**

"Hidden messages" in *Black Enterprise* (Vol. 32, No. 7, February 2002, pp. 56) **[4685]**, **[6473]**, **[22248]**, **[23028]**, **[53316]**

"Hidden Net Treasures" in *Inc.* (November 15, 2000, pp. 110) **[14111]**

"Hidden treasure" in *Entrepreneur* (Vol. 30, No. 2, February 2002, pp. 56) **[32472]**, **[44546]**, **[48909]**, **[55662]**

Hidden Treasures: A Collector's Guide to Antique and Vintage Jewelry of the 19th and 20th Centuries **[1351]**

"The Hidden Value of Slow Sellers" in *Inc.* (October 2005, pp. 36) **[11626]**, **[30877]**, **[34005]**, **[51179]**, **[51667]**

"Hide and Click: Optio S4 is Small but Powerful" in *Black Enterprise* (Vol. 34, No. 7, February 2004, pp. 54) **[4188]**, **[49070]**

Hideaways Newsletter **[24757]**, **[25293]**

Higginsville Chamber of Commerce **[61974]**

"High-Adventure Past, High-Speed Future" in *Success* (Vol. 47, No. 4, September 2000, pp. 44) **[13755]**, **[35504]**

"The high cost of lost trust." in *Harvard Business Review* (Vol. 80, No. 9, September 2002, pp. 18) **[34930]**, **[45238]**

"The High Cost of Penny-Ante Scams" in *Business Week Online* (September 25, 2003) **[30229]**

"High Court Hears Case Pitting Property Rights Against Redevelopment" in *Chicago Tribune* (February 23, 2005) **[7358]**, **[29287]**

"High-Definition TV Coming Slowly into View, Officials at Broadcasters Expo Say" in *Las Vegas Review-Journal* (April 11, 2003) **[24415]**

High Desert Hispanic Chamber of Commerce **[57543]**

High Desert Ventures, Inc. **[62721]**

"High designs: the architect's career is taking flight" in *Black Enterprise* (Vol. 33, No. 3, October 2002, pp. 74) **[1516]**, **[1519]**, **[3433]**, **[3539]**, **[34386]**, **[36283]**, **[48212]**, **[48862]**

"High and Dry? A New Federal Contract Program May Not Be an Oasis After All" in *Entrepreneur* (Vol. 32, No. 4, April 2004, pp. 20) **[22249]**, **[40040]**, **[53774]**

"High-end home sales falter in North Fulton" in *Atlanta Business Chronicle* (Vol. 25, December 6, 2002, No. 26, pp. 3A) **[7359]**, **[20523]**, **[20892]**, **[28275]**

"A High-Flying Time: Ronald Mays Zips Through the Air with Jets of His Own" in *Black Enterprise* (Vol. 34, No. 2, September 2003) **[950]**, **[36284]**, **[52543]**

"High Hopes: Ralph Mitchell's Picks Have Growth Potential" in *Black Enterprise* (Vol. 37, February 2007, No. 7, pp. 42) **[7360]**, **[11883]**, **[15080]**, **[28276]**, **[38117]**

High-Impact Communication Skills for Women **[27251]**

High Income Consulting: How to Build & Market Your Professional Practice **[3540]**, **[31167]**

"High On Energy, Wary of Inflation" in *Business Week Online* (February 8, 2005) **[10000]**, **[15081]**, **[38118]**

High Peaks Venture Partners, LLC / Berkshires Capital Invest **[61081]**

High Performance Business Plan (Canada) **[27252]**

High Performance Business Writing (Canada) **[27253]**

High Performance Hiring **[42261]**

High Performance Selling **[51668]**

High Plains Technology Center **[64142]**

High Point Chamber of Commerce **[63386]**

High Probability Selling **[52001]**

"High Profit in Play" in *Small Business Opportunities* (Vol. 16, No. 1, January 2004, pp. 62, 64) **[24816]**, **[28277]**, **[32156]**, **[37682]**, **[46313]**

"High-Quality Relationships Succeed Where Incentives Fall Short" in *Incentive* (Vol. 174, No. 9, September 2000, pp. 76) **[31168]**, **[45239]**, **[47070]**

"High resolution" in *Entrepreneur* (Vol. 30, No. 2, February 2002, pp. 35) **[3541]**, **[27396]**, **[29288]**, **[34006]**

"A High ROI Weapon" in *Ingram's* (Vol. 28, No. 5, May 2002, pp. 29) **[33112]**, **[51669]**

"High-Speed Web Access" in *Black Enterprise* (Vol. 35, February 2005, No. 7, pp. 162) **[6675]**, **[14112]**, **[34007]**, **[49071]**

High Springs Chamber of Commerce **[58857]**

High Street Capital **[59737]**

"A high-tech domino effect: as dot-coms go, so go the e-commerce consultants" in *The New York Times* (December 16, 2000, pp. B1, C1) **[14113]**, **[28278]**, **[31169]**, **[34008]**, **[41736]**

High-Tech Enterprise Solutions Inc. **[49432]**

High-Tech Entrepreneurship: Managing Innovation in a World of Uncertainty **[36285]**, **[41737]**

High Tech, High Hope: Turning Your vision of Technology into Business Success **[41738]**

"High Tech, High Sales" in *Small Business Opportunities* (Vol. 13, No. 5, September 2001, pp. 76, 78) **[4686]**, **[41461]**, **[47071]**

"High-tech, low-tech methods can help cut costs for training" in *Crain's Detroit Business* (Vol. 19, No. 17, April 28, 2003, pp. 12) **[33113]**, **[41739]**

The High Tech Marketing Machine: Applying the Power of Coputers to Out-Smart the Competition **[47072]**

High-Tech Materials Alert **[42134]**

The High-Tech News **[6423]**, **[24346]**

High Tech Start Up **[41462]**

"High-Tech Trade Shows" in *Sales and Marketing.com* (Vol. 147, No. 2, February 2004, pp. 12) **[24947]**, **[41740]**, **[47073]**

"High-Tech Trash" in *Kiplinger's Personal Finance Magazine* (Vol. 55, No. 1, January, 2001, pp. 98) **[54201]**, **[54589]**

High Technology Careers Magazine **[4416]**, **[23407]**

High Technology Market Place Directory **[41741]**

"High Tech's Unwavering Champion" in *Hispanic Business* (March 2002, pp. 24-26) **[28279]**, **[41742]**

High Touch - High Tech **[15737]**

High Trust Selling: Make More Money, in Less Time, with Less Stress **[27397]**, **[51670]**

High Volume Printing **[2841]**, **[18956]**, **[19911]**

"High-Wired Competition" in *Inc.* (November 15, 2000, pp. 26) **[30878]**, **[41743]**

High Yield Report **[15646]**

Highbar Ventures **[58034]**

"Higher Gas Prices Lead to More Hybrid Car Sales in Portland, Maine, Area" in *Portland Press Herald* (September 13, 2005) **[18056]**, **[37294]**

"Higher Revenue Boosts Call for Tax Cut" in *Boston Globe* (February 2, 2005) **[28280]**, **[40438]**, **[54590]**

Highland Area Chamber of Commerce **[57544]**

Highland Capital Partners **[61082]**

Highland Chamber of Commerce **[59538]**, **[59941]**

Highland County Chamber of Commerce **[63698]**, **[65913]**

"Highland Park, Budco are happy together" in *Crain's Detroit Business* (Vol. 19, No. 6, Feb. 10, 2003, pp. 16) **[16814]**, **[47074]**, **[50606]**

Highland Park Chamber of Commerce **[59539]**

Highlands Area Chamber of Commerce **[63387]**

"HighRankings.com: www.highrankings.com" in *Entrepreneur* (Vol. 31, No. 12, December 2003, pp. 8) **[14114]**, **[25864]**, **[34009]**

HighTech Weight Loss **[26053]**

hightechbiz.com **[3729]**, **[16618]**, **[31372]**, **[46044]**, **[47868]**, **[50499]**

"Highway Robbery? You Can Make Renting a Car Easier on the Company Budget" in *Entrepreneur* (Vol. 31, No. 10, October 2003, pp. 26) **[2077]**, **[27135]**

Highway Safety Directions **[8728]**

Highway Vehicles Safety Database **[2106]**, **[18209]**

Hilbren Consulting Services Inc. **[17463]**

Guy C. Hill, G H Associates **[38543]**

Hill International, Inc.–Library **[7686]**

Hilliard Area Chamber of Commerce **[63699]**

Hillier Architecture **[49613]**

Hillman Area Chamber of Commerce **[61332]**

Hills Chamber of Commerce **[59540]**

Hills Consulting Group Inc. **[3730]**, **[31373]**, **[31973]**, **[33347]**, **[47869]**, **[48830]**, **[51001]**

Hillsboro Area Chamber of Commerce **[59541]**

Hillsboro Chamber of Commerce **[60349]**, **[64228]**, **[65307]**

Hillsborough Chamber of Commerce **[62422]**

Hillsborough/Orange County Chamber of Commerce **[63388]**

Hillsdale County Chamber of Commerce **[61333]**

Hillside Chamber of Commerce **[62516]**

Hillwood Museum & Gardens–Library **[1656]**, **[13728]**

Hilmar Chamber of Commerce **[57545]**

Hilton Head Island Bluffton Chamber of Commerce **[64759]**

"Hilton Suit Reveals More Mold Problems" in *Pacific Business News* (Vol. 41, No. 24, August 22, 2003, pp. 1) **[3234]**, **[7361]**, **[9362]**, **[12562]**

Hinckley, Allen, & Snyder–Law Library **[9532]**

Hinds Community College
SBDC Business Assistance Center at Pearl **[61748]**

Small Business Development Center/International Trade Center **[61749]**

"Hines blends architecture, environmental awareness" in *Atlanta Business Chronicle* (Vol. 25, December 6, 2002, No. 26, pp. 5C) **[1517]**, **[13647]**, **[18547]**, **[20524]**, **[37295]**

C. W. Hines and Associates Inc. **[38544]**, **[42971]**, **[46045]**, **[47870]**, **[50500]**

Hinsdale Chamber of Commerce **[59542]**

Hinton Chamber of Commerce **[64013]**

"HIPAA hysteria" in *Atlanta Business Chronicle* (Vol. 25, November 29, 2002, No. 25, pp. 1C) **[6253]**, **[13322]**, **[14115]**, **[22250]**, **[40439]**, **[43215]**

"Hipper Than Thou" in *Business 2.0* (Vol. 6, July 2005, No. 6, pp. 56) **[2713]**, **[2836]**

"Hire for Attitude, Train for Skills" in *Rough Notes* (Vol. 145, No. 9, September 2002, pp. 106) **[42262]**, **[45240]**

"Hire Diversity: Diversity Leaders" in *Hispanic Business* (October 2004, pp. 130) **[42263]**, **[48213]**, **[48556]**

"Hire Education" in *Hispanic Business* (May 2005, pp. 56) **[33114]**, **[39838]**, **[42264]**

"Hire Ground" in *Entrepreneur* (Vol. 33, March 2005, No. 3, pp. 28) **[18775]**, **[42265]**, **[45241]**

"Hire Learning" in *Entrepreneur* (Vol. 32, November 2004, No. 11, pp. 100) **[33115]**, **[42266]**

"Hire Power" in *Entrepreneur* (Vol. 33, March 2005, No. 3, pp. 128) **[14116]**, **[42267]**

"Hire purpose" in *Entrepreneur* (Vol. 31, No. 4, April 2003, pp. 56) **[42268]**, **[54591]**

"Hired Guns: Is Enlisting Bloggers the Wave of the Future in Marketing?" in *Entrepreneur* (Vol. 31, No. 9, September 2003, pp. 30) **[660]**, **[14117]**, **[34010]**, **[47075]**

HireDiversity.com **[23427]**

"HireDiversity.com Named a Top Site" in *Hispanic Business* (Vol. 24, No. 1/2, January/February 2002, pp. 60) **[4398]**, **[9211]**, **[9561]**, **[22044]**, **[42269]**

"Hiring an Accountant" in *Crain's Detroit Business* (Vol. 19, No. 49, December 8, 2003, pp. 14) **[25874]**, **[26252]**, **[42270]**

Hiring the Best! **[42271]**

"Hiring a guide just to find the camp" in *The New York Times* (February 20, 2000, pp. A39) **[31170]**

"Hiring Employees With Disabilities" in *Inc.* (October 2005, pp. 29-32) **[10511]**, **[16016]**, **[42272]**, **[46314]**, **[54202]**

Hiring & Firing **[42482]**, **[42909]**, **[42927]**

The Hiring, Firing and Everything in Between Personnel Forms Book **[42273]**, **[42862]**

Hiring Handbook Special Report: Avoiding Employee Lawsuits **[42274]**

"Hiring, Hollywood Style" in *Inc.* (January 1, 2004) **[42275]**, **[45242]**

Hiring: More Than a Gut Feeling **[42276]**

Hiring Right: A Practical Guide **[42277]**

"Hiring the Right People to Rep Your Products" in *Black Enterprise* (Vol. 35, November 2004, No. 4, pp. 54) **[32157]**, **[42278]**, **[51671]**

"Hiring is Slow Despite Optimism About Economy" in *Wall Street Journal* (August 12, 2003, pp. B9) **[32473]**, **[42279]**

Hiring Strategies for Long-Term Success: How to Hire the Best People & Keep Them! **[42280]**

"Hiring True Believers" in *Sacramento Bee* (November 14, 2005) **[42281]**, **[51180]**, **[51672]**, **[52357]**

Hiring Winners **[42282]**

"His Brother's Keeper: a Mentor Learns the True Meaning of Leadership" in *Black Enterprise* (Vol. 37, December 2006, No. 5, pp. 69) **[33116]**, **[36286]**, **[45243]**

"His stand on football: Reginald Rutledge creates a stadium rush" in *Black Enterprise* (Vol. 33, No. 6, January 2003, pp. 89) **[5908]**, **[36287]**, **[48214]**

"His Rock Club Was In Ruins. His Partnership Was Crumbling" in *Inc.* (May 1, 2006) **[2340]**, **[2388]**, **[47612]**, **[49978]**

"His Word is Law" in *Fast Company* (November 2001, pp. 66) **[36288]**, **[37147]**

"Hispanic Auto Dealers Form Group" in *Hispanic Business* (Vol. 24, No. 4, April 2002, pp. 14) **[18057]**, **[48215]**

"Hispanic Banking Initiatives" in *Hispanic Business* (October 2002, pp. 14) **[44547]**, **[48216]**

Hispanic Business **[48491]**

Hispanic Business (April 2005, pp. 14); "$1 Billion Outreach" in **[12511]**, **[48013]**, **[48518]**, **[56107]**

"Hispanic Business 100 Influentials" in *Hispanic Business* (October 2003) **[36289]**, **[48217]**

"Hispanic Business 500 Directory" in *Hispanic Business* (June 2005) **[48218]**

"The Hispanic Business 500" in *Hispanic Business* (June 2002, pp. 44, 46, 48, 50, 52, 54, 56, 58, 60, 62, 64) **[28281]**, **[48219]**

"The Hispanic Business 2002 Top 50 Exporters" in *Hispanic Business* (November 2002, pp. 38-39) **[43695]**, **[48220]**

Hispanic Business (January/February 2004, pp. 36, 38, 40, 42, 44, 46); "2004 Corporate Elite Directory" in **[35752]**, **[44867]**, **[48016]**

Hispanic Business (January/February 2005, pp. 22); "2005 Corporate Elite Directory" in **[44868]**, **[48017]**, **[53574]**

Hispanic Business (April 2005, pp. 54); "2005 Elite Women" in **[44869]**, **[53335]**, **[56110]**

Hispanic Business (September 2006, pp. 40, 42, 44, 48, 50); "2006 Hispanic Business Diversity Report: Employment" in **[42163]**, **[48019]**

Hispanic Business (Vol. 22, No. 10, October 2000, pp. 94); "A secure net for agriculture" in **[33487]**

Hispanic Business (December 2003, pp. 24, 26); "A Bicultural Bias" in **[48058]**, **[48524]**

Hispanic Business (October 2002, pp. 30-32, 34); "A College Lockout?" in **[33045]**, **[45012]**

Hispanic Business (October 2003, pp. 32, 34); "A Contracting Conundrum" in **[39804]**, **[40000]**

Hispanic Business (June 2005, pp. 32, 34, 36, 38); "A Cool $2 Billion" in **[7302]**, **[20845]**, **[35973]**

Hispanic Business (July/August 2004, pp. 42, 44); "A Decade of NAFTA" in **[40304]**, **[43615]**

Hispanic Business (October 2003, pp. 42); "A Decade Well Spent" in **[33066]**, **[54166]**

Hispanic Business (September 2003, pp. 30, 32); "A Diversity Plan Turns 100" in **[18014]**, **[28042]**, **[46899]**, **[48135]**

Hispanic Business (October 2004, pp. 50, 52, 54); "A Fight for Rights" in **[29239]**, **[32429]**, **[54178]**

Hispanic Business (Vol. 23, No. 10, October, 2001, pp. 98); "A Generally Beneficial Law" in **[40404]**, **[54567]**

Hispanic Business (Vol. 24, No. 4, April 2002, pp. 22); "A Growing Market for Talk" in **[12886]**, **[20122]**, **[24943]**, **[27387]**, **[28244]**, **[48191]**

Hispanic Business (Vol. 23, No. 11, November 2001, pp. 38, 40); "A Home Court Advantage" in **[7366]**, **[16520]**, **[48237]**, **[56265]**

Hispanic Business (October 2004, pp. 28); "A Home of Their Own" in **[17391]**, **[20534]**, **[32483]**

Hispanic Business (December 2003, pp. 34-36, 38, 40); "A House Divided" in **[665]**, **[20317]**, **[24417]**, **[47090]**

Hispanic Business (December 2006, pp. 44); "A Lifetime of Perseverance" in **[694]**, **[56304]**

Hispanic Business (January/February 2005, pp. 24, 26, 28); "A Macro View at Microsoft" in **[4720]**, **[6718]**, **[23071]**, **[41823]**, **[47214]**, **[48278]**, **[53357]**

Hispanic Business (December 2003, pp. 20-21); "A Melting Pot with Flavor" in **[47277]**, **[48289]**

Hispanic Business (December 2002, pp. 22, 24, 26); "A Meta-Study of the Market" in **[721]**, **[47281]**, **[53852]**

Hispanic Business (November 2002, pp. 22-23); "A Minority Role in the Homeland" in **[22298]**, **[48310]**

Hispanic Business (Vol. 24, No. 1/2, January/February 2002, pp. 14, 16); "A Mixed Forecast for 2002" in **[28494]**, **[32575]**

Hispanic Business (July/August 2002, pp. 64-66); "A Model Chamber Tackles Complex Issues" in **[40538]**, **[48313]**

Hispanic Business (Vol. 22, No. 3, March 2000, pp. 54); "A New Century for Start-ups" in **[29752]**, **[35582]**, **[55747]**

Hispanic Business (September 2004, pp. 86, 88); "A New Tone" in **[5067]**, **[41866]**, **[49165]**

Hispanic Business (January/February 2004, pp. 30, 34); "A Passion for the Work" in **[36604]**, **[48355]**

Hispanic Business (July/August 2002, pp. 18, 20); "A Peek Inside a Public Organization" in **[15346]**, **[32625]**

Hispanic Business (March 2002, pp. 56); "A Place for More Hispanics?" in **[40614]**, **[48591]**

Hispanic Business (March 2003, pp. 42, 44); "A Plan for Today's Money Market" in **[29755]**, **[44434]**, **[47973]**, **[56069]**

Hispanic Business (Vol. 23, No. 5, May 2001, pp. 56); "A Profile in Success" in **[35027]**, **[36652]**, **[48369]**

Hispanic Business (Vol. 22, No. 9, September 2000, pp. 20); "A labor in progress" in **[33149]**

Hispanic Business (Vol. 22, No. 11, November 2000, pp. 36); "A time of lower returns" in **[43843]**, **[48439]**

Hispanic Business (June 2005, pp. 80, 82); "A Rich New Niche" in **[15422]**, **[38325]**

Hispanic Business (Vol. 22, No. 6, June 2000, pp. 42); "A launching point to the next step" in **[31096]**, **[35544]**, **[39970]**, **[48268]**

Hispanic Business (Vol. 22, No. 3, March 2000, pp. 18); "A heritage of success" in **[44307]**, **[45233]**, **[48209]**

Hispanic Business (June 2002, pp. 104); "A Tasty Blend of the Old and New" in **[24734]**, **[25253]**, **[30422]**, **[45712]**

Hispanic Business (Vol. 23, No. 11, November 2001, pp. 68); "A Time to Donate" in **[54263]**, **[54835]**

Hispanic Business (July/August 2004, pp. 52, 54, 56, 58, 62, 66); "A Toast to Success" in **[18942]**, **[48443]**

Hispanic Business (October 2002, pp. 26, 28); "A Tough Row to Hoe" in **[26549]**, **[40776]**, **[48452]**

Hispanic Business (December 2006, pp. 48); "A Tough Sell" in **[4124]**, **[24453]**, **[30975]**

Hispanic Business (November 2003, pp. 32, 34); "A Whole New Chamber" in **[39681]**, **[48482]**

Hispanic Business (Vol. 23, No. 5, May 2001, pp. 78); "A Wireless Decision" in **[42123]**, **[49367]**

Hispanic Business (September 2004, pp. 46); "Access to Capital: Closing the 'Gap'" in **[44460]**, **[48021]**

Hispanic Business (September 2004, pp. 44); "Access to Capital: Government Financiers" in **[9804]**, **[14720]**, **[44461]**, **[48022]**

Hispanic Business (October 2004, pp. 98-100); "Access to Capital: Money to Grow" in **[9805]**, **[44462]**, **[48023]**

Hispanic Business (Vol. 24, No. 5, May 2002, pp. 14); "Accessing Minority Markets" in **[27750]**, **[46649]**, **[48024]**

Hispanic Business (Vol. 24, No. 1/2, January/February 2002, pp. 60); "Accounting Group Gets a New Name" in **[23876]**

Hispanic Business (Vol. 23, No. 7/8, July/August 2001, pp. 29); "Action Yet in Need of Affirming" in **[39978]**, **[40145]**, **[48025]**

Hispanic Business (December 2002, pp. 30, 32-34, 36, 38); "Ad Spending Heats Up" in **[531]**, **[46655]**

Hispanic Business (July/August 2002, pp. 14); "Advertising/Marketing" in **[46663]**, **[53579]**

Hispanic Business (Vol. 24, No. 1/2, January/February 2002, pp. 18-20, 22); "Advocate or Competitor?" in **[30777]**, **[48027]**

Hispanic Business (June 2002, pp. 16); "Aegis of Success" in **[39979]**, **[46186]**, **[48028]**

Hispanic Business (March 2003, pp. 20, 22, 24); "Affirmative Action Front and Center" in **[32991]**, **[40147]**, **[48029]**

Hispanic Business (September 2003, pp. 40-42, 44); "Affirmative Action on Trial" in **[32992]**, **[39135]**, **[40148]**, **[48520]**

Hispanic Business (December 2003, pp. 30, 32); "Affluence in Two Cultures" in **[32235]**, **[46666]**

Hispanic Business (September 2003, pp. 24, 26, 28); "Agency with a Small Focus" in **[39136]**, **[39786]**

Hispanic Business (March 2002, pp. 56-58); "Agendas Cross in SHCC Boardroom" in **[32238]**, **[35757]**

Hispanic Business (January/February 2003, pp. 14); "AHAA: Computer Manufacturers Missing the Boat" in **[4591]**, **[6575]**, **[22908]**

Hispanic Business (March 2003, pp. 18); "Alarcon Backs McCain Bill" in **[20299]**, **[40152]**, **[48031]**

Hispanic Business (Vol. 24, No. 4, April 2002, pp. 20-21); "Alchemist Among the Vines" in **[23453]**, **[35761]**, **[37584]**, **[48032]**

Hispanic Business (December 2006, pp. 46-47, 49); "All Eyes on Univision" in **[4084]**, **[24374]**

Hispanic Business (March 2002, pp. 28, 30-31); "An Era of Downsized Expectations" in **[9938]**, **[14960]**, **[32417]**

Hispanic Business (October 2003, pp. 40); "An Evening with the Brain Trust" in **[28123]**, **[40354]**, **[48151]**

Hispanic Business (June 2002, pp. 20); "An Inspirational Launch" in **[24349]**, **[47962]**

Hispanic Business (Vol. 23, No. 5, May 2001, pp. 74); "An Oasis of Luxury" in **[30288]**

Hispanic Business (Vol. 24, No. 1/2, January/February 2002, pp. 24, 26); "Any Room on the Board?" in **[48035]**, **[48521]**

Hispanic Business (Vol. 23, No. 10, October, 2001, pp. 104); "Arlington the Site of HD Career Expo" in **[39149]**, **[42169]**, **[48036]**

Hispanic Business (October 2003, pp. 92, 94, 96); "Assembling a Crack Sales Team" in **[44905]**, **[51558]**

Hispanic Business (July/August 2004, pp. 26); "At Top Speed" in **[27796]**, **[32254]**, **[48039]**

Hispanic Business (March 2005, pp. 42, 44, 46, 48); "Auto Review" in **[17968]**, **[53592]**

Hispanic Business (Vol. 22, No. 6, June 2000, pp. 100); "Automotive Dealers Move Wheels" in **[17973]**, **[27802]**, **[35794]**, **[48043]**

Hispanic Business (May 2000, pp. 50); "B-to-b goes online: e-commerce among companies is rapidly changing the nature of procurement" in **[33555]**, **[48045]**

Hispanic Business (July/August 2002, pp. 32, 34); "B2G Supplies Revenue Gains" in **[27806]**, **[37106]**, **[39985]**, **[48046]**

Hispanic Business (October 2004, pp. 126); "Bankable Skills" in **[9830]**, **[44914]**

Hispanic Business (November 2006, pp. 74, 76); "Banking on Diversity" in **[42177]**, **[48523]**

Hispanic Business (October 2002, pp. 36, 38); "Banks: Big vs. Small" in **[35807]**, **[44477]**

Hispanic Business (Vol. 24, No. 4, April 2002, pp. 62); "Bargain Season Begins" in **[30291]**, **[32267]**

Hispanic Business (March 2004, pp. 42); "Battle of the Wily Worms" in **[6160]**, **[13837]**, **[22179]**, **[33565]**

Hispanic Business (December 2003, pp. 58); "Beat Those Bouncing Checks" in **[8375]**, **[31513]**, **[33568]**

Hispanic Business (Vol. 23, No. 11, November 2001, pp. 62-64); "Beauty and the Beast" in **[17977]**, **[48054]**

Hispanic Business (Vol. 24, No. 5, May 2002, pp. 40-41); "Behind the Curve" in **[33569]**, **[41539]**, **[48055]**, **[53214]**, **[53602]**

Hispanic Business (June 2002, pp. 32, 34, 36); "Best of the Best" in **[35822]**, **[44927]**, **[48056]**

Hispanic Business (December 2002, pp. 57); "Betting on Business" in **[12521]**, **[22470]**, **[24668]**, **[24893]**, **[25156]**, **[30296]**

Hispanic Business (June 2005, pp. 98); "Betting on Growth" in **[14788]**, **[27834]**, **[37914]**

Hispanic Business (Vol. 22, No. 6, June 2000, pp. 14); "Betting on the Net" in **[33574]**, **[37107]**

Hispanic Business (December 2002, pp. 55); "Beware the Dotted Line" in **[29124]**, **[37390]**

Hispanic Business (December 2002, pp. 50-52); "Beyond Big Macs" in **[21447]**, **[35832]**, **[48057]**

Hispanic Business (March 2003, pp. 25); "Big Box vs. Online" in **[31012]**, **[33583]**, **[48959]**, **[51071]**

Hispanic Business (March 2002, pp. 5052); "Big Boxes of the Road" in **[17978]**, **[39176]**

Hispanic Business (Vol. 22, No. 6, June 2000, pp. 102); "Big Clients Push Construction Boom" in **[7254]**, **[27837]**, **[48059]**

Hispanic Business (January/February 2003, pp. 46, 48); "Big Goals, Small Steps" in **[39988]**, **[48060]**

Hispanic Business (October 2003, pp. 102); "Billing Bad Debt" in **[88]**, **[8376]**, **[9848]**, **[14796]**, **[26169]**, **[31515]**

Hispanic Business (December 2001, pp. 41, 44, 46, 48); "Billings Bonanza" in **[89]**, **[46720]**

Hispanic Business (Vol. 23, No. 11, November 2001, pp. 70); "BizWare" in **[4607]**, **[13852]**, **[22928]**, **[25801]**, **[35338]**, **[48061]**, **[53219]**

Hispanic Business (January/February 2003, pp. 17); "Blockbuster Stores Get Hispanic Theme" in **[9697]**, **[48525]**

Hispanic Business (October 2004, pp. 106); "Boosting Access" in **[17361]**, **[20437]**

Hispanic Business (April 2005, pp. 14); "Boosting Corporate Diversity" in **[30800]**, **[33018]**, **[42182]**, **[44949]**, **[48526]**, **[53614]**

Hispanic Business (October 2004, pp. 108, 110, 112); "Breaking Into the Chains" in **[38612]**, **[47943]**

Hispanic Business (December 2001, pp. 54, 56); "Bringing the Noise" in **[91]**, **[46749]**

Hispanic Business (March 2005, pp. 14); "Broadband Access" in **[13858]**, **[27877]**, **[33610]**, **[41569]**

Hispanic Business (Vol. 22, No. 11, November 2000, pp. 12); "Bromley, AHAA shine at Confab" in **[46750]**, **[55071]**

Hispanic Business (December 2001, pp. 66); "Bruised but Unbowed" in **[35877]**, **[39184]**

Hispanic Business (December 2002, pp. 64); "Building Business Leaders" in **[35347]**

Hispanic Business (Vol. 23, No. 7/8, July/August 2001, pp. 116); "Building the Minority High-Tech Work Force" in **[41574]**, **[42185]**, **[48075]**, **[56147]**

Hispanic Business (Vol. 23, No. 5, May 2001, pp. 28, 30); "Building the Perfect Tech CEO" in **[6927]**, **[35882]**, **[41575]**, **[48076]**

Hispanic Business (March 2004, pp. 44-45); "Building a Professional Pipeline" in **[33023]**, **[39187]**, **[44963]**

Hispanic Business (October 2006, pp. 24, 26); "Bumpy Ride" in **[20446]**, **[32288]**

Hispanic Business (March 2003, pp. 18); "Burying the Hatchet" in **[17985]**, **[48079]**, **[49830]**

Hispanic Business (Vol. 23, No. 10, October, 2001, pp. 22); "Bush Backs Contracting Program" in **[39993]**, **[40211]**, **[48080]**

Hispanic Business (November 2002, pp. 32); "Business Primer for Legislators" in **[35894]**, **[39199]**, **[40217]**

Hispanic Business (September 2006, pp. 14); "CAFTA Action" in **[12948]**, **[40228]**, **[43571]**

Hispanic Business (December 2001, pp. 64); "Calm After the Storm" in **[573]**, **[20307]**, **[46772]**

Hispanic Business (July/August 2004, pp. 68, 70, 72, 74); "Capital Access" in **[35914]**, **[48082]**

Hispanic Business (March 2002, pp. 44, 46, 48, 50, 52); "Capital Crunch" in **[27927]**, **[40238]**

Hispanic Business (March 2005, pp. 25-26, 28, 30, 34, 36); "Capital Ideas" in **[14831]**, **[37942]**

Hispanic Business (March 2003, pp. 30-34, 36-38); "Captains of Capital" in **[35915]**, **[44490]**, **[48085]**

Hispanic Business (Vol. 23, No. 5, May 2001, pp. 12); "Cardenas' Star on the Rise" in **[35916]**, **[48086]**

Hispanic Business (April 2003, pp. 62, 64); "Career Quarterly" in **[33649]**, **[42192]**

Hispanic Business (October 2003, pp. 104, 106); "Caribbean Charisma" in **[24675]**, **[25168]**, **[30307]**

Hispanic Business (Vol. 22, No. 10, October 2000, pp. 24); "Cartel Creativo wins army contract" in **[577]**, **[39996]**, **[48088]**

Hispanic Business (Vol. 24, No. 5, May 2002, pp. 52); "Cashing In on Bad Debts" in **[31519]**, **[54480]**

Hispanic Business (June 2005, pp. 90); "Catering to Fickle Customers" in **[52512]**

Hispanic Business (Vol. 23, No. 5, May 2001, pp. 20); "Caucus Decries Bush Plan" in **[48090]**, **[54482]**

Hispanic Business (December 2002, pp. 58-60); "Celebrating Business Heroes" in **[35927]**, **[46791]**, **[48093]**

Hispanic Business (September 2003, pp. 34, 36, 38); "Celebration of Culture and Commerce" in **[46792]**, **[48094]**

Hispanic Business (November 2002, pp. BG4); "CEO Buyer's Guide: Computers" in **[48983]**

Hispanic Business (November 2002, pp. BG18-BG19); "CEO Buyer's Guide: Office" in **[48984]**

Hispanic Business (November 2002, pp. BG8, BG10); "CEO Buyer's Guide: Telecom" in **[4946]**

Hispanic Business (November 2002, pp. BG14); "CEO Buyer's Guide: Travel" in **[30308]**

Hispanic Business (November 2002, pp. BG12-13); "CEO Buyers's Guide: Financial" in **[9870]**, **[14842]**, **[37951]**

Hispanic Business (November 2003, pp. 22); "CEO Confidence on the Rise" in **[27937]**, **[32313]**

Hispanic Business (May 2005, pp. 72, 74); "Chain Lightening" in **[38736]**, **[48095]**, **[53640]**

Hispanic Business (Vol.22, July-Aug. 2000); "Chamber trouble: organizations in California and Texas suffer high-profile resignations" in **[48097]**, **[53641]**

Hispanic Business (Vol. 24, No. 1/2, January/February 2002, pp. 57); "Changing of the Guard" in **[40252]**, **[48099]**

Hispanic Business (March 2003, pp. 16); "Citigroup, NCLR Announce $105 million Revitalization Pact" in **[17369]**, **[20464]**, **[20831]**, **[49856]**

Hispanic Business (Vol. 23, No. 10, October, 2001, pp. 96); "City of Angels" in **[30312]**

Hispanic Business (March 2004, pp. 54, 56); "Clicking with Hispanics" in **[6610]**, **[46806]**, **[54158]**

Hispanic Business (Dec. 1999, pp. 60); "Clicking online: mergers, consolidations predicted for Hispanic targeted Web sites in 2000" in **[13903]**, **[14866]**, **[33677]**, **[48105]**, **[49860]**

Hispanic Business (March 2003, pp. 54-56); "Company Crisis: CEO Under Fire" in **[35961]**, **[45017]**

Hispanic Business (Vol. 24, No. 5, May 2002, pp. 50); "Computer-Assisted Consulting" in **[3513]**, **[4622]**, **[22945]**, **[29830]**, **[46828]**, **[51594]**, **[53240]**

Hispanic Business (Vol. 23, No. 7/8, July/August 2001, pp. 44, 46, 48, 50, 52, 54, 56); "Construction in the Fast Mode" in **[7298]**, **[27974]**, **[48109]**

Hispanic Business (January/February 2004, pp. 64); "Contacts for Contracts" in **[7301]**, **[7867]**, **[39999]**, **[40150]**, **[41678]**, **[43594]**, **[48110]**, **[48642]**, **[49874]**, **[51112]**, **[52836]**

Hispanic Business (December 2001, pp. 10); "Continuing to Shine" in **[9197]**, **[24520]**, **[49687]**, **[53661]**

Hispanic Business (April 2005, pp. 12); "Controversial Ruling on Cuban Trade" in **[26495]**, **[43595]**

Hispanic Business (June 2005, pp. 78); "Cooking Again" in **[10619]**, **[37618]**

Hispanic Business (January/February 2005, pp. 50, 52, 54); "Corporate Diversity" in **[29835]**, **[39257]**, **[48530]**

Hispanic Business (January/February 2005, pp. 30, 32, 34, 38, 40, 42); "Corporate Elite" in **[45026]**, **[48112]**, **[56177]**

Hispanic Business (March 2002, pp. 36); "Cream of the Crop" in **[29183]**, **[33059]**, **[45032]**

Hispanic Business (December 2001, pp. 16-17); "Creating Their Own Niche: 2001 Entrepreneurial Spirit Awards" in **[593]**, **[1504]**, **[3126]**, **[5976]**, **[7888]**, **[15840]**, **[19389]**, **[35987]**

Hispanic Business (May 2005, pp. 14); "Cropping Up" in **[26498]**, **[33062]**, **[48117]**, **[48532]**

Hispanic Business (Vol. 22, No. 3, March 2000, pp. 14); "Crossing the clothesline" in **[5531]**, **[5649]**, **[48533]**

Hispanic Business (Vol. 22, No. 6, June 2000, pp. 52); "Crossing the finish line at full speed" in **[40294]**

Hispanic Business (Vol. 22, No. 4, April 2000, pp. 38); "Cuba's prosperous future" in **[27992]**, **[43606]**

Hispanic Business (Vol. 23, No. 5, May 2001, pp. 6); "Cultural Access Moves into Medical Research" in **[31134]**, **[46860]**, **[48119]**

Hispanic Business (June 2005, pp. 86); "Culture Cash" in **[32149]**, **[48120]**

Hispanic Business (Vol. 22, No. 11, November 2000, pp. 44); "Cyber-battle for a piece of the pie" in **[33728]**, **[43611]**

Hispanic Business (Vol. 22, No. 6, June 2000, pp. 122); "Cyber contracting" in **[13946]**, **[28002]**, **[33729]**

Hispanic Business (June 2005, pp. 22, 24); "Dark Dollar Signs" in **[14904]**, **[32345]**

Hispanic Business (Vol. 23, No. 7/8, July/August 2001, pp. 112, 114); "Data Disposal Questions" in **[39272]**, **[49495]**

Hispanic Business (Vol. 23, No. 5, May 2001, pp. 20); "De la Torre Named to Hall of Fame" in **[18865]**, **[36001]**, **[48124]**, **[56183]**

Hispanic Business (Vol. 22, No. 10, October 2000, pp. 20); "Dealt a double blow" in **[40004]**, **[48125]**

Hispanic Business (Vol. 23, No. 11, November 2001, pp. 68); "Deductible Gifts" in **[54512]**

Hispanic Business (March 2005, pp. 64); "Delayed Obsolescence" in **[4633]**, **[22961]**, **[53251]**, **[53682]**

Hispanic Business (Vol. 22, No. 6, June 2000, pp. 106); "Demand surges in manufacturing" in **[46262]**, **[48127]**

Hispanic Business (January/February 2003, pp. 54-55); "Designing Woman" in **[5536]**, **[36008]**

Hispanic Business (June 2005, pp. 92); "Destination" in **[18010]**, **[48128]**, **[53688]**

Hispanic Business (Vol. 22, No. 6, June 2000, pp. 20); "Destined for success" in **[24793]**, **[35386]**, **[47951]**, **[56720]**

Hispanic Business (October 2002, pp. 14); "Dialing Up Market Share" in **[4972]**, **[13966]**, **[28034]**

Hispanic Business (Vol. 24, No. 5, May 2002, pp. 36, 38); "Dialtone's Unlikely Arc" in **[13740]**, **[35388]**, **[47952]**

Hispanic Business (Vol. 22, No. 9, September 2000, pp. 12); "Discrimination's new name" in **[40006]**, **[48132]**

Hispanic Business (June 2002, pp. 80); "Diversity in the Big City" in **[42220]**, **[48538]**, **[53692]**

Hispanic Business (January/February 2003, pp. 64, 66); "Diversity Defined" in **[42221]**, **[48133]**, **[48540]**

Hispanic Business (Vol. 22, No. 7-8, July-August 2000, pp. 24); "Doing well by doing good: Latino Health Care" in **[13270]**, **[43161]**

Hispanic Business (Vol. 23, No. 11, November 2001, pp. 52, 54); "Dollars in the Deals" in **[12955]**, **[28049]**, **[43628]**

Hispanic Business (Vol. 23, No. 10, October, 2001, pp. 42, 44); "Merger Fever" in **[720]**, **[15257]**, **[43750]**, **[48290]**, **[50075]**

Hispanic Business (November 2003, pp. 72); "Merger Finally Gets Green Light" in **[15258]**, **[24432]**, **[50076]**

Hispanic Business (Vol. 23, No. 10, October, 2001, pp. 28, 30); "Mexican Industries Goes Under" in **[1947]**, **[37730]**, **[48291]**

Hispanic Business (Vol. 22, No. 5, May 2000, pp. 14); "Mexican grocery gets wired" in **[11642]**, **[34192]**, **[48292]**

Hispanic Business (October 2002, pp. 86); "Miami Upstart Goes National" in **[14241]**, **[28480]**, **[41468]**, **[47967]**

Hispanic Business (March 2002, pp. 16); "Microlending - Arizona Style" in **[39868]**, **[44586]**, **[48915]**, **[54224]**

Hispanic Business (Vol. 23, No. 5, May 2001, pp. 46); "Microsoft Sees 'Untapped Territory'" in **[33173]**, **[48294]**

Hispanic Business (Vol. 22, No. 6, June 2000, pp. 22); "Might of the roundtable" in **[48295]**

Hispanic Business (Vol. 23, No. 7/8, July/August 2001, pp. 108); "Mile-High Vacation" in **[30377]**

Hispanic Business (May 2005, pp. 16); "Minding the Money" in **[13386]**, **[15266]**, **[38223]**, **[43278]**

Hispanic Business (Vol. 22, No. 9, September 2000, pp. 14); "Minorities meet opportunities" in **[48297]**, **[55124]**

Hispanic Business (March 2002, pp. 10); "Minority Biz of the Year" in **[46374]**, **[48302]**

Hispanic Business (July/August 2004, pp. 14); "Minority Home Gaps" in **[17407]**, **[20590]**

Hispanic Business (July/August 2002, pp. 50, 52, 54); "Missing Part of the Equation" in **[37168]**, **[48311]**, **[52153]**

Hispanic Business (November 2003, pp. 60, 62, 64); "Money that Binds from Afar" in **[10091]**, **[15269]**, **[28499]**, **[32578]**, **[43756]**

Hispanic Business (June 2002, pp. 70); "Money-Counting for Growth" in **[10092]**, **[15271]**, **[38231]**

Hispanic Business (September 2004, pp. 34-36, 38, 40, 42); "Money Rules" in **[10094]**, **[44594]**, **[48314]**

Hispanic Business (Vol. 23, No. 7/8, July/August 2001, pp. 30); "More Checks in the Mail" in **[27152]**, **[39481]**

Hispanic Business (Dec. 1999, pp.56); "More steady growth: Hispanic ad expenditures increase 11 percent to reach nearly $1.9 billion" in **[28505]**, **[34210]**, **[47295]**, **[48315]**

Hispanic Business (June 2002, pp. 76); "More Than Smart Talk" in **[27445]**, **[45444]**

Hispanic Business (November 2002, pp. 14); "Mortgage Lending Disparities" in **[17417]**

Hispanic Business (November 2006, pp. 42, 44, 46, 48); "Motor City Mayhem" in **[18092]**, **[46379]**

Hispanic Business (Vol. 23, No. 5, May 2001, pp. 66, 68); "Moving Pictures" in **[5948]**, **[6450]**, **[9670]**, **[25758]**, **[35574]**, **[47971]**

Hispanic Business (Vol. 23, No. 7/8, July/August 2001, pp. 74, 76, 78); "Mr. Prime Time" in **[9731]**, **[28520]**

Hispanic Business (Vol. 24, No. 4, April 2002, pp. 58, 60); "Multiculturalism Grows Up" in **[42352]**, **[48317]**, **[48584]**, **[53870]**

Hispanic Business (March 2005, pp. 15); "Multilingual Execs in Demand" in **[42353]**, **[48585]**, **[53871]**

Hispanic Business (January/February 2003, pp. 28); "Muscling in on the Hispanic Market" in **[729]**, **[18094]**, **[47302]**

Hispanic Business (Vol. 23, No. 10, October, 2001, pp. 104); "NAHREP Set to Host Confab" in **[20604]**, **[20948]**, **[47312]**

Hispanic Business (Vol. 22, No. 5, May 2000, pp. 38); "Netting a bigger piece of the action" in **[1953]**, **[14279]**, **[18605]**, **[19751]**, **[34246]**, **[48321]**

Hispanic Business (Vol. 24, No. 4, April 2002, pp. 26); "Networking for Success" in **[27453]**, **[48323]**, **[56338]**

Hispanic Business (Vol.22,No.7-8, July-Aug. 2000); "New DOE contracts: small business is the focus of several new agency initiatives" in **[39872]**, **[40064]**

Hispanic Business (Vol. 23, No. 7/8, July/August 2001, pp. 104, 106); "New Dynamic for Nonprofits" in **[36536]**, **[48327]**, **[54230]**

Hispanic Business (Vol. 22, No. 1/2, January/February, pp. 24, 26); "New Economy Creates New Markets" in **[28536]**, **[32588]**, **[55132]**

Hispanic Business (Vol. 23, No. 10, October, 2001, pp. 32, 34); "New Face at the SBA" in **[39873]**, **[40065]**, **[48328]**, **[53877]**

Hispanic Business (June 2005, pp. 20); "New Foundation" in **[731]**, **[33187]**, **[47326]**, **[48330]**

Hispanic Business (Vol. 23, No. 7/8, July/August 2001, pp. 24); "New Group Seeks Greater Hispanic Influence" in **[28540]**, **[32589]**, **[53878]**

Hispanic Business (January/February 2005, pp. 14); "New Political Players on the Scene" in **[40557]**, **[48333]**, **[48587]**

Hispanic Business (March 2003, pp. 14); "New TV Network on the Launch Pad" in **[736]**, **[4116]**, **[24437]**, **[47336]**, **[48334]**

Hispanic Business (March 2002, pp. 58); "New War Means New Contracts" in **[22310]**, **[40567]**, **[49718]**

Hispanic Business (Vol. 23, No. 7/8, July/August 2001, pp. 14); "New World Border" in **[32595]**, **[40568]**, **[48337]**

Hispanic Business (Vol. 23, No. 7/8, July/August 2001, pp. 26); "Next Round on Adarand" in **[39494]**, **[40067]**

Hispanic Business (January/February 2004, pp. 20, 22, 24); "Night of Stars" in **[36554]**, **[48340]**

Hispanic Business (September 2003, pp. 20); "NMAC Settles Suit" in **[18100]**, **[29418]**, **[32050]**

Hispanic Business (Vol. 23, No. 10, October, 2001, pp. 22); "NMSDC Confab" in **[39501]**, **[48341]**

Hispanic Business (January/February 2005, pp. 16); "NMSDC Honors PepsiCo, Toyota" in **[1954]**, **[18101]**, **[46393]**, **[48342]**

Hispanic Business (July/August 2002, pp. 28, 30); "No Slam Dunk" in **[15305]**, **[23727]**, **[24439]**

Hispanic Business (November 2003, pp. 58, 64); "North-South Power Balance" in **[12999]**, **[43766]**

Hispanic Business (Vol. 24, No. 5, May 2002, pp. 56); "Northwest Bounty" in **[30390]**

Hispanic Business (March 2004, pp. 16); "On the Road" in **[12609]**, **[24716]**, **[25229]**

Hispanic Business (Vol. 21, No. 12, December 1999, pp. 70); "On the Same Page: Newspaper Advertising is Generally Flat" in **[18920]**, **[47363]**, **[53899]**

Hispanic Business (December 2001, pp. 60, 62); "On With the Show" in **[745]**, **[24441]**, **[47366]**

Hispanic Business (Vol. 22, No. 10, October 2000, pp. 100); "One size doesn't fit all" in **[26866]**

Hispanic Business (October 2002, pp. 40); "100 Most Influential Hispanics" in **[36581]**, **[48345]**

Hispanic Business (January/February 2003, pp. 50, 52); "Online Rivals' Market Plays" in **[14319]**, **[47373]**

Hispanic Business (October 2002, pp. 92); "Online Trading Primer" in **[10123]**, **[14323]**, **[34304]**, **[38265]**

Hispanic Business (Vol. 23, No. 7/8, July/August 2001, pp. 66); "Opening the Door to VC" in **[44614]**, **[55766]**

Hispanic Business (Vol. 24, No. 5, May 2002, pp. 17); "Opposition to Auto Group Grows" in **[18107]**, **[48348]**

Hispanic Business (December 2002, pp. FRG12-FRG14); "OSDBU Directory" in **[36594]**, **[39882]**, **[40073]**, **[41516]**, **[48349]**

Hispanic Business (May 2005, pp. 6); "Our So-Called Economic Recovery" in **[28602]**, **[32622]**

Hispanic Business (Vol. 22, No. 6, June 2000, pp. 48); "Out of the box and onto the Web" in **[34317]**, **[37177]**, **[48350]**

Hispanic Business (March 2003, pp. 40-41); "Overseas Lender of First Resort" in **[43778]**, **[44615]**

Hispanic Business (Vol. 22, No. 9, September 2000, pp. 82); "Painting by numbers" in **[18710]**, **[38874]**, **[45512]**

Hispanic Business (March 2003, pp. 24); "Panasonic Tunes In Hispanic Market" in **[752]**, **[47386]**, **[48352]**, **[49196]**, **[53907]**

Hispanic Business (March 2004, pp. 12); "Panel to Monitor Minority Contracts" in **[40074]**, **[48353]**

Hispanic Business (May 2005, pp. 64, 66); "Partners in Style" in **[4119]**, **[11797]**, **[28612]**, **[44618]**, **[48354]**

Hispanic Business (March 2002, pp. 64); "Pearl by the Sea" in **[12614]**, **[25231]**, **[30400]**

Hispanic Business (April 2005, pp. 26, 28); "Pension Performer" in **[15348]**, **[26875]**

Hispanic Business (Vol. 24, No. 4, April 2002, pp. 16, 18); "Perfect Storm Strikes CEOs" in **[13417]**, **[41079]**, **[43311]**, **[48358]**

Hispanic Business (Vol. 23, No. 11, November 2001, pp. 24-25, 28); "Perfecting the Growth Spurt" in **[22323]**, **[28621]**, **[36618]**, **[48359]**

Hispanic Business (March 2003, pp. 64); "Perked-Up Flyers" in **[30401]**

Hispanic Business (May 2005, pp. 80); "Personal Style" in **[1612]**, **[11270]**, **[24443]**, **[36621]**, **[44124]**, **[49535]**

Hispanic Business (Vol. 23, No. 7/8, July/August 2001, pp. 6); "Pharmed Wins for Innovation" in **[28623]**, **[39524]**, **[48360]**

Hispanic Business (Vol. 22, No. 7-8, July-August 2000, pp. 44); "Pick a niche and fill it" in **[41902]**, **[45534]**, **[48361]**

Hispanic Business (Vol. 22, No. 3, March 2000, pp. 60); "Picking apart company reports" in **[38282]**

Hispanic Business (March 2003, pp. 30-31, 34, 36, 38, 40-42, 44, 46, 48, 50, 52, 54, 56-57); "Pioneers in a Wider World" in **[48364]**, **[56366]**

Hispanic Business (March 2002, pp. 64); "Pizza Hut" in **[19636]**, **[38881]**

Hispanic Business (June 2005, pp. 88); "Playing the Fuel" in **[25405]**, **[32630]**

Hispanic Business (March 2005, pp. 12); "Power and Influence on the Hill" in **[40621]**, **[48365]**

Hispanic Business (March 2005, pp. 16, 18); "Power PACs" in **[40622]**, **[48366]**

Hispanic Business (July/August 2002, pp. 68, 70, 72); "Predicting Success" in **[33211]**

Hispanic Business (December 2002, pp. FRG10); "Procurement: Federal File" in **[40076]**, **[48367]**

Hispanic Business (Vol. 23, No. 7/8, July/August 2001, pp. 6); "Productive Lessons from a Tech Meltdown" in **[36648]**, **[47425]**, **[48368]**

Hispanic Business (June 2002, pp. 96); "Profit or Paycheck?" in **[38296]**, **[54713]**

Hispanic Business (March 2005, pp. 20, 22, 24); "Profiting in a Sideways Market" in **[15379]**, **[28653]**, **[32642]**

Hispanic Business (March 2003, pp. 20); "Program Boosts Minority Supplier Chain" in **[1962]**, **[18113]**, **[48370]**

Hispanic Business (October 2006, pp. 28, 30); "Prospecting in Cuba" in **[13005]**, **[43790]**

Hispanic Business (Vol. 23, No. 7/8, July/August 2001, pp. 110); "Protecting What's Yours" in **[26891]**, **[43328]**

Hispanic Business (Vol. 22, No. 6, June 2000, pp. 116); "Public companies push the envelope" in **[15383]**, **[48373]**, **[50147]**

Hispanic Business (Vol. 22, No. 5, May 2000, pp. 36); "Putting the 'E' in Your Business" in **[34384]**, **[37181]**, **[48374]**

Hispanic Business (September 2004, pp. 20); "Putting Hispanics Behind the Wheel" in **[18114]**, **[53929]**

Hispanic Business (November 2003, pp. 38, 40); "Putting Pension Funds to Work" in **[10146]**, **[15389]**, **[38298]**, **[48375]**

Hispanic Business (July/August 2004, pp. 14); "Putting Research on the Map" in **[16823]**, **[18928]**, **[50948]**

Hispanic Business (Vol. 22, No. 6, June 2000, pp. 112); "Putting the brakes on transportation" in **[25406]**, **[48376]**, **[50152]**

Hispanic Business (January/February 2003, pp. 14); "Radio Broadcasters Rip Arbitron's Language-Weighting Policy" in **[20330]**

Hispanic Business (Vol. 23, No. 5, May 2001, pp. 38, 40); "The Essential Tech Toolbox" in **[4982]**, **[14021]**, **[22986]**, **[41672]**, **[49020]**

Hispanic Business (Vol. 23, No. 10, October, 2001); "The Fed Connection: 100 Most Influential Hispanics" in **[36149]**, **[39329]**

Hispanic Business (Vol. 22, No. 3, March 2000, pp. 40); "The 51 percent rule fallout" in **[40377]**, **[48160]**, **[53724]**

Hispanic Business (Vol. 21, No. 12, December 1999, pp. 74); "The 51 Percent Solution" in **[40378]**, **[48161]**

Hispanic Business (Vol. 22, No. 5, May 2000, pp. 60); "The Franchising Formula" in **[2076]**, **[19875]**, **[21517]**, **[38804]**, **[48169]**

Hispanic Business (Vol. 24, No. 1/2, January/February 2002, pp. 64); "The Good Life by the Bay" in **[25191]**, **[30339]**

Hispanic Business (Vol. 24, No. 4, April 2002, pp. 64); "The Great Software Equalizer" in **[4680]**, **[23021]**, **[53304]**

Hispanic Business (July/August 2004, pp. 28); "The 'Guerrilla' Approach" in **[5007]**, **[41725]**, **[48196]**

Hispanic Business (Vol. 21, No. 12, December 1999, pp. 22); "The new fact of HACR" in **[28539]**, **[48329]**

Hispanic Business (June 2002, pp. 44, 46, 48, 50, 52, 54, 56, 58, 60, 62, 64); "The Hispanic Business 500" in **[28281]**, **[48219]**

Hispanic Business (November 2002, pp. 38-39); "The Hispanic Business 2002 Top 50 Exporters" in **[43695]**, **[48220]**

Hispanic Business (November 2003, pp. 56-57); "The Hispanic Business 2003 Top 50 Exporters" in **[13009]**, **[43840]**

Hispanic Business (March 2002, pp. 38, 40, 42); "The Hispanic Business Top 10 Business Schools" in **[33117]**, **[45244]**

Hispanic Business (March 2002, pp. 44, 46, 48); "The Hispanic Business Top 10 Law Schools" in **[29289]**, **[33118]**

Hispanic Business (March 2003, pp. 50-52); "The Hispanic Market Goes Wireless" in **[661]**, **[5012]**, **[14118]**, **[47076]**, **[49072]**

Hispanic Business (December 2001, pp. 21-22, 26, 28, 30, 32); "The Hispanic Middle Class Comes of Age" in **[32476]**

Hispanic Business (January/February 2004, pp. 48-50); "The Honored Few" in **[36293]**, **[48239]**

Hispanic Business (Vol. 22, No. 6, June 2000, pp. 146); "The Internet vs. the travel agent" in **[25199]**, **[30354]**, **[34084]**

Hispanic Business (Vol. 23, No. 10, October, 2001, pp. 90, 92); "The Internship Edge" in **[33135]**, **[42309]**, **[48565]**

Hispanic Business (November 2006, pp. 26, 28, 30); "The 'IT' Factor" in **[28887]**, **[30971]**, **[42062]**

Hispanic Business (July/August 2004, pp. 46); "The Long Road to Free Trade" in **[40522]**, **[43737]**

Hispanic Business (January/February 2003, pp. 24, 26); "The Man Who Started It All" in **[39455]**, **[48285]**

Hispanic Business (December 2001, pp. FG1-FG2); "The Moment You Least Expect It" in **[22299]**, **[36506]**

Hispanic Business (Vol. 23, No. 7/8, July/August 2001, pp. 28); "The Myth of Benign 'Resistance'" in **[40061]**, **[48318]**

Hispanic Business (January/February 2003, pp. 22, 24); "The New Chairman" in **[39489]**, **[48325]**

Hispanic Business (July/August 2004, pp. 36, 38); "The New Frontier" in **[4114]**, **[48331]**

Hispanic Business (November 2003, pp. 26, 28, 30); "The New Hispanic Information Economy" in **[32591]**, **[49162]**, **[50933]**

Hispanic Business (January/February 2003, pp. 62); "The Newest Cell Phones" in **[5070]**, **[49166]**

Hispanic Business (Vol. 22, No. 10, October 2000, pp. 30); "The 100 most influential Hispanics" in **[36580]**, **[48344]**

Hispanic Business (October 2002, pp. 90); "The Online Lawyer" in **[14316]**, **[29427]**, **[34294]**, **[40594]**

Hispanic Business (Vol. 22, No. 7-8, July-August 2000, pp. 68); "The Perfect Niche" n **[25466]**, **[34341]**, **[35606]**

Hispanic Business (March 2005, pp. 38, 40); "The Perfect Pitch" in **[15350]**, **[36617]**, **[55775]**

Hispanic Business (Vol. 23, No. 7/8, July/August 2001, pp. 94, 96); "The Place That Gump Built" in **[9736]**, **[33206]**

Hispanic Business (October 2002, pp. 22, 24); "The Privatization Question" in **[40627]**

Hispanic Business (Vol. 22, No. 1/2, January/February, pp. 18, 20, 22); "The Race to Reach Critical Mass" in **[30588]**, **[47447]**

Hispanic Business (June 2005, pp. 26, 28, 30); "The Rich Get Richer" in **[28712]**, **[48389]**

Hispanic Business (July-Aug.2000, pp.72); "The Right Recipe: Successful E-Commerce Sites have Three Essential Ingredients in Common" in **[33482]**, **[37075]**

Hispanic Business (December 2002, pp. 56); "The Second-Home Tax Shelter" in **[20663]**, **[54739]**

Hispanic Business (December 2001, pp. 50, 52); "The Sky's the Limit" in **[252]**, **[47537]**

Hispanic Business (March 2004, pp. 20, 22); "The Social Movement That Grew Up" in **[18935]**, **[32065]**, **[32700]**

Hispanic Business (Vol. 23, No. 10, October, 2001, pp. 36, 38); "The Social Security Conundrum" in **[39602]**, **[40705]**, **[48414]**

Hispanic Business (June 2002, pp. 66); "The Strategic Planning Payoff" in **[30011]**, **[48422]**

Hispanic Business (November 2002, pp. 36); "The Struggle for Sales Overseas" in **[28837]**, **[43828]**, **[48425]**, **[51851]**

Hispanic Business (Vol. 21, No. 12, December 1999, pp. 26); "The chemistry of super-growth" in **[27944]**, **[48101]**

Hispanic Business (January/February 2005, pp. 56, 58); "The Tech Track" in **[10205]**, **[28870]**, **[42047]**, **[42433]**, **[46457]**, **[52598]**

Hispanic Business (Vol. 22, No. 10, October 2000, pp. 26); "The changing face of technology" in **[41599]**, **[48098]**

Hispanic Business (Vol.22, No.6, June 2000, pp. 66); "The 2000 Hispanic Business 500 Directory" in **[48460]**

Hispanic Business (March 2004, pp. 36-37); "The VC Process" in **[44683]**, **[48467]**, **[55888]**

Hispanic Business (March 2002, pp. 20, 22, 24, 26, 28, 30, 32, 34, 36); "The Wealthiest Hispanics" in **[36924]**

Hispanic Business (January/February 2005, pp. 60, 62); "The Year Ahead" in **[29034]**, **[32804]**

Hispanic Business (Vol. 23, No. 11, November 2001, pp. 66); "Therapy Island" in **[12647]**, **[17915]**, **[25255]**, **[30425]**

Hispanic Business (July/August 2002, pp. 16); "Thumbs Up" in **[39942]**, **[48438]**

Hispanic Business (June 2002, pp. 78); "Time for an Upgrade" in **[6840]**, **[49320]**

Hispanic Business (May 2005, pp. 46, 48); "Titans Tune In" in **[6842]**, **[42070]**, **[48441]**

Hispanic Business (July/August 2002, pp. 36, 38, 42, 44, 46, 48); "To Fill A Widening Niche" in **[28903]**, **[48442]**

"The Hispanic Business Top 10 Business Schools" in *Hispanic Business* (March 2002, pp. 38, 40, 42) **[33117]**, **[45244]**

Hispanic Business (September 2004, pp. 78, 80, 82, 84); "Top 10 Business Schools for Hispanics" in **[32275]**, **[33256]**, **[35536]**, **[36874]**, **[39633]**, **[45748]**, **[48401]**, **[48445]**

"The Hispanic Business Top 10 Law Schools" in *Hispanic Business* (March 2002, pp. 44, 46, 48) **[29289]**, **[33118]**

Hispanic Business (September 2004, pp. 70, 72, 74, 76); "Top 10 Law Schools for Hispanics" in **[29551]**, **[30210]**, **[33257]**, **[36875]**, **[48402]**, **[48446]**

Hispanic Business (December 2003, pp. 42, 44, 46, 48, 50); "Top 25 Hispanic Ad Agencies" in **[816]**, **[47653]**, **[48447]**

"Hispanic Business Top 50 Companies for Diversity" in *Hispanic Business* (September 2006, pp. 32-34) **[39383]**, **[48223]**

Hispanic Business (July/August 2004, pp. 50, 51); "Top 50 Exporters" in **[13011]**, **[43845]**, **[56017]**

Hispanic Business (Vol. 22, No. 9, September 2000, pp. 42); "Top-down diversity" in **[47656]**, **[54265]**

Hispanic Business (September 2006, pp. 76, 78, 80); "Top Ten Schools for Hispanics: Engineering" in **[33260]**, **[48449]**

Hispanic Business (September 2006, pp. 70, 72, 74); "Top Ten Schools for Hispanics MBA" in **[33261]**, **[48450]**

Hispanic Business (September 2006, pp. 82, 84, 86); "Top Ten Schools for Hispanics: Medical" in **[33262]**, **[41119]**, **[48451]**

Hispanic Business (March 2004, pp. 46-49); "Tough Luxury" in **[18146]**

Hispanic Business (April 2005, pp. 14); "Towering Goal" in **[20690]**, **[21026]**, **[54268]**

Hispanic Business (September 2002, pp. 8); "Toyota's Opportunity Exchange" in **[46462]**, **[48453]**

Hispanic Business (Vol. 23, No. 10, October, 2001, pp. 40); "Tracking the Hispanic Traveler" in **[24737]**, **[25259]**, **[28913]**

Hispanic Business (Vol. 22, No. 4, April 2000, pp. 77); "Tracking T&E deductions" in **[30428]**, **[54842]**

Hispanic Business (Vol. 22, No. 5, May 2000, pp. 100); "Transforming online car buying" in **[18149]**, **[34621]**

Hispanic Business (Vol. 22, No. 7-8, July-August 2000, pp. 14); "Transforming TV" in **[4125]**, **[34622]**, **[43852]**

Hispanic Business (Vol. 22, No. 9, September 2000, pp. 80); "Trends in organization management" in **[47667]**

Hispanic Business (Vol. 23, No. 10, October, 2001, pp. 20); "Trouble in Little Cuba" in **[40783]**, **[48455]**

Hispanic Business (October 2002, pp. 18); "Trouble in Tennessee" in **[40104]**, **[48456]**

Hispanic Business (December 2006, pp. 52); "Tuned In" in **[20342]**, **[48458]**

Hispanic Business (Vol. 21, No. 12, December 1999, pp. 52); "Tuning in to the stock market: Two Hispanic radio firms launch IPOs" in **[15548]**, **[20344]**, **[50228]**

Hispanic Business (March 2004, pp. 24-26, 28-29); "Turning the Silver Screen Gold" in **[9745]**, **[10221]**, **[15551]**, **[48459]**

Hispanic Business (October 2006, pp. 16); "Two Growing Hispanic Radio Companies Broadcast Expansion Plans" in **[15552]**, **[20346]**, **[28928]**, **[50232]**

Hispanic Business (June 2002, pp. 22); "Uncle Sam, Paralegal" in **[29078]**, **[35708]**, **[39781]**, **[40129]**, **[47984]**

Hispanic Business (Vol. 23, No. 5, May 2001, pp. 58); "Under the Big Top" in **[38941]**

Hispanic Business (November 2006, pp. 58, 60, 62); "Unhealthy Costs" in **[13507]**, **[41126]**, **[43411]**

Hispanic Business (January/February 2005, pp. 8); "U.S. Hispanic Market Has Special Character" in **[43863]**, **[48463]**

Hispanic Business (Vol. 23, No. 11, November 2001, pp. 20); "U.S.-Mexico Relations Remain on Front Burner" in **[43864]**, **[48464]**

Hispanic Business (July/August 2002, pp. 58, 60, 62); "Unrealized Potential" in **[43865]**, **[48465]**

Hispanic Business (September 2006, pp. 18, 20); "Urban Pioneers" in **[7508]**, **[21033]**, **[51398]**

Hispanic Business (Vol. 23, No. 10, October, 2001, pp. 12); "Valor on the Front Lines" in **[4894]**, **[47985]**

Hispanic Business (March 2003, pp. 16); "Verizon Breaks New Ads" in **[826]**, **[47690]**, **[48470]**

Hispanic Business (Vol. 23, No. 7/8, July/August 2001, pp. 32-33); "Voice of Experience" in **[36918]**, **[48472]**

Hispanic Business (July/August 2002, pp. 10); "Volvo Opens Supplier Diversity Office" in **[1984]**, **[46478]**, **[48473]**

Hispanic Business (December 2003, pp. 56); "Wall Street Performers" in **[829]**, **[20347]**, **[24459]**

Hispanic Business (March 2002, pp. 34); "Wary of Economic Instability" in **[10235]**, **[15591]**, **[32783]**

Hispanic Business (March 2003, pp. 12); "Washington Insider: Hispanics Crash House Small-Biz Groups" in **[40812]**, **[48475]**

Hispanic Business (July/August 2004, pp. 12); "Washington Insider: Issues Count More Than Affiliation" in **[40813]**, **[48476]**

Hispanic Business (March 2003, pp. 16); "Washington Insider: Small Business Overlooked?" in **[36920]**, **[39659]**, **[40814]**, **[48477]**

Hispanic Business (September 2003, pp. 46); "Which School is Right?" in **[29581]**, **[33281]**, **[39678]**, **[45835]**

Hispanic Business (July/August 2004, pp. 16); "Who Are We?" in **[32795]**, **[48481]**

Hispanic Business (Vol. 22, No. 6, June 2000, pp. 114); "Wholesaler plans Web expansion" in **[7749]**, **[34715]**, **[56021]**

Hispanic Business (January/February 2004, pp. 14-16, 18); "Why Bright Star Shines" in **[5178]**, **[32167]**, **[36967]**, **[48483]**

Hispanic Business (Vol. 23, No. 11, November 2001, p. 22); "Why Small Firms Can't Do Their Part" in **[40108]**, **[40844]**, **[54080]**

Hispanic Business (November 2003, pp. 74); "Why Wi-Fi?" in **[34724]**, **[54082]**

Hispanic Business (Vol. 22, No. 5, May 2000, pp. 80); "Wired generation: polls indicate Hispanics are at home in the online market" in **[34733]**

Hispanic Business (Vol. 22, No. 7-8, July-August 2000, pp. 70); "Wiring the border" in **[14629]**, **[34738]**, **[39959]**, **[43879]**

"Hispanic Business - Woman of the Year: Making the Case for Small Business" in *Hispanic Business* (March 2003, pp. 26-28) **[48224]**, **[56263]**

Hispanic Business (May 2005, pp. 58); "Words Fail Them" in **[25097]**, **[41139]**, **[54282]**

Hispanic Business (October 2004, pp. 116, 118); "Working on Thin Air" in **[5190]**, **[6873]**, **[30454]**, **[49376]**

Hispanic Business (December 2006, pp. 54); "World Cup Kicks Print Media Into High Gear" in **[842]**, **[47762]**

Hispanic Business (Vol. 22, No. 7-8, July-August 2000, pp. 106); "Wrestling for Web dominance" in **[15613]**, **[34751]**, **[37213]**, **[43886]**, **[50271]**

Hispanic Business (June 2005, pp. 18); "WSJ Honors Economist" in **[15614]**, **[31256]**, **[32802]**, **[45875]**, **[56520]**

Hispanic Business (Vol. 23, No. 10, October, 2001, pp. 26); "Yes to English, No to Espanol?" in **[33287]**, **[39699]**

Hispanic Business (Vol. 22, No. 1/2, January/February, pp. 88); "Your PC Post Office" in **[49384]**, **[49570]**

Hispanic Business (March 2003, pp. 57); "You're Deposing Me?" in **[29592]**

"Hispanic Chamber of Commerce creates venture fund" in *Wall Street Journal* (February 22, 2000, pp. B2) **[48225]**, **[55663]**

Hispanic Chamber of Commerce of Hawaii **[59247]**

Hispanic Chamber of Commerce of Minnesota **[61602]**

Hispanic Chamber of Commerce of Orange County **[57546]**

Hispanic Chamber of Commerce of Santa Barbara **[57547]**

Hispanic Chamber of Commerce of Sonoma County **[57548]**

Hispanic Chamber of Commerce Yakima County **[66116]**

"Hispanic Employment Program Managers Directory" in *Hispanic Business* (December 2001, pp. FG8, FG10 FG12) **[42283]**, **[48557]**

"The Hispanic Market Goes Wireless" in *Hispanic Business* (March 2003, pp. 50-52) **[661]**, **[5012]**, **[14118]**, **[47076]**, **[49072]**

Hispanic Metropolitan Chamber of Commerce **[64229]**

"The Hispanic Middle Class Comes of Age" in *Hispanic Business* (December 2001, pp. 21-22, 26, 28, 30, 32) **[32476]**

"Hispanic Outreach Takes Off" in *Hispanic Business* (March 2003, pp. 62, 64) **[40041]**, **[42284]**

"Hispanic women taking the reins" in *Hispanic Business* (Vol. 22, No. 6, June 2000, pp. 118) **[48226]**, **[56264]**

"Hispanic market pioneer retires" in *Hispanic Business* (Vol. 22, No. 1-2, January-February 2000, pp. 30) **[13323]**, **[47077]**, **[56012]**

"HispanicBusiness.com, AOL Team Up" in *Hispanic Business* (Vol. 23, No. 7/8, July/August 2001, pp. 72) **[14119]**, **[48227]**

"HispanicBusiness.com Expands" in *Hispanic Business* (Vol. 23, No. 5, May 2001, pp. 18) **[14120]**, **[28283]**, **[34011]**, **[48228]**

"Hispanics who write the checks" in *Hispanic Business* (Vol. 22, No. 11, November 2000, pp. 74) **[48229]**

"Hispanics Flocking to the Web" in *Hispanic Business* (March 2002, pp. 12) **[14121]**, **[34012]**

"Hispanics Gravitating Toward the 'Net" in *Hispanic Business* (March 2003, pp. 24) **[14122]**, **[34013]**, **[48230]**

"Hispanics Now Top Minority" in *Hispanic Business* (March 2003, pp. 16) **[47078]**, **[48231]**

"Hispanics on Wall Street" in *Hispanic Business* (Vol. 23, No. 10, October, 2001, pp. 14) **[15082]**, **[48232]**

Hispano Chamber of Commerce de Las Cruces **[62696]**

HispanTelligence **[48500]**

"Hispantelligence quarterly" in *Hispanic Business* (March 2003, pp. 10) **[28284]**, **[48233]**

"Hispantelligence Report" in *Hispanic Business* (December 2006, pp. 12) **[662]**, **[10001]**, **[11627]**, **[15083]**, **[15562]**, **[16125]**, **[17387]**, **[20525]**, **[27760]**, **[28285]**, **[32477]**, **[33567]**, **[42285]**, **[45952]**, **[48234]**, **[48558]**, **[49045]**, **[49173]**, **[50169]**, **[51181]**

"Hispantelligence Reports" in *Hispanic Business* (June 2005, pp. 12) **[15084]**, **[28286]**, **[32478]**, **[48235]**

Hissong Associates Inc. **[31974]**

Historic Annapolis Foundation–Research Center **[11093]**

Historic Exterior Paint Colors Consulting **[1557]**, **[7610]**, **[18715]**

"Historic Redevelopment Pushes Kirtland, Ohio Ice Cream Shop to Relocate" in *Willoughby News-Herald* (September 13, 2002) **[12780]**, **[37683]**, **[52681]**

Historic Silver Valley Chamber of Commerce **[59308]**

Historic Sonora Chamber of Commerce **[57549]**

"Historical Architectural Review Board Recently Awarded Nancy Noll, the Historic Rehabilitation Award" in *Roofing Contractor* (Aug. 03) **[2436]**

Historical Roller Skating Overview **[22837]**

History of Aviation **[976]**

"History Bears Fruit for Maine Family's Apple Orchard" in *Portland Press Herald* (October 7, 2005) **[26514]**, **[37684]**

"History Lesson" in *Entrepreneur* (Vol. 33, September 2005, No. 9, pp. 19) **[1320]**, **[37685]**, **[51182]**

"History Recycled" in *Crain's Detroit Business* (Vol. 21, October 3, 2005, No. 43, pp. 11) **[1321]**, **[1518]**, **[13648]**, **[21237]**

A History of Small Business in America **[26515]**, **[32479]**, **[39384]**, **[46315]**, **[51673]**, **[52544]**

"Hit Discriminators Where it Hurts" in *Black Enterprise* (Vol. 34, No. 4, November 2003, pp. 28) **[32031]**, **[32480]**, **[48236]**

"Hit the Mark" in *My Business* (August/September 2002, pp. 28-35) **[26825]**, **[28287]**, **[31732]**, **[34014]**, **[47079]**, **[49073]**, **[53775]**

"Hit Parade" in *Venture Capital Journal* (September 1, 2005) **[55664]**

"Hit the Road" in *Entrepreneur* (Vol. 31, No. 10, October 2003, pp. 87) **[47080]**, **[50607]**, **[54203]**

"Hit the Road: Itching to Throw Your Business Into High Gear?" in *Entrepreneur* (Vol. 32, December 2004, No. 12, pp. 37) **[18058]**, **[27136]**

Hitchcock Chamber of Commerce **[65308]**

"Hitting the Links" in *Small Business Opportunities* (Vol. 13, No. 5, September 2001, pp. 84) **[14123]**, **[25865]**, **[34015]**

Hive Lights **[2472]**

H.J. Wings & Things **[21841]**

HME News **[17123]**

HMS Group **[58035]**

HMS Hawaii Management Partners **[59259]**

Ho-Lee-Chow **[12087]**

HO2 Partners **[65609]**

Hobart Chamber of Commerce **[59942]**, **[64014]**

Hobbs Chamber of Commerce **[62697]**

Hobby Greenhouse **[11464]**

Hobby Greenhouse Association **[11411]**

Hobby Industry Association Annual Convention and Trade Show **[8085]**, **[8241]**, **[24847]**

Hobby Merchandiser **[8211]**

Hobby Merchandiser Annual Trade Directory **[8168]**

Hobbytown USA **[8248]**

Hobe Sound Chamber of Commerce **[58858]**

"The HOC 100" in *Home Office Computing* (Vol. 18, No. 12, December 2000, pp. 52) **[49074]**

Hock Shop Inc. **[7182]**

"Hockeytown Cafe Adds Motorcycles to Mix" in *Crain's Detroit Business* (Vol. 21, November 7, 2005, No. 45, pp. 18) **[2341]**, **[21530]**

Hoffman Estates Chamber of Commerce **[59543]**

"Hogan's Inferno" in *Entrepreneur* (Vol. 28, No. 8, August 2000, pp. 48) **[6170]**, **[49075]**

Hogi Yogi **[12828]**

Hoisington Chamber of Commerce **[60350]**

Hoisington Koegler Group Inc. **[1558]**

Hola Amigos Boxed Set **[33318]**

Hola Amigos: Spanish for Kids **[5387]**

Holbrook Chamber of Commerce **[57044]**

Holcomb Gallagher Adams Advertising Inc. **[47871]**, **[50726]**

"Hold On Tight" in *Entrepreneur* (Vol. 31, No. 8, August 2003, pp. 66) **[36290]**, **[42863]**, **[45245]**

"Hold That Bid on eBay" in *Fortune* (Vol. 151, February 21, 2005, No. 4, pp. 125) **[1823]**, **[15085]**

"Hold Your Tongue" in *Black Enterprise* (Vol. 34, No. 3, October 2003, pp. 54) **[42286]**, **[45246]**

"Hold'Em" in *Entrepreneur* (Vol. 28, No. 7, July 2000, pp. 78) **[35505]**, **[37837]**, **[44417]**, **[55392]**

Holden Arboretum–Warren H. Corning Library **[11522]**

Holden Area Chamber of Commerce **[60961]**

Holden Chamber of Commerce **[61975]**

Holdenville Chamber of Commerce **[64015]**

Holding Capital Group, Inc. **[63108]**

"Holding a Job, Having a Life: The Next Level in Work" in *Employment Relations Today* (Vol. 27, No. 2, Summer 2000, pp. 29) **[34931]**, **[53776]**

"Holding Pattern" in *Entrepreneur* (Vol. 33, September 2005, No. 9, pp. 26) **[31582]**, **[32481]**, **[40482]**, **[42287]**, **[53777]**

"Holding pattern: It's not time to go 3G quite yet" in *Entrepreneur* (Vol. 30, No. 2, February 2002, pp. 31) **[5013]**, **[41744]**, **[49076]**

"Holding onto talent: the best defense is a preemptive strike" in *Wall Street Journal* (March 14, 2000, pp. B1) **[45247]**

Holdrege Area Chamber of Commerce **[62271]**

"Holiday Bonus" in *Entrepreneur* (Vol. 33, September 2005, No. 9, pp. 48) **[32994]**, **[34016]**, **[47081]**, **[51674]**

Holiday Centerpieces **[8227]**, **[10592]**

"Holiday Crush Never Stops for Nazareth, Pa., Bed & Breakfast's Owners" in *Morning Call* (December 1, 2003) **[2437]**

Holiday Fair **[5473]**, **[8086]**, **[8242]**

"Holiday Headache" in *The Record* (November 14, 2005) **[26826]**, **[42288]**

Holiday Market **[5474]**, **[8087]**

Holiday Showcase **[1752]**

"Holiday Week Can Be Extra-Productive for Some Sacramento, Calif.-Area Workers" in *Sacramento Bee* (December 28, 2005) **[20022]**, **[52358]**, **[54951]**

Holistic Chamber of Commerce **[65309]**

Holistic Management International **[9467]**

Holistic Massage-The Caring Touch **[17021]**

Holland Area Chamber of Commerce **[61334]**

Holland - Springfield Chamber of Commerce **[63700]**

"Holliday Fenoglio Begins Buyout of Lend Lease" in *South Florida Business Journal* (Vol. 23, No. 48, July 4, 2003, pp. 4) **[20526]**, **[20893]**, **[49980]**

Hollinger Capital **[63109]**

"Hollinger Contacts VC Giant" in *Crain's Chicago Business* (Vol. 26, No. 50, December 15, 2003, pp. 1) **[15086]**, **[18882]**, **[49981]**, **[55665]**

"Hollinger Contacts VC Giant; Hicks Muse Could See Synergies with Radio Here" in *Crains Chicago Business* (Vol. 26, No. 50) **[15087]**, **[18883]**, **[49982]**, **[55666]**

"Hollinger VC Unit has Family Ties; Black's Nephew has Few Hits, Many Misses With Fund" in *Crains Chicago Business* (Vol. 26, No. 51) **[15088]**, **[37686]**, **[49983]**, **[55667]**

"Hollinger VC Unit has Family Ties" in *Crain's Chicago Business* (Vol. 26, No. 51, December 22, 2003, pp. 3) **[15089]**, **[37687]**, **[49984]**, **[55668]**

Hollingsworth & Associates **[24118]**, **[38545]**

"Hollister wins business praise" in *Crain's Detroit Business* (Vol. 18, No. 51, December 23, 2002, pp. 7) **[28288]**, **[32482]**

"Hollister priorities: Loan, training programs" in *Crain's Detroit Business* (Vol. 19, No. 3, January 20, 2003, pp. 24) **[35506]**, **[39769]**, **[44418]**

Holly Area Chamber of Commerce **[61335]**

Holly Hill Chamber of Commerce **[58859]**

Holly Springs Chamber of Commerce **[61799]**

Hollywood Chamber of Commerce **[57550]**

Hollywood Directors and Their Craft **[9763]**

Hollywood Distributors Directory **[24465]**

Hollywood Film Archive–Library **[17549]**, **[25614]**

"Hollywood, Fla., Men's Shop is Tailor-Made for Success" in *South Florida Sun-Sentinel* (January 3, 2005) **[18997]**, **[37688]**, **[51183]**

"Hollywood Opens Ahead Of Schedule" in *Mississippi Business Journal* (Vol. 28, September 2006, No. 36, pp. 20) **[10869]**, **[28289]**, **[39385]**

Hollywood Radio and Television Society **[20289]**, **[24361]**

"Hollywood Redux" in *My Business* (April/May 2004, pp. 52) **[5669]**, **[7166]**

The Hollywood Reporter **[17540]**

Hollywood Representation Directory **[23827]**

"Hollywood, Silicon Valley at odds over digital piracy bills" in *Atlanta Business Chronicle* (Vol. 25, No. 21, Nov. 1, 2002, pp. 10B) **[9719]**, **[17745]**, **[25592]**, **[34017]**, **[41745]**, **[44057]**

Holmes Community College–SBDC **[61750]**

Holmes County Chamber of Commerce **[58860]**, **[63701]**

Genese Holmes **[2985]**

H.H. Holmes Testing Laboratories Inc. **[7611]**

Holstein Chamber of Commerce **[60150]**

Holt Capital **[3731]**, **[16619]**, **[31374]**, **[38546]**, **[46046]**, **[53095]**

Holton Chamber of Commerce **[60351]**

Holtville Chamber of Commerce **[57551]**

"The Holy Wafer" in *Red Herring* (No. 99, June 15 & July 1, 2001, pp. 106-107) **[41746]**, **[50887]**

Holyoke Chamber of Commerce **[58383]**

Home Accents Today (Vol. 18, No. 9, August 2003, pp. 26); "Bed & Breakfast" in **[2425]**

"Home Alone: Make an Effort to Fight Loneliness" in *My Business* (October/November 2002, pp. 45) **[35507]**, **[42516]**

Home-Alyze **[3274]**

The Home-Based Entrepreneur: The Complete Guide to Working at Home **[42633]**

"Home-Based Entrepreneurs Still Rely Most on the 4 F's" in *Home Business* (Vol. 12, March/April 2005, No. 2, pp. 78) **[42520]**, **[44419]**

Home Based & Mail Order Business **[16441]**

"Home-Based Microbiz" in *Small Business Opportunities* (Vol. 16, No. 2, March 2004, pp. 12, 168) **[42521]**

Home-Based Newsletter Publishing: A Success Guide for Entrepreneurs **[18230]**

"Home-Based Resources" in *Small Business Opportunities* (Vol. 16, No. 2, March 2004, pp. 184) **[39839]**, **[42634]**

Home-Based Travel Agent, 5th Edition **[24645]**, **[25118]**, **[42522]**

Home-Based Working Moms **[42776]**

"Home Builder Falls Under SEC Scrutiny" in *Orlando Business Journal* (Vol. 20, No. 10, August 22, 2003, pp. 1) **[7309]**, **[7362]**, **[14881]**, **[15090]**, **[29290]**, **[30257]**, **[40440]**, **[40543]**, **[47619]**, **[49985]**

Home Builders Network Inc. **[7612]**

"Home-building firms post double-digit profits, but Wall Street remains unimpressed" in *Daily Business Review* (Vol. 77, Jan. 7, 2003) **[7363]**, **[10002]**, **[15091]**, **[28290]**, **[38119]**

"Home Building at Record High" in *Tampa Tribune* (October 27, 2005) **[7364]**, **[20527]**, **[28291]**

Home Business (Vol. 12, March/April 2005, No. 2, pp. 92); "12 Steps to Preventing Identity Theft" in **[22159]**

Home Business (Vol. 12, March/April 2005, No. 2, pp. 16, 20-23, 26-29, 100-101, 104-105); "250 Unleash the Entrepreneur Within You!" in **[35311]**, **[38599]**, **[42499]**

Home Business (Vol. 12, March/April 2005, No. 2, pp. 78); "2005 Standard Mileage Rates" in **[55]**, **[2861]**, **[23873]**, **[42571]**, **[54420]**

Home Business (Vol. 13, January/February 2006, No. 1, pp. 81); "A Chance at a Second Career" in **[3309]**, **[35933]**, **[37609]**

Home Business (Vol. 12, October 2005, No. 5, pp. 40); "A Full House" in **[5545]**, **[9624]**, **[22762]**, **[36193]**, **[37661]**

Home Business (Vol. 12, October 2005, No. 5, pp. 86); "A Little Equation that Creates Big Results" in **[36449]**, **[54966]**

Home Business (Vol. 12, March/April 2005, No. 2, pp. 46, 94); "Add Some Magic to Your Marketing" in **[42573]**, **[46659]**

Home Business (Vol. 12, October 2005, No. 5, pp. 74); "Are You Ready for Your Accounts?" in **[73]**, **[2866]**, **[23884]**

Home Business (Vol. 12, March/April 2005, No. 2, pp. 48); "Back in the Saddle" in **[31112]**, **[42574]**

Home Business (Vol. 12, October 2005, No. 5, pp. 76); "Beating the Cash Flow Blues" in **[82]**, **[27087]**

Home Business (Vol. 12, March/April 2005, No. 2, pp. 81); "Beauty and the Bugs" in **[19019]**, **[35814]**, **[42576]**, **[56132]**

Home Business to Big Business: How to Launch Your Home Business and Make it a Success **[42635]**

Home Business (Vol. 12, October 2005, No. 5, pp. 68); "Book Publishing for Entrepreneurs" in **[2632]**, **[8589]**, **[42502]**

Home Business (Vol. 13, January/February 2006, No. 1, pp. 58, 60); "Build Your Business with eBay" in **[1787]**, **[13864]**, **[27883]**, **[33620]**, **[46754]**

Home Business (Vol. 12, October 2005, No. 5, pp. 16, 18-22, 102, 104); "Build Your Dream Home Business" in **[29714]**, **[35346]**, **[39030]**, **[42503]**, **[44390]**, **[46561]**

Home Business (Vol. 12, October 2005, No. 5, pp. 88, 90-91); "Build Your Own Web Site" in **[13865]**, **[25806]**, **[46755]**

Home Business (Vol. 12, October 2005, No. 5, pp. 71); "Business is Bouncin'" in **[21313]**, **[42585]**, **[56150]**

Home Business (Vol. 12, October 2005, No. 5, pp. 72); "Business Budgeting Basics" in **[7]**, **[27071]**

Home Business (Vol. 12, March/April 2005, No. 2, pp. 68); "Can Your Product Make It In Mail Order?" in **[16408]**

Home Business (Vol. 13, January/February 2006, No. 1, pp. 71); "Competing with the Big Guys" in **[16809]**, **[30820]**, **[42593]**, **[46825]**, **[56169]**

Home Business (Vol. 13, January/February 2006, No. 1, pp. 64); "Develop a Mission Statement for Your Business" in **[29848]**, **[36011]**

Home Business (Vol. 12, March/April 2005, No. 2, pp. 40, 42-43); "Discovering a Spin-Off Business" in **[28040]**, **[36018]**, **[42602]**

Home Business (Vol. 12, October 2005, No. 5, pp. 62); "Doing Your Homework" in **[29725]**, **[35395]**, **[39047]**, **[42509]**

Home Business (Vol. 12, March/April 2005, No. 2, pp. 90); "Employee Matters" in **[42227]**, **[42610]**

Home Business (Vol. 12, March/April 2005, No. 2, pp. 44); "Entrepreneurship on the Rise" in **[36110]**, **[48149]**, **[56208]**

Home Business (Vol. 12, March/April 2005, No. 2, pp. 74); "Finding Investors" in **[35453]**, **[42514]**, **[44410]**, **[49766]**

Home Business (Vol. 12, March/April 2005, No. 2, pp. 82, 84-87); "Fitting Home Offices Into Small Spaces" in **[13642]**, **[18543]**, **[42616]**, **[49499]**

Home Business (Vol. 13, January/February 2006, No. 1, pp. 24, 26-27, 54-55); "Franchise Fever" in **[38637]**

Home Business (Vol. 12, March/April 2005, No. 2, pp. 96); "From Tee to Green" in **[11262]**, **[42620]**, **[44049]**

Home Business (Vol. 12, March/April 2005, No. 2, pp. 32, 34-35); "Generate More Revenue with a Bottom-Up Marketing Plan" in **[28198]**, **[42621]**, **[47004]**

Home Business (Vol. 12, March/April 2005, No. 2, pp. 58); "Grassroots Marketing" in **[645]**, **[35490]**, **[42516]**, **[46570]**

Home Business (Vol. 13, January/February 2006, No. 1, pp. 88, 90-91); "Growing Pains" in **[28245]**, **[42253]**, **[42627]**

Home Business (Vol. 13, January/February 2006, No. 1, pp. 40); "Healthy, Wealthy and Wise" in **[12008]**, **[19407]**, **[36271]**, **[42631]**, **[51662]**

Home Business (Vol. 12, March/April 2005, No. 2, pp. 78); "Home-Based Entrepreneurs Still Rely Most on the 4 F's" in **[42520]**, **[44419]**

Home Business (Vol. 12, October 2005, No. 5, pp. 52); "How to Advertise with Flyers" in **[666]**, **[47095]**

Home Business (Vol. 13, January/February 2006, No. 1, pp. 52); "How to Make Tough Sales Without Pressure" in **[51682]**

Home Business (Vol. 13, January/February 2006, No. 1, pp. 82, 84); "How to Prepare Your Home Business for a Natural Disaster" in **[13328]**, **[29902]**, **[43223]**

Home Business (Vol. 12, October 2005, No. 5, pp. 32, 34, 95); "How to Vitalize a Home-Based Operation" in **[28312]**, **[29908]**, **[42662]**

Home Business (Vol. 12, March/April 2005, No. 2, pp. 44); "Howdy Partner!" in **[36327]**, **[49994]**

Home Business (Vol. 13, January/February 2006, No. 1, pp. 92); "In the Right Field" in **[26517]**

Home Business (Vol. 12, March/April 2005, No. 2, pp. 88); "Internet Firewalls" in **[4700]**, **[6694]**, **[22264]**, **[23048]**, **[42665]**, **[53336]**

Home Business (Vol. 12, March/April 2005, No. 2, pp. 76); "It's Tax Time - Again" in **[179]**, **[2923]**, **[23975]**, **[42667]**, **[54629]**

Home Business (Vol. 12, October 2005, No. 5, pp. 64, 66); "Joining Forces" in **[28363]**, **[42668]**, **[50029]**

Home Business (Vol. 12, March/April 2005, No. 2, pp. 62); "Lending a Helping Hand Even When Off Duty" in **[33155]**, **[36436]**, **[42674]**

Home Business (Vol. 12, October 2005, No. 5, pp. 48, 50-51); "Loyal Clients Boost Revenue" in **[28440]**, **[31764]**

Home Business Made Easy: How to Select & Start a Home Business That Fits Your Interests, Lifestyles & Pocketbook **[42636]**

Home Business (Vol. 13, January/February 2006, No. 1, pp. 70); "Magic Moments" in **[42675]**, **[47219]**

Home Business (Vol. 12, March/April 2005, No. 2, pp. 44); "Major Contributions to the Community" in **[36463]**, **[54221]**

Home Business (Vol. 12, March/April 2005, No. 2, pp. 70); "Making Cents of It All" in **[24819]**, **[37720]**, **[56754]**

Home Business (Vol. 13, January/February 2006, No. 1, pp. 28, 30-31, 95); "Managing Creativity in a Progressive Home Business" in **[29932]**, **[42677]**

Home Business (Vol. 12, October 2005, No. 5, pp. 42, 44-45); "Market Planning 101" in **[29750]**, **[39772]**, **[42543]**, **[44426]**, **[46579]**, **[49771]**, **[52367]**

Home Business (Vol. 12, October 2005, No. 5, pp. 24, 26-27, 54-55); "Marketing Strategies for Your New Home-Based Business" in [42544], [46581]

Home Business (Vol. 13, January/February 2006, No. 1, pp. 94); "Medical Coverage Options for the Self-Employed" in [13383], [43275]

Home Business (Vol. 12, March/April 2005, No. 2, pp. 44); "Military Service Equips Future Business Owners" in [35565], [53565]

Home Business (Vol. 13, January/February 2006, No. 1, pp. 78); "Money Corner" in [38230], [39870], [51249], [54662]

Home Business News [63903]

Home Business (Vol. 13, January/February 2006, No. 1, pp. 98); "News and Reviews" in [4740], [23099], [34261], [42877], [47342], [48770], [49167], [53386]

Home Business (Vol. 13, January/February 2006, No. 1, pp. 38-39); "Newsstand" in [6265], [6741], [18607], [29414], [32598], [34262], [36550], [42687], [47345], [49521], [50101], [51272], [54676]

Home Business (Vol. 12, October 2005, No. 5, pp. 41; "On Her Best Behavior" in [27461], [36573], [39512]

Home Business (Vol. 13, January/February 2006, No. 1, pp. 92); "On Top of the World" in [8177], [24717], [34283], [36577]

The Home Business Report [42777]

Home Business (Vol. 13, January/February 2006, No. 1, pp. 56); "Reporting for Boot Camp" in [3576], [16528], [36687]

Home Business (Vol. 12, March/April 2005, No. 2, pp. 63); "Rich in Tradition" in [8018], [8181], [42717], [56386]

Home Business (Vol. 12, October 2005, No. 5, pp. 57; "Saying Goodbye to the Standardized Test Prep Blues" in [25467], [33227]

Home Business (Vol. 13, January/February 2006, No. 1, pp. 41); "Scrubs in Vogue" in [5568], [56397]

Home Business (Vol. 12, October 2005, No. 5, pp. 82, 84); "Setting Up a Productive Home Office" in [42550], [48933], [49475], [53148]

Home Business (Vol. 12, March/April 2005, No. 2, pp. 66); "Sharpening the Saw When You Work as a Consultant" in [3582], [31215], [33233]

Home Business (Vol. 13, January/February 2006, No. 1, pp. 32, 34, 66, 68); "Silver (and Gold) in Senior Services" in [9671], [9779], [12354], [16109], [17152], [18423], [19348], [23810], [31098], [42552], [52499]

Home Business (Vol. 12, October 2005, No. 5, pp. 93); "Smooth Operator" in [2398], [34505], [51362]

Home Business (Vol. 12, October 2005, No. 5, pp. 92); "Spy Moms" in [19978], [42726], [56415]

Home Business (Vol. 12, October 2005, No. 5, pp. 28, 30-31, 78-79); "Start-Up Funding Options" in [42554], [44442], [48891]

Home Business (Vol. 13, January/February 2006, No. 1, pp. 36, 100); "Success Within Your Reach" in [2746], [36817], [45687]

Home Business (Vol. 12, March/April 2005, No. 2, pp. 50, 52-53); "Survey Your Customers" in [23772], [31868], [47590]

Home Business (Vol. 12, March/April 2005, No. 2, pp. 80); "Tackling the Competition" in [4832], [23219], [23738], [30968], [53499]

Home Business (Vol. 13, January/February 2006, No. 1, pp. 72, 74-75); "Tapping Into Your Warm Market" in [44669], [48925]

Home Business Tax Deductions: Keep What You Earn [23959], [42637], [54592]

Home Business (Vol. 12, March/April 2005, No. 2, pp. 71); "The Art Auctioneer" in [1595], [1774]

Home Business (Vol. 12, October 2005, No. 5, pp. 56); "The Bumpy Road to Success" in [22475], [35886]

Home Business (Vol. 13, January/February 2006, No. 1, pp. 16, 18-22, 102, 104); "The Crash of 2006" in [32339], [42597]

Home Business (Vol. 12, October 2005, No. 5, pp. 58, 60); "The Design of an Ideal Business" in [29722], [35383], [39046]

Home Business (Vol. 12, March/April 2005, No. 2, pp. 64); "The Four Questions" in [29064], [35466], [44414]

Home Business (Vol. 12, October 2005, No. 5, pp. 70); "The Knight's Still Young" in [5511], [56724]

Home Business (Vol. 12, October 2005, No. 5, pp. 46); "The Power of Permission-Based Prospecting" in [51770]

Home Business (Vol. 13, January/February 2006, No. 1, pp. 42, 44-45); "The Value of Networking" in [28955], [47689], [51890]

Home Business (Vol. 12, March/April 2005, No. 2, pp. 78); "Top 25 Overlooked Tax Deductions" in [284], [2969], [24063], [42741], [54838]

Home Business (Vol. 13, January/February 2006, No. 1, pp. 62); "Turning Your Services Into a Product" in [3601], [31238]

Home Business (Vol. 12, October 2005, No. 5, pp. 36, 100); "Unforgettable as Usual" in [42746], [51886]

Home Business (Vol. 12, March/April 2005, No. 2, pp. 36, 38, 60-61); "Use Webcasting to Grow Your Home Business" in [14561], [25993], [34642], [42747], [47686], [51888]

Home Business (Vol. 12, March/April 2005, No. 2, pp. 48); "Virtual Company Achieves Actual Savings" in [14567], [16536], [31243], [34648], [42748], [56466]

Home Business (Vol. 13, January/February 2006, No. 1, pp. 80); "Wearing Her Work on Her Sleeve" in [34662], [42751], [49562], [51405]

Home Business (Vol. 12, March/April 2005, No. 2, pp. 56); "What is the Most Effective Way to Advertise?" in [834], [47720]

Home Business (Vol. 13, January/February 2006, No. 1, pp. 76); "What To Do When Your Client Declares Bankruptcy" in [10245], [31604], [38455], [42755]

Home Business (Vol. 13, January/February 2006, No. 1, pp. 56); "When It Comes to Shopping, Safety Comes First" in [44176], [51411], [56477]

Home Business (Vol. 12, March/April 2005, No. 2, pp. 54); "Why Do So Many Salespeople Fail to Get It?" in [36969], [42762], [51912]

The Home Buyer's Inspection Guide: Making Investments in Your Home That Pay for Themselves [3235]

"Home-Buying Fair Appeals to First-Time Purchasers" in *Sun Herald* (February 10, 2005) [7365], [10003], [17388], [20528], [24948], [55099]

Home Care Assistance [12422]

Home Channel News [11902]

Home Cleaning Business: Your Step by Step Business Plan [8685]

Home Cleaning Centers of America [8703]

Home Computer Business Guide [42638]

"A Home Court Advantage" in *Hispanic Business* (Vol. 23, No. 11, November 2001, pp. 38, 40) [7366], [16520], [48237], [56265]

Home Decorating Combo [12234], [26079]

"Home Depot looks to succeed in Detroit where Kmart didn't" in *Crain's Detroit Business* (Vol. 19, No. 16, April 21, 2003, pp. 23) [11884], [16305]

"Home Depot Offers Expensive Lesson in Curbing Execs' Pay" in *Crain's Chicago Business* (Vol. 30, January 2007, No. 3, pp. 13) [11885], [12288], [30556], [31171], [45248]

"Home Depot" in *Sales & Marketing Management* (Vol. 159, January-February 2007, No. 1, pp. 15) [11886], [33119], [34018], [47082], [51675]

"Home Depot Swings into Spring Hiring Season" in *Altanta Journal-Constitution* (January 30, 2007) [11887], [42289], [51184]

"Home Designers Have Women in Mind" in *Chicago Tribune* (March 6, 2005) [1519], [7367], [13649]

Home Entertainment Retail Expo [9766]

Home Entertainment Show [8088], [8243], [11122], [11187], [55219]

Home Fashion Products Association [2561], [12177], [13624]

"A Home is the Foundation for Wealth" in *Black Enterprise* (Vol. 34, No. 6, January 2004) [20529], [20894], [38120]

Home Furnishings International Association [12262]

Home Furnishings Retailer [12328]

The Home Gardener [16126]

The Home Gardener, Revised Edition [16127]

Home Health Care [12373]

Home Health Care: An Annotated Bibliography [12374]

Home Health Care Management and Practice [12390], [41218]

"Home Health Care Poised to Grow Despite Obstacles" in *Kiplinger Business Forecasts* (January 20, 2005) [447], [18326]

Home Health Care Services Quarterly [1704], [12391], [41219]

Home Health Line [12392]

Home Health Nursing: Nursing Diagnosis in the Home Health Setting [12402]

Home Health Nursing Practice Concepts and Application [12375]

Home Health and Rehabilitation: Concepts of Care [12376]

Home Healthcare Agency & Chains Directory [12431]

Home Healthcare Nurse [12393]

Home Helpers [12423]

"Home, cheap home" in *Entrepreneur* (Vol. 30, No. 9, September 2002, pp. 32) [663], [47083]

"Home Improvement: Black Homeownership Is Up, But at What Cost?" in *Black Enterprise* (Vol. 35, November 2004, No. 4, pp. 34) [7368], [20530]

Home Improvement: Decorating [12235]

Home Improvement: Interior Projects [12236]

The Home Improvement Market [11897]

Home Improvement Retailing [11903], [12232], [12329]

Home Improvement Videos [12237]

"Home Improvements" in *Entrepreneur* (Vol. 32, No. 1, January 2004, pp. 210) [3314], [7369], [11217], [13650], [26073], [38828]

"Home In on Your Image" in *My Business* (June/July 2002, pp. 15) [5989], [47084], [50608]

The Home Inspection Business from A to Z On-Site Checklist: The Narrative Checklist the Others Don't Have! [3236]

The Home Inspection Business from A to Z: The Real Facts Other Books Don't Tell You! [3237]

Home Instead Senior Care [18389]

"Home Instead Senior Care" in *Small Business Opportunities* (Vol. 16, November 2004, No. 6, pp. 112) [448], [38829]

"Home Invasion" in *Business Week* (No. 3666, January 31, 2000, pp. F8) [42639], [56564]

Home Lighting & Accessories [9117]

Home Lighting & Accessories-Suppliers Directory Issue [9110]

Home Magazine [13692]

"Home Market Deflates" in *Milwaukee Journal Sentinel* (December 15, 2005) [20531], [20895]

Home Media Retailing [25602]

Home Office Association of America [42566]

Home Office Computing (Vol. 18, No. 8, August 2000, pp. 36); "Accounting Moves to the Web" in [66], [53197]

Home Office Computing (Vol. 19, No. 1, January 2001, pp. 24); "Add An 'Inc' And Get Some Respect" in [33516], [35754], [42572], [53578]

Home Office Computing (Vol. 18, No. 10, October 2000, pp. 64); "An Office With Ambiance" in [42695], [49531]

Home Office Computing (Vol. 18, No. 7, July 2000, pp. 16); "Are the Tax-Free Net's Days Numbered?" in [33541], [40160], [51053], [53588], [54430]

Home Office Computing (Vol. 18, No. 10, October 2000, pp. 94); "Back to School" in [6159], [33003]

Home Office Computing (Vol. 18, No. 10, October 2000, pp. 19); "Bigger Office, Bigger Breaks" in [42582], [54449]

Home Office Computing (Vol. 18, No. 9, September 2000, pp. 92); "Brave New World" in [2686], [8605], [9132], [46743], [50563]

Home Office Computing (Vol. 18, No. 12, December 2000, pp. 66); "Bring the New Economy Home" in **[32283]**, **[42583]**, **[49677]**, **[53620]**

Home Office Computing (Vol. 18, No. 12, December 2000, pp. 99); "Business by the Book" in **[40214]**, **[42584]**, **[44010]**

Home Office Computing (Vol. 18, No. 11, November 2000, pp. 52); "Business to E-Business" in **[25810]**, **[33626]**, **[42586]**, **[46761]**

Home Office Computing (Vol. 18, No. 11, November 2000, pp. 20); "Can you be a merchant vendor?" in **[31517]**, **[33645]**

Home Office Computing (Vol. 18, No. 10, October 2000, pp. 92); "Checking Inn at the Office" in **[44995]**, **[49491]**

Home Office Computing (Vol. 18, No. 12, December 2000, pp. 102); "Cultivating Teleworkers" in **[14898]**, **[34859]**, **[42212]**, **[42599]**, **[53674]**

Home Office Computing (Vol. 19, No. 1, January 2001, pp. 92); "Dare to Disconnect" in **[30316]**, **[42600]**

Home Office Computing (Vol. 18, No. 9, September 2000, pp. 73); "Desktop Publishing" in **[8607]**, **[53254]**

Home Office Computing (Vol. 19, No. 1, January 2001, pp. 77); "Digital Video Editing" in **[53256]**

Home Office Computing (Vol. 18, No. 8, August 2000, pp. 20); "Distance Makes a Difference" in **[45067]**, **[53691]**

Home Office Computing (Vol. 18, No. 11, November 2000, pp. 19); "DSL Users Brace for Bumpy Ride" in **[33787]**, **[42605]**, **[49016]**

Home Office Computing (Vol. 18, No. 12, December 2000, pp. 48); "E-Mail Secrets Revealed" in **[33814]**, **[53264]**

Home Office Computing (Vol. 18, No. 10, October 2000, pp. 16); "Farming IT Out" in **[33881]**, **[42612]**, **[49028]**, **[49694]**

Home Office Computing (Vol. 18, No. 7, July 2000, pp. 48); "Find Anything on the Web" in **[33893]**, **[42615]**

Home Office Computing (Vol. 18, No. 10, October 2000, pp. 20); "Finding Permanence in Temporary Assignments" in **[24524]**, **[42238]**

Home Office Computing (Vol. 18, No. 9, September 2000, pp. 13); "For Sale by (Home Office) Owner" in **[42617]**

Home Office Computing (Vol. 18, No. 12, December 2000, pp. 45); "Free Reign" in **[33924]**, **[42619]**, **[46984]**

Home Office Computing (Vol. 18, No. 11, November 2000, pp. 88); "Getting Personal" in **[31725]**

Home Office Computing (Vol. 18, No. 10, October 2000, pp. 87); "Going Global" in **[25860]**, **[33959]**, **[42623]**, **[43678]**, **[53752]**

Home Office Computing (Vol. 18, No. 11, November 2000, pp. 90); "Going Once, Going Twice..." in **[1816]**, **[33962]**

Home Office Computing (Vol. 18, No. 8, August 2000, pp. 54); "Grow Your Client BASE" in **[28237]**, **[42625]**, **[47040]**

Home Office Computing (Vol. 18, No. 10, October 2000, pp. 52); "Grow Your Technology" in **[3536]**, **[25861]**, **[33981]**, **[42626]**, **[49058]**

Home Office Computing (Vol. 18, No. 7, July 2000, pp. 54); "Home Office, Simplified" in **[42642]**, **[49507]**, **[54952]**

Home Office Computing (Vol. 18, No. 12, December 2000, pp. 24); "Home Offices as Status Symbol" in **[42645]**, **[53779]**

Home Office Computing (Vol. 19, No. 1, January 2001, pp. 94); "How to Tame a COBRA" in **[26830]**

Home Office Computing (Vol. 18, No. 9, September 2000, pp. 87); "I'll Trade You..." in **[26713]**, **[34052]**, **[53799]**

Home Office Computing (Vol. 18, No. 10, October 2000, pp. 86); "In the Family Way" in **[8998]**, **[42663]**

Home Office Computing (Vol. 19, No. 2, February 2001, pp. 73); "Keep 'Em Clicking" in **[25880]**, **[31043]**, **[31749]**, **[34116]**

Home Office Computing (Vol. 18, No. 10, October 2000, pp. 89); "Keep It Professional" in **[42669]**, **[49513]**

Home Office Computing (Vol. 18, No. 8, August 2000, pp. 22); "Keeping Customers Clueless?" in **[31750]**, **[34118]**, **[53823]**

Home Office Computing (Vol. 17, No. 1, January 1999, pp. 67); "Kick the Habit" in **[4712]**, **[20023]**, **[23062]**, **[42670]**, **[49113]**, **[53347]**, **[54961]**

Home Office Computing (Vol. 19, No. 1, January 2001, pp. 104); "Leave It at the Office" in **[54964]**

Home Office Computing (Vol. 18, No. 12, December 2000, pp. 21); "Magna Carta for the Virtual Age" in **[39446]**, **[53844]**

Home Office Computing (Vol. 18, No. 9, September 2000, pp. 40); "Manners Matter" in **[31772]**

Home Office Computing (Vol. 18, No. 10, October 2000, pp. 26); "Microsoft Windows Millennium Edition" in **[42679]**, **[49146]**, **[53372]**

Home Office Computing (Vol. 18, No. 8, August 2000, pp. 15); "New OSHA Rules to Reduce Injuries" in **[40555]**, **[42686]**, **[56574]**

Home Office Computing (Vol. 19, No. 1, January 2001, pp. 11); "Nothing is Unworkable" in **[36565]**, **[42692]**

Home Office Computing (Vol. 18, No. 8, August 2000, pp. 42); "Office Down Below" in **[42693]**, **[49525]**, **[52707]**

Home Office Computing (Vol. 18, No. 8, August 2000, pp. 24); "OnLine Job Sites, Take Two" in **[22047]**, **[34293]**

Home Office Computing (Vol. 18, No. 12, December 2000, pp. 97); "Out of the Zone" in **[40600]**, **[42704]**

Home Office Computing (Vol. 18, No. 11, November 2000, pp. 40); "Post It and They Will Come" in **[28639]**, **[34360]**, **[42709]**

Home Office Computing (Vol. 18, No. 9, September 2000, pp. 13); "Q&A" in **[12907]**, **[25942]**, **[27479]**, **[27670]**, **[29456]**, **[30358]**, **[31206]**, **[32856]**, **[33348]**, **[34388]**, **[35565]**, **[40628]**, **[42711]**, **[51301]**, **[52578]**, **[54715]**, **[54983]**

Home Office Computing (Vol. 18, No. 10, October 2000, pp. 46); "Remote Control" in **[35046]**, **[42714]**, **[45592]**, **[49227]**

Home Office Computing (Vol. 19, No. 1, January 2001, pp. 22); "Savings in the Mall" in **[49241]**, **[53953]**

Home Office Computing (Vol. 19, No. 1, January 2001, pp. 22); "SBA Offers Free E-Commerce CD" in **[34435]**, **[40670]**, **[53448]**

Home Office Computing (Vol. 18, No. 11, November 2000, pp. 12); "Secret Shopper" in **[31845]**, **[34445]**

Home Office Computing (Vol. 18, No. 11, November 2000, pp. 28); "Send E-Mail Securely" in **[34456]**, **[53456]**

Home Office Computing (Vol. 18, No. 10, October 2000, pp. 90); "Setting Up Shop" in **[25957]**, **[34459]**, **[44244]**, **[47516]**, **[52588]**

Home Office Computing (Vol. 18, No. 11, November 2000, pp. 85); "Show Me the Money" in **[7199]**, **[42551]**, **[55427]**

Home Office Computing (Vol. 19, No. 1, January 2001, pp. 20); "Site Watch for Home Workers" in **[30890]**, **[34482]**, **[35875]**, **[37856]**, **[42723]**, **[43381]**, **[47533]**, **[49547]**

Home Office Computing (Vol. 19, No. 1, January 2001, pp. 17); "Sleepy Little Towns Turn High Tech" in **[28768]**, **[30175]**, **[41990]**, **[52728]**, **[53967]**

Home Office Computing (Vol. 18, No. 11, November 2000, pp. 58); "Strength in Numbers" in **[30964]**, **[50194]**, **[51335]**, **[52323]**, **[54004]**

Home Office Computing (Vol. 18, No. 10, October 2000, pp. 42); "Stretching Room" in **[42729]**, **[49283]**, **[49552]**

Home Office Computing (Vol. 18, No. 9, September 2000, pp. 79); "Tap Into the Corporate LAN" in **[42730]**, **[49297]**, **[54024]**

Home Office Computing (Vol. 18, No. 10, October 2000, pp. 18); "Tapping Foreign Markets" in **[42731]**, **[43836]**, **[54025]**

Home Office Computing (Vol. 18, No. 10, October 2000, pp. 37); "Telephony Rising" in **[5144]**, **[34582]**, **[40759]**

Home Office Computing (Vol. 19, No. 1, January 2001, pp. 18); "Telework Lowers Office Expense" in **[42737]**, **[54030]**

Home Office Computing (Vol. 19, No. 1, January 2001, pp. 88); "The Cash Flow Crunch" in **[27096]**, **[33651]**

Home Office Computing (Vol. 18, No. 11, November 2000, pp. 98); "The Check's in the Mail" in **[31521]**

Home Office Computing (Vol. 18, No. 10, October 2000, pp. 58); "The Healthy Home Office" in **[42630]**, **[56563]**

Home Office Computing (Vol. 18, No. 12, December 2000, pp. 52); "The HOC 100" in **[49074]**

Home Office Computing (Vol. 18, No. 12, December 2000, pp. 26); "The IRS Wants You-Online" in **[34090]**, **[53813]**, **[54623]**

Home Office Computing (Vol. 18, No. 12, December 2000, pp. 89); "The Networked Home" in **[42685]**, **[49157]**

Home Office Computing (Vol. 19, No. 1, January 2001, pp. 85); "The Path of Lease Resistance" in **[49198]**, **[53405]**

Home Office Computing (Vol. 18, No. 7, July 2000, pp. 42); "The Spirit of Independence" in **[14472]**, **[30004]**, **[34524]**, **[38367]**, **[42725]**

Home Office Computing (Vol. 19, No. 1, January 2001, pp. 90); "The Telework Puzzle" in **[31228]**, **[49744]**, **[53510]**

Home Office Computing (Vol. 18, No. 10, October 2000, pp. 11); "The Web: Land of Opportunists" in **[1865]**, **[30264]**, **[34670]**

Home Office Computing (Vol. 18, No. 11, November 2000, pp. 92); "The Work-at-Home Hook" in **[35159]**, **[42469]**, **[42766]**

Home Office Computing (Vol. 18, No. 9, September 2000, pp. 52); "Time To Hire" in **[42440]**, **[42739]**

Home Office Computing (Vol. 18, No. 12, December 2000, pp. 107); "Tuning In to Telework" in **[20343]**, **[42742]**, **[54049]**

Home Office Computing (Vol. 18, No. 8, August 2000, pp. 40); "Twice as Nice" in **[42743]**, **[49331]**

Home Office Computing (Vol. 18, No. 9, September 2000, pp. 44); "2001 : A Home Office Odyssey" in **[42745]**, **[49332]**

Home Office Computing (Vol. 18, No. 12, December 2000, pp. 16); "VPNs Go Mainstream" in **[42749]**, **[49347]**, **[54063]**

Home Office Computing (Vol. 18, No. 11, November 2000, pp. 71); "Web-based Accounting" in **[291]**, **[23253]**, **[26398]**, **[34665]**, **[42752]**, **[53532]**

Home Office Computing (Vol. 18, No. 10, October 2000, pp. 14); "What Price Time?" in **[31247]**, **[42754]**, **[52608]**, **[55001]**

Home Office Computing (Vol. 18, No. 8, August 2000, pp. 81); "What's in a Domain Name?" in **[26015]**, **[30040]**, **[34698]**

Home Office Computing (Vol. 18, No. 9, September 2000, pp. 18); "When Business is Personal" in **[31904]**

Home Office Computing (Vol. 18, No. 8, August 2000, pp. 22); "Who Wants to be an Expert?" in **[31252]**, **[34714]**

Home Office Computing (Vol. 19, No. 1, January 2001, pp. 20); "Wireless Phones Get Organized" in **[5184]**, **[7149]**, **[49369]**

Home Office Computing (Vol. 18, No. 11, November 2000, pp. 37); "Wireless Web Boom" in **[5186]**, **[34736]**, **[42764]**

Home Office Computing (Vol. 18, No. 12, December 2000, pp. 23); "Workers Simply Want to Be Organized" in **[23266]**, **[42771]**, **[49568]**, **[54088]**

"The Home Office Deduction" in *My Business* (October/November 2002, pp. 46) **[42640]**, **[54593]**

The Home Office Money and Tax Guide: Bringing Professional Business Practices Home **[42641]**

"Home Office, Simplified" in *Home Office Computing* (Vol. 18, No. 7, July 2000, pp. 54) **[42642]**, **[49507]**, **[54952]**

The Home Office and Small Business Answer Book: Solutions to the Most Frequently Asked Questions about Starting and Running Home Offices **[42643]**, **[52863]**

Home Office - Small Office Quick Planner **[49508]**

"Home Office vs. the Field" in *Sales & Marketing Management* **[26827]**, **[30347]**, **[42644]**, **[45249]**, **[51676]**, **[51703]**, **[53778]**

"Home Office vs. the Field" in *Sales and Marketing.com* (Vol. 156, No. 3, March 2004, pp. 13) **[45250]**, **[51677]**

"Home Offices as Status Symbol" in *Home Office Computing* (Vol. 18, No. 12, December 2000, pp. 24) **[42645]**, **[53779]**

"Home auctions quadruple as sales option for owners" in *Business First Columbus* (Vol. 18, No. 26, February 15, 2002, pp. 38) **[1824]**, **[20532]**

"Home Plate: Learning How to Let Go by Delegating" in *Crain's Detroit Business* (Vol. 19, No. 49, December 8, 2003, pp. 18) **[36291]**, **[43222]**, **[45251]**

"Home remedies: feisty mom-and-pops of Gotham strike back at drugstore chains" in *Wall Street Journal* (, pp.) **[8787]**

"Home Rules" in *Business Week* (No. 3667, February 7, 2000, pp. 53) **[40441]**, **[42646]**

Home Satellite TV Installation and Troubleshooting Manual **[22086]**

Home Sewing Association **[7985]**, **[22723]**

The Home Shop Machinist **[8044]**

"Home Smart Home" in *Entrepreneur* (Vol. 33, October 2005, No. 10, pp. 39) **[7731]**, **[13560]**, **[13651]**

The Home Star Group **[7613]**

"The Home Stretch" in *Entrepreneur* (Vol. 33, January 2005, No. 1, pp. 52) **[17389]**, **[38121]**, **[48910]**

"Home Sweet Equity" in *Hispanic Business* (October 2004, pp. 102, 104, 106) **[17390]**, **[20533]**, **[36292]**, **[48238]**

"Home, Sweet Office" in *Entrepreneur* (Vol. 31, No. 11, November 2003, pp. 72) **[162]**, **[23960]**, **[26253]**, **[42647]**, **[54594]**

"Home Sweet Office: Giving to Charity" in *Sales & Marketing Management* (Vol. 157, January 2005, No. 1, pp. 52) **[52864]**, **[54204]**

"Home Sweet Office: Stress Relievers" in *Sales and Marketing.com* (Vol. 156, No. 3, March 2004, pp. 66) **[42648]**

"Home Sweet Office: The Pitch for Telecommuting" in *Sales and Marketing.com* (Vol. 153, No. 3, March 2004, pp. 50) **[42649]**

"A Home of Their Own" in *Hispanic Business* (October 2004, pp. 28) **[17391]**, **[20534]**, **[32483]**

"Home crafting stimulates togetherness" in *Retail Merchandiser* (Vol. 42, No. 11, Nov. 2002, pp. 33) **[8169]**, **[32484]**, **[53780]**

Home Ventilating Institute **[999]**

"Home base and knowledge management in international ventures" in *Journal of Business Venturing* (Vol. 17, No. 2, March 2002, pp. 99) **[43462]**, **[44267]**

Home Video Hits: Great Ideas for Creating Better Home Videos **[4215]**

Home Visits: The Nursing Bag **[12403]**

"Home: Where the Money Is" in *Small Business Opportunities* (Vol. 14, No. 1, January 2002, pp. 86) **[3295]**, **[35508]**, **[38652]**, **[42523]**

Home Wine and Beer Trade Association **[3119]**

"Home Work" in *Black Enterprise* (Vol. 37, October 2006, No. 3, pp. 78) **[22041]**, **[42524]**, **[52775]**

Home, Yard & Garden Pest Newsletter **[19031]**

"Home2NetServices Announces a Revolutionary New Way of Insuring Personal Property" in *PR Newswire* (January 20, 2005) **[13324]**, **[19964]**, **[22251]**, **[43216]**

The Homebased Business Book **[42650]**

"Homebased Moneymakers" in *Small Business Opportunities* (Vol. 12, No. 5, September 2000, pp. 74, 76) **[1762]**, **[8503]**, **[15979]**, **[19813]**, **[33445]**, **[42525]**, **[52491]**

"Homebuilders Pony Up with Incentives for Home Buyers" in *Memphis Business Journal* (Vol. 25, No. 19, September 5, 2003, pp. 1) **[7370]**, **[47085]**

Homecare Administrative HORIZONS **[466]**, **[12394]**, **[30273]**, **[41220]**

Homecare DIRECTION **[467]**, **[12395]**, **[17263]**

HomeCare Magazine **[12396]**

HOMECAExpo **[12406]**

Homedale Chamber of Commerce **[59309]**

HomeFixology **[4505]**

"Homegrown Business" in *Mail Tribune* (February 21, 2005) **[11330]**, **[12148]**, **[56266]**

"Homeless entrepreneurs swap shopping carts" in *Red Herring* (No. 76, March 2000, pp. 58) **[13756]**, **[33446]**, **[35509]**

"Homeless Group Seeks to Buy Denver Hotel Property" in *Denver Post* (April 11, 2003) **[20535]**, **[20896]**, **[54205]**

Homemade Business **[42651]**

Homemade Money **[42652]**

Homeowners Concept, Inc. **[20750]**

"Homeownership up, but home equity declining" in *Business First Columbus* (Vol. 18, No. 26, February 15, 2002, pp. 39) **[20536]**, **[32485]**

Homer Chamber of Commerce **[56965]**

Homerville - Clinch County Chamber of Commerce **[59125]**

Homes & Land Magazine **[18979]**

Homes Magazine **[20718]**

"Homesites still sell big in S. Florida" in *Daily Business Review* (Vol. 77, No. 187, March 7, 2003, pp. A1) **[7371]**, **[20537]**, **[20897]**

Homestart **[883]**, **[47922]**

The Homesteader **[18980]**, **[42797]**

The Hometeam Inspection Services, Inc. **[3275]**

Hometown Hearth & Grill **[51459]**

"Hometown Heroes: Doing Good by Doing Well" in *My Business* (November/December 2001, pp. 26-30, 33-35) **[39386]**, **[54206]**

Hometown Threads **[11203]**, **[22741]**

HomeVestors of America, Inc. **[21102]**

Homewatch Caregivers & Homewatch International, Inc. **[478]**

Homewood Area Chamber of Commerce **[59544]**

Homewood Chamber of Commerce **[56866]**

"Homewood Gets a $7M Hilton" in *Birmingham Business Journal* (Vol. 20, No. 29, July 18, 2003, pp. 1) **[12563]**, **[28292]**

"Homework 2001" in *Small Business Opportunities* (Vol. 13, No. 5, September 2001, pp. 72-73) **[7372]**, **[42653]**, **[49509]**, **[53781]**

Hominy Chamber of Commerce **[64016]**

Hondo Area Chamber of Commerce **[65310]**

Honest-1 Auto Care, Inc. **[22677]**

Honest Business: A Superior Strategy for Starting & Maintaining Your Own Business **[37455]**, **[45252]**

Honey Grove Chamber of Commerce **[65311]**

Honey, I Want to Start My Own Business: A Planning Guide for Couples **[52865]**

"Honey Rhymes with Money" in *Small Business Opportunities* (Vol. 12, No. 2, March 2000, pp. 104) **[2463]**, **[35510]**, **[54206]**

The Honeybaked Ham Co. and Cafe **[11715]**, **[21842]**, **[23565]**

Honeywell–Federal Manufacturing Technologies–Technical Information Center **[51018]**

Honeywell, Inc.–Air Transport Systems–Engineering Library **[989]**

Hong Kong Trade Development Council **[43502]**

Honolulu Japanese Chamber of Commerce **[59248]**

Honolulu Japanese Junior Chamber of Commerce **[59249]**

Honolulu Minority Business Development Center **[59258]**

Honolulu SBDC **[59231]**

"Honor Thy Self" in *Black Enterprise* (Vol. 35, February 2005, No. 7, pp. 156) **[35511]**, **[56052]**

"The Honored Few" in *Hispanic Business* (January/February 2004, pp. 48-50) **[36293]**, **[48239]**

"Honoring the Profit" in *PC Computing* (April, 2000, pp. 58) **[32486]**, **[53782]**

The Honors Learning Center **[5431]**

Hood River County Chamber of Commerce **[64230]**

Hoohobbers **[2139]**, **[5306]**

"Hook up" in *Entrepreneur* (Vol. 30, No. 1, January 2002, pp. 43) **[6676]**, **[6942]**, **[41747]**, **[49077]**

"Hooked Up to Profit" in *Small Business Opportunities* (Vol. 17, May 2005, No. 3, pp. 92) **[7732]**, **[17520]**, **[24416]**, **[37689]**, **[52545]**

Hooker Chamber of Commerce **[64017]**

Hooker & Holcombe Inc. **[27035]**

Hooks and Lines **[2181]**

"Hooray for R. and D. It's time to make a popular and effective tax credit permanent" in *Time Inc.* (Vol. 156, No. 13, Sept. 25, 2000) **[54595]**

The Hoosier Genealogist **[10965]**

Hooters of America, Inc. **[10642]**, **[21843]**

Hoover Chamber of Commerce **[56867]**

Hoover Institution on War, Revolution and Peace **[24206]**

"Hoover's Introduces Competitive Intelligence and Media Monitoring Service" in *Information Today* (Vol. 17, No. 11, Dec. 2000, pp. 31) **[27398]**, **[30879]**, **[44309]**, **[47086]**, **[50448]**

Hope College–Carl Frost Center for Social Science Research **[23786]**

Hope Foundation Inc.–Margaret L. Tyler Library **[1357]**, **[3076]**

Hope-Hempstead County Chamber of Commerce **[57181]**

Hopewell-Prince George Chamber of Commerce **[65914]**

"Hoping for a Bad Winter" in *Forbes* (Vol. 175, January 10, 2005, No. 1, No. 13, pp. 153) **[1938]**, **[15092]**, **[49986]**

Hopkins County Chamber of Commerce **[65312]**

Hopkinsville-Christian County Chamber of Commerce **[60525]**

Horicon Chamber of Commerce **[66425]**

Horizon Consulting Services **[30089]**

Horizon Ventures **[58036]**

Horizons **[326]**, **[8212]**

The Horn Book Magazine **[2768]**

Horn Lake Chamber of Commerce **[61800]**

Hornberger & Associates **[3732]**, **[31375]**, **[47872]**, **[48831]**

Horror Writers Association **[8960]**

The Horse **[1202]**, **[12464]**

Horse Industry Directory **[12461]**

Horseback **[12467]**

Horsemanship Safety Association **[12446]**

Horsemanship, Vol. 1-3 **[12468]**

Horseshoe Bend Area Chamber of Commerce **[57182]**

Horticultural Research Institute **[11551]**

Horticultural Society of New York–Library **[12163]**, **[16094]**

Horticulture **[11465]**, **[16040]**

Horticulture Review **[11466]**

HortIdeas **[11467]**

Horton Chamber of Commerce **[60352]**

Horwath International Association **[26430]**, **[54890]**

The Hosiery Association **[16210]**

Hospital Home Health **[12397]**

Hospital News Canada **[41221]**

Hospital Telephone Directory **[17091]**

Hospital Topics **[41222]**

Hospitality Design **[12662]**, **[13693]**, **[21684]**

Hospitality Facilities Management and Design **[12564]**

Hospitality Financial and Technology Professionals **[12502]**

"Hospitality Hobnobber" in *Crain's New York Business* (Vol. 23, January 29, 2007, No. 5, pp. F10) **[10004]**, **[15093]**, **[20898]**, **[36294]**, **[38122]**, **[45253]**

"Hospitality Industry Continues Rough Ride in 2003" in *Atlanta Business Chronicle* (Vol. 25, January 10, 2003, No. 31, pp. 16A) **[12565]**, **[30348]**

"Hospitality Industry" in *Rough Notes* (Vol. 146, No. 4, April 2003, pp. 84) **[12566]**, **[13325]**, **[43217]**

"Hospitality in Kansas City" in *Ingram's* (Vol. 28, No. 2, February 2002, pp. 25) **[12567]**, **[28293]**

Hospitality Law **[12663]**

Hospitality Product News **[12664]**, **[21685]**

Hospitality Sales and Marketing Association
International **[12503]**
    Sales & Marketing Research Library
    [12744]
"Hospitality, tourism up, but not in Atlanta market"
in *Atlanta Business Chronicle* (Vol. 25, No. 22,
November 8, 2002, pp. 8C) **[22511]**, **[24694]**,
[24949], **[25195]**
"Hospitals Across Long Island Shift to Digital
Imaging Technology" in *Long Island Business
News* (February 20, 2004) **[41030]**, **[41748]**
"Hospitals Turn to Ads as the Rx for Blahs" in *San
Francisco Business Times* (Vol. 17, No. 51, July
25, 2003, pp. 20) **[41031]**, **[47087]**
Host Midwest Expo **[2375]**, **[2461]**, **[4260]**, **[7790]**,
[12682], **[21703]**
Host Site in Transition–Small Business Technology
Development Center **[61195]**
"Host a Virtual Meeting: Collaborate with a Video
Link and a Whiteboard" in *Journal of
Accountancy* (Vol. 199, February 2005, No. 2)
[4687], **[14124]**, **[23029]**, **[27399]**, **[53783]**
"Host With the Most" in *Small Business
Opportunities* (Vol. 13, No. 5, September 2001,
pp. 58) **[14125]**, **[25866]**, **[34019]**, **[52373]**
Hostline **[12695]**, **[21722]**
"Hot 100" in *Entrepreneur* (Vol. 31, No. 6, June
2003, pp. 64) **[501]**, **[10659]**, **[25356]**, **[27725]**,
[32487], **[35512]**, **[46573]**, **[48656]**, **[52492]**
"Hot Bets in the Cold North" in *Business Week*
(December 19, 2005, No. 3964, pp. 24)
[50888], **[52119]**, **[53784]**
"Hot commodities" in *WorkingWoman* (Vol. 25, No.
2, February 2000, pp. 40) **[9562]**, **[42290]**,
[56267]
"Hot housing areas start to cool: Sales slow; prices
keep rising" in *Atlanta Business Chronicle* (Vol.
25, No. 21, Nov. 1, 2002) **[20538]**, **[20899]**
"Hot Disks" in *Entrepreneur* (Vol. 32, September
2004, No. 9, pp. 46) **[4688]**, **[4924]**, **[5014]**,
[6171], **[6254]**, **[6644]**, **[6677]**, **[14126]**,
[15257], **[22252]**, **[22981]**, **[23030]**, **[23826]**,
[23833], **[25774]**, **[26254]**, **[34020]**, **[46741]**,
[47088], **[49073]**, **[49078]**, **[50673]**, **[53317]**,
[54953]
Hot Dog on a Stick **[21844]**
"Hot Fiscal Issues" in *Small Business Opportunities*
(Vol. 16, November 2004, No. 6, pp. 70-71)
[26828], **[37690]**
"Hot Kicks, Cool Price" in *Black Enterprise* (Vol. 37,
December 2006, No. 5, pp. 34) **[5670]**, **[9625]**,
[22763], **[44232]**, **[48744]**, **[51185]**
Hot Line to Sales **[24301]**
"The Hot List" in *Black Enterprise* (Vol. 34, No. 5,
December 2003) **[36295]**, **[41749]**
Hot N' Now LLC **[21845]**
"Hot or Not?" in *Inc.* (Volume 28, January 2006, No.
1, pp. 102-105) **[15094]**, **[39387]**, **[44548]**
Hot Philly Steak & Fries **[23566]**
"Hot Product" in *Pittsburgh Business Times* (Vol.
22, No. 52, July 11, 2003, pp. 3) **[48745]**
"Hot Property" in *Entrepreneur* (Vol. 31, No. 8,
August 2003, pp. 57) **[13326]**, **[43218]**
"Hot Resort Market May Aid Sale of 2 Isle Hotels"
in *Pacific Business News* (Vol. 41, No. 23,
August 15, 2003, pp. 1) **[12568]**, **[20539]**,
[20900]
Hot Rod Detailing **[2029]**
"Hot Scoop" in *Small Business Opportunities*
(March 2005) **[12781]**, **[38830]**
"Hot Seat: Bruce Schneier" in *PC Computing* (April
2000, pp. 42) **[14127]**, **[22253]**, **[34021]**,
[36296]
"Hot Shots: 200 Up And Coming Companies" in
Forbes (Vol. 172, No. 9, October 27, 2003, pp.
139) **[10005]**, **[15095]**, **[28294]**, **[39388]**,
[52866]
"Hot Shots: U.S. Top 15" in *Forbes* (Vol. 6, No. 20,
October 27, 2003, pp. 53) **[28295]**, **[39389]**,
[52867]
"Hot Spots" in *Entrepreneur* (Vol. 33, October 2005,
No. 10, pp. 68) **[28296]**, **[29420]**, **[30150]**,
[52682]
Hot Springs Area Chamber of Commerce **[64826]**
Hot Springs Chamber of Commerce **[62175]**
Hot Springs, Mineral Waters **[3084]**, **[24758]**

Hot Stop **[15956]**
"Hot Stuff" in *Entrepreneur* (Vol. 32, No. 2,
February 2004, pp. 43) **[2592]**, **[7892]**, **[10564]**,
[11628], **[11888]**, **[12009]**, **[23484]**, **[34022]**,
[51186]
Hot Stuff Pizza, LLC **[19675]**
"Hot on Their Trail: How to Use the Net to Track
Offline Customers" in *Entrepreneur* (Vol. 32,
December 2004, No. 12, pp. 94) **[664]**, **[25867]**,
[34023], **[47089]**
"Hot Tip: Limo as Mobile Office" in *Inc.* (November
15, 2000, pp. 26) **[3315]**, **[49510]**, **[54954]**
"Hot Tips" in *Inc.* (May 2000, pp. 161) **[42291]**,
[45254]
Hot Under the Collar: Dealing with Angry Customers
[31933]
Hotchkiss Chamber of Commerce **[58384]**
Hotel Brokers International **[12504]**
Hotel Business **[12665]**
"Hotel Consultant Finds Room at the Top" in
Crain's New York Business (Vol. 21, January
31, 2005, No. 5, pp. 18) **[3542]**, **[12569]**,
[31172]
Hotel Electronic Distribution Network Association
[12505]
Hotel and Motel Management **[12570]**, **[12666]**
Hotel and Motel Management and Operations
[12571]
Hotel & Travel Index **[12572]**
Hotel & Travel Index-International Edition **[24759]**
Hotelier **[12667]**
HOTELS **[12668]**, **[21686]**
"Hotels Fill Rooms with Memphis Vacation Package
Offers" in *Memphis Business Journal* (Vol. 25,
No. 10, July 4, 2003, pp. 22) **[12573]**, **[24695]**,
[24950], **[25196]**
"Hotels & Motels" in *Entrepreneur* (Vol. 32, No. 1,
January 2004, pp. 216) **[12574]**, **[24696]**,
[25197]
"Hotels skip surcharges, focus on conservation" in
Atlanta Business Chronicle (Vol. 24, No. 14,
September 7, 2001, pp. S6) **[12575]**, **[37296]**,
[53785]
"Hotels With a Sweaty Twist On Room Service" in
Inc. (May 1, 2005) **[12576]**, **[29600]**, **[30349]**
"Hotlist 05" in *Black Enterprise* (Vol. 36, December
2005, No. 5, pp. 102) **[36297]**, **[56268]**
Houghton Lake Chamber of Commerce **[61336]**
Houghton Mifflin Company–School Division
Research Center **[2815]**
Houma-Terrebonne Chamber of Commerce **[60648]**
Housatonic Community College **[58628]**
House Beautiful **[13694]**
House of Bread **[2302]**
"House of Cards? Home-Equity Borrowing Could be
Risky Business as Interest Rates Rise" in
Entrepreneur (Vol. 31, October 2003) **[17392]**,
[32488]
"A House Divided" in *Hispanic Business* (December
2003, pp. 34-36, 38, 40) **[665]**, **[20317]**,
[24417], **[47090]**
House Doctors Handyman Service **[4506]**
House Ear Institute **[12127]**
"House Exempts Small Businesses From
Superfund" in *Atlanta Business Chronicle* (Vol.
23, No. 51, May 25, 2001, pp. 7A) **[37297]**,
[40442]
House Menders **[7664]**
"House Party" in *Hispanic Business* (June 2005, pp.
84) **[7373]**, **[20540]**
"House Party Over? High Cost of Living in New
Jersey Continues" in *The Record* (November
16, 2005) **[20541]**, **[32489]**
"House Rules: Before You Let Your People Work at
Home, Find Out What You're Liable For-And
Cover Your Bases" in *Entrepreneur* (Vol. 32)
[13327], **[40443]**, **[43219]**
"The House That Knowledge Built" in *Fortune* (Vol.
142, No. 7, October 2, 2000, pp. 278+) **[44310]**
"House Wants Bigger Business-Tax Cut" in *Crain's
Detroit Business* (Vol. 21, October 31, 2005,
No. 44, pp. 6) **[41750]**, **[52120]**, **[54596]**
Household Furniture Market **[12318]**
Housemaster **[3276]**
HouseWall Garage System **[20040]**

Housing Association of Delaware Valley–Library
[20086]
Housing Economics **[7554]**
"Housing, Immigration Called Keys to the Future" in
Boston Globe (January 31, 2005) **[7374]**,
[20542], **[48559]**
Housing Market Report **[7555]**
"Housing Market Slowdown Will Weaken California
Economy, Forecasters Say" in *Sacramento Bee*
(December 7, 2005) **[7375]**, **[20543]**, **[32490]**
"Housing Pilot Plan Updated" in *Mississippi
Business Journal* (Vol. 29, January 2007, No. 4,
pp. 8) **[32491]**, **[39840]**
"Housing Program Breaks Mortgage Lending
Record" in *Milwaukee Journal Sentinel*
(December 2, 2005) **[17393]**, **[20544]**, **[20901]**,
[28297]
"Housing Project" in *Entrepreneur* (Vol. 31, No. 7,
July 2003, pp. 50) **[34932]**, **[42292]**
"Housing to Rise on CSX Yard" in *Crain's Chicago
Business* (Vol. 26, No. 50, December 15, 2003,
pp. 1) **[7376]**, **[17394]**
"Housing to Rise on CSX Yard; South Loop Boom
Goes on With Plans for 1,500 Units" in *Crains
Chicago Business* (Vol. 26, No. 50) **[7377]**,
[17395]
"Housing market at high risk" in *Atlanta Business
Chronicle* (Vol. 25, January 10, 2003, No. 31,
pp. 1A) **[7378]**, **[17396]**, **[20545]**, **[20902]**,
[28298], **[32492]**
Housing for Seniors Report **[1705]**, **[18356]**
Houston Area Chamber of Commerce **[61976]**
"Houston-Based ChaseCom L.P." in *Black
Enterprise* (Vol. 35, December 2004, No. 5, pp.
38) **[5015]**, **[14128]**, **[28299]**, **[31733]**, **[41751]**,
[52546]
"Houston-based GC Services Adds 100 Jobs in
Oklahoma City" in *Journal Record* (February 5,
2004) **[152]**, **[163]**, **[2912]**, **[2996]**, **[23961]**,
[24800], **[25877]**, **[26255]**, **[28300]**, **[30874]**,
[31734]
"Houston-Based Restaurant Chain Uses Mystery
Shoppers to Ensure Quality" in *Beaumont
Enterprise* (January 24, 2005) **[10006]**, **[12577]**,
[17521], **[21324]**, **[21531]**, **[29291]**, **[31035]**,
[31735], **[51187]**
Houston Business **[65668]**
Houston Business Journal (Vol. 34, No. 13, August
8, 2003, pp. 3); "Anadarko Laying Off 400
Workers to Cut Costs" in **[26152]**, **[32245]**
Houston Business Journal (Vol. 34, No. 14, August
15, 2003, pp. 3); "Anadarko Seeks Bidders for
Possible Buyout" in **[14739]**, **[26153]**, **[32246]**,
[49786]
Houston Business Journal (Vol. 33, No. 49, April 18,
2003, pp. 2A); "Andrews & Kurth goes high-tech
with ex-Brobeck attorneys" in **[29097]**, **[41514]**
Houston Business Journal (Vol. 33, No. 48, April 11,
2003, pp. 2A); "Animal porter escapes
economic dog days in shipshape" in **[16178]**,
[35771]
Houston Business Journal (Vol. 34, No. 13, August
8, 2003, pp. 1); "Apache on the Rise, Anadarko
in Decline" in **[26155]**, **[29789]**, **[44889]**
Houston Business Journal (Vol. 34, No. 13, August
8, 2003, pp. 2); "Banker Right on the Money
with Financial Powerhouse" in **[9831]**, **[14772]**,
[29798], **[37901]**, **[44915]**, **[46705]**
Houston Business Journal (Vol. 34, No. 14, August
15, 2003, pp. 17); "Beating Strong" in **[17254]**,
[29800], **[30135]**, **[44923]**
Houston Business Journal (Vol. 33, No. 51, May 2,
2003, pp. 2A); "Blade server firm sharpens up
with funding" in **[41556]**
Houston Business Journal (Vol. 34, No. 10, July 18,
pp. 19); "Bloom Bloom" in **[11421]**
Houston Business Journal (Vol. 34, No. 18,
September 12, 2003, pp. 1); "Buyers Check Out
Telecom Hotel" in **[12530]**, **[20449]**, **[20818]**
Houston Business Journal (Vol. 34, No. 14, August
15, 2003, pp. 1); "Citgo Mulls Relocation to
Houston" in **[30138]**, **[32315]**, **[54494]**
Houston Business Journal (Vol. 34, No. 19,
September 19, 2003, pp. 1B); "Design Turns
Theater-Going Into a Grand Night Out" in
[1509], **[17514]**

Houston Business Journal (Vol. 34, No. 13, August 8, 2003, pp. 1); "Dividends Gushing from Tax Cut" in [9916], [14922], [38010], [54516]

Houston Business Journal (Vol. 34, No. 14, August 15, 2003, pp. 3); "Dresser to Close Plant Eliminate 244 Jobs" in [32366], [46268]

Houston Business Journal (Vol. 34, No. 9, July 11, pp. 1); "Drypers Co-Founder Gets Fresh Start" in [7336], [20499], [20865]

Houston Business Journal (Vol. 33, No. 51, May 2, 2003, pp. 1A); "EC Outlook returns from Ohio." in [4647], [22977], [53269]

Houston Business Journal (Vol. 34, No. 15, August 22, 2003, pp. 1A); "Enterprising Union Creates $100M Bank" in [14955], [49918]

Houston Business Journal (Vol. 33, No. 48, April 11, 2003, pp. 1A); "Finance vets bank on bypassed businesses" in [44520], [55606]

Houston Business Journal (Vol. 34, No. 7, June 27, 2003, pp. 19A); "Gallery of Growth" in [12285], [28196]

Houston Business Journal (Vol. 34, No. 7, June 27, 2003, pp. 27A); "Houston Leads Research in Superconducting Wire" in [41752], [50889], [52121]

Houston Business Journal (Vol. 33, No. 48, April 11, 2003, pp. 19A); "Industrious solution" in [9218], [9568], [24529], [56278]

Houston Business Journal (Vol. 34, No. 11, July 25, pp. 19); "Inside Out" in [29920], [30890], [45304]

Houston Business Journal (Vol. 34, No. 18, September 12, 2003, pp. 17); "It's a Snap" in [19302], [29923], [36376]

Houston Business Journal (Vol. 34, No. 8, July 4, 2003, pp. 1); "JP Morgan Rolls Out Tech-Heavy Branches" in [10047], [15191], [15924], [34107], [41789]

Houston Business Journal (Vol. 34, No. 15, August 22, 2003, pp. 17); "King of the Hill" in [21546], [28380], [30564], [30899]

Houston Business Journal (Vol. 33, No. 51, May 2, 2003, pp. 1A); "Lender forecloses on historic hotel" in [7399], [12591], [28404]

Houston Business Journal (Vol. 34, No. 9, July 11, pp. 1); "Libraries Turn Page on Subscription Disruption" in [18896], [52555]

Houston Business Journal (Vol. 34, No. 9, July 11, pp. 2); "Microcinema Owner Puts Unique Lens on Houston" in [17522]

Houston Business Journal (Vol. 34, No. 9, July 11, 2003, pp. 17); "Moving Up" in [17557]

Houston Business Journal (Vol. 34, No. 18, September 12, 2003, pp. 1); "NASA Logs on for Team Encounter in Space" in [40062], [41856], [50932], [52158]

Houston Business Journal (Vol. 34, No. 8, July 4, 2003, pp. 15); "Party Time" in [4551], [18730], [21342]

Houston Business Journal (Vol. 33, No. 49, April 18, 2003, pp. 1A); "Plans afoot to revive world trade center" in [7450], [24998]

Houston Business Journal (Vol. 34, No. 19, September 19, 2003, pp. 1A); "Power Firms Poised to Recharge National Grid" in [9075]

Houston Business Journal (Vol. 34, No. 17, September 5, 2003, pp. 1); "Qcorps Scores Military Coup" in [17558], [30934], [40080]

Houston Business Journal (Vol. 33, No. 48, April 11, 2003, pp. 10A); "Reliant's refinancing package could be a model for industry" in [38313], [44632]

Houston Business Journal (Vol. 34, No. 7, June 27, 2003, pp. 2A); "Restaurateur's Answer to Construction is a Second Eatery" in [21611], [29981]

Houston Business Journal (Vol. 33, No. 46, March 28, 2003, pp. 17A); "Seeds of success" in [10573], [16028], [45629], [56399]

Houston Business Journal (Vol. 34, No. 11, July 25, pp. 1); "Soft Market Stall Apartments" in [1379], [20672], [21011], [32703], [47556]

Houston Business Journal (Vol. 34, No. 14, August 15, 2003, pp. 7); "Sonic Shifts Momentum With Purchase of 12 Car Dealerships" in [18125], [30000]

Houston Business Journal (Vol. 34, No. 8, July 4, 2003, pp. 1); "South Texas Builders Head for Houston's Border" in [7483], [30177]

Houston Business Journal (Vol. 34, No. 12, August 1, 2003, pp. 7); "Southwest May Put Stock in Dividends" in [10187], [15466]

Houston Business Journal (Vol. 34, No. 19, September 19, 2003, pp. 1A); "Sports Authority Faces Fourth Down" in [23736], [40713]

Houston Business Journal (Vol. 34, No. 11, July 25, pp. 7); "Sterling Makes a Mint on Sale of Single-Family Mortgage Business" in [17444], [20677], [47578]

Houston Business Journal (Vol. 34, No. 19, September 19, 2003, pp. 2A); "Stewart & Stevenson Treads Through Tough Times" in [38375], [46443]

Houston Business Journal (Vol. 34, No. 19, September 19, 2003, pp. 17A); "Striking Up the Brand Band" in [47581], [50682]

Houston Business Journal (Vol. 33, No. 49, April 18, 2003, pp. 31A); "The world's a stage" in [22582], [25053]

Houston Business Journal (Vol. 34, No. 14, August 15, 2003, pp. 2A); "Toyota Center Bypasses Ticketmaster" in [3954], [52393]

Houston Business Journal (Vol. 34, No. 16, August 29, 2003, pp. 2); "W. Alabama a Sweet Home - and Office - for Retailers" in [42750], [51401], [52749]

Houston Chronicle (April 11, 2003); "Airline Slump Hurts Houston-Based Maker of Tow Tractors" in [32240], [46188]

Houston Chronicle (April 11, 2003); "Continental Airlines' Deb Rating Suffers Another Blow" in [27975], [32330]

Houston Chronicle (April 11, 2003); "Corporate Scandals Inspire Texas Fraud Bill" in [29168], [30209], [37411], [40284]

Houston Chronicle (October 6, 2002); "Houston Microbrewery Has Cult Following" in [3128], [31736]

Houston Chronicle (April 11, 2003); "In Corporate-Fraud Cases, Lawyer's Approval Can Let Client Avoid Charges" in [29304], [37464], [40457]

Houston Chronicle (April 11, 2003); "Organizers Say Houston Will Be Ready for XXXVIII" in [23732], [50649]

Houston Chronicle (April 11, 2003); "Texas Doctors Take Pains to Follow Privacy Rules" in [29544], [40761]

Houston Ear Research Foundation [12128]

Houston International Trade Center–Small Business Development Center [65038]

Houston JobBank [23392]

"Houston Leads Research in Superconducting Wire" in *Houston Business Journal* (Vol. 34, No. 7, June 27, 2003, pp. 27A) [41752], [50889], [52121]

"Houston Microbrewery Has Cult Following" in *Houston Chronicle* (October 6, 2002) [3128], [31736]

Houston Minority Business Council [65580]

Houston Museum of Decorative Arts–Library [1358]

Houston North Forest Chamber of Commerce [65313]

Houston Northwest Chamber of Commerce [65314]

Houston Partners / Houston Venture Partners [65610]

Houston Public Library–Clayton Library–Center for Genealogical Research [11036]

"Houston Super Bowl XXXVIII Host Committee" in *Black Enterprise* (Vol. 34, No. 6, January 2004, pp. 51) [23725]

Houston West Chamber of Commerce [65315]

"Hover craft" in *Entrepreneur* (Vol. 30, No. 1, January 2002, pp. 18) [22791], [47091]

"How About a Little Browser Branding?" in *Sales & Marketing Management* (Vol. 159, January-February 2007, No. 1, pp. 45) [34024], [47092], [51678]

How to Achieve Zero-Defect Marketing [47093]

"How to Acquire Customers on the Web" in *Harvard Business Review* (Vol. 78, No. 3, May 2000, pp. 179) [34025], [47094]

"How Adobe is Pushing Quark Off the Page" in *Business 2.0* (Vol. 6, September 2005, No. 8, pp. 56) [4689], [8615], [18231], [18884], [23031], [50674], [53318]

"How to Advertise with Flyers" in *Home Business* (Vol. 12, October 2005, No. 5, pp. 52) [666], [47095]

How to Advertise a Small Business: Step by Step Guide to Starting Your Own Business [667], [47096]

"How newspaper overcame loss of big advertisers" in *Wall Street Journal* (January 25, 2002, pp. A13) [18885], [47097]

"How well is Appeals doing?" in *Tax Notes* (Vol. 96, No. 12, September 16, 2002, pp. 1564-1567) [40444], [54597]

"How ASPs Can Accelerate Your E-Business" in *E-business Advisor* (Vol. 18, No. 3, March 2000, pp. 20) [23032], [34026], [44311], [53319]

"How to Avoid Auction Scams" in *New York Times* (March 20, 2004, pp. C2) [1825], [18648], [30230], [34027]

How to Avoid Patent, Marketing and Invention Company Scams: Wow! What a Great Idea. Now What? [44058]

"How to Be a Better Googler" in *My Business* (December/January 2004, pp. 24) [14129], [34028]

How to Be a Better Trainer [33319]

How to Be an Entrepreneur and Keep Your Sanity: The African-American Guide to Owning, Building and Maintaining Successfully Your Own Small Business [36298], [48240]

How to Be an Entrepreneur: The Six Secrets of Self-Made Success [36299]

"How to Be a Good Listener" in *Women in Business* (Vol. 54, No. 5, September-October 2002, pp. 17) [36300], [45255]

How to Be a Great Communicator: The Complete Guide to Mastering Internal Communications [27400]

How to Be the Kid with the Perfect Swing [23660]

How to Be the Life of the Podium: Openers, Closers & Everything in Between to Keep Them Listening [45256]

How to Be a Second Mortgage Loan Broker [17397]

How to Be a Successful Computer Consultant [6474]

How to Be Your Own Contractor [7379], [18707]

How to Beat the Odds [54317]

How to Become a Successful Consultant in Your Own Field [9363], [31173]

How to Become a Successful Weekend Entrepreneur: Secrets of Making an Extra $100 or More Each Week Using Your Spare Time [49762]

"How to beat the big-box retailers" in *Hispanic Business* (Vol. 22, No. 6, June 2000, pp. 110) [48241], [51188]

"How to build a blockbuster" in *Harvard Business Review* (Vol. 80, No. 10, October 2002, pp. 18) [47098], [48746], [50609]

"How Blue Will Christmas Be? As sales keep plunging, retailers are panicking" in *Fortuneit* (Vol. 146, No. 9, Nov. 11, 2002, pp. 127) [28301], [32493], [51189]

"How Bluetooth Works" in *PC Computing* (April, 2000, pp. 87) [5016], [7137], [14130], [34029]

"How to Boost Your Portfolio's Performance" in *Black Enterprise* (Vol. 34, No. 4, November 2003) [10007], [15096], [38123]

How to Build a More Positive Work Environment (Canada) [44758]

How to Build a Profitable Consulting Practice 1 & 2 [9400], [31262]

How to Build Resilience in Your Staff and Yourself [44759]

How to Build a Successful One-Person Business: A Common-Sense Guide to Starting & Growing a Company [42654]

"How can you find the elusive prospect hot button" in *Atlanta Business Chronicle* (Vol. 24, No. 14, September 7, 2001, pp. 6B) [51679]

How to Buy and/or Sell a Small Business for Maximum Profit: A Step-by-Step Guide [30681], [52428]

How and When to Be Your Own Lawyer: A Step-by-Step Guide to Effectively Using Our Legal System **[29294]**

"How to Win Big and Get Ahead Fast" in *Inc.* (September 1, 2003) **[29910]**, **[36326]**

How to Win at Everything: Experts Reveal the Fine Art of Beating the Competition **[30885]**

How to Win Marketing Wars in the 1990s **[48677]**

"How to Win a Marquee Account" in *Sales and Marketing.com* (Vol. 156, No. 3, March 2004, pp. 72) **[41033]**, **[47115]**, **[51683]**, **[52123]**

How to Win at Work **[34944]**

How to Work Most Effectively with Your Boss **[27258]**, **[34795]**

"How resilience works" in *Harvard Business Review* (Vol. 80, No. 5, May 2002, pp. 46) **[45276]**, **[52893]**

How to Write an Affirmative Action Plan **[42821]**

How to Write a Business Plan **[29911]**, **[39397]**

How to Write a Business Plan 4.4 **[29912]**

How to Write a Great Business Plan for Your Small Business in 60 Minutes or Less **[29913]**, **[31557]**, **[38132]**, **[39398]**, **[45277]**, **[47116]**

How to Write Macintosh Software: The Debugging Reference for the Macintosh **[23035]**

How to Write and Prepare Training Materials **[34945]**

How to Write a Successful Advertising Plan **[47117]**

How to Write a Successful Business Plan: Step-by-Step Guide to Business Success **[29914]**

How to Write Training Materials **[33125]**

How to Write a Winning Business Plan **[29915]**

"How You Can Hire Gray Hairs" in *FSB* (Vol. 10, No. 9, December 1, 2000, pp. 79) **[42300]**

How You Can Make $25,000 a Year with Your Camera **[19301]**

How You Can Start, Build, Manage, or Turn Around Any Business **[37037]**

"How to identify your enemies before they destroy you" in *Harvard Business Review* (Vol. 80, No. 10, October 2002, pp. 115) **[41756]**, **[49079]**

How You Too Can Make at Least $1 Million in the Mail-Order Business **[16449]**

"How Your CFO should Raise Money: What the Experts Say" in *Inc.* (April 2000, pp. 123) **[45278]**, **[55675]**

Howard County Center for Business and Technology Development–SBDC Central Region **[60798]**

Howard County Chamber of Commerce **[60838]**

Howard High School of Technology–Media Center **[4460]**

Howard Johnson International Inc. **[12714]**, **[21846]**

Howard University
Office of University Research and Planning **[58685]**
School of Business–Library **[2995]**
Small Business Development Center **[58660]**

Howard University School of Business–Small Business Development Center **[58661]**

"Howard University's School of Communications has Been Named After John H. Johnson" in *Black Enterprise* (Vol. 34, No. 6, January 2004) **[18886]**, **[20076]**, **[45961]**, **[48243]**

"Howdy, Partner" in *Entrepreneur* (Vol. 32, October 2004, No. 10, pp. 104) **[13758]**, **[33450]**, **[35519]**, **[49767]**

"Howdy Partner!" in *Home Business* (Vol. 12, March/April 2005, No. 2, pp. 44) **[36327]**, **[49994]**

Howe Chamber of Commerce **[65316]**

Howell Area Chamber of Commerce **[61337]**

Howell Chamber of Commerce **[62517]**

Howell County–SBDC Extension Center **[61867]**

"Howell Twp. May Get Import Motor Mall" in *Crain's Detroit Business* (Vol. 21, January 31, 2005, No. 5, pp. 40) **[18059]**, **[38833]**

Howick Associates **[31975]**

"Howle turns to new tech start-up" in *Atlanta Business Chronicle* (Vol. 24, No. 14, September 7, 2001, pp. 3A) **[6916]**, **[37062]**, **[49768]**

Hoxie Area Chamber of Commerce and EDC **[60353]**

"HP iPAQ h6315 Pocket PC Phone Edition" in *Black Enterprise* (Vol. 35, December 2004, No. 5, pp. 71) **[5022]**, **[49080]**

HP World Directory **[6680]**

HPAC Engineering-Info-Dex **[1022]**

HPAC (Heating-Plumbing-Air Conditioning Magazine) **[1039]**, **[19761]**

"HQ Hotel Idea Irks Industry" in *Washington Business Journal* (Vol. 22, No. 11, July 18, 2003, pp. 1) **[12579]**, **[22516]**, **[24953]**

HR Advice.com **[42972]**

HR Answers Inc. **[42973]**

"HR Battles to Conquer" in *Hispanic Business* (June 2002, pp. 72) **[28313]**, **[42301]**

The HR Book: Human Resources Management for Small Business **[42302]**, **[42864]**

The HR Dept. **[42974]**

HR First Contact **[3884]**

HR Manager's Legal Reporter **[42910]**

HR Reporter **[48616]**

Tim W. Hrastar Associates **[27587]**

HRD Press **[61164]**

HRD in Small Organizations: Research and Practice **[39399]**, **[42865]**

HRMagazine **[42911]**

HRX **[31491]**

"HSAs-A Growing Trend In Health Benefits for Businesses and Individuals" in *Entrepreneur* (Vol. 32, December 2004, No. 12, pp. 67) **[13329]**, **[26831]**, **[43224]**, **[53788]**, **[54603]**

"HSB Sees Growth in Monoline Equipment Breakdown Due to Hard Market" in *Rough Notes* (Vol. 145, No. 9, September 2002, pp. 14) **[13330]**, **[43225]**

HSMAI Affordable Meetings Exposition and Conference **[25068]**

HSMAI - Affordable Meetings West **[4565]**, **[12683]**, **[47820]**, **[55220]**

HTML Publishing on the Internet for Windows: Great-Looking Documents Online: Home Pages, Newsletters, Catalogs, Ads & Forums **[18233]**

"HTVN Files for Bankruptcy" in *Hispanic Business* (March 2002, pp. 12) **[24419]**, **[28314]**

Huber Heights Chamber of Commerce **[63702]**

Huddle House **[21847]**

"Huddle Up" in *Entrepreneur* (Vol. 27, No. 12, December 1999, pp. 131) **[34946]**, **[45279]**

Huddleston, Bolen LLP–Law Library **[10401]**, **[15801]**, **[24180]**

Hudson Area Chamber of Commerce **[61338]**, **[63703]**

Hudson Area Chamber of Commerce and Tourism Bureau **[66426]**

Hudson Chamber of Commerce **[60151]**

Hudson County Chamber of Commerce **[62518]**

Hudson County Improvement Authority–Library **[9441]**

Hudson Falls-Kingsbury Chamber of Commerce **[62933]**

Hudson Valley Business Journal **[63233]**

Hudson Valley Gateway Chamber of Commerce **[62934]**

Hudson Venture Partners **[63110]**

Hudson's Grill of America, Inc. **[21848]**

Hudsonville Area Chamber of Commerce **[61339]**

Hueytown Chamber of Commerce **[56868]**

Hughes Springs Chamber of Commerce **[65317]**

Hughson Chamber of Commerce **[57552]**

Hugo Chamber of Commerce **[64018]**

Hugoton Area Chamber of Commerce **[60354]**

Huguenot Society of America–Library **[11037]**

Huguenot Society of South Carolina–Library **[11038]**

Hulbert Financial Digest **[15647]**

Human Capital Research Corp. **[38547]**

Human Factors in Ergonomics and Manufacturing **[42912]**, **[45889]**, **[46507]**

Human Factors and Ergonomics Society Bulletin **[18567]**

Human Mutation **[52267]**

Human Networks Inc. **[42975]**

Human Resource Development: The Field **[42866]**

Human Resource Executive's Market Resource **[42867]**

Human Resource Executive's Survival Guide to the Americans with Disabilities Act **[32033]**

Human Resource Management: A Guide to Personnel Management in the Hotel and Catering Industry **[4545]**, **[12580]**

Human Resource Planning Society **[42810]**, **[54925]**

Human Resource Solutions Inc. **[48638]**

Human Resource Specialties Inc. **[16620]**, **[31376]**, **[42976]**, **[46047]**

Human Resources Group Ltd. **[32116]**

Human Resources Management: Ideas and Trends Newsletter **[42913]**

Human Resources Measurements **[42914]**

Human Resources Report **[43006]**, **[55326]**, **[55339]**

Human Resources Research Organization **[15907]**, **[42811]**

Human Resources for Small Business Made Easy **[39400]**, **[42868]**

"Humana battles for growth" in *Atlanta Business Chronicle* (Vol. 25, January 3, 2003, No. 30, pp. 3A) **[13331]**, **[26832]**, **[28315]**, **[30886]**, **[43226]**

Humana Venture Capital **[60581]**

Humane News **[1254]**

Humanics ErgoSystems Inc. **[49614]**, **[56666]**

Humanities Full Text **[8110]**

"Humanize Your Web Customer Service" in *E-business Advisor* (Vol. 18, No. 8, August 2000, pp. 12) **[25870]**, **[31741]**, **[34039]**

"Humanizing Leaders" in *Fast Company* (March 2005, No. 92, pp. 82) **[33126]**, **[36328]**, **[45280]**

Humble Area Chamber of Commerce **[65318]**

"Humble Beginning" in *Entrepreneur* (Vol. 33, March 2005, No. 3, pp. 131) **[1376]**, **[21325]**, **[37695]**

Humboldt Chamber of Commerce **[60355]**, **[64929]**

Humboldt County Chamber of Commerce **[62353]**

Humboldt-Dakota City Chamber of Commerce **[60152]**

Humboldt State University–Institute for Study of Alternative Dispute Resolution **[17079]**

Humboldt State University Foundation **[58205]**

Humitech Franchise Corp. **[23339]**

Hummel Collectors Club **[5887]**

Humphreys County Area Chamber of Commerce **[64930]**

Humpty's Restaurants International Inc. **[21849]**

Hungry Howie's Pizza, Inc. **[19676]**

"Hungry Howie's Plans 50 Stores" in *Crain's Detroit Business* (Vol. 19, No. 49, December 8, 2003, pp. 3) **[19632]**, **[21533]**, **[38834]**

"Hungry for More: With Four Food Franchises on His Plate, This Owner Reveals His Recipe for Success" in *Entrepreneur* (August 2004) **[21534]**, **[38835]**

"Hungry for Success" in *Black Enterprise* (Vol. 34, No. 7, February 2004, pp. 137) **[10508]**, **[10622]**, **[45962]**, **[48244]**

"The Hungry Wolf Syndrome" in *Rough Notes* (Vol. 145, No. 1, January 2003, pp. 92) **[13332]**, **[37459]**, **[43227]**

Hunt-Scanlon Publishing **[58634]**

Hunt-Scanlon's Executive Recruiters of North America - Contingency Firms **[9212]**, **[9563]**

Hunt-Scanlon's Select Guide to Finance Executives **[9213]**, **[9564]**

Hunt-Scanlon's Select Guide to Human Resource Executives **[9214]**, **[9565]**

Hunt-Scanlon's Select Guide to Information Technology Executives **[9215]**, **[9566]**

Hunt-Scanlon's Select Guide to Sales & Marketing Executives **[9216]**, **[9567]**

Hunter Arts Publishing **[58261]**

"Hunter Fans May Buy Rights to Interchangeable Light Product" in *Memphis Business Journal* (Vol. 25, No. 16, August 15, 2003, pp. 18) **[9111]**, **[12190]**, **[12290]**

Hunter Museum of American Art–Library **[1359]**

Hunterdon County Chamber of Commerce **[62519]**

Hunterdon Historical Newsletter **[10966]**

"Hunting Season: Feds Try to Protect the Little Guy From Payroll Tax Predators" in *Entrepreneur* (Vol. 32, September 2004, No. 9) **[165]**, **[18777]**, **[23962]**, **[26257]**, **[29295]**, **[40447]**, **[54604]**

Huntingburg Chamber of Commerce **[59943]**

Huntington Beach Chamber of Commerce **[57553]**

Huntington County Chamber of Commerce **[59944]**

Huntington Learning Centers, Inc. **[25478]**

Huntington Regional Chamber of Commerce [66280]

Huntington Township Chamber of Commerce [62935]

Huntley Area Chamber of Commerce and Industry [59545]

Huntsville Chamber of Commerce [57183]

Hurley Area Chamber of Commerce [66427]

"Huron to Announce $25M Deal, Eyes New $250M Fund" in *Crain's Detroit Business* (Vol. 23, No. 3, January 15, 2007, pp. 26) [28316], [52894], [55676]

Huron Chamber of Commerce [63704]

Huron County Economic Development Corp.–Small Business Development Center [61196]

Huron Shores Chamber of Commerce [61340]

Huron Township Chamber of Commerce [61341]

Huron Valley Chamber of Commerce [61342]

Hurricane Valley Chamber of Commerce [65714]

"Hurricane Watch:Whether the Market's Boisterous or Becalmed, the Web's the Place to Vent and Pontificate" in *Barron's* (July 28, 2003) [10013], [14137], [15108], [34040], [38133]

"Hurricane Won't Blow Down State Economy" in *Crain's Detroit Business* (Vol. 21, October 3, 2005, No. 43, pp. 48) [28317], [32501]

Hurst - Euless - Bedford Chamber of Commerce [65319]

Hutchinson Area Chamber of Commerce [61603]

Hutchinson/Reno County Chamber of Commerce [60356]

Galen O. Hutchison [5486]

Hutto Chamber of Commerce [65320]

Huxford Genealogical Society, Inc.–Huxford Library [11039]

HVAC Technician: Start and Run a Money-Making Business [1023]

The H.W. Wilson Co. [63251]

HWL International L.L.P. [18577]

Hy-Tech Weight Loss [26054]

"Hy-Vee Hall Des Moines, IA" in *Tradeshow Week* (Vol. 34, November 29, 2004, No. 48, pp. S6) [22517], [24954], [55101]

Hyannis Area Chamber of Commerce [60962]

"Hybrid Phones Hold Promise of Cellular, VoIP" in *Boston Globe* (March 7, 2005) [5023], [49081]

Hyde Park Chamber of Commerce [59546], [62936]

Hydro Physics Pipe Inspection Corp. [4507]

Hydro-Quebec Capitech Inc. [66770]

"Hydrogen: The Next Fuel for Laptops?" in *San Jose Mercury News* (March 2, 2005) [6681], [48749], [50892], [52124]

Hydrography: For the Surveyor and Engineer [23764]

Hydroshield [7758]

HYDRO■WIRE [9390], [40865]

HyettPalma Inc. [32829]

Beverly Hyman and Associates [27588]

"Hyper business or just...hyperbusy?" in *Women in Business* (Vol. 53, No. 3, May-June, 2001, pp. 12) [39401], [53789]

HyperClick Online Services [34776]

"Hypermediation: Commerce as Clickstream" in *Harvard Business Review* (Vol. 78, No. 1, January 2000, pp. 46) [34041], [51194]

The Hysen Group [21723]

I

"I-5 Corridor: Nurturing Its Economic Potential" in *San Fernando Valley Business Journal* (Vol. 11, December 2006, No. 25, pp. 35) [32502], [39402]

I-70 Corridor Chamber of Commerce [58385]

I-94 West Chamber of Commerce [61604]

"I Bought It Through the Grapevine" in *Success* (Vol. 47, No. 4, September 2000, pp. 4) [23441], [25757], [33451], [37063]

"I want to start my own business" in *Women in Business* (Vol. 54, No. 5, September-October 2002, pp. 14) [35520], [56054]

I Can Do It! Ed Lewis [37038]

I Can Do It! Judi Wineland [25317]

I Can Do It! Stew Leonard [53057]

"I Can't Seem to Hire the Right Bookkeeper. Should I Try Using a Personality Test?" in *Inc.* (October 2005, pp. 62) [2914], [26258], [42303], [53790]

"I Consider Myself the Visionary Still" in *Business Week* (December 19, 2005, No. 3964, pp. 54, 56) [36329], [56274]

"I Did It My Way" in *Entrepreneur* (Vol. 31, No. 8, August 2003, pp. 112) [29747], [35521]

"I Do" Weddings: A Guide to Starting Your Own Wedding Consulting Business [3167]

"I Feel Your Pain" in *Forbes* (Vol. 174, December 27, 2004, No. 13, pp. 38) [53791]

"I Fulfilled My Family Dream" in *Success* (Vol. 47, No. 5, October 2000, pp. 22) [23036], [37696]

"I was greedy, too" in *Harvard Business Review* (Vol. 81, No. 2, February 2003, pp. 38) [166], [14138], [26259], [33127], [36330], [37460]

I-Hatch Ventures, LLC [63111]

"I Have One Life, and It Must Come Together" in *Inc.* (October 1, 2003) [36331], [39403]

I Love People...It's Customers I Can't Stand [31936]

"I Spy With My Little Wi-Fi: Wireless Video Cameras can Mean More Security" in *Entrepreneur* (Vol. 32, No. 1, January 2004, pp. 38) [4189], [22254]

"I Spy...: Workplace Surveillance is Coming to Small and Midsize Businesses" in *Entrepreneur* (Vol. 31, No. 8, August 2003, pp. 20) [22255], [53792], [56566]

"I Think I'll Pass: Do Women Have a Tougher Time Delegating Tasks?" in *Entrepreneur* (Vol. 32, October 2004, No. 10, pp. 44) [36332], [45281], [56275]

"I Think We're Up to the Challenge" *Business Week Online* (March 16, 2002) [4692], [23037], [53322]

"I Tune, You Tune" in *Forbes* (Vol. 175, January 31, 2005, No. 2, pp. 60) [17746], [41757]

"I Want My Cell TV" in *Entrepreneur.com* (Vol. 34, February 2006, No. 2, pp. 42) [5024], [6682], [41758], [49082]

"I Want My meVC!: the armchair venture capitalist" in *Fortune* (Vol. 142, No. 1, June 26, 2000, pp. 294) [55396]

"I Want my WTV" in *Entrepreneur* (Vol. 32, No. 1, January 2004, pp. 22) [7733], [15109], [49083]

i9 Sports [23753]

IAA National & World News [854]

IAAM Guide to Members and Services [48869]

"IACVB Considers Changing Its Name" in *Tradeshow Week* (Vol. 34, December 20, 2004, No. 51, pp. 3) [22518], [24955], [47118], [55102]

IAEI News [9083]

"IAEM Commission To Oversee Audits: Exhibitors To Constitute a Majority; Body Will Enforce Audit Standards" in *Tradeshow Week* (Vol. 34) [167], [22519], [24956], [26260], [55103]

IAEM Membership Directory and Buyer's Guide [24957]

IAHI, The Owners' Association [12506]

IBA News [1451]

Ibelay [58453]

Iberville Chamber of Commerce [60649]

IBEX Publishers Inc. [60898]

IBIS/Business Information Services, International [58262]

IBJS Capital Corp. [63112]

IBM Canada, Ltd.–Research Information Centre [49470]

IBM Corporation
    Bur Technical Library [6448], [6544], [23317]
    Library/Information Resource Center [6545], [23318]

"IBM Corp." in *PC Magazine* (March 7, 2000, pp. 158) [34042], [49084], [53323]

IBM on Demand Technology for the Growing Business: How to Optimize Your Computing Environment for Today and Tomorrow [6683], [41759], [49085], [53793]

"IBM Has A Vision Too! Here's its answer to all those frustrated tech customers" in *Fortuneit* (Vol. 146, Nov. 25, 2002, pp. 158) [6172], [6476], [14139], [34043], [37150], [39404]

IBM Journal of Research and Development [52268]

"IBM readies Linux suite" in *InfoWorld* (Vol. 22, No. 45, November 6, 2000, pp. 5) [14140], [25871], [53324]

"IBM gives Lotus the muscle to punch above its weight" in *PC Magazine* (Vol. 9, No. 5, May 2000, pp. 34) [44315], [53325]

"IBM, Microsoft, others plan alliance to help conduct business online" in *Wall Street Journal* (February 6, 2002, pp. B4) [34044], [49995], [53794]

"IBM Readies Linux Suite for Small Biz" in *Network World* (November 6, 2000, pp. NA) [34045], [49086], [53326], [53795]

IBM Systems Journal (Vol. 42, No. 3, September 2003, pp. 498); "Experimental Games for the Design of Reputation Management Systems" in [1812], [12881], [20117], [32419], [45124]

"IBM Unveils Intel-Based Servers to Improve Business Security and Efficiency" in *Internet Wire* (February 14, 2005) [6684], [6943], [22256], [41760]

"IBOC Grows in Oklahoma" in *Hispanic Business* (September 2004, pp. 20) [10014], [48245], [49996]

ICA Update [4373]

ICCM - Incoming Call Center Management [24313], [24327]

ICDI Inc. [17464], [20737], [21084]

Ice Cream Churn [12829]

Ice Cream and Economics: Ben and Jerry's Homemade [12798]

Ice Cream Reporter (Vol. 14, No. 2, January 20, 2001, pp. 2); "Elan Frozen Yogurt returns to New York" in [12775], [46927]

"Ice cream shop does its best to satisfy its customers' Cravings" in *Sarasota Herald Tribune* (November 21, 2002, pp. H12) [11331], [12782], [37697]

Ice Fishing Secrets I [2195]

Ice Magic Franchising Inc. [1637]

Ice Skating Institute [22830]

Iceberg Ventures [60582]

Icebox/Soupbox [21850]

ICFF - International Contemporary Furniture Fair [12333]

ICG Magazine [9755], [19236]

Icon Venture Advisors / Icon Ventures [58037]

ICOP, Business Management Consultant [46048]

ICP Report [12398]

ICPA Reporter [54343]

ICS Cleaning Specialist [10522], [25541]

ICTA Update [25294]

ICTs and SMEs Antecedents and Consequences of Technology Adoption [39405], [41761]

"I'd Like to Buy Machinery From China" in *Inc.* (September 2005, pp. 53) [16370], [29296], [43700], [44062], [46316]

"I'd Rather Be Flying (Myself)" in *Inc.* (January 1, 2002) [30351], [53796]

Idabel Chamber of Commerce and Agriculture [64019]

The Idaho Business Review [59356]

Idaho Department of Commerce [59355], [66862]

Idaho Department of Commerce and Labor–Department of Economic Development [59280]

Idaho Innovation Center, Inc. [59343]

Idaho Procurement Technical Assistance Center–Idaho Department of Commerce [59339]

Idaho Sportsmen's Show [21191]

Idaho Springs Chamber of Commerce [58386]

Idaho State Library [66863]

Idaho State University
    Center for Business Research [32854]
    Center for Business Research and Services [66864]
    College of Technology [59352]
    Idaho Museum of Natural History–Stirton-Kelson Library [12164]

Idaho State University (Region V)–Small Business Development Center [59276]

Idaho State University (Region VI)–Small Business Development Center [59277]

Idaho State University Research Park [59344]

Idanta Partners, Ltd. (San Diego) [58038]

Master Index

IDDBA Legis-Letter [2265], [10629], [12795]

IDEA Health and Fitness Association [19362]

IDEA Personal Trainer [19456]

Ideal Image [7935]

"Ideal PR consultant knows to keep pitches clear and simple" in *Boston Business Journal* (Vol. 22, No. 14, May 10, 2002, pp. 44) [20124], [47119]

Idealab! [58039]

IDEAlliance - International Digital Enterprise Alliance [19845], [25768]

"Ideas on demand: you don't have to wait for inspiration" in *Entrepreneur* (Vol. 31, No. 4, April 2003, pp. 78) [36333], [45282]

Ideas To Go Inc. [867]

The Ident-A-Kid Program [52626]

"Identify All Possible Exits" in *Business Week Online* (Dec. 6, 2002) [29748], [30485], [35522]

"Identifying and Developing Measures of Information Technology Ethical Work Climates" in *Journal of Business Ethics* (Sept. 15, 2003) [34046], [37461]

Identifying the UN/DOT Hazard Classes: Labels and Placards (Revised) [56633]

"Identity crisis" in *Entrepreneur* (Vol. 31, No. 4, April 2003, pp. 24) [22257], [39406], [44316]

"Identity Theft Still Top Fraud Complaint" in *Kansas City Star* (February 2, 2005) [22258], [29297], [30231]

"Identity Theft" in *The Economist* (Vol. 376, July 16-22, 2005, No. 8435, pp. 59) [22259], [44317]

"Ideology, Politics & the Bench" in *Hispanic Business* (June 2002, pp. 18) [29298], [32034]

IDG Ventures (San Francisco) [58040]

Idi-Supply Inc. [3733], [16621], [31377], [38548], [43925], [46049], [53096]

"The idol life" in *Entrepreneur* (Vol. 30, No. 1, January 2002,) [36334]

IDRS, Inc. [4508]

Idyllwild Chamber of Commerce [57554]

IE News: Ergonomics [18568]

IEEE–Information Center [9098]

IEEE Computational Science and Engineering [52269]

IEEE Software [23283]

IEG Venture Management, Inc. [59738]

Iemerge Ventures [62085]

IEQ Strategies [1079]

"If At First You Don't Succeed" in *Inc.* (July 1, 2003) [36335]

"If BlackBerry Gets Smushed..." in *Business Week* (January 9, 2006, No. 3966, pp. 16) [27404], [27645], [34047], [41762], [44063], [49087]

If at First: Overcoming the Fear of Failure [35191], [37039]

"If at First You Don't Succeed..." in *Black Enterprise* (Vol. 34, No. 4, Nov. 2003, pp. 48) [5316], [35523], [49769], [56055]

"If the Gene Fits" in *Fast Company* (November 2001, pp. 140) [50893]

"If you want honesty, break some rules" in *Harvard Business Review* (Vol. 80, No. 4, April 2002, pp. 42) [34947], [45283]

"If I had had more experience, if I was more careful, if I was more competent" in *Fast Company* (June 2001, pp. 161) [15110], [29299], [40448]

"If I Had an E-Hammer" in *Success* (Vol. 47, No. 3, July 2000, pp. 24) [11870], [33452], [35524]

"If I knew then what I know now" in *WorkingWoman* (Vol. 25, No. 7, August 2000, pp. 48) [30887], [36336], [56276]

"If Members Think Items are Overpriced, They'll Blame Barter Trust's Economy, says CEO Mike Edelhart" in *Inc.* (October 2000, pp. 58) [26712], [34048], [36337]

"If Not the Word, What? Leaders Speak" in *Tradeshow Week* (Vol. 34, November 29, 2004, No. 48, pp. 20) [22520], [24958], [49997], [55104]

"If you seek ways to pay, look about you" in *Crain's Detroit Business* (Vol. 18, No. 23, June 10, 2002, pp. 8) [25703]

"If you want something done right, delegate it" in *Women in Business* (Vol. 53, No. 7, January-February 2002, pp. 13) [27405], [45284], [54958]

"If Telemarketers Paid For Your Time" in *Forbes* (April 15, 2002, p. 225) [47120], [53797]

"If You Build It" in *Entrepreneur* (Vol. 31, No. 8, August 2003, pp. 30) [25872], [34049], [51195]

"If You Build It, They Might Not Come" in *Business Week* (February 20, 2006, No. 3972, pp. 40) [7381], [20550], [20904]

"If You Built It" in *Entrepreneur* (Vol. 31, Oct. 2003) [7382], [54605]

"If the spirit moves you" in *Fast Company* (May 2001, pp. 54) [30352], [53798]

"If You Have Rules, You Have To Be Prepared to Stick With Them-Even When It's Hard" in *Inc.* (May 1, 2005) [40498], [42304], [45285]

"If You Market, They Will Come" in *Success* (Vol. 47, No. 1, January 2000, pp. 50) [34050], [47121], [51196]

"If You Want Business, Answer Your Phone" in *Crain's Detroit Business* (Vol. 19, No. 45, November 10, 2003, pp. 8) [5025], [5177], [30882], [31742]

If You're Clueless about Starting Your Own Business & Want to Know More [52895]

IFAC News [327]

IFMA's Annual Conference & Expo, World Workplace [20070]

iFranchise Group [3885], [29627], [39006]

IGA Grocergram [11696]

IGM CorporateWatch [10378], [15760]

The Ignite Group / Ignite Associates, LLC [58041]

"IGT: In Search of the Next Jackpot" in *Business Week* (February 14, 2005, No. 3920, pp. 58) [10870], [28318]

IH/M & RS - International Hotel/Motel & Restaurant Show [12684], [21704]

IHA Membership Directory [12222]

IHOP [21851]

I.H.R. Solutions [3734], [3972], [16622], [31378], [42140], [42977], [46050]

IIE Solutions (Vol. 34, No. 12, Dec. 2002, pp. 34); "The right place for a bottleneck" in [3134], [29982]

I.I.I. Insurance Daily [13584]

IIMI–Information Center [16894]

IIT Research Institute [48847]

Ilium Associates Inc. [16869], [47873]

"I'll Trade You" in *Black Enterprise* (Vol. 33, No. 6, January 2003, pp. 43) [14141], [34051]

"I'll Trade You..." in *Home Office Computing* (Vol. 18, No. 9, September 2000, pp. 87) [26713], [34052], [53799]

"Illicit Affairs?" in *Entrepreneur* (Vol. 32) [29300], [31038], [40449], [43701]

Illini Hospital–Perlmutter Library of the Health Sciences [18399]

Illinois Agricultural Association–Illinois Farm Bureau Information Research Center [26660]

Illinois Association of Chamber of Commerce Executives [59547]

Illinois Bureau of the Budget–Office of Management and Budget [66867]

"Illinois Businesses Anxious about Governor's Plans on Fees, Taxes" in *Chicago Tribune* (April 11, 2003) [40450], [54606]

Illinois CPA Society–Business Research Library [421], [24181]

Illinois Department of Commerce and Community Affairs

   Illinois Enterprise Zone Program [59397]
   Small Business Development Center [59360]
   Small Business Office [59398]

Illinois Department of Commerce and Economic Opportunity–Small Business Division [59399]

Illinois Early Childhood Intervention Clearinghouse–Library [5456]

Illinois Eastern Community College–Small Business Development Center [59373]

The Illinois Financial Institutions Directory & Fact Book [44550]

"Illinois Gov. Pushes More Pension Reform" in *Venture Capital Journal* (October 1, 2005) [26833], [40451]

Illinois-Indiana Sea Grant Program [10487]

Illinois Institute of Art/Schaumburg–Learning Resource Center [5613], [5762], [13729]

Illinois Issues [50364]

Illinois Procurement Technical Assistance Center–State of Illinois Department of Commerce & Community Affairs [59768]

Illinois Quad City Chamber of Commerce [59548]

"Illinois Regulators Investigate Possible Title Insurance Kickbacks" in *Chicago Tribune* (February 23, 2005) [7383], [13333], [17400], [40452], [43228]

Illinois River Area Chamber of Commerce [59549]

Illinois State Board of Education–Data Analysis and Progress Reporting Division [33390]

Illinois State Chamber of Commerce [59550]

Illinois State University

   Census and Data User Services [66868]
   University Research Office [59780]

"Illinois Tax Scofflaws Land on New Internet List" in *Chicago Tribune* (March 2, 2005) [14142], [54607]

Illinois Valley Area Chamber of Commerce and Economic Development [59551]

Illinois Valley Community College–Small Business Development Center [59374]

Illinois Waste Management & Research Center Library [9442], [11979]

Illuminated Concepts Inc. [49615]

The Illustrated Handbook of Furniture Restoration [10832]

"I'm with the Band" in *Entrepreneur* (Vol. 31, No. 11, November 2003, pp. 132) [17595], [24420], [52547]

"I'm Game: What Hot, New Pastime is Inspiring Entrepreneurs to Launch Businesses?" in *Entrepreneur* (Vol. 32, September 2004) [15111], [24794], [26261], [35525], [53563]

"I'm O.K., You're Not" in *Business Week* (No. 3694, August 14, 2000, pp. F10) [32503], [53800]

"I'm Stuck. Can You Pass the Play-Doh?" in *Inc.* (August 2005, pp. 68) [34948], [45286]

"IM: When Time Matters" in *Hispanic Business* (November 2002, pp. 34) [4693], [23038], [27406], [49088], [53801]

"Image-Building Needs to Include Problem-Solving" in *St. Louis Post-Dispatch* (February 18, 2005) [12887], [20125], [52684]

Image Depot [8289]

"Image is Everything" in *Entrepreneur* (Vol. 32, September 2004, No. 9, pp. 106) [12888], [20126], [22521], [24959], [47122], [50610], [55105], [56277]

"Image is Everything" in *Red Herring* (No. 99, June 15 & July 1, 2001, pp. 114, 116) [4190], [41464], [50793]

"Image Feels Tower's Pain" in *San Fernando Valley Business Journal* (Vol. 11, November 2006, No. 24, pp. 10) [15112], [32158]

Image Industry Council International/Institute for Image Management [12864]

Image Sun Tanning Centers [23845]

ImageFirst Healthcare Laundry Specialists [8933]

ImageMaker [19912]

Images 4 Kids [19326]

"The Imagination Gap" in *Internet World* (Vol. 7, No. 1, January 15, 2001, pp. 8) [14143], [30558], [34053]

Imaginative Events for Training [33128]

Imagine Canada–John Hodgson Library [10778]

Imagine That [5432]

Imagine This Sold [51460]

Imagineria [5388]

"Imaging: Changing the Way We Do Business" in *Rough Notes* (Vol. 146, No. 3, March 2003, pp. 56) [13334], [31743], [49089]

Imaging News [19913], [25499]

"Imagining the Google Future" in *Business 2.0* (Vol. 7, January/February 2006, No. 1, pp. 78-80) [14144], [34054]

"Imagining a Web Beyond the Browser: a new kind of dot" in *Fortune* (Vol. 141, No. 4, February 21, 2000, pp. 274+) [14145], [34055], [52896]

Imaginit [5389]

IMC Consulting & Training [868], [3735], [3973], [16623], [31379], [46051], [47874]

IMC Internet [49433], [49616]

IMinds [58042]

Immedia Technologies [9408]

Inc. (August 2005, pp. 24-25); "Don't Bet Your Life On It" in **[13272]**, **[26790]**, **[40321]**, **[43163]**, **[54519]**

Inc. (September 2005, pp. 124-131); "Dov Charney, Like It Or Not" in **[5540]**, **[5654]**, **[28060]**

Inc. (February 1, 2002); "Downhill and Dirty" in **[23589]**, **[35399]**

Inc. (September 1, 2003); "Drives Provide New Electronics Avenue" in **[7723]**, **[41648]**

Inc. (November 15, 2000, pp. 98); "E-Strategies" in **[2245]**, **[13998]**, **[33821]**

Inc. (January 1, 2005); "Earning Your Wings" in **[44511]**, **[55585]**

Inc. (April 1, 2005); "EBay Springs a Price Increase on eBay Store Owners" in **[1808]**, **[18442]**, **[18642]**, **[33838]**

Inc. (January 1, 2005); "Entrepreneur of the Year: Bob Baron" in **[35416]**, **[41452]**

Inc. (January 1, 2005); "Entrepreneur of the Year: Frank Altman" in **[9775]**, **[35417]**, **[44402]**

Inc. (January 1, 2005); "Entrepreneur of the Year: Peter Provenzano" in **[10674]**, **[17312]**, **[25382]**, **[35418]**

Inc. (January 1, 2005); "Entrepreneur of the Year: Shoba Purushothaman" in **[4102]**, **[24404]**, **[35419]**, **[56040]**

Inc. (January 1, 2005); "Entrepreneur of the Year: The Ceja Family" in **[23436]**, **[35420]**, **[37562]**

Inc. (May 1, 2005); "Even as the M&A Market Heats Up, Unloading a Company Gets Trickier" in **[9836]**, **[9939]**, **[14760]**, **[14964]**, **[47562]**, **[49920]**, **[53716]**

Inc. (September 2005, pp. 42, 45); "Everyone's a CFO" in **[138]**, **[2898]**, **[26223]**, **[45115]**

Inc. (October 2005, pp. 113-117, 119, 122); "Everything You Ever Wanted to Know About Email" in **[27364]**, **[27636]**, **[33865]**

Inc. (Volume 27, July 2005, No. 7, pp. 112); "Exaggeration Nation" in **[28128]**, **[37440]**

Inc. (October 2005, pp. 80-81); "Exit Strategy" in **[29869]**, **[36131]**

Inc. (July 1, 2003); "Facing the Online Music" in **[17741]**, **[29229]**, **[33876]**, **[36136]**, **[40363]**, **[44295]**

Inc. (August 1, 2003); "Failure of Genius" in **[26505]**, **[36137]**, **[45130]**

Inc. (Volume 27, July 2005, No. 7, pp. 26); "Family Partnerships Under Scrutiny" in **[37649]**, **[49926]**, **[54546]**

Inc. (January 1, 2005); "Fancy-Sounding Tax Hurts S Corps" in **[54547]**

Inc. (July 1, 2003); "Faster Tech Transfer" in **[29231]**, **[35445]**, **[41680]**, **[44041]**, **[44297]**

Inc. (December 1, 2004); "Fax Regs Rethought" in **[29233]**, **[40367]**, **[46952]**

Inc. (August 2005, pp. 24); "Federal Contracts Draw New Scrutiny" in **[29234]**, **[40019]**, **[40369]**

Inc. (Volume 27, June 2005, No. 6, pp. 21-23); "Fifty States, a Thousand New Tax Laws" in **[40379]**, **[54552]**

Inc. (November 15, 2000, pp. 110); "Finding It Online" in **[14040]**

Inc. (October 1, 2003); "Finding the Right Keyword" in **[625]**, **[14042]**, **[33898]**, **[46959]**

Inc. (December 1, 2004); "Firms Turn to Perks in Lieu of Bonus Checks" in **[26806]**, **[34902]**, **[53732]**

Inc. (Volume 27, July 2005, No. 7, pp. 92-99); "Five Angels With Angles" in **[44525]**, **[55617]**

Inc. (October 1, 2004); "Five Ideas to Watch" in **[7055]**, **[11259]**, **[24408]**, **[52532]**

Inc. (July 1, 2004); "Five Ideas to Watch" in **[619]**, **[628]**, **[4663]**, **[6650]**, **[11612]**, **[12005]**, **[12548]**, **[21508]**, **[23000]**, **[24340]**, **[24686]**, **[25182]**, **[33904]**, **[41010]**, **[46408]**, **[46969]**, **[48679]**, **[48731]**

Inc. (August 2005, pp. 44-45); "For Cash-Strapped Cloudveil, It Was a Very Hard Offer to Refuse" in **[23619]**, **[52422]**

Inc. (April 1, 2005); "For Offering Hope and Help to the Parents of Autistic Children" in **[33914]**, **[39309]**, **[41012]**, **[53440]**, **[56227]**

Inc. (September 1, 2003); "For-Your-Own-Good Innovation" in **[4667]**, **[18037]**, **[23004]**, **[31548]**, **[44043]**, **[53287]**

Inc. (May 1, 2005); "Forget About Bartering. For Start-Ups, It's All About the Freebies" in **[26704]**, **[33916]**, **[44413]**, **[46977]**

Inc. (Oct, 2006, pp. 41-42); "Found in Translation" in **[34906]**, **[48549]**

Inc. (Volume 27, June 2005, No. 6, pp. 24, 26); "Franchising, Franchising" in **[38644]**, **[55631]**

Inc. (April 1, 2005); "Frank Robinson Robinson Helicopter for Whipping an Entire Industry Into Shape" in **[46295]**

Inc. (January 1, 2005); "From Mushing to Management" in **[36187]**, **[42853]**, **[45167]**, **[56234]**

Inc. (January 1, 2002); "Frozen Assets" in **[10621]**, **[21521]**

Inc. (September 1, 2004); "Geography is Destiny" in **[20776]**, **[30865]**

Inc. (July 1, 2003); "Getting Away and Meaning It" in **[24690]**, **[25188]**, **[30336]**, **[36203]**

Inc. (November 15, 2000, pp. 26); "Getting in on the E-Signature Game" in **[33949]**, **[40408]**

Inc. (Volume 27, March 2005, No. 3, pp. 48, 51); "Getting Started" in **[13646]**, **[18544]**, **[49502]**

Inc. (October 1, 2003); "Getting To No" in **[45188]**, **[51652]**

Inc. (November 1, 2004); "Giving Back" in **[11112]**, **[36212]**, **[54187]**

Inc. (September 2005, pp. 48, 50); "Global Entrepreneur" in **[6938]**, **[36215]**, **[43669]**

Inc. (October 1, 2004); "Going After Nike" in **[22749]**, **[35483]**

Inc. (Volume 27, December 2005, No. 12, pp. 77-78); "Going Medium-Tech" in **[28214]**, **[41715]**

Inc. (July 1, 2004); "Gone Fishing" in **[25190]**, **[36223]**

Inc. (January 1, 2002); "Good-bye Doesn't Mean Forever" in **[4677]**, **[6252]**, **[23016]**, **[42250]**, **[53301]**

Inc. (November 2006, pp. 35,38); "Goodbye, Retainers" in **[38101]**, **[47032]**, **[50446]**

Inc. (September 1, 2003); "Goodwill for Your Ex" in **[29270]**, **[39368]**

Inc. (January 1, 2004); "Google Update Draws Criticism from Small Biz" in **[644]**, **[33971]**, **[47033]**

Inc. (October 2005, pp. 34); "Granting Options Like It's 1999" in **[158]**, **[2909]**, **[15051]**, **[23955]**, **[26249]**, **[26820]**

Inc. (September 1, 2003); "Grants for Rural Biz" in **[26512]**, **[39832]**, **[50884]**, **[52114]**

Inc. (May 2000, pp. 94); "Gray Might be a Geek, thought DeVeau, but he was a Geek with Vision" in **[13753]**, **[29742]**, **[52639]**

Inc. (October 1, 2004); "Grist: A Passport to America" in **[27383]**, **[28235]**, **[52860]**

Inc. (January 1, 2005); "Grist: An Entrepreneurs Resolutions" in **[28236]**, **[36236]**, **[53763]**

Inc. (July 1, 2004); "Grist: Beyond the Vale of Smiles" in **[34917]**, **[45203]**

Inc. (December 1, 2004); "Grist: Micromanagers, Unite!" in **[36237]**, **[45204]**

Inc. (August 1, 2003); "Grist: More Power Than Point" in **[4681]**, **[23022]**, **[49055]**, **[53306]**, **[53764]**

Inc. (October 1, 2003); "Grist: The Inevitable Rise of the Entrepreneur" in **[32460]**, **[36238]**

Inc. (October 2000, pp. 20); "Growing Pains" in **[28246]**, **[36248]**, **[54950]**

Inc. (November 2000, pp. 78); "Growth Strategies" in **[2488]**, **[27724]**, **[35492]**, **[46571]**

Inc. (October 1, 2003); "Guerrilla Tactic Targets Golfers" in **[11267]**, **[47049]**, **[50601]**

Inc. (November 2006, pp. 69-70); "Guest Speaker. The Saltshaker Theory" in **[34920]**, **[42858]**, **[45214]**

Inc. (August 2005, pp. 29-30); "Hands On" in **[652]**, **[7729]**, **[27391]**, **[27643]**, **[29065]**, **[33992]**, **[35498]**, **[43194]**, **[43689]**, **[45218]**, **[46310]**, **[47054]**, **[51660]**, **[53562]**

Inc. (Volume 27, July 2005, No. 7, pp. 86-91); "He Came. He Saw. He Took On the Whole Power-Tool Industry" in **[11882]**, **[16369]**, **[36266]**, **[44056]**, **[48743]**

Inc. (Volume 27, December 2005, No. 12, pp. 59-60); "Her Line of Credit Was in Default. Her Partnership With Her Mom Was Faltering" in **[31555]**, **[37679]**, **[38114]**

Inc. (November 15, 2000, pp. 110); "Hidden Net Treasures" in **[14111]**

Inc. (November 15, 2000, pp. 26); "High-Wired Competition" in **[30878]**, **[41743]**

Inc. (October 2005, pp. 29-32); "Hiring Employees With Disabilities" in **[10511]**, **[16016]**, **[42272]**, **[46314]**, **[54202]**

Inc. (January 1, 2004); "Hiring, Hollywood Style" in **[42275]**, **[45242]**

Inc. (May 1, 2006); "His Rock Club Was In Ruins. His Partnership Was Crumbling" in **[2340]**, **[2388]**, **[47612]**, **[49978]**

Inc. (Volume 28, January 2006, No. 1, pp. 102-105); "Hot or Not?" in **[15094]**, **[39387]**, **[44548]**

Inc. (November 15, 2000, pp. 26); "Hot Tip: Limo as Mobile Office" in **[3315]**, **[49510]**, **[54954]**

Inc. (May 2000, pp. 161); "Hot Tips" in **[42291]**, **[45254]**

Inc. (May 1, 2005); "Hotels With a Sweaty Twist On Room Service" in **[12576]**, **[29600]**, **[30349]**

Inc. (Volume 27, June 2005, No. 6, pp. 48); "How Can I Find the Right Business Contacts in China?" in **[12977]**, **[39841]**, **[43696]**

Inc. (Volume 27, March 2005, No. 3, pp. 70-80, 84); "How China Will Change Your Business" in **[12978]**, **[43697]**, **[53786]**

Inc. (Volume 27, March 2005, No. 3); "How David Steinberg Wins Friends, Influences People, and Moves a Whole Lot of Cell Phones" in **[5017]**, **[14131]**, **[36301]**, **[51680]**

Inc. (April 1, 2006); "How Don Zacharia Turned a Mom-and-Pop Liquor Store Into a Wine-Retailing Juggernaut" in **[16232]**, **[23485]**, **[37691]**

Inc. (February 1, 2002); "How to Get Your Book Published" in **[2637]**

Inc. (Volume 27, July 2005, No. 7, pp. 80-82); "How I Did It" in **[5018]**, **[5990]**, **[12149]**, **[12189]**, **[12289]**, **[12980]**, **[14133]**, **[15098]**, **[20546]**, **[20903]**, **[23486]**, **[25593]**, **[28303]**, **[34033]**, **[35046]**, **[36304]**, **[44313]**, **[47103]**, **[51190]**, **[53476]**, **[54207]**, **[56270]**

Inc. (September 1, 2004); "How I Did It: Amber Chand" in **[1588]**, **[37567]**, **[54117]**, **[56053]**

Inc. (January 1, 2005); "How I Did It: Randy Slager" in **[35515]**, **[41463]**

Inc. (January 1, 2004); "How I Did It: Roxanne Quimby" in **[2593]**, **[7893]**, **[56271]**

Inc. (August 1, 2004); "How I Learned to Stop Worrying and Love the Death Tax" in **[54598]**

Inc. (Volume 27, July 2005, No. 7, pp. 49, 51); "How to Lose Customers" in **[30883]**, **[31739]**, **[51681]**

Inc. (October 1, 2003); "How to Make Friends" in **[34035]**, **[36306]**, **[39391]**

Inc. (October 1, 2004); "How To Assemble a Board of Directors" in **[29905]**, **[36313]**, **[52892]**

Inc. (October 1, 2004); "How To Be a Great Boss" in **[34943]**, **[36314]**, **[45269]**

Inc. (October 1, 2004); "How To Conduct Due Diligence" in **[15104]**, **[36315]**, **[49991]**

Inc. (October 1, 2004); "How To Crack Big-Box Retail" in **[28310]**, **[51192]**

Inc. (October 1, 2004); "How To Fire Decisively" in **[36317]**, **[45270]**

Inc. (October 1, 2004); "How To Get the Kids On Your Side" in **[36318]**

Inc. (October 1, 2004); "How To Give Your Money Away" in **[36319]**, **[54209]**

Inc. (October 1, 2004); "How To Groom a No. 2 (Or, Gasp, a Successor)" in **[29906]**, **[45271]**

Inc. (October 1, 2004); "How To Hire Wisely" in **[42299]**, **[45272]**

Inc. (August 2005, pp. 80-85); "How To Raise an Entrepreneur" in **[36320]**, **[37693]**

Inc. (October 1, 2004); "How To Spot Trouble in Your Financials" in **[10010]**, **[15105]**, **[36321]**, **[38130]**

Inc. (October 1, 2004); "How To Star in an Ad (Without Looking Like an Idiot)" in **[673]**, **[47114]**

Inc. (August 1, 2003); "On the Waterfront" in [35594], [52710]

Inc. (October 2005, pp. 32); "One Man's Alien is Another's Employee" in [32616], [42371], [48590]

Inc. (July 1, 2004); "Onward, Christian Marketer" in [748], [9735], [14326], [34308], [47376]

Inc. (September 1, 2003); "Opening the Kimono" in [27466], [36587], [45500]

Inc. (November 1, 2004); "Opening Up the Baghdad Office" in [12203], [12306], [36588], [43775]

Inc. (September 2005, pp. 46); "...Or Your Money Back" in [31809], [51759]

Inc. (November 2006, pp. 39-40); "Our Companies, Ourselves" in [45503]

Inc. (May1,2006); "Our Rankings Are Derived From 3-Month Rolling Averages of US Bureau of Labor Statistics Unadjusted Employment Data" in [32621], [33702], [40561], [42373]

Inc. (September 1, 2003); "Out of Control" in [14331], [20233], [23115], [34316], [36596], [45504], [52445], [53401]

Inc. (Volume 27, December 2005, No. 12, pp. 55-56); "Outsource the Outsourcing" in [49722], [53903]

Inc. (July 1, 2004); "Overtime Reform Overdoses on Politics" in [29431], [40601], [55306]

Inc. (October 17, 2000, pp. 115); "Overview: The List" in [18658], [28607], [34324]

Inc. (January 1, 2002); "Pat Croce's Bottom Line" in [19428], [36606], [45518]

Inc. (February 1, 2002); "Penny-Wise, Site-Foolish" in [14344], [25932], [34337], [52384]

Inc. (July 1, 2004); "Perspective: Doing Well By Doing Nothing" in [35021], [45531]

Inc. (January 1, 2002); "Pork Chaps" in [4552], [21585]

Inc. (September 2005, pp. 30); "Pregnancy Claim Settlements Rise" in [29447], [32052]

Inc. (November 2000, pp. 78); "Preoccupied with what's working-or what's not-many CEOs see only linear paths to growth" in [28643], [45559]

Inc. (Volume 27, March 2005, No. 3, pp. 23-26, 28, 30); "Priority" in [10691], [15370], [32638], [33212], [34365], [38290], [39535], [39890], [42382], [44127], [56373]

Inc. (November 2006, pp. 23-24); "Priority. Fast, Cheap, and Ready To Move-in." in [14363], [20629], [20969], [52716]

Inc. (October 2005, pp. 84); "Private Lives" in [36646], [55784]

Inc. (October 1, 2004); "Property Tax Woes Hit Indiana" in [35615], [54714]

Inc. (Volume 27, July 2005, No. 7, pp. 28); "Proving That You Have the Right Stuff" in [40078], [41922]

Inc. (Volume 27, March 2005, No. 3, pp. 62-63); "Pursuits" in [4774], [12619], [24723], [25236], [33214], [36661], [53423], [54242]

Inc. (Volume 28, January 2006, No. 1, pp. 39, 42); "Put a Hacker to Work" in [4775], [6770], [22337], [23140], [42385], [53424]

Inc. (September 2006, pp. 44-45); "Put Some Wow In Your Website" in [25940], [27478], [34382], [41927]

Inc. (November 2006, pp. 95-98, 100, 102, 104, 106); "Rating the Governors" in [29460], [39893]

Inc. (July 1, 2003); "Ray-gulation" in [23838], [40630]

Inc. (October 2005, pp. 41-42, 44, 46); "Ready, Set Strategize" in [29973], [39550]

Inc. (September 1, 2004); "Real Estate Now" in [20645]

Inc. (Volume 28, January 2006, No. 1, pp. 70-77); "(Re)Born To Be Wild" in [17489], [28675]

Inc. (September 2005, pp. 154-159); "Rebuilding Shangri-la" in [12620], [21593], [33218], [35039]

Inc. (August 2005, pp. 53-54); "Reconnaissance" in [36680], [39554]

Inc. (Volume 27, July 2005, No. 7, pp. 57-58); "Recreation" in [31832], [35042], [42389], [45582]

Inc. (October 17, 2000, pp. 17); "Red-Tape Brainstorms" in [35621]

Inc. (August 1, 2004); "Reeling In the Big One" in [27733], [46587], [51504], [52783]

Inc. (October 17, 2000, pp. 98); "Regrets" in [29977], [30591]

Inc. (November 1, 2004); "Reining In Office Rumors" in [45587], [51791]

Inc. (October 2000, pp. 23); "Rembrandts in the Attic" in [1613], [34407], [36684], [37074]

Inc. (September 1, 2003); "Respect Your Elders" in [42396], [53941]

Inc. (March 2000, pp. 88); "Retail Holdouts - But at What Price" in [34411], [51313]

Inc. (September 1, 2003); "Rich Man, Politician" in [36698], [40650]

Inc. (November 15, 2000, pp. 33); "Road Warrior" in [49233]

Inc. (January 1, 2004); "Safer Harbors, Higher Fees" in [13007], [22354], [43805]

Inc. (Volume 27, March 2005, No. 3, pp. 38); "Sales" in [29477], [32678], [40662], [47485], [51814], [51821]

Inc. (October 2005, pp. 156); "Save the Founder" in [28743], [36716], [53952]

Inc. (August 1, 2003); "SBA Finds Another Billion for Loans" in [39909], [44642]

Inc. (Vol. 27, July 2005); "Scammers Have Been Downloading Software From My Website Using Stolen PayPal Accounts. What Can I Do?" in [8320], [8397], [22358], [29479], [30252], [34437], [53449]

Inc. (Volume 28, January 2006, No. 1, pp. 29-31); "Scenes From the Talent Wars" in [42406], [42889], [53954]

Inc. (January 1, 2002); "Sea Change" in [36725], [47505], [50671]

Inc. (January 1, 2002); "Search" in [16533], [45624]

Inc. (Volume 27, June 2005, No. 6, pp. 26); "SEC Acts to Curb Cash Flow Shenanigans" in [241], [2953], [24029], [26344], [38340]

Inc. (August 2005, pp. 57-58); "Security Lapse" in [6284], [22370], [34449]

Inc. (October 1, 2004); "Seed Capital for Farm Communities" in [26448], [44436], [55425]

Inc. (October 2005, pp. 124-125, 128); "Self-Service" in [4792], [22376], [23165], [27495], [27675], [34453], [53455]

Inc. (August 1, 2004); "Senate Targets Payroll Tax Scam" in [245], [2956], [24033], [29484], [40686], [54744]

Inc. (August 1, 2003); "Senators Call for Small-Biz Refunds" in [246], [2957], [24034], [26348], [54745]

Inc. (October 2005, pp. 75-76); "Service With a Smile" in [31850], [41978]

Inc. (August 1, 2003); "Severe Storm Watch" in [13460], [39575], [43356]

Inc. (September 1, 2004); "Singh-ing His Praises" in [49734], [53964]

Inc. (October 1, 2003); "Small Biz Barges into Cuba" in [10697], [36748], [43812]

Inc. (September 1, 2004); "Small Biz Braces for Life on the High (Priced) Seas" in [22380], [43813]

Inc. (July 1, 2003); "Small-Biz Owners' Wild Mood Swings" in [28770], [32688], [36749]

Inc. (September 2000, pp. 107); "Small or Not, It's the Law" in [29075], [40128], [53567]

Inc. (November 1, 2003); "Smart Set" in [30176], [33239], [41992], [52729]

Inc. (September 2005, pp. 69, 72); "Smarter Than You" in [36764], [45653]

Inc. (September 2005, pp. 75-76); "Somebody's Watching You" in [12910], [14461], [20156], [25968], [34513], [50469], [50508]

Inc. (September 1, 2003); "Space Centered" in [13670], [18560], [49550]

Inc. (November 15, 2000, pp. 110); "Staffing" in [14477], [42423]

Inc. (December 1999, pp. 92); "Start a Business at Home? You've Got to be Kidding" in [29763], [42553]

Inc. (February 1, 2002); "Start with Nothing" in [4584], [22890], [29764], [35664], [51505], [53151]

Inc. (January 1, 2002); "Start Up the Band" in [35665]

Inc. (July 1, 2004); "States Target Outsourcing" in [29516], [40730], [49737], [54001]

Inc. (November 1, 2003); "Stopping Office Snoops" in [36797], [37510], [39607]

Inc. (Volume 27, March 2005, No. 3, pp. 33-34); "Strategies, Let's Be Friends" in [30962], [36801], [45674]

Inc. (August 2000, pp. 37); "Street Smarts" in [29767], [30494], [31074], [35676]

Inc. (November 2006, pp. 61-62); "Street Smarts. Are You Listening to Me?" in [31223], [36803], [45675]

Inc. (January 1, 2005); "Street Smarts: Don't Sign Anything Yet" in [29076], [29766], [35675], [52788]

Inc. (September 1, 2004); "Street Smarts: Hidden Assets" in [20678], [22822]

Inc. (November 1, 2004); "Street Smarts: Just Say Yes" in [36804], [45676]

Inc. (September 2006, pp. 57-58); "Street Smarts. Keep Your Customers" in [31866], [45677]

Inc. (December 1, 2004); "Street Smarts: Pennies From Heaven" in [27184], [45678]

Inc. (October 1, 2004); "Street Smarts: Presumed Guilty" in [29520], [36805], [45679]

Inc. (December 1, 2003); "Street Smarts: The Capacity Trap II" in [30963], [45680]

Inc. (July 1, 2003); "Street Smarts: The King and I" in [36807], [39610]

Inc. (August 1, 2004); "Street Smarts: The Myths About Niches" in [29077], [46593], [52789]

Inc. (November 1, 2003); "Street Smarts: Ya Gotta Love It" in [6814], [37786], [42728]

Inc. (Volume 28, January 2006, No. 1, pp. 34-36); "Striking Out with VCs?" in [15491], [55850]

Inc. (November 2006, pp. 44,46); "Student Teachers" in [38384], [42428], [45684]

Inc. (October 1, 2003); "Sued Over the Dress Code" in [5719], [29524]

Inc. (July 1, 2004); "Sued Over an Employee's Cell Phone" in [5124], [29525]

Inc. (October 1, 2003); "Surviving the New Economy" in [14499], [25977], [30702], [32735], [34553], [45695], [52460]

Inc. (September 2005, pp. 132-138); "Surviving Sarbanes-Oxley" in [29531], [54782]

Inc. (August 1, 2003); "Take It Or Leave It: The Only Guide to Negotiating You Will Ever Need" in [27510], [36825], [45700]

Inc. (August 1, 2003); "Take a Seat" in [18562], [18614], [49553]

Inc. (January 1, 2005); "Taking the Pain Out of Payday" in [18793], [26380], [27189]

Inc. (December 1, 2003); "Talking the Talk" in [27512], [27680]

Inc. (September 2005, pp. 30); "Tax Breaks for Angels" in [54794], [55854]

Inc. (December 1999, pp. 92); "Taxing Matters" in [42733], [54828]

Inc. (November 15, 2000, pp. 128-129); "Techniques: Microcases" in [49304], [53509]

Inc. (October 1, 2003); "Telecommuter Denied Jobless Benefits" in [26928], [29542], [40758]

Inc. (January 1, 2004); "Temp Hiring Signals Economic Recovery" in [9238], [24537], [32741], [42434]

Inc. (Nov. 15, 2000); "Thanks to the Xerox, the company reduced its outsourcing by 77.6 percent for the first six months of the year" in [49746], [53009]

Inc. (August 1, 2003); "The '4 2 Formula' For Success" in [29781], [30500], [35745]

Inc. (Volume 27, December 2005, No. 12, pp. 104); "The $2.6 Billion Men" in [4905], [13794]

Inc. (October 1, 2003); "The 90-Day Difference" in [44864]

Inc. (July 1, 2003); "The Activist Ingredient" in [27753], [34805], [44876]

Inc. (Volume 27, June 2005, No. 6, pp. 59-60); "The 'Always On' Economy" in [4911], [32243], [33528], [41509]

Inc. (September 2005, pp. 116-123, 160, 162, 164, 168); "The Anatomy of a Sale" in [18849], [52405]

Center for Studies of Law in Action [54400]
Center for the Study of Institutions, Population, and Environmental Change [33393]
Indiana Business Research Center [32855]
Indiana University of Pennsylvania
Small Business Development Center [64329]
Small Business Incubator–SBDC [64330]
Indiana University-Purdue University at Indianapolis
Center for Alzheimer's Disease and Related Disorders [17244]
Center for American Studies [33394]
Center for Law and Health [41375]
Center on Philanthropy [10781]
Center for the Study of Religion and American Culture [33395]
CyberLab [33396]
Indiana AIDS Clinical Trials Unit [41376]
Mead Johnson Mass Spectrometry Laboratory [18524]
Nuclear Magnetic Resonance Laboratory [33397]
Peirce Edition Project [33398]
Indianapolis Business Journal (Vol. 25, December 27, 2004, No. 43, pp. 21); "Center Is One-Stop Shop for Brides" in [3165], [7152]
Indianapolis Business Journal (Vol. 21, No. 15, June 26, 2000, pp. 33A); "Estate tax huge headache for small business owners" in [54541]
Indianapolis Business Journal (Vol. 25); "Sailing On the Crest of the Home Health Care Wave" in [457], [18335], [56391]
Indianapolis Business Journal (September 27, 2004); "Shopping For Good Health: Perception Strategies Adds 'Mystery' to Medicine" in [31852], [41098]
"Indianapolis Indoor Day-Care Center Turns Dog's Life Into One of Fun" in *Indianapolis Star* (October 31, 2004) [19075], [53807]
Indianapolis-Marion County Public Library–Business, Science and Technology Service Section [7831]
Indianapolis Star (September 24, 2002); "Central Indiana's High-Tech Incubator Lands First Tenant" in [41597], [43049], [52074]
Indianapolis Star (October 31, 2004); "Indianapolis Indoor Day-Care Center Turns Dog's Life Into One of Fun" in [19075], [53807]
Indiana's Midwest Builders Convention [7592]
Indianola Chamber of Commerce [60154], [61801]
Indiantown Western Martin County Chamber of Commerce [58863]
Indigo Joe's Sports Pub & Restaurant [21852]
Indinapolis Business Journal (Vol. 25, November 29, 2004, No. 38, pp. 15); "Windshields Go Sporty" in [11222], [18163]
Indio Chamber of Commerce [57558]
Indosuez Ventures [58044]
"Industrial Cleanser" in *Entrepreneur* (Vol. 28, No. 1, January 2000, pp. 132) [37300], [46317]
Industrial Computer Control [6359]
Industrial Council of Nearwest Chicago–Small Business Development Center [59375]
Industrial Fabrics Association International Expo [22738]
Industrial Health Foundation, Inc.–Library [56686]
Industrial Heating Buyers Guide & Reference Handbook [1024]
Industrial Hygiene Made Easy: A Checklist Approach to Recognizing, Evaluating & Controlling Workplace Hazards [56567]
Industrial Hygiene News [41223]
Industrial Laser Solutions [46508]
Industrial Management Services [46540]
"Industrial Metamorphosis" in *The Economist* (Vol. 377, October 1-7, 2005, No. 8446, pp. 69-70) [28326], [46318], [53808]
Industrial Patent Activity in the United States Parts 1 and 2, 1974-1998 [29666], [44212]
Industrial Property Directory [32229]
Industrial Safety [56634]
Industrial Safety and Hygiene News [56598]
Industrial Technology Consultants [16870]

"Industrious solution" in *Houston Business Journal* (Vol. 33, No. 48, April 11, 2003, pp. 19A) [9218], [9568], [24529], [56278]
Industry Council for Tangible Assets [5806]
Industry Economic Development–Western Regional Office [66696]
Industry Economic Development and Mines–Technology Commercialization Program [66697]
"Industry Experts Expect Mergers to Remain Strong Among Banks" in *Long Island Business News* (February 13, 2004) [10023], [15123], [50000]
"Industry Fights Law on Violent Video Games" in *Crain's Detroit Business* (Vol. 21, October 24, 2005, No. 43, pp. 1) [1110], [4696], [23043], [29310], [40464], [51203]
Industry Magazine [18981]
Industry Manufacturers Council [57559]
"Industry News; Coinstar Expands Self-Service Kiosk Line" in *National Petroleum News* (Vol. 95, No. 13, December 2003, pp. 46) [5028], [7778], [15922], [34064]
Industry Pulse [5205]
"Industry standards set a base for family pay range" in *Business First Columbus* (Vol. 18, No. 25, February 8, 2002, pp. B9) [37700], [53809]
"An Industry Resource: Thee Direct Selling Association Membership List" in *Success* (Vol. 47, No. 6, November 2000, pp. 74) [51694]
Industry Ventures (Newburyport) [61083]
Industry Week (Vol. 252, No. 1, January 2003, pp. 19); "E-waste Reuse" in [4981], [6638], [7724], [21228], [24338]
Indy Lube and Indy Lube Express [20270]
"InDyne's $440M Launch Pad" in *Washington Business Journal* (Vol. 22, No. 12, July 25, 2003, pp. 1) [40043]
Infant and Juvenile Manufacturers Association [5268]
"Infectious Agents: A Growing Number of Uninvited Guests Are Pushing Their Way Onto Your PCs. Here Are the Latest Antidotes" in *Entrepreneur* [6688], [14149], [22263], [34065]
Infinity Capital LLC [58045]
"Inflation Woes: Secure Your Portfolio Against Rising Prices" in *Black Enterprise* (Vol. 37, January 2007, No. 6, pp. 40) [10024], [15124], [20907], [38140]
Influence without Authority [36345], [45298]
"Influence-Peddling" in *Business Week* (January 16, 2006, No. 3967, pp. 32) [29311], [39412], [40465]
Influence and Removal: Organics in Drinking Water Treatment [25704]
Info Franchise Newsletter [38958]
Info-Link [7556], [13695]
"Info Overload" in *Small Business Opportunities* (Vol. 13, No. 6, November 2001, pp. 82) [13760], [33453], [37064]
Info Press Inc. [63252]
InfoComm International [9680], [25587]
Infoline [33299]
InfoLines [9248], [24542], [33300]
"Informal Partnership gives Agents Clout" in *Rough Notes* (Vol. 145, No. 1, January 2003, pp. 34) [13336], [50001]
The Information Advisor [13098]
Information Broker [13099]
Information Broker's Handbook [13078]
Information Display-Directory of the Display Industry Issue [3399]
Information First [44201]
Information Group [63115]
Information Industry Directory [3400], [6257], [6944], [25876]
Information International [66006]
The Information Machine [6360]
Information Management [13100]
Information Resources Center–Library [50738]
Information & Responsibility: The Ethical Challenge [37465]
Information Services Inc. [3888], [31492], [39008]
Information Sources [6258], [6945], [13079]
Information Sources for the Press and Broadcast Media [18234]
Information Standards Quarterly [13101]

Information Storage Industry Consortium [6231]
Information Systems Project Management (Canada) [44766]
Information Technology Adviser [6198]
Information Technology Association of America [53153]
Information Technology Association of Canada [13061]
Information Technology Industry Council [6571], [18594]
"Information Technology" in *Ingram's* (Vol. 27, No. 7, July 2001, pp. 76) [28327], [37151]
Information Technology for the Non-IT Manager [41491]
Information Technology Project Management [42776], [44767]
Information Technology for the Small Business: How to Make IT Work For Your Company [6259], [6689], [14150], [27409], [27648], [34066], [41766]
"Information Technology Software" in *Business Week* (January 23, 2006, No. 3968, pp. 65-66) [4697], [15125], [23044], [45299], [50002], [53331]
Information Technology Ventures [58046]
Information Today [13102], [13118], [14647]
Information Today (Vol. 17, No. 7, July 2000, pp. 53); "AIP's OJPS to Host ASME International's Journals" in [2675], [9130], [18848]
Information Today (Vol. 17, No. 11, December 2000, pp. 6); "BountyQuest Introduces New Service to Help Strengthen U.S. Patent System" in [33605], [44003]
Information Today (Vol. 17, No. 11, December 2000, pp. 14); "Business.com Pushes Portal Envelope" in [13874], [33634]
Information Today (Vol. 17, No. 11, December 2000, pp. 8); "CSA Acquires Political Science Abstracts" in [5], [39267]
Information Today (Vol. 17, No. 11, December 2000, pp. 41); "ebrary Snags Key Investors for Pay-Per-Use Service" in [33840], [49913]
Information Today (Vol. 17, No. 10, November 2000, pp. 39); "EBSCO Expands Book Services, Creates E-Journal Licensing Web Site" in [3039], [33841]
Information Today (Vol. 20, No. 3, March 2003, pp. 26); "Elsevier launches e-Book program" in [2700], [3041], [9139]
Information Today (Vol. 17, No. 7, July 2000, pp. 7); "Emerging Opportunities from the Evolving Book" in [2701], [9140]
Information Today (Vol. 19, No. 10, November 2002, pp. 44); "Fictionwise announces e-book lending solution for libraries" in [2703], [9141], [14035], [33892]
Information Today (Vol. 17, No. 11, Dec. 2000, pp. 31); "Hoover's Introduces Competitive Intelligence and Media Monitoring Service" in [27398], [30879], [44309], [47086], [50448]
Information Today (Vol. 17, No. 11, December 2000, pp. 23); "Ingenta, Inc. Announces 19 New Publisher Portal Partnerships" in [34067], [50896]
Information Today (Vol. 17, No. 11, December 2000, pp. 28); "Internet World Fall 2000 Conference" in [14162], [34085], [55106]
Information Today (Vol. 17, No. 10, November 2000, pp. 42); "Linking Policies for Public Web Sites" in [25885], [34138], [44088]
Information Today (Vol. 20, No. 1, Jan. 2003, pp. 44); "Net Crimes & Misdemeanors" in [13084], [14273], [34239], [37481]
Information Today (Vol. 17, No. 10, November 2000, pp. 32); "NEXIS Finally Goes Dot-Com" in [34263], [49169]
Information Today (Vol. 19, No. 5, May 2002, pp. 41); "OverDrive Introduces Digital Kiosk" in [2731], [4756], [9152], [14335], [17763], [23117], [34323]
Information Today (Vol. 17, No. 10, November 2000, pp. 44); "Sagent Technology Unveils New Enterprise Information Portal" in [34428], [53445]

Ingram's (Vol. 27, No. 2, February 2001, pp. 28); "Planning is everything" in **[35023]**, **[45541]**

Ingram's (Vol. 29, No. 1, January 2003, pp. 10); "Players-Accomplishments of the Area's Most Significant Producers" in **[36633]**

Ingram's (Vol. 28, No. 5, May 2002, pp. 28); "Protecting the Dream" in **[26890]**, **[29455]**, **[29965]**, **[38297]**, **[39541]**

Ingram's (Vol. 28, No. 6, June 2002, pp. 22); "Protecting your intellectual property" in **[22336]**, **[44356]**

Ingram's (Vol. 27, No. 8, August 2001, pp. 19); "Rebuilding Your Business With Former and Current Customers" in **[28677]**, **[31830]**, **[35040]**

Ingram's (Vol. 29, No. 1, January 2003, pp. 13); "Reimagining Union Station" in **[7463]**, **[28695]**, **[52717]**

Ingram's (Vol. 28, No. 5, May 2002, pp. 31); "Retirement Plans for Small Business" in **[15417]**, **[26902]**, **[38322]**

Ingram's (Vol. 29, No. 1, January 2002, pp. 31); "Run To The Spot J. Gilbert's" in **[21614]**

Ingram's (Vol. 27, No. 6, June 2001, pp. 23); "Sales & Marketing: The Power of Brand" in **[31841]**, **[47488]**, **[50665]**, **[51817]**

Ingram's (Vol. 27, No. 5, May 2001, pp. 28); "Sales & Marketing: Why Advertise Anyway?" in **[27170]**, **[29984]**, **[47489]**, **[50666]**, **[51818]**

Ingram's (Vol. 29, No. 7, July 2003, pp. 42); "Shopping for Investment Advice" in **[10181]**, **[15450]**, **[38347]**

Ingram's (Vol. 28, No. 3, March 2002, pp. 62); "Should banks be allowed to broker real estate?" in **[20669]**, **[21007]**

Ingram's (Vol. 27, No. 5, May 2001, pp. 25); "Small Business Advisor: A Customer for All Seasons" in **[31855]**, **[47538]**

Ingram's (Vol. 28, No. 2, February 2002, pp. 53); "Smarter highways to revolutionize the way we drive" in **[7481]**, **[41993]**

Ingram's (Vol. 29, No. 1, January 2003, pp. 29); "Souping Up Your January" in **[21630]**

Ingram's (Vol. 28, No. 6, June 2002, pp. 53); "Talking tiger, hidden classroom" in **[6335]**, **[6486]**, **[33247]**, **[34566]**

Ingram's (Vol. 29, No. 1, January 2003, pp. 19); "Tax Law Changes Mean Money for Education and Retirement" in **[26927]**, **[32739]**, **[54806]**

Ingram's (Vol. 28, No. 5, May 2002, pp. 25); "The City Market" in **[20465]**, **[20832]**

Ingram's (Vol. 28, No. 9, September 2002, pp. 62); "The Evolution of E-Mail" in **[14024]**, **[27365]**, **[33866]**

Ingram's (Vol. 27, No. 8, August 2001, pp. 20); "The Power of Ideas" in **[36636]**, **[47413]**

Ingram's (Vol. 28, No. 3, March 2002, pp. 61); "The current spin on REIT spin-offs" in **[20480]**, **[20851]**

Ingram's (Vol. 28, No. 3, March 2002, pp. 74); "Thinking outside the big box" in **[20059]**, **[51387]**

Ingram's (Vol. 28, No. 6, June 2002, pp. 27); "This little drug went to the market" in **[48801]**, **[52219]**, **[55864]**

Ingram's (Vol. 29, No. 9, September 2003, pp. 52); "Tips to Keep Your Medical Renewal Cost Under Control" in **[13495]**, **[26939]**, **[41117]**, **[43399]**

Ingram's (Vol. 29, No. 7, July 2003, pp. 24); "To Manage Growth, Embrace Change" in **[28905]**, **[30028]**, **[30618]**

Ingram's (Vol. 28, No. 9, September 2002, pp. 29); "Top Area Advertising Agencies" in **[817]**, **[47654]**, **[50696]**

Ingram's (Vol. 29, No. 1, January 2003, pp. 32); "Top Area Staffing Agencies" in **[9239]**, **[9580]**, **[24539]**, **[42441]**

Ingram's (Vol. 29, No. 1, January 2003, pp. 27); "Top Area Stock Brokerage Firms" in **[10213]**, **[15531]**, **[38418]**

Ingram's (Vol. 28, No. 9, September 2002, pp. 42); "Top MBA Programs (MO&KS)" in **[33258]**, **[45753]**

Ingram's (Vol. 29, No. 7, July 2003, pp. 20); "Top Venture Capital Companies" in **[55871]**

Ingram's (Vol. 28, No. 6, June 2002, pp. 25); "Trading in intelligence" in **[22407]**, **[44376]**

Ingram's (Vol. 29, No. 1, January 2003, pp. 47); "2003 Economic Forecast" in **[32757]**

Ingram's (Vol. 28, No. 2, February 2002, pp. 23); "Uncle Sam says Turbo Charge your future" in **[54848]**

Ingram's (Vol. 29, No. 1, January 2003, pp. 23); "What About TIF?" in **[21037]**, **[54863]**

Ingram's (Vol. 29, No. 1, January 2003, pp. 24); "What a Long Strange Trip It's Been...Where We Have Been" in **[10243]**, **[15596]**, **[38452]**

Ingram's (Vol. 29, No. 8, August 2003, pp. S6); "What Makes Topeka Unique" in **[52750]**

Ingram's (Vol. 28, No. 9, September 2002, pp. 15); "What the One Hand Giveth" in **[32790]**, **[40824]**

Ingram's (Vol. 29, No. 1, January 2003, pp. 4); "Where Have the Leaders Gone?" in **[29001]**, **[32793]**

Ingram's (Vol. 29, No. 1, January 2003, pp. 15); "Why Kansas City Needs a New Downtown Arena" in **[7513]**, **[29007]**, **[52753]**

Ingram's (Vol. 29, No. 8, August 2003, pp. 21); "Wining & Dining" in **[21667]**, **[23524]**

Ingram's (Vol. 28, No. 9, September 2002, pp. 69); "Wyandotte County" in **[32803]**

Ingram's (Vol. 27, No. 7, July 2001, pp. 19); "Your Business needs to be E-Commerce - so what now?" in **[34766]**, **[45882]**, **[47773]**, **[51919]**, **[53036]**

"Inheriting business as challenging as starting one" in *Atlanta Business Chronicle* (Vol. 24, No. 13, August 24, 2001, pp. 5B) **[8687]**, **[37701]**, **[38837]**, **[45300]**, **[50003]**

"Initial Public Optimism" in *Business Week* (No. 3670, February 28, 2000, pp. f6) **[15126]**, **[50004]**

"Injections of 'Anti-Aging' Human Growth Hormone Carry Serious Side Effects" in *Sacramento Bee* (November 13, 2002) **[17898]**

"Injector Gadget" in *Inc.* (February 1, 2002) **[17099]**, **[41767]**

"Ink turns crimson at Clover" in *Crain's Detroit Business* (Vol. 19, No. 4, January 27, 2003, pp. 3) **[6946]**, **[48249]**

Ink, Inc. **[4173]**

"Inking the Deal" in *Kiplinger's Personal Finance Magazine* (Vol. 54, No. 12, December 2000, pp. 26) **[19882]**, **[34068]**, **[47140]**, **[51204]**

"Inking Up: Now Coming to a Printer Near You-Files From a Cell Phone or PDA" in *Entrepreneur* (Vol. 31, No. 7, July 2003, pp. 37) **[5029]**, **[6690]**, **[41768]**, **[49096]**

Inkster Chamber of Commerce **[61344]**

InkTec Zone **[19933]**

Inland Empire Hispanic Chamber of Commerce **[57561]**

Inland Empire North SBDC–Satellite Center **[57262]**

Inland Empire SBDC Coachella Valley SBDC–Coachella Valley Satellite Center **[57263]**

Inland Empire Small Business Development Center **[57264]**

Inland Seas Education Association **[16716]**

Inlet Information Office **[62937]**

Inman and Bowman **[58048]**

"The inn crowd" in *Black Enterprise* (Vol. 32, No. 5, December 2001, pp. 126) **[2441]**, **[48250]**

Inn Room Visitors Magazine **[2457]**

"Inn Vogue" in *Black Enterprise* (Vol. 35, November 2004, No. 4, pp. 124) **[2442]**, **[12581]**, **[37702]**

"Inn Vogue" in *Time* (Vol. 162, No. 14, November 3, 2003, pp. G1) **[2443]**

Inner Circle **[3889]**

"Inner-City Innovation" in *Entrepreneur* (Vol. 28, No. 2, February 2000, pp. 136) **[35533]**, **[39770]**, **[40124]**

"Inner-City Light" in *Hispanic Business* (September 2006, pp. 28, 30) **[39413]**, **[54211]**

innkeeping **[2458]**

Innocal Venture Capital **[58049]**

"Innotrac tries to get back on track after telecom woes" in *Atlanta Business Chronicle* (Vol. 25, November 29, 2002, No. 25, pp. 3A) **[6260]**, **[28328]**, **[41769]**

Innov and Entrepren in Biotech **[36346]**, **[41770]**, **[44066]**

"Innovating for Cash" in *Harvard Business Review* (Vol. 81, No. 9, September 2003, pp. 76) **[48752]**

"Innovating a Classic at Airstream" in *Harvard Business Review* (Vol. 81, No. 10, October 2003, pp. 18) **[21172]**, **[47141]**, **[48753]**

Innovation Canada Inc. **[66752]**

Innovation Center & Technology Transfer Office–Ohio University **[63877]**

"The Innovation Conversation" in *Fast Company* (July 2001, pp. 70) **[28329]**, **[39414]**, **[44067]**

"Innovation drain" in *Crain's Detroit Business* (Vol. 19, No. 1, Jan. 6, 2003, pp. 3) **[1940]**, **[18062]**, **[30889]**, **[31040]**, **[43707]**

Innovation and Entrepreneurship **[32509]**, **[35084]**, **[36347]**, **[42112]**, **[44068]**

Innovation and Entrepreneurship: Practice and Principles **[36348]**, **[44069]**

"Innovation and Incentives: VCs Find Partner in Quebec" in *Venture Capital Journal* (Vol. 42, No. 5, May 2002, pp. 47) **[43708]**, **[50897]**, **[55678]**

"Innovation at the speed of information" in *Harvard Business Review* (Vol. 79, No. 1, January 2001, pp. 149) **[48754]**

Innovation in Iowa **[60250]**

Innovation Methodologies in Enterprise Research **[39415]**, **[44070]**, **[50898]**

Innovation Norway - United States **[43503]**

Innovation Ontario Corporation–Information Centre **[55995]**

Innovation Park **[58991]**

Innovation Place **[66783]**

"Innovation To Go" in *Fast Company* (July 2001, pp. 39) **[5030]**, **[37152]**

"The innovation toolkit" in *Entrepreneur* (Vol. 31, No. 5, May 2003, pp. 52) **[36349]**, **[45301]**

Innovation Works, Inc. **[64554]**

Innovative Leader **[16547]**, **[45890]**

Innovative Lease Services, Inc. **[55986]**

Innovative Reward Systems for the Changing Workplace **[30736]**

Innovative Scientific Analysis & Computing **[3737]**, **[31381]**, **[52342]**

"The Innovator" in *Forbes* (Vol. 175, January 10, 2005, No. 1, pp. 150) **[13337]**, **[15127]**, **[43230]**

"Innovators ride rough road in Detroit area" in *Crain's Detroit Business* (Vol. 16, No. 21, May 22, 2000, pp. 9) **[44071]**

"The Innovator's Next Bestseller?" in *Inc.* (September 1, 2004) **[44072]**, **[48755]**

Innovest Group, Inc. **[64555]**

Inroads Capital Partners, L.P. **[59739]**

"The ins and outs: Sales Force: Answering the eternal question" in *Entrepreneur* (Vol. 30, No. 3, March 2002, pp. 87) **[34954]**, **[47142]**, **[51695]**

"Inside the box: Buyer's guide: New software slowing you down?" in *Entrepreneur* (Vol. 30, No. 1, January 2002, pp. 44) **[4698]**, **[6691]**, **[23045]**, **[49097]**, **[53332]**

Inside Business Today **[2786]**, **[5390]**, **[9262]**, **[12674]**, **[17541]**, **[20734]**, **[21697]**, **[25318]**, **[53060]**

Inside Business Today...The '90s **[53061]**

"Inside Business" in *Tribune* (March 9, 2005) **[7385]**, **[56279]**

Inside Cal/EPA **[9391]**, **[37346]**

"Inside the Care Crisis" in *Hispanic Business* (June 2002, pp. 24, 26, 28) **[13338]**, **[43231]**

"Inside the Customer-Focused Company" in *Harvard Business Review* (Vol. 78, No. 3, May 2000, pp. S20) **[31095]**, **[31623]**, **[35534]**, **[52776]**

"Inside Intel" in *Business Week* (January 9, 2006, No. 3966, pp. 46-52, 54) **[5031]**, **[6692]**, **[7734]**, **[36350]**, **[41034]**, **[41771]**, **[45302]**, **[46319]**

"Inside Job" in *Entrepreneur* (Vol. 33, March 2005, No. 3, pp. 132) **[12291]**, **[13653]**, **[51205]**

Inside MBS & ABS **[17452]**

"Inside Microsoft. Balancing Creativity and Discipline" in *Harvard Business Review* (Vol. 80, No. 1, January 2002, pp. 73) **[28330]**, **[29919]**, **[45303]**

Intensive Review of Grammar [8979]

Intent vs. Impact [32091]

"Intention, adaptation and annexation" in *Rough Notes* (Vol. 146, No. 4, April 2003, pp. 74) [13348], [21327], [43239]

Intentional Integrity [37466]

Inter-American University of Puerto Rico–Puerto Rico SBDC [66644]

Inter-Industry Conference on Auto Collision Repair [22594]

Inter/Port [16757]

Interactive Global News [47790]

Interactive TV Investor [24473]

"Interactive TV: What's In the Cards?" in *Business Week* (January 31, 2005, pp. 32) [4109], [24342], [46320]

Interamerican Accounting Association [36]

Interax Corp. [46055]

Interbike [2516]

Intercoiffure America [11773]

Intercollegiate Horse Show Association [12447]

Intercultural Communication Institute [48650]

InterEquity Capital Partners, L.P. [63117]

"Interest Alone May Not Be Enough" in *Hispanic Business* (November 2003, pp. 79) [10026], [15131], [38145]

"Interest in Commercial Brownfield Properties High, but Action Still on Hold" in *Long Island Business News* (March 12, 2004) [7335], [7387], [38793], [40470]

"Interest Increases in Wedding Coordinator as Potential Career" in *Daily Record* (June 28, 2004) [3186], [33132]

"Interest Paid as an Administrative Expense" in *Journal of Accountancy* (Vol. 198, December 2004, No. 6, pp. 95) [172], [2919], [23967], [26266], [27141], [54612]

Interest Rate & Currency Swaps: The Markets, Products and Applications [15132]

Interest Rate Futures and Options [15133]

"Interest Rate Speculation May Be Fueling Home Buying in Denver Area" in *Denver Post* (January 26, 2005) [20553], [32511]

Interest Rate Spreads & Market Analysis: Tools for Managing and Reducing Rate Exposure in Global Markets [15134]

Interest Rate Swaps: A Self-Study Guide to Mastering and Applying Interest Rate Swaps [15135]

Interface Computer Associates [49435]

Interface Financial Group [10224], [10357]

Interface Tech News [39721]

Interfase Capital Partners LP [65611]

Interim Health Care [41343]

Interim HomeStyle Services [9272]

Interior Construction [7557]

Interior Design [13696], [18569], [22823]

Interior Design Business [13619], [42537]

The Interior Design Business Handbook: A Complete Guide to Profitability [13654]

Interior Design-Buyers Guide Issue [13655]

Interior Design Management [13656]

Interior Design Society [13625]

Interior Design Sourcebook [13680]

Interior Door Replacement Co. [4509]

Interior Landscapes: Gardens and the Domestic Environment [13657]

Interior Magic International, LLC [25557]

Interior Service Center–Business Utilization and Development Specialist–Branch of Acquisitions, Fiscal and Property Services [67632]

"Interiors By Design" in *Black Enterprise* (Vol. 35, October 2004, No. 3, pp. 54) [13658], [28336], [36355], [42664], [56281]

Interiors by Decorating Den [42798]

Interlac [5888]
　　Library [5939]

Interlochen Area Chamber of Commerce [61345]

Interlochen Center for the Arts–Frederick and Elizabeth Ludwig Fennell Music Library [17680]

Intermarket Agency Network [519], [50528]

Intermediate Finance and Accounting for Non-Financial Managers (Canada) [37857]

Intermediate Fundamentals of Finance and Accounting for Non-Financial Managers (Canada) [37858]

Intermountain Contractor [7558]

"Intern affairs: more and more companies are hiring virtual interns." in *Entrepreneur* (Vol. 31, No. 6, June 2003, pp. 74) [34071], [42307]

"Intern Burn: Hired the Ultimate Intern from Hell?" in *Entrepreneur* (Vol. 32, November 2004, No. 11, pp. 96) [42308], [45307]

Internal Auditor (Vol. 58, No. 5, October 2001, pp. 47); "Training as a Retention Tool" in [26391], [35125]

International Academy of Compounding Pharmacists [8765]

International Advertising Association [520], [50529]
　　Worldwide Service Center [911]

International Affiliation of Independent Accounting Firms-Update [329]

International Aloe Science Council [2390]

International Animated Film Association - Canada [9681]

International Assistance Center–SBDC [65039]

International Association of Administrative Professionals [25509]

International Association of Air Travel Couriers [4526]
　　Library [990]

International Association of Amusement Parks and Attractions [1127]

International Association of Amusement Parks and Attractions Annual Convention and Trade Show [1145]

International Association of Amusement Parks and Attractions-International Directory and Buyer's Guide [1133]

International Association of Assessing Officers–Research and Technical Services Department [24208]

International Association of Association Management Companies-Directory [1734]

International Association of Astacology [10443]

International Association of Audio Visual Communicators [9682]

International Association of Business Communicators [27226], [27604]

International Association for Business Organizations [39116], [43504]

International Association of Commercial Collectors [8369]

International Association for Computer Information Systems [6155], [6324]

International Association of Conference Center Administrators [24865]

International Association of Conference Centers [24866]

International Association of Corporate and Professional Recruitment [42159]

International Association of Counseling Services [4388]

International Association for Creative Dance [8442]

International Association of Credit Card Investigators-Membership Directory [8297], [8373]

International Association of Culinary Professionals [7807]

International Association for Exhibition Management [24867]

International Association of Fairs and Expositions Trade Show [1146], [7097], [18285], [23835], [25069]

International Association of Financial Crimes Investigators [8370]

International Association of Food Industry Suppliers-Directory of Membership, Products and Services [8513]

International Association of Infant Massage [16999]

International Association for Jazz Education [17573]

International Association of Lighting Designers [9104], [13626], [49478]

International Association of Optometric Executives [25631]

International Association of Piano Builders and Technicians [17835]

International Association of Plumbing and Mechanical Officials [1000], [23790]

International Association of Printing House Craftsmen [19846]

International Association of Professional Security Consultants [22149], [35276]

International Association of Refrigerated Warehouses [20206]

International Association of Speakers Bureaus [22457]

International Association for Time Use Research [3495], [16494]

International Association of Tour Managers - North American Region [24651], [25130]

"International Association of Virtual Office Assistants" in *Entrepreneur* (Vol. 31, No. 8, August 2003, pp. 6) [173], [2920], [3949], [18778], [23968], [25523], [26094]

International Association of Workforce Professionals [9185]

International Auto Sound Challenge Association [4340]

International BBSing and Electronic Communications Corporation [3395]

International Bedding Exposition [12242]

International Bedding Plant Conference and Trade Show [11491]

International Big R Show [2004]

International Black Writers and Artists [8961]

International Book Trade Directory [3024]

International Bottled Water Association [3078]

International Bottled Water Association Convention and Trade Show [3085]

International Bowl Expo [3111]

International Budget Project of the Center on Budget and Policy Priorities [37], [26114], [27073]

International Business [12988], [43709]

International Business Aviation Council [940], [30278]

International Business Handbook [43710]

International Business & Management Institute [58264]

International Business Opportunities [3891]

International Business Resource Guide DFW: Free Low cost Assistant to Start or Expand Your International Business [43711]

International Career Development Conference [4443]

International Cartridge Recycling Association [21206]

International Carwash Association [4370]

International Carwash Association Annual Convention and Exhibition [4375]

International Cemetery and Funeral Association [10791]

International Center for Entrepreneurial Development, Inc. [3892], [39010]

International Center of Photography–Library [19214], [19338]

International Cheese Classics [23548]

International Chiropractic Pediatric Association [17882]

International Civil Aviation Organization [941]

International Claim Association [17155]

International Clown Hall of Fame and Research Center, Inc. [18748]

International Coatings Expo [18692]

International Collectors Guild [5889]

International Communications Agency Network [521], [50530]

International Computer Music Association [17574], [22899]

International Conference of Building Officials-Membership Directory [3239]

International Conference on Fundraising [10757], [55222]

International Council of Grocery Manufacturers Associations [11585]

International Council on Hotel, Restaurant, and Institutional Education [7808], [12507]

International Council of Kinetography Laban [8443]

International Council for Small Business [39117], [44712], [62114]

International Customer Service Association [31625]

International Dairy-Deli-Bakery Association [8506], [23449]

International Dancesport Studios [8489]

International Data Corp.
　　IDC Library [3408], [7042], [14687]

International Society of Arboriculture Annual Conference and Industrial Trade Show **[16062]**

International Society of Certified Electronics Technicians **[6402]**, **[24333]**

International Society of Certified Employee Benefit Specialists **[26729]**

International Society of Financiers **[9791]**

International Society of Stress Analysts **[19950]**

International Society for the Study of Ghosts and Apparitions **[17883]**

International Society for the Study of Time **[54928]**

International Spa Association **[2576]**, **[7872]**

International Spa and Pool Expo and Conference **[23800]**

International Sport Summit **[23750]**, **[55223]**

International Sporthorse Registry **[1173]**

International Sports Directory **[23710]**

International Sports Massage Federation **[17000]**

International Spotted Horse Registry Association **[1174]**

International Stamp and Coin Collectors Society–Library **[5870]**

International Swimming Hall of Fame–Henning Library **[23809]**

International Tap Association **[8444]**

International Tax and Public Finance **[10277]**, **[24090]**

International Television and Video Almanac **[4110]**, **[23828]**, **[25594]**

International Tennis Hall of Fame **[24560]**

International Tennis Hall of Fame and Tennis Museum–Library **[24579]**

International Textile & Apparel Association-Membership Directory **[5550]**

International Thermographers Association **[19849]**

International Trade Administration
  Office of Public Affairs **[67180]**
  U.S. and Foreign Commercial Service–Export Assistance Center (Anchorage) **[67182]**
  U.S. and Foreign Commercial Service–Export Assistance Center (Austin) **[67258]**
  U.S. and Foreign Commercial Service–Export Assistance Center (Baltimore) **[67215]**
  U.S. and Foreign Commercial Service–Export Assistance Center (Birmingham) **[67181]**
  U.S. and Foreign Commercial Service–Export Assistance Center (Boise) **[67204]**
  U.S. and Foreign Commercial Service–Export Assistance Center (Boston) **[67217]**, **[67697]**
  U.S. and Foreign Commercial Service–Export Assistance Center (Buffalo) **[67232]**
  U.S. and Foreign Commercial Service–Export Assistance Center (Carmel) **[67209]**
  U.S. and Foreign Commercial Service–Export Assistance Center (Charleston) **[67252]**
  U.S. and Foreign Commercial Service–Export Assistance Center (Charlotte) **[67236]**
  U.S. and Foreign Commercial Service–Export Assistance Center (Chicago) **[67205]**
  U.S. and Foreign Commercial Service–Export Assistance Center (Cincinnati) **[67238]**
  U.S. and Foreign Commercial Service–Export Assistance Center (Clearwater) **[67198]**
  U.S. and Foreign Commercial Service–Export Assistance Center (Cleveland) **[67239]**
  U.S. and Foreign Commercial Service–Export Assistance Center (Columbia) **[67253]**
  U.S. and Foreign Commercial Service–Export Assistance Center (Columbus) **[67240]**

U.S. and Foreign Commercial Service–Export Assistance Center (Dallas) **[67259]**

U.S. and Foreign Commercial Service–Export Assistance Center (Denver) **[67196]**

U.S. and Foreign Commercial Service–Export Assistance Center (Des Moines) **[67210]**

U.S. and Foreign Commercial Service–Export Assistance Center (Detroit) **[67218]**

U.S. and Foreign Commercial Service–Export Assistance Center (Eugene) **[67244]**

U.S. and Foreign Commercial Service–Export Assistance Center (Ft. Worth) **[67260]**

U.S. and Foreign Commercial Service–Export Assistance Center (Gaithersburg) **[67216]**

U.S. and Foreign Commercial Service–Export Assistance Center (Grand Rapids) **[67219]**

U.S. and Foreign Commercial Service–Export Assistance Center (Greensboro) **[67237]**

U.S. and Foreign Commercial Service–Export Assistance Center (Harrisburg) **[67246]**

U.S. and Foreign Commercial Service–Export Assistance Center (Highland Park) **[67206]**

U.S. and Foreign Commercial Service–Export Assistance Center (Honolulu) **[67203]**

U.S. and Foreign Commercial Service–Export Assistance Center (Houston) **[67261]**

U.S. and Foreign Commercial Service–Export Assistance Center (Jackson) **[67223]**

U.S. and Foreign Commercial Service–Export Assistance Center (Kansas City) **[67224]**

U.S. and Foreign Commercial Service–Export Assistance Center (Knoxville) **[67255]**

U.S. and Foreign Commercial Service–Export Assistance Center (Little Rock) **[67184]**

U.S. and Foreign Commercial Service–Export Assistance Center (Long Beach) **[67185]**

U.S. and Foreign Commercial Service–Export Assistance Center (Long Island) **[67233]**

U.S. and Foreign Commercial Service–Export Assistance Center (Los Angeles) **[67186]**

U.S. and Foreign Commercial Service–Export Assistance Center (Louisville) **[67212]**

U.S. and Foreign Commercial Service–Export Assistance Center (Memphis) **[67256]**

U.S. and Foreign Commercial Service–Export Assistance Center (Miami) **[67199]**

U.S. and Foreign Commercial Service–Export Assistance Center (Middletown) **[67197]**

U.S. and Foreign Commercial Service–Export Assistance Center (Milwaukee) **[67269]**

U.S. and Foreign Commercial Service–Export Assistance Center (Minneapolis) **[67222]**

U.S. and Foreign Commercial Service–Export Assistance Center (Monterey) **[67187]**

U.S. and Foreign Commercial Service–Export Assistance Center (Montpelier) **[67264]**

U.S. and Foreign Commercial Service–Export Assistance Center (Nashville) **[67257]**

U.S. and Foreign Commercial Service–Export Assistance Center (Newark) **[67229]**

U.S. and Foreign Commercial Service–Export Assistance Center (Newport Beach) **[67188]**

U.S. and Foreign Commercial Service–Export Assistance Center (Novato) **[67189]**

U.S. and Foreign Commercial Service–Export Assistance Center (Oakland) **[67190]**

U.S. and Foreign Commercial Service–Export Assistance Center (Oklahoma City) **[67242]**

U.S. and Foreign Commercial Service–Export Assistance Center (Omaha) **[67226]**

U.S. and Foreign Commercial Service–Export Assistance Center (Orlando) **[67200]**

U.S. and Foreign Commercial Service–Export Assistance Center (Philadelphia) **[67247]**

U.S. and Foreign Commercial Service–Export Assistance Center (Phoenix) **[67183]**

U.S. and Foreign Commercial Service–Export Assistance Center (Pittsburgh) **[67248]**

U.S. and Foreign Commercial Service–Export Assistance Center (Pontiac) **[67220]**

U.S. and Foreign Commercial Service–Export Assistance Center (Portland, ME) **[67214]**

U.S. and Foreign Commercial Service–Export Assistance Center (Portland, OR) **[67245]**

U.S. and Foreign Commercial Service–Export Assistance Center (Portsmouth) **[67228]**

U.S. and Foreign Commercial Service–Export Assistance Center (Providence) **[67251]**

U.S. and Foreign Commercial Service–Export Assistance Center (Reno) **[67227]**

U.S. and Foreign Commercial Service–Export Assistance Center (Richmond) **[67265]**

U.S. and Foreign Commercial Service–Export Assistance Center (Rochester) **[67234]**

U.S. and Foreign Commercial Service–Export Assistance Center (Rockford) **[67207]**

U.S. and Foreign Commercial Service–Export Assistance Center (Sacramento) **[67191]**

U.S. and Foreign Commercial Service–Export Assistance Center (St. Louis) **[67225]**

U.S. and Foreign Commercial Service–Export Assistance Center (Salt Lake City) **[67263]**

U.S. and Foreign Commercial Service–Export Assistance Center (San Antonio) **[67262]**

U.S. and Foreign Commercial Service–Export Assistance Center (San Diego) **[67192]**

U.S. and Foreign Commercial Service–Export Assistance Center (San Francisco) **[67193]**

U.S. and Foreign Commercial Service–Export Assistance Center (San Jose) **[67194]**

U.S. and Foreign Commercial Service–Export Assistance Center (San Juan) **[67250]**

U.S. and Foreign Commercial
Service–Export Assistance Center
(Santa Clara) [67195]
U.S. and Foreign Commercial
Service–Export Assistance Center
(Santa Fe) [67231]
U.S. and Foreign Commercial
Service–Export Assistance Center
(Savannah) [64763], [67202]
U.S. and Foreign Commercial
Service–Export Assistance Center
(Scranton) [67249]
U.S. and Foreign Commercial
Service–Export Assistance Center
(Seattle) [67266]
U.S. and Foreign Commercial
Service–Export Assistance Center
(Sioux Falls) [67254]
U.S. and Foreign Commercial
Service–Export Assistance Center
(Somerset) [67213]
U.S. and Foreign Commercial
Service–Export Assistance Center
(Spokane) [67267]
U.S. and Foreign Commercial
Service–Export Assistance Center
(Tallahassee) [67201]
U.S. and Foreign Commercial
Service–Export Assistance Center
(Toledo) [67241]
U.S. and Foreign Commercial
Service–Export Assistance Center
(Trenton) [67230]
U.S. and Foreign Commercial
Service–Export Assistance Center
(Tulsa) [67243]
U.S. and Foreign Commercial
Service–Export Assistance Center
(Westchester) [67235]
U.S. and Foreign Commercial
Service–Export Assistance Center
(Wheaton) [67208]
U.S. and Foreign Commercial
Service–Export Assistance Center
(Wheeling) [67268]
U.S. and Foreign Commercial
Service–Export Assistance Center
(Wichita) [67211]
U.S. and Foreign Commercial
Service–Export Assistance Center
(Ypsilanti) [67221]
International Trade Assistance–Clarion
University–Small Business Development Center
[64331]
International Trade Center for East
Tennessee–SBDC [64858]
International Trade Center for Middle
Tennessee–SBDC [64859]
International Trade Center for West
Tennessee–SBDC [64860]
International Trade Commission
Office of Economics [67270]
Office of Industries [67271]
Office of Operations [67272]
Office of Tariff Affairs and Trade
Agreements [67273]
Office of Unfair Import Investigations
[67274]
International Trade Council [43505]
International Trade Exhibitions in France [24868]
The International Trade Journal [43898]
International Trade Office–Governor's office of
International Trade [58316]
International Trade Reporter [13033], [13040],
[32819], [43899], [43936]
International Trade Reporter Decisions [43900]
International Trade and Trade Policy [43720]
International Trademark Association [43976],
[63253]
The International Trader [10278], [13034], [43901]
International Traders' Mailbag [43902]
International Traders Newsletter [43903]
International Traditional Karate Federation [16905]
International Training and Management Co. [55254]
International Truck Parts Association [25362]
International Trucking Show [25449]

International Union of Allied Novelty and Production
Workers [18275]
International Union of Bricklayers and Allied
Craftsworkers [16932]
International Union of Nutritional Sciences [18432]
International Union of Operating
Engineers–Research Department–Library
[56688]
International Union of Operating Engineers -
Training Center–Local 68, 68A, 68B–Library
[1064]
International Vision Expo and Conference/West
[25663]
International Vital Records Handbook [10944]
International Warehouse Logistics Association
[20207]
*International Warehouse Logistics Association-
Roster of Members* [20226]
International Wealth Success [13035], [37018]
International Wealth Success Inc. [63254]
International Wildlife Carving Association [7987]
International Wildlife Coalition - Canada [9327]
International Window Film Association [11213]
International Women Pilots [966]
International Women's Writing Guild-Network [9032]
International Wood Products Association [16288]
International Wood Products Association-Directory
[16306]
Internationalist [13036], [15649], [32820], [43904]
*The Internationalization of Asset Ownership in
Europe* [10027], [15136], [43721]
"The Internationalization of new and small firms" in
Journal of Business Venturing (Vol. 16, No. 4,
July 2001, pp. 333) [43722], [52898]
The Internet 6471, 6647
Internet Alliance [33503]
"Internet Auctions Rank High in U.S. Complaints
about Online Fraud" in *Atlanta Journal-
Constitution* (April 11, 2003) [1828], [30232],
[34073]
"Internet Banking Can Improve Your Cash
Management" in *Ingram's* (Vol. 28, No. 1,
January 2002, pp. 42) [26267], [34074]
Internet Buyer's Guide [25683]
"Internet Companies Learn How to Personalize
Service" in *The New York Times* (August 28,
2000, pp. C8(L)) [14152], [34075], [47146],
[51699]
"Internet or Desktop" in *PC Magazine* (February 20,
2001, pp. 145) [174], [26268], [34076], [53335]
"Internet Facilities Defined Contribution Model For
Employer-Sponsored Health Benefits" in
Employee Benefit Plan Review (Vol. 55, No.12)
[14153], [26834], [41035], [43240]
"Internet Firewalls" in *Home Business* (Vol. 12,
March/April 2005, No. 2, pp. 88) [4700], [6694],
[22264], [23048], [42665], [53336]
Internet Gateway Environments and Technology
[14660]
The Internet for Genealogists [10945]
"The Internet giveth, and it can also taketh away" in
Wall Street Journal (May 23, 2000, pp. B2)
[14154], [34077]
"Internet Incubators Rethink Strategies, Become
Pickier" in *Wall Street Journal* (May 2, 2000, pp.
B2) [14155], [43055]
Internet Industry Almanac [13791], [18649]
"Internet Law Arena Marked by Issues About Spam,
Pop-Up Ads, Domain Names, and File Sharing"
in *Long Island Business News* (Feb.6, 2004)
[14156], [29313], [34078], [40473], [47147]
Internet Law & Regulation [34787]
Internet Marketing [37093]
"Internet Marketing Focusing on Search Engines" in
Atlanta Business Chronicle (Vol. 24, No. 14,
September 7, 2001, pp. 4A) [14157], [25877],
[34079], [47148]
Internet Marketing Group [14673]
Internet Marketing Report [14648], [16837], [47791]
Internet Media Investor [4138], [24474]
Internet Medicine [14649]
The Internet Newsroom [14650]
"Internet Opens World of Sales" in *Roanoke Times*
(January 21, 2005) [1829], [14158], [47149],
[51208]

"Internet Privacy" in *Success* (Vol. 47, No. 4,
September 2000, pp. 64) [14159]
Internet Regulation Alert [40866]
*Internet Resources and Services for International
Real Estate Information* [20554]
Internet Society [13789], [18634]
"Internet Tax Won't Be Collected Anytime Soon" in
Crain's Detroit Business (Vol. 17, No. 44,
October 22, 2001, pp. 3) [14160], [16450],
[34080], [51209], [54613]
"Internet Technologies-The constantly evolving Web
is being driven by ever-growing human needs"
in *PC Magazine* (Aug. 8, 2000, pp. 144)
[34081], [53810]
Internet Telephone [5206], [14651]
"Internet To Go" in *Kiplinger's Personal Finance
Magazine* (Vol. 54, No. 12, December 2000, pp.
150) [5032], [34082], [41773]
"Internet Use by Manufacturers is Small for
Business-to-Business Commerce" in *Wall Street
Journal* (February 23, 2000, pp. B11C) [14161],
[34083], [46321]
"The Internet vs. the travel agent" in *Hispanic
Business* (Vol. 22, No. 6, June 2000, pp. 146)
[25199], [30354], [34084]
Internet Week (August 9, 2002); "Briefing Book: E-
Procurement" in [33609]
Internet Wire (October 30, 2001, pp. 100); "Find Out
How To Reduce The Cost of Email" in [14037],
[33895], [34901]
Internet Wire (February 14, 2005); "Flowfinity
Wireless and Partners Extend Microsoft
Business Solutions to BlackBerry" in [6652],
[14049], [49033]
Internet Wire (February 14, 2005); "IBM Unveils
Intel-Based Servers to Improve Business
Security and Efficiency" in [6684], [6943],
[22256], [41760]
Internet Wire (February 10, 2005); "MailFrontier
Addresses Growing Threat of Enterprise
Phishing at RSA" in [14218], [19967], [22289]
Internet Wire (October 26, 2004); "National
Shopping Service Announces 150,000th
Mystery Shopper" in [31794], [51262]
Internet Wire (August 20, 2003); "TouchSystems
Launches Mighty Touch, All-In-One Wireless
Kiosk Terminal Offers Flexibility" in [15944]
Internet Wire (September 24, 2002); "Wal-Mart
Helps Warm Up America At Crochet and Knit-
Out Event" in [8187], [54272]
Internet World (Vol. 6, No. 6, March 15, 2000, pp.
60); "A Talk With the Net's Financiers" in
[33495], [37080], [43044], [55438]
Internet World (Vol. 7, No. 1, January 15, 2001, pp.
48); "B2B Exchanges Survival Guide" in
[27805], [29797], [33557]
Internet World (Vol. 7, No. 2, January 15, 2001, pp.
30); "David Wetherell" in [13953], [33740]
Internet World Fall [14661]
"Internet World Fall 2000 Conference" in
Information Today (Vol. 17, No. 11, December
2000, pp. 28) [14162], [34085], [55106]
Internet World (Vol. 6, No. 13, July 1, 2000, pp. 60);
"Flip Flipowski" in [13749], [33439], [55385]
Internet World (Vol. 7, No. 1, January 15, 2001, pp.
56); "Getting Unwired" in [5001], [14075],
[33952]
Internet World (Vol. 6, No. 12, June 15, 2000, pp.
31); "Making Ideas Fly" in [33457], [43040],
[55402]
Internet World (Vol. 7, No. 1, January 15, 2001, pp.
41); "Mark Hoffman" in [28460], [34173],
[37165]
Internet World (Vol. 7, No. 1, January 15, 2001, pp.
60); "Mix and Match" in [25897], [53378],
[53856]
Internet World (Vol. 7, No. 1, January 15, 2001, pp.
28); "Of Two Minds: Is Consumer fraud a
serious threat to online auctions?" in [1840],
[30244]
Internet World (Vol. 6, No. 7, April 1, 2000, pp. 94);
"Sky Dayton" in [33490], [37078], [43043],
[55431]
Internet World Spring [14662]

"The investors next door: trying to figure out the best moves in today's market?" in *Black Enterprise* (Vol. 33, Oct. 2002, pp. 134) **[10036]**, **[15162]**, **[38161]**

Investors' Property Services **[20081]**

"Investors Retrench with Bond in Shaky Market" in *Atlanta Business Chronicle* (Vol. 25, No. 20, October 25, 2002, pp. 3C) **[10037]**, **[15163]**, **[32514]**, **[38162]**

"Investors Sue Montana-Based Coffee Kiosk Businesses Alleging Financial Fraud" in *Billings Gazette* (August 23, 2003) **[5767]**, **[11332]**, **[15923]**

"Investors Suit up" in *Daily Business Review* (Vol. 77, No. 146, Jan. 7, 2003, pp. A1) **[10038]**, **[15164]**

"Investors Wary of IPOs as New Charges Emerge" in *Atlanta Business Chronicle* (Vol. 25, No. 20, October 25, 2002, pp. 7C) **[10039]**, **[15165]**, **[38163]**

"Invisible Inc." in *Crain's Detroit Business* (Vol. 19, No. 3, January 20, 2003, pp. 10) **[19883]**, **[28344]**

"Invoice-buying deals thrive on one thing: The cash factor" in *Crain's Detroit Business* (Vol. 17, No. 44, October 22, 2001, pp. 22) **[44554]**, **[48911]**

Iola Area Chamber of Commerce **[60358]**

Iola - Scandinavia Area Chamber of Commerce **[66428]**

ION **[19951]**

Ionia Area Chamber of Commerce **[61346]**

"IOP Aftermarket" in *Venture Capital Journal* (Vol. 42, No. 10, Oct. 2002, pp. 54) **[15166]**, **[55686]**

Iowa Central Community College–SBDC **[60056]**

Iowa City Area Chamber of Commerce **[60155]**

Iowa Department of Economic Development
    Department of Economic Development **[60068]**
        International Division **[60069]**
        Small Business Services **[60070]**

Iowa Department of Education–Census Data Center **[66876]**

Iowa Education Department–Financial and Information Services Division–Planning, Research and Evaluation Bureau **[33400]**

Iowa Falls Chamber of Commerce - Main Street **[60156]**

Iowa Great Lakes Area Chamber of Commerce **[60157]**

Iowa Grocer **[4064]**, **[11697]**

Iowa Home-based Business Directory **[42666]**

Iowa Human Services Department–Research, Analysis and Statistics Bureau **[29058]**

Iowa Lakes Community College (Estherville) **[60246]**

Iowa Lakes Community College (Spencer)–Small Business Development Center **[60057]**

Iowa Park Chamber of Commerce **[65322]**

Iowa Pork Producers **[1203]**

Iowa Procurement Outreach Center **[60239]**

Iowa Procurement Technical Assistance Center–Outreach Center **[60240]**

Iowa SBDC–Iowa State University **[60051]**

Iowa Senate Committee on Small Business, Economic Development and Tourism **[60248]**

Iowa State University
    Census Services **[66877]**
    Small Business Development Center **[60052]**, **[60058]**

Iowa State University Research Park **[60241]**

Iowa State University of Science and Technology
    Center for Industrial Research and Service **[48849]**
    Family and Consumer Sciences Research Institute **[5624]**
    Institute for International Cooperation in Animal Biologics **[1285]**
    ISU Foundation **[60242]**
    Midwest Agribusiness Trade Research and Information Center **[26688]**
    Veterinary Diagnostic Laboratory **[1286]**

Iowa Western Community College–Small Business Development Center **[60059]**

IPA The Association of Graphic Solutions Providers **[19850]**

IPI (Insta-Plak, Inc.) **[4217]**, **[19327]**

The IPM Practitioner **[19032]**

"IPO Aftermarket: I'm a Bull! No, I'm a Bear! Wait, I'm a ... Blear!" in *Venture Capital Journal* (Vol. 42, No. 9, Sept. 2002, pp. 46) **[10040]**, **[15167]**, **[50010]**, **[55687]**

"IPO Aftermarket: New Issues Could Start to Gather Momentum in Spring" in *Venture Capital Journal* (Vol. 42, No. 5, May 2002, pp. 59) **[15168]**, **[50011]**, **[55688]**

"IPO Aftermarket: New Issues Struggle to Overcome the Enron Effect" in *Venture Capital Journal* (Vol. 42, No. 8, August 2002, pp. 50) **[15169]**, **[50012]**, **[55689]**

"IPO Aftermarket" in *Venture Capital Journal* (Vol. 40, No. 10, October 2000, pp. 78-79) **[402]**, **[403]**, **[2121]**, **[2122]**, **[2397]**, **[2398]**, **[15170]**, **[50013]**, **[55690]**

"IPO illusions" in *WorkingWoman* (Vol. 25, No. 6, June 2000, pp. 36) **[15171]**, **[50014]**

"IPO an Inner City 100 First" in *Inc.* (October 1, 2003) **[15172]**, **[41036]**, **[50015]**

"IPO Monitor" in *Venture Capital Journal* (Vol. 40, No. 10, October 2000, pp. 75-77) **[2124]**, **[2400]**, **[15173]**, **[15709]**, **[50016]**, **[55691]**

"IPO Review" in *Red Herring* (No. 99, June 15 & July 1, 2001, pp. 61) **[15174]**, **[44555]**, **[50017]**, **[55692]**

"IPO Revival Not a Sure Thing" in *Business Journal-Milwaukee* (Vol. 20, No. 52, September 12, 2003, pp. A1) **[15175]**, **[50018]**, **[53812]**

"IPO Scandal Means Venture Capitalists Need To Be More Vigilant" in *Venture Capital Journal* (Vol. 42, No. 10, October 2002, pp. 50) **[15176]**, **[29315]**, **[40475]**, **[50019]**, **[55693]**

"The iPod Squad" in *Entrepreneur* (Vol. 33, February 2005, No. 2, pp. 40) **[4702]**, **[6695]**, **[23051]**, **[49099]**, **[53339]**

"IPOs/Recent Issues" in *Venture Capital Journal* (Vol. 41, No. 8, August 2000, pp. 42-45) **[408]**, **[2127]**, **[7390]**, **[14659]**, **[14957]**, **[15177]**, **[15367]**, **[17258]**, **[33139]**, **[37154]**, **[42816]**, **[46323]**, **[46599]**, **[46824]**, **[50020]**, **[50903]**, **[52052]**, **[52132]**, **[55694]**

"IPOs Take a Break After a Big Year" in *Venture Capital Journal* (January 1, 2005) **[15178]**, **[28345]**, **[55695]**

"IPOs: Things of the Past" in *Crain's New York Business* (Vol. 23, January 1, 2007, No. 1, pp. 14) **[15179]**, **[28346]**, **[30560]**, **[38164]**, **[50021]**

IPS Industrial Promotion Services, Ltd. **[66724]**

IRA - Stocks **[15653]**

Irasville Incubator & Storage LLC–Irasville Business Park–SBDC **[65763]**

"Irby Buys Two Companies" in *Mississippi Business Journal* (Vol. 29, January 2007, No. 4, pp. 8) **[41777]**, **[47153]**, **[50022]**

IRC Newsletter **[55328]**

"The Ire Next Time" in *Business Week* (March 27, 2000, pp. F28) **[42311]**, **[42870]**

Ireland Chamber of Commerce **[64457]**

Irell & Manella–Library **[9533]**

IRI Design Associates Inc. **[49617]**

IRI Research Institute **[26461]**

"The Iridian Authenticam" in *PC Magazine* (February 6, 2001, pp. 26) **[22265]**, **[41778]**

"iRise: Real Promise in Simulations" in *Business Week Online* (February 2, 2005) **[4703]**, **[23052]**, **[53340]**

Irish Dance **[8477]**

Irish Families **[10968]**

Irish Records **[10946]**

Irish Water Spaniel Club of America Newsletter **[1204]**

Iron County Chamber of Commerce **[61347]**

Ironwood Area Chamber of Commerce **[61348]**

"IRS changes and finalizes 2000 cafeteria plan rules" in *Employee Benefit Plan Review* (Vol. 55, No. 8, February 2001, pp. 13) **[26835]**, **[40476]**, **[41037]**, **[43242]**

IRS Advisor Report **[24092]**

"IRS Agrees to Pursue Legislative Changes to Section 6103" in *Tax Notes* (Vol. 102, No. 3, January 19, 2004, pp. 295-298) **[175]**, **[18779]**, **[23969]**, **[26271]**, **[48566]**, **[54614]**

"IRS Allows Statistical Sampling for M&E Costs: New Procedure May Increase Taxpayer Deductions" in *Journal of Accountancy* (Vol. 198) **[176]**, **[2921]**, **[23970]**, **[26272]**, **[27143]**

"IRS Boosts Enforcement Collections" in *The Record* (November 4, 2005) **[40477]**, **[54615]**

"IRS to aid businesses, but tax code is a problem" in *Birmingham Business Journal* (Vol. 17, No. 22, June 2, 2000, pp. 10) **[40478]**, **[54616]**

"IRS Compliance Audits Will Affect 30,000 Small Businesses" in *My Business* (February/March 2003, pp. 19) **[23971]**, **[54617]**

"IRS Cuts Mileage Rates for Deductions" in *Milwaukee Journal Sentinel* (December 6, 2005) **[177]**, **[23972]**, **[54618]**

"IRS Errors Snag Entrepreneurs" in *Inc.* (October 1, 2003) **[54619]**

"The IRS Goes Fishin'" in *Inc.* (July 1, 2003) **[39417]**, **[54620]**

"IRS informants: everything you ever wanted to know about taxes" in *Entrepreneur* (Vol. 30, No. 12, December 2002, pp. 75) **[23973]**, **[54621]**

IRS Practice and Procedure **[24141]**, **[54903]**

IRS Publication 334: Tax Guide for Small Business **[24142]**, **[29667]**

"IRS intent on stopping tax avoidance schemes, officials say" in *Tax Notes* (Vol. 96, No. 14, September 30, 2002, pp. 1833-1834) **[54622]**

IRS Tax Practitioner Mail List **[392]**, **[24143]**

"The IRS Wants You-Online" in *Home Office Computing* (Vol. 18, No. 12, December 2000, pp. 26) **[34090]**, **[53813]**, **[54623]**

"IRS Will Remove Tax Trap for One-Person S Corporations" in *Kiplinger Letter* (Vol. 82, January 12, 2007, No. 1) **[13350]**, **[41038]**, **[43243]**, **[51489]**, **[54624]**

Irvine Chamber of Commerce **[57562]**

Irvington Chamber of Commerce **[62520]**, **[65915]**

Irwin 59810

The Irwin International Almanac 1994 **[43723]**

Irwin Ventures LLC / Irwin Ventures Incorporated **[60031]**

Irwindale Chamber of Commerce **[57563]**

IRZ Consulting **[7614]**

"Is Anybody in Charge?" in *Fast Company* (June 2001, pp. 52) **[36361]**, **[45309]**

"Is Anyone Listening?" in *Fortune* (Vol. 142, No. 2, July 10, 2000, pp. 200B+) **[43244]**, **[54625]**

"Is a Condo Right For You?" in *Black Enterprise* (Vol. 35, November 2004, No. 4, pp. 37) **[7391]**, **[20558]**

"Is Division of an IRA a Taxable Event?" in *Journal of Accountancy* (Vol. 199, February 2005, No. 2, pp. 78) **[54626]**

"Is Employer-Sponsored Health Insurance On Its Way Out?" in *Kiplinger Letter* (Vol. 84, January 26, 2007, No. 4) **[13351]**, **[26836]**, **[42871]**, **[43245]**, **[54627]**

"Is 'Equitable Remedy' Settlement Excludable from Gross Income?" in *Journal of Accountancy* (Vol. 198, December 2004, No. 6, pp. 94) **[178]**, **[2922]**, **[23974]**, **[26273]**, **[27144]**, **[29316]**, **[54628]**

"Is Excite@Home The AOL of Broadband?" in *Fortune* (Vol. , No. 11, December 6, 1999, pp. 156+) **[14165]**, **[34091]**, **[50023]**

"Is GM on the Road to a Board Fight?" in *Business Week* (January 23, 2006, No. 3968, pp. 35) **[18063]**, **[45310]**, **[46324]**

"The I's Have It: A More Secure Wireless Standard Is On Its Way" in *Entrepreneur* (Vol. 32, November 2004, No. 11, pp. 59) **[6696]**, **[22266]**, **[41779]**

"Is the Internet Second Nature" in *Fast Company* (July 2001, pp. 145) **[14166]**, **[28347]**, **[34092]**

"Is the iPod a Computer Security Threat?" in *Inc.* (April 1, 2005) **[6663]**, **[6697]**, **[21955]**, **[22267]**

"Is it time to consolidate IRAs?" in *Women in Business* (Vol. 53, No. 5, September-October, 2001, pp. 46) **[15180]**, **[38165]**

Is It Sexual Harassment? **[32092]**

"Is It Time for the Fed to Take a Good, Long Vacation?" in *Barron's* (August 18, 2003, pp. 14) **[10041]**, **[15181]**, **[40479]**

"Is that Kosher? Here's a Food Niche You May Not Have Considered" in *Entrepreneur* (Vol. 32, No. 2, February 2004, pp. 27) **[2249]**, **[8514]**, **[11630]**, **[23488]**, **[37703]**

"Is a Minority Share Really Worth It?" in *Automotive News* (Vol. 79, February 28, 2005, No. 6136, pp. 12) **[18064]**, **[46325]**

"Is My Partnership Fair?" in *Inc.* (July 1, 2004) **[29067]**, **[30486]**, **[35536]**, **[49100]**, **[49770]**

"Is Pearl Headed for a Fall?" in *Business Journal-Portland* (Vol. 20, No. 22, August 1, 2003, pp. 1) **[20559]**, **[20653]**, **[20912]**, **[21800]**, **[31611]**, **[32515]**

"Is your price right?" in *Atlanta Business Chronicle* (Vol. 24, No. 13, August 31, 2001, pp. 41A) **[31041]**

"Is it theft, or is it freedom? 7 views of the Web's impact on culture clashes" in *The New York Times* (Sept. 20, 2000, pp. D40, H40) **[14167]**, **[34093]**

Is There a Book Inside You? How to Successfully Author a Book Alone or Through Collaboration **[9001]**

"Is There a Cure?" in *My Business* (June/July 2004, pp. 30-34) **[13352]**, **[43246]**

"Is There a Secret to Happiness in Retirement?" in *Women In Business* (Vol. 52, No. 3, May 2000, pp. 9) **[36362]**, **[56285]**

"Is This Any Way to Run a Family" in *Inc.* (Volume 27, December 2005, No. 12, pp. 122-131) **[25200]**, **[36363]**, **[37704]**

"Is Your Mate Ready For Your Success?" in *Black Enterprise* (Vol. 34, July 2004, No. 12, pp. 139) **[36364]**, **[45311]**

"Is Your Phone System Moving You Forward Or Chaining You Down?" in *Ingram's* (Vol. 29, No. 8, August 2003, pp. 15) **[5033]**, **[34094]**, **[49101]**

Isaksen Foodservice Consultants Inc. **[2285]**, **[12696]**, **[21724]**

ISC Chicago **[19989]**, **[22438]**

ISDA - Association of Storage and Retrieval Professionals **[18595]**

ISGS Newsletter **[10969]**

Ishpeming Office of Lake Superior Community Partnership **[61349]**

The ISI EDGE **[22838]**

Islamorada Chamber of Commerce **[58864]**

Island Hearing Services **[12116]**

Island Ink-Jet Systems Inc. **[18623]**

Island Pond Chamber of Commerce **[65787]**

"Island View Opening" in *Mississippi Business Journal* (Vol. 28, September 2006, No. 36, pp. 22) **[10872]**, **[54305]**

Isle of Wight - Smithfield - Windsor Chamber of Commerce **[65916]**

Isleton Chamber of Commerce **[57564]**

Islip Chamber of Commerce **[62938]**

ISM Annual International Supply Management Conference **[50772]**

The ISO 9000 Almanac, 1994-1995 Edition **[45312]**

ISO 9000: Meeting the New International Standards **[43724]**

ISO 9000: Motivating the People, Mastering the Process, Achieving Registration **[34956]**

ISO 9000 for Small Businesses **[49102]**

ISO Healthcare Consulting **[38972]**

"The isolation process: a powerful path to more sales" in *Atlanta Business Chronicle* (Vol. 25, November 15, 2002, No. 23 pp. 4B) **[51700]**

ISold It **[18673]**

ISP Business **[14653]**

"ISPs Need To Keep Moving Against Spam" in *eWeek* (February 3, 2005) **[14168]**, **[30234]**, **[34095]**

ISSA/Interclean **[3337]**, **[8428]**

Issues & Answers in Sales Management **[51924]**

Issues in Employment Law (Canada) **[29082]**

Issues in Ethics **[37540]**

Issues in Homecare Nursing **[41313]**

ISTVS Newsletter **[21182]**

The ISVA Directory of Members & Member Firms **[1769]**

"It Even Makes Calls!" in *Fortune* (Vol. 151, January 10, 2005, No. 1, pp. 55) **[5034]**, **[41780]**, **[49103]**

"It figures" in *Entrepreneur* (Vol. 31, No. 5, May 2003, pp. 32) **[14169]**, **[28348]**, **[32516]**, **[34096]**, **[35272]**, **[36365]**, **[39418]**, **[56286]**

I.T. Financial Management Association **[6459]**

IT Forecaster **[6510]**

"The IT Hot List: Leading VCs Say Where the Smart Money is Headed" in *Venture Capital Journal* (Vol. 40, No. 10, October 2000, pp. 4-46) **[55696]**

"IT Risk Assessment: Who Needs It?" in *Ingram's* (Vol. 29, No. 7, July 2003, pp. 23) **[40480]**, **[41781]**, **[49104]**, **[53814]**

"It looks as if they got it right this time" in *Crain's Detroit Business* (Vol. 18, No. 50, December 16, 2002, pp. 8) **[20560]**, **[20913]**, **[28349]**, **[52685]**

Italian-American Chamber of Commerce **[43506]**

Italian Genealogical Group **[10918]**

Italo's Pizza Shop, Inc. **[19677]**

Italy-America Chamber of Commerce **[43507]**

Itasca Development Corp.–Small Business Development Center **[61522]**

Itawamba Community College–Small Business Development Center **[61751]**

Itawamba County Development Council **[61802]**

"Itching to Make Your Mark?" in *Inc.* (February 1, 2002) **[46326]**, **[52433]**

ITEC Inc. **[48639]**

Itex Corp. **[26720]**

ITG Journal **[17790]**

It'll Be O.K. on the Day **[55187]**

"It'll Cost Ya: Know How Your Lawyer Tallies Up Your Legal Tab" in *Entrepreneur* (Vol. 32, July 2004, No. 7, pp. 76) **[27145]**, **[29317]**

"It's 2006! Whatcha Gonna Do About It?" in *Inc.* (Volume 28, January 2006, No. 1, pp. 78-85, 113) **[10042]**, **[15182]**, **[20561]**, **[20914]**, **[27410]**, **[32517]**, **[34097]**, **[38166]**, **[39419]**, **[49707]**, **[53815]**

It's A Grind Coffee House **[11387]**

"It's Alive! New Software You Play Dr. Frankenstein" in *Black Enterprise* (Vol. 35, November 2004, No. 4, pp. 64) **[4704]**, **[5993]**, **[23053]**, **[41782]**, **[52133]**, **[53341]**

"It's All About Convenience" in *Success* (Vol. 47, No. 6, November 2000, pp. 88) **[52550]**, **[54959]**

"It's All About the Image" in *Crain's New York Business* (Vol. 22, December 11, 2006, No. 50, pp. 26) **[681]**, **[14170]**, **[25878]**, **[31179]**, **[47154]**, **[50612]**

"It's All About Results" in *Entrepreneur* (Vol. 32, October 2004, No. 10, pp. 92) **[682]**, **[34098]**, **[47155]**

"It's All Coming Together: A Hybrid Cradle Saves You Wireless Phone Minutes" in *Entrepreneur* (Vol. 32, No. 2, February 2004, pp. 38) **[5035]**, **[27146]**

"It's All in the Family for Craig Schnuck" in *St. Louis Post-Dispatch* (November 5, 2004) **[11631]**, **[37705]**

"It's All in the Family" in *Kansas City Star* (March 8, 2005) **[1444]**, **[15847]**, **[37706]**

"It's All In Your Head" in *Entrepreneur* (Vol. 33, January 2005, No. 1, pp. 58) **[28350]**, **[32518]**

"It's All Relative" in *Entrepreneur* (Vol. 33, March 2005, No. 3, pp. 74) **[36367]**, **[37707]**

"It's All Talk" in *Entrepreneur* (Vol. 33, September 2005, No. 9, pp. 44) **[5004]**, **[5036]**, **[29318]**, **[49105]**, **[51119]**

"It's in the Bag, Baby" in *Entrepreneur.com* (Vol. 34, February 2006, No. 2, pp. 110) **[2127]**, **[56287]**

"It's Business...and Personal" in *Black Enterprise* (Vol. 34, July 2004, No. 12, pp. 38) **[5674]**, **[13353]**, **[15183]**, **[29922]**, **[30561]**, **[36368]**, **[43247]**

"It's in the card" in *BlackEnterprise* (Vol. 31, No. 12, July 2001, pp. 50) **[39066]**, **[44422]**, **[47963]**, **[52777]**

"It's Cheaper to Keep 'Em" in *Black Enterprise* (Vol. 36, February 2006, No. 7, pp. 72) **[34957]**, **[45313]**

"It's a Chic Thing: Boutique Hotel Chains Are Going Strong With Cheap, Stylish Offerings" in *Entrepreneur* (Vol. 32, September 2004) **[12584]**, **[38840]**

"It's Down to a Waiting Game" in *Tampa Tribune* (December 24, 2005) **[51210]**

"It's Fall, And The Shopping Is Easy" in *Fortune* (Vol. 142, No. 10, October 30, 2000, pp. 208) **[28351]**, **[49106]**

"It's a Given" in *Entrepreneur* (Vol. 28, No. 9, September 2000, pp. 142) **[45314]**

"It's a 'go' in Detroit" in *BlackEnterprise* (Vol. 32, No. 2, September 2001, pp. 50) **[21539]**, **[38841]**, **[39844]**

"It's Good to be King" in *Inc.* (December 1, 2003) **[36369]**, **[39420]**

"It's a Good Time to Scare Up Business" in *St. Louis Post-Dispatch* (October 11, 2004) **[7392]**, **[13659]**, **[36370]**

"It's Important to Be Proactive about Risk Issues" in *Atlanta Business Chronicle* (Vol. 24, No. 9, August 3, 2001, pp. 9B) **[26274]**, **[30894]**, **[36371]**, **[43248]**, **[45315]**

"It's an investment: Events require funds, planning" in *Atlanta Business Chronicle* (Vol. 24, No. 14, September 7, 2001, pp. S17) **[34958]**, **[51211]**, **[51701]**

"It's the Law" in *Entrepreneur* (Vol. 30, No. 3, March 2002, pp. 42) **[29319]**, **[34099]**, **[40481]**

It's in the Mail: Techniques for Collecting Debts **[31615]**

"It's a Matter of Style" in *Rough Notes* (Vol. 146, No. 9, September 2003, pp. 60) **[13354]**, **[31747]**

"It's all mine" in *Black Enterprise* (Vol. 32, No. 6, January 2002, pp. 42) **[44080]**, **[44322]**

"It's only rock 'n' roll" in *Atlanta Business Chronicle* (Vol. 25, No. 21, November 1, 2002, pp. 6A) **[7090]**

"It's Never E-nough" in *Business Week* (No. 3689, July 10, 2000, pp. F14) **[14171]**, **[34100]**, **[36372]**, **[49512]**, **[49708]**, **[53816]**

"It's a New Game: Killerspin Pushes Table Tennis to Extreme Heights" in *Black Enterprise* (Vol. 37, October 2006, No. 3, pp. 73) **[9725]**, **[14172]**, **[18650]**, **[18890]**, **[23622]**, **[25879]**, **[34101]**, **[36373]**, **[47156]**

"It's Not Easy Being Green" in *Inc.* (November 1, 2004) **[36374]**, **[50024]**

"It's Not Enough" in *Entrepreneur* (Vol. 28, No. 8, August 2000, pp. 30) **[44556]**

"It's Not the First Time" in *Entrepreneur* (Vol. 30, No. 2, February 2002, pp. 53) **[35537]**, **[44423]**, **[55399]**

It's Not Just Courtesy-It's the Law **[32093]**

"It's Not about Money" in *Wall Street Journal* (May 22, 2000, pp. R18) **[36375]**

"It's Not Personal" in *Entrepreneur* (Vol. 33, September 2005, No. 9, pp. 94) **[40482]**, **[42872]**

"It's OK If You Shop Til You Drop" in *Tampa Tribune* (November 19, 2005) **[41039]**, **[51212]**, **[53817]**

"It's On Us: On Your Next Trip, Let Your Hotel Pick Up the Tab For Extras" in *Entrepreneur* (Vol. 31, No. 8, August 2003, pp. 20) **[12585]**, **[30356]**

"It's Optional: What Do You Really Need, and What Can You Live Without?" in *Entrepreneur* (Vol. 31, No. 7, July 2003, pp. 26) **[18065]**, **[38167]**

It's Party Time **[18757]**

"It's really Pretty Simple" in *Rough Notes* (Vol. 146, No. 3, March 2003, pp. 49) **[13355]**, **[43249]**, **[47157]**

"It's a Scream" in *Incentive* (Vol. 174, No. 9, September 2000, pp. 92) **[34959]**

"It's the Service, Stupid! Want Repeat Business?" in *Sales and Marketing.com* (Vol. 156, No. 3, March 2004, pp. 8) **[31748]**, **[51702]**

"It's Settled: A New Law Makes it Easier to Reach Settlements" in *Entrepreneur* (Vol. 33, February 2005, No. 2, pp. 74) **[29320]**, **[32037]**, **[39421]**

"It's a Snap" in *Houston Business Journal* (Vol. 34, No. 18, September 12, 2003, pp. 17) **[19302]**, **[29923]**, **[36376]**

"It's Son of NAFTA" in *Inc.* (Volume 27, July 2005, No. 7, pp. 26-27) **[12990]**, **[30895]**, **[40483]**, **[43725]**

"It's the Sound Bite, Stupid" in *Inc.* (Volume 27, June 2005, No. 6, pp. 128) **[27411]**, **[27649]**, **[36377]**, **[45316]**

"It's a Stretch" in *Entrepreneur* (Vol. 30, No. 1, January 2002, pp. 48) **[28352]**, **[44557]**, **[52134]**, **[55697]**

"It's Swing Time" in *Inc.* (September 1, 2004) **[36378]**, **[45317]**

"It's Tax Time - Again" in *Home Business* (Vol. 12, March/April 2005, No. 2, pp. 76) **[179]**, **[2923]**, **[23975]**, **[42667]**, **[54629]**

"It's a Team Thing" in *Black Enterprise* (Vol. 35, December 2004, No. 5, pp. 67) **[4705]**, **[23054]**, **[34960]**, **[41783]**, **[45318]**, **[53342]**

"It's That Time of Season" in *Entrepreneur* (Vol. 31, No. 8, August 2003, pp. 75) **[18998]**, **[34102]**, **[51213]**, **[51703]**

"It's The Business Model, Stupid!" in *Fortune* (Vol. 143, No. 1, January 8, 2001, pp. 54) **[29924]**, **[52899]**

"It's a Three-Ring Circus and Then Some" in *Crain's Detroit Business* (Vol. 22, January 16, 2006, No. 4, pp. 8) **[18066]**, **[24960]**, **[46327]**, **[55107]**

"It's Time For Venture Capital Firms To Grow Up" in *Venture Capital Journal* (Vol. 42, No. 8, August 2002, pp. 38-39) **[28353]**, **[45698]**

"It's a Trap! Watch Your Step-Pharming Scams Are Lurking Around Every Corner" in *Entrepreneur* (Vol. 33, August 2005, No. 8, pp. 40) **[6152]**, **[6174]**, **[21956]**, **[22268]**, **[27650]**, **[29321]**, **[34103]**, **[36093]**, **[37467]**

"It's got wings!" in *Entrepreneur* (Vol. 30, No. 12, December 2002, pp. 61) **[4706]**, **[23055]**, **[49107]**

"It's a Woman's World" in *Black Enterprise* (Vol. 36, November 2005, No. 4, pp. 80) **[12890]**, **[20128]**, **[47158]**, **[48756]**

It's Your Choice **[31937]**

It's Your Life! **[41040]**

"It's all about the profits (you're the boss)" in *Black Enterprise* (Vol. 33, No. 3, October 2002, pp. S3) **[10043]**, **[10266]**, **[15184]**, **[31042]**, **[32054]**, **[38168]**, **[53921]**, **[56746]**

The Itty Bitty Guide to Business Travel **[25201]**, **[30357]**

"Ivan Allen Jr. helped build, and heal Atlanta" in *Atlanta Business Chronicle* (Vol. 25, No. 22, November 8, 2002, pp. 4C) **[24697]**, **[25202]**, **[36379]**

"I've got an idea" in *Atlanta Business Chronicle* (Vol. 25, January 3, 2003, No. 30, pp. 2B) **[9776]**, **[13762]**, **[35538]**

Ivey Publishing **[66753]**

Ivins, Phillips, Barker–Library **[27063]**

Ivy Software Inc. **[66007]**

Ivy Tech State College of Indiana
　　Columbus **[60043]**
　　Fort Wayne **[60044]**
　　Gary **[60045]**

"IXL Enterprises to merge with Scient Corp." in *Atlanta Business Chronicle* (Vol. 24, No. 9, August 3, 2001, pp. 12A) **[15185]**, **[37155]**, **[50025]**

J

"J. Crew Sees No Objection to Bridal Line" in *WWD* (January 26, 2004, pp. 4) **[3187]**, **[5551]**

J. K. Lasser's Small Business Taxes: Your Complete Guide to a Better Bottom Line **[54630]**

J-U-B Engineers Inc. **[16783]**

J. Walter Thompson (Canada)–Information Services **[912]**

"Ja-Da must make its plan more palatable" in *Crain's Detroit Business* (Vol. 16, No. 49, December 4, 2000, pp. 41) **[21540]**, **[38169]**

J.A. Hall Publications **[66684]**

Jabooka Jooce **[12830]**

Jacadi **[5307]**

"Jack of All Trades" in *Hispanic Business* (Vol. 23, No. 5, May 2001, pp. 70-71) **[10044]**, **[15186]**, **[36380]**

"Jack on Jack" in *Harvard Business Review* (Vol. 80, No. 2, February 2002, pp. 88) **[36381]**, **[45319]**

Jack O'Dwyer's Newsletter **[20169]**

"Jackmont Hospitality Acquires Four T.G.I. Friday's Restaurants" in *Black Enterprise* (Vol. 35, September 2004, No. 2, pp. 32) **[15187]**, **[21541]**, **[50026]**

Jacksboro Chamber of Commerce **[65323]**

Jackson Area Chamber of Commerce **[61606]**, **[63706]**, **[64931]**

Jackson - Beldon Chamber of Commerce **[63707]**

Jackson - Breathitt County Chamber of Commerce **[60526]**

Jackson Business Development Center–SBDC **[61197]**

"Jackson CEO: company growing from within" in *Atlanta Business Chronicle* (Vol. 25, No. 20, October 25, 2002, pp. 26A) **[10045]**, **[15188]**, **[38170]**, **[48253]**

Jackson Chamber of Commerce **[56869]**, **[61978]**

Jackson County Area Chamber of Commerce **[59126]**

Jackson County Chamber of Commerce **[58865]**, **[61803]**, **[63389]**

Jackson County Public Library–Indiana & Jackson County History and Genealogy Collection **[11040]**

Jackson Enterprise Center **[61848]**

Jackson Hewitt Tax Service **[24131]**

Jackson Hole Chamber of Commerce **[66614]**

C. E. Jackson, Jr. **[7615]**

Jackson - Madison County African American Chamber of Commerce **[64932]**

Jackson Parish Chamber of Commerce **[60650]**

Jackson State Community College–Small Business Development Center **[64861]**

Jackson State University
　　Bureau of Business and Economic Research **[51499]**
　　Small Business Development Center **[61752]**

Jacksonville Area Chamber of Commerce **[59552]**

Jacksonville Chamber of Commerce **[65324]**

Jacksonville Chamber of Commerce and Visitors' Information **[64231]**

Jacksonville - Onslow Chamber of Commerce **[63390]**

Jacksonville Regional Chamber of Commerce **[58866]**

Jacksonville Regional Chamber of Commerce - Beaches Division **[58867]**

Jacksonville State University
　　Center for Economic Development **[32857]**
　　Small Business Development Center–College of Commerce and Business Administration **[56782]**

Jacobs Institute of Women's Health **[41380]**

Jacobs-Schneider Interior Design Inc. **[49618]**

Jacques Pepin's Cooking Techniques **[7822]**

"Jadi's Journey; Move to OU Incubator Could Lead to Funding" in *Crain's Detroit Business* (Vol. 22, January 9, 2006, No. 2, pp. 3) **[15189]**, **[39845]**, **[40044]**, **[41784]**, **[50027]**, **[55699]**

Jafco Ventures **[58054]**

Jaffrey Chamber of Commerce **[62423]**

JAGEN UND FISCHEN - International Exhibition for Hunters, Fishermen and Marksmen **[1485]**, **[23688]**, **[55224]**

Jaguar Ventures **[66214]**

Jake's Pizza Enterprises, Inc. **[19678]**

Jamaica Business Resource Center–Queens/Brooklyn Minority Development Center **[63047]**

Jamaica Chamber of Commerce **[62939]**

James A. Garfield Historical Society–Library **[11041]**

James B. Kobak & Co. **[58596]**

James B. Sheets, Attorney at Law **[29628]**

"James Bronce Henderson III" in *Crain's Detroit Business* (Vol. 19, No. 1, January 6, 2003, pp. 11) **[36382]**, **[45320]**

"James L. Knight International Center Miami, FL" in *Tradeshow Week* (Vol. 34, November 29, 2004, No. 48, pp. S7) **[22522]**, **[24961]**, **[55108]**

"James L. McNeil" in *Entrepreneur* (Vol. 31, No. 10, October 2003, pp. 30) **[2718]**, **[3546]**, **[22269]**, **[25088]**, **[36383]**, **[44323]**

James Madison University
　　Carrier Library–Special Collections **[9100]**
　　Shenandoah Valley SBDC **[65823]**

Jamestown Area Chamber of Commerce **[63526]**

Jamestown Center–SBDC **[60885]**, **[63495]**

Jamestown Community College–Small Business Development Center **[62761]**

The Kaleel Jamison Consulting Group Inc. **[32117]**

"Jamul Plans $200 Million Facility" in *San Diego Business Journal* (Vol. 28, January 1, 2007, No. 1, pp. 8) **[10873]**, **[28354]**

Jancis Robinson's Wine Course **[23549]**

Janco Associates Inc. **[58265]**

Jane Applegate's Strategies for Small Business Success **[52900]**

Jane Rule...Writing **[9047]**

Jane's Aero-Engines **[977]**

Jane's Aircraft Upgrades **[978]**

Jane's Airports and Handling Agents Library **[979]**

Jane's Helicopter Markets and Systems **[980]**

Jane's Merchant Ships **[9420]**

Jane's Unmanned Aerial Vehicles and Targets **[981]**

Jane's World Airlines **[982]**

Jani-King Canada **[8704]**

Jani-King International, Inc. **[3368]**

Janitize America **[3369]**

"Janitors at Safeway Seek Union Contract" in *Sacramento Bee* (November 23, 2005) **[3316]**, **[11632]**, **[55296]**

Janta de Planificacion–Oficina del Censo **[66970]**

"January Retail Sales Will Exaggerate Consumer Spending Strength" in *Kiplinger Letter* (Vol. 78, January 19, 2007, No. 2) **[32519]**, **[51214]**

Japan Aikido Association U.S.A. **[16906]**

Japan Camera 1 Hour Photo **[4218]**

Japan External Trade Organization **[43508]**

Japanese Chamber of Commerce and Industry of New York **[43509]**, **[62940]**

Japanese Chamber of Commerce of Southern California **[57565]**

Jarlett Consulting **[30649]**

Jasneek Medical Staffing **[23422]**

Jasper Chamber of Commerce **[59947]**

Jasper County Chamber of Commerce **[59553]**, **[64760]**

Jasper Lake Sam Rayburn Area Chamber of Commerce **[65325]**

Jatotech Management LLC **[65613]**

"Java anyone?" in *Black Enterprise* (Vol. 31, No. 5, December 2000, pp. 178) **[11333]**, **[48254]**

Java Dave's Coffee **[51461]**

"Java Enabled" in *Entrepreneur* (Vol. 32, December 2004, No. 12, pp. 164) **[11334]**, **[36384]**, **[51215]**

Java Hut and Photo Expresso **[11388]**

Java Joe's Inc. **[11389]**

Java for Non-Programmers **[32940]**

Java Report **[6511]**

JavaScript for Non-Programmers **[25774]**

JavaServer Pages for Nonprogrammers **[53176]**

JAX FAX-Travel Marketing Magazine **[24698]**, **[25296]**

Jay Chamber of Commerce **[64020]**

Jazz Education Journal **[17619]**

Jazz Greats from Louis Armstrong to Duke Ellington **[17657]**

"Jazzed About Work" in *Fast Company* (May 2001, pp. 193) **[23056]**, **[53343]**

Jazzin' across the Floor **[8478]**

"Jazzin' Up the Chips" in *Red Herring* (No. 99, June 15 & July 1, 2001, pp. 118) **[6948]**, **[41785]**, **[50904]**

Jazzman's Cafe **[11390]**

"JBHM Education Group, LLC" in *Mississippi Business Journal* (Vol. 29, January 2007, No. 4, pp. 6) **[7393]**, **[31180]**, **[33140]**, **[45321]**

JC Ventures Inc. **[38973]**

"J.C. Watts First Black John Deere Dealer" in *Black Enterprise* (Vol. 37, November 2006, No. 4, pp. 36) **[18067]**, **[28355]**, **[30562]**, **[48255]**

"JCI Auto Chief" in *Crain's Detroit Business* (Vol. 22, January 30, 2006, No. 5, pp. 35) **[1942]**, **[46328]**

"JCJC, SMG Partner" in *Mississippi Business Journal* (Vol. 29, January 2007, No. 4, pp. 9) **[15892]**, **[33141]**, **[41786]**

The JCK International Jewelry Show/Orlando **[15874]**

J.D. Byrider **[18203]**

"J.D. Power Study: Hispanics Prefer Imports" in *Hispanic Business* (March 2003, pp. 18) **[18068]**, **[48256]**, **[53818]**

JDE Construction Management Ltd. **[7616]**

JDI Cleaning Systems **[3370]**

Jean Mayer U.S.D.A. Human Nutrition Research Center on Aging at Tufts University–Nutrition Information Office **[488]**, **[18501]**

Jeanerette Chamber of Commerce **[60651]**

"Jeep Adds to Legacy of Federal Program Gone Well" in *San Diego Business Journal* (Vol. 28, January 8, 2007, No. 2, pp. 12) **[18069]**, **[39846]**, **[46329]**

"Jeepers, Creepers" in *Entrepreneur* (Vol. 32, July 2004, No. 7, pp. 75) **[8365]**, **[22270]**, **[52686]**

"Jeff Jonas" in *Entrepreneur* (Vol. 32, September 2004, No. 9, pp. 24) **[4707]**, **[23057]**, **[40045]**, **[44081]**, **[53344]**

Jefferson Area Chamber of Commerce **[60158]**, **[63708]**

Jefferson Capital Fund, Ltd. **[56911]**

Jefferson Chamber of Commerce **[60652]**, **[66429]**

Jefferson City Area Chamber of Commerce **[61979]**

Jefferson College–Extended Learning **[62104]**

Jefferson College of Health Sciences–Learning Resource Center **[1718]**

Jefferson Community College–Small Business Development Center **[62762]**

Jefferson County Chamber of Commerce **[59127]**, **[59554]**, **[63709]**, **[64933]**, **[66281]**
    Ohio SBDC **[63559]**

Jefferson Park Chamber of Commerce **[59555]**

Jefferson Partners **[66725]**

Jeffersontown Chamber of Commerce **[60527]**

Jeffrey Lant Associates Inc. **[61165]**

Jegi Capital, LLC **[63118]**

Jenam Securities Inc. **[50320]**, **[55975]**

Jenkins County Chamber of Commerce and Development Authority **[59128]**

Jenkins & Gilchrist Parker Chapin LLP–Library **[9534]**

Jenkins Group Inc. **[61507]**

Jenks Chamber of Commerce **[64021]**

Jenks Subacute Business Report **[10279]**, **[15654]**

Jennifer MAXX **[11763]**

Jennings County Chamber of Commerce **[59948]**

Jenny Craig Weight Loss & Management Centres **[26056]**

Jensen Beach Chamber of Commerce **[58868]**

Jeppson Galleries **[1636]**

Jerome Capital LLC **[58597]**

Jerome Chamber of Commerce **[57045]**, **[59310]**

Jerome Hill Library **[25615]**

JerQ'Zine **[19679]**

"Jerry's Diner is One Man's Business Vision Come True" in *Miami Herald* (March 10, 2005) **[4546]**, **[21542]**, **[30563]**

Jerry's Subs and Pizza **[19680]**, **[21853]**

Jersey County Business Association **[59556]**

Jersey Mike's Subs **[8553]**

Jerusalem Venture Partners /JVP **[63119]**

Jessamine County Chamber of Commerce **[60528]**

Jest for the Health of It Services **[3741]**, **[31386]**, **[41333]**

Jesup Chamber of Commerce **[60159]**

Jet-Black World's Most Beautiful Driveway's & Parking Lots **[22077]**

"Jet Stream E-Mail" in *Inc.* (September 1, 2003) **[14173]**, **[27651]**, **[30358]**, **[34104]**

"Jetblue Outlines Massive Logan Expansion" in *Boston Globe* (February 3, 2005) **[28356]**, **[30359]**, **[42312]**

Jewelers of America **[15824]**

Jewelers' Circular-Keystone **[15866]**

Jewelers International Showcase **[15875]**

Jewelers' Security Alliance **[1433]**, **[15825]**, **[22151]**

Jewelers Vigilance Committee **[15826]**

Jewell Chamber of Commerce **[60359]**

Jewellers Vigilance Canada **[15827]**

The Jewelry Appraiser **[1452]**, **[15867]**

"Jewelry Designer Gets Chance to Shine" in *Crain's New York Business* (Vol. 21, January 31, 2005, No. 5, pp. 28) **[8012]**, **[15848]**

Jewelry and Gems: The Buying Guide, How to Buy Diamonds, Pearls, Precious and Other Popular Gems with Confidence and Knowledge **[15849]**

Jewelry Information Center **[15828]**

Jewelry Kleen & See Kleer **[15885]**

"Jewelry Lines Picked Up" in *Mississippi Business Journal* (Vol. 29, January 2007, No. 4, pp. 12) **[14174]**, **[15850]**, **[18651]**, **[50028]**

"Jewelry Mixes Fashion and Healing Energies" in *Marketing to Women* (Vol. 19, November 2006, No. 11, pp. 5) **[9626]**, **[15851]**, **[47159]**, **[48757]**, **[56288]**

Jewelry Newsletter International **[15868]**

Jewett Area Chamber of Commerce **[65326]**

Jewish Board of Family and Children's Services, Inc.–Child Development Center **[5459]**

The Jewish Century **[36386]**, **[48567]**

Jewish Funeral Directors of America **[10792]**

Jewish Historical Society of New York, Inc.–Library **[11042]**

JF Robinson Research & Demographics **[47876]**

Jiffy Lube International, Inc. **[20271]**

Jim Castello Marketing Consultants **[3742]**, **[11289]**, **[23752]**, **[31387]**

Jim Thorpe Chamber of Commerce **[64458]**

Jimmy John's Gourmet Sandwiches **[8554]**

Jim's Mowing Canada Inc. **[16153]**

J.J. Keller & Associates, Inc.–Editorial Resource Center–Research & Technical Library **[56689]**

JK Lasser's Small Business Taxes 2077: Your Complete Guide to a Better Bottom Line **[23976]**, **[54631]**

JK&B Capital **[59740]**

JKM Associates **[21725]**

J.L. Albright Venture Partners **[66726]**

JLA Publications **[61166]**

J.M. Davis Arms & Historical Museum–Research Library **[11745]**

"J.M. Neil and Associates: Primary Vendor IT and Network contract with International Communications Company" in *Ingram's* (Vol. 27,No. 7) **[9219]**, **[45322]**

JMB International **[46057]**

JMW Group Inc. **[63255]**

JND Enterprises Message on Hold **[884]**

"Job Board for NAIA Looks Like a Winner" in *Kansas City Star* (February 8, 2005) **[9220]**, **[9569]**, **[14175]**, **[42313]**

"Job Flight: Is it Real: Evidence is Scant, but a Shift Would be Welcome" in *Barron's* (August 11, 2003, pp. 26) **[42314]**, **[43726]**, **[53819]**

"Job Growth Encouraging in Silicon Valley, Nationwide" in *San Jose Mercury News* (March 5, 2005) **[28357]**, **[46330]**

"Job Growth in State Catching Up to Nation" in *San Jose Mercury News* (February 26, 2005) **[28358]**, **[32520]**

Job Hotlines USA **[23394]**

Job Hunt **[4431]**

"Job Inside" in *Fast Company* (September 2001, pp. 177) **[14176]**, **[43951]**, **[49709]**

"Job Market for 2004 Show Improvement, but Not Higher Starting Salaries" in *Hispanic Business* (January/February 2004, pp. 57) **[42315]**

"Job Market May Be Turning Around" in *Hispanic Business* (October 2003, pp. 111) **[32521]**, **[42316]**

"Job Market Thaw" in *Sales and Marketing.com* (Vol. 156, No. 3, March 2004, pp. 24) **[7394]**, **[10046]**, **[15190]**, **[20562]**, **[20915]**, **[25393]**, **[41041]**, **[41787]**, **[42317]**, **[51704]**, **[52551]**

"Job Outlook Stays Bright in Florida" in *Tampa Tribune* (December 16, 2005) **[28359]**, **[32522]**, **[42318]**

Job Performance and Chemical Dependency **[54335]**

"The job site evolution" in *Rough Notes* (Vol. 146, No. 3, March 2003, pp. 173) **[13356]**, **[34105]**, **[42319]**, **[43250]**

"Job Titles of the Future: Chief Academic Officer" in *Fast Company* (September 2001, pp. 60) **[33142]**, **[39422]**

"Job Titles of the Future" in *Fast Company* (July 2001, pp. 50) **[5037]**, **[12891]**, **[16523]**, **[20129]**, **[22272]**, **[45323]**, **[50613]**

"Job Titles of the Future: Project Meanie" in *Fast Company* (September 2001, pp. 70) **[4708]**, **[23058]**, **[45324]**

"Job Training Serious Play" in *Crain's Detroit Business* (Vol. 19, No. 17, April 28, 2003, pp. 11) **[33143]**, **[45325]**

"A Job Well Done" in *My Business* (June/July 2004, pp. 46) **[34961]**, **[45326]**

The JobBank Guide to Computer and High-Tech Companies **[9190]**

The JobBank Guide to Health Care Companies **[9191]**

"Jobless Claims Data Not As Bad As Feared by Economists" in *Atlanta Journal-Constitution* (April 11, 2003) **[28360]**, **[32523]**

"Jobless benefits on family leave? Not here" in *Crain's Detroit Business* (Vol. 16, No. 32, August 7, 2000, pp. 7) **[26837]**, **[40484]**

JobMart **[9250]**

"Jobs Are Back; Too Bad Wages Aren't" in *Fortune* (Vol. 149, No. 9, May 3, 2004, pp. 40) **[13357]**, **[26838]**, **[32524]**, **[42320]**

Jobs for the Future **[6325]**

Jobs In Horticulture Inc. **[4449]**, **[11499]**, **[16070]**

"Jobs Increase in Milwaukee Area" in *Milwaukee Journal Sentinel* (December 22, 2005) **[28361]**, **[42321]**, **[46331]**

Joe Corbi's Pizza Kit Fundraising Program **[10770]**

Joe Loue Tout/Rent All **[21381]**

Joey Pagoda's Oriental Express **[21854]**

John A. Logan College–Small Business Development Center **[59376]**

John Bollinger's Capital Growth Letter **[15655]**

John Brown University–Music Library **[17681]**, **[17820]**

John C. Stennis Space Center–Institute for Technology Development **[61849]**

John Casablanca's Modeling and Career Centers **[17343]**

"John Chambers after the deluge" in *Fast Company* (July 2001, pp. 100) **[14177]**, **[34106]**, **[36387]**

"John Deere Named In Discrimination Suit" in *Black Enterprise* (Vol. 35, August 2004, No. 1, pp. 30) **[26518]**, **[29322]**, **[32038]**, **[36388]**, **[48257]**

John E. Allen, Inc.–Motion Picture Archives **[17550]**

"John Ladaga" in *Hispanic Business* (January/February 2005, pp. 56) **[41788]**, **[48258]**, **[48568]**

The John Liner Letter **[13549]**, **[43434]**

John Markham & Associates **[66685]**

John Michael Kohler Arts Center–Resource Center **[8262]**

John R. Mohr **[29629]**

John T's Unique Gifts **[11204]**

John Tyler Community College **[65997]**

John Wiley and Sons, Inc.–Information Center **[2816]**

Johnny Rockets Group Inc. **[21855]**

Johnny Tremain **[33321]**

Johns Hopkins University
    Center for Hospital Finance and Management **[41381]**
    Health Services Research and Development Center **[41382]**

Johnson, Butler & Co. **[50321]**

Johnson City Chamber of Commerce **[65327]**

Johnson City - Jonesboro - Washington County Chamber of Commerce **[64934]**

Johnson County Chamber of Commerce **[64935]**

Johnson County Community College
    Office of Institutional Research **[60444]**
    Small Business Development Center **[60261]**

"Johnson County, Missouri" in *Ingram's* (Vol. 29, No. 9, September 2003, pp. 34) **[28362]**, **[32525]**

Johnson Creek Area Chamber of Commerce **[66430]**

Johnson and Johnson Consumer and Personal Products Worldwide–Library **[2416]**, **[2628]**

Johnson & Johnson Pharmaceutical Research & Development–Hartman Library **[8867]**

Johnson & Wales College–Harborside Culinary Library **[4574]**, **[7832]**, **[12745]**
Johnson and Wales University **[64682]**
Rhode Island SBDC **[64638]**
Johnson and Wales University Charleston Campus–Barry L. Gleim Library **[4575]**, **[12746]**, **[24782]**, **[25349]**
Johnsonburg Chamber of Commerce **[64459]**
Johnston Associates, Inc. **[62599]**
Johnston Chamber of Commerce **[60160]**
Johnston Co. **[3743]**, **[16626]**, **[31388]**, **[38551]**, **[46058]**, **[53099]**
Johnston County Chamber of Commerce **[64022]**
Johnstown-Milliken Chamber of Commerce **[58387]**
"Join the club?" in *Black Enterprise* (Vol. 33, No. 6, January 2003, pp. 87) **[51216]**, **[53820]**
"Join the club: launching your first product" in *Entrepreneur* (Vol. 31, No. 5, May 2003, pp. 132) **[43962]**, **[46576]**, **[48686]**
"Join Hands" in *Entrepreneur* (Vol. 33, September 2005, No. 9, pp. 138) **[18477]**, **[18683]**, **[18708]**, **[44082]**, **[47160]**, **[48758]**, **[50731]**
"Joining Forces" in *Home Business* (Vol. 12, October 2005, No. 5, pp. 64, 66) **[28363]**, **[42668]**, **[50029]**
"Joining Forces" in *Sales & Marketing Management* **[11633]**, **[12010]**, **[46332]**, **[47161]**, **[50030]**
"Joining Forces" in *Washington Business Journal* (Vol. 22, No. 15, August 15, 2003, pp. 20) **[12892]**, **[20130]**, **[33144]**
"Joining the Ranks" in *Entrepreneur* (Vol. 33, October 2005, No. 10, pp. 89) **[42322]**, **[43294]**, **[45327]**
The Joint Commission Journal on Quality Improvement **[41230]**
Joint Industry Group **[12929]**, **[43510]**
Joint Oceanographic Institutions **[58686]**
Jojacks Inc. **[7665]**
Joliet Junior College–Small Business Development Center **[59377]**
Joliet Region Chamber of Commerce and Industry **[59557]**
Jolson Merchant Partners Group, LLC **[58055]**
"Jolting Joe" in *Washington Business Journal* (Vol. 22, No. 12, July 25, 2003, pp. 23) **[11335]**, **[40485]**, **[51217]**, **[56013]**
"Jonathan Hoffman Was Sure a Former Staffer Had Stolen His Company's Ideas" in *Inc.* (September 2005, pp. 55-56) **[29323]**, **[33145]**, **[35281]**, **[44324]**
Keith R. Jones, Consulting Arborist **[16071]**
Richard J. Jones Consulting Services **[16627]**
Jones County Chamber of Commerce **[61804]**
Jones County Junior College–SBDC **[61753]**
Jonesboro Regional Chamber of Commerce **[57184]**
Joplin Area Chamber of Commerce **[61980]**
The Jordan Edmiston Group Inc. **[63120]**
Jordan International Enterprises **[46059]**
"Jordanian delegation looks to expand business ties" in *Crain's Detroit Business* (Vol. 18, No. 50, December 16, 2002, pp. 22) **[28364]**, **[43727]**
Joseph Chamber of Commerce **[64232]**
Joseph J. Walczak, P.C. **[29630]**
Josephberg, Grosz and Co., Inc. **[63121]**
Josephson Institute of Ethics **[37550]**
Joshua Area Chamber of Commerce **[65328]**
Joshua Tree Chamber of Commerce **[57566]**
Jourdanton Community Chamber of Commerce **[65329]**
The Journal **[43435]**
Journal of Accountacncy; "Amortization of Certain Intangible Assets" in **[70]**, **[2865]**, **[23881]**, **[26150]**, **[27079]**, **[38709]**, **[43986]**, **[54428]**
Journal of Accountacy; "What CPAs Need to Know About Separately Managed Accounts" in **[294]**, **[2971]**, **[10240]**, **[15595]**, **[24070]**, **[27198]**
Journal of Accountancy **[330]**
Journal of Accountancy (Vol. 198, November 2004); "20 Steps for Pricing a Patent: To Value an Invention You Have to Understand It" in **[54]**, **[2860]**, **[23872]**, **[26137]**, **[27074]**, **[43981]**
Journal of Accountancy "Accounting Education; Response to Corporate Scandals: Helping the Profession Find Opportunity in Crisis" in **[60]**, **[2863]**, **[23875]**, **[26143]**, **[27077]**, **[32988]**
Journal of Accountancy (January 2005); "Accumulated Earnings Tax: Deductibility of Paid But Contested Liabilities" in **[67]**, **[2864]**, **[23878]**, **[26148]**, **[27078]**, **[54421]**
Journal of Accountancy (January 2005); "Automate Excel Functions: Easy-to-Create Macros Can Take Over Many Manual Processes" in **[76]**, **[2867]**, **[23886]**, **[26158]**, **[27081]**, **[53594]**
Journal of Accountancy; "Avoid the Payroll Tax Trap: Using Withheld Payroll Taxes for Other Purposes Can be a Dangerous and Expensive Game" in **[78]**, **[2868]**, **[18770]**, **[23888]**, **[26160]**, **[27082]**, **[54435]**
Journal of Accountancy; "Avoid the Tax Trap When Repaying Shareholder Loans" in **[79]**, **[2869]**, **[23889]**, **[26161]**, **[27083]**, **[54436]**
Journal of Accountancy (Vol. 198, December 2004, No. 6, pp. 30); "Become Famous for What You Do" in **[83]**, **[2873]**, **[9841]**, **[14782]**, **[23894]**, **[27088]**
Journal of Accountancy (Vol. 199, January 2005, No. 1, pp. 78); "Buying Long-Term-Care Insurance: A Security Blanket for Old Age" in **[96]**, **[2880]**, **[12531]**, **[23902]**, **[43111]**
Journal of Accountancy (Vol. 198); "Capturing the Potential: How CPA Firms are Building Successful Financial Services Practices" in **[99]**, **[2882]**, **[23905]**, **[26182]**, **[27095]**, **[37944]**
Journal of Accountancy (Vol. 199, January 2005, No. 1, pp. 29); "Caveats to Selling Financial Services" in **[102]**, **[2884]**, **[9868]**, **[14840]**, **[23907]**, **[26185]**, **[27098]**, **[51584]**
Journal of Accountancy (Vol. 199, January 2005); "Class-Based Pensions: A Cost-Saving Alternative for Companies of All Sizes" in **[106]**, **[2885]**, **[23911]**, **[26189]**, **[26769]**, **[27099]**
Journal of Accountancy (Vol. 199, January 2005, No. 1, pp. 75); "Commuting Expenses: What is a 'Metropolitan Area'?" in **[107]**, **[2886]**, **[23912]**, **[26191]**, **[27103]**, **[54496]**
Journal of Accountancy (Vol. 198, December 2004, No. 6, pp. 93); "Court Review of IRS Abuse of Discretion" in **[113]**, **[2888]**, **[23917]**, **[26198]**, **[27106]**, **[54504]**
Journal of Accountancy; "Damages Aren't Always Patently Obvious" in **[119]**, **[2889]**, **[23923]**, **[26205]**, **[27109]**, **[44023]**, **[44286]**
Journal of Accountancy (Vol. 198, September 2004, No. 3, pp. 80); "Debt Allocation and LLCs" in **[123]**, **[2890]**, **[23924]**, **[26209]**, **[27110]**
Journal of Accountancy (Vol. 198, December 2004, No. 6, pp. 92); "Deducting the Cost of Laser Eye Surgery" in **[125]**, **[2891]**, **[23926]**, **[26211]**, **[27111]**, **[40994]**, **[54513]**
Journal of Accountancy (Vol. 198, October 2004, No. 4, pp. 102); "Deemed Substantiation of Business Travel Expenses" in **[126]**, **[2892]**, **[23927]**, **[26212]**, **[27112]**, **[30317]**
Journal of Accountancy (Vol. 190, No. 3, September 2000, pp. 94); "Determination of a profit motive" in **[40308]**, **[54514]**
Journal of Accountancy (Vol. 199, February 2005, No. 2, pp. 89); "Directory of AICPA Selected Services" in **[131]**, **[2894]**, **[23930]**, **[26216]**, **[27113]**
Journal of Accountancy (Vol. 198, September 2004); "Employer-Provided Education Benefits: Section 132(d) is Worth a Second Look" in **[134]**, **[2896]**, **[23935]**, **[26220]**, **[26795]**, **[27115]**, **[54532]**
Journal of Accountancy (Vol. 198, September 2004, No. 3, pp.); "Encourage General Ledger Efficiency" in **[135]**, **[2897]**, **[23936]**, **[26221]**, **[27116]**
Journal of Accountancy (Vol. 199, January 2005); "Explore the Art of Consultative Selling" in **[140]**, **[2899]**, **[9944]**, **[14970]**, **[23938]**, **[26226]**, **[27119]**, **[31147]**, **[51630]**
Journal of Accountancy (Vol. 198); "Financial Reporting Goes Global: International Standards Affect U.S. Companies and GAAP" in **[145]**, **[2901]**, **[23941]**, **[26233]**, **[27122]**
Journal of Accountancy (Vol. 199, February 2005, No. 2, pp. 75); "Firm-and-Fixed-Plan Rule Reaffirmed" in **[2902]**, **[3531]**, **[14992]**, **[23942]**, **[29240]**, **[54555]**
Journal of Accountancy; "Fraud Risk: Are You Prepared? The Mission: To Create Stronger Support for an Ethically Sound Business Environment" in **[153]**, **[2905]**, **[23946]**, **[26243]**, **[27124]**, **[29255]**, **[30225]**
Journal of Accountancy (October 2004); "Get the Raise You Deserve: A Step-by-Step Guide to Negotiating the Right Pay Package" in **[156]**, **[2907]**, **[23951]**, **[26247]**, **[27129]**, **[45180]**
Journal of Accountancy (Vol. 199, January 2005, No. 1, pp. 108); "Grow Your Own Executive Team" in **[33110]**, **[34919]**, **[45207]**
Journal of Accountancy (Vol. 199, February 2005, No. 2); "Hedge Fund Investing: Current Advice for Financial Advisers and Planners" in **[161]**, **[2911]**, **[9995]**, **[15073]**, **[23957]**, **[27133]**
Journal of Accountancy (Vol. 199, February 2005, No. 2); "Host a Virtual Meeting: Collaborate with a Video Link and a Whiteboard" in **[4687]**, **[14124]**, **[23029]**, **[27399]**, **[53783]**
Journal of Accountancy (Vol. 198, September 2004, No. 3, pp.); "Impact of Self-Employment Loss on Earned Income" in **[168]**, **[2915]**, **[23963]**, **[26262]**, **[27137]**
Journal of Accountancy (Vol. 198, December 2004, No. 6, pp. 22); "Increasing Transparency in Peer Review: Members Speak Out" in **[170]**, **[2917]**, **[23965]**, **[26264]**, **[27139]**
Journal of Accountancy (Vol. 198); "Install Your Own Wireless Networks" in **[171]**, **[2918]**, **[6947]**, **[14151]**, **[23966]**, **[26265]**, **[27140]**
Journal of Accountancy (Vol. 198, December 2004, No. 6, pp. 95); "Interest Paid as an Administrative Expense" in **[172]**, **[2919]**, **[23967]**, **[26266]**, **[27141]**, **[54612]**
Journal of Accountancy (Vol. 198); "IRS Allows Statistical Sampling for M&E Costs: New Procedure May Increase Taxpayer Deductions" in **[176]**, **[2921]**, **[23970]**, **[26272]**, **[27143]**
Journal of Accountancy (Vol. 199, February 2005, No. 2, pp. 78); "Is Division of an IRA a Taxable Event?" in **[54626]**
Journal of Accountancy (Vol. 198, December 2004, No. 6, pp. 94); "Is 'Equitable Remedy' Settlement Excludable from Gross Income?" in **[178]**, **[2922]**, **[23974]**, **[26273]**, **[27144]**, **[29316]**, **[54628]**
Journal of Accountancy (Vol. 199, February 2005, No. 2); "Jump-Start Success: How to Set Up a World-Class Internal Audit Function" in **[180]**, **[2924]**, **[23977]**, **[26275]**, **[27147]**
Journal of Accountancy (Vol. 190, No. 4, October 2000, pp. 113); "LMSB Deputy Commissioner stresses fairness for taxpayers" in **[40517]**, **[53839]**, **[54648]**
Journal of Accountancy (Vol. 198, October 2004); "Make the Most of Buy-Sell Agreements: These Complex Contracts Solve Many Problems" in **[188]**, **[2927]**, **[23985]**, **[26284]**, **[27149]**
Journal of Accountancy (Vol. 198, November 2004); "Nonindividual QTP Contributions: How Employers Can Help Workers Save for College" in **[208]**, **[2938]**, **[24001]**, **[26304]**, **[26863]**, **[27157]**
Journal of Accountancy (Vol. 199, January 2005, No. 1, pp. 76); "Ohio Investment Tax Credit Struck Down" in **[212]**, **[2942]**, **[24006]**, **[26309]**, **[27159]**, **[54685]**
Journal of Accountancy (Vol. 199, January 2005, No. 1, pp. 73); "Partnership Terminations" in **[220]**, **[2944]**, **[15342]**, **[24011]**, **[26317]**, **[27161]**, **[50125]**
Journal of Accountancy (Vol. 199, February 2005, No. 2, pp. 108); "Practical Ideas for Improving Your Business" in **[4768]**, **[6764]**, **[23131]**, **[28642]**, **[45555]**, **[53416]**
Journal of Accountancy; "Price Equals Value Plus Terms" in **[227]**, **[2946]**, **[24018]**, **[26329]**, **[27165]**, **[50138]**
Journal of Accountancy; "Radio Frequency Identification" in **[234]**, **[2949]**, **[24022]**, **[26336]**, **[27167]**, **[41931]**, **[44241]**
Journal of Accountancy (January 2005); "Renewing a Great Profession: Esteemed Professions Initiate Change - For Their Own Good" in **[237]**, **[2952]**, **[24024]**, **[26339]**, **[27168]**

Master Index

Journal Record (February 5, 2004); "Okla. Restaurant Assn. Gets New Slate of Officers and New Set of Industry Challenges" in [21577], [22311]

Journal Record (June 24, 2003); "Oklahoma Business Roundtable Elects Officers" in [39508], [40925]

Journal Record (Oklahoma City, OK) (February 5, 2007); "After Eight Years of Dreaming, Tulsa Woman Opens Wedding Chapel" in [3164], [56027]

Journal Record (Oklahoma City, OK) (February 8, 2007); "Client Surveys Slow to Catch on as a Legal Marketing Tool" in [29153], [46809]

Journal Record (Oklahoma City, OK) (February 2, 2007); "Commentary: Fresh-Air Shopping" in [20838], [51104]

Journal Record (Oklahoma City, OK) (February 6, 2007); "Former Manager Files Suit Against OKC-based Hudiburg Auto Group" in [18042], [29252]

Journal Record (Oklahoma City, OK) (February 6, 2007); "Heller Family Pays $4.1M for Warehouse" in [15076], [20224], [28270], [38825]

Journal Record (Oklahoma City, OK) (October 2003); "Helping You Realize Your Potential...on eBay" in [1822], [34004]

Journal Record (Oklahoma City, OK) (February 6, 2007); "Lawmaker in Okla. Seeks to Discourage Fines for Tax Preparers" in [183], [2926], [23981], [26278]

Journal Record (Oklahoma City, OK) (February 1, 2007); "Manufacturing Sector Expects Improvement After Slow January" in [28456], [46363]

Journal Record (Oklahoma City, OK) (February 8, 2007); "OKC-based Devon Energy's Fourth-Quarter Profits Dip 40 Percent" in [15314], [38254]

Journal Record (Oklahoma City, OK) (February 8, 2007); "OKC-based The Benham Cos. Lands Military Housing Contract" in [7445], [40069]

Journal Record (Oklahoma City, OK) (February 5, 2007); "OKC Man Charged in Connection With Identity Theft Ring" in [1956], [22317], [29424], [44346]

Journal Record (Oklahoma City, OK) (February 5, 2007); "SBA Hearing Scheduled" in [39911], [40666]

Journal Record (Oklahoma City, OK) (February 7, 2007); "Scaramucci Sets Up Gift Shop in Skirvin Hilton in Downtown OKC" in [11167], [12632]

Journal Record (Oklahoma City, OK) (February 6, 2007); "Stillwater-Based Southwest Bancorp Inc. to Buy Bank of Kansas" in [10189], [15476], [50190]

Journal Record (Oklahoma City, OK) (February 7, 2007); "Tobacco Sales to Minors Decline In Oklahoma" in [24610], [29550]

Journal Record (Oklahoma City, OK) (February 5, 2007); "Tulsa-based Dollar Thrifty Automotive Group Buys Franchise" in [15546], [21358], [38935], [50226]

Journal Record (Oklahoma City, OK) (February 8, 2007); "Tulsa-Based Dollar Thrifty Automotive Group Inc. to Outsource Call Center" in [21359], [31888], [49749]

Journal Record (Oklahoma City, OK) (February 8, 2007); "Tulsa-based SpiritBank Reconsiders Future of Branching" in [10218], [28922]

Journal Record (Oklahoma City, OK) (February 1, 2007); "Tulsa Home Sales See Another Record Year" in [7502], [20693], [21029], [28923]

Journal Record (Oklahoma City, OK) (February 8, 2007); "Tulsa Insurance Company Sues Kansas-based Bank" in [10219], [29556], [43407]

Journal Record (Oklahoma City, OK) (February 1, 2007); "Tulsan Reflects on 35 Years of Polishing Shoes" in [22745], [36892]

Journal Record (Oklahoma City, OK) (February 8, 2007); "Workers' Comp Claims Filed Have Decreased in Okla., Statistics Show" in [40853], [42902]

Journal Record (February 5, 2004); "Oklahoma Insurance Commissioner Orders Tribal Companies Out of State" in [40589], [42055], [43298]

Journal Record (June 24, 2003); "Rhino Products Device Keeps Ladders Stationary" in [42178], [44135], [56565], [56585]

Journal Record (June 24, 2003); "Sonic Profits, Sales Up for Quarter" in [21629], [23055], [38913], [40439]

Journal Record (February 5, 2004); "South Okla. City Chamber Seeks to Attract Large Bookstore" in [3048], [52730], [54981]

Journal Record (February 4, 2004); "Spam Law Proposed in State House of Representatives" in [14466], [15018], [34516], [35696], [40710], [40792]

Journal Record (June 25, 2003); "Third Degree Advertising Names VP for Solomon Inc." in [47633], [49535], [50692], [50764]

Journal Record (February 4, 2004); "Tulsa-based Dollar Thrifty Buys Franchises" in [15547], [16058], [21360], [22081], [38936], [39389], [47818], [50227]

Journal Record (February 4, 2004); "Twenty Nine Percent of State's Farmers are Female" in [26551], [27460], [53637], [56452]

Journal Record (February 5, 2004); "Two Identity-Theft Bills Filed In Oklahoma House of Representatives" in [22408], [23121], [28891], [29557], [40787], [41776]

Journal Record (June 24, 2003); "Urban Renewal May Hire Contractor to Evaluate Skirvin Proposals" in [12649], [13163], [28947], [29886]

Journal of Relationship Marketing [31916], [47795]

Journal for Research in Music Education [17621]

Journal of Scholarly Publishing [2771]

Journal of School Health [41250]

Journal of Small Business Management [13051], [45895]

Journal of Small Business Management; "Access to Capital and Terms of Credit: A Comparison of Men- and Women-Owned Small Businesses" in [31510], [55478], [56113]

Journal of Small Business Management (Vol. 38, No. 3); "Career Patterns of the Self-Employed: Career Motivations and Career Outcomes" in [35917]

Journal of Small Business Management (Vol. 38, No. 3, July 2000, pp. 1); "Crime and Small Business" in [33061], [35278]

Journal of Small Business Management (Vol. 41, No. 4, October 2003); "Critical Success Factors for Manufacturing Networks..." in [46254]

Journal of Small Business Management (Vol. 44, October 2006, No. 4, pp. 563); "Differentiating Legal Issues by Business Type" in [28035], [29197], [29849], [33073], [36016], [45063], [52843]

Journal of Small Business Management (Vol. 41, No. 4, October 2003, pp. 366); "Does the Franchisor Provide Value to Franchisees?" in [28046], [38756]

Journal of Small Business Management; "Environmental and Ownership Characteristics of Small Businesses and their Impact on Development" in [28122], [29864], [30145], [30537], [30677], [32416]

Journal of Small Business Management (Vol. 38, No. 2, April 2000, pp. 48); "Ethnic Enterprises and their Clientele" in [48150]

Journal of Small Business Management (Vol. 41, July 2003); "Failure Rates for Female-Controlled Businesses: Are They Any Different?" in [28140], [56212]

Journal of Small Business Management (Vol. 41, No. 3, July 2003, pp. 233); "Health and Female Self-Employment" in [36269], [56258]

Journal of Small Business Management (Vol. 38, No. 38, April 2000, pp. 1); "How to Plan as a Small Scale Business Owner" in [29899], [30557], [45264]

Journal of Small Business Management (Vol.38, No.1, Jan. 2000); "Market Orientation and Other Potential Influences on Performance..." in [44336], [45418], [46367]

Journal of Small Business Management (Vol. 41, No. 3, July 2003); "Raising Response Rates In Mail Surveys of Small Business Owners" in [39546]

Journal of Small Business Management (Vol. 41, No. 4, October 2003); "Small Business Growth: Intention, Ability, and Opportunity" in [28777], [29931], [39584], [40991]

Journal of Small Business Management (Vol. 44, October 2006, No. 4, pp. 493); "Small Firm Bankruptcy" in [28787], [32695], [33238], [44363], [45652], [52955], [53975]

Journal of Small Business Management (Vol. 38, No. 4, October 2000, pp. 1); "Small Firms' Motivation for Exporting" in [43816]

Journal of Small Business Management (Vol. 41, No. 4, October 2003, pp. 346); "Support for Rapid-Growth Firms" in [28845], [39620], [40744]

Journal of Small Business Management (Vol. 38, No. 4, Oct. 2000); "The International Process of Small and Medium-sized Enterprises" in [43719]

Journal of Small Business Management; "Toward the Development of Measures of Distinctive Competencies among Small Independent Retailers" in [30976], [51394], [53014]

Journal of Small Business Management (Vol. 41, No. 4, October 2003, pp. 385); "Uncertainty and Information Search Activities" in [36897], [42083], [45776], [46469]

Journal of Small Business Management (Vol. 38, No. 3, July 2000, pp. 27); "Workforce Diversity in Small Business" in [42470], [45868], [48608]

Journal of Social Service Research [41251]

Journal of the Society of Architectural Historians (JSAH) [1540]

Journal of the Society of Pediatric Nurses [41252]

Journal of Spiritual Bodywork [17013], [17931]

Journal Star (November 25, 2003); "Peoria, Ill., Woodcraft Store Gets Kiosk" in [15934]

Journal Star (August 24, 2004); "Pet Sitting a Growing Business Nationwide" in [19080], [53917]

Journal of State Taxation [24094]

The Journal of Supply Chain Management [50764]

The Journal of Taxation [24095]

Journal of Technical Writing and Communication [9033]

Journal of Turbomachinery [52301]

Journal of Vegetable Crop Production [9488], [11698], [26598], [37347]

Journal of Visualization and Computer Animation [52302]

Journal of Waterway, Port, Coastal, and Ocean Engineering [52303]

Journeywoman Online Magazine [24760], [25297]

Joy Carpet Dry Cleaning [25558]

"The Joy of Conflict" in *Inc.* (August 2005, pp. 112) [34962], [45328]

"The Joy Factory" in *WorkingWoman* (Vol. 25, No. 4, April 2000, pp. 48) [9003], [20319], [24422], [36389], [56289]

"The Joy of Quitting" in *Fortune* (Vol. 141, No. 3, February 7, 2000, pp. 199+) [32526], [52901], [53821]

Joy Reisinger, Certified Genealogist–Library [11043]

Joy of Stocks: The Forbes Guide to the Stock Market [15704]

"Joyless recovery based on Georgia Economic Outlook" in *Atlanta Business Chronicle* (Vol. 25, January 10, 2003, No. 31, pp. 23A) [28365], [32527]

J.P. Morgan Capital Corp. [63122]

"JP Morgan Rolls Out Tech-Heavy Branches" in *Houston Business Journal* (Vol. 34, No. 8, July 4, 2003, pp. 1) [10047], [15191], [15924], [34107], [41789]

"JPMorgan Chase Helps LI Crisis Center" in *Long Island Business News* (February 20, 2004) [10048], [15192], [54213]

"JPMorgan Chase Regional Economist Forecasts Long Island Growth for 2004" in *Long Island Business News* (January 30, 2004) **[28366]**, **[32528]**, **[46333]**, **[52552]**

"'JR still starts with W; Ratings up and Smith's re-upped" in *Crain's Detroit Business* (Vol. 19, No. 4, January 27, 2003, pp. 1) **[20320]**, **[28367]**

"JSU Receives Record Funding" in *Mississippi Business Journal* (Vol. 28, September 2006, No. 36, pp. 23) **[39847]**, **[52135]**, **[55700]**

Jubilee Centre for Agricultural Research **[26689]**

"Jubilee! JAM Returning June 2007" in *Mississippi Business Journal* (Vol. 29, January 2007, No. 1, pp. 3) **[24962]**, **[50031]**

Judah L. Magnes Museum–Western Jewish History Center **[11044]**

"Judge Halts Initial Step in Auto-Insurance Revamp" in *Boston Globe* (February 2, 2005) **[13358]**, **[43251]**

"Judge, Jury, and Spam Executioner" in *Black Enterprise* (Vol. 34, No. 7, February 2004, pp. 53) **[14178]**, **[22273]**, **[34108]**

"Judge, Jury, and Spam Executioner: Tech Exec Sets His Sights On Fighting E-Mail Menaces" in *Black Enterprise* (Vol. 34, No. 7) **[14179]**, **[22274]**, **[34109]**

"Judge Rejects Effort to Keep Billing Records for Boston's Big Dig a Secret" in *Boston Globe* (April 11, 2003) **[29324]**, **[37468]**, **[40486]**

"Judge Stays Implementation of Massachusetts Governor's Auto Insurance Plan" in *Boston Globe* (February 2, 2005) **[13359]**, **[40487]**, **[43252]**

Judicial News **[29668]**

"The Juggling Act" in *My Business* (October/November 2003, pp. 36-39) **[28368]**, **[36390]**, **[39423]**

Jugo Juice International Inc. **[21856]**

Juice Gallery Multimedia **[58266]**

"A Juice Guy Changes Lanes" in *Inc.* (December 1, 2003) **[11634]**, **[23489]**, **[36391]**

Juice Heaven **[12831]**

Juice It Up! Franchise Corp. **[12832]**

"The Juice is Loose" in *My Business* (April/May 2004, pp. 16) **[28369]**, **[36392]**

Juilliard School–Lila Acheson Wallace Library **[1658]**

Julian Chamber of Commerce **[57567]**

Julie Ann's Frozen Custard **[12833]**

"Jump-Start Success: How to Set Up a World-Class Internal Audit Function" in *Journal of Accountancy* (Vol. 199, February 2005, No. 2) **[180]**, **[2924]**, **[23977]**, **[26275]**, **[27147]**

Jump Start Your Business Brain: Ideas, Advice and Insights for Immediate Marketing and Innovation Success **[28370]**, **[44083]**, **[45329]**, **[47162]**

"Jump-starting broadband" in *Barron's* (Vol. 82, No. 54, January 20, 2003, pp. T1) **[5038]**, **[14180]**, **[30896]**, **[40488]**

JumpBunch **[5433]**

Jump.Net Ventures **[65614]**

Junction City Area Chamber of Commerce **[60360]**

Junction City-Harrisburg Chamber of Commerce **[64233]**

June Lake Chamber of Commerce **[57568]**

Juneau Chamber of Commerce **[56966]**, **[66431]**

Juneau SBDC–University of Alaska at Anchorage **[56938]**

"The jungle" in *Wall Street Journal* (May 7, 2002, pp. B12) **[9221]**, **[9570]**, **[45330]**

Juniata Valley Area Chamber of Commerce **[64460]**

"Junkyard Blues" in *Forbes* (October 30, 2000, pp. 282) **[44558]**, **[55701]**

Jupiter-Tequesta-Juno Beach Chamber of Commerce **[58869]**

Jurupa Chamber of Commerce **[57569]**

"Jury Finds 2 Guilty of Scamming Investors" in *St. Louis Post-Dispatch* (February 3, 2005) **[1831]**, **[10049]**, **[14181]**, **[15193]**, **[29325]**, **[30235]**

"Jury is still out: Is the bar ready for virtual law firms?" in *Boston Business Journal* (Vol. 22, No. 3, February 22, 2002, pp. 27) **[29326]**, **[34110]**

Just-A-Buck **[7794]**

"Just Ask: Use e-mail to start a conversation with online buyers" in *My Business* (October/November 2002, pp. 17) **[14182]**, **[27652]**, **[34111]**, **[47163]**

"Just down the block" in *Entrepreneur* (Vol. 30, No. 1, January 2002, pp. 18) **[4709]**, **[23059]**, **[34112]**, **[47164]**, **[53345]**

"Just Browsing" in *Entrepreneur* (Vol. 32, November 2004, No. 11, pp. 66) **[14183]**, **[22275]**, **[34113]**

"Just Call Him George W. Reagan" in *Business Week Online* (Jan. 8, 2003) **[40489]**, **[54632]**

"Just Can't Hack It" in *Entrepreneur* (Vol. 28, No. 11, November 2000, pp. 30) **[14184]**, **[34114]**

Just Compensation **[30737]**

"Just for shows with a new design, these booths are gonna walk all over you" in *Entrepreneur* (Vol. 30, No. 1, January 2002, pp. 26) **[24963]**, **[47165]**

"Just Desserts" in *Small Business Opportunities* (Vol. 12, No. 3, May 2000, pp. 54) **[2223]**, **[30487]**, **[35539]**, **[37569]**

"Just Do It" in *Entrepreneur* (Vol. 28, No. 17, July 2000, pp. 162) **[43963]**, **[55400]**

Just the Facts Learning Series: The Great American State Quiz **[33322]**

Just Fresh **[21857]**

"Just for Her" in *Inc.* (April 1, 2005) **[6698]**, **[30360]**

"Just for kicks: Every car you buy doesn't have to go to work with you" in *Entrepreneur* (Vol. 30, No. 1, January 2002, pp. 20) **[18070]**, **[45331]**

Just Kidstuff - A Division of the New York International Gift Fair **[2134]**, **[5298]**, **[24848]**

Just Kidstuff - A Division of the San Francisco International Gift Fair **[2135]**, **[5299]**

"Just a Little Bit Public" in *Inc.* (August 2005, pp. 32, 34) **[15194]**, **[38171]**, **[41790]**, **[55702]**

"Just a Mirage? Proposed Legislation May Expand SBIC Financing-Someday" in *Entrepreneur* (Vol. 31, No. 8, August 2003, pp. 24) **[39848]**, **[40490]**, **[44559]**

Just Promoted: How to Survive and Thrive in Your First 12 Months as a Manager **[45332]**

"Just Say Om" in *Inc.* (July 1, 2003) **[17899]**, **[19409]**, **[30897]**

The Just So Stories, Vol. 1 **[5391]**

The Just So Stories, Vol. 2 **[5392]**

The Just So Stories, Vol. 3 **[5393]**

"Just the Tax" in *Entrepreneur* (Vol. 32, December 2004, No. 12, pp. 39) **[23978]**, **[54633]**

"Just Teasing: A- Ads" in *Entrepreneur* (Vol. 31, No. 9, September 2003, pp. 88) **[683]**, **[47166]**

"Just the Tiqit" in *Red Herring* (January 2003, pp. 26) **[6699]**, **[28371]**, **[41791]**, **[48759]**, **[52136]**

"Just 'To-Do' It: Having Trouble Getting Organized? Start by Getting a Grip on Your To-Do List" in *Entrepreneur* (August 2004) **[36393]**, **[54960]**

"Just Woo It: It's Possible to Flirt with Success After All" in *Entrepreneur* (Vol. 32, No. 4, April 2004, pp. 29) **[44084]**, **[47167]**

"Just Zip It: A Confidentiality Agreement Can Give You the Upper Hand" in *Entrepreneur* (Vol. 32, November 2004, No. 11, pp. 96) **[39424]**, **[44325]**

Justice Management Division–Procurement Services Staff **[67638]**

Justice Research Association **[19952]**

"Justice's warning" in *Black Enterprise* (Vol. 33, No. 198, March 24, 2003, pp. A3) **[32529]**, **[40491]**

JWU Larry Friedman International Center for Entrepreneurship–Providence Metro SBDC **[64648]**

K

K–Kentucky Highlands Investment Corporation **[60583]**

K & N Mobile Distribution Systems **[7759]**

K & T Training **[30090]**, **[31389]**, **[35235]**, **[46060]**

"Ka-Boom! Looks Like the Economy is Finally Growing-And Guess What's Leading the Way?" in *Entrepreneur* (Vol. 32, August 2004) **[28372]**, **[32530]**, **[41792]**

KaBloom **[10603]**

Kahala Investments, Inc. **[65615]**

"Kahiki Launches Frozen Meals, Refrigerated Rice Bowls" in *Frozen Food Age* (Vol. 51, No. 12, July 2003, pp. 40) **[11635]**, **[23490]**

Kahoka - Clark County Chamber of Commerce **[61981]**

Kailua Chamber of Commerce **[59250]**

"Kaiser Getting a Transplant" in *San Francisco Business Times* (Vol. 18, No. 1, August 15, 2003, pp. 1) **[41042]**, **[50905]**

Kaiser Group Inc. **[46061]**

Kaiser Permanente Center for Health Research **[41383]**

Kaiser Permanente Medical Care Program–Division of Research **[41384]**

Kaiser-Permanente Medical Center–Health Sciences Library **[1719]**

Kaiser Permanente Ventures **[58056]**

Kajioka Design Associates **[49619]**

Kalama Chamber of Commerce **[66117]**

Kalamazoo College–Small Business Technology Development Center **[61198]**

Kalamazoo Regional Chamber of Commerce **[61350]**

"Kaleidoscope Yarns recently opened its doors at 15 Pearl Street" in *Vermont Business Magazine* (Vol. 30, No. 9, Aug. 2002, pp. 18) **[8129]**, **[53564]**

Kalin Associates Inc. **[7617]**

Kalispell Area Chamber of Commerce **[62176]**

Kalispell Small Business Development Center–Kalispell Area Chamber of Commerce **[62124]**

Kalkaska Area Chamber of Commerce **[61351]**

Kalona Area Chamber of Commerce **[60161]**

Kamiah Chamber of Commerce **[59311]**

KampGround Owners Association **[4227]**

Kampgrounds of America, Inc **[4262]**

Kanab Chamber of Commerce **[65715]**

Kanabec Area Chamber of Commerce **[61607]**

Kane Chamber of Commerce **[64461]**

Kankakee Community College–Small Business Development Center **[59378]**

Kankakee River Valley Chamber of Commerce **[59558]**

Kanouse & Walker, P.A. **[29631]**, **[39012]**

Kansas Agri-Business Expo **[26603]**

Kansas Chamber of Commerce and Industry **[60361]**

Kansas City Business Journal **[62109]**

Kansas City Business Journal (Vol. 18, No. 21, January 28, 2000, pp. 4); "Office tech allows 'knowledge management'" in **[44345]**

Kansas City Business Journal (Vol. 18, No. 21, January 28, 2000, pp. 21); "Puncturing Myths" in **[17874]**, **[35616]**

Kansas City Business Journal (Vol. 18, No. 22, February 4, 2000, pp. 6); "Web-based publisher books investment from local sources" in **[2640]**, **[9125]**, **[33497]**

"Kansas City Cardiology Works Towards Advancements" in *Ingram's* (Vol. 29, No. 9, September 2003, pp. 24) **[50906]**, **[52137]**

Kansas City Equity Partners **[62087]**

Kansas City, Kansas Area Chamber of Commerce **[60362]**

Kansas City Minority Business Development Center–KCMO Of-DHCD-Small Business Division **[62072]**

Kansas City Sportshow **[23689]**

Kansas City Star (February 6, 2005); "At Your Service" in **[9815]**, **[13826]**, **[27298]**, **[27617]**

Kansas City Star (February 1, 2005); "Bits and Bytes" in **[4926]**, **[30297]**, **[52509]**

Kansas City Star (February 15, 2005); "Chili Shack Draws Interest" in **[19627]**, **[21470]**, **[38741]**, **[44014]**

Kansas City Star (March 8, 2005); "Contest Challenges Teens to Consider Entrepreneurship" in **[30827]**, **[35375]**, **[56034]**, **[56719]**

Kansas City Star (March 8, 2005); "Corporate Coffers Full of Cash" in **[14889]**, **[27979]**, **[32335]**, **[37983]**

Kansas City Star (February 16, 2005); "E-Trade Financial Cuts Prices of Many Online Transactions" in **[14941]**, **[33824]**, **[38024]**

Kansas City Star (February 8, 2005); "Edgy Bistro Mixes Fancy and Casual" in **[21395]**, **[37561]**

Kansas City Star (March 4, 2005); "Fabric Flower Brooches, a 1930s-Era Wooden Crib, Dustpans Made Out of Old License Plates" in **[1513]**, **[5275]**, **[7164]**, **[12186]**, **[12280]**

Kansas City Star (February 2, 2005); "Identity Theft Still Top Fraud Complaint" in **[22258]**, **[29297]**, **[30231]**

Kansas City Star (March 8, 2005); "It's All in the Family" in **[1444]**, **[15847]**, **[37706]**

Kansas City Star (February 8, 2005); "Job Board for NAIA Looks Like a Winner" in **[9220]**, **[9569]**, **[14175]**, **[42313]**

Kansas City Star (January 23, 2005); "Last Year Was Good to Investors in the American Century Value Fund" in **[15205]**, **[38180]**

Kansas City Star (March 11, 2005); "Late Buying Boosts Crops" in **[26519]**, **[28392]**

Kansas City Star (March 8, 2005); "Local Labs are Working to Perfect DNA Probes" in **[41048]**, **[44089]**, **[50912]**, **[52143]**

Kansas City Star (March 8, 2005); "Loss-Limit Repeal May be Tied to Tax Boost" in **[10877]**, **[40524]**, **[54649]**

Kansas City Star (February 8, 2005); "New Group Tries to Gain OK for River Falls Casino Plan" in **[10881]**, **[20949]**

Kansas City Star (February 9, 2005); "New Rules Cut Health Risks from Lead in Children's Jewelry" in **[12998]**, **[15855]**, **[40559]**, **[46388]**, **[51269]**

Kansas City Star (February 4, 2005); "Progressive Dinner, Segway-Style" in **[21591]**, **[47428]**

Kansas City Star (February 24, 2005); "QuikTrip Policy Points to Dismissal" in **[6772]**, **[41929]**, **[45577]**

Kansas City Star (March 11, 2005); "Restaurant Patrons Can Now Peruse the Menus and Prices of 110 Kansas City Area Restaurants..." in **[2739]**, **[10750]**, **[21601]**, **[54246]**

Kansas City Star (February 4, 2005); "Services Offer Unlimited Music Rentals for a Monthly Fee" in **[4793]**, **[17768]**, **[21350]**, **[23167]**, **[53458]**

Kansas City Star (January 23, 2005); "Think You Know How Much Your Home Is Worth?" in **[10207]**, **[17445]**

Kansas City Star (February 25, 2005); "Three Bars in One" in **[2352]**

Kansas City Star (February 22, 2005); "Union Paychecks Could Be Bigger in 2005, But At a Cost" in **[13509]**, **[26947]**, **[43413]**, **[55316]**

Kansas City Star (December 24, 2004); "Virus Dangers Lurk if Cell Phones Get Too Smart, Experts Warn" in **[5163]**, **[14568]**, **[22415]**

Kansas City Star (February 6, 2005); "Want to Improve Your Hiring and Promotion Odds?" in **[42452]**, **[45795]**

Kansas City Star (January 20, 2005); "Workplace Column" in **[26963]**, **[35165]**

Kansas Department of Administration–Division of Purchases **[60443]**

Kansas Department of Commerce
Agriculture Marketing **[60269]**
Business Development Division **[60270]**
Division of Trade Development **[60271]**
Kansas Technology Enterprise Corp. **[60272]**
Office of Minority Business **[60438]**

Kansas Division of the Budget **[66881]**

Kansas House Standing Committee on Economic Development **[60451]**

"Kansas Investigators Target Wichita Dating Service in Credit-Card Fraud Probe" in *Wichita Eagle* (February 13, 2004) **[7060]**, **[29327]**, **[30236]**, **[31560]**

Kansas Sports, Boat, & Travel Show **[16776]**, **[21192]**, **[23690]**, **[25323]**

Kansas (State) Department of Transportation–Library **[2111]**, **[8738]**, **[16197]**, **[24255]**

Kansas State University
Center for Leadership **[46162]**
Department of Sociology–Population and Research Laboratory **[66882]**

John C. Pair Horticultural Center **[16170]**
Office of the Vice Provost for Research **[60445]**
Richard L.D. and Marjorie J. Morse Department of Special Collections **[7964]**

Kansas State University Research Foundation **[60446]**

Kansas State University, Salina–Libraries **[6547]**

Kansas Technology Enterprise Corporation **[60441]**

Kansas Venture Capital, Inc. **[60442]**

Kaplan Area Chamber of Commerce **[60653]**

"Kar Nut Products Gets New HQ; Snack-Maker Cites Growth for Need for Space" in *Crain's Detroit Business* (Vol. 21, January 10, 2005) **[11636]**, **[28373]**, **[30152]**, **[52687]**

"Karaoke Nation" in *Entrepreneur* (Vol. 31, No. 8, August 2003, pp. 6) **[36394]**

Karl Kardel Consultancy **[1560]**

Karen Voight: Energy Sprint **[19475]**

Karen Voight: Strong & Smooth Moves **[19476]**

Karma Cards: A New Age Guide to Your Future Through Astrology **[17900]**

Karn Charuhas Chapman & Twohey **[1561]**

Karnes City Community Chamber of Commerce **[65330]**

Karpeles Manuscript Library
Buffalo Museum **[1360]**
Charleston Museum **[1361]**
Duluth Museum **[9443]**
Jacksonville Museum **[1362]**
Montecito Exhibit Halls **[1363]**
Santa Barbara Museum **[1364]**
Tacoma Museum **[1365]**

Drew A. Kartiganer, Architect **[1562]**

Arden Kashishian **[26632]**

Kaskaskia College–Small Business Development Center **[59379]**

Katahdin Area Chamber of Commerce **[60755]**

Katalyst Venture Partners **[64556]**

"Kate and Andy Spade Are That Rare Thing: A Great Husband-and-Wife Business Team" in *Fast Company* (March 2005, No. 92, pp. 44) **[5552]**, **[5675]**, **[9627]**, **[36395]**, **[37708]**

"Katrina Cottages At Lowe's" in *Mississippi Business Journal* (Vol. 28, September 2006, No. 36, pp. 23) **[3317]**, **[7395]**, **[48760]**, **[50032]**, **[51218]**

"Katrina Relief Bill May Produce Windfall For a Few Nonprofits" in *Crain's Detroit Business* (Vol. 21, November 7, 2005, No. 45) **[10736]**, **[40492]**

"Katrina's Impact On Insurance Rippling Northward From Coast" in *Mississippi Business Journal* (Vol. 29, January 2007, No. 4, pp. 3) **[13360]**, **[43253]**

Katy Area Chamber of Commerce **[65331]**

"Kauai Businesses Prepare to Welcome Cruise Visitors" in *Pacific Business News* (Vol. 41, No. 26, September 5, 2003, pp. 10) **[24699]**, **[25203]**

Kauai Chamber of Commerce **[59251]**

Kaua'i Community College–Small Business Development Center **[59232]**

Kauffman Center for Entrepreneurial Leadership **[35739]**

Kauffman & Drebing Registered Investment Advisors **[15731]**

Kaufman Global L.L.C. **[3744]**

"Kay Wagner" in *San Diego Business Journal* (Vol. 28, January 15, 2007, No. 3, pp. 34) **[36396]**, **[56290]**

Kay's You Can Have It All: Practical Advice for Doing Well by Doing Good; Mary **[56319]**

KB Partners LLC **[59741]**

KBL Healthcare Ventures **[63123]**

"K.C. Hopps, Ltd." in *Ingram's* (Vol. 28, No. 5, May 2002, pp. 38) **[3130]**, **[21543]**, **[36397]**

"KCBS-KCAL Studio Center Complex" in *San Fernando Valley Business Journal* (Vol. 12, January 2007, No. 1, pp. 12) **[2147]**, **[11336]**, **[21544]**, **[24423]**, **[28374]**, **[32531]**

KCS Applications Inc. **[3371]**

KCS Computer Technology Inc. **[49436]**, **[49620]**

Kean University–Small Business Development Center **[62456]**

Kearney Area Chamber of Commerce **[62273]**

Kearney Chamber of Commerce **[61982]**

Keck & Co. **[26633]**, **[30091]**, **[31390]**, **[47877]**

Burke Keegan **[10762]**

"Keen.com links experts to users via phone" in *InfoWorld* (Vol. 23, No. 5, January 29, 2001, pp. 44) **[5039]**, **[34115]**

Keene State College–Small Business Development Center **[62387]**

Keeneland Association–Library **[12479]**

"Keep it coming" in *Entrepreneur* (Vol. 30, No. 3, March) **[40493]**, **[44560]**

"Keep 'Em Clicking" in *Home Office Computing* (Vol. 19, No. 2, February 2001, pp. 73) **[25880]**, **[31043]**, **[31749]**, **[34116]**

"Keep them flying" in *BlackEnterprise* (Vol. 31, No. 11, June 2001, pp. 74) **[39771]**, **[47964]**, **[52494]**

"Keep fit for free: personal training advice on the Web" in *Black Enterprise* (Vol. 33, No. 3, October 2002, pp. 179) **[14185]**, **[14400]**, **[19410]**, **[20793]**, **[34117]**, **[35558]**

"Keep Hand Injuries at Arm's Length" in *San Jose Mercury News* (February 28, 2005) **[37301]**, **[49108]**

"Keep It Professional" in *Home Office Computing* (Vol. 18, No. 10, October 2000, pp. 89) **[42669]**, **[49513]**

"Keep It Simple" in *Forbes* (Vol. 171, No. 2, January 20, 2003, pp. 108) **[29925]**, **[44561]**

"Keep It Up! Need Some Motivation? Someone To Show You the Ropes?" in *Entrepreneur.com* (Vol. 34, February 2006, No. 2, pp. 98) **[3547]**, **[31181]**

"Keep Large and Small in the Mix" in *Black Enterprise* (Vol. 34, No. 2, September 2003, pp. 36) **[10050]**, **[15195]**, **[38172]**

"Keep their feet to the fire to get moving" in *Crain's Detroit Business* (Vol. 19, No. 14, April 7, 2003, pp. 8) **[10874]**, **[12586]**

"Keep it Simple" in *Entrepreneur.com* (Vol. 34, February 2006, No. 2, pp. 60) **[181]**, **[15196]**, **[23979]**, **[28375]**, **[29926]**, **[31561]**, **[38173]**, **[39425]**, **[41793]**, **[45333]**, **[49109]**, **[50033]**, **[54634]**

"Keep The Ball Rolling" in *Rough Notes* (Vol. 145, No. 2, February 2002, pp. 79) **[13361]**, **[43254]**, **[45334]**, **[51705]**

"Keep in Touch: Be Sure to Reconnect with Your Key Clients" in *Entrepreneur* (Vol. 32, No. 1, January 2004, pp. 79) **[27412]**, **[27653]**

"Keep in Touch...Even in the Air. These New Tech Features Are Ready for Takeoff" in *Entrepreneur* (Vol. 32, December 2004, No. 12) **[5040]**, **[14186]**, **[24424]**, **[30361]**

"Keep on Truckin'" in *Hispanic Business* (Vol. 23, No. 11, November 2001, pp. 56-58) **[18071]**, **[48259]**, **[53822]**

Keep on Truckin News **[25436]**

"Keep on Truckin': These Powerful Trucks Help Keep Your Business Going" in *Entrepreneur* (Vol. 32, October 2004, No. 10, pp. 42) **[18072]**, **[25394]**

Keep Up to Date on Accounts Payable **[26413]**

Keep Up to Date on Payroll **[18795]**

"Keeping America safe" in *Black Enterprise* (Vol. 32, No. 5, Decembe) **[3548]**, **[13081]**, **[22276]**, **[36398]**, **[41794]**, **[44326]**, **[48260]**

"Keeping Art Alive" in *Birmingham Business Journal* (Vol. 20, No. 29, July 18, 2003, pp. 11) **[1687]**, **[20916]**

"Keeping the Balls Rolling" in *Entrepreneur* (Vol. 30, No. 10, October 2002, pp. 39) **[4295]**, **[36399]**

Keeping the Books: Basic Recordkeeping and Accounting for the Small Business **[182]**, **[2925]**, **[23980]**, **[26276]**

"Keeping Customers Clueless?" in *Home Office Computing* (Vol. 18, No. 8, August 2000, pp. 22) **[31750]**, **[34118]**, **[53823]**

Keeping Customers Happy **[31751]**

"Keeping Employees" in *Success* (Vol. 47, No. 5, October 2000, pp. 12) **[37709]**, **[42323]**, **[52434]**

"Keeping an Eye on Corporate America" in *Fortuneit* (Vol. 146, No. 11, November 25, 2002, pp. 44) **[37469]**, **[39426]**

"Keeping to the fairway" in *Harvard Business Review* (Vol. 81, No. 4, April 2003, pp. 29) **[11268]**, **[34963]**, **[54214]**

"Keeping it all in the family" in *BlackEnterprise* (Vol. 31, No. 6, January 2001, pp. 40) **[3318]**, **[37710]**, **[48261]**, **[52553]**

"Keeping It All in the Family" in *Black Enterprise* (Vol. 31, No. 5, December 2000, pp. 66) **[36400]**, **[37711]**, **[48262]**

"Keeping It Legal" in *Small Business Opportunities* (Vol. 12, No. 2, March 2000, pp. 76) **[684]**, **[29328]**, **[40494]**, **[47168]**

"Keeping It Positive" in *Small Business Opportunities* (Vol. 17, May 2005, No. 3, pp. 18, 20) **[28376]**, **[34964]**, **[36401]**

"Keeping It Simple" in *Entrepreneur* (Vol. 28, No. 8, August 2000, pp. 94) **[27148]**, **[45335]**

"Keeping It Together: Maryland Family's Home is a Hub of Tech Activity" in *Black Enterprise* (Vol. 35, November 2004, No. 4, pp. 66) **[13362]**, **[25204]**, **[41795]**

"Keeping Mums" in *Entrepreneur* (Vol. 33, February 2005, No. 2, pp. 71) **[685]**, **[34965]**, **[45336]**, **[47169]**, **[50450]**

"Keeping your computer safe" in *Women in Business* (Vol. 53, No. 7, January-February 2002, pp. 21) **[4710]**, **[6175]**, **[22277]**, **[23060]**, **[49110]**

"Keeping Score" in *Wall Street Journal* (September 12, 2002, pp. B8) **[56747]**

"Keeping pace with technology" in *Women in Business* (Vol. 54, No. 2, March-April 2002, pp. 22) **[33146]**, **[49111]**, **[49514]**

"Keeping Their Options Open" in *Boston Business Journal* (Vol. 23, No. 26, August 1, 2003, pp. 3) **[4711]**, **[23061]**, **[30898]**, **[32532]**, **[38174]**, **[41796]**, **[53346]**

"KeepMedia Inc.: www.keepmedia.com" in *Entrepreneur* (Vol. 31, No. 12, December 2003, pp. 8) **[18891]**, **[34119]**

Keg Restaurants Ltd. **[21858]**

Keiei Senryaku Corp. **[3745]**, **[16628]**, **[30092]**, **[31391]**, **[38552]**, **[46062]**, **[52002]**, **[53100]**

Keizer Chamber of Commerce and Visitor Center **[64234]**

"Keller Graduate School of Management of DeVry University" in *Ingram's* (Vol. 29, No. 8, August 2003, pp. 59) **[33147]**, **[45337]**

Keller and Heckman LLP–Law Firm Library **[8868]**, **[9444]**

Robert J. Keller **[3406]**, **[14666]**

Kellett Investment Group **[66215]**

Kelley, Drye & Warren LLP–Law Library **[9535]**

Kelleys Island Chamber of Commerce **[63710]**

Kellogg Company–Kellogg Information Center **[18502]**

"Kelly Thinks Globally and Earns Locally; International Sales Up 50 Percent Over 2 Years" in *Crain's Detroit Business* (Vol. 21) **[9222]**, **[28377]**, **[43728]**

Kelly's Cajun Grill Franchise Corp. **[21859]**

Kelly's Coffee & Fudge Factory **[11391]**

The Kelsey Group, Inc. **[21860]**, **[34778]**, **[47878]**

Hub Kelsh Inc. **[35300]**

Kelso Longview Chamber of Commerce **[66118]**

Kemmerer/Diamondville Area Chamber of Commerce **[66615]**

Kemper Ventures **[62600]**

The Ken Blanchard Cos. **[35236]**

"Ken Burns's Jeffersonian Pavilion" in *Inc.* (January 1, 2002) **[36402]**, **[45338]**

"Ken Chenault: Dealing Out the Cards" in *Business Week* (February 14, 2005, No. 3920, pp. 42) **[8311]**, **[15197]**, **[30362]**

"Ken Evoy and Neil Tarvin on E-Book PDF Page Formatting" in *Web Marketing Today* (No. 121, February 5, 2003) **[2719]**, **[9148]**

"Ken & Jennifer Miller: 43, 40, Co-Founders of Thousand Mile, in Vista, California" in *Entrepreneur* (Vol. 31, No. 9, September 2003) **[5553]**, **[5676]**

Kenai Chamber of Commerce **[56967]**

Kenai Peninsula Small Business Development Center **[56939]**

Kendall College of Art & Design–Library **[10850]**

Kendallville Area Chamber of Commerce **[59949]**

Kendallville Chamber of Commerce–SBDC Satellite Office **[59827]**

Kenderdine Art Gallery–Archive **[1659]**

Kenmare Association of Commerce **[63527]**

Kenmore-Town of Tonawanda Chamber of Commerce **[62941]**

Kennebec Valley Chamber of Commerce **[60756]**

Kennebunk-Kennebunkport Chamber of Commerce **[60757]**

James O. Kennedy & Co. **[47879]**

Kennedy Group Inc. **[19581]**

Kennesaw State University
　Cox Family Enterprise Center **[37582]**
　Small Business Development Center **[59030]**

Kennett Chamber of Commerce **[61983]**

Kenosha Area Chamber of Commerce **[66432]**

Kent Area Chamber of Commerce **[63711]**

Kent Chamber of Commerce **[58544]**, **[66119]**

Kent County Chamber of Commerce **[60839]**

Kent State University
　Exercise Physiology Lab **[19547]**
　Graduate School of Management **[63890]**

Kent State University Portage Campus–SBDC **[63560]**

Kent State University/Salem Campus–Columbiana County/Salem Small Business Development Center **[63561]**

Kent State University/Stark Campus–Kent/Stark Small Business Development Center **[63562]**

Kent State University at Tuscarawas City–Tuscarawas Small Business Development Center **[63563]**

Kentland Area Chamber of Commerce **[59950]**

Kentucky Cabinet for Economic Development
　Business and Entrepreneurship Development Division **[60469]**
　Community Development Department–Small and Minority Business Division **[60579]**
　International Trade Division–Department for Existing Business Development **[60470]**
　New Business Development Division **[60471]**
　Office of Business Technology **[60472]**
　Small & Minority Business Div. **[60599]**
　Small and Minority Business Division–Office of Export Development **[60473]**
　Small and Minority Business Division–Small and Minority Business Division **[60474]**

Kentucky Chamber of Commerce **[60529]**

Kentucky Department for Libraries and Archives–State Library Division **[66887]**

Kentucky Financial Institutions Directory **[44562]**

Kentucky Highlands Investment Corporation **[60584]**

Kentucky Procurement Assistance Program **[60586]**

Kentucky SBDC–University of Kentucky–Kentucky SBDC **[60453]**

Kentucky (State) Department for Environmental Protection–EPIC Library **[25731]**

Kentucky & Tennessee Procurement Center **[60587]**

Kentucky Transportation Center–Library **[2112]**, **[8739]**, **[16198]**, **[24256]**

Kentucky's Growing Gold **[16328]**

Kentwood Chamber of Commerce **[60654]**

"Kenworth Dealership in Works" in *Birmingham Business Journal* (Vol. 20, No. 37, September 12, 2003, pp. 1) **[18073]**, **[25395]**

Kenyon College–Olin Library–Visual Image Collection **[1660]**, **[17682]**, **[17821]**

KEOGH Consulting Inc. **[20246]**

Keokuk Area Chamber of Commerce **[60162]**

Keon Mitchell B Architectural Lighting Consultants **[49621]**

Kerens Chamber of Commerce **[65332]**

The Kerf **[9489]**

Kerman District Chamber of Commerce **[57570]**

Kermit Chamber of Commerce **[65333]**

Kern River Valley Chamber of Commerce **[57571]**

Kernal's Popcorn Limited **[23567]**

Kernersville Chamber of Commerce **[63391]**

Kernville Chamber of Commerce **[57572]**

Kerr Center for Sustainable Agriculture, Inc. **[19055]**

Kerrville Area Chamber of Commerce **[65334]**

Kersey Area Chamber of Commerce **[58388]**

Aantia Kersey Phd & Associates **[54368]**

Kershaw County Applied Technology Education Campus–Vocational-Technical Library **[4462]**

Kershaw County Chamber of Commerce and Visitors' Center **[64761]**

Kessler Associates **[44204]**

Harold L. Kestenbaum P.C. **[16871]**, **[38974]**

Kestrel Venture Management / Corning Venture Management **[61084]**

Ketab Bookstore **[58267]**

Ketchum Advertising–Library Services **[50739]**

Kettering - Moraine - Oakwood Chamber of Commerce **[63712]**

Kettle Falls Area Chamber of Commerce **[66120]**

Kettle Partners **[59742]**

Kettleman City Chamber of Commerce **[57573]**

Kettleman's Bagel Co. **[21861]**

Kewanee Chamber of Commerce **[59559]**

Kewaunee Area Chamber of Commerce **[66433]**

Keweenaw Peninsula Chamber of Commerce **[61352]**

Key Biscayne Chamber of Commerce **[58870]**

"Key Bored? Innovative Alternatives to the Old QWERTY Keyboard" in *Entrepreneur* (Vol. 33, January 2005, No. 1, pp. 27) **[6700]**, **[49112]**

The Key to Cleanliness **[21698]**

Key Communications Group Inc. **[30093]**, **[31392]**, **[31977]**, **[38553]**, **[47880]**, **[48833]**, **[53101]**

Key Equity Capital Corp. **[63852]**

Key Largo Chamber of Commerce **[58871]**

Key Management Strategies **[31978]**

"Key is getting region's leaders at one table" in *Crain's Detroit Business* (Vol. 19, No. 17, April 28, 2003, pp. 8) **[28378]**, **[32533]**

Key West Chamber of Commerce **[58872]**

KeyCite **[29669]**, **[40896]**

"KeyCorp Named Top SBA Lender" in *Hispanic Business* (January/February 2003, pp. 14) **[44563]**, **[48263]**

KEYGroup **[42980]**

KeyLAN Consulting Inc. **[49437]**, **[49622]**

Keynotes **[16264]**

"Keys to Communication" in *Small Business Opportunities* (Vol. 16, November 2004, No. 6, pp. 10) **[27413]**, **[36403]**

"Keys to Motivation" in *Small Business Opportunities* (Vol. 12, No. 2, March 2000, pp. 94, 96, 146) **[34966]**, **[45339]**

"Keys to Successful Multiple-Unit Franchising" in *Black Enterprise* (Vol. 34, No. 4, November 2003, pp. 157) **[27846]**, **[28379]**, **[37376]**, **[38842]**

Keystone Minority Capital Fund, L.P. **[64557]**

Keystone Venture Capital Management Co. **[64558]**

KFA Services **[50322]**

KFC-Canada **[21862]**

"KFC Forms Moms' Advisory Board" in *Marketing to Women* (Vol. 19, October 2006, No. 10, pp. 3) **[14187]**, **[21545]**, **[41797]**, **[47170]**, **[54215]**

KI Systems Inc. **[6041]**

Kiamichi Area Vo-Tech-Atoka **[64143]**

Kiamichi Technology Center **[64144]**

Kiamichi Technology Center-Stigler **[64145]**

Kibel Green Inc. **[50323]**

"Kick Back and Relax" in *Entrepreneur* **[35540]**, **[54920]**

"Kick the Habit" in *Home Office Computing* (Vol. 17, No. 1, January 1999, pp. 67) **[4712]**, **[20023]**, **[23062]**, **[42670]**, **[49113]**, **[53347]**, **[54961]**

Kick Start Your Dream Business: Getting it Started and Keeping You Going **[39067]**

"Kid-Friendly Business Sources" in *Black Enterprise* (Vol. 37, January 2007, No. 6, pp. 40) **[14188]**, **[25881]**, **[36404]**, **[48264]**, **[52902]**, **[56748]**

"Kid from the capital makes good" in *Hispanic Business* (Vol. 22, No. 11, November 2000, pp. 20) **[14189]**, **[36405]**, **[48265]**

Kid to Kid **[65434]**

"Kid power! Adults need not apply" in *Black Enterprise* (Vol. 32, No. 9, April 2002, pp. 135) **[35541]**, **[56723]**

"Kid stuff: want to light your child's entrepreneurial fire?" in *Entrepreneur* (Vol. 31, No. 5, May 2003, pp. 24) **[36406]**, **[56749]**

Kidbiz: Everything You Need to Start Your Own Business **[56750]**

Kiddie Academy Child Care Learning Centers [5435]

The Kiddie Kobbler Limited [22774]

Kidfacts Research [16872]

"Kids get 411 on Healthy Habits from Moms" in *Marketing to Women* (Vol. 19, October 2006, No. 10, pp. 3) [686], [11637], [12011], [12056], [47171]

"Kids @ Work" in *My Business* (October/November 2002, pp. 42) [42671], [54962]

The Kids' Business Book [56751]

Kids Coach [5436]

Kids Creations [5293]

KiDS CREATION-Buyers' Guide Issue [5286]

Kids Make Puppets: Easy Scarf Marionettes [8228]

Kids Play Harmonica Overnight [17634]

Kids Shots [19328]

Kidspark [5437]

Kidstage [17546]

KidzArt [33366]

Kidzone [29632]

Kiel Area Association of Commerce [66434]

Kies Intelligence Agency [35301]

Kilgore Chamber of Commerce [65335]

Kilgore College [65666]
  SBDC [65040]

"Kill a Brand, Keep a Customer" in *Harvard Business Review* (Vol. 81, No. 12, December 2003, pp. 86) [47172], [48761]

"Kill the Commissions" in *Inc.* (August 1, 2004) [51706]

"Kill The Estate Tax! World War I is over" in *Time Inc.* (Vol. 156, No. 7, August 14, 2000, pp. B20) [54635]

"The Killer Ad Machine" in *Forbes* (December 11, 2000, pp. 168) [34120], [47173]

"Killer Apps for Rent" in *Success* (Vol. 47, No. 3, July 2000, pp. 22) [14190], [36407]

Killer Tactics: Survival Guide for Choosing, Running, Marketing a Small Business in the '90s [47174]

Killington Chamber of Commerce [65788]

Killingworth Chamber of Commerce [58545]

"KILO still rockin' after 25 years in the business" in *Colorado Springs Business Journal* (February 28, 2003) [20321], [36408]

Kilwin's Chocolates and Ice Cream [4334]

Kimball - Banner County Chamber of Commerce [62274]

Kimble County Chamber of Commerce [65336]

Kimmel & Associates [11967]

Kinderdance International, Inc. [5438]

The Kindess Revolution: The Company-Wide Culture Shift That Inspires Phenomenal Customer Service [31752], [45340]

Kinetic Ventures LLC [60873]

KINETIDEX System [8855], [12432], [17235]

King Bear Auto Services Centers, Inc. [24596]

King Chamber of Commerce [63392]

King City and Southern Monterey Chamber of Commerce and Agriculture [57574]

King George County Chamber of Commerce [65917]

"King of the Hill" in *Houston Business Journal* (Vol. 34, No. 15, August 22, 2003, pp. 17) [21546], [28380], [30564], [30899]

"King: 'It's not a recession. It's a disaster'" in *Atlanta Business Chronicle* (Vol. 25, No. 21, November 1, 2002, pp. 6C) [20563], [20917], [32534]

"King Kullen Freshening Up Image" in *Long Island Business News* (May 7, 2004) [11638], [12893], [20131], [30900], [50451], [50614]

King of Prussia Chamber of Commerce at Valley Forge [64462]

Kingdom of Callaway Chamber of Commerce [61984]

Kingfisher Chamber of Commerce [64023]

Kingman Area Chamber of Commerce [57046], [60363]

Kings County Museum–Library [11045]

Kings Mountain - Branch of Cleveland County Chamber of Commerce [63393]

Kings Park Chamber of Commerce [62942]

Kingsburg District Chamber of Commerce [57575]

Kingsbury Associates [58057]

Kingsland - Lake LBJ Chamber of Commerce [65337]

Kingsport Area Chamber of Commerce [64936]

Kingsville Chamber of Commerce [65338]
  Small Business Development Center [65041]

Kingwood Center–Library [12165]

Kinney County Chamber of Commerce [65339]

Kinship Partners [58455]

Kinston-Lenoir County Chamber of Commerce [63394]

"Kiosk Makes Paying Court Fines Easier in McAllen, Texas, But Few Are Using It" in *The Monitor* (September 10, 2003) [15925]

Kiplinger Books and Tapes [58693]

Kiplinger Business Forecasts (January 20, 2005); "Home Health Care Poised to Grow Despite Obstacles" in [447], [18326]

Kiplinger California Letter (Vol. 38, No. 17, September 4, 2002); "Alameda high-tech incubator is expanding" in [39760], [41440], [43034], [55484]

Kiplinger Letter (Vol. 78, January 5, 2007, No. 1); "Businesses Have Faith in the Economy's Resiliency" in [27910], [32295]

Kiplinger Letter (Vol. 78, January 19, 2007, No. 2); "Can Harry Potter Carry the Day for the Book and Film Industries?" in [2688], [9699]

Kiplinger Letter (Vol. 78, January 19, 2007, No. 2); "Clearer Regs on Wellness Programs in the Workplace" in [26770], [40263], [42837]

Kiplinger Letter (Vol. 84, January 26, 2007, No. 4); "Employers Can Expect More Legal Challenges from Workers" in [29220], [42849]

Kiplinger Letter (Vol. 78, January 19, 2007, No. 2); "Firms Will Spend Less on Buildings and Equipment This Year" in [32434], [41688], [49031], [49498]

Kiplinger Letter (Vol. 82, January 12, 2007, No. 1); "Fixing the Alternative Minimum Tax" in [54556]

Kiplinger Letter (Vol. 78, January 19, 2007, No. 2); "Grocery Prices in 2007" in [11624], [32461]

Kiplinger Letter (Vol. 82, January 12, 2007, No. 1); "IRS Will Remove Tax Trap for One-Person S Corporations" in [13350], [41038], [43243], [51489], [54624]

Kiplinger Letter (Vol. 84, January 26, 2007, No. 4); "Is Employer-Sponsored Health Insurance On Its Way Out?" in [13351], [26836], [42871], [43245], [54627]

Kiplinger Letter (Vol. 78, January 19, 2007, No. 2); "January Retail Sales Will Exaggerate Consumer Spending Strength" in [32519], [51214]

Kiplinger Letter (Vol. 78, January 19, 2007, No. 2); "Laws Mandating Paid Sick Leave Will Pass in Several States" in [26840], [29348], [40505], [42873]

Kiplinger Letter (Vol. 78, January 19, 2007, No. 2); "Lawyers on War-Path Filing Wage and Hour Lawsuits" in [14195], [29353], [34129], [42874]

Kiplinger Letter (Vol. 78, January 19, 2007, No. 2); "Mortgage Delinquencies in 2007" in [17412], [38234]

Kiplinger Letter (Vol. 78, January 19, 2007, No. 2); "Peanut Growers to Ramp Up Research Work" in [26528], [50944], [52172]

Kiplinger Letter (Vol. 78, January 5, 2007, No. 1); "Postal Rate Hikes" in [759], [16464], [27669], [40619]

Kiplinger Letter (Vol. 84, January 26, 2007, No. 4); "Prices, Wages in 2007" in [32636], [42883]

Kiplinger Letter (Vol. 78, January 19, 2007, No. 2); "Research Funding New Uses for Eggs, Prune Juice" in [26533], [50956], [52188]

Kiplinger Letter (Vol. 82, January 12, 2007, No. 1); "Retail Stores Taking Health Care Debit Cards Must Upgrade Systems" in [8318], [41089], [51316]

Kiplinger Letter (Vol. 78, January 19, 2007, No. 2); "Semiconductor Industry's Growth Will Slow" in [28753], [41973], [46428]

Kiplinger Letter (Vol. 84, January 26, 2007, No. 4); "Small Businesses Looking to Bolster Web Presence Are in Luck" in [788], [14446], [25965], [47547]

Kiplinger Letter (Vol. 78, January 19, 2007, No. 2); "Small Firms Seeking Government Contracts Will Get More Help" in [39932], [40095], [44660]

Kiplinger Letter (Vol. 78, January 19, 2007, No. 2); "U.S.-Canada Agricultural Trade to Get Stickier in 2007" in [13014], [22409], [26554], [43860]

Kiplinger Letter (Vol. 78, January 19, 2007, No. 4); "U.S. Cotton Farmers Waiting Out the Market for Better Prices" in [13015], [26555], [43861]

Kiplinger Letter (Vol. 78, January 5, 2007, No. 1); "U.S. Exports in 2007" in [13016], [28938], [32763], [43862]

Kiplinger Letter (Vol. 78, January 5, 2007, No. 1); "USDA Plans to Charge Farm Commodity Groups a Fee for Research" in [40801], [50986], [52223]

Kiplinger's Personal Finance Magazine (Vol. 54, No. 8, August 2000, pp. 21); "A Crash Diet for Dot-Coms" in [13935], [27985], [33716], [42598], [53670]

Kiplinger's Personal Finance Magazine (Vol. 55, No. 1, January, 2001, pp. 97); "A Fire Wall for Unwanted E-Mail" in [14043], [33901]

Kiplinger's Personal Finance Magazine (Vol. 54, No. 9, September 2000, pp. 94); "A Risky Business" in [35629], [37076], [56761]

Kiplinger's Personal Finance Magazine (Vol. 54, No. 10, October 2000, pp. 106); "A Simple Choice for Small Firms" in [26911]

Kiplinger's Personal Finance Magazine (Vol. 58, No. 5, May 2004, pp. 21); "A Singular Hookup" in [5109], [17010], [50179]

Kiplinger's Personal Finance Magazine (Vol. 55, No. 1, January, 2001, pp. 128); "A World at their Feet" in [22750], [35732]

Kiplinger's Personal Finance Magazine (Vol. 55, No. 1, January, 2001, pp. 24); "Battle of the Sexes" in [43088]

Kiplinger's Personal Finance Magazine (Vol. 54, No. 12, December 2000, pp. 28); "Buying Tunes Online" in [6136], [17732], [33639], [40263], [44011]

Kiplinger's Personal Finance Magazine (Vol. 55, No. 1, January, 2001, pp. 26); "Closing the Book on Public Records" in [13906], [29154], [33682]

Kiplinger's Personal Finance Magazine (Vol. 54, No. 12, December 2000, pp. 30); "Deals on Wheels" in [46873], [51610]

Kiplinger's Personal Finance Magazine (Vol. 54, No. 10, October 2000, pp. 118); "Disappearing Ink" in [33765], [40314]

Kiplinger's Personal Finance Magazine (Vol. 55, No. 1, January, 2001, pp. 28); "Don't Fall for these Numbers" in [30215], [42604]

Kiplinger's Personal Finance Magazine (Vol. 58, No. 5, May 2004, pp. 20); "Great Time to Go It Alone" in [28230], [32456], [35491]

Kiplinger's Personal Finance Magazine (Vol. 54, No. 10, October 2000, pp. 96); "Have Your Job and Leave It, Too" in [26823]

Kiplinger's Personal Finance Magazine (Vol. 55, No. 1, January, 2001, pp. 98); "High-Tech Trash" in [54201], [54589]

Kiplinger's Personal Finance Magazine (Vol. 54, No. 12, December 2000, pp. 26); "Inking the Deal" in [19882], [34068], [47140], [51204]

Kiplinger's Personal Finance Magazine (Vol. 54, No. 12, December 2000, pp. 150); "Internet To Go" in [5032], [34082], [41773]

Kiplinger's Personal Finance Magazine (Vol. 54, No. 11, November 2000, pp. 98); "Many Ways to Lose" in [30239], [43271]

Kiplinger's Personal Finance Magazine (Vol. 55, No. 1, January, 2001, pp. 26); "Point and Sniff" in [14358], [34358]

Kiplinger's Personal Finance Magazine (Vol. 54, No. 11, November 2000, pp. 130); "Retailers' Siren Song" in [51326], [51798]

Kiplinger's Personal Finance Magazine (Vol. 54, No. 12, January, 2001, pp. 25); "Saving Will Get Sweeter" in [26908], [54735]

Kiplinger's Personal Finance Magazine (Vol. 58, No. 5, May 2004, pp. 21); "Scam Alert" in [30251]

Kiplinger's Personal Finance Magazine (Vol. 54, No. 12, December 2000, pp. 94); "Selling Yourself" in **[34455]**, **[42548]**

Kiplinger's Personal Finance Magazine (Vol. 55, No. 1, January, 2001, pp. 20); "Slower, but Still Strong" in **[32687]**

Kiplinger's Personal Finance Magazine (Vol. 54, No. 12, December 2000, pp. 32); "The Big, Bad Wolf Meets His Match" in **[7253]**, **[16298]**

Kiplinger's Personal Finance Magazine (Vol. 54, No. 9, September 2000, pp. 24); "Why Clip When You Can Clip?" in **[34718]**, **[47745]**

Kiplinger's Personal Finance Magazine (Vol. 54, No. 10, October 2000, pp. 32); "Working at Home" in **[26962]**

Kirby Tours Inc. **[24777]**

Kirbyville Chamber of Commerce **[65340]**

"Kirco buys apartment complex from Beaumont Hospital" in *Crain's Detroit Business* (Vol. 19, No. 10, March 10, 2003, pp. 35) **[1377]**, **[20564]**, **[20918]**

"Kirkland's, Gap Will Close At Leases' End" in *Bradenton Herald* (January 22, 2005) **[28381]**, **[51219]**

Dr. Donald Kirkpatrick **[55040]**

Kirksville Area Chamber of Commerce **[61985]**

Kirkus Reviews **[2772]**

Kirkwood Area Chamber of Commerce **[61986]**

Kirkwood Community College–Small Business Development Center **[60060]**

Kirlan Venture Capital, Inc. **[66216]**

Kirtland Community College–SBDC **[61199]**

"Kiss Privacy Goodbye" in *Fortune* (Vol. 151, January 10, 2005, No. 1, pp. 55) **[22278]**, **[29329]**, **[40495]**, **[41798]**

Kissimmee - Osceola County Chamber of Commerce **[58873]**

Kitchen Cabinet Manufacturers Association **[12268]**

Kitchen Capers **[5394]**

Kitchen Gardener **[12154]**

Kitchen Solvers **[4510]**

Kitchen Table Entrepreneurs: How Eleven Women Escaped Poverty and Became Their Own Bosses **[36409]**, **[56291]**

"Kitchen Table Entrepreneurs" in *Small Business Opportunities* (Vol. 16, November 2004, No. 6, pp. 134) **[36410]**, **[56292]**

The Kitchen Table Millionaire: Home-Based Money-Making Strategies to Build Financial Independence Today **[42672]**

Kitchen Tune-Up, Inc. **[4511]**

Kitchen Wizards **[12249]**

Kittochtinny Historical Society–Library **[11046]**

Kitty Hawk Capital **[63460]**, **[66139]**

Klamath County Chamber of Commerce **[64235]**

"Kleiner Perkins Adds Lane As New GP" in *Venture Capital Journal* (Vol. 40, No. 10, October 2000, pp. 34) **[34121]**, **[44564]**, **[55703]**

Kleiner Perkins Caufield & Byers (Menlo Park) **[58058]**

The Kleper Report on Digital Publishing **[8636]**

Kline Hawkes & Co. **[58059]**

KLM Capital Group **[58060]**

Kluger & Associates Inc. **[7039]**

"Kmart cuts 46 jobs at Troy HQ" in *Crain's Detroit Business* (Vol. 16, No. 49, December 4, 2000, pp. 4) **[51220]**

"Kmart scurries to tie loose ends as approval of Ch. 11 plan nears" in *Crain's Detroit Business* (Vol. 19, No. 15, April 14, 2003) **[29330]**, **[51221]**

"Kmart closings to take another slice from Little Caesar" in *Crain's Detroit Business* (Vol. 19, No. 4, January 27, 2003, pp. 7) **[19634]**, **[28382]**, **[51222]**

"Kmart Makes Branding Pro Its New Chief" in *Black Enterprise* (Vol. 35, December 2004, No. 5, pp. 33) **[12894]**, **[20132]**, **[47175]**, **[50615]**, **[51223]**

KMWorld **[8637]**

"A Knack for Macs" in *Entrepreneur* (Vol. 31, No. 10, October 2003, pp. 56) **[6701]**, **[49114]**

Knifemakers' Guild **[7988]**

Knifex **[48508]**

Knight-Ridder/Tribune Business News (October 28, 2001); "After 70 Years, It's Still a Treat Texas Company to Sell Chick-O-Sticks" in **[4275]**

Knight-Ridder/Tribune Business News (April 11, 2002, pp. ITEM02101008); "Chocolate Maker Plans New Plant in Pauls Valley, Okla" in **[4282]**, **[30519]**, **[48103]**

Knight-Ridder/Tribune Business News (September 25,2001); "Dunkirk, N.Y.-Based Ice Cream Manufacturer Files for Bankruptcy" in **[12774]**

Knight-Ridder/Tribune Business News (March 30, 2002, pp. ITEM02089101); "Easter Is Big Business for Pennsylvania Candy Companies" in **[4287]**, **[28076]**

Knight-Ridder/Tribune Business News (July 29, 2001); "Groups Working on Conflict Resolution for Stock Analysts, Investment Bankers" in **[15059]**, **[17053]**, **[27386]**

Knight-Ridder/Tribune Business News (October 23, 2001, pp. ITEM01296031); "Richmond Times-Dispatch, Va., Business Briefs Column" in **[39900]**, **[44635]**, **[48923]**

Knight-Ridder/Tribune Business News (October 26, 2001, pp. ITEM01299024); "Russell Stover Candies to Close Clarksville, Va. Facility" in **[4307]**

Knight-Ridder/Tribune Business News (Melissa L. Jones, pp. ITEM02087067); "Sandy, Ore., Candy Farm Produces All Things Chocolate" in **[4308]**, **[28741]**

Knight-Ridder/Tribune Business News (October 29, 2001); "Stockton, Calif., Chocolate Company Recognized for Quick Growth" in **[4311]**, **[28828]**

"Knight Ridder's Happy Ending?" in *Business Week* (February 20, 2006, No. 3972, pp. 26) **[15198]**, **[18892]**, **[30685]**, **[50034]**, **[52435]**

Knightdale Chamber of Commerce **[63395]**

Knights Franchise Systems, Inc. **[12716]**

"The Knight's Still Young" in *Home Business* (Vol. 12, October 2005, No. 5, pp. 70) **[5511]**, **[56724]**

Knightstown Indiana Chamber of Commerce **[59951]**

Stan Knipe & Associates **[51442]**

"Knit Loss, Knit Income: Ashworth Inc." in *San Diego Business Journal* (Vol. 28, January 15, 2007, No. 3, pp. 38) **[5554]**, **[5677]**

"Knit One, Stitch Too" in *Charlotte Business Journal* (Vol. 16, No. 17, July 27, 2001, pp. 48) **[8130]**

"Knitting a Close Bond with Dogs" in *Chicago Tribune* (February 16, 2005) **[8013]**, **[8170]**

The Knitting Guild Association **[7989]**

Knob Noster Chamber of Commerce **[61987]**

"Knock on Wood: Lumber Prices Uncertain after 'inventory rally'" in *Barron's* (July 7, 2003, pp. MW11) **[7396]**, **[16307]**, **[44233]**

Knock Your Socks Off Selling **[30901]**, **[51707]**

"Know your limits" in *Entrepreneur* (Vol. 31, No. 6, June 2003, pp. 73) **[29331]**, **[40496]**, **[53824]**

"Know the Rules" in *Black Enterprise* (Vol. 35, December 2004, No. 5, pp. 56) **[29332]**, **[40497]**, **[42673]**, **[54636]**

"Know Thy Customer: How CRM Software Helps One Company Deliver" in *My Business* (October/November 2003, pp. 46) **[4713]**, **[23063]**, **[31753]**, **[53348]**

"Know Thy Worth" in *Entrepreneur.com* (Vol. 34, February 2006, No. 2, pp. 50) **[31182]**, **[39427]**, **[52375]**

Know What You're Selling **[8531]**

Know-Who Based Entrepreneurship from Knowledge Creation to Business Implementation **[36411]**, **[44327]**

"Know Your Customers" in *PC Computing* (April 2000, pp. 94) **[34122]**, **[47176]**, **[53349]**

"Know Your Way Around?" in *Entrepreneur.com* (Vol. 34, January 2006, No. 1, pp. 22) **[18074]**, **[49115]**

Knowing the Prospect **[10310]**, **[15705]**, **[51961]**

"Knowing the Score About False Notes" in *Business Week* (Sept. 11, 2002) **[30237]**

"Knowing What Customers Want" in *Inc.* (August 2005, pp. 22-23) **[31754]**

"Knowing When It's Time" in *Black Enterprise* (Vol. 35, December. 2004, No. 5, pp. 65) **[36412]**, **[38175]**

"Knowledge helped company bounce back" in *Crain's Detroit Business* (Vol. 19, No. 11, March 17, 2003, pp. 14) **[3549]**, **[4714]**, **[23064]**, **[28383]**, **[45341]**

"Knowledge Management: Know What You Know" in *PC Magazine* (July 1, 2000, pp. 165) **[44328]**, **[53825]**

"Knowledge Networks: Making the Brand" in *Venture Capital Journal* (Vol. 41, No. 8, August 2000, pp. 18) **[31755]**, **[44329]**, **[47177]**, **[50616]**

"Knowledge On Demand" in *PC Computing* (March 2000, pp. 128) **[33148]**, **[34123]**

"Knowledge is power" in *The Economist* (Vol. 356, No. 8189, September 23, 2000, pp. NA) **[44330]**

Knowledge, Technology & Policy **[13105]**

Knox City Chamber of Commerce **[65341]**

Knox College–Center for the Fine Arts Music Library **[17683]**

Knox County Chamber of Commerce **[59952]**, **[60530]**

Knoxville Area Chamber Partnership **[64937]**

Knoxville Business College–Library **[12747]**, **[53133]**

Knoxville Chamber of Commerce and Economic Development **[60163]**

Knoxville News-Sentinel (November 30, 2003); "Couple First to Open Bed-and-Breakfast Under New Knoxville, Tenn. Rules" in **[2435]**, **[37619]**

Koach Enterprises **[38975]**

Koch Group Inc. **[3746]**, **[16629]**, **[31393]**, **[47881]**

Koch Ventures **[57090]**

Kocham Business Directory **[43729]**

Kochman Mavrelis Associates Inc. **[48640]**

Kodaly Envoy **[17622]**

Kodaly Society of Canada, Alla Breve **[17623]**

Kodiak Area Chamber of Commerce **[56968]**

The Koffee Kiosk **[15926]**

"Kohl's Announces Plans to Open Its First Baltimore County, Md. Store" in *Baltimore Sun* (April 11, 2003) **[28384]**, **[51224]**

"Kohl's, Lowe's Set to Move into WNY" in *Business First Buffalo* (Vol. 19, No. 47, August 15, 2003, pp. 1) **[11890]**, **[12891]**, **[51225]**, **[52688]**, **[53448]**, **[53731]**

Kohn Engineering **[3259]**, **[7618]**

Kohr Bros. Frozen Custard & Smoothie Station **[12834]**

Kokomo - Howard County Chamber of Commerce **[59953]**

Kokopelli Mexican Grill **[21863]**

Kolache Factory, Inc. **[2303]**

Komei Inc. **[27590]**

Kona Kohala Chamber of Commerce **[59252]**

Konawa Chamber of Commerce **[64024]**

T. Kondos Associates **[49623]**

The Konlin Letter **[15657]**

Kora Management Ltd. **[7619]**

"Koran-Friendly Lenders" in *Business Week* (February 14, 2005, No. 3920, pp. 12) **[10051]**, **[17401]**

Korea Trade Promotion Center **[43511]**

Korean Chamber of Commerce **[57576]**

Kosciusko-Attala Chamber of Commerce **[61805]**

Kostka & Company Inc. **[3747]**, **[16630]**, **[31394]**, **[46063]**

Kott Koatings, Inc. **[19787]**

Kountze Chamber of Commerce **[65342]**

Kouts Chamber of Commerce **[59954]**

Koya Japan **[21864]**

KPMG

    Research Centre **[423]**, **[2996]**, **[24182]**

    Resource Centre **[424]**

KPMG L.L.P.

    Library **[2997]**

    Resource Centre **[2998]**

Kraft Foods, Inc.–Technical Information Center **[18503]**

"Kraft Not Alone" in *Crain's Chicago Business* (Vol. 30, February 2007, No. 6, pp. 8) **[37470]**, **[47178]**, **[50452]**, **[50617]**

Steven E. Kramer C.P.A. **[372]**

L.G. Kranick & Associates **[50324]**

Krantz Marketing Services L.L.C. **[47882]**

Kremmling Area Chamber of Commerce and Economic Development Commission **[58389]**

Krieger's Pub & Grill [21865]

Kroll Zolfo Cooper L.L.C. [373], [3748], [3977], [16631], [26431], [31395]

Charles A. Krueger [26432], [38554]

Krupin's Toll-Free Environmental Directory [9365], [37302]

The Krystal Co. [21866]

KSBDC Lead Center–Fort Hays State University [60255]

K.T. Analytics, Inc.–Library [24257]

KTB Ventures / KTB Venture Capital [58061]

Kubba Consultants Inc. [3749], [31396], [47883], [48834], [51002]

William E. Kuhn & Associates [3750], [16632], [31397], [35237], [38555], [42981], [46064], [52003]

Kumon Canada Inc. [25479]

Kumon North America, Inc. [33367]

Kuna Chamber of Commerce [59312]

Kung Fu Workout [19477]

Kushell Associates Inc. [38976]

Kutler Consultants [31979]

Kutztown University–Small Business Development Center [64332]

KV Marketing Inc. [12247], [12337]

Kwicksilver Systems, LLC [2052], [22678]

Kwik Dry Carpet & Upholstery Cleaning [25559]

Kwik Kerb [16079]

Kwik Kloset [20041]

Kwik Kopy Business Centers [885], [6051], [7857], [19934]

Kwik-Kopy Printing Canada [19935]

Kyle Area Chamber of Commerce and Visitors' Bureau [65343]

Kyocera International, Inc. [58062]

KZF Design Inc. [1149]

L

L. Michael Schwartz, P.A. [31495], [39013]

L & W Investigations, Inc. [19994]

La Barge Chamber of Commerce [66616]

La Boxing Franchise Corp. [19513]

La Canada - Flintridge Chamber of Commerce [57577]

La Conner Chamber of Commerce [66121]

L.A. County Arboretum and Botanic Garden–Plant Science Library [11523]

"L.A. County Econowatch" in *San Fernando Valley Business Journal* (Vol. 12, January 2007, No. 1, pp. 23) [10052], [15199], [32535], [38176]

La Crescent Chamber of Commerce [61608]

La Crosse Area Chamber of Commerce [66435]

La Crosse Chamber of Commerce [60364]

"L.A. Fitness Works on Second Long Island Location" in *Long Island Business News* (February 13, 2004) [19411]

La Grange Area Chamber of Commerce [65344]

La Habra Area Chamber of Commerce [57578]

"La Habra, Calif., Entrepreneur Starts Errand-Running Service for Busy Workers" in *San Gabriel Valley Tribune* (July 8, 2004) [19076], [47179], [51226], [56293]

"La Habra, Calif., Resident Builds Needlework Empire" in *Orange County Register* (February 12, 2001) [8131], [16412], [33455], [42538], [56058]

L.A. Italian Kitchen Franchise Corp. [19681]

La Jolla Town Council [57579]

La Jolla Village News [18959]

La Junta Chamber of Commerce [58390]

La Junta SBDC–Otero Junior College [58305]

La Mirada Chamber of Commerce [57580]

"A La Modem" in *Entrepreneur* (Vol. 31, No. 8, August 2003, pp. 46) [6702], [14191], [49116]

La Paletera Franchise Systems, Inc. [12835]

La Palma Chamber of Commerce [57581]

La Pine Chamber of Commerce [64236]

La Porte-Bayshore Chamber of Commerce [65345]

La Porte City Chamber of Commerce [60164]

La Quinta Chamber of Commerce [57582]

La Rabida Children's Hospital and Research Center [41385]

La Salsa [21867]

L.A. Shapes, Inc. [19514]

"La-Van Hawkins Linked to Philadelphia Corruption Probe" in *Black Enterprise* (Vol. 35, September 2004, No. 2) [29333], [36413], [40498]

La Verne Chamber of Commerce [57583]

La Veta/Cuchara Chamber of Commerce [58391]

L.A. Weight Loss Centers, Inc. [26057]

La-Z-Boy Inc. [12348]

Laban/Bartenieff Institute of Movement Studies [8501]

Labanon/Wilson County Chamber of Commerce–Satellite Office of Memphis Tennessee State University–SBDC [64862]

Label Letter [55329]

Labette Community College [60449]

Labmedica [17207]

Labor Arbitration in Government [17066]

Labor Center Reporter [55330]

"Labor and delivery" in *WorkingWoman* (Vol. 25, No. 2, February 2000, pp. 28) [28385]

"Labor Department Seeks Repeal of Regulation Threatening UI Reserves" in *My Business* (February/March 2003, pp. 19) [26839], [40499]

Labor and Employment Law Library [29670]

Labor and Employment Relations Association [55347]

Labor Finders International, Inc. [9273]

"A labor in progress" in *Hispanic Business* (Vol. 22, No. 9, September 2000, pp. 20) [33149]

"Labor of Love" in *Entrepreneur* (Vol. 31, No. 9, September 2003, pp. 110) [20259], [23765], [31756], [36414], [38843]

"A Labor of Love: Have You Lost That Lovin' Feeling For Your Business?" in *Entrepreneur* (Vol. 32, November 2004, No. 11, pp. 130) [30565], [36415]

Labor Management [55335]

"Labor pains: if immigration laws tighten, all entrepreneurs could feel the squeeze" in *Entrepreneur* (Vol. 31, No. 5, May 2003) [29334], [40500], [42324]

Labor Relations and Collective Bargaining [55297]

Labor Relations: Development, Structure, Process [55298]

"Labor Relations" in *Inc.* (Volume 27, December 2005, No. 12, pp. 34) [29335], [55299]

Labor Relations Week [55331], [55340]

Labor Research Association [55348]

Labor Union Congress of Quebec [55275]

Laboratory Compliance Insider [17208]

Laboratory Conditions: Using Chemicals Safely [17220], [56635]

Laboratory Medicine [17209]

Laboratory Product News [17210]

Laboratory Technician Training [17221]

"Labor's Fate Tied to Delphi's" in *Crain's Detroit Business* (Vol. 21, October 10, 2005, No. 43, pp. 1) [1943], [55300]

Laborwatch [29601]

Labrador Ventures [58063]

Lac Du Flambeau Chamber of Commerce [66436]

Lacey Thurston County Chamber of Commerce [66122]

"Lack of Lease Could Cost US Airways" in *Pittsburgh Business Times* (Vol. 23, No. 5, August 22, 2003, pp. 3) [30363], [39849]

"Lack o' tax: the return from these funds all yours" in *Entrepreneur* (Vol. 30, No. 3, March 2002, pp. 66) [15200], [38177], [54637]

Lackawanna Area Chamber of Commerce [62943]

Lacloche Manitoulin Business Assistance Corp. [38556]

Ladies Apparel Contractors Association [16212]

Ladies Professional Golf Association [11247]

Ladies Workout Express [19515]

Ladonia Chamber of Commerce [65346]

Lady of America [19516]

Lady Lake Area Chamber of Commerce [58874]

Ladybug Organics [9496], [16154]

LaFarge Canada Inc.–Technical Library [16989]

"Lafayette 148 Had High Hopes For Its New Chinese Factory" in *Inc.* (Volume 27, December 2005, No. 12, pp. 62, 66) [5555], [12991], [40501], [43730]

Lafayette Chamber of Commerce [57584], [58392]

Lafayette County Chamber of Commerce [58875]

Lafayette - West Lafayette Chamber of Commerce [59955]

"Lagging behind? Get ahead of jet lag before it gets the best of you" in *Entrepreneur* (Vol. 31, No. 6, June 2003, pp. 24) [30364]

Lago Vista Area Chamber of Commerce [65347]

Lagrange County Chamber of Commerce [59956]

LaGrange - Troup County Chamber of Commerce [59129]

LaGuardia Community College–SBDC [62763]

Laguna Beach Chamber of Commerce [57585]

Laguna Niguel Chamber of Commerce [57586]

LaJunta Small Business Development Center [58306]

Lake Alfred Chamber of Commerce [58876]

Lake Arrowhead Communities Chamber of Commerce [57587]

Lake Benton Area Chamber of Commerce and Convention and Visitors Bureau [61609]

Lake Buchanan - Inks Lake Chamber of Commerce and Tourist Center [65348]

Lake Capital Partners, Inc. [59743]

Lake Champlain Islands Chamber of Commerce [65789]
    SBDC [65764]

Lake Champlain Region Chamber of Commerce [65790]

Lake Chelan Chamber of Commerce [66123]

Lake Cities Chamber of Commerce [65349]

Lake City Area Chamber of Commerce [61353], [61610]

Lake City Betterment Association [60165]

Lake City - Columbia County Chamber of Commerce [58877]

Lake City - Hinsdale County Chamber of Commerce [58393]

Lake County Chamber of Commerce [59560], [64237]

Lake County Economic Development Center–SBDC [63564]

Lake Crystal Area Chamber of Commerce [61611]

Lake Elsinore Valley Chamber of Commerce [57588]

Lake Erie Islands Historical Society–Library [11047]

Lake Forest - Lake Bluff Chamber of Commerce [59561]

Lake Gaston Chamber of Commerce [63396]

Lake George Regional Chamber of Commerce [62944]

Lake Gogebic Area Chamber of Commerce [61354]

Lake Granbury Area Chamber of Commerce [65350]

Lake Guntersville Chamber of Commerce [56870]

Lake Havasu Area Chamber of Commerce [57047]

Lake Los Angeles Chamber of Commerce [57589]

Lake Michigan College Satellite Office–Small Business Development Center–Corporate and Community Involvement [61200]

Lake Mills Area Chamber of Commerce [66437]

Lake Minnetonka Chamber of Commerce [61612]

Lake Norman Chamber and Convention and Visitors Bureau [63397]

Lake Oswego Chamber of Commerce [64238]

Lake of the Ozarks West Chamber of Commerce [61988]

Lake Park Area Chamber of Commerce and Visitors Center [59130]

Lake Placid Chamber of Commerce [58878], [62945]

Lake Placid Satellite–Essex City Business Council–North Country SBDC [62764]

Lake Region State College [63545]

Lake Shore Capital Partners [59744]

Lake Station Chamber of Commerce [59957]

"Lake Success Based Astoria Financial Finds Fewer Acquisition Opportunities..." in *Long Island Business News* (Mar. 5, 2004) [10053], [15201], [32536], [50035]

Lake Tahoe Community College [58231]

Lake Tawakoni Area Chamber of Commerce and CVB [65351]

Lake Township Chamber of Commerce [63713]

Lake Vermilion Area Chamber of Commerce [61613]

Lake View East Chamber of Commerce [59562]

Lake Village Chamber of Commerce [57185]

Lake Wales Area Chamber of Commerce [58879]

Lake Weir Chamber of Commerce [58880]

Lake Whitney Chamber of Commerce [65352]

Lake Wisconsin Chamber of Commerce [66438]

Lake Wylie Chamber of Commerce [64762]

Lake Zurich Area Chamber of Commerce [59563]

Lakehead University–Resource Centre for Occupational Health and Safety [56690]

Lakeland Area Chamber of Commerce [58881]

"Lakeland-Based Harrell's Fertilizer Establishes Itself as a National Supplier" in *Ledger* (March 6, 2005) [16114]

"Lakeland, Fla.-Based Health Club Chain Survives 20 Years in Changing Business" in *Lakeland Ledger* (August 15, 2002) [2342], [28386]

Lakeland Ledger (August 15, 2002); "Lakeland, Fla.-Based Health Club Chain Survives 20 Years in Changing Business" in [2342], [28386]

Lakeport Regional Chamber of Commerce [57590]

Lakes Area Chamber of Commerce [61355]

Lakeshore Chamber of Commerce [59958], [61356]

Lakeside Chamber of Commerce [57591], [64239]

Lakeside-Somers Chamber of Commerce [62177]

Lakeview Area Chamber of Commerce [61357]

Lakeview Center, Inc.–Library [54382]

"Lakeway Inn Gets $1.5 M Remodel" in *Bellingham Business Journal* (January 2007, pp. A1) [12587], [28387], [30365]

Lakewood Area Chamber of Commerce [66439]

Lakewood Chamber of Commerce [62521], [63714], [66124]

"Lakewood Hotel Draws Lofty Rating From Chain" in *Bradenton Herald* (February 3, 2005) [12588], [25205], [30366]

Lakewood Small Business Development Center–Denver satellite Office [58307]

Lam Partners Inc. [49624]

Lamar Chamber of Commerce [58394]

Lamar Community College [58478]

Lamar County Chamber of Commerce [65353]

Lamar State College at Port Arthur–Small Business Development Center [65042]

Lamar University

    Mary and John Gray Library–Justice Cookery Collection [7833]

    Small Business Development Center [65043]

Lamar's Donuts [2304]

The Lambda Funds [63124]

Lambda Philatelic Journal [5846]

"Lambeau Leap" in *Business Journal-Milwaukee* (Vol. 20, No. 52, September 12, 2003, pp. A15) [7397]

Lambertville Area Chamber of Commerce [62522]

Lamesa Area Chamber of Commerce [65354]

Laminating Design and Technology [10835], [12330]

Lamoille Economic Development Corp.–SBDC [65765]

Lampasas County Chamber of Commerce [65355]

LAN Solutions [49438], [49625]

Lancaster Area Chamber of Commerce [62946], [66440]

Lancaster Chamber of Commerce [65356]

Lancaster Chamber of Commerce and Industry [64463]

Lancaster County Chamber of Commerce [64763], [65918]

Lancaster Fairfield County Chamber of Commerce [63715]

Lancaster Mennonite Historical Society [10919]

Lancaster New Era (January 8, 2004); "Lancaster, Pa.-Area Restaurateur Markets Business with Internet-Based Kiosk" in [15927], [21547], [34124]

"Lancaster, Pa.-Area Restaurateur Markets Business with Internet-Based Kiosk" in *Lancaster New Era* (January 8, 2004) [15927], [21547], [34124]

Lancet Capital / Caduceus Capital Partners [64559]

The Lancz Letter [15658]

LAND [16041]

"Land Bank South Distributes $3 Million" in *Mississippi Business Journal* (Vol. 29, January 2007, No. 2, pp. 8) [38178]

"Land use requires regional cooperation" in *Crain's Detroit Business* (Vol. 19, No. 14, April 7, 2003, pp. 9) [28388], [37303]

"Land of the Free" in *Fast Company* (May 2001, pp. 125) [32537], [39428]

Land Line [25437]

Land O'Lakes Chamber of Commerce [66441]

Land Survey Calculator [23780]

Land Survey Review Manual [23766]

Land Surveyor-in-Training Sample Examination [23767]

LandaJob Advertising Staffing Specialists [6042]

Landauer Realty Group, Inc.–Information Center [20767], [21111]

Lander Area Chamber of Commerce [66617]

"Landing the big fish" in *Crain's Detroit Business* (Vol. 19, No. 6, February 10, 2003, pp. 3) [36416], [51708]

"Landlords keep on plugging" in *San Francisco Business Times* (Vol. 16, No. 42, May 24, 2002, pp. 3) [20054], [20565], [20919], [41799]

"Landlords may design leases to deter subleasing" in *Atlanta Business Chronicle* (Vol. 25, No. 21, November 1, 2002, pp. 11C) [20566], [20920], [21329]

"Landlords shaking up broker teams" in *Atlanta Business Chronicle* (Vol. 25, January 3, 2003, No. 30, pp. 3A) [20567], [20921], [21330]

Landmark Partners, Inc. [58598]

Landor Associates [6043]

The Landplan Collaborative Ltd. [10601]

Landscape Architect and Specifier News [16042]

Landscape Architecture [16043]

Landscape Architecture Foundation [15995], [16101]

The Landscape Contractor [16044]

Landscape Design: An International Survey [16018]

Landscape Detailing [16019]

Landscape Ecology [16045]

Landscape Equipment Safety for the 90s [16057], [16128]

"Landscape shifts to exclude midsize firms" in *Atlanta Business Chronicle* (Vol. 25, November 15, 2002, No. 23 pp. S8) [16816], [20133], [47180]

Landscape Industry Show [16063]

Landscape Journal [16046]

The Landscape Lighting Book [16020]

Landscape Management [16047], [16121]

Landscape Management Greenbook-Buyers Guide Issue [16021]

Landscape Nursery Council [11412], [15964], [15996]

Landscape Tools: Use and Safety [16058], [16129]

Landscape Trades [11468], [15969], [16048]

Landscapers Supply Franchise Corp. [16155]

Landscaping Business [15982], [34125], [42539], [47181]

Landscaping & Ground Covers [16130]

Landscaping New Homes [16022]

Landscaping: Principle and Practices [16023]

Landscaping for Small Spaces [16024]

Landscaping with Wildflowers: An Environmental Approach to Gardening [16025]

Lane Community College

    Oregon SBDC [64159]

    Oregon SBDC–State Network Office [64160]

Lane County Area Chamber of Commerce [60365]

Lang Michener LLP–Library [29698]

Langenwalter Carpet Dyeing [25560]

Langley South Whidbey Chamber of Commerce [66125]

Langston University–Small Business Development Center [63913]

"The Language of Business" in *My Business* (November/December 2001, pp. 17) [27414], [43731]

"Language Is a Virus" in *PC Computing* (March 2000, pp. 62) [14192], [27415], [34126]

Language Leaders Franchising L.L.C. [25110], [33368]

"Language and Markets in the U.S." in *Hispanic Business* (December 2002, pp. 16, 18, 20) [687], [47182], [53826]

"Language of the Middle Class" in *Hispanic Business* (December 2003, pp. 28-30, 32) [36417], [47183]

"The language of safety" in *Rough Notes* (Vol. 146, No. 4, April 2003, pp. 24) [13363], [43255], [48569], [56568]

The Language of Real Estate [20568]

"The Language of Sales" in *My Business* (October/November 2003, pp. 43) [688], [47184]

The Language Workshop for Children [25480]

Languages Inc. [25102]

Lansing Chamber of Commerce [59564]

Lansing Community College–Small Business Development Center [61201]

Lansing Regional Chamber of Commerce [61358]

Jeffrey Lant Associates Inc. [10763], [16487], [47884], [50501]

Lantis Fireworks & Lasers [24778]

"Lap of Luxury" in *Small Business Opportunities* (Vol. 14, No. 1, January 2002, pp. 90) [21300], [35542]

Lapeer Area Chamber of Commerce [61359]

Lapeer Development Corp.–Small Business Development Center [61202]

Lapels Dry Cleaning [8934]

Lapidary Journal-Annual Buyers' Directory Issue [15852]

"Lapping It Up" in *Entrepreneur* (Vol. 33, September 2005, No. 9, pp. 48) [6669], [6703], [49117], [51133]

Laptop Training Solutions [6378]

Laramie Area Chamber of Commerce [66618]

Laramie SBDC–Region IV Satellite Office [66598]

Laredo Development Foundation–Small Business Development Center [65044]

Laredo - Webb County Chamber of Commerce [65357]

"Large industrial gas companies setting sights on Detroit" in *Crain's Detroit Business* (Vol. 19, No. 4, January 27, 2003, pp. 21) [28389], [30153], [50036]

Large and Midrange Systems and Software 6471, 6647

"Large Potential in Small Companies" in *Forbes* (Vol. 172, No. 13, December 22, 2003, pp. 220) [10054], [15202], [38179]

"Largest Nonprofits; Based on 2004 Gross Receipts, Figures in Millions" in *Crain's Detroit Business* (Vol. 21, Nov. 7, 2005, No. 45) [10737]

"Largest Shareholder Urges Knight Ridder to Sell Itself" in *Sacramento Bee* (November 2, 2005) [15203], [18893], [50037], [52436]

Larimer County Small Business Development Center–Front Range Community College [58308]

"The Lark" in *Crain's Detroit Business* (Vol. 21, November 7, 2005, No. 45, pp. 16) [21548], [30902], [37712]

Larkspur Chamber of Commerce [57592]

Larned Area Chamber of Commerce [60366]

Larry Chase's Web Digest for Marketers (WDFM) [14654], [16839], [47796]

"Larry Nelson" in *Black Enterprise* (Vol. 34, No. 5, December 2003, pp. 68) [21549], [38844], [39282], [45342]

Larry's Giant Subs [8555]

LaRue County Chamber of Commerce [60531]

Las Animas - Bent County Chamber of Commerce [58395]

Las Vegas Chamber of Commerce [62355]

"Las Vegas Hotel Revenues Surge as Casino Earnings Slump" in *Las Vegas Review-Journal* (February 17, 2004) [10875], [12589], [24700], [25206], [28390]

Las Vegas Insider [10899]

Las Vegas Review-Journal (November 6, 2003); "Automotive Aftermarket Products Show in Las Vegas Is Gaining in Popularity" in [1909], [24890]

Las Vegas Review-Journal (April 11, 2003); "Construction Defect Bill Is Progressing in Nevada, Lobbyist Says" in [7296], [13242], [29163], [40280], [43134]

Las Vegas Review-Journal (December 21, 2004); "Henderson, Nev., Boot Camp Teaches How to Combat Hackers" in **[14109]**, **[22247]**, **[36275]**

Las Vegas Review-Journal (April 11, 2003); "High-Definition TV Coming Slowly into View, Officials at Broadcasters Expo Say" in **[24415]**

Las Vegas Review-Journal (February 17, 2004); "Las Vegas Hotel Revenues Surge as Casino Earnings Slump" in **[10875]**, **[12589]**, **[24700]**, **[25206]**, **[28390]**

Las Vegas-San Miguel Chamber of Commerce **[62698]**

"Las Vegas Sands Sets IPO Strike Price" in *Tradeshow Week* (Vol. 34, December 13, 2004, No. 50, pp. 3) **[10876]**, **[15204]**, **[22523]**, **[24964]**, **[50038]**, **[55109]**

Las Vegas SBDC–SBDC **[62327]**

LaSalle Capital Group, Inc. **[59745]**

"Laser 'Breakthrough': Changing the Silicon Game" in *San Jose Mercury News* (March 7, 2005) **[7735]**, **[41800]**, **[50907]**, **[52138]**

"Laser Business Fails to Shine" in *Orlando Business Journal* (Vol. 20, No. 5, July 18, 2003, pp. 1) **[40046]**, **[40050]**, **[40195]**, **[41801]**

"Laser pointers" in *Entrepreneur* (Vol. 30, No. 2, February 2002, pp. 36) **[6704]**, **[49118]**

Laser Stop Hair Removal and Cosmetic Clinics of Canada **[7936]**

Lassen County Chamber of Commerce **[57593]**

Last Best Hope: How to Start & Grow Your Own Business **[52903]**

"Last But Not Least" in *Entrepreneur* (Vol. 27, No. 12, December 1999, pp. 144) **[51709]**

"The Last Frontier of Beer" in *Success* (Vol. 47, No. 5, October 2000, pp. 32) **[3113]**, **[35543]**

"Last-Minute Shoppers Boost Holiday Retail Sales" in *Sacramento Bee* (December 29, 2005) **[28391]**, **[51227]**, **[52359]**

"The last thing you should do is panic" in *Fast Company* (May 2001, pp. 90) **[29927]**, **[32538]**

"Last Year Was Good to Investors in the American Century Value Fund" in *Kansas City Star* (January 23, 2005) **[15205]**, **[38180]**

"Late Buying Boosts Crops" in *Kansas City Star* (March 11, 2005) **[26519]**, **[28392]**

"Later Easter, War Crimp March Retail Sales" in *Atlanta Journal-Constitution* (April 11, 2003) **[28393]**, **[51228]**

Lateral Marketing: New Techniques for Finding Breakthrough Ideas **[689]**, **[47185]**

"Laterals keep coming" in *Black Enterprise* (Vol. 33, No. 198, March 24, 2003, pp. AA2) **[29336]**, **[32539]**

"Laterals keep coming" in *Daily Business Review* (Vol. 77, No. 198, March 24, 2003, pp. AA2) **[29337]**, **[50039]**, **[53827]**

"Laterals? Pass" in *Daily Business Review* (Vol. 77, No. 146, Jan. 7, 2003, pp. A8) **[29338]**, **[50040]**, **[53828]**

"The Latest and Greatest Disease" in *Fortune* (Vol. 142, No. 9, October 16, 2000, pp. 312X) **[49119]**, **[53350]**

The Latest Scoop **[2086]**

Lathrop Chamber of Commerce **[57594]**

Debra F. Latimer Nutrition Associates **[18481]**

William Latimore Associates **[21085]**

Latin American Chamber of Commerce **[59714]**
Latin American Chamber of Commerce **[59769]**
Small Business Development Center **[59380]**

Latin American Markets: A Guide to Company and Industry Sources **[43732]**

"Latin Americans Continue to Snap Up Condo Supply" in *South Florida Business Journal* (Vol. 23, No. 48, July 4, 2003, pp. 6) **[7398]**, **[20569]**, **[20922]**

Latin Business Association **[47999]**

Latin Chamber of Commerce of Nevada **[62356]**

Latin Chamber of Commerce of U.S.A. **[43512]**

"Latin Food Boom" in *Hispanic Business* (March 2005, pp. 15) **[21550]**, **[53829]**

"Latinas' Businesses and Earnings are Seeing Major Growth" in *Marketing to Women* (Vol. 19, October 2006, No. 10, pp. 2) **[28394]**, **[47186]**, **[48266]**, **[48570]**, **[56294]**

Latino American Management Association **[48000]**

Latino Income Tax **[24132]**

"Latinocare Goes Public" in *Hispanic Business* (June 2002, pp. 28) **[13364]**, **[15206]**, **[43256]**, **[48267]**, **[50041]**

Latrobe Area Chamber of Commerce **[64464]**

Latterell Venture Partners **[58064]**

Lauderdale By The Sea Chamber of Commerce **[58882]**

Lauderdale County Chamber of Commerce **[64938]**

"Laugh track" in *Entrepreneur* (Vol. 30, No. 2, February 2002) **[3550]**, **[17901]**, **[36418]**, **[45343]**

"Laughing All the Way to the Bank" in *Harvard Business Review* (Vol. 81, No. 9, September 2003, pp. 16) **[38181]**, **[45344]**

Laughing Bear Newsletter **[2773]**

Robert J. Laughlin & Associates **[49626]**

Laughlin Chamber of Commerce **[62357]**

"The Launch" in *Inc.* (October 17, 2000, pp. 57) **[28395]**, **[52904]**, **[55704]**

Launchcyte LLC **[64560]**

Launching a Business on the Web **[37156]**

Launching New Ventures **[29928]**

Launching Onto the Web: A Small Business View **[37065]**

"A launching point to the next step" in *Hispanic Business* (Vol. 22, No. 6, June 2000, pp. 42) **[31096]**, **[35544]**, **[39970]**, **[48268]**

Launching onto the Web: A Small Business View **[37157]**

Launching Your First Small Business: Make the Right Decisions During Your First 90 Days **[52905]**

Launchworks Inc. **[66665]**

Laund-Ur-Mutt **[19097]**

Laundries: Are They a Good Business to Get into? **[8907]**

Laurel Chamber of Commerce **[62178]**

"Laurel County, Ga., Bed and Breakfast Promises Relaxation in Scenic Spot" in *Macon Telegraph* (March 8, 2004) **[2445]**, **[25207]**

Laurel Highlands Chamber of Commerce **[64465]**

"Laurel Touby" in *Entrepreneur* (Vol. 30, No. 2, February 2002, pp. 18) **[14193]**, **[35545]**, **[50908]**

Laurens Chamber of Commerce **[60166]**

Laurentian Chamber of Commerce **[61614]**

The Laurier Institute **[66754]**

Laurinburg - Scotland County Area Chamber of Commerce **[63398]**

Lava Hot Springs Chamber of Commerce **[59313]**

Laval University
Centre for Entrepreneurship and Small Business **[53143]**
Human Nutrition Research Group **[18525]**

Laverne Area Chamber of Commerce **[64025]**

Lavista Area Chamber of Commerce **[62275]**

Lavonia Chamber of Commerce **[59131]**

"Law Away" in *Entrepreneur* (Vol. 31, No. 8, August 2003, pp. 53) **[10055]**, **[15207]**, **[38182]**

The Law of Corporations, Partnerships, & Sole Proprietorships Instructor's Guide **[51490]**, **[54306]**

The Law Digest **[29671]**

Law Firm Inc. (December 2004); "Accounting for the Budget" in **[59]**, **[26140]**, **[27076]**

Law Firm Inc. (October 2004); "Moving Daze" in **[20600]**, **[29389]**, **[30160]**, **[52701]**

Law Firm Inc. (August 2004); "Out Of Pocket, Out Of Mind" in **[27160]**, **[29430]**, **[31053]**, **[31810]**

Law Firm Inc. (August 2004); "Patrick Tisdale, Chief Information Officer" in **[29436]**, **[33204]**, **[45519]**

Law Firm Inc. (October 2004); "Printing in the Privacy of Your Hotel Room" in **[6766]**, **[19891]**, **[30406]**, **[49537]**

Law Firm Inc. (August 2004); "The Economics" in **[29214]**, **[49691]**

Law Firm Inc. (August 2004); "The Importance of Well-Crafted Terms" in **[29301]**, **[41763]**, **[44064]**, **[49706]**, **[49998]**

Law Firm Inc. (October 2004); "When Leadership Means Letting Go" in **[29579]**, **[36950]**, **[45827]**, **[47735]**

"Law Firm Recruiters Face Hurdles in Pay, Local Economy" in *Crain's Detroit Business* (Vol. 22, November 27, 2006, No. 48, pp. 18) **[29339]**, **[34967]**, **[42325]**

Law Firm Services Association **[39]**, **[26116]**

"Law Firms Beef Up Extranets to Handle Complex Deals" in *Crain's Detroit Business* (Vol. 23, January 29, 2007, No. 5, pp. 26) **[6705]**, **[6949]**, **[20570]**, **[20923]**, **[29340]**, **[34127]**, **[41802]**

"Law firm creates privacy group" in *Atlanta Business Chronicle* (Vol. 24, No. 8, July 27, 2001, pp. 3A) **[14194]**, **[22279]**, **[34128]**

Law (in Plain English) for Small Business **[29341]**, **[39429]**

"Law of the Land" in *Entrepreneur* (Vol. 33, October 2005, No. 10, pp. 89) **[25899]**, **[26277]**, **[38183]**

"Law-Less Approach" in *Pittsburgh Business Times* (Vol. 23, No. 9, September 19, 2003, pp. 1) **[29342]**, **[44331]**

The Law and Occupational Injury, Disease, and Death **[56569]**

Law Office of James F. McLaughlin **[29633]**

Law Office of Suzanne C. Cummings & Associates, P.C. **[29634]**

Law for the Small Business Owner **[29343]**

Law for the Small and Growing Business **[20924]**, **[28396]**, **[29344]**, **[38184]**, **[56570]**

"Law Talent" in *Entrepreneur* (Vol. 32, October 2004, No. 10, pp. 98) **[29345]**, **[45345]**

"Law provides more protection for whistle-blowers" in *Atlanta Business Chronicle* (Vol. 25, November 15, 2002, No. 23 pp. SS3) **[10056]**, **[15208]**, **[29346]**

"Lawmaker in Okla. Seeks to Discourage Fines for Tax Preparers" in *Journal Record (Oklahoma City, OK)* (February 6, 2007) **[183]**, **[2926]**, **[23981]**, **[26278]**

"Lawmakers to tackle e-waste issue" in *Waste News* (Vol. 8, No. 20, January 6, 2002, pp. 15) **[6706]**, **[21240]**, **[40502]**

"Lawmakers take aim at living-wage laws" in *Crain's Detroit Business* (Vol. 19, No. 8, February 24, 2003, pp. 7) **[25575]**, **[29347]**, **[39850]**, **[40503]**

"Lawmakers Tackle Loan Lender Rates" in *Atlanta Journal-Constitution* (March 4, 2005) **[10057]**, **[18075]**, **[44565]**

"Lawmakers Working on Insurance Issues" in *Miami Herald* (March 10, 2005) **[13365]**, **[40504]**, **[43257]**

Lawn America **[16156]**

Lawn Care for the North American Gardener **[16131]**

Lawn Doctor, Inc. **[16157]**

Lawn and Garden **[16132]**

Lawn and Garden Marketing and Distribution Association **[11413]**

Lawn & Landscape Magazine **[16049]**, **[16122]**

"Lawn Ranger" in *My Business* (September/October 2001, pp. 54) **[16413]**, **[35546]**

"Lawn Tractor Manufacturer Relocates From Wisconsin to Portland, Maine" in *Portland Press Herald* (August 17, 2005) **[30154]**, **[46334]**

Lawndale Chamber of Commerce **[57595]**

Lawns **[16059]**, **[16133]**

Lawns: Planting and Maintenance **[16134]**

Lawntamers **[16158]**

Lawrence Chamber of Commerce **[60367]**

Lawrence County Chamber of Commerce **[56871]**, **[59565]**, **[61806]**, **[64466]**, **[64939]**
Small Business Development Center **[63565]**

Lawrence Financial Group **[58065]**

Lawrence Krieger, Attorney at Law **[29635]**

Lawrence Siegel-Consultant **[7620]**

Lawrence University–Seeley G. Mudd Library–Music Collections **[17684]**, **[17822]**

"Laws Mandating Paid Sick Leave Will Pass in Several States" in *Kiplinger Letter* (Vol. 78, January 19, 2007, No. 2) **[26840]**, **[29348]**, **[40505]**, **[42873]**

"Lawsuit: EPA ignored impact of lead regulation" in *Atlanta Business Chronicle* (Vol. 23, No. 46, April 20, 2001, pp. 11A) **[29349]**, **[40506]**

"Lawsuit against Masco alleges predatory pricing" in *Crain's Detroit Business* (Vol. 19, No. 10, March 10, 2003, pp. 32) **[29350]**, **[30903]**, **[31044]**, **[46335]**

"Lawsuit, Tax Lien Plague Post-Bankruptcy Orbcomm" in *Washington Business Journal* (Vol. 22, No. 9, July 4, 2003, pp. 5) **[29351]**, **[38185]**, **[54638]**

Lawton - Fort Sill Chamber of Commerce and Industry **[64026]**

Lawyer Locator **[29672]**

"Lawyering Up" in *Boston Business Journal* (Vol. 23, No. 30, August 29, 2003, pp. 1) **[9223]**, **[29352]**, **[32540]**, **[42326]**

"Lawyers on War-Path Filing Wage and Hour Lawsuits" in *Kiplinger Letter* (Vol. 78, January 19, 2007, No. 2) **[14195]**, **[29353]**, **[34129]**, **[42874]**

A Layman's Guide to New Age and Spiritual Terms **[17902]**

"Layoffs, no tax hike in city's proposed budget" in *Atlanta Business Chronicle* (Vol. 25, No. 21, November 1, 2002, pp. 2A) **[28397]**, **[54639]**

Layout Software Basics **[53177]**

Lazard Technology Partners **[63125]**

Lazaris: Forgiving Yourself **[12404]**

Lazerquick **[7858]**

"The Laziness Factor in Loyalty" in *American Banker* (Vol. 170, September 5, 2006, No. 170, pp. 4A) **[10058]**, **[15209]**, **[30904]**

"LBA event draws a crowd" in *Hispanic Business* (Vol. 22, No. 11, November 2000, pp. 14) **[28398]**, **[48269]**, **[55110]**

LBC Networks **[49439]**, **[49627]**

The LBMAO Reporter **[7560]**, **[16329]**

LBOs and Fraudulent Conveyances **[30274]**

LC MARC: Books All **[2808]**, **[3071]**

LC39 Venture Group LLC **[63126]**

LCT **[16190]**

LD-A **[9118]**

LD-A-Lighting Equipment Accessories Directory Issue **[9112]**

LDB Interior Textiles **[12233]**, **[13697]**

LDB Interior Textiles Annual Buyers' Guide **[12191]**

LDG Associates **[35238]**

"LDM Technologies makes play for bankrupt Soo Plastics" in *Crain's Detroit Business* (Vol. 18, No. 50, December 16, 2002, pp. 5) **[1944]**, **[15210]**, **[50042]**

"LDMI gets $15 million in venture capital funding" in *Crain's Detroit Business* (Vol. 16, No. 15, April 10, 2000, pp. 26) **[55705]**

Le Chef du Service Alimentaire **[12066]**

Le Coq Roti **[21868]**

Le Cordon Bleu II **[4563]**, **[7823]**

Le Sueur Area Chamber of Commerce **[61615]**

Lea County Economic Development Corporation **[62728]**

Lead Area Chamber of Commerce **[64827]**

"Lead Generator: Quick Ideas for Better Sales Leads" in *Sales and Marketing.com* (Vol. 156, No. 3, March 2004, pp. 9) **[47187]**, **[51710]**

"Lead Generator: Quick Ideas For Better Sales Leads" in *Sales & Marketing Management* (Vol. 157, January 2005, No. 1, pp. 11) **[28399]**, **[51711]**

"Lead Softly, but Carry a Big Baton" in *Fast Company* (July 2001, pp. 46) **[39430]**, **[47188]**

"Lead the Way: New Gadgets Blaze Trails for Mobile Workers" in *Entrepreneur* (Vol. 31, No. 9, September 2003, pp. 39) **[6707]**, **[10680]**, **[14196]**, **[49120]**

The Leader for Agriculture **[26599]**

"Leader of the Pack" in *Entrepreneur* (Vol. 32, November 2004, No. 11, pp. 106) **[6097]**, **[36419]**, **[38845]**, **[56295]**

Leader's Edge **[334]**, **[61500]**

"Leaders for the Long Haul" in *Fast Company* (July 2001, pp. 56) **[25396]**, **[39431]**, **[45346]**

"Leaders Make Deal on Business Taxes" in *Crain's Detroit Business* (Vol. 21, November 7, 2005, No. 45, pp. 6) **[46336]**, **[54640]**

"Leaders Prepare for Lean Times" in *Hispanic Business* (Vol. 23, No. 11, November 2001, pp. 14) **[28400]**, **[32541]**, **[48270]**

Leadership 101: What Every Leader Needs to Know **[30566]**, **[36420]**, **[45347]**

Leadership: Building Rainbows **[37040]**

Leadership Development Center **[46065]**

The Leadership Edge **[37041]**

"A Leadership Evolution" in *Employment Relations Today* (Vol. 26, No. 4, Winter 2000, pp. 73) **[45348]**

"Leadership and followership" in *Physician Executive* (Vol. 28, No. 1, January-February 2002, pp. 91) **[36421]**, **[45349]**

"Leadership that Gets Results" in *Harvard Business Review* (Vol. 78, No. 2, March 2000, pp. 78) **[45350]**

"Leadership" in *Harvard Business Review* (Vol. 79, No. 11, December 2001, pp. 121) **[27416]**, **[45351]**

"The leadership journey" in *Harvard Business Review* (Vol. 80, No. 10, October 2002, pp. 42) **[36422]**, **[45352]**

Leadership Library on CD-ROM **[39851]**

Leadership and Management in Engineering **[46144]**

Leadership Management, Inc. **[27221]**

The Leadership Secrets of Colin Powell **[36423]**, **[45353]**

Leadership Skills by Aaron Alejandro **[45927]**

Leadership Skills for Supervisors (Canada) **[44769]**

Leadership Skills for Women **[56296]**

Leadership Strategies **[45896]**

Leadership and Team Development for Managerial Success **[44770]**

Leadership and Team Development for Managerial Success (Canada) **[34796]**

Leadership Training Associates **[55041]**

"Leadership Training" in *Black Enterprise* (Vol. 37, January 2007, No. 6, pp. 56) **[33150]**, **[34968]**, **[36424]**, **[45354]**, **[50043]**

"Leadership Training in Uniform" in *Hispanic Business* (Vol. 23, No. 7/8, July/August 2001, pp. 20) **[39432]**, **[45355]**

"Leadership in a combat zone" in *Harvard Business Review* (Vol. 79, No. 11, December 2001, pp. 107) **[27417]**, **[45356]**

"Leading Indicators: Continued Growth" in *My Business* (December/January 2004, pp. 50) **[28401]**, **[32542]**

"Leading Indicators; Slow (But Steady) Growth" in *My Business* (December/January 2003, pp. 48) **[28402]**, **[39433]**

"Leading from the slow lane" in *Incentive* (Vol. 174, No. 9, September 2000, pp. 33) **[45357]**

"Leading Lenders Shift as 2006 Activity Slows" in *Crain's New York Business* (Vol. 22, December 11, 2006, No. 50, pp. 28) **[32543]**, **[44566]**, **[52906]**

"Leading the Pack" in *Black Enterprise* (Vol. 34, No. 4, November 2003, pp. 82) **[11114]**, **[18894]**, **[36425]**, **[41803]**, **[56752]**

Leading a Service Team **[35192]**

"Leading in Times of Trauma" in *Harvard Business Review* (Vol. 80, No. 1, January 2002, pp. 55) **[39434]**, **[45358]**

"Leading for value" in *Harvard Business Review* (Vol. 81, No. 4, April 2003, pp. 41) **[36426]**, **[45359]**

Leading Virtual and Remote Teams **[44771]**

"Leading the Way" in *Black Enterprise* (Vol. 35, February 2005, No. 7, pp. 57) **[41804]**, **[44234]**, **[48271]**, **[56297]**

Leading With Emotional Intelligence (Canada) **[44772]**

Leadssolutions.com **[55987]**

Leadville/Lake County Chamber of Commerce **[58366]**

League of American Bicyclists **[2492]**

League of California Cities **[24209]**

The League Letter **[12112]**, **[17264]**, **[41253]**

Leake County Chamber of Commerce **[61807]**

Lean Manufacturing (Canada) **[46177]**, **[46225]**

"'Lean manufacturing' consultant moves south" in *Atlanta Business Chronicle* (Vol. 25, November 29, 2002, No. 25, pp. 5A) **[3551]**, **[46337]**

"The Lean Service Machine" in *Harvard Business Review* (Vol. 81, No. 10, October 2003, pp. 123) **[45360]**, **[52554]**

Lean Six Sigmas That Works: A Powerful Action Plan for Dramatically Improving Quality, Increasing Speed, and Reducing Waste **[39435]**, **[45361]**, **[54963]**

Lean Teen **[19478]**

Lean Trimmings **[4065]**

"The Leap: A Memoir of Love and Madness in the Internet Gold Rush" in *Harvard Business Review* (Vol. 78, No. 4, July 2000, pp. 152) **[13763]**, **[33456]**, **[37158]**

"Leap of Faith" in *Entrepreneur* (Vol. 32, October 2004, No. 10, pp. 21) **[15211]**, **[50044]**

"Leap Wireless Talks Merger with MetroPCS" in *San Diego Business Journal* (Vol. 28, January 15, 2007, No. 3, pp. 10) **[5041]**, **[15212]**, **[50045]**

Leapfrog Ventures **[58066]**

"Lear won't take a back seat" in *Fast Company* (June 2001, pp. 179) **[37159]**, **[46338]**

Learn to Dance Overnight **[8479]**

Learn to Dance Overnight Vol. 2 **[8480]**

Learn by Doing: A Step-by-Step How-To Guide about Multi-Level Marketing **[48657]**

Learn & Earn with Calligraphy **[4175]**

"Learn to lead with a little help from your friends" in *Women In Business* (Vol. 52, No. 2, March 2000, pp. 24) **[3552]**, **[45362]**

"Learn and Grow Rich" in *Black Enterprise* (Vol. 32, No. 10, May 2002, pp. 106) **[33151]**, **[36427]**

"Learn the Importance of Being Perfect" in *Women In Business* (Vol. 52, No. 2, March 2000, pp. 28) **[36428]**

"Learn Your ABC" in *Hispanic Business* (December 2001, pp. 68) **[184]**, **[23982]**, **[26279]**

"Learn Your Lines" in *Entrepreneur* **[27418]**, **[47189]**, **[51712]**

The Learning Annex Guide to Starting Your Own Import-Export Business **[12992]**

"Learning Curve" in *Entrepreneur* (Vol. 33, September 2005, No. 9, pp. 126) **[32189]**, **[33152]**, **[36429]**, **[37648]**

"Learning Curves: How to Avoid 3 First-Time Mistakes" in *My Business* (December/January 2004, pp. 48) **[19344]**, **[28403]**, **[35547]**

Learning Edge Publishing **[66246]**

The Learning Experience **[25481]**

Learning Express **[24852]**

Learning Forum **[58268]**

"Learning the Game of Hard Knocks" in *Hispanic Business* (October 2003, pp. 36, 38) **[35548]**, **[46577]**, **[47965]**

Learning about Honesty **[5395]**

"Learning business was key" in *Crain's Detroit Business* (Vol. 19, No. 13, March 31, 2003, pp. 13) **[25882]**, **[41466]**, **[44424]**, **[45363]**, **[48885]**

"Learning to lead" in *Incentive* (Vol. 174, No. 9, September 2000, pp. 32) **[34969]**, **[44332]**, **[45364]**

Learning Leadership **[45365]**

Learning and Leading with Technology **[6346]**

"Learning across lines. The secret to more efficient factories" in *Harvard Business Review* (Vol. 80, No. 10, October 2002, pp. 107) **[33153]**, **[46339]**

Learning Resources Network **[6326]**

"Learning the Ropes" in *Entrepreneur* (Vol. 33, October 2005, No. 10, pp. 99) **[1]**, **[13138]**, **[21827]**, **[22139]**, **[23538]**, **[23859]**, **[28440]**, **[29068]**, **[37199]**, **[38656]**, **[41164]**, **[43063]**

"Learning to Walk; E-waste stewardship takes first tentative steps" in *Waste News* (Vol. 8, No. 10, September 16, 2002, pp. 10) **[21241]**, **[37304]**

LearningRX Franchise Corp. **[33369]**

"Lease reviews can help avoid extra expenses" in *Business First Columbus* (Vol. 18, No. 28, March 1, 2002, pp. B13) **[20055]**, **[40507]**

"Lease Is More" in *Inc.* (August 1, 2003) **[12590]**, **[14197]**, **[21331]**, **[25883]**, **[34130]**

"Lease Lessons" in *Entrepreneur* (Vol. 32, December 2004, No. 12, pp. 106) **[20925]**, **[21332]**, **[52689]**

"Lease on Life?" in *Entrepreneur* (Vol. 32, November 2004, No. 11, pp. 98) **[9224]**, **[18780]**, **[24530]**, **[26280]**, **[29354]**, **[40508]**

"Leasing 101: need a new fleet but low on dough? Leasing may be the key" in *Entrepreneur* (Vol. 30, No. 12, December 2002, pp. 43) [18076], [49515], [49710]

Leasing Sourcebook: The Directory of the U.S. Capital Equipment Leasing Industry [21333]

"Leasingsecrets.com" in *Entrepreneur* (Vol. 31, No. 8, August 2003, pp. 6) [21334], [49121]

"The least lease" in *Entrepreneur* (Vol. 30, No. 3, March 2002, pp. 65) [20571], [20926], [32544], [52690]

Leather Apparel Association [16268]

"Leather Bound: Jim Metellus On Preserving a Fashionable Fabric" in *Black Enterprise* (Vol. 35, October 2004, No. 3, pp. 208) [5556], [16272]

Leather Industries of America [16269]

The Leather Manufacturer [16277]

Leather Manufacturer Directory [16273]

Leather Medic [10842], [16281]

"Leave small business alone!" in *My Business* (April/May 2002, pp. 51) [39436], [40509]

"Leave It at the Office" in *Home Office Computing* (Vol. 19, No. 1, January 2001, pp. 104) [54964]

"Leave It To Them: Make Sure Your Family Gets What It Needs by Including a Disclaimer Provision in Your Estate Plan" in *Entrepreneur* [29355], [54641]

"Leave a Legacy" in *Ingram's* (Vol. 27, No. 12, December 2001, pp. 71) [54216]

"Leave Me Alone!" in *Entrepreneur* (Vol. 32, August 2004, No. 8, pp. 31) [690], [31757], [47190]

Leaven [41254]

Leavenworth Chamber of Commerce [66126]

Leavenworth County Historical Society and Museum–Library [11048]

Leavenworth-Lansing Area Chamber of Commerce [60368]

Leaverton Auto [22679]

Leaves Class and Events Magazine [11469]

"Leaving a legacy" in *Women In Business* (Vol. 52, No. 4, July 2000, pp. 24) [36430], [56298]

"Leaving their Mark" in *Entrepreneur* (Vol. 32, December 2004, No. 12, pp. 8) [36431], [39437]

Leawood Chamber of Commerce [60369]

The Leawood Group Ltd. [20247]

Lebanon Area Chamber of Commerce [61989], [63716]

Lebanon Chamber of Commerce [59566], [62424]

Lebanon Hub Club [60370]

Lebanon-Marion County Chamber of Commerce [60532]

Lebanon Valley Chamber of Commerce [64467]

Lebanon/Wilson County Chamber of Commerce [64940]

LeBoeuf, Lamb, Greene & MacRae–Law Library [13600]

LECG, LLC–Library [29699], [32835]

"Led poisoning" in *Entrepreneur* (Vol. 30, No. 1, January 2002, pp. 18) [36432], [45366]

Ledger (February 20, 2005); "After a Bumpy Period, Local Industry Seems to Be Soaring" in [25145], [32236]

Ledger (March 6, 2005); "Berridge Confident of Evolving Work Force" in [41541], [50821], [52045]

Ledger (February 26, 2005); "GEICO Pays 24.2 Percent In Worker Bonuses" in [12557], [13293], [26813], [43181]

Ledger (March 6, 2005); "Lakeland-Based Harrell's Fertilizer Establishes Itself as a National Supplier" in [16114]

Ledger (February 24, 2005); "Lennar Corp. Expands With Five Polk Projects" in [7400], [28406]

Ledger (February 27, 2005); "More Area Employers Seeking Spanish-Speaking Workers" in [48582], [53867]

Ledger (February 19, 2005); "Polk Job Growth Boomed in 2004" in [28634], [32632]

Ledger (March 1, 2005); "Publix Stock Reaches Record High" in [11656], [15385]

Ledger (March 2, 2005); "Rousches Celebrate 35 Years in Lawn Mower Business" in [16115], [37772]

Ledo Pizza Systems [19682]

Lee and Baldauf Consulting Engineers Inc. [7621]

Lee College–Small Business Development Center [65045]

Lee County Area Chamber of Commerce [65919]

Lee County Chamber of Commerce and Visitors Center [64764]

Lee Hecht Harrison–Business Information Center [4463]

Lee Munder Venture Partners [61085]

Lee Myles Transmissions [22680]

Lee Resources International Inc. [16339]

Lee Vining Chamber of Commerce [57596]

Leech Lake Area Chamber of Commerce [61616]

Leeds Clark Inc. [1563]

John Leeke [1564]

Leelanau Peninsula Chamber of Commerce [61360]

Leesburg Area Chamber of Commerce [58883]

Leetonia-Washingtonville Area Chamber of Commerce [63717]

Leeward Oahu Junior Chamber of Commerce [59253]

"Left Unsaid: How Ignoring Internal Conflict Can Kill Your Small Business" in *My Business* (April/May 2004, pp. 36-39) [34970], [36433], [45367]

"A Leg Up on Legal Fees" in *My Business* (October/November 2002, pp. 52) [29356], [34131]

Legacy Venture [58067]

"Legal Aid: Sample Legal Documents can Lower Your Attorney Fees" in *Black Enterprise* (Vol. 37, October 2006, No. 3, pp. 210) [14198], [25884], [29357], [39438], [52376]

The Legal Aspects of Purchasing and Supply Chain Management [29083], [50751]

Legal & Corporate Forms for Small Business [29358]

"Legal Eagle?" in *Entrepreneur* (Vol. 32, October 2004, No. 10, pp. 89) [691], [4715], [22280], [23065], [24290], [29359], [40510], [47191], [53351]

"Legal Ease" in *My Business* (December/January 2004, pp. 53) [29360], [34132]

Legal Environmental Assistance Foundation [9328]

Legal Forms for Starting & Running a Small Business Vol. 2 [53830]

Legal Guide for Starting and Running a Small Business [21301], [29069], [30655], [35549], [39068], [42156], [43964], [52402], [54409]

Legal Help for Your Business [29361]

The Legal Investigator [19985]

Legal-Legislative Reporter [30755]

"Legal News Publisher Sells His Interest in Company" in *Crain's Detroit Business* (Vol. 22, February 13, 2006, No. 7, pp. 26) [15213], [18895], [29362], [50046]

LegalEase: Legal Description Writer [23781]

"Legally bound" in *Crain's Detroit Business* (Vol. 19, No. 17, April 28, 2003, pp. 3) [29363], [33154], [53831]

"Legendary Entrepreneur" in *Small Business Opportunities* (Spring 2005) [11639], [36434], [54217]

"Legends at Cascades" in *San Fernando Valley Business Journal* (Vol. 12, January 2007, No. 1, pp. 12) [20572], [20927]

"Legends" in *Inc.* (Volume 27, December 2005, No. 12, pp. 30, 32) [36435], [39439]

"Legislation aims to tax Internet sales" in *Crain's Detroit Business* (Vol. 19, No. 1, January 6, 2003, pp. 20) [14199], [34133], [40511], [51229], [54642]

Legislative Watch [29602], [40867]

"Legislature considers energy tax breaks" in *Crain's Detroit Business* (Vol. 18, No. 16, April 22, 2002, pp. 23) [37305], [40512], [41805], [54643]

Legislature Of the Virgin Islands–Virgin Islands Senate Standing Committee on Economic Development Center [66664]

Lehigh Acres Chamber of Commerce [58884]

Lehigh University
    Institute for Metal Forming [16407]
    Office of Research and Sponsored Programs [64609]

Small Business Development Center [37054], [64333]

Lehman College–Small Business Development Center [62765]

Lehman College SBDC [62766]

Lehrer Financial and Economic Advisory Services [20738]

Leipsic Area Chamber of Commerce [63718]

Leland Chamber of Commerce [61808]

Lemko Housing Organization [18306]

Lemmon Area Chamber of Commerce [64828]

"Lemon Aid" in *WorkingWoman* (Vol. 25, No. 8, September 2000, pp. 94) [30367], [56299]

Lemon Grove Chamber of Commerce [57597]

Lemon Tree Family Hair Salon [11835]

Lemont Area Chamber of Commerce [59567]

Lemoore District Chamber of Commerce [57598]

Lemstone Christian Stores [3064], [17809]

Lena Community Development Corp. [66442]

Lenawee County Chamber of Commerce [61361]

"Lender forecloses on historic hotel" in *Houston Business Journal* (Vol. 33, No. 51, May 2, 2003, pp. 1A) [7399], [12591], [28404]

The Lender Liability Deskbook [55706]

"Lenders rebuke SBA plan to address 7(a) shortfall" in *Business First Columbus* (Vol. 18, No. 18, March 1, 2002, A14) [39852], [44567]

"Lenders wary of plan to make up SBA program shortfall" in *Wall Street Journal* (March 19, 2002, pp. B2) [39853], [44568]

"Lending a Helping Hand Even When Off Duty" in *Home Business* (Vol. 12, March/April 2005, No. 2, pp. 62) [33155], [36436], [42674]

"Lending Tree earns first profit, branches out" in *Atlanta Business Chronicle* (Vol. 25, No. 22, November 8, 2002, pp. 8A) [17402], [20573], [20928], [28405], [38186]

Lenexa Chamber of Commerce [60371]

"Lennar Corp. Expands With Five Polk Projects" in *Ledger* (February 24, 2005) [7400], [28406]

Lenora Chamber of Commerce [60372]

Lenow International Inc. [19990], [22439]

Lenox Chamber of Commerce [60963]

Lenox Library Association–Music Department [17685]

"Lentek Lands in Chapter 11" in *Orlando Business Journal* (Vol. 20, No. 5, July 18, 2003, pp. 1) [28711], [29364], [36751], [38187]

Lentz USA Service Centers [22681]

Leo A. Daly Company–Library [13730]

"Leo Rivera" in *Entrepreneur* (Vol. 32, No. 4, April 2004, pp. 22) [11793], [36437]

Leon Chamber of Commerce [60167]

Leon Gottlieb USA/Int'l Franchise/Restaurant Consultants [3894], [31496], [39014]

Leonard Chamber of Commerce [65358]

Leonard Mautner Associates [58068]

Leonard Reed's Shim Sham Shimmy [8481]

Leonard's Guide-International Air Cargo Directory [12993]

Leonard's Guide National Warehouse and Distribution Directory [20227]

Lepercq Capital Management, Inc. / Lepercq de Neuflize in [63127]

Les Franchises Panda Ltee/Panda Franchises Ltd. [22775]

"Less Bang For Your Buck" in *Black Enterprise* (Vol. 36, November 2005, No. 4, pp. 168) [24701], [25208], [30368]

"Less than Half of Small Firms Offer Health Plans" in *Wall Street Journal* (November 4, 2003, pp. B9) [13366], [26841], [41043], [43258]

"Less Is More: Believe It Or Not" in *Entrepreneur* (Vol. 31, No. 8, August 2003, pp. 114) [8171], [46578], [48687]

"Less Is More" in *Entrepreneur* (Vol. 33, October 2005, No. 10, pp. 100) [29857], [30656], [37200], [38657]

"A less taxing bite on small business" in *Black Enterprise* (Vol. 33, No. 6, January 2003, pp. 38) [185], [23983], [54644]

"A Less Taxing Way to Invest" in *Black Enterprise* (Vol. 35, December 2004, No. 5, pp. 48) [15214], [38188], [54645]

The Less Than Perfect Rider: Overcoming Common Riding Problems [12462]

"A Lesson Learned" in *Black Enterprise* (Vol. 34, No. 2, September 2003, pp. S2) **[36438]**, **[56753]**

"Lesson Plan: Cashing in Online" in *Orlando Sentinel* (February 1, 2005) **[1832]**, **[14200]**, **[33156]**

"Lessons from the 8(A) Leaders" in *Hispanic Business* (March 2005, pp. 54, 56) **[7401]**, **[40047]**, **[48272]**

"Lessons From Katrina on Prepaid Cards" in *American Banker* (Vol. 170, September 30, 2005, No. 189, pp. 11) **[8312]**, **[8387]**, **[10059]**, **[18781]**, **[31562]**

"Lessons From the Past: Entrepreneur Takes the Old World Approach to Business" in *Black Enterprise* (Vol. 34, No. 3, October 2003) **[22281]**, **[36439]**, **[44569]**

"Lessons learned in a changing industry" in *My Business* (August/September 2002, pp. 48) **[24702]**, **[25209]**

"Lessons Learned: The franchising road can be hard, expensive" in *My Business* (August/September 2002, pp. 46) **[5678]**, **[38846]**

"Lessons from the Sandbox" in *Small Business Opportunities* (Vol. 12, No. 5, September 2000, pp. 106) **[36440]**, **[47192]**

Lessons in Service From Charlie Trotter **[21551]**, **[39440]**

"Let the games begin" in *Red Herring* (No. 106, October 15, 2001, pp. 30) **[1111]**, **[14201]**, **[23066]**, **[28407]**

"Let Freedom Ring: The Internet is a Powerful Force for Telephone Deregulation" in *Barron's* (July 7, 2003, pp. 30) **[5042]**, **[14202]**, **[34134]**, **[40513]**

"Let Go" in *My Business* (December/January 2003, pp. 35-37) **[45368]**, **[54965]**

"Let It Roll: Reginald Bowser Bends Over Backward to Create Convenient 401(k) Transfers" in *Black Enterprise* (Vol. 34, December 2003) **[10060]**, **[10414]**, **[15215]**, **[15983]**, **[36753]**, **[38189]**, **[51933]**, **[54646]**

"Let the (Political) Games Begin" in *Inc.* (Volume 27, June 2005, No. 6, pp. 51-52, 54, 56) **[29365]**, **[40514]**

"Let it rain" in *Ingram's* (Vol. 28, No. 3, March 2002, pp. 35) **[28408]**, **[29366]**

"Let The Buyer Beware" in *Small Business Opportunities* (Vol. 13, No. 6, November 2001, pp. 20) **[30238]**, **[49516]**

"Let Them Eat Cake: When It Comes to Small Business, a New Tax-Cut Bill is Half-Baked" in *Entrepreneur* (Vol. 32, November 2004) **[186]**, **[23984]**, **[26281]**, **[46340]**, **[54647]**

"Let Your Fingers Do the Locking: Forgotten That Password?" in *Fortune* (Vol. 151, January 24, 2005, No. 2, pp. 42) **[4716]**, **[6708]**, **[22282]**, **[23067]**, **[41806]**, **[49122]**, **[53352]**, **[53832]**

"Let Your Stuff Tell a Story: How to Edit Your Accessories to Showcase Your Personality" in *Charlotte Observer* (February 8, 2007) **[12895]**, **[13660]**, **[18550]**

Letcher County Chamber of Commerce **[60533]**

Let's Buy a Company: How to Accelerate Growth Through Acquisitions **[15216]**, **[28409]**, **[30686]**, **[50047]**

"Let's celebrate! Use performance evaluations as a time to praise" in *Black Enterprise* (Vol. 32, No. 6, January 2002, pp. 45) **[34971]**, **[45369]**

Let's Create for Halloween **[5396]**

Let's Create for Thanksgiving **[5397]**

"Lets get creative: creativity is what makes the world go round." in *Entrepreneur* (Vol. 30, No. 10, Oct. 2002, pp. 42) **[36441]**

"Let's make a deal" in *Atlanta Business Chronicle* (Vol. 24, No. 9, August 3, 2001, pp. B1) **[20574]**, **[52691]**

"Let's Do Launch" in *Entrepreneur* (Vol. 32, No. 4, April 2004, pp. 26) **[18077]**, **[39441]**

"Let's Do Lunch: Giving New Meaning to the Term 'Power Lunch'" in *Entrepreneur* (Vol. 32, November 2004, No. 11, pp. 34) **[27419]**, **[36442]**, **[39442]**

Let's Eat **[10643]**

Let's Face It USA **[2660]**, **[8965]**, **[40939]**

"Let's Hang Together" in *Ingram's* (Vol. 29, No. 7, July 2003, pp. 83) **[28410]**

"Let's Have Some Funds!" in *Entrepreneur* (Vol. 32, July 2004) **[55707]**, **[56300]**

"Let's Make a Deal" in *Business Journal-Milwaukee* (Vol. 20, No. 47, August 8, 2003, pp. A23) **[15217]**, **[43733]**, **[46341]**, **[50048]**

"Let's Make a Dual" in *Entrepreneur* (Vol. 32, November 2004, No. 11, pp. 70) **[15218]**, **[50049]**

Let's Make Wine **[51462]**

"Let's Move" in *Black Enterprise* (Vol. 34, No. 6, January 2004, pp. 46) **[49116]**, **[49123]**

"Let's roll up our sleeves" in *Crain's Detroit Business* (Vol. 18, No. 50, December 16, 2002, pp. 8) **[20575]**, **[20929]**, **[28411]**, **[52692]**

"Let's Talk About Sexism: Do Sexist Attitudes Still Exist in Business? Women Sound Off" in *Entrepreneur* (Vol. 32, No. 4, April 2004) **[32039]**, **[45370]**, **[56301]**

"A letter to the chief executive" in *Harvard Business Review* (Vol. 80, No. 10, October 2002, pp. 94) **[36443]**, **[45371]**

"Letters count at keypadding design firm Digit Wireless" in *Boston Business Journal* (Vol. 22, No. 14, May 10, 2002, pp. 19) **[5043]**, **[40048]**, **[49124]**

Letterspace **[6023]**, **[19914]**, **[25500]**

"Letting A Store's Expert Do Shopping Can Make Choices Easier, Quicker" in *Orange County Register* (December 23, 2004) **[18999]**, **[51230]**

Marilyn LeVasseur **[12411]**

"Level Playing Field" in *Entrepreneur* (Vol. 32, No. 2, February 2004, pp. 28) **[30905]**, **[40049]**

Levelland Area Chamber of Commerce **[65359]**

"Leveraged growth. Expanding sales without sacrificing profits" in *Harvard Business Review* (Vol. 80, No. 10, October 2002, pp. 68) **[15219]**, **[28412]**, **[50050]**, **[51713]**

The Levison Letter **[50485]**

"Levitt on the street" in *Harvard Business Review* (Vol. 81, No. 4, April 2003, pp. 22) **[10061]**, **[15220]**, **[38190]**

R.J. Levulis & Associates **[44260]**

Lewes Chamber of Commerce **[58650]**

Lewis-Clark State College–School of Technology **[59353]**

Lewis-Clark State College (Region II)–Small Business Development Center **[59278]**

Lewis County Chamber of Commerce **[62947]**, **[64941]**, **[66282]**

Lewiston Area Chamber of Commerce **[61362]**

Lewiston Chamber of Commerce **[59314]**

Lewistown Area Chamber of Commerce **[62179]**

Lewistown Chamber of Commerce **[59568]**

Lewisville Area Chamber of Commerce **[65360]**

Lexecon, Inc.–Library **[10403]**, **[15803]**

"Lexicon Leads Advertising Pack Wireless Plans, Consumer Products Also Big" in *Hispanic Business* (December 2006, pp. 36, 38, 40, 42) **[692]**, **[47193]**

Lexington Area Chamber of Commerce **[61990]**, **[62276]**

Lexington Area Small Business Development Center **[60458]**

Lexington Chamber of Commerce **[60964]**, **[64765]**

Lexington Community College–Learning Resource Center **[49471]**

Lexington Herald-Leader (August 28, 2002); "Women's Club Leads to Profitable Business" in **[2359]**, **[24838]**

Lexington Medical Center–LMC Health Library **[8869]**, **[18400]**

Lexington-Rockbridge County Chamber of Commerce **[65920]**

LEXIS/NEXIS Technical Library **[14688]**

LexisNexis Patent & Trademark File History Services **[44213]**

LF International, Inc. **[58069]**

"LI Banks $2 Million in State Environmental Grants for Waterfront Projects" in *Long Island Business News* (March 12, 2004) **[7402]**, **[7669]**, **[35942]**, **[37306]**, **[39854]**, **[39995]**

"Liar, Liar: In the Race to Make Money, Some American Businesses Have Been Lying Their Pants Off" in *Entrepreneur* (Vol. 31, Oct. 2003) **[29367]**, **[37471]**

Libby Area Chamber of Commerce **[62180]**

Liberal Area Chamber of Commerce **[60373]**

Liberty Area Chamber of Commerce **[61809]**, **[61991]**

Liberty Bidco Investment Corporation **[61458]**

Liberty Business Strategies Ltd. **[3751]**, **[31398]**, **[46066]**, **[47885]**

Liberty-Casey County Chamber of Commerce **[60534]**

Liberty County Chamber of Commerce **[58885]**, **[59132]**, **[62181]**

Liberty-Dayton Area Chamber of Commerce **[65361]**

Liberty Environmental Partners **[58070]**

Liberty Net **[49440]**

Liberty Publishing Company Inc. **[59020]**

Liberty Tax Service **[24133]**

Liberty - Union County Chamber of Commerce **[59959]**

Liberty Venture Partners, Inc. **[64561]**

"The Librarian's Internet Survival Guide" in *Information Today* (Vol. 20, No. 1, Jan. 2003, pp. 44) **[13082]**, **[14203]**, **[34135]**

"Libraries Turn Page on Subscription Disruption" in *Houston Business Journal* (Vol. 34, No. 9, July 11, pp. 1) **[18896]**, **[52555]**

Library Binding Institute **[2830]**

Library in a Book-Sexual Harassment **[32040]**

Library of the Chicago Botanic Garden **[11524]**

Library of Congress **[67275]**
    Humanities and Social Sciences
        Division–Local History & Genealogy
        Reading Room **[11049]**
    Motion Picture, Broadcasting & Recorded
        Sound Division **[20380]**
    Music Division **[17686]**
    Prints & Photographs Division **[6068]**

Library Literature **[13083]**

Library Literature & Information Science Full Text **[13120]**, **[23428]**

The Library at the Mariners' Museum **[16789]**

The Library of Michigan–Government Documents Service **[66898]**

Library Times International **[13106]**

Library Trends (Vol. 51, No. 2, Fall 2002, pp. 199); "Aspects of dealing with digital information" in **[13067]**

Library of Virginia–Collection Management Division **[67002]**

"License to Bill?" in *Black Enterprise* (Vol. 34, No. 4, November 2003, pp. 48) **[29070]**, **[42540]**, **[52778]**

License! (Vol. 6, No. 6, July 2003, pp. 22); "Manny, Moe, & Jack Are In the Driver's Seat" in **[1946]**, **[2724]**, **[5684]**, **[24820]**, **[44094]**, **[51241]**

License! (Vol. 6, No. 7, August 2003, pp. 14); "Mother Lode" in **[5691]**

"License to Thrive" in *Entrepreneur* (Vol. 33, October 2005, No. 10, pp. 22) **[44085]**, **[48762]**, **[50734]**, **[53833]**

"License To Thrive" in *Inc.* (August 2005, pp. 38) **[44086]**, **[50051]**, **[51714]**

"License to Upgrade" in *Entrepreneur* (Vol. 32, September 2004, No. 9, pp. 44) **[4717]**, **[23068]**, **[44087]**, **[53353]**

"Licensed massage therapist helps high performers" in *Colorado Springs Business Journal* (February 28, 2003) **[17005]**, **[17903]**

Licking County Art Gallery–Library **[1661]**

"The Lid On Spam Is Still Loose" in *Business Week* (February 7, 2005, No. 3919, pp. 10) **[14204]**, **[22283]**, **[27420]**, **[29368]**, **[34136]**

Lieber & Associates **[31980]**

"Life After Enron" in *Black Enterprise* (Vol. 34, No. 4, November 2003) **[187]**, **[37472]**, **[38191]**

"Life after bankruptcy: there are still pitfalls in folding a business" in *Black Enterprise* (Vol. 33, No. 3, October 2002, pp. 58) **[29369]**, **[30059]**, **[45372]**, **[47131]**

"Life after business" in *Women in Business* (Vol. 53, No. 2, March-April, 2001, pp. 38) **[30369]**, **[56302]**

"Life after business" in *Women In Business* (Vol. 52, No. 2, March 2000, pp. 25) **[14205]**, **[34137]**, **[53354]**, **[56303]**

The Life Cycle of Entrepreneurial Ventures **[36444]**, **[39443]**

"A Life Experience is Part of the Package" in *Sacramento Bee* (November 21, 2005) **[693]**, **[24703]**, **[25210]**, **[47194]**, **[52360]**

"Life Is What You Make It" in *Entrepreneur.com* (Vol. 34, February 2006, No. 2, pp. 28) **[10062]**, **[36445]**

"The Life of a Landlord: Acquiring the Building is Just the Beginning." in *Black Enterprise* (Vol. 35, August 2004, No. 1, pp. 94) **[20930]**, **[21335]**, **[33157]**, **[36446]**

"Life in the slow lane" in *Entrepreneur* (Vol. 30, No. 3, March 2002,) **[17314]**, **[30906]**, **[53834]**

Life of the Party: A Guide to Building Your Party Plan Business **[18758]**

"Life is just a bowl of jelly beans and so is sales" in *Atlanta Business Chronicle* (Vol. 24, No. 13, August 31, 2001, pp. 36A) **[51715]**

"The Life Sciences Building Boom" in *Boston Globe* (January 31, 2005) **[7403]**, **[28413]**, **[50909]**, **[52139]**

"Life Sciences Industry Outlook" in *Ingram's* (Vol. 28, No. 6, June 2002, pp. 65) **[41807]**, **[52140]**

"Life Sciences Span The Globe: U.S. VCs Like to Spend Money in their Backyards" in *Venture Capital Journal* (October 1, 2004) **[43734]**, **[49711]**, **[50910]**, **[52141]**, **[55708]**

Life Untangled Publishing **[66755]**

Life Work Insight L.L.C. **[63904]**

Lifelines: A Career Profile Study **[4432]**

Life's a Game So Fix the Odds: How to Be More Persuasive and Influential in Your Personal and Business **[27421]**, **[36447]**

"LifeSecure Goes National" in *Crain's Detroit Business* (Vol. 23, January 29, 2007, No. 5, pp. 17) **[13367]**, **[28414]**, **[43259]**, **[50052]**

Lifestar **[58485]**

"Lifestyle, research drugs cloud benefit decisions" in *Business First Columbus* (Vol. 18, No. 40, May 24, 2002, pp. B8) **[41044]**, **[43260]**

"Lifestyle: Innovated accoutrements for discerning executives" in *Hispanic Business* (March 2003, pp. 45) **[6709]**, **[18078]**, **[49125]**

Lifestyle Media-Relations Reporter **[20170]**

Lifestyles Furniture: A Sole Proprietorship Merchandising Business Practice Set **[12292]**

"A Lifetime of Perseverance" in *Hispanic Business* (December 2006, pp. 44) **[694]**, **[56304]**

Lifting Properly **[56636]**

Lifts for Your Choreography: From Beginner to Spectacular, Vol. 1 **[8482]**

Liggett & Myers Tobacco Co.–Information Services **[24635]**

Light Lines **[17932]**

"Light Rider" in *Success* (Vol. 47, No. 1, January 2000, pp. 13) **[2022]**, **[35550]**

Light and Shade **[4213]**, **[19309]**

"A Light Touch" in *Entrepreneur* (Vol. 32, July 2004, No. 7, pp. 46) **[6710]**, **[49126]**

The Lightbulb/Invent! Journal **[44186]**

"Lighten Up! Weighed Down By Your Portable PC?" in *Entrepreneur* (Vol. 31, October. 2003) **[6711]**, **[49127]**

The Lighten Up! Weight Loss Program **[26058]**

"Lightening the Workload: Entrepreneurs Should Know When It's Time to Delegate" in *Black Enterprise* (Vol. 34, No. 2, September 2003) **[36448]**, **[45373]**

Lighthouse Capital Partners **[58071]**

Lighthouse Inspection Canada Limited **[3278]**

"Lighthouse starts sign biz to boost revenue, people" in *Crain's Detroit Business* (Vol. 18, No. 20, May 20, 2002, pp. 18) **[22780]**, **[38847]**

Lighting Design Collaborative **[49628]**

Lighting Dimensions **[9119]**

Lighting Research Institute, Inc. **[49670]**

"Lighting Their Way" in *Crain's Detroit Business* (Vol. 21, October 3, 2005, No. 43, pp. 22) **[18079]**, **[20931]**, **[37713]**

"Lightning Speed" in *Entrepreneur* (Vol. 28, No. 3, March 2000, pp. 26) **[14206]**, **[41808]**, **[52556]**

"Lights, Camera, Action! Do You Dream of Promoting Your Business On Oprah Or the Today Show, But Don't Know Where To Start?" in *Entrepreneur* **[695]**, **[13661]**, **[24343]**, **[47195]**, **[50618]**

"Lights, camera, action" in *Entrepreneur* (Vol. 31, No. 4, April 2003, pp. 126) **[24425]**, **[47196]**, **[50619]**, **[51231]**, **[51716]**

"Lights, Camera, Trauma!" in *Crain's Chicago Business* (Vol. 26, No. 50, December 15, 2003, pp. 1) **[24426]**, **[41045]**, **[50620]**

"Lightspeed GPs Set To Launch New Fund" in *Venture Capital Journal* (October 1, 2005) **[55401]**

Lightspeed Venture Partners / Weiss, Peck and Greer **[58072]**

"Lightweight Newsprint Could Bring Cost Savings to Heavyweight Papers" in *Los Angeles Business Journal* (Vol. 27, Feb. 7, 2005) **[18897]**, **[19884]**

Ligonier Chamber of Commerce **[59960]**

"Like Hair, Barbers' Ranks Thinning" in *Chicago Tribune* (February 17, 2005) **[11794]**, **[53835]**

"Like It or Not...Culture Matters" in *Employment Relations Today* (Vol. 27, No. 2, Summer 2000, pp. 43) **[34972]**, **[45374]**

Lil' Angels Photography **[19329]**

Li'l Dino Deli & Grille **[8556]**

Lille D'Easum Library–SPEC Library **[9445]**

Lillington Area Chamber of Commerce **[63399]**

Lil'Pals Pet Photography **[19330]**

Lima/Allen County Chamber of Commerce **[63719]**

Lima Technical College–Small Business Development Center **[63566]**

Limestone Area Chamber of Commerce **[59569]**

"Limestone brick can cut construction expenses" in *Business First Columbus* (Vol. 18, No. 26, February 15, 2002, pp. 24) **[1520]**, **[7404]**

Limited Liability Companies: Tax & Business Law **[54904]**

"The Limo Jet: Its Time is Coming" in *Business Week* (December 11, 2000, pp. 5) **[30370]**

Limon Chamber of Commerce **[58397]**

Limousine Industry Manufacturers Organization **[16176]**

LIMRA International **[9792]**
    InfoCenter **[13601]**

LIMRA International Inc. **[13575]**

LIMS/Letter **[13107]**

Linc Capital, Inc. **[59746]**

Lincoln Area Chamber of Commerce **[57599]**, **[60374]**

Lincoln Chamber of Commerce **[62277]**

Lincoln City Chamber of Commerce **[64240]**

Lincoln County Chamber of Commerce **[60535]**

Lincoln Environmental Inc. **[9409]**

Lincoln Heights Chamber of Commerce **[57600]**

Lincoln Lakes Region Chamber of Commerce **[60758]**

Lincoln Land Community College–Small Business Development Center **[59381]**

Lincoln - Logan County Chamber of Commerce **[59570]**

Lincoln Park Chamber of Commerce **[59571]**, **[61363]**

Lincoln Service Center–Small Business Development Center **[62222]**

Lincoln Valley Chamber of Commerce **[62182]**

Lincoln Women's Chamber of Commerce **[62278]**

Lincoln-Woodstock Chamber of Commerce **[62425]**

Lincolnton-Lincoln County Chamber of Commerce **[63400]**

Lincolnton - Lincoln County Chamber of Commerce and Development Authority **[59133]**

Lincolnwood Chamber of Commerce and Industry **[59572]**

Lindale Area Chamber of Commerce **[65362]**

Linden Area Chamber of Commerce **[65363]**

Linden Argentine Chamber of Commerce **[61364]**

Linden-Peters Chamber of Commerce **[57601]**

Lindenhurst - Lake Villa Chamber of Commerce **[59573]**

Lindsay Chamber of Commerce **[57602]**, **[64027]**

Lindsborg Chamber of Commerce **[60375]**

"A line in the sand" in *InfoWorld* (Vol. 23, No. 5, January 29, 2001, pp. 1) **[29370]**

Line-X Spray-On Truck Bedliners **[2053]**

Link Staffing Services **[24548]**

Link-Up **[13108]**, **[14655]**

"Linking 'Em Up" in *Incentive* (Vol. 174, No. 10, October 2000, pp. 109) **[26843]**, **[34973]**, **[53836]**

"Linking Policies for Public Web Sites" in *Information Today* (Vol. 17, No. 10, November 2000, pp. 42) **[25885]**, **[34138]**, **[44088]**

Linking Ring **[18735]**

Linn-Benton Community College–Small Business Development Center **[64168]**

Linn's Stamp News **[5847]**

Linton Industrial Development Corporation **[63528]**

Linton-Stockton Chamber of Commerce **[59961]** SBDC **[59828]**

"Linux gaining admirers, users" in *Crain's Detroit Business* (Vol. 19, No. 15, April 14, 2003, pp. 1) **[6176]**, **[6477]**

Linux Business Week **[62628]**

Linux Buyer's Guide **[2720]**, **[6878]**, **[23272]**, **[51423]**

Linux Global Partners **[63128]**

The Lion And Rose Pub **[21869]**

Lip Service vs. Customer Service: Making Customer Cents for Customer Sense **[31758]**

Linda Lipsky Restaurant Consultants Inc. **[3752]**, **[12084]**, **[31399]**

Liqui-Green Lawn Care Corp. **[16159]**

"Liquidity Events" in *Fast Company* (March 2005, No. 92, pp. 28) **[14207]**, **[55709]**

Lisbon Area Chamber of Commerce **[62426]**, **[63720]**

Lisle Chamber of Commerce **[59574]**

A List" in *Entrepreneur* (Vol. 31, No. 8, August 2003, pp. 65); "The **[35109]**, **[42896]**

List of Journals and Other Serials **[18898]**

"Listen and Judge" in *Black Enterprise* (Vol. 36, November 2005, No. 4, pp. 66) **[17747]**, **[21142]**, **[34139]**

"Listen Up! Get the Scoop on Bluetooth Headsets With This Guide" in *Entrepreneur.com* (Vol. 34, February 2006, No. 2, pp. 34) **[5044]**, **[41809]**, **[49128]**

"Listen Up! If You're Not Advertising on Internet Radio, You Could Be Missing Out" in *Entrepreneur* (Vol. 32, November 2004, No. 11) **[696]**, **[14208]**, **[20322]**, **[34140]**, **[47197]**

"Listen While You Work" in *Entrepreneur* (Vol. 31, No. 10, October 2003, pp. 120) **[17748]**, **[20323]**, **[34141]**

"Listening Begins at Home" in *Harvard Business Review* (Vol. 81, No. 11, November 2003, pp. 106) **[47198]**, **[48666]**

"Listening for opportunity" in *Hispanic Business* (Vol. 22, No. 9, September 2000, pp. 16) **[34142]**, **[40050]**, **[48273]**

Listening Skills **[27569]**

Listening and Writing: Building a Better Foundation for Better Communication **[27265]**

Litchfield Chamber of Commerce **[59575]**, **[61365]**, **[61617]**

Lite For Life **[26059]**, **[31497]**

Literary Market Place **[2721]**, **[8618]**, **[25495]**

Literary Press Group of Canada **[2661]**

Literary Translators' Association of Canada **[25078]**

Lithography: How to Paint and Sell Lithographs **[6027]**, **[8066]**

Litigation Management & Training Services Inc. **[32118]**

"Litigation's price boosts arbitration's appeal" in *Atlanta Business Chronicle* (Vol. 25, November 15, 2002, No. 23 pp. SS15) **[29371]**, **[42327]**

Paul J. Litteau Consulting Services **[15732]**

"A Little Bit Goes a Long Way" in *My Business* (September/October 2001, pp. 46) **[44570]**, **[48912]**

Little Brothers - Friends of the Elderly **[437]**

Little Caesars Pizza **[19683]**

Little Dreamers Preschool **[5439]**, **[33370]**

"A Little Equation that Creates Big Results" in *Home Business* (Vol. 12, October 2005, No. 5, pp. 86) **[36449]**, **[54966]**

"Little Extras: Get More From Your Insurance Company than Just Coverage" in *Entrepreneur* (Vol. 33, January 2005, No. 1, pp. 52) **[13368]**, **[43261]**

Little Falls Area Chamber of Commerce **[61618]**
"A Little Friendly Advice: Exhibitor Advisory
Committees Can Make a Difference" in
Tradeshow Week (Vol. 34, December 6, 2004,
No. 49) **[22524]**, **[24965]**, **[45375]**, **[55111]**
"The Little Guys Spy a Slowdown" in *Business
Week* (No. 3691, July 24, 2000, pp. 26)
[28415], **[42328]**, **[53837]**
The Little Gym International **[5440]**
"Little urgency seen over HIPAA" in *Crain's Detroit
Business* (Vol. 18, No.) **[13369]**, **[40515]**,
[41046], **[43262]**
Little King **[8557]**
Little Leaf Press Inc. **[61736]**
"Little things mean a lot" in *Rough Notes* (Vol. 146,
No. 3, March 2003, pp. 118) **[27654]**, **[31759]**,
[45376]
Little River Chamber of Commerce **[57186]**, **[64766]**
Little Rock Regional Chamber of Commerce
[57187]
Little Scientists **[5441]**
"Little Things Make a Big Difference at NanoOpto"
in *Venture Capital Journal* (Vol. 42, No. 10,
October 2002, pp. 33-34) **[15221]**, **[37160]**,
[52142], **[55710]**
Littlefield Chamber of Commerce **[65364]**
Littlerock Chamber of Commerce **[57603]**
Littlestown Area Chamber of Commerce **[64468]**
Littleton Area Chamber of Commerce **[62427]**
Littleton Small Business Development Center
[62388]
"Live Long and Prosper: New Life Insurance
Policies Offer Refunds" in *Entrepreneur* (Vol.
32, December 2004, No. 12, pp. 66) **[13370]**,
[43263]
Live Oak District Chamber of Commerce **[57604]**
The Live Oak Press L.L.C. **[2797]**, **[8653]**
"Live Wire: Online Seminars Show 'Em What
You've Got" in *Entrepreneur* (Vol. 31, No. 10,
October 2003, pp. 91) **[22525]**, **[24966]**,
[34143]
Liveoak Equity Partners **[59200]**
Livermore Chamber of Commerce **[57605]**
Livestock Marketing Association **[1766]**
"LiveWell Center Opens" in *Mississippi Business
Journal* (Vol. 29, January 2007, No. 2, pp. 10)
[18441], **[41047]**
"Livin' la vida promo" in *Incentive* (Vol. 174, No. 10,
October 2000, pp. 28) **[47199]**, **[53838]**
"Living on the Hedge" in *Entrepreneur* (Vol. 31, No.
7, July 2003, pp. 49) **[10063]**, **[15222]**, **[38192]**
"Living High on the Blog" in *Entrepreneur* (Vol. 33,
February 2005, No. 2, pp. 65) **[3553]**, **[27422]**,
[31183], **[34144]**, **[47200]**, **[50453]**, **[50621]**
"Living the Lifestyle of the Successful
Businessperson" in *Hispanic Business*
(January/February 2005, pp. 63, 64) **[6712]**,
[15853], **[26520]**, **[30371]**, **[36450]**, **[45377]**,
[48274], **[49129]**, **[56305]**
Living Lighting **[9120]**
"Living with Linux" in *PC Magazine* (February 6,
2001, pp. 63) **[34145]**, **[49130]**
"Living wage lands on death row; Legislature nears
ban on ordinances" in *Crain's Detroit Business*
(Vol. 16, No. 49, Dec. 4, 2000) **[40516]**
Livingston Area Chamber of Commerce **[62183]**,
[62523]
Livingston County Chamber of Commerce **[62948]**
Livingston County Economic Development
Center–SBDC Satellite Office **[61203]**
Livingston Enterprise **[62216]**
Livingston - Overton County Chamber of Commerce
[64942]
Livingston-Polk County Chamber of Commerce
[65365]
Livonia Chamber of Commerce **[61366]**
"Liz Claiborne Acquires Urban Sportswear Brand
Enyce" in *Black Enterprise* (Vol. 34, No. 7,
February 2004, pp. 29) **[5557]**, **[5679]**, **[50053]**
"L.L. Bean Chooses a New Advertising Agency" in
Portland Press Herald (October 1, 2005) **[697]**,
[5680], **[23623]**
Llano County Chamber of Commerce **[65366]**
Lloyd Staffing **[23423]**
"Lloyd Ward: Victim or Villan?" in *Black Enterprise*
(Vol. 34, No. 6, January 2004, pp. 60) **[45378]**

LM Capital Corp. **[58972]**
LMI Canada Inc. **[46142]**
"LMSB Deputy Commissioner stresses fairness for
taxpayers" in *Journal of Accountancy* (Vol. 190,
No. 4, October 2000, pp. 113) **[40517]**, **[53839]**,
[54648]
Loan Brokers Association–Information Services
[8338], **[8362]**, **[8417]**, **[31618]**, **[55996]**
Loan Express **[55994]**
"Loan guarantees: costs of default and benefits to
small firms" in *Journal of Business Venturing*
(Vol. 16, No. 6, Nov. 2001, pp. 595) **[44571]**,
[52907], **[55711]**
"Loan Stars" in *Hispanic Business* (March 2004, pp.
38, 40) **[10064]**, **[39855]**, **[44572]**, **[48275]**
"A Loan Time" in *Entrepreneur* (Vol. 32, November
2004, No. 11, pp. 69) **[10065]**, **[44573]**
"Loan Will Go To Help Old Area" in *Sacramento
Bee* (December 20, 2005) **[28416]**, **[32545]**
"LoanGiant.com Files for Chapter 11" in *Crain's
Detroit Business* (Vol. 21, October 10, 2005,
No. 43, pp. 3) **[10066]**, **[17403]**, **[29372]**,
[40518]
"Loans, grants, and more" in *BlackEnterprise* (Vol.
32, No. 2, September 2001, pp. 46) **[39856]**,
[40051], **[44574]**, **[48913]**
"Loans can be more than just the numbers" in
Atlanta Business Chronicle (Vol. 23, No. 52,
June 1, 2001, pp. 52A) **[39444]**, **[44575]**
Loansforbusiness.Com **[3895]**
"Loanworthy Women" in *Business Week* (June 12,
2000, pp. F8) **[39857]**, **[44576]**, **[56306]**
Local Area Networks 6471, 6647
"Local Business Bankruptcies Outpace Nation" in
Boston Business Journal (Vol. 22, No. 16, May
24, 2002, pp. 1) **[28417]**, **[32546]**
"Local Business Changes Name" in *Bellingham
Business Journal* (January 2007, pp. 3) **[698]**,
[3188], **[14209]**, **[18652]**, **[25886]**, **[28418]**,
[34146], **[56307]**
"Local Businesses Discover There's No Place Like
Home" in *Bradenton Herald* (February 7, 2005)
[28419], **[36451]**, **[52693]**
"Local Companies Position Themselves Following
News of Stargate Sale" in *Pittsburgh Business
Times* (Vol. 23, No. 7, September 5, 2003)
[3554], **[15223]**
"Local Courses Try to Stay Chipper after Weak
Year" in *Crain's Detroit Business* (Vol. 19, No.
14, April 7, 2003, pp. 14) **[11269]**, **[28420]**,
[32547]
"Local Daily Papers Hit Hard by Declining
Circulation" in *Crain's Detroit Business* (Vol. 22,
December 4, 2006, No. 49, pp. 3) **[18236]**,
[29929], **[48863]**
Local Development Corporation of East New
York–East Brooklyn Enterprise Center **[63199]**
"Local Economy to Do Better Than State, Nation in
'07" in *San Diego Business Journal* (Vol. 28,
January 1, 2007, No. 1, pp. 1) **[28421]**, **[32548]**
*Local Enterprises in the Global Economy: Issues of
Governance and Upgrading* **[28422]**, **[32549]**,
[43735], **[45379]**
"Local Entrepreneurs cash in on trend in women-
only health clubs" in *Westchester County
Business Journal* (Jan. 21, 2002, pp. 1)
[19412], **[53840]**
"Local Filmmaker Directs Smoking Ads" in
Milwaukee Journal Sentinel (December 13,
2005) **[699]**, **[9726]**, **[54218]**
"Local Gelato King is Getting Ready to Expand His
Empire" in *Bellingham Business Journal*
(January 2007, pp. A4) **[12783]**, **[28423]**,
[30567], **[52908]**
"Local tech firms mine for government gold" in
Atlanta Business Chronicle (Vol. 25, November
15, 2002, No. 23 pp. 6C) **[37161]**, **[40052]**
"Local Hero: Ken Enright of MFS Bets on
Underdogs-and Usually Wins" in *Barron's*
(September 8, 2003) **[10067]**, **[15224]**, **[38193]**
"Local Investors Eye Chip Plant" in *Orlando
Business Journal* (Vol. 20, No. 11, August 29,
2003, pp. 1) **[15010]**, **[15225]**, **[40058]**, **[41810]**,
[50911], **[53115]**

"Local ISPs NAS, Open Access Join Forces" in
Bellingham Business Journal (January 2007, pp.
A6) **[14210]**, **[41811]**, **[50054]**
"Local Labs are Working to Perfect DNA Probes" in
Kansas City Star (March 8, 2005) **[41048]**,
[44089], **[50912]**, **[52143]**
Local Merchant Display Centers **[886]**
"Local Motion: For a Competitive Edge, Offer Items
Made Locally" in *Entrepreneur* (Vol. 32,
November 2004, No. 11, pp. 90) **[24967]**,
[30907], **[46342]**, **[55112]**
"Local Paradox" in *Atlanta Business Chronicle* (Vol.
23, No. 40, March 9, 2001, pp. 1B) **[28424]**,
[47201]
"Local execs buy ad agency from parent" in *Crain's
Detroit Business* (Vol. 19, No. 15, April 14,
2003, pp. 25) **[700]**, **[15226]**, **[47202]**, **[50055]**
"Local nonprofits benefit from polluter-pay rulings"
in *Crain's Detroit Business* (Vol. 19, No. 1,
January 6, 2003, pp. 19) **[37307]**, **[40519]**,
[46343]
"Local Realty Firm's Owner Confident In Strength of
Real Estate Market" in *Bradenton Herald*
(January 28, 2005) **[20576]**, **[28425]**
"Local Restaurants Report Sales Decline since
Sept. 11" in *Crain's Detroit Business* (Vol. 18,
No. 17, April 29, 2002, pp. 16) **[21552]**, **[28426]**
"Local Truckers Cheer an Upsurge in Business" in
Birmingham Business Journal (Vol. 20, No. 28,
July 11, 2003, pp. 15) **[25397]**, **[28427]**
"Localizing the Brand" in *Inc.* (October 2005, pp.
54-56) **[12994]**, **[23491]**, **[40520]**, **[43736]**
"Location of Huge Development Depends on
Interchange Site" in *St. Louis Post-Dispatch*
(January 6, 2005) **[7405]**, **[20228]**, **[46344]**
"Location, Location, Location" in *Black Enterprise*
(Vol. 36, November 2005, No. 4, pp. 64) **[5681]**,
[52694], **[54970]**
"Location, Location, Location" in *Inc.* (October 17,
2000, pp. 57) **[28428]**, **[52695]**
"Location, Location, Location" in *Sales & Marketing
Management* (Vol. 159, January-February 2007,
No. 1, pp. 28) **[47203]**, **[51717]**
"Lock it Away" in *Entrepreneur* (Vol. 31, No. 11,
November 2003, pp. 62) **[6261]**, **[22284]**,
[34147], **[44333]**
Lock Haven University of Pennsylvania
SBDC Outreach Center **[64334]**
Small Business Development Center
[64335]
Lock Museum of America **[16259]**
Lock Museum of America Inc.–Library **[16267]**
"Locker Room Tactics" in *Hispanic Business*
(October 2002, pp. 76) **[3555]**, **[32041]**,
[34974], **[45380]**, **[48571]**, **[53841]**
Lockhart Chamber of Commerce **[65367]**
Lockheed Martin–Manassas Library **[6548]**
Lockheed Martin Orincon Corp. **[7001]**
Lockheed Martin Utility Services, Inc.–Portsmouth
Gaseous Diffusion Plant–X-710 Library MS-
2206 **[56691]**
Lockney Chamber of Commerce **[65368]**
Lockport Chamber of Commerce **[59576]**
"Lockport, N.Y.-Based First Niagara Financial to
Open More Branches, Buy Bank" in *The Buffalo
News* (April 11, 2203) **[10068]**, **[38194]**,
[44577], **[50056]**
"Lockport Tops Eastern Niagara List" in *Business
First Buffalo* (Vol. 19, No. 44, July 25, 2003, pp.
1) **[27889]**, **[28429]**, **[52696]**, **[53738]**
Locksmith Ledger's Security Register **[16262]**,
[22285]
Lodging Magazine **[12670]**
*Lodging Magazine-American Hotel and Motel
Association Buyers Guide* **[12592]**
Lodi Area Chamber of Commerce **[63721]**
"Lodi, Calif., Couple Combines Winery with Bed and
Breakfast" in *The Record* (August 25, 2003)
[2446], **[23492]**
Lodi Chamber of Commerce **[57606]**, **[66443]**
"Lodi Twp. Development Homes To Start at $1 M;
Project Would Be First in County" in *Crain's
Detroit Business* (January 17, 2005) No **[7406]**
Loeb & Loeb LLP–Law Library **[9536]**
Loeb Partners Corp. **[63129]**
Loeb Retail Letter **[51429]**

"Loehmann's New Owner Keeps the Faith" in *Fortune* (Vol. 151, February 7, 2005, No. 3, pp. 26) [15227], [28430], [36452], [51232], [52557]

"Loft, Condo Projects Planned in Birmingham, Ferndale" in *Crain's Detroit Business* (Vol. 22, December 18, 2006, No. 51, pp. 16) [7407], [20056], [47204]

"Log on for work" in *Black Enterprise* (Vol. 33, No. 3, October 2002, pp. 74) [9225], [9571], [9930], [14211], [15338], [34148], [35587], [37425], [42329]

Logan Chamber of Commerce [60168]

Logan County Area Chamber of Commerce [63722]

Logan County Chamber of Commerce [58398], [60536], [66283]

Logan Farms Honey Glazed Hams [4073]

Logan - Hocking Chamber of Commerce [63723]

Logansport - Cass County Chamber of Commerce [59962]

Logansport Chamber of Commerce [60655]

"Logged on; Moon Valley Furniture's New Owner Expanding Biz." in *Crain's Detroit Business* (Vol. 23, January 29, 2007, No. 5, pp. 3) [12293], [28431], [29930], [47205]

LOGIBASE [6908]

"Logitech MX Revolution Cordless Laser Mouse" in *Sales & Marketing Management* (Vol. 159, January-February 2007, No. 1, pp. 42) [6713], [49131]

"Logo design reflects on your business; so take it seriously" in *San Antonio Business Journal* (Vol. 15, No. 4, Feb. 16, 2001, pp. 18) [5994], [50622]

"Logos That Turn Heads" in *Inc.* (December 1, 2003) [12896], [20134], [47206], [50454]

"LoJack's Stronger Signal" in *Business Week* (January 16, 2006, No. 3967, pp. 50) [1945], [4341], [18080], [22286]

Loleta Chamber of Commerce [57607]

Loma Linda Chamber of Commerce [57608]

Loma Linda University–Del E. Webb Memorial Library [1720]

Lombard Area Chamber of Commerce and Industry [59577]

Lomira Area Chamber of Commerce [66444]

Lomita Chamber of Commerce [57609]

Lompoc Valley Chamber of Commerce and Visitors' Bureau [57610]

London-Laurel County Chamber of Commerce [60537]

Lone Pine Chamber of Commerce [57611]

Lone Star Chamber of Commerce [65369]

"Lonely at the Top: Blacks Are a Fraction of Top Editors at Mainstream Magazines" in *Black Enterprise* (Vol. 35, September 2004, No. 2) [18899], [48572], [53842]

Long Beach Area Chamber of Commerce [57612]

Long Beach Chamber of Commerce [62949]

Long Beach Public Library–Performing Arts Department [4176]

Long Island Association [62950]

"Long Island Banks Compete for Customers by Offering 'Pay Less' ATMs" in *Long Island Business News* (February 13, 2004) [10069], [31760], [47207]

"Long Island Banks Upgrade IT to Improve Service, Sales" in *Long Island Business News* (February 13, 2004) [6714], [10070], [31761], [41812]

Long Island Better Business Bureau [62809]

"Long Island Builders Institute Responds to the Need for More Affordable Housing" in *Long Island Business News* (February 6, 2004) [7408], [20577]

Long Island Business News [63234]

Long Island Business News (February 27, 2004); "A Computer on Every Desk: Online Learning Takes Off" in [4623], [6613], [13917], [22947], [33050], [33696]

Long Island Business News (April 2, 2004); "AcutionASAP: Another eBay But Without All the Hassles" in [1772], [7157], [18636], [33512]

Long Island Business News (February 13, 2004); "Advisory Board Members Help Students Understand Market and Customers" in [31634], [46664]

Long Island Business News (March 12, 2004); "After Bitter Dot-Com Pill, Market Sweetens for Office Suite Operators" in [20204], [20416], [20788], [21307], [22563], [27303], [27757]

Long Island Business News (May 7, 2004); "Albany Eyes Real Estate Transfer Tax" in [20419], [20790], [54425]

Long Island Business News (March 5, 2004); "Alternative Minimum Tax has Expanded Annually to Include More and More Taxpayers" in [53581], [54427]

Long Island Business News (February 27, 2004); "Amityville-Based Napco Security Systems Back in Good With Nasdaq" in [14738], [22167]

Long Island Business News (May 7, 2004); "An E-Mail from the IRS? Don't Believe It" in [13993], [27352], [27627], [30217], [33810], [54526]

Long Island Business News (February 27, 2004); "Andrea Electronics Completes Stage 1 of Restructuring" in [7714], [44886]

Long Island Business News (March 12, 2004); "Applebee Int'l Sets Up Loans for Remodeling by Franchises" in [21439], [22178], [37253], [38710], [44470]

Long Island Business News (February 27, 2004); "Arbor Realty Provides $35M in Financing" in [20424], [20797], [27784], [51052]

Long Island Business News (February 20, 2004); "Arrow Electronics Moves to Cut Costs, Reports 4Q Income" in [7716], [14746]

Long Island Business News (February 20, 2004); "Bank and Thrift Stocks Report Solid 4th Quarter" in [9829], [14770]

Long Island Business News (March 5, 2004); "Bethpage-based Cablevision Systems to Complete an Internal Accounting Review" in [85], [86], [4076], [4086], [25793], [26166]

Long Island Business News (March 12, 2004); "Brookhaven Revising Commercial Development Codes After Developer Backlash" in [7268], [7536], [38554], [40206]

Long Island Business News (March 12, 2004); "Cablevision Systems Corp. Tops 1M Interactive Optimum Customers" in [4086], [4097], [27917]

Long Island Business News (February 27, 2004); "Cablevision in Talks to Sell Fox Sports Stake to Comcast" in [14822], [24390], [49834]

Long Island Business News (Feb.27,2004); "California based Robeks Fruit Smoothies Sets Expansion in NY Metro..." in [12051], [21461], [27919], [38733]

Long Island Business News (February 27, 2004); "Carle-Based Pliskin Realty & Dev. Brokers Space for All State and Carvel" in [20456], [20825]

Long Island Business News (February 27, 2004); "CB Richard Ellis Nabs Leasing Contract of 175 Fulton Ave. in Hempstead" in [20460], [20827], [21315], [52651]

Long Island Business News (February 6, 2004); "CFO's Exit Returns CPI Aerostructures Inc. to Recruiting Market" in [42199], [44989]

Long Island Business News (February 27, 2004); "Commentary: 'About Us' Pages Spell Good Business, Consumer Confidence" in [13913], [25818], [33690], [46816], [53653]

Long Island Business News (February 6, 2004); "Commentary: Departure of Jobs Hurts National Security" in [22195], [32321], [46245], [49684]

Long Island Business News (March 12, 2004); "Commentary: For Women in Management, Communication is King" in [27320], [28260], [43011], [45013], [56165], [58712]

Long Island Business News (February 6, 2004); "Commentary: Is America Ill Positioned for Global Economy?" in [32322], [43590], [49685]

Long Island Business News (February 13, 2004); "Commentary: Mergers: A Meeting of the Minds" in [9892], [14876], [49867]

Long Island Business News (February 20, 2004); "Commentary: 'Opportunity Calls': Networking With an Agenda" in [46817], [51592]

Long Island Business News (February 20, 2004); "Commentary: Real Estate Binders: Are They Enforceable?" in [20470], [20839], [29157], [40268]

Long Island Business News (January 30, 2004); "Commentary: Research is Key To Getting Hired in 'Jobless Recovery'" in [42205], [53654]

Long Island Business News (March 12, 2004); "Commentary: Testimonials-Let Your Customers Do the Talking" in [31664], [33691], [46818], [50577]

Long Island Business News (March 12, 2004); "Commentary: Testimonials-Let Your Customers Do the Talking" in [31665], [33692], [46819], [50578]

Long Island Business News (February 13, 2004); "Commentary: Three Steps to Becoming a Business Leader in Your Field" in [35954], [45014], [56166]

Long Island Business News (January 30, 2004); "Commentary: Turning Job Losses to Indian Into Gains" in [22196], [43591], [53655]

Long Island Business News (March 12, 2004); "Connecticut's Biggest Bank Heading to Long Island" in [9896], [10746], [30142], [31120], [47519], [49871]

Long Island Business News (Feb. 13, 2004); "Consumer Bankers Assn. Files Petition With FCC Seeking Clarification About Do Not Call" in [24283], [40281]

Long Island Business News (March 5, 2004); "Corporate Image-Maker Sees Hope for Symbol, Pain for Computer Associates" in [111], [6589], [6620], [12878], [13345], [19889], [20114], [26196], [27120], [30293], [31132], [41619], [48014], [50434]

Long Island Business News (March 12, 2004); "CPI Aerostructures Wins $3M Contract for Assemblies" in [27981], [28949], [44186], [46252]

Long Island Business News (March 12, 2004); "Dawson on Board at Melville-based Fala Direct Marketing" in [44744], [45044], [46777], [46872]

Long Island Business News (February 27, 2004); "Deer Park-Based Cannillo Motorsports Sells High-End Cars for the Masses" in [1799], [18007], [28011]

Long Island Business News (February 27, 2004); "East End PR Firm Helps Give Webshots One More Shot" in [4184], [19229], [19297], [46925], [48664]

Long Island Business News (January 30, 2004); "Ethanol Additive Pushes Long Island Gas Prices Up In January" in [22612]

Long Island Business News (Feb.6, 2004); "Farmingdale-based THM Scientific Introduces Product Line Based on Sustainable Agriculture" in [16012], [26508], [48728], [49927], [50872], [52097]

Long Island Business News (February 13, 2004); "Federal Legislation Lays Groundwork for Electronic Check Exchange" in [9948], [31546], [40372]

Long Island Business News (January 30, 2004); "Federal Trade Comm. Report Says Long Island a Favorite of Scam Artists" in [29236], [30220]

Long Island Business News (February 13, 2004); "Financial Advisors Give Last-Minute Tax Tips for Small Businesses" in [143], [14983], [23940], [54554]

Long Island Business News (February 27, 2004); "For Acclaim, Business as Brutal as a Video Game" in [1104], [4666], [23003]

Long Island Business News (May 7, 2004); "For Auditors, Gain From All That Pain" in [150], [2903], [23944], [26239]

Long Island Business News (March 12, 2004); "For Big-Box Retailers, It's Market, Market, Market" in [48689], [50076], [51165], [52673]

Long Island Business News (March 12, 2004); "For Riesterer's Bake Shops, Low-Carb Diets are Just Another Fad" in [2248], [2291], [11228], [11326], [11920], [12007], [12054], [13073]

Long Island Business News (Jan. 30, 2004); "Former Computer Associates Executive Pleads Guilty in U.S. District Court in Brooklyn" in **[152]**, **[2904]**, **[23945]**, **[26242]**, **[29250]**, **[40397]**

Long Island Business News (March 12, 2004); "Former Information Warrior D'Amico Now Fighting Cyberwarfare" in **[22234]**, **[22961]**, **[33917]**, **[34477]**, **[42328]**, **[44298]**, **[53290]**, **[55600]**

Long Island Business News (February 6, 2004); "Franchisees of Huntington Station-based Relax the Back Find Success on Long Island" in **[37657]**, **[38796]**, **[51167]**

Long Island Business News (February 27, 2004); "Frank Otto Named EDO's COO" in **[40024]**, **[41698]**, **[45161]**, **[52103]**

Long Island Business News (May 7, 2004); "Green Energy Co. Goes Public" in **[15054]**, **[16304]**, **[28232]**

Long Island Business News (February 13, 2004); "Hamptons Newspapers Vie for Spanish Readership" in **[18880]**, **[25086]**

Long Island Business News (Mar.5,2004); "Hauppauge-Based Robert Martin Advertising Attracts Customers in the Same Way It Helps Them" in **[654]**, **[47059]**

Long Island Business News (Jan.30,2004); "Hauppauge-based Spellman High Voltage Electronics Doubles the Size of Its Bohemia Facility" in **[7730]**, **[28268]**, **[41729]**, **[46311]**

Long Island Business News (January 30, 2004); "Health Savings Accounts Not Getting Much Attention from Garden City-Area Employers" in **[13318]**, **[41024]**, **[43211]**

Long Island Business News (February 20, 2004); "Hedge Funds Beat S&P 500 Index's Return in January 2004" in **[9996]**, **[15074]**, **[32471]**

Long Island Business News (February 27, 2004); "Henry Schein Expands Office Space in Melville" in **[8786]**, **[28271]**, **[41028]**

Long Island Business News (Feb. 20, 2004); "Hicksville-Based KeySpan Trains Managers to Take Over Blue-Collar/Clerical Jobs..." in **[45237]**, **[55295]**

Long Island Business News (February 20, 2004); "Hospitals Across Long Island Shift to Digital Imaging Technology" in **[41030]**, **[41748]**

Long Island Business News (March 5, 2004); "In Accounting, Number of Registered Sole Practitioners Decreasing" in **[169]**, **[2916]**, **[23964]**, **[26263]**, **[53803]**, **[54304]**

Long Island Business News (February 13, 2004); "Industry Experts Expect Mergers to Remain Strong Among Banks" in **[10023]**, **[15123]**, **[50000]**

Long Island Business News (March 12, 2004); "Interest in Commercial Brownfield Properties High, but Action Still on Hold" in **[7335]**, **[7387]**, **[38793]**, **[40470]**

Long Island Business News (Feb.6, 2004); "Internet Law Arena Marked by Issues About Spam, Pop-Up Ads, Domain Names, and File Sharing" in **[14156]**, **[29313]**, **[34078]**, **[40473]**, **[47147]**

Long Island Business News (March 5, 2004); "Introduction by TS Provides Personal Matchmaking for Long Island and NYC Clientele" in **[7059]**, **[56283]**, **[58839]**

Long Island Business News (February 20, 2004); "JPMorgan Chase Helps LI Crisis Center" in **[10048]**, **[15192]**, **[54213]**

Long Island Business News (January 30, 2004); "JPMorgan Chase Regional Economist Forecasts Long Island Growth for 2004" in **[28366]**, **[32528]**, **[46333]**, **[52552]**

Long Island Business News (May 7, 2004); "King Kullen Freshening Up Image" in **[11638]**, **[12893]**, **[20131]**, **[30900]**, **[50451]**, **[50614]**

Long Island Business News (February 13, 2004); "L.A. Fitness Works on Second Long Island Location" in **[19411]**

Long Island Business News (Mar. 5, 2004); "Lake Success Based Astoria Financial Finds Fewer Acquisition Opportunities..." in **[10053]**, **[15201]**, **[32536]**, **[50035]**

Long Island Business News (March 12, 2004); "LI Banks $2 Million in State Environmental Grants for Waterfront Projects" in **[7402]**, **[7669]**, **[35942]**, **[37306]**, **[39854]**, **[39995]**

Long Island Business News (February 13, 2004); "Long Island Banks Compete for Customers by Offering 'Pay Less' ATMs" in **[10069]**, **[31760]**, **[47207]**

Long Island Business News (February 13, 2004); "Long Island Banks Upgrade IT to Improve Service, Sales" in **[6714]**, **[10070]**, **[31761]**, **[41812]**

Long Island Business News (February 6, 2004); "Long Island Builders Institute Responds to the Need for More Affordable Housing" in **[7408]**, **[20577]**

Long Island Business News (March 5, 2004); "Long Island Development Corp. Steps Up Loan Programs in 2003" in **[39858]**, **[41262]**, **[42600]**, **[44578]**

Long Island Business News (March 5, 2004); "Long Island Financial Briefs: March 5, 2004" in **[17404]**, **[40521]**

Long Island Business News (February 6, 2004); "Long Island Law Firm Takes Steps To Increase Pro Bono Work" in **[29373]**, **[54219]**

Long Island Business News (March 5, 2004); "Long Island's East End to Get a New TV Station" in **[24096]**, **[24427]**, **[50057]**, **[50094]**

Long Island Business News (February 20, 2004); "Long Island's Industrial Agencies Spend $733 Million in 2003 on Economic Incentives" in **[28432]**, **[46345]**, **[52697]**

Long Island Business News (March 12, 2004); "Long Island's Newsday Fields Post-Redesign Reactions" in **[18696]**, **[18900]**, **[30901]**, **[31762]**

Long Island Business News (March 5, 2004); "Long Island's Patent Production Falls Nearly 20 Percent Since 1988" in **[4718]**, **[23069]**, **[28433]**, **[32550]**, **[40053]**, **[44090]**, **[50913]**, **[52144]**, **[53355]**

Long Island Business News (January 30, 2004); "Longislandwinecountry.com Challenges the Long Island Wine Council's Trademark" in **[23493]**, **[44091]**

Long Island Business News (February 6, 2004); "Manhattan-based Terra Holdings Acquires Dunemere Associates" in **[15248]**, **[20583]**, **[20934]**, **[50069]**

Long Island Business News (February 6, 2004); "Martin Family Estate Sells the Knole to Development Interest for $11M" in **[7420]**, **[20585]**, **[20936]**

Long Island Business News (March 5, 2004); "Medfone Expanding Its Wantagh Headquarters" in **[41054]**, **[41110]**, **[47379]**, **[49716]**, **[49982]**, **[52562]**

Long Island Business News (February 6, 2004); "Melville-Based DealerTrack Inc. Sue Rival Mich.-Based RouteOne" in **[10086]**, **[18090]**, **[29381]**, **[31564]**, **[34189]**, **[44096]**

Long Island Business News (February 20, 2004); "Michael Witt Hired as Long Island Partnership 'Concierge'" in **[28481]**, **[52700]**

Long Island Business News (February 6, 2004); "Microsoft Makes Security Vow" in **[4727]**, **[22294]**, **[23080]**, **[53367]**

Long Island Business News (March 5, 2004); "Mortgage Warehouse in Melville Announces Staffing Changes" in **[196]**, **[17419]**, **[26295]**, **[45445]**

Long Island Business News (February 6, 2004); "Motorola Foundation Funds 'Road Map' for Employers Who Hire People With Disabilities" in **[42351]**, **[54229]**

Long Island Business News (March 5, 2004); "Nassau County Executive Tom Suozzi Proposes Empire Zone" in **[29431]**, **[30161]**, **[50104]**, **[52703]**

Long Island Business News (March 5, 2004); "Nassau County's New Taxi and Limousine Commission to Begin its Work Soon" in **[15953]**, **[16183]**, **[23907]**, **[24236]**

Long Island Business News (March 12, 2004); "Nassau Democrats Propose Reforms to Prevent Mismanagement" in **[32583]**, **[40543]**

Long Island Business News (February 13, 2004); "Nathan's Reverses Loss, Posts Third Quarter Profit" in **[21570]**, **[36521]**

Long Island Business News (January 30, 2004); "National Survey Finds More Small-Business Owners Planning to Increase Their Staffs" in **[10099]**, **[15287]**, **[28526]**, **[42355]**, **[53873]**

Long Island Business News (January 30, 2004); "New Chain 'Drug Stores' in Long Island Fill the Gap..." in **[8795]**, **[51264]**

Long Island Business News (February 20, 2004); "New Rochelle-Based Simone Development Increases its Long Island Holdings" in **[28549]**, **[46387]**

Long Island Business News (February 6, 2004); "New York Community Bancorp Renames All of Its Branches..." in **[10108]**, **[47339]**, **[50646]**

Long Island Business News (February 27, 2004); "Newsday Suit Lawyer Enlists 'Big Firms'" in **[18916]**, **[29413]**

Long Island Business News (March 12, 2004); "Nikon's Newly Created Long Island Unit to Scout Tech Trends for the Home Office" in **[4178]**, **[4193]**, **[42688]**, **[42821]**, **[49170]**, **[50171]**

Long Island Business News (February 20, 2004); "North Fork Bancorp Acquires GreenPoint Financial" in **[15307]**, **[50108]**

Long Island Business News (March 12, 2004); "North Fork Bancorp to Trim Employees of Two Acquisitions" in **[10112]**, **[10483]**, **[15308]**, **[50109]**, **[51140]**

Long Island Business News (Jan.30,2004); "North Massapequa-based Love 'n' Care Pet Sitting Service Walks, Trains, and Cares for Pets" in **[19077]**, **[19114]**, **[19194]**

Long Island Business News (February 6, 2004); "Northeast's Largest Independent Accounting Firm Comes to Long Island" in **[209]**, **[2939]**, **[24002]**, **[26305]**

Long Island Business News (March 5, 2004); "Northrop Grumman in Bethpage Celebrates National Engineers Week..." in **[41876]**, **[52163]**

Long Island Business News (Mar. 5, 04); "Northrop Grumman in Bethpage Celebrates National Engineers Week with Paper Airplane Contest" in **[41877]**, **[52164]**

Long Island Business News (February 6, 2004); "NY Bankruptcy Courts Shift to Online Filing" in **[29422]**, **[34275]**, **[40583]**

Long Island Business News (February 20, 2004); "NY Metro Gets $388M in Fourth-Quarter Venture Funds, Survey Says" in **[28577]**, **[55759]**

Long Island Business News (February 13, 2004); "NY State Attorney General Cracks Down on Auto and Credit Complaints" in **[10117]**, **[18105]**, **[31571]**

Long Island Business News (February 13, 2004); "NY State Senator Introduces Bill to Obtain Federal Funding for Genetic Research" in **[40068]**, **[40584]**, **[50938]**, **[52165]**

Long Island Business News (February 20, 2004); "NYC Eyes Taxes on 'Luxury' Items" in **[54683]**

Long Island Business News (Feb.20, 2004); "Oakdale Based Skills Unlimited Helps Long Island's Disabled Develop Skills and Find Work" in **[42367]**, **[54235]**

Long Island Business News (March 12, 2004); "One Liberty Properties Snaps Up San Diego Area Cinema for $11.5M" in **[17329]**, **[17528]**, **[20384]**, **[20616]**, **[20957]**

Long Island Business News (February 13, 2004); "Optimum Online Launches Online Arcade Service" in **[24825]**, **[34313]**

Long Island Business News (February 6, 2004); "Orbit International Corp. Expects $1M in UPS Orders" in **[40072]**, **[46398]**

Long Island Business News (February 13, 2004); "OSI Pharmaceuticals Hopes to Get FDA Approval for Its Cancer Drug" in **[8796]**, **[50940]**, **[52167]**

Long Island Business News (Feb. 13, 2004); "Owner of Panama Hatties in Huntington Station Plays Roles of Chef and Business Manager" in **[21579]**, **[45510]**

Long Island Business News (February 20, 2004); "Pall Corp. Plans to Sell New Bacteria-Detection System to Blood Banks" in **[41075]**, **[41894]**, **[50942]**, **[52169]**

Long Island Business News (February 6, 2004); "Patriot Ford in Copiague Driven to Bankruptcy Protection" in **[18108]**, **[28613]**

Long Island Business News (January 30, 2004); "PC Maker Systemax Launches Software Unit" in **[4761]**, **[6753]**, **[23122]**, **[53406]**

Long Island Business News (March 5, 2004); "Plato's Closet, a Retail Outlet, Sells Teenagers Brand-Name Labels for Less" in **[5564]**, **[5703]**, **[7170]**, **[9634]**, **[38882]**, **[51291]**

Long Island Business News (February 13, 2004); "Private Investors Purchase a Controlling Stake at Ecoboard Holdings" in **[10141]**, **[15373]**, **[16318]**, **[46409]**, **[50140]**, **[55783]**

Long Island Business News (February 20, 2004); "Professional Financial Planners in Garden City Appoints Steiger Financial..." in **[15378]**, **[47426]**

Long Island Business News (May 7, 2004); "Rep. Israel: Extend Terrorism Reinsurance Program Through '06" in **[13444]**, **[22344]**, **[43339]**

Long Island Business News (March 5, 2004); "Researchers Test Bioterrorism Sensors in Greenwich Village and on Long Island" in **[40175]**, **[41943]**, **[50958]**, **[51995]**, **[52190]**, **[54399]**

Long Island Business News (March 5, 2004); "Restaurant Depot Expanding in Bohemia" in **[21295]**, **[21597]**, **[28700]**

Long Island Business News (March 12, 2004); "St. Catherine of Siena Medical Center Seeks to Block LIRR" in **[10581]**, **[10695]**, **[28816]**, **[29476]**, **[38975]**, **[40661]**

Long Island Business News (February 27, 2004); "School Career Centers Think Outside the Box" in **[33229]**, **[42407]**, **[45620]**

Long Island Business News (March 12, 2004); "Scientific Industries Acquires New Assets from Spectrum Labs" in **[15203]**, **[15433]**, **[47772]**, **[49637]**, **[50170]**, **[52198]**

Long Island Business News (February 27, 2004); "SEC Opens Inquiry Linked to Newsday Circulation" in **[18932]**, **[29481]**

Long Island Business News (May 7, 2004); "Service Franchises Hold Advantages Over Retail Operations" in **[38676]**, **[51036]**, **[52497]**

Long Island Business News (February 13, 2004); "Several Queen's Advertisers File $100M Lawsuit Against Newsday" in **[783]**, **[29486]**

Long Island Business News (March 12, 2004); "Small Business Protests Loan Program Shift" in **[38292]**, **[39012]**, **[39928]**, **[40700]**, **[44659]**

Long Island Business News (Feb. 20, 2004); "Smithtown-based LuminNet Helps Small Businesses Design and Market Their Own Web Sites" in **[25967]**, **[34504]**, **[47553]**

Long Island Business News (March 5, 2004); "Southampton Town Board Approves a $20 Million Affordable Housing Development Plan" in **[7422]**, **[7484]**, **[28214]**, **[28800]**

Long Island Business News (March 5, 2004); "Suffolk County Executive Names Andrea Lohneiss as Commissioner of Economic Development" in **[32729]**, **[34169]**

Long Island Business News (March 5, 2004); "Summit Plastics Pursues Acquisition of Industrial Property in Bay Shore" in **[7904]**, **[22495]**, **[22802]**, **[44359]**, **[46449]**

Long Island Business News (Feb. 13, 2004); "Survey Projects that Nation's Banks Will Spend More on Information Technology in 2004" in **[10196]**, **[13089]**, **[44371]**, **[54012]**

Long Island Business News (Feb. 27, 2004); "...Survey Shows Employees Using Work Computers for Romantic/Sexual Activity" in **[40746]**, **[45693]**

Long Island Business News (Feb. 6, 2004); "Susan McMillan Appointed Executive Director of the Long Island Better Business Bureau" in **[29532]**, **[39622]**, **[56424]**

Long Island Business News (January 30, 2004); "Swezey's Department Store Sites Sought By a Diversity of Businesses" in **[51376]**, **[52736]**

Long Island Business News (February 6, 2004); "Symbol Technologies Appoints Steinberg as CTO and VP of Its Mobility Solutions Group" in **[5127]**, **[42023]**, **[45696]**

Long Island Business News (March 5, 2004); "Symbol Technologies Inc. Hires Former IBM Executive" in **[40248]**, **[42024]**, **[45697]**, **[46325]**, **[48888]**, **[51378]**

Long Island Business News (January 30, 2004); "Symbol Technologies Wins Landmark Lawsuit in Nevada Federal Court" in **[29534]**, **[44158]**, **[51379]**

Long Island Business News (February 20, 2004); "Systemax Pares U.S., LI Staff" in **[6819]**, **[28853]**

Long Island Business News (February 6, 2004); "TGIFridays to Open Restaurant at Islip MacArthur Airport" in **[21645]**, **[28880]**, **[38926]**

Long Island Business News (February 27, 2004); "Tritec Deal is a Symbol of Commercial Real Estate Market Strength" in **[20691]**, **[21027]**, **[21357]**

Long Island Business News (February 13, 2004); "Two Companies Find Investment at Long Island VC Forum" in **[44679]**, **[55876]**

Long Island Business News (February 27, 2004); "Union-Based Del Labs Has Strong Fourth Quarter" in **[2609]**, **[7907]**, **[8804]**

Long Island Business News (February 27, 2004); "U.S. CFOs Bullish on Hiring" in **[42447]**, **[45779]**, **[54052]**

Long Island Business News (March 12, 2004); "U.S. District Court of Appeals Sides with Baby Bells Over 1996 Telecommunications Act" in **[5159]**, **[5542]**, **[29563]**, **[30495]**, **[30979]**, **[31616]**, **[39097]**, **[40794]**

Long Island Business News (March 5, 2004); "U.S. District Court Issues Injunction to Prevent Hi-Tech Pharmacal..." in **[8805]**, **[29564]**, **[44175]**

Long Island Business News (February 13, 2004); "Used Car Dealers' Business Held Up by NY Department of Motor Vehicles" in **[18155]**, **[40802]**

Long Island Business News (February 13, 2004); "Voom Direct-Broadcast Satellite Service Offers High Definition News" in **[24458]**, **[42101]**

Long Island Business News (February 13, 2004); "Wi-Fi is a Must for New Office Space on Long Island" in **[5179]**, **[14623]**, **[34725]**, **[42118]**, **[49365]**, **[52754]**

Long Island Business News (February 27, 2004); "Woman Car Dealership Owner Brings Fresh Outlook to Male-Oriented Business" in **[18164]**, **[56485]**

Long Island Business News (February 20, 2004); "Woodbury-Based Bankers Life of New York Reports Record Sales" in **[13521]**, **[43424]**

Long Island Business News (February 6, 2004); "World Savings Bank Opens First LI Location" in **[10256]**, **[29031]**, **[51418]**

Long Island Business News (Vol. 50, No. 14, March 28, 2003, pp. 23A); "Yoga Instructor finds peace in classroom" in **[17923]**, **[19450]**, **[56522]**

"Long Island Development Corp. Steps Up Loan Programs in 2003" in *Long Island Business News* (March 5, 2004) **[39858]**, **[41262]**, **[42600]**, **[44578]**

"Long Island Financial Briefs: March 5, 2004" in *Long Island Business News* (March 5, 2004) **[17404]**, **[40521]**

Long Island High Technology Incubator **[63200]**

"Long Island Law Firm Takes Steps To Increase Pro Bono Work" in *Long Island Business News* (February 6, 2004) **[29373]**, **[54219]**

Long Island Lighting Company–Resource Center **[11980]**, **[21291]**

Long Island Magazine **[63235]**

Long Island University
  Center for Business Research **[3939]**
  Development Services **[63201]**

Long Island University at Southhampton/Southampton Outreach Center–SBDC **[62767]**

"Long Island's East End to Get a New TV Station" in *Long Island Business News* (March 5, 2004) **[24096]**, **[24427]**, **[50057]**, **[50094]**

"Long Island's Industrial Agencies Spend $733 Million in 2003 on Economic Incentives" in *Long Island Business News* (February 20, 2004) **[28432]**, **[46345]**, **[52697]**

"Long Island's Newsday Fields Post-Redesign Reactions" in *Long Island Business News* (March 12, 2004) **[18696]**, **[18900]**, **[30901]**, **[31762]**

"Long Island's Patent Production Falls Nearly 20 Percent Since 1988" in *Long Island Business News* (March 5, 2004) **[4718]**, **[23069]**, **[28433]**, **[32550]**, **[40053]**, **[44090]**, **[50913]**, **[52144]**, **[53355]**

Long John Silver's **[21870]**

Long & Levit–Library **[29700]**, **[43457]**

"Long Live the New King of Bonds" in *Business Week* (January 16, 2006, No. 3967, pp. 68, 70) **[15228]**, **[38195]**, **[45381]**

Long Prairie Area Chamber of Commerce **[61619]**

"The Long Road to Free Trade" in *Hispanic Business* (July/August 2004, pp. 46) **[40522]**, **[43737]**

Long & Silverman Publishing Inc. **[62384]**

"Long-term bunker: Louis A. Holland thinks more turbulence is ahead" in *Black Enterprise* (Vol. 33, No. 3, Oct. 2002, pp. 48) **[10071]**, **[15229]**, **[32551]**, **[38196]**

"Long-Term Bunker: Louis A. Holland Thinks More Turbulence Is Ahead" in *Black Enterprise* (Vol. 33, No. 3, Oct. 2002, pp. 48) **[10072]**, **[15230]**, **[32552]**, **[38197]**

Long Term Care **[18357]**

"Long-Term Care Insurance is Growing Option Among Munster, Ind.-Area Families" in *The Times* (July 4, 2004) **[449]**, **[13371]**, **[18327]**, **[39859]**, **[43264]**

"Long-term dare" in *WorkingWoman* (Vol. 25, No. 7, August 2000, pp. 36) **[38198]**, **[56308]**

"Long-Term Technology" in *Black Enterprise* (Vol. 34, No. 4, November 2003, pp. 34) **[10073]**, **[15231]**, **[38199]**, **[41813]**, **[50914]**

"Long-Time Music Publisher Sings" in *San Fernando Valley Business Journal* (Vol. 11, November 2006, No. 24, pp. 26) **[2722]**, **[37714]**, **[46346]**, **[50058]**

"Long in the Tooth" in *Red Herring* (January 2003, pp. 72) **[10074]**, **[15232]**, **[28434]**, **[41814]**

"Long & Winding Road" in *Small Business Opportunities* (Vol. 12, No. 5, September 2000, pp. 84) **[3043]**, **[37162]**

Longboat Key Chamber of Commerce **[58886]**

"Longislandwinecountry.com Challenges the Long Island Wine Council's Trademark" in *Long Island Business News* (January 30, 2004) **[23493]**, **[44091]**

Longmont Area Chamber of Commerce **[58399]**

"Longtime Pitchmen Started Chain" in *Tampa Tribune* (November 17, 2005) **[21553]**, **[36453]**, **[37715]**, **[38848]**

Longview Partnership **[65370]**

Longwood Gardens, Inc.–Library **[11525]**

Longwood University - Crater SBDC **[65824]**

Longwood University at Farmville–Small Business Development Center **[65825]**

Longwood University SBDC at Martinsville **[65826]**

Longwood University SBDC at South Boston **[65827]**

Longworth Venture Partners, L.P. **[61086]**

Longy School of Music–Bakalar Music Library **[17687]**

Lonoke Area Chamber of Commerce **[57188]**

Look Before You Leap: Market Research Made Easy **[50915]**

"Look at the Big Economic Picture." in *Black Enterprise* (Vol. 35, September 2004, No. 2, pp. 38) **[10075]**, **[15233]**, **[32553]**

"Look for Early Stage Returns to Surge" in *Venture Capital Journal* (September 1, 2005) **[55712]**

"The Look of Fashion" in *Black Enterprise* (Vol. 34, No. 7, February 2004, pp. 45) **[5558]**, **[5682]**, **[9628]**

"The Look of Fashion: With a Splash of Paint and a Vision, Four Friends Became Entrepreneurs" in *Black Enterprise* (Vol. 34, No. 7) **[5559]**, **[5683]**, **[9629]**

"Look to the Future" in *Atlanta Business Chronicle* (Vol. 25, No. 20, October 25, 2002, pp. 1) **[7409]**, **[28435]**, **[41815]**

"Look before you lay off" in *Harvard Business Review* (Vol. 80, No. 4, April 2002, pp. 20) **[26282]**, **[32554]**, **[45382]**

"Look for the Pony" in *Forbes* (May 29, 2000, pp. 104) **[28436]**

"Look for a Sign" in *Entrepreneur* (Vol. 31, No. 8, August 2003, pp. 44) **[5045]**, **[6715]**, **[14212]**, **[41816]**

"Looking ahead" in *Black Enterprise* (Vol. 32, No. , , pp.) **[11640]**, **[32159]**, **[48276]**

Looking Ahead: Preparing to Meet the Future **[42929]**

"Looking for Attention" in *Entrepreneur* (Vol. 28, No. 11, November 2000, pp. 30) **[14213]**, **[18653]**, **[47208]**

"Looking For Winning Small Businesses" in *Crain's Detroit Business* (Vol. 23, February 5, 2007, No. 6, pp. 27) **[36454]**, **[50623]**, **[52909]**

"Looking Good" in *Small Business Opportunities* (Vol. 16, No. 1, January 2004, pp. 88) **[2594]**, **[7894]**

"Looking Into the Sun" in *Inc.* (Volume 27, July 2005, No. 7, pp. 76-79) **[7736]**, **[9366]**, **[36455]**, **[37308]**

Looking at It from Every Angle **[45928]**

"Looking for Leverage" in *Hispanic Business* (Vol. 23, No. 5, May 2001, pp. 32, 34, 36) **[3556]**, **[31184]**, **[31763]**, **[34149]**, **[41817]**, **[44334]**

"Looking for a bull market" in *BlackEnterprise* (Vol. 32, No. 3, October 2001, pp. 38) **[15234]**, **[38200]**, **[48277]**

"Looking for a club that's more than just for fun?" in *Women in Business* (Vol. 53, No. 1, January-February, 2001, pp. 41) **[15235]**, **[38201]**

"Looking for The Prevailing Wind The bulls and bears are both blowing plenty of hot air these days" in *Fortune* (May 15, 2000, p. 441) **[32555]**, **[52910]**

"The Lookout: It's time to play some war games" in *Red Herring* (No. 103, September 1, 2001, pp. 94) **[41818]**, **[50059]**

"The Lookout: New trading system will pay off for Nyfix" in *Red Herring* (No. 105, October 1, 2001, pp. 94) **[6950]**, **[15236]**

"Looks do matter" in *Black Enterprise* (Vol. 32, No. 9, April 2002, pp. 114) **[14214]**, **[25887]**, **[34150]**

"Looming Large: Are Small-Business Contracts Really Going to the Big Guys?" in *Entrepreneur* (Vol. 31, No. 9, September 2003, pp. 22) **[40054]**

Loomis Basin Chamber of Commerce **[57613]**

Loomsong **[8045]**

"Looting Luggage: Safeguarding Your Valuables Against Airport Employee Theft" in *Black Enterprise* (Vol. 34, No. 6, January 2004) **[22287]**, **[23016]**, **[29621]**, **[30372]**

"Lop Legal Costs" in *My Business* (April/May 2002, pp. 16) **[29374]**, **[38202]**

Lopatka Franchise Services **[29636]**

Lopez Island Chamber of Commerce **[66127]**

Lorain County Chamber of Commerce **[63724]** SBDC **[63567]**

Lord Fairfax Community College–Lord Fairfax SBDC at Middletown **[65828]**

Lord Fairfax SBDC at Fauquier–Lord Fairfax Community College–Lord Fairfax SBDC **[65829]**

"Lord and Taylor Exit Leave Hole" in *Pittsburgh Business Times* (Vol. 23, No. 2, August 1, 2003, pp. 1) **[28437]**, **[51233]**

Lordsburg - Hidalgo County Chamber of Commerce **[62699]**

"Lori & Ryan Pacchiano" in *Entrepreneur* (Vol. 31, No. 7, July 2003, pp. 23) **[19140]**, **[35551]**, **[37570]**

Lorillard Tobacco Company–Library **[24636]**

Loris Chamber and Visitors and Convention Bureau **[64767]**

Los Alamitos Area Chamber of Commerce **[57614]**

Los Alamos Chamber of Commerce **[62700]**

Los Alamos Commerce and Development Corporation **[62701]**

Los Alamos Commerce and Economic Development Corp. **[62729]**

Los Alamos National Laboratory–Advanced Computing Laboratory **[6394]**

Los Altos Chamber of Commerce **[57615]**

Los Angeles Advertising Agencies Association **[50531]**

Los Angeles Area Chamber of Commerce **[57616]**

Los Angeles Business Journal (Vol. 27, Feb. 7, 2005); "Lightweight Newsprint Could Bring Cost Savings to Heavyweight Papers" in **[18897]**, **[19884]**

Los Angeles Business Journal (Vol. 25, No. 7, February 17, 2003, pp. 30); "Old fashioned hobby returns to textile shop" in **[8176]**, **[53895]**

Los Angeles Business Journal (July 5, 2004); "Pala Mesa Resort: A True Tranquil Setting and an Easy Drive from Orange County" in **[3190]**, **[12612]**

Los Angeles County/Harbor-UCLA Medical Center–A.F. Parlow Library of the Health Sciences **[1721]**

Los Angeles County Museum of Art–Research Library **[7965]**

"Los Angeles Grabs Furniture Shows" in *Tradeshow Week* (Vol. 34, December 20, 2004, No. 51, pp. 3) **[12192]**, **[12294]**, **[22526]**, **[24968]**, **[55113]**

Los Angeles JobBank **[23395]**

Los Angeles Metro Minority Business Development Center **[57891]**

Los Angeles Minority Business Opportunity Committee–Mayor's Office of Economic Development **[57892]**

Los Angeles Public Library–Arts, Music and Recreation Department **[8493]**

"Los Angeles Redevelopment Agency Will See Major Restructuring" in *Daily News* (April 11, 2003) **[28438]**

Los Angeles Region SBDC–Long Beach Community College District **[57245]**

Los Banos Chamber of Commerce **[57617]**

Los Cabos Magazine **[12671]**

Los Fresnos Chamber of Commerce **[65371]**

Los Osos/Baywood Park Chamber of Commerce **[57618]**

"Lose weight for charity!" in *Bellingham Business Journal* (January 2003, pp. C4) **[19413]**, **[54220]**

"Lose Weight, Get a Toaster" in *Inc.* (January 1, 2005) **[13372]**, **[41049]**, **[43265]**

"Losing the race: is the Patent Office's slowness putting U.S. innovation at risk?" in *Entrepreneur* (Vol. 31, No. 5, May 2003) **[40523]**, **[44092]**

"Losing Stream: Smart Moves: Is Your Business Leaking Profits?" in *Entrepreneur* (Vol. 31, No. 9, September 2003, pp. 77) **[38203]**, **[45383]**

"Loss-Limit Repeal May be Tied to Tax Boost" in *Kansas City Star* (March 8, 2005) **[10877]**, **[40524]**, **[54649]**

The Loss of a Pet **[19102]**

Loto-Quebec–Centre de Documentation **[10906]**

Lottery, Parimutuel & Casino Regulation **[10900]**

Lotus Bloom Publishing Pte. Ltd. **[66247]**

Lotus Software **[6313]**, **[6391]**, **[7013]**

Lotusea Wellness Group **[19517]**

"Lou Fusz Cultivates Returns on Car-Selling Business" in *St. Louis Post-Dispatch* (July 23, 2004) **[18081]**, **[37716]**, **[51718]**

"Loud and Clear: CEO Hopes to Find International Audience For Multimedia Services" in *Black Enterprise* (Vol. 35, September 2004) **[4111]**, **[9727]**, **[14215]**, **[17749]**, **[20324]**, **[24428]**, **[34151]**, **[43738]**

Loudon County Chamber of Commerce **[64943]**

Loudonville - Mohican Area Convention and Visitor's Bureau **[63725]**

Loudoun County Chamber of Commerce **[65921]**

Loudoun County SBDC **[65830]**

Lougheed Resource Group Inc. **[1150]**, **[21159]**, **[51443]**

Louis Navellier's Emerging Growth **[15659]**

Louis Rukeyser's Wall Street Investment Seminar **[15706]**

Louisa County Chamber of Commerce **[65922]**

Louisburg Chamber of Commerce **[60376]**

Louise-Hillje Chamber of Commerce **[65372]**

Louisiana Chamber of Commerce **[61992]**

Louisiana SBDC–University of Louisiana at Monroe **[60600]**

Louisville Area Chamber of Commerce **[63726]**

Louisville Chamber of Commerce **[58400]**

Louisville Sport, Boat, RV & Vacation Show **[5252]**, **[23691]**, **[24773]**, **[25324]**

Louisville-Winston County Chamber of Commerce **[61810]**

Loup City Chamber of Commerce **[62279]**

Love Boutique **[51463]**

"Love of Country" in *Entrepreneur* (Vol. 33, March 2005, No. 3, pp. 62) **[39860]**, **[44579]**

Love County Chamber of Commerce **[64028]**

Love and Profit: The Art of Caring Leadership **[37042]**, **[45929]**

"Love Story" in *Entrepreneur* (Vol. 28, No. 8, August 2000, pp. 142) **[29749]**, **[35552]**

Lovejoy's MarketBrief Hotline **[15660]**

Lovelady Consulting **[8654]**

Loveland Area Chamber of Commerce **[63727]**

Loveland Chamber of Commerce and Visitors Center **[58401]**

Loveland Info Chamber of Commerce **[58402]**

Lovell Area Chamber of Commerce **[66619]**

Lovelock/Pershing County Chamber of Commerce **[62358]**

Loves Park - Machesney Park Chamber of Commerce **[59578]**

"Love's Rewards" in *Success* (Vol. 47, No. 1, January 2000, pp. 63) **[7048]**, **[38658]**

Lovett Miller & Co. Incorporated **[58973]**

"Loving the IPO Comeback" in *Inc.* (July 1, 2004) **[15237]**, **[50060]**

Lovington Chamber of Commerce **[62702]**

Low-Budget Online Marketing for Small Business **[34152]**, **[47209]**, **[52558]**

"Low-Cost Teleconferencing" in *My Business* (February/March 2004, pp. 17) **[4719]**, **[6716]**, **[23070]**, **[27423]**, **[34153]**, **[36456]**, **[45384]**, **[49132]**, **[53356]**

"The Low Down" in *My Business* (June/July 2004, pp. 46) **[42330]**, **[45385]**

"Low-Income Residents First to Access Free Internet Services" in *San Diego Business Journal* (Vol. 28, January 8, 2007, No. 2, pp. 6) **[14216]**, **[34154]**

"Low-key expansion expected for manufacturers" in *Atlanta Business Chronicle* (Vol. 25, January 10, 2003, No. 31, pp. 24A) **[28439]**, **[46347]**

Low Priced Stocks **[15661]**

Low Profile Selling **[51719]**

"Low Rates Drive 25 Percent Increase in Denver-Area Home Construction" in *Denver Post* (April 11, 2003) **[7410]**, **[20578]**, **[20932]**

Low-Slope Roofing Materials Guide **[22065]**

Low Voltage Safety **[9087]**

"Low-Volume Chevy Dealers Criticize Incentive Program" in *Automotive News* (Vol. 79, February 7, 2005, No. 6133, pp. 42) **[18082]**, **[38849]**, **[46348]**

"Lowcost Launch" in *Small Business Opportunities* (Vol. 16, November 2004, No. 6, pp. 76) **[3319]**, **[8689]**, **[56309]**

Lowell Area Chamber of Commerce **[61367]**

Lowell Chamber of Commerce **[59963]**

Lower Bucks County Chamber of Commerce **[64469]**

"Lower Fees, Higher Returns" in *Black Enterprise* (Vol. 34, No. 3, October 2003, pp. 82) **[10076]**, **[15238]**, **[38204]**

Lower Keys Chamber of Commerce **[58887]**

"Lower prices boost southside sales" in *Atlanta Business Chronicle* (Vol. 25, November 8, 2002, No. 22 pp. 3A) **[17405]**, **[20579]**

"Lowest bid is not always best for hiring contractor" in *Business First Columbus* (Vol. 18, No. 25, February 8, 2002, pp.) **[42331]**, **[49712]**, **[52377]**

Lox of Bagels **[2174]**, **[11392]**

"Loyal Clients Boost Revenue" in *Home Business* (Vol. 12, October 2005, No. 5, pp. 48, 50-51) **[28440]**, **[31764]**

"Loyal Customers can't be Strangers" in *Microsoft Executive Circle* (Vol. 1, No. 2, Q2 2001, pp. 8-10) **[31765]**

Loyalhanna Venture Fund **[64562]**

Loyalist Gazette **[10970]**

Loyola University Chicago
        Center for Ethics and Social Justice **[37551]**
        Center for Organization Development **[35272]**
        School of Professional Studies **[59798]**

"L.P. Confidential" in *Venture Capital Journal* (Vol. 42, No. 8, August 2002, pp. 18-29) **[15239]**, **[50061]**, **[55713]**

"The LP Report Card" in *Venture Capital Journal* (October 1, 2005) **[15240]**, **[50062]**

"LP Sales Put Restructuring on Schedule" in *Business Journal-Portland* (Vol. 20, No. 26, August 29, 2003, pp. 1) **[16085]**, **[16308]**

LPD Enterprises **[8655]**

"LPs Carry Their Weight Beyond Venture Capital" in *Venture Capital Journal* (Vol. 42, No. 9, September 2002, pp. 10-11) **[37163]**, **[55714]**

"LPs Give Redpoint $1.25B Green Light" in *Venture Capital Journal* (Vol. 40, No. 10, October 2000, pp. 16, 17) **[41819]**, **[44580]**, **[55715]**

"LP's Loans to Executives Raises Issues" in *Business Journal-Portland* (Vol. 20, No. 27, September 5, 2003, pp. 1) **[16086]**, **[16309]**, **[26844]**, **[27769]**, **[38205]**, **[39625]**

"LPs Reconsider the Value of IRRs" in *Venture Capital Journal* (Vol. 42, No. 5, May 2002, pp. 5-6) **[15241]**, **[50063]**, **[55716]**

LRP Publications **[42982]**

LSA Associates Inc. **[52764]**

"LSW Architects receives entrepreneurial spirit award in construction category" in *Vancouver, WA Business Journal* (February 28, 2003) **[1488]**, **[7197]**, **[35553]**

LTD Shippers Association **[32133]**, **[46171]**

LTI Ventures Leasing Corp. **[58599]**

Lubar & Co. **[66565]**

Lubbock Chamber of Commerce **[65373]**

Lubepro's International, Inc. **[20272]**

Luby's International Buyer's Guide **[2523]**, **[3104]**

Lucas Area Chamber of Commerce **[60377]**

Lucent Venture Partners, Inc. **[58073]**

Lucerne Valley Chamber of Commerce **[57619]**

Lucille Roberts Fitness Express **[19518]**, **[26060]**

"Luck of the Draw: A Windfall Helps One Man's Small Business Dream Come True" in *Entrepreneur* (Vol. 31, No. 10, October 2003) **[21404]**, **[30488]**, **[55554]**, **[38659]**

"Lucky Charms" in *Small Business Opportunities* (Vol. 14, No. 1, January 2002, pp. 12) **[47210]**, **[51720]**

"A Lucky journey" in *Crain's Detroit Business* (Vol. 19, No. 10, March 10, 2003, pp. 34) **[17599]**, **[17750]**, **[36457]**, **[37717]**

Lucrative List Building **[47211]**, **[51721]**

Ludington Area Chamber of Commerce **[61368]**

Lufkin - Angelina County Chamber of Commerce **[65374]**

May Toy Lukens **[3753]**, **[3978]**, **[16633]**, **[31400]**, **[35239]**

Luling Area Chamber of Commerce **[65375]**

Lum, Danzis, Drasco, Positan, & Kleinberg–Law Library **[9537]**

Lumber and Building Materials Association of Ontario **[11874]**

The Lumber Co-Operator **[16330]**

"Lumber Company Purchases Store Location in Gulfport, Miss." in *Sun Herald* (April 11, 2003) **[7411]**, **[16310]**

Lumbermen's Association of Texas Convention and Buying Market **[16336]**

Lumberton Area Chamber of Commerce **[63401]**

Lumberton Chamber of Commerce **[65376]**

Luminations Inc. **[49629]**

Luna Community College–Small Business Development Center **[62647]**

Lunch Couples of America **[7078]**

The Lunch Lady Group Inc. **[10644]**

Lundquist, Killeen, Potvin and Bender Inc. **[1058]**, **[7622]**, **[9095]**, **[19771]**

Lupfer & Associates **[3754]**, **[16634]**, **[31401]**, **[35240]**, **[38977]**, **[46067]**, **[47886]**

Luray-Page County Chamber of Commerce **[65923]**

"The Lure of Bay State Technology" in *Boston Globe* (February 7, 2005) **[15242]**, **[41820]**, **[43739]**, **[50064]**, **[52145]**, **[55717]**

"Luring MP3ers Back to the Mall" in *Business 2.0* (Vol. 7, January/February 2006, No. 1, pp. 32) **[17751]**, **[51234]**

Luverne Area Chamber of Commerce **[61620]**

Luxemburg Chamber of Commerce **[66445]**

Luxury Bath Systems **[4025]**

"Luxury for the Little People" in *Inc.* (August 1, 2003) **[47212]**, **[48763]**

"Luxury for the masses" in *Harvard Business Review* (Vol. 81, No. 4, April 2003, pp. 48) **[701]**, **[28441]**, **[30908]**, **[47213]**

"Luxury Travel Firm Driven for Success" in *Providence Business News* (Vol. 18, No. 11, June 30, 2003, pp. 10) **[24704]**, **[25211]**

Lycos Ventures **[64563]**

Lyle Tuttle Tattooing–Tattoo Art Museum–Library **[23858]**

Lynchburg - Moore County Chamber of Commerce **[64944]**

Lynchburg Regional Chamber of Commerce **[65924]**

Lynden Chamber of Commerce **[66128]**

Lyndon Area Chamber of Commerce **[65791]**

Lyndon Chamber of Commerce **[60378]**

Lyndon State College–Continuing Education Department **[65811]**

Lynn Area Chamber of Commerce **[60965]**

Lynwood Chamber of Commerce **[57620]**

"Lyon Twp. apple orchard eyed for $70M development" in *Crain's Detroit Business* (Vol. 19, No. 13, March 31, 2003, pp. 6) **[7412]**, **[28442]**, **[51235]**

Lyons Chamber of Commerce **[58403]**, **[62951]**

Lyons Hollis Associates Inc. **[50325]**

M

M Art Now Gallery Guide-International Edition 1600

M/C Venture Partners **[61087]**

"M/C Venture Partners Close on $550M" in *Venture Capital Journal* (Vol. 40, No. 10, November 2000, pp. 24, 26) **[41821]**, **[55718]**

"M-commerce: does 'streaming media' give you the screaming meemies?" in *The New York Times Magazine* (March 19, 2000, pp. 32) **[5046]**, **[14217]**, **[27424]**, **[34155]**

M & M Meat Shops, Ltd. **[4074]**

M & M and Sons Enterprises **[4379]**, **[19799]**

"M-protection" in *Entrepreneur* (Vol. 30, No. 1, January 2002, pp. 40) **[5047]**, **[22288]**, **[41822]**

M R&D Contracts Monthly 50984

M-Squared Inc. **[53102]**

M Street Radio Directory **[20325]**

M Thomson International Bank Directory 38409

M31 Ventures, LLC **[63130]**

Maaco Collision Repair & Auto Painting **[2054]**, **[22682]**

Maaco Systems Canada Inc. **[2055]**

Mac Interiors **[13719]**

"The mac pack: some entrepreneurs would rather switch than fight" in *Entrepreneur* (Vol. 31, No. 5, May 2003, pp. 23) **[6717]**, **[49133]**, **[53843]**

Mac Repair and Troubleshooting II **[32941]**

MacGregors Market **[21871]**

Machine Design **[52304]**

Machine Embroidery **[9303]**

Machine Monogramming **[9304]**

Machine Monogramming & Embroidery Combo **[9305]**

Machine Shop Fundamentals **[16371]**

Machine Tool Practices **[16372]**

Machine Tool Sales Co. **[16404]**

Machinery Information Management Open Systems Alliance **[44713]**

Machining Science and Technology **[16396]**

Machinist's Workshop **[8046]**

MacInn **[12737]**

Macintosh Computer Consultants **[8656]**

Mackenzie Smith Lewis Michell & Hughes–Law Library **[9538]**

Mackinac Island Tourism Bureau **[61369]**

Mackinaw City Chamber of Commerce **[61370]**

"MACM To Issue Refunds" in *Mississippi Business Journal* (Vol. 29, January 2007, No. 3, pp. A8) **[13373]**, **[43266]**

Macmillan Online USA **[60050]**

Macomb Area Chamber of Commerce & Downtown Development Corporation **[59579]**

Macomb Area Economic Development Corporation **[59781]**

Macomb Chamber **[61371]**

Macomb Community College
        Center for Continuing Education-Macomb Community College–SBDC **[61204]**
        SBDC **[61205]**

Macomb County Department of Planning and Economic Development–Small Business Technology Development Center **[61206]**

Macon Area Chamber of Commerce **[61993]**

Macon County Chamber of Commerce **[64945]**

Macon Telegraph (January 31, 2005); "Father/Daughter Duo Finds Success in Classic Car Business" in **[1813]**, **[14032]**, **[18031]**, **[37652]**

Macon Telegraph (March 8, 2004); "Laurel County, Ga., Bed and Breakfast Promises Relaxation in Scenic Spot" in **[2445]**, **[25207]**

"Macro Money Maker" in *Forbes* (Vol. 174, December 27, 2004, No. 13, pp. 121) **[10077]**, **[15243]**, **[38206]**

"A Macro View at Microsoft" in *Hispanic Business* (January/February 2005, pp. 24, 26, 28) **[4720]**, **[6718]**, **[23071]**, **[41823]**, **[47214]**, **[48278]**, **[53357]**

"MacroChem Advances Relaunch of Viagra Rival" in *Boston Business Journal* (Vol. 23, No. 31, September 5, 2003, pp. 1) **[8789]**, **[41050]**, **[48764]**, **[50916]**

Macrocosm USA **[8594]**

Macromedia Authorware I **[32942]**

Macromedia Authorware II **[53178]**

Macromedia Authorware III **[32943]**

Macromedia Captivate **[27266]**, **[53179]**

Macromedia ColdFusion I **[25775]**

Macromedia ColdFusion II **[53180]**

Macromedia Director I **[32944]**

Macromedia Director II **[32945]**

Macromedia Director III: Intensive **[32946]**

Macromedia Dreamweaver I **[25776]**

Macromedia Dreamweaver II **[25777]**

Macromedia Dreamweaver III **[25778]**

Macromedia Fireworks I **[25779]**

Macromedia Fireworks II **[53181]**

Macromedia Flash I **[32947]**

Macromedia Flash II **[32948]**

Macromedia Flash III **[53182]**

Macromedia HomeSite **[32949]**

"Macromedia Inc. Strikes Gold Worth $55M HQ Buy" in *San Francisco Business Times* (Vol. 18, No. 2, August 22, 2003, pp. 1) **[3557]**, **[3950]**, **[30155]**, **[53358]**

MACS Service Reports **[1041]**

MacTech Magazine **[6513]**, **[23284]**

"Macy's Adds a Restaurant" in *Sacramento Bee* (December 20, 2005) **[21554]**, **[51236]**

Macy's Vision Express **[25664]**

The Mad Matter **[10537]**

The Mad Science Group **[33371]**

"Mad skills" in *Entrepreneur* (Vol. 31, No. 4, April 2003, pp. 79) **[27425]**, **[36458]**, **[45386]**

"Madame chairman" in *WorkingWoman* (Vol. 25, No. 5, May 2000, pp. 30) **[29375]**, **[48573]**

"Made in America?" in *Entrepreneur* (Vol. 31, No. 10, October 2003, pp. 72) **[31045]**, **[38207]**, **[43740]**, **[46349]**

Made in Japan Teriyaki Experience **[21872]**

Made to Measure **[5739]**

"Made in the Shade" in *Small Business Opportunities* (Vol. 17, May 2005, No. 3, pp. 102-103) **[23624]**, **[24570]**, **[46350]**

Madelia Area Chamber of Commerce **[61621]**

Madeline Island Chamber of Commerce [66446]
Madera Chamber of Commerce [57621]
Madison - Anson Chamber of Commerce [60759]
Madison Area Chamber of Commerce [59964], [60379], [61622]
Madison Chamber of Commerce [58546], [61811], [62524], [64946], [65925]
Madison County Chamber of Commerce [58888], [60169], [63728], [65377]
Madison County Chamber of Commerce and Industrial Authority [59134]
Madison County Historical Society [11050]
Madison Dearborn Partners LLC [59747]
Madison Enterprise Center [66571]
Madison Heights - Hazel Park Chamber of Commerce [61372]
Madison Investment Partners, Inc. [63131]
Madison-Morgan County Chamber of Commerce [59135]
Madison - Perry Area Chamber of Commerce [63729]
"Madison, Wis., University Research Park Expands Again" in *Milwaukee Journal Sentinel* (December 1, 2005) [28443], [50794], [52020]
Madisonville-Hopkins County Chamber of Commerce [60538]
"Madler: Local Venues Replace Exotic Locales" in *San Fernando Valley Business Journal* (Vol. 12, January 2007, No. 2, pp. 43) [41824], [55114]
Madonna Grimes Cardio Sculpt [19479]
Madonna Grimes Hip Hop Dance Workout [19480]
Madras-Jefferson County Chamber of Commerce [64241]
MadScam: Kick-Ass Advertising Without the Madison Avenue Price Tag [702], [47215]
Madson Group Inc. [58269]
The Magazine Antiques [1348]
The Magazine Article: How to Think It, Plan It, Write It [18901]
"Magazine Covers Anti-Aging Treatments" in *Marketing to Women* (Vol. 19, October 2006, No. 10, pp. 5) [7895], [12593], [18902], [47216]
The Magazine: Everything You Need to Know to Make It in the Magazine Business [18903]
"A Magazine on the Move" in *Tampa Tribune* (December 22, 2005) [18904], [36459]
Magazine Publishers of America [18835] Information Center [18989]
Magazines Canada [18836]
"Magazines Snare More Dot-Com Ad Dollars" in *Folio: the Magazine for Magazine Management* (Vol. 30, No. 1, January 2001, pp. 7) [28444], [47217]
Magdalena Chamber of Commerce [62703]
Magee Chamber of Commerce [61812]
Maggie Valley Area Chamber of Commerce and Convention and Visitors' Bureau [63402]
MaggieMoo's Ice Cream & Treatery [12836]
Magic [18736]
"Magic Carpet Ride" in *Small Business Opportunities* (Vol. 17, May 2005, No. 3, pp. 46, 48) [12193], [12295], [36460]
"Magic Markets: The Experts Use Marketing Mojo on Our Tech Makeover Winner" in *Entrepreneur* (Vol. 32, December 2004, No. 12, pp. 106) [25888], [47218]
"Magic Moments" in *Home Business* (Vol. 13, January/February 2006, No. 1, pp. 70) [42675], [47219]
"The Magic Number" in *Inc.* (September 1, 2003) [28445], [39445]
Magic: The Sleeveless Way [18738]
Magic Venture Capital LLC [58074]
Magic Wok, Inc. [21873]
Magicuts [11836]
Magis Fund Raising Specialists Services For Non-Profits [10771]
"Magna Carta for the Virtual Age" in *Home Office Computing* (Vol. 18, No. 12, December 2000, pp. 21) [39446], [53844]
"Magna Rating Adjusted" in *Mississippi Business Journal* (Vol. 29, January 2007, No. 2, pp. 8) [13374], [28446], [43267]
MAGNET–Information Resource Center [6549]
Magnet Marketing & Sales [47797]
Magnetic Resonance Imaging Center 61151

Magnolia Chamber of Commerce [66129]
Magnolia-Columbia County Chamber of Commerce [57189]
Maharishi Global Construction L.L.C. [7623]
Maharishi University of Management–Agriculture Institute [26690]
Mahomet Chamber of Commerce [59580]
Maid Brigade [8705]
Maid & Butler Service Directory [8690]
Maid to Perfection [8706]
Maidpro [8707]
MAIDS ETC. [8708]
The Maids Home Services [8709]
Mail Boxes Etc.–MBEC Communications, Inc. [4026]
"Mail call" in *Entrepreneur* (Vol. 31, No. 5, May 2003, pp. 38) [4721], [23072], [53359]
"Mail Carriers Bring Home the Goods for Holiday Online Shoppers" in *Portland Press Herald* (December 22, 2005) [16451], [34156], [51237]
Mail & Grow Rich: How to Get Rich Quickly in "Mail Order" in the Information Age! [16414]
Mail & More [6121]
"Mail Order 500" in *Small Business Opportunities* (Vol. 17, September 2005, No. 5, pp. 22, 24, 26, 28, 30, 32, 36, 38, 40, 42, 120) [16415], [42541]
Mail Order Business Directory [16452]
Mail Order Legal Guide [16453]
Mail-Order Marketing News [16483]
"Mail-Order Medical Suppliers Combined" in *Tampa Tribune* (November 23, 2005) [8790], [16454], [50065]
Mail Order Millions: It Worked for Me...It Will Work for You. [16455]
Mail Order Riches Success Kit [16456]
Mail Order Selling: How to Market Almost Anything by Mail [16457]
Mail Order Success Secrets: How to Create a $1,000,000-a-Year Business Starting from Scratch [16458]
Mail Service Pharmacy Market [16476]
Mail Tribune (February 21, 2005); "Homegrown Business" in [11330], [12148], [56266]
Mail Tribune (February 2, 2005); "OnlineAuction.com Ready for Return, Rematch With eBay" in [1842], [14325], [30925], [31050]
"MailFrontier Addresses Growing Threat of Enterprise Phishing at RSA" in *Internet Wire* (February 10, 2005) [14218], [19967], [22289]
Mailing and Fulfillment Service Association [522], [46613], [50532]
Main Line Chamber of Commerce [64470]
Main SBDC Outreach Office at Limestone–ATDC Agriculture–Maine's Applied Technology Development Centers [60689]
Main Street Chamber of Commerce - Adel Partners [60170]
Main Street Coalition for Postal Fairness [6092]
"Main Street Moves Online" in *Business Week* (No. 3678, April 24, 2000, pp. F10) [30909], [34157]
Maine Aquaculture Innovation Center [10488]
Maine Coalition For Safe Kids Inc. [11712]
"Maine Debate Imposing Stricter Standards for Auto Emissions" in *Portland Press Herald* (October 7, 2005) [18083], [40525], [46351]
Maine Department of Economic and Community Development [60717]
    Office of Business Development [60718]
Maine Department of Labor–Division of Economic Analysis and Research [66889]
Maine Development Foundation [60719]
"Maine Executives Give State's Economy 'Worst' Rating" in *Portland Press Herald* (May 27, 2005) [32556], [45387]
"Maine Faces Slow Population Growth, Aging Workforce" in *Portland Press Herald* (May 6, 2005) [28447], [32557], [39447]
"Maine Family Rolls Out 100 Flavors of Ice Cream" in *Portland Press Herald* (July 15, 2005) [12784], [37718]
"Maine Fishermen Welcome Amendment to Preserve Wharf Tax Rates" in *Portland Press Herald* (November 10, 2005) [26521], [54650]

"Maine Home Sales Fall 4 Percent" in *Portland Press Herald* (November 30, 2005) [7413], [20580], [32558]
Maine International Trade Center [60720]
"Maine International Trade Center Adds China Desk" in *Portland Press Herald* (September 23, 2005) [12995], [43741]
"Maine Lawyer Launches Personal Chef and Catering Service" in *Portland Press Herald* (August 9, 2002) [4520], [35555], [42542]
Maine Lobstermen's Association [10419]
Maine Maritime Academy–Nutting Memorial Library [16790]
"Maine Office of Innovation Releases Plan for Research Development" in *Portland Press Herald* (November 4, 2005) [39861], [50917], [52146]
Maine Procurement Technical Assistance Center–Eastern Maine Development Corporation–Market Development Center [60786]
"Maine Program Helps Businesses Apply for Federal Grants" in *Portland Press Herald* (September 23, 2005) [39862], [44581]
"Maine Program Merges On-The-Job Trainings with College Education" in *Portland Press Herald* (August 30, 2005) [5342], [7414], [16736], [33158], [39863]
"Maine Reweaves Thread of Former Textile Industry Into Artistry" in *Portland Press Herald* (September 6, 2005) [1521], [8014], [24969], [46352], [55115]
"Maine Says Flooring Companies Need to Pay Subcontractor Taxes" in *Portland Press Herald* (April 8, 2005) [10512], [49713], [54651]
Maine SBCD Service Center at Midcoast East–Coastal Enterprises, Inc. [60690]
Maine SBDC Outreach Office at Belfast–Hutchinson Center [60691]
Maine SBDC Outreach Office at Bingham–Municipal Bldg., Town of Bingham [60692]
Maine SBDC Outreach Office at Bridgton–Greater Bridgton Lakes Region Chamber of Commerce [60693]
Maine SBDC Outreach Office at Bucksport–Bucksport Town Hall [60694]
Maine SBDC Outreach Office at Calais–Washington County Community College [60695]
Maine SBDC Outreach Office at Dover-Foxcroft–Penquis Higher Education Center [60696]
Maine SBDC Outreach Office at Fort Kent–Aroostock County Registry of Deeds [60697]
Maine SBDC Outreach Office at Houlton–Ward Log Homes Executive Suites [60698]
Maine SBDC Outreach Office at Rumford–ATD Manufacturing [60699]
Maine SBDC Outreach Office at Saco–Biddeford-Saco Area Economic Development–SBDC [60700]
Maine SBDC Outreach Office at Skowhegan–University of Maine Cooperative Extension [60701]
Maine SBDC Outreach Office at South Paris–Oxford Hills Chamber of Commerce [60702]
Maine SBDC Outreach Office at Wilton–Career Center [60703]
Maine SBDC Outreach Office at York–York Chamber of Commerce–SBDC [60704]
Maine SBDC Service Center at Bangor–Eastern Maine Development Corp. (EMDC) [60705]
Maine SBDC Service Center at Ellsworth [60706]
Maine SBDC Service Center at Fairfield–CEI at Kennebec Valley Council of Governments [60707]
Maine SBDC Service Center at Gardiner–Maine Technology Institute [60708]
Maine SBDC Service Center at Machias–Sunrise County Economic Council–SBDC [60709]
Maine SBDC Service Center at Midcoast-West–CEI at MidCoast Council for Business Development and Planning [60710]
Maine SBDC Service Center at Portland–University of Southern Maine [60711]

Maine SBDC Service Center at Sanford/Springvale–Southern Maine Regional Planning Commission **[60712]**

Maine State Chamber of Commerce **[60760]**

Maine State Library **[66890]**

Maine State Office of Substance Abuse–Information and Resource Center **[54383]**

"Maine Thing: Camden Tries New Approach" in *American Banker* (Vol. 172, January 18, 2007, No. 12, pp. 1) **[10078]**, **[15244]**, **[28448]**, **[38208]**, **[44582]**

"Maine Tourism Bureau Awards Account to New York Firm" in *Portland Press Herald* (September 20, 2005) **[703]**, **[24705]**, **[25212]**, **[47220]**

"Maine Tribes Express Interest in Naval Base Redevelopment Project" in *Portland Press Herald* (December 17, 2005) **[21242]**, **[37309]**, **[40055]**, **[46353]**, **[48574]**

"Maine Women's Fund Makes a Difference With Women Entrepreneurs" in *Portland Press Herald* (April 26, 2005) **[36461]**, **[44425]**, **[56310]**

Mainstay Suites **[12717]**

MainStream **[25715]**

Mainstream fashions, Inc. **[5308]**, **[5755]**

"Maintaining Momentum" in *Hispanic Business* (October 2003, pp. 86) **[3320]**, **[36462]**, **[48279]**, **[56311]**

"Maintenance" in *Entrepreneur* (Vol. 32, No. 1, January 2004, pp. 218) **[3321]**, **[38850]**

"Maintenance-Free Condos Offer Stunning Views" in *Bradenton Herald* (February 3, 2005) **[20581]**, **[28449]**

Maintenance Made Simple **[7666]**

Maintenance Management Newsletter **[3331]**

Maintenance and Show Grooming **[1215]**, **[19088]**

Maintenance and Show Grooming for Your Cat **[19089]**

Maintenance Supplies **[3332]**

Maitland Area Chamber of Commerce **[58889]**

"Major Contributions to the Community" in *Home Business* (Vol. 12, March/April 2005, No. 2, pp. 44) **[36463]**, **[54221]**

Major Electric Supply Inc. **[49630]**

Major Financial Institutions of the World **[10079]**

Major Food & Drink Companies of the World **[4531]**, **[11589]**, **[23452]**

"Major League Baseball Signs Partnership Pacts" in *Hispanic Business* (March 2002, pp. 12) **[48280]**, **[50066]**

"The Major Leagues: Have Front-Office Positions Opened Up for Blacks?" in *Black Enterprise* (Vol. 37, February 2007, No. 7, pp.) **[23726]**, **[48281]**, **[53845]**

"Major food company backs trendy sandwich shop" in *Colorado Springs Business Journal* (March 7, 2003) **[8515]**, **[12057]**, **[21555]**

Major Studies of Minority Business: A Bibliographic Review **[48282]**

Major Wingfield Historical Society **[24561]**

Make it Big in the $100 Billion Outsource Contracting Industry: Turn Your Knowledge Experience & Commitment into Lifetime Strategic Partnerships **[49714]**

"Make the Change Today" in *Black Enterprise* (Vol. 34, No. 6, January 2004, pp. 53) **[20582]**, **[38209]**

"Make Corporate America Work for You" in *Inc.* (July 1, 2003) **[31766]**, **[39448]**

"Make Driving Less Taxing" in *My Business* (April/May 2003, pp. 10) **[26283]**, **[54652]**

"Make sure that employee ranking systems are effective" in *Atlanta Business Chronicle* (Vol. 24, No. 13, August 24, 2001, pp. 6B) **[32042]**, **[45388]**

"Make 'Em an Offer: Entrepreneurs Can Save Big Bucks Bidding for Equipment on eBay. Learn Which Strategies Work Best" in *Entrepreneur* **[1833]**, **[14219]**, **[34158]**, **[49134]**

Make It A Winning Life **[3625]**, **[16550]**, **[45897]**

Make It Big With Yuvi: How to Achieve Poolside Living by Growing Your Small Business **[36464]**, **[39449]**

"Make It Usable" in *PC Magazine* (February 6, 2001, pp. 1a) **[25889]**, **[34159]**

Make It Your Business: The Definitive Guide to Launching, Managing, & Succeeding in Your Own Business **[52779]**

Make Landscaping Your Business **[16026]**

"Make a List, Check it Twice: Can You Check Off All the Items on Your List?" in *Entrepreneur* (Vol. 33, February 2005, pp. 92) **[10080]**, **[36465]**, **[39450]**, **[55719]**

"Make a List, Check it Twice: Ever Wonder What's on Other Entrepreneurs' To-Do Lists?" in *Entrepreneur* (Vol. 32, December 2004) **[36466]**, **[39451]**

Make Money with Your PC! **[52911]**

Make More Money by Setting Goals/Rick Barrera **[30639]**

"Make the Most of Buy-Sell Agreements: These Complex Contracts Solve Many Problems" in *Journal of Accountancy* (Vol. 198, October 2004) **[188]**, **[2927]**, **[23985]**, **[26284]**, **[27149]**

"Make No Mistake" in *My Business* (June/July 2002, pp. 34-35, 38-39) **[37719]**

"Make Over Magic" in *Entrepreneur* (Vol. 31, No. 7, July 2003, pp. 49) **[39864]**, **[44583]**

"Make Room for Mickey; Disney Plans Radio Station for Detroit" in *Crain's Detroit Business* (Vol. 21, January 17, 2005, No. 3, pp. 1) **[20280]**

"Make Small Devices A Corporate Asset" in *E-business Advisor* (Vol. 18, No. 3, March 2000, pp. 10) **[5048]**, **[7138]**, **[34160]**

Make Sure It's Deductible **[23986]**, **[54653]**

"Make Sure You Take Advantage of the Repatriation Tax Break Just Like the Big Boys" in *Inc.* (April 1, 2005) **[23987]**, **[54654]**

"Make That To Go" in *Entrepreneur* (Vol. 31, No. 8, August 2003, pp. 34) **[6719]**, **[49135]**

"Make Them Pay!" in *Inc.* (August 1, 2003) **[31563]**, **[43742]**, **[44584]**

Make Training Worth Every Penny: On-Target Evaluation **[33159]**

"Make your layoff list and check it twice" in *BlackEnterprise* (Vol. 32, No. 3, October 2001, pp. 70) **[26285]**, **[32559]**, **[45389]**

"Make Up Your Mind" in *Black Enterprise* (Vol. 36, February 2006, No. 7, pp. 164) **[36467]**, **[45390]**

"Make Vroom" in *Inc.* (July 1, 2004) **[17486]**

Make Your Business Survive and Thrive! 100+ Proven Marketing Methods to Help You Beat the Odds **[28450]**, **[36468]**, **[39452]**, **[42676]**, **[47221]**

"Make Your Company an Idea Factory" in *Fortune* (Vol. 141, No. 12, June 12, 2000, pp. 264N+) **[36469]**, **[55720]**

Make Your Life Tax Deductible: Easy Techniques to Reduce Your Taxes and Start Building Wealth Immediately **[23988]**, **[54655]**

Make Your Mark Onsite Computer Security **[6217]**, **[22445]**

"Make Your Office Fun Place to Be in 2007" in *San Diego Business Journal* (Vol. 28, January 1, 2007, No. 1, pp. 12) **[18551]**, **[49517]**

"Make Your Website Pop" in *Black Enterprise* (Vol. 36, November 2005, No. 4, pp. 70) **[25890]**, **[34161]**

"Makeover Magic: The Experts Work Their Mojo on Our 'Biz 101' Tech Makeover Winners Outdated Web Site" in *Entrepreneur* (July 2004) **[6720]**, **[25891]**, **[49136]**

Making the ADA Work for You **[32094]**

Making Advances: What You Can Do about Sexual Harassment at Work **[32043]**

"Making B2B Better" in *E-business Advisor* (Vol. 18, No. 5, May 2000, pp. 10) **[34162]**, **[50067]**

"Making Book" in *Entrepreneur* (Vol. 33, February 2005, No. 2, pp. 37) **[189]**, **[4722]**, **[23073]**, **[26286]**, **[53360]**

"Making the Call" in *Hispanic Business* (May 2005, pp. 42) **[5049]**, **[14220]**, **[44585]**

"Making sense of corporate venture capital" in *Harvard Business Review* (Vol. 80, No. 3, March 2002, pp. 90) **[55721]**

"Making Cents of It All" in *Home Business* (Vol. 12, March/April 2005, No. 2, pp. 70) **[24819]**, **[37720]**, **[56754]**

"Making a Clean Break" in *Atlanta Business Chronicle* (Vol. 25, December 6, 2002, No. 26, pp. 1B) **[27426]**, **[45391]**, **[50068]**

"Making a Comeback" in *Entrepreneur* (Vol. 32, August 2004, No. 8, pp. 71) **[31185]**, **[42332]**, **[45392]**

Making Connections: Adult Day Health Care for People with AIDS **[450]**

"Making Contact" in *Entrepreneur* (Vol. 33, August 2005, No. 8, pp. 42) **[5017]**, **[5050]**, **[49138]**, **[52559]**

"The Making of a Corporate Athlete" in *Harvard Business Review* (Vol. 79, No. 1, January 2001, pp. 120) **[36470]**, **[45393]**

"Making ethical business decisions" in *Women in Business* (Vol. 53, No. 2, March-April, 2001, pp. 22) **[37473]**, **[56312]**

"Making a Dent" in *The Record* (November 7, 2005) **[2030]**, **[22615]**, **[33160]**

Making Diversity Work **[48621]**

"Making Dough: Warren Brown is Baking His Way to Success" in *Black Enterprise* (Vol. 35, September 2004, No. 2, pp. 45) **[2250]**, **[28451]**

"Making E-Mail Work" in *Sales and Marketing.com* (Vol. 156, No. 3, March 2004, pp. 18) **[27655]**, **[34163]**, **[47222]**

"Making an Educated Decision" in *Business Week Online* (February 16, 2006) **[33161]**, **[37721]**

Making Effective Presentations **[22588]**

"Making Entrepreneurship Job One" in *Black Enterprise* (Vol. 32, No. 10, May 2002, pp. 12) **[36471]**, **[48283]**

"Making Family Leave Family-Friendly; California is considering subsidizing parental leave" in *Business Week Online* (Sept. 20, 2002) **[26845]**, **[40526]**

"Making Fast Food Faster" in *Altanta Journal-Constitution* (January 23, 2007) **[14221]**, **[21556]**, **[34164]**, **[38851]**

"Making a case for a four-day work week" in *Business First Columbus* (Vol. 18, No. 26, February 15, 2002, pp. A30) **[34975]**, **[39453]**

"Making the grade" in *Entrepreneur* (Vol. 31, No. 5, May 2003, pp. 96) **[5317]**, **[35556]**, **[56059]**

"Making the Grade" in *Hispanic Business* (March 2004, pp. 51) **[23989]**, **[54656]**

"Making the Grade: Want to Create a Team of 'A' Players?" in *Sales and Marketing.com* (Vol. 156, No. 3, March 2004, pp. 24) **[34976]**, **[51722]**

"Making Ideas Fly" in *Internet World* (Vol. 6, No. 12, June 15, 2000, pp. 31) **[33457]**, **[43040]**, **[55402]**

Making It Better: How Everyone Can Create a Safer Workplace **[56637]**

Making It! Careers Newsmagazine **[4419]**

Making It in the Construction Business: The Contractor's Survival Guide **[7415]**

Making It Live **[10311]**, **[15707]**, **[51962]**

Making It in Public Relations: An Insider's Guide to Career Opportunities **[20135]**

"Making it" in *Wall Street Journal* (Dec. 9, 2002, pp. R5) **[8172]**, **[14222]**, **[34165]**, **[41825]**

"Making Lemonade" in *Entrepreneur* (Vol. 33, October 2005, No. 10, pp. 83) **[18937]**, **[19152]**, **[28723]**, **[29376]**, **[42364]**, **[44093]**, **[44335]**

"Making Life Easier Overseas; Export Assistance" in *Crain's New York Business* (Vol. 22, November 13, 2006, No. 46, pp. 22) **[12996]**, **[33162]**, **[43743]**, **[55722]**

"The Making of a Mediator: Developing Artistry in Practice" in *Dispute Resolution Journal* (Vol. 56, No. 1, February-April 2001, pp. 88) **[17054]**, **[27427]**

Making Millions in the Export-Import Market **[12997]**

Making Money in Cyberspace: The Inside Information You Need to Start or Take Your Own Business On-Line **[14223]**, **[25892]**

Making Money in the Fitness Business **[19414]**

Making Money in the Novelty Telegram Business **[18728]**

Making Money from Writing: How to Become a Freelance Writer **[8619]**, **[9004]**, **[18237]**

Making Money with Your Computer at Home **[6478]**

Making Money with Your Creative Paint Finishes **[8015]**

"Making the Most Of It" in *Sales & Marketing Management* **[24970]**, **[47223]**, **[51723]**, **[55116]**

"Making the Most of What You Have" in *Success* (Vol. 47, No. 6, November 2000, pp. 26) **[55723]**

"Making the Most of Your Network" in *Women In Business* (Vol. 52, No. 4, July 2000, pp. 20) **[36472]**, **[56313]**

"Making New Memories at Little Cheese Shop" in *Business Journal-Milwaukee* (Vol. 20, No. 45, July 25, 2003, pp. A15) **[12897]**, **[20136]**, **[23494]**, **[37722]**, **[47224]**, **[50624]**

"Making Partner: A Mentor's Guide to the Psychological Journey" in *Harvard Business Review* (Vol. 78, No. 2, March 2000, pp. 147) **[45394]**

"Making Pro Formas Perform" in *Harvard Business Review* (Vol. 81, No. 10, October 2003, pp. 24) **[190]**, **[10081]**, **[15245]**, **[26287]**, **[29377]**

The Making of a Salesman **[10312]**, **[15708]**, **[51963]**

"Making a scene: your special event won't be so special if nobody hears about it." in *Entrepreneur* (Vol. 31, No. 5, May 2003, pp. 79) **[704]**, **[47225]**, **[50625]**

"Making Scents" in *Small Business Opportunities* (Vol. 17, November 2005, No. 6, pp. 68) **[2595]**, **[7896]**

"Making Sense of Scanner Data" in *Harvard Business Review* (Vol. 78, No. 2, March 2000, pp. 24) **[46354]**, **[51238]**

"Making Sense of Stocks" in *Black Enterprise* (Vol. 31, No. 5, December 2000, pp. 147) **[38210]**

"Making Strides in Building Jobs" in *Milwaukee Journal Sentinel* (December 3, 2005) **[7416]**, **[33163]**, **[42333]**

"Making strides, but losing ground?" in *Black Enterprise* (Vol. 32, No. April 2002, 9, pp. 30) **[48284]**, **[56314]**

"Making a Success of Failure" in *Success* (Vol. 47, No. 4, September 2000, pp. 58) **[33458]**, **[37066]**

Making Teams Work: A Guide to Creating and Managing Teams **[34977]**

"Making Their 'Book' Mark" in *Boston Business Journal* (Vol. 22, No. 16, May 24, 2002, pp. 28) **[2723]**, **[36473]**

Making the Transition to Management **[44773]**

Making the Transition to Management (Canada) **[44774]**

Making the Transition from Staff Member to Supervisor **[44775]**

Making the Transition from Staff Member to Supervisor (Canada) **[44776]**

"Making the upgrade" in *Working Woman* (Vol. 25, No. 6, June 2000, pp. 114) **[30373]**, **[56315]**

Making a Video Program **[9764]**

"Making Waves: For the Brothers Who Made the Fish Taco a Million Dollar Industry, It's All Relative" in *Entrepreneur* (Vol. 32) **[21557]**, **[37723]**

"Making waves" in *San Francisco Business Times* (Vol. 16, No. 43) **[25119]**, **[33459]**

"Making Your Case: Think Client Testimonials are Just Icing on the Cake?" in *Entrepreneur* (Vol. 33, January 2005, No. 1, pp. 64) **[31767]**, **[47226]**, **[51724]**

Malakoff Chamber of Commerce **[65378]**

"Malan Realty to sell 15 shopping centers for $94M" in *Crain's Detroit Business* (Vol. 18, No. 24, June 17, 2002, pp. 4) **[20933]**

"The Malaria Fighter" in *Business 2.0* (Vol. 7, January/February 2006, No. 1, pp. 116-118, 120, 122, 124) **[36474]**, **[50918]**, **[52147]**

"Malcolm Alexander" in *Entrepreneur* (Vol. 31, No. 5, May 2003, pp. 19) **[5909]**, **[36475]**

Malcolm Pirnie, Inc.–Virtual Library/LSSI **[25732]**

Malden Chamber of Commerce **[60966]**, **[61994]**

"Male and female in organizational behavior" in *Journal of Organizational Behavior* (Vol. 23, No. 2, March 2002, pp. 149) **[39454]**, **[45395]**

Malibu Chamber of Commerce **[57622]**

"Mall Makeover" in *South Florida Business Journal* (Vol. 23, No. 52, August 1, 2003, pp. 35) **[7417]**, **[51239]**

"Malley's Chocolates opens first Summit County store" in *Crain's Cleveland Business* (Vol. 22, No. 42, October 15, 2001, pp. 11) **[4296]**, **[37724]**

Malone Chamber of Commerce **[62952]**

Malone Satellite–North Country SBDC Outreach Office–OneWorkSource **[62768]**

Malta Area Chamber of Commerce **[62184]**

Malvern and Hot Springs County Chamber of Commerce **[57190]**

Mamaroneck Chamber of Commerce **[62953]**

Mamma Ilardo's **[19684]**

"Man Behind the News" in *Hispanic Business* (July/August 2002, pp. 22, 24, 26) **[24429]**, **[48575]**

Man Hunt **[42489]**

"Man in the Mirror" in *Incentive* (Vol. 174, No. 10, October 2000, pp. 93) **[2596]**, **[7897]**, **[53846]**

The Man from OSHA **[56638]**

"Man Power: Tips To Get Male Shoppers Spending in Your Store" in *Entrepreneur* (Vol. 32, October 2004, No. 10, pp. 91) **[47227]**, **[51240]**

"Man for all Seasons" in *Small Business Opportunities* (Vol. 12, No. 3, May 2000, pp. 102-103) **[13620]**, **[15983]**, **[35557]**

"The Man Who Launched 4,000 Businesses" in *Fortune* (Vol. 143, No. 3, February 5, 2001, pp. 180) **[35558]**, **[38660]**

"The Man Who Started It All" in *Hispanic Business* (January/February 2003, pp. 24, 26) **[39455]**, **[48285]**

"Man With the Golden Touch" in *Black Enterprise* (Vol. 35, October 2004, No. 3, pp. 53) **[705]**, **[5995]**, **[25893]**, **[36476]**, **[47228]**, **[50626]**

"Man With a Plan" in *My Business* (December/January 2004, pp. 56) **[29931]**, **[36477]**

"Manage with care" in *Black Enterprise* (Vol. 32, No. 5, December 2001, pp. 61) **[34978]**, **[45396]**

Manage to the Individual, If You Want to Know How, Ask!: A Story about the Belief System of Motivation and Performance **[34979]**

"Manage Projects in Real Time" in *PC Magazine* (February 20, 2001, pp. 37) **[53361]**, **[54967]**

Manage Your Time to Build Your Territory **[51964]**, **[55021]**

Managed Care Quarterly **[41255]**

Managed Care Week **[13552]**, **[41256]**

"Managed Care's Poor Health" in *Rough Notes* (Vol. 145, No. 2, February 2002, pp. 36) **[10082]**, **[13375]**, **[26846]**, **[28452]**, **[32560]**

Managed Healthcare Executive **[41257]**

Management 21 Inc. **[31981]**

Management Accounts: How to Use Them To Control Your Business **[38211]**

Management Action Program **[45930]**

Management Action Programs Inc. **[38978]**

Management Advisory Associates Inc. **[35241]**

Management of Alcohol & Drug-Related Issues in the Workplace **[54336]**

Management Concepts Inc. **[66008]**

Management Consultants International, Inc.–Library **[16692]**

Management Consulting 1996 **[16524]**

Management Consulting: Theory & Tools for Small Business Interventions **[16525]**, **[31186]**

The Management Course (Canada) **[44777]**

The Management Course: Finance **[44778]**

The Management Course: Leadership **[44779]**

The Management Course: Marketing **[44780]**

Management Course for Supervisors (Canada) **[44781]**

Management: Emphasize Your Strengths **[45931]**

"Management commitment to innovation and ESOP stock concentration" in *Journal of Business Venturing* (Vol. 15, No. 5-6, Sept.-Nov. 2000) **[26847]**, **[45397]**

"Management to Go" in *Success* (Vol. 47, No. 6, November 2000, pp. 54) **[14224]**, **[47229]**, **[49715]**

Management Growth Institute **[37829]**, **[46068]**

Management House Inc. **[46069]**

"Management Liability at the Speed of Light" in *Rough Notes* (Vol. 145, No. 38, June 2002, pp. 38) **[13376]**, **[43268]**, **[45398]**

"Management Makes a Difference: Bill Thomason Managed His Way to Outstanding Gains" in *Black Enterprise* (Vol. 34, No. 4, November 2003) **[9971]**, **[10083]**, **[15030]**, **[15246]**, **[38212]**, **[39632]**

Management Mastery: Accelerating Your Management Potential (Canada) **[44782]**

Management Mess-Ups: 57 Pitfalls You Can Avoid (& Stories of Those Who Didn't) **[45399]**

Management Methods Inc. **[46070]**

The Management Network Group Inc. **[3755]**, **[46071]**

Management Now **[1750]**

"Management by whose objectives?" in *Harvard Business Review* (Vol. 81, No. 1, January 2003, pp. 107) **[36478]**, **[45400]**

Management 1 **[45932]**

Management Problems of the Technical Person in a Leadership Role **[44783]**

Management Recruiters International Inc. **[9274]**, **[9593]**

Management Report for Nonunion Organizations **[16551]**, **[45898]**

Management Resource Center Inc. **[50326]**

Management Resource Partners **[3756]**, **[16635]**, **[31402]**, **[38557]**, **[46072]**, **[53103]**

Management Services & Development Ltd. **[52479]**

Management Skills for Administrative Professionals **[44784]**

Management Skills for Administrative Professionals (Canada) **[44785]**

Management Skills for New Managers (Canada) **[44786]**

Management Skills for New Supervisors **[44787]**

Management Skills for New Supervisors (Canada) **[42797]**, **[44788]**

Management for the Small Design Firm: Handling Your Practice, Personnel, Finances, & Projects **[706]**, **[5996]**

Management Strategies **[3757]**, **[16636]**, **[30094]**, **[31403]**, **[46073]**, **[47887]**

Management Teams: Why They Succeed or Fail **[34980]**

Management Techniques That Work **[45933]**

Management Technology Associates Ltd. **[46074]**

Management and Technology Conferences - ASAE Annual Meeting **[1753]**

Management of Time **[55022]**

The Management of Work **[45934]**

"Manager in a box" in *Hispanic Business* (Vol. 22, No. 10, October 2000, pp. 114) **[26288]**, **[53362]**

"Managerial Rudeness: Bad Attitudes Can Demoralize Your Staff" in *Black Enterprise* (Vol. 37, January 2007, No. 6, pp. 58) **[34981]**, **[45401]**

Managerial Skills of the New Supervisors **[44789]**

Managerial and Team-building Skills for Project Managers **[44790]**

Managerial and Team-building Skills for Project Managers (Canada) **[44791]**

A Manager's Guide to Globalization: Six Keys to Success in a Changing World **[43744]**

A Manager's Guide to OSHA **[56571]**

The Manager's Guide to Rewards: What You Need to Know to Get the Best of – and from – Your Employees **[34982]**, **[45402]**

The Manager's Intelligence Report **[45899]**

Manager's Legal Bulletin **[32075]**

Manager's Official Guide to Team Working **[34983]**

Managing Business Ethics: Straight Talk about How to Do It Right **[37474]**

Managing Business Growth: Get a Grip on the Numbers That Count **[28453]**, **[38213]**, **[45403]**

"Managing in the Cappuccino Economy" in *Harvard Business Review* (Vol. 78, No. 2, March 2000, pp. 177) **[31187]**, **[45404]**

Managing Chaos: Dynamic Time Management, Recall, Reading, and Stress **[44792]**

Managing Chaos: Dynamic Time Management, Recall, Reading, and Stress Management Skills for Administrative Professionals (Canada) **[54932]**

Managing Chaos: How to set Priorities And Make Decisions Under Pressure **[44793]**

Managing Chaos: How to set Priorities and make Decisions Under Pressure (Canada) **[44794]**

Managing Chaos: How to Set Priorities and Make Decisions Under Pressure (Canada) **[44795]**

Managing Chaos: How to Set Priorities and Make Decisions Under Pressure (Canada) **[44796]**

Managing Communications in a Crisis **[44797]**

Managing Complexity and Change in SMEs Frontiers in European Research **[43745]**, **[46355]**

"Managing Creativity in a Progressive Home Business" in *Home Business* (Vol. 13, January/February 2006, No. 1, pp. 28, 30-31, 95) **[29932]**, **[42677]**

Managing Credit, Receivables, and Collections **[8333]**

Managing Cultural Differences **[48622]**

Managing for Customer Care **[31938]**

Managing Difficult Customers 1...2...3 **[31939]**

Managing the Distributor Sales Network **[44798]**, **[51525]**

Managing the Distributor Sales Network (Canada) **[44799]**

Managing Diversity **[48623]**

Managing Diversity in Organizations **[48576]**

Managing Diversity: The Complete Desk Reference **[48577]**

Managing a Drug-Free Work Environment **[54353]**

Managing the Emerging Company **[3630]**, **[30058]**, **[39732]**

Managing Emotions in the Workplace: Strategies for Success **[27267]**

Managing Emotions in the Workplace Strategies for Success (Canada) **[27268]**, **[28221]**

Managing Enterprise-wide Projects **[44800]**

"Managing emotional fallout" in *Harvard Business Review* (Vol. 80, No. 2, February 2002, pp. 55) **[39456]**, **[45405]**

Managing the Family Business **[37725]**

Managing Frontline Service **[42490]**

Managing Generation X: How to Bring Out the Best in Young Talent **[34984]**

Managing Globally: A Complete Guide to Competing Worldwide **[43746]**

Managing to Have Profits: The Secret Japan Learned but the U.S. Forgot **[45406]**

Managing Health Benefits in Small and Mid-Sized Organizations **[13377]**, **[26848]**, **[41051]**, **[43269]**

Managing India's Small Industrial Economy: The Catalytic Role of Industrial Counselors and Policy Makers **[31188]**, **[32561]**, **[43747]**

Managing International Teams **[43748]**

Managing to Keep the Customer: How to Achieve and Maintain Superior Customer Service Throughout the Organization **[31768]**

Managing Knock Your Socks Off Service **[31769]**

Managing Labour in Small Firms **[39457]**, **[45407]**

Managing Learning in Organizations **[33164]**

Managing Managers: Bridging Strategy and Implementation **[44801]**

"Managing a Multicultural Workforce" in *BlackEnterprise* (Vol. 31, No. 12, July 2001, pp. 120) **[30910]**, **[48578]**

Managing Nonprofit Organizations in the 21st Century **[1735]**

Managing by the Numbers: Financial Essentials for the Growing Business **[26289]**, **[38214]**

Managing Older Workers **[32044]**

"Managing information overload" in *Women In Business* (Vol. 52, No. 2, March 2000, pp. 20) **[45408]**

Managing Payroll Systems: Payroll Accounting **[18782]**

Managing People and Organizations **[45409]**

Managing the Publications Department **[2671]**

Managing Quality Customer Service **[31770]**

Managing for Results **[36479]**, **[45410]**

Managing Risk with Financial Futures: Pricing, Hedging and Arbitrage **[15247]**

Managing Sales Stress **[51965]**

Managing Scientists in Industry **[44802]**

Managing a Small Business Made Easy **[31771]**, **[36480]**, **[38215]**, **[39458]**, **[45411]**

Managing Small Businesses **[45412]**

Managing Systematic and Ethical Public Relations **[20137]**

Managing Technical Professionals (Canada) **[44803]**

"Managing for the next big thing" in *Harvard Business Review* (Vol. 79, No. 1, January 2001, pp. 131) **[6262]**, **[36481]**, **[45413]**

Managing Time **[55023]**

Managing Today's IT and Technical Professionals (Canada) **[44804]**

"Managing to Win" in *Small Business Opportunities* (Vol. 17, November 2005, No. 6, pp. 10, 20) **[22290]**, **[34985]**, **[45414]**

Managing Work and Family Inc. **[27037]**

Managing a World-Class IT Department **[44805]**

Managing a World-Class IT Department (Canada) **[44806]**

Managing Your Business: Milady's Guide to the Salon **[11795]**

"Managing Your IT Managers" in *Ingram's* (Vol. 28, No. 5, May 2002, pp. 26) **[6177]**, **[14225]**, **[34166]**, **[45415]**

Managing Your Marketing Communications Mix: An Integrated Strategy **[46632]**

Managing Your Marketing Communications Mix for Better Bottom-Line Results **[44807]**

Managing Your Marketing Communications Mix for Better Bottom-Line Results (Canada) **[44808]**

Managing Your Personal Finances **[10313]**

Managing Your Time **[55024]**

Managing Your Working Capital: How to Keep Your Assets Moving and Growing **[37859]**

"Manatee Boat Makers Are Hiring, But Workers Aren't Plentiful" in *Bradenton Herald* (February 4, 2005) **[16737]**, **[28454]**, **[42334]**, **[46356]**

Manatee Chamber of Commerce **[58890]**

Manatee Community College–Small Business Development Center **[58708]**

"Manatee County, Fla. New Home Permits Up 13 Percent in 2004" in *Bradenton Herald* (January 5, 2005) **[7418]**, **[28455]**

Manawa Area Chamber of Commerce **[66447]**

Mancelona Area Chamber of Commerce **[61373]**

Manchester Area Chamber of Commerce **[60171]**, **[61374]**, **[64947]**

Manchester College–Peace Studies Institute–Program in Conflict Resolution **[50788]**

Manchester Humphreys, Inc. **[64676]**

Manchester and the Mountains Regional Chamber of Commerce **[65792]**

Manchester Small Business Development Center **[62389]**

Manchu Wok (Canada) Inc. **[21874]**

Mancino's, Samuel Italian Eatery **[10645]**

Mandalay Associates L.L.C. **[33349]**, **[35242]**

Mandarin Restaurant Franchise Corp. **[21875]**

M&M/Mars Research Library **[4338]**

"Mane Attraction" in *Inc.* (August 1, 2003) **[4297]**, **[36482]**, **[56316]**

"Maneuver warfare: Can modern military strategy lead you to victory?" in *Harvard Business Review* (Vol. 80, No. 4, April 2002, pp. 57) **[30911]**, **[45416]**

Manhasset Chamber of Commerce **[62954]**

Manhattan Area Chamber of Commerce **[60380]**, **[62185]**

Manhattan Area Chamber of Commerce (MACC)–Small Business Development Center **[60262]**

"Manhattan-based Terra Holdings Acquires Dunemere Associates" in *Long Island Business News* (February 6, 2004) **[15248]**, **[20583]**, **[20934]**, **[50069]**

Manhattan Beach Chamber of Commerce **[57623]**

Manhattan Chamber of Commerce **[59581]**, **[62955]**

The Manhattan Consulting Group Inc. **[46542]**

Manhattan School of Music–Frances Hall Ballard Library **[17688]**

Manheim Area Chamber of Commerce **[64471]**

Manistee Area Chamber of Commerce **[61375]**

Manito Area Chamber of Commerce **[59582]**

Manitoba Automobile Injury Compensation Appeal Commission Decisions **[29673]**, **[30765]**, **[43454]**

Manitoba Beekeeper **[2473]**

Manitoba Crafts Museum & Library–Gladys Chown Memorial Library **[8117]**, **[8263]**

Manitoba Department of Labour–Manitoba Labour Board–Library **[55343]**

Manitoba Department of Labour & Immigration–Workplace Safety and Health Division–Client Resource Centre **[56692]**

Manitoba Genealogical Society Inc.–Library **[11051]**

Manitoba Industry, Trade and Tourism–Canada Manitoba Business Service Center–Women's Entrepreneurial Programs **[66701]**

Manitoba Intergovernmental Affairs and Trade Community Economic Development Branch **[66698]**
    Rural Economic Development Initiative **[66699]**

Manitoba Tax Assistance Office **[66700]**

Manitoba Telecom Services–Corporate Library **[5231]**, **[8671]**

Manitoba Trucking Association–Library **[25457]**

Manitou Springs Chamber of Commerce **[58404]**

Manitou Ventures, LLC **[58075]**

Manitowish Waters Chamber of Commerce **[66448]**

Manitowoc/Two Rivers Area Chamber of Commerce **[66449]**

Mankato Chamber of Commerce **[60381]**

Mankind Research Foundation **[3758]**, **[31404]**, **[52343]**

JG Manley and Associates **[42983]**

"Mann to Lead Builders" in *Charlotte Observer* (January 31, 2007) **[7419]**, **[20584]**, **[20935]**

Mann Publishing Group **[62450]**

"Manners Matter" in *Home Office Computing* (Vol. 18, No. 9, September 2000, pp. 40) **[31772]**

Manners at Work **[27570]**

Mannes College of Music–Harry Scherman Music Library **[17689]**

Mannford Chamber of Commerce **[64029]**

Manning Chamber of Commerce **[60172]**

"Manny, Moe, & Jack Are In the Driver's Seat" in *License!* (Vol. 6, No. 6, July 2003, pp. 22) **[1946]**, **[2724]**, **[5684]**, **[24820]**, **[44094]**, **[51241]**

Manoa Innovation Center (MIC) **[59260]**

"Manpower Inc. Will Move Headquarters to Downtown Milwaukee" in *Milwaukee Journal Sentinel* (December 22, 2005) **[9226]**, **[9572]**, **[24531]**

"A Man's World?" in *Entrepreneur* (Vol. 31, No. 8, August 2003, pp. 26) **[34167]**, **[36483]**, **[41826]**, **[52560]**, **[56317]**

Mansfield Area Chamber of Commerce **[65379]**

Mansfield-Richland Area Chamber of Commerce **[63730]**

Mansfield Stock Chart Service **[10283]**, **[15662]**

Manson Economic Development Corp. and Chamber of Commerce **[60173]**

Manteca Chamber of Commerce **[57624]**

"Manufacturer AmerTac Buys Night Light Maker" in *The Record* (November 8, 2005) **[9113]**, **[15249]**, **[46357]**, **[50070]**

Manufacturers' Agents for the Foodservice Industry **[16696]**

Manufacturers' Agents National Association **[16697]**

Manufacturers' Agents National Association-Directory of Manufacturers' Sales Agencies **[16704]**

Manufacturer's Directory **[46358]**

"Manufacturers Group Wants End to Spam" in *Crain's Detroit Business* (Vol. 19, No. 10, March 10, 2003, pp. 6) **[14226]**, **[34168]**, **[40527]**, **[46359]**

Manufacturer's Mart **[46509]**

Manufacturers Representatives of America **[16698]**

Manufacturers Representatives of America-Newsline **[16706]**

Manufacturers Representatives Educational Research Foundation **[16699]**, **[16710]**

Manufacturing Automation **[46510]**

Manufacturing Confectioner-Directory of Ingredients, Equipment and Packaging **[4298]**

Manufacturing Control in the Small Plant (7MP-J01) **[46528]**

"Manufacturing History: Tales of Turning Points in Factory Jobs are Just That" in *Barron's* (July 28, 2003, pp. 30) **[32562]**, **[42335]**, **[46360]**

"Manufacturing: Industrial Strength Integration" in *Microsoft Executive Circle* (Vol. 1, No. 2, Q2 2001, pp. 56-58) **[14227]**, **[41827]**, **[42336]**, **[46361]**, **[53847]**

Manufacturing Jewelers and Suppliers of America **[15829]**, **[46172]**

"Manufacturing Job Losses Hit Other Sectors" in *Crain's Detroit Business* (Vol. 22, November 20, 2006,No. 47, pp. 3) **[29933]**, **[42337]**, **[46362]**

Manufacturing Management Associates **[3896]**, **[16683]**

Manufacturing Market Insider **[46511]**

The Manufacturing Report **[46512]**

"Manufacturing Sector Expects Improvement After Slow January" in *Journal Record (Oklahoma City, OK)* (February 1, 2007) **[28456]**, **[46363]**

"Manufacturing Sector Strengthening" in *Milwaukee Journal Sentinel* (December 1, 2005) **[28457]**, **[32563]**, **[46364]**

Manufacturing Technology **[46513]**

Manufacturing and Technology News **[46514]**

Manulife Capital Corporation **[61088]**

Manulife Financial–Canadian Division–Law Library **[13602]**

"Many firms don't know they can deduct premiums" in *Birmingham Business Journal* (Vol. 17, No. 36, September 8, 2000, pp. 14) **[43270]**

"Many Eggs, Many Baskets" in *Crain's Chicago Business* (Vol. 30, January 2007, No. 3, pp. 18) **[707]**, **[14228]**, **[24430]**, **[25894]**, **[47230]**

"Many federal contractors ignore subcontracting goals" in *Atlanta Business Chronicle* (Vol. 25, No. 22, November 8, 2002, pp. 5B) **[40056]**, **[40528]**

"Many Healthy Returns" in *Entrepreneur* (Vol. 31, No. 9, September 2003, pp. 116) **[4547]**, **[23495]**, **[37726]**

"Many things matter, and here's what matters most" in *Fast Company* (June 2001, pp. 70) **[39459]**

"Many analysts think the old-style expensive portal deals deserve more scrutiny from e-tailers" in *The New York Times* (May 1, 2000) **[34169]**, **[47231]**

"Many small firms are unaware of pension-plan options" in *Wall Street Journal* (May 30, 2000, pp. B2) **[26849]**

"Many unhappy returns" in *Entrepreneur* (Vol. 31, No. 6, June 2003, pp. 74) **[31773]**, **[51242]**

"Many happy returns" in *WorkingWoman* (Vol. 25, No. 2, February 2000, pp. S8) **[42678]**, **[54657]**, **[56318]**

"Many Ways to Lose" in *Kiplinger's Personal Finance Magazine* (Vol. 54, No. 11, November 2000, pp. 98) **[30239]**, **[43271]**

Map Guide to the U.S. Federal Censuses, 1790-1920 **[10947]**

"Map your Next Location" in *PC Computing* (April 2000, pp. 91) **[52698]**

"MAPICS Implements Web-based Self Service Tool to Enhance Customer Service For High Tech Manufacturers" in *PR Newswire* (Oct. 29, 2001) **[14229]**, **[31774]**, **[34170]**, **[37164]**, **[46365]**

Maple City Business and Technology Center Incubator–Technology Center Incubator **[59782]**

The Maple Leaflet **[10971]**

Maplewood Chamber of Commerce **[62525]**

"Maponics: www.maponics.com" in *Entrepreneur* (Vol. 32, November 2004, No. 11, pp. 6) **[14230]**, **[34171]**, **[47232]**, **[51725]**

"Mapping the World of Customer Satisfaction" in *Harvard Business Review* (Vol. 78, No. 3, May 2000, pp. 30) **[28458]**, **[31775]**, **[52912]**

"Maps on Tap" in *Entrepreneur.com* (Vol. 34, February 2006, No. 2, pp. 38) **[5051]**, **[30374]**, **[34172]**

Maquoketa Area Chamber of Commerce **[60174]**

Marad Fine Art International **[1696]**, **[19836]**

Marana Chamber of Commerce **[57048]**

maranGraphics Inc. **[66756]**

Marble Falls - Lake LBJ Chamber of Commerce **[65380]**

Marble Institute of America **[16933]**

Marble Slab Creamery **[12837]**

Marblehead Chamber of Commerce **[60967]**

Marblehead Peninsula Chamber of Commerce **[63731]**

MarbleLife **[10538]**

E.F. Marburger and Son Inc. **[49631]**

Marceline Chamber of Commerce **[61995]**

"March Is National Craft Month" in *PR Newswire* (March 7, 2003) **[8173]**, **[28459]**, **[53848]**

Marco Island Area Chamber of Commerce **[58891]**

Marconi Designs **[18578]**, **[49632]**

Marconi Ventures **[61089]**

Marco's Pizza **[19685]**

"Marcus Buckingham Thinks Your Boss Has an Attitude Problem" in *Fast Company* (August 2001, pp. 88) **[31189]**, **[45417]**

Marenghi Public Relations Inc. **[50502]**

Marengo Chamber of Commerce **[60175]**

Marengo-Union Chamber of Commerce **[59583]**

Marfa Chamber of Commerce **[65381]**

Margiloff & Associates **[40117]**, **[44205]**, **[51003]**

Maricopa County Community College–Arizona Small Business Development Center–Lead Center **[56989]**

Maricopa County Procurement Technical Assistance Center–APTAN - Bid Source **[57096]**

Marietta Area Chamber of Commerce **[63732]**

Marietta College–SBDC **[63568]**

Marina Chamber of Commerce **[57625]**

Marine Business Journal **[5246]**

Marine City Chamber of Commerce **[61376]**

Marine Museum at Fall River, Inc.–Library **[16791]**

"Marine One, Sikorsky Zero" in *Business Week* (February 14, 2005, No. 3920, pp. 40) **[40057]**, **[46366]**

Marine Products Directory **[16738]**

Marine Retailers Association of America **[16718]**

Marine Textiles and Upholstery Journal-Buyers Guide Issue **[25539]**

Marinette Area Chamber of Commerce **[66450]**

Marion Area Chamber of Commerce **[61377]**, **[63733]**

　　SBDC **[63569]**

Marion Area Genealogical Society–Library **[11052]**

Marion Chamber of Commerce **[57191]**, **[59584]**, **[64768]**

Marion County Chamber of Commerce **[64948]**, **[65382]**, **[66284]**

Marion County Development Partnership **[61813]**

Marion-Grant County Chamber of Commerce **[59965]**

Mariposa County Chamber of Commerce **[57626]**

Maristeth Ventures, LLC **[66217]**

Maritime College of Forest Technology–Library **[9446]**

Maritz Inc. **[16873]**

Maritz Travel Company–Resource Center **[30471]**

"Mark to sell 9 Weight Watchers franchises" in *Crain's Detroit Business* (Vol. 19, No. 10, March 10, 2003, pp. 1) **[19415]**, **[38852]**

Mark A. Adams Inc. **[63256]**

Mark Amtower's B-to-Government Report **[40114]**

"Mark Hoffman" in *Internet World* (Vol. 7, No. 1, January 15, 2001, pp. 41) **[28460]**, **[34173]**, **[37165]**

Mark-to-Market: Managing the Portfolio Under FASB 115 **[15250]**

Mark Twain Lake Chamber of Commerce **[61996]**

Mark W. Carnes & Associates Inc. **[4027]**, **[39015]**

Mark West Area Chamber of Commerce **[57627]**

Marked Tree Chamber of Commerce **[57192]**

The Market for Bakery Products **[2251]**

The Market for Dental Equipment and Supplies **[17108]**

Market Discoveries Inc. **[8537]**, **[21726]**

"Market Drifts While Tech Stocks Wilt" in *Barron's* (August 11, 2003, pp. MW3) **[10084]**, **[15251]**, **[32564]**, **[41828]**

"A Market-Driven Approach to Retaining Talent" in *Harvard Business Review* (Vol. 78, No. 1, January 2000, pp. 103) **[26850]**, **[30738]**, **[34986]**

"Market Driver" in *Hispanic Business* (April 2005, pp. 30-31) **[708]**, **[18084]**, **[47233]**

Market Focus **[30095]**, **[46075]**, **[47888]**

Market Guide **[3465]**, **[15761]**

"Market Guru Does a Reality Check on Forecasting" in *St. Louis Post-Dispatch* (January 14, 2005) **[15252]**, **[38216]**

The Market for Lawn, Garden, & Snow Equipment **[11447]**

Market for Medical Waste Management **[11942]**

The Market for Musical Instruments **[17781]**

"A Market of One" in *Black Enterprise* (Vol. 34, July 2004, No. 12, pp. 140) **[2638]**, **[18816]**

"Market Orientation and Other Potential Influences on Performance..." in *Journal of Small Business Management* (Vol.38, No.1, Jan. 2000) **[44336]**, **[45418]**, **[46367]**

The Market Outlook for Bakery Products **[2259]**

Market Outlook for Footwear **[22769]**

The Market Outlook for Leisure and Recreational Vehicles **[21179]**

The Market for Physical Fitness Equipment **[19452]**

"Market Planning 101" in *Home Business* (Vol. 12, October 2005, No. 5, pp. 42, 44-45) **[29750]**, **[39772]**, **[42543]**, **[44426]**, **[46579]**, **[49771]**, **[52367]**

The Market Planning Guide: Creating a Plan to Successfully Market Your Business, Products or Service **[29934]**

Market Potential Mapping **[4028]**, **[31498]**

Market Research: How to Get the Right Data to Make the Right Decisions **[46633]**

Market Research: How to get the Right Data to Make the Right Decisions **[46634]**

Market Resource Guide **[12296]**

Market for Roofing and Siding **[22069]**

Market Street Capital, LLC **[60874]**

The Market for Toiletries and Cosmetics: A Product-by-Product Marketing Analysis and Computer Profile **[2597]**

"Market Upswing" in *Black Enterprise* (Vol. 34, No. 5, December 2003) **[10085]**, **[15253]**, **[38217]**

The Market for Value-Added Fresh Produce **[11682]**

"Market Values: The virtue of unselfishness" in *Red Herring* (No. 106, October 15, 2001, pp. 42) **[36847]**

"Market Watch" in *Entrepreneur* (Vol. 28, No. 1, January 2000, pp. 46) **[14231]**, **[28461]**, **[34174]**

Market Ways International Corp. **[47889]**

Marketcorp Venture Associates, L.P. (MCV) **[58600]**

Marketemps–Marketing Intelligence Center **[16895]**

"Marketers Hang Their Hopes on Holiday Promotions" in *Sacramento Bee* (December 21, 2005) **[709]**, **[12898]**, **[20138]**, **[47234]**, **[51243]**, **[52361]**

"Marketers, a Lawyer, And a Techie-Cheap" in *FSB* (Vol. 10, No. 9, December 1, 2000, pp. 118) **[31190]**, **[34175]**

Marketing **[47815]**, **[48678]**

Marketing and Advertising Global Network **[523]**, **[50533]**

Marketing Agencies Association Worldwide **[51511]**

Marketing Communications for Non-Marketers **[32950]**, **[46635]**

Marketing for Dummies **[16817]**, **[31191]**, **[47235]**

"Marketing for Dummies" in *Inc.* (October 2005, pp. 70-72) **[710]**, **[47236]**

"Marketing E-Coaches" in *Entrepreneur* (Vol. 28, No. 10, October 2000, pp. 30) **[14232]**, **[47237]**, **[51726]**

"Marketing" in *Entrepreneur* (Vol. 27, No. 12, December 1999, pp. 40) **[27428]**

The Marketing Glossary: Key Terms, Concepts, and Applications **[47238]**

Marketing Health Services **[41258]**

"Marketing: How to Get Some Attention" in *Business Week Online* (October 18, 2002) **[47239]**, **[50627]**

"Marketing" in *Inc.* (Volume 27, March 2005, No. 3, pp. 36) **[47240]**, **[50628]**

"Marketing Know-How" in *Black Enterprise* (Vol. 30, No. 5, December 1999, pp. 42) **[27726]**, **[46580]**, **[52780]**

"A marketing leader is made of life's experiences" in *Atlanta Business Chronicle* (Vol. 24, No. 9, August 3, 2001, pp. 2B) **[36485]**, **[47241]**

Marketing Leverage Inc. **[3759]**, **[16637]**, **[30096]**, **[31405]**, **[31982]**, **[47890]**, **[48835]**

Marketing Magazine **[16840]**

Marketing Management **[16841]**

Marketing Masters: Secrets of America's Best Companies **[47242]**

Marketing Methods Press **[57107]**

Marketing Myths **[47243]**, **[50629]**

Marketing Myths That Are Killing Business: The Cure for Death Wish Marketing **[47244]**

Marketing News **[16842]**, **[47798]**

Marketing News-Software Directory **[47245]**

Marketing in the Not-for-Profit Sectors **[47246]**, **[50630]**

Marketing Perspectives **[47816]**

Marketing Plus **[47891]**

"Marketing in the Portable Age" in *Crain's Detroit Business* (Vol. 19, No. 45, November 10, 2003, pp. 28) **[5052]**, **[5228]**, **[45066]**, **[47247]**

"Marketing Quandary: VCs See a Growing Need for Differentiation" in *Venture Capital Journal* (Vol. 41, No. 8, August 2000, pp. 31-33) **[47248]**, **[50631]**, **[55724]**

The Marketing Report **[47799]**

Marketing Research **[16843]**, **[16848]**, **[48679]**

Marketing Research Association **[16797]**, **[47934]**

Marketing Resource Group **[47892]**, **[52004]**

Marketing Resources Group **[3897]**, **[31499]**, **[39016]**

Marketing Resources Group Franchise Consulting **[38979]**

"Marketing budgets may rise" in *Atlanta Business Chronicle* (Vol. 25, January 10, 2003, No. 31, pp. 3A) **[711]**, **[16818]**, **[47249]**

"Marketing and sales" in *Boston Business Journal* (Vol. 22, No. 14, May 10, 2002, pp. 22) **[28462]**, **[47250]**, **[51727]**

Marketing and Selling Design Services: The Designer-Client Relationship **[13662]**

Marketing & Selling Your Film Around the World: A Guide for Independent Filmmakers **[9728]**

Marketing for Service-driven Organizations **[46636]**

"Marketing Spreads Hawaiian Message" in *Pacific Business News* (Vol. 41, No. 22, August 8, 2003, pp. 1) **[39460]**, **[40529]**, **[47251]**

Marketing Strategies for Small Businesses **[47252]**

"Marketing Strategies for Your New Home-Based Business" in *Home Business* (Vol. 12, October 2005, No. 5, pp. 24, 26-27, 54-55) **[42544]**, **[46581]**

Marketing Strategy **[48680]**

Marketing Technology Assistance Center 54110

Marketing in Travel and Tourism **[24706]**, **[25213]**

"Marketing: Use 2003 As a Building Year" in *Atlanta Business Chronicle* (Vol. 25, No. 20, October 25, 2002, pp. 10B) **[47253]**, **[48765]**

Marketing with Video: How to Create a Winning Video for Your Small Business or Non-Profit **[47254]**

Marketing Without Advertising **[47255]**, **[50632]**

Marketing Without Money for Small and Midsize Businesses: 300 FREE and Cheap Ways to Increase Your Sales **[712]**, **[34176]**, **[47256]**, **[51728]**

Marketing to Women (Vol. 19, October 2006, No. 10, pp. 1); "Arts and Crafts are Big with Women" in **[1682]**, **[8150]**, **[46686]**

Marketing to Women (Vol. 20, January 2007, No. 1, pp. 6); "Boom: Marketing to the Ultimate Power Consumer" in **[564]**, **[27859]**, **[46726]**

Marketing to Women (Vol. 19, October 2006, No. 10, pp. 8); "Boomer Women Need Financial Advisors" in **[9852]**, **[27091]**, **[37926]**, **[46728]**

Marketing to Women (Vol. 19, November 2006, No. 11, pp. 5); "Chatom Offers Wines With Cause Tie-Ins" in **[23465]**, **[46797]**, **[48712]**, **[54155]**, **[56161]**

Marketing to Women (Vol. 20, January 2007, No. 1, pp. 3); "City Guide for Moms Launched" in **[584]**, **[3943]**, **[13901]**, **[41603]**, **[46804]**, **[52370]**

Marketing to Women (Vol. 20, January 2007, No. 1, pp. 7); "Conference Calendar" in **[24911]**, **[46829]**, **[55078]**, **[56170]**

Marketing to Women (Vol. 19, October 2006, No. 10, pp. 7); "Fashion Sense Dictates Where Women Shop" in **[5658]**, **[9619]**, **[28148]**, **[46946]**

Marketing to Women (Vol. 19, October 2006, No. 10, pp. 5); "First Women's Sports Talk Show Launches" in **[627]**, **[20316]**, **[23617]**, **[23719]**, **[46966]**

Marketing to Women (Vol. 19, November 2006, No. 11, pp. 11); "Full-Figured Women are Avid Online Shoppers" in **[5665]**, **[14059]**, **[16214]**, **[41703]**, **[46997]**

Marketing to Women (Vol. 19, December 2006, No. 12, pp. 5); "Girls Learn to Ride" in **[14078]**, **[23722]**, **[47018]**

Marketing to Women (Vol. 19, October 2006, No. 10, pp. 5); "Glam Media Launches Fashion Week Site" in **[5547]**, **[5667]**, **[14079]**, **[25858]**, **[41712]**, **[47021]**

Marketing to Women (Vol. 19, December 2006, No. 2, pp. 8); "Glass Ceiling Persists in the Board Room" in **[28207]**, **[30549]**, **[34915]**, **[39358]**, **[45191]**, **[47022]**

Marketing to Women (Vol. 20, January 2007, No. 1, pp. 8); "Golf School Caters to Women" in **[11265]**, **[23620]**, **[33107]**, **[47028]**

Marketing to Women (Vol. 20, January 2007, No. 1, pp. 8); "Guide Advises Would-Be Entrepreneurs" in **[2710]**, **[29892]**, **[30554]**, **[36253]**, **[47051]**, **[56254]**

Marketing to Women (Vol. 20, January 2007, No. 1, pp. 4); "In Entertainment Men Out-Earn Women" in **[9721]**, **[28320]**, **[47126]**

Marketing to Women (Vol. 19, November 2006, No. 11, pp. 5); "Jewelry Mixes Fashion and Healing Energies" in **[9626]**, **[15851]**, **[47159]**, **[48757]**, **[56288]**

Marketing to Women (Vol. 19, October 2006, No. 10, pp. 3); "KFC Forms Moms' Advisory Board" in **[14187]**, **[21545]**, **[41797]**, **[47170]**, **[54215]**

Marketing to Women (Vol. 19, October 2006, No. 10, pp. 3); "Kids get 411 on Healthy Habits from Moms" in **[686]**, **[11637]**, **[12011]**, **[12056]**, **[47171]**

Marketing to Women (Vol. 19, October 2006, No. 10, pp. 2); "Latinas' Businesses and Earnings are Seeing Major Growth" in **[28394]**, **[47186]**, **[48266]**, **[48570]**, **[56294]**

Marketing to Women (Vol. 19, October 2006, No. 10, pp. 5); "Magazine Covers Anti-Aging Treatments" in **[7895]**, **[12593]**, **[18902]**, **[47216]**

Marketing to Women (Vol. 20, January 2007, No. 1, pp. 4); "Media Habits of Working Moms" in **[717]**, **[14234]**, **[47270]**

Marketing to Women (Vol. 19, October 2006, No. 10, pp. 5); "Meredith Debuts Mag for Cancer Survivors" in **[18907]**, **[47279]**, **[54222]**

Marketing to Women (Vol. 20, January 2007, No. 1, pp. 5); "Moms Have Their Own Generation Gap" in **[726]**, **[28497]**, **[47290]**

Marketing to Women (Vol. 19, November 2006, No. 11, pp. 3); "Moms Say Missing Their Babies is Hardest Part of Returning to Work" in **[28498]**, **[47291]**, **[54970]**

Marketing to Women (Vol. 19, October 2006, No. 10, pp. 3); "Moms Want Ads to Address Them as Women" in **[727]**, **[47292]**, **[50456]**

Marketing to Women (Vol. 19, October 2006, No. 10, pp. 12); "More Women Than Men Have Home Offices" in **[14253]**, **[27446]**, **[27660]**, **[28509]**, **[42681]**, **[47296]**, **[56326]**

Marketing to Women (Vol. 19, November 2006, No. 11, pp. 11); "Most Women Make Electronics Buying Choices" in **[728]**, **[7738]**, **[28512]**, **[47297]**

Marketing to Women (Vol. 19, November 2006, No. 11, pp. 5); "Motherhood Maternity Debuts Canadian Site" in **[2128]**, **[5692]**, **[14254]**, **[25900]**, **[41846]**, **[47299]**

Marketing to Women (Vol. 20, January 2007, No. 1, pp. 8); "MSN Signs DIY Expert With Female Focus" in **[14259]**, **[25902]**, **[47301]**, **[50089]**

Marketing to Women (Vol. 20, January 2007, No. 1, pp. 8); "New Shade of Vodka Targets Women" in **[2347]**, **[16233]**, **[47331]**

Marketing to Women (Vol. 20, January 2007, No. 1, pp. 8); "New Site Sells Women's Self-Defense Wares" in **[14289]**, **[22307]**, **[47332]**

Marketing to Women (Vol. 20, January 2007, No. 1, pp. 8); "New Website for Women's Clothes" in **[5698]**, **[14293]**, **[34260]**, **[47338]**, **[56346]**

Marketing to Women (Vol. 19, November 2006, No. 11, pp. 5); "News Blog Highlights Women's Careers" in **[14294]**, **[27455]**, **[27663]**, **[41868]**, **[42361]**, **[47341]**

Marketing to Women (Vol. 19, November 2006, No. 22, pp. 8); "News on Women" in **[737]**, **[5699]**, **[28561]**, **[47343]**

Marketing to Women (Vol. 20, January 2007, No. 1, pp. 8); "Nike Develops Brand for Women" in **[22764]**, **[47348]**, **[48772]**, **[50104]**

Marketing to Women (Vol. 20, January 2007, No. 1, pp. 3); "Playskool Makes Product for Moms" in **[2732]**, **[47404]**, **[50131]**

Marketing to Women (Vol. 19, October 2006, No. 10, pp. 5); "Podcast Network Focuses on Wedding Plans" in **[3191]**, **[14356]**, **[25934]**, **[41908]**, **[47405]**

Marketing to Women (Vol. 19, November 2006, No. 11, pp. 5); "Prepaid Card Benefits Breast Cancer Research" in **[8317]**, **[31579]**, **[47421]**, **[48778]**, **[50136]**, **[54240]**

Marketing to Women (Vol. 20, January 2007, No. 1, pp. 5) "School's out; Working Moms are Worried" in **[28746]**, **[47499]**, **[54987]**

Marketing to Women (Vol. 19, December 2006, No. 2, pp. 6); "Shattered Magazine: A Monthly for the Global Businesswoman" in **[18933]**, **[27497]**, **[28758]**, **[30598]**, **[38906]**, **[47522]**, **[56400]**

Marketing to Women (Vol. 19, November 2006, No. 11, pp. 3); "Similac Launches Online Moms' Community" in **[14435]**, **[41988]**, **[47530]**

Marketing to Women (Vol. 19, October 2006, No. 10, pp. 9); "Simon Group Offers Cobranded Giftcard" in **[8321]**, **[31585]**, **[47531]**, **[50178]**, **[54256]**

Marketing to Women (Vol. 20, January 2007, No. 1, pp. 3); "TodaysMama.com Relaunches Website" in **[815]**, **[3953]**, **[14543]**, **[42071]**, **[47650]**, **[50218]**, **[52392]**

Marketing to Women (Vol. 19, October 2006, No. 10, pp. 9); "Tomboy Tools Ties in With Pink Hammer" in **[11895]**, **[14545]**, **[47651]**, **[50219]**, **[54264]**

Marketing to Women (Vol. 19, October 2006, No. 10, pp. 5); "Website Offers Family Pages and Networking" in **[14589]**, **[26007]**, **[47706]**

Marketing to Women (Vol. 20, January 2007, No. 1, pp. 2); "What I Think of Pink" in **[832]**, **[42108]**, **[47718]**

Marketing to Women (Vol. 19, November 2006, No. 1, pp. 2); "What I've Learned About Women" in **[833]**, **[28988]**, **[47719]**, **[50703]**

Marketing to Women (Vol. 20, January 2007, No. 1, pp. 5); "What Women Want at Work" in **[28993]**, **[33276]**, **[47726]**

Marketing to Women (Vol. 19, November 2006, No. 11, pp. 12); "Women Business Owners Get Credit Easily" in **[8327]**, **[29023]**, **[30706]**, **[31607]**, **[47753]**, **[56490]**

Marketing to Women (Vol. 19, December 2006, No. 2, pp. 8); "Women Business Owners Seek Financing" in **[30631]**, **[30707]**, **[31608]**, **[38472]**, **[39690]**, **[44687]**, **[47754]**, **[48927]**, **[56491]**

Marketing to Women (Vol. 19, October 2006, No. 10, pp. 11); "Women Favor Discounters for Back-to-School" in **[5730]**, **[29024]**, **[47755]**

Marketing to Women (Vol. 19, December 2006, No. 2, pp. 8); "Women Want More Info on Wellness" in **[29025]**, **[47756]**, **[55004]**

Marketing to Women (Vol. 19, October 2006, No. 10, pp. 5); "Women's Firms Reach Nearly $2 Trillion in Sales" in **[29026]**, **[47757]**, **[56508]**

Marketing to Women (Vol. 19, October 2006, No. 10, pp. 5); "Women's Talk Radio Network Launches" in **[20349]**, **[27540]**, **[47758]**

Marketing that Works: How Entrepreneurial Marketing Can Add Sustainable Value to Any Sized Company **[36486]**, **[47257]**

Marketing Works: Unlock Big Company Strategies for Small Business **[713]**, **[47258]**

Marketing Your Consulting and Professional Services **[9367]**

"Marketing Your Consulting Service by Elaine Biech: www.josseybass.com" in *Entrepreneur* (Vol. 31, No. 10, October 2003, pp. 6) **[28463]**, **[47259]**

Marketing Your Invention **[44095]**

Marketing Your Product **[34177]**, **[47260]**

Marketing Your Service Business: Plan a Winning Strategy **[52561]**

Marketing Your Small Business for Big Profits **[714]**, **[47261]**

"MarketingExperiments.com: www.marketingexperiments.com" in *Entrepreneur* (Vol. 32, November 2004, No. 11, pp. 6) **[715]**, **[14233]**, **[47262]**

"Marketingfix: www.marketingfix.com" in *Entrepreneur* (Vol. 31, No. 10, October 2003, pp. 6) **[716]**, **[34178]**, **[47263]**

"MarketingSherpa: www.marketingsherpa.com" in *Entrepreneur* (Vol. 33, February 2005, No. 2, pp. 8) **[18238]**, **[34179]**, **[47264]**

Marketnews **[7752]**

The Markets Directory **[16819]**

A. Marks & Associates **[47893]**

Marks & Associates, Attorneys-at-Law **[29637]**

MarkSearch **[44214]**

Marksville Chamber of Commerce **[60656]**

Marlborough Regional Chamber of Commerce **[60968]**

Marleau Lemire, Inc. **[66772]**

Marlin Chamber of Commerce **[65383]**

Marlow Chamber of Commerce **[64030]**

Marple's Pacific Northwest Letter **[39724]**

C.E. Marquardt Lighting Design **[49633]**

Marquette Area Chamber of Commerce- Lake Superior Community Partnership **[61378]**

Marquette Venture Partners **[59748]**

"Marriage of Expedience" in *Red Herring* (No. 99, June 15 & July 1, 2001, pp. 108) **[6951]**, **[41829]**, **[50919]**

Married & Making a Living: Couples Who Own Small Franchise Businesses **[37727]**

"Married With Business" in *My Business* (February/March 2003, pp. 28-32, 34) **[37728]**

Marringa International Co. **[43927]**

"Marsh Mac Settles Up" in *Business Week* (February 14, 2005, No. 3920, pp. 42) **[13378]**, **[29378]**, **[43272]**

Marsha Scott's Hair Loss Clinic For Women **[11764]**

Marshall Area Chamber of Commerce **[59585]**, **[61379]**, **[61623]**

Marshall Chamber of Commerce **[61997]**

Marshall Community & Technical College–Small Business Development Center **[66258]**

Marshall County Chamber of Commerce **[60539]**, **[64031]**, **[64949]**, **[66285]**

Marshall Craft Associates Inc. **[49634]**

The Marshall Group Executive Search Corp. **[9594]**

Marshall Heights Community Development Organization–SBDC **[58662]**

Marshall Texas Chamber of Commerce **[65384]**

Marshall University–Research Committee **[66314]**

Marshall University Research Corp. **[41386]**

Marshalltown Area Chamber of Commerce **[60176]**

Marshalltown Community College **[60247]**

Marshfield Area Chamber of Commerce and Industry **[66451]**

Marshville Chamber of Commerce **[63403]**

The Martha Rules: 10 Essentials for Achieving Success as You Start, Build, or Manage a Business **[36487]**, **[39461]**, **[45419]**

The Martha Rules: 10 Essentials for Achieving Success as You Start, Grow, or Manage a Business **[36488]**, **[39462]**, **[45420]**

Martha's Vineyard Chamber of Commerce **[60969]**

Martin County Chamber of Commerce **[59966]**, **[63404]**

"Martin Family Estate Sells the Knole to Development Interest for $11M" in *Long Island Business News* (February 6, 2004) **[7420]**, **[20585]**, **[20936]**

"Martin Van Der Werf Column" in *St. Louis Post-Dispatch* (December 10, 2004) **[2343]**, **[21558]**

Martin/Williams Advertising Inc.–Library **[50740]**

Martindale-Hubbell International Dispute Resolution Directory **[17040]**

"Martindale's Calculators On-Line Center" in *Entrepreneur* (Vol. 33, September 2005, No. 9, pp. 6) **[46801]**, **[49139]**

Martinez Area Chamber of Commerce and Visitors and Information Center **[57628]**

Martinizing Dry Cleaning **[8935]**

Martins Ferry Area Chamber of Commerce **[63734]**

Martinsburg-Berkeley County Chamber of Commerce **[66286]**

Martinsville Chamber of Commerce **[59586]**

Martinsville - Henry County Chamber of Commerce **[65926]**

Marwit Capital, LLC **[58076]**

Mary Browns Inc. **[21876]**

"Mary Engelbreit: My Biggest Mistake" in *Inc.* (November 2000, pp. 97) **[5997]**, **[11566]**, **[36489]**

Mary Kay Inc.–Knowledge Resources **[2417]**, **[2629]**, **[7947]**

Mary Kay's You Can Have It All: Practical Advice for Doing Well by Doing Good **[56319]**

Mary Washington College–Center for Historic Preservation **[1583]**

Maryland Advanced Development Laboratory **[60886]**

"Maryland-based Hotel Chains Step Up Efforts in Pursuit of Business Travelers" in *Daily Record* (January 28, 2005) **[7139]**, **[12594]**, **[30375]**

Maryland Chamber of Commerce **[60840]**

Maryland Department of Business and Economic Development–Business Development Division **[60803]**

Maryland Department of Business and Economic Development Center–Administration Division–Contracts and Procurement Office **[60883]**

Maryland Economic Development Corp. **[60804]**

Maryland Heights Chamber of Commerce **[61998]**

Maryland Municipal League Convention **[50375]**, **[55225]**

Maryland Office of Planning **[66893]**

Maryland Pharmacists Association–Library **[8870]**

Maryland RV Show **[21193]**

Maryland Small Business Development Center **[60792]**

    University of Maryland **[60793]**

Maryland Small Business Development Center (SBDC) **[66894]**

Maryland Technology Extension Service **[60887]**

Maryland Venture Capital Trust **[60875]**

Marysville Appeal-Democrat (January 26, 2003); "Former Female Weightlifter Opens Yuba City, Calif., Women-Only Fitness Center" in **[19399]**, **[36176]**, **[56228]**

Marysville Appeal-Democrat (January 26, 2003); "Marysville, Calif., Downtown Building Gets New Look, New Name" in **[19416]**, **[19635]**, **[28464]**, **[52699]**

Marysville Appeal-Democrat (August 25, 2002); "Marysville, Calif., Woman Runs Personal Chef Service" in **[4548]**, **[56320]**

"Marysville, Calif., Downtown Building Gets New Look, New Name" in *Marysville Appeal-Democrat* (January 26, 2003) **[19416]**, **[19635]**, **[28464]**, **[52699]**

"Marysville, Calif., Woman Runs Personal Chef Service" in *Marysville Appeal-Democrat* (August 25, 2002) **[4548]**, **[56320]**

Marysville Chamber of Commerce **[60382]**, **[61380]**

Maryville Chamber of Commerce **[61999]**

"Masco Corp. (NYSE:MAS)" in *Crain's Detroit Business* (Vol. 16, No. 46, November 13, 2000, pp. 4) **[28465]**

"Masco hopes Home Depot deals, new product line build growth" in *Crain's Detroit Business* (Vol. 19, No. 7, Feb. 17, 2003, pp. 4) **[11891]**, **[28466]**

"Masco Installs Two Subsidiaries in Deals Worth $719M" in *Crain's Detroit Business* (Vol. 16, No. 49, December 4, 2000, pp. 3) **[50071]**

"Masco to Reduce Jobs, Businesses" in *Crain's Detroit Business* (Vol. 21, November 7, 2005, No. 45, pp. 41) **[46368]**, **[52437]**

Maskmaking with Clay **[8067]**

Mason Area Chamber of Commerce **[61381]**

Mason City Area Chamber of Commerce **[60177]**

Mason Contractors Association of America **[16934]**

Mason County Area Chamber of Commerce **[66287]**

Mason County Chamber of Commerce **[65385]**

Mason Wells Private Equity / M&I Ventures **[66566]**

Masonry Block Explained **[16973]**

Masonry Construction (Vol. 16, No. 1, January 2003, pp. 17); "CSDA creates a new Web site" in **[1505]**, **[7305]**, **[27340]**

Masonry: Design and Construction, Problems and Repair **[16951]**

Masonry Design and Detailing: For Architects, Engineers, and Contractors **[16952]**

Masonry Estimating **[16953]**

Masonry Heater Association of North America **[1003]**

Masonry Skills **[16954]**

The Masonry Society **[16935]**

Masonry Society Journal **[7561]**, **[16968]**

Masonry Specification Sheets **[16955]**

Masonry Walls: Design & Specification **[16956]**

Mass Merchandisers & Off-Price Apparel Buyers **[9630]**

Mass Storage News **[6301]**

Massachusetts Administration and Finance Executive Office–Human Resources Division–Research/Survey Office **[50403]**

Massachusetts Capital Resource Co. **[61090]**

Massachusetts College of Art–Design Research Unit **[50744]**

Massachusetts Export Center–Small Business Development Center Network **[60906]**

Massachusetts Export Center (Headquarters)–Trade Development Unit–Massachusetts Small Business Export Program **[60911]**

Massachusetts Horticultural Society–Library **[11526]**

"Massachusetts House Plan Seeks More Excise Tax for Newer Cars" in *Boston Globe* (April 11, 2003) **[18085]**, **[54658]**

Massachusetts Institute for Social and Economic Research (MISER) **[66896]**

Massachusetts Institute of Technology

    CADLAB **[23323]**

    Center for Coordination Science **[6395]**

    Center for Real Estate **[21115]**

    Center for Technology, Policy and Industrial Development–International Motor Vehicle Program **[33401]**

    Japan Program **[33402]**

    Laboratory for Computer Science–Programming Methodology Group **[6558]**

    Media Laboratory **[24511]**

    Office of Sponsored Programs **[61142]**

    Program on the Pharmaceutical Industry **[33403]**

    Real Estate Office **[61143]**

    Technology Licensing Office **[61144]**

Massachusetts International Auto Show **[926]**

"Massachusetts Jobless Insurance Trust Fund May Need Federal Help" in *Boston Globe* (April 11, 2003) **[28467]**, **[32565]**, **[39865]**

Massachusetts Office of Business Development **[60912]**

Massachusetts Office of International Trade and Investment **[60913]**

Massachusetts Society for the Prevention of Cruelty to Animals (MSPCA)–Angell Memorial Animal Hospital Veterinary Library **[1278]**

Massachusetts Technology Development Corp. (MTDC) **[61091]**

Massachusetts Water Resources Authority–Library **[25733]**

Massage: A Career At Your Fingertips **[17012]**

Massage: A Career at Your Fingertips **[17006]**

Massage Envy **[17028]**

Massage for Health **[17022]**

Massage Therapy Journal **[41259]**

MassBay Community College **[61155]**

Massey Burch Capital Corp. **[64997]**

Massillon Area Chamber of Commerce **[63735]**

Massinnovation, LLC **[61145]**

"Massport Drops Metal Recycling Facility Plan" in *Boston Globe* (March 5, 2005) **[21243]**

MAST (Mailing Systems Technology) **[6115]**, **[10716]**

MASTA notes **[17624]**, **[17791]**

Master Brewers Association of the Americas [3120]

"Master Builder" in *Success* (Vol. 47, No. 5, October 2000, pp. 26) [35559]

Master Care [3372]

"Master of Disaster" in *Fast Company* (November 2001, pp. 46) [3558], [31192], [36490]

"Master of your domain" in *WorkingWoman* (Vol. 25, No. 4, April 2000, pp. 54) [13764], [29071], [33460], [37067]

Master Gardener Series [16060]

Master Guide [19207], [19237]

"Master of Her Retail Space" in *Crain's New York Business* (Vol. 23, January 29, 2007, No. 5, pp. F11) [20586], [20937], [33165], [36491], [45421], [48579]

Master Keys for Making Profits in Lapidary [15854]

The Master Mechanic Inc. [22683]

"The Master Negotiator: How To Use the Power of Persuasion to Raise Dollars" in *Black Enterprise* (Vol. 34, No. 2, September 2003) [27429], [44585], [48914]

Master Organizational Politics, Influence and Alliances [44809]

"Mastering Agency Management" in *Rough Notes* (Vol. 146, No. 9, September 2003, pp. 52) [13379], [45422]

Mastering Business Growth and Change Made Easy [28468], [39463]

Mastering Change Management: Turning Obstacles into Opportunities [45423]

Mastering the Complex Sales: How to Compete and Win When the Stakes Are High! [30912], [51729]

Mastering CorelDRAW Newsletter [26025]

Mastering Diversity [48580]

Mastering Information Overload: Speed Reading and Memory Skills [32951]

Mastering Organizational Politics, Influence and Alliance: The Winning Formula for Experienced Managers (Canada) [44810]

Mastering Organizational Politics, Influence and Alliances: The Winning Formula for Experienced Managers [44811], [46519]

Masthead Venture [61092]

Mat-su–Small Business Development Center [56940]

Matanuska-Susitna College [56984]

Matawan - Aberdeen Chamber of Commerce [62526]

"Match Made in Heaven" in *Hispanic Business* (June 2002, pp. 82) [42338], [48581]

"A Match Made in Hormones" in *Business 2.0* (Vol. 7, January/February 2006, No. 1, pp. 24) [7061], [34180]

"Matchmaker" in *Forbes* (Vol. 175, February 28, 2005, No. 4, pp. 48) [42339], [42875]

Matco Tools [11914]

Materia Venture Associates, L.P. [66218]

Materials Advisory Group Inc. [7624]

Materials Handling and Management Society [20208]

Materials Management in Health Care [17161], [41260]

Maternal and Child Health [41052]

"Math Will Rock Your World" in *Business Week* (January 23, 2006, No. 3968, pp. 54-58, 60, 62) [36492], [47265], [53849]

Mathews County Chamber of Commerce [65927]

Mathis Area Chamber of Commerce [65386]

Mathnasium Learning Centers [25482], [33372]

Stuart Matlins Associates [46076]

Maton Venture [58077]

Matrix Partners [61093]

Matrix Partners (Menlo Park) [58078]

Matrix System Automotive Finishes, Inc. [2056], [32184]

Matson & Associates [10764], [20187]

"A matter of safety" in *Black Enterprise* (Vol. 32, No. 9, April 2002) [35560], [43965], [48688]

"A Matter of Opinion" in *Entrepreneur* (Vol. 31, No. 8, August 2003, pp. 72) [31776], [47266], [48667], [51244]

"A Matter of Taste" in *Fast Company* (March 2005, No. 92, pp. 35) [48766], [50920], [52148]

Matteson Area Chamber of Commerce [59587]

Matthew Bender and Company Inc. [63257]

Matthews CATV Directory [4112], [22088]

Matthews Chamber of Commerce [63405]

Matthews Media Directory [20326], [24431]

Mattituck Chamber of Commerce [62956]

Mattoon Chamber of Commerce [59588]

"Mattresses Beneath His Wings" in *Sacramento Bee* (October 10, 2005) [12194], [12297], [36493]

Maui Chamber of Commerce [59254]

Maui Research and Technology Park [59261]

Maui Small Business Development Center [59233]

"Maui Wowi Fresh Hawaiian Blends" in *Small Business Opportunities* (Vol. 16, November 2004, No. 6, pp. 112) [12012], [23496], [38853]

Maui Wowi Hawaiian Coffees & Smoothies [12838]

Mauldin Area Chamber of Commerce [64769]

Maumee Chamber of Commerce [63736]

Maumee Valley Planning Organization
    Northwest Small Business Development Center [63570]
    SBDC [63571]

Maumelle Area Chamber of Commerce [57193]

Maury Alliance [64950]

Maury County Alliance–Satellite Office of Middle Tennessee State University–SBDC [64863]

"Mavericks" in *Success* (Vol. 47, No. 2, June 2000, pp. 18) [28469], [35561]

"The Maw of the Law" in *Success* (Vol. 47, No. 5, October 2000, pp. 42) [27150], [29379]

Max Muscle [51464]

"Max Polaner" in *Entrepreneur* (Vol. 30, No. 3, March 2002, pp. 22) [23442], [35562]

Max S. Hayes Vocational School–Library [2063]

Max Sacks International [52005]

Maxdeco Interior Design Inc. [49635]

"Maximize Your Resources" in *Small Business Opportunities* (Vol. 13, No. 6, November 2001, pp. 12, 133) [6332], [33166], [49140]

"Maximizing Employee Performance: Grow Your Business by Empowering Your Workforce" in *Black Enterprise* (Vol. 35, February 2005, No. 7) [34987], [36494], [45424]

"Maximizing the Plus-Size Potential" in *WWD* (August 4, 2003, pp. 19) [5685], [9631]

Maximum Marketing, Minimum Dollars: The Top 50 Ways to Grow Your Small Business [28470], [34181], [47267], [51730]

Maximum PC [6199], [6884], [23285]

Maximum Performance Leadership (Canada) [44812]

Maximum Response Marketing [10765], [47894]

Max's Deli and Restaurant/David & Bernies [8558], [21877]

"May I Help You?" in *Inc.* (Volume 28, January 2006, No. 1, pp. 31-32) [4723], [23074], [34182], [53363]

George S. May International Co. [46077]

Maya Collection [1633]

"Maybe it's time to batten down the hatches" in *Crain's Detroit Business* (Vol. 19, No. 11, March 17, 2003, pp. 8) [32566]

Daniel F. Mayer [26634]

Mayeri Research Inc. [16874]

Mayfield Fund [58079]

Mayfield-Graves County Chamber of Commerce [60540]

Mayo Biomedical Imaging Resource–Library [6550]

Mayo Medical Ventures [61702]

Mayor's Office of Planning–Data Services Division [66846]

Maysville Chamber of Commerce [64032]

Maysville-Mason County Area Chamber of Commerce [60541]

Mayville Area Chamber of Commerce [66452]

Mayville - Chatauqua Area Chamber of Commerce [62957]

Maywood Chamber of Commerce [57629], [59589], [62527]

"Mazda's Minority Dealers" in *Minority Business Journal* (Vol. 17, No. 5, September/October 2001, pp. 2) [18086], [48286]

Mazomanie Chamber of Commerce [66453]

Mazzio's Italian Eatery [19686]

MB Venture Partners, LLC [64998]

MBA-Management Basics in Action [45935]

"MBA Programs That Work for the Working Professional" in *Ingram's* (Vol. 29, No. 8, August 2003, pp. 53) [33167], [45425]

MBA Venture Group [65616]

"MBDA's new horizons" in *Hispanic Business* (Vol. 22, No. 11, November 2000, pp. 18) [28471], [48287]

MBW Management Inc. [62601]

MC Capital, Inc. [63132]

"MC, MMA Offering Manufacturing Management Program" in *Mississippi Business Journal* (Vol. 29, January 2007, No. 3, pp. A15) [33168], [45426], [46369], [55117]

MCAA Reporter [1042], [19763]

MCAA's Masonry Showcase & MCAA Annual Convention [16975]

McAlester Area Chamber of Commerce and Agriculture [64033]

McAlester Economic Development Service Inc.–Incubator [64124]

McAlester Industrial Incubator–Kiamichi Technology Center-McAlester [64125]

McAlister's Deli [8559]

McAllen Chamber of Commerce [65387]

McAllen Memorial Library–McAllen Genealogical Society Collection [11053]

MCBA Newsletter [2842]

McBain Area Chamber of Commerce [61382]

McCall Area Chamber of Commerce [59315]

McCamey Chamber of Commerce [65388]

McCann-Erickson Advertising of Canada Ltd.–Information Centre [913], [50741]

Edward F. McCartan Publishing Consultant [2798]

McCarthy Tetrault–Library [29701]

"McClatchy Among Possible Suitors for Knight Ridder" in *Sacramento Bee* (December 9, 2005) [15254], [18905], [50072]

"McClatchy-Owned Minneapolis Newspaper Settles Advertiser Lawsuit" in *Sacramento Bee* (December 21, 2005) [18906], [29380]

McCleary Community Chamber of Commerce [66130]

McCloud Chamber of Commerce [57630]

McClure Associates Inc. [48641]

McCook Area Chamber of Commerce [62280]

McCormick County Chamber of Commerce [64770]

McCown De Leeuw and Co. (Menlo Park) [58080]

McCown, De Leeuw and Co. (New York) [63133]

McCoy's Cake and Pie Shop Franchise Corp. [2305]

McCreary County Chamber of Commerce [60542]

McCreight & Company Inc. [3760], [16638], [30097], [31406], [42984]

McDargh Communications [31983]

Mcdermott, Will & Emery [29638]

McDonald Consulting Group Inc. [3761], [16639], [30098], [31407], [46078]

"McDonald's goes to church" in *BlackEnterprise* (Vol. 32, No. 2, September 2001, pp. 24) [21405], [38661]

McDonald's Corp. [21878]

McDonald's Restaurants of Canada Ltd. [21879]

McDowell Chamber of Commerce [63406]

McFarland Chamber of Commerce [66454]

Scott McGarvey Associates [47895]

Jerome W. McGee & Associates [30099], [44206], [46079], [49441]

McGehee Chamber of Commerce [57194]

McGill University
    Environmental Engineering Laboratory [25743]
    International Centre for Youth Gambling Problems and High-Risk Behaviors [10909]
    McGill Finance Research Centre [10410]
    Office of Technology Transfer [66776]

McGoodwin James & Co. [58081]

The McGraw-Hill Companies Inc. [63258]
    Business Information Center [2817]

McGraw-Hill Guide to Starting Your Own Business: A Step-by-Step Blueprint [52913]

McGraw-Hill Inc. [63259]

McGraw-Hill/Irwin [59810]

McGraw-Hill Machining and Metalworking Handbook [16373]

The McGraw-Hill Recycling Handbook [21244]

The McGraw-Hill Thirty-Six Hour Course in Finance for Nonfinancial Managers [38218]

McGraw-Hill Trade [63260]

McGraw-Hill Ventures /McGraw-Hill Capital Corp. [63134]

McGregor Chamber of Commerce [65389]

McGregor/Marquette Chamber of Commerce [60178]

McGrow Consulting [3898], [31500]

McGruff Safe Kids Total Identification System [19519]

McHenry Area Chamber of Commerce [59590]

McHenry County College–Small Business Development Center [59382]

McIntosh County Chamber of Commerce [59136]

McKay/Moore Consultants [7625]

McKee & Co. [57091]

McKenna Long & Aldridge LLP–Law Library [8871], [9447], [13603]

McKenzie River Chamber of Commerce and Information Center [64242]

McKinleyville Chamber of Commerce [57631]

McKinney Chamber of Commerce [65390]

McKinnon, Allen & Associates Western Ltd. [26635]

McKinsey & Company, Inc.–Information Centre [4051]

McKnight's Long-Term Care News [18358], [41261]

McLean County Chamber of Commerce [59591], [60543]

McLean Watson Capital Inc. [66727]

McLennan Community College–Small Business Development Center [65046]

McLeod Associates Inc. [7040]

Mcloud Chamber of Commerce [64034]

McMaster University
　　Health Sciences Library [1722]
　　Office of Research Services [66737]

McMinnville Area Chamber of Commerce [64243]

McMinnville - Warren County Chamber of Commerce [64951]

McMullen Valley Chamber of Commerce [57049]

"McMullouch Has Had Busy Telecommunications Career" in *Mississippi Business Journal* (Vol. 29, January 2007, No. 4, pp. 10) [5053], [27430], [45427]

McNairy County Chamber of Commerce [64952]

MCNC Research and Development [63474]

MCNC Ventures LLC [63461]

McNeil Consumer and Specialty Pharmaceuticals–Pharmaceutical Research Center [8872]

McNeilly Business Center [64610]

McPherson Chamber of Commerce [60383]

MCR Capital Advisors L.L.P. [46080]

McShane Group Inc. [3762], [16640], [30100], [31408], [38558], [46081]

James V. McTevia & Associates [50327]

"M.D. Hodges changes strategy" in *Atlanta Business Chronicle* (Vol. 25, December 6, 2002, No. 26, pp. 7C) [20938], [21336], [28472], [32567]

MD Pluckers Wing Factory & Grill [21880]

MDA Engineering Inc. [7626]

"MDC Homes expanding in North Carolina" in *Atlanta Business Chronicle* (Vol. 25, No. 22, November 8, 2002, pp. 25A) [7421], [28473]

MDR Telecom Timeshare Multiple Listing Service [20587]

MDS Discovery Venture Management, Inc. [66681]

"M.D.s, business group seek to shape patients' bill" in *Atlanta Business Chronicle* (Vol. 24, No. 8, July 27, 2001, pp. 8A) [13380], [40530]

MDT Advisers, Inc. [61094]

ME-Mobile Entertainment [4346]

Me-n-Ed's Pizzerias [19687]

Meade Chamber of Commerce [60384]

Meade County Area Chamber of Commerce [60544]

Meadowlands Regional Chamber of Commerce [62528]

Meadville - Western Crawford County Chamber of Commerce [64472]

J.L. Meaher & Associates Inc. [9410]

Mealey's Emerging Insurance Disputes [32076]

Mealey's Insurance Supplement [13553]

Mealey's Litigation Report: Insurance Bad Faith [13554]

Mealey's Litigation Report: Insurance Fraud [13555]

Mealey's Managed Care Liability Report [17126], [17162], [17211], [17265], [41262]

Mean Gene's Burgers [21881]

Meaning of Masonry [16957]

Means Labor Rates for the Construction Industry [7519]

"Measure Twice, Cut Once" in *Milwaukee Journal Sentinel* (December 14, 2005) [16311], [30687]

"Measure twice, cut once" in *Incentive* (Vol. 174, No. 9, September 2000, pp. 74) [47268]

"Measurement of Human Potential" in *Employment Relations Today* (Vol. 27, No. 2, Summer 2000, pp. 15) [33169]

MeasureNet [3763]

"Measuring the Car Market" in *Hispanic Business* (November 2003, pp. 66, 68, 70) [18087], [47269]

Measuring Customer Satisfaction [31777]
　　Crisp Learning–Thomson Learning [31993]

"Measuring Progress: A Look at the Economic Strides of African Americans in Recent Decades" in *Black Enterprise* (Vol. 34, No. 5) [31659], [32568], [38219], [39640]

Measuring Team Performance: Tracking Team Success [34988]

Meat Goat Monthly News [1205]

Meat Industry Suppliers Association [4057]

Meat & Poultry [4066]

Mechanical Contractors Association of America [1004]

Mechanical Contractors Association of Canada [7221]

"Mechanical Minds" in *Red Herring* (No. 105, October 1, 2001, pp. 64-69) [37166], [50921]

"Mechanically inclined" in *Entrepreneur* (Vol. 31, No. 4, April 2003, pp. 168) [36495], [41830], [50922]

Mechanicville Area Chamber of Commerce [62958]

Mecosta County Area Chamber of Commerce [61383]

"Med Mal in Crisis Mode" in *Rough Notes* (Vol. 145, No. 9, September 2002, pp. 66) [13381], [43273]

"Med Tech Carl Goldfischer" in *Venture Capital Journal* (January 1, 2005) [41053], [41831], [50923], [52149], [55725]

Medallion Healthy Homes of Canada [3279]

"MEDC Showcases Michigan's Automotive Brainpower at Auto Show Symposium" in *Crain's Detroit Business* (Vol. 21, December 19, 2005) [18088], [32569], [46370]

"Medfone Expanding Its Wantagh Headquarters" in *Long Island Business News* (March 5, 2004) [41054], [41110], [47379], [49716], [49982], [52562]

Medford Area Chamber of Commerce [66455]

Medford Chamber of Commerce [60970], [64035]

Media Communications Association International [9685]

Media Computing [3403], [4871], [6200], [6347], [6885], [23286]

The Media Guys Inc. [20188]

"Media Habits of Working Moms" in *Marketing to Women* (Vol. 20, January 2007, No. 1, pp. 4) [717], [14234], [47270]

"Media, Mid-Perm" in *Inc.* (October 1, 2003) [718], [11796], [47271]

"Media Planning: The Seven 'Undeniable Truths'" in *Ingram's* (Vol. 28, No. 9, September 2002, pp. 27) [47272], [50633]

Media Publications [64306]

Media Relations in Your Spare Time: A Step-by-Step Guide for Anyone in Business [50455]

Media Review Digest [9729]

Media Sports Business [23746]

Media Technology Ventures [58082]

Media Venture Partners [58083]

"A Mediation on Risk" in *Fortune* (Vol. 152, October 3, 2005, No. 7, pp. 50) [39464], [40531]

"Mediation for Small Business: Cheaper and Faster Than The Courts" in *My Business* (February/March 2003, pp. 16) [3559], [27431], [34183]

"Mediation Year 2051?" in *Dispute Resolution Journal* (Vol. 56, No. 1, February-April 2001, pp. 24) [17055], [23075], [27432], [37167]

MEDIAWEEK (Vol. 11, No. 4, January 22, 2001, pp. 65); "Enterprising Moves" in [2702], [28106], [53712]

"Medicaid HMOs seek cure for what ails them" in *Crain's Detroit Business* (Vol. 19, No. 15, April 14, 2003, pp. 13) [13382], [26851], [43274]

Medicaid Long-Term Care: Successful State Efforts to Expand Home Services While Limiting Costs [18328]

Medical Benefits [26988]

Medical Care [17127], [17163], [17212], [17266], [17303], [41263]

Medical College of Wisconsin
　　Center for the Study of Bioethics [48651]
　　MCW Research Foundation [66572]

"Medical Coverage Options for the Self-Employed" in *Home Business* (Vol. 13, January/February 2006, No. 1, pp. 94) [13383], [43275]

Medical Device Register [17259], [17286]

Medical Devices, Diagnostics & Instrumentation Reports - The Gray Sheet [17128]

Medical Directory of the Dakotas & Montana [41055]

"Medical Emergency" in *Hispanic Business* (May 2005, pp. 76, 78) [41056], [48288]

Medical Environment Update Newsletter [41264]

"Medical Events' Popularity on the Rise" in *Tradeshow Week* (Vol. 34, November 29, 2004, No. 48, pp. 6) [22527], [24971], [55118]

Medical and Health Information Directory [8791], [12377], [17189], [41057]

Medical & Healthcare Marketplace Guide [17100], [17260]

Medical Imaging [17129]

Medical Imaging Consultants Inc. [3764], [16641], [31409], [46082], [47896], [48836], [51004]

Medical Innovation Partners [61703]

Medical Laboratory Management and Supervision: A Study Guide [17190]

Medical Laboratory Observer (MLO) [17213]

"Medical Lessons: What Can Collision Repair Shops Learn About Insurance From the Health Care Industry?" in *Automotive Body Repair News* [11218], [13384], [22616], [43276]

Medical Needles & Syringes Market [17261]

Medical Outcomes Management Inc. [3765], [16642], [31410], [46083]

Medical Science Partners [61095]

Medical Staffing Consultants (MSC) [9275], [42799]

Medical Technology and Practice Patterns Institute, Inc. [41387]

Medical Transcription for Health Information Managers [17298]

Medical Transcription Self-Assessment [17299]

The Medical Transcriptionist: Independent Contractor or Employee? [17300]

The Medical Transcriptionist's Handbook [17301]

Medical Transcriptions [17302]

Medical Venture Holdings, Inc. [63135]

Medicap Pharmacy [8845]

Medicare & You Handbook [41058]

MEDIchair Ltd. [17141]

"Medicine meets the alternatives" in *Georgia Trend* (Vol. 18, No. 3, November 2002, pp. 30) [17904], [19417]

Medicine Lodge Area Chamber of Commerce [60385]

"Medicine Man" in *Forbes* (June 10, 2002, p. 146) [13385], [41059], [43277]

Medicine on the Net [14656], [41265]

The Medicine Shoppe [8846]

Medicine Shoppe Canada [8847]

Medicus Venture Partners (Burlingame) [58084]

"Medieval or Modern? A Scholastic's View of Business Ethics, circa 1430" in *Journal of Business Ethics* (Vol. 28, No. 2, Nov. 15, 2000) [37475]

Medina Area Chamber of Commerce [63737]

"Mediocre Middle Management" in *Entrepreneur* (Vol. 28, No. 2, February 2000, pp. 38) [45428]

Mediphase Venture Partners / EHealth Technology Fund [61096]

Merchant Magazine-Buyers Guide [16312]

"A (mercifully) brief history of Kansas City's epicurean vote" in Ingram's (Vol. 28, No. 6, June 2002, pp. 32) [21559]

Merck Frosst Canada Ltd.–Research Library and Information Centre [8873]

Mercy College–SBDC Outreach [62769]

Mercy Medical Center–Health Sciences Library [18401]

Meredith Area Chamber of Commerce [62428]

Meredith Chamber of Commerce [62429]

"Meredith Debuts Mag for Cancer Survivors" in Marketing to Women (Vol. 19, October 2006, No. 10, pp. 5) [18907], [47279], [54222]

Mergent Company Snapshots [15762]

Merger and Acquisition Sourcebook [3420]

"Merger with Advo May Mean Shift in Business for Valassis" in Crain's Detroit Business (Vol. 232, January 8, 2007, No. 2, pp. 4) [28476], [47280], [50074]

"Merger Fever" in Hispanic Business (Vol. 23, No. 10, October, 2001, pp. 42, 44) [720], [15257], [43750], [48290], [50075]

"Merger Finally Gets Green Light" in Hispanic Business (November 2003, pp. 72) [15258], [24432], [50076]

"Merger to Form Nation's Largest Freight Consolidator" in Chicago Tribune (March 1, 2005) [10681], [15259], [50077]

"Merger to Join Cambridge, Mass., Rivals in Anti-Aging Work" in Boston Globe (January 14, 2003) [17872], [49772], [55726]

Mergers and Acquisitions from A to Z [191], [15260], [26290], [29383], [30688], [50078], [52438], [54659]

Mergers & Acquisitions Reports [3466], [15763], [29674]

Meridian Chamber of Commerce [59316]

Meridian Consulting Group Inc. [7627]

Meridian Technology Center [64146]

Meridian Technology Center for Business Development Center [64126]

Meridian Venture Partners (MVP) [64565]

"Merit Networks offshoot draws $5M in venture capital funding" in Crain's Detroit Business (Vol. 16, No. 37, Sept. 11, 2000, pp. 55) [41467], [55403]

Merita Capital Ltd. [57092]

Meritage Private Equity Funds [58456]

Meriwether County Chamber of Commerce [59137]

Merkel Chamber of Commerce [65394]

Merle Norman Cosmetics Studio [7937]

Merlin 200,000 Mile Shops [22685]

Merriam-Webster's Vocabulary Builder [25111]

Merrill Area Chamber of Commerce [66460]

"Merrill Lynch Phones Ahead" in Fast Company (November 2001, pp. 156) [5055], [14239], [15261], [49143], [53851]

Merrill Pickard Anderson & Eyre [58087]

Merrillville Chamber of Commerce [59968]

Merrimac Associates Inc. [38561]

Merrimack Chamber of Commerce [62430]

Merrimack Valley Chamber of Commerce [60972]

Merritt & Harris Inc. [21086]

"The Merry Go-Round" in The Economist (Vol. 377, October 1-7, 2005, No. 8446, pp. 60) [40533], [41061], [50924], [52150]

Merry Maids [8710]

Merry Maids of Canada [8711]

Mertz Associates Inc. [50328], [52480]

Mesa Chamber of Commerce [57050]

Mesa House Publishing [65674]

Mesalands Community College–Small Business Development Center [62648]

MESBIC Ventures Holding Co. [65618]

Mesick Area Chamber of Commerce [61385]

Mesirow Private Equity Investments, Inc. [59749]

Mesquite Area Chamber of Commerce [62359]

Mesquite Chamber of Commerce and Convention and Visitors Bureau [65395]

"A Message About Managing Email" in Fast Company (August 2001, pp. 38) [14240], [54968]

"The Messenger" in Black Enterprise (Vol. 30, No. 12, July 2000, pp. 55) [27727], [33463]

Messenger Courier Association of America-Network Guide and Membership Directory [10682]

Messenger Courier Association of the Americas [17310]

"The Messengers' Chooses Peavey" in Mississippi Business Journal (Vol. 28, September 2006, No. 37, pp. 10) [9730], [24433]

"A Meta-Study of the Market" in Hispanic Business (December 2002, pp. 22, 24, 26) [721], [47281], [53852]

Metal Architecture [7562]

Metal Construction News-Metal Architecture Building Systems Product File and Directory Issue [7422]

Metal Maintenance Services International [16405]

Metal Processing Institute 61151

METALFORM [16403]

Metalforming [16397]

Metalines Chamber of Commerce [66132]

Metascience Foundation–Library [17945]

Metcalf & Eddy, Inc.–Harry L. Kinsel Library [11981]

Methodist Research Institute [41388]

"Methodology" in Inc. (May 2000, pp. 61) [29935]

Metro Accounting Services Inc. [38562]

Metro Atlanta Chamber of Commerce [59138]

"Metro firms maintain pay for called-up reservists" in Crain's Detroit Business (Vol. 19, No. 14, April 7, 2003, pp. 1) [26852], [39468], [53853], [54223]

Metro East Chamber of Commerce [61386]

Metro North Chamber of Commerce [58406]

"Metro homes become harder to sell" in Atlanta Business Chronicle (Vol. 25, January 10, 2003, No. 31, pp. 1A) [17406], [20588], [20939], [28477]

Metro South Chamber of Commerce [60973]

Metro Vocational Technical School [64147]

Metro Washington DC JobBank [23396]

Metrocrest Chamber of Commerce [65396]

MetroFarm: The Guide to Growing for Big Profit on a Small Parcel of Land [26522]

MetroHartford Chamber of Commerce [58547]

MetroJackson Chamber of Commerce [61815]

Metromedia Family Steakhouses - Ponderosa & Bonanza [21884]

MetroNorth Chamber of Commerce [61625]

Metropolis Area Chamber of Commerce [59594]

Metropolitan Boston Regional Office–Boston College SBDC [60907]

Metropolitan Council Research–Metropolitan Council Data Center [66902]

Metropolitan Economic Development Association [61689]

Metropolitan Economic Development Association (MEDA)–Procurement Techical Assistance Center [61712]

Metropolitan Evansville Chamber of Commerce [59969]

Metropolitan Home [13698]

Metropolitan Life Insurance Company–Corporate Information Center & Library [13604]

Metropolitan Milwaukee Association of Commerce [66461]

Metropolitan Museum of Art–Irene Lewisohn Costume Reference Library [5614], [7966]

Metropolitan Venture Partners (METVP) [63136]

Metropolitan Washington Council of Governments [66800], [66847]

MetroWest Chamber of Commerce [60974]

Metter-Candler Chamber of Commerce [59139]

Metuchen Area Chamber of Commerce [62530]

Mexia Area Chamber of Commerce [65397]

Mexicali Rosa's Franchise Co. [21885]

Mexican Arts and Technology Network [43513]

"Mexican Industries Goes Under" in Hispanic Business (Vol. 23, No. 10, October, 2001, pp. 28, 30) [1947], [37730], [48291]

"Mexican grocery gets wired" in Hispanic Business (Vol. 22, No. 5, May 2000, pp. 14) [11642], [34192], [48292]

Mexico Area Chamber of Commerce [62000]

Mexico Consensus Economic Forecast [43907]

"Mexico Resort Brings 'Paradise' to the Overweight" in Travel Weekly (Vol. 62, No. 29, July 21, 2003, pp. 32) [12595], [24707], [25214]

Mexico Watch [27557], [29042]

Meyer, Duffy & Associates [58602]

Richard Meyerhoff [31414]

The MFP Report [46516]

MFV Expositions [3899]

"MGM Mirage Expands: New Project CityCenter Set to Include Space for Convention Meetings" in Tradeshow Week (Vol. 34, December 6, 2004) [10878], [12596], [21560], [22530], [24974], [55121]

"MGM Taking Bids for Two Casinos in Detroit" in Crain's Detroit Business (Vol. 21, February 7, 2005, No. 6, pp. 3) [10879], [29384], [40534], [52439]

M.H. Chew & Associates–Corporate Library [9448], [9501]

"MHV Opens 100th SONIC" in Mississippi Business Journal (Vol. 28, September 2006, No. 36, pp. 8) [21561], [28478], [38854]

"Miami-Area Professional Organizer Rescues Clients Drowning in Paper" in Miami Herald (November 3, 2001) [20024], [52563]

Miami Beach Chamber of Commerce [58893]

"Miami strikes back in bid for trade capital" in Atlanta Business Chronicle (Vol. 25, No. 19, October 18, 2002) [28479], [43751]

Miami Chamber of Commerce [64036]

Miami-Dade County Chamber of Commerce [58894]

Miami Herald (March 10, 2005); "Aetna to Expand to Pompano Beach" in [13178], [16422], [40955], [43068]

Miami Herald (November 11, 2002); "CEO of Fort Lauderdale, Fla., Women's Fitness Chain Creates Smaller Outlets" in [19386], [27938], [38735]

Miami Herald (March 10, 2005); "Clouds Pass and Tourism Forecast is Sunny as Ever" in [12536], [24677], [25171]

Miami Herald (March 1, 2004); "Florida Online Dating Service Tries to Find Love Link for Urban Professionals" in [7056], [18727], [18755], [33908], [36164], [56222]

Miami Herald (December 2, 2003); "Hallandale Beach, Fla., City Leaders Criticize Dating Service Company" in [7058], [29282], [53770]

Miami Herald (March 10, 2005); "Jerry's Diner is One Man's Business Vision Come True" in [4546], [21542], [30563]

Miami Herald (March 10, 2005); "Lawmakers Working on Insurance Issues" in [13365], [40504], [43257]

Miami Herald (November 3, 2001); "Miami-Area Professional Organizer Rescues Clients Drowning in Paper" in [20024], [52563]

Miami Herald (March 10, 2005); "Musicians in South Florida Have Variety of Places to Buy New, Used Instruments" in [17760], [17843]

Miami Herald (June 28, 2004); "Pampering Pets Makes Miami-Area Groomer, Salon Owner Happy" in [19078], [56362]

Miami Herald (March 9, 2005); "Pines Tract Plans Unveiled" in [20964], [28626], [51289]

Miami Herald (June 28, 2004); "South Florida Developers Combine Capitalism, Charity in Bottled-Water Company" in [3080], [15465], [21013], [50185], [54260]

Miami Herald (June 28, 2004); "South Florida Farmers Attempt to Broaden Market for Tropical Fruits" in [11663], [26541], [28799]

Miami Herald (June 24, 2004); "Study: Women Executives Want Corner Office, Too" in [36813], [39615], [45685], [56418]

Miami Herald (June 29, 2004); "Supreme Court Rules Regal Entertainment's Style is Unfair to Disabled Customers" in [17531], [29528], [40745]

Miami Herald (November 2003, 2003); "With the Right Guidance, Philanthropists Choose Best Way to Give" in [54279]

The Miami Home Design & Remodeling Show [12334], [13709]

Miami International Boat Show and Strictly Sail [16777]

Miami Model Agency Directory [17334], [23821]

Miami Subs Grill [8560]

Mid-Atlantic Technology Applications Center **[64345]**

Mid-Atlantic Venture Funds / Nepa Management Corp. **[64566]**

The Mid-Career Entrepreneur: How to Start a Business and Be Your Own Boss **[52915]**

Mid-Columbia Medical Center–Planetree Health Resource Center **[18402]**

Mid-East States Regional Print Competition and Exhibition and Trade Show **[19261]**

Mid-Hudson Better Business Bureau **[62810]**

Mid-Hudson Region SBDC at Kingston **[62770]**

Mid-Maine Chamber of Commerce **[60761]**

Mid-Miami Valley Chamber of Commerce **[63740]**

Mid Michigan Community College **[61495]**

> Small Business Technology Development Center **[61208]**

Mid-Ohio Small Business Development Center–Mansfield-Richland Business Incubator **[63572]**

Mid-Ohio Valley Regional Council **[66309]**

Mid-Plains Community College–SBDC **[62223]**

Mid-South Farm and Gin Supply Exhibit **[26604]**

Mid-South Jewelry & Accessories Fair Fall **[8090]**

Mid-South Jewelry & Accessories Fair Spring **[15877]**

Mid-Town Manhattan Outreach Center–Baruch College–SBDC **[62771]**

Mid Valley Chamber of Commerce **[57635]**

Mid-West Truckers Association **[25363]**

Midas **[22686]**

"Middays of Thunder" in *Inc.* (January 1, 2002) **[31780]**, **[39470]**, **[47282]**

Middle Atlantic Fisheries Association **[10420]**

Middle Department Inspection Agency Inc. **[3260]**

Middle Rio Grande Development Council–Small Business Development Center **[65047]**

"Middle of the Road" in *Black Enterprise* (Vol. 31, No. 5, December 2000, pp. 44) **[38221]**

Middle Tennessee State University–Small Business Development Center **[64865]**

Middle Township Chamber of Commerce **[62531]**

Middlefield Capital Fund **[66728]**

Middlefield Chamber of Commerce **[63741]**

Middlesex County Chamber of Commerce **[58548]**

> Small Business Development Center **[58497]**

Middlesex County Regional Chamber of Commerce **[62532]**

Middlesex West Chamber of Commerce **[60975]**

Middleton Chamber of Commerce **[66462]**

Middletown Chamber of Commerce **[60546]**

Midland Area Chamber of Commerce **[61388]**

Midland Chamber of Commerce **[65398]**

> SBDC Satellite Office **[61209]**

Midland Economic Development Council **[61234]**

Midland Park Chamber of Commerce **[62533]**

Midlothian Chamber of Commerce **[65399]**

Midlothian SBDC **[65048]**

"Midsize suppliers will buy others or be bought" in *Crain's Detroit Business* (Vol. 19, No. 4, January 27, 2003, pp. 20) **[1948]**, **[50083]**

Midstate College–Barbara Fields Memorial Library–Special Collections **[25350]**

Midvale Area Chamber of Commerce **[65716]**

Midwest City Chamber of Commerce **[64037]**

Midwest City Chamber of Commerce Foundation for Progress **[64038]**

The Midwest Clinic An International Band and Orchestra Conference **[17653]**, **[17848]**

Midwest Computer Group L.L.C. **[374]**, **[3769]**, **[16646]**, **[20189]**, **[31415]**

Midwest Contractor **[7563]**

Midwest Food Network **[12067]**

Midwest Research Institute **[3770]**, **[31416]**, **[51019]**, **[52344]**

Midwest Travel Writers Association-Membership Directory **[9005]**

Midwest Truck Show **[25451]**

Midwest Winter Sports Representatives Association **[22845]**

Midwestern State University–Small Business Development Center **[65049]**

"Might mascots" in *Entrepreneur* (Vol. 31, No. 6, June 2003, pp. 79) **[722]**, **[47283]**

"Might of the roundtable" in *Hispanic Business* (Vol. 22, No. 6, June 2000, pp. 22) **[48295]**

Mighty Distributing System of America **[22687]**

MIIX Healthcare Group **[46085]**

"Mike and Wendy Sign, Seal and Deliver $450,000 a Year Sending Greeting Cards..." in *Small Business Opportunities* (Vol. 17, May 2005) **[4733]**, **[7141]**, **[11567]**, **[23087]**, **[37731]**, **[53376]**

Mikes Restaurants Inc. **[8561]**

Margaret L. Mikkola **[18482]**

Milaca Chamber of Commerce **[61626]**

Milady's Art and Science of Nail Technology **[17855]**

Milady's Guide to Owning and Operating a Nail Salon **[17856]**

Milan Area Chamber of Commerce **[61389]**

Milan Chamber of Commerce **[64954]**

Milbank Area Chamber of Commerce **[64829]**

"Mile-High Vacation" in *Hispanic Business* (Vol. 23, No. 7/8, July/August 2001, pp. 108) **[30377]**

MileMaker **[10722]**

Miles City Area Chamber of Commerce **[62186]**

"Miles to go: when an airline goes bust, do your points take flight?" in *Entrepreneur* (Vol. 31, No. 5, May 2003, pp. 22) **[30378]**

Milestone Inc. **[30102]**, **[33350]**

Milestone Venture Partners **[63137]**

"A "Milestone" for Web Services: Microsoft's Dan'l Lewin Talks About Indigo" in *Business Week Online* (February 8, 2005) **[4734]**, **[14245]**, **[23088]**, **[53377]**

Milex Tune-up & Brake **[22688]**

Milford Area Chamber of Commerce **[60976]**

Milford Area Historical Society–Library **[11055]**

Milford Chamber of Commerce **[58549]**

"Milford DDA to Redevelop Former TRW Plant" in *Crain's Detroit Business* (Vol. 21, November 7, 2005, No. 45, pp. 36) **[7423]**, **[12598]**, **[28486]**

Milford - Miami Township Chamber of Commerce **[63742]**

"Military Base Closures Could Have Big Impact on California Economy" in *San Jose Mercury News* (February 17, 2005) **[32572]**

"Military Detail" in *Entrepreneur* (Vol. 32, No. 1, January 2004, pp. 26) **[47284]**

"Military leave" in *Ingram's* (Vol. 27, No. 12, December 2001, pp. 24) **[40535]**, **[42342]**

"Military Now One of the Big Guns in Tech Financing" in *Washington Business Journal* (Vol. 22, No. 16, August 22, 2003, pp. 30) **[40058]**, **[41835]**, **[48916]**

"Military Service Equips Future Business Owners" in *Home Business* (Vol. 12, March/April 2005, No. 2, pp. 44) **[35565]**, **[53565]**

Mill Valley Chamber of Commerce **[57636]**

Millbrae Chamber of Commerce **[57637]**

Millburn-Short Hills Chamber of Commerce **[62534]**

Millcreek Community Hospital–Medical Library **[18403]**

Milledgeville-Baldwin County Chamber of Commerce **[59140]**

"Millennial Madness" in *Entrepreneur* (Vol. 32, August 2004, No. 8, pp. 74) **[34990]**, **[45435]**

Millennium Hanson **[58088]**

Millennium Three Venture Group LLC **[62374]**

Miller Agricultural Consulting Services **[26637]**

Dawn Miller and Associates **[42986]**

Miller Brewing Company–Scientific and Technical Information Facility **[3162]**

Miller Capital Corp. **[57093]**

Miller Civic and Commerce Association **[64830]**

Miller/Cook & Associates Inc. **[38563]**, **[46086]**

Miller, Hellwig Associates **[3771]**, **[16647]**, **[27591]**, **[31417]**, **[35243]**, **[46087]**, **[51005]**, **[53106]**

Bentley Miller Lights Inc. **[24497]**

Miller Thomson–Library **[29702]**

Miller Thomson LLP **[29639]**

Millicare Commercial Carpet Care **[4512]**

"Millinery Magic" in *Small Business Opportunities* (Vol. 13, No. 6, November 2001, pp. 62, 122) **[11917]**, **[42545]**, **[56060]**

Milling & Baking News **[2155]**, **[2268]**

Millington Chamber of Commerce **[64955]**

Million-Dollar Guide to Business & Real Estate Loan Sources **[44588]**

Million Dollar Mailings **[16459]**

"The Million-Dollar Post-it Note" in *Inc.* (February 1, 2002) **[44427]**, **[48886]**

"Million-dollar home sales smash record" in *San Francisco Business Times* (Vol. 16, No. 43, May 31, 2002, pp. 1) **[20589]**, **[20940]**

Million Dollar Sales Strategy **[51966]**

Millionaire Republican **[38222]**

Millionaire Upgrade: Lessons in Success from Those Who Travel at the Sharp End of the Plane **[36502]**

Mills College–F.W. Olin Library–Special Collections **[2849]**

Mills County, Goldthwaite Area Chamber of Commerce **[65400]**

Milpitas Chamber of Commerce **[57638]**

Milton Area Chamber of Commerce **[66463]**

Milton S. Eisenhower Foundation **[48001]**

Miltonvale Chamber of Commerce **[60386]**

Milwaukee Area Technical College–Rasche Memorial Library **[6069]**

Milwaukee Art Museum–Library **[6070]**

"Milwaukee Businesswoman Opens Plus-Size Clothing Store to Fill Need" in *Milwaukee Journal Sentinel* (November 16, 2003) **[5687]**, **[48296]**, **[51246]**, **[56322]**

Milwaukee Grill **[21886]**

"Milwaukee Harley Shifts Gears" in *Business Journal-Milwaukee* (Vol. 20, No. 46, August 1, 2003, pp. A3) **[15265]**, **[17487]**, **[44589]**, **[50084]**

Milwaukee Institute of Art & Design–Library **[6071]**

Milwaukee Journal Sentinel (December 13, 2005); "$1 Million Grant Program Aims to Boost Renewable Energy" in **[21213]**, **[39976]**, **[41492]**, **[50800]**, **[52028]**

Milwaukee Journal Sentinel (December 15, 2005); "A Brand to Unify the Region" in **[27868]**, **[32281]**, **[52823]**

Milwaukee Journal Sentinel (December 19, 2005); "Airport Industrial Sites in Demand" in **[7237]**, **[20215]**, **[27760]**, **[32138]**, **[32241]**, **[46189]**

Milwaukee Journal Sentinel (December 20, 2005); "Angel Investors Take a Plunge" in **[44467]**, **[55489]**

Milwaukee Journal Sentinel (December 12, 2005) "'Angels' Seek to Expand Territory; Investors Begin to Target Waukesha County" in **[41515]**, **[44468]**, **[50811]**, **[52039]**, **[55490]**

Milwaukee Journal Sentinel (December 13, 2005); "Apartments Planned Downtown" in **[2328]**, **[7243]**, **[21309]**, **[21438]**

Milwaukee Journal Sentinel (December 1, 2005); "Appleton, Wis.-Based Construction Company Settles Racial Harassment Suit" in **[7244]**, **[29099]**, **[32006]**

Milwaukee Journal Sentinel (December 1, 2005); "Authentic Bavarian Beer Hall to Open" in **[2330]**, **[21443]**

Milwaukee Journal Sentinel (December 1, 2005); "Authors Defend Study on Great Lakes Shipping Value" in **[10668]**, **[12944]**, **[43553]**

Milwaukee Journal Sentinel (December 4, 2005); "Breadth of World Housing Boom Stuns Analysts" in **[7264]**, **[20439]**, **[20809]**, **[27869]**

Milwaukee Journal Sentinel (December 7, 2005); "Brookfield, Wis., Staffing Firm to Get $3 Million Venture-Capital Infusion" in **[9195]**, **[9553]**, **[24519]**, **[55524]**

Milwaukee Journal Sentinel (December 17, 2005); "Butler, Wis., Printing Plant Expands Operations" in **[19868]**, **[27912]**, **[37607]**

Milwaukee Journal Sentinel (December 21, 2005); "Cherry to Move 100 Jobs to Mexico" in **[7720]**, **[43579]**, **[46232]**

Milwaukee Journal Sentinel (December 21, 2005); "Cleanup Delays Lessens Katrina's Economic Toll, Economist Says" in **[7287]**, **[27954]**, **[32317]**

Milwaukee Journal Sentinel (December 6, 2005); "Cold Remedy Control has Pharmacies on Hot Seat" in **[7772]**, **[8778]**, **[11600]**, **[29156]**, **[40267]**, **[51100]**

Milwaukee Journal Sentinel (December 9, 2005); "Company Tied to Style, Success" in **[5528]**, **[5647]**, **[9614]**, **[46248]**

Milwaukee Journal Sentinel (December 17, 2005); "Copper Prices Hover Near Record Highs" in **[46249]**

Milwaukee Journal Sentinel (December 3, 2005); "Corporate Present-Giving Looking Up After Slow Stretch" in **[31672]**, **[53666]**

Milwaukee Journal Sentinel (December 6, 2005); "Cracking Down On Copycats" in **[16735]**, **[29182]**, **[46253]**

Milwaukee Journal Sentinel (December 12, 2005); "Developer Sets His Sights On the East Side" in **[7324]**, **[28031]**

Milwaukee Journal Sentinel (December 13, 2005); "Employment Will Be Stable, Survey Says" in **[28100]**, **[32406]**, **[42229]**

Milwaukee Journal Sentinel (December 14, 2005); "Engineer Turned Winemaker Became Toast of State Industry" in **[23475]**, **[36062]**

Milwaukee Journal Sentinel (December 14, 2005); "Fed Bumps Rate to 4.25 Percent" in **[28154]**, **[32425]**

Milwaukee Journal Sentinel (December 10, 2005); "GM Hopes Boosting Mileage Will Slow Big Models' Sales Drain" in **[18045]**, **[28209]**, **[51654]**

Milwaukee Journal Sentinel (December 20, 2005); "Harley's '06 Models Revving Sales" in **[17484]**, **[28263]**

Milwaukee Journal Sentinel (December 15, 2005); "Home Market Deflates" in **[20531]**, **[20895]**

Milwaukee Journal Sentinel (December 2, 2005); "Housing Program Breaks Mortgage Lending Record" in **[17393]**, **[20544]**, **[20901]**, **[28297]**

Milwaukee Journal Sentinel (December 6, 2005); "IRS Cuts Mileage Rates for Deductions" in **[177]**, **[23972]**, **[54618]**

Milwaukee Journal Sentinel (December 22, 2005); "Jobs Increase in Milwaukee Area" in **[28361]**, **[42321]**, **[46331]**

Milwaukee Journal Sentinel (December 13, 2005); "Local Filmmaker Directs Smoking Ads" in **[699]**, **[9726]**, **[54218]**

Milwaukee Journal Sentinel (December 1, 2005); "Madison, Wis., University Research Park Expands Again" in **[28443]**, **[50794]**, **[52020]**

Milwaukee Journal Sentinel (December 3, 2005); "Making Strides in Building Jobs" in **[7416]**, **[33163]**, **[42333]**

Milwaukee Journal Sentinel (December 22, 2005); "Manpower Inc. Will Move Headquarters to Downtown Milwaukee" in **[9226]**, **[9572]**, **[24531]**

Milwaukee Journal Sentinel (December 1, 2005); "Manufacturing Sector Strengthening" in **[28457]**, **[32563]**, **[46364]**

Milwaukee Journal Sentinel (December 14, 2005); "Measure Twice, Cut Once" in **[16311]**, **[30687]**

Milwaukee Journal Sentinel (November 16, 2003); "Milwaukee Businesswoman Opens Plus-Size Clothing Store to Fill Need" in **[5687]**, **[48296]**, **[51246]**, **[56322]**

Milwaukee Journal Sentinel (December 8, 2005); "Milwaukee Mayor Says Federal Business Development Program Will Create Jobs" in **[27728]**, **[35566]**, **[39773]**

Milwaukee Journal Sentinel (December 14, 2005); "Milwaukee, Wis., to Host Biotech Finance Gathering in 2007" in **[24975]**, **[41836]**, **[48767]**, **[50926]**, **[52152]**, **[55122]**, **[55727]**

Milwaukee Journal Sentinel (December 8, 2005); "Modine Manufacturing Unit to Provide Cooling System for Video-Game Computers" in **[1113]**, **[6726]**, **[24822]**, **[46376]**

Milwaukee Journal Sentinel (December 18, 2005); "Paper-Run Web Sites Prosper" in **[18922]**, **[34326]**, **[53908]**

Milwaukee Journal Sentinel (December 1, 2005); "Potawatomi Would Take Hit From Kenosha Casino" in **[10882]**

Milwaukee Journal Sentinel (December 14, 2005); "Retailers' Outlook 'Rosy'" in **[28707]**, **[51325]**

Milwaukee Journal Sentinel (December 2, 2005); "Small Business Owners are Less Optimistic" in **[28779]**, **[32691]**

Milwaukee Journal Sentinel Sports Show **[23693]**

Milwaukee Journal Sentinel (December 21, 2005); "Taxes Set a Record in 2005" in **[54825]**

Milwaukee Journal Sentinel (December 7, 2005); "Upscale Restaurant, Tavern Chain to Enter Milwaukee Market" in **[2354]**, **[21657]**

Milwaukee Journal Sentinel (December 11, 2005); "Wanted" in **[30986]**, **[42455]**, **[46481]**

Milwaukee Journal Sentinel (December 13, 2005); "Wisconsin is Among States With Best Savers" in **[10254]**, **[15607]**, **[38471]**

Milwaukee Journal Sentinel (December 8, 2005); "Wisconsin Biotech Aims to Create Artificial Heart Tissue" in **[39960]**, **[42127]**, **[50994]**, **[52230]**, **[52755]**

Milwaukee Journal Sentinel (December 8, 2005); "Wisconsin Economic Development Programs Could be Hurt by Tax Fight" in **[29018]**, **[32800]**, **[54875]**

Milwaukee Journal Sentinel (December 1, 2005); "Wisconsin Grants Economic Assistance to Four Companies, One Technical College" in **[29019]**, **[33283]**, **[39961]**

Milwaukee Journal Sentinel (December 16, 2005); "Wisconsin Job Market Continues to Grow Despite Shrinking Labor Force" in **[29020]**, **[42468]**

"Milwaukee Mayor Says Federal Business Development Program Will Create Jobs" in *Milwaukee Journal Sentinel* (December 8, 2005) **[27728]**, **[35566]**, **[39773]**

Milwaukee Minority Chamber of Commerce **[66464]**

Milwaukee School of Engineering–Applied Technology Center **[66573]**

"Milwaukee, Wis., to Host Biotech Finance Gathering in 2007" in *Milwaukee Journal Sentinel* (December 14, 2005) **[24975]**, **[41836]**, **[48767]**, **[50926]**, **[52152]**, **[55122]**, **[55727]**

"MIMlist Draws Eclectic Crowd: Online Forums" in *Tradeshow Week* (Vol. 34, November 29, 2004, No. 48, pp. 52) **[14246]**, **[22531]**, **[24976]**, **[27438]**, **[34196]**, **[41837]**, **[55123]**

Minco Chamber of Commerce **[64039]**

"Mind Games: Jump-Start Your Problem-Solving Skills for a Better Business" in *Entrepreneur* (Vol. 31, No. 10, October 2003, pp. 34) **[36503]**, **[39471]**, **[45436]**

"Mind over manners" in *Entrepreneur* (Vol. 31, No. 5, May 2003, pp. 118) **[27439]**, **[39472]**

"Mind over Matter" in *Entrepreneur* (Vol. 28, No. 9, September 2000, pp. 42) **[14247]**, **[34197]**, **[44337]**, **[53855]**

"Mind Over Market" in *Entrepreneur* (Vol. 33, March 2005, No. 3, pp. 66) **[723]**, **[47285]**

"Mind Over Matter" in *Entrepreneur* (Vol. 33, August 2005, No. 8, pp. 37) **[19216]**, **[19419]**, **[34991]**, **[45437]**

"Mind Your Manners" in *Inc.* (September 2005, pp. 51) **[27440]**, **[43752]**

"Mind Your Manners" in *Sales & Marketing Management* **[27441]**, **[27657]**, **[45438]**, **[51732]**

Mind Your Own Business: Getting Started As an Entrepreneur **[36504]**

Mind Your Own Business and Keep It in the Family **[37732]**

"Mind Your Pricing Cues" in *Harvard Business Review* (Vol. 81, No. 9, September 2003, pp. 96) **[47286]**, **[51247]**

"Mind Your P's and Q's" in *Entrepreneur* (Vol. 32, September 2004, No. 9, pp. 77) **[724]**, **[27658]**, **[39473]**

"Mind Your P's and Q's" in *Rough Notes* (Vol. 145, No. 2, February 2003, pp. 43) **[27442]**, **[27659]**, **[39474]**

Minden Chamber of Commerce **[62281]**

Minden/South Webster Chamber of Commerce **[60657]**

"Minding Her Bees-Ness" in *Small Business Opportunities* (Vol. 12, No. 5, September 2000, pp. 108) **[2571]**, **[7864]**, **[35567]**, **[54225]**

Minding the Kids: A Practical Guide to Employing Nannies, Caregivers, Baby Sitters, and Au Pairs **[17867]**

"Minding the Money" in *Hispanic Business* (May 2005, pp. 16) **[13386]**, **[15266]**, **[38223]**, **[43278]**

MindLabs.net **[49442]**, **[49637]**

Mineola Chamber of Commerce **[62959]**

Mineral Area College–SBDC **[61868]**

Mineral County Chamber of Commerce **[62187]**, **[62360]**, **[66288]**

Mineral County High School–SBDC **[62328]**

Mineral Point Chamber of Commerce **[66465]**

Mineral Wells Area Chamber of Commerce **[65401]**

Minerals Management Service
Alaska OCS **[67619]**
Business Utilization and Development Specialist–Division of Procurement and Contracts **[67622]**
Business Utilization and Development Specialist–Western ASC Procurement and Contracts **[67621]**
Pacific Region OCS **[67620]**

Minerva Area Chamber of Commerce **[63743]**

"MingleMatch Reaches Half-Million Member Milestone" in *PR Newswire* (January 12, 2004) **[7062]**, **[34198]**

"Mingling at Business Holiday Parties Made Easier for Some" in *Sacramento Bee* (November 29, 2005) **[39475]**, **[45439]**, **[52362]**

Mini-Cassia Chamber of Commerce **[59317]**

"The Mini-K Advantage" in *Rough Notes* (Vol. 144, No. 12, December 2001, pp. 80) **[26853]**, **[40536]**, **[43279]**, **[54660]**

Mini Maid **[8712]**

Mini Melts **[12839]**

Mini Movie Reviews **[25611]**

Mini-Tankers Canada Ltd. **[22689]**

Miniature Donkey Talk **[1206]**, **[1257]**, **[19117]**

"Miniature Golf" in *Small Business Opportunities* (Winter 2005) **[17318]**

Minimaid Service Systems of Canada **[8713]**

"Minimize Your Legal Risks" in *Folio: the Magazine for Magazine Management* (Vol. 30, No. 1, January 2001, pp. 25) **[18908]**, **[29386]**

"Minimizing the Risk of Violence in the Workplace" in *Employment Relations Today* (Vol. 27, No. 1, Spring 2000, pp. 83) **[56572]**

"Minimum Credit Payments Will Rise" in *Sacramento Bee* (October 16, 2005) **[8313]**, **[8353]**, **[8388]**, **[38224]**

"Minimum Wage Hikes Eyed Nationwide" in *Inc.* (October 1, 2004) **[194]**, **[18783]**, **[26293]**, **[40537]**

"Mining venture capital" in *Black Enterprise* (Vol. 32, No. 7, February 2002,) **[35568]**, **[44428]**, **[55404]**

"Mining a Company's Mother Lode of Talent" in *Business Week* (No. 3696, August 28, 2000, pp. 135) **[44338]**, **[44349]**

"Mining Mars" in *CMA Management* (Vol. 76, No. 6, Sept. 2002, pp. 38) **[41838]**, **[43056]**

"Mining Online for the Bottom Line" in *Success* (Vol. 47, No. 4, September 2000, pp. 82) **[34199]**, **[38856]**, **[47287]**

Minneapolis Area Chamber of Commerce **[60387]**

Minneapolis College of Art and Design–Library **[6072]**, **[7967]**

Minneapolis Community and Technical College–Business Management Program **[61726]**

"Minneapolis" in *Entrepreneur* (Vol. 28, No. 4, April 2000, pp. 162) **[30489]**, **[35569]**, **[43041]**

Minneapolis Home & Garden Show **[11493]**

Minneapolis International Motorcycle Show **[2006]**, **[17501]**, **[55230]**

Minneapolis Regional Chamber of Commerce **[61627]**

Minneapolis-St. Paul City Business (Vol. 19, No. 15, September 14, 2001, pp. 12); "Establish strong team with game plan, feedback" in **[34893]**

Minnesota Airport Directory & Travel Guide **[951]**

Minnesota American Indian Chamber of Commerce **[61628]**

Minnesota Bank Directory **[44590]**

"Minnesota-Based Developer Seeks Funds for Shingle Springs, Calif., Casino" in *Sacramento Bee* (December 25, 2005) **[10880]**, **[28487]**

Minnesota Department of Education–Education Resource Center **[66903]**

Minnesota Department of Employment and Economic Development **[61540]**
  Business and Community Development Division and Trade **[61541]**
  Minnesota Trade Office **[61542]**

Minnesota Department of Trade and Economic Development–Small Business Development Center **[61511]**

Minnesota Labor and Industry Department–Research and Statistics Office **[29059]**

Minnesota Planning–State Demographic Center **[66904]**

Minnesota Procurement Technical Assistance Center
  Metropolitan Economic Development Association (MEDA) **[61713]**
  Minnesota Project Innovation, Inc. **[59083]**, **[61714]**
  Minnesota Project Innovation, Inc.–Hennepin Technical College **[61715]**

Minnesota Project Innovation–Small Business Development Center **[61523]**

Minnesota SBDC–Minnesota Small Business Development Center **[61512]**

Minnesota Small Business Management Program **[61727]**

Minnesota State Chamber of Commerce **[61629]**

Minnesota State Community and Technical College
  Detroit Lakes **[61728]**
  Fergus Falls **[61729]**

Minnesota Technology, Inc.
  Minnesota Department of Trade and Economic Development Center **[61732]**
  Small Business Development Center **[61524]**

Minnesota University–Small Business Development Center **[61525]**

Minnesota West Community & Technical College **[61730]**

Minocqua - Arbor Vitae - Woodruff Chamber of Commerce **[66466]**

"Minorities meet opportunities" in *Hispanic Business* (Vol. 22, No. 9, September 2000, pp. 14) **[48297]**, **[55124]**

"Minorities Push to Keep Supplier Program" in *Plastics News* (Vol. 16, July 12, 2004, No. 19, pp. 10) **[1949]**, **[46373]**, **[48298]**

"Minority Architects Say Reaching Out to Youth Will Help Add Diversity" in *Crain's Detroit Business* (Vol.16, No.31,July 31,2000, pp.35) **[48299]**, **[54226]**, **[56323]**

"Minority Banks are Called to Account" in *Inc.* (October 1, 2003) **[10088]**, **[32045]**, **[48300]**

"Minority Banks are Thriving: Deposits Jumped 213 percent in Five Years" in *Atlanta Business Chronicle* (Vol. 25, Jan. 10, 2003, pp.1A) **[10089]**, **[38225]**, **[48301]**

"Minority Biz of the Year" in *Hispanic Business* (March 2002, pp. 10) **[46374]**, **[48302]**

Minority Business Center–SBDC **[60908]**

Minority Business Development Agency **[67276]**
  Atlanta Regional Office **[67277]**
  Chicago Regional Office **[67278]**
  Dallas Regional Office **[67279]**
  New York Regional Office **[67280]**
  San Francisco Regional Office **[67281]**
  Washington, DC, Regional Office **[67282]**

Minority Business Development Agency-Directory of Regional & District Offices and Funded Organizations **[48303]**

Minority Business Development Agency District Office (Boston) **[67285]**

Minority Business Development Agency District Office (Los Angeles) **[67283]**

Minority Business Development Agency District Office (Miami) **[67284]**

Minority Business Development Agency District Office (Philadelphia) **[67286]**

Minority Business Development Center **[58963]**

Minority Business Entrepreneur **[13052]**, **[48492]**

"Minority Business Group Looks to Cement Ties with Foreign Automakers" in *Crain's Detroit Business* (Vol. 19, No. 40, October 13, 2003) **[1950]**, **[1963]**, **[17891]**, **[18091]**, **[41816]**, **[43753]**, **[46016]**, **[46375]**, **[47143]**, **[48304]**

Minority Business Journal (Vol. 17, No. 5, September/October 2001, pp. 2); "Free Entrepreneurial Workshop" in **[32883]**, **[35471]**

Minority Business Journal (Vol. 17, No. 5, September/October 2001, pp. 2); "Mazda's Minority Dealers" in **[18086]**, **[48286]**

Minority Business Journal (Vol. 17, No. 5, September/October 2001, pp. 3, 6-7); "The Growth of Minority Car Dealerships" in **[18052]**, **[28252]**, **[48194]**

Minority Business Journal (Vol. 17, No. 5, September/October 2001, pp. 4); "Why Must China Die?" in **[40843]**, **[43877]**

"Minority Businesses Look For a Boost From Super Bowl and Beyond" in *Crain's Detroit Business* (Vol. 21, October 10, 2005, No. 43) **[28488]**, **[48305]**, **[56324]**

"Minority Certification Needs Examination" in *Crain's Detroit Business* (Vol. 18, No. 20, May 20, 2002, pp. 8) **[28489]**, **[48306]**, **[50085]**

"Minority-certified paper company sets up shop in Canton Twp." in *Crain's Detroit Business* (Vol. 19, No. 16, April 21, 2003, pp. 6) **[46166]**, **[47968]**

Minority Enterprise in the Nineties: A Questionable Future? **[48307]**

Minority Health Resources Directory **[41062]**

"Minority Home Gaps" in *Hispanic Business* (July/August 2004, pp. 14) **[17407]**, **[20590]**

"Minority-Owned Businesses Up" in *Inc.* (April 2000, pp. 145) **[28490]**, **[48308]**

"Minority Report" in *Entrepreneur* (Vol. 32, October 2004, No. 10, pp. 59) **[48309]**, **[55728]**, **[56325]**

"A Minority Role in the Homeland" in *Hispanic Business* (November 2002, pp. 22-23) **[22298]**, **[48310]**

Minot Area Chamber of Commerce **[63530]**

Minot Regional Service Center–SBDC **[63496]**

Min's New Media Report **[8638]**, **[20003]**

Mint Condition Franchising, Inc. **[8714]**

Minuteman Press **[19936]**

MIOSHA News **[61501]**

Miracle Auto Painting **[2057]**

Miracle Ear **[12117]**

Miracle Method Bath And Kitchen Restoration **[12250]**

MiracleLink **[25103]**

Mirage Tanning Centers **[23846]**

Miralta Capital, Inc. **[66666]**

Miramar-Pembroke Pines Regional Chamber of Commerce **[58895]**

"Mirra, Mirra" in *Entrepreneur* (Vol. 32, No. 1, January 2004, pp. 38) **[6725]**, **[41839]**, **[49148]**

MIS Quarterly **[6514]**

"Misclassifying Workers Can Cost You, Big Time" in *Inc.* (November 2000, pp. 97) **[42343]**, **[45440]**

Mishicot Area Growth and Improvement Committee **[66467]**

"A Misleading Predictor of Inflation" in *Business Week* (January 23, 2006, No. 3968, pp. 28) **[28491]**, **[32573]**

"The Mismanagement of Advertising" in *Harvard Business Review* (Vol. 78, No. 1, January 2000, pp. 22) **[725]**, **[47288]**

"The Missing Link?" in *Entrepreneur* (Vol. 33, September 2005, No. 9, pp. 88) **[25555]**, **[25896]**, **[34200]**, **[47289]**, **[51733]**

"Missing Part of the Equation" in *Hispanic Business* (July/August 2002, pp. 50, 52, 54) **[37168]**, **[48311]**, **[52153]**

"Mission accomplish: manage multiple projects and meet deadlines" in *Women In Business* (Vol. 52, No. 2, March 2000, pp. 38) **[54969]**

Mission Ventures **[58089]**

Mississippi Action for Community Education, Inc. (MACE) **[61850]**

"Mississippi Association Of Realtors" in *Mississippi Business Journal* (Vol. 29, January 2007, No. 2, pp. 6) **[20591]**, **[20941]**

Mississippi Business Journal (Vol. 28, September 2006, No. 36, pp. 28); "Arts Group Adopts New Name, Look, Enhanced Agenda" in **[20099]**, **[27294]**, **[39153]**

Mississippi Business Journal (Vol. 29, January 2007, No. 4, pp. 6); "Baker, Donelson, Bearman, Caldwell & Berkowitz, PC" in **[29111]**, **[39158]**, **[40965]**

Mississippi Business Journal (Vol. 29, January 2007, No. 4, pp. 11); "Banners Tout Development" in **[12868]**, **[20103]**, **[30507]**, **[32266]**, **[46709]**, **[50553]**

Mississippi Business Journal (Vol. 29, January 2007, No. 4, pp. 6); "Barnes-Pettey Financial Advisors, LLC" in **[9838]**, **[14777]**, **[37910]**, **[39163]**

Mississippi Business Journal (Vol. 28, January 2007, No. 36, pp. 34); "Bean Enjoys Expanding Eat With Us Restaurants, Franchises" in **[21446]**, **[27822]**, **[37593]**

Mississippi Business Journal (Vol. 29, January 2007, No. 2, pp. 7); "Beau Restoration Complete" in **[10860]**, **[17510]**

Mississippi Business Journal (Vol. 29, January 2007, No. 2, pp. 6); "Beau Rivage Resort And Casino" in **[555]**, **[5969]**, **[46711]**, **[50554]**

Mississippi Business Journal (Vol. 28, September 2006, No. 36, pp. 6); "Belhaven College" in **[33009]**, **[35818]**

Mississippi Business Journal (Vol. 29, January 2007, No. 4, pp. 5); "Big Success Can Start With a Few Steps" in **[2581]**, **[32277]**, **[35842]**, **[39178]**

Mississippi Business Journal (Vol. 29, January 2007, No. 2, pp. 9); "Bio Solutions Acquisition" in **[26484]**, **[48702]**, **[49819]**

Mississippi Business Journal (Vol. 28, September 2006, No. 36, pp. 12); "Biz Travelers Adapting To Ever-Changing Security Measures" in **[22186]**, **[40196]**

Mississippi Business Journal (Vol. 28, September 2006, No. 36, pp. 23); "Broaddus Opens Office" in **[3503]**, **[7267]**, **[9347]**, **[31114]**, **[44959]**

Mississippi Business Journal (Vol. 29, January 2007, No. 2, pp. 8); "Bryson Buys Two Agencies" in **[27879]**, **[37929]**, **[43105]**, **[49826]**

Mississippi Business Journal (Vol. 29, January 2007, No. 3, pp. A6); "Cadence Bank" in **[39215]**, **[44975]**

Mississippi Business Journal (Vol. 28, September 2006, No. 36, pp. 24); "Callon Adds Inventory" in **[39217]**, **[49838]**

Mississippi Business Journal (Vol. 29, January 2007, No. 3, pp. A10); "CAN Forms In Capital City" in **[15890]**, **[40977]**

Mississippi Business Journal (Vol. 29, January 2007, No. 2, pp. 30); "Capital City Beverage To Distribute Energy Drink" in **[32147]**, **[39220]**, **[49839]**

Mississippi Business Journal (Vol. 29, January 2007, No. 2, pp. 3); "Cigar Company Promoting Hand-Rolled Products, Delta Blues" in **[5478]**, **[24608]**, **[48714]**

Mississippi Business Journal (Vol. 28, January 2007, No. 36, pp. 29); "Community Theaters Mean More Than Just Entertainment" in **[17513]**, **[37404]**, **[39240]**

Mississippi Business Journal (Vol. 29, January 2007, No. 2, pp. 28); "ConventionSouth Honors Jackson CVB" in **[7126]**, **[7774]**, **[24915]**, **[30674]**

Mississippi Business Journal (Vol. 29, January 2007, No. 2, pp. 8); "D&PL Reports Loss" in **[26500]**, **[28007]**, **[39271]**

Mississippi Business Journal (Vol. 29, January 2007, No. 4, pp. 6); "Delta Industries Inc" in **[39279]**, **[45054]**

Mississippi Business Journal (Vol. 29, January 2007, No. 2, pp. 13); "Denbury Selects Digital Oilfield" in **[6469]**, **[43015]**, **[49892]**

Mississippi Business Journal (Vol. 28, September 2006, No. 36, pp. 6); "Duckworth Realty Inc." in **[20500]**, **[20866]**, **[36037]**

Mississippi Business Journal (Vol. 29, January 2007, No. 4, pp. 9); "EastGroup Buys Buildings" in **[20502]**, **[20869]**, **[28077]**, **[32373]**, **[49910]**

Mississippi Business Journal (Vol. 29, January 2007, No. 2, pp. 8); "Fitness 24 Buys DAC Club" in **[10461]**, **[19397]**, **[30678]**, **[49939]**

Mississippi Business Journal (Vol. 29, January 2007, No. 2, pp. 19); "FNC, HomeSafe Team Up" in **[12549]**, **[41692]**, **[44526]**, **[49941]**

Mississippi Business Journal (Vol. 29, January 2007, No. 2, pp. 17); "Furniture Market Adapting Strategy to Combat Competition" in **[10831]**, **[12282]**, **[37662]**

Mississippi Business Journal (Vol. 28, September 2006, No. 36, pp. 22); "Garner Debuts New Site" in **[634]**, **[14063]**, **[25853]**, **[47003]**

Mississippi Business Journal (Vol. 29, January 2007, No. 3, pp. A6); "Godwin Group" in **[30679]**, **[39360]**, **[45194]**

Mississippi Business Journal (Vol. 28, September 2006, No. 36, pp. 20); "Hollywood Opens Ahead Of Schedule" in **[10869]**, **[28289]**, **[39385]**

Mississippi Business Journal (Vol. 29, January 2007, No. 4, pp. 8); "Housing Pilot Plan Updated" in **[32491]**, **[39840]**

Mississippi Business Journal (Vol. 29, January 2007, No. 4, pp. 8); "Irby Buys Two Companies" in **[41777]**, **[47153]**, **[50022]**

Mississippi Business Journal (Vol. 28, September 2006, No. 36, pp. 22); "Island View Opening" in **[10872]**, **[54305]**

Mississippi Business Journal (Vol. 29, January 2007, No. 4, pp. 6); "JBHM Education Group, LLC" in **[7393]**, **[31180]**, **[33140]**, **[45321]**

Mississippi Business Journal (Vol. 29, January 2007, No. 4, pp. 9); "JCJC, SMG Partner" in **[15892]**, **[33141]**, **[41786]**

Mississippi Business Journal (Vol. 29, January 2007, No. 4, pp. 12); "Jewelry Lines Picked Up" in **[14174]**, **[15850]**, **[18651]**, **[50028]**

Mississippi Business Journal (Vol. 28, September 2006, No. 36, pp. 23); "JSU Receives Record Funding" in **[39847]**, **[52135]**, **[55700]**

Mississippi Business Journal (Vol. 29, January 2007, No. 1, pp. 3); "Jubilee! JAM Returning June 2007" in **[24962]**, **[50031]**

Mississippi Business Journal (Vol. 28, September 2006, No. 36, pp. 23); "Katrina Cottages At Lowe's" in **[3317]**, **[7395]**, **[48760]**, **[50032]**, **[51218]**

Mississippi Business Journal (Vol. 29, January 2007, No. 4, pp. 3); "Katrina's Impact On Insurance Rippling Northward From Coast" in **[13360]**, **[43253]**

Mississippi Business Journal (Vol. 29, January 2007, No. 2, pp. 8); "Land Bank South Distributes $3 Million" in **[38178]**

Mississippi Business Journal (Vol. 29, January 2007, No. 2, pp. 10); "LiveWell Center Opens" in **[18441]**, **[41047]**

Mississippi Business Journal (Vol. 29, January 2007, No. 3, pp. A8); "MACM To Issue Refunds" in **[13373]**, **[43266]**

Mississippi Business Journal (Vol. 29, January 2007, No. 2, pp. 8); "Magna Rating Adjusted" in **[13374]**, **[28446]**, **[43267]**

Mississippi Business Journal (Vol. 29, January 2007, No. 3, pp. A15); "MC, MMA Offering Manufacturing Management Program" in **[33168]**, **[45426]**, **[46369]**, **[55117]**

Mississippi Business Journal (Vol. 29, January 2007, No. 4, pp. 10); "McMullouch Has Had Busy Telecommunications Career" in **[5053]**, **[27430]**, **[45427]**

Mississippi Business Journal (Vol. 28, September 2006, No. 36, pp. 8); "MHV Opens 100th SONIC" in **[21561]**, **[28478]**, **[38854]**

Mississippi Business Journal (Vol. 29, January 2007, No. 2, pp. 6); "Mississippi Association Of Realtors" in **[20591]**, **[20941]**

Mississippi Business Journal (Vol. 29, January 2007, No. 4, pp. 6); "Mississippi Children's Home Services" in **[27443]**, **[39476]**, **[52916]**

Mississippi Business Journal (Vol. 28, September 2006, No. 36, pp. 6); "Northwest Mississippi Community College" in **[33194]**, **[36561]**

Mississippi Business Journal (Vol. 28, September 2006, No. 37, pp. 20); "NW Miss. Firms Merge To Meet Growing Needs Of Region" in **[29421]**, **[50114]**

Mississippi Business Journal (Vol. 29, January 2007, No. 4, pp. 9); "Posecai's To Open" in **[20057]**, **[21587]**, **[29959]**

Mississippi Business Journal (Vol. 29, January 2007, No.4, pp. 9); "Prewitt With Prudential" in **[20628]**, **[20968]**, **[38886]**, **[50137]**

Mississippi Business Journal (Vol. 29, January 2007, No. 2, pp. 21); "Program Off To A Great Start Providing Capital for Gazelles" in **[15380]**, **[28654]**, **[41919]**

Mississippi Business Journal (Vol. 28, September 2006, No. 36, pp. 22); "Rapiscan Opens Plant" in **[41932]**, **[48780]**

Mississippi Business Journal (Vol. 29, January 2007, No. 3, pp. A10); "RenaLab Acquired" in **[17192]**, **[41088]**, **[50160]**

Mississippi Business Journal (Vol. 28, September 2006, No. 36, pp. 3); "Rotary Club Of Jackson Invests In Metro Students" in **[32676]**, **[33225]**, **[56762]**

Mississippi Business Journal (Vol. 29, January 2007, No. 2, pp. 22); "Silverado's Clean Coal Technology Coming To Choctaw County" in **[9371]**, **[41987]**, **[48791]**, **[50969]**

Mississippi Business Journal (Vol. 28, September 2006, No. 28, pp. 31); "Site Attracting Jobseekers" in **[14437]**, **[15894]**, **[25962]**, **[33234]**

Mississippi Business Journal (Vol. 28, September 2006, No. 37, pp. 30); "The Excellence Group Helping Good Schools Become Great." in **[31145]**, **[33092]**, **[36127]**

Mississippi Business Journal (Vol. 28, September 2006, No. 37, pp. 10); "The Messengers' Chooses Peavey" in **[9730]**, **[24433]**

Mississippi Business Journal (Vol. 29, January 2007, No. 2, pp. 8); "The Pantry Expands Presence" in **[7781]**, **[28888]**, **[50207]**, **[53012]**

Mississippi Business Journal (Vol. 29, January 2007, No. 2, pp. 1); "Time Right For Tech Upgrade? That Depends" in **[6185]**, **[6417]**, **[53013]**, **[53517]**

Mississippi Business Journal (Vol. 29, January 2007 , No. 29, pp. 4); "Time Right To Let Sun Shine On AG, Outside Attorneys" in **[29548]**, **[37516]**, **[40770]**

Mississippi Business Journal (Vol. 28, September 2006, No. 36, pp. 24); "Titan May Build Plant" in **[21259]**, **[50215]**, **[55867]**

Mississippi Business Journal (Vol. 29, January 2007, No. 2, pp. 6); "Vector Marketing" in **[39654]**, **[48673]**, **[51891]**

Mississippi Business Journal (Vol. 28, September 2006, No. 36, pp. 24); "Viking Adds Rangetops" in **[1418]**, **[46475]**, **[48807]**

Mississippi Business Journal (Vol. 29, January 2007, No. 3, pp. A8); "Vivid Buys Amerigos, Char" in **[21659]**, **[47693]**, **[50247]**

Mississippi Business Journal (Vol. 28, September 2006, No. 36, pp. 24); "Web Site Retooled" in **[14584]**, **[26001]**

"Mississippi Children's Home Services" in *Mississippi Business Journal* (Vol. 29, January 2007, No. 4, pp. 6) **[27443]**, **[39476]**, **[52916]**

Mississippi Contract Procurement Center–SBDC **[61754]**

Mississippi Contract Procurement Center, Inc.
  Delta Contract Procurement Center, Inc. (DCPC) **[61844]**
  Northeast Mississippi Contract Procurement Center, Inc. (NMCPC) **[61845]**
  South Mississippi Contract Procurement Center, Inc. (SMCPC) **[61846]**

"Mississippi-Corporate Partnership Boosts Shipyards" in *Sun Herald* (April 11, 2003) **[10683]**, **[28492]**, **[50086]**

Mississippi Delta Community College–Small Business Development Center **[61755]**

Mississippi Department of Economic and Community Development–Industry Resource Bureau–Mississippi Development Authority **[66905]**

Mississippi Development Authority **[61843]**
  Mississippi Department of Economic and Community Development–**[61765]**

Mississippi Enterprise for Technology–Mississippi Technology Transfer Office **[61766]**

Mississippi Gulf Coast Chamber of Commerce **[61816]**

Mississippi Gulf Coast Community College–SBDC **[61756]**

Mississippi Lumber Manufacturers Association Convention and Trade Show **[16337]**

Mississippi News Media Directory **[18909]**, **[20327]**, **[24434]**

Mississippi Research and Technology Park **[61851]**

Mississippi SBDC–University of Mississippi **[61739]**

Mississippi State University
  Agricultural & Forestry Experiment Station–Delta Research and Extension Center **[26663]**
  Carl Small Town Center **[1584]**
  Office of the Vice President for Research and Graduate Studies **[61852]**
  Small Business Development Center **[61757]**

Mississippi University for Women–Career Services **[61767]**

Mississippi Valley State University–Affiliate SBDC **[61758]**

Missoula Area Chamber of Commerce **[62188]**

Missouri Association of Insurance Agents Exhibition - Annual Convention **[13571]**

Missouri Botanical Garden–Library **[11528]**

Missouri Botanical Garden Annals **[11470]**

Missouri Business **[62110]**

Missouri Department of Economic Development Business Services **[61894]**
  Economic Development Office **[62106]**
  Office of International Marketing **[61895]**
  Office of Minority Business **[62073]**

Missouri Enterprise Business Center **[62096]**

Missouri Grocers Association Annual Convention and Trade Show **[11708]**

Missouri Historical Society–Archives–Architecture Collection **[7688]**

Missouri Municipal Review **[50366]**

Missouri PAC - Southeastern Missouri State University–SBDC **[61869]**

Missouri Procurement Technical Assistance Center **[62089]**
  Western Region PTAC–University of Missouri, Kansas City **[62090]**

Missouri SBDC–University of Missouri–SBDC **[61855]**

Missouri Small Business Development Centers **[66908]**

Missouri Southern State College–Small Business Development Center **[61870]**

Missouri Southern State University–Heartland Procurment Technical Assistance Center–Institute for Procurement Assistance **[62091]**

Missouri State Genealogical Association Journal **[10972]**

Missouri (State) Highway and Transportation Department–Division of Materials–Library **[2113]**, **[8740]**, **[16199]**, **[24258]**

Missouri State Library–Library Development **[66909]**

Missouri State Office of Administration **[66910]**

Missouri State Office of Social and Economic Data Analysis–University of Missouri-Columbia **[66911]**

Missouri Valley Chamber of Commerce **[60179]**

Missouri Veterinary Medical Association Annual Convention **[1265]**

"Missouri's System of Higher Education: the New Rules for the Knowledge Economy" in *Ingram's* (Vol. 29, No. 8, August 2003, pp. 75) **[32574]**, **[33174]**, **[44339]**

Mistake-Free Grammar & Proofreading **[27269]**

Mister Bar-B-Que **[21887]**

Mr. Boston's Official Video Bartender's Guide **[2372]**

Mister Front End **[22690]**

Mister Mobile, On-Site Oil Changes **[22691]**

Mister Money - USA **[5262]**

Mister Softee, Inc. **[12840]**

Mister Transmission (International) Limited **[22692]**

Misys Laboratory **[17239]**

"Mitch Siegler: 41 President of Sovietski collection in San Diego" in *Entrepreneur* (Vol. 30, No. 1, January 2002, pp. 19) **[5910]**, **[11157]**, **[43754]**, **[51248]**

Mitchell Area Chamber of Commerce **[64831]**

Mitchell County Chamber of Commerce **[63407]**

Mitchell J. Kassoff, Esq. (Attorney) **[29640]**

Mitchell Office (Region V)–Small Business Development Center **[64806]**

Mitchell Technical Institute **[64845]**

Mitchell & Titus L.L.P. **[24119]**, **[26433]**, **[38564]**

Mitsui and Co. Venture Partners (MCVP) **[63138]**

Mix **[17792]**, **[21151]**

"Mix and Match" in *Internet World* (Vol. 7, No. 1, January 15, 2001, pp. 60) **[25897]**, **[53378]**, **[53856]**

"Mix it Up" in *Entrepreneur* (Vol. 32, No. 2, February 2004, pp. 47) **[15267]**, **[38226]**

"A Mixed Blessing" in *Entrepreneur* (Vol. 31, No. 7, July 2003, pp. 68) **[38227]**, **[39477]**

"Mixed Fate for Black Law Firms" in *Black Enterprise* (Vol. 34, No. 4, November 2003, pp. 27) **[28493]**, **[29387]**, **[48312]**

"A Mixed Forecast for 2002" in *Hispanic Business* (Vol. 24, No. 1/2, January/February 2002, pp. 14, 16) **[28494]**, **[32575]**

"Mixed Grill: A Quarter's Menu: Good-and Some Bad-News" in *Barron's* (July 7, 2003, pp. 22) **[10090]**, **[15268]**, **[32576]**, **[38228]**, **[53857]**, **[54661]**

"Mixed Signals" in *Entrepreneur* (Vol. 33, September 2005, No. 9, pp. 18) **[5844]**, **[5879]**, **[24821]**, **[31667]**, **[32577]**

"Mixed-use development deserves a good look" in *Crain's Detroit Business* (Vol. 16, No. 49, December 4, 2000, pp. 8) **[52917]**

Mixin' **[2368]**

"Mixing Books with Business" in *Black Enterprise* (Vol. 34, No. 2, September 2003, pp. S1) **[18910]**, **[56755]**

"Mixing it up is recipe for successful event menus" in *Atlanta Business Chronicle* (Vol. 24, No. 14, September 7, 2001, pp. S14) **[4549]**, **[24977]**

MJSA Benchmark **[15869]**

MJSA Expo Providence **[15878]**

MLM Consultants **[65675]**

MMA Cycles Report **[15663]**

Moab Area Chamber of Commerce **[65717]**

Moapa Valley Chamber of Commerce **[62361]**

Mobil Travel Guide **[12736]**

Mobile Air Conditioning Society Worldwide **[1005]**

Mobile Air Conditioning Society Worldwide Convention and Trade Show **[1046]**, **[48505]**

Mobile Area Chamber of Commerce **[56872]**

Mobile Automotive Window Service Business Guide **[11219]**

Mobile Data Report **[5207]**

"Mobile Gaming Sector Growing, and Middletown, Conn. Firm Wants to be Player" in *Hartford Courant* (December 19, 2004) **[1112]**, **[5057]**, **[17324]**, **[23089]**

"Mobile Moguls" in *Small Business Opportunities* (Vol. 12, No. 3, May 2000, pp. 120) **[49149]**

Mobile Radio Technology **[5208]**, **[48504]**

"Mobile Situation UT Starcom Soars" in *Barron's* (July 21, 2003, pp. 16) **[5058]**, **[14248]**, **[41840]**, **[43755]**

Mobile Tire Guys **[22693]**, **[24597]**

Mobility **[23408]**

Mobility Scooters Franchising, LLC **[17277]**

"Mobilize! These Businesses Get Moving" in *My Business* (August/September 2002, pp. 38-41) **[2031]**, **[30914]**, **[31781]**, **[53858]**

Mobius Venture Capital / Softbank Venture Capital **[58090]**

Mobridge Chamber of Commerce **[64832]**

Mocha Delites Inc. **[11393]**

Mode Accessories International Exposition **[9656]**

Model Airplane News **[8213]**

"Model behavior" in *Entrepreneur* (Vol. 30, No. 3, March 2002, pp. 68) **[29936]**, **[44591]**, **[55729]**

"A Model Chamber Tackles Complex Issues" in *Hispanic Business* (July/August 2002, pp. 64-66) **[40538]**, **[48313]**

"A model occupation: who says you can't turn business into play?" in *Entrepreneur* (Vol. 31, No. 4, April 2003, pp. 102) **[8132]**, **[35570]**, **[37571]**, **[38662]**

Model Railroad Industry Association **[8145]**

Model Railroader **[8214]**

Model Retailer **[8215]**

Modeling, Commercials, & Acting **[17340]**

Modeling Made Easy **[17341]**

Modeling (The Basics) **[17342]**

Modern Art Museum of Fort Worth–Library **[6073]**

Modern Baking **[2156]**

"Modern Bed and Breakfast Slated for Boynton Beach, Fla." in *South Florida Sun-Sentinel* (August 1, 2003) **[2447]**

Modern Brewery Age **[2369]**, **[3150]**, **[16242]**

Modern Brewery Age Tabloid Edition **[3151]**

Modern Bride **[3206]**

Modern Bulk Transporter **[25438]**

Modern Bulk Transporter-Buyers Guide Issue **[25398]**

Modern Business Statistics **[28495]**

Modern Casting Magazine **[16398]**

Modern Healthcare **[12399]**, **[41267]**

Modern Materials Handling (Vol. 58, No. 7, July 2003, pp. 60); "UPS-Compliant Shipping Software" in **[6104]**, **[23242]**, **[53522]**

Modern Metalworking **[16374]**

Modern Plastics (Vol. 79, Dec. 2002, pp. 65); "Plastics recovery technology developer tackles post-consumer electronics scrap" in **[6758]**, **[21250]**, **[24344]**, **[41907]**

Modern Press **[56934]**

Modern Purchasing **[50765]**

Modern Real Estate Practice **[20592]**

Modern Salon **[11809]**

Modern Tire Dealer-Facts/Directory Issue **[24585]**

Modern Woodworking **[4486]**, **[8047]**

Modernistic Cleaning Services **[25561]**

"A Modest Defense of the Cubicle" in *Inc.* (September 1, 2004) **[49518]**, **[53859]**

"A Modest Manifesto for Shattering the Glass Ceiling" in *Harvard Business Review* (Vol. 78, No. 1, January 2000, pp. 127) **[45441]**, **[53860]**

Modesto Bee (January 22, 2003); "Health Crisis Inspires Medesto, Calif. Woman to Open Needlework Store" in **[8126]**, **[19548]**, **[35502]**, **[42518]**, **[56050]**

Modesto Chamber of Commerce **[57639]**

Modesto Junior Chamber of Commerce **[57640]**

"Modine Manufacturing Unit to Provide Cooling System for Video-Game Computers" in *Milwaukee Journal Sentinel* (December 8, 2005) **[1113]**, **[6726]**, **[24822]**, **[46376]**

Modular Building Institute **[48503]**

"Modular Home Center Opens in Arcadia" in *Charlotte Observer* (February 1, 2007) **[7424]**, **[20593]**, **[40539]**, **[46377]**

Modus Vivendi Inc. **[66778]**

Moe's Italian Sandwiches **[8562]**

Moe's Southwest Grill **[21888]**

Mofa Inc. **[20273]**

"MoGo Mouse BT" in *Sales & Marketing Management* (Vol. 159, January-February 2007, No. 1, pp. 42) **[5059]**, **[6727]**, **[49150]**

Mohave Community College–Small Business Development Center **[56995]**

Mohave Valley Chamber of Commerce **[57051]**

"Mohawk to Introduce Retail Kiosk" in *HFN The Weekly Newspaper for the Home Furnishing Network* (Jul. 14, 2003) **[12196]**, **[12299]**, **[15928]**

Mohawk Valley Chamber of Commerce **[62960]**

"Mohr, Davidow Names New Partner, East Coast Presence" in *Venture Capital Journal* (Vol. 40, No. 10, October 2000, pp. 34) **[28496]**, **[55730]**

Mohr Davidow Ventures (Menlo Park) **[58091]**

"Mohyr, Davidow Hires AOL Exec." in *Venture Capital Journal* (Vol. 40, No. 10, November 2000, pp. 36) **[14249]**, **[23090]**, **[34201]**, **[41841]**, **[55731]**

Mokena Chamber of Commerce **[59595]**

Molalla Area Chamber of Commerce **[64244]**

Molecular Physics **[52307]**

Molluscan Shellfish Institute **[10445]**

Molly Maid, Inc. **[8715]**

"Molly Maid franchise owners have own site" in *Crain's Detroit Business* (Vol. 16, No. 34, August 21, 2000, pp. E-6) **[8691]**, **[34202]**, **[38857]**

Moloka'i Chamber of Commerce **[59255]**

"Mom & Pop: Please Read" in *Inc.* (September 1, 2003) **[37733]**

"Mom and Pop Psychology" in *Inc.* (December 1, 2003) **[29937]**, **[36505]**, **[39478]**

"Mom and pop's retail secret: doggie in the window" in *Wall Street Journal* (December 22, 1999, pp. B1) **[53861]**

"MomandPop.com" in *PC Magazine* (January 16, 2001, pp. 131) **[31193]**, **[31834]**, **[34203]**

Momence Chamber of Commerce **[59596]**

"The Moment You Least Expect It" in *Hispanic Business* (December 2001, pp. FG1-FG2) **[22299]**, **[36506]**

Mom's Bake at Home Pizza **[19688]**

"Moms Have Their Own Generation Gap" in *Marketing to Women* (Vol. 20, January 2007, No. 1, pp. 5) **[726]**, **[28497]**, **[47290]**

"Moms Say Missing Their Babies is Hardest Part of Returning to Work" in *Marketing to Women* (Vol. 19, November 2006, No. 11, pp. 3) **[28498]**, **[47291]**, **[54970]**

"Moms Want Ads to Address Them as Women" in *Marketing to Women* (Vol. 19, October 2006, No. 10, pp. 3) **[727]**, **[47292]**, **[50456]**

Mon Valley Regional Chamber of Commerce **[64474]**

Monahans Chamber of Commerce **[65402]**

Monart School of The Arts **[19520]**

Monday Morning Moms **[5442]**

Monett Chamber of Commerce **[62001]**

Money **[3435]**

Money in America **[38499]**

"Money that Binds from Afar" in *Hispanic Business* (November 2003, pp. 60, 62, 64) **[10091]**, **[15269]**, **[28499]**, **[32578]**, **[43756]**

"Money to Burn? Before You Go On a Spending Spree With Your Surplus Cash, Get Your Priorities Straight" in *Entrepreneur* (July 2004) **[15270]**, **[38229]**

The Money Connection: Where & How to Apply for Business Loans & Venture Capital **[44592]**

"Money Corner" in *Home Business* (Vol. 13, January/February 2006, No. 1, pp. 78) **[38230]**, **[39870]**, **[51249]**, **[54662]**

"Money-Counting for Growth" in *Hispanic Business* (June 2002, pp. 70) **[10092]**, **[15271]**, **[38231]**

Money for Entrepreneurs **[55732]**

"Money From Thin Air" in *Small Business Opportunities* (Vol. 16, No. 1, January 2004, pp. 70) **[992]**, **[1068]**, **[35571]**

Money Fund Report **[15664]**

"Money Is Out There, But Where?" in *Crain's Chicago Business* (Vol. 30, January 2007, No. 1, pp. 12) **[14250]**, **[25898]**, **[33175]**, **[48917]**, **[52564]**, **[52918]**, **[55733]**

Money Mailer, Inc. **[887]**

Money-Making 900 Numbers: How Entrepreneurs Use the Telephone to Sell Information **[8666]**

"Money & Manners" in *Small Business Opportunities* (Vol. 17, September 2005, No. 5, pp. 12) **[27444]**, **[28500]**, **[39479]**, **[51734]**

"Money Master" in *Entrepreneur* (Vol. 28, No. 9, September 2000, pp. 60) **[37840]**, **[56061]**

"Money Matters" in *Small Business Opportunities* (Vol. 13, No. 5, September 2001, pp. 10) **[39871]**, **[44593]**, **[55734]**

"Money-Preneuring" in *Small Business Opportunities* (Vol. 16, No. 3, May 2004, pp. 62, 64) **[10093]**, **[15272]**, **[15802]**, **[23497]**, **[26854]**, **[37734]**, **[38232]**, **[39653]**, **[40540]**, **[42344]**, **[50927]**, **[54663]**

"Money Rules" in *Hispanic Business* (September 2004, pp. 34-36, 38, 40, 42) **[10094]**, **[44594]**, **[48314]**

Money Smart Secrets for the Self-Employed **[2929]**, **[26294]**, **[38233]**

Money Source Financial Services Inc. **[27038]**

"Money well spent" in *Rough Notes* (Vol. 146, No. 3, March 2003, pp. 148) **[13387]**, **[43280]**

"Money strategies: What to know about multi-state taxation" in *Atlanta Business Chronicle* (Vol. 25, No. 22, November 8, 2002, pp. 6B) **[195]**, **[23991]**, **[54664]**

"Money talks" in *Black Enterprise* (Vol. 32, No. 9, April 2002, pp. 52) **[41842]**, **[54227]**

"Money Talks; Here's Message to Michigan" in *Crain's Detroit Business* (Vol. 22, November 20, 2006, No. 47, pp. 9) **[28501]**, **[30569]**, **[43757]**

"Money Talks to New Economy Firms: More Startups Choose Chicago for Home Base" in *Crain's Chicago Business* (Vol. 23, Nov. 27, 2000) **[52640]**, **[55735]**

Money in Your Mailbox: How to Start and Operate a Successful Mail-Order Business **[16460]**

The Moneychanger **[15665]**

The MoneyLetter **[15666]**

"Moneymaker Without Walls" in *Tampa Tribune* (December 17, 2005) **[4299]**, **[15929]**

Moneysoft Inc. **[30103]**, **[53553]**

The Monitor (September 10, 2003); "Kiosk Makes Paying Court Fines Easier in McAllen, Texas, But Few Are Using It" in **[15925]**

"Monitor and Manage Your Web Server" in *E-business Advisor* (Vol. 18, No. 1, January 2000, pp. 38) **[23091]**, **[34204]**, **[53379]**

"Monitor Your E-Business Systems' Health" in *E-business Advisor* (Vol. 17, No. 12, December 1999, pp. 22) **[23092]**, **[34205]**, **[53380]**

"Monitoring Your Carriers" in *Rough Notes* (Vol. 145, No. 2, February 2003, pp. 72) **[13388]**, **[43281]**

"Monkey Business" in *Entrepreneur* (Vol. 28, No. 1, January 2000, pp. 26) **[34206]**

Monmouth Area Chamber of Commerce **[59597]**

Monmouth-Independence Chamber of Commerce **[64245]**

Monon Chamber of Commerce **[59971]**

Monona Chamber of Commerce **[66468]**

Monroe Chamber of Commerce **[58550]**, **[60658]**, **[66133]**

Monroe Chamber of Commerce and Industry **[66469]**

Monroe City Area Chamber of Commerce **[62002]**

Monroe County Chamber of Commerce **[61390]**, **[61817]**, **[63744]**, **[64956]**

Monroe County Extension Center–Small Business Development Center **[61871]**

Monroe County Industrial Development Corp.–SBDC **[61210]**

Monroeville Area Chamber of Commerce **[56873]**, **[64475]**

Monrovia Chamber of Commerce **[57641]**

Monster Mini Golf **[17331]**

Mont Clare - Elmwood Park Chamber of Commerce **[59598]**

Montana Chamber of Commerce **[62189]**

"Montana Champion Again, Joins F-of-F" in *Venture Capital Journal* (Vol. 40, No. 10, November 2000, pp. 8, 9) **[35572]**, **[55736]**

Montana Community Development Corporation–Missoula Small Business Development Center **[62125]**

Montana Department of Administration–Procurement Bureau **[62209]**

Montana Department of Agriculture–Agriculture Development Division **[62128]**

Montana Department of Commerce
  Business Resources Division **[62129]**
  Census and Economic Information Center **[62130]**, **[66914]**
  Certified Communities Program **[62131]**
  Economic Development Division–Marketing Assistance and Made in Montana Program **[62132]**
  International Trade Program **[62133]**
  Montana SBDC **[62116]**
  Montana Science and Technology Alliance Division **[62134]**
  Small Business Development Center **[62117]**

Montana Land Magazine **[21052]**

Montana Magazine **[62217]**

Montana Mike's Steakhouse **[21889]**

"Montana Mountain High" in *Business Week* (February 20, 2006, No. 3972, pp. 86) **[12599]**, **[24708]**, **[25216]**

Montana Procurement Technical Assistance Center Government Marketing Assistance Group–Big Sky Economic Development Authority **[62210]**
  Great Falls Development Authority **[62211]**

Montana Standard (July 20, 2003); "Butte, Montana, Luxury Home Turned into European-Style Bed and Breakfast" in **[2432]**

Montana (State) Department of Transportation–Library **[2114]**, **[8741]**, **[16200]**, **[24259]**

Montana State Library–Digital Library Division **[66915]**

Montana State University-Bozeman Information Technology Center **[23324]**
  Office of Vice President for Research, Creativity, and Technology Transfer **[62214]**

Montana Tech of the University of Montana–Montana Tech Library **[56693]**

Montana's Cookhouse Saloons **[21890]**

Montcalm Community College **[61496]**

Montclair Chamber of Commerce **[57642]**

Montco Chamber of Commerce **[64476]**

Monte Rio Chamber of Commerce **[57643]**

Monte Vista Chamber of Commerce **[58407]**

Monteagle Mountain Chamber of Commerce **[64957]**

Montebello Chamber of Commerce **[57644]**

Montello Area Chamber of Commerce **[66470]**

Monterey Media Inc. **[58271]**

Monterey Park Chamber of Commerce **[57645]**

Monterey Peninsula Chamber of Commerce **[57646]**

Montesano Chamber of Commerce and Visitor Information Center **[66134]**

Montevallo Chamber of Commerce **[56874]**

Montevideo Area Chamber of Commerce **[61630]**

Montgomerie, Huck & Co. **[66710]**

Montgomery Area Center for Economic - Small Business Incubator **[56922]**

Montgomery Area Chamber of Commerce **[56875]**

Montgomery Associates, Inc. **[58092]**

Montgomery City Area Chamber of Commerce **[62003]**

Montgomery County Chamber of Commerce **[60841]**, **[63408]**, **[65928]**

Montgomery County Chamber of Commerce at Guy Park Manor **[62961]**

Montgomery County Extension–Small Business Development Center **[61872]**

The Montgomery County (KS) Genealogy Society–Library **[11056]**

Montgomery's Inn Museum–Heritage Resource Centre **[11057]**

"The Month in Review: Who Made News?" in *Venture Capital Journal* (Vol. 42, No. 5, May 2002, pp. 15, 16-17) **[10095]**, **[15273]**, **[50087]**, **[55737]**

"Monthly Report - December 1999" in *Small Business Economic Trends* (December 1999, pp. COV) **[42345]**, **[53862]**

"Monthly report-December 2001" in *Small Business Economic Trends* (December 2001, pp. 1) **[28502]**, **[32579]**

"Monthly Report - January 2000" in *Small Business Economic Trends* (January 2000, pp. COV) **[42346]**, **[53863]**

"Monthly report-January 2002" in *Small Business Economic Trends* (January 2002, pp. 1) **[28503]**, **[32580]**

"Monthly Report - July 2000" in *Small Business Economic Trends* (July 2000, pp. 1) **[53864]**

"Monthly Report - June 2000" in *Small Business Economic Trends* (June 2000, pp. 1) **[26855]**, **[42347]**, **[53865]**

"Monthly Report - March 2000" in *Small Business Economic Trends* (March 2000, pp. COV) **[42348]**, **[53866]**

Monticello Area Chamber of Commerce **[60180]**, **[61631]**

Monticello Chamber of Commerce **[59599]**, **[65718]**

Monticello Drew County Chamber of Commerce **[57197]**

Monticello-Jasper County Chamber of Commerce **[59141]**

Monticello-Jefferson County Chamber of Commerce **[58896]**

Monticello/Wayne County Chamber of Commerce **[60547]**

Montpelier Area Chamber of Commerce **[63745]**

"Montreal: A Fertile Ground For VC Exploration" in *Venture Capital Journal* (Vol. 42, No. 5, May 2002, pp. 54) **[41469]**, **[50795]**, **[52021]**, **[55405]**

Montreal International Auto Show **[927]**

Montreal Spring Gift Show **[11189]**

Montrose Chamber of Commerce **[58408]**

Montrose-Verdugo City Chamber of Commerce **[57647]**

Montville Township Chamber of Commerce **[62535]**

Monument Advisors, Inc. **[60032]**

Monument Builders of North America **[10793]**

"Mood Music" in *Entrepreneur* (Vol. 31, No. 9, July 2003, pp. 79) **[51250]**, **[51735]**

"The moonlighter" in *Harvard Business Review* (Vol. 80, No. 11, November 2002, pp. 33) **[37476]**, **[45442]**

"Moonlighting" in *Forbes* (January 24, 2000, pp. 138) **[37068]**

Moore & Associates **[64116]**

Moore Chamber of Commerce **[64040]**

W.S. Moore Consulting **[16145]**

Moore County Chamber of Commerce **[63409]**

Moore Norman Technology Center **[64149]**

Moore Stephens North America **[40]**

Mooresville Chamber of Commerce **[59972]**

Mooresville-South Iredell Chamber of Commerce **[63410]**

Moorhead Associates Inc. **[40118]**

Jane Moosbruker, Organization Development Consultant **[35244]**

Moose Lake Area Chamber of Commerce **[61632]**

Moosehead Lake Region Chamber of Commerce **[60762]**

Moraine Valley Community College–Small Business Development Center **[59383]**

"The Moral Intensity of Privacy: An Empirical Study of Webmasters' Attitudes" in *Journal of Business Ethics* (Vol. 46, Sept. 15, 2003) **[14251]**, **[22300]**, **[25899]**, **[34207]**, **[37477]**

Moral Issues in Business **[37478]**

Moral Management: Integrating Ethics **[37479]**

"Morale Boost Payoff" in *Small Business Opportunities* (Vol. 17, September 2005, No. 5, pp. 10, 20) **[34992]**

Morbidity and Mortality Weekly Report **[41268]**

"More Area Employers Seeking Spanish-Speaking Workers" in *Ledger* (February 27, 2005) **[48582]**, **[53867]**

More Awkward Customers **[10314]**, **[15709]**

"More bang" in *Entrepreneur* (Vol. 30, No. 2, February) **[27151]**, **[34993]**, **[36507]**, **[39480]**, **[47293]**, **[51736]**

"More Bang for Your Buck" in *Entrepreneur* (Vol. 32) **[1834]**, **[2395]**, **[7737]**, **[9632]**, **[11158]**, **[12013]**, **[24823]**, **[24978]**, **[34208]**, **[47294]**, **[51251]**, **[55125]**

"More apartments headed for Buckhead" in *Atlanta Business Chronicle* (Vol. 25, January 3, 2003, No. 30, pp. 1A) **[7425]**, **[20594]**, **[20942]**, **[21337]**

"More Cell Phone Providers Using Stealthy Approach to Erecting Towers" in *Chicago Tribune* (March 4, 2005) **[5060]**, **[28504]**

"More Change For IAEM: New Magazine Planned, Foundation Mothballed As Unification Talks Continue" in *Tradeshow Week* (Vol. 34) **[22532]**, **[24979]**, **[55126]**

"More fly charter, wing it themselves" in *Crain's Detroit Business* (Vol. 19, No. 9, March 3, 2003, pp. 18) **[30379]**, **[53868]**

"More Checks in the Mail" in *Hispanic Business* (Vol. 23, No. 7/8, July/August 2001, pp. 30) **[27152]**, **[39481]**

"More condos, lofts in pipeline for Detroit" in *Crain's Detroit Business* (Vol. 19, No. 10, March 10, 2003, pp. 37) **[20595]**, **[20943]**

Motivation & a Positive Attitude [35196]

The Motivational Manager [45900]

"Motivator Vehicles" in *Sacramento Bee* (October 31, 2005) [3560], [31194], [34997], [45446]

Motivision Media [58272]

MotoPhoto [19212], [19331]

MotoPhoto (Canada) [19213], [19332]

Motor Age [22633]

Motor Age (Vol. 122, No. 11, November 2003, pp. 86); "Aftermarket Auto Parts Alliance" in [1892], [32137]

Motor Age (Vol. 122, No. 9, September 2003, pp. 100); "Automotive Aftermarket Suppliers Association (AASA)" in [1910]

Motor Age (Vol. 122, No. 11, November 2003, pp. 86); "Web Site Guides Activists" in [1985], [34675], [54064]

"Motor City Mayhem" in *Hispanic Business* (November 2006, pp. 42, 44, 46, 48) [18092], [46379]

Motor and Equipment Manufacturers Association [1887]

Motor Magazine [22634]

Motor Trend [18181]

The Motor Vehicle Parts Aftermarket [1989]

Motor Vehicle Regulation [924]

Motorcycle Industry Council [17481]

Motorcycle Industry Magazine [17498]

The Motorcyclist's Post [17499]

"Motorola to Cut 3,500 Jobs" in *Crain's Chicago Business* (Vol. 30, January 2007, No. 4, pp. 12) [39482], [41847]

"Motorola Foundation Funds 'Road Map' for Employers Who Hire People With Disabilities" in *Long Island Business News* (February 6, 2004) [42351], [54229]

Motorola, Inc.–Information Resource Center [5232]

Motorola Ventures [59751], [62436]

"Motorola's Cell Slide Resumes" in *Crain's Chicago Business* (Vol. 26, No. 50, December 15, 2003, pp. 3) [5063], [28513]

"Motorola's Cell Slide Resumes; Rivals with Camera Phones Steal Marketshare" in *Crains Chicago Business* (Vol. 26, No. 50) [5064], [28514]

Motorsport Dealer & Trade [17500]

Moulton Chamber of Commerce and Agriculture [65404]

R.E. Moulton Inc. [3772], [16648], [20190], [31418], [42987], [46088]

Moultrie-Colquitt County Chamber of Commerce [59142]

Mound City Chamber of Commerce [60388], [62004]

Moundridge Community Chamber of Commerce [60389]

Mount Adams Chamber of Commerce [66137]

Mount Angel Chamber of Commerce [64246]

Mount Carroll Chamber of Commerce [59603]

Mount Desert Chamber of Commerce [60763]

Mount Dora Area Chamber of Commerce [58897]

Mount Greenwood Chamber of Commerce [59604]

Mount Holyoke College Library–Music and Dance Library [17690]

Mount Hood Area Chamber of Commerce [64247]

Mount Hood Community College [64301] Small Business Development Center [64169]

Mount Horeb Area Chamber of Commerce [66472]

Mount Ida Area Chamber of Commerce [57199]

Mt. Ida College–Division of Continuing Education [61156]

Mount Juliet - West Wilson County Chamber of Commerce [64959]

Mount Kisco Chamber of Commerce [62962]

Mount Lebanon Dormont Area Chamber of Commerce [64477]

Mount Olive Area Chamber of Commerce [62537], [63412]

Mount Pleasant Area Chamber of Commerce [60181], [61391]

Mount Pleasant Main Street Comm. [65719]

Mount Pleasant/Titus County Chamber of Commerce and Convention and Visitors' Bureau [65405]

Mount Prospect Chamber of Commerce [59605]

Mount St. Helens Chamber of Commerce [66138]

Mt. San Antonio College SBDC [57265]

Mount Shasta Chamber of Commerce [57651]

Mount Sinai School of Medicine of City University of New York–International Longevity Center [41390]

Mount Snow Valley Chamber of Commerce [65793]

Mount Sterling-Montgomery County Chamber of Commerce [60551]

Mount Vernon Area Chamber of Commerce [60182]

Mount Vernon Chamber of Commerce [62005], [62963], [66139]

Mount Vernon - Knox County Chamber of Commerce [63747]

Mount Vernon - Lee Chamber of Commerce [65929]

Mt. Vernon Skagit Valley College–Small Business Development Center [66019]

Mount Washington Valley Chamber of Commerce and Visitor's Bureau [62431]

Mount Washington Valley SCORE [62394]

Mount Zion Chamber of Commerce [59606]

Mountain Bike Magazine [2510]

Mountain Empire Community College [65998] Mountain Empire SBDC [65831]

The Mountain Gardener [11471], [16050]

Mountain Grove Chamber of Commerce [62006]

Mountain Home Area Chamber of Commerce [57200]

Mountain Home Chamber of Commerce [59319]

Mountain Mike's Pizza [19689], [21891]

Mountain Realty Inc. [49444]

Mountain View Chamber of Commerce [62007], [64041]

Mountainair Chamber of Commerce [62706]

Mountainwest Golf [11281], [23649]

The Mouser Report [856]

"Move over, Charlotte" in *Atlanta Business Chronicle* (Vol. 25, December 6, 2002, No. 26, pp. 1A) [28515], [32582]

"Move Over" in *Entrepreneur* (Vol. 33, September 2005, No. 9, pp. 55) [28516], [29429], [30159]

"Move Over, Internet Explorer; Why the Rush to Foxfire?" in *Business Week* (February 7, 2005, No. 3919, pp. 89) [14255], [22302], [34214]

"Move to expense stock options get mixed results" in *Atlanta Business Chronicle* (Vol. 25, November 15, 2002, No. 23 pp. SS4) [197], [10096], [15280], [26296]

MovieEntertainment Feature [4139]

"Movin' On Up" in *Entrepreneur* (Vol. 31, No. 9, September 2003, pp. 68) [6729], [49151]

"Movin' on up" in *Crain's Detroit Business* (Vol. 19, No. pp. 11) [2344], [7428], [11337], [20599], [20945], [21564]

Moving Ahead: Breaking Destructive Behavior Patterns That Hold You Back [32963]

"Moving Daze" in *Law Firm Inc.* (October 2004) [20600], [29389], [30160], [52701]

Moving Freely: A Creative Dance Class [5398]

"Moving mountains" in *Harvard Business Review* (Vol. 81, No. 1, January 2003, pp. 41) [34998], [36511], [45447]

"Moving On: Ex-Apprentices Find Life After 'The Donald' is All Business" in *Entrepreneur* (Vol. 32, October 2004, No. 10, pp. 28) [1835], [5560], [15281], [20601], [20946], [31566], [36512]

Moving from an Operational Manager to a Strategic Leader [44814]

Moving from an Operational Manager to a Strategic Thinker [44815]

Moving from Operational Manager to Strategic Thinker (Canada) [44816]

"Moving Out: When to Outsource Your Server Operations" in *My Business* (December/January 2004, pp. 42) [3951], [6952], [49152], [49717], [52378]

"Moving Pictures" in *Hispanic Business* (Vol. 23, No. 5, May 2001, pp. 66, 68) [5948], [6450], [9670], [25758], [35574], [47971]

"Moving from one product was their prize" in *Crain's Detroit Business* (Vol. 19, No. 13, March 31, 2003, pp. 13) [14256], [25901], [28517], [34215], [41848]

"Moving Up" in *Houston Business Journal* (Vol. 34, No. 9, July 11, 2003, pp. 17) [17557]

The Moving World [17562]

MPM Capital / MPM Asset Management LLC [61099]

Mr. Appliance [52627]

"Mr. Cashman, You're On" in *Inc.* (Volume 27, July 2005, No. 7, pp. 100-102, 104) [44598], [55739]

"Mr. Clean" in *Crain's New York Business* (Vol. 23, January 8, 2007, No. 2, pp. 23) [19968], [35282], [36513]

"Mr. Clean" in *Forbes* (Vol. 175, January 10, 2005, No. 1, pp. 140) [3322], [15282], [21565]

Mr. Electric Corp. [9097]

"Mr. Fix-It" in *Entrepreneur* (Vol. 28, No. 8, August 2000, pp. 192) [3561], [14257]

Mr. Goodcents Subs & Pastas [8563], [21892]

Mr. Greek Express [21893]

Mr. Greek Jr. [21894]

Mr. Greek Mediterranean Grill [21895]

Mr. Handyman [8716]

Mr. Handyman of Canada [52628]

Mr. Hero Restaurants [21896]

"Mr. Koogle's Failed Return" in *Red Herring* (January 2003, pp. 69) [35575], [41470]

Mr. Lube Canada Limited Partnership [22694]

Mr. Mikes West Coast Grill [21897]

Mr. Payroll Check Cashing [15957]

"Mr. Pita legal woes haven't put a wrap on expansion" in *Crain's Detroit Business* (Vol. 18, No. 24, June 17, 2002, pp. 22) [21566], [28518], [29390], [38859]

Mr. Pita/Pita Depot [8564]

"Mr. Pita Wagons Rolling Along" in *Crain's Detroit Business* (Vol. 22, February 6, 2006, No. 6, pp. 21) [21567], [28519], [38860]

Mr. Plant [11500], [42800]

"Mr. Prime Time" in *Hispanic Business* (Vol. 23, No. 7/8, July/August 2001, pp. 74, 76, 78) [9731], [28520]

Mr. Rooter Plumbing [19779]

Mr. Sandless Inc. [10539]

Mr. SUB [21898]

Mr. Subb [21899]

Mr. Transmission/Transmission USA [22695]

"Mr. Yoshida's Opus" in *Small Business Opportunities* (Vol. 14, No. 1, January 2002, pp. 56) [23443], [35576]

MRA Blue Book Research Services Directory [47300]

"MRI and the national defense" in *Ingram's* (Vol. 28, No. 6, June 2002, pp. 73) [22303], [41849], [52154]

"Mrs. D & I are cool (handle your business)" in *Black Enterprise* (Vol. 33, No. 3, October 2002, pp. S9) [33176], [34258]

Mrs. Field's Original Cookies, Inc. [2307]

"Mrs., Mom, and CEO" in *Black Enterprise* (Vol. 32, No. 9, April 2) [24235], [36514], [37737], [42682], [48316], [52565], [56327]

Mrs. Powell's Bakery Eatery [8565]

Mrs. Vanellis Fresh Italian Foods [21900]

"MSA Withdrawals: Rules on Tax Exclusion" in *Employee Benefit Plan Review* (Vol. 55, No. 12, June 2001, pp. 8) [26856], [41063], [43283], [54666]

"MSCI-Red Herring Index" in *Red Herring* (January 2003, pp. 72) [2725], [3562], [4735], [5065], [6730], [14258], [18912], [23093], [24435], [28521], [34216], [41850], [44342]

"MSN Signs DIY Expert With Female Focus" in *Marketing to Women* (Vol. 20, January 2007, No. 1, pp. 8) [14259], [25902], [47301], [50089]

"MSU Enlists Biz Help On $1B Isotope Project Bid" in *Crain's Detroit Business* (Vol. 21, January 24, 2005, No. 4, pp. 1) [40060], [50928], [52155]

MSU SBDC Business Assistance Center–Meridian Community College at Webb Center [61759]

"MTDC 'speaks' for itself" in *Women In Business* (Vol. 52, No. 4, July 2000, pp. 35) [33177], [45448]

MTM Association for Standards and Research [18537]

MTO Cleaning Services, Inc. [8717]

"Much Higher Learning: Exploring the Benefits Of an Academic Career" in *Black Enterprise* (Vol. 34, July 2004, No. 12, pp. 61) [33178], [45449]

Muenster Chamber of Commerce [65406]

Mueser Rutledge Consulting Engineers **[7628]**

Mukwonago Area Chamber of Commerce and Tourism Center **[66473]**

Muleshoe Chamber of Commerce and Agriculture **[65407]**

Mullaney Publishing Group **[65676]**

Mullens Area Chamber of Commerce **[66290]**

Multi-Ad Builder **[904]**

Multi-Housing Laundry Association **[8897]**

Multi-Housing News **[7564]**

Multi-Level Marketing International Association **[46614]**, **[48659]**

Multi-Level Money: The Complete Guide to Generating, Closing & Working with All the Prospects You Need to Make Real Money Every Month in Network **[48668]**

Multi-Media Publications Inc. **[66757]**

Multi-Menu **[32185]**

"A Multi-Sensory Booth Attraction" in *Tradeshow Week* (Vol. 34, December 6, 2004, No. 49, pp. S10) **[22533]**, **[24981]**, **[55128]**

"Multibillion-Dollar Project Gets Key OK" in *San Francisco Business Times* (Vol. 17, No. 51, July 25, 2003, pp. 1) **[7429]**, **[20602]**, **[20947]**

Multicultural Customer Service **[31783]**

Multicultural Education, Training, and Advocacy **[48515]**

Multicultural Marketing News **[48493]**, **[56529]**

"Multiculturalism Grows Up" in *Hispanic Business* (Vol. 24, No. 4, April 2002, pp. 58, 60) **[42352]**, **[48317]**, **[48584]**, **[53870]**

"Multifaceted Motoring" in *Sacramento Bee* (December 9, 2005) **[18093]**, **[46380]**

"Multilingual Execs in Demand" in *Hispanic Business* (March 2005, pp. 15) **[42353]**, **[48585]**, **[53871]**

MultiMedia Internetscholarshipools **[6887]**, **[33302]**

"Multiple Building Business Warrants Careful Attention To Loss of Earnings Exposure" in *Rough Notes* (Vol. 146, No. 3, March 2003) **[7430]**, **[13390]**

"Multiple Stakeholder Judgments of Employee Behaviors" in *Journal of Business Ethics* (Vol. 46, No. 3, September 2003, pp. 235) **[34999]**, **[37480]**, **[45450]**

Multiply Your Profits: A Common-Sense Approach for Small to Midsize Businesses **[28522]**

Multistate Transmission **[22696]**

"Multitasking" in *Business First Columbus* (Vol. 18, No. 26, February 15, 2002, pp. A17) **[36515]**, **[38861]**

Mulvane Chamber of Commerce **[60390]**

Munchville Billiards & Arcade **[2536]**

Munchville International Cafe **[21901]**

Muncie-Delaware County Chamber of Commerce **[59973]**

Munday Chamber of Commerce and Agriculture **[65408]**

Municipal Art Society Newsletter **[1541]**

Municipal Cable TV and Telecommunications News **[4140]**

Municipal Futures Data-Line **[10380]**, **[15765]**

Municipal Leader **[50367]**

Municipal Market Data-Line **[10381]**, **[15766]**

"Municipal Wi-Fi: Let's Keep It Local" in *eWeek* (February 3, 2005) **[14260]**, **[34217]**, **[41851]**

Municipal World **[50368]**

Munsey Music **[66758]**

Munster Chamber of Commerce **[59974]**

Muppet Sales: Make-a-Buck **[35197]**

"Murdoch's Bid for DirecTV Parent May Lead to Launch of New Networks" in *Boston Globe* (April 11, 2003) **[4113]**, **[15283]**, **[24436]**, **[50090]**

"Murdock Carrousel Sold" in *Charlotte Observer* (January 31, 2007) **[30689]**, **[51255]**, **[52440]**

The Murdock Group Holding Corp. **[42988]**

Murfreesboro Chamber of Commerce **[63413]**

Murphree Venture Partners **[65619]**

P. Murphy & Associates Inc. **[49445]**

Murphy/Jahn–Library **[7689]**

Murphy and Partners, L.P. **[63140]**

Richard D. Murphy **[49446]**

Murphysboro Chamber of Commerce **[59607]**

Murray Area Chamber of Commerce **[65720]**

Murray-Calloway County Chamber of Commerce **[60552]**

J. Stewart Murray **[26638]**

Murray State University
  Bureau of Business and Economic Research **[50404]**
  Owensboro SBDC **[60462]**
  Small Business Development Center **[52401]**
  West Kentucky SBDC **[60463]**

Murray State University (Hopkinsville)–Small Business Development Center **[60464]**

Murrieta Chamber of Commerce **[57652]**

Muscle & Fitness **[19458]**

"Muscling in on the Hispanic Market" in *Hispanic Business* (January/February 2003, pp. 28) **[729]**, **[18094]**, **[47302]**

Muscular Development **[19459]**

Musea **[1628]**

Musee McCord d'histoire Canadienne–Archives and Documentation Centre **[1663]**

Museum of the City of New York–Department of Collections Access **[7968]**

Museum of Classical Chinese Furniture–Library **[1664]**

Museum of Independent Telephony–Archives Collection **[5233]**, **[24329]**

Museum of International Folk Art **[8269]**

Museum of Television and Radio–Research Services **[20381]**

Museum of Western Colorado–Loyd Files Research Library **[5941]**

"Music" in *Business Week* (December 19, 2005, No. 3964, pp. 40) **[17752]**, **[31047]**, **[34218]**

"Music to his Ears" in *Small Business Opportunities* (Vol. 12, No. 5, September 2000, pp. 88, 90) **[21128]**, **[35577]**

Music Educators Journal **[17625]**

Music Gigs & Auditions U.S.A. **[17339]**, **[23409]**, **[23833]**

Music-Go-Round **[17810]**

"Music-Go-Round: Webcasters Reach Tentative Agreement with RIAA, DiMA" in *Black Enterprise* (Vol. 34, No. 4, November 2003, pp. 52) **[14261]**, **[17753]**, **[20328]**, **[34219]**, **[44097]**

Music Inc. **[6141]**, **[17793]**

The Music Index **[6142]**

Music Industries Association of Canada **[17727]**

"Music Instructor Gives Students Confidence to Get Up On Stage" in *The Record* (November 13, 2005) **[17600]**, **[56328]**

"Music Like Water" in *Forbes* (Vol. 175, January 31, 2005, No. 2, pp. 42) **[17754]**, **[34220]**, **[44098]**

Music Notation Modernization Association **[17576]**, **[32897]**

Music Product Directory-Piano and Electronic Keyboard Editions **[17755]**

Music Publishers' Association of the United States **[17577]**

Music Teachers National Association **[17578]**

"Music To Her Ears: Lamonica Thomas Taps Into the Digital Greeting Card Market" in *Black Enterprise* (Vol. 34, No. 3, October 2003) **[11159]**, **[11569]**

"Music To Your Ears" in *Entrepreneur.com* (Vol. 34, February 2006, No. 2, pp. 113) **[17756]**, **[37738]**, **[44099]**

Music Trades **[17626]**, **[17794]**

Music Trades-Purchaser's Guide to the Music Industry Issue **[17607]**, **[17757]**

"Musical cases" in *Crain's Detroit Business* (Vol. 19, No. 10, March 10, 2003, pp. 34) **[17601]**, **[17758]**, **[29391]**, **[44100]**

Musical Merchandise Review-Music Industry Directory Issue **[17602]**, **[17780]**

"Musical sales? You better, you better, you bet" in *Atlanta Business Chronicle* (Vol. 25, November 29, 2002, No. 25, pp. 2B) **[17759]**, **[51739]**

Musicians Hotline **[17795]**, **[17847]**

"Musicians in South Florida Have Variety of Places to Buy New, Used Instruments" in *Miami Herald* (March 10, 2005) **[17760]**, **[17843]**

Muskego Area Chamber of Commerce **[66474]**

Muskegon Area Chamber of Commerce **[61392]**

Muskegon Community College–Allen G. Umbreit Library–Special Collections **[9297]**

Muskegon Economic Growth Alliance–Small Business Development Center Satellite Office **[61211]**

Muskingum Valley Area Chamber of Commerce **[63748]**

"Mussel Farmer's Expansion Plan Worries Island Lobster Fishermen" in *Portland Press Herald* (October 11, 2005) **[10462]**, **[26523]**

Musselshell Valley Chamber of Commerce **[62190]**

Must Be Heaven Franchise Corp. **[8566]**

"Must Love Wing Tips; Executives Tend to List Eyes as Their Best Feature" in *Business Week* (February 20, 2006, No. 3972, pp. 84) **[7063]**, **[45451]**

Mustang Area Chamber of Commerce **[64042]**

"Mutual Attraction: Despite the Headlines, Mutual Funds are Still a Good Thing" in *Entrepreneur* (Vol. 32, July 2004, No. 7, pp. 32) **[15284]**, **[38236]**

Mutual Fund Activity **[15767]**

"The Mutual Fund Trading Scandals: Implications for CPAs and Their Clients" in *Journal of Accountancy* (Vol. 198, December 2004) **[198]**, **[2930]**, **[10097]**, **[15285]**, **[23992]**, **[27153]**

Mutual Funds Database **[10382]**, **[15768]**

Mutual Funds, Options, Commodities, & Collectibles **[15710]**

MVS Update **[6515]**

MVTL Laboratories Inc. **[11968]**

MW Corp. **[35245]**

MW Megawatt Markets **[47802]**

MWV Capital Partners **[60033]**

"My Bad! Playing the Blame Game is Out." in *Entrepreneur* (Vol. 33, March 2005, No. 3, pp. 94) **[39483]**, **[45452]**

"My Best Practices: Do you want to sell smarter and don't know how?" in *Fortune* (Vol. 142, No. 14, December 18, 2000, pp. 292B) **[3563]**, **[14262]**, **[25903]**, **[49153]**

"My Best Practices: Sell smarter. Streamline your office. Work better. Crush competition" in *FSB* (Vol. 10, No. 9, Dec. 1, 2000, pp. 54) **[30774]**, **[48932]**

My Big Idea: 30 Successful Entrepreneurs Reveal How They Found Inspiration **[36516]**

My Business (December/January 2004, pp. 14); "5 Moves to Make Before the New Year" in **[17959]**, **[48936]**, **[54127]**, **[54415]**

My Business (February/March 2004, pp. 38); "5 Steps to Audit-Free Returns" in **[53]**, **[2859]**, **[23871]**, **[54416]**

My Business (December/January 2004, pp. 45); "5 Tips to Make Your Web Site Work" in **[25782]**, **[33504]**, **[46644]**

My Business (December/January 2004, pp. 46); "6 Secrets of eBay Sales Success" in **[1770]**, **[18635]**, **[33505]**, **[51540]**

My Business (September/October 2001, pp. 47); "A flat road ahead" in **[28164]**, **[32435]**

My Business (August/September 2002, pp. 16); "A Crisis Waiting to Happen?" in **[29840]**, **[39264]**

My Business (August/September 2002, pp. 47); "A Good Man(ager) is Hard to Find" in **[21524]**, **[36229]**, **[38818]**

My Business (June/July 2004, pp. 46); "A Job Well Done" in **[34961]**, **[45326]**

My Business (October/November 2002, pp. 52); "A Leg Up on Legal Fees" in **[29356]**, **[34131]**

My Business (September/October 2001, pp. 46); "A Little Bit Goes a Long Way" in **[44570]**, **[48912]**

My Business (February/March 2004, pp. 40); "A Road Less Taxed" in **[239]**, **[24026]**, **[51491]**, **[54307]**, **[54727]**

My Business (June/July 2004, pp. 45); "A Rose by No Name" in **[10168]**, **[10570]**, **[37771]**

My Business (June/July 2004, pp. 50); "A Woman's Job" in **[38947]**, **[56489]**

My Business (April/May 2004, pp. 20); "Air-Tight Technology For the Business Traveler" in **[16271]**, **[30284]**

My Business (February/March 2004, pp. 41); "All About Me" in **[68]**, **[23880]**, **[26740]**, **[35762]**, **[54426]**

My Business (October/November 2003, pp. 45); "Almost Famous: Market Yourself as an Expert" in **[30779]**, **[46672]**, **[50548]**, **[51546]**

My Business (February/March 2003, pp. 54); "Special Delivery" in [5633], [16416], [33492], [56077]

My Business (October/November 2003, pp. 46); "Spread the News: Communicate with Customers" in [18247], [27678], [47564]

My Business (June/July 2004, pp. 44); "Start Your Engines" in [795], [14482], [34535], [47573]

My Business (December/January 2003, pp. 14); "Staying in the Loop: Continuing Education for Entrepreneurs" in [33242], [36792]

My Business (October/November 2002, pp. 39); "Steady Economic Growth" in [28823], [32715]

My Business (October/November 2003, pp. 12); "Stuck in Mud?" in [36809], [45683]

My Business (December/January 2004, pp. 28-33, 52); "Success: What's Your Definition?" in [36816], [39617]

My Business (December/January 2004, pp. 12); "Sweet Victory" in [4317], [31871], [52735], [54015]

My Business (June/July 2002, pp. 46); "Swimgear Web Site Crosses Oceans" in [5722], [31872], [34556]

My Business (December/January 2003, pp. 17); "Taking Stock of Your Intellectual Property Assets" in [22392], [44160], [44372]

My Business (August/September 2002, pp. 15); "Tax-Free College Savings" in [26926], [40753], [54804]

My Business (June/July 2002, pp. 24); "Technology Can't Replace Your Best Asset: People" in [36839], [49305]

My Business (April/May 2003, pp. 32); "10 Rules for Bouncing Back" in [28877], [36842]

My Business (October/November 2003, pp. 26); "The 2003 Tax Relief Act: What Does It Mean for You?" in [39131], [54419]

My Business (February/March 2003, pp. 36-38); "The ABSc of ESOPs" in [40140], [52403]

My Business (April/May 2002, pp. 48); "The outside advantage" in [42705], [52712]

My Business (June/July 2004, pp. 48); "The Attention Getter" in [551], [1904], [4350], [38713], [46691]

My Business (June/July 2004, pp. 13); "The Bulls are Back" in [14814], [32287], [37931]

My Business (February/March 2003, pp. 15); "The Change Up: Find New Uses for Your Products" in [46795], [48711], [50572], [50846], [51585]

My Business (April/May 2003, pp. 26-28, 30-32); "The Great Comeback" in [28229], [36233]

My Business (October/November 2002, pp. 46); "The Home Office Deduction" in [42640], [54593]

My Business (October/November 2003, pp. 36-39); "The Juggling Act" in [28368], [36390], [39423]

My Business (April/May 2004, pp. 16); "The Juice is Loose" in [28369], [36392]

My Business (November/December 2001, pp. 17); "The Language of Business" in [27414], [43731]

My Business (October/November 2003, pp. 43); "The Language of Sales" in [688], [47184]

My Business (June/July 2004, pp. 46); "The Low Down" in [42330], [45385]

My Business (October/November 2002, pp. 49); "The Need for Tort Reform" in [8794], [29395], [40544], [42684]

My Business (April/May 2002, pp. 36-39); "The Root of the Business: Drawing on one's ethnicity leads to a passionate niche" in [35630], [52784]

My Business (April/May 2004, pp. 28-34); "The Secret Life of a Tightwad" in [27171], [36727]

My Business (April/May 2004, pp. 14); "The Time is Now" in [32747], [35116], [45742]

My Business (November/December 2001, pp. 13-14); "They'll Get Your Goat (Milk)" in [4267], [23445], [35694]

My Business (June/July 2004, pp. 45); "They've Got Mail - From You" in [47629], [51868]

My Business (September/October 2001, pp. 50); "Think Happy Thoughts" in [28891], [32742]

My Business (June/July 2002, pp. 26-32); "3 Ways to improve your business by getting a life" in [36859], [54994]

My Business (April/May 2002, pp. 18); "Throwing Money at Technology Isn't the Solution" in [45738], [49318]

My Business (June/July 2004, pp. 54); "Time Saver" in [12313], [34603]

My Business (October/November 2003, pp. 11); "To Fax or Not to Fax?" in [814], [40773], [47648]

My Business (October/November 2003, pp. 56); "Top-Heavy: The Pitfalls of Overhiring" in [42442], [45752]

My Business (February/March 2004); "Trailblazing Entrepreneurs Prove that Hot Businesses Aren't Always Found in Industry Hotbeds" in [35704], [39639]

My Business (June/July 2002, pp. 45); "Truly 'Small' Business" in [4319], [34629], [37805], [56769]

My Business (October/November 2003, pp. 58); "Uncommon Enterprise: A Tall Order" in [12211], [12312], [36831]

My Business (November/December 2001, pp. 54); "Uncommon Enterprise: An inn that's down to earth" in [12491], [35709]

My Business (June/July 2004, pp. 56); "Uncommon Enterprise: Breaking Up is Easy to Do" in [7072], [37806]

My Business (April/May 2003, pp. 54); "Uncommon Enterprise: Chasing Business" in [36900], [38940], [52601]

My Business (April/May 2002, pp. 54); "Uncommon Enterprise: Coffee, Tea or Fax?" in [7847], [9666], [11357], [15946]

My Business (February/March 2004, pp. 52); "Uncommon Enterprise: Feed Me!" in [10576]

My Business (June/July 2002, pp. 54); "Uncommon Enterprise: On the Map" in [9646], [37807]

My Business (December/January 2004, pp. 58); "Uncommon Enterprise: Rain Man" in [25707], [36901], [52602]

My Business (December/January 2003, pp. 54); "Uncommon Enterprise: Sinking Ships" in [16747], [56455]

My Business (April/May 2002, pp. 54); "Uncommon Enterprise: Sweet Dreams" in [26553]

My Business (April/May 2004, pp. 12-13); "Up Front: Broad Brand" in [47683], [50698]

My Business (February/March 2004, pp. 10-11); "Up Front: Seeking Help" in [42448], [45781]

My Business (December/January 2004, pp. 10-11); "Up Front: Stacking Up Sales Overseas" in [3138], [36904], [43866]

My Business (October/November 2003, pp. 10-11); "Up Front: Supersize It? No Thanks!" in [11672], [36905], [46470], [56458]

My Business (April/May 2003, pp. 8-9); "Up Front: Thinking Outside the Box" in [28944], [47684], [50699]

My Business (June/July 2002, pp. 13-14); "Upfront: Be Flexible or Fold" in [30035], [36907], [45783], [48466], [56459]

My Business (April/May 2002, pp. 13-14); "Upfront: Don't Say That" in [3603], [47685], [50700], [56460]

My Business (October/November 2002, pp. 13-14); "Upfront: Saddle Up" in [31895], [36908]

My Business (December/January 2004, pp. 40); "Wants vs. Needs: How to Shop Wisely for Technology" in [5168], [6853], [49352], [49561]

My Business (December/January 2003, pp. 24); "Weighing Wireless Options" in [6190], [6855], [49353]

My Business (June/July 2004, pp. 36-40); "Well Connected" in [34689], [36929]

My Business (October/November 2003, pp. 43); "What Makes You Great? Close Deals by Selling Value" in [51900]

My Business (November/December 2001, pp. 47); "What to Pay" in [35139], [42459], [45812]

My Business (April/May 2003, pp. 16); "What Works For You?" in [13516], [43420]

My Business (February/March 2003, pp. 42); "What's New for 2002 Returns?" in [40829], [54867]

My Business (February/March 2003, pp. 44); "What's Your Fiscal Year" in [40831], [54869]

My Business (February/March 2003, pp. 24); "What's Your 'ROI?" in [4856], [23258], [49358]

My Business (November/December 2001, pp. 48); "When a partner doesn't work out" in [39674], [50259]

My Business (June/July 2004, pp. 41); "When You Speak, Lawmakers Listen" in [8326], [26957], [29580], [31606], [39676], [40834], [50261]

My Business (April/May 2003, pp. 46); "Where Are You Going?" in [28999], [30044], [30628], [36953], [47738]

My Business (December/January 2003, pp. 47); "Where Small Business Stands: Your Voice Sends A Clear Message to Lawmakers" in [40836], [54872]

My Business (October/November 2003, pp. 55); "Why I Love My Lawyer" in [29584]

My Business (December/January 2003, pp. 28-31); "Why Image Matters" in [3614], [4321], [4480], [7512], [11221], [12919], [20163], [39685], [47746], [50708]

My Business (August/September 2002, pp. 54); "Working out the Bugs" in [4322]

My Business (April/May 2003, pp. 14); "Working With Women" in [36989], [45871], [56516]

My Business (June/July 2004, pp. 51); "You Should Be the Boss of Them" in [37003], [45880]

My Business (October/November 2002, pp. 35-37); "Yours, Mine, Ours" in [43047], [49476]

"My Favorite Fiascos" in *Fast Company* (November 2001, pp. 38) [36517], [47306], [51256]

My First Haircut [11815]

"My First Home" in *Black Enterprise* (Vol. 35, January 2005, No. 6) [17421], [20603]

"My Focus Is My Children" in *Inc.* (October 1, 2003) [21568], [36518], [56329]

My Friend's Place [8567]

"My Gadget" in *My Business* (August/September 2002, pp. 24-25) [6731], [25576], [25705], [27661], [31788], [34221], [36519], [47307], [49154], [49519], [51175], [51257]

My Girlfriend's Kitchen [7795], [8290]

My Gym Children's Fitness Center [19521]

My Herbal Water Cure: An Encyclopedia of Herbology [12150]

My Homemade Business [25904], [34222], [47308]

"My Kind of Town" in *Entrepreneur* (Vol. 33, January 2005, No. 1, pp. 27) [44101], [52702]

"My Life as a Blogger: A Growing Number of VCs Are Opening Themselves Up in Online Diaries" in *Venture Capital Journal* (Jan. 1, 2005) [14263], [34223], [53872], [55740]

"My, Oh, Miami" in *Entrepreneur* (Vol. 30, No. 2, February 2002, pp. 20) [25217], [30380]

"My Own Private Way to Go" in *Working Woman* (Vol. 25, No. 7, August 2000, pp. 86) [952], [30381], [56330]

"My Short, Unhappy Life as an E-Tailer" in *Fortune* (Vol. 140, No. 11, December 6, 1999, pp. 313+) [18629], [33464]

"My 'Won't Do' List" in *My Business* (February/March 2003, pp. 49) [36520], [39484], [54971]

"MyDoom Computer Worm Strikes Again" in *St. Louis Post-Dispatch* (February 18, 2005) [6732], [14264], [22304]

Mykytyn Consulting Group Inc. [3773], [3979], [16649], [30104], [31419], [46089]

"Myms, pings and vortals" in *The New York Times* (March 27, 2000, pp. D4, H4) [14265], [27447], [34224]

"MyPayNet" in *Entrepreneur.com* (Vol. 34, January 2006, No. 1, pp. 6) [199], [2931], [4736], [23094], [26297], [31567], [34225], [53381]

Myrtle Beach Area–Small Business Development Center [64695]

Myrtle Beach Area Chamber of Commerce [64771]

"MySay: Hiring Help" in *My Business* (December/January 2003, pp. 49) [20229], [42354], [45453]

"MySpace for Business: Are You Connected?" in *Sales & Marketing Management* (Vol. 158, November-December 2006, No. 11, pp. 20) [34226], [47309], [51740]

"The Mystery of ERM" in *Rough Notes* (Vol. 145, No. 1, January 2003, pp. 52) [13391], [43284]

"Mystery Shopper Reports Lead to Several Firings at Roanoke, Va., Theater" in *Roanoke Times* (July 13, 2004) [17524], [31789]

"Mystery Shoppers Enjoy Being Spies" in *Atlanta Journal-Constitution* (January 29, 2005) [12600], [21569], [31048], [31790], [51258]

"Mystery Shoppers Help Provide Certainty for Several Major Companies" in *Chicago Tribune* (July 4, 2004) [31791], [51259]

"Mystery Shoppers Keep Eye on Customer Service" in *Washington Times* (July 8, 2004) [31792], [51260]

"Mystery Shoppers Take a Second Glance at Customer Service" in *Business Record* (Vol. 22, August 30, 2004, No. 35, pp. 1) [19420], [31793], [47310], [51261]

Mystic Chamber of Commerce [58551]

Mystic Seaport Museum, Inc.–G.W. Blunt White Library [16792]

"MyTechTool" in *My Business* (June/July 2002, pp. 24) [11160], [34227], [42683], [56331]

"The Myth of Benign 'Resistance'" in *Hispanic Business* (Vol. 23, No. 7/8, July/August 2001, pp. 28) [40061], [48318]

"The Myth of the Superstar CEO" in *Venture Capital Journal* (November 1, 2004) [4737], [23095], [29392], [45454], [53382], [55741]

N

N-Hance [10540]

NA - The Material Handling & Logistics Show & Conference [11958]

NAA Reporter [5483]

NAACLS News [17214]

NAADAC The Association for Addiction Professionals [54325]

"Nab your Niche" in *Entrepreneur* (Vol. 31, No. 6, June 2003, pp. 100) [7431], [47311], [50638]

NAB Radio Show and World Media Expo [24485]

NAB RadioWeek [20356]

NAB TV Today [24475]

NAB World [24476]

NABJ Update [9034]

Nach-O Fast–Corn Dog Factory Intl. [21902]

Nicholas J. Naclerio and Associates Inc. [8657]

NACO Update on Job Training [15900], [33303]

Nacogdoches County Chamber of Commerce [65409]

NACOMEX Insider [335], [10284], [29043], [38492]

NACS [7788]

"NADA Was a Success and Then Some" in *Automotive News* (Vol. 79, February 7, 2005, No. 6133, pp. 12) [18095], [46381]

NADA's AutoExec Magazine [18182]

Nadasdy Ferenc Museum–Library [25351], [30472]

NAEB Bulletin [50766]

NAEMT News [1090]

The NAFE Guide to Starting Your Own Business: A Handbook for Entrepreneurial Women [56332]

NAGMR [2391], [3411], [16700]

NAHC Report [12400]

"NAHREP Set to Host Confab" in *Hispanic Business* (Vol. 23, No. 10, October, 2001, pp. 104) [20604], [20948], [47312]

NAHWW Newsletter [9035]

NAI McCabe-Henley [21087]

"NAIAS Spotlight Shines on Design" in *Crain's Detroit Business* (Vol. 23, January 1, 2007, No. 1, pp. 1) [28523], [29939], [55129]

Nail Manufacturers Council [17851]

"Nail the Sale: Need Some Surefire Ways to Seal the Deal with Customers?" in *Entrepreneur* (Vol. 33, March 2005, No. 3, pp. 86) [51741]

"NAIOP Awards" in *Atlanta Business Chronicle* (Vol. 25, December 6, 2002, No. 26, pp. 12C) [1522], [7432], [18552]

"Naked at Work: Psst! The Boss is Watching" in *Black Enterprise* (Vol. 34, No. 5, December 2003, pp. 55) [22305], [23034], [41852], [42883], [49155], [51176]

Nalco Company–Library [25734]

"Nall Launches Video Game Co." in *San Fernando Valley Business Journal* (Vol. 11, December 2006, No. 25, pp. 27) [9732], [14266], [32160]

NALS, the Association for Legal Professionals [25510]

NAMA National Expo - National Automatic Merchandising Association [51437]

NAMA Spring Expo [51438]

"Name that Domain" in *Entrepreneur* (Vol. 33, March 2005, No. 3, pp. 53) [14267], [24709], [25218], [25905]

"The Name Game" in *Entrepreneur* (Vol. 33, January 2005, No. 1, pp. 72) [29393], [47313], [50639]

"The Name Game-Spending millions on a domain name?" in *PC Computing* (April 2000, pp. 108) [14268], [34228]

"The Name Game" in *Venture Capital Journal* (Vol. 42, No. 10, October 2002, pp. 35-37) [35578], [39069]

"Name Grab-Cypersquaters, once a mere nuisance, now can go to prison for violating your trademark" in *PC Computing* (April 2000, pp. 40) [29394], [34229], [44102]

The Name Principle [47817]

"Name Your Price" in *Entrepreneur* (Vol. 33, September 2005, No. 9, pp. 108) [30214], [31049]

"Named Insured Wording: Doing It Right" in *Rough Notes* (Vol. 146, No. 3, March 2003, pp. 78) [13392], [43285]

NAMES News Today [17132]

Naming Your Business and Its Products and Services [44103]

NAMM International Music Market [17805], [21154]

NAMM, the International Music Products Association [17579]

NAMM PlayBack [17796]

NAMM - Summer Session [21155]

Nampa Chamber of Commerce [59320]

NAMS News Online [23775]

NAMSB News [5740]

The NAMSB Show [5747]

Nancy's Pizzeria [19690]

Nando's Chicken [21903]

"Nanomaterials: The Road to Lilliput" in *Red Herring* (No. 99, June 15 & July 1, 2001, pp. 48-50) [41853], [50929]

"Nanotech Grows" in *Red Herring* (No. 99, June 15 & July 1, 2001, pp. 46-47) [28524], [41854], [50930]

"Nanotech Steve Jurvetson" in *Venture Capital Journal* (January 1, 2005) [40542], [41855], [52156], [55742]

"Nanotechnology sector analysis" in *Red Herring* (March 2003, pp. 62) [28525], [46382], [50931], [52157]

Nantucket Island Chamber of Commerce [60977]

Napa Chamber of Commerce [57653]

Napa Valley College–Small Business Development Center [57266]

Napa Valley Genealogical & Biographical Society–Library [11058]

Napa Valley Wine Library Association–Library [23583]

Naperville Area Chamber of Commerce [59608]

Napoleon - Henry County Chamber of Commerce [63749]

Nappanee Area Chamber of Commerce [59975]

"The Napsterization of B2B" in *Harvard Business Review* (Vol. 78, No. 6, November-December 2000, pp. 18) [34230]

NAQP News [7851]

Narcotics Anonymous [54326]

Narcotics and Drug Abuse [54337]

NARDA Independent Retailer [7753]

NARHA Strides [12465]

Narragansett Chamber of Commerce [64669]

"Narrowing the divide" in *Black Enterprise* (Vol. 32, No. 10, May 2002, pp. 26) [14269], [34231]

NARSA National Newsletter [22635]

NASA Industrial Applications Center (Los Angeles) [67299]

NASA Industrial Applications Center (Pittsburgh) [67306]

"NASA Logs on for Team Encounter in Space" in *Houston Business Journal* (Vol. 34, No. 18, September 12, 2003, pp. 1) [40062], [41856], [50932], [52158]

"NASA Offers Free Rocket Scientists" in *Inc.* (August 1, 2004) [35579], [41471], [52022]

NASA/Southern Technology Applications Center [58720]

"NASA Training Program" in *Black Enterprise* (Vol. 30, No. 10, May 2000, pp. 52) [30918], [33180], [48319]

"NASD Ruling 'Unprecedented' in Duncan-Williams Victory" in *Memphis Business Journal* (Vol. 25, No. 16, August 15, 2003, pp. 1) [10098], [15286]

The Nash & Cibinic Report [27558], [40115], [40868]

Nashoba Valley Chamber of Commerce [60978]

Nashville Area Chamber of Commerce [64960]

Nashville-Berrien Chamber of Commerce [59143]

Nashville Business Journal [65016]

Nashville Minority Business Development Center [64989]

NASPO Newsletter [50767]

"Nassau County Executive Tom Suozzi Proposes Empire Zone" in *Long Island Business News* (March 5, 2004) [29431], [30161], [50104], [52703]

"Nassau County's New Taxi and Limousine Commission to Begin its Work Soon" in *Long Island Business News* (March 5, 2004) [15953], [16183], [23907], [24236]

"Nassau Democrats Propose Reforms to Prevent Mismanagement" in *Long Island Business News* (March 12, 2004) [32583], [40543]

NASSCO - Setting the Industry Standards for the Rehabilitation of Underground Utilities [22715]

Nasus Publishing [61737]

Natchez-Adams County Chamber of Commerce [61819]

Natchitoches Area Chamber of Commerce [60659]

Nathan's [21904]

"Nathan's Reverses Loss, Posts Third Quarter Profit" in *Long Island Business News* (February 13, 2004) [21570], [36521]

Nation-wide General Rental Centers, Inc. [21382]

National Academy of Arbitrators [17038]

National Academy of Opticianry [25632]

National Academy of Public Administration [50350]

National Academy of Recording Arts and Sciences [21135]

National Accounts Management [51526]

National Accrediting Agency for Clinical Laboratory Sciences [17179]

National Accrediting Commission of Cosmetology Arts and Sciences [11774]

National Adult Day Services Association [438]

National Advertising Review Board [524], [50534]

National Aeronautics and Space Administration
    Ames Research Center–Small Business Specialist [67288]
    Goddard Space Flight Center–Small Business Specialist [67289]
    Jet Propulsion Laboratory–Contractor Capabilities Office [67290]
    Johnson Space Center–Small Business Specialist [67291]
    Kennedy Space Center–Small Business Specialist [67292]
    Langley Research Center–Small Business Specialist [67293]
    Marshall Space Flight Center–Small Business Specialist [67294]
    Office of Small and Disadvantaged Business Utilization [67287]
    Resident Office-JPL–Small Business Specialist [67295]
    Small Business Innovation Research Office [67296]
    John C. Stennis Space Center–Small Business Specialist–Procurement Office [67297]

National Aeronautics and Space Administration (NASA)–John H. Glenn Research Center at Lewis Field–Small Business Specialist [67298]

National Agri-Marketing Association-Directory of Members [26524]

National Agricultural Aviation Association-Membership Directory [48864]

National Agricultural Bankers Conference [10332], [38507], [55231]

National Air Carrier Association [942]

National Air Transportation Association [943]

National Air Transportation Association-Aviation Business Resource Book and Official Membership Directory [953]

"National Alliance Promotes Professionalism Through Education" in *Rough Notes* (Vol. 145, No. 9, September 2002, pp. 112) [20605], [33181]

National Animal Control Association–Research Library [1223], [1279], [19135]

National Animal Damage Control Association [19016]

National Antique and Art Dealers Association of America [1308]

National Antique & Art Dealers Association of America-Membership Directory [1325]

National Apartment Association [20782]

National Appliance Parts Suppliers Association [1406]

National Appliance Parts Suppliers Association Annual Convention [1423]

National Appliance Parts Suppliers Association-Membership Roster [1414]

National Appliance Service Association [1407]

National Art Materials Trade Association [1680]

National Asphalt Pavement Association [2540]
    Charles R. Foster Technical Library [2551]

National Association of Addiction Treatment Providers [54327]

National Association of Bar and Tavern Owners [2326]

National Association of Barber Boards of America [11775]

National Association of Beverage Importers [16224]

National Association of Black Accountants [41]

"National Association of Black Accountants" in *Black Enterprise* (Vol. 35, December 2004, No. 5, pp. 86) [200], [12601], [26298], [48320]

National Association of Black Accountants-News Plus [336]

National Association of Boards of Examiners of Long Term Care Administrators [18307]

National Association of Boards of Pharmacy–Library [8874]

National Association of Broadcasters [20291], [24363]
    Information Resource Center [20382]

National Association of Business Consultants [3496]

National Association for Business Economics [58694]

National Association Business Economics Annual Meeting [32827]

National Association for Business Organizations [3942], [39118], [42567], [52803]

National Association of Casino Party Operators [10854], [18750]

National Association of Catering Executives [4527]

National Association of Chain Drug Stores [8767]
    Resource Center [8875]

National Association of Child Care Professionals [5325]

National Association of College Stores [3022]

National Association of Colleges and Employers [9186]
    Information Center [4464]

National Association of Colleges and Employers-Spotlight [9253]

National Association of Competitive Mounted Orienteering [12450]

National Association of Computer Consultant Businesses [6156], [6460]

National Association of Concessionaires [7083]

National Association of Convenience Stores [7767]
    NACS Information Center [7801]

National Association of Credit Management [8343], [8371], [31509]

National Association of Cruise-Oriented Agencies [25133]

National Association of Development Companies [44455], [55469]

National Association of Development Organizations Research Foundation [32218]

National Association of Diaper Services [8674]

National Association of Directors of Nursing Administration in Long Term Care [18308]

National Association of Display Industries [26071], [49479]

National Association of Dog Obedience Instructors [19107]

National Association for Drama Therapy-Membership List [48865]

National Association on Drug Abuse Problems [54328]

National Association for the Education of Young Children [5326]

National Association for the Education of Young Children Annual Conference [5416]

National Association of Electrical Distributors [9058]

National Association of Entrepreneurial Parents [39119]

National Association of Equity Source Banks [55470]

"National Association for the Exchange of Industrial Resources" in *Entrepreneur* (Vol. 33, August 2005, No. 8, pp. 4) [39485], [40904], [42271], [44235], [46383], [54667]

National Association of Executive Recruiters [9548], [42160]

National Association of Executive Secretaries Annual Conference [25529]

National Association of Export Companies [12930], [43515]

National Association of Federally Licensed Firearms Dealers [11721]

National Association for Female Executives [56098]

National Association of Fleet Administrators [2068]
    Fleet Information Resources Center [18215]

National Association of Fleet Resale Dealers [17953]

National Association of Flood and Storm Water Management Agencies [8420]

National Association of Floor Covering Distributors [10502]

National Association of Floor Covering Distributors-Membership Directory [10513]

National Association of Floor Covering Distributors-News and Views [10523]

National Association of Foreign-Trade Zones [43516]

National Association of General Merchandise Representatives Annual Convention [16709]

National Association of Government Guaranteed Lenders [39783]

National Association of Health Underwriters [13165]

National Association of Hispanic Publications [18837], [48002]

National Association of Home Based Businesses [42568]

National Association of Home Based Businesses Convention [42783]

National Association of Home Builders [7222]

National Association for Home Care and Hospice [12364]

National Association of Independent Fee Appraisers [1434]

National Association of Independent Fee Appraisers-National Membership Directory [1445]

National Association of Independent Lighting Distributors [9105]

National Association of Independent Publishers [2662], [8595]

National Association of Independent Resurfacers [3097]

National Association for Industry-Education Cooperation [32898], [42813]
    Library [33387]

National Association of Insurance Commissioners–NAIC Support and Services Office–Research Library [13605]

National Association of Insurance and Financial Advisors [13166]

National Association of Insurance Women International [13167]

National Association of Investigative Specialists [19953]

National Association of Investment Companies [48003], [55471]

National Association of Jewelry Appraisers [1435], [15830]

National Association of Legal Investigators [19954]

National Association of Limited Edition Dealers [5890], [18276]

National Association of Litho Clubs [19851]

National Association of Manufacturers [46173]

National Association of Master Appraisers [1436], [20405]

National Association of Master Appraisers-Membership Directory [1446]

National Association Meeting Planners & Conference/Convention Directors [1736], [24982]

National Association for Membership Development [33331]

National Association of Minority Automobile Dealers [17954], [48004]

National Association of Mortgage Brokers [17349]

National Association of Nurse Massage Therapists [17001]

National Association of Off-Track Betting [10855]

National Association of Optometrists and Opticians [25633]

National Association of Part-Time and Temporary Employees [49761]

National Association of Personal Financial Advisors [9793]

National Association of Personnel Services [9187], [24516]

National Association of Postmasters of the United States Convention [6119]

National Association of Printing Ink Manufacturers [19852]

National Association for Printing Leadership [19853]

National Association of Private Enterprise [52804]

National Association of Professional Background Screeners [19955]

National Association of Professional Band Instrument Repair Technicians [17836]

National Association of Professional Employer Organizations [24517]

National Association of Professional Geriatric Care Managers [18309]

National Association of Professional Insurance Agents [13168]
    Library [43458]

National Association of Professional Mortgage Women [17350]

National Association of Professional Pet Sitters [19067], [19190]

National Association of Professional Process Servers [17311]

National Association of Property Inspectors [3230]

National Association of Public Sector Equal Opportunity Officers [48516], [54123]

National Association of Publishers' Representatives [50535]

National Association of Quick Printers-Roster [19886]

National Association of Real Estate Appraisers [1437]

National Association of Real Estate Appraisers Annual Conference [1456], [20735]

National Association of Real Estate Brokers [17351], [20406]

National Association of Real Estate Buyer Brokers [17352]

National Association of Real Estate Companies [20783]

National Association of Real Estate Investment Trusts [20784]

National Association of Realtors [20407], [20785]
    Information Central [20768]

National Association of Realtors Trade Exposition [20736]

National Association of Recording Merchandisers [6135], [21136]

National Association of Rehabilitation Professionals in the Private Sector Annual Conference [19578]

National Association of Resale and Thrift Shops [7155]

National Association for Retail Marketing Services [51044]

National Association of Review Appraisers and Mortgage Underwriters **[17353]**, **[20408]**

National Association of Review Appraisers and Mortgage Underwriters Convention - National Conference & Expo **[17461]**

National Association of RV Parks and Campgrounds **[4228]**

National Association of RV Parks & Campgrounds-Buyers Guide and Membership Directory **[4237]**

National Association of School Music Dealers **[17580]**, **[17728]**

National Association of Schools of Dance **[8445]**

National Association of Schools of Music **[17581]**

National Association of Schools of Music-Directory **[17603]**

National Association of Security Companies **[22152]**

National Association for the Self-Employed **[52805]**, **[54297]**

National Association of Service Dealers **[6403]**

National Association of Small Business Investment Companies **[39120]**, **[55472]**

National Association for the Specialty Food Trade **[12000]**, **[23450]**

National Association of Sporting Goods Wholesalers **[22846]**, **[23597]**

National Association of Sporting Goods Wholesalers-Membership Directory **[23646]**

National Association of State Boards of Accountancy **[42]**

National Association of State Development Agencies **[43517]**

National Association of State Units on Aging **[18310]**

National Association for the Study and Performance of African-American Music **[17582]**

National Association of Tax Professionals **[43]**, **[23865]**

National Association of Teachers' Agencies-Membership Directory **[23376]**

National Association of Teachers of Singing **[17583]**

National Association of Television Program Executives **[24364]**

National Association of Theatre Owners **[17509]**

National Association for Variable Annuities **[13169]**

National Association of Video Distributors **[25588]**

National Association of Vision Professionals **[25634]**

National Association of Wholesaler-Distributors **[32134]**, **[56005]**

    Distribution Research and Education Foundation **[32186]**

National Association of Women Artists, Inc. News **[1629]**

National Association of Women Business Owners **[56099]**

National Association of Women in Construction **[7223]**

National Association of Women MBAs **[56100]**

National Auctioneers Association **[1767]**, **[9545]**

National Auctioneers Association National Convention **[1869]**

National Audubon Society–Aullwood Audubon Center and Farm–Library **[9502]**

National Auto Auction Association **[1768]**, **[17955]**

National Auto Auction Association-Membership Directory **[1836]**

National Auto Body Council **[22596]**

National Automatic Merchandising Association **[25571]**

National Automobile Dealers Association **[17956]**

National Automotive Radiator Service Association **[22597]**

National Automotive Radiator Service Association Annual Trade Show and Convention **[22654]**

National Ayurvedic Medical Association **[19559]**

National Ballroom and Entertainment Association **[8446]**

National Barbecue Association **[4528]**, **[21425]**

National Beauty Culturists' League **[7873]**, **[11776]**

National Beauty Show - HAIRWORLD **[7927]**, **[11817]**

National Bed-and-Breakfast Association **[2420]**

National Beer Wholesalers Association **[16225]**

National Beer Wholesalers Association Convention and Exposition **[3154]**

National Bicycle Dealers Association **[2493]**

National Bicycle League **[2494]**

National Black Child Development Institute **[5327]**

National Black Masters of Business Administration Annual Conference and Exposition **[48632]**

National Black MBA Association **[32899]**, **[48005]**

National Black McDonald's Operators Association **[21426]**

National Board for Certified Counselors and Affiliates **[4389]**

National Board of Examiners in Optometry **[25635]**

The National Bowling Association **[3098]**

National Bridal Market **[3221]**

National Brotherhood of Skiers **[22847]**

National Bulk Vendors Association **[25572]**

National Bureau of Certified Consultants Inc. **[3774]**, **[3980]**, **[16650]**, **[31420]**, **[46090]**

National Bureau of Economic Research **[24210]**

National Burglar and Fire Alarm Association **[22153]**

National Bus Trader **[24761]**

National Bus Traffic Association **[24226]**

National Business Association **[52806]**

National Business Aviation Association **[944]**

National Business Aviation Association Annual Meeting & Convention **[971]**

National Business and Disability Council **[9188]**

National Business Education Association **[32900]**

National Business Incubation Association **[13046]**, **[52807]**

National Business Travel Association **[30279]**

National Cable and Telecommunications Association **[4080]**, **[24365]**

National Cable Television Institute **[4081]**, **[24366]** Resource Center **[4158]**

National Career Development Association **[4390]**

National Caricaturist Network **[5957]**

National Cartoon Museum–Library **[5942]**

National Catholic Cemetery Conference **[10794]**

National Catholic Pharmacists Guild of the United States **[8768]**

National Cattlemen's Beef Association **[4058]** Library **[4076]**

National Center for Appropriate Technology–Library **[1576]**, **[7690]**

National Center for Bicycling and Walking **[2495]**

National Center for Home Equity Conversion **[17354]**

National Center for Manufacturing Sciences **[46551]**

National Center for Mediation Education **[17039]**

National Center for Policy Analysis **[24211]**

National Center for Public Policy Research **[3775]**, **[31421]**, **[50379]**

National Center for Technology Planning **[42145]**

National Chimney Sweep Guild **[5463]**

National Chincoteague Pony Association **[1175]**

National Christmas Tree Association **[5477]**

National Citizens Coalition for Nursing Home Reform **[18311]**

National City Chamber of Commerce **[57654]**

National City Equity Partners, Inc. **[63854]**

National Clearinghouse for Alcohol and Drug Information–Library **[54384]**

The National Clothesline **[8920]**

National Coalition for Campus Children's Centers **[5328]**

National Coalition for Cancer Research **[40940]**

National Coffee Association of U.S.A. **[5765]**, **[11308]**

National College of Appraisal and Property Management **[3307]**

National College of Business and Technology **[60593]**

National College of Naturopathic Medicine–Library **[18504]**

National Committee on Planned Giving **[10729]**

National Community Pharmacists Association **[8769]**

National Community Pharmacists Association Convention and Exhibition **[8838]**

National Concierge Association **[7116]**

National Concrete Burial Vault Association **[10795]**

National Concrete Masonry Association **[16936]** Library **[16990]**

    Research and Development Laboratory **[16991]**

National Confectioners Association All Candy Expo **[4329]**

National Confectioners Association of the U.S. **[4271]**

National Confectionery Sales Association **[4272]**

National Conference on the Advancement of Research **[51020]**

National Conference of CPA Practitioners **[44]**

National Conference on Peacemaking and Conflict Resolution **[50775]**

National Conference of State Liquor Administrators-Official Directory **[2345]**

National Conference of States on Building Codes & Standards-Membership Directory **[3240]**

National Congress of Inventor Organizations **[44207]**

National Contact Lens Examiners **[25636]**

National Contract Management Association **[39975]**

National Convenience Store Distributors Association **[32135]**

National Cooperative Bank, Corporate Banking Div. **[38980]**

National Coordinating Committee for Multiemployer Plans **[26730]**

National Cosmetology Association **[7874]**, **[11777]**, **[17852]**

National Costumers Association **[7954]**

National Costumers Association Annual Convention **[5600]**, **[7956]**

National Council of Acoustical Consultants-Directory **[48866]**

National Council for Advanced Manufacturing **[46174]**

National Council Against Health Fraud **[40941]**

National Council on the Aging **[439]**

National Council of Agricultural Employers **[26462]**

National Council of Chain Restaurants **[10617]**, **[21427]**

National Council on Ethics in Human Research **[37381]**

National Council of Exchangors **[20409]**

National Council of the Housing Industry **[7224]**

National Council for Interior Design Qualification **[13629]**

National Council on International Trade Development **[43518]**

National Council of Investigation and Security Services **[19956]**, **[22154]**

National Council of Less Commonly Taught Languages **[25079]**

National Council on Problem Gambling **[10856]**

National Council of Self-Insurers **[43064]**

National Court Reporters Association **[25511]**

National Credentialing Agency for Laboratory Personnel **[17180]**

National Credit Union Administration–Office of Small and Disadvantaged Business Utilization **[67312]**

National Credit Union Administration (Region 1)–Albany Regional Office **[67307]**

National Credit Union Administration (Region 2)–Alexandria Regional Office **[67308]**

National Credit Union Administration (Region 3)–Atlanta Regional Office **[67309]**

National Credit Union Administration (Region 4)–Austin Regional Office **[67310]**

National Credit Union Administration (Region 5)–Tempe Regional Office **[67311]**

The National Culinary Review **[4561]**, **[21688]**, **[23537]**

National Custom Applicator Exposition **[26605]**

National Customs Brokers and Forwarders Association of America **[10662]**

National Customs Brokers & Forwarders Association of America-Membership Directory **[10684]**

National Dance Association **[8447]**

National Delinquency Survey **[20721]**

National Demolition Association **[7225]**

National Development Council **[32219]**

The National Dipper **[12796]**

National Directory of Adult Day Care Centers **[451]**

National Directory for Employment in Education **[23377]**

National Directory of Magazines **[5498]**

National Directory of Minority-Owned Business Firms **[48501]**

National Directory of Private Social Agencies **[41064]**

National Directory of Safety Consultants **[56573]**

National Directory of Woman-Owned Business Firms **[56333]**, **[56546]**

National Dog Groomers Association of America [19068]

National Drug Code Directory [8793]

National E-mail and Fax Directory [9665]

National Eating Disorder–Information Centre [18505], [26067]

National Eating Disorder Information Centre [18433]

National Economic Development and Law Center [32220]

National Electrical Contractors Association [9059]

National Electrical Manufacturers Association [9060]

National Electrical Manufacturers Representatives Association [9061]

National Electrical Manufacturers Representatives Association-Locator [9074]

National Electronic Distributors Association-Membership Directory [7739]

National Electronics Service Dealers Association [6404], [7711]

National Employment Counseling Association [4391]

"National" in *Entrepreneur* (Vol. 28, No. 10, October 2000, pp. 138) [35580], [46583]

National Environmental Balancing Bureau [1006]

National Environmental Health Association–Library [9503]

National Export Assistance Center–University of South Carolina–Small Business Development Center [64696]

National Eye Research Foundation [25676] Library [25671]

National Families in Action–Library [41354]

National Family Business Council [37581]

National Farm Medicine Center [56712]

National Federation of Abstracting and Information Services [13062]

National Federation of Community Broadcasters [20292]

National Federation of Filipino American Associations [35740]

National Federation of Hispanic Owned Newspapers [18838], [48006]

National Federation of Independent Business [40131]

National Federation of Professional Trainers [19366]

National Field Archery Association [1469]

National Financing Law Digest [10285]

National Fire Safety Engineering Inc. [3261]

National Fisheries Institute [10446]

National Fisherman [10469]

National Floor Trends Magazine [10524], [25542]

National Food Laboratory [7107]

National Food Service Management Institute [18434]

National Foreign Trade Council [12931]

National Forest Recreation Association [4229]

National Forum for Black Public Administrators [50351]

National Foundation for Credit Counseling [8344] Library [8363]

National Foundation for Teaching Entrepreneurship [35741], [56731]

National Frame Builders Association [7226]

National Franchise Associates Inc. [3902], [38981], [39017]

National Franchise Consultants [3903]

National Franchise Resources, Inc. [7667]

National Franchise Sales [3904], [38982]

National Frozen Food Convention [11709]

National Frozen Pizza Institute [19623]

National Frozen and Refrigerated Foods Association [11586]

National Frozen and Refrigerated Foods Association-Membership Directory [11644]

National Fund Raiser [10755]

National Funeral Directors Association [10796] Howard C. Raether Library [10818]

National Funeral Directors and Morticians Association [10797]

National Gardening Association [11414] Library [11530]

National Genealogical Society [10920] Library [11059]

National Genealogical Society Quarterly [10973]

National Glass Association [11214]

National Glaucoma Research Report [25657]

National Golf Foundation [11248], [17319]

National Green Pages [9485], [21246]

National Grocers Association [7768], [11587]

National Grocers Co. Ltd.–ISD Technical Library [11718]

National Guide to Funding in Arts and Culture [10738]

National Guide to Funding for Children, Youth and Families [10739]

National Guide to Funding for the Environment and Animal Welfare [10740]

National Guide to Funding in Health [10741]

National Guide to Funding in Higher Education [10742]

National Guide to Funding for Women and Girls [10743]

National Guide to Vehicle Leasing Suppliers and Services [2078]

National Guild of Community Schools of the Arts-Membership Directory [8453]

National Guild of Decoupeurs-Dialogue [8048]

National Guild of Professional Paperhangers [18699]

National Hardware Show - Lawn and Garden World [11909]

National Hardwood Lumber Association [16289] Library [16341]

National Hardwood Lumber Association-Members [16314]

National Head Start Association [5329]

National Health Council [12365]

National Health Policy Forum [40942]

National Highway and Airway Carriers Directory [25399]

National Hispanic Corporate Council [48007]

National Hispanic Council on Aging -News [1706]

National Home Buyers Assistance - NHBA [44696]

National Home Equity Mortgage Association [17355]

National Home Furnishings Association [12269]

National Honey Packers and Dealers Association [2467]

National Housing Endowment [7227]

National Housing Law Project [1399]

National Hunters Association, Inc.–Library [11746]

National Ice Cream Retailers Association [12762]

National Independent Automobile Dealers Association [17957]

National Indian Gaming Association [10857]

National Industrial Transportation League [10663]

National Information Infrastructure News [24477]

National Information Standards Organization [2663]

National Institute for Automotive Service Excellence [22598]

National Institute of Building Sciences [7703]

National Institute on Community-Based Long-Term Care [18312]

National Institute of Enviromental Heath Sciences–Small Business Administation [63471]

National Institute for Fitness and Sport [19607]

National Institute of Governmental Purchasing, Inc.–Specifications/Searchable Forms/Documents [40123]

National Institute of Pension Administrators [26731]

National Institute for Rehabilitation Engineering [19608]

National Institute of Relationship Enhancement [50789]

National Institute of Senior Housing [18313]

National Institutes of Health
Division of Contracts and Grants–Small and Disadvantaged Business Utilization Specialist [67536]
Stanford University–Center for Information Technology [13128]

National Insulation Association [7228], [13132]

National Insulation Association-Membership Directory and Resource Guide [13135]

National Insurance Association-Member Roster [13393]

National Insurance Professionals Corp. [3776], [13576]

National - Interstate Council of State Boards of Cosmetology [7875], [11778]

National Inventors Foundation [43980]

National Investment Company Service Association [14704]

National Investment Management, Inc. [58093]

National Investor Relations Institute [14705]

National Jeweler [15870]

National JobBank [23397]

National Kitchen and Bath Association [12270], [13630]

National Labor Relation Board (Region 30)–Milwaukee Regional Office [67313]

National Labor Relations Board [67314]
Office of Small and Disadvantaged Business Utilization [67315]

National Labor Relations Board (Region 1)–Boston Regional Office [67316]

National Labor Relations Board (Region 2)–New York Regional Office [67317]

National Labor Relations Board (Region 3)–Buffalo Regional Office [67318]

National Labor Relations Board (Region 4)–Philadelphia Regional Office [67319]

National Labor Relations Board (Region 6)–Pittsburgh Regional Office [67320]

National Labor Relations Board (Region 7)–Detroit Regional Office [67321]

National Labor Relations Board (Region 8)–Cleveland Regional Office [67322]

National Labor Relations Board (Region 9)–Cincinnati Regional Office [67323]

National Labor Relations Board (Region 10)–Atlanta Regional Office [67324]

National Labor Relations Board (Region 11)–Winston-Salem Regional Office [67325]

National Labor Relations Board (Region 12)–Tampa Regional Office [67326]

National Labor Relations Board (Region 13)–Chicago Regional Office [67327]

National Labor Relations Board (Region 14)–St. Louis Regional Office [67328]

National Labor Relations Board (Region 16)–Ft. Worth Regional Office [67329]

National Labor Relations Board (Region 17)–Overland Park Regional Office [67330]

National Labor Relations Board (Region 18)–Minneapolis Regional Office [67331]

National Labor Relations Board (Region 19)–Seattle Regional Office [67332]

National Labor Relations Board (Region 20)–San Francisco Regional Office [67333]

National Labor Relations Board (Region 21)–Los Angeles Regional Office [67334]

National Labor Relations Board (Region 22)–Newark Regional Office [67335]

National Labor Relations Board (Region 24)–Hato Rey Regional Office [67336]

National Labor Relations Board (Region 25)–Indianapolis Regional Office [67337]

National Labor Relations Board (Region 26)–Memphis Regional Office [67338]

National Labor Relations Board (Region 27)–Denver Regional Office [67339]

National Labor Relations Board (Region 28)–Phoenix Regional Office [67340]

National Labor Relations Board (Region 29)–Brooklyn Regional Office [67341]

National Labor Relations Board (Region 31)–Los Angeles Regional Office [67342]

National Labor Relations Board (Region 32)–Oakland Regional Office [67343]

National Labor Relations Board (Region 34)–Hartford Regional Office [67344]

National Labor Relations (Region 5)–Baltimore Regional Office [67345]

National Landscape Association [15997]

The National Law Journal [29675]

National League for Nursing [12366]

National Lighting Bureau [9106]

National Limousine Association [16177]

National Locksmith [16265]

National Luggage Dealers Association [16270]

National Lumber and Building Material Dealers Association [11875], [16290]

National Management Association [44714]

National Marine Bankers Association [16719]

National Marine Distributors Association [16720]

National Marine Electronics Association [16721]

National Marine Manufacturers Association [16722]

National Marine Representatives Association-Directory [16739]

National Meals on Wheels Foundation [440]
National Mechanical Contractors Council [7229]
National Minority Business Council [48008]
National Minority Supplier Development Council [48009]
National Mortgage News [17458]
National MultiCultural Institute [48517], [48652]
National Museum of Roller Skating–Archives [22842]
The National Needle Arts Association [8146], [22724]
National Needlework Association Trade Show [8091]
National Newspaper Publishers Association [18839]
National Occupational Competency Testing Institute Area Test Center Coordinators [15893]
National Office Paper Recycling Project [37230]
National Oil and Acrylic Painters' Society [5958]
National Opera Association-Membership Directory [17604]
National Optometric Association [25637]
National Paint and Coatings Association [18676], [18700]
National Park Service
    Business Utilization and Development Specialist–Alaska Region [67623]
    Business Utilization and Development Specialist–Business and Economic Development Program [67626]
    Business Utilization and Development Specialist–Intermountain Region [67625]
    Business Utilization and Development Specialist–Midwest Region [67629]
    Business Utilization and Development Specialist–National Capitol Region [67627]
    Business Utilization and Development Specialist–Northeast Region [67630]
    Business Utilization and Development Specialist–Pacific Northwest Region [67631]
    Business Utilization and Development Specialist–Pacific West Region [67624]
    Business Utilization and Development Specialist–Southeast Region [67628]
National Partnership for Social Enterprise [54124]
National Pavement Maintenance Exposition and Conference [2548]
National Pawnbrokers Association [18766]
National Pediculosis Association Inc. [33351]
The National Perspective [5357]
National Pest Management Association–Library [19048]
National Pest Management Association International [19017]
National Pesticide Information Retrieval System [19046]
National Petroleum News (Vol. 95, No. 13, December 2003, pp. 46) "Industry News; Coinstar Expands Self-Service Kiosk Line" in [5028], [7778], [15922], [34064]
National Petroleum News (Vol. 95, No. 11, October 2003, pp. 57); "Planar Monitors Address Kiosk and POS Applications" in [15935]
National Plumbing Codes Handbook [19750]
National Poker Association [10858]
National Prepared Food Festival [21707]
National Press Club–Eric Friedheim Library & News Information Center [9055], [24507]
National Prevention Network-Directory [54338]
National Private Truck Council [25364]
National Professional Service Convention and Trade Show [7755]
National Property Inspections [3280]
National Property Law Digests [20722], [21053]
National Property Management Association [20044]
National Public Radio–Broadcast Library [20383]
National Public Records Research Association [10921]
National Purchasing Institute [50747]
National Quartz Producers Council [16937]
National Quotation Service [15667]
National Real Estate Investor [20723], [21054]
The National Registry [20761], [21106]

National Research Council Canada
    Industrial Materials Institute [48850]
    Institute for Information Technology [7023]
    Social Sciences and Humanities Research Council of Canada [66738]
National Resource Center 41362
National Resource Center for Health and Safety in Child Care [5330]
National Restaurant Association [7084], [8507], [12050]
    Information Services and Library [22036]
    Quality Assurance Executive Study Group [10655]
National Restaurant Association Educational Foundation [7809], [10618], [21428]
National Restaurant Association Multi-Unit Architects, Engineers and Construction Officers [21429]
National Restauraunt Association Restaurant and Hotel-Motel Show [12685]
National Retail Federation [5638], [51045]
National Retail Hardware Association [11876]
National Rifle Association of America [1470]
    National Firearms Museum–Library [11747]
    NRA-ILA Library [11748]
    NRA Technical Library [1487]
National Roofing Contractors Association [22057]
National Roofing Contractors Association Annual Convention and Exhibit [22073]
National Roofing Contractors Association-Membership Directory [22066]
National Roofing Foundation [22058]
The National RV Trade Show [21195]
National Safe Workplace Institute/SafeSpaces.com [56548]
National Safety Council [56549]
    Library [56694]
National Safety Management Society [56550]
National Sash and Door Jobbers Association Bulletin [4487]
National Sash and Door Jobbers Association Convention [11229]
National School Supply & Equipment Association Fall Show [24278]
National Science Foundation
    Office of Small and Disadvantaged Business Utilization [67346]
    Small Business Innovation Research Programs [67347]
    Small Business Technology Transfer Program [67348]
National Search & Discovery [9276]
National Shaving Mug Collectors Association [1309], [5809]
National Shellfisheries Association [10447]
National Shoe Retailers Association [22752]
    Library [22778]
"National Shopping Service Announces 150,000th Mystery Shopper" in *Internet Wire* (October 26, 2004) [31794], [51262]
National Ski Patrol System [22848]
National Ski and Snowboard Retailers Association [22849], [23598]
National Small Business Association [39121], [52808], [58695]
National Small Business Benefits Association–Library [53134]
National Snow Industries Association [22850]
National Society of Accountants [45], [23866]
National Society of Accountants for Cooperatives [46]
National Society of Compliance Professionals [14706]
National Society of Environmental Consultants [9329]
National Society for Graphology [11855]
National Society of Hispanic MBAs [48010]
National Society of Professional Surveyors [23760]
National Society of Public Accountants Annual Convention [361], [26416]
National Society of the Sons of the American Revolution–Genealogy Library [11060]
National Society of the Sons of Utah Pioneers–Library [11061]
National Soft Drink Association–NSDA Information Center [7105], [22037]

National Solid Wastes Management Association [11928]
National Speakers Association [22458], [22589]
National Sporting Clays Association [1471]
National Sporting Goods Association [22851], [23599]
National Sporting Goods Association-Buying Guide [23627]
National Staff Development Council [23364]
National Standard Plumbing Code Committee [19739]
National Stationery Show [11574]
National Sugar Ingredient Marketing Association [3412]
"National Survey Finds More Small-Business Owners Planning to Increase Their Staffs" in *Long Island Business News* (January 30, 2004) [10099], [15287], [28526], [42355], [53873]
National Swimming Pool Foundation [23791]
National Tabletop and Giftware Association [11139], [12179]
National Tank Truck Carrier Directory [25400]
National Tank Truck Carriers [25365]
National Tattoo Association [23852]
National Tattoo Association Convention [23857]
National Tax Association - Tax Institute of America [47], [23867]
National Telephone Cooperative Association Annual Meeting & Expo [19808]
National Tenant Network [8413]
National Terrazzo and Mosaic Association [16938]
National Toll-Free 800 Guide to Real Estate Publications and Publishers [20606]
National Topical Stamp Show [5861]
National Tour Association [24654], [25134]
National Towing News [4364]
National Trade and Professional Associations of the U.S. [1737]
National Training Center of Polygraph Science [19991]
    Library [19995]
National Training and Simulation Association [15889]
"National Treasure" in *Entrepreneur* (Vol. 33, October 2005, No. 10, pp. 26) [36522], [37743], [39486]
National Truck Equipment Association [1888], [25366]
National Truck Equipment Association-Membership Roster & Product Directory [25401]
National Truck Leasing System [2069]
National Truck Rate Report [25439]
National Trust Company–Reference Library [9539]
National Underwriter Life & Health/Financial Services Edition [13586]
National Underwriter Life & Health-Financial Services Edition (Vol. 105, No. 42); "Small Businesses Now Can Afford Big Benefits" in [24042], [39931], [54763]
National Underwriter Property and Casualty/Risk and Benefits Management [13556]
National Underwriter Property & Casualty/Risk and Benefits Management Edition [13587]
"National Urban League: State of Black America" in *Black Enterprise* (Vol. 34, July 2004, No. 12, pp. 28) [7433], [28527], [32584], [33182]
National Vehicle Leasing Association [2070]
National Venture Capital Association [55473]
National Venture Capital Association-Membership Directory [55743]
"National trends in Webcast advertising" in *Crain's Detroit Business* (Vol. 16, No. 46, November 13, 2000, pp. 15) [14270], [34232], [47314]
National Wellness Institute-Member Directory [41065]
National Women's Business Council [56101]
"National Womens Business Council" in *Black Enterprise* (Vol. 34, No. 4, November 2003, pp. 62) [53534], [56334]
National Women's Sailing Association [5238]
National Writers Association [8966]
The National Yellow Book of Funeral Directors [10803]
Nations Bank–Business Resource Center [53135]

"Nation's busiest airports expand to ease delays" in *Atlanta Business Chronicle* (Vol. 25, No. 22, November 8, 2002, pp. 13C) **[30382]**

The Nation's Health **[41269]**

Nation's Restaurant News (Vol. 37, No. 45, November 10, 2003, pp. 47); "Star Quality: Celebrity Chefs Add Luster to Hotel Dining" in **[12638]**, **[21634]**

Nationwide Floor and Window Coverings **[10541]**, **[26083]**

Nationwide Franchise Marketing Services **[3905]**, **[38983]**

Native American Business Development Center **[61690]**

Native American Economic Development Project–Yankton Sioux Tribe **[64843]**

Native Americans for a Clean Environment–Resource Office Native Americans for a Clean Environment **[9504]**

Native Hawaiian Chamber of Commerce **[59256]**

Native Indian/Inuit Photographers' Association **[19287]**

Native Spirit **[19482]**

Native Venture Capital Co., Ltd. **[66667]**

NATSO–Membership Directory **[25402]**

Natural Foods Merchandiser **[12027]**

Natural Fruit Corp. **[12842]**

Natural Gas Partners (NGP) **[65620]**

"Natural Gas Prices Pinch Businesses" in *Tampa Tribune* (October 28, 2005) **[27154]**, **[39487]**

Natural Hazards Observer **[8425]**

Natural Hazards Research and Applications Information Center **[8421]**

"Natural Hedge" in *The Economist* (Vol. 377, October 1-7, 2005, No. 8446, pp. 72) **[15288]**, **[38237]**

"Natural Instinct" in *Entrepreneur* (Vol. 31, No. 8, August 2003, pp. 90) **[4053]**, **[11303]**, **[12151]**, **[12757]**, **[26447]**, **[35581]**

Natural Products Association **[12001]**

Natural Products Expo East **[9491]**, **[12077]**, **[55232]**

Natural Products Expo West **[9492]**

Natural Products Marketing Council **[9330]**, **[9479]**

Natural Resources Commission **[66919]**

"Natural Selection" in *Forbes* (Vol. 175, January 10, 2005, No. 1, pp. 144) **[12015]**, **[15289]**

Natural Waste Water Treatment **[25721]**

Naturalawn of America **[16160]**

"Nature Brings Uncertainty and Opportunity" in *Venture Capital Journal* (October 1, 2005) **[28528]**, **[55744]**

The Nature Conservancy
    Maine Chapter **[16102]**
    New Jersey Chapter Office **[39020]**
    Ohio Chapter **[11987]**

Nature Stone **[8718]**

"Nature's Way" in *Crain's Detroit Business* (Vol. 18, No. 19, May 13, 2002, pp) **[13663]**, **[18553]**, **[18604]**, **[49520]**

Naugatuck Chamber of Commerce **[58552]**

Nautilus Aerobics Plus: High Impact Aerobics **[19483]**

Nautilus Aerobics Plus: Low Impact Aerobics **[19484]**

Nauvoo Chamber of Commerce **[59609]**

Navajo-Churro Sheep Association **[1176]**

Naval Technical Representative Office (Laurel) **[67430]**

Navarre Beach Area Chamber of Commerce **[58898]**

Navarro College–Small Business Development Center **[65050]**

Navarro, Kim & Associates **[3777]**, **[3981]**, **[16651]**, **[27707]**, **[31422]**, **[46091]**, **[48642]**

"Navigate the Application Framework Terrain" in *E-business Advisor* (Vol. 18, No. 1, January 2000, pp. 16) **[23096]**, **[25906]**, **[34233]**, **[53383]**

Navigating with Marine Electronics: A Guide to DC **[16767]**

"Navigation-Technology Startup Seeks Investors" in *Portland Press Herald* (August 5, 2005) **[41857]**, **[55745]**

Navigator **[9394]**, **[45901]**

Navigator Research Group Inc. **[19992]**, **[35302]**

Navigator Technology Ventures / NTV **[61100]**

Navis Pack & Ship Centers **[6122]**

Navis Partners **[64677]**

"Navteq Corp." in *Crain's Chicago Business* (Vol. 30, January 2007, No. 4, pp. 36) **[14271]**, **[50091]**

Navy Inventory Control Point **[64583]**

"Navy assesses small-biz impact of intranet deal" in *Network World* (April 3, 2000, pp. NA) **[40063]**, **[43952]**

NAW Report **[56024]**

"NAWBO honors top business women" in *Crain's Detroit Business* (Vol. 16, No. 10, March 6, 2000, pp. 21) **[56335]**

The NAWIC Image **[7565]**

Nazareth Area Chamber of Commerce **[64478]**

Nazem and Co. **[63141]**

NBBJ **[6044]**

NBC Universal–Information Resource Center **[20384]**

NC Small Business and Technology Development Center–University of North Carolina **[63270]**

NCBA Newsletter **[17627]**

NCCLS-Update/Standards Status **[17215]**

NCPA Newsletter **[8825]**

NCPD National Update **[41270]**

"NCR Spinoff Hits Home" in *San Diego Business Journal* (Vol. 28, January 15, 2007, No. 3, pp. 38) **[6264]**, **[20230]**, **[29940]**, **[50092]**

NCSL - National Conference of State Legislatures Annual Meeting and Exhibition **[50376]**, **[55233]**

ND/SD Realtors Convention **[1390]**, **[55234]**

"NEA Fund 10 $2B Hard Cap" in *Venture Capital Journal* (Vol. 40, No. 10, October 2000, pp. 18, 20, 22) **[41858]**, **[44599]**, **[55746]**

Neal-Schuman Guide to Finding Legal and Regulatory Information on the Internet **[29086]**, **[40135]**

"Nearly Three Years Into an Economic Recovery" in *St. Louis Post-Dispatch* (October 15, 2004) **[32585]**, **[38238]**

NEARSBDC–University of Alabama at Huntsville–NE Alabama Regional Small Business Development Center **[56783]**

The Neatest Little FundLetter **[10286]**

Nebagamon Community Association **[66475]**

Nebraska Business Development Center **[33404]**

Nebraska Chamber of Commerce and Industry **[62282]**

Nebraska City Tourism and Commerce **[62283]**

Nebraska Department of Administration Services–The Central Data Processing Division **[66920]**

Nebraska Department of Economic Development–Industrial Training Programs **[62316]**

Nebraska Department of Labor **[66921]**

Nebraska Library Commission–Federal Document Librarian **[66922]**

Nebraska Ombudsman's Office **[62231]**

Nebraska Policy Research Office **[66923]**

Nebraska Procurement Technical Assistance Center–Nebraska Business Development Center **[62312]**

"NEC Solutions (America) Inc." in *Black Enterprise* (Vol. 34, No. 3, October 2003, pp. 58) **[45455]**

The NECA Show **[9090]**

"Neck and Neck" in *Entrepreneur* (Vol. 32, No. 1, January 2004, pp. 134) **[36523]**, **[38862]**

Neckwear Association of America **[9609]**

NEDA Business Consultants–New Mexico Statewide Minority Business Enterprise Center **[62719]**

Nederland Area Chamber of Commerce **[58409]**

Nederland Chamber of Commerce and Tourist Bureau **[65410]**

"Need to Boost Morale? Try Good Food, Fitness and Communication" in *Wall Street Journal* (May 28, 2002, pp. B1) **[27448]**, **[35000]**, **[45456]**

"The need for more, not less, quicker, not slower tax guidance" in *Tax Executive* (Vol. 52, No. 4, July 2000, pp. 323) **[54668]**

"The need for privacy" in *Crain's Detroit Business* (Vol. 18, No. 24, June) **[30383]**, **[53874]**

"Need Help? Don't Call Us" in *Inc.* (August 2005, pp. 36) **[31795]**, **[34234]**

"Need Money?" in *Inc.* (November 2006, pp.25-26) **[37841]**, **[55406]**

"The Need for Separate Accounts" in *Black Enterprise* (Vol. 35, October 2004, No. 3, pp. 48) **[201]**, **[2932]**, **[23993]**, **[26299]**

"The Need for Speed in New Millennium Leadership Styles" in *Employment Relations Today* (Vol. 27, No. 1, Spring 2000, pp. 61) **[34235]**, **[45457]**, **[53875]**

"The Need for Tort Reform" in *My Business* (October/November 2002, pp. 49) **[8794]**, **[29395]**, **[40544]**, **[42684]**

"Needbucks.com" in *Forbes* (January 10, 2000, pp. 188) **[29751]**, **[55407]**

"Needed on the Frontline" in *Pittsburgh Business Times* (Vol. 23, No. 8, September 12, 2003, pp. 19) **[41066]**, **[48768]**, **[56336]**

"Needful things?" in *Entrepreneur* (Vol. 30, No. 12, December 2002, pp. 109) **[36524]**, **[47315]**, **[51742]**

Needham Asset Management **[63142]**

Needles Area Chamber of Commerce **[57655]**

Needlework and Accessories Trade Show/Charlotte **[8092]**, **[8246]**, **[19828]**

Needlework Retailer **[1691]**, **[8216]**

"Needs Toner: Facing Rivals, Lexmark Shares Could Go Lower" in *Barron's* (July 28, 2003, pp. 15) **[6733]**, **[10100]**, **[15290]**, **[30919]**, **[46384]**

"Negotiate from Strength" in *Success* (Vol. 47, No. 3, July 2000, pp. 74) **[27449]**, **[51743]**

"Negotiating the spirit of a deal" in *Harvard Business Review* (Vol. 81, No. 2, February 2003, pp. 66) **[27450]**, **[45458]**

"Negotiating without a net. A conversation with the NYPD's Dominick J. Misino" in *Harvard Business Review* (Vol. 80, Oct. 2002, pp. 49) **[27451]**, **[36525]**, **[45459]**

Negotiating Profitable Sales **[51967]**

Negotiating the Purchase or Sale of a Business **[30690]**, **[52441]**

"Negotiating Tips" in *Black Enterprise* (Vol. 37, December 2006, No. 5, pp. 70) **[2726]**, **[3044]**, **[33183]**, **[35001]**, **[45460]**

Negotiating to Win **[27270]**

Negotiating to Win (Canada) **[27271]**

"Neighborhood Mortgage Announces Office Expansion" in *Bellingham Business Journal* (December 2006, pp. 2) **[17422]**, **[28529]**, **[30162]**, **[30571]**

Neillsville Area Chamber of Commerce **[66476]**

Nelson Capital Corp. **[64999]**

Raymond Nelson Distribution Consultants **[20248]**

The Nelson Group Ltd. **[3778]**, **[16652]**, **[30105]**, **[31423]**, **[35246]**, **[38565]**, **[46092]**, **[53107]**

Nelson Information's Directory of Investment Research **[15291]**

"Nemes Allen Merges with Wisconsin Firm; Accountants to Pursue Middle-Market Clients" in *Crain's Detroit Business* (Vol. 19, No. 44) **[202]**, **[2933]**, **[23994]**, **[50093]**

"Nemes Allen Merges with Wisconsin Firm" in *Crain's Detroit Business* (Vol. 19, No. 44, November 3, 2003, pp. 1) **[203]**, **[2934]**, **[23995]**, **[50094]**

Nenana Chamber of Commerce **[56969]**

Neocarta Ventures, Inc. **[61101]**

NeoCon South **[10529]**, **[13710]**

"Neon Sign Makers Light Up Reading, Pa. Area" in *Reading Eagle* (September 21, 2003) **[1952]**, **[22793]**

Neponset Valley Chamber of Commerce **[60979]**

NERAC, Inc. **[67300]**

"Nervous About Bidding on eBay?" in *New York Times* (November 17, 2003, pp. C7) **[1837]**, **[13394]**, **[34236]**, **[43286]**

Nesbitt Burns **[59752]**

Ness City Chamber of Commerce **[60391]**

Ness County Historical Society–Library **[11062]**

Nestle Toll House Cafe by Chip **[2308]**

"Nestle pushes a gooey popcorn treat" in *Wall Street Journal* (February 5, 2003, pp. B4B) **[4300]**, **[17525]**

"Net Attacks to Plague Small and Midsize Firms" in *Network World* (October 16, 2000, pp. 108) **[34237]**, **[53876]**

"Net Company: Don't Shout, Listen" in *Fast Company* (August 2001, pp. 129) [14272], [31796], [34238], [47316], [50640]

"Net Crimes & Misdemeanors" in *Information Today* (Vol. 20, No. 1, Jan. 2003, pp. 44) [13084], [14273], [34239], [37481]

"Net Data Seller Can Be Sued in Stalking-Murder Case" in *Daily Business Review* (Vol. 77, No. 190, March 12, 2003, pp. A7) [14274], [29396], [34240]

"Net Deposits" in *Entrepreneur* (Vol. 33, October 2005, No. 10, pp. 54) [34241], [38239]

"Net Gains" in *Incentive* (Vol. 174, No. 10, October 2000, pp. 9) [14275], [24983], [34242], [55130]

"Net Profits" in *Entrepreneur* (Vol. 27, No. 12, December 1999, pp. 48) [14276], [30240], [34243]

Net Transforms Inc. [49447], [49638]

Netcap Franchise Consultants [3906]

Netcatalyst [58094]

NetExpo Washington [34773]

Netfuel Inc. [58095]

Netherlands Chamber of Commerce in the United States [43519]

NetKnowledge Technologies L.L.C. [31617], [49448]

"NetNose: www.netnose.com" in *Entrepreneur* (Vol. 31, No. 12, December 2003, pp. 8) [14277], [25907], [34244]

"Netscape unveils Web site aimed at small firms" in *Wall Street Journal* (September 13, 2000, pp. B5) [14278], [34245]

Netspace [14674], [26030]

"Netting a bigger piece of the action" in *Hispanic Business* (Vol. 22, No. 5, May 2000, pp. 38) [1953], [14279], [18605], [19751], [34246], [48321]

"Network for a greater good in 2002" in *Women in Business* (Vol. 54, No. 2, March-April 2002, pp. 33) [27452], [45461]

Network Consulting & Associates Inc. [25687]

"Network It" in *Entrepreneur* (Vol. 33, March 2005, No. 3, pp. 48) [6734], [14280], [49156]

Network Marketing [47317]

"Network Marketing or Pyramid Scheme?" in *Black Enterprise* (Vol. 35, November 2004, No. 4, pp. 102) [29397], [30241], [47318]

"The network of relationships between the economic environment and the entrepreneurial culture firms" in *Journal of Business Venturing* [32586], [36526], [52919]

Network World (September 18, 2000, pp. 12); "AOL woos small businesses with e-comm plan " in [33536], [53209]

Network World (December 6, 1999, pp. NA); "BorderWare to ship e-commerce gateways for small business use" in [33603], [53221], [53615]

Network World (July 24, 2000, pp. NA); "Cisco, SBA announce online learning program" in [33039], [33670], [39798]

Network World (October 24, 2000, pp. NA); "Dell and NetObjects make small business play" in [33745], [49006], [53253], [53683]

Network World (November 6, 2000, pp. NA); "IBM Readies Linux Suite for Small Biz" in [34045], [49086], [53326], [53795]

Network World (September 18, 2000, pp. NA); "Intuit launches small business marketplace" in [26269], [34087], [53337]

Network World (September 25, 2000, pp. NA); "Microsoft Launches Small Business Web Services" in [34194], [49145], [53365]

Network World (April 3, 2000, pp. NA); "Navy assesses small-biz impact of intranet deal" in [40063], [43952]

Network World (October 16, 2000, pp. 108); "'Net Attacks to Plague Small and Midsize Firms" in [34237], [53876]

"The Networked Home" in *Home Office Computing* (Vol. 18, No. 12, December 2000, pp. 89) [42685], [49157]

"Networked incubators: Hothouses of the new economy" in *Harvard Business Review* (Vol. 78, No. 5, September-October 2000, pp. 51) [43057]

Networked Solutions Inc. [49449], [49639]

Networkers of the Costa Mesa Chamber of Commerce [57656]

Networking [32964]

Networking Alternatives for Publishers, Retailers and Artists [17884]

"Networking is a Click Away" in *Black Enterprise* (Vol. 34, No. 6, January 2004, pp. 101) [24984], [36527], [48322], [55131]

"Networking know-how" in *Women in Business* (Vol. 53, No. 7, January-February 2002, pp. 40) [45462], [56337]

"Networking Made Easy; Three Quick Tips for Setting Up a Wired Connection" in *Black Enterprise* (Vol. 34, No. 2, September 2003) [6735], [6953], [49158]

"Networking Nice" in *Success* (Vol. 47, No. 1, January 2000, pp. 54) [47319]

"Networking Provides Partnership's Funding" in *Wall Street Journal* (October 14, 2003, pp. B4) [36528], [44600], [48919], [50095]

"Net.Working" in *Small Business Opportunities* (Vol. 12, No. 2, March 2000, pp. 80) [34247], [36529], [47320]

"Networking for Success" in *Hispanic Business* (Vol. 24, No. 4, April 2002, pp. 26) [27453], [48323], [56338]

"Networking for Success: It Takes More Than Just Handling Out Business Cards" in *Black Enterprise* (Vol. 34, No. 4, Nov. 2003, pp. 72) [36530]

Networking for Your Personal & Financial Growth [10315]

"Neuburger Outgrows Pajamas" in *San Francisco Business Times* (Vol. 17, No. 51, July 25, 2003, pp. 1) [5693], [47321], [51263]

Neumeier Consulting Inc. [21727]

Neurobiology of Learning and Memory [52308]

Neuroventures Capital [65976]

Neutral Networks in Finance and Investing: Using Artificial Intelligence to Improve Real-World Performance [15292]

Nevada Bob's Golf [11293]

Nevada Chamber of Commerce [60183]

Nevada Chamber of Commerce Association [62362]

Nevada City Chamber of Commerce [57657]

Nevada Commission on Economic Development
    Procurement Outreach Program–Northern Nevada Regional Office [62375]
    Procurement Outreach Program–Southern Nevada Regional Office [62376]

Nevada Department of Business and Industry–DEAL WITH VARIOUS ISSUES OF SMALL BUSINESSES [62336]

Nevada Manufacturers Register [46385]

Nevada Procurement Technical Assistance Center–Economic Development [62377]

Nevada Small Business Development Center–University of Nevada at Reno [62319]

Nevada State Library–Department of Cultural Affairs [66924]

Nevada-Vernon County Chamber of Commerce [62008]

Never Bet the Farm [38240], [39488]

"Never say die: how a family beat the odds (and the weather) to improve a franchise" in *Entrepreneur* (Vol. 30, No. 12, Dec. 2002) [37739], [38863]

Never Eat Alone: And Other Secrets to Success, One Relationship at a Time [36531], [45463]

"Never say 'NO'" in *Women in Business* (Vol. 54, No. 2, March-April 2002, pp. 27) [31797]

"A New Abacus for Pensions" in *Business Week* (January 9, 2006, No. 3966, pp. 91) [204], [2935], [13395], [15293], [23996], [26300], [26857], [29398], [40545], [41067], [43287]

New Account Selling [51926]

"New Adult-Home Reforms Announced" in *Westchester County Business Journal* (Vol. 43, July 5, 2004, No. 27, pp. 16) [452], [18330], [40546]

New Age Marketing Opportunities Newsletter [17933]

"New theme park for Atlanta?" in *Atlanta Business Chronicle* (Vol. 24, No. 13, August 31, 2001, pp. 1A) [1134]

"The New Atlantic Century" in *Harvard Business Review* (Vol. 78, No. 1, January 2000, pp. 17) [28530]

New Bedford Area Chamber of Commerce [60980]

New Beginnings [41271]

"New Beginnings for VIBE" in *Black Enterprise* (Vol. 37, November 2006, No. 4, pp. 34) [18913], [28531], [30572], [36532], [50757]

New Berlin Chamber of Commerce and Visitors Bureau [66477]

New Bern Area Chamber of Commerce [63414]

New Bethlehem Area Chamber of Commerce [64479]

"New Biscotti Company Gets Cooking" in *Bellingham Business Journal* (December 2006, pp. A5) [4550], [11338], [28532], [36533], [56339]

New Boston Chamber of Commerce [65411]

"The New Brands in Town" in *WWD* (January 2, 2003, pp. 9) [5561], [5694], [19421]

"A New Breed of Entrepreneurs" in *Black Enterprise* (Vol. 37, November 2006, No. 4, pp. 16) [36534], [42356], [48324], [48586]

New Britain Chamber of Commerce [58553]

New Brunswick Translation Bureau–Library [25112]

"New Burdens on Home Builders Hurt Local Government" in *Atlanta Business Chronicle* (Vol. 25, December 6, 2002, No. 26, pp. 38A) [7434], [40547], [54669]

New Business Capital Fund, Ltd. [62722]

"New Business on Champion Street Uncorks a New Trend" in *Bellingham Business Journal* (January 2007, pp. A4) [23498], [28533], [29941], [36535], [52920]

The New Business Landscape: Taking Your Business into the Twenty-First Century [30573]

"New Business Owners Learn the Ropes in 2006" in *Bellingham Business Journal* (January 2007, pp.) [730], [5695], [7167], [28534], [47322]

"New Campaign Aims to Educate Californians About Fake Insurance Policies" in *Sacramento Bee* (October 1, 2005) [13396], [30242], [33184], [43288]

New Canaan Chamber of Commerce [58554]

New Canaan Historical Society [10922]

"New Career Center Opens at Right Time: Laid-Off Freightliner Workers Will Need Help" in *Charlotte Observer* (February 1, 2007) [33185], [42876]

"A New Career for You Might Start at Franchise U" in *Success* (Vol. 47, No. 3, July 2000, pp. 82) [38663]

New Castle Area Chamber of Commerce [58410]

New Castle County Chamber of Commerce [58651]

New Castle-Henry County Chamber of Commerce [59976]

"New disease has businesses cautious, but few effects seen" in *Crain's Detroit Business* (Vol. 19, No. 14, April 7, 2003, pp. 46) [41068], [43758]

New Century Consultants [50329]

"A New Century for Start-ups" in *Hispanic Business* (Vol. 22, No. 3, March 2000, pp. 54) [29752], [35582], [55747]

The New Century Venture Center [65988]

"New CEO: So What is Moto, Anyway?" in *Crain's Chicago Business* (Vol. 26, No. 51, December 22, 2003, pp. 20) [5066], [5240], [12816], [12900], [19925], [20140], [40103], [41859], [43419], [45126], [45464], [47323], [50641], [52812]

"New Chain 'Drug Stores' in Long Island Fill the Gap..." in *Long Island Business News* (January 30, 2004) [8795], [51264]

"The New Chairman" in *Hispanic Business* (January/February 2003, pp. 22, 24) [39489], [48325]

"The New China?" in *Entrepreneur.com* (Vol. 34, February 2006, No. 2, pp. 17) [43759], [46386]

New Choices for Writers: How to Get Published in the New Age Market [8984]

New City Chamber of Commerce [62964]

"New Clothing Store in Augusta, Ga., Features High-End Brands" in *Augusta Chronicle* (February 17, 2004) [5562], [5696]

"New Computer Sellers Bite Into Market..." in *Crain's Chicago Business* (Vol. 26, No. 50, December 15, 2003) **[6736]**, **[49159]**, **[51265]**

"New Computer Sellers Bite Into Market; MDG, Fry's Set to Debut, While CompUSA Grows Again" in *Crains Chicago Business* (Vol. 26) **[6737]**, **[49160]**, **[51266]**

"New Congress may give business some gains" in *Atlanta Business Chronicle* (Vol. 25, November 15, 2002, No. 23 pp. 7A) **[40548]**, **[54670]**

"New 'corporate sheriff' starts touch talk" in *Atlanta Business Chronicle* (Vol. 25, No. 21, November 1, 2002, pp. 3A) **[205]**, **[23997]**, **[26301]**, **[37482]**

"The new culture of criticism is hurting you and your company" in *Fast Company* (May 2001, pp. 102) **[47324]**, **[50642]**

"New Curves franchise serves up fast fitness" in *Sarasota Herald Tribune* (August 12, 2002, pp. 8) **[10498]**, **[17873]**, **[19345]**, **[21406]**, **[38664]**

"A New Deal for SBK-Brooks: B.E. Investment Bank Completes $233 Million Bond Offering" in *Black Enterprise* (Vol. 34, December 2003) **[10101]**, **[10892]**, **[15294]**, **[15824]**

"New Deli Destination Coming to Town" in *Bellingham Business Journal* (December 2006, pp. A3) **[8516]**, **[14281]**, **[25908]**, **[34248]**, **[52921]**, **[56340]**

"New Detroit survey targets metro area minority business" in *Crain's Detroit Business* (Vol. 16, No. 7, February 14, 2000, pp. 37) **[48326]**, **[52922]**

The New Direct Marketing: How to Implement a Profit-Driven Database Marketing Strategy **[47325]**, **[50643]**

"New DOE contracts: small business is the focus of several new agency initiatives" in *Hispanic Business* (Vol.22,No.7-8, July-Aug. 2000) **[39872]**, **[40064]**

"New Dynamic for Nonprofits" in *Hispanic Business* (Vol. 23, No. 7/8, July/August 2001, pp. 104, 106) **[36536]**, **[48327]**, **[54230]**

New Dynamics Associates **[48643]**

"The New Economic World Order" in *Red Herring* (No. 102, August 15, 2001, pp. 16) **[28535]**, **[32587]**

"New Economy Creates New Markets" in *Hispanic Business* (Vol. 22, No. 1/2, January/February, pp. 24, 26) **[28536]**, **[32588]**, **[55132]**

"New Economy" in *Inc.* (November 2000, pp. 37) **[32189]**, **[35583]**, **[56726]**

"The new economy's currency is stock, stock, and stock" in *The New York Times* (March 27, 2000, pp. D12, H12) **[25909]**, **[28537]**, **[34249]**

"The New Edition" in *Internet World* (Vol. 7, No. 2, January 15, 2001, pp. 20) **[9149]**, **[28538]**, **[34250]**

"New EEOC and OFCCP Issues for the Year 2000 and Beyond" in *Employment Relations Today* (Vol. 26, No. 4, Winter 2000, pp. 99) **[29399]**, **[32047]**, **[40549]**

"New dean has expensive plans for Emory Law" in *Atlanta Business Chronicle* (Vol. 25, November 15, 2002, No. 23 pp. SS7) **[29400]**, **[33186]**

New Employment Issues in the Electronic Workplace **[49161]**

The New England Antiques Journal **[1349]**

New England Apparel Club **[5748]**

New England Bride **[3207]**

New England Connexion **[10974]**

New England Conservatory of Music–Harriet M. Spaulding Library **[17691]**

New England Economic Review **[61159]**

New England Fisheries Development Association **[10421]**, **[10448]**

New England Gerontological Association **[18314]**

New England Historical and Genealogical Register **[10975]**

New England Hot Dog Company, LLC **[21905]**

New England Human Resource Group **[27040]**, **[42989]**

New England International Auto Show **[18194]**

New England Manufacturers Directory **[16701]**

New England Partners **[61102]**

New England Real Estate Journal **[21055]**

New England Wholesalers Association–Lending Library **[19782]**

New Enterprise Associates (Baltimore) **[60876]**

New Enterprise Associates (Menlo Park) **[58096]**

"New Entrepreneurs Arise from Bad Breaks" in *Atlanta Journal-Constitution* (January 20, 2007) **[10568]**, **[36537]**, **[56341]**

The New Era of Investment Banking: Industry Structure, Trends and Performance **[15295]**

"New Ethics or No Ethics? Questionable behavior is Silicon Valley's next big thing" in *Fortune* (Vol. 141, No. 6, Mar. 20, 2000, pp. 82) **[37483]**, **[55748]**

"New Face at the SBA" in *Hispanic Business* (Vol. 23, No. 10, October, 2001, pp. 32, 34) **[39873]**, **[40065]**, **[48328]**, **[53877]**

"The new fact of HACR" in *Hispanic Business* (Vol. 21, No. 12, December 1999, pp. 22) **[28539]**, **[48329]**

"New developments in business forecasting: debunking executive conventional wisdom" in *Journal of Business Forecasting* (Vol. 19, No. 2) **[30574]**

"New Foundation" in *Hispanic Business* (June 2005, pp. 20) **[731]**, **[33187]**, **[47326]**, **[48330]**

"New Franchise Offers Customers Web Design Tech Without the Hassles" in *Small Business Opportunities* (March 2005) **[14282]**, **[25910]**, **[34251]**, **[38864]**

"The New Frontier" in *Hispanic Business* (July/August 2004, pp. 36, 38) **[4114]**, **[48331]**

"New frontiers" in *Entrepreneur* (Vol. 31, No. 6, June 2003, pp. 34) **[3564]**, **[9990]**, **[10102]**, **[15079]**, **[15296]**, **[36538]**, **[38241]**, **[43760]**

"New Frontiers to Explore" in *Fast Company* (September 2001, pp. 76) **[38242]**, **[39490]**

"A New Game for Johnson: BET Founder Looking to Acquire Baseball Franchise" in *Black Enterprise* (Vol. 33, No. 7, Feb. 2003, pp. 19) **[36540]**, **[48332]**

"A New Game Plan for C Players" in *Harvard Business Review* (Vol. 80, No. 1, January 2002, pp. 81) **[35002]**, **[42357]**, **[45465]**

"New pottery studio preserves a legacy of generosity" in *Sarasota Herald Tribune* (September 13, 2002, pp. BC4) **[8174]**, **[8274]**

New Glarus Chamber of Commerce **[66478]**

The New Graphic Communications Trade Customs and Business Practices **[5998]**

"New Group Creating Opportunities for Women" in *Atlanta Business Chronicle* (Vol. 25, November 15, 2002, No. 23 pp. 10A) **[35584]**, **[44429]**, **[56063]**

"New Group Plan Offers 'Free-Agent' Workers Affordable Health Benefits" in *Boston Globe* (March 3, 2005) **[13397]**, **[26858]**, **[43289]**

"New Group Seeks Greater Hispanic Influence" in *Hispanic Business* (Vol. 23, No. 7/8, July/August 2001, pp. 24) **[28540]**, **[32589]**, **[53878]**

"New Group Tries to Gain OK for River Falls Casino Plan" in *Kansas City Star* (February 8, 2005) **[10881]**, **[20949]**

"New Group Weighs Solutions" in *Crain's Detroit Business* (Vol. 19, No. 16, April 21, 2003, pp. 25) **[32590]**

"New Growth in the Garden State" in *Fast Company* (August 2001, pp. 36) **[27662]**, **[39491]**

"New Habits Die Hard" in *Red Herring* (No. 102, August 15, 2001, pp. 48-50, 52-53) **[14283]**, **[28541]**

"New Hampshire Attorney General Probes Mall's Ouster of Diamond Kiosk" in *The Telegraph* (December 18, 2003) **[15930]**, **[29401]**

New Hampshire Business Review **[62447]**

New Hampshire Department of Resources and Economic Development–Business Resource Center **[62393]**

New Hampshire Department of Resources and Economic Development-Agenda **[62448]**

New Hampshire Office of Energy and Planning **[66925]**

New Hampshire Procurement Technical Assistance Center–State of New Hampshire–Economic Development **[62442]**

New Hampshire Sea Grant College Program **[10490]**

New Hampshire Small Business Development Center **[62451]**

New Hampshire State Library **[66926]**

New Hampshire Technical Institute, Concord–Library **[39746]**

New Hartford Chamber of Commerce **[62965]**

New Haven Chamber of Commerce **[59977]**

"New 'Heads in Beds' in Suburban Hotels" in *Boston Business Journal* (Vol. 23, No. 21, June 27, 2003, pp. 1) **[12602]**, **[25219]**, **[30384]**

The New High-Yield Bond Market: Investment Opportunities, Strategies and Analysis **[15297]**

"The New Hispanic Information Economy" in *Hispanic Business* (November 2003, pp. 26, 28, 30) **[32591]**, **[49162]**, **[50933]**

New Holstein Area Chamber of Commerce **[66479]**

"New Home Construction Reaches 21-Year-High Pace in January" in *Chicago Tribune* (February 17, 2005) **[7435]**, **[20607]**, **[28542]**

"New-Home Sales Drop 9.2 Percent" in *Atlanta Journal-Constitution* (March 1, 2005) **[7436]**, **[20608]**, **[32592]**

"A New Hope" in *Entrepreneur* (Vol. 30, No) **[7049]**, **[12758]**, **[21407]**, **[26036]**, **[35585]**, **[38665]**

New Horizons **[11472]**, **[41272]**

New Horizons-Chamber/MainStreet **[60184]**

New Horizons Computer Learning Centers, Inc.-Entrepreneur.com **[6379]**

New Horizons Venture Capital **[65977]**

"New house, new food, new life" in *Ingram's* (Vol. 28, No. 2, February 2002, pp. 38) **[7814]**, **[54231]**

The New How to Advertise: Expanded, Updated, and Completely Revised for the '90s **[47327]**

"New Issues: There's a Side Door into the Public Markets" in *Red Herring* (No. 99, June 15 & July 1, 2001, pp. 138) **[15298]**, **[32593]**, **[38242]**, **[50096]**

New Jersey Accounting, Business & Technology Show & Conference **[362]**, **[2983]**, **[24115]**

"New Jersey Acting Governor Seeks Deal to Ban Smoking in Bars, Eateries" in *The Record* (November 18, 2005) **[2346]**, **[21571]**, **[40550]**

New Jersey Attorney General's Office–Law and Public Safety Department–Research Services **[40903]**

"New Jersey-Based Arts, Crafts Chain to Open Store in Erie, Pa" in *Erie Times-News* (March 4, 2002) **[8175]**, **[28543]**

"New Jersey Builder Hovnanian Enters Chicago Home Market" in *Chicago Tribune* (March 3, 2005) **[7437]**, **[15299]**, **[50097]**

New Jersey Business **[62630]**

New Jersey Commerce Economic Growth and Tourism Commission
    Office of Business Advocate **[62460]**
    Office of Business Services **[62461]**
    Office of International Trade **[62462]**
    Office of Marketing **[62463]**

New Jersey Data Center–New Jersey Department of Labor–Division of Labor Market and Demographic Research **[66928]**

New Jersey Department of Commerce and Economic Development
    Division of Small, Women, and Minority Business **[62577]**
    Set-Aside and Certification Office **[62578]**

New Jersey Economic Development Department **[62464]**, **[62794]**

"New Jersey Firm Busy Westbrook, Maine, Online Classified Company" in *Portland Press Herald* (December 7, 2005) **[732]**, **[18914]**, **[30691]**, **[42358]**, **[52442]**

New Jersey Flower & Patio Show **[15971]**, **[16065]**

New Jersey Health and Senior Services Department–Health Planning and Regulation–Health Care Systems Analysis–Research and Development **[41391]**

New Jersey Institute of Technology–Center for Architecture and Building Science Research **[49671]**

New York State Office of Science Technology and Academic Research
New York Science and Technology Foundation **[62797]**
New York Science and Technology Foundation–Technology Development Organizations **[62798]**

New York State Offices General Services–Minority and Women-Owned Business **[63049]**

"New York State Officials May Allow Wine Sales in Supermarkets" in *Buffalo News* (April 11, 2003) **[11647]**, **[16234]**, **[23500]**, **[40570]**

New York State School Music Association Winter Conference **[17654]**, **[17806]**

New York State Science & Technology Foundation **[63143]**

New York State Small Business Development Center–Research Network **[53136]**

New York State Turf and Landscape Association **[15965]**, **[15998]**

"New York Stories" in *Venture Capital Journal* (Vol. 42, No. 9, September 2002, pp. 21, 22-23) **[36549]**, **[39493]**

The New York Times (December 16, 2000, pp. B1, C1); "A high-tech domino effect: as dot-coms go, so go the e-commerce consultants" in **[14113]**, **[28278]**, **[31169]**, **[34008]**, **[41736]**

The New York Times (June 7, 2000, pp. D34, H34); "A wary welcome for the Net from Kentucky artisans" in **[8023]**, **[34656]**

The New York Times (September 3, 2000, pp. BU10); "Accentuating the accent" in **[42164]**, **[44873]**

The New York Times (March 21, 2000, pp. C1); "Agreement on Internet taxes eludes deeply divided commission" in **[13807]**, **[33522]**, **[54423]**

The New York Times(Sept25,2000); "As Web sites seek an attractive mix of content, a new type of business is providing the right stuff"in **[13824]**, **[25792]**, **[33544]**

The New York Times (April 5, 2000, pp. C2); "Attorney General to offer olive branch to Silicon Valley" in **[13829]**, **[29106]**, **[40165]**

The New York Times (September 20, 2000, pp. D44, H44); "Automated advice sites turning up the heat on planners" in **[9819]**, **[33553]**

The New York Times (December 13, 2000, pp. D13, H13); "Betty Crocker: can she cook in cyberspace?" in **[33575]**

The New York Times Book Review **[3059]**

The New York Times (July 25, 2000, pp. C6); "BP Amoco wants to sell much more than gas at its new stations" in **[22609]**, **[33606]**, **[50558]**, **[51075]**

The New York Times (October 30, 2000, pp. C1); "Bricks-and-Clicks World Needs Commercial Space" in **[13856]**, **[20220]**, **[33607]**

The New York Times (September 1, 2000, pp. C2); "California bill on Web sales tax" in **[33643]**, **[40232]**, **[54470]**

New York Times (August 31, 2001); "Campaigns for several products are shifting their focus from 'women only' to include 'real men'" in **[2585]**, **[7884]**, **[12765]**, **[46774]**

The New York Times (May 15,2000, pp.C16); "Catalog companies show the upstarts that they know a thing or two about Internet retailing" in **[33652]**, **[46785]**, **[51581]**

The New York Times (March 9, 2000, pp. D1, G1); "Clicks, not licks, as Green Stamps go digital" in **[31660]**, **[33680]**, **[46808]**

New York Times (March 25, 2001, pp. BU13); "Conflict resolution, made simple" in **[27326]**

The New York Times; "Content sites find a way to keep e-tailer marketing booths on their page-without having lured their visitors away" in **[33701]**, **[46836]**

The New York Times (September 28, 2000, pp. D8); "CueCat links printed ads to Web, but skeptics are wary" in **[597]**, **[33721]**, **[46859]**

The New York Times (December 8, 2000, pp. C3); "Cutbacks at another consultant" in **[27997]**, **[31136]**, **[33727]**

The New York Times (February 17, 2000, pp. D4, G4); "Delegating the dirty work of cleaning up" in **[13958]**, **[33744]**, **[42215]**

The New York Times (December 13, 2000, pp. D4, H4); "Digitally speaking, builders remain on the ground floor" in **[7331]**, **[33760]**

The New York Times (September 27, 2000, pp. B14, F7); "Dream of Zinfandel, delivered to the door" in **[23474]**, **[33786]**

The New York Times (July 10, 2000, pp. C12); "E-retailers turn to the printed page to put their wares before consumers" in **[33819]**, **[46924]**, **[51139]**

The New York Times (July 4, 2000, pp. C1); "E-signing law seen as a boon to e-business" in **[28070]**, **[29210]**, **[33820]**

The New York Times (December 4, 2000, pp. C1); "Executives see trouble spreading" in **[28131]**, **[31146]**, **[41675]**

New York Times (December 31, 2003, pp. C1); "FedEx Moves to Expand With Purchase of Kinko's" in **[9949]**, **[14980]**, **[17313]**, **[19873]**, **[49929]**

The New York Times (May 15, 2000, pp. C4); "Finding deals, small businesses buy more online" in **[14038]**, **[33896]**, **[53727]**

The New York Times (March 27, 2000, pp. D9); "For the small retailer, life on the Internet is one big bazaar" in **[14053]**, **[51166]**

The New York Times (March 27, 2000, pp. D3, H3); "Free-for-all on the name exchange" in **[14056]**, **[33921]**, **[46983]**

The New York Times (December 13 2000, pp. D3, H3); "From big idea to big bust: the wild ride of Boo.com" in **[14058]**, **[33927]**, **[37138]**

The New York Times (February 9, 2000, pp. G1); "Harmony and bottom line: hm..." in **[34925]**, **[45224]**

The New York Times (December 13, 2000, pp. D10, H10); "He knows if you've been naughty, but you can still send him e-mail" in **[28269]**, **[34000]**

The New York Times (March 27, 2000, pp. D18, H18); "Help! My brain's being eaten by a zillion dot-com ads!" in **[657]**, **[34003]**, **[47063]**

New York Times (November 2, 2003, pp. 1); "Helping the Economy, One Snip at a Time" in **[11791]**, **[39836]**, **[44543]**, **[48908]**

The New York Times (February 20, 2000, pp. A39); "Hiring a guide just to find the camp" in **[31170]**

New York Times (March 20, 2004, pp. C2); "How to Avoid Auction Scams" in **[1825]**, **[18648]**, **[30230]**, **[34027]**

The New York Times (May 7, 2000, pp. BU1); "How Killer B-to-B's Slid to the Endangered List" in **[14134]**, **[28306]**, **[34034]**

The New York Times (December 13, 2000, pp. D6, H6); "How Much Am I Bid for This Imperfect Marketplace" in **[1826]**, **[34036]**

The New York Times (August 17, 2000, pp. D8, G8); "In Online Auctions of the Future, It'll Be Bot vs Bot vs. Bot." in **[1827]**, **[23041]**, **[34060]**

The New York Times (December 13, 2000, pp. D8, H8); "Insurance Sites Aren't Closing the Sale" in **[13343]**, **[34069]**

The New York Times (August 28, 2000, pp. C8(L)); "Internet Companies Learn How to Personalize Service" in **[14152]**, **[34075]**, **[47146]**, **[51699]**

The New York Times (Sept. 20, 2000, pp. D40, H40); "Is it theft, or is it freedom? 7 views of the Web's impact on culture clashes" in **[14167]**, **[34093]**

The New York Times Magazine (March 19, 2000, pp. 32); "M-commerce: does 'streaming media' give you the screaming meemies?" in **[5046]**, **[14217]**, **[27424]**, **[34155]**

The New York Times Magazine (Jan. 9, 2000); "The downside of the upside of the downside: these days nothing succeeds like failure" in **[13742]**, **[33430]**, **[35400]**

The New York Times (May 1, 2000); "Many analysts think the old-style expensive portal deals deserve more scrutiny from e-tailers" in **[34169]**, **[47231]**

The New York Times (July 4, 2000, pp. C1); "Mother, I'm the boss now: Internet executives hire their parents and traditions fall" in **[34213]**, **[36510]**, **[37736]**

The New York Times (March 27, 2000, pp. D4, H4); "Myms, pings and vortals" in **[14265]**, **[27447]**, **[34224]**

New York Times (November 17, 2003, pp. C7); "Nervous About Bidding on eBay?" in **[1837]**, **[13394]**, **[34236]**, **[43286]**

The New York Times (March 27, 2000, pp. D9, H9); "Now that they've come, what can we sell them?" in **[34273]**, **[51749]**

The New York Times (December 13, 2000, pp. D8, H8); "Or you could call it schadenfreude.com" in **[28600]**, **[34314]**

The New York Times (March 9, 2000, pp. C1); "Out there in never-Bell land, where phone service is way above average, and competitive" in **[5081]**, **[30928]**

The New York Times (March 22, 2000, pp. D28, H28); "Panel on taxing Internet sales ends its meetings in disagreement" in **[14336]**, **[34325]**, **[54693]**

New York Times (November 12, 2006, pp. 15); "Pinstriped Populist" in **[15356]**, **[32627]**, **[39526]**, **[41080]**, **[43784]**, **[49727]**

The New York Times (March 27, 2000, pp. D3, H3); "Putting their money where the future is" in **[34386]**, **[55788]**

The New York Times (December 13, 2000, pp. D1, H1); "Reaching for less than the sky: as boldest fall, modest dreamers fly on" in **[14385]**, **[29972]**, **[34398]**, **[37184]**

The New York Times (May 22, 2000, pp. C4); "Renting software and the skills to go with it" in **[23149]**, **[53435]**, **[53938]**

The New York Times; "Report proposes update of copyright act: panel seeks liability for violations by Internet access services" in **[14393]**, **[40639]**, **[44132]**

The New York Times (March 3, 2000, pp. A25, A21); "Saga of an online pioneer" in **[13776]**, **[33484]**

The New York Times (April 5, 2000, pp. B2(L)); "Selling guns: a tradition and a dilemma" in **[11728]**, **[37775]**

New York Times (January 14, 2007, pp. 15); "Setting the Table: The Transforming Power of Hospitality in Business" in **[21410]**, **[35637]**

The New York Times (September 20, 2000, pp. D8, H8); "She's only code and pixels, but she can help you shop" in **[10574]**, **[34465]**

The New York Times (November 11, 2000, pp. A1); "Shopping in palm of the hand is making its holiday debut" in **[5105]**, **[14428]**, **[34469]**, **[51834]**

The New York Times (October 8, 2000, pp. WK2); "Sign right here" in **[14432]**, **[29491]**, **[34473]**

The New York Times (Sept. 4, 2000, pp. C5); "Sporting Goods Web Sites, Last Year's Costly Rage, Are Turned Over tothe Professionals" in **[23637]**, **[34525]**, **[47563]**

The New York Times (December 13, 2000, pp. D13, H13); "Sure, it would be easier on the Web - but let's haggle" in **[34550]**, **[51857]**

The New York Times (June 7, 2000, pp. D3, H3); "10 months, 10 minutes, $10 million" in **[35692]**, **[55441]**

The New York Times (April 6, 2000, pp. D1); "That online religion with shopping, too" in **[14528]**, **[17914]**, **[34585]**

The New York Times (May 26, 2000, pp. A23, A19); "The sticky road to a killer app" in **[14487]**

New York Times (December 31, 2006, pp. 14); "The Bleeding-Heart Rationalist: William Morris b. 1911" in **[6592]**, **[27850]**, **[33015]**, **[35851]**, **[39181]**, **[46216]**

The New York Times (March 27, 2000, pp. D12, H12); "The new economy's currency is stock, stock, and stock" in **[25909]**, **[28537]**, **[34249]**

The New York Times (December 18, 2000, pp. C16); "The art of making a plan and making it happen" in **[29705]**, **[35320]**, **[52768]**

The New York Times(Jul.12,2000, pp.C6); "The direct marketing industry hopes to get Internet retailers to see things in an old light"in **[33763]**, **[46893]**

New York Times (February 4, 2007, pp. 7); "The Real Pepsi Challenge" in **[26894]**, **[47455]**

New York Times (October 27, 2002, pp. 81); "The sweet spot: a cathedral to candy brings together two very different worshipers" in **[4315]**, **[37793]**

The New York Times (May 31, 2000, pp. C1); "The Wisdom of Thoughtfulness: In Tight Labor Market, Bosses Find Value in Being Nice" in **[35157]**, **[45858]**, **[54084]**

The New York Times (November 12, 2000, pp. BU14); "Two $10,000 Questions for Small Business" in **[28930]**

The New York Times (October 15, 2000, pp. BU1); "Venture capitalists, venturing beyond capital" in **[55448]**

New York Times (November 5, 2006, pp. 109); "Vintage Chic" in **[23516]**, **[56465]**

The New York Times (July 6, 2000, pp. G1); "Voyeur-cams come to home furnishings: the idea is to check out the wares" in **[12215]**, **[12315]**, **[34651]**

The New York Times (August 14, 2000, pp. C8); "Wacky, fake Web sites grab attention, while only slyly referring to their sponsors" in **[34652]**, **[47695]**

The New York Times (June 7, 2000, pp. D35, H35); "What Conservatives, Liberals, Stores and States Share" in **[34690]**, **[54864]**

The New York Times (August 24, 2000, pp. C2); "When Commerce Moves Online, Competition Can Work in Strange Ways" in **[34706]**

The New York Times (December 13, 2000, pp. D14, H14); "Where Ads Aimed at Kids Come to Life" in **[34708]**, **[47737]**

The New York Times (December 18, 2000, pp. C28); "With dot-coms no longer soaring, financial backers get back to basics" in **[14631]**, **[34740]**, **[55958]**

The New York Times (July 2, 2000, pp. BU10); "You paid that bill with a single click. Or did you?" in **[26409]**, **[34761]**

New York University
 Berkley Center for Entrepreneurial Studies **[37055]**
 Conservation Center **[1675]**
 Glucksman Institute **[15810]**
 National Center on Philanthropy and the Law **[10782]**
 Office of Sponsored Programs **[63202]**
 Salomon Center for the Study of Financial Institutions **[3004]**

New Yorktown Chamber of Commerce **[62968]**

"New to You?" in *Entrepreneur* (Vol. 28, No. 9, September 2000, pp. 50) **[39877]**, **[40571]**, **[44604]**

"The New You" in *Entrepreneur* (Vol. 32, October 2004, No. 10, pp. 100) **[31799]**, **[47340]**

Newark Chamber of Commerce **[57658]**, **[62969]**

Newark Minority Business Development Center **[62579]**

Newark Public Library
 Arts & Humanities Center **[7969]**
 Special Collections Division of the Special Collections Department **[2850]**

Newberry Area Chamber of Commerce **[58899]**, **[61393]**

Newberry County Chamber of Commerce **[64772]**

"Newbie Rules" in *Entrepreneur* (Vol. 28, No. 8, August 2000, pp. 34) **[42360]**

Newbury Ventures **[58098]**

Newcastle Area Chamber of Commerce **[66620]**

Newcastle Chamber of Commerce **[64043]**

Newcomb Chamber of Commerce **[62970]**

Newcomerstown Chamber of Commerce **[63750]**

Robert Newell Lighting Design **[49640]**

"The Newest Cell Phones" in *Hispanic Business* (January/February 2003, pp. 62) **[5070]**, **[49166]**

Newfound Region Chamber of Commerce **[62433]**

Newfoundland Department of Industry, Trade and Technology–Registry **[53137]**

Newington Chamber of Commerce **[58555]**

Newkirk Chamber of Commerce **[64044]**

The Newly Promoted African-American Manager and Supervisor: Making the Transition **[44817]**

"Newly revived yoga, Pilates show promise over long stretch" in *DSN Retailing Today* (Vol. 41, No. 19, October 7, 2002, pp. 23) **[17710]**, **[17905]**, **[19424]**, **[20140]**

Newman Chamber of Commerce **[57659]**

Newmarket Capital Advisors **[55976]**

Newnan-Coweta Chamber of Commerce **[59144]**

Newport Area Chamber of Commerce **[62434]**

Newport/Cocke County Chamber of Commerce **[64961]**

Newport County Chamber of Commerce **[64670]**
 E. Bay Small Business Development Center **[64649]**

Newport Harbor Area Chamber of Commerce **[57660]**

Newport News Daily Press (August 20, 2002); "Smithfield, Va., Candy Shop Pleases Children, Adults" in **[2254]**, **[4310]**

"Newport, N.H., Couple Soon to Open Bed and Breakfast" in *Eagle Times* (August 3, 2003) **[2448]**

Newport - Oldtown Chamber of Commerce **[66140]**

NewRoad Publishing **[63486]**

"News Blog Highlights Women's Careers" in *Marketing to Women* (Vol. 19, November 2006, No. 11, pp. 5) **[14294]**, **[27455]**, **[27663]**, **[41868]**, **[42361]**, **[47341]**

News-Herald, Willoughby (April 3, 2004); "Northeast Ohio Cottage Industry of eBay Drop-Off Stores Emerges" in **[1839]**, **[7169]**, **[18655]**, **[34270]**, **[52570]**

News-Herald (August 21, 2004); "Willoughby, Ohio-Area Wedding Coordinators Look for Ways to Reduce Final Bill" in **[3202]**

News Media Yellow Book **[4117]**

News & Observer (February 1, 2004); "Raleigh, N.C.-Area Employers Decline to Offer Dating Service as Perk" in **[7067]**, **[26893]**, **[35036]**, **[37765]**

"News and Reviews" in *Home Business* (Vol. 13, January/February 2006, No. 1, pp. 98) **[4740]**, **[23099]**, **[34261]**, **[42877]**, **[47342]**, **[48770]**, **[49167]**, **[53386]**

"News from the Small Business Front" in *My Business* (June/July 2002, pp. 14) **[26860]**, **[28070]**, **[29412]**, **[35589]**, **[40572]**, **[49168]**

News Tribune (March 2, 2005); "Business Briefs" in **[7280]**, **[13216]**, **[29134]**, **[43107]**

News Tribune (April 11, 2003); "Diplomat Sells Trade with China at Tacoma, Wash., Symposium" in **[24921]**, **[43624]**

News Tribune (April 11, 2003) "Study Foresees End of Boeing's Commercial Work; Company Calls Report Flawed" in **[28840]**, **[43830]**, **[46448]**

News Tribune (April 11, 2003); "Washington State Apple Commission Shuts Down Soon after Ruling on Fees" in **[26559]**, **[40815]**

"News on Women" in *Marketing to Women* (Vol. 19, November 2006, No. 22, pp. 8) **[737]**, **[5699]**, **[28561]**, **[47343]**

News of the World **[10525]**

NewsAccount **[337]**

The NewsBank NewsFile Collection **[18986]**

Newsday (March 8, 2005); "Newsday's Weekday, Saturday Circulation Drops 2 Percent" in **[18917]**, **[28562]**

Newsday (August 22, 2004); "Saks Offers Complimentary 'Personal Shopper' Service in Long Island Store" in **[19006]**, **[51340]**

"Newsday Suit Lawyer Enlists 'Big Firms'" in *Long Island Business News* (February 27, 2004) **[18916]**, **[29413]**

"Newsday's Weekday, Saturday Circulation Drops 2 Percent" in *Newsday* (March 8, 2005) **[18917]**, **[28562]**

NewsEdge Insight **[3932]**

NewsEdge Live **[3933]**, **[39743]**

Newsletter Communications **[18257]**

Newsletter Design **[18239]**

Newsletter and Electronic Publishers Association **[18217]**

The Newsletter on Newsletters **[18258]**

"Newsletter company to nearly double in size" in *Atlanta Business Chronicle* (Vol. 25, January 10, 2003, No. 31, pp. 5A) **[8620]**, **[16820]**, **[18240]**, **[47344]**, **[50647]**

Newsletters in Print **[5499]**, **[18241]**

Newsline **[12672]**, **[22431]**

Newspaper Abstracts National **[5506]**

"Newspaper Relocates" in *Bellingham Business Journal* (January 2007, pp. A5) **[738]**, **[18918]**, **[30164]**

Newspring Ventures **[64567]**

"Newsstand" in *Home Business* (Vol. 13, January/February 2006, No. 1, pp. 38-39) **[6265]**, **[6741]**, **[18607]**, **[29414]**, **[32598]**, **[34262]**, **[36550]**, **[42687]**, **[47345]**, **[49521]**, **[50101]**, **[51272]**, **[54676]**

Newtek Ventures **[58099]**

Newton Area Chamber of Commerce and Visitors Bureau **[60392]**

Newton Chamber of Commerce **[61820]**

Newton County Chamber of Commerce **[65412]**

"Newton Furniture Shutters Stores" in *Crain's Detroit Business* (Vol. 21, October 31, 2005, No. 44, pp. 30) **[12200]**, **[12303]**

"Newton Gets Whiff of Success in Bottles: Glass Factory Makes Vials for Perfumes" in *Altanta Journal-Constitution* (January 29, 2007) **[2599]**, **[7899]**, **[46391]**

Newton - Needham Chamber of Commerce **[60981]**

The NewYork Times (March 27, 2000, pp. D28, H28); "1,000 Crates of Sprinkles With That" in **[34285]**, **[47370]**

"NEXIS Finally Goes Dot-Com" in *Information Today* (Vol. 17, No. 10, November 2000, pp. 32) **[34263]**, **[49169]**

"The next best thing to being there?" in *E-business Advisor* (Vol. 18, No. 10, October 2000, pp. 11) **[9734]**, **[34264]**, **[48771]**

"The next big e-thing" in *WorkingWoman* (Vol. 25, No. 5, May 2000, pp. 72) **[34265]**

"The Next Big Idea is Already Here" in *Automotive News* (Vol. 79, January 24, 2005, No. 79, pp. 12) **[18099]**, **[47346]**

"The Next Big Market" in *Success* (Vol. 47, No. 5, October 2000, pp. 36) **[47347]**, **[53884]**

"The Next Big Things: Nothing is more profitable than an investment idea whose time has come" in *Fortune* (Vol. 140, December 20, 1999) **[38246]**, **[53885]**

"The Next Big Trend: Cutting Mgmt. Fees" in *Venture Capital Journal* (Vol. 42, No. 9, September 2002, pp. 6, 8-9) **[28563]**, **[53886]**, **[55754]**

"The Next Generation. Planning Ahead" in *San Francisco Business Times* (Vol. 17, No. 48, July 4, 2003, pp. 15) **[2252]**, **[29943]**, **[37743]**

"The Next Management Revolution" in *Inc.* (July 1, 2004) **[36551]**, **[45471]**

Next Point Partners, L.P. **[58676]**

"Next Round on Adarand" in *Hispanic Business* (Vol. 23, No. 7/8, July/August 2001, pp. 26) **[39494]**, **[40067]**

"Next step: Bricks and mortar" in *Crain's Detroit Business* (Vol. 19, No. 10, March 10, 2003, pp. 11) **[41869]**, **[44104]**, **[50102]**, **[52160]**

"NextEnergy gets $2M from feds" in *Crain's Detroit Business* (Vol. 19, No. 10, March 10, 2003, pp. 29) **[40573]**, **[41870]**, **[44605]**, **[50936]**, **[52161]**

"NextEnergy May Get HQ" in *Crain's Detroit Business* (Vol. 22, February 6, 2006, No. 6, pp. 11) **[41871]**, **[52704]**

NextGen Partners LLC **[58100]**

Nextreme Ventures **[58101]**

"NextWave to Buy Go Networks, Lists on Nasdaq" in *San Diego Business Journal* (Vol. 28, January 8, 2007, No. 2, pp. 5) **[17008]**, **[41872]**, **[50103]**

Nextwave Computers **[6441]**

NFCC Directory of Members **[8355]**, **[8389]**

NFDA Bulletin **[10812]**

NFDA Directory of Members and Resource Guide **[10804]**

"NFIB Building on Tax Cut Victory for Members" in *My Business* (September/October 2001, pp. 18) **[32599]**, **[54677]**

"NFIB Education Foundation: small business economic survey" in *Small Business Economic Trends* (August 2000, pp. 1) **[53887]**

"NFIB Lays Groundwork for 108th Congress" in *My Business* (February/March 2003, pp. 18) **[39495], [40574]**

"NFIB Report From The State Capitals" in *My Business* (August/September 2002, pp. 20-22) **[29415], [40575]**

"NFIB Report From The State Capitols" in *My Business* (December/January 2003, pp. 20-23) **[39496], [40178], [40576], [41179]**

"NFIB Report from the State Capitals" in *My Business* (April/May 2002, pp. 22-25) **[29416], [35110], [39497], [40577], [41180], [42042]**

"NFIB Report from the State Capitols" in *My Business* (November/December 2001, pp. 20-22) **[1500], [39498], [40578], [40610], [53888]**

"NFL Reaches Out" in *Crain's Detroit Business* (Vol. 21, January 3, 2005, No. 1, pp. 12) **[36552], [48339], [56347]**

The NGA Show: America's Glass Expo (GlassBuild) **[11230]**

NGDC Geologic Hazards Photos **[9421]**

NGS Newsmagazine **[10976]**

Niagara County Community College International Trade Center–SBDC **[62772]** SBDC **[62773]**

Niagara County Community College at Sanborn–Small Business Development Center **[62774]**

Niagara University–Library–Rare Book Room Collection **[1367]**

Niagara USA Chamber **[62971]**

"Nice Girls Don't Ask" in *Harvard Business Review* (Vol. 81, No. 10, October 2003, pp. 14) **[45472], [56348]**

"Nice work If You Can Get It" in *Fortune* (Vol. 140, No. 11, December 6, 1999, pp. 177+) **[55410]**

"Nice meeting you!" in *Entrepreneur* (Vol. 30, No. 12, December 2002, pp. 111) **[27456], [36553], [39499]**

Niceville-Valparaiso Bay Area Chamber of Commerce **[58900]**

Nicholas Brealey Publishing **[59811]**

Nicholby's Franchise Systems Inc. **[51465]**

Nichols College–Conant Library **[26445], [38595], [46153]**

Nick-N-Willy's World Famous Take-N-Bake Pizza **[19692]**

"Nicknamed 'nag' she's just doing her job" in *Wall Street Journal* (May 14, 2002, pp. B1) **[45473]**

Nicoma Park Chamber of Commerce **[64045]**

NIF Ventures USA, Inc. **[58102]**

"Night of Stars" in *Hispanic Business* (January/February 2004, pp. 20, 22, 24) **[36554], [48340]**

Nightclub & Bar/Beverage Retailer/Food and Beverage Convention & Tradeshow **[2376], [21709]**

Nightingale Associates **[3780], [16653], [30106], [31425], [42990], [43928], [46093]**

Nightly Business Report: How Wall Street Works-The NBR Guide to Investing in the Financial Markets **[15711]**

"A Night's Sleep, Ultracheap" in *Business Week* (January 23, 2006, No. 3968, pp. 73) **[12603], [30388], [43765]**

"Nike Develops Brand for Women" in *Marketing to Women* (Vol. 20, January 2007, No. 1, pp. 8) **[22764], [47348], [48772], [50104]**

Nike HealthWalking Training System **[19485]**

Nikki Safety Consultants **[1151]**

Nikmal Financial Services **[10344]**

"Nikon's Newly Created Long Island Unit to Scout Tech Trends for the Home Office" in *Long Island Business News* (March 12, 2004) **[4178], [4193], [42688], [42821], [49170], [50171]**

Niland Chamber of Commerce **[57661]**

Niles Chamber of Chamber of Commerce and Industry **[59611]**

Nimark Group Inc. **[50330]**

"Nina Zagat: My Biggest Mistake" in *Inc.* (April 2000, pp. 145) **[2727], [14295], [25914], [52379]**

"9/11 Call: When Crisis Hit, Business Owners Answered" in *Entrepeneur* (Vol. 30, No. 2, February 2002, pp. 46) **[36555], [39500]**

"9/11 Calls: Wireless Devices in the Post-Attacks Era"in *Entrepeneur* (Vol. 30, No. 1, January 2002, pp. 39) **[5071], [27457], [41873]**

900 Know-How: How to Succeed with Your Own 900 Number Business **[8667]**

Nine Lives Associates **[19957], [22155]**

Nine Lives Associates-Membership Directory **[19970], [22313]**

The 9to5 Guide to Combating Sexual Harassment: Candid Advice from 9to5, the National Association of Working Women **[32049]**

"9 Ways to be More Frugal" in *My Business* (September/October 2001, pp. 43) **[27155]**

"Nine Ways to Slash Your Insurance Costs, From Health Savings Accounts to Getting Tough With Your Broker To Joining Purchasing Pools" in *Inc.* **[13401], [43293]**

"Nine Ways to Slash Your Insurance Costs" in *Inc.* (April 1, 2005) **[13402], [43294]**

1998 Plumber's Business Planner **[19752], [22717]**

1995-96 Greeting Card Industry Directory: A Comprehensive Guide to the Products & Services of the Greeting Card Industry **[11570]**

"1999 McKinsey Awards" in *Harvard Business* (Vol. 78, No. 1, January 2000, pp. 137) **[31800], [46392], [52923]**

1997 Valuation Survey of A E P & Environmental Consulting Firms **[9369]**

"90 percent of laid-off hotel workers back on the job" in *Boston Business Journal* (Vol. 22, No. 16, May 24, 2002, pp. 7) **[12604], [32600], [42362]**

Ninety Six Chamber of Commerce **[64773]**

90 Telemarketing Selling Skills for the '90s **[24302]**

90 Telemarketing Skills in 90 Minutes **[24303]**

93M in Development Planned for South Lyon" in *Crain's Detroit Business* (V. 19, No. 7, 2/17/03, pp. 22); "$ **[7441]**

Niobrara Chamber of Commerce **[66621]**

"Nip It In the Bud" in *Entrepreneur* (Vol. 32, November 2004, No. 11, pp. 95) **[29417], [45474]**

Nipawin School Division–Education Resource Centre **[17692], [17823]**

Nipomo Chamber of Commerce **[57662]**

Nirvana in a Cup: The Founding of Oregon Chai **[11340], [36556], [37744]**

"The Nirve of These Guys" in *Success* (Vol. 47, No. 6, November 2000, pp. 20) **[18630], [23590], [33466]**

Nisonger Associates Inc. **[12697], [21728]**

Nisswa Chamber of Commerce **[61636]**

Nite Time Decor **[9121], [15972], [16080]**

NiteLites Franchise Systems, Inc. **[16161]**

Nitrogreen Professional Lawn & Tree Care **[16081], [16162]**

Nixa Area Chamber of Commerce **[62010]**

Nixon Peabody LLP–Law Library **[9540]**

"NLRB Finds California Almond Growers Engaged in Anti-Union Activity" in *Sacramento Bee* (November 1, 2005) **[26525], [55302]**

"NMAC Settles Suit" in *Hispanic Business* (September 2003, pp. 20) **[18100], [29418], [32050]**

NMBC Business Report **[48494]**

NMMA Boat Show News **[5247]**

"NMSDC Confab" in *Hispanic Business* (Vol. 23, No. 10, October, 2001, pp. 22) **[39501], [48341]**

"NMSDC Honors PepsiCo, Toyota" in *Hispanic Business* (January/February 2005, pp. 16) **[1954], [18101], [46393], [48342]**

NMW - National Manufacturing Week **[46530]**

"No Ad Recession for Hispanic Marketers" in *Business Week Online* (February 19, 2002) **[739], [47349]**

"No Bad Days: Sherry Williams excels as a Mary Kay sales pro while battling breast cancer" in *Black Enterprise* (Oct. 2002, pp. 175) **[2600], [2635], [7900], [7955], [40840], [42689], [56349]**

"No Bankruptcy Break for Hurricane Victims" in *Credit Union Journal* (Vol. 9, October 3, 2005, No. 39, pp. 12) **[29419], [31568], [40579]**

"No Biz Like Show Biz" in *Small Business Opportunities* (Vol. 13, No. 6, November 2001, pp. 18) **[24986], [55134]**

"No Boundaries" in *Rough Notes* (Vol. 145, No. 9, September 2002, pp. 54) **[13403], [43295]**

"No more boxes" in *Black Enterprise* (Vol. 32, No. 9, April 2002, pp. 54) **[4741], [23100]**

"No Brainer: Simple Ways to Solve Your Own Tech Problems" in *My Business* (October/November 2002, pp. 44) **[42690], [49171]**

"No coddling? Work-site day care, once the rage, falls under pressures" in *Wall Street Journal* (April 2, 2002, pp. A1) **[5343], [26861]**

"No Credit? No Problem! Here's How to Get Good Credit If You Don't Have Any" in *Black Enterprise* (Vol. 35, February 2005, No. 7) **[8315], [8356], [8390], [31569]**

"No Escape? Even the Internet May Not Be Able to Avoid Taxes" in *Entrepreneur* (Vol. 31, No. 4, April 2003, pp. 17) **[14296], [34266], [54678]**

"No Fast Cash Class" in *Black Enterprise* (Vol. 37, December 2006, No. 5, pp. 72) **[10109], [33191], [38247]**

"No Free Lunch" in *Entrepreneur* (Vol. 32, October 2004, No. 10, pp. 107) **[12785], [37745], [38866]**

"No Guts, Some Glory" in *Entrepreneur* (Vol. 31, No. 10, October 2003, pp. 60) **[10110], [15303], [38248]**

"No Husband, No Loan" in *Entrepreneur* (Vol. 28, No. 11, November 2000, pp. 40) **[44606]**

"No IPO market? No problem. Call Ravisent" in *Red Herring* (No. 106, October 15, 2001, pp. 94) **[4742], [14297], [15304], [23101], [50105]**

"No sweet deal for Key" in *Baltimore Business Journal* (Vol. 19, No. 19, October 5, 2001, pp. 3) **[4301]**

"No Line At 6 a.m. Black Friday" in *Tampa Tribune* (December 7, 2005) **[30920], [47350], [51273]**

"No mercy: are VCs sucking the life out of your business?" in *Entrepreneur* (Vol. 30, No. 12, December 2002, pp. 79) **[32601], [55755]**

"No Money Down" in *Forbes* (Vol. 175, January 10, 2005, No. 1, pp. 44) **[17424], [20611]**

No Money down Financing for Franchising **[38867]**

No More Cold Calls **[52568]**

"No More Debt" in *Black Enterprise* (Vol. 37, November 2006, No. 4, pp. 159) **[31570], [38249]**

"No More Free Rides: It's the End of the Free Lunch on the Web" in *Black Enterprise* (Vol. 32, No. 6, January 2002, pp. 39) **[14298], [25915], [28565], [34267]**

No More Frogs to Kiss **[56350]**

"No More Ms. NiceGuy: Do Nice Girls Really Finish Last in the Business World" in *Entrepreneur* (Vol. 33, February 2005, No. 2, pp. 34) **[45475], [56351]**

"No More Postdating: New Bill Allows Banks to Process Your Checks at Warp Speed" in *Black Enterprise* (Vol. 35, January 2005, No. 6) **[207], [2937], [10111], [26303]**

"No More Waiting" in *Electronic Publishing* (Vol. 27, No. 7, July 2003, pp. 4) **[15931], [18242]**

"No experience necessary" in *Entrepreneur* (Vol. 30, No. 12, December 2002, pp. 109) **[42363], [51745]**

"No Pain, All Gain" in *Success* (Vol. 47, No. 3, July 2000, pp. 24) **[17250], [33467]**

"No Pain, No Gain" in *Entrepreneur* (Vol. 28, No. 4, April 2000, pp. 42) **[14299], [34268]**

The No-Pain Resume Workbook: A Complete Guide to Job-Winning Resumes **[22046]**

"No Place Like Home" in *Entrepreneur* (Vol. 32, December 2004, No. 12, pp. 108) **[453], [19002], [37746], [52569]**

No Place Like Home: Organizing Home-Based Labor in the Era of Structural Adjustment **[42691], [55303]**

"No Recovery for Disabled?" in *Wall Street Journal* (April 16, 2002, pp. B1) **[42364]**

"No Refuge" in *Entrepreneur* (Vol. 33, October 2005, No. 10, pp. 56) **[51965], [54679]**

"No Respect: ONI Systems is the ugly stepchild of the networking market" in *Red Herring* (No. 105, October 1, 2001, pp. 92) **[6954]**, **[28566]**, **[37171]**

"No Room for Mediocrity" in *Fast Company* (September 2001, pp. 160) **[12605]**, **[31801]**

No Salt Week-The Newsletter **[7821]**, **[12028]**, **[12068]**, **[12155]**, **[18453]**

"No Slam Dunk" in *Hispanic Business* (July/August 2002, pp. 28, 30) **[15305]**, **[23727]**, **[24439]**

"No Slowdown Likely for Rising Health Costs" in *Crain's Detroit Business* (Vol. 22, November 27, 2006, No. 48, pp. 21) **[29944]**, **[39878]**, **[41069]**

"No Small Change" in *Black Enterprise* (Vol. 32, No. 8, March 2002, pp. 64) **[14300]**, **[25916]**, **[34269]**, **[48343]**, **[56352]**

"No Small Plans" in *Inc.* (December 1, 2004) **[10514]**, **[36557]**, **[54233]**

"No Surrender" in *Entrepreneur* (Vol. 33, January 2005, No. 1, pp. 63) **[45476]**, **[51746]**

"No Sweat" in *Entrepreneur* (Vol. 32, December 2004, No. 12, pp. 126) **[5563]**, **[9633]**, **[23628]**

"No, They Can't Do It Themselves" in *Inc.* (July 1, 2004) **[18919]**, **[28567]**, **[30921]**, **[50106]**

"No Ticket to Easy Street" in *Black Enterprise* (Vol. 31, No. 4, November 2000, pp. 62) **[35590]**, **[38666]**

"No Train, No Gain?" in *Entrepreneur* (Vol. 32, October 2004, No. 10, pp. 96) **[27156]**, **[33192]**

"No Vacancies" in *Black Enterprise* (Vol. 36, December 2005, No. 5, pp. 62) **[20612]**, **[20952]**

"No Wonder Market Shares are Falling" in *Automotive News* (Vol. 79, February 21, 2005, No. 6135, pp. 12) **[18102]**, **[28568]**, **[46394]**

"No-Work Wonders" in *Small Business Opportunities* (Vol. 16, No. 2, March 2004, pp. 140) **[33468]**

Noble and Associates–Library **[914]**, **[2321]**, **[4576]**, **[5784]**, **[7106]**, **[7691]**, **[8588]**, **[10653]**, **[22038]**

Noble Chamber of Commerce **[64046]**

Noble County Chamber of Commerce **[63751]**

"Noble International to Buy Laser Welding International" in *Crain's Detroit Business* (January 26, 2004, pp. 20) **[15306]**, **[18103]**, **[46395]**

Noble Roman's Pizza **[19693]**, **[21908]**

Noblesville Chamber of Commerce **[59979]**

Nobody Gets Rich Working for Somebody Else: An Entrepreneur's Guide **[52924]**

Nobody's Business but Your Own **[35591]**

"Nobody's Fool? Health Insurance Scams Target Entrepreneurs" in *Entrepreneur* (Vol. 32, August 2004, No. 8, pp. 21) **[13404]**, **[26862]**, **[30243]**, **[41070]**, **[43296]**

Nobody's Perfect: Managing the Team **[45936]**

Nocona Area Chamber of Commerce **[65413]**

Nogales-Santa Cruz County Chamber of Commerce **[57052]**

Noguska L.L.C. **[63905]**

"Nokia 9300 SmartPhone" in *Black Enterprise* (Vol. 35, December 2004, No. 5, pp. 70) **[5072]**, **[49172]**

Nokia Venture Partners **[58103]**

Nome Chamber of Commerce **[56970]**

"NOM's Moms" in *WWD* (November 3, 2003, pp. 12) **[5700]**

Non-Thermal Plasma Techniques for Pollution Control **[1071]**

Non-Verbal Communication **[51969]**

"Nonindividual QTP Contributions: How Employers Can Help Workers Save for College" in *Journal of Accountancy* (Vol. 198, November 2004) **[208]**, **[2938]**, **[24001]**, **[26304]**, **[26863]**, **[27157]**

"Nonprofit groups provide banking for bankless" in *Wall Street Journal* (October 3, 2000, pp. B1) **[44607]**

"Nonprofit Consolidation to Increase" in *Crain's Detroit Business* (Vol. 22, November 27, 2006, No. 48, pp. 20) **[38250]**, **[48920]**, **[50107]**

"The Nonprofit Motive" in *Fortune* (Vol. 148, No. 8, October 13, 2003, pp. 214) **[6955]**, **[36558]**, **[50937]**

A Nonprofit Organization Operating Manual: Planning for Survival and Growth **[1738]**

"Nonprofit Seminar is March 13" in *Crain's Detroit Business* (Vol. 22, February 13, 2006, No. 7, pp. 26) **[10744]**, **[24987]**, **[55135]**

The NonProfit Times **[10756]**

"Nonprofits shift strategy to personal appeals" in *Atlanta Business Chronicle* (Vol. 25, December 6, 2002, No. 26, pp. 5A) **[27664]**, **[54234]**

"Nonprofits Eye New Revenue Ideas as Gifts, Grants Dwindle" in *Boston Business Journal* (Vol. 23, No. 31, September 5, 2003, pp. 1) **[10745]**, **[32602]**, **[38251]**

"Nonstop Innovation" in *Inc.* (Volume 27, July 2005, No. 7, pp. 34) **[35004]**, **[36559]**, **[44105]**

"The nontraditional student in you" in *Women In Business* (Vol. 52, No. 4, July 2000, pp. 14) **[33193]**

Norco Chamber of Commerce **[57663]**

Nord & Demand **[29641]**

Nordonia Hills Chamber of Commerce **[63752]**

Norfolk Area Chamber of Commerce **[62284]**

Norfolk Botanical Garden Society–Frederic Heutte Memorial Library **[11532]**

Norfolk Historical Society–Archives **[11064]**

Norman Chamber of Commerce **[64047]**

Normandale Associates Inc. **[21088]**

Normandale Community College **[61731]**

Normandale Community College (Bloomington)–Small Business Development Center **[61526]**

Noro-Moseley Partners **[59201]**

"Norquist Sees Antitax Crusade as Cornerstone of GOP Domination" in *Tax Notes* (Vol. 102, No. 3, January 19, 2004, pp. 307-317) **[54680]**

NORTEL–Information Resource Network **[26033]**

"Nortel Net-telephony package aims at small businesses" in *InfoWorld* (Vol. 22, No. 27, July 3, 2000, pp. 46) **[49173]**

Nortext Multimedia Inc. (Iqaluit) **[66713]**

Nortext Multimedia Inc. (Ottawa) **[66759]**

North America Investment Corp. **[66654]**

North American Association of Food Equipment Manufacturers **[21430]**

North American Association of State and Provincial Lotteries Conference and Trade Show **[10902]**, **[55237]**

North American Bookdealers Exchange **[64313]**

North American Brewers Resource Directory **[3131]**

North American Broadcasters Association **[20293]**, **[24367]**

North American Building Material Distribution Association **[7230]**

North American Building Material Distribution Association-Membership Directory **[16315]**

North American Business Development Co., L.L.C. **[58975]**

North American-Chilean Chamber of Commerce **[43520]**

North American Family Campers Association **[4230]**

North American Flowerbulb Wholesalers Association **[11415]**, **[15966]**, **[15999]**

North American Gaming Regulators Association **[10859]**

North American Graphic Arts Suppliers Association **[5959]**, **[19854]**

North American Horsemen's Association **[12451]**

North American Insulation Manufacturers Association **[13133]**

North American International Auto Show **[18195]**

North American Journal of Aquaculture **[10470]**

North American Journal of Economics and Finance **[10287]**, **[32822]**, **[38493]**

North American Manufacturing Research Institution **[46552]**

North American Radio Archives–Tape and Printed Materials Libraries **[20385]**

North American Radio Archives (NARA)–Library **[20386]**

North American Securities Administrators Association **[14708]**

North American Snowsports Journalists Association **[8967]**, **[18840]**

North American Wholesale Lumber Association **[16291]**

North American Wholesale Lumber Association-Distribution Directory **[16316]**

North Atlantic Capital Corporation **[60785]**

North Attleboro and Plainville Chamber of Commerce **[60982]**

North Augusta Chamber of Commerce **[64774]**

North Baldwin Chamber of Commerce **[56876]**

North Baltimore Area Chamber of Commerce **[63753]**

North Branch Area Chamber of Commerce **[61637]**

North Bridge Venture Partners **[61103]**

North Business and Industrial Council (NORBIC)–SBDC **[59384]**

North Canton Area Chamber of Commerce **[63754]**

North Carolina A&T State University
    Division of Research **[63475]**
    Small Business and Technology Development Center **[63279]**

North Carolina Association of Plumbing, Heating, and Cooling Contractors Annual Trade Show **[1047]**, **[19767]**

North Carolina Department of Administration–Purchase and Contract Division–State Purchasing Office **[63472]**

North Carolina Department of Agriculture and Consumer Services–Sandhills Research Station **[16172]**

North Carolina Department of Agriculture and Consumers Services–Division of Marketing **[63291]**

North Carolina Department of Commerce–Business/Industry Development Division **[63292]**

North Carolina Department of Community Colleges–Small Business Center Network **[63293]**

North Carolina Department of Environment and Natural Resources–DENR Library **[9505]**

The North Carolina Enterprise Fund, L.P. **[63462]**

North Carolina Fair Share **[3781]**, **[31426]**, **[50380]**

North Carolina Genealogical Society Journal **[10977]**

North Carolina Medical Society Annual Meeting **[17272]**

North Carolina Office of State Budget and Management **[66943]**

North Carolina Rural Economic Development Center–Micro Enterprise Loan Program **[63294]**

North Carolina SBDTC–University of North Carolina **[63271]**

North Carolina School of the Arts–Semans Library **[1665]**, **[8495]**, **[9773]**, **[17693]**, **[17824]**

North Carolina Small Business Partnership **[63295]**

North Carolina Small Business and Technology Development Center–Western Carolina Small Business and Technology Development Center **[63296]**

North Carolina (State) Department of Labor–Charles H. Livengood, Jr. Memorial Labor Library **[56697]**

North Carolina (State) Department of Transportation–Research and Development Library **[2116]**, **[8743]**, **[16202]**, **[24261]**

North Carolina State University
    Industrial Extension Service **[63297]**
    Libraries–D.H. Hill Library - Special Collections Research Center **[7692]**
    Research Stations Division **[26692]**

North Carolina Technological Development Authority–First Flight Venture Center **[63476]**

North Carolina Technological Development Authority, Inc. **[63463]**

North Carolina Wesleyan College–SBDC **[63280]**

North Central Chamber of Commerce **[64671]**

North Central Connecticut Chamber of Commerce **[58556]**

North Central Idaho Business Technology Incubator **[59345]**

North Central Indiana–Small Business Development Center **[59829]**

North Central Massachusetts Chamber of Commerce **[60983]**

North Central Michigan College **[61497]**

North Central Pennsylvania Regional Planning and Devolvment Commission **[64611]**

North Central Regional Aquaculture Center **[10432]**

North Central Texas College–Small Business Development Center **[65051]**

North Channel Area Chamber of Commerce **[65414]**

North Charles Mental Health Research and Training Foundation, Inc. **[54401]**

North Clackamas County Chamber of Commerce **[64248]**

North Coast–Small Business Development Center **[57267]**

North Coast Regional Chamber of Commerce **[63755]**

"North Cobb office market healthier than most" in *Atlanta Business Chronicle* (Vol. 25, December 6, 2002, No. 26, pp. 20C) **[20613]**, **[20953]**, **[28569]**, **[52705]**

North Conway Institute–Resource Center - Alcohol and Drugs **[54385]**

North Country Chamber of Commerce **[62435]**

North County Chamber of Commerce **[62011]**

North Dade Regional Chamber of Commerce **[58901]**

North Dakota Agriculture Department–Research, Information and Policy Development **[26693]**

North Dakota Department of Commerce–Department of Economic Development and Finance **[63502]**

North Dakota Economic Development and Finance Department–Procurement Division **[63542]**

The North Dakota Financial Institutions Directory **[44608]**

North Dakota SBDC–University of North Carolina **[63487]**

North Dakota (State) Department of Transportation–Materials and Research Division–Library **[2117]**, **[8744]**, **[16203]**, **[24262]**

North Dakota State Library **[66946]**

North Dakota State University
Institute for Business and Industry Development **[32859]**
North Dakota State Data Center **[66947]**
Transportation Technology Transfer Center **[63543]**

North Dallas Chamber of Commerce **[65415]**

North East Area Chamber of Commerce **[64480]**

North East Chamber of Commerce **[60842]**

North Essex Chamber of Commerce **[62538]**

North Florida Regional Chamber of Commerce **[58902]**

"North Fork Bancorp Acquires GreenPoint Financial" in *Long Island Business News* (February 20, 2004) **[15307]**, **[50108]**

"North Fork Bancorp to Trim Employees of Two Acquisitions" in *Long Island Business News* (March 12, 2004) **[10112]**, **[10483]**, **[15308]**, **[50109]**, **[51140]**

North Fork Chamber of Commerce **[57664]**

North Fort Myers Chamber of Commerce **[58903]**

North Galveston County Chamber of Commerce **[65416]**

North Harris Montgomery–Community College District SBDC **[65052]**

North Harris Montgomery Community College District–Small Business Development Center **[65053]**

North Haven Gardens **[16146]**

North Hennepin Area Chamber of Commerce **[61638]**

"North Highland creates transportation service" in *Atlanta Business Chronicle* (Vol. 25, No. 21, November 1, 2002, pp. 10A) **[3566]**, **[16526]**, **[41874]**

North Hill Ventures **[61104]**

North Houston-Greenspoint Chamber of Commerce **[65417]**

North Idaho Business Journal **[59357]**

North Idaho College–Professional - Technical Education **[59354]**

North Idaho College (Region 1)–Small Business Development Center **[59279]**

North Iowa Area–Small Business Development Center **[60061]**

North Jersey Regional Chamber of Commerce **[62539]**

North Kingstown Chamber of Commerce **[64672]**

North Las Vegas Chamber of Commerce **[62363]**

North Las Vegas Small Business Development Center **[62329]**

North Little Rock Chamber of Commerce **[57201]**

North Manchester Chamber of Commerce **[59980]**

North Mason Chamber of Commerce **[66141]**

"North Massapequa-based Love 'n' Care Pet Sitting Service Walks, Trains, and Cares for Pets" in *Long Island Business News* (Jan.30,2004) **[19077]**, **[19114]**, **[19194]**

North Miami Beach Chamber of Commerce **[58904]**

North Monterey County Chamber of Commerce **[57665]**

North Myrtle Beach Chamber of Commerce **[64775]**

North Newton Area Chamber of Commerce **[59981]**

North Olmsted Chamber of Commerce **[63756]**

North Pacific Anadromous Fish Commission **[10449]**

North Palm Beach County Chamber of Commerce **[58905]**

North Park Chamber of Commerce **[58411]**

North Penn Chamber of Commerce **[64481]**

North Phoenix Chamber of Commerce **[57053]**

North Platte Area Chamber of Commerce **[62285]**

North Platte Center–Small Business Development Center **[62224]**

North Port Area Chamber of Commerce **[58906]**

North Quabbin Chamber of Commerce **[60984]**

North of the River Chamber of Commerce **[57666]**

North Royalton Chamber of Commerce **[63757]**

North Sacramento Chamber of Commerce **[57667]**

North San Antonio Chamber of Commerce **[65418]**

North Santiam Chamber of Commerce **[64249]**

North Shore Chamber of Commerce **[60985]**

"North-South Power Balance" in *Hispanic Business* (November 2003, pp. 58, 64) **[12999]**, **[43766]**

North Suburban Chamber of Commerce **[60986]**

North Tampa Chamber of Commerce **[58907]**

North Texas MESBIC, Inc. **[65621]**

"North market merchants selling Valentine's package" in *Business First Columbus* (Vol. 18, No. 25, February 8, 2002, pp. A12) **[21576]**, **[47351]**

North Valley Regional Chamber of Commerce **[57668]**

North Webster - Tippecanoe Township Chamber of Commerce **[59982]**

North York Central Library–Canadiana Department **[11065]**

Northampton Area Chamber of Commerce **[64482]**

Northampton Community College **[64626]**
Paul and Harriett Mack Library **[10819]**

Northampton County Chamber of Commerce **[65932]**

Northbrook Chamber of Commerce and Industry **[59612]**

Northcoast Environmental Center–Library **[9449]**

Northeast Alabama Entrepreneurial System **[56923]**

Northeast Cincinnati Chamber of Commerce **[63758]**

Northeast Floral Expo **[10597]**

Northeast Indiana Regional Office–Small Business Development Center **[59830]**

Northeast Iowa–Small Business Development Center **[60062]**

Northeast Johnson County Chamber of Commerce **[60393]**

Northeast Kingdom Chamber of Commerce **[65794]**

Northeast Mississippi Community College–SBDC **[61760]**

"Northeast Ohio Cottage Industry of eBay Drop-Off Stores Emerges" in *News-Herald, Willoughby* (April 3, 2004) **[1839]**, **[7169]**, **[18655]**, **[34270]**, **[52570]**

Northeast Ohio Procurement Technical Assistance Center–Lake County Economic Development Center **[63863]**

Northeast San Fernando Valley Chamber of Commerce **[57669]**

Northeast Sustainable Energy Association–Library **[23349]**

Northeast Tarrant Chamber of Commerce **[65419]**

Northeast Technology Center **[64150]**

Northeast Texarkana–Small Business Development Center **[65054]**

Northeast Ventures **[58603]**

Northeast Ventures Corporation **[61704]**

Northeastern Connecticut Chamber of Commerce **[58557]**

Northeastern Illinois Planning Commission–Data Research and Forcasting **[66869]**

Northeastern Lumber Manufacturers Association **[16292]**

Northeastern Oklahoma A&M–Miami Satellite–SBDC **[63914]**

Northeastern Oklahoma State University–Small Business Development Center–Tahlequah Satellite Office **[63915]**

Northeastern Regional Aquaculture Center **[10433]**

Northeastern State University–Small Business Development Center **[63916]**

Northeastern University
Center for Nano and Microcontamination Control **[1084]**
Division of Research Management **[61146]**

Northeastern Vermont Development Association–Small Business Development Center **[65766]**

"Northeast's Largest Independent Accounting Firm Comes to Long Island" in *Long Island Business News* (February 6, 2004) **[209]**, **[2939]**, **[24002]**, **[26305]**

Northern Allegheny County Chamber of Commerce **[64483]**

Northern Anne Arundel County Chamber of Commerce **[60843]**

Northern Arizona Genealogical Society Bulletin **[10978]**

Northern Arizona University–College of Business Administration **[66823]**

"Northern Bounty" in *Black Enterprise* (Vol. 36, December 2005, No. 5, pp. 45) **[10113]**, **[15309]**

Northern Dakota County Chamber of Commerce **[61639]**

"Northern Exposure: American Entrepreneurs are Finding Success by Heading for the Border" in *Entrepreneur* (Vol. 31, August 2003) **[36560]**, **[43767]**, **[55756]**

Northern Gateway Chamber of Commerce **[62436]**

Northern Illinois University
The Regional Development Institute (RDI)–Center for Governmental Studies **[66870]**
Technology Commercialization Office **[59784]**

Northern Kathadin Valley Region Chamber of Commerce **[60764]**

Northern Kentucky Chamber of Commerce **[60553]**

Northern Kentucky University–SBDC **[60465]**

Northern Kentucky University Foundation Inc. **[60589]**

Northern Lakes Economic Alliance–SBDC **[61212]**

Northern Maine Development Commission–Maine SBDC Service Center at Caribou **[60713]**

Northern Monmouth Chamber of Commerce **[62540]**

Northern New Mexico College–Small Business Development Center **[62654]**

Northern New Mexico Community College **[62737]**

Northern Pike: The Water World **[2196]**

Northern Rhode Island Chamber of Commerce **[64673]**
SBDC **[64650]**

Northern Tier Chamber of Commerce **[62972]**

"Northern Trust Close To an Outsourcing Foothold in Britain" in *American Banker* (Vol. 170, February 3, 2005, No. 23, pp. 2) **[10114]**, **[15310]**, **[43768]**, **[49719]**

Northern Virginia Community College **[65999]**

Northern Westmoreland Chamber of Commerce **[64484]**

Northern White Mountain Chamber of Commerce **[62437]**

Northfield Area Chamber of Commerce **[61640]**

Northfield Enterprise Center–SBDC for Rice County **[61527]**

"Northfield Hits Blood-Test Hurdle" in *Wall Street Journal* (Vol. 248, December 2006, No. 145, pp. A10) **[41875]**, **[52162]**

Northlake Chamber of Commerce **[59613]**

Northland Pioneer College–Small Business Development Center **[56996]**

Northland Regional Chamber of Commerce **[62012]**

"Northrop Grumman in Bethpage Celebrates National Engineers Week..." in *Long Island Business News* (March 5, 2004) **[41876]**, **[52163]**

"Northrop Grumman in Bethpage Celebrates National Engineers Week with Paper Airplane Contest" in *Long Island Business News* (Mar. 5, 04) [41877], [52164]

Northrop Grumman Mission Systems–Technology Library [7020]

"Northside ends exclusive insurer contracts" in *Atlanta Business Chronicle* (Vol. 24, No. 15, September 14, 2001, pp. 14A) [13405], [26864]

Northville Chamber of Commerce [61394]

"Northwest seeks to cut $1.5B, but little impact felt at Metro for now" in *Crain's Detroit Business* (Vol. 19, No. 7, Feb. 17, 2003) [28570], [30389]

"Northwest Accord To Allow Flying For Other Carriers" in *Wall Street Journal* (Vol. 248, December 2006, No. 149, pp. B2) [47352], [50110]

Northwest Alabama Junior Chamber of Commerce [56877]

Northwest Aquifer Surveying [23779]

Northwest Atlantic Fisheries Organization [10450]

"Northwest Bounty" in *Hispanic Business* (Vol. 24, No. 5, May 2002, pp. 56) [30390]

Northwest Chamber of Commerce [62013], [64048]

Northwest Farm Managers Association [26463]

Northwest Fisheries Association [10422]

Northwest Florida Daily News (November 18, 2002); "Southern Living Profiles Niceville, Fla.-Based Personal Chef Business" in [4555], [54261]

"Northwest Herbs & Extracts opens in Vancouver's Uptown Village" in *Vancouver, WA Business Journal* (February 28, 2003) [12152], [17906], [51274]

Northwest Indiana Regional Development Company–Small Business Development Center [59831]

Northwest Indiana SBDC [59832]

"Northwest may be next with low-cost subsidiary" in *Crain's Detroit Business* (Vol. 19, No. 6, February 10, 2003, pp. 1) [28571], [30391]

Northwest Marine Trade Association [16723]

Northwest Michigan Council of Governments–Small Business Development Center [61213]

Northwest Mississippi Community College–SBDC [61761]

"Northwest Mississippi Community College" in *Mississippi Business Journal* (Vol. 28, September 2006, No. 36, pp. 6) [33194], [36561]

Northwest Missouri State University–Small Business Development Center [61873]

Northwest Ohio Venture Fund [63855]

"Northwest worries labor could harm on-time record" in *Crain's Detroit Business* (Vol. 16, No. 50, December 11, 2000, pp. 21) [55304]

"Northwest sees friendlier skies; Detroit called key to strategy" in *Crain's Detroit Business* (Vol. 19, No. 1, Jan. 6, 2003, pp. 18) [28572]

Northwest Sportshow [23694]

Northwest Suburban Chamber of Commerce [61641]

Northwest Tarrant Chamber of Commerce [65420]

Northwest Technical College–SBDC [61528]

Northwest Trade Adjustment Assistance Center [46543]

Northwest Valley Chamber of Commerce [57054]

Northwest Venture Associates, Inc. / Spokane Capital MGMT [66219]

Northwest Yachting [5248], [16758]

Northwestern Building Products Expo [11910], [16338]

Northwestern Lumber Association [16293]

Northwestern Michigan College MTEC–Small Business Development Center [61214]

Northwestern Oklahoma State University–Small Business Development Center [63917]

Northwestern Scene [16332]

Northwestern University
    Center for Retail Management [47935]
    Dispute Resolution Research Center [17080]
    Evanston Research Park [59785]
    Guthrie Center for Real Estate Research [21116]
    Institute for Health Services Research and Policy Studies [41394]

    Office for Research [59786]
    The Technology Innovation Center [59787]

Northwood Area Chamber of Commerce [60185]

Northwood Ventures [63144]

Norton Area Chamber of Commerce [60394]

Norwalk Area Chamber of Commerce [60186], [63759]

Norwalk Chamber of Commerce [57670]

"Norwalk, Conn., Businessman Looks to Build Rooftop Miniature Golf Course" in *Stamford Advocate* (February 2, 2005) [1114], [17326]

Norwalk - The Furniture Idea [12350], [22742]

Norwegian American Chamber of Commerce - New York City [43521]

Norwegian-American Historical Association–Archives [11066]

Norwegian Forest Cat Breed Council [1177]

Norwest Equity Partners [61105], [61705]

Norwest Venture Partners [58104]

Norwin Chamber of Commerce [64485]

Norwood Park Chamber of Commerce and Industry [59614]

Norwood Venture Corp. [63145]

Nostradamus Advertising [8658]

"Not just for a rainy day" in *Black Enterprise* (Vol. 33, No. 6, Jan. 2003, pp. 87) [10115], [15311], [38252]

"Not Every Small Business will be able to (or should) Jump on Linux Immediately" in *Inc.* (June 2000, pp. 100) [49174], [49522]

"Not so fast!: Studies show many of you aren't looking before you leap" in *Entrepreneur* (Vol. 31, No. 6, June 2003, pp. 30) [30575], [36562], [39502]

"Not hiring" in *Entrepreneur* (Vol. 30, No. 12, December 2002, pp. 103) [29420], [42365]

"Not In My Inbox: Moving Large Files Is As Easy AS FTP" in *Black Enterprise* (Vol. 34, No. 3, October 2003, pp. 51) [25524], [26095], [49175]

Not by Jeans Alone [5595]

"Not Just Telenovelas" in *The Record* (November 12, 2005) [740], [4118], [24440], [48588], [53889]

"Not Just Window Dressing: the Art of Hanging a Great Curtain" in *Black Enterprise* (Vol. 35, February 2005, No. 7, pp. 170) [12201], [12304]

"Not Lost in Translation" in *Entrepreneur* (Vol. 32, December 2004, No. 12, pp. 16) [741], [47353]

"Not On His Watch" in *Entrepreneur.com* (Vol. 34, January 2006, No. 1, pp. 35) [4743], [6742], [22314], [23102], [53387], [56756]

"Not for Profit" in *Inc.* (April 2000, pp. 74) [14301], [25917]

"Not for sale" in *BlackEnterprise* (Vol. 32, No. 3, October 2001, pp. 165) [31802], [40580]

"Not So Fast! Raising Money: Seeking an Investor?" in *Entrepreneur* (Vol. 31, No. 9, September 2003, pp. 55) [20614], [20954], [44609], [55757]

"The Not-So-Golden state? Economic optimism is gathering steam across most of the country" in *Business Week Online* (April 25, 2002) [28573], [32603]

"Not So Swift" in *Forbes* (Vol. 175, January 10, 2005, No. 1, pp. 38) [15312], [25403]

"The Not-So-Talented Tenth" in *Sales & Marketing Management* (Vol. 158, November-December 2006, No. 11, pp. 16) [10116], [33195], [47354], [51747]

"A not-so-taxing CHANGE" in *Pittsburgh Business Times* (Vol. 20, No. 53, July 20, 2001, pp. 25) [24003], [39879], [54681]

"Not Your Arena?" in *Entrepreneur* (Vol. 31, No. 8, August 2003, pp. 22) [23728], [36563]

"Not Your Father's Business Card" in *Success* (Vol. 47, No. 2, June 2000, pp. 12) [49176]

"Not Your Ordinary Perks" in *My Business* (April/May 2004, pp. 14) [35005], [45477]

"Not Your Typical Agency" in *Rough Notes* (Vol. 145, No. 2, February 2003, pp. 18) [13406], [43297]

Notables [8361]

Notari Associates [49641]

"Note to Staff" in *My Business* (April/May 2004, pp. 44) [29945], [36564], [45478]

"Nothing to fear? White House seeks cheerleaders for the economy" in *Wall Street Journal* (May 31, 2002, pp. A4) [32604]

"Nothing but Net" in *Fast Company* (November 2001, pp. 36) [37172], [53890]

"Nothing but Net" in *Success* (Vol. 47, No. 4, September 2000, pp. 80) [34271], [51748]

"Nothing Personal" in *Entrepreneur* (Vol. 31, No. 10, October 2003, pp. 85) [27458], [39503]

"Nothing to Sneeze At" in *Success* (Vol. 47, No. 2, June 2000, pp. 58) [33469], [37069]

"Nothing is Unworkable" in *Home Office Computing* (Vol. 19, No. 1, January 2001, pp. 11) [36565], [42692]

Nova Scotia Business, Inc.–Business Services Center [66707]

Nova Scotia Department of Education–Drug Dependency Services Division–Library [54386]

Nova Scotia Economic Development [66708]

Novacor Ltd. [21909]

Novak Biddle Venture Partners, L.P. [60877]

Novato Chamber of Commerce [57671]

"Novel microarray applications" in *Small Business Economic Trends* (February 2002, pp. 1) [4744], [17191], [23103], [41878], [53388]

"Novel Ideas: Two Entrepreneurs Write Books About Their Experiences-And Learn Something in the Process" in *Entrepreneur* (Vol. 32) [2601], [2728], [7901], [11161], [16461], [46396], [51275], [56353]

Novelists, Inc. [8968]

Noveltek Venture Corp. [63146]

Novi Chamber of Commerce [61395]

Novidian Corp. [3907]

Novon [11473]

Novotel Canada [12720]

Novus Auto Glass Repair & Replacement [11235]

Novus Ventures [58105]

"Now in 3-D" in *Entrepreneur* (Vol. 33, October 2005, No. 10, pp. 18) [25571], [25918], [34272]

"Now Boarding" in *Inc.* (Volume 28, January 2006, No. 1, pp. 66) [28574], [30392], [43769]

"Now Boarding: Small Business" in *Business Week* (May 22, 2000, pp. F54) [30393]

"Now Playing" in *Entrepreneur* (Vol. 33, March 2005, No. 3, pp. 87) [742], [17527], [47355]

"Now Presenting..." in *Entrepreneur* (Vol. 32, No. 1, January 2004, pp. 46) [4194], [6743], [22535], [49177], [53389]

"Now, on to the Really Big Time" in *Inc.* (October 17, 2000, pp. 88) [50111], [52443]

"Now Showing: Hard At Work" in *My Business* (April/May 2002, pp. 44) [743], [5999], [25919], [47356], [52706]

"Now Showing: Win Partners by Letting Them See What You're Made Of" in *Entrepreneur* (Vol. 31, No. 9, September 2003) [44106], [50112]

"Now that they've come, what can we sell them?" in *The New York Times* (March 27, 2000, pp. D9, H9) [34273], [51749]

"Now, ear this" in *Black Enterprise* (Vol. 33, No. 6, January 2003, pp. 43) [5073], [49178]

"Now You See It: Payroll Tax is Likely the Tax You Most Want to Have Cut, But Will It Ever Happen?" in *Entrepreneur* (Vol. 31, Aug.2003) [210], [2940], [24004], [26306], [54682]

"Now you've done it! Real deal" in *Entrepreneur* (Vol. 30, No. 3, March 2002, pp.) [27459], [47357]

Nowata Area Chamber of Commerce [64049]

Noxubee County Chamber of Commerce [61821]

NPES - The Association for Suppliers of Printing, Publishing and Converting Technologies [19855]

NQB Monthly Price Report [15668]

NQB Price Digest [15669]

NRH Nutrition Consultants Inc. [18483]

NRI Relocation Inc. [30198]

"The NSA" in *Business Week* (January 23, 2006, No. 3968, pp. 62) [22315], [42366]

NSBE Magazine [23410]

NSCA Bulletin [19460]

NSDJA Newsletter [7566]

NSFRE Directory [10746]

nSight Inc. [2800]
NSS News Bulletin [1630]
NSSRA Newsletter [23650], [51430]
The NTC Group [58604]
NTEA News [4365]
NTEA Technical Report [25440]
"Nth Power Energizes New $120M Fund" in *Venture Capital Journal* (Vol. 40, No. 10, November 2000, pp. 26, 28) [41879], [55758]
Nu Capital Access Group, Ltd. [58106]
Nu-Look 1-Hour Cleaners [8936]
"Nuance Gains Voice in Noisy Speech Market" in *San Francisco Business Times* (Vol. 18, No. 2, August 22, 2003, pp. 3) [4745], [15313], [23104], [41880], [50113], [53390]
Nucla-Naturita Area Chamber of Commerce [58412]
Nuclear Power: The Hot Debate [37356]
Nueces Canyon Chamber of Commerce [65421]
The Nugget and CGS News [10979]
"No. 1 Company Succeeds in Rehabilitating Malls" in *San Fernando Valley Business Journal* (Vol. 11, November 2006, No. 24, pp. 22) [20955], [28575]
"The Number Cruncher Versus the Vision Guy" in *Inc.* (Volume 28, January 2006, No. 1, pp. 90-93, 96, 99) [39504]
The Number Express [5399]
"Number-Portability Change to Increase Wireless Competition" in *Crain's Detroit Business* (Vol. 19, No. 45, November 10, 2003, pp. 28) [5074], [5225], [40581], [42047]
"The Numbers" in *Fortune* (Vol. 140, No. 12, December 20, 1999 pp. 52) [28576], [32605], [52925]
"Numbers Game" in *Entrepreneur* (Vol. 32, December 2004, No. 12, pp. 46) [18104], [39505], [40582], [41881], [48589]
"Numbers Prove Accountants Are On a Roll" in *The Record* (November 10, 2005) [211], [2941], [24005], [26307]
Numerical Heat Transfer, Part A: Applications [52309]
Numismatic News [5848]
Numismatics International [5810]
Library [5871]
The Numismatist [5849]
Nursery and Landscape Association Executives of North America [11416]
Nursery/Landscape Expo [10598], [11494], [19727]
Nursery Management: Administration and Culture [11437]
Nursery News [11474]
"A Nursery Tale" in *Inc.* (June 2000, pp. 96) [5344], [35006], [36566]
Nursing Education Perspectives [41273]
"Nurun Transforms Loews Hotels Website Into a More User-Friendly Experience" in *Canadian Corporate News* (February 7, 2007) [12606], [34274], [47358]
Nutley Chamber of Commerce [62541]
Nutri-Lawn [16082], [16163]
Nutrients Catalog [18442]
Nutrition Action Healthletter [12029]
Nutrition for Better Health [18465]
Nutrition in a Box: Video Food Quiz [18466]
The Nutrition Club [12034], [14675], [26061]
Nutrition: Eat and Be Healthy [18467]
Nutrition Entrepreneurs [18383]
Nutrition Facts: The New Food Label with Supermarket Savvy's Leni Reed [18468]
The Nutrition Funding Report [18443]
Nutrition House Canada Inc. [8848]
Nutrition & Mental Health [41274]
Nutrition for Optimal Health Association [18435]
Nutrition Reviews [18454]
Nutrition Today [18455], [41275]
Nutrition for Wellness [18469]
Nutrition for You [18470]
Nutritional Aspects of the AIDS Patient [18471]
Nutritional Assessment of the Elderly [18472]
Nutty Monkey Frozen Custard [12443]
"NW Miss. Firms Merge To Meet Growing Needs Of Region" in *Mississippi Business Journal* (Vol. 28, September 2006, No. 37, pp. 20) [29421], [50114]

"NY Bankruptcy Courts Shift to Online Filing" in *Long Island Business News* (February 6, 2004) [29422], [34275], [40583]
"NY Metro Gets $388M in Fourth-Quarter Venture Funds, Survey Says" in *Long Island Business News* (February 20, 2004) [28577], [55759]
"NY State Attorney General Cracks Down on Auto and Credit Complaints" in *Long Island Business News* (February 13, 2004) [10117], [18105], [31571]
"NY State Senator Introduces Bill to Obtain Federal Funding for Genetic Research" in *Long Island Business News* (February 13, 2004) [40068], [40584], [50938], [52165]
"NYC Eyes Taxes on 'Luxury' Items" in *Long Island Business News* (February 20, 2004) [54683]
"NYC Hotels Register Gains; Occupancy Hits 85-Percent for March" in *Crain's New York Business* (Vol. 20, No. 16, April 19, 2004, pp. 4) [12607], [28578], [32606]
"NYC Increases Hotel Security" in *The Record* (November 11, 2005) [12608], [22316]
Nyikos Associates Inc. [1152]
NYNEX Telecommunications Center [64651]
NYSE Weekly Stock Buys [15670]
Nyssa Chamber of Commerce and Agriculture [64250]

O

O & A Marketing News [20263]
"O-Web Design Firm Makes Case for Student Startups" in *Crain's Cleveland Business* (Vol. 26, January 10, 2005, No. 2, pp. 7) [25920], [56757]
"O2 Interactive Realizes Profits as it Builds Relationships" in *San Diego Business Journal* (Vol. 28, January 8, 2007, No. 2, pp. 9) [4746], [7442], [23105], [28579], [53391]
OAG Business Travel Planner [24713], [25224]
OAG Flight-Finder Asia Pacific Plus [24762], [25299]
OAG Travel Planner European Edition [24714], [25225]
"Oahu Apartment Inventory Down, Rents Up" in *Pacific Business News* (Vol. 41, No. 19, July 18, 2003, pp. 1) [21339], [32607]
Oak Brook Area Association of Commerce and Industry [59615]
Oak Business Center [61485]
Oak Cliff Chamber of Commerce [65422]
Oak Forest Chamber of Commerce [59616]
Oak Grove Chamber of Commerce [62014]
Oak Harbor Area Chamber of Commerce [63760]
Oak Investment Partners [58605]
Oak Investment Partners (Minneapolis) [61706]
Oak Investment Partners (Palo Alto) [58107]
Oak Lawn Chamber of Commerce [59617]
Oak Park-River Forest Chamber of Commerce [59618]
Oak Ridge Chamber of Commerce [64962]
Oak Ridge National Laboratory–Toxicology Information Response Center [8876]
Oakdale Area Chamber of Commerce [60660]
"Oakdale Based Skills Unlimited Helps Long Island's Disabled Develop Skills and Find Work" in *Long Island Business News* (Feb.20, 2004) [42367], [54235]
Oakdale District Chamber of Commerce [57672]
Oakdales Olde Towne Veterinary Hospital [46094]
Oakes Area Chamber of Commerce [63531]
Oakesdale Chamber of Commerce [66142]
Oakhurst Area Chamber of Commerce [57673]
Oakland African-American Chamber of Commerce [57674]
"Oakland cities try to reinvigorate neglected areas" in *Crain's Detroit Business* (Vol. 19, No. 1, Jan. 6, 2003, pp. 7) [7443], [28580]
"Oakland, Calif., Port Agrees to Manage West Sacramento Shipping Facility" in *Sacramento Bee* (December 21, 2005) [10686], [13000], [43770]
Oakland Chamber of Commerce [62542]
Oakland Chinatown Chamber of Commerce [57675]
Oakland Metropolitan Chamber of Commerce [57676]

Oakland University–School of Education and Human Services–Educational Resources Laboratory [25490]
Oakley Area Chamber of Commerce [60395]
Oakley Chamber of Commerce [57677]
Oakridge - Westfir Chamber of Commerce [64251]
Oakville Chamber of Commerce [66143]
OAS Staff Association [23365]
"OASIS Overhauls Intellectual Property Rights Policy" in *eWeek* (February 7, 2005) [14302], [44107], [44344]
Oasis Press 64316
Oatman-Goldroad Chamber of Commerce [57055]
Ober, Kaler, Grimes & Shriver–Library [9541]
Oberlin Area Chamber of Commerce [63761]
Oberlin Chamber of Commerce [60661]
"Obesity costing billions" in *Atlanta Business Chronicle* (Vol. 24, No. 14, September 7, 2001, pp. 1A) [39506], [41071]
"Obesity Whets VC Appetites" in *Inc.* (Volume 27, June 2005, No. 6, pp. 26) [11995], [40905], [53891], [55760]
Obion County Chamber of Commerce [64963]
"Obits" in *Inc.* (September 2000, pp. 29) [16740], [45479]
Object-Oriented Programming (OOP) Boot Camp [53185]
Objection Handling: Overcoming the Hurdles [31940]
"Objectivity, Consensus Key For Survival of Family Biz" in *Crain's Detroit Business* (Vol. 21, October 10, 2005, No. 43, pp. 23) [37747], [45480]
M.C. O'Brien Inc. [21089]
Obtaining Venture Financing: Principles & Practices [55761]
Ocala-Marion County Chamber of Commerce [58908]
Ocapt Business Books [66760]
"OCC Starts Negotiations With Unions" in *Crain's Detroit Business* (Vol. 22, January 23, 2006, No. 4, pp. 5) [55305]
Occidental Chamber of Commerce [57678]
Occupational & Environmental Health Consulting Services [3782], [31427], [41334]
Occupational and Environmental Medical Association of Canada [40943]
Occupational Hazards [41276], [56600]
Occupational Hazards-Annual Directory Issue [56576]
Occupational Health & Safety [56601]
Occupational Outlook Handbook [9227]
Occupational Outlook Quarterly [9254]
Occupational Safety and Health Administration
Office of Communications [67349]
Office of Small Business Assistance–Directorate of Cooperative and State Programs [67350]
Occupational Safety and Health Administration (OSHA) [67351]
"The Occupational Safety & Health Administration (OSHA)" in *Entrepreneur* (Vol. 32, No. 1, January 2004, pp. 10) [39880], [56577]
Occupational Safety and Health Standards for General Industry [56578]
Occupational Therapy in Health Care [41277]
Occusafe Inc. [37362]
Ocean City Chamber of Commerce [60844], [62543]
Ocean City Hotel, Motel, and Restaurant Trade Exposition [12686]
Ocean Futures Society [25696]
Ocean Grove Chamber of Commerce [62544]
Ocean Park Area Chamber of Commerce [66144]
Ocean Pines Area Chamber of Commerce [60845]
Ocean Resource Conservation Alliance–Library [10480]
Ocean Shores Chamber of Commerce [66145]
Ocean Springs Chamber of Commerce [61822]
Oceana County Economic Development Corp.–SBDC [61215]
Oceanic Institute [10491]
Oceanside Chamber of Commerce [57679], [62973]

"Oceanside: Chamber Gets in Networking Fast Lane" in *San Diego Business Journal* (Vol. 28, January 15, 2007, No. 3, pp. 16) [27665], [39507]

"Oceanside In Play" in *San Diego Business Journal* (Vol. 28, January 8, 2007, No. 2, pp. 30) [7444], [23729]

O'Charley's Restaurants [21910]

Ocilla - Irwin Chamber of Commerce [59145]

OCLC Name-Address Directory [13085]

OCLC Newsletter [13109]

OCLC WorldCat [2809], [3072]

Oconee County Chamber of Commerce [59146]

O'Connor Associates Environmental Inc.–Library [9450]

Oconomowoc Area Chamber of Commerce [66483]

Oconto Area Chamber of Commerce [66484]

Oconto Falls Area Chamber of Commerce [66485]

"October Recap" in *Sales & Marketing Management* (Vol. 159, January-February 2007, No. 1, pp. 48) [35007], [45481], [51750]

"October Winner" in *Sales & Marketing Management* (Vol. 159, January-February 2007, No. 1, pp. 48) [47359], [51751]

Octoclean [3373]

"Ode to a Server" in *Entrepreneur.com* (Vol. 34, February 2006, No. 2, pp. 38) [6266], [6744], [49179]

Odessa Chamber of Commerce [62015], [66146]

Odin Capital Group [62311]

O'Dwyer's Directory of Public Relations Firms [20142], [50459]

O'Dwyer's New York Public Relations Directory [20096], [46642], [50544]

Oelwein Chamber and Area Development [60187]

"Of Growing Interest" in *Ingram's* (Vol. 28, No. 1, January 2002, pp. 35) [44610]

"Of Mouse and Men" in *Crain's Detroit Business* (Vol. 18, No. 24, June 17, 2002) [6333], [33196]

"Of One Mind: Keep Employees by Getting on the Same Page From the Get-Go" in *Entrepreneur* (Vol. 31, No. 8, August 2003, pp. 23) [42368], [45482]

"Of Two Minds: Is Consumer fraud a serious threat to online auctions?" in *Internet World* (Vol. 7, No. 1, January 15, 2001, pp. 28) [1840], [30244]

OFA Short Course [10599], [19728]

O'Fallon Chamber of Commerce [59619], [62016]

"OFCCP Contractor Survey; New Worker Economic Opportunity Law" in *Employment Relations Today* (Vol. 27, No. 2, Summer 2000, pp. 81) [32051], [40585]

Off the Beaten Path L.L.C. [30468]

Off the Grill Franchising, LLC [10646], [21911]

"Off the Wall: Keith Collins' Larger-Than-Life Designs" in *Black Enterprise* (Vol. 37, February 2007, No. 7, pp. 138) [8016], [36567]

Offfice Of Goverment Contacting [60884]

Office of Aircraft Services
Business Utilization and Development Specialist–Division of Contracting [67633]
Business Utilization and Development Specialist–Division of Contracting–Aviation Management Directorate [67634]

Office Automation: A Systems Approach [49180]

Office of Civil Rights–Office of Small and Disadvantaged Business Utilization [67420]

Office Design [49523]

Office Design That Really Works! Design for the 90s [49524]

Office Design: The Complete Process from Concept to Move-In [18554]

"Office Down Below" in *Home Office Computing* (Vol. 18, No. 8, August 2000, pp. 42) [42693], [49525], [52707]

Office of Economic Analysis [66960]

Office of Economic and Community Development–Office of Economic Development [61147]

Office of Economic Initiatives–SBDC [62390]

"The Office" in *Entrepreneur* (Vol. 33, October 2005, No. 10, pp. 76) [47185], [49526], [52238], [54972]

Office Equal Opportunities [63838]

Office of Financial Management–Forecasting Division [66801]

"Office Furniture Dealers" in *San Diego Business Journal* (Vol. 28, January 8, 2007, No. 2, pp. 13) [12305], [18608], [49527]

Office Furniture Market [18619]

Office of the Govener–Econmic Development Torist Division–Economic Information Clearinghouse [16798]

Office of the Governor–Legislative Liaison Office [60594]

Office of Intergovernmental Assistance [66948]

Office of Justice Programs–Information Systems Division [67639]

"Office tech allows 'knowledge management'" in *Kansas City Business Journal* (Vol. 18, No. 21, January 28, 2000, pp. 4) [44345]

"Office Makeover Contest Winner" in *My Business* (December/January 2003, pp.32) [5701], [49528]

"Office Offers" in *Entrepreneur* (Vol. 31, No. 11, November 2003, pp. 60) [4747], [23106], [49181], [53392]

"An Office of One's Own" in *Entrepreneur* (Vol. 31, No. 9, September 2003, pp. 105) [42694], [49529]

"Office Optional" in *Inc.* (Volume 27, December 2005, No. 12, pp. 42, 44) [3567], [31196], [49530], [53892]

Office of Personnel Management
Center for National Security–Office of Operations [67352]
Division for Human Capital Leadership and Merit System Accountability [67353]
Office of Communications and Public Liaison [67354]
Office of Small and Disadvantaged Business Utilization–Contracting Division [67355]

Office Pride Commercial Cleaning Services [3374]

Office of Real Property Services [66940]

Office Safety and Workplace Ergonomics [56639]

"Office Search Engine" in *Success* (Vol. 47, No. 1, January 2000, pp. 23) [33470], [49474]

Office of the Secretary of the Army–Office of Small and Disadvantaged Business Utilization [67424]

"Office Space: It's better to rent than own" in *Red Herring* (No. 103, September 1, 2001, pp. 85) [26308], [27158], [52708]

Office of Surface Mining Reclamation and Enforcement
Appalachian Regional Office [67597]
Mid-Continent Regional Office [67598]
Western Regional Office [67599]

Office Systems: People, Procedures, and Technology [49182]

Office Technology [7033]

Office of the Under Secretary of the Navy–Director of Small and Disadvantaged Business Utilization [67425]

"Office vacancies, lease perks pile up" in *Crain's Detroit Business* (Vol. 19, No. 4, January 27, 2003, pp. 3) [20615], [20956], [21340], [28581]

"An Office With Ambiance" in *Home Office Computing* (Vol. 18, No. 10, October 2000, pp. 64) [42695], [49531]

"OfficeMax launches e-book store" in *Publishers Weekly* (Vol. 249, No. 37, September 16, 2002, pp. 14) [2729], [9150], [14303], [34276]

Offices: A Briefing and Design Guide [18555]

The Official American International Toy Fair Directory [24824]

Official Board Markets (Vol. 77, No. 35, September 1, 2001, pp. 14); "Detergent Exhibit Cleanses Female Stereotypes" in [5978], [46882]

Official Export Guide [10687], [13001]

Official Hotel Guide [25226]

The Official Internet World Internet Mall [37173]

Official Recycled Products Guide [21268]

Official Summary of Security Transactions and Holdings [3436]

Official Tour Directory [24715], [25227]

"Officials discuss deferred comp, guidance and legislation for EOs" in *Tax Notes* (Vol. 96, No. 13, September 23, 2002, pp. 1693-1697) [40586], [54684]

"Officials Hope Testing Center Spurs More International Investment" in *Crain's Detroit Business* (Vol. 21, October 10, 2005, No. 43) [1955], [32608], [43771]

Offinger's Handcrafted Marketplace [11192]

Offinger's Handcrafted Marketplace Directory [11173]

Offshore Funds [38591]

"Offshoring Could Boost Your Career" in *Fortune* (Vol. 151, January 24, 2005, No. 2, pp. 36) [41882], [43772], [45483], [49720], [53893]

"Offshoring Isn't Such a Sure Thing" in *Inc.* (September 2005, pp. 32, 34) [43773], [49721]

Ogallala - Keith County Chamber of Commerce [62286]

Ogden Roemer Wilkerson Architecture, AIA [13714]

Ogden/Weber Chamber of Commerce [65721]

Ogunquit Chamber of Commerce [60765]

"Oh So Good" in *My Business* (August/September 2002, pp. 44) [2253], [6098], [8692], [38868]

Ohio Bell–Corporate Information Resource Center [5234], [24330]

Ohio Business [39725]

Ohio Center for Prevention Studies–Ohio Safe Schools Center [54387]

Ohio Chamber of Commerce [63762]

Ohio County Chamber of Commerce [60554]

Ohio Department of Development
Minority Contractors and Business Assistance Program [63839]
Office of Strategic Research [66952]
Ohio SBDC [63550]
Small Business Development [63840]
Small Business Development Center [63551]
Small and Developing Business Division [63587]
Technology Division [63588]

Ohio Entrepreneur [39726]

The Ohio Financial Institutions Directory & Fact Book [44611]

Ohio Florists Association Bulletin [10587]

Ohio Genealogical Society
Coshocton County Chapter–Library [11067]
Perry County, Ohio Chapter (OGS)–Library [11068]

Ohio House Economic Development and Small Business Committee [63893]

Ohio Insurance Department–Research and Policy [43459]

Ohio International Motorcycle Show [17502]

"Ohio Investment Tax Credit Struck Down" in *Journal of Accountancy* (Vol. 199, January 2005, No. 1, pp. 76) [212], [2942], [24006], [26309], [27159], [54685]

Ohio-Israel Chamber of Commerce [63763]

The Ohio JobBank [9291]

Ohio Jurisprudence on Westlaw [29677]

Ohio Manufacturing SBDC at Central Ohio [63573]

Ohio Occupational Information Coordinating Commission–Ohio Bureau of Employment Services–Division of Labor Market Information [66953]

Ohio Partners [63856]

Ohio Procurement Technical Assistance Center [63864]
Cincinnati Procurement Outreach Center [63865]
Mahoning Valley Technical Procurement Center–MVEDC [63866]
Ohio University–Procurement Technical Assistance Program [63867]
Procurement Technical Assistance Program [63868]

Ohio Safety Congress and Expo [56650]

Ohio SBDC at SBDC, Inc. [63574]

Ohio (State) Bureau of Workers' Compensation–BWC Library [56698]

Ohio State Journal on Dispute Resolution [17067]

Ohio State University
A. Sophie Rogers Laboratory for Child and Family Studies [5460]

Advanced Computing Center for the Arts and Design [6560]
Agricultural Technical Institute [11552]
C. Wayne Ellett Plant and Pest Diagnostic Clinic [19733]
Career Connection [4465]
Cartoon Research Library [5943]
Center for Real Estate Education and Research [20774]
Engineering Research Center for Net Shape Manufacturing [46553]
Gould Food Industries Center [18526]
Journalism Library [20199]
Laboratory for Pest Control Application Technology [19056]
National Regulatory Research Institute [19809]
Office of Research [63879]
Ohio Manufacturing & Technology SBDC [63575]
Science and Technology Campus Corp. [63880]
Water Resources Center [25745]
Ohio State University Library–Census Data Center [66954]
Ohio State University Research Foundation [63881]
Ohio Statewide Minority Business Development Center–Cincinnati Business Development Services, Inc. [63841]
Ohio United Way Legislative Bulletin [63894]
Ohio University
Innovation Center [63882]
Institute for Local Government Administration and Rural Development [50405]
Office of Research and Sponsored Programs [63883]
Small Business Development Center [63576]
Ohio Veterinary Medical Association/Midwest Veterinary Conference [1266]
Ohio Wesleyan University
Kinnison Music Library [17694], [17825]
L.A. Beeghly Library–Archives/Special Collections [1368]
Ohlone College [58232]
OI Publishing [61508]
Oil Butler International, Corp. [20274]
Oil Can Henry's [20275]
Oil City Area Chamber of Commerce [64486]
"Oil changers may face oversight" in Crain's Detroit Business (Vol. 18, No. 17, April 29, 2002, pp. 6) [20260], [22617], [40587]
"Oil Slicks" in Inc. (October 1, 2003) [29423], [40588], [45484], [50115]
Ojai Valley Chamber of Commerce [57680]
"Ok, let's review" in Entrepreneur (Vol. 30, No. 10, October 2002, pp. 91) [45485], [51752]
Okaloosa-Walton Community College–Small Business Development Center [58709]
Okanogan Chamber of Commerce [66147]
Okawville Chamber of Commerce [59620]
"OKC-based Advanced Financial Solutions Releases New Check Image Exchange System" in Journal Record (February 4,2004) [36809], [38253]
"OKC-based Devon Energy's Fourth-Quarter Profits Dip 40 Percent" in Journal Record (Oklahoma City, OK) (February 8, 2007) [15314], [38254]
"OKC-based Dobson Communications Subscribers Up 14,400" in Journal Record (February 4, 2004) [5075], [5226], [28582]
"OKC-based The Benham Cos. Lands Military Housing Contract" in Journal Record (Oklahoma City, OK) (February 8, 2007) [7445], [40069]
"OKC Chamber of Commerce Finds Many Firms Interested in City" in Journal Record (February 4, 2004) [28583], [52709], [54961]
"OKC Man Charged in Connection With Identity Theft Ring" in Journal Record (Oklahoma City, OK) (February 5, 2007) [1956], [22317], [29424], [44346]
"OKC Rotary Club Elects First Female President" in Journal Record (June 24, 2003) [9228], [10007], [24197], [24532], [53550], [56354]
Okeechobee Chamber of Commerce [58909]

Okeene Chamber of Commerce [64050]
Okefenokee Chamber of Commerce and Folkston and Charlton County Development Authority [59147]
Okemah Chamber of Commerce [64051]
Okhai - Diagnostics L.L.C. [66761]
"Okla. City-based BancFirst Plans $25M Public Offering" in Journal Record (February 5, 2004) [15097], [15315], [47728], [50116]
"Okla. Restaurant Assn. Gets New Slate of Officers and New Set of Industry Challenges" in Journal Record (February 5, 2004) [21577], [22311]
"Oklahoma-Based Company to Renovate Rancho Cordova, Calif., Tax Board Buildings" in Sacramento Bee (December 28, 2005) [6267], [20231], [54686]
"Oklahoma Business Roundtable Elects Officers" in Journal Record (June 24, 2003) [39508], [40925]
Oklahoma Center for the Advancement of Science Technology–Oklahoma Inventor's Assistance Service [63923]
Oklahoma City Minority Business Enterprise Center [64111]
Oklahoma Department of Agriculture–Market Development Services Division [63924]
Oklahoma Department of Career and Technology Education
Bid Assistance Centers [64119]
Oklahoma State Department of Vocational and Technical Education–Training for Industry Program [63925]
Oklahoma Department of Commerce
Administration and Central Services [63926]
Business Development Division [63927]
Business Development Division–Minority Business Office [64112]
Export Assistance Program [63928]
Global Business Solutions [63929]
Oklahoma Small Business Conference [64156]
Oklahoma State Data Center [66958]
Oklahoma Department of Libraries–U.S. Government Information Division [66959]
Oklahoma Family Policy Council [41395]
Oklahoma Fishery Research Laboratory–Library [10481]
Oklahoma Genealogical Society Quarterly [10980]
"Oklahoma Insurance Commissioner Orders Tribal Companies Out of State" in Journal Record (February 5, 2004) [40589], [42055], [43298]
Oklahoma Native American Business Development Center [64113]
Oklahoma Procurement Technical Assistance Center–Tribal Government Institute [64120]
Oklahoma State University
Center for Local Government Technology [50406]
Ecotoxicology and Water Quality Research Laboratory [25746]
Ecotoxicology and Water Quality Research Laboratory–Library [25735]
Surgical Laser Laboratory [1287]
Oklahoma Tackle Show [2212]
Oklahoma Technology Transfer Center [63930]
Okmulgee Chamber of Commerce [64052]
Okolona Area Chamber of Commerce-Main Street Program [61823]
Olathe Chamber of Commerce [60396]
"Old Cell Phones" in Black Enterprise (Vol. 34, No. 5, December 2003, pp. 60) [5076], [5464], [21247], [21962], [37312], [38616]
Old Dominion Petro Food Expo [11710]
"The Old Economy Meets the New Economy" in Fast Company (November 2001, pp. 70) [28584], [30576], [31803], [37174], [39509]
"An old-fashioned fate: it takes the tax collector to really ruin somebody" in Barron's (Vol. 82, No. 58, February 17, 2003, pp. 31) [213], [24007], [26310], [37484], [54687]
"The Old Guard" in Venture Capital Journal (Vol. 42, No. 10, October 2002, pp. 24-30) [15316], [36568], [55762]
Old Hippy Wood Products [46546]
Old-House Interiors [13699]
Old House/New House Home Show [1391], [55238]

"Old King Coal Comes Back: Actually, It Never Really Left" in Fortune (Vol. 151, February 21, 2005, No. 4, pp. 114) [15317], [28585], [52926], [53894]
"Old Media's Mobile Future" in Business Week (January 16, 2006, No. 3967, pp. 20) [5077], [14304], [41883]
"Old becomes new; Wave of practicality poses challenge to retailers this holiday season" in Crain's Detroit Business (Vol. 16, No. 49) [51276]
Old Orchard Beach Chamber of Commerce [60766]
Old Saybrook Chamber of Commerce [58558]
Old School [22867]
"Old fashioned hobby returns to textile shop" in Los Angeles Business Journal (Vol. 25, No. 7, February 17, 2003, pp. 30) [8176], [53895]
Old-Stuff-Directory of Shops Section [1326], [5911]
"Olddebts.com: www.olddebts.com" in Entrepreneur (Vol. 31, No. 10, October 2003, pp. 6) [31572]
Oldenburg Registry N.A. [1178]
"Older CEOs Plan to Work Past Age 65. They May Find That Harder Than They Expect" in Inc. (September 2005, pp. 27-29) [36569], [45486], [53896]
"Older firm gets venture funds" in Wall Street Journal (March 25, 2003, pp. B4) [50117], [55763]
"Older is seen as better in small-business owners" in Wall Street Journal (August 20, 2002, pp. B4) [36570], [39510]
Oldham County Chamber of Commerce [60555]
Oldsmar/Upper Tampa Bay Regional Chamber of Commerce [58910]
Olive Branch Chamber of Commerce [61824]
Olivia Area Chamber of Commerce [61642]
Olney Chamber of Commerce [60846], [65423]
Olney and the Greater Richland County Chamber of Commerce [59621]
G.V. Olsen Associates [26639]
Olson Research Associates Inc. [10345]
Olton Chamber of Commerce and Agriculture [65424]
Olver Incorporated–Library [25736]
Olympic College [66238]
Omaha Business and Technology Center–Procurement Technical Assistance Center–SBDC [62225]
Omaha Chamber of Commerce [65425]
Omak Chamber of Commerce [66148]
"Omanoff Eyes Lange Expansion" in Brandweek (Vol. 44, No. 27, July 14, 2003, pp. 30) [5702]
OMB Watcher [27208]
O'Melveny & Myers LLP–Library [44221]
Omex Office Maintenance Experts [3375]
OMI Government Relations Inc. [11969]
Omnimed Corp. [65622]
Omninet Capital, LLC [58108]
"Omniplex on the Case" in Black Enterprise (Vol. 37, December 2006, No. 5, pp. 38) [30922], [39511], [40590], [52571], [56579]
Omohundro Institute of Early American History and Culture–Kellock Library [2818]
Omro Area Chamber of Commerce [66486]
"On A Shoestring" in Birmingham Business Journal (Vol. 20, No. 28, July 11, 2003, pp. 11) [1327], [1415], [5912], [15856]
"On the Agenda" in Entrepreneur (Vol. 30, No. 2, February 2002, pp. 39) [34277], [40591]
On Assignment: A Video Series for Photographers [19259]
"On a Bank Roll" in Black Enterprise (Vol. 33, No. 6, Jan. 2003, pp. 31) [10118], [15318], [38255]
"On Boss Day, We Praise and Pan" in Sacramento Bee (October 17, 2005) [35008], [36571], [45487]
"On the Business of Life" in Forbes (Vol. 175, January 31, 2005, No. 2, pp. 156) [27460], [27666], [36572]
"On the Cheap: Creative Ways to Stretch Your Marketing Dollar" in Sales and Marketing.com (Vol. 156, No. 3, March 2004, pp. 10) [47360], [51753]
"On the Cheap" in Sales & Marketing Management (Vol. 158, November-December 2006, No. 11, pp. 14) [744], [23730], [47361], [51754]

"One of a kind? Make your product conform to break away from the norm" in *Entrepreneur* (Vol. 30, No. 12, December 2002, pp. 144) **[43966]**, **[46585]**, **[48773]**

"One Liberty Properties Snaps Up San Diego Area Cinema for $11.5M" in *Long Island Business News* (March 12, 2004) **[17329]**, **[17528]**, **[20384]**, **[20616]**, **[20957]**

"One Life To Live: They say starting up is hard to do" in *Fortune* (Vol. 142, No. 8, October 9, 2000, pp. 180+) **[55413]**

"One Man's Alien is Another's Employee" in *Inc.* (October 2005, pp. 32) **[32616]**, **[42371]**, **[48590]**

"One More For the Road" in *Sales & Marketing Management* (January 2005) **[13410]**, **[29426]**, **[36582]**, **[40593]**, **[43302]**, **[45494]**, **[47367]**, **[51758]**

"One More Time: How Do You Motivate Employees?" in *Harvard Business Review* (Vol. 81, No. 1, January 2003, pp. 87) **[35011]**, **[36583]**, **[45495]**

"The One Number You Need to Grow" in *Harvard Business Review* (Vol. 81, No. 12, December 2003, pp. 46) **[28593]**, **[31806]**

The One to One Future **[47368]**

One One Wheel **[2511]**

The One Page Business Plan: Start with a Vision, Build a Company! **[29950]**

"One of Portland, Maine's Fastest Growing Tech Companies is Sold" in *Portland Press Herald* (December 20, 2005) **[30693]**, **[41073]**, **[41886]**, **[52444]**

"One Site Does Not Fit All" in *Business 2.0* (Vol. 6, July 2005, No. 6, pp. 110-111) **[12610]**, **[24718]**, **[25230]**, **[30398]**, **[35012]**

One Small Step **[45937]**

"One Smart Customer" in *Fast Company* (September 2001, pp. 68) **[31807]**, **[34284]**

One Stop Capital Shop (Atlanta) **[67358]**

One Stop Capital Shop (Baltimore) **[67361]**

One Stop Capital Shop (Bismarck) **[67367]**

One Stop Capital Shop (Detroit) **[67363]**

One Stop Capital Shop (Edinburg) **[67370]**

One Stop Capital Shop (Glendale) **[67356]**

One Stop Capital Shop (Houston)–U.S. General Store **[67371]**

One Stop Capital Shop (Hugo) **[67368]**

One Stop Capital Shop (Jamaica) **[67365]**

One Stop Capital Shop (Kansas City) **[67359]**

One Stop Capital Shop (Mississippi Mid-Delta) **[67364]**

One Stop Capital Shop (New York) **[67366]**

One Stop Capital Shop (Oakland) **[67357]**

One Stop Capital Shop (Philadelphia/Camden) **[67369]**

One Stop Capital Shop (Roxbury) **[67362]**

One Stop Capital Shop (Somerset) **[67360]**

One Stop Capital Shop (Tacoma) **[67372]**

"A One-Stop Marketing Shop" in *Entrepreneur* (Vol. 31, No. 10, October 2003, pp. 112) **[47369]**, **[48658]**, **[48669]**, **[51033]**

"One-stop shop? Brokerage firms make a play for your bank business, too" in *Entrepreneur* (Vol. 31, No. 5, May 2003, pp. 48) **[10122]**, **[15324]**, **[38263]**

"1,000 Crates of Sprinkles With That" in *The New York Times* (March 27, 2000, pp. D28, H28) **[34285]**, **[47370]**

One Thousand One Businesses You Can Start from Home **[42700]**

1,001 Ways to Market Yourself & Your Small Business **[47371]**, **[50648]**

"One To Watch: Danger looms large for the Blackberry" in *Red Herring* (No. 99, June 15 & July 1, 2001, pp. 36, 38) **[14311]**, **[44108]**

"One Tough Lesson Plan" in *Forbes* (Vol. 170, No. 9, October 28, 2002, pp. 238) **[33199]**, **[36584]**, **[45496]**

"One-Track Mind" in *Entrepreneur.com* (Vol. 34, February 2006, No. 2, pp. 33) **[4750]**, **[6270]**, **[23110]**, **[53397]**, **[56359]**

1-2-3: Advanced Features **[6529]**

"One to Watch: A Russian entrepreneur scores a wireless hit with teenagers" in *Red Herring* (No. 103, September 1, 2001, pp. 26) **[35595]**, **[41472]**

"One to Watch: Alpiri hopes to win the name game in e-commerce" in *Red Herring* (No. 105, October 1, 2001, pp. 26) **[33473]**, **[35596]**

"One to Watch: KnowNow tackles two-way computing" in *Red Herring* (No. 102, August 15, 2001, pp. 24) **[6918]**, **[13768]**, **[35597]**, **[41473]**

"One World Seeking to Expand Beyond Its Local Universe" in *San Diego Business Journal* (Vol. 28, January 15, 2007, No. 3, pp. 12) **[23501]**, **[38869]**

OneDisc **[393]**, **[24144]**, **[29678]**, **[54905]**

OneDisc Research Library **[394]**, **[24145]**

O'Neill Area Chamber of Commerce **[62287]**

OneLiberty Ventures **[61106]**

"OneLiberty Ventures Wraps On $200M" in *Venture Capital Journal* (Vol. 40, No. 10, October 2000, pp. 26) **[44613]**, **[55764]**

"The Ones That Get Away" in *The Economist* (Vol. 376, July 30-August 5, 2005, No. 8437, pp. 65-66) **[214]**, **[26311]**

Onex Corp. **[66730]**

Online **[6202]**, **[6302]**, **[6348]**, **[6516]**, **[6888]**, **[6988]**, **[14657]**, **[18671]**, **[26026]**

"Online Appraisals Yield Ballpark Prices for Owners" in *Business First Columbus* (Vol. 18, No. 26, February 15, 2002, pp. 26) **[20617]**, **[34286]**

"Online APPS and Quotes for E&O" in *Rough Notes* (Vol. 145, No. 9, September 2002, pp. 49) **[13411]**, **[34287]**, **[43303]**

"Online Banking is Evolution...Not Revolution" in *Ingram's* (Vol. 29, No. 1, January 2003, pp. 20) **[14312]**, **[34288]**, **[38264]**

"Online Banking - The Revolution That Really Is" in *Ingram's* (Vol. 29, No. 1, January 2003, pp. 65) **[14313]**, **[34289]**

"Online Comics: Superheroes Take The ITunes Route" in *Wall Street Journal* (Vol. 248, December 2006, No. 142, pp. P2) **[5913]**, **[14314]**, **[18656]**, **[25922]**

"Online Content Reaches Bottom Line" in *Crain's New York Business* (Vol. 20, No. 12, March 22, 2004, pp. 4) **[746]**, **[18921]**, **[34290]**, **[47372]**

Online (Vol. 26, No. 5, September-October 2002, pp. 6); "E-book report from the field" in **[2695]**, **[9133]**

Online (Vol. 26, No. 5, September-October 2002, pp. 6); "E-book poll, results" in **[2697]**, **[9136]**

"Online Education: Global Questions, Local Answers" in *Journal of Business Communication* (Vol. 44, January 2007, No. 1, pp. 96) **[14315]**, **[27463]**, **[33200]**, **[41887]**

"Online Employee Surveys Slow to Catch on" in *Atlanta Business Chronicle* (Vol. 25, No. 19, October 18, 2002, pp. 12C) **[34291]**, **[45497]**

"Online In A Flash" in *Small Business Opportunities* (Vol. 13, No. 5, September 2001, pp. 12, 130) **[13769]**, **[33474]**, **[37072]**

"Online Insurance Exchanges Fail to Connect" in *Atlanta Business Chronicle* (Vol. 25, No. 19, October 18, 2002, pp. 6C) **[13412]**, **[34292]**, **[43304]**

"OnLine Job Sites, Take Two" in *Home Office Computing* (Vol. 18, No. 8, August 2000, pp. 24) **[22047]**, **[34293]**

"The Online Lawyer" in *Hispanic Business* (October 2002, pp. 90) **[14316]**, **[29427]**, **[34294]**, **[40594]**

Online Marketing and Search Engine Optimization **[32965]**, **[46637]**

"Online Markets for Private Equity Enter Second Season" in *Venture Capital Journal* (Vol. 40, No. 10, November 2000, pp. 50) **[14317]**, **[34295]**, **[55765]**

"Online Moneymakers" in *Small Business Opportunities* (Vol. 16, No. 3, May 2004, pp. 102, 110, 120) **[1763]**, **[25923]**, **[33475]**

"Online Office" in *Entrepreneur* (Vol. 32, No. 1, January 2004, pp. 47) **[4751]**, **[23111]**, **[27464]**, **[34296]**, **[53398]**

"The Online Office" in *Success* (Vol. 47, No. 3, July 2000, pp. 18) **[3952]**, **[14318]**, **[49190]**

The Online Outpost **[14676]**

"Online Publisher Seeks Dismissal of Apple's Trade-Secret Lawsuit" in *San Jose Mercury News* (March 8, 2005) **[6749]**, **[8621]**, **[29428]**, **[34297]**, **[44348]**

"Online Resources: Consultant Keeps Computers Well" in *My Business* (December/January 2003, pp. 52) **[6179]**, **[56360]**

"Online Retail Sales Jumper 13.1 Percent in Fourth Quarter" in *Wall Street Journal* (February 21, 2002, pp. B6) **[28594]**, **[34298]**

Online Retrieval: A Dialogue of Theory and Practice **[13086]**

"Online Rivals' Market Plays" in *Hispanic Business* (January/February 2003, pp. 50, 52) **[14319]**, **[47373]**

"Online Sales Booming; Retailers Rethink Web Biz as Sales Increase" in *Crain's Detroit Business* (Vol. 19, No. 1, Jan. 6, 2003, pp. 3) **[14320]**, **[25924]**, **[28595]**, **[34299]**, **[51279]**

"Online Sales Continue To Climb at L.L. Bean, Other Retailers" in *Portland Press Herald* (December 13, 2005) **[28596]**, **[34300]**, **[51280]**

"Online Self-Publishing Services" in *Black Enterprise* (Vol. 37, November 2006, No. 4, pp. 90) **[2730]**, **[8622]**, **[14321]**, **[25925]**, **[36585]**, **[52382]**

"Online Shoppers Begin Their Quest in Earnest" in *Sacramento Bee* (November 28, 2005) **[34301]**, **[51281]**

"Online Sites are Registering with Couples" in *HFN* (January 26, 2004, pp. 22) **[3189]**, **[12202]**, **[18657]**, **[34302]**, **[51282]**

"Online Success: Go Fetch More Money!" in *My Business* (June/July 2002, pp. 41) **[14322]**, **[25926]**, **[34303]**

Online Trading Academy **[33373]**

"Online Trading Primer" in *Hispanic Business* (October 2002, pp. 92) **[10123]**, **[14323]**, **[34304]**, **[38265]**

Online Training Solutions Inc. **[66248]**

"Online Video Ads Get Ready to Grab You" in *Business 2.0* (Vol. 6, May 2005, No. 4, pp. 25-26) **[747]**, **[34305]**, **[47374]**

"OnlineAuction.com Makes Bid for Outraged eBay Sellers" in *PR Newswire* (January 18, 2005) **[1841]**, **[14324]**, **[30924]**

"OnlineAuction.com Ready for Return, Rematch With eBay" in *Mail Tribune* (February 2, 2005) **[1842]**, **[14325]**, **[30925]**, **[31050]**

Only Doors and Windows, Inc, **[11236]**

"Only a Few Sea Turtles Survive" in *Forbes* (February 21, 2000, pp. 96) **[35598]**, **[41474]**, **[55414]**

"The Only Question That Matters" in *Business 2.0* (Vol. 6, September 2005, No. 8, pp. 50) **[23768]**, **[31808]**, **[45165]**, **[47375]**

"Only Time Will Tell" in *My Business* (June/July 2004, pp. 22) **[4752]**, **[23112]**, **[49191]**, **[53399]**

Onondaga Community College–Small Business Development Center **[62775]**

Onondaga Venture Capital Fund, Inc. **[63147]**

Onset Ventures **[58109]**

Ontario Association of Landscape Architects–Library **[16096]**

Ontario Chamber of Commerce **[57681]**, **[62974]**, **[64252]**

Ontario Crafts Council–Craft Resource Centre **[8118]**, **[8264]**

Ontario Duct Cleaning Ltd. **[1078]**

The Ontario Land Surveyor **[23776]**

Ontario Ministry of Community and Correctional Services–Centre of Forensic Sciences **[11749]**

Ontario Ministry of Economic Development and Trade–InfoSource **[32836]**, **[43943]**, **[46154]**

Ontario Nature **[9331]**

Ontario Regulations and Rules of Court **[29679]**

Ontario Teachers' Pension Plan Board–Library **[10404]**, **[15804]**

Ontonagon County Chamber of Commerce **[61396]**

"Ontrackfitness.com Introduces the Fitness Accountability Trainer Service" in *PR Newswire* (Nov. 25, 2003) **[19426]**, **[34306]**

"Onvia Business Builder" in *Entrepreneur* (Vol. 33, October 2005, No. 10, pp. 6) **[34307]**, **[40071]**

Oregon Health Sciences University–Oregon Hearing Research Center [12125]
Oregon Housing and Community Services Department [66962]
The Oregon Innovation Center (OIC) [64296]
Oregon Institute of Technology–Small Business Development Center [64171]
Oregon Lodging Association–Materials Library [12748]
Oregon Office of Minority, Women, and Emerging Small Businesses [64287]
Oregon Procurement Technical Assistance Center–The Organization for Economic Initiatives [64294]
Oregon Publisher [8639], [18259]
Oregon Research Institute [54402]
Oregon Resource and Technology Development Fund [64289]
Oregon State Library [66963]
Oregon State University
    Kiewit Center for Infrastructure and Transportation [2556]
    Office of Vice Provost for Research [64297]
    Seafoods Research Laboratory–Library [10431]
Oregon Thoroughbred Breeders Association–Library [1224]
"Oreo Woes Bringing Kraft Down" in *Crain's Chicago Business* (Vol. 26, No. 50, December 15, 2003, pp. 4) [11648], [30926], [31051]
"Oreo Woes Bringing Kraft Down; Fat Fears, Price Hikes, Private-Label Brands Sap Sales" in *Crains Chicago Business* (Vol. 26, No. 50) [11649], [30927], [31052]
The Organic Food and Beverage Market [12022]
The Organic Gardener's Handbook of Natural Insect and Disease Control: A Complete, Problem-Solving Guide to Keeping Your Garden and Yard... [11438]
Organic Gardening [11475]
Organic Inc. [34779]
Organic Trade Association [9480]
Organization of American Kodaly Educators [17584]
Organization of Black Designers [5523], [5960], [13631]
Organization for Competitive Markets [26464]
Organization Counselors Inc. [3784], [16654], [27592], [31428], [35247], [46095], [53108]
Organization Design Forum [44715]
Organization Development Institute [46163]
Organization of Pakistani Entrepreneurs of North America [41489]
Organization Plus [55042]
Organization for the Promotion and Advancement of Small Telecommunications Companies [4900]
Organization of Women in International Trade [43522]
Organizational Consulting Services Inc. [46096]
Organizational Futures [3785], [16655], [30107], [31429], [32830], [35248], [46097], [51006]
Organizational Improvement Associates [3786], [31430], [50782]
Organizational Synergies [42991]
Organizational Systems Research Association [49473]
Organizational Transactions [45938]
Organizational Transformations [35249]
"Organizations" in *Black Enterprise* (Vol. 34, No. 5, December 2003, pp. S5) [35599], [53903], [56727]
"Organizations award performers" in *Atlanta Business Chronicle* (Vol. 25, December 6, 2002, No. 26, pp. 2C) [1525], [7448], [13664], [18557], [20621], [20960]
"Organize Yourself" in *Fast Company* (September 2001, pp. 60) [14329], [36593]
"Organizer's Laud Bigger Javits" in *Tradeshow Week* (Vol. 34) [22538], [24989], [40598], [55137]
"Organizers Say Houston Will Be Ready for XXXVIII" in *Houston Chronicle* (April 11, 2003) [23732], [50649]
Organizing Your Home Office for Success: Expert Strategies That Can Work for You [42701]
Orick Chamber of Commerce [57687]
Orien Ventures [58606], [64290]

Origin Partners [62604]
The Original Basket Boutique [42801]
The Original Woodwork Shop & School [8291], [33374]
Orinda Chamber of Commerce [57688]
Orion Area Chamber of Commerce [61397]
Orion Blue Book [4342], [17762], [18609]
Orland Area Chamber of Commerce [57689]
Orland Park Area Chamber of Commerce [59623]
Orlando Business Journal (Vol. 20, No. 8, August 8, 2003, pp. 2); "Cancer Scans a Lifesaver for Crystal Maker" in [39870], [41590], [48394], [50843], [52045], [52070]
Orlando Business Journal (Vol. 20, No. 13, September 12, 2003, pp. 3); "Center Braces for New Wave of Business" in [22166], [22481], [24904], [25749]
Orlando Business Journal (Vol. 20, No. 2, June 27, 2003, pp. 1); "Charging an Arm and a Leg?" in [39281], [40982]
Orlando Business Journal (Vol. 20, No. 2, June 27, 2003, pp. 26); "Cooking Up a Winner in Manny Garcia's Kitchen" in [21186], [21478], [45022], [45610]
Orlando Business Journal (Vol. 20, No. 2, June 27, 2003, pp. 1); "Ex-TV Exec Sues Over Lentek Deal" in [24405], [25226], [29228]
Orlando Business Journal (Vol. 20, No. 10, August 22, 2003, pp. 1); "Home Builder Falls Under SEC Scrutiny" in [7309], [7362], [14881], [15090], [29290], [30257], [40440], [40543], [47619], [49985]
Orlando Business Journal (Vol. 20, No. 5, July 18, 2003, pp. 1); "Laser Business Fails to Shine" in [40046], [40050], [40195], [41801]
Orlando Business Journal (Vol. 20, No. 5, July 18, 2003, pp. 1); "Lentek Lands in Chapter 11" in [28711], [29364], [36751], [38187]
Orlando Business Journal (Vol. 20, No. 11, August 29, 2003, pp. 1); "Local Investors Eye Chip Plant" in [15010], [15225], [40058], [41810], [50911], [53115]
Orlando Business Journal (Vol. 20, No. 7, August 1, 2003, No. pp. 1); "Philly Firm Launches Lawsuit over 'Space'" in [1084], [1137], [29439], [30119]
Orlando Business Journal (Vol. 20, No. 8, August 8, 2003, pp. 28); "Pizam: Hospitality Business Showing Signs of Life" in [24720], [24893], [25233], [25549]
Orlando Business Journal (Vol. 20, No. 6, July 25, 2003, pp. 31); "R&G: Growing Branches Through New Acquisitions" in [10149], [15393], [47760], [50155]
Orlando Business Journal (Vol. 20, No. 13, September 12, 2003, pp. 32); "Regional Leaders Search for Solutions to Water Problems" in [39557]
Orlando Business Journal (Vol. 20, No. 13, September 12, 2003, pp. 1); "Study: Insurance Fraud Thriving" in [13388], [13477], [29523], [30456], [43381], [45053]
Orlando Regional Chamber of Commerce [58911]
Orlando Sentinel (February 9, 2005); "Companies Adapt to Elder Care Needs" in [443], [18320], [53656]
Orlando Sentinel (October 11, 2004); "Devoted Shopper Resurrects Jacobson's Department Store in Central Florida" in [18994], [51132]
Orlando Sentinel (February 1, 2005); "Lesson Plan: Cashing in Online" in [1832], [14200], [33156]
Orlando Sentinel (January 6, 2005); "New Owners of Daytona Beach, Fla. Water Park Ride Second Wave of Optimism" in [1135], [17325]
Orleans Chamber of Commerce [59983], [62289]
Orleans County Chamber of Commerce [62976]
Ormond Beach Chamber of Commerce [58912]
Ornamental Concrete Producers Association [11417]
Ornamental Outlook [11476]
Oroville Area Chamber of Commerce [57690]
Oroville Chamber of Commerce [66149]
"Orthodontist turns inventor of breast prothesis" in *Atlanta Business Chronicle* (Vol. 25, November 29, 2002, No. 25, pp. 4C) [44109], [48774]
OrthoKineticReview [17267]

Orthopaedic Section, American Physical Therapy Association [19560]
Osage Chamber of Commerce [60190]
Osage City Chamber of Commerce [60397]
Osawatomie Chamber of Commerce [60398]
Osborn Capital LLC [61107]
Osborne Area Chamber of Commerce [60399]
Osceola Area Chamber of Commerce [66487]
Osceola Chamber of Commerce [60191]
Osceola-South Mississippi County Chamber of Commerce [57202]
"OSDBU Directory" in *Hispanic Business* (December 2002, pp. FRG12-FRG14) [36594], [39882], [40073], [41516], [48349]
OSH-DB [56675]
OSHA Compliance Advisor [56602]
OSHA Confined Space Entry [56640]
OSHA Electrical Safety for Non-Electrical Workers [56641]
OSHA Handbook for Small Businesses [56580]
"OSHA Ushers Itself Out" in *Business Week* (March 27, 2000, pp. F6) [42702], [56581]
"OSHA's Proposed Ergonomic Standard and Clarification on Home Work Policy" in *Employment Relations Today* (Vol. 27, No. 1, Spring 2000) [40599], [42703]
OSHAWeek [56603]
Oshkosh Chamber of Commerce [66488]
"OSI Pharmaceuticals Hopes to Get FDA Approval for Its Cancer Drug" in *Long Island Business News* (February 13, 2004) [8796], [50940], [52167]
Oskaloosa Area Chamber and Development Group [60192]
Osler, Hoskin & Harcourt LLP [3908]
Osprey Ventures, L.P. [58113]
Osteoporosis Canada [40945]
Osteoporosis International [41279]
Oswego Chamber of Commerce [59624]
Oswego Chamber of Commerce and Visitors Center [60400]
Oswego State University–SBDC Oswego Outreach [62776]
Otay Mesa Chamber of Commerce [57691]
OTC Insight [10288]
"Other Comments" in *Forbes* (Vol. 170, No. 6, September 30, 2002, pp. 36) [5080], [32620], [34315], [41892]
Other Essentials of Business Ownership [36595], [45502]
Other Mothers, Inc. [2140], [5309]
"Other People's Money: A Pension Fund Learns About Soft Dollars-the Hard Way" in *Barron's* (July 7, 2003, pp. L7) [10126], [15331], [26868], [38268], [53902]
The Other Woman [8719]
Otis College of Art and Design–Millard Sheets Library [5615]
Otsego Area Chamber of Commerce [61398]
Otsego County Chamber of Commerce [62977]
Ottawa Area Chamber of Commerce [60401], [63764]
Ottawa Area Chamber of Commerce and Industry [59625]
Ottawa County Economic Development Office, Inc.–Small Business Development Center [61216]
Ottawa Letter [13037], [13110], [22094], [40869], [43908]
Ottawa Wine and Food Show [4567], [21710], [23554]
Ottumwa Area Chamber of Commerce [60193]
"Our Companies, Ourselves" in *Inc.* (November 2006, pp. 39-40) [45503]
"Our Kinda Town" in *Entrepreneur* (Vol. 28, No. 1, January 2000, pp. 26) [3484], [13770], [33476], [35600]
Our Place [42778]
"Our Rankings Are Derived From 3-Month Rolling Averages of US Bureau of Labor Statistics Unadjusted Employment Data" in *Inc.* (May1,2006) [32621], [33702], [40561], [42373]
"Our So-Called Economic Recovery" in *Hispanic Business* (May 2005, pp. 6) [28602], [32622]
Our Town America, A Franchising Corp. [888]

"Pace Exec Taking Creative Route to Expand Bus Service" in *Crain's Chicago Business* (Vol. 26, No. 51, December 22, 2003, pp. 12) [15955], [16185], [23909], [24238]

PACE International Union–Irene Glaus Memorial Library [56699]

Pace University–Small Business Development Center [62777]

Pacific Area Chamber of Commerce [62019]

Pacific Asia Travel Association [25136]

Pacific Basin Economic Council - Canadian Committee [32221]

Pacific Boating Almanac [16741]

Pacific Builder & Engineer [7567]

Pacific Business News [59269]

Pacific Business News (Vol. 41, No. 24, August 22, 2003, pp. 10); "ATMs Keep Evolving as Part of Customers' Everyday Life" in [31641], [53590]

Pacific Business News (Vol. 41, No. 20, July 25, 2003, pp. 1); "Billion-Dollar Plan in Limbo" in [7256], [29125], [40191]

Pacific Business News (Vol. 41, No. 23, August 15, 2003, pp. 1); "Biotech Takes Heart in Potential New Drug" in [8775], [41554], [50832], [52060]

Pacific Business News (Vol. 41, No. 16, June 27, 2003, pp. 12); "City Bank Expands as Merger Bid Threatens Branches" in [9886], [14861], [27951], [49858]

Pacific Business News (Vol. 41, No. 16, June 27, 2003, pp. 1); "Disabled Rise Up As Entrepreneurs" in [36017], [39807]

Pacific Business News (Vol. 41, No. 19, July 18, 2003, pp. 23); "Hawaii's Growers Wake Up and Sell the Coffee" in [11329], [26513], [47061]

Pacific Business News (Vol. 41, No. 24, August 22, 2003, pp. 1); "Hilton Suit Reveals More Mold Problems" in [3234], [7361], [9362], [12562]

Pacific Business News (Vol. 41, No. 23, August 15, 2003, pp. 1); "Hot Resort Market May Aid Sale of 2 Isle Hotels" in [12568], [20539], [20900]

Pacific Business News (Vol. 41, No. 19, July 18, 2003, pp. 12); "Insurance Firms Forecast Profitable Year" in [13342], [28333], [32510], [43235]

Pacific Business News (Vol. 41, No. 26, September 5, 2003, pp. 10); "Kauai Businesses Prepare to Welcome Cruise Visitors" in [24699], [25203]

Pacific Business News (Vol. 41, No. 22, August 8, 2003, pp. 1); "Marketing Spreads Hawaiian Message" in [39460], [40529], [47251]

Pacific Business News (Vol. 41, No. 23, August 15, 2003, pp. 1); "New Rules Stall Foreign Vessels" in [10685], [25220], [40561]

Pacific Business News (Vol. 41, No. 19, July 18, 2003, pp. 1); "Oahu Apartment Inventory Down, Rents Up" in [21339], [32607]

Pacific Business News (Vol. 41, No. 19, July 18, 2003, pp. 3); "Software Translates Old Hawaiian to Modern" in [4819], [23205], [25092]

Pacific Business News (Vol. 41, No. 17, July 4, 2003, pp. 9); "Stock Basics Offer Insights on Value of Local Bank Merger" in [15477], [50191]

Pacific Business News (Vol. 41, No. 16, June 27, 2003, pp. 1); "Summer Could Help Lick Tourism Slump" in [24731], [25251], [47587], [50684]

Pacific Business News (Vol. 41, No. 19, July 18, 2003, pp. 10); "Travel Agency Business All Over the Map" in [24739], [25261], [32753], [34623]

Pacific Century Group Ventures Ltd. [55977]

Pacific Coast Nurseryman and Garden Supply Dealer [11477], [15970]

Pacific Coast Shellfish Growers Association [10451]

Pacific Gas and Electric Company–Energy Resource Center [7693]

Pacific Grove Chamber of Commerce [57693]

"Pacific Growth, Others Bank on Emerging Firms" in *San Francisco Business Times* (Vol. 17, No. 50, July 18, 2003, pp. 1) [10128], [15338], [28609], [30165]

Pacific Health Research Institute [41396]

Pacific Islands Small Business Development Center–University of Guam [66641]

"Pacific Life Insurance Committed to Secondaries" in *Venture Capital Journal* (Vol. 41, No. 8, August 2000, pp. 41) [15339], [43307], [55769]

Pacific Magazine with Islands Business [59266]

Pacific Northwest Christmas Tree Association Buy-Sell Directory [5480]

Pacific Northwest Partners SBIC, L.P. [66221]

Pacific Palisades Chamber of Commerce [57694]

Pacific Research Institute for Public Policy [41397]

Pacific Resource Development Group Inc. [32119]

Pacific Salmon Commission [10452]

Pacifica Chamber of Commerce and Visitor Center [57695]

Pacifica Fund [58115]

Paciugo Italian Gelato Renaissance [12844]

"Pack a Punch" in *Entrepreneur* (Vol. 31, No. 11, November 2003, pp. 102) [751], [6752], [22540], [47385], [49195]

"Package deal" in *Entrepreneur* (Vol. 31, No. 4, April 2003, pp. 22) [28610], [32623], [38873], [39518], [40602], [54692]

Packaging and Converting Hotline [6116]

Packaging and Shipping Specialists [6123]

The Packer [11699]

The Packet [46517]

Pacrim Venture Management [58116]

Padgett Business Services [382], [4029], [24134]

Padows's Hams & Deli [10647]

Paducah Area Chamber of Commerce [60558]

Paducah Chamber of Commerce [65428]

Page Communications Inc. [24498]

Barry Page Consulting [17226]

Page-Lake Powell Chamber of Commerce [57056]

Page & Turners Bookstores [3065]

Pageland Chamber of Commerce [64777]

Pagosa Springs Area Chamber of Commerce [58414]

Pahokee Chamber of Commerce [58913]

Pahrump Valley Chamber of Commerce [62364]

"Paid family leave better if voluntary" in *Crain's Detroit Business* (Vol. 16, No. 5, January 31, 2000, pp. 8) [26869], [40603]

Paier College of Art, Inc.–Library [6074]

"Pain-Free Patching" in *Entrepreneur* (Vol. 32, November 2004, No. 11, pp. 62) [4757], [23118], [44110], [53403]

"A pain in the supply chain" in *Harvard Business Review* (Vol. 80, No. 5, May 2002, pp. 31) [44237], [46400], [51760]

"Pain Medicine May Keep Jobs in Ann Arbor, Pfizer CEO Says" in *Crain's Detroit Business* (Vol. 22, February 13, 2006, No. 7, pp. 1) [50941], [52168]

Painesville Area Chamber of Commerce [63767]

Paint & Decorating Retailer Magazine [18691], [22824]

Paint and Decorating Retailers Association [13632], [18701]

"Paint Hustle: New Orleans Artist Went from the Streets to Mainstream" in *Black Enterprise* (Vol. 35, December 2004, No. 5, pp. 77) [8017], [36600], [48351]

Paint Medic [2100]

Paint Works [8049]

The Painted Penguin, LLC [8107]

Painting [8050]

Painting Contractor: Start and Run a Money-Making Business [18709]

Painting and Decorating Contractors of America [13633], [18702]

"Painting by numbers" in *Hispanic Business* (Vol. 22, No. 9, September 2000, pp. 82) [18710], [38874], [45512]

Painting & Wallcovering Contractor [18714]

Painting and Wallcovering Contractor-PDCA Roster [18711]

Paints and Coatings [18689]

The Paints & Coatings Industry [18684]

Paintsville - Johnson County Chamber of Commerce [60559]

Pajaro Valley Chamber of Commerce [57696]

Pak Mail [6124], [9667], [14677]

Pak Mail Centres (Canada) Ltd. [6125]

"Pala Mesa Resort: A True Tranquil Setting and an Easy Drive from Orange County" in *Los Angeles Business Journal* (July 5, 2004) [3190], [12612]

"Palace Goes Ultra-Luxury With Suites, Club" in *Crain's Detroit Business* (Vol. 21, October 24, 2005, No. 43, pp. 27) [23733]

Palacios Chamber of Commerce [65429]

Paladin Consultants L.L.C. [49450]

Paladin Partners [66222]

Palatine Area Chamber of Commerce [59626]

Palestine Area Chamber of Commerce [65430]

Palestine Chamber of Commerce [59627]

Palestine Development Association [59628]

Palisade Chamber of Commerce [58415]

"Pall Corp. Plans to Sell New Bacteria-Detection System to Blood Banks" in *Long Island Business News* (February 20, 2004) [41075], [41894], [50942], [52169]

Palm Beach Chamber of Commerce [58914]

"Palm Beach County Convention Center West Palm Beach, FL" in *Tradeshow Week* (Vol. 34, November 29, 2004, No. 48, pp. S4) [22541], [24991], [55139]

Palm Beach County Resource Center, Inc. [58964]

Palm Beach Mega Tan [23847]

Palm Beach Post (April 11, 2003); "Tenet Healthcare Ends Fight over Heart Program at Stuart, Fla. Medical Center" in [42060], [52217]

Palm City Chamber of Commerce [58915]

Palm Desert Chamber of Commerce [57697]

Palm Springs Chamber of Commerce [57698]

Palm Ventures [58117]

"Palmdale, Calif., Hampton Inn to House Business Travelers to Sports Fans" in *Daily News* (February 17, 2004) [12613], [30399]

Palmdale Chamber of Commerce [57699]

John C. Palmer Associates Inc. [17139]

Palmer Partners, L.P. [61108]

Palmerton Chamber of Commerce [64488]

Palmetto Business Group [42992]

Palmetto Poultry Life [1207]

Palms West Chamber of Commerce [58916]

Palmyra Area Chamber of Commerce [66489]

Palo Alto Chamber of Commerce [57700]

Palo Alto Venture Partners / 21VC Oartners [58118]

Palomar Ventures [58119]

Palomino Horse Breeders of America–Library [12480]

Palos Hills Chamber of Commerce [59629]

Palos Verdes Peninsula Chamber of Commerce [57701]

Palouse Chamber of Commerce [66150]

The Pampered Chef [7815], [21581]

"Pampering Pets Makes Miami-Area Groomer, Salon Owner Happy" in *Miami Herald* (June 28, 2004) [19078], [56362]

Pana Chamber of Commerce [59630]

Panache Magazine [18982]

Panago Pizza Inc. [19694]

"Panasonic Tunes In Hispanic Market" in *Hispanic Business* (March 2003, pp. 24) [752], [47386], [48352], [49196], [53907]

Panchero's Mexican Grill [21914]

Pandini's [21915]

"Panel Chief Set To Reopen SBA Budget Debate" in *American Banker* (Vol. 171, November 30, 2006, No. 229, pp. 1) [10129], [15340], [39883], [44617]

"Panel on taxing Internet sales ends its meetings in disagreement" in *The New York Times* (March 22, 2000, pp. D28, H28) [14336], [34325], [54693]

"Panel to Monitor Minority Contracts" in *Hispanic Business* (March 2004, pp. 12) [40074], [48353]

"Panel Seeks to Put Organic Loophole Out to Pasture" in *Chicago Tribune* (March 3, 2005) [12016], [26526], [40604]

Panel World [7568], [16333]

Panel World-Directory and Buyers' Guide Issue [16317]

Panfish Patterns [2197]

Panguitch Chamber of Commerce [65722]

Panhandle Area Council–Business Center for Innovation and Development [59346]

Panhandle Chamber of Commerce [65431]

The Panhandler [11205], [12251]

Panigas Group [7629]

Pannell Kerr Forster–Library [24783]

Panola County Chamber of Commerce [65432]

Panola Partnership [61826]

"Panorama Place" in *San Fernando Valley Business Journal* (Vol. 12, January 2007, No. 1, pp. 13) [20961], [51283], [52932]

The Pantry Hospitality Corp. [21916]

Paola Chamber of Commerce [60403]

Paoli Chamber of Commerce [59985]

B. Paolucci Inc. [18972]

Paonia Chamber of Commerce [58416]

Papa & Associates Inc. [3788], [16657], [31432], [42993], [46099]

Papa John's International, Inc. [19695]

Papa Murphy's Take 'N' Bake Pizza [19696]

Papa's Pizza To-Go, Inc. [19697]

"The Paper Chase" in *Small Business Opportunities* (Vol. 12, No. 5, September 2000, pp. 66) [27667]

Paper Crafts Magazine [8051]

"Paper Jam: Curtis Sherrod's Hip-Hop History Session" in *Black Enterprise* (Vol. 34, No. 5, December 2003, pp. 147) [9229], [10008], [36601], [37818]

"Paper Mountain" in *Boston Business Journal* (Vol. 22, No. 15, May 17, 2002) [6271], [28611]

"Paper, Printing & Profit" in *Small Business Opportunities* (Vol. 16, No. 2, March 2004, pp. 70) [18610], [19887], [31054], [31812], [56015]

"Paper-Run Web Sites Prosper" in *Milwaukee Journal Sentinel* (December 18, 2005) [18922], [34326], [53908]

Papermaking & Bookbinding [2843]

"Papermaster in startup mode" in *Austin Business Journal* (Vol. 22, No. 28, September 27, 2002, pp. 1) [4758], [23119], [41895], [43058], [55770]

"Papers Away: Tax Records Weighing You Down? Switch to Electronic Storage" in *Entrepreneur* (Vol. 32, October 2004, No. 10, pp. 60) [219], [22321], [24010], [26316], [54694]

Pappajohn Capital Resources [60238]

PAR Enterprises Inc. [27042]

Par-T-Perfect Party Planners [42802]

Par-T-Zone [18745], [48509]

Parachute Computer Services Inc. [49451], [49642]

Paradigm Accounting: Computerized Payroll Procedures [18784]

Paradigm Capital Partners, LLC [65000]

Paradise Ridge Chamber of Commerce [57702]

Paragon Venture Partners [58120]

Paragould - Greene County Chamber of Commerce [57204]

Paragraphs on Translation [25089]

Paramount Chamber of Commerce [57703]

Parcel Plus [17317]

Pardeeville Area Business Association [66490]

Parent and Preschooler Newsletter [5358]

"Parent Trap?" in *Entrepreneur* (Vol. 33, March 2005, No. 3, pp. 96) [35303], [36602], [37820], [42374], [52239], [54973]

"Parents and tots share exercise fun at new Gymboree facility" in *Vancouver, WA Business Journal* (February 28, 2003) [19427]

"Parents for hire" in *Entrepreneur* (Vol. 31, No. 4, April 2003, pp. 76) [36603], [42375], [45513]

Paribas Principal, Inc. [63150]

Paris Area Chamber of Commerce [57205], [62020]

Paris Area Chamber of Commerce and Tourism [59631]

Paris-Bourbon County Chamber of Commerce [60560]

Paris/Henry County Chamber of Commerce [64964]

Paris Junior College–Small Business Development Center [65055]

Park City Chamber of Commerce [65723]

Park Falls Area Chamber of Commerce [66491]

Park Hills Chamber of Commerce [62021]

Park Rapids Area Chamber of Commerce [61644]

Park Ridge Chamber of Commerce [59632]

Parke County Chamber of Commerce [59986]

Parker Area Chamber of Commerce [57057]

Glenn M. Parker Associates Inc. [35251]

Parker Chamber of Commerce [58417]

Parker Consultants Inc. [3789], [16658], [31433], [31984], [35252], [46100], [53109]

Parker Finch Management [383], [16684]

Parker, Smith & Feek, Inc.–Library [13606]

"Parking Kiosk Failure Gives Denver Shoppers Break" in *Denver Post* (October 24, 2003) [15932]

Parking Products & Services Directory [2546]

Parks Pavilion [1155]

"Parlez-vous e-Commerce? Here's How To Give Your Website International Appeal" in *Black Enterprise* (Vol. 35, October 2004, No. 3) [25090], [34327], [43779]

Parlier Chamber of Commerce [57704]

Parma Area Chamber of Commerce [63768]

"Parrish, Fla. Farmland Sells for $6.5 Million" in *Bradenton Herald* (January 20, 2005) [7449], [20962], [26527]

Parsippany Area Chamber of Commerce [62545]

Parsons Chamber of Commerce [60404]

Parsons School of Design–Adam & Sophie Gimbel Design Library [5616], [6075], [8119]

"Part-Time Assignments" in *Black Enterprise* (Vol. 37, December 2006, No. 5, pp. 70) [42376], [45514], [53909]

Partech International [58121]

Participative Dynamics Inc. [35253]

Particulate Science and Technology [52310]

"Partnering for Success" in *Rough Notes* (Vol. 146, No. 4, April 2003, pp. 32) [13415], [43308], [50123]

Partnering: The Heart of Selling Today [31942]

Partnering With Your Boss: Strategic Skills for Administrative Professionals (Canada) [25517]

Partnering with Your Boss: Strategic Skills for Administrative Professionals [34799]

"PartnerMD Finds Customers Willing to Pay More for Individualized Health Care" in *Richmond Times-Dispatch* (February 7, 2005) [7142], [41076]

"Partners in Branding" in *Sales and Marketing.com* (Vol. 156, No. 3, March 2004, pp. 10) [30929], [47387], [50124]

Partners in Contracting Corporation–Partners in Contracting Corporation [60035]

Partners for Market Leadership Inc. [3790], [16659], [31434], [38566], [48839], [53110]

"Partners in Style" in *Hispanic Business* (May 2005, pp. 64, 66) [4119], [11797], [28612], [44618], [48354]

Partners at Work and at Home: How Couples Can Build a Successful Business Together without Killing Each Other [37752], [42706]

Partnership for AiR Transportation Noise and Emissions Reduction [9468]

"Partnership: Cisco, SBA team on online learning" in *InfoWorld* (Vol. 22, No. 30, July 24, 2000, pp. 20) [14337], [33203], [39884]

Partnership for New York City [62979]

Partnership Series [50280]

Partnership: Small Business Start-Up Kit [15341], [29072], [39071], [49774]

Partnership Tax Planning & Practice [24096]

"Partnership Terminations" in *Journal of Accountancy* (Vol. 199, January 2005, No. 1, pp. 73) [220], [2944], [15342], [24011], [26317], [27161], [50125]

Partnership for Tomorrow [64778]

Partnerwerks Inc. [35254]

PartSource [1874]

Party America [52629]

Party Land [11206], [18746]

Party & Paper Retailer [11181]

"Party Planning Can Make Memories" in *Crain's Detroit Business* (Vol. 21, October 3, 2005, No. 43, pp. 14) [18729], [18759]

"Party Time" in *Houston Business Journal* (Vol. 34, No. 8, July 4, 2003, pp. 15) [4551], [18730], [21342]

Pasadena Chamber of Commerce [65433]

Pasadena Chamber of Commerce and Civic Association [57705]

Pasco-Hernando County SCORE - Chapter 439 [58721]

Paso Robles Chamber of Commerce [57706]

Pass Your Plate [8292]

Passaic County Department of Community and Economic Development [62636]

Passenger Vessel Association [5239]

"Passing the Baton" in *Sales & Marketing Management* (Vol. 157, January 2005, No. 1, pp. 34) [49726], [51761], [53910]

"Passing the Buck" in *Entrepreneur* (Vol. 32) [5082], [14338], [49197]

"Passing the bucks" in *WorkingWoman* (Vol. 25, No. 4, April 2000, pp. 28) [38274], [56363]

"Passing Marks?" in *Entrepreneur* (Vol. 31, No. 11, November 2003, pp. 70) [221], [24012], [26318], [40605], [54695]

"Passing the baton the importance of sequence, timing, technique and communication in executive succession" in *Journal of Business Venturing* [37753], [46401]

"Passing the Torch" in *Entrepreneur* (Vol. 31, No. 11, November 2003, pp. 97) [45515], [51762]

Passing the Torch: Succession, Retirement, and Estate Planning for Owners of Family Businesses [37754]

Passing Your Family Business on to Your Family: Creating a Lifetime Succession Plan to Meet Your Changing Tax, Estate and Business Needs [37755]

A Passion for Planning [45516]

The Passion Profit Co. [63262]

"A Passion for the Work" in *Hispanic Business* (January/February 2004, pp. 30, 34) [36604], [48355]

Passport Health, Inc. [479]

Passport Inn [12721]

Passport to International Detroit-Services [43780]

"Password Protection" in *Entrepreneur* (Vol. 32, December 2004, No. 12, pp. 52) [4759], [22322], [23120], [53404]

Past Due!: A Debt Collecting Manual for Collections Professionals, Accounts Receivable Personnel & Small Business Owners [8393]

"Past due, and getting soaked" in *Crain's Detroit Business* (Vol. 17, No. 43, October 15, 2001, pp. 1) [26319], [31575]

"Past Track to the Future" in *Fast Company* (May 2001, pp. 166) [36605], [45517]

Pastry Art & Design [2269], [21689]

"Pat Croce's Bottom Line" in *Inc.* (January 1, 2002) [19428], [36606], [45518]

PATCA Journal [6203]

Patent Attorneys and Agents Registered to Practice before the United States Patent and Trademark Office [44111]

"Patent a key victory for Catuity, but smart-card wait continues" in *Crain's Detroit Business* (Vol. 19, No. 3, Jan. 20, 2003, pp. 12) [4760], [23121], [44112]

"Patent Chutzpah" in *Forbes* (November 13, 2000, pp. 58) [13771], [33477], [35602], [43967]

"The Patent Epidemic" in *Business Week* (January 9, 2006, No. 3966, pp. 60-62) [29433], [40606], [44113]

"Patent expiration to hit MSU" in *Crain's Detroit Business* (Vol. 19, No. 14, April 7, 2003, pp. 3) [44114], [50943], [52170]

"Patent Pending" in *Entrepreneur* (Vol. 33, October 2005, No. 10, pp. 28) [28778], [29434], [44115]

"Patent Pitfalls for Early Stage Investors" in *Venture Capital Journal* (November 1, 2004) [44116], [55771]

Patent Reexamination and Small Business Innovation: Congressional Hearing [29435], [40607], [44117]

Patent Term & Patent Disclosure Legislation: Hearing Before the Committee on Small Business, U.S. House of Representatives [44118]

Patent, Trademark & Copyright Journal [44215]

Patent and Trademark Office

> Board of Patent Appeals and Inferences [67373]

> Office of Enforcement [67374]

> Office of Enrollment and Discipline [67375]

> Office of Initial Patent Examination [67376]

> Office of International Relations [67377]

> Office of Patent and Cooperation Operations (PCT) [67378]

Office of Patent Publication [67379]
Office of Petitions [67380]
Office of Procurement [67381]
Office of Public Affairs [67382]
"A Patently Obvious Strategy" in *Success* (Vol. 47, No. 3, July 2000, pp. 61) [44119], [44350]
Patents Handbook [44120]
Patents Handbook: A Guide for Inventors and Researchers to Searching Patent Documents and Preparing and Making an Application [44121]
"Paternal Instincts" in *Entrepreneur* (Vol. 32, October 2004, No. 10, pp. 102) [753], [47388]
PATH Associates [42994]
"The Path of Lease Resistance" in *Home Office Computing* (Vol. 19, No. 1, January 2001, pp. 85) [49198], [53405]
Path to Profit [2277], [51971]
Pathfinder Venture Capital Funds (Menlo Park) [58122]
Pathfinder Venture Capital Funds (Minneapolis) [61707]
"Pathmark Adds Online Shopping Middletown, N.J., Store" in *The Record* (November 10, 2005) [11650], [34328]
Pathogen Control Associates Inc. [1075]
Pathways Education & Training Centers, Inc. [33376]
Pathways To Wellness [3791], [3983], [19582], [31435], [41335]
Pathways Unlimited Inc. [7002]
"Patient Capital: How Life Sciences Investments Touch Us All" in *Venture Capital Journal* (December 1, 2004) [41896], [52171], [55772]
Patient Rights: The Art of Caring [41314]
"Patio Appeal" in *Birmingham Business Journal* (Vol. 20, No. 28, July 11, 2003, pp. 11) [12204], [12307]
Paton Press L.L.C. [58274]
"Patriarch Adds $7 Million Auto Supplier to its Holdings" in *Crain's Detroit Business* (Vol. 22, February 6, 2006, No. 6, pp. 3) [1957], [15343], [50126]
Patrick County Chamber of Commerce [65934]
"Patrick Tisdale, Chief Information Officer" in *Law Firm Inc.* (August 2004) [29436], [33204], [45519]
Patricof & Co. Ventures, Inc. [64569]
Patricof & Co. Ventures, Inc. (New York) [63151]
Patricof & Co. Ventures, Inc. (Palo Alto) [58123]
"Patriot Acts: Should You Play Up the 'Made in the USA' Angle?" in *Entrepreneur* (Vol. 32, December 2004, No. 12, pp. 93) [754], [47389]
Patriot Associates [21090]
"Patriot Ford in Copiague Driven to Bankruptcy Protection" in *Long Island Business News* (February 6, 2004) [18108], [28613]
Patriot-News (April 11, 2003); "York, Pa.-Based Company Plans to Build Ethanol Plant in Northeast" in [26563], [52231]
Patron Saint Productions Inc. [66249]
"Pattern Behavior" in *Entrepreneur* (Vol. 28, No. 11, November 2000, pp. 22) [14339], [29437], [44122]
"Patterns of Disruption in Retailing" in *Harvard Business Review* (Vol. 78, No. 1, January 2000, pp. 42) [34329], [51284]
Patterson Chamber of Commerce [62980]
James G. Patterson - The Cogent Communicator [27593], [47898]
Patterson-Westley Chamber of Commerce [57707]
Paul Davis Restoration [43448]
Paul Davis Systems Canada, Ltd. [13582]
Paul Hornsby & Co. [21091]
Paul Jones, Barrister, Solicitor, & Trademark Agent [29642]
Paul Revere's Pizza [19698]
Paul Smith's College of Arts and Sciences–Joan Weill Adirondack Library [7834], [12749]
Paulding Chamber of Commerce [59148]
Paul's Professional Window Washing Franchise Inc. [43449]
Paul's Restorations [43450]
Pauls Valley Chamber of Commerce [64055]

"Paulson Changes Name of Business" in *Bellingham Business Journal* (January 2007, pp. A19) [10130], [27469], [28614], [38275], [56364]
Pavco Talks [16399]
Pavement [7569]
"Paving the Cow Path" in *Rough Notes* (Vol. 146, No. 9, September 2003, pp. 40) [13416], [30580], [34330], [43309], [47390], [53911]
Pawhuska Chamber of Commerce [64056]
Pawling Chamber of Commerce [62981]
Pawnee Community Chamber of Commerce [64057]
Pawtucket Business Resource Center–Pawtucket and Central Falls SBDC [64652]
Pawtuxet Valley Chamber of Commerce [64674]
Paxton Area Chamber of Commerce [59633]
"Pay Attention" in *Entrepreneur* (Vol. 32, September 2004, No. 9, pp. 80) [18785], [36607]
"Pay you back: your employees may be better off driving their own cars" in *Entrepreneur* (Vol. 30, No. 10, October 2002, pp. 38) [26870], [30739]
"Pay Dirt! Finally Making a Profit? Put It Where It Belongs-Back in Your Business" in *Entrepreneur* (Vol. 31, No. 11, November 2003) [26320], [38276]
"The Pay-for-Performance Fallacy" in *Business 2.0* (Vol. 6, July 2005, No. 6, pp. 64) [26871], [35015], [45520]
"Pay For Play" in *Rough Notes* (Vol. 145, No. 9, September 2002, pp. 120) [1115], [1136]
"Pay Per Sale" in *The Economist* (Vol. 377, October 1-7, 2005, No. 8446, pp. 62) [755], [1844], [34331], [47391]
"Pay Up" in *PC Computing* (April 2000, pp. 37) [31576], [34332], [37178]
"Pay as You Click" in *Crain's New York Business* (Vol. 22, December 11, 2006, No. 50, pp. 19) [14340], [25930], [28615], [30930], [34333], [43029]
"Payback Time: Mutual Funds are Paying the Price, But Will You Get Your Fair Share?" in *Entrepreneur* (Vol. 32, August 2004, No. 8) [15344], [38277], [40608]
"Paying off in the end" in *BlackEnterprise* (Vol. 31, No. 11, June 2001, pp. 71) [35016], [36608], [45521]
"Paying the piper for Internet access" in *Red Herring* (No. 105, October 1, 2001, pp. 38) [14341], [34334], [54696]
"Paying in Kind" in *Entrepreneur.com* (Vol. 34, February 2006, No. 2, pp. 82) [31813], [45522]
"Paying to lose" in *Sarasota Herald Tribune* (Nov. 11, 2002, pp. 10) [19429], [38875], [53912]
"Paying your respects" in *Entrepreneur* (Vol. 31, No. 5, May 2003, pp. 70) [35017], [45523]
"Paying Your Dues" in *Entrepreneur* (Vol. 32) [5083], [41897], [44619]
"Paying for Your Mistakes: Are You Overlooking Allowable Deductions in Your Business?" in *My Business* (February/March 2003, pp. 43) [40609], [54697]
Payless Car Rental [2101]
PayMaster Hospitality [22028]
Payne's Publications on Family Law [29680]
Paynesville Area Chamber of Commerce [61645]
"PayPal" in *Cardline* (Vol. 4, No. 13, March 26, 2004, pp. 1) [1845], [18659], [34335], [52574]
"PayPal Founders Banking on New VC Firm" in *Venture Capital Journal* (September 1, 2005) [13772], [55416]
"PayPal Pushes For Business Use; A Hit With Consumers" in *Investor's Business Daily* (October 24, 2003, pp. A04) [18786], [34336], [50127], [51285]
Payroll I [18808]
Payroll Legal Alert [18796]
Payroll Manager's Letter [18797]
"Payroll Piggy Bank?" in *Entrepreneur* (Vol. 31, No. 9, September 2003, pp. 61) [222], [18787], [29438], [54698]
Payroll Toolkit: Nuts & Bolts Techniques to Managing Your Payroll [18788]
Payson Chamber of Commerce [65724]
Payteam, LLC. [3909]
P.B.Loco Peanutbutterlicious Cafes [21917]

PC AI Online [6517]
PC Business Products [53545]
PC Computing (April 2000, pp. 44); "A New Pain in the Neck-OSHA lays down ergonomic standards for businesses great and small" in [29404], [40556], [56575]
PC Computing (April 2000, pp. 112); "Beyond dot.com" in [13846], [33578]
PC Computing (March 2000, pp. 104); "Buried Alive-There's no such thing as a paperless office" in [48968], [53227]
PC Computing (March 2000, pp. 159); "Business Services" in [7109], [13871], [33419], [33630]
PC Computing (April, 2000, pp. 74); "E-Mail and Communications" in [4980], [7129], [13992], [33809]
PC Computing (April 2000, pp. 117); "E-Mail the Way it Should Be" in [33815], [49690]
PC Computing (March 2000, pp. 128); "Get All Your Work Done in Half the Time, Be the Office Hero...and Go Home Early" in [33101], [54946]
PC Computing (April 2000, pp. 108); "Get a Piece of the Action" in [14068], [33940]
PC Computing (April 2000, pp. 97); "Get There Faster" in [5000], [7133], [14070], [33943]
PC Computing (March 2000, pp. 137); "Groom Your Workforce" in [33109], [33980], [34918], [53765]
PC Computing (April 2000, pp. 100); "Grow Your Market" in [47041], [51659], [53308]
PC Computing (April, 2000, pp. 58); "Honoring the Profit" in [32486], [53782]
PC Computing (April 2000, pp. 42); "Hot Seat: Bruce Schneier" in [14127], [22253], [34021], [36296]
PC Computing (April, 2000, pp. 87); "How Bluetooth Works" in [5016], [7137], [14130], [34029]
PC Computing (April 2000, pp. 94); "Know Your Customers" in [34122], [47176], [53349]
PC Computing (March 2000, pp. 128); "Knowledge On Demand" in [33148], [34123]
PC Computing (March 2000, pp. 62); "Language Is a Virus" in [14192], [27415], [34126]
PC Computing (April 2000, pp. 91); "Map your Next Location" in [52698]
PC Computing (April 2000, pp. 40); "Name Grab-Cypersquaters, once a mere nuisance, now can go to prison for violating your trademark" in [29394], [34229], [44102]
PC Computing (April 2000, pp. 117); "Outsourced e-mail" in [28605], [34318], [49723], [53904]
PC Computing (April 2000, pp. 185); "Outsourcing" in [34319], [49725], [52573]
PC Computing (April 2000, pp. 37); "Pay Up" in [31576], [34332], [37178]
PC Computing (April 2000, pp. 35); "Protect Yourself" in [30246], [53925]
PC Computing (April 2000, pp. 100); "Push Your Plans Through" in [28660], [29968]
PC Computing (April 2000, pp. 90); "Scout New Business" in [34438], [47502]
PC Computing (April 2000); "Secrets of the Great White North-The world's hush-hush 3-commerce powerhouse is just a few miles away" in [34446], [43808], [51347]
PC Computing (March 2000, pp. 42); "Smile: Your Company's Under Attack" in [31858], [34503], [50676]
PC Computing (April 2000, pp. 44); "Stressed Out" in [29521], [40737], [56590]
PC Computing (March 2000, pp. 146); "The Anywhere Office" in [7118], [33535], [53586]
PC Computing (April 2000, pp. 114); "The Big Deals" in [13848], [33585]
PC Computing (March 2000, pp. 94); "The Feds Are Following You" in [13075], [33888]
PC Computing (April 2000, pp. 108); "The Name Game-Spending millions on a domain name?" in [14268], [34228]
PC Computing (April 2000, pp. 64); "The 10 Least Wired Industries" in [3137], [7493], [8910], [10806], [15517], [34584], [50206]
PC Computing (April 2000, pp. 78); "The Wireless Web" in [5187], [7150], [14628], [34737]
PC Computing (April 2000, pp. 95); "Ward off Competitors" in [30988], [47697], [53531]

"Peer Pressure" in *Red Herring* (No. 103, September 1, 2001, pp. 62-65) **[14343]**, **[25931]**, **[41898]**

"Peering In" in *Entrepreneur* (Vol. 33, January 2005, No. 1, pp. 70) **[35018]**, **[42377]**, **[45524]**

Pekin Area Chamber of Commerce **[59634]**

Pele Productions **[58276]**

Pelham Chamber of Commerce **[59150]**, **[62982]**

Pelican Lake Chamber of Commerce **[66492]**

Pelican Rapids Area Chamber of Commerce **[61646]**

Pella Chamber of Commerce **[60194]**

Pellet Fuels Institute **[37231]**

Pellissippi State Technical Community College Knoxville Area Chamber Partnership–SBDC **[64866]**

Tennessee Small Business Development Center–Knoxville Area Chamber Partnership **[64867]**

Pembina Institute for Appropriate Development **[9332]**, **[37232]**

"A Penchant for Profits" in *Entrepreneur* (Vol. 33, August 2005, No. 8, pp. 53) **[4741]**, **[4762]**, **[22814]**, **[23124]**, **[28048]**, **[28617]**, **[36612]**, **[50760]**, **[53407]**

"Pendleton Braces for Fight." in *Business Journal-Portland* (Vol. 20, No. 26, August 29, 2003, pp. 1) **[43781]**, **[46402]**

Pendleton Chamber of Commerce **[64254]**

Pendleton County Chamber of Commerce **[60561]**

Penfund Partners, Inc. **[66731]**

"Peninsula Alliance for Economic Development Place Information Kiosk in Airport" in *Dolan's Virginia Business Observer* (June 30, 2003) **[15933]**, **[28618]**

Peninsula Chamber of Commerce **[57709]**

Peninsula Equity Partners **[58124]**

Penn Foster Career School **[6406]**, **[64627]**

Penn Hills Chamber of Commerce **[64489]**

The Penn-Janney Fund, Inc. **[64570]**

Penn & Pearl Publishers L.L.C. **[56935]**

Penn State University at Harrisburg–Pennsylvania State Data Center–Institute of State and Regional Affairs **[66966]**

Penn Station East Coast Subs **[8569]**

Pennell Venture Partners **[63152]**

"Penney" in *Business Week* (January 9, 2006, No. 3966, pp. 82, 84) **[28619]**, **[45525]**, **[51286]**

Pennridge Chamber of Commerce **[64490]**

Pennsylvania Chamber of Business and Industry **[64491]**

Pennsylvania College of Optometry–Gerard Cottet Library **[25672]**

Pennsylvania Department of Community and Economic Development

Center for Business Financing–Site Development Division **[64346]**

Center Entrepreneurial Assistance **[64347]**

Loans Division **[64348]**

Office of International Business Development **[64349]**

Pennsylvania Industrial Development Authority **[64350]**

Technology Innovation–Ben Franklin Partnership **[64351]**

Pennsylvania Department of General Services–Bureau of Minority and Women's Business Opportunities (BMWBO) **[64538]**

"Pennsylvania" in *Entrepreneur* (Vol. 28, No. 6, June 2000, pp. 155) **[35604]**, **[39774]**, **[40125]**, **[54410]**

Pennsylvania Environmental Council–Library **[11982]**, **[21292]**

Pennsylvania Family Institute **[10910]**

The Pennsylvania Financial Institutions Directory & Fact Book **[44620]**

"Pennsylvania Governor Says Business Taxes May Aid City of Pittsburgh Bailout" in *Pittsburgh Post-Gazette* (April 11, 2003) **[28620]**, **[54700]**

Pennsylvania Growth Fund **[64571]**

Pennsylvania Horticultural Society–McLean Library **[11533]**, **[12168]**

Pennsylvania.& Maryland Procurement Center **[64584]**

Pennsylvania Minority Business Development Authority **[64539]**

Pennsylvania Procurement Center **[64585]** 2155802771 **[64586]**

Pennsylvania Procurement Technical Assistance Center **[64587]**

Government Agency Coordination Office–California University of Pennsylvania **[64588]**

Indiana University of Pennsylvania–Government Contracting Assistance Program **[64589]**

Johnstown Area Regional Industries **[64590]**

North Central Pennsylvania Regional Planning & Development Commission **[64591]**

Northeastern Pennsylvania Alliance **[64592]**

Northern Tier Regional Planning & Development Commission **[64593]**

SEDA Council of Governments **[64594]**

Southwestern Pennsylvania Commission **[64595]**

"Pennsylvania RV Show Hits the Road" in *Tradeshow Week* (Vol. 34) **[21173]**, **[22542]**, **[24992]**, **[55140]**

Pennsylvania Small Business Development Centers **[54109]**

Pennsylvania State Library **[66967]**

Pennsylvania State University

Center for Research in Conflict and Negotiation **[17081]**

Center for the Study of Higher Education–NCTLA Project **[33405]**

Institute for the Study of Business Markets **[48851]**

Network for Policy Research **[41398]**

Research and Graduate Studies Office **[64612]**

Research and Technology Transfer Organization **[64613]**

Risk Management Research Center **[27066]**

Technical Assistance Program **[64352]**

Pennsylvania State University at Harrisburg–Pennsylvania State Data Center **[14692]**

Penny & Associates Inc. **[376]**, **[26434]**, **[38567]**

Penny Lane Parnters **[62605]**

"A Penny Not Saved" in *Entrepreneur* (Vol. 31, No. 8, August 2003, pp. 30) **[38278]**, **[53913]**

"Penny wise, pound foolish" in *Black Enterprise* (Vol. 32, No. 10, May 2002, pp. 44) **[26322]**, **[36613]**, **[48357]**

"Penny-Wise, Site-Foolish" in *Inc.* (February 1, 2002) **[14344]**, **[25932]**, **[34337]**, **[52384]**

Penobscot Bay Regional Chamber of Commerce **[60768]**

Pensacola Area Chamber of Commerce **[58917]**

Pensacola Beach Chamber of Commerce and Visitor Information Center **[58918]**

Pension & Benefits Daily **[27058]**

Pension & Benefits Reporter **[27059]**, **[30766]**

Pension Consultants & Administrators Inc. **[27043]**

Pension Fund Investment Management: A Handbook for Sponsors and Their Advisors **[15347]**

"Pension Funds Prod Firms to Show Management Compensation Packages" in *Sacramento Bee* (December 22, 2005) **[26872]**, **[45526]**

"Pension Liabilities Threaten Suppliers' Credit Ratings" in *Crain's Detroit Business* (Vol. 19, No. 17, April 28, 2003, pp. 27) **[1958]**, **[26873]**

"Pension Pain" in *Forbes* (Vol. 170, No. 4, September 2, 2002, pp. 144) **[224]**, **[24014]**, **[26323]**, **[26874]**, **[40611]**

"Pension Performer" in *Hispanic Business* (April 2005, pp. 26, 28) **[15348]**, **[26875]**

Pension Plan Guide **[26989]**

Pension Plan Guide-Summary **[26990]**

"Pension Reform Enhances Sponsored Retirement Plans" in *San Diego Business Journal* (Vol. 22, No. 41, October 8, 2001, pp. 16) **[24015]**, **[26876]**, **[39885]**, **[54701]**

"Penske Eyes Russia, China" in *Crain's Detroit Business* (Vol. 23, January 22-28, 2007, No. 4, pp. 3, 20) **[1959]**, **[50128]**

Pentwater Chamber of Commerce **[61400]**

"People Growers Deals With Personal Growing Pains" in *Business Journal-Portland* (Vol. 20, No. 22, August 1, 2003, pp. 3) **[39371]**, **[41077]**, **[42707]**, **[52575]**, **[53560]**, **[56365]**

"People" in *Ingram's* (Vol. 28, No. 5, May 2002, pp. 49) **[3132]**, **[36614]**

People Investment: How to Make Your Hiring Decisions Pay off for Everyone **[42378]**

People in Management **[4433]**

"People who need people" in *Entrepreneur* (Vol. 31, No. 5, May 2003, pp. 76) **[51763]**

People, Performance & Pay: Dynamic Compensation for Changing Organizations **[30740]**

"People Smarts: Human touch needed to manage knowledge" in *Atlanta Business Chronicle* (Vol. 25, No. 21, November 1, 2002, pp. 3B) **[44351]**, **[45527]**

People Who Help: Health Careers **[4434]**

People Who Sell Things **[4435]**

People Who Work in Manufacturing **[4436]**

People Who Work with People **[4437]**

"PeopleProfileUSA" in *Entrepreneur* (Vol. 32, No. 1, January 2004, pp. 10) **[16822]**, **[34338]**, **[47393]**

People's Medical Society **[40946]**

Peoria Area Chamber of Commerce **[59635]**

Peoria Chamber of Commerce **[57059]**

Peoria Heights Chamber of Commerce **[59636]**

"Peoria, Ill., Woodcraft Store Gets Kiosk" in *Journal Star* (November 25, 2003) **[15934]**

Pepe's Mexican Restaurants **[21918]**

Pepsico Beverages & Foods–The Information Center **[18507]**

"Perceived risks and choices in entrepreneurs' new venture decisions" in *Journal of Business Venturing* (Vol.15, No.4, Jul.2000, pp.305) **[35605]**, **[55417]**

Perceptive Technology Corp. **[49452]**, **[49643]**

Percussion News **[17628]**

Percussive Arts Society–Library **[17696]**

"Perdue's home-work plan has failed past" in *Atlanta Business Chronicle* (Vol. 25, November 29, 2002, No. 25, pp. 1A) **[14345]**, **[34339]**, **[42708]**, **[53914]**

Perennial Ventures / Tredegar Investments **[66223]**

"A Perfect Brainstorm" in *Inc.* (October 1, 2003) **[30581]**, **[36615]**, **[52173]**

"The Perfect Connection" in *Small Business Opportunities* (Vol. 16, No. 3, May 2004, pp. 72) **[14346]**, **[31814]**, **[34340]**

"A Perfect Match?" in *Entrepreneur* (Vol. 31, No. 10, October 2003, pp. 60) **[11341]**, **[15349]**, **[36616]**, **[37756]**, **[55774]**

"The Perfect Niche" n *Hispanic Business* (Vol. 22, No. 7-8, July-August 2000, pp. 68) **[25466]**, **[34341]**, **[35606]**

"A perfect pair" in *Entrepreneur* (Vol. 30, No. 3, March 2002, pp. 37) **[5084]**, **[34342]**, **[49201]**

The Perfect Pita **[21919]**

"The Perfect Pitch" in *Hispanic Business* (March 2005, pp. 38, 40) **[15350]**, **[36617]**, **[55775]**

"Perfect Proposals" in *Sales & Marketing Management* (Vol. 159, January-February 2007, No. 1, pp. 9) **[31197]**, **[47394]**, **[51764]**

The Perfect Sale **[10317]**, **[15713]**, **[51972]**

"The Perfect Storm? Employers Need Navigation Tools For The Newest Set of Health Cost Waves" in *Employee Benefit Plan Review* (Vol. 55) **[26324]**, **[26877]**, **[41078]**, **[43310]**

"Perfect Storm Strikes CEOs" in *Hispanic Business* (Vol. 24, No. 4, April 2002, pp. 16, 18) **[13417]**, **[41079]**, **[43311]**, **[48358]**

"The Perfect System" in *Small Business Opportunities* (Vol. 14, No. 1, January 2002, pp. 70, 104) **[14347]**, **[31815]**, **[47395]**

"A Perfect Visual PIM-for Some" in *PC Magazine* (February 20, 2001, pp. 52) **[44352]**, **[53408]**

The Perfect Wedding Guide, Inc. **[18983]**

"Perfecting the Growth Spurt" in *Hispanic Business* (Vol. 23, No. 11, November 2001, pp. 24-25, 28) **[22323]**, **[28621]**, **[36618]**, **[48359]**

The Perfectionist **[8720]**

A Perfectly Normal Day **[55025]**

Performance Appraisal **[42930]**

Pets Welcome California Edition [12615]

Pets Welcome Southern Edition [12616]

Pettis County–Extension Center–Central Missouri Region [61874]

Petty Capitalists and Globalization: Flexibility, Entrepreneurship, and Economic Development [32626], [36626], [39523], [43783]

Pewaukee Chamber of Commerce [66493]

PGA Merchandise Show [11287]

"PGI Closes Offices, Lays Off 50 Employees" in Tradeshow Week (Vol. 34, December 20, 2004, No. 51, pp. 3) [22544], [24994], [55142]

Pharmaceutical Approvals Monthly [8826]

Pharmaceutical Care Management Association [8770]

Pharmaceutical Law & Industry Report [29681]

Pharmaceutical Marketers Directory [8797]

Pharmaceutical News Index [2623]

Pharmaceutical Research and Manufacturers of America [8771]

"Pharmacies Fight Mail-Order Purchases, Medicaid Tax" in Crain's Detroit Business (Vol. 19, No. 43, October 27, 2003, pp. 6) [8798], [9430], [13418], [13923], [16245], [16463], [43312], [44983], [54702]

Pharmacy Connection [8827]

Pharmacy & Therapeutics Forum [8828]

Pharmacy Times [8829]

Pharmacy Today [8830]

Pharmacy Week [8831]

"Pharmed Wins for Innovation" in Hispanic Business (Vol. 23, No. 7/8, July/August 2001, pp. 6) [28623], [39524], [48360]

Pharr Chamber of Commerce [65438]

PHC Profit Report [1043], [19725]

Phelan Chamber of Commerce [57712]

Phelps Chamber of Commerce [66494]

Phenix City-Russell County Chamber of Commerce [56881]

Philadelphia Business Journal (Vol. 19, No. 36, October 13, 2000, pp. 6); "Pa. comes in at No. 24 in small business study" in [28608], [54691]

Philadelphia Corporation for Aging–Library [489]

Philadelphia Inquirer (October 16, 2006); "Building on History" in [26072], [34837], [35881], [46220]

Philadelphia Inquirer (February 6, 2007); "Fattah's Plan for Small Business" in [39820], [42614], [44516]

Philadelphia Inquirer (November 13, 2006); "SAP AG Starting Unit to Target Small, Medium-Sized Firms" in [4788], [23159], [28742], [53446]

Philadelphia Minority Business Development Center [64540]

Philadelphia University–Paul J. Gutman Library [5617]

Philadelphia Ventures, Inc. [64572]

"Philanthropy Award Winners" in Crain's Detroit Business (Vol. 21, November 7, 2005, No. 45, pp. 25) [10747], [54237]

Philatelic Foundation–Archives and Library [5872]

Philatelic Literature Review [5850]

Philip Kotler on Competitive Marketing [48681]

Philip Morris–Corporate Library [24638], [47931]

Philippine-American Chamber of Commerce [43523]

Philips County Chamber of Commerce [57206]

Philipsburg Chamber of Commerce [62191]

Phillip B. Chute Corp. [58277]

Phillips Area Chamber of Commerce [66495]

Phillips-Smith Specialty Retail Group [65623]

Phillips University–Small Business Development Center [63918]

Phillips Wireless Industry Directory [2484]

Phillipsburg Area Chamber of Commerce [60405], [62547]

The Philly Connection [21921]

"Philly Firm Launches Lawsuit over 'Space'" in Orlando Business Journal (Vol. 20, No. 7, August 1, 2003, No. 1) [1084], [1137], [29439], [30119]

Philomath Area Chamber of Commerce [64255]

"Phoenix Awards" in Atlanta Business Chronicle (Vol. 25, November 15, 2002, No. 23 pp. S13) [12902], [20144]

Phoenix Bird Collectors of America [1310], [5811]

"Phoenix tops list of fertile areas for small companies" in Wall Street Journal (December 7, 1999, pp. B2) [28624], [30166]

"Phoenix Gold Investor Not At All Pleased" in Business Journal-Portland (Vol. 20, No. 29, September 19, 2003, pp. 1) [1946], [1960], [4343]

Phoenix Growth Capital [58125]

Phoenix JobBank [23401]

The Phoenix Partners [66224]

Phoenix Public Library–Burton Barr Central Library–Vehicle and Appliance Repair Collection [2064]

"Phoenix" in Sales & Marketing Management (Vol. 159, January-February 2007, No. 1, pp. 41) [22545], [24995], [28625], [52714]

Phoenixville Area Chamber of Commerce [64494]

"Phone Calls Destined to be Sent Like E-Mail, as Packets of Data" in San Jose Mercury News (March 4, 2005) [5086], [14351]

"Phone, Camera, Action!(Wireless)" in Entrepreneur (Vol. 31, No. 8, August 2003, pp. 43) [4195], [5087], [49206]

"Phone Home" in My Business (April/May 2004, pp. 44) [36627], [45533]

"Phone on the Range" in Entrepreneur (Vol. 33, October 2005, No. 10, pp. 40) [5088], [46866], [49207]

Phoning for Profits [24304]

"A Phony Cure; Shifting Class Actions to Federal Courts Is No Reform" in Business Week (February 7, 2005, No. 3919, pp. 33) [29440], [40612]

Photo Business Careers [19205]

Photo Marketing [19208]

Photo Marketing Association International [4180], [19204]

Photo Marketing Newsline (Aug. 13, 03); "AAA Imaging & Supplies Has Become the Exclusive U.S. Distributor of Oblo Multimedial Kiosk" in [15915]

The Photo Review [19238]

Photo Screen Printing [22127]

Photo Techniques [19310]

PhotoBulletin-Weekly [19239]

PhotoDaily [19240], [19311]

The Photograph Collector [1631]

The Photographer's Guide to Marketing and Self-Promotion [19303]

Photographer's Market [19304]

Photographic Manufacturers & Distributors Association-Membership Directory [19233]

Photographic Society of America [19222], [19288]

Photographic Video Trade News [19209]

Photographing People for Stock [19231]

Photography [19322]

Photography 101 [19260]

Photography Collections Online [19270]

Photography Quarterly [19241]

Photoimaging Manufacturers and Distributors Association [4181]

PhotoPro [19242], [19312]

PhotoSource Book [19234]

PhotoSource International [19264]

PhotoStock Notes/Plus [19243]

PhotoStockNotes [19244]

Physical Medicine and Rehabilitation Clinics [18359], [19569]

Physical & Occupational Therapy in Geriatrics [19570]

Physical and Occupational Therapy in Pediatrics [19571], [41282]

Physical Therapists [19564]

Physical Therapy [19572]

Physical Therapy Assistant License Exam [19565]

Physical Therapy Market [19566]

Physical Therapy Products [17268], [19573]

Physical Therapy Reimbursement News [19574]

Physician Executive [41283]

Physician Executive (Vol. 28, No. 1, January-February 2002, pp. 91); "Leadership and followership" in [36421], [45349]

Physician Insurers Association of America [13170]

Physician Magazine [41284]

The Physician & Sportsmedicine [19534]

Physicians Committee for Responsible Medicine [40947]

Physicians Weight Loss Centers of America, Inc. [26062]

The Physiological Effects of Cocaine [54354]

Piano Guild Notes [17629]

Piano Manufacturers Association International [17837]

Piano for Quitters [17635]

Piano Servicing, Tuning, and Rebuilding: For the Professional, the Student, the Hobbyist [17844]

Piano Technicians Guild [17838]

"Pick A Topic" in Entrepreneur (Vol. 28, No. 3, March 2000, pp. 220) [34347]

"Pick a niche and fill it" in Hispanic Business (Vol. 22, No. 7-8, July-August 2000, pp. 44) [41902], [45534], [48361]

"Pick of the Pack" in Black Enterprise (Vol. 34, No. 3, October 2003, pp. 30) [10133], [15353], [38281]

Pick Up Stix [21922]

Pick Ups Plus [2016]

"Pick Your Battles" in Entrepreneur (Vol. 31, No. 11, November 2003, pp. 95) [36628], [45535]

"Pick Your Startup Tool" in Black Enterprise (Vol. 36, November 2005, No. 4, pp. 74) [1189], [22856], [26326], [29754], [31055], [39073], [47401], [53410]

Pickerington Area Chamber of Commerce [63771]

Pickerman's Soup & Sandwiches [8570]

Picket Fence Preview [20751]

"Picking a 529 College Savings Plan" in Black Enterprise (Vol. 37, February 2007, No. 7, pp. 46) [15354], [26880]

"Picking apart company reports" in Hispanic Business (Vol. 22, No. 3, March 2000, pp. 60) [38282]

"Picking Up the Pace of the Space Tourism Race" in Business Week (February 7, 2005, No. 3919, pp. 81) [24719], [25232], [41903]

"Picking Up the Pieces" in Black Enterprise (Vol. 32, No. 9, April 2002, pp. 44) [41904], [45536], [48362]

Pickles & Ice Cream Franchising, Inc. [5756]

Pico Rivera Chamber of Commerce [57713]

Pictorial Photographers of America [19223]

Picture Framing Magazine [19826]

"Picture Perfect " in Entrepreneur (Vol. 32) [4196], [49208]

"Picture This" in Entrepreneur (Vol. 32, July 2004, No. 7, pp. 46) [4197], [4763], [6000], [6756], [23125], [49209], [53411]

PIDA Bulletin [19163]

A Piece of the Pie [39525], [39886]

Piedmont Area Chamber of Commerce [62023]

Piedmont Chamber of Commerce [64060]

Piedmont Technical College
   Continuing Education [64800]
   Library [53138]

Piedmont Venture Partners [63464]

Pierce County Chamber of Commerce [59152]

"Pierogi Power" in Frozen Food Age (Vol. 52, No. 3, October 2003, pp. 36) [11651], [23502]

Pierre Area Chamber of Commerce [64833]

Pierre Small Business Development Center (Region II) [64807]

PIERS Exports (Latin America) [43937]

PIERS Imports (Latin America) [43938]

The Pie's The Limit [2309]

Piet Mondrian: Mr. Boogie-Woogie Man [1692]

Pigeon Chamber of Commerce [61402]

Pigeon Forge Chamber of Commerce [64965]

Piggaso's Barbeque [21923]

Piggott Chamber of Commerce [57207]

"Pigtails & Crewcuts" in Small Business Opportunities (Vol. 16, November 2004, No. 6, pp. 112) [11798], [38878]

Pike County Chamber of Commerce [56882], [59638], [59989], [60562], [63772], [64495]

Pike County Chamber of Commerce and Economic Development District [61828]

Pike in the Dead Zone [2198]

"Pikesville-Based SafeDate and Dating Service Industry as a Whole Experiencing Growth" in Daily Record (July 18, 2003) [7050], [33478], [35609]

"Pizza Hut" in *Hispanic Business* (March 2002, pp. 64) **[19636]**, **[38881]**

Pizza Inn, Inc. **[19701]**

Pizza Man **[19702]**

Pizza Nova Take Out Ltd. **[19703]**

Pizza One **[19704]**

"Pizza makers to add online orders" in *Crain's Detroit Business* (Vol. 16, No. 16, April 17, 2000, pp. 16) **[19637]**, **[34348]**, **[53918]**

The Pizza Pipeline **[19705]**

Pizza Pit **[19706]**

Pizza Pizza Limited **[19707]**

Pizza Ranch, Inc. **[21927]**

Pizza Salvatore **[21928]**

Pizza Schimizza **[19708]**

"Pizza Schmizza Ready to Take on Puget Sound" in *Business Journal-Portland* (Vol. 20, No. 22, August 1, 2003, pp. 7) **[19638]**, **[20360]**, **[28628]**, **[29798]**, **[30262]**, **[30582]**, **[30932]**, **[31943]**, **[43489]**, **[45537]**

Pizza Today-Pizza Industry Buyer's Guide Issue **[19639]**

Pizzaville, Inc. **[19709]**

Pizzicato Gourmet Pizza **[19710]**

PJ Materials Consultants Ltd. **[7630]**

PKF Consulting **[21092]**

Library **[12750]**

"PL chocolates" in *Private Label Buyer* (Vol. 16, No. 4, April 2002, pp. 47) **[4302]**, **[10748]**, **[48775]**

"A Place in the Heart" in *Ingram's* (Vol. 28, No. 9, September 2002, pp. 32) **[757]**, **[47402]**

"A Place for More Hispanics?" in *Hispanic Business* (March 2002, pp. 56) **[40614]**, **[48591]**

"The Place That Gump Built" in *Hispanic Business* (Vol. 23, No. 7/8, July/August 2001, pp. 94, 96) **[9736]**, **[33206]**

Placentia Chamber of Commerce **[57718]**

Plain and Simple Books **[64315]**

Plainfield Area Chamber of Commerce **[59640]**

Plainfield Chamber of Commerce **[59990]**

Plains-Paradise Chamber of Commerce **[62192]**

Plainview Chamber of Commerce **[62290]**, **[65440]**

Plainwell Chamber of Commerce **[61404]**

"Plan to Avoid Confusion When Passing the Torch" in *Atlanta Business Chronicle* (Vol. 23, No. 49, May 11, 2001, pp. 10B) **[29953]**, **[37757]**, **[45538]**

"Plan B from Cyberspace: A growing number of websites are going back to the future" in *Time Inc.* (Vol. 157, No. 1, Jan. 8, 2001, pp.57) **[19819]**, **[19888]**, **[34349]**

"Plan for a comfortable retirement while you save for your children's education" in *Black Enterprise* (Vol.33, No.3, Oct. 2002, pp.103) **[10135]**, **[15357]**, **[15883]**, **[38283]**, **[39702]**

"Plan Events that Will Fill Seats" in *Women In Business* (Vol. 52, No. 2, March 2000, pp. 32) **[45539]**, **[54975]**, **[56367]**

"Plan a legacy for your business and your family" in *Black Enterprise* (Vol. 33, No. 3, October 2002, pp. 104) **[28852]**, **[29954]**, **[30583]**, **[31258]**, **[35722]**, **[37758]**

"Plan May Need Overhaul to Maintain Growth" in *Crain's Detroit Business* (Vol. 21, January 17, 2005, No. 3, pp. 18) **[28629]**, **[29955]**, **[46404]**

"Plan would gut MEDC to fund scholarships" in *Crain's Detroit Business* (Vol. 19, No. 14, April 7, 2003, pp. 1) **[33207]**, **[40615]**, **[54703]**

Plan Sponsor **[10290]**

"A Plan for Today's Money Market" in *Hispanic Business* (March 2003, pp. 42, 44) **[29755]**, **[44434]**, **[47973]**, **[56069]**

"Plan Would Share Wealth From $1B Fund" in *Crain's Detroit Business* (Vol. 21, October 24, 2005, No. 43, pp. 26) **[9737]**, **[22325]**, **[24721]**, **[25234]**, **[26529]**, **[39887]**, **[41905]**, **[46405]**, **[52175]**

"Planar Monitors Address Kiosk and POS Applications" in *National Petroleum News* (Vol. 95, No. 11, October 2003, pp. 57) **[15935]**

"Planes, Tractors and Automobiles" in *Tradeshow Week* (Vol. 34, November 29, 2004, No. 48, pp. 64) **[22546]**, **[24996]**, **[45540]**, **[55143]**

Planet Cash **[14678]**

PLANET News **[19726]**

Planet Smoothie, LLC **[12846]**

Planetary Association for Clean Energy **[37233]**

Planetree–Institute for Health and Healing–Library **[18508]**

Plank Road Chamber of Commerce **[62984]**

"Planned obsolescence, the tech way" in *Recycling Today* (Vol. 40, No. 19, September 2002, pp. 4) **[6757]**, **[21249]**, **[41906]**

"Planned transition" in *Business First Columbus* (Vol. 1) **[3568]**, **[12787]**, **[29956]**, **[37759]**

"Planners say the best defense is preparation" in *Atlanta Business Chronicle* (Vol. 24, No. 14, September 7, 2001, pp. S7) **[24997]**, **[39527]**

"Planning Ahead: Steven Taylor Mulls a Second Career After Retirement" in *Black Enterprise* (Vol. 37, November 2006, No. 4, pp. 82) **[10136]**, **[15358]**, **[38284]**

Planning for Business Owners & Professionals **[29957]**

Planning and Developing New Products (Canada) **[46638]**, **[47242]**

"Planning is everything" in *Ingram's* (Vol. 27, No. 2, February 2001, pp. 28) **[35023]**, **[45541]**

"Planning for Gold" in *Entrepreneur* (Vol. 32, November 2004, No. 11, pp. 112) **[29756]**, **[30933]**, **[35610]**, **[55777]**

"Planning Made Easy" in *Incentive* (Vol. 174, No. 10, October 2000, pp. 150) **[3569]**, **[26881]**, **[31198]**

Planning and Managing Organizational Change **[44822]**

"Planning in Pittsburgh, Chicago has produced results" in *Crain's Detroit Business* (Vol. 19, No. 17, April 28, 2003, pp. 19) **[28630]**, **[32629]**

"Planning productive programs" in *Women In Business* (Vol. 52, No. 4, July 2000, pp. 28) **[45542]**, **[56368]**

Planning a Project and Building Your Project Team **[35198]**

Planning and Visual Education Partnership **[49480]**, **[51046]**

Planning a Wedding to Remember **[3209]**

"Planning Your Exit Strategy: Three Ways To Go" in *My Business* (October/November 2003, pp. 30-35) **[29958]**, **[30584]**, **[36629]**

Planning Your Future **[33208]**

Planning Your Wedding, Vol. 1: Selecting Your Formal Wear **[3210]**

Planning Your Wedding, Vol. 2: A Visit to Your Caterer **[3211]**

Planning Your Wedding, Vol. 3: Selecting Your Wedding Cake **[3212]**

Planning Your Wedding, Vol. 4: Selecting Your Photographer **[3213]**

Planning Your Wedding, Vol. 5: Visiting Your Travel Agent **[3214]**

Planning Your Wedding, Vol. 6: Meeting with Your Financial Advisor **[3215]**

Planning Your Wedding, Vol. 7: Visiting with Your Jeweler **[3216]**

Planning Your Wedding, Vol. 8: Meeting with Your Minister **[3217]**

Planning Your Wedding, Vol. 9: Selecting Your Flowers **[3218]**

Planning Your Wedding, Vol. 10: Meeting with Your Bridal Consultant **[3219]**

Plano Chamber of Commerce **[65441]**

Plano Commerce Association **[59641]**

"Plans afoot to revive world trade center" in *Houston Business Journal* (Vol. 33, No. 49, April 18, 2003, pp. 1A) **[7450]**, **[24998]**

Plans and Solutions Inc. **[29050]**, **[30113]**, **[31441]**, **[43929]**, **[51007]**

The Plant Care Manual: The Essential Guide to Caring for and Rejuvenating Over 300 Garden Plants **[11439]**

The Plant Cell **[52311]**

"Plant Manager Urges Lockheed Martin Employees Not to Strike" in *Atlanta Journal-Constitution* (March 5, 2005) **[43314]**, **[46406]**, **[55307]**

The Plant Works **[49645]**

"Plantation, Fla., Mayor Blasts Aggressive Mall Kiosk Sales Tactics" in *South Sun-Sentinel* (October 10, 2003) **[15936]**, **[51290]**

Planting Fields Arboretum–The Garden Library **[11534]**

Plantkeeper Inc. **[49646]**

Plants & Gardens News **[11478]**

Plants Sites & Parks **[21057]**, **[30189]**

Plantscape Inc. **[16147]**

Plastic Recycling Update **[21273]**

Plastics News (Vol. 16, July 12, 2004, No. 19, pp. 10); "Minorities Push to Keep Supplier Program" in **[1949]**, **[46373]**, **[48298]**

"Plastics recovery technology developer tackles post-consumer electronics scrap" in *Modern Plastics* (Vol. 79, Dec. 2002, pp. 65) **[6758]**, **[21250]**, **[24344]**, **[41907]**

The Platinum Group, Inc. **[63154]**

The Platinum Rule for Small Business Success **[36630]**, **[39528]**

Plato's Closet **[7184]**

"Plato's Closet, a Retail Outlet, Sells Teenagers Brand-Name Labels for Less" in *Long Island Business News* (March 5, 2004) **[5564]**, **[5703]**, **[7170]**, **[9634]**, **[38882]**, **[51291]**

Platte City Chamber of Commerce **[62024]**

Platte County Chamber of Commerce **[66623]**

Platteville Chamber of Commerce **[66496]**

Plattsburg Chamber of Commerce **[62025]**

Plattsburgh - North Country Chamber of Commerce **[62985]**

Plattsburgh State University of New York–Technical Assistance Center **[32860]**

Plattsmouth Chamber of Commerce **[62291]**

Platypus Publisher **[66671]**

Play it Again Sports **[7185]**, **[23706]**

Play Blues Piano Overnight **[17636]**

Play Guitar Overnight-Rock **[17637]**

Play Harmonica Overnight **[17638]**

"Play Keyboard for Cash" in *Entrepreneur* (Vol. 28, No. 11, November 2000, pp. 38) **[11799]**, **[14352]**, **[15359]**, **[34350]**

Play N Trade Franchise Inc. **[52631]**

"Play Nice" in *Entrepreneur* (Vol. 32, September 2004, No. 9, pp. 32) **[36631]**, **[54976]**

Play Piano Overnight **[17639]**

"Playbook" in *Business 2.0* (Vol. 6, May 2005, No. 4, pp. 121-122, 126-127) **[28631]**, **[36632]**, **[45543]**

"Players-Accomplishments of the Area's Most Significant Producers" in *Ingram's* (Vol. 29, No. 1, January 2003, pp. 10) **[36633]**

The Players Connection, Inc. **[11294]**

"Playing the Business-to-Business Odds" in *Success* (Vol. 47, No. 1, January 2000, pp. 22) **[34351]**

Playing and Coaching Winning Baseball and Softball **[23661]**

"Playing Cupid: These Matchmaking Sisters Aim to Give Busy Singles a Fast-and-Fun-Way to Date" in *Entrepreneur* (September 2004) **[7066]**, **[37760]**, **[38883]**

"Playing games with customers" in *Harvard Business Review* (Vol. 81, No. 4, April 2003, pp. 21) **[7758]**, **[47403]**, **[51765]**

"Playing e-Detective" in *Entrepreneur* (Vol. 30, No.) **[34352]**, **[42379]**

"Playing favorites" in *Entrepreneur* (Vol. 31, No. 4, April 2003, pp. 22) **[4581]**, **[22887]**, **[34353]**, **[35611]**, **[36634]**, **[39529]**, **[45544]**, **[55418]**, **[56369]**

"Playing the Fuel" in *Hispanic Business* (June 2005, pp. 88) **[25405]**, **[32630]**

"Playing It Safe: Security on the Road is in Your Own Hands" in *Sales and Marketing.com* (Vol. 156, No. 3, February 2004, pp. 53) **[12617]**, **[22326]**, **[30402]**

"Playing It Safe: What Can You Do to Protect Your E-Commerce Site From Fraud?" in *Entrepreneur* (Vol. 32, No. 4, April 2004, pp. 35) **[14353]**, **[22327]**, **[34354]**

"Playing the Money Game" in *Washington Business Journal* (Vol. 22, No. 8, June 27, 2003, pp. 26) **[10137]**, **[15360]**, **[38285]**

"Playskool Makes Product for Moms" in *Marketing to Women* (Vol. 20, January 2007, No. 1, pp. 3) **[2732]**, **[47404]**, **[50131]**

Playthings **[24854]**

Playtime Piano Instruction **[25483]**

Pleasant Hill Chamber of Commerce **[57719]**

Pleasanton Chamber of Commerce **[57720]**, **[65442]**

Pleasanton Publishing [58278]

"Please stay! You have the hotels rights where you want them" in *Entrepreneur* (Vol. 30, No. 10, October 2002, pp. 34) [12618], [30403]

Pleasure Island, Carolina Beach, and Kure Beach Chamber of Commerce [63417]

"Plexus Finds Success in Helping Manufacturers with Cost-Cutting Software" in *Crain's Detroit Business* (Vol. 22, January 16, 2006) [4764], [23126], [46407], [53412]

The Plotkin Group [31986], [42996]

"Plugging In: Networking Skills That Promise Success" in *Black Enterprise* (Vol. 34, No. 7, February 2004, pp. 61) [39530], [40202], [47742], [50132]

"Plugging Into the Future with New Wave of Communication Services" in *Boston Globe* (March 7, 2005) [5089], [14354]

"Plumbing Business Moves to Hannegan" in *Bellingham Business Journal* (December 2006, pp. A6) [11893], [19753], [28632], [30167]

Plumbing Contractor: Start and Run a Money Making Business [19754]

Plumbing and Drainage Institute [19740]

Plumbing Engineer [19764]

Plumbing Engineer-Product Directory Issue [19755], [22718]

Plumbing-Heating-Cooling Contractors Association [1007], [19741]

Plumbing & HVAC Product News [19765]

Plumbing Manufacturers Institute [19742]

"Plumbing Web Connection" in *Harvard Business Review* (Vol. 81, No. 9, September 2003, pp. 18) [4765], [23127], [25933], [34355], [53413]

"The Plumtree Software Soap Opera" in *Forbes* (May 29, 2000, pp. 96) [23128], [45545]

"Plunkett's E-Commerce & Internet Business Almanac 2001-2002" in *Business Information Alert* (Vol. 14, No. 9, October 2002, pp. 9) [14355], [28633], [34356]

Plunkett's Employers Internet Sites with Careers Information [9192], [9550]

"A Pluralistic Account of Intellectual Property" in *Journal of Business Ethics* (Vol. 46, No. 4, September 15, 2003, pp. 319) [29441], [44353]

Plymouth Area Chamber of Commerce [59991], [60988]

Plymouth Chamber of Commerce [62438], [66497]

Plymouth Community Chamber of Commerce [61405]

"Plymouth land rising again as residential" in *Crain's Detroit Business* (Vol. 19, No. 12, March 24, 2003, pp. 3) [7451], [20623], [20965]

Plymouth State College–Small Business Development Center [62391]

PM Directory & Reference Issue [1025]

PM USA–Library [24639]

PMA Independent [2776]

PMA - Independent Book Publishers Association [2665]

PMA - Photo Marketing Association International Annual Convention and Trade Show [4216]

PMCA: An International Association of Confectioners [4273]

PMCA - an International Association of Confectioners–Bibliography of Technical Papers Collection [4339]

PMDS - Plant Maintenance and Design Engineering Show/Montreal [46531]

"PMMI Debuts Contracting Service: By Taking Over Services, PACK EXPO Intl" in *Tradeshow Week* (Vol. 34) [22547], [24999], [46408], [55144]

Pocahontas Chamber of Commerce [60196]

The Pocket Change Investor [24097]

The Pocket Guide to Clinical Laboratory Instrumentation [17101]

"Pocket protector" in *Entrepreneur* (Vol. 30, No. 1, January 2002, pp. 44) [6759], [49211]

"Pocketbook Issues: The 2000 election brings some of small business's biggest issues to the forefront" in *Time Inc.* (Vol.155, May 2000) [26882], [54704]

Pocomoke City Chamber of Commerce [60848]

Pocono Mountains Chamber of Commerce [64497]

Pocono Mountains Chamber of Commerce/Women in Business [64498]

"Podcast Network Focuses on Wedding Plans" in *Marketing to Women* (Vol. 19, October 2006, No. 10, pp. 5) [3191], [14356], [25934], [41908], [47405]

"Podcast Startups Look Doomed from the Start" in *Venture Capital Journal* (October 1, 2005) [14357], [33479], [41475], [55419]

Poetalk [9037]

Kevin L. Pohle [27044], [30763], [38568]

"Point, Click, File a Lawsuit" in *Sacramento Bee* (December 11, 2005) [29442], [34357]

Point-of-Purchase Advertising International [50537] Information Center [52014]

Point Pleasant Beach Chamber of Commerce [62549]

Point Roberts Chamber of Commerce [66151]

"Point of Sale: Software Giants Focus on Selling to Small Businesses" in *Entrepreneur* (Vol. 32, November 2004, No. 11, pp. 26) [4766], [23129], [53414]

"Point and Sniff" in *Kiplinger's Personal Finance Magazine* (Vol. 55, No. 1, January, 2001, pp. 26) [14358], [34358]

Point Venture Partners [64573]

Points for Profit [889]

The Polar Bear ROARS [18764], [19313]

Polaris Venture Partners [61109]

Polaroid Corporation–Research Library [19215]

Polestar Capital, Inc. [59755]

Police & Security News [22432]

"Policy Follies: Fiscal and Monetary Levers Lose their Power" in *Barron's* (August 18, 2003, pp. 28) [32631]

"Policy: The future of telecom lies at the steps of Capitol Hill" in *Red Herring* (No. 106, October 15, 2001, pp. 24-25) [5090], [14359], [37179], [40616]

Polish Genealogical Society-Journal [10982]

Political Risk Letter [43909]

"Politics of Design" in *San Francisco Business Times* (Vol. 18, No. 1, August 15, 2003, pp. 15) [1526], [7452], [40617]

"Politics as Usual?" in *Sales and Marketing.com* (Vol. 156, No. 3, March 2004, pp. 14) [27471], [51766]

Polk County Board of County Commissioners–Small and Minority Business Development Center [58710]

Polk County Chamber of Commerce [63418]

"Polk County Convention Complex Des Moines, IA" in *Tradeshow Week* (Vol. 34, November 29, 2004, No. 48, pp. S6) [22548], [25000], [55145]

"Polk Job Growth Boomed in 2004" in *Ledger* (February 19, 2005) [28634], [32632]

Pollution Probe [9334], [37234]

Pollution Reduction and Contaminant Control [37316]

"Pollution Rules to Cost Illinois Firms" in *Chicago Tribune* (March 11, 2005) [11937], [40618]

Polo Chamber of Commerce [59642]

Polsinelli Shalton Welte–Law Library [20769], [21112], [24183]

Polson Chamber of Commerce [62193]

Poly Ventures [63155]

Polygraph Update [19986]

Polytechnic University–Institute for Technology and Enterprise [52349]

Pomeroy Appraisal Associates Inc. [52765]

"Pomona, Calif., Aftermarket Auto Firm Goes After Markets in Midwest" in *Business Press* (September 3, 2003) [1961], [28635]

Pomona Capital [63156]

Pomona Chamber of Commerce [57721]

Pompton Lakes Chamber of Commerce [62550]

Ponca City Area Chamber of Commerce [64061]

Ponce Minority Business Development Center [66651]

Ponce and Southern Puerto Rico Chamber of Commerce [66649]

Ponchatoula Chamber of Commerce [60663]

Pond Creek Chamber of Commerce [64062]

"Pond Venture Partners Closes $78M Fund II" in *Venture Capital Journal* (Vol. 40, No. 10, October 2000, pp. 24, 26) [41909], [44621], [55778]

Pontiac Area Chamber of Commerce [59643]

"Pontiac-GMC Dealers are Excited About New Products" in *Automotive News* (Vol. 9, January 31, 2005, No. 3, pp. 24) [18112], [48776]

Pontiac Regional Chamber [61406]

Pontotoc County Chamber of Commerce [61829]

Pool 1: Pool School [2528]

Pool 2: Power Pool [2529]

Pool 3: Trick Shots [2530]

Pool Maintenance: Complete Guide to Spa & Hot Tub [23798]

Pool & Spa Marketing [23797]

Poolesville Area Chamber of Commerce [60849]

"Poor Health" in *Entrepreneur* (Vol. 28, No. 4, April 2000, pp. 114) [43315]

"Pop Quiz: A Quick Test Of Your Managerial Skills" in *Sales & Marketing Management* (Vol. 157, January 2005, No. 1, pp. 17) [45546], [51767]

"Pop Quiz: A Quick Test of Your Managerial Skills" in *Sales & Marketing Management* (Vol. 158, November-December 2006, No. 11, pp. 17) [31199], [45547], [47406], [51768]

"Pop Quiz: A Quick Test of Your Managerial Skills" in *Sales and Marketing.com* (Vol. 156, No. 3, March 2004, pp. 13) [45548], [46162], [51769]

Pope & Associates Inc. [48644]

Popeyes Chicken & Biscuits [21929]

"Popping Perfection" in *Black Enterprise* (Vol. 35, February 2005, No. 7, pp. 52) [11652], [23503]

"Popular Lance Armstrong Wristbands Spawn Counterfits" in *Boston Globe* (January 28, 2005) [30245], [54238]

Popular Photography and Imaging [19314]

"Population Boom" in *Forbes* (Vol. 175, January 10, 2005, No. 1, pp. 152) [24444], [53919]

Porcelain Enamel Institute [19783]

"Pork Chaps" in *Inc.* (January 1, 2002) [4552], [21585]

"Port Adopts 2007 Strategic Budget" in *Bellingham Business Journal* (December 2006, pp. A3) [14360], [27163], [28636], [30585], [32633], [54705]

Port Allegany Chamber of Commerce [64499]

Port Aransas Chamber of Commerce [65443]

Port Arthur Chamber of Commerce [65444]

"Port of Call? Port Authority in Talks to Reopen Detroit Marine Terminal" in *Crain's Detroit Business* (Vol. 21, February 7, 2005) [10689], [43785]

Port Chester - Rye Brook Chamber of Commerce [62986]

Port City Java [51468]

Port Gibson-Claiborne County Chamber of Commerce [61830]

Port Hueneme Chamber of Commerce [57722]

Port Isabel Chamber of Commerce [65445]

Port Lavaca-Calhoun County Chamber of Commerce and Agriculture [65446]

Port Ludlow Chamber of Commerce [66152]

Port Mansfield Chamber of Commerce [65447]

Port Neches Chamber of Commerce [65448]

Port O'Connor Chamber of Commerce [65449]

Port Orange/South Daytona Chamber of Commerce [58920]

Port Orchard Chamber of Commerce [66153]

Port Orford and North Curry Chamber of Commerce [64256]

"Port of Pittsburgh to Start Weekday Water Taxi Service" in *Pittsburgh Business Times* (Vol. 23, No. 8, September 12, 2003, pp. 1) [24239], [39888]

Port of Subs [8571], [21930]

Port Townsend Chamber of Commerce [66154]

Port Washington Chamber of Commerce [62987], [66498]

"The portable CEO" in *WorkingWoman* (Vol. 25, No. 2, February 2000, pp. 54) [49728], [53920]

Portable Computer and Communications Association [6405], [22901]

The Portable Financial Analyst: What Practitioners Need to Know [15361]

"Portable lite" in *Entrepreneur* (Vol. 31, No. 5, May 2003, pp. 35) [6760], [49212]

Portable Practitioner: Opportunities in the Healing Arts [17014]

Portage Area Chamber of Commerce [66499]

Portage County Business Council [66500]

Portage Park Chamber of Commerce **[59644]**

Portage Venture Partners / Graystone Venture Partners **[59756]**

Portageville Chamber of Commerce **[62026]**

"Portals battle for businesses' attention" in *Crain's Detroit Business* (Vol. 16, No. 47, November 13, 2000, pp. 17) **[25935]**

"Portals popping up again as links to customers" in *Atlanta Business Chronicle* (Vol. 25, No. 21, November 1, 2002, pp. 5A) **[25936]**, **[34359]**, **[47407]**

Portbook **[16742]**

Porter Henry & Co. **[52006]**

Porterville Chamber of Commerce **[57723]**

"Portfolio D&O Insurance Can Leave Outside Directors in the Cold" in *Venture Capital Journal* (October 1, 2005) **[13420]**, **[43316]**, **[55779]**

Portland Area Chamber of Commerce **[59992]**, **[61407]**

Portland Boat Show **[16778]**

Portland Business Alliance **[64257]**

Portland Cement Association–Library **[7694]**

Portland Chamber of Commerce **[64967]**, **[65450]**

Portland Community College
    Small Business Development Center **[64172]**
    Small Business International Trade Program **[64173]**

"Portland Considered for Maine Hydrogen Development Site" in *Portland Press Herald* (November 10, 2005) **[10690]**, **[52715]**

"Portland, Maine-Based Amato's Sandwich Shops Spread Across New England" in *Portland Press Herald* (September 16, 2005) **[8520]**, **[21586]**, **[38884]**

"Portland, Maine-Based L.L. Bean Ranks High In Customer Loyalty" in *Portland Press Herald* (April 8, 2005) **[5704]**, **[23629]**, **[31820]**

"Portland, Maine, Surplus Store Sells Clothes From Flooded Mississippi Mall" in *Portland Press Herald* (September 20, 2005) **[5705]**, **[51292]**, **[54239]**

"Portland, Maine, Woman Builds Successful Child-Care Business" in *Portland Press Herald* (June 10, 2005) **[5345]**, **[12308]**, **[38885]**, **[56370]**

"Portland, Maine, Women's Clothing Store Still Going Strong After 20 Years" in *Portland Press Herald* (April 15, 2005) **[5706]**, **[9635]**

Portland Minority Business Development Center **[64288]**

Portland Press Herald (December 23, 2005); "Americans Have Grown Very Attached to Their Gadgets, Survey Finds" in **[4912]**, **[6578]**, **[7713]**, **[41510]**, **[53582]**

Portland Press Herald (April 29, 2005); "Anjon's Sauces May Take the Lead" in **[11591]**, **[21437]**, **[23454]**, **[37586]**

Portland Press Herald (September 17, 2005); "Antiques Dealers Converge For Show in Portland, Maine" in **[1313]**, **[24883]**, **[55064]**

Portland Press Herald (December 3, 2005); "Army Extends Contract With Maine Company to Improve Armor On Humvees" in **[39983]**, **[46198]**

Portland Press Herald (June 17, 2005); "Artascope Carves Out Niche In Arts and Crafts" in **[7997]**, **[8149]**, **[8271]**, **[56119]**

Portland Press Herald (April 20, 2005); "Author, Expert to Discuss Socially Responsible Business Methods" in **[39156]**, **[54135]**

Portland Press Herald (October 15, 2005); "Bath Iron Works Wins Contract for Tri-Hulled Navy Warship" in **[16361]**, **[39987]**

Portland Press Herald (November 18, 2005); "Biddeford, Maine, Cord Business Weathers Trials of Domestic Textile Industry" in **[27835]**, **[35835]**, **[46212]**

Portland Press Herald (July 8, 2005); "Biddeford, Maine, Partners Highlight Weirdest eBay Auctions on New Web Site" in **[1781]**, **[33581]**, **[49814]**

Portland Press Herald (October 14, 2005); "Bill Proposes Tax for Maine's Bottled Water Industry" in **[3079]**, **[54450]**

Portland Press Herald (November 2, 2005); "Biomedical, Marine Research Funds Could Grow If Voters Approve Seed Money" in **[39791]**, **[41548]**, **[50828]**, **[52054]**

Portland Press Herald (November 8, 2005); "Burger King Franchisees, Parent Squabble Over Firm's Declining Fortunes" in **[21455]**, **[29132]**, **[38728]**

Portland Press Herald (April 22, 2005); "Clean-Water Company Begins a Growth Spurt" in **[14864]**, **[25698]**, **[27953]**, **[49859]**

Portland Press Herald (September 28, 2005); "Close Shave" in **[11786]**, **[37611]**, **[53649]**

Portland Press Herald (November 15, 2005); "Cod Limits Worry Maine Fishermen" in **[5242]**, **[10425]**, **[10458]**, **[26492]**

Portland Press Herald (May 17, 2005); "Credit Unions Share Branches to Compete with Bigger, National Banks" in **[9901]**, **[30833]**, **[37988]**

Portland Press Herald (November 16, 2005); "Cruise Ships Boost Business in Portland, Maine" in **[24679]**, **[25173]**

Portland Press Herald (December 1, 2005); "Damariscotta, Maine, Merchants Worry About Wal-Mart" in **[30834]**, **[51121]**

Portland Press Herald (April 7, 2005); "Developer Proposes Westin Hotel, Condos for Former Meat Plant Site" in **[7320]**, **[12544]**

Portland Press Herald (June 17, 2005); "Economist Says Focus on Emerging Markets to Boost Foreign Trade" in **[12957]**, **[32386]**, **[43632]**

Portland Press Herald (December 16, 2005); "Experts Advise Office Workers on the Fine Art of Holiday Gift-Giving" in **[39323]**, **[45126]**

Portland Press Herald (November 4, 2005); "First Slot Machines To Start Cranking in Maine Today" in **[10865]**

Portland Press Herald (May 20, 2005); "Harrison, Maine, Homeland Security Consultant Telecommutes Around the Globe" in **[22246]**, **[31162]**, **[36262]**

Portland Press Herald (September 13, 2005); "Higher Gas Prices Lead to More Hybrid Car Sales in Portland, Maine, Area" in **[18056]**, **[37294]**

Portland Press Herald (October 7, 2005); "History Bears Fruit for Maine Family's Apple Orchard" in **[26514]**, **[37684]**

Portland Press Herald (December 2, 2005); "Institute for Financial Literacy Thrives Teaching Adults to Manage Money" in **[10025]**, **[33131]**, **[38144]**

Portland Press Herald (August 17, 2005); "Lawn Tractor Manufacturer Relocates From Wisconsin to Portland, Maine" in **[30154]**, **[46334]**

Portland Press Herald (October 1, 2005); "L.L. Bean Chooses a New Advertising Agency" in **[697]**, **[5680]**, **[23623]**

Portland Press Herald (December 22, 2005); "Mail Carriers Bring Home the Goods for Holiday Online Shoppers" in **[16451]**, **[34156]**, **[51237]**

Portland Press Herald (October 7, 2005); "Maine Debate Imposing Stricter Standards for Auto Emissions" in **[18083]**, **[40525]**, **[46351]**

Portland Press Herald (May 27, 2005); "Maine Executives Give State's Economy 'Worst' Rating" in **[32556]**, **[45387]**

Portland Press Herald (May 6, 2005); "Maine Faces Slow Population Growth, Aging Workforce" in **[28447]**, **[32557]**, **[39447]**

Portland Press Herald (July 15, 2005); "Maine Family Rolls Out 100 Flavors of Ice Cream" in **[12784]**, **[37718]**

Portland Press Herald (November 10, 2005); "Maine Fishermen Welcome Amendment to Preserve Wharf Tax Rates" in **[26521]**, **[54650]**

Portland Press Herald (November 30, 2005); "Maine Home Sales Fall 4 Percent" in **[7413]**, **[20580]**, **[32558]**

Portland Press Herald (September 23, 2005); "Maine International Trade Center Adds China Desk" in **[12995]**, **[43741]**

Portland Press Herald (August 9, 2002); "Maine Lawyer Launches Personal Chef and Catering Service" in **[4520]**, **[35555]**, **[42542]**

Portland Press Herald (November 4, 2005); "Maine Office of Innovation Releases Plan for Research Development" in **[39861]**, **[50917]**, **[52146]**

Portland Press Herald (September 23, 2005); "Maine Program Helps Businesses Apply for Federal Grants" in **[39862]**, **[44581]**

Portland Press Herald (August 30, 2005); "Maine Program Merges On-The-Job Trainings with College Education" in **[5342]**, **[7414]**, **[16736]**, **[33158]**, **[39863]**

Portland Press Herald (September 6, 2005); "Maine Reweaves Thread of Former Textile Industry Into Artistry" in **[1521]**, **[8014]**, **[24969]**, **[46352]**, **[55115]**

Portland Press Herald (April 8, 2005); "Maine Says Flooring Companies Need to Pay Subcontractor Taxes" in **[10512]**, **[49713]**, **[54651]**

Portland Press Herald (September 20, 2005); "Maine Tourism Bureau Awards Account to New York Firm" in **[703]**, **[24705]**, **[25212]**, **[47220]**

Portland Press Herald (December 17, 2005); "Maine Tribes Express Interest in Naval Base Redevelopment Project" in **[21242]**, **[37309]**, **[40055]**, **[46353]**, **[48574]**

Portland Press Herald (April 26, 2005); "Maine Women's Fund Makes a Difference With Women Entrepreneurs" in **[36461]**, **[44425]**, **[56310]**

Portland Press Herald (October 11, 2005); "Mussel Farmer's Expansion Plan Worries Island Lobster Fishermen" in **[10462]**, **[26523]**

Portland Press Herald (August 5, 2005); "Navigation-Technology Startup Seeks Investors" in **[41857]**, **[55745]**

Portland Press Herald (December 7, 2005); "New Jersey Firm Busy Westbrook, Maine, Online Classified Company" in **[732]**, **[18914]**, **[30691]**, **[42358]**, **[52442]**

Portland Press Herald (July 4, 2003); "New Portland, Maine, Boutique Sells High-End Maternity Clothes" in **[5697]**, **[56344]**

Portland Press Herald (December 20, 2005); "One of Portland, Maine's Fastest Growing Tech Companies is Sold" in **[30693]**, **[41073]**, **[41886]**, **[52444]**

Portland Press Herald (December 13, 2005); "Online Sales Continue To Climb at L.L. Bean, Other Retailers" in **[28596]**, **[34300]**, **[51280]**

Portland Press Herald (September 2, 2005); "Pest-Control Companies Increasingly Rely on Non-Chemical Techniques" in **[19024]**, **[37315]**

Portland Press Herald (November 10, 2005); "Portland Considered for Maine Hydrogen Development Site" in **[10690]**, **[52715]**

Portland Press Herald (September 16, 2005); "Portland, Maine-Based Amato's Sandwich Shops Spread Across New England" in **[8520]**, **[21586]**, **[38884]**

Portland Press Herald (April 8, 2005); "Portland, Maine-Based L.L. Bean Ranks High In Customer Loyalty" in **[5704]**, **[23629]**, **[31820]**

Portland Press Herald (September 20, 2005); "Portland, Maine, Surplus Store Sells Clothes From Flooded Mississippi Mall" in **[5705]**, **[51292]**, **[54239]**

Portland Press Herald (June 10, 2005); "Portland, Maine, Woman Builds Successful Child-Care Business" in **[5345]**, **[12308]**, **[38885]**, **[56370]**

Portland Press Herald (April 15, 2005); "Portland, Maine, Women's Clothing Store Still Going Strong After 20 Years" in **[5706]**, **[9635]**

Portland Press Herald (December 13, 2005); "Portland Seeks Biotech Park to Stimulate New Business" in **[28637]**, **[41910]**, **[50945]**, **[52176]**

Portland Press Herald (December 23, 2005); "Portland's Small Retailers Launch 'Independents' Day' Campaign to Buy Locally" in **[47408]**, **[51293]**

Portland Press Herald (October 21, 2005); "Publisher Evolves With Technology, Entrepreneurial Talent" in **[2735]**, **[8624]**, **[36658]**, **[56377]**

Portland Press Herald (April 19, 2005); "Saco's Downtown Merchants Say Big-Box Retailers Are Hurting Businesses" in **[28729]**, **[30939]**, **[51338]**

Portland Press Herald (May 6, 2005); "SBA's Small Business Person of the Year Shares Her Story" in **[36718]**, **[56396]**

Portland Press Herald (July 27, 2005); "Senate Debates Bill That Shields Gunmakers From Some Lawsuits" in **[11729]**, **[40684]**, **[46430]**

Portland Press Herald (August 2, 2005); "'Serial Inventor' Seeks Patent for Wireless Directory Network" in **[6793]**, **[14426]**, **[44144]**

Portland Press Herald (June 22, 2005); "Shipbuilders Labor Union Threatens Management Over Layoff Plans in Bath, Maine" in **[3325]**, **[16382]**, **[45637]**, **[55311]**

Portland Press Herald (August 16, 2005); "South Portland, Maine, College Develops Small-Business Incubator" in **[35657]**, **[39088]**

Portland Press Herald (October 27, 2005); "South Portland, Maine, Company Brings Innovation to Recycling Centers" in **[21255]**

Portland Press Herald (May 18, 2005); "Study" in **[10194]**, **[15492]**, **[38385]**

Portland Press Herald (March 25, 2005); "Study Says Change Tax Laws to Help Forest Products Industry Stay Competitive" in **[16320]**, **[26544]**, **[30965]**, **[54780]**

Portland Press Herald (April 6, 2005); "Task Force Recommends Strategies to Improve Maine's Forest Products Industry" in **[16321]**, **[26547]**, **[39936]**

Portland Press Herald (November 22, 2005); "Trade Mission to France Nets $5 Million in Projected Sales" in **[13012]**, **[25032]**, **[43846]**

Portland Press Herald (March 29, 2005); "U.S. Postal Service Offers Free At-Home Pickups for eBay Sellers" in **[1864]**, **[10703]**, **[16473]**, **[30980]**

Portland Press Herald (September 24, 2005); "Voters May Rule on Export Tax for Maine's Drinking Water" in **[3081]**, **[40807]**, **[54855]**

Portland Press Herald (August 26, 2005); "Wells, Maine, Duo Start Custom Electronics Business" in **[5170]**, **[6856]**, **[7748]**, **[14595]**, **[36931]**, **[50257]**

Portland Press Herald (March 24, 2005); "Young Entrepreneur of the Year Works Round the Clock" in **[2258]**, **[37005]**

Portland Public Library–Art/Audiovisual Department **[17697]**

"Portland Seeks Biotech Park to Stimulate New Business" in *Portland Press Herald* (December 13, 2005) **[28637]**, **[41910]**, **[50945]**, **[52176]**

Portland State University–Center for Population Research and Census **[66964]**

Portland VA Research Foundation, Inc. **[41399]**

"Portland's Small Retailers Launch 'Independents' Day' Campaign to Buy Locally" in *Portland Press Herald* (December 23, 2005) **[47408]**, **[51293]**

Portrait Avenue **[19333]**

A Portrait of the U.S. Appliance Industry **[1416]**

Portsmouth Area Chamber of Commerce **[63774]**

"Portsmouth, Va., Couple Turns Yacht into Floating Bed and Breakfast" in *Virginian-Pilot* (July 23, 2003) **[2450]**

Portuguese Trade Commission **[43524]**

"Posecai's To Open" in *Mississippi Business Journal* (Vol. 29, January 2007, No. 4, pp. 9) **[20057]**, **[21587]**, **[29959]**

Posey County Chamber of Commerce **[59993]**

"Position in management doesn't equal leadership" in *Atlanta Business Chronicle* (Vol. 24, No. 14, September 7, 2001, pp. 2B) **[45549]**

"Positioning properties: Top office owners map plans for 2003" in *Atlanta Business Chronicle* (Vol. 25, No. 21, Nov. 1, 2002, pp. 1C) **[20624]**, **[20966]**, **[28638]**

Positive Impact Consulting **[35260]**

Positive Leadership **[45902]**

"Positive defense for networks" in *Red Herring* (January 2003, pp. 60) **[22328]**, **[41911]**, **[52177]**

"Positive Peer Pressure" in *My Business* (December/January 2004, pp. 34-37) **[36635]**, **[45550]**, **[53921]**

Positive Potentials **[57108]**

Post Card and Souvenir Distributors Association **[11140]**, **[11554]**

"Post founder trying to buy bankrupt energy company" in *Atlanta Business Chronicle* (Vol. 25, January 10, 2003, No. 31, pp. 3A) **[15362]**, **[50133]**

Post and Courier (January 20, 2005); "eBay Fees Cause Vendor to Bid Adieu" in **[1804]**, **[5905]**, **[8166]**, **[14005]**

Post Falls Chamber of Commerce **[59321]**

"Post It and They Will Come" in *Home Office Computing* (Vol. 18, No. 11, November 2000, pp. 40) **[28639]**, **[34360]**, **[42709]**

Postage Stamp Mega Event Fall **[5862]**

"Postage unpaid" in *Entrepreneur* (Vol. 30, No. 12, December 2002, pp. 77) **[24016]**, **[53922]**, **[54706]**

Postal Bulletin **[6117]**

Postal History Society of Canada **[5812]**

"Postal Rate Hikes" in *Kiplinger Letter* (Vol. 78, January 5, 2007, No. 1) **[759]**, **[16464]**, **[27669]**, **[40619]**

Postalannex+ **[6126]**

Postcard History Society **[5927]**

"Postcard perfect" in *Incentive* (Vol. 174, No. 10, October 2000, pp. 146) **[27164]**, **[27472]**

"Postcards with an Edge" in *Small Business Opportunities* (Vol. 12, No. 5, September 2000, pp. 52-53) **[47409]**

"Postcards From The Edge" in *Forbes* (Vol. 174, December 27, 2004, No. 13, pp. 54) **[760]**, **[47410]**

Posterity Press **[60899]**

The Posthorn **[5851]**

"The Postmodern Shift in Values and Jobs and the Implications for HR" in *Employment Relations Today* (Vol. 26, No. 4, Winter 2000) **[37489]**, **[42882]**

PostNet **[6127]**

Pot Pourri Accent **[12252]**

Potatoes Plus **[21931]**

"Potawatomi Would Take Hit From Kenosha Casino" in *Milwaukee Journal Sentinel* (December 1, 2005) **[10882]**

Poteau Chamber of Commerce **[64063]**

Poteau Kiamichi Technology Center–Incubator **[64128]**

Poteet Chamber of Commerce **[65451]**

The Potential of Herbs as a Cash Crop: How to Make a Living in the Country **[12153]**

"Potential Landfill Study Raises Radiation Concerns" in *Bradenton Herald* (January 27, 2005) **[37317]**

"The potential of actuarial decision models: can they improve the venture capital investment decision" in *Journal of Business Venturing* **[55780]**

Potomac Chamber of Commerce **[60850]**

Potomac Ventures **[58677]**

Potosi - Tennyson Area Chamber of Commerce **[66501]**

Potsdam Chamber of Commerce **[62988]**

"Pottery from Albuquerque, N.M., Designer Puts Area Color on Clay" in *Albuquerque Journal* (January 24, 2003) **[8178]**, **[8275]**

"Pottery studio offers a form of self-expression" in *Sarasota Herald Tribune* (December 19, 2002, pp. H1) **[8179]**, **[8276]**, **[11342]**, **[37761]**

"Pottery school expansion to put more behind the wheel" in *Crain's Cleveland Business* (Vol. 23, No. 42, October 21, 2002, pp. 14) **[8180]**, **[8277]**

Pottstown SCORE No. 594 **[64353]**

Potty Doctor Plumbing Service **[19780]**

Potty Training One, Two, Three **[5401]**

Poughkeepsie Area Chamber of Commerce **[62989]**

Poultry - U.S. **[4061]**

Poway Chamber of Commerce **[57724]**

Powder **[22861]**

Powder River Chamber of Commerce **[62194]**

Powell Area Chamber of Commerce **[63775]**

Powell County Chamber of Commerce **[62195]**

Powell SBDC–Region II **[66599]**

Powell Valley Chamber of Commerce **[66624]**

"The Power 50" in *Fortune* (Vol. 142, No. 9, October 16, 2000, pp. 139+) **[45551]**

"Power Agent Puts More Power in Agents' Hands" in *South Florida Business Journal* (Vol. 23, No. 48, July 4, 2003, pp. 31) **[4767]**, **[23130]**, **[24722]**, **[25235]**, **[53415]**

"Power Broker Gets 7 1/2 Years in Prison" in *Black Enterprise* (Vol. 35, January 2005, No. 6, pp. 28) **[15363]**, **[29443]**, **[40620]**

Power Budd LLP–Law Library **[15805]**, **[24184]**

"Power to the Buyer With Group Buying Sites" in *E-business Advisor* (Vol. 18, No. 2, February 2000, pp. 10) **[31821]**, **[34361]**, **[47411]**, **[53923]**

The Power of Customer Service **[31943]**

Power Direct Marketing: How to Make It Work for You **[47412]**

The Power of Exhibit Marketing: How to Make Money at Trade or Consumer Shows **[25001]**

"Power Firms Poised to Recharge National Grid" in *Houston Business Journal* (Vol. 34, No. 19, September 19, 2003, pp. 1A) **[9075]**

"The Power of the Group" in *Black Enterprise* (Vol. 34, No. 4, November 2003, pp. 165) **[50758]**, **[51294]**

"Power House" in *Entrepreneur* (Vol. 32, No. 1, January 2004, pp. 37) **[6761]**, **[7741]**, **[41912]**

"The Power of Ideas" in *Ingram's* (Vol. 27, No. 8, August 2001, pp. 20) **[36636]**, **[47413]**

"Power and Influence on the Hill" in *Hispanic Business* (March 2005, pp. 12) **[40621]**, **[48365]**

Power Interviewing: A Headhunter's Guide to Getting Hired in the '90s **[4438]**

Power Kickbox **[19524]**

"Power Living: Teresa Kay-Aba Kennedy Says Executives Don't Get Enough S.E.X." in *Black Enterprise* (Vol. 34, No. 6, January 2004) **[19430]**, **[35336]**, **[36637]**, **[45552]**, **[47328]**

"Power Lunch" in *St. Louis Post-Dispatch* (February 25, 2005) **[5091]**, **[15364]**, **[21588]**, **[27473]**, **[50134]**

Power Marketing for Small Business **[47414]**

"Power is the great motivator" in *Harvard Business Review* (Vol. 81, No. 1, January 2003, pp. 117) **[36638]**, **[45553]**

Power and Motoryacht **[16759]**

Power Multi-Level Marketing **[48670]**

"The Power of the Pack" in *Sales & Marketing Management* (Vol. 159, January-February 2007, No. 1, pp. 45) **[31200]**, **[33209]**, **[42380]**

Power-Packed Selling **[3631]**

"Power PACs" in *Hispanic Business* (March 2005, pp. 16, 18) **[40622]**, **[48366]**

"Power to the People" in *Incentive* (Vol. 174, No. 8, August 2000, pp. 18) **[35024]**, **[42381]**, **[45554]**

"The Power of Permission-Based Prospecting" in *Home Business* (Vol. 12, October 2005, No. 5, pp. 46) **[51770]**

The Power of Personal Sales: 501 Ways to Turn Self-Promotion into Profit **[51771]**

"Power Play" in *Entrepreneur* (Vol. 32, August 2004, No. 8, pp. 42) **[4198]**, **[6762]**, **[6957]**, **[7026]**, **[30404]**, **[46872]**, **[49213]**

The Power of Positive and Effective Communication **[42932]**

Power Real Estate Advertising: The Complete Guide for Professionals **[20625]**

"Power Shopping" in *Entrepreneur* (Vol. 28, No. 4, April 2000, pp. 62) **[36639]**, **[51295]**, **[56371]**

Power Show Ohio **[7593]**

"The Power of Spin" in *The Economist* (Vol. 377, October 1-7, 2005, No. 8446, pp. 76-77) **[37318]**, **[44125]**, **[48777]**, **[50946]**, **[52178]**

The Power of Team Building: Using Ropes Techniques **[35025]**

Power Thinking for powerful Results **[34800]**

"The Power of Touch" in *Entrepreneur* (Vol. 28, No. 9, September 2000, pp. 26) **[29960]**, **[32634]**

"Power Up!" in *Entrepreneur* (Vol. 31, No. 9, September 2003, pp. 20) **[28640]**, **[39531]**

Power Up Your Small-Medium Business: A Guide to Enabling Network Technologies **[5092]**, **[6410]**, **[6480]**, **[6763]**, **[6958]**, **[41913]**, **[49214]**

"The Power of Your Reputation Equals Profits Can Be a Tangible Business Strategy" in *Black Enterprise* (Vol. 35, August 2004, No. 1) **[6001]**, **[12903]**, **[20145]**, **[29961]**, **[50650]**

Power2BE Media **[58279]**

Powerboat Magazine **[16760]**

"Powerful forces" in *Black Enterprise* (Vol. 32, No. 6, January 2002, pp. 69) **[41476]**, **[47974]**, **[56070]**

Powerful Persuasion Skills for Technical Professionals **[26856]**, **[27272]**

Powerful Persuasion Skills for Technical Professionals (Canada) **[27612]**

"Powerhouse Tech Companies Merge" in *Black Enterprise* (Vol. 35, November 2004, No. 4, pp. 28) **[22329]**, **[40075]**, **[41914]**, **[50135]**

"Powering the imagination" in *Red Herring* (No. 103, September 1, 2001, pp. 74) **[41915]**, **[52179]**

PowerplayUSA **[14679]**

Powhatan Chamber of Commerce **[65936]**

Poynette Chamber of Commerce **[66502]**

Poynter Center Newsletter **[37541]**

PPC's Guide to Audits of Small Businesses **[38286]**

PPC's Guide to Audits of Small Businesses, Vol. 3 **[225]**, **[26327]**

PPC's Guide to Choosing Retirement Plans for Small Businesses **[15365]**, **[26883]**

PPC's Guide to Compensation Planning for Small Business **[26884]**, **[39532]**

PPC's Guide to Small Business Consulting Engagements **[3570]**, **[27474]**, **[31201]**

PPC's Guide to Small Business Consulting Engagements, Vol. 2 **[3571]**, **[31202]**

PPC's Guide to Small Business Consulting Engagements, Vol. 3 **[3572]**, **[31203]**

PPC's Small Business Tax Guide **[29444]**, **[54707]**

PPC's Small Business Tax Guide, Vol. 2 **[29445]**, **[54708]**

"PR advertising" in *Atlanta Business Chronicle* (Vol. 25, Nov. 15, 2002, No. 23 pp. S1) **[761]**, **[12904]**, **[20146]**, **[47415]**

"PR Exec: Agencies Share Blame for Crash" in *Atlanta Business Chronicle* (Vol. 24, No. 13, August 31, 2001, pp. 3A) **[14361]**, **[20147]**, **[28641]**, **[34362]**

"PR Firms Tout the Value of 'Buzz' Marketing" in *Atlanta Business Chronicle* (Vol. 25, November 15, 2002, No. 23 pp. S12) **[20148]**, **[34363]**, **[47416]**

"PR Leads www.prleads.com" in *Entrepreneur* (Vol. 32, No. 1, January 2004, pp. 10) **[47417]**, **[50460]**, **[50651]**

PR Newswire **[50731]**

PR Newswire (Dec. 9, 2003); "12.1 Inch SVGA Modules From Toshiba..." in **[7712]**, **[15914]**, **[41495]**

PR Newswire (January 16, 2003); "Americans Still 'Searching' for the Perfect Way to Lose Weight" in **[13811]**, **[19372]**

PR Newswire; "Blue From American Express(R) Re-Launches Blue PLAY(R) Site With Real-Time Online Auctions That Money Can't Buy" in **[1784]**, **[13854]**

PR Newswire (October 29, 2001, pp. NA); "CELLIT Technologies Empowers CB Richard Ellis to Deliver Superior Customer Service" in **[20461]**, **[20828]**, **[31657]**

PR Newswire (March 25, 2004); "CollectiveGood and eBay Team Up to Recycle Cell Phones for Charity" in **[1796]**, **[4955]**, **[33686]**, **[54159]**

PR Newswire (February 14, 2005); "College Students Take on eBay: CollegeJunktion.com, Where Your Junk Becomes Treasure" in **[1797]**, **[13908]**

PR Newswire (January 12, 2005); "ConversionCenter.com Specializes in Customer Service and Conversion Van Sales on Website" in **[7127]**, **[18001]**

PR Newswire (December 2, 2003); "eBay Auction Integration Will be a Major Player with Irun's Website Builder Tools" in **[1802]**, **[1846]**, **[25840]**, **[33832]**, **[53268]**

PR Newswire (November 13, 2003); "eBay Phenomenon Embraced by Online Piano Company" in **[1806]**, **[17740]**, **[17840]**, **[33836]**

PR Newswire (March 15, 2004); "Exbayer Online Trading Assistant Helps You Sell Items on eBay with New Store" in **[1811]**, **[7163]**, **[10675]**, **[18644]**, **[33868]**

PR Newswire (January 20, 2005); "Fairmont Hotels and Resorts Offers Help Asking Life's Most Important Question" in **[3181]**, **[7130]**, **[12547]**

PR Newswire (Feb. 24, 2004); "Free Online Bridal Registry Service Offers Total Flexibility to Add Any Gift..." in **[3183]**, **[18646]**, **[33922]**

PR Newswire (Jan. 5, 2004) "FriendFinder Online Dating Far Outranks the Competition; Multiple Awards Bestowed..." in **[7057]**, **[33925]**

PR Newswire (January 20, 2005); "Has eBay Finally Gone Too Far? EBay's Arrogance Paves the Way for the Competition" in **[1821]**, **[30873]**

PR Newswire (January 20, 2005); "Home2NetServices Announces a Revolutionary New Way of Insuring Personal Property" in **[13324]**, **[19964]**, **[22251]**, **[43216]**

PR Newswire (Oct. 29, 2001); "MAPICS Implements Web-based Self Service Tool to Enhance Customer Service For High Tech Manufacturers" in **[14229]**, **[31774]**, **[34170]**, **[37164]**, **[46365]**

PR Newswire (March 7, 2003); "March Is National Craft Month" in **[8173]**, **[28459]**, **[53848]**

PR Newswire (January 12, 2004); "MingleMatch Reaches Half-Million Member Milestone" in **[7062]**, **[34198]**

PR Newswire (March 8, 2004) "New Online Dating Service Uses Psychoanalytic Approach; Dr. Freud: Log On!" in **[7064]**, **[34253]**

PR Newswire (January 18, 2005); "OnlineAuction.com Makes Bid for Outraged eBay Sellers" in **[1841]**, **[14324]**, **[30924]**

PR Newswire (Nov. 25, 2003); "Ontrackfitness.com Introduces the Fitness Accountability Trainer Service" in **[19426]**, **[34306]**

PR Newswire (Nov. 17, 2003) "Perquest Brings Payroll Industry Into 21st Century; PayPal Founder Seeds Silicon Valley Startups" in **[18789]**, **[26325]**, **[34344]**

PR Newswire (Mar. 29, 2004); "QuikDrop Authorized by State of Illinois and State of MI to Offer eBay Drop-Off Store Franchises" in **[1847]**, **[7172]**, **[18661]**, **[38890]**, **[52581]**

PR Newswire (January 13, 2003) "Renowned Scientist's Research on Aging Delivers Anti-Aging Supplement; Juvenon Energy Formula" in **[17909]**, **[52186]**

PR Newswire (April 1, 2004); "SGS Automotive Services Offering Vehicle Inspections on eBay" in **[1852]**, **[4352]**, **[34462]**, **[52589]**

PR Newswire (January 17, 2005); "Sideways Wines on Auction at WineBid.com" in **[1854]**, **[14431]**, **[23506]**

PR Newswire (January 6, 2003); "Skinnyguy.com Rekindles America's Love to Barter" in **[6138]**, **[14439]**, **[17772]**, **[25598]**, **[26715]**, **[34485]**

PR Newswire; "SteelSalvor Chooses Lois Paul & Partners to Kick Start Public Relations, Strategic Communications Initiative" in **[1856]**, **[14486]**, **[46441]**, **[47577]**, **[50471]**

PR Newswire (January 5, 2004); "The First Wedding Planning Board Game to Help Lower Divorce" in **[3182]**, **[24810]**

PR Newswire (April 30, 2002, pp. CLTU00330042002); "Velvet Ice Cream Welcomes Return of Spring" in **[12794]**, **[37809]**

PR Newswire (Jan. 29, 2003); "Who Says Sunshine and Anti-Aging Don't Mix? " in **[16832]**, **[17919]**, **[25049]**

PR Newswire (January 25, 2005); "WholeSecurity Selected as Finalist for SC Magazine Global Awards 2005" in **[14618]**, **[19981]**, **[22423]**

PR Newswire (December 23, 2002); "Widespread Ignorance of Regulation and Labeling of Vitamins, Minerals and Food Supplements" in **[17920]**, **[40845]**

PR Newswire (November 11, 2003); "With So Many Bed and Breakfast Values on the Internet, Why Stay Home for the Holidays?" in **[2455]**, **[34742]**

"PR Power" in *Entrepreneur* (Vol. 31, No. 11, November 2003, pp. 97) **[47418]**, **[50461]**, **[50652]**

PR Week (August 18, 2003, pp. 3); "Yahoo! Hooks Up with H&S to Promote Dating Service" in **[7074]**, **[34759]**

The Practical Accountant **[338]**

Practical Approaches to Counseling in Careers Guidance **[4401]**

Practical Behavior-Based Safety: Step-by-Step Methods to Improve Your Workplace **[56582]**

The Practical Book of Greenhouse Gardening **[11440]**

Practical Business Ethics **[37490]**

Practical Debt Collecting for Small Companies and Traders **[8394]**, **[31578]**

A Practical Guide to Aerial Photography: With an Introduction to Surveying **[23769]**

A Practical Guide for Translators **[25091]**

"Practical Ideas for Improving Your Business" in *Journal of Accountancy* (Vol. 199, February 2005, No. 2, pp. 108) **[4768]**, **[6764]**, **[23131]**, **[28642]**, **[45555]**, **[53416]**

Practical Marketing Research **[47419]**

The Practical Real Estate Lawyer **[20724]**

The Practical Tax Lawyer **[24098]**

Practical Tax Strategies **[339]**, **[24099]**

Practical Tax Strategies (Vol. 67, No. 1, July 2001, pp. 30); "New Law Offers Tax Relief for Individuals - But Only Temporarily" in **[23998]**, **[39874]**, **[54671]**

Practical Taxidermy **[24269]**

Practical Time Management **[54977]**

Practical Time Management: How to Get More Things Done in Less Time **[54978]**

Practical Welding Today **[16400]**

Practice Beef Quality Grading II **[4068]**

Practice Development Counsel **[3797]**, **[31442]**, **[50381]**

"Practice List Hygiene for Healthy Business" in *Folio: the Magazine for Magazine Management* (Vol. 30, No. 1, January 2001, pp. 9) **[44354]**

Practice Periodical on Structural Design and Construction **[7571]**

Practice Retail Cut Identification II **[4069]**

Practice Retail Cut Identification III **[4070]**

Practice Retail Cut Identification IV **[4071]**

The Practicing CPA **[340]**

A Pragmatic Approach to Business Ethics **[37491]**

Prague Chamber of Commerce **[64064]**

Prairie Agricultural Machinery Institute **[26694]**

Prairie County Chamber of Commerce **[62196]**

Prairie Du Chien Area Chamber of Commerce **[66503]**

Prairie Grove Chamber of Commerce **[57208]**

Prairie View A&M University–Small Business Development Center **[65056]**

Prairie View Chamber of Commerce **[65452]**

Cedric Prange Associates Inc. **[19583]**

Pratt Area Chamber of Commerce **[60407]**

Joanne H. Pratt Associates **[42784]**

Prattville Area Chamber of Commerce **[56883]**

Praxis Media Inc. **[3798]**, **[31443]**, **[50382]**

PRC News **[25603]**

"Pre-Nups for Small Business" in *Black Enterprise* (Vol. 30, No. 7, February 2000, pp. 65) **[29962]**, **[45556]**

Pre- and Post-Natal Fitness **[19486]**

"Pre-Showtime class on the art of selling space" in *Atlanta Business Chronicle* (Vol. 25, No. 21, November 1, 2002, pp. 9C) **[20626]**, **[20967]**, **[33210]**, **[47420]**, **[51772]**

Precast/Prestressed Concrete Institute **[16939]**

Precious and Fashion Jewelry Markets: Past Performance, Current **[15863]**

Precision Concrete Cutting **[16983]**

Precision Door Service **[52632]**

Precision Metalforming Association **[16353]**

Precision Shooting **[1479]**

Precision Tune Auto Care, Inc. **[20276]**, **[22697]**

Precision Valley Development Corp. **[65809]**

"Predatory Towing" in *San Fernando Valley Business Journal* (Vol. 12, January 2007, No. 2, pp. 37) **[4361]**, **[29446]**, **[40623]**

"Predictable surprises: The disasters you should have seen coming" in *Harvard Business Review* (Vol. 81, No. 3, March 2003, pp. 72) **[226]**, **[26328]**, **[45557]**

"Predicting the outcome of a sale is easy. Sort of" in *Atlanta Business Chronicle* (Vol. 25, January 10, 2003, No. 31, pp. 8B) **[51773]**

"Predicting Success" in *Hispanic Business* (July/August 2002, pp. 68, 70, 72) **[33211]**

"Preferred Club Program Sits Atop The Leader Board" in *Rough Notes* (Vol. 146, No. 3, March 2003, pp. 90) **[13421]**, **[43317]**

"Pregnancy Claim Settlements Rise" in *Inc.* (September 2005, pp. 30) **[29447]**, **[32052]**

Prejudice: A Lesson to Forget **[48625]**

"Premier Execs Collar National SBA Honors" in *Pet Product News* (Vol. 57, No. 11, November 2003, pp. 1) **[19156]**

Premier One Low Price Cleaners **[8938]**

PremierGarage **[19789]**

"Premium pain" in *Boston Business Journal* (Vol. 22, No. 16, Ma) **[13422]**, **[41081]**, **[43318]**

"Premium Pain Relief" in *Business Week* (June 12, 2000, pp. F14) **[43319]**

"Premium RX? Consumer-driven health plans" in *Atlanta Business Chronicle* (Vol. 25, No. 19, October 18, 2002, pp. 5C) **[13423]**, **[26885]**, **[43320]**

"Premiums to climb at double-digit rate-again" in *Atlanta Business Chronicle* (Vol. 24, No. 13, August 31, 2001, pp. 14A) **[13424]**, **[26886]**

Premont Chamber of Commerce **[65453]**

Prentice Hall Business Publishing **[62637]**

Prentice Hall Press **[62638]**

Prentice Hall Small Business Management Handbook **[45558]**

The Prentice Hall Small Business Survival Guide: A Blueprint for Success **[52933]**

"Preoccupied with what's working-or what's not-many CEOs see only linear paths to growth" in *Inc.* (November 2000, pp. 78) **[28643]**, **[45559]**

"Prepaid Card Benefits Breast Cancer Research" in *Marketing to Women* (Vol. 19, November 2006, No. 11, pp. 5) **[8317]**, **[31579]**, **[47421]**, **[48778]**, **[50136]**, **[54240]**

"Preparation key to conquering overseas exhibits" in *Atlanta Business Chronicle* (Vol. 24, No. 14, September 7, 2001, pp. S16) **[25002]**, **[43786]**, **[55146]**

"Prepare for takeoff" in *Entrepreneur* (Vol. 31, No. 6, June 2003, pp. 124) **[30586]**, **[36640]**

"Prepare for Y2K Litigation" in *E-business Advisor* (Vol. 17, No. 12, December 1999, pp. 36) **[29448]**, **[34364]**, **[40624]**

Prepared Foods (Vol. 171, No. 5, May 2002, pp. 83); "Bulk chocolate" in **[4276]**, **[48709]**

"Preparing for evil" in *Harvard Business Review* (Vol. 81, No. 4, April 2003, pp. 109) **[36641]**, **[45560]**

Preparing for Leadership: What It Takes to Take the Lead (Canada) **[44823]**

"Preparing for national leadership" in *Women in Business* (Vol. 53, No. 4, July-August, 2001, pp. 20) **[36642]**, **[56372]**

Preparing a Successful Business Plan: A Practical Guide for Small Business **[29963]**

Preparing Your Business for Sale: Sell Your Business for the Most Money! **[52446]**

Preparing Your Family Business for Strategic Change **[37762]**

Preplayed **[51469]**

Prescient Capital **[58126]**

Prescott Area Chamber of Commerce **[66504]**

Prescott Chamber of Commerce **[57061]**

Prescott Valley Chamber of Commerce **[57062]**

Prescription for Complaints **[10318]**, **[15714]**, **[51973]**

"Prescription Drug Cost Containment" in *Rough Notes* (Vol. 145, No. 2, February 2003, pp. 76) **[13425]**, **[26887]**, **[43321]**

"Prescription for Profit" in *Small Business Opportunities* (Vol. 13, No. 6, November 2001, pp. 84, 86, 138) **[17151]**, **[37073]**, **[42546]**

"Present Perfect" in *Fast Company* (September 2001, pp. 164) **[30405]**, **[31822]**

"Present Perfect" in *Incentive* (Vol. 174, No. 9, September 2000, pp. 65) **[7143]**, **[11115]**, **[31204]**

Presenting the Story **[10319]**, **[15715]**, **[51974]**

Preserving the Legacy of a Small Business Family: Estate Planning & Business Succession **[37763]**

"Preserving Tradition, Embracing Progress" in *Rough Notes* (Vol. 145, No. 2, February 2003, pp. 26) **[13426]**, **[36643]**, **[43322]**, **[45561]**

"President signs tax cut bill with pension reform" in *Employee Benefit Plan Review* (Vol. 56, No. 1, July 2001, pp. 10) **[24017]**, **[26888]**, **[39889]**, **[54709]**

Presidential Families Gazette **[10983]**

Presidio Chamber of Commerce **[65454]**

Presque Isle Area Chamber of Commerce **[60769]**

Presque Isle Chamber of Commerce **[66505]**

"Press Conference: You've Worked Hard to Land That Media Interview-So Don't Blow Your Opportunity" in *Entrepreneur* **[22549]**, **[27475]**, **[47422]**, **[50653]**

Pressed 4 Time **[8939]**

"Pressure on appraisers creates risk for fraud" in *Atlanta Business Chronicle* (Vol. 24, No. 13, August 31, 2001, pp. 4B) **[1447]**, **[20627]**, **[37492]**

"Pressure mounting for terrorism insurance relief" in *Atlanta Business Chronicle* (Vol. 25, No. 21, November 1, 2002, pp. 5C) **[13427]**, **[22330]**, **[40625]**, **[43323]**

Preston Chamber of Commerce **[59322]**

Preston County Chamber of Commerce **[66291]**

"Pretty Picture" in *Entrepreneur.com* (Vol. 34, January 2006, No. 1, pp. 40) **[6765]**, **[49215]**

Pretzel Time, Inc. **[2310]**

The Pretzel Twister **[23569]**

Pretzelmaker, Inc. **[7101]**

Pretzels Plus **[23570]**

"The Prevaricator" in *Barron's* (July 28, 2003, pp. 7) **[10138]**, **[15366]**, **[37493]**

Preventing Sexual Harassment: A Management Responsibility **[32095]**

Preventing Sexual Harassment: A Shared Responsibility **[32096]**

Prevention Research Center–Library **[54388]**

The Prevention Researcher **[41285]**, **[54345]**

"Prewitt With Prudential" in *Mississippi Business Journal* (Vol. 29, January 2007, No.4, pp. 9) **[20628]**, **[20968]**, **[38886]**, **[50137]**

"Price Equals Value Plus Terms" in *Journal of Accountancy* **[227]**, **[2946]**, **[24018]**, **[26329]**, **[27165]**, **[50138]**

"Price Fix" in *Entrepreneur* (Vol. 33, September 2005, No. 9, pp. 56) **[30221]**, **[31056]**, **[51296]**

Price Guide for Desktop Services **[8623]**

"The Price Makes the Stock" in *Forbes* (Vol. 175, February 14, 2005, No. 3, pp. 138) **[10139]**, **[15367]**, **[38287]**

"Price for News Was $25 Million" in *Crain's Detroit Business* (Vol. 21, October 10, 2005, No. 43, pp. 20) **[15368]**, **[18923]**, **[50139]**

Price-Pottenger Nutrition Foundation–Library **[12043]**, **[18509]**

"Price is Right: 114 Franchises You Can Buy for Less than $25,000" in *Entrepreneur* (Vol. 31, No. 10, October 2003, pp. 94) **[38887]**

"The Price is Right" in *Black Enterprise* (Vol. 31, No. 5, December 2000, pp. 56) **[38288]**

"The Price is Right" in *Inc.* (July 1, 2003) **[4769]**, **[23132]**, **[31057]**, **[38289]**, **[53417]**

"The price slice" in *Crain's Detroit Business* (Vol. 18, No. 49, Dec. 9, 2002, pp. 11) **[31058]**

The Price: Update **[50281]**

Price Waterhouse–Library **[2999]**

"Priced to Sell" in *Entrepreneur.com* (Vol. 34, February 2006, No. 2, pp. 100) **[31059]**, **[47423]**

Priceenergy.com Franchising, LLC. **[23340]**

Pricele$$ Rent-A-Car **[21383]**

Prices, Cycles & Growth **[32635]**

"Prices, Wages in 2007" in *Kiplinger Letter* (Vol. 84, January 26, 2007, No. 4) **[32636]**, **[42883]**

"PriceSmart Doubles Profits: PriceSmart Inc." in *San Diego Business Journal* (Vol. 28, January 15, 2007, No. 3, pp. 10) **[20234]**, **[51297]**

PricewaterhouseCoopers
North Toronto Research Centre **[3000]**
Research Centre **[425]**, **[24185]**

"Pricey Playthings" in *Tampa Tribune* (December 19, 2005) **[19431]**, **[23630]**

"Pricing and the psychology of consumption" in *Harvard Business Review* (Vol. 80, No. 9, September 2002, pp. 90) **[31060]**, **[31823]**

Pride Publications Inc. **[59813]**

Pridestaff **[9278]**, **[9596]**, **[24550]**

Bill J. Priest Institute for Economic Development–Dallas SBDC **[65057]**

Priest Lake Chamber of Commerce **[59323]**

Priest River Chamber of Commerce **[59324]**

James J. Prihoda & Associates **[47899]**, **[52007]**

"Primal Leadership: The hidden driver of great performance" in *Harvard Business Review* (Vol. 79, No. 11, December 2001, pp. 42) **[36644]**, **[45562]**

"Primal Need" in *Entrepreneur.com* (Vol. 34, February 2006, No. 2, pp. 20) **[51298]**

Primavera Systems Inc. **[46105]**

Primaxis Technology Ventures Inc. **[66732]**

Prime Capital Management Co., Inc. **[58608]**

Prime Restaurants **[21932]**

Prime Time Walleye Locations **[2199]**

Primer for Graphic Arts Profitability **[6002]**

"Primer for Profit" in *Small Business Opportunities* (Vol. 13, No. 6, November 2001, pp. 52, 56) **[18696]**, **[35612]**, **[38670]**

Primeurs **[4141]**

Primrose School Franchising Co. **[5445]**

"Primus Fund V Eyes $250M Close" in *Venture Capital Journal* (Vol. 40, No. 10, October 2000, pp. 22, 24) **[14362]**, **[41916]**, **[44622]**, **[55781]**

Primus Venture Partners, Inc. **[63857]**

Prince Edward Island Food Technology Centre–Information Services **[7835]**, **[22039]**

Prince George's Chamber of Commerce **[60851]**

Prince George's County Minority Business Opportunities Commission–Suburban Washington Region Small Business Development Center **[60799]**

"Prince of Management" in *Entrepreneur* (Vol. 27, No. 12, December 1999, pp. 20) **[45563]**

Prince Ventures **[58609]**, **[59757]**

Prince of Wales Chamber of Commerce **[56972]**

Prince William County - Greater Manassas Chamber of Commerce **[65937]**

Prince William Regional Chamber of Commerce **[65938]**

Princess Anne Chamber of Commerce **[60852]**

Princeton Area Chamber of Commerce **[59994]**, **[61650]**, **[65455]**

Princeton Area Chamber of Commerce and Main Street **[59645]**

Princeton-Caldwell County Chamber of Commerce **[60563]**

Princeton Community Hospital–Library **[18404]**

Princeton Health Systems Inc. **[27045]**

Princeton-Mercer County Chamber of Commerce **[66292]**

Princeton Regional Chamber of Commerce **[62551]**

Princeton University
Bendheim Center for Finance **[10411]**
Council of the Humanities **[62617]**
Firestone Library–Social Science Reference Center–Data and Statistical Services **[66930]**
Office of Research and Project Administration **[62618]**
Princeton Forrestal Center **[62619]**
Research Program in Development Studies **[32861]**

Principal Financial Group–Corporate Library **[10405]**

Principle Publications Inc. **[65677]**

Principles of Management **[45941]**

Principles of Private Firm Valuation **[15369]**, **[39533]**, **[54710]**

Principles of Professional Selling **[51527]**

Principles of Professional Selling Level 2 **[51528]**

Principles of Professional Selling - Level 2 (Canada) **[48214]**, **[51529]**

Principles of Small Business **[52934]**

Principles of Water Quality Control **[25706]**

Prindle Hinds Environmental Inc. **[37363]**

Prineville-Crook County Chamber of Commerce [64258]

"Pringle to Chinese: Bring It On" in *Business Journal-Milwaukee* (Vol. 20, No. 44, July 18, 2003, pp. A9) [1026], [43787], [44126]

Print Council of America [19814]

Print Ontario [7854], [19925]

Print Solutions [7034], [39727]

Print Solutions-Buyers' Guide Issue [39534]

Print Three Franchising Corp. [19266], [19938]

Printers Inc. [19942]

Printer's Ink [19915]

"Printers producing plenty of red ink" in *Crain's Detroit Business* (Vol. 19, No. 3, January 20, 2003, pp. 10) [19889], [28644], [32637]

PrintImage International [5961], [19856]

Printing [22128]

Printing Basics for Non-Printers 1: An Abridged Guide to Printing Fundamentals [22129]

Printing Brokerage/Buyers Association [3413], [19857], [25493]
  Library [6076]

Printing Impressions [19916]

Printing Impressions-Top 500 Printers Issue [19890]

Printing Industries of America [18842], [19858]

Printing Industries of America/Graphic Arts Technical Foundation–Edward H. Wadewitz Memorial Library [6077], [8665]

"Printing in the Privacy of Your Hotel Room" in *Law Firm Inc.* (October 2004) [6766], [19891], [30406], [49537]

PrintMedia Magazine [2777], [18260], [18960]

Prints [22130]

Print's Best Typography [19892]

Printwear Xpress Franchising [22134]

Printworld Directory of Contemporary Prints and Prices [19820]

PrintWorthy Publishing Co. [64158]

Prior Lake Area Chamber of Commerce [61651]

"Prioritizing a Hectic Schedule" in *Sales & Marketing Management* (Vol. 157, January 2005, No. 1, pp. 52) [31205], [47424], [54979]

"Priority packets pay to fly first class" in *Red Herring* (No. 87, December 18, 2000, pp. 44, 46) [27731], [36645], [41477]

"Priority. Fast, Cheap, and Ready To Move-in." in *Inc.* (November 2006, pp. 23-24) [14363], [20629], [20969], [52716]

"Priority" in *Inc.* (Volume 27, March 2005, No. 3, pp. 23-26, 28, 30) [10691], [15370], [32638], [33212], [34365], [38290], [39535], [39890], [42382], [44127], [56373]

"Priority Mail" in *Entrepreneur* (Vol. 28, No. 1, January 2000, pp. 38) [14364], [31824], [34366]

Priority Process Associates Inc. [26435], [27218], [33352], [46106], [49453], [53555]

Priority Response Restoration Services [4030]

Prism Capital [59758]

PRISM International - Professional Records and Information Services Management [6233]

Prism Venture Partners [61110]

Prisoners of Advertising [857]

"Privacy, the workplace and the Internet" in *Journal of Business Ethics* (Vol. 28, No. 3, December 1, 2000, pp. 255) [22331], [34367]

Privacy in the Workplace: Unreasonable Intrusion or Legitimate Interest? [37545]

Private Capital Corp. [56912]

"Private Company Profiles" in *Red Herring* (No. 99, June 15 & July 1, 2001, pp. 124, 126) [1694], [4770], [6273], [6959], [14365], [23133], [41917], [50947], [52180]

"Private firms surviving downturn" in *Atlanta Business Chronicle* (Vol. 25, November 8, 2002, No. 22 pp. 3A) [7453], [20630], [21589], [28645], [32639]

"Private Equity Firms Help Hurricane Victims" in *Buyouts* (October 3, 2005) [15371], [54241], [55782]

Private Eyes [19971]

"Private investors manage for the long haul" in *Crain's Detroit Business* (Vol. 19, No. 15, April 14, 2003, pp. 9) [10140], [15372], [38291]

Private Industry Council–Procurement Information Center of Westmoreland/Fay [64596]

Private Investigative Agency Start-Up Manual [19972]

"Private Investors Purchase a Controlling Stake at Ecoboard Holdings" in *Long Island Business News* (February 13, 2004) [10141], [15373], [16318], [46409], [50140], [55783]

Private Label Buyer (Vol. 16, No. 4, April 2002, pp. 47); "PL chocolates" in [4302], [10748], [48775]

Private Label Directory [20001]

Private Label Manufacturers Association [19998]

Private Label Marketing in the 1990s: The Evolution of Price Labels into Global Brands [20002]

"Private Lives" in *Inc.* (October 2005, pp. 84) [36646], [55784]

"Private Matters" in *Red Herring* (No. 87, December 18, 2000, pp. 228-233) [15374], [50141]

"Private Matters: Retail Alert: Keep an Eye on New RFID Privacy Legislation" in *Entrepreneur* (Vol. 32, October 2004, No. 10, pp. 38) [22332], [29449], [40626], [41918], [51299]

"Private venture capital sources in Michigan" in *Crain's Detroit Business* (Vol. 16, No. 19, May 8, 2000, pp. 17) [55785]

Private Motor Truck Council of Canada [25368]

Private Placements and Other Private Financings [3440]

Private Practice Section/American Physical Therapy Association [19561]

"Private Sector Soldiers" in *Fortune* (Vol. 149, No. 9, May 3, 2004, pp. 33) [7454], [56583]

Private Security Case Law Reporter [35286]

Private Security and the Investigative Process [19973]

Private Security Law Case Studies [19974]

"A private space race" in *Wall Street Journal* (Feb. 5, 2003, pp. B1) [35613], [41478], [52023], [55420]

"Private-to-Private Corruption" in *Journal of Business Ethics* (Vol. 47, No. 3, October 15, 2003, pp. 253) [29450], [37494]

"Private Web hubs let companies build ties with their key buyers" in *Crain's Detroit Business* (Vol. 16, No. 46, Nov. 13, 2000, pp. 19) [14366], [34368]

"The Privatization Question" in *Hispanic Business* (October 2002, pp. 22, 24) [40627]

Priveq Capital Funds [66733]

"Prized Package: DHL Hub Could Deliver 500 Jobs" in *South Florida Business Journal* (Vol. 23, No. 52, August 1, 2003, pp. 1) [10692], [28646]

Pro [16051], [16123]

Pro Cuts [11837]

Pro Golf Discount [11295]

PRO, President's Resource Organization [3911]

Pro Sound News [21152]

Pro Windows Small Business Server 2003 [6180], [6274], [6767], [6960], [49216]

Pro2Net [52], [2858], [23870]

ProActive English [3984], [27595], [31444], [33353], [42141], [48645]

Probabilistic Press [65678]

"The Problem: Getting Stung by a B" in *St. Louis Post-Dispatch* (January 16, 2005) [15375], [38292]

"The Problem of Perceptions: Reasons for Outsourcing the Sexual Harassment Investigation" in *Employment Relations Today* (Vol.27, No.1) [32053], [42884], [49729]

Problem Solving: A Process for Managers [45942]

Problem Solving and Decision Making Workshop [44824]

"The Problem With Confidence" in *Inc.* (September 2005, pp. 176) [36647], [39536]

Procedures for the Automated Office [49217]

"Proceed With Caution" in *Black Enterprise* (Vol. 35, December 2004, No. 5, pp. 44) [10142], [15376], [38293]

Process Management: Applying Process Mapping to Analyze and Improve [44825]

Process Management: Applying Process Mapping to Analyze and Improve Your Operation (Canada) [44826]

Process Management Process Mapping and Work Simplification [44827]

"Process Online Payments Quickly and Effectively" in *E-business Advisor* (Vol. 18, No. 6, June 2000, pp. 34) [228], [26330], [31580], [34369], [53418]

Processing of Polymeric Composites and Injection Molding [46518]

"ProcessLibrary.com" in *Entrepreneur* (Vol. 33, September 2005, No. 9, pp. 6) [6411], [14215], [14367], [22333]

Procter & Gamble Pharmaceuticals–Research & Development Library [8877]

Procurement Assistance Center–SBDC [63497]

Procurement Center Representative [58682]

"Procurement: Federal File" in *Hispanic Business* (December 2002, pp. FRG10) [40076], [48367]

Procurement Technical Assistance Center–Lawrence Economic Development Corporation [63869]

ProdigalPen Publishing Inc. [59814]

"Producer compensation linked to agency size" in *Rough Notes* (Vol. 146, No. 3, March 2003, pp. 16) [13428], [26889], [35026], [43324]

"Producers as Consultants" in *Rough Notes* (Vol. 145, No. 12, December 2002, pp. 124) [3573], [13429], [43325]

"The Producers: Fixed Payouts Mimic Yield. But Will the Hit Keep Playing?" in *Barron's* (August 25, 2003, pp. F2) [10143], [15377], [38294], [54711]

Producing Effective Government Publications: The Plain-Language Approach [8980]

"Producing excellence" in *Black Enterprise* (Vol. 31, No. 5, December 2000, pp. 80) [25937]

Product Alert [2401]-[12021], [48814]

Product Costs: What's In Them [31082]

Product Design and Development [48815]

Product Safety & Liability Reporter [40897], [48816]

Product Strategy: All the Right Moves [30059], [37043]

"Production Co. Enters Familiar Chapter: 11" in *Washington Business Journal* (Vol. 22, No. 17, August 29, 2003, pp. 1) [28647], [32640], [38259]

Production and Inventory Control Handbook [44238]

Production and Inventory Management [44239]

Production Planning, Scheduling and Activity Control Workshop [46178]

Production Planning, Scheduling and Activity Control Workshop (Canada) [46179]

Production Techniques and Technology [2672]

Production Technology News [16401]

"Productive Lessons from a Tech Meltdown" in *Hispanic Business* (Vol. 23, No. 7/8, July/August 2001, pp. 6) [36648], [47425], [48368]

Productive Publications [66763]

Productivity Press [59815], [63263]

Productivity Software [6204], [16552], [23287]

PRODUCTSCAN [48843]

"Professional athlete credits ABWA with the right 'assist'" in *Women in Business* (Vol. 54, No. 5, September-October 2002, pp. 10) [36649], [56374]

Professional Agent [13558], [43436]

Professional Alternatives Inc. [54369]

Professional Apartment Management [1383]

Professional Apparel Association [5639]

Professional Association of Custom Clothiers [5524]

Professional Association of Resume Writers and Career Coaches [22042]

Professional Awning Manufacturers Association-Membership Directory [7517]

Professional Beauty Association [2392], [11779]

Professional Bowlers Association of America [3099]

Professional Builder [7572]

Professional Careers Sourcebook [4402]

Professional Carpet Systems, Inc. [25562]

Professional Carwashing & Detailing [2035], [4374]

The Professional Chef: The Business of Doing Business As a Personal Chef [4521], [35614]

Professional Construction Estimators Association of America [7231]

Professional Convention Management Association [24869]

Professional Counseling Centers of Indiana [3799], [31445], [41336]

Property Casualty Insurers Association of America [13171]
  Library [13607]
Property Damage Appraisers, Inc. [1459]
"Property Firm Off to a Strong Start" in *Atlanta Business Chronicle* (Vol. 26, No. 11, August 22, 2003, pp. 3A) [20631], [20971]
Property Management Association [20045]
Property Management Association-Bulletin [20066]
Property Management Association-Directory [20058]
"Property Tax Woes Hit Indiana" in *Inc.* (October 1, 2004) [35615], [54714]
PropertyGuys.com Inc. [20752]
Prophetstown-Lyndon Area Chamber of Commerce [59646]
"Proposed Apartments Meant For Those With Below-Median Income" in *Bradenton Herald* (January 26, 2005) [7455], [20972], [21344], [37764]
ProQuest General Periodicals [13121]
Proquest Investments [62606]
"Proquest's Slimdown Has Little Effect on Local Jobs" in *Crain's Detroit Business* (Vol. 23, January 29, 2007, No. 5, pp. 13) [15381], [29964], [50145]
Proshop Retail [11296]
Proshred Security [4032]
Prospect Chamber of Commerce [58560]
Prospect Street Ventures [63157]
Prospect Venture Partners / Prospect Management LLC [58127]
"Prospecting in Cuba" in *Hispanic Business* (October 2006, pp. 28, 30) [13005], [43790]
Prospecting: The Key to Sales Success [51777]
"Prospects are dim for entry-level employment" in *Atlanta Business Chronicle* (Vol. 25, No. 21, November 1, 2002, pp. 13C) [20632], [20973], [42383]
"Prospects improve for toolmakers, but cash crunch may hurt" in *Crain's Detroit Business* (Vol. 19, No. 9, March 3, 2003, pp. 26) [16377], [28656]
Prosper Area Chamber of Commerce [65456]
J.P. Prosser & Associates Inc. [20082]
Prosser Chamber of Commerce [66155]
Protape, Inc.–Library [426], [13608], [20770], [24186]
"Protect Company Info" in *Small Business Opportunities* (Vol. 16, No. 2, March 2004, pp. 86) [29453], [44355]
"Protect Customer's Web Privacy" in *E-business Advisor* (Vol. 18, No. 4, April 2000, pp. 28) [22334], [34374]
Protect Painters [18719]
"Protect the Source" in *Entrepreneur* (Vol. 33, February 2005, No. 2, pp. 46) [4772], [6769], [22335], [23136], [53421]
"Protect your computer from potential viruses" in *Women In Business* (Vol. 52, No. 3, May 2000, pp. 39) [14369], [53422]
Protect Your Business: Top Cops Help You Safeguard Against Shoplifting, Employee Theft and More [35283]
"Protect Your Profits" in *Small Business Opportunities* (Vol. 12, No. 2, March 2000, pp. 20) [51300], [56584]
"Protect Yourself From Lawsuits" in *My Business* (November/December 2001, pp. 42) [29454]
"Protect Yourself" in *PC Computing* (April 2000, pp. 35) [30246], [53925]
"Protect Yourself: Records to store off-site" in *My Business* (April/May 2002, pp. 17) [20235], [45569]
Protecting Animals [1258]
"Protecting copyrights: how e-books will be like parking meters" in *Wall Street Journal* (September 11, 2000, pp. B1) [9153]
"Protecting the Dream" in *Ingram's* (Vol. 28, No. 5, May 2002, pp. 28) [26890], [29455], [29965], [38297], [39541]
"Protecting Ideas" in *Black Enterprise* (Vol. 35, February 2005, No. 7, pp. 54) [14370], [34375], [44129]
"Protecting your intellectual property" in *Ingram's* (Vol. 28, No. 6, June 2002, pp. 22) [22336], [44356]

"Protecting your company from high turnover" in *Women in Busines s* (Vol. 53, No. 2, March-April, 2001, pp. 30) [35031], [42384], [45570], [56376]
"Protecting What's Yours" in *Hispanic Business* (Vol. 23, No. 7/8, July/August 2001, pp. 110) [26891], [43328]
"Protecting Your Idea From Bigmouths, and Calling All CFOs" in *Fortune* (Vol. 142, No. 7, October 2, 2000, pp. 284) [43968]
Protection Management Associates Inc. [12698], [18385], [22440]
"Protocol: Coming Soon: Ethernet as business model" in *Red Herring* (No. 102, August 15, 2001, pp. 68-69) [6961], [14371], [36655]
Protocol, LLC. [25586]
"Prove Your Worth: Forget the Stock Market." in *Entrepreneur* (Vol. 31, No. 7, July 2003, pp. 64) [29966], [36656]
Proven Promotions for Kitchen & Bathroom Businesses [7456], [47432], [50655]
Proventure [3912]
Providence Business News [64683]
Providence Business News (Vol. 18, No. 20, September 1, 2003, pp. 2); "Amgen Looking to Develop Medicines with Competitors" in [8774], [14737], [48695], [49785], [50810], [52038]
Providence Business News (Vol. 18, No. 15, July 28, 2003, pp. 1); "Amgen's Profit Up 58 Percent in 2nd Quarter" in [27770], [46676]
Providence Business News (Vol. 17, No. 27, October 21, 2002, pp. 18); "An entertainment hybrid finds an audience" in [2338], [17516], [21499]
Providence Business News (Vol. 18, No. 16, August 4, 2003, pp. 3); "Aquaculture Becoming Big Business in Rhode Island" in [10424], [10457], [26480], [50813], [52041]
Providence Business News (Vol. 18, No. 23, September 22, 2003, pp. 1); "Blue Cross Ties Healthy Living to Lower Rates" in [13205], [43095]
Providence Business News (Vol. 18, No. 11, June 30, 2003, pp. 4); "Bristol Firm Focuses on Innovative Sailboat Masts" in [16731]
Providence Business News (Vol. 18, No. 24, September 29, 2003, pp. 1); "Commercial Real Estate Buoyed by Health Care" in [14877], [20472], [20841]
Providence Business News (Vol. 18, No. 13, July 14, 2003, pp. 3); "Customers Wary of Online Banking Security Breeches" in [30211], [33725], [37991]
Providence Business News (Vol. 18, No. 20, September 1, 2003, pp. 1); "Cyberkinetics Plans for Clinical Trials" in [8780], [48719], [50854], [52080]
Providence Business News (Vol. 18, No. 19, August 25, 2003, pp. 1); "Dairy Co-Op Targets R.I. Consumers" in [11605], [26499]
Providence Business News (Vol. 18, No. 23, September 22, 2003, pp. 1) "Fishermen's Days Numbered; New Regs Would Cut Time at Sea" in [10426], [10460], [26510], [40384]
Providence Business News (Vol. 18, No. 11, June 30, 2003, pp. 10); "Luxury Travel Firm Driven for Success" in [24704], [25211]
Providence Business News (Vol. 18, No. 15, July 28, 2003, pp. 3); "Raytheon, SRM Awarded U.S. Navy Contracts" in [40081]
Providence Business News (Vol. 18, No. 17, August 11, 2003, pp. 2); "Roomier Recreational Trailers Becoming More Popular" in [21175], [28722]
Providence Business News (Vol. 18, No. 20, September 1, 2003, pp. 1); "Telemarketers Plan to Do-Not-Call" in [39626], [47617]
Providence Business News (Vol. 18, No. 18, August 25, 2003, pp. 10); "The Competition has Nuttin' on this Business" in [11602], [23468], [26493], [30824]
Providence Business News (Vol. 18, No. 19, August 25, 2003, pp. 4); "Tuning In to LIN TV" in [24455]
Providence Equity Partners, Inc. /Providence Ventures [64678]
Providence Journal Bulletin [64684]

Provider [41286]
Provider-LTC Buyers' Guide Issue [18332]
Provincetown Chamber of Commerce [60989]
Provincial Drug Benefit Programs [8833]
"Proving That You Have the Right Stuff" in *Inc.* (Volume 27, July 2005, No. 7, pp. 28) [40078], [41922]
Provo-Orem Chamber of Commerce [65725]
"Proxity Electronic Commerce System" in *Entrepreneur* (Vol. 33, August 2005, No. 8, pp. 4) [34376], [35554], [40079]
PRstore LLC [18625]
Prudential Relocation Intercultural Services [30201]
Pryor Area Chamber of Commerce [64065]
"PS Cleaning Products, Lightning Join to Promote Line" in *Tampa Tribune* (December 23, 2005) [762], [47433], [50146]
PSA Journal [19246], [19316]
PSExtreme [18961], [23288]
PSI Research Inc./Oasis Press/Hellgate Press [64316]
"PSI Uses Technology to Keep Call-Center Biz in U.S." in *Crain's Detroit Business* (Vol. 21, December 19, 2005, No. 51, pp. 10) [45571], [49730], [52577]
Psychiatry in the Nursing Home [18333]
Psychoanalytic Dialogues [1397]
Psychoanalytic Social Work [41287]
Psychological Insights Inc. [16878]
The Psychology of Entrepreneurship [36657]
The Psychology of Technical Analysis: Profiting from Crowd Behavior and the Dynamics of Price [15382]
PT, Magazine of Physical Therapy [19575], [41288]
Ptek Ventures [59202]
PTN (Photographic Trade News) [19247]
"Pub grub grows up" in *Restaurant Business* (Vol. 101, No. 15, Sept. 15, 2002, pp. 76) [3133], [21592], [53926]
PubCom & i-Imagery [8659]
PubEasy [63264]
Public Accounting Report [341]
Public Administration Review [50370]
Public Administration Service [3800], [31446], [50383]
Public Affairs Report [50371]
Public Broadcasting Management Association [24368]
Public Budgeting and Finance [27209]
Public Citizen–Health Research Group [41400]
"Public Company Profiles" in *Red Herring* (No. 105, October 1, 2001, pp. 90) [4773], [6275], [14372], [23137], [41923], [52181]
"Public companies push the envelope" in *Hispanic Business* (Vol. 22, No. 6, June 2000, pp. 116) [15383], [48373], [50147]
Public Health Institute [17245]
Public Human Services Directory [41084]
Public Library of Cincinnati and Hamilton County–Public Documents and Patents Department [44222]
"The Public Library: Technology Lets You Browse the Stacks from Your Home Office" in *Black Enterprise* (Vol. 34, No. 4, Nov. 2003) [9154], [34377], [42710], [45572], [47434]
Public Management (PM) [50372]
"Public opinion" in *Entrepreneur* (Vol. 30, No. 10, October 2002, pp. 76) [15384], [50148], [55787]
Public Personnel Management [23411]
Public Policy Communications [3801], [31447], [50384]
Public/Private Ventures [50407]
Public Relations Cases [50462]
Public Relations-More Than Publicity [32969], [50423]
Public Relations Practices: Managerial Case Studies and Problems [20149]
Public Relations: Principles & Practice [12905], [20150]
Public Relations Review [20171]
Public Relations Society of America [20093], [50422]
Public Relations: Strategies for Success [50424]
Public Relations: Strategies for Success (Canada) [50425]

Public Relations Strategist [50486]

Public Relations Student Society of America [20094]

Public Relations Tactics [20172]

Public Relations Tactics-Member Services Directory-The Blue Book [20151], [50463]

The Public Relations Writer's Handbook [20152], [50464]

Public Risk Management Association [42814]

Public Sector Consultants Inc. [3802], [31448], [50385]

"Public Transit Works for Wendel Deuchscherer" in *Business First Buffalo* (Vol. 19, No. 48, August 22, 2003, pp. 32) [1527], [1528], [15957], [16187]

"Publicis throws a few Curves" in *ADWEEK New England Edition* (Vol. 39, No. 50, December 16, 2002, pp. 6) [763], [19432], [47435]

The Publicity Hound [20173], [47807], [50716]

Publicity Power: A Practical Guide to Effective Promotion [50656]

Publish Now! [2733]

"Publish or Perish" in *Forbes* (November 13, 2000, pp. 252) [18924], [34378], [47436]

"Publish Thyself: More and more, book authors are using the Web" in *Time* (Vol. 155, No. 3, January 24, 2000, pp. B7) [2734], [9155], [14373]

"Publisher Evolves With Technology, Entrepreneurial Talent" in *Portland Press Herald* (October 21, 2005) [2735], [8624], [36658], [56377]

Publishers' Catalogues [2736]

Publishers Directory [2737], [3046], [9007]

Publishers, Distributors, and Wholesalers of the United States [2738], [23138]

Publishers Information Bureau [18844]

Publishers Weekly [2779], [3060], [16255]

Publishers Weekly-Calendar Roundup Issue [11163]

Publishers Weekly (Vol. 249, No. 19, November 21, 2002, pp. 3); "Check out our new book-What E-sourcing Means to You" in [13894], [33665]

Publishers Weekly (Vol. 249, No. 40, October 7, 2002, pp. 12); "E-Book vendors look to libraries for growth" in [2696], [4641], [9134], [13986], [22970], [33789]

Publishers Weekly (Vol. 249, No. 36, September 9, 2002, pp. 12); "E-book users surveyed online, in college" in [9135]

Publishers Weekly (Vol. 249, No. 50, December 16, 2002, pp. 14); "E-book writer for print" in [2698], [9137]

Publishers Weekly (Vol. 250, No. 17, April 28, 2003, pp. 18); "Firm offers new way to secure digital content" in [2704], [9142], [24407], [25591]

Publishers Weekly (Vol. 249, No. 47, November 25, 2002, pp. 18); "Gemstar may unload e-book assets (Who will Buy?)" in [2708], [9143], [14065]

Publishers Weekly (Vol. 249, No. 37, September 16, 2002, pp. 14); "OfficeMax launches e-book store" in [2729], [9150], [14303], [34276]

Publishers Weekly (Vol. 250, No. 2, January 13, 2003, pp. 15); "OverDrive Inks Library, Yahoo! E-book Deals" in [9151], [14334], [34322]

Publishers Weekly (Vol. 250, No. 15, April 14, 2003, pp. 10); "Rosetta gets dozens of Random e-book licenses" in [2740], [9157]

Publishers Weekly (Vol. 249, No. 49, Dec. 9, 2002, pp. 9); "Rosetta, Random House settle e-book lawsuit" in [2741], [9158], [44138]

Publishers Weekly (Vol. 249, No. 35, September 2, 2002, pp. 18); "Seattle Book Co. offers e-book conversion" in [2742], [9159], [14417], [34444]

"Publishing" in *Business Week* (January 9, 2006, No. 3966, pp. 29-30) [764], [18925], [34379], [47437], [53927]

Publishing Poynters [2780]

"Publix building on 3.5 acres acquired for almost $4 million" in *Daily Business Review* (Vol. 77, No. 146, January 7, 2003, pp. A4) [20633], [20974]

"Publix Alliances Upend Payment-Fee Models" in *American Banker* (Vol. 170, February 4, 2005, No. 24, pp. 1) [10145], [11654]

"Publix chief leads quietly" in *Atlanta Business Chronicle* (Vol. 24, No. 13, August 31, 2001, pp. 3A) [11655], [14374], [28657], [45573], [50149]

"Publix Stock Reaches Record High" in *Ledger* (March 1, 2005) [11656], [15385]

Puckmasters Hockey Training Centers [23754]

Pudgie's Famous Chicken [21933]

Pueblo Business Journal (February 28, 2003); "New mortgage company looks past the numbers" in [17344], [37572], [44430]

Pueblo Business Journal (February 28, 2003); "Pueblo Economic Development Corp. names operations director" in [28658], [32643]

Pueblo Business Journal (February 28, 2003); "Women of Courage International to hold second women's conference" in [25051], [54280], [56493]

Pueblo Business and Technology Center [58471]

Pueblo Chieftain (January 9, 2003); "Pueblo, Colo., Center Offers Relationship Classes, Yoga, Massage" in [17907], [19433]

"Pueblo, Colo., Center Offers Relationship Classes, Yoga, Massage" in *Pueblo Chieftain* (January 9, 2003) [17907], [19433]

"Pueblo Convention Center Pueblo, CO" in *Tradeshow Week* (Vol. 34, November 29, 2004, No. 48, pp. S7) [22550], [25003], [55147]

"Pueblo Economic Development Corp. names operations director" in *Pueblo Business Journal* (February 28, 2003) [28658], [32643]

Pueblo Small Business Development Center–Pueblo Community College [58309]

Puerto Rico Business Review [43910]

Puerto Rico Chamber of Commerce [66650]

Puerto Rico House Standing Committee on Industry and Commerce [66656]

Puerto Rico Minority Business Development Center [66652], [67136]

Puerto Rico Procurement Technical Assistance Center–Commonwealth of Puerto Rico [66655]

Puerto Rico Small Business Development Center [66645]

Puff Pastry Dough [2278]

Puget Sound Business Journal (Vol. 21, No. 3, May 26, 2000, pp. 20); "Sharp Turn" in [17910], [43358]

Puget Sound Council of Governments [67007]

Pulaski Area Chamber of Commerce [66506]

Pulaski County Chamber of Commerce [65939]

Pulaski - Eastern Shore Chamber of Commerce [62990]

"Pull the Plug on Stress" in *Harvard Business Review* (Vol. 81, No. 7, July 2003, pp. 102) [39542]

"Pulling together" in *Crain's Detroit Business* (Vol. 19, No. 17, April 28, 2003, pp. 14) [28659], [32644]

Pullman Chamber of Commerce [66156]

Pulse [1259]

Pulse Newsletter [26600]

"The Pulse" in *Sales & Marketing Management* (Vol. 159, January-February 2007, No. 1, pp. 9) [41924], [47438], [49220], [51778]

Puma Publishing Co. [58280]

"The Pump-and-Dump Economy" in *Wall Street Journal* (Vol. 248, January 2007, No. 146, pp. A16) [15386], [29967], [30587], [50150]

"Pump 'em up at the office" in *Incentive* (Vol. 174, No. 10, October 2000, pp. 149) [35032], [51779]

Pump It Up - The Inflatable Party Zone [5446]

"Pump it Up" in *Entrepreneur* (Vol. 32, No. 2, February 2004, pp. 73) [36659], [51780]

"Pump Up with PR" in *Small Business Opportunities* (Vol. 16, No. 2, March 2004, pp. 10) [765], [12906], [20153], [25004], [47439], [50465], [50657]

Pumping Iron After Fifty [19487]

"Punching the Time Card" in *Incentive* (Vol. 174, No. 8, August 2000, pp. 75) [14375], [34380], [54981]

"Puncturing Myths" in *Kansas City Business Journal* (Vol. 18, No. 21, January 28, 2000, pp. 21) [17874], [35616]

Pundmann & Company Inc. [30718]

"Punta Gorda Interested in Wi-Fi Internet" in *Charlotte Observer* (February 1, 2007) [14376], [34381], [41925]

Punxsutawney Area Chamber of Commerce [64500]

Purcell Chamber of Commerce [64066]

"Purchase Cements Metaldyne Chassis Biz" in *Crain's Detroit Business* (January 26, 2004, pp. 28) [15387], [46411], [47158]

Purchase and Sale of Commercial Real Estate [21066]

Purchase and Sale of Small Businesses: Tax and Legal Aspects [30694], [52447]

Purchasing Contract Management: How to Avoid Legal Pitfalls [29084]

The Purchasing Department [3803], [23416], [31449]

Purchasing Magazine [50770]

"Purchasing Power" in *Small Business Opportunities* (Spring 2005) [38671], [49539]

Purchasing and Supply Management [50752]

Purdue Research Foundation [60037]

Purdue Research Park [60038]

Purdue University
  Center for Customer-Driven Quality [31995]
  Center for Food and Agricultural Business [26695]
  Center for Urban and Industrial Pest Management [19057]
  Dauch Center for the Management of Manufacturing Enterprises [46554]
  Division of Sponsored Program Development [60039]
  SBDC [59834]
  Southeast-Purdue Agricultural Center [5489]
  Technical Assistance Program [59852]

Purdue University Libraries-CFS–Consumer and Family Sciences Library [5618], [12751], [18510], [22040]

Purdue University Libraries-KRAN–Management and Economics Library [26665]

Purified Water Store Corp. [3089]

Puroclean - The Paramedics of Property Damage [43451]

Purple Directory [10805]

The Pursuit of Happyness [15388], [36660], [39543]

"Pursuits" in *Inc.* (Volume 27, March 2005, No. 3, pp. 62-63) [4774], [12619], [23139], [24723], [25236], [33214], [36661], [53423], [54242]

PUSH Commerical Division [48011]

"Push Your Plans Through" in *PC Computing* (April 2000, pp. 100) [28660], [29968]

"Pushbutton Pizza; Livonia Company Markets Vending-Machine Pies" in *Crain's Detroit Business* (Vol. 21, October 17, 2005) [19640], [25577]

"Pushing Green Building into Mainstream" in *Crain's Detroit Business* (Vol. 22, November 20, 2006, No. 47, pp. 16) [1528], [7457], [37319]

"Pushing the Right Buttons" in *Crain's Detroit Business* (Vol. 23, January 15,2007, No. 3, pp. 11) [5093], [27477], [41926], [54982]

Pushmataha County Chamber of Commerce [64067]

"Put a Hacker to Work" in *Inc.* (Volume 28, January 2006, No. 1, pp. 39, 42) [4775], [6770], [22337], [23140], [42385], [53424]

Put-in-Bay Chamber of Commerce [63776]

"Put It In Drive" in *Entrepreneur.com* (Vol. 34, February 2006, No. 2, pp. 34) [39544], [49540], [53928]

"Put Some Wow In Your Website" in *Inc.* (September 2006, pp. 44-45) [25940], [27478], [34382], [41927]

"Put sales last to succeed" in *Rough Notes* (Vol. 146, No. 3, March 2003, pp. 124) [13433], [51781]

"Put Your Finger On It" in *Entrepreneur* (Vol. 33, January 2005, No. 1, pp. 20) [6771], [22338], [49221]

Put Your Show on the Road [2374]

"Put Your Web Applications to the Test" in *E-business Advisor* (Vol. 18, No. 7, July 2000, pp. 44) [34383], [49222], [53425]

Putnam County Chamber of Commerce [58921], [66293]

Putnam County Chamber of Commerce - South Putnam Branch [58922]

Putnam Lovell NBF Capital Partners, L.P. [58128]

Putney, Twombly, Hall & Hirson–Law Library [9542]

Puttin' on Your Lips [7922]

Putting the ADA to Work for You [32097]

"Putting the 'E' in Your Business" in *Hispanic Business* (Vol. 22, No. 5, May 2000, pp. 36) [34384], [37181], [48374]

"Putting Focus on 4 Famed Firms" in *Crain's New York Business* (Vol. 22, November 27, 2006, No. 48, pp. 17) [5565], [5707], [11657], [14377], [18926], [25941], [28661], [43030], [47440], [50151]

"Putting the Heat on Spam" in *Entrepreneur* (Vol. 32, No. 4, April 2004, pp. 34) [14378], [22339], [34385]

"Putting Hispanics Behind the Wheel" in *Hispanic Business* (September 2004, pp. 20) [18114], [53929]

"Putting their money where the future is" in *The New York Times* (March 27, 2000, pp. D3, H3) [34386], [55788]

"Putting Pen to Paper: Teen Publisher Uses Poetry to Touch Hearts" in *Black Enterprise* (Vol. 34, No. 2, September 2003, pp. S6) [18927], [56759]

"Putting Pension Funds to Work" in *Hispanic Business* (November 2003, pp. 38, 40) [10146], [15389], [38298], [48375]

"Putting Research on the Map" in *Hispanic Business* (July/August 2004, pp. 14) [16823], [18928], [50948]

"Putting the Screws to Google" in *Business Week* (January 23, 2006, No. 3968, pp. 24) [766], [14379], [34387], [47441]

"Putting signage on shirts is a cinch for sign-a-Rama's founder" in *Entrepreneur* (Vol. 30, No. 3, March 2002, pp. 106) [22728], [22794], [36662], [38888]

"Putting the brakes on transportation" in *Hispanic Business* (Vol. 22, No. 6, June 2000, pp. 112) [25406], [48376], [50152]

"Puzzleman to the Rescue" in *My Business* (December/January 2003, pp. 12-13) [24826], [36663], [47442], [50658], [56378]

"PVC Index" in *Venture Capital Journal* (Vol. 42, No. 10, October 2002, pp. 55-59) [13859], [14629], [15390], [15432], [15911], [42578], [50153], [55752], [55789], [56822], [56916], [58277]

PWAContact [9038]

"Pygmalion in management" in *Harvard Business Review* (Vol. 81, No. 1, January 2003, pp. 97) [35033], [36664], [45574]

"Pyrotechnics fire up the crowd at meetings" in *Atlanta Business Chronicle* (Vol. 24, No. 14, September 7, 2001, pp. S15) [25005], [35034], [47443], [50154]

Q

Q Lube, Inc. [20277]

Q Ventures [65624]

"QA: Shopping for Capital" in *Black Enterprise* (Vol. 35, January 2005, No. 6, pp. 44) [44623], [48377]

"Q&A: Forecasts from Five New York Real Estate Experts" in *Crain's New York Business* (Vol. 23, January 15, 2007, No. 3, pp. 40) [17428], [20634], [20975], [32645]

"Q&A" in *Home Office Computing* (Vol. 18, No. 9, September 2000, pp. 13) [12907], [25942], [27479], [27670], [29456], [30358], [31206], [32856], [33348], [34388], [35565], [40628], [42711], [51301], [52578], [54715], [54983]

"Q&A: Jack Bamberger" in *Folio: the Magazine for Magazine Management* (Vol. 30, No. 1, January 2001, pp. 18) [18929], [28662], [34389]

"Qcorps Scores Military Coup" in *Houston Business Journal* (Vol. 34, No. 17, September 5, 2003, pp. 1) [17558], [30934], [40080]

Qdoba Mexican Grill [21934]

"QEK's Intranet keeps life organized" in *Crain's Detroit Business* (Vol. 16, No. 34, August 21, 2000, pp. E-8) [34390], [43953]

"Q401 Will it Matter?" in *Red Herring* (No. 105, October 1, 2001, pp. 58-59) [28663], [32646]

Quaboag Valley Chamber of Commerce [60990]

Quad City Boat and Vacation Show [5254], [25326]

Quadra Pacific Consultants Ltd. [1059], [7631], [19772]

"Qualified state tuition programs: EGTRRA update" in *The Tax Adviser* (Vol. 32, No. 10, October 2001, pp. 672) [24019], [33215], [39891], [54716]

Qualitative Health Research [41289]

Qualitative Research Consultants Association-Membership Directory [16824]

Quality Bakers of America Cooperative Laboratory [2176]

Quality Business: Quality Issues & Smaller Firms [52935]

Quality Care Advocate [18360]

Quality Control in Publications [2673]

Quality Customer Service [31826]

Quality Inns, Hotels & Resorts [12722]

Quality Interviewing [42386]

Quality Management in Health Care (QMHC) [41290]

Quality Management Journal [45903]

Quality Manager's Alert [45904]

Quality Service: Frontline Commitment [31944]

Quality of Service: Making It Really Work [52579]

Quality Service: The Three R's for Managers [31945]

Quality Specialists [46108]

The Quality Technician's Handbook [16378]

"Quality Time: Not Getting What You Want Out of Your Sales Meeting? Here are 5 Tips to Point You in the Right Direction" in *Entrepreneur* [27480], [35035], [45575], [51782]

Quanah Chamber of Commerce [65457]

Quantum Capital Partners [58976]

"A quantum leap" in *Red Herring* (January 2003, pp. 54) [22340], [41928]

QuarkXPress I [32970]

QuarkXPress II [32971]

QuarkXPress III [32972]

The Quarter Racing Journal [23747]

Quarterly Financial Report [3467], [15771]

Quarterly Journal of Business & Economics [10292], [32823], [38494]

"Quarterly Report - February 2000" in *Small Business Economic Trends* (February 2000, pp. COV) [42387], [53930]

"Quarterly report-February 2002" in *Small Business Economic Trends* (February 2002, pp. 1) [28664], [32647]

"Quarterly Report - May 2000" in *Small Business Economic Trends* (May 2000, pp. COV) [53931]

The Quarterly Review of Biology [52313]

Quartz Hill Chamber of Commerce [57725]

Quartzsite Chamber of Commerce [57063]

"QuatRx uses $10M in venture capital for psoriasis drug" in *Crain's Detroit Business* (Vol. 19, No. 12, March 24, 2003, pp. 12) [50949], [52182], [55790]

Quebec Province Communications et Societe-Centre de Documentation [4159]

"The Quebec Story: Low Cost, Low Risk, Tremendous Opportunity" in *Venture Capital Journal* (Vol. 42, No. 5, May 2002, pp. 48, 50) [41479], [43464], [50796], [52024], [55421]

"Quebec's Competitive Edge" in *Venture Capital Journal* (Vol. 42, No. 5, May 2002, pp. 51-52) [30775], [43465], [55422]

Queen Anne's County Chamber of Commerce [60853]

Queens Borough Public Library-Information Services Division [14689]

Queens Business Consulting [3804], [31005], [38569]

Queens College of City University of New York Office of Research and Sponsored Programs [63203]
  Speech and Hearing Center [12129]

Queen's University at Kingston-Institute of Intergovernmental Relations [50408]

Queensborough [63228]

Quest Capital [58458]

"Quest for the Next Great Search Company" in *Venture Capital Journal* (December 1, 2004) [14380], [34391], [55791]

The Quest for Quality: Prescriptions for Service Excellence [31827]

"The Quest for Resilience" in *Harvard Business Review* (Vol. 81, No. 9, September 2003, pp. 52) [28665], [29969], [52936]

Quest Small Business Development Center [66020]

Quest Ventures [58129]

"A Question of Character" in *Entrepreneur* (Vol. 28, No. 8, August 2000, pp. 30) [44624]

Quick Caller Area Air Cargo Directory QC [10693]

"Quick Drop Franchise Opens in Virginia Beach, Va., for Storefront eBay Sales" in *Virginian-Pilot* (March 16, 2004) [1846], [7171], [18660], [34392], [38889], [52580]

"Quick Fix: Do SBA Express Loans Really Shortchange Entrepreneurs?" in *Entrepreneur* (Vol. 32, No. 4, April 2004, pp. 27) [36665], [39892], [44625], [46412], [51302], [56016]

"Quick fix: Help your IT staff save time and energy with PC Pinpoint" in *Entrepreneur* (Vol. 30, No. 2, February 2002, pp. 34) [6412], [34393]

"Quick and lightening" in *WorkingWoman* (Vol. 25, No. 6, June 2000, pp. 120) [49223], [49541]

"Quick Pick" in *Entrepreneur* (Vol. 32, No. 1, January 2004, pp. 79) [767], [3574], [8625], [18244], [18930], [20329], [24445], [29970], [47378], [47444], [48369], [50659], [53426]

Quick Printing [7852], [19917]

"A Quick Test of Your Managerial Skills" in *Sales & Marketing Management* (Vol. 158, October 2006, No. 10, pp. 19) [45576], [47445], [51783]

Quick Topics Newsletter [4326]

QuickBooks All-in-One Desk Reference for Dummies [229], [2947], [4776], [23141], [24020], [26331], [53427]

QuickBooks for the New Bean Counter: Business Owner's Guide 2006 [230], [1190], [22857], [26332], [53428]

QuickBooks Simple Start for Dummies [231], [2948], [4777], [23142], [24021], [26333], [53429], [54717]

QuickBooks X on Demand [232], [4778], [23143], [26334], [53430]

QuickBooks X for Dummies [233], [4779], [18790], [23144], [26335], [27166], [51303], [53431], [54718]

"A Quickened Pace; Lender Powers through Rapid Growth" in *Crain's Detroit Business* (Vol. 19, No. 42, October 20, 2003, pp. 1) [17429], [28666]

"A Quickened Pace; Lender Powers through Rapid Growth, Prepares for Interest Rates to Rise" in *Crain's Detroit Business* (Vol. 19) [17430], [28667]

"Quicker SBA Loans" in *Business Week* (No. 3698, September 11, 2000, pp. F6) [48378], [52937], [55792]

QuickFit Health Centers, Inc. [19525]

"QuickSeek" in *Entrepreneur* (Vol. 33, September 2005, No. 9, pp. 6) [708], [768], [28668], [34394], [35572], [45226], [47446]

"Quid Pro Quo: Bartering Is a Cashless Alternative to Conducting Business" in *Black Enterprise* (Vol. 35, September 2004, No. 2) [26714], [44240]

"Quiet Riot" in *Fast Company* (May 2001, pp. 50) [18558], [49542]

Patrick B Quigley & Associates Inc. [49647]

Quik Internet [14680]

Quikava [11394]

"QuikDrop Authorized by State of Illinois and State of MI to Offer eBay Drop-Off Store Franchises" in *PR Newswire* (Mar. 29, 2004) [1847], [7172], [18661], [38890], [52581]

"QuikTrip Policy Points to Dismissal" in *Kansas City Star* (February 24, 2005) [6772], [41929], [45577]

"The quilted picker-upper: Celebrating the highs (and the lows) of dotcom culture with a needle and thread" in *Entrepreneur* (Vol. 30) [14381], [22729], [34395]

Quimby's Cruising Guide [16743]

Quincy Area Chamber of Commerce [59647]

Quincy Business News [61157]

Quincy Chamber of Commerce [57726], [61408]

Quincy Valley Chamber of Commerce [66157]

Quinebaug Valley Community College–CSBDC Danielson–Small Business Development Center [58498]

James Quinn Agency Inc. [17465]

Quinnipiac Chamber of Commerce [58561]

Quinter Chamber of Commerce [60408]

Quirk's Marketing Research Review Data Processing and Statistical Analysis Directory Issue [16799]

Quirk's Marketing Research Review-Directory of Customer Satisfaction Research Providers Issue [16800]

Quit Your Day Job!: Develop a Successful Career As a Freelance Writer [8626], [9008], [18245]

Quitman-Brooks County Chamber of Commerce [59154]

"Quitting time!" in *Incentive* (Vol. 174, No. 10, October 2000, pp. 142) [54984]

Quizno's Canada Corp. [21935]

Quizno's Subs [8572], [21936]

Quma Learning Systems Inc. [55043]

"Qwest's Napoleonic Ambitions" in *Red Herring* (No. 106, October 15, 2001, pp. 47-50, 52) [5094], [14382], [37182]

R

R & D Magazine [52314]

"R and D Spending Jumps as Firms Foresee Recovery" in *Atlanta Business Chronicle* (Vol. 26, No. 10, August 15, 2003, pp. 1) [32648], [41930], [50950], [52183]

"R-E-S-P-E-C-T: The Changing Attitudes Toward Home-Based Businesses" in *My Business* (October/November 2002, pp. 45) [29971], [42712], [53932]

"Rabbi trusts give execs a false sense of security" in *Atlanta Business Chronicle* (Vol. 25, No. 20, October 25, 2002, pp. 2C) [10147], [15391], [26892], [38299]

"Rabbit on a Run" in *Business 2.0* (Vol. 7, January/February 2006, No. 1, pp. 69) [30935], [46413]

RAB.com [20377]

Rabun County Chamber of Commerce [59155]

"Race-Conscious Agenda: Poll Shows Most African Americans Want Affirmative Action Reform" in *Black Enterprise* (Vol. 34, Nov. 2003) [48379], [48592], [53933]

"Race Matters: Studies Show Race, Even Black-Sounding Names, Causes Doors To Shut" in *Black Enterprise* (Vol. 34, February 2004) [32054], [42388]

"The Race to Reach Critical Mass" in *Hispanic Business* (Vol. 22, No. 1/2, January/February, pp. 18, 20, 22) [30588], [47447]

Rachel Carson Council, Inc.–Library [19049]

"Racial divisions still hang over efforts to foster cooperation" in *Crain's Detroit Business* (Vol. 19, No. 17, April 28, 2003) [28669], [32649], [48593]

Racine Area Manufacturers and Commerce [66507]

"Racing for growth: an interview with Perkin Elmer's Greg Summe" in *Harvard Business Review* (Vol. 78, No. 6, Nov. - Dec. 2000, pp. 14) [28670]

Racquet and Tennis Club–Library [24580]

Radcliff-Hardin County Chamber of Commerce [60564]

Radford Chamber of Commerce [65940]

"Radiant heat company markets hotproduct" in *Business First of Buffalo* (Vol. 18, No. 46, August 12, 2002, pp. 15) [1027], [48779]

Radiation Safety Institute of Canada–Library [20394]

Radiator Reporter [22637]

The Radical New Road to Wealth: How to Raise Venture Capital for a New Business [55793]

"Radical Rendezvous: Bye-Bye Boring" in *Entrepreneur* (Vol. 31, No. 9, July 2003, pp. 79) [22551], [25006], [51784]

"Radical Sabbaticals" in *Success* (Vol. 47, No. 3, July 2000, pp. 68) [36666]

Radio Advertising Bureau [20294], [50539]
 Marketing Information Center [20387]

"Radio Broadcasters Rip Arbitron's Language-Weighting Policy" in *Hispanic Business* (January/February 2003, pp. 14) [20330]

"Radio Frequency Identification" in *Journal of Accountancy* [234], [2949], [24022], [26336], [27167], [41931], [44241]

"Radio weaves a web of listeners; Internet helps stations build an audience and advertising" in *Crain's Detroit Business* [14383], [20331], [47448]

The Radio Power Book [20298]

Radio Programming Profile [20332]

Radio-Television News Directors' Association [20295], [24369]

Radio-Television News Directors Association International Conference & Exhibition [20361], [24486]

Radio and Television Research Council [50745]

Radio World [20357]

RadioShack [7760]

Radiotechniques Engineering Corp. [20374]

Raeford - Hoke Chamber of Commerce [63419]

RAF Netventures / RAF Ventures [64574]

Rafters [12253]

"Raging Beauty: One-Time Female Boxing Champ is Winning Bouts in Sports" in *Black Enterprise* (Vol. 35, December 2004, No. 5, pp. 55) [23734], [56379]

"Rah-Rah rides" in *Entrepreneur* (Vol. 30, No. 2, February 2002, pp. 96) [1880], [35617]

Railroad Model Craftsman [8218]

Rainbow International [3378]

Rainbow Network Communications [22104]

Rainbow Station [5447]

"Raines Stays Cool Under Fire" in *Black Enterprise* (Vol. 35, December 2004, No. 5, pp. 34) [17431], [29457], [40629], [45578]

"Rainfall Helps Growers" in *Tribune* (March 2, 2005) [26530]

Rainsville Chamber of Commerce [56884]

Rainwater-Gish & Associates [38570]

Rainy River Community College–Small Business Development Center [61531]

"Raise Your Voice: A New Committee Promises to Give Small Businesses a Say in Accounting Standards. But Will It Help?" in *Entrepreneur* [235], [2950], [26337]

"Raising the Bar Again" in *Hispanic Business* (October 2002, pp. 72, 74) [12017], [36667]

"Raising the Bar" in *Hispanic Business* (June 2005, pp. 104, 106) [29458], [48380]

Raising Capital [44626], [48921], [55794]

Raising Capital: How to Write a Financing Proposal to Raise Venture Capital [55795]

Raising Capital in Turbulent Times [48931]

Raising Capital for Your Business: By Using Private Placement Offerings, Direct Public Offerings [55796]

"Raising children and working can be a challenge" in *Atlanta Business Chronicle* (Vol. 24, No. 13, August 31, 2001, pp. 38A) [36668], [39545]

Raising Money to Start of Expand Your Business Through a SCOR [38300], [55797]

"Raising Response Rates In Mail Surveys of Small Business Owners" in *Journal of Small Business Management* (Vol. 41, No. 3, July 2003) [39546]

"Raising the Roof: Cincinnati Realtor Undaunted by Race Riots" in *Black Enterprise* (Vol. 35, November 2004, No. 4, pp. 51) [20635], [20976], [47449]

"Raising the Woof: Make No Bones About It-This Bakery Takes Dog Food to a Whole New Level" in *Entrepreneur* (Vol. 32, July 2004) [2224], [19141], [37573], [38672], [56071]

Raising Your Dog with the Monks of New Skete [19126], [19169]

"Raleigh, N.C.-Area Employers Decline to Offer Dating Service as Perk" in *News & Observer* (February 1, 2004) [7067], [26893], [35036], [37765]

Ralls Chamber of Commerce [65458]

"A Rally Deferred" in *Black Enterprise* (Vol. 34, No. 2, September 2003, pp. 38) [10148], [15392], [38301]

Rally's Hamburgers [21937]

Ralph W. Miller Golf Library/Museum–Library [11298]

Ralph Wilson Equity Fund LLC [61459]

"Ralphs Grocery Co. Indicted on Charges Related to Hiring Striking Union Workers" in *Sacramento Bee* (December 16, 2005) [11658], [55308]

Ralston Area Chamber of Commerce [62292]

Ramada Franchise Systems, Inc. [12723]

Richard Ramis [16193]

Ramona Chamber of Commerce [57727]

Rampant Lion Publishers Inc. [58281]

"Ramps to Riches" in *Small Business Opportunities* (Vol. 17, May 2005, No. 3, pp. 66) [1963], [38891], [42713]

Ranch 1 [21938]

"Ranch Project Hailed as Farmland Preservation Model" in *Sacramento Bee* (December 8, 2005) [26531]

Rancho Cordova Chamber of Commerce [57728]

Rancho Cucamonga Chamber of Commerce [57729]

Rancho Mirage Chamber of Commerce [57730]

Rancho Santa Ana Botanic Garden–Library [11535]

Rand Capital Corporation [63158]

"R&D comes to services: Bank of America's pathbreaking experiments" in *Harvard Business Review* (Vol. 81, No. 4, April 2003, pp. 70) [44627], [50951], [52582]

R&D Village [60888]

"R&G: Growing Branches Through New Acquisitions" in *Orlando Business Journal* (Vol. 20, No. 6, July 25, 2003, pp. 31) [10149], [15393], [47760], [50155]

Randleman Chamber of Commerce [63420]

Randolph Area Chamber of Commerce [62552]

Randolph Chamber of Commerce [65795], [66508]

Randolph County Chamber of Commerce [57209]

Randolph County Convention and Visitors Bureau [66294]

Randolph County Economic Development Foundation–SBDC [59835]

Randolph Metrocom Chamber of Commerce [65459]

The Random House Guide to Business Writing [27671]

Random Lengths Weekly Report [16334]

Random Structures & Algorithms [52315]

R&S Design Computer Services Inc. [49454], [49648]

The Rangefinder [19248], [19317]

Rangeley Lakes Region Chamber of Commerce [60770]

Rangely Area Chamber of Commerce [58418]

Ranger Chamber of Commerce [65460]

Rank and File [5962]

Rankin County Chamber of Commerce [61831]

"Ranks of Banker-Brokers Growing at Local Banks" in *Business Journal-Portland* (Vol. 20, No. 22, August 1, 2003, pp. 3) [10033], [10150], [15168], [15394], [38302], [39084]

"Ranks are thinning in concierge industry" in *Denver Business Journal* (Vol. 52, No. 1, August 18, 2000, pp. 15A) [7144]

Ransford [3805], [29051]

Rantoul Area Chamber of Commerce [59648]

"A Rap for Manners: Angelo Ellerbee Refines the Rough on Urban Artist" in *Black Enterprise* (Vol. 34, No. 5, December 2003, pp. 66) [12908], [13375], [20154], [21424], [48224], [50466], [50660]

Rapid City Area Chamber of Commerce [64834]

Rapid City Small Business Development Center (Region I) [64808]

Rapid Communications in Mass Spectrometry [52316]

"Rapid Motion" in *Fast Company* (August 2001, pp. 102) [5095], [37183]

Rapid Refill Ink [7761]

"Rapid Response" in *Rough Notes* (Vol. 145, No. 9, September 2002, pp. 74) [13434], [14384], [34396], [43329]

Rapid Software Deployment [23145]

Rapid Team Deployment [35037]

"Rapiscan Opens Plant" in *Mississippi Business Journal* (Vol. 28, September 2006, No. 36, pp. 22) [41932], [48780]

Rappahannock Region SBDC at Fredericksburg **[65833]**

Rappahannock Region SBDC at Warsaw–University of Mary Washington **[65834]**

"Rapport & Revenue" in *Small Business Opportunities* (July 2005) **[27481]**, **[31828]**

Raspberry Junction **[8250]**

Rat **[19038]**

"The Rat Pack" in *Forbes* (Vol. 170, No. 9, October 28, 2002, pp. 228) **[1191]**, **[28671]**, **[36669]**

"Rate Increases Nail Homebuilding Sector" in *Business Journal-Portland* (Vol. 20, No. 26, August 29, 2003, pp. 18) **[7398]**, **[7458]**, **[13435]**, **[13917]**, **[29459]**, **[30385]**, **[43330]**, **[43467]**

"Rating the Governors" in *Inc.* (November 2006, pp. 95-98, 100, 102, 104, 106) **[29460]**, **[39893]**

Rating Guide to Franchises **[38892]**

"Rating reasonable risks" in *Women in Business* (Vol. 53, No. 4, July-August, 2001, pp: 18) **[30589]**, **[39547]**

"The Ratings Game" in *Entrepreneur* (Vol. 31, No. 8, August 2003, pp. 45) **[25943]**, **[34397]**, **[47450]**, **[51304]**

Rauch Guide to the U.S. Paint Industry **[18678]**

"Rave Reviews" in *My Business* (April/May 2003, pp. 42) **[36670]**, **[45579]**

Ravenna Area Chamber of Commerce **[62293]**, **[63777]**

Raving Fans: A Revolutionary Approach to Customer Service **[31829]**

"Raw Deal: Avoid These Consumer Scams at all Costs" in *Black Enterprise* (Vol. 35, September 2004, No. 2, pp. 185) **[22341]**, **[29461]**, **[30247]**

"Raw Deal" in *Forbes* (December 25, 2000, pp. 238) **[19641]**, **[38893]**

"Raw-Material Costs Put Squeeze on JCI" in *Crain's Detroit Business* (Vol. 21, January 24, 2005, No. 4, pp. 7) **[1964]**, **[18115]**, **[46414]**

Rawlins-Carbon County Chamber of Commerce **[66625]**

Rawlins County Genealogical Society–Library **[11070]**

"Ray-gulation" in *Inc.* (July 1, 2003) **[23838]**, **[40630]**

"Ray of hope?" in *Entrepreneur* (Vol. 31, No. 5, May 2003, pp. 45) **[44628]**, **[55798]**

Raymore Chamber of Commerce **[62027]**

Rayne Chamber of Commerce **[60664]**

"Raytheon, SRM Awarded U.S. Navy Contracts" in *Providence Business News* (Vol. 18, No. 15, July 28, 2003, pp. 3) **[40081]**

Raytown Area Chamber of Commerce **[62028]**

RBC Ventures, Inc. **[64117]**

"RBS Takes Stake in Home Developer" in *Crain's Detroit Business* (Vol. 21, January 10, 2005, No. 2, pp. 5) **[7459]**, **[20636]**, **[50156]**

RCT Bioventures NE LLC **[61111]**

R.D. Network Inc. **[11713]**, **[12412]**, **[13577]**, **[18484]**, **[21729]**

RDS Associates Inc. **[58635]**

Re-Bath, LLC **[10542]**, **[19790]**

Re/Max **[20753]**

Re-News **[21274]**

REA/OPB–Executive Office of the Governor–Florida State Data Center **[66851]**

"Reaching For Financial Success" in *Black Enterprise* (Vol. 34, No. 5, December 2003, pp. 71) **[10151]**, **[15395]**, **[38303]**

"Reaching For Financial Success: Our 2002 Financial Fitness Contest Winners Are Achieving Their Goals" in *Black Enterprise* (Vol. 34) **[10152]**, **[15396]**, **[38304]**

"Reaching Out: Finding Good Leads Takes More Than Just Making a Few Phone Calls." in *Entrepreneur* (Vol. 32, December 2004, No. 12) **[51785]**

"Reaching Out to Low-Wage Countries" in *Washington Business Journal* (Vol. 22, September 26, 2003) **[41933]**, **[43791]**, **[48594]**

"Reaching the silver screen" in *Black Enterprise* (Vol. 32, No. 5, December 20) **[9738]**, **[48381]**

"Reaching for less than the sky: as boldest fall, modest dreamers fly on" in *The New York Times* (December 13, 2000, pp. D1, H1) **[14385]**, **[29972]**, **[34398]**, **[37184]**

"Reaching the Small Business Accounting Market" in *Accounting Today* (Vol. 14, No. 12, July 10, 2000, pp. 41) **[23146]**, **[26338]**, **[34399]**, **[53432]**

"Reaching for the Stars" in *Black Enterprise* (Vol. 34, No. 2, September 2003, pp. 48) **[11762]**, **[11800]**, **[48922]**

"Reaching Their Potential" in *Rough Notes* (Vol. 146, No. 3, March 2003, pp. 42) **[13436]**, **[43331]**

"ReachLocal" in *Entrepreneur* (Vol. 33, August 2005, No. 8, pp. 4) **[709]**, **[769]**, **[34400]**, **[45231]**, **[47451]**

"Read My Bytes" in *Success* (Vol. 47, No. 3, July 2000, pp. 22) **[9156]**

"Read fine print yearly to avoid costly contractual obligations" in *Boston Business Journal* (Vol. 22, No. 14, May 10, 2002, pp. 42) **[29462]**

"Read a plant-fast" in *Harvard Business Review* (Vol. 80, No. 5, May 2002, pp. 105) **[46415]**

"Read the fine print" in *Black Enterprise* (Vol. 33, No. 7, February 2003, pp. 6) **[40631]**, **[48382]**

"Read Smart, Grow Smart" in *Fast Company* (May 2001, pp. 202) **[6276]**, **[13773]**, **[14386]**, **[27732]**, **[33480]**, **[35618]**

Reader's Digest–Marketing Information Center **[50742]**

Reader's Digest Association–Editorial Research Library **[18990]**

Reading Chamber of Commerce **[63778]**

Reading Eagle (September 21, 2003); "Neon Sign Makers Light Up Reading, Pa. Area" in **[1952]**, **[22793]**

Reading Financial Reports: The Income Statement **[38500]**

Reading Friends Franchise Co. **[5448]**

Reading-North Reading Chamber of Commerce **[60991]**

"Reading for retention" in *Women in Business* (Vol. 53, No. 4, July-August, 2001, pp. 26) **[33216]**, **[39548]**

"Reading, writing, and protection" in *Black Enterprise* (Vol. 32, No. 5,) **[29463]**, **[39549]**

"Ready Business: www.ready.gov" in *Entrepreneur* (Vol. 33, February 2005, No. 2, pp. 8) **[14387]**, **[22342]**

Ready Decks Franchise Systems Inc. **[4513]**

"Ready For Launch" in *My Business* (June/July 2002, pp. 16) **[46586]**, **[48689]**, **[50511]**

"Ready-for-Prime-Time Players" in *Hispanic Business* (Vol. 23, No. 10, October, 2001, pp. 22) **[24446]**

"Ready to land" in *Crain's Detroit Business* (Vol. 19, No. 16, April 21, 2003, pp. 11) **[6773]**, **[14388]**, **[30407]**, **[34401]**, **[41934]**

"Ready for Progress" in *Hispanic Business* (January/February 2005, pp. 44, 46, 48) **[40632]**, **[48383]**

"Ready? Set? Search! Rev Up Your Sales With Comparison-Shopping Engines" in *Entrepreneur* (Vol. 31, No. 9, September 2003, pp. 87) **[31061]**, **[34402]**, **[47452]**, **[51786]**

"Ready, Set Strategize" in *Inc.* (October 2005, pp. 41-42, 44, 46) **[29973]**, **[39550]**

"Ready To Go: How An Online Tool Helped One Company Speed Distribution of Marketing Materials To Reps" in *Sales & Marketing Management* **[13437]**, **[14389]**, **[43332]**, **[47453]**, **[51787]**, **[54985]**

Real-Comp Inc.–RPMW (Real Comp) **[20253]**

"The Real Deal" in *Entrepreneur* (Vol. 33, September 2005, No. 9, pp. 74) **[28806]**, **[29464]**, **[29974]**, **[30590]**, **[36671]**, **[41853]**, **[43792]**, **[47454]**

"Real Estate Ambitions" in *Black Enterprise* (Vol. 37, January 2007, No. 6, pp. 101) **[7460]**, **[20637]**, **[20977]**, **[33217]**, **[36672]**, **[50952]**

Real Estate Analyzer **[20764]**

Real Estate Bar Association for Massachusetts–Library **[20771]**, **[21113]**

Real Estate Broker's Insider **[20726]**, **[21059]**

"Real Estate" in *Business Week* (December 19, 2005, No. 3964, pp. 30-32) **[20638]**, **[20978]**

"Real Estate Company Expands, Changes Name" in *Bellingham Business Journal* (January 2007, pp. 3) **[20639]**, **[28672]**, **[30169]**, **[32650]**

Real Estate Financing **[21067]**

Real Estate Forum **[20727]**

Real Estate Home Inspection: A Comprehensive Study **[3241]**

Real Estate Home Inspection: Mastering the Profession **[3242]**

"Real Estate Horrors" in *Black Enterprise* (Vol. 32, No. 6, January 2002, pp. 86) **[17432]**, **[20640]**, **[20979]**, **[30248]**

"Real Estate Insiders to Reveal Forecasts for the Coming Year" in *Crain's Detroit Business* (Vol. 19, No. 1, January 6, 2003, pp. 6) **[20641]**, **[20980]**, **[28673]**, **[43793]**

The Real Estate Investors Tax Guide **[20981]**

Real Estate Law Report **[20728]**

Real Estate Loopholes: Secrets of Successful Real Estate Investing **[20642]**, **[20982]**

Real Estate New York **[1384]**

"Real Estate on New York Business.com" in *Crain's New York Business* (Vol. 22, December 4, 2006, No. 49, pp. 22) **[3421]**, **[14390]**, **[20643]**, **[20983]**, **[25944]**, **[43031]**

"Real Estate Niches Continue as Bright Spots" in *Crain's Detroit Business* (Vol. 22, November 27, 2006, No. 48, pp. 18) **[20644]**, **[20984]**, **[32651]**, **[52938]**, **[53934]**

"Real Estate Now" in *Inc.* (September 1, 2004) **[20645]**

"Real Estate One unites luxury sales under Max Broock name" in *Crain's Detroit Business* (Vol. 19, No. 14, April 7, 2003, pp. 46) **[20646]**, **[20985]**

The Real Estate Pro's Internet Edge - Agent's Edition: Maximizing Your Business on the World Wide Web **[20647]**

"Real Estate Reality Check" in *Black Enterprise* (Vol. 35, September 2004, No. 2, pp. 42) **[15397]**, **[20648]**, **[20986]**

Real Estate Research Institute **[21117]**

Real Estate Review **[20729]**

"Real Estate" in *Sarasota Herald Tribune* (January 20, 2003, pp. 5) **[19346]**, **[38673]**

Real Estate Software Directory and Catalog **[20709]**

The Real Estate Success Series **[51975]**

Real Estate Weekly **[20730]**

"The Real New Economy" in *Harvard Business Review* (Vol. 81, No. 10, October 2003, pp. 104) **[32652]**

"The Real Pepsi Challenge" in *New York Times* (February 4, 2007, pp. 7) **[26894]**, **[47455]**

Real Selling: How to Increase Sales in Growing Companies **[51976]**

"A real steal" in *Entrepreneur* (Vol. 31, No. 5, May 2003, pp. 45) **[30249]**, **[31581]**

"Reality Check: Even the Best Execs Can Blow It When They Lose Tough" in *Entrepreneur* (Vol. 31, No. 8, August 2003, pp. 25) **[29975]**, **[33481]**

"Reality Check" in *InfoWorld* (Vol. 27, May 16, 2005, No. 20, pp. 22) **[6277]**, **[29976]**, **[39551]**

"Reality check: threat of lawsuit changes discriminatory payment practices" in *Black Enterprise* (Vol. 33, No. 3, Oct. 2002, pp. 178) **[29465]**, **[30399]**, **[32055]**, **[51305]**, **[53533]**

"Reality Checker" in *Forbes* (February 19, 2001, pp. 95) **[31207]**, **[36673]**, **[55799]**

"Reality TV for Business" in *Hispanic Business* (September 2003, pp. 74) **[6774]**, **[27482]**, **[41935]**, **[49224]**

"Realizing the Spirit and Impact of Adam Smith's Capitalism through Entrepreneurship" in *Journal of Business Ethics* (Vol.46, Sept.03) **[36674]**, **[39552]**

Realtor Magazine **[20731]**, **[21060]**

Realtor Magazine (Vol. 35, No. 9, September 2002, pp. 22); "Trust toppers" in **[39642]**

Realtors Land Institute **[20410]**

Realtors Land Institute Newsletter **[20732]**

Realty Direct **[17467]**

Realty Executives International **[20754]**

"Reap What You Grow" in *Entrepreneur.com* (Vol. 34, February 2006, No. 2, pp. 52) **[15398]**, **[38305]**

"Rearrangement: Sellers of office furniture go through changes" in *Crain's Detroit Business* (Vol. 18, No. 19, May 13, 2002, pp. 13) **[18559]**, **[18611]**, **[28674]**

"A Reason for Ranting" in *Black Enterprise* (Vol. 36, November 2005, No. 4, pp. 161) **[27483]**, **[36675]**

"A Reason to Smile" in *Black Enterprise* (Vol. 34, No. 2, September 2003, pp. 62) **[36676]**, **[41085]**, **[56380]**

"Reasons to celebrate" in *Incentive* (Vol. 174, No. 9, September 2000, pp. 96) **[35038]**

"Reawakening your passion for work" in *Harvard Business Review* (Vol. 80, No. 4, April 2002, pp. 86) **[39553]**

Rebok Memorial Library **[54389]**

"(Re)Born To Be Wild" in *Inc.* (Volume 28, January 2006, No. 1, pp. 70-77) **[17489]**, **[28675]**

"Rebound Continues" in *My Business* (October/November 2003, pp. 50) **[28676]**, **[32653]**

"Rebound or Release?" in *Black Enterprise* (Vol. 34, No. 3, October 2003, pp. 69) **[10153]**, **[15399]**, **[38306]**

"Rebuilding Interest; Bank One Brings in New Credit Chief to Ease Lending Rules, Win Back Middle-Market Business" in *Crain's Detroit Business* **[38307]**, **[44629]**

"Rebuilding Interest" in *Crain's Detroit Business* (Vol. 19, No. 45, November 10, 2003, pp. 1) **[38308]**, **[44630]**

"Rebuilding and Revitalizing Lower Manhattan" in *Venture Capital Journal* (Vol. 42, No. 9, September 2002, pp. 32) **[36677]**, **[55800]**

"Rebuilding Shangri-la" in *Inc.* (September 2005, pp. 154-159) **[12620]**, **[21593]**, **[33218]**, **[35039]**

"Rebuilding Your Business With Former and Current Customers" in *Ingram's* (Vol. 27, No. 8, August 2001, pp. 19) **[28677]**, **[31830]**, **[35040]**

Rec Room Publishing Inc. **[66250]**

Receil it Professional Ceiling Restoration **[52633]**

"Recent State Legislative Developments Concerning Employment Discrimination..." in *Employment Relations Today* (Summer 2000, pp. 89) **[32056]**, **[40633]**

"Recession session" in *Entrepreneur* (Vol. 30, No. 3, March 2002, pp.) **[28678]**, **[32654]**, **[36678]**, **[38309]**, **[41936]**, **[45580]**, **[47456]**

"Recession takes its toll" in *Black Enterprise* (Vol. 33, No. 6, Jan. 2003, pp. 26) **[28679]**, **[32655]**

"Recharge Life and Business With a Vacation" in *Crain's Detroit Business* (Vol. 22, December 18, 2006, No. 51, pp. 14) **[35041]**, **[42885]**, **[45581]**

Recinto Universitario De Mayaguez–Universidad de Puerto Rico **[66971]**

"Recipe for Disaster?" in *Entrepreneur* (Vol. 32, November 2004, No. 11, pp. 75) **[13438]**, **[43333]**

"Recipe for Growth" in *Fast Company* (November 2001, pp. 40) **[1417]**, **[28680]**, **[44130]**

"Recipe for success in construction mediation" in *Dispute Resolution Journal* (Vol. 56, No. 2, May-July 2001, pp. 16) **[7461]**, **[17056]**, **[27484]**

"A Recipe for Perfection" in *Inc.* (July 1, 2003) **[12621]**, **[31831]**

"Recipe for Profit" in *Small Business Opportunities* (Fall 2005) **[2225]**, **[38894]**

"Recipe for Riches" in *Small Business Opportunities* (Vol. 16, No. 1, January 2004, pp. 72) **[8504]**, **[21409]**, **[37574]**, **[38674]**

"A Recipe for Success" in *Black Enterprise* (Vol. 36, February 2006, No. 7, pp. 165) **[21594]**, **[54243]**

"Recipe for Success: Smart Partnering Can Transform a Lone Inventor Into a Market Force" in *Entrepreneur* (Vol. 32, September 2004) **[12205]**, **[44131]**

Reckitt Benckiser, Inc.–Knowledge Resource Center **[7948]**

Recognition Review **[9302]**

"Recognition for Volunteer" in *San Diego Business Journal* (Vol. 28, January 15, 2007, No. 3, pp. 33) **[20649]**, **[56381]**

"Recognize this Voice? Speech Recognition Reduces Keyboard Tedium" in *Black Enterprise* (Vol. 36, February 2006, No. 7, pp. 68) **[4780]**, **[6775]**, **[23147]**, **[49225]**, **[53433]**

"Recognizing Gifted Entrepreneurs" in *Black Enterprise* (Vol. 34, No. 3, October 2003, pp. 150) **[36679]**, **[48384]**

Recon For Investors (RFI) **[10293]**, **[13111]**, **[29044]**

"Reconnaissance" in *Inc.* (August 2005, pp. 53-54) **[36680]**, **[39554]**

The Record (November 6, 2005); "A Refreshing Way to Make a Living" in **[11343]**, **[26896]**, **[35045]**

The Record (November 8, 2005); "AIG Plans to Cut 27 Jobs at Neptune, N.J., Offices" in **[13181]**, **[26739]**, **[27759]**, **[32239]**, **[43072]**

The Record (February 17, 2004); "Arson Charges Spotlight Downtown Bergenfield, N.J., Business Slump" in **[2520]**, **[11312]**, **[27787]**

The Record (December 23, 2002); "Business Briefs" in **[95]**, **[8451]**, **[10799]**, **[11784]**, **[19381]**, **[24230]**

The Record (November 8, 2005); "Cablevision Plans Faster Internet Service Without Raising Price" in **[4096]**, **[13880]**, **[31016]**

The Record (November 18, 2005); "CO-OP Network Makes Deal With 7-Eleven" in **[7771]**, **[9889]**, **[49864]**

The Record (February 12, 2005); "Customers Must Look Out for Themselves in 'Phishing' E-mail Situations" in **[13943]**, **[22208]**, **[30210]**

The Record (November 9, 2005); "Cuts in Retail, Manufacturing Hurt Northern New Jersey's Job Growth" in **[28000]**, **[42214]**, **[46256]**, **[51120]**

The Record (November 13, 2005); "Department-Store Chain Boosts N.J. Index" in **[14914]**, **[28016]**, **[51127]**

The Record (November 8, 2005); "Divide and Prosper" in **[12545]**, **[20493]**, **[25177]**

The Record (November 4, 2005); "Expanding Its Menu and Changing Its Business Strategy Have Helped IHOP" in **[21501]**, **[38769]**

The Record (November 21, 2005); "Greenhouse Gas Limits are Called Affordable" in **[37290]**, **[40423]**

The Record (November 18, 2005); "Hazlet, N.J., Firm Stays Ahead of Real Estate Trends" in **[20223]**, **[20889]**, **[36265]**

The Record (November 14, 2005); "Holiday Headache" in **[26826]**, **[42288]**

The Record (November 16, 2005); "House Party Over? High Cost of Living in New Jersey Continues" in **[20541]**, **[32489]**

The Record (November 4, 2005); "IRS Boosts Enforcement Collections" in **[40477]**, **[54615]**

The Record (August 25, 2003); "Lodi, Calif., Couple Combines Winery with Bed and Breakfast" in **[2446]**, **[23492]**

The Record (November 7, 2005); "Making a Dent" in **[2030]**, **[22615]**, **[33160]**

The Record (November 8, 2005); "Manufacturer AmerTac Buys Night Light Maker" in **[9113]**, **[15249]**, **[46357]**, **[50070]**

The Record (November 13, 2005); "Music Instructor Gives Students Confidence to Get Up On Stage" in **[17600]**, **[56328]**

The Record (November 18, 2005); "New Jersey Acting Governor Seeks Deal to Ban Smoking in Bars, Eateries" in **[2346]**, **[21571]**, **[40550]**

The Record (November 18, 2005); "New Jersey Jobless Rate Down, But Jobs Lost" in **[28544]**, **[42359]**

The Record (November 12, 2005); "Not Just Telenovelas" in **[740]**, **[4118]**, **[24440]**, **[48588]**, **[53889]**

The Record (November 10, 2005); "Numbers Prove Accountants Are On a Roll" in **[211]**, **[2941]**, **[24005]**, **[26307]**

The Record (November 11, 2005); "NYC Increases Hotel Security" in **[12608]**, **[22316]**

The Record (November 10, 2005); "Pathmark Adds Online Shopping Middletown, N.J., Store" in **[11650]**, **[34328]**

The Record (January 13, 2003); "Professional Organizer Gives Tips on Cleaning Up Messy Desks" in **[20025]**, **[52576]**

"Record Profits Lead to Record Bonus for Goldman Sachs CEO" in *San Diego Business Journal* (Vol. 28, January 15, 2007, No. 3, pp. 10) **[10154]**, **[15400]**, **[28681]**

The Record (November 19, 2005); "Restaurants are Hiring Workers Faster than Other Economic Sectors" in **[21607]**, **[28701]**, **[42397]**

The Record (November 4, 2005); "Retailers Helped by Chill, Gas Price Dip" in **[32668]**, **[51323]**

The Record (November 3, 2005); "Retirement Communities Grow in Popularity in New Jersey" in **[7471]**, **[53943]**

The Record (November 5, 2002); "Second 'Mix-In' Ice Cream Shop Comes to Stockton, Calif." in **[12788]**, **[30945]**

"Record setting: music industry veteran forms a label for Latin music performers who sing in English" in *Hispanic Business* (Jul-Aug2000) **[21129]**, **[35619]**

The Record (November 12, 2005); "Spotlight on Retailing" in **[5281]**, **[7174]**, **[51366]**, **[56413]**

The Record (November 6, 2005); "This Marketing Pro's Aim is to Clear the Clutter" in **[20027]**, **[47634]**

The Record (November 5, 2005); "Towns, Counties Grow With Interest" in **[10215]**, **[15538]**, **[38423]**, **[40778]**

The Record (November 17, 2005); "Verizon Told to Widen Service" in **[5161]**, **[28967]**, **[40804]**

The Record (November 15, 2005); "Workplace Air 'Unfit'" in **[2360]**, **[10892]**, **[21670]**, **[56592]**

The Record (November 13, 2005); "Y Stay Put? Generation Y Bounces From Job to Job" in **[42473]**, **[54093]**

Recording Industry Association of America **[21137]** Reference Library **[21164]**

ReCourses Inc. **[869]**, **[20191]**, **[30650]**

"Recover Deleted E-Mail" in *PC World* (Vol. 23, April 2005, No. 4, pp. 150) **[27672]**, **[53434]**

"Recovering from Tragedy - How Alta Has Coped with Losses" in *Venture Capital Journal* (Vol. 42, No. 9, September 2002, pp. 24-25) **[36681]**, **[54244]**, **[55801]**

"Recovering Yuppie turns yoga hobby into a business" in *Sarasota Herald Tribune* (September 9, 2002, pp. 9) **[17875]**, **[35620]**

Recovery Communications Inc. **[54370]**

"Recovery Continues" in *My Business* (June/July 2002, pp. 49) **[28682]**, **[32656]**

"Recovery for Some; Chicago's Economy Will Lag the State and Nation Next Year" in *Crains Chicago Business* (Vol. 26, No. 51) **[10037]**, **[10155]**, **[12622]**, **[13080]**, **[15174]**, **[15401]**, **[20020]**, **[20236]**, **[25237]**, **[26070]**, **[28683]**, **[29656]**, **[30314]**, **[30408]**, **[31298]**, **[31737]**, **[32161]**, **[32657]**, **[38310]**, **[39734]**

"Recovery driving shaky growth in transportation" in *Atlanta Business Chronicle* (Vol. 25, January 10, 2003, No. 31, pp. 20A) **[25407]**, **[28684]**, **[32658]**

"Recovery Will Have to Wait" in *Washington Business Journal* (Vol. 22, No. 18, September 5, 2003, pp. 1) **[20650]**, **[20987]**, **[32659]**

"Recovery Will Probably Take a While Yet" in *Crain's Detroit Business* (Vol. 19, No. 42, October 20, 2003, pp. 8) **[28685]**, **[29626]**, **[31740]**, **[32660]**

"Recreation" in *Entrepreneur* (Vol. 32, No. 1, January 2004, pp. 234) **[5914]**, **[8908]**, **[12206]**, **[12309]**, **[23631]**, **[38895]**

"Recreation" in *Inc.* (Volume 27, July 2005, No. 7, pp. 57-58) **[31832]**, **[35042]**, **[42389]**, **[45582]**

Recreation Vehicle Dealers Association of America **[21167]**

Recreation Vehicle Industry Association **[21168]**

Recreation Vehicle Industry Association-Membership Directory and Industry Buyer's Guide **[21174]**

Recreation Vehicle Rental Association **[2071]**, **[21169]**

"Recreational/Personal Watercraft Market" in *Rough Notes* (Vol. 145, No. 2, February 2003, pp. 48) **[13439]**, **[16744]**, **[28686]**, **[32661]**, **[43334]**

Red Herring (No. 105, October 1, 2001, pp. 82-83); "Explained: iSCSI: SAN of the times" in **[6246]**, **[22989]**

Red Herring (Jan. 2003, pp. 42); "Exposed!" in **[44515]**, **[55599]**

Red Herring (March 2003, pp. 52); "Extreme hunter scores big with tiny funds" in **[41677]**, **[46281]**, **[50868]**, **[52094]**

Red Herring (No. 99, June 15 & July 1, 2001, pp. 110, 112-113); "Fabricating Photons" in **[6935]**, **[41679]**, **[50871]**

Red Herring (No. 76, March 2000, pp. 92); "Five things to remember when raising money" in **[55383]**

Red Herring (March 2003, pp. 66); "For some companies, it pays to be private" in **[39340]**, **[51484]**, **[53739]**

Red Herring (No. 99, June 15 & July 1, 2001, pp. 34-35); "Forward: Patents" in **[29253]**, **[41697]**, **[44044]**

Red Herring (No. 102, August 15, 2001, pp. 22-23); "Forward: Startups: Network-chip makers may be in danger of extinction" in **[6912]**, **[15013]**, **[41454]**, **[49948]**

Red Herring (No. 105, October 1, 2001, pp. 30-31); "Forward: Thomas Middelhoff faces the music at Bertelsmann" in **[17743]**, **[33918]**, **[55628]**

Red Herring (No. 103, September 1, 2001, pp. 36); "From the Ground Floor: From hosted applications to Web services" in **[6913]**, **[13750]**

Red Herring (No. 99, June 15 & July 1, 2001, pp. 42, 44); "From the Ground Floor: The business paths to nanotech" in **[41455]**, **[44415]**, **[55387]**

Red Herring (No. 106, October 15, 2001, pp. 18); "Gadget: Danger Hiptop" in **[4993]**, **[6936]**, **[49041]**

Red Herring (No. 103, September 1, 2001, pp. 18); "Gadget: Why I Wi-Fi" in **[6937]**, **[14062]**, **[41704]**

Red Herring (January 2003, pp. 23); "GeoPhoenix is ready for its close-up" in **[4994]**, **[48737]**

Red Herring (No. 103, September 1, 2001, pp. 54-58, 60); "Good Health is Just a Costly Way to Die" in **[17186]**, **[52113]**

Red Herring (No. 106, October 15, 2001, pp. 35); "Good night, sweetheart" in **[28221]**, **[37142]**

Red Herring (No. 103, September 1, 2001, pp. 28); "Graphiti: Eking out e-commerce" in **[14091]**, **[28226]**, **[33978]**, **[51172]**

Red Herring (No. 102, August 15, 2001, pp. 26); "Graphiti: Online demographics" in **[14092]**, **[28227]**

Red Herring (No. 99, June 15 & July 1, 2001, pp. 40-41); "Graphiti: commercial real estate retrenches" in **[20518]**, **[20883]**

Red Herring (No. 106, October 15, 2001, pp. 92); "Greed Is Bad" in **[29275]**, **[37143]**, **[44053]**, **[44305]**

Red Herring (No. 87, December 18, 2000, pp. 88-92, 94); "Hatching a Better Incubator" in **[43054]**, **[55658]**

Red Herring (No. 76, March 2000, pp. 58); "Homeless entrepreneurs swap shopping carts" in **[13756]**, **[33446]**, **[35509]**

Red Herring (No. 105, October 1, 2001, pp. 78-79); "How Data Mining Makes Businesses Smarter" in **[4690]**, **[6255]**, **[23033]**, **[31738]**

Red Herring (No. 103, September 1, 2001, pp. 72-73); "How microturbines generate megawatts" in **[37298]**, **[41753]**

Red Herring (No. 99, June 15 & July 1, 2001, pp. 114, 116); "Image is Everything" in **[4190]**, **[41464]**, **[50793]**

Red Herring (No. 99, June 15 & July 1, 2001, pp. 140); "Introducing the art of second-derivative investing" in **[15138]**, **[38146]**

Red Herring (No. 102, August 15, 2001, pp. 25); "Invention: Scientist puts circuits on paper" in **[41775]**, **[44077]**, **[50900]**

Red Herring (No. 102, August 15, 2001, pp. 82-83); "Investor: Advance Notification" in **[15154]**, **[50008]**, **[52432]**

Red Herring (No. 99, June 15 & July 1, 2001, pp. 130, 132); "Investor: Boarding School" in **[26270]**, **[27142]**, **[38156]**, **[53811]**

Red Herring (No. 103, September 1, 2001, pp. 82-83); "Investor: Earnings projections for technology are still too lofty" in **[28342]**, **[41776]**

Red Herring (No. 106, October 15, 2001, pp. 36); "Investors don't want their MeVC" in **[55685]**

Red Herring (No. 99, June 15 & July 1, 2001, pp. 61); "IPO Review" in **[15174]**, **[44555]**, **[50017]**, **[55692]**

Red Herring (No. 99, June 15 & July 1, 2001, pp. 118); "Jazzin' Up the Chips" in **[6948]**, **[41785]**, **[50904]**

Red Herring (January 2003, pp. 26); "Just the Tiqit" in **[6699]**, **[28371]**, **[41791]**, **[48759]**, **[52136]**

Red Herring (No. 106, October 15, 2001, pp. 30); "Let the games begin" in **[1111]**, **[14201]**, **[23066]**, **[28407]**

Red Herring (January 2003, pp. 72); "Long in the Tooth" in **[10074]**, **[15232]**, **[28434]**, **[41814]**

Red Herring (No. 106, October 15, 2001, pp. 42); "Market Values: The virtue of unselfishness" in **[36484]**

Red Herring (No. 99, June 15 & July 1, 2001, pp. 108); "Marriage of Expedience" in **[6951]**, **[41829]**, **[50919]**

Red Herring (No. 105, October 1, 2001, pp. 64-69); "Mechanical Minds" in **[37166]**, **[50921]**

Red Herring (No. 103, September 1, 2001, pp. 73); "Microeconomics" in **[28484]**, **[37310]**, **[41834]**

Red Herring (No. 105, October 1, 2001, pp. 94); "More Money: Bankers focus on follow-ons" in **[15276]**, **[44596]**

Red Herring (January 2003, pp. 69); "Mr. Koogle's Failed Return" in **[35575]**, **[41470]**

Red Herring (January 2003, pp. 72); "MSCI-Red Herring Index" in **[2725]**, **[3562]**, **[4735]**, **[5065]**, **[6730]**, **[14258]**, **[18912]**, **[23093]**, **[24435]**, **[28521]**, **[34216]**, **[41850]**, **[44342]**

Red Herring (No. 99, June 15 & July 1, 2001, pp. 48-50); "Nanomaterials: The Road to Lilliput" in **[41853]**, **[50929]**

Red Herring (No. 99, June 15 & July 1, 2001, pp. 46-47); "Nanotech Grows" in **[28524]**, **[41854]**, **[50930]**

Red Herring (March 2003, pp. 62); "Nanotechnology sector analysis" in **[28525]**, **[46382]**, **[50931]**, **[52157]**

Red Herring (No. 102, August 15, 2001, pp. 48-50, 52-53); "New Habits Die Hard" in **[14283]**, **[28541]**

Red Herring (No. 99, June 15 & July 1, 2001, pp. 138); "New Issues: There's a Side Door into the Public Markets" in **[15298]**, **[32593]**, **[38242]**, **[50096]**

Red Herring (No. 106, October 15, 2001, pp. 94); "No IPO market? No problem. Call Ravisent" in **[4742]**, **[14297]**, **[15304]**, **[23101]**, **[50105]**

Red Herring (No. 105, October 1, 2001, pp. 92); "No Respect: ONI Systems is the ugly stepchild of the networking market" in **[6954]**, **[28566]**, **[37171]**

Red Herring (No. 103, September 1, 2001, pp. 85); "Office Space: It's better to rent than own" in **[26308]**, **[27158]**, **[52708]**

Red Herring (No. 106, October 15, 2001, pp. 62-64, 66); "On the Edge" in **[4580]**, **[4892]**, **[6917]**, **[22886]**, **[37071]**, **[55411]**

Red Herring (No. 75, February 2000, pp. 148-150, 152, 154, 156, 158); "On the Internet Nobody Knows You're Not a VC" in **[13766]**, **[33472]**, **[35592]**, **[55412]**

Red Herring (No. 99, June 15 & July 1, 2001, pp. 36, 38); "One To Watch: Danger looms large for the Blackberry" in **[14311]**, **[44108]**

Red Herring (No. 103, September 1, 2001, pp. 26); "One to Watch: A Russian entrepreneur scores a wireless hit with teenagers" in **[35595]**, **[41472]**

Red Herring (No. 105, October 1, 2001, pp. 26); "One to Watch: Alpiri hopes to win the name game in e-commerce" in **[33473]**, **[35596]**

Red Herring (No. 102, August 15, 2001, pp. 24); "One to Watch: KnowNow tackles two-way computing" in **[6918]**, **[13768]**, **[35597]**, **[41473]**

Red Herring (Jan. 2003); "Operation no safe haven: there's $400 billion in unregulated money stashed in offshore hedge accounts" in **[216]**, **[24008]**, **[26313]**, **[29429]**, **[37486]**, **[54688]**

Red Herring (March 2003, pp. 50); "Opportunities emerge in a new age of miracle materials. (Nanotechnology)" in **[41889]**, **[46397]**, **[50939]**, **[52166]**

Red Herring (No. 102, August 15, 2001, pp. 86); "Optics' Second Wave: Test-and-measurement stocks burn brightly" in **[6956]**, **[14327]**, **[28598]**, **[41890]**

Red Herring (No. 105, October 1, 2001, pp. 38); "Paying the piper for Internet access" in **[14341]**, **[34334]**, **[54696]**

Red Herring (No. 103, September 1, 2001, pp. 62-65); "Peer Pressure" in **[14343]**, **[25931]**, **[41898]**

Red Herring (No. 102, August 15, 2001, pp. 35); "Peter Drucker, still essential" in **[39522]**, **[45532]**

Red Herring (No. 106, October 15, 2001, pp. 24-25); "Policy: The future of telecom lies at the steps of Capitol Hill" in **[5090]**, **[14359]**, **[37179]**, **[40616]**

"The Red Herring Portfolio: Another market false start" in *Red Herring* (No. 105, October 1, 2001, pp. 102) **[15402]**, **[28687]**

"The Red Herring Portfolio: Going nowhere fast" in *Red Herring* (No. 103, September 1, 2001, pp. 96) **[28688]**, **[41937]**

"The Red Herring Portfolio: Not a stellar performance" in *Red Herring* (No. 105, October 1, 2001, pp. 104) **[15403]**, **[28689]**

"The Red Herring Portfolio" in *Red Herring* (No. 99, June 15 & July 1, 2001, pp. 146) **[15404]**, **[28690]**

"The Red Herring Portfolio: Stuck inside a sideways pattern with the market" in *Red Herring* (No. 102, August 15, 2001, pp.96) **[28691]**, **[41938]**

Red Herring (January 2003, pp. 60); "Positive defense for networks" in **[22328]**, **[41911]**, **[52177]**

Red Herring (No. 103, September 1, 2001, pp. 74); "Powering the imagination" in **[41915]**, **[52179]**

Red Herring (No. 87, December 18, 2000, pp. 44, 46); "Priority packets pay to fly first class" in **[27731]**, **[36645]**, **[41477]**

Red Herring (No. 99, June 15 & July 1, 2001, pp. 124, 126); "Private Company Profiles" in **[1694]**, **[4770]**, **[6273]**, **[6959]**, **[14365]**, **[23133]**, **[41917]**, **[50947]**, **[52180]**

Red Herring (No. 87, December 18, 2000, pp. 228-233); "Private Matters" in **[15374]**, **[50141]**

Red Herring (No. 103, September 1, 2001, pp. 38, 40); "Profile: Alan Patricof as entrepreneurial curmudgeon" in **[36650]**, **[55786]**

Red Herring (No. 105, October 1, 2001, pp. 44); "Profile: Don Green reigns as the don of optical networking" in **[36651]**, **[37180]**

Red Herring (No. 102, August 15, 2001, pp. 68-69); "Protocol: Coming Soon: Ethernet as business model" in **[6961]**, **[14371]**, **[36655]**

Red Herring (No. 105, October 1, 2001, pp. 90); "Public Company Profiles" in **[4773]**, **[6275]**, **[14372]**, **[23137]**, **[41923]**, **[52181]**

Red Herring (No. 105, October 1, 2001, pp. 58-59); "Q401 Will it Matter?" in **[28663]**, **[32646]**

Red Herring (No. 106, October 15, 2001, pp. 47-50, 52); "Qwest's Napoleonic Ambitions" in **[5094]**, **[14382]**, **[37182]**

Red Herring (No. 102, August 15, 2001, pp. 84-85); "Resistance is Futile: EDS has been on a buying binge" in **[15411]**, **[30695]**, **[50161]**

Red Herring (No. 105, October 1, 2001, pp. 58-63); "Revenge of the neurons" in **[8801]**, **[50797]**

Red Herring (No. 103, September 1, 2001, pp. 84-85); "Risky Business: Hedge fund chic is both undeserved - and dangerous" in **[15423]**, **[38326]**

Red Herring (No. 103, September 1, 2001, pp. 67); "Saving our energy" in **[37324]**, **[41962]**

Red Herring (No. 103, September 1, 2001, pp. 25-26); "Security: Messaging Gets Serious" in **[14422]**, **[22371]**, **[27493]**

Red Herring (No. 99, June 15 & July 1, 2001, pp. 21-22); "Seeing the future in real time" in **[14424]**, **[32682]**, **[41970]**

Red Herring (No. 105, October 1, 2001, pp. 88-89); "Shrinking Surplus: George W. Bush, technology CEO?" in **[32685]**, **[54747]**

Red Herring (No. 105, October 1, 2001, pp. 80); "Software: A Rising Middle Class Takes on Wireless" in **[5113]**, **[14455]**, **[23187]**

Red Herring (No. 102, August 15, 2001, pp. 18); "Software Is Back - Sort of" in **[14456]**, **[23199]**, **[53982]**

Red Herring (March 2003, pp. 17); "Stand by NASA research" in **[28809]**, **[42006]**, **[50972]**, **[52209]**

Red Herring (No. 103, September 1, 2001, pp. 34); "Startups: Microsoft matters again" in **[6966]**, **[14484]**, **[25973]**, **[55845]**

Red Herring (No. 105, October 1, 2001, pp. 78, 80-81); "Storage titans would rather fight than connect" in **[6229]**, **[22892]**, **[35674]**

Red Herring (No. 105, October 1, 2001, pp. 100-101); "Storage Showdown: Hitachi is now a big thorn in EMC's side" in **[6289]**, **[30961]**

Red Herring (No. 105, October 1, 2001, pp. 76-77); "Storage: With the dumb dot-com money gone, the space race begins in earnest" in **[6290]**, **[28829]**

Red Herring (No. 105, October 1, 2001, pp. 102); "Tactics: Semiconductors will lead the tech recovery" in **[28854]**, **[37194]**

Red Herring (No. 103, September 1, 2001, pp. 88); "Tactics: Technology's earnings riddle" in **[28855]**, **[42025]**

Red Herring (No. 102, August 15, 2001, pp. 94); "Tactics: Will better be good enough?" in **[28856]**, **[42026]**

Red Herring (No. 105, October 1, 2001, pp. 24-25); "Telecom: As companies go bankrupt, buyout firms lick their chops" in **[28873]**, **[50205]**

Red Herring (No. 106, October 15, 2001, pp. 74-75); "Telecom Services: Finding new life in a troubled industry" in **[5140]**, **[14521]**, **[37201]**

Red Herring (No. 106, October 15, 2001, pp. 86-87); "Telecommunications Sector Analysis" in **[6416]**, **[23228]**, **[37202]**

Red Herring (No. 106, October 15, 2001, pp. 28); "Terrorism: After attacks, survivors use the Internet to say 'I'm OK'" in **[14524]**, **[37203]**

Red Herring (January 2003, pp. 70); "The cycle turns for technology in 2003" in **[28004]**, **[41626]**

Red Herring (No. 103, September 1, 2001, pp. 16); "The Angler: With more opportunities comes more isolation" in **[13814]**, **[41516]**

Red Herring (March 2003, pp. 56); "The true believer" in **[31076]**, **[42076]**, **[46466]**, **[50982]**, **[52220]**

Red Herring (No. 103, September 1, 2001, pp. 42-43); "The energy roller coaster" in **[27117]**, **[39302]**

Red Herring (No. 102, August 15, 2001, pp. 88); "The Contrarian: Want a hot tip? Avoid JagNotes.com" in **[13924]**, **[27976]**

Red Herring (No. 102, August 15, 2001, pp. 58-59); "The Digital Disruptors" in **[2692]**, **[9704]**, **[13971]**, **[17735]**, **[20314]**, **[24403]**, **[41636]**, **[44030]**, **[46888]**

Red Herring (No. 106, October 15, 2001, pp. 54-58, 60); "The Game of War" in **[1106]**, **[30864]**

Red Herring (No. 102, August 15, 2001, pp. 40-45); "The Giant that would be King" in **[14076]**, **[28206]**, **[53561]**

Red Herring (No. 106, October 15, 2001, pp. 25-26); "The Hague: Laws without Borders" in **[14099]**, **[29281]**, **[33989]**, **[37144]**, **[40430]**, **[43687]**, **[44055]**

Red Herring (No. 99, June 15 & July 1, 2001, pp. 106-107); "The Holy Wafer" in **[41746]**, **[50887]**

Red Herring (March 2003, pp. 34); "The case of the obsolete inventory" in **[100]**, **[23906]**, **[26183]**, **[37401]**, **[44228]**

Red Herring (No. 103, September 1, 2001, pp. 94); "The Lookout: It's time to play some war games" in **[41818]**, **[50059]**

Red Herring (No. 105, October 1, 2001, pp. 94); "The Lookout: New trading system will pay off for Nyfix" in **[6950]**, **[15236]**

Red Herring (No. 102, August 15, 2001, pp. 16); "The New Economic World Order" in **[28535]**, **[32587]**

Red Herring (March 2003, pp. 28); "The operators" in **[5079]**, **[41888]**

Red Herring (No. 106, October 15, 2001, pp. 16); "The end of the PC world as we know it" in **[6642]**, **[28102]**, **[49018]**

Red Herring (March 2003, pp. 54); "The fabric of consumer reality" in **[31027]**, **[41678]**, **[46283]**, **[50870]**, **[52096]**

Red Herring (No. 99, June 15 & July 1, 2001, pp. 146); "The Red Herring Portfolio" in **[15404]**, **[28690]**

Red Herring (No. 105, October 1, 2001, pp. 102); "The Red Herring Portfolio: Another market false start" in **[15402]**, **[28687]**

Red Herring (No. 103, September 1, 2001, pp. 96); "The Red Herring Portfolio: Going nowhere fast" in **[28688]**, **[41937]**

Red Herring (No. 105, October 1, 2001, pp. 104); "The Red Herring Portfolio: Not a stellar performance" in **[15403]**, **[28689]**

Red Herring (No. 102, August 15, 2001, pp.96); "The Red Herring Portfolio: Stuck inside a sideways pattern with the market" in **[28691]**, **[41938]**

Red Herring (No. 99, June 15 & July 1, 2001, pp. 102, 104-105); "The Silicon Killer" in **[41985]**, **[50968]**

Red Herring (No. 99, June 15 & July 1, 2001, pp. 142, 144); "The semi swing" in **[15445]**, **[41972]**

Red Herring (No. 99, June 15 & July 1, 2001, pp. 72, 74); "The Top 25 Investment Banks of 2000" in **[15534]**, **[44676]**

Red Herring (No 99, June 15 & July 1, 2001, pp. 62, 64); "The Top 25 IPOs of 2000" in **[15535]**, **[44677]**, **[50220]**, **[55869]**

Red Herring (No. 99, June 15 & July 1, 2001, pp. 68, 70); "The Top 25 VC Firms of 2000" in **[28909]**, **[55870]**

Red Herring (No. 102, August 15, 2001, pp. 33); "The technology trade-off" in **[14516]**, **[42054]**

Red Herring (January 2003, pp. 58); "The microbe warrior. (Bioterrorism)" in **[22291]**, **[39867]**, **[41832]**, **[50925]**, **[52151]**

Red Herring (No. 99, June 15 & July 1, 2001, pp. 134); "There's No There There" in **[15521]**, **[42063]**, **[54034]**

Red Herring (January 2003, pp. 67); "Thrift: working at home or hardly working?" in **[6838]**, **[28899]**

Red Herring (No. 105, October 1, 2001, pp. 36); "Trading Private Equity Publicly May not fly" in **[15540]**, **[50224]**, **[55873]**

Red Herring (No. 105, October 1, 2001, pp. 30); "Trading Takes a Breather" in **[15542]**, **[28915]**, **[38424]**

Red Herring (No. 99, June 15 & July 1, 2001, pp. 120); "Truth or Consequences" in **[6973]**, **[23241]**, **[42078]**, **[50983]**

Red Herring (No. 103, September 1, 2001, pp. 78); "VC Whispers: Glowing optimism" in **[28958]**, **[42092]**, **[55891]**

Red Herring (No. 102, August 15, 2001, pp. 76); "VC Whispers: Optical components shine brightly in a dreary market" in **[6976]**, **[14563]**, **[42093]**, **[55892]**

Red Herring (No. 105, October 1, 2001, pp. 86); "VC Whispers: Putting cash into stash" in **[6294]**, **[55893]**

Red Herring (No. 105, October 1, 2001, pp. 84); "VC Whispers: Software surges ahead" in **[4586]**, **[6451]**, **[13785]**, **[22893]**, **[25764]**, **[55446]**

Red Herring (No. 87, December 18, 2000, pp. 40); "Venture Capital: Arthritic corporations get a chance at a second childhood" in **[14565]**, **[34646]**, **[55909]**

Red Herring (No. 105, October 1, 2001, pp. 38-39); "Venture Capital: First-round investments: now for the small and the brave" in **[28962]**, **[37206]**, **[55912]**

Red Herring (No. 102, August 15, 2001, pp. 32); "Venture Capital: Its' hip to be old" in **[54059]**, **[55914]**

Red Herring (January 2003, pp. 68); "Venture investors start lending a hand" in **[35712]**, **[44446]**, **[55449]**

Red Herring (No. 105, October 1, 2001, pp. 96-97); "Web Retailing: The prodigal e-commerce sites return" in **[34672]**, **[51406]**

Red Herring (No. 105, October 1, 2001, pp. 82); "Web Services: Connection established" in **[14583]**, **[23254]**, **[34673]**

Red Herring (No. 102, August 15, 2001, pp. 100); "Webvan, Microsoft, and the second-mover advantage" in **[28980]**, **[39662]**, **[47707]**

Red Herring (March 2003, pp. 24); "What the Internet can do for the record labels" in **[14600]**, **[17777]**, **[34694]**

Red Herring (No. 99, June 15 & July 1, 2001, pp. 122); "When the Chips are Down" in **[6978]**, **[42113]**, **[50990]**, **[55943]**

Red Herring (No. 76, pp. 185-186, 188, 192, 194, 198-200, 202, 204); "Why the Small-Business Market is the Internet's new frontier" in **[14621]**, **[34722]**, **[47748]**, **[55954]**

Red Herring (No. 106, October 15, 2001, pp. 34-35); "Wireless security catches the eye of venture capitalists" in **[37211]**, **[55957]**

Red Hook Area Chamber of Commerce **[62991]**

Red Kangaroo Franchise **[23571]**

Red Lodge Area Chamber of Commerce **[62197]**

Red Oak Chamber of Commerce **[60197]**

Red River Area Technology Center **[64152]**

Red River Chamber of Commerce **[62707]**

Red River County Chamber of Commerce **[65461]**

Red River Regional Planning Council SBDC–SBDC–SBDC **[63498]**

Red Rock Chili Co. **[21939]**

Red Rock Ventures **[58130]**

Red Roof Inn. **[12724]**

"Red-Tape Brainstorms" in *Inc.* (October 17, 2000, pp. 17) **[35621]**

Red Wheel Fundraising **[3913]**

Red Wing Area Chamber of Commerce **[61652]**

"Redefining my role" in *My Business* (June/July 2002, pp. 48) **[10156]**, **[36682]**, **[37766]**

"Redefining Sick Days" in *Sales & Marketing Management* (Vol. 157) **[26895]**, **[35044]**, **[47457]**, **[53935]**

Redevelopment Authority of the City of Meadville **[64614]**

Redfield Area Chamber of Commerce **[64835]**

Redford Township Chamber of Commerce **[61409]**

Redlands Chamber of Commerce **[57732]**

Redland's Daily Facts **[18962]**

Redleaf Group, Inc. **[58131]**

"Redleaf, UPenn Launch PenNetWorks" in *Venture Capital Journal* (Vol. 40, No. 10, October 2000, pp. 6, 8) **[41939]**, **[50157]**, **[55802]**

Redmond Chamber of Commerce **[64259]**

Redmond Technology Press **[66251]**

Redondo Beach Chamber of Commerce and Visitors Bureau **[57733]**

Redrock Ventures **[58132]**

"Reduce your tax bill" in *Women In Business* (Vol. 52, No. 2, March 2000, pp. 37) **[38311]**

"Reducing Turnover" in *Automotive News* (Vol. 79, January 24, 2005, No. 6131, pp. 38) **[18116]**, **[51789]**, **[53936]**

Redwood Area Chamber and Tourism **[61653]**

Redwood Empire–Small Business Development Center **[57269]**

"Reebok Rolls Out Marketing Device" in *Boston Globe* (February 10, 2005) **[770]**, **[22765]**, **[47458]**

"Reed Acquires Manufacturing Shows" in *Tradeshow Week* (Vol. 34, December 13, 2004, No. 50, pp. 3) **[15405]**, **[22552]**, **[25007]**, **[41940]**, **[46416]**, **[50158]**, **[55148]**

Reed Business Information–Frederic G. Melcher Library **[2819]**

Reed City Area Chamber of Commerce **[61410]**

Reed Construction Data **[7632]**

"Reed Jumps Onto the Medical Bandwagon " in *Tradeshow Week* (Vol. 3) **[22553]**, **[25008]**, **[28692]**, **[33219]**, **[41086]**, **[55149]**

Reed Royalty Public Affairs Inc. **[3806]**, **[31450]**, **[50386]**

Reedsburg Area Chamber of Commerce **[66509]**

Reedsburg Area Medical Center–Medical Library **[18405]**

Reed–Sendecke–Krebsbach Inc. **[55256]**

Reedsport - Winchester Bay Chamber of Commerce **[64260]**

"Reel to Real" in *Success* (Vol. 47, No. 2, June 2000, pp. 28) **[36683]**

Reelfoot Area Chamber of Commerce **[64968]**

"Reeling in the Big Ones" in *Entrepreneur* (Vol. 28, No. 1, January 2000, pp. 138) **[35622]**, **[51503]**

"Reeling In the Big One" in *Inc.* (August 1, 2004) **[27733]**, **[46587]**, **[51504]**, **[52783]**

Reengineering the Corporation: A Manifesto for Business Revolution **[45585]**

Reese Chamber of Commerce **[61411]**

"Refer madness" in *Entrepreneur* (Vol. 30, No. 3, March 2002, pp. 87) **[34403]**, **[47459]**, **[51790]**

Reference Book For Metalworking Machinery **[16379]**

"Reference Library" in *Small Business Opportunities* (Vol. 17, May 2005, No. 3, pp. 54, 56) **[42395]**, **[45586]**

"Refinancing fuels growth in home renovations" in *Atlanta Business Chronicle* (Vol. 25, January 10, 2003, No. 31, pp. 19A) **[4479]**, **[7462]**, **[17433]**

Refinishing Furniture with Bob Flexner **[10836]**

Reflexology Association of America **[17885]**

"Reforming pro forma" in *Entrepreneur* (Vol. 31, No. 5, May 2003, pp. 50) **[236]**, **[2951]**, **[24023]**, **[29466]**, **[38312]**, **[40634]**

"A Refreshing Way to Make a Living" in *The Record* (November 6, 2005) **[11343]**, **[26896]**, **[35045]**

Refrigerated & Frozen Foods (Vol. 14, No. 7, July 2003, pp. 19); "Clear Sailing" in **[11597]**, **[23467]**, **[27955]**

Refrigerated & Frozen Foods (Vol. 14, No. 7, July 2003, pp. 12); "Crunch Time!" in **[11604]**, **[23469]**

Refrigerating Engineers and Technicians Association **[1008]**

Refrigeration Service Engineers Society **[1009]** Library **[1065]**

"Reg Complexity Fuels Demand for ABA Institute" in *American Banker* (Vol. 170, February 3, 2005, No. 23, pp. 3) **[10157]**, **[33220]**

Regal Mortgage.Com **[17468]**

Regal Nails, Salon & Spa **[11838]**

ReGENERATION Partners **[37831]**

"The Regenerative Organization" in *Employment Relations Today* (Vol. 27, No. 1, Spring 2000, pp. 19) **[42887]**, **[43794]**

Regenstrief Institute, Inc. **[41401]**

Regent Capital Management **[63159]**

Regent International Ltd. **[6381]**

Regina Economic Development Authority **[66780]**

Region 2000 SBDC **[65835]**

Region Nine Development Commission–SBDC **[61532]**

Regional Business Alliance **[64501]**

"Regional Center Serves Seniors" in *Sarasota Herald-Tribune* **[456]**, **[18334]**

Regional Contracting Assistance Center **[66310]** Ranson **[60885]** Robert C. Byrd Institute–Huntington **[66311]**

Regional Contracting Assistant Center–Princeton **[66312]**

Regional Directory: National **[46182]**

Regional Industrial Directory **[16702]**

"Regional Insurers Thrive" in *Rough Notes* (Vol. 145, No. 2, February 2003, pp. 78) **[13440]**, **[28693]**, **[43335]**

"Regional Leaders Search for Solutions to Water Problems" in *Orlando Business Journal* (Vol. 20, No. 13, September 12, 2003, pp. 32) **[39557]**

Regional Research and Development Services–Southern Illinois University at Edwardsville **[66871]**

Registry of Utah Financial Institutions **[44631]**

"Regrets" in *Inc.* (October 17, 2000, pp. 98) **[29977]**, **[30591]**

"Regulation Nation" in *Entrepreneur* (Vol. 32, October 2004, No. 10, pp. 32) **[28694]**, **[29467]**, **[40635]**

"Regulatory Rescue" in *Entrepreneur* (Vol. 31, No. 8, August 2003, pp. 24) **[39896]**, **[40636]**

Regulatory Spending Soars: An Analysis of the US Budget for 2003 **[40857]**

Regulus International Capital Co., Inc. **[58610]**

Regus Business Centres **[4033]**

Rehabilitation Institute of Chicago–Sensory Motor Performance Program **[19609]**

Rehabilitation Institute of Michigan **[19610]**

"Rehashing Fashion: Consignment Shops Do It All" in *Birmingham Business Journal* (Vol. 20, No. 27, July 4, 2003, pp. 1) **[5630]**, **[7153]**, **[9605]**

The Rehmann Group **[50331]**

Rehoboth Beach-Dewey Beach Chamber of Commerce **[58652]**

Rei America Inc. **[59021]**

Reid and Riege, PC–Library **[24187]**

Reiki Alliance **[17886]**

"Reimagining Union Station" in *Ingram's* (Vol. 29, No. 1, January 2003, pp. 13) **[7463]**, **[28695]**, **[52717]**

Reimbursement Advisor **[17164]**

Reinforced Masonry Design **[16959]**

"Reinforcing Ethical Decision Making Through Organizational Structure" in *Journal of Business Ethics* (Vol. 28, No. 1, Nov. 1, 2000) **[37496]**

"Reining in the Forces of Change" in *Hispanic Business* (December 2001, pp. 12) **[3575]**, **[4781]**, **[7464]**, **[23148]**

"Reining in activist funds" in *Harvard Business Review* (Vol. 81, No. 3, March 2003, pp. 22) **[10158]**, **[15406]**, **[26897]**

"Reining In Office Rumors" in *Inc.* (November 1, 2004) **[45587]**, **[51791]**

Reinsurance News **[13559]**

"Reinsurance" in *Rough Notes* (Vol. 146, No. 9, September 2003, pp. 94) **[13441]**, **[43336]**

"Reinventing the wheel" in *Hispanic Business* (Vol. 22, No. 4, April 2000, pp. 12) **[14391]**, **[34404]**, **[47460]**

The Reinvestment Fund (TRF) **[64575]**

Reisterstown - Owings Mills - Glyndon Chamber of Commerce **[60854]**

"Relationship Advice" in *Entrepreneur* (Vol. 32, No. 1, January 2004, pp. 47) **[31833]**, **[34405]**, **[51792]**

"The relationship between quality, time and cost" in *Women in Business* (Vol. 53, No. 2, March-April, 2001, pp. 34) **[51306]**, **[52385]**

"Relationship builder" in *Pittsburgh Business Times* (Vol. 22, No. 46, May 30, 2003, pp. 15) **[12909]**, **[20155]**, **[50467]**, **[50661]**

"Relationship-marketing ventures take toll on Valassis' earnings" in *Crain's Detroit Business* (Vol. 19, No. 9, March 3, 2003, pp. 4) **[771]**, **[47461]**

Relationship Selling: Building Trust to Sell Your Service **[51793]**

"Relative power and influence strategy" in *Journal of Organizational Behavior* (Vol. 23, No. 2, March 2002, pp. 167) **[33221]**, **[45588]**

Relax the Back **[17278]**

"Relax Your Grip" in *Black Enterprise* (Vol. 36, February 2006, No. 7, pp. 71) **[45589]**, **[51794]**

"Relaxed fit: Tailor your travel for less stress and maximum chill" in *Entrepreneur* (Vol. 30, No. 3, March 2002, pp. 24) **[3047]**, **[17009]**, **[25595]**, **[30409]**

Relaxing Touch: A Guide to the Healing Art of Massage Therapy **[17023]**

"Relaxing their Way to Profits" in *Black Enterprise* (Vol. 31, No. 5, December 2000, pp. 62) **[17908]**

"Release the Hounds " in *Entrepreneur* **[772]**, **[14392]**, **[34406]**, **[47462]**

"Reliant's refinancing package could be a model for industry" in *Houston Business Journal* (Vol. 33, No. 48, April 11, 2003, pp. 10A) **[38313]**, **[44632]**

"Relief Is Finally Coming with A Rise in M&A" in *Venture Capital Journal* (July 1, 2003) **[15407]**, **[50159]**, **[55803]**

"Relief Valve? Done Right, a Private Investment in Public Equity, Or Pipe, Could Bring Your Business Much-Needed Cash" in *Entrepreneur* **[10159]**, **[15408]**, **[38314]**

"Relief on Wheels? Mall Strollers Play DVDs" in *Tampa Tribune* (November 23, 2005) **[51307]**, **[53937]**

Relocating Your Workplace **[30170]**

"Relocation Tools: What You Need To Know About Moving To a New Town" in *Black Enterprise* (Vol. 35, August 2004, No. 1, pp. 68) **[30171]**

REMAN Newsletter **[46519]**

Rembrandt Venture Partners **[58133]**

"Rembrandts in the Attic" in *Inc.* (October 2000, pp. 23) **[1613]**, **[34407]**, **[36684]**, **[37074]**

Remedies in Employment Discrimination Law **[32057]**

Remedy Intelligent Staffing **[24551]**

"A Remedy for Malpractice Malaise" in *Business Week* (February 7, 2005, No. 3919, pp. 38) **[13442]**, **[41087]**, **[43337]**

"Remember Service With a Smile?" in *Microsoft Executive Circle* (Vol. 1, No. 2, Q2 2001, pp. 16-18, 21) **[31834]**

"Remember The Nanny Tax? Now It's the Granny Tax" in *Fortune* (Vol. 141, No. 1, January 10, 2000, pp. 218) **[12379]**, **[40637]**, **[54719]**

"Remember Y2K threat at small firms? Forget it" in *Wall Street Journal* (January 4, 2000, pp. A4) **[29978]**

Remerica Real Estate **[20756]**

Remgro Recycling Equipment Marketing News **[21277]**

Remodeling **[7573]**

"Remodeling Riches" in *Small Business Opportunities* (Vol. 12, No. 2, March 2000, pp. 126) **[7198]**, **[35623]**

"The Remote Control CEO" in *Inc.* (October 2005, pp. 96-101, 144, 146) **[12018]**, **[26532]**, **[36685]**, **[45590]**

"Remote Control" in *Entrepreneur* (Vol. 33, February 2005, No. 2, pp. 56) **[36686]**, **[45591]**, **[51795]**

Remote Control Hobbies **[8251]**

"Remote Control" in *Home Office Computing* (Vol. 18, No. 10, October 2000, pp. 46) **[35046]**, **[42714]**, **[45592]**, **[49227]**

"Remote Control" in *My Business* (February/March 2004, pp. 14) **[41941]**, **[52386]**, **[52583]**

"Renaissance hopes $20M primes pump" in *Crain's Detroit Business* (Vol. 19, No. 10, March 10, 2003, pp. 3) **[7465]**, **[20651]**, **[20988]**

Renaissance Capital Corp. **[59203]**

Renaissance Executive Forums, Inc. **[3914]**

Renaissance Leadership **[35262]**

Renaissance Ventures **[65979]**

"Renal Solutions" in *Pittsburgh Business Times* (Vol. 22, No. 51, July 4, 2003, pp. 1) **[50953]**, **[52184]**, **[55804]**

"RenaLab Acquired" in *Mississippi Business Journal* (Vol. 29, January 2007, No. 3, pp. A10) **[17192]**, **[41088]**, **[50160]**

Rend Lake College **[59799]** Small Business Development Center **[59385]**

Renew America–Library **[9506]**

Renew the Earth **[23332]**

"Renewed Biotech Interest Boosts BioCryst" in *Birmingham Business Journal* (Vol. 20, No. 35, August 29, 2003, pp. 1) **[8800]**, **[15409]**, **[38315]**, **[41942]**, **[50954]**, **[52185]**

"Renewed Effort for Reintroduced Rural Credit Bill" in *American Banker* (Vol. 170, February 2, 2005, No. 22, pp. 5) **[10160]**, **[40638]**, **[54720]**

"Renewing a Great Profession: Esteemed Professions Initiate Change - For Their Own Good" in *Journal of Accountancy* (January 2005) **[237]**, **[2952]**, **[24024]**, **[26339]**, **[27168]**

Reno-Sparks Chamber of Commerce **[62366]**

"Renovations of old buildings" in *Rough Notes* (Vol. 145, No. 1, January 2003, pp. 16) **[1529]**, **[7466]**, **[13443]**, **[43338]**

"Renowned Scientist's Research on Aging Delivers Anti-Aging Supplement; Juvenon Energy Formula" in *PR Newswire* (January 13, 2003) **[17909]**, **[52186]**

"Restaurant Depot Expanding in Bohemia" in *Long Island Business News* (March 5, 2004) **[21295]**, **[21597]**, **[28700]**

Restaurant Financial Management System **[22029]**

Restaurant Hospitality **[12070]**, **[21691]**

"Restaurant King, Hotel Developer to Hook Up" in *Atlanta Journal-Constitution* (January 31, 2007) **[12626]**, **[21598]**, **[50163]**

"Restaurant chains look for bite of local market" in *Crain's Detroit Business* (Vol. 18, No. 19, May 13, 2002, pp. 1) **[21599]**, **[38897]**

Restaurant Marketing for Owners and Managers **[21600]**, **[47464]**

Restaurant Normandin **[21941]**

"Restaurant Patrons Can Now Peruse the Menus and Prices of 110 Kansas City Area Restaurants..." in *Kansas City Star* (March 11, 2005) **[2739]**, **[10750]**, **[21601]**, **[54246]**

The Restaurant Planning Guide: Starting and Managing a Successful Restaurant **[21602]**

Restaurant Publishing **[58486]**

"Restaurant Riches" in *Small Business Opportunities* (Vol. 17, November 2005, No. 6, pp. 76, 86) **[21603]**, **[36692]**

The Restaurant Start-Up Guide **[21604]**

Restaurant Success **[21605]**

"Restaurants stay hot commodities despite downturn" in *Boston Business Journal* (Vol. 22, No. 15, May 17, 2002, pp. 13) **[21606]**, **[32666]**

"Restaurants are Hiring Workers Faster than Other Economic Sectors" in *The Record* (November 19, 2005) **[21607]**, **[28701]**, **[42397]**

Restaurants & Institutions **[21692]**

"Restaurants, retail attracted by neighborhood" in *Atlanta Business Chronicle* (Vol. 25, No. 20, October 25, 2002, pp. 3) **[21608]**, **[28702]**

"Restaurants Watch Helplessly As Wait Staff Applications Dry Up" in *Bradenton Herald* (January 31, 2005) **[21609]**, **[40646]**, **[42398]**, **[54723]**

"Restaurateur Inks Subway Deal for Eastern Wayne County" in *Crain's Detroit Business* (Vol. 19, No. 45, November 10, 2003, pp. 44) **[8521]**, **[21610]**, **[23039]**, **[38898]**

"Restaurateur's Answer to Construction is a Second Eatery" in *Houston Business Journal* (Vol. 34, No. 7, June 27, 2003, pp. 2A) **[21611]**, **[29981]**

Reston Consulting Group Inc. **[25688]**

"Reston's $399M Blowout" in *Washington Business Journal* (Vol. 22, No. 9, July 4, 2003, pp. 1) **[20657]**, **[20996]**

Restoration **[2036]**, **[22638]**

"Restored 1948 warehouse home to studio, architects" in *Business First Columbus* (Vol. 18, No. 26, Febr) **[42716]**, **[49543]**

Restyle **[7186]**

Resume Preparation **[4439]**

Resume Pro: The Professional's Guide **[22048]**

The Resume Writer: Writing It Right **[22049]**

Resumes! Resumes! Resumes! **[22050]**

Resumes That Mean Business **[22051]**

"Retail" in *Business 2.0* (Vol. 6, July 2005, No. 6, pp. 30) **[5708]**, **[9636]**, **[51310]**, **[53942]**

The Retail Challenge **[51431]**

Retail Confectioners International **[4274]**

Retail Confectioners International-Membership Directory and Buyers' Guide **[4304]**

"Retail" in *Entrepreneur* (Vol. 32, No. 1, January 2004, pp. 238) **[10694]**, **[19821]**, **[38899]**, **[51311]**

"Retail Exec Stays in Style" in *Crain's New York Business* (Vol. 23, January 29, 2007, No. 5, pp. F3) **[5709]**, **[28703]**, **[30593]**, **[36693]**

"Retail Experts Laud Costco's Shopping Strategy" in *Business Journal-Portland* (Vol. 20, No. 22, August 1, 2003, pp. 11) **[31747]**, **[32667]**, **[45598]**, **[46210]**, **[47465]**, **[48050]**, **[51312]**, **[53540]**

"Retail Holdouts - But at What Price" in *Inc.* (March 2000, pp. 88) **[34411]**, **[51313]**

"Retail/Hospitality" in *Microsoft Executive Circle* (Vol. 1, No. 2, Q2 2001, pp. 34-37) **[21612]**, **[31835]**, **[41948]**

Retail Info Systems News **[51432]**

"Retail Kiosk" in *Black Enterprise* (Vol. 36, November 2005, No. 4, pp. 64) **[15937]**, **[51314]**

Retail Management Consultants **[31987]**

Retail Merchandiser (Vol. 43, No. 10, October, 2003, pp. 38); "Auto Aftermarket Targets Tech Savvy Shoppers" in **[1905]**

Retail Merchandiser (Vol. 42, No. 11, Nov. 2002, pp. 33); "Home crafting stimulates togetherness" in **[8169]**, **[32484]**, **[53780]**

"Retail Rut: Sears Holders Might Get a $10 Payout. But Don't Expect Much More from the Stock" in *Barron's* (July 21, 2003, pp. 15) **[8395]**, **[10162]**, **[15413]**, **[38317]**, **[50164]**, **[51315]**

Retail Safety Consortium **[56667]**

"Retail Stores Taking Health Care Debit Cards Must Upgrade Systems" in *Kiplinger Letter* (Vol. 82, January 12, 2007, No. 1) **[8318]**, **[41089]**, **[51316]**

Retail Technology **[51439]**

Retail Tobacco Dealers of America **[24603]**

Retail Traffic **[21062]**

Retailer and Marketing News **[51927]**

"Retailer Torrid Looks to Tap into Plus-Size Apparel Market for Teenagers" in *Tampa Tribune* (August 8, 2003) **[5710]**, **[51317]**

Retailer's Bakery Association **[2234]**

The Retailer's Bakery Association Marketplace **[2158]**, **[2284]**

"Retailers Beginning to Get Holiday Spirit" in *Crain's Detroit Business* (Vol. 19, No. 42, October 20, 2003, pp. 1) **[28704]**, **[51318]**

"Retailers Beginning to Get Holiday Spirit; Many Boost Inventory in Hopes of Strong Sales" in *Crain's Detroit Business* (Vol. 19) **[28705]**, **[51319]**

"Retailers, Beware" in *Entrepreneur* (Vol. 28, No. 4, April 2000, pp. 58) **[31836]**, **[51320]**

"Retailers Draw Link Between Halloween, Christmas Sales" in *Sacramento Bee* (October 30, 2005) **[51321]**, **[51797]**, **[52363]**

Retailers Forum Magazine **[7179]**

"Retailers Have Disappointing March" in *Baltimore Sun* (April 11, 2003) **[28706]**, **[51322]**

"Retailers Helped by Chill, Gas Price Dip" in *The Record* (November 4, 2005) **[32668]**, **[51323]**

"Retailers Optimistic They Can Compete for Slice of Macomb" in *Crain's Detroit Business* (Vol. 21, October 31, 2005, No. 44, pp. 3) **[30937]**, **[51324]**, **[52718]**

"Retailers' Outlook 'Rosy'" in *Milwaukee Journal Sentinel* (December 14, 2005) **[28707]**, **[51325]**

"Retailers' Siren Song" in *Kiplinger's Personal Finance Magazine* (Vol. 54, No. 11, November 2000, pp. 130) **[51326]**, **[51798]**

"Retailers Welcome Valentine's Day Gift Binge" in *Bradenton Herald* (February 5, 2005) **[4305]**, **[11164]**, **[51327]**, **[51799]**

"Retailing Experts See Rise in Label-Conscious Male Shoppers" in *Atlanta Journal-Constitution* (February 17, 2004) **[47466]**, **[51328]**

Retailing Management **[51329]**

"Retailing Your Personal Lines Accounts" in *Rough Notes* (Vol. 146, No. 9, September 2003, pp. 56) **[13446]**, **[31837]**, **[47467]**, **[51800]**

"Retention Rate Can Be Enhanced" in *Morgage Servicing News* (Vol. 5, No. 10, November 2001, pp. 4) **[10163]**, **[23151]**, **[31838]**, **[47468]**

"Rethinking Refinancing" in *Black Enterprise* (Vol. 34, No. 5, December 2003, pp. 33) **[17434]**, **[38318]**

"Rethinking Refinancing: With Mortgage Rates on the Rise, Does It Still Make Sense to Refinance?" in *Black Enterprise* (Vol. 34) **[17435]**, **[38319]**

"Retire Rich" in *Entrepreneur* (Vol. 33, September 2005, No. 9, pp. 68) **[15186]**, **[15414]**, **[36694]**, **[38320]**

"Retired Couple Open Gift Shop, Bed-and-Breakfast in Jacksonville, Texas" in *Tyler Morning Telegraph* (February 10, 2004) **[2451]**, **[11165]**, **[13666]**, **[37767]**

"Retired exec finds leisure time less than idle" in *Atlanta Business Chronicle* (Vol. 25, December 6, 2002, No. 26, pp. 26A) **[36695]**, **[45599]**

"Retirees face waning insurance contributions" in *Atlanta Business Chronicle* (Vol. 25, No. 19, October 18, 2002, pp. 7C) **[13447]**, **[26899]**, **[43341]**

"Retirement Benefits More Important to Workers" in *Wall Street Journal* (January 14, 2003, pp. B5) **[26900]**, **[35047]**

"Retirement Communities Grow in Popularity in New Jersey" in *The Record* (November 3, 2005) **[7471]**, **[53943]**

"Retirement-Plan Administer To Be Bought For $115 Million" in *Wall Street Journal* (Vol. 248, December 2006, No. 149, pp. C5) **[39561]**, **[43342]**, **[50165]**

"Retirement Plan Shopping" in *Hispanic Business* (Vol. 23, No. 5, May 2001, pp. 76) **[15415]**, **[38321]**

"Retirement Plans: Choosing from the Alphabet Soup" in *My Business* (December/January 2003, pp. 16) **[10164]**, **[15416]**, **[26901]**

Retirement Plans Report **[30756]**

"Retirement Plans for Small Business" in *Ingram's* (Vol. 28, No. 5, May 2002, pp. 31) **[15417]**, **[26902]**, **[38322]**

"Retiring Minds" in *Hispanic Business* (March 2005, pp. 50) **[42399]**, **[45600]**, **[48387]**

"Retiring boomers to cut start-up launches, study says" in *Wall Street Journal* (March 14, 2000, pp. B4) **[53944]**

Retiring to Your Own Business: How You Can Launch a Satisfying, Productive and Prosperous Second Career **[52484]**

The Retort **[27559]**

Retro Fitness **[19526]**

"Return of the Agent" in *Entrepreneur.com* (Vol. 34, January 2006, No. 1, pp. 19) **[24725]**, **[25239]**, **[30410]**, **[34412]**

"The Return of the Black Entrepreneur" in *Business Week Online* (Oct. 8, 2002) **[28708]**, **[36696]**, **[48388]**

"The Return of the Global Brand" in *Harvard Business Review* (Vol. 81, No. 8, August 2003, pp. 22) **[28709]**, **[32669]**, **[43798]**, **[47469]**

Return on Investment **[38501]**

"Return of the Kings" in *Forbes* (Vol. 175, February 14, 2005, No. 3, pp. 88) **[10165]**, **[14399]**, **[15418]**

"Return To Me" in *Entrepreneur* (Vol. 33, September 2005, No. 9, pp. 28) **[28710]**, **[47470]**

Reunion Planner **[18760]**

Reuse/Recycle **[21280]**

The Reuter Guide to Official Interest Rates **[15419]**

Reuters Business Briefing **[3468]**, **[4041]**

"Revamped Retiring Plans" in *My Business* (April/May 2002, pp. 15) **[26903]**, **[40647]**, **[54724]**

"Revamping a Retirement Plan" in *Black Enterprise* (Vol. 35, October 2004, No. 3, pp. 43) **[15420]**, **[36697]**, **[38323]**, **[56385]**

"Revamping Roth" in *Entrepreneur* (Vol. 33, October 2005, No. 10, pp. 60) **[10048]**, **[10166]**, **[15193]**, **[15421]**, **[38324]**

Revay and Associates Ltd. **[7633]**

Revelations of Awareness **[17934]**

"Revenge of the neurons" in *Red Herring* (No. 105, October 1, 2001, pp. 58-63) **[8801]**, **[50797]**

"Revenue-Raising Ideas Could Hit Financial Services" in *American Banker* (Vol. 170, February 2, 2005, No. 22, pp. 4) **[10167]**, **[54725]**

"Revenue Upswing" in *Hispanic Business* (December 2002, pp. 40-41) **[773]**, **[20333]**, **[47471]**

Revere Chamber of Commerce **[60992]**

"Reverence for radicals" in *Fast Company* (June 2001, pp. 48) **[45601]**, **[47472]**

"Reveries" in *Entrepreneur* (Vol. 31, No. 8, August 2003, pp. 6) **[47473]**

"The Reverse Greenhouse Effect: Why pay another to gardener to cultivate your stock?" in *Fortune* (Vol.141, No.7, Apr. 3, 2000, pp.302) **[43059]**, **[55807]**

"Reverse auctions online" in *Hispanic Business* (Vol. 22, No. 11, November 2000, pp. 94) **[1848]**, **[34413]**

"The Right Tool for the Job" in *Inc.* (Volume 27, December 2005, No. 12, pp. 136) **[49232]**, **[49544]**

"Righting the Digital Ship" in *Black Enterprise* (Vol. 36, February 2006, No. 7, pp. 63) **[31840]**, **[45604]**

The Rights of Employees & Union Members: The Basic ACLU Guide to the Rights of Employees & Union Members **[55309]**

Rights and Respect: What You Need to Know about Gender Bias and Sexual Harassment **[32058]**

Rim Country Regional Chamber of Commerce **[57064]**

"Ring Bearers: Some Would-Be Grooms Need a Little Direction in Finding the Perfect Diamond. Here Comes the Guides" in *Entrepreneur* **[3192]**, **[15857]**, **[37769]**

"Ring It Up. Way Systems Helps Convert Cell Phones into Portable Cash Registers" in *Boston Business Journal* (Vol. 23, Aug. 22, 2003) **[5097]**, **[41953]**, **[48782]**

"Ringing Up Profits" in *Small Business Opportunities* (Vol. 16, No. 3, May 2004, pp. 12) **[5098]**, **[27169]**

"Ringing Up Sales" in *Small Business Opportunities* (Vol. 12, No. 2, March 2000, pp. 52) **[51808]**

Ringling School of Art and Design–Verman Kimbrough Memorial Library **[6078]**, **[19276]**

Ringwood Chamber of Commerce **[62554]**

Rinksider **[22839]**

Rio Grande Valley Chamber of Commerce **[65463]**

Rio Linda-Elverta Chamber of Commerce **[57738]**

Rio Rancho Chamber of Commerce **[62708]**

Rio Salado Community College **[57103]**

Rio Vista Chamber of Commerce **[57739]**

Riordan Lewis & Haden **[58135]**

"Riparian Unveils Village Ventures' R.I. Fund" in *Venture Capital Journal* (Vol. 40, No. 10, November 2000, pp. 20) **[41954]**, **[55811]**

Ripley County Chamber of Commerce **[59997]**, **[62031]**

Ripon Area Chamber of Commerce **[66513]**

Ripon Chamber of Commerce **[57740]**

"Ripple Effects" in *Hispanic Business* (May 2005, pp. 68, 70) **[39901]**, **[40653]**

"Rise of China's Consumer Class Excites California Ag Industry" in *Sacramento Bee* (December 19, 2005) **[13006]**, **[26534]**, **[43800]**

"Rising Drug Costs" in *Venture Capital Journal* (October 1, 2204) **[32672]**, **[43801]**, **[49731]**, **[50959]**, **[52192]**, **[55812]**

"Rising Gas Costs Create Pricing Pressure" in *Tradeshow Week* (Vol. 34, November 29, 2004, No. 48, pp. 4) **[22556]**, **[25011]**, **[25408]**, **[55152]**

"Rising money" in *Entrepreneur* (Vol. 30, No. 1, January 2002, pp. 36) **[35627]**, **[44435]**, **[48889]**, **[55423]**

"Rising to the Top" in *Black Enterprise* (Vol. 35, November 2004, No. 4, pp. 183) **[20335]**, **[36701]**, **[40654]**

"Rising health premiums mean more uninsured" in *Atlanta Business Chronicle* (Vol. 25, No. 19, October 18, 2002, pp. 10C) **[13450]**, **[26906]**, **[43345]**

"Risk of Debit-Card Fraud Rises" in *Sacramento Bee* (November 12, 2005) **[8319]**, **[8358]**, **[8396]**, **[22347]**

"Risk at your Fingertips" in *Small Business Opportunities* (Vol. 16, No. 1, January 2004, pp. 86, 130) **[6780]**, **[22348]**

Risk-Free Entrepreneur **[36702]**, **[46419]**, **[47479]**, **[48783]**, **[48924]**

"Risk is His Business" in *Fortune* (Vol. 152, October 3, 2005, No. 7, pp. 61) **[13451]**, **[43346]**

Risk & Insurance Magazine's Managing Risk for Loss Prevention and Cost Control **[43437]**

Risk and Insurance Management Society **[13172]**

"Risk Is a Wonderful Thing" in *Success* (Vol. 47, No. 6, November 2000, pp. 24) **[35628]**

Risk Management Association **[44456]**

"Risk Management on the Farm" in *Hispanic Business* (November 2002, pp. 33) **[13452]**, **[26535]**, **[43347]**

Risk Management for Project Managers **[44838]**

Risk Management Resource Guide **[19567]**

Risk Management Strategies and Tactics for Business **[36467]**, **[37860]**

The Risk Report **[13561]**

"Risky Business: Hedge fund chic is both undeserved - and dangerous" in *Red Herring* (No. 103, September 1, 2001, pp. 84-85) **[15423]**, **[38326]**

"Risky business: on the lookout for business insurance?" in *Entrepreneur* (Vol. 31, No. 6, June 2003, pp. 73) **[13453]**, **[43348]**, **[53946]**

"A Risky Business" in *Kiplinger's Personal Finance Magazine* (Vol. 54, No. 9, September 2000, pp. 94) **[35629]**, **[37076]**, **[56761]**

"Risky Business: Staff Smarts" in *Entrepreneur* (Vol. 31, No. 9, September 2003, pp. 78) **[31582]**, **[42401]**

"Risky Business: Wacky Marketing Moves Put These Businesses on the Map" in *Entrepreneur* (Vol. 32, August 2004, No. 8, pp. 26) **[47480]**, **[50663]**

Rita's Ices - Cones - Shakes and Other Cool Stuff **[12847]**

Rittman Area Chamber of Commerce **[63780]**

"Ritz-Carlton Offers Henry Ford Patients a Place to Recuperate" in *Crain's Detroit Business* (Vol. 21, October 10, 2005, No. 43) **[12628]**, **[41091]**

Ritzville Area Chamber of Commerce **[66159]**

"Rivaling a Giant" in *Boston Business Journal* (Vol. 23, No. 30, August 29, 2003, pp. 3) **[6963]**, **[30938]**, **[41955]**, **[47481]**, **[48784]**

River Capital **[59204]**

River Cities Regional Chamber of Commerce **[61413]**

River East Corp. **[63884]**

River Falls Area Chamber of Commerce and Tourism Bureau **[66514]**

River Heights Chamber of Commerce **[61655]**

River Oaks - Sansom Park Area Chamber of Commerce **[65464]**

River Valley Chamber of Commerce **[60771]**

River Walleye Location Secrets **[2200]**

River Walleye Presentation Secrets **[2201]**

Riverbank Chamber of Commerce **[57741]**

Riverdale Chamber of Commerce **[59650]**

Riverfront Research Park **[64298]**

Riverhead Chamber of Commerce **[62995]**

Riverside Chamber of Commerce **[59651]**

Riverton Chamber of Commerce **[66626]**

Rivervest Venture Partners **[62088]**

"Riverview, Trenton try to salvage riverfront dreams" in *Crain's Detroit Business* (Vol. 16, No. 49, December 4, 2000, pp. 41) **[25409]**, **[52940]**

Rivier College–Small Business Development Center **[62392]**

R.J. Boar's Barbecue **[21943]**

RLG Focus **[13112]**

RMA Annual Statement Studies **[309]**, **[849]**, **[956]**, **[1032]**, **[1141]**, **[1419]**, **[1990]**, **[2082]**, **[2260]**, **[2364]**, **[2402]**, **[2506]**, **[2756]**, **[3052]**, **[3105]**, **[3328]**, **[4212]**, **[4371]**, **[4481]**, **[5195]**, **[5348]**, **[5468]**, **[5733]**, **[6011]**, **[6492]**, **[6880]**, **[7520]**, **[7750]**, **[7785]**, **[7849]**, **[8189]**, **[8810]**, **[8911]**, **[9079]**, **[9243]**, **[9753]**, **[10516]**, **[10578]**, **[10710]**, **[10807]**, **[11175]**, **[11448]**, **[11683]**, **[11806]**, **[11898]**, **[12024]**, **[12319]**, **[12380]**, **[12658]**, **[13530]**, **[15864]**, **[16032]**, **[16188]**, **[16237]**, **[16276]**, **[16323]**, **[16388]**, **[16477]**, **[16543]**, **[16752]**, **[16966]**, **[17109]**, **[17196]**, **[17493]**, **[17536]**, **[17560]**, **[17782]**, **[18167]**, **[18344]**, **[18620]**, **[18690]**, **[18713]**, **[18949]**, **[19028]**, **[19206]**, **[19307]**, **[19453]**, **[19760]**, **[19898]**, **[19982]**, **[20240]**, **[20711]**, **[21180]**, **[21365]**, **[21674]**, **[22070]**, **[22429]**, **[22623]**, **[22770]**, **[22804]**, **[22835]**, **[23273]**, **[23648]**, **[23795]**, **[24245]**, **[24541]**, **[24839]**, **[25276]**, **[25417]**, **[25496]**, **[25581]**, **[25600]**, **[25651]**, **[46495]**, **[51424]**, **[56022]**

RMA (Risk Management Association)–Information Center **[8418]**

"The Road to Healthy Sales " in *Sales & Marketing Management* **[4783]**, **[23152]**, **[51809]**, **[53438]**

"A Road Less Taxed" in *My Business* (February/March 2004, pp. 40) **[239]**, **[24026]**, **[51491]**, **[54307]**, **[54727]**

"Road-money halt slows $172.5M Oakland plan" in *Crain's Detroit Business* (Vol. 19, No. 17, April 28, 2003, pp. 1) **[28716]**, **[32673]**

The Road to Self-Employment: A Practical Guide to Microbusiness Development **[52941]**

"Road Signs" in *Entrepreneur* (Vol. 33, September 2005, No. 9, pp. 85) **[775]**, **[47482]**

Road & Track **[18183]**

"Road Warrior" in *Inc.* (November 15, 2000, pp. 33) **[49233]**

"Road Warriors" in *BlackEnterprise* (Vol. 32, No. 2, September 2001, pp. 106) **[30411]**, **[49234]**

"Road Weary No More" in *Hispanic Business* (Vol. 24, No. 1/2, January/February 2002, pp. 10) **[40655]**, **[43802]**

The Road to Wise Money Management: Planning, Credit, and Your First Paycheck **[10320]**

"Roamin' Holiday: Let a Vacation Put You On the Road to a Great Start-Up Idea" in *Entrepreneur* (Vol. 31, No. 9, September 2003) **[9637]**, **[36703]**

Roane County Chamber of Commerce **[64969]**, **[66296]**

Roanoke Regional Chamber of Commerce **[65942]**

Roanoke Regional Small Business Development Center **[65836]**

Roanoke Times (January 21, 2005); "Internet Opens World of Sales" in **[1829]**, **[14158]**, **[47149]**, **[51208]**

Roanoke Times (July 13, 2004); "Mystery Shopper Reports Lead to Several Firings at Roanoke, Va., Theater" in **[17524]**, **[31789]**

Roanoke Valley Chamber of Commerce **[63422]**

Robbinex Inc. **[50333]**

"Robbins Bros. Executive to Manage Growth" in *San Fernando Valley Business Journal* (Vol. 11, December 2006, No. 25, pp. 16) **[15858]**, **[37770]**

Robbinsdale Chamber of Commerce **[61656]**

Robeks Fruit Smoothies & Healthy Eats **[12035]**, **[12848]**

"Robert L. Johnson" in *Black Enterprise* (Vol. 36, November 2005, No. 4, pp. 34) **[4120]**, **[24447]**, **[36704]**, **[56389]**

Robert W. Neill Companies **[21093]**

"Robert Wagner Hosts The Litigation Explosion" in *Entrepreneur* (Vol. 33, January 2005, No. 1, pp. 104) **[22349]**, **[29470]**, **[31209]**, **[38327]**, **[54728]**

Robert Weinstein Maritime Historical Collection **[16793]**

Roberta - Crawford County Chamber of Commerce **[59156]**

A.E. Roberts Co. **[27046]**, **[43442]**

Douglas F. Roberts **[47901]**

"Roberts' Internet venture to set up shop in Detroit" in *Crain's Detroit Business* (Vol. 16, No. 16, April 17, 2000, pp. 34) **[13775]**, **[33483]**, **[47975]**, **[52641]**

Robertson Personal Injury NetLetter **[29682]**, **[30767]**

Robertson-Stephens Co. **[58136]**

Norman A. Robins Consulting **[29052]**

Robin's Donuts **[2311]**

Fred J. Robinson & Associates Inc. **[16148]**

Robot Times **[42137]**

Robotic Ventures **[59759]**

Rochelle Area Chamber of Commerce **[59652]**

Rochester Area Chamber of Commerce **[61657]**

Rochester Business Alliance **[62996]**

Rochester Business Alliance, Women's Council **[62997]**

Rochester Business Journal **[63236]**

Rochester Business Magazine **[63237]**

Rochester Civic Garden Center–Library **[11536]**

Rochester Community and Tech. College–Small Business Development Center **[61533]**

Rochester Institute of Technology
    Center for Integrated Manufacturing Studies **[46555]**
    Melbert B. Cary, Jr. Graphic Arts Collection **[2851]**, **[4177]**, **[6079]**, **[25507]**

Rochester and Lake Manitou Chamber of Commerce **[59998]**

"Rochester OKs plans for $30M, 140-room hotel" in *Crain's Detroit Business* (Vol. 18, No. 51, December 23, 2002, pp. 1) **[12629]**

Rock Beach Press **[63265]**

Rock Falls Chamber of Commerce **[59653]**

Rock Hill Ventures, Inc. / Hillman Medical Ventures, Inc. **[64576]**

Rock Island County Illinois Genealogical Society–Library **[11071]**

Rock Port Chamber of Commerce **[62032]**

Rock Rapids Community Affairs Corporation **[60198]**

Rock Springs Chamber of Commerce **[66627]**

Rock Springs SBDC–Region I **[66600]**

Rock Valley Chamber of Commerce **[60199]**

Rock Valley College **[59800]**
   Small Business Development Center **[59386]**

Rockburn Institute **[41402]**

Rockdale Chamber of Commerce **[65465]**

Nelson A. Rockefeller Institute of Government **[66941]**

"Rocket Science Retailing Is Almost Here Are You Ready?" in *Harvard Business Review* (Vol. 78, No. 4, July 2000, pp. 115) **[34419]**, **[51334]**

Rocket Ventures **[58137]**

Rockford Area Chamber of Commerce **[61414]**

Rockford Regional Chamber of Commerce **[59654]**

Rockford Regional Chamber of Commerce Business Women's Council **[59655]**

Rockhurst College–Small Business Development Center **[61875]**

Rockin'Baja Lobster **[21944]**

Rockland Chamber of Commerce **[60993]**, **[62998]**

Rockland Community College–Small Business Development Center **[62779]**

Rockland Satellite–SBDC **[60714]**

Rocklin Area Chamber of Commerce **[57742]**

Rockmountain Ventures **[58459]**

Rockport-Camden-Lincolnville Chamber of Commerce **[60772]**

Rockport-Fulton Area Chamber of Commerce **[65466]**

Rockport capital Partners **[61112]**

Rockton Chamber of Commerce **[59656]**

Rockville Centre Chamber of Commerce **[62999]**

Rockville Chamber of Commerce **[60855]**

Rockwall County Chamber of Commerce **[65467]**

Rockwell City Chamber and Development **[60200]**

Rocky Ford Chamber of Commerce **[58420]**

Rocky Hill Chamber of Commerce **[58563]**

Rocky Mount Area Chamber of Commerce **[63423]**

Rocky Mountain Chocolate Factory, Inc. **[4335]**

Rocky Mountain Publishing Professionals Guild-Directory **[2753]**, **[18254]**

Rocky Mountain Snowmobile & Icefishing Expo **[23697]**, **[55243]**

"Rocky Mountain Steel Mill, a decade and counting" in *Colorado Springs Business Journal* (March 7, 2003) **[46420]**

Rocky River Chamber of Commerce **[63781]**

Rodale Inc.–Library **[11537]**

Rodale Institute **[12171]**

Rodale's All-New Encyclopedia of Organic Gardening: The Indispensable Resource for Every Gardener **[11441]**

Rodale's Illustrated Encyclopedia of Perennials **[11442]**

Rodan Jewellers **[15886]**

Rodeway Inn **[12726]**

Guy Rodgers & Associates Inc. **[10766]**, **[20192]**

Earl Rodney **[26437]**

Roeder Design **[49650]**

"Rofin-Sinar sales rise 61 percent" in *Crain's Detroit Business* (Vol. 16, No. 46, November 13, 2000, pp. 4) **[16380]**, **[28717]**

"Roger Cass the Last Optimist" in *Fast Company* (July 2001, pp. 88) **[36705]**, **[39564]**

Rogers City Chamber of Commerce **[61415]**

Rogers Lowell Area Chamber of Commerce **[57211]**

Rogue Community College–Small Business Development Center **[64174]**

Rogue River Area Chamber of Commerce **[64261]**

Rohnert Park Chamber of Commerce **[57743]**

"ROI Drive Spurs New Models: More Choices" in *Tradeshow Week* (Vol. 34, November 29, 2004, No. 48, pp. 58) **[22557]**, **[25012]**, **[55153]**

"The ROI On Your MBA" in *Business 2.0* (Vol. 6, September 2005, No. 8, pp. 99) **[33223]**, **[45605]**

"Role of Coach Critical to Success of New Producer" in *Rough Notes* (Vol. 145, No. 9, September 2002, pp. 30) **[13454]**, **[33224]**, **[43349]**, **[53947]**

"The Role of Integrity as a Mediator in Strategic Leadership" in *Journal of Business Ethics* (Vol. 46, No. 1, Aug. 2003, pp. 31) **[36706]**, **[37498]**, **[45606]**

The Role of the Non-Executive Director in the Small to Medium-Sized Business **[36707]**, **[45607]**

Roll A Way Storm and Security Shutters **[22446]**

"Roll On: Davin Enjoys Just Spinning Your Wheels" in *Black Enterprise* (Vol. 34, No. 4, November 2003, pp. 180) **[1966]**, **[28718]**, **[36708]**, **[48394]**

Rolla Area Chamber of Commerce **[62033]**

Rolla Chamber of Commerce **[63532]**

Rollaway Bay Publications Inc. **[58487]**

Roller Skating Association Convention and Trade Show **[22841]**

Roller Skating Association International **[22832]**

Rollerz **[21945]**

"Rolling the Dice on Hedge Funds" in *Business 2.0* (Vol. 6, May 2005, No. 4, pp. 34) **[15424]**, **[38328]**

"Rolling dough: do you go with original butter and salt or almond crunch?" in *Entrepreneur* (Vol. 31, No. 6, June 2003, pp. 106) **[20179]**, **[38900]**

Rolling Hills Publishing **[60900]**

Rolling Meadows Chamber of Commerce **[59657]**

Rollins College–Center for Enterprise Management **[43012]**

"Rollups Redux" in *Business Week* (No. 3666, January 31,, 2000 pp. 6) **[52448]**

Roly Poly The Original Rolled Sandwich **[21946]**

Romanian-U.S. Business Council **[43525]**

"Romar Group Newest NASCAR Licensee" in *Black Enterprise* (Vol. 35, November 2004, No. 4, pp. 32) **[5567]**, **[5712]**, **[23735]**, **[44136]**, **[48395]**

Rome Area Chamber of Commerce **[63000]**

Romeo-Washington Chamber of Commerce **[61416]**

Romeoville Chamber of Commerce **[59658]**

Rommett Floor-Barre Technique: A Method to Develop and Refine Ballet Technique **[8483]**

"Romney, Businesses Wrangle On 'Loopholes'" in *Boston Globe* (January 31, 2005) **[40656]**, **[54729]**

"Romney Set To Unveil Jobs Program" in *Boston Globe* (February 3, 2005) **[39902]**, **[40657]**, **[42402]**

Ronzio Pizza **[21947]**

Roof Coatings Manufacturers Association **[22059]**

Roof Consultants Institute **[22060]**

Roof Patch Man **[22078]**

Roofing Contractor **[7574]**, **[13136]**

Roofing Contractor (Aug. 03); "Historical Architectural Review Board Recently Awarded Nancy Noll, the Historic Rehabilitation Award" in **[2436]**

Roofing Contractor-Single Ply Systems Index Issue **[22067]**

Roofing Materials Science and Technology **[22076]**

Roofing and Siding **[22071]**

"Rookie Season" in *Incentive* (Vol. 174, No. 10, October 2000, pp. 130) **[35054]**

"Room Glut Has Hotels Unsettled" in *Atlanta Business Chronicle* (Vol. 25, December 6, 2002, No. 26, pp. 1) **[12630]**, **[22558]**, **[25013]**, **[25241]**, **[28719]**, **[30412]**, **[32674]**

"Room to Grow" in *Entrepreneur* (Vol. 32, November 2004, No. 11, pp. 64) **[6279]**, **[49235]**

"Room to Grow: yes, even in the most stagnant economy, it's possible to expand" in *Entrepreneur* (Vol. 31, No. 6, June 2003, pp. 28) **[16530]**, **[28720]**, **[32675]**

"Room for Growth in the Big Apple" in *Black Enterprise* (Vol. 31, No. 5, December 2000, pp. 64) **[28721]**, **[34420]**, **[48396]**

"Room for More" in *Business First Columbus* (Vol. 18, No. 38, May) **[17559]**, **[39565]**, **[54248]**

"Room at the table" in *Boston Business Journal* (Vol. 22, No. 14, May 10, 2002, pp. 21) **[3578]**, **[16531]**, **[45608]**

"Roomier Recreational Trailers Becoming More Popular" in *Providence Business News* (Vol. 18, No. 17, August 11, 2003, pp. 2) **[21175]**, **[28722]**

Roosevelt County Chamber of Commerce **[62709]**

Roosters - Men's Grooming Centers **[11839]**

"The Root of the Business: Drawing on one's ethnicity leads to a passionate niche" in *My Business* (April/May 2002, pp. 36-39) **[35630]**, **[52784]**

Root Cause Analysis and Problem Solving (Canada) **[46180]**

Rooter-Man **[22720]**

"The Roots of a Home" in *Crain's Detroit Business* (Vol. 22, February 6, 2006, No. 6, pp. 19) **[20659]**, **[20998]**, **[54730]**

Rootstown Area Chamber of Commerce **[63782]**

Ropers Majeski Kohn & Bentley–Library **[13609]**

Rosalia Chamber of Commerce **[66160]**

Roscoe-Rockland Chamber of Commerce **[63001]**

Rose Bowl Collectors **[1311]**, **[5815]**

"A rose by any other name" in *Harvard Business Review* (Vol. 81, No. 3, March 2003, pp. 29) **[46421]**, **[51335]**

Rose & Crangle Ltd. **[3808]**, **[3985]**, **[10346]**, **[16663]**, **[31452]**, **[46110]**, **[53112]**

Rose Marketing on a Daisy Budget: Learn the Secrets to Blooming Profits **[10569]**

"A Rose by No Name" in *My Business* (June/July 2004, pp. 45) **[10168]**, **[10570]**, **[37771]**

The Rose Sheet **[2615]**, **[7918]**

Rose State College
   Oklahoma Small Business Development Center–Procurement Center **[64121]**
   SBDC **[63919]**

"A Rose With Another Name" in *Forbes* (Vol. 174, December 27, 2004, No. 13, pp. 51) **[6003]**, **[9301]**, **[10571]**, **[11659]**, **[19893]**, **[44137]**

Rosebud Chamber of Commerce and Agriculture **[65468]**

Roseburg Area Chamber of Commerce **[64262]**

Roselle Chamber of Commerce and Industry **[59659]**

Rosemead Chamber of Commerce **[57744]**

Rosen Numismatic Advisory **[5853]**

Sam Rosenbaum & Co. **[50334]**

Rosenberg - Richmond Area Chamber of Commerce **[65469]**

Roser Ventures LLC **[58460]**

"Rosetta gets dozens of Random e-book licenses" in *Publishers Weekly* (Vol. 250, No. 15, April 14, 2003, pp. 10) **[2740]**, **[9157]**

"Rosetta, Random House settle e-book lawsuit" in *Publishers Weekly* (Vol. 249, No. 49, Dec. 9, 2002, pp. 9) **[2741]**, **[9158]**, **[44138]**

Rosetta Stone Associates **[25104]**

"RosettaNet: The Key to Supply Chain Efficiency?" in *E-business Advisor* (Vol. 17, No. 12, December 1999, pp. 16) **[23153]**, **[28723]**, **[34421]**, **[53439]**

"Roseville, Calif., Gourmet Gift Firm Puts Buyout on Hold" in *Sacramento Bee* (October 21, 2005) **[4306]**, **[15425]**, **[23504]**, **[30696]**, **[50166]**, **[52364]**, **[52449]**

Roseville Chamber of Commerce **[57745]**

Rosevine Winery **[23572]**

Rosewood Capital, L.P. **[58138]**

Ross County Genealogical Society–Library **[11072]**

Ross & McBride–Library **[54918]**

Ross Products Division–Abbott Laboratories–Resource Center **[18511]**

Ross University–School of Veterinary Medicine–Stanley Mark Dennis Veterinary Library **[1280]**

Roswell Chamber of Commerce **[62710]**

Roswellness **[41293]**

"A rosy sales picture" in *Crain's Detroit Business* (Vol. 19, No. 7, February 17, 2003, pp. 25) **[10572]**, **[51336]**

ROTA.GENE **[10985]**

"Rotary Club Of Jackson Invests In Metro Students" in *Mississippi Business Journal* (Vol. 28, September 2006, No. 36, pp. 3) **[32676]**, **[33225]**, **[56762]**

Rotelli Pizza & Pasta **[19711]**

Rothman Consulting Group Inc. **[23307]**

Rothschild Strategies Unlimited L.L.C. **[3809]**, **[3986]**, **[16664]**, **[30114]**, **[31453]**, **[46111]**, **[53113]**

Rothschild Ventures, Inc. **[63160]**

The Rottweiler Quarterly **[1208]**

"Rouge Industries' Russian Suitor Promises New Furnace" in *Crain's Detroit Business* (Vol. 19, No. 43, October 27, 2003, pp. 17) **[46422]**, **[47769]**, **[48260]**, **[50167]**

"Rough-Cut Dimon" in *Forbes* (May 13, 2002, p. 64) **[28724]**, **[45609]**

Rough Notes (Vol. 145, No. 1, January 2003, pp. 84); "A Balancing Act" in **[13198]**, **[43086]**

Rough Notes (Vol. 145, No. 1, January 2003, pp. 54); "A Consistent Social Services Market For Over 20 Years" in **[13241]**, **[43133]**

Rough Notes (Vol. 146, No. 4, April 2003, pp. 58); "A classical gas" in **[13236]**, **[16734]**, **[17996]**, **[43127]**

Rough Notes (Vol. 145, No. 2, February 2003, pp. 44); "A Silver Lining For the Nursing Home Industry" in **[13462]**, **[18337]**, **[43359]**

Rough Notes (Vol. 146, No. 3, March 2003, pp. 30); "Accountants on the Move" in **[57]**, **[13175]**, **[26139]**, **[43067]**

Rough Notes (Vol. 146, No. 3, March 2003, pp. 128); "Accounting for intangible assets" in **[58]**, **[13176]**, **[40143]**

Rough Notes (Vol. 145, No. 9, September 2002, pp. 38); "Agent of Change" in **[6328]**, **[13179]**, **[32994]**, **[35758]**, **[43069]**

Rough Notes (Vol. 145, No. 12, December 2002, pp. 127); "Agents Urged to Answer the Call" in **[13180]**, **[43071]**, **[51544]**

Rough Notes (Vol. 146, No. 3, March 2003, pp. 54); "All Offices Are Not Created Equal" in **[13183]**, **[43074]**

Rough Notes (Vol. 146, No. 3, March 2003, pp. 38); "Alternative Market Grows As Rates Harden" in **[13184]**, **[43075]**

Rough Notes (Vol. 145, No. 9, September 2002, pp. 82); "Alternative Markets and Risk Financing" in **[13185]**, **[43076]**

Rough Notes (Vol. 145, No. 2, February 2003, pp. 66); "Anatomy of a Merger" in **[13186]**, **[29788]**, **[43077]**, **[49788]**

Rough Notes (Vol. 146, No. 4, April 2003, pp. 18); "Answer the phone and have a good time" in **[7240]**, **[13187]**, **[40960]**, **[41517]**, **[43078]**

Rough Notes (Vol. 145, No. 2, February 2002, pp. 50); "Appraising The Agency" in **[3497]**, **[13189]**, **[43079]**

Rough Notes (Vol. 145, No. 1, January 2003, pp. 82); "Automation Accountability" in **[3499]**, **[13195]**, **[48952]**, **[49486]**

Rough Notes (Vol. 145, No. 9, September 2002, pp. 62); "Becoming a Great Agency: Part One" in **[13200]**, **[43089]**

Rough Notes (Vol. 145, No. 12, December 2002, pp. 110); "Boosting Morale with Work/Life Benefits" in **[13213]**, **[26753]**, **[34833]**, **[43103]**

Rough Notes (Vol. 146, No. 3, March 2003, pp. 106); "Builders Risk Options" in **[7275]**, **[13215]**

Rough Notes (Vol. 146, No. 3, March 2003, pp. 82); "Business Interruption Insurance Required Rethinking" in **[13218]**, **[43109]**

Rough Notes (Vol. 145, No. 1, January 2003, pp. 108); "C-DHP: Where Is The Movement Headed" in **[13221]**, **[27316]**, **[33028]**, **[43112]**

Rough Notes (Vol. 145, No. 1, January 2003, pp. 78); "Captive Agents Face Off Against Their Captors" in **[13227]**, **[29144]**, **[43119]**

Rough Notes (Vol. 146, No. 9, September 2003, pp. 16); "Captives Should Broaden their Focus" in **[13228]**, **[26765]**, **[43120]**

Rough Notes (Vol. 146, No. 3, March 2003, pp. 98); "Carrier Services Centers" in **[13229]**, **[43121]**

Rough Notes (Vol. 145, No. 2, February 2003, pp. 65); "Changing Times Require Changes in Recruiting Styles" in **[9873]**, **[13231]**, **[31658]**, **[42200]**, **[44992]**

Rough Notes (Vol. 146, No. 4, April 2003, pp. 104); "Clear as mud" in **[13237]**, **[43128]**

Rough Notes (Vol. 145, No. 9, September 2002, pp. 18); "Committed to Independence" in **[13239]**, **[20473]**, **[20842]**, **[43130]**

"Rough Notes presents Community Service Award" in *Rough Notes* (Vol. 146, No. 4, April 2003, pp. 98) **[13455]**, **[43350]**, **[54249]**

Rough Notes (Vol. 145, No. 1, January 2003, pp. 98); "Construction Risk Management: Facing the Fire" in **[3515]**, **[7300]**, **[13243]**, **[37615]**

Rough Notes (Vol. 145, No. 1, January 2003, pp. 64); "Contractors Market" in **[13245]**, **[43136]**, **[49688]**

Rough Notes (Vol. 145, No. 1, January 2003, pp. 10); "Court Decisions - Privacy coverage differs from patent infringement" in **[13247]**, **[29174]**, **[43138]**, **[44021]**

Rough Notes (Vol. 145, No. 9, September 2002, pp. 52); "Covering Contractors" in **[13248]**, **[43139]**

Rough Notes (Vol. 146, No. 3, March 2003, pp. 52); "Create a Client Loyalty Program" in **[13252]**, **[31675]**, **[45033]**

Rough Notes (Vol. 145, No. 2, February 2003, pp. 90); "Credit Score Providers Address Concerns" in **[31533]**

Rough Notes (Vol. 145, No. 2, February 2003, pp. 40); "Cyber Theft" in **[13072]**, **[13255]**, **[22209]**, **[43144]**, **[53676]**

Rough Notes (Vol. 145, No. 1, January 2003, pp. 110); "Cybersecurity: Opportunities for Agents" in **[13256]**, **[13950]**, **[22210]**, **[22957]**, **[28003]**, **[33734]**, **[43145]**, **[53677]**

Rough Notes (Vol. 145, No. 9, September 2002, pp. 71); "D&O: Hard and Getting Harder" in **[13257]**, **[37417]**, **[43146]**

Rough Notes (Vol. 145, No. 9, September 2002, pp. 34); "Debit Cards Ease FSA Administration Burden" in **[122]**, **[26208]**, **[37995]**, **[40303]**, **[53681]**

Rough Notes (Vol. 146, No. 9, September 2003, pp. 62); "Delivering the Right Technology at the Right Time" in **[4634]**, **[13261]**, **[22962]**, **[53252]**

Rough Notes (Vol. 146, No. 4, April 2003, pp. 30); "Employee theft on the rise - Fidelity coverage is crucial" in **[13274]**, **[22221]**, **[43165]**, **[45100]**

Rough Notes (Vol. 146, No. 9, September 2003, pp. 68); "Engaging Before Merger" in **[13278]**, **[49917]**

Rough Notes (Vol. 145, No. 5, May 2002, pp. 53); "Enterprise Risk Management-A Fading Fad?" in **[9934]**, **[13280]**, **[22222]**, **[43170]**

Rough Notes (Vol. 145, No. 1, January 2003, pp. 44); "Equipment Maintenance Insurance Coverage" in **[13281]**, **[43171]**, **[46276]**

Rough Notes (Vol. 146, No. 3, March 2003, pp. 116); "ERM to the rescue" in **[36119]**, **[45112]**

Rough Notes (Vol. 146, No. 2, February 2003, pp. 68); "Everyone's a Winner at the Chub Charity Challenge" in **[11257]**, **[54173]**

Rough Notes (Vol. 146, No. 3, March 2003, pp. 18); "Everything designed with the customer in mind" in **[13282]**, **[31713]**, **[43172]**

Rough Notes (Vol. 146, No. 3, March 2003, pp. 114); "Fighting alcohol abuse can benefit insurers" in **[13284]**, **[41008]**

Rough Notes (Vol. 146, No. 3, March 2003, pp. 68); "Financial Services Market Changing" in **[9956]**, **[13285]**, **[38063]**, **[49933]**

Rough Notes (Vol. 145, No. 9, September 2002, pp. 46); "Finding Prospects By Using The Internet" in **[13286]**, **[14041]**, **[33897]**, **[43175]**, **[51635]**

Rough Notes (Vol. 146, No. 9, September 2003, pp. 50); "Fire Loss Illustrates Adjustment Terms" in **[13287]**, **[43176]**

Rough Notes (Vol. 145, No. 1, January 2003, pp. 20); "14th Annual Rough Notes Marketing Agency of the Year Candidate" in **[3533]**, **[13290]**, **[16813]**, **[46980]**

Rough Notes (Vol. 146, No. 3, March 2003, pp. 28); "Gaining Access to Middle Market Environmental Business" in **[13292]**, **[43180]**

Rough Notes (Vol. 146, No. 9, September 2003, pp. 44); "Gulf Team With Corpedia on Ethics Course" in **[13303]**, **[33986]**, **[34922]**, **[37452]**, **[43193]**, **[47053]**

Rough Notes (Vol. 145, No. 6, June 2002, pp. 50); "Hartford Expands Small Commercial Offerings" in **[13307]**, **[28265]**, **[43198]**

Rough Notes (Vol. 145, No. 9, September 2002, pp. 106); "Hire for Attitude, Train for Skills" in **[42262]**, **[45240]**

Rough Notes (Vol. 146, No. 4, April 2003, pp. 84); "Hospitality Industry" in **[12566]**, **[13325]**, **[43217]**

Rough Notes (Vol. 145, No. 9, September 2002, pp. 14); "HSB Sees Growth in Monoline Equipment Breakdown Due to Hard Market" in **[13330]**, **[43225]**

Rough Notes (Vol. 146, No. 3, March 2003, pp. 56); "Imaging: Changing the Way We Do Business" in **[13334]**, **[31743]**, **[49089]**

Rough Notes (Vol. 146, No. 4, April 2003, pp. 40); "IMMS lessens market woes" in **[13335]**, **[43229]**

Rough Notes (Vol. 145, No. 1, January 2003, pp. 34); "Informal Partnership gives Agents Clout" in **[13336]**, **[50001]**

Rough Notes (Vol. 145, No. 1, January 2003, pp. 38); "Inspection By Insurer Is Valuable But Doesn't Constitute A Warranty" in **[13339]**, **[43232]**

Rough Notes (Vol. 145, No. 12, December 2001, pp. 70); "Integrated consulting services offered by Allegent" in **[3545]**, **[13347]**, **[16522]**

Rough Notes (Vol. 146, No. 4, April 2003, pp. 74); "Intention, adaptation and annexation" in **[13348]**, **[21327]**, **[43239]**

Rough Notes (Vol. 146, No. 9, September 2003, pp. 60); "It's a Matter of Style" in **[13354]**, **[31747]**

Rough Notes (Vol. 146, No. 3, March 2003, pp. 49); "It's really Pretty Simple" in **[13355]**, **[43249]**, **[47157]**

Rough Notes (Vol. 145, No. 2, February 2002, pp. 79); "Keep The Ball Rolling" in **[13361]**, **[43254]**, **[45334]**, **[51705]**

Rough Notes (Vol. 146, No. 3, March 2003, pp. 118); "Little things mean a lot" in **[27654]**, **[31759]**, **[45376]**

Rough Notes (Vol. 145, No. 2, February 2002, pp. 36); "Managed Care's Poor Health" in **[10082]**, **[13375]**, **[26846]**, **[28452]**, **[32560]**

Rough Notes (Vol. 145, No. 38, June 2002, pp. 38); "Management Liability at the Speed of Light" in **[13376]**, **[43268]**, **[45398]**

Rough Notes (Vol. 146, No. 9, September 2003, pp. 52); "Mastering Agency Management" in **[13379]**, **[45422]**

Rough Notes (Vol. 145, No. 9, September 2002, pp. 66); "Med Mal in Crisis Mode" in **[13381]**, **[43273]**

Rough Notes (Vol. 145, No. 2, February 2003, pp. 43); "Mind Your P's and Q's" in **[27442]**, **[27659]**, **[39474]**

Rough Notes (Vol. 146, No. 3, March 2003, pp. 148); "Money well spent" in **[13387]**, **[43280]**

Rough Notes (Vol. 145, No. 2, February 2003, pp. 72); "Monitoring Your Carriers" in **[13388]**, **[43281]**

Rough Notes (Vol. 146, No. 3, March 2003); "Multiple Building Business Warrants Careful Attention To Loss of Earnings Exposure" in **[7430]**, **[13390]**

Rough Notes (Vol. 146, No. 3, March 2003, pp. 78); "Named Insured Wording: Doing It Right" in **[13392]**, **[43285]**

Rough Notes (Vol. 145, No. 9, September 2002, pp. 112); "National Alliance Promotes Professionalism Through Education" in **[20605]**, **[33181]**

Rough Notes (Vol. 145, No. 1, January 2003, pp. 40); "New NAPSLO President Helm" in **[13399]**, **[43291]**, **[53880]**

Sacramento Hispanic Chamber of Commerce [57750]

Sacramento Metro Chamber of Commerce [57751]

Sacramento SBDC–California State University at Chico [57270]

"Sacrificing a profitable account in favor of growth" in *Atlanta Business Chronicle* (Vol. 24, No. 13, August 31, 2001, pp. 40A) [28733]

Saddle & Bridle Magazine [12466]

Saddleback College [58233]

Saderling Ventures [58140]

Sadoff Investment Management [15673]

SAE International - Society of Automotive Engineers [22600]

SAE Online Roster [919]

SAE Ventures [58612]

"A Safe Bet" in *Entrepreneur* (Vol. 31, No. 7, July 2003, pp. 42) [22350], [34425], [49238]

Safe Driver [16191], [24249]

"Safe Keeping" in *Washington Business Journal* (Vol. 22, No. 17, August 29, 2003, pp. 26) [10171], [22351]

Safe Laboratories: Principle, Practices, Design, and Remodeling [17193]

Safe Not Sorry [3283]

"Safe Seats Don't Make Sound Politics" in *Hispanic Business* (Vol. 24, No. 5, May 2002, pp. 26, 28) [40660], [48398]

"Safe and Secure" in *Business First Columbus* (Vol. 18, No. 26, February 15, 2002, pp. A21) [22352], [41957], [52194]

"Safeguard your financial legacy" in *BlackEnterprise* (Vol. 32, No. 3, October 2001, pp. 75) [29983], [37773], [38331]

"Safeguarding your critical business information" in *Harvard Business Review* (Vol. 80, No. 2, February 2002, pp. 20) [6281], [6482], [22353], [44360]

"Safekeeping for Software" in *Business 2.0* (Vol. 7, January/February 2006, No. 1, pp. 30) [4785], [23155], [44141], [53441]

Safekidscard [33377]

"Safer Harbors, Higher Fees" in *Inc.* (January 1, 2004) [13007], [22354], [43805]

Safety in the Auto Shop [22651]

Safety Compliance Alert [56604]

"Safety Dance: Get Policies in Place Now, and Avoid Liability Later" in *Entrepreneur* (Vol. 31, No. 11, November 2003, pp. 93) [13456], [43352], [56586]

The Safety Deck [56643]

"Safety First" in *Entrepreneur* (Vol. 31, No. 11, November 2003, pp. 60) [4786], [22355], [23156], [49239], [53442]

Safety Harbor Chamber of Commerce [58924]

Safety & Health (Vol. 163, No. 3, March 2001, pp. 282); "Adapting to a multicultural workforce" in [48519], [56552]

Safety, Health & Environmental Hazards in the Workplace [56587]

Safety Is Caring About Identifying Hazards [56644]

Safety & Loss Control Associates [54371]

Safety Management Services [40891], [56668]

Safety Matters! Childproofing Services [5449]

"Safety Measures" in *Washington Business Journal* (Vol. 22, No. 16, August 22, 2003, pp. 18) [4787], [22356], [23157], [30414], [34426], [41958], [43806], [53443]

Safety: Not By Accident [56645]

Safety Orientation for Construction Contractors [7586]

Safety and the Supervisor [56605]

Safety Update [56606]

"Safeway gets in shape for food fight" in *San Francisco Business Times* (Vol. 16, No. 42, May 24, 2002, pp. 1) [11660], [30940], [51339]

Saffire Systems & Development Inc. [7003]

Sag Harbor Chamber of Commerce [63003]

"Saga of an online pioneer" in *The New York Times* (March 3, 2000, pp. A25, A21) [13776], [33484]

Sage [13588]

"Sage Advice" in *Entrepreneur* (Vol. 33, September 2005, No. 9, pp. 86) [27059], [27489], [47484]

"Sage unveils big plans for small business" in *Accounting Today* (Vol. 14, No. 13, July 24, 2000, pp. 29) [23158], [26342], [34427], [48786], [53444]

Sage Management Group [61115]

Sage Public Administration Abstracts [50373]

Sagebrook Technology [65626]

"Sagent Technology Unveils New Enterprise Information Portal" in *Information Today* (Vol. 17, No. 10, November 2000, pp. 44) [34428], [53445]

Saginaw Area Chamber of Commerce [65478]

Saginaw County Chamber of Commerce [61417] SBDC [61218]

Saginaw Future, Inc.–Small Business Development Center [61219]

Saginaw Valley State University–Small Business Development Center [61220]

"Said The Spider" in *Entrepreneur* (Vol. 28, No. 4, April 2000, pp. 149) [31210], [51810]

Sail Tall Ships! [16745]

Sailboat Buyers Guide [16746]

"Sailing On the Crest of the Home Health Care Wave" in *Indianapolis Business Journal* (Vol. 25) [457], [18335], [56391]

Sailing World [16762]

St. Albans Area Chamber of Commerce [66297]

St. Ansgar Chamber of Commerce [60201]

"St. Catherine of Siena Medical Center Seeks to Block LIRR" in *Long Island Business News* (March 12, 2004) [10581], [10695], [28816], [29476], [38975], [40661]

St. Charles Area Chamber of Commerce [59662]

"St. Charles Builders React to Steel Crisis" in *St. Charles Business Record* (May 3, 2004) [7473], [28734]

St. Charles Business Record (May 4, 2004); "Blossom Antique Shop Opens in Frenchtown" in [1292], [56028]

St. Charles Business Record (May 3, 2004); "St. Charles Builders React to Steel Crisis" in [7473], [28734]

St. Charles Business Record (May 7, 2004); "SBA Creates Contracting Opportunities for Disabled Veterans" in [39908], [40085]

St. Charles Business Record (May 7, 2004); "State Dept. of Economic Development Reports Strong Growth" in [28815], [32708]

St. Charles Business Record (September 30, 2004); "Westinn Kennels: A Phenomenal Growth Story" in [19085], [56474]

St. Charles Chamber of Commerce [62034]

"St. Charles Convention Center St. Charles, MO" in *Tradeshow Week* (Vol. 34, November 29, 2004, No. 48, pp. S5) [11344], [22559], [25015], [55154]

St. Charles County–SBDC University of Missouri Extension Center [61876]

St. Charles County Business Record, MO (Sept.2,03); "Investment Group Considers St. Charles as Home for Floating Bed and Breakfast" in [2444], [21538]

St. Charles County Business Record (February 2, 2005); "New St. Peters-based Company Helps Customers Take Care of Day-to-Day Errands" in [19001], [52566]

Saint Cinnamon Bake Shoppe [2312]

St. Clair Area Chamber of Commerce [62035]

St. Clair Shores Public Library–Local History Center [11074]

St. Clare's Hospital and Health Center–Spellman Center for HIV-Related Disease [17246]

St. Cloud Area Chamber of Commerce [61658]

St. Cloud Greater Osceola County Chamber of Commerce [58925]

St. Cloud State University
    Learning Resource Services–Special Collections [1666]
    Minnesota Real Estate Research Center [21118]
    Small Business Development Center [61534]

St. Croix Chamber of Commerce [66662]

St. Croix Falls Chamber of Commerce [66515]

St. Croix Valley Chamber of Commerce [60773]

St. Francis Area Chamber of Commerce [60411]

Saint Francis College–Small Business Development Center [64336]

St. Francis Xavier University–Coady International Institute [51500]

Ste. Genevieve Chamber of Commerce [62036]

St. George Area Chamber of Commerce [65726]

St. Germain Chamber of Commerce [66516]

St. Helena Chamber of Commerce [57752]

St. Ignace Chamber of Commerce [61418]

St. James Chamber of Commerce [62037], [63004]

The St. James Encyclopedia of Mortgage & Real Estate Finance [20661]

St. James Guide to Black Artists [6005], [8019]

St. John Chamber of Commerce [60000]

St. Johns Area Chamber of Commerce [61419]

St. Johns Regional Chamber of Commerce [57065]

St. Johns River Community College [59002]

St. Joseph Area Chamber of Commerce [62038]

St. Joseph Chamber of Commerce [61659]

St. Joseph Station [60040]

St. Joseph's University
    Academy of Food Marketing [11719]
    Academy of Food Marketing–Campbell Library [23584]

St. Lawrence County Chamber of Commerce [63005]

Saint Louis Bread/Panera Bread [2313]

St. Louis Business Journal [62111]

St. Louis Business Journal (Vol. 20, No. 40, June 12, 2000, pp. 23); "Small Business Owners Want Tax Cuts, Less Regulation" in [40699], [54753]

St. Louis Community College–Institute for Continuing Education [62105]

St. Louis County–Extension Center [61877]

St. Louis County Economic Council [62092]

St. Louis Franchise Limited [21949]

St. Louis Genealogical Society–Library [11075]

St. Louis Minority Business Council [62074]

St. Louis Post-Dispatch (December 8, 2004); "Business Briefs" in [26489], [50841], [52068]

St. Louis Post-Dispatch (August 27, 2004); "Business Incubator Has a Fish Wriggling Off of the Hook" in [35352], [41444], [52636], [55363], [56031]

St. Louis Post-Dispatch (February 23, 2005); "CABIR Phone Virus is Bad, But Not That Bad" in [4935], [13878], [22190]

St. Louis Post-Dispatch (December 6, 2004); "Can Firms Ban Weapons?" in [29140], [40235], [44979]

St. Louis Post-Dispatch (September 17, 2004); "Cardwell's at the Plaza is on the Plus Side of Ledger" in [21464], [27317]

St. Louis Post-Dispatch (February 17, 2005); "Company Looks to Link Rural Firms with City Buyers" in [3511], [31124], [39801], [46247]

St. Louis Post-Dispatch (September 24, 2004); "David Nicklaus Column" in [9905], [14905], [17370], [20482], [32346], [37993], [40299], [44398], [49888], [51123], [55368]

St. Louis Post-Dispatch (November 19, 2004); "Developer Sees a Bright Future for Downtown St. Louis" in [7323], [28030], [52664]

St. Louis Post-Dispatch (November 3, 2004); "Dialogue Picks Up on St. Louis' Status in IT and Biotech" in [41634], [50858], [52083], [55572]

St. Louis Post-Dispatch (January 9, 2005); "Fare Cuts Might Signal End to Airlines as We Know Them" in [28146], [30324]

St. Louis Post-Dispatch (December 17, 2004) "Firefox Is Hot; Thunderbird's Not" in [4660], [14044], [22996], [33902], [53283]

St. Louis Post-Dispatch (December 19, 2004) "Forget the Series; St. Louis has Bragging Rights for Job Growth" in [15011], [28178], [32444], [49946]

St. Louis Post-Dispatch (January 9, 2005); "Here's a Late Resolution, But One to Be Taken Seriously" in [27395], [34929], [39381], [45232]

St. Louis Post-Dispatch (March 9, 2005); "How High Can Low Go Without Adverse Effects on Economy?" in [32496], [42293]

Sales & Marketing Management (Vol. 157, January 2005, No. 1, pp. 50); "How I Got Here" in **[45260]**, **[47104]**

Sales & Marketing Management; "Joining Forces" in **[11633]**, **[12010]**, **[46332]**, **[47161]**, **[50030]**

Sales & Marketing Management (Vol. 157, January 2005, No. 1, pp. 11); "Lead Generator: Quick Ideas For Better Sales Leads" in **[28399]**, **[51711]**

Sales & Marketing Management (Vol. 159, January-February 2007, No. 1, pp. 28); "Location, Location, Location" in **[47203]**, **[51717]**

Sales & Marketing Management (Vol. 159, January-February 2007, No. 1, pp. 42); "Logitech MX Revolution Cordless Laser Mouse" in **[6713]**, **[49131]**

Sales & Marketing Management; "Making the Most Of It" in **[24970]**, **[47223]**, **[51723]**, **[55116]**

Sales & Marketing Management; "Mind Your Manners" in **[27441]**, **[27657]**, **[45438]**, **[51732]**

Sales & Marketing Management (Vol. 159, January-February 2007, No. 1, pp. 42); "MoGo Mouse BT" in **[5059]**, **[6727]**, **[49150]**

Sales & Marketing Management (Vol. 158, November-December 2006, No. 11, pp. 20); "MySpace for Business: Are You Connected?" in **[34226]**, **[47309]**, **[51740]**

Sales & Marketing Management (Vol. 159, January-February 2007, No. 1, pp. 48); "October Recap" in **[35007]**, **[45481]**, **[51750]**

Sales & Marketing Management (Vol. 159, January-February 2007, No. 1, pp. 48); "October Winner" in **[47359]**, **[51751]**

Sales & Marketing Management (Vol. 158, November-December 2006, No. 11, pp. 14); "On the Cheap" in **[744]**, **[23730]**, **[47361]**, **[51754]**

Sales & Marketing Management (Vol. 157, February 2005); "On the Fast Track: How Technology Is Speeding Incentive Delivery" in **[4749]**, **[6747]**, **[14305]**, **[23108]**, **[41884]**, **[49185]**, **[51755]**, **[53394]**

Sales & Marketing Management (Vol. 157, Jan. 2005); "On the Same Page: Gain Competitive Edge With a Company-Wide Focus on Customers" in **[30923]**, **[31804]**, **[51756]**

Sales & Marketing Management (January 2005); "One More For the Road" in **[13410]**, **[29426]**, **[36582]**, **[40593]**, **[43302]**, **[45494]**, **[47367]**, **[51758]**

Sales & Marketing Management (Vol. 157, January 2005, No. 1, pp. 34); "Passing the Baton" in **[49726]**, **[51761]**, **[53910]**

Sales & Marketing Management (Vol. 159, January-February 2007, No. 1, pp. 9); "Perfect Proposals" in **[31197]**, **[47394]**, **[51764]**

Sales & Marketing Management (Vol. 159, January-February 2007, No. 1, pp. 42); "Perific Wireless Dual Mouse" in **[6754]**, **[49202]**

Sales & Marketing Management (Vol. 159, January-February 2007, No. 1, pp. 41); "Phoenix" in **[22545]**, **[24995]**, **[28625]**, **[52714]**

Sales & Marketing Management (Vol. 157, January 2005, No. 1, pp. 17); "Pop Quiz: A Quick Test Of Your Managerial Skills" in **[45546]**, **[51767]**

Sales & Marketing Management (Vol. 158, November-December 2006, No. 11, pp. 17); "Pop Quiz: A Quick Test of Your Managerial Skills" in **[31199]**, **[45547]**, **[47406]**, **[51768]**

Sales & Marketing Management (Vol. 157, January 2005, No. 1, pp. 52); "Prioritizing a Hectic Schedule" in **[31205]**, **[47424]**, **[54979]**

Sales & Marketing Management (Vol. 157, Jan. 2005); "Promoting Praise: Incorporating Client Feedback Into Your Motivation Efforts" in **[31825]**, **[47430]**, **[51776]**

Sales & Marketing Management; "Ready To Go: How An Online Tool Helped One Company Speed Distribution of Marketing Materials To Reps" in **[13437]**, **[14389]**, **[43332]**, **[47453]**, **[51787]**, **[54985]**

Sales & Marketing Management (Vol. 157, February 2005, No. 2, pp. 16); "Recruit From Another Industry" in **[42390]**, **[45583]**, **[51788]**

Sales & Marketing Management (Vol. 157); "Redefining Sick Days" in **[26895]**, **[35044]**, **[47457]**, **[53935]**

Sales & Marketing Management (Vol. 159, January-February 2007, No. 1, pp. 45); "Repackage Your Words" in **[4782]**, **[6776]**, **[23150]**, **[27485]**, **[53436]**

Sales & Marketing Management (Vol. 157, February 2005); "Rewards For Recruiting: Incentivize Your Reps For Bringing In New Hires" in **[26904]**, **[42400]**, **[51804]**

Sales & Marketing Management (Vol. 158, November-December 2006, No. 11, pp. 20); "S&MM Pulse" in **[14409]**, **[22357]**, **[27491]**, **[31842]**, **[34433]**, **[45615]**, **[47491]**, **[49292]**, **[51824]**

Sales & Marketing Management (Vol. 158, October 2006, No. 10, pp. 15); "Say It and Sell It" in **[27492]**, **[47496]**, **[51825]**

Sales & Marketing Management (Vol. 157); "Staying Interactive: Web Presentation Success Requires More Than Just Technical Skills" in **[14485]**, **[27507]**, **[47576]**

Sales & Marketing Management (Vol. 157, February 2005, No. 2, pp. 11); "Substitute Presenter" in **[45686]**, **[51852]**

Sales & Marketing Management (Vol. 157, January 2005, No. 1, pp. 54); "T & E Report" in **[2080]**, **[21354]**, **[30419]**, **[47595]**

Sales & Marketing Management (Vol. 159, January-February 2007, No. 1, pp. 33); "Table Talk" in **[43833]**, **[47596]**, **[51858]**

Sales & Marketing Management (Vol. 158, October 2006, No. 10, pp. 16); "Take-Aways" in **[47597]**, **[51859]**

Sales & Marketing Management (Vol. 157, January 2005, No. 1, pp. 23); "Tech Watch: BlackBerry 7100t" in **[5136]**, **[49302]**

Sales & Marketing Management (Vol. 157, February 2005, No. 2, pp. 22); "Technophobe Help Desk" in **[5138]**, **[6293]**, **[6834]**, **[14517]**, **[16828]**, **[22397]**, **[25983]**, **[34576]**, **[42056]**, **[47616]**, **[49308]**, **[51865]**

Sales & Marketing Management (Vol. 157, February 2005, No. 2, pp. 18); "The Extra Mile: Customer Service That's a Step Beyond" in **[14027]**, **[22225]**, **[30856]**, **[31715]**, **[45127]**, **[46942]**, **[51632]**

Sales & Marketing Management (Vol. 158, November-December 2006, No. 11, pp. 16); "The Not-So-Talented Tenth" in **[10116]**, **[33195]**, **[47354]**, **[51747]**

Sales & Marketing Management (Vol. 159, January-February 2007, No. 1, pp. 45); "The Power of the Pack" in **[31200]**, **[33209]**, **[42380]**

Sales & Marketing Management (Vol. 159, January-February 2007, No. 1, pp. 9); "The Pulse" in **[41924]**, **[47438]**, **[49220]**, **[51770]**

Sales & Marketing Management; "The Road to Healthy Sales " in **[4783]**, **[23152]**, **[51809]**, **[53438]**

Sales & Marketing Management (Vol. 157, January 2005, No. 1, pp. 9); "The Technology Discrepancy" in **[49307]**, **[51864]**

Sales & Marketing Management (Vol. 157, January 2005); "To the Extreme: Watch Sales Grow by Making a Positive Lasting Impression" in **[2032]**, **[12915]**, **[20160]**, **[47647]**, **[50474]**, **[51873]**

Sales & Marketing Management (Vol. 158, October 2006, No. 10, pp. 52); "Truly Personal Entertainment" in **[30434]**, **[42077]**

Sales & Marketing Management (Vol. 159, January-February 2007, No. 1, pp. 9); "Trying to Reach a Senior Level Executive?" in **[31235]**, **[47670]**, **[51882]**

Sales & Marketing Management (Vol. 157, February 2005); "Up and Running: Energize Salespeople To Get Out Of a First-Quarter Slump" in **[45782]**, **[51887]**

Sales & Marketing Management (Vol. 158, October 2006, No. 10, pp. 18); "Wanted: Brainy in Business" in **[42454]**, **[47696]**, **[51894]**

Sales & Marketing Management (Vol. 158, October 2006, No. 10, pp. 15); "Warm Up to Cold Calls" in **[24295]**, **[47698]**, **[51895]**

Sales & Marketing Management (Vol. 157, Jan. 20, 2005); "Warp Speed" in **[3605]**, **[16538]**, **[31244]**, **[42456]**, **[45799]**, **[51896]**

Sales & Marketing Management (Vol. 159, January-February 2007, No. 1, pp. 11); "What Customer Relationship?" in **[31900]**, **[47713]**, **[51897]**

Sales & Marketing Management (Vol. 159, January-February 2007, No. 1, pp. 17); "What is Del.icio.us and How Is It Used?" in **[26012]**, **[34691]**, **[47715]**, **[51898]**

Sales & Marketing Management; "What Should I Do? Last Year's Poor Performance Can Push This Year's Quotas Higher" in **[28990]**, **[51901]**

Sales & Marketing Management; "Where Everyone's a Winner: Sure, the Annual Trip to Hawaii Is a Great Reward For Your Top Performers" in **[26959]**, **[35143]**, **[45831]**, **[51906]**

Sales & Marketing Management (Vol. 158, October 2006, No. 10, pp. 54); "Why Johnny Can't Sell...And What to Do About It" in **[45853]**, **[47747]**, **[51914]**

Sales & Marketing Management (Vol. 157, February 2005, No. 2, pp. 14); "Yellow Pages Association" in **[843]**, **[47767]**

Sales & Marketing Report **[51929]**

Sales and Marketing Success **[19918]**

"Sales & Marketing: The Power of Brand" in *Ingram's* (Vol. 27, No. 6, June 2001, pp. 23) **[31841]**, **[47488]**, **[50665]**, **[51817]**

"Sales & Marketing: Why Advertise Anyway?" in *Ingram's* (Vol. 27, No. 5, May 2001, pp. 28) **[27170]**, **[29984]**, **[47489]**, **[50666]**, **[51818]**

Sales and Marketing.com (Vol. 156, No. 3, March 2004); "A Thorough Assessment: Want to Evaluate Your Management Skills?" in **[45734]**, **[51869]**

Sales and Marketing.com (Vol. 156, No. 3, March 2004, pp. 48); "A Touch of Class: Teaching Can Give Your Career a Boost" in **[45755]**

Sales and Marketing.com (Vol. 156, No. 3, March 2004, pp. 19); "A View From the Top" in **[45789]**, **[51893]**

Sales and Marketing.com (Vol. 156, No. 3, March 2004, pp. 22); "Are Customers Selling For You?" in **[46683]**, **[51551]**

Sales and Marketing.com (Vol. 153, No. 3, March 2004, pp. 52); "Ask the Etiquette Doctor" in **[27296]**, **[51555]**

Sales and Marketing.com (Vol. 147, No. 2, February 2004, pp. 16); "Balancing Act" in **[34821]**, **[46701]**, **[51561]**, **[53599]**

Sales and Marketing.com (Vol. 153, No. 3, March 2004, pp. 47); "Beating Burnout" in **[32269]**

Sales and Marketing.com (Vol. 156, No. 3, March 2004, pp. 7); "Channel Surfing" in **[44993]**, **[51586]**

Sales and Marketing.com (Vol. 156, No. 3, March 2004, pp. 40); "CRM: Buy or Rent?" in **[4629]**, **[22955]**, **[31681]**, **[53247]**

Sales and Marketing.com (Vol. 147, No. 2, February 2004, pp. 7); "Dealing With Bonus Backlash" in **[34861]**, **[45046]**, **[51608]**

Sales and Marketing.com (Vol. 156, No. 3, March 2004, pp. 12); "Dealing With a Slumping Rep" in **[45047]**, **[51609]**

Sales and Marketing.com (Vol. 147, No. 2, February 2004, pp. 8); "Digging Deeper" in **[46887]**, **[51614]**

Sales and Marketing.com (Vol. 147, No. 2, February 2004, pp. 14); "Does Your Team Need a Hug or a Prod?" in **[34873]**, **[45073]**

Sales and Marketing.com (Vol. 156, No. 3, March 2004, pp. 9); "Done Deal: How One Sales Pro Closed a Big Customer" in **[46909]**, **[48663]**

Sales and Marketing.com (Vol. 156, No. 3, March 2004, pp. 18); "E-Train" in **[4645]**, **[16513]**, **[22975]**, **[33078]**, **[33825]**, **[45086]**, **[53266]**

Sales and Marketing.com (Vol. 156, No. 3, March 2004, pp. 63); "Feedback Needed" in **[45136]**

Sales and Marketing.com (Vol. 156, No. 3, March 2004, pp. 11); "Five Questions" in **[33905]**, **[45152]**, **[46972]**

Sales and Marketing.com (Vol. 156, No. 3, March 2004, pp. 32); "Forward Thinking" in **[46978]**

Sales and Marketing.com (Vol. 156, No. 3, March 2004, pp. 20); "Good References, Easy to Find" in **[33966]**, **[51658]**

Sales and Marketing.com (Vol. 147, No. 2, February 2004, pp. 12); "High-Tech Trade Shows" in **[24947]**, **[41740]**, **[47073]**

Sales and Marketing.com (Vol. 156, No. 3, March 2004, pp. 13); "Home Office vs. the Field" in **[45250]**, **[51677]**

Sales and Marketing.com (Vol. 156, No. 3, March 2004, pp. 66); "Home Sweet Office: Stress Relievers" in **[42648]**

Sales and Marketing.com (Vol. 153, No. 3, March 2004, pp. 50); "Home Sweet Office: The Pitch for Telecommuting" in **[42649]**

Sales and Marketing.com (Vol. 156, No. 3, March 2004, pp. 72); "How to Win a Marquee Account" in **[41033]**, **[47115]**, **[51683]**, **[52123]**

Sales and Marketing.com (Vol. 156, No. 3, March 2004, pp. 8); "It's the Service, Stupid! Want Repeat Business?" in **[31748]**, **[51702]**

Sales and Marketing.com (Vol. 156, No. 3, March 2004, pp. 24); "Job Market Thaw" in **[7394]**, **[10046]**, **[15190]**, **[20562]**, **[20915]**, **[25393]**, **[41041]**, **[41787]**, **[42317]**, **[51704]**, **[52551]**

Sales and Marketing.com (Vol. 156, No. 3, March 2004, pp. 9); "Lead Generator: Quick Ideas for Better Sales Leads" in **[47187]**, **[51710]**

Sales and Marketing.com (Vol. 156, No. 3, March 2004, pp. 18); "Making E-Mail Work" in **[27655]**, **[34163]**, **[47222]**

Sales and Marketing.com (Vol. 156, No. 3, March 2004, pp. 24); "Making the Grade: Want to Create a Team of 'A' Players?" in **[34976]**, **[51722]**

Sales and Marketing.com (Vol. 156, No. 3, March 2004, pp. 10); "On the Cheap: Creative Ways to Stretch Your Marketing Dollar" in **[47360]**, **[51753]**

Sales and Marketing.com (Vol. 156, No. 3, March 2004, pp. 48); "On the Road" in **[18106]**, **[38261]**, **[45489]**

Sales and Marketing.com (Vol. 156, No. 3, March 2004, pp. 10); "Partners in Branding" in **[30929]**, **[47387]**, **[50124]**

Sales and Marketing.com (Vol. 156, No. 3, February 2004, pp. 53); "Playing It Safe: Security on the Road is in Your Own Hands" in **[12617]**, **[22326]**, **[30402]**

Sales and Marketing.com (Vol. 156, No. 3, March 2004, pp. 14); "Politics as Usual?" in **[27471]**, **[51766]**

Sales and Marketing.com (Vol. 156, No. 3, March 2004, pp. 13); "Pop Quiz: A Quick Test of Your Managerial Skills" in **[45548]**, **[46162]**, **[51769]**

Sales and Marketing.com (Vol. 156, No. 3, March 2004, pp. 10); "S&MM Pulse" in **[34434]**, **[47492]**

Sales and Marketing.com (Vol. 156, No. 3, March 2004, pp. 56); "Selling Innovation" in **[4582]**, **[22888]**, **[47510]**, **[51350]**

Sales and Marketing.com (Vol. 156, No. 3, March 2004, pp. 20); "Serving Your Client-And Yourself" in **[31851]**, **[47514]**, **[51830]**, **[52587]**

Sales and Marketing.com (Vol. 156, No. 3, March 2004, pp. 12); "Shifting Into Growth Mode" in **[28760]**, **[45636]**, **[51833]**

Sales and Marketing.com (Vol. 156, No. 3, March 2004, pp. 16); "Show Me the Money" in **[28762]**, **[51836]**

Sales and Marketing.com (Vol. 156, No. 3, March 2004, pp. 40); "Site Matters" in **[51837]**

Sales and Marketing.com (Vol. 156, No. 3, March 2004, pp. 9); "Surprise, It's the CEO" in **[45691]**

Sales and Marketing.com (Vol. 156, No. 3, March 2004, pp. 68); "T&E Report" in **[30421]**

Sales and Marketing.com (Vol. 153, No. 3, March 2004, pp. 49); "The Art and Science of Networking" in **[39152]**, **[42170]**

Sales and Marketing.com (Vol. 156, No. 3, March 2004); "The Sales Auction: Is Bidding for Leads the Sales Trend of the Future" in **[45614]**, **[51811]**, **[53949]**

Sales and Marketing.com (Vol. 156, No. 3, March 2004, pp. 68); "Time For a Checkup" in **[10208]**, **[15526]**, **[38413]**, **[45740]**

Sales and Marketing.com (Vol. 147, No. 2, February 2004, pp. 90); "Turning Chaos Into Order" in **[55000]**

Sales and Marketing.com (Vol. 156, No. 3, March 2004, pp. 8); "What Should You Do" in **[45814]**, **[51902]**

Sales and Marketing.com (Vol. 156, No. 3, March 2004, pp. 30); "Whistle Blowers" in **[35146]**, **[51907]**

"Sales Picture Brightens for Sparks Exhibits and Environments" in *Tradeshow Week* (Vol. 34, December 6, 2004, No. 49, pp. 2) **[22560]**, **[25016]**, **[28737]**, **[55155]**

The Sales Professionals: Building Your Clients' Confidence **[51978]**

Sales Professionals USA **[51513]**

"Sales, Profits Surge for Jabil" in *Tampa Tribune* (December 21, 2005) **[7742]**, **[28738]**

Sales Promotion Essentials: The 10 Basic Sales Promotion Techniques...& How to Use Them **[51819]**

"Sales Report: Once Tainted by Get-Rich-Quick Schemes, the Direct-Sales Industry is Changing its Image" in *Entrepreneur* (July 2004) **[51342]**, **[51820]**, **[53950]**

"Sales of Scooters Get in the Fast Lane" in *Chicago Tribune* (February 21, 2005) **[2503]**, **[17490]**, **[53951]**

"Sales Secrets" in *Atlanta Business Chronicle* (Vol. 25, Nov. 8, 2002, No. 22 pp. 2B) **[28739]**, **[51821]**

"Sales Secrets: Persistence is key to building your brand" in *Atlanta Business Chronicle* (Vol. 25, No. 21, November 1, 2002, pp. 2B) **[47490]**, **[50667]**, **[51822]**

"Sales Strategies" in *Small Business Opportunities* (Vol. 17, November 2005, No. 6, pp. 64) **[27490]**, **[51823]**

Sales Systems Specialists **[47903]**

Salina Area Chamber of Commerce **[60412]**

Salinas Valley Chamber of Commerce **[57753]**

Saline Area Chamber of Commerce **[61420]**

Saline County Chamber of Commerce **[59663]**

Salisbury Area Chamber of Commerce **[60857]**

Salisbury By the Sea Chamber of Commerce **[60995]**

Salisbury State University–Eastern SBDC **[60800]**

Salix Ventures **[65001]**

Sallisaw Chamber of Commerce **[64068]**

Kurt Salmon Associates **[51444]**

Salmon River Chamber of Commerce **[59327]**

Salmon Valley Chamber of Commerce **[59328]**

Salon 2.0 - Salon and Spa Managment Software **[11758]**, **[11848]**

The Salon Biz: Tips for Success **[11801]**, **[17850]**

Salon Today Magazine **[11810]**

Salsa Rico **[21952]**

Salsarita's Fresh Cantina **[21953]**

Salt Lake Chamber **[65727]**

Salt Lake City Small Business Development Center–Salt Lake Community College **[65681]**

Salt Lake Community College
Redwood Road Campus **[65748]**
Sandy SBDC **[65686]**
Small Business Development Center **[65682]**

Salt Lake Tribune (March 5, 2005); "30 of 32 Condos Offered at Solitude Auction Sale" in **[1771]**, **[12512]**, **[20414]**, **[20787]**

Salt Lake Tribune (February 24, 2005); "Business Briefs" in **[2687]**, **[20221]**, **[20816]**, **[21456]**, **[39994]**, **[41577]**, **[46221]**

Salt Lake Tribune (February 24, 2005); "Business Digest" in **[12527]**, **[27898]**

Saluda County Chamber of Commerce **[64779]**

"Salvation Army Picks Center Site" in *Crain's Detroit Business* (Vol. 21, October 24, 2005, No. 43, pp. 24) **[7474]**, **[52720]**, **[54250]**

Sam Houston State University–Small Business Development Center **[65058]**

"Same Markets, New Marketplaces" in *Black Enterprise* (Vol. 35, September 2004, No. 2, pp. 34) **[32679]**, **[36713]**, **[48399]**, **[56392]**

Samford University–Institute of Genealogy and Historical Research **[11094]**

Sammy J. Peppers Restaurant & Lounge **[21954]**

"Sample business plans" in *Crain's Detroit Business* (Vol. 18, No. 49, December 9, 2002, pp. 17) **[29985]**, **[30594]**

Samurai Sam's Teriyaki Grill **[21955]**

San Angelo Chamber of Commerce **[65480]**

San Anselmo Chamber of Commerce **[57754]**

San Antonio Business Journal (Vol. 15, No. 4, Feb. 16, 2001, pp. 18) "Logo design reflects on your business; so take it seriously" in **[5994]**, **[50622]**

San Antonio Express-News (November 12, 2004); "Stained-Glass Specialty Evolved Into Inviting Entryways for San Antonio Artist" in **[8022]**, **[11220]**

San Antonio Express-News (January 23, 2005); "Using Security Consultants is Playing It Safe" in **[19980]**, **[22413]**, **[31240]**

San Antonio Hispanic Chamber of Commerce **[65481]**

San Antonio Minority Business Development Enterprise–University of Texas at San Antonio, Downtown **[65581]**

San Antonio Women's Chamber of Commerce of Texas **[65482]**

San Augustine County Chamber of Commerce **[65483]**

San Benito Chamber of Commerce **[65484]**

San Benito County Chamber of Commerce **[57755]**

San Bernardino Area Chamber of Commerce **[57756]**

San Bruno Chamber of Commerce **[57757]**

San Carlos Chamber of Commerce **[57758]**

San Clemente Chamber of Commerce **[57759]**

San Diego Association of Governments **[66832]**

"San Diego: Baja a Prudent Choice for Realty Company" in *San Diego Business Journal* (Vol. 28, January 8, 2007, No. 2, pp. 29) **[20662]**, **[21000]**, **[52721]**

San Diego Business Journal **[58244]**

San Diego Business Journal (Vol. 28, January 15, 2007, No. 3, pp. 11); "A Dose of News: Neurocrine Biosciences Inc." in **[50861]**, **[52086]**

San Diego Business Journal; "A Web of Attacks: Companies Increasing Their Security Measures to Prevent Viruses on Computer Networks" in **[6189]**, **[14579]**, **[22419]**, **[23252]**

San Diego Business Journal (Vol. 28, January 15, 2007, No. 3, pp. 20); "Accounting Firms" in **[62]**, **[26145]**

San Diego Business Journal (Vol. 28, January 15, 2007, No. 3, pp. 11); "Bio-Pharmaceutical Emphasis" in **[50825]**, **[52051]**

San Diego Business Journal (Vol. 28, January 15, 2007, No. 3, pp. 16); "Carlsbad: SkinMedica Has New Treatment for Acne" in **[2586]**, **[7885]**

San Diego Business Journal (Vol. 28, January 8, 2007, No. 2, pp. 27); "Carlsbad: Weevil Bugs $900M Nursery Industry" in **[11422]**, **[26491]**

San Diego Business Journal (Vol. 28, January 8, 2007, No. 2, pp. 27); "Chula Vista: Dobson's Has Designs on Eastlake" in **[21472]**, **[27948]**

San Diego Business Journal (Vol. 28, January 15, 2007, No. 3, pp. 33); "Combined Health Agencies" in **[40987]**, **[54160]**

San Diego Business Journal (Vol. 21, No. 8, February 21, 2000, pp. 16); "Companies Embrace Modern Ways of Communicating" in **[44281]**

San Diego Business Journal (Vol. 28, January 15, 2007, No. 3, pp. 17); "Coronado: Program Looks to Empower Restaurateurs" in **[21479]**, **[49876]**

San Diego Business Journal (Vol. pp.); "Despite Push for Diversity, Hotels Struggle to Find Qualified Applicants" in **[12542]**, **[48535]**

San Diego Business Journal (Vol. pp.); "Despite Stability in Fuel Prices, Airfares Predicted to Climb this Year" in **[26787]**

San Diego Business Journal (Vol. 23, No. 51, December 23, 2002, pp. 16); "Do-it-yourself Ceramics store offers homey touch" in **[8163]**, **[8272]**

San Diego Business Journal (Vol. 28, January 8, 2007, No. 2, pp. 31); "Eat, Drink and Be Merry, Trans Fats or No" in **[11323]**, **[53704]**

San Fernando Valley Business Journal (Vol. 12, January 2007, No. 1, pp. 12); "Firm Suiting Up for New Space Flights" in **[40382]**, **[41685]**, **[52100]**, **[55614]**

San Fernando Valley Business Journal (Vol. 11, November 2006, No. 24, pp. 48); "Firm's New President to Push Digital Experience" in **[9715]**, **[41687]**

San Fernando Valley Business Journal (Vol. 12, January 2007, No. 2, pp. 37); "Guards Unionize" in **[19963]**, **[55294]**

San Fernando Valley Business Journal (Vol. 11, December 2006, No. 25, pp. 35); "I-5 Corridor: Nurturing Its Economic Potential" in **[32502]**, **[39402]**

San Fernando Valley Business Journal (Vol. 11, November 2006, No. 24, pp. 10); "Image Feels Tower's Pain" in **[15112]**, **[32158]**

San Fernando Valley Business Journal (Vol. 12, January 2007, No. 1, pp. 12); "KCBS-KCAL Studio Center Complex" in **[2147]**, **[11336]**, **[21544]**, **[24423]**, **[28374]**, **[32531]**

San Fernando Valley Business Journal (Vol. 12, January 2007, No. 1, pp. 23); "L.A. County Econowatch" in **[10052]**, **[15199]**, **[32535]**, **[38176]**

San Fernando Valley Business Journal (Vol. 12, January 2007, No. 1, pp. 12); "Legends at Cascades" in **[20572]**, **[20927]**

San Fernando Valley Business Journal (Vol. 11, November 2006, No. 24, pp. 26); "Long-Time Music Publisher Sings" in **[2722]**, **[37714]**, **[46346]**, **[50058]**

San Fernando Valley Business Journal (Vol. 12, January 2007, No. 2, pp. 43); "Madler: Local Venues Replace Exotic Locales" in **[41824]**, **[55114]**

San Fernando Valley Business Journal (Vol. 11, December 2006, No. 25, pp. 27); "Nall Launches Video Game Co." in **[9732]**, **[14266]**, **[32160]**

San Fernando Valley Business Journal (Vol. 11, December 2006, No. 25, pp. 14); "New Newspaper Set for N. Valley Launch" in **[14286]**, **[18915]**, **[25911]**

San Fernando Valley Business Journal (Vol. 11, November 2006, No. 24, pp. 22); "No. 1 Company Succeeds in Rehabilitating Malls" in **[20955]**, **[28575]**

San Fernando Valley Business Journal (Vol. 12, January 2007, No. 2, pp. 33); "Opus Seen In Talks To Buy Rare Westlake Property" in **[20620]**, **[20959]**, **[40596]**

San Fernando Valley Business Journal (Vol. 12, January 2007, No. 1, pp. 13); "Panorama Place" in **[20961]**, **[51283]**, **[52932]**

San Fernando Valley Business Journal (Vol. 12, January 2007, No. 2, pp. 37); "Predatory Towing" in **[4361]**, **[29446]**, **[40623]**

San Fernando Valley Business Journal (Vol. 11, November 2006, No. 24, pp. 6); "Residential Units at Noho Commons Open" in **[7470]**, **[20994]**

San Fernando Valley Business Journal (Vol. 11, December 2006, No. 25, pp. 16); "Robbins Bros. Executive to Manage Growth" in **[15858]**, **[37770]**

San Fernando Valley Business Journal (Vol. 12, January 2007, No. 2, pp. 32); "Vacancy Squeeze" in **[20700]**, **[21035]**, **[28954]**

San Fernando Valley Business Journal (Vol. 11, December 2006, No. 25, pp. 25); "Valley Econowatch" in **[10227]**, **[15568]**, **[32777]**, **[38434]**

San Fernando Valley Business Journal (Vol. 11, November 2006, No. 24, pp. 1); "Valley Record Label Goes Back to Future" in **[30621]**, **[32166]**, **[42089]**

San Fernando Valley Business Journal (Vol. 11, December 2006, No. 25, pp. 1); "West L.A. CPA Firm Opening Valley Office" in **[292]**, **[26399]**, **[28982]**, **[30442]**, **[38450]**

San Fernando Valley Business Journal (Vol. 12, January 2007, No. 2, pp. 1); "Young Professional Share Ideas" in **[37008]**, **[47772]**, **[50709]**

San Fernando Valley Business Journal (Vol. 12, January 2007, No. 2, pp. 51); "Younger But Wiser Than You Might Think" in **[37009]**, **[39701]**

San Francisco Bay Area JobBank **[23402]**

San Francisco Bulletin **[32824]**

San Francisco Business Times (Vol. 16, No. 42, May 24, 2002); "Ambitious business women search for mentors during challenging times" in **[35317]**, **[54130]**, **[56115]**

San Francisco Business Times (Vol. 15, No. 2, August 18, 2000, pp. 29); "Area HMOs get the point about acupuncture" in **[17888]**, **[43080]**

San Francisco Business Times (Vol. 18, No. 6, September 19, 2003, pp. 19); "Banking on California" in **[9832]**, **[14773]**, **[27811]**, **[30787]**, **[49806]**

San Francisco Business Times (Vol. 18, No. 6, September 19, 2003, pp. 22); "Banks Reaching Out to New Communities" in **[9836]**, **[37908]**, **[46707]**

San Francisco Business Times (Vol. 17, No. 53, August 8, 2003, pp. 27); "Bean Counter" in **[11314]**, **[27821]**, **[37592]**

San Francisco Business Times (Vol. 16, No. 43, May 31, 2002, pp. 19); "Board the Linux love boat" in **[30298]**, **[33017]**

San Francisco Business Times (Vol. 16, No. 43, May 31, 2002, pp. 3); "Bus deal stalls as Oakland's council fumes" in **[15917]**, **[22787]**

San Francisco Business Times (Vol. 17, No. 48, July 4, 2003, pp. 3); "Carrying Off the Gold" in **[20457]**, **[35921]**

San Francisco Business Times (Vol. 17, No. 48, July 4, 2003, pp. 18); "Engineering a Structure that's Lasted Generations" in **[29856]**, **[37632]**

San Francisco Business Times (Vol. 16, No. 42, May 24, 2002,); "Game for more" in **[1105]**, **[4670]**, **[23009]**

San Francisco Business Times (Vol. 16, No. 42, May 24, 2002, pp. S4); "Generation next" in **[26814]**, **[36196]**, **[56236]**

San Francisco Business Times (Vol. 16, No. 43, May 31, 2002, pp. 16); "Hard times push Sun to go soft" in **[4682]**, **[6167]**, **[6941]**, **[23025]**

San Francisco Business Times (Vol. 17, No. 50, July 18, 2003, pp. 1); "Health Care Battle Heats Up" in **[13310]**, **[30874]**, **[41019]**, **[43202]**

San Francisco Business Times (Vol. 17, No. 51, July 25, 2003, pp. 20); "Hospitals Turn to Ads as the Rx for Blahs" in **[41031]**, **[47087]**

San Francisco Business Times (Vol. 18, No. 1, August 15, 2003, pp. 1); "Kaiser Getting a Transplant" in **[41042]**, **[50905]**

San Francisco Business Times (Vol. 16, No. 42, May 24, 2002, pp. 3); "Landlords keep on plugging" in **[20054]**, **[20565]**, **[20919]**, **[41799]**

San Francisco Business Times (Vol. 18, No. 2, August 22, 2003, pp. 1); "Macromedia Inc. Strikes Gold Worth $55M HQ Buy" in **[3557]**, **[3950]**, **[30155]**, **[53358]**

San Francisco Business Times (Vol. 16, No. 43); "Making waves" in **[25119]**, **[33459]**

San Francisco Business Times (Vol. 16, No. 43, May 31, 2002, pp. 1); "Million-dollar home sales smash record" in **[20589]**, **[20940]**

San Francisco Business Times (Vol. 17, No. 51, July 25, 2003, pp. 1); "Multibillion-Dollar Project Gets Key OK" in **[7429]**, **[20602]**, **[20947]**

San Francisco Business Times (Vol. 17, No. 51, July 25, 2003, pp. 1); "Neuburger Outgrows Pajamas" in **[5693]**, **[47321]**, **[51263]**

San Francisco Business Times (Vol. 18, No. 2, August 22, 2003, pp. 3); "Nuance Gains Voice in Noisy Speech Market" in **[4745]**, **[15313]**, **[23104]**, **[41880]**, **[50113]**, **[53390]**

San Francisco Business Times (Vol. 16, No. 43, May 31, 2002, pp. 1); "Oracle chief puts CEOs to the test" in **[41891]**, **[45501]**

San Francisco Business Times (Vol. 17, No. 48, July 4, 2003, pp. 1); "Oracle's Security Guard. Exec Vying to Put Lock on Hot Market" in **[4754]**, **[22320]**, **[23114]**, **[44349]**

San Francisco Business Times (Vol. 17, No. 50, July 18, 2003, pp. 1); "Pacific Growth, Others Bank on Emerging Firms" in **[10128]**, **[15338]**, **[28609]**, **[30165]**

San Francisco Business Times (Vol. 18, No. 1, August 15, 2003, pp. 15); "Politics of Design" in **[1526]**, **[7452]**, **[40617]**

San Francisco Business Times (Vol. 16, No. 42, May 24, 2002, pp. 1); "Safeway gets in shape for food fight" in **[11660]**, **[30940]**, **[51339]**

San Francisco Business Times (Vol. 17, No. 53, August 8, 2003, pp. 1); "S.F. Slashes Economic Development" in **[28757]**, **[32684]**

San Francisco Business Times (Vol. 16, No. 42, May 24, 2002, pp. 3); "Slump wipes 228 eateries off S.F. menu" in **[21627]**, **[28769]**

San Francisco Business Times (Vol. 18, No. 2, August 22, 2003, pp. 38); "Soup's On" in **[23507]**, **[30001]**, **[45655]**

San Francisco Business Times (Vol. 18, No. 6, September 19, 2003, pp. 1); "State Investigates 'Tribal Coverage'" in **[29515]**, **[40722]**, **[48599]**

San Francisco Business Times (Vol. 16, No. 43, May 21, 2002, pp. 3); "The education of Clint Reilly" in **[20872]**, **[31143]**

San Francisco Business Times (Vol. 17, No. 48, July 4, 2003, pp. 15); "The Next Generation. Planning Ahead" in **[2252]**, **[29943]**, **[37743]**

San Francisco Business Times (Vol. 16, No. 42, May 24, 2002, pp. 1); "VCs raid biotechs, nab talent" in **[42094]**, **[52224]**, **[55895]**

San Francisco Business Times (Vol. 16, No. 43, May 31, 2002, pp. 3); "Wine country's pinot push is bearing fruit" in **[23520]**, **[29014]**

San Francisco Camerawork **[19226]**, **[19291]**

San Francisco Chamber of Commerce **[57766]**

"A San Francisco Chronicle: George Dewey's View of the Bay" in *Black Enterprise* (Vol. 34, No. 3, October 2003, pp. 142) **[30172]**, **[52722]**

San Francisco Conservatory of Music–Library **[17699]**

"San Francisco Job Applicants Do Not Have to Admit to Former Convictions" in *Sacramento Bee* (October 26, 2005) **[40663]**, **[42405]**

San Francisco Observer **[18963]**

San Francisco Oven **[19712]**

San Francisco Planning and Urban Research Association **[1400]**

San Francisco Public Library
    Bernard Osher Foundation–Art & Music Center **[1668]**, **[8266]**, **[17700]**, **[17827]**, **[19277]**
    Wallace Stegner Environmental Center **[9454]**

San Francisco SBDC **[57272]**
    Northern California SBDC Lead Center–Humboldt State University **[57246]**

San Francisco State University–Office of Research and Sponsored Programs **[58207]**

San Francisco State University Foundation, Inc. **[58208]**

San Francisco Winter Home Furnishings Market **[10530]**, **[12245]**, **[12335]**, **[13711]**

San Gabriel Chamber of Commerce **[57767]**

San Gabriel Valley Tribune (July 8, 2004); "La Habra, Calif., Entrepreneur Starts Errand-Running Service for Busy Workers" in **[19076]**, **[47179]**, **[51226]**, **[56293]**

San Jacinto College–Small Business Development Center **[65059]**

San Joaquin Delta College–Small Business Development Center **[57273]**

"San Jose, Calif., Woman is Secret Shopper Evaluating Quality of Business" in *San Jose Mercury News* (August 10, 2004) **[21617]**, **[30941]**, **[31064]**, **[51343]**

San Jose Mercury News (February 17, 2005); "145,000 Americans' Identity Data Stolen" in **[22160]**

San Jose Mercury News (March 10, 2005); "A Wealth of Choices: Automakers Try to Create Excitement with New Releases" in **[18160]**, **[46484]**

SCORE Kokomo/Howard Counties [59858]
SCORE Lafayette [60604]
SCORE Lake Charles [60605]
SCORE Lake Havasu [57001]
SCORE Lake Ozark [61899]
SCORE Lake-Sumter [58730]
SCORE Lancaster [64361]
SCORE Las Cruces [62667]
SCORE Las Vegas [62337]
SCORE Lawton [63933]
SCORE Lehigh Valley [64362]
SCORE Lewiston-Auburn [60724]
SCORE Lexington [60475]
SCORE Lincoln [62234]
SCORE Little Rock [57122]
SCORE Logansport [59859]
SCORE Los Angeles [57291]
SCORE Maine Coastal [60725]
SCORE Manasota [58731]
SCORE Marion/Grant Co [59860]
SCORE McPherson [60277]
SCORE Merrimack Valley, NH, Chapter 199 [62396]
SCORE Mid Missouri [61900]
SCORE Midlands [64714]
SCORE Minneapolis [61545]
SCORE Minot [63506]
SCORE Missoula [62143]
SCORE Mobile [56797]
SCORE Mon-Valley [64363]
SCORE Monadnock [62397]
SCORE Monterey Bay [57292]
SCORE Muskegon [61239]
SCORE Naples of Collier [58732]
SCORE New Haven [58507]
SCORE New Ulm Area [61546]
SCORE Newark [62465]
SCORE North Alabama [56798]
SCORE North Central Kansas [60278]
SCORE North Central PA [64364]
SCORE North Coast [57293]
SCORE North Platte [62235]
SCORE Northeast [62803]
SCORE Northeast Alabama [56799]
SCORE Northeast Iowa [60078]
SCORE Northeast Louisiana [60606]
SCORE Northeast Massachusetts [60918]
SCORE Northern Arizona [57002]
SCORE Northern Illinois [59404]
SCORE Northern Nevada [62338]
SCORE Northshore [60607]
SCORE Northwest Arkansas [57123]
SCORE Ocala [58733]
SCORE Old Saybrook [58508]
SCORE Omaha [62236]
SCORE Orange City [57294]
SCORE Orlando [58734]
SCORE Outer Banks [63307]
SCORE Oxford Hills [60726]
SCORE Ozark-Gateway [61901]
SCORE Paducah [60476]
SCORE Palm Beach [58735]
SCORE Palm Springs [57295]
SCORE Panhandle [62237]
SCORE Peoria [59405]
SCORE Petoskey [61240]
SCORE Philadelphia [64365]
SCORE Phoenix [57003]
SCORE Piedmont [64715]
SCORE Pittsburgh [64366]
SCORE Poplar Bluff Area [61902]
SCORE Portland [60727], [64187]
SCORE Pueblo [58320]
SCORE Puerto Rico and Virgin Islands [66647]
SCORE Quad Cities [59406]
SCORE Quincy Tri-State [59407]
SCORE Raleigh [63308]
SCORE River City [60079]
SCORE Sacramento [57296]
SCORE St. Joseph [61903]
SCORE St. Louis [61904]
SCORE St. Paul [61547]
SCORE Salisbury [60808]
SCORE San Francisco [57297]
SCORE San Luis Obispo [57298]
SCORE Sandhills Area - No. 364 [63309]

SCORE Santa Barbara [57299]
SCORE Savannah [59045]
"Score Savvy: Business Credit Scores are on the Horizon" in *Entrepreneur* (Vol. 31, Oct. 2003) [31583], [38339], [44651]
SCORE Shasta [57300]
SCORE Shreveport [60608]
SCORE Silicon Valley [57301]
SCORE Sioux City [60080]
SCORE Somerset [62466]
SCORE South Bend [59861]
SCORE South Broward [58736]
SCORE South Central [57124], [60081]
SCORE South Central Indiana [59862]
SCORE South East Indiana [59863]
SCORE South Metro [61548]
SCORE South Palm Beach [58737]
SCORE Southeast Arkansas [57125]
SCORE Southeast Massachusetts [60919]
SCORE Southern Illinois [59408]
SCORE Southern Maryland [60809]
SCORE Southwest Florida [58738]
SCORE Southwest Kansas [60279]
SCORE Space Coast [58739]
SCORE Springfield [59409], [61905]
SCORE Stockton [57302]
SCORE Suncoast/Pinellas [58740]
SCORE SW Illinois [59410]
SCORE Syracuse [62804]
SCORE Tallahassee [58741]
SCORE Topeka [60280]
SCORE Traverse City [61241]
SCORE Treasure Coast [58742]
SCORE Treasure Valley [59282]
SCORE Tucson [57004]
SCORE Tuolumne County [57303]
SCORE Tuscaloosa [56800]
SCORE Uniontown [64367]
SCORE Upper Red River [63507]
SCORE Upper Shore [60810]
SCORE Ventura [57304]
SCORE Vista [60082]
SCORE Volusia/Flagler Co [58743]
SCORE Washington DC [58665]
SCORE Waterloo [60083]
SCORE Westchester [62805]
SCORE Western Mountains [60728]
SCORE Westmoreland County [64368]
SCORE Wilkes-Barre [64369]
SCORE Wilmington [58643], [63310]
SCORE Worcester [60920]
SCORE York [64370]
SCORE Yosemite [57305]
"Scorecard & Blueprint" in *Hispanic Business* (Vol. 24, No. 5, May 2002, pp. 48) [40089], [40676], [49732]
"Scoring Big Goals" in *Small Business Opportunities* (Vol. 17, September 2005, No. 5, pp. 74) [23632], [36723]
Scott City Area Chamber of Commerce [60414]
Scott County Chamber of Commerce [64971], [65944]
Scott Stamp Monthly [5854]
Scottdale Area Chamber of Commerce [64506]
Scottish Fold Cats: Everything about Acquisition, Care, Nutrition, Behavior, Health Care, and Breeding [1192]
Scottish Inns, Red Carpet Inns, Master Hosts Inns [12727]
Scott's Canadian Dental Directory [17104]
Scott's Canadian Pharmacists Directory [8808]
Scott's Directories [16703], [46183], [46426]
Scotts Lawn Service- Entrepreneur.com [16164]
Scotts Valley Chamber of Commerce [57796]
Scottsbluff - Gering United Chamber of Commerce [62297]
Scottsbluff Small Business Development Center–SBDC [62227]
Scottsdale Area Chamber of Commerce [57066]
Scottsville-Allen County Chamber of Commerce [60567]
Scottsville Community Chamber of Commerce [65945]
Scottville Area Chamber of Commerce [61423]
"Scout New Business" in *PC Computing* (April 2000, pp. 90) [34438], [47502]

"Scouting employment in the major leagues" in *BlackEnterprise* (Vol. 32, No. 2, September 2001, pp. 66) [9231], [9575], [42408]
"Scouting a Perfect Site" in *My Business* (October/November 2003, pp. 49) [38901], [52723]
SCP Journal [17935]
Scrap [21281]
Scrap & Stamp Arts [8219]
Scrapbooking for Profit: Cashing in on Retail, Home-Based and Internet Opportunities [7976], [8134], [33485], [42547], [51034], [56002]
"Screen Dream" in *Entrepreneur* (Vol. 33, February 2005, No. 2, pp. 42) [6785], [49244]
"Screen Gems" in *Fast Company* (March 2005, No. 92, pp. 39) [9739], [17529], [25596], [35059], [36724], [45623]
"Screen Play" in *Hispanic Business* (December 2006, pp. 28-30, 32, 34) [778], [34439], [47503]
Screen Printing [22125]
Screen Printing-Buyer's Guide Issue [22117], [22123]
Screen Printing-Distributor/Dealer Directory Section [22124]
Screen Printing Technical Foundation [5963], [19859], [22112]
"Screen Test" in *Success* (Vol. 47, No. 1, January 2000, pp. 18) [15434], [29986], [50171]
"Screen Test: Time for a Monitor Upgrade?" in *Entrepreneur* (Vol. 32, October 2004, No. 10, pp. 54) [6786], [49245]
Screening Industry [46520]
The Screenmobile [26084]
Screenprinting: Water-Based Techniques [22118]
Screenz Computing Centers [6902], [11395], [23826]
Screven County Chamber of Commerce [59158]
Scripps Ventures [63162]
Scroll [26103]
"Scrubs in Vogue" in *Home Business* (Vol. 13, January/February 2006, No. 1, pp. 41) [5568], [56397]
Scrubway [3379]
SCS Engineers–Library [9456]
Scuba ExtaSea Expo [23698], [55244]
Scudder, Stevens & Clark–Library [15807]
Sculptor's Society of Canada–Canadian Sculpture Centre–Archives [1670]
"?Se Habla Espanol? If you don't already, it's time to start. " in *Entrepreneur* (Vol. 31, No. 6, June 2003) [779], [47504]
"SE Tools" in *Entrepreneur* (Vol. 33, October 2005, No. 10, pp. 6) [25594], [25951], [33396], [34440]
SEA-ARM Consulting Associates [26641]
"A Sea Change for Artificial Bones" in *Business Week* (February 20, 2006, No. 3972, pp. 65) [48788], [50964], [52200]
"Sea Change" in *Inc.* (January 1, 2002) [36725], [47505], [50671]
Seaboard Franchise Services Co. [31501]
Seacoast Capital [55978], [61117]
Seacoast SCORE Chapter 185 [62398]
Seaflower Ventures [61118]
Seaflower Ventures (Fowlerville) [61460]
Seafood Price-Current [10429]
Seagoville Chamber of Commerce [65491]
Seagraves Area Chamber of Commerce [65492]
Seal Beach Chamber of Commerce, California [57797]
Sealmaster [7669]
Sealy Chamber of Commerce [65493]
SeaMaster Cruises [25343], [42803]
Seapoint Ventures [66225]
"Search Engine Strategies" in *My Business* (October/November 2002, pp. 24) [14413], [25952], [34441]
"Search Engines Help Shoppers To Buy Locally" in *Wall Street Journal* (Vol. 248, January 2007, No. 148, pp. B1-B3) [14414], [25953], [51345], [51826]
"Search" in *Inc.* (January 1, 2002) [16533], [45624]
"Search Party" in *Entrepreneur* (Vol. 33, September 2005, No. 9, pp. 28) [33980], [35060], [53955]
"Search party" in *WorkingWoman* (Vol. 25, No. 5, May 2000, pp. 48) [14415]

"The Search for Top Talent" in *Success* (Vol. 47, No. 4, September 2000, pp. 90) **[9232]**, **[9576]**, **[42409]**

The Searcher **[10986]**

"Searching for a city" in *BlackEnterprise* (Vol. 32, No. 3, October 2001, pp. 32) **[48405]**, **[52724]**

"Searching for Relief" in *My Business* (April/May 2003, pp. 49) **[3580]**, **[31211]**, **[52388]**

"Searching for Signs of Intelligent Life" in *Barron's* (August 11, 2003, pp. T1) **[7069]**, **[10175]**, **[14416]**, **[15435]**, **[25954]**, **[28747]**, **[30944]**, **[34442]**

"Searching the sky" in *Atlanta Business Chronicle* (Vol. 25, Nov. 15, 2002, No. 23 pp. 38A) **[780]**, **[45625]**, **[47506]**

Searcy Chamber of Commerce **[57213]**

Searcy County Chamber of Commerce **[57214]**

Sears Commercial Janitorial Services **[3380]**

"Sears, Dell Unplug Kiosk Venture" in *United Press International* (June 24, 2003) **[15938]**

Sears Disaster restoration Services **[4035]**

Sears Home Cleaning Services **[8721]**

Seaside-Sand City Chamber of Commerce **[57798]**

"Seasonal Wonder" in *Small Business Opportunities* (Vol. 12, No. 2, March 2000, pp. 68) **[35632]**, **[52496]**

"Seasoned Professional Offers Holiday Gift of Stress-Free Shopping" in *Boston Globe* (December 5, 2004) **[19007]**

"Season's Ho! Ho! Turns No! No! No!" in *Atlanta Business Chronicle* (Vol. 25, January 3, 2003, No. 30, pp. 3B) **[28748]**, **[34443]**, **[51346]**

"Seattle Book Co. offers e-book conversion" in *Publishers Weekly* (Vol. 249, No. 35, September 2, 2002, pp. 18) **[2742]**, **[9159]**, **[14417]**, **[34444]**

Seattle International Boat Show **[16779]**

Seattle International Motorcycle Show **[17503]**

Seattle JobBank **[23403]**

Seattle Sutton's Franchise Corp. **[21957]**

Seattle Times (February 18, 2004); "Silvana, Wash., Entrepreneur Designs Coffeepot-Shaped Kiosk" in **[5768]**, **[7091]**, **[15939]**, **[44146]**

Seattle Times (November 16, 2004); "Slow Economic Recovery Prompts More Firms to Turn to 'Just-in-Time' Employment" in **[7145]**, **[32686]**

Seaworthy **[5249]**

Sebago Lakes Region Chamber of Commerce **[60775]**

Sebastian River Area Chamber of Commerce **[58931]**

Sebastopol Area Chamber of Commerce and Visitors Center **[57799]**

Sebewaing Chamber of Commerce **[61424]**

Sebree Chamber of Commerce **[60568]**

"SEC Acts to Curb Cash Flow Shenanigans" in *Inc.* (Volume 27, June 2005, No. 6, pp. 26) **[241]**, **[2953]**, **[24029]**, **[26344]**, **[38340]**

"SEC Comes Down Hard On Unregistered Stock Giveaways" in *Venture Capital Journal* (Vol. 40, No. 10, November 2000, pp. 5) **[14418]**, **[15436]**, **[40677]**

"SEC, FBI Bring Fraud Charges Against Former Brocade Management" in *Hispanic Business* (September 2006, pp. 12) **[15437]**, **[29480]**

"SEC Offers Small Banks Internal Controls Leeway" in *American Banker* (Vol. 171, December 14, 2006, No. 239, pp. 3) **[10176]**, **[15438]**, **[39566]**, **[40678]**

SEC Online **[10385]**, **[15772]**

"SEC Opens Inquiry Linked to Newsday Circulation" in *Long Island Business News* (February 27, 2004) **[18932]**, **[29481]**

"A Second Act for CRM" in *Inc.* (Volume 27, March 2005, No. 3, pp. 40, 42) **[4790]**, **[23162]**, **[31844]**, **[53450]**

"Second Act" in *Entrepreneur* (Vol. 32, December 2004, No. 12, pp. 42) **[18119]**, **[38341]**

Second Amendment Foundation–Library **[11751]**

"Second Bank Set To Offer Small-Business Job Incentives" in *Boston Globe* (February 13, 2005) **[10177]**, **[44652]**

"Second Base: Getting the Right Accountant Can Pay Big Dividends" in *Crain's Detroit Business* (Vol. 19, No. 49, December 8, 2003) **[235]**, **[242]**, **[25961]**, **[26345]**

Second Chance Animal Center–Library **[1225]**, **[1281]**

"Second Chance" in *Entrepreneur* (Vol. 33, September 2005, No. 9, pp. 58) **[23701]**, **[24030]**, **[38991]**, **[40679]**, **[52019]**, **[54738]**

"Second Chances" in *Black Enterprise* (Vol. 34, No. 2, September 2003, pp. 58) **[6787]**, **[49246]**

The Second Cup Ltd. **[11396]**

"The Second-Home Tax Shelter" in *Hispanic Business* (December 2002, pp. 56) **[20663]**, **[54739]**

"Second 'Mix-In' Ice Cream Shop Comes to Stockton, Calif." in *The Record* (November 5, 2002) **[12788]**, **[30945]**

"Second Time Around" in *Entrepreneur* (Vol. 31, No. 7, July 2003, pp. 24) **[13777]**, **[33486]**, **[35633]**, **[41480]**

"Second Time Around" in *Small Business Opportunities* (Vol. 12, No. 3, May 2000, pp. 18) **[29987]**, **[37774]**

"Second wind" in *Entrepreneur* (Vol. 31, No. 4, April 2003, pp. 18) **[6788]**, **[49247]**, **[53956]**

"Secondaries Jay Pierrepont" in *Venture Capital Journal* (January 1, 2005) **[32681]**, **[55817]**

"Secondaries Ready For The Big Leagues" in *Venture Capital Journal* (July 1, 2003) **[15439]**, **[28749]**, **[50172]**, **[55818]**

The Secondary Mortgage Market: Strategies for Surviving and Thriving in Today's Challenging Markets **[17438]**

The Secret of Exiting Your Business Under Your Terms! **[1849]**, **[15440]**, **[30697]**, **[39567]**, **[50173]**, **[52451]**, **[54740]**

The Secret Language of Competitive Intelligence: How to See Through and Stay Ahead of Business Disruptions, Distortions, Rumors, and Smoke **[30946]**, **[36726]**

"The Secret Life of a Tightwad" in *My Business* (April/May 2004, pp. 28-34) **[27171]**, **[36727]**

"Secret Shopper" in *Home Office Computing* (Vol. 18, No. 11, November 2000, pp. 12) **[31845]**, **[34445]**

Secret of Training Dogs **[19127]**

"Secret Weapon: Synopsys is Thriving Behind the Scenes in the Semiconductor Business" in *Barron's* (August 11, 2003, pp. 16) **[4791]**, **[23163]**, **[41966]**, **[53451]**

Secrets to Enliven Learning: How to Develop Extraordinary Self-Directed Training Materials **[33231]**

Secrets of Entrepreneurial Leadership: Building Top Performance Through Trust & Teamwork **[35061]**, **[45626]**

"Secrets of the Great White North-The world's hush-hush 3-commerce powerhouse is just a few miles away" in *PC Computing* (April 2000) **[34446]**, **[43808]**, **[51347]**

The Secrets of Locating Past-Due Debtors **[8412]**

The Secrets of Magic and Illusion **[8232]**

Secrets of Millionaire Moms **[36728]**, **[56398]**

Secrets to Running a Successful Business **[42720]**, **[52945]**

"Secrets to Success" in *Small Business Opportunities* (Vol. 17, November 2005, No. 6, pp. 74, 86) **[19976]**, **[22359]**, **[36729]**

Secrets of Success for Today's Interior Designers and Decorators: Easily Sell the Job, Plan it Correctly and Keep the Customer Coming Back **[13667]**

"Secrets to Success: Yes, You Can Be a Successful Franchisee in 2003" in *Entrepreneur* (Vol. 31, No. 9, July 2003, pp. 86) **[35634]**, **[38675]**

Secrets of Successful Direct Mail **[16465]**

Secrets of a Successful Entrepreneur: How to Start & Succeed at Running Your Own Business **[36730]**

Secrets of Successful Selling **[51827]**

Secrets of Telemarketing Scripts **[24305]**

Secrets of the Walleye Trail **[2202]**

"SEC's Harness Might Help Hedge Funds More Than it Hurts" in *St. Louis Post-Dispatch* (October 31, 2004) **[15441]**, **[38342]**

"Section 404 Compliance in the Annual Report" in *Journal of Accountancy* **[243]**, **[2954]**, **[24031]**, **[26346]**, **[27172]**, **[45627]**, **[54741]**

Section for Women in Public Administration **[50352]**

"Secure access; Carriersnet building Web-based system to track worldwide cargo" in *Crain's Detroit Business* (Jan. 13, 2003, pp. 3) **[10696]**, **[14419]**, **[22360]**, **[34447]**

"Secure Fortune" in *Small Business Opportunities* (Vol. 16, No. 3, May 2004, pp. 54, 56) **[22361]**, **[36731]**, **[54251]**

"A secure net for agriculture" in *Hispanic Business* (Vol. 22, No. 10, October 2000, pp. 94) **[33487]**

"Secure your network" in *PC Magazine* (June 27, 2000, pp. 183) **[49248]**, **[53452]**

"Secure Your Database" in *E-business Advisor* (Vol. 18, No. 12, December 2000, pp. 34) **[22362]**, **[34448]**

"Secure Your Wireless" in *My Business* (August/September 2002, pp. 24) **[6789]**, **[14420]**, **[49249]**

The Secured Lender **[15674]**

Securities and Exchange Commission
   Atlanta District Office **[67384]**
   Boston District Office **[67385]**
   Central Regional Office (Denver) **[67386]**
   Fort Worth District Office **[67387]**
   Midwest Regional Office (Chicago) **[67388]**
   Northeast Regional Office (New York) **[67389]**
   Office of Small Business Policy–Small Business Ombudsman **[67383]**
   Pacific Regional Office (Los Angeles) **[67390]**
   Philadelphia District Office **[67391]**
   Salt Lake District Office **[67392]**
   San Francisco District Office **[67393]**
   Southeast Regional Office **[67394]**

Securities Industry Association **[14709]**

Securities Law Daily **[10386]**, **[15773]**, **[17476]**

Securities Pro **[48495]**

Securities Regulation & Law Report **[10387]**, **[15774]**

Securities Week **[10388]**, **[15775]**

Security **[22433]**

"Security Blanket" in *Entrepreneur* (Vol. 33, March 2005, No. 3, pp. 46) **[1193]**, **[14421]**, **[22363]**, **[23164]**, **[53453]**

"Security Blanket: Terrorists changed your employees" in *Entrepreneur* (Vol. 30, No. 3, March 2002, pp. 19) **[35062]**, **[45628]**, **[53957]**

"Security Breach? New Laws Could Change How You Handle Customer Info" in *Entrepreneur* (Vol. 33, October 2005, No. 10, pp. 24) **[6283]**, **[22364]**, **[28821]**, **[29482]**

"Security Companies Expect War to Increase Business" in *Crain's Detroit Business* (Vol. 19, No. 12, March 24, 2003, pp. 24) **[22365]**, **[28750]**, **[41967]**

"Security Company Gets Olympics-Related Job in Utah" in *Atlanta Business Chronicle* (Vol. 24, No. 9, August 3, 2001, pp. 24A) **[22366]**

Security/Firewalls Buyers' Guide **[6157]**

"Security at the Forefront" in *Women in Business* (Vol. 54, No. 3, May-June 2002, pp. 38) **[22367]**, **[42410]**

"Security Guide for Small Business" in *Entrepreneur.com* (Vol. 34, February 2006, No. 2, pp. 6) **[6790]**, **[22368]**, **[53454]**

Security Hardware Distributors Association **[16260]**

"The Security-Industrial Complex" in *Forbes* (Vol. 174, November 29, 2004, No. 11, pp. 44) **[15442]**, **[22369]**, **[28751]**, **[41968]**

Security Industry Association **[22156]**

"Security Lapse" in *Inc.* (August 2005, pp. 57-58) **[6284]**, **[22370]**, **[34449]**

Security Letter **[35287]**

Security & Loss Prevention Associates Inc. **[35303]**

Security Management **[22434]**

"Security: Messaging Gets Serious" in *Red Herring* (No. 103, September 1, 2001, pp. 25-26) **[14422]**, **[22371]**, **[27493]**

Security Sales **[4347]**, **[22435]**

"Senators Call for Small-Biz Refunds" in *Inc.* (August 1, 2003) **[246]**, **[2957]**, **[24034]**, **[26348]**, **[54745]**

"Send in the Clones" in *Entrepreneur* (Vol. 31, No. 9, September 2003, pp. 128) **[30948]**, **[44143]**

"Send E-Mail Securely" in *Home Office Computing* (Vol. 18, No. 11, November 2000, pp. 28) **[34456]**, **[53456]**

Send 'Em One White Sock: 67 Outrageously Simple Ideas from Around the World for Building Your Business **[28754]**, **[52946]**

"Send In the Robots!" in *Fortune* (Vol. 151, January 24, 2005, No. 2, pp. 140) **[41976]**, **[46431]**, **[53959]**

Send Me a Memo: A Handbook of Model Memos **[27676]**

"Send Out the Search Party" in *Entrepreneur* (Vol. 33, January 2005, No. 1, pp. 47) **[6792]**, **[23166]**, **[53457]**

"Sending Out an SOS: Our Franchisees Just Hit an Iceberg in Negotiating Their Land Deal" in *Entrepreneur* (Vol. 31, No. 9, July 2003) **[20665]**, **[37776]**, **[38902]**

"Sending the Right Messages: How to Make Staff Meetings More Effective" in *Black Enterprise* (Vol. 35, November 2004, No. 4, pp. 74) **[27496]**, **[45632]**

Seneca Chamber of Commerce **[60416]**

Seneca County Chamber of Commerce **[63013]**

SENES Consultants Ltd. **[37365]**

Michael Senew & Associates **[11970]**

Senior Housing South **[472]**, **[18376]**

"Senior In-Home Care a Burgeoning Business" in *Colorado Springs Business Journal* (July 23, 2004) **[458]**, **[18336]**, **[38903]**

Senior Project Management **[44839]**

Senior Project Management (Canada) **[44840]**

"Seniority Rules" in *Entrepreneur* (Vol. 31, No. 10, October 2003, pp. 88) **[47511]**, **[51351]**

"Senkbeil: increasing equity will mean stable markets" in *Atlanta Business Chronicle* (Vol. 24, No. 9, August 3, 2001, pp. 9C) **[20666]**, **[21002]**, **[44654]**

Senmed Medical Ventures **[63859]**

"Sense and reliability: A conversation with celebrated psychologist Karl E. Weick" in *Harvard Business Review* (Vol. 81, No. 4, Apr. 2003) **[36735]**, **[39570]**, **[45633]**

"Sense & Sensibility" in *Small Business Opportunities* (Vol. 12, No. 2, March 2000, pp. 18) **[28755]**, **[30597]**, **[31213]**

"Sensing the System Is Being Abused, Congress Passed a Bill in March to Help Creditors Recover More Debt From Businesses That Have Filed Bankruptcy" i **[31584]**, **[40688]**

Sensor Technology **[42139]**, **[52319]**

Sentinel Chamber of Commerce **[64074]**

Sentron Medical Inc.–Senmed Medical Ventures Library **[8881]**, **[17147]**, **[44223]**, **[55997]**

"Separation Anxiety" in *Entrepreneur* (Vol. 28, No. 6, June 2000, pp. 170) **[19284]**, **[30129]**, **[42549]**

SEPCO **[1153]**

"September 11, 2001. A CEO's story" in *Harvard Business Review* (Vol. 80, No. 10, October 2002, pp. 58) **[36736]**, **[39571]**, **[45634]**, **[54252]**

Sequel Venture Partners **[58462]**

Sequim-Dungeness Valley Chamber of Commerce **[66164]**

Sequoia Capital **[58147]**

SER Network Directory **[23379]**

"'Serial Inventor' Seeks Patent for Wireless Directory Network" in *Portland Press Herald* (August 2, 2005) **[6793]**, **[14426]**, **[44144]**

"Series A, For Arthritis: Proprius Pharmaceuticals Inc." in *San Diego Business Journal* (Vol. 28, January 15, 2007, No. 3, pp. 38) **[50966]**, **[52202]**, **[55822]**

Serious Sportsman Taxidermy for Beginners **[24270]**

Serious Surveillance for the Private Investigator **[19977]**

"Server it Right" in *Entrepreneur* (Vol. 31, No. 11, November 2003, pp. 57) **[6964]**, **[41977]**, **[49250]**

Serves You Right! **[31846]**, **[39572]**

Service 800 **[52399]**

Service Corps of Retired Executives-Chapter 6 **[59864]**

"Service that truly makes a difference" in *Rough Notes* (Vol. 146, No. 4, April 2003, pp. 114) **[13459]**, **[31847]**, **[43355]**

The Service Edge: 101 Companies That Profit from Customer Care **[31848]**

Service Excellence **[31946]**

"Service Franchises Hold Advantages Over Retail Operations" in *Long Island Business News* (May 7, 2004) **[38676]**, **[51036]**, **[52497]**

"Service Lets Customers Trade DVDs for 99 Cents a Transaction" in *San Jose Mercury News* (March 10, 2005) **[21349]**, **[25597]**

Service One Janitorial **[3284]**

"Service Providers" in *Crain's Detroit Business* (Vol. 16, No. 50, December 11, 2000, pp. E-13) **[29989]**, **[36737]**, **[37495]**, **[39924]**

Service Quality Institute **[31988]**

Service Sells/Phil Wexler **[31947]**

Service, Service, Service...The Key to Winning and Keeping Customers for Life **[31849]**

"Service with a smile" in *Entrepreneur* (Vol. 30, No. 2, February 2002, pp. 66) **[29485]**, **[39573]**, **[40689]**

Service Specialists Association Annual Convention [2007] **[2042]**, **[2090]**, **[18197]**, **[25452]**

Service Station Dealers of America/National Coalition of Petroleum Retailers and Allied Trades **[22601]**

Service-Tech Corp. **[3381]**

Service That Sells **[2279]**, **[31948]**, **[51984]**

"Service To A Tee" in *Entrepreneur* (Vol. 28, No. 4, April 2000, pp. 172) **[31214]**, **[47512]**

"Service With a Smile" in *Inc.* (October 2005, pp. 75-76) **[31850]**, **[41978]**

Servicemaster of Canada Limited **[52634]**

ServiceMaster Residential and Commercial Services, L.P. **[8722]**

Services **[3333]**, **[8695]**

"Services" in *Entrepreneur* (Vol. 32, No. 1, January 2004, pp. 242) **[3243]**, **[17767]**, **[17845]**, **[21619]**, **[38904]**, **[52585]**

"Services finalists" in *Crain's Detroit Business* (Vol. 16, No. 26, June 26, 2000, pp. E-15) **[45635]**, **[52586]**

"Services Offer Unlimited Music Rentals for a Monthly Fee" in *Kansas City Star* (February 4, 2005) **[4793]**, **[17768]**, **[21350]**, **[23167]**, **[53458]**

"Servicing Pitfalls: How To Avoid Having Your REMIC Disqualified" in *Banking & Financial Services Policy Report* (Vol. 23, August 2004) **[17439]**, **[21003]**, **[54746]**

"Serving Fine Fare, Cafe Alters the Course of At-Risk Youth" in *Chicago Tribune* (February 22, 2005) **[12634]**, **[21620]**, **[54253]**

"Serving Up Success: There's Something to be Said for Doing Things Your Way" in *Entrepreneur* (Vol. 31, No. 11, November 2003, pp. 86) **[11346]**, **[21621]**, **[36738]**, **[47513]**

"Serving the world's poor, profitably" in *Harvard Business Review* (Vol. 80, No. 9, September 2002, pp. 48) **[43809]**, **[54254]**

"Serving Your Client-And Yourself" in *Sales and Marketing.com* (Vol. 156, No. 3, March 2004, pp. 20) **[31851]**, **[47514]**, **[51830]**, **[52587]**

Servpro **[8429]**, **[8723]**, **[25563]**

"Set up shop" in *Entrepreneur* (Vol. 30, No. 3, March 2002, pp. 40) **[4794]**, **[14427]**, **[23168]**, **[25956]**, **[34457]**, **[53459]**

"Set Up Shop in Europe" in *E-business Advisor* (Vol. 18, No. 2, February 2000, pp. 16) **[34458]**, **[43810]**

"Set Up a Voice Mail and Fax System-Give your company the appearance of corporate professionalism" in *PC Magazine* (Mar.21,2000, pp.115) **[49251]**, **[53460]**

Seton Hall University–Center for Public Service **[41408]**

Seton Hill University's E-magnify **[56102]**

"Setting out on your own" in *BlackEnterprise* (Vol. 32, No. 3, October 2001, pp. 37) **[15446]**

"Setting Sail" in *Crain's New York Business* (Vol. 23, January 15, 2007, No. 3, pp. 25) **[20667]**, **[21004]**, **[30173]**, **[52725]**

"Setting aside a reliance on set-asides" in *Washington Business Journal* (Vol. 22, No. 3, May 23, 2003, pp. 35) **[41979]**, **[48406]**, **[48597]**

"Setting Sights on the Hispanic Buyer" in *Hispanic Business* (November 2002, pp. 49, 52, 54) **[18121]**, **[30949]**, **[47515]**

Setting the Table **[21622]**, **[36739]**

Setting the Table: The Transforming Power of Hospitality in Business **[36740]**, **[39574]**

"Setting the Table: The Transforming Power of Hospitality in Business" in *New York Times* (January 14, 2007, pp. 15) **[21410]**, **[35637]**

"Setting Up a Productive Home Office" in *Home Business* (Vol. 12, October 2005, No. 5, pp. 82, 84) **[42550]**, **[48933]**, **[49475]**, **[53148]**

"Setting Up Shop" in *Black Enterprise* (Vol. 35, February 2005, No. 7, pp. 60) **[5631]**, **[25761]**, **[33488]**, **[35638]**

"Setting Up Shop" in *Home Office Computing* (Vol. 18, No. 10, October 2000, pp. 90) **[25957]**, **[34459]**, **[44244]**, **[47516]**, **[52588]**

Setting Up a Telemarketing Program **[24307]**

Setting Up Your Ceramic Studio: Ideas and Plans from Working Artists **[7977]**, **[8135]**, **[8270]**

Settlement Music School–Blanche Wolf Kohn Library **[17701]**

7-Eleven Inc. **[7796]**

Seven Habits of Highly Effective People **[37044]**

Seven Imperatives for Fair, Legal & Productive Interviewing: A Guide for Anyone Who Makes or Influences Hiring Decision **[42411]**

"The Seven Laws of E-Commerce Strategy" in *Journal of Business Strategies* (Vol. 21, No. 5, September 2000, pp. 8) **[34460]**

"7 Questions to Ask Before You Hire an Accountant" in *My Business* (February/March 2003, pp. 44) **[247]**, **[24035]**, **[26349]**

Seven Steps to a Successful Business Plan (Canada) **[44841]**

"7 Ways You Can Use E-Books to Build Your Business" in *Web Marketing Today* (No. 121, February 5, 2003) **[782]**, **[9160]**, **[47517]**

Seventh-Day Adventist Dietetic Association **[18436]**

Seventh Generation Strategies Inc. **[7636]**

"Several restaurants to be added to Boston's menu" in *Boston Business Journal* (Vol. 22, No. 16, May 24, 2002, pp. 10) **[21623]**, **[28756]**

"Several buildings may change hands in coming months" in *Crain's Detroit Business* (Dec. 16, 2002, pp. 17) **[20668]**, **[21005]**, **[30174]**, **[52726]**

"Several Queen's Advertisers File $100M Lawsuit Against Newsday" in *Long Island Business News* (February 13, 2004) **[783]**, **[29486]**

"Severe Storm Watch" in *Inc.* (August 1, 2003) **[13460]**, **[39575]**, **[43356]**

"Severed Ties" in *Entrepreneur* (Vol. 33, October 2005, No. 10, pp. 30) **[28826]**, **[29487]**, **[36895]**, **[38344]**

Sevierville Chamber of Commerce **[64972]**

Sevin Rosen Management Co. / Sevin Rosen Funds **[65629]**

Sew News **[5586]**, **[22735]**

"Sew What?" in *Black Enterprise* (Vol. 36, February 2006, No. 7, pp. 68) **[22730]**, **[23814]**, **[34461]**

Seward Area Chamber of Commerce **[62298]**

Seward Chamber of Commerce **[56974]**

Seward County Community College–Small Business Development Center **[60264]**

Sex-Based Employment Discrimination **[32060]**

"Sex, Drugs, and Career Choices" in *Fortune* (Vol. 141, No. 7, April 3, 2000, pp. 68) **[55310]**

Sextant Publishing **[66672]**

"Sexton Hoping to Hit the Jackpot for Viejas Casino" in *San Diego Business Journal* (Vol. 28, January 8, 2007, No. 2, pp. 16) **[10883]**, **[47518]**

Sexual Harassment **[32061]**

Sexual Harassment: Crossing the Line **[32098]**

Sexual Harassment: Handling the Complaint **[32099]**

Sexual Harassment: It's Hurting People **[32100]**

Sexual Harassment on the Job [32062]

Sexual Harassment: Serious Business [32101]

Sexual Harassment: Walking the Corporate Fine Line [32102]

Sexual Harassment: What You Need to Know [32063]

Sexual Harassment in the Workplace [32064]

Sexual Harassment in the Workplace...Identify. Stop. Prevent. [32103]

"Sexy Or Sensible? What You Buy To Drive May Not Be What You're Driven To Buy" in *Business Week* (January 16, 2006, No. 3967) [18122], [47519]

Seybold San Francisco Conference and Exposition [8650]

Seymour Chamber of Commerce [65496]

SF Camerawork–Reference Library [19279]

"S.F. Slashes Economic Development" in *San Francisco Business Times* (Vol. 17, No. 53, August 8, 2003, pp. 1) [28757], [32684]

SG Capital [55979]

SGIA/DPI Conference [22132]

"SGS Automotive Services Offering Vehicle Inspections on eBay" in *PR Newswire* (April 1, 2004) [1852], [4352], [34462], [52589]

"The Shadow Knows" in *Entrepreneur* (Vol. 28, No. 1, January 2000, pp. 110) [44361]

"Shady Business" in *Entrepreneur* (Vol. 30, No. 2, February 2002, pp. 22) [41980], [49252]

Shady Grove Life Sciences Center 60888

Chris Shaff Consulting [49656]

Shafter Chamber of Commerce [57801]

Shakamak Chamber of Commerce [60002]

Shake-A-Paw Puppy and Pet Supply Stores [1217]

"Shake 'Em Up" in *Forbes* (Vol. 175, February 14, 2005, No. 3, pp. 58) [41096], [50967], [52203]

Shake Hands with Your Computer [6364]

Shake's Frozen Custard [12850]

Shakespeare Composites & Electronics [1568]

Shakey's Pizza & Buffet [21959]

Shakopee Chamber of Commerce [61665]

Shamrock Chamber of Commerce [65497]

Shane's Office Supply [18626]

Shanghai International Jewellery Fair [15880]

"Shankz Opens New Location in California" in *Tourist Attractions and Parks* (Vol. 35, January 2005, No. 1, pp. 12) [17327], [21624]

The Shannon Management Group. [42997], [47906], [50505]

Shape [19461], [26045]

"Shape Up!" in *Entrepreneur* (Vol. 31, No. 10, October 2003, pp. 100) [29757], [35639]

"Shaping Up" in *Entrepreneur* (Vol. 33, September 2005, No. 9, pp. 100) [19233], [19437], [38905]

Share [41295]

"Share the Health: When Encouraging Healthy Living, You've Got to Walk the Walk" in *Entrepreneur* (Vol. 33, January 2005, No. 1) [41097], [50356]

"Share Safely" in *Entrepreneur* (Vol. 32, November 2004, No. 11, pp. 62) [6794], [22377], [49253]

"Share the Wealth" in *Entrepreneur* (Vol. 32, November 2004, No. 11, pp. 90) [51831]

"Sharebuilder 401(k)" in *Entrepreneur.com* (Vol. 34, February 2006, No. 2, pp. 6) [248], [4795], [18791], [23169], [24036], [26909], [53461]

"ShareBuilder by Netstock" in *Black Enterprise* (Vol. 33, No. 7, February 2003, pp. 6) [10179], [15447], [38345]

Shared Ventures, Inc. [61709]

"Sharing Digital Shots Snap with Picasa 2.0" in *Tampa Tribune* (January 24, 2005) [4202], [4796], [23170], [49254], [53462]

Sharing Ideas News Magazine [22583], [25061]

"Sharing Marketing Expenses" in *Rough Notes* (Vol. 145, No. 9, September 2002, pp. 80) [13461], [43357], [47520], [50175]

Sharing Solutions [25659]

"Sharing the wealth: never mind the dismal economy." in *Entrepreneur* (Vol. 31, No. 5, May 2003, pp. 88) [52498]

"Sharing the Wealth" in *Hispanic Business* (March 2003, pp. 46, 48, 50) [48407], [54255]

"Sharing the Wealth: Want to Get a Piece of the eBay Pie?" in *Entrepreneur* (Vol. 33, February 2005, No. 2, pp. 40) [784], [1853], [34463], [47521]

Sharkey's Cuts For Kids, Franchising Co., LLC [3285]

Sharonville Chamber of Commerce [63784]

"Sharp costs hurt pizza biz" in *Atlanta Business Chronicle* (Vol. 24, No. 9, August 3, 2001, pp. A1) [19642], [21625]

"A Sharp Focus on Fuzzy Thinking" in *Business Week Online* (February 2) [3485], [29758], [44145]

"Sharp Turn" in *Puget Sound Business Journal* (Vol. 21, No. 3, May 26, 2000, pp. 20) [17910], [43358]

Richard Sharpe Associates P.C. [1569]

Sharpen Your Sales Presentation: Make It a Winner [51985]

"Sharpening the Saw When You Work as a Consultant" in *Home Business* (Vol. 12, March/April 2005, No. 2, pp. 66) [3582], [31215], [33233]

"Sharper Image: Smartphones are the Brainier Mobile Choice" in *Entrepreneur* (Vol. 32, October 2004, No. 10, pp. 49) [5104], [53960]

"Shattered Magazine: A Monthly for the Global Businesswoman" in *Marketing to Women* (Vol. 19, December 2006, No. 2, pp. 6) [18933], [27497], [28758], [30598], [38906], [47522], [56400]

Shattuck Chamber of Commerce [64075]

Irving Shaw and Associates [32181]

Shaw Venture Partners / Shaw Glasgow Partners [64292]

Shawano Area Chamber of Commerce [66520]

Shawmut Capital Partners [61119]

"Shawn Fanning's New Tune" in *Business 2.0* (Vol. 6, May 2005, No. 4, pp. 38, 41) [17769], [34464]

Shawnee Area Chamber of Commerce [60417]

Shawnee Community College–Small Business Development Center [59388]

"She Said Yes!" in *Black Enterprise* (Vol. 34, No. 7, February 2004, pp. 12) [3194]

Shealy & Associates [46114]

Sheboygan County Chamber of Commerce and Convention and Visitors Bureau [66521]

Sheboygan Falls Chamber Main Street [66522]

"Shed Some Light on Your Work" in *My Business* (April/May 2002, pp. 47) [49546], [56588]

Sheet Metal and Air Conditioning Contractors' National Association [1010]

Sheet Metal and Air-Conditioning Contractors National Association Convention/Exhibition Forum [1048]

Sheet Metal Forming [46522]

Sheet Music Magazine [17797]

Shefield Gourmet [24632]

Shelburne Museum, Inc.–Research Library [1369]

Shelby Area Chamber of Commerce [62198]

Shelby Chamber of Commerce [63785]

Shelby County Chamber of Commerce [60003], [60203], [60569], [65498]

Shelby Report of the Southeast [11701]

Shelby Report of the Southwest [11702]

"Shelby Supervisor Hopes Township Plan Can Spur More Growth" in *Crain's Detroit Business* (Vol. 21, January 31, 2005, No. 5, pp. 35) [7477], [17530], [28759], [51352]

Shelbyville Area Chamber of Commerce [59667]

Shelbyville-Bedford County Chamber of Commerce [64973]

Sheldon Chamber and Development Corp. [60204]

Sheldon Jackson College–Stratton Library–Rare Book and Archives Room [1370]

"Shelf-Determination" in *Forbes* (April 15, 2002, p. 130) [11661], [47523]

Shell Lake Chamber of Commerce [66523]

"Shell Shock?" in *Entrepreneur* (Vol. 32, December 2004, No. 12, pp. 15) [15448], [40690], [50176]

Shelley Chamber of Commerce [59329]

Sheltie Pacesetter [1210]

The Shelton Companies, Inc. [63466]

Shelton-Mason County Chamber of Commerce [66165]

Shenandoah Chamber and Industry Association [60205]

Shenandoah County Library–Local History and Genealogy Collection [11077]

Shenandoah Valley SBDC–Blue Ridge Community College [65839]

Shenango Valley Chamber of Commerce [64507]

Shepherd College–Small Business Development Center [66259]

Sherbrooke University–Research Centre on Aging [18418]

Sheridan County Chamber of Commerce [62199], [66629]

Sherman Chamber of Commerce [65499]

Sherpa Partners LLC [61710]

Sherwin-Williams Automotive Finishes Corporation–Library [18695], [18720]

Sherwood Chamber of Commerce [57215], [64265]

"She's Got a Brand New Bag: TV Producer's Designs Express Her Inner Child" in *Black Enterprise* (Vol. 35, August 2004, No. 1, pp. 133) [5514], [9606], [12173], [18675], [56073]

"She's not afraid to flex her sales muscles" in *Selling* (October 2002, pp. 15) [19438], [38907], [56401]

"She's only code and pixels, but she can help you shop" in *The New York Times* (September 20, 2000, pp. D8, H8) [10574], [34465]

Shetland Properties Limited Partnership [59788]

Shhh! I'm Finding a Job: The Library and Your Self-Directed Job Search [9263]

"Shh...It's a Secret" in *Entrepreneur.com* (Vol. 34, February 2006, No. 2, pp. 82) [29488], [30950], [44362]

Shiatsu Massage [17024]

Shiawassee Regional Chamber of Commerce [61425]

SHIELD Security Systems [22447]

"Shielding Your Home from Lawsuits" in *Hispanic Business* (October 2003, pp. 90) [29489], [29990], [36741]

"Shift in business strategy helps Littlearth turn around financials" in *Pittsburgh Business Times* (Vol. 22, No. 42, May 2, 2003) [9638], [31066], [51832]

"Shift to Military Contracts Could Help Excel Stay Afloat" in *Crain's Detroit Business* (Vol. 21, October 10, 2005, No. 43, pp. 36) [1967], [40093]

"Shifting Fortunes" in *Black Enterprise* (Vol. 35, October 2004, No. 3, pp. 114) [10180], [15449], [38346]

"Shifting gears: Suit and tie gone, passion becomes his business" in *Crain's Detroit Business* (Vol. 18, No. 16, April 22, 2002, pp. 3) [17479], [35640]

"Shifting Into Growth Mode" in *Sales and Marketing.com* (Vol. 156, No. 3, March 2004, pp. 12) [28760], [45636], [51833]

Tom Shillock Consulting [27596], [47907], [50506]

The Shine Factory [2058], [4380]

Shiner Chamber of Commerce [65500]

Shingle Springs/Cameron Park Chamber of Commerce [57802]

"Shipbuilders Labor Union Threatens Management Over Layoff Plans in Bath, Maine" in *Portland Press Herald* (June 22, 2005) [3325], [16382], [45637], [55311]

Shippensburg Area Chamber of Commerce [64508]

Shippensburg University of Pennsylvania–Office of Extended Studies [3005]

"Shipping out" in *Entrepreneur* (Vol. 31, No. 6, June 2003, pp. 42) [31067], [34466], [51353]

Shoals Chamber of Commerce [56887]

"Shock Treatment" in *My Business* (April/May 2002, pp. 46) [42721], [49255]

"Shock Value: A Belief in the Power of Batteries Charged This Couple Up for Franchise Ownership" in *Entrepreneur* (Vol. 32, Oct. 2004) [37777], [38908]

Shoe Factory Buyer's Guide [22766]

Shoe Repair & Clothing Alterations [19013]

Shoe Retailing Today [22771]

Shoe Service Institute of America [22744]

"Shoe-String Your Site" in *My Business* (June/July 2002, pp. 43) [25958], [34467]

Shoeless Joe's Limited [21960]

Shoes-n-Feet [22776]

"Shoestring Marketing: Web Research: Is This Fantasy or Reality?" in *Atlanta Business Chronicle* (Vol. 25, No. 21, Nov. 1, 2002) [25959], [34468], [47524]

"Shoestring Start-Ups" in *Small Business Opportunities* (Vol. 16, November 2004, No. 6, pp. 22, 24, 26, 28, 30-32, 34, 36, 38, 40) [503], [6568], [9299], [10612], [11130], [11210], [12257], [15859], [15959], [16108], [16467], [19188], [19347], [22141], [25762], [27734], [30491], [33489], [34527], [35641], [37588], [39074], [51037], [52785]

The SHOOT Directory for Commercial Production and Postproduction [9740]

Shooter's Bible [11730]

Shooting Federation of Prince Edward Island–Library [11752]

"Shooting from the hip" in *Entrepreneur* (Vol. 31, No. 5, May 2003, pp. 75) [47525]

Shooting Industry [1481], [11737]

Shooting Industry-Buyers Guide Issue [1475], [11731]

Shooting Times [1482]

"Shop Around: Getting Estimates Can Save You a Bundle" in *Black Enterprise* (Vol. 34, No. 4, November 2003, pp. 166) [52389]

"Shop Around: This Technology Can Help You Comparison Shop for Low Fares" in *Entrepreneur* (Vol. 32, July 2004, No. 7, pp. 28) [25243], [30416], [31068]

"Shop Shifting" in *Hispanic Business* (April 2005, pp. 18, 20) [785], [47526], [48408]

"Shop for Success" in *Small Business Opportunities* (Vol. 12, No. 3, May 2000, pp. 46-48) [23591], [30492], [35642]

Shop Talk [22639]

Shopkeeper Software [65679]

Shoplifting Prevented [51435]

Shoppers Drug Mart [8849]

"Shopping Centers That Sizzle: Entertainment Elements Enliven Malls" in *Tourist Attractions and Parks* (Vol. 35, January 2005, No. 1) [17328], [51354]

"Shopping in palm of the hand is making its holiday debut" in *The New York Times* (November 11, 2000, pp. A1) [5105], [14428], [34469], [51834]

"Shopping For Good Health: Perception Strategies Adds 'Mystery' to Medicine" in *Indianapolis Business Journal* (September 27, 2004) [31852], [41098]

Shopping for Health [18473]

"Shopping for Investment Advice" in *Ingram's* (Vol. 29, No. 7, July 2003, pp. 42) [10181], [15450], [38347]

"Shopping List" in *Entrepreneur* (Vol. 32, September 2004, No. 9, pp. 44) [4203], [6795], [6965], [7285], [7341], [41981], [46912], [49256], [50271]

"Shopping List: Thin is When It Comes to Monitors. Try These Models for Size" in *Entrepreneur* (Vol. 32, October 2004, No. 10, pp. 56) [6796], [49257]

"Shopping Magazines Gain Popularity by Telling Readers Exactly Where to Buy" in *San Diego Union-Tribune* (October 14, 2004) [14429], [18934], [19008], [51355], [53961]

"Shopping Pals" in *Entrepreneur* (Vol. 27, No. 8, August 2000, pp. 20) [3583], [34470]

"Shopping for the Right Database" in *Business Week Online* (December 13, 2001) [6483], [9370], [23171], [52390], [53463]

"Shopping Spies Help Retail Businesses Keep Eye on Service" in *Charlotte Observer* (October 10, 2004) [31069], [31853], [51356]

"Shopping Spree; Ramco-Gershenson Rings Up $500M in Acquisitions in 2004" in *Crain's Detroit Business* (Vol. 21, January 31, 2005) [15451], [21006], [50177]

"Shopping for Value" in *Forbes* (Vol. 175, January 31, 2005, No. 2, pp. 110) [10182], [15452], [38348]

SHOPtalk [22640]

Shoreline Chamber of Commerce [66166]

Shoreline General Contractors Inc. [7637]

Shoreline Venture Management, LLC [58148]

Short Elliott Hendrickson Inc. [23803]

Short Story Writers [9009]

"Short and Sweet" in *Entrepreneur* (Vol. 32, No. 2, February 2004, pp. 74) [28761], [51835]

"Short Takes" in *Crain's Cleveland Business* (Vol. 24, No. 41, October 13, 2003, pp. 21) [2452]

"Short of Time? Call a Wedding Planner" in *Fairfield County Business Journal* (Vol. 43, November 1, 2004, No. 44, pp. 20) [3195]

SHOT SHOW - The Shooting, Hunting, and Outdoor Trade Show [1486], [11742], [23699]

Shotgun News [11738]

"Should Doctors Own Hospitals?" in *Business Week* (February 20, 2006, No. 3972, pp. 63) [41099], [53962]

"Should banks be allowed to broker real estate?" in *Ingram's* (Vol. 28, No. 3, March 2002, pp. 62) [20669], [21007]

"Should you take the money...and run?" in *Women in Business* (Vol. 54, No. 3, May-June 2002, pp. 40) [26910], [42412]

"Should You Get Incubated?" in *E-business Advisor* (Vol. 18, No. 10, October 2000, pp. 18) [43042], [53566]

"Shout It Out" in *Entrepreneur* (Vol. 33, September 2005, No. 9, pp. 128) [36742]

Show Low Regional Chamber of Commerce [57068]

"Show Me the Money" in *Black Enterprise* (Vol. 34, No. 3, October 2003, pp. 40) [39776], [44437]

"Show Me the Money" in *Entrepreneur* (Vol. 33, September 2005, No. 9, pp. 102) [12047], [21411], [37220], [38677], [44438]

"Show Me the Money" in *Home Office Computing* (Vol. 18, No. 11, November 2000, pp. 85) [7199], [42551], [55427]

"Show Me the Money" in *Sales and Marketing.com* (Vol. 156, No. 3, March 2004, pp. 16) [28762], [51836]

"Show Me the Money!" in *Success* (Vol. 47, No. 6, November 2000, pp. 60) [29991], [36743], [55823]

Show Me PCs [6382]

"Show me the money" in *Entrepreneur* (Vol. 31, No. 6, June 2003, pp. 108) [37778], [38909], [52727]

"The Show Must Go On" in *Atlanta Business Chronicle* (Vol. 25, No. 21, November 1, 2002, pp. 1B) [22561], [25017]

Show off Your Dog-Grooming Basics [19170]

Showcase of Interior Design: International Commercial Edition [13668]

Showcase of Interior Design: Pacific Edition [13669]

"Showcase Your Talent" in *Black Enterprise* (Vol. 36, February 2006, No. 7, pp. 66) [17770], [21144], [34471]

"Showdown at the Apollo" in *Black Enterprise* (Vol. 33, No. 6, January 2003, pp. 55) [9741], [24448]

"Showing Products In a Better Light" in *Business 2.0* (Vol. 6, September 2005, No. 8, pp. 62) [48868], [51357]

"Showtime's networking a draw for dealmakers" in *Atlanta Business Chronicle* (Vol. 25, No. 21, November 1, 2002, pp. 8C) [20670], [21008], [25018]

"Shred of evidence: learn a lesson from Arthur Anderson" in *Entrepreneur* (Vol. 30, No. 12, December 2002, pp. 106) [249], [26350], [29490], [37501]

Shred-It [21287]

Shrimp Notes [10430]

Shriner-Midland Co. [39737]

Shrinking the Globe into Your Company's Hands: The Step-by-Step International Trade Guide for Small Businesses [43811]

"Shrinking Surplus: George W. Bush, technology CEO?" in *Red Herring* (No. 105, October 1, 2001, pp. 88-89) [32685], [54747]

Shutterbug [19250], [19319]

SI Ventures [58977]

SIA Member Update [22862]

SIA Snow Sports Book [22858]

The SIA SnowSports Show [22872]

SIAM Journal on Optimization [52320]

SIAM Journal on Scientific Computing [52321]

SibJewelry - International Exhibition of Jewelry, Precious Stones, Equipment for Treatment and Manufacturing [15881]

Sibley Chamber of Commerce [60206]

"Sibleys Shores Inc. History" in *Crain's Detroit Business* (Vol. 19, No. 49, December 8, 2003, pp. 3) [22767]

Sid Cato's Newsletter on Annual Reports [27695]

"Side Lines" in *Forbes* (Vol. 170, No. 3, August 12, 2002, pp. 22) [40691]

Side Pockets [21961]

"Sides Vie to Regulate Internet-Based Service; Michigan Wants to Play Role" in *Crain's Detroit Business* (Vol. 21, January 24, 2005) [5106], [14430], [34472], [40692], [41982]

"Sideways Wines on Auction at WineBid.com" in *PR Newswire* (January 17, 2005) [1854], [14431], [23506]

Sidney Area Chamber of Commerce and Agriculture [62200]

Sidney Chamber of Commerce [60207], [63014]

Siebrand-Wilton Associates Inc. [27048], [37547], [42998], [50335]

SIECUS Report [41296]

Sienna Ventures / Sienna Holdings Inc. [58149]

Sierra Club of Canada [9337]

Sierra College–Small Business Development Center [57274]

Sierra Legal Defence Fund [9338]

Sierra Madre Chamber of Commerce [57803]

Sierra Ventures [58150]

Siesta Key Chamber of Commerce [58933]

SIGACT News [6518]

Sight Survey Professional Version 3 [23782]

SIGIR Forum [6303]

Sigma Capital Corp. [58978]

Sigma Partners (Menlo Park) [58151]

SIGN-A-RAMA [22810]

Sign Association of Canada [525]

Sign Biz, Inc. [892], [6052]

Sign Business [22805]

"Sign right here" in *The New York Times* (October 8, 2000, pp. WK2) [14432], [29491], [34473]

"Sign Replacement Process Still Sluggish Months After Hurricanes" in *Bradenton Herald* (January 26, 2005) [22795]

"Sign of the Times: Are You Missing Out on This Simple, Inexpensive Marketing Tool?" in *Entrepreneur* (Vol. 33, January 2005, No. 1) [27677], [34474], [47527]

"Sign of the Times" in *Entrepreneur* (Vol. 28, No. 10, October 2000, pp. 29) [14433], [34475], [40693]

"A Sign of the Times" in *Small Business Opportunities* (Vol. 14, No. 1, January 2002, pp. 82, 84) [22796], [50673]

Signal Graphics Business Centers [22811]

Signal Hill Chamber of Commerce [57804]

Signal Lake Management LLC [58614]

"Signal Strength" in *Entrepreneur* (Vol. 33, March 2005, No. 3, pp. 18) [31216], [47528], [55824]

Signature Alert Security [22448]

SignCraft [22806]

Signia Ventures [58152]

Significant Earthquakes Database [9422]

"Signing Internet Noncompetes And Working From Home" in *Fortune* (Vol. 141, No. 5, March 6, 2000, pp. 430) [14434], [34476], [37186], [42722]

Signs First [22812]

"Signs of Life? You'll Need Plenty of Patience to Profit from M-Commerce" in *Entrepreneur* (Vol. 31, No. 10, October 2003, pp. 28) [5107], [28763], [34477], [36744], [41983], [53963]

Signs Now [22813]

Signs of the Times [22807], [47810]

Signs of the Times Magazine-Buyers' Guide Issue [22797]

Signs of the Times Magazine-Neon Directory Section [22798]

Signs of the Times Magazine-Sign Erection and Maintenance Directory Section [22799]

Signs of the Times Magazine-Sign Supply Distributors Directory Section [22800]

Signs of the Times & Screen Printing en Espanol [19919]

Skilled Nursing Facility Management: New Directions in Long Term Care [18338]

SkillSearch [9294], [9602]

"Skin Deep" in *Entrepreneur* (Vol. 33, January 2005, No. 1, pp. 21) [2605], [56406]

Skin Inc. [2407], [2616], [7919]

The Skincare Market [2403]

"The Skinflint Goes Shopping" in *Forbes* (December 24, 2001, p. 100) [31070], [34484], [51361]

Skinned Knuckles [22641]

"The Skinny" in *Entrepreneur* (Vol. 32, September 2004, No. 9, pp. 42) [6798], [49259]

"Skinny Jeans Sticking Around for Fall" in *Charlotte Observer* (February 5, 2007) [5570], [5715], [53965]

"Skinnyguy.com Rekindles America's Love to Barter" in *PR Newswire* (January 6, 2003) [6138], [14439], [17772], [25598], [26715], [34485]

"Skip the links and head to the gym or the spa" in *Crain's Chicago Business* (Vol. 25, No. 42, October 21, 2002, pp. SR11) [2349], [11802], [19440], [56407]

Sklar & Associates [3813], [3989], [16667], [30115], [31458], [46115], [53114], [54098]

Skokie Chamber of Commerce [59668]

"Skokie Taxed by School-Business Rift" in *Chicago Tribune* (March 9, 2005) [28767], [54749]

Harvey C. Skoog [27219], [30719], [30764], [31459], [38572], [47908], [53115], [54893]

Skowhegan Area Chamber of Commerce [60776]

"Sky Dayton" in *Internet World* (Vol. 6, No. 7, April 1, 2000, pp. 94) [33490], [37078], [43043], [55431]

Sky Link Internet Plus [14682]

Sky Ranch Grill [21964]

Sky Valley Chamber of Commerce [66169]

Skyline Chili, Inc. [21965]

Skyline Ventures [58154]

"The Sky's the Limit" in *Hispanic Business* (December 2001, pp. 50, 52) [252], [47537]

"Sky's the Limit: Think Your Product has Limited Appeal?" in *Entrepreneur* (Vol. 32, No. 4, April 2004, pp. 132) [12258], [35645], [43969]

"Slack Off" in *Fast Company* (August 2001, pp. 27) [31217], [35072], [37187], [54988]

Slaton Chamber of Commerce [65503]

Slats Blind Cleaning [2569]

Michael Slavitch Consulting [49460]

Slayton Area Chamber of Commerce [61666]

Sleep [41297]

Sleep Inn [12728]

"Sleep-state visualization in five easy steps" in *Black Enterprise* (Vol. 33, No. 6, January 2003, pp. 84) [30599], [36747]

"Sleep tight" in *Entrepreneur* (Vol. 30, No. 2, February 2002, pp. 20) [12635], [30417]

Sleeping Bear Area Chamber of Commerce [61427]

"Sleeping On the Job" in *Incentive* (Vol. 174, No. 10, October 2000, pp. 1S8) [26912], [35073], [53966]

Sleepy Eye Area Chamber of Commerce [61667]

Sleepy Hollow Chamber of Commerce [63016]

"Sleepy Little Towns Turn High Tech" in *Home Office Computing* (Vol. 19, No. 1, January 2001, pp. 17) [28768], [30175], [41990], [52728], [53967]

Slender Lady, Inc. [26063]

"A Slice of Happiness" in *Small Business Opportunities* (Vol. 17, September 2005, No. 5, pp. 72, 138) [19622], [21414], [38680]

"A Slice of Life" in *Entrepreneur* (Vol. 32, December 2004, No. 12, pp. 18) [19643], [21626], [37781]

"Slick Trick" in *Tampa Tribune* (December 2, 2005) [18123], [50970], [52204]

"Slick Tricks" in *Entrepreneur* (Vol. 31, No. 7, July 2003, pp. 73) [5110], [14440], [29492], [34486], [37502], [40695]

"Slim Down: Sick of Your Bulky PC? A Desktop Replacement Notebook Could Be the Answer" in *Entrepreneur* (Vol. 32, July 2004, No. 7) [6799], [49260]

Slim and Tone 30 Minute Workout for Women [19527]

"Slow Down and Back Up" in *My Business* (October/November 2003, pp. 12) [22379], [49261]

"Slow Economic Recovery Prompts More Firms to Turn to 'Just-in-Time' Employment" in *Seattle Times* (November 16, 2004) [7145], [32686]

"Slower, but Still Strong" in *Kiplinger's Personal Finance Magazine* (Vol. 55, No. 1, January, 2001, pp. 20) [32687]

"Slump wipes 228 eateries off S.F. menu" in *San Francisco Business Times* (Vol. 16, No. 42, May 24, 2002, pp. 3) [21627], [28769]

"Smack Down! Show Those Numbers Who's Boss With a New Accounting Software Program" in *Entrepreneur* (Vol. 31, No. 10, October 2003) [253], [2959], [4798], [23174], [24038], [26352], [53466]

"SmaL Camera Technologies Snaps Up $13.5M in V.C." in *Boston Business Journal* (Vol. 23, No. 27, August 8, 2003, pp. 21) [4204], [55826]

"Small and midsize concerns are facing boosts up to 15 percent for their insurance" in *Wall Street Journal* (March 20, 2000, pp. A2) [43360]

"Small businesses fret over delays in eliminating an unpopular 1999 law" in *Wall Street Journal* (July 19, 2000, pp. A1) [29493], [52454]

"Small businesses holding out on panic attack" in *Atlanta Business Chronicle* (Vol. 24, No. 13, August 31, 2001, pp. 2B) [42413], [53968]

"Small Biz Barges into Cuba" in *Inc.* (October 1, 2003) [10697], [36748], [43812]

"Small Biz Braces for Life on the High (Priced) Seas" in *Inc.* (September 1, 2004) [22380], [43813]

"Small-Biz Leaders Mixed on Retirement Proposal" in *Crain's Detroit Business* (Vol. 22, January 30, 2006, No. 5, pp. 6) [26913], [40696]

"Small-Biz Owners' Wild Mood Swings" in *Inc.* (July 1, 2003) [28770], [32688], [36749]

"Small Biz Survivors" in *Small Business Opportunities* (Vol. 13, No. 6, November 2001, pp. 74-76, 80) [3487], [33236], [35074], [36750]

"Small Biz Tentative about Testing Web Waters" in *Crain's Detroit Business* (Vol. 19, No. 9, March 3, 2003, pp. 29) [14441], [34487], [53969]

"Small is Bountiful" in *Business Week* (May 22, 2000, pp. 126) [44655]

Small Business Access and Alternatives to Health Care: Congressional Hearing [13463], [41100], [43361]

Small Business Access to Health Care: Congressional Hearing [29494], [40697], [41101]

Small Business Accountant [26353]

Small Business Accounting [254], [2960], [24039]

Small Business Accounting Systems [26415]

Small Business Administration [61136]
    Reference Library [54103]

"Small Business Adviser: Aim resources at biggest accounts" in *Crain's Chicago Business* (Vol. 23, October 9, 2000, pp. 23) [19822], [19894], [52455]

The Small Business Advisor [37020], [53047]

"Small Business Advisor: A Customer for All Seasons" in *Ingram's* (Vol. 27, No. 5, May 2001, pp. 25) [31855], [47538]

"Small Business Advisor: A pressing matter" in *Crain's Chicago Businesss* [19823], [19895], [28771], [52947]

"Small Business Advisor: Choose kids' or collectors' market" in *Crain's Chicago Business* (Vol. 23, November 13, 2000, pp. SB17) [28772], [52948], [55827]

"Small Business Advisor: Dialing for dollars" in *Crain's Chicago Business* (Vol. 23, December 11, 2000, pp. SB16) [24291], [31218], [31856], [33237]

"Small Business Advisor: Focus effort on receptive audience" in *Crain's Chicago Business* (Vol. 23, December 11, 2000, pp. SB17) [42414]

"Small Business Advisor: Identify and protect your niches" in *Crain's Chicago Business* (Vol. 23, October 9, 2000, pp. SB15) [19824], [19838], [28773], [52949]

"Small Business Advisor: Toy Story: Sharon P. John's Toy Company is Relaunching the Dawn Doll" in *Crain's Chicago Business* (Vol. 23) [24829], [36751], [46432]

The Small Business Advocate [40872]

Small Business: An Entrepreneur [36752]

Small Business: An Entrepreneur's Business Plan [29993], [36753], [39578]

Small Business: An Entrepreneur's Plan [36754], [39579], [54308]

Small Business Barriers & Battlefields: Adding Reality to the American Dream [45641]

The Small Business Bible: Everything You Need to Know to Succeed in Your Small Business [255], [787], [2961], [26354], [38350], [39580], [47539], [50674]

Small Business, Big Life: Five Steps to Creating a Great Life with Your Own Small Business [36755], [39581]

"Small Business, Big Losses" in *Journal of Accountancy* (Vol. 19) [256], [2962], [24040], [26355], [27174], [29495]

"Small Business on the Big Screen" in *My Business* (November/December 2001, pp. 36-39) [36756], [39582]

Small Business in a Big World [32826], [53063]

Small Business Cash Flow: Strategies for Making Your Business a Financial Success [27175], [28774], [38351]

"Small-Business Centers: E-Biz for Everyone" in *PC Magazine* (July 1, 2000, pp. 189) [34488]

"Small-Business Centers" in *PC Magazine* (June 6, 2000, pp. 141) [14442], [34489]

Small Business Clustering Technology: Applications in Marketing, Management, Finance, and IT [27176], [32689], [34490], [38352], [41991], [45642], [47540]

The Small Business Computer Book: A Guide in Plain English [49262]

Small Business Computing for Dummies [4799], [23175]

Small Business Council of America [40132]

Small Business Council of America-Alert [54884]

Small Business Council of the Chamber of Commerce of Hawaii [59257]

"Small business" in *Crain's Detroit Business* (Vol. 18, No. 45, November 11, 2002, pp. 23) [28775], [31071], [47541]

The Small Business Credit & Collection Guide [8398], [31586]

"Small Business: Crunching numbers via the Internet" in *Crain's Detroit Business* (Vol. 16, May 29, 2000, pp. 54) [23176], [26356], [34491]

Small Business Desk Reference [257], [21415], [26357], [29496], [29994], [30699], [31100], [31857], [37503], [38353], [38910], [39583], [43362], [47542], [51038], [51841], [52500], [54750]

Small Business Development Center
    Alabama State University–College of Business Administration [56784]
    Culverhouse College of Commerce–The University of Alabama [56785]
    Gainesville Technology Enterprise Center [58712]
    University of South Carolina [64686]
    UWSP Continuing Education–University of Wisconsin-Stevens Point [66559]

Small Business Development Center (Columbia) [64868]

Small Business Development Center for Enterprise Excellence–SBDC [65060]

Small Business Development Center at SUNY Brockport [62780]

The Small Business Directory [52950]

Small Business for Dummies [34492], [39075]

"Small-Business e-Loan" in *Hispanic Business* (March 2002, pp. 60) [34493], [39925], [44656]

Small Business Economic Trends (December 1999, pp. COV); "Monthly Report - December 1999" in [42345], [53862]

Small Business Economic Trends (December 2001, pp. 1); "Monthly report-December 2001" in [28502], [32579]

Small Business Economic Trends (January 2000, pp. COV); "Monthly Report - January 2000" in **[42346]**, **[53863]**

Small Business Economic Trends (January 2002, pp. 1); "Monthly report-January 2002" in **[28503]**, **[32580]**

Small Business Economic Trends (July 2000, pp. 1); "Monthly Report - July 2000" in **[53864]**

Small Business Economic Trends (June 2000, pp. 1); "Monthly Report - June 2000" in **[26855]**, **[42347]**, **[53865]**

Small Business Economic Trends (March 2000, pp. COV); "Monthly Report - March 2000" in **[42348]**, **[53866]**

Small Business Economic Trends (August 2000, pp. 1); "NFIB Education Foundation: small business economic survey" in **[53887]**

Small Business Economic Trends (February 2002, pp. 1); "Novel microarray applications" in **[4744]**, **[17191]**, **[23103]**, **[41878]**, **[53388]**

Small Business Economic Trends (April 2000, pp. 1); "Overview-small business optimism" in **[53905]**

Small Business Economic Trends (February 2000, pp. COV); "Quarterly Report - February 2000" in **[42387]**, **[53930]**

Small Business Economic Trends (February 2002, pp. 1); "Quarterly report-February 2002" in **[28664]**, **[32647]**

Small Business Economic Trends (May 2000, pp. COV); "Quarterly Report - May 2000" in **[53931]**

Small Business ED, MS Office 97 for Dummies **[4800]**, **[23177]**

Small Business Entrepreneur: Launching a New Venture and Managing a Business on a Day-to-Day Basis **[35646]**, **[39076]**

Small Business or Entrepreneurial Related Newsletters and Periodicals **[53970]**

Small Business Executive Report **[45906]**

Small Business Exporters Association of the United States **[12932]**

"Small-Business Exports Show Big Growth" in *Hispanic Business* (Vol. 22, No. 1/2, January/February, pp. 16) **[28776]**, **[53971]**

Small Business Finance **[38354]**

Small Business Financing: How & Where to Get It **[38355]**, **[55828]**

"Small Business Gets Big Squeeze From Property Insurance Rates" in *Tampa Tribune* (February 6, 2007) **[13464]**, **[30952]**, **[43363]**

"Small Business Groups Intensify Efforts to Repeal a Recently Enacted Law" in *Wall Street Journal* (January 19, 2000, pp. A1) **[29497]**

"Small Business Groups and Lawyers Step Up Efforts to Erase a 1999 law" in *Wall Street Journal* (April 12, 2000, pp. A1) **[29498]**

"Small Business Growth: Intention, Ability, and Opportunity" in *Journal of Small Business Management* (Vol. 41, No. 4, October 2003) **[28777]**, **[29931]**, **[39584]**, **[40991]**

Small Business Guide to Borrowing Money **[55829]**

A Small Business Guide to Direct Mail: Build Your Customer Base and Boost Profits **[47543]**

The Small Business Guide to HSAs **[39926]**, **[41102]**, **[53972]**

A Small Business Handbook **[39585]**, **[52951]**

Small Business Handbook: Laws, Regulations & Technical Assistance Services - U.S. Department of Labor **[40698]**

"Small Business: Houman Jewelry Design" in *San Diego Business Journal* (Vol. 28, January 8, 2007, No. 2, pp. 26) **[15860]**, **[36757]**

"Small Business Index Falls as Sales Growth Slows" in *Wall Street Journal* (July 17, 2000, pp. A2) **[28778]**

Small Business Innovative Research Awards **[51012]**, **[55990]**

Small Business Innovative Research Current Solicitations **[39967]**, **[48502]**, **[51013]**, **[53123]**, **[55991]**

Small Business Innovative Research Past Solicitations **[51014]**, **[55992]**

Small Business Innovative Research Solicitations and Awards **[51015]**, **[55993]**

Small Business Insiders Guide to Bankers **[38356]**

Small Business Internet Connections for Dummies **[37188]**

Small Business Internet Directory for Dummies **[37189]**

Small Business Investment Company Directory & Handbook **[13048]**, **[43060]**

"Small Business: Just When Hopes Were High" in *Business Week* (January 8, 2007) **[32690]**, **[52952]**

Small Business Kit for Dummies **[52953]**

The Small Business Legal Kit **[29499]**

Small Business Legal Smarts **[29500]**

Small Business Legal Strategies **[29501]**, **[39586]**

Small Business Legal Tool Kit **[29073]**, **[39077]**, **[44147]**, **[54751]**

Small Business Legislative Council **[40133]**, **[53572]**

Small Business Loan Program Kit **[39927]**, **[44657]**, **[48409]**

Small Business Management **[27177]**, **[29502]**, **[29995]**, **[34494]**, **[35647]**, **[36758]**, **[37504]**, **[43590]**, **[44245]**, **[44658]**, **[44703]**, **[45643]**, **[54752]**

Small Business Management: A Planning Approach **[45644]**

Small Business Management: An Entrepreneur's Guide to Success **[45645]**

Small Business Management Fundamentals **[45646]**

Small-Business Management Guide: Advice from the Brass-Tacks Entrepreneur **[36759]**, **[45647]**

Small Business Management: Launching and Managing New Ventures **[39078]**, **[44704]**

Small Business Marketing for Dummies **[47544]**

The Small Business Money Guide: How to Get It, Use It, Keep It **[38357]**, **[55830]**

"The Small-Business Network" in *PC Magazine* (August 1, 2000, pp. 101) **[49263]**

Small Business Opportunities **[8282]**, **[13053]**, **[53048]**

Small Business Opportunities (Vol. 17, May 2005, No. 3); "4Smartphone's Mobility Solution for Small and Medium Size Businesses" in **[4903]**, **[48935]**

Small Business Opportunities (Vol. 16, No. 1, January 2004, pp. 12, 20); "20 Keys to Leadership" in **[35744]**, **[44862]**

Small Business Opportunities (Vol. 16, November 2004, No. 6, pp. 12, 20); "20 Words That Sell" in **[27288]**, **[51541]**

Small Business Opportunities (Fall 2005); "25 Biz for Kids" in **[1676]**, **[5311]**, **[8121]**, **[8430]**, **[9668]**, **[18721]**, **[19216]**, **[19283]**, **[19812]**, **[22110]**

Small Business Opportunities (Vol. 13, No. 6, November 2001, pp. 38, 40); "A Billion in Baskets" in **[35845]**, **[37597]**, **[46214]**, **[56139]**

Small Business Opportunities (Vol. 13, No. 5, September 2001, pp. 22-24, 26, 28, 30, 32, 34, 36, 40); "A Fortune From Home" in **[16410]**, **[27720]**, **[29735]**

Small Business Opportunities (Vol. 14, No. 1, January 2002, pp. 82, 84); "A Sign of the Times" in **[22796]**, **[50673]**

Small Business Opportunities (Vol. 17, September 2005, No. 5, pp. 48, 50); "A Sizzling Fortune" in **[21412]**, **[38678]**

Small Business Opportunities (Vol. 17, September 2005, No. 5, pp. 72, 138); "A Slice of Happiness" in **[19622]**, **[21414]**, **[38680]**

Small Business Opportunities (Vol. 16, November 2004, No. 6, pp. 48, 50); "A Toast to Innovation" in **[23513]**, **[38932]**, **[44169]**

Small Business Opportunities (Vol. 12, No. 3, May 2000, pp. 43); "A Walk in the Park" in **[24646]**, **[35715]**

Small Business Opportunities (Vol. 14, No. 1, January 2002, pp. 10); "Anti-Recession Strategies" in **[32250]**, **[39147]**

Small Business Opportunities (Vol. 12, No. 2, March 2000, pp. 12); "Appearances Count" in **[27615]**, **[51550]**

Small Business Opportunities (Vol. 16, November 2004, No. 6, pp. 90); "Armed for Profit-Taking" in **[1098]**, **[35776]**, **[43987]**

Small Business Opportunities (Vol. 12, No. 3, May 2000, pp. 70, 72, 74, 76, 78, 80-82, 84); "At Your Service" in **[6]**, **[433]**, **[2853]**, **[6319]**, **[7108]**, **[10610]**, **[15974]**, **[18749]**, **[24222]**, **[38605]**, **[42501]**, **[52488]**

Small Business Opportunities (Vol. 13, No. 6, November 2001, pp. 66, 68); "Automatic Riches" in **[17946]**, **[33413]**, **[35324]**, **[37058]**

Small Business Opportunities (Vol. 16, No. 3, May 2004, pp. 46, 48); "Ballooning Riches" in **[20102]**, **[22779]**, **[46703]**, **[50428]**, **[50552]**

Small Business Opportunities (July 2005); "Be Your Own Boss" in **[496]**, **[1758]**, **[1876]**, **[4265]**, **[11300]**, **[17721]**, **[19061]**, **[19137]**, **[19186]**, **[21197]**, **[23435]**, **[23588]**, **[25616]**, **[35328]**, **[39028]**, **[55999]**

Small Business Opportunities (Vol. 16, November 2004, No. 6, pp. 100, 104); "Beating Travel Stress" in **[25155]**, **[30293]**

Small Business Opportunities (Vol. 14, No. 1, January 2002, pp. 96, 103); "Big Bucks in Big Mouth" in **[21393]**, **[46558]**, **[47940]**, **[50509]**

Small Business Opportunities (Vol. 17, September 2005, No. 5, pp. 126-127); "Big Bucks in Boats" in **[16729]**, **[37596]**

Small Business Opportunities (Vol. 16, No. 2, March 2004, pp. 76-79); "Big Bucks in Bojangles" in **[21450]**, **[38609]**

Small Business Opportunities (Winter 2005); "Big Bucks in Little Gym" in **[19376]**, **[38610]**

Small Business Opportunities (Vol. 16, No. 1, January 2004, pp. 92); "Big Ideas for Small Biz" in **[27841]**, **[31648]**, **[34827]**, **[35840]**, **[39177]**

Small Business Opportunities (Vol. 12, No. 2, March 2000, pp. 64, 66); "Bird Biz Takes Off" in **[35336]**, **[37556]**, **[51021]**

Small Business Opportunities (Vol. 17, September 2005, No. 5, pp. 58, 60); "Biz By the Book" in **[3010]**, **[46560]**, **[49820]**, **[56142]**

Small Business Opportunities (Vol. 14, No. 1, January 2002, pp. 50-51, 54); "Biz Paved With Gold" in **[7188]**, **[38611]**

Small Business Opportunities (Vol. 14, No. 1, January 2002, pp. 52-53); "Blazing Profit" in **[7189]**, **[31621]**, **[35339]**

Small Business Opportunities (Vol. 16, November 2004, No. 6, pp. 72); "Bloopers & Blunders" in **[29803]**, **[30512]**, **[35853]**, **[44943]**, **[49822]**

Small Business Opportunities (Vol. 12, No. 2, March 2000, pp. 120); "Brainstorming" in **[29805]**, **[30514]**, **[35867]**

Small Business Opportunities (Vol. 16, No. 1, January 2004, pp. 58, 110); "Bright Biz Idea" in **[5464]**, **[9056]**, **[15975]**

Small Business Opportunities (Vol. 16, No. 3, May 2004, pp. 70); "Bright Idea Takes Off" in **[9102]**, **[33417]**

Small Business Opportunities (Vol. 17, May 2005, No. 3, pp. 12); "Building Your Business" in **[27888]**, **[38726]**, **[40210]**, **[46758]**, **[54146]**, **[56009]**

Small Business Opportunities (Vol. 16, No. 2, March 2004, pp. 180); "Business Bookshelf" in **[9859]**, **[13868]**, **[14815]**, **[15976]**, **[20447]**, **[20815]**, **[30233]**, **[32291]**, **[33024]**, **[33624]**, **[34779]**, **[35890]**, **[37394]**, **[39191]**, **[40681]**, **[54464]**, **[56149]**

Small Business Opportunities (Vol. 16, No. 2, March 2004, pp. 22); "Cash In At Home" in **[38616]**, **[42504]**

Small Business Opportunities (Vol. 13, No. 5, September 2001, pp. 44); "Cash In On Coupons" in **[497]**, **[46783]**

Small Business Opportunities (Vol. 12, No. 5, September 2000, pp. 58-59); "Check's in the Mail" in **[16429]**, **[52517]**

Small Business Opportunities (Vol. 12, No. 3, May 2000, pp. 60); "Cleaning Up" in **[3289]**, **[35365]**, **[38619]**

Small Business Opportunities (Vol. 17, May 2005, No. 3, pp. 22-24, 26-28, 30, 32, 34, 36, 38, 40, 42, 44); "Click on a Fortune" in **[441]**, **[1794]**, **[3036]**, **[4953]**, **[7123]**, **[17322]**, **[18318]**, **[18993]**, **[20835]**, **[24855]**, **[33674]**, **[38620]**, **[38743]**, **[39039]**, **[41607]**, **[52519]**, **[55050]**

Small Business Opportunities (Vol. 17, May 2005, No. 3, pp. 72); "Club Planet Takes Off" in **[2335]**, **[33683]**, **[46812]**

Small Business Opportunities (Vol. 17, November 2005, No. 6, pp. 100, 104); "Collectibles Cash-In" in **[1315]**, **[1795]**, **[5896]**, **[33685]**, **[51101]**

Small Business Opportunities (Vol. 12, No. 3, May 2000, pp. 108, 130); "Computing Riches" in **[35374]**

Small Business Opportunities (Vol. 12, No. 5, September 2000, pp. 70); "Creative Celebrations" in **[4516]**

Small Business Opportunities (Vol. 13, No. 6, November 2001, pp. 90, 138); "Creative Recruiting" in **[42211]**

Small Business Opportunities (Summer 2005); "Critical Mass" in **[35991]**, **[39265]**, **[45036]**

Small Business Opportunities (Vol. 16, No. 3, May 2004, pp. 18, 20); "Customer Loyalty" in **[46864]**, **[51604]**

Small Business Opportunities (Vol. 12, No. 2, March 2000, pp. 108, 146); "Cybercafe Cash-In" in **[11301]**, **[13947]**, **[33731]**

Small Business Opportunities (Vol. 12, No. 5, September 2000, pp. 44); "Database Dollars" in **[46870]**, **[52841]**, **[53250]**

Small Business Opportunities (Vol. 17, May 2005, No. 3, pp. 126); "Deciding to Sell Your Business" in **[52420]**

Small Business Opportunities (Vol. 16, No. 2, March 2004, pp. 110, 112); "Decorating Dollars" in **[13616]**, **[38625]**, **[42601]**, **[56184]**

Small Business Opportunities (Vol. 17, November 2005, No. 6, pp. 72, 106); "Designs on Success" in **[3521]**, **[5507]**, **[12880]**, **[20116]**, **[31138]**, **[35385]**, **[42508]**

Small Business Opportunities (Vol. 13, No. 6, November 2001, pp. 58, 60); "Direct Success" in **[499]**, **[35391]**, **[46567]**

Small Business Opportunities (Vol. 16, No. 3, May 2004, pp. 58, 120); "Documenting Profit" in **[29062]**, **[37559]**, **[38627]**

Small Business Opportunities (Vol. 17, November 2005, No. 6, pp. 52, 54); "Dramatic Success" in **[32878]**, **[38628]**

Small Business Opportunities (Vol. 16, No. 3, May 2004, pp. 92, 130); "Drawing Attention" in **[1677]**, **[5946]**, **[38629]**, **[42510]**

Small Business Opportunities (Vol. 12, No. 3, May 2000, pp. 86, 130); "Dressed for Success" in **[5508]**, **[5625]**, **[35401]**, **[37560]**, **[38759]**, **[42511]**

Small Business Opportunities (Vol. 12, No. 5, September 2000, pp. 18); "E-Brand Lessons" in **[33790]**, **[51138]**

Small Business Opportunities (Vol. 14, No. 1, January 2002, pp. 16); "E-Commerce Complaints" in **[31706]**, **[33799]**

Small Business Opportunities (Vol. 13, No. 6, November 2001, pp. 92, 94); "E-Learning Takes Off!" in **[13990]**, **[33076]**, **[33806]**

Small Business Opportunities (Vol. 13, No. 5, September 2001, pp. 100, 102); "E-Mail Marketing" in **[13994]**, **[33812]**, **[46923]**

Small Business Opportunities (Vol. 16, November 2004, No. 6, pp. 134); "eBay Motors the Smart Way" in **[1805]**, **[18021]**

Small Business Opportunities (Vol. 17, September 2005, No. 5, pp. 100, 104); "Eco-Preneuring" in **[2590]**, **[2657]**, **[3478]**, **[7890]**, **[8141]**, **[8905]**, **[9481]**, **[10611]**, **[11994]**, **[12172]**, **[12254]**, **[15811]**, **[16282]**, **[21198]**, **[31092]**, **[31622]**, **[34308]**, **[35405]**, **[36633]**, **[37211]**, **[37265]**, **[37922]**, **[53705]**, **[54115]**, **[54154]**, **[54168]**, **[56721]**

Small Business Opportunities (Vol. 13, No. 6, November 2001, pp. 108); "Electric Avenue" in **[7708]**, **[35406]**, **[56000]**, **[56038]**

Small Business Opportunities (Vol. 12, No. 2, March 2000, pp. 86, 88); "Empire Blossoms" in **[15977]**, **[35409]**

Small Business Opportunities (Vol. 16, November 2004, No. 6, pp. 116, 120-121); "Exercise in Profit" in **[19395]**

Small Business Opportunities (Vol. 16, November 2004, No. 6, pp. 62, 64, 138); "Expanding an Empire" in **[8893]**, **[28132]**, **[38631]**

Small Business Opportunities (Vol. 14, No. 1, January 2002, pp. 62-64); "Explosive Success" in **[27718]**, **[35438]**, **[37563]**, **[56043]**

Small Business Opportunities (Vol. 17, November 2005, No. 6, pp. 126-128); "Express to Success" in **[9175]**, **[37637]**, **[38632]**

Small Business Opportunities (Vol. 12, No. 3, May 2000, pp. 62, 64); "Feline Fortunes" in **[19138]**, **[35448]**

Small Business Opportunities (Vol. 13, No. 5, September 2001, pp. 20); "Find the Perfect Biz" in **[3530]**, **[30654]**, **[31150]**, **[38633]**

Small Business Opportunities (Vol. 13, No. 5, September 2001, pp. 52-54); "Finding Millions in the Trash" in **[9307]**, **[31151]**, **[37276]**

Small Business Opportunities (Vol. 13, No. 5, September 2001, pp. 66, 80); "First-Class Delivery" in **[6096]**, **[49695]**

Small Business Opportunities (Vol. 12, No. 3, May 2000, pp. 20); "Flying Solo" in **[29734]**, **[35458]**

Small Business Opportunities (Vol. 14, No. 1, January 2002, pp. 44); "Food Frenzy" in **[21397]**, **[35459]**

Small Business Opportunities (Vol. 13, No. 6, November 2001, pp. 54-55); "Football Fever" in **[35460]**, **[51028]**, **[55094]**, **[56046]**

Small Business Opportunities (Vol. 13, No. 6, November 2001, pp. 72); "Fore Profit Biz" in **[11241]**, **[22748]**, **[35463]**

Small Business Opportunities (Vol. 12, No. 3, May 2000, pp. 52-53); "Form Follows Function" in **[49500]**

Small Business Opportunities (Vol. 17, May 2005, No. 3, pp. 72); "Former Flight Attendant Starts Biz & Soars To $1.5 Million" in **[17296]**, **[56229]**

Small Business Opportunities (Vol. 14, No. 1, January 2002, pp. 126); "Franchise Finds" in **[1425]**, **[1878]**, **[1889]**, **[2221]**, **[2242]**, **[3291]**, **[7195]**, **[8502]**, **[11766]**, **[11924]**, **[12255]**, **[12754]**, **[18590]**, **[19062]**, **[19621]**, **[19792]**, **[21398]**, **[22881]**, **[23437]**, **[24259]**, **[32881]**, **[34319]**, **[36527]**, **[38639]**, **[51029]**

Small Business Opportunities (Vol. 17, May 2005, No. 3, pp. 80, 84); "Fraud Alert" in **[29254]**, **[30224]**

Small Business Opportunities (Vol. 17, November 2005, No. 6, pp. 48, 50); "Fresh-Tossed Profits" in **[21401]**, **[38647]**

Small Business Opportunities (Vol. 17, May 2005, No. 3); "From Dream to Reality: Inventor Takes Invention from Prototype to Product" in **[24813]**, **[44045]**

Small Business Opportunities (May 2005); "From Idea to Marketplace" in **[24857]**, **[43961]**, **[44046]**, **[44847]**, **[46296]**, **[46992]**, **[48735]**, **[55051]**

Small Business Opportunities (Vol. 14, No. 1, January 2002, pp. 92, 124); "Get the Mojo Working" in **[34910]**

Small Business Opportunities (Vol. 16, No. 1, January 2004, pp. 22); "Get Rich in 2004" in **[434]**, **[2021]**, **[2635]**, **[3224]**, **[3294]**, **[5465]**, **[7196]**, **[8591]**, **[10546]**, **[11103]**, **[16106]**, **[18292]**, **[19105]**, **[19343]**, **[19793]**, **[26070]**, **[38650]**, **[51030]**

Small Business Opportunities (Vol. 12, No. 5, September 2000, pp. 12); "Get the Word Out" in **[33945]**, **[47012]**

Small Business Opportunities (Vol. 12, No. 3, May 2000, pp. 22-24, 26, 28, 30, 32); "Getrich.com: Join America's Newest Gold Rush" in **[33441]**

Small Business Opportunities (Vol. 16, No. 2, March 2004, pp. 60); "Getting Organized" in **[51651]**, **[54948]**

Small Business Opportunities (Vol. 16, No. 2, March 2004, pp. 162-163); "Getting Set for Success" in **[35480]**, **[39060]**

Small Business Opportunities (Vol. 12, No. 3, May 2000, pp. 110); "Getting Set for Success with Your Own Small Business" in **[29739]**, **[30482]**, **[35481]**

Small Business Opportunities (Vol. 13, No. 5, September 2001, pp. 18); "Give Advice? Get Protected!" in **[29263]**, **[43185]**

Small Business Opportunities (Vol. 13, No. 6, November 2001, pp. 114); "Go With the Flow" in **[27130]**, **[38096]**

Small Business Opportunities (Fall 2005); "Goal Tending" in **[29889]**, **[36219]**, **[39359]**

Small Business Opportunities (Vol. 16, No. 3, May 2004, pp. 76, 130); "Graduating with Wings" in **[21402]**, **[38651]**

Small Business Opportunities (Vol. 12, No. 2, March 2000, pp. 70, 72); "Graphically Speaking" in **[5947]**, **[37566]**

Small Business Opportunities (Vol. 13, No. 5, September 2001, pp. 60, 64); "Green Acres" in **[15978]**, **[49760]**

Small Business Opportunities (Vol. 16, No. 3, May 2004, pp. 80, 84); "Growing a Business" in **[11434]**, **[28240]**, **[36245]**

Small Business Opportunities (Vol. 12, No. 3, May 2000, pp. 44); "Hall of Mirrors" in **[30483]**, **[35494]**

Small Business Opportunities (Vol. 12, No. 2, March 2000, pp. 58, 60); "Handling Critics" in **[35496]**

Small Business Opportunities (Vol. 12, No. 3, May 2000, pp. 10, 130); "Healthcare Options" in **[26721]**, **[43062]**

Small Business Opportunities (Vol. 12, No. 5, September 2000, pp. 10, 130); "Help Wanted" in **[42860]**, **[49703]**

Small Business Opportunities (Vol. 16, No. 1, January 2004, pp. 62, 64); "High Profit in Play" in **[24816]**, **[28277]**, **[32156]**, **[37682]**, **[46313]**

Small Business Opportunities (Vol. 13, No. 5, September 2001, pp. 76, 78); "High Tech, High Sales" in **[4686]**, **[41461]**, **[47071]**

Small Business Opportunities (Vol. 13, No. 5, September 2001, pp. 84); "Hitting the Links" in **[14123]**, **[25865]**, **[34015]**

Small Business Opportunities (Vol. 16, No. 2, March 2004, pp. 12, 168); "Home-Based Microbiz" in **[42521]**

Small Business Opportunities (Vol. 16, No. 2, March 2004, pp. 184); "Home-Based Resources" in **[39839]**, **[42634]**

Small Business Opportunities (Vol. 16, November 2004, No. 6, pp. 112); "Home Instead Senior Care" in **[448]**, **[38829]**

Small Business Opportunities (Vol. 14, No. 1, January 2002, pp. 86); "Home: Where the Money Is" in **[3295]**, **[35508]**, **[38652]**, **[42523]**

Small Business Opportunities (Vol. 12, No. 5, September 2000, pp. 74, 76); "Homebased Moneymakers" in **[1762]**, **[8503]**, **[15979]**, **[19813]**, **[33445]**, **[42525]**, **[52491]**

Small Business Opportunities (Vol. 13, No. 5, September 2001, pp. 72-73); "Homework 2001" in **[7372]**, **[42653]**, **[49509]**, **[53781]**

Small Business Opportunities (Vol. 12, No. 2, March 2000, pp. 104); "Honey Rhymes with Money" in **[2463]**, **[35510]**, **[42526]**

Small Business Opportunities (Vol. 17, May 2005, No. 3, pp. 92); "Hooked Up to Profit" in **[7732]**, **[17520]**, **[24416]**, **[37689]**, **[52545]**

Small Business Opportunities (Vol. 13, No. 5, September 2001, pp. 58); "Host With the Most" in **[14125]**, **[25866]**, **[34019]**, **[52373]**

Small Business Opportunities (Vol. 16, November 2004, No. 6, pp. 70-71); "Hot Fiscal Issues" in **[26828]**, **[37690]**

Small Business Opportunities (March 2005); "Hot Scoop" in **[12781]**, **[38830]**

Small Business Opportunities (Vol. 12, No. 5, September 2000, pp. 100); "Import an Income" in **[12925]**, **[30353]**, **[35527]**

Small Business Opportunities (Vol. 13, No. 6, November 2001, pp. 82); "Info Overload" in **[13760]**, **[33453]**, **[37064]**

Small Business Opportunities (Vol. 12, No. 3, May 2000, pp. 54); "Just Desserts" in **[2223]**, **[30487]**, **[35539]**, **[37569]**

Small Business Opportunities (Vol. 12, No. 2, March 2000, pp. 76); "Keeping It Legal" in **[684]**, **[29328]**, **[40494]**, **[47168]**

Small Business Start-Up Workbook: A Step-by-Step Guide to Starting the Business You've Dreamed Of **[35649]**, **[39083]**, **[45650]**, **[47546]**

"Small Business Strains to Provide Health Care" in *Bradenton Herald* (December 6, 2006) **[41103]**, **[43364]**

Small Business Success **[58245]**

Small Business Survival Guide **[39588]**

Small Business Survival Guide: Starting, Protecting, and Securing Your Business for Long-Term Success **[259]**, **[26359]**, **[29503]**, **[30953]**, **[31588]**, **[36761]**, **[39589]**, **[54756]**

Small Business Systems **[49387]**

Small Business Tax Deductions 2006 **[24041]**, **[54757]**

Small Business Tax Guide: Guide to Small Business Tax **[54758]**

Small Business Taxation **[29504]**, **[54759]**

Small Business Taxes 2006: Your Complete Guide to a Better Bottom Line **[39590]**, **[54760]**

Small Business Taxes Made Easy: How to Increase Your Deductions, Reduce What You Owe, and Boost Your Profits **[34496]**, **[39591]**, **[54761]**

Small Business Taxes and Management **[45907]**, **[54885]**

Small Business and Technology Development Center at Raleigh–Capital Region SBTDC–SBDC **[63272]**

Small Business Turnaround **[28783]**, **[39592]**

"Small Business and the Use of Accrual Accounting" in *Accounting Today* (Vol. 14, No. 16, September 4, 2000, pp. 10) **[26360]**

The Small Business Valuation Book **[38359]**

Small Business Web Strategies for Dummies **[37190]**

Small Business Windows 95 for Dummies **[4801]**, **[23178]**

Small Business Windows 98 for Dummies **[4802]**, **[23179]**

"Small-Business Wonder:SmartOnline.com provides the tools and experti se to take the trepidation out of launching a new business"in *PCMagazine* **[35650]**, **[52786]**

"Small Businesses Are Engine to American Economy" in *Atlanta Business Chronicle* (Vol. 24, No. 9, August 3, 2001, pp. 10B) **[28784]**, **[32692]**, **[39593]**, **[48410]**, **[54762]**, **[56409]**

"Small Businesses Are Raising Prices, in Latest Sign Inflation is Heating Up" in *Wall Street Journal* (May 2, 2000, pp. B2) **[53973]**

"Small Businesses Don't Have to Spend Big for Web Sites" in *Crain's Detroit Business* (Vol. 18, No. 49, December 9, 2002, pp. 18) **[14445]**, **[25964]**, **[34497]**

"Small Businesses Driving for 'Fast Track' on Trade" in *Atlanta Business Chronicle* (Vol. 24, No. 9, August 3, 2001, pp. 11B) **[40701]**, **[43814]**

"Small Businesses Fuel Growth" in *Success* (Vol. 47, No. 3, July 2000, pp. 16) **[28785]**, **[32693]**, **[35651]**, **[47977]**, **[56075]**

"Small Businesses Looking to Bolster Web Presence Are in Luck" in *Kiplinger Letter* (Vol. 84, January 26, 2007, No. 4) **[788]**, **[14446]**, **[25965]**, **[47547]**

"Small Businesses Now Can Afford Big Benefits" in *National Underwriter Life & Health-Financial Services Edition* (Vol. 105, No. 42) **[24042]**, **[39931]**, **[54763]**

Small Businesses and Workplace Fatality Risk: An Exploratory Analysis **[39594]**, **[56589]**

"Small But Special" in *Entrepreneur* (Vol. 28, No. 9, September 2000, pp. 170) **[2639]**, **[8592]**, **[33491]**, **[37079]**

"Small banks may draw buyers' interest" in *Atlanta Business Chronicle* (Vol. 24, No. 13, August 24, 2001, pp. 3A) **[15456]**, **[50180]**

Small Cap Stocks: Investment and Portfolio Strategies for the Institutional Investor **[15457]**

"Small Caps, Big Value" in *Black Enterprise* (Vol. 35, November 2004, No. 4, pp. 40) **[10185]**, **[15458]**, **[38360]**

"Small Caps Gain Affection" in *Black Enterprise* (Vol. 31, No. 5, December 2000, pp. 48) **[38361]**

"Small business tax cuts 'complement' Bush plan" in *Atlanta Business Chronicle* (Vol. 23, No. 35, February 2, 2001, pp. 53A) **[54764]**

"Small business package passes Congress" in *BlackEnterprise* (Vol. 31, No. 10, May 2001, pp. 22) **[39084]**, **[39778]**, **[40127]**, **[55432]**

"Small Deals, Big Business" in *Washington Business Journal* (Vol. 22, No. 17, August 29, 2003, pp. 17) **[4803]**, **[23180]**, **[28786]**, **[47548]**, **[53467]**, **[53974]**

"Small business could reap dividends" in *Wall Street Journal* (January 22, 2003, pp. B4C) **[54309]**, **[54765]**

Small Engines **[22652]**

A Small Enterprise **[39595]**, **[45651]**

"Small Exporters in a Big World" in *Hispanic Business* (November 2003, pp. 42-43, 46, 48, 50) **[13008]**, **[30954]**, **[32694]**, **[43815]**, **[48411]**

Small Farm News **[45908]**

"Small Firm Bankruptcy" in *Journal of Small Business Management* (Vol. 44, October 2006, No. 4, pp. 493) **[28787]**, **[32695]**, **[33238]**, **[44363]**, **[45652]**, **[52955]**, **[53975]**

Small Firm Finance: An Entrepreneurial Analysis **[38362]**

"Small Firms, Consumers Have PWBA Health Care Benefit Tools" in *Employee Benefit Plan Review* (Vol. 55, No. 8, February 2001, pp. 40) **[26914]**, **[40702]**, **[41104]**, **[43365]**

Small Firms and Economic Growth **[32696]**, **[52956]**

"Small Firms Emphasize Trade-Show Marketing" in *Crain's Detroit Business* (Vol. 21, February 7, 2005, No. 6, pp. 24) **[25019]**, **[30955]**, **[36762]**, **[47549]**, **[50675]**, **[51843]**, **[55157]**

Small Firms: Entrepreneurship in the '90s **[36763]**

"Small Firms Flock to Remote Deposit Service" in *American Banker* (Vol. 172, January 16, 2006, No. 10, pp. 6A) **[10186]**, **[15459]**, **[26361]**

Small Firms in Global Competition **[30956]**

Small Firms, Large Concerns: The Development of Small Business in Comparative Perspective **[52957]**

"Small Firms' Motivation for Exporting" in *Journal of Small Business Management* (Vol. 38, No. 4, October 2000, pp. 1) **[43816]**

"Small Firms Seeking Government Contracts Will Get More Help" in *Kiplinger Letter* (Vol. 78, January 19, 2007, No. 2) **[39932]**, **[40095]**, **[44660]**

"Small Firms Slow to Board E-com Boat" in *Accounting Today* (Vol. 14, No. 14, August 7, 2000, pp. 27) **[34498]**, **[53976]**

"Small Firms Still Strain for Space: Outlook Brighter for Companies in Need of More Room" in *Crain's Chicago Business* (Vol.23, Dec. 11) **[28788]**, **[53977]**

"Small Firms Turn to Financial Futures for Fuel" in *Wall Street Journal* (November 3, 2003, pp. A2) **[26362]**, **[53978]**

"Small Fry" in *Entrepreneur* (Vol. 33, January 2005, No. 1, pp. 44) **[6801]**, **[49266]**

"Small businesses are starting to sweat a little about the future" in *Wall Street Journal* (April 4, 2000, pp. B2) **[30600]**

Small Giants: Companies that Choose to Be Great Instead of Big **[39596]**

"Small-Group Reform, Blue Changes on Hold" in *Crain's Detroit Business* (Vol. 18, No. 50, December 16, 2002, pp. 6) **[13465]**, **[40703]**, **[43366]**

"Small-group insurance reforms are in works" in *Crain's Detroit Business* (Vol. 19, No. 16, April 21, 2003, pp. 7) **[13466]**, **[40704]**, **[43367]**

"Small firms cut hires, inventory, capital plans" in *Wall Street Journal* (November 15, 2000, pp. B17) **[29996]**, **[42416]**, **[44246]**

"Small Is Big" in *Forbes* (May 27, 2002, p. 88) **[26363]**, **[53468]**

"Small Manufacturers Aren't Using the Internet" in *Wall Street Journal* (July 3, 2000, pp. B6) **[14447]**, **[34499]**, **[46433]**

Small Manufacturing SIG Newsletter **[46523]**

Small and Medium-Sized Enterprises in Countries in Transition **[39597]**, **[43817]**

Small & Minority Business - OSMB–Department of General Services–Small and Minority Business Office **[57893]**

"Small or Not, It's the Law" in *Inc.* (September 2000, pp. 107) **[29075]**, **[40128]**, **[53567]**

"Small-Office Firewalls" in *PC Magazine* (June 27, 2000, pp. 198) **[49267]**, **[53469]**

"Small Office/Home Office" in *Hispanic Business* (Vol. 22, No. 1/2, January/February, pp. 92) **[42724]**, **[43368]**, **[44148]**, **[49268]**

"Small Office Space: Tear Down Those Walls" in *My Business* (April/May 2002, pp. 43) **[49549]**

" Small business owners' outlook soars on sales prospects " in *Wall Street Journal* (February 29, 2000, pp. B2) **[30601]**

"Small Package" in *Fast Company* (August 2001, pp. 44) **[14448]**, **[37191]**

"The Small Picture: How Does the Federal Deficit Affect Your Business?" in *Entrepreneur* (Vol. 31, No. 6, June 2003, pp. 26) **[28789]**, **[32697]**

"A Small Price to Pay" in *Inc.* (September 1, 2003) **[13467]**, **[43369]**

Small Project/Task Management for Team Members (Canada) **[30499]**

Small Publishers Association of North America **[2666]**, **[8596]**

"Small businesses dissatisfied with SBA" in *Black Enterprise* (Vol. 31, No. 5, December 2000, pp. 29) **[39598]**, **[39933]**, **[40096]**, **[48412]**

Small Shop Tips and Techniques **[4494]**

"Small can be beautiful for two sporting-goods retailers" in *Wall Street Journal* (November 14, 2000, pp. B2) **[23633]**

Small Talk **[13562]**

"Small businesses fight to repeal tax-law change" in *Crain's Detroit Business* (Vol. 16, No. 16, April 17, 2000, pp. 32) **[52456]**, **[54766]**

Small Time Operator: How to Start Your Own Business, Keep Your Books, Pay Your Taxes, and Stay Out of Trouble **[29505]**, **[39085]**, **[54767]**

Small Time Operator: How to Start Your Own Small Business, Keep Your Books, Pay Your Taxes, & Stay out of Trouble! **[26364]**, **[52958]**, **[54768]**

Small Time Operator: The Software **[52959]**

"Small Town Car Dealers Survive" in *Business First Buffalo* (Vol. 19, No. 46, August 8, 2003, pp. 1B) **[18124]**, **[19079]**, **[28790]**, **[29732]**

"Small, Yes-But With A Big Back Office" in *Business Week* (No. 3853, October 13, 2003, pp. 86) **[4804]**, **[23181]**, **[28791]**, **[30957]**, **[53470]**

"Smaller firms see biggest jump in health-care costs" in *Wall Street Journal* (August 29, 2000, pp. B2) **[43370]**

"Smaller companies plan to build up inventories" in *Wall Street Journal* (February 15, 2002, pp. B6) **[44247]**, **[53979]**

"Smaller, greener jobs dominate remodeling" in *Atlanta Business Chronicle* (Vol. 24, No. 13, August 31, 2001, pp. 5B) **[7480]**, **[28792]**, **[53980]**

"Smaller Shopping Centers Adopt Larger Style" in *Crain's Detroit Business* (Vol. 22, December 4, 2006, No. 49, pp. 33) **[29997]**, **[47550]**

"Smaller Venture Funds Drive Interest in FoFs" in *Venture Capital Journal* (October 1, 2005) **[55833]**

Smallmouth Bass: America's Greatest Sportfish **[2203]**

Smart Access **[6349]**

"Smart Answers" in *Business Week* (No. 3694, August 14, 2000, pp. F14) **[25244]**, **[29998]**, **[37782]**, **[49269]**

SMART Body Shop Talk: Paint Tips **[2038]**

"Smart Business Tools" in *Black Enterprise* (Vol. 32, No. 9, April 2002, pp. 54) **[4805]**, **[23182]**, **[29760]**, **[35652]**

"Smart Businesses See Value, and Profit, in Promoting Women" in *Crain's Chicago Business* (Vol. 30, February 2007, No. 6, pp. 30) **[39599]**, **[50357]**, **[50468]**

Smart Cartridge Canada **[7861]**, **[51472]**

"Smart growth advocates push for change" in *Atlanta Business Chronicle* (Vol. 24, No. 14, September 7, 2001, pp. 10C) **[28793]**, **[39600]**

"Smart Content Management" in *E-business Advisor* (Vol. 18, No. 6, June 2000, pp. 28) **[25966]**, **[34500]**

Smart Customer Service **[31917]**

"Smart customers, dumb companies" in *Harvard Business Review* (Vol. 78, No. 6, November-December 2000, pp. 187) **[14449]**, **[34501]**

"Smart Design" in *Entrepreneur* (Vol. 30, No. 3, March 2002, pp. 40) **[4806]**, **[6007]**, **[23183]**, **[53471]**

Smart Hiring for Your Business: Everything You Need to Know to Find & Hire the Best Employees **[42417]**, **[42893]**

"Smart inventory: start electing superior filing options now" in *Barron's* (Vol. 82, No. 59, February 24, 2003, pp. 23) **[260]**, **[15460]**, **[24043]**, **[26365]**, **[29506]**, **[54310]**, **[54769]**

Smart Mail **[10698]**

"Smart Marketing Can Make Your Fortune" in *Success* (Vol. 47, No. 5, October 2000, pp. 30) **[47551]**

"Smart Money: Where to Spend Your Marketing Dollars When a Product Isn't Selling" in *Entrepreneur* (Vol. 33, January 2005, No. 1) **[47552]**, **[51844]**

"Smart patents" in *Harvard Business Review* (Vol. 80, No. 4, April 2002, pp. 18) **[29507]**, **[44149]**, **[44364]**

"Smart Set" in *Inc.* (November 1, 2003) **[30176]**, **[33239]**, **[41992]**, **[52729]**

Smart Start your Arizona Business **[60790]**

Smart Start your Arkansas Business **[61733]**

Smart Start your Colorado Business **[58482]**

Smart Start your Connecticut Business **[60682]**

Smart Start your Florida Business **[61854]**

Smart Start your Georgia Business **[62381]**

Smart Start your Hawaii Business **[59270]**

Smart Start your Illinois Business **[59804]**

Smart Start your Indiana Business **[60049]**

Smart Start your Iowa Business **[60251]**

Smart Start your Kentucky Business **[60597]**

Smart Start your Maryland Business **[60895]**

Smart Start your Massachusetts Business **[61160]**

Smart Start your Michigan Business **[61504]**

Smart Start your Missouri Business **[62112]**

Smart Start your New Hampshire Business **[62449]**

Smart Start your New Jersey Business **[62632]**

Smart Start your New Mexico Business **[62740]**

Smart Start your New York Business **[63238]**

Smart Start your North Carolina Business **[63483]**

Smart Start your Ohio Business **[63900]**

Smart Start your Oregon Business **[64308]**

Smart Start your Pennsylvania Business **[64628]**

Smart Start your South Carolina Business **[64802]**

Smart Start your Tennessee Business **[65017]**

Smart Start your Texas Business Guide **[65672]**

Smart Start your Virginia Business **[66001]**

Smart Start your Washington Business **[66244]**

Smart Start your Washington D.C. Business **[60452]**

Smart Start your Wisconsin Business **[66584]**

Smart Start Your Arizona Business **[52960]**

Smart Start Your Arkansas Business **[52961]**

Smart Start Your California Business **[52962]**, **[62218]**

Smart Start Your Colorado Business **[52963]**

Smart Start Your Connecticut Business **[52964]**

Smart Start Your Florida Business **[52965]**

Smart Start Your Georgia Business **[52966]**

Smart Start Your Hawaii Business **[52967]**

Smart Start Your Illinois Business **[52968]**

Smart Start Your Indiana Business **[52969]**

Smart Start Your Kentucky Business **[52970]**

Smart Start Your Maryland Business **[52971]**

Smart Start Your Massachusetts Business **[52972]**

Smart Start Your Michigan Business **[52973]**

Smart Start Your New Jersey Business **[52974]**

Smart Start Your New York Business **[52975]**

Smart Start Your North Carolina Business **[52976]**

Smart Start Your Ohio Business **[52977]**

Smart Start Your Oregon Business **[52978]**

Smart Start Your Pennsylvania Business **[52979]**

Smart Start Your South Dakota Business **[64846]**

Smart Start Your Tennessee Business **[52980]**

Smart Start Your Texas Business **[52981]**

Smart Start Your Utah Business **[65749]**

Smart Start Your Vermont Business **[65812]**

Smart Start Your Virginia Business **[52982]**

Smart Start Your Washington Business **[52983]**

Smart Start Your Washington, D.C. Business **[52984]**

Smart Start Your West Virginia Business **[66319]**

Smart Start Your Wisconsin Business **[52985]**

Smart Start Your Wyoming Business **[66640]**

"Smart Tech Solutions For Small Businesses" in *Black Enterprise* (Vol. 35, August 2004, No. 1, pp. 61) **[6802]**, **[14450]**, **[27179]**, **[49270]**, **[53472]**

"The Smart Way to Hire Superstars" in *Fortune* (Vol. 142, No. 2, July 10, 2000, pp. 200V+) **[9577]**, **[42418]**

Smart Ways to Work **[46116]**, **[55044]**

The Smart Women's Guide to Starting a Business **[56410]**

Smart Workplace Practices **[42917]**

"Smarten Up" in *Entrepreneur* (Vol. 32, August 2004, No. 8, pp. 42) **[5111]**, **[14451]**

"Smarter highways to revolutionize the way we drive" in *Ingram's* (Vol. 28, No. 2, February 2002, pp. 53) **[7481]**, **[41993]**

"Smarter Than You" in *Inc.* (September 2005, pp. 69, 72) **[36764]**, **[45653]**

"A smarter way to sell commodities" in *Harvard Business Review* (Vol. 80, No. 4, April 2002, pp. 24) **[30958]**, **[31072]**, **[51845]**

SMARTRISK **[40948]**

"Smarty pants" in *Entrepreneur* (Vol. 30, No. 3, March 2002, pp. 42) **[6182]**, **[49271]**

Smash Hit Subs **[8574]**, **[15958]**

SME Cluster Development: A Dynamic View on Survival Clusters in Developing Countries **[39601]**, **[43818]**

SMEs and New Technologies: Learning E-Business and Development **[14452]**, **[34502]**, **[41994]**

"SMG cooking up new uses for convention center" in *Business First Columbus* (Vol. 18, No. 28, March 1, 2002, pp. A8) **[25020]**

"Smile: Your Company's Under Attack" in *PC Computing* (March 2000, pp. 42) **[31858]**, **[34503]**, **[50676]**

Smith, Bridges & Associates **[6046]**

Smith Center Chamber of Commerce **[60418]**

Smith College–Office of Institutional Research **[61148]**

S.B. Smith Consulting Group Inc. **[3814]**

Smith County Chamber of Commerce **[64974]**

Smith, Dawson & Andrews **[20193]**

Smith-Emery Co. **[7638]**

Michael John Smith **[49658]**

Smith Mountain Lake Chamber of Commerce/Partnership **[65946]**

"Smith & Nephew's local spark" in *Boston Business Journal* (Vol. 22, No. 15, May 17, 2002, p) **[17105]**, **[36765]**

Smith, Turner & Reeves P.A. **[46117]**

"Smithfield, Va., Candy Shop Pleases Children, Adults" in *Newport News Daily Press* (August 20, 2002) **[2254]**, **[4310]**

John Smithkey, III, RN **[32120]**, **[56669]**

Smithsonian Institute–Office of Small and Disadvantaged Business Utilization **[67395]**

Smithsonian Institution

    Smithsonian American Art Museum–National Portrait Gallery Library **[6081]**, **[19280]**

    Smithsonian American Art Museum–Photograph Archives **[6082]**

Smithsonian Institution Libraries–National Postal Museum Library **[5873]**

"Smithtown-based LuminNet Helps Small Businesses Design and Market Their Own Web Sites" in *Long Island Business News* (Feb. 20, 2004) **[25967]**, **[34504]**, **[47553]**

Smithtown Chamber of Commerce **[63017]**

Smithville Area Chamber of Commerce **[65504]**

Smithville - DeKalb County Chamber of Commerce **[64975]**

Smitty's **[21966]**

Smocking Arts Guild of America **[7990]**

"Smoke screening" in *Entrepreneur* (Vol. 30, No. 9, September 2002, pp. 30) **[45654]**, **[54257]**

Smoke in Your Eyes **[24631]**

Smokeless Tobacco Council **[24604]**

Smokin' Donut Books **[64685]**

Smoking Cessation Research Institute **[26069]**

Smoking and Health Database **[17236]**, **[19535]**

"Smooth Operator" in *Home Business* (Vol. 12, October 2005, No. 5, pp. 93) **[2398]**, **[34505]**, **[51362]**

"Smooth Selling" in *My Business* (September/October 2001, pp. 34-37) **[30700]**, **[52457]**

"Smoother Ice Cream From Winter Wheat" in *Business Week* (No. 3772, March 4, 2002, pp.73) **[12789]**, **[48793]**

The Smoothie Kiosk Business Plan **[15940]**

"Smoothie Operators" in *Small Business Opportunities* (Vol. 16, No. 2, March 2004, pp. 82) **[15910]**, **[38682]**

SMOR Chamber of Commerce **[57069]**

Smugglers' Notch Area Chamber of Commerce **[65797]**

"Smurfit-Stone Narrows Losses" in *St. Louis Post-Dispatch* (January 26, 2005) **[46434]**

Smyth Fivenson Co. **[11971]**, **[37366]**

Snackology: Have Your Snacks and Eat Them Too **[18474]**

Snake River Territory Convention and Visitors Bureau **[59330]**

Snap Fitness Inc. **[19528]**

"Snap n' Print" in *Entrepreneur* (Vol. 32, November 2004, No. 11, pp. 18) **[4205]**, **[49272]**

Snap-on Tools Co. **[11915]**

Snap-On Tools Of Canada Ltd. **[4359]**

Snappy Tomato Pizza **[19714]**

Snare Drum for Beginners **[17641]**

"Snare and Share Alike: Here's a Quick and Easy Way to Capture Video" in *Black Enterprise* (Vol. 34, No. 6, January 2004, pp. 46) **[4807]**, **[9742]**, **[10153]**, **[23184]**, **[49273]**, **[50820]**, **[53473]**

"Snatching Victory from Defeat" in *Hispanic Business* (September 2006, pp. 58, 60, 62) **[42419]**, **[48413]**

Snelling Staffing, LLC **[9282]**

Snip-Its **[3286]**

Snip N' Clip Haircut Shops **[11840]**

"Snipers, Stalkers, and Nibblers: Online Auction Business Ethics" in *Journal of Business Ethics* (Vol. 46, No. 2, Aug. 15, 2003) **[1855]**, **[34506]**, **[37505]**

Snips Magazine **[1044]**

SNL DataSource Banking Module **[3469]**, **[15776]**

SNL Financial Services Daily **[15675]**

SNL Real Estate DataSource **[3470]**, **[15777]**

SNL REIT Weekly **[21063]**

SNL Weekly Bankfax **[343]**

Snohomish Chamber of Commerce **[66170]**

Snoqualmie Valley Chamber of Commerce **[66171]**

Snow Angels Ice Cream & Hot Dog Shops **[12851]**

"Snow, rain and sleet lead to weather delay claims" in *Business First Columbus* (Vol. 18, No. 25, February 8, 2002, pp. 17) **[7482]**, **[29508]**

Snow College–Small Business Development Center **[65687]**

Snow Hill Chamber of Commerce **[60858]**

Thomas J. Snow **[25105]**

"Snowboarding Secrets" in *Forbes* (Vol. 175, February 14, 2005, No. 3, pp. 78) **[14453]**, **[23634]**, **[34507]**, **[36766]**

Snowdon's Official International Protocols: The Definitive Guide to the Business and Social Customs of the World **[43819]**

Snowflake - Taylor Chamber of Commerce **[57070]**

Snowmass Village Resort Association **[58423]**

SnowSports Industries America **[22853]**

Snyder Chamber of Commerce **[65505]**

"So Close...Yet so Far" in *Entrepreneur* (Vol. 28, No. 10, October 2000, pp. 38) **[30657]**, **[44440]**

"So Long, Stage Fright" in *Success* (Vol. 47, No. 2, June 2000, pp. 70) **[27500]**

"So Many Lenders, So Few Takers" in *Business Week* (January 9, 2006, No. 3966, pp. 79-80) **[17440]**, **[20671]**, **[21010]**, **[32698]**

So Smart **[5410]**

So That's Who Used to Be!: A Reunion Planning Guide **[18761]**

"So What's Your Story?" in *Forbes* (October 30, 2000, pp. 274) **[3585]**, **[15461]**, **[38363]**

Solar Energy Industries Association [23333]

Solar Rating and Certification Corporation [23334]

Solar Today [7576]

"Sold for $20 Million" in *Black Enterprise* (Vol. 31, No. 5, December 2000, pp. 30) [34511], [37192], [52458]

"Soldiers of fortune" in *Entrepreneur* (Vol. 31, No. 5, May 2003, pp. 27) [14458], [36771], [41997]

"A Soldier's Story" in *Black Enterprise* (Vol. 34, No. 6, January 2004, pp. 91) [2729], [2745], [40098], [41544]

Sole Proprietorship [54311]

SOLE - The International Society of Logistics [20212]

Solid Waste Information Clearinghouse–Library [11984]

Solid Waste Report (Vol. 34, No. 1, January 10, 2003); "CIWMB wants e-waste law signed, looks at zero waste, landfills" in [21223], [40262]

Solid Waste Report (Vol. 33, No. 39, December 27, 2002); "E-waste Bill in Oregon" in [6636], [21226], [24337], [40330]

Solid Waste Report (Vol. 33, No. 32, September 20, 2002); "E-waste Management Muddled as Agencies Grope for Solutions" in [6637], [21227], [40331]

Solid Waste Report (Vol. 33, No. 37, November 29, 2002); "Flourishing programs give rise to businesses' recycling interest" in [6651], [21232]

Solid Waste Report (Vol. 33, No. 32, September 20, 2002); "More E-waste" in [6728], [21245]

Solid Waste Report (Vol. 33, No. 36, November 15, 2002); "Watchdog groups say evidence shows Canada continues to export e-waste" in [6854], [21263], [40816]

"Solo Mission: Paul Stannard used to make software for other companies" in *Entrepreneur* (Vol. 30, No. 3, March 2002, pp. 160) [4583], [22889], [35653], [53150]

Solo Private Practice: A Step by Step Guide to Opening Your Private Practice [39086], [40906]

Solo Success [36772]

Warren Solodar [19211], [19323]

SoloDining.com [31260]

"Soloella.com to launch" in *Hispanic Business* (Vol. 22, No. 4, April 2000, pp. 78) [14459], [34512]

Solon Chamber of Commerce [63786]

Solstice Capital [61121]

Solvang Chamber of Commerce [57807]

"Solving the regional puzzle" in *Crain's Detroit Business* (Vol. 19, No. 17, April 28, 2003, pp. 1) [32704], [39603]

Somatic Cell and Molecular Genetics [52323]

"Some small biz markets underserved by CPAs" in *Journal of Accountancy* (Vol. 190, No. 6, December 2000, pp. 30) [261], [52391], [53983]

"Some D.C. Health enters Quietly Filling Urgent Needs" in *Washington Business Journal* (Vol. 22, No. 8, June 27, 2003, pp. 34) [41105]

Some Dude's Playground [18747]

"Some outplacement firms benefit in down economy" in *Boston Business Journal* (Vol. 22, No. 14, May 10, 2002, pp. 38) [32705], [49735], [53984]

"Some ideas to entertain: how to host a memorable party" in *Utah Business* (Vol. 16, No. 9, September 2002, pp. 50) [4554], [53985]

"Some prison program deals not using inmates" in *Atlanta Business Chronicle* (Vol. 25, No. 21, November 1, 2002, pp. 11B) [40099], [40706]

"Some Local Firms Find Opportunity in Telecom" in *Atlanta Business Chronicle* (Vol. 25, November 15, 2002, No. 23 pp. 11C) [5114], [14460], [28795]

"Some Relief Over End of Pixelworks Merger" in *Business Journal-Portland* (Vol. 20, No. 23, August 8, 2003, pp. 8) [15464], [41998], [43606], [47784], [50184]

"Some Service-Related Businesses Surge Ahead" in *Atlanta Business Chronicle* (Vol. 25, January 10, 2003, No. 31, pp. 21A) [28796], [52592]

"Some Suppliers Expanding Biz" in *Crain's Detroit Business* (Vol. 22, January 16, 2006, No. 3, pp. 3) [1969], [28797], [43822]

"Some "Unlikely" Losses Worth Mentioning To Business Owners" in *Rough Notes* (Vol. 145, No. 9, September 2002, pp. 86) [13468], [43371]

"Some Wichita listeners misled by radio spots" in *Atlanta Business Chronicle* (Vol. 25, November 15, 2002, No. 23 pp. S10) [790], [20337], [47557]

"Somebody's Watching You" in *Inc.* (September 2005, pp. 75-76) [12910], [14461], [20156], [25968], [34513], [50469], [50677]

"Someone switching careers could be the perfect match" in *Atlanta Business Chronicle* (Vol. 24, No. 8, July 27, 2001, pp. 6B) [42421]

Somerset Area Chamber of Commerce [66524]

Somerset County Chamber of Commerce [64509]

Somerset Historical Center–Historical and Genealogical Society of Somerset County [11095]

Somerset-Pulaski County Chamber of Commerce [60570]

Somerville Chamber of Commerce [60998]

"Something Different" in *Entrepreneur* (Vol. 28, No. 2, February 2000, pp. 40) [29999], [30602]

"Something to Prove" in *Crain's Detroit Business* (Vol. 22, January 2, 2006, No. 1, pp. 8) [14462]

Something Special [8253], [33324]

"Something's fishy: More Captain D's coming" in *Atlanta Business Chronicle* (Vol. 25, No. 21, November 1, 2002, pp. 8A) [21628], [38912]

Sommers Consultants Inc. [38984]

SON Systems International Inc. [49461]

Sona Laser Centers, Inc. [17279]

Sona MedSpa [17280]

Sona Medspa International [7938]

Sonic Drive In [21967]

"Sonic Profits, Sales Up for Quarter" in *Journal Record* (June 24, 2003) [21629], [23055], [38913], [40439]

"Sonic Shifts Momentum With Purchase of 12 Car Dealerships" in *Houston Business Journal* (Vol. 34, No. 14, August 15, 2003, pp. 7) [18125], [30000]

"SoniqCast Element" in *Black Enterprise* (Vol. 35, December 2004, No. 5, pp. 70) [6804], [49276]

Sonitrol Corp. [22449]

Sonitrol Distribution Canada Inc. [22450]

Sonoita - Elgin Chamber of Commerce [57071]

"Sonoma County, Calif., Voters Set to Decide Whether to Ban Biotech Crops" in *Sacramento Bee* (November 2, 2005) [26540], [40707], [41999]

"Sonoma County Wine Country B&Bs Go Boutique" in *Travel Weekly* (Vol. 62, No. 29, July 21, 2003, pp. 48) [12636]

Sonoma Valley Chamber of Commerce [57808]

Sonora Chamber of Commerce [65506]

Son's [12852]

Sony Ericsson WTA Tour [24563]

"Sony Ericsson's T310/T316 Mobile Phone" in *Black Enterprise* (Vol. 34, No. 5, December 2003, pp. S6) [5080], [5115], [49277], [50131]

Sonz–Sonz Franchising, Inc. [19529]

"Soothe operator: word-of-mouth was the cure for discouragement" in *Entrepreneur* (Vol. 30, No. 12, December 2002, pp. 112) [2572], [50798], [56076]

Soperton - Treutlen Chamber of Commerce [59159]

Sorcia Inc. [3815]

"A Sore Site for Eyes" in *Entrepreneur* (Vol. 28, No. 10, October 2000, pp. 38) [14463], [34514], [55838]

Sorrento Ventures [58156]

"Sorting out Enron mess pumps up Plante & Moran" in *Crain's Detroit Business* (Vol. 19, No. 17, April 28, 2003, pp. 30) [262], [24044], [26366]

S.O.S. Kids: Infant/Child Emergency Life Saving Video [5411], [41315]

SOS Mole Trappers [16165]

Souhegan Valley Chamber of Commerce [62439]

Soul Fixins Restaurant [21968]

"Soul Progress" in *Fast Company* (August 2001, pp. 22) [5116], [14464], [25969], [35654]

Soul Proprietor: 101 Lessons from a Lifestyle Entrepreneur [8136], [35655], [39087]

Soul Works [35263]

Sound & Communications Magazine [5211]

Sound Current Music & Books [66687]

Sound Healers Association [19562]

Sound & Music Studio [21145]

The Sound Studio [21146]

Sound Success [9765]

Sound & Video Contractor [21153]

Sounding the Alarm: Awareness Level Training [56646]

Sounding Board [1707]

Soundings [16763]

Soundings Trade Only [16764]

"Sounds Like Success" in *Small Business Opportunities* (Vol. 13, No. 5, September 2001, pp. 50, 103) [17723], [35656]

Soundview Financial Group, Inc. [58615]

"Souping Up Your January" in *Ingram's* (Vol. 29, No. 1, January 2003, pp. 29) [21630]

"Soup's On" in *San Francisco Business Times* (Vol. 18, No. 2, August 22, 2003, pp. 38) [23507], [30001], [45655]

"Sour forecasts reach fruition; Local companies' 3Q profits fall 26.8 percent from '99" in *Crain's Detroit Business* (Vol. 16, No. 47) [28798]

"Sour Lake, Texas, Looks to Bed and Breakfast to Help Revive Downtown" in *Beaumont Enterprise* (November 6, 2003) [2453]

The Source [10949]

"Source Interlink, Batanga Ink Distribution Pact" in *Hispanic Business* (March 2003, pp. 24) [17773], [18936], [32162]

Source One GSA [7676]

SourceBook [19896]

Sourcebooks Inc. [59816]

South Atlantic Venture Funds, L.P. [58979]

South Baldwin Chamber of Commerce [56888]

South Beach Franchising, LLC [17281]

South Belt - Ellington Chamber of Commerce [65507]

South Bend Area SBDC [59836]

South Bend Chocolate Co. [4337]

South Boston Satellite Office of Longwood–Small Business Development Center [65840]

South Carolina Chamber of Commerce [64781]

South Carolina Department of Commerce [64709]

"South Carolina Duo Cashes in By Buying Ugly Houses as Fixer-Uppers" in *Sun News* (January 9, 2005) [791], [20673], [21012], [38914], [47558]

South Carolina Export Consortium–University of South Carolina–Small Business Development Center [64697]

South Carolina Jobs-Economic Development Authority [64710]

South Carolina Office of Small and Minority Business Assistance [64711]

South Carolina Procurement Technical Assistance Center–University of South Carolina Procurement Center [64793]

South Carolina Procurement Technical Assistance Program–Small Business Development Center [64698]

South Carolina Research Authority–Charleston Research Park [64796]

South Carolina State Budget and Control Board–Office of Research and Statistical Services [66979]

South Carolina (State) Department of Alcohol and Other Drug Abuse Services–The Drugstore Information Clearinghouse [54392]

South Carolina (State) Department of Mental Health–Earle E. Morris, Jr. Alcohol & Drug Addiction Treatment Center–Library [54393]

South Carolina (State) Department of Transportation–Library [2118], [8745], [16204], [24263]

South Carolina State Library [66980]

South Carolina State University–Small Business Development Center [64699]

South Carolina Statewide Minority Business Development Center [62258], [64790]

South Carolina Wildlife [23748]

South Central Indiana [59837]

South Central Indiana SBDC [59838]

South Charleston Chamber of Commerce [66298]

Master Index

South College **[63481]**

South Columbia County Chamber of Commerce **[64268]**

South County SBDC **[64653]**

South Dakota Department of Health–Director of Administration **[66981]**

South Dakota Department of Labor–Labor Market Information Center **[66982]**

South Dakota Governor's Office of Economic Development **[64812]**
　　　　Export, Trade, and Marketing Division **[64813]**

South Dakota Procurement Technical Assistance Center **[64844]**

South Dakota State Library–Documents Department **[66983]**

South Dakota State University
　　　　Rural Sociology Department **[66984]**
　　　　Water Resources Institute **[25747]**

South DeKalb Business Incubator **[59218]**

South Eastern Chamber United in Business **[66525]**

South Fairfax SBDC of the Community Business Partnership **[65841]**

"South Florida Braces From New Overtime Law" in *South Florida Business Journal* (Vol. 23, No. 47, June 27, 2003, pp. 1) **[40708]**, **[55312]**

South Florida Business Journal (Vol. 23, No. 48, July 4, 2003, pp. 1); "Adversity Leads to Creativity in Tourism" in **[12514]**, **[24660]**, **[25144]**, **[46660]**

South Florida Business Journal (Vol. 23, No. 47, June 27, 2003, pp. 2); "Ameribank Plans Branch in Palm Beach Gardens" in **[9810]**, **[27768]**, **[37873]**

South Florida Business Journal (Vol. 23, No. 48, July 4, 2003, pp. 31); "Bald is Beautiful. Concierge Makes Any Wish Come True" in **[7121]**, **[30134]**

South Florida Business Journal (Vol. 23, No. 53, August 8, 2003, pp. 1A); "Bankers' Gaze Turns Northward" in **[27810]**, **[37902]**

South Florida Business Journal (Vol. 23, No. 47, June 27, 2003, pp. 6); "Brickell is Crown Jewel Setting for Emerald" in **[20440]**, **[20810]**

South Florida Business Journal (Vol. 23, No. 48, July 4, 2003, pp. 1); "Building Boom Hits Homestead" in **[7276]**, **[27885]**

South Florida Business Journal (Vol. 24, No. 1, August 15, 2003, pp. 1); "Cybercare's Offices Empty Out Amid Tardy Filings" in **[33732]**, **[40993]**

South Florida Business Journal (Vol. 23, No. 47, June 27, 2003, pp. 1); "Deposit-Rich Boca Raton has Few Banks of its Own" in **[9911]**

South Florida Business Journal (Vol. 23, No. 53, August 8, 2003, pp. 1A); "Developers See Trouble in Petitions" in **[7328]**, **[20490]**, **[20859]**, **[40311]**

South Florida Business Journal (Vol. 23, No. 52, August 1, 2003, pp. 1); "Doctors Form Insurance Company" in **[13269]**, **[43160]**

South Florida Business Journal (Vol. 24, No. 7, September 26, 2003, pp. 1); "Factor Hurt by Funding Investments" in **[9945]**, **[14972]**, **[38044]**

South Florida Business Journal (Vol. 23, No. 48, July 4, 2003, pp. 4); "Holliday Fenoglio Begins Buyout of Lend Lease" in **[20526]**, **[20893]**, **[49980]**

South Florida Business Journal (Vol. 23, No. 48, July 4, 2003, pp. 6); "Latin Americans Continue to Snap Up Condo Supply" in **[7398]**, **[20569]**, **[20922]**

South Florida Business Journal (Vol. 23, No. 52, August 1, 2003, pp. 35); "Mall Makeover" in **[7417]**, **[51239]**

South Florida Business Journal (Vol. 23, No. 48, July 4, 2003, pp. 31); "Power Agent Puts More Power in Agents' Hands" in **[4767]**, **[23130]**, **[24722]**, **[25235]**, **[53415]**

South Florida Business Journal (Vol. 23, No. 52, August 1, 2003, pp. 1); "Prized Package: DHL Hub Could Deliver 500 Jobs" in **[10692]**, **[28646]**

South Florida Business Journal (Vol. 23, No. 47, June 27, 2003, pp. 1); "South Florida Braces From New Overtime Law" in **[40708]**, **[55312]**

South Florida Business Journal (Vol. 24, No. 7, September 26, 2003, pp. 1); "Vending Machines Get an Audit" in **[4850]**, **[23247]**, **[25579]**, **[53524]**

"South Florida Developers Combine Capitalism, Charity in Bottled-Water Company" in *Miami Herald* (June 28, 2004) **[3080]**, **[15465]**, **[21013]**, **[50185]**, **[54260]**

"South Florida Farmers Attempt to Broaden Market for Tropical Fruits" in *Miami Herald* (June 28, 2004) **[11663]**, **[26541]**, **[28799]**

South Florida Sun-Sentinel (December 23, 2002); "Chocolate Makes a Success Story for Boca Raton Fla. Shop" in **[4283]**, **[16430]**, **[42592]**

South Florida Sun-Sentinel (November 5, 2003); "Former Model Opens Hollywood, Fla. Maternity Clothes Boutique" in **[5662]**, **[56230]**

South Florida Sun-Sentinel (January 3, 2005); "Hollywood, Fla., Men's Shop is Tailor-Made for Success" in **[18997]**, **[37688]**, **[51183]**

South Florida Sun-Sentinel (August 1, 2003); "Modern Bed and Breakfast Slated for Boynton Beach, Fla." in **[2447]**

South Florida Sun-Sentinel (October 24, 2004); "Right Tone Separates Reliable Post-Disaster Vendors from Bottom Feeders" in **[22346]**, **[30250]**

South Fork Chamber of Commerce and Visitors Center **[58424]**

South Fulton Chamber of Commerce **[59160]**

South Gate Chamber of Commerce **[57809]**

South Grand Lake Area Chamber of Commerce **[64077]**

South Hadley Chamber of Commerce **[60999]**

South Hill Chamber of Commerce **[65947]**

South Hills Chamber of Commerce **[64510]**

South Kansas City Chamber of Commerce **[62045]**

South Kingstown Chamber of Commerce **[64675]**

South Lake Chamber of Commerce **[58934]**

South Lake Tahoe Chamber of Commerce **[57810]**

South Los Angeles Minority Business Development Center **[57894]**

South Lyon Area Chamber of Commerce **[61428]**

South Metro Denver Chamber of Commerce **[58425]**

South Metro Regional Chamber of Commerce **[63787]**

South Metro Small Business Development Center **[58310]**

South Montgomery County - Woodlands Chamber of Commerce **[65508]**

"South Okla. City Chamber Seeks to Attract Large Bookstore" in *Journal Record* (February 5, 2004) **[3048]**, **[52730]**, **[54981]**

South Oklahoma City Chamber of Commerce **[64078]**

South Orange Chamber of Commerce **[62558]**

South Orange County Regional Chambers of Commerce **[57811]**

South Padre Island Chamber of Commerce **[65509]**

"South Park gives birth to two upscale boutiques" in *San Diego Business Journal* (Vol. 23, No. 47, November 25, 2002, pp. 13) **[11664]**, **[17911]**, **[19441]**

South Platte Area Chamber of Commerce **[58426]**

"South Portland, Maine, College Develops Small-Business Incubator" in *Portland Press Herald* (August 16, 2005) **[35657]**, **[39088]**

"South Portland, Maine, Company Brings Innovation to Recycling Centers" in *Portland Press Herald* (October 27, 2005) **[21255]**

South Puget Sound Community College–Small Business Development Center **[66021]**

South Salt Lake Chamber of Commerce **[65729]**

South San Antonio Chamber of Commerce **[65510]**

South San Francisco Chamber of Commerce **[57812]**

South Seattle Community College **[66239]**
　　　　Duwamish Industrial Education Center–Small Business Development Center **[66022]**

South Shore Chamber of Commerce **[61000]**

South Sioux City Area Chamber of Commerce **[62299]**

South Snohomish County Chamber of Commerce **[66173]**

South Sun-Sentinel (October 10, 2003); "Plantation, Fla., Mayor Blasts Aggressive Mall Kiosk Sales Tactics" in **[15936]**, **[51290]**

South Tampa Chamber of Commerce **[58935]**

South Tarrant County Chamber of Commerce **[65511]**

"South Texas Builders Head for Houston's Border" in *Houston Business Journal* (Vol. 34, No. 8, July 4, 2003, pp. 1) **[7483]**, **[30177]**

South Texas Minority Business Opportunity Committee **[65582]**

South Tipton County Chamber of Commerce **[64976]**

South Valley SBDC–SBDC **[62658]**

South West Texas Border Region SBDC–University of Texas at San Antonio **[65061]**

Southampton Chamber of Commerce **[63019]**

"Southampton Town Board Approves a $20 Million Affordable Housing Development Plan" in *Long Island Business News* (March 5, 2004) **[7422]**, **[7484]**, **[28214]**, **[28800]**

Southaven - Horn Lake Area Chamber of Commerce **[61833]**

Southeast Community College - Bell County Campus–SBDC **[60466]**

Southeast Dallas Chamber of Commerce **[65512]**

Southeast Minnesota Development Corp.–SBDC **[61535]**

Southeast Missouri State University–Small Business Development Center **[61880]**

Southeast Roofing and Sheet Metal Spectacular Trade Exposition **[1049]**, **[22074]**

Southeast Tennessee Development District–Small Business Development Center **[64869]**

Southeast Volusia Chamber of Commerce **[58936]**

Southeastern Applied Technology College–Small Business Development Center **[65688]**

Southeastern Association of Fish and Wildlife Agencies **[10423]**

Southeastern Business College **[63891]**

Southeastern Butler County Chamber of Commerce **[63788]**

Southeastern Community College–Small Business Development Center **[60063]**

Southeastern Connecticut Enterprise Region–Connecticut Procurement Center **[58621]**

Southeastern Fabric, Notions and Crafts Association **[7992]**

Southeastern Fisheries Association **[10453]**

Southeastern Franklin County Chamber of Commerce **[63789]**

Southeastern Illinois College–Small Business Development Center **[59389]**

Southeastern Indiana SBDC **[59839]**

Southeastern Indiana SBDC at Connersville–Satellite Office **[59840]**

Southeastern Lumber Manufacturers Association **[16294]**

Southeastern Massachusetts Regional Office–Small Business Development Center **[60909]**

Southeastern Montana Development Corporation–Colstrip Small Business Development Center **[62126]**

Southeastern Oklahoma State University
　　　　Oklahoma SBDC **[63908]**
　　　　Small Business Development Center **[63909]**

Southeastern Technology Fund **[56914]**

Southeastern University–Library **[46155]**, **[54919]**

Southern Alleghenies Planning and Development Commission **[64597]**

Southern Arkansas University–Small Business Development Center **[57117]**

Southern Berkshire Chamber of Commerce **[61001]**

Southern Beverage Journal **[16243]**

Southern California Association of Governments **[66833]**

Southern California College of Optometry–M.B. Ketchum Memorial Library **[25673]**

Southern California International Motorcycle Show **[17504]**

Southern California Senior Life [1708]
Southern California Ventures [58157]
Southern Capitol Ventures [63467]
Southern Chester County Chamber of Commerce [64511]
Southern Christmas Show [5475], [8094]
Southern Colorado Women's Chamber of Commerce [58427]
Southern Dutchess Chamber of Commerce–SBDC Outreach Center [62781]
Southern Early Childhood Association [5331]
"Southern Expansion" in *Frozen Food Age* (Vol. 51, No. 12, July 2003, pp. 34) [11665], [23508]
Southern Festivals [2459], [24763], [25301], [30464]
Southern Fish Culturists Inc. [10474]
A Southern Greeting [893]
"Southern gentleman sparks downtown growth" in *Atlanta Business Chronicle* (Vol. 25, No. 22, November 8, 2002, pp. 5C) [24728], [25245], [28801]
Southern Illinois Research Park Inc. [59789]
Southern Illinois University at Carbondale
    Center for Rural Health and Social Service Development [41409]
    Office of Research Development and Administration [59790]
    Small Business Development Center [59390]
Southern Illinois University at Edwardsville
    Office of Research and Projects [59791]
    Small Business Development Center [59391]
Southern Illinois University at St. Louis [59392]
Southern Indiana Chamber of Commerce [60004]
"Southern Living Profiles Niceville, Fla.-Based Personal Chef Business" in *Northwest Florida Daily News* (November 18, 2002) [4555], [54261]
Southern Maid Donuts [2314]
Southern Maine Regional Planning Commission–Small Business Development Center [60715]
Southern Medical Association Annual Scientific Assembly [17273]
Southern Methodist University
    Caruth Institute of Entrepreneurship [37056]
    Center for Research in Real Estate and Land Use Economics [21119]
    Cox School of Business–Business Information Center [39747]
    Office of Research Administration [65653]
Southern Midcoast Maine Chamber [60777]
Southern Monmouth Chamber of Commerce [62559]
Southern New Hampshire University–Shapiro Library [5619]
Southern Ocean County Chamber of Commerce [62560]
Southern Ohio Genealogical Society–Reference Library [11079]
Southern Oregon University–Small Business Development Center [64175]
Southern Piscataquis County Chamber of Commerce [60778]
Southern Plantations Group Inc. [26643]
Southern Public Administration Education Foundation [50353]
Southern Regional Aquaculture Center [10434]
Southern Saratoga County Chamber of Commerce [63020]
Southern Technology Applications Center [67301]
Southern Ulster County Chamber of Commerce [63021]
Southern Utah University–Small Business Development Center [65689]
Southern Wayne County Regional Chamber [61429]
Southern Wayne Regional Chamber of Commerce [64512]
Southern West Virginia Community and Technical College [66316]
Southern Windsor County Incubator–SBDC [65768]
Southfield Area Chamber of Commerce [61430]
Southlake Chamber of Commerce [65513]
Southport-Oak Island Area Chamber of Commerce [63427]

Southport-Oak Island Chamber of Commerce [63428]
"Southwest Adds Chicago Flight" in *Sacramento Bee* (October 28, 2005) [25246], [28802], [30418]
Southwest Exotic Plant Mapping Project [11503]
Southwest Florida Hispanic Chamber of Commerce [58937]
Southwest Georgia Chamber of Commerce [59161]
Southwest Health Center–Medical Library [8882], [18407]
Southwest International Veterinary Symposium Expo [1267]
Southwest King County Chamber of Commerce [66174]
"Southwest May Put Stock in Dividends" in *Houston Business Journal* (Vol. 34, No. 12, August 1, 2003, pp. 7) [10187], [15466]
Southwest Minnesota State University–Southwest Minnesota Historical Center [11096]
Southwest Mississippi Community College–SBDC [61763]
Southwest Missouri State University–College of Business Administration–Small Business Development Center [61881]
Southwest Performance Group [3916]
Southwest Region University Transportation Center [24266]
Southwest State University–Small Business Development Center [61536]
Southwest Valley Chamber of Commerce [57072], [65730]
Southwest Venture Group [65630]
The Southwest Venture Partnerships [65631]
Southwest Virginia Community College–Southwest Small Business Development Center [65842]
Southwestern Area Commerce and Industry Association (SACIA)–Small Business Development Center [58499]
Southwestern Auglaize County Chamber of Commerce [63790]
Southwestern College [58235]
    Small Business Development and International Trade Center [57276]
Southwestern Community College–Small Business Development Center [60064]
Southwestern Financial Directory [44662]
Southwestern Indiana Regional Small Business Development Center [59841]
Southwestern Madison County Chamber of Commerce [59669]
Southwestern Michigan College–Business Development and Corporate Services [61498]
Southwestern Michigan Economic Growth Alliance, Inc. [61486]
Southwestern Michigan Technical Assistance Center–Western Michigan University [61473]
Southwestern Oklahoma State University–Small Business Development Center [63920]
Southwestern Oregon Community College [64302]
    Small Business Development Center [64176]
Southwestern Retailer [11904]
Miles F. Southworth, Consultant to the Graphic Arts [6047]
Souvenirs, Gifts, & Novelties Magazine [11182], [18281]
Souvenirs, Gifts & Novelties Magazine-Buyer's Guide Issue [18280]
"Sowing seeds for growth" in *Women In Business* (Vol. 52, No. 1, January-February 2000, pp. 20) [56411]
Spa Destinations [24764], [25302]
Spa Magazine [24765], [25303]
Spa Management [11811], [12673], [17015], [23839]
"Space Case" in *Entrepreneur* (Vol. 32, November 2004, No. 11, pp. 67) [6286], [6805]
"Space Centered" in *Inc.* (September 1, 2003) [13670], [18560], [49550]
Space Cowboys: Dysfunctional Superheroes II [22869], [23664]
Space Management Programs Inc. [7639], [52767]
"Space and Technology" in *The Economist* (Vol. 376, July 16-22, 2005, No. 8435, pp. 75-76) [42000], [52207]

"Space Trade" in *Crain's New York Business* (Vol. 22, November 27, 2006, No. 48, pp. 33) [30603], [50186]
Spacevest [65980]
Spacial Design [49659]
"Spacing Out: There's Plenty of Elbow Room in these Cargo-Friendly Minivans" in *Entrepreneur* (Vol. 32, August 2004, No. 8, pp. 23) [18126]
Spack Architects; Cox Graae [1550]
Spain-United States Chamber of Commerce [43527]
"Spam Could be a Scam: Internet Tricks Are Becoming High Crimes" in *Black Enterprise* (Vol. 35, August 2004, No. 1, pp. 30) [14465], [22383], [29510], [30253], [34515], [40709]
"Spam Law Proposed in State House of Representatives" in *Journal Record* (February 4, 2004) [14466], [15018], [34516], [35696], [40710], [40792]
"A Spam Law That Slams Small Business" in *Business Week Online* (November 5, 2003) [30254], [34517], [37508]
"Spam Stopper" in *Entrepreneur* (Vol. 32, November 2004, No. 11, pp. 62) [14467], [22384], [34518]
"Spam Uncanned: Why the Recent Anti-Spam Legislation Isn't Protecting You" in *Entrepreneur* (Vol. 32, July 2004, No. 7, pp. 72) [14468], [30255], [34519], [40711]
"Spam wars" in *Entrepreneur* (Vol. 31, No. 4, April 2003, pp. 48) [20261], [34520]
"SpamCheck http://spamcheck.sitesell.com" in *Entrepreneur* (Vol. 32, No. 1, January 2004, pp. 10) [27502], [34521]
"Spanish Firm Hopes U.S. Is In the Bag" in *Crain's Chicago Business* (Vol. 26, No. 51, December 22, 2003, pp. 14) [9641], [10458], [30178], [30840], [43823], [45482], [51364], [53594]
Spanish Fork Area Chamber of Commerce [65731]
"Spanish-Language Radio Mogul Buys 24th Station" in *Sacramento Bee* (October 14, 2005) [20338], [30701]
Sparkle Carpet Cleaning [25564]
"Sparkle Plenty" in *Success* (Vol. 47, No. 4, September 2000, pp. 20) [9607], [35658]
Sparkle Wash [19800]
Sparks Chamber of Commerce [62367]
Sparkventures, LLC [61122]
Sparkworks Media [50507]
Sparta Area Chamber of Commerce [59670], [66526]
Sparta - White County Chamber of Commerce [64977]
Spartanburg Area Chamber of Commerce [64782]
Spartanburg Area SBDC–Spartanburg Human Resources Center [64700]
Spartanburg Chamber of Commerce–Small Business Development Center [64701]
Spartanburg Small Business Development Center [64702]
Spartanburg Technical College–Industry and Business Training [64801]
"Spatial Concerns" in *Small Business Opportunities* (Vol. 16, No. 2, March 2004, pp. 68) [20237], [20674], [52731], [53986]
"Speak Easy" in *Fast Company* (March 2005, No. 92, pp. 30) [22562], [36773], [45656]
"Speak employees' language to build their loyalty" in *Atlanta Business Chronicle* (Vol. 24, No. 3, June 22, 2001, pp. 62A) [48598], [53987]
"Speak and Slide: Siemens' Small Phone Packs in Big Features" in *Black Enterprise* (Vol. 34, No. 7, February 2004, pp. 54) [5082], [5117], [49278], [50132]
"Speak and spell" in *Entrepreneur* (Vol. 30, No. 1, January 2002, pp. 31) [5118], [49279]
"Speak Up: Hate to Negotiate? That's Still No Excuse to Avoid Learning This Skill" in *Entrepreneur* (Vol. 32, September 2004) [27503], [36774], [45657]
"Speak Up! The Ins and Outs of Hiring a Spokesperson" in *Entrepreneur* (Vol. 32, No. 2, February 2004, pp. 75) [12911], [20157], [47559], [48671], [50470], [50678]
"Speak up!" in *Women in Business* (Vol. 54, No. 2, March-April 2002, pp. 38) [22563], [27504]
Leland Speakes & Associates. [21096]

"The State of Small Business: Confident, yet cautious, in 2001" in *Crain's Chicago Business* (Vol. 23, December 11, 2000, pp. SB1) [28818], [32711], [54000]

"State Stocks Show Generally Strong 3Q, Despite Auto Woes" in *Crain's Detroit Business* (Vol. 21, October 10, 2005, No. 43, pp. 43) [15472], [18131], [32712], [46439]

State Street Bank & Trust Co. [59205]

State Tax Notes [396], [24148], [29684], [54908]

The State Tax OneDisc [397], [24149], [29685], [54909]

State Tax Today [398], [24150], [29686], [54910]

State Telephone Regulation Report [19806]

"State Tells Poker Rooms to Fold 'Em" in *Tampa Tribune* (November 11, 2005) [10885], [40727]

State of The Industry [19899]

"State Turns Up Heat on Green" in *Crain's Detroit Business* (Vol. 22, November 20, 2006, No. 47, pp. 11) [30007], [37328], [40728]

"State, U.S. Housing Sales Hit New Highs in 2004" in *Boston Globe* (January 26, 2005) [7486], [17442], [20675], [28819]

State University College at Cortland–Memorial Library [19540]

State University Institute of Technology at Utica/Rome–Small Business Development Center [62782]

State University of New York
    New York SBDC [62742]
    New York Small Business Development Center [62743]
    SUNY College at Plattsburgh–North Country SBDC [62783]

State University of New York at Albany–Small Business Development Center [62784]

State University of New York at Binghamton
    Division of Research [63208]
    Institute for Materials Research [52351]

State University of New York at Buffalo
    Center for Executive Development [24789]
    Music Library [17702]
    Research Institute on Addictions [54405]
    Small Business Development Center [62785]
    University Development–Library [10779]
    Vice President for Research [63209]

State University of New York College at Cortland–Office of Sponsored Programs [63210]

State University of New York College at Fredonia–Grants Administration/Research Services Office [63211]

State University of New York College at Oneonta–Center for Economic and Community Development [32863]

State University of New York Downstate Medical Center–Scientific and Medical Instrumentation Center [17292]

State University of New York Health Science Center at Brooklyn–Office of Research Administration [63212]

State University of New York at Plattsburgh–Economic Development and Technical Assistance [62799]

State University of New York at Stony Brook
    Department of Technology and Society [63213]
    Living Marine Resources Institute [10492]

"State, Utilities to Debate How to Meet Power Needs" in *Crain's Detroit Business* (Vol. 22, November 27, 2006, No. 48, pp. 14) [39934], [40729], [52594]

"State to seek VC to ease biotech cuts" in *Crain's Detroit Business* (Vol. 19, No. 8, February 24, 2003, pp. 1) [42009], [52210], [55846]

State Wildlife Laws Handbook [9372]

Staten Island Chamber of Commerce [63022]

"State's asking price for Detroit building drops from $8.5M to $2M" in *Crain's Detroit Business* (Vol. 19, No. 11, March 17, 2003) [20676], [21014]

"State's Economy to Join Recovery by Third Quarter of Next Year" in *Crain's Detroit Business* (Vol. 19, No. 45, November 10, 2003) [31788], [32713]

"State's Independent Wineries Are Facing Tough Road" in *Sacramento Bee* (September 30, 2005) [23509], [26542]

"State's Jobs Up 1.7 Percent" in *Sacramento Bee* (October 5, 2005) [28820], [32714]

States Organization for Boating Access [5240]

"States' aid for tech start-ups: more talk than action" in *Wall Street Journal* (January 4, 2000, pp. B2) [39779], [41483]

"States Target Outsourcing" in *Inc.* (July 1, 2004) [29516], [40730], [49737], [54001]

Statesboro-Bulloch Chamber of Commerce [59162]

Statice Franchising, LLC [5757]

"Stats of the Month" in *Business Week* (No. 3761, December 10, 2001, pp. SB9) [28821], [52999]

"Status Quota? Without Trade Quotas, U.S. Textile-Makers Struggle" in *Entrepreneur* (Vol. 33, September 2005, No. 9, pp. 23) [30129], [30960], [43826], [46440]

"Status Symbols, Bargain Prices" in *Hispanic Business* (June 2002, pp. 84) [18132], [48419]

"Status Woe: Contractors' Illegal Workers Could Put You in a Legal Pickle" in *Entrepreneur* (Vol. 32, No. 4, April 2004, pp. 23) [7487], [29517], [40731], [48600]

Staubs Business Services [30116]

Staunton Chamber of Commerce [59671]

Stay Clean, Stay Safe [2281]

"Stay In Touch" in *Entrepreneur* (Vol. 33, September 2005, No. 9, pp. 44) [266], [2948], [2964], [4825], [23212], [23716], [24046], [25984], [26369], [53492]

"Stay Out of Foreclosure: Here's What to Do If You Miss a Mortgage Payment" in *Black Enterprise* (Vol. 35, February 2005, No. 7) [17443], [38372]

"Stay in Touch" in *Entrepreneur* (Vol. 32, December 2004, No. 12, pp. 52) [4826], [5122], [6811], [23213], [53493]

"Staying Afloat" in *Black Enterprise* (Vol. 30, No. 10, May 2000, pp. 50) [38373]

"Staying Afloat: VCs Raise Annex Funds to Buoy Waning Portfolios" in *Venture Capital Journal* (Vol. 41, No. 8, August 2000, pp. 27-30) [28822], [55847]

"Staying Ahead of the Curve" in *Fortune International* (Vol. 146, No. 4, March 3, 2003, pp. 41) [35077], [45666]

"Staying Interactive: Web Presentation Success Requires More Than Just Technical Skills" in *Sales & Marketing Management* (Vol. 157) [14485], [27507], [47576]

"Staying in the Loop: Continuing Education for Entrepreneurs" in *My Business* (December/January 2003, pp. 14) [33242], [36792]

"Staying Out of Court" in *Business Week* (No. 3702, October 9, 2000, pp. F16) [29518], [40732], [54002]

"Staying power" in *Black Enterprise* (Vol. 32, No. 9, April 2002, pp. 108) [39606], [45667]

"Staying within their niche yields success for winners" in *Atlanta Business Chronicle* (Vol. 23, No. 48, May 4, 2001, pp. 70A) [9179], [35670], [39096]

Stayton - Sublimity Chamber of Commerce [64270]

"Steady Economic Growth" in *My Business* (October/November 2002, pp. 39) [28823], [32715]

Steak and Ale [21969]

The Steak Escape [21970]

Steak 'N Shake [21971]

"Steal This Customer" in *Internet World* (Vol. 7, No. 1, January 15, 2001, pp. 32) [31862], [34539], [51368]

"Stealing the Show: Exhibitors and Show Managers Fight Suitcasing" in *Tradeshow Week* (Vol. 34, December 6, 2004, No. 49, pp. S3) [22565], [25023], [27183], [32716], [55160]

"A stealthier way to raise money" in *Harvard Business Review* (Vol. 78, No. 5, September-October 2000, pp. 18) [35671], [48892], [55436]

Steam Brothers [25566]

Steamatic, Inc. [3382]

Steamboat Springs Chamber Resort Association [58429]

Stearns History Museum [11098]

Stearns Weaver Miller et al.–Library [15808]

Stedman's Medical Equipment Words [17106]

Steel Recycling Institute [21210]

Steel Valley Chamber of Commerce [64513]

"SteelSalvor Chooses Lois Paul & Partners to Kick Start Public Relations, Strategic Communications Initiative" in *PR Newswire* [1856], [14486], [46441], [47577], [50471]

Steelville Chamber of Commerce [62047]

Steep-Slope Roofing Materials Guide [22068]

Steep Snow [22870], [23665]

Steeps Tea Inc. [21972]

Gary Steffy Lighting Design [49660]

Steilacoom Chamber of Commerce [66178]

Steinmann Facility Development Consultants [7640]

Stelle & Associates Inc. [9411], [20194]

R.F. Stengel & Company Inc. [3816], [16668], [30117], [31460], [46119]

"A Step Beyond" in *Entrepreneur* (Vol. 32, July 2004, No. 7, pp. 44) [6812], [33243], [53494]

Step-by-Step Bookkeeping: The Complete Handbook for the Small Business [26370], [38374]

"A Step Toward Independence" in *Black Enterprise* (Vol. 35, September 2004, No. 2, pp. 37) [15473], [21015]

Stephen F. Austin State University–Office of Research and Sponsored Programs [65654]

Stephens Chamber of Commerce [57219]

Stephenville Chamber of Commerce [65517]

"Stepping down" in *Entrepreneur* (Vol. 30, No. 2, February 2002, pp. 64) [32717], [45668], [54003]

"Stepping On It: Will New Measures Really Rev Up U.S. Manufacturers' Engines?" in *Entrepreneur* (Vol. 32, July 2004, No. 7, pp. 35) [28824], [40733], [46442]

Stepping Up to Leadership: A Course for Administrative Professionals [44844]

Stepping Up to Leadership: A Course for Administrative Professionals (Canada) [44845]

Steps to Small Business Start-Up [35672], [39097]

Steps to Small Business Start-Up: Everything You Need to Know to Turn Your Idea into a Successful Business [53000]

Sterling Capital Limited [60879]

Sterling/Carl Marks Capital / Sterling Capital [63169]

Sterling Chamber of Commerce [60421]

Sterling Executive Counselors Inc. [26644]

Sterling Heights Area Chamber of Commerce [61431]

Sterling Heights Chamber of Commerce–Small Business Development Center [61221]

"Sterling Makes a Mint on Sale of Single-Family Mortgage Business" in *Houston Business Journal* (Vol. 34, No. 11, July 25, pp. 7) [17444], [20677], [47578]

Sterling Management Systems [377]

Sterling Optical [25666]

Sterling Strategies Corp. [34782]

"Sterling Venture, Set to Close Fund I" in *Venture Capital Journal* (Vol. 40, No. 10, October 2000, pp. 24) [35673], [42010], [44664], [55848]

Sternhill Partners [65633]

Stern's Management Review [46145], [54099]

Stetson University–Roland and Sara George Investments Institute [10413]

"Steve Richardson" in *Entrepreneur* (Vol. 30, No. 9, September 2002, pp. 25) [24830], [36793]

"Steven Clem heads two TVS winning projects" in *Atlanta Business Chronicle* (Vol. 25, December 6, 2002, No. 26, pp. 15C) [1532], [13672], [18561]

Steven Winter Associates–Library [20087]

Greg Stevens & Co. [10767], [20195]

Stevens Institute of Technology–Office of Research [62622]

Stevens Technology Ventures Incubator [62623]

Stevenson Real Estate Group Ltd. [21097]

Stewart County Chamber of Commerce [64980]

Stewart/Laurence Associates Inc. [24500]

Strategies for Developing Effective Presentation Skills (Canada) **[27278]**

Strategies for Effective Problem Solving and Decision Making: Good Decisions, Good Solutions **[44848]**

Strategies of Effective Writing **[27279]**

Strategies for Growth in SMEs: The Role of Information and Information Systems **[6291]**, **[28831]**, **[44369]**

"Strategies Keep Business Warm When Weather Cools" in *Crain's Detroit Business* (Vol. 21, December 19, 2005, No. 51, pp. 15) **[16029]**, **[28832]**

"Strategies, Let's Be Friends" in *Inc.* (Volume 27, March 2005, No. 3, pp. 33-34) **[30962]**, **[36801]**, **[45674]**

Strategies for Selecting and Verifying Hearing Aid Fittings **[12109]**

Strategies for Selling Technical/Industrial Products **[51536]**

"Strategize your e-mail newsletter to realize more grins than groans" in *The Business Journal* (Vol. 18, No. 10, June 30, 2000, pp. 41) **[9162]**, **[14491]**, **[34546]**

Strategizing, Disequilibrium, and Profit **[30013]**, **[39609]**

"Strategy for a Weak Market" in *Forbes* (Vol. 175, January 31, 2005, No. 2, pp. 144) **[10192]**, **[15488]**, **[38381]**

Stratford Area Chamber of Commerce **[66531]**

Stratford Capital Partners, L.P. / Stratford Equity Partners **[65634]**

Stratford Chamber of Commerce **[64084]**, **[65519]**

"Strather Launches Hitsville Gaming-But Not in U.S." in *Crain's Detroit Business* (Vol. 22, December 18, 2006, No. 5, pp. 3) **[36802]**, **[42013]**, **[44154]**

Stratis Business Centers **[18585]**, **[49668]**

"Straub's Doesn't Fill its Baskets With a Lot of Gimmicks" in *St. Louis Post-Dispatch* (October 29, 2004) **[11667]**, **[28833]**, **[37785]**

Straw Hat Pizza **[19715]**

Strawberry Point Chamber of Commerce **[60214]**

Strawberry Shortcake Chat Group **[5820]**, **[24797]**

Stream Trout Tactics **[2204]**

Streamwood Chamber of Commerce **[59672]**

Streator Area Chamber of Commerce and Industry **[59673]**

Street Corner **[7798]**

"Street Smarts. Are You Listening to Me?" in *Inc.* (November 2006, pp. 61-62) **[31223]**, **[36803]**, **[45675]**

"Street Smarts: Don't Sign Anything Yet" in *Inc.* (January 1, 2005) **[29076]**, **[29766]**, **[35675]**, **[52788]**

"Street Smarts: Hidden Assets" in *Inc.* (September 1, 2004) **[20678]**, **[22822]**

"Street Smarts" in *Inc.* (August 2000, pp. 37) **[29767]**, **[30494]**, **[31074]**, **[35676]**

"Street Smarts: Just Say Yes" in *Inc.* (November 1, 2004) **[36804]**, **[45676]**

"Street Smarts. Keep Your Customers" in *Inc.* (September 2006, pp. 57-58) **[31866]**, **[45677]**

"Street Smarts: Pennies From Heaven" in *Inc.* (December 1, 2004) **[27184]**, **[45678]**

"Street Smarts: Presumed Guilty" in *Inc.* (October 1, 2004) **[29520]**, **[36805]**, **[45679]**

Street Smarts: Real Life Lessons from a Successful Entrepreneur **[36806]**

"Street Smarts: The Capacity Trap II" in *Inc.* (December 1, 2003) **[30963]**, **[45680]**

"Street Smarts: The King and I" in *Inc.* (July 1, 2003) **[36807]**, **[39610]**

"Street Smarts: The Myths About Niches" in *Inc.* (August 1, 2004) **[29077]**, **[46593]**, **[52789]**

"Street Smarts: Ya Gotta Love It" in *Inc.* (November 1, 2003) **[6814]**, **[37786]**, **[42728]**

"Street Talk" in *Barron's* (July 21, 2003, pp. 7) **[13782]**, **[41484]**

Streetsboro Chamber of Commerce **[63795]**

"Streetscapes to be improved" in *Crain's Detroit Business* (Vol. 19, No. 10, March 10, 2003, pp. 37) **[20679]**, **[21016]**

Streetwise Finance and Accounting for Entrepreneurs: Set Budgets, Manage Costs, Keep Your Business Profitable **[267]**, **[26371]**, **[27185]**, **[38382]**

Streetwise Motivating and Rewarding Employees: New and Better Ways to Inspire Your People **[35081]**, **[45681]**

Streetwise Small Business Book of Lists: Hundreds of Lists to Help You Reduce Costs, Increase Revenues, and Boost Your Profits! **[268]**, **[26372]**, **[27186]**, **[28834]**, **[39611]**, **[51849]**

"Strength in diversity" in *Hispanic Business* (Vol. 22, No. 7-8, July-August 2000, pp. CA4) **[46445]**, **[48423]**, **[52595]**

"Strength in Numbers" in *Home Office Computing* (Vol. 18, No. 11, November 2000, pp. 58) **[30964]**, **[50194]**, **[51335]**, **[52323]**, **[54004]**

"Strength in numbers" in *Washington Business Journal* (Vol. 22, No. 3, May 23, 2003, pp. 3) **[6815]**, **[28835]**, **[32722]**, **[42014]**

Strengthening Technology Incubation System for Creating High Technology-Based Enterprises in Asia and the Pacific **[32723]**, **[41485]**, **[43466]**

"Stress Case? Is the Pressure to 'Get the Sale' Getting to You? Keep Your Cool With These Stress-Busters" in *Entrepreneur* (Vol. 32) **[35082]**, **[51850]**

Stress Management for Women **[32973]**

"Stress free home office" in *WorkingWoman* (Vol. 25, No. 8, September 2000, pp. 72) **[42555]**, **[56078]**

"Stress Relief" in *Entrepreneur.com* (Vol. 34, February 2006, No. 2, pp. 104) **[38683]**, **[56079]**

"Stressed Industries Drive Demand for Temporary Execs" in *Crain's Detroit Business* (Vol. 22, January 2, 2006, No. 1, pp. 22) **[9234]**, **[9579]**, **[10193]**, **[15489]**, **[18134]**, **[24534]**, **[31590]**, **[46446]**

"Stressed Out" in *PC Computing* (April 2000, pp. 44) **[29521]**, **[40737]**, **[56590]**

"Stresses of Elder Care Hitting the Workplace" in *Boston Globe* (July 11, 2004) **[459]**, **[18339]**, **[54005]**

"Stretch Your Limits" in *Entrepreneur* (Vol. 32, December 2004, No. 12, pp. 108) **[19350]**, **[38684]**, **[54006]**

"Stretching Room" in *Home Office Computing* (Vol. 18, No. 10, October 2000, pp. 42) **[42729]**, **[49283]**, **[49552]**

"Stretching for the inner yogi" in *WWD* (Vol. 184, No. 78, October 17, 2002, pp. 8) **[5574]**, **[5718]**, **[17912]**, **[19442]**

"Strictly Business" in *Entrepreneur* (Vol. 28, No. 1, January 2000, pp. 118) **[37787]**, **[45682]**

Strides Woman's Fitness **[26064]**

"Strike a Balance" in *Entrepreneur.com* (Vol. 34, February 2006, No. 2, pp. 50) **[15490]**, **[38383]**

"Strike it Rich!" in *Small Business Opportunities* (Vol. 16, No. 3, May 2004, pp. 22-24, 26, 28, 30, 32, 34, 36, 38, 40-42, 44, 98) **[2023]**, **[3299]**, **[8681]**, **[9309]**, **[11211]**, **[12355]**, **[18992]**, **[19285]**, **[19797]**, **[25531]**, **[35677]**, **[38685]**, **[52501]**

"Strike Up the Brand" in *Small Business Opportunities* (Vol. 16, November 2004, No. 6, pp. 92, 94) **[36808]**, **[51373]**

"Strike While the Iron's Red Hot!" in *Success* (Vol. 47, No. 2, June 2000, pp. 92) **[38686]**

"Striking Out with VCs?" in *Inc.* (Volume 28, January 2006, No. 1, pp. 34-36) **[15491]**, **[55850]**

"Striking Up the Brand Band" in *Houston Business Journal* (Vol. 34, No. 19, September 19, 2003, pp. 17A) **[47581]**, **[50682]**

Strings Italian Cafe/Strings Italian Express **[21973]**

"Striving for 'Critical Mass'" in *Hispanic Business* (Vol. 23, No. 10, October, 2001, pp. 16) **[29522]**, **[40738]**, **[48424]**

"Strong Demand for Home Products Gives Masco Record Numbers" in *Crain's Detroit Business* (Vol. 19, No. 45, November 10, 2003, pp. 4) **[12210]**, **[12311]**, **[12660]**, **[12765]**

"Strong Demand Is Firing Up U.S. Factories" in *Business Week* (January 31, 2005, pp. 23) **[28836]**, **[44248]**, **[46447]**

"Strong Future Brewing" in *Small Business Opportunities* (Spring 2005) **[5764]**, **[7081]**, **[11351]**, **[15912]**, **[38687]**, **[51041]**

"Strong Medicine" in *Hispanic Business* (June 2005, pp. 40, 42) **[13476]**, **[43380]**

"Strong Signal Cuts Through Turmoil" in *Hispanic Business* (December 2003, pp. 52, 54) **[20340]**, **[24449]**

"Strong Structure" in *Black Enterprise* (Vol. 34, July 2004, No. 12, pp. 48) **[29768]**, **[35678]**, **[49775]**, **[51480]**, **[52790]**

"Strong demand for fine wine but oenophiles seek value" in *Atlanta Business Chronicle* (Vol. 25, No. 22, November 8, 2002, pp. 17C) **[21637]**, **[23510]**

Strongland Chamber of Commerce **[64514]**

Strongsville Chamber of Commerce **[63796]**

Stroud Chamber of Commerce **[64085]**

Structural Design of Masonry **[16964]**

Structured Query Language (SQL) I **[53186]**

Structured Query Language (SQL) II **[53187]**

"The Struggle for Sales Overseas" in *Hispanic Business* (November 2002, pp. 36) **[28837]**, **[43828]**, **[48425]**, **[51851]**

"The Struggle to Sell the Economy's Sizzle" in *Business Week* (January 23, 2006, No. 3968, pp. 43) **[32724]**

Strutters **[21974]**

Strutter's Complete Guide to Clown Makeup **[18731]**

"Strutting Your Cyber Stuff" in *Folio: the Magazine for Magazine Management* (Vol. 30, No. 1, January 2001, pp. 15) **[9163]**, **[18940]**, **[34547]**

Strybing Arboretum Society–Helen Crocker Russell Library of Horticulture **[11539]**

Stuart-Martin County Chamber of Commerce **[58938]**

"Stuck in Mud?" in *My Business* (October/November 2003, pp. 12) **[36809]**, **[45683]**

"Stuck in a Storm of Controversy" in *Fortune* (Vol. 152, October 17, 2005, No. 8, pp. 41) **[35962]**, **[37329]**, **[40739]**

Student Lamps of the Victorian Era **[1329]**

"Student Loan Firm Will Add 170 Jobs" in *Tampa Tribune* (November 29, 2005) **[28838]**, **[42427]**, **[44666]**

"Student teachers" in *Entrepreneur* (Vol. 30, No. 10, October 2002, pp. 93) **[33244]**, **[39612]**

"Student Teachers" in *Inc.* (November 2006, pp. 44,46) **[38384]**, **[42428]**, **[45684]**

"Students of Enterprise" in *Entrepreneur* (Vol. 32, November 2004, No. 11, pp. 108) **[8522]**, **[21638]**, **[36810]**, **[38916]**, **[56764]**

"Students help biz with marketing, consulting" in *Crain's Detroit Business* (Vol. 18, No. 24, June 17, 2002, pp. 12) **[3590]**, **[47582]**

"Studies push for analysis of quality in health care" in *Business First Columbus* (Vol. 18, No. 40, May 24, 2002, pp. B7) **[41108]**

"Studies probe cost to clean, fix Book Cadillac" in *Crain's Detroit Business* (Vol. 19, No. 10, March 10, 2003, pp. 14) **[12639]**

Studies of Entrepreneurship, Business and Government in Hong Kong: The Economic Development of a Small Open Economy **[32725]**, **[36811]**, **[40740]**, **[43829]**

"Studies keep coming in response to down market" in *Atlanta Business Chronicle* (Vol. 25, No. 21, November 1, 2002, pp. 22C) **[20680]**, **[21017]**

Studio 6 **[12729]**

Studio City Chamber of Commerce **[57817]**

"Study" in *Crain's Detroit Business* (Vol. 18, No. 18, May 6, 2002, pp. 6) **[39613]**, **[52732]**

"Study focuses on improving Dallas' taxi system" in *Atlanta Business Chronicle* (Vol. 25, No. 20, October 25, 2002, pp. 16A) **[24241]**, **[25024]**, **[25250]**

"Study: Detroit Second in Number of Cell-Phone Users" in *Crain's Detroit Business* (Vol. 19, No. 42, October 20, 2003, pp. 15) **[5123]**, **[5274]**, **[54007]**, **[56385]**

"Study shows businesses are slow to embrace e-commerce" in *Black Enterprise* (Vol. 32) **[14492]**, **[25975]**, **[28839]**, **[34548]**, **[42015]**, **[48426]**, **[49284]**

"Study Foresees End of Boeing's Commercial Work; Company Calls Report Flawed" in *News Tribune* (April 11, 2003) **[28840]**, **[43830]**, **[46448]**

"Study: Insurance Fraud Thriving" in *Orlando Business Journal* (Vol. 20, No. 13, September 12, 2003, pp. 1) **[13388]**, **[13477]**, **[29523]**, **[30456]**, **[43381]**, **[45053]**

"Study: Language Worsens Hispanic Healthcare Crisis" in *Hispanic Business* (March 2003, pp. 12) **[13478]**, **[43382]**

"Study Looks at Benefits of Nonprofits Teaming Up to Buy Health Insurance" in *Pittsburgh Business Times* (Vol. 23, August 8, 2003) **[13479]**, **[41109]**, **[43383]**

"Study" in *Portland Press Herald* (May 18, 2005) **[10194]**, **[15492]**, **[38385]**

"Study Says Change Tax Laws to Help Forest Products Industry Stay Competitive" in *Portland Press Herald* (March 25, 2005) **[16320]**, **[26544]**, **[30965]**, **[54780]**

"Study Says Corporate Relocations Don't Impact California Economy" in *Sacramento Bee* (October 26, 2005) **[30179]**, **[32726]**

"Study: State 12th-best for small biz" in *Crain's Detroit Business* (Vol. 17, No. 44, October 22, 2001, pp. 20) **[36812]**, **[39614]**, **[52733]**

"Study: Women Executives Want Corner Office, Too" in *Miami Herald* (June 24, 2004) **[36813]**, **[39615]**, **[45685]**, **[56418]**

"Studying Molecules to Build a Better Grape" in *Business Week* (February 20, 2006, No. 3972, pp. 65) **[23511]**, **[50974]**, **[52211]**

Stueven Engineering Consultants **[1061]**, **[7641]**, **[19773]**

Stuft Pizza, Stuft Pizza Bar & Grill, Stuft Pizza Pronto **[19716]**

"Stump the slump" in *Entrepreneur* (Vol. 30, No. 2, February 2002, pp. 90) **[29769]**, **[32727]**, **[35679]**, **[44443]**

"Stumping in Cyberspace" in *Hispanic Business* (June 2005, pp. 100, 102) **[14493]**, **[34549]**

Sturgis Area Chamber of Commerce **[61432]**, **[64838]**

Sturgis Chamber of Commerce **[60572]**

Stuttgart Chamber of Commerce **[57220]**

Style Summit **[27280]**

Style Summit: Editorial Evolution in the Internet Era **[32974]**

Stylus Publishing L.L.C. **[66009]**

Sub Connection **[21975]**

"Sub chains target Detroit: Quizno's, Panera want bite of market" in *Crain's Detroit Business* (Vol. 16, No. 6, February 7, 2000, pp. 3) **[21639]**, **[38917]**

Sub Station II **[8575]**, **[21976]**

"Subcontractors on the hook in fight over stadium overruns" in *Crain's Detroit Business* (Vol. 19, No. 5, February 3, 2003, pp. 1) **[7488]**, **[49739]**

Subject Guide to Children's Books in Print 2689, 3035

"Sublease steals kick-starting leasing in Portland" in *Atlanta Business Chronicle* (Vol. 25, December 6, 2002, No. 26, pp. 31C) **[20681]**, **[21018]**, **[21353]**, **[52734]**

Sublette County Chamber of Commerce **[66631]**

Subscriber Bulletin **[15680]**

Substance Abuse: Everyone's Problem **[54355]**

Substance Abuse Funding Week **[54346]**

Substance Abuse Librarians and Information Specialists **[54329]**

Substance Abuse in the Workplace **[54339]**

Substantive Editing I **[27281]**

Substantive Editing II **[27282]**

"Substitute Presenter" in *Sales & Marketing Management* (Vol. 157, February 2005, No. 2, pp. 11) **[45686]**, **[51852]**

Suburban Chamber of Commerce **[62562]**

Suburban Cylinder Express **[42804]**

Suburban Essex Chamber of Commerce **[62563]**

Suburban Horsham Willow Grove Chamber of Commerce **[64515]**

Suburban Lodge **[12730]**

Subway **[8576]**

Succeeding as a Self-Managed Team: Operating as a Self-Managed Work Team **[35083]**

Succeeding in Small Business: The 101 Toughest Problems and How to Solve Them **[39616]**, **[53001]**

"Succeeding in adversity makes success all the sweeter" in *Fast Company* (May 2001, pp. 84) **[36814]**, **[56419]**

Success (Vol. 47, No. 3, July 2000, pp. 82); "A New Career for You Might Start at Franchise U" in **[38663]**

Success (Vol. 47, No. 3, July 2000, pp. 80); "A New Vision for Network Marketing" in **[34258]**, **[36546]**, **[47337]**

Success (Vol. 47, No. 3, July 2000, pp. 61); "A Patently Obvious Strategy" in **[44119]**, **[44350]**

Success (Vol. 47, No. 2, June 2000, pp. 50); "Addicted to Success" in **[35755]**

Success (Vol. 47, No. 3, July 2000, pp. 84); "Ahead of Her Time" in **[35760]**, **[56114]**

Success (Vol. 47, No. 6, November 2000, pp. 74); "An Industry Resource: Thee Direct Selling Association Membership List" in **[51694]**

Success (Vol. 47, No. 3, July 2000, pp. 50); "Back from the Brink" in **[35799]**

Success (Vol. 47, No. 3, July 2000, pp. 59); "Be a Loan Shark" in **[35326]**, **[55360]**

Success (Vol. 47, No. 3, July 2000, pp. 28); "Beating the Odds" in **[32270]**, **[40176]**

Success (Vol. 47, No. 6, November 2000, pp. 42); "Beware of Love at First Byte" in **[13844]**, **[25799]**, **[33576]**

"Success a Big Seller: N. Carolina, Duke Coaches Cash in as Marketers' Dreams" in *Charlotte Observer* (February 7, 2007) **[798]**, **[47583]**

Success (Vol. 47, No. 4, September 2000, pp. 22); "Blood is Thicker than Ink" in **[19867]**, **[37599]**

Success (Vol. 47, No. 2, June 2000, pp. 80); "Building Downline...Online" in **[33622]**, **[46757]**

Success (Vol. 47, No. 6, November 2000, pp. 58); "Can Brand Management Help You Succeed?" in **[46775]**

Success (Vol. 47, No. 2, June 2000, pp. 25); "Can Your Company Get VC Funding?" in **[55531]**

Success (Vol. 47, No. 5, October 2000, pp. 6); "Change is Good" in **[38737]**

Success (Vol. 47, No. 5, October 2000, pp. 46); "Common Cents" in **[37978]**

Success (Vol. 47, No. 6, November 2000, pp. 62); "Cover Your Assets" in **[13932]**, **[53245]**

Success (Vol. 47, No. 2, June 2000, pp. 69); "Culture Vultures Go Online" in **[33425]**, **[35378]**

Success (Vol. 47, No. 2, June 2000, pp. 60); "Customer Driven" in **[18003]**, **[33723]**

Success (Vol. 47, No. 3, July 2000, pp. 52); "Designing Women" in **[4889]**, **[35384]**, **[41446]**

Success (Vol. 47, No. 5, October 2000, pp. 18); "Doing Away With the Old Resume" in **[9203]**, **[9557]**, **[33772]**

Success (Vol. 47, No. 5, October 2000, pp. 52); "dot-com or dot-bomb?" in **[25835]**, **[37126]**

Success (Vol. 47, No. 3, July 2000, pp. 36); "Dynamic Duo" in **[35402]**

Success (Vol. 47, No. 2, June 2000, pp. 22); "E-commerce: Too Valuable to Tax" in **[33802]**, **[54525]**

Success (Vol. 47, No. 1, January 2000, pp. 58); "Early-Bird Special" in **[38762]**

Success (Vol. 47, No. 2, June 2000, pp. 12); "Even Privacy Has Its Price" in **[14022]**, **[16811]**

Success from Failure (August 2000); "Counterpoint: Why So Many Mergers & Acquisitions Fail" in **[14890]**, **[49878]**

Success from Failure (August 2000); "Creative Accounting? Don't laugh!" in **[26201]**, **[27989]**

Success from Failure (August 2000); "How to Survive When You've Lost Your Monopoly" in **[28308]**, **[52891]**

Success from Failure (August 2000); "Selling into the Middle Market on the Downswing Can Be Costly" in **[52453]**

Success from Failure (August 2000); "Taking the Emotions out of Business Decisions" in **[30610]**, **[36828]**

Success from Failure (August 2000); "There's no place in business for these 4-letter words" in **[36850]**

Success from Failure (August 2000); "Through Grieving" in **[3597]**, **[36860]**, **[37800]**, **[56438]**

Success (Vol. 47, No. 1, January 2000, pp. 80); "Faith, Determination, and a Little Marinara Sauce" in **[19619]**, **[35441]**

Success (Vol. 47, No. 1, January 2000, pp. 26); "Fare Game" in **[30325]**

Success (Vol. 47, No. 5, October 2000, pp. 34); "Finding Success in a Haystack" in **[24808]**, **[43958]**

Success (Vol. 47, No. 6, November 2000, pp. 46); "For Love of the Game" in **[35461]**, **[43960]**

Success (Vol. 47, No. 2, June 2000, pp. 88); "Former Collection Attorney Needs Consultants to Offer Bulletproof Asset Protection" in **[29249]**, **[31154]**, **[38079]**

Success (Vol. 47, No. 5, October 2000, pp. 58); "Franchise Gold 200" in **[38788]**

Success (Vol. 47, No. 3, July 2000, pp. 90); "Franchisee Satisfaction Critical to Success" in **[38795]**

Success (Vol. 47, No. 4, September 2000, pp. 62); "Generation W" in **[55389]**, **[56048]**

Success (Vol. 47, No. 3, July 2000, pp. 55); "Get Hooked on an Intranet" in **[14067]**, **[49043]**

Success (Vol. 47, No. 1, January 2000, pp. 20); "Gilded Paper Route" in **[2709]**, **[19818]**, **[19878]**, **[36208]**

Success (Vol. 47, No. 1, January 2000, pp. 30); "Gluttons for Punishment" in **[45192]**

Success (Vol. 47, No. 4, September 2000, pp. 69); "Going by the Handbook" in **[42857]**, **[45195]**

Success (Vol. 47, No. 6, November 2000, pp. 38); "Going Places" in **[13751]**, **[25117]**, **[33444]**, **[35485]**

Success (Vol. 47, No. 6, November 2000, pp. 18); "Got Fit?" in **[9177]**, **[35487]**, **[52490]**

Success (Vol. 47, No. 6, November 2000, pp. 68); "Got Ideas? Book 'Em" in **[14089]**, **[33974]**, **[44303]**

Success (Vol. 47, No. 6, November 2000, pp. 34); "Handled Like a Pro" in **[7351]**, **[36258]**, **[37676]**

Success (Vol. 47, No. 4, September 2000, pp. 66); "Harley's Angels" in **[55390]**

Success (Vol. 47, No. 2, June 2000, pp. 52); "Healthy Transition" in **[29897]**, **[37677]**

Success (Vol. 47, No. 4, September 2000, pp. 44); "High-Adventure Past, High-Speed Future" in **[13755]**, **[35504]**

Success (Vol. 47, No. 1, January 2000, pp. 25); "How to Hire A Workers" in **[42294]**

Success (Vol. 47, No. 6, November 2000, pp. 28); "How iWon Won the Web" in **[35516]**, **[55395]**

Success (Vol. 47, No. 4, September 2000, pp. 4); "I Bought It Through the Grapevine" in **[23441]**, **[25757]**, **[33451]**, **[37063]**

Success (Vol. 47, No. 5, October 2000, pp. 22); "I Fulfilled My Family Dream" in **[23036]**, **[37696]**

Success (Vol. 47, No. 3, July 2000, pp. 24); "If I Had an E-Hammer" in **[11870]**, **[33452]**, **[35524]**

Success (Vol. 47, No. 1, January 2000, pp. 50); "If You Market, They Will Come" in **[34050]**, **[47121]**, **[51196]**

Success (Vol. 47, No. 4, September 2000, pp. 64); "Internet Privacy" in **[14159]**

Success (Vol. 47, No. 4, September 2000, pp. 78); "Invasion of the Privacy Snatchers" in **[16815]**, **[34089]**, **[47151]**

Success (Vol. 47, No. 3, July 2000, pp. 32); "Investing in tomorrow" in **[37153]**, **[54212]**

Success (Vol. 47, No. 6, November 2000, pp. 88); "It's All About Convenience" in **[52550]**, **[54959]**

Success (Vol. 47, No. 5, October 2000, pp. 12); "Keeping Employees" in **[37709]**, **[42323]**, **[52434]**

Success (Vol. 47, No. 3, July 2000, pp. 22); "Killer Apps for Rent" in **[14190]**, **[36407]**

Success (Vol. 47, No. 1, January 2000, pp. 13); "Light Rider" in **[2022]**, **[35550]**

"Success line" in *Success* (Vol. 47, No. 3, July 2000, pp. 78) **[35680]**, **[39780]**, **[43970]**, **[47978]**, **[55437]**, **[56080]**

Success (Vol. 47, No. 1, January 2000, pp. 63); "Love's Rewards" in **[7048]**, **[38658]**

Sugarloaf Crafts Festival Fort Washington [8097]

Sugarloaf Crafts Festival Fort Washington, Fall [8098]

Sugarloaf Crafts Festival Gaithersburg, Fall [8099]

Sugarloaf Crafts Festival Gaithersburg, Spring [8100]

Sugarloaf Crafts Festival Manassas, Fall [8101]

Sugarloaf Crafts Festival Somerset [8102]

Sugarloaf Crafts Festival Somerset, Fall [8103]

Sugarloaf Crafts Festival Timonium, Fall [8104]

Sugarloaf Crafts Festival Timonium, Spring [8105]

Suggestive Selling 101 [51987]

Suhaila Unveiled [8484]

"Suit May Cost Post Unit its Trademark" in *Washington Business Journal* (Vol. 22, No. 15, August 15, 2003, pp. 3) [29526], [30966], [44155]

"Suit May Force SBC Refunds" in *Atlanta Journal-Constitution* (February 17, 2004) [5125], [29527], [40741]

"Suiting Up; Yes, You're Smart, But Can You Look the Part" in *Crain's Chicago Business* (Vol. 30, February 2007, No. 6, pp. 39) [5720], [15493], [50759]

"Suits Mount Against Salons" in *San Jose Mercury News* (March 5, 2005) [17857], [40742], [41110]

Suki Hana Franchise Corp. [21977]

Sul Ross State University–Big Bend SBDC Satellite [65062]

Sullivan Area Chamber of Commerce [62050]

Sullivan Chamber and Economic Development [59674]

Sullivan County Chamber of Commerce [60007], [63024], [64516]

Sulphur Chamber of Commerce [64086]

Sulphur Springs Community Chamber of Commerce [57221]

Sylvia M. Sultenfuss [43001]

Sumerford Software and Marketing [16881]

Sumiton Chamber of Commerce [56890]

A Summary of the Law of Patents for Useful Inventions with Forms [44156]

Summer and Casual Furniture Manufacturers Association [12271]

"Summer Could Help Lick Tourism Slump" in *Pacific Business News* (Vol. 41, No. 16, June 27, 2003, pp. 1) [24731], [25251], [47587], [50684]

"Summerford, Dixon Odom Cite Sarbanes in Breakup" in *Birmingham Business Journal* (Vol. 20, No. 31, August 1, 2003, pp. 1) [271], [2966], [24048], [26376], [40743]

Summers County Chamber of Commerce [66299]

Summersville Area Chamber of Commerce [66300]

Summersville Chamber of Commerce [62051]

Summit Capital Group [60585]

Summit County Chamber of Commerce [58430]

Summit Group [66764]

Summit Partners [61126]

Summit Partners (Palo Alto) [58160]

"Summit Plastics Pursues Acquisition of Industrial Property in Bay Shore" in *Long Island Business News* (March 5, 2004) [7904], [22495], [22802], [44359], [46449]

Sump and Sewage Pump Manufacturers Association [22716]

Sumter County Chamber of Commerce [58939]

Sun Books - Sun Publishing [62741]

Sun City Center Area Chamber of Commerce [58940]

"Sun CTO: New License Protects Developer Rights" in *eWeek* (February 7, 2005) [4828], [23215], [44157], [54009]

Sun Herald (January 11, 2004); "Bed, Breakfast House in Arcadia, Miss., Reopens with New Owner" in [2426], [42577], [56133]

Sun Herald (November 12, 2004); "Biloxi, Miss.-Area Pet Sitting Services Offer Alternative to Kennel Boarding" in [19072], [56140]

Sun Herald (January 7, 2004); "Biloxi, Miss., Bed, Breakfast Law Upheld" in [2429], [3177], [29126], [40193]

Sun Herald (August 15, 2003); "Biloxi, Miss., Historic Bed and Breakfast Up For Sale" in [2430]

Sun Herald (February 10, 2005); "Home-Buying Fair Appeals to First-Time Purchasers" in [7365], [10003], [17388], [20528], [24948], [55099]

Sun Herald (April 11, 2003); "Lumber Company Purchases Store Location in Gulfport, Miss." in [7411], [16310]

Sun Herald (April 11, 2003); "Mississippi-Corporate Partnership Boosts Shipyards" in [10683], [28492], [50086]

"Sun Microsystems Remakes Its Sales Force" in *Wall Street Journal* (Vol. 248, December 2006, No. 149, pp. B3) [6968], [15895], [42016], [51856]

Sun News (January 9, 2005); "South Carolina Duo Cashes in By Buying Ugly Houses as Fixer-Uppers" in [791], [20673], [21012], [38914], [47558]

Sun Publications [58284]

"Sun Sets on H-1B Visa Provision" in *Hispanic Business* (December 2003, pp. 12) [42429], [48601]

Sun Valley Area Chamber of Commerce [57818]

Sun Valley-Ketchum Chamber and Visitors Bureau [59333]

Sun Valley Ventures (Ketchum) [59338]

SunBanque Island Tanning [23848]

Sunbelt Business Brokers [3453], [3918]

Sunbelt Foodservice [12071]

Sunbrook Academy [5450]

Sunbury - Big Walnut Area Chamber of Commerce [63797]

Suncare - U.S. Report [2405]

SunCoach Inc. [55045]

Sundance Area Chamber of Commerce [66632]

Sundance Venture Partners, L.P. [58161]

Sunday Best! [8940]

Sunglass Association of America [9610]

Sunland-Tujunga Chamber of Commerce [57819]

Sunnyside Chamber of Commerce [66179]

Sunnyvale Chamber of Commerce [57820]

Sunriver Area Chamber of Commerce [64271]

Sunset Grill [21978]

Sunshine Artist [8221]

Sunshine Cafe Restaurants [21979]

Sunshine Pack & Ship Retail Centers [6130]

"Sunshine State Summit" in *Hispanic Business* (March 2003, pp. 26, 28) [28842], [48427]

Suntanning Association for Education [23836]

Sunwestern Investment Group [65635]

SUNY Canton College [62787], [63224]

SUNY College of Environmental Science and Forestry–Randolph G. Pack Environmental Institute [9470]

SUNY Geneseo Outreach Center–SBDC [62788]

SUNY at Oswego–Center for Business and Community Development–SBDC [62789]

SUNY at Stony Brook–State University of New York–SBDC [62790]

Super 8 Motels, Inc. [12731]

"Super Bowl Sundae" in *Entrepreneur* (Vol. 32, October 2004, No. 10, pp. 107) [12791], [18732], [18762], [38918]

"Super Cell" in *Forbes* (Vol. 175, February 14, 2005, No. 3, pp. 46) [6816], [24831], [42017]

"The Super-Cheap Supercomputer" in *Business 2.0* (Vol. 6, May 2005, No. 4, pp. 30) [6817], [6969], [49285]

Super Family Vacations [24732]

"Super Sales in Service" in *Small Business Opportunities* (Vol. 17, September 2005, No. 5, pp. 76, 86) [2606], [9643], [31867], [56420]

"A Super Selling Point" in *Crain's Detroit Business* (Vol. 22, February 13, 2006, No. 7, pp. 11) [12640], [21640], [25027], [55164]

The Super Show Official Show Directory and Sports Product Guide [23639]

"Super Success in Spas" in *Small Business Opportunities* (Vol. 16, No. 2, March 2004, pp. 92, 95) [23787], [37790], [38688], [54262]

"A Super superhighway" in *Incentive* (Vol. 174, No. 9, September 2000, pp. 14) [3591], [14495], [33324]

Super Suppers [8293]

Super Wash [4381]

Super Zoo [19091], [19174]

Superbrokers, A Yacht Brokers Franchise Group, Inc. [15738]

SuperComm [5221]

SuperCoups, Inc. [894]

Supercuts [11843], [12332]

Superior Area Chamber of Commerce [62300]

The Superior Business Center Inc. [66574]

Superior Chamber of Commerce [57074]

"Superior Consultant Holdings sees demand for health care IT" in *Crain's Detroit Business* (Vol. 19, No. 13, March 31, 2003, pp. 4) [4829], [6485], [23216], [41111], [42018], [53496]

Superior - Douglas County Chamber of Commerce [66532]

Superior Senior Care [41344]

Supermarket Promotion Show [12246], [24849]

Supermarkets Transformed: Understanding Organizational and Technological Innovations [11668]

"Supersize It!" in *Small Business Opportunities* (Vol. 12, No. 5, September 2000, pp. 56) [16470]

Supervising the Drug-Free Workplace [42933]

Supervising Employees with Disabilities [32066]

Supervisor's Guide to Employment Practices [42918]

Supervisor's Infobank: 1000 Quick Answers to Your Toughest Problems [45690]

Supervisors Legal Update [45909]

Supervisory Series [3335]

Supper Thyme USA [21980]

"Supplier Diversity" in *Hispanic Business* (September 2004, pp. 18) [48428], [55165]

"Supplier Innovation Key to Industry Future, Exec Says" in *Crain's Detroit Business* (Vol. 21, January 24, 2005, No. 4, pp. 5) [1971], [18135], [28843], [42019]

Supplier Selection and Management Report [50771]

"Supplier Takes Care to Shield Business" in *Crain's Detroit Business* (Vol. 21, October 17, 2005, No. 43, pp. 33) [1972], [30016]

"Suppliers Called On To Boost Minority Deals" in *Crain's Detroit Business* (Vol. 21, October 3, 2005, No. 43) [18136], [46450], [48429]

"Suppliers Picked for Pilot Program" in *Crain's Detroit Business* (Vol. 21, January 24, 2005, No. 4, pp. 18) [1973], [18137], [46451], [48795]

"Suppliers: Price cuts aren't a winning long-term strategy" in *Crain's Detroit Business* (Vol. 19, No. 3, Jan. 20, 2003, pp. 21) [1974], [18138]

"Supply Chain Challenges: Building Relationships" in *Harvard Business Review* (Vol. 81, No. 7, July 2003, pp. 64) [28844], [50195], [53003]

Supply Master USA [2017]

"Supply Side Economics" in *Small Business Opportunities* (Vol. 16, No. 2, March 2004, pp. 64, 68) [18591], [38689]

"Support the Advocate!" in *Bellingham Business Journal* (December 2006, pp. 3) [799], [18941], [27509], [47588], [50196]

"Support for Rapid-Growth Firms" in *Journal of Small Business Management* (Vol. 41, No. 4, October 2003, pp. 346) [28845], [39620], [40744]

Support Services Alliance [52810]

Supramolecular Science [52325]

"Supreme Court Rules Regal Entertainment's Style is Unfair to Disabled Customers" in *Miami Herald* (June 29, 2004) [17531], [29528], [40745]

Sure-Hire Resumes [22052]

Sure Print & Copy Centers [7862]

"Sure, it would be easier on the Web - but let's haggle" in *The New York Times* (December 13, 2000, pp. D13, H13) [34550], [51857]

SureSlim Wellness Clinic [26065]

Surf City Squeeze [12853]

Surface Doctor Kitchen and Bath Restoration [4514], [10543]

Surface Specialists [19791]

Surface Technologies Inc. [10531], [25546]

"Surfing the Tongues" in *Business Week* (December 11, 2000, pp. 18) [14496], [34551]

"Surfing the Virtual Wave" in *Business 2.0* (Vol. 6, May 2005, No. 4, pp. 116-118) [5126], [42020]

"Sworn to secrecy" in *Women in Business* (Vol. 53, No. 4, July-August, 2001, pp. 22) **[37513]**, **[39624]**

Swyrich Corp. **[10988]**, **[23313]**, **[33380]**

Sybase, Inc. **[58163]**

Sycamore Chamber of Commerce **[59676]**

"Sycuan" in *San Diego Business Journal* (Vol. 28, January 1, 2007, No. 1, pp. 8) **[10886]**, **[28852]**

Sydney Morning Herald Small Business Show **[39736]**

Syed Hussayn TMCI **[38576]**, **[46123]**, **[47911]**, **[50727]**, **[52008]**

Sylacauga Chamber of Commerce **[56891]**

Sylvan Learning Center **[25485]**

Sylvania Area Chamber of Commerce **[63799]**

"Symbol Technologies Appoints Steinberg as CTO and VP of Its Mobility Solutions Group" in *Long Island Business News* (February 6, 2004) **[5127]**, **[42023]**, **[45696]**

"Symbol Technologies Inc. Hires Former IBM Executive" in *Long Island Business News* (March 5, 2004) **[40248]**, **[42024]**, **[45697]**, **[46325]**, **[48888]**, **[51378]**

"Symbol Technologies Wins Landmark Lawsuit in Nevada Federal Court" in *Long Island Business News* (January 30, 2004) **[29534]**, **[44158]**, **[51379]**

"Symbolism with a Bottom Line" in *Hispanic Business* (Vol. 23, No. 7/8, July/August 2001, pp. 16) **[29535]**, **[40747]**, **[48432]**

Symmes Maini & McKee Associates **[49661]**

Syndication News **[4143]**, **[24478]**

"Syndication: The Emerging Model for Business in the Internet Era" in *Harvard Business Review* (Vol. 78, No. 3, May 2000, pp. 85) **[30967]**, **[34558]**, **[54016]**

Synergy Homecare **[12425]**

Synopsys, Inc. **[58164]**

"Synthetic funds draw scrutiny from regulators" in *Crain's Detroit Business* (Vol. 16, No. 46, November 13, 2000, pp. 22) **[38391]**, **[40748]**

Syosset Chamber of Commerce **[63025]**

Syracuse-Hamilton County Chamber of Commerce **[60423]**

Syracuse University
    Center for Technology and Information Policy **[52352]**
    Program on the Analysis and Resolution of Conflicts **[17082]**

Syracuse-Wawasee Chamber of Commerce **[60008]**

System-built advantage **[7577]**

System4 **[3384]**

Systematic Analysis in Dispute Resolution **[17060]**

"Systemax Pares U.S., LI Staff" in *Long Island Business News* (February 20, 2004) **[6819]**, **[28853]**

Systems Alternatives International L.L.C. **[49462]**, **[49662]**

Systems and Computers in Japan **[52326]**

The Systems Development Series (27-0XX) **[6993]**

Systems Paving Franchising Inc. **[16984]**

The Systems Series **[6994]**

Systems Service Enterprises Inc. **[8662]**

T

"T & E Report" in *Sales & Marketing Management* (Vol. 157, January 2005, No. 1, pp. 54) **[2080]**, **[21354]**, **[30419]**, **[47595]**

T. Rowe Price Threshold Partnerships **[60880]**

"The T. Rowe Small-Cap Gauge" in *Forbes* (Vol. 175, January 31, 2005, No. 2, pp. 102) **[10198]**, **[15498]**, **[38392]**

TA Associates, Inc. (Boston) **[61127]**

TA Associates, Inc. (Menlo Park) **[58165]**

Taag International, Inc. **[3919]**, **[20083]**, **[54896]**

The Tab **[1484]**

Table Centerpieces **[8234]**, **[10594]**

Table for Eight **[7080]**

Table Rock Lake - Kimberling City Area Chamber of Commerce **[62052]**

"Table Talk" in *Sales & Marketing Management* (Vol. 159, January-February 2007, No. 1, pp. 33) **[43833]**, **[47596]**, **[51858]**

Table Time for Tots **[5412]**, **[33326]**

"The Tablet PC" in *Rough Notes* (Vol. 145, No. 1, January 2003, pp. 90) **[6820]**, **[13480]**, **[49287]**

"Tablet Tools" in *Entrepreneur* (Vol. 31, No. 10, October 2003, pp. 57) **[4831]**, **[6821]**, **[23218]**, **[49288]**, **[53498]**

Tabletop Market **[12224]**

"Tackle Your International Logistics Obstacles" in *E-business Advisor* (Vol. 18, No. 12, December 2000, pp. 22) **[34559]**, **[43834]**

"Tackling the Competition" in *Home Business* (Vol. 12, March/April 2005, No. 2, pp. 80) **[4832]**, **[23219]**, **[23738]**, **[30968]**, **[53499]**

Taco Bell of Canada **[21982]**

Taco Casa **[21983]**

Taco Grande, Inc. **[21984]**

Taco John's International, Inc. **[21985]**

The Taco Maker, Inc. **[21986]**

Taco Mayo **[21987]**

Taco Palace **[21988]**

Taco Time **[21989]**

Taco Time Canada Inc. **[21990]**

"Taco Treasure" in *Small Business Opportunities* (Vol. 16, November 2004, No. 6, pp. 84, 86) **[21641]**, **[38919]**

Taco Villa **[21991]**

Tacoma Business Assistance Center–Small Business Development Center **[66023]**

Tacoma Community College–Business and Industry Resource Center **[66241]**

Tacoma Dome Boat Show **[16780]**

Tacoma Home and Garden Show **[11497]**

Tacoma-Pierce County Chamber of Commerce **[66180]**

Tacoma RV Show **[21196]**

"Tactics: Semiconductors will lead the tech recovery" in *Red Herring* (No. 105, October 1, 2001, pp. 102) **[28854]**, **[37194]**

"Tactics: Technology's earnings riddle" in *Red Herring* (No. 103, September 1, 2001, pp. 88) **[28855]**, **[42025]**

"Tactics: Will better be good enough?" in *Red Herring* (No. 102, August 15, 2001, pp. 94) **[28856]**, **[42026]**

The Tactix Group **[25329]**, **[47912]**, **[52009]**

Tae Kwon Do: The Ultimate Reference Guide to the World's Most Popular Martial Art **[16913]**

James S. Taffae Associates Inc. **[21731]**

Taft Chamber of Commerce **[65522]**

Taft District Chamber of Commerce **[57822]**

"Tag Sale" in *Business 2.0* (Vol. 7, January/February 2006, No. 1, pp. 34, 37) **[25979]**, **[34560]**

Tahlequah Area Chamber of Commerce and Tourism Council **[64087]**

T'ai Chi **[16917]**

"Take-Aways" in *Sales & Marketing Management* (Vol. 158, October 2006, No. 10, pp. 16) **[47597]**, **[51859]**

Take Back Your Power: A Working Woman's Response to Sexual Harassment **[32067]**

Take Back Your Time: How to Regain Control of Work, Information and Technology **[45698]**, **[54990]**

"Take a bow" in *Atlanta Business Chronicle* (Vol. 25, November 8, 2002, No. 22 pp. 1B) **[18733]**, **[37514]**, **[38920]**

"Take Cover: No Need to Panic-We've Got Tips to Help You Cut Your Car Insurance Costs" in *Entrepreneur* (Vol. 33, March 2005, No. 3) **[13481]**, **[43384]**

"Take a virtual drive" in *Hispanic Business* (Vol. 22, No. 3, March 2000, pp. 58) **[34561]**, **[49289]**

"Take It to the Bank" in *Washington Business Journal* (Vol. 22, No. 15, August 15, 2003, pp. 3) **[10199]**, **[30017]**, **[38393]**, **[45699]**, **[47598]**

"Take It For Granted" in *Entrepreneur* (Vol. 33, January 2005, No. 1, pp. 50) **[39935]**, **[42027]**, **[44667]**, **[48796]**, **[50976]**, **[52213]**

"Take It Or Leave It: The Only Guide to Negotiating You Will Ever Need" in *Inc.* (August 1, 2003) **[27510]**, **[36825]**, **[45700]**

Take It from the Top: The Business of Business Success **[39733]**

"Take a hard look, and do the right thing" in *Crain's Detroit Business* (Vol. 19, No. 5, February 3, 2003, pp. 9) **[273]**, **[2967]**, **[24049]**, **[26378]**, **[29536]**, **[37515]**, **[40749]**

"Take it from me" in *Entrepreneur* (Vol. 31, No. 4, April 2003, pp. 26) **[3592]**, **[28857]**, **[36826]**, **[45701]**, **[56429]**

"Take Me To Your Leaders: A New Research Tool Helps You Find Leading Mutual Funds" in *Entrepreneur* (Vol. 31, No. 9, September 2003) **[10200]**, **[15499]**, **[38394]**

Take a Minute: The Organized Call **[31949]**

"Take No For an Answer: Don't Dismiss Naysayers-Ask For Advice, and Turn It Into a Tool for Success" in *Entrepreneur* (October 2004) **[3593]**, **[31225]**, **[36827]**

"Take Note: Document Incidents Now, and Avoid Lawsuits Later" in *Entrepreneur* (Vol. 32, October 2004, No. 10, pp. 64) **[13482]**, **[29537]**, **[43385]**

"Take One Tablet" in *Black Enterprise* (Vol. 34, No. 4, November 2003, pp. 55) **[6822]**, **[49290]**

"Take One Tablet: Buyer's Guide" in *Entrepreneur* (Vol. 31, No. 9, September 2003, pp. 46) **[5128]**, **[6823]**, **[14501]**

"Take Our Outfit - Please! How do you start a small business?" in *Business Week Online* (December 23, 2002) **[35684]**, **[50198]**

"Take a Peek: What Does Congress Have in Mind for 2005?" in *Entrepreneur* (Vol. 33, January 2005, No. 1, pp. 27) **[39625]**, **[40750]**

"Take your pick" in *Entrepreneur* (Vol. 31, No. 5, May 2003, pp. 69) **[13483]**, **[26921]**, **[41112]**, **[43386]**

"Take the Plunge" in *Entrepreneur* (Vol. 32, November 2004, No. 11, pp. 93) **[801]**, **[47599]**, **[50687]**

"Take the Plunge! Teetering on the Edge of Unemployment?" in *Entrepreneur* (Vol. 31, No. 11, November 2003, pp. 118) **[35685]**, **[53568]**

"Take a Seat" in *Inc.* (August 1, 2003) **[18562]**, **[18614]**, **[49553]**

"Take a SIP" in *Entrepreneur* (Vol. 33, October 2005, No. 10, pp. 46) **[5129]**, **[46947]**, **[49291]**

"Take a peek at tech site" in *Crain's Detroit Business* (Vol. 16, No. 49, December 4, 2000, pp. 9) **[14502]**, **[42028]**

Take This Job and Love It **[42934]**

Take Two ... for Safety **[56647]**

"Take a vacation" in *Women in Business* (Vol. 54, No. 2, March-April 2002, pp. 20) **[15500]**, **[38395]**

"Take the Work Home" in *Black Enterprise* (Vol. 36, December 2005, No. 5, pp. 72) **[45702]**, **[54017]**

"Take Your Life for a Spin" in *Fast Company* (July 2001, pp. 52) **[15501]**, **[45703]**

"Take Your Pick: Palm OS or Pocket PC?" in *Entrepreneur* (Vol. 31, No. 11, November 2003, pp. 58) **[6824]**, **[49292]**

"Takeover Offer Is Accepted By Parent Of Argo-Tech" in *Wall Street Journal* (Vol. 248, December 2006, No. 152, pp. A7) **[30609]**, **[46454]**, **[50199]**

"Takes the cake" in *Black Enterprise* (Vol. 32, No. 10, May 2002, pp. 58) **[45704]**, **[47600]**, **[48797]**, **[50688]**

"Taking ABWA to the office" in *Women in Business* (Vol. 53, No. 2, March-April, 2001, pp. 28) **[56430]**

Taking Action: Substance Abuse in the Workplace **[54356]**

Taking Action 2: Frontline Against Drugs **[54357]**

"Taking Advantage of Technology" in *Black Enterprise* (Vol. 31, No. 4, November 2000, pp. 57) **[34562]**, **[54018]**, **[54991]**

"Taking stock in Atlanta public companies" in *Atlanta Business Chronicle* (Vol. 25, December 6, 2002, No. 26) **[15502]**

"Taking the mystery out of investor behavior" in *Harvard Business Review* (Vol. 80, No. 9, September 2002, pp. 68) **[10201]**, **[15503]**, **[38396]**

"Taking Boutique Hotels to the Extreme" in *Fortune* (Vol. 151, February 21, 2005, No. 4, pp. 36) **[12643]**, **[24733]**, **[25252]**

"Taking care of business" in *BlackEnterprise* (Vol. 31, No. 12, July 2001, pp. 46) **[4367]**, **[8894]**, **[11767]**, **[35686]**, **[47979]**, **[52502]**

"Taking Care of Baby?" in *Entrepreneur* (Vol. 32, July 2004, No. 7, pp. 78) **[26922]**, **[35085]**

"Taking Care of Business: Downloadable Programs For Your Enterprise" in *Black Enterprise* (Vol. 34, July 2004, No. 12, pp. 145) **[274]**, **[4833]**, **[15504]**, **[22391]**, **[23220]**, **[26379]**, **[38397]**, **[49293]**, **[53500]**

"Taking a Chance" in *Atlanta Business Chronicle* (Vol. 26, No. 13, September 5, 2003, pp. 1A) **[4834]**, **[10887]**, **[23221]**

"Taking the fear out of buying a personal computer" in *Women in Business* (Vol. 53, No. 3, May-June, 2001, pp. 22) **[49294]**, **[49554]**

"Taking credit" in *Entrepreneur* (Vol. 30, No) **[8322]**, **[31591]**, **[54019]**

"Taking Credit" in *Small Business Opportunities* (Vol. 13, No. 5, September 2001, pp. 68) **[31592]**

"Taking the 'dis' out of disability" in *Black Enterprise* (Vol. 32, No. 9, March 2002, pp. 102) **[35687]**, **[46594]**, **[47980]**, **[56081]**

"Taking a Dive: A Federally Chartered Insurer of Pensions has Fallen on Hard Times. Taxpayers, Beware" in *Barron's* (July 21, 2003) **[13484]**, **[26923]**, **[40751]**, **[43387]**, **[54786]**

"Taking the Emotions out of Business Decisions" in *Success from Failure* (August 2000) **[30610]**, **[36828]**

"Taking Flight: Angel Investors are Flocking Together to Your Advantage" in *Entrepreneur* (Vol. 32, October 2004, No. 10, pp. 34) **[44668]**, **[50200]**, **[55852]**

Taking on Greater Responsibility: Step-up Skills for Nonmanagers. **[41879]**, **[42862]**, **[44853]**

"Taking the Hospitality Test" in *Crain's Detroit Business* (Vol. 21, October 10, 2005, No. 43, pp. 11) **[12914]**, **[20159]**, **[31873]**, **[50473]**, **[52597]**

"Taking It Outside: Outsourcing Can Be a Great Time Saver-But Mind the Costs" in *Black Enterprise* (Vol. 34, No. 5, December 2003) **[38921]**, **[49741]**

"Taking It Outside: Outsourcing Can Be a Great Time Saver-But Mind the Costs" in *Black Enterprise* (Vol. 34, No. 5, December 2003) **[38922]**, **[49742]**

"Taking the Leap. Minority Staffing Services Owner Proves He Can Make It in MA" in *Boston Business Journal* (Vol. 23, Aug. 22, 2003) **[9235]**, **[24535]**, **[48433]**

"Taking License: It Pays to Do Your Homework Before Signing a Licensing Agreement" in *Entrepreneur* (Vol. 32, December 2004, No. 12) **[7489]**, **[9076]**, **[9114]**, **[29538]**, **[44159]**

Taking Money Out of Your Corporation: Perfectly Legal Methods to Maximize Your Income **[38398]**

"Taking the Net by Storm" in *Entrepreneur* (Vol. 28, No. 1, January 2000, pp. 50) **[14503]**, **[34563]**, **[54020]**

"Taking Off" in *Washington Business Journal* (Vol. 22, No. 20, September 19, 2003, pp. 34) **[28858]**, **[30420]**

"Taking On the Energy Crunch" in *Fortune* (Vol. 151, February 7, 2005, No. 3, pp. 97) **[21257]**, **[27188]**, **[53005]**, **[54021]**

"Taking Our Affluence For Granted" in *Black Enterprise* (Vol. 34, No. 3, October 2003, pp. 12) **[32736]**, **[47601]**

"Taking the Pain Out of Payday" in *Inc.* (January 1, 2005) **[18793]**, **[26380]**, **[27189]**

"Taking charge in a new leadership role" in *Women in Business* (Vol. 53, No. 5, September-October, 2001, pp. 32) **[45705]**

"Taking Sides" in *Entrepreneur* (Vol. 33, September 2005, No. 9, pp. 26) **[53006]**, **[54022]**

"Taking Spiritual E-Path" in *Crain's New York Business* (Vol. 23, November 20, 2006, No. 47, pp. 29) **[802]**, **[14504]**, **[25980]**, **[30611]**, **[36829]**, **[47602]**

"Taking Stock" in *Fast Company* (May 2001, pp. 44) **[15505]**, **[37195]**, **[38399]**

"Taking stock" in *Harvard Business Review* (Vol. 81, No. 1, January 2003, pp. 19) **[10202]**, **[15506]**, **[28859]**, **[38400]**, **[45706]**

"Taking Stock of Your Intellectual Property Assets" in *My Business* (December/January 2003, pp. 17) **[22392]**, **[44160]**, **[44372]**

"Taking it to the Street" in *Hispanic Business* (March 2004, pp. 30, 32, 34) **[15507]**, **[41113]**, **[50201]**

"Taking Technology Curbside and Beyond" in *Black Enterprise* (Vol. 35, October 2004, No. 3, pp. 63) **[6825]**, **[12644]**, **[14505]**, **[42029]**

Taking Your Business Global: Your Small Business Guide to Successful International Trade **[43835]**

"A tale of 25 Cities" in *Entrepreneur* (Vol. 28, No. 10, October 2000, pp. 86) **[30018]**, **[36830]**

"A Tale of Two Cities" in *Fast Company* (May 2001, pp. 143) **[14506]**, **[23222]**, **[37196]**, **[52737]**, **[54023]**

"A Tale of Two Cities: Livin' La Vida Boca" in *Fast Company* (May 2001, pp. 155) **[14507]**, **[23223]**, **[37197]**, **[52738]**

"Talent" in *Business Week* (January 9, 2006, No. 3966, pp. 26-28) **[35086]**, **[45707]**

Talent Tree Crystal, Inc. **[24553]**

"Talented work force credited for right ideas" in *Crain's Detroit Business* (Vol. 19, No. 13, March 31, 2003, pp. 14) **[4835]**, **[23224]**, **[42030]**, **[42430]**, **[48798]**, **[53501]**

Talihina Chamber of Commerce **[64088]**

"The Talk About VoIP is Ringing Off the Hook" in *San Jose Mercury News* (March 9, 2005) **[5130]**, **[14508]**

"Talk America Plans $40M State Expansion" in *Crain's Detroit Business* (Vol. 21, January 24, 2005, No. 4, pp. 12) **[5131]**, **[28860]**

"Talk Direct" in *PC Magazine* (February 6, 2001, pp. 26) **[5132]**, **[27511]**, **[53502]**

"The Talk of the Inc. 500" in *Inc.* (October, 2000, pp. 13) **[28861]**, **[32737]**, **[34564]**, **[46455]**

Talk Show Hosts.com **[20296]**

Talk Show Yearbook **[23829]**

"A Talk With the Net's Financiers" in *Internet World* (Vol. 6, No. 6, March 15, 2000, pp. 60) **[33495]**, **[37080]**, **[43044]**, **[55438]**

Talkeetna Chamber of Commerce **[56976]**

Talking Book World **[3066]**, **[21388]**

"Talking heads" in *Entrepreneur* (Vol. 31, No. 6, June 2003, pp. 84) **[803]**, **[47603]**

"Talking Shop: Where Should You Focus Your Online Marketing? Try the Office" in *Entrepreneur* (Vol. 31, No. 9, July 2003, pp. 83) **[34565]**, **[47604]**

"Talking Shop: Wonder What Makes Shoppers Tick?" in *Entrepreneur* (Vol. 31, No. 9, September 2003, pp. 62) **[31874]**, **[51380]**

"Talking the talk" in *Black Enterprise* (Vol. 32, No. 9, April 2002, pp. 123) **[22454]**, **[35688]**

"Talking the Talk" in *Inc.* (December 1, 2003) **[27512]**, **[27680]**

"Talking tiger, hidden classroom" in *Ingram's* (Vol. 28, No. 6, June 2002, pp. 53) **[6335]**, **[6486]**, **[33247]**, **[34566]**

"Talking trash" in *Incentive* (Vol. 174, No. 9, September 2000, pp. 34) **[22567]**

"Tall Order" in *Entrepreneur* (Vol. 32, December 2004, No. 12, pp. 58) **[5133]**, **[49295]**

"Uncommon Enterprise: A Tall Order" in *My Business* (October/November 2003, pp. 58) **[12211]**, **[12312]**, **[36831]**

Tallahassee Democratic (October 3, 2002); "Gold's Buys Gym, Converts to Women's Facility in Tallahassee, Fla." in **[19402]**, **[53754]**

Tallmadge Chamber of Commerce **[63800]**

Tallwood Venture Capital **[58166]**

Tama/Toledo Area Chamber of Commerce **[60215]**

"TAMACC Launches Leadership School" in *Hispanic Business* (July/August 2002, pp. 10) **[32885]**, **[35689]**

Tamaqua Area Chamber of Commerce **[64518]**

Tamayo Consulting Inc. **[30120]**, **[33356]**, **[35265]**, **[46124]**

"Taming of the Crew: What Lion Tamers Teach Us About Team Management" in *Entrepreneur* (Vol. 33, January 2005, No. 1, pp. 26) **[30969]**, **[31875]**, **[35087]**, **[36832]**, **[45708]**

"Taming the Techno Beast" in *Business Week* (May 22, 2000, pp. F30) **[49296]**

Tampa Bay Beaches Chamber of Commerce **[58942]**

"Tampa, Fla.-Area Housing Downshifts" in *Tampa Tribune* (December 24, 2005) **[7490]**, **[20682]**, **[32738]**

"Tampa, Fla.-Area Project Gets Grant to Put Medical Data Online" in *Tampa Tribune* (December 22, 2005) **[6292]**, **[41114]**

"Tampa, Fla.-Based Fitness Club Company Expands Manatee County Operations" in *Bradenton Herald* (September 12, 2002) **[19443]**, **[28862]**

"Tampa, Fla., Bike Shop Turns Off Its Engine" in *Tampa Tribune* (November 5, 2005) **[1975]**, **[17491]**, **[36833]**, **[56431]**

Tampa Tribune (November 22, 2005); "2 Companies' Scrap Equals 392,649 Tons of Cargo for Port of Tampa" in **[12942]**, **[21214]**

Tampa Tribune (December 22, 2005); "2 Lawsuits Challenge State's Canker Policy" in **[26467]**, **[40136]**

Tampa Tribune (November 30, 2005); "A Bumper Crop of Worries" in **[26488]**, **[30806]**, **[53625]**

Tampa Tribune (December 22, 2005); "A Magazine on the Move" in **[18904]**, **[36459]**

Tampa Tribune (November 30, 2005); "Airfares Increase Amid High Demand" in **[30285]**

Tampa Tribune (November 28, 2005); "Albany's High-Tech Park Already Creating Jobs" in **[6576]**, **[41503]**, **[50806]**, **[52034]**

Tampa Tribune (November 9, 2005); "As Home Prices Soar, People Renovate To Move Up But Not Out" in **[4477]**, **[7247]**, **[9108]**, **[10506]**, **[23792]**

Tampa Tribune (December 3, 2005); "Better Ingredients for Better Ads" in **[557]**, **[16802]**, **[19624]**, **[46714]**

Tampa Tribune (November 22, 2005); "Budget Sportswear Store Coming to Tampa, Fla." in **[5643]**, **[23609]**, **[51080]**

Tampa Tribune (December 12, 2005); "Builder Bandits" in **[7271]**, **[30805]**, **[32285]**, **[42184]**

Tampa Tribune (December 28, 2005); "Busch Gardens Sees 2005 Attendance Grow" in **[1131]**, **[27892]**

Tampa Tribune (November 3, 2005); "Businesses' Cost From Flu Are Nothing To Sneeze At" in **[39211]**, **[40976]**

Tampa Tribune (November 28, 2005); "Carry Your Memory" in **[6603]**, **[48982]**

Tampa Tribune (December 23, 2005); "Churn Plagues Wal-Mart Labor Effort" in **[51095]**, **[55285]**

Tampa Tribune (December 15, 2005); "Citizens Rates Set to Rise Yet Again" in **[13235]**, **[43126]**

Tampa Tribune (November 27, 2005); "Clearwater Man Puts Technology To Work" in **[41605]**, **[50850]**, **[52078]**

Tampa Tribune (November 16, 2005); "Company Tracks Shoppers, Issues Coupons on Tendencies" in **[11601]**, **[16808]**, **[46823]**, **[51106]**

Tampa Tribune (October 4, 2002); "Directors of High-Tech Incubator in Tampa, Fla., Vote to Shut Down" in **[41639]**, **[43050]**

Tampa Tribune (December 9, 2005); "Dry Cleaning Dons a Corporate Veneer" in **[8904]**, **[30842]**, **[38760]**

Tampa Tribune (November 8, 2005); "Eateries Fend Off Nutrition Labels" in **[21494]**, **[40334]**

Tampa Tribune (November 22, 2005); "Employee Health Costs Rose 6.1 Percent" in **[26792]**, **[41005]**

Tampa Tribune (November 28, 2005); "Farmers Faithful to Their Fields" in **[20505]**, **[20874]**, **[26506]**

Tampa Tribune (November 2, 2005); "Film Producer Casts Self in a New Role" in **[9712]**, **[9951]**, **[14982]**

Tampa Tribune (December 22, 2005); "Florida is Fastest-Growing State in U.S." in **[28166]**, **[32436]**, **[52672]**

Tampa Tribune (December 10, 2005); "Go For Fir or Spruce Up, But It Could Cost You" in [5479], [11430]

Tampa Tribune (October 27, 2005); "Home Building at Record High" in [7364], [20527], [28291]

Tampa Tribune (December 24, 2005); "It's Down to a Waiting Game" in [51210]

Tampa Tribune (November 19, 2005); "It's OK If You Shop Til You Drop" in [41039], [51212], [53817]

Tampa Tribune (December 16, 2005); "Job Outlook Stays Bright in Florida" in [28359], [32522], [42318]

Tampa Tribune (November 17, 2005); "Longtime Pitchmen Started Chain" in [21553], [36453], [37715], [38848]

Tampa Tribune (November 23, 2005); "Mail-Order Medical Suppliers Combined" in [8790], [16454], [50065]

Tampa Tribune (December 17, 2005); "Moneymaker Without Walls" in [4299], [15929]

Tampa Tribune (October 28, 2005); "Natural Gas Prices Pinch Businesses" in [27154], [39487]

Tampa Tribune (December 7, 2005); "No Line At 6 a.m. Black Friday" in [30920], [47350], [51273]

Tampa Tribune (December 19, 2005); "Pricey Playthings" in [19431], [23630]

Tampa Tribune (December 23, 2005); "PS Cleaning Products, Lightning Join to Promote Line" in [762], [47433], [50146]

Tampa Tribune (November 23, 2005); "Relief on Wheels? Mall Strollers Play DVDs" in [51307], [53937]

Tampa Tribune (August 8, 2003); "Retailer Torrid Looks to Tap into Plus-Size Apparel Market for Teenagers" in [5710], [51317]

Tampa Tribune (December 21, 2005); "Sales, Profits Surge for Jabil" in [7742], [28738]

Tampa Tribune (January 24, 2005); "Sharing Digital Shots Snap with Picasa 2.0" in [4202], [4796], [23170], [49254], [53462]

Tampa Tribune (December 2, 2005); "Slick Trick" in [18123], [50970], [52204]

Tampa Tribune (February 6, 2007); "Small Business Gets Big Squeeze From Property Insurance Rates" in [13464], [30952], [43363]

Tampa Tribune (December 21, 2005); "StarShip Gets 30 More Years at Channelside" in [21635], [24730]

Tampa Tribune (November 24, 2005); "State Farm Rate Boost Approved" in [13473], [43377]

Tampa Tribune (November 11, 2005); "State Tells Poker Rooms to Fold 'Em" in [10885], [40727]

Tampa Tribune (November 29, 2005); "Student Loan Firm Will Add 170 Jobs" in [28838], [42427], [44666]

Tampa Tribune (December 24, 2005); "Tampa, Fla.-Area Housing Downshifts" in [7490], [20682], [32738]

Tampa Tribune (December 22, 2005); "Tampa, Fla.-Area Project Gets Grant to Put Medical Data Online" in [6292], [41114]

Tampa Tribune (November 5, 2005); "Tampa, Fla., Bike Shop Turns Off Its Engine" in [1975], [17491], [36833], [56431]

Tampa Tribune (February 28, 2005); "Technology Column" in [5137], [6832], [7084], [14514], [22395], [30423], [31084], [49306], [49318]

Tampa Tribune (November 25, 2005); "Their Life's Work" in [31880], [35112], [45724]

Tampa Tribune (October 27, 2005); "Theme Parks Go From One Extreme to Another to Scare Up Customers On Halloween" in [1139], [54033]

Tampa Tribune (November 21, 2005); "Through the Grape Vine" in [23512], [45737]

Tampa Tribune (November 17, 2005); "Vendors Help Seniors Sort Out Medicare Options" in [13512], [43415]

Tampa Tribune (November 17, 2005); "Women Roll Out Cigar Magazine" in [18947], [24612], [56502]

The Tan Sheet [12030], [18456], [40873]

Tan & Tone America [23849]

"T&E Report" in *Sales and Marketing.com* (Vol. 156, No. 3, March 2004, pp. 68) [30421]

Tandem, Staffing for Industry [24554]

Taney County Extension SBDC [61882]

"Tangled Web" in *Hispanic Business* (December 2001, pp. 58) [14509], [34567], [48434]

Robert H. Tanner, P.E. Acoustics [17543]

Tao of Karate [16923]

The Tao of Teams: A Guide to Team Success [35088]

Taos County Chamber of Commerce [62714]

Tap Dancin' [8485]

"Tap into Expert Input" in *Black Enterprise* (Vol. 30, No. 12, July 2000, pp. 47) [30019], [30949], [38262], [43388], [45709]

"Tap Into the Corporate LAN" in *Home Office Computing* (Vol. 18, No. 9, September 2000, pp. 79) [42730], [49297], [54024]

"Tap WAP for Enterprise Mobile Solutions?" in *E-business Advisor* (Vol. 18, No. 5, May 2000, pp. 12) [5134], [34568]

"Tape Backup isn't the sexiest technology on the network, but it is one of the most essential" in *PC Magazine* (April 4, 2000, pp. 155) [49298], [53503]

Tapioca Express Inc. [11397]

Tappahannock-Essex County Chamber of Commerce [65950]

Tappan Zee Capital Corp. [62608]

Tappin' across the Floor [8486]

Tappin' Rhythm [8487]

"Tapping the Ethnic Marketplace Without Getting Lost in Translation" in *Sacramento Bee* (November 20, 2005) [25093], [48602]

"Tapping Foreign Markets" in *Home Office Computing* (Vol. 18, No. 10, October 2000, pp. 18) [42731], [43836], [54025]

Tapping the Government Grapevine: The User-Friendly Guide to U.S. Government Information Sources [13090]

"Tapping Into Your Warm Market" in *Home Business* (Vol. 13, January/February 2006, No. 1, pp. 72, 74-75) [44669], [48925]

"Tapping local markets can pay off" in *Wall Street Journal* (May 14, 2002, pp. B4) [45710], [47605], [51860]

"Tapping the Potential of Employee Ranks; Human Resources" in *Crain's New York Business* (Vol. 22, November 13, 2006, No. 46, pp. 32) [33248], [42431], [42895], [54787]

"Tapping the Talent Pool of Hispanic Affluence" in *Hispanic Business* (Vol. 24, No. 1/2, January/February 2002, pp. 6) [34569], [43837], [45711], [47606], [48435]

Taranto & Associates Inc. [49463]

Tarboro - Edgecombe Chamber of Commerce [63432]

Tarbutton Associates Inc. [12699], [38985]

Target Marketing for the Small Business: Researching, Reaching and Retaining Your Target Market [47607]

"Target Practice" in *Entrepreneur* (Vol. 31, No. 8, August 2003, pp. 72) [47608], [51861]

Target Smart: Database Marketing for the Small Business [47609], [50689]

Target Success: How You Can Become a Successful Entrepreneur-Regardless of Your Background [36834]

"Target plans superstores" in *Crain's Detroit Business* (Vol. 19, No. 14, April 7, 2003, pp. 48) [11670], [28863], [51381]

"A targeted approach" in *Pittsburgh Business Times* (Vol. 22, No. 39, April 11, 2003, pp. 24) [46456]

"Targeting Options Threatens Innovation and Growth" in *Venture Capital Journal* (Vol. 42, No. 5, May 2002, pp. 42) [15508], [28864], [30612], [36835], [55853]

"Targeting Success" in *Small Business Opportunities* (Vol. 12, No. 5, September 2000, pp. 60, 64) [16471], [47610]

"Targeting a Tighter Audience" in *Hispanic Business* (Vol. 22, No. 1/2, January/February, pp. 90) [34570], [47611]

Targets [51933]

Tarleton State University
    Small Business Development Center [65063]
    Texas Institute for Applied Environmental Research [37375]

Tarpon Springs Chamber of Commerce [58943]

The Tarrance Group [20196]

Tarrant County College–Small Business Development Center [65064]

Tarrant/Pinson Valley Chamber of Commerce [56892]

Tarzana Chamber of Commerce [57823]

"Task Force Recommends Strategies to Improve Maine's Forest Products Industry" in *Portland Press Herald* (April 6, 2005) [16321], [26547], [39936]

A Taste Above [23574]

"Taste, Bud" in *Fast Company* (July 2001, pp. 62) [12793], [47612], [48799]

Tastee-Freez [12854], [21992]

"Tastes Differ" in *Crain's New York Business* (Vol. 22, December 11, 2006, No. 50, pp. 24) [804], [24450], [47613], [50690], [53007]

"Tastes great? Less taxing?" in *Barron's* (Vol. 82, No. 57, February 10, 2003, pp. T4) [275], [4836], [24050], [26381], [38401], [54880]

"A Tasty Blend of the Old and New" in *Hispanic Business* (June 2002, pp. 104) [24734], [25253], [30422], [45712]

Tate County Chamber of Commerce [61835]

Tattoo [23856]

"Tattoo Shop Moves to Cornwall Avenue" in *Bellingham Business Journal* (January 2007, pp. A5) [23854], [28865], [30180]

Tatum Chamber of Commerce [62715]

"Taubman Plans Spur Optimism" in *Crain's Detroit Business* (Vol. 22, November 27, 2006, No. 48, pp. 20) [51382], [52739]

"Taubman-Simon battle employs an army of high-priced advisers" in *Crain's Detroit Business* (Vol. 19, No. 17, April 28, 2003, pp. 4) [276], [7491], [15509], [29539], [50202], [51383]

Taunton Area Chamber of Commerce [61005]

Tavy Stone Fashion Library [5620], [5763], [7950]

Tawas Area Chamber of Commerce [61435]

"The Tax Act of 2001" in *Hawaii Business* (Vol. 47, No. 2, August 2001, pp. 208) [24051], [39937], [54788]

"A Tax Act" in *Entrepreneur* (Vol. 31, No. 8, August 2003, pp. 55) [40752], [54789]

The Tax Adviser (Vol. 32, No. 10, October 2001, pp. 668); "Are sec. 529 plans a better choice than education IRAs?" in [23883], [32997], [39787], [54429]

The Tax Adviser (Vol. 32, No. 10, October 2001, pp. 677); "EGTRRA lowers rates and expands credits, education benefits" in [23934], [39814], [54530]

The Tax Adviser (Vol. 32, No. 10, October 2001, pp. 672); "Qualified state tuition programs: EGTRRA update" in [24019], [33215], [39891], [54716]

"Tax time is approaching" in *Black Enterprise* (Vol. 33, No. 7, February 2003, pp. 6) [277], [26382], [54790]

"Tax Benefit is Worth Keeping" in *Crain's New York Business* (Vol. 23, November 20, 2006, No. 47, pp. 10) [7492], [20683], [21020], [26924], [54791]

"Tax Bill Doesn't Repeal Estate Tax Uncertainty" in *Atlanta Business Chronicle* (Vol. 24, No. 1, June 8, 2001, pp. 5A) [37795], [54792]

"A tax break as big as a big SUV" in *Wall Street Journal* (May 27, 2003, pp. D2) [18140], [54793]

"Tax Breaks for Angels" in *Inc.* (September 2005, pp. 30) [54794], [55854]

"Tax Breaks: Don't Forget Your Home Office" in *Business Week* (No. 3666, January 31, 2000, pp. 124E4) [42732], [54795]

"Tax Breaks May Aid Dealers Pummeled by Katrina; Bush Official Also Touts 'Investment Opportunity'" in *Automotive News* (September 2006) [18141], [54796]

"Tax plan could prompt corporations to move to C" in *Crain's Detroit Business* (Vol. 19, No. 5, Feb. 3, 2003, pp. 13) [51493], [54797]

Tax Centers of America [24135]

Tel-Advise **[33357]**

"Telecom: As companies go bankrupt, buyout firms lick their chops" in *Red Herring* (No. 105, October 1, 2001, pp. 24-25) **[28873]**, **[50205]**

Telecom Asia **[27560]**, **[49389]**

"Telecom recession may have hit bottom" in *Atlanta Business Chronicle* (Vol. 25, January 3, 2003, No. 30, pp. 3A) **[5139]**, **[14520]**, **[28874]**, **[34579]**, **[42057]**

Telecom Business Opportunities: The Entrepreneur's Guide to Making Money in the Telecommunications Revolution **[6184]**

Telecom Made Easy: Money-Saving, Profit-Building Solutions for Home Businesses, Telecommuters & Small Organizations **[42735]**

The Telecom Manager's Voice Report **[5227]**

Telecom & Network Security Review **[5212]**, **[19987]**

Telecom Partners / Telecom Management LLC **[58463]**

Telecom Perspectives **[25686]**

"Telecom Rewrite Has New Rules for Wireless" in *Crain's Detroit Business* (Vol. 21, October 17, 2005, No. 43, pp. 7) **[40757]**, **[42058]**

"Telecom Services: Finding new life in a troubled industry" in *Red Herring* (No. 106, October 15, 2001, pp. 74-75) **[5140]**, **[14521]**, **[37201]**

"Telecom Trickle-Up" in *Washington Business Journal* (Vol. 22, No. 11, July 18, 2003, pp. 27) **[5141]**, **[14522]**, **[34580]**

Telecommunications 6471, 6647

Telecommunications Community Resource Center–University of Missouri Extension–Small Business Development Center **[61883]**

Telecommunications Consultants of America **[24328]**

Telecommunications Development Fund (TDF) **[58678]**

Telecommunications Directory **[5142]**, **[22089]**, **[25684]**

Telecommunications Industry Association **[4902]**, **[25682]**

Telecommunications Research and Action Center **[19810]**

"Telecommunications Sector Analysis" in *Red Herring* (No. 106, October 15, 2001, pp. 86-87) **[6416]**, **[23228]**, **[37202]**

"Telecommuter Denied Jobless Benefits" in *Inc.* (October 1, 2003) **[26928]**, **[29542]**, **[40758]**

The Telecommuter's Advisor: Working in the Fast Lane **[42736]**, **[49309]**

"Telecom's transformation continues in Georgia" in *Atlanta Business Chronicle* (Vol. 25, January 10, 2003, No. 31, pp. 17A) **[5143]**, **[14523]**, **[28875]**, **[34581]**, **[42059]**

The Telegraph (December 18, 2003); "New Hampshire Attorney General Probes Mall's Ouster of Diamond Kiosk" in **[15930]**, **[29401]**

"Telemarketers Plan to Do-Not-Call" in *Providence Business News* (Vol. 18, No. 20, September 1, 2003, pp. 1) **[39626]**, **[47617]**

Telemarketing: Applications and Opportunities **[24293]**, **[47618]**

Telemarketing Basics **[47619]**

Telemarketing & Call Center Solutions **[24299]**

Telemarketing Skills in Minutes **[24308]**

Telephone Courtesy and Customer Service–Crisp Learning–Thomson Learning **[31994]**

Telephone Doctor **[3920]**

Telephone IP News **[8669]**

Telephone Manners **[24309]**, **[24326]**

Telephone Prospecting and Selling Report **[24300]**

Telephone Selling: A New Approach **[24310]**

Telephone Techniques: A Complete Program for the Insurance Professional **[13568]**

Telephone Terrific! Facts, Fun and 103 "How-To" Tips for Phone Success **[31878]**

"Telephony Rising" in *Home Office Computing* (Vol. 18, No. 10, October 2000, pp. 37) **[5144]**, **[34582]**, **[40759]**

TelephonyOnline **[5213]**

Teleselling: High Performance Business-to-Business Phone Selling Techniques **[24294]**

Television Bureau of Advertising **[24370]**, **[50541]**

Television Bureau of Canada–Library **[915]**

Television & Cable Action Update **[4144]**, **[24479]**

Television & Cable Factbook **[4122]**, **[24451]**

Television Operators Caucus **[24371]**

TelevisionWeek **[4145]**, **[20359]**

"Telework Lowers Office Expense" in *Home Office Computing* (Vol. 19, No. 1, January 2001, pp. 18) **[42737]**, **[54030]**

"The Telework Puzzle" in *Home Office Computing* (Vol. 19, No. 1, January 2001, pp. 90) **[31228]**, **[49744]**, **[53510]**

Telfair County Chamber of Commerce **[59164]**

"Tell-A-Friend Wizard" in *Entrepreneur* (Vol. 33, September 2005, No. 9, pp. 6) **[34583]**, **[47620]**, **[50691]**

"Tell me no secrets" in *Entrepreneur* (Vol. 31, No. 5, May 2003, pp. 48) **[30022]**, **[55860]**

Tellus Institute **[9516]**

Telos Venture Partners **[58172]**

Telsoft Ventures **[66775]**

Temecula Valley Chamber of Commerce **[57824]**

"Temp help" in *Black Enterprise* (Vol. 33, No. 7, February 2003, pp. 16) **[9237]**, **[24536]**

"Temp Hiring Signals Economic Recovery" in *Inc.* (January 1, 2004) **[9238]**, **[24537]**, **[32741]**, **[42434]**

Tempaco, Inc. **[3921]**

Tempe Chamber of Commerce **[57075]**

Tempest Co. **[7644]**

Temping, Freelancing & Entrepreneurial Opportunities **[24538]**

Temple Chamber of Commerce **[64090]**, **[65525]**

Temple City Chamber of Commerce **[57825]**

Temple University
    Esther Boyer College of Music–New School Institute - Alice Tully Library **[17704]**
    Office of the Vice President for Research and Graduate Studies **[64616]**
    Small Business Development Center **[64339]**
    Temple University Libraries–Blitman Resource Center **[20388]**

Temple University Small Business Development Center–Temple University **[64598]**

Templeton Chamber of Commerce **[57826]**

"Temporary Nursing" in *BlackEnterprise* (Vol. 31, No. 6, January 2001, pp. 41) **[18293]**, **[24513]**

The Ten Best Opportunities for Starting a Home Business Today **[42738]**

The Ten Commandments of Networking **[29046]**, **[53064]**

10 Easy Ways to Keep Your Job **[54288]**

The Ten Faces of Innovation **[36841]**, **[39627]**

"10 ways to improve small business cash flow" in *Journal of Accountancy* (Vol. 189, No. 3, March 2000, pp. 14) **[38406]**

"The Ten Hottest New Franchises" in *Success* (Vol. 47, No. 2, June 2000, pp. 82) **[38925]**

Ten Keys to Sales & Financial Success for Small Business **[38407]**

"The 10 Least Wired Industries" in *PC Computing* (April 2000, pp. 64) **[3137]**, **[7493]**, **[8910]**, **[10806]**, **[15517]**, **[34584]**, **[50206]**

"10 months, 10 minutes, $10 million" in *The New York Times* (June 7, 2000, pp. D3, H3) **[35692]**, **[55441]**

"10 Names that Drive the Game" in *Crain's Detroit Business* (Vol. 19, No. 14, April 7, 2003, pp. 11) **[11273]**, **[28876]**

"10 Rules for Bouncing Back" in *My Business* (April/May 2003, pp. 32) **[28877]**, **[36842]**

$10,000 -a-Day Business Opportunities: Seminars, Newsletters, Cassettes, Software & More **[28878]**

10 til 2 **[9283]**

Tender Loving Care **[12426]**

"Tenet Healthcare Ends Fight over Heart Program at Stuart, Fla. Medical Center" in *Palm Beach Post* (April 11, 2003) **[42060]**, **[52217]**

Tenino Chamber of Commerce and Economic Development Commission **[66181]**

Tennessee Board of Regents–Tennessee Small Business Development Center **[64847]**

Tennessee Chamber of Commerce and Industry **[64981]**

Tennessee Department of Agriculture–Market Development **[64874]**

Tennessee Department of Economic and Community Development
    Business Enterprise Resource Office **[64875]**
        International Development Group **[64876]**
        Research Division **[66986]**

Tennessee Department of Economic and Community Development Center–Business Enterprise Resource Office (BERO) **[64990]**

Tennessee Economic Development Quarterly **[65013]**

Tennessee JobBank **[23404]**

Tennessee Procurement Technical Assistance Center–Center for Industrial Services **[65005]**

Tennessee SBDC–Middle Tennessee State University **[64848]**

Tennessee (State) Human Rights Commission–Resource Library **[32125]**

Tennessee State University
    Institute of Government **[50410]**
    Small Business Development Center **[64871]**

Tennessee Technological University
    Center for Energy Systems Research **[9101]**
    Center for the Management, Utilization and Protection of Water Resources **[25748]**
    Center for Manufacturing Research **[46556]**
    SBDC **[64872]**

Tennessee Town & City **[50374]**

Tennessee Valley Authority **[67396]**
    Minority Economic and Small Business Development **[67397]**
    TVA Environmental Research Center–TVA Research Library **[26667]**

Tennis Magazine **[24575]**

"Tennis Player Serves Mexican Meals" in *Crain's New York Business* (Vol. 21, January 31, 2005, No. 5, pp. 25) **[21643]**, **[36843]**

Tennis Week **[24576]**

Tent Rental Directory **[18763]**

Tenting Directory **[4239]**

Tera Capital Corp. **[66735]**

Teratogenesis, Carcinogenesis and Mutagenesis **[52327]**

Teratology **[52328]**

Teriyaki Stix **[21993]**

"Termination reasons key to workers' comp claims" in *Business First Columbus* (Vol. 18, No. 40, May 24, 2002, pp. B6) **[26929]**, **[45719]**

Terminix International **[19042]**

Terminix Termite & Pest Control **[19043]**

Terra Community College–Small Business Development Center **[63577]**

Terrazzo Tile and Marble Association of Canada **[10504]**

Terrell Chamber of Commerce **[65526]**

Terrell County Chamber of Commerce **[59165]**

Terrier Type **[1211]**

Terri's New & Consigned Furnishings **[7187]**

"Terrorism: After attacks, survivors use the Internet to say 'I'm OK'" in *Red Herring* (No. 106, October 15, 2001, pp. 28) **[14524]**, **[37203]**

"Terrorism Backup Legislation Raises Many Questions" in *Rough Notes* (Vol. 145, No. 2, February 2003, pp. 34) **[13486]**, **[22398]**, **[29543]**, **[40760]**, **[43390]**

"Terrorism Insurance" in *The Economist* (Vol. 376, July 16-22, 2005, No. 8435, pp. 71) **[13487]**, **[39940]**, **[43391]**

"Testing, 1-2-3: Wondering If You Can Really Get Any Work Done at a Wi-Fi Hot Spot?" in *Entrepreneur* (Vol. 31, No. 9, September 2003) **[11353]**, **[12645]**, **[14525]**, **[21644]**

"Teton wins construction award with speed, safety" in *Atlanta Business Chronicle* (Vol. 25, December 6, 2002, No. 26, pp. 14C) **[1533]**, **[7494]**, **[18563]**

Teton Valley Chamber of Commerce **[59334]**

Tetra Tech NUS, Inc.–Technical Information Center **[9458]**, **[9508]**

"Tewksbury Firm Cashes in as Internet Calling Grows" in *Boston Globe* (March 7, 2005) **[5145]**, **[14526]**, **[28879]**

Texarkana Chamber of Commerce **[65527]**

"There is no correlation at all between success and hours worked" in *Fast Company* (June 2001, pp. 76) **[36849]**, **[54993]**

"There's no place in business for these 4-letter words" in *Success from Failure* (August 2000) **[36850]**

"There's Life In Life Science" in *Venture Capital Journal* (Vol. 42, No. 8, August 2002, pp. 32-35) **[50799]**, **[52026]**, **[55442]**

"There's More to E-Business Than Point and Click" in *Journal of Business Strategies* (Vol. 21, No. 5, September 2000, pp. 11) **[34587]**, **[47627]**

"There's More Than One Way to Bust a Trust" in *Inc.* (Volume 27, December 2005, No. 12, pp. 24) **[6835]**, **[14530]**, **[29546]**, **[40765]**, **[53512]**

"There's No Perk Like Home" in *Inc.* (December 1, 2003) **[26932]**, **[35113]**, **[45725]**

"There's No There There" in *Red Herring* (No. 99, June 15 & July 1, 2001, pp. 134) **[15521]**, **[42063]**, **[54034]**

There's Someplace Like Home: Developing an Adult Day Care Center in Your Church **[435]**

"There's Something About Harry" in *Venture Capital Journal* (Vol. 42, No. 5, May 2002, pp. 18-19) **[15522]**, **[36851]**, **[50208]**, **[55861]**

Thermopolis - Hot Springs Chamber of Commerce **[66633]**

"These Days, Who Isn't a Venture Capitalist?" in *Fortune* (Vol. 141, No. 8, April 17, 2000, pp. 532) **[55862]**

TheWorldCo.Com **[14683]**

"They Almost Changed the World" in *Forbes* (Vol. 170, No. 13, December 23, 2002, pp. 217) **[36852]**, **[44164]**

"They Bought In. Now They Want to Bail Out" in *Harvard Business Review* (Vol. 81, No. 12, December 2003, pp. 28) **[4841]**, **[23230]**, **[31881]**, **[45726]**, **[53513]**

"They clicked, they left: why aren't your web site visitors buying?" in *Entrepreneur* (Vol. 31, No. 4, April 2003, pp. 85) **[806]**, **[25985]**, **[34588]**, **[47628]**

"They Hate You...They Really, Really Hate You" in *Entrepreneur* (Vol. 28, No. 8, August 2000, pp. 99) **[14531]**, **[45727]**

"They Have the Goods" in *Spokesman-Review* (January 29, 2005) **[1857]**, **[7176]**, **[14532]**

"They Just Can't Stop Themselves" in *Inc.* (Volume 27, March 2005, No. 3, pp. 98-104) **[35693]**, **[39101]**

"They Want You" in *Inc.* (Volume 27, June 2005, No. 6, pp. 32) **[28890]**, **[36853]**

"They'll Get Your Goat (Milk)" in *My Business* (November/December 2001, pp. 13-14) **[4267]**, **[23445]**, **[35694]**

"They're Certifiable" in *Entrepreneur* (Vol. 28, No. 10, October 2000, pp. 36) **[48926]**, **[55863]**

"They're not employees, they're people" in *Harvard Business Review* (Vol. 80, No. 2, February 2002, pp. 70) **[35114]**, **[42897]**, **[45728]**, **[49747]**

"They're all round, but..." in *Crain's Detroit Business* (Vol. 19, No. 10, March 10, 2003, pp. 33) **[6836]**, **[49312]**

"They've Got Mail - From You" in *My Business* (June/July 2004, pp. 45) **[47629]**, **[51868]**

Thibodaux Chamber of Commerce **[60671]**

Thief River Falls Chamber of Commerce **[61670]**

"Thiel Design" in *The Business Journal-Milwaukee* (Vol. 18, No. 24, March 2, 2001, pp. 33) **[6009]**

Thimband **[58488]**

Thimband-The Newsletter **[33306]**

Thin Book Publishing **[64318]**

"Things I Can't Live Without" in *Inc.* (September 1, 2004) **[807]**, **[2399]**, **[11169]**, **[12212]**, **[13675]**, **[21648]**, **[36854]**, **[37798]**, **[38067]**, **[38225]**, **[47630]**, **[56436]**

"Things I Can't Live Without: Marcy Zambelli" in *Inc.* (July 1, 2004) **[37799]**, **[45729]**, **[46458]**

"Think Ahead" in *Entrepreneur* (Vol. 32, October 2004, No. 10, pp. 40) **[30024]**, **[36855]**, **[44165]**, **[54035]**

"Think fast" in *Entrepreneur* (Vol. 31, No. 5, May 2003, pp. 82) **[38927]**

"Think Fast: Take Advantage of Faster Depreciation" in *Entrepreneur* (Vol. 32, December 2004, No. 12, pp. 62) **[282]**, **[24061]**, **[26386]**, **[54833]**

"Think Happy Thoughts" in *My Business* (September/October 2001, pp. 50) **[28891]**, **[32742]**

"Think Small" in *Entrepreneur* (Vol. 31, No. 10, October 2003, pp. 50) **[6837]**, **[49313]**

"Think Small. No, Smaller" in *Inc.* (January 1, 2002) **[45730]**

"Think Small" in *PC Magazine* (November 21, 2000, pp. 5a) **[34589]**, **[49314]**

"Think Tech; Automation Alley" in *Crain's Detroit Business* (Vol. 21, October 3, 2005, No. 43, pp. 1) **[28892]**, **[42064]**, **[42436]**, **[52218]**

"Think You Know How Much Your Home Is Worth?" in *Kansas City Star* (January 23, 2005) **[10207]**, **[17445]**

"The thinker: Watch Out! Your car may be getting smarter than you" in *Entrepreneur* (Vol. 30, No. 2, February 2002, pp. 19) **[5148]**, **[18143]**

"Thinking About Security" in *PC Magazine* (January 4, 2000, pp. 191) **[49315]**, **[53514]**

"Thinking Ahead" in *Entrepreneur* (Vol. 33, September 2005, No. 9, pp. 62) **[13490]**, **[26529]**, **[26933]**, **[43394]**

"Thinking outside the big box" in *Ingram's* (Vol. 28, No. 3, March 2002, pp. 74) **[20059]**, **[51387]**

"Thinking Inside the Box" in *Inc.* (July 1, 2004) **[4123]**, **[24452]**

"Thinking Out of the Clamshell" in *Business 2.0* (Vol. 6, July 2005, No. 6, pp. 58) **[44166]**, **[46459]**, **[51388]**

"Thinking Outside the Box" in *E-business Advisor* (Vol. 18, No. 10, October 2000, pp. 8) **[30615]**, **[34590]**

"Thinking Pink? Think Again" in *Entrepreneur* (Vol. 32, No. 2, February 2004, pp. 12) **[808]**, **[47631]**, **[56437]**

"Thinking Small: Coca-Cola Shows How the 20'x20' Exhibit Is Done" in *Tradeshow Week* (Vol. 34, December 6, 2004, No. 49, pp. S6) **[22569]**, **[25030]**, **[47632]**, **[55167]**

Thinking Through Safety: The Job Safety and Healthy Analysis **[56648]**

Thinking Translation: A Course in Translation Method **[25094]**

Thinnes & Dutton P.C. **[1271]**

"Third Base: Hiring Employees Can Free Owner to Help Business Grow" in *Crain's Detroit Business* (Vol. 19, No. 49, December 8, 2003) **[40619]**, **[42437]**, **[43671]**, **[45731]**

Third Coast Capital **[59760]**

"Third Degree Advertising Names VP for Solomon Inc." in *Journal Record* (June 25, 2003) **[47633]**, **[49535]**, **[50692]**, **[50764]**

Third Indicator **[13113]**

"Third time's the charm" in *BlackEnterprise* (Vol. 32, No. 2, September 2001, pp. 53) **[6919]**, **[13783]**, **[25763]**, **[35695]**, **[37082]**, **[47982]**

Thirteen-One, Inc. **[31502]**

"This Biz Delivers!!" in *Small Business Opportunities* (Vol. 12, No. 5, September 2000, pp. 22-24, 26, 28, 30, 32, 34, 36, 38, 40) **[16418]**

"This Biz is Growing by Leaps and Bounds" in *Small Business Opportunities* (Vol. 16, November 2004, No. 6, pp. 90) **[21649]**, **[28893]**, **[38928]**

"This Biz Is Smokin'" in *Small Business Opportunities* (Vol. 13, No. 6, November 2001, pp. 102, 122) **[21416]**, **[35696]**

This Business of Writing **[9013]**

"This Call May Be Monitored" in *Inc.* (Volume 27, June 2005, No. 6, pp. 29-30) **[31882]**, **[54036]**

"This Detective has Rediscovered a Lost Art" in *Fortune* (Vol. 149, No. 9, May 3, 2004, pp. 58) **[1614]**, **[1858]**, **[19979]**, **[50209]**

"This just in" in *Crain's Detroit Business* (Vol. 19, No. 17, April 28, 2003, pp. 1) **[39628]**, **[50210]**

"This Is Not About Charity" in *Forbes* (August 21, 2000, pp. 70) **[30616]**, **[36856]**, **[56767]**

This Is Not Your Parents' Retirement: A Revolutionary Guide for a Revolutionary Generation **[15523]**, **[26934]**, **[39629]**

"This Is a Test" in *Entrepreneur* (Vol. 32, December 2004, No. 12, pp. 97) **[27191]**, **[38408]**

"This Isn't Your Teenage Daughter's Diary: Web Logs Are a Big Hit With Everyone..." in *Black Enterprise* (Vol. 34, December 2003) **[4842]**, **[14533]**, **[23231]**, **[34591]**, **[53515]**, **[54037]**

"This Just In" in *Crain's Detroit Business* (Vol. 21, January 24, 2005, No. 4, pp. 1) **[809]**, **[7432]**, **[7495]**, **[7727]**, **[10699]**, **[10888]**, **[13584]**, **[13676]**, **[14534]**, **[17446]**, **[18564]**, **[19226]**, **[20685]**, **[21022]**, **[21650]**, **[24735]**, **[25256]**, **[28294]**, **[28894]**, **[29645]**, **[32743]**, **[34592]**, **[44369]**, **[44374]**, **[46460]**, **[48307]**, **[48437]**, **[50211]**

"This little drug went to the market" in *Ingram's* (Vol. 28, No. 6, June 2002, pp. 27) **[48801]**, **[52219]**, **[55864]**

"This Marketing Pro's Aim is to Clear the Clutter" in *The Record* (November 6, 2005) **[20027]**, **[47634]**

"This Means War" in *Entrepreneur* (Vol. 31, No. 11, November 2003, pp. 94) **[22399]**, **[34593]**

This is Mini Golf **[17329]**

"This will keep you up at night" in *E-business Advisor* (Vol. 18, No. 10, October 2000, pp. 10) **[34594]**, **[47635]**

"This Phone Connects" in *Fast Company* (September 2001, pp. 70) **[5149]**, **[49316]**

"This is a Test: Just How Effective are Puzzle Interviews When It Comes to Singling Out the Best Candidates for the Job?" in *Entrepreneur* **[42438]**, **[45732]**

This Time **[8056]**

"This V-Day, Money Can Buy You Love" in *Fortune* (Vol. 151, February 7, 2005, No. 3, pp. 32) **[7070]**, **[14535]**, **[34595]**

"This VC Firm's Motto: Make Money, Not War" in *Fortune* (Vol. 142, No. 3, July 24, 2000, pp. 54) **[41488]**, **[43045]**, **[55443]**

"This is War" in *Entrepreneur* (Vol. 28, No. 2, February 2000, pp. 96) **[36857]**

"This Week: McD's Eyes Ad Plan, Shifts Breakfast Biz" in *Crain's Chicago Business* (Vol. 30, February 2007, No. 6, pp. 1) **[810]**, **[21651]**, **[47636]**

"This Week: McD's Tests Trans-Free Oil in 1,200 Locations" in *Crain's Chicago Business* (Vol. 29, December 2006, No. 50, pp. 1) **[21652]**, **[30972]**, **[40766]**, **[47637]**, **[50981]**

"This Week: Raising the Roof at North Pier?" in *Crain's Chicago Business* (Vol. 29, December 2006, No. 51, pp. 1) **[21023]**, **[28895]**

"This job guarantees a good workout" in *Wall Street Journal* (April 15, 2003, pp. B7) **[19444]**, **[45733]**

"This Yogi Is Hot-And Bothered" in *Fortune International* (Vol. 147, No. 6, March 31, 2003, pp. 42) **[17916]**, **[19445]**

Thole Associates **[8843]**, **[11714]**

Thoma Cressey Equity Partners **[59761]**

Thomas Chamber of Commerce **[64091]**

Thomas College–Waterville Satellite–SBDC **[60716]**

The Thomas Hill Enterprise Center **[62098]**

Thomas Hill Enterprise Satellite Center–Southeast Missouri State University–SBDC **[61884]**

Thomas Investigative Publications–Library **[19996]**

Thomas Jefferson University–Center for Research in Medical Education and Health Care **[41413]**

R. G. Thomas **[1062]**, **[7645]**

Thomas Raddall Research Centre–Archives **[11081]**

Thomaston - Upson Chamber of Commerce **[59166]**

Thomasville Area Chamber of Commerce **[63433]**

Thomasville-Thomas County Chamber of Commerce **[59167]**

Thompson Clive & Partners Limited (Menlo Park) **[58173]**

Thompson Falls Chamber of Commerce **[62202]**

Thomson Bank Directory **[38409]**

Thomson Crisp Learning **[58285]**

Thomson Delmar Learning–Solitaire Publishing **[59023]**

Thomson Gale **[61510]**

Thomson Legal & Regulatory **[61738]**

Thomson North American Financial Institutions Directory **[38410]**

Thomson Physicians World–Knowledge Management & Medical Library **[8883]**

Thomson World Bank Directory **[44670]**

Thorndale Area Chamber of Commerce **[65531]**

Thornton Financial FNIC **[10348]**

"A Thorough Assessment: Want to Evaluate Your Management Skills?" in *Sales and Marketing.com* (Vol. 156, No. 3, March 2004) **[45734]**, **[51869]**

Thoroughbred Racing Associations of North America-Directory and Record Book **[10889]**

"Those China Franchises are Risky" in *Automotive News* (Vol. 78, July 5, 2004, No. 6101, pp. 12) **[18144]**, **[38929]**, **[43842]**

"Those Weren't the Days?" in *Inc.* (August 1, 2003) **[32744]**

"Thoughts On the Business of Life" in *Forbes* (Vol. 170, No. 13, December 23, 2002, pp. 396) **[36858]**, **[45735]**

"A thousand bottles of beer on the wall" in *Washington Business Journal* (Vol. 22, No. 3, May 23, 2003, pp. 31) **[2351]**, **[26387]**, **[38411]**, **[45736]**

Thousand Oaks - Westlake Village Regional Chamber of Commerce **[57827]**

"A Thousand to One" in *Entrepreneur* (Vol. 28, No. 11, November 2000, pp. 22) **[25578]**, **[54038]**

Thousand Palms Chamber of Commerce **[57828]**

Threads **[5587]**, **[8057]**

"Threat Level" in *Entrepreneur* (Vol. 31, No. 8, August 2003, pp. 28) **[3596]**, **[22400]**, **[31230]**, **[34596]**, **[42065]**

"3.5 Trillion Miles...and Counting" in *Fast Company* (September 2001, pp. 166) **[30426]**

"Three Bars in One" in *Kansas City Star* (February 25, 2005) **[2352]**

"Three questions you need to ask about your brand" in *Harvard Business Review* (Vol. 80, No. 9, September 2002, pp. 80) **[30973]**, **[47638]**, **[50693]**

"Three Cheers for Bankruptcy" in *Fortune* (Vol. 152, October 17, 2005, No. 8, pp. 33) **[36957]**, **[38412]**, **[40767]**

Three Forks Chamber of Commerce **[62203]**

Three House Publishing **[62115]**

301 Great Ideas for Using Technology to Grow Your Business **[28896]**, **[42066]**, **[49317]**

"365-day forecast" in *Entrepreneur* (Vol. 30, No. 1, January 2000) **[28897]**, **[32745]**

The 3-Point Contact **[7587]**

Three Rivers Area Chamber of Commerce **[61436]**

Three Rivers Chamber of Commerce **[61006]**, **[65532]**

"Three Scary Words: Buy it Used" in *Inc.* (September 2006, pp. 29-31) **[1859]**, **[14536]**, **[28898]**, **[34597]**, **[47639]**

"Three Trends for 2005" in *Forbes* (Vol. 175, January 31, 2005, No. 2, pp. 39) **[34598]**, **[35697]**, **[54039]**

"3 Ways to improve your business by getting a life" in *My Business* (June/July 2002, pp. 26-32) **[36859]**, **[54994]**

"3G Wireless Networks: Worth the Wait?" in *E-business Advisor* (Vol. 18, No. 7, July 2000, pp. 12) **[5150]**, **[34599]**, **[48802]**

"Three's Company: American Carriers Are Finally Bringing 3G Cellular Service to a Phone Near You" in *Entrepreneur* (September 2004) **[5151]**, **[50212]**

"Thrift: working at home or hardly working?" in *Red Herring* (January 2003, pp. 67) **[6838]**, **[28899]**

"Thrifts adrift? Mortgage slowdown would hurt the industry" in *Barron's* (Vol. 82, No. 59, February 24, 2003, pp. T6) **[7496]**, **[17447]**, **[20686]**, **[28900]**

"The thrifty boss" in *Forbes* (Vol. 6, No. 5, March 2003, pp. 46) **[4843]**, **[23232]**, **[44250]**, **[50760]**

Thrifty Car Sales Inc. **[18206]**

Thrifty Clean, Inc. **[21390]**

Thrifty Rent-A-Car System, Inc. **[2102]**

ThriftyTraveling.com **[30465]**

"The Thrill of the Chase" in *Entrepreneur* (Vol. 31, No. 7, July 2003, pp. 56) **[44671]**, **[55865]**

"Thriving Locally in the Global Economy" in *Harvard Business Review* (Vol. 81, No. 8, August 2003, pp. 119) **[28901]**, **[32746]**

Throne & Co. **[50338]**

Through the Gears Trucking Magazine **[6118]**, **[10717]**

"Through the Grape Vine" in *Tampa Tribune* (November 21, 2005) **[23512]**, **[45737]**

"Through the grapevine: E-mail newsletter has owners tasting profits" in *Entrepreneur* (Vol. 31, No. 6, June 2003, pp. 81) **[27516]**, **[27682]**, **[31883]**, **[34600]**

"Through Grieving" in *Success from Failure* (August 2000) **[3597]**, **[36860]**, **[37800]**, **[56438]**

"Through a Wall, Clearly" in *Business 2.0* (Vol. 7, January/February 2006, No. 1, pp. 28) **[42067]**

"Throwing money away" in *Incentive* (Vol. 174, No. 9, September 2000, pp. 8) **[26935]**, **[35115]**

"Throwing a Line to Uninsured Workers" in *Business Week* (No. 3853, October 13, 2003, pp. 88) **[26936]**

"Throwing Money at Technology Isn't the Solution" in *My Business* (April/May 2002, pp. 18) **[45738]**, **[49318]**

"Throwing a Tea Party" in *Success* (Vol. 47, No. 4, September 2000, pp. 38) **[11354]**, **[35698]**

"Thumbs Up" in *Hispanic Business* (July/August 2002, pp. 16) **[39942]**, **[48438]**

"Thumbs Up! Rave Reviews Could be All the Advertising You Need" in *Entrepreneur* (Vol. 32, July 2004, No. 7, pp. 71) **[811]**, **[4844]**, **[23233]**, **[25986]**, **[47640]**, **[50694]**, **[53516]**

Thundercloud Subs **[8577]**, **[12856]**

Thurston County Chamber of Commerce **[66182]**

"Thwarting Office Theft, and Making the Most of Revolving Credit Lines" in *Inc.* (May 1, 2005) **[22087]**, **[22401]**

Tiburon Peninsula Chamber of Commerce **[57829]**

"Ticker Takes: Jmar Technologies" in *San Diego Business Journal* (Vol. 28, January 15, 2007, No. 3, pp. 10) **[15524]**, **[42068]**

"Ticket Resellers Aim to Be Top Draws" in *Business Week Online* (February 3, 2005) **[14537]**, **[30974]**, **[34601]**

"Tickle Makes a Match With SendTec" in *ADWEEK Western Edition* (December 24, 2003) **[7071]**, **[47641]**

Ticonderoga Area Chamber of Commerce **[63026]**

Ticonderoga Capital Inc. **[58174]**

"Tiered pricing plans have benefits and disadvantages" in *Business First Columbus* (Vol. 18, No. 40, May 24, 2002, pp. B11) **[13491]**, **[31075]**, **[41116]**, **[43395]**

"Ties That Bind" in *Entrepreneur* (Vol. 31, No. 10, October 2003) **[29547]**, **[42439]**

Tiffin Area Chamber of Commerce **[63801]**

Tigard Area Chamber of Commerce **[64274]**

Tiger Hills Arts Association–Music Resource Library **[17705]**

"Tiger Power" in *Rough Notes* (Vol. 146, No. 9, September 2003, pp. 32) **[13492]**, **[43396]**, **[45739]**, **[47642]**

"Tight-Lipped Banks" in *Entrepreneur* (Vol. 28, No. 7, July 2000, pp. 40) **[39943]**, **[40768]**, **[44672]**

"Tight buyout financing may boost use of employee stock plans" in *Wall Street Journal* (April 30, 2002, pp. B6) **[15525]**, **[26937]**, **[50213]**

Tijuana Flats Burrito Co. **[21994]**

Tilden Car Care Centers **[22702]**

Tile Council of North America **[16940]**

Tile Outlet Always in Stock **[7670]**

Tile Roofing Institute **[22061]**

Tillamook Bay Community College–Small Business Development Center **[64177]**

Tillamook Chamber of Commerce **[64275]**

Tillman's Corner Chamber of Commerce **[56893]**

Tim Hortons **[2316]**

Timber Framing **[1542]**, **[7578]**

Timberline Venture Partners **[66226]**

Time (Vol. 156, No. 14, October 2, 2002, pp. 68); "A Crisis of Content: It's not just pop music." in **[13940]**, **[33719]**, **[44022]**, **[44285]**, **[53671]**

Time (Vol. 133, No. 23, June 5, 1989, pp. 56); "Angling For Bass and Bucks" in **[2177]**, **[18850]**, **[20011]**, **[23712]**

"Time for a Change?" in *Entrepreneur* (Vol. 33, February 2005, No. 2, pp. 76) **[35699]**

"Time to Change" in *Entrepreneur.com* (Vol. 34, January 2006, No. 1, pp. 27) **[6839]**, **[49319]**

"Time to Collect? Tacking Taxes Onto Internet Sales Could Soon Become Mandatory" in *Entrepreneur.com* (Vol. 34, February 2006, No. 2) **[24062]**, **[34602]**, **[40769]**, **[51389]**, **[54834]**

"A Time to Donate" in *Hispanic Business* (Vol. 23, No. 11, November 2001, pp. 68) **[54263]**, **[54835]**

"Time For a Checkup" in *Sales and Marketing.com* (Vol. 156, No. 3, March 2004, pp. 68) **[10208]**, **[15526]**, **[38413]**, **[45740]**

"The time for talk is over" in *Rough Notes* (Vol. 146, No. 4, April 2003, pp. 16) **[283]**, **[13493]**, **[26388]**, **[36861]**, **[43397]**, **[45741]**

Time Inc. (Vol. 156, No. 3, July 17, 2000, pp. B13); "Focus on Prohibitive Health-Care Costs: Government help may be on the way" in **[26808]**, **[40388]**

Time Inc. (Vol. 156, No. 13, Sept. 25, 2000); "Hooray for R. and D. It's time to make a popular and effective tax credit permanent" in **[54595]**

Time Inc. (Vol. 156, No. 7, August 14, 2000, pp. B20); "Kill The Estate Tax! World War I is over" in **[54635]**

Time Inc. (Vol. 157, No. 1, Jan. 8, 2001, pp.57); "Plan B from Cyberspace: A growing number of websites are going back to the future" in **[19819]**, **[19888]**, **[34349]**

Time Inc. (Vol.155, May 2000); "Pocketbook Issues: The 2000 election brings some of small business's biggest issues to the forefront" in **[26882]**, **[54704]**

Time Inc. (Vol. 156, No. 3, July 17, 2000, pp. B7); "The Big Issues for Small Concerns: Listen up, candidates" in **[40185]**, **[54445]**

Time (Vol. 162, No. 14, November 3, 2003, pp. G1); "Inn Vogue" in **[2443]**

Time Is Money! **[51988]**, **[55028]**

"The Time Machine" in *Birmingham Business Journal* (Vol. 20, No. 30, July 25, 2003, pp. 11) **[5917]**, **[36862]**

Time Management **[54995]**

Time Management (Canada) **[54933]**

Time Management: Conquering the Clock **[54996]**

Time Management: Keeping the Monkey off Your Back **[55029]**

Time Management for Managers **[55030]**

Time Management for Managers and Professionals (41-1XX) **[55031]**

Time Management for Women **[55032]**, **[56538]**

Time Masters - The Institute for Personal Excellence **[55047]**

"The Time is Now" in *My Business* (April/May 2004, pp. 14) **[32747]**, **[35116]**, **[45742]**

"A time of lower returns" in *Hispanic Business* (Vol. 22, No. 11, November 2000, pp. 36) **[43843]**, **[48439]**

The Time of Our Lives **[55033]**

Time (Vol. 155, No. 3, January 24, 2000, pp. B7); "Publish Thyself: More and more, book authors are using the Web" in **[2734]**, **[9155]**, **[14373]**

"The Time is Right For A Binder Authority Review" in *Rough Notes* (Vol. 145, No. 9, September 2002, pp. 78) **[13494]**, **[43398]**

"Time Right For Tech Upgrade? That Depends" in *Mississippi Business Journal* (Vol. 29, January 2007, No. 2, pp. 1) **[6185]**, **[6417]**, **[53013]**, **[53517]**

"Time Right To Let Sun Shine On AG, Outside Attorneys" in *Mississippi Business Journal* (Vol. 29, January 2007 , No. 29, pp. 4) **[29548]**, **[37516]**, **[40770]**

"Time Saver" in *My Business* (June/July 2004, pp. 54) **[12313]**, **[34603]**

"A Time to Sell?" in *Black Enterprise* (Vol. 35, September 2004, No. 2, pp. 95) **[10209]**, **[15527]**, **[38414]**

Time Share Systems **[61718]**

"A Time to Shine: Awards Celebration Spotlights Today's Successful Entrepreneurs" in *Black Enterprise* (Vol. 34, No. 4, November 2003) **[36863]**, **[37397]**, **[45743]**, **[47544]**, **[48440]**, **[49166]**

Time and Territory Management **[51989]**

Time and Territory Management for Salespeople **[51537]**

"A Toast to Innovation" in *Small Business Opportunities* (Vol. 16, November 2004, No. 6, pp. 48, 50) **[23513]**, **[38932]**, **[44169]**

"A Toast to Success" in *Hispanic Business* (July/August 2004, pp. 52, 54, 56, 58, 62, 66) **[18942]**, **[48443]**

"Toasting High Profits" in *Small Business Opportunities* (July 2005) **[23514]**, **[38933]**

The Toastmaster **[22585]**

Tobacco Association of the U.S. **[24605]**

Tobacco Barometer: Cigarettes, Cigars, Little Cigars **[24621]**

Tobacco Barometer: Smoking, Chewing, and Snuff **[24622]**

Tobacco Industry Litigation Reporter **[24623]**

Tobacco International **[24624]**

Tobacco International Buyers' Guide & Directory **[24609]**

Tobacco Merchants Association **[24606]**

Tobacco Merchants Association of the U.S.–Howard S. Cullman Library **[24640]**

"Tobacco Sales to Minors Decline In Oklahoma" in *Journal Record (Oklahoma City, OK)* (February 7, 2007) **[24610]**, **[29550]**

Tobacco Trade Barometer: Imports **[24625]**

Tobacconists' Association of America **[24607]**

Today's Facility Manager **[18570]**

Today's HR Professional: From Technician to Strategist (Canada) **[42824]**

Today's Insurance Professionals **[13564]**

"Today's Specialist" in *Entrepreneur* (Vol. 33, August 2005, No. 8, pp. 28) **[22920]**, **[23235]**, **[32273]**, **[33254]**, **[50865]**, **[53519]**

Today's Window Fashions **[26085]**

"TodaysMama.com Relaunches Website" in *Marketing to Women* (Vol. 20, January 2007, No. 1, pp. 3) **[815]**, **[3953]**, **[14543]**, **[42071]**, **[47650]**, **[50218]**, **[52392]**

"Todd Brown" in *Black Enterprise* (Vol. 34, No. 5, December 2003, pp. 68) **[10211]**, **[36961]**, **[38416]**, **[45746]**

Tog on Software Design **[23236]**

Together! **[35203]**

Together Inc. **[55257]**

Together We Can! **[35204]**

Togo's Eatery **[8578]**

Tok Chamber of Commerce **[56977]**

Tokyo Stock Exchange Inc. **[63268]**

"Told You So" in *Entrepreneur* (Vol. 28, No. 6, June 2000, pp. 90) **[27735]**, **[35702]**

Tole World **[8058]**

Toledo Area Chamber of Commerce **[63803]**

Toledo Business Journal **[63901]**

Toledo Business Journal (Vol. 19, No. 2, February 2003, pp. 23); "EISC partners start-up with unique technology" in **[39765]**, **[41450]**, **[50791]**, **[52018]**

Toledo Business and Technology Center **[63885]**

Toledo Chamber of Commerce–Ohio SBDC–Lead Center (Region 2) **[63552]**

"Toll Bros. Plans $313M Luxury Push in Oakland Twp." in *Crain's Detroit Business* (Vol. 21, January 10, 2005, No. 2, pp. 1) **[7498]**

Tolland County Chamber of Commerce **[58567]**

"Tollhouses & cookies" in *Entrepreneur* (Vol. 30, No. 2,) **[14544]**, **[34613]**, **[40774]**, **[44170]**

"Tom McConnell: At Service to the Venture Community" in *Venture Capital Journal* (Vol. 41, No. 8, August 2000, pp. 35-36) **[36872]**, **[55868]**

Tom Thompson Memorial Art Gallery–Archives **[1672]**

Tomahawk Regional Chamber of Commerce **[66534]**

"Tomato Shortage Is Now a Glut In Florida" in *Bradenton Herald* (January 19, 2005) **[26548]**

Tomball Area Chamber of Commerce **[65533]**

"Tomboy Tools Ties in With Pink Hammer" in *Marketing to Women* (Vol. 19, October 2006, No. 10, pp. 9) **[11895]**, **[14545]**, **[47651]**, **[50219]**, **[54264]**

Tombstone Chamber of Commerce **[57076]**

TOMES Plus System **[29692]**, **[40899]**

Tompkins County Chamber of Commerce **[63028]**

Tompkinsville - Monroe County Chamber of Commerce **[60574]**

Toms River - Ocean County Chamber of Commerce **[62566]**

"TomTom GO910: On the Road Again" in *Black Enterprise* (Vol. 37, January 2007, No. 6, pp. 52) **[6844]**, **[7746]**, **[30427]**, **[42072]**, **[48803]**

Tonasket Chamber of Commerce **[66183]**

Tonkawa Chamber of Commerce **[64093]**

Tonopah Chamber of Commerce **[62368]**

Tony Alessandra, Ph.D.: On Collaborative Selling **[51990]**

Tony Alessandra, Ph.D.: On Customer-Driven Service **[31950]**

Tony Roma's, Famous for Ribs **[21995]**

"Tony Thompson Believes in Playing the Cards He Was Dealt" in *St. Louis Post-Dispatch* (March 4, 2005) **[7499]**, **[31231]**

"Too High a Price for Black Ink" in *Business Week* (January 23, 2006, No. 3968, pp. 25) **[15530]**, **[51392]**

"Too old to learn?" in *Harvard Business Review* (Vol. 78, No. 6, November-December 2000, pp. 37) **[13499]**, **[33255]**, **[45747]**

"Too Much Information?" in *Black Enterprise* (Vol. 37, December 2006, No. 5, pp. 59) **[10212]**, **[31593]**, **[36873]**, **[38417]**, **[44675]**, **[47652]**, **[48444]**, **[50695]**, **[56440]**

"Too Much Too Soon?" in *Inc.* (November 1, 2003) **[28906]**, **[38934]**

"Too Sensible to Survive" in *The Economist* (Vol. 377, October 22-28, 2005, No. 8449, pp. 33-34) **[40775]**, **[54837]**

Tooele County Chamber of Commerce **[65732]**

Tooling & Production **[16402]**

Tooling & Production (Vol. 69, No. 1, January 2003, pp. 10); "AMTDA members can self-update info online" in **[6234]**, **[16360]**, **[33531]**

Tools for Team Excellence: A Practical Handbook for Making Teams Work: Building, Assessing, and Team Performance **[35119]**

Toombs-Montgomery Chamber of Commerce **[59168]**

"Top 10 Business Schools for Hispanics" in *Hispanic Business* (September 2004, pp. 78, 80, 82, 84) **[32275]**, **[33256]**, **[35536]**, **[36874]**, **[39633]**, **[45748]**, **[48401]**, **[48445]**

"The top 10 business women of ABWA" in *Women In Business* (Vol. 52, No. 1, January-February 2000, pp. 16) **[56441]**

"Top 10 characteristics of Cintas' top salesperson" in *Atlanta Business Chronicle* (Vol. 24, No. 8, July 27, 2001, pp. 2B) **[51875]**

"Top 10 Law Schools for Hispanics" in *Hispanic Business* (September 2004, pp. 70, 72, 74, 76) **[29551]**, **[30210]**, **[33257]**, **[36875]**, **[48402]**, **[48446]**

"The Top 25" in *Entrepreneur* (Vol. 31, No. 10, October 2003, pp. 22) **[28907]**, **[36876]**, **[52742]**

"Top 25 Hispanic Ad Agencies" in *Hispanic Business* (December 2003, pp. 42, 44, 46, 48, 50) **[816]**, **[47653]**, **[48447]**

"Top 25 Overlooked Tax Deductions" in *Home Business* (Vol. 12, March/April 2005, No. 2, pp. 78) **[284]**, **[2969]**, **[24063]**, **[42741]**, **[54838]**

"Top 50 Exporters" in *Hispanic Business* (July/August 2004, pp. 50, 51) **[13011]**, **[43845]**, **[56017]**

The Top 100 List **[16847]**

"The top 500 women-owned businesses" in *WorkingWoman* (Vol. 25, No. 6, June 2000, pp. 51) **[56442]**

"Top ten business women of ABWA!" in *Women in Business* (Vol. 53, No. 7, January-February 2002, pp. 14) **[45749]**, **[56443]**

"Top Area Advertising Agencies" in *Ingram's* (Vol. 28, No. 9, September 2002, pp. 29) **[817]**, **[47654]**, **[50696]**

"Top Area Staffing Agencies" in *Ingram's* (Vol. 29, No. 1, January 2003, pp. 32) **[9239]**, **[9580]**, **[24539]**, **[42441]**

"Top Area Stock Brokerage Firms" in *Ingram's* (Vol. 29, No. 1, January 2003, pp. 27) **[10213]**, **[15531]**, **[38418]**

"A top brand won't happen without top leadership" in *Atlanta Business Chronicle* (Vol. 24, No. 10, August 10, 2001, pp. 43A) **[36877]**, **[47655]**

"Top Cities For African Americans: The Results Are In." in *Black Enterprise* (Vol. 34, July 2004, No. 12, pp. 78) **[48448]**, **[52743]**

"Top Coffee Has Concord Ties" in *Charlotte Observer* (February 7, 2007) **[11355]**, **[21653]**

"Top Cop" in *Forbes* (Vol. 175, January 10, 2005, No. 1, pp. 154) **[4846]**, **[15532]**, **[22406]**, **[23237]**, **[38419]**, **[53520]**

"Top Dog Enterprise" in *Small Business Opportunities* (Vol. 16, No. 2, March 2004, pp. 134, 138) **[19064]**, **[56444]**

"Top Dollar" in *Entrepreneur* (Vol. 32, No. 1, January 2004, pp. 78) **[51393]**

"Top-down diversity" in *Hispanic Business* (Vol. 22, No. 9, September 2000, pp. 42) **[47656]**, **[54265]**

"Top-drawer advice: new software tells you how much your charitable contributions are worth" in *Barron's* (Vol.82, Feb.17, 2003, pp.T7) **[285]**, **[4847]**, **[23238]**, **[24064]**, **[26390]**, **[38420]**, **[54266]**, **[54839]**

"Top Drawer" in *Forbes* (Vol. 174, December 27, 2004, No. 13, pp. 156) **[1861]**, **[5826]**, **[10214]**, **[15533]**, **[38421]**

"Top Drawers" in *Entrepreneur* (Vol. 33, September 2005, No. 9, pp. 118) **[5681]**, **[5724]**, **[9645]**

"Top Executives Set the Tone for Treating Employees Well" in *St. Louis Post-Dispatch* (January 16, 2005) **[35120]**, **[45750]**

"Top of the Heap" in *Business 2.0* (Vol. 6, May 2005, No. 4, pp. 54) **[1978]**, **[34614]**

"Top-Heavy: Is it Time to Thin Out Your Management Pool" in *Entrepreneur* (Vol. 32, No. 1, January 2004, pp. 30) **[36878]**, **[42898]**, **[45751]**

"Top-Heavy: The Pitfalls of Overhiring" in *My Business* (October/November 2003, pp. 56) **[42442]**, **[45752]**

Top of the Line Fragrance Franchise **[2621]**, **[7939]**

Top of the Line Fragrances **[7940]**

"Top MBA Programs (MO&KS)" in *Ingram's* (Vol. 28, No. 9, September 2002, pp. 42) **[33258]**, **[45753]**

The Top One Hundred Coffee Recipes: A Cookbook for Coffee Drinkers **[11356]**

"Top Secrets: Psst! Think You Know Everything About Sales?" in *Entrepreneur* (Vol. 31, No. 8, August 2003, pp. 62) **[51876]**

Top Tax Saving Ideas for Today's Small Business: A Fresh Look after Tax Reform Legislation **[54840]**

Top Tax Savings Ideas: How to Survive in Today's Tough Tax Environment **[24065]**, **[54841]**

"Top Ten Program Offers Many Possibilities for Women" in *Women in Business* (Vol. 53, No. 1, January-February, 2001, pp. 16) **[33259]**, **[56445]**

"Top Ten Schools for Hispanics: Engineering" in *Hispanic Business* (September 2006, pp. 76, 78, 80) **[33260]**, **[48449]**

"Top Ten Schools for Hispanics MBA" in *Hispanic Business* (September 2006, pp. 70, 72, 74) **[33261]**, **[48450]**

"Top Ten Schools for Hispanics: Medical" in *Hispanic Business* (September 2006, pp. 82, 84, 86) **[33262]**, **[41119]**, **[48451]**

"Top 25 Cities" in *Entrepreneur* (Vol. 30, No, 10, October 2002, pp. 30) **[28908]**, **[52744]**

"The Top 25 Investment Banks of 2000" in *Red Herring* (No. 99, June 15 & July 1, 2001, pp. 72, 74) **[15534]**, **[44676]**

"The Top 25 IPOs of 2000" in *Red Herring* (No 99, June 15 & July 1, 2001, pp. 62, 64) **[15535]**, **[44677]**, **[50220]**, **[55869]**

"The Top 25 VC Firms of 2000" in *Red Herring* (No. 99, June 15 & July 1, 2001, pp. 68, 70) **[28909]**, **[55870]**

Top Value Car & Truck Service Centers **[2018]**

"Top Venture Capital Companies" in *Ingram's* (Vol. 29, No. 7, July 2003, pp. 20) **[55871]**

Topics in Clinical Nutrition (TICN) **[18457]**, **[41302]**

Topics in Geriatric Rehabilitation (TGR) **[18361]**

Topline **[860]**

Toppenish Chamber of Commerce **[66184]**

Topper's Pizza **[21996]**

"Topping the Charts" in *Black Enterprise* (Vol. 36, November 2005, No. 4, pp. 104) **[17775]**, **[21147]**

TOPS Club (Take Off Pounds Sensibly) **[26039]**

TOPS News **[26046]**

Toronto International Home Furnishings Market **[12336]**

Toronto Real Estate Board–Library **[20772]**

Toronto Reference Library–Performing Arts Centre **[8497]**, **[17706]**

Toronto Rehabilitation Institute–Library **[18408]**

Toronto Ski, Snowboard and Travel Show **[22874]**

Torrance Area Chamber of Commerce Foundation **[57830]**

Tortas The Original Mexican Sub **[21997]**

"Toshiba Qosmio E15-AV Notebook PC" in *Black Enterprise* (Vol. 35, December 2004, No. 5, pp. 71) **[6845]**, **[49324]**

The Total Business Plan: How to Write, Rewrite, and Revise **[30029]**

Total Design **[66688]**

Total Improvement Management: How to Coordinate Diverse Improvement Efforts for Maximum Gain **[45754]**

"Total Recall" in *Entrepreneur* (Vol. 31, No. 11, November 2003, pp. 100) **[818]**, **[47657]**

The Total Tattoo Book **[23855]**

"Total Tech LLC" in *San Diego Business Journal* (Vol. 28, January 15, 2007, No. 3, pp. 34) **[36879]**, **[42073]**

"Total Tote (Tech Toy)" in *Entrepreneur* (Vol. 31, No. 8, August, 2003, pp. 18) **[6846]**, **[49325]**

Total Travel Management **[30469]**

Harvey Toub Engineering **[3264]**

Toucan Capital **[60881]**

"A Touch of Class" in *Entrepreneur* (Vol. 28, No. 10, October 2000, pp. 29) **[14546]**, **[34615]**, **[37204]**, **[47658]**

"A Touch of Class: Teaching Can Give Your Career a Boost" in *Sales and Marketing.com* (Vol. 156, No. 3, March 2004, pp. 48) **[45755]**

Touch for Health **[17026]**

"A touch of the Pointes" in *Crain's Detroit Business* (Vol. 19, No. 14, April 7, 2003, pp. 20) **[20689]**, **[21025]**

"Touchdown!" in *Rough Notes* (Vol. 145, No. 2, February 2002, pp. 92) **[13500]**, **[45756]**, **[51877]**

"Touched by an Angel" in *BlackEnterprise* (Vol. 31, No. 11, June 2001, pp. 242) **[44445]**, **[47983]**, **[48893]**, **[55445]**

"TouchSystems Launches Mighty Touch, All-In-One Wireless Kiosk Terminal Offers Flexibility" in *Internet Wire* (August 20, 2003) **[15944]**

"Tough times force banks to own other businesses" in *Crain's Detroit Business* (Vol. 18, No. 22, June 3, 2002, pp. 1) **[28910]**, **[32750]**

Tough Choices: A Memoir **[36880]**, **[45757]**, **[56446]**

"Tough choices" in *Entrepreneur* (Vol. 31, No. 5, May 2003, pp. 70) **[35121]**, **[36881]**, **[42443]**, **[45758]**

"Tough Luxury" in *Hispanic Business* (March 2004, pp. 46-49) **[18146]**

"Tough Mama" in *Forbes* (December 25, 2000, pp. 232) **[15536]**, **[37803]**, **[50221]**

"A tough review" in *Black Enterprise* (Vol. 32, No. 10, May 2002, pp. 107) **[35122]**, **[45759]**

"A Tough Row to Hoe" in *Hispanic Business* (October 2002, pp. 26, 28) **[26549]**, **[40776]**, **[48452]**

"Tough Sell" in *Black Enterprise* (Vol. 37, October 2006, No. 3, pp. 92) **[31232]**, **[39634]**, **[42444]**

"A Tough Sell" in *Hispanic Business* (December 2006, pp. 48) **[4124]**, **[24453]**, **[30975]**

"Tough Talk" in *Entrepreneur.com* (Vol. 34, February 2006, No. 2, pp. 100) **[27518]**, **[45760]**

"Tough Times build character" in *Fast Company* (May 2001, pp. 86) **[15537]**, **[36882]**, **[39635]**

"The tough work of turning around a team" in *Harvard Business Review* (Vol. 78, No. 6, November-December 2000, pp. 179) **[35123]**

"Tougher rules likely to dry up boardroom candidates" in *Crain's Detroit Business* (Vol. 19, No. 6, February 10, 2003, pp. 14) **[37517]**, **[45761]**

"Tougher Test for Bankruptcy" in *Black Enterprise* (Vol. 36, November 2005, No. 4, pp. 56) **[29552]**, **[38422]**, **[40777]**

"Tourism foundation falters, plans tasty comeback" in *Washington Business Journal* (Vol. 21, No. 49, April 4, 2003, pp. 5) **[22570]**, **[25031]**, **[25258]**

Tourism Industry Association of Canada **[24655]**, **[25137]**

Tourism Saskatchewan **[66781]**

Tourist Attractions and Parks (Vol. 35, January 2005, No. 1, pp. 47); "Get Involved in Your Association" in **[636]**, **[47008]**

Tourist Attractions & Parks Magazine **[7096]**

Tourist Attractions and Parks (Vol. 35, January 2005, No. 1, pp. 12); "Shankz Opens New Location in California" in **[17327]**, **[21624]**

Tourist Attractions and Parks (Vol. 35, January 2005, No. 1); "Shopping Centers That Sizzle: Entertainment Elements Enliven Malls" in **[17328]**, **[51354]**

"The Tournament" in *Inc.* (January 1, 2002) **[35124]**, **[54267]**

Touro College
　　Bensonhurst Library **[39748]**
　　Boro Park (53rd Street) Library **[39749]**
　　Brighton Beach Library **[39750]**
　　Flushing Library **[39751]**
　　Forest Hills Library **[39752]**
　　Lander College for Men Library **[39753]**, **[46157]**
　　Midtown Library **[39754]**
　　Midwood (Flatbush) Library **[39755]**
　　Starrett City Library **[39756]**
　　Sunset Park Library **[39757]**

Tow Times' Annual Sourcebook **[4362]**

"Toward the Development of Measures of Distinctive Competencies among Small Independent Retailers" in *Journal of Small Business Management* **[30976]**, **[51394]**, **[53014]**

"Toward Transparency" in *Venture Capital Journal* (October 1, 2005) **[50222]**, **[55872]**

"Tower Automotive Plans to Cut More Jobs, Close More Plants" in *Crain's Detroit Business* (Vol. 22, January 16, 2006, No. 4, pp.) **[1979]**, **[28911]**, **[46461]**

Tower Cleaning Systems **[3386]**

"Tower of label" in *Entrepreneur* (Vol. 30, No. 3, March 2002, pp. 47) **[14547]**, **[25987]**, **[34616]**

"Towering Goal" in *Hispanic Business* (April 2005, pp. 14) **[20690]**, **[21026]**, **[54268]**

Towers Perrin
　　Information Centre **[4052]**, **[27064]**, **[30770]**, **[43008]**
　　Western Canada Information Centre **[27065]**, **[43009]**

Towing and Recovery Association of America **[4360]**

Towing and Recovery Footnotes **[4366]**

Town of Conconully Chamber of Commerce **[66185]**

Town of Hunter Chamber of Commerce **[63029]**

Town of Los Gatos Chamber of Commerce **[57831]**

Town of Montgomery Chamber of Commerce **[63030]**

Town of Portland Chamber of Commerce **[58568]**

Towneley Capital Management Inc. **[15735]**

"Towns, Counties Grow With Interest" in *The Record* (November 5, 2005) **[10215]**, **[15538]**, **[38423]**, **[40778]**

Towns County Chamber of Commerce **[59169]**

Townsend Area Chamber of Commerce **[62204]**

R. L. Townsend & Associates Inc. **[7646]**

Township of Richland Chamber of Commerce **[64520]**

Towson University
　　Baltimore County Small Business Development Center **[60801]**
　　Office of University Research Services **[60891]**

"Toxic mold" in *Boston Business Journal* (Vol. 22, No. 3, February 22, 2002, pp. S4) **[9374]**, **[20061]**, **[37331]**

Toxics Law Reporter **[29693]**

The Toy Book **[18282]**, **[24843]**

Toy Industry Association **[18277]**, **[24798]**

Toy Shop **[24844]**

"Toying with new ideas" in *Entrepreneur* (Vol. 31, No. 4, April 2003, pp. 81) **[24835]**, **[47659]**, **[48804]**

"Toyota Center Bypasses Ticketmaster" in *Houston Business Journal* (Vol. 34, No. 14, August 15, 2003, pp. 2A) **[3954]**, **[52393]**

"Toyota-eBay Deal Opens Floodgates" in *Automotive News* (Vol. 78, No. 6086, March 29, 2004, pp. 20B) **[819]**, **[1862]**, **[18147]**, **[18666]**, **[25988]**, **[34617]**, **[47660]**

"Toyota's Opportunity Exchange" in *Hispanic Business* (September 2002, pp. 8) **[46462]**, **[48453]**

"Toyota's Plans Get Suppliers Worked Up; U.S. Expansion Drives Scramble for Business" in *Crain's Detroit Business* (Vol. 21) **[1980]**, **[18148]**, **[28912]**, **[46463]**

Toys and Games **[24841]**, **[24845]**

Toys & Games-Buyer's Guide Issue **[2129]**

"TPA business for self-funded plans balanced in 2000" in *Employee Benefit Plan Review* (Vol. 56, No. 1, July 2001, pp. 18) **[26942]**, **[41120]**, **[43403]**

TPMC Realty Services Group **[31503]**

The TQM Almanac, 1994-1995 Edition **[45762]**

TQM Consulting **[3822]**

TQM for Training **[33263]**

TR Wireless **[5214]**

Trace **[6024]**

Tracing, Charting and Writing Your Family History **[10951]**

"Tracing It" in *Pittsburgh Business Times* (Vol. 22, No. 51, July 4, 2003, pp. 17) **[42445]**, **[44375]**

Tracing Your Irish Ancestors **[10952]**

Tracing Your Scottish Ancestry **[10953]**

"Tracking the Hispanic Traveler" in *Hispanic Business* (Vol. 23, No. 10, October, 2001, pp. 40) **[24737]**, **[25259]**, **[28913]**

"Tracking T&E deductions" in *Hispanic Business* (Vol. 22, No. 4, April 2000, pp. 77) **[30428]**, **[54842]**

"Tracking Tech Time" in *Inc.* (November 15, 2000, pp. 26) **[14548]**, **[23239]**, **[31233]**

"Tracking a trend" in *Entrepreneur* (Vol. 30, No. 1, January 2002, pp. 24) **[30429]**

Tracy Area Chamber of Commerce **[61671]**

Tracy Chamber of Commerce **[57832]**

Trade Association of Paddlesports **[23604]**

Trade Card Collectors Association **[5891]**

Trade Dimensions-Directory of Convenience Stores **[7782]**

"Trade Group Endorsements For Every Specialty" in *Rough Notes* (Vol. 145, No. 9, September 2002, pp. 88) **[13501]**, **[43404]**, **[50223]**

Trade Inc. **[13039]**

"Trade Mission to France Nets $5 Million in Projected Sales" in *Portland Press Herald* (November 22, 2005) **[13012]**, **[25032]**, **[43846]**

"Trade Policy" in *The Economist* (Vol. 376, July 30-August 5, 2005, No. 8437, pp. 66) **[13013]**, **[40779]**, **[43847]**

Trade Secrets **[11844]**

The Trade Show Advantage **[25065]**, **[55189]**

Trade Show Exhibiting: The Insider's Guide for Entrepreneurs **[25033]**, **[47661]**, **[55168]**

Trade Show and Exhibition Calendars: A Where to Find or Locate Workbook **[25034]**

Trade Show Exhibitors Association **[24870]**, **[46616]**, **[55053]**

Trade Show Exhibitors Association-Membership Directory and Industry Buyer's Guide **[25035]**

"Trade Show Exhibitors Association: www.tsea.org" in *Entrepreneur* (Vol. 31, No. 12, December 2003, pp. 8) **[22571]**, **[55169]**

Trade Show Ideas **[25062]**

Trade Shows: The Small Business Guide to Successful Exhibiting **[25036]**, **[47662]**, **[55170]**

Trade Shows Worldwide **[47663]**, **[55171]**

Tri-Cities Chamber of Commerce **[56894]**

Tri-Cities Enterprise Center **[66233]**

Tri-Cities Industrial Development Council (TRIDEC)–Small Business Development Center **[66024]**

Tri-City Better Business Bureau **[66039]**

Tri-City Chamber of Commerce **[60575]**

Tri-City Regional Chamber of Commerce **[66186]**

Tri-Color Franchise Systems, Inc. **[25567]**

Tri-Community Area Chamber of Commerce **[61007]**

Tri-County Area Chamber of Commerce **[60424]**, **[64521]**

Tri-County Area Vo-Tech **[64153]**

Tri-County Development Authority–Small Business Development Center **[62332]**

Tri-County Economic Development Center–Incubator **[64131]**

Tri-county Economic Development Corp.–Fargo Regional Small Business Development Center **[63499]**

Tri-County Heritage Society–Reference Library **[1577]**

Tri-County Regional Chamber of Commerce **[64783]**

Tri-Lakes Chamber of Commerce **[58431]**

Tri-M News **[17630]**

Tri-Meridian, Inc.–MEDSEARCH Division Library **[8884]**

Tri-Ology **[11480]**, **[19037]**

Tri-State Better Business Bureau **[59870]**

Tri-State Chamber of Commerce **[58569]**, **[63031]**

Tri-Town Chamber of Commerce **[61008]**, **[62567]**

"Triad venture firms invest in Charlotte companies" in *Charlotte Business Journal* (Vol. 18, No. 1, April 4, 2003, pp. 7) **[55875]**

Triad Strategies **[10768]**, **[20197]**

Triad Studios **[21160]**

Triad Ventures, LTD–AM Fund **[65637]**

"Trial By Fire" in *Entrepreneur* (Vol. 33, October 2005, No. 10, pp. 112) **[48806]**, **[50775]**

Triangles **[17937]**

Tribune (February 3, 2004); "Business Buzz" in **[570]**, **[2333]**, **[24673]**, **[25165]**, **[27895]**, **[30302]**, **[46759]**, **[54147]**

The Tribune (November 25, 2003); "Chandler, Ariz., PostNet Among Chain's Stores that has eBay-Selling Service" in **[1791]**, **[10671]**, **[33659]**, **[37115]**

Tribune (March 9, 2005); "Inside Business" in **[7385]**, **[56279]**

Tribune (March 8, 2005); "New Market to Open" in **[7779]**, **[8517]**, **[11645]**

Tribune (March 2, 2005); "Rainfall Helps Growers" in **[26530]**

Tribune (March 11, 2005); "The Dream of Homeownership" in **[17375]**, **[20498]**

Tribune (February 23, 2004); "Upscale Garden Offerings" in **[11444]**, **[16116]**

Tribune Ventures **[59763]**

Tribune (February 15, 2005); "Work Space" in **[11172]**, **[17921]**, **[19724]**, **[52612]**, **[56513]**

"The Trick is to Live" in *Journal of Political Economy* (Vol. 111, No. 6, December 2003, pp. 18) **[37804]**, **[54845]**

"Trickle Up: Small Companies Slowly Build Momentum in the Job Market" in *Wall Street Journal* (December 4, 2003, pp. A1) **[7500]**, **[28917]**, **[32754]**, **[41121]**

"Tricks of the Trade" in *Small Business Opportunities* (Vol. 12, No. 5, September 2000, pp. 46, 48, 102-103) **[34628]**, **[47668]**

Trimark Master Franchise **[896]**

Trinidad-Las Animas Chamber of Commerce **[58432]**

Trinidad Small Business Development Center **[58311]**

Trinity County Chamber of Commerce **[57833]**, **[65534]**

Trinity Peninsula Chamber of Commerce **[65535]**

"Trinity Potter celebrates 15th anniversary behind strong commitment to quality" in *Gifts & Decorative Accessories* (Jan. 2003, pp.190) **[8185]**, **[8278]**, **[11170]**, **[31886]**

Trinity Valley Community College–Small Business Development Center **[65071]**

Trinity Ventures **[58175]**

Triodyne Consulting Engineers and Scientists–Safety Information Center **[56700]**

Trionics International Inc. **[60791]**

"Triple sport star: Steve Mills scores for the Knicks, Rangers, and the Liberty" in *Black Enterprise* (Vol.33, No.3, Oct. 2002, pp. 72) **[35544]**, **[36885]**, **[45766]**, **[45785]**

"Tripped up" in *Atlanta Business Chronicle* (Vol. 25, No. 19, October 18, 2002, pp. 1C) **[13503]**, **[26943]**, **[43406]**

"Tritec Deal is a Symbol of Commercial Real Estate Market Strength" in *Long Island Business News* (February 27, 2004) **[20691]**, **[21027]**, **[21357]**

Triton Ventures **[65638]**

Triune Capital **[58176]**

Trombone for Beginners **[17642]**

Trophy Lake Trout Tactics **[2205]**

Tropi Tan **[23850]**

Tropical Fish Hobbyist **[1465]**

Tropical Plant Industry Exhibition **[10600]**

Tropical Smoothie Cafe **[12858]**

Tropicana Smoothies, Juices & More! **[12037]**

Tropik Sun Fruit & Nut **[21998]**

Trost Publishing **[60683]**

Trott Communications Group Inc. **[5224]**

Trotwood Chamber of Commerce **[63804]**

"Trouble Ahead For Stocks" in *Fortune* (Vol. 151, February 21, 2005, No. 4, pp. 124) **[10217]**, **[15544]**, **[28918]**

"Trouble on the horizon...isn't going away" in *Fast Company* (May 2001, pp. 85) **[36886]**, **[45767]**

"Trouble In PDA Paradise" in *Entrepreneur* (Vol. 31, No. 7, July 2003, pp. 44) **[5156]**, **[42075]**, **[49328]**

"The trouble I've seen" in *Harvard Business Review* (Vol. 80, No. 3, March 2002, pp. 42) **[39641]**, **[45768]**

"Trouble in Little Cuba" in *Hispanic Business* (Vol. 23, No. 10, October, 2001, pp. 20) **[40783]**, **[48455]**

"Trouble in Tennessee" in *Hispanic Business* (October 2002, pp. 18) **[40104]**, **[48456]**

"The Trouble With Lifestyle Entrepreneurs" in *Inc.* (Volume 27, July 2005, No. 7, pp. 21-23) **[28919]**, **[32755]**, **[36887]**, **[43855]**

The Trouble with Words **[42935]**

Troubleshooting the IBM PC **[6426]**

Troubleshooting the IBM PC II **[6427]**

Troup Chamber of Commerce **[65536]**

Trout Unlimited Canada **[9340]**

Troutdale Area Chamber of Commerce **[64276]**

Troy Area Chamber of Commerce **[59678]**, **[62056]**, **[63805]**

"Troy plan draws interest from big-name developers" in *Crain's Detroit Business* (Vol. 19, No. 9, March 3, 2003, pp. 3) **[7501]**, **[12648]**, **[20692]**, **[21028]**, **[22573]**, **[25042]**, **[28920]**

Troy Chamber of Commerce **[61438]**

Troy State University–Small Business Development Center **[56786]**

TR's Last-MileTelecom Report **[19807]**

Truck Cover and Tarp Association Membership Directory **[1987]**

Truck-Frame and Axle Repair Association **[22604]**

Truck Frame & Axle Repair Association-Membership Directory **[4363]**, **[25410]**

Truck Parts & Service **[22643]**

Truck Renting and Leasing Association **[2072]**

Truck Sales & Leasing Magazine **[2087]**, **[21185]**

"Truck stop" in *Crain's Detroit Business* (Vol. 19, No. 12, March 24, 2003, pp. 1) **[1981]**, **[18150]**, **[25411]**, **[43856]**, **[46465]**

Truck & SUV Performance **[18184]**

Truck and Van Service Manual 1990-94 **[22619]**

Truck West **[25444]**

Truckee-Donner Chamber of Commerce **[57834]**

Truckee Meadows Community College–Institute for Business and Industry **[62380]**

Trucker's Connection **[25445]**

"Trucking firms hope bridge lanes cut shipping costs" in *Crain's Detroit Business* (Vol. 18, No. 19, May 13, 2002, pp. 28) **[25412]**, **[43857]**, **[54999]**

"Trucking Industry Faces Driver Shortage" in *Inc.* (November 1, 2004) **[25413]**, **[42446]**

Trucking Management, Inc. **[25371]**

"Trucking Stocks: Downshifting Soon?" in *Business Week Online* (February 9, 2005) **[15545]**, **[25414]**

Truckload Carriers Association **[25372]**, **[25453]**

"The true believer" in *Red Herring* (March 2003, pp. 56) **[31076]**, **[42076]**, **[46466]**, **[50982]**, **[52220]**

"True Blue" in *Entrepreneur* (Vol. 31, No. 8, August 2003, pp. 46) **[6848]**, **[49329]**

True to Yourself: Leading a Values-Based Business **[28921]**, **[36888]**, **[45769]**

Truepilot, LLC **[63469]**

TruePresence **[14684]**, **[42805]**

TruePresence LLC **[26031]**

TrueStar for Women **[19530]**

Trufant Area Chamber of Commerce **[61439]**

Truly Nolen **[19044]**

"Truly Personal Entertainment" in *Sales & Marketing Management* (Vol. 158, October 2006, No. 10, pp. 52) **[30434]**, **[42077]**

"Truly 'Small' Business" in *My Business* (June/July 2002, pp. 45) **[4319]**, **[34629]**, **[37805]**, **[56769]**

Truman State University–Small Business Development Center **[61885]**

Trumann Area Chamber of Commerce **[57222]**

Truman's Scientific Guide to Pest Control Operations **[19027]**

Trumbull County Law Library Association–Library **[24189]**

Trump University Entrepreneurship 101 **[33269]**, **[36889]**

Trumpet for Beginners **[17643]**

Trussville Area Chamber of Commerce **[56895]**

"The Trust Factor" in *Small Business Opportunities* (Vol. 16, No. 2, March 2004, pp. 18, 20) **[51881]**

"Trust is a must" in *Entrepreneur* (Vol. 30, No. 10, October 2002, pp. 70) **[36890]**, **[37518]**

"Trust toppers" in *Realtor Magazine* (Vol. 35, No. 9, September 2002, pp. 22) **[39642]**

Trust Your Team **[35205]**

"Trustbuster" in *Forbes* (Vol. 175, February 14, 2005, No. 3, pp. 86) **[24611]**, **[40784]**

Trustee **[41303]**

"Trusting Credit Counselors" in *Black Enterprise* (Vol. 34, No. 7, February 2004, pp. 140) **[8359]**, **[8400]**, **[8646]**, **[31594]**

"Trusting Your Instincts: Crystal Winslow Followed Her Heart to Become an Author" in *Black Enterprise* (Vol. 34, No. 7, February 2004) **[2733]**, **[2749]**, **[56451]**, **[59015]**

Trussville Chamber of Commerce **[56896]**

"Truth or Consequences" in *Red Herring* (No. 99, June 15 & July 1, 2001, pp. 120) **[6973]**, **[23241]**, **[42078]**, **[50983]**

Truth or Consequences/Sierra County Chamber of Commerce **[62716]**

"The Truth Is Out There" in *Entrepreneur* (Vol. 33, August 2005, No. 8, pp. 8) **[820]**, **[36142]**, **[37519]**, **[47669]**

"Try Again: Business Fell Flat? No Use Whining About It." in *Entrepreneur* (Vol. 32, December 2004, No. 12, pp. 102) **[36891]**

TRY US National Minority Business Directory **[48457]**

"Trying to Play their Cards Right" in *Crain's New York Business* (Vol. 20, No. 12, March 22, 2004, pp. 20) **[8803]**, **[40785]**, **[41122]**

"Trying to Reach a Senior Level Executive?" in *Sales & Marketing Management* (Vol. 159, January-February 2007, No. 1, pp. 9) **[31235]**, **[47670]**, **[51882]**

"Trying Times: Every Once in a While, You'll Meet Difficult Customers" in *Entrepreneur* (Vol. 31, No. 9, July 2003, pp. 80) **[31887]**, **[51883]**

TS2 - The Trade Show About Trade Shows **[55248]**

TSG Capital Group, L.L.C. **[58617]**

TTC Ventures **[61128]**

TTouch for Dogs and Puppies **[19130]**

Tualatin Chamber of Commerce **[64277]**

Tuality Health–Information Resource Center **[19541]**

Tuba for Beginners **[17644]**

Tubac Chamber of Commerce **[57077]**

Tubby's Sub Shops, Inc. **[8580]**, **[21999]**

Tuckerman Chamber of Commerce **[57223]**

"Tucson, Ariz., Senior Citizen Keeps Moving with Dance Studio" in *Arizona Daily Star* (October 7, 2002) **[8454]**, **[52486]**

Tucson Metropolitan Chamber of Commerce **[57078]**

Tucson Pima Public Library–Grants and Nonprofit Information Collection **[10780]**

Tucumcari-Quay County Chamber of Commerce **[62717]**

Tudor's Biscuit World **[22000]**

Tuesday **[24767]**

Tuffy Auto Service Centers **[22705]**

Tufts-New England Medical Center–Division of Clinical Care Research **[41414]**

Tufts University
Hirsh Health Sciences Library **[18513]**
Office of the Associate Provost for Research **[61149]**

Tug Valley Chamber of Commerce **[66302]**

"A Tug of War: Real Deal: You Can't Have It All." in *Entrepreneur* (Vol. 31, No. 9, September 2003, pp. 81) **[27520]**, **[45770]**

Tulare Chamber of Commerce **[57835]**

Tulia Chamber of Commerce **[65537]**

Tullahoma Area Chamber of Commerce **[64982]**

"Tulsa-based Dollar Thrifty Automotive Group Buys Franchise" in *Journal Record (Oklahoma City, OK)* (February 5, 2007) **[15546]**, **[21358]**, **[38935]**, **[50226]**

"Tulsa-Based Dollar Thrifty Automotive Group Inc. to Outsource Call Center" in *Journal Record (Oklahoma City, OK)* (February 8, 2007) **[21359]**, **[31888]**, **[49749]**

"Tulsa-based Dollar Thrifty Buys Franchises" in *Journal Record* (February 4, 2004) **[15547]**, **[16058]**, **[21360]**, **[22081]**, **[38936]**, **[39389]**, **[47818]**, **[50227]**

"Tulsa-based SpiritBank Reconsiders Future of Branching" in *Journal Record (Oklahoma City, OK)* (February 8, 2007) **[10218]**, **[28922]**

Tulsa Better Business Bureau **[63935]**

Tulsa Community College **[64154]**

"Tulsa Home Sales See Another Record Year" in *Journal Record (Oklahoma City, OK)* (February 1, 2007) **[7502]**, **[20693]**, **[21029]**, **[28923]**

"Tulsa Insurance Company Sues Kansas-based Bank" in *Journal Record (Oklahoma City, OK)* (February 8, 2007) **[10219]**, **[29556]**, **[43407]**

Tulsa Metro Chamber **[64094]**

Tulsa Satellite Office–Small Business Development Center **[63921]**

Tulsa World (March 12, 2004); "New Shop in Tulsa, Okla., Helps Customers Sell Merchandise on eBay" in **[1838]**, **[7168]**, **[18654]**, **[52567]**

"Tulsan Reflects on 35 Years of Polishing Shoes" in *Journal Record (Oklahoma City, OK)* (February 1, 2007) **[22745]**, **[36892]**

Tumble Town **[19531]**

Tumwater Area Chamber of Commerce **[66187]**

Tune Up America: Detailing **[2039]**

"Tuned In" in *Hispanic Business* (December 2006, pp. 52) **[20342]**, **[48458]**

Tunex Automotive Specialists **[22706]**

Tunica County Chamber of Commerce **[61836]**

"Tuning In?" in *Entrepreneur* (Vol. 32, No. 4, April 2004, pp. 26) **[17776]**, **[40786]**

"Tuning In to LIN TV" in *Providence Business News* (Vol. 18, No. 19, August 25, 2003, pp. 4) **[24455]**

"Tuning In to Telework" in *Home Office Computing* (Vol. 18, No. 12, December 2000, pp. 107) **[20343]**, **[42742]**, **[54049]**

"Tuning in to the stock market: Two Hispanic radio firms launch IPOs" in *Hispanic Business* (Vol. 21, No. 12, December 1999, pp. 52) **[15548]**, **[20344]**, **[50228]**

Tuolumne County Chamber of Commerce **[57836]**

Tupper Lake Chamber of Commerce **[63032]**

Turbo Leadership Systems Ltd. **[3924]**, **[16686]**, **[35268]**

Turbo Reading Dynamics **[22817]**

TURF **[16124]**

Turf News **[16125]**

Turf Notes **[16053]**

Turf and Ornamental Communicators Association **[16002]**

"Turf wars" in *Crain's Detroit Business* (Vol. 19, No. 15, April 14, 2003, pp. 3) **[16030]**, **[23641]**, **[50229]**

TurfGrass TRENDS **[11481]**

"Turing the Page" in *Business 2.0* (Vol. 6, July 2005, No. 6, pp. 98-100) **[7846]**, **[42079]**, **[45771]**

Turkish American Chamber of Commerce **[59679]**

Turlock Chamber of Commerce **[57837]**

"Turn Back the Hands of Time: Travel to the Past with Windows' System Restore" in *Black Enterprise* (Vol. 34, No. 7, February 2004) **[49330]**, **[49347]**

"Turn Customer Input into Innovation" in *Harvard Business Review* (Vol. 80, No. 1, January 2002, pp. 91) **[28924]**, **[31889]**, **[47671]**

"Turn classmates into customers" in *Black Enterprise* (Vol. 33, No. 3, October 2002, pp. S2) **[47672]**, **[50697]**, **[50770]**, **[53943]**, **[56770]**

"Turn It Off!" in *Entrepreneur* (Vol. 31, No. 9, September 2003, pp. 77) **[5157]**, **[45772]**, **[54050]**

"Turn It Up" in *Entrepreneur* (Vol. 32, No. 1, January 2004, pp. 80) **[821]**, **[20345]**, **[47673]**

Turn of Phrase **[27708]**

"Turn Public Problems into Private Account" in *Harvard Business Review* (Vol. 81, No. 8, August 2003, pp. 129) **[39643]**, **[54269]**

Turnagain Enterprises Ltd. **[66689]**

Turnaround Inc. **[3824]**, **[3993]**, **[16674]**, **[31467]**, **[37835]**, **[46128]**, **[53118]**

Turnaround Management Association **[16496]**

Turner Consulting Group **[1154]**

Joe Turner **[7648]**, **[31989]**

J. Ed Turner Real Estate **[21098]**

"The Turning of Atlanta" in *Harvard Business Review* (Vol. 81, No. 12, December 2003, pp. 18) **[28925]**, **[52394]**

"Turning Chaos Into Order" in *Sales and Marketing.com* (Vol. 147, No. 2, February 2004, pp. 90) **[55000]**

"Turning Corn Into Clothing" in *Forbes* (Vol. 175, January 31, 2005, No. 2, pp. 98) **[5576]**, **[5725]**, **[15549]**, **[22731]**, **[50230]**

"Turning Designers Into Managers" in *Business Week* (No. 3761, December 10, 2001, pp. 60EU1) **[1615]**, **[33270]**, **[36893]**

"Turning Market Pain Into Prosperity" in *Black Enterprise* (Vol. 34, No. 3, October 2003, pp. 32) **[10220]**, **[15550]**, **[38427]**

"Turning an industry inside out: a conversation with Robert Redford" in *Harvard Business Review* (Vol. 80, No. 5, May 2002, pp. 57) **[9744]**

"Turning Receivables Into Received" in *Black Enterprise* (Vol. 34, No. 7, February 2004, pp. 46) **[286]**, **[3599]**, **[8401]**, **[26392]**, **[31236]**, **[31595]**

"Turning Receivables Into Received: Don't Let Your Collections Process Fall Through the Cracks" in *Black Enterprise* (Vol. 34, No. 7) **[287]**, **[3600]**, **[8402]**, **[26393]**, **[31237]**, **[31596]**

"Turning the Silver Screen Gold" in *Hispanic Business* (March 2004, pp. 24-26, 28-29) **[9745]**, **[10221]**, **[15551]**, **[48459]**

"Turning South; Sterling Heights Pushes Redevelopment of Older Areas as Vacant Land Dries Up" in *Crain's Detroit Business* (Vol. 21) **[7503]**, **[28926]**, **[42080]**, **[51396]**

"Turning the Tables: You Worked for Them, and Now You Want Them to 'Work' for You" in *Entrepreneur* (Vol. 32, December 2004, No. 12) **[35705]**, **[46596]**

"Turning Vendors Into Partners" in *Inc.* (August 2005, pp. 94-98, 100) **[50231]**

"Turning Your Services Into a Product" in *Home Business* (Vol. 13, January/February 2006, No. 1, pp. 62) **[3601]**, **[31238]**

Turok's Choice **[6143]**

Turtle Jack's Grillhouse Restaurant Inc. **[22001]**

Tuscarawas County Chamber of Commerce **[63806]**

Tuscola Chamber of Commerce **[59680]**

Tuscola County Economic Development Corp.–Small Business Development Center **[61224]**

Tuskegee University–Center for Biomedical Research - RCMI Carver Research Foundation **[56924]**

Tustin Chamber of Commerce **[57838]**

Tustin Women in Chamber of Commerce **[57839]**

Tutoring Club LLC **[25486]**

TV Blueprint **[4146]**

"TV to Go" in *Entrepreneur* (Vol. 32, October 2004, No. 10, pp. 24) **[7747]**, **[14551]**, **[24345]**, **[42081]**

TV Guide **[4147]**, **[24480]**

TV International Daily **[4148]**, **[24481]**

"TV One Auditions District for HQ" in *Washington Business Journal* (Vol. 22, No. 9, July 4, 2003, pp. 1) **[24456]**, **[47674]**, **[52746]**

TV Ontario–Library **[24509]**

TV Technology **[24347]**, **[24482]**

TVM Techno Venture Management **[61129]**

Twain Harte Area Chamber of Commerce **[57840]**

TWD & Associates **[46129]**, **[55048]**

Tweed-Weber Inc. **[46130]**

Twelve Steps to Superior Customer Service **[31951]**

20 Active Training Programs **[33271]**

21st Century Manufacturing Enterprise Strategy, Vol. I: An Industry-Led View **[46467]**

21st Century Manufacturing Enterprise Strategy, Vol. II: Infrastructure **[46468]**

25 Activities for Teams **[35127]**

"$25M to Aid Slow Border Crossings on Fast Track" in *Crain's Detroit Business* (V. 17, No. 44, 10/22/2001) **[39644]**, **[43858]**

Twenty-Five Tips for Customer Service: An Action Plan for Service Success **[31890]**

The Twenty-Minute Counselor: Transforming Brief Conversations into Effective Helping Experience **[4404]**

"Twenty Nine Percent of State's Farmers are Female" in *Journal Record* (February 4, 2004) **[26551]**, **[27460]**, **[53637]**, **[56452]**

"23 Unsold Condos Financed in Coral Gables" in *Daily Business Review* (Vol. 77, No. 146, January 7, 2003, pp. A4) **[17448]**, **[20694]**

"20 Top Biz for 2002" in *Small Business Opportunities* (V. 14, No. 1, 1/2002, pp. 22-24, 26, 28, 30, 32, 34, 36, 38, 40, 130) **[2024]**, **[2227]**, **[6399]**, **[7115]**, **[8431]**, **[8682]**, **[11768]**, **[11996]**, **[13054]**, **[15913]**, **[15987]**, **[17308]**, **[20009]**, **[22783]**, **[35706]**, **[38691]**, **[39102]**, **[52503]**

Twenty Ways to Improve Customer Service **[31891]**

The 21st Century Manger **[16556]**

Twentynine Palms Chamber of Commerce **[57841]**

TWICE **[25604]**

"Twice as Nice" in *Home Office Computing* (Vol. 18, No. 8, August 2000, pp. 40) **[42743]**, **[49331]**

Twin Cities North Chamber of Commerce **[61672]**

Twin Cities Quorum **[61673]**

Twin Cities Regional Office–University of St. Thomas–College of Business–Small Business Development Center **[61537]**

Twin City Area Chamber of Commerce **[62057]**

Twin City Chamber of Commerce **[63807]**

Twin Falls Area Chamber of Commerce **[59335]**

"Twin Picks" in *Entrepreneur* (Vol. 32, December 2004, No. 12, pp. 95) **[822]**, **[30978]**, **[47675]**

Twinsburg Chamber of Commerce **[63808]**

TwinWest Chamber of Commerce **[61674]**

Twisp Chamber of Commerce **[66188]**

"Two projects worth $27M planned for Royal Oak" in *Crain's Detroit Business* (Vol. 19, No. 16, April 21, 2003, pp. 3) **[7504]**, **[20695]**, **[21030]**, **[28927]**

"Two Au Bon Pain Restaurants in Baltimore Provide Nutritional Information on Computer Kiosk" in *Daily Record (Baltimore)* (Nov.17,2003) **[15945]**, **[21654]**

Two Blonds & A Brunette Gift Co. **[42806]**

Two-Can Publishing **[62639]**

"Two Companies Find Investment at Long Island VC Forum" in *Long Island Business News* (February 13, 2004) **[44679]**, **[55876]**

"Two Detroit Riverfront Projects Win Tax Breaks" in *Crain's Detroit Business* (Vol. 22, November 27, 2006, No. 48, pp. 25) **[21031]**, **[32756]**, **[39947]**, **[54846]**

U

Understanding Business Valuation: A Practical Guide to Valuing Small to Medium-Sized Businesses **[38429]**

Understanding Cats **[19171]**

Understanding Desktop Publishing **[8646]**

Understanding EEOC, Part 1-3 **[42936]**, **[48626]**

Understanding Financial Statements **[38430]**

Understanding and Managing Financial Information: The Non-financial Manager's Guide **[38431]**

Understanding the New Age **[17917]**

Understanding the New Security and Compliance Regulations for Export/Import: What Every Supply Chain manager Needs to Know **[29085]**

Understanding Novelty: Information, Technological Change, and the Patent System **[44174]**

Understanding Small Business **[29562]**, **[36902]**

"Understanding Women is Key to Biz Success, Author Says" in *Crain's Detroit Business* (Vol. 22, November 20, 2006, No. 47, pp. 6) **[28936]**, **[30034]**, **[47681]**, **[56457]**

Understanding Workers Compensation **[26945]**

Understanding Workers' Compensation: A Guide for Safety & Health Professionals **[30742]**

"Understanding Your Risk Portfolio" in *Rough Notes* (Vol. 145, No. 9, September 2002, pp. 58) **[13506]**, **[43410]**

Underwriting the Self-Employed Borrower Correspondence Course **[44681]**

"Unemployment higher in 2002, but rate of job loss slowed" in *Crain's Detroit Business* (Vol. 19, No. 9, March 3, 2003, pp. 1) **[28937]**, **[32762]**

Unemployment Compensation: A Cost You Can Cut **[30743]**

Unemployment Insurance Reports with Social Security **[43438]**

"Unemployment changes are 'mixed bag' for business, labor" in *Crain's Detroit Business* (Vol. 18, No. 15, 2002, pp. 6) **[39651]**, **[40790]**

"Unemployment, workers' comp may split again" in *Crain's Detroit Business* (Vol. 19, No. 5, February 3, 2003, pp. 7) **[40791]**

"Unfinished business: the disappearing Tax Act of 2001" in *Tax Notes* (Vol. 91, No. 11, June 4, 2001, pp. 1652-1653) **[24066]**, **[39949]**, **[54850]**

"Unforgettable as Usual" in *Home Business* (Vol. 12, October 2005, No. 5, pp. 36, 100) **[42746]**, **[51886]**

"Unhappy LPs Pass on New Mayfield Fund" in *Venture Capital Journal* (September 1, 2005) **[50476]**, **[55880]**

"Unhealthy Costs" in *Hispanic Business* (November 2006, pp. 58, 60, 62) **[13507]**, **[41126]**, **[43411]**

"Unhelpful critique" in *Waste News* (Vol. 7, No. 16, December 10, 2001, pp. 8) **[6186]**, **[6418]**, **[6849]**, **[21260]**, **[37332]**, **[54051]**

Unicash Financial Centres **[5263]**

Uniclean Systems **[3387]**

Unicoi County Chamber of Commerce **[64983]**

Uniglobe Travel (USA), LLC **[25345]**

Unilever Bestfoods
  Library/Information Center **[11402]**
  Technical Center–Information Center **[7837]**, **[18514]**

Unilever HPC NA–Research Library **[7951]**

"Uninsured: a Vexing Problem" in *Crain's New York Business* (Vol. 23, January 15, 2007, No.3, pp. 12) **[13508]**, **[26946]**, **[43412]**

"Union-Based Del Labs Has Strong Fourth Quarter" in *Long Island Business News* (February 27, 2004) **[2609]**, **[7907]**, **[8804]**

Union of Canadian Transportation Employees **[55278]**

Union Chamber of Commerce **[61837]**, **[62058]**

Union City Chamber of Commerce **[57842]**, **[60010]**

Union Communication Services Inc. **[60902]**

Union County Chamber of Commerce **[59681]**, **[63434]**, **[63809]**, **[64279]**, **[64784]**

Union Labor Report Weekly Newsletter **[55334]**

"Union, Nursing Home Owners in Tense Negotiations" in *Chicago Tribune* (March 2, 2005) **[460]**, **[18341]**, **[41127]**, **[55315]**

Union Parish Chamber of Commerce **[60672]**

"Union Paychecks Could Be Bigger in 2005, But At a Cost" in *Kansas City Star* (February 22, 2005) **[13509]**, **[26947]**, **[43413]**, **[55316]**

Union Springs/Bullock County Chamber of Commerce **[56897]**

"Union Station Has the Blues Over Loss of Hockey, Low Sales" in *St. Louis Post-Dispatch* (January 13, 2005) **[11171]**, **[15947]**, **[21656]**, **[39652]**

Union Township Chamber of Commerce **[62568]**

Union Venture Corp. **[58177]**

"Unions Buying Amalgamated; CFL, Other Groups Take Stake in Bank Long Tied to Labor" in *Crains Chicago Business* (Vol. 26, No. 51) **[10222]**, **[15555]**, **[50235]**, **[55317]**

"Unions Buying Amalgamated" in *Crain's Chicago Business* (Vol. 26, No. 51, December 22, 2003, pp. 3) **[10223]**, **[15556]**, **[50236]**, **[55318]**

"Union's Job is to Protect Due Process, Not Bad Teachers" in *Crain's Chicago Business* (Vol. 29, December 2006, No. 51, pp.) **[40792]**, **[55319]**

"Unions shouldn't labor in financial secrecy" in *Crain's Detroit Business* (Vol. 18, No. 16, April 22, 2002, pp. 8) **[40793]**, **[55320]**

Uniplex: A Guide to Integrated Office Automation **[49334]**

Unique 3-in-1 Research & Development Directory **[50984]**

UNISYS Corporation
  Corporate Library **[6552]**
  Technical Information Center **[6553]**, **[23320]**
  West Coast Information Center **[6554]**, **[23321]**

UNITE HERE **[12509]**

United Agribusiness League **[26465]**

United American Healthcare Corp. **[12414]**

United Capital Mortgage Assistance, L.L.C. **[20758]**

United Cat Federation **[1182]**

United Chamber of Commerce **[61009]**

United Check Cashing **[5264]**

United Dairy Industry Association **[12763]**

"United Front" in *Entrepreneur* (Vol. 33, January 2005, No. 1, pp. 47) **[14555]**, **[27521]**, **[34636]**, **[49335]**

United Insurance Consultants Inc. **[43444]**

The United Insurance Group **[43452]**

United Kennel Club **[1183]**

United Library Services Inc. **[66674]**

United Marketing Solutions **[897]**, **[47923]**

United Methodist Association of Health and Welfare Ministries **[40952]**

United Motorcoach Association **[24229]**

United Nations Association of Southern Arizona–Education Resource Center **[9459]**

United Press International (December 5, 2003); "Dating Service: Don't Call Anymore" in **[7053]**

United Press International (June 24, 2003); "Sears, Dell Unplug Kiosk Venture" in **[15938]**

United Professional Horsemen's Association **[12452]**

United Shipping Solutions **[10721]**

U.S. Agency for International Development
  Freedom of Information Act Request–Bureau for Management/Information and Records Division **[66786]**
  Office of the Inspector General **[66787]**
  USAID Library **[66788]**
  USAID Office of Procurement **[66789]**

United States Amateur Confederation of Roller Skating **[22834]**

U.S. Armed Forces - School of Music–Reference Library **[17707]**

U.S. Army
  Center for Health Promotion & Preventive Medicine–Library **[56701]**
  Engineer Research and Development Center–Airfields, Pavements, and Mobility Information Analysis Center **[2553]**
  Engineer Research and Development Center–Research Library **[2554]**

United States Association for Small Business and Entrepreneurship **[35742]**

U.S. Austrian Chamber of Commerce **[43529]**

U.S. Bancorp Piper Jaffray Private Capital **[61711]**

U.S. Banker Online **[17477]**

U.S. Bistro **[8581]**

U.S. Book Publishing Industry **[2758]**

United States Bowling Congress **[3100]**

The U.S. Bread Market **[2261]**

U.S. Bureau of Alcohol, Tobacco and Firearms
  National Laboratory Library **[11753]**, **[24641]**
  Reference Library **[24642]**

U.S. Bureau of Mines–Twin Cities Research Center–Library **[56702]**

U.S. Business Directory File **[39744]**

"U.S.-Canada Agricultural Trade to Get Stickier in 2007" in *Kiplinger Letter* (Vol. 78, January 19, 2007, No. 2) **[13014]**, **[22409]**, **[26554]**, **[43860]**

United States and Canadian Academy of Pathology Convention & Exhibits **[17225]**

"U.S. CFOs Bullish on Hiring" in *Long Island Business News* (February 27, 2004) **[42447]**, **[45779]**, **[54052]**

U.S. Child Day Care Services: An Industry Analysis 6th Edition **[5349]**

United States Commission on Minority Business Development, Final Report **[48462]**

United States Competitive Aerobics Federation **[19367]**

U.S. Composting Council **[21211]**

"U.S. Cotton Farmers Waiting Out the Market for Better Prices" in *Kiplinger Letter* (Vol. 78, January 19, 2007, No. 4) **[13015]**, **[26555]**, **[43861]**

United States Council for International Business **[12933]**, **[43530]**

U.S. Credit Bureau and Collections Agencies: An Industry Analysis **[8408]**

United States Cutting Tool Institute **[16356]**

United States Cycling Federation **[2496]**

U.S. Department of Agriculture
  Administrative Services Division–Farmers Home Administration–Office of Small and Disadvantaged Business Utilization Coordinator **[67399]**
  Administrative Services Division–Food and Nutrition Service–Office of Small and Disadvantaged Business Utilization Coordinator **[67400]**
  Administrative Services Division–Rural Electrification Administration–Office of Small and Disadvantaged Business Utilization Coordinator **[67401]**
  Administrative Services Division–U.S. Forest Service–Office of Small and Disadvantaged Business Utilization Coordinator **[67402]**
  Agricultural Research Service–Office of Small and Disadvantaged Business Utilization **[67403]**
  Agricultural Research Service–Western Regional Research Center Library **[18515]**
  Contracting and Acquisition Management Division–Agricultural Stabilization and Conservation Service–Office of Small and Disadvantaged Business Utilization Coordinator **[67404]**
  Contracts and Procurement Branch–Office of the Inspector General–Office of Small and Disadvantaged Business Utilization Coordinator **[67405]**
  Cooperative State Research, Education, and Extension Service (CSREES)–Small Business Innovation Research Representative **[67406]**
  Economic Research Service–ERS Reference Center **[26668]**
  Management Services Branch–Extension Service–Office of Small and Disadvantaged Business Utilization Coordinator **[67407]**
  Management Services Division–Animal and Plant Health Inspection Service–Office of Small and Disadvantaged Business Utilization Coordinator **[67408]**
  Management Services Division–Farm Service Agency–Office of Small and Disadvantaged Business Utilization Coordinator **[67409]**

Management Services Division–Natural Resources Conservation Service–Office of Small and Disadvantaged Business Utilization Coordinator [67410]

National Agricultural Library–Food and Nutrition Information Center [12045], [18516]

National Agricultural Library–Rural Information Center [32837], [53140]

Office of Small and Disadvantaged Business Utilization [67398]

Procurement Division–Office of Operations–Office of Small and Disadvantaged Business Utilization Coordinator [67411]

Procurement and Property Branch–Food Safety and Inspection Service [67412]

Procurement, Property and Space–Economics Management Staff [67413]

Resources Management Staff–Office of Communications [67414]

U.S.D.A. Forest Service–Forest Products Laboratory–Library [16344]

U.S. Department of Commerce
Economic Development Administration [67416]
Library & Information Services [29056]
Office of Business Liaison [67417]
Office of Small and Disadvantaged Business Utilization [67415]

U.S. Dept. of Defense
Central Repository for Military Working Dog Records–Archives [1226], [19136]
Office of Small and Disadvantaged Business Utilization [67421]

U.S. Department of Education
Assistant Secretary for Educational Research and Improvement–Small Business Innovation Research Program Coordinator [67479]
Office of Small and Disadvantaged Business Utilization [67478]

U.S. Department of Energy
Alaska Power Administration [67515]
Albuquerque Operations Office [67487]
Amarillo Field Office [67495]
Argonne Area Office [67501]
Argonne National Laboratory (West)–Idaho Operations Office [67480]
Atlanta Support Office [67511]
Bartlesville Project Office [67512]
Bettis Atomic Power Laboratory [67481]
Bonneville Power Administration [67516]
Boston Regional Office [67502]
Brookhaven Area Office [67503]
Carlsbad Field Office [67496]
Chicago Operations Office [67488]
Chicago Regional Office [67504]
Denver Regional Office [67510]
Energy Efficiency and Renewable Energy–Golden Field Office [67505]
Energy Library [23351]
Firmi Site Office [67506]
Idaho Operations Office [67489]
Kirtland Area Office [67497]
Los Alamos Area Office [67498]
Morgantown Energy Technology Center [67513]
National Energy Technology Laboratory (NETL-MGN) [67482]
Nevada Operations Office [67490]
Oak Ridge Operations Office [67491]
Oakland Operations Office [67492]
Office of Kansas City Site Operations [65060], [67499]
Philadelphia Regional Support Office [67507]
Pinellas Area Office [67500]
Pittsburgh Energy Technology Center [67514]
Pittsburgh Naval Reactors (PNR) [67483]
Princeton Area Office [67508]
Richland Operations Office [67493]
Savannah River Operations Office [67494]
Schenectady Navel Reactors Office [67484]

Southeastern Power Administration [67517]
Southwestern Power Administration [67518]
U.S. Department of Homeland Security–Environmental Measurements Lab [67509]
Western Area Power Administration [67519]

U.S. Department of Energy, Headquarters–Office of Small and Disadvantaged Business Utilization [67486]

U.S. Department of Health and Human Services
Office for Civil Rights–Equal Employment Opportunity/Affirmation Action Coordinator [67522]
Office of Small and Disadvantaged Business Utilization [67521]

U.S. Department of Health and Human Services (Region 1) [67526]

U.S. Department of Health and Human Services (Region 2) [67527]

U.S. Department of Health and Human Services (Region 3) [67528]

U.S. Department of Health and Human Services (Region 4) [67529]

U.S. Department of Health and Human Services (Region 5) [67530]

U.S. Department of Health and Human Services (Region 6) [67531]

U.S. Department of Health and Human Services (Region 7) [67532]

U.S. Department of Health and Human Services (Region 8) [67533]

U.S. Department of Health and Human Services (Region 9) [67534]

U.S. Department of Health and Human Services (Region 10) [67535]

U.S. Department of Homeland Security
Office for Domestic Preparedness (ODP) [67138]
Office of Procurement Operations [67139]
Office of Small and Disadvantaged Business Utilization [67140]
U.S. Citizenship and Immigration Services–Procurement Division [67141]

U.S. Department of Housing and Urban Development
Deputy Assistant Secretary for Economic Development–Grants Management Division [67542]
Library [7697]
Office of the Chief Procurement Officer [67543]
Office of Departmental Operations and Coordination [67544]
Office of Healthy Homes and Lead Hazard [67545]
Office of Security and Emergency Planning [67546]
Office of Small and Disadvantaged Business Utilization [67547], [67548]
Southeast/Caribbean–Library [20088]

U.S. Department of Housing and Urban Development (Region 1) [67549]

U.S. Department of Housing and Urban Development (Region 2) [67550]

U.S. Department of Housing and Urban Development (Region 3) [67551]

U.S. Department of Housing and Urban Development (Region 4) [67552]

U.S. Department of Housing and Urban Development (Region 5) [67553]

U.S. Department of Housing and Urban Development (Region 6) [67554]

U.S. Department of Housing and Urban Development (Region 7) [67555]

U.S. Department of Housing and Urban Development (Region 8) [67556]

U.S. Department of Housing and Urban Development (Region 9) [67557]

U.S. Department of Housing and Urban Development (Region 10) [67558]

U.S. Department of the Interior
Office of Small and Disadvantaged Business Utilization [67559], [67561]
Office of the Solicitor [67560]

U.S. Department of Justice
Federal Bureau of Investigation–Seattle Field Office [67635]
Office of Small and Disadvantaged Business Utilization [67636]

U.S. Dept. of Labor
Occupational Safety and Health Administration–Region VIII Library [56703]
Office of Small Business and Minority Affairs [67646]
OSHA–Billings Area Office Library [56704]
OSHA–Region III Library [56705]
OSHA–Region X Library [56706]
OSHA–Technical Data Center [56707]
OSHA - Office of Training & Education–H. Lee Saltsgaver Library [56708]

U.S. Department of State
Bureau of Diplomatic Security–Office of Foreign Missions [67647]
Office of Civil Rights [67648]
Office of the Inspector General [67649]
Office of Small and Disadvantaged Business Utilization [67650]

U.S. Department of Transportation
Coast Guard–Procurement Management Division–Minority Business Program [67659]
Federal Aviation Administration–Small Business Utilization Office [67660]
Federal Highway Administration–Central Federal Lands Highway Division [67651]
Federal Highway Administration–Eastern Federal Lands Highway Division–Small and Disadvantaged Business Utilization Liaison [67661]
Federal Highway Administration–Federal Lands Highway Division [67652]
Federal Highway Administration–Small and Disadvantaged Business Utilization Liaison [67662]
Federal Highway Administration–Western Federal Lands Highway Division [67653]
Federal Railroad Administration–Small and Disadvantaged Business Utilization Liaison [67663]
Federal Transit Administration–Small and Disadvantaged Business Utilization Liaison [67664]
John A. Volpe National Transportation Center–Office of Management Services–Contracts and Small Business Programs Branch [67654]
Maritime Administration–Small and Disadvantaged Business Utilization Liaison–Office of Acquisition [67665]
National Highway Traffic Safety Administration–Small and Minority Business Utilization Liaison–Office of Contracts and Procurement [67666]
Office of Small and Disadvantaged Business Utilization [67658]
Pipeline and Hazardous Materials Safety Administration [67655]
Research and Innovative Technology Administration (RITA) [67656]
Research and Special Programs Administration–Office of Contracts and Administration [67667]
St. Lawrence Seaway Development Corporation–Office of the Associate Administrator [67668]
Transportation Safety Institute–Operations Support Division [67657]

U.S. Department of the Treasury
Austin Financial Center [67689]
Birmingham Financial Center [67690]
Bureau of Alcohol, Tobacco Tax and Trade (TTB) [67670]
Bureau of Engraving and Printing [67671]
Bureau of the Public Debt [67672]
Chicago Financial Center [67691]
Comptroller of the Currency [67673]

Departmental Offices–Procurement Services Division **[67674]**
Federal Law Enforcement Training Center **[67675]**
Financial Management Service **[67676]**
Internal Revenue Service **[67682]**
Internal Revenue Service–Detroit Computing Center **[67687]**
Internal Revenue Service–Martinsburg Computing Center **[67688]**
Internal Revenue Service–Mid-States Region **[67683]**
Internal Revenue Service–Northeast Region **[67684]**
Internal Revenue Service–Southeast Region **[67685]**
Internal Revenue Service–Western Region **[67686]**
Kansas City Financial Center **[67692]**
Office of Small and Disadvantaged Business Utilization **[67669]**
Office of Thrift Supervision **[67677]**
Philadelphia Financial Center **[67693]**
San Francisco Financial Center **[67694]**
Treasury Library **[427]**, **[24190]**
U.S. Customs Service **[67678]**
U.S. Customs Service–Field Procurement Services **[67679]**
U.S. Mint **[67680]**
U.S. Secret Service **[67681]**
U.S. Department of Veterans Affairs
Office of Small and Disadvantaged Business Utilization **[67695]**
Public Health and Environmental Hazards **[67696]**
"U.S. District Court of Appeals Sides with Baby Bells Over 1996 Telecommunications Act" in *Long Island Business News* (March 12, 2004) **[5159]**, **[5542]**, **[29563]**, **[30495]**, **[30979]**, **[31616]**, **[39097]**, **[40794]**
"U.S. District Court Issues Injunction to Prevent Hi-Tech Pharmacal..." in *Long Island Business News* (March 5, 2004) **[8805]**, **[29564]**, **[44175]**
United States Dressage Federation **[12453]**
U.S. Drug Enforcement Administration
Library **[54394]**
Office of Procurement **[67640]**
U.S. Environmental Protection Agency
Andrew W. Breidenbach Environmental Research Center Library **[19050]**
Headquarters Library **[9460]**, **[9509]**, **[11985]**
Library **[9461]**, **[9510]**
National Enforcement Investigations Center–Environmental Forensics Library **[19051]**
U.S. Equal Employment Opportunity Commission–Library **[32126]**
United States Equestrian Federation **[12454]**
United States Eventing Association **[12455]**
U.S. Export Assistance–North Seattle Community College–Small Business Development Center **[66025]**
"U.S. Exports in 2007" in *Kiplinger Letter* (Vol. 78, January 5, 2007, No. 1) **[13016]**, **[28938]**, **[32763]**, **[43862]**
U.S. Exports of Merchandise **[13041]**
"U.S. Fails to Deal with Threat of Cyberattack, Experts Says" in *San Jose Mercury News* (February 17, 2005) **[22410]**, **[40795]**
U.S. Farm News (Vol. 25, No. 3, Autumn 2001, pp. 7); "Congress Debates Fate of U.S. Agriculture" in **[26494]**, **[40275]**
U.S. Farm News (Vol. 25, No. 3, Autumn 2001, pp. 6-7); "Will Congress Act to Preserve Family Type Farming?" in **[26561]**, **[37814]**, **[40846]**
U.S. Federal Aviation Administration–Mike Monroney Aeronautical Center Library **[991]**
U.S. Federal Bureau of Investigation–Administrative Services Division–Property Procurement and Management **[67641]**
U.S. Federal Communications Commission–Library **[5236]**, **[8672]**
U.S. Federal Prisons Industries/UNICOR–Procurement Division **[67642]**

U.S. Fish and Wildlife Service
Budget and Administration Division–Region 5–Northeast Regional Office **[67600]**
Business Utilization and Development Specialist–Branch of Construction Contracting **[67601]**
Business Utilization and Development Specialist–Division of Contracting and General Services **[67602]**
Contracting & General Services Chief–Region 4 **[67603]**
Contracting & General Services Chief–Region 7 **[67604]**
Contracting & General Services Officer–Region 2 **[67605]**
Contracting Officer–Region 6 **[67606]**
Contracting & Procurement Officer–Region 3 **[67607]**
Policy, Management and Budget–Alaska Region **[67609]**
Policy, Management and Budget–Great Lakes, Big Rivers Region **[67610]**
Policy, Management and Budget–Mountain Prairie Region **[67611]**
Policy, Management and Budget–Northeast Regional Office **[67612]**
Policy, Management and Budget–Pacific Region **[67613]**
Policy, Management and Budget–Southeast Region **[67614]**
Policy, Management and Budget–Southwest Region **[67615]**
Procurement Assistant–Region 1 **[67608]**
U.S. Food & Drug Administration
Center for Devices & Radiological Health–Library HFZ-46 **[17291]**
Center for Food Safety & Applied Nutrition–CFSAN Branch Library **[7952]**, **[18517]**
Division of Contracts and Grants Management–Office of Management **[67537]**
Division of Contracts and Grants Management–Small and Disadvantaged Business Utilization Specialist **[67538]**
Office of Small Business, Scientific, and Trade Affairs **[67539]**
U.S. Geological Survey
Business Utilization and Development Specialist **[67616]**, **[67618]**
Business Utilization and Development Specialist–Central Region **[67617]**
United States Golf Association **[11250]**, **[17321]**
Library **[11299]**
U.S. Government Management Policy **[40900]**
The United States Government Manual **[39950]**
The U.S. Greeting Cards Market **[11571]**
U.S. Hardware Industry Association **[11877]**
United States Harness Writers' Association **[8974]**
U.S. Health Care Financing Administration–Equal Employment Opportunity Office **[67523]**
U.S. Health Resources Services Administration–Grants and Procurement Management Division–Contracts Policies and Operations **[67540]**
United States Hispanic Chamber of Commerce **[48012]**
"U.S. Hispanic Market Has Special Character" in *Hispanic Business* (January/February 2005, pp. 8) **[43863]**, **[48463]**
U.S. Immigration and Naturalization Service–Human Resources and Administrative Services Division–Procurement Policy and Evaluation **[67643]**
U.S. International Trade Commission–National Library of International Trade **[13044]**
United States International Trade in Goods and Services **[43939]**
"The U.S. Is In Decline-And That's a Good Thing" in *Fortune* (Vol. 151, February 21, 2005, No. 4, pp. 58) **[28939]**, **[32764]**
United States-Italy Trade Directory **[13017]**
United States Judo Association **[16907]**
The U.S. Kids' Foods Market **[11685]**
The U.S. Lawn and Garden Market, 5th Edition **[11449]**

U.S. Lawns Inc. **[16168]**
The U.S. Lighting Fixtures Industry **[9115]**
U.S. Liquor Market **[15847]**, **[16238]**
The U.S. Market for Bottled, Enhanced and Flavored Water - 3rd Edition **[25712]**
The U.S. Market for Pleasure Boats **[16753]**
The U.S. Market for Vitamin, Minerals, and Herbal Supplements **[17926]**
U.S. Marshals Service–Procurement Policy and Oversight Team **[67644]**
U.S. Media, Inc. **[3926]**
U.S. Medical Resources Corp. **[63860]**
United States-Mexico Chamber of Commerce **[43531]**
"U.S.-Mexico Relations Remain on Front Burner" in *Hispanic Business* (Vol. 23, No. 11, November 2001, pp. 20) **[43864]**, **[48464]**
U.S. National Arboretum–Library **[10608]**, **[11541]**, **[16097]**
U.S. National Highway Traffic Safety Administration–Technical Information Services **[929]**, **[8746]**
United States National Institute of Dance **[8450]**
U.S. National Institute for Occupational Safety & Health–Library C-21 **[56709]**
U.S. National Oceanic & Atmospheric Administration–Library and Information Services Division–Central Library **[10482]**
U.S. National Park Service–Blue Ridge Parkway–Archives **[7698]**, **[16098]**
U.S. National Ski Hall of Fame and Museum–Roland Palmedo National Ski Library **[22876]**
"U.S. Needs Help from the Private Sector to Combat Terrorism" in *Venture Capital Journal* (Vol. 42, No. 9, September 2002, pp. 40) **[22411]**, **[37205]**, **[52221]**, **[55881]**
U.S. News & World Report: Building Your Fortune **[10323]**
U.S. Nuclear Regulatory Commission–Office of Small and Disadvantaged Business Utilization/Civil Rights **[67702]**
U.S. Nuclear Regulatory Commission (Region 1)–King of Prussia Regional Office **[67698]**
U.S. Nuclear Regulatory Commission (Region 2)–Atlanta Regional Office **[67699]**
U.S. Nuclear Regulatory Commission (Region 3)–Lisle Regional Office **[67700]**
U.S. Nuclear Regulatory Commission (Region 4)–Arlington Regional Office **[67701]**
U.S. Operator Services and Card Calling Markets **[19804]**
U.S. Pan Asian American Chamber of Commerce **[43532]**
The U.S. Pasta Market **[23531]**
U.S. PatentImages **[44216]**
United States Patents Quarterly **[44188]**
U.S. Payment Solutions **[4036]**
The U.S. Pizza Market **[19644]**
United States Pony Clubs **[12456]**
U.S. Postal Service
Administrative Operations–Information Technology Division **[67703]**
Chicago Service Center **[67704]**
Environmental and MRO Category Management Center **[67705]**
Field Operations - East **[67706]**
Field Operations - South **[67707]**
Field Operations - West **[67708]**
General Counsel–Business Services **[67709]**
Intelligent Mail and Address Quality **[67710]**
Investigations and Security–Dangerous Mail Investigations and Homeland Security **[67711]**
Memphis Purchasing Service Center **[67712]**
Office of the Inspector General **[67713]**
Office of Operations **[67714]**
Office of Small and Disadvantaged Business Utilization **[67718]**
San Francisco Purchasing Service Center **[67715]**
United States Postal Inspection Service **[67716]**

Master Index

"U.S. Soldier Returns from Iraq to Find How His Business Fared" in *Small Business Opportunities* (January 2006) **[36903]**, **[39653]**

U.S. Source Book of R & D Spenders **[50985]**, **[52222]**

U.S. Sources & Resources Volume: Alabama-New York 10935

U.S. Sources & Resources Volume: North Carolina-Wyoming 10935

United States Sports Massage Federation **[17002]**

United States Squash Racquets Association **[24567]**

The U.S. Tabletop Market **[12225]**

U.S. Taekwondo Union **[16908]**

U.S. Tax Court–Library **[428]**, **[24191]**

United States Tennis Association **[24568]**

United States Tour Operators Association **[24656]**, **[25139]**

U.S. Travel Data Center **[25140]**

U.S. Trout Farmers Association **[10454]**

U.S. Tuna Foundation **[10435]**, **[10455]**

U.S. Venture Partners **[58178]**

United States Water Fitness Association **[19369]**

U.S. Weekly Statistics **[10394]**, **[15783]**, **[17478]**

United Steelworkers of America - Canadian Branch **[55279]**

United Systems Software **[1461]**

United Way 2-1-1–Information & Referral Service **[491]**, **[18409]**

United Way of Rhode Island **[66978]**

"UnitedAuto seeks $250M for more acquisitions" in *Crain's Detroit Business* (Vol. 16, No. 50, December 11, 2000, p. 4) **[18151]**, **[28940]**

"UnitedAuto Dealerships Sued" in *Crain's Detroit Business* (Vol. 19, No. 45, November 10, 2003, pp. 4) **[18152]**, **[29565]**, **[30498]**

"UnitedAuto Sells Properties" in *Crain's Detroit Business* (January 26, 2004, pp. 20) **[15557]**, **[18153]**, **[38942]**

Universal City-North Hollywood Chamber of Commerce **[57843]**

"Universal connectivity" in *Entrepreneur* (Vol. 30, No. 1, January 2002, pp. 43) **[6850]**, **[6974]**, **[42084]**, **[49336]**

Universite de Montreal–Bibliotheque de Kinesiologie et d'Education Physique **[19542]**

University of Akron **[63892]**
  Fisher Institute for Professional Selling **[52015]**

University of Alabama
  Alabama International Trade Center **[56793]**
  Center for Business and Economic Research **[66818]**
  Environmental Institute **[11988]**
  Garner Center for Current Accounting Issues **[3006]**
  Office for Sponsored Programs **[56925]**
  Research Advisory Committee **[56926]**

University of Alabama at Birmingham
  Alabama Small Business Development Consortium–Small Business Development Center **[56787]**
  Lister Hill Center for Health Policy **[41415]**
  Office of Grants and Contracts Administration **[56927]**

University of Alaska - Anchorage **[66803]**
  Small Business Development Center **[56937]**, **[56981]**

University of Alaska Fairbanks
  Office of Sponsored Programs **[56983]**
  Procurement Technical Assistance Center Program **[56982]**
  Small Business Development Center **[56941]**

University at Albany, State University of New York–Institute for Informatics, Logics, and Security Studies **[6562]**

University of Alberta
  Canadian Circumpolar Institute–Northern Resources Research Centre **[9472]**
  Devonian Botanic Garden–Library **[11542]**, **[16099]**
  Institute for Public Economics **[32865]**

University of Arizona
  Architecture Research Laboratory **[1585]**
  Arizona Center on Aging **[18419]**
  Center for Creative Photography **[19339]**

Computer Engineering Research Laboratory **[14693]**
  Economic and Business Research Program–College of Business and Public Administration **[66824]**
  Karsten Turfgrass Research Facility **[16173]**
  Native American Research and Training Center **[41416]**
  Office of Vice President for Research and Graduate Studies **[57100]**

University of Arizona Foundation **[57101]**

University of Arkansas
  Arkansas Center for Technology Transfer **[57238]**
  Research Support and Sponsored Programs **[57239]**
  Small Business Development Center **[57118]**

University of Arkansas at Little Rock
  Institute for Economic Advancement **[24216]**
  Small Business Development Center **[57113]**, **[57119]**
  State Data Center **[66827]**

University of Arkansas - Monticello–Small Business Development Center–College of Technology - McGehee **[57120]**

University of Arkansas at Pine Bluff–Agriculture Research Center **[26696]**

University Associates Training Technologies **[33272]**

University Auxiliary Services, Inc. **[58215]**

University of Baltimore
  Information Systems Research Center **[13129]**
  Merrick School of Business **[60893]**

University of British Columbia
  Botanical Garden **[19734]**
  Bureau for Research on Applications of Information Technology **[43013]**
  Centre for Operations Excellence **[46164]**
  Fine Arts Division **[5621]**
  Fisheries Centre **[10493]**
  W. Maurice Young Entrepreneurship and Venture Capital Research Centre **[37057]**
  Wine Research Centre **[23587]**

University of Calgary
  Human Performance Laboratory **[19611]**
  Office of the Vice President, Research **[66670]**
  Vision and Aging Laboratory **[25677]**
  World Tourism Education and Research Centre **[24790]**

University of California
  California Institute for Energy and Environment **[1067]**
  Office of Technology Transfer **[58216]**
  State Governmental Relations Office **[58217]**

University of California at Berkeley
  Berkeley Roundtable on International Economy **[42147]**
  Botanical Garden–Library **[11543]**
  Center for Labor Research and Education **[41417]**
  Environmental Chemistry and Toxicology Laboratory **[19058]**
  Fisher Center for Real Estate and Urban Economics **[1401]**
  Giannini Foundation of Agricultural Economics–Research Library **[26669]**
  Institute of Governmental Studies **[50411]**
  Institute of Human Development–Harold E. Jones Child Study Center **[5461]**
  Marian Koshland Bioscience and Natural Resources Library **[18518]**
  School of Public Health–Labor Occupational Health Program Library **[56710]**
  Sponsored Projects Office **[58218]**
  UC Data Archive and Technical Assistance **[66834]**

University of California, Davis
  Agricultural and Resource Economics Library **[26670]**
  AIDS Virus Diagnostic Laboratory **[17247]**
  Air Quality Group **[1085]**

Arboretum–Library **[11544]**
  Center for Companion Animal Health **[1288]**
  Center for Equine Health **[12485]**
  Information Center for the Environment **[37376]**
  Office of Research **[58219]**
  University Libraries–Special Collections **[2481]**, **[3163]**, **[23585]**
  Veterinary Genetics Laboratory **[1229]**

University of California, Irvine
  Distributed Real-time Ever Available Microcomputing Laboratory **[6563]**
  Office of Research and Graduate Studies **[58220]**
  Office of Technology Alliances **[58221]**

University of California, Los Angeles
  Accounting Research Program **[431]**
  Department of Education & Information Studies–Multimedia & Information Technology Lab **[13127]**
  Department of Special Collections **[5944]**
  Grunwald Center for the Graphic Arts **[6090]**
  Harold and Paulina Price Center for Entrepreneurial Studies **[37218]**
  Jules Stein Eye Institute **[25678]**
  Music Library **[17708]**
  Research Program in Takeovers and Corporate Restructuring **[31006]**
  UCLA Film and Television Archive–Research and Study Center **[24510]**

University of California, San Diego
  The Arts Libraries **[1673]**
  Office of Contract and Grant Administration **[58222]**

University of California, San Francisco
  California AIDS Research Center **[17248]**
  Center for AIDS Prevention Studies **[17249]**
  Institute for Health Policy Studies **[41418]**
  San Francisco Injury Center **[1096]**

University of California, Santa Barbara–Office of Research **[58223]**

University of Central Florida
  Dick Pope, Sr. Institute for Tourism Studies **[24791]**
  Florida Solar Energy Center **[23357]**
  Kissimmee/Osceola Chamber of Commerce–Small Business Development Center **[58713]**
  Office of Research and Commercialization **[58993]**
  Small Business Development Center **[58714]**

University of Central Oklahoma–Small Business Development Center **[63922]**

University of Chicago–Center for Research in Security Prices **[10414]**

University of Cincinnati
  College Conservatory of Music–Gorno Memorial Music Library **[8498]**, **[17709]**
  Design, Architecture, Art & Planning Library **[5622]**
  SBDC **[63578]**
  Southwest Ohio Regional Data Center–Institute for Policy Research **[66956]**

University City Science Center **[64617]**

University of Colorado at Boulder
  Business Research Division **[24792]**
  Business Research Division–Graduate School of Business Administration **[66838]**
  Carl McGuire Center for International Studies **[32866]**
  Environmental Program **[9517]**
  Research Park **[58472]**
  Technology Transfer Office **[58473]**
  William M. White Business Library **[53141]**

University of Colorado-Denver
  Center for Health Services Research **[41419]**
  Center for Human Investment Policy **[41420]**

University of Connecticut
Center for International Community Health Studies [41421]
Connecticut Center for Economic Analysis [32867]
Connecticut Small Business Development Center [54110]
Environmental Research Institute [11989]
Institute for Teaching and Learning [33408]
Research Foundation [58626]
Small Business Development Center [58491]
University Center for Instructional Media and Technology [42148]
University of Connecticut (Greater Hartford Campus)–Small Business Development Center [58500]
University of Dayton–Research Institute [63886]
University of Delaware [67477]
Center for Molecular and Engineering Thermodynamics [52353]
College of Urban Affairs and Public Policy [66845]
Delaware Education Research and Development Center [33409]
Delaware SBDC Network [58639]
Delaware Small Business Development Center Network [58637]
Halophyte Biotechnology Center [26697]
Human Performance Laboratory [19612]
Institute for Public Administration [50412]
Office of the Vice Provost for Research [58655]
Small Business Development Center [58640]
University of Delaware Research Foundation [58656]
University of Denver
Penrose Library–Special Collections & Archives [7838]
School of Real Estate and Construction Management–Software Testing Center [20775]
University of Detroit-Mercy
Small Business Development Center Satellite Office [61225]
Sponsored Research Administration [61487]
University of District of Columbia–D.C. Water Resources Research Center–Library [25737]
University Film and Video Association [9686]
University Film and Video Association-Membership Directory [9746]
University of Florida
Biotechnology Development Incubator [58994]
Center for Applied Philosophy and Ethics in the Professions [54292]
Center for Exercise Science [19613]
Center for Nutritional Sciences [18527]
Center for Real Estate Studies [21121]
Database Systems Research and Development Center [6318]
Division of Sponsored Research [58995]
Florida Center for Solid and Hazardous Waste Management [11990]
Horse Research Center [12486]
Institute of Food and Agricultural Sciences [26698]
Institute of Food and Agricultural Sciences–Florida Medical Entomology Laboratory [19059]
Powell Center for Construction and Environment [37377]
Research and Education Center for Architectural Preservation [1586]
Solar Energy and Energy Conversion Laboratory [23358]
University of Georgia
Attapulgus Research Farm [10609]
Carl Vinson Institute of Government [50413]
Center for Insurance Education and Research [13615]
Center for Remote Sensing and Mapping Science [6564]

Institute for Behavioral Research–Center for Family Research [5462]
Office of Vice President for Research [59219]
Small Business Development Center [59025]
University of Georgia - Albany Office–Small Business Development Center [59031]
University of Georgia - Augusta Office–Small Business Development Center [59032]
University of Georgia - Brunswick Office–Small Business Development Center [59033]
University of Georgia - Columbus Office–Small Business Development Center [59034]
University of Georgia - Decatur Office–Small Business Development Center [59035]
University of Georgia - Gainesville Office–Small Business Development Center [59036]
University of Georgia Libraries–Government Documents Department [66857]
University of Georgia - Macon Office–Small Business Development Center [59037]
University of Georgia - Savannah Office–Small Business Development Center [59038]
University of Guam
Guam Small Business Development Center [66642]
Robert F. Kennedy Memorial Library–Instructional Media Division [4887], [6084]
University of Guelph
Arboretum [16103]
Guelph Turfgrass Institute [16174]
University of Hartford
Acoustics and Vibrations Laboratory [17849]
Construction Institute [7704]
William H. Mortensen Library–Anne Bunce Cheney Library [8120], [8267]
University of Hawaii
John A. Burns School of Medicine–Health Sciences Library [18519]
Pacific Business Center Program [59237]
University of Hawaii at Hilo
Hawaii SBDC [59229]
Small Business Development Center [59234]
University of Hawaii at Manoa
Hawaii Real Estate Research and Education Center [21122]
Water Resources Research Center–Library [25738]
University of Houston
African American Studies Program [48653]
Division of Research [65660]
Fort Bend County SBDC [65073]
Southeastern Texas Small Business Development Center [65019]
Texas Information Procurement Service–Small Business Development Center [65074]
Texas Manufacturing Assistance Center–TMAC Gulf Coast–SBDC [65075]
University of Houston Coastal Plains–Small Business Development Center [65076]
University of Houston-Victoria–Small Business Development Center [65077]
University of Idaho
Aquaculture Research Institute [10494]
Idaho Research Foundation [59347]
Sandpoint Research and Extension Center [5491]
University Research Office [59348]
University of Illinois
Applied Life Studies Library [19543]
Communications Library [20200]
Funk Library of Agricultural, Consumer and Environmental Sciences Library [26671]
Health Systems Research [41422]
University of Illinois at Chicago
Electronic Visualization Laboratory [23326]
Institute for Health Research and Policy–Center for Health Services Research [41423]
Office of Research Services [59792]

Office of Technology Management [59793]
University of Illinois Extension at Decatur–SBDC [59393]
University of Illinois at Urbana-Champaign
Building Research Council [7705]
Center for Reliable and High Performance Computing [7025]
Office of Real Estate Research [21123]
Office of Technology Management [59794]
Technology Commercialization Laboratory [42149]
University of Iowa
Center for Health Effects of Environmental Contamination [11991]
Division of Sponsored Programs [60243]
Iowa Social Science Institute [66879]
RSM McGladrey Institute of Accounting Education and Research [3007]
Small Business Development Center [60065]
Technology Innovation Center [60244]
Translation Laboratory [25113]
The University of Kansas
Institute for Public Policy and Business Research [66884]
Small Business Development Center [60265]
University of Kentucky
Business & Economics Information Center [429], [16695], [26446], [32838], [38597], [47932]
Center for Business Development [60454]
Center on Drug and Alcohol Research [54406]
Center for Real Estate Studies [21124]
Gluck Equine Research Center–John A. Morris Memorial Library [12481]
Horse Research Farm [12487]
University of Kentucky (Elizabethtown)–Small Business Development Center [60467]
University Licensable Technologies and Patents [44217]
University of Louisville
College of Business and Public Administration–Urban Studies Institute [66888]
Information Technology Resource Center [25692]
Labor-Management Center [55349]
National Crime Prevention Institute [22451]
Sponsored Program Development [60590]
University of Maine–Office of the Vice President for Research [60788]
University of Maine at Machias [60789]
University of Manitoba
Manitoba Nursing Research Institute [41424]
Technology Transfer Office [66702]
W.R. McQuade Laboratory [16992]
University of Maryland
Biotechnology Institute [60892]
Center on Aging [41425]
Center on Drugs and Public Policy [8887]
Crane Aquaculture Facility [10495]
Department of Computer Science [66895]
Institute for Advanced Computer Studies [7026]
Institute for Systems Research [7027]
Nutrition Laboratory [18528]
University of Maryland at College Park
Center for Global Business [43947]
Center for International Economics [32868]
Center for Project Management [7706]
Dingman Center for Entrepreneurship [51501]
Institute for Governmental Service [50414]
International Communications and Negotiations Simulations [43948]
University of Maryland, College Park
Libraries–Hornbake Library–Library of American Broadcasting [20389]
University of Massachusetts
Massachusetts Institute for Social and Economic Research [66897]
Massachusetts SBDC [60903]

Small Business Development Center
[60904], [60914]
University of Massachusetts at Amherst
Massachusetts Water Resources Research
Center [25750]
Office of Research Affairs [61150]
University of Massachusetts at Boston–Gerontology
Institute [18420]
University of Memphis
Center for Health Services Research
[41426]
Ecological Research Center [10496]
Tennessee SBDC [64873]
University of Miami
Clean Energy Research Institute [23359]
Institute for the Study of Culture and
Nursing [18421]
Laboratory of Clinical and Applied
Physiology [19614]
Office of Research [58996]
University of Michigan
Business and Industrial Assistance Division
[61488]
Center for Ergonomics [56713]
Center for National Truck and Bus Statistics
[25459]
Collaboratory for Research on Electronic
Work [6398]
College of Engineering–Office of
Technology Transfer–Industrial
Development Division [61489]
Division of Research Development and
Administration [61490]
Health Management Research Center
[41427]
Information and Library Studies Library
[14690]
Kresge Hearing Research Institute [12130]
Kresge Hearing Research Institute–Auditory
Anatomy Laboratory [12131]
Matthaei Botanical Gardens–Library [11545]
Nichols Arboretum [16104]
Office of Tax Policy Research [24217]
Upjohn Center for Clinical Pharmacology
[8888]
University of Minnesota
Business Library [6315]
Center for the Development of
Technological Leadership [61719]
Charles Babbage Institute–Center for the
History of Information Technology
[6316]
Charles Babbage Institute for the History of
Information Technology [3409]
Children's Literature Research Collections
[5945]
Division of Health Policy and Management
[41428]
Eric Sevareid Journalism Library [6085]
Hubert H. Humphrey Institute of Public
Affairs–Conflict and Change Center
[17083]
Minnesota Landscape Arboretum–Andersen
Horticultural Library [11546]
Office of Sponsored Projects Administration
[61720]
Office for Technology Commercialization
[61721]
University of Minnesota, Crookston–Media
Resources [12482]
University of Minnesota, Duluth
Center for Community and Regional
Research [50415]
Small Business Development Center
[61538]
University of Minnesota, St. Paul–Magrath Library
[26672]
The University of Mississippi
Center for Population Studies [66906]
Small Business Development Center
[54111], [61740]
University of Missouri
Missouri Research Park [62099]
SBDC Extension Center–Phelps County
[61886]

University of Missouri-Columbia
Journalism Library [20201]
Office of Research Administration [62100]
Power Electronics Research Center [48853]
Small Business Development Center
[61856], [61887], [61896]
University of Missouri Extension–Camden
County–Small Business Development Center
[61888]
University of Missouri Extension at Camden
County–SBDC [61889]
University of Missouri-Kansas City
Center for Economic Information [66912]
Office of Research Services [62101]
University of Missouri-Rolla–Small Business
Research and Information Center [61897]
University of Missouri-St. Louis
Center for Business and Industrial Studies
[48854]
Office of Research Administration [62102]
University of Moncton–Centre for Acadians Studies
[11099]
University of Montana
Bureau of Business and Economic
Research [66917]
Montana Business Connection [62135]
University of Montreal
Health and Prevention Social Research
Group [56714]
International Centre for Comparative
Criminology [35304]
University of Nebraska at Kearney
Nebraska Business Development Center
[44698]
Nebraska Career and Technical Education
Resource Center [7839]
SBDC [62228]
University of Nebraska at Lincoln
Center for Entrepreneurship [62317]
C.Y. Thompson Library [18520]
Office of Sponsored Programs [62314]
University of Nebraska at Omaha
Center for Management of Information
Technology [19811]
Nebraska Business Development Center
[30128]
Nebraska Small Business Development
Center [59603], [62219]
Small Business Development Center
[62229]
University of Nebraska Technology Park [62315]
University of Nevada, Las Vegas
Architecture Studies Library [1578], [7699],
[13731], [16100]
Lied Institute for Real Estate Studies
[21125]
Music Library [17710], [17829]
Small Business Development Center
[62333]
Special Collections–Gaming Studies
Collection [10907]
University of Nevada, Reno
Nutrition Education and Research Program
[18529]
Small Business Development Center
[62320]
University Library–Business and
Government Information Center [39758]
University of New Brunswick
New Brunswick Cooperative Fish and
Wildlife Research Unit [9473]
Nexfor/Bowater Forest Watershed Research
Centre [9474]
Transportation Group [25460]
University of New Hampshire
New Hampshire Small Business
Development Center [54112]
Office of Biometrics [66927]
Office of Vice President for Research and
Public Service [62443]
Small Business Development Center
[59766], [62385]
University of New Haven–Bureau of Business
Research [3008]

University of New Mexico
Bureau of Business and Economic
Research–Business and Industrial Data
Center [66936]
Office of Vice Provost Research [62733]
University of New Mexico at Gallup–Small Business
Development Center [62659]
University of New Mexico at Los Alamos–Small
Business Development Center [62660]
University of New Mexico at Valencia–Small
Business Development Center [62661]
University of North Alabama–Small Business
Development Center [56788]
University of North Carolina
Odum Institute for Research in Social
Science [66945]
SBDC [63281]
University of North Carolina at Chapel Hill
Cecil G. Sheps Center for Health Services
Research [27067]
Central Carolina Regional Small Business
Development Center [63282]
Frank Hawkins Kenan Institute of Private
Enterprise [35274]
Highway Safety Research Center [8750]
Institute for Economic Development [32869]
Institute of Government [50416]
University of North Carolina at Charlotte
Small Business and Technology
Development Center (Southern
Piedmont Region) [63283]
University Research Park [63478]
University of North Carolina at Greensboro
Special Collections & Rare Books, Jackson
Library–Cello Music Collections [17711]
Special Collections & Rare Books, Jackson
Library–Dance Collection [8499]
Special Collections & Rare Books, Jackson
Library–Physical Education History
Collection [19544]
University of North Carolina at Pembroke–SBTDC
[63284]
University of North Carolina/SBTDC–Small Buisness
Technical Development Center [63473]
University of North Carolina at Wilmington–Small
Business Technology Development Center
[63285]
University of North Dakota
Center for Innovation [63503]
Department of Geography [66949]
North Dakota SBDC [63500]
North Dakota Small Business Development
Center [63488]
Vice President for Research [63544]
Workforce Development [63546]
University of North Florida
Center for Community Initiatives [50417]
First Coast Technology Park [58997]
Institute of Police Technology and
Management [23327]
Ocala Small Business Development Center
[58715]
Small Business Development Center
[58716]
University of North Texas
Center for Economic Development and
Research [32870]
Office for Research Services [65661]
University of Northern Colorado–Library
Government Publics [66839]
University of Northern Iowa
Center for Social and Behavioral Research
[66880]
Iowa Waste Reduction Center [11992]
Small Business Development Center
[60066]
University of Notre Dame
Fanning Center for Business
Communication [27713]
Office of Research of The Graduate School
[60041]
University of Oklahoma
Center for Financial Studies [38598]
Keys Speech and Hearing Center [12132]
Not A Working Number [63931]
Office of Research Services [64132]

University Airpark [64133]
University of Oregon
    Career Center Library [4467]
    Office of Research Services and
        Administration [64299]
    Solar Energy Center [23360]
University of Oregon Library–Documents and
    Microforms Department [66965]
University of Pennsylvania
    Center for Technology Transfer [64618]
    Leonard Davis Institute of Health
        Economics [41429]
    Morris Arboretum [16105]
    Morris Arboretum Library [11547]
    Office of Research Services [64619]
    Pennsylvania SBDC [64321]
    Pension Research Council [27068]
    Rodney L. White Center for Financial
        Research [10415]
    Samuel Zell and Robert Lurie Real Estate
        Center at Wharton [21126]
    SEI Center for Advanced Studies in
        Management [48855]
    Small Business Development Center
        [64322]
University of Pittsburgh–Small Business
    Development Center [64340]
University of Puerto Rico–Library System–Arts
    Collection [6086]
University of Puerto Rico at Mayaguez–Small
    Business Development Center [64646]
University of Quebec at Montreal–Centre for Study
    of Biological Interactions Between Environment
    and Health [49673]
University of Quebec at Trois-Rivieres–Research
    Institute on Small and Medium Sized
    Businesses [53144]
University of Redlands–Armacost Library - Special
    Collections [17712]
University Resources [17238], [51016]
University of Rhode Island
    Exercise Science Laboratories [19615]
    Research Center in Business and
        Economics [3009]
University of Rochester–Office of Research and
    Project Administration [63214]
University of St. Thomas–College of
    Business–SBDC [61513]
University of Scranton–Small Business
    Development Center [64341]
University of South Alabama–Small Business
    Development Center [56789]
University of South Carolina
    Career Center–Library [4468]
    The Moore School of Business–Elliot White
        Springs Business Library [29057],
        [30651]
    Small Business Development Center
        [64687]
University of South Carolina at Aiken–Small
    Business Development Center [64703]
University of South Carolina at Beaufort–Small
    Business Development Center [64704]
University of South Carolina at Columbia
    Office of Sponsored Programs and
        Research [64797]
    South Carolina Real Estate Center [21127]
University of South Carolina at Hilton Head–Small
    Business Development Center [64705]
University of South Carolina at Sumter–Small
    Business Development Center [64706]
University of South Dakota
    Christian P. Lommen Health Sciences
        Library [19591]
    Government Research Bureau [50418]
    School of Business–Business Research
        Bureau [66985]
    Small Business Development Center
        [64803]
    Vermillion Lead Office [64804]
University of South Florida
    Center for HIV Education and Research
        [41430]
    College of Medicine–Suncoast Gerontology
        Center - The Eastern Star Library on
        Alzheimer's Disease [18410]

    Office of Research [58998]
    Small Business Development Center
        [37219], [58717]
University of South Florida, Saint
    Petersburg–Nelson Poynter Memorial
    Library–Special Collections [37549]
University of Southern California
    Center for Effective Organizations [35275]
    Information Sciences Institute [6565]
    Library–Cinema-Television Library and
        Archives of Performing Arts [17552]
    Office of Technology Licensing [58224]
University of Southern Maine
    Maine SBDC State Office [60684]
    Maine State Data Center–Center for
        Business and Economic Research
        [66891]
    Small Business Development Center
        [60685]
University of Southern Mississippi
    National Food Service Management
        Institute–Applied Research Division
        [18530]
    Small Business Development Center
        [61764]
    Sponsored Programs Administration
        [61853]
University Technology Center (Minneapolis) [61722]
University of Tennessee
    College of Business Administration–Center
        for Business and Economic Research
        [66987]
    Drug Information Center [8889]
University of Tennessee at Chattanooga–Center of
    Excellence for Computer Applications [7044]
University of Tennessee Health Science
    Center–Research Administration [65009]
University of Tennessee, Knoxville
    Energy, Environment and Resources Center
        [23361]
    Office of Research [65010]
    Society for the Study of Social Problems,
        Inc. [41431]
University of Texas [65662]
University of Texas at Arlington
    Center for Information Technologies
        Management [7045]
    Center for Research on Organizational and
        Managerial Excellence [23433]
    Construction Research Center [7707]
    Human Performance Institute [19616]
    Office of Research [65663]
    Women and Minorities Research and
        Resource Center [48654]
University of Texas at Austin
    Bureau of Business Research [32871]
    Center for American Architecture and
        Design [1587]
    Center for Transportation Research [2558]
    Drug Dynamics Institute [8890]
    Faculty Development Program [65664]
    Solar Energy Laboratory [23362]
University of Texas at Dallas
    Bruton Center for Development Studies
        [41432]
    Center for Translation Studies [25115]
    Center for Translation Studies–Translation
        Library [25114]
University of Texas (Downtown San Antonio)–South
    Texas Border SBDC [65078]
University of Texas-Houston Health Science
    Center–Hermann Eye Center [25679]
University of Texas-Pan American
    Center for Entrepreneurship and Economic
        Development [32872]
    Small Business Development Center–Rio
        Grande Valley Empowerment Zone
        [65079]
University of Texas-Permian Basin–Small Business
    Development Center [65080]
University of Texas Southwestern Medical Center at
    Dallas–Center for Human Nutrition [18531]
University of Toronto
    Centre for Research in Information Studies
        [2824]

    Institute for the History and Philosophy of
        Science and Technology [52354]
    Institute for Policy Analysis [24218]
    Ontario Institute for Studies in
        Education–Centre for Teacher
        Development [33410]
    Ontario Institute for Studies in
        Education–International Centre for
        Educational Change [33411]
University of Toronto Innovation Foundation [66740]
University of Tulsa–Mary K. Chapman Center for
    Communicative Disorders [12133]
University of Utah
    Bureau of Economic and Business
        Research [32873], [66995]
    Center for Public Policy and Administration
        [50419]
    Garn Institute of Finance [10416]
    Human Performance Research Laboratory
        [19617]
    Rocky Mountain Center for Occupational
        and Environmental Health [56715]
    Technology Commercialization Office
        [65744]
    University of Utah Research Park [65745]
University of Vermont
    Center for Rural Studies [66998]
    McClure Musculoskeletal Research Center
        [19618]
    Office of Sponsored Programs [65810]
University of the Virgin Islands
    Eastern Caribbean Center [66992]
    Small Business Development Center
        [66658]
    USVI Small Business Development Center
        [66660]
University of the Virgin Islands at Charlotte
    Amalie–Small Business Development Center
    [66661]
University of Virginia
    Center for Public Service [67003]
    Office of Sponsored Programs [65990]
    Office of Vice President for Research and
        Graduate Studies [65991]
    Olsson Center for Applied Ethics [54293]
    Shannon Center for Advanced Studies
        [65992]
University of Washington
    Addictive Behaviors Research Center
        [54407]
    Alcohol & Drug Abuse Institute–Library
        [54395]
    Center for Urban Horticulture–Elisabeth C.
        Miller Horticulture Library [11548]
    CSSCR [67008]
    UW TechTransfer [66234]
University of Waterloo
    Centre for Accounting Research and
        Education [18815]
    Ergonomics and Safety Consulting Services
        [56716]
    Institute of Insurance and Pension
        Research [30772]
    Office of Research–Contract Section
        [66741]
    Technology Transfer and Licensing Office
        [66742]
University of West Alabama–Small Business
    Development Center [56790]
University of West Florida
    Florida SBDC [58698]
    Office of Research and Sponsored
        Programs [58999]
    Small Business Development Center
        [58718]
University of West Georgia–Richards College of
    Business [59223]
University of Wisconsin–Wisconsin SBDC [66320]
University of Wisconsin-Eau Claire–Eau Claire Area
    Research Center [11100]
University of Wisconsin-Extension–Small Business
    Development Center [66321]
University of Wisconsin-Green Bay
    Area Research Center [11101]
    Small Business Development Center
        [66322]

Small Business Sourcebook ■ **22nd Edition**

University of Wisconsin-La Crosse–Small Business Development Center [66323]
University of Wisconsin - Madison
Applied Population Laboratory–Department of Rural Sociology [67019]
Center for Health System Research and Analysis [41433]
Hancock Agricultural Research Station [5492]
Land Tenure Collection [26673]
Medical Instrumentation Laboratory [17150]
Ruth Ketterer Harris Library–Helen Louise Allen Textile Collection [7970]
School of Human Ecology–Helen Louise Allen Textile Collection [7971]
Small Business Development Center [66324]
Solar Energy Laboratory [23363]
Steenbock Memorial Library [26674]
University Research Park [66575]
University of Wisconsin-Milwaukee
Institute on Race and Ethnicity [48655]
Small Business Development Center [66325]
University of Wisconsin-Oshkosh–Small Business Development Center [66326]
University of Wisconsin-Parkside
Archives and Area Research Center [11102]
Kenosha Area Business Association–Small Business Development Center [66327]
University of Wisconsin at Stevens Point–Small Business Development Center [66328]
University of Wisconsin-Stout
Library Learning Center [24786]
Research Services [66576]
University of Wisconsin-Superior
Northern Center for Community and Economic Development [32874]
Small Business Development Center [66329]
University of Wisconsin-Whitewater
Small Business Development Center [66330]
Wisconsin Innovation Service Center [44225]
Wisconsin Innovation Service Center–SBDC [66331]
University of Wyoming
Division of Research Support [66637]
Office of Research [66638]
Survey Research Center [67021]
Wyoming State Veterinary Laboratory [1289]
"Unleash the Power of Leasing" in *Success* (Vol. 47, No. 4, September 2000, pp. 76) [26948], [27193], [28941]
"Unleash the Wireless Future" in *Microsoft Executive Circle* (Vol. 1, No. 2, Q2 2001, pp. 28-29, 31) [6187], [6975], [42085], [49337], [54053]
"Unleashing The Millennium" in *Fortune* (Vol. 141, No. 5, March 6, 2000, pp. 16+) [32765], [53018]
"The Unlevel Playing Field: At Some Mutual Funds, Big Investors Got Big Breaks" in *Barron's* (September 8, 2003, pp. F2) [10224], [15558], [38432]
Unlimited Future, Inc. [66315]
Unlimited Learning Publications [66675]
Unlimited Results, Inc. [3927]
Unlimited Success Enterprises [46131]
"Unlock Information, Unleash the Future" in *Microsoft Executive Circle* (Vol. 1, No. 2, Q2 2001, pp. 14-15) [31894]
"Unlocking the Hidden Value in Organizations" in *Employment Relations Today* (Vol. 27, No. 2, Summer 2000, pp. 63) [54054]
Unlocking the Value of Your Business: How to Increase It, Measure It & Negotiate a Sale Price - In Easy, Step-by-Step Terms [52465]
Uno Chicago Grill [8582]
The Unofficial Business Traveler's Pocket Guide: 249 Tips Even the Best Business Traveler May Not Know [30436]
The Unofficial Guide to Starting a Business [53019]

The Unofficial Guide to Starting a Small Business [16830], [29771], [39104], [46597]
The Unorganized Salesperson [51991]
"Unpredictable Flight Path" in *Washington Business Journal* (Vol. 22, No. 18, September 5, 2003, pp. 3) [10704], [32766]
"Unrealized Potential" in *Hispanic Business* (July/August 2002, pp. 58, 60, 62) [43865], [48465]
"Unselfish Teamwork Helps Gibson Insurance Agency Grow" in *Rough Notes* (Vol. 146, No. 9, September 2003, pp. 18) [13510], [28942], [35129], [45780]
"An Unsure Thing: Can't Pay Your Federal Tax Bill?" in *Entrepreneur* (Vol. 31, No. 7, July 2003, pp. 55) [39951], [54851]
"Up Against the Ropes: A Professional Coach May Help" in *Black Enterprise* (Vol. 37, December 2006, No. 5, pp. 72) [15896], [31239], [33273]
"Up in the Air: Dotcom Stocks Could be Poised for a Comeback" in *Entrepreneur* (Vol. 31, No. 10, October 2003, pp. 38) [10225], [14556], [15559], [28943], [34637]
"Up in Arms: Prepare for Litigation With These Weapons of Mass Discussion" in *Entrepreneur* (Vol. 33, January 2005, No. 1, pp. 70) [27522], [29566]
Up Beat Daily [17798]
"Up & Comers" in *Success* (Vol. 47, No. 2, June 2000, pp. 20) [14557], [34638]
"Up Front: Broad Brand" in *My Business* (April/May 2004, pp. 12-13) [47683], [50698]
"Up Front" in *Business Week* (January 16, 2006, No. 3967, pp. 11-12, 14) [7507], [14558], [18154], [30981], [34639], [51397]
"Up Front: Seeking Help" in *My Business* (February/March 2004, pp. 10-11) [42448], [45781]
"Up Front: Stacking Up Sales Overseas" in *My Business* (December/January 2004, pp. 10-11) [3138], [36904], [43866]
"Up Front: Supersize It? No Thanks!" in *My Business* (October/November 2003, pp. 10-11) [11672], [36905], [46470], [56458]
"Up Front: Thinking Outside the Box" in *My Business* (April/May 2003, pp. 8-9) [28944], [47684], [50699]
"Up and away to better health" in *BlackEnterprise* (Vol. 32, No. 3, October 2001, pp. 168) [30437], [41128]
"Up and Running: Energize Salespeople To Get Out Of a First-Quarter Slump" in *Sales & Marketing Management* (Vol. 157, February 2005) [45782], [51887]
Up and Running: Opening a Chiropractic Office [39105], [40907]
"Up to Speed? Wireless Could be Just What the Lagging Tech Market Needs to Get Moving Again" in *Entrepreneur* (Vol. 31, August, 2003) [5160], [14559], [34640], [42086]
"Up To the Challenge" in *Entrepreneur.com* (Vol. 34, February 2006, No. 2, pp. 64) [28945], [36906]
"Up-to-date" in *Black Enterprise* (Vol. 31, No. 5, December 2000, pp. 76) [25992], [54055]
Update Publicare Co. [58489]
"Updates on sugar, peanut reform" in *Candy Industry* (Vol. 167, No. 2, February 2002, pp. 18) [4320], [40796]
"Upfront: Be Flexible or Fold" in *My Business* (June/July 2002, pp. 13-14) [30035], [36907], [45783], [48466], [56459]
"Upfront: Don't Say That" in *My Business* (April/May 2002, pp. 13-14) [3603], [47685], [50700], [56460]
"Upfront: Saddle Up" in *My Business* (October/November 2002, pp. 13-14) [31895], [36908]
Upholstered Furniture Action Council [12272]
Upholstering [25537]
Upholstering a Dining Room Chair [25544]
Upholstering Methods [25538]
Upholstery Journal [25543]
Upland Chamber of Commerce [57844], [60011]
"Uplifting" in *Pittsburgh Business Times* (Vol. 23, No. 5, August 22, 2003, pp. 1) [28946], [30438]

UPMC Braddock–Health Sciences Library [18411]
Upper Arlington Area Chamber of Commerce [63810]
Upper Bucks Chamber of Commerce [64524]
Upper Kanawha Valley Chamber of Commerce and Economic Development Corporation [66303]
Upper Kennebec Valley Chamber of Commerce [60779]
Upper Midwest Electrical Expo [9091]
Upper Midwest Hospitality, Restaurant, and Lodging Show - UP Show [12687]
Upper St. Clair Chamber of Commerce [64525]
Upper Sandusky Area Chamber of Commerce [63811]
Upper Savannah Council of Government–Small Business Development Center [64707]
Upper Tampa Bay Regional Chamber of Commerce [58946]
Upper Valley Bi-State Regional Chamber of Commerce [65802]
Upper Valley Joint Vocational School–Small Business Development Center [63579]
Upper Valley SCORE [62399]
"Upping the Minimum Wage: Small Business Bust or Low-Income Boost?" in *Black Enterprise* (Vol. 35, October 2004, No. 3, pp. 60) [32767], [40797], [42449]
Uppy, Inc. [5452]
"UPS to Buy 27 Boeing Craft" in *Altanta Journal-Constitution* (February 6, 2007) [6103], [10705], [43867]
"UPS-Compliant Shipping Software" in *Modern Materials Handling* (Vol. 58, No. 7, July 2003, pp. 60) [6104], [23242], [53522]
"Ups & downs" in *Entrepreneur* (Vol. 30, No. 2, February 2002, pp. 66) [13511], [32768], [43414]
"UPS Drives Changes to Postal Service" in *Atlanta Business Chronicle* (Vol. 26, No. 12, August 29, 2003, pp. 1) [10706], [40798]
The UPS Store / Mail Boxes Etc. [6131]
UPS Strategic Enterprise Fund [59207]
"Upscale Garden Offerings" in *Tribune* (February 23, 2004) [11444], [16116]
"Upscale Restaurant, Tavern Chain to Enter Milwaukee Market" in *Milwaukee Journal Sentinel* (December 7, 2005) [2354], [21657]
"The Upside and Downside of Outsourcing" in *Business Week* (February 20, 2006, No. 3972, pp. 18) [26556], [32769], [46471], [49750], [52603], [54056]
The Upstart Guide to Owning & Managing a Mail Order Business [16474]
The Upstart Guide to Owning & Managing a Newsletter [18252]
The Upstart Small Business Legal Guide: How to Understand Legal Issues & Protect Your Small Business Complete with Forms [29567]
"An Uptick In the Local Tech Index" in *Sacramento Bee* (November 25, 2005) [15560], [42087]
Uptown Chamber of Commerce [59682]
Uptown Shelby Association Inc. [1571]
Upwrite Press [66591]
Urban Information Center–University of Missouri-St. Louis [66913]
Urban Land Magazine [52762]
"Urban Legend: Do 90 Percent of Startups Really Fail to Make It Past Their First Year?" in *Entrepreneur* (Vol. 31, No. 8, Aug., 2003) [27736], [35710], [53569]
"Urban Media CTO pushes broadband envelope" in *InfoWorld* (Vol. 22, No. 23, June 5, 2000, pp. 32) [14560], [34641], [49338]
"Urban Pioneers" in *Hispanic Business* (September 2006, pp. 18, 20) [7508], [21033], [51398]
"Urban Renewal May Hire Contractor to Evaluate Skirvin Proposals" in *Journal Record* (June 24, 2003) [12649], [13163], [28947], [29886]
"An Urban Survivor Poised for Better Times" in *Crain's Chicago Business* (Vol. 26, No. 50, December 15, 2003, pp. 8) [28948], [29887], [31838], [32770]
Urbandale Chamber of Commerce [60218]
"The Urge to Merge" in *Black Enterprise* (Vol. 35, August 2004, No. 1, pp. 50) [15561], [28949], [50238]

"The Urge to Merge" in *Fortune* (Vol. 151, February 21, 2005, No. 4, pp. 21) **[10226]**, **[15562]**, **[28950]**, **[50239]**

"The Urge to Unbundle" in *Fast Company* (February 2005, No. 91, pp. 23) **[12862]**, **[20090]**, **[31101]**

Urner Barry's Meat and Poultry Directory **[4060]**

URS–Library **[1082]**, **[9511]**

"US Airways Stock Up 5 Percent on Day Merger Try Ends" in *Charlotte Observer* (February 1, 2007) **[15563]**, **[50240]**

"U.S." in *Business Week* (February 20, 2006, No. 3972, pp. 29) **[15564]**, **[28951]**, **[32771]**, **[40799]**

US-China Business Council **[12934]**

US Market Access Center **[58225]**

The U.S. Market for Pet Supplies and Pet Care Products, 5th Edition **[19159]**

US SBA Office of Government Contracting for Maine and New Hampshire **[60787]**

"U.S.: Signs That Inflation Is Losing Its Fangs" in *Business Week* (February 7, 2005, No. 3919, pp. 25) **[30982]**, **[32772]**, **[43868]**

US Small Business Administration **[62616]**

US Small Business Administration **[59212]**

"US Supreme Court Rules on Punitive Damages in Title VII Discrimination Cases" in *Employment Relations Today* (Vol.27, No.1, Spring2000) **[32068]**, **[40800]**

"U.S.: The Fed: Trying To Shift Into Neutral" in *Business Week* (February 14, 2005, No. 3920, pp. 23) **[15565]**, **[28952]**, **[32773]**

US Tobacco Trade Barometer: Exports **[24626]**

US Trust Private Equity **[63170]**

US West Communications–Learning Systems/Employee Development–Library **[46158]**

U.S.A. - Business and Industry Advisory Committee to the OECD **[43534]**

USA Engage **[32224]**

U.S.A. Karate Federation **[16909]**

USA Table Tennis Magazine **[23655]**

U.S.A. Toy Library Association **[5332]**, **[24799]**

USAquatics Inc. **[7649]**

"USDA Plans to Charge Farm Commodity Groups a Fee for Research" in *Kiplinger Letter* (Vol. 78, January 5, 2007, No. 1) **[40801]**, **[50986]**, **[52223]**

"The Use of Criminal Record in Employment Decisions" in *Journal of Business Ethics* (Vol. 47, No. 3, Oct. 15, 2003, pp. 237) **[42450]**, **[45784]**

"Use the index: The scoop on fully tradable ETFs" in *Entrepreneur* (Vol. 30, No. 2, February 2002, pp. 54) **[15566]**, **[38433]**

"Use It or Lose It: Is Your Business Usable-or Disposable? Figure It Out Before Your Competitors Gain an Edge" in *Entrepreneur* (Vol.32) **[30983]**, **[41129]**, **[50987]**

"Use It Or Lose It" in *The Economist* (Vol. 377, October 1-7, 2005, No. 8446, pp. 37) **[24457]**, **[55321]**

"Use Webcasting to Grow Your Home Business" in *Home Business* (Vol. 12, March/April 2005, No. 2, pp. 36, 38, 60-61) **[14561]**, **[25993]**, **[34642]**, **[42747]**, **[47686]**, **[51888]**

"Use XML to Speed Application Development" in *E-business Advisor* (Vol. 18, No. 9, September 2000, pp. 40) **[23243]**, **[25994]**, **[34643]**

"Use Your Intuition" in *Entrepreneur* (Vol. 33, March 2005, No. 3, pp. 85) **[5726]**, **[56461]**

Used Car Dealer **[18185]**

"Used Car Dealers' Business Held Up by NY Department of Motor Vehicles" in *Long Island Business News* (February 13, 2004) **[18155]**, **[40802]**

Used Machinery Buyer's Guide **[16383]**

Used Tire Recycling and Resource Recovery **[24587]**

Used Truck Association **[17958]**

"Useful Web sites for owners of small businesses" in *Crain's Detroit Business* (Vol. 16, No. 50, December 11, 2000, pp. E-6) **[13784]**, **[35711]**

"UserLand Software Inc." in *Inc.* (November 15, 2000, pp. 145) **[14562]**, **[23244]**, **[25995]**, **[34644]**

Users First Inc. **[4884]**, **[23311]**

"Users inch to security outsourcers" in *InfoWorld* (Vol. 23, No. 5, January 29, 2001, pp. 10) **[22412]**, **[34645]**, **[49751]**

"Users Size Up Tax Software: Product Ratings Gain, But Vendor Support Slips" in *Journal of Accountancy* (Vol. 198, October 2004) **[288]**, **[2970]**, **[23245]**, **[24067]**, **[26394]**, **[27194]**, **[53523]**

USG Corporation–USG Research and Technology Center Library **[7700]**

"Using the right bait" in *Crain's Detroit Business* (Vol. 19, No. 6, February 10, 2003, pp. 3) **[51889]**

Using a Balanced Scorecard to Implement a Strategic Plan (Canada) **[27286]**

Using Computer Bulletin Boards **[3401]**

Using Information Technology **[6995]**

Using Microsoft Office 97: Small Business Edition **[4849]**, **[23246]**

Using and Modifying CGI Scripts **[25780]**

Using Others to Save Time **[55037]**

"Using a Reverse RFP Process to Assess Your Outsourcing Options" in *Employment Relations Today* (Vol. 27, No. 2, Summer 2000, pp. 7) **[44377]**, **[49752]**

"Using Security Consultants is Playing It Safe" in *San Antonio Express-News* (January 23, 2005) **[19980]**, **[22413]**, **[31240]**

"Using intuition at work" in *Women in Business* (Vol. 54, No. 3, May-June 2002, pp.) **[45785]**

USPTA Membership Directory **[24572]**

USVP-Schlein Marketing Fund **[58179]**

Utah Business (Vol. 16, No. 9, September 2002, pp. 50); "Some ideas to entertain: how to host a memorable party" in **[4554]**, **[53985]**

Utah Community and Economic Development Department
    International Development Office **[65694]**
    Office of Asian Affairs **[65735]**
    Office of BL Affairs **[65736]**
    Office of Hispanic Affairs **[65737]**
    Office of Indian Affairs **[65738]**

Utah Computer & Business Show/Tech 20/20 **[49395]**

Utah Department of Community and Economic Development **[66996]**

Utah Department of Community and Economic Development Department–Procurement Technical Assistance Center **[65742]**

Utah Department of Workforce Services Workforce Information **[32825]**

Utah Foundation **[24219]**

Utah Manufacturers Register **[46472]**

Utah Office of Planning and Budget **[66997]**

Utah SBDC–Salt Lake Community College **[65683]**

Utah State University **[65690]**
    Central Utah Veterinary Diagnostic Laboratory **[1290]**
    Office of Research Services **[65746]**
    Small Business Development Center **[65691]**
    Utah State University Innovation Campus **[65747]**
    Utah Water Research Laboratory **[25751]**

Utah Valley State College–Utah Small Business Development Center **[65692]**

Utah Ventures II LP **[64293]**, **[65740]**

"Utilities Boost Companies; Utility Services" in *Crain's New York Business* (Vol. 22, November 13, 2006, No. 46, pp. 36) **[28953]**, **[30183]**, **[30704]**, **[32774]**, **[39952]**, **[52747]**, **[53020]**, **[54852]**

Utilities Telecommunications News **[4149]**, **[5215]**, **[40874]**

Utility Automation **[45910]**

Utillaje **[16386]**

Uvalde Chamber of Commerce **[65540]**

UWC - Strategic Services on Unemployment and Workers' Compensation **[30726]**

V

V2K Window Decor & More **[26086]**

"Vacancies up but investors still high on retail" in *Atlanta Business Chronicle* (Vol. 25, December 13, 2002, No. 27, pp. A5) **[20697]**, **[21034]**, **[21361]**, **[44682]**, **[51399]**, **[52748]**, **[54057]**

"Vacancy Rates Begin to Ease; Companies' Unused Space Likely to Slow Rebound in Office Market" in *Crain's Detroit Business* (Vol. 19) **[20698]**, **[21362]**, **[32775]**

"Vacancy Rates Begin to Ease" in *Crain's Detroit Business* (Vol. 19, No. 42, October 20, 2003, pp. 3) **[20699]**, **[21363]**, **[32776]**

"Vacancy Squeeze" in *San Fernando Valley Business Journal* (Vol. 12, January 2007, No. 2, pp. 32) **[20700]**, **[21035]**, **[28954]**

Vacation Rental Managers Association **[20046]**

"Vacation Research Made Easy" in *Black Enterprise* (Vol. 36, November 2005, No. 4, pp. 168) **[24743]**, **[25267]**, **[30439]**

"Vacaville, Calif.-Based Biotech Firm Ends Operations" in *Sacramento Bee* (December 23, 2005) **[26557]**, **[42088]**, **[46473]**

Vacaville Chamber of Commerce **[57845]**

Vaccari & Associates Inc. **[32123]**, **[43002]**, **[56670]**

Vaccine and Infectious Disease Organization **[1235]**

Vacuvent Air Duct Cleaning **[3388]**

"Vail Cascade Resort & Spa" in *Black Enterprise* (Vol. 35, September 2004, No. 2, pp. 198) **[12650]**, **[24744]**, **[25268]**

"Valassis Buys N'West Center; Refines Plans for $30M Livonia Campus" in *Crain's Detroit Business* (Vol. 21, January 31, 2005, No. 5) **[825]**, **[15567]**, **[47687]**

Valdosta-Lowndes County Chamber of Commerce **[59170]**

Valdosta State University–Small Business Development Center **[59039]**

Vale Chamber of Commerce **[64280]**

Valentine Chamber of Commerce **[62303]**

Validating Your Training **[35130]**

Validation Times **[8834]**

Vallecito Lake Chamber of Commerce **[58433]**

Vallejo Chamber of Commerce **[57846]**

Valley Calligraphy Guild Newsletter **[4174]**

Valley Capital Corp. **[65003]**

Valley Center Chamber of Commerce **[57847]**, **[60425]**

Valley City Area Chamber of Commerce/CVB **[63535]**

Valley City Chamber of Commerce **[63812]**

"Valley Econowatch" in *San Fernando Valley Business Journal* (Vol. 11, December 2006, No. 25, pp. 25) **[10227]**, **[15568]**, **[32777]**, **[38434]**

Valley Falls Chamber of Commerce **[60426]**

"Valley Record Label Goes Back to Future" in *San Fernando Valley Business Journal* (Vol. 11, November 2006, No. 24, pp. 1) **[30621]**, **[32166]**, **[42089]**

Valley Ventures / Arizona Growth Partners, L.P. **[57094]**

"Valor on the Front Lines" in *Hispanic Business* (Vol. 23, No. 10, October, 2001, pp. 12) **[4894]**, **[47985]**

Valpak Direct Marketing Systems Inc. **[898]**

Valtek Consultants Inc. **[3448]**

Valu Muffler & Brake **[22707]**

"Valuable Cargo" in *Small Business Opportunities* (Vol. 16, November 2004, No. 6, pp. 122) **[10707]**, **[44253]**, **[56462]**

"Valuable Goods" in *Black Enterprise* (Vol. 31, No. 5, December 2000, pp. 46) **[38435]**

Valuation of Companies (Canada) **[30659]**

Valuation of Companies: The Practical Aspects **[30660]**

"Valuation" in *Inc.* (November 2000, pp. 125) **[27195]**

Valuation of Information Technology: How to Measure and Create Value from Your IT Investment **[26135]**

Valuation Researcher **[24111]**

Value Added Customer Service: The Employees Guide to Creating Satisfied Customer **[31896]**

"Value Added: Here's a Midcap Fund that's More than Just Middle of the Road" in *Entrepreneur* (Vol. 31, No. 11, November 2003, pp. 72) **[10228]**, **[15569]**

Venture Capital Journal (Vol. 42, No. 10, Oct. 2002, pp. 47-48); "GPs Say Valuation Standard Is 'Important' But Can't Agree on one" in **[15050]**, **[49967]**, **[55648]**

Venture Capital Journal (September 1, 2005); "Granite Ventures Chisels Out Its Own Identity" in **[55649]**

Venture Capital Journal (February 1, 2006); "Guest Article" in **[40428]**, **[55654]**

Venture Capital Journal (September 1, 2005); "Has the Free Software Paradox Been Solved?" in **[4683]**, **[23026]**, **[53313]**, **[55657]**

Venture Capital Journal (Vol. 42, No. 9, September 2002, pp. 31); "Have Faith, Not Fear" in **[36263]**, **[55659]**

Venture Capital Journal (September 1, 2005); "Hit Parade" in **[55664]**

Venture Capital Journal (July 1, 2003); "How Not To Get Tripped Up by UBTI" in **[54599]**, **[55670]**

Venture Capital Journal (July 1, 2003); "How Partnerships Can Avoid Tax Surprises" in **[49988]**, **[54600]**, **[55671]**

Venture Capital Journal (January 1, 2005); "How To Create an Entrepreneurial Infrastructure" in **[36316]**, **[55672]**

Venture Capital Journal (Vol. 42, No. 9, September 2002, pp. 5-6); "How To Pick Through the Optics Fire Sale" in **[37149]**, **[55673]**

Venture Capital Journal (Vol. 42, No. 10, October 2002, pp. 40-42); "How VCs Can Limit Their Liabilities in a Down Round" in **[10012]**, **[15107]**, **[55674]**

Venture Capital Journal (October 1, 2005); "Illinois Gov. Pushes More Pension Reform" in **[26833]**, **[40451]**

Venture Capital Journal (Vol. 42, No. 5, May 2002, pp. 47); "Innovation and Incentives: VCs Find Partner in Quebec" in **[43708]**, **[50897]**, **[55678]**

Venture Capital Journal (December 1, 2004); "Intellectual Property and Licensing Pitfalls" in **[44074]**, **[44320]**, **[55679]**

Venture Capital Journal (Vol. 40, No. 10, October 2000, pp. 16); "InterWest Fund VIII Nears $750M Mark" in **[41774]**, **[44553]**, **[55680]**

Venture Capital Journal (November 1, 2004); "Investing in Training Will Yield a Powerful ROI" in **[30892]**, **[33137]**, **[55681]**

Venture Capital Journal (Vol. 41, No. 8, August 2000, pp. 14, 16); "Investment Firms Forge Partnerships" in **[15148]**, **[50007]**, **[55683]**

Venture Capital Journal; "Investment Pace Starts To Return to Normal" in **[28341]**, **[55684]**

Venture Capital Journal (Vol. 42, No. 10, Oct. 2002, pp. 54); "IOP Aftermarket" in **[15166]**, **[55686]**

Venture Capital Journal (Vol. 40, No. 10, October 2000, pp. 78-79); "IPO Aftermarket" in **[402]**, **[403]**, **[2121]**, **[2122]**, **[2397]**, **[2398]**, **[15170]**, **[50013]**, **[55690]**

Venture Capital Journal (Vol. 42, No. 9, Sept. 2002, pp. 46); "IPO Aftermarket: I'm a Bull! No, I'm a Bear! Wait, I'm a ... Blear!" in **[10040]**, **[15167]**, **[50010]**, **[55687]**

Venture Capital Journal (Vol. 42, No. 5, May 2002, pp. 59); "IPO Aftermarket: New Issues Could Start to Gather Momentum in Spring" in **[15168]**, **[50011]**, **[55688]**

Venture Capital Journal (Vol. 42, No. 8, August 2002, pp. 50); "IPO Aftermarket: New Issues Struggle to Overcome the Enron Effect" in **[15169]**, **[50012]**, **[55689]**

Venture Capital Journal (Vol. 40, No. 10, October 2000, pp. 75-77); "IPO Monitor" in **[2124]**, **[2400]**, **[15173]**, **[15709]**, **[50016]**, **[55691]**

Venture Capital Journal (Vol. 42, No. 10, October 2002, pp. 50); "IPO Scandal Means Venture Capitalists Need To Be More Vigilant" in **[15176]**, **[29315]**, **[40475]**, **[50019]**, **[55693]**

Venture Capital Journal (Vol. 41, No. 8, August 2000, pp. 42-45); "IPOs/Recent Issues" in **[408]**, **[2127]**, **[7390]**, **[14659]**, **[14957]**, **[15177]**, **[15367]**, **[17258]**, **[33139]**, **[37154]**, **[42816]**, **[46323]**, **[46599]**, **[46824]**, **[50020]**, **[50903]**, **[52052]**, **[52132]**, **[55694]**

Venture Capital Journal (January 1, 2005); "IPOs Take a Break After a Big Year" in **[15178]**, **[28345]**, **[55695]**

Venture Capital Journal (Vol. 42, No. 8, August 2002, pp. 38-39); "It's Time For Venture Capital Firms To Grow Up" in **[28353]**, **[55698]**

Venture Capital Journal (Vol. 40, No. 10, October 2000, pp. 34); "Kleiner Perkins Adds Lane As New GP" in **[34121]**, **[44564]**, **[55703]**

Venture Capital Journal (Vol. 41, No. 8, August 2000, pp. 18); "Knowledge Networks: Making the Brand" in **[31755]**, **[44329]**, **[47177]**, **[50616]**

Venture Capital Journal (October 1, 2004); "Life Sciences Span The Globe: U.S. VCs Like to Spend Money in their Backyards" in **[43734]**, **[49711]**, **[50910]**, **[52141]**, **[55708]**

Venture Capital Journal (October 1, 2005); "Lightspeed GPs Set To Launch New Fund" in **[55401]**

Venture Capital Journal (Vol. 42, No. 10, October 2002, pp. 33-34); "Little Things Make a Big Difference at NanoOpto" in **[15221]**, **[37160]**, **[52142]**, **[55710]**

Venture Capital Journal (September 1, 2005); "Look for Early Stage Returns to Surge" in **[55712]**

Venture Capital Journal (Vol. 42, No. 8, August 2002, pp. 18-29); "L.P. Confidential" in **[15239]**, **[50061]**, **[55713]**

Venture Capital Journal (Vol. 42, No. 9, September 2002, pp. 10-11); "LPs Carry Their Weight Beyond Venture Capital" in **[37163]**, **[55714]**

Venture Capital Journal (Vol. 40, No. 10, October 2000, pp. 16, 17); "LPs Give Redpoint $1.25B Green Light" in **[41819]**, **[44580]**, **[55715]**

Venture Capital Journal (Vol. 42, No. 5, May 2002, pp. 5-6); "LPs Reconsider the Value of IRRs" in **[15241]**, **[50063]**, **[55716]**

Venture Capital Journal (Vol. 40, No. 10, November 2000, pp. 24, 26); "M/C Venture Partners Close on $550M" in **[41821]**, **[55718]**

Venture Capital Journal (Vol. 41, No. 8, August 2000, pp. 31-33); "Marketing Quandary: VCs See a Growing Need for Differentiation" in **[47248]**, **[50631]**, **[55724]**

Venture Capital Journal (January 1, 2005); "Med Tech Carl Goldfischer" in **[41053]**, **[41831]**, **[50923]**, **[52149]**, **[55725]**

Venture Capital Journal (Vol. 40, No. 10, October 2000, pp. 34); "Mohr, Davidow Names New Partner, East Coast Presence" in **[28496]**, **[55730]**

Venture Capital Journal (Vol. 40, No. 10, November 2000, pp. 36); "Mohyr, Davidow Hires AOL Exec." in **[14249]**, **[23090]**, **[34201]**, **[41841]**, **[55731]**

Venture Capital Journal (Vol. 40, No. 10, November 2000, pp. 8, 9); "Montana Champion Again, Joins F-of-F" in **[35572]**, **[55736]**

Venture Capital Journal (Vol. 42, No. 5, May 2002, pp. 54); "Montreal: A Fertile Ground For VC Exploration" in **[41469]**, **[50795]**, **[52021]**, **[55405]**

Venture Capital Journal (Jan. 1, 2005); "My Life as a Blogger: A Growing Number of VCs Are Opening Themselves Up in Online Diaries" in **[14263]**, **[34223]**, **[53872]**, **[55740]**

Venture Capital Journal (January 1, 2005); "Nanotech Steve Jurvetson" in **[40542]**, **[41855]**, **[52156]**, **[55742]**

Venture Capital Journal (October 1, 2005); "Nature Brings Uncertainty and Opportunity" in **[28528]**, **[55744]**

Venture Capital Journal (Vol. 40, No. 10, October 2000, pp. 18, 20, 22); "NEA Fund 10 $2B Hard Cap" in **[41858]**, **[44599]**, **[55746]**

Venture Capital Journal (Vol. 40, No. 10, October 2000, pp. 52-53); "New Media Venture Partners" in **[14285]**, **[28547]**, **[55749]**

Venture Capital Journal (Vol.40, No.10, Oct. 2000); "New SEC Rules Regarding Selective Disclosure and Insider Trading Increase Risks" in **[871]**, **[29407]**, **[40563]**, **[55751]**

Venture Capital Journal (Vol. 42, No. 9, September 2002, pp. 21, 22-23); "New York Stories" in **[36549]**, **[39493]**

Venture Capital Journal (Vol. 40, No. 10, November 2000, pp. 26, 28); "Nth Power Energizes New $120M Fund" in **[41879]**, **[55758]**

Venture Capital Journal (Vol. 40, No. 10, October 2000, pp. 26); "OneLiberty Ventures Wraps On $200M" in **[44613]**, **[55764]**

Venture Capital Journal (Vol. 40, No. 10, November 2000, pp. 50); "Online Markets for Private Equity Enter Second Season" in **[14317]**, **[34295]**, **[55765]**

Venture Capital Journal (Vol. 41, No. 8, August 2000, pp. 41); "Pacific Life Insurance Committed to Secondaries" in **[15339]**, **[43307]**, **[55769]**

Venture Capital Journal (November 1, 2004); "Patent Pitfalls for Early Stage Investors" in **[44116]**, **[55771]**

Venture Capital Journal (December 1, 2004); "Patient Capital: How Life Sciences Investments Touch Us All" in **[41896]**, **[52171]**, **[55772]**

Venture Capital Journal (September 1, 2005); "PayPal Founders Banking on New VC Firm" in **[13772]**, **[55416]**

Venture Capital Journal (July 1, 2003); "PE Returns Set To Turn Up in 2nd Half" in **[55773]**

Venture Capital Journal (October 1, 2005); "Podcast Startups Look Doomed from the Start" in **[14357]**, **[33479]**, **[41475]**, **[55419]**

Venture Capital Journal (Vol. 40, No. 10, October 2000, pp. 24, 26); "Pond Venture Partners Closes $78M Fund II" in **[41909]**, **[44621]**, **[55778]**

Venture Capital Journal (October 1, 2005); "Portfolio D&O Insurance Can Leave Outside Directors in the Cold" in **[13420]**, **[43316]**, **[55779]**

Venture Capital Journal (Vol. 40, No. 10, October 2000, pp. 22, 24); "Primus Fund V Eyes $250M Close" in **[14362]**, **[41916]**, **[44622]**, **[55781]**

Venture Capital Journal (Vol. 42, No. 10, October 2002, pp. 55-59); "PVC Index" in **[13859]**, **[14629]**, **[15390]**, **[15432]**, **[15911]**, **[42578]**, **[50153]**, **[55752]**, **[55789]**, **[56822]**, **[56916]**, **[58277]**

Venture Capital Journal (Vol. 42, No. 5, May 2002, pp. 51-52); "Quebec's Competitive Edge" in **[30775]**, **[43465]**, **[55422]**

Venture Capital Journal (December 1, 2004); "Quest for the Next Great Search Company" in **[14380]**, **[34391]**, **[55791]**

Venture Capital Journal (Vol. 42, No. 9, September 2002, pp. 32); "Rebuilding and Revitalizing Lower Manhattan" in **[36677]**, **[55800]**

Venture Capital Journal (Vol. 42, No. 9, September 2002, pp. 24-25); "Recovering from Tragedy - How Alta Has Coped with Losses" in **[36681]**, **[54244]**, **[55801]**

Venture Capital Journal (Vol. 40, No. 10, October 2000, pp. 6, 8); "Redleaf, UPenn Launch PenNetWorks" in **[41939]**, **[50157]**, **[55802]**

Venture Capital Journal (July 1, 2003); "Relief Is Finally Coming with A Rise in M&A" in **[15407]**, **[50159]**, **[55803]**

Venture Capital Journal (January 1, 2005); "RFID Due Diligence: RFID Technologies Hold Great Promise for VCs" in **[41949]**, **[55808]**

Venture Capital Journal (Vol. 40, No. 10, November 2000, pp. 20); "Riparian Unveils Village Ventures' R.I. Fund" in **[41954]**, **[55811]**

Venture Capital Journal (October 1, 2204); "Rising Drug Costs" in **[32672]**, **[43801]**, **[49731]**, **[50959]**, **[52192]**, **[55812]**

Venture Capital Journal (November 1, 2004); "Sarbanes-Oxley: A Guide for Venture Capitalists" in **[54732]**, **[55814]**

Venture Capital Journal (January 1, 2005); "SBA Suspends VC Program, Future in Doubt" in **[39920]**, **[40672]**, **[55815]**

Venture Capital Journal (Vol. 40, No. 10, November 2000, pp. 24); "SBV Venture Partners Eyes $75M First Fund" in **[41963]**, **[55816]**

Venture Capital Journal (Vol. 40, No. 10, November 2000, pp. 5); "SEC Comes Down Hard On Unregistered Stock Giveaways" in **[14418]**, **[15436]**, **[40677]**

Venture Capital Journal (January 1, 2005); "Secondaries Jay Pierrepont" in **[32681]**, **[55817]**

"Venture Capital is Not For Girlie Men" in *Fortune* (Vol. 152, October 17, 2005, No. 8, pp. 38) **[44684]**, **[55915]**

Venture Capital Sourcebook: The Definitive Guide to Finding Start-Up Fuds & Growth Capital **[55916]**

"Venture Capitalism Inspires Hope in the Face of Tragedy" in *Venture Capital Journal* (Vol. 42, No. 9, September 2002, pp. 30) **[36910]**, **[55917]**

"Venture capitalists, venturing beyond capital" in *The New York Times* (October 15, 2000, pp. BU1) **[55448]**

"A Venture Capitalist's View of 9-11" in *Venture Capital Journal* (Vol. 42, No. 9, September 2002, pp. 28-29) **[32779]**, **[36911]**, **[55918]**

"Venture capitalists get 'clawed'" in *Wall Street Journal* (December 10, 2002, pp. 35) **[55919]**

Venture Economics Inc. **[30720]**, **[55982]**

Venture Financing: Raising Capital in Wisconsin **[66586]**

Venture First Associates (Acworth) **[59208]**

Venture Funding, Ltd. **[61461]**

Venture Growth Associates **[58183]**

"Venture investors start lending a hand" in *Red Herring* (January 2003, pp. 68) **[35712]**, **[44446]**, **[55449]**

"Venture capitalists show hope" in *Wall Street Journal* (February 28, 2003, pp. C5) **[55920]**

Venture Investment Management Company LLC (VIMAC) **[61132]**

Venture Investors LLC **[66567]**

"Venture funding down sharply from June" in *Atlanta Business Chronicle* (Vol. 24, No. 11, August 17, 2001, pp. 11B) **[37083]**, **[55450]**

"Venture Lender Lighthouse Attracts $336M" in *Venture Capital Journal* (July 1, 2003) **[15576]**, **[55921]**

Venture Marketing Associates **[3928]**

Venture Marketing Association, Business Development Services **[38986]**, **[53120]**

"Venture Michigan Makes First Investment Commitments" in *Crain's Detroit Business* (Vol. 23, January 29, 2007, No. 5, pp. 17) **[28964]**, **[38440]**, **[48868]**, **[55922]**

Venture Opportunities Corp. **[63175]**

"Venture funding keeps up pace: First quarter blows away 1999 start" in *Crain's Detroit Business* (Vol. 16, No. 21, May 22, 2000, pp. 3) **[55923]**

"Venture Philanthropist" in *Harvard Business Review* (Vol. 78, No. 4, July 2000, pp. 26) **[14566]**, **[36912]**, **[54271]**

Venture Planning Associates Inc. **[55983]**

VenturEdge Corp. **[30122]**, **[38581]**, **[44383]**, **[46133]**

"Venturelab Launches $50M Targeted Fund" in *Venture Capital Journal* (Vol. 40, No. 10, November 2000, pp. 22) **[34647]**, **[42096]**, **[55924]**

Ventures **[61133]**

"Ventures' valuations decline" in *Wall Street Journal* (June 3, 2003, pp. C5) **[28965]**, **[55925]**

Ventures Medical Associates **[65640]**

Ventures West Management, Inc. **[66682]**

VentureTrac: Complete Business Development Program **[53023]**

"Venturing Forward?" in *Boston Business Journal* (Vol. 23, No. 33, September 19, 2003, pp. 40) **[28966]**, **[54060]**, **[55926]**

"Venus's Designs" in *Inc.* (September 1, 2003) **[13677]**, **[48469]**, **[56463]**

Vera Institute of Justice, Inc.–Research Department **[35305]**

Verbit & Co. **[38582]**, **[43003]**, **[46134]**, **[49464]**

"Verdi and Me" in *Inc.* (February 1, 2002) **[36913]**, **[42097]**

"Verifiers Try New Tactics To Counter Check Decline" in *American Banker* (Vol. 170, February 4, 2005, No. 24, pp. 12) **[8404]**, **[10230]**, **[54061]**

"Verizon Breaks New Ads" in *Hispanic Business* (March 2003, pp. 16) **[826]**, **[47690]**, **[48470]**

Verizon Bryant Center–Bryant University–Small Business Development Center **[64654]**

"Verizon Taps Strigl To Become President, Chief Operating Officer" in *Wall Street Journal* (Vol. 248, December 2006, No. 145, pp. B10) **[24325]**, **[30705]**, **[42098]**

"Verizon Told to Widen Service" in *The Record* (November 17, 2005) **[5161]**, **[28967]**, **[40804]**

Verk Consultants Inc. **[40892]**, **[56671]**

Verlo Mattress Factory Stores **[12351]**

Vermeer: Light, Love, and Silence **[1693]**

Vermilion Advantage-Chamber of Commerce Division **[59684]**

Vermilion Chamber of Commerce **[63814]**

Vermillion Area Chamber of Commerce and Development Company **[64839]**

Vermillion County Chamber of Commerce **[60013]**

Vermont Business Magazine (Vol. 30, No. 9, Aug. 2002, pp. 18); "Kaleidoscope Yarns recently opened its doors at 15 Pearl Street" in **[8129]**, **[53564]**

Vermont Chamber of Commerce **[65803]**

Vermont Community and Technical Colleges Library **[26675]**

Vermont Department of Libraries **[66999]**

Vermont Office of Policy Research and Coordination **[67000]**

Vermont Small Business Development Center Economic Development Department–Vermont Small Business Development Center **[65775]** Vermont Technical College **[65752]**

Vermont (State) Agency of Transportation–Policy and Planning Division–Library **[2119]**, **[8747]**, **[16205]**, **[24264]**

Vermont Tech Enterprise Center Incubator–SBDC **[65770]**

Vermont Technical College–Small Business Development Center **[65753]**

Vermont Travel Department **[67001]**

Vermont World Trade Office, Inc.–Economic Development Department–Export Development Program **[65776]**

Vernal Area Chamber of Commerce **[65733]**

Vernon Chamber of Commerce **[56898]**, **[57850]**, **[62569]**, **[65544]**

Verona Area Chamber of Commerce **[66535]**

Versailles Area Chamber of Commerce **[62060]**

Versar Inc. **[37367]**

Vert Peak Fitness Centers **[19532]**

Vertex Consultants Inc. **[16883]**

The Vertical Group **[62609]**

Vertical Systems Analysis Inc. **[1572]**

"A Very British Compromise" in *Red Herring* (No. 105, October 1, 2001, pp. 50-53) **[43871]**, **[55927]**

Very Important Post Cards LLC **[899]**

Vestavia Hills Chamber of Commerce **[56899]**

Vesterheim Genealogical Center and Naeseth Library **[11082]**

"Veteran CEO: Don't Fall for These Five Lines" in *Venture Capital Journal* (Vol. 42, No. 5, May 2002, pp. 38-39) **[36914]**, **[55928]**

"Veteran GPs Launch Maven" *Venture Capital Journal* (February 1, 2006) **[5162]**, **[42099]**, **[55929]**

Veterans Affairs Medical Center **[41436]**

Veterinarians Billing Manager **[1273]**

Veterinarians Equipment & Supplies Directory **[1239]**

Veterinary Clinics **[1261]**

Veterinary Pharmaceuticals and Biologicals **[1240]**

VetLogic **[1274]**

"Vets, Your Best Bet?" in *Entrepreneur* (Vol. 31, No. 11, November 2003, pp. 92) **[42451]**

VFDA Update **[7789]**

VHS Duplication Directory **[9751]**

Via Media Publishing Co. **[64634]**

Via Nova Consulting **[3826]**, **[16676]**, **[31469]**, **[46135]**, **[48842]**, **[51008]**

"The Vice Squad" in *Incentive* (Vol. 174, No. 10, October 2000, pp. 30) **[827]**, **[47691]**

Vickers Weekly Insider Report **[15687]**, **[38592]**

Vicksburg-Warren County Chamber of Commerce **[61838]**

Victor Chamber of Commerce **[63033]**

Victoria Chamber of Commerce **[65545]**

Victorian Crafts Video Vol. 1 **[8235]**

Victorian and Edwardian Furniture: Price Guide and Reasons for Values **[1330]**

Victorian Furniture: Our American Heritage **[1331]**

Victorian Interior Decoration: American Interiors, 1830-1900 **[13678]**

Victorian Jewelry: Unexplored Treasures **[15861]**

Victorville Chamber of Commerce **[57851]**

The Victory Studios **[24502]**

Vidalia Chamber of Commerce **[60673]**

The Video Career Library **[4441]**

Video for Fun & Profit **[9747]**

Video Investor **[25606]**

Video Software Dealers Association **[25589]**

Video Source Book **[25599]**

Video Store Controller **[25612]**

Video Systems **[9759]**

"Video Terminals Could Cut Off Indian Casino Money, Officials Say" in *Crain's Detroit Business* (Vol. 19, No. 45, November 10, 2003) **[10891]**, **[11264]**, **[15948]**, **[16469]**

"Video To Go" in *Entrepreneur* (Vol. 31, No. 9, September 2003, pp. 32) **[27523]**, **[49339]**

"Video Ventures" in *Small Business Opportunities* (Vol. 17, September 2005, No. 5, pp. 52, 54) **[9748]**, **[33274]**, **[56464]**

Video Watchdog **[25607]**

Videography **[9760]**

Videomaker Magazine **[9761]**

Videomasters Inc. **[9769]**

Videoway Communications Inc.–Operations-Customer Services Publications **[4160]**

Vidor Chamber of Commerce **[65546]**

Vienna-Tysons Regional Chamber of Commerce **[65952]**

"Vietnam Primed for VC Growth" in *Venture Capital Journal* (February 1, 2006) **[43872]**, **[55930]**

Vietnam Travel Newsletter **[25313]**

Vietnamese Chamber of Commerce **[57852]**

"A View From the Top" in *Sales and Marketing.com* (Vol. 156, No. 3, March 2004, pp. 19) **[45789]**, **[51893]**

"View Master" in *Fast Company* (September 2001, pp. 72) **[31241]**, **[36915]**

"Viewer's Choice" in *Entrepreneur* (Vol. 30, No. 3, March 2002, pp. 44) **[4208]**, **[27524]**, **[36916]**, **[49340]**, **[54062]**

"Viewpoint: Rule on Race, Gender Data Has Outlived Its Intent" in *American Banker* (Vol. 171, December 15, 2006, No. 240, pp. 11) **[828]**, **[10231]**, **[15577]**, **[40805]**, **[47692]**, **[48605]**

"Viewpoint: Timing Is Right for Digital Content" in *Venture Capital Journal* (July 1, 2003) **[15578]**, **[55931]**

Views **[25098]**

Viewtech Market Research & Analysis **[47914]**

"Viking Adds Rangetops" in *Mississippi Business Journal* (Vol. 28, September 2006, No. 36, pp. 24) **[1418]**, **[46475]**, **[48807]**

Vilas County Chamber of Commerce **[66536]**

Villa Park Chamber of Commerce **[59685]**

Villa Pizza, Inc. **[19717]**, **[22002]**

Village of Itasca Chamber of Commerce **[59686]**

"The Village Vanguard: Two new-economy entrepreneurs aim to jump-start businesses in college towns" in *Fortune* (July 10, 2000, pp.154) **[29772]**, **[35713]**, **[55451]**

Villager Franchise Systems, Inc. **[12733]**

Villages Chamber of Commerce **[58948]**

Villanova University Falvey Memorial Library–Special Collections **[1372]**, **[3077]** Office of Research and Sponsored Projects **[64620]**

Ville Platte Chamber of Commerce **[60674]**

"The Villians of Currency" in *Wall Street Journal* (Vol. 249, January 2007, No. 5, pp. B1-B2) **[15579]**, **[30261]**

Villisca Chamber of Commerce **[60219]**

Vince Emery Productions **[58286]**

Vincennes University **[3101]**

The Vineyard–Real Estate, Shopping Center & Urban Development Information Center **[16899]**

Vinita Area Chamber of Commerce **[64095]**

Vinotizie Italian Wine Newsletter **[23539]**

"Vintage Chic" in *New York Times* (November 5, 2006, pp. 109) **[23516]**, **[56465]**

Vintage Stock **[51475]**

"Vintage Vehicles: Manufacturers' Inspection Programs Make It Worth Your While to Buy Used" in *Entrepreneur* (Vol. 31, Oct. 2003) **[4354]**, **[18156]**

Vintage Wine Book **[23517]**

Vinton Area Chamber of Commerce **[65953]**

Vinton County Chamber of Commerce **[63815]**

Viola for Beginners **[17645]**

Violin for Beginners **[17646]**

Virgin Islands Department of Economic Development **[66993]**

Virgin Islands SBDC–University of the Virgin Islands **[66659]**

Virginia Association of Chamber of Commerce Executives **[65954]**

Virginia Biotechnology Research Park **[65993]**

Virginia Business **[66002]**

Virginia Capital **[65982]**

Virginia Chamber of Commerce **[65955]**

Virginia City/Gold Hill Chamber of Commerce **[62369]**

Virginia Commonwealth University
Center for Public Policy **[50420]**
Virginia Center on Aging–Information Resources Center **[492]**, **[12435]**, **[18412]**, **[52487]**

Virginia Department of Agriculture and Consumer Services–Office of International Marketing **[65848]**

Virginia Department of Business Assistance
Small Business Development Division **[65849]**
Small Business and Financing Authority **[65850]**

Virginia Department of General Services–Division of Purchases and Supply–Procurement Assistance **[65984]**

Virginia Department of Minority Business Enterprise **[65964]**

Virginia Economic Development Partnership–Trade Division **[65851]**

Virginia Employment Commission **[67004]**

Virginia Health Care Association Annual Convention and Trade Show **[41322]**, **[55249]**

Virginia Highlands SBDC–Virginia Highlands Community College **[65843]**

Virginia Institute of Marine Science–Library **[2220]**

The Virginia JobBank **[9295]**

Virginia Native Plant Society Bulletin **[16054]**

Virginia Peninsula Chamber of Commerce **[65956]**

Virginia Polytechnic Institute and State University
Center for High Performance Manufacturing **[48856]**
Center for Wireless Telecommunications **[2487]**
Environmental Engineering and Sciences Program **[25752]**
Marion Du Pont Scott Equine Medical Center **[1291]**
Virginia Tech Corporate Research Center **[65994]**

Virginia Procurement Center–Defense Supply Center-Richmond **[65985]**

Virginia Procurement Technical Assistance Center–Crater Planning District Commission **[65986]**

Virginia Procurement Technical Assistance Program–George Mason University **[65987]**

Virginia SBDC Network–George Mason University **[65815]**

Virginia Senate Committee on Commerce and Labor **[66000]**

Virginia Small Business Development Center **[65844]**
Commonwealth of Virginia–Department of Economic Development **[65816]**

Virginia Tech University–Art & Architecture Library **[7701]**

Virginia Travel Conference and Hospitality Expo **[12688]**, **[24775]**, **[25328]**

Virginian-Pilot (September 9, 2004); "EBay Shippers Receive Special Service at Virginia Beach, Va., Post Office" in **[1807]**, **[14006]**, **[39812]**

Virginian-Pilot (July 23, 2003); "Portsmouth, Va., Couple Turns Yacht into Floating Bed and Breakfast" in **[2450]**

Virginian-Pilot (March 16, 2004); "Quick Drop Franchise Opens in Virginia Beach, Va., for Storefront eBay Sales" in **[1846]**, **[7171]**, **[18660]**, **[34392]**, **[38889]**, **[52580]**

Virology **[52330]**

"Virtual Assistants A Reality: Now You Can Outsource an Assistant's Job to A Remote Provider" in *Broker Magazine* (Vol. 7) **[7146]**, **[17449]**, **[49754]**, **[52604]**

"Virtual Assistants Become Real Help as more U.S. Firms Use Outsourced Aides" in *Chicago Tribune* (October 3, 2004) **[7147]**, **[31242]**

"Virtual Camcorder" in *PC Magazine* (April 4, 2000, pp. 61) **[49341]**

"Virtual Company Achieves Actual Savings" in *Home Business* (Vol. 12, March/April 2005, No. 2, pp. 48) **[14567]**, **[16536]**, **[31243]**, **[34648]**, **[42748]**, **[56466]**

"Virtual proving ground" in *Crain's Detroit Business* (Vol. 18, No. 50, Dec. 16, 2002, pp. 11) **[4851]**, **[23248]**

"Virtual Money Chain: Company Changes the Rules of Wire Transfers Through the Internet" in *Black Enterprise* (Vol.34, No.4, Nov. 2003) **[34649]**, **[38441]**, **[48606]**

"A Virtual, Personal HR" in *PC Magazine* (December 19, 2000, pp. 7a) **[26949]**, **[53525]**

"Virtual Private Networks: Editors' Hot Links" in *PC Magazine* (January 4, 2000, pp. 146) **[49342]**, **[53526]**

"Virtual Private Networks" in *PC Magazine* (January 4, 2000, pp. 146) **[49343]**, **[53527]**

"Virtual reality, chief whatiffer...this is EDS?" in *Crain's Detroit Business* (Vol. 18, No. 22, June 3, 2002, pp. 22) **[35132]**, **[49560]**

"A Virtual Wallet" in *PC Magazine* (December 14, 1999, pp. 12) **[34650]**, **[49344]**

Virtual Word Publishing **[59024]**

"Virtually Yours" in *Black Enterprise* (Vol. 36, November 2005, No. 4, pp. 116) **[25526]**, **[26098]**, **[52605]**

"The virtue matrix" in *Harvard Business Review* (Vol. 80, No. 3, March 2002, pp. 69) **[37521]**, **[45790]**

"Virtue Theory as a Dynamic Theory of Business" in *Journal of Business Ethics* (Vol. 28, No. 2, November 15, 2000, pp. 159) **[37522]**

"A Virtuous Cycle" in *Forbes* (Vol. 170, No. 13, December 23, 2002, pp. 248) **[36917]**, **[37523]**, **[45791]**

"Virus Blockers" in *Entrepreneur* (Vol. 31, No. 7, July 2003, pp. 40) **[4852]**, **[22414]**, **[23249]**, **[53528]**

"Virus Dangers Lurk if Cell Phones Get Too Smart, Experts Warn" in *Kansas City Star* (December 24, 2004) **[5163]**, **[14568]**, **[22415]**

"Virus hunter" in *Fast Company* (June 2001, pp. 62) **[14569]**, **[23250]**

"Viruses, not snooping, top companies' worries" in *Atlanta Business Chronicle* (Vol. 25, November 15, 2002, No. 23 pp. 47A) **[6188]**, **[22416]**

The Visa Approval Backlog and Its Impact on American Small Business: Congressional Hearing **[8323]**, **[8405]**, **[31599]**

"Visa Rolls Out Business Card" in *American Banker* (Vol. 171, September 27, 2006, No. 186, pp. 7) **[8324]**, **[31600]**

Visalia Chamber of Commerce **[57853]**

Visibooks **[66010]**

Vision Council of America **[25642]**

Vision: How Leaders Develop It, Share It, & Sustain It **[30622]**

Vision Management **[3827]**, **[16677]**, **[30123]**, **[31470]**, **[35266]**, **[38583]**, **[46136]**

"A Vision for Recycling" in *Business Journal-Milwaukee* (Vol. 20, No. 51, September 5, 2003, pp. A14) **[21261]**, **[48471]**, **[50246]**, **[56467]**

"Vision and the Right Team Made This Dream Happen" in *Success* (Vol. 47, No. 2, June 2000, pp. 27) **[35714]**

Visionaire **[5588]**

The Visioneering Institute **[3828]**

Visions International Publishing **[66676]**

Visiting Angels **[12427]**

Vista **[65670]**

Vista Chamber of Commerce **[57854]**

"Vista: Dave's Seeks Fame, Fortune in North County" in *San Diego Business Journal* (Vol. 28, January 15, 2007, No. 3, pp. 17) **[21658]**, **[38943]**

Vista Environmental Inc. **[37368]**

"Visteon CEO" in *Crain's Detroit Business* (Vol. 21, October 3, 2005, No. 43, pp. 4) **[18157]**, **[46476]**

"Visteon Plans to Close, Fix or Sell 23 Plants" in *Crain's Detroit Business* (Vol. 22, January 16, 2006, No. 3, pp. 4) **[18158]**, **[46477]**

"Visteon's new HQ to start rising in April" in *Crain's Detroit Business* (Vol. 19, No. 7, February 17, 2003, pp. 23) **[1982]**, **[28968]**

"Visteon's 'pay to play' is the wrong strategy" in *Crain's Detroit Business* (Vol. 19, No. 9, March 3, 2003, pp. 8) **[1983]**, **[31601]**

Visual Basic I **[32975]**

Visual Basic II **[32976]**

Visual Merchandising and Store Design **[26078]**

Visual Merchandising & Store Design-Buyers' Guide Issue **[13681]**, **[26075]**, **[51400]**

Visual Thinking I **[8599]**

Visual Thinking II: Color Theory **[8600]**

Visual Thinking III: Design Principles and Typography **[8601]**

Vitality Juice, Java & Smoothie Bar **[12089]**

"VitalMed Absorbs Doctors' Paperwork" in *Birmingham Business Journal* (Vol. 20, No. 20, July 4, 2003, pp. 1) **[16537]**, **[41131]**

"Vitamin Outlet Gets New Owner, New Name, More Products" in *Crain's Detroit Business* (Vol. 19, No. 45, November 10, 2003, pp. 35) **[8806]**, **[12020]**

VIV Poultry Yutav **[26607]**

"Vive les funds" in *WorkingWoman* (Vol. 25, No. 8, September 2000, pp. 24) **[38442]**

"Vivid Buys Amerigos, Char" in *Mississippi Business Journal* (Vol. 29, January 2007, No. 3, pp. A8) **[21659]**, **[47693]**, **[50247]**

VK Ventures **[58184]**

Vladimir Ashkenazy **[17647]**, **[17800]**

VMC Consulting Service **[54372]**

VMI Research Laboratories **[65995]**

VMS Inc. **[6050]**

Vocam **[56672]**

Vocational Visions Career Series **[4442]**

Vocelli Pizza **[19718]**

"Voice of America" in *Fortune* (Vol. 151, June 27, 2005, No. 13 pp. F184) **[39655]**, **[40806]**

Voice for Animals, Inc.–Library **[1227]**, **[1282]**, **[12046]**, **[12098]**

"Voice of Experience" in *Hispanic Business* (Vol. 23, No. 7/8, July/August 2001, pp. 32-33) **[36918]**, **[48472]**

The Voice of Leadership: How Leaders Inspire, Influence, and Achieve Results **[44856]**

The Voice of Leadership: How Leaders Inspire, Influence and Achieve Results (Canada) **[44857]**

The Voice Newspaper **[19197]**

Voice of the Pharmacist Newsletter **[8835]**

"Voices carry" in *Entrepreneur* (Vol. 31, No. 6, June 2003, pp. 80) **[27525]**, **[45792]**, **[49345]**

"The Voices In Your Head" in *Entrepreneur* (Vol. 28, No. 7, July 2000, pp. 105) **[3604]**

"Voices of Innovation" in *Business Week* (January 23, 2006, No. 3968, pp. 20) **[4853]**, **[23251]**, **[48524]**, **[49662]**, **[50989]**, **[52226]**, **[53529]**

"VoIP; After Years of Hype, a Real Market has Emerged for Voice Over IP." in *Venture Capital Journal* (December 1, 2004) **[5164]**, **[14570]**, **[27526]**, **[55932]**

"VoIP Lessons: Learn How to Get Around Potential Problems" in *Entrepreneur* (Vol. 33, January 2005, No. 1, pp. 26) **[5165]**, **[14571]**, **[49346]**

Volatility and Credit Risk in the Capital Markets: Assessing and Managing Financial Instrument Risk and Off-Balance Sheet Operations **[15580]**

Volcanoes: Cauldrons of Fury **[33329]**

Volta Voices **[12113]**

Voluntary Protection Programs Participants' Association **[56551]**

Wall Street Journal (December 17, 2001, pp. A18); "Engler's tax web" in **[14012]**, **[33848]**, **[54537]**

Wall Street Journal (Vol. 248, December 2006, No. 149, pp. B4); "Entrepreneur Seeks Riches In Pixels-Again" in **[614]**, **[14016]**, **[25843]**, **[33853]**

Wall Street Journal (May 7, 2002, pp. B6); "Entrepreneurs test start-ups-on the side" in **[35426]**, **[44403]**, **[48878]**, **[53559]**, **[55377]**

Wall Street Journal (October 1, 2002, pp. B4); "Entrepreneurship, too, has its economic limits" in **[29732]**, **[35433]**

Wall Street Journal (February 3, 2003, pp. B6); "Executive who was dismissed accuses firm of inflating profit" in **[37441]**, **[39322]**

Wall Street Journal (Vol. 248, December 2006, No. 149, pp. A2); "Exxon Damages for Valdez Spill Are Cut In Half" in **[40362]**, **[44294]**

Wall Street Journal (June 12, 2000, pp. A6); "FedEx to launch service that allows small companies to build online stores" in **[18645]**, **[33887]**

Wall Street Journal (Vol. 248, December 2006, No. 145, pp. B1); "Filmmakers Face Some Big Challenges On Tiny Cellphones" in **[4986]**, **[9714]**, **[48729]**, **[50590]**

Wall Street Journal (April 23, 2002, pp. B5); "Finding the potential in down and dirty jobs" in **[36152]**, **[52530]**

Wall Street Journal (December 17, 2002, pp. B7); "Firms rate terrorist attack as No. 1 concern" in **[39334]**, **[45143]**

Wall Street Journal (June 13, 2000, pp. B4); "Forum helps firms headed by women raise capital" in **[55627]**, **[56231]**

Wall Street Journal (May 16, 2002, pp. D1); "From office catnaps to lunchtime jogs" in **[34907]**, **[45166]**, **[54945]**

Wall Street Journal (January 24, 2002, pp. A1); "Get ready for spikes in gasoline prices, as supplies tighten" in **[32447]**

Wall Street Journal (Vol. 249 January 2007, No. 5, pp. A2); "GlitzyShow, Worry Galore" in **[30871]**, **[43665]**, **[46300]**

Wall Street Journal (February 16, 2000, pp. A6); "GOP tells business owners that effort to finance fights against OSHA is lost" in **[40414]**

Wall Street Journal (February 5, 2003, pp. B4A); "Group sees beauty in an attempt to revive BeOS operating system" in **[6666]**, **[6940]**, **[49056]**

Wall Street Journal (Vol. 248, December 2006, No. 149, pp. A1); "Hewlett-Packard Was Far From First To Try 'PreTexting'" in **[30228]**, **[37454]**, **[40436]**, **[51665]**

Wall Street Journal (August 12, 2003, pp. B9); "Hiring is Slow Despite Optimism About Economy" in **[32473]**, **[42279]**

Wall Street Journal (February 22, 2000, pp. B2); "Hispanic Chamber of Commerce creates venture fund" in **[48225]**, **[55663]**

Wall Street Journal (March 14, 2000, pp. B1); "Holding onto talent: the best defense is a preemptive strike" in **[45247]**

Wall Street Journal (, pp.); "Home remedies: feisty mom-and-pops of Gotham strike back at drugstore chains" in **[8787]**

Wall Street Journal (January 25, 2002, pp. A13); "How newspaper overcame loss of big advertisers" in **[18885]**, **[47097]**

Wall Street Journal (April 22, 2003, pp. A22); "How owners see themselves on the job" in **[36305]**

Wall Street Journal (April 9, 2002, pp. B1); "How Managers Can Keep From Being Ambushed by the Boss" in **[45261]**

Wall Street Journal (March 17, 2003, pp. R3); "How do you narrow your product options?" in **[41754]**, **[47109]**, **[48747]**, **[52122]**

Wall Street Journal (February 6, 2002, pp. B4); "IBM, Microsoft, others plan alliance to help conduct business online" in **[34044]**, **[49995]**, **[53794]**

Wall Street Journal (September 24, 2002, pp. B6); "In critical decisions, often sole adviser is kin" in **[37699]**, **[39407]**, **[45288]**

Wall Street Journal (April 10, 2002, pp. B1); "In office of the future, we'll all be scanned like a can of beans" in **[39408]**, **[53805]**

Wall Street Journal (Jan. 24, 2003, pp. A1); "In a tough market, a tech executive chooses to gamble" in **[35530]**, **[41465]**

Wall Street Journal (May 8, 2002, pp. D1); "In Search of the Operator" in **[31745]**, **[52374]**

Wall Street Journal (May 2, 2000, pp. B2); "Internet Incubators Rethink Strategies, Become Pickier" in **[14155]**, **[43055]**

Wall Street Journal (February 23, 2000, pp. B11C); "Internet Use by Manufacturers is Small for Business-to-Business Commerce" in **[14161]**, **[34083]**, **[46321]**

Wall Street Journal (May 22, 2000, pp. R18); "It's Not about Money" in **[36375]**

Wall Street Journal (September 12, 2002, pp. B8); "Keeping Score" in **[56747]**

Wall Street Journal (March 19, 2002, pp. B2); "Lenders wary of plan to make up SBA program shortfall" in **[39853]**, **[44568]**

Wall Street Journal (November 4, 2003, pp. B9); "Less than Half of Small Firms Offer Health Plans" in **[13366]**, **[26841]**, **[41043]**, **[43258]**

Wall Street Journal (Dec. 9, 2002, pp. R5); "Making it" in **[8172]**, **[14222]**, **[34165]**, **[41825]**

Wall Street Journal (May 30, 2000, pp. B2); "Many small firms are unaware of pension-plan options" in **[26849]**

Wall Street Journal (February 14, 2000, pp. B8); "Microsoft and market expect slower start for Windows 2000 sales" in **[23084]**, **[28485]**

Wall Street Journal (December 22, 1999, pp. B1); "Mom and pop's retail secret: doggie in the window" in **[53861]**

Wall Street Journal (February 5, 2003, pp. B10); "More limited form of mold insurance emerges" in **[9368]**, **[13389]**, **[43282]**

Wall Street Journal (June 13, 2000, pp. B4); "More than luck was required to remake San Diego's economy" in **[28507]**, **[41844]**

Wall Street Journal (October 8, 2002, pp. B4); "More protection means less worry over suits" in **[29388]**, **[40541]**

Wall Street Journal (March 13, 2003, pp. B10); "Mortgage assistance" in **[7426]**, **[17409]**

Wall Street Journal (October 16, 2000, pp. A4); "Most small businesses say credit access is good" in **[38235]**

Wall Street Journal (May 28, 2002, pp. B1); "Need to Boost Morale? Try Good Food, Fitness and Communication" in **[27448]**, **[35000]**, **[45456]**

Wall Street Journal (February 5, 2003, pp. B4B); "Nestle pushes a gooey popcorn treat" in **[4300]**, **[17525]**

Wall Street Journal (September 13, 2000, pp. B5); "Netscape unveils Web site aimed at small firms" in **[14278]**, **[34245]**

Wall Street Journal (October 14, 2003, pp. B4); "Networking Provides Partnership's Funding" in **[36528]**, **[44600]**, **[48919]**, **[50095]**

Wall Street Journal (May 14, 2002, pp. B1); "Nicknamed 'nag' she's just doing her job" in **[45473]**

Wall Street Journal (April 2, 2002, pp. A1); "No coddling? Work-site day care, once the rage, falls under pressures" in **[5343]**, **[26861]**

Wall Street Journal (April 16, 2002, pp. B1); "No Recovery for Disabled?" in **[42364]**

Wall Street Journal (October 3, 2000, pp. B1); "Nonprofit groups provide banking for bankless" in **[44607]**

Wall Street Journal (Vol. 248, December 2006, No. 145, pp. A10); "Northfield Hits Blood-Test Hurdle" in **[41875]**, **[52162]**

Wall Street Journal (Vol. 248, December 2006, No. 149, pp. B2); "Northwest Accord To Allow Flying For Other Carriers" in **[47352]**, **[50110]**

Wall Street Journal (May 31, 2002, pp. A4); "Nothing to fear? White House seeks cheerleaders for the economy" in **[32604]**

Wall Street Journal (March 25, 2003, pp. B4); "Older firm gets venture funds" in **[50117]**, **[55763]**

Wall Street Journal (August 20, 2002, pp. B4); "Older is seen as better in small-business owners" in **[36570]**, **[39510]**

Wall Street Journal (June 29, 2000, pp. A1); "On the Same Page: Small Booksellers Unite Online" in **[3045]**, **[14308]**, **[34282]**

Wall Street Journal (January 2, 2002, pp. A7); "One Company Founder Learned the Hard Way" in **[36578]**

Wall Street Journal (Vol. 248, December 2006, No. 142, pp. P2); "Online Comics: Superheroes Take The ITunes Route" in **[5913]**, **[14314]**, **[18656]**, **[25922]**

Wall Street Journal (February 21, 2002, pp. B6); "Online Retail Sales Jumper 13.1 Percent in Fourth Quarter" in **[28594]**, **[34298]**

Wall Street Journal (April 30, 2002, pp. B6); "Owners find credit a bit harder to get" in **[31574]**, **[44616]**

Wall Street Journal (December 17, 2002, pp. B7); "Peer group provides expertise firms lack" in **[36611]**, **[39520]**

Wall Street Journal (December 7, 1999, pp. B2); "Phoenix tops list of fertile areas for small companies" in **[28624]**, **[30166]**

Wall Street Journal (September 11, 2000, pp. B9); "Pimco, a big manager in fixed income, seeks more business with small investors" in **[15355]**

Wall Street Journal (September 11, 2000, pp. B1); "Protecting copyrights: how e-books will be like parking meters" in **[9153]**

Wall Street Journal (January 4, 2000, pp. A4); "Remember Y2K threat at small firms? Forget it" in **[29978]**

Wall Street Journal (Vol. 248, December 2006, No. 149, pp. D1-D3); "Renters Gloat Over Housing Slump" in **[20989]**, **[31062]**

Wall Street Journal (Vol. 248, December 2006, No. 153, pp. C9); "Report of Big Oil-Inventory Drop Appears To Correct An Error" in **[15410]**, **[22618]**, **[46417]**

Wall Street Journal (January 14, 2003, pp. B5); "Retirement Benefits More Important to Workers" in **[26900]**, **[35047]**

Wall Street Journal (Vol. 248, December 2006, No. 149, pp. C5); "Retirement-Plan Administer To Be Bought For $115 Million" in **[39561]**, **[43342]**, **[50165]**

Wall Street Journal (March 14, 2000, pp. B4); "Retiring boomers to cut start-up launches, study says" in **[53944]**

Wall Street Journal (December 13, 1999, pp. A2); "SBA Head Opposes Relaxing 'Minority' Terms" in **[39910]**, **[48402]**

Wall Street Journal (August 1, 2000, pp. B2); "SBA Program Falls Short on Helping Firms Win Jobs" in **[39916]**, **[40671]**

Wall Street Journal (March 12, 2002, pp. B2); "SBA's main loan program faces deep cut for fiscal 2003" in **[39921]**, **[44650]**

Wall Street Journal (Vol. 248, January 2007, No. 148, pp. B1-B3); "Search Engines Help Shoppers To Buy Locally" in **[14414]**, **[25953]**, **[51345]**, **[51826]**

Wall Street Journal (December 1, 2003, pp. A2); "Self-Employed Boost the Economic Recovery" in **[32683]**, **[39569]**

Wall Street Journal (March 20, 2000, pp. A2); "Small and midsize concerns are facing boosts up to 15 percent for their insurance" in **[43360]**

Wall Street Journal (July 19, 2000, pp. A1); "Small businesses fret over delays in eliminating an unpopular 1999 law" in **[29493]**, **[52454]**

Wall Street Journal (January 19, 2000, pp. A1); "Small Business Groups Intensify Efforts to Repeal a Recently Enacted Law" in **[29497]**

Wall Street Journal (April 12, 2000, pp. A1); "Small Business Groups and Lawyers Step Up Efforts to Erase a 1999 law" in **[29498]**

Wall Street Journal (July 17, 2000, pp. A2); "Small Business Index Falls as Sales Growth Slows" in **[28778]**

Wall Street Journal (May 2, 2000, pp. B2); "Small Businesses Are Raising Prices, in Latest Sign Inflation is Heating Up" in **[53973]**

Wall Street Journal (January 22, 2003, pp. B4C); "Small business could reap dividends" in [54309], [54765]

Wall Street Journal (November 3, 2003, pp. A2); "Small Firms Turn to Financial Futures for Fuel" in [26362], [53978]

Wall Street Journal (April 4, 2000, pp. B2); "Small businesses are starting to sweat a little about the future" in [30600]

Wall Street Journal (November 15, 2000, pp. B17); "Small firms cut hires, inventory, capital plans" in [29996], [42416], [44246]

Wall Street Journal (July 3, 2000, pp. B6); "Small Manufacturers Aren't Using the Internet" in [14447], [34499], [46433]

Wall Street Journal (February 29, 2000, pp. B2); " Small business owners' outlook soars on sales prospects " in [30601]

Wall Street Journal (November 14, 2000, pp. B2); "Small can be beautiful for two sporting-goods retailers" in [23633]

Wall Street Journal (August 29, 2000, pp. B2); "Smaller firms see biggest jump in health-care costs" in [43370]

Wall Street Journal (February 15, 2002, pp. B6); "Smaller companies plan to build up inventories" in [44247], [53979]

Wall Street Journal (January 4, 2000, pp. B2); "States' aid for tech start-ups: more talk than action" in [39779], [41483]

Wall Street Journal (April 9, 2002, pp. B6); "Stimulus plan offers some firms tax windfall" in [40734], [54777]

Wall Street Journal (Vol. 248, December 2006, No. 149, pp. B3); "Sun Microsystems Remakes Its Sales Force" in [6968], [15895], [42016], [51856]

Wall Street Journal (Vol. 248, December 2006, No. 152, pp. A7); "Takeover Offer Is Accepted By Parent Of Argo-Tech" in [30609], [46454], [50199]

Wall Street Journal (May 14, 2002, pp. B4); "Tapping local markets can pay off" in [45710], [47605], [51860]

Wall Street Journal (January 26, 2000, pp. C1) "Tax Rule Crimps Small Business Deals; Firms Get Creative in Seeking Remedy" in [40755], [54812]

Wall Street Journal (April 9, 2002, pp. D3); "Tax test" in [4837], [23225], [53504], [54817]

Wall Street Journal (July 18, 2000, pp. B2); "Tea, anyone? Competition is brewing for coffee bars" in [11352], [30970]

Wall Street Journal (April 22, 2002, pp. B1); "Tech firms' juicy new prospect" in [4838], [23226], [42037], [53507]

Wall Street Journal (April 16, 2002, pp. B1); "The employee strikes back" in [34880], [42228], [53709]

Wall Street Journal (May 28, 2002, pp. B5); "The perils of starting a service firm" in [29753], [36619], [52495]

Wall Street Journal (Vol. 248, December 2006, No. 142, pp. S1); "The Individual Investor And The Power Of Research" in [10206], [15519], [28886], [30023]

Wall Street Journal (May 23, 2000, pp. B2); "The Internet giveth, and it can also taketh away" in [14154], [34077]

Wall Street Journal (May 7, 2002, pp. B12); "The jungle" in [9221], [9570], [45330]

Wall Street Journal (Vol. 248, January 2007, No. 146, pp. A16); "The Pump-and-Dump Economy" in [15386], [29967], [30587], [50150]

Wall Street Journal (Vol. 249, January 2007, No. 5, pp. B1-B2); "The Villians of Currency" in [15579], [30261]

Wall Street Journal (April 15, 2003, pp. B7); "This job guarantees a good workout" in [19444], [45733]

Wall Street Journal (April 30, 2002, pp. B6); "Tight buyout financing may boost use of employee stock plans" in [15525], [26937], [50213]

Wall Street Journal (February 27, 2003, pp. B1); "Time for marketers to grow up?" in [812], [47643]

Wall Street Journal (March 26, 2003, D1); "Training for retirement" in [19446]

Wall Street Journal (December 4, 2003, pp. A1); "Trickle Up: Small Companies Slowly Build Momentum in the Job Market" in [7500], [28917], [32754], [41121]

Wall Street Journal (May 13, 2003, pp. B7); "Two women's drive opens a closed door" in [11274], [56453]

Wall Street Journal (April 29, 2003, pp. C5); "Venture-capital investing fell to five-year low in 1st quarter" in [28963], [55913]

Wall Street Journal (December 10, 2002, pp. 35); "Venture capitalists get 'clawed'" in [55919]

Wall Street Journal (February 28, 2003, pp. C5); "Venture capitalists show hope" in [55920]

Wall Street Journal (June 3, 2003, pp. C5); "Ventures' valuations decline" in [28965], [55925]

Wall Street Journal (Vol. 248, December 2006, No. 145, pp. B10); "Verizon Taps Strigl To Become President, Chief Operating Officer" in [24325], [30705], [42098]

Wall Street Journal (October 17, 2000, pp. C1); "Vulture capital gains spotlight after swoon of dot-coms" in [55933]

Wall Street Journal (Vol. 248, December 2006, No. 142, pp. B1); "WaMu Whiplash: Fast Expansion Yields Problems" in [10233], [15587], [38445], [39656]

Wall Street Journal (November 1, 2000, pp. A1); "Washington gridlock worries small business groups" in [29571], [40811], [54860]

Wall Street Journal (April 25, 2000, pp. B2); "Web Sites Help Small Companies Open Internet Stores" in [18633], [33498]

Wall Street Journal (December 10, 2001, pp. B1); "What Do You Risk Using a Credit Card to Shop on the Net?" in [14598], [22420], [34692]

Wall Street Journal (February 27, 2003, pp. C1); "What will Wall Street do on a red alert?" in [22421], [40826]

Wall Street Journal (May 28, 2002, pp. B12); "What's the best way to get noticed by an executive-search firm?" in [9583], [45818]

Wall Street Journal (April 10, 2002, pp. B10); "When is using a property manager appropriate?" in [20062], [52396]

Wall Street Journal (February 16, 2000, pp. B1); "When it's time to retire, who will mind the gay-owned store?" in [30043]

Wall Street Journal (April 8, 2002, pp. A17); "Where Are They Now? Working, but More Calmly" in [34709], [36952]

Wall Street Journal (July 18, 2000, pp. B2); "Who's small enough to get SBA aid? Some ceilings are raised" in [39957], [40839], [44686]

Wall Street Journal (March14,2000); "With employee retention a headache, a small business builds entertainment into the work routine" in [35158], [45859]

Wall Street Journal (March 14, 2000, pp. B4); "Young Entrepreneurs Give the U.S. Mint Their Two Cents" in [37006], [56773]

Wall Street Journal (Dec. 5, 2002, pp. A1); "Yuppie joblessness brings new perk: great deals on yoga" in [17925], [32811]

"Wall Street Performers" in *Hispanic Business* (December 2003, pp. 56) [829], [20347], [24459]

"Wall Street wooing wary investors with reforms" in *Atlanta Business Chronicle* (Vol. 25, No. 20, October 25, 2002, pp. 11C) [10232], [15585], [37525], [38444]

"Wall Street Rogues: Fast Cars, Women, and Cash. These Financial Whizzes Had It All" in *Black Enterprise* (Vol. 35, August 2004, No. 1) [15586], [29570], [40808], [48474]

Wall Street Week: An Investment Primer [15719]

"Wall-To-Wall: Wireless Jacks are the 'In' Thing for Networking" in *Entrepreneur* (Vol. 33, January 2005, No. 1, pp. 41) [6851], [42103], [49350]

Walla Walla Community College–SBDC [66026]

Walla Walla Valley Chamber of Commerce [66190]

Wallace Chamber of Commerce [59336], [63436]

Wallace County Area Chamber of Commerce [60428]

Wallcoverings Association [18677], [18703]

"Walled In" in *Entrepreneur* (Vol. 32, No. 4, April 2004, pp. 34) [6852], [14573], [22417], [34653], [49351]

Waller Area Chamber of Commerce [65547]

Wallingford Chamber of Commerce [66191]

Wallowa County Chamber of Commerce [64282]

Wallpapers & Wallcovering Retail Directory [18685]

Walls & Ceilings [16971]

Walnut Capital Corp. (Vienna) [65983]

Walnut Chamber of Commerce [59688]

Walnut Creek Chamber of Commerce [57855]

The Walnut Group [63861]

Walnut Ridge/Lawrence County Chamber of Commerce [57226]

Walnut Valley Chamber of Commerce [57856]

Walpole Chamber of Commerce [61012]

Walsh Bishop Associates [18583]

"Walsh College offers business information-technology degree" in *Crain's Detroit Business* (Vol. 19, No. 17, April 28, 2003, pp. 13) [6337], [33275]

Walt Disney World–Information Services Technical Resource Center [6227], [6449], [6555], [6910], [43011]

Walterboro-Colleton Chamber of Commerce [64785]

Walters Chamber of Commerce [64097]

Walthall County Chamber of Commerce [61839]

Waltham West Suburban Chamber of Commerce [61013]

Walther Cancer Institute, Inc.–Mary Margaret Walther Program for Cancer Care Research [41437]

Walton Chamber of Commerce [63035]

Walton County Chamber of Commerce [58950], [59172]

"Waltraud Prechter" in *Crain's Detroit Business* (Vol. 19, No. 1, January 6, 2003, pp. 12) [54273]

Walt's Auto World Inc. [1875]

"Walz wants to extend NAIOP's reach" in *Atlanta Business Chronicle* (Vol. 25, December 6, 2002, No. 26, pp. 9C) [1534], [7510], [18566], [40809]

Wamego Area Chamber of Commerce [60429]

"WaMu Whiplash: Fast Expansion Yields Problems" in *Wall Street Journal* (Vol. 248, December 2006, No. 142, pp. B1) [10233], [15587], [38445], [39656]

"Wanda Wen" in *Entrepreneur* (Vol. 30, No. 10, October 2002, pp. 32) [11133], [11553], [35716], [56083]

"Waning Risk Tolerance Haunts Tech IPOs" in *Venture Capital Journal* (Vol. 42, No. 5, May 2002, pp. 6, 8, 10-11) [15588], [37084], [50251], [55452]

"Wanna trade? Tax Talk" in *Entrepreneur* (Vol. 30, No. 2, February 2002, pp. 59) [54858]

"Want to Be an Event Planner?" in *Black Enterprise* (Vol. 36, November 2005, No. 4, pp. 132) [22575], [25044], [55177]

"Want a Facial With That Steak?" in *Charlotte Observer* (February 5, 2007) [2610], [7908], [17011], [21660], [56468]

"Want to Improve Your Hiring and Promotion Odds?" in *Kansas City Star* (February 6, 2005) [42452], [45795]

"Want List" in *Crain's Detroit Business* (Vol. 19, No. 49, December 8, 2003, pp. 1) [46480], [48329]

"Want New Customers? Go Guerrilla: Ad campaigns can be expensive" in *Business Week Online* (April 29, 2002) [4895], [42557], [46598]

"Wanted: A Few Good Hackers" in *Business Week* (December 11, 2000, pp. 14) [14574], [34654]

"Wanted: African American Professional for Hire" in *Black Enterprise* (Vol. 37, November 2006, No. 4, pp. 93) [9581], [42453], [42900], [45796], [48607]

"Wanted" in *Black Enterprise* (Vol. 32, No. 6, January 2002, pp. 3) [3488], [33496], [42157], [44447], [47986], [55453]

Washington Business Journal (Vol. 22, No. 17, August 29, 2003, pp. 17); "Small Deals, Big Business" in **[4803]**, **[23180]**, **[28786]**, **[47548]**, **[53467]**, **[53974]**

Washington Business Journal (Vol. 22, No. 8, June 27, 2003, pp. 34); "Some D.C. Health enters Quietly Filling Urgent Needs" in **[41105]**

Washington Business Journal (Vol. 21, No. 49, April 4, 2003, pp. 16); "Spurred 1Q lease activity recovers lost ground in '02" in **[21352]**

Washington Business Journal (Vol. 22, No. 3, May 23, 2003, pp. 3); "Strength in numbers" in **[6815]**, **[28835]**, **[32722]**, **[42014]**

Washington Business Journal (Vol. 22, No. 15, August 15, 2003, pp. 3); "Suit May Cost Post Unit its Trademark" in **[29526]**, **[30966]**, **[44155]**

Washington Business Journal (Vol. 22, No. 15, August 15, 2003, pp. 3); "Take It to the Bank" in **[10199]**, **[30017]**, **[38393]**, **[45699]**, **[47598]**

Washington Business Journal (Vol. 22, No. 20, September 19, 2003, pp. 34); "Taking Off" in **[28858]**, **[30420]**

Washington Business Journal (Vol. 22, No. 11, July 18, 2003, pp. 27); "Telecom Trickle-Up" in **[5141]**, **[14522]**, **[34580]**

Washington Business Journal (Vol. 22, No. 17, August 29, 2003, pp. 20); "The Great Hyped Hope" in **[646]**, **[47036]**

Washington Business Journal (Vol. 21, No. 49, April 4, 2003, pp. 5); "Tourism foundation falters, plans tasty comeback" in **[22570]**, **[25031]**, **[25258]**

Washington Business Journal (Vol. 22, No. 9, July 4, 2003, pp. 1); "TV One Auditions District for HQ" in **[24456]**, **[47674]**, **[52746]**

Washington Business Journal (Vol. 22, No. 18, September 5, 2003, pp. 3); "Unpredictable Flight Path" in **[10704]**, **[32766]**

Washington Business Journal (Vol. 21, No. 44, Feb. 28, 2003, pp. 2,6); "Whose drug is it, anyway?" in **[29582]**, **[40841]**, **[44178]**, **[50993]**, **[52228]**

Washington Business Journal (Vol. 22, No. 9, July 4, 2003); "Young Banks Hurting as Nation Celebrates Interest Rate Cuts" in **[10262]**, **[32806]**

Washington Calligraphers Guild **[4164]**

Washington Chamber of Commerce **[59689]**, **[60222]**

Washington Coast Chamber of Commerce **[66192]**

Washington County Chamber of Commerce **[58951]**, **[59175]**, **[63439]**, **[64527]**, **[65548]**, **[65958]**

Washington County Historical & Genealogical Society–Library **[11085]**

Washington County SBDC Extension **[61891]**

Washington, DC, Metropolitan Area Procurement Center–Department of Transportation **[58683]**

Washington Department of Revenue **[66031]**

Washington Department of Trade and Economic Development–International Trade Division **[66032]**

Washington District Office–Business Information Center–SBDC **[58663]**

Washington Gift Show **[5933]**, **[11127]**, **[11196]**

"Washington gridlock worries small business groups" in *Wall Street Journal* (November 1, 2000, pp. A1) **[29571]**, **[40811]**, **[54860]**

"Washington Insider: Hispanics Crash House Small-Biz Groups" in *Hispanic Business* (March 2003, pp. 12) **[40812]**, **[48475]**

"Washington Insider: Issues Count More Than Affiliation" in *Hispanic Business* (July/August 2004, pp. 12) **[40813]**, **[48476]**

"Washington Insider: Small Business Overlooked?" in *Hispanic Business* (March 2003, pp. 16) **[36920]**, **[39659]**, **[40814]**, **[48477]**

Washington Island Chamber of Commerce **[66538]**

"Washington a Leader in Organic Cereal Market" in *Business Journal-Portland* (Vol. 20, No. 24, August 15, 2003, pp. 14) **[11674]**, **[26558]**

Washington Procurement Technical Assistance Center

Bellingham Whatcom Economic Development Council **[66228]**

Metropolitan Development Center **[66229]**

Snohomish Conunty Economic Development Council–PTAC **[66230]**

Washington State University Tri-City Business LINK **[66231]**

Washington Research Council **[24220]**

Washington Restaurant and Hospitality Show **[21711]**

Washington SBDC–Washington State University **[66011]**

Washington Small Business Development Center at Seattle **[66027]**

Washington Sportmen's Show **[23701]**

"Washington State Apple Commission Shuts Down Soon after Ruling on Fees" in *News Tribune* (April 11, 2003) **[26559]**, **[40815]**

Washington State Department of Community, Trade, and Economic Development

Business Development Division **[66033]**

Product Export Development Division **[66034]**

Washington State Department of Natural Resources–Public Land Survey Office **[23785]**

Washington State Division of Banking-Annual Report **[10236]**

Washington State Library–Government Publics Division **[67009]**

Washington State Office of Financial Management–Forecasting Division **[67010]**

Washington State Office of Minority and Women's Business Enterprises **[66205]**

Washington State University

Extension Economist **[67011]**

Research and Technology Park **[66235]**

Small Business Development Center **[54113]**, **[66012]**

Social Research Center–Department of Rural Sociology **[67012]**

Washington State University at Pullman–Small Business Development Center **[66028]**

Washington State University at Spokane–Small Business Development Center **[66029]**

Washington State Veterinary Medical Association Convention **[1268]**

Washington Suburban Sanitary Commission–Library **[9462]**

Washington Tariff & Trade Letter **[43912]**

Washington Technology Center **[42150]**, **[66236]**

Washington Times (July 8, 2004); "Mystery Shoppers Keep Eye on Customer Service" in **[31792]**, **[51260]**

Washington Times (February 4, 2005); "Personal Shopper, Concierge Service Removes Clients' Stress" in **[7113]**, **[18991]**, **[56068]**

Washington University–Center for Air Pollution Impact and Trend Analysis–Library **[1083]**

Washington University in St. Louis

Computer and Communications Research Center **[7028]**

Office of Technology Management **[62103]**

Washington Weekly **[15689]**

Washington-Wilkes Chamber of Commerce **[59176]**

Washington Writer **[9042]**

Washoe County Law Library **[10908]**

Washtenaw Community College–SBDC **[61227]**

Wasserstein, Perella & Co. Inc. **[63177]**

Waste Age **[11950]**

Waste Isolation Pilot Plant **[67485]**

Waste Minimization and Recycling **[21262]**

Waste News (Vol. 10, January 17, 2005, No. 21, pp. 1); "EBay Tackles E-Waste" in **[1809]**, **[21229]**

Waste News (Vol. 8, No. 10, September 16, 2002, pp. 12); "Federal agencies generate most e-waste" in **[21231]**, **[40370]**

Waste News (Vol. 8, No. 8, August 19, 2002, pp. 1) "Follow that bill; E-waste and landfill policies just some of new changes" in **[21233]**, **[40390]**

Waste News (Vol. 7, No. 16, December 10, 2001, pp. 1); "Grading confusion: Computer makers balk at report card's methods" in **[6164]**, **[6409]**, **[6662]**, **[21234]**, **[37283]**, **[53760]**

Waste News (Vol. 8, No. 20, January 6, 2002, pp. 15); "Lawmakers to tackle e-waste issue" in **[6706]**, **[21240]**, **[40502]**

Waste News (Vol. 8, No. 10, September 16, 2002, pp. 10) "Learning to Walk; E-waste stewardship takes first tentative steps" in **[21241]**, **[37304]**

Waste News (Vol. 8, No. 10, September 16, 2002, pp. 11); "State, local bodies work to police e-waste" in **[6809]**, **[21256]**, **[40720]**

Waste News (Vol. 7, No. 16, December 10, 2001, pp. 8); "Unhelpful critique" in **[6186]**, **[6418]**, **[6849]**, **[21260]**, **[37332]**, **[54051]**

Waste Recovery Report **[21282]**

WASTEC Directory of Member Products and Services Directory **[11940]**

Wastewater Treatment **[25722]**

Watch & Clock Review **[15871]**

Watch It! Inc. **[18288]**, **[51476]**

"Watch Out!" in *Entrepreneur* (Vol. 28, No. 11, November 2000, pp. 40) **[38447]**

"Watch Out For Career Scams" in *Black Enterprise* (Vol. 34, No. 3, October 2003, pp. 53) **[4405]**, **[30262]**, **[31245]**, **[42457]**

"Watch your step" in *Entrepreneur* (Vol. 31, No. 6, June 2003, pp. 55) **[290]**, **[24069]**, **[26397]**, **[50252]**, **[51494]**, **[54861]**

"Watch That Bird's Rear" in *The Economist* (Vol. 376, July 16-22, 2005, No. 8435, pp. 30) **[26560]**, **[29572]**, **[37333]**

"Watchdog groups say evidence shows Canada continues to export e-waste" in *Solid Waste Report* (Vol. 33, No. 36, November 15, 2002) **[6854]**, **[21263]**, **[40816]**

"Watching baby grow" in *WorkingWoman* (Vol. 25, No. 4, April 2000, pp. 32) **[28975]**, **[56471]**

Water Conditioning & Purification **[25717]**

Water Conditioning & Purification-Buyers Guide Issue **[25708]**

Water Depot **[3090]**

Water Desalination Report **[25718]**

Water Policy Report **[9395]**, **[25719]**, **[37349]**, **[40875]**

Water Quality Association **[25697]**

Water Quality Association-Directory **[25709]**

Water Sports Industry Association **[23605]**

Water Technology **[25720]**

Water Treatment Plant Design **[25710]**

Water Treatment Specification Manual **[25711]**

"Water Wagons" in *Forbes* (Vol. 175, January 31, 2005, No. 2, pp. 58) **[18159]**, **[46482]**

Waterbury Regional Chamber **[58570]**

Waterford Area Chamber of Commerce **[66539]**

"Waterfront, Airport on Top of List For Port" in *Bellingham Business Journal* (January 2007, pp. B5) **[27527]**, **[28976]**, **[30036]**, **[30623]**, **[53025]**

The Waterfront Center **[26706]**

Waterloo Chamber of Commerce **[59690]**, **[66540]**

WATERNET Bibliographic Database **[3091]**, **[25726]**

Waters Instruments Inc. **[49465]**, **[49664]**

Watertown Area Chamber of Commerce **[64840]**, **[66541]**

Watertown - Belmont Chamber of Commerce **[61014]**

Watertown Small Business Development Center (Region IV) **[64810]**

Waterville Area Chamber of Commerce **[63818]**

Waterville Chamber of Commerce **[60430]**, **[66193]**

Waterville Valley Region Chamber of Commerce **[62440]**

Watford City Area Chamber of Commerce **[63538]**

Watkins Institute College of Art & Design–Library **[1674]**, **[9774]**, **[13732]**

Watonga Chamber of Commerce **[64099]**

Watseka Area Chamber of Commerce **[59691]**

Watson Chamber of Commerce **[57228]**

Scott M. Watson Inc. **[49665]**

The Watts Corp. **[27599]**

Waubonsee Community College (Aurora Campus)–Small Business Development Center **[59394]**

Wauconda Chamber of Commerce **[59692]**

Waukesha County Chamber of Commerce **[66542]**

Waukon Chamber of Commerce **[60223]**

Waunakee/Westport Chamber of Commerce **[66543]**

Waupaca Area Chamber of Commerce **[66544]**

Waupun Area Chamber of Commerce **[66545]**

Waurika Chamber of Commerce **[64100]**

Wausau/Marathon County Chamber of Commerce **[66546]**

Wausaukee Area Business Association **[66547]**

Wauseon Chamber of Commerce **[63819]**

"Websites" in *Black Enterprise* (Vol. 34, No. 5, December 2003, pp. S8) **[3606]**, **[14591]**, **[15146]**, **[25641]**, **[26010]**, **[31246]**, **[32279]**, **[33633]**, **[34686]**, **[35580]**, **[36927]**, **[56771]**, **[59370]**

Webster Area Chamber of Commerce **[66549]**

Arnold H. Webster **[16149]**

Webster Chamber of Commerce **[63038]**

Webster City Area Association of Business and Industry **[60225]**

Webster Groves-Shrewsbury Area Chamber of Commerce **[62066]**

"Webvan, Microsoft, and the second-mover advantage" in *Red Herring* (No. 102, August 15, 2001, pp. 100) **[28980]**, **[39662]**, **[47707]**

"Webwise Service" in *Small Business Opportunities* (Vol. 13, No. 6, November 2001, pp. 10) **[14592]**, **[34687]**

Wedbush Capital Partners **[58186]**

Wedding and Event Videographers Association International **[3173]**, **[9687]**

Wedding Music: An Index to Collections **[3199]**

Wedding Photography Monthly **[19251]**, **[19320]**

"The Wedding Planner" in *Everett Business Journal* (Vol. 6, No. 12, December 2003, pp. A9) **[3200]**, **[25045]**, **[47708]**

"Wedding Planner Sets Up Shop at Pan Pacific" in *Travel Weekly* (Vol. 62, No. 46, November 17, 2003, pp. 27) **[3201]**

Wedding and Portrait Photographers International **[3174]**, **[19292]**

Wedding Wishes/Anniversary Dreams **[3222]**

Weed Chamber of Commerce **[57858]**

Weed Man **[16169]**

"Week In Review" in *Crain's Detroit Business* (Vol. 16, No. 49, December 4, 2000, pp. 46) **[23256]**, **[50254]**

Weekend Decorating Projects **[13700]**

Weekend Small Business Start **[35720]**, **[39106]**

"Weekend warrior" in *Entrepreneur* (Vol. 31, No. 6, June 2003, pp. 160) **[5578]**, **[56473]**

Weekly Insiders Turkey Letter **[4067]**

Weekly Outlook **[13038]**, **[26601]**, **[43913]**

Weekly Perspectives **[1709]**, **[18362]**

"The Wegman's Way" in *Fortune* (Vol. 151, January 24, 2005, No. 2, pp. 62) **[11675]**, **[30989]**, **[35136]**

Weich & Bilotti Inc. **[3831]**, **[3994]**, **[6216]**, **[10349]**, **[16678]**, **[30124]**, **[31472]**, **[46138]**

Weichert Real Estate Affiliates Inc. **[20759]**

"Weigh your opt-ins" in *Entrepreneur* (Vol. 30, No. 10, October 2002, pp. 96) **[27530]**, **[27683]**, **[31899]**, **[47709]**

Weigh USA **[19533]**

"Weighing Wireless Options" in *My Business* (December/January 2003, pp. 24) **[6190]**, **[6855]**, **[49353]**

Weill Institute SBDC at Bakersfield **[57278]**

Weill-Lenya Research Center **[17714]**, **[17830]**

Weimar Area Chamber of Commerce **[65551]**

The Weinberg Group–Washington Information Resources Library **[9463]**

Weiner Area Chamber of Commerce **[57229]**

Weirton Area Chamber of Commerce **[66304]**

Kenneth D. Weiss **[26646]**

"Weiss, Peck & Greer Venture Partners Vanishes in Lightspeed" in *Venture Capital Journal* (Vol. 40, No. 10, November 2000, pp. 16, 18) **[50255]**, **[54275]**, **[55935]**

Welch Area Chamber of Commerce **[66305]**

"Welcome Back, Mom and Pop" in *Harvard Business Review* (Vol. 78, No. 3, May 2000, pp. 24) **[51407]**, **[54065]**

"Welcome to the Big Leagues" in *Small Business Opportunities* (Vol. 16, November 2004, No. 6, pp. 52, 55-56) **[23642]**, **[23739]**

"Welcome aboard (but don't change a thing)" in *Harvard Business Review* (Vol. 80, No. 10, October 2002, pp. 32) **[36928]**, **[45801]**

"Welcome to the Doll Factory" in *Inc.* (Volume 28, January 2006, No. 1, pp. 26-27) **[9749]**, **[46485]**

"Welcome to the New Economy: Act III" in *Inc.* (November 15, 2000, pp. 139) **[14593]**, **[34688]**, **[47710]**

Welcome to the Team: Disability Etiquette in the Workplace **[32104]**

"Welcome to the Valley of the Damned.Com" in *Fortune* (Vol. 143, No. 1, January 8, 2001, pp. 52) **[14594]**, **[30037]**, **[30990]**

Welfare Research, Inc. **[41438]**

"Well Connected" in *My Business* (June/July 2004, pp. 36-40) **[34689]**, **[36929]**

"'Well dones' shouldn't be rare" in *BlackEnterprise* (Vol. 32, No. 3, October 2001, pp. 67) **[35137]**, **[45802]**

The Well-Run Theatre: Forms and Systems for Daily Operation **[17533]**

"Well-Suited Profits" in *Small Business Opportunities* (Vol. 12, No. 2, March 2000, pp. 48-49) **[7178]**, **[36930]**

"We'll drink to that! " in *Entrepreneur* (Vol. 31, No. 4, April 2003, pp. 112) **[2323]**, **[11997]**, **[35721]**, **[48690]**

"Well, Well, Well: Hawaii's Warm Toast to Good Health" in *Black Enterprise* (Vol. 34, No. 5, December 2003, pp. 148) **[12569]**, **[12652]**, **[17918]**, **[18988]**, **[24410]**, **[24745]**, **[24931]**, **[25269]**

Wellbrock Inc. **[50343]**

Wellesley Chamber of Commerce **[61015]**

Wellesley Inn & Suites **[12734]**

Wellfleet Chamber of Commerce **[61016]**

Wellington Area Chamber of Commerce **[60431]**, **[63821]**

Wellington Chamber of Commerce **[58952]**

Wellmax, Inc. **[61462]**

"Wellness programs" in *Rough Notes* (Vol. 146, No. 3, March 2003, pp. 134) **[26951]**, **[41134]**

Wells Area Chamber of Commerce **[61679]**

Wells Chamber of Commerce **[60780]**, **[62370]**

Wells County Chamber of Commerce **[60019]**

"Wells Fargo to Buy Southwest Community Bank Parent" in *San Diego Business Journal* (Vol. 28, January 15, 2007, No. 3, pp. 5) **[10238]**, **[15594]**, **[50256]**

"Wells, Maine, Duo Start Custom Electronics Business" in *Portland Press Herald* (August 26, 2005) **[5170]**, **[6856]**, **[7748]**, **[14595]**, **[36931]**, **[50257]**

Wellsboro Area Chamber of Commerce **[64530]**

Wellsburg Chamber of Commerce **[66306]**

Wellston Chamber of Commerce **[64103]**

Wellsville Area Chamber of Commerce **[60432]**, **[63039]**

Welsh, Carson, Anderson, & Stowe **[63178]**

Welsh Chamber of Commerce **[60675]**

Ann Welsh Communications Inc. **[27600]**

Wenatchee Business Journal (Vol. 15, No. 5, May 2001, pp. A9); "Frozen yogurt is sweet deal for Planet Sun" in **[12055]**, **[12777]**, **[23837]**, **[25186]**

Wenatchee Valley Chamber of Commerce **[66194]**

Wendell Chamber of Commerce **[63441]**

"Wendy's beefs up its salad offerings" in *Business First Columbus* (Vol. 18, No. 25, February 8, 2002, pp. A12) **[21662]**, **[48810]**

Wendy's Old Fashioned Hamburgers **[22005]**

Wendy's Restaurants of Canada Inc. **[22006]**

Wentzville Chamber of Commerce **[62067]**

We're Rolling Pretzel Co. **[23575]**

Wes Watkins Technology Center–Incubator **[64134]**

Weslaco Area Chamber of Commerce **[65552]**

Wesley-Kind Associates Inc. **[20251]**, **[32182]**

Wesson Chamber of Commerce **[61840]**

West Allis/West Milwaukee Chamber of Commerce **[66550]**

West Anne Arundel County Chamber of Commerce **[60859]**

West Baton Rouge Chamber of Commerce **[60676]**

West Bend Area Chamber of Commerce **[66551]**

West Bend Chamber of Commerce **[60226]**

West Branch Area Chamber of Commerce **[61441]**

West Branch Chamber of Commerce **[60227]**

West Carroll Chamber of Commerce **[60677]**

West Central Georgia Regional Hospital–Library **[54396]**

West Central Indiana SBDC **[59844]**

West Chamber of Commerce **[65553]**

West Chamber of Commerce Serving Jefferson County **[58434]**

West Chambers County Chamber of Commerce **[65554]**

West Chester University–SBDC **[64342]**

West Chicago Chamber of Commerce and Industry **[59693]**

West Coast Commercial Credit **[3929]**

West Columbia Chamber of Commerce **[65555]**

West Covina Chamber of Commerce **[57859]**

"West Dearborn Rising" in *Crain's Detroit Business* (Vol. 21, October 31, 2005, No. 44, pp. 11) **[12653]**, **[21663]**, **[28981]**

West Des Moines Chamber of Commerce **[60228]**

West Ex: The Rocky Mountain Regional Hospitality Exposition **[12079]**, **[12689]**, **[21712]**, **[55250]**

West Fargo Chamber of Commerce **[63539]**

West Hants Historical Society–Genealogies Collections **[11086]**

West Hartford Chamber of Commerce **[58571]**

West Haven Chamber of Commerce **[58572]**

West I-10 Chamber of Commerce **[65556]**

West Jordan Chamber of Commerce **[65734]**

"West L.A. CPA Firm Opening Valley Office" in *San Fernando Valley Business Journal* (Vol. 11, December 2006, No. 25, pp. 1) **[292]**, **[26399]**, **[28982]**, **[30442]**, **[38450]**

West Lawn Chamber of Commerce **[59694]**

West Liberty Chamber of Commerce **[60229]**

West Los Angeles Chamber of Commerce **[57860]**

West Marin Chamber of Commerce **[57861]**

West Metro Chamber of Commerce **[64786]**

West Milford Chamber of Commerce **[62571]**

West Monroe-West Ouachita Chamber of Commerce **[60678]**

West New York Chamber of Commerce **[62572]**

West Orange Chamber of Commerce **[58953]**

West Pasco Chamber of Commerce **[58954]**

West Plains Chamber of Commerce **[66195]**

West Plains Satellite Center–Missouri State University–Small Business Development Center **[61892]**

West Point Chamber of Commerce **[60576]**, **[62306]**

West Point - Tri-Rivers Chamber of Commerce **[65959]**

West Sacramento Chamber and Visitors Bureau **[57862]**

West St. Louis County Chamber of Commerce **[62068]**

West Seattle Chamber of Commerce **[66196]**

West Seneca Chamber of Commerce **[63040]**

West Shore Chamber of Commerce **[63822]**, **[64531]**

West Shore Community College–Small Business Development Center **[61229]**

West Shores Chamber of Commerce of the Salton Sea **[57863]**

West Side Chamber of Commerce **[63041]**

West Side Charlies Bar and Billiards **[2537]**

West Suburban Chamber of Commerce **[66552]**

West Suburban Chamber of Commerce and Industry **[59695]**

West Texas A&M University–Small Business Development Center **[65081]**

West Union Chamber of Commerce **[60230]**

West Unity Area Chamber of Commerce **[63823]**

West Virginia Chamber of Commerce **[66307]**

West Virginia Development Office
    Business and Industrial Development Division **[66268]**
    Research and Strategic Planning Division **[67015]**
    Small Business Development Center **[66253]**
    West Virginia SBDC **[66254]**

West Virginia Development Office at Logan–Small Business Development Center **[66260]**

West Virginia Flatwoods Area–Small Business Development Center **[66261]**

West Virginia Institute of Technology–Small Business Development Center **[66262]**

West Virginia International Auto Show **[18198]**

West Virginia Junior College–Library **[4469]**

West Virginia Northern Community College–Small Business Development Center **[66263]**

West Virginia Northern Community College (Wheeling) **[66317]**

West Virginia Procurement Technical Assistance Center **[66313]**

West Virginia SBDC at Pineville - Welch Area [66264]

West Virginia SBDC at Summersville [66265]

West Virginia Society of Osteopathic Medicine Primary Care Update [8841]

West Virginia State Library Commission–Reference Library [67016]

West Virginia University
  College of Business and Economics–Bureau of Business and Economic Research [32839]
  Institute for Labor Studies and Research [27069]
  Institute of Occupational and Environmental Health [56717]
  Safety and Environmental Management Program [37378]
  Small Business Development Center [66266]

West Virginia University Health Science Center–Office of Health Services Research [67017]

West Virginia University (Parkersburg) [66318]
  Small Business Development Center [66267]

West Yellowstone Chamber of Commerce [62205]

West Yuma County Chamber of Commerce [58435]

Westar Capital (Costa Mesa) [58187]

WestCap Partners Inc. [38584]

Westchester Chamber of Commerce [59696]

Westchester County Business Journal [63239]

Westchester County Business Journal (Vol. 44, January 31, 2005, No. 5, pp. 3); "Company Unveils Program to Evaluate Car Dealerships" in [17999], [51107]

Westchester County Business Journal (Jan. 21, 2002, pp. 1); "Local Entrepreneurs cash in on trend in women-only health clubs" in [19412], [53840]

Westchester County Business Journal (Vol. 43, July 5, 2004, No. 27, pp. 16); "New Adult-Home Reforms Announced" in [452], [18330], [40546]

Westchester-LAX/ Marina del Rey Chamber of Commerce [57864]

Westchester SBDC [62791]

"Western Airlines Announces Inaugural Flight Schedule" in *Bellingham Business Journal* (January 2006, pp. A5) [25270], [28983], [30443]

Western Arborists Inc. [16072], [16150]

Western Association of Chamber Executives [57865]

Western Association of Venture Capitalists-Directory of Members [55936]

Western Builder [7581]

Western Building Material Association [16295]

Western Canada Testing [26699]

Western Canada Wilderness Committee [9341]

Western Capital Holdings Inc. [30125], [38585], [55984]

Western Carolina University–Small Business and Technology Development Center (Western Region) [63286]

Western Chester County Chamber of Commerce [64532]

Western Colorado Business Development Corp. [58474]

Western Connecticut State University–Music Library [17715]

Western Connection [31990]

Western Douglas County Chamber of Commerce [62307]

Western-English Industry Report [51433]

Western Fairs Association [7086]

Western Food Industry Expo [11711]

Western Food Service & Hospitality Expo Los Angeles [12080], [55251]

Western Hi-Tech Companies Database [42105], [46486]

Western Illinois Area Agency on Aging–Greta J. Brook Elderly Living and Learning Facility [493], [18413]

Western Illinois University
  Office of Sponsored Projects [59795]
  Small Business Development Center [59395]

Western Iowa Tech Community College–Small Business Development Center [60067]

Western Itasca Review & Deerpath Shopper [21695]

Western Kentucky University (Warren County)–Bowling Green Small Business Development Center [60468]

Western Maryland Public Libraries–Regional Library [1373], [22714], [26676]

Western Maryland Region–Small Business Development [60802]

Western Massachusetts Regional Office–Scibelli Enterprise Center [60910]

Western Medical Services [12429]

Western Michigan University
  Center for the Study of Ethics in Society [37553]
  Human Performance Institute [18588]
  Office of the Vice President for Research [61492]
  Paper and Imaging [22135]

Western Monmouth Chamber of Commerce [62573]

Western New Mexico University–Small Business Development Center [62662]

Western New York Gift Show [11128], [11197]

Western New York Technology Development Center [63215]

Western Oklahoma Technology Center–Burnes Flat Campus [64155]

Western Pharmacy Education Faire [8842]

Western Red Cedar Lumber Association [16296]

Western Region Hazardous Substance Research Center [11993]

Western Regional Aquaculture Center [10497]

Western Rental Equipment Expo [21372]

Western Research Institute [2559]

Western Rockingham Chamber of Commerce [63442]

Western Sizzlin [22007]

Western State Psychiatric Center–Library [54397]

Western States Investment Group [58188]

Western Technology Investment [58189]

Western Veterinary Conference [1269]

Western Washington University–Demographic Research Laboratory–Department of Sociology [67013]

Western Winter Sports Representatives Association [22854]

Western Wood Products Association [16297]

Westerville Area Chamber of Commerce [63824]

Westfield [17799]

Westfield Area Chamber of Commerce [62574]

Westfield Chamber of Commerce [66553]

Westfield Washington Chamber of Commerce [60020]

Westford Technology Ventures, L.P. [62610]

"Westinghouse software program finds a market" in *Pittsburgh Business Times* (Vol. 22, No. 42, May 2, 2003, pp. 1) [4855], [6857], [6977], [23257], [53534]

"Westinn Kennels: A Phenomenal Growth Story" in *St. Charles Business Record* (September 30, 2004) [19085], [56474]

Westland Chamber of Commerce [61442]

Westminster Chamber of Commerce [57866], [64787]

Westminster Choir College–Rider University–Talbott Library [17716]

The Westminster Kennel Club Dog Care Guide [1216]

Westminster Small Business Development Center–Front Range Community College [58312]

Westmont Chamber of Commerce and Tourism Bureau [59697]

Westmoreland Chamber of Commerce [64533]

Weston Area Chamber of Commerce [58955]

Westport-Grayland Chamber of Commerce [66197]

Westport/Weston Chamber of Commerce [58573]

Westridge Chamber of Commerce [59698]

Westville Area Chamber of Commerce [60021]

WestWayne/Tampa [47915]

Westwood Area Chamber of Commerce [57867]

Wethersfield Chamber of Commerce [58574]

Wetmore Associates [38586]

Wetumka Chamber of Commerce [64104]

Wetumpka Area Chamber of Commerce [56900]

Wetzel's Pretzels [22008], [23576]

"We've Got To Get Our Hands on Some Workers" in *Business Week* (No. 3666, January 31, 2000, pp. 4) [42458], [54066]

Wewoka Chamber of Commerce [64105]

Weyauwega Area Chamber of Commerce [66554]

Weyerhaeuser Company–Archives NP-190 [16345]

W.G. Grinders [8584]

Wharton Chamber of Commerce [65557]

Wharton Small Business Development Center [64343]

"What About Debt Management?" in *Black Enterprise* (Vol. 35, August 2004, No. 1, pp. 44) [8406], [10239]

"What are you complaining about?" in *Fast Company* (May 2001, pp. 66) [35138], [39663], [45803]

"What About TIF?" in *Ingram's* (Vol. 29, No. 1, January 2003, pp. 23) [21037], [54863]

"What arbitration agreement? Compelling non-signatories to arbitrate" in *Dispute Resolution Journal* (Vol. 56, May-July 2001, pp. 40) [17062], [27531], [29574]

"What Ales You?" in *Entrepreneur.com* (Vol. 34, February 2006, No. 2, pp. 73) [2356], [3140], [19645], [21664], [28984]

"What Am I Worth? How to Increase Your Value to Your Company" in *Black Enterprise* (Vol. 36, November 2005, No. 4, pp. 76) [36932], [39664]

"What Are You Worth?" in *Fortune* (Vol. 141, No. 12, June 12, 2000, pp. 264B+) [45804]

"What Becomes an Icon Most" in *Harvard Business Review* (Vol. 81, No. 3, March 2003, pp. 43) [47711], [50701]

What Business Must Know about the ADA: 1992 Compliance Guide [32069]

"What Can Consultants, Doctors, Lawyers, and Accountants do Online Besides Boast about Their Skills?" in *Inc.* (Nov. 15, 2000, pp. 130) [293], [14597], [26011], [47712]

"What is venture capital?" in *Crain's Detroit Business* (Vol. 19, No. 12, March 24, 2003, pp. 12) [44449], [55456], [55937]

"What dreams may come" in *Entrepreneur* (Vol. 31, No. 6, June 2003, pp. 32) [3607], [30624]

"What Comes Next" in *Business Week* (No. 3658, December 6, 1999, pp. F30) [40820], [43418], [54067]

"What Conservatives, Liberals, Stores and States Share" in *The New York Times* (June 7, 2000, pp. D35, H35) [34690], [54864]

"What CPAs Need to Know About Separately Managed Accounts" in *Journal of Accountacy* [294], [2971], [10240], [15595], [24070], [27198]

"What Customer Relationship?" in *Sales & Marketing Management* (Vol. 159, January-February 2007, No. 1, pp. 11) [31900], [47713], [51897]

What Customers Want [31952]

"What a deal!" in *Entrepreneur* (Vol. 30, No. 2, February 2002, pp. 71) [16831], [47714]

"What a Deal! You Can Keep Hotel Costs Down-If You Know What To Look For" in *Entrepreneur* (Vol. 33, January 2005, No. 1, pp. 22) [12654], [27199], [30444]

"What is Del.icio.us and How Is It Used?" in *Sales & Marketing Management* (Vol. 159, January-February 2007, No. 1, pp. 17) [26012], [34691], [47715], [51898]

What to Do Before the Money Runs Out: A Roadmap for America's Automobile Dealers [18161]

"What Do You Risk Using a Credit Card to Shop on the Net?" in *Wall Street Journal* (December 10, 2001, pp. B1) [14598], [22420], [34692]

"What Do Your Customers See?" in *Inc.* (February 1, 2002) [44255], [47716], [50702], [52395]

What Does it Cost: Web Sites [25781]

"What Drives Inspiration?" in *Entrepreneur* (Vol. 32, October 2004, No. 10, pp. 22) **[28985]**, **[30625]**, **[31901]**, **[35586]**, **[36933]**, **[37245]**, **[42107]**, **[45805]**

"What Eliot Spitzer's Investigations Mean For You" in *Inc.* (May 1, 2005) **[10241]**, **[13514]**, **[26547]**, **[26952]**, **[36987]**, **[38451]**, **[40821]**, **[43419]**, **[54068]**

"What Empowerment Requires" in *Black Enterprise* (Vol. 33, No. 7, February 2003, pp. 9) **[36934]**, **[39665]**

"What Every Executive Needs to Know About Global Warming" in *Harvard Business Review* (Vol. 78, No. 4, July 2000, pp. 129) **[37334]**

What Every Manager Needs to Know: AMA's Tool Kit for Success **[44858]**

What Every Programmer Should Know about Object-Oriented Design **[6489]**

"What is science good for?" in *Harvard Business Review* (Vol. 79, No. 1, January 2001, pp. 159) **[45806]**

"What Gives?" in *Entrepreneur* (Vol. 28, No. 9, September 2000, pp. 20) **[39954]**, **[40822]**, **[48479]**

"What is a Global Manager?" in *Harvard Business Review* (Vol. 81, No. 8, August 2003, pp. 101) **[43873]**, **[45807]**

"What Goes Up: Now There's a New Way to Track Small Business's Ups and Downs" in *Entrepreneur* (Vol. 32, No. 1, January 2004, pp. 30) **[13018]**, **[28986]**, **[31603]**, **[39666]**, **[43874]**

"What a Governance Referee Thinks" in *Journal of Accountancy* (Vol. 199, February 2005, No. 2, pp. 43) **[295]**, **[2972]**, **[24071]**, **[26400]**, **[27200]**, **[29575]**, **[40823]**

"What makes great boards great." in *Harvard Business Review* (Vol. 80, No. 9, Sept. 2002, pp. 106) **[27532]**, **[45808]**

What Handwriting Indicates: An Analytical Graphology **[11861]**

"What Happened to the Paperless Society?" in *Automotive News* (Vol. 20, December 6, 2004, No. 49, pp. 8) **[14599]**, **[34693]**, **[47717]**

What Has EX-IM Bank Done for Small Business Lately?: Congressional Hearing **[10242]**, **[13019]**

"What I Know Now" in *Fast Company* (March 2005, No. 92, pp. 96) **[7848]**, **[45809]**

"What I Think of Pink" in *Marketing to Women* (Vol. 20, January 2007, No. 1, pp. 2) **[832]**, **[42108]**, **[47718]**

"What the Internet can do for the record labels" in *Red Herring* (March 2003, pp. 24) **[6139]**, **[14600]**, **[17777]**, **[34694]**

What Is a Computer? **[6366]**

"What Is the New Economics?" in *Fast Company* (September 2001, pp. 118) **[14601]**, **[32788]**

"What Is Really Fueling This Economy, and Confounding the Grand Pooh-Bahs of the Old One" in *Inc.* (November 2000, pp. 37) **[36935]**

What Is Salesmanship? **[51992]**

What Is Telemarketing and How Do I Get Started? **[24311]**

"What It Says on the Tag" in *Inc.* (July 1, 2003) **[22576]**, **[25046]**

"What It Takes to be a Successful Intrapreneur" in *Black Enterprise* (Vol. 36, December 2005, No. 5, pp.) **[28987]**, **[45810]**, **[54069]**

"What I've Learned About Women" in *Marketing to Women* (Vol. 19, November 2006, No. 1, pp. 2) **[833]**, **[28988]**, **[47719]**, **[50703]**

"What Leaders Really Do" in *Harvard Business Review* (Vol. 79, No. 11, December 2001, pp. 85) **[30991]**, **[36936]**, **[45811]**

"What a Lightweight!" in *Entrepreneur* (Vol. 31, No. 8, August 2003, pp. 36) **[4209]**, **[22577]**, **[49354]**, **[51899]**

"What a Long Strange Trip It's Been...Where We Have Been" in *Ingram's* (Vol. 29, No. 1, January 2003, pp. 24) **[10243]**, **[15596]**, **[38452]**

"What Makes Global Firms Resilient?" in *Harvard Business Review* (Vol. 81, No. 7, July 2003, pp. 14) **[32789]**, **[43875]**

"What Makes a High Quality Customer Service Team?" in *Rough Notes* (Vol. 146, No. 9, September 2003, pp. 74) **[13515]**, **[31902]**

"What Makes Owning a Business Fun? A Lesson Learned" in *Black Enterprise* (Vol. 34, No. 5, December 2003, pp. S2) **[36937]**, **[37249]**, **[56772]**, **[59371]**

"What Makes Topeka Unique" in *Ingram's* (Vol. 29, No. 8, August 2003, pp. S6) **[52750]**

"What Makes You Great? Close Deals by Selling Value" in *My Business* (October/November 2003, pp. 43) **[51900]**

"What is the Most Effective Way to Advertise?" in *Home Business* (Vol. 12, March/April 2005, No. 2, pp. 56) **[834]**, **[47720]**

What No Ever Tells You About Starting Your Own Business: Real-Life Start-Up Advice from 101 Successful Entrepreneurs **[29773]**, **[35722]**, **[39107]**, **[46599]**

What No One Ever Tells You about Starting Your Own Business: Real Life Start-Up Advice from 101 Successful Entrepreneurs **[29774]**, **[35723]**

"What Not To Do in a Press Release" in *Inc.* (January 1, 2004) **[36938]**, **[47721]**, **[50704]**

"What Office?" in *Entrepreneur* (Vol. 33, October 2005, No. 10, pp. 94) **[28372]**, **[28989]**, **[34695]**

"What the One Hand Giveth" in *Ingram's* (Vol. 28, No. 9, September 2002, pp. 15) **[32790]**, **[40824]**

"What One Man Can Do" in *Inc.* (September 2005, pp. 144-153) **[38944]**, **[54276]**

"What does 'open source' mean?" in *Crain's Detroit Business* (Vol. 19, No. 15, April 14, 2003, pp. 1) **[6191]**, **[6490]**

"What to Pay" in *My Business* (November/December 2001, pp. 47) **[35139]**, **[42459]**, **[45812]**

"What Price Time?" in *Home Office Computing* (Vol. 18, No. 10, October 2000, pp. 14) **[31247]**, **[42754]**, **[52608]**, **[55001]**

"What Rate Hike?" in *Business Week* (No. 3658, December 6, 1999, pp. F9) **[38453]**

"What Really Works" in *Harvard Business Review* (Vol. 81, No. 7, July 2003, pp. 42) **[45813]**, **[53027]**

"What a Relief!" in *Entrepreneur* (Vol. 31, No. 8, August 2003, pp. 57) **[49355]**, **[54865]**

"What a relief! New tax laws mean more money stays in your business" in *Entrepreneur* (Vol. 30, No. 12, December 2002, pp. 74) **[24072]**, **[54866]**

What Self-Made Millionaires Really Think, Know and Do: A Straight-Talking Guide to Business Success and Personal Riches **[30038]**, **[36939]**, **[47722]**, **[56084]**

"What Should I Do? Last Year's Poor Performance Can Push This Year's Quotas Higher" in *Sales & Marketing Management* **[28990]**, **[51901]**

"What Should You Do" in *Sales and Marketing.com* (Vol. 156, No. 3, March 2004, pp. 8) **[45814]**, **[51902]**

"What about Small Business?" in *Success* (Vol. 47, No. 1, January 2000, pp. 15) **[36940]**, **[40825]**

"What a Smile Means" in *Inc.* (October 1, 2003) **[27533]**, **[47723]**

"What to do when bad news hits your stocks" in *Women in Business* (Vol. 53, No. 3, May-June, 2001, pp. 20) **[15597]**, **[38454]**

"What Taboo?" in *Entrepreneur* (Vol. 28, No. 10, October 2000, pp. 18) **[54277]**

What Tadoo **[41316]**

What They Don't Teach You at Harvard Business School **[39734]**

"What the Titans Can Teach Us" in *Harvard Business Review* (Vol. 79, No. 11, December 2001, pp. 70) **[28991]**, **[30626]**, **[36941]**, **[45815]**, **[47724]**

"What To Do as Interest Rates Rise" in *Black Enterprise* (Vol. 35, September 2004, No. 2, pp. 88) **[10244]**, **[21038]**

"What To Do When Your Client Declares Bankruptcy" in *Home Business* (Vol. 13, January/February 2006, No. 1, pp. 76) **[10245]**, **[31604]**, **[38455]**, **[42755]**

"What Took You So Long To Call?" in *Fast Company* (November 2001, pp. 165) **[5172]**, **[14602]**, **[28992]**

"What Venture Trends Can Tell You" in *Harvard Business Review* (Vol. 81, No. 7, July 2003, pp. 18) **[54070]**, **[55938]**

"What will Wall Street do on a red alert?" in *Wall Street Journal* (February 27, 2003, pp. C1) **[22421]**, **[40826]**

What Went Wrong? **[45944]**

"What Will Remain of PGE" in *Business Journal-Portland* (Vol. 20, No. 29, September 19, 2003, pp. 1) **[296]**, **[39128]**, **[40827]**

"What Women Want" in *Entrepreneur* (Vol. 32, No. 2, February 2004, pp. 54) **[47725]**, **[51903]**

"What Women Want at Work" in *Marketing to Women* (Vol. 20, January 2007, No. 1, pp. 5) **[28993]**, **[33276]**, **[47726]**

"What Works" in *Business 2.0* (Vol. 6, May 2005, No. 4, pp. 49-51) **[6859]**, **[42109]**

"What Works For You?" in *My Business* (April/May 2003, pp. 16) **[13516]**, **[43420]**

"What Works: Start Last, Finish First" in *Business 2.0* (Vol. 7, January/February 2006, No. 1, pp. 41-43) **[35724]**, **[39108]**

"What Works and What Doesn't - A Job Hunter's Primer to Looking for a Job on the Internet" in *Women in Business* (Vol.54, No.3 May-Jun.) **[14603]**, **[26013]**, **[34696]**, **[42460]**

"What You Look Like Online" in *Black Enterprise* (Vol. 37, January 2007, No. 6, pp. 56) **[9241]**, **[9582]**, **[14604]**, **[26014]**, **[42461]**, **[47727]**, **[50705]**

"What You Need to Know About Stock Options" in *Harvard Business Review* (Vol. 78, No. 2, March 2000, pp. 121) **[26953]**

"What Your Country Can Do For You" in *Inc.* (July 1, 2003) **[40107]**

"Whatcom E-View Moving to New Space" in *Bellingham Business Journal* (December 2006, pp. A3) **[14605]**, **[27534]**, **[30184]**, **[34697]**

"Whatever it takes" in *BlackEnterprise* (Vol. 32, No. 3, October 2001, pp. 54) **[39667]**, **[47728]**, **[49563]**, **[50706]**

W.J. Whatley Inc. **[1573]**

What's the Big Idea?: How to Win with Outrageous Ideas (That Sell) **[835]**

"What's the Biggest Problem in American Business? An Excess of Loyalty" in *Inc.* (May 1, 2005) **[39668]**, **[45816]**

"What's Brewing at Starbucks?" in *Black Enterprise* (Vol. 35, August 2004, No. 1, pp. 25) **[11358]**, **[28994]**

"What's your real cost of capital?" in *Harvard Business Review* (Vol. 80, No. 10, October 2002, pp. 114) **[30039]**, **[39669]**

"What's a Clawback?" in *Venture Capital Journal* (September 1, 2005) **[55939]**

"What's a Company Worth? It Depends on Which GP You Ask" in *Venture Capital Journal* (Vol. 42, No. 5, May 2002, pp. 40-41) **[15598]**, **[50258]**, **[55940]**

"What's Cookin'?" in *Entrepreneur* (Vol. 32, December 2004, No. 12, pp. 30) **[29576]**, **[38945]**, **[40828]**

"What's the Deal?" in *Entrepreneur* (Vol. 31, No. 10, October 2003, pp. 34) **[3608]**, **[27535]**, **[39670]**, **[45817]**

"What's in a Domain Name?" in *Home Office Computing* (Vol. 18, No. 8, August 2000, pp. 81) **[26015]**, **[30040]**, **[34698]**

What's Ethical in Business? **[37529]**

"What's the best way to get noticed by an executive-search firm?" in *Wall Street Journal* (May 28, 2002, pp. B12) **[9583]**, **[45818]**

"What's For Dinner?" in *Entrepreneur* (Vol. 31, No. 8, August 2003, pp. 148) **[4522]**, **[7803]**, **[35725]**, **[56084]**

"What's In a Name?" in *Entrepreneur* (Vol. 32) **[836]**, **[14606]**, **[26016]**, **[34699]**, **[47729]**

"What's In a Name?" in *Inc.* (July 1, 2004) **[12918]**, **[20162]**, **[30041]**, **[36942]**, **[47730]**, **[50479]**

"What's In a Name? Often Overlooked, Choosing the Right Business Moniker is Key" in *Black Enterprise* (Vol. 34, No. 4, Nov. 2003) **[29775]**, **[46600]**

"What's In a Name? Quite a Lot, Actually" in *Crain's Detroit Business* (Vol. 21, October 3, 2005, No. 43, pp. 8) **[56475]**

"What's In Store? Get Ahead of the Game with the Latest Retail Trends" in *Entrepreneur* (Vol. 33, September 2005, No. 9, pp. 84) **[51401]**, **[51408]**, **[54071]**

"What's In Your Wallet? The Smartcard Is Emerging as a Major E-Commerce Tool" in *Black Enterprise* (Vol. 36, November 2005, No. 4) **[8325]**, **[34700]**, **[54072]**

"What's In Your Wallet?" in *Tradeshow Week* (Vol. 34, December 13, 2004, No. 50, pp. 1) **[22578]**, **[25047]**, **[45819]**, **[55178]**

"What's It Worth? Get Your Prices Right, Or It'll Cost You" in *Entrepreneur* (Vol. 32, December 2004, No. 12, pp. 92) **[31077]**, **[51409]**

"What's New for 2002 Returns?" in *My Business* (February/March 2003, pp. 42) **[40829]**, **[54867]**

What's New in Benefits & Compensation **[26992]**

"What's New" in *Entrepreneur.com* (Vol. 34, February 2006, No. 2, pp. 104) **[14696]**, **[38456]**, **[38693]**

"What's Next" in *Business 2.0* (Vol. 6, July 2005, No. 6, pp. 27-28) **[5173]**, **[24462]**, **[42110]**

"What's Next: Data Disasters" in *Inc.* (November 1, 2003) **[27684]**, **[29577]**, **[34701]**

"What's Next? Hardware that Can Straddle Wireless LANs and Cellular Networks" in *Entrepreneur* (Vol. 32, December 2004, No. 12, pp. 49) **[5174]**, **[6860]**, **[42111]**, **[49356]**

"What's Next" in *Inc.* (Volume 27, March 2005, No. 3, pp. 59-60) **[28995]**, **[42112]**

"What's Next: Internet Phone Service is Here" in *Inc.* (October 1, 2003) **[5175]**, **[14607]**, **[34702]**

"What's Next? Mistakes Were Made" in *Inc.* (November 2006, pp. 65-66) **[27536]**, **[42901]**, **[45820]**

"What's Next: Power Surge" in *Inc.* (July 1, 2003) **[14608]**, **[54073]**

"What's Next for The Internet" in *Venture Capital Journal* (July 1, 2003) **[14609]**, **[28996]**, **[34703]**, **[55941]**

"What's Next: They've Got Your Number" in *Inc.* (August 1, 2003) **[22422]**, **[29578]**, **[30265]**

"What's the Plan? How President Bush's Second-Term Agenda Will Affect You" in *Entrepreneur* (Vol. 33, January 2005, No. 1, pp. 24) **[26954]**, **[39671]**, **[40830]**, **[54868]**

"What's the Plan? Need a Marketing Plan?" in *Entrepreneur* (Vol. 32, December 2004, No. 12, pp. 94) **[837]**, **[47731]**

"What's your problem?" in *Entrepreneur* (Vol. 31, No. 5, May 2003, pp. 126) **[9]**, **[838]**, **[1535]**, **[2854]**, **[7511]**, **[18767]**, **[23860]**, **[31508]**, **[35726]**, **[42756]**, **[47732]**

"What's your problem? People don't open junk mail, so send a postcard" in *Entrepreneur* (Vol. 30, No. 3, March 2002, pp. 142) **[47733]**, **[51904]**

"What's the Secret to Successful CRM?" in *E-business Advisor* (Vol. 18, No. 8, August 2000, pp. 41) **[26017]**, **[31903]**, **[34704]**

"What's Something H20 Plus Founder Cindy Melk Can't Live Without? (Hint)" in *Inc.* (May 1, 2005) **[2611]**, **[7909]**

What's Stopping You?: Attitude Adjustment for the About-to-Be Entrepreneur **[36943]**

"What's That Bad Odor at Innovation Skunkworks?" in *Fortune* (Vol. 140, No. 12, December 20, 1999, pp. 338) **[45821]**

"What's That Ringing in iPod's Ears?" in *Business Week* (January 16, 2006, No. 3967, pp. 70-71) **[5176]**, **[17778]**, **[49357]**

"What's Up Doc?" in *Entrepreneur* (Vol. 28, No. 10, October 2000, pp. 132) **[13786]**, **[37087]**, **[48894]**

"What's Up Doc? They May Not be Old Enough for Medical School, But Now Kids Can Look the Part" in *Entrepreneur* (Vol. 32, July 2004) **[5579]**, **[5728]**, **[46487]**, **[56476]**

"What's a VC Doing on a Public Board?" in *Venture Capital Journal* (Vol. 42, No. 8, August 2002, pp. 5-6) **[55942]**

"What's the word? (Extra: Commercial Vehicle Guide)" in *Entrepreneur* (Vol. 30, No. 12, December 2002, pp. 43) **[18162]**, **[49564]**

What's Working for American Companies in International Sales & Marketing **[47811]**, **[51934]**

What's Working in Credit & Collections **[31614]**

What's Working in Human Resources **[42919]**

What's Working in Sales Management **[51935]**

"What's Wrong with Computer-Generated Images of Perfection in Advertising?" in *Journal of Business Ethics* (Vol. 45, No. 3, July 2003) **[37530]**, **[47734]**

"What's Wrong with Executive Compensation" in *Harvard Business Review* (Vol. 81, No. 1, January 2003, pp. 69) **[26955]**, **[36944]**, **[45822]**

"What's on Your Agenda?" in *Fast Company* (June 2001, pp. 85) **[39672]**, **[45823]**

"What's Your Angle? Get Fresh Ideas When You Change Your Perspective" in *Entrepreneur* (Vol. 31, No. 9, September 2003, pp. 81) **[3609]**, **[36945]**, **[45824]**

"What's Your Company Worth Now?" in *Inc.* (July 1, 2003) **[38457]**, **[39673]**

"What's Your Fiscal Year" in *My Business* (February/March 2003, pp. 44) **[40831]**, **[54869]**

"What's Your Problem? A Mobile Photography Business Can Go a Long Way If You Know Where You're Going" in *Entrepreneur* (July 2004) **[19286]**, **[37577]**

"What's Your Problem?" in *Entrepreneur* (Vol. 33, October 2005, No. 10, pp. 97) **[8327]**, **[8407]**, **[23643]**, **[23740]**, **[30042]**, **[30185]**, **[30751]**, **[31605]**, **[40832]**, **[42757]**, **[54870]**

"What's Your Problem?" in *Entrepreneur.com* (Vol. 34, February 2006, No. 2, pp. 102) **[42560]**, **[44450]**, **[48895]**

"What's Your Problem? So You Want to Start a Secretarial Service" in *Entrepreneur* (Vol. 31, No. 10, October 2003, pp. 109) **[25527]**, **[26099]**

"What's Your Problem? When to Tell Customers You Work From Your Home" in *Entrepreneur* (Vol. 32, December 2004, No. 12, pp. 104) **[36946]**, **[42758]**

"What's Your Problem? Your Store May Not Be a Big, City-Slicker Business" in *Entrepreneur* (Vol. 31, No. 9, July 2003, pp. 104) **[5729]**, **[9648]**, **[11805]**, **[51410]**

"What's Your Project's Real Price Tag?" in *Harvard Business Review* (Vol. 81, No. 9, September 2003, pp. 20) **[297]**, **[26401]**

What's Your Risk? **[56649]**

"What's Your 'ROI?'" in *My Business* (February/March 2003, pp. 24) **[4856]**, **[23258]**, **[49358]**

Wheaton Area Chamber of Commerce **[61680]**

Wheaton Chamber of Commerce **[59699]**

"The Wheel Deal" in *Fast Company* (September 2001, pp. 168) **[16275]**, **[30445]**

Wheel Fun Rentals **[21392]**

Wheelchair Getaways, Inc. **[2103]**

Wheeler & Associates **[43004]**

Wheeler Chamber of Commerce and Economic Development Corporation **[65558]**

Wheeler County Chamber of Commerce **[59178]**

Wheeler and Young Inc. **[3832]**, **[6533]**, **[16679]**, **[31473]**, **[46139]**

Wheelers RV Resort & Campground Guide **[4241]**

Wheeling Area Chamber of Commerce **[66308]**

Wheeling - Prospect Heights Area Chamber of Commerce and Industry **[59700]**

Wheels 4 Rent Used Car Rentals **[2104]**

Wheels America Advertising **[900]**

"Wheels of Fortune" in *Entrepreneur* (Vol. 33, March 2005, No. 3, pp. 128) **[2505]**, **[36947]**

"Wheels in Motion: Ian Hardman Takes Rims to the Next Level" in *Black Enterprise* (Vol. 34, No. 5, December 2003, pp. S9) **[1986]**

Wheels of Time **[2088]**, **[25446]**

"When is using a property manager appropriate?" in *Wall Street Journal* (April 10, 2002, pp. B10) **[20062]**, **[52396]**

"When diamonds aren't forever" in *Black Enterprise* (Vol. 31, No. 5, December 2000, pp. 169) **[1866]**

"When company values backfire" in *Harvard Business Review* (Vol. 80, No. 11, November 2002, pp. 18) **[28997]**, **[30627]**, **[37531]**

"When your good sales go bad: Ask, don't whine" in *Atlanta Business Chronicle* (Vol. 24, No. 13, August 24, 2001, pp. 3B) **[51905]**

"When small firms work from big-name locations" in *Boston Business Journal* (Vol. 22, No. 3, February 22, 2002, pp. S6) **[20063]**, **[52751]**

"When a BlackBerry Is Overkill: The Phones Are Fine for Reading, But Not Writing e-Mails" in *Business Week* (January 31, 2005, pp. 20) **[4857]**, **[5177]**, **[14610]**, **[23259]**, **[49359]**, **[53535]**

"When BlackBerry Use Causes Pain" in *San Jose Mercury News* (February 28, 2005) **[6861]**, **[37335]**, **[49360]**

"When the Boss Won't Budge" in *Harvard Business Review* (Vol. 78, No. 1, January 2000, pp. 25) **[45825]**

"When Bots Collide" in *Harvard Business Review* (Vol. 78, No. 4, July 2000, pp. 17) **[14611]**, **[34705]**

"When Business is Personal" in *Home Office Computing* (Vol. 18, No. 9, September 2000, pp. 18) **[31904]**

"When your computer goes bye, make sure data stays put" in *Crain's Detroit Business* (Vol. 18, No. 22, June 3, 2002, pp. 57) **[6419]**, **[21264]**, **[49361]**

"When the Chips are Down" in *Red Herring* (No. 99, June 15 & July 1, 2001, pp. 122) **[6978]**, **[42113]**, **[50990]**, **[55943]**

"When Commerce Moves Online, Competition Can Work in Strange Ways" in *The New York Times* (August 24, 2000, pp. C2) **[34706]**

"When a Customer Believes in You...They'll Stick with You Almost No Matter What" in *Fast Company* (June 2001, pp. 138) **[31905]**

"When Does Bending Rules Become Breaking Rules?" in *Atlanta Business Chronicle* (Vol. 24, No. 10, August 10, 2001, pp. 46A) **[37532]**, **[45826]**

"When a partner doesn't work out" in *My Business* (November/December 2001, pp. 48) **[39674]**, **[50259]**

"When in Doubt Grab a Mouse, or a Phone" in *Crain's Chicago Business* (Vol. 30, January 2007, No. 1, pp. 12) **[14612]**, **[26018]**, **[36948]**, **[39955]**, **[52609]**, **[53028]**

"When in Doubt, Outsource" in *PC Magazine* (January 4, 2000, pp. 146) **[49362]**, **[49756]**

"When Duty Calls" in *Entrepreneur* (Vol. 28, No. 3, March 2000, pp. 127) **[39675]**, **[40833]**

"When Egos Collide" in *Entrepreneur* (Vol. 28, No. 7, July 2000, pp. 113) **[37810]**

"When Everything Isn't Half Enough" in *Harvard Business Review* (Vol. 78, No. 2, March 2000, pp. 28) **[36949]**

"When the Going Gets Tough...many turn to financial counselors" in *Business Week Online* (November 15, 2002) **[10246]**, **[32791]**, **[38458]**

When Good Projects go Bad...and How to Fix Them (Canada) **[44859]**

When Good Projects Go Bad...and How to Fix Them **[44860]**

"When an Incubator Goes Cold" in *Business Week Online* () **[15599]**, **[32792]**, **[43061]**, **[55944]**

"When Investor Trust is Shaken: Retaining Client Confidence in a Time of Investment Scandals" in *Journal of Accountancy* (Vol. 198) **[298]**, **[2973]**, **[10247]**, **[15600]**, **[24073]**, **[27201]**

"When Is the Price Right?" in *Black Enterprise* (Vol. 34, July 2004, No. 12, pp. 42) **[31078]**, **[44256]**

"When It Comes to Shopping, Safety Comes First" in *Home Business* (Vol. 13, January/February 2006, No. 1, pp. 56) **[44176]**, **[51411]**, **[56477]**

"When it's time to retire, who will mind the gay-owned store?" in *Wall Street Journal* (February 16, 2000, pp. B1) **[30043]**

"When It's Time to Market that Matters Most" in *Inc.* (July 2000, pp. 92) **[13787]**, **[33500]**, **[43046]**

"When Leadership Means Letting Go" in *Law Firm Inc.* (October 2004) **[29579]**, **[36950]**, **[45827]**, **[47735]**

"When Life Happens: A New Trend In Employee Benefits" in *Rough Notes* (Vol. 145, No. 1, January 2003, pp. 46) **[13517]**, **[26956]**, **[35140]**, **[43421]**

"When the Love is Gone: How to Reignite Passion for the Job" in *Black Enterprise* (Vol. 35, January 2005, No. 6, pp. 54) **[35141]**, **[36951]**, **[45828]**

"When planning to landscape a property, earlier is better" in *Boston Business Journal* (Vol.) **[16031]**, **[20064]**

"When to Put the Brakes on Learning." in *Harvard Business Review* (Vol. 81, No. 2, February 2003, pp. 20) **[33277]**, **[35142]**, **[45829]**

"When to Roll Over" in *Black Enterprise* (Vol. 37, November 2006, No. 4, pp. 50) **[10248]**, **[15601]**, **[38459]**

"When a turnaround stalls" in *Harvard Business Review* (Vol. 80, No. 2, February 2002, pp. 45) **[28998]**, **[30992]**

"When Taking Candy From Babies Makes Sense" in *Fortune* (Vol. 141, No. 17, April 3, 2000, pp. 304) **[37811]**, **[50260]**, **[54074]**

"When Technology Runs Amok" in *Inc.* (Volume 27, July 2005, No. 7, pp. 53-54) **[6192]**, **[6420]**, **[42114]**

"When those at the Thanksgiving table are your team" in *Business First Columbus* (Vol. 18, No. 25, February 8, 2002, pp. B6) **[37812]**, **[45830]**

"When Will 'Content of Character' Count?" in *Black Enterprise* (Vol. 34, No. 6, January 2004, pp. 12) **[32070]**, **[33167]**, **[42462]**, **[44116]**

"When Wolfe Hires Someone for a Job Working a Cash Register or Cutting Meat, odds are, that Person was a Customer First" in *Inc.*(May2000) **[33278]**, **[42463]**

"When You Really Lose Customers" in *Entrepreneur* (Vol. 30, No. 1) **[14613]**, **[31906]**, **[34707]**, **[47736]**

"When You Speak, Lawmakers Listen" in *My Business* (June/July 2004, pp. 41) **[8326]**, **[26957]**, **[29580]**, **[31606]**, **[39676]**, **[40834]**, **[50261]**

"When You Want a Low Share Price" in *Inc.* (May 2000, pp. 171) **[26958]**

"When Your Job Really Makes You Sick" in *Black Enterprise* (Vol. 34, No. 5, December 2003, pp. 63) **[3610]**, **[16539]**, **[31248]**, **[42759]**, **[56478]**

"When Your Job Really Makes You Sick: Why You Need to Develop a High Adversity Quotient" in *Black Enterprise* (Vol. 34, December 2003) **[3611]**, **[16540]**, **[31249]**, **[42760]**, **[56479]**

"When You're no Longer Home Alone" in *Inc.* (December 1999, pp. 92) **[40835]**, **[42464]**, **[42761]**

When You're Turned Down-Turn On! **[10324]**, **[15720]**, **[51993]**

"Where Ads Aimed at Kids Come to Life" in *The New York Times* (December 13, 2000, pp. D14, H14) **[34708]**, **[47737]**

"Where Are the 529 Plans?" in *Black Enterprise* (Vol. 34, No. 5, December 2003, pp. 40) **[32292]**, **[33279]**, **[38460]**, **[54871]**

"Where Are They Now? Working, but More Calmly" in *Wall Street Journal* (April 8, 2002, pp. A17) **[34709]**, **[36952]**

"Where Are You Going?" in *My Business* (April/May 2003, pp. 46) **[28999]**, **[30044]**, **[30628]**, **[36953]**, **[47738]**

"Where Are You Headed?" in *Women in Business* (Vol. 53, No. 7, January-February 2002, pp. 22) **[36954]**, **[56480]**

Where to Buy Hardwood Plywood, Veneer, and Engineered Hardwood Flooring **[16322]**

"Where Do I E-Sign?" in *Black Enterprise* (Vol. 31, No. 5, December 2000, pp. 61) **[34710]**

"Where Do You Go From Here" in *Black Enterprise* (Vol. 31, No. 5, December 2000, pp. 87) **[38461]**, **[48480]**

"Where Everyone's a Winner: Sure, the Annual Trip to Hawaii Is a Great Reward For Your Top Performers" in *Sales & Marketing Management* **[26959]**, **[35143]**, **[45831]**, **[51906]**

"Where to Find Bits of History For Your Home" in *Crain's Detroit Business* (Vol. 21, October 3, 2005, No. 43, pp. 11) **[1334]**, **[1536]**, **[13679]**, **[21265]**

"Where to Find Business Answers; Advice and Education" in *Crain's New York Business* (Vol. 22, November 13, 2006, No. 46, pp. 24) **[29000]**, **[30045]**, **[33280]**, **[36955]**, **[47739]**, **[53029]**

Where to Find Venture Capital: A Resource Guide **[55945]**

"Where Fiorina Went Wrong; A Charismatic Leader, She Helped Make HP a Powerful Marketer" in *Business Week Online* (February 10, 2005) **[6862]**, **[45832]**

Where to Get the Money & Management Help for New Business Start-Ups & Small Business Growth: East-North Central Region, IL, IN, MI, OH, WI **[38462]**, **[55946]**

Where to Get the Money & Management Help for New Business Start-Ups & Small-Business Growth: East-South Central Region, AL, KY, MS, TN **[50991]**, **[55947]**

Where to Get the Money & Management Help for New Business Start-Ups & Small Business Growth: Mountain Region, AZ, CO, ID, MT, NV, NM, UT, WY **[38463]**, **[55948]**

Where to Get the Money & Management Help for New Business Start-Ups & Small Business Growth: Pacific Region, AK, CA, HI, OR, WA **[38464]**, **[55949]**

Where to Get the Money & Management Help for New Business Start-Ups & Small Business Growth: South Atlantic Region, DE, DC, FL, GA, MD, NC, SC, VA, WV **[38465]**, **[45833]**

Where to Get the Money & Management Help for New Business Start-Ups & Small Business Growth: West-North Central Region, IA, KS, MN, MO, NE, ND, SD **[38466]**, **[55950]**

Where to Get the Money & Management Help for New Business Start-Ups & Small Growth: West-South Central Region, AR, LA, OK, TX **[38467]**, **[55951]**

Where to Go When the Bank Says No: Alternatives for Financing Your Business **[44685]**

"Where Have the Leaders Gone?" in *Ingram's* (Vol. 29, No. 1, January 2003, pp. 4) **[29001]**, **[32793]**

"Where can you improve? Get the numbers" in *Crain's Detroit Business* (Vol. 19, No. 3, January 20, 2003, pp. 14) **[39677]**, **[55003]**

"Where is the new frontier of innovation?" in *Fast Company* (September 2001, pp. 128) **[35144]**, **[37210]**, **[44381]**, **[50992]**

"Where It's a Woman's World" in *Inc.* (January 1, 2004) **[36956]**, **[56481]**

"Where the Jobs Are" in *Black Enterprise* (Vol. 32, No. 7, February 2002, pp. 95) **[29002]**, **[32794]**

"Where the Jobs Are" in *Business Week* (January 16, 2006, No. 3967, pp. 42-43) **[42465]**, **[49757]**, **[54075]**

"Where Jobs Are Plenty, Challenge is Finding Right People" in *Crain's Detroit Business* (Vol. 22, November 27, 2006, No. 48, pp. 17) **[35145]**, **[37336]**, **[42466]**

Where to Make Money: A Rating Guide to Opportunities in America's Metro Areas **[29003]**

"Where Seed Money Really Comes From" in *Inc.* (August 1, 2003) **[44451]**, **[48896]**, **[55457]**

"Where Segway Finds Traction" in *Inc.* (September 1, 2003) **[44177]**, **[48811]**

"Where Small Business Stands: Your Voice Sends A Clear Message to Lawmakers" in *My Business* (December/January 2003, pp. 47) **[40836]**, **[54872]**

"Where There's Smoke...One Entrepreneur Feels the Heat of Anti-Smoking Laws" in *Entrepreneur* (Vol. 32, No. 2, February 2004, pp. 32) **[2357]**, **[21665]**, **[40837]**

Where There's a Will...(Leadership and Motivation) **[35206]**, **[45945]**

"Where To Go Next" in *Adweek* (Vol. 45, October 11, 2004, No. 38, pp. 24) **[839]**, **[47740]**

The Where-to-Sell-It Directory **[1335]**

Where to Write for Vital Records: Births, Death, Marriages & Divorces **[10954]**

"Wherefore Art Thou Board Member?" in *Entrepreneur* (Vol. 31, No. 10, October 2003, pp. 64) **[10249]**, **[15602]**, **[45834]**

"Where's the Beef? Has Your Business Lost Momentum?" in *Entrepreneur* (Vol. 31, No. 11, November 2003, pp. 92) **[29004]**, **[36957]**

"Where's Big Brother? Orwell's Nightmare Won't Be Coming to the Internet Anytime Soon" in *Entrepreneur* (Vol. 31, No. 7, July 2003) **[14614]**, **[34711]**

"Where's the Love?" in *Entrepreneur* (Vol. 31, No. 10, October 2003) **[30629]**, **[36958]**

Which Business?: Help in Selecting Your New Venture **[52397]**

"Which School is Right?" in *Hispanic Business* (September 2003, pp. 46) **[29581]**, **[33281]**, **[39678]**, **[45835]**

"Which Switch? Speed Up Your Network's Performance With a Fast Ethernet Switch" in *Entrepreneur* (Vol. 33, August 2005, No. 8, pp. 46) **[6818]**, **[6863]**, **[6979]**, **[49363]**, **[51430]**

Which Wich (Superior Sandwiches) **[8585]**

"While I'm Gone: Transitioning Into-and Back From-Family and Medical Leave" in *Black Enterprise* (Vol. 35, September 2004, No. 2) **[26960]**, **[41135]**

"Whipping up a great meeting" in *Black Enterprise* (Vol. 31, No. 5, December 2000, pp. 82) **[27537]**, **[45836]**

Whisper on Wall Street **[15690]**

"Whistle Blowers" in *Sales and Marketing.com* (Vol. 156, No. 3, March 2004, pp. 30) **[35146]**, **[51907]**

"Whistle Shop: Turn Your Store Into a Destination by Making Shopping an Event" in *Entrepreneur* (Vol. 33, March 2005, No. 3, pp. 86) **[31250]**, **[51412]**

White Bear Area Chamber of Commerce **[61681]**

White Center Chamber of Commerce **[66198]**

White Cloud Area Chamber of Commerce **[61443]**

White County Chamber of Commerce and Development Authority **[59179]**

White Glove Placement, Inc. **[9285]**

White Hall Chamber of Commerce **[57230]**

White Hen Pantry, Inc. **[2218]**, **[7800]**

White House Area Chamber of Commerce **[64986]**

White, Hutchinson, Leisure & Learning Group **[20739]**

"White Joins Pequot, Heads West Coast Ops." in *Venture Capital Journal* (Vol. 40, No. 10, November 2000, pp. 34, 36) **[42115]**, **[55952]**

White Lake Area Chamber of Commerce **[61444]**

White Mountain Publications **[66767]**

White, Nelson & Company L.L.P. **[50344]**

White Pine Chamber of Commerce **[62371]**

White Pines Management, L.L.C. **[61463]**

White Plains Outreach–Westchester Small Business Development Center **[62792]**

White Rock Publishing **[66779]**

White Settlement Area Chamber of Commerce **[65559]**

White Spot Restaurants **[22009]**

Whitefish Chamber of Commerce **[62206]**

Whitehall Area Chamber of Commerce **[63825]**, **[66555]**

Whitehall Chamber of Commerce **[63042]**

Whitehouse Area Chamber of Commerce **[65560]**

Whites City Chamber of Commerce **[62718]**

Whitesboro Area Chamber of Commerce **[65561]**

Whitewater Area Chamber of Commerce **[66556]**

Whiting - Robertsdale Chamber of Commerce **[60022]**

Whitney and Co. **[58618]**

Whittier Area Chamber of Commerce **[57868]**

C B Richard Ellis Whittier Partners **[21099]**

Whizard Academy For Mathematics & English **[25487]**, **[33381]**

"Who Are the Gurus' Gurus? One Thing is Clear: They're Not the Usual Suspects" in *Harvard Business Review* (Vol. 81, No. 12, Dec. 2003) **[36959]**, **[45837]**

"Who Are We?" in *Hispanic Business* (July/August 2004, pp. 16) **[32795]**, **[48481]**

"Why the Union Can't Win" in *Inc.* (Volume 27, March 2005, No. 3, pp. 55) **[55322]**

"Why the Valley Way is Here to Stay" in *Fortune* (Vol. 141, No. 11, May 29, 2000, pp. 36+) **[32798]**, **[53031]**

Why Value Diversity? **[48629]**

"Why We Misread Motives" in *Harvard Business Review* (Vol. 81, No. 1, January 2003) **[33282]**, **[35151]**, **[36971]**, **[45854]**

"Why Wi-Fi?" in *Hispanic Business* (November 2003, pp. 74) **[34724]**, **[54082]**

Why Work?: Motivating the New Workforce **[35152]**

"Why You're Hiring All Wrong" in *Inc.* (February 1, 2002) **[31253]**, **[35153]**, **[42467]**

"Wi-Fi is a Must for New Office Space on Long Island" in *Long Island Business News* (February 13, 2004) **[5179]**, **[14623]**, **[34725]**, **[42118]**, **[49365]**, **[52754]**

"Wi-Fi Reloaded: Maybe All Your 802.11B Network Needs is a Boost" in *Entrepreneur* (Vol. 31, No. 7, July 2003, pp. 38) **[4860]**, **[5180]**, **[6865]**, **[6980]**, **[23263]**, **[42119]**, **[53537]**

"Wi-Fi, Where Are You? Where to Find the Nearest Free Hot Spot" in *Entrepreneur.com* (Vol. 34, February 2006, No. 2, pp. 19) **[6866]**, **[12655]**, **[13112]**, **[30448]**, **[42120]**

"Wi-Fi wherever" in *Entrepreneur* (Vol. 31, No. 5, May 2003, pp. 35) **[5181]**, **[7783]**, **[14624]**, **[21666]**, **[22621]**, **[34726]**, **[42121]**

Wibaux County Chamber of Commerce **[62207]**

Wichita Area Chamber of Commerce **[60433]**

Wichita Eagle (February 13, 2004); "Kansas Investigators Target Wichita Dating Service in Credit-Card Fraud Probe" in **[7060]**, **[29327]**, **[30236]**, **[31560]**

Wichita Falls Board of Commerce and Industry **[65562]**

Wichita Genealogical Society–Library **[11087]**

Wichita State University
　　　Center for Economic Development and Business Research **[66885]**
　　　Center for Entrepreneurship **[60450]**
　　　Center for Technology Application (MAMTC) **[60273]**
　　　Small Business Development Center **[60256]**, **[60267]**

Wickenburg Chamber of Commerce **[57079]**

Wickliffe Area Chamber of Commerce **[63826]**

Wicks 'N' Sticks **[11207]**

"Widespread Ignorance of Regulation and Labeling of Vitamins, Minerals and Food Supplements" in *PR Newswire* (December 23, 2002) **[17920]**, **[40845]**

Wienerschnitzel/Tastee Freez **[22010]**

Donald Wigal **[2804]**

Wikinomics: How Mass Collaboration Changes Everything **[39686]**, **[50265]**

Wilber Area Chamber of Commerce **[62308]**

Wilbur Chamber of Commerce **[66199]**

Wilbur Sings the Classics **[5413]**

Wilburton Chamber of Commerce **[64106]**

Wild Bird Center **[19184]**

Wild Bird Centers of America **[51477]**, **[56545]**

Wild Birds Unlimited, Inc. **[19185]**

"A Wild Ride: The Twists and Turns of Running Your Own Business Can Throw You for a Loop" in *Entrepreneur* (Vol. 31, October 2003) **[29010]**, **[36972]**

Wildomar Chamber of Commerce **[57869]**

Thomas Wilds Associates Inc. **[6306]**

Wilkes Chamber of Commerce **[63443]**

Wilkes University
　　　Foundations and Grants Management **[64622]**
　　　Small Business Development Center **[64344]**

Wilkinsburg Chamber of Commerce **[64534]**

"Will disruptive innovations cure health care?" in *Harvard Business Review* (Vol. 78, No. 5, September-October 2000, pp. 102) **[29011]**, **[49366]**

"Will Congress Act to Preserve Family Type Farming?" in *U.S. Farm News* (Vol. 25, No. 3, Autumn 2001, pp. 6-7) **[26561]**, **[37814]**, **[40846]**

Will County Center for Economic Development **[59701]**

"Will E-Commerce Erode Liberty?" in *Harvard Business Review* (Vol. 78, No. 3, May 2000, pp. 189) **[34727]**, **[40847]**

"'Will He Be a Friend or Foe?'" in *Fortune* (Vol. 142, No. 11, November 13, 2000, pp. F384V+) **[29012]**, **[32799]**

"Will I Lose If I Beat the Boss At Racquetball?" in *Fortune* (Vol. 151, January 24, 2005, No. 2, pp. 36) **[30994]**, **[45855]**

"Will journal publishers perish?" in *The Economist* (Vol. 355, No. 8170, May 13, 2000, pp. 81) **[2751]**, **[9168]**, **[18946]**

"Will Power: Build Flexibility Into Your Estate Plan so Heirs Can Avoid the Pitfalls of Changing Tax Laws" in *Entrepreneur* (Vol. 32) **[38470]**, **[54873]**

"Will Power: What Would You Do If You Suddenly Inherited a Business?" in *Entrepreneur* (Vol. 32, September 2004, No. 9, pp. 28) **[36973]**, **[39687]**

"Will Presentment Growth Enliven Online Bill Pay?" in *American Banker* (Vol. 170, February 2, 2005, No. 22, pp. 17) **[7032]**, **[10253]**, **[34728]**

Willamette Institute for Biological Control **[19060]**

Willamette Management Associates–Library **[10407]**, **[24192]**

Willapa Harbor Chamber of Commerce **[66200]**

Willard Area Chamber of Commerce **[63827]**

Willcox Chamber of Commerce and Agriculture **[57080]**

William Blair Capital Partners **[59765]**

William Paterson University of New Jersey–Office of Institutional Research and Assessment **[62624]**

Ralph E. Williams & Associates **[26647]**

Williams Coffee Pub Inc. **[5783]**

Williams College
　　　Center for Development Economics **[32875]**
　　　Center for Environmental Studies–Matt Cole Memorial Library **[9464]**, **[9512]**
　　　Chapin Library **[6088]**

Williams-Grand Canyon Chamber of Commerce **[57081]**

Horace Williams **[48649]**

"Williams-Sonoma Tries a New Recipe: Pottery Barn Kids is a hit" in *Business Week* (May 6, 2002, pp. 36) **[29013]**, **[51416]**

Williamsburg Chamber of Commerce **[60231]**

Williamsburg HomeTown Chamber of Commerce **[64788]**

Williamsburg Minority Business Development Center–Opportunity Development Association (ODA) **[63050]**

Williamsburg SBDC/Hampton Roads SBDC–Thomas Nelson Community College/Hampton Roads Chamber of Commerce **[65845]**

Williamson County - Franklin Chamber of Commerce **[64987]**

Williamson Imagineering **[44261]**

Williamsport-Lycoming Chamber of Commerce **[64535]**

Williamston Area Chamber of Commerce **[61445]**

Williamstown Chamber of Commerce **[61017]**

Williston Area Chamber of Commerce **[58956]**, **[63540]**

Williston Service Center–SBDC **[63501]**

Willits Chamber of Commerce **[57870]**

Willkie Farr & Gallagher–Library **[9544]**

Willmar Lakes Area Chamber of Commerce **[61682]**

Willoughby Area Chamber of Commerce **[63828]**

Willoughby News-Herald (December 17, 2002); "Global Fitness, Weight-Loss Franchise Opens Sites in Willoughby, Ohio Area" in **[19401]**, **[38816]**

Willoughby News-Herald (September 13, 2002); "Historic Redevelopment Pushes Kirtland, Ohio Ice Cream Shop to Relocate" in **[12780]**, **[37683]**, **[52681]**

"Willoughby, Ohio-Area Wedding Coordinators Look for Ways to Reduce Final Bill" in *News-Herald* (August 21, 2004) **[3202]**

Willow Chamber of Commerce **[56978]**

Willow Creek Chamber of Commerce **[57871]**

Willow Springs Area Chamber of Commerce **[62069]**

Willowbrook - Burr Ridge Chamber of Commerce and Industry **[59702]**

Willowick Chamber of Commerce **[63829]**

Willows Area Chamber of Commerce **[57872]**

Wills Point Chamber of Commerce **[65563]**

Willy Dog **[7102]**

Wilmette Chamber of Commerce **[59703]**

Wilmington Chamber of Commerce **[57873]**, **[59704]**, **[61018]**

Wilmington - Clinton County Chamber of Commerce **[63830]**

Wilmington Minority Business Enterprise Office **[58653]**

Wilshire Center Chamber of Commerce **[57874]**

Wilson Biographies **[17658]**

Wilson Chamber of Commerce **[63444]**

Steve Wilson & Co. **[35267]**

Wilson Technical Community College–Small Business Center **[63482]**

Wilsonville Chamber of Commerce **[64283]**

Wilton Appreciation Series 100—Grades K-4 **[5414]**

Wilton Chamber of Commerce **[58575]**, **[60232]**

Wimberley Chamber of Commerce **[65564]**

"Win Consumers with Better Usability" in *E-business Advisor* (Vol. 18, No. 6, June 2000, pp. 16) **[26019]**, **[34729]**

Win Government Contracts for Your Small Business **[30995]**, **[38465]**, **[40109]**

WIN Home Inspection **[3287]**

Win-Win Negotiations: An Overview (Canada) **[27613]**

Winchester Area Chamber of Commerce **[60023]**

Winchester Chamber of Commerce **[61019]**

Winchester-Clark County Chamber of Commerce **[60577]**

Winchester-Frederick County Chamber of Commerce **[65960]**

Winco Window Cleaning & Janitorial **[3390]**

Wind Energy Weekly **[9396]**, **[23337]**, **[37350]**

Wind Point Partners (Chicago) **[59766]**

Windom Area Chamber of Commerce and Visitors Bureau **[61683]**

Window Brigade **[3391]**

Window Covering Manufacturers Association **[2563]**, **[13636]**

Window and Door Manufacturers Association **[4474]**

Window Gang **[19801]**

Window Genie **[3392]**, **[19802]**

Window King **[3393]**

Window Master **[52635]**

"Window of Opportunity" in *Small Business Opportunities* (Summer 2005) **[3327]**, **[19798]**, **[42763]**

Window Works **[26087]**

"Windows 98 Lives" in *Black Enterprise* (Vol. 34, No. 3, October 2003, pp. 51) **[6867]**, **[25528]**, **[26100]**, **[31908]**

Windows to a View: Chris Reis **[1634]**

"Winds of Change" in *Entrepreneur* (Vol. 33, October 2005, No. 10, pp. 82) **[31044]**, **[31909]**, **[51915]**

"Windshields Go Sporty" in *Indianapolis Business Journal* (Vol. 25, November 29, 2004, No. 38, pp. 15) **[11222]**, **[18163]**

Windsor Area Chamber of Commerce **[62070]**

Windsor/Bertie County Chamber of Commerce **[63445]**

Windsor Chamber of Commerce **[58436]**, **[58576]**

Windsor Chamber of Commerce and Visitors Center **[57875]**

Windsor Locks Chamber of Commerce **[58577]**

The Windsor Press Inc. **[64635]**

Windstar Wildlife Garden Weekly **[9397]**, **[40876]**

"'Windtunnel' Vision: Air Out Some New Ideas with This Technique" in *Entrepreneur* (Vol. 31, No. 6, June 2003, pp. 76) **[45856]**, **[47750]**

Windward Holdings **[58619]**

Windward Ventures (Westlake Village) **[58190]**

The Wine Advocate **[23540]**

"Wine Battle May Be Aging Toward Compromise" in *Crain's Detroit Business* (Vol. 21, October 10, 2005, No. 43, pp. 42) **[6105]**, **[10708]**, **[23518]**, **[40848]**

"Wise Up! When It Comes to Inventing a Successful Product, Experience May Be Your Best Asset" in *Entrepreneur* (Vol. 31, October 2003) **[6870]**, **[49370]**

"Wish I'd Thought Of That! Aim small to make it big? You bet." in *Fortune* (Vol. 141, No. 10, May 15, 2000, pp. F372C+) **[14630]**, **[34739]**, **[47752]**

"Wish List: What Do People Want Most in a Cell Phone" in *Entrepreneur* (Vol. 32, No. 1, January 2004, pp. 37) **[4210]**, **[5188]**, **[49371]**

"Wish You Were Here. Oh-You Are" in *Business Week* (January 23, 2006, No. 3968, pp. 84-85) **[24746]**, **[25272]**

"With the Big Dogs" in *Crain's Detroit Business* (Vol. 21, December 19, 2005, No. 51, pp. 3) **[19157]**, **[29021]**, **[38946]**, **[51417]**

"With dot-coms no longer soaring, financial backers get back to basics" in *The New York Times* (December 18, 2000, pp. C28) **[14631]**, **[34740]**, **[55958]**

"With Great Power Tools Comes Great Responsibility" in *Inc.* (May 1, 2005) **[16163]**, **[16384]**, **[56484]**

"With employee retention a headache, a small business builds entertainment into the work routine" in *Wall Street Journal* (March14,2000) **[35158]**, **[45859]**

"With large chains and specialty stores looking to expand their markets, Detroit becomes a Grocery Battleground" in *Crain's Detroit Business* **[11677]**, **[29022]**

"With Revenue Flattening, David Galbenski Needed a Bold New Plan" in *Inc.* (Volume 28, January 2006, No. 1, pp. 44-46) **[9242]**, **[9584]**, **[24540]**, **[29585]**, **[43880]**

"With the Right Guidance, Philanthropists Choose Best Way to Give" in *Miami Herald* (November 2003, 2003) **[54279]**

"With Rootlevel closed, Carriersnet to revise shipping-software project" in *Crain's Detroit Business* (Vol. 19, No. 16, Apr. 21, 2003) **[4861]**, **[6106]**, **[10709]**, **[23264]**, **[34741]**

"With So Many Bed and Breakfast Values on the Internet, Why Stay Home for the Holidays?" in *PR Newswire* (November 11, 2003) **[2455]**, **[34742]**

With These Hands **[8068]**

"Witness to history...and tragedy: a Wall Street veteran reflects on his 9/11 loss" in *Barron's* (Vol. 82, Sept. 9, 2002, pp. 26) **[10255]**, **[15608]**, **[36978]**, **[37816]**

"Witness protection" in *Entrepreneur* (Vol. 31, No. 4, April 2003, pp. 78) **[29586]**, **[37534]**, **[40850]**

"Witness Systems adopts anti-takeover plan" in *Atlanta Business Chronicle* (Vol. 25, November 15, 2002, No. 23 pp. 3A) **[15609]**, **[37212]**, **[50268]**

Wittenberg Area Chamber of Commerce **[66558]**

"WKR-Small Business" in *Entrepreneur* (Vol. 28, No. 2, February 2000, pp. 38) **[20348]**, **[36979]**

WLH & Associates **[31504]**

WMB and Associates **[47916]**

"WNET discovers 'virtual' solution to storage needs" in *InfoWorld* (Vol. 23, No. 5, January 29, 2001, pp. 56) **[49372]**

WNF Consulting Inc. **[49466]**, **[49666]**

Wok To U Express **[12090]**, **[22015]**

Franz Wolf **[7650]**

Wolf Point Chamber of Commerce and Agriculture **[62208]**

Wolf Ventures / Wolf Asset Management Corp. **[58464]**

Wolfe City Chamber of Commerce **[65568]**

Wolfforth Area Chamber of Commerce and Agriculture **[65569]**

"Woman Car Dealership Owner Brings Fresh Outlook to Male-Oriented Business" in *Long Island Business News* (February 27, 2004) **[18164]**, **[56485]**

Woman Entrepreneur: Do You Have What it Takes? **[56539]**

The Woman Entrepreneur-Out of Your Mind and into the Marketplace **[56486]**

The Woman Entrepreneur: 33 Personal Stories of Success **[56487]**

Woman to Woman: Street Smarts for Women Entrepreneurs **[56488]**

"A Woman's Job" in *My Business* (June/July 2004, pp. 50) **[38947]**, **[56489]**

Woman's Life Insurance Society **[26732]**

Wome n in Business (Vol. 53, No. 1, January-February 2001, pp. 42) "Developing a working relationship with your supervisor" in **[34866]**, **[45061]**

Women in Agribusiness **[26466]**

Women in B usiness (Vol. 53, No. 2, March-April, 2001, pp. 34) "The relationship between quality, time and cost" in **[51306]**, **[52385]**

Women in Busines s (Vol. 53, No. 2, March-April, 2001, pp. 30) "Protecting your company from high turnover" in **[35031]**, **[42384]**, **[45570]**, **[56376]**

Women in Business **[56530]**

Women in Business (Vol. 54, No. 5, September-October 2002, pp. 18) "ABWA entrepreneurs are making fun their business!" in **[2327]**, **[2422]**, **[5877]**, **[56112]**

Women in Business (Vol. 54, No. 2, March-April 2002, pp. 32) "Building visibility" in **[27309]**, **[44964]**

Women in Business (Vol. 54, No. 5, September-October 2002, pp. 11) "Bus or bust" in **[16180]**, **[22476]**, **[24898]**, **[56148]**

Women in Business (Vol. 54, No. 5, Sept.-Oct. 2002, pp. 28) "Business Owners: Are You Getting Your Share of Investment Capital?" in **[35893]**, **[44488]**, **[55528]**, **[56151]**

Women in Business (Vol. 53, No. 5, September-October, 2001, pp. 12) "Can You 'Pass' on Passion?" in **[34846]**, **[35911]**, **[44984]**

Women in Business (Vol. 53, No. 4, July-August, 2001, pp. 38) "Career smarts" in **[35919]**, **[39224]**

Women in Business (Vol. 53, No. 1, January-February, 2001, pp. 26) "Career smarts: Bouncing back from career setbacks" in **[35918]**, **[39223]**

Women in Business (Vol. 54, No. 2, March-April 2002, pp. 24) "Changing for the better through conferences and conventions" in **[24906]**, **[44991]**, **[56159]**

Women in Business (Vol. 54, No. 5, September-October 2002, pp. 12) "Changing times: tax relief for women business owners" in **[37954]**, **[40253]**, **[54488]**, **[56160]**

Women in Business (Vol. 54, No. 5, September-October 2002, pp. 41) "Clear leadership" in **[30520]**, **[35950]**, **[45004]**

Women in Business (Vol. 53, No. 5, September-October, 2001, pp. 34) "Cybersecretary" in **[7128]**, **[54939]**

Women in Business (Vol. 53, No. 3, May-June, 2001, pp. 26) "Designing web sites that work" in **[13963]**, **[25829]**, **[46880]**

Women in Business (Vol. 53, No. 3, May-June, 2001, pp. 8) "Developing performers" in **[34865]**, **[36012]**, **[45060]**

Women in Business (Vol. 54, No. 5, September-October 2002, pp. 30) "Eureka! I have an idea - how a business is born" in **[35435]**, **[56042]**

Women in Business (Vol. 53, No. 2, March-April, 2001, pp. 36) "Evaluating promotion opportunities" in **[34894]**, **[39317]**

Women in Business (Vol. 53, No. 7, January-February 2002, pp. 27) "Free yourself from taxes" in **[15016]**, **[54562]**

Women in Business (Vol. 53, No. 1, January-February, 2001, pp. 22) "Getting Noticed at Work" in **[27380]**, **[39354]**

Women in Business (Vol. 53, No. 5, September-October, 2001, pp. 5) "Handling people with tact and skill" in **[34924]**, **[45217]**

Women in Business (Vol. 53, No. 7, January-February 2002, pp. 9) "Helping each other - one woman at a time" in **[45230]**, **[56262]**

Women in Business (Vol. 54, No. 5, September-October 2002, pp. 17) "How to Be a Good Listener" in **[36300]**, **[45255]**

Women in Business (Vol. 53, No. 3, May-June, 2001, pp. 16) "How to beat the Monday blues" in **[39392]**, **[54956]**

Women in Business (Vol. 53, No. 3, May-June, 2001, pp. 12) "Hyper business or just...hyperbusy?" in **[39401]**, **[53789]**

Women in Business (Vol. 54, No. 5, September-October 2002, pp. 14) "I want to start my own business" in **[35520]**, **[56054]**

Women in Business (Vol. 53, No. 7, January-February 2002, pp. 13) "If you want something done right, delegate it" in **[27405]**, **[45284]**, **[54958]**

Women in Business (Vol. 54, No. 2, March-April 2002, pp. 11) "In Search of a Leader" in **[36343]**, **[45296]**

Women in Business (Vol. 53, No. 2, March-April, 2001, pp. 26) "Investment Chat Rooms Can Be Hazardous" in **[14164]**, **[15145]**, **[30233]**, **[38152]**

Women in Business (Vol. 53, No. 5, September-October, 2001, pp. 46) "Is it time to consolidate IRAs?" in **[15180]**, **[38165]**

Women in Business (Vol. 53, No. 7, January-February 2002, pp. 21) "Keeping your computer safe" in **[4710]**, **[6175]**, **[22277]**, **[23060]**, **[49110]**

Women in Business (Vol. 54, No. 2, March-April 2002, pp. 22) "Keeping pace with technology" in **[33146]**, **[49111]**, **[49514]**

Women in Business (Vol. 53, No. 2, March-April, 2001, pp. 38) "Life after business" in **[30369]**, **[56302]**

Women in Business (Vol. 53, No. 1, January-February, 2001, pp. 41) "Looking for a club that's more than just for fun?" in **[15235]**, **[38201]**

Women in Business (Vol. 53, No. 2, March-April, 2001, pp. 22) "Making ethical business decisions" in **[37473]**, **[56312]**

Women in Business (Vol. 54, No. 2, March-April 2002, pp. 33) "Network for a greater good in 2002" in **[27452]**, **[45461]**

Women in Business (Vol. 53, No. 7, January-February 2002, pp. 40) "Networking know-how" in **[45462]**, **[56337]**

Women in Business (Vol. 54, No. 2, March-April 2002, pp. 27) "Never say 'NO'" in **[31797]**

Women in Business (Vol. 54, No. 2, March-April 2002, pp. 30) "On the road to fitness" in **[30394]**, **[45488]**, **[56355]**

"Women Business Owners Get Credit Easily" in *Marketing to Women* (Vol. 19, November 2006, No. 11, pp. 12) **[8327]**, **[29023]**, **[30706]**, **[31607]**, **[47753]**, **[56490]**

"Women Business Owners Seek Financing" in *Marketing to Women* (Vol. 19, December 2006, No. 2, pp. 8) **[30631]**, **[30707]**, **[31608]**, **[38472]**, **[39690]**, **[44687]**, **[47754]**, **[48927]**, **[56491]**

Women Business Owners: Selling to the Federal Government **[56492]**

Women in Business (Vol. 53, No. 4, July-August, 2001, pp. 20) "Preparing for national leadership" in **[36642]**, **[56372]**

Women in Business (Vol. 54, No. 5, September-October 2002, pp. 10) "Professional athlete credits ABWA with the right 'assist'" in **[36649]**, **[56374]**

Women in Business (Vol. 53, No. 4, July-August, 2001, pp. 18) "Rating reasonable risks" in **[30589]**, **[39547]**

Women in Business (Vol. 53, No. 4, July-August, 2001, pp. 26) "Reading for retention" in **[33216]**, **[39548]**

Women in Business Roundtable **[57877]**

Women in Business (Vol. 53, No. 2, March-April, 2001, pp. 32) "Running on empty?" in **[36711]**, **[56390]**

Women in Business (Vol. 54, No. 3, May-June 2002, pp. 38) "Security at the Forefront" in **[22367]**, **[42410]**

Women in Business (Vol. 54, No. 3, May-June 2002, pp. 40) "Should you take the money...and run?" in **[26910]**, **[42412]**

Women in Business (Vol. 54, No. 2, March-April 2002, pp. 38) "Speak up!" in **[22563]**, **[27504]**

Women's and Children's Apparel and Accessories Mart [2136], [5300], [5749], [9658], [16221]

Women's & Children's Wear Buyers [5282], [5731]

"Women's Club Leads to Profitable Business" in *Lexington Herald-Leader* (August 28, 2002) [2359], [24838]

The Women's Conference [32979]

Women's Council of Realtors [20412]

Women's Division of the Lancaster Chamber of Commerce [63831]

"Women's Firms Reach Nearly $2 Trillion in Sales" in *Marketing to Women* (Vol. 19, October 2006, No. 10, pp. 12) [29026], [47757], [56508]

"Women's Fitness Chains Pour on 24 More Stores" in *Sacramento Business Journal* (Vol. 19, No. 25, August 30, 2002, pp. 1) [19447], [29027]

Women's Global Business Alliance L.L.C. [47917]

Womens Growth Capital Fund [58681]

Women's Health Boutique [2622], [7941], [11765]

Women's Health Concerns Sourcebook [41138]

Women's Healthy Environments Network [9342], [37240], [54126]

Women's Jewelry Association [15831]

Women's National Book Association [2670], [3023]

Women's Network for Entrepreneurial Training (WNET)–University of South Carolina–Small Business Development Center [64688]

Women's Organization for Mentoring, Entrepreneurship & Networking–(WOMEN) & Women's Network Inc.–Small Business Development Center [63580]

Women's Regional Publications of America [46617], [56106]

"Women's Talk Radio Network Launches" in *Marketing to Women* (Vol. 19, October 2006, No. 10, pp. 5) [20349], [27540], [47758]

Women's Ventures, Women's Visions: 29 Inspiring Stories from Women Who Started Their Own Business [56509]

Women's Yellow Pages "Referral Guide" [58288]

A Wonderful Wedding [18984]

"Won't You Be My Neighbor?" in *Entrepreneur* (Vol. 32, August 2004, No. 8, pp. 52) [44690], [55959]

WOOD [8059]

Wood County Small Business Development Center [63581]

Wood Dale Chamber of Commerce [59707]

Wood Design & Building [7582]

Wood Digest [4488]

Wood Lebois [7583]

Wood Moulding and Millwork Producers Association [4475]

Wood Re New [3394]

Wood & Wood Products [4489]

Woodall's Campground Directory [4243]

Woodall's Camping Guide for Canada [4244]

Woodall's Camping Guide for Far West [4245]

Woodall's Camping Guide for Frontier West [4246]

Woodall's Camping Guide for Great Lakes States [4247]

Woodall's Camping Guide for Great Plains & Mountain States [4248]

Woodall's Camping Guide for Mid-Atlantic States [4249]

Woodall's Camping Guide for New York & New England [4250]

Woodall's Camping Guide for Southern States [4251]

WOODALL's Northeast Outdoors [4257], [21186], [24768], [25314]

WOODALL'S Southern RV [21187]

Woodbridge Metro Chamber of Commerce [62575]

Woodburn Area Chamber of Commerce [64285]

"Woodbury-Based Bankers Life of New York Reports Record Sales" in *Long Island Business News* (February 20, 2004) [13521], [43424]

Woodbury Chamber of Commerce [61686]

Woodbury University–Library [5623], [13733], [43944], [46159]

Woodcraft Franchise Corp. [11916]

WoodenBoat [8060], [16765]

Woodford County Chamber of Commerce [60578]

Woodframe Furniture Restoration [10833]

The Woodhouse Day Spa [2413]

Woodland Area Chamber of Commerce [57878]

Woodland Chamber of Commerce [66202]

Woodland Hills Chamber of Commerce [57879]

Woodplay [23707]

Woodridge Area Chamber of Commerce [59708]

Woodshop News [4490], [8061]

Woodside Fund [58191]

Woodsmith [8062]

Woodson County Chamber of Commerce [60437]

Woodstock Area Chamber of Commerce [65804]

Woodstock Chamber of Commerce [65962]

Woodstock Chamber of Commerce and Arts [63043]

Woodstock Chamber of Commerce and Industry [59709]

Woodward Chamber of Commerce [64107]

Woodwork [4491], [8063]

Woodworker's Journal [8223]

Woodworking [4495]

Woody's Bar-B-Q [22016]

Wool Gathering [8064]

Wooster Area Chamber of Commerce [63832]

Worcester Business Journal [61161]

Worcester County Horticultural Society–Library [11549]

Worcester Polytechnic Institute–Division of Academic Affairs [61151]

Worcester Regional Chamber of Commerce [61021]

Word Engines Press Inc. [66677]

"Word games" in *Entrepreneur* (Vol. 31, No. 6, June 2003, pp. 76) [29587]

"Word Menu" in *Entrepreneur* (Vol. 31, No. 8, August 2003, pp. 6) [4862], [23265], [27541], [53538]

Word Processing/Desktop Publishing/Graphics Library [8647]

Word Processing Profits at Home: A Complete Business Plan for the Self-Employed Word Crafter [26101]

Word Processing Service Directory [26102]

"Word to the Wise" in *Entrepreneur* (Vol. 32, July 2004, No. 7, pp. 82) [38695]

WordPerfect 5.0 [49393]

WordPerfect for Desktop Publishing [8648]

"Words Fail Them" in *Hispanic Business* (May 2005, pp. 58) [25097], [41139], [54282]

Words From Woody [4492], [7584]

"Words of Wisdom Reap Huge Rewards" in *Success* (Vol. 47, No. 6, November 2000, pp. 50) [15610], [50269]

"Words from the Wise" in *Entrepreneur* (Vol. 28, No. 1, January 2000, pp. 42) [3615], [43971], [45863], [55458], [56510]

"Words to the Wise: Has Your Marketing Copy Lost Its Punch?" in *Entrepreneur* (Vol. 31, No. 10, October 2003, pp. 91) [841], [47759]

Work in America Institute, Inc. [23434]

"Work Area Clutter is Not a Problem Unless It's a Problem" in *St. Louis Post-Dispatch* (January 30, 2005) [3616], [31254], [49566]

"A Work of Art" in *Entrepreneur* (Vol. 32, December 2004, No. 12, pp. 24) [3617], [36984], [44179]

"Work At Home" in *Black Enterprise* (Vol. 34, July 2004, No. 12, pp. 145) [14632], [34744], [42561]

"The Work-At-Home Diaries" in *Inc.* (February 1, 2002) [30267], [42765]

"The Work-at-Home Hook" in *Home Office Computing* (Vol. 18, No. 11, November 2000, pp. 92) [35159], [42469], [42766]

"Work-At-Home Scheme" in *Black Enterprise* (Vol. 35, October 2004, No. 3, pp. 200) [30268], [42767]

Work From Home Jobs Directory [42768]

"Work Gear" in *St. Louis Post-Dispatch* (August 27, 2004) [5189], [6871], [18616], [30452], [49373], [49567]

Work of Her Own: A Woman's Guide to Success off the Career Track [56511]

"Work at Home? First, Get Real" in *Business Week* (No. 3699, September 18, 2000, pp. 112) [42769]

"Work at Home-More bandwidth means better performance for an important business tool called a virtual private network" in *PC Magazine* [34745], [42770]

Work Improvement Through Redesign and Simplification (Canada) [32980]

"Work, Interrupted: Think Work Distractions Are a Pain? Top CEOs Tend to Disagree" in *Entrepreneur* (Vol. 32, September 2004, No. 9) [20029], [36985], [45864], [55005]

"Work It" in *Entrepreneur* (Vol. 33, October 2005, No. 10, pp. 34) [35730], [39109]

"Work It! Score Great Deals With the Best-Kept Travel Secrets Around" in *Entrepreneur* (Vol. 32, August 2004, No. 8, pp. 28) [25273], [30453]

Work/Life Today [26993]

"Work Like an Insurance Company to Save Money" in *Journal of Accountancy* [302], [2974], [24076], [26405], [27202], [45865]

"Work with Me! Resolving Everyday Conflicts in Your Organization" in *Dispute Resolution Journal* (Vol. 56, No. 1, February-April 2001) [17063], [27542], [45866]

"Work with me" in *WorkingWoman* (Vol. 25, No. 6, June 2000, pp. 40) [34746], [50270], [56512]

Work & Motivation [35160]

"The work of leadership" in *Harvard Business Review* (Vol. 79, No. 11, December 2001, pp. 131) [35161], [45867]

"Work and Play" in *Fast Company* (November 2001, pp. 48) [39692], [49374]

The Work Prejudice Film [48630]

Work Smarter, Not Harder, the Service that Sells Workbook for Family Dining Operation [37817]

"Work Space" in *Tribune* (February 15, 2005) [11172], [17921], [19724], [52612], [56513]

Work Span [26994], [30759]

Work & Stress [56608]

"Work This Way" in *Entrepreneur* (Vol. 28, No. 6, June 2000, pp. 170) [6401], [7154]

The Work Truck Show and Annual NTEA Convention [25454]

"Workaholic Cooks Up Site" in *Crain's New York Business* (Vol. 23, January 29, 2007, No. 5, pp. F3) [14633], [21669], [26020], [34747], [36986], [52466]

WorkAmerica [15903]

"Workers as Assets: A Good Start But..." in *Employment Relations Today* (Vol. 27, No. 1, Spring 2000, pp. 1) [54086], [54283]

"Workers' Comp Claims Filed Have Decreased in Okla., Statistics Show" in *Journal Record* (Oklahoma City, OK) (February 8, 2007) [40853], [42902]

"Workers' Comp Rates to Fall" in *Sacramento Bee* (November 29, 2005) [13522], [43425], [54087]

Workers Compensation Insurance: Profiles of the State Systems [43426]

Worker's Compensation Insurance: The Survival Guide for Business [30744], [43427]

Workers' Compensation Monitor [30760]

"Workers' Con" in *Forbes* (Vol. 175, February 28, 2005, No. 4, pp. 34) [26961], [40854]

"Workers Simply Want to Be Organized" in *Home Office Computing* (Vol. 18, No. 12, December 2000, pp. 23) [23266], [42771], [49568], [54088]

Workers" in *Success* (Vol. 47, No. 1, January 2000, pp. 25); "How to Hire A [42294]

"Workforce Board Seeks To Improve Jobs" in *Bradenton Herald* (January 28, 2005) [29028], [33284], [35162], [52756]

Workforce Diversity [9256], [23413], [42920]

"Workforce Diversity in Small Business" in *Journal of Small Business Management* (Vol. 38, No. 3, July 2000, pp. 27) [42470], [45868], [48608]

Workforce Stability Alert [3626], [42921]

Work@home: A Practical Guide for Women Who Want to Work from Home [42562], [56085]

"Workin' the show" in *BlackEnterprise* (Vol. 32, No. 2, September 2001, pp. 58) [14634], [23267], [25052], [55181]

Working the Booth: Trade Show Success [25066], [55190]

"Working out the Bugs" in *My Business* (August/September 2002, pp. 54) [4322]

Working Drug Free [54358]

Master Index

Worksight [41305]

"Workspace Wonders" in *Small Business Opportunities* (Vol. 16, No. 2, March 2004, pp. 80) [18617], [42773], [49569]

WorkTalk Communications [27601], [27709]

Workteams and the Wizard of Oz [35210]

Worland Area Chamber of Commerce [66634]

"The World According to Clark" in *Business 2.0* (Vol. 6, May 2005, No. 4, pp. 88) [22818], [36991]

World AgExpo [26608]

World Airlines Clubs Association [945]

The World of ASP [16919]

World Association of Community Radio Broadcasters [20297]

World Association of Document Examiners-Membership Directory [11862]

"The World Bank's Innovation Market" in *Harvard Business Review* (Vol. 80, No. 11, November 2002, pp. 104) [44180], [44691], [48812], [54284]

World Beer Hunter [3158]

World Business Desk Reference: How to Do Business with 192 Countries by Phone, Fax, and Mail [43881]

"World Cities Alliance: www.worldcitiesalliance.com" in *Entrepreneur* (Vol. 31, No. 12, December 2003, pp. 8) [29030], [43882]

World Class Production and Inventory Management [44258]

World Class: Thriving Locally in the Global Economy [53033]

World Coin News [5859]

World of Concrete [16977]

World Confederation of Productivity Science [44719]

"World Cup Kicks Print Media Into High Gear" in *Hispanic Business* (December 2006, pp. 54) [842], [47762]

World Databases in Biosciences and Pharmacology [8857]

World Databases in Management [46146]

"A World of Difference" in *Entrepreneur* (Vol. 32, October 2004, No. 10, pp. 78) [36992], [50481], [54285]

The World Directory of Custom Bullet Makers [11732]

World Economic Processing Zones Association [57111]

World Economy (Vol. 24); "Conflicts and Conflict Resolution in International Anti-trust: Do We Need International Competition Rules?" in [14882], [27328], [43593], [49870]

World Energy Engineering Congress [23338]

World Exonumia [59817]

World Federation of Direct Selling Associations [51514]

"A World at their Feet" in *Kiplinger's Personal Finance Magazine* (Vol. 55, No. 1, January, 2001, pp. 128) [22750], [35732]

World Fishing and Outdoor Exposition [2213], [23702]

World Floor Covering Association [10505]

World Franchise Consultants [31505]

World Gaming Congress and Expo [10903], [55252]

World Gumbo Publishing [65680]

"The world in your backyard" in *WorkingWoman* (Vol. 25, No. 2, February 2000, pp. 72) [43883], [47763], [48613], [55323]

World Industrial Reporter-International Buyers' Guide Issue [13020]

World International Nail and Beauty Association [11780], [17853]

The World Is Flat: A Brief History of the Twenty-First Century [39694]

World Jewish Genealogy Organization–Library [11088]

World Jurist Association [54114]

World Life Research Institute [18533]

World Links [22017]

World M&A Network [3422]

World Maritime Directory [16748]

The World Markets Desk Book: A Region-by-Region Survey of Global Trade Opportunities [43884]

World Markets for Tires and Rubber [24589]

World Martial Arts Association [16910]

World Organization for Early Childhood Education [5333]

World Organization of Webmasters [13790]

World Packaging Directory [6107]

World Resources Volume 10935

The World Satellite Marketplace [22103]

"World Savings Bank Opens First LI Location" in *Long Island Business News* (February 6, 2004) [10256], [29031], [51418]

World Sign Associates [22785]

World Tire Conference and Exhibition [24593]

World Tourism Directory [24747], [25274]

World Trade Centers Association [12935]

World Trade Centre Montreal [32225]

World Trade Centre Vancouver [32226]

World Trade Connection [43914]

World Trade and Convention Centre Halifax [32227]

World Trade Network, Inc. [4038]

World Waterpark Association [1129]

"World of Wi-Fi" in *Entrepreneur* (Vol. 31, No. 8, August 2003, pp. 30) [5191], [49378]

World Wide Pet Industry Association [1464], [19147]

"World Wide Technology Expands" in *Black Enterprise* (Vol. 37, December 2006, No. 5, pp. 34) [29032], [42129], [43033]

WorldatWork [30727]

WorldatWork Journal [26995]

Worldgram Newsletter [3955], [14658]

"The world's a stage" in *Houston Business Journal* (Vol. 33, No. 49, April 18, 2003, pp. 31A) [22582], [25053]

The World's Emerging Stock Markets: Structure, Developments, Regulations & Opportunities [15611]

The World's Greatest Walleye Lure [2206]

The World's Largest Market: A Business Guide to Europe 1992 [43885]

The World's Showcase of Horticulture [11498], [19729]

Worldview Technology Partners [58192]

Worldwide Express [6133]

Worldwide Internet Music Resources [21161]

Worldwide Merchandise [42807], [56026]

Worldwide Riches Opportunities [13021]

Worldwide Tax Daily [24112]

Worldwide Videotex Update [22098]

Worm Digest [9398]

"Worried on Woodward; Police Caucus on Robbers of Oakland Businesses" in *Crain's Detroit Business* (Vol. 21, January 31, 2005, No. 5) [22424], [29589], [39695]

"Worst-case scenario" in *Entrepreneur* (Vol. 30, No. 2, February 2) [30052], [39696]

"Worth the Drive? Your Company Cars Could Be Gulping More than Just Gas if You Don't Know What Your Ownership Costs Are" in *Entrepreneur* [303], [13523], [26406], [27203], [38473], [43428]

"Worth His Weight" in *Entrepreneur* (Vol. 31, No. 8, August 2003, pp. 96) [19448], [26041], [38949]

"Worth a Try" in *Entrepreneur* (Vol. 31, No. 8, August 2003, pp. 71) [47764], [48674]

Worthington Area Chamber of Commerce [61687], [63833]

"Would You Buy a Chinese Car From This Man?" in *Inc.* (Volume 27, July 2005, No. 7, pp. 68-72, 74) [18165], [36993], [46490]

"Would You Like a Franchise With That?" in *Entrepreneur* (Vol. 33, January 2005, No. 1, pp. 120) [30708], [38950]

Would You Put That in Writing? [27686]

"Would You Recommend Us? Perfect Your Service By Asking The Only Question That Matters." in *Inc.* (September 2006, pp. 40, 42) [30632], [31912]

Wrangell Chamber of Commerce [56979]

Wrap Daddy's [7103]

"Wrap It Up Right" in *Entrepreneur* (Vol. 32, December 2004, No. 12, pp. 68) [24077], [54877]

WrapUp [2270], [10630], [12797]

Wray Chamber of Commerce [58438]

"Wrestling with the bear" in *Black Enterprise* (Vol. 33, No. 3, Oct. 2002, pp. 46) [10257], [10315], [15114], [15612], [37008], [38474], [48486]

"Wrestling for Web dominance" in *Hispanic Business* (Vol. 22, No. 7-8, July-August 2000, pp. 106) [15613], [34751], [37213], [43886], [50271]

Wright Area Chamber of Commerce [66635]

Wright City Area Chamber of Commerce [62071]

Donald C. Wright [26439], [27052], [38587], [46140], [54894]

Wright State University–SBDC [63582]

Wright State University at Lake Campus–Small Business Development Center [63583]

Robert E. Wright Tax and Accounting [50345]

Wrightsville - Johnson County Chamber of Commerce [59180]

Wrightwood Chamber of Commerce [57880]

Write It Well [27710]

Write Job Inc. [4885]

"Write On" in *Entrepreneur* (Vol. 33, March 2005, No. 3, pp. 94) [27543], [27687]

"Write Stuff" in *Crain's New York Business* (Vol. 23, January 15, 2007, No. 3, pp. 47) [4169], [36994], [42774], [56518]

"The Write Stuff: Entrepreneurs Find Success with a New Take on a Familiar Product" in *Entrepreneur* (Vol. 32, November 2004, No. 11) [36995], [46491]

"The Write Stuff: What Does it Take to Launch a Brand-New Product?" in *Entrepreneur* (Vol. 32, December 2004, No. 12, pp. 104) [47765], [48813]

The Writer Magazine [9043]

Writer's Digest [9044], [16257]

The Writer's Digest Handbook of Making Money Freelance Writing [8630], [9014], [18253]

Writer's Guide to Book Editors, Publishers, and Literary Agents [2752], [9015], [16251]

The Writer's Handbook [9016], [16252]

Writers Union of Canada Newsletter [9045]

The Writer's Voice [61502]

"Writing a Business Plan" in *Crain's Detroit Business* (Vol. 15, No. 50, December 13, 1999, pp. E-7) [30053]

Writing Business Proposals and Reports [27688]

Writing a Convincing Business Plan [30054]

Writing Creative Nonfiction [9017]

"Writing her own e-ticket" in *WorkingWoman* (Vol. 25, No. 8, September 2000, pp. 20) [34752], [45874], [56519]

Writing Effective News Releases: How to Get Free Publicity for Yourself, Your Business, or Your Organization [50482]

Writing Effectively in Business [27689]

Writing and Implementing a Marketing Plan [47766]

Writing Localizable Software for the Macintosh [23268]

Writing News [18219]

"Writing the big ones: Part Two" in *Rough Notes* (Vol. 146, No. 4, April 2003, pp. 46) [13524], [43429]

"Writing the big ones" in *Rough Notes* (Vol. 146, No. 3, March 2003, pp. 126) [13525], [43430], [51918]

Writing the Perfect Business E-Mail [27614], [32981]

Writing and Selling Your First Screenplay [9048]

Writing That Works [27696]

Writing for the Web [37098]

Writing for the Web II [27287], [53192]

WSI Internet [14685]

"WSJ Honors Economist" in *Hispanic Business* (June 2005, pp. 18) [15614], [31256], [32802], [45875], [56520]

WSPA World [3405], [9399]

WTA Tour Players Association [24569]

"WTC mission is 'call to service' for Ann Arbor biotech firm" in *Crain's Detroit Business* (Vol. 18, No. 18, May 6, 2002, pp. 1) [4863], [22425], [23269], [42130], [53539]

WWD (November 20, 2003, pp. 12); "3 Companies Dip Into Swim" in [5640]

WWD (Vol. 184, No. 59, September 20, 2002, pp. S1); "Beauty's new age" in [2580], [7880], [17890], [27824]

WWD (September 24, 2003, pp. 14); "Failing to Rise to Women's Size" in [5656]

WWD (January 26, 2004, pp. 4); "J. Crew Sees No Objection to Bridal Line" in [3187], [5551]

WWD (August 4, 2003, pp. 19); "Maximizing the Plus-Size Potential" in [5685], [9631]

WWD (Oct. 17, 2002, pp. S60); "More than a store: independent specialty stores are adding art installations, yoga classes" in [1611], [5690], [51254]

WWD (November 3, 2003, pp. 12); "NOM's Moms" in [5700]

WWD (Vol. 184, No. 78, October 17, 2002, pp. 8); "Stretching for the inner yogi" in [5574], [5718], [17912], [19442]

WWD (January 2, 2003, pp. 9); "The New Brands in Town" in [5561], [5694], [19421]

"www.circles.com" in *Entrepreneur* (Vol. 28, No. 9, September 2000, pp. 145) [7151], [52614]

"Wyandotte County" in *Ingram's* (Vol. 28, No. 9, September 2002, pp. 69) [32803]

Wyanet Chamber of Commerce [59710]

Wyatt-MacKenzie Publishing Inc. [64320]

Wyckoff Chamber of Commerce [62576]

Walter S. Wydro Consultants [24503]

Wyeth Pharmaceuticals Collegeville–Library [8885]

Wylie Chamber of Commerce [65571]

Bruce D. Wyman Co. [46141]

Wynnewood Chamber of Commerce [64108]

Wyoming Administration and Information Department–Procurement Services [66636]

Wyoming County Chamber of Commerce [63044]

Wyoming Department of Commerce–Wyoming Business Council [66601]

Wyoming Kentwood Area Chamber of Commerce [61446]

Wyoming Small Business Development Center–State Office [66592]

Wytheville Community College–Wytheville Small Business Development Center [65846]

Wytheville SBDC–Wytheville Community College [65847]

Wytheville-Wythe-Bland Chamber of Commerce [65963]

X

"XBRL Revisited: Grasp the Fundamentals to See How Businesses Use XBRL Today" in *Journal of Accountancy* (Vol. 199, February 2005) [304], [2975], [4864], [10258], [15615], [23270], [24078], [26407], [27204], [54092]

Xela Enterprises Ltd. [22018]

Xenia Area Chamber of Commerce [63834]

Xerox Corporation
    Technical Information Center [7863]
    Wilsonville Library [6556]

"Xign's Order-to-Pay Service Aims to Save Time, Money" in *eWeek* (February 2, 2005) [14637], [31609], [34753]

XL Global Services–Corporate Library [13612]

Xlibris Corp. [64636]

"XML for All" in *Entrepreneur* (Vol. 28, No. 11, November 2000, pp. 28) [14638], [34754], [49379]

XML and Databases [32982]

XML Development I [53193]

XML Development II [53194]

XML Development III [50556], [53195]

"XML offers flexibility, ebXML sorts it out" in *Crain's Detroit Business* (Vol. 16, No. 47, November 13, 2000, pp. 18) [34755], [53034]

"XML: The Only Chance for a Worldwide Standard" in *E-business Advisor* (Vol. 18, No. 4, April 2000, pp. 10) [34756], [43887], [53035]

"XML: What's Still Needed for B2B?" in *E-business Advisor* (Vol. 18, No. 5, May 2000, pp. 44) [22426], [26022], [34757], [49380]

Xpedior Inc. [34784]

Xpert Business Brokers Inc. [3456]

Y

"Y Stay Put? Generation Y Bounces From Job to Job" in *The Record* (November 13, 2005) [42473], [54093]

"Y2K disasters? Never mind: Glitch fixers head for e-commerce opportunities" in *Crain's Detroit Business* (Vol. 16, No. 3, Jan. 17, 2000) [34758]

Yachats Area Chamber of Commerce [64286]

Yacht and Brokerage Show [16781]

Yachting [16766]

Yadkin County Chamber of Commerce [63446]

Yadkin Valley Chamber of Commerce [63447]

"Yahoo! Hooks Up with H&S to Promote Dating Service" in *PR Week* (August 18, 2003, pp. 3) [7074], [34759]

Yahoo! Internet Life [6206], [6889], [23295]

Yakety Yak Wireless [5226]

Yakima County Hispanic Chamber of Commerce [66203]

Yakima Valley Community College–Small Business Development Center [66030]

"Yaknow?" in *Entrepreneur* (Vol. 28, No. 10, October 2000, pp. 15) [33286], [34760], [37214]

Yale Chamber of Commerce [64109]

Yale University
    Arts of the Book Collection (Arts Library) [2852], [4179], [25508]
    Drama Library (Arts Library) [7973]
    Office of Cooperative Research [58627]

"Yamacraw fund broadens its focus" in *Atlanta Business Chronicle* (Vol. 24, No. 8, July 27, 2001, pp. 3A) [4078], [37088], [55459]

"Yamaha Sued Over Imports" in *Sacramento Bee* (December 20, 2005) [13022], [17492], [43888]

The Yamamoto Forecast [15691]

Yancey County/Burnsville Chamber of Commerce [63448]

William J. Yang & Associates [3995]

Yankeetek Ventures [61134]

Yankton Area Chamber of Commerce [64842]

Yankton Small Business Development Center (Region V) [64811]

Yard & Garden [11445], [11482], [16117]

Yarmouth Chamber of Commerce [60781]

Yarnell - Peeples Valley Chamber of Commerce [57083]

Yavapai College–Small Business Development Center [56998]

Yaya's Flame Broiled Chicken [22019]

"Yazam Taps Coleman, Opens DC Office" in *Venture Capital Journal* (Vol. 40, No. 10, October 2000, pp. 36) [44692], [55960]

Yazoo County Chamber of Commerce [61841]

YB News [10813]

Ybor City Chamber of Commerce [58958]

"The Year 2000 Top Inc. 500" in *Inc.* (October 17, 2000 pp. 57) [29033], [54094]

"A Year of Advice is Prize in Woman-Owned Program" in *Crain's Detroit Business* (Vol. 21, December 12, 2005, No. 50, pp. 2) [46492], [51419], [52615], [56521]

"The Year Ahead" in *Hispanic Business* (January/February 2005, pp. 60, 62) [29034], [32804]

"The Year of the Convertible" in *Forbes* (Vol. 175, February 14, 2005, No. 3, pp. 134) [10259], [15616], [32805], [38475]

"Year-End Bonus Points" in *Inc.* (November 1, 2003) [26964], [35168]

"Year-End Tax Tips" in *Black Enterprise* (Vol. 31, No. 5, December 2000, pp. 125) [54878]

"Year In Review Fund-Raising" in *Venture Capital Journal* (February 1, 2006) [39697], [55961]

"Year In Review IPO Market" in *Venture Capital Journal* (February 1, 2006) [6874], [42131], [55962]

"Year In Review People" in *Venture Capital Journal* (February 1, 2006) [36996], [55963]

"A Year Into The Job, He's Making Progress Slowly But Surely" in *Fortuneit* (Vol. 146, No. 12, December 9, 2002, pp. 217) [39698], [39966]

"Year to Success" in *Small Business Opportunities* (Vol. 17, May 2005, No. 3, pp. 126) [36997], [44181], [45876]

"Year's biggest industrial deal months in making" in *Atlanta Business Chronicle* (Vol. 25, December 13, 2002, No. 27, pp. A3) [7516], [32168], [52757]

Yeast [52331]

Yello Dyno Child Protection Programs [5453]

The Yellow Balloon [11846]

"Yellow Pages Association" in *Sales & Marketing Management* (Vol. 157, February 2005, No. 2, pp. 14) [843], [47767]

Yellow Pages for Stamp Collectors [5828]

Yellow Springs Chamber of Commerce [63835]

Yellville Area Chamber of Commerce [57231]

Yelm Area Chamber of Commerce [66204]

"Yes, you can" in *Black Enterprise* (Vol. 31, No. 5, December 2000, pp. 64) [29776], [30495], [35733], [47987], [52791]

"Yes to English, No to Espanol?" in *Hispanic Business* (Vol. 23, No. 10, October, 2001, pp. 26) [33287], [39699]

"Yes, No, Maybe So" in *Inc.* (August 1, 2003) [27544], [36998], [45877]

"Yes, You Can!" in *Entrepreneur* (Vol. 32, No. 1, January 2004, pp. 32) [30633], [36999]

"Yes, You Still Can Go Public" in *Inc.* (Volume 27, July 2005, No. 7, pp. 38) [15617], [50272]

"Yessian Music hires Detroit producer, wins contract for ads" in *Crain's Detroit Business* (Vol. 18, No. 50, Dec. 16, 2002, pp. 16) [844], [17606], [17779], [37818], [47768]

"Yesterday & Today: How DFJ Went From Shrimp to Whale" in *Venture Capital Journal* (Vol. 42, No. 5, May 2002, pp. 12) [35734], [37089], [55460]

Yesterday's Furniture and Country Store [12352]

Yeung's Lotus Express Franchise Corp. [22020]

Yield/Revenue Management: New Strategies for Boosting Profits [26136]

"Yielding to Yoga" in *Crain's Chicago Business* (Vol. 25, No. 49, Dec. 9, 2002, pp. SB1) [17922], [19449], [29035]

Yipes Stripes, Inc. [2060]

YMCA Resident Camp Directory [4252]

Yoakum Area Chamber of Commerce [65572]

Yoga to Go with Misty Carey Volume 2: Strength [19489]

Yoga to Go with Misty Carey Volume 3: Health [19490]

"Yoga Instructor finds peace in classroom" in *Long Island Business News* (Vol. 50, No. 14, March 28, 2003, pp. 23A) [17923], [19450], [56522]

"Yoga Studio to Open in Greeley, Colo." in *Greeley Tribune* (November 5, 2002) [17924], [19451]

Yogen Fruz Worldwide Inc. [12859]

Yogi Bear's Jellystone Park Camp-Resorts [4263], [12735]

Yogurt & Such Cafe [22021]

Yogurteria [12860]

Yogurty's Yogurt Discovery [12861]

Yonkers Chamber of Commerce [63045]

Yorba Linda Chamber of Commerce [57881]

York Chamber of Commerce [60782]

York College/City University of New York–Small Business Development Center [62793]

York County Chamber of Commerce [64536]

York County Regional Chamber of Commerce [64789]

"York, Pa.-Based Company Plans to Build Ethanol Plant in Northeast" in *Patriot-News* (April 11, 2003) [26563], [52231]

York Publishing Co. [63907]

York Technical College–Anne Springs Close Library [49472]

York University
    Centre for Research in Work and Society [17075], [55344]
    Office of Research Service [66743]

York University, Glendon Campus Counselling & Career Centre [4470]

Yorktown Chamber of Commerce [65573]

Yorkville Area Chamber of Commerce [59711]

Yoshi's [22022]

"You Are What You Charge" in *Journal of Accountancy* (Vol. 198, November 2004, No. 5, pp. 20) [305], [2976], [24079], [26408], [27205], [31081], [47769]

"You better shop around" in *Atlanta Business Chronicle* (Vol. 23, No. 46, April 20, 2001, pp. 65A) [21417], [39782], [44453]

You Can Be a Columnist: Writing and Selling Your Way to Prestige [9018]

"You Can Build It, But They Might Not Come" in *Inc.* (July 1, 2004) **[17534]**, **[48487]**

"You Can Count on Me: A Friend Can Make the Best Kind of Business Partner" in *Entrepreneur* (Vol. 32, November 2004, No. 11, pp. 36) **[12920]**, **[20164]**, **[37000]**, **[47770]**, **[50273]**, **[50483]**

You Can Make Money from Your Hobby: Building a Business Doing What You Love **[8188]**

"You Can Quote Him" in *Fast Company* (July 2001, pp. 66) **[15618]**, **[37001]**

"You Can Run" in *Entrepreneur* (Vol. 31, No. 6, June 2003, pp. 39) **[5192]**, **[6875]**, **[14639]**, **[42132]**, **[49381]**

"You Can Take It With You: Use Your Mobile Phone Even While Abroad" in *Entrepreneur* (Vol. 32, July 2004, No. 7, pp. 43) **[5193]**, **[30455]**, **[43889]**

"You Can Take It with You: Clubs that Let the Stocks Travel with Individual Owners" in *Black Enterprise* (Vol. 33, Oct. 2002, pp. 43) **[10260]**, **[15619]**, **[38476]**

"You can't lead without making sacrifices" in *Fast Company* (June 2001, pp. 106) **[39700]**, **[45878]**

"You paid that bill with a single click. Or did you?" in *The New York Times* (July 2, 2000, pp. BU10) **[26409]**, **[34761]**

"You Data, Naked On the Net; What's Jeopardizing Your Privacy?" in *Business Week* (February 20, 2006, No. 3972) **[6296]**, **[14640]**, **[22427]**, **[34762]**

"You Don't Know Jackalope" in *Success* (Vol. 47, No. 4, September 2000, pp. 18) **[27737]**, **[30496]**, **[35735]**

"You Don't Say" in *Entrepreneur* (Vol. 31, No. 10, October 2003, pp. 81) **[27545]**, **[27690]**

"You First: An Opening Move May Make or Break a Deal-So Step Lightly" in *Entrepreneur* (Vol. 33, March 2005, No. 3, pp. 96) **[37002]**, **[45879]**

"You need to know" in *BlackEnterprise* (Vol. 31, No. 12, July 2001, pp. 45) **[29080]**, **[29777]**

"You Know My Name (Don't Call My Number)" in *Inc.* (July 1, 2003) **[24296]**, **[29590]**, **[40855]**

You & the Law **[29604]**

"You Must Be Crazy" in *Entrepreneur.com* (Vol. 34, February 2006, No. 2, pp. 18) **[15620]**, **[38477]**

"You Need a Break" in *Success* (Vol. 47, No. 1, January 2000, pp. 14) **[30456]**, **[54879]**

"You Should Be the Boss of Them" in *My Business* (June/July 2004, pp. 51) **[37003]**, **[45880]**

"You think that's funny?" in *Entrepreneur* (Vol. 30, No. 12, December 2002, pp. 101) **[27546]**, **[27691]**

"You Win! Poor You!" in *Entrepreneur* (Vol. 28, No. 10, October 2000, pp. 82) **[37004]**

"You hire them to do the tough work, but how easy is it to work with them?" in *E-business Advisor* (Vol. 18, No. 10, Oct. 2000, pp. 12) **[31257]**, **[49382]**

"You can take it with you: clubs that let the stocks travel with individual owners" in *Black Enterprise* (Vol. 33, Oct. 2002, pp. 43) **[10261]**, **[15621]**, **[38478]**

Young & Associates Inc. **[16885]**, **[53121]**

"Young Banks Hurting as Nation Celebrates Interest Rate Cuts" in *Washington Business Journal* (Vol. 22, No. 9, July 4, 2003) **[10262]**, **[32806]**

Young Children **[5360]**

"Young Entrepreneur of the Year Works Round the Clock" in *Portland Press Herald* (March 24, 2005) **[2258]**, **[37005]**

"Young Entrepreneurs Give the U.S. Mint Their Two Cents" in *Wall Street Journal* (March 14, 2000, pp. B4) **[37006]**, **[56773]**

Young Entrepreneur's Guide to Creating What Matters Most: Building Attitudes, Behaviors & an Action Plan for Success in Your Own Business **[56774]**

"Young, Female, and Demanding" in *Inc.* (Volume 28, January 2006, No. 1, pp. 27) **[54095]**, **[56523]**

"Young Guns" in *Success* (Vol. 47, No. 1, January 2000, pp. 24) **[42474]**

"Young at Heart: Are you Making the Mistake of Lumping Older Baby Boomers with Seniors in Your Marketing Campaign?" in *Entrepreneur* **[845]**, **[47771]**

"Young Millionaires: Class of 2004" in *Entrepreneur* (Vol. 32, November 2004, No. 11, pp. 77) **[846]**, **[2361]**, **[2612]**, **[7911]**, **[12316]**, **[20705]**, **[23645]**, **[24748]**, **[25275]**, **[33288]**, **[34763]**, **[37007]**, **[46493]**

Young Naturalists' Circle **[9343]**

"Young is old" in *Entrepreneur* (Vol. 30, No. 9, September 2002, pp. 28) **[42475]**

Young Presidents' Organization **[56732]**

"Young Professional Share Ideas" in *San Fernando Valley Business Journal* (Vol. 12, January 2007, No. 2, pp. 1) **[37008]**, **[47772]**, **[50709]**

Young Rembrandts, A Children's Drawing Program **[33383]**

The Young Vegetarian's Companion **[18444]**

"Younger But Wiser Than You Might Think" in *San Fernando Valley Business Journal* (Vol. 12, January 2007, No. 2, pp. 51) **[37009]**, **[39701]**

Youngstown Business Incubator **[63887]**

Youngstown/Warren–Small Business Development Center **[63584]**

Youngstown/Warren Regional Chamber of Commerce **[63836]**

Youngstown/Warren Satellite–Small Business Development Center **[63585]**

Yountville Chamber of Commerce **[57882]**

"Your Annual Business Tune-Up" in *Business Week* (December 28, 2006) **[14641]**, **[26023]**, **[30634]**, **[37010]**

"Your Best Interest" in *Entrepreneur* (Vol. 32, July 2004, No. 7, pp. 52) **[306]**, **[10263]**, **[26410]**

"Your Best M&A Strategy" in *Harvard Business Review* (Vol. 81, No. 3, March 2003, pp. 16) **[15622]**, **[32807]**, **[50274]**

"Your Boss is Watching" in *PC Computing* (March 2000, pp. 86) **[34764]**, **[45881]**, **[53540]**, **[54096]**

"Your Browser is Selling You Out" in *PC Computing* (March 2000, pp. 90) **[13093]**, **[34765]**

"Your Business needs to be E-Commerce - so what now?" in *Ingram's* (Vol. 27, No. 7, July 2001, pp. 19) **[34766]**, **[45882]**, **[47773]**, **[51919]**, **[53036]**

"Your Business" in *Entrepreneur* (Vol. 27, No. 12, December 1999, pp. 119) **[42476]**

Your Business Plan **[64309]**

Your Business, Your Future: How to Predict and Harness Growth **[29036]**, **[37011]**

"Your Butt On The Line" in *Entrepreneur* (Vol. 28, No. 7, July 2000, pp. 70) **[55461]**

"Your Career: Take Charge and Find Peace of Mind" in *Atlanta Business Chronicle* (Vol. 25, No. 20, October 25, 2002, pp. 8B) **[32808]**

Your Company Safety & Health Manual: Programs, Policies & Procedures for Preventing Accidents & Injuries in the Workplace **[56594]**

Your Dog **[1262]**, **[19118]**

Your Dollar Store With More Inc. **[51478]**

"Your Employees" in *Small Business Opportunities* (Vol. 14, No. 1, January 2002, pp. 76, 78) **[35169]**, **[39702]**

Your Family Business-A Success Guide for Growth and Survival **[37819]**

"Your Father's Bank" in *Inc.* (September 1, 2004) **[10264]**, **[30996]**, **[38479]**

"Your Feature Presentation" in *Entrepreneur* (Vol. 28, No. 9, September 2000, pp. 82) **[55462]**

Your First Business Plan: A Simple Question-and-Answer Format Designed to Help You Write Your Own Plan **[29037]**, **[29081]**, **[39111]**

Your First Business Plan: Learn the Critical Steps to Writing a Winning Business Plan **[30055]**

"Your career can still thrive in an age of flux" in *Black Enterprise* (Vol. 33, No. 3, October 2002, pp. 163) **[29038]**, **[29760]**, **[42477]**, **[43530]**

Your International Business Plan **[64310]**

"Your Kind of News: Free Personalized Information for the Public" in *Black Enterprise* (Vol. 34, No. 7, February 2004, pp. 140) **[37012]**, **[38480]**, **[39784]**, **[47039]**, **[49383]**

Your Lawyer: An Owner's Manual **[29591]**, **[39703]**

"Your Loss? Don't Risk Losing Your Laptop (or PDA or Phone) on Your Next Flight" in *Entrepreneur* (Vol. 31, No. 9, September 2003) **[30457]**, **[35284]**

"Your Loss Is Your Gain" in *Entrepreneur* (Vol. 31, No. 5, May 2003, pp. 50) **[32809]**, **[51495]**

"Your Man On The Hill" in *Fortune* (Vol. 142, No. 9, October 16, 2000, pp. 312B) **[40856]**, **[53037]**

Your Marketing Plan **[64311]**

"Your money: be sure you have access to your cash" in *Atlanta Business Chronicle* (Vol. 25, No. 20, October 25, 2002, pp. 6B) **[10265]**, **[38481]**

Your Money Series **[15721]**

Your New Business: A Personal Plan for Success **[53038]**

"Your New Neighborhood" in *Small Business Opportunities* (Vol. 17, May 2005, No. 3, pp. 10) **[29039]**, **[47672]**, **[47774]**, **[51420]**

Your New Pryor Report Managers Edge **[3627]**, **[16553]**, **[45911]**

Your Own Shop: How to Open and Operate a Successful Retail Business **[51421]**

"Your Own Style" in *Entrepreneur* (Vol. 33, January 2005, No. 1, pp. 43) **[4865]**, **[6876]**, **[23271]**, **[27692]**, **[53541]**

"Your PC Post Office" in *Hispanic Business* (Vol. 22, No. 1/2, January/February, pp. 88) **[49384]**, **[49570]**

"Your Personal/Virtual Mentor" in *Small Business Opportunities* (Vol. 12, No. 5, September 2000, pp. 68) **[33289]**, **[53542]**

"Your Phone Kiosk May Vary" in *PC World* (Vol. 21, No. 9, September 2003, pp. 43) **[4211]**, **[15949]**, **[19306]**

"Your space is the place" in *Fast Company* (May 2001, pp. 60) **[20706]**, **[30056]**, **[42478]**, **[52758]**

"Your Recovery Rights" in *Small Business Opportunities* (Vol. 12, No. 2, March 2000, pp. 90) **[31610]**

"Your Retail Riches" in *Small Business Opportunities* (Winter 2005) **[1765]**, **[33502]**, **[51042]**

"Your Safety Is What Drives Us: Auto Safety Tips from Allstate" in *Black Enterprise* (Vol. 34, No. 6, January 2004, pp. 59) **[13435]**, **[13526]**, **[41518]**, **[43431]**

"Your Secret Weapon" in *Small Business Opportunities* (Vol. 16, No. 3, May 2004, pp. 10, 120) **[45883]**, **[51920]**

Your Specialty Store: How to Start & Run a Money-Making Store **[23446]**

"Your Story Here" in *Black Enterprise* (Vol. 36, February 2006, No. 7, pp. 57) **[20350]**, **[24463]**, **[34767]**, **[47775]**, **[50484]**, **[50710]**

Your Successful Real Estate Career, 5h Edition **[20707]**, **[21040]**

"Your own time" in *BlackEnterprise* (Vol. 32, No. 3, October 2001, pp. 162) **[39704]**, **[55007]**

"Your Vote Really Does Count: Changing Political Dynamics of an Evenly Divided Congress" in *Venture Capital Journal* (Vol. 40, No. 10) **[39705]**, **[55964]**

Your Way: Starting Your Own Business in Rural South Dakota **[53039]**

Your Writing Partner **[31991]**

"You're the Boss: There Are Some Things Beyond Your Control..." in *Entrepreneur* (Vol. 31, No. 9, September 2003, pp. 90) **[37013]**, **[38951]**

"You're Deposing Me?" in *Hispanic Business* (March 2003, pp. 57) **[29592]**

"You're Fired!" in *Forbes* (Vol. 174, December 13, 2004, No. 12, pp. 89) **[3620]**, **[31258]**, **[32073]**, **[42479]**, **[42903]**

You're Hired: Employers Give Tips For Successful Interviewing **[42480]**

"You're the Inspiration" in *Entrepreneur* (Vol. 33, September 2005, No. 9, pp. 96) **[43972]**, **[46603]**, **[48691]**, **[50667]**

"Yours, Mine, Ours" in *My Business* (October/November 2002, pp. 35-37) **[43047]**, **[49476]**

"Yourshop@Black Enterprise.com" in *Black Enterprise* (Vol. 31, No. 2, September 2000, pp. 215) **[31913]**, **[34768]**, **[47776]**, **[51921]**